75TH EDITION

AMERICAN LIBRARY DIRECTORY™

2022-2023

American Library Directory™
75th Edition

Publisher
Thomas H. Hogan

Director, ITI Reference Group
Owen O'Donnell

Consulting Editor
Stephen L. Torpie

Associate Editor
Jennifer Williams

Operations Manager, Tampa Editorial
Debra James

Project Coordinator, Tampa Editorial
Carolyn Victor

75TH EDITION

AMERICAN LIBRARY DIRECTORY™

2022-2023

VOL. 1

ALABAMA–PENNSYLVANIA

Information Today, Inc.

ISSN 0065-910X

Set ISBN: 978-1-57387-580-6

Library of Congress Catalog Card Number: 23-3581

Information Today, Inc.
143 Old Marlton Pike
Medford, NJ 08055-8750
Phone: 800-300-9868 (Customer Service)
800-409-4929 (Editorial)
Fax: 609-654-4309
E-mail: custserv@infotoday.com (Customer Service)
jwilliams@infotoday.com (Editorial)
Web Site: www.infotoday.com

Printed and bound in the United States of America

US $411.05

ISBN 978-1-57387-580-6

CONTENTS

VOLUME 1

VOLUME 2

PREFACE

Welcome to the 75th edition of the *American Library Directory*, now in its 113th year. The *American Library Directory* is edited and compiled by Information Today, Inc. of New Providence, New Jersey.

ARRANGEMENT AND COVERAGE

The major section of the directory contains listings of public, academic, government, and special libraries in the United States and in Canada. Listings are arranged geographically by the U.S. and Canada, then alphabetized by states, provinces, cities, and finally by the library or organization name.

Each state and province chapter opens with statistical information regarding public libraries. These statistics were supplied by the state or provincial library authorities. Some are derived from public sources.

Entries include the name and address of the library, names of key personnel, and information on the library's holdings. In addition, the entries for the majority of libraries provide information on some or all of these additional areas: Income; Expenditures including salaries; E-Mail; Subject Interests; Special Collections; Automation; and Publications. Also included in each entry is a Standard Address Number (SAN), a unique address identification code used to expedite billing, shipping, and electronic ordering. For SAN assignments or questions, contact SAN@bowker.com. See the sample entry on page xi for a comprehensive guide to information that can be included in each entry.

Each library was provided its data to update via an e-mail and web data interchange application. If an update was not returned, the data were verified, as much as possible, through telephone outreach, direct e-mail, and web research. Entries verified from public sources are indicated by an asterisk (*) following the library name.

Non-listed libraries that have come to our attention since the previous edition are provided with questionnaires. If the library returns sufficient information, it is included. Entries new to the directory, are indicated by a section icon (§) to the left of the classification letter that precedes the entry.

Each library listed is identified by a code that indicates the type of library it is. The following codes are used:

- A — Armed Forces
- C — College or University
- E — Electronic
- G — Government, from local to federal
- J — Community College
- L — Law
- M — Medical
- P — Public and State Libraries
- R — Religious
- S — Special, including industry and company libraries as well as libraries serving associations, clubs, foundations, institutes, and societies.

ADDITIONAL SECTIONS

Library Award Recipients 2021. This section includes awards for outstanding librarianship or services, major development grants, and research projects.

Volume 2 of the directory provides auxiliary information to the Library industry, and includes a variety of specialized information:

1. *Networks, Consortia, and Other Cooperative Library Organizations* includes automation networks, statewide networking systems, book processing and purchasing centers, and other specialized cooperating organizations. Entries indicate the number of members and the primary functions of each.

2. *Library Schools and Training Courses* includes a variety of college, and university library science programs. Entries include entrance requirements, tuition, type of training, degrees and hours offered, and special courses offered. A dagger icon (†) indicates a program accredited by the American Library Association Committee on Accreditation.

3. *Library Systems* provides a listing of all state and provincial library systems as provided directly by those authorities. A brief statement indicating system functions within the state or province precedes the alphabetically arranged list of the state or

province's systems. Cities are also included so that the user can locate a system's entry in the Library Section of the directory, or in cases where the state is followed by (N), in the Network Section of the directory.

4. *Libraries for the Blind and Physically Handicapped* provides a listing of all libraries designated by the National Library Service for the Blind and Physically Handicapped as regional and subregional libraries serving print handicapped patrons. It also includes other specialty libraries and those with a significant amount of specialized equipment and services in these areas.

5. *Libraries Serving the Deaf and Hearing Impaired* provides a similar listing of all libraries that have a significant commitment to patrons whoare deaf or hearing impaired as evidenced by the specialized equipment and services they have available. The list is arranged by state and then by library name. The city is included so the user can find the entry in the Library Section and determine the specialized sesrvices by reading the paragraph "Special Services for the Deaf" included in the library's entry.

6. *State and Provincial Public Library Agencies* indicates name, address, person-in-charge, and telephone number of the state agency that is responsible for public libraries.

7. *State School Library Agencies* indicates the same information for the state agency that is responsible for elementary and high school programs.

8. The *Interlibrary Loan Code for the United States* is reprinted with the kind permission of the American Library Association.

9. The *Organization Index* provides an alphabetical listing of all libraries, schools, and networks with the page number reference.

10. The *Personnel Index* is an alphabetical listing of individuals who are included within entries for libraries, consortia, and library schools. Entries include name, title, organization, location, and page number reference.

RELATED SERVICES

American Library Directory is also available online at **www.americanlibrarydirectory.com**. You can search and identify all libraries that meet certain specialty criteria such as legal, medical, religious, etc. You can also search by geographic criteria, vendors, holdings, staff size, expenditures, income, and more with a single search. We invite you to visit the site and take advantage of our free trial offer.

The editors and researchers have made every effort to include all material submitted as accurately and completely as possible within the confines of format and scope. However, the publishers do not assume and hereby disclaim any liability to any party for any loss or damage caused by errors or omissions in the *American Library Directory* whether such errors and omissions resulted from negligence, accident, or any other cause. In the event of a publication error, the sole responsibility of the publisher will be the entry of corrected information in succeeding editions.

ACKNOWLEDGEMENTS

The editors wish to thank all of those who responded to our requests for information; without their efforts, the *American Library Directory* could not be published.

The editors also wish to express their appreciation for the cooperation of the officers of the state, regional, and provincial libraries who have provided statistics and other information concerning libraries in their jurisdictions.

Stephen L. Torpie
Consulting Editor

Return this form by e-mail or mail to:

aldsupport@infotoday.com

Information Today, Inc.

American Library Directory
Suite G-20
121 Chanlon Road
New Providence, NJ 07974-2195

AMERICAN LIBRARY DIRECTORY EDITORIAL REVISION FORM

☐ Please check here if you are nominating this library for a new listing in the directory

☐ Please check if this library is already listed

Library Name: ______________________

Address: ______________________

City: ____________ State or Province: ________ Postal Code: ________

E-Mail: ____________ Web Site: ____________

Phone: ____________ Fax: ____________

Brief Description of Library: ______________________

Personnel

☐ Addition ☐ Deletion ☐ Correction

First Name: ________ Last Name: ________ Title: ________

☐ Addition ☐ Deletion ☐ Correction

First Name: ________ Last Name: ________ Title: ________

☐ Addition ☐ Deletion ☐ Correction

First Name: ________ Last Name: ________ Title: ________

(Continued on back)

Other Information

Indicate other information to be added to or corrected in this listing. Please be as specific as possible, noting erroneous data to be corrected or deleted.

____

____

____

____

____

____

____

Verification

Data for this listing will not be updated without the following information.

Your Name: ______________ Your Title: ______________

Organization Name: ______________

Address: ______________

City: ______________ State or Province: ______________ Postal Code: ______________

E-Mail: ______________ Web Site: ______________

Indicate if you are a: ☐ Representative of this organization ☐ User of this directory ☐ Other

If other, please specify: ______________

Thank you for helping Information Today, Inc. maintain the most up-to-date information available.

SAMPLE ENTRY

(fictional)

[1]**P** [2]McNeil & Foster, [3]Prescott Memorial Library, [4]500 Terra Cotta Dr, 85005-3126. [5]SAN 360-9070. [6]Tel: 602-839-9108. Toll Free Tel: 800-625-3848. FAX: 602-839-2020. TDD: 602-839-9202. E-mail: mcneilfoster@prescott.org. Web Site: www.prescottlib.com. [7]*Dir* Michelle Trozzo; Tel: 602-839-5522; *Asst Dir* Brie Goodwin; *Tech Serv* Nina Silva; *Pub Servs* Katie Joyce. Subject Specialists: *Bus* Axel Abraham; *Folklore* Benjamin Torpie; *Mythology* Casey Joyce.

[8]Staff 20 (MLS 15, Non-MLS 5)

[9]Founded 1903. Pop served 92,540; Circ 210,000

[10]July 2020-Jun 2021 Income (Main Library and Branch(es)) $750,500, State $600,000, City $150,500. Mats Exp $118,400, Books $53,400, Per/Ser (Incl. Access Fees) $60,000, Micro $2,000, AV Equip $3,000. Sal $53,000 (Prof $44,000)

[11]**Library Holdings:** Bk Vols 90,000; Bk Titles 87,000; Per subs 145

[12]**Special Collections:** Local History (Lehi College)

[13]**Subject Interests:** Child psychology, genetics

[14]**Automation Activity & Vendor Info:** (Acquisitions) Innovative Interfaces Inc.; (Cataloging) Innovative Interfaces Inc.; (Circulation) Gaylord

[15]Wireless access

[16]Mem of Southwestern Library System

[17]Partic in Amigos Library Services, Inc.; Library Interchange Network (LINK)

[18]Special Services for the Deaf-TDD. Staff member who knows sign language; projector & captioned films

[19]Friends of Library Group

[20]**Bookmobiles:** 1

[21]**Branches:** 1

EASTSIDE, 9807 Post St, 85007-3184. SAN 360-9083. Tel 602-839-9178; *Librn* Emily Trozzo

Library Holdings: Bk Vols 23,000

1. Classification key (see "Arrangement & Coverage" in the Preface for explanation).
2. Official library name.
3. Other name by which library may be known.
4. Address.
5. SAN (Standard Address Number).
6. Communication information.
7. Personnel.
8. Number and professional status of staff.
9. Library background—Data on enrollment and the highest degree offered are included for academic libraries.
10. Income figures—Library income is broken down by source when reported.
    Expenditure figures—Material expenditure figures are requested for AV equipment, books, electronic reference materials (including access fees), manuscripts and archives, microforms, other print materials, periodicals/serials (including access fees), and preservation. In addition, salary figures are broken down by professional status when given.
11. Library holdings.
12. Special collections.
13. Subject interests.
14. Automation activity and vendor.
15. Library with wireless access.
16. Library system to which the library belongs.
17. Networks in which the library participates.
18. Special services.
19. Friends of Library Group.
20. Bookmobiles.
21. Branches (or departmental libraries for academic libraries)—Entries include library name, address, name of librarian, and number of book volumes. Branch libraries are listed under the library of which they are a part.

LIBRARY COUNT

Provided here are totals for major types of libraries in the United States and Canada. Included are counts for public, academic, armed forces, government, and special libraries. Excluded from the counts are branch, departmental, and divisional libraries not listed with a full address in the directory. Some categories, such as academic, provide counts for specialized libraries such as law or medical libraries. As counts for only certain types of libraries are given, these subcategories do not add up to the total count for each type of library.

PUBLIC—Each public library is counted once and then each branch is counted separately. Because the organization of systems varies from state to state, the method of counting these libraries varies also. In some cases, the libraries forming the systems were designated as member libraries, while in others they were given as branch libraries. In yet other instances, systems maintain branches as well as member libraries. If listed in this directory as a branch, the library was recorded in the branch count; however, member libraries were counted independently and recorded in the number of public libraries. Special public libraries are also included in the Total Special Libraries count.

ACADEMIC—The figure for academic libraries includes all libraries listed in the directory as part of academic institutions, whether they are main, departmental, or special. Specialized libraries and library departments at these colleges, such as law, medical, religious, or science libraries, are also counted in the Total Special Libraries figure.

GOVERNMENT and ARMED FORCES—Counts include all government and armed forces-related libraries listed in the directory, including specialized ones. Those libraries that are also defined as special libraries are included in the Total Special Libraries figure.

SPECIAL—The special libraries count includes only specialized libraries that are not public, academic, armed forces, or government institutions. The Total Special Libraries count includes all law, medical, religious, business, and other special libraries found in the *American Library Directory* regardless of who operates them.

LIBRARIES IN THE UNITED STATES

A. PUBLIC LIBRARIES....................*16,967
- Public Libraries, excluding Branches....................9,638
  - Main Public Libraries that have branches....................1,439
- Public Library Branches....................7,329

B. ACADEMIC LIBRARIES....................*3,501
- Community College Libraries....................1,082
  - Departmental....................243
  - Medical....................5
  - Religious....................5
- University & College....................2,419
  - Departmental....................1,137
  - Law....................190
  - Medical....................238
  - Religious....................247

C. ARMED FORCES LIBRARIES....................*225
- Air Force....................62
  - Medical....................3
- Army....................103
  - Medical....................21
- Marine....................12
- Navy....................48
  - Law....................1
  - Medical....................9

D. GOVERNMENT LIBRARIES....................*801
- Law....................349
- Medical....................108

E. SPECIAL LIBRARIES (Excluding Public, Academic, Armed Forces, and Government)....................*4,396
- Law....................626
- Medical....................778
- Religious....................349

F. TOTAL SPECIAL LIBRARIES (Including Public, Academic, Armed Forces, and Government)....................5,572
- Total Law....................1,166
- Total Medical....................1,162
- Total Religious....................762

G. TOTAL LIBRARIES COUNTED (*)....................25,890

LIBRARIES IN REGIONS ADMINISTERED BY THE UNITED STATES

A. PUBLIC LIBRARIES......*18
Public Libraries, excluding Branches......9
Main Public Libraries that have branches......3
Public Library Branches......9

B. ACADEMIC LIBRARIES......*38
Community College Libraries......3
Departmental......1
University & College......35
Departmental......18
Law......3
Medical......3
Religious......1

C. ARMED FORCES LIBRARIES......*2
Air Force......1
Army......1

D. GOVERNMENT LIBRARIES......*3
Law......1
Medical......1

E. SPECIAL LIBRARIES (Excluding Public, Academic, Armed Forces, and Government)......*4
Law......3
Religious......1

F. TOTAL SPECIAL LIBRARIES (Including Public, Academic, Armed Forces, and Government)......13
Total Law......7
Total Medical......4
Total Religious......2

G. TOTAL LIBRARIES COUNTED (*)......65

LIBRARIES IN CANADA

A. PUBLIC LIBRARIES......*2,216
Public Libraries, excluding Branches......799
Main Public Libraries that have branches......159
Public Library Branches......1,417

B. ACADEMIC LIBRARIES......*316
Community College Libraries......75
Departmental......14
Religious......1
University & College......241
Departmental......169
Law......16
Medical......11
Religious......31

C. GOVERNMENT LIBRARIES......*154
Law......25
Medical......4

D. SPECIAL LIBRARIES (Excluding Public, Academic, Armed Forces, and Government)......*501
Law......85
Medical......117
Religious......20

E. TOTAL SPECIAL LIBRARIES (Including Public, Academic, Armed Forces, and Government)......589
Total Law......126
Total Medical......132
Total Religious......66

F. TOTAL LIBRARIES COUNTED (*)......3,187

SUMMARY

TOTAL UNITED STATES LIBRARIES......25,890

TOTAL LIBRARIES ADMINISTERED BY THE UNITED STATES......65

TOTAL CANADIAN LIBRARIES......3,187

GRAND TOTAL OF LIBRARIES LISTED......29,142

Library Award Recipients 2021

Listed below are major awards given to libraries and librarians in the calendar year 2021. These entries were selected from the more inclusive list of scholarships and grant awards found in the *Library and Book Trade Almanac*, 67th edition (Information Today, Inc., 2022). Included here are awards for outstanding librarianship or service, development grants, and research projects larger than an essay or monograph. Awards are listed alphabetically by organization.

American Association of School Librarians (AASL)

AASL/ABC-CLIO LEADERSHIP GRANT (up to $1,750). To AASL affiliates for planning and implementing leadership programs at state, regional, or local levels. Donor: ABC-CLIO. Winner: Oklahoma School Librarians, a division of the Oklahoma Library Association.

American Library Association (ALA)

ALA/INFORMATION TODAY, INC. LIBRARY OF THE FUTURE AWARD ($1,500). For a library, consortium, group of librarians, or support organization for innovative planning for, applications of, or development of patron training programs about information technology in a library setting. Donors: Information Today, Inc., and IIDA. Winner: Plano (Texas) Public Library for its innovative use of technology to provide one-on-one tech training to seniors, Brain Injury Network of Dallas club members, and ESL students.

BETA PHI MU AWARD ($1,000). For distinguished service in library education. Donor: Beta Phi Mu International Library and Information Science Honorary Society. Winner: Marcia Rapchak, teaching assistant professor, School of Computing and Information, University of Pittsburgh.

EQUALITY AWARD ($1,000). To an individual or group for an outstanding contribution that promotes equality in the library profession. Donor: Rowman & Littlefield. Winner: Joint Council of Librarians of Color.

ELIZABETH FUTAS CATALYST FOR CHANGE AWARD ($1,000). A biennial award to recognize a librarian who invests time and talent to make positive change in the profession of librarianship. Donor: Elizabeth Futas Memorial Fund. Winner (2020): Nora Wiltse.

GALE, A CENGAGE COMPANY, FINANCIAL DEVELOPMENT AWARD ($2,500). To a library organization for a financial development project to secure new funding resources for a public or academic library. Donor: Gale, a Cengage Company. Winner: Not awarded in 2021.

MARY V. GAVER SCHOLARSHIP ($3,000). To a student pursuing an MLS degree and specializing in youth services. Winner: Monet Raquel Hardison.

KEN HAYCOCK AWARD FOR PROMOTING LIBRARIANSHIP ($1,000). For significant contribution to public recognition and appreciation of librarianship through professional performance, teaching, or writing. Winner: Steven Yates, assistant director and assistant professor, School of Library and Infor-mation Studies (SLIS), University of Alabama.

JOHN AMES HUMPHRY/OCLC/FOREST PRESS AWARD ($1,000). To one or more individuals for significant contributions to international librarianship. Donor: OCLC/Forest Press. Winner: Janet Lee.

LEMONY SNICKET PRIZE FOR NOBLE LIBRARIANS FACED WITH ADVERSITY ($3,000 plus a $1,000 travel stipend to enable attendance at the ALA Annual Conference). To honor a librarian who has faced adversity with integrity and dignity intact. Sponsor: Lemony Snicket (author Daniel Handler). Winner: Janet Eldred, Hollidaysburg Area (Pennsylvania) Public Library.

JOSEPH W. LIPPINCOTT AWARD ($1,500). For distinguished service to the library profession. Donor: Joseph W. Lippincott III. Winner: Newlen Robert.

Association for Library Collections and Technical Services (ALCTS)

ROSS ATKINSON LIFETIME ACHIEVEMENT AWARD ($3,000). To recognize the contribution of an ALCTS member and library leader who has demonstrated exceptional service to ALCTS and its areas of interest. Donor: EBSCO. Winner: Not awarded in 2021.

ESTHER J. PIERCY AWARD ($1,500). To a librarian with no more than ten years' experience for contributions and leadership in the field of library collections and technical services. Donor: YBP Library Services. Winner: Not awarded in 2021.

Association for Library Service to Children (ALSC)

ALSC/BAKER & TAYLOR SUMMER READING PROGRAM GRANT ($3,000). For implementation of an outstanding public library summer reading program for children. Donor: Baker & Taylor. Winner: New Brunswick (New Jersey) Free Public Library.

ALSC/CANDLEWICK PRESS "LIGHT THE WAY: LIBRARY OUTREACH TO THE UNDERSERVED" GRANT ($3,000). To a library conducting exemplary outreach to underserved populations. Donor: Candlewick Press. Winner: Madison (Ohio) Public Library.

Association of College and Research Libraries (ACRL)

ACRL ACADEMIC OR RESEARCH LIBRARIAN OF THE YEAR AWARD ($5,000). For outstanding contribution to academic and research librarianship and library development. Donor: YBP Library Services. Winner: Julia M. Gelfand, University of California-Irvine.

ACRL/CLS INNOVATION IN COLLEGE LIBRARIANSHIP AWARD ($3,000). To academic librarians who show a capacity for innovation in the areas of programs, services, and operations; or creating innovations for library colleagues that facilitate their ability to better serve the library's community. Winner: Not awarded in 2021.

ACRL/EBSS DISTINGUISHED EDUCATION AND BEHAVIORAL SCIENCES LIBRARIAN AWARD ($2,500). To an academic librarian who has made an outstanding contribution as an education and/or behavioral sciences librarian through accomplishments and service to the profession. Donor: John Wiley & Sons. Winner: Kaya van Beynen, Associate Dean of Library Research & Instruction, University of South Florida.

EXCELLENCE IN ACADEMIC LIBRARIES AWARDS ($3,000). To recognize outstanding college and university libraries. Donor: YBP Library Services. Winners: (university) Loyola Marymount University, Santa Clara, California; (college) Davidson (North Carolina) College; (community college) Tulsa (Oklahoma) Community College.

INSTRUCTION SECTION INNOVATION AWARDS ($5,000). To librarians or project teams in recognition of a project that demonstrates creative, innovative, or unique approaches to information literacy instruction or programming. Donor: ProQuest. Winners: Alexandria Chisholm and Sarah Hartman-Caverly, Reference and Instruction Librarians, Penn State Berks, for their Digital Shred Privacy Literacy Initiative project.

Black Caucus of the American Library Association (BCALA)

DEMCO/BCALA EXCELLENCE IN LIBRARIANSHIP AWARD. To a librarian who has made significant contributions to promoting the status of African Americans in the library profession. Winner: Not awarded in 2021.

Ethnic and Multicultural Information and Exchange Round Table (EMIERT)

DAVID COHEN MULTICULTURAL AWARD ($300). To recognize articles of significant research and publication that increase understanding and promote multiculturalism in North American libraries. Donor: Routledge. Winners: Denice Adkins, Jenny Bossaller, Heather Moulaison Sandy, School of Information Science & Learning Technologies, University of Missouri.

EMIERT Distinguished Librarian Award. Given biennially to recognize significant accomplishments in library services that are national or international in scope and that include improving, spreading, and promoting multicultural librarianship. Winner: K.C. Boyd.

Library Leadership and Management Association (LLAMA)

JOHN COTTON DANA LIBRARY PUBLIC RELATIONS AWARDS ($10,000). To libraries or library organizations of all types for public relations programs or special projects ended during the preceding year. Donors: H. W. Wilson Foundation and EBSCO. Winners: Anchorage (Alaska) Public Library; Chicago (Illinois) Public Library; Cincinnati & Hamilton County (Ohio) Public Library; Edmonton (Alberta) Public Library; Fort Worth (Texas) Public Library; Los Angeles (California) County Library; Spartanburg County (South Carolina) Public Libraries; Whatcom County (Washington) Library System.

Public Library Association (PLA)

EBSCO EXCELLENCE IN SMALL AND/OR RURAL PUBLIC SERVICE AWARD ($1,000). Honors a library serving a population of 10,000 or fewer that demonstrates excellence of service to its community as exemplified by an overall service program or a special program of significant accomplishment. Donor: EBSCO. Winner: Not awarded in 2021.

ALLIE BETH MARTIN AWARD ($3,000). To honor a public librarian who has demonstrated extraordinary range and depth of knowledge about books or other library materials and has distinguished ability to share that knowledge. Donor: Baker & Taylor. Winner: Not awarded in 2021.

ROMANCE WRITERS OF AMERICA LIBRARY GRANT ($4,500). To a library to build or expand a fiction collection and/or host romance fiction programming. Donor: Romance Writers of America. Winner: Not awarded in 2021.

Reference and User Services Association (RUSA)

ISADORE GILBERT MUDGE AWARD ($5,000). For distinguished contributions to reference librarianship. Donor: Credo Reference. Winner: R. David Lankes, School of Information Science, University of South Carolina.

KEY TO SYMBOLS AND ABBREVIATIONS

KEY TO SYMBOLS

A - Armed Forces libraries
C - College and University libraries
E - Electronic libraries
G - Government libraries
J - Community College libraries
L - Law libraries
M - Medical libraries
P - Public and State libraries
R - Religious libraries
S - Special libraries
* - No response received directly from the library; data gathered from other sources
§ - New library and/or listed for the first time
† - Library school program accredited by the American Library Association Committee on Accreditation

KEY TO ABBREVIATIONS

A-tapes - Audio Tapes
Acad - Academic, Academy
Acctg - Accounting
Acq - Acquisition Librarian, Acquisitions
Actg - Acting
Ad - Adult Services Librarian
Add - Address
Admin - Administration, Administrative
Adminr - Administrator
Adv - Adviser, Advisor, Advisory
Advan - Advanced, Advancement
Aeronaut - Aeronautics
AFB - Air Force Base
Agr - Agricultural, Agriculture
Ala - Alabama
Alta - Alberta
Am - America, American
Ann - Annual, Annually
Anthrop - Anthropology
APO - Air Force Post Office, Army Post Office
Approp - Appropriation
Approx - Approximate, Approximately
Appt - Appointment
Archaeol - Archaeology
Archit - Architecture
Ariz - Arizona
Ark - Arkansas
Asn - Association
Assoc - Associate
Asst - Assistant
AV - Audiovisual, Audiovisual Materials
Ave - Avenue
BC - British Columbia
Bd - Binding, Bound
Behav - Behaviorial
Bibliog - Bibliographic, Bibliographical, Bibliography
Bibliogr - Bibliographer
Biog - Biographer, Biographical, Biography
Biol - Biology
Bk(s) - Book(s)
Bkmobile - Bookmobile
Bldg - Building
Blvd - Boulevard
Bot - Botany
Br - Branch, Branches
Bro - Brother
Bur - Bureau
Bus - Business
Calif - California
Can - Canada, Canadian
Cap - Capital
Cat(s) - Cataloging Librarian, Cataloging, Catalog(s)
Cent - Central
Ch - Children, Children's Librarian, Children's Services
Chem - Chemical, Chemistry
Chmn - Chairman
Cht(s) - Chart(s)
Circ - Circulation
Cler - Clerical Staff
Co - Company
Col - College
Coll - Collection, Collections
Colo - Colorado
Commun - Community
Comn - Commission
Comt - Committee
Conn - Connecticut
Conserv - Conservation
Consult - Consultant
Coop - Cooperates, Cooperating, Cooperation, Cooperative
Coord - Coordinating
Coordr - Coordinator
Corp - Corporation
Coun - Council
CP - Case Postale
Ct - Court
Ctr - Center, Centre
Curric - Curriculum
DC - District of Columbia
Del - Delaware
Den - Denominational
Dent - Dentristry
Dep - Deputy, Depository
Dept - Department
Develop - Development
Dir - Director
Div - Division
Doc - Document, Documents
Dr - Doctor, Drive
E - East
Econ - Economic
Ed - Edited, Edition, Editor
Educ - Education, Educational
Elem - Elementary
Eng - Engineering
Enrl - Enrollment
Ent - Entrance
Environ - Environmental
Equip - Equipment
Est - Estimate, Estimation
Estab - Established
Excl - Excluding
Exec - Executive
Exp - Expenditure
Ext - Extension of Telephone
Fac - Faculty, Facilities
Fed - Federal
Fedn - Federation
Fel - Fellowship
Fla - Florida
Flr - Floor
Found - Foundation
FPO - Fleet Post Office
Fr - French
Ft - Fort
FT - Full Time

FTE - Full Time Equivalent
Ga - Georgia
Gen - General, Generated
Geog - Geographical, Geography
Geol - Geological, Geology
Govt - Government
Grad - Graduate
Hist - Historical, History
Hort - Horticulture
Hq - Headquarters
Hrs - Hours
Hwy - Highway, Highways
Hydrol - Hydrology
Ill - Illinois
ILL - Interlibrary Loan
Illustr - Illustrator, Illustration
Inc - Income, Incorporated
Incl - Including
Ind - Indiana
Indust - Industrial, Industry
Info - Information
Ins - Insurance
Inst - Institute, Institutions
Instrul - Instructional
Instr - Instructor
Intl - International
Jr - Junior
Juv - Juvenile
Kans - Kansas
Ky - Kentucky
La - Louisiana
Lab - Laboratories, Laboratory
Lang(s) - Language(s)
Lectr - Lecturer
Legis - Legislative, Legislature
Libr - Libraries, Library
Librn - Librarian
Lit - Literary, Literature
Ltd - Limited
Mag(s) - Magazine(s)
Man - Manitoba
Mass - Massachusetts
Mat(s) - Material(s)
Math - Mathematical, Mathematics
Md - Maryland
Med - Medical, Medicine
Media - Media Specialist
Mem - Member
Metaphys - Metaphysical, Metaphysics
Metrop - Metropolitan
Mgr - Manager, Managerial
Mgt - Management
Mich - Michigan
Micro - Microform
Mil - Military
Misc - Miscellaneous
Miss - Mississippi
Minn - Minnesota
Mkt - Marketing
Mo - Missouri
Ms - Manuscript, Manuscripts
Mus - Museum
N - North
NASA - National Aeronautics & Space Administration
Nat - National
NB - New Brunswick
NC - North Carolina
NDak - North Dakota
NE - Northeast, Northeastern
Nebr - Nebraska
Nev - Nevada
New Eng - New England
Newsp - Newspaper, Newspapers
Nfld - Newfoundland
NH - New Hampshire
NJ - New Jersey
NMex - New Mexico
Nonfict - nonfiction
NS - Nova Scotia
NW - Northwest, Northwestern
NY - New York
Oceanog - Oceanography
Off - Office
Okla - Oklahoma
Ont - Ontario
OPAC - Open Public Access Catalog
Ore - Oregon
Ornith - Ornithology
Pa - Pennsylvania
Pac - Pacific
Partic - Participant, Participates
Per(s) - Periodical(s)
Pharm - Pharmacy
Philos - Philosophical, Philosophy
Photog - Photograph, Photography
Phys - Physical
Pkwy - Parkway
Pl - Place
PO - Post Office
Polit Sci - Political Science
Pop - Population
PR - Puerto Rico
Prep - Preparation, Preparatory
Pres - President, Presidents
Presv - Preservation
Proc - Process, Processing
Prof - Professional, Professor
Prog - Program, Programming
Prov - Province, Provincial
Psychiat - Psychiatrist, Psychiatry, Psychiatric
Psychol - Psychological, Psychology
PT - Part Time
Pub - Public
Pub Rel - Public Relations Head
Publ(s) - Publisher, Publishing, Publication(s)
Pvt - Private
Qtr - Quarter
Que - Quebec
R&D - Research & Development
Rd - Road
Read - Readable
Rec - Record, Recording, Records
Ref - Reference
Relig - Religion, Religious
Rep - Representative
Reprod - Reproduction
Req - Requirement
Res - Research, Resource, Resources
RI - Rhode Island
Rm - Room
Rpt(s) - Report(s)
RR - Rural Route
Rte - Route
S - South
Sal - Salary
SAN - Standard Address Number
Sask - Saskatchewan
SC - South Carolina
Sch - School
Sci - Science, Scientific
Sci Fict - Science Fiction
SDak - South Dakota
SE - Southeast, Southeastern
Secy - Secretary
Sem - Semester, Seminary
Ser - Serials, Serials Librarian
Serv(s) - Service(s)
Soc - Social, Society, Societies
Sociol - Sociology
Spec - Special, Specialist
Sq - Square
Sr - Senor, Senior, Sister
St - Saint, Street
Sta - Station
Sub(s) - Subscription(s)
Subj - Subject, Subjects
Sup - Supplies
Supv - Supervising, Supervision
Supvr - Supervisor
Supvry - Supervisory
SW - Southwest, Southwestern
Syst - System, Systems
TDD - Telecomm. Device for the Deaf
Tech - Technical, Technician, Technology
Tel - Telephone
Tenn - Tennessee
Tex - Texas
Theol - Theological, Theology
Tpk - Turnpike
Treas - Treasurer
TTY - Teletypewriter
TV - Television
UN - United Nations
Undergrad - Undergraduate
Univ - University
US - United States
VPres -Vice President
V-tapes - Video Tapes
Va - Virginia
Vet - Veteran
VF - Vertical Files
VI - Virgin Islands
Vis - Visiting
Vols - Volumes, Volunteers
Vt - Vermont
W - West
Wash - Washington
Wis - Wisconsin
WVa - West Virginia
Wyo - Wyoming
YA - Young Adult Librarian, Young Adult Services
Zool - Zoology

75TH EDITION

AMERICAN LIBRARY DIRECTORY™

2022-2023

LIBRARIES IN THE UNITED STATES

ALABAMA

Date of Statistics: FY 2020
Population, 2020 U.S. Census: 4,921,532
Population Served by Public Libraries: 4,921,532
Total Volumes in Public Libraries: 21,477,980
Volumes Per Capita: 4.36
Total Public Library Circulation: 20,623,917
Circulation Per Capita: 3.14
Income and Expenditures:
Total Public Library Income: $114,400,939
Source of Income: Mainly public funds
Expenditures Per Capita: $21.96
Number of County & Multi-county Public Library Systems: 15
Counties Served: 67
Grants-in-Aid to Public Libraries:
State: $5,428,505
Federal: $986,090
Information provided courtesy of: Stephanie Taylor, Library Consultant; Alabama Public Library Service

ABBEVILLE

P ABBEVILLE MEMORIAL LIBRARY*, 301 Kirkland St, 36310. SAN 330-2822. Tel: 334-585-2818. FAX: 334-585-2819. E-mail: abbevillelibrary@gmail.com. Web Site: www.abbevillelibrary.org. *Dir*, Paul McNamara
Library Holdings: Bk Vols 25,534
Automation Activity & Vendor Info: (Cataloging) Book Systems; (Circulation) Book Systems; (OPAC) Book Systems
Wireless access
Open Mon, Wed & Fri 9-5, Tues & Thurs 10-6
Friends of the Library Group

ADAMSVILLE

P ADAMSVILLE PUBLIC LIBRARY, 4825 Main St, 35005-1947. (Mail add: PO Box 309, 35005-0309), SAN 376-7620. Tel: 205-674-3399. FAX: 205-674-5405. Web Site: adamsville.lib.al.us. *Dir*, Sandra Vatani; E-mail: svatani@bham.lib.al.us; Staff 1 (MLS 1)
Library Holdings: Bk Vols 14,000
Wireless access
Function: 24/7 Online cat, Audiobks on Playaways & MP3, Audiobks via web, Bks on CD, Computers for patron use, E-Readers, Free DVD rentals, Genealogy discussion group, Homework prog, ILL available, Instruction & testing, Internet access, Magazines, Music CDs, Notary serv, Online cat, Outside serv via phone, mail, e-mail & web, OverDrive digital audio bks, Photocopying/Printing, Printer for laptops & handheld devices, Scanner, Tax forms, Wheelchair accessible
Open Mon-Fri 9-5

AKRON

P AKRON PUBLIC LIBRARY*, 207 First Ave S, 35441. (Mail add: PO Box 8, 35441-0008), SAN 300-0001. Tel: 205-372-3148. FAX: 205-372-3198. E-mail: townofakron2013@gmail.com. *Interim Dir*, Diann Taylor; Staff 14 (MLS 5, Non-MLS 9)
Pop 356
Library Holdings: Bk Vols 1,000; Per Subs 10
Open Mon-Thurs 10-4

ALABASTER

P ALBERT L SCOTT LIBRARY*, 100 Ninth St NW, 35007-9172. SAN 371-9332. Tel: 205-664-6822. FAX: 205-664-6839. Web Site: cityofalabaster.com/221/Library. *Dir*, Nan Abbott; E-mail: nabbott@shelbycounty-al.org; Staff 8 (MLS 4, Non-MLS 4)
Pop 31,545; Circ 164,504
Library Holdings: Per Subs 117; Talking Bks 1,658; Videos 534
Special Collections: Alabama Coll
Subject Interests: Cooking, Decorating, Gardening, Local hist
Automation Activity & Vendor Info: (Circulation) Innovative Interfaces, Inc; (OPAC) Innovative Interfaces, Inc
Wireless access
Function: 24/7 Online cat, Activity rm, Adult bk club, After school storytime
Mem of Harrison Regional Library System
Open Mon, Tues & Thurs 9-7:50, Wed 10-5:50, Fri 9-5:50, Sat 10-4:50, Sun 1-4:50
Friends of the Library Group

ALBERTVILLE

P ALBERTVILLE PUBLIC LIBRARY*, 200 Jackson St, 35950. (Mail add: PO Box 430, 35950-0008), SAN 300-001X. Tel: 256-891-8290. FAX: 256-891-8295. Web Site: www.albertvillelibrary.org. *Dir*, Reagan Deason; E-mail: rdeason@albertvillelibrary.org; *Circ*, Teri Barnard; Staff 5 (MLS 1, Non-MLS 4)
Pop 80,000; Circ 150,095
Library Holdings: Bk Titles 85,000; Per Subs 100
Special Collections: Civil War Coll; Rare Books Room; War Between the States
Automation Activity & Vendor Info: (Cataloging) Book Systems; (Circulation) Book Systems; (OPAC) Book Systems
Mem of Marshall County Cooperative Library
Open Mon 10-7, Tues-Fri 8-5, Sat 9-1
Friends of the Library Group

ALEXANDER CITY

J CENTRAL ALABAMA COMMUNITY COLLEGE*, Learning Resources Center, 1675 Cherokee Rd, 35010. SAN 330-0005. Tel: 256-234-6346. Circulation Tel: 256-215-4290. FAX: 256-234-0384. Web Site: www.cacc.edu. *Librn*, Denita Oliver; Tel: 256-215-4293, E-mail: doliver@cacc.edu; *Cat, Ref (Info Servs)*, Marty Cook; Tel: 256-215-4291, E-mail: mcook@cacc.edu; Staff 3 (MLS 1, Non-MLS 2)
Founded 1965. Enrl 2,000; Fac 60; Highest Degree: Associate
Library Holdings: CDs 71; DVDs 71; e-books 8,601; Bk Titles 19,625; Bk Vols 11,024; Per Subs 52
Special Collections: Alabama & Local History (Alabama Room)
Automation Activity & Vendor Info: (Cataloging) Follett Software; (Circulation) Follett Software; (OPAC) Follett Software
Wireless access
Open Mon-Thurs 7:30am-7pm, Fri 7:30am-11:30am
Friends of the Library Group
Departmental Libraries:
CHILDERSBURG CAMPUS LIBRARY, 34091 US Hwy 280, Childersburg, 35044, SAN 370-4548. Tel: 256-378-2041. FAX: 256-378-2040. *Librn*, Deborah Waller; Tel: 256-378-5576, Ext 2041; Staff 2 (MLS 1, Non-MLS 1)
Founded 1989. Enrl 2,365; Fac 75; Highest Degree: Associate
Library Holdings: CDs 55; DVDs 55; e-books 8,600; Per Subs 60; Videos 246
Open Mon-Thurs 7:30-7, Fri 7:30-11:30
Restriction: Open to students, fac & staff

P ADELIA M RUSSELL LIBRARY*, 318 Church St, 35010-2516. SAN 376-5601. Tel: 256-329-6796. FAX: 256-329-6797. Web Site: alexandercityal.gov/library. *Dir,* Amy Huff; E-mail: amy.huff@alexandercityal.gov
Library Holdings: Bk Vols 38,000; Per Subs 87
Automation Activity & Vendor Info: (Cataloging) Book Systems; (Circulation) Book Systems; (OPAC) Book Systems
Wireless access
Mem of Horseshoe Bend Regional Library
Open Mon-Fri 8:30-5, Sat 9-1
Branches: 1
MAMIE'S PLACE CHILDREN'S LIBRARY & LEARNING CENTER, 284 Church St, 35010. Tel: 256-234-4644. *Ch,* Kathryn Reed
Library Holdings: Bk Vols 400,000
Open Mon-Thurs 8-7, Fri 8-5, Sat 8-12

ALICEVILLE

P ALICEVILLE PUBLIC LIBRARY, 416 Third Ave N, 35442. SAN 300-0028. Tel: 205-373-6691. FAX: 205-373-3731. E-mail: apl@nctv.com. Web Site: alicevillelibrary.wordpress.com. *Dir,* Melanie Wood
Founded 1955. Pop 3,227; Circ 12,000
Library Holdings: Bk Titles 20,000
Automation Activity & Vendor Info: (Acquisitions) Follett Software; (Cataloging) Follett Software; (Circulation) Follett Software; (ILL) OCLC WorldShare Interlibrary Loan
Wireless access
Function: ILL available, Music CDs, Photocopying/Printing, Prog for children & young adult, Summer reading prog, Tax forms, VHS videos
Mem of Pickens County Cooperative Library
Open Mon-Wed & Fri 10-5, Thurs 1-7
Friends of the Library Group

ANDALUSIA

P ANDALUSIA PUBLIC LIBRARY*, 212 S Three Notch St, 36420. SAN 300-0036. Tel: 334-222-6612. FAX: 334-222-6612. Web Site: www.cityofandalusia.com/leisure-services/library.html. *Dir,* Karin Taylor; E-mail: Karin.Taylor@cityofandalusia.com; *Ch Serv,* Betty Harrelson; *Ref (Info Servs),* La Ferne D Griggs; *Tech Serv,* Joan Herring
Founded 1920. Pop 8,000; Circ 50,000
Library Holdings: Bk Titles 53,000; Per Subs 48
Special Collections: American Ancestors, bks, micro; One Hundred Years of County Newspapers, micro. Oral History
Automation Activity & Vendor Info: (Acquisitions) TLC (The Library Corporation); (Cataloging) TLC (The Library Corporation); (Circulation) TLC (The Library Corporation); (OPAC) TLC (The Library Corporation)
Open Mon-Fri 8-5, Sat 8-12

J LURLEEN B WALLACE COMMUNITY COLLEGE LIBRARY*, 1000 Dannelly Blvd, 36420. (Mail add: PO Box 1418, 36420-1418), SAN 300-0044. Tel: 334-881-2265. Interlibrary Loan Service Tel: 334-881-2269. Administration Tel: 334-881-2266. FAX: 334-881-2300. Web Site: www.lbwcc.edu/library.aspx. *Dir, Learning Res,* Hugh Carter; E-mail: hcarter@lbwcc.edu; Staff 2 (MLS 1, Non-MLS 1)
Founded 1969. Enrl 1,585; Fac 51; Highest Degree: Associate
Oct 2013-Sept 2014 Income $298,855. Mats Exp $37,490, Books $12,965, Per/Ser (Incl. Access Fees) $17,000, AV Mat $7,525
Library Holdings: AV Mats 1,331; e-books 25,299; Bk Titles 33,774; Bk Vols 39,616
Special Collections: Alabama Coll; LBW Community College Archives
Automation Activity & Vendor Info: (Acquisitions) Auto-Graphics, Inc; (Cataloging) Auto-Graphics, Inc; (Circulation) Auto-Graphics, Inc; (Course Reserve) Auto-Graphics, Inc; (ILL) Auto-Graphics, Inc; (Media Booking) Auto-Graphics, Inc; (OPAC) Auto-Graphics, Inc; (Serials) Auto-Graphics, Inc
Wireless access
Publications: Annual Report
Partic in LYRASIS
Open Mon-Thurs 7:45am-8pm, Fri 8-Noon

ANNISTON

M NORTHEAST ALABAMA REGIONAL MEDICAL CENTER*, William Bruce Mitchell Medical Library, 400 E Tenth St, 36207. SAN 324-5950. Tel: 256-235-5224. Web Site: rmccares.org/hospitals/rmc-anniston. *Coordr,* Donna Black; E-mail: dblack@rmccares.org
Founded 1940
Library Holdings: e-books 50; e-journals 52; Per Subs 3
Wireless access
Special Services for the Deaf - ADA equip
Restriction: Staff use only

R PARKER MEMORIAL BAPTIST CHURCH LIBRARY, 1205 Quintard Ave, 36207. (Mail add: PO Box 2140, 36202), SAN 300-0052. Tel: 256-236-5628. FAX: 256-236-5441. E-mail: kaparkermemorial@gmail.com. Web Site: parkermemorial.com.
Founded 1951
Library Holdings: Bk Vols 7,500
Wireless access

P PUBLIC LIBRARY OF ANNISTON-CALHOUN COUNTY*, 108 E Tenth St, 36201. SAN 330-003X. Tel: 256-237-8501. FAX: 256-238-0474. E-mail: library@publiclibrary.cc. Web Site: www.anniston.lib.al.us. *Dir,* Teresa Kiser; E-mail: tkiser@publiclibrary.cc; *Spec Coll Librn,* Tom Mullins; E-mail: alroom@publiclibrary.cc; *Bus Mgr,* Angie White; E-mail: awhite@publiclibrary.cc; *Adult Serv,* Beth Cason; E-mail: bcason@publiclibrary.cc; Staff 19 (MLS 4, Non-MLS 15)
Founded 1965. Pop 75,527; Circ 171,995
Oct 2016-Sept 2017 Income (Main & Associated Libraries) $835,652, State $66,487, City $550,000, County $107,065, Locally Generated Income $112,100
Library Holdings: Audiobooks 2,087; AV Mats 57,642; CDs 2,087; DVDs 3,696; e-books 29,171; Electronic Media & Resources 60; Bk Vols 85,896; Per Subs 225
Special Collections: Alabama History; Andrea Coll (Alabama Room); Anniston Room Coll; Genealogy (Alabama Room)
Subject Interests: Genealogy, Local hist
Automation Activity & Vendor Info: (Cataloging) ByWater Solutions; (Circulation) ByWater Solutions; (OPAC) ByWater Solutions
Wireless access
Function: 24/7 Electronic res, 24/7 Online cat, Activity rm, Adult bk club, Archival coll
Publications: Serendipity (Newsletter)
Open Mon-Fri 8:30-6, Sat & Sun 1:30-5
Friends of the Library Group
Branches: 1
CARVER BRANCH, 722 W 14th St, 36201, SAN 330-0099. Tel: 256-237-7271. FAX: 256-237-7271. E-mail: carver@publiclibrary.cc. *Librn,* Lillie Brown; E-mail: lbrownpubliclibrary.cc
Open Tues-Thurs 12:30-5
Friends of the Library Group
Bookmobiles: 1. Librn, Linda Levens. Bk vols 5,542

ARAB

P ARAB PUBLIC LIBRARY, 325 Second St NW, 35016-1999. SAN 300-0060. Tel: 256-586-3366. FAX: 256-586-5638. E-mail: library@arabcity.org. Web Site: www.arabpubliclibrary.com. *Dir,* Tanya Alexander; Staff 7 (Non-MLS 7)
Founded 1963. Circ 71,269
Library Holdings: CDs 1,600; DVDs 1,900; Bk Vols 50,000; Per Subs 40
Subject Interests: Alabama, Civil War
Automation Activity & Vendor Info: (Cataloging) Book Systems; (Circulation) Book Systems; (OPAC) Book Systems
Wireless access
Function: 24/7 Electronic res, 24/7 Online cat, Accelerated reader prog, Archival coll, Audiobks via web, Bks on CD, Children's prog, Computers for patron use, Free DVD rentals, ILL available, Internet access, Magazines, Magnifiers for reading, Meeting rooms, Music CDs, Online cat, Preschool reading prog, Story hour, Summer & winter reading prog, Summer reading prog, Winter reading prog
Open Mon-Wed & Fri 10-5, Sat 10-2
Friends of the Library Group

ARLEY

P ARLEY PUBLIC LIBRARY, 6788 Hwy 41, 35541. (Mail add: PO Box 146, 35541), SAN 300-0079. Tel: 205-387-0129. FAX: 205-384-0031. E-mail: arleypubliclibrary@gmail.com. *Librn,* Jennifer Stewart
Founded 1974
Library Holdings: Bk Vols 3,800
Wireless access
Mem of Carl Elliott Regional Library System
Open Mon-Fri 10-5

ASHLAND

P ASHLAND CITY LIBRARY*, 113 Second Ave N, 36251. (Mail add: PO Box 296, 36251-0296), SAN 376-561X. Tel: 256-354-3427. FAX: 256-354-3427. E-mail: ashlibrary@centurytel.net. Web Site: www.cityofashlandal.com/library. *Librn,* Tina Nolen
Library Holdings: Bk Vols 14,000
Automation Activity & Vendor Info: (Cataloging) Follett Software; (Circulation) Follett Software
Wireless access
Mem of Cheaha Regional Library
Open Mon-Fri 9-5
Friends of the Library Group

ASHVILLE

P ASHVILLE PUBLIC LIBRARY*, 195 Sixth Ave, 35953. (Mail add: PO Box 187, 35953), SAN 330-3241. Tel: 205-594-7954. E-mail: ashvillepubliclibrary@gmail.com. Web Site: www.ashvillepubliclibrary.org. *Librn,* Paula Ballard
Library Holdings: Bk Vols 16,000
Wireless access
Open Tues-Fri 10-5:30

ATHENS

P ATHENS-LIMESTONE PUBLIC LIBRARY*, 603 S Jefferson St, 35611. SAN 300-0087. Tel: 256-232-1233. FAX: 256-232-1250. E-mail: librarydirector@alcpl.org. Web Site: www.ALCPL.org. *Actg Dir,* Laura Poe; Staff 9 (MLS 3, Non-MLS 6)
Founded 1970. Pop 90,787
Oct 2015-Sept 2016 Income $521,825, State $70,000, City $130,000, County $80,000, Locally Generated Income $156,825, Other $85,000. Mats Exp $28,000, Books $2,000, Electronic Ref Mat (Incl. Access Fees) $6,000, Presv $20,000. Sal $52,528
Automation Activity & Vendor Info: (Acquisitions) Innovative Interfaces, Inc; (Cataloging) Innovative Interfaces, Inc; (Circulation) Innovative Interfaces, Inc; (OPAC) Innovative Interfaces, Inc
Wireless access
Function: Activity rm, Adult bk club, Art exhibits, Audiobks via web, AV serv, Bk club(s), Bks on CD, Children's prog, Computer training, Computers for patron use, E-Readers, E-Reserves, Free DVD rentals, Homebound delivery serv, Homework prog, ILL available, Instruction & testing, Internet access, Life-long learning prog for all ages, Magazines, Mail & tel request accepted, Movies, Notary serv, Online cat, OverDrive digital audio bks, Photocopying/Printing, Preschool outreach, Preschool reading prog, Prog for adults, Prog for children & young adult, Ref & res, Ref serv available, Senior computer classes, Spanish lang bks, Spoken cassettes & CDs, Spoken cassettes & DVDs, Story hour, Study rm, Summer reading prog, Teen prog, Telephone ref, Wheelchair accessible, Workshops, Writing prog
Special Services for the Deaf - Bks on deafness & sign lang; Closed caption videos
Special Services for the Blind - Bks on CD; Home delivery serv; Large print bks; Ref serv
Open Mon, Wed & Fri 10-5, Tues & Thurs 10-8, Sat 10-4
Friends of the Library Group

C ATHENS STATE UNIVERSITY, Kares Library, 407 E Pryor St, 35611. (Mail add: 300 N Beaty St, 35611), SAN 300-0095. Tel: 256-216-6650. FAX: 256-216-6674. E-mail: refdesk@athens.edu. Web Site: www.athens.edu/library. *Dir,* Toni Carter; Tel: 256-216-6659; *Acq & Coll Develop Librn,* Jennifer Williams; Tel: 256-216-6667, E-mail: jennifer.williams@athens.edu; *Cat Librn,* Mary Aquila; E-mail: mary.aquila@athens.edu; *Ref Librn,* Jennifer Wolfe; Tel: 256-216-6668, E-mail: jennifer.wolfe@athens.edu; *Circ Supvr,* Amber Skantz; Tel: 256-216-6664, E-mail: Amber.Skantz@athens.edu; *Circ, ILL, Libr Support Spec,* Robby King; Tel: 256-216-6662, E-mail: Robby.King@athens.edu; *Univ Archivist,* Dakota Cotton; Tel: 256-216-6663, E-mail: dakota.cotton@athens.edu; Staff 8 (MLS 5, Non-MLS 3)
Founded 1842. Enrl 3,947; Fac 86; Highest Degree: Master
Library Holdings: e-books 92,000; Bk Vols 123,000; Per Subs 317
Subject Interests: Local hist, Rare bks
Automation Activity & Vendor Info: (Cataloging) Innovative Interfaces, Inc; (Circulation) Innovative Interfaces, Inc; (ILL) OCLC; (OPAC) Innovative Interfaces, Inc
Wireless access
Partic in LYRASIS; Network of Alabama Academic Libraries; OCLC Online Computer Library Center, Inc
Open Mon-Thurs 8am-9pm, Fri 8-5, Sun 1-9

ATMORE

P ATMORE PUBLIC LIBRARY, 700 E Church St, 36502. SAN 330-0153. Tel: 251-368-5234. FAX: 251-368-7064. E-mail: atmorelibrary@gmail.com. Web Site: www.atmorepubliclibrary.com. *Dir,* Hope Lassiter; E-mail: director@atmorelibrary.com; Staff 1 (MLS 1)
Founded 1923. Pop 15,000; Circ 54,927
Library Holdings: Bk Titles 50,000; Per Subs 54
Special Collections: Cancer & Heart Coll; Forestry (Atmores Industries Coll); Scout Books Coll
Automation Activity & Vendor Info: (Cataloging) Follett Software; (Circulation) Follett Software; (OPAC) Follett Software
Wireless access
Mem of Escambia County Cooperative Library System
Open Mon-Fri 8-5, Sat 9-1
Friends of the Library Group

P ESCAMBIA COUNTY COOPERATIVE LIBRARY SYSTEM*, 700 E Church St, 36502. SAN 324-0754. Tel: 251-368-4130. E-mail: escolib@frontiernet.net. Web Site: www.escambiacountylibrary.com. *Adminr,* Geri Lynn Albritton; Staff 2 (Non-MLS 2)
Founded 1980
Library Holdings: Bk Vols 10,000; Per Subs 14
Function: Homebound delivery serv
Member Libraries: Atmore Public Library; Brewton Public Library; Flomaton Public Library
Special Services for the Blind - Talking bks
Open Mon-Fri 7:30-3:30

ATTALLA

P ATTALLA-ETOWAH COUNTY PUBLIC LIBRARY, 604 N Fourth St, 35954. SAN 300-0109. Tel: 256-538-9266. FAX: 256-538-9223. Web Site: www.attallacity.org/attalla-public-library-2. *Dir,* Renae Bush; E-mail: renaebush20@gmail.com; *Asst Librn,* Connie Beddingfield
Founded 1967. Pop 8,000; Circ 14,284
Library Holdings: Bk Vols 26,000; Per Subs 72
Wireless access
Open Mon-Fri 9-5

AUBURN

P AUBURN PUBLIC LIBRARY, 749 E Thach Ave, 36830. SAN 300-0117. Tel: 334-501-3190. Reference Tel: 334-501-3195. E-mail: weblibrary@auburnalabama.org. Web Site: www.auburnalabama.org/library. *Libr Dir,* Tyler Whitten; E-mail: twhitten@auburnalabama.org; *Pub Serv,* Samantha Godsy; E-mail: sgodsy@auburnalabama.org; Staff 9 (MLS 5, Non-MLS 4)
Pop 42,987; Circ 167,338
Library Holdings: AV Mats 2,608; High Interest/Low Vocabulary Bk Vols 62; Large Print Bks 5,000; Bk Vols 70,000; Per Subs 135; Talking Bks 850
Special Collections: English as a Second Language
Automation Activity & Vendor Info: (Cataloging) Innovative Interfaces, Inc; (Circulation) Innovative Interfaces, Inc; (OPAC) Innovative Interfaces, Inc
Wireless access
Function: AV serv, ILL available, Magnifiers for reading, Photocopying/Printing, Prog for children & young adult, Ref serv available, Summer reading prog, Telephone ref, Wheelchair accessible
Publications: What's New? (Newsletter)
Mem of Horseshoe Bend Regional Library
Special Services for the Blind - Aids for in-house use; Assistive/Adapted tech devices, equip & products; Bks available with recordings; Bks on cassette; Bks on CD; Computer with voice synthesizer for visually impaired persons; Copier with enlargement capabilities; HP Scan Jet with photo-finish software; Info on spec aids & appliances; Large print bks; Large screen computer & software; Networked computers with assistive software; PC for people with disabilities; Reader equip; Screen enlargement software for people with visual disabilities; Screen reader software; Talking bks
Open Mon-Thurs 8:30-8, Fri & Sat 8:30-5, Sun 1-6
Friends of the Library Group

AUBURN UNIVERSITY
C RALPH BROWN DRAUGHON LIBRARY*, 231 Mell St, 36849. Tel: 334-844-4500. Circulation Tel: 334-844-1701. Interlibrary Loan Service Tel: 334-844-1728. Reference Tel: 334-844-1737. Administration Tel: 334-844-1741. Toll Free Tel: 800-446-0387. FAX: 334-844-4424. Web Site: www.lib.auburn.edu/. *Dean, Libr Serv,* Bonnie MacEwan; Tel: 334-844-1715, E-mail: macewbj@auburn.edu; *Asst Dean, Coll Develop,* Glenn Anderson; *Head, Acq,* Paula Sullenger; Tel: 334-844-1725; *Head Archivist, Head, Spec Coll,* Dwayne Cox; Tel: 334-844-1707; *Head, Syst,* Aaron Trehub; Tel: 334-844-1716, E-mail: trehuaj@auburn.edu; *Outreach Serv Librn,* Linda Thornton; *Mgr,* Bob Yerkey; Tel: 334-844-2704; *Cat,* Helen Goldman; Tel: 334-844-0241; *Circ, Reserves,* Susan Hinds; Tel: 334-844-1579; *Digital Serv,* Gary Hawkins; *Doc Delivery,* Pambanisha King. Subject Specialists: *Bus,* Bob Yerkey; Staff 47 (MLS 47)
Founded 1856. Enrl 23,547; Fac 1,142; Highest Degree: Doctorate
Library Holdings: e-books 285,137; e-journals 13,850; Bk Vols 3,016,986; Per Subs 36,395
Special Collections: Alabama Coll; Architecture Coll, slides; Auburn University Coll; US Government Publications; USGS Map Reference Coll. US Document Depository
Subject Interests: Genealogy, Relig hist, Sports
Automation Activity & Vendor Info: (Acquisitions) Ex Libris Group; (Cataloging) Ex Libris Group; (Circulation) Ex Libris Group; (Course Reserve) Docutek; (ILL) Ex Libris Group; (OPAC) Ex Libris Group; (Serials) Ex Libris Group
Partic in Association of Research Libraries; CAS Online; LYRASIS; NAAL; Nat Ground Water; National Network of Libraries of Medicine

Region 2; Network of Alabama Academic Libraries; Proquest Dialog; Research Libraries Information Network; SDC Info Servs; USDC
Open Mon-Thurs 7:45-2, Fri 7:45am-9pm, Sat 9-9, Sun 1pm-2am

C THE LIBRARY OF ARCHITECTURE, DESIGN & CONSTRUCTION*, Dudley Hall Commons, 36849. Tel: 334-844-1752. FAX: 334-844-1756. Web Site: www.lib.auburn.edu/architecture/. *Librn,* Boyd Childress
Library Holdings: Bk Vols 36,500
Open Mon-Thurs 7:45am-Midnight, Fri 7:45-5, Sat 9-6, Sun 1-Midnight

CM VETERINARY MEDICAL*, 101 Greene Hall, 36849-5606. Tel: 334-844-1749. Administration Tel: 334-844-1750. FAX: 334-844-1758. *Librn,* Bob Buchanan; E-mail: buchara@auburn.edu; Staff 3 (MLS 1, Non-MLS 2)
Library Holdings: Bk Vols 30,000
Partic in National Network of Libraries of Medicine Region 2
Open Mon-Thurs 7:30am-10:30pm, Fri 7:30-6, Sat 10-2, Sun 1-10:30

G UNITED STATES FOREST SERVICE, Forest Engineering Research Library, George W Andrews Forestry Sciences Lab, 521 Devall Dr, 36849-5418. SAN 373-3777. Tel: 334-826-8700, Ext 123. FAX: 334-821-0037. Web Site: srs.fs.usda.gov/forestops. *Project Leader,* Dana Mitchell; E-mail: dana.mitchell@usda.gov
Library Holdings: Bk Vols 12,000
Special Collections: Foreign publications; Forest Engineering; Forest operations literature
Subject Interests: Forestry
Open Mon-Fri 8-4:30

BAY MINETTE

P BAY MINETTE PUBLIC LIBRARY, 205 W Second St, 36507. SAN 300-0133. Tel: 251-580-1648. FAX: 251-937-0339. Web Site: www.cityofbayminette.org/Library. *Libr Dir,* Joanna M Bailey; E-mail: jbailey@ci.bay-minette.al.us; Staff 7 (Non-MLS 7)
Founded 1922. Pop 8,000; Circ 25,000
Library Holdings: Bk Vols 36,000; Per Subs 60
Subject Interests: Alabama, Genealogy
Automation Activity & Vendor Info: (Acquisitions) TLC (The Library Corporation); (Cataloging) TLC (The Library Corporation); (Circulation) TLC (The Library Corporation)
Mem of Baldwin County Library Cooperative, Inc
Open Mon-Fri 9-6, Sat 10-2
Friends of the Library Group

J COASTAL ALABAMA COMMUNITY COLLEGE*, Austin R Meadows Library, 1900 Hwy 31 S, 36507. SAN 300-0141. Tel: 251-580-2145. Web Site: www.coastalalabama.edu/students/library/bay_minettefairhopegulf_shores. *Dir, Libr Serv,* Ms Rheena Elmore; Tel: 251-580-2159, E-mail: rheena.elmore@coastalalabama.edu; Staff 5 (MLS 1, Non-MLS 4)
Founded 1965. Enrl 4,500; Fac 120; Highest Degree: Associate
Library Holdings: AV Mats 2,500; Bks on Deafness & Sign Lang 30; High Interest/Low Vocabulary Bk Vols 30; Bk Titles 65,815; Bk Vols 68,343; Per Subs 200
Special Collections: Baldwin Coll
Automation Activity & Vendor Info: (Cataloging) Book Systems; (Circulation) Book Systems; (OPAC) Book Systems
Wireless access
Open Mon-Thurs 7:30am-8:30pm, Fri 7:30-3:30

Departmental Libraries:

ATMORE CAMPUS LIBRARY, 2967 AL Hwy 21, Atmore, 36502. Tel: 251-368-7610, 251-809-1594. *Dir, Libr Serv,* Jeffrey Faust; Tel: 251-809-1581, E-mail: jeffrey.faust@coastalalabama.edu
Open Mon-Thurs 7:30-5, Fri 7:30-1:30

FAIRHOPE LEARNING RESOURCES CENTER, 440 Fairhope Ave, Fairhope, 36532. Tel: 251-580-2159, 251-990-0420. *Dir, Libr Serv,* Ms Rheena Elmore; E-mail: rheena.elmore@coastalalabama.edu
Open Mon-Thurs 8-8, Fri 8-4

JOHN DENNIS FORTE LIBRARY, 2800 S Alabama Ave, Monroeville, 36460, SAN 300-1547. Tel: 251-575-8207. *Dir, Libr Serv,* Alisha Linam; Tel: 251-575-8271, E-mail: alisha.linam@coastalalabama.edu
Founded 1965. Enrl 1,218
Library Holdings: Bk Vols 34,741; Per Subs 36
Special Collections: Alabamiana Coll; Professional Coll
Subject Interests: Careers
Automation Activity & Vendor Info: (Cataloging) Book Systems; (Circulation) Book Systems
Open Mon-Thurs 7:30-5, Fri 7:30-1:30

GULF SHORES LEARNING RESOURCES CENTER, 3301 Gulf Shores Pkwy, Gulf Shores, 35642. Tel: 251-580-2159, 251-968-3104. *Dir, Libr Serv,* Ms Rheena Elmore; E-mail: rheena.elmore@coastalalabama.edu
Open Mon-Thurs 8-8, Fri 8-4

LEIGH LIBRARY, 220 Alco Dr, Brewton, 36426, SAN 300-0508. Tel: 251-809-1584. *Dir, Libr Serv,* Jeffrey Faust; Tel: 251-809-1581, E-mail: jeffrey.faust@coastalalabama.edu; *Tech Serv,* Kim Coale; Tel: 251-809-1582, E-mail: kim.coale@coastalalabama.edu; Staff 3 (MLS 2, Non-MLS 1)
Founded 1965. Enrl 1,200
Library Holdings: Bk Titles 33,500; Per Subs 218
Special Collections: Alabama Coll
Automation Activity & Vendor Info: (OPAC) LibraryWorld, Inc
Function: ILL available
Partic in National Network of Libraries of Medicine Region 2
Open Mon-Thurs 7:30-7, Fri 7:30-1:30

H PAT LINDSAY LIBRARY, 251 College St, Gilbertown, 36908. Tel: 334-843-4427. *Dir, Libr Serv,* Alisha Linam; E-mail: alisha.linam@coastalalabama.edu
Library Holdings: Bk Vols 33,500; Per Subs 60
Open Mon-Thurs 9-5

KATHRYN TUCKER WINDHAM LIBRARY & MUSEUM, 30755 Hwy 43, Thomasville, 36784-2519, SAN 322-8827. Tel: 334-637-3147. *Dir, Libr Serv,* Alisha Linam; E-mail: alisha.linam@coastalalabama.edu; *Librn,* Deborah Robinson; Tel: 334-637-3146; Staff 4 (MLS 2, Non-MLS 2)
Enrl 1,100; Fac 40
Library Holdings: Bk Vols 47,000; Per Subs 60
Open Mon-Thurs 7:30-5, Fri 7:30-1:30

BESSEMER

P BESSEMER PUBLIC LIBRARY, 400 19th St N, 35020. SAN 300-0168. Tel: 205-428-7882. FAX: 205-428-5479. E-mail: bessemerlibrary@gmail.com. Web Site: www.bessemer.lib.al.us. *Libr Dir,* Venedia Wallace; E-mail: vwallace@bham.lib.al.us; *Adult Serv,* Deidre Sims; Staff 12 (MLS 2, Non-MLS 10)
Founded 1908. Pop 29,672; Circ 112,903
Library Holdings: AV Mats 4,065; Bk Titles 71,622; Per Subs 124; Talking Bks 2,448
Wireless access
Partic in Jefferson County Libr Coop
Open Mon-Fri 9-2

J LAWSON STATE COMMUNITY COLLEGE LIBRARY*, Bessemer Campus, 1100 Ninth Ave SW, 35022. Tel: 205-929-3434, 205-929-6333. Administration Tel: 205-929-3490. Web Site: www.library.lawsonstate.edu. *Dir, Libr & Media Serv,* Julie Kennedy; E-mail: jkennedy@lawsonstate.edu; *Extended Day Librn,* Sheryl Howard; E-mail: swhoward@lawsonstate.edu; *AV Tech,* Harold Dennard; E-mail: hdennard@lawsonstate.edu; *Automation Spec,* LeighAnn Carroll; E-mail: lcarroll@lawsonstate.edu
Founded 1949. Enrl 3,500; Fac 167; Highest Degree: Associate
Library Holdings: Audiobooks 80; AV Mats 1,196; CDs 758; DVDs 322; e-books 26,000; Bk Titles 53,516; Bk Vols 55,000; Per Subs 160; Videos 847
Automation Activity & Vendor Info: (Acquisitions) SirsiDynix; (Cataloging) SirsiDynix; (Circulation) SirsiDynix; (Course Reserve) SirsiDynix; (OPAC) SirsiDynix
Wireless access
Function: Art exhibits
Partic in LYRASIS
Open Mon-Thurs 8am-8:30pm, Fri 8-4

BIRMINGHAM

S ALABAMA POWER CO*, Research Services, 600 N 18th St, 35203-2206. (Mail add: PO Box 2641, 35291-0277), SAN 300-0184. Tel: 205-257-4466. FAX: 205-257-2075. E-mail: w2xaplib@southernco.com. *Coordr,* Elizabeth Beasley; E-mail: ebbeasle@southernco.com; *Research Librn,* Lisa Mitchell; E-mail: lrmitche@southernco.com; Staff 3 (MLS 2, Non-MLS 1)
Founded 1925
Library Holdings: Audiobooks 300; Bk Titles 7,500; Bk Vols 8,000; Per Subs 30; Videos 500
Subject Interests: Bus & mgt, Computer sci, Electric utilities, Engr
Automation Activity & Vendor Info: (Cataloging) EOS International; (Circulation) EOS International; (OPAC) EOS International; (Serials) EOS International
Function: Bks on CD, ILL available, Internet access, Microfiche/film & reading machines, Online cat, Res libr
Partic in LYRASIS
Restriction: Access for corporate affiliates, Circulates for staff only, Co libr, Employees only, External users must contact libr

M AMERICAN SPORTS MEDICINE INSTITUTE*, Sports Medicine Library, 833 St Vincent's Dr, Ste 205, 35205. SAN 327-0327. Tel: 205-918-2130. Administration Tel: 205-918-2135. FAX: 205-918-2178. Administration FAX: 205-918-2177. Web Site: www.asmi.org. *Med Librn,* Susan McWhorter; E-mail: susan@asmi.org; *Asst Librn,* DeBora Hall; E-mail: deborah@asmi.org
Library Holdings: Bk Titles 500; Bk Vols 700; Per Subs 95

Subject Interests: Orthopedics
Partic in Alabama Health Libraries Association, Inc; Medical Library Association; SEND

L BALCH & BINGHAM LLP LIBRARY*, 1901 Sixth Ave N, Ste 1500, 35203. SAN 300-0192. Tel: 205-251-8100. FAX: 205-226-8798. E-mail: libraryreferencedesk@balch.com. *Mgr, Res Serv,* Mrs Rebecca M Carnley; E-mail: bcarnley@balch.com; Staff 3 (MLS 3)
Subject Interests: State law
Restriction: Private libr

S BIRMINGHAM MUSEUM OF ART*, Clarence B Hanson Jr Library, 2000 Rev Abraham Woods Jr Blvd, 35203-2278. SAN 300-0214. Tel: 205-297-8065. E-mail: library@artsbma.org. Web Site: artsbma.org.
Founded 1966
Library Holdings: Bk Titles 31,000; Per Subs 50
Special Collections: Buten Wedgwood Coll; Chellis Wedgwood Coll; The Dwight & Lucille Beeson Wedgwood Coll
Subject Interests: Art
Automation Activity & Vendor Info: (Cataloging) ByWater Solutions; (OPAC) ByWater Solutions
Wireless access
Function: For res purposes, ILL available, Telephone ref
Restriction: In-house use for visitors, Non-circulating, Open by appt only

P BIRMINGHAM PUBLIC LIBRARY*, Central, 2100 Park Pl, 35203-2744. SAN 330-0307. Tel: 205-226-3600. Circulation Tel: 205-226-3602. Interlibrary Loan Service Tel: 205-226-3730. Administration Tel: 205-226-3610. FAX: 205-226-3743. Web Site: www.bplonline.org. *Exec Dir,* Floyd G Council, Sr; E-mail: bpldirector@cobpl.org; *Dir, Pub Relations,* Roy L Williams, Sr; E-mail: roy.williams@cobpl.org; *Dep Dir,* Janine Langston; E-mail: janine.langston@cobpl.org; *Regional Libr Mgr,* Yolanda Hardy; E-mail: yolanda.hardy@cobpl.org; *Regional Coordr,* Felita Hawkins; E-mail: felita.hawkins@cobpl.org; Staff 75 (MLS 65, Non-MLS 10)
Founded 1902. Pop 656,700; Circ 1,217,148
Library Holdings: AV Mats 82,159; CDs 17,810; Large Print Bks 19,471; Music Scores 2,362; Bk Vols 899,404; Per Subs 2,500; Talking Bks 15,848; Videos 48,501
Special Collections: Affiliate Agency-Alabama Data Center; Ballet, Dance (Collins Coll of the Dance), bks, photog, programs; Cartography (Agee-Woodward Coll), bks, maps; Drama Coll; Early Children's Books (Hardie Coll); Foundation Center New York (Cooperating Coll); Genealogy, Southern History (Tutwiler Coll), bks, micro, pamphlets, per, VF; Philately (Scruggs Coll), bks, stamps, pamphlets; Rare Books (Bowron Coll). UN Document Depository; US Document Depository
Subject Interests: Genealogy
Automation Activity & Vendor Info: (Acquisitions) Innovative Interfaces, Inc; (Cataloging) Innovative Interfaces, Inc; (Circulation) Innovative Interfaces, Inc; (OPAC) Innovative Interfaces, Inc; (Serials) Innovative Interfaces, Inc
Wireless access
Partic in Jefferson County Libr Coop
Special Services for the Deaf - TDD equip
Open Mon & Tues 9-8, Wed-Sat 9-6, Sun 2-6
Friends of the Library Group

Branches: 18

AVONDALE, 509 40th St S, 35222-3309, SAN 330-0390. Tel: 205-226-4000. Circulation Tel: 205-226-4001. FAX: 205-595-5824. *Librn,* Felita Yarbrough Hawkins; Staff 18 (MLS 5, Non-MLS 13)
Founded 1913
Library Holdings: CDs 723; DVDs 1,028; Large Print Bks 841; Bk Vols 37,160; Talking Bks 1,297; Videos 2,170
Open Mon & Tues 9-8, Wed-Sat 9-6, Sun 2-6

EAST ENSLEY BRANCH, 900 14th St, Ensley, 35218-1206, SAN 330-0455. Tel: 205-787-1928. FAX: 205-786-7219. *Librn,* Christopher Hare
Founded 1965
Library Holdings: CDs 76; DVDs 596; Large Print Bks 19; Bk Vols 16,569; Talking Bks 90; Videos 955
Open Mon, Tues, Thurs & Fri (Summer) 9-12 & 1-6, Wed 1-6; Mon, Tues, Thurs & Fri (Winter) 8-12 & 1-5, Wed 1-5
Friends of the Library Group

EAST LAKE, Five Oporto-Madrid Blvd S, 35206-4800, SAN 330-048X. Tel: 205-836-3341. FAX: 205-833-8055. *Librn,* William Darby
Founded 1927
Library Holdings: Bk Vols 17,585
Open Mon-Sat 9-1 & 2-6

EASTWOOD, 4500 Montevallo Rd, 35210, SAN 330-0498. Tel: 205-591-4944. FAX: 205-956-2503. *Librn,* Brandon Smith; Staff 7 (MLS 1, Non-MLS 6)
Founded 1982
Library Holdings: CDs 6; Large Print Bks 412; Bk Vols 7,571; Per Subs 50; Talking Bks 623
Open Mon-Sat 9-1 & 2-6

ENSLEY BRANCH, 1201 25th St, Ensley, 35218-1944, SAN 330-051X. Tel: 205-785-2625. FAX: 205-785-6625. *Librn,* Alisha Johnson
Founded 1911
Library Holdings: DVDs 630; Large Print Bks 17; Bk Vols 11,728; Videos 591
Open Mon, Tues, Thurs & Fri (Summer) 9-12 & 1-6, Wed 1-6; Mon, Tues, Thurs & Fri (Winter) 8-12 & 1-5, Wed 1-5

FIVE POINTS WEST, 4812 Avenue W, 35208-4726, SAN 330-0528. Tel: 205-226-4013. Circulation Tel: 205-226-4014. FAX: 205-780-8152. *Regional Mgr,* Janine Langston; Staff 4 (MLS 4)
Library Holdings: CDs 618; DVDs 1,346; Large Print Bks 778; Bk Vols 48,232; Talking Bks 1,310; Videos 1,618
Open Mon & Tues 9-8, Wed-Sat 9-6, Sun 2-6

INGLENOOK, 4100 N 40th Terrace N, 35217-4162, SAN 330-0595. Tel: 205-849-8739. FAX: 205-841-2551. *Librn,* Karnecia Williams
Founded 1979
Library Holdings: DVDs 560; Large Print Bks 2; Bk Vols 7,715; Videos 648
Open Mon, Tues, Thurs & Fri (Summer) 9-12 & 1-6, Wed 1-6; Mon, Tues, Thurs & Fri (Winter) 8-12 & 1-5, Wed 1-5

NORTH AVONDALE, 501 43rd St N, 35222-1417, SAN 330-0544. Tel: 205-592-2082. FAX: 205-595-9871. *Librn,* Saundra Ross; Staff 3 (MLS 1, Non-MLS 2)
Founded 1961
Library Holdings: CDs 269; DVDs 610; Bk Vols 10,906; Talking Bks 80; Videos 1,175
Open Mon, Tues, Thurs & Fri (Summer) 9-12 & 1-6, Wed 1-6; Mon, Tues, Thurs & Fri (Winter) 8-12 & 1-5, Wed 1-5

NORTH BIRMINGHAM, 2501 31st Ave N, 35207-4423, SAN 330-0633. Tel: 205-226-4025. FAX: 205-250-0725. Web Site: www.bplonline.org/locations/branch/NorthBirmingham. *Librn,* Sandra Crawley
Founded 1926
Library Holdings: CDs 670; DVDs 970; Large Print Bks 7; Bk Vols 33,530; Talking Bks 968; Videos 1,680
Open Mon & Tues 9-8, Wed-Sat 9-6, Sun 2-6

POWDERLY, 3301 Jefferson Ave SW, 35221-1241, SAN 330-0684. Tel: 205-925-6178. FAX: 205-925-1276. *Br Mgr,* Loretta Bitten
Founded 1979
Library Holdings: Bks-By-Mail 7,401; CDs 259; DVDs 592; Large Print Bks 932; Bk Vols 13,424; Talking Bks 497; Videos 1,077
Open Mon, Tues, Thurs & Fri (Summer) 9-12 & 1-6, Wed 1-6; Mon, Tues, Thurs & Fri (Winter) 8-12 & 1-5, Wed 1-5

PRATT CITY BRANCH, 509 Dugan Ave, 35214-5224, SAN 330-0692. Tel: 205-791-4997. *Br Mgr,* Deborah Drake-Blackman
Founded 2014
Library Holdings: CDs 230; DVDs 622; Large Print Bks 126; Bk Vols 22,013; Talking Bks 570; Videos 2,000
Open Mon-Sat 9-1 & 2-6

SMITHFIELD, One Eighth Ave W, 35204-3724, SAN 330-0757. Tel: 205-324-8428. FAX: 205-254-8851. *Librn,* Yolanda T Hardy
Founded 1956
Library Holdings: CDs 257; DVDs 628; Large Print Bks 21; Bk Vols 25,017; Talking Bks 278; Videos 898
Open Mon-Sat 9-1 & 2-6

SOUTHSIDE, 1814 11th Ave S, 35205-4808, SAN 330-0668. Tel: 205-933-7776. FAX: 205-918-0723. *Librn,* Teresa Ceravolo; Staff 1 (MLS 1)
Founded 1945
Library Holdings: Audiobooks 600; CDs 300; DVDs 1,700; Large Print Bks 500; Bk Vols 23,394; Videos 60
Special Services for the Deaf - Closed caption videos; High interest/low vocabulary bks
Special Services for the Blind - Large print bks
Open Mon-Sat 9-1 & 2-6
Friends of the Library Group

SPRINGVILLE ROAD, 1224 Springville Rd, 35215-7512, SAN 330-0579. Tel: 205-226-4081. Circulation Tel: 205-226-4082. FAX: 205-856-0825. *Librn,* Ms Kelly Laney
Founded 1981
Library Holdings: CDs 738; DVDs 1,114; Large Print Bks 2,474; Bk Vols 58,938; Talking Bks 2,880; Videos 3,283
Open Mon & Tues 9-8, Wed-Sat 9-6, Sun 2-6

TITUSVILLE, Two Sixth Ave SW, 35211-2909, SAN 330-0781. Tel: 205-322-1140. FAX: 205-328-2149. *Librn,* Darlene Worford
Founded 1957
Library Holdings: Bk Vols 21,000; Talking Bks 400
Open Mon-Sat 9-1 & 2-6

WEST END, 1348 Tuscaloosa Ave SW, 35211-1948, SAN 330-0811. Tel: 205-226-4089. FAX: 205-785-6260. *Br Head,* Maya N Jones; Staff 3 (MLS 1, Non-MLS 2)
Library Holdings: CDs 175; DVDs 527; Bk Vols 16,000; Per Subs 25; Talking Bks 150
Special Services for the Deaf - Bks on deafness & sign lang; Staff with knowledge of sign lang

Open Mon-Sat 9-1 & 2-6
Friends of the Library Group
WOODLAWN, 5709 First Ave N, 35212-1603, SAN 330-0846. Tel: 205-595-2001. FAX: 205-595-9654. *Librn,* Pamela Jessie
Founded 1905
Library Holdings: CDs 373; DVDs 650; Large Print Bks 424; Bk Vols 16,550; Videos 1,549
Open Mon, Tues, Thurs & Fri (Summer) 9-12 & 1-6, Wed 1-6; Mon, Tues, Thurs & Fri (Winter) 8-12 & 1-5, Wed 1-5
WYLAM BRANCH, 4300 Seventh Ave, 35224-2624, SAN 330-0870. Tel: 205-785-0349. FAX: 205-781-6571. *Librn,* Jean Shanks
Founded 1921
Library Holdings: CDs 45; DVDs 2,000; Bk Vols 11,000; Videos 75
Open Mon, Tues, Thurs & Fri (Summer) 9-12 & 1-6, Wed 1-6; Mon, Tues, Thurs & Fri (Winter) 8-1 & 1-5, Wed 1-5

C BIRMINGHAM-SOUTHERN COLLEGE*, Charles Andrew Rush Learning Center & N E Miles Library, 900 Arkadelphia Rd, 35254. (Mail add: PO Box 549020, 35254-0001), SAN 300-0230. Circulation Tel: 205-226-4740. Interlibrary Loan Service Tel: 205-226-4748. Reference Tel: 205-226-4766. Administration Tel: 205-226-4742. FAX: 205-226-4743. Web Site: library.bsc.edu. *Dir,* Dr Tiffany Norris; E-mail: tdnorris@bsc.edu; *Archives Librn, Digital Initiatives,* GK Armstrong; E-mail: gkarmstr@bsc.edu; *Electronic Res Librn,* Scott Hill; E-mail: sehill@bsc.edu; *Cat, ILL Librn,* Janice J Poplau; E-mail: jpoplau@bsc.edu; *Research Librn,* Dasha Maye; Tel: 205-226-4749, E-mail: dcmaye@bsc.edu; *Circ Supvr,* Eric Kennedy; E-mail: ekennedy@bsc.edu; *Ref Serv Coordr,* Pam Sawallis; E-mail: psawalli@bsc.edu; *Acq Asst,* Sherrie Coston; Tel: 205-226-4745, E-mail: scoston@bsc.edu; *Circ Asst,* Tracy Duncan; E-mail: tdduncan@bsc.edu; *ILL Asst,* Jimmie Chicarello; E-mail: jchicare@bsc.edu. Subject Specialists: *Info sci,* Dr Tiffany Norris; Staff 9.5 (MLS 5.5, Non-MLS 4)
Founded 1856. Enrl 1,284; Fac 107; Highest Degree: Bachelor
Jun 2017-May 2018. Mats Exp $1,041,565. Sal $443,484
Library Holdings: AV Mats 39,000; e-books 183,672; e-journals 700; Bk Titles 239,850; Per Subs 5,715; Videos 5,325
Special Collections: Alabama Authors; Alabama History; Alabama Methodism. US Document Depository
Subject Interests: Americana
Automation Activity & Vendor Info: (Acquisitions) OCLC Worldshare Management Services; (Cataloging) OCLC Worldshare Management Services; (Circulation) OCLC Worldshare Management Services; (Discovery) EBSCO Discovery Service; (ILL) OCLC WorldShare Interlibrary Loan; (Serials) OCLC Worldshare Management Services
Wireless access
Partic in Associated Colleges of the South; LYRASIS; Network of Alabama Academic Libraries
Open Mon-Thurs 8am-Midnight, Fri 8-5, Sat 9-5, Sun 2-Midnight

L BRADLEY LLP*, Law Library, One Federal Pl, 1819 Fifth Ave N, 35203. SAN 300-0249. Tel: 205-521-8000. FAX: 205-521-8800. Web Site: www.bradley.com/offices/birmingham. *Dir, Res,* Lori D Martin; E-mail: lmartin@bradley.com
Library Holdings: Bk Vols 27,000
Partic in Proquest Dialog
Restriction: Private libr

L BURR & FORMAN LIBRARY*, 420 N 20th St, Ste 3400, 35203. SAN 300-0419. Tel: 205-251-3000. FAX: 205-458-5100. Web Site: www.burr.com. *Mgr, Libr Serv,* Helen Walker
Library Holdings: Bk Vols 18,000; Per Subs 25
Special Collections: Labor, Corporate law
Restriction: Staff use only

SR INDEPENDENT PRESBYTERIAN CHURCH*, John N Lukens Library, 3100 Highland Ave S, 35205. SAN 328-5138. Tel: 205-933-1830. FAX: 205-933-1836. Web Site: ipc-usa.org. *Librn,* Ginni Robertson
Library Holdings: Bk Vols 4,500; Per Subs 10
Subject Interests: Relig, Theol
Open Mon-Fri 8:30-4:30

GL JEFFERSON COUNTY LAW LIBRARY*, Jefferson County Court House, Ste 530, 716 Richard Arrington Jr Blvd N, 35203. SAN 300-029X. Tel: 205-325-5628. Web Site: lawlib.jccal.org. *Law Librn,* Amanda Haddin; E-mail: haddina@jccal.org; *Law Libr Asst,* Karen W Bussey; E-mail: busseyk@jccal.org; Staff 2 (MLS 1, Non-MLS 1)
Founded 1885
Subject Interests: Law
Wireless access
Partic in American Association of Law Libraries
Open Mon-Fri 8:30-4:40
Restriction: Non-circulating to the pub

J JEFFERSON STATE COMMUNITY COLLEGE*, James B Allen Library, 2601 Carson Rd, 35215. SAN 300-0303. Tel: 205-856-8524. FAX: 205-856-8512. Web Site: library.jeffersonstate.edu. *Librn,* Dusty Folds; Tel: 205-856-7786, E-mail: dfolds@jeffersonstate.edu; Staff 6 (MLS 3, Non-MLS 3)
Founded 1965. Enrl 7,400; Highest Degree: Associate
Library Holdings: AV Mats 2,931; Bk Vols 70,207; Per Subs 294
Special Collections: US Document Depository
Automation Activity & Vendor Info: (Cataloging) SirsiDynix; (Circulation) SirsiDynix
Wireless access
Publications: LRC Quarterly
Open Mon-Thurs 7:30am-9pm, Fri 7:30-4, Sat 9-Noon

J LAWSON STATE COMMUNITY COLLEGE LIBRARY*, Birmingham Campus, 3060 Wilson Rd SW, 35221. SAN 320-5487. Tel: 205-929-6333. Circulation Tel: 205-929-2068. FAX: 205-925-3716. Web Site: www.library.lawsonstate.edu. *Dir of Libr/Media Serv,* Julie Kennedy; E-mail: jkennedy@lawsonstate.edu; *Ref & Instruction Librn,* Sabrina Dyck; E-mail: sdyck@lawsonstate.edu; *Circ,* Derick Embry; E-mail: dembry@lawsonstate.edu
Founded 1965. Enrl 2,000
Library Holdings: Bk Vols 31,000; Per Subs 165
Special Collections: Martin Luther King Jr Afro-American Coll
Automation Activity & Vendor Info: (Acquisitions) SirsiDynix; (Cataloging) SirsiDynix; (Circulation) SirsiDynix; (Course Reserve) SirsiDynix; (OPAC) SirsiDynix
Wireless access
Publications: Annual Report; Booktalk (Newsletter); Policy Manual; Student Handbook
Open Mon-Thurs 8am-8:30pm, Fri 8-4, Sat 8-Noon
Friends of the Library Group

S THE LIBRARY AT BIRMINGHAM BOTANICAL GARDENS, 2612 Lane Park Rd, 35223. SAN 324-0061. Tel: 205-414-3920. E-mail: thelibrary@bbgardens.org. Web Site: www.bbgardens.org/library. *Libr Dir,* Hope Long; Tel: 205-414-3931, E-mail: hlong@bbgardens.org; *Archivist,* Jason Kirby; Tel: 205-414-3967, E-mail: jkirby@bbgardens.org; Staff 2 (MLS 1, Non-MLS 1)
Founded 1973
Library Holdings: Audiobooks 10; AV Mats 200; CDs 30; DVDs 50; Electronic Media & Resources 20; Per Subs 60; Videos 125
Special Collections: Japanese Artifacts, Rare Botanical/Horticultural books
Subject Interests: Beekeeping, Botany, Children's bks, Cooking, Environ, Floral design, Food, Garden design, Gardening, Hort, Nature, Plants, Teacher res ctr
Automation Activity & Vendor Info: (Circulation) Innovative Interfaces, Inc; (OPAC) Innovative Interfaces, Inc
Wireless access
Function: 24/7 Online cat, Adult bk club, Art exhibits, Art programs, Audio & video playback equip for onsite use, Audiobks on Playaways & MP3, Audiobks via web, Bk club(s), Bks on CD, Butterfly Garden, CD-ROM, Children's prog, Computers for patron use, Digital talking bks, E-Reserves, Electronic databases & coll, Free DVD rentals, Holiday prog, Home delivery & serv to seniorr ctr & nursing homes, Homebound delivery serv, ILL available, Internet access, Life-long learning prog for all ages, Magazines, Mail & tel request accepted, Mail loans to mem, Mango lang, Movies, Music CDs, Online cat, Outreach serv, OverDrive digital audio bks, Photocopying/Printing, Prog for adults, Prog for children & young adult, Ref & res, Ref serv available, Res assist avail, Res libr, Scanner, Senior outreach, STEM programs, Telephone ref, VHS videos, Visual arts prog, Wheelchair accessible, Workshops
Publications: Garden Dirt (Newsletter)
Partic in Jefferson County Libr Coop
Open Mon-Fri 9-4

L MAYNARD, COOPER & GALE*, Law Library, Regions Harbert Plaza, Ste 2400, 1901 Sixth Ave N, 35203. SAN 372-2627. Tel: 205-254-1000. FAX: 205-254-1999. Web Site: www.maynardcooper.com/birmingham. *Law Librn,* Shawn Reese; Staff 2 (MLS 1, Non-MLS 1)
Library Holdings: Bk Titles 10,000
Restriction: Staff use only

P NORTH SHELBY COUNTY LIBRARY*, 5521 Cahaba Valley Rd, 35242. SAN 371-9367. Tel: 205-439-5500. Reference Tel: 205-439-5510. Administration Tel: 205-439-5555. FAX: 205-439-5503. Web Site: www.northshelbylibrary.org. *Dir, Libr Serv,* Katie Bailey; Tel: 205-439-5540, E-mail: KBailey@shelbycounty-al.org; Staff 10 (MLS 7, Non-MLS 3)
Pop 60,000; Circ 250,000
Library Holdings: Bk Vols 63,000; Per Subs 95
Automation Activity & Vendor Info: (Acquisitions) Innovative Interfaces, Inc; (Cataloging) Innovative Interfaces, Inc; (Circulation) Innovative Interfaces, Inc; (OPAC) Innovative Interfaces, Inc
Wireless access

Mem of Harrison Regional Library System
Open Mon & Thurs 10-8, Tues, Wed & Fri 10-6, Sat 10-4, Sun 1-5
Friends of the Library Group
Branches: 1
MT LAUREL LIBRARY, 111 Olmsted St, 35242. Tel: 205-991-1660. E-mail: mtlaurel@shelbycounty-al.org. Web Site: www.mtlaurellibrary.org. *Libr Dir,* Katie Bailey; Tel: 205-439-5540, E-mail: KBailey@shelbycounty-al.org
Friends of the Library Group

M SAINT VINCENT'S HOSPITAL*, Cunningham Wilson Library & Resource Center, 810 St Vincent's Dr, 35205. SAN 324-5306. Tel: 205-939-7830. FAX: 205-930-2182. *Libr Spec,* Sister Anne Marie Schreiner
Library Holdings: e-books 20; e-journals 250; Bk Titles 2,000; Per Subs 120; Videos 100
Subject Interests: Career develop, Consumer health, Nursing, Spiritual life
Partic in Alabama Health Libraries Association, Inc; SEND
Open Mon-Fri 8-4:30

C SAMFORD UNIVERSITY LIBRARY*, 800 Lakeshore Dr, 35229. SAN 330-0900. Tel: 205-726-2846. Circulation Tel: 205-726-2748. Interlibrary Loan Service Tel: 205-726-2983. Reference Tel: 205-726-2196. FAX: 205-726-4009. E-mail: library@samford.edu. Web Site: library.samford.edu, www.samford.edu/library. *Dean,* Kimmetha Herndon; E-mail: kherndon@samford.edu; *Assoc Dean, Chair, Coll Develop & Acq,* Lori Northrup; Tel: 205-726-2518, E-mail: lanorthr@samford.edu; *Chair, Cat,* Jaro Szurek; Tel: 205-726-4136, E-mail: jszurek@samford.edu; *Chair, Circ,* Cheryl Cecil; Tel: 205-726-2699, E-mail: cscecil@samford.edu; *Chair, Ref & Res Serv,* Carla Waddell; Tel: 205-726-2755, E-mail: ctwaddel@samford.edu; *Chair, Spec Coll,* Jennifer Taylor; Tel: 205-726-4103, E-mail: jrtaylor@samford.edu; *Automation Syst Coordr,* Ed Cherry; Tel: 205-726-2506, E-mail: cecherry@samford.edu; Staff 29 (MLS 14, Non-MLS 15)
Founded 1841. Enrl 5,493; Highest Degree: Doctorate
Library Holdings: e-books 121,086; e-journals 109,841; Microforms 663,779; Bk Vols 639,845; Per Subs 13,204
Special Collections: Alabama History & Literature, bks, ms, maps, microfilm, newsp; Baptist History, bks, ms, microfilm; Douglas McMurtrie Coll, bks, pamphlets; Genealogy Coll, bks, ms, per; Hearn Coll; History & Genealogy (Casey Coll), bks, ms, maps; Irish Coll; John Ruskin First Edition Books; Masefield First Edition Books & Critical Works; Tennyson First Edition Books & Critical Works. Oral History; US Document Depository
Automation Activity & Vendor Info: (Acquisitions) Innovative Interfaces, Inc - Sierra; (Cataloging) Innovative Interfaces, Inc - Sierra; (Circulation) Innovative Interfaces, Inc - Sierra; (Discovery) EBSCO Discovery Service; (ILL) OCLC ILLiad; (OPAC) Innovative Interfaces, Inc - Sierra; (Serials) Innovative Interfaces, Inc - Sierra
Wireless access
Function: 24/7 Online cat, Archival coll, Art exhibits, Audio & video playback equip for onsite use, Audiobks on Playaways & MP3, Audiobks via web, Computers for patron use, Doc delivery serv, Electronic databases & coll, Govt ref serv, ILL available, Instruction & testing, Internet access, Mail & tel request accepted, Mail loans to mem, Music CDs, Notary serv, Online cat, Online info literacy tutorials on the web & in blackboard, Online ref, Orientations, Outreach serv, Photocopying/Printing, Ref & res, Ref serv available, Res libr, Scanner, Spoken cassettes & DVDs, Tax forms, Telephone ref, VHS videos, Wheelchair accessible
Publications: Folklore in the Samford University Library; History of Marion, Alabama, by Samuel A Townes, reprint of 1844 Edition; Ireland, The Albert E Casey Coll & Other Irish Materials in the Samford University Library; Maps in the Samford University Library; Maud McLure Kelly, Alabama's First Woman Lawyer, by C Newman (Samford University Library Research Series, paper No 6); Samford University Library Research Series, paper No 7
Partic in LYRASIS; Network of Alabama Academic Libraries
Restriction: Open to students, fac & staff, Open to students, fac, staff & alumni
Friends of the Library Group
Departmental Libraries:
CL LUCILLE STEWART BEESON LAW LIBRARY, 800 Lakeshore Dr, 35229, SAN 330-0994. Tel: 205-726-2714. FAX: 205-726-2644. Web Site: lawlib.samford.edu. *Dir,* Gregory K Laughlin; E-mail: glaughli@samford.edu; *Acq Librn,* Cherie Feenker; E-mail: cdfeenke@samford.edu; *Cat Librn,* Rebecca Hutto; E-mail: rmhutto@samford.edu; *IT Librn,* Grace Simms; E-mail: glsimms@samford.edu; *Ref Librn,* Edward L Craig, Jr; E-mail: elcraig@samford.edu; Staff 14 (MLS 7, Non-MLS 7)
Founded 1847. Enrl 494; Fac 24
Library Holdings: Bk Titles 37,991; Bk Vols 202,951; Per Subs 2,029
Partic in Southeastern Chapter of the American Association of Law Libraries
Restriction: Open to researchers by request, Open to students, fac & staff
Friends of the Library Group
CENTER FOR HEALTH INNOVATION AND PATIENT OUTCOMES RESEARCH, Ingalls Bldg, 800 Lakeshore Dr, 35229, SAN 330-0935. Tel: 205-726-2891. FAX: 205-726-4012. Web Site: www.samford.edu/pharmacy/CHIPOR/default. *Mgr,* Sandra Boyken; E-mail: spboyken@samford.edu
Library Holdings: Bk Vols 900; Per Subs 80
Open Mon-Wed 8am-9pm, Thurs & Fri 8-4:30
CURRICULUM MATERIALS CENTER, Beeson Education Bldg, 800 Lakeshore Dr, 35229, SAN 330-096X. Tel: 205-726-2558. FAX: 205-726-2068. Web Site: www.samford.edu/education/curriculum-materials-and-technology-center. *Dir,* Michele Haralson; Tel: 205-726-2987, E-mail: mkharals@samford.edu
Library Holdings: Bk Titles 5,000; Per Subs 12
Open Mon-Thurs 7:30am-Midnight, Fri 7:30am-8pm, Sat 10-7, Sun 1pm-Midnight
Friends of the Library Group

L SIROTE & PERMUTT PC*, Law Library, 2311 Highland Ave S, 35205-2792. (Mail add: PO Box 55727, 35255-5727), SAN 326-3088. Tel: 205-930-5233. FAX: 205-930-5101. *Librn,* William Preston Peyton; E-mail: ppeyton@sirote.com
Founded 1946
Wireless access
Restriction: Staff use only

R TEMPLE EMANU-EL*, Engel Library, 2100 Highland Ave, 35205. SAN 300-0397. Tel: 205-933-8037, Ext 238. FAX: 205-933-8099. *Library Contact,* William Lehman
Founded 1914
Library Holdings: Bk Vols 4,500
Open Mon-Fri 8:30-4

M UAB CALLAHAN EYE HOSPITAL, John E Meyer Eye Library, 1720 University Blvd, 35233-1895. SAN 324-6523. Tel: 205-325-8507. FAX: 205-325-8200. *Prog Coordr,* Harriett Holmes; E-mail: hholmes@uab.edu
Library Holdings: Bk Titles 1,650; Per Subs 42
Subject Interests: Ophthalmology
Wireless access
Partic in National Network of Libraries of Medicine Region 2
Open Mon-Fri 7:30-4

UNIVERSITY OF ALABAMA AT BIRMINGHAM
CM DEPARTMENT OF ANESTHESIOLOGY LIBRARY*, 619 19th St S, J965, 35249-6810, SAN 324-5284. Tel: 205-975-0158. FAX: 205-975-5963. Web Site: medicine.uab.edu/anesthesiology. *Librn,* A J Wright; E-mail: ajwright@uab.edu; Staff 1 (MLS 1)
Founded 1979
Library Holdings: CDs 125; DVDs 60; Bk Vols 3,348
Special Collections: Alice McNeal, MD Coll, bks & other mats related to first dept Chair, 1946-1964; Anesthesia History Coll, bks & other mats; Departmental History Coll, correspondence, photog & other mats, 1946 to present
Subject Interests: Anesthesia, Critical care, Pain mgt
Partic in National Network of Libraries of Medicine Region 2
Open Mon-Fri 7-5
CM LISTER HILL LIBRARY OF THE HEALTH SCIENCES*, 1700 University Blvd, 35294-0013. (Mail add: 1720 Second Ave S, 35294-0013), SAN 330-1176. Tel: 205-934-5460. Circulation Tel: 205-934-3306. Interlibrary Loan Service Tel: 205-934-2356. Information Services Tel: 205-934-2230. FAX: 205-934-3545. Information Services FAX: 204-975-8313. Web Site: www.uab.edu/lister. *Dir,* T Scott Plutchak; E-mail: tscott@uab.edu; *Assoc Dir, Hist Coll,* Mike Flannery; E-mail: flannery@uab.edu; *Assoc Dir, Pub Serv,* Patricia Higginbottom; E-mail: phiggin@uab.edu; *Asst Dir, Access & Doc Delivery,* Michael Fitts; E-mail: fitts@uab.edu; *Head, Cat,* Valerie Gordon; E-mail: vgordon@uab.edu; *Syst Librn,* Lisa Ennis; E-mail: scorbett@uab.edu; *Archivist,* Tim Pennycuff; E-mail: tpenny@uab.edu; *Ser,* Sylvia McAphee; E-mail: smcaphee@uab.edu; Staff 40 (MLS 19, Non-MLS 21)
Founded 1945. Highest Degree: Doctorate
Library Holdings: Bk Vols 337,728
Special Collections: Alabama Museum of the Health Sciences; Reynolds Historical Library; UAB Archives
Subject Interests: Allied health, Dentistry, Med, Nursing, Optometry, Pub health
Automation Activity & Vendor Info: (Acquisitions) SirsiDynix; (Cataloging) SirsiDynix; (Circulation) SirsiDynix; (ILL) OCLC ILLiad; (OPAC) SirsiDynix; (Serials) SirsiDynix
Partic in Network of Alabama Academic Libraries
Publications: Lister Hill Letter; Newsletter of the Reynolds Library Assocs
Friends of the Library Group

C MERVYN H STERNE LIBRARY*, 917 13th St S, 35205. (Mail add: 1720 Second Ave S, SL 172, 35294-0014). Tel: 205-934-6364. Circulation Tel: 205-934-4338. Interlibrary Loan Service Tel: 205-934-6365. Administration Tel: 205-934-6360. Interlibrary Loan Service FAX: 205-975-6230. Administration FAX: 205-934-0238. Web Site: www.mhsl.uab.edu. *Inaugural Dean of Libr & Prof of UAB Libr,* John M Meador, Jr; Tel: 205-934-5460, E-mail: jmmj@uab.edu; *Head, Cat & Coll Mgt,* Carolyn Walden; Tel: 205-934-0633, E-mail: cwalden@uab.edu; *Head, Ref,* Linda Harris; E-mail: lharris@uab.edu; *Head, User Serv/Circ,* Dr Fred J Olive, III; E-mail: folive@uab.edu; *Digital Res/Presv Librn,* Yan Wang; Tel: 205-934-6357, E-mail: yanwang3@uab.edu; *Electronic Res Librn,* Peggy Kain; Tel: 205-934-9939, E-mail: pkain@uab.edu; *Ref Librn,* Craig Beard; E-mail: cbeard@uab.edu; *Ref Librn,* Brooke Becker; E-mail: babecker@uab.edu; *Ref Librn,* Jeffery Graveline; E-mail: jgraveli@uab.edu; *Ref Librn,* Dana Hettich; E-mail: dhettich@uab.edu; *Ref Librn,* Jennifer Long; E-mail: jmlong@uab.edu; *Ref Librn,* Heather Martin; E-mail: hmartin@uab.edu; *Ref Librn,* Imelda Vetter; E-mail: ivetter@uab.edu; *Ref Librn, Instruction & Outreach,* Delores Carlito; E-mail: delo@uab.edu; *Cataloger,* Tony Schimizzi; Tel: 205-934-3512, E-mail: senecas@uab.edu; *Cataloger,* Laura Simpson; E-mail: simle@uab.edu; *Cataloger,* Irina Stanishevskaya; E-mail: istan@uab.edu; *ILL,* Eddie Luster; E-mail: eluster@uab.edu. Subject Specialists: *Engr,* Craig Beard; *Behav sci, Soc sci,* Brooke Becker; *Bus, Govt doc, Legal,* Jeffery Graveline; *Math, Sci,* Jennifer Long; *Arts, Humanities,* Heather Martin; *Educ,* Imelda Vetter; Staff 25 (MLS 17, Non-MLS 8)
Founded 1966. Enrl 17,999; Fac 2,322; Highest Degree: Doctorate
Oct 2012-Sept 2013 Income $5,555,795, State $3,819,487, Locally Generated Income $27,075, Parent Institution $1,609,682, Other $99,551. Mats Exp $1,797,041, Books $232,989, Per/Ser (Incl. Access Fees) $708,440, Other Print Mats $4,699, AV Mat $8,296, Electronic Ref Mat (Incl. Access Fees) $822,910, Presv $19,707. Sal $2,513,046 (Prof $1,111,569)
Library Holdings: AV Mats 10,565; CDs 9,594; e-books 80,620; e-journals 4,221; Microforms 1,267,569; Bk Titles 1,120,007; Bk Vols 1,159,102; Per Subs 20,846; Videos 6,844
Special Collections: Proust Coll. Oral History
Automation Activity & Vendor Info: (Acquisitions) Ex Libris Group; (Cataloging) Ex Libris Group; (Circulation) Ex Libris Group; (Course Reserve) Ex Libris Group; (ILL) OCLC ILLiad; (OPAC) Ex Libris Group; (Serials) Ex Libris Group
Partic in Association of Southeastern Research Libraries; Consortium of Southern Biomedical Libraries; LYRASIS; Network of Alabama Academic Libraries; OCLC Online Computer Library Center, Inc
Publications: Mervyn H Sterne Library Directions (Newsletter)
Open Mon-Thurs 7:30am-2am, Fri 7:30-7, Sat 9-5, Sun 1pm-2am
Friends of the Library Group

BLOUNTSVILLE

P BLOUNTSVILLE PUBLIC LIBRARY*, 65 Chestnut St, 35031. (Mail add: PO Box 219, 35031-0219), SAN 300-0443. Tel: 205-429-3156. FAX: 205-429-4806. E-mail: blountsvillelib@hotmail.com. Web Site: www.blountsvillepubliclibrary.info. *Dir,* Yvonne Murphree; *Asst Librn,* Dorothy Yarbrough
Pop 1,400; Circ 23,000
Library Holdings: Bk Titles 22,000; Bk Vols 23,000; Per Subs 40
Subject Interests: Local hist
Automation Activity & Vendor Info: (Cataloging) Follett Software; (Circulation) Follett Software
Open Mon & Thurs 9-7, Tues, Wed & Fri 9-5, Sat 9-2
Friends of the Library Group

BOAZ

P BOAZ PUBLIC LIBRARY, 404 Thomas Ave, 35957. SAN 300-0451. Tel: 256-593-3000, 256-593-8056. FAX: 256-593-8153. E-mail: library@cityofboaz.org. Web Site: www.cityofboaz.org/247/Library. *Dir,* Lynn Burgess; Staff 1 (Non-MLS 1)
Founded 1971. Pop 8,000; Circ 10,000
Library Holdings: Bk Titles 55,000; Bk Vols 60,000; Per Subs 100
Special Collections: Paperback Coll
Subject Interests: Alabama, Genealogy
Automation Activity & Vendor Info: (Cataloging) Follett Software; (Circulation) Follett Software; (OPAC) Follett Software
Wireless access
Mem of Marshall County Cooperative Library
Open Mon-Thurs 9-7, Fri 9-5, Sat 9-3
Friends of the Library Group

J SNEAD STATE COMMUNITY COLLEGE*, Virgil B McCain Jr Learning Resource Center, 102 Elder St, 35957. (Mail add: PO Box 734, 35957-0734), SAN 300-046X. Tel: 256-840-4173. Administration Tel: 256-840-4195. FAX: 256-593-3098. Web Site: www.snead.edu/library.aspx. *Librn,* Gary Bodine; E-mail: gbodine@snead.edu; *Librn,* John M Miller; E-mail: jmiller@snead.edu; Staff 4 (MLS 1, Non-MLS 3)
Founded 1935. Enrl 1,472; Fac 40
Library Holdings: AV Mats 1,038; e-books 50,000; Bk Titles 38,044; Bk Vols 50,000; Per Subs 172
Special Collections: Alabama Authors (Borden Deal, Babs Deal, William B Huie, William Heath, Elise Sanguinetti, Thomas Wilkerson); Alabama Coll; College Archives
Automation Activity & Vendor Info: (Cataloging) Innovative Interfaces, Inc; (Circulation) Innovative Interfaces, Inc; (OPAC) Innovative Interfaces, Inc
Wireless access
Partic in Library Management Network, Inc
Restriction: Open to pub for ref & circ; with some limitations, Open to students, fac & staff

BRANTLEY

P BRANTLEY PUBLIC LIBRARY*, Ten MLK Dr, 36009. (Mail add: PO Box 45, 36009-0045), SAN 300-0478. Tel: 334-527-8624. FAX: 334-527-3216. E-mail: brantleypublib@hotmail.com. *Dir,* Davina Mount
Pop 1,151; Circ 4,207
Library Holdings: Large Print Bks 300; Bk Vols 3,600; Per Subs 24
Wireless access
Open Mon-Thurs 1-5

BREWTON

P BREWTON PUBLIC LIBRARY*, 206 W Jackson St, 36426. SAN 300-0494. Tel: 251-867-4626. FAX: 251-809-1749. Web Site: www.brewtonpubliclibrary.org, www.cityofbrewton.org/library. *Dir,* Lynn Likely; E-mail: llikely@cityofbrewton.org; Staff 10 (MLS 1, Non-MLS 9)
Founded 1960. Pop 5,498; Circ 91,000
Library Holdings: AV Mats 5,848; Bks on Deafness & Sign Lang 4; Large Print Bks 3,200; Bk Titles 49,061; Per Subs 60
Special Collections: Rare Books Coll; Wildflowers of Escambia County
Automation Activity & Vendor Info: (Cataloging) Follett Software; (Circulation) Follett Software; (OPAC) Follett Software
Wireless access
Function: Home delivery & serv to seniorr ctr & nursing homes, Homebound delivery serv, ILL available, Photocopying/Printing, Prog for children & young adult, Summer reading prog, Wheelchair accessible
Mem of Escambia County Cooperative Library System
Partic in National Network of Libraries of Medicine Region 2
Open Mon-Fri 9-6, Sat-9-1
Restriction: Circ limited
Friends of the Library Group

BRIDGEPORT

P LENA CAGLE PUBLIC LIBRARY, 401 Alabama Ave, 35740. (Mail add: PO Box 875, 35740-0875). Tel: 256-495-2259. FAX: 256-495-2119. E-mail: lenacaglelibrary@bellsouth.net. *Librn,* Miranda Hambrick; Staff 1 (Non-MLS 1)
Founded 1993. Pop 3,000
Library Holdings: Bk Vols 7,600; Per Subs 23
Automation Activity & Vendor Info: (Acquisitions) Follett Software; (Cataloging) Follett Software; (Circulation) Follett Software
Open Tues-Thurs 9-12 & 1-4
Friends of the Library Group

G RUSSELL CAVE NATIONAL MONUMENT LIBRARY*, 3729 County Rd 98, 35740. SAN 323-6927. Tel: 256-495-2672. FAX: 256-495-9220. Web Site: www.nps.gov/ruca. *Superintendent,* Steve Black; E-mail: steve_black@nps.gov
Founded 1962
Library Holdings: Bk Titles 600
Subject Interests: Archaeology
Open Mon-Sun 8-4:30

BRUNDIDGE

P TUPPER LIGHTFOOT MEMORIAL LIBRARY, Brundidge Public Library, 164 S Main St, 36010. SAN 330-2911. Tel: 334-735-2145. FAX: 334-735-2147. Web Site: tupperlightfootbrundidgelib.org. *Libr Dir,* Theresa Trawick; E-mail: tlmldirector@troycable.net; Staff 4.3 (MLS 0.5, Non-MLS 3.8)
Founded 1940. Pop 6,026; Circ 11,941
Library Holdings: Audiobooks 57; DVDs 1,650; e-books 42,000; Large Print Bks 1,800; Bk Vols 15,000; Per Subs 28
Subject Interests: Genealogy, Local hist
Automation Activity & Vendor Info: (Cataloging) Book Systems; (Circulation) Book Systems; (OPAC) Book Systems
Wireless access
Function: 24/7 Electronic res, 24/7 Online cat, Accelerated reader prog, Activity rm, Adult bk club, Adult literacy prog, Archival coll, Art

programs, Audiobks on Playaways & MP3, Bk club(s), Children's prog, Computer training, Computers for patron use, E-Readers, Electronic databases & coll, Family literacy, Free DVD rentals, Holiday prog, Homework prog, Internet access, Laminating, Large print keyboards, Life-long learning prog for all ages, Magazines, Magnifiers for reading, Mail & tel request accepted, Meeting rooms, Movies, Online cat, Orientations, Outreach serv, Outside serv via phone, mail, e-mail & web, OverDrive digital audio bks, Photocopying/Printing, Preschool outreach, Preschool reading prog, Printer for laptops & handheld devices, Prog for adults, Prog for children & young adult, Ref serv available, Scanner, Spanish lang bks, Study rm, Summer & winter reading prog, Summer reading prog, Tax forms, Teen prog, Telephone ref, Wheelchair accessible, Winter reading prog
Special Services for the Deaf - High interest/low vocabulary bks
Special Services for the Blind - Accessible computers; Extensive large print coll
Open Mon-Fri 9-6, Sat 9-12
Friends of the Library Group

BUTLER

P CHOCTAW COUNTY PUBLIC LIBRARY*, 124 N Academy Ave, 36904. SAN 330-1206. Tel: 205-459-2542. E-mail: choctaw.library@gmail.com. *Dir,* Emily Knowles
Founded 1954. Pop 15,000; Circ 62,646
Oct 2018-Sept 2019 Income (Main & Associated Libraries) $83,500
Library Holdings: Bk Vols 75,000; Per Subs 30
Subject Interests: Alabama
Automation Activity & Vendor Info: (Cataloging) Follett Software; (Circulation) Follett Software; (OPAC) Follett Software
Wireless access
Function: Computers for patron use, Electronic databases & coll, Summer reading prog, Tax forms
Open Wed-Fri 10-6
Friends of the Library Group
Branches: 1
SILAS BRANCH, 130 Indian Way, Silas, 36919. (Mail add: PO Box 92, Silas, 36919), SAN 330-1265. Tel: 251-542-9379. *Br Mgr,* Patsy Ray
Open Mon & Wed 9:30-4:30
Friends of the Library Group

CALERA

P ROY DOWNS MEMORIAL CALERA LIBRARY, 9700 Hwy 25, 35040. SAN 371-9340. Tel: 205-668-7200. FAX: 205-668-3515. Web Site: cityofcalera.org/102/library. *Dir,* Allison Powers; E-mail: apowers@calera.org
Pop 4,000
Library Holdings: Bk Vols 16,000; Per Subs 13
Automation Activity & Vendor Info: (Cataloging) Innovative Interfaces, Inc; (Circulation) Innovative Interfaces, Inc; (ILL) Innovative Interfaces, Inc; (OPAC) Innovative Interfaces, Inc
Wireless access
Mem of Harrison Regional Library System
Open Mon & Tues 8-7, Wed & Thurs 8-6, Fri 8-4, Sat 9-1

CAMDEN

P WILCOX COUNTY LIBRARY*, 100 Broad St, 36726-1702. SAN 324-0738. Tel: 334-682-4355. FAX: 334-682-5437. E-mail: wilcoxlibrary@frontiernet.net. *Dir,* Bettie Morgan; E-mail: betmorgan@frontiernet.net; Staff 3 (MLS 1, Non-MLS 2)
Founded 1979. Pop 14,000
Library Holdings: Bk Titles 36,444; Per Subs 60
Special Collections: Census Records Coll, micro. State Document Depository
Subject Interests: Alabama, Genealogy
Automation Activity & Vendor Info: (Acquisitions) Biblionix/Apollo; (Cataloging) Biblionix/Apollo; (Circulation) Biblionix/Apollo; (Course Reserve) Biblionix/Apollo; (ILL) Biblionix/Apollo; (OPAC) Biblionix/Apollo; (Serials) Biblionix/Apollo
Wireless access
Open Mon 9-6, Tues-Fri 8-5

CARBON HILL

P CARBON HILL CITY LIBRARY, 215 Second St NW, 35549. (Mail add: PO Box 116, 35549), SAN 300-0524. Tel: 205-924-4254. E-mail: carbonhillpubliclibrary@gmail.com. Web Site: www2.youseemore.com/cerl/Default.asp. *Librn,* Nancy Stewart; Staff 1 (MLS 1)
Founded 1931. Pop 5,000
Library Holdings: AV Mats 24; Bk Titles 7,000; Per Subs 20
Wireless access
Mem of Carl Elliott Regional Library System
Open Mon-Thurs 1-4:30

CARROLLTON

P CARROLLTON PUBLIC LIBRARY*, 225 Commerce Ave, 35447. (Mail add: PO Box 92, 35447-0092), SAN 325-1551. Tel: 205-367-2142. FAX: 205-367-2142. E-mail: cpl@nctv.com. Web Site: www.pickenslibrary.com/carrollton.html. *Dir,* Larance Hale
Founded 1981. Pop 963; Circ 6,010
Library Holdings: Bk Vols 10,500
Automation Activity & Vendor Info: (Cataloging) Follett Software; (Circulation) Follett Software
Mem of Pickens County Cooperative Library
Open Mon & Wed 12-5, Tues 9-3, Thurs 12-8, Sat 9-12

P PICKENS COUNTY COOPERATIVE LIBRARY*, Service Ctr Bldg, 155 Reform St, Rm 120, 35447. (Mail add: PO Box 489, 35447-0489). Tel: 205-367-8407. E-mail: pccl@nctv.com. Web Site: pickenslibrary.com. *Dir,* Nelda B Hudgins; Staff 1 (Non-MLS 1)
Library Holdings: Bk Vols 50,000
Special Collections: Pickens County Historical Coll
Automation Activity & Vendor Info: (Acquisitions) Book Systems; (Cataloging) Book Systems; (Circulation) Book Systems
Wireless access
Member Libraries: Aliceville Public Library; Carrollton Public Library; Reform Public Library; Ruth Holliman Public Library
Open Mon-Thurs 8-4
Restriction: Not a lending libr, Ref only to non-staff

CENTRE

P CHEROKEE COUNTY PUBLIC LIBRARY*, 310 Mary St, 35960. SAN 300-0532. Tel: 256-927-5838. FAX: 256-927-2800. E-mail: ccplincentre@gmail.com. Web Site: www.cheaharegionallibrary.org/member_libraries/cherokee_county_public_library. *Dir,* Elaine J Henry; Staff 1 (MLS 1)
Founded 1946. Pop 18,200; Circ 28,295
Library Holdings: Bk Titles 24,000; Bk Vols 27,000; Per Subs 20
Automation Activity & Vendor Info: (Cataloging) Book Systems; (Circulation) Book Systems; (OPAC) Book Systems
Wireless access
Mem of Cheaha Regional Library
Open Mon, Tues, Thurs & Fri 8-5, Wed 8-12

CENTREVILLE

P BRENT-CENTREVILLE PUBLIC LIBRARY*, 20 Library St, 35042. SAN 300-0486. Tel: 205-926-4736. FAX: 205-926-4736. E-mail: bcpl.read@gmail.com. Web Site: www.brentcentlib.com/. *Dir,* Tracy Griffin
Pop 16,000
Library Holdings: Bk Vols 20,000; Per Subs 55
Automation Activity & Vendor Info: (Cataloging) Follett Software; (Circulation) Follett Software
Special Services for the Deaf - Captioned film dep
Open Mon 9-8, Tues-Fri 9-5, Sat 9-12
Friends of the Library Group

CHATOM

P WASHINGTON COUNTY PUBLIC LIBRARY*, 14102 Saint Stephens Ave, 36518. (Mail add: PO Box 1057, 36518), SAN 300-0540. Tel: 251-847-2097. FAX: 251-847-2098. E-mail: info@wcpls.org. Web Site: www.wcpls.net. *Dir,* Jessica Ross; E-mail: jross@wcpls.org; Staff 1 (MLS 1)
Founded 1956. Pop 18,000; Circ 43,275
Library Holdings: Bk Vols 55,000; Per Subs 116
Special Collections: African Artifacts (Dr Paul Petcher Coll); Washington County History Coll
Subject Interests: Consumer health, Gardening
Automation Activity & Vendor Info: (Acquisitions) Book Systems; (Cataloging) Book Systems; (Circulation) Book Systems; (Course Reserve) Book Systems; (ILL) Book Systems; (Media Booking) Book Systems; (OPAC) Book Systems; (Serials) Book Systems
Function: Accelerated reader prog, Adult literacy prog, Archival coll, Art exhibits, Audio & video playback equip for onsite use, Audiobks via web, AV serv, Bk club(s), Bk reviews (Group), Bks on cassette, Bks on CD, CD-ROM, Children's prog, Citizenship assistance, Computer training, Computers for patron use, Distance learning, Doc delivery serv, E-Reserves, Electronic databases & coll, Family literacy, Games & aids for people with disabilities, Genealogy discussion group, Health sci info serv, Holiday prog, Home delivery & serv to seniorr ctr & nursing homes, Homebound delivery serv, Homework prog, ILL available, Instruction & testing, Internet access, Jail serv, Learning ctr, Literacy & newcomer serv, Magnifiers for reading, Mail & tel request accepted, Mail loans to mem, Music CDs, Online cat, Online info literacy tutorials on the web & in blackboard, Online ref, Orientations, Outreach serv, Outside serv via phone, mail, e-mail & web, Photocopying/Printing, Preschool outreach,

Prof lending libr, Prog for adults, Prog for children & young adult, Ref & res, Ref serv available, Res libr, Res performed for a fee, Satellite serv, Scanner, Senior computer classes, Senior outreach, Serves people with intellectual disabilities, Specialized serv in classical studies, Spoken cassettes & CDs, Spoken cassettes & DVDs, Story hour, Summer reading prog, Tax forms, Teen prog, Telephone ref, VHS videos, Visual arts prog, Wheelchair accessible, Workshops, Writing prog
Partic in Ohio Public Library Information Network; Serving Every Ohioan Library Center; Southeast Regional Library System
Special Services for the Blind - Web-Braille
Open Mon & Wed-Fri 9-5, Tues 9-7
Friends of the Library Group
Branches: 1
MCINTOSH BRANCH, Melva Jean Daughtery Bldg, 83 Olin Rd, McIntosh, 36553. (Mail add: PO Box 55, McIntosh, 36553). Tel: 251-944-2047. FAX: 251-944-2041. E-mail: mcintoshpubliclibrary@hotmail.com. *Libr Asst,* Faye Johnson
Open Mon, Wed & Thurs 10-6
Bookmobiles: 1

CHELSEA

P CHELSEA PUBLIC LIBRARY*, 16623 US 280, 35043. Tel: 205-847-5750. E-mail: chelsealibrary.al@gmail.com. Web Site: www.cityofchelsea.com/225/Library-Home. *Libr Dir,* Dana Polk; E-mail: dpolk@shelbycounty-al.org; *Asst Dir, Vols Coordr,* Amanda Fenton; E-mail: cplvolunteer41@gmail.com; *Children's Dir, Programming Dir,* Emily Sims; E-mail: chelsealibraryprogramming@gmail.com
Wireless access
Mem of Harrison Regional Library System
Open Mon-Thurs 9-7, Fri 9-5, Sat 9-4
Friends of the Library Group

CHEROKEE

P CHEROKEE PUBLIC LIBRARY*, 118 Church St, 35616. (Mail add: PO Box 333, 35616-0333). Tel: 256-359-4384. FAX: 256-359-4385. E-mail: cpl@cherokeetel.net. *Dir,* Alice Whitaker; Staff 1 (Non-MLS 1)
Circ 2,850
Library Holdings: Bk Vols 20,000
Automation Activity & Vendor Info: (Cataloging) Book Systems; (Circulation) Book Systems
Wireless access
Function: Bks on CD, Children's prog, Computers for patron use, Free DVD rentals
Special Services for the Blind - Bks on CD; Large print bks
Open Tues & Wed 12-5, Thurs 12-5:45, Fri 10-2
Friends of the Library Group

CHICKASAW

P CHICKASAW PUBLIC LIBRARY, Ina Pullen Smallwood Memorial Library, 224 Grant St, 36611. (Mail add: PO Box 11449, 36671-0449), SAN 300-0559. Tel: 251-452-6465. FAX: 251-452-6465. E-mail: chickasawlibrarystaff@gmail.com. Web Site: cityofchickasaw.org/residents/library. *Libr Operations Coordr,* Amber L Johnson
Founded 1948. Pop 6,649; Circ 35,126
Library Holdings: Bk Vols 20,000; Per Subs 75
Automation Activity & Vendor Info: (Cataloging) Book Systems; (Circulation) Book Systems; (OPAC) Book Systems
Wireless access
Open Mon-Fri 12-6
Friends of the Library Group

CHILDERSBURG

P EARLE A RAINWATER MEMORIAL LIBRARY*, 124 Ninth Ave SW, 35044. SAN 300-0567. Tel: 256-378-7239. FAX: 256-378-7287. *Dir,* Susan Carpenter; E-mail: scarpenter@childersburg.org; Staff 5 (Non-MLS 5)
Founded 1946. Pop 5,068; Circ 36,243
Oct 2015-Sept 2016 Income $171,699, State $5,134, City $106,560, County $34,146, Locally Generated Income $25,859. Mats Exp $23,000. Sal $77,673
Library Holdings: Bk Vols 58,351; Per Subs 20; Talking Bks 4,599
Special Collections: Army Ordinance Works Records. US Document Depository
Subject Interests: World War II power plant
Automation Activity & Vendor Info: (Acquisitions) Book Systems; (Cataloging) Book Systems; (Circulation) Book Systems; (OPAC) Book Systems; (Serials) Book Systems
Wireless access
Mem of Cheaha Regional Library
Open Mon-Fri 9-6, Sat 8-1
Restriction: Circ to mem only

CITRONELLE

P CITRONELLE MEMORIAL LIBRARY, 7855 State St, 36522. SAN 300-0575. Tel: 251-866-7319. FAX: 251-866-5210. E-mail: clib4@yahoo.com. Web Site: www.cityofcitronelle.com/library.asp. *Head Librn,* Deborah Craft; *Librn,* Tina Bender
Founded 1893. Pop 5,000; Circ 23,177
Library Holdings: Bk Titles 24,000; Per Subs 20
Automation Activity & Vendor Info: (Cataloging) Book Systems; (Circulation) Book Systems; (OPAC) Book Systems
Wireless access
Open Mon, Tues & Thurs 11-7, Fri 11-5, Sat 9-1

CLANTON

P CHILTON CLANTON PUBLIC LIBRARY*, 100 First Ave, 35045. SAN 300-0583. Tel: 205-755-1768. FAX: 205-755-1374. Web Site: www.chiltonclantonlibrary.org. *Dir,* Darlene Brock; E-mail: darlene@chiltonclantonlibrary.org; Staff 5 (Non-MLS 5)
Founded 1963. Pop 40,516
Library Holdings: AV Mats 625; Bk Titles 70,100; Per Subs 25
Subject Interests: Genealogy
Automation Activity & Vendor Info: (Cataloging) Follett Software; (Circulation) Follett Software; (OPAC) Follett Software
Wireless access
Open Mon-Thurs 8-6, Fri 8-4
Branches: 2
JEMISON PUBLIC LIBRARY, 160 Main St, Jemison, 35085, SAN 300-127X. Tel: 205-576-6760.
Founded 1945. Pop 1,828; Circ 3,669
Open Mon-Fri 8-4
MAPLESVILLE PUBLIC LIBRARY, 9400 AL Hwy 22, Maplesville, 36750, SAN 300-1377. Tel: 334-366-4211.
Pop 680; Circ 3,099
Restriction: Staff use only

CLAYTON

P TOWN & COUNTY PUBLIC LIBRARY*, 45 N Midway St, 36016. (Mail add: PO Box 518, 36016-0518), SAN 330-2946. Tel: 334-775-3506. FAX: 334-775-3538. E-mail: town.library@yahoo.com. *Libr Dir,* Dorothy Lang
Library Holdings: Bk Vols 18,000; Per Subs 8
Special Collections: Genealogical Resources
Automation Activity & Vendor Info: (Cataloging) Book Systems; (Circulation) Book Systems; (OPAC) Book Systems
Wireless access
Open Mon-Fri 12-5
Friends of the Library Group

COLLINSVILLE

P COLLINSVILLE PUBLIC LIBRARY, 151 Main St, 35961. (Mail add: PO Box 743, 35961-0743), SAN 376-740X. Tel: 256-524-2323. FAX: 256-524-5119. E-mail: collinsvillelibrary@gmail.com. Web Site: www.collinsvillealabama.net/library. *Librn,* Jennifer Wilkins; E-mail: jencollib@hotmail.com; Staff 2 (Non-MLS 2)
Pop 2,500; Circ 4,000
Library Holdings: Bk Vols 9,832; Talking Bks 30; Videos 1,037
Special Collections: Adult bks in Spanish
Automation Activity & Vendor Info: (Cataloging) Book Systems; (Circulation) Book Systems; (OPAC) Book Systems
Wireless access
Open Mon, Tues & Thurs 11-6, Fri 11-5, Sat 10-3

COLUMBIANA

P COLUMBIANA PUBLIC LIBRARY*, 50 Lester St, 35051. (Mail add: PO Box 1459, 35051-1459), SAN 321-6063. Tel: 205-669-5812. FAX: 205-669-5803. Web Site: www.shelbycounty-al.org. *Dir,* Shelia Gallups; E-mail: cpldirector@shelbycounty-al.org; Staff 8 (MLS 6, Non-MLS 2)
Founded 1963. Pop 4,200; Circ 70,000
Library Holdings: AV Mats 1,500; Bk Titles 26,000; Per Subs 24; Talking Bks 1,200
Automation Activity & Vendor Info: (Acquisitions) Innovative Interfaces, Inc; (Cataloging) Innovative Interfaces, Inc; (Circulation) Innovative Interfaces, Inc; (ILL) Innovative Interfaces, Inc; (Media Booking) Innovative Interfaces, Inc; (OPAC) Innovative Interfaces, Inc; (Serials) Innovative Interfaces, Inc
Wireless access
Function: 24/7 Electronic res, Adult bk club, Adult literacy prog, After school storytime, Archival coll, Audiobks via web, AV serv, Bk club(s), Bks on CD, Children's prog, Computers for patron use, E-Reserves, Electronic databases & coll, Family literacy, Free DVD rentals, Holiday prog, Home delivery & serv to seniorr ctr & nursing homes, Homework prog, ILL available, Internet access, Laminating, Magazines, Mail & tel request accepted, Meeting rooms, Microfiche/film & reading machines,

Movies, Online ref, OverDrive digital audio bks, Photocopying/Printing, Prog for adults, Prog for children & young adult, Ref serv available, Spanish lang bks, Spoken cassettes & CDs, Spoken cassettes & DVDs, Story hour, Summer reading prog, Tax forms, Telephone ref, Wheelchair accessible
Mem of Harrison Regional Library System
Special Services for the Deaf - Bks on deafness & sign lang; Staff with knowledge of sign lang
Open Mon, Wed & Fri 9-5, Tues & Thurs 9-8, Sat 9-1
Friends of the Library Group

P HARRISON REGIONAL LIBRARY SYSTEM*, 50 Lester St, 35051. SAN 330-129X. Tel: 205-669-3910. Reference Tel: 205-669-3893. Administration Tel: 205-669-3891. FAX: 205-669-3940. Web Site: www.shelbycounty-al.org. *Dir,* Kathy Davis; E-mail: kdavis@shelbycounty-al.org; *Head, Cat,* Cindy Reed; E-mail: creed@shelbycounty-al.org; *ILL Librn,* Kala Petric; E-mail: hrlill@shelbycounty-al.org; Staff 6 (MLS 1, Non-MLS 5)
Founded 1940. Pop 213,605; Circ 1,327,633
Special Collections: Alabama & Shelby County History Coll; George Washington Museum & Coll
Automation Activity & Vendor Info: (Acquisitions) Innovative Interfaces, Inc; (Cataloging) Innovative Interfaces, Inc; (Circulation) Innovative Interfaces, Inc; (ILL) Innovative Interfaces, Inc; (OPAC) Innovative Interfaces, Inc; (Serials) Innovative Interfaces, Inc
Wireless access
Function: 24/7 Electronic res, 24/7 Online cat, Home delivery & serv to seniorr ctr & nursing homes, Homebound delivery serv, ILL available, Internet access, Online cat, Online ref, Outreach serv, OverDrive digital audio bks, Ref serv available, Senior outreach, Telephone ref, Wheelchair accessible
Member Libraries: Albert L Scott Library; Chelsea Public Library; Columbiana Public Library; Jane B Holmes Public Library; Lallouise Florey McGraw Public Library; North Shelby County Library; Parnell Memorial Library; Pelham Public Library; Roy Downs Memorial Calera Library; Vernice Stoudenmire Public Library
Open Mon-Fri 8-4

COURTLAND

P COURTLAND PUBLIC LIBRARY, 215 College St, 35618. SAN 376-7639. Tel: 256-522-8035. E-mail: courtland315@gmail.com. *Dir,* Sherry Hamilton
Library Holdings: Bk Vols 16,000
Wireless access
Open Mon-Thurs 12-4
Friends of the Library Group

CROSSVILLE

P CROSSVILLE PUBLIC LIBRARY*, 80 Gaines St, 35962. (Mail add: PO Box 308, 35962-0308). Tel: 256-528-2628. E-mail: cplib@farmerstel.com. Web Site: aplsws1.apls.state.al.us/crossville. *Librn,* Elizabeth Hearn
Founded 1971. Pop 1,506
Library Holdings: Bk Vols 9,000
Automation Activity & Vendor Info: (Acquisitions) Brodart; (Cataloging) Brodart
Wireless access
Open Mon-Thurs 9-5, Fri 9-3, Sat 9-1
Friends of the Library Group

CULLMAN

P CULLMAN COUNTY PUBLIC LIBRARY SYSTEM*, 200 Clark St NE, 35055. SAN 330-1567. Tel: 256-734-1068. E-mail: cullmanpubliclibrary@gmail.com. Web Site: www.ccpls.com. *Dir,* Sharon Townson; E-mail: townsonsd@ccpls.com; Staff 4 (MLS 3, Non-MLS 1)
Founded 1928. Pop 77,000; Circ 121,000
Library Holdings: AV Mats 4,800; Bks on Deafness & Sign Lang 15; CDs 1,500; DVDs 300; e-books 45,000; Large Print Bks 3,500; Bk Titles 70,000; Bk Vols 87,615; Per Subs 167; Videos 2,000
Special Collections: Archival (W C Bates Coll, City of Cullman Records, Geo Parker Diaries, Pittman Gin Records, Memorabilia Coll, Coterie Club Records); Genealogy (Daughters of the American Revolution Coll, United Daughters of the Confederacy Coll); Maps (Fuller Coll, Dan J Scott Coll); Photographs (Cullman-Johnson Coll, Hazel Karter-Daniel Coll). Oral History
Subject Interests: Alabama, Civil War
Automation Activity & Vendor Info: (Cataloging) Book Systems; (Circulation) Book Systems; (ILL) OCLC Connexion; (OPAC) Book Systems
Wireless access
Function: Adult literacy prog, Archival coll, Art exhibits, Audio & video playback equip for onsite use, AV serv, Computer training, Doc delivery serv, E-Reserves, Electronic databases & coll, Equip loans & repairs, Family literacy, Govt ref serv, Health sci info serv, Home delivery & serv to seniorr ctr & nursing homes, Homework prog, ILL available, Internet access, Learning ctr, Mail & tel request accepted, Music CDs, Orientations, Photocopying/Printing, Preschool outreach, Prog for adults, Prog for children & young adult, Ref & res, Ref serv available, Senior computer classes, Serves people with intellectual disabilities, Spoken cassettes & CDs, Spoken cassettes & DVDs, Summer reading prog, Tax forms, Telephone ref, VHS videos, Wheelchair accessible
Partic in OCLC Online Computer Library Center, Inc
Open Mon, Wed & Fri 9-6, Tues & Thurs 9-8, Sat 9-1
Restriction: Non-resident fee
Friends of the Library Group
Branches: 4
TOM BEVILL PUBLIC, Colony Education Complex, 151 Byars Rd, Hanceville, 35077, SAN 330-1621. Tel: 256-287-1573. FAX: 256-287-1573. *Librn,* Brenda Johnson
Founded 1996. Pop 298
Library Holdings: Bk Vols 1,500; Per Subs 12
Subject Interests: Adult educ, African-Am
Open Tues-Thurs 11-4, Fri 9-Noon
Friends of the Library Group
GARDEN CITY PUBLIC, Municipal Bldg, 501 First Ave S, Garden City, 35070, SAN 330-1591. Tel: 256-352-4552. *Librn,* Mary Griffin; E-mail: marygriffin45@yahoo.com
Founded 1946. Pop 604; Circ 5,504
Subject Interests: Local hist
Open Mon-Thurs 12-5
Friends of the Library Group
HANCEVILLE PUBLIC, 200 Commercial St SE, Hanceville, 35077, SAN 377-7812. Tel: 256-352-0685. FAX: 256-352-1111. E-mail: hanceville@ccpls.com. *Librn,* Shirley Burden
Open Tues-Fri 8-12 & 1-5, Sat 9-1
Friends of the Library Group
GUY HUNT PUBLIC, 60 Lions Park Rd, Holly Pond, 35083. Tel: 256-796-5226. E-mail: guyhuntlibrary@gmail.com. *Librn,* Melody Camp
Open Tues & Thurs 9-5, Wed & Fri 1-5, Sat 9-1
Friends of the Library Group
Bookmobiles: 2. Coordr, Extension Servs, Jeremy Weissend. Bk titles 3,000

DADEVILLE

P DADEVILLE PUBLIC LIBRARY*, 205 N West St, 36853. SAN 300-0613. Tel: 256-825-7820. Toll Free FAX: 866-450-1944. E-mail: dadevillelibrary@gmail.com. Web Site: dadevillepubliclibrary.com. *Dir,* Shelley Macon; Staff 3 (MLS 1, Non-MLS 2)
Founded 1907. Pop 3,212; Circ 18,684
Library Holdings: Bk Vols 10,300; Per Subs 12
Wireless access
Function: ILL available
Mem of Horseshoe Bend Regional Library
Open Mon, Tues, Thurs & Fri 9-5, Wed 2-6, Sat 9-12
Friends of the Library Group

P HORSESHOE BEND REGIONAL LIBRARY*, 207 N West St, 36853. SAN 300-0621. Tel: 256-825-9232. FAX: 256-825-4314. E-mail: horseshoebend@bellsouth.net. Web Site: www.horseshoebendlibrary.org. *Dir,* Deja Ruddick; *Asst Dir,* Regina Strickland; Staff 2 (MLS 2)
Founded 1940. Pop 178,200
Library Holdings: AV Mats 2,992; Bk Vols 119,644; Per Subs 32
Automation Activity & Vendor Info: (Cataloging) Brodart; (Circulation) Brodart
Function: Home delivery & serv to seniorr ctr & nursing homes, Homebound delivery serv, ILL available, Ref serv available
Member Libraries: Adelia M Russell Library; Auburn Public Library; Dadeville Public Library; Eclectic Public Library; Goodwater Public Library; Lewis Cooper Junior Memorial Library; Millbrook Public Library; Rockford Public Library; Tallassee Community Library; Wetumpka Public Library
Open Mon-Thurs 8-5
Bookmobiles: 3

DALEVILLE

P DALEVILLE PUBLIC LIBRARY*, 308 Donnell Blvd, 36322. SAN 330-3004. Tel: 334-503-9119. FAX: 334-503-9119. E-mail: dalevillepubliclibrary@troycable.net. Web Site: www.dalevilleal.com/CityServices/PublicLibrary.aspx, www.dalevillepubliclibrary.com. *Libr Dir,* Kathryn Brown
Library Holdings: Bk Vols 18,000; Per Subs 20
Automation Activity & Vendor Info: (Cataloging) Evergreen; (Circulation) Evergreen; (OPAC) Evergreen
Wireless access
Open Mon-Thurs 10-6, Fri & Sat 10-3
Friends of the Library Group

DAPHNE

P DAPHNE PUBLIC LIBRARY*, 2607 US Hwy 98, 36526. (Mail add: PO Drawer 1225, 36526-1225), SAN 300-063X. Tel: 251-620-2500. FAX: 251-621-3086. Web Site: www.daphnelibrary.org. *Libr Dir,* Tonja Young; E-mail: tyoung@daphneal.com; Staff 10 (MLS 3, Non-MLS 7)
Founded 1969. Pop 18,600; Circ 270,871
Library Holdings: Audiobooks 4,330; AV Mats 12,507; Bks on Deafness & Sign Lang 50; Braille Volumes 100; CDs 648; DVDs 3,275; Electronic Media & Resources 89; Large Print Bks 2,548; Bk Vols 51,374; Per Subs 91; Talking Bks 7,045; Videos 4,254
Special Collections: Ecology & Environmental Sciences (Earth Matters Environmental Resource Coll); Local History, Oral History & Alabama Authors (Daphne Special Coll); Small Business Resource Center
Automation Activity & Vendor Info: (Circulation) TLC (The Library Corporation)
Wireless access
Function: Adult bk club, After school storytime, Archival coll, Art exhibits, Audio & video playback equip for onsite use, Bk club(s), Bks on cassette, Bks on CD, Children's prog, Computer training, Computers for patron use, Electronic databases & coll, Family literacy, Free DVD rentals, Govt ref serv, Holiday prog, ILL available, Instruction & testing, Internet access, Large print keyboards, Magnifiers for reading, Music CDs, Online cat, Outreach serv, Photocopying/Printing, Preschool outreach, Prog for adults, Prog for children & young adult, Ref serv available, Senior computer classes, Senior outreach, Story hour, Summer reading prog, Tax forms, Teen prog, VHS videos, Wheelchair accessible, Workshops
Mem of Baldwin County Library Cooperative, Inc
Special Services for the Deaf - Bks on deafness & sign lang
Special Services for the Blind - Aids for in-house use; Audio mat; Bks & mags in Braille, on rec, tape & cassette; Bks on cassette; Bks on CD; Braille bks; Cassettes; Children's Braille; Closed circuit TV; Computer access aids; Extensive large print coll; IBM screen reader; Large print bks; Large screen computer & software; Low vision equip; Magnifiers; Newsletter (in large print, Braille or on cassette); Recorded bks; Screen enlargement software for people with visual disabilities; Sound rec; Variable speed audiotape players; Videos on blindness & physical disabilties; ZoomText magnification & reading software
Open Mon-Thurs 9-8, Fri 9-5, Sat 9-2
Restriction: Non-resident fee
Friends of the Library Group

S UNITED STATES SPORTS ACADEMY*, Robert Block Library, One Academy Dr, 36526. SAN 324-5098. Tel: 251-626-3303. FAX: 251-626-1149. E-mail: library@ussa.edu. Web Site: ussa.edu/students/library-resources. *Libr Dir,* Dr Vandy Pacetti-Donelson; E-mail: vpacettidonelson@ussa.edu
Library Holdings: Bk Titles 10,000; Per Subs 247
Special Collections: Foreign Countries (International Coll), bks, flms, vf
Subject Interests: Fitness, Sport coaching, Sport mgt, Sport res, Sports med
Wireless access
Publications: Shelflist (Acquisition list)
Partic in LYRASIS; National Network of Libraries of Medicine Region 2; Network of Alabama Academic Libraries; OCLC Online Computer Library Center, Inc
Open Mon-Fri 8-5

DAUPHIN ISLAND

G DEPARTMENT OF CONSERVATION & NATURAL RESOURCES, Marine Resources Division, Two North Iberville St, 36528-0189. (Mail add: PO Box 189, 36528), SAN 327-8883. Tel: 251-861-2882. FAX: 251-861-8741. *Library Contact,* John Mareska; E-mail: john.mareska@dcnr.alabama.gov
Library Holdings: Bk Vols 500
Open Mon-Fri 8-5

DECATUR

J CALHOUN COMMUNITY COLLEGE*, Albert P Brewer Library, Hwy 31 N, 35609. (Mail add: PO Box 2216, 35609-2216), SAN 330-1656. Tel: 256-306-2774. Reference Tel: 256-306-2777. Administration Tel: 256-306-2784. FAX: 256-306-2780. E-mail: reference@calhoun.edu. Web Site: www.calhoun.edu/student-resources/library. *Dir, Libr Serv,* James Loyd; E-mail: james.loyd@calhoun.edu; *Ref Librn, Tech Serv,* Brenda P Parris; Tel: 256-306-2778, E-mail: brenda.parris@calhoun.edu
Founded 1965. Highest Degree: Associate
Special Collections: Alabama Coll; Center for the Study of Southern Political Culture
Automation Activity & Vendor Info: (Cataloging) SirsiDynix; (Circulation) SirsiDynix; (ILL) OCLC WorldShare Interlibrary Loan; (OPAC) SirsiDynix
Wireless access
Special Services for the Blind - Screen enlargement software for people with visual disabilities
Open Mon-Thurs 7:45am-8pm, Fri 7:45am-11:45am

Departmental Libraries:

HUNTSVILLE CAMPUS LIBRARY, 102-B Wynn Dr, Huntsville, 35805. (Mail add: PO Box 2216, 35609-2216). Tel: 256-890-4774. Reference Tel: 256-890-4777. FAX: 256-890-4713. *Head Librn,* Gerald D Jackson; Tel: 256-890-4771, E-mail: gerald.jackson@calhoun.edu
Open Mon-Thurs 7:45am-8pm, Fri 7:45am-11:45am

P DECATUR PUBLIC LIBRARY*, 504 Cherry St NE, 35601. SAN 300-0656. Tel: 256-353-2993. FAX: 256-350-6736. Web Site: mydpl.org. *Dir,* Sherry Sakovich; Tel: 256-353-2993, Ext 102, E-mail: ssakovich@mydpl.org; Staff 16 (MLS 1, Non-MLS 15)
Founded 1905
Oct 2020-Sept 2021 Income $849,109, State $98,951, City $441,936, County $65,000, Locally Generated Income $13,016, Other $230,206. Mats Exp $849,109, Books $61,828, Per/Ser (Incl. Access Fees) $4,030, AV Mat $8,004, Electronic Ref Mat (Incl. Access Fees) $13,779. Sal $443,220 (Prof $56,000)
Library Holdings: Audiobooks 3,138; AV Mats 8,474; DVDs 5,153; e-books 44,950; Electronic Media & Resources 17; Large Print Bks 4,085; Bk Titles 85,350; Bk Vols 91,909; Per Subs 25
Special Collections: Genealogy & local history
Automation Activity & Vendor Info: (Acquisitions) Koha; (Cataloging) Koha; (Circulation) Koha; (OPAC) Koha
Wireless access
Function: 24/7 Electronic res, 24/7 Online cat, Adult bk club, Audiobks via web, AV serv, Bk club(s), Bks on CD, Children's prog, Computer training, Computers for patron use, Electronic databases & coll, Holiday prog, Internet access, Life-long learning prog for all ages, Magazines, Meeting rooms, Movies, Online cat, OverDrive digital audio bks, Photocopying/Printing, Prog for adults, Prog for children & young adult, Ref serv available, Scanner, Senior computer classes, Spanish lang bks, Story hour, Summer reading prog, Tax forms, Workshops
Publications: INDEX-Friends of the Library (Newsletter)
Open Mon-Thurs 10-6, Fri 10-5, Sat 10-4
Friends of the Library Group

P LINDA DURAN PUBLIC LIBRARY*, 1612 S Bethel Rd, 35603-5408. Tel: 256-584-0230. FAX: 256-584-0230. Web Site: townofpriceville.com/town-services/library. *Librn,* Paula Hensley; E-mail: PaulaHensley@townofpriceville.com
Library Holdings: Bk Vols 15,200; Per Subs 15
Open Mon, Tues & Thurs 9-7, Fri 9-5

DEMOPOLIS

P DEMOPOLIS PUBLIC LIBRARY*, 211 E Washington, 36732. SAN 300-0664. Tel: 334-289-1595. E-mail: demopolislibrary@gmail.com. Web Site: www.demopolislibrary.info. *Dir,* Kathy Owings; E-mail: library.director@demopolisal.gov; *Circ Mgr,* Connie Lawson; E-mail: dplconstance@gmail.com
Founded 1922. Pop 8,000; Circ 41,170
Library Holdings: Bk Vols 25,000; Per Subs 66
Special Collections: Demopolis History Coll
Subject Interests: Genealogy
Automation Activity & Vendor Info: (Cataloging) Book Systems; (Circulation) Book Systems; (OPAC) Book Systems
Wireless access
Open Mon-Fri 9-5
Friends of the Library Group

DOTHAN

M ALABAMA COLLEGE OF OSTEOPATHIC MEDICINE*, Medical Library, 445 Health Sciences Blvd, Hwy 84 E, 36303. (Mail add: PO Box 6987, 36302-6987), SAN 320-362X. Tel: 334-699-2266. FAX: 334-699-2268. E-mail: lrc.ask@acomedu.org. Web Site: www.acom.edu/library. *Libr Dir,* Lisa Ennis; E-mail: lennis@acom.edu; *Sr Assoc, Tech Serv,* Michelle Miller; E-mail: mmiller@acom.edu
Founded 1964
Library Holdings: Bk Titles 705; Per Subs 100
Subject Interests: Clinical med
Wireless access
Partic in SE-Atlantic Regional Med Libr Servs
Restriction: Staff use only

P DOTHAN HOUSTON COUNTY LIBRARY SYSTEM*, Downtown Branch - Headquarters, 445 N Oates St, 36303. SAN 330-1710. Tel: 334-793-9767. E-mail: dhcls@dhcls.org, main@dhcls.org. Web Site: www.dhcls.org. *Libr Dir,* Jason LeDuc; E-mail: director@dhcls.org; *Mgr, Resources & Digital Strategy,* Terah Harris; *Ch Serv,* Kristin North; E-mail: childrens@dhcls.org; *Br Mgr,* Michael Mitchell; Staff 11 (MLS 4, Non-MLS 7)

Founded 1900. Pop 90,000; Circ 317,074
Library Holdings: Large Print Bks 9,357; Bk Vols 192,000; Per Subs 116; Talking Bks 1,066; Videos 2,634
Automation Activity & Vendor Info: (Cataloging) SirsiDynix; (Circulation) SirsiDynix; (OPAC) SirsiDynix
Wireless access
Open Mon, Tues & Thurs 10-8, Wed & Fri 10-6, Sat 10-5, Sun 1-5
Branches: 2
ASHFORD BRANCH, 305 Sixth Ave, Ashford, 36312, SAN 330-1745. Tel: 334-899-3121. *Librn,* Anna Todd
Library Holdings: Bk Vols 17,384
Open Mon 10-3, Tues -Thurs 1-6, Fri 10-6, Sat 10-2
WESTGATE BRANCH, 535 Recreation Rd, 36303. Tel: 334-699-2950. E-mail: westgate@dhcls.org. *Br Mgr,* Kim Driskell
Open Mon, Tues & Thurs 10-8, Wed & Fri 10-6, Sat 10-5, Sun 1-5
Bookmobiles: 1

C TROY UNIVERSITY*, Dothan Library, 502 University Dr, 36304. SAN 300-0885. Tel: 334-983-6556, Ext 1320. Circulation Tel: 334-983-6556, Ext 1331. Interlibrary Loan Service Tel: 334-983-6556, Ext 1323. Reference Tel: 334-983-6556, Ext 1321. FAX: 334-983-6327. Web Site: troy.edu/libraries/index.html. *Dir, Libr Serv,* Position Currently Open; *Spec Coll & Archives Librn,* Tina Bernath; Tel: 334-983-6556, Ext 1324, E-mail: tbernath@troy.edu; *Tech Serv Librn,* Olga Casey; Tel: 334-983-6556, Ext 1325, E-mail: oknyaz@troy.edu; *Archivist,* Dr Martin Olliff; Tel: 334-983-6556, Ext 1327, E-mail: molliff@troy.edu; *Archives Asst,* Diane Sowell; E-mail: lsowell@troy.edu; *Circ, Libr Asst,* Mary B McCruter; E-mail: mmccruter@troy.edu; *Tech Serv,* Susan Echols; E-mail: sechols@troy.edu; Staff 7 (MLS 3, Non-MLS 4)
Founded 1973. Enrl 1,200; Fac 95; Highest Degree: Doctorate
Library Holdings: e-books 40,000; Bk Vols 102,000; Per Subs 410
Special Collections: Wiregrass History Coll
Subject Interests: Bus & mgt, Computer sci, Criminal law & justice, Educ, Hist
Automation Activity & Vendor Info: (Cataloging) SirsiDynix; (Circulation) SirsiDynix; (Course Reserve) SirsiDynix; (OPAC) SirsiDynix; (Serials) SirsiDynix
Wireless access
Partic in LYRASIS; Network of Alabama Academic Libraries
Open Mon-Thurs 8am-9pm, Fri 8-Noon, Sat 10-2, Sun 1-5

J WALLACE COMMUNITY COLLEGE*, Phillip J Hamm Library-LRC, 1141 Wallace Dr, 36303. SAN 300-0680. Tel: 334-556-2217. Administration Tel: 334-556-2217, Ext 2225. Web Site: www.wallace.edu/student_services/learning_resources_center.aspx. *Dir,* A P Hoffman; E-mail: ahoffman@wallace.edu; Staff 1 (MLS 1)
Founded 1965. Enrl 3,500; Fac 90; Highest Degree: Associate
Library Holdings: AV Mats 350; e-books 40,000; Bk Titles 35,000; Bk Vols 40,000; Per Subs 170; Talking Bks 50
Subject Interests: Alabama, Allied health, Children's educ, Nursing
Automation Activity & Vendor Info: (Acquisitions) Ex Libris Group; (Cataloging) Ex Libris Group; (Circulation) Ex Libris Group; (Course Reserve) Ex Libris Group; (OPAC) Ex Libris Group; (Serials) Ex Libris Group
Wireless access

DOUBLE SPRINGS

P DOUBLE SPRINGS PUBLIC LIBRARY, 637 Blake Dr, 35553. (Mail add: PO Box 555, 35553-0555), SAN 300-0699. Tel: 205-489-2412. E-mail: doublespringspubliclibrary@live.com. Web Site: www.townofdoublesprings.com/?page_id=63. *Librn,* Beth Kendrick; E-mail: bekendrick@hotmail.com
Library Holdings: AV Mats 2,000; Bk Vols 9,000
Wireless access
Mem of Carl Elliott Regional Library System
Open Mon-Fri 8:30-1:30 & 2-5

ECLECTIC

P ECLECTIC PUBLIC LIBRARY*, 50 Main St, 36024. Tel: 334-639-4727. E-mail: eclecticpubliclibrary@live.com. Web Site: aplsws1.apls.state.al.us/eclectic/home. *Librn,* Betty Coker
Founded 2009
Library Holdings: DVDs 600; Bk Vols 12,500
Wireless access
Mem of Horseshoe Bend Regional Library
Open Mon, Tues & Thurs 1-5, Sat 9-1

ELBA

P ELBA PUBLIC LIBRARY*, 406 Simmons St, 36323. SAN 300-0710. Tel: 334-897-6921. FAX: 334-897-6921. E-mail: elbalibrary@elbaal.gov. Web Site: www.elbapubliclibrary.com. *Dir,* Jennifer F Amlong; E-mail: jamlong@elbaal.gov; Staff 1 (MLS 1)
Pop 4,355; Circ 18,525
Library Holdings: CDs 222; Bk Titles 12,682; Per Subs 24; Talking Bks 643; Videos 429
Automation Activity & Vendor Info: (Cataloging) Book Systems; (Circulation) Book Systems; (OPAC) Book Systems
Wireless access
Open Mon, Tues, Thurs & Fri 8-5, Wed 8-2

ELBERTA

P ELBERTA PUBLIC LIBRARY*, 13052-A Main St, 36530. Tel: 251-986-3069. E-mail: elbertalibrary@yahoo.com. Web Site: www.facebook.com/elbertalibrary/. *Dir,* Betty Wood; E-mail: elbertalibrary@yahoo.com; Staff 1 (Non-MLS 1)
Founded 2016. Pop 1,714; Circ 2,421
Library Holdings: Audiobooks 123; CDs 36; DVDs 545; Large Print Bks 216; Bk Titles 8,685; Bk Vols 8,719; Videos 15
Automation Activity & Vendor Info: (Cataloging) TLC (The Library Corporation); (Circulation) TLC (The Library Corporation); (ILL) OCLC WorldShare Interlibrary Loan; (OPAC) TLC (The Library Corporation)
Function: Bks on CD, Children's prog, Computers for patron use, Electronic databases & coll, Free DVD rentals, ILL available, Internet access, Movies, Music CDs, Online cat, Photocopying/Printing, Prog for children & young adult, Summer reading prog, Tax forms, Wheelchair accessible
Mem of Baldwin County Library Cooperative, Inc
Open Mon, Wed & Fri 9-Noon,Tues & Thurs 1-5

ENTERPRISE

P ENTERPRISE PUBLIC LIBRARY*, 101 E Grubbs St, 36330. SAN 300-0729. Tel: 334-347-2636. FAX: 334-393-6477. Web Site: www.enterpriselibrary.org. *Libr Dir,* Sheila Harris; E-mail: director@enterpriselibrary.org; *Youth Librn,* Chrissy Crump; *Circ Mgr,* Kay Knop; *Cat, Coll,* Jo Thompson
Founded 1923. Pop 21,176; Circ 116,000
Library Holdings: AV Mats 175; Large Print Bks 500; Bk Vols 110,000; Per Subs 9; Talking Bks 500
Special Collections: Audio Books, Large Print, Videos
Subject Interests: Alabama
Automation Activity & Vendor Info: (Acquisitions) TLC (The Library Corporation); (Cataloging) TLC (The Library Corporation); (Circulation) TLC (The Library Corporation); (ILL) OCLC; (OPAC) TLC (The Library Corporation)
Wireless access
Special Services for the Blind - Audio mat; Large print bks
Open Mon, Wed & Fri 9-5:30, Tues & Thurs 9-7, Sat 9-2
Friends of the Library Group
Bookmobiles: 1

J ENTERPRISE STATE COMMUNITY COLLEGE*, Learning Resources Center, 600 Plaza Dr, 36330. (Mail add: PO Box 1300, 36331-1300), SAN 300-0737. Tel: 334-347-2623, Ext 2271. FAX: 334-347-0146. Web Site: www.escc.edu/about-escc/Library. *Librn, Tech Proc,* Linda Henderson; Tel: 334-347-2623, Ext 2301; *Exec Secy,* Rebecca Stephens; Tel: 334-347-2623, Ext 2271, E-mail: bstephens@escc.edu; *Libr Asst,* Amy Willis; Tel: 334-347-2623, Ext 2237, E-mail: awillis@escc.edu; Staff 6 (MLS 2, Non-MLS 4)
Founded 1966. Enrl 1,900; Fac 100; Highest Degree: Associate
Library Holdings: Bks on Deafness & Sign Lang 10; CDs 50; DVDs 150; e-books 5,000; Bk Vols 80,000; Per Subs 150
Special Collections: Genealogy. US Document Depository
Subject Interests: Genealogy
Automation Activity & Vendor Info: (Cataloging) SirsiDynix-WorkFlows; (Circulation) SirsiDynix-WorkFlows; (Discovery) SirsiDynix-WorkFlows; (ILL) OCLC FirstSearch; (OPAC) SirsiDynix; (Serials) EBSCO Discovery Service
Wireless access
Partic in LYRASIS; OCLC Online Computer Library Center, Inc
Open Mon, Tues & Thurs 7:45-7, Wed 7:45-5, Fri 7:45-1

EUFAULA

P EUFAULA CARNEGIE LIBRARY*, 217 N Eufaula Ave, 36027. SAN 330-3039. Tel: 334-687-2337. Administration Tel: 334-687-8190. FAX: 334-687-8143. Web Site: aplsnew-web.apls.state.al.us:10129/eufaula/web/. *Dir,* Ronnie Smith; E-mail: dir_ecl@yahoo.com; Staff 9 (MLS 1, Non-MLS 8)
Founded 1904. Pop 26,985
Oct 2018-Sept 2019 Income $500,822, State $13,067, City $79,075, Federal $5,000, Locally Generated Income $375,497, Other $28,183. Sal $212,349 (Prof $54,834)
Library Holdings: Audiobooks 1,021; DVDs 2,594; e-books 370,225; Bk Vols 31,671; Per Subs 63
Special Collections: Local History & Genealogy Coll

Automation Activity & Vendor Info: (Cataloging) Book Systems; (Circulation) Book Systems; (OPAC) Book Systems
Wireless access
Function: 24/7 Electronic res, 24/7 Online cat, Children's prog, Computers for patron use, Electronic databases & coll, Free DVD rentals, Home delivery & serv to seniorr ctr & nursing homes, Magazines, Online cat, Outreach serv
Open Mon & Wed 9-6, Tues & Thurs 9-8, Fri 9-5, Sat 9-2
Friends of the Library Group

J WALLACE COMMUNITY COLLEGE*, Sparks Campus Learning Resources Center, 3235 S Eufaula Ave, 36027-3542. (Mail add: PO Drawer 580, 36072-0580). Tel: 334-687-3543. Toll Free Tel: 800-543-2426. FAX: 334-687-0255. Web Site: www.wallace.edu/student_services/learning_resources_center.aspx. *Dir,* A P Hoffman; E-mail: ahoffman@wallace.edu; Staff 1 (Non-MLS 1)
Founded 2000. Enrl 640; Fac 32; Highest Degree: Associate
Library Holdings: CDs 50; DVDs 36; e-books 49,070; e-journals 56; Bk Vols 6,000; Per Subs 32; Videos 437
Open Mon-Thurs 7:30am-9pm, Fri 7:30am-12:15pm

EUTAW

P JAMES C POOLE JR MEMORIAL LIBRARY*, 420 Prairie Ave, 35462-1165. Tel: 205-372-9026. FAX: 205-372-9026. E-mail: greene.library@yahoo.com. *Librn,* Marilyn Gibson
Pop 9,880
Library Holdings: Bk Vols 15,000; Per Subs 22
Automation Activity & Vendor Info: (Cataloging) Book Systems; (Circulation) Book Systems; (Course Reserve) Book Systems; (ILL) Book Systems; (Media Booking) Book Systems
Wireless access
Open Mon-Fri 9-5, Sat 9-Noon

EVA

P EVA PUBLIC LIBRARY*, 4549 Hwy 55 E, 35621. (Mail add: PO Box 99, 35621-0099), SAN 376-7647. Tel: 256-796-8638. FAX: 256-796-8638. E-mail: evalibrary@att.net. *Head Librn,* Joyce Woodall; *Librn,* Judy Burrow; *Librn,* Pam Morgan
Founded 1980
Library Holdings: Bk Vols 12,000; Per Subs 6
Wireless access
Open Mon 3-7, Tues & Sat 10-1, Wed & Fri 2-5, Thurs 2-6
Friends of the Library Group

EVERGREEN

P EVERGREEN PUBLIC LIBRARY*, 119 Cemetery Ave, 36401. SAN 300-0753. Tel: 251-578-2670. FAX: 251-578-2316. E-mail: evergreenpubliclibrary@mediacombb.net. *Dir,* Diann Lee
Pop 14,500; Circ 30,000
Library Holdings: Bk Vols 35,000; Per Subs 10
Special Collections: Lucy C Warren Heritage Section
Subject Interests: Genealogy
Automation Activity & Vendor Info: (Cataloging) Book Systems; (Circulation) Book Systems; (ILL) OCLC WorldShare Interlibrary Loan; (OPAC) Book Systems
Open Mon-Fri 9-5, Sat 9-Noon

FAIRFIELD

P WALTER J HANNA MEMORIAL LIBRARY, 4615 Gary Ave, 35064. SAN 300-0761. Tel: 205-783-6007. FAX: 205-783-6041. Web Site: www.fairfield.lib.al.us. *Dir,* Lora R Perry; E-mail: lora.perry@fairfield.lib.al.us
Circ 12,179
Library Holdings: Bk Vols 37,000; Per Subs 33
Automation Activity & Vendor Info: (Cataloging) Innovative Interfaces, Inc; (Circulation) Innovative Interfaces, Inc; (OPAC) Innovative Interfaces, Inc
Wireless access
Function: Music CDs, Prog for children & young adult, Summer reading prog, VHS videos
Open Mon-Fri 10-2

C MILES COLLEGE*, C A Kirkendoll Learning Resources Center, 5500 Myron Massey Blvd, 35064. (Mail add: PO Box 39800, Birmingham, 35208-0937), SAN 300-0311. Tel: 205-929-1709, 205-929-1714. Reference Tel: 205-929-1748. FAX: 205-929-1635. Web Site: www.miles.edu/library. *Dir,* Dr Geraldine Bell; Tel: 205-929-1715; *Circ Mgr,* Lynne Bobbs; Tel: 205-929-1710, E-mail: lbobbs@miles.edu; *Cataloger,* Candice Murdock; Tel: 205-929-1748, E-mail: cmurdock@miles.edu; *Library Contact,* Emma Sloan; E-mail: esloan@miles.edu; *Ser,* Helen Tutt; Tel: 205-929-1711, E-mail: htutt@miles.edu; Staff 9 (MLS 3, Non-MLS 6)
Founded 1978. Enrl 1,875; Fac 110; Highest Degree: Bachelor
Library Holdings: AV Mats 2,473; Bk Vols 100,000; Per Subs 400
Special Collections: Afro-American Coll; Children's Coll
Automation Activity & Vendor Info: (Acquisitions) Innovative Interfaces, Inc; (Cataloging) Innovative Interfaces, Inc; (Circulation) Innovative Interfaces, Inc; (Course Reserve) Innovative Interfaces, Inc; (ILL) Innovative Interfaces, Inc; (OPAC) Innovative Interfaces, Inc; (Serials) Innovative Interfaces, Inc
Wireless access
Function: ILL available, Ref serv available
Partic in HBCU Library Alliance; LYRASIS
Open Mon-Thurs 8am-Midnight, Fri 8-5, Sat 1-5, Sun 1-10
Friends of the Library Group

FAIRHOPE

P FAIRHOPE PUBLIC LIBRARY, 501 Fairhope Ave, 36532. SAN 300-0788. Tel: 251-928-7483. Administration Tel: 251-929-0366. FAX: 251-928-9717. Web Site: www.fairhopelibrary.org. *Dir,* Tamara Dean; E-mail: director@fairhopelibrary.org; *Head, Ref,* Trista Lackey; E-mail: reference@fairhopelibrary.org; *Circ,* Robert Gourlay; E-mail: circulation@fairhopelibrary.org; *Tech Serv,* Susan Diemert; E-mail: cataloguer@fairhopelibrary.org; *Youth Serv,* Brooke Arnold; Tel: 251-990-0209, E-mail: youthservices@fairhopelibrary.org; Staff 8 (MLS 5, Non-MLS 3)
Founded 1894. Pop 9,425; Circ 224,312
Special Collections: Alabama Poetry (Frances Ruffin Durham); Area History Coll; Local Authors Coll. Oral History
Subject Interests: Local hist, Theosophy
Automation Activity & Vendor Info: (Cataloging) TLC (The Library Corporation); (Circulation) TLC (The Library Corporation); (OPAC) TLC (The Library Corporation)
Wireless access
Function: 24/7 Electronic res, 24/7 Online cat, 3D Printer, Accelerated reader prog, Activity rm, Adult bk club, After school storytime, Audiobks on Playaways & MP3, Audiobks via web, Bk club(s), Bk reviews (Group), Bks on CD, Children's prog, Citizenship assistance, Computer training, Computers for patron use, Digital talking bks, Distance learning, E-Readers, Electronic databases & coll, Family literacy, Free DVD rentals, Genealogy discussion group, Holiday prog, Homework prog, ILL available, Internet access, Life-long learning prog for all ages, Magazines, Magnifiers for reading, Mail & tel request accepted, Makerspace, Mango lang, Meeting rooms, Movies, Music CDs, Notary serv, Online cat, Outreach serv, OverDrive digital audio bks, Photocopying/Printing, Preschool reading prog, Printer for laptops & handheld devices, Prog for adults, Prog for children & young adult, Ref & res, Ref serv available, Res assist avail, Scanner, Senior computer classes, Spanish lang bks, Spoken cassettes & CDs, Spoken cassettes & DVDs, STEM programs, Story hour, Study rm, Summer & winter reading prog, Summer reading prog, Tax forms, Teen prog, Telephone ref, Wheelchair accessible, Winter reading prog
Mem of Baldwin County Library Cooperative, Inc
Open Mon, Tues & Thurs 9-8, Wed 1-6, Fri 9-5, Sat 9-3
Restriction: Authorized patrons, Borrowing requests are handled by ILL, Circ limited, ID required to use computers (Ltd hrs), In-house use for visitors, Lending limited to county residents, Non-circulating of rare bks, Non-circulating to the pub
Friends of the Library Group

FALKVILLE

P FALKVILLE PUBLIC LIBRARY*, Seven N First Ave, 35622. (Mail add: PO Box 407, 35622-0407), SAN 376-737X. Tel: 256-784-5822. FAX: 256-784-5525. E-mail: falkvillepubliclibrary@yahoo.com. Web Site: www.falkville.org/FalkvillePublicLibrary.aspx, www.falkvillepubliclibrary.us. *Dir,* Jennifer Asherbranner
Founded 1989. Pop 1,109
Library Holdings: DVDs 500; e-books 22,000; Large Print Bks 1,000; Bk Vols 11,000
Automation Activity & Vendor Info: (Acquisitions) Biblionix; (Cataloging) Biblionix; (Circulation) Biblionix
Wireless access
Open Mon, Tues, Thurs & Fri 8-12 & 1-5, Wed 8-12

FAYETTE

J BEVILL STATE COMMUNITY COLLEGE*, Learning Resources Center, 2631 Temple Ave N, 35555. SAN 300-0796. Tel: 205-932-3221, Ext 5141. FAX: 205-932-8821. Web Site: www.bscc.edu. *Head Librn,* Marry Harris; E-mail: mharris@bscc.edu; Staff 1 (MLS 1)
Founded 1969. Enrl 1,600; Fac 30
Library Holdings: Bk Vols 40,000
Special Collections: Albert P Brewer Coll. State Document Depository; US Document Depository
Automation Activity & Vendor Info: (Cataloging) Follett Software; (Circulation) Follett Software; (OPAC) Follett Software
Publications: BSCC LRC Handbook
Open Mon-Thurs 7:30am-8:30pm, Fri 7:30-3:30

P FAYETTE COUNTY MEMORIAL LIBRARY*, 326 Temple Ave N, 35555. SAN 300-080X. Tel: 205-932-6625. FAX: 205-932-4152. E-mail: webmaster@fcml.org. Web Site: www.fcml.org. *Dir,* Jessica Crowe; E-mail: jessie@fcml.org; Staff 1 (MLS 1)
Founded 1922. Pop 17,182; Circ 34,890
Special Collections: Alabama Room, including Census Records through 1920; Genealogy Coll
Automation Activity & Vendor Info: (Cataloging) Book Systems; (Circulation) Book Systems; (OPAC) Book Systems
Wireless access
Function: Bks on cassette, Bks on CD, Computer training, Computers for patron use, Electronic databases & coll, Free DVD rentals, Homework prog, Microfiche/film & reading machines, Online cat, OverDrive digital audio bks, Photocopying/Printing, Preschool reading prog, Printer for laptops & handheld devices, Prog for children & young adult, Ref serv available, Spoken cassettes & CDs, Story hour, Summer reading prog, Tax forms, VHS videos
Open Mon-Thurs 9-6, Fri 9-5, Sat 9-12

FLOMATON

P FLOMATON PUBLIC LIBRARY*, 436 Dr Van Ave, 36441. SAN 300-0818. Tel: 251-296-3552. FAX: 251-296-3355. Web Site: www.flomatonpubliclibrary.org. *Libr Dir,* Kaci Boutwell; E-mail: kboutwell@flomatonal.org
Pop 15,033; Circ 25,238
Library Holdings: Bk Titles 22,000; Per Subs 30
Automation Activity & Vendor Info: (Cataloging) Follett Software; (Circulation) Follett Software; (OPAC) Follett Software
Mem of Escambia County Cooperative Library System
Open Mon-Thurs 7:30-5:30, Fri 8-5

FLORALA

P FLORALA PUBLIC LIBRARY*, 1214 Fourth St, 36442. SAN 300-0826. Tel: 334-858-3525. FAX: 334-858-3525. Web Site: aplsws1.apls.state.al.us/florala. *Dir,* Sherry Simpson; E-mail: fpldirector@fairpoint.net
Founded 1934. Pop 2,011; Circ 22,681
Library Holdings: Audiobooks 80; AV Mats 964; CDs 287; DVDs 1,619; Large Print Bks 100; Bk Vols 18,251; Per Subs 43; Talking Bks 345; Videos 285
Special Collections: Historic Photographs of Florala, Ala
Wireless access
Open Mon-Fri 8:30-5

FLORENCE

P FLORENCE-LAUDERDALE PUBLIC LIBRARY*, 350 N Wood Ave, 35630. SAN 300-0834. Tel: 256-764-6564. FAX: 256-764-6629. E-mail: events@flpl.org. Web Site: flpl.org. *Interim Exec Dir,* Abby Carpenter; E-mail: abby@flpl.org; *Coll Develop & Automation Serv Librn,* Elisabeth G South; E-mail: esouth@flpl.org; *Tech Librn,* James Mitchell; E-mail: Jmitchell@flpl.org; *Daily Operations & Tech Serv Supvr,* Melissa Dial; E-mail: mdial@flpl.org; Staff 19.5 (MLS 4.5, Non-MLS 15)
Founded 1945. Pop 80,000; Circ 275,000
Special Collections: Digital Archive of Local History
Subject Interests: Genealogy, Local hist
Automation Activity & Vendor Info: (Acquisitions) Innovative Interfaces, Inc; (Cataloging) Innovative Interfaces, Inc; (Circulation) Innovative Interfaces, Inc; (ILL) OCLC; (OPAC) Innovative Interfaces, Inc
Wireless access
Function: 3D Printer, Activity rm
Open Mon-Thurs 10-7, Fri & Sat 10-5, Sun 1-5
Friends of the Library Group

C UNIVERSITY OF NORTH ALABAMA*, Collier Library, One Harrison Plaza, Box 5028, 35632-0001. SAN 300-0850. Tel: 256-765-4241. Circulation Tel: 256-765-4469. Interlibrary Loan Service Tel: 256-765-4308. FAX: 256-765-4438. Web Site: www.una.edu/library. *Assoc Prof, Univ Librn,* Derek Malone; E-mail: dmalone3@una.edu; *Head, Acq & Electronic Res,* Amy Butler; Tel: 256-765-4266; *Head, Cat,* Darlene Townsend; Tel: 256-765-4473; *Head, Circ, Head, Per,* Doris McDaniel; *Instrul Serv Librn,* D Leigh Thompson; Tel: 256-765-4466; *Ref & ILL Serv Coordr,* Celia Reynolds; Tel: 256-765-4625; *Tech Coordr,* Jonathan Simms; Tel: 256-765-4470; *Web Coordr,* Phillip Oliver; Tel: 256-765-4559; Staff 11.5 (MLS 10.5, Non-MLS 1)
Founded 1830. Enrl 7,260; Fac 348; Highest Degree: Master
Library Holdings: AV Mats 13,303; CDs 1,756; DVDs 3,635; e-books 241,784; e-journals 3,408; Electronic Media & Resources 137; Bk Titles 277,016; Bk Vols 398,512; Per Subs 3,815; Videos 5,968
Special Collections: Alabama Historical Coll; Congressman Flippo Coll; Film Script Archives; Local History Archives. US Document Depository
Subject Interests: Bus & mgt, Educ, Hist, Humanities, Nursing, Soc sci & issues
Automation Activity & Vendor Info: (Acquisitions) Ex Libris Group; (Cataloging) Ex Libris Group; (Circulation) Ex Libris Group; (Course Reserve) Ex Libris Group; (ILL) Ex Libris Group; (Media Booking) Ex Libris Group; (OPAC) Ex Libris Group; (Serials) Ex Libris Group
Wireless access
Function: ILL available
Publications: Pathfinder Series Finding Aids (Reference guide)
Partic in LYRASIS; Network of Alabama Academic Libraries
Open Mon-Thurs 7:30am-1am, Fri 7:30-4:30, Sat 9-5, Sun 2pm-1am

FOLEY

P FOLEY PUBLIC LIBRARY, 319 E Laurel Ave, 36535. SAN 300-0869. Tel: 251-943-7665. FAX: 251-943-8637. E-mail: foleylibrary@gmail.com. Web Site: www.foleylibrary.org. *Dir,* John Jackson; E-mail: jjackson@cityoffoley.org; *Ch,* Kelley Wansley; E-mail: kwansley@cityoffoley.org; Staff 18 (MLS 1, Non-MLS 17)
Founded 1923. Pop 19,700; Circ 14,776
Library Holdings: Bk Vols 86,500; Per Subs 81
Subject Interests: Alabama, Genealogy
Automation Activity & Vendor Info: (Cataloging) TLC (The Library Corporation); (Circulation) TLC (The Library Corporation); (OPAC) TLC (The Library Corporation)
Wireless access
Function: 24/7 Electronic res, 24/7 Online cat, Activity rm, Adult bk club, Adult literacy prog, Archival coll, Art programs, Audiobks via web, AV serv, Bks on CD, Children's prog, Computers for patron use, E-Readers, Electronic databases & coll, Free DVD rentals, Homework prog, ILL available, Instruction & testing, Internet access, Magazines, Meeting rooms, Microfiche/film & reading machines, Movies, Music CDs, Online cat, Outreach serv, OverDrive digital audio bks, Photocopying/Printing, Preschool reading prog, Prog for adults, Prog for children & young adult, Ref & res, Scanner, Senior computer classes, Senior outreach, Spoken cassettes & CDs, STEM programs, Story hour, Study rm, Summer reading prog, Tax forms, Teen prog, Wheelchair accessible, Workshops
Mem of Baldwin County Library Cooperative, Inc
Open Mon, Tues & Wed 9-8, Thurs 1-8, Fri & Sat 9-5
Friends of the Library Group

FORT PAYNE

P DEKALB COUNTY PUBLIC LIBRARY*, 504 Grand Ave NW, 35967. SAN 300-0877. Tel: 256-845-2671. FAX: 256-845-2671. Web Site: dekalbcountypubliclibrary.wordpress.com. *Dir,* Cynthia Hancock; E-mail: chancock@dekalbcountyal.us; *Asst Librn,* Yvonne Toombs
Circ 102,000
Library Holdings: Bk Vols 81,000; Per Subs 34
Special Collections: Indian Coll
Subject Interests: Indians, Local hist
Automation Activity & Vendor Info: (Cataloging) Innovative Interfaces, Inc; (Circulation) Innovative Interfaces, Inc; (OPAC) Innovative Interfaces, Inc
Wireless access
Partic in Library Management Network, Inc
Open Mon 10-8, Tues-Fri 10-6, Sat 10-3
Branches: 1
HENAGAR BRANCH, 17163 Alabama Hwy 75, Henagar, 35978. Tel: 256-657-1380. E-mail: books@farmerstel.com. *Br Mgr,* Donna Carlin
Open Tues & Thurs 1-5, Sat 9-1
Bookmobiles: 1

FORT RUCKER

UNITED STATES ARMY

A AVIATION TECHNICAL LIBRARY*, Bldg 9204, Fifth Ave, 36362, SAN 330-1923. Tel: 334-255-2944. Interlibrary Loan Service Tel: 334-255-3177. Administration Tel: 334-255-3912.
Founded 1955
Special Collections: Army Regulations; DTIC Technical Reports
Subject Interests: Aviation, Mil hist
Automation Activity & Vendor Info: (Cataloging) SirsiDynix; (Circulation) SirsiDynix; (OPAC) SirsiDynix
Partic in National Network of Libraries of Medicine Region 2

A CENTER LIBRARY*, Bldg 212, Corner of Ruf Ave & Novosel, 36362-5000, SAN 330-1869. Tel: 334-255-3885. FAX: 334-255-1567. *Head Librn,* Alfred Edwards; E-mail: al.edwards@us.army.mil; *Tech Serv Librn,* Laurie Richardson; Staff 6 (MLS 2, Non-MLS 4)
Founded 1954
Library Holdings: AV Mats 4,500; Bks on Deafness & Sign Lang 22; High Interest/Low Vocabulary Bk Vols 212; Large Print Bks 450; Bk Titles 63,500; Bk Vols 65,000; Per Subs 112
Special Collections: Christian Fiction Coll; German Language Coll; World War II Coll
Automation Activity & Vendor Info: (Acquisitions) Baker & Taylor; (Cataloging) SirsiDynix; (Circulation) SirsiDynix; (Media Booking) Baker & Taylor; (Serials) EBSCO Online

Function: Story hour
Partic in Federal Library & Information Network; Western New York Library Resources Council
Special Services for the Blind - Talking bks
Open Mon & Fri 9-5, Tues-Thurs 9-7, Sat Noon-5
Restriction: Open to authorized patrons

FULTONDALE

P FULTONDALE PUBLIC LIBRARY, 500 Byrd Lane, 35068. SAN 300-0893. Tel: 205-849-6335. FAX: 205-841-3620. Web Site: www.fultondale.lib.al.us. *Dir,* Jessica Allen; E-mail: jessica.allen@fultondale.lib.al.us
Pop 7,000; Circ 42,000
Library Holdings: Bk Vols 25,000; Per Subs 52
Automation Activity & Vendor Info: (Cataloging) Innovative Interfaces, Inc; (Circulation) Innovative Interfaces, Inc; (OPAC) Innovative Interfaces, Inc
Open Mon-Fri 8-4

GADSDEN

P GADSDEN PUBLIC LIBRARY*, 254 S College St, 35901. SAN 330-1958. Tel: 256-549-4699. Web Site: gadsdenlibrary.org. *Libr Dir,* Craig Scott; E-mail: craig@gadsdenlibrary.org; *IT Mgr,* Jacob Blackwood; E-mail: jacob@gadsdenlibrary.org; *Cat,* Debbie Walker; E-mail: debbie@gadsdenlibrary.org; *Circ,* Paulette Makary; E-mail: gplill@gadsdenlibrary.org; *ILL,* Amy McCary; E-mail: amy@gadsdenlibrary.org; Staff 29 (MLS 3, Non-MLS 26)
Founded 1906. Pop 103,975; Circ 237,188
Library Holdings: Bk Titles 166,285; Bk Vols 202,166
Special Collections: Alabama History Coll. US Document Depository
Subject Interests: Genealogy
Automation Activity & Vendor Info: (Cataloging) Book Systems; (Circulation) Book Systems; (ILL) Book Systems; (OPAC) Book Systems
Wireless access
Function: 24/7 Electronic res, 24/7 Online cat, Accelerated reader prog, Activity rm, Adult bk club, Adult literacy prog, After school storytime, Archival coll, Art exhibits, Audio & video playback equip for onsite use, Audiobks on Playaways & MP3, AV serv, Bilingual assistance for Spanish patrons, Bk club(s), Bks on CD, Bus archives, CD-ROM, Chess club, Children's prog, Citizenship assistance, Computer training, Computers for patron use, Distance learning, E-Reserves, Electronic databases & coll, Family literacy, For res purposes, Free DVD rentals, Games & aids for people with disabilities, Genealogy discussion group, Govt ref serv, Health sci info serv, Homework prog, ILL available, Instruction & testing, Internet access, Jail serv, Learning ctr, Life-long learning prog for all ages, Literacy & newcomer serv, Magazines, Magnifiers for reading, Mail & tel request accepted, Mango lang, Meeting rooms, Microfiche/film & reading machines, Movies, Notary serv, Online cat, Online info literacy tutorials on the web & in blackboard, Online ref, Orientations, Outreach serv, Outside serv via phone, mail, e-mail & web, OverDrive digital audio bks, Photocopying/Printing, Preschool outreach, Preschool reading prog, Prog for adults, Prog for children & young adult, Ref & res, Ref serv available, Res assist avail, Res libr, Scanner, Senior computer classes, Senior outreach, Serves people with intellectual disabilities, STEM programs, Story hour, Study rm, Summer & winter reading prog, Summer reading prog, Tax forms, Teen prog, Telephone ref, Visual arts prog, Wheelchair accessible, Winter reading prog, Workshops, Writing prog
Open Mon, Tues & Thurs 10-7, Wed & Fri 9-5, Sat 1-5
Restriction: Borrowing requests are handled by ILL, Closed stack, Non-resident fee
Friends of the Library Group
Branches: 2
EAST GADSDEN BRANCH, 809 E Broad St, 35903, SAN 330-2016. Tel: 256-549-4691. *Br Mgr,* LaShunda Williams; Staff 2 (Non-MLS 2)
Library Holdings: Bk Vols 5,000
Function: 24/7 Online cat, Accelerated reader prog, Activity rm, Adult bk club, Adult literacy prog, Ref serv available, Res libr
Open Mon-Fri 9-5
Friends of the Library Group
WARSHAM-JUNKINS ALABAMA CITY GENEALOGY BRANCH, 2700 W Meighan Blvd, 35904, SAN 330-1982. Tel: 256-549-4688. *Br Mgr,* Kevin Graves. Subject Specialists: *Genealogy,* Kevin Graves; Staff 3 (Non-MLS 3)
Library Holdings: Bk Vols 2,725
Function: 24/7 Online cat, Activity rm, Genealogy discussion group, Govt ref serv
Open Mon-Fri 9-5
Friends of the Library Group

J GADSDEN STATE COMMUNITY COLLEGE*, Meadows Library, 1001 George Wallace Dr, 35902. (Mail add: PO Box 227, 35902-0227), SAN 324-3435. Tel: 256-549-8333. FAX: 256-549-8401. Web Site: lmn-verso.auto-graphics.com/MVC. *Dean, Libr Serv,* Bridget Burney; Tel: 256-549-8245; *Ref Librn,* Julie Kennedy; E-mail: jkennedy@gadsdenstate.edu; *Tech Serv Librn,* Dorothy Burgess; Tel: 256-549-8496, E-mail: dmburgess@gadsdenstate.edu; *Ref,* Phillip Burgess; E-mail: pburgess@gadsdenstate.edu; *Ref,* Sarah Cooper; E-mail: scooper@gadsdenstate.edu; *Ref,* Alexandria Sims; E-mail: asims@gadsdenstate.edu. Subject Specialists: *Cherokee Indians,* Julie Kennedy; Staff 9 (MLS 4, Non-MLS 5)
Founded 1965. Enrl 3,500; Fac 125; Highest Degree: Associate
Library Holdings: Bk Vols 110,000; Per Subs 282
Special Collections: Gadsden State Archives; Mary Cooper Coll
Subject Interests: Alabama, Law, Southern lit
Automation Activity & Vendor Info: (Cataloging) Auto-Graphics, Inc; (Circulation) Auto-Graphics, Inc; (Discovery) EBSCO Discovery Service; (ILL) Auto-Graphics, Inc; (OPAC) Auto-Graphics, Inc
Wireless access
Function: For res purposes
Publications: Faculty Handbook; Library Skills Handbook; New-Acquisitions (annual); Student Handbook
Partic in Library Management Network, Inc
Special Services for the Blind - Low vision equip
Open Mon-Thurs 7am-6pm, Fri 7:30am-11:30am
Departmental Libraries:
PIERCE C CAIN LEARNING RESOURCE CENTER, Ayers Campus, 1801 Coleman Rd, Anniston, 36207-6858. (Mail add: PO Box 1647, Anniston, 36202-1647). Tel: 256-835-5436. FAX: 256-835-5476. Web Site: gadsdenstate.libguides.com/ayers. *Pub Serv Librn,* Michael Gibson; Tel: 256-835-5432, E-mail: mgibson@gadsdenstate.edu; *Ref Librn,* Wanda Yates
Library Holdings: Bk Titles 14,000; Per Subs 40
Function: AV serv, Satellite serv
Open Mon-Thurs 7:30am-6pm
MCCLELLAN CENTER, 100 Gamecock Dr, Anniston, 36205. Tel: 256-238-9352. *Ref Librn,* Melinda Harvey; E-mail: mharvey@gadsdenstate.edu; *Librn,* Tim Moon; Tel: 256-238-9352, E-mail: tmoon@gadsdenstate.edu; *Libr Asst,* Edna Pickles; Tel: 256-238-9352, E-mail: epickles@gadsdenstate.edu
Automation Activity & Vendor Info: (Cataloging) Auto-Graphics, Inc; (Discovery) EBSCO Discovery Service; (OPAC) Auto-Graphics, Inc
Open Mon-Thurs 8-7
VALLEY STREET CAMPUS, 600 Valley St, 35901. Tel: 256-439-6887. *Librn,* Linda Sosebee; E-mail: lsosebee@gadsdenstate.edu
Automation Activity & Vendor Info: (Cataloging) Auto-Graphics, Inc; (Circulation) Auto-Graphics, Inc; (Discovery) EBSCO Discovery Service; (OPAC) Auto-Graphics, Inc

GARDENDALE

P GARDENDALE - MARTHA MOORE PUBLIC LIBRARY, 995 Mt Olive Rd, 35071. SAN 300-0958. Tel: 205-631-6639. FAX: 205-631-0146. Web Site: www.gardendalelibrary.org. *Dir,* Connie Smith; E-mail: connie.smith@gardendalelibrary.org; *Adult Serv,* Lisa Keith; E-mail: lisa.keith@gardendalelibrary.org; *Adult Serv,* Gina Robertson; E-mail: gina.robertson@gardendalelibrary.org; *Ch Serv,* Ashley Kimbrough; E-mail: ashley.kimbrough@gardendalelibrary.org
Founded 1959. Pop 15,000; Circ 193,303
Library Holdings: Bk Vols 51,261; Per Subs 120
Automation Activity & Vendor Info: (Cataloging) Innovative Interfaces, Inc - Sierra; (Circulation) Innovative Interfaces, Inc - Sierra; (OPAC) Innovative Interfaces, Inc - Sierra
Wireless access
Partic in Jefferson County Libr Coop
Open Mon, Tues & Thurs 9-8, Wed & Fri 9-5, Sat 9-2

GENEVA

P EMMA KNOX KENAN LIBRARY*, 312 S Commerce St, 36340. (Mail add: PO Box 550, 36340-0550), SAN 300-0966. Tel: 334-684-2459. FAX: 334-219-4223. E-mail: genevapubliclibrary@gmail.com. Web Site: www.genevapubliclibrary.org. *Dir,* Marian Wynn; Staff 1 (Non-MLS 1)
Founded 1904. Pop 8,401; Circ 15,000
Library Holdings: Bk Vols 15,000; Per Subs 25
Automation Activity & Vendor Info: (Acquisitions) Book Systems; (Cataloging) Book Systems; (Circulation) Book Systems; (ILL) OCLC WorldShare Interlibrary Loan
Wireless access
Function: Computers for patron use, Summer reading prog, Tax forms
Open Mon-Fri 10-5

GERALDINE

P GERALDINE PUBLIC LIBRARY*, 13543 Alabama Hwy 227, 35974. (Mail add: PO Box 183, 35974-0183), SAN 376-6454. Tel: 256-659-6663. FAX: 256-659-6663. Web Site: www.townofgeraldineal.com/library. *Dir,* Diane Maddox; E-mail: maddox1043@yahoo.com
Founded 1987. Pop 900; Circ 3,661
Library Holdings: Bk Titles 34,534

Special Collections: Civil war
Special Services for the Blind - Audio mat; Bks available with recordings
Open Mon-Fri 8:30-4

GOODWATER

P GOODWATER PUBLIC LIBRARY*, 62 Coosa County Rd, 66, 35072. (Mail add: PO Box 140, 35072-0140), SAN 300-0974. Tel: 256-839-5741. FAX: 256-839-5741. E-mail: gplibrary2003@yahoo.com. *Dir,* Shirley Thompson; *Asst Librn,* Bonnie Rogers
Founded 1945. Pop 1,550; Circ 2,932
Library Holdings: Bk Titles 10,000
Function: Activity rm, Bks on cassette, Bks on CD, Children's prog, Computers for patron use, Free DVD rentals, ILL available, Internet access, Magazines, Meeting rooms, Movies, Online cat, Online info literacy tutorials on the web & in blackboard, Photocopying/Printing, Ref serv available, Scanner, Summer reading prog, Tax forms, VHS videos, Wheelchair accessible
Mem of Horseshoe Bend Regional Library
Open Mon, Wed & Fri 9-5, Tues & Thurs 9-6

GORDO

P RUTH HOLLIMAN PUBLIC LIBRARY*, 287 Main St, 35466. (Mail add: PO Box 336, 35466-0336), SAN 300-0982. Tel: 205-364-7148. FAX: 205-364-7148. E-mail: justbooksmelba@gmail.com. Web Site: pickenslibrary.com/gordo.html. *Dir,* Shelia Spencer
Pop 4,250; Circ 10,500
Library Holdings: Bk Vols 12,500
Automation Activity & Vendor Info: (Cataloging) Follett Software; (Circulation) Follett Software
Mem of Pickens County Cooperative Library
Open Mon, Thurs & Fri 12-5, Tues 10-5, Wed 12-3, Sat 8-12
Friends of the Library Group

GRANT

P GRANT PUBLIC LIBRARY, 5379 Main St, 35747. (Mail add: PO Box 401, 35747-0401), SAN 376-5628. Tel: 256-728-5128. E-mail: readme@nehp.net. Web Site: www.grantpubliclibrary.com. *Librn,* Vicki Chaney
Library Holdings: Bk Vols 15,000
Wireless access
Mem of Marshall County Cooperative Library
Open Tues, Thurs & Fri 9-4, Wed & Sat 9-Noon

GRAYSVILLE

P GRAYSVILLE PUBLIC LIBRARY*, 315 S Main St, 35073. SAN 300-0990. Tel: 205-674-3040. FAX: 205-674-3296. Web Site: www.graysvillecity.com/library. *Dir,* Debbie Alexander; E-mail: dalexander@bham.lib.al.us
Founded 1978. Pop 2,112; Circ 60,000
Library Holdings: Bk Vols 24,000; Per Subs 45
Automation Activity & Vendor Info: (Cataloging) Innovative Interfaces, Inc; (Circulation) Innovative Interfaces, Inc; (OPAC) Inmagic, Inc.
Partic in Jefferson County Libr Coop
Open Mon-Fri 8-5

GREENSBORO

P HALE COUNTY PUBLIC LIBRARY*, 1103 Main St, 36744. (Mail add: PO Box 399, 36744-0399), SAN 300-1008. Tel: 334-624-3409. FAX: 334-624-3409. E-mail: halecountylibrar@bellsouth.net. Web Site: www.hcplgreensboro.org. *Libr Dir,* Carolyn Hemstreet; *Asst Librn,* Twanisha Jones; Staff 1.4 (Non-MLS 1.4)
Founded 1925. Pop 6,560; Circ 10,000
Oct 2015-Sept 2016 Income $42,100, State $5,155, City $4,000, County $5,433, Locally Generated Income $15,786, Other $11,724. Mats Exp $3,566, Books $1,913, Per/Ser (Incl. Access Fees) $657, Other Print Mats $300, Electronic Ref Mat (Incl. Access Fees) $995. Sal $24,392
Library Holdings: Audiobooks 576; Bks on Deafness & Sign Lang 2; CDs 13; DVDs 441; e-books 537; High Interest/Low Vocabulary Bk Vols 100; Large Print Bks 327; Bk Titles 15,330; Per Subs 25; Videos 527
Special Collections: Alabama History & Literature Coll; Genealogy Coll (area families)
Automation Activity & Vendor Info: (Cataloging) Book Systems; (Circulation) Book Systems; (OPAC) Book Systems
Wireless access
Function: 24/7 Online cat, Accelerated reader prog, Bilingual assistance for Spanish patrons, Bks on CD, Children's prog, Computer training, Computers for patron use, Electronic databases & coll, ILL available, Internet access, Magazines, Magnifiers for reading, Mail & tel request accepted, Microfiche/film & reading machines, Online cat, Orientations, Photocopying/Printing, Printer for laptops & handheld devices, Prog for adults, Prog for children & young adult, Ref & res, Ref serv available, Scanner, Senior computer classes, Study rm, Summer reading prog, Tax forms, Telephone ref, VHS videos, Wheelchair accessible
Open Mon-Wed & Fri 10-5:15, Sat 9-12
Friends of the Library Group

GREENVILLE

G BUTLER COUNTY HISTORICAL-GENEALOGICAL SOCIETY LIBRARY*, 309 Fort Dale Rd, 36037. (Mail add: PO Box 561, 36037-0561), SAN 375-8346. Tel: 334-383-9564. E-mail: ButlerCoALHistory@gmail.com. Web Site: sites.rootsweb.com/~albchgs. *VPres,* Annie Crenshaw
Library Holdings: Bk Titles 600; Per Subs 50
Function: Ref serv available

P GREENVILLE-BUTLER COUNTY PUBLIC LIBRARY*, 309 Ft Dale St, 36037. Tel: 334-382-3216. E-mail: library@greenville-bcpl.org. Web Site: www.greenville-bcpl.org. *Dir,* Kevin Pearcy
Library Holdings: Bk Vols 40,000; Per Subs 20
Automation Activity & Vendor Info: (Cataloging) Book Systems; (Circulation) Book Systems
Wireless access
Open Mon-Fri 9-5:30, Sat 9-2

GROVE HILL

P GROVE HILL PUBLIC LIBRARY, 108 Dubose Ave, 36451-9502. SAN 300-1016. Tel: 251-275-8157. FAX: 251-275-8157. E-mail: ghpldesk@tds.net. Web Site: sites.google.com/site/grovehilllibrary. *Librn,* Betsy West; E-mail: betsywest43@yahoo.com
Pop 2,266; Circ 10,800
Library Holdings: Bk Vols 19,000; Per Subs 25
Special Collections: Census Rec; Family Research
Wireless access
Open Mon-Fri 9-4:30

GULF SHORES

P THOMAS B NORTON PUBLIC LIBRARY*, 221 W 19th Ave, 36542. SAN 300-1024. Tel: 251-968-1176. FAX: 251-968-1184. Web Site: www.gulfshoresal.gov/924/Library. *Managing Librn,* Wendy Congiardo; E-mail: wcongiardo@gulfshoresal.gov; *Ad,* Deanne Fincher; E-mail: dfincher@gulfshoresal.gov; *Ref Librn,* Vern Cresap; E-mail: vcresap@gulfshoresal.gov; *Youth Serv Librn,* Amy Maliska; E-mail: amaliska@gulfshoresal.gov; Staff 5 (MLS 2, Non-MLS 3)
Founded 1963
Library Holdings: AV Mats 1,926; High Interest/Low Vocabulary Bk Vols 34; Large Print Bks 1,300; Bk Vols 35,419; Per Subs 110
Special Collections: Alabama Room
Subject Interests: Hist
Automation Activity & Vendor Info: (Acquisitions) TLC (The Library Corporation); (Cataloging) TLC (The Library Corporation); (Circulation) TLC (The Library Corporation); (OPAC) TLC (The Library Corporation)
Wireless access
Function: Adult bk club, Art exhibits, Audiobks via web, Bks on cassette, Bks on CD, CD-ROM, Children's prog, Computer training, Computers for patron use, Electronic databases & coll, Free DVD rentals, Holiday prog, ILL available, Instruction & testing, Internet access, Magnifiers for reading, Microfiche/film & reading machines, Music CDs, Notary serv, Online cat, Online ref, Orientations, Photocopying/Printing, Prog for adults, Prog for children & young adult, Ref serv available, Scanner, Senior computer classes, Spanish lang bks, Summer reading prog, Tax forms, Teen prog, VHS videos, Wheelchair accessible, Workshops, Writing prog
Mem of Baldwin County Library Cooperative, Inc
Open Mon & Tues 10-8, Wed-Fri 10-6, Sat 10-3
Friends of the Library Group

GUNTERSVILLE

P GUNTERSVILLE PUBLIC LIBRARY*, 1240 O'Brig Ave, 35976. SAN 300-1032. Tel: 256-571-7595. FAX: 256-571-7596. E-mail: books@guntersvillelibrary.org. Web Site: www.guntersvillelibrary.org. *Dir,* Beth Dean; *Asst Dir,* Marie Harmon; *Ch,* Mandy Broadhurst; E-mail: mandyb@guntersvillelibrary.org; Staff 4 (MLS 2, Non-MLS 2)
Founded 1947. Pop 10,343; Circ 75,400
Library Holdings: AV Mats 300; DVDs 300; Large Print Bks 500; Bk Vols 50,000; Per Subs 65; Talking Bks 600; Videos 2,000
Special Collections: Genealogical materials of Marshall County; Historical Coll of Guntersville's newspapers
Publications: Friends Newsletter; Library Notes (Newsletter)
Mem of Marshall County Cooperative Library
Open Tues 9-8, Wed-Fri 9-6, Sat 9-2
Friends of the Library Group

P MARSHALL COUNTY COOPERATIVE LIBRARY*, 19348 Hwy 431 N, 35976. (Mail add: 424 Blount Ave, Ste 305, 35976), SAN 324-1424. Tel: 256-878-8523. E-mail: bookmobile@marshallco.org. Web Site: www.marshallco.org/bookmobile. *Dir,* Debra Slaton
Founded 1974
Library Holdings: Bk Vols 7,000
Member Libraries: Albertville Public Library; Boaz Public Library; Grant Public Library; Guntersville Public Library
Open Mon-Thurs 8-1
Bookmobiles: 1

HALEYVILLE

P HALEYVILLE PUBLIC LIBRARY*, 913 20th St, 35565. SAN 300-1040. Tel: 205-486-7450. FAX: 205-486-7450. E-mail: library@cityofhaleyville.com. *Librn,* Waldrup Carla; *Asst Librn,* SuzzAne Fowler
Library Holdings: Bk Vols 12,000; Per Subs 45
Mem of Carl Elliott Regional Library System
Open Mon-Fri 8-5, Sat 9-12

HAMILTON

J BEVILL STATE COMMUNITY COLLEGE*, Hamilton Campus Library, 1481 Military St S, 35570. (Mail add: PO Box 9, 35570-0009). Tel: 205-921-3177, Ext 5313. Toll Free Tel: 800-648-3271. FAX: 205-952-9617. Web Site: www.bscc.edu. *Librn,* Tammy Sanders; Tel: 205-921-3177, Ext 5356, E-mail: tammy.sanders@bscc.edu
Library Holdings: Bk Vols 13,500
Wireless access
Function: ILL available, Photocopying/Printing, Ref serv available
Open Mon-Thurs 7:30am-8:30pm, Fri 7:30am-11:30am

HANCEVILLE

J WALLACE STATE COLLEGE*, Hanceville Campus Library, 801 Main St NW, 35077. (Mail add: PO Box 2000, 35077-2000). Tel: 256-352-8260. FAX: 256-352-8254. E-mail: library@wallacestate.edu. Web Site: www.wallacestate.edu. *Head Librn,* Lisa Hullett; E-mail: lisa.hullett@wallacestate.edu
Library Holdings: Bk Vols 55,000; Per Subs 167
Automation Activity & Vendor Info: (Cataloging) Follett Software; (Circulation) Follett Software; (OPAC) Follett Software
Function: AV serv
Open Mon-Thurs 7:30am-8:30pm, Fri 7:30am-2pm, Sat 8-2

HARTFORD

P MCGREGOR-MCKINNEY PUBLIC LIBRARY*, Hartford Public Library, 101 E Fulton St, 36344. SAN 300-1059. Tel: 334-588-2384. FAX: 334-588-2384. Web Site: webmini.apls.state.al.us/apls_web/Hartford/index.html. *Dir,* Stephanie Riley; E-mail: librarydirector@hartfordpubliclibrary.org
Pop 2,649; Circ 14,280
Library Holdings: Audiobooks 1,100; Large Print Bks 2,100; Bk Vols 19,000; Per Subs 35; Videos 450
Automation Activity & Vendor Info: (Cataloging) Book Systems; (Circulation) Book Systems; (OPAC) Book Systems
Wireless access
Function: Prog for children & young adult, Summer reading prog
Partic in LYRASIS
Open Mon & Wed-Fri 8-5, Tues 8-5:30

HARTSELLE

P WILLIAM BRADFORD HUIE LIBRARY OF HARTSELLE*, 152 NW Sparkman St, 35640. SAN 300-1067. Tel: 256-773-9880. FAX: 256-773-2257. E-mail: mblaylock@hartselle.org. *Libr Mgr,* Michelle Blaylock; E-mail: mblaylock@hartselle.org; *Libr Asst,* Patricia Poe; E-mail: ppoe@hartselle.org
Pop 10,860; Circ 47,280
Library Holdings: Bk Vols 29,000; Per Subs 20
Special Collections: William Bradford Huie Coll
Wireless access
Open Mon-Thurs 9:30-5:30, Fri 9:30-5
Friends of the Library Group

HAYNEVILLE

P HAYNEVILLE-LOWNDES COUNTY PUBLIC LIBRARY*, 215 E Tuskeena St, Ste B, 36040. (Mail add: PO Box 425, 36040-0425). Tel: 334-548-2686. FAX: 334-548-5427. E-mail: hayneville123@gmail.com. *Dir,* Rutha Davis-Bonner
Founded 1988. Pop 9,000
Library Holdings: Audiobooks 25; Bks on Deafness & Sign Lang 2; High Interest/Low Vocabulary Bk Vols 300; Large Print Bks 50; Bk Vols 24,000; Per Subs 7
Wireless access
Function: Art exhibits, Bks on cassette, Citizenship assistance, Internet access, Online ref, Photocopying/Printing, Ref serv available, Summer reading prog, Tax forms, Wheelchair accessible, Workshops
Open Tues-Fri 9-4

HEADLAND

P BLANCHE R SOLOMON MEMORIAL LIBRARY*, 17 Park St, 36345. SAN 330-3063. Tel: 334-693-2706. FAX: 334-693-5023. E-mail: headlandlibrary@gmail.com. Web Site: www.headlandlibrary.org. *Libr Dir,* Joan Moulton
Pop 3,523
Library Holdings: Bk Vols 48,461; Per Subs 43
Automation Activity & Vendor Info: (Cataloging) Book Systems; (Circulation) Book Systems; (OPAC) Book Systems
Wireless access
Open Mon-Fri 9-5

HEFLIN

P CHEAHA REGIONAL LIBRARY*, 935 Coleman St, 36264. SAN 320-1430. Tel: 256-463-7125. FAX: 256-463-7125. E-mail: cheaharegionallibrary@yahoo.com. Web Site: www.cheaharegionallibrary.org. *Dir,* Sherry Poe
Founded 1976. Pop 65,000
Library Holdings: Audiobooks 5,681; Bks on Deafness & Sign Lang 243; CDs 862; DVDs 358; e-books 2,985; e-journals 12; Electronic Media & Resources 98; High Interest/Low Vocabulary Bk Vols 8,594; Large Print Bks 7,948; Bk Vols 35,489; Talking Bks 24
Automation Activity & Vendor Info: (Acquisitions) Book Systems; (Cataloging) Book Systems; (Circulation) Book Systems; (OPAC) Book Systems
Wireless access
Member Libraries: Annie L Awbrey Public Library; Ashland City Library; Cherokee County Public Library; Earle A Rainwater Memorial Library; Lincoln Public Library; Lineville City Library; Lucile L Morgan Public Library
Special Services for the Deaf - Bks on deafness & sign lang; High interest/low vocabulary bks; TDD equip
Special Services for the Blind - Braille bks; Home delivery serv; Talking bks
Open Mon-Fri 8:30-4:30
Bookmobiles: 2. Librn, Kayron Triplett

P LUCILE L MORGAN PUBLIC LIBRARY*, 541 Ross St, 36264. SAN 300-1075. Tel: 256-463-2259. FAX: 256-463-2259. E-mail: llmorganlibrary@gmail.com. Web Site: cheaharegionallibrary.org/member_libraries/lucile_morgan_public_library. *Librn,* Joyce Dryden
Founded 1964. Pop 3,014; Circ 5,691
Library Holdings: AV Mats 82; Large Print Bks 146; Bk Vols 14,500; Per Subs 25; Talking Bks 130
Special Collections: Old Book Coll
Mem of Cheaha Regional Library
Open Mon-Fri 1-5, Sat 10-1

HELENA

P JANE B HOLMES PUBLIC LIBRARY, 230 Tucker Rd, 35080-7036. SAN 371-9359. Tel: 205-664-8308. FAX: 205-664-4593. Web Site: cityofhelena.org/public-library. *Dir,* Daniel Dearing; E-mail: ddearing@shelbycounty-al.org; Staff 5 (Non-MLS 5)
Founded 1960. Pop 21,000
Library Holdings: Bk Vols 26,000; Per Subs 20
Automation Activity & Vendor Info: (Cataloging) Innovative Interfaces, Inc; (Circulation) Innovative Interfaces, Inc; (OPAC) Innovative Interfaces, Inc
Wireless access
Mem of Harrison Regional Library System
Open Mon & Thurs 10-7, Tues & Wed 10-6, Fri 10-5, Sat 10-2
Friends of the Library Group

HOMEWOOD

P HOMEWOOD PUBLIC LIBRARY*, 1721 Oxmoor Rd, 35209-4085. SAN 300-1083. Tel: 205-332-6600. FAX: 205-802-6424. Web Site: www.homewoodpubliclibrary.org. *Dir,* Deborah Fout; E-mail: dfout@bham.lib.al.us; *Head, Adult Serv,* Leslie West; Tel: 205-332-6620, E-mail: lwest@bham.lib.al.us; *Head, Children's Servx,* Laura Tucker; Tel: 205-332-6616, E-mail: ltucker@bham.lib.al.us; *Head, Circ Serv,* Lonnie Jones; Tel: 205-332-6611, E-mail: ljones@bham.lib.al.us; *Head, Circ Serv,* Lonnie Jones; Tel: 205-332-6600, E-mail: ljones@bham.lib.al.us; *Librn,*

Judith Wright; Tel: 205-332-6622, E-mail: jrwright@bham.lib.al.us; *Spec Projects Librn,* Heather Cover; Tel: 205-332-6621, E-mail: hcover@bham.lib.al.us; *IT Mgr,* Brooks Fancher; Tel: 205-332-6630, E-mail: bfancher@bham.lib.al.us; *Webmaster,* Rob Harris; Tel: 205-332-6631, E-mail: rharris@bham.lib.al.us; Staff 33.1 (MLS 9.4, Non-MLS 23.7)
Founded 1941. Pop 25,262; Circ 519,683
Library Holdings: Audiobooks 5,590; AV Mats 327; CDs 2,901; DVDs 15,770; e-books 4,991; Electronic Media & Resources 77; Large Print Bks 2,397; Bk Vols 73,301; Per Subs 220
Automation Activity & Vendor Info: (Cataloging) Innovative Interfaces, Inc - Millennium; (Circulation) Innovative Interfaces, Inc - Millennium; (OPAC) Innovative Interfaces, Inc
Wireless access
Function: 24/7 Electronic res, Adult bk club, After school storytime, Art exhibits, Audiobks via web, Bk club(s), Bks on CD, Chess club, Children's prog, Computer training, Computers for patron use, E-Readers, E-Reserves, Electronic databases & coll, Free DVD rentals, Holiday prog, ILL available, Internet access, Life-long learning prog for all ages, Magazines, Mango lang, Movies, Music CDs, Notary serv, Online cat, Online ref, Outreach serv, OverDrive digital audio bks, Photocopying/Printing, Preschool outreach, Printer for laptops & handheld devices, Prog for adults, Prog for children & young adult, Scanner, Senior outreach, Serves people with intellectual disabilities, Spanish lang bks, Story hour, Study rm, Summer reading prog, Tax forms, Teen prog, Telephone ref, Wheelchair accessible, Workshops
Partic in Jefferson County Libr Coop
Open Mon, Tues & Thurs 9-9, Wed, Fri & Sat 9-6, Sun 2-6
Friends of the Library Group

HOOVER

P HOOVER PUBLIC LIBRARY*, 200 Municipal Dr, 35216. SAN 329-1839. Tel: 205-444-7810. Circulation Tel: 205-444-7800. FAX: 205-444-7878. Web Site: www.hooverlibrary.org. *Dir,* Amanda Borden; *Children's Coordr,* Jeremy Davis; *Coordr,* Theresa Davis; *Circ Coordr,* Pam Wilson; *Fine Arts Coord,* Matina Johnson; *Non-Fiction Coor,* Ashley Davidson; *Tech Coordr,* Carrie Steinmehl. Subject Specialists: *Fiction,* Theresa Davis; Staff 74.1 (MLS 25.9, Non-MLS 48.2)
Founded 1983. Pop 84,353; Circ 1,479,073
Oct 2018-Sept 2019 Income $7,297,284, State $53,851, City $7,063,988, Federal $10,605, Locally Generated Income $168,840
Automation Activity & Vendor Info: (Cataloging) Innovative Interfaces, Inc; (Circulation) Innovative Interfaces, Inc; (OPAC) Innovative Interfaces, Inc
Wireless access
Function: 24/7 Electronic res, 24/7 Online cat, Activity rm, Adult bk club, Adult literacy prog, After school storytime, Archival coll, Art exhibits, Audio & video playback equip for onsite use, Audiobks on Playaways & MP3, Audiobks via web, AV serv, Bilingual assistance for Spanish patrons, Bk club(s), Bks on cassette, Bks on CD, Bus archives, CD-ROM, Children's prog, Computer training, Computers for patron use, Doc delivery serv, E-Readers, E-Reserves, Electronic databases & coll, Equip loans & repairs, For res purposes, Free DVD rentals, Govt ref serv, Health sci info serv, Holiday prog, Homework prog, ILL available, Internet access, Life-long learning prog for all ages, Literacy & newcomer serv, Magazines, Magnifiers for reading, Mango lang, Meeting rooms, Microfiche/film & reading machines, Movies, Music CDs, Online cat, Online ref, Outreach serv, Outside serv via phone, mail, e-mail & web, OverDrive digital audio bks, Photocopying/Printing, Preschool outreach, Preschool reading prog, Printer for laptops & handheld devices, Prog for adults, Prog for children & young adult, Ref & res, Ref serv available, Scanner, Senior computer classes, Senior outreach, Spanish lang bks, Story hour, Study rm, Summer reading prog, Tax forms, Teen prog, Telephone ref, VHS videos, Visual arts prog, Wheelchair accessible, Workshops, Writing prog
Publications: Bi-monthly calendar
Partic in Jefferson County Libr Coop
Open Mon-Thurs 9-9, Fri 9-6, Sat 10-6, Sun 1-6
Friends of the Library Group

HUEYTOWN

P HUEYTOWN PUBLIC LIBRARY*, 1372 Hueytown Rd, 35023-2443. SAN 300-1091. Tel: 205-491-1443. FAX: 205-491-6319. Web Site: www.hueytownlibrary.org. *Dir,* Jeff Parsons; E-mail: jdparsons@bham.lib.al.us; Staff 6 (MLS 1, Non-MLS 5)
Founded 1969. Pop 15,734; Circ 61,053
Library Holdings: Bk Vols 45,000; Per Subs 42
Special Collections: Alabama and Local History; Local Authors
Subject Interests: Alabama
Automation Activity & Vendor Info: (Cataloging) Innovative Interfaces, Inc - Sierra; (Circulation) Innovative Interfaces, Inc - Sierra; (OPAC) Innovative Interfaces, Inc - Sierra
Wireless access
Function: 24/7 Electronic res, 24/7 Online cat, Adult bk club, Audiobks via web, Bilingual assistance for Spanish patrons, Bk club(s), Bks on CD, Children's prog, Computer training, Computers for patron use, E-Readers, E-Reserves, Electronic databases & coll, For res purposes, Free DVD rentals, Govt ref serv, ILL available, Internet access, Magazines, Mail & tel request accepted, Meeting rooms, Microfiche/film & reading machines, Movies, Music CDs, Notary serv, Online cat, Online info literacy tutorials on the web & in blackboard, Outreach serv, Outside serv via phone, mail, e-mail & web, OverDrive digital audio bks, Photocopying/Printing, Preschool reading prog, Prog for adults, Prog for children & young adult, Ref & res, Ref serv available, Res assist avail, Serves people with intellectual disabilities, Spanish lang bks, STEM programs, Story hour, Summer reading prog, Tax forms, Telephone ref, Wheelchair accessible, Workshops
Partic in Jefferson County Libr Coop
Open Mon-Fri 10-6, Sat 9-1
Friends of the Library Group

HUNTSVILLE

J DRAKE STATE COMMUNITY & TECHNICAL COLLEGE, S C O'Neal Library & Technology Center, 3421 Meridan St N, 35811-1544. Tel: 256-551-3120, 256-551-5218. Reference Tel: 256-551-5207. Toll Free Tel: 888-413-7253. FAX: 256-551-3134. Web Site: www.drakestate.edu. *Dir, Libr Serv,* Carla Clift; E-mail: carla.clift@drakestate.edu; *Asst Dir,* Dennis Borden; E-mail: dennis.borden@drakestate.edu; Staff 2 (MLS 2)
Founded 1961. Enrl 695; Highest Degree: Associate
Library Holdings: Bk Vols 21,000; Per Subs 150
Special Collections: Black Coll
Automation Activity & Vendor Info: (Cataloging) Innovative Interfaces, Inc - Sierra; (Circulation) Innovative Interfaces, Inc - Sierra; (Course Reserve) EBSCO Online; (OPAC) Innovative Interfaces, Inc - Sierra; (Serials) Innovative Interfaces, Inc - Sierra
Wireless access
Function: AV serv, Photocopying/Printing
Open Mon-Thurs 7:30-7, Fri 7:30am-11:30am
Friends of the Library Group

P HUNTSVILLE-MADISON COUNTY PUBLIC LIBRARY*, 915 Monroe St, 35801. (Mail add: PO Box 443, 35804-0443), SAN 330-2105. Tel: 256-532-5940. Circulation Tel: 256-532-5984. Interlibrary Loan Service Tel: 256-532-5967. Administration Tel: 256-532-5950. Automation Services Tel: 256-532-5963. FAX: 256-532-5997. E-mail: askus@hmcpl.org. Web Site: hmcpl.org. *Interim Exec Dir,* Cindy Hewitt; E-mail: chewitt@hmcpl.org; *Actg Dep Dir,* Connie Chow; E-mail: cchow@hmcpl.org
Founded 1818. Pop 350,299; Circ 2,094,469
Oct 2014-Sept 2015 Income (Main & Associated Libraries) $5,945,792. Mats Exp $812,194. Sal $3,832,454
Library Holdings: AV Mats 106,422; e-books 7,786; Electronic Media & Resources 86; Bk Vols 403,227; Per Subs 555
Special Collections: Civil War & Southern History (Zeitler Room Coll), bks, maps & newsp; Foreign Language Materials; Genealogy & Local History (Heritage Room Coll), bks, micro & ms
Subject Interests: Foreign lang
Automation Activity & Vendor Info: (Acquisitions) Koha; (Cataloging) Koha; (Circulation) Koha; (ILL) OCLC; (OPAC) Koha; (Serials) Koha
Wireless access
Publications: Cover to Cover (Newsletter)
Special Services for the Blind - Assistive/Adapted tech devices, equip & products; Bks & mags in Braille, on rec, tape & cassette; Bks on cassette; Braille & cassettes; Braille equip; Talking bks & player equip
Open Mon-Thurs 9-9, Fri & Sat 9-5, Sun 1-5
Friends of the Library Group
Branches: 12
BAILEY COVE LIBRARY, 1409 Weatherly Plaza SE, 35803, SAN 377-6581. Tel: 256-881-0257. E-mail: bcove@hmcpl.org. *Br Mgr,* Patsy Ducote
Open Mon-Thurs 9-8, Fri & Sat 9-5, Sun 1-5
Friends of the Library Group
ELIZABETH CARPENTER PUBLIC LIBRARY OF NEW HOPE, 5498 Main St, New Hope, 35760, SAN 329-6148. Tel: 256-723-2995. E-mail: newhope@hmcpl.org. *Br Mgr,* Amanda Porter
Founded 1989
Library Holdings: Bk Vols 20,930
Open Mon & Tues 10-5, Wed 12-6, Thurs 10-6, Fri 12-5, Sat 10-2
Friends of the Library Group
CAVALRY HILL PUBLIC LIBRARY, 2800 Poplar Ave, 35816. Tel: 256-970-6313. E-mail: cavalry@hmcpl.org. *Br Mgr,* Courtney Braggs
Library Holdings: Bk Vols 800
Friends of the Library Group
GURLEY PUBLIC LIBRARY, 225 Walker St, Gurley, 35748, SAN 329-6121. Tel: 256-776-2102. E-mail: gurley@hmcpl.org. *Br Mgr,* Position Currently Open
Library Holdings: Bk Vols 9,849

Open Mon, Tues & Thurs 12-7, Wed 10-5, Fri 12-5, Sat 10-2
Friends of the Library Group
TILLMAN D HILL PUBLIC LIBRARY, 131 Knowledge Dr, Hazel Green, 35750, SAN 372-5103. Tel: 256-828-9529. E-mail: hazelgr@hmcpl.org. *Br Mgr,* Vickie Mares
Library Holdings: Bk Vols 29,000
Open Mon, Wed & Thurs 10-6, Tues 10-8, Fri & Sat 10-5
Friends of the Library Group
MADISON PUBLIC LIBRARY, 142 Plaza Blvd, Madison, 35758, SAN 330-2229. Tel: 256-461-0046. E-mail: madison@hmcpl.org. *Br Mgr,* Sarah Sledge
Library Holdings: Bk Vols 80,000
Open Mon-Thurs 9-8, Fri & Sat 9-5, Sun 1-5
Friends of the Library Group
MONROVIA PUBLIC LIBRARY, 254 Allen Drake Dr, 35806, SAN 377-6603. Tel: 256-489-3392. E-mail: monrovia@hmcpl.org. *Br Mgr,* Mandy Farley
Library Holdings: Bk Vols 11,127
Open Mon-Thurs 9-8, Tues, Fri & Sat 9-5
Friends of the Library Group
ELEANOR E MURPHY LIBRARY, 7910 Charlotte Dr SW, 35802, SAN 330-2164. Tel: 256-881-5620. E-mail: murphy@hmcpl.org. *Br Mgr,* Annie Phillips
Open Mon-Thurs 9-7, Fri & Sat 9-5
Friends of the Library Group
BESSIE K RUSSELL BRANCH LIBRARY, 3011 C Sparkman Dr, 35810, SAN 330-2253. Tel: 256-859-9050. E-mail: russell@hmcpl.org. *Br Mgr,* Patti Ehmen
Founded 1962
Open Mon-Thurs 10-6, Fri & Sat 10-5
Friends of the Library Group
R SHOWERS CENTER, 4600 Blue Spring Rd, 35810, SAN 377-6964. Tel: 256-851-7492. E-mail: showers@hmcpl.org. *Br Mgr,* Lillie Cawthron
Library Holdings: Bk Vols 6,835
Open Mon-Thurs 9-6, Fri 9-5
Friends of the Library Group

P SUBREGIONAL LIBRARY FOR THE BLIND & PHYSICALLY HANDICAPPED, 915 Monroe St, 35801-5007. (Mail add: PO Box 443, 35804-0443). Tel: 256-532-5980. E-mail: bphdept@hmcpl.org. *Librn,* Amanda Trawick
Founded 1967
Open Mon-Fri 9-4:30
TRIANA PUBLIC LIBRARY, 357 Record Rd, Madison, 35756, SAN 376-8937. Tel: 256-772-9943. E-mail: triana@hmcpl.org. *Br Mgr,* Blanche Orr
Open Mon-Thurs 10-6, Fri 10-5, Sat 10-2
Friends of the Library Group
Bookmobiles: 2

CR OAKWOOD UNIVERSITY, Eva B Dykes Library, (Formerly Oakwood College), 7000 Adventist Blvd NW, 35896. SAN 300-1164. Tel: 256-726-7246. FAX: 256-726-7538. Web Site: library.oakwood.edu. *Dir,* Dr Ruth Swan; Tel: 256-726-7250, E-mail: rswan@oakwood.edu; *E-Resources Librn, Media Librn,* Rebecca Brothers; Tel: 256-726-7253, E-mail: rbrothers@oakwood.edu; *Acq, Tech,* Elaine Parker; Tel: 256-726-7251, E-mail: eparker@oakwood.edu; *Archivist,* Dr Barbara Stovall; Tel: 256-726-7249, E-mail: bstovall@oakwood.edu; *Cat,* Odalys Miranda; E-mail: omiranda@oakwood.edu; *Circ,* Evaline Otieno; E-mail: eotieno@oakwood.edu; *ILL, Tech Serv,* Stella Mbyirukira; Tel: 256-726-8389, E-mail: smbyirukira@oakwood.edu; *Ref (Info Servs),* Jeshua Hinton; E-mail: jhinton@oakwood.edu. Subject Specialists: *Allied health, Nursing,* Rebecca Brothers; *Biology, Chemistry, Educ,* Odalys Miranda; *Bus, Polit sci, Theol,* Jeshua Hinton; Staff 7 (MLS 4, Non-MLS 3)
Founded 1896. Enrl 1,700; Fac 105; Highest Degree: Bachelor
Library Holdings: Bk Vols 135,000; Per Subs 200
Special Collections: Black Studies; Oakwood College History; Seventh-Day Adventist Black History. Oral History
Automation Activity & Vendor Info: (Acquisitions) SirsiDynix; (Cataloging) SirsiDynix; (Circulation) SirsiDynix; (Course Reserve) SirsiDynix-WorkFlows; (Discovery) EBSCO Discovery Service; (ILL) OCLC WorldShare Interlibrary Loan; (OPAC) SirsiDynix-WorkFlows; (Serials) SirsiDynix
Wireless access
Function: Archival coll
Partic in LYRASIS; Network of Alabama Academic Libraries
Special Services for the Deaf - ADA equip; Assisted listening device; Assistive tech
Special Services for the Blind - Accessible computers; Assistive/Adapted tech devices, equip & products
Open Mon-Thurs 7:30am-11pm, Fri 7:30-1, Sun 1-10
Restriction: Authorized patrons, Borrowing privileges limited to fac & registered students, By permission only, In-house use for visitors

S US SPACE & ROCKET CENTER, Von Braun Library & Archives, One Tranquility Base, 35805-3399. SAN 327-9340. Tel: 256-721-5401, 256-721-7148. FAX: 256-722-5600. *Coll Mgr, Curator,* Audrey Glasgow; E-mail: audreyg@spacecamp.com; Staff 3 (Non-MLS 3)
Founded 1970
Library Holdings: Bk Vols 4,500
Wireless access
Function: Archival coll
Restriction: Access at librarian's discretion, Authorized scholars by appt, Limited access based on advanced application, Open by appt only, Researchers by appt only

C UNIVERSITY OF ALABAMA IN HUNTSVILLE*, M Louis Salmon Library, 4700 Holmes Ave, 35899. SAN 300-1199. Tel: 256-824-6530. Interlibrary Loan Service Tel: 256-890-6124. Reference Tel: 256-824-6529. Administration Tel: 256-824-6540. Circulation FAX: 256-824-6552. E-mail: library@uah.edu. Web Site: www.uah.edu/library. *Dir,* David Moore; E-mail: david.moore@uah.edu; *Head, ILL,* Charlotte Olson; Tel: 256-824-6522, E-mail: Charlotte.Olson@uah.edu; *Head, Tech Serv,* Susan McCreless; Tel: 256-824-6537, E-mail: Susan.Mccreless@uah.edu; *Ref Librn,* Belinda Ong; Tel: 256-824-6432, E-mail: Belinda.Ong@uah.edu; *Syst Librn,* Jack Drost; Tel: 256-824-7407, E-mail: Jack.Drost@uah.edu; *Archivist,* David Hanning; Tel: 256-824-7407, E-mail: dlh0029@uah.edu; *Archives,* Reagan Grimsley; Tel: 256-824-5781, E-mail: rlg0020@uah.edu; Staff 33 (MLS 8, Non-MLS 25)
Founded 1967. Enrl 6,200; Fac 301; Highest Degree: Doctorate
Library Holdings: e-books 46,172; e-journals 17,500; Bk Titles 283,948; Bk Vols 329,686; Per Subs 1,044
Special Collections: Harvie Jone Architectural Coll; Robert E Jones Congressional Papers; Robert Forward Space Coll; Saturn V History Documentation Coll; Skylab Space Station Coll; Willy Ley Space Coll. US Document Depository
Subject Interests: Bus, Engr
Automation Activity & Vendor Info: (Acquisitions) SirsiDynix; (Cataloging) SirsiDynix; (Circulation) SirsiDynix; (Course Reserve) SirsiDynix; (ILL) SirsiDynix; (OPAC) SirsiDynix; (Serials) SirsiDynix
Wireless access
Function: For res purposes, Ref serv available, Res libr, Wheelchair accessible
Publications: Guide to the Salmon Library (Library handbook)
Partic in LYRASIS; Network of Alabama Academic Libraries; OCLC Online Computer Library Center, Inc
Special Services for the Blind - Assistive/Adapted tech devices, equip & products; Computer with voice synthesizer for visually impaired persons

IDER

P IDER PUBLIC LIBRARY*, 10808 Alabama Hwy 75, 35981. (Mail add: PO Box 202, 35981-0202), SAN 376-5636. Tel: 256-657-2170. FAX: 256-657-3178. E-mail: iderpl1@farmerstel.com. *Dir,* Sandra Roberts
Founded 1992
Library Holdings: Bk Vols 12,000
Function: Adult bk club, After school storytime
Open Mon-Fri 12:30-5, Sat 9-Noon
Friends of the Library Group

IRONDALE

P IRONDALE PUBLIC LIBRARY*, 105 20th St S, 35210. SAN 300-1210. Tel: 205-951-1415. FAX: 205-951-7715. E-mail: Librarian@irondalelibrary.org. Web Site: www.irondalelibrary.org. *Dir,* Madelyn M Wilson; E-mail: del.wilson@irondalelibrary.org; Staff 5.5 (MLS 2, Non-MLS 3.5)
Founded 1951. Pop 9,704; Circ 67,367
Library Holdings: Audiobooks 1,025; DVDs 1,896; Bk Vols 41,313; Per Subs 85
Automation Activity & Vendor Info: (Cataloging) Innovative Interfaces, Inc; (Circulation) Innovative Interfaces, Inc; (OPAC) Innovative Interfaces, Inc
Wireless access
Partic in Jefferson County Libr Coop
Open Mon, Tues & Thurs 9:30-7, Wed 9:30-6, Fri 9-1, Sat 11-3, Sun 2-5
Friends of the Library Group

IRVINGTON

P CITY OF BAYOU LA BATRE PUBLIC LIBRARY*, 12747 Padgett Switch Rd, 36544. SAN 300-015X. Tel: 251-824-4213. FAX: 251-824-3196. E-mail: cityofbayoulabatrepubliclibrary@yahoo.com. Web Site: www.cityofbayoulabatre.com/public_library/index.php. *Dir,* Patricia Sebert; Staff 1 (Non-MLS 1)
Pop 2,558; Circ 35,533
Library Holdings: Bk Vols 23,971; Per Subs 10
Automation Activity & Vendor Info: (Cataloging) Book Systems; (Circulation) Book Systems; (OPAC) Book Systems
Friends of the Library Group

JACKSON

P WHITE SMITH MEMORIAL LIBRARY, 213 College Ave, 36545. (Mail add: PO Box 265, 36545), SAN 300-1229. Tel: 251-246-4962. FAX: 251-246-9791. E-mail: wsmlibrary@yahoo.com. Web Site: whitesmithlibrary.org. *Dir, Pub Relations,* Debra Grayson
Founded 1937. Pop 10,000; Circ 29,521
Library Holdings: Large Print Bks 200; Bk Titles 18,500; Bk Vols 21,000; Per Subs 15
Special Collections: Video Coll
Automation Activity & Vendor Info: (Cataloging) Book Systems; (Circulation) Book Systems; (OPAC) Book Systems
Wireless access
Open Mon & Thurs 9-6, Tues, Wed & Fri 9-5

JACKSONVILLE

P JACKSONVILLE PUBLIC LIBRARY*, 200 Pelham Rd S, 36265. SAN 300-1245. Tel: 256-435-6332. FAX: 256-435-4459. E-mail: lotsabooks@hotmail.com. Web Site: www.jacksonvillepubliclibrary.org. *Dir,* Barbara Rowell; *Computer Tech,* Christy Wallace; Staff 9 (MLS 1, Non-MLS 8)
Founded 1957. Pop 9,000; Circ 94,000
Library Holdings: Audiobooks 677; DVDs 2,447; e-books 3,249; Bk Vols 58,216; Per Subs 61
Special Collections: Col John Pelham Papers; Jacksonville History Museum Coll; John Francis Papers (Civil War Roster & Letters)
Automation Activity & Vendor Info: (Cataloging) SirsiDynix; (Circulation) SirsiDynix; (OPAC) SirsiDynix
Wireless access
Open Tues-Fri 8-5:45, Sat 8-3:45

C JACKSONVILLE STATE UNIVERSITY LIBRARY*, Houston Cole Library, 700 Pelham Rd N, 36265. SAN 300-1237. Tel: 256-782-5758. Reference Tel: 256-782-8034. FAX: 256-782-5872. Web Site: www.jsu.edu/library. *Dean, Libr Serv,* John-Bauer Graham; E-mail: jgraham@jsu.edu; *Head, Tech Serv,* Jodi Poe; *Sr Cat Librn,* Kim Stevens; *Cat Librn,* Arland Henning; *Electronic Res Librn,* Bethany Latham; *Health Sci Librn,* Paula Barnett-Ellis; *Acq, Per Librn,* Mary Bevis; *Ref & Instruction Librn,* Charlcie Pettway Vann; *Ref Librn,* Carley Knight; *Ref Librn,* Harry Nuttall; *Ref Librn,* Hanrong Wang; *Electronic Res Mgr,* Yingqi Tang. Subject Specialists: *Math, Sci,* Paula Barnett-Ellis; *Art, Lang arts, Music,* Carley Knight; *Lit,* Harry Nuttall; *Law, Tech,* Hanrong Wang; Staff 18 (MLS 15, Non-MLS 3)
Founded 1883. Enrl 9,000; Fac 453; Highest Degree: Master
Library Holdings: AV Mats 38,940; e-books 19,067; Bk Vols 714,960; Per Subs 1,802
Special Collections: Alabama; Old & Rare Books. Oral History; US Document Depository
Automation Activity & Vendor Info: (Acquisitions) Ex Libris Group; (Cataloging) Ex Libris Group; (Circulation) Ex Libris Group; (OPAC) Ex Libris Group; (Serials) Ex Libris Group
Wireless access
Partic in LYRASIS; Network of Alabama Academic Libraries
Open Mon-Thurs 7:30am-11pm, Fri 7:30-4:30, Sat 9-5, Sun 3-11
Friends of the Library Group

JASPER

J BEVILL STATE COMMUNITY COLLEGE*, Irma D Nicholson Library, 1411 Indiana Ave, 35501. SAN 300-1261. Tel: 205-387-0511, Ext 5748. FAX: 205-387-5190. Web Site: bscc.libguides.com, www.bscc.edu/students/student-resources/library. *Librn,* Rebecca E Whitten; E-mail: rebecca.whitten@bscc.edu; *Libr Asst,* Pat Bowden; E-mail: pat.bowden@bscc.edu; Staff 2 (MLS 2)
Enrl 1,000; Highest Degree: Associate
Library Holdings: Bk Vols 25,930; Per Subs 85
Automation Activity & Vendor Info: (Cataloging) Follett Software; (Circulation) Follett Software; (OPAC) Follett Software
Wireless access
Open Mon-Thurs 7-5

P CARL ELLIOTT REGIONAL LIBRARY SYSTEM*, 98 E 18th St, 35501. SAN 300-1253. Tel: 205-221-2568. E-mail: contact@carlelliottregionallibrary.com. Web Site: www.youseemore.com/cerl. *Dir,* Sandra Underwood; *Adminr, Info Tech,* Stephen Underwood; E-mail: sunderwood@carlelliottregionallibrary.org; *Tech Serv Librn,* Christy Frazier
Founded 1957. Pop 95,000; Circ 165,000
Library Holdings: Bk Titles 87,000; Bk Vols 98,000; Per Subs 132
Special Collections: Literature (Musgrove Coll)
Automation Activity & Vendor Info: (Cataloging) TLC (The Library Corporation); (Circulation) TLC (The Library Corporation); (OPAC) TLC (The Library Corporation)
Wireless access
Publications: Regional Messenger
Member Libraries: Arley Public Library; Carbon Hill City Library; Double Springs Public Library; Haleyville Public Library; Sumiton Public Library
Open Mon-Fri 9-5

P JASPER PUBLIC LIBRARY, 98 18th St E, 35501. SAN 320-8915. Tel: 205-221-2568, 205-221-8512. E-mail: jasperpubliclibrary@hotmail.com. Web Site: www2.youseemore.com/cerl. *Dir,* Sandra Underwood; E-mail: sandraunderwood@carlelliottregionallibrary.org
Library Holdings: Bk Titles 60,000; Per Subs 124
Open Mon-Thurs 9-4:30

KILLEN

P KILLEN PUBLIC LIBRARY*, 325 J C Malden Hwy, 35645. SAN 376-5644. Tel: 256-757-5471. FAX: 256-757-5471. E-mail: killenlibrary@bellsouth.net. Web Site: webmini.apls.state.al.us/apls_web/killen. *Dir,* Linda Baskins
Library Holdings: CDs 67; DVDs 78; Large Print Bks 3,467; Bk Titles 19,000; Bk Vols 20,000; Talking Bks 145
Automation Activity & Vendor Info: (Acquisitions) Book Systems; (Cataloging) Book Systems; (Circulation) Book Systems; (OPAC) Book Systems
Wireless access
Open Mon-Fri 9-5, Sat 9-1
Friends of the Library Group

LEEDS

P LEEDS JANE CULBRETH PUBLIC LIBRARY, 8104 Parkway Dr, 35094. SAN 300-130X. Tel: 205-699-5962. FAX: 205-699-6843. Web Site: www.leedslibrary.com. *Dir,* Melanie Carden; E-mail: mcarden@bham.lib.al.us; Staff 4 (MLS 1, Non-MLS 3)
Founded 1923. Pop 10,455; Circ 95,786
Library Holdings: AV Mats 4,068; e-books 472; Bk Vols 31,424; Per Subs 92; Talking Bks 1,570
Subject Interests: Alabama
Automation Activity & Vendor Info: (Circulation) Innovative Interfaces, Inc
Function: Ref serv available
Partic in Jefferson County Libr Coop
Special Services for the Deaf - Staff with knowledge of sign lang
Special Services for the Blind - Bks on cassette
Open Mon & Thurs 9:30-7, Tues, Wed & Fri 9:30-5:30, Sat 9:30-1:30
Friends of the Library Group

LEIGHTON

P LEIGHTON PUBLIC LIBRARY*, 8740 Main St, 35646. (Mail add: PO Box 484, 35646-0484), SAN 300-1318. Tel: 256-446-5380. FAX: 256-446-5380. E-mail: leightonpubliclibrary8@gmail.com. *Librn,* Sheri Childress
Pop 988; Circ 7,100
Library Holdings: Bk Vols 10,000; Per Subs 22
Wireless access
Open Tues-Fri 12:30-5, Sat 11-3
Friends of the Library Group

LEXINGTON

P LEXINGTON PUBLIC LIBRARY, Burchell Campbell Memorial Library, 11075 Hwy 101, 35648-0459. SAN 376-7590. Tel: 256-229-5579. FAX: 256-667-5551. E-mail: lexingtonlibrary101@gmail.com. Web Site: lexingtonal.org/library. *Dir,* Paula Newton; Staff 1 (Non-MLS 1)
Pop 750
Library Holdings: Bk Vols 7,500
Wireless access
Open Mon-Fri 10-4
Friends of the Library Group

LILLIAN

P LILLIAN PERDIDO BAY LIBRARY, 34081 Ickler Ave N, 36549. (Mail add: PO Box 237, 36549-0237). Tel: 251-962-4700. FAX: 251-962-4700. *Librn,* Michelle Cooke
Founded 1993
Library Holdings: CDs 188; DVDs 41; Large Print Bks 277; Bk Vols 16,269; Talking Bks 360; Videos 634
Wireless access
Open Tues & Thurs 10-2 & 4-6, Wed, Fri & Sat 10-2

LINCOLN

P LINCOLN PUBLIC LIBRARY, 47475 US Hwy 78, 35096. SAN 376-5520. Tel: 205-763-4080. FAX: 205-763-7244. E-mail: lincolnpubliclibrary@lincolnal.org. Web Site: www.lincolnalabama.com/Default.asp?ID=179&pg=Library. *Dir,* Robin Bishop; E-mail: robin.bishop@lincolnal.org
Founded 1975. Pop 4,800
Library Holdings: AV Mats 300; Large Print Bks 283; Bk Vols 19,000; Per Subs 6; Talking Bks 186
Automation Activity & Vendor Info: (Cataloging) Book Systems; (Circulation) Book Systems; (OPAC) Book Systems
Wireless access
Mem of Cheaha Regional Library
Partic in Minuteman Library Network
Open Mon, Tues, Thurs & Fri 8-6, Sat 9-Noon

LINDEN

P MARENGO COUNTY PUBLIC LIBRARY*, 210 N Shiloh St, 36748. SAN 300-1326. Tel: 334-295-2246. FAX: 334-295-2265. E-mail: marengocounty933@bellsouth.net. *Dir,* Sarah Dailey
Founded 1941. Pop 23,819; Circ 60,069
Library Holdings: Audiobooks 281; Bk Vols 9,770
Automation Activity & Vendor Info: (Acquisitions) Book Systems; (Cataloging) Book Systems; (Circulation) Book Systems; (OPAC) Book Systems
Wireless access
Function: 24/7 Electronic res, Bks on CD, Children's prog, Computers for patron use, Homebound delivery serv, Internet access, Outreach serv, Photocopying/Printing, Prof lending libr, Prog for children & young adult, Ref & res, Spoken cassettes & CDs, Summer reading prog, Wheelchair accessible
Open Mon-Fri 10-5
Restriction: Authorized patrons, Circ to mem only, In-house use for visitors, Lending limited to county residents, Open to pub for ref & circ; with some limitations

LINEVILLE

P LINEVILLE CITY LIBRARY, 60119 Hwy 9, 36266. (Mail add: PO Box 482, 36266-0482); SAN 376-7388. Tel: 256-396-5162. FAX: 256-901-8078. E-mail: linevillelibrary@gmail.com. Web Site: www.cheaharegionallibrary.org/member_libraries/lineville_city_library. *Dir,* Julie Siverson
Library Holdings: Bk Vols 10,000
Wireless access
Mem of Cheaha Regional Library
Open Mon-Fri 9:30-4:30

LIVINGSTON

P SUMTER COUNTY LIBRARY SYSTEM*, 201 Monroe St, 35470. (Mail add: PO Drawer U, 35470-0377), SAN 324-0746. Tel: 205-652-2349. E-mail: rptlibrary35470@gmail.com. *Dir,* Kelly Tarply; Staff 1 (MLS 1)
Founded 1979. Pop 14,500
Automation Activity & Vendor Info: (Cataloging) Book Systems; (Circulation) Book Systems
Wireless access
Member Libraries: Ruby Pickens Tartt Public Library
Open Mon, Tues & Thurs 9-6, Wed & Fri 9-5, Sat 9-12

P RUBY PICKENS TARTT PUBLIC LIBRARY*, 201 Monroe St, 35470. (Mail add: PO Drawer U, 35470), SAN 300-1342. Tel: 205-652-2349. FAX: 205-652-6688. E-mail: rptlibrary35470@gmail.com. Web Site: www.cityoflivingstonal.com/library. *Dir,* Kelly Tarpley; Staff 3 (MLS 1, Non-MLS 2)
Founded 1905. Pop 14,500; Circ 31,715
Library Holdings: Audiobooks 1,032; DVDs 521; Bk Vols 31,214; Per Subs 40
Automation Activity & Vendor Info: (Acquisitions) Book Systems; (Cataloging) Book Systems; (Circulation) Book Systems
Wireless access
Mem of Sumter County Library System
Open Mon, Tues & Thurs 9-6, Wed & Fri 9-5, Sat 9-12
Friends of the Library Group

C UNIVERSITY OF WEST ALABAMA, Julia Tutwiler Library, UWA Station 12, 35470. SAN 300-1334. Tel: 205-652-3613. Interlibrary Loan Service Tel: 205-652-3842. Administration Tel: 205-652-3614. FAX: 205-652-2332. Web Site: www.uwa.edu/library. *Dir & Univ Librn,* Dr Neil Snider; E-mail: nsnider@uwa.edu; Staff 5 (MLS 3, Non-MLS 2)
Founded 1835. Enrl 3,500; Fac 110; Highest Degree: Doctorate
Oct 2020-Sept 2021. Mats Exp $234,000, Books $12,000, Electronic Ref Mat (Incl. Access Fees) $203,500, Presv $1,500. Sal $439,940
Library Holdings: Bk Titles 130,000; Bk Vols 250,000; Per Subs 200
Special Collections: Alabama Room; Folklore (Ruby Pickens Tartt Coll), ms; Microfiche Coll
Automation Activity & Vendor Info: (Acquisitions) Ex Libris Group; (Cataloging) Ex Libris Group; (Circulation) Ex Libris Group; (Course Reserve) Ex Libris Group; (ILL) Ex Libris Group; (Media Booking) Ex Libris Group; (OPAC) Ex Libris Group; (Serials) Ex Libris Group
Wireless access
Function: 24/7 Electronic res, 24/7 Online cat
Partic in LYRASIS
Open Mon-Thurs 7:30am-11:45pm, Fri 7:30-4:45, Sat 9-4:45, Sun 2-11:45

LOUISVILLE

P LOUISVILLE PUBLIC LIBRARY*, 1951 Main St, 36048. (Mail add: PO Box 125, 36048), SAN 330-3098. Tel: 334-266-5210. FAX: 334-266-5630. *Librn,* Debra Vinson
Pop 618
Library Holdings: Bk Vols 5,500; Videos 17
Wireless access
Open Mon-Wed & Fri 8-3

LOXLEY

P LOXLEY PUBLIC LIBRARY, 1001 Loxley Ave, 36551. SAN 300-1350. Tel: 251-964-5695. E-mail: loxleylibrary@yahoo.com. Web Site: www.townofloxley.com/departments/library. *Libr Dir,* Patricia Hudson
Circ 3,760
Library Holdings: Bk Vols 8,000
Wireless access
Mem of Baldwin County Library Cooperative, Inc
Open Tues 9-5, Sat 10-2

LUVERNE

P LUVERNE PUBLIC LIBRARY*, 148 E Third St, 36049. SAN 300-1369. Tel: 334-335-5326. FAX: 334-335-6402. E-mail: luvernepubliclibrary@gmail.com. Web Site: www.luvernepubliclibrary.com. *Dir,* Kathryn Tomlin; *Asst Dir,* Jody A Foote; Staff 2 (Non-MLS 2)
Founded 1954. Pop 10,242; Circ 13,424
Library Holdings: Audiobooks 747; AV Mats 1,181; CDs 323; DVDs 581; Large Print Bks 114; Bk Vols 13,823; Per Subs 33
Automation Activity & Vendor Info: (Cataloging) Book Systems; (Circulation) Book Systems; (ILL) OCLC WorldShare Interlibrary Loan; (OPAC) Book Systems
Wireless access
Function: Bks on cassette, Bks on CD, CD-ROM, Children's prog, Computers for patron use, Electronic databases & coll, Free DVD rentals, Holiday prog, ILL available, Internet access, Music CDs, Online cat, Online info literacy tutorials on the web & in blackboard, Photocopying/Printing, Prog for adults, Prog for children & young adult, Ref serv available, Summer reading prog, Tax forms, Wheelchair accessible
Open Mon-Fri 10-6

MARION

C JUDSON COLLEGE*, Bowling Library, 306 E Dekalb St, 36756. SAN 300-1393. Tel: 334-683-5182. Reference Tel: 334-683-5283. Web Site: libguides.judson.edu. *Dir, Libr Serv,* Dr George Washburn; Tel: 334-683-5281, E-mail: gwashburn@judson.edu; *Librn,* Andrea Abernathy; E-mail: aabernathy@judson.edu
Founded 1838. Enrl 425; Fac 37; Highest Degree: Bachelor
Library Holdings: Bk Titles 58,000; Bk Vols 72,000; Per Subs 429
Special Collections: Alabama Women's Hall of Fame Coll
Subject Interests: British hist, Relig
Automation Activity & Vendor Info: (Cataloging) Ex Libris Group; (Circulation) Ex Libris Group; (OPAC) Ex Libris Group
Wireless access
Partic in LYRASIS; NAAL
Open Mon-Thurs 8-6 & 7-10, Fri 8-12 & 1-4, Sun 6pm-10pm

J MARION MILITARY INSTITUTE*, Baer Memorial Library, 1101 Washington St, 36756. SAN 300-1407. Tel: 334-683-2371. E-mail: librarian@marionmilitary.edu. Web Site: marionmilitary.edu/academics/library, sites.google.com/site/baermemorial. *Dir,* Ashley Plummer; E-mail: aplummer@marionmilitary.edu; Staff 2 (MLS 1, Non-MLS 1)
Founded 1887. Enrl 325
Library Holdings: Bk Titles 22,853; Bk Vols 32,131; Per Subs 60
Automation Activity & Vendor Info: (Cataloging) Book Systems; (Circulation) Book Systems; (OPAC) Book Systems
Wireless access
Restriction: Authorized patrons, Open to students, fac & staff

P MARION-PERRY COUNTY LIBRARY*, 202 Washington St, 36756. SAN 300-1415. Tel: 334-683-6411. E-mail: librar_p@bellsouth.net. Web Site: marionperrycountylibrary.webs.com. *Dir,* Kim Stewart
Founded 1934. Pop 14,872
Library Holdings: Bk Vols 20,000; Per Subs 2
Special Collections: Genealogy, filmstrips, audiobooks, videos
Subject Interests: Art
Open Mon-Thurs 9-1 & 2-5
Friends of the Library Group

MAXWELL AFB

UNITED STATES AIR FORCE

A AIR UNIVERSITY - MUIR S FAIRCHILD RESEARCH INFORMATION CENTER*, 600 Chennault Circle, 36112-6010, SAN 300-1431. Tel: 334-953-2606. Circulation Tel: 334-953-2230. Interlibrary Loan Service Tel: 334-953-7223. Reference Tel: 334-953-2888. Web Site: www.au.af.mil/au/aul/aul.htm. *Dir,* Dr Jeff Luzius; E-mail: jeff.luzius@us.af.mil; *Head, Reader Serv,* Terry Hawkins; Tel: 334-953-2237, Fax: 334-953-2329, E-mail: terry.hawkins@us.af.mil; *Head, Ref,* Ron Dial; Tel: 334-953-2347, E-mail: ron.dial@us.af.mil; *Head, Syst,* Martha M McCrary; Tel: 334-953-2474, E-mail: martha.mccrary@us.af.mil; *Head, Tech Serv,* Tyler S Evans; Tel: 334-953-7691, E-mail: tyler.evans.1@us.af.mil; *Acq,* Deborah Barone; Tel: 334-953-2410, E-mail: deborah.barone@us.af.mil; *Automation Syst Coordr,* Wendy Ng; Tel: 334-953-6498, E-mail: wendy.ng@us.af.mil; *Bibliographer,* Kimberly Hunter; Tel: 334-953-9811, E-mail: kimberly.hunter@us.af.mil; *Cat,* Amanda Haldy; Tel: 334-953-2190, E-mail: amanda.haldy@us.af.mil; *Electronic Serv,* Dr Stephanie Rollins; Tel: 334-953-8301, E-mail: stephanie.rollins@us.af.mil; Staff 31 (MLS 31)
Founded 1946. Enrl 8,593; Highest Degree: Master
Library Holdings: AV Mats 769; CDs 1,090; e-books 46,816; Microforms 959,522; Bk Titles 564,911; Per Subs 1,255; Videos 2,326
Special Collections: Air University Coll, rare bks & per related to flight
Subject Interests: Bus & mgt, Econ, Educ, Foreign relations, Hist, Mil sci
Automation Activity & Vendor Info: (Acquisitions) Ex Libris Group; (Cataloging) Ex Libris Group; (Circulation) Ex Libris Group; (Course Reserve) Ex Libris Group; (ILL) Ex Libris Group; (OPAC) Ex Libris Group; (Serials) Ex Libris Group
Partic in Association of Southeastern Research Libraries; Central New York Library Resources Council; LYRASIS; Military Education Coordination Conference; Network of Alabama Academic Libraries; Panhandle Library Access Network
Publications: Air University Library Index to Military Periodicals; Air University Library Master List of Periodicals; Special Bibliography Series
Open Mon-Thurs 7:30am-9pm, Fri 7:30-5, Sat 11-5
Restriction: Pub use on premises

A HISTORICAL RESEARCH AGENCY*, AFHRA, 600 Chennault Circle, Bldg 1405, 36112-6424, SAN 330-2288. Tel: 334-953-2395. FAX: 334-953-4096. E-mail: afhranews@maxwell.af.mil. Web Site: afhra.maxwell.af.mil. *Archivist,* Lynn Gamma; E-mail: lynn.gamma@maxwell.af.mil
Founded 1942
Special Collections: End of Tour Reports; German Air Force (Karlsruhe Document Coll) & GAF Monograph Series, doc, micro; Gulf War Coll; Historical Monographs; Histories of Air Force Organizations; Personal Papers of Air Force Leaders USAF (Individual Aircraft Record Card Coll), doc, micro. Oral History

A MAXWELL AIR FORCE BASE LIBRARY FL3300*, FL 3300, Bldg 28, 355 Kirkpatrick Ave E, 36112, SAN 330-2075. Tel: 334-953-6484. FAX: 334-953-7643.
Founded 1958. Pop 6,800
Library Holdings: Bk Vols 68,000; Per Subs 275
Partic in Federal Library & Information Network; Medical Library Association

A MAXWELL GUNTER COMMUNITY LIBRARY SYSTEM*, MSD/MSEL, 481 Williamson St, Bldg 1110 Gunter Annex, 36114, SAN 330-2342. Tel: 334-416-3179. FAX: 334-416-2949. *Dir,* Bernadette Roche; Staff 8 (MLS 1, Non-MLS 7)
Library Holdings: Bk Vols 41,000

MIDLAND CITY

P MARY BERRY BROWN MEMORIAL LIBRARY, 1318 Hinton Waters Ave, 36350. (Mail add: PO Box 713, 36350-0713), SAN 330-2881. Tel: 334-983-9999. FAX: 334-983-9999. E-mail: mbbmidlandcitylibrary@gmail.com. *Dir & Librn,* Ms Lee Creel; *Libr Asst,* Joyce York; Staff 2 (Non-MLS 2)
Founded 1973
Library Holdings: Bk Vols 10,000; Per Subs 10
Function: 24/7 Electronic res, Accelerated reader prog, Archival coll, Audio & video playback equip for onsite use, Bks on cassette, Bks on CD, Children's prog, Computers for patron use, Distance learning, Doc delivery serv, Electronic databases & coll, Free DVD rentals, Govt ref serv, Holiday prog, Homework prog, Internet access, Magazines, Magnifiers for reading, Mail & tel request accepted, Meeting rooms, Movies, Outside serv via phone, mail, e-mail & web, Photocopying/Printing, Printer for laptops & handheld devices, Prog for children & young adult, Ref serv available, Story hour, Study rm, Summer reading prog
Open Mon-Fri 10-5
Restriction: Access at librarian's discretion, Authorized patrons, Authorized personnel only, ID required to use computers (Ltd hrs), In-house use for visitors, Non-circulating of rare bks, Photo ID required for access, Pub ref by request, Pub use on premises

MILLBROOK

P MILLBROOK PUBLIC LIBRARY, 3650 Grandview Rd, 36054. (Mail add: PO Box 525, 36054-0525), SAN 300-144X. Tel: 334-285-6688. FAX: 334-285-0152. E-mail: millbrooklib@elmore.rr.com. Web Site: www.library.cityofmillbrook.org. *Dir,* Linda Moore; Tel: 334-285-6688, Ext 101; *Ch Serv,* Angela Dewberry; Tel: 334-285-6688, Ext 102; *Circ Librn,* Kimberly Breen; E-mail: kimberly.breen@cityofmillbrook-al.gov; *Circ Librn,* Christian Long; E-mail: christian.long@cityofmillbrook-al.gov; Staff 3 (Non-MLS 3)
Founded 1964. Pop 20,000; Circ 76,737
Library Holdings: Bk Vols 33,000; Per Subs 60
Special Collections: Oral History
Automation Activity & Vendor Info: (Cataloging) Book Systems; (Circulation) Book Systems; (ILL) OCLC; (OPAC) Book Systems
Wireless access
Function: 24/7 Online cat, Accelerated reader prog, Adult literacy prog, Audiobks via web, Bk club(s), Bks on cassette, Bks on CD, Children's prog, Computers for patron use, Electronic databases & coll, Free DVD rentals, Holiday prog, ILL available, Internet access, Large print keyboards, Magazines, Mail & tel request accepted, Movies, Music CDs, Online cat, OverDrive digital audio bks, Photocopying/Printing, Preschool reading prog, Printer for laptops & handheld devices, Prog for adults, Prog for children & young adult, Scanner, Spoken cassettes & CDs, Spoken cassettes & DVDs, Story hour, Study rm, Summer reading prog, Tax forms, VHS videos, Wheelchair accessible, Writing prog
Mem of Horseshoe Bend Regional Library
Open Mon, Wed & Fri 8-5, Tues & Thurs 8-6, Sat 8-3
Friends of the Library Group

MOBILE

J BISHOP STATE COMMUNITY COLLEGE*, Minnie Slade Bishop Library, 351 N Broad St, 36603-5898, SAN 300-1512. Administration Tel: 251-405-7113. Web Site: www.bishop.edu/student-services/library. *Dir, Libr Serv,* Marsha Mickles; E-mail: mmickles@bishop.edu
Founded 1943
Library Holdings: Bk Vols 53,883; Per Subs 207
Special Collections: Black Coll
Automation Activity & Vendor Info: (Cataloging) Follett Software; (Circulation) Follett Software; (OPAC) Follett Software
Special Services for the Deaf - Captioned film dep; Staff with knowledge of sign lang
Open Mon-Thurs 8-7, Fri 8-2, Sat 9-2

Departmental Libraries:

BAKER-GAINES CENTRAL CAMPUS, 1365 Dr Martin Luther King Jr Ave, 36603-5362. Tel: 251-405-4423. FAX: 251-405-4423.
Founded 1995
Library Holdings: Bk Vols 4,442; Per Subs 25
Open Mon-Thurs 8-7, Fri 8-2, Sat 9-2

CARVER CAMPUS, 414 Stanton St, 36617-2399. Tel: 251-662-5390.
Founded 1991
Library Holdings: Bk Vols 6,979; Per Subs 33
Open Mon-Thurs 8-5, Fri 8-2

SOUTHWEST CAMPUS, 925 Dauphin Island Pkwy, 36605-3299. Tel: 251-665-4091.
Founded 1954
Library Holdings: Bk Vols 1,479; Per Subs 24
Open Mon-Thurs 8-5, Fri 8-2

S HISTORIC MOBILE PRESERVATION SOCIETY*, Minnie Mitchell Archives, 300 Oakleigh Pl, 36604. SAN 327-8654. Tel: 251-432-1281. E-mail: hmps@bellsouth.net. Web Site: www.historicmobile.org/archives. *Archivist,* Bob Peck
Founded 1936
Library Holdings: Bk Vols 800
Special Collections: 19th Century Original Documents, deeds, letters, newsp; Civil War Diaries; George Rogers Library Coll; Local History Coll; Wilson Photograph Coll
Subject Interests: 19th Century
Function: Archival coll, Ref & res
Open Mon-Fri 10-3 by appointment

S HISTORY MUSEUM OF MOBILE, Reference Library, 111 S Royal St, 36602-3101. (Mail add: PO Box 2068, 36602-2068), SAN 300-1504. Tel: 251-208-7569. E-mail: museumrelations@historymuseumofmobile.com. Web Site: www.historymuseumofmobile.com. *Dir,* Meg McCrummen Fowler; E-mail: meg.fowler@historymuseumofmobile.com; *Historian,* Charles Torrey; E-mail: torrey@historymuseumofmobile.com
Founded 1962
Library Holdings: Bk Titles 3,000
Subject Interests: City hist, Civil War
Wireless access
Restriction: Open by appt only

GL MOBILE COUNTY PUBLIC LAW LIBRARY*, Mobile Government Plaza, 205 Government St, 36644-2308. SAN 300-1482. Tel: 251-574-8436. FAX: 251-574-4757. E-mail: mobilecolawlibrary@gmail.com. *Librn,* Patricia Evans
Library Holdings: Bk Titles 500; Bk Vols 60,000; Per Subs 59
Partic in LexisNexis
Open Mon-Fri 8-5

P MOBILE PUBLIC LIBRARY*, Ben May Main Library, 701 Government St, 36602. (Mail add: 700 Government St, 36602), SAN 330-2407. Tel: 251-340-1534. Interlibrary Loan Service Tel: 251-340-1448. FAX: 251-333-8185. Circulation E-mail: circulation@mplonline.org. Web Site: mobilepubliclibrary.org/index.php. *Dir,* Scott Kinney; Tel: 251-545-3570, E-mail: director@mplonline.org; *Asst Dir,* Margie Calhoun; Tel: 251-545-3552, E-mail: asstdirector@mplonline.org; *Mgr,* Sara McGough; Tel: 251-340-1532, E-mail: smcgough@mplonline.org; Staff 33 (MLS 33)
Founded 1928. Pop 400,236; Circ 1,335,076
Library Holdings: Bk Vols 417,737; Per Subs 800
Special Collections: Mobile History, 1702-present; Mobile Mardi Gras Coll, misc
Subject Interests: Genealogy
Automation Activity & Vendor Info: (Acquisitions) SirsiDynix; (Cataloging) SirsiDynix; (Circulation) SirsiDynix; (OPAC) SirsiDynix
Wireless access
Publications: Library Connections (Newsletter)
Partic in National Network of Libraries of Medicine Region 2
Special Services for the Deaf - Bks on deafness & sign lang; Staff with knowledge of sign lang; TTY equip
Open Mon-Thurs 9-8, Fri & Sat 9-6, Sun (Sept-May) 1-5
Friends of the Library Group
Branches: 8
MOORER/SPRING HILL BRANCH, Four McGregor Ave, 36608, SAN 330-2466. Tel: 251-470-7770. FAX: 251-470-7774. *Br Mgr,* Stephen Prager
Library Holdings: Bk Vols 36,894
Open Mon, Wed, Fri & Sat 9-6, Tues & Thurs 9-8
Friends of the Library Group
PARKWAY BRANCH, 1924-B Dauphin Island Pkwy, 36605-3004, SAN 330-2490. Tel: 251-470-7766. FAX: 251-470-7712. E-mail: parkwaybranch@mplonline.org. *Br Mgr,* Gloria Williams
Library Holdings: Bk Vols 36,894
Open Mon, Wed, Fri & Sat 9-6, Tues & Thurs 12-8
Friends of the Library Group
SARALAND PUBLIC LIBRARY, 111 Saraland Loop, Saraland, 36571-2418, SAN 330-2520. Tel: 251-675-2879. FAX: 251-675-2879. E-mail: saralandbranch@mplonline.org. *Br Mgr,* Sheryl Somathilake
Library Holdings: Bk Vols 24,181
Open Mon, Wed, Fri & Sat 10-6, Tues & Thurs 12-9
Friends of the Library Group
SEMMES BRANCH, 9150 Moffett Rd, Semmes, 36575. Tel: 251-645-6840. FAX: 251-645-6856. E-mail: sembranch@mplonline.org. *Mgr,* Heather Williams
Open Mon & Wed 10-6, Tues & Thurs Noon-7:30, Sat 10-5
Friends of the Library Group
VIRGINIA DILLARD SMITH/TOULMINVILLE BRANCH, 601 Stanton Rd, 36617-2209, SAN 330-2555. Tel: 251-438-7075. FAX: 251-438-7058. E-mail: tvlebranch@mplonline.org. *Br Mgr,* Betty Kidd
Library Holdings: Bk Vols 45,000
Open Mon & Thurs 9-8, Tues, Wed, Fri & Sat 9-6
Friends of the Library Group
THEODORE OAKS BRANCH, 5808 Hwy 90 W, Ste E, Theodore, 36582. Tel: 251-653-5012. FAX: 251-653-8176. E-mail: theodoreoaksbranch@mplonline.org. *Mgr,* Gina Wilson
Open Mon & Tues 10-7, Wed-Sat 10-5
Friends of the Library Group
TRINITY GARDENS COMMUNITY LIBRARY, 2668 Berkley Ave, 36610. Tel: 251-457-5954. FAX: 251-457-5954. E-mail: trincir@mplonline.org.
Open Mon-Wed (Winter) 11-4; Tues-Thurs (Summer) 9-2
Friends of the Library Group
WEST REGIONAL LIBRARY, 5555 Grelot Rd, 36609, SAN 330-2431. Tel: 251-340-8555. FAX: 251-304-2160. E-mail: westregionalbranch@mplonline.org. *Br Mgr,* Position Currently Open; *Asst Mgr,* Geraldine Wells
Library Holdings: Bk Vols 190,000
Open Mon-Thurs 9-8, Fri & Sat 9-6
Friends of the Library Group
Bookmobiles: 1. Mgr, Elaine Crook

CR SPRING HILL COLLEGE, Marnie & John Burke Memorial Library, 4000 Dauphin St, 36608. SAN 300-1520. Tel: 251-380-3870. Interlibrary Loan Service Tel: 251-380-4178. Reference Tel: 251-380-3660. Administration Tel: 251-380-3871. FAX: 251-460-2107. Web Site: libguides.shc.edu/burkelibrary. *Dir,* Gentry L Holbert; E-mail: gholbert@shc.edu; *Tech Serv Librn,* Janie Mathews; E-mail: jmathews@shc.edu; Staff 8 (MLS 5, Non-MLS 3)
Founded 1830. Enrl 1,093; Fac 83; Highest Degree: Master
Library Holdings: Bk Titles 99,500; Bk Vols 173,000; Per Subs 543
Special Collections: Jesuitica Coll; Mobiliana Coll. US Document Depository
Subject Interests: Rare bks
Automation Activity & Vendor Info: (Acquisitions) OCLC Worldshare Management Services; (Cataloging) OCLC Worldshare Management Services; (Circulation) OCLC Worldshare Management Services; (Course Reserve) OCLC Worldshare Management Services; (Discovery) OCLC Worldshare Management Services; (ILL) OCLC ILLiad; (OPAC) OCLC Worldshare Management Services; (Serials) OCLC Worldshare Management Services
Wireless access
Function: Archival coll
Publications: Friends of the Library Newsletter
Partic in Association of Jesuit Colleges & Universities; LYRASIS; Network of Alabama Academic Libraries; OCLC Online Computer Library Center, Inc
Friends of the Library Group

A UNITED STATES ARMY CORPS OF ENGINEERS*, Mobile District Library, 109 Saint Joseph St, 36602. (Mail add: PO Box 2288, 36628-0001). Tel: 251-690-3182. E-mail: CESAM-Library@sam.usace.army.mil. Web Site: www.sam.usace.army.mil/library. *Librn,* Cheryl Martin
Library Holdings: Bk Vols 7,800; Per Subs 15
Subject Interests: Sci, Tech
Wireless access
Restriction: Staff use only

C UNIVERSITY OF MOBILE, J L Bedsole Library, 5735 College Pkwy, 36613-2842. SAN 330-2377. Tel: 251-442-2242. Circulation Tel: 251-442-2246. Interlibrary Loan Service Tel: 251-442-2423. Toll Free Tel: 800-946-7267. FAX: 251-442-2515. E-mail: umlibrary@umobile.edu. Web Site: umobile.edu/library. *Dir, Libr Serv,* Jeffrey D Calametti; Tel: 251-442-2243, E-mail: jcalametti@umobile.edu; *Asst Dir, Tech Serv Librn,* Donna Ramer; Tel: 251-442-2478, E-mail: dramer@umobile.edu; *Tech Serv,* Haley Rodgers; Tel: 251-442-2479, E-mail: hrodgers@umobile.edu; Staff 5 (MLS 2, Non-MLS 3)
Founded 1961. Enrl 1,509; Fac 92; Highest Degree: Master
Library Holdings: AV Mats 1,833; e-books 39,944; e-journals 33,294; Bk Titles 62,350; Bk Vols 71,341; Per Subs 323
Special Collections: Southern Baptist History
Subject Interests: Alabama, Civil War, Educ, Local hist, Relig
Automation Activity & Vendor Info: (Cataloging) TLC (The Library Corporation); (Circulation) TLC (The Library Corporation); (Course Reserve) TLC (The Library Corporation); (OPAC) TLC (The Library Corporation)
Wireless access
Partic in LYRASIS; Network of Alabama Academic Libraries; OCLC Online Computer Library Center, Inc; Southern Baptist Libr Asn
Open Mon-Fri 7:30am-Midnight, Sat 10am-Midnight, Sun 1pm-Midnight

C UNIVERSITY OF SOUTH ALABAMA LIBRARIES*, Marx Library, 5901 USA Drive N, 36688. Tel: 251-460-7021. Circulation Tel: 251-460-7028. Interlibrary Loan Service Tel: 251-460-7034. Information Services Tel: 251-460-7025. FAX: 251-460-7181. Interlibrary Loan Service FAX: 251-460-7636. Web Site: southalabama.edu/departments/library/. *Exec Dir, Libr Serv,* E Lorene Flanders; *Libr Dir,* Dr Angela Rand; Tel: 251-460-7028, E-mail: arand@southalabama.edu; *Assoc Univ Librn, Coll Mgt & Syst Librn,* Mary Duffy; E-mail: mduffy@southalabama.edu; *Asst Univ Librn, Coll,* Kathy Wheeler; Tel: 251-460-7938, E-mail: kwheeler@southalabama.edu; *Head, Cat,* Muriel Nero; Tel: 251-460-2837, E-mail: mnero@southalabama.edu; *Head, Govt Doc & Ser,* Vicki Tate; Tel: 251-460-2822, E-mail: vtate@southalabama.edu; *ILL,* Deborah Cobb; E-mail: dcobb@southalabama.edu, Subject Specialists: *Educ,* Dr Angela Rand; *Math, Statistics,* Kathy Wheeler; Staff 37 (MLS 15, Non-MLS 22)
Founded 1964. Fac 833; Highest Degree: Doctorate

Special Collections: Charles M. Baugh Biomedical Library; Health Information Resource Center, USA Medical Center; Joseph & Rebecca Mitchell Learning Center, Mitchell College of Business; McCall Rare Book and Manuscript Library. State Document Depository; US Document Depository
Subject Interests: Alabama, Archives, Hist, Local hist
Automation Activity & Vendor Info: (Acquisitions) Ex Libris Group; (Cataloging) Ex Libris Group; (Circulation) Ex Libris Group; (Course Reserve) Ex Libris Group; (Discovery) EBSCO Discovery Service; (ILL) OCLC Online; (OPAC) Ex Libris Group; (Serials) Ex Libris Group
Wireless access
Function: Art exhibits, Computers for patron use, Internet access, Online cat, Photocopying/Printing, Ref serv available, Wheelchair accessible
Partic in Consortium of Southern Biomedical Libraries; LYRASIS; Network of Alabama Academic Libraries

Departmental Libraries:

CM BIOMEDICAL LIBRARY, Biomedical Library Bldg, 5791 USA Dr N, 36688-0002, SAN 330-258X. Tel: 251-460-7043. Interlibrary Loan Service Tel: 251-460-7850. Reference Tel: 251-460-7044. FAX: 251-460-6958. Interlibrary Loan Service FAX: 251-460-7638. Web Site: biomedicallibrary.southalabama.edu/library. *Dir,* Geneva Staggs; *Asst Dir, Coll Mgt,* Jie Li; Tel: 251-460-6890; *Asst Dir, Strategic Serv,* Clista Clanton; Staff 26 (MLS 9, Non-MLS 17)
Founded 1972. Enrl 2,862; Fac 236; Highest Degree: Doctorate
Oct 2013-Sept 2014 Income $2,785,460. Mats Exp $968,000, Books $39,000, Per/Ser (Incl. Access Fees) $929,000. Sal $1,052,931
Library Holdings: Bk Titles 21,606
Publications: Biofeedback (Newsletter)
Open Mon-Thurs 7:15am-10:45pm, Fri 7:15-6, Sat 9-6, Sun 1-9:45

CM HEALTH INFORMATION RESOURCE CENTER, USA Medical Center, 2451 Fillingim St, 36617. Tel: 251-471-7855. *Libr Supvr,* Nancy Pugh; E-mail: npugh@southalabama.edu; *Circ, Ser, Tech Asst,* Jessica Medema; E-mail: jmedema@southalabama.edu; Staff 2 (Non-MLS 2)
Function: Photocopying/Printing, Study rm
Open Mon-Fri 8-5
Restriction: Badge access after hrs

DOY LEALE MCCALL RARE BOOK & MANUSCRIPT LIBRARY, Marx Library, 3rd Flr, Ste 300, 5901 USA Dr N, 36688. Tel: 251-341-3900. Web Site: southalabama.edu/libraries/mccallarchives. *Dir,* Carol Ellis; E-mail: cellis@southalabama.edu; *Asst Librn,* Deborah Gurt; E-mail: dgurt@southalabama.edu; *Tech Asst II,* Kristina Polizzi; *Tech Asst,* Michael Campbell
Special Collections: Architectural & Portrait Colls, photographs; Civil Rights & Political Colls; History of Mobile, Alabama Black Belt & Southwest Alabama Coll; Holocaust Survivors Coll, papers; McCall Papers

JOSEPH & REBECCA MITCHELL LEARNING RESOURCE CENTER, Mitchell College of Business, Rm 240, 5811 USA Dr S, 36688. Tel: 251-414-8067. E-mail: buscirc@southalabama.edu. *Dir,* Amia Baker; Tel: 251-460-7998, E-mail: amiabaker@southalabama.edu; Staff 3 (MLS 1, Non-MLS 2)

MONROEVILLE

P MONROE COUNTY PUBLIC LIBRARY*, 121 Pineville Rd, 36460. SAN 300-1539. Tel: 251-743-3818. FAX: 251-575-7357. E-mail: monroli2@frontiernet.net. Web Site: moncolib.org.
Founded 1927. Pop 25,043; Circ 62,000
Library Holdings: CDs 40; DVDs 10; Large Print Bks 265; Bk Vols 26,091; Per Subs 27; Talking Bks 1,077; Videos 552
Special Collections: Alabama Coll; Forestry Coll; Genealogy Coll; Paperback Coll
Automation Activity & Vendor Info: (Acquisitions) Baker & Taylor; (Cataloging) Follett Software; (Circulation) Follett Software
Partic in Midwest Collaborative for Library Services
Open Mon-Fri 9-5
Friends of the Library Group

MONTEVALLO

P PARNELL MEMORIAL LIBRARY*, 277 Park Dr, 35115-3882. SAN 321-5660. Tel: 205-665-9207. FAX: 205-665-9214. E-mail: parnellibrary@shelbycounty-al.org. Web Site: parnellmemoriallibrary.org. *Dir,* Savannah Kitchens; E-mail: skitchens@shelbycounty-al.org; Staff 1 (Non-MLS 1)
Founded 1958. Pop 4,500; Circ 25,866
Library Holdings: CDs 180; Bk Titles 17,356; Talking Bks 291; Videos 640
Special Collections: Alabama Authors Coll; Large Print Coll
Automation Activity & Vendor Info: (Cataloging) Innovative Interfaces, Inc; (Circulation) Innovative Interfaces, Inc; (OPAC) Innovative Interfaces, Inc
Function: ILL available, Music CDs, Photocopying/Printing, Prog for children & young adult, Summer reading prog, VHS videos, Wheelchair accessible
Mem of Harrison Regional Library System
Open Mon-Wed & Fri 10-5, Thurs 4pm-8pm

C UNIVERSITY OF MONTEVALLO*, Oliver Cromwell Carmichael Library, Bloch St, 35115. SAN 300-1555. Tel: 205-665-6100. Circulation Tel: 205-665-6101. FAX: 205-665-6112. E-mail: library@montevallo.edu. Web Site: libguides.montevallo.edu, www.montevallo.edu/academic/library. *Libr Dir,* Charlotte Ford; E-mail: cford6@montevallo.edu; *Head, Ref, Head, User Experience,* Kathleen Lowe; E-mail: lowek@montevallo.edu; *Head, Tech Serv,* Amanda Melcher; Tel: 205-665-6104, E-mail: melcheras@montevallo.edu; *Archivist, Spec Coll Librn,* Carey Heatherly; Tel: 205-665-6107, E-mail: heatherlycw@montevallo.edu; Staff 12.7 (MLS 7, Non-MLS 5.7)
Founded 1896. Enrl 2,494; Fac 168; Highest Degree: Master
Library Holdings: Bk Titles 156,531; Bk Vols 252,120; Per Subs 738
Special Collections: Alabama Authors; Alabama History & Descriptions
Partic in LYRASIS; Network of Alabama Academic Libraries; OCLC Online Computer Library Center, Inc
Open Mon, Tues & Wed 7:30am-1am, Thurs 7:30-Midnight, Fri 7:30-5, Sat 1-5, Sun 2pm-1am

MONTGOMERY

S ALABAMA DEPARTMENT OF ARCHIVES & HISTORY RESEARCH ROOM, 624 Washington Ave, 36130. (Mail add: PO Box 300100, 36130-0100), SAN 300-1571. Tel: 334-242-4435. Interlibrary Loan Service Tel: 334-353-3287. FAX: 334-240-3433. Web Site: www.archives.alabama.gov. *Dir, Div Archives,* Mary Jo Scott; Tel: 334-353-4694, E-mail: maryjo.scott@archives.alabama.gov; *Head, Res Serv,* Courtney Pinkard; Tel: 334-353-9272, E-mail: courtney.pinkard@archives.alabama.gov; Staff 6 (MLS 6)
Founded 1901
Library Holdings: Bk Vols 40,000
Special Collections: Alabama Newspapers; Historical Records of State of Alabama, bks, ms, maps, pamphlets & photog; Private Manuscript Coll. State Document Depository
Subject Interests: State govt, State hist
Automation Activity & Vendor Info: (Cataloging) Ex Libris Group; (OPAC) Ex Libris Group
Wireless access
Function: 24/7 Online cat, Archival coll, Computers for patron use, Electronic databases & coll, For res purposes, ILL available, Internet access, Online cat, Outside serv via phone, mail, e-mail & web, Ref & res, Res assist avail, Res libr, Workshops
Open Tues-Sat 8:30-4:30
Restriction: Non-circulating coll
Friends of the Library Group

G ALABAMA LEAGUE OF MUNICIPALITIES LIBRARY*, 535 Adams Ave, 36104. (Mail add: PO Box 1270, 36102). Tel: 334-262-2566. FAX: 334-263-0200. Web Site: www.alalm.org. *Librn,* Rachel Wagner; Tel: 334-262-2566, Ext 131
Library Holdings: Bk Titles 1,500; Per Subs 42
Restriction: Mem only

P ALABAMA PUBLIC LIBRARY SERVICE*, 6030 Monticello Dr, 36130. SAN 330-2644. Tel: 334-213-3900. Reference Tel: 334-213-3950. Automation Services Tel: 334-213-3938. Toll Free Tel: 800-723-8459 (Alabama only). FAX: 334-213-3993. Reference FAX: 334-213-3960. TDD: 334-213-3905. Web Site: aplsws1.apls.state.al.us/aplsnew/. *Dir,* Nancy Pack; E-mail: npack@apls.state.al.us; *Financial Serv,* Jeann Price; Tel: 334-213-3629; Staff 30 (MLS 12, Non-MLS 18)
Founded 1959. Pop 4,802,740
Library Holdings: Bk Titles 137,893; Bk Vols 147,026; Per Subs 1,249; Talking Bks 306,212
Subject Interests: Alabama
Automation Activity & Vendor Info: (Acquisitions) Evergreen; (Cataloging) Evergreen; (Circulation) Evergreen; (Course Reserve) Evergreen; (ILL) Evergreen; (OPAC) Evergreen; (Serials) Evergreen
Wireless access
Function: Audio & video playback equip for onsite use, Games & aids for people with disabilities, Govt ref serv, ILL available, Internet access, Ref serv available, Summer reading prog, Telephone ref, Wheelchair accessible, Workshops
Publications: APLSeed (Online only); What's Line (Quarterly)
Partic in Association for Rural & Small Libraries
Special Services for the Deaf - Assistive tech; Bks on deafness & sign lang; TDD equip
Special Services for the Blind - Accessible computers; Assistive/Adapted tech devices, equip & products; Bks & mags in Braille, on rec, tape & cassette; Bks on cassette; Bks on flash-memory cartridges; Daisy reader; Digital talking bk; Digital talking bk machines; Free checkout of audio mat; Home delivery serv; Newsline for the Blind; Spec cats; Talking bks; Talking bks & player equip; Volunteer serv
Open Mon-Fri 8-5

Branches: 1
ALABAMA REGIONAL LIBRARY FOR THE BLIND & PHYSICALLY HANDICAPPED
See Separate Entry

P ALABAMA PUBLIC LIBRARY SERVICE*, Alabama Regional Library for the Blind & Physically Handicapped, 6030 Monticello Dr, 36130. SAN 300-1598. Tel: 334-213-3906. Administration Tel: 334-213-3921. Information Services Tel: 334-213-3909. Toll Free Tel: 800-392-5671. FAX: 334-213-3993. E-mail: bph@alps.state.al.us. Web Site: aplsws1.apls.state.al.us/aplsnew/content/bphmain. *Regional Dir,* Angela Fisher-Hall; E-mail: afisherhall@apls.state.al.us; *Librn,* Amanda Trawick; *Pub Info Officer,* Ryan Godfrey; Staff 5 (MLS 4, Non-MLS 1)
Founded 1978. Pop 5,496; Circ 138,508
Library Holdings: Bks on Deafness & Sign Lang 50; Braille Volumes 2,265; Talking Bks 390,000
Special Collections: Alabamiana Coll; Blindness & Physically Handicapped (Core Coll)
Subject Interests: Adaptive tech, Braille
Automation Activity & Vendor Info: (Cataloging) Keystone Systems, Inc (KLAS); (Circulation) Keystone Systems, Inc (KLAS); (ILL) Keystone Systems, Inc (KLAS); (Serials) Keystone Systems, Inc (KLAS)
Wireless access
Function: Accelerated reader prog, Audiobks via web, Bks on cassette, Children's prog, Computers for patron use, Digital talking bks, Equip loans & repairs, Games & aids for people with disabilities, ILL available, Mail & tel request accepted, Mail loans to mem, Photocopying/Printing, Prog for adults, Prog for children & young adult, Wheelchair accessible
Publications: What's Line (Newsletter)
Partic in Network of Alabama Academic Libraries
Special Services for the Deaf - Closed caption videos; Coll on deaf educ; Deaf publ; Spec interest per; Staff with knowledge of sign lang; TDD equip
Special Services for the Blind - Accessible computers; Assistive/Adapted tech devices, equip & products; Bks & mags in Braille, on rec, tape & cassette; Bks on cassette; Braille & cassettes; Braille alphabet card; Braille bks; Cassette playback machines; Cassettes; Children's Braille; Digital talking bk; Info on spec aids & appliances; Machine repair; Musical scores in Braille & large print; Newsline for the Blind; PC for people with disabilities; Tel Pioneers equip repair group; Web-Braille; ZoomText magnification & reading software
Open Mon-Fri 8-5
Restriction: Closed stack

C ALABAMA STATE UNIVERSITY*, Levi Watkins Learning Resource Center, 915 S Jackson St, 36104. (Mail add: PO Box 271, 36101-0271), SAN 300-161X. Tel: 334-229-4106. Circulation Tel: 334-229-4109. Interlibrary Loan Service Tel: 334-229-5108. Reference Tel: 334-229-4110. FAX: 334-229-4940. Web Site: www.lib.alasu.edu. *Dean,* Dr Janice R Franklin; E-mail: jfranklin@alasu.edu; *Acq Librn,* Madhu Kadiyala; E-mail: mkadiyala@alasu.edu; *Pub Serv Coordr,* Jian Zhang; E-mail: jzhang@alasu.edu; *Info Literacy,* Natasha Jenkins; E-mail: njenkins@alasu.edu; *Spec Coll,* Linda Harvey; E-mail: lkharvey@alasu.edu; Staff 33 (MLS 16, Non-MLS 17)
Founded 1921. Enrl 5,565; Fac 427; Highest Degree: Doctorate
Library Holdings: Bk Titles 209,149; Bk Vols 417,404; Per Subs 2,082
Special Collections: E D Nixon Coll; Ollie L Brown Afro-American Heritage Coll, bks, micro
Subject Interests: Acctg, Biol sci, Educ, Health sci
Automation Activity & Vendor Info: (Acquisitions) Ex Libris Group; (Cataloging) Ex Libris Group; (Circulation) Ex Libris Group; (Course Reserve) Ex Libris Group; (ILL) Ex Libris Group; (Media Booking) Ex Libris Group; (OPAC) Ex Libris Group; (Serials) Ex Libris Group
Wireless access
Publications: Libretto
Partic in LYRASIS; Montgomery Higher Education Librs; National Network of Libraries of Medicine Region 2; Network of Alabama Academic Libraries
Open Mon-Thurs 8-10, Fri 8-5, Sat 10-4, Sun 2-9
Friends of the Library Group

GL ALABAMA SUPREME COURT & STATE LAW LIBRARY, Heflin-Torbert Judicial Bldg, 300 Dexter Ave, 36104. SAN 300-1628. Tel: 334-229-0578. Circulation Tel: 334-229-0563. Interlibrary Loan Service Tel: 334-229-0570. Toll Free Tel: 800-236-4069. FAX: 334-229-0543. Reference FAX: 334-229-0545. Reference E-mail: ALSCReference@gmail.com. Web Site: judicial.alabama.gov/library. *Dir, State Law Librn,* Timothy A Lewis; E-mail: tim.lewis@alappeals.gov; *Pub Serv Librn,* Alma Surles; Tel: 334-229-0569, E-mail: asurles@alappeals.gov; *Tech Serv Librn,* Myra Sabel; Tel: 334-229-0580, E-mail: msabel@alappeals.gov; *Asst Pub Serv Librn,* Marilyn Floyd; E-mail: marilyn.floyd@alappeals.gov; *Curator,* Mr Hall Copeland; Tel: 334-229-0564, E-mail: hall.copeland@alappeals.gov; Staff 8 (MLS 4, Non-MLS 4)
Founded 1828
Library Holdings: AV Mats 342; Bk Titles 58,847; Bk Vols 235,834; Per Subs 776
Special Collections: Alabama Supreme Court Briefs (1965-present); Judicial College Papers. State Document Depository; US Document Depository
Subject Interests: Alabama, Law
Automation Activity & Vendor Info: (Acquisitions) Innovative Interfaces, Inc; (Cataloging) Innovative Interfaces, Inc; (Circulation) Innovative Interfaces, Inc; (Course Reserve) Innovative Interfaces, Inc; (ILL) OCLC; (OPAC) Innovative Interfaces, Inc; (Serials) Innovative Interfaces, Inc
Wireless access
Function: 24/7 Electronic res, 24/7 Online cat, Archival coll, AV serv, Computers for patron use, Doc delivery serv, Electronic databases & coll, For res purposes, Govt ref serv, ILL available, Internet access, Legal assistance to inmates, Mail & tel request accepted, Meeting rooms, Microfiche/film & reading machines, Notary serv, Online cat, Photocopying/Printing, Ref serv available, Study rm
Publications: Court Brief (Newsletter); The Rotunda (Newsletter)
Partic in LYRASIS; Network of Alabama Academic Libraries; OCLC Online Computer Library Center, Inc
Open Mon-Fri 8-5

CR AMRIDGE UNIVERSITY LIBRARY*, 1200 Taylor Rd, 36117. SAN 371-9936. Tel: 334-387-7541. Toll Free Tel: 800-790-8080, Ext 6. FAX: 334-387-3878. E-mail: library@amridgeuniversity.edu. Web Site: www.amridgeuniversity.edu/academics/library. *Libr Dir,* Terence Sheridan; Staff 5 (MLS 2, Non-MLS 3)
Founded 1967. Enrl 700; Highest Degree: Doctorate
Library Holdings: AV Mats 800; Bk Titles 80,000; Per Subs 1,200
Subject Interests: Counseling, Theol
Automation Activity & Vendor Info: (Cataloging) Book Systems; (Circulation) Book Systems; (OPAC) Book Systems
Wireless access
Function: Online cat
Open Mon-Thurs 8-5, Fri 8-Noon

C AUBURN UNIVERSITY, Montgomery Library, 7440 East Dr, 36117. (Mail add: PO Box 244023, 36124-4023), SAN 300-1636. Tel: 334-244-3200. Circulation Tel: 334-244-3416, 334-244-3647. Interlibrary Loan Service Tel: 334-244-3447. Reference Tel: 334-244-3649. Automation Services Tel: 334-244-3420. FAX: 334-244-3720. Reference E-mail: Reference@aum.edu. Web Site: aumnicat.aum.edu. *Dean of Libr,* Phill Johnson; E-mail: pjohns23@aum.edu; *Head, Libr Tech,* Tim Bailey; E-mail: tbailey1@aum.edu; *Head, Pub Serv,* Jessica Hayes; E-mail: jhayes11@aum.edu; *Head, Tech Serv,* John Gantt; E-mail: jgantt2@aum.edu; *Access Serv/ILL Librn,* Karen Williams; E-mail: kwilli16@aum.edu; *Archives & Spec Coll Librn, Libr Instruction Coordr,* Samantha McNeilly; E-mail: smcneill@aum.edu; *Coll Develop Librn,* Rickey D Best; E-mail: rbest@aum.edu; *Web Serv & Emerging Tech Librn,* Daniel Moody; E-mail: dmoody2@aum.edu; Staff 21 (MLS 8, Non-MLS 13)
Founded 1969. Enrl 4,255; Fac 246; Highest Degree: Doctorate
Oct 2020-Sept 2021 Income $1,992,540. Mats Exp $470,219, Books $31,514, Per/Ser (Incl. Access Fees) $434,204, AV Mat $4,401, Presv $100. Sal $1,021,700 (Prof $524,350)
Library Holdings: CDs 1,628; DVDs 1,001; e-books 65,500; e-journals 256; Bk Vols 500,000; Per Subs 432
Special Collections: Local & Regional Studies; University Archives. US Document Depository
Subject Interests: Genealogy
Automation Activity & Vendor Info: (Acquisitions) Ex Libris Group; (Cataloging) Ex Libris Group; (Circulation) Ex Libris Group; (Course Reserve) Ex Libris Group; (ILL) Ex Libris Group; (Media Booking) Ex Libris Group; (OPAC) Ex Libris Group; (Serials) Ex Libris Group
Wireless access
Partic in Association of Southeastern Research Libraries; LYRASIS; Montgomery Higher Education Librs; OCLC Online Computer Library Center, Inc
Special Services for the Blind - Accessible computers; Copier with enlargement capabilities; Large screen computer & software
Open Mon-Thurs 7:30am-11pm, Fri 7:30-6, Sat 1-6, Sun 1-11
Friends of the Library Group

CR FAULKNER UNIVERSITY*, Gus Nichols Library, 5345 Atlanta Hwy, 36109-3398. SAN 300-1563. Tel: 334-386-7207. Administration Tel: 334-386-7299. Web Site: www.faulkner.edu/current/nichols-library. *Dir,* Barbara Kelly; E-mail: bkelly@faulkner.edu; *Asst Dir,* Angie Moore; E-mail: almoore@faulkner.edu; *Coll Develop,* Jim Womack; E-mail: jwomack@faulkner.edu; *Extended Serv,* Donna Itson; E-mail: ditson@faulkner.edu; *Tech Serv,* Deidre Herring-Cole; E-mail: dherring@faulkner.edu; Staff 10 (MLS 5, Non-MLS 5)
Founded 1944. Enrl 2,300; Fac 75; Highest Degree: Doctorate
Library Holdings: Bk Vols 107,000; Per Subs 504
Special Collections: Churches of Christ Materials

Subject Interests: Art & archit, Bus & mgt, Econ, Educ, Health sci, Hist, Lit, Math, Natural sci, Psychol, Relig, Soc sci & issues
Automation Activity & Vendor Info: (Acquisitions) Innovative Interfaces, Inc; (Cataloging) Innovative Interfaces, Inc; (Circulation) Innovative Interfaces, Inc; (OPAC) Innovative Interfaces, Inc; (Serials) Innovative Interfaces, Inc
Wireless access
Function: Archival coll, ILL available, Photocopying/Printing, Ref serv available, Res libr
Partic in Christian Col Libr; LYRASIS; Montgomery Higher Education Libra; Network of Alabama Academic Libraries; OCLC Online Computer Library Center, Inc
Restriction: In-house use for visitors, Open to students, fac & staff

J H COUNCILL TRENHOLM STATE TECHNICAL COLLEGE LIBRARY*, 3086 Mobile Hwy, 36108. (Mail add: 1225 Air Base Blvd, 36108). Tel: 334-420-4357. Circulation Tel: 334-420-4455. Reference Tel: 334-420-4456. FAX: 334-420-4458. E-mail: libstaff@trenholmstate.edu. Web Site: www.trenholmstate.edu/future-students/student-resources/library. *Head Librn,* Paul Blackmon; E-mail: pblackmon@trenholmstate.edu; *Ref & Info Literacy Librn,* Amy Smith; E-mail: asmith@trenholmstate.edu; Staff 3 (MLS 2, Non-MLS 1)
Enrl 1,134; Highest Degree: Associate
Library Holdings: AV Mats 395; e-books 25,000; Bk Titles 5,425; Bk Vols 7,123; Per Subs 101
Special Collections: Archives
Subject Interests: Voting rights
Automation Activity & Vendor Info: (Cataloging) OCLC Online; (Circulation) Follett Software; (Course Reserve) Follett Software; (Media Booking) Follett Software; (OPAC) Follett Software; (Serials) Follett Software
Function: Archival coll, Photocopying/Printing, Ref serv available, Telephone ref, Wheelchair accessible
Open Mon-Thurs 7:30am-8pm, Fri 7:30am-11:30pm
Restriction: In-house use for visitors, Open to pub for ref only

C HUNTINGDON COLLEGE*, Houghton Memorial Library, 1500 E Fairview Ave, 36106. SAN 300-1660. Tel: 334-833-4421. Interlibrary Loan Service Tel: 334-833-4537. Reference Tel: 334-833-4560. Administration Tel: 334-833-4512. FAX: 334-263-4465. Web Site: libguides.huntingdon.edu/website. *Dir, Libr Serv,* Eric A Kidwell; E-mail: ekidwell@hawks.huntingdon.edu; *Access Serv Librn,* Paige Crumbley; Tel: 334-833-4422, E-mail: paige.crumbley@hawks.huntingdon.edu; *Instruction Librn, ILL,* Nordis Smith; E-mail: nosmith@huntingdon.edu; *Syst/Electronic Res Librn,* Brenda Kerwin; Tel: 334-833-4529, E-mail: bkerwin@huntingdon.edu; *Archives Mgr,* Sharon Tucker; Tel: 334-833-4413, E-mail: stucker@huntingdon.edu; *Asst Archivist,* Jill Tucker; Tel: 334-833-4418, E-mail: jtucker@huntingdon.edu; Staff 4 (MLS 4)
Founded 1854. Enrl 995; Fac 57; Highest Degree: Bachelor
Library Holdings: AV Mats 4,543; DVDs 2,303; e-books 78,595; e-journals 15,000; Microforms 64,674; Bk Vols 101,596; Per Subs 189; Videos 1,536
Special Collections: Alabama-West Florida Conference of the United Methodist Church; Alabamiana; Archives & History of United Methodist Church; Autographed Book Coll; College Archives; Rare Book Coll
Automation Activity & Vendor Info: (Acquisitions) OCLC; (Cataloging) OCLC; (Circulation) OCLC; (OPAC) OCLC; (Serials) OCLC
Wireless access
Publications: LibGuides (Research guide)
Partic in LYRASIS; Montgomery Higher Education Librs; Network of Alabama Academic Libraries
Open Mon-Thurs 7:30am-11pm, Fri 7:30-4:45, Sat 12-4:45, Sun 5pm-11pm

P MONTGOMERY CITY-COUNTY PUBLIC LIBRARY SYSTEM*, Library Administration, 245 High St, 36104. SAN 330-2709. Tel: 334-240-4300. FAX: 334-240-4977. Web Site: www.mccpl.lib.al.us. *Libr Dir,* Jaunita McClain Owes; Tel: 334-240-4989, E-mail: jowes@mccpl.lib.al.us; *Asst Libr Dir,* Karen Preuss; Tel: 334-240-4922, E-mail: kpreuss@mccpl.lib.al.us; *Coll Develop Librn,* Thomas Anderson; Tel: 334-240-4975, E-mail: tanderson@mccpl.lib.al.us; *Youth Serv Coordr,* Sarah Foster; Tel: 334-625-4984, E-mail: sfoster@mccpl.lib.al.us; Staff 66.5 (MLS 25, Non-MLS 41.5)
Founded 1899. Pop 230,149; Circ 435,477
Oct 2016-Sept 2017 Income (Main & Associated Libraries) $4,790,075, City $3,227,670, Federal $50,000, County $1,075,890, Locally Generated Income $260,310, Other $176,205. Mats Exp $442,255, Books $361,297, Other Print Mats $8,791, Electronic Ref Mat (Incl. Access Fees) $72,167. Sal $2,366,330
Automation Activity & Vendor Info: (Acquisitions) SirsiDynix; (Cataloging) OCLC; (Circulation) SirsiDynix; (ILL) OCLC; (OPAC) SirsiDynix
Wireless access
Function: Outreach serv
Publications: Black History Month Program Guide (Annual); Guide to Services & Programs (Library handbook); MCCPL Staff Read Into the Holidays (Annual); Montgomery City-County Public Library Annual Report; National Library Week Program Guide (Annual); Summer Reading Program Guide (Annual); Things to Do @ Your Library (Monthly bulletin)
Open Mon-Fri 8-5
Friends of the Library Group
Branches: 10
COLISEUM BOULEVARD BRANCH LIBRARY, 840 Coliseum Blvd, 36109. SAN 330-2768. Tel: 334-271-7005. FAX: 334-244-5754. E-mail: coliseumcirc@mccpl.lib.al.us. Web Site: www.mccpl.lib.al.us/locations_coliseum.asp. *Head Librn,* Sharon Phillips; Staff 4.5 (MLS 1, Non-MLS 3.5)
Circ 46,386
Special Collections: US Dep of Transportation Plume Investigation Reports, Dec 1999 to present
Function: 24/7 Electronic res, 24/7 Online cat, Adult bk club, After school storytime, Art exhibits, Art programs, AV serv, Bk club(s), Bks on cassette, Bks on CD, Children's prog, Computer training, Computers for patron use, Electronic databases & coll, Homework prog, Internet access, Life-long learning prog for all ages, Magazines, Meeting rooms, Outreach serv, Preschool reading prog, Prog for adults, Prog for children & young adult, STEM programs, Story hour, Summer reading prog, Tax forms, Wheelchair accessible
Special Services for the Deaf - Staff with knowledge of sign lang
Open Mon-Fri 9-6
Friends of the Library Group
GOVERNORS SQUARE BRANCH LIBRARY, 2885-B E South Blvd, 36116. (Mail add: 2885-B E S Blvd, 36116), SAN 330-2725. Tel: 334-284-7929. FAX: 334-240-4839. E-mail: govercirc@mccpl.lib.al.us. Web Site: www.mccpl.lib.al.us/locations_govsquare.asp. *Head Librn,* Jonathan Darby; Tel: 334-284-7929, E-mail: jdarby@mccpl.lib.al.us; *Librn I,* Anita Berry; Tel: 334-284-7929, E-mail: aberry@mccpl.lib.al.us; Staff 4.5 (MLS 2, Non-MLS 2.5)
Circ 26,698
Function: 24/7 Electronic res, 24/7 Online cat, Adult bk club, After school storytime, Bk club(s), Children's prog, Computers for patron use, Electronic databases & coll, Holiday prog, Homework prog, Internet access, Life-long learning prog for all ages, Magazines, Meeting rooms, Movies, Online cat, Photocopying/Printing, Preschool outreach, Preschool reading prog, Prog for adults, Prog for children & young adult, Story hour, Summer reading prog, Tax forms, Wheelchair accessible
Open Mon-Fri 9-6
Friends of the Library Group
HAMPSTEAD BRANCH LIBRARY, 5251 Hampstead High St, Ste 107, 36116. Tel: 334-244-5771. FAX: 334-244-5773. E-mail: hampsteadcirc@mccpl.lib.al.us. Web Site: www.mccpl.lib.al.us/locations_hampstead.asp. *Head Librn,* Marsha Taylor; *Librn,* Elizabeth McCord; E-mail: emccord@mccpl.lib.al.us; Staff 3 (MLS 2, Non-MLS 1)
Function: 24/7 Electronic res, 24/7 Online cat, Children's prog, Computers for patron use, Electronic databases & coll, Holiday prog, Magazines, Online cat, Outreach serv, Photocopying/Printing, Preschool outreach, Preschool reading prog, Prog for children & young adult, STEM programs, Story hour, Summer reading prog, Tax forms
Open Mon-Fri 9-6
Friends of the Library Group
RUFUS A LEWIS REGIONAL LIBRARY, 3095 Mobile Hwy, 36108, SAN 374-6860. Tel: 334-240-4848. FAX: 334-240-4847. E-mail: lewiscirc@mccpl.lib.al.us. Web Site: www.mccpl.lib.al.us/locations_lewis.asp. *Head Librn,* Glenda Walker; E-mail: gwalker@mccpl.lib.al.us; Staff 5.5 (MLS 2, Non-MLS 3.5)
Function: 24/7 Electronic res, 24/7 Online cat, Adult bk club, Art programs, Chess club, Children's prog, Computer training, Computers for patron use, Electronic databases & coll, Holiday prog, Homework prog, ILL available, Magazines, Meeting rooms, Movies, Online cat, Photocopying/Printing, Preschool outreach, Preschool reading prog, Prog for adults, Prog for children & young adult, Senior computer classes, Senior outreach, Story hour, Summer reading prog, Tax forms, Teen prog, Writing prog
Open Mon & Tues 9-9, Wed-Fri 9-6, Sat 9-1
Friends of the Library Group
E L LOWDER REGIONAL BRANCH LIBRARY, 2590 Bell Rd, 36117, SAN 374-6879. Tel: 334-244-5717. FAX: 334-240-4893. E-mail: lowdercirc@mccpl.lib.al.us. Web Site: www.mccpl.lib.al.us/locations_lowder.asp. *Head Librn,* Julia-Ann Jenkins; E-mail: jjenkins@mccpl.lib.al.us; Staff 5.5 (MLS 2, Non-MLS 3.5)
Function: 24/7 Electronic res, 24/7 Online cat, Adult bk club, Art programs, Bk club(s), Chess club, Children's prog, Computer training, Computers for patron use, Electronic databases & coll, Holiday prog, Homework prog, ILL available, Internet access, Magazines, Meeting rooms, Movies, Online cat, Outreach serv, Photocopying/Printing, Preschool outreach, Preschool reading prog, Prog for adults, Prog for children & young adult, STEM programs, Story hour, Summer reading prog, Tax forms, Teen prog
Open Mon & Wed 9-9, Tues, Thurs & Fri 9-6, Sat 9-1
Friends of the Library Group

JULIETTE HAMPTON MORGAN MEMORIAL LIBRARY, 245 High St, 36104. Tel: 334-240-4999. Circulation Tel: 334-240-4997, 334-240-4998. Reference Tel: 334-240-4982, 334-240-4992. FAX: 334-240-4980. E-mail: maincirc@mccpl.lib.al.us. Web Site: www.mccpl.lib.al.us/locations_morgan.asp. *Head Librn,* Position Currently Open; *Head, Circ Serv,* Zella'Ques S Holmes; Tel: 334-240-4999, E-mail: zholmes@mccpl.lib.al.us; *Head, Ref & Info Serv,* Suzanne Horton; Tel: 334-240-4992, E-mail: shorton@mccpl.lib.al.us; *Ref Librn,* James Cannon; Tel: 334-240-4992, E-mail: jcannon@mccpl.lib.al.us; *Ref Librn,* Brenda Davis; Tel: 334-240-4992, E-mail: bdavis@mccpl.lib.al.us; *Computer Lab Mgr, Ref Librn, Webmaster,* LaRuth Martin; Tel: 334-240-4994, E-mail: lmartin@mccpl.lib.al.us; *Ch, Librn II,* Fredriatta Brown-Green; Tel: 334-240-4991, E-mail: fbrown@mccpl.lib.al.us. Subject Specialists: *Hist,* Suzanne Horton; *Hist,* James Cannon; *Educ,* Brenda Davis; Staff 25 (MLS 8, Non-MLS 17)

Pop 230,149; Circ 115,818

Library Holdings: Audiobooks 36,452; DVDs 7,890; e-books 48,000; e-journals 116; Electronic Media & Resources 89; Bk Vols 582,062; Per Subs 540

Special Collections: Alabama Journal Newspaper Coll, June 1952 to April 1993, microfilm; Alabamiana & Rare Book Coll; Arms & Military Coll; Descriptive Video Coll; Montgomery Advertiser, March 1952 to present, microfilm; New York Times Newspaper Coll, Jan 1972 to present, microfilm; Wall Street Journal, Jan 1972 to present, microfilm

Automation Activity & Vendor Info: (Acquisitions) Baker & Taylor; (Cataloging) OCLC; (Circulation) SirsiDynix; (ILL) OCLC WorldShare Interlibrary Loan; (OPAC) SirsiDynix; (Serials) SirsiDynix

Function: 24/7 Electronic res, 24/7 Online cat, 3D Printer, Accelerated reader prog, Activity rm, Adult bk club, Adult literacy prog, After school storytime, Archival coll, Art exhibits, Audio & video playback equip for onsite use, Audiobks on Playaways & MP3, Audiobks via web, AV serv, Bk club(s), Bks on cassette, Bks on CD, Chess club, Children's prog, Computer training, Computers for patron use, E-Reserves, Electronic databases & coll, Health sci info serv, Holiday prog, Home delivery & serv to seniorr ctr & nursing homes, Homework prog, ILL available, Internet access, Life-long learning prog for all ages, Magazines, Mail & tel request accepted, Meeting rooms, Microfiche/film & reading machines, Movies, Music CDs, Online cat, Online ref, OverDrive digital audio bks, Photocopying/Printing, Preschool outreach, Preschool reading prog, Prog for adults, Prog for children & young adult, Ref & res, Ref serv available, Res assist avail, Scanner, Senior computer classes, Serves people with intellectual disabilities, Spanish lang bks, Story hour, Summer reading prog, Tax forms, Teen prog, Telephone ref, VHS videos, Wheelchair accessible

Publications: Reference Notes (Reference guide)

Special Services for the Deaf - TTY equip

Special Services for the Blind - Bks on cassette; Descriptive video serv (DVS); Large print bks; Ref serv

Open Mon-Wed 9-9, Thurs & Fri 9-6, Sat 9-1, Sun 2-6

Restriction: In-house use for visitors, Non-circulating of rare bks, Non-resident fee, Restricted borrowing privileges

Friends of the Library Group

PIKE ROAD BRANCH LIBRARY, 9585 Vaughn Rd, Pike Road, 36064-2292. (Mail add: PO Box 640036, Pike Road, 36064-0036), SAN 378-1720. Tel: 334-244-8679. FAX: 334-240-4887. E-mail: pikeroadcirc@mccpl.lib.al.us. Web Site: www.mccpl.lib.al.us/locations_pikeroad.asp. *Head Librn,* Marsha Taylor; *Librn,* Charles Matthew Williams; E-mail: cmwilliams@mccpl.lib.al.us; Staff 3 (MLS 2, Non-MLS 1)

Function: 24/7 Electronic res, 24/7 Online cat, Children's prog, Computers for patron use, Electronic databases & coll, Holiday prog, Internet access, Magazines, Meeting rooms, Online cat, Outreach serv, Photocopying/Printing, Preschool outreach, Preschool reading prog, Prog for adults, Prog for children & young adult, Story hour, Summer reading prog, Tax forms

Open Mon-Fri 9-6

Friends of the Library Group

PINTLALA BRANCH LIBRARY, 255 Federal Rd, Pintlala, 36043-9781, SAN 378-1704. Tel: 334-281-8069. FAX: 334-281-9784. E-mail: pintlalacirc@mccpl.lib.al.us. Web Site: www.mccpl.lib.al.us/locations_pintlala.asp. *Head Librn,* Marsha Taylor; *Librn,* Sandra S Berry; E-mail: ssavage@mccpl.lib.al.us; Staff 3 (MLS 1, Non-MLS 2)

Function: 24/7 Electronic res, 24/7 Online cat, Adult bk club, Art programs, Bk club(s), Children's prog, Computers for patron use, Electronic databases & coll, Holiday prog, Magazines, Online cat, Outreach serv, Photocopying/Printing, Preschool reading prog, Prog for adults, Prog for children & young adult, Story hour, Summer reading prog, Tax forms

Open Mon-Fri 9-6

Friends of the Library Group

RAMER BRANCH LIBRARY, 5444 State Hwy 94, Ramer, 36069-5008, SAN 330-2741. Tel: 334-562-3364. FAX: 334-562-3889. E-mail: ramercirc@mccpl.lib.al.us. Web Site: www.mccpl.lib.al.us/locations_ramer.asp. *Head Librn,* James A Greer; E-mail: jgreer@mccpl.lib.al.us; Staff 2 (MLS 2)

Function: 24/7 Electronic res, 24/7 Online cat, Activity rm, Bk club(s), Children's prog, Computers for patron use, Electronic databases & coll, Holiday prog, Magazines, Movies, Online cat, Photocopying/Printing, Preschool outreach, Preschool reading prog, Prog for adults, Prog for children & young adult, Senior outreach, Story hour, Summer reading prog, Tax forms

Open Mon-Fri 9-6

Friends of the Library Group

BERTHA PLEASANT WILLIAMS LIBRARY - ROSA L PARKS AVENUE BRANCH, 1276 Rosa L Parks Ave, 36108, SAN 330-2733. Tel: 334-240-4979. FAX: 334-240-4925. E-mail: rosacirc@mccpl.lib.al.us. Web Site: www.mccpl.lib.al.us/locations_rosaparks.asp. *Head Librn,* Glenda Walker; E-mail: gwalker@mccpl.lib.al.us; *Librn,* Amy Campbell; E-mail: acampbell@mccpl.lib.al.us; Staff 3.5 (MLS 2, Non-MLS 1.5)

Function: 24/7 Electronic res, 24/7 Online cat, Activity rm, Adult bk club, Bk club(s), Children's prog, Computers for patron use, Electronic databases & coll, Holiday prog, Internet access, Magazines, Meeting rooms, Movies, Online cat, Outreach serv, Photocopying/Printing, Preschool outreach, Preschool reading prog, Prog for adults, Prog for children & young adult, Story hour, Summer reading prog, Tax forms

Open Mon-Fri 9-6

Friends of the Library Group

GL MONTGOMERY COUNTY LAW LIBRARY, 251 S Lawrence St, 36104. SAN 300-1679. Tel: 334-832-1394. FAX: 334-265-9536. Web Site: montgomery.alacourt.gov/law-library. *Librn,* Suzanne Duffey; E-mail: teachduff@aol.com

Library Holdings: Bk Titles 215

Open Mon-Fri 8:30-4:30

Restriction: Ref only to non-staff

C SOUTH UNIVERSITY LIBRARY, Montgomery Campus, 5355 Vaughn Rd, 36116-1120. SAN 375-4383. Tel: 334-395-8800. FAX: 334-395-8859. Web Site: www.southuniversity.edu/montgomery. *Libr Dir,* Rachel Cotney; Staff 3 (MLS 2, Non-MLS 1)

Enrl 580; Highest Degree: Master

Library Holdings: Audiobooks 50; AV Mats 976; CDs 296; DVDs 500; e-books 50,000; Bk Vols 20,000; Per Subs 22

Special Collections: Fiction & Non-Fiction by Alabama Authors (Alabama Coll); Law Coll

Subject Interests: Bus, Counseling, Info tech, Law, Med, Phys therapy

Automation Activity & Vendor Info: (Acquisitions) Ex Libris Group; (Cataloging) Ex Libris Group; (Circulation) Ex Libris Group; (Course Reserve) Ex Libris Group; (ILL) Ex Libris Group; (OPAC) Ex Libris Group; (Serials) Ex Libris Group

Wireless access

Function: Audio & video playback equip for onsite use, Bks on cassette, Bks on CD, CD-ROM, Computers for patron use, Distance learning, Electronic databases & coll, Free DVD rentals, ILL available, Instruction & testing, Internet access, Mail & tel request accepted, Notary serv, Online cat, Orientations, Photocopying/Printing, Ref & res, Ref serv available, Spoken cassettes & CDs, Spoken cassettes & DVDs, Telephone ref, Workshops

Open Mon-Thurs 8am-9:30pm, Fri & Sat 8:30-4:30

C TROY UNIVERSITY, MONTGOMERY CAMPUS, Rosa Parks Library, 252 Montgomery St, 36104-3425. SAN 300-1709. Tel: 334-241-9576. Interlibrary Loan Service Tel: 334-241-9784. Reference Tel: 334-241-8605. FAX: 334-241-9590. E-mail: libhelp@troy.edu. Web Site: www.troy.edu/student-life-resources/arts-culture/rosa-parks-museum/library. *Actg Dir,* Rachel Hooper; Tel: 334-670-3269, E-mail: hooperr@troy.edu; *Circ, Ref Librn,* Kent E Snowden; Tel: 334-241-9783, E-mail: kesnowden@troy.edu; *Ref & Instruction Librn,* Alyssa Martin; Tel: 334-241-8601, E-mail: almartin@troy.edu; Staff 3 (MLS 3)

Founded 1964. Enrl 2,000; Fac 100; Highest Degree: Doctorate

Library Holdings: AV Mats 800; e-books 75,000; Bk Vols 40,000; Per Subs 49

Subject Interests: Bus, Nursing

Automation Activity & Vendor Info: (Acquisitions) OCLC Worldshare Management Services; (Cataloging) OCLC Worldshare Management Services; (Circulation) OCLC Worldshare Management Services; (ILL) OCLC WorldShare Interlibrary Loan; (OPAC) OCLC Worldshare Management Services; (Serials) OCLC Worldshare Management Services

Wireless access

Partic in Montgomery Higher Education Librs; Network of Alabama Academic Libraries

Open Mon-Thurs 8-5:30, Fri 8-Noon

Restriction: Borrowing privileges limited to fac & registered students

S VALIDATA COMPUTER & RESEARCH CORP LIBRARY*, 600 S Court St, 36104. (Mail add: PO Box 4774, 36103-4774), SAN 373-3831. Tel: 334-834-2324. FAX: 334-262-5648. E-mail: helpdesk@validata.org. Web Site: www.validata.com.
Library Holdings: Bk Vols 7,000; Per Subs 10
Restriction: Not open to pub

MOODY

P DORIS STANLEY MEMORIAL LIBRARY, 300 Bookmark Circle, 35004. SAN 325-402X. Tel: 205-640-2517. FAX: 205-640-2534. E-mail: dsml@moodyalabama.gov. Web Site: www.moodypubliclibr.org. *Libr Dir,* Patsy Spradley
Open Mon-Fri 9-6

MOULTON

P LAWRENCE COUNTY PUBLIC LIBRARY*, 401 College St, 35650. SAN 300-1733. Tel: 256-974-0883. FAX: 256-974-0890. E-mail: info@lawrencecpl.org. Web Site: sites.google.com/site/lawrencecpl01. *Libr Dir,* M Rex Bain; Staff 4 (MLS 1, Non-MLS 3)
Founded 1961. Pop 34,800
Library Holdings: DVDs 362; Large Print Bks 707; Bk Titles 37,241; Talking Bks 845; Videos 1,371
Automation Activity & Vendor Info: (Acquisitions) Follett Software; (Cataloging) Follett Software; (ILL) OCLC Online
Wireless access
Function: ILL available, Photocopying/Printing, Prog for children & young adult, Summer reading prog, Telephone ref
Partic in Tenn-Share
Open Mon-Thurs 9:30-6, Fri 9:30-3:30
Friends of the Library Group

MOUNDVILLE

P MOUNDVILLE PUBLIC LIBRARY*, 279 Market St, 35474. (Mail add: PO Box 336, 35474-0336), SAN 300-1741. Tel: 205-371-2283. FAX: 205-371-2238. E-mail: moundvillepubliclibrary@gmail.com. Web Site: www.moundvillepubliclibrary.com. *Dir,* Lindsey Mullins
Pop 6,000; Circ 4,700
Library Holdings: Bk Vols 8,500; Per Subs 10
Special Collections: Alabamaian Coll
Automation Activity & Vendor Info: (Acquisitions) Book Systems; (Cataloging) Book Systems; (Circulation) Book Systems; (ILL) Book Systems; (OPAC) Book Systems; (Serials) Book Systems
Wireless access
Open Tues-Fri 9-5:30, Sat 9-12

MOUNT VERNON

P MOUNT VERNON PUBLIC LIBRARY*, 19180 Shepard Lake Rd, 36560. Tel: 251-829-9497. E-mail: mvlib@mountvernonal.org. Web Site: www.mtvernonal.com/Library.html. *Dir,* Darryl Pennywell
Library Holdings: Bk Vols 8,000; Per Subs 30
Wireless access
Open Mon & Wed 1-8, Tues & Thurs 10-6, Sat 4-8

MOUNTAIN BROOK

P EMMET O'NEAL LIBRARY, 50 Oak St, 35213. SAN 300-1768. Tel: 205-879-0459. Reference Tel: 205-445-1121. Administration Tel: 205-445-1192. FAX: 205-879-5388. E-mail: info@oneallibrary.org. Web Site: www.oneallibrary.org. *Dir,* Lindsy Gardner; E-mail: lgardner@oneallibrary.org; *Head, Adult Serv,* Katie Moellering; E-mail: kmoellering@oneallibrary.org; *Head, Children's Servx,* Gloria Repolesk; E-mail: grepolesk@oneallibrary.org; *Head, Circ,* Daniel Daughhetee; E-mail: ddaughhetee@oneallibrary.org; *Head, Tech Serv,* Nancy D Sexton; E-mail: nsexton@oneallibrary.org; *Ref Librn,* Holley Wesley; E-mail: hwesley@oneallibrary.org; Staff 5 (MLS 3, Non-MLS 2)
Founded 1964. Pop 20,183; Circ 327,189
Library Holdings: Bk Titles 106,044; Bk Vols 123,638; Per Subs 132
Special Collections: Gardening Coll; Travel Coll
Subject Interests: Gardening
Automation Activity & Vendor Info: (Cataloging) Innovative Interfaces, Inc; (Circulation) Innovative Interfaces, Inc; (OPAC) Innovative Interfaces, Inc
Wireless access
Publications: Friends of the Library Bookends
Partic in Jefferson County Libr Coop
Open Mon-Sat 10-6
Friends of the Library Group

MUSCLE SHOALS

S IFDC LIBRARY*, Travis P Hignett Memorial Library, TVA Reservation Rd, COMPLEX F, 35661. (Mail add: PO Box 2040, 35662-2040), SAN 325-9072. Tel: 256-381-6600. FAX: 256-381-7408. E-mail: librarian@ifdc.org. Web Site: ifdc.org. *Archivist, Managing Librn,* Joyce L Fedeczko; Staff 1 (MLS 1)
Founded 1977
Library Holdings: Bk Titles 23,500; Per Subs 25
Special Collections: Audio Visuals; Country File; International Agricultural Organization File; Organization File; Training Programs; TVA Fertilizer Coll
Subject Interests: Agr, Agr bus, Develop countries, Fertilizers, Mkt
Automation Activity & Vendor Info: (Cataloging) SoutronGLOBAL; (Circulation) SoutronGLOBAL; (ILL) OCLC; (OPAC) SoutronGLOBAL; (Serials) SoutronGLOBAL
Wireless access
Function: 24/7 Online cat, Archival coll, Doc delivery serv, For res purposes, ILL available, Internet access, Mail & tel request accepted, Online cat, Ref & res, Ref serv available, Res libr, Res performed for a fee
Open Mon-Fri 7:30-4:15
Restriction: Authorized patrons, Authorized personnel only, Authorized scholars by appt, Borrowing requests are handled by ILL, External users must contact libr, Fee for pub use, Open to pub by appt only, Open to researchers by request, Pub by appt only, Pub use on premises, Visitors must make appt to use bks in the libr

P MUSCLE SHOALS PUBLIC LIBRARY*, 1918 E Avalon, 35661. SAN 300-1776. Tel: 256-386-9212. FAX: 256-386-9211. E-mail: mspl@muscleshoals.lib.al.us. Web Site: youseemore.com/muscleshoals. *Libr Mgr,* Denita Lester; E-mail: dlester@muscleshoals.lib.al.us; *Acq,* Anna Cathernine Thompson; *Ch Serv,* Kelsey Sherron; *Circ,* Christina Johnson; *Tech Asst,* Melanie Emerson; Staff 1 (MLS 1)
Pop 17,589; Circ 241,547
Library Holdings: Bk Vols 46,000; Per Subs 50
Automation Activity & Vendor Info: (Acquisitions) TLC (The Library Corporation); (Cataloging) TLC (The Library Corporation); (Circulation) TLC (The Library Corporation); (OPAC) TLC (The Library Corporation); (Serials) TLC (The Library Corporation)
Wireless access
Function: 24/7 Electronic res, 24/7 Online cat, Archival coll, Audiobks on Playaways & MP3, Audiobks via web, Bks on CD, Children's prog, Computer training, Computers for patron use, Digital talking bks, E-Readers, E-Reserves, Electronic databases & coll, Free DVD rentals, Home delivery & serv to seniorr ctr & nursing homes, ILL available, Internet access, Magazines, Mail & tel request accepted, Microfiche/film & reading machines, Movies, Music CDs, Online cat, Photocopying/Printing, Printer for laptops & handheld devices, Prog for adults, Prog for children & young adult, Scanner, Senior outreach, Serves people with intellectual disabilities, Summer reading prog, Tax forms, Teen prog
Open Mon 12-5, Tues & Thurs 10-7, Wed, Fri & Sat 10-5
Restriction: Open to pub upon request
Friends of the Library Group

J NORTHWEST-SHOALS COMMUNITY COLLEGE*, Larry W McCoy Learning Resource Center, 800 George Wallace Blvd, 35661-3206. (Mail add: PO Box 2545, 35662-2545). Tel: 256-331-5283. FAX: 256-331-5269. Web Site: www.nwscc.edu/current-students/library. *Dir,* Rachel Trapp; E-mail: rachel.trapp@nwscc.edu; *Librn,* John Foust; E-mail: john.foust@nwscc.edu; *Librn,* Debbie Nale; *Librn,* Claudia Smith; E-mail: claudias@nwscc.edu; *Asst Librn,* Teresa Colvin; E-mail: colvint@nwscc.edu
Library Holdings: Bk Vols 30,000; Per Subs 150
Wireless access
Function: ILL available
Open Mon-Thurs 7:30am-9pm, Fri 7:30-Noon

NEWTON

P NEWTON PUBLIC LIBRARY & AGRICULTURAL MUSEUM*, 209 Oates Dr, 36352. SAN 330-3128. Tel: 334-299-3316. E-mail: NewtonLibraryMuseum@gmail.com. Web Site: aplsws1.apls.state.al.us/newton. *Dir & Curator,* Ms Terry Rust
Library Holdings: Bk Vols 12,000
Automation Activity & Vendor Info: (Cataloging) Evergreen; (Circulation) Evergreen
Wireless access
Open Tues-Fri 8-5, Sat 10-2

NORMAL

C ALABAMA A&M UNIVERSITY*, Joseph F Drake Memorial Learning Resources Center, 4900 Meridian St N, 35762. SAN 300-1792. Tel: 256-372-4712. FAX: 256-372-5768. E-mail: info@aamu.edu. Web Site: alabamam.sdp.sirsi.net. *Dir,* Annie Payton, PhD; Tel: 256-372-5007,

E-mail: annie.payton@aamu.edu; *Asst Dir, Res Info Serv,* Mr Sammie Johnson; Tel: 256-372-4719, E-mail: sammie.johnson@aamu.edu; *Acq Librn, Educ Librn,* Mrs Thedis Bryant; Tel: 256-372-4724, E-mail: thedis.bryant@aamu.edu; *Cat,* Delorise Pruitt; Tel: 256-372-4730, E-mail: delorise.pruitt@aamu.edu; Staff 21 (MLS 11, Non-MLS 10)
Founded 1875. Enrl 6,500; Fac 280; Highest Degree: Doctorate
Library Holdings: Bk Titles 254,000; Per Subs 1,600
Special Collections: Archival & Historical Colls; Audio Visual Coll; Black Coll; Carnegie-Mydral Coll; Curriculum Coll; ERIC Coll; Government Documents Coll; International Studies Coll; J F Kennedy Memorial Coll; Schomburg Coll; Textbook Coll; YA Coll. Oral History; US Document Depository
Subject Interests: Agr, Art & archit, Bus & mgt, Econ, Educ, Engr, Food sci, Forestry, Hist, Humanities, Music, Natural sci, Physics, Soc sci & issues, Urban planning
Automation Activity & Vendor Info: (Acquisitions) SirsiDynix; (Cataloging) SirsiDynix; (Circulation) SirsiDynix; (Serials) SirsiDynix
Wireless access
Publications: Bulldogbytes (Newsletter)
Partic in LYRASIS; Network of Alabama Academic Libraries
Open Mon-Thurs (Sept-June) 8am-11pm, Fri 8-5, Sat 11-3, Sun 1-10
Friends of the Library Group

ODENVILLE

P ODENVILLE PUBLIC LIBRARY*, 200 Alabama St, 35120. SAN 330-3276. Tel: 205-629-5901. E-mail: odenlib@windstream.net. Web Site: aplsws1.apls.state.al.us/odenville. *Libr Dir,* Betty Corley; E-mail: b.corley@cityofodenville.net
Founded 1960
Library Holdings: Audiobooks 185; DVDs 910; e-books 259; Large Print Bks 447; Bk Vols 18,000; Per Subs 9; Spec Interest Per Sub 3
Automation Activity & Vendor Info: (Acquisitions) Biblionix; (Cataloging) Biblionix; (Circulation) Biblionix; (OPAC) OCLC
Wireless access
Open Tues-Fri 9-12 & 1-6
Friends of the Library Group

ONEONTA

P ONEONTA PUBLIC LIBRARY*, 221 Second St S, 35121. SAN 300-1806. Tel: 205-274-7641. FAX: 205-274-7643. E-mail: oplib@otelco.net. Web Site: www.oneontapubliclibrary.org. *Dir,* Ricky Statham; *Asst Dir,* Kay Butts; *Head, Circ,* Amy Woods; *Programming Librn,* Cassandra Brindle; *Cat,* Pam Guin; Staff 7 (MLS 2, Non-MLS 5)
Founded 1948. Circ 50,867
Library Holdings: Bk Vols 40,000; Per Subs 100
Subject Interests: Genealogy, Rare bks, Video
Automation Activity & Vendor Info: (Cataloging) Book Systems; (Circulation) Book Systems; (OPAC) Book Systems
Wireless access
Special Services for the Deaf - Bks on deafness & sign lang
Special Services for the Blind - Aids for in-house use; Audio mat; Bks on CD; Closed circuit TV; Copier with enlargement capabilities; Large print bks; Large screen computer & software; Micro-computer access & training
Open Mon & Thurs 9-7, Tues, Wed & Fri 9-5, Sat 9-2
Friends of the Library Group

OPELIKA

P LEWIS COOPER JUNIOR MEMORIAL LIBRARY*, 200 S Sixth St, 36801. SAN 300-1814. Tel: 334-705-5380. FAX: 334-705-5381. E-mail: library@opelika-al.gov. Web Site: www.cooperlibrary.com. *Libr Dir,* Rosanna McGinnis; E-mail: rmcginnis@opelika-al.gov; Staff 12 (MLS 3, Non-MLS 9)
Founded 1941. Pop 34,000
Library Holdings: Audiobooks 5,000; CDs 1,000; DVDs 5,000; Large Print Bks 1,000; Microforms 100; Bk Titles 61,000; Bk Vols 65,000; Per Subs 60; Videos 1,000
Special Collections: Alabama Coll
Subject Interests: Genealogy
Automation Activity & Vendor Info: (Cataloging) Innovative Interfaces, Inc; (Circulation) Innovative Interfaces, Inc; (OPAC) Innovative Interfaces, Inc
Wireless access
Function: 24/7 Electronic res, 24/7 Online cat, Accelerated reader prog, Activity rm, Adult bk club, Audiobks on Playaways & MP3, Audiobks via web, Bk club(s), Bks on CD, Children's prog, Computers for patron use, Electronic databases & coll, Free DVD rentals, ILL available, Instruction & testing, Internet access, Magazines, Mail & tel request accepted, Mango lang, Microfiche/film & reading machines, Movies, Notary serv, Online cat, OverDrive digital audio bks, Photocopying/Printing, Preschool reading prog, Prog for adults, Prog for children & young adult, Ref & res, Ref serv available, Scanner, Spanish lang bks, STEM programs, Story hour, Study rm, Summer reading prog, Tax forms, Teen prog, Wheelchair accessible
Mem of Horseshoe Bend Regional Library
Open Mon & Tues 8:30-7:30, Wed 8:30-5, Sat 9-5, Sun 1-5
Friends of the Library Group

OPP

P OPP PUBLIC LIBRARY, 1604 N Main St, 36467. SAN 300-1830. Tel: 334-493-6423. FAX: 334-493-6423. E-mail: opppubliclibrary@gmail.com. Web Site: www.opplibrary.com. *Dir,* Courtney Smart; *Head Librn,* Janet L Davis; *Asst Librn,* Kourtnee Bradley; Staff 2 (Non-MLS 2)
Founded 1937. Pop 12,946; Circ 31,753
Library Holdings: CDs 150; DVDs 50; Large Print Bks 575; Bk Vols 18,444; Per Subs 23; Talking Bks 210; Videos 265
Automation Activity & Vendor Info: (Cataloging) Book Systems; (Circulation) Book Systems; (ILL) OCLC FirstSearch; (OPAC) Book Systems; (Serials) EBSCO Online
Wireless access
Function: Art exhibits, Audio & video playback equip for onsite use, Bk club(s), CD-ROM, Computer training, E-Reserves, Electronic databases & coll, Homework prog, ILL available, Magnifiers for reading, Music CDs, Photocopying/Printing, Preschool outreach, Prog for children & young adult, Senior computer classes, Spoken cassettes & CDs, Summer reading prog, Tax forms, VHS videos, Wheelchair accessible
Special Services for the Deaf - TTY equip
Open Mon-Fri 9-5
Restriction: Open to pub for ref & circ; with some limitations
Friends of the Library Group

ORANGE BEACH

P ORANGE BEACH PUBLIC LIBRARY*, 26267 Canal Rd, 36561-3917. (Mail add: PO Box 1649, 36561-1649), SAN 373-7004. Tel: 251-981-2923. FAX: 251-981-2920. E-mail: askobpl@orangebeachal.gov. Web Site: www.orangebeachlibrary.org. *Dir,* Steven A Gillis; E-mail: sgillis@orangebeachal.gov; *IT/Tech Serv Librn,* Meagan Bing; Tel: 251-981-2360, E-mail: mbing@cityoforangebeach.com; *Circ Supvr,* Sherry Brandler; *Adult Serv,* Dustin McDowell; E-mail: dmcdowell@cityoforangebeach.com; *Ch Serv,* Cassie Chenoweth; Tel: 251-981-8120, E-mail: cchenoweth@cityoforangebeach.com; *Circ,* Rachel Bobo; E-mail: rbobo@cityoforangebeach.com; *Ref,* Lisa Leinhos; Tel: 251-981-8179, E-mail: lleinhos@cityoforangebeach.com. Subject Specialists: *Adult prog, Hist,* Dustin McDowell; *Sustainability,* Rachel Bobo; *Computer, Tech,* Lisa Leinhos; Staff 9 (MLS 6, Non-MLS 3)
Founded 1992. Pop 5,441; Circ 110,674
Jan 2016-Dec 2016 Income $645,289, State $4,509, City $605,780, Federal $4,000, Locally Generated Income $31,000. Mats Exp $41,700, Books $26,000, Per/Ser (Incl. Access Fees) $1,400, Other Print Mats $2,000, AV Equip $4,700, AV Mat $7,000, Electronic Ref Mat (Incl. Access Fees) $600. Sal $238,012 (Prof $224,012)
Library Holdings: Audiobooks 4,221; AV Mats 5,426; Bks on Deafness & Sign Lang 20; CDs 2,653; DVDs 3,227; e-books 28,100; Large Print Bks 1,928; Bk Vols 37,462; Per Subs 12; Talking Bks 2,199; Videos 636
Automation Activity & Vendor Info: (Cataloging) TLC (The Library Corporation); (Circulation) TLC (The Library Corporation); (Course Reserve) TLC (The Library Corporation); (OPAC) TLC (The Library Corporation)
Wireless access
Function: 24/7 Electronic res, 24/7 Online cat, Accelerated reader prog, Adult bk club, Audio & video playback equip for onsite use, Audiobks via web, Bk club(s), Bks on cassette, Bks on CD, Butterfly Garden, Children's prog, Computer training, Computers for patron use, Digital talking bks, Distance learning, E-Readers, Electronic databases & coll, Free DVD rentals, Homebound delivery serv, Homework prog, ILL available, Instruction & testing, Internet access, Large print keyboards, Magazines, Mail & tel request accepted, Meeting rooms, Movies, Music CDs, Notary serv, Online cat, Online ref, Outreach serv, Outside serv via phone, mail, e-mail & web, OverDrive digital audio bks, Photocopying/Printing, Preschool reading prog, Printer for laptops & handheld devices, Prog for adults, Prog for children & young adult, Ref serv available, Res libr, Scanner, Senior computer classes, Senior outreach, Serves people with intellectual disabilities, Spoken cassettes & CDs, Spoken cassettes & DVDs, Story hour, Summer & winter reading prog, Summer reading prog, Tax forms, Teen prog, Telephone ref, VHS videos, Wheelchair accessible, Winter reading prog, Workshops
Mem of Baldwin County Library Cooperative, Inc
Partic in National Network of Libraries of Medicine Region 2
Special Services for the Deaf - Bks on deafness & sign lang
Special Services for the Blind - Bks on CD; Home delivery serv; Large print bks; Recorded bks
Open Mon, Tues & Fri 9-6, Wed & Thurs 9-8, Sat 9-3
Friends of the Library Group

OXFORD

P OXFORD PUBLIC LIBRARY*, 110 E Sixth St, 36203. SAN 300-1849. Tel: 256-831-1750. FAX: 256-835-0138. Web Site: www.oxfordpl.org. *Dir,* Amy Henderson; E-mail: amy.henderson@oxfordal.gov; *Asst Dir,* Jeanna

McEwen; E-mail: jeanna.mcewen@oxfordal.gov; *Ad,* Darlene Horton; E-mail: darlene.horton@oxfordal.gov; *Ch,* Elisabeth Mayes; E-mail: elisabeth.mayes@oxfordal.gov
Founded 1927. Pop 14,592; Circ 37,311
Library Holdings: Bk Vols 24,000; Per Subs 35
Automation Activity & Vendor Info: (Cataloging) Book Systems; (Circulation) Book Systems; (OPAC) Book Systems
Wireless access
Partic in Connecticut Library Consortium; Evergreen Indiana Consortium
Open Mon-Fri 9-5, Sat 9-1, Sun 1-5

OZARK

P OZARK DALE COUNTY LIBRARY, INC, 416 James St, 36360. SAN 330-2970. Tel: 334-774-2399, 334-774-5480. E-mail: olibrary@troycable.net. Web Site: ozarklibrary.com, www.odcpl.com. *Dir,* Karen A Speck; *Ch,* Brenan Martin; *Ref Serv,* Joni Wood; Staff 6 (Non-MLS 6)
Founded 1945. Pop 37,106
Library Holdings: AV Mats 4,619; DVDs 1,103; Large Print Bks 2,066; Bk Titles 22,881; Per Subs 36; Talking Bks 1,041
Special Collections: Autry Religious Coll; Creel R Richardson Genealogy Coll
Automation Activity & Vendor Info: (Cataloging) Book Systems; (Circulation) Book Systems; (OPAC) Book Systems
Wireless access
Function: Prog for adults, Prog for children & young adult
Open Tues-Thurs 10-7, Fri & Sat 10-5
Friends of the Library Group

PELHAM

P PELHAM PUBLIC LIBRARY*, 2000 Ball Park Rd, 35124. (Mail add: PO Box 1627, 35124-5627), SAN 325-0407. Tel: 205-620-6418. FAX: 205-620-6469. Web Site: pelhamlibraryal.gov/576/Library. *Dir,* Mary Campbell; E-mail: mcampbell@pelhamalabama.gov; Staff 17 (MLS 5, Non-MLS 12)
Founded 1975. Pop 17,000; Circ 200,000
Library Holdings: Bk Vols 50,000; Per Subs 50
Automation Activity & Vendor Info: (Cataloging) Innovative Interfaces, Inc; (Circulation) Innovative Interfaces, Inc; (OPAC) Innovative Interfaces, Inc
Wireless access
Mem of Harrison Regional Library System
Open Mon-Thurs 9-8, Fri 9-5, Sat 10-5

PELL CITY

P PELL CITY LIBRARY, 1000 Bruce Etheredge Pkwy, Ste 100, 35128. SAN 330-3306. Tel: 205-884-1015. FAX: 205-814-4798. E-mail: pclibrary@epell.net. Web Site: www.pellcitylibrary.com. *Dir,* Danny Stewart; E-mail: dstewart@cityofpellcity.net; *Asst Dir,* Susan Mann
Pop 25,000
Library Holdings: Bk Vols 36,000
Special Collections: Oral History
Automation Activity & Vendor Info: (Cataloging) Book Systems; (Circulation) Book Systems; (OPAC) Book Systems
Wireless access
Open Mon-Fri 9-6
Friends of the Library Group

PHENIX CITY

J CHATTAHOOCHEE VALLEY COMMUNITY COLLEGE*, Learning Resource Center, Owen Hall, 2602 College Dr, 36869. Tel: 334-291-4978. FAX: 334-291-4980. Web Site: www.cv.edu/learning-resource-center-lrc. *Dir, Learning Res Ctr,* Elizabeth Bradsher; E-mail: elizabeth.bradsher@cv.edu
Founded 1981. Enrl 2,000
Library Holdings: AV Mats 300; e-books 8,000; Bk Vols 46,000; Per Subs 50
Special Collections: Southern States Genealogy Coll
Automation Activity & Vendor Info: (Acquisitions) SirsiDynix; (Circulation) SirsiDynix; (Course Reserve) SirsiDynix; (OPAC) SirsiDynix
Wireless access
Function: ILL available
Partic in LYRASIS
Open Mon-Thurs 7:30am-9pm, Fri 7:30-2, Sun 2-6

P PHENIX CITY-RUSSELL COUNTY LIBRARY*, 1501 17th Ave, 36867. SAN 300-1857. Tel: 334-297-1139. FAX: 334-298-8452. E-mail: phenixcitylibrary@gmail.com. Web Site: phenixcitylibrary.com. *Dir,* Michele Squier Kilday; E-mail: mkilday@phenixcityal.us; Staff 4 (Non-MLS 4)
Founded 1957. Pop 52,000; Circ 99,352
Library Holdings: Audiobooks 501; Bks on Deafness & Sign Lang 10; DVDs 1,516; Large Print Bks 1,862; Bk Titles 38,279; Per Subs 91; Talking Bks 513; Videos 572
Automation Activity & Vendor Info: (Cataloging) Book Systems; (Circulation) Book Systems; (OPAC) Book Systems
Wireless access
Function: 24/7 Electronic res, 24/7 Online cat, Activity rm
Special Services for the Deaf - Bks on deafness & sign lang
Special Services for the Blind - Extensive large print coll
Open Mon & Wed-Fri 9:30-6, Tues 9:30-8, Sat 10-2, Sun 1-5
Restriction: Authorized scholars by appt
Friends of the Library Group

PHIL CAMPBELL

J NORTHWEST-SHOALS COMMUNITY COLLEGE*, James A Glasgow Library, 2080 College Rd, 35581. (Mail add: PO Box 2545, Muscle Shoals, 35662), SAN 300-1865. Tel: 256-331-6271. FAX: 256-331-6202. E-mail: library@nwscc.edu. Web Site: www.nwscc.edu/current-students/library. *Chair,* Rachel Trapp; E-mail: rachel.trapp@nwscc.edu; *Asst Librn,* Teresa Colvin; E-mail: covint@nwscc.edu; Staff 2 (MLS 1, Non-MLS 1)
Founded 1963. Enrl 1,700; Fac 33
Library Holdings: Bk Vols 31,100; Per Subs 210
Special Collections: Alabama Professional; Alabama Room Coll, bks, microflm; Children's Coll; Nursing Coll, multi media mat
Subject Interests: Lang arts, Nursing, Soc sci & issues
Automation Activity & Vendor Info: (Cataloging) SirsiDynix; (Circulation) SirsiDynix; (OPAC) SirsiDynix
Function: ILL available
Publications: AV Catalog; Policy & Procedures Manual
Partic in Library Management Network, Inc
Open Mon-Thurs 7:30am-9pm, Fri 8-3:30

PIEDMONT

P PIEDMONT PUBLIC LIBRARY*, 106 N Main St, 36272. SAN 300-1873. Tel: 256-447-3369. FAX: 256-447-3383. Web Site: www.publiclibrary.cc/piedmont. *Libr Dir,* Tessa Maddox; E-mail: tessa.maddox@piedmontcity.org
Founded 1969. Circ 40,000
Library Holdings: Bk Vols 35,000; Per Subs 40
Automation Activity & Vendor Info: (Cataloging) SirsiDynix; (Circulation) SirsiDynix; (OPAC) SirsiDynix
Wireless access
Open Mon, Tues, Thurs & Fri 8-4, Wed 8-Noon

PLEASANT GROVE

P PLEASANT GROVE PUBLIC LIBRARY, 501 Park Rd, 35127. SAN 324-122X. Tel: 205-744-1731. FAX: 205-744-5479. Web Site: www.pleasantgrove.lib.al.us. *Actg Dir,* Jennie Patterson; E-mail: jennie.patterson@jclc.org
Founded 1948. Pop 7,102; Circ 30,228
Library Holdings: Bk Vols 30,000; Per Subs 21
Automation Activity & Vendor Info: (Cataloging) Innovative Interfaces, Inc; (Circulation) Innovative Interfaces, Inc; (OPAC) Innovative Interfaces, Inc
Wireless access
Open Mon-Thurs 8-5:30, Fri & Sat 8-12

PRATTVILLE

P AUTAUGA PRATTVILLE PUBLIC LIBRARY*, 254 Doster St, 36067-3933. SAN 300-1903. Tel: 334-365-3396. FAX: 334-365-3397. Web Site: www.appl.info. *Libr Dir,* Lindsey Milam; E-mail: lmilam@appl.info; *Asst Dir,* Stevie Sowell; E-mail: ssowell@appl.info; *Adult Prog Coordr, Children's Prog Coordr,* Rachael Parlier; E-mail: rparlier@appl.info; Staff 5 (MLS 2, Non-MLS 3)
Founded 1956. Pop 54,000; Circ 120,000
Library Holdings: Bk Vols 85,000; Per Subs 145
Special Collections: Local History & Genealogical Materials for Autauga County & Surrounding Alabama Counties (Alabama History Coll)
Automation Activity & Vendor Info: (Cataloging) SirsiDynix; (Circulation) SirsiDynix
Wireless access
Function: Accelerated reader prog, Audiobks via web, Bk club(s), Bks on CD, Children's prog, Computers for patron use, Genealogy discussion group, ILL available, Notary serv, Photocopying/Printing, Preschool outreach, Preschool reading prog, Ref serv available, Story hour
Publications: APPLe Newsletter (Online only)
Open Mon, Tues & Thurs 9-7, Wed, Fri & Sat 9-5
Friends of the Library Group

Branches: 3
AUTAUGAVILLE PUBLIC, 207 N Taylor St, Autaugaville, 36003, SAN 300-0125. Tel: 334-361-2096. *Br Mgr,* Cliff Harker
Open Mon-Wed 8-5
Friends of the Library Group
BILLINGSLEY PUBLIC, 2021 Office St, Billingsley, 36006, SAN 300-0176. Tel: 205-755-9809. *Br Mgr,* Dakota Leach
Open Mon & Thurs 8-5
MARBURY COMMUNITY, 205 County Rd 20 E, Marbury, 36051, SAN 300-1385. Tel: 205-755-8575. *Br Mgr,* Emma Tyus; *Outreach & Children's Serv,* Susan Akins
Open Tues-Thurs 9-5
Friends of the Library Group

PRICHARD

P PRICHARD PUBLIC LIBRARY*, 300 W Love Joy Loop, 36610. SAN 300-1911. Tel: 251-452-7847. FAX: 251-452-7935. E-mail: 171@apls.net. Web Site: www.thecityofprichard.org/residents/prichard-public-library. *Dir,* Autherine Caponis; E-mail: autherinecaponis@bellsouth.net
Pop 22,659
Library Holdings: Bk Vols 68,077; Per Subs 150
Wireless access
Open Mon, Tues & Thurs 10-6, Fri 10-4

RAGLAND

P RAGLAND PUBLIC LIBRARY, 26 Providence Rd, 35131. SAN 330-3330. Tel: 205-472-2007. FAX: 205-472-2007. Web Site: www.townofragland.org/Default.asp?ID=51&pg=Public+Library. *Librn,* Sandi Maroney; E-mail: sandi.maroney@townofragland.org
Library Holdings: Audiobooks 524; DVDs 2,168; Bk Vols 15,994
Open Mon 8-3, Tues, Thurs & Fri 1-6, Sat 8-Noon

RAINBOW CITY

P RAINBOW CITY PUBLIC LIBRARY*, 3702 Rainbow Dr, 35906. SAN 374-4604. Tel: 256-442-8477. E-mail: library@rbcalabama.com. Web Site: www.rbclibrary.org. *Dir,* Tina M Brooks; *Cat,* Joan Roark; Staff 8 (MLS 1, Non-MLS 7)
Founded 1981. Pop 9,611; Circ 62,792
Library Holdings: Audiobooks 2,884; DVDs 2,955; e-books 45,844; Large Print Bks 1,750; Bk Vols 49,074; Per Subs 58
Automation Activity & Vendor Info: (Cataloging) Book Systems; (Circulation) Book Systems; (ILL) OCLC; (OPAC) Book Systems
Wireless access
Open Mon-Thurs 9-7, Fri & Sat 9-5

RAINSVILLE

J NORTHEAST ALABAMA COMMUNITY COLLEGE*, Cecil B Word Learning Resources Center, 138 Alabama Hwy 35, 35986. (Mail add: PO Box 159, 35986-0159), SAN 300-192X. Tel: 256-228-6001, 256-638-4418. FAX: 256-228-4350. Circulation E-mail: nac_circ@lmn.lib.al.us. Web Site: www.nacc.edu. *Dir, Libr Serv,* Julia B Everett; Tel: 256-228-6001, Ext 226, E-mail: everettj@nacc.edu; *Librn,* Lori White; E-mail: whitel@nacc.edu; Staff 5 (MLS 3, Non-MLS 2)
Founded 1965. Enrl 2,500; Fac 135; Highest Degree: Associate
Library Holdings: Bk Vols 60,000; Per Subs 120
Automation Activity & Vendor Info: (Cataloging) Innovative Interfaces, Inc; (Circulation) Innovative Interfaces, Inc; (OPAC) Innovative Interfaces, Inc
Wireless access
Function: ILL available
Partic in Library Management Network, Inc
Open Mon-Thurs 7:30am-9:30pm, Fri 7:30-3

P RAINSVILLE PUBLIC LIBRARY*, 941 Main St E, 35986. (Mail add: PO Box 509, 35986), SAN 300-1938. Tel: 256-638-3311. FAX: 256-638-3314. E-mail: rpl1@farmerstel.com. Web Site: www.rainsvillepubliclibrary.com. *Dir,* Sarah Cruce; *Asst Dir,* Carolyn Wooten
Founded 1968. Pop 9,900; Circ 38,000
Library Holdings: Bk Vols 42,000; Per Subs 35
Automation Activity & Vendor Info: (Cataloging) Follett Software; (Circulation) Follett Software; (OPAC) Follett Software
Open Mon, Wed, Thurs & Fri 8-5, Tues 8-7, Sat 8-Noon

REDSTONE ARSENAL

UNITED STATES ARMY
A REDSTONE ARSENAL FAMILY & MWR LIBRARY*, 3323 Redeye Rd, 35898, SAN 330-3454. Tel: 256-876-4741. FAX: 256-876-3949. Web Site: www.redstonemwr.com. *Dir,* Gail M Alden; E-mail: gail.alden@us.army.mil; *Head, Tech Serv,* Martha A Burns; E-mail: martha.a.burns@us.army.mil; *Ref Librn,* Barbara McGroary; E-mail: barbara.s.mcgroary@us.army.mil; *Ref Librn,* Sara Kate Roberts; E-mail: sara.kate.roberts@us.army.mil; Staff 6 (MLS 3, Non-MLS 3)
Founded 1952
Library Holdings: DVDs 9,990; Bk Vols 34,000; Per Subs 30; Talking Bks 2,500
Automation Activity & Vendor Info: (Cataloging) OCLC Connexion; (Circulation) Innovative Interfaces, Inc - Millennium; (ILL) OCLC Connexion; (OPAC) Innovative Interfaces, Inc - Millennium
Open Tues-Sat 10-6:30
Restriction: Authorized patrons

A REDSTONE SCIENTIFIC INFORMATION CENTER*, Bldg 4484, Martin Rd, 35898-5000, SAN 330-342X. Tel: 256-876-9309. Interlibrary Loan Service Tel: 256-842-1268. Reference Tel: 256-876-5181. Information Services Tel: 256 876-5195. FAX: 256-842-7415. Reference FAX: 256-876-6000. E-mail: usarmy.redstone.amrdec.mbx.rsic-gov@mail.mil. *Libr Dir,* Elizabeth Lloyd; Staff 8 (MLS 6, Non-MLS 2)
Founded 1949
Library Holdings: Bk Vols 263,000
Special Collections: Guidance & Control; Helicopter; Peenemuende Papers; Rocket Technology; Space Defense
Subject Interests: Aeronaut, Aviation, Chem, Computer sci, Electrical engr, Electronics, Mechanical engr, Nuclear sci, Physics
Automation Activity & Vendor Info: (Cataloging) SirsiDynix; (Circulation) SirsiDynix; (OPAC) SirsiDynix
Function: Electronic databases & coll, ILL available, Microfiche/film & reading machines, Online cat, Ref serv available
Open Mon-Thurs 8-4
Restriction: Authorized personnel only

REFORM

P REFORM PUBLIC LIBRARY*, 302 First St S, 35481. (Mail add: PO Box 819, 35481-0819), SAN 324-0630. Tel: 205-375-6240. FAX: 205-375-6240. E-mail: rpl@nctv.com. Web Site: pickenslibrary.com/reform. *Dir,* Curtis Wheat; Staff 1 (Non-MLS 1)
Founded 1975. Pop 2,100; Circ 5,030
Library Holdings: Bk Vols 12,000; Per Subs 27
Automation Activity & Vendor Info: (Cataloging) Follett Software; (Circulation) Follett Software
Wireless access
Mem of Pickens County Cooperative Library
Open Mon, Tues, Thurs & Fri 9-4
Friends of the Library Group

ROANOKE

P ANNIE L AWBREY PUBLIC LIBRARY, 736 College St, 36274-1616. SAN 300-1946. Tel: 334-863-2632. FAX: 334-863-8997. E-mail: annielawbrey@yahoo.com. Web Site: www.cheaharegionallibrary.org/member_libraries/annie_l_awbrey_public_library. *Dir,* Margaret Calhoun; Staff 1 (MLS 1)
Founded 1934. Pop 20,400
Library Holdings: Bk Titles 21,000; Bk Vols 22,500; Per Subs 50
Special Collections: Adult Readers
Automation Activity & Vendor Info: (Cataloging) Follett Software; (Circulation) Follett Software
Wireless access
Mem of Cheaha Regional Library
Open Mon-Fri 9-12 & 1-5, Sat 9-12
Friends of the Library Group

ROBERTSDALE

P BALDWIN COUNTY LIBRARY COOPERATIVE, INC, 22251 Palmer St, 36567. (Mail add: PO Box 399, 36567-0399), SAN 300-1954. Tel: 251-970-4010. FAX: 251-970-4011. Web Site: baldwincountylibrary.org. *Dir, Tech Serv,* Elizabeth Webb; E-mail: director@baldwincountylibrary.org; *Asst Dir, ILL,* Amanda Burgett; E-mail: assistantdirector@baldwincountylibrary.org; *Cataloger, Circ Asst,* Kimberly Smith; E-mail: cataloger@baldwincountylibrary.org; *Circ Asst, Tech Serv,* Montie Mann; E-mail: circulation@baldwincountylibrary.org; *Financial Serv Adminr,* Ellen Ginn; E-mail: finadmin@baldwincountylibrary.org; Staff 3 (Non-MLS 3)
Founded 1966. Pop 102,040
Oct 2021-Sept 2022 Income $236,035, State $114,598, County $100,000, Other $21,436. Mats Exp $22,000, Books $2,000, Electronic Ref Mat (Incl. Access Fees) $20,000. Sal $181,000
Library Holdings: Audiobooks 8,219; DVDs 1,645; Large Print Bks 2,284; Per Subs 3
Subject Interests: Adult educ
Automation Activity & Vendor Info: (Cataloging) TLC (The Library Corporation); (Circulation) TLC (The Library Corporation); (ILL) OCLC WorldShare Interlibrary Loan; (OPAC) TLC (The Library Corporation)
Wireless access
Function: 24/7 Electronic res, 24/7 Online cat, Art exhibits, Audiobks on Playaways & MP3, Audiobks via web, Bks on CD, Computers for patron

use, Digital talking bks, Doc delivery serv, Electronic databases & coll, Free DVD rentals, Govt ref serv, Home delivery & serv to seniorr ctr & nursing homes, Homebound delivery serv, Homework prog, ILL available, Internet access, Laminating, Magazines, Magnifiers for reading, Mail & tel request accepted, Meeting rooms, Movies, Music CDs, Online cat, Online info literacy tutorials on the web & in blackboard, Outside serv via phone, mail, e-mail & web, OverDrive digital audio bks, Photocopying/Printing, Printer for laptops & handheld devices, Prof lending libr, Ref serv available, Res assist avail, Scanner, Senior outreach, Serves people with intellectual disabilities, Spanish lang bks, Summer reading prog, Tax forms, Telephone ref, Wheelchair accessible
Member Libraries: Bay Minette Public Library; Daphne Public Library; Elberta Public Library; Fairhope Public Library; Foley Public Library; Loxley Public Library; Orange Beach Public Library; Oscar Johnson Memorial Library; Robertsdale Public Library; Thomas B Norton Public Library
Open Tues-Thurs 8-4:30
Bookmobiles: 1. Charles Middleton

P ROBERTSDALE PUBLIC LIBRARY*, 18301 Pennsylvania St, 36567. SAN 300-1962. Tel: 251-947-8960. FAX: 251-947-5521. E-mail: rdalelib@gulftel.com. Web Site: www.robertsdale.org/library. *Dir,* Cynthia Nall; *Asst Librn,* Joyce Allen; *Asst Librn,* Joyce Nims
Founded 1914. Pop 3,600; Circ 51,000
Library Holdings: Bk Titles 30,000; Per Subs 60
Automation Activity & Vendor Info: (Cataloging) TLC (The Library Corporation); (Circulation) TLC (The Library Corporation); (OPAC) TLC (The Library Corporation)
Wireless access
Mem of Baldwin County Library Cooperative, Inc
Open Mon & Wed 9-6, Tues & Thurs 9-8, Fri 9-5, Sat 9-1

ROCKFORD

P ROCKFORD PUBLIC LIBRARY, 100 Main St, 35136. (Mail add: PO Box 128, 35136-0128), SAN 300-1970. Tel: 256-377-4911. FAX: 256-377-4489. E-mail: rockfordpl@wwisp.com. *Dir,* Glenda Cardwell
Founded 1962. Pop 480; Circ 5,140
Library Holdings: AV Mats 70; Bk Vols 4,600; Per Subs 19
Wireless access
Mem of Horseshoe Bend Regional Library
Open Mon-Fri 7-5

ROGERSVILLE

P ROGERSVILLE PUBLIC LIBRARY*, 74 Bank St, 35652. (Mail add: PO Box 190, 35652-0190), SAN 300-1989. Tel: 256-247-0151. FAX: 256-247-0144. E-mail: information@rogersvillelibrary.org. Web Site: www.rogersvillelibrary.org. *Libr Dir,* Teresa Garner; E-mail: tgarner@rogersvillelibrary.org; Staff 4 (MLS 1, Non-MLS 3)
Pop 11,000; Circ 35,359
Library Holdings: Bk Vols 26,000; Per Subs 32
Subject Interests: Genealogy
Automation Activity & Vendor Info: (Cataloging) Book Systems; (Circulation) Book Systems; (OPAC) Book Systems
Wireless access
Open Tues 9-7, Wed & Fri 9-5, Thurs 11-7, Sat 9-3
Friends of the Library Group

RUSSELLVILLE

P RUSSELLVILLE PUBLIC LIBRARY*, 110 E Lawrence St, 35653. SAN 330-4175. Tel: 256-332-1535. E-mail: ruslib110@yahoo.com. Web Site: www.russellvilleal.org/library-. *Libr Dir,* Ashley Copeland Cummins
Pop 25,000
Library Holdings: Bk Vols 16,500
Wireless access
Open Tues-Fri 10-5, Sat 10-2
Friends of the Library Group

SAMSON

P SAMSON PUBLIC LIBRARY*, 200 N Johnson St, 36477-2006. SAN 300-2012. Tel: 334-898-7806. FAX: 334-898-7806. E-mail: samsonpubliclibrary@gmail.com. Web Site: www.cityofsamson.com/library.html. *Interim Dir,* Teresa Bryant
Founded 1928. Pop 5,722; Circ 3,022
Library Holdings: CDs 154; Electronic Media & Resources 72; Large Print Bks 555; Bk Vols 8,641; Per Subs 15; Videos 75
Special Collections: 1500 Centenniel Photos Coll
Wireless access
Open Mon-Fri 10-12 & 1-5

SARDIS CITY

P SARDIS CITY PUBLIC LIBRARY*, 1310 Church St, 35956-2200. (Mail add: 1335 Sardis Dr, 35956-2862). Tel: 256-593-5634. FAX: 256-593-6258. E-mail: sardislibrary@charter.net. *Librn,* Georgia Lipscomb; E-mail: glipscomb@sardiscityal.gov
Library Holdings: Large Print Bks 200; Bk Vols 9,500; Per Subs 10
Wireless access
Partic in LYRASIS
Open Tues, Wed & Fri 1-5, Thurs & Sat 9-1

SATSUMA

P SATSUMA PUBLIC LIBRARY*, 5466 Old Hwy 43, 36572. Tel: 251-679-0700, 251-679-0866. FAX: 251-679-0973. Web Site: www.satsumalibrary.org. *Libr Dir,* Tiphani Clearman; E-mail: splibdir@bellsouth.net
Founded 1994
Library Holdings: Bk Titles 11,900; Bk Vols 13,000; Per Subs 21
Automation Activity & Vendor Info: (Acquisitions) Book Systems; (Cataloging) Book Systems; (Circulation) Book Systems; (Course Reserve) Book Systems; (OPAC) Book Systems
Wireless access
Open Mon, Wed & Fri 10-5, Tues & Thurs 10-6, Sat 9-2
Friends of the Library Group

SCOTTSBORO

P SCOTTSBORO PUBLIC LIBRARY*, 1002 S Broad St, 35768. SAN 300-2039. Tel: 256-574-4335. FAX: 256-259-4457. E-mail: publiclibraryscottsboro@gmail.com. Web Site: www.scottsborolibrary.org. *Dir,* Laura Pitts; *Librn,* Martha Avans
Founded 1929. Pop 49,900; Circ 101,183
Library Holdings: Bk Vols 42,000; Per Subs 105
Special Collections: Alabama Genealogy Coll
Automation Activity & Vendor Info: (Cataloging) Innovative Interfaces, Inc; (Circulation) Innovative Interfaces, Inc; (OPAC) Innovative Interfaces, Inc
Wireless access
Open Mon-Thurs 9-6, Fri 9-5, Sat 9-1
Friends of the Library Group

SELMA

P PUBLIC LIBRARY OF SELMA & DALLAS COUNTY*, 1103 Selma Ave, 36703-4498. SAN 300-2055. Tel: 334-874-1725. FAX: 334-874-1742. E-mail: admin@selmalibrary.org. Web Site: www.selmalibrary.org. *Dir,* Becky Nichols; E-mail: becky@selmalibrary.org
Founded 1903. Pop 45,000; Circ 142,586
Library Holdings: Bk Titles 72,568; Bk Vols 72,701; Per Subs 61
Subject Interests: Local hist
Automation Activity & Vendor Info: (Cataloging) SirsiDynix; (Circulation) SirsiDynix; (OPAC) SirsiDynix
Wireless access
Open Mon-Sat 9-5
Friends of the Library Group

C SELMA UNIVERSITY*, Stone-Robinson Library, 1501 Lapsley St, 36701. SAN 300-2063. Tel: 334-872-2628. FAX: 334-872-7746. E-mail: selmau4@bellsouth.net. Web Site: www.selmauniversity.edu/library.html. *Librn,* Edna Green
Founded 1959. Highest Degree: Master
Library Holdings: Bk Titles 23,000; Per Subs 154
Special Collections: Black Studies Coll
Wireless access
Open Mon & Wed 8-8, Tues & Thurs 8-9, Fri 8-5, Sat 9-2

J WALLACE COMMUNITY COLLEGE, Selma Library, 3000 Earl Goodwin Pkwy, 36701. (Mail add: PO Box 2530, 36702-2530), SAN 300-2047. Tel: 334-876-9344, 334-876-9345. FAX: 334-876-9314. Web Site: www.wccs.edu/library. *Dir, Libr Serv,* Minnie Carstarphen; E-mail: minnie.carstarphen@wccs.edu; *Asst Librn,* Lefloris Jemison; E-mail: Lefloris.Jemison@wccs.edu; *Asst Librn,* Brenda Powell; E-mail: brenda.powell@wccs.edu; Staff 4 (MLS 4)
Founded 1974. Enrl 1,976; Fac 60; Highest Degree: Associate
Oct 2020-Sept 2021 Income $166,232. Mats Exp $29,775, Books $22,003, Per/Ser (Incl. Access Fees) $3,072, Other Print Mats $1,200, AV Mat $100, Electronic Ref Mat (Incl. Access Fees) $3,400. Sal $125,620
Library Holdings: AV Mats 1,201; CDs 120; e-books 80; Bk Titles 24,550; Per Subs 26; Videos 630
Subject Interests: Lit, Nursing, Soc sci & issues
Automation Activity & Vendor Info: (Cataloging) MITINET, Inc; (Circulation) Follett Software; (OPAC) Follett Software
Wireless access
Function: Res libr

Publications: Audio-Visual Catalog; Library Handbook; Nursing Video Catalog; Periodical Catalog
Open Mon-Thurs 7am-8:30pm, Fri 7-Noon
Restriction: Open to students, fac & staff

SHEFFIELD

P SHEFFIELD PUBLIC LIBRARY*, 316 N Montgomery Ave, 35660. SAN 300-2101. Tel: 256-386-5633. FAX: 256-386-5608. E-mail: sheffieldlibrary@sheffield.lib.al.us. Web Site: www1.youseemore.com/sheffieldpl. *Dir,* Beth Ridgeway; *Cat,* Sandy Kirsch; *Ch Serv,* Lynne Martin; *Tech Serv,* Evallou Richardson
Founded 1963. Pop 15,000; Circ 52,125
Library Holdings: e-books 27,000; Bk Vols 57,000; Per Subs 50
Special Collections: Local History & Genealogy Coll
Automation Activity & Vendor Info: (Cataloging) Innovative Interfaces, Inc; (Circulation) Innovative Interfaces, Inc; (OPAC) Innovative Interfaces, Inc
Wireless access
Open Mon-Fri 9-5
Friends of the Library Group

SILVERHILL

P OSCAR JOHNSON MEMORIAL LIBRARY, 21967 Sixth St, 36576. (Mail add: PO Box 309, 36576-0309). Tel: 251-945-5201. E-mail: ojmlib@gmail.com. Web Site: silverhillalabama.com/library. *Librn,* Shirley Stevens; Staff 1 (Non-MLS 1)
Founded 1907. Pop 630; Circ 3,050
Library Holdings: Bk Vols 10,000
Mem of Baldwin County Library Cooperative, Inc
Open Mon-Fri 1-4

SLOCOMB

P SLOCOMB PUBLIC LIBRARY, 134 S Dalton St, 36375. (Mail add: PO Box 1026, 36375-1026), SAN 376-7418. Tel: 334-886-9009. E-mail: slocombpl@gmail.com. *Librn,* Esther Pryor
Founded 1985
Library Holdings: Large Print Bks 200; Bk Vols 8,000
Automation Activity & Vendor Info: (Cataloging) Evergreen; (Circulation) Evergreen
Wireless access
Function: Accelerated reader prog, Adult literacy prog, Children's prog, Computers for patron use, Internet access, Laminating, Scanner, Summer reading prog, Wheelchair accessible
Open Mon-Fri 1-5

SPRINGVILLE

S ALABAMA DEPARTMENT OF CORRECTIONS*, St Clair Correctional Facility Library, 1000 Saint Clair Rd, 35146. Tel: 205-467-6111. Web Site: www.doc.state.al.us/facility.aspx?loc=21.
Founded 1983
Library Holdings: Bk Vols 7,000
Restriction: Not open to pub

P SPRINGVILLE PUBLIC LIBRARY*, 6315 US Hwy 11, 35146. SAN 374-6526. Tel: 205-467-2339. FAX: 205-467-0160. Web Site: www.springvillealabama.org/library. *Dir,* Jamie Twente
Library Holdings: Bk Vols 19,565; Per Subs 11
Automation Activity & Vendor Info: (Acquisitions) Book Systems; (Cataloging) Book Systems; (Circulation) Book Systems; (OPAC) Book Systems
Wireless access
Open Tues-Thurs 9-6:30, Fri 9-4:30, Sat 10-1
Friends of the Library Group

STEELE

P STEELE PUBLIC LIBRARY*, 78 Hillview St, 35987. (Mail add: PO Box 548, 35987). Tel: 256-538-0811. FAX: 256 538-0855. E-mail: steelepubliclibrary@gmail.com. *Librn,* Lynda Fann
Pop 1,248; Circ 3,301
Library Holdings: DVDs 447; Bk Titles 8,840
Wireless access
Open Mon-Thurs 9-4:30

STEVENSON

P STEVENSON PUBLIC LIBRARY*, 102 W Main St, 35772. SAN 374-4507. Tel: 256-437-3008. FAX: 256-437-0031. E-mail: spl0031@gmail.com. Web Site: www.cityofstevensonalabama.com/Library.html. *Libr Dir,* Monica Davis
Library Holdings: Bk Vols 12,000; Per Subs 40
Automation Activity & Vendor Info: (Cataloging) Book Systems; (Circulation) Book Systems
Wireless access
Open Mon-Wed & Fri 12-4, Thurs 8am-1pm

SUMITON

J BEVILL STATE COMMUNITY COLLEGE*, Sumiton Campus Library, 101 S State St, 35148. (Mail add: PO Box 800, 35148-0800). Tel: 205-648-3271. Information Services Tel: 205-648-3271, Ext 5238. Toll Free Tel: 800-648-3271. FAX: 205-648-7152. Web Site: www.bscc.edu/admissions/current-students/library. *Asst Dean of Libr,* Tyrone Webb; E-mail: twebb@bscc.edu
Founded 1965. Enrl 1,800; Fac 75; Highest Degree: Associate
Library Holdings: AV Mats 1,250; Bk Titles 25,000; Per Subs 75; Talking Bks 54
Automation Activity & Vendor Info: (Cataloging) Follett Software; (Circulation) Follett Software; (OPAC) Follett Software
Wireless access
Function: ILL available, Photocopying/Printing, Ref serv available
Open Mon-Thurs (Fall & Spring) 7:30am-8:30pm, Fri 7:30am-11:30am; Mon-Thurs (Summer) 7am-7:30pm

P SUMITON PUBLIC LIBRARY*, Town Hall, 416 State St, 35148. (Mail add: PO Box 10, 35148-0010), SAN 300-2136. Tel: 205-648-7451. FAX: 205-648-7451. E-mail: sumitonpubliclibrary@gmail.com. Web Site: www.thecityofsumiton.com/city-services.html, www2.youseemore.com/cerl. *Librn,* Lori Jackson; *Asst Librn,* Vicki Nichols
Pop 4,000
Library Holdings: e-books 4,000; Bk Titles 9,000
Wireless access
Mem of Carl Elliott Regional Library System
Open Mon-Fri 8-4

SYLACAUGA

P B B COMER MEMORIAL LIBRARY*, 314 N Broadway, 35150-2528. SAN 300-2144. Tel: 256-249-0961. FAX: 256-401-2492. E-mail: comerlibrary@bbclibrary.net. Web Site: www.bbcomerlibrary.net. *Dir,* Tracey Thomas; E-mail: tthomas@bbclibrary.net; Staff 3 (MLS 1, Non-MLS 2)
Founded 1939
Sept 2014-Aug 2015 Income $704,000
Library Holdings: Bk Vols 100,000; Per Subs 170
Special Collections: Alabama History Coll
Subject Interests: Genealogy
Automation Activity & Vendor Info: (Cataloging) Innovative Interfaces, Inc; (Circulation) Innovative Interfaces, Inc; (OPAC) Innovative Interfaces, Inc
Wireless access
Open Mon-Thurs 8:30-6, Fri 8:30-5, Sat 9-3

TALLADEGA

P ALABAMA INSTITUTE FOR THE DEAF & BLIND, Library & Resource Center for the Blind & Print Disabled, 705 South St E, 35160. (Mail add: PO Box 698, 35161), SAN 300-2152. Tel: 256-761-3237. FAX: 256-761-3561. Toll Free FAX: 800-848-4722. Web Site: www.aidb.org. *Dir,* Caitlin Cox; E-mail: cox.caitlin@aidb.org; *Reader Serv,* Ben Payne; E-mail: Payne.Ben@aidb.org; Staff 2 (MLS 1, Non-MLS 1)
Founded 1965. Circ 20,000
Library Holdings: Bk Vols 60,000; Per Subs 62
Special Collections: Alabama History, cassettes
Automation Activity & Vendor Info: (Acquisitions) Book Systems; (Cataloging) Book Systems; (Circulation) Book Systems; (Course Reserve) Book Systems; (ILL) Book Systems; (Media Booking) Book Systems; (OPAC) Book Systems; (Serials) Book Systems
Wireless access
Function: 24/7 Online cat, Accelerated reader prog, Activity rm
Publications: Newsletter (irregular)
Special Services for the Blind - Bks on cassette; Braille bks; Large print bks
Open Mon-Fri 8-4:30
Restriction: Registered patrons only
Friends of the Library Group

P ARMSTRONG-OSBORNE LIBRARY*, 202 South St E, 35160. SAN 300-2187. Tel: 256-362-4211. FAX: 256-362-0653. E-mail: talladeg@yahoo.com. Web Site: www.talladegalibrary.com. *Librn,* Vickie Harkins; Staff 7 (MLS 1, Non-MLS 6)
Founded 1906. Pop 72,601; Circ 118,641
Library Holdings: Bk Vols 100,000; Per Subs 100
Special Collections: Talladega History & Alabana History
Automation Activity & Vendor Info: (Cataloging) Book Systems; (Circulation) Book Systems
Wireless access

Open Mon-Thurs 9-6, Fri 9-4, Sat 9-3
Friends of the Library Group

C TALLADEGA COLLEGE*, Savery Library, 627 Battle St W, 35160. SAN 300-2160. Tel: 256-761-6284. FAX: 256-362-0497. E-mail: tclibrary@talladega.edu. Web Site: talladega.libguides.com, www.talladega.edu. *Libr Dir,* Caitlin Cox; Tel: 256-761-6377, E-mail: cmcox@talladega.edu; Staff 2 (MLS 2)
Founded 1939. Enrl 706; Fac 30; Highest Degree: Bachelor
Library Holdings: Bk Titles 120,687; Per Subs 211
Special Collections: Amistad Mutiny - Murals; Black Studies; Talladega Historical Coll. Oral History
Automation Activity & Vendor Info: (Acquisitions) Innovative Interfaces, Inc; (Cataloging) Innovative Interfaces, Inc; (Circulation) Innovative Interfaces, Inc; (OPAC) Innovative Interfaces, Inc
Wireless access
Publications: New Acquisitions; Student Handbook
Partic in LYRASIS; Network of Alabama Academic Libraries
Open Mon-Thurs 7am-10pm, Fri 7-5, Sat & Sun 11-8

GL TALLADEGA COUNTY LAW LIBRARY*, Talladega County Judicial Bldg, 148 East St N, 2nd Flr, 35161. (Mail add: PO Box 459, 35161-0459), SAN 300-2179. FAX: 256-480-5293. *Librn,* Cindy Haynes; Tel: 256-761-2110
Founded 1955
Library Holdings: Bk Vols 35,000; Per Subs 100
Wireless access
Open Mon-Fri 8-5

TALLASSEE

P TALLASSEE COMMUNITY LIBRARY*, 99 Freeman Ave, 36078. SAN 300-2195. Tel: 334-283-2732. FAX: 334-283-2732. E-mail: checkit-out.tclibrary@gmail.com. Web Site: www.tallasseeal.gov/library. *Librn,* Margaret Lumpkin; *Asst Librn,* Laura Pardue
Pop 5,500; Circ 18,750
Library Holdings: Bk Titles 20,000; Per Subs 15
Automation Activity & Vendor Info: (Cataloging) Follett Software; (Circulation) Follett Software
Wireless access
Mem of Horseshoe Bend Regional Library
Open Mon & Fri 9-5, Tues-Thurs 9-6, Sat 9-1

TARRANT

P TARRANT PUBLIC LIBRARY*, 1143 Ford Ave, 35217. SAN 300-2209. Tel: 205-841-0575. Web Site: www.tarrant.lib.al.us. *Dir,* Patrick Coleman; E-mail: pcoleman@bham.lib.al.us
Founded 1930. Pop 8,046
Library Holdings: Bk Vols 31,000; Per Subs 66
Special Collections: Arrowhead Coll; Petrified Wood; Shell Coll
Subject Interests: Alabama
Automation Activity & Vendor Info: (Cataloging) Innovative Interfaces, Inc; (Circulation) Innovative Interfaces, Inc; (OPAC) Innovative Interfaces, Inc
Publications: Newsletter
Open Mon-Fri 8-5

THOMASVILLE

P THOMASVILLE PUBLIC LIBRARY, 1401 Mosley Dr, 36784. SAN 300-2225. Tel: 334-636-5343. FAX: 334-636-4305. E-mail: tvillelibrary@gmail.com. Web Site: www.thomasvillepubliclibrary.org. *Dir,* Nichole Stinson; *Tech Coordr,* Chris Trull; E-mail: tpltech@bellsouth.net; *Youth Serv Coordr,* Liz Megginson; E-mail: tplkids@bellsouth.net; Staff 6 (MLS 1, Non-MLS 5)
Pop 8,900; Circ 41,000
Oct 2014-Sept 2015 Income $264,984, State $8,089, City $227,228, Federal $8,313, Locally Generated Income $21,354
Automation Activity & Vendor Info: (Acquisitions) Book Systems; (Cataloging) Book Systems; (Circulation) Book Systems; (ILL) OCLC FirstSearch; (OPAC) Book Systems
Wireless access
Function: 24/7 Electronic res, 24/7 Online cat, Accelerated reader prog, Activity rm, Adult bk club, Adult literacy prog, After school storytime, Archival coll, Art exhibits, Audio & video playback equip for onsite use, Audiobks on Playaways & MP3, Audiobks via web, AV serv, Bk club(s), Bks on CD, Bus archives, CD-ROM, Children's prog, Citizenship assistance, Computer training, Computers for patron use, Digital talking bks, Distance learning, Doc delivery serv, E-Readers, Electronic databases & coll, Family literacy, For res purposes, Free DVD rentals, Games & aids for people with disabilities, Holiday prog, Home delivery & serv to seniorr ctr & nursing homes, Homework prog, ILL available, Instruction & testing, Internet access, Learning ctr, Life-long learning prog for all ages, Literacy & newcomer serv, Magazines, Mail & tel request accepted, Meeting rooms, Movies, Online cat, Online info literacy tutorials on the web & in blackboard, Online ref, Orientations, Outreach serv, Outside serv via phone, mail, e-mail & web, OverDrive digital audio bks, Photocopying/Printing, Preschool outreach, Printer for laptops & handheld devices, Prog for adults, Prog for children & young adult, Ref & res, Ref serv available, Scanner, Senior computer classes, Senior outreach, Serves people with intellectual disabilities, Story hour, Summer & winter reading prog, Summer reading prog, Tax forms, Teen prog, Telephone ref, Wheelchair accessible, Winter reading prog, Workshops
Open Mon, Wed & Fri 9-5, Tues & Thurs 9-7, Sat 9-1
Friends of the Library Group

TROY

P TROY PUBLIC LIBRARY*, 500 E Walnut St, 36081. SAN 330-3152. Tel: 334-566-1314. Web Site: troycitylibrary.org. *Dir,* William White; *Asst Dir,* Gynene Terry; E-mail: gterry@troycitylibrary.org; Staff 8 (MLS 1, Non-MLS 7)
Pop 29,605
Library Holdings: AV Mats 528; Large Print Bks 3,342; Bk Titles 75,000; Per Subs 136; Talking Bks 2,771
Subject Interests: Antiques, Genealogy, State hist
Automation Activity & Vendor Info: (Cataloging) Book Systems; (Circulation) Book Systems; (OPAC) Book Systems
Wireless access
Open Mon-Thurs 9-5:45, Fri 9-4:45, Sat 9-2:45
Friends of the Library Group

C TROY UNIVERSITY LIBRARY, 309 Wallace Hall, 36082. SAN 330-3489. Tel: 334-670-3256. Reference Tel: 334-670-3255. Reference FAX: 334-670-3955. E-mail: libhelp@troy.edu. Web Site: www.troy.edu/libraries. *Dean, Univ Libr,* Dr Chris Shaffer; Tel: 334-670-3694, E-mail: shafferc@troy.edu; *Bus Librn, Head, Pub Serv,* Rachel Hooper; Tel: 334-670-3269, E-mail: hooperr@troy.edu; *Acq, Head, Tech Serv,* Jana Slay; E-mail: jslay@troy.edu; *Educ Librn, Instrul Media Serv Librn,* Lisa Vardaman; Tel: 334-670-3262, E-mail: lisavardaman@troy.edu; *Govt Doc Librn, Soc Sci Librn,* Rodney Lawley; Tel: 334-670-3198, E-mail: rlawley@troy.edu; *Humanities Librn,* Debbie West; Tel: 334-808-6344, E-mail: debwest@troy.edu; *Sci Librn,* Position Currently Open; *ILL Spec,* Mr Kelly Reeves; Tel: 334-670-3257, E-mail: jreeves157554@troy.edu; *Cataloger,* Ruth E Elder; Tel: 334-670-3874, E-mail: relder71917@troy.edu; Staff 10 (MLS 9, Non-MLS 1)
Founded 1887. Enrl 7,500; Fac 524; Highest Degree: Doctorate
Oct 2020-Sept 2021 Income $10,000
Library Holdings: Audiobooks 369; AV Mats 42,809; Bks on Deafness & Sign Lang 160; CDs 960; DVDs 4,745; e-books 278,000; e-journals 200,000; Microforms 1,217,631; Music Scores 1,830; Bk Titles 205,000; Per Subs 74; Talking Bks 15
Special Collections: Alabamiana. US Document Depository
Subject Interests: Educ, Indians
Automation Activity & Vendor Info: (Acquisitions) OCLC Worldshare Management Services; (Cataloging) OCLC Connexion; (Circulation) OCLC Worldshare Management Services; (Course Reserve) OCLC Worldshare Management Services; (ILL) OCLC Tipasa; (OPAC) OCLC Worldshare Management Services; (Serials) OCLC Worldshare Management Services
Wireless access
Function: Wheelchair accessible
Partic in LYRASIS; NAAL; OCLC Online Computer Library Center, Inc
Open Mon-Wed 7:30am-2am, Thurs 7:30am-11pm, Fri 7:30-6, Sat 10-5, Sun 2pm-2am

TRUSSVILLE

P TRUSSVILLE PUBLIC LIBRARY*, 201 Parkway Dr, 35173. SAN 300-2241. Tel: 205-655-2022. Web Site: www.trussvillelibrary.com. *Dir,* Emily Tish; E-mail: etish@bham.lib.al.us
Circ 50,000
Library Holdings: Bk Vols 60,000; Per Subs 95
Special Collections: Trussville & Alabama History Coll
Automation Activity & Vendor Info: (Cataloging) Innovative Interfaces, Inc; (Circulation) Innovative Interfaces, Inc; (OPAC) Innovative Interfaces, Inc
Wireless access
Open Mon & Tues 9-8, Wed-Fri 9-6, Sat 10-4, Sun 1-5
Friends of the Library Group

TUSCALOOSA

G GEOLOGICAL SURVEY OF ALABAMA LIBRARY*, Walter Bryan Jones Hall, Rm 200, 420 Hackberry Lane, 35401. (Mail add: PO Box 869999, 35486-6999), SAN 300-2322. Tel: 205-247-3634. FAX: 205-349-2861. E-mail: library@gsa.state.al.us. Web Site: www.gsa.state.al.us. *Interim Librn,* Camilla Musgrove; Staff 1 (MLS 1)
Founded 1873
Library Holdings: Bk Titles 150,911
Special Collections: Aerial Photography; Satellite Imagery for Alabama

Subject Interests: Geol, Paleontology
Wireless access
Publications: Bibliographies; publications of the Geological Survey of Alabama & State Oil & Gas Board
Open Mon-Fri 8-12 & 1-4 by appointment

R GRACE PRESBYTERIAN CHURCH*, Ann Inglett Library, 113 Hargrove Rd, 35401. SAN 300-2276. Tel: 205-758-5422. FAX: 205-758-5422. E-mail: office@gracetuscaloosa.org. Web Site: www.gracetuscaloosa.org. *Librn,* Nancy DuPree
Founded 1964
Library Holdings: Bk Vols 4,000; Per Subs 10
Subject Interests: Biblical studies, Relig, Sociol, Theol

J SHELTON STATE COMMUNITY COLLEGE, Brooks-Cork Library, Martin Campus, 9500 Old Greensboro Rd, 35405. SAN 300-225X. Tel: 205-391-3925. Administration Tel: 205-391-2268. Web Site: www.sheltonstate.edu/instruction-workforce-development/library-services/. *Head Librn,* Kelly Ann Griffiths; Tel: 205-391-2268, E-mail: kgriffiths@sheltonstate.edu; *Cat Librn,* Jennifer Cabanero; Tel: 205-391-2971, E-mail: jcabanero@sheltonstate.edu; *Librn,* Elena Hodgson; Tel: 205-391-2285, E-mail: ehodgson@sheltonstate.edu; *Librn,* Tracy Williams; Tel: 205-391-2203, E-mail: twilliams@sheltonstate.edu; *AV,* Jean Epps; Tel: 205-391-2970, E-mail: jepps@sheltonstate.edu; *Outreach Serv,* Tamara Okafor; Tel: 205-391-2248, E-mail: tokafor@sheltonstate.edu; *Archivist, Libr Support Spec,* Alex Smith; Tel: 205-391-2245, E-mail: asmith@sheltonstate.edu; Staff 8 (MLS 4, Non-MLS 4)
Founded 1979. Enrl 5,072; Fac 95; Highest Degree: Associate
Library Holdings: AV Mats 3,000; DVDs 175; e-books 17,000; Bk Vols 50,000; Per Subs 375; Videos 1,600
Special Collections: Lon Alexander Sr Coll; Phifer Family Coll
Automation Activity & Vendor Info: (Acquisitions) OCLC; (Cataloging) OCLC; (Circulation) OCLC; (Course Reserve) OCLC; (ILL) OCLC; (Media Booking) OCLC; (OPAC) OCLC
Wireless access
Partic in HBCU Library Alliance; LYRASIS; OCLC Online Computer Library Center, Inc
Special Services for the Deaf - ADA equip
Special Services for the Blind - Accessible computers
Open Mon-Thurs 7:30am-8pm, Fri 8-Noon

C STILLMAN COLLEGE*, William H Sheppard Library, 3601 Stillman Blvd, 35403. (Mail add: PO Box 1430, 35403-1430), SAN 300-2268. Tel: 205-366-8850. FAX: 205-247-8042. E-mail: librarian@stillman.edu. Web Site: stillman.edu/student-life/sheppard-library. *Dean,* Robert Heath; Tel: 205-366-8851, E-mail: rheath@stillman.edu; Staff 5 (MLS 4, Non-MLS 1)
Founded 1876. Enrl 1,065; Fac 71; Highest Degree: Bachelor
Library Holdings: Bk Vols 118,000
Special Collections: Afro-American Coll; Black History & Literature, 19th Century & Early 20th Century (microfilm). Oral History
Subject Interests: Relig
Automation Activity & Vendor Info: (Cataloging) Ex Libris Group; (Circulation) Ex Libris Group; (OPAC) Ex Libris Group
Wireless access
Partic in OCLC Online Computer Library Center, Inc
Open Mon-Thurs 8am-10pm, Fri 8-5, Sat 10-2, Sun 6pm-10pm

P TUSCALOOSA PUBLIC LIBRARY*, 1801 Jack Warner Pkwy, 35401-1027. SAN 330-3519. Tel: 205-345-5820. FAX: 205-758-1735. Reference E-mail: info@tuscaloosa-library.org. Web Site: www.tuscaloosa-library.org. *Exec Dir,* Richard Freemon; Tel: 205-345-5820, Ext 1102, E-mail: execdirector@tuscaloosa-library.org; *Mkt & Pub Relations Dir,* Vince Bellofatto; Tel: 205-345-5820, Ext 1110, E-mail: vbellofatto@tuscaloosa-library.org; Staff 48 (MLS 11, Non-MLS 37)
Founded 1921. Pop 202,000
Library Holdings: Bk Vols 186,595; Per Subs 700
Subject Interests: Genealogy, Local hist
Automation Activity & Vendor Info: (Acquisitions) Innovative Interfaces, Inc - Sierra; (Cataloging) Innovative Interfaces, Inc - Sierra; (Circulation) Innovative Interfaces, Inc - Sierra; (ILL) Innovative Interfaces, Inc - Sierra; (OPAC) Innovative Interfaces, Inc - Sierra; (Serials) Innovative Interfaces, Inc - Sierra
Wireless access
Open Mon-Thurs 9-9, Fri 12-5, Sat 9-5, Sun 2-6
Friends of the Library Group
Branches: 2
BROWN LIBRARY, 300 Bobby Miller Pkwy, 35405. Tel: 205-391-9989. FAX: 205-391-9355. *Head Librn,* Kelly Butler; Staff 3 (MLS 1, Non-MLS 2)
Open Mon, Wed & Thurs 10-6, Tues 1-8, Fri 1-5
WEAVER-BOLDEN LIBRARY, 2522 Lanier Ave, 35401, SAN 330-3578. Tel: 205-758-8291. FAX: 205-464-0906. *Head Librn,* Marti Ball
Open Mon-Thurs 9-7, Fri 1-5
Friends of the Library Group
Bookmobiles: 2

UNIVERSITY OF ALABAMA

CL SCHOOL OF LAW LIBRARY*, 101 Paul Bryant Dr, 35487. (Mail add: Box 870383, 35487-0383), SAN 330-3969. Tel: 205-348-5925. Reference Tel: 205-348-1114. FAX: 205-348-1112. Web Site: www.law.ua.edu. *Dir,* James Leonard; E-mail: jleonard@law.ua.edu; *Assoc Dir,* Robert Marshall; *Asst Dir,* Ruth Weeks; *Head, Ref (Info Serv),* Iain Barksdale; *Cat,* Julie Griffith-Kees; *Coll Develop,* Paul Pruitt; *Computer Serv,* David Lowe; *Curator of Archival Coll,* David Durham; *Ref (Info Servs),* Penny Gibson; Staff 9 (MLS 8, Non-MLS 1)
Founded 1872. Enrl 592; Fac 35; Highest Degree: Doctorate
Library Holdings: Bk Titles 134,603; Bk Vols 438,444; Per Subs 3,368
Special Collections: Former US Senator Howell Heflin; Former US Supreme Court Justice Hugo L Black
Automation Activity & Vendor Info: (Acquisitions) Innovative Interfaces, Inc; (Cataloging) Innovative Interfaces, Inc; (Circulation) Innovative Interfaces, Inc; (Course Reserve) Innovative Interfaces, Inc; (OPAC) Innovative Interfaces, Inc; (Serials) Innovative Interfaces, Inc
Partic in Association of Research Libraries; NAAL; Proquest Dialog; Southeastern Chapter of the American Association of Law Libraries
Publications: CASE; User Guides Series
Open Mon-Fri 7:30am-Midnight, Sat 9am-10pm, Sun 10am-Midnight

C UNIVERSITY LIBRARIES*, University of Alabama Campus, Capstone Dr, 35487. (Mail add: Box 870266, 35487-0266), SAN 330-3845. Tel: 205-348-7561. Circulation Tel: 205-348-9748. Interlibrary Loan Service Tel: 205-348-6345. Reference Tel: 205-348-6047. Automation Services Tel: 205-348-4608. FAX: 205-348-8833. Interlibrary Loan Service FAX: 205-348-9564. Reference FAX: 205-348-0760. Web Site: www.lib.ua.edu. *Dean of Libr,* Donald A Gilstrap; *Assoc Dean,* Karen Croneis; Tel: 205-348-5569; *Head, Acq,* Beth Holley; Tel: 205-348-1493, Fax: 205-348-6358, E-mail: bholley@bama.ua.edu; *Curator,* Clark Center; Tel: 205-348-0513, Fax: 205-348-1699, E-mail: ccenter@bama.ua.edu; Staff 46 (MLS 40, Non-MLS 6)
Founded 1831. Enrl 23,878; Fac 811; Highest Degree: Doctorate
Library Holdings: e-books 40,389; e-journals 73,449; Bk Vols 2,175,700; Per Subs 29,374
Special Collections: 17th & 18th Century Cartography (Warner Map Coll); Alabama & Southern Manuscripts & University Archives; Confederate Imprints Coll; David Walker Lupton African American Cookbook Coll; First Editions (19th Century Literature Coll); Rucker Agee Coll of Alabamiana; Sheet Music Coll; Southern Americana Coll; Southern History & Culture (Wade Hall Coll), photogs, sound rec; William Campbell March & Numerous Southern Authors Coll; World War II Armed Services Editions. State Document Depository; US Document Depository
Automation Activity & Vendor Info: (Acquisitions) Ex Libris Group; (Cataloging) Ex Libris Group; (Circulation) Ex Libris Group; (Course Reserve) Ex Libris Group; (OPAC) Ex Libris Group; (Serials) Ex Libris Group
Partic in Association of Southeastern Research Libraries; LYRASIS
Publications: Library Horizons (Newsletter)
Special Services for the Deaf - TTY equip
Special Services for the Blind - Assistive/Adapted tech devices, equip & products
Open Mon-Thurs 7:45am-Midnight, Sat 10-8, Sun 1pm-Midnight
Friends of the Library Group

CM UNIVERSITY OF ALABAMA COLLEGE OF COMMUNITY HEALTH SCIENCES, Health Sciences Library, 850 Peter Bryce Blvd, 35401. (Mail add: Box 870326, 35487), SAN 330-3608. Tel: 205-348-1360. FAX: 205-348-9563. E-mail: library@cchs.ua.edu. Web Site: cchs.ua.edu/library. *Libr Dir,* Nelle Williams; Tel: 205-348-1364, E-mail: ntwilliams1@ua.edu; *Clinical Librn, Tech Serv Librn,* Andrea Wright; Tel: 205-348-1335, E-mail: alwright1@ua.edu; Staff 3 (MLS 2, Non-MLS 1)
Founded 1973. Highest Degree: Doctorate
Subject Interests: Med, Rural health
Automation Activity & Vendor Info: (Cataloging) Ex Libris Group; (Circulation) Ex Libris Group; (Discovery) EBSCO Discovery Service; (OPAC) Ex Libris Group
Wireless access
Partic in Docline; National Network of Libraries of Medicine Region 2; Network of Alabama Academic Libraries; OCLC Online Computer Library Center, Inc
Open Mon-Fri 8-4:45

TUSCUMBIA

P HELEN KELLER PUBLIC LIBRARY, 511 N Main St, 35674. SAN 300-2292. Tel: 256-383-7065. FAX: 256-389-9057. E-mail: info@hkpl.org. Web Site: cityoftuscumbia.org/?page_id=1965, www.hkpl.org. *Dir,* Elisabeth South; E-mail: esouth@hkpl.org; Staff 3 (MLS 1, Non-MLS 2)
Founded 1893. Pop 9,137; Circ 48,220

Library Holdings: Audiobooks 947; DVDs 3,700; e-books 28,000; Bk Vols 24,700; Per Subs 10
Automation Activity & Vendor Info: (Cataloging) Book Systems; (Circulation) Book Systems; (OPAC) Book Systems
Wireless access
Open Mon-Fri 10-5
Friends of the Library Group

TUSKEGEE

P MACON COUNTY-TUSKEGEE PUBLIC LIBRARY*, 302 S Main St, 36083. SAN 330-3667. Tel: 334-727-5192. FAX: 334-727-5989. E-mail: info@mctpl.us. Web Site: www.mctpl.us. *Libr Dir,* Mr Petre Bridges; Staff 2 (Non-MLS 2)
Founded 1968. Pop 25,000
Library Holdings: Bk Vols 26,000; Per Subs 63
Special Collections: Children's Literature (Sammy Young Coll), A-tapes, fs, flm
Wireless access
Publications: American Libraries; Library Journal; Library Scene
Open Mon-Thurs 8:30-5, Fri 8:30-3:30
Friends of the Library Group

C TUSKEGEE UNIVERSITY*, Ford Motor Company Library, 1200 W Old Mongtomery Rd, Ford Motor Company Library, 36088. SAN 330-3721. Tel: 334-727-8892, 334-727-8894. Circulation Tel: 334-724-4744, 334-727-8900. Interlibrary Loan Service Tel: 334-724-4688, 334-727-8895. Reference Tel: 334-724-4231, 334-727-8896. Automation Services Tel: 334-724-4740. FAX: 334-727-9282. Web Site: www.tuskegee.edu/libraries. *Dir, Libr Serv - Univ Archives & Mus,* Juanita M Roberts; Tel: 334-727-8894, E-mail: jroberts@tuskegee.edu; *Head, Cat & Tech Serv,* Deborah Haile; Tel: 334-727-8898; *Head, Circ & Reserves,* Position Currently Open; *Head, Ref Serv,* Eunice G Samuel; E-mail: gbanks@mytu.tuskegee.edu; *Archit Librn,* Thomas Kaufmann; Tel: 334-727-4572; *Eng Librn,* Position Currently Open; *Govt Doc/Ref Librn,* Asteria Ndulute; Tel: 334-727-8891; *Media/Ser/ILL Librn,* Rose Frazier; *Veterinary Med Librn,* Margaret Alexander; Tel: 334-727-8780, Fax: 334-727-8442; *Curator,* Dr Jontyule Robinson; Tel: 334-727-8888, Fax: 334-725-2400; *Info Literacy,* Jonathan Underwood; Tel: 334-727-8676; *Spec Coll,* Position Currently Open; *Univ Archivist,* Dana Chandler; Staff 9 (MLS 9)
Founded 1881. Enrl 3,000; Highest Degree: Doctorate
Library Holdings: Bk Vols 310,000; Per Subs 1,500
Special Collections: Blacks (Washington Coll). US Document Depository
Automation Activity & Vendor Info: (Acquisitions) SirsiDynix; (Cataloging) SirsiDynix; (Circulation) SirsiDynix; (ILL) SirsiDynix; (OPAC) SirsiDynix; (Serials) SirsiDynix
Wireless access
Partic in Coop Col Libr Ctr, Inc; NAAL
Open Mon-Thurs 8am-10pm, Fri 8-4:30, Sat 1-5, Sun 2-10

UNION SPRINGS

P UNION SPRINGS PUBLIC LIBRARY*, 103 Prairie St N, 36089. SAN 330-3187. Tel: 334-738-2760. FAX: 334-738-2780. E-mail: unionspringslibrary@yahoo.com. Web Site: aplsws1.apls.state.al.us/unionsprings. *Librn,* Frances Brown
Library Holdings: Bk Vols 10,000; Per Subs 31
Wireless access
Open Mon-Fri 11-5

UNIONTOWN

P UNIONTOWN PUBLIC LIBRARY*, PO Box 637, 36786-0637. Tel: 334-628-6681. FAX: 334-628-6683. E-mail: uniontownbookworm@yahoo.com. Web Site: www.uniontownal.org/library. *Librn,* Detre Langhorne
Library Holdings: Bk Vols 1,500
Open Mon-Fri 11-4

VALLEY

P H GRADY BRADSHAW CHAMBERS COUNTY LIBRARY*, 3419 20th Ave, 36854. SAN 320-1155. Tel: 334-768-2161. FAX: 334-768-7272. E-mail: aksus@chamberscountylibrary.org. Web Site: www.chamberscountylibrary.org. *Dir,* Mary H Hamilton; E-mail: maryhamilton@chamberscountylibrary.org; *Asst Dir,* Tabitha Truitt; *Head, Pub Serv,* Cathy Wright; Staff 9 (MLS 4, Non-MLS 5)
Founded 1976. Pop 34,200; Circ 90,633
Library Holdings: Bk Titles 52,808; Bk Vols 62,912; Per Subs 153
Special Collections: Cobb Memorial Archives. Oral History
Subject Interests: Genealogy
Wireless access
Open Mon-Fri (Summer) 10-6, Sat 10-2; Mon & Tues (Winter) 10-7, Wed-Fri 10-6
Friends of the Library Group

Branches: 1
LAFAYETTE PILOT PUBLIC LIBRARY, 198 First St SE, Lafayette, 36862, SAN 300-1288. Tel: 334-864-0012. E-mail: lafayette@chamberscountylibrary.org. *Dir,* Mary Hamilton; *Br Mgr,* Rachel Johnson; E-mail: racheljohnson@chamberscountylibrary.org
Circ 8,299
Library Holdings: Bk Vols 8,418; Per Subs 25
Open Mon-Fri 12:30-5, Sat 9-12
Friends of the Library Group

VESTAVIA HILLS

P VESTAVIA HILLS LIBRARY IN THE FOREST, 1221 Montgomery Hwy, 35216. SAN 300-2349. Tel: 205-978-0155. Administration Tel: 205-978-0162. FAX: 205-978-0156. Web Site: www.vestavialibrary.org. *Dir,* Taneisha K Tucker; E-mail: tyoung@bham.lib.al.us
Founded 1969. Pop 20,384; Circ 131,238
Library Holdings: Bk Vols 82,000; Per Subs 135
Special Collections: American Heritage, National Geographic, 1955-82, Readers Digest
Automation Activity & Vendor Info: (Cataloging) Innovative Interfaces, Inc; (Circulation) Innovative Interfaces, Inc; (OPAC) Innovative Interfaces, Inc
Wireless access
Publications: American Libraries; Booklist
Partic in Jefferson County Libr Coop
Open Mon-Sat 9-6
Friends of the Library Group

VINCENT

P LALLOUISE FLOREY MCGRAW PUBLIC LIBRARY, 42860 Hwy 25, 35178-6156. (Mail add: PO Box 3, 35178-0003), SAN 371-9375. Tel: 205-672-2749. FAX: 205-672-2749. E-mail: vincentlibrary@shelbycounty-al.org. Web Site: cityofvincental.com/library.aspx. *Librn,* Sandra Carden-Berry
Library Holdings: Bk Vols 10,500
Automation Activity & Vendor Info: (Cataloging) Innovative Interfaces, Inc. - Polaris; (Circulation) Innovative Interfaces, Inc. - Polaris; (OPAC) Innovative Interfaces, Inc. - Polaris
Wireless access
Mem of Harrison Regional Library System
Open Mon, Wed & Thurs 9-5, Tues 10-6

WADLEY

J SOUTHERN UNION STATE COMMUNITY COLLEGE*, McClintock-Ensminger Library, 750 Robert St, 36276. SAN 300-2357. Tel: 256-395-2211. Web Site: www.suscc.edu. *Dir,* Kathy E Reynolds; Tel: 256-395-2211, Ext 5130, E-mail: kreynolds@suscc.edu; *Tech Serv,* John Carlisle; Tel: 256-395-2211, Ext 5132, E-mail: jcarlisle@suscc.edu; *Tech Serv,* Amy Smith; Tel: 256-395-2211, Ext 5131, E-mail: asmith@suscc.edu; Staff 7 (MLS 2, Non-MLS 5)
Founded 1922
Library Holdings: Bk Vols 90,000; Per Subs 370
Special Collections: Alabama History Coll
Automation Activity & Vendor Info: (Acquisitions) SirsiDynix; (Cataloging) SirsiDynix; (Circulation) SirsiDynix; (OPAC) SirsiDynix; (Serials) SirsiDynix
Publications: A/V Catalog; Student Handbook
Partic in Alabama Libr Asn
Open Mon-Thurs 7:30am-8pm, Fri 7:30am-12:15pm
Departmental Libraries:
OPELIKA CAMPUS, 1701 Lafayette Pkwy, Opelika, 36801. Tel: 334-745-6437. FAX: 334-749-5505. *Dir,* Kathy E Reynolds; E-mail: kreynolds@suscc.edu; *Librn,* Michelle Wimbish; Tel: 334-745-6437, Ext 5322, E-mail: mwimbish@suscc.edu
Open Mon-Thurs 7:30am-8:30pm, Fri 7:30am-12:15pm
VALLEY CAMPUS, 321 Fob James Dr, Valley, 36854, SAN 300-1296. Tel: 334-756-4151. FAX: 334-756-5183. *Dir,* Kathy Reynolds; E-mail: kreynolds@suscc.edu
Open Mon-Thurs 9:30-1:30 & 2:45-8:45

WALNUT GROVE

P WESTSIDE PUBLIC LIBRARY*, 5151 Walnut Grove Rd, 35990. (Mail add: PO Box 100, 35990-0100), SAN 374-5678. Tel: 205-589-6699. FAX: 205-589-6699. E-mail: walnutgrove219@gmail.com. *Dir,* Vickie Dobbins; *Head Librn,* Stacy Richards; Staff 2 (MLS 1, Non-MLS 1)
Founded 1991. Pop 3,500
Library Holdings: Bk Vols 7,500; Per Subs 20
Automation Activity & Vendor Info: (Cataloging) Book Systems; (Circulation) Book Systems; (OPAC) Book Systems
Wireless access
Open Mon & Thurs 11-7, Tues 9-2, Fri 9-1

WARRIOR

P WARRIOR PUBLIC LIBRARY, Ten First St, 35180. SAN 376-5539. Tel: 205-647-3006. FAX: 205-647-9280. Web Site: warriorpubliclibrary.org. *Librn,* Karen Moody; E-mail: karen.moody@jclc.org
Library Holdings: Bk Titles 16,000
Automation Activity & Vendor Info: (Cataloging) Innovative Interfaces, Inc; (Circulation) Innovative Interfaces, Inc; (OPAC) Innovative Interfaces, Inc
Wireless access
Partic in Jefferson County Libr Coop
Open Mon, Wed & Fri 9-5, Tues & Thurs 9-7, Sat 9-12
Friends of the Library Group

WEST BLOCTON

P WEST BLOCTON PUBLIC LIBRARY*, 109 Florida St, 35184. (Mail add: PO Box 292, 35184-0292). Tel: 205-938-3570. FAX: 205-938-7803. E-mail: wbplibrary@bellsouth.net. *Librn,* Rebecca Paulene
Library Holdings: Bk Vols 15,000
Wireless access
Open Tues 10-2, Wed 12-4, Thurs 1-5, Fri 12-3, Sat 10-1

WETUMPKA

P WETUMPKA PUBLIC LIBRARY, 212 S Main St, 36092. (Mail add: PO Box 249, 36092-0005), SAN 300-2365. Tel: 334-567-1308. FAX: 334-567-1309. E-mail: library@cityofwetumpka.com. Web Site: www.wetumpkalibrary.com. *Dir,* Susan Hayes; Staff 5 (MLS 1.5, Non-MLS 3.5)
Founded 1957. Pop 6,528; Circ 76,000
Library Holdings: Bk Vols 23,000; Per Subs 55
Special Collections: Local Artists Art Coll
Wireless access
Function: Bk club(s), Bks on CD, Children's prog, Computers for patron use, Free DVD rentals, ILL available, Music CDs, Photocopying/Printing, Story hour, Summer reading prog, Tax forms
Mem of Horseshoe Bend Regional Library
Open Mon-Fri 8-6, Sat 9-5
Friends of the Library Group

WHITEHALL

P WHITE HALL PUBLIC LIBRARY, 640 Freedom Rd, 36040. Tel: 334-874-7323. *Dir,* Ethel J Williams; E-mail: e.williams@mindspring.com
Library Holdings: High Interest/Low Vocabulary Bk Vols 3,000; Bk Vols 20,000
Automation Activity & Vendor Info: (Acquisitions) Evergreen; (Cataloging) Evergreen; (Circulation) Evergreen; (ILL) Evergreen; (Serials) Evergreen
Wireless access
Open Tues-Thurs 9:30-4

WILSONVILLE

P VERNICE STOUDENMIRE PUBLIC LIBRARY*, PO Box 70, 35186-0070. SAN 371-9383. Tel: 205-669-6180. FAX: 205-669-6205. E-mail: wpl@shelbycounty-al.org. *Librn,* Joyce Saxon
Pop 1,750
Library Holdings: Bk Titles 5,500
Wireless access
Function: 24/7 Electronic res, Activity rm
Mem of Harrison Regional Library System
Open Mon 1-5, Tues 11-5, Wed 10-5, Thurs 10-6, Fri 1-6
Restriction: Access at librarian's discretion, Authorized patrons, Borrowing requests are handled by ILL, Co libr, Non-resident fee

WINFIELD

P NORTHWEST REGIONAL LIBRARY*, 185 Ashwood Dr, 35594-5436. (Mail add: PO Box 1527, 35594-1527), SAN 330-4027. Tel: 205-487-2330. FAX: 205-487-5146. E-mail: library@winfieldcity.org. *Dir,* Regina Sperry; E-mail: rsperry@northwestregional.net
Founded 1961
Library Holdings: Bk Vols 80,176; Per Subs 10
Automation Activity & Vendor Info: (Cataloging) Follett Software; (Circulation) Follett Software; (OPAC) Follett Software
Open Mon-Thurs 8-4
Branches: 8
MARY WALLACE COBB MEMORIAL LIBRARY, 44425 Hwy 17, Vernon, 35592. (Mail add: PO Box 357, Vernon, 35592-0357), SAN 330-423X. Tel: 205-695-6123. FAX: 205-695-1006. Web Site: webmini.apls.state.al.us/apls_web/northwest/?q=wallace. *Libr Dir,* Amanda Glasgow
Circ 16,000
Library Holdings: Bk Vols 5,454
Open Mon-Fri 9-5:30
KENNEDY PUBLIC LIBRARY, 17885 Hwy 96, Kennedy, 35574. (Mail add: PO Box 70, Kennedy, 35574-0070), SAN 330-4086. Tel: 205-596-3670. FAX: 205-596-3956. *Librn,* James Vice
Circ 800
Library Holdings: Bk Vols 4,595
Open Mon, Tues, Thurs & Fri 8-12 & 1-5
MCHS COMMUNITY LIBRARY, 8115 US Hwy 43, Guin, 35563. (Mail add: PO Box 549, Guin, 35563-0549), SAN 330-4116. Tel: 205-468-2544. FAX: 205-468-2544. *Librn,* Margaret Masengale
Pop 3,000; Circ 20,400
Library Holdings: Bk Vols 15,938; Per Subs 83
MILLPORT PUBLIC LIBRARY, 920 Black St, Millport, 35576. (Mail add: PO Box 159, Millport, 35576-0159), SAN 330-4124. Tel: 205-662-4286. E-mail: millportlibrary@bamacomm.com. Web Site: webmini.apls.state.al.us/apls_web/northwest/?q=millport. *Libr Dir,* Sue Atkins
Circ 2,500
Library Holdings: Bk Vols 7,460
Open Mon & Wed 9-Noon, Tues, Thurs & Fri 9-12 & 1-5
Friends of the Library Group
CLYDE NIX PUBLIC LIBRARY, 350 Bexar Ave W, Hamilton, 35570. (Mail add: PO Box 1944, Hamilton, 35570-1944), SAN 330-4051. Tel: 205-921-4290. FAX: 205-921-4290. E-mail: clydenix@yahoo.com. *Librn,* Starr Homer
Circ 33,400
Library Holdings: Bk Vols 15,646; Per Subs 29
Open Mon, Tues, Thurs & Fri 10-5, Wed 12-4, Sat 10-12
Friends of the Library Group
SULLIGENT PUBLIC LIBRARY, 514 Elm St, Sulligent, 35586-9053. (Mail add: PO Box 215, Sulligent, 35586-0215), SAN 330-4205. Tel: 205-698-8631. FAX: 205-698-0232. E-mail: sullpl@yahoo.com. *Librn,* Cathy Collins
Circ 13,000
Library Holdings: Bk Vols 11,948
Open Mon 9-6, Tues-Fri 9-5, Sat 9-12
WEATHERFORD PUBLIC LIBRARY, 307 Fourth Ave, Red Bay, 35582. (Mail add: PO Box 870, Red Bay, 35582-0870), SAN 330-4140. Tel: 256-356-9255. E-mail: rblibrary@bellsouth.net. *Librn,* Linda Ezzeal
Founded 1974. Circ 13,300
Library Holdings: Bks on Deafness & Sign Lang 10; Bk Vols 9,703; Per Subs 10
Subject Interests: Biographies, Fiction
Open Mon & Wed 1-5, Tues 10-5, Thurs & Fri 12-5
WINFIELD PUBLIC LIBRARY, 185 Ashwood Dr, 35594. (Mail add: PO Box 688, 35594-0688), SAN 330-4264. Tel: 205-487-2484. FAX: 205-487-5146. E-mail: library@winfieldcity.org. *Dir & Librn,* Regina Sperry
Circ 43,000
Library Holdings: Bk Vols 27,000; Per Subs 44
Open Mon & Thurs 9-6, Tues & Fri 9-5, Wed 12-5, Sat 9-Noon
Friends of the Library Group

WOODVILLE

P WOODVILLE PUBLIC LIBRARY, 26 Venson St, 35776. (Mail add: PO Box 116, 35776-0116), SAN 325-4402. Tel: 256-776-2796. FAX: 256-776-3294. E-mail: publicw@bellsouth.net. *Dir,* Karen Chambers
Founded 1985. Pop 775; Circ 787
Library Holdings: CDs 15; DVDs 181; Large Print Bks 575; Bk Vols 10,380; Per Subs 4
Subject Interests: Genealogy
Automation Activity & Vendor Info: (Acquisitions) OCLC; (Cataloging) OCLC; (Circulation) OCLC; (Course Reserve) OCLC; (Discovery) OCLC; (ILL) OCLC; (Media Booking) OCLC; (OPAC) OCLC; (Serials) OCLC
Wireless access
Function: Preschool reading prog
Partic in National Network of Libraries of Medicine Region 2
Open Tues-Fri 9-5

YORK

P HIGHTOWER MEMORIAL LIBRARY*, 630 Ave A, 36925. SAN 300-2373. Tel: 205-392-2004. E-mail: hmlibrary@att.net. *Librn,* Edna Williams
Pop 5,859; Circ 11,514
Library Holdings: AV Mats 217; Bk Vols 12,000; Per Subs 20
Open Mon & Wed 10-12 & 1-4, Tues & Thurs 10-12 & 1-6, Fri 10-1, Sat 9-Noon

ALASKA

Date of Statistics: FY 2021
Population, 2020 U.S. Census: 731,158
Population Served by Public Libraries: 634,557
Total Volumes in Public Libraries: 2,780,969 (print)
Total Public Library Circulation: 4,552,378
Digital Resources:
Total e-books: 1,406,794
Total audio items (physical & downloadable units): 909,359
Total video items (physical & downloadable units): 336,281
Total computers for use by the public: 681
Total annual wireless sessions: 455,770
Income and Expenditures:
Public Library Income:
Operating Revenue: $39,546,366
Operating Expenditures: $34,914,866
Capital Revenue: $6,612,326
Capital Expenditures: $6,612,326
Number of County Libraries: Alaska is divided into 19 organized boroughs and one unorganized borough. Twelve boroughs fund borough-wide service.
Public Library Assistance & Interlibrary Cooperation Grants: Continuing to offer these grants, as well as Continuing Education Grants.
State Appropriations: $889,800
Information provided courtesy of: Patience Frederiksen, Alaska State Librarian; Alaska State Library

ANCHOR POINT

P ANCHOR POINT PUBLIC LIBRARY*, 34020 N Fork Rd, 99556. (Mail add: PO Box 129, 99556-0129). Tel: 907-235-5692. FAX: 907-235-5692. E-mail: anchorpointlibrary@gmail.com. Web Site: www.anchorpointlibrary.com. *Dir,* Lora L Craig; Staff 1 (Non-MLS 1)
Founded 1947. Pop 2,500
Jul 2019-Jun 2020. Mats Exp $3,600, Books $3,500, Per/Ser (Incl. Access Fees) $100. Sal $4,800
Library Holdings: Bk Vols 20,000; Per Subs 5
Subject Interests: Alaskana
Automation Activity & Vendor Info: (Acquisitions) Follett Software; (Cataloging) Follett Software; (Circulation) Follett Software
Wireless access
Function: Art exhibits, Bks on CD, Computers for patron use, ILL available, Internet access, Movies, Online cat, Photocopying/Printing, Preschool outreach, Scanner, Story hour, Summer & winter reading prog, Wheelchair accessible
Open Mon, Wed & Fri 10-5, Sat 11-5
Friends of the Library Group

ANCHORAGE

G ALASKA DEPARTMENT OF NATURAL RESOURCES DIVISION OF MINING, LAND & WATER LIBRARY*, 550 W Seventh Ave, Ste 1070, 99501-3579, SAN 320-8095. Tel: 907-269-8600. FAX: 907-269-8904. TDD: 907-269-8411.
Library Holdings: Bk Vols 500; Per Subs 10
Special Collections: Coal Application Permits for Alaska; Division Reports; Geology & Mining Magazines; Large Mine Applications & Permitting in Alaska; US Bureaus of Mines Reports on Southeast Alaska
Subject Interests: Alaska
Open Mon-Fri 8-4:30

G PUBLIC INFORMATION CENTER*, 550 W Seventh Ave, Ste 1260, 99501, SAN 374-602X. Tel: 907-269-8400. FAX: 907-269-8901. TDD: 907-269-8411. E-mail: dnr.pic@alaska.gov. Web Site: dnr.alaska.gov. *Mgr,* Kathy Johnson
Publications: Fact Sheets; Pamphlets on ADNR programs
Special Services for the Deaf - TTY equip
Open Mon-Fri 10-5

S ALASKA HERITAGE MUSEUM & LIBRARY AT WELLS FARGO*, 301 W Northern Lights Blvd, K3212-051, 99503. SAN 329-7209. Tel: 907-265-2834. Web Site: www.wellsfargohistory.com/museums/anchorage. *Curator,* Tom D Bennett; E-mail: tom.d.bennett@wellsfargo.com; *Mus Asst,* Walter Van Horn; Staff 2 (Non-MLS 2)
Founded 1968
Library Holdings: AV Mats 24; Bk Titles 2,500
Special Collections: Alaskan History
Subject Interests: Alaska
Function: Ref serv available
Publications: Heritage of Alaska
Partic in Alaska Libr Asn
Open Mon-Fri 12-4 or by appointment

S ALASKA HOUSING FINANCE CORP*, Research Information Center Library, 4300 Boniface Pkwy, 99504. (Mail add: PO Box 101020, 99510), SAN 321-446X. Tel: 907-330-8166. FAX: 907-330-8247. Web Site: www.ahfc.us. *Librn,* Betty Hall; E-mail: bhall@ahfc.us
Founded 1984
Library Holdings: Bk Titles 6,000; Per Subs 20
Wireless access
Open Mon-Fri 8-5

S ALASKA MASONIC LIBRARY & MUSEUM*, 518 E 14th Ave, 99501. Tel: 907-561-1477. *Curator,* Roger Hansen
Library Holdings: Bk Vols 2,000
Restriction: Open by appt only

M ALASKA NATIVE MEDICAL CENTER*, Bonnie Williams Memorial Library, 4315 Diplomacy Dr, 99508-5999. Tel: 907-729-2943. E-mail: library@anthc.org.
Founded 1959
Wireless access
Function: ILL available
Restriction: Med staff only

G ALASKA OIL & GAS CONSERVATION COMMISSION LIBRARY, 333 W Seventh Ave, Ste 100, 99501. SAN 373-3335. Tel: 907-279-1433. FAX: 907-276-7542. Web Site: www.aogcc.alaska.gov. *Tech Librn,* Abby Bell; Tel: 907-793-1225, E-mail: abby.bell@alaska.gov
Library Holdings: Bk Vols 3,000; Per Subs 10
Open Mon-Fri 8-4:30

G ALASKA RESOURCES LIBRARY & INFORMATION SERVICES*, Library Bldg, 3211 Providence Dr, Ste 111, 99508-4614. SAN 377-841X. Tel: 907-272-7547. FAX: 907-786-7652. Interlibrary Loan Service FAX: 907-786-7680. Reference E-mail: reference@arlis.org. Web Site: www.arlis.org. *Librn,* Juli Braund-Allen; Tel: 907-786-7666, E-mail: jebraundallen@alaska.edu; *Coll Develop Coordr,* Celia Rozen; Tel: 907-786-7676, E-mail: celia@arlis.org; *Ref Serv Coordr,* Helen Woods; Tel: 907-786-7660, E-mail: helen@arlis.org; Staff 15 (MLS 6, Non-MLS 9)
Founded 1997
Library Holdings: Bk Titles 90,000; Bk Vols 200,000; Per Subs 700
Special Collections: US Document Depository
Subject Interests: Cultural res, Natural res
Automation Activity & Vendor Info: (Cataloging) OCLC; (Circulation) SirsiDynix; (ILL) OCLC; (OPAC) SirsiDynix
Function: Doc delivery serv, Govt ref serv, ILL available, Outside serv via phone, mail, e-mail & web, Ref serv available, Res libr, Wheelchair accessible
Partic in OCLC Online Computer Library Center, Inc; OCLC-LVIS

Open Mon-Fri 8-5
Friends of the Library Group

GL ALASKA STATE COURT LAW LIBRARY*, 303 K St, 99501. SAN 300-2381. Tel: 907-264-0585. Toll Free Tel: 888-282-2082. FAX: 907-264-0733. E-mail: library@akcourts.us. Web Site: www.courts.alaska.gov/library. *State Law Librn,* Susan Falk; E-mail: sfalk@akcourts.us; *Pub Serv Librn,* Ashley Stewart; E-mail: astewart@akcourts.us; *Tech Serv Librn,* Nancy Tileston; E-mail: ntileston@akcourts.us
Founded 1959
Library Holdings: Bk Vols 363,735; Per Subs 328
Special Collections: US Document Depository
Automation Activity & Vendor Info: (Acquisitions) EOS International; (Cataloging) EOS International; (Circulation) EOS International; (OPAC) EOS International; (Serials) EOS International
Wireless access
Open Mon-Thurs 8-6, Fri 8-Noon, Sun Noon-5
Branches:
FAIRBANKS BRANCH, 101 Lacey St, Fairbanks, 99701. Tel: 907-452-9241. FAX: 907-458-9345. *Librn,* Tamara Borgen; E-mail: tborgen@akcourts.us
Open Mon-Thurs 8-6, Fri 8-12
JUNEAU BRANCH, Dimond Court Bldg, 123 Fourth St, Juneau, 99811. (Mail add: PO Box 114100, Juneau, 99811-4100). Tel: 907-463-4761. FAX: 907-463-4784. *Librn,* Danielle Devore; E-mail: ddevore@akcourts.us
Open Mon-Thurs 8-6, Fri 8-12

S ANCHORAGE MUSEUM*, Atwood Alaska Resource Center, 625 C St, 99501. SAN 300-242X. Tel: 907-929-9235. FAX: 907-929-9233. E-mail: resourcecenter@anchoragemuseum.org. Web Site: www.anchoragemuseum.org. *Librn, Ref Spec,* Zane Treesh; *Archivist,* Sara Piasecki; Staff 3 (MLS 3)
Founded 1968
Library Holdings: Bk Titles 15,000; Per Subs 45
Special Collections: ADAK Coll (Adak Historical Society); Alaska Railroad Coll, photog; Alexander Creek (Fred Winters Coll), diaries; Barrow & Diomede Islands (Eide Coll), photog; Otto Goetze Coll; Reindeer Herding (Ickes Coll), photog; Steve McCutcheon Coll, photog; Valdez History (Crary-Henderson Coll), photog; Vern Brickley Coll; Ward Wells Coll, photog
Subject Interests: Alaskana, Art, Ethnology, Hist, Sci
Automation Activity & Vendor Info: (Acquisitions) SirsiDynix; (Cataloging) SirsiDynix; (Circulation) SirsiDynix; (ILL) OCLC WorldShare Interlibrary Loan; (OPAC) SirsiDynix; (Serials) SirsiDynix
Wireless access
Function: Archival coll, ILL available, Mail & tel request accepted, Online cat, Telephone ref
Partic in Alaska Library Network
Open Tues-Fri 10-2
Restriction: Circulates for staff only, In-house use for visitors, Non-circulating to the pub

P ANCHORAGE PUBLIC LIBRARY*, Z J Loussac Public Library, 3600 Denali St, 99503. SAN 330-4329. Tel: 907-343-2975. Interlibrary Loan Service Tel: 907-343-2826. FAX: 907-343-2930. TDD: 907-563-0872. Web Site: libguides.anchoragelibrary.org/Loussac, www.anchoragelibrary.org. *Dir,* Mary Jo Torgeson; Tel: 907-343-2892, E-mail: torgesonmj@muni.org; *Coll Develop Coordr,* Laura Baldwin; Tel: 907-343-2980, E-mail: baldwinls@muni.org; *Adult Serv Coordr,* Stacia McGourty; Tel: 907-343-2856, E-mail: mcgourtysa@muni.org; *Youth Serv,* Elizabeth Nicolai; Tel: 907-343-2840, E-mail: nicolaiel@muni.org; Staff 78.9 (MLS 20.6, Non-MLS 58.3)
Founded 1945. Pop 301,134; Circ 1,876,368
Jan 2013-Dec 2013 Income (Main & Associated Libraries) $11,226,490, State $320,250, City $10,448,481, Locally Generated Income $111,000, Other $337,750. Mats Exp $1,152,300, Books $649,934, Per/Ser (Incl. Access Fees) $50,813, Other Print Mats $16,732, AV Mat $236,379, Electronic Ref Mat (Incl. Access Fees) $198,442. Sal $6,068,101 (Prof $6,068,101)
Library Holdings: Audiobooks 46,845; AV Mats 63,779; e-books 9,150; Bk Vols 481,861; Per Subs 751
Special Collections: Alaska Coll, bks, ms, maps, micro, newsp clippings, personal papers, photos; Loussac Children's Literature Coll; Patent & Trademark. Oral History; State Document Depository; US Document Depository
Subject Interests: Alaskana
Automation Activity & Vendor Info: (Acquisitions) SirsiDynix; (Cataloging) SirsiDynix; (Circulation) SirsiDynix
Wireless access
Function: Adult bk club, After school storytime, Art exhibits, Audiobks via web, Bks on CD, Children's prog, Computers for patron use, Digital talking bks, Electronic databases & coll, Family literacy, Free DVD rentals, Genealogy discussion group, Holiday prog, Homework prog, ILL available, Magnifiers for reading, Mail & tel request accepted, Music CDs, Outside serv via phone, mail, e-mail & web, OverDrive digital audio bks, Photocopying/Printing, Preschool outreach, Prog for adults, Prog for children & young adult, Ref serv available, Senior outreach, Story hour, Summer reading prog, Teen prog, Telephone ref, Wheelchair accessible, Workshops
Publications: Activities Calendar (Monthly); Annual Report
Partic in Alaska Library Network; OCLC Online Computer Library Center, Inc
Special Services for the Deaf - Adult & family literacy prog; Sign lang interpreter upon request for prog; Staff with knowledge of sign lang; TDD equip
Special Services for the Blind - BiFolkal kits; Bks available with recordings; Bks on CD; Large print bks; Magnifiers; Playaways (bks on MP3); Sound rec
Open Mon-Thurs 10-9, Fri & Sat 10-6, Sun 1-5
Friends of the Library Group
Branches: 4
CHUGIAK-EAGLE RIVER BRANCH, Eagle River Town Ctr, 12001 Business Blvd, No 176, Eagle River, 99577, SAN 330-4353. Tel: 907-343-1530. FAX: 907-694-2955. E-mail: LibraryChugiakEagleRiver@muni.org. Web Site: libguides.anchoragelibrary.org/ChugiakEagleRiver. *Br Mgr,* Nancy Clark; Tel: 907-343-1533, E-mail: clarkne@muni.org
Open Tues 12-7, Wed 11-7, Thurs-Sat 10-6
Friends of the Library Group
SCOTT & WESLEY GERRISH LIBRARY, 250 Egloff Dr, Girdwood, 99587. (Mail add: PO Box 169, Girdwood, 99587-0169), SAN 330-4388. Tel: 907-343-4024. FAX: 907-783-3118. E-mail: LibraryGirdwood@muni.org. Web Site: libguides.anchoragelibrary.org/Girdwood. *Br Mgr,* Claire Agni; Tel: 907-343-4074, E-mail: AgniCL@muni.org
Open Tues & Thurs-Sat 10-6, Wed 1-8
Friends of the Library Group
MOUNTAIN VIEW BRANCH, 120 Bragaw St, 99508. Tel: 907-343-2818. E-mail: LibraryMountainView@muni.org. Web Site: libguides.anchoragelibrary.org/MountainView. *Br Mgr,* Virginia McClure; Tel: 907-343-2907, E-mail: McClureVC@muni.org
Automation Activity & Vendor Info: (Acquisitions) SirsiDynix; (Cataloging) SirsiDynix; (Circulation) SirsiDynix
Special Services for the Deaf - Sign lang interpreter upon request for prog; Staff with knowledge of sign lang
Special Services for the Blind - BiFolkal kits; Bks on CD; Cassettes; Large print bks; Playaways (bks on MP3); Recorded bks; Sound rec; Talking bks from Braille Inst
Open Tues & Wed-Fri 11-7, Thurs 11-6, Fri & Sat 10-6
Friends of the Library Group
MULDOON BRANCH, 1251 Muldoon Rd, Ste 158, 99504, SAN 325-4380. Tel: 907-343-4223. Circulation Tel: 907-343-4032. FAX: 907-337-2122. E-mail: LibraryMuldoon@muni.org. Web Site: libguides.anchoragelibrary.org/Muldoon. *Br Mgr,* Jim Curran; Tel: 903-343-4030, E-mail: CurranJM@muni.org
Publications: Business & Company ASAP; Computer Database; General Reference Center (Index to periodicals); Health Reference Center; National Newspapers Index
Open Tues & Wed 11-7, Thurs & Fri 10-6, Sat 11-6
Friends of the Library Group

L COOK INLET PRE-TRIAL FACILITY LIBRARY*, 1300 E Fourth Ave, 99501. Tel: 907-269-0943. FAX: 907-269-0905. *Educ Coordr,* Robert Bailey; E-mail: robert.bailey@alaska.gov
Library Holdings: Bk Vols 1,000
Restriction: Not open to pub

S SPECIAL EDUCATION SERVICE AGENCY LIBRARY, 3501 Denali St, Ste 101, 99503. SAN 371-7720. Tel: 907-334-1301. FAX: 907-562-0545. TDD: 907-563-8284, Web Site: sesa.org. *Librn,* Anne Freitag; E-mail: afreitag@sesa.org; Staff 1 (MLS 1)
Founded 1987
Library Holdings: Audiobooks 1; AV Mats 473; Bks-By-Mail 3,432; Bks on Deafness & Sign Lang 552; Braille Volumes 258; CDs 234; DVDs 474; e-books 42; e-journals 11; High Interest/Low Vocabulary Bk Vols 46; Large Print Bks 34; Music Scores 6; Bk Titles 3,432; Bk Vols 4,643; Per Subs 26; Spec Interest Per Sub 26; Videos 794
Special Collections: Alaska Autism Resource Center; Assistive Technology Equipment
Subject Interests: Autism Spectrum disorders & related topics, Blindness, Deafness, Emotional disabilities, Hearing impaired, Low vision, Spec educ
Automation Activity & Vendor Info: (Acquisitions) LibraryWorld, Inc; (Cataloging) LibraryWorld, Inc; (Circulation) LibraryWorld, Inc; (OPAC) LibraryWorld, Inc; (Serials) LibraryWorld, Inc
Wireless access
Function: 24/7 Online cat, Audio & video playback equip for onsite use, CD-ROM, Computers for patron use, Digital talking bks, Distance learning,

E-Readers, Electronic databases & coll, Free DVD rentals, Games & aids for people with disabilities, Health sci info serv, Internet access, Magazines, Magnifiers for reading, Mail & tel request accepted, Mail loans to mem, Online cat, Online ref, Orientations, Outside serv via phone, mail, e-mail & web, Photocopying/Printing, Printer for laptops & handheld devices, Ref serv available, Scanner, Study rm, Telephone ref, Wheelchair accessible
Partic in Alaska Library Network; OCLC Online Computer Library Center, Inc
Special Services for the Deaf - Am sign lang & deaf culture; Assistive tech; Bks on deafness & sign lang; Closed caption videos; Coll on deaf educ; High interest/low vocabulary bks; Spec interest per; TTY equip; Videos & decoder
Special Services for the Blind - Assistive/Adapted tech devices, equip & products; Braille bks; Braille equip; Braille paper; Cassette playback machines; Children's Braille; Closed circuit TV magnifier; Computer access aids; Daisy reader; Home delivery serv; Info on spec aids & appliances; Inspiration software; Large type calculator; Lending of low vision aids; Low vision equip; Magnifiers; Talking calculator; Videos on blindness & physical disabilties
Restriction: Open to pub by appt only

GL UNITED STATES COURTS LIBRARY*, 222 W Seventh Ave, Rm 181, 99513-7586. SAN 300-2470. Tel: 907-271-5655. FAX: 907-271-5640. E-mail: anchoragelibrary@lb9.uscourts.gov. Web Site: www.akd.uscourts.gov/united-states-federal-court-library. *Librn,* Anna Russell; E-mail: anna_russell@lb9.uscourts.gov; Staff 1 (MLS 1)
Library Holdings: Bk Titles 9,000; Bk Vols 26,000; Per Subs 12
Special Collections: Alaska District Court Historical Records; Alaska National Interest Lands Conservation Act; Alaska Native Claims Settlement Act & other Alaska Titles
Subject Interests: Law
Automation Activity & Vendor Info: (Cataloging) OCLC; (OPAC) SirsiDynix
Wireless access
Function: Res libr
Publications: Audio Visual Holdings List; Microfiche Holdings List; Pathfinders; Periodicals List
Partic in OCLC Online Computer Library Center, Inc
Open Mon-Fri 9-3
Restriction: Restricted access

C UNIVERSITY OF ALASKA ANCHORAGE CONSORTIUM LIBRARY*, 3211 Providence Dr, 99508-8176, SAN 300-2497. Tel: 907-786-1871. Reference Tel: 907-786-1848. FAX: 907-786-1834. Web Site: www.consortiumlibrary.org. *Dean of Libr,* Stephen Rollins; Tel: 907-786-1825, E-mail: sjrollins@uaa.alaska.edu; *Head, Admin Budget,* Kate Gordon; Tel: 907-786-1903; *Head, Alaska Med Libr,* Kathy Murray; Tel: 907-786-1870; *Head, Archives & Spec Coll,* Arlene Schmuland; Tel: 907-786-1849; *Head, Circ, Head, ILL,* Robin Hanson; Tel: 907-786-1871; *Acq, Head, Coll Develop,* Jodee Kuden; Tel: 907-786-1875; *Head, Libr Syst,* Mike Robinson; Tel: 907-786-1001; *Govt Doc Librn, Head, Tech Serv,* Rebecca Moorman; Tel: 907-786-1974; *Head, Ref & Instruction,* Page Brannon; Tel: 907-786-1873, E-mail: ayref@uaa.alaska.edu; *Med Ref Librn,* Sally Bremner; *Web Librn,* Coral Sheldon-Hess; *Archives,* Megan Friedel; *Archivist,* Mariecris Gatlabayan; *E-Res Mgt,* Christie Ericson; Tel: 907-786-1990; *Ref & Instruction,* Anna Bjartmarsdottir; *Ref & Instruction,* Juli Braund-Allen; *Ref & Instruction,* Daria Carle; *Ref & Instruction,* Christina Carter; *Ref & Instruction,* Ralph Courtney; *Ref & Instruction,* Judy Green; *Ref & Instruction,* Kevin Keating; *Ref & Instruction,* Deborah Mole; *Ref Serv,* Nancy Lesh. Subject Specialists: *Engr,* Kate Gordon; *Health sci,* Kathy Murray; *Culinary, Phys educ, Recreation,* Robin Hanson; *Computer sci,* Mike Robinson; *Govt doc,* Rebecca Moorman; *Justice,* Page Brannon; *Health sci,* Sally Bremner; *Engr,* Coral Sheldon-Hess; *Women's studies,* Mariecris Gatlabayan; *Foreign lang,* Christie Ericson; *English,* Anna Bjartmarsdottir; *Art, Philos, Relig,* Juli Braund-Allen; *Sciences,* Daria Carle; *Bus,* Christina Carter; *Anthrop, Music, Soc sci,* Ralph Courtney; *Educ,* Judy Green; *Hist, Polit sci,* Kevin Keating; *Communications,* Deborah Mole; *Alaskana,* Nancy Lesh; Staff 21 (MLS 21)
Founded 1973. Enrl 11,650; Fac 576; Highest Degree: Master
Library Holdings: e-books 13,266; e-journals 48,952; Music Scores 1,500; Bk Titles 499,697; Bk Vols 789,648; Per Subs 3,700
Special Collections: Alaskana & Polar Regions Coll; Archives & Manuscripts Coll; Music Coll. State Document Depository; US Document Depository
Subject Interests: Alaskana, Health sci
Automation Activity & Vendor Info: (Acquisitions) SirsiDynix; (Cataloging) SirsiDynix; (Circulation) SirsiDynix; (Course Reserve) SirsiDynix; (ILL) OCLC; (OPAC) SirsiDynix; (Serials) SirsiDynix
Function: Archival coll, Art exhibits, Audiobks via web, Computers for patron use, Distance learning, Doc delivery serv, Electronic databases & coll, Govt ref serv, Health sci info serv, ILL available, Microfiche/film & reading machines, Music CDs, Online cat, Online ref, Photocopying/Printing, Scanner, Wheelchair accessible
Partic in Alaska Library Network

C ENVIRONMENT & NATURAL RESOURCES INSTITUTE ARCTIC ENVIRONMENT & DATA INFORMATION CENTER LIBRARY*, 707 A St, 99501, SAN 300-2500. Tel: 907-257-2732. FAX: 907-257-2707. *Info Spec,* Judy Alward; E-mail: anjaa@uaa.alaska.edu
Founded 1972
Library Holdings: Bk Titles 8,800
Special Collections: Alaska Department of Transportation & Public Facilities Statewide Research, rpts; Alaska Native Regional Corporations Annual Reports; Alaska Oil & Gas Association Reports; Alaska Oil Spill Commission Coll; Alyeska's Port Valdez Environmental Monitoring Studies; ARCO Arctic Environmental Reports; Arctic Petroleum Operators Association Publications; Climatological Data for Alaska; Depository for Arctic Petroleum Operators Association & for Alaska Oil & Gas Association; National Association of Corrosion Engineers, Alaska Section, Corrosion Book & Technical Reports Coll; Report Series of Various State Agencies; University of Alaska Institute Reports. State Document Depository; US Document Depository
Subject Interests: Alaska climate res, Alaska environ studies, Arctic res, Natural sci
Publications: Bibliographies; Climate & Environmental Atlases; Maps; Pamphlets; Posters; Technical Reports

BARROW

P TUZZY CONSORTIUM LIBRARY*, 5421 North Star St, 99723. (Mail add: PO Box 2130, 99723-2130), SAN 376-3609. Tel: 907-852-4050. Toll Free Tel: 800-478-6916. FAX: 907-852-4059. E-mail: tuzzy@tuzzy.org. Web Site: www.tuzzy.org. *Libr Dir,* Tess Williams; E-mail: teressa.williams@tuzzy.org; *Engagement Librn, Outreach Librn,* Jasmine Templet; E-mail: jasmine.templet@tuzzy.org; *Archivist, Tech Serv Librn,* Jason Russell; E-mail: jason.russell@tuzzy.org; Staff 2 (MLS 2)
Founded 1989. Pop 7,481; Circ 36,094. Sal $346,814 (Prof $153,335)
Library Holdings: CDs 1,300; DVDs 4,000; e-books 4,803; Bk Titles 50,903; Bk Vols 55,000; Per Subs 153; Talking Bks 335; Videos 6,498
Special Collections: Arctic Related Rare Books
Automation Activity & Vendor Info: (Cataloging) SirsiDynix; (Circulation) SirsiDynix; (Course Reserve) SirsiDynix; (ILL) OCLC FirstSearch; (OPAC) SirsiDynix-iBistro; (Serials) SirsiDynix
Wireless access
Partic in Alaska Library Network
Open Mon, Fri & Sat 12-6, Tues-Thurs 9-8
Friends of the Library Group

BETHEL

P KUSKOKWIM CONSORTIUM LIBRARY, Yupiit Picirarait Cultural Ctr, 420 State Hwy, 99559. (Mail add: PO Box 368, 99559-0368), SAN 300-2535. Tel: 907-543-4516. Administration Tel: 907-543-4517. FAX: 907-543-4503. E-mail: bethel.library@alaska.edu. Web Site: www.uaf.edu/bethellibrary. *Libr Dir,* Theresa Quiner; E-mail: tquiner@alaska.edu; *Adult Serv Coordr,* Eleanor Oser; *Youth Serv Coordr,* Mikayla Miller; Staff 3 (MLS 1, Non-MLS 2)
Founded 1970. Pop 15,000
Library Holdings: Bk Vols 35,700; Per Subs 63; Talking Bks 2,454; Videos 1,405
Special Collections: Alaska History
Automation Activity & Vendor Info: (Cataloging) SirsiDynix; (Circulation) SirsiDynix; (ILL) OCLC; (OPAC) SirsiDynix
Wireless access
Partic in Alaska Library Network
Friends of the Library Group

S YUKON-KUSKOKWIM CORRECTIONAL CENTER LIBRARY, 1000 Chief Eddie Hoffman Hwy, 99559. (Mail add: PO Box 400, 99559). Tel: 907-543-8491. FAX: 907-543-4475. Web Site: doc.alaska.gov/institutions/yukon-kuskokwim. *Educ Coordr,* Hugh Dyment; E-mail: hugh.dyment@alaska.gov
Library Holdings: Bk Titles 250
Special Collections: Alaska Native
Subject Interests: Fiction, How-to-do-it info, Substance abuse prevention & treatment

BIG LAKE

P BIG LAKE PUBLIC LIBRARY*, 3140 S Big Lake Rd, 99652. (Mail add: PO Box 520829, 99652-0829), SAN 376-3625. Tel: 907-861-7635. FAX: 907-892-6546. E-mail: biglake.library@matsugov.us. Web Site: www.matsugov.us/msln/biglake. *Librn,* Jo Cassidy; E-mail: jcassidy@matsugov.us
Founded 1986. Pop 25,615; Circ 74,041
Library Holdings: AV Mats 1,342; Large Print Bks 257; Bk Titles 18,769; Per Subs 58; Talking Bks 1,238

Automation Activity & Vendor Info: (Cataloging) SirsiDynix; (Circulation) SirsiDynix; (ILL) SirsiDynix; (OPAC) SirsiDynix
Wireless access
Partic in Alaska Library Network
Open Mon, Wed & Fri 10-6, Tues & Thurs 10-8, Sat 11-6
Friends of the Library Group

CANTWELL

P CANTWELL COMMUNITY-SCHOOL LIBRARY*, Mile 133-5 Denali Hwy & Second Ave, 99729. (Mail add: PO Box 29, 99729-0029). Tel: 907-768-2372. FAX: 907-768-2500. Web Site: www.dbsd.org/CS/1130-Library.html. *Dir,* JoElla Blanchard; *Sch Librn,* Joanna Cockman; E-mail: joannacockman@dbsd.org
Library Holdings: Bk Vols 11,312; Per Subs 30
Automation Activity & Vendor Info: (Cataloging) Chancery SMS; (Circulation) Chancery SMS; (OPAC) Chancery SMS
Partic in Alaska Library Network
Open Mon & Tues 4-9, Sat 2-5

CHINIAK

P CHINIAK PUBLIC LIBRARY*, 43318 Spruce Way, 99615. (Mail add: PO Box 5610, 99615-5610), SAN 376-3641. E-mail: chiniaklibrary@gmail.com. Web Site: chiniaklibrary.org. *Co-Dir,* Susan Baker
Pop 75
Library Holdings: DVDs 100; Videos 300
Wireless access
Open Thurs 4:30-7:30

COFFMAN COVE

§P COFFMAN COVE COMMUNITY LIBRARY, 113 NW Denali Ally, 99918. Tel: 907-329-2080. Web Site: www.facebook.com/coffmancovelibrary.
Founded 2002
Partic in Alaska Library Network
Open Mon 9-4 & 5-7, Tues 11-2 & 5-7, Wed 9-1 & 5-7, Thurs 12-3:30 & 4-5:30, Fri 10-2, Sat 10-Noon, Sun 11-1

COOPER LANDING

P COOPER LANDING COMMUNITY LIBRARY*, 18511 Bean Creek Rd, 99572. (Mail add: PO Box 517, 99572-0517), SAN 322-8460. Tel: 907-595-1241. FAX: 907-595-1241. E-mail: cooperlandinglibrary@gmail.com. Web Site: www.cooperlandinglibrary.com. *Dir,* Kay Thomas; Tel: 907-599-1643, E-mail: qenqay@arctic.net; Staff 20 (Non-MLS 20)
Founded 1983. Pop 300
Jul 2020-Jun 2021. Mats Exp $5,200, Books $3,500, Per/Ser (Incl. Access Fees) $50, AV Mat $750, Electronic Ref Mat (Incl. Access Fees) $900
Library Holdings: Bks-By-Mail 400; DVDs 600; Bk Titles 3,500
Subject Interests: Alaskana
Wireless access
Function: 24/7 Online cat, Adult bk club
Partic in Alaska Library Network
Open Mon & Tues 1-3, Wed 12-3, Thurs 12:30-3 & 5-7, Fri 1-5, Sat 11-3
Friends of the Library Group

COPPER CENTER

P THE FRANCES KIBBLE KENNY LAKE PUBLIC LIBRARY*, Mile 5 Edgerton Hwy, 99573. (Mail add: HC 60, Box 223, 99573-0223). Tel: 907-822-3015. E-mail: kennylakelibrary@yahoo.com. *Librn,* Lil Gilmore; *Librn,* Ruth McHenry
Pop 410; Circ 3,802
Library Holdings: AV Mats 1,300; Bk Vols 6,000
Wireless access
Partic in Alaska Library Network
Open Mon & Thurs-Sat 1-4, Tues 4-7
Friends of the Library Group

CORDOVA

P CORDOVA PUBLIC LIBRARY*, 601 First St, 99574. (Mail add: PO Box 1170, 99574-1170), SAN 300-2543. Tel: 907-424-6667. FAX: 907-424-6668. Web Site: www.cordovalibrary.org.
Founded 1908. Pop 3,000; Circ 27,397
Library Holdings: Bk Titles 25,000; Per Subs 70
Special Collections: State Document Depository
Subject Interests: Alaskana, Arts & crafts, Educ, Local hist, Natural sci
Wireless access
Partic in Alaska Library Network
Open Tues-Thurs 10-8, Fri 10-6, Sat & Sun 12-5
Friends of the Library Group

CRAIG

P CRAIG PUBLIC LIBRARY*, 504 Third St, 99921. (Mail add: PO Box 769, 99921-0769), SAN 300-2551. Tel: 907-826-3281. FAX: 907-826-3280. E-mail: library@craigak.com. Web Site: craigak.com/library. *Libr Dir,* Angela Matthews; *Asst Librn,* Michelle Winrod
Founded 1934. Pop 5,000; Circ 14,000
Library Holdings: Bk Titles 10,900; Per Subs 73
Subject Interests: Alaska
Automation Activity & Vendor Info: (Cataloging) OCLC WorldShare Interlibrary Loan; (Circulation) Follett Software; (OPAC) Follett Software
Wireless access
Partic in Alaska Library Network
Open Mon 12-5 & 7-9, Tues-Thurs 10-5 & 7-9, Fri 10-5, Sat 11-3
Friends of the Library Group

P HOLLIS PUBLIC LIBRARY*, PO Box 764, 99921. SAN 376-3595. Tel: 907-530-7112. E-mail: hollispubliclibrary@gmail.com. *Dir,* Sandy Curtis
Founded 1985
Library Holdings: Bk Titles 9,500; Bk Vols 16,000
Wireless access
Partic in Alaska Library Network
Open Mon & Fri 3-7, Tues 1-4, Wed 8-2, Sat 10-2
Friends of the Library Group

DEERING

P IPNATCHIAQ PUBLIC LIBRARY*, 59 Main St, 99736. (Mail add: PO Box 36070, 99736-0070). Tel: 907-363-2136. FAX: 907-363-2156. *Librn,* Nellie M Brown
Founded 1983. Pop 158; Circ 467
Library Holdings: Bk Titles 6,434; Bk Vols 8,184; Per Subs 21
Special Collections: Oral History
Open Mon-Sat 6pm-8pm

DELTA JUNCTION

P DELTA COMMUNITY LIBRARY, 2291 Deborah St, 99737. (Mail add: PO Box 229, 99737-0229). Tel: 907-895-4102. FAX: 907-895-4457. E-mail: deltalibrary@wildak.net. Web Site: deltajunction.us/delta-community-library. *Libr Dir,* Tiki Levinson; Staff 1 (Non-MLS 1)
Founded 1960. Pop 4,500
Jul 2021-Jun 2022 Income $247,149, State $7,000, City $235,149, Locally Generated Income $6,500, Other $12,000. Mats Exp $23,625, Books $10,000, Per/Ser (Incl. Access Fees) $450, AV Equip $1,500, AV Mat $1,500, Electronic Ref Mat (Incl. Access Fees) $2,000, Presv $175. Sal $134,283 (Prof $65,719)
Library Holdings: Audiobooks 615; Bks on Deafness & Sign Lang 21; DVDs 3,448; High Interest/Low Vocabulary Bk Vols 35; Large Print Bks 15; Bk Titles 6,698; Bk Vols 7,400; Per Subs 12; Spec Interest Per Sub 3
Special Collections: Local Alaskana; Newspapers (Walker's Weekly, Midnight Sun & Delta Paper). Municipal Document Depository
Subject Interests: Alaskana
Automation Activity & Vendor Info: (Cataloging) Follett Software; (Circulation) Follett Software; (OPAC) Follett Software; (Serials) EBSCO Discovery Service
Wireless access
Function: 24/7 Electronic res, 24/7 Online cat, Adult bk club, Audiobks via web, Bk club(s), Bks on CD, Children's prog, Computers for patron use, E-Readers, Electronic databases & coll, Family literacy, Free DVD rentals, Holiday prog, Homebound delivery serv, ILL available, Internet access, Laminating, Large print keyboards, Life-long learning prog for all ages, Magazines, Magnifiers for reading, Mail & tel request accepted, Mango lang, Movies, Notary serv, Online cat, OverDrive digital audio bks, Photocopying/Printing, Preschool outreach, Preschool reading prog, Printer for laptops & handheld devices, Prog for adults, Prog for children & young adult, Ref serv available, Scanner, Spanish lang bks, Story hour, Summer & winter reading prog, Summer reading prog, Tax forms, Telephone ref, Wheelchair accessible, Winter reading prog, Workshops
Partic in Alaska Library Network
Special Services for the Deaf - Closed caption videos
Special Services for the Blind - Accessible computers; Bks on CD; Copier with enlargement capabilities; Home delivery serv; Internet workstation with adaptive software; Magnifiers
Open Mon-Fri 10-6, Sat 11-5
Friends of the Library Group

DILLINGHAM

P DILLINGHAM PUBLIC LIBRARY*, 306 D St W, 99576. (Mail add: PO Box 870, 99576-0870), SAN 322-6557. Tel: 907-842-5610. FAX: 907-842-4237. E-mail: librarian@dillinghamak.us. Web Site: www.dillinghamak.us. *Librn,* Sonja Marx; Staff 1 (Non-MLS 1)
Founded 1949. Pop 2,413

Automation Activity & Vendor Info: (Acquisitions) ComPanion Corp; (Circulation) ComPanion Corp; (OPAC) ComPanion Corp
Wireless access
Partic in Alaska Library Network
Special Services for the Deaf - Bks on deafness & sign lang
Open Mon, Tues & Thurs 12-5, Wed 10-5:30, Fri 2-5:30, Sat 10-2
Friends of the Library Group

EAGLE

P EAGLE PUBLIC LIBRARY*, Second & Amundsen, 99738. (Mail add: PO Box 45, 99738), SAN 376-7957. Tel: 907-547-2334. *Dir,* Trish Nix; E-mail: epldirector@outlook.com
Library Holdings: AV Mats 1,840; Bk Vols 10,000; Per Subs 40
Wireless access
Partic in Alaska Library Network
Open Mon 2-8, Thurs 3-9, Sat 1-4

EAGLE RIVER

S ALASKA STATE DEPARTMENT OF CORRECTIONS*, Hiland Mountain Correctional Center Library, 9101 Hesterberg Rd, 99577. SAN 321-026X. Tel: 907-694-9511, 907-696-9188. FAX: 907-694-4507. Web Site: www.correct.state.ak.us/institutions/hiland-mountain. *Educ Coordr,* Karen Jenkins; E-mail: karen.jenkins@alaska.gov; *Educ Coordr,* Michael Clark; E-mail: michael.clark@alaska.gov; Staff 1 (Non-MLS 1)
Founded 1974
Library Holdings: Bk Titles 6,200; Bk Vols 6,500; Per Subs 27
Wireless access
Restriction: Not open to pub

EGEGIK

P EGEGIK VILLAGE LIBRARY*, 289 Airport Rd, 99579. (Mail add: PO Box 29, 99579-0029), SAN 376-6535. Tel: 907-233-2211. E-mail: egegikvillage2013@yahoo.com. *Dir,* Michelle Olsen
Library Holdings: AV Mats 690; Bk Vols 4,500; Per Subs 126
Wireless access
Open Mon-Fri 9-5, Sat 1-5; Tues-Fri (Summer) 9-7, Sat 1-5

EIELSON AFB

A UNITED STATES AIR FORCE*, Eielson Air Force Base Library, 2518 Central Ave, Bldg 3310, 99702. SAN 330-4620. Tel: 907-377-3174. FAX: 907-377-1683. E-mail: eielsonafblibrary@gmail.com. Web Site: www.eielsonafblibrary.org. *Supvry Librn,* Mrs Ashley Mayer; E-mail: ashley.mayer.1@us.af.mil; Staff 6 (MLS 1, Non-MLS 5)
Founded 1946
Library Holdings: AV Mats 3,700; e-books 11; Bk Vols 29,800; Per Subs 63
Special Collections: Arctic Coll; Professional Military Education
Automation Activity & Vendor Info: (Cataloging) SirsiDynix; (Circulation) SirsiDynix; (OPAC) SirsiDynix
Wireless access
Restriction: Not open to pub

ELIM

P ELIM COMMUNITY LIBRARY*, Ernest Nylin Memorial Library, 101 Hillside St, 99739. (Mail add: PO Box 39009, 99739). Tel: 907-890-3441. *Librn,* Position Currently Open
Pop 300
Library Holdings: Bk Titles 7,201; Bk Vols 7,445; Per Subs 38
Function: Audio & video playback equip for onsite use, CD-ROM, Digital talking bks, Distance learning, ILL available, Internet access, Music CDs, Photocopying/Printing, Spoken cassettes & CDs, Summer reading prog, VHS videos, Wheelchair accessible
Library is temporarily closed for repairs 2018-
Open Mon & Fri 1-3, Tues & Thurs 7:30pm-10pm

FAIRBANKS

G BUREAU OF LAND MANAGEMENT LIBRARY*, Fairbanks District Office, 1150 University Ave, 99709-3844. SAN 300-256X. Tel: 907-474-2200. FAX: 907-474-2280, 907-474-2282. E-mail: FairbanksDistrict@blm.gov. Web Site: aurora.ak.blm.gov. *Natural Res Mgr,* Elliott Lowe; Tel: 907-474-2307
Library Holdings: Bk Vols 3,000
Special Collections: Alaska Statutes Coll; Department of the Interior Decisions Coll; Interior Board of Land Appeals (IBLA) decisions; United States Codes of Federal Regulations Coll; United States Statutes at Large Coll
Subject Interests: Natural res mgt
Partic in Federal Library & Information Network
Restriction: Non-circulating to the pub

SR CATHOLIC DIOCESE OF FAIRBANKS*, Library Resource Center, Chancery Bldg, 1316 Peger Rd, 99709-5199. Tel: 907-374-9500. FAX: 907-374-9580. E-mail: library@cbna.org. Web Site: dioceseoffairbanks.org. *Archives Coordr,* David Schienle; Tel: 907-374-9555
Library Holdings: Bk Vols 4,541
Special Collections: Alaskana Coll
Subject Interests: Theol
Open Mon-Fri 8:30-4:30

S FAIRBANKS CORRECTIONAL CENTER LIBRARY*, 1931 Eagan Ave, 99701. Tel: 907-458-6700, 907-458-6739. FAX: 907-458-6751. Web Site: www.correct.state.ak.us/institutions/fairbanks. *Educ Coordr,* Ms C Howard
Restriction: Not open to pub

M FAIRBANKS MEMORIAL HOSPITAL LIBRARY*, 1650 Cowles St, 99701-5998. Tel: 907-458-5580. E-mail: fhpeducation@foundationhealth.org. *Librn,* Corlis Taylor; Staff 1 (MLS 1)
Library Holdings: Bk Vols 1,000; Per Subs 150
Function: Doc delivery serv, Electronic databases & coll, For res purposes, Health sci info serv, ILL available, Internet access, Mail & tel request accepted, Orientations, Photocopying/Printing, Ref serv available
Restriction: Hospital employees & physicians only, Not open to pub, Prof mat only

P FAIRBANKS NORTH STAR BOROUGH LIBRARIES*, Noel Wien Library, 1215 Cowles St, 99701. SAN 300-2578. Tel: 907-459-1020. Circulation Tel: 907-459-1048. FAX: 907-459-1024. E-mail: circulation@fnsb.us. Web Site: fnsblibrary.org. *Libr Dir,* Melissa Harter; E-mail: mharter@fnsblibrary.us
Founded 1909. Pop 87,650; Circ 561,979
Library Holdings: AV Mats 32,096; e-journals 25; Bk Vols 293,609; Per Subs 999
Special Collections: State Document Depository
Subject Interests: Alaska
Automation Activity & Vendor Info: (Acquisitions) SirsiDynix; (Serials) SirsiDynix
Wireless access
Partic in Alaska Library Network
Open Mon-Thurs 10-9, Fri 10-6, Sat 10-5, Sun (Sept-May) 1-5
Friends of the Library Group
Branches: 1
NORTH POLE BRANCH, 656 NPHS Blvd, North Pole, 99705, SAN 324-2463. Tel: 907-488-6101. FAX: 907-488-8465. E-mail: northpole@fnsblibrary.us. *Libr Dir,* Melissa Harter
Open Tues & Wed 11-9, Thurs & Fri 11-6, Sat 11-5
Friends of the Library Group

S GEOPHYSICAL INSTITUTE*, Keith B Mather Library, Int Arctic Research Ctr, 2156 Koyukuk Dr, 99775. (Mail add: PO Box 757320, 99775), SAN 330-4833. Tel: 907-474-7503. Administration Tel: 907-474-7512. E-mail: uaf-gi-library@alaska.edu. Web Site: www.gi.alaska.edu/services/mather-library. *Libr Tech,* Robin Nicholson; E-mail: rnichol3@alaska.edu; Staff 1.5 (MLS 1.5)
Founded 1945
Library Holdings: Bk Vols 68,000
Special Collections: Alaska Department of Transportation Library; International Association of Volcanology & Chemistry of the Earth's Interior Coll; International Geophysical Year (IGY) Coll
Subject Interests: Atmospheric sci, Geophysics, Glaciology, Remote sensing, Seismology, Space sci, Volcanology
Wireless access
Open Mon-Fri 9-5

C UNIVERSITY OF ALASKA FAIRBANKS*, Elmer E Rasmuson Library, 1732 Tanana Dr, 99775. (Mail add: PO Box 756800, 99775-6800), SAN 330-4779. Tel: 907-474-7481. Reference Tel: 907-474-7482. FAX: 907-474-6841. Web Site: www.library.uaf.edu. *Interim Dean of Libr,* Kit Shannon; Tel: 907-474-6194, E-mail: kmshannon@alaska.edu; *Mgr, Coll Serv,* Marie Johnson; Tel: 907-474-7024, E-mail: mhjohnson@alaska.edu; *Fiscal Mgr,* Wendy Frandsen; Tel: 907-474-6696, E-mail: wlfrandsen@alaska.edu; *IT Mgr,* Bob Forshaw; Tel: 907-474-7921, E-mail: raforshaw@alaska.edu; *Pub Serv Coordr,* Paul Adasiak; Tel: 907-474-5354, E-mail: pfadasiak@alaska.edu; *Bibliographer, Curator, Rare Bks & Maps,* Katherine Arndt; Tel: 907-474-6671, E-mail: klarndt@alaska.edu; *Asst Archivist,* Becky Butler; Tel: 907-474-6688, E-mail: rlbutler3@alaska.edu; *Circ,* Robin Andrews; Tel: 907-474-6699, E-mail: randrews@alaska.edu; *Coll Develop Officer,* Karen Jensen; Tel: 907-474-6695, E-mail: kljensen@alaska.edu; *Curator, Oral Hist,* Leslie McCartney; Tel: 907-474-7737, E-mail: lmccartney@alaska.edu; *Film Archivist,* Angela Schmidt; Tel: 907-474-5357, E-mail: ajschmidt@alaska.edu; *ILL,* Colleen Sullivan; Tel: 907-474-5348, E-mail: cmsullivan@alaska.edu. Subject Specialists: *Video,* Marie Johnson; Staff 66 (MLS 12, Non-MLS 54)
Founded 1917. Enrl 5,423; Fac 622; Highest Degree: Doctorate

Library Holdings: Audiobooks 417; AV Mats 27,880; CDs 2,301; DVDs 5,150; Electronic Media & Resources 55,086; Microforms 163,910; Music Scores 6,079; Bk Vols 809,372; Per Subs 7,716; Videos 17,312
Special Collections: Alaska and Polar Regions. Oral History; State Document Depository; US Document Depository
Subject Interests: Alaska & Polar regions, Alaskana
Automation Activity & Vendor Info: (Circulation) SirsiDynix; (Course Reserve) Docutek; (ILL) OCLC; (OPAC) SirsiDynix
Wireless access
Function: Archival coll, Audio & video playback equip for onsite use, Bus archives, CD-ROM, Distance learning, Doc delivery serv, E-Reserves, Electronic databases & coll, Equip loans & repairs, Govt ref serv, ILL available, Music CDs, Photocopying/Printing, Ref & res, VHS videos, Wheelchair accessible
Partic in Alaska Library Network; EPSCoR Science Information Group; Minitex
Special Services for the Deaf - TTY equip
Open Mon-Fri (Winter) 8-6, Sat & Sun 12-6; Mon-Thurs (Spring) 7:30am-10pm. Fri 7:30-7, Sat 11-7, Sun 1-10

FORT RICHARDSON

A FORT RICHARDSON POST LIBRARY*, IMPA-FRA-HRE PL, Bldg 7, Chilkoot Ave, 99505-0055. SAN 376-6314. Tel: 907-384-1648. FAX: 907-384-7534. E-mail: jber.library@gmail.com. Web Site: jberlife.com/library. *Dir,* Pamela Medolo; *Head, Tech Serv,* Jody Evans; Staff 4 (MLS 1, Non-MLS 3)
Founded 1950
Library Holdings: Bk Titles 50,000; Per Subs 125
Special Collections: Artic Coll
Subject Interests: Arctic
Automation Activity & Vendor Info: (Circulation) Horizon; (OPAC) Horizon
Wireless access
Open Mon-Fri 9-8, Sat 10-5

FORT WAINWRIGHT

UNITED STATES ARMY

AM BASSET ARMY HOSPITAL MEDICAL LIBRARY*, 1060 Gaffney Rd, No 7440, 99703-7440. Tel: 907-361-5194. FAX: 907-361-4845. *Libr Tech,* Thomas Bracher
Library Holdings: Bk Titles 1,800; Bk Vols 2,000; Per Subs 119
Subject Interests: Obstetrics & gynecology, Orthopedics, Surgery

A FORT WAINWRIGHT POST LIBRARY*, Santiago Ave, Bldg 3700, 99703. (Mail add: 1060 Gaffney Rd, No 6600, 99703-6600), SAN 330-4957. Tel: 907-353-2642. Administration Tel: 907-353-2645. FAX: 907-353-2609. *Supvr,* Joann Ogreenc; Staff 5 (MLS 1, Non-MLS 4)
Founded 1951
Library Holdings: CDs 1,121; DVDs 1,529; Bk Vols 41,097; Per Subs 75; Talking Bks 556; Videos 2,816
Special Collections: Alaskana; Children's Coll
Function: Audio & video playback equip for onsite use, Bks on cassette, Bks on CD, Children's prog, Computers for patron use, Electronic databases & coll, ILL available, Mail & tel request accepted, Music CDs, Online cat, Photocopying/Printing, Ref serv available, Scanner, Story hour, Summer reading prog, VHS videos, Wheelchair accessible
Partic in OCLC Online Computer Library Center, Inc
Open Mon-Thurs 10-7, Fri 10-6, Sat 10-4
Restriction: Authorized patrons

A MILITARY OCCUPATIONAL SPECIALTY LIBRARY*, Bldg 2110, Montgomery Rd, 99703. (Mail add: 1060 Gaffnee Rd, Box 6600, 99703). Tel: 907-353-7297. FAX: 907-353-7472. *Librn,* Nikki Tuck
Library Holdings: Bk Vols 5,000; Per Subs 100
Restriction: Mil only

GALENA

P CHARLES EVANS COMMUNITY LIBRARY*, 299 Antoski Dr, 99741. (Mail add: PO Box 299, 99741-0299), SAN 376-6934. Tel: 907-656-1883, Ext 127. FAX: 907-656-1368. Web Site: library.galenaalaska.org. *Librn,* Ayla Kalke; E-mail: ayla.kalke@galenanet.com; Staff 2 (Non-MLS 2)
Founded 1976. Pop 675; Circ 6,852
Library Holdings: AV Mats 175; DVDs 300; Bk Vols 25,000; Per Subs 25; Videos 400
Automation Activity & Vendor Info: (Cataloging) Follett Software; (Circulation) Follett Software; (OPAC) Follett Software
Open Mon-Thurs 4:30pm-6:45pm, Sun 10-3

GLENNALLEN

P COPPER VALLEY COMMUNITY LIBRARY*, Mile 186 Glenn Hwy, 99588. (Mail add: PO Box 173, 99588-0173), SAN 372-5316. Tel: 907-822-5427. Automation Services Tel: 907-259-8526. FAX: 907-822-5427. E-mail: cvcla@cvinternet.net. Web Site: www.coppervalleylibrary.org. *Coordr,* Sharron Ables
Founded 1954. Pop 2,037; Circ 18,000
Library Holdings: Bk Vols 18,523; Per Subs 29
Automation Activity & Vendor Info: (Acquisitions) Follett Software; (Cataloging) Follett Software; (Circulation) Follett Software
Wireless access
Function: 24/7 Electronic res, 24/7 Online cat, Art exhibits, Audiobks on Playaways & MP3, Audiobks via web, Bks on CD, Children's prog, Computers for patron use, Digital talking bks, Free DVD rentals, Holiday prog, ILL available, Internet access, Laminating, Magazines, Magnifiers for reading, Mango lang, Meeting rooms, Movies, Online cat, Online ref, Outside serv via phone, mail, e-mail & web, OverDrive digital audio bks, Photocopying/Printing, Scanner, Study rm, Summer reading prog, Tax forms, Wheelchair accessible
Partic in Alaska Library Network
Open Tues-Thurs 1-6, Fri 12-7, Sat 11-6

GUSTAVUS

P GUSTAVUS PUBLIC LIBRARY, PO Box 279, 99826-0279. Tel: 907-697-2350. FAX: 907-697-2249. E-mail: librarian@gustavus.lib.ak.us. Web Site: cms.gustavus-ak.gov/library. *Admin Dir,* Jessie Soder; *Libr Serv Dir,* LeAnn Weikle
Library Holdings: Bk Vols 8,200; Per Subs 30
Wireless access
Partic in Alaska Library Network
Open Mon & Wed 1:30-4:30 & 7-9, Tues & Fri 1:30-4:30, Thurs 10-12 & 1:30-4:30, Sat 11-3

S NATIONAL PARK SERVICE, Glacier Bay National Park & Preserve Library, PO Box 140, 99826-0140. Tel: 907-697-2230. FAX: 907-697-2654. Web Site: www.nps.gov/glba. *Chief, Admin,* Elizabeth Withers; E-mail: elizabeth_withers@nps.gov
Library Holdings: Bk Vols 2,000
Subject Interests: Archaeology, Ethnography, Geol, Glaciology, Hist, Marine biol
Function: Res libr
Open Mon-Fri 8-4:30

HAINES

P HAINES BOROUGH PUBLIC LIBRARY, 111 Third Ave, 99827. (Mail add: PO Box 1089, 99827-1089), SAN 300-2632. Tel: 907-766-6420. FAX: 907-766-2551. E-mail: frontdesk@haineslibrary.org. Web Site: haineslibrary.org. *Dir,* Carolyn Goolsby; E-mail: director@haineslibrary.org; *Asst Dir,* Rebecca Heaton; E-mail: operations@haineslibrary.org; Staff 6 (MLS 1, Non-MLS 5)
Founded 1928. Pop 2,534
Library Holdings: Bk Titles 25,450; Per Subs 97
Special Collections: Alaska Coll, Tlingit
Subject Interests: Alaskana
Automation Activity & Vendor Info: (Cataloging) OCLC; (Circulation) SirsiDynix-WorkFlows; (ILL) OCLC CatExpress; (OPAC) SirsiDynix
Wireless access
Function: 24/7 Electronic res, 24/7 Online cat, Adult bk club, After school storytime, Art exhibits, Audio & video playback equip for onsite use, Audiobks on Playaways & MP3, Audiobks via web, Bk club(s), Bks on cassette, Bks on CD, Chess club, Children's prog, Computer training, Computers for patron use, Digital talking bks, Distance learning, E-Readers, E-Reserves, Electronic databases & coll, Equip loans & repairs, Free DVD rentals, Govt ref serv, Holiday prog, Homework prog, ILL available, Instruction & testing, Internet access, Large print keyboards, Life-long learning prog for all ages, Magazines, Magnifiers for reading, Mail loans to mem, Mango lang, Meeting rooms, Movies, Music CDs, Online cat, Online ref, Orientations, Outside serv via phone, mail, e-mail & web, OverDrive digital audio bks, Photocopying/Printing, Preschool outreach, Prog for adults, Scanner, Senior computer classes, Story hour, Summer reading prog, Tax forms, VHS videos, Wheelchair accessible, Workshops
Partic in Alaska Library Network
Open Mon-Thurs 10-8, Fri 10-6, Sat & Sun 12:30-4:30
Friends of the Library Group

S SHELDON MUSEUM & CULTURAL CENTER LIBRARY*, 11 Main St, 99827. (Mail add: PO Box 269, 99827), SAN 329-1995. Tel: 907-766-2366. FAX: 907-766-2368. Web Site: www.sheldonmuseum.org. *Dir,* Helen Alten; Staff 2 (MLS 2)
Founded 1925
Library Holdings: Bk Titles 1,100; Bk Vols 1,150
Subject Interests: Local hist, State hist, Tlingit art, Tlingit culture
Wireless access
Function: Archival coll, AV serv, Res libr
Restriction: Not a lending libr, Open by appt only

HEALY

P TRI-VALLEY COMMUNITY LIBRARY, Suntrana Rd, 99743. (Mail add: PO Box 518, 99743-0518), SAN 376-3404. Tel: 907-683-2507. Web Site: www.tvclibrary.org. *Libr Dir,* Ticee Graham; E-mail: tvcl.director@gmail.com; Staff 2 (Non-MLS 2)
Founded 1980. Pop 1,000
Library Holdings: Bk Vols 16,900
Automation Activity & Vendor Info: (Cataloging) Chancery SMS; (Circulation) Chancery SMS; (OPAC) Chancery SMS
Wireless access
Partic in Alaska Library Network

HOMER

P HOMER PUBLIC LIBRARY, 500 Hazel Ave, 99603. SAN 320-1414. Tel: 907-235-3180. FAX: 907-235-3136. E-mail: circ@ci.homer.ak.us. Web Site: www.cityofhomer-ak.gov/library. *Libr Dir,* David Berry; Tel: 907-435-3151, E-mail: dberry@ci.homer.ak.us; Staff 9 (MLS 1, Non-MLS 8)
Founded 1944. Pop 13,016; Circ 118,157
Library Holdings: Audiobooks 2,597; DVDs 2,451; Bk Vols 39,954; Per Subs 145
Automation Activity & Vendor Info: (Acquisitions) Evergreen; (Cataloging) Evergreen; (Circulation) Evergreen; (ILL) Clio; (OPAC) Evergreen; (Serials) Evergreen
Wireless access
Function: 24/7 Electronic res, 24/7 Online cat, Adult bk club, Archival coll, Art exhibits, Audiobks via web, AV serv, Bilingual assistance for Spanish patrons, Bks on CD, Children's prog, Computer training, Computers for patron use, Digital talking bks, E-Reserves, Electronic databases & coll, Equip loans & repairs, Family literacy, Free DVD rentals, Games & aids for people with disabilities, Genealogy discussion group, Govt ref serv, Holiday prog, Homebound delivery serv, ILL available, Instruction & testing, Internet access, Life-long learning prog for all ages, Magazines, Magnifiers for reading, Mail & tel request accepted, Mango lang, Meeting rooms, Microfiche/film & reading machines, Movies, Music CDs, Online cat, Online info literacy tutorials on the web & in blackboard, Outreach serv, OverDrive digital audio bks, Photocopying/Printing, Preschool outreach, Preschool reading prog, Prof lending libr, Prog for adults, Prog for children & young adult, Ref serv available, Res libr, Scanner, Senior computer classes, Serves people with intellectual disabilities, Spoken cassettes & CDs, Spoken cassettes & DVDs, Story hour, Study rm, Summer reading prog, Tax forms, Teen prog, Telephone ref, Wheelchair accessible
Partic in Alaska Library Network
Special Services for the Deaf - Sorenson video relay syst
Open Mon, Wed, Fri & Sat 10-6, Tues & Thurs 10-8
Friends of the Library Group

HYDER

P HYDER PUBLIC LIBRARY, 50 Main St, 99923. (Mail add: PO Box 50, 99923-0050), SAN 328-0381. Tel: 250-636-2637.
Circ 1,517
Library Holdings: AV Mats 550; Bk Titles 5,961; Bk Vols 15,000; Per Subs 70
Wireless access

JUNEAU

GL ALASKA DEPARTMENT OF LAW*, Attorney General's Library, PO Box 110300, 99811-0300. SAN 371-0270. Tel: 907-465-3600. FAX: 907-465-2417. Web Site: www.law.state.ak.us. *Librn,* Marinke Van Gelder
Library Holdings: Bk Vols 2,500; Per Subs 35
Open Mon-Fri 8-4

G ALASKA STATE LEGISLATURE, Legislative Reference Library, State Capitol, 99801-1182. SAN 321-074X. Tel: 907-465-3808. Web Site: w3.akleg.gov. *Head Librn,* Jennifer Fletcher; E-mail: jennifer.fletcher@akleg.gov; Staff 2 (MLS 2)
Special Collections: Alaska State Legislature Committee Records; Alaska State Legislature Publications Coll
Wireless access
Open Mon-Fri 8-5

P ALASKA STATE LIBRARY*, 395 Whittier St, 99801. (Mail add: PO Box 110571, 99811-0571), SAN 330-4981. Tel: 907-465-2920. Interlibrary Loan Service Tel: 907-465-2988. Reference Tel: 907-465-2921. Administration Tel: 907-465-2910. FAX: 907-465-2665. Administration FAX: 907-465-2151. E-mail: asl@alaska.gov. Web Site: library.alaska.gov. *Dir, Libr, Archives & Mus,* Patience Frederiksen; Tel: 907-465-2911, E-mail: patience.frederiksen@alaska.gov; *Head, Info Serv,* Freya Anderson; E-mail: freya.anderson@alaska.gov; *Digital Projects Librn,* Anastasia Tarmann; *Electronic Res Librn,* Kate Dunn; E-mail: kate.dunn@alaska.gov; *Librn,* Sorrel Goodwin; *Govt Pub Librn,* Kathleen Fearer; E-mail: kathleen.fearer@alaska.gov; *Outreach Serv Librn,* Claire Imamura; E-mail: claire.imamura@alaska.gov; *Tech Serv Librn,* Virginia Jacobs; E-mail: virginia.jacobs@alaska.gov; *Div Mgr, Operations,* Lisa Golisek-Nankerv; E-mail: lisa.golisek@alaska.gov; *Continuing Educ Coordr,* Julie Niederhauser; E-mail: julie.niederhauser@alaska.gov; *Grants Coordr,* Position Currently Open; *Sch Libr Coordr,* Janet Madsen; E-mail: Janet.Madsen@alaska.gov; *Tech Coordr,* Daniel Cornwall; E-mail: daniel.cornwall@alaska.gov; Staff 27 (MLS 15, Non-MLS 12)
Founded 1957. Pop 741,894
Library Holdings: AV Mats 835; Bk Vols 115,150; Per Subs 300
Special Collections: Alaska History (Wickersham Coll of Alaskana), photos; Alaska Marine History (L H Bayers Coll), doc; Can, Calif & Wash; Salmon Canneries (Alaska Packers Association Records), flm; Trans-Alaska Pipeline Impact, slides. Oral History; State Document Depository; US Document Depository
Subject Interests: Alaskana, Educ, Hist, Libr & info sci, State govt
Automation Activity & Vendor Info: (Cataloging) SirsiDynix; (Circulation) SirsiDynix; (OPAC) SirsiDynix; (Serials) SirsiDynix
Wireless access
Function: 24/7 Electronic res, 24/7 Online cat, Activity rm, Archival coll, Art exhibits, Audiobks via web, Computers for patron use, Digital talking bks, Electronic databases & coll, For res purposes, Govt ref serv, Holiday prog, Homework prog, ILL available, Internet access, Life-long learning prog for all ages, Magazines, Magnifiers for reading, Mail & tel request accepted, Meeting rooms, Microfiche/film & reading machines, Online cat, Online ref, Outreach serv, Outside serv via phone, mail, e-mail & web, OverDrive digital audio bks, Photocopying/Printing, Printer for laptops & handheld devices, Prof lending libr, Prog for adults, Prog for children & young adult, Ref & res, Ref serv available, Res assist avail, Res libr, Scanner, Summer reading prog, Tax forms, Telephone ref, Wheelchair accessible, Workshops
Publications: Indexes to Collection; Information Empowered; Statistics of Alaska Public Libraries
Partic in Alaska Library Network; OCLC Online Computer Library Center, Inc
Special Services for the Blind - Talking bks
Open Mon-Fri 10-4
Friends of the Library Group
Branches: 2
ALASKA HISTORICAL COLLECTIONS, 395 Whittier St, 99801. (Mail add: PO Box 110571, 99811-0571), SAN 300-2667. Tel: 907-465-2925. FAX: 907-465-2990. E-mail: asl.historical@alaska.gov. Web Site: library.alaska.gov/hist/hist.html, www.eed.state.ak.us/lam. *Hist Coll Librn,* James Simard; Tel: 907-465-2926, E-mail: james.simard@alaska.gov; Staff 9 (MLS 5, Non-MLS 4)
Founded 1900
Library Holdings: Bk Vols 37,000
Special Collections: Alaska Juneau Mining Company Records; Alaska Packers Association Records; Alaska-Artic Research; Alaskana (Wickersham Coll); Juneau Area Mining Records; Marine History (L H Bayers), doc; Russian American Coll; Russian History-General & Military (Dolgopolov Coll); Salmon Canneries; Trans-Alaska Pipeline Impact; Vinokouroff Coll; Winter & Pond Photograph Coll. State Document Depository; US Document Depository
Subject Interests: Alaska, Arctic
Function: Res libr
Partic in OCLC Online Computer Library Center, Inc
Publications: Alaska Historical Monograph Series; Alaska Newspapers on Microfilm, 1866-1998; Some Books About Alaska Received (annual)
Open Tues-Fri 10-4
Restriction: Non-circulating to the pub
Friends of the Library Group
TALKING BOOK CENTER
See separate entry under Alaska State Library, Anchorage

P ALASKA STATE LIBRARY, Talking Book Center, 395 Whittier St, 99801. (Mail add: PO Box 110571, 99811-0571), SAN 300-2403. Tel: 907-465-1315. Toll Free Tel: 888-820-4525 (Alaska only). FAX: 907-465-2151. E-mail: tbc@alaska.gov. Web Site: lam.alaska.gov/tbc. *Regional Librn,* Freya Anderson; E-mail: freya.anderson@alaska.gov; Staff 2 (MLS 1, Non-MLS 1)
Founded 1968
Library Holdings: Large Print Bks 2,700; Talking Bks 79,000
Wireless access
Function: ILL available
Special Services for the Blind - Braille alphabet card; Cassette playback machines; Cassettes; Digital talking bk; Digital talking bk machines; Extensive large print coll; Volunteer serv
Open Mon-Fri 8-4:30
Restriction: Registered patrons only

P JUNEAU PUBLIC LIBRARIES*, 292 Marine Way, 99801. SAN 330-5104. Tel: 907-586-5249. FAX: 907-586-6278. E-mail: reference@juneau.org. Web Site: www.juneau.org/library. *Dir,* Robert Barr;

Network Adminr, Dan Coleman; *Circ,* Shari Kitchin; *Coll Develop,* Catherine Melville; *Electronic Serv,* Andi Hirsh; *Info Serv,* Jenna Guenther; *ILL,* Kate Enge; *Youth Serv,* M.J. Grande; *Webmaster,* Patrick McGonegal; Staff 5 (MLS 5)
Founded 1913. Pop 32,000; Circ 300,000
Library Holdings: Bk Vols 122,383; Per Subs 364
Subject Interests: Alaska
Automation Activity & Vendor Info: (Cataloging) SirsiDynix; (Circulation) SirsiDynix; (OPAC) SirsiDynix
Wireless access
Partic in Alaska Library Network
Open Mon-Thurs 11-8, Fri 1-5, Sat-Sun 12-5
Friends of the Library Group
Branches: 2
DOUGLAS PUBLIC, 1016 Third St, Douglas, 99824, SAN 330-5139. Tel: 907-364-2378. FAX: 907-364-2627. *Br Mgr,* LouAnn Gagne
Open Mon-Wed 2-8, Thurs 11-5, Fri-Sun 1-5
Friends of the Library Group
MENDENHALL VALLEY, 3025 Dimond Park Loop, 99801, SAN 330-5163. Tel: 907-789-0125. FAX: 907-790-2213. *Br Mgr,* Shari Kitchin
Open Mon-Thurs 10-8, Fri 10-7, Sat 10-6, Sun 12-5
Friends of the Library Group

C UNIVERSITY OF ALASKA SOUTHEAST*, William A Egan Library, 11066 Auke Lake Way, BE1, 99801. SAN 300-2691. Tel: 907-796-6300. Interlibrary Loan Service Tel: 907-796-6470. Reference Tel: 907-796-6502. FAX: 907-796-6249. Administration FAX: 907-796-6302. E-mail: uas.eganlibrary@alaska.edu. Web Site: www.uas.alaska.edu/library. *Regional Libr Dir,* Elise Tomlinson; Tel: 907-796-6467, E-mail: elise.tomlinson@alaska.edu; *Info Literacy Librn,* Megan J Watson; Tel: 907-796-6515, E-mail: mjwatson4@alaska.edu; *Outreach Serv Librn,* Jennifer Ward; Tel: 907-796-6285, E-mail: jdbrown@alaska.edu; *Pub Serv Librn,* Jonas Lamb; Tel: 907-796-6440, E-mail: j.lamb@alaska.edu; *Tech Serv Librn,* David B Cox, II; Tel: 907-796-6345, E-mail: dbcoxii@alaska.edu; *ILL,* Beatrice Franklin; E-mail: bsfranklin@alaska.edu. Subject Specialists: *Bus, Educ,* Jennifer Ward; *Sciences,* Jonas Lamb; Staff 12 (MLS 5, Non-MLS 7)
Founded 1956. Enrl 1,760; Fac 88; Highest Degree: Master
Library Holdings: e-books 36,938; Electronic Media & Resources 6,350; Bk Titles 142,000; Bk Vols 154,500; Per Subs 465
Special Collections: US Document Depository
Automation Activity & Vendor Info: (Cataloging) SirsiDynix; (Circulation) SirsiDynix; (ILL) OCLC ILLiad; (OPAC) SirsiDynix
Wireless access
Partic in Alaska Library Network; Leian
Open Mon-Thurs 8am-10pm, Fri 8-5, Sat 11-5, Sun 11-8

KAKE

§P SHIRLY JACKSON COMMUNITY LIBRARY, Kake City School District, 175 Library Way, 99830. Tel: 907-785-3741. E-mail: library@kakeschools.com. Web Site: www.facebook.com/kakecommunitylibrary.
Pop 600
Automation Activity & Vendor Info: (Cataloging) LibraryWorld, Inc; (OPAC) LibraryWorld, Inc
Wireless access
Partic in Alaska Library Network
Restriction: External users must contact libr

KASILOF

P KASILOF PUBLIC LIBRARY*, 5800 Sterling Hwy, 99610. (Mail add: PO Box 176, 99610-0176), SAN 320-4650. Tel: 907-252-5886. E-mail: kasiloflibrary@gmail.com. *Libr Dir,* Robin Moore; Staff 1 (MLS 1)
Founded 1962. Pop 1,132; Circ 7,000
Library Holdings: Bk Vols 14,000
Special Collections: Alaska Coll
Automation Activity & Vendor Info: (Acquisitions) ComPanion Corp; (Cataloging) ComPanion Corp; (Circulation) ComPanion Corp; (OPAC) ComPanion Corp
Wireless access
Open Mon-Thurs (Winter) 2-6; Tues-Thurs (Summer) 12-5

KENAI

P KENAI COMMUNITY LIBRARY*, 163 Main St Loop, 99611. SAN 300-2705. Tel: 907-283-4378. FAX: 907-283-2266. E-mail: kenailibrary@kenai.city. Web Site: www.kenailibrary.org. *Libr Dir,* Katja Wolfe; E-mail: kwolfe@kenai.city; *Asst Dir,* Hannah Meyer; E-mail: hmeyer@kenai.city; *Ch,* James Adcox; E-mail: jadcox@kenai.city; *ILL,* Janina Efta; E-mail: jefta@ci.kenai.ak.us; Staff 8 (MLS 2, Non-MLS 6)
Founded 1949. Pop 13,560; Circ 123,000
Library Holdings: AV Mats 1,664; Bks on Deafness & Sign Lang 45; High Interest/Low Vocabulary Bk Vols 350; Bk Titles 65,185; Bk Vols 77,772; Per Subs 275
Subject Interests: Alaska, Fishing, Genealogy
Automation Activity & Vendor Info: (Cataloging) SirsiDynix; (Circulation) SirsiDynix; (ILL) OCLC Connexion; (OPAC) SirsiDynix-iBistro
Wireless access
Function: AV serv, ILL available, Ref serv available
Partic in Alaska Library Network
Open Mon-Thurs 9-7, Fri 9-6, Sat 9-5, Sun (Winter) 1-4
Friends of the Library Group

S WILDWOOD CORRECTIONAL COMPLEX LIBRARY*, Ten Chugach Ave, 99611. Tel: 907-260-7200. FAX: 907-260-7229. Web Site: www.correct.state.ak.us/institutions/wildwood. *Educ Coordr,* Mary Rowley; E-mail: mary.rowley@alaska.gov
Restriction: Not open to pub

S WILDWOOD PRE-TRIAL FACILITY LIBRARY*, Five Chugach Ave, 99611. Tel: 907-260-7265. FAX: 907-260-7224. Web Site: www.correct.state.ak.us/institutions/wildwood-pretrial-facility. *Educ Coordr,* Mary Rowley; E-mail: mary.rowley@alaska.gov
Restriction: Not open to pub

KETCHIKAN

P KETCHIKAN PUBLIC LIBRARY*, 1110 Copper Ridge Lane, 99901. SAN 300-2721. Tel: 907-225-3331. E-mail: library@firstcitylibraries.org. Web Site: www.ketchikanpubliclibrary.org. *Dir,* Lisa Pearson; E-mail: lisap@firstcitylibraries.org. Subject Specialists: *Alaskana, Maritime,* Lisa Pearson; Staff 13 (MLS 3, Non-MLS 10)
Founded 1901. Pop 13,787; Circ 167,969
Jan 2014-Dec 2014 Income $1,393,555, State $6,600, City $711,056, Federal $4,000, County $395,000, Locally Generated Income $10,400, Parent Institution $215,596, Other $50,903. Mats Exp $138,028, Books $58,089, Per/Ser (Incl. Access Fees) $7,814, Manu Arch $43,021, Other Print Mats $44, AV Mat $23,511, Electronic Ref Mat (Incl. Access Fees) $5,549. Sal $953,356
Library Holdings: Audiobooks 2,996; Bks-By-Mail 360; CDs 5,474; DVDs 6,100; e-books 13,177; Electronic Media & Resources 10,424; Large Print Bks 2,415; Microforms 332; Bk Vols 59,459; Per Subs 183; Spec Interest Per Sub 3; Talking Bks 338; Videos 705
Special Collections: Alaskana (SE Alaska History); Maritime. Municipal Document Depository
Subject Interests: Alaskana
Automation Activity & Vendor Info: (Acquisitions) SirsiDynix-WorkFlows; (Cataloging) SirsiDynix-WorkFlows; (Circulation) SirsiDynix-WorkFlows; (ILL) OCLC WorldShare Interlibrary Loan; (OPAC) SirsiDynix; (Serials) EBSCO Online
Wireless access
Function: 24/7 Electronic res, Accelerated reader prog, Activity rm, Audio & video playback equip for onsite use, Audiobks via web, AV serv, Bks on CD, Children's prog, Citizenship assistance, Computer training, Computers for patron use, Digital talking bks, E-Reserves, Electronic databases & coll, Equip loans & repairs, Family literacy, Free DVD rentals, Games & aids for people with disabilities, Holiday prog, Home delivery & serv to seniorr ctr & nursing homes, ILL available, Internet access, Large print keyboards, Life-long learning prog for all ages, Magazines, Magnifiers for reading, Mango lang, Microfiche/film & reading machines, Movies, Online cat, Orientations, Outreach serv, OverDrive digital audio bks, Photocopying/Printing, Preschool outreach, Preschool reading prog, Prog for adults, Prog for children & young adult, Ref serv available, Scanner, Senior outreach, Serves people with intellectual disabilities, Spoken cassettes & CDs, Story hour, Study rm, Summer reading prog, Tax forms, Teen prog, Telephone ref, VHS videos, Wheelchair accessible, Winter reading prog
Partic in Alaska Library Network; Association for Rural & Small Libraries; First City Libraries
Special Services for the Deaf - ADA equip; Assistive tech; Bks on deafness & sign lang; Closed caption videos
Special Services for the Blind - Aids for in-house use; Assistive/Adapted tech devices, equip & products; Bks available with recordings; Bks on CD; Extensive large print coll; Home delivery serv; Large screen computer & software; Lending of low vision aids; Magnifiers; Rental typewriters & computers; Screen enlargement software for people with visual disabilities; Talking bks & player equip
Open Mon-Sat 10-6
Restriction: ID required to use computers (Ltd hrs), Photo ID required for access
Friends of the Library Group

S TONGASS HISTORICAL MUSEUM*, Reference Room, 629 Dock St, 99901. SAN 327-6805. Tel: 907-225-5600. Web Site: www.ktn-ak.us/tongass-historical-museum. *Dir,* Anita Maxwell; E-mail:

anitam@ktn-ak.us; *Curator,* Hayley Chambers; E-mail: hayleyc@ktn-ak.us; Staff 3 (Non-MLS 3)
Founded 1961
Library Holdings: Bk Vols 2,500
Subject Interests: Ethnology
Publications: Bibliography of Ketchikan History
Open Tues (Winter) 1-5, Sat 10-4; Mon-Fri (Summer) 8-5

C UNIVERSITY OF ALASKA SOUTHEAST, Ketchikan Campus Library, 2600 Seventh Ave, 99901. SAN 300-2713. Tel: 907-228-4567. Toll Free Tel: 888-550-6177. FAX: 907-228-4520. Web Site: www.ketch.alaska.edu/library. *Libr Mgr,* Kathy Bolling; Tel: 907-228-4517, E-mail: kjbolling3@alaska.edu; *Libr Asst,* Michelle Lampton; Tel: 907-228-4567, E-mail: mlampton@alaska.edu. Subject Specialists: *Libr instruction,* Kathy Bolling; Staff 3 (MLS 1, Non-MLS 2)
Founded 1954
Library Holdings: Bk Vols 30,000; Per Subs 100
Subject Interests: Native people, Western Americana
Wireless access
Partic in First City Libraries
Open Mon-Fri 9-5

KODIAK

C KODIAK COLLEGE*, Carolyn Floyd Library, 117 Benny Benson Dr, 99615. SAN 320-5517. Tel: 907-486-1238. FAX: 907-486-1257. Web Site: www.koc.alaska.edu/students/library. *Libr Mgr,* Mike Trussell; E-mail: mjtrussell@alaska.edu; Staff 2 (MLS 1, Non-MLS 1)
Library Holdings: DVDs 1,200; Bk Titles 27,000; Per Subs 12
Special Collections: Alaskana Coll
Wireless access
Open Mon-Thurs 11-8, Fri 11-5, Sat Noon-5

P KODIAK PUBLIC LIBRARY*, 612 Egan Way, 99615. SAN 300-273X. Tel: 907-486-8686. FAX: 907-486-8681. Web Site: www.city.kodiak.ak.us. *Dir,* Katie Baxter; E-mail: kbaxter@city.kodiak.ak.us; Staff 7 (MLS 1, Non-MLS 6)
Founded 1946. Pop 14,041; Circ 95,000
Library Holdings: CDs 5,517; DVDs 300; Bk Vols 67,681; Per Subs 275; Videos 2,670
Special Collections: Alaska. Oral History
Subject Interests: Fisheries
Automation Activity & Vendor Info: (Cataloging) SirsiDynix; (Circulation) SirsiDynix; (OPAC) SirsiDynix
Function: 24/7 Electronic res, 24/7 Online cat, Activity rm, Adult bk club, Adult literacy prog, Archival coll, Art exhibits, Audio & video playback equip for onsite use, Audiobks via web, AV serv, Bilingual assistance for Spanish patrons, Bk club(s), Bks on CD, CD-ROM, Children's prog, Citizenship assistance, Computer training, Computers for patron use, Digital talking bks, Doc delivery serv, E-Readers, Electronic databases & coll, Equip loans & repairs, Family literacy, For res purposes, Free DVD rentals, Games & aids for people with disabilities, Govt ref serv, Health sci info serv, Holiday prog, Home delivery & serv to seniorr ctr & nursing homes, Homework prog, ILL available, Instruction & testing, Internet access, Life-long learning prog for all ages, Literacy & newcomer serv, Magazines, Magnifiers for reading, Mail loans to mem, Mango lang, Meeting rooms, Microfiche/film & reading machines, Movies, Music CDs, Online cat, Orientations, Outreach serv, OverDrive digital audio bks, Photocopying/Printing, Preschool outreach, Printer for laptops & handheld devices, Prof lending libr, Prog for adults, Prog for children & young adult, Ref & res, Ref serv available, Scanner, Senior computer classes, Senior outreach, Serves people with intellectual disabilities, Spanish lang bks, Spoken cassettes & CDs, Story hour, Study rm, Summer & winter reading prog, Summer reading prog, Tax forms, Teen prog, Telephone ref, Visual arts prog, Wheelchair accessible, Winter reading prog, Workshops, Writing prog
Publications: Library Lines (Monthly); Lively Lib Chat; DogSpots for Dog Eared ReadsRadio Broadcast
Partic in Alaska Library Network
Open Mon-Fri 10-9, Sat 10-5, Sun 1-5
Friends of the Library Group

R SAINT HERMAN ORTHODOX THEOLOGICAL SEMINARY LIBRARY*, 414 Mission Rd, 99615. SAN 320-5525. Tel: 907-486-3524. FAX: 907-486-5935. E-mail: info@sthermanseminary.org. Web Site: www.sthermanseminary.org. *Librn,* Irenaios Anderson; E-mail: doulos00@gmail.com; Staff 1 (Non-MLS 1)
Founded 1973. Fac 6
Library Holdings: Bk Vols 15,000; Per Subs 100
Subject Interests: Alaskan native studies, Orthodox theol, Rare bks, Relig hist
Automation Activity & Vendor Info: (Cataloging) Follett Software
Wireless access
Restriction: Open to students, fac & staff

KOTZEBUE

C UNIVERSITY OF ALASKA FAIRBANKS, Chukchi Consortium Library, 604 Third Ave, 99752. (Mail add: PO Box 297, 99752-0297), SAN 376-3560. Tel: 907-442-2410. Toll Free Tel: 800-478-3402. FAX: 907-442-2322. Web Site: www.uaf.edu/chukchi/chukchi-consortium-librar. *Libr Dir,* Mae Mendenhall; E-mail: mgmendenhall@alaska.edu
Library Holdings: AV Mats 1,400; Bk Titles 14,000; Bk Vols 20,000; Per Subs 120; Talking Bks 275
Automation Activity & Vendor Info: (Acquisitions) SirsiDynix; (Cataloging) SirsiDynix; (Circulation) SirsiDynix; (Course Reserve) SirsiDynix; (ILL) SirsiDynix; (Media Booking) SirsiDynix; (OPAC) SirsiDynix; (Serials) SirsiDynix
Wireless access
Partic in Alaska Library Network
Open Tues-Fri Noon-8, Sat 10-6

MCGRATH

P MCGRATH COMMUNITY LIBRARY*, 12 Chinana Ave, 99627. (Mail add: PO Box 249, 99627-0249), SAN 374-437X. Tel: 907-524-3843. FAX: 907-524-3335. E-mail: mcgrathlibrarian@gmail.com. Web Site: mcgrathlibrary.com. *Mgr,* Kellie Pierce; Staff 3 (MLS 1, Non-MLS 2)
Founded 1942. Pop 466; Circ 3,291
Library Holdings: Bk Titles 12,000; Per Subs 12
Special Collections: Alaskana, bks, per, res papers & v-tapes
Automation Activity & Vendor Info: (Acquisitions) Follett Software; (Cataloging) Follett Software; (Circulation) Follett Software; (OPAC) Follett Software
Partic in Alaska Library Network
Open Mon 3-5 & 7-9, Sun 2-5

MOOSE PASS

P MOOSE PASS PUBLIC LIBRARY*, 33675 Depot Rd, 99631. (Mail add: PO Box 154, 99631). Tel: 907-288-3111. FAX: 907-288-3111. E-mail: bookmoose@gmail.com. Web Site: www.moosepasslibrary.webs.com. *Librn,* Deanna Thomas; *IT Tech,* Kindra Leaders; Staff 1 (Non-MLS 1)
Pop 375
Library Holdings: AV Mats 700; Bk Vols 6,000; Per Subs 10
Special Collections: Alaskana
Wireless access
Partic in Alaska Library Network
Open Mon 10-2 & 5:30-6:30, Wed 11-6, Thurs 2-8, Fri & Sat 2-6
Friends of the Library Group

NAKNEK

P BRISTOL BAY BOROUGH LIBRARIES*, Martin Monsen Regional Library, 101 Main St, 99633. (Mail add: PO Box 147, 99633-0147). Tel: 907-246-4465. Web Site: www.bristolbayboroughak.us/adminstration/libraries/index.php.
Pop 1,257
Library Holdings: Bks on Deafness & Sign Lang 20; Bk Vols 10,000; Per Subs 24
Automation Activity & Vendor Info: (Cataloging) Biblionix/Apollo; (Circulation) Biblionix/Apollo
Wireless access
Partic in Alaska Library Network
Open Tues & Thurs 10-6, Wed, Fri & Sat 9-5
Branches: 1
SOUTH NAKNEK BRANCH, One School Rd, South Naknek, 99670. (Mail add: PO Box 70086, South Naknek, 99670). Tel: 907-246-6513. E-mail: southnakneklibrary@bbbak.us.
Library Holdings: Bk Vols 5,000; Per Subs 12
Open Tues-Fri 1-5:30, Sat 1-5

NENANA

P NENANA PUBLIC LIBRARY, 106 E Second St, 99760. (Mail add: PO Box 40, 99760-0040). Tel: 907-832-5812. *Dir,* Adrianne Coffey; E-mail: acoffeyfolibrary@gmail.com; Staff 1 (Non-MLS 1)
Founded 1981. Pop 549
Library Holdings: CDs 310; DVDs 113; Bk Titles 13,307; Per Subs 12; Talking Bks 290; Videos 1,580
Special Collections: Nenana Historical Coll. Oral History
Automation Activity & Vendor Info: (Cataloging) TinyCat; (Circulation) Follett Software; (ILL) OCLC; (OPAC) Follett Software
Wireless access
Function: CD-ROM, Homebound delivery serv, ILL available, Photocopying/Printing, Prog for children & young adult, Serves people with intellectual disabilities, Summer reading prog, Telephone ref, VHS videos
Special Services for the Blind - Computer with voice synthesizer for visually impaired persons

Open Wed 11-2, Thurs-Sat 12-4
Friends of the Library Group

NIKOLAI

P NIKOLAI PUBLIC LIBRARY*, PO Box 90, 99691-0090. SAN 376-0090. Tel: 907-293-2427. FAX: 907-293-2214. *Principal,* Tara Wiggins; *Librn,* Stephanie Petruska; E-mail: stephaniepetruska@iditarodsd.org
Library Holdings: Bk Vols 1,000
Open Mon-Thurs & Sat 3-5

NINILCHIK

P NINILCHIK COMMUNITY LIBRARY, 15850 Sterling Hwy, 99639. (Mail add: PO Box 39165, 99639-0165), SAN 325-3031. Tel: 907-567-3333. E-mail: nincomlib@alaska.net. Web Site: www.ninilchiklibrary.org. *Librn,* Becky Hamilton; Staff 1 (Non-MLS 1)
Founded 1952. Pop 780; Circ 21,000
Wireless access
Partic in Alaska Library Network
Open Mon-Sat 1-5

NOME

P KEGOAYAH KOZGA PUBLIC LIBRARY, Richard Foster Bldg, 100 W Seventh Ave, 99762. (Mail add: PO Box 1168, 99762-1168), SAN 300-2756. Tel: 907-443-6628. FAX: 907-443-3762. E-mail: library@nomealaska.org. Web Site: www.nomealaska.org/library. *Dir,* Marguerite La Riviere
Founded 1902. Pop 3,508
Library Holdings: AV Mats 993; Bk Titles 17,000; Bk Vols 18,372; Per Subs 50
Special Collections: Alaskana Rare Book Coll (Kozga); Alice Green Coll; Bilingual Inupiat; Bilingual Inupiat/English; Elders Conference Recordings for the Inupiat Eskimo; Seward Peninsula; Siberian Yupik/English
Subject Interests: Local hist
Automation Activity & Vendor Info: (Circulation) Follett Software; (OPAC) Follett Software
Wireless access
Partic in Alaska Library Network
Open Mon-Thurs 12-7, Fri & Sat 12-6

OUZINKIE

S OUZINKIE TRIBAL COUNCIL*, Media Center, 130 Third St, 99644. (Mail add: PO Box 130, 99644). Tel: 907-680-2323. FAX: 907-680-2214. E-mail: library@ouzinkie.org. Web Site: www.ouzinkie.org. *Librn,* Rebecca Anderson
Library Holdings: Bk Vols 2,000; Per Subs 10
Wireless access
Open Mon-Fri 9-4

PALMER

CR ALASKA BIBLE COLLEGE LIBRARY*, 248 E Elmwood Ave, 99645. SAN 300-2616. Tel: 907-745-3201. E-mail: library@akbible.edu. *Libr Dir,* Noel Maxwell; E-mail: library@akbible.edu; Staff 1 (Non-MLS 1)
Founded 1966. Enrl 35; Fac 8; Highest Degree: Bachelor
Library Holdings: AV Mats 381; Per Subs 54
Special Collections: Alaska-Arctic
Subject Interests: Relig

PALMER CORRECTIONAL CENTER

S MEDIUM SECURITY FACILITY LIBRARY*, PO Box 919, 99645-0919. Tel: 907-746-8270. FAX: 907-746-8222.
Library Holdings: Bk Vols 2,000
Open Mon-Sun 8am-9pm

S MINIMUM SECURITY FACILITY LIBRARY*, PO Box 919, 99645-0919. Tel: 907-746-8250. FAX: 907-746-8248.
Library Holdings: Bk Vols 2,700
Open Mon-Sun 8am-9pm

P PALMER PUBLIC LIBRARY, 655 S Valley Way, 99645. SAN 300-2772. Tel: 907-745-4690. Web Site: www.palmerak.org/library. *Libr Dir,* Beth Skow; E-mail: bskow@palmerak.org; *Libr Serv Coordr,* Katie Schweisthal; E-mail: kschweisthal@palmerak.org; Staff 5 (MLS 1, Non-MLS 4)
Founded 1945. Pop 17,000; Circ 100,000
Library Holdings: AV Mats 625; Large Print Bks 625; Bk Titles 41,700; Bk Vols 45,000; Talking Bks 600
Special Collections: Jewish Holocaust Memorial Coll; Matanuska Valley Pioneer, Valley Settler & Matanuska Valley Record; Matanuska Valley Settlement Newspapers (1937-1959)
Automation Activity & Vendor Info: (Cataloging) SirsiDynix; (Circulation) SirsiDynix
Wireless access
Function: 24/7 Electronic res, 24/7 Online cat, Audiobks on Playaways & MP3, Audiobks via web, Bks on CD, Children's prog, Computers for patron use, Digital talking bks, E-Readers, Electronic databases & coll, Free DVD rentals, Holiday prog, ILL available, Internet access, Magnifiers for reading, Mail & tel request accepted, Movies, Music CDs, Online cat, Online info literacy tutorials on the web & in blackboard, Online ref, Photocopying/Printing, Preschool outreach, Preschool reading prog, Printer for laptops & handheld devices, Prog for adults, Prog for children & young adult, Scanner, Spoken cassettes & CDs, Spoken cassettes & DVDs, STEM programs, Story hour, Summer & winter reading prog, Summer reading prog, Tax forms, Teen prog, Telephone ref, VHS videos, Wheelchair accessible, Winter reading prog
Publications: Friends of the Library Newsletter (Quarterly)
Partic in Alaska Library Network
Open Tues-Thurs 10-5, Fri & Sat 10-4
Restriction: Residents only
Friends of the Library Group

C UNIVERSITY OF ALASKA ANCHORAGE, MAT-SU COLLEGE*, Alvin S Okeson Library, 8295 E College Dr, 99645. (Mail add: PO Box 2889, 99645-2889), SAN 300-2780. Tel: 907-745-9740. Interlibrary Loan Service Tel: 907-745-9735. FAX: 907-745-9777. Web Site: matsu.alaska.edu/library. *Dir,* Craig Ballain; E-mail: ceballain@matsu.alaska.edu; Staff 6 (MLS 2, Non-MLS 4)
Founded 1961
Library Holdings: AV Mats 4,800; e-books 20,000; Bk Vols 49,000; Per Subs 93
Special Collections: Local History. Oral History
Subject Interests: Art, Educ, Renewable energy, Soc sci
Wireless access
Partic in OCLC Online Computer Library Center, Inc
Open Mon-Thurs 8:30-8, Fri 8:30-6, Sat 9-4

PELICAN

P PELICAN PUBLIC LIBRARY*, 166 Salmon Way, 99832. (Mail add: PO Box 712, 99832-0712), SAN 376-7302. Tel: 907-735-2500. FAX: 907-735-2258. *Dir,* Linda Ady
Library Holdings: Bk Vols 8,000; Per Subs 35
Wireless access
Partic in Alaska Library Network
Open Mon & Fri (June-Aug) 5:30-7:30, Tues & Thurs 7:30pm-9:30pm, Wed 2:30-5:30, Sat 2:30-5:30
Friends of the Library Group

PETERSBURG

P PETERSBURG PUBLIC LIBRARY*, 14 S Second St, 99833. (Mail add: PO Box 549, 99833-0549), SAN 300-2799. Tel: 907-772-3349. FAX: 907-772-3759. E-mail: library@petersburgak.gov. Web Site: psglib.org. *Libr Dir,* Tara Alcock; E-mail: talcock@petersburgak.gov; *Tech Serv,* Chris Weiss
Founded 1913. Pop 3,200; Circ 28,000
Library Holdings: Bk Vols 33,036; Per Subs 72
Automation Activity & Vendor Info: (Cataloging) SirsiDynix; (Circulation) SirsiDynix; (OPAC) SirsiDynix
Wireless access
Publications: Petersburg, Heritage of the Sea
Partic in Alaska Library Network; OCLC Online Computer Library Center, Inc
Open Tues-Thurs 11-8, Fri & Sat 11-6
Friends of the Library Group

PORT LIONS

P JESSIE WAKEFIELD MEMORIAL LIBRARY*, 207 Spruce Dr, 99550. (Mail add: PO Box 49, 99550-0049). Tel: 907-454-8185. FAX: 907-454-2420. E-mail: portlions.jwml@gmail.com. *Head Librn,* Angel Sanders
Circ 3,495
Library Holdings: AV Mats 260; Bk Vols 11,356; Per Subs 20
Wireless access

SELDOVIA

P SELDOVIA PUBLIC LIBRARY*, 260 Seldovia St, 99663. (Mail add: PO Box H, 99663-0190), SAN 376-3390. Tel: 907-234-7662. E-mail: seldovia.library@gmail.com. *Libr Dir,* Sara Nichols; Staff 13 (Non-MLS 13)
Founded 1935. Pop 500
Library Holdings: Audiobooks 331; AV Mats 2,262; CDs 132; Bk Titles 8,336; Per Subs 16; Videos 1,799
Subject Interests: Alaskana
Automation Activity & Vendor Info: (Cataloging) JayWil Software Development, Inc; (Circulation) JayWil Software Development, Inc
Wireless access

Function: 24/7 Electronic res, 24/7 Online cat, Activity rm, After school storytime, Archival coll, Art exhibits, Audio & video playback equip for onsite use, AV serv, Bks on cassette, Bks on CD, CD-ROM, Children's prog, Citizenship assistance, Computer training, Computers for patron use, Distance learning, Electronic databases & coll, For res purposes, Free DVD rentals, Govt ref serv, Holiday prog, ILL available, Instruction & testing, Internet access, Large print keyboards, Learning ctr, Magazines, Magnifiers for reading, Mail & tel request accepted, Meeting rooms, Movies, Music CDs, Online cat, Online ref, Outside serv via phone, mail, e-mail & web, Photocopying/Printing, Preschool outreach, Preschool reading prog, Prog for adults, Prog for children & young adult, Ref & res, Ref serv available, Scanner, Senior outreach, Spoken cassettes & CDs, Story hour, Summer reading prog, Teen prog, Telephone ref, VHS videos, Wheelchair accessible
Open Mon & Sat 2-4, Tues & Thurs 2-6, Wed 12-2

SEWARD

J ALASKA VOCATIONAL TECHNICAL CENTER*, Jack Werner Memorial Library, 809 Second Ave, 99664. (Mail add: PO Box 889, 99664-0889). Tel: 907-224-6114. FAX: 907-224-4406. Web Site: avtec.edu/department/learning-resources. *Librn,* Jamie Hall; E-mail: jamie.hall@avtec.edu
Founded 1970. Enrl 250; Fac 50
Library Holdings: Bk Vols 8,000
Subject Interests: Alaska, Prof
Automation Activity & Vendor Info: (Cataloging) Follett Software; (Circulation) Follett Software; (ILL) OCLC; (OPAC) Follett Software
Wireless access
Open Mon-Thurs 11:30-1 & 3:30-10, Fri-Sun 4-9

P SEWARD COMMUNITY LIBRARY & MUSEUM, 239 Sixth Ave, 99664. (Mail add: PO Box 2389, 99664-2389), SAN 300-2802. Tel: 907-224-4082. Administration Tel: 907-224-4008. FAX: 907-224-3521. E-mail: libmus@cityofseward.net. Web Site: www.cityofseward.us/departments/library-museum. *Dir,* Valarie Kingsland; E-mail: vkingsland@cityofseward.net; *Prog Coordr,* Position Currently Open; *Curator,* Elana Yanusz; Tel: 907-224-4007, E-mail: eyanusz@cityofseward.net; Staff 6 (MLS 1, Non-MLS 5)
Founded 1933. Pop 7,529; Circ 54,020
Library Holdings: High Interest/Low Vocabulary Bk Vols 50; Bk Titles 27,000; Bk Vols 30,000; Per Subs 75
Special Collections: Local Historical Photo Coll
Subject Interests: Alaskana, Japanese
Wireless access
Function: 24/7 Online cat, Adult bk club, Archival coll, Art exhibits, Audio & video playback equip for onsite use, Audiobks on Playaways & MP3, Audiobks via web, Bi-weekly Writer's Group, Bk club(s), Bks on CD, Children's prog, Citizenship assistance, Computer training, Computers for patron use, Digital talking bks, Distance learning, Electronic databases & coll, Equip loans & repairs, Free DVD rentals, Govt ref serv, Holiday prog, Homebound delivery serv, ILL available, Instruction & testing, Internet access, Jail serv, Laminating, Magazines, Mail & tel request accepted, Meeting rooms, Microfiche/film & reading machines, Movies, Museum passes, Music CDs, Notary serv, Online cat, Outreach serv, Outside serv via phone, mail, e-mail & web, OverDrive digital audio bks, Passport agency, Photocopying/Printing, Preschool reading prog, Printer for laptops & handheld devices, Prog for adults, Prog for children & young adult, Ref serv available, Scanner, Serves people with intellectual disabilities, Spanish lang bks, Story hour, Summer & winter reading prog, Summer reading prog, Tax forms, Telephone ref, Wheelchair accessible, Winter reading prog, Writing prog
Publications: Index to the Seward Gateway (1904-1910); Seward Gateway Prosperity, 1925 ed reprint
Partic in Alaska Library Network
Friends of the Library Group

S SPRING CREEK CORRECTIONAL CENTER LIBRARY*, 3600 Bette Cato Rd, 99664. (Mail add: PO Box 2109, 99664). Tel: 907-224-8143. FAX: 907-224-8062. Web Site: www.correct.state.ak.us/institutions/spring-creek. *Educ Coordr,* Vernon Willet; E-mail: vernon.willet@alaska.gov
Restriction: Not open to pub

SITKA

S NATIONAL PARK SERVICE*, Sitka National Historical Park Library, 103 Monastery St, 99835-7603. SAN 323-8784. Tel: 907-747-6281. Web Site: www.nps.gov/sitk. *Library Contact,* Position Currently Open
Founded 1950
Library Holdings: Bk Titles 2,400
Special Collections: Russian American History, bks, tapes, film; SE Alaska Native Coll; Tlingit Indian Culture. Oral History
Restriction: Open by appt only

P SITKA PUBLIC LIBRARY, 320 Harbor Dr, 99835-7553. SAN 300-2810. Tel: 907-747-4020, 907-747-4021. FAX: 907-747-8755. E-mail: library@cityofsitka.org. Web Site: www.cityofsitka.com/government/departments/library. *Dir,* Jessica Ieremia; E-mail: jessica.ieremia@cityofsitka.org; *Youth Serv Librn,* Maite Lorente Rial; Tel: 907-747-4022, E-mail: maite.lorente@cityofsitka.org; Staff 10 (MLS 1, Non-MLS 9)
Founded 1923. Pop 8,835; Circ 131,021
Library Holdings: AV Mats 9,940; Bk Titles 56,293; Bk Vols 59,767; Per Subs 283
Special Collections: Local History (Louise Brightman Room), bk, micro
Automation Activity & Vendor Info: (Cataloging) SirsiDynix; (Circulation) SirsiDynix
Wireless access
Function: 24/7 Electronic res, 24/7 Online cat
Open Mon-Sat 11-6, Sun 12-4
Friends of the Library Group

SKAGWAY

P SKAGWAY PUBLIC LIBRARY, 769 State St, 99840. (Mail add: PO Box 394, 99840-0394), SAN 300-2837. Tel: 907-983-2665. FAX: 907-983-2666. E-mail: library@skagway.org. Web Site: www.skagway.org/library. *Dir,* Jennifer Sasselli; E-mail: j.sasselli@skagway.org
Pop 811; Circ 17,290
Library Holdings: Music Scores 16; Bk Titles 106,000; Per Subs 67; Talking Bks 200
Automation Activity & Vendor Info: (Circulation) Follett Software; (ILL) OCLC; (OPAC) Follett Software
Wireless access
Partic in Alaska Library Network
Open Mon-Fri (Winter) 1-8, Sat & Sun 1-5; Mon-Fri (Summer) 10-9, Sat & Sun 1-5

G UNITED STATES NATIONAL PARK SERVICE*, Klondike Gold Rush International Historical Park Library, Park Headquarters, Second Ave Broadway, 99840. (Mail add: PO Box 517, 99840-0517), SAN 372-7157. Tel: 907-983-9200. FAX: 907-983-9249. Web Site: www.nps.gov/klgo. *Historian,* Karl Gurcke; Tel: 907-983-9214, E-mail: karl_gurcke@nps.gov
Founded 1976
Library Holdings: Bk Titles 1,000
Special Collections: Dyea & the Chilkoot Trail; Klondike Gold Rush, especially Skagway & the White Pass
Special Services for the Deaf - TDD equip
Open Mon-Fri 8-5

SOLDOTNA

C ALASKA CHRISTIAN COLLEGE*, Learning Resource Center, 35109 Royal Pl, 99669. Tel: 907-260-7422. FAX: 907-260-6722. Web Site: alaskacc.edu/academics/learning-resource-center. *Dir, Learning Res,* Lindsay Hallam; E-mail: lhallam@alaskacc.edu; *Coordr,* Amy Adcox; E-mail: aadcox@alaskacc.edu; Staff 1.5 (MLS 1, Non-MLS 0.5)
Founded 2000. Enrl 40; Fac 7; Highest Degree: Associate
Library Holdings: AV Mats 100; Electronic Media & Resources 35; Bk Vols 14,000; Per Subs 40
Automation Activity & Vendor Info: (Circulation) Follett Software; (OPAC) Follett Software
Wireless access
Partic in Christian Library Consortium; OCLC Online Computer Library Center, Inc
Open Mon-Fri 9-9, Sat 1-9, Sun 6:30pm-9pm

C KENAI PENINSULA COLLEGE LIBRARY*, 156 College Rd, 99669. SAN 300-2845. Tel: 907-262-0385. FAX: 907-262-0386. Web Site: kpc.alaska.edu/academics/library. *Dir,* Jane E Fuerstenau; E-mail: jefuerstenau@alaska.edu; *Libr Tech,* Meagan Zimpelmann; Tel: 907-262-0384, E-mail: mazimpelmann@alaska.edu; Staff 2 (MLS 2)
Founded 1964. Enrl 700; Fac 23; Highest Degree: Bachelor
Library Holdings: Bk Vols 23,000; Per Subs 30
Subject Interests: Alaska
Automation Activity & Vendor Info: (Cataloging) SirsiDynix; (Circulation) SirsiDynix
Wireless access
Function: Art exhibits, Audio & video playback equip for onsite use, AV serv, Computers for patron use, Electronic databases & coll, Magnifiers for reading, Music CDs, Online cat, Online ref, Ref & res, Scanner, VHS videos, Wheelchair accessible
Open Mon-Fri 8-8
Restriction: Open to pub for ref & circ; with some limitations

P SOLDOTNA PUBLIC LIBRARY, Joyce Carver Memorial Library, 235 N Binkley St, 99669. SAN 300-2853. Tel: 907-262-4227. Toll Free FAX: 866-596-2993. E-mail: circ@soldotna.org, library@soldotna.org. Web Site:

www.soldotna.org/departments/library. *City Librn,* Rachel Nash; E-mail: rnash@soldotna.org
Founded 1965. Pop 4,000; Circ 100,345
Library Holdings: Bk Titles 43,930; Per Subs 95
Automation Activity & Vendor Info: (Circulation) Follett Software
Wireless access
Partic in Alaska Library Network; Association for Rural & Small Libraries
Open Mon, Wed, Fri & Sat 10-6, Tues & Thurs 10-8
Friends of the Library Group

SUTTON

P SUTTON PUBLIC LIBRARY, 11301 N Chickaloon Way, 99674. (Mail add: PO Box 266, 99674-0266), SAN 376-7329. Tel: 907-861-7640. FAX: 907-745-1057. E-mail: sutton.library@matsugov.us. Web Site: www.matsugov.us/msln/sutton. *Librn,* Juli Buzby; E-mail: juli.buzby@matsugov.us; Staff 2 (Non-MLS 2)
Pop 52,322
Library Holdings: Bk Titles 9,976; Bk Vols 10,206; Per Subs 35
Automation Activity & Vendor Info: (Cataloging) SirsiDynix; (Circulation) SirsiDynix; (ILL) OCLC FirstSearch; (OPAC) SirsiDynix
Wireless access
Function: After school storytime, ILL available, Photocopying/Printing, Prog for adults, Prog for children & young adult, Ref serv available, Spoken cassettes & CDs, Summer reading prog, Telephone ref, VHS videos, Wheelchair accessible
Partic in Alaska Library Network
Open Tues-Fri 10-7, Sat 11-4
Friends of the Library Group

TALKEETNA

P TALKEETNA PUBLIC LIBRARY*, 24645 S Talkeetna Spur Rd, 99676. (Mail add: PO Box 768, 99676), SAN 376-3706. Tel: 907-861-7645. FAX: 907-733-3017. Web Site: www.matsugov.us/msln/talkeetna. *Libr Mgr,* Hugh Leslie; Tel: 907-861-7868, E-mail: hugh.leslie@matsugov.us
Library Holdings: Audiobooks 965; Bk Titles 14,588; Per Subs 39; Videos 2,025
Automation Activity & Vendor Info: (Acquisitions) SirsiDynix; (Cataloging) SirsiDynix; (Circulation) SirsiDynix; (Media Booking) SirsiDynix; (OPAC) SirsiDynix
Partic in Alaska Library Network; Matanuska-Susitna Library Network
Open Mon-Sat 11-6
Friends of the Library Group

TANANA

P TANANA COMMUNITY-SCHOOL LIBRARY*, 89 Front St, 99777. (Mail add: PO Box 109, 99777-0109). Tel: 907-366-7211. FAX: 907-366-7201. E-mail: talcomlib@hotmail.com. *Librn,* Barbara Martin
Pop 233; Circ 1,215
Library Holdings: Bk Vols 9,875; Per Subs 20
Open Mon 4-8, Wed & Fri 5-8

TENAKEE SPRINGS

P DERMOTT O'TOOLE MEMORIAL LIBRARY*, 707 W Tenakee Ave, 99841. SAN 376-7965. Tel: 907-736-2248. E-mail: domltke@gmail.com. Web Site: www.tenakeespringsak.com/dermott-otoole-memorial-library.html. *Chair,* Kim Rivera
Pop 104
Library Holdings: Bk Titles 8,500
Wireless access
Partic in Alaska Library Network
Open Tues & Wed 1-3, Thurs 6-8, Sat 12-2, Sun 2-4
Friends of the Library Group

THORNE BAY

P THORNE BAY PUBLIC LIBRARY, 120 Freeman Dr, 99919. Tel: 907-828-3303. E-mail: library@thornebay-ak.gov. *Dir,* Laura Clark
Founded 2001. Pop 500
Library Holdings: AV Mats 300; Bk Titles 4,000; Per Subs 10
Special Collections: Alaskana Section
Subject Interests: Local hist
Wireless access
Partic in Alaska Library Network
Open Mon & Thurs-Sun 10-5, Tues & Wed 10-8
Friends of the Library Group

TOK

P TOK COMMUNITY LIBRARY*, Mile 1314 Alaska Hwy, 99780. (Mail add: PO Box 227, 99780-0227), SAN 322-7669. Tel: 907-883-5623. FAX: 907-883-5623. E-mail: library@tokak.us. Web Site: www.tokak.us/library. *Librn,* Kathy Morgan; Tel: 907-940-0046, E-mail: kathy@tokak.us
Founded 1955. Pop 1,367; Circ 3,005
Jul 2016-Jun 2017 Income $16,900, State $6,900, Locally Generated Income $5,000, Other $5,000. Mats Exp $3,959, Books $2,731, AV Mat $728, Electronic Ref Mat (Incl. Access Fees) $500
Library Holdings: Audiobooks 7,089; AV Mats 1,163; Large Print Bks 108; Music Scores 1; Bk Titles 7,204; Bk Vols 7,092; Per Subs 5; Videos 1,163
Subject Interests: Alaskana
Automation Activity & Vendor Info: (Acquisitions) LibraryWorld, Inc; (Cataloging) LibraryWorld, Inc; (Circulation) LibraryWorld, Inc; (OPAC) LibraryWorld, Inc
Wireless access
Function: 24/7 Online cat, Audiobks on Playaways & MP3, Bks on cassette, Bks on CD, Children's prog, Computers for patron use, Free DVD rentals, ILL available, Instruction & testing, Internet access, Laminating, Mail & tel request accepted, Music CDs, Online cat, Photocopying/Printing, Ref & res, Ref serv available, Scanner, Spoken cassettes & CDs, Summer reading prog, VHS videos, Wheelchair accessible
Partic in Alaska Library Network
Special Services for the Blind - Accessible computers
Open Mon 1-4, Tues 3-5, Wed 4-8, Thurs 10-4, Sat 10-2, Sun 10-2
Restriction: In-house use for visitors, Non-resident fee, Registered patrons only

TRAPPER CREEK

P TRAPPER CREEK PUBLIC LIBRARY, 8901 E Devonshire Dr, 99683. (Mail add: PO Box 13388, 99683-0388), SAN 376-6497. Tel: 907-861-7650. FAX: 907-733-1548. Web Site: www.matsugov.us/msln/trappercreek. *Libr Mgr,* Jennie Earles; E-mail: jennie.earles@matsugov.us
Library Holdings: Bk Vols 10,500; Per Subs 20
Subject Interests: Alaska
Automation Activity & Vendor Info: (Acquisitions) SirsiDynix; (Cataloging) SirsiDynix; (Circulation) SirsiDynix; (OPAC) SirsiDynix; (Serials) SirsiDynix
Wireless access
Partic in Alaska Library Network
Open Mon & Wed 11-6, Thurs 10-3, Sat 12-6
Friends of the Library Group

TULUKSAK

P TULUKSAK SCHOOL-COMMUNITY LIBRARY*, Yupiit School District, 115 Main Rd, 99679. SAN 376-6926. Tel: 907-695-5636. *Head Librn,* Dora Napoka; E-mail: DNapoka@yupiit.org
Library Holdings: CDs 300; Large Print Bks 75; Bk Vols 3,000
Automation Activity & Vendor Info: (Cataloging) Follett Software; (Circulation) Follett Software; (OPAC) Follett Software
Wireless access
Open Mon-Fri 10-3:30

UNALAKLEET

P TICASUK LIBRARY*, PO Box 28, 99684-0028. Tel: 907-624-3053. FAX: 907-624-3130.
Founded 1982. Pop 780; Circ 2,474
Library Holdings: Bk Vols 4,537; Per Subs 18
Special Collections: Oral History
Subject Interests: Ethnography
Wireless access
Open Wed-Sat 1-5

UNALASKA

P UNALASKA PUBLIC LIBRARY, 64 Eleanor Dr, 99685. (Mail add: PO Box 1370, 99685-1370). Tel: 907-581-5060. FAX: 907-581-5266. Web Site: www.ci.unalaska.ak.us/library. *Librn,* Karen Kresh; E-mail: kkresh@ci.unalaska.ak.us
Founded 1995. Pop 4,376; Circ 228,841
Library Holdings: Audiobooks 71; Bks on Deafness & Sign Lang 142; DVDs 17,940; Electronic Media & Resources 51; High Interest/Low Vocabulary Bk Vols 4,492; Bk Titles 34,241; Bk Vols 35,847; Per Subs 135; Videos 8,491
Special Collections: Alaskana Coll; Aleutian Region Newspaper Coll
Automation Activity & Vendor Info: (Acquisitions) Baker & Taylor; (Cataloging) OCLC FirstSearch; (Circulation) SirsiDynix; (Course Reserve) SirsiDynix; (ILL) OCLC WorldShare Interlibrary Loan; (OPAC) SirsiDynix; (Serials) SirsiDynix

Wireless access
Function: After school storytime
Partic in Alaska Library Network
Special Services for the Deaf - TDD equip
Open Mon-Fri 10-9, Sat & Sun 12-6
Restriction: Non-circulating of rare bks
Friends of the Library Group

VALDEZ

P VALDEZ CONSORTIUM LIBRARY, 212 Fairbanks St, 99686. (Mail add: PO Box 609, 99686-0609), SAN 300-2861. Tel: 907-835-4632. FAX: 907-835-4876. Web Site: www.valdezak.gov/148/library. *Head Librn,* Mollie Good; E-mail: mgood@valdezak.gov; *Circ Supvr,* Sara Baker; E-mail: sbaker@valdezak.gov; Staff 1 (MLS 1)
Founded 1930. Pop 4,036; Circ 48,442
Library Holdings: Bks on Deafness & Sign Lang 111; DVDs 64; High Interest/Low Vocabulary Bk Vols 54; Large Print Bks 140; Bk Titles 44,750; Bk Vols 45,786; Per Subs 136; Talking Bks 1,700; Videos 1,455
Special Collections: Alaska Coll
Automation Activity & Vendor Info: (Acquisitions) SirsiDynix; (Cataloging) SirsiDynix; (Circulation) SirsiDynix; (OPAC) SirsiDynix
Wireless access
Partic in Alaska Library Network
Open Mon-Fri 10-6, Sat 12:30-4:30

WASILLA

P WASILLA PUBLIC LIBRARY, 500 N Crusey St, 99654. SAN 300-287X. Tel: 907-864-9170. FAX: 907-376-2347. E-mail: library@ci.wasilla.ak.us. Web Site: www.cityofwasilla.com/services/departments/library. *Dir,* Zane Treesh; E-mail: ztreesh@ci.wasilla.ak.us; *User Serv Librn,* Ivory VanZant; Tel: 907-864-9177, E-mail: ivanzant@ci.wasilla.ak.us; *Youth Serv Librn,* Sara Saxton; Tel: 907-864-9173, E-mail: ssaxton@ci.wasilla.ak.us; Staff 12 (MLS 3, Non-MLS 9)
Founded 1938. Pop 39,736; Circ 169,567. Sal $463,684
Library Holdings: Audiobooks 2,112; e-books 6,280; Electronic Media & Resources 7,871; Bk Titles 55,277; Bk Vols 53,914; Per Subs 79; Videos 2,985
Special Collections: Municipal Document Depository
Subject Interests: Alaskana
Automation Activity & Vendor Info: (Cataloging) SirsiDynix; (Circulation) SirsiDynix; (ILL) OCLC WorldShare Interlibrary Loan; (OPAC) SirsiDynix
Wireless access
Function: Art exhibits, Audiobks via web, Bks on cassette, Bks on CD, Children's prog, Computers for patron use, Digital talking bks, Doc delivery serv, Electronic databases & coll, Free DVD rentals, Homework prog, ILL available, Internet access, Microfiche/film & reading machines, Music CDs, Online cat, Outside serv via phone, mail, e-mail & web, OverDrive digital audio bks, Photocopying/Printing, Preschool reading prog, Printer for laptops & handheld devices, Prog for adults, Prog for children & young adult, Ref serv available, Serves people with intellectual disabilities, Story hour, Summer & winter reading prog, Summer reading prog, Tax forms, Teen prog, Telephone ref, VHS videos, Wheelchair accessible, Winter reading prog
Partic in Alaska Library Network; Matanuska-Susitna Library Network
Open Mon 2-6, Tues & Thurs 10:30-7, Wed & Fri 10:30-6, Sat 1-5
Friends of the Library Group

WILLOW

P WILLOW PUBLIC LIBRARY, 23557 W Willow Community Center Circle, 99688. (Mail add: PO Box 129, 99688-0129), SAN 320-4677. Tel: 907-861-7655. Administration Tel: 907-861-7656. FAX: 907-495-5014. E-mail: willow.library@matsugov.us. Web Site: matsugov.us/msln/willow. *Librn,* Julie Mitchell; E-mail: jmitchell@matsugov.us; *Asst Librn,* LeaAnn Nichols; Staff 2 (Non-MLS 2)
Founded 1967. Circ 33,377
Library Holdings: Audiobooks 1,345; DVDs 2,091; Bk Vols 23,306; Per Subs 55
Special Collections: Alaskana
Automation Activity & Vendor Info: (Acquisitions) SirsiDynix; (Cataloging) SirsiDynix; (ILL) SirsiDynix; (OPAC) Innovative Interfaces, Inc
Wireless access
Function: 24/7 Electronic res, 24/7 Online cat, Activity rm, Adult bk club, Art programs, Audiobks via web, Bk club(s), Bks on CD, Children's prog, Computer training, Computers for patron use, Electronic databases & coll, Free DVD rentals, Govt ref serv, Holiday prog, Homework prog, ILL available, Internet access, Life-long learning prog for all ages, Magazines, Mail & tel request accepted, Meeting rooms, Movies, Music CDs, Notary serv, Online cat, Online info literacy tutorials on the web & in blackboard, Outside serv via phone, mail, e-mail & web, OverDrive digital audio bks, Photocopying/Printing, Preschool reading prog, Prog for adults, Prog for children & young adult, Ref & res, Ref serv available, Scanner, Senior computer classes, Spanish lang bks, Story hour, Study rm, Summer & winter reading prog, Summer reading prog, Tax forms, Teen prog, Telephone ref, Wheelchair accessible
Partic in Alaska Library Network
Open Mon, Tues & Thurs 12-8, Wed & Fri 10-6, Sat 10-3:30
Friends of the Library Group

WRANGELL

P IRENE INGLE PUBLIC LIBRARY*, Wrangell Public Library, 124 Second Ave, 99929. (Mail add: PO Box 679, 99929-0679), SAN 300-2888. Tel: 907-874-3535. FAX: 907-874-2520. E-mail: wrangelllibrary@gci.net. Web Site: www.wrangell.com/library. *Libr Dir,* Margaret Villarma; *Libr Asst,* Sarah Scambler; Staff 2 (Non-MLS 2)
Founded 1921. Pop 2,348; Circ 40,209
Jul 2012-Jun 2013 Income $292,590, State $6,250, City $280,340, Federal $6,000. Mats Exp $286,340
Library Holdings: Bk Titles 28,000; Per Subs 62
Subject Interests: Alaska
Automation Activity & Vendor Info: (Acquisitions) The Library Co-Op, Inc; (Cataloging) The Library Co-Op, Inc; (Circulation) The Library Co-Op, Inc; (ILL) OCLC FirstSearch; (OPAC) The Library Co-Op, Inc
Wireless access
Partic in Alaska Library Network
Open Mon & Fri 10-12 & 1-5, Tues-Thurs 1-7, Sat 9-5
Friends of the Library Group

ARIZONA

Date of Statistics: FY 2020
Population, 2020 U.S. Census: 7,421,401
Population Served by Public Libraries: 7,294,587
Total Volumes in Public Libraries: 8,797,074
Volumes Per Capita: 1.21
Total Public Library Circulation: 45,886,475
Digital Resources:
Total computers for use by the public: 4,749
Total annual wireless sessions: 8,797,074
Successful Retrieval of Electronic Information: 9,822,450
Library Visits Per Year: 16,287,783
Circulation Per Capita: 6.29
Income and Expenditures:
Total Public Library Income: $216,340,710
Number of County Libraries: 15
Counties Served: 15
Number of Bookmobiles in State: 10
Grants-in-Aid to Public Libraries: (FY 2020-2021)
Federal: $1,499,636
State Aid: $1,514,876
Information provided courtesy of: Chris Guerra, Project Specialist & State Data Coordinator; Arizona State Library, Archives and Public Records

APACHE JUNCTION

P APACHE JUNCTION PUBLIC LIBRARY*, 1177 N Idaho Rd, 85119. SAN 300-290X. Tel: 480-474-8555. FAX: 480-671-8037. Web Site: www.ajpl.org. *Libr Dir,* Pam Harrison; Tel: 480-474-8615, E-mail: pstandhart@ajcity.net; *Librn,* Linda Konopitski; Tel: 480-474-8562, E-mail: lkonopitski@ajcity.net; *Adult Serv Supvry Librn,* Vicki Ann Duraine; Tel: 480-474-8561; *Youth Serv Supvry Librn,* Position Currently Open; *Libr Mgr,* Tracie Curtis; Tel: 480-474-8563, E-mail: tcompton@ajcity.net; *Libr Supvr,* Trish Pelletier; Tel: 480-474-8558, E-mail: tp@ajcity.net. Subject Specialists: *Adult prog,* Vicki Ann Duraine; *Circ & libr serv,* Trish Pelletier; Staff 6 (MLS 5, Non-MLS 1)
Founded 1965. Pop 37,263; Circ 578,126
Jul 2013-Jun 2014 Income $1,118,952, City $1,093,952, County $25,000
Library Holdings: AV Mats 34,402; e-books 27,626; Bk Titles 92,310; Bk Vols 122,022; Per Subs 127
Special Collections: Arizona Coll; Superstition Mountain Reserve Coll. US Document Depository
Automation Activity & Vendor Info: (Acquisitions) Innovative Interfaces, Inc; (Cataloging) Innovative Interfaces, Inc; (Circulation) Innovative Interfaces, Inc; (OPAC) Innovative Interfaces, Inc
Wireless access
Mem of Pinal County Library District
Special Services for the Deaf - TDD equip; Videos & decoder
Special Services for the Blind - Bks on cassette; Bks on CD; Large print bks; Magnifiers; Screen enlargement software for people with visual disabilities; ZoomText magnification & reading software
Open Mon-Thurs 9-8, Fri & Sat 9-5
Friends of the Library Group

C CENTRAL ARIZONA COLLEGE*, Superstition Mountain Campus Learning Resource Center, 805 S Idaho Rd, 85119. Tel: 480-677-7747. FAX: 480-677-7738. *Librn,* Heidi Greathouse; E-mail: heidi.greathouse@centralaz.edu; *Librn,* Melanie Schneeflock; E-mail: melanie.schneeflock@centralaz.edu
Library Holdings: Bk Vols 10,000; Per Subs 10
Wireless access
Open Mon-Thurs 8-6

ARIZONA CITY

P ARIZONA CITY COMMUNITY LIBRARY*, 13254 Sunland Gin Rd, 85123. (Mail add: PO Box 118, 85223-0118), SAN 300-2918. Tel: 520-466-5565. FAX: 520-466-6050.
Founded 1963. Pop 5,000; Circ 9,942
Library Holdings: AV Mats 600; Bk Vols 22,000; Talking Bks 450
Special Collections: Arizona Coll
Automation Activity & Vendor Info: (Cataloging) Horizon; (Circulation) Horizon; (OPAC) Horizon
Wireless access
Publications: Newsletter
Mem of Pinal County Library District
Special Services for the Blind - Audio mat; Talking bks
Open Mon, Tues, Thurs & Fri 9-1, Sat 10-2
Friends of the Library Group

AVONDALE

P AVONDALE PUBLIC LIBRARY*, Sam Garcia Western Avenue Library, 495 E Western Ave, 85323. SAN 300-2926. Tel: 623-333-2602. E-mail: emailLibrary@avondale.org. Web Site: www.avondalelibrary.org. *Libr Mgr,* Ava Gutwein; E-mail: agutwein@avondale.org
Founded 1930. Pop 60,000; Circ 150,000
Library Holdings: Bk Vols 45,000; Per Subs 52
Subject Interests: Spanish (Lang)
Automation Activity & Vendor Info: (Cataloging) Innovative Interfaces, Inc; (Circulation) Innovative Interfaces, Inc; (OPAC) Innovative Interfaces, Inc
Wireless access
Open Mon-Thurs 11-7, Fri & Sun 1-5, Sat 11-5
Friends of the Library Group
Branches: 1
AVONDALE CIVIC CENTER LIBRARY, 11350 W Civic Ctr Dr, 85323. Tel: 623-333-2602. *Libr Mgr,* Jesse Caufield; E-mail: jcaufield@avondale.org
Founded 2007
Open Mon-Thurs 11-7, Fri 1-5, Sat 11-5
Friends of the Library Group

J ESTRELLA MOUNTAIN COMMUNITY COLLEGE LIBRARY, 3000 N Dysart Rd, 85392. SAN 374-7417. Tel: 623-935-8191. FAX: 623-935-8060. Web Site: www.estrellamountain.edu/library. *Div Chair,* Terry Meyer; *Librn,* Nikol Price; E-mail: nikol.price@estrellamountain.edu; *Librn,* Elisabeth Rodriguez; E-mail: elisabeth.rodriquez@estrellamountain.edu; *Librn,* Jennifer Wong; Staff 9 (MLS 5, Non-MLS 4)
Founded 1992. Enrl 5,000; Fac 92; Highest Degree: Associate
Library Holdings: Bk Titles 24,000; Per Subs 30
Automation Activity & Vendor Info: (Acquisitions) SirsiDynix; (Cataloging) SirsiDynix; (Circulation) SirsiDynix; (Course Reserve) SirsiDynix; (ILL) OCLC ILLiad; (Serials) SirsiDynix
Wireless access
Open Mon-Thurs 7am-10pm, Fri 7-4:30, Sat 8-3

BENSON

P BENSON PUBLIC LIBRARY*, 300 S Huachuca St, 85602-6650. SAN 300-2934. Tel: 520-586-9535. E-mail: bensonpubliclibrary@cityofbenson.com. Web Site: www.cityofbenson.com/index.asp?SEC=1006AE7A-E93F-46BA-9EDA-2134A0439EDF&Type=B_BASIC (www.cityofbenson.com/index.asp?SEC=1006AE7A-E93F-46BA-9EDA-2134A0439EDF&Type=B_BASIC). *Senior Asst Dir,* Kelli Jeter; E-mail: kjeter@bensonaz.gov; Staff 7 (Non-MLS 7)

Founded 1916. Pop 8,000; Circ 74,000
Library Holdings: Bk Vols 36,625; Per Subs 51
Special Collections: Arizoniana
Subject Interests: Arizona, Gen fiction
Automation Activity & Vendor Info: (Cataloging) SirsiDynix; (Circulation) SirsiDynix
Wireless access
Function: ILL available, Photocopying/Printing, Prof lending libr, Ref serv available, Telephone ref
Mem of Cochise County Library District
Partic in Prairielands Library Exchange
Special Services for the Deaf - Bks on deafness & sign lang; Spec interest per
Special Services for the Blind - Bks on cassette
Open Mon-Thurs 10-6, Fri 10-5
Friends of the Library Group

BISBEE

S BISBEE MINING & HISTORICAL MUSEUM*, Lemuel C Shattuck Memorial Archival Library, Five Copper Queen Plaza, 85603. (Mail add: PO Box 14, 85603-0014), SAN 300-2942. Tel: 520-432-7071, Ext 2. E-mail: info@bisbeemuseum.org. Web Site: bisbeemuseum.org. *Dir,* Carrie Gustavson; E-mail: carrie@bisbeemuseum.org; Staff 4 (MLS 1, Non-MLS 3)
Founded 1974
Library Holdings: AV Mats 450; Bk Titles 1,200
Special Collections: Bisbee Newspapers 1898-1970, microfilm; City of Bisbee Voter Registration Records; Cochise County Original Geological Survey Maps; County Great Registers & County Census for 1880 (1882 Special Census), 1900 & 1910; Historic Image Photographic Coll; Historic Preservation & Restoration File; Hospital Records, pre-1900; Manuscript Coll; Tombstone Newspapers 1877-1901. Municipal Document Depository; Oral History
Subject Interests: Geol, Local hist, Mining
Wireless access
Open Mon-Sun 10-4
Restriction: Non-circulating
Friends of the Library Group

GL COCHISE COUNTY LAW LIBRARY*, 100 Quality Hill Rd, 85603. (Mail add: PO Box 204, 85603-0204), SAN 300-2950. Tel: 520-432-8513. Administration Tel: 520-432-8500. FAX: 520-432-2630. Web Site: www.cochise.az.gov. *Librn,* Veronica Olivares; E-mail: volivares@cochise.az.gov
Founded 1930
Library Holdings: Bk Titles 27,000
Open Mon-Fri 8-5

P COCHISE COUNTY LIBRARY DISTRICT*, 100 Clawson Ave, 85603. (Mail add: PO Drawer AK, 85603-0099), SAN 330-5228. Tel: 520-432-8930. Toll Free Tel: 800-231-1574. FAX: 520-432-7339. Web Site: cochiselibrary.org. *Libr Dir,* Amadee Ricketts; Tel: 520-432-8935, E-mail: aricketts@cochise.az.gov; *Syst Adminr,* Larry Scritchfield; E-mail: lscritch@cochisecold.lib.az.us; *Tech Serv,* April McKinney; E-mail: amckinney@cochisecold.lib.az.us; Staff 9 (MLS 4, Non-MLS 5)
Founded 1970. Pop 135,000
Library Holdings: Bk Titles 70,000; Bk Vols 120,000
Automation Activity & Vendor Info: (Cataloging) SirsiDynix; (Circulation) SirsiDynix; (ILL) SirsiDynix; (OPAC) SirsiDynix
Wireless access
Function: Homebound delivery serv
Member Libraries: Benson Public Library; Copper Queen Library; Douglas Public Library; Elsie S Hogan Community Library; Huachuca City Public Library; Sierra Vista Public Library; Tombstone City Library
Open Mon-Fri 8-5
Friends of the Library Group
Branches: 5
ELFRIDA LIBRARY, 10552 N Hwy 191, Elfrida, 85610-9021. (Mail add: PO Box 98, Elfrida, 85610-0098). Tel: 520-642-1744. FAX: 520-642-1744. Web Site: cochiselibrary.org/client/en_US/elfrida. *Br Mgr,* Stephanie Fulton; E-mail: sfulton@cochise.az.gov; Staff 1 (Non-MLS 1)
Pop 1,200; Circ 9,434
Library Holdings: Bk Vols 6,440
Function: Prog for children & young adult, Summer reading prog
Open Tues 12-7, Wed 10-2, Thurs 9-12 & 2-5, Fri 1-5, Sat 9-12
Friends of the Library Group
MYRTLE KRAFT LIBRARY, 2393 S Rock House Rd, Portal, 85632. (Mail add: PO Box 16552, Portal, 85632-6552), SAN 330-5430. Tel: 520-558-2468. FAX: 520-558-2468. Web Site: cochiselibrary.org/client/en_US/portal. *Br Mgr,* Kathleen Talbot; E-mail: ktalbot@cochise.az.gov; Staff 1 (Non-MLS 1)
Founded 1979. Pop 300; Circ 4,913
Library Holdings: Bk Vols 4,800
Function: Summer reading prog
Open Tues-Sat 10-2
Friends of the Library Group
JIMMIE LIBHART LIBRARY, 201 N Central Ave, Bowie, 85605. (Mail add: PO Box 417, Bowie, 85605-0417), SAN 325-3910. Tel: 520-847-2522. FAX: 520-847-2522. Web Site: cochiselibrary.org/client/en_US/bowie. *Br Mgr,* Richard Bergquist; E-mail: rbergquist@cochise.az.gov; Staff 1 (Non-MLS 1)
Founded 1985. Pop 300; Circ 5,070
Library Holdings: Bk Vols 4,897
Function: Prog for children & young adult, Summer reading prog
Open Mon, Tues & Thurs-Sat 10-3
SUNSITES COMMUNITY LIBRARY, 210 N Ford Rd, Pearce, 85625. (Mail add: PO Box 544, Pearce, 85625-0544), SAN 330-5252. Tel: 520-826-3866. FAX: 520-826-3866. Web Site: cochiselibrary.org/client/en_US/sunsites. *Br Mgr,* Sharon Arthur; E-mail: sarthur@cochise.az.gov; Staff 1 (Non-MLS 1)
Founded 1979. Pop 1,200; Circ 13,290
Library Holdings: Bk Vols 10,166
Function: Prog for children & young adult, Summer reading prog
Open Mon, Wed & Fri 9:30-4:30, Thurs 12-7, Sat 9:30-11:30
Friends of the Library Group
ALICE WOODS SUNIZONA LIBRARY, Ash Creek School, 6460 E Hwy 181, Pearce, 85625, SAN 330-549X. Tel: 520-824-3145. FAX: 520-824-3145. Web Site: cochiselibrary.org/client/en_US/sunizona. *Br Mgr,* Marian Baker Gierlach; E-mail: mbakergierlach@cochise.az.gov; Staff 1 (Non-MLS 1)
Founded 1979. Pop 300; Circ 9,639
Library Holdings: Bk Vols 9,536
Function: Summer reading prog
Open Tues 2-4, Wed 9:30-11:30, Thurs 9-11:30, Fri 11:30-5, Sat 9-12

P COPPER QUEEN LIBRARY*, Bisbee City Library, Six Main St, 85603. (Mail add: PO Box 1857, 85603-2857), SAN 300-2969. Tel: 520-432-4232. FAX: 520-432-7061. E-mail: CopperQueenLibrary@BisbeeAz.gov. Web Site: www.bisbeeaz.gov/2155/Copper-Queen-Library. *Libr Mgr,* Jason Macoviak; *Prog Coordr,* Allison Williams; Staff 4 (MLS 1, Non-MLS 3)
Founded 1882. Pop 6,090; Circ 42,196
Library Holdings: Bk Vols 30,000; Per Subs 40
Special Collections: Southwest & Arizona Coll
Automation Activity & Vendor Info: (Cataloging) SirsiDynix; (Circulation) SirsiDynix
Wireless access
Mem of Cochise County Library District
Open Mon & Tues Noon-7, Wed-Fri 10-5
Friends of the Library Group

BOUSE

P BOUSE PUBLIC LIBRARY*, 44031 Plomosa Rd, 85325. (Mail add: PO Box 840, 85325-0840). Tel: 928-851-1023. FAX: 928-851-2758. E-mail: bplbouse@co.la-paz.az.us. Web Site: www.bousepubliclibrary.com, www.parkerpubliclibrary.com/bouse.html. *Libr Mgr,* Sharon Hillhouse; E-mail: shillhouse@co.la-paz.az.us; Staff 1 (Non-MLS 1)
Automation Activity & Vendor Info: (Acquisitions) Follett Software; (Cataloging) Follett Software; (Circulation) Follett Software; (ILL) OCLC CatExpress; (OPAC) Follett Software
Wireless access
Function: 24/7 Electronic res, 24/7 Online cat, Activity rm, Adult bk club, Adult literacy prog
Open Mon 10-6, Tues, Wed & Thurs 9-4
Friends of the Library Group

BUCKEYE

S ARIZONA DEPARTMENT OF CORRECTIONS - ADULT INSTITUTIONS*, Arizona State Prison Complex - Lewis Library, 26700 S Hwy 85, 85326. (Mail add: PO Box 70, 85326-0070), Tel: 623-386-6160. FAX: 623-386-7332. Web Site: corrections.az.gov/location/98/lewis. *Librn,* Steve Latto; E-mail: slatto@azadc.gov
Library Holdings: Bk Vols 30,000

P BUCKEYE PUBLIC LIBRARY SYSTEM*, Downtown Library, 310 N Sixth St, 85326-2439. SAN 300-2977. Tel: 623-349-6300. FAX: 623-349-6310. E-mail: library@buckeyeaz.gov. Web Site: www.buckeyeaz.gov/residents/library. *Dir,* Christine Larson; E-mail: clarson@buckeyeaz.gov; Staff 9.8 (MLS 2, Non-MLS 7.8)
Founded 1956. Pop 54,000
Library Holdings: Bk Vols 25,000; Per Subs 60
Special Collections: Arizona History & Culture (Southwest Coll)
Automation Activity & Vendor Info: (Cataloging) Innovative Interfaces, Inc; (Circulation) Innovative Interfaces, Inc; (OPAC) Innovative Interfaces, Inc
Wireless access
Open Mon, Wed & Fri 9-6, Tues & Thurs 9-7, Sat 9-4
Friends of the Library Group

Branches: 1
COYOTE BRANCH, 21699 W Yuma Rd, Ste 116, 85326, SAN 991-3165.
Open Mon & Wed 11-7, Tues, Thurs & Fri 10-6, Sat 9-4
Friends of the Library Group
Bookmobiles: 1

CAMP VERDE

P CAMP VERDE COMMUNITY LIBRARY, 130 N Black Bridge Rd, 86322. SAN 323-7850. Tel: 928-554-8380. E-mail: library@campverde.az.gov. Web Site: www.campverde.az.gov/departments/community-library. *Libr Dir,* Kathy D Hellman; Tel: 928-554-8381, E-mail: kathy.hellman@campverde.az.gov; *Youth Serv Librn,* Leticia Ancira; Tel: 928-554-8387, E-mail: leticia.ancira@campverde.az.gov; *Circ Spec,* Alice R Gottschalk; Tel: 928-554-8383, E-mail: alice.gottschalk@campverde.az.gov; *Adult Serv, Libr Spec,* Carson Ralston; E-mail: carson.ralston@campverde.az.gov; *Libr Spec - Teens,* Zack Garcia; E-mail: zachary.garcia@campverde.az.gov; *Ref Spec,* Wendy Cook-Roberts; E-mail: wendy.roberts@campverde.az.gov; *Tech Serv Spec,* Jaye Valles; Tel: 928-554-8388, E-mail: jaye.valles@campverde.az.gov; Staff 7 (MLS 2, Non-MLS 5)
Founded 1958. Pop 12,000; Circ 63,976
Jul 2020-Jun 2021 Income $571,880, City $460,880, County $86,000, Locally Generated Income $25,000. Mats Exp $26,700, Books $17,700, Other Print Mats $1,700, AV Mat $7,300. Sal $288,279 (Prof $81,557)
Library Holdings: Audiobooks 1,260; AV Mats 16; CDs 649; DVDs 4,077; e-books 77; Large Print Bks 2,904; Bk Titles 27,121; Per Subs 46
Special Collections: Southwest US Information & Culture
Automation Activity & Vendor Info: (Cataloging) SirsiDynix; (Circulation) SirsiDynix; (ILL) OCLC WorldShare Interlibrary Loan; (OPAC) SirsiDynix
Wireless access
Function: 24/7 Electronic res, 24/7 Online cat, 3D Printer, Accelerated reader prog, Activity rm, Adult bk club, Adult literacy prog, Art exhibits, Audiobks on Playaways & MP3, Audiobks via web, AV serv, BA reader (adult literacy), Bilingual assistance for Spanish patrons, Bk club(s), Bk reviews (Group), Bks on CD, Butterfly Garden, Children's prog, Citizenship assistance, Computer training, Computers for patron use, Digital talking bks, E-Readers, Electronic databases & coll, Family literacy, Free DVD rentals, Games & aids for people with disabilities, Health sci info serv, Holiday prog, Home delivery & serv to seniorr ctr & nursing homes, Homebound delivery serv, Homework prog, ILL available, Instruction & testing, Internet access, Laminating, Learning ctr, Life-long learning prog for all ages, Literacy & newcomer serv, Magazines, Magnifiers for reading, Mail & tel request accepted, Mango lang, Meeting rooms, Movies, Music CDs, Online cat, Outreach serv, Outside serv via phone, mail, e-mail & web, OverDrive digital audio bks, Photocopying/Printing, Preschool outreach, Preschool reading prog, Printer for laptops & handheld devices, Prof lending libr, Prog for adults, Prog for children & young adult, Ref & res, Ref serv available, Scanner, Senior computer classes, Senior outreach, Spanish lang bks, STEM programs, Story hour, Study rm, Summer reading prog, Tax forms, Teen prog, Telephone ref, Wheelchair accessible, Workshops, Writing prog
Publications: Subject Handouts
Partic in Association for Rural & Small Libraries; Yavapai Libr Network
Open Mon-Thurs 9-8, Fri & Sat 9-5
Friends of the Library Group

CASA GRANDE

P CASA GRANDE PUBLIC LIBRARY*, 449 N Drylake St, 85222. SAN 300-2993. Tel: 520-421-8710. FAX: 520-421-8701. E-mail: cglibrary@casagrandeaz.gov. Web Site: casagrandeaz.gov/library. *Libr Mgr,* Amber Kent; E-mail: AKent@ci.casa-grande.az.us; *Circ Supvr,* Ella Kubrick; E-mail: Ella_Kubrick@ci.casa-grande.az.us; Staff 12 (MLS 4, Non-MLS 8)
Founded 1958. Pop 42,455; Circ 230,000
Library Holdings: AV Mats 8,365; CDs 494; DVDs 696; Electronic Media & Resources 12; High Interest/Low Vocabulary Bk Vols 100; Large Print Bks 3,241; Bk Titles 75,433; Per Subs 312; Talking Bks 100; Videos 6,933
Special Collections: Municipal Document Depository
Subject Interests: Local hist
Automation Activity & Vendor Info: (Acquisitions) Innovative Interfaces, Inc; (Cataloging) Innovative Interfaces, Inc; (Circulation) Innovative Interfaces, Inc; (Course Reserve) Innovative Interfaces, Inc; (ILL) Innovative Interfaces, Inc; (Media Booking) Innovative Interfaces, Inc; (OPAC) Innovative Interfaces, Inc; (Serials) Innovative Interfaces, Inc
Wireless access
Function: Archival coll, Art exhibits, Audiobks via web, BA reader (adult literacy), Bk club(s), Bks on cassette, Bks on CD, Children's prog, Computer training, Computers for patron use, Digital talking bks, E-Reserves, Electronic databases & coll, Family literacy, Free DVD rentals, Holiday prog, Homebound delivery serv, Homework prog, ILL available, Instruction & testing, Internet access, Learning ctr, Music CDs, Online cat, Outside serv via phone, mail, e-mail & web, OverDrive digital audio bks, Photocopying/Printing, Ref & res, Ref serv available, Res libr, Senior computer classes, Senior outreach, Spoken cassettes & CDs, Spoken cassettes & DVDs, Story hour, Summer reading prog, Tax forms, Teen prog, Telephone ref, VHS videos, Wheelchair accessible
Mem of Pinal County Library District
Special Services for the Deaf - TTY equip
Open Mon-Thurs 9-7, Fri 9-5, Sun 1-5
Friends of the Library Group
Branches: 1
VISTA GRANDE LIBRARY, 1556 N Arizola Rd, 85122. Tel: 520-421-8652. FAX: 520-836-0819. *Mgr,* Amber Kent
Library Holdings: AV Mats 10,000; Bk Vols 30,000; Per Subs 50
Open Mon-Fri 8-5, Sat 9-5
Friends of the Library Group
Bookmobiles: 1. Librn, Chuck Okafor

S CASA GRANDE VALLEY HISTORICAL SOCIETY*, Museum of Casa Grande Museum Library, 110 W Florence Blvd, 85122. SAN 327-7089. Tel: 520-836-2223. E-mail: info@tmocg.org. Web Site: www.tmocg.org. *Library Contact,* Erin Henderson
Founded 1964
Library Holdings: Bk Titles 200
Subject Interests: Local hist
Wireless access
Open Thurs-Sun Noon-4
Restriction: Non-circulating to the pub

CAVE CREEK

P DESERT FOOTHILLS LIBRARY, 38443 N Schoolhouse Rd, 85331. SAN 376-8414. Tel: 480-488-2286. FAX: 480-595-8353. Web Site: dfla.org. *Exec Dir,* Anne Johnson; E-mail: ajohnson@dfla.org; *Acq Librn,* Sara Zapotocky; E-mail: szapotocky@dfla.org; *Youth & Teen Serv Librn,* Heather Wurr; E-mail: hwurr@dfla.org; *Pub Serv Mgr,* Ashley Ware; E-mail: aware@dfla.org; *Support Serv Mgr,* Terri Engebretson; E-mail: tengebretson@dfla.org; Staff 7 (MLS 5, Non-MLS 2)
Founded 1953. Pop 5,676; Circ 90,000
Jul 2017-Jun 2018 Income $845,500, Federal $5,000, County $63,000, Locally Generated Income $777,500. Mats Exp $67,000, Books $43,500, Per/Ser (Incl. Access Fees) $4,000, AV Mat $19,500. Sal $402,473 (Prof $135,000)
Library Holdings: Audiobooks 3,617; AV Mats 5,300; DVDs 7,818; e-books 5,000; Large Print Bks 1,200; Bk Vols 52,526; Per Subs 100
Special Collections: Southwest Coll
Automation Activity & Vendor Info: (Acquisitions) Baker & Taylor; (Cataloging) Baker & Taylor; (ILL) OCLC WorldShare Interlibrary Loan
Wireless access
Function: 24/7 Electronic res, 24/7 Online cat, Accelerated reader prog, Activity rm, Adult bk club, Adult literacy prog, Art exhibits, Audiobks via web, Bks on CD, Children's prog, Citizenship assistance, Computer training, Computers for patron use, Digital talking bks, Electronic databases & coll, Free DVD rentals, Homebound delivery serv, ILL available, Internet access, Magazines, Movies, Museum passes, Music CDs, Notary serv, Online cat, Online ref, Orientations, OverDrive digital audio bks, Passport agency, Photocopying/Printing, Prog for adults, Prog for children & young adult, Senior computer classes, Senior outreach, Spanish lang bks, Story hour, Study rm, Summer reading prog, Tax forms, Teen prog, Wheelchair accessible, Workshops
Open Mon, Wed & Fri 9-5, Tues & Thurs 9-6, Sat 10-4

CHANDLER

J CHANDLER-GILBERT COMMUNITY COLLEGE LIBRARY*, 2626 E Pecos Rd, 85225-2499. Tel: 480-857-5100. Circulation Tel: 480-857-5102. Web Site: www.cgc.maricopa.edu/library. *Div Chair,* Carol Dichtenberg; Tel: 480-857-5133, E-mail: carol.dichtenberg@cgc.edu; *Access Serv,* Theresa Santa Cruz; Tel: 480-857-5116, E-mail: Theresa.Santacruz@cgc.edu; Staff 9 (MLS 4, Non-MLS 5)
Founded 1987. Enrl 12,000; Highest Degree: Associate
Library Holdings: Bk Vols 27,000; Per Subs 180
Automation Activity & Vendor Info: (Acquisitions) SirsiDynix; (Cataloging) SirsiDynix; (Circulation) SirsiDynix; (ILL) OCLC ILLiad; (OPAC) SirsiDynix
Wireless access
Open Mon-Thurs 7:30am-9pm, Fri 7:30-2, Sat 8-2

P CHANDLER PUBLIC LIBRARY*, 22 S Delaware, 85225. (Mail add: MS601, PO Box 4008, 85244-4008), SAN 300-3000. Tel: 480-782-2800. FAX: 480-782-2823. TDD: 800-367-8939. Web Site: www.chandlerlibrary.org. *Libr Mgr,* Daniel Lee; Tel: 480-782-2813, E-mail: dan.lee@chandleraz.gov; *Asst Libr Mgr,* Mary Sagar; Tel: 480-782-2820, E-mail: mary.sagar@chandleraz.gov; *Asst Libr Mgr, Pub Serv,* Kris Sherman; Tel: 480-782-2818, E-mail: kris.sherman@chandleraz.gov; *Admin Librn, Br Mgr, Main Libr,* Abigail Nersesian; Tel: 480-782-2804, E-mail:

abigail.nersesian@chandleraz.gov; *Admin Librn, Coll Develop,* Marybeth Gardner; Tel: 480-782-2816, E-mail: marybeth.gardner@chandleraz.gov; Staff 38 (MLS 10, Non-MLS 28)
Founded 1954. Pop 250,000
Automation Activity & Vendor Info: (Acquisitions) Innovative Interfaces, Inc; (Cataloging) Innovative Interfaces, Inc; (Circulation) Innovative Interfaces, Inc; (Course Reserve) Innovative Interfaces, Inc; (Discovery) Innovative Interfaces, Inc; (ILL) Innovative Interfaces, Inc; (Media Booking) Innovative Interfaces, Inc; (OPAC) Innovative Interfaces, Inc; (Serials) Innovative Interfaces, Inc
Wireless access
Function: Adult bk club, Homebound delivery serv, Homework prog, ILL available, Summer reading prog, Telephone ref
Open Mon-Wed 9-9, Thurs-Sat 9-5, Sun 1-5
Friends of the Library Group
Branches: 3
BASHA, 5990 S Val Vista Dr, 85249. (Mail add: MS 920, PO Box 4008, 85244-4008). FAX: 480-782-2855. *Admin Librn,* Jess Hawkins; Tel: 480-782-2856, E-mail: jessica.hawkins@chandleraz.gov; Staff 10 (MLS 5, Non-MLS 5)
Founded 2003
Function: 24/7 Electronic res, 24/7 Online cat, Adult literacy prog, Electronic databases & coll, Photocopying/Printing, Prog for adults, Prog for children & young adult, Summer reading prog
Open Mon-Wed 7:30-8, Thurs & Fri 7:30-5, Sat 10-2
Friends of the Library Group
HAMILTON, 3700 S Arizona Ave, 85248-4500. (Mail add: MS917, PO Box 4008, 85244-4008). FAX: 480-782-2833. *Admin Librn,* Phyllis Saunders; Tel: 480-782-2831, E-mail: phyllis.saunders@chandleraz.gov; Staff 9 (MLS 4, Non-MLS 5)
Function: Adult bk club, Photocopying/Printing
Open Mon-Wed 7:30am-8pm, Thurs & Fri 7:30-5, Sat 1-5
Friends of the Library Group
SUNSET, 4930 W Ray Rd, 85226-6219. (Mail add: MS918, PO Box 4008, 85244-4008). FAX: 480-782-2848. *Admin Librn,* Susan Van Horne; E-mail: susan.vanhorne@chandleraz.gov; Staff 16 (MLS 6, Non-MLS 10)
Function: 24/7 Electronic res, 24/7 Online cat, Activity rm, Adult bk club, After school storytime, Audiobks via web, Bilingual assistance for Spanish patrons, Bk club(s), Bks on CD, Children's prog, Computers for patron use, Digital talking bks, E-Reserves, Electronic databases & coll, Family literacy, ILL available, Internet access, Life-long learning prog for all ages, Magazines, Mango lang, Meeting rooms, Movies, Museum passes, Music CDs, Online cat, Online ref, Photocopying/Printing, Preschool outreach, Preschool reading prog, Printer for laptops & handheld devices, Prog for adults, Prog for children & young adult, Ref & res, Ref serv available, Scanner, Story hour, Summer & winter reading prog, Summer reading prog, Tax forms, Teen prog, Wheelchair accessible
Open Mon-Wed 7:30am-8pm, Thurs & Fri 7:30-5, Sat 1-5
Friends of the Library Group

CHINO VALLEY

P CHINO VALLEY PUBLIC LIBRARY, 1020 W Palomino Rd, 86323-5500. SAN 323-7877. Tel: 928-636-2687. E-mail: library@chinoaz.net. Web Site: www.chinoaz.net/214/Library. *Libr Dir,* Scott A Bruner; E-mail: sbruner@chinoaz.net; *Libr Mgr,* Stacey Johnson; E-mail: sjohnson@chinoaz.net; *Ch Serv,* Rebecca Laurence; Tel: 928-636-9115, E-mail: rlaurence@chinoaz.net; Staff 11 (MLS 2, Non-MLS 9)
Founded 1983
Wireless access
Partic in Libr Network of Arizona; Yavapai Libr Network
Open Mon-Fri 9-6, Sat 10-2
Friends of the Library Group

CIBECUE

P CIBECUE COMMUNITY LIBRARY*, Six W Third St, 85911. (Mail add: PO Box 80008, 85911), SAN 376-6047. Tel: 928-332-2621. FAX: 928-332-2442. E-mail: cbqlibrary@wmat.us. *Dir,* Verna Cromwell
Library Holdings: Bk Vols 3,200
Wireless access
Mem of Navajo County Library System
Open Mon-Thurs 9-4:45

CLAY SPRINGS

P CLAY SPRINGS PUBLIC LIBRARY, 2106 Granite Rd, 85923. (Mail add: PO Box 428, 85923-0428), SAN 377-0737. Tel: 928-535-7142. E-mail: clayspringslibrary@gmail.com. *Dir,* Doris Reidhead
Library Holdings: AV Mats 215; Large Print Bks 50; Bk Titles 2,000; Bk Vols 3,500; Talking Bks 60
Wireless access
Mem of Navajo County Library System
Open Mon-Thurs 1:30-5:30

CLIFTON

P CLIFTON PUBLIC LIBRARY*, 588 Turner Ave, 85533. (Mail add: PO Box 1226, 85533-1226), SAN 300-3027. Tel: 928-865-2461. FAX: 928-865-3014. Web Site: www.greenleelibraries.org/Pages/Index/70876/clifton-library-information. *Libr Dir,* Sabrina Dumas; E-mail: dumas@townofclifton.com; Staff 1 (Non-MLS 1)
Founded 1941. Pop 9,000
Library Holdings: Bk Vols 17,500; Per Subs 15
Special Collections: Arizona Coll
Wireless access
Mem of Greenlee County Library System
Open Mon-Fri 9-5

COOLIDGE

C CENTRAL ARIZONA COLLEGE*, Signal Peak Library, 8470 N Overfield Rd, 85128. SAN 300-3043. Tel: 520-494-5286. FAX: 520-494-5284. *Librn,* Jonathan Osmer; E-mail: jonathan.osmer@centralaz.edu; Staff 9 (MLS 5, Non-MLS 4)
Founded 1969. Highest Degree: Associate
Library Holdings: Bk Vols 90,000; Per Subs 105
Special Collections: US Document Depository
Automation Activity & Vendor Info: (Acquisitions) SirsiDynix; (Cataloging) SirsiDynix; (Circulation) SirsiDynix; (Course Reserve) SirsiDynix; (ILL) SirsiDynix; (Media Booking) SirsiDynix; (OPAC) SirsiDynix; (Serials) SirsiDynix
Wireless access
Partic in Amigos Library Services, Inc; OCLC Online Computer Library Center, Inc
Special Services for the Blind - Accessible computers; Audio mat; Bks on CD; Copier with enlargement capabilities; Large screen computer & software; Low vision equip
Open Mon-Thurs 8-7
Departmental Libraries:
ARAVAIPA CAMPUS LEARNING RESOURCE CENTER
See Separate Entry in Winkelman

C ARAVAIPA CAMPUS LEARNING RESOURCE CENTER, 80440 E Aravaipa Rd, Winkelman, 85192. Tel: 520-357-2821. FAX: 520-357-2832. Web Site: www.centralaz.edu/current-students/student-support/library. *Dir,* Adriana Saavedra; E-mail: adriana.saavedra@centralaz.edu; *Librn,* Rebecca Swift; E-mail: rebecca.swift1@centralaz.edu
Enrl 260; Fac 6; Highest Degree: Associate
Library Holdings: Bk Vols 35,000
Function: AV serv
Special Services for the Deaf - Assistive tech
Open Mon-Thurs 8-6

C MARICOPA CAMPUS LEARNING RESOURCE CENTER, 17945 N Regent Dr, Maricopa, 85138. Tel: 520-494-6431. *Librn,* Scott Snellman; Tel: 520-494-6407, E-mail: scott.snellman@centralaz.edu
Open Mon-Thurs 8-7

C SAN TAN CAMPUS LEARNING RESOURCE CENTER, 3736 E Bella Vista Rd, San Tan Valley, 85143. Tel: 480-677-7844, 480-677-7861. *Librn,* Brandi Faulkner; Tel: 480-677-7841, E-mail: brandi.faulkner@centralaz.edu
Open Mon-Thurs 8-7
SUPERSTITION MOUNTAIN CAMPUS LEARNING RESOURCE CENTER
See Separate Entry in Apache Junction

P COOLIDGE PUBLIC LIBRARY*, 160 W Central Ave, 85128. SAN 300-3051. Tel: 520-723-6030. FAX: 520-723-7026. E-mail: library@coolidgeaz.com. Web Site: www.coolidgeaz.com/library. *Libr Mgr,* Joyce Baker; E-mail: joyce.baker@pinalcountyaz.gov; Staff 2 (MLS 2)
Pop 13,000; Circ 75,000
Library Holdings: Bk Titles 27,775; Per Subs 40
Special Collections: Large Print Coll
Automation Activity & Vendor Info: (Cataloging) Innovative Interfaces, Inc; (Circulation) Innovative Interfaces, Inc; (OPAC) Innovative Interfaces, Inc
Wireless access
Function: 24/7 Electronic res, 24/7 Online cat, Adult bk club
Mem of Pinal County Library District
Open Mon-Fri 8-6, Sat 8-1
Friends of the Library Group

COTTONWOOD

P COTTONWOOD PUBLIC LIBRARY*, 100 S Sixth St, 86326. SAN 300-306X. Tel: 928-634-7559. Reference Tel: 928-634-7559, Ext 100. FAX: 928-634-0253. Web Site: www.ctwpl.info. *Libr Mgr,* Ryan Bigelow; Tel: 928-340-2780, E-mail: rbigelow@cottonwoodaz.gov; Staff 5 (MLS 2, Non-MLS 3)
Founded 1960. Pop 40,000; Circ 349,783

Library Holdings: Audiobooks 750; CDs 830; DVDs 1,806; Large Print Bks 6,283; Bk Titles 83,559; Per Subs 60; Videos 3,244
Automation Activity & Vendor Info: (Circulation) SirsiDynix
Wireless access
Function: 24/7 Online cat, Activity rm, Adult bk club, Art programs, Audiobks on Playaways & MP3, Audiobks via web, AV serv, Bk club(s), Bks on CD, Chess club, Children's prog, Computer training, Computers for patron use, E-Readers, Electronic databases & coll, Free DVD rentals, Homebound delivery serv, Homework prog, ILL available, Instruction & testing, Internet access, Jail serv, Large print keyboards, Magazines, Magnifiers for reading, Mango lang, Meeting rooms, Movies, Music CDs, Online cat, Outreach serv, OverDrive digital audio bks, Photocopying/Printing, Preschool outreach, Preschool reading prog, Prog for adults, Prog for children & young adult, Ref & res, Scanner, Spanish lang bks, STEM programs, Story hour, Study rm, Summer reading prog, Tax forms, Teen prog, Wheelchair accessible, Workshops
Partic in Yavapai Libr Network
Open Mon & Sat 10-2, Tues-Fri 8:30-6
Friends of the Library Group

M VERDE VALLEY MEDICAL CENTER*, David G Wells MD Memorial Library, 269 S Candy Lane, 86326. Tel: 928-639-6444. Administration Tel: 928-634-2251. FAX: 928-639-6457. Web Site: nahealth.com/family-friends-services/our-medical-library-verde-valley. *Libr Assoc,* Laura Patterson; E-mail: laura.patterson@nahealth.com
Founded 1996
Library Holdings: Bk Titles 300
Open Mon-Fri 8-4:30
Restriction: Not a lending libr

DOUGLAS

G ARIZONA DEPARTMENT OF CORRECTIONS*, Arizona State Prison Complex - Douglas, 6911 N BDI Blvd, 85608. (Mail add: PO Drawer 3867, 85608-3867). Tel: 520-364-7521, Ext 34522. FAX: 520-805-5971. *Librn III,* Kathleen Fry; E-mail: kfry@azadc.gov; *Librn II,* Deliz Nunez; E-mail: dnunez1@azadc.gov
Library Holdings: Audiobooks 198; DVDs 93; Large Print Bks 402; Bk Vols 32,641; Per Subs 16; Videos 37

J COCHISE COLLEGE LIBRARY*, Charles Di Peso Library, Bldg 300, 4190 W Hwy 80, 85607. SAN 330-5643. Tel: 520-417-4082. FAX: 520-417-4120. E-mail: library@cochise.edu. Web Site: www.cochise.edu/library. *Dir, Libr Serv,* Dr John Walsh; E-mail: walshj@cochise.edu; *Librn,* Karly Scarbrough; Staff 12 (MLS 3, Non-MLS 9)
Founded 1964. Enrl 5,000; Fac 105; Highest Degree: Associate
Library Holdings: AV Mats 3,000; Bk Vols 66,950; Per Subs 325; Talking Bks 230; Videos 2,400
Subject Interests: Aviation, Hist, Nursing
Automation Activity & Vendor Info: (Cataloging) OCLC; (Circulation) SirsiDynix; (Course Reserve) SirsiDynix; (ILL) OCLC; (Media Booking) SirsiDynix; (OPAC) SirsiDynix
Wireless access
Function: For res purposes, Homebound delivery serv, ILL available, Magnifiers for reading, Outside serv via phone, mail, e-mail & web, Photocopying/Printing, Ref serv available, Telephone ref
Publications: Annual Report; Monthly Acquisitions Report; Periodical Holdings List
Partic in Amigos Library Services, Inc
Open Mon-Thurs 8-8, Fri 8-4
Restriction: In-house use for visitors, Residents only, Students only
Friends of the Library Group

Departmental Libraries:

ANDREA CRACCHIOLO LIBRARY, Bldg 900, 901 N Colombo Ave, Sierra Vista, 85635, SAN 300-4295. Tel: 520-515-5320. FAX: 520-515-5464. *Dir, Libr Serv,* John Walsh; E-mail: walshj@cochise.edu; *Librn,* Alexandra Felton; *Librn,* Tetima Parnprome; Staff 5 (MLS 4, Non-MLS 1)
Founded 1974. Enrl 4,600; Fac 100; Highest Degree: Associate
Automation Activity & Vendor Info: (Cataloging) SirsiDynix; (Serials) EBSCO Online
Function: Art exhibits, Audio & video playback equip for onsite use, AV serv, Bks on CD, Computers for patron use, Distance learning, Doc delivery serv, Electronic databases & coll, Equip loans & repairs, Free DVD rentals, Instruction & testing, Internet access, Mail & tel request accepted, Online cat, Photocopying/Printing, Ref & res, Tax forms, VHS videos, Wheelchair accessible
Open Mon-Thurs 8am-9pm, Fri 8-4, Sat 10-4, Sun 12-5; Mon-Thurs (Summer) 8-8
Restriction: Authorized patrons, ID required to use computers (Ltd hrs), In-house use for visitors, Open to students, fac & staff
Friends of the Library Group

P DOUGLAS PUBLIC LIBRARY, 560 E Tenth St, 85607. SAN 300-3078. Tel: 520-417-7352. FAX: 520-805-5503. E-mail: DPL@douglasaz.gov. Web Site: www.douglasaz.gov/301/Library. *City Librn, Libr Mgr,* Margaret White; E-mail: Margaret.White@douglasaz.gov; Staff 7 (MLS 1, Non-MLS 6)
Founded 1902. Pop 21,000; Circ 72,302
Library Holdings: AV Mats 3,949; Bk Vols 42,500; Per Subs 102
Special Collections: Arizona Coll; Spanish Language Coll
Wireless access
Mem of Cochise County Library District
Open Mon-Thurs 10-6, Fri 10-5, Sat 10-1
Friends of the Library Group

DRAGOON

S AMERIND MUSEUM LIBRARY, Fulton-Hayden Memorial Library, 2100 N Amerind Rd, 85609. (Mail add: PO Box 400, 85609-0400), SAN 300-3086. Tel: 520-586-3666. FAX: 520-586-4679. E-mail: libros@amerind.org. Web Site: www.amerind.org. *Librn,* Sally Newland
Founded 1962
Library Holdings: Bk Titles 25,000; Spec Interest Per Sub 20
Special Collections: El Archivo de Hidalgo del Parral, 1631-1821, micro; Facsimile Editions of Major Mesoamerican Codices; North American Exploration & Native American-European Contact (William Shirley Fulton Coll), rare bks; Records of the Colonial Period of New Spain (Northern Mexico); Southwest Americana
Subject Interests: Anthrop, Archaeology
Automation Activity & Vendor Info: (Cataloging) LibraryWorld, Inc; (Course Reserve) LibraryWorld, Inc; (Discovery) LibraryWorld, Inc; (ILL) LibraryWorld, Inc; (Media Booking) LibraryWorld, Inc; (OPAC) LibraryWorld, Inc; (Serials) LibraryWorld, Inc
Wireless access
Function: 24/7 Electronic res, 24/7 Online cat, Archival coll, Audio & video playback equip for onsite use, Scanner
Restriction: Access at librarian's discretion, Authorized personnel only, Authorized scholars by appt, By permission only, Circulates for staff only, External users must contact libr, Internal circ only, Internal use only, Non-circulating of rare bks, Non-circulating to the pub, Open by appt only, Open to pub upon request, Open to qualified scholars, Open to researchers by request, Pub by appt only, Pub ref by request, Researchers by appt only, Secured area only open to authorized personnel, Staff use, pub by appt, Visitors must make appt to use bks in the libr

DUNCAN

P DUNCAN PUBLIC LIBRARY*, 122 N Hwy 75, 85534. (Mail add: PO Box 115, 85534-0115), SAN 300-3094. Tel: 928-359-2094. FAX: 928-359-2094. E-mail: duncanlibrary@vtc.net. Web Site: www.greenleelibraries.org/Pages/Index/70877/duncan-library-information. *Libr Serv Dir,* Ashley Germaine; Staff 1 (Non-MLS 1)
Founded 1947. Pop 850
Library Holdings: Bk Titles 12,259
Special Collections: Southwest Coll
Subject Interests: Native Americans
Automation Activity & Vendor Info: (Acquisitions) Follett Software; (Cataloging) Follett Software; (Circulation) Follett Software
Wireless access
Function: ILL available, Photocopying/Printing, Prog for children & young adult, Summer reading prog
Mem of Greenlee County Library System
Open Mon & Wed 1-6, Tues & Thurs 9-5, Fri 1-5

P GREENLEE COUNTY LIBRARY SYSTEM*, 22 Blue Jay Dr, 85534. Web Site: www.greenleelibraries.org. *County Librn,* Karen Soohy; E-mail: ksoohy@greenlee.az.gov
Member Libraries: Clifton Public Library; Duncan Public Library

ELOY

P ELOY SANTA CRUZ LIBRARY, 1000 N Main St, 85131. SAN 300-3116. Tel: 520-466-3814. FAX: 520-466-4433. Web Site: eloyaz.gov/202/Library. *Dir, Commun Serv,* Paul Anchondo; E-mail: panchondo@eloyaz.gov; *Assoc Librn,* Vivianna Flores; E-mail: Vivianna.Flores@pinalcountyaz.gov; Staff 4.5 (MLS 1, Non-MLS 3.5)
Founded 1952. Pop 11,000; Circ 35,687
Library Holdings: Audiobooks 114; CDs 700; DVDs 3,494; e-books 2,000; Electronic Media & Resources 100; Large Print Bks 500; Bk Vols 17,605; Per Subs 72
Special Collections: Adult Literacy Coll; African-American & Hispanic Coll; Arizona Coll; Audio Visual Coll; Southwest Coll
Automation Activity & Vendor Info: (Acquisitions) Innovative Interfaces, Inc; (Cataloging) Innovative Interfaces, Inc; (Circulation) Innovative Interfaces, Inc; (Discovery) EBSCO Discovery Service; (ILL) OCLC WorldShare Interlibrary Loan; (OPAC) Innovative Interfaces, Inc
Wireless access

Function: Art exhibits, Audiobks via web, CD-ROM, Children's prog, Computer training, Computers for patron use, Digital talking bks, E-Reserves, Electronic databases & coll, Family literacy, Free DVD rentals, ILL available, Internet access, Music CDs, Online cat, Photocopying/Printing, Prog for adults, Prog for children & young adult, Ref serv available, Scanner, Spanish lang bks, Spoken cassettes & DVDs, Summer reading prog, Tax forms, Teen prog, Wheelchair accessible
Mem of Pinal County Library District
Open Mon-Fri 7:30-6
Friends of the Library Group

FLAGSTAFF

S THE ARBORETUM AT FLAGSTAFF LIBRARY, 4001 S Woody Mountain Rd, 86005. SAN 373-3866. Tel: 928-774-1442. FAX: 928-774-1441. E-mail: info@thearb.org. Web Site: www.thearb.org. *Education Program Mgr,* Helena Murray; E-mail: helena.murray@thearb.org
Founded 1981
Library Holdings: Bk Titles 1,650
Subject Interests: Botany, Colorado Plateau, Ecology, Environ educ, Forestry, Hort, Natural hist, Nonprofit mgt
Function: For res purposes, Res libr
Restriction: By permission only, Circulates for staff only, Open by appt only, Staff & prof res

S ARIZONA HISTORICAL SOCIETY LIBRARY*, Northern Arizona Division, 2340 N Fort Valley Rd, 86001. Tel: 928-774-6272. E-mail: AHSFlagstaff@azhs.gov. Web Site: arizonahistoricalsociety.org. *Dep Dir, COO,* Bill Ponder; E-mail: bponder@azhs.gov; *Curator,* Joseph M Meehan
Library Holdings: Bk Vols 50,000
Open Mon-Sat 9-5

GL COCONINO COUNTY LAW LIBRARY & SELF-HELP CENTER, 200 N San Francisco St, 86001. SAN 300-3124. Tel: 928-679-7540. Toll Free Tel: 877-806-3187. Web Site: www.coconino.az.gov/lawlibrary. *Law Librn,* Gretchen Hornberger; E-mail: ghornberger@coconino.az.gov
Function: Res libr
Open Mon-Fri 8-5
Restriction: Not a lending libr

P FLAGSTAFF CITY-COCONINO COUNTY PUBLIC LIBRARY SYSTEM*, 300 W Aspen Ave, 86001. SAN 330-5678. Tel: 928-213-2331. Circulation Tel: 928-213-2333. Interlibrary Loan Service Tel: 928-213-2379. Administration Tel: 928-213-2351. FAX: 928-774-9573. Web Site: www.flagstaffpubliclibrary.org. *Dir,* Jared Tolman; E-mail: jared.tolman@flagstaffaz.gov; Staff 11 (MLS 7, Non-MLS 4)
Founded 1890. Pop 106,000; Circ 752,724
Library Holdings: Bk Vols 207,000; Per Subs 400
Subject Interests: Arizona, Local hist, SW
Automation Activity & Vendor Info: (Acquisitions) SirsiDynix; (Cataloging) SirsiDynix; (Circulation) SirsiDynix; (Course Reserve) SirsiDynix; (ILL) SirsiDynix; (Media Booking) SirsiDynix; (OPAC) SirsiDynix; (Serials) SirsiDynix
Wireless access
Publications: The Friends of the Library (Newsletter)
Member Libraries: Fredonia Public Library; Page Public Library; Sedona Public Library; Williams Public Library
Partic in OCLC Online Computer Library Center, Inc
Special Services for the Deaf - High interest/low vocabulary bks; Spec interest per
Special Services for the Blind - Closed circuit TV; Magnifiers; Reader equip; Talking bks
Open Mon-Thurs 10-9, Fri 10-7, Sat 10-6, Sun 10-2
Friends of the Library Group
Branches: 4
EAST FLAGSTAFF COMMUNITY LIBRARY, 3000 N Fourth St, Ste 5, 86004, SAN 330-5767. Tel: 928-213-2348. *Br Mgr,* Barbara Tait; E-mail: barbara.tait@flagstaffaz.gov; Staff 10 (MLS 1, Non-MLS 9)
Library Holdings: Bk Vols 18,000
Open Mon-Thurs 9-9, Fri 9-6, Sat 9-1, Sun 1-5
Friends of the Library Group
FOREST LAKES COMMUNITY LIBRARY, 417 Old Rim Rd, Forest Lakes, 85931. (Mail add: PO Box 1799, Forest Lakes, 85931-1799), SAN 376-320X. Tel: 928-535-9125. E-mail: FLlibraryaz@gmail.com. Web Site: www.forestlakescommunitylibrary.org. *Br Mgr,* Bryan Hawk; E-mail: bryan.hawk@flagstaffaz.gov
Library Holdings: Bk Titles 5,500; Bk Vols 7,700
Open Tues-Fri 9-5, Sat 9-3
Friends of the Library Group
GRAND CANYON-TUSAYAN COMMUNITY LIBRARY, 11 Navajo St, Grand Canyon, 86023. (Mail add: PO Box 518, Grand Canyon, 86023), SAN 300-3310. Tel: 928-638-2718. E-mail: gccl518@yahoo.com. Web Site: www.grandcanyoncommunitylibrary.org. *Br Mgr,* Mindy Karlsberger; E-mail: mindy.karlsberger@flagstaffaz.gov; Staff 4 (Non-MLS 4)
Founded 1932. Pop 3,000; Circ 20,000
Library Holdings: Audiobooks 150; DVDs 10,000; Bk Vols 18,000; Per Subs 30
Subject Interests: SW
Automation Activity & Vendor Info: (Cataloging) SirsiDynix; (Circulation) SirsiDynix; (OPAC) Follett Software
Function: 24/7 Online cat, Activity rm
Open Mon-Sat 10:30-5
Friends of the Library Group
TUBA CITY PUBLIC LIBRARY, 78 Main St, Tuba City, 86045. (Mail add: PO Box 190, Tuba City, 86045-0190), SAN 300-4465. Tel: 928-283-5856. FAX: 928-283-6188. Web Site: www.tubacitypubliclibrary.org. *Br Mgr,* Pearl Goldtooth; E-mail: pearl.goldtooth@yahoo.com
Founded 1957. Pop 10,000; Circ 14,031
Library Holdings: Bk Vols 12,000; Per Subs 30
Special Collections: Navaho History & Culture
Subject Interests: Native Am
Open Mon-Thurs 10-7, Sun 1-5
Friends of the Library Group
Bookmobiles: 2

S FLAGSTAFF MEDICAL CENTER, John B Jamison MD Memorial Library, 1200 N Beaver St, 86001. SAN 374-8235. Tel: 928-773-2418. FAX: 928-773-2253. Web Site: www.nahealth.com/hospital-patients/medical-libraries/our-medical-library-flagstaff-medical-center. *Coordr,* Suzanne Tackitt; E-mail: suzanne.tackitt@nahealth.com; Staff 1 (MLS 1)
Library Holdings: Bk Vols 1,000
Function: Computer training, Electronic databases & coll, ILL available, Mail & tel request accepted, Online ref, Photocopying/Printing, Ref serv available, Spoken cassettes & CDs, Telephone ref, VHS videos
Partic in Arizona Health Information Network
Open Mon-Fri 8-4:30
Restriction: Hospital staff & commun, In-house use for visitors

S LOWELL OBSERVATORY LIBRARY, 1400 W Mars Hill Rd, 86001. SAN 300-3132. Tel: 928-774-3358. FAX: 928-774-6296. Web Site: library.lowell.edu/Research/library. *Librn & Archivist,* Lauren Amundson; Tel: 928-714-7083, E-mail: amundson@lowell.edu; Staff 1 (MLS 1)
Founded 1894
Library Holdings: Bk Titles 7,000; Per Subs 30
Subject Interests: Astronomy, Math, Physics
Wireless access
Restriction: Open to staff only, Staff use only

S MUSEUM OF NORTHERN ARIZONA, Harold S Colton Memorial Library, 3100 N Fort Valley Rd, 86001. SAN 300-3140. Tel: 928-774-5211, Ext 269. FAX: 928-779-1527. E-mail: library@musnaz.org. Web Site: musnaz.org/collections/our-collections/library-and-archives/home. *Archivist,* Melissa Lawton; E-mail: mlawton@musnaz.org; *Dir of Coll,* Elaine Hughes; E-mail: ehughes@musnaz.org; Staff 1 (MLS 1)
Founded 1928
Subject Interests: Archaeology, Botany, Cultural hist, Ethnology, Fine arts, Geol, Mus studies, Natural hist, Paleontology, Regional hist, Zoology
Automation Activity & Vendor Info: (Cataloging) ResourceMATE; (Circulation) ResourceMATE; (OPAC) ResourceMATE
Wireless access
Function: Ref serv available, Res libr
Restriction: Circulates for staff only, Closed stack, Non-circulating, Open by appt only

C NORTHERN ARIZONA UNIVERSITY, Cline Library, Bldg 28, 1001 S Knoles Dr, 86011. (Mail add: PO Box 6022, 86011-6022), SAN 300-3159. Tel: 928-523-2173. Administration Tel: 928-523-6802. Toll Free Tel: 800-247-3380 (Arizona only). E-mail: cline.library@nau.edu. Administration E-mail: library.administration@nau.edu. Web Site: nau.edu/library. *Dean & Univ Librn,* Cynthia Childrey; E-mail: cynthia.childrey@nau.edu; *Asst Dean,* Jill Friedmann; Tel: 928-523-3253, E-mail: jill.friedmann@nau.edu; *Asst Dean,* Laura Rose Taylor; Tel: 928-523-6189, E-mail: laura.taylor@nau.edu; *Head Research, Teaching & Learning,* John Doherty; Tel: 928-523-1491, E-mail: john.doherty@nau.edu; *Head, Spec Coll & Archives,* Peter J Runge; Tel: 928-523-6502, E-mail: peter.runge@nau.edu; *Delivery Serv Mgr, Head, User Serv,* Andrew See; Tel: 928-523-9929, E-mail: andrew.see@nau.edu; *Commun Engagement Librn,* Kevin Ketchner; Tel: 928-523-3710, E-mail: Kevin.Ketchner@nau.edu; Staff 31 (MLS 29, Non-MLS 2)
Founded 1912. Enrl 29,569; Fac 998; Highest Degree: Doctorate
Jul 2019-Jun 2020 Income (Main Library Only) $7,050,809. Mats Exp $2,834,199. Sal $7,050,809
Library Holdings: AV Mats 49,478; e-books 245,056; e-journals 123,990; Bk Vols 617,779; Per Subs 6,146
Special Collections: Arizona History (Historical Society Coll), archives, photos; Bill Belknap Coll; Bruce Babbitt Coll; Emery Kolb Coll; Fred

Harvey Coll; George Billingsley Coll; Harvey Butchart Coll; James J Hanks Coll; John Running Coll; Josef Muench Coll, photos; Katie Lee Coll; Martin Litton Coll; Milton Snow (Hopi Tribe) Coll; NAU Archives; Norm Nevills Coll; Peter Huntoon Coll; Philip Johnston Coll; PT Reilly Coll; Sue Bennett Coll; Tad Nichols Coll. Oral History; US Document Depository
Subject Interests: Colorado Plateau, Culture, Environ sci, Hist, Land use & develop, Native Am hist, Regional
Automation Activity & Vendor Info: (Acquisitions) Ex Libris Group; (Cataloging) Ex Libris Group; (Circulation) Ex Libris Group; (Course Reserve) Blackboard Inc; (Discovery) Ex Libris Group; (ILL) OCLC ILLiad; (Media Booking) Ex Libris Group; (OPAC) Ex Libris Group; (Serials) Ex Libris Group
Wireless access
Publications: Library Insights (Newsletter)
Partic in Ariz Univ Librs Coun; Arizona Health Information Network; Midwest Collaborative for Library Services; OCLC Online Computer Library Center, Inc
Special Services for the Deaf - Assistive tech; Closed caption videos; TTY equip
Special Services for the Blind - Assistive/Adapted tech devices, equip & products; Braille equip; Internet workstation with adaptive software; Scanner for conversion & translation of mats; Screen enlargement software for people with visual disabilities; Screen reader software; ZoomText magnification & reading software

G US GEOLOGICAL SURVEY LIBRARY*, 2255 N Gemini Dr, 86001. SAN 300-3167. Tel: 928-556-7272. FAX: 928-556-7237. E-mail: flag_lib@usgs.gov. *Librn,* Position Currently Open
Founded 1964
Library Holdings: Bk Vols 60,000
Special Collections: Astro-Geology Coll
Subject Interests: Earth sci, Geol, Space sci
Open Mon-Fri 8-4:30

FLORENCE

S ARIZONA DEPARTMENT OF CORRECTIONS*, Arizona State Prison Complex - Eyman, 4374 Butte Ave, 85232. (Mail add: PO Box 3500, 85232-3500). Tel: 520-868-0201. *Supvr,* Stephanie Johnson
Library Holdings: Bk Vols 28,952
Restriction: Not open to pub

S ARIZONA STATE PRISON COMPLEX FLORENCE LIBRARIES*, 1305 E Butte Ave, 85132. (Mail add: PO Box 629, 85132-3013), SAN 324-1130. Tel: 520-868-4011, Ext 6010. FAX: 520-868-8288. *Librn,* Kathleen Pettit; E-mail: kpettit@azadc.gov; *Librn II,* Vincent Parker; E-mail: vparker@azadc.gov
Founded 1914
Library Holdings: Bk Titles 60,000; Per Subs 28
Special Services for the Deaf - Bks on deafness & sign lang; Staff with knowledge of sign lang

P FLORENCE COMMUNITY LIBRARY*, 778 N Main St, 85132. (Mail add: PO Box 2670, 85132), SAN 300-3175. Tel: 520-868-8311. Web Site: www.florenceaz.gov/library. *Libr Mgr,* Jasper Halt; E-mail: jasper.halt@florenceaz.gov; Staff 6 (Non-MLS 6)
Pop 11,540; Circ 19,718
Library Holdings: Bk Titles 26,000; Per Subs 38
Automation Activity & Vendor Info: (Cataloging) Innovative Interfaces, Inc; (Circulation) Innovative Interfaces, Inc; (OPAC) Innovative Interfaces, Inc
Wireless access
Function: ILL available
Mem of Pinal County Library District
Open Mon-Thurs 9-8, Fri 9-5, Sat 12-4
Friends of the Library Group

S PINAL COUNTY HISTORICAL SOCIETY, INC LIBRARY*, 715 S Main St, 85132. (Mail add: PO Box 851, 85132-0851), SAN 328-672X. Tel: 520-868-4382. E-mail: florenceazmuseum@gmail.com. Web Site: www.pinalcountyhistoricalmuseum.org. *Exec Dir,* Stephanie Joyner
Founded 1958
Library Holdings: Bk Titles 1,000; Bk Vols 1,500; Per Subs 3; Spec Interest Per Sub 3; Videos 35
Special Collections: 1870-1950's Arizona State Prisoner Ledgers, microfilm; Arizona History, doc; Arizona State Prison & Pinal County (Della Meadows Coll); Florence Historic Pioneer Letters, doc; Southwest Native American Coll. Oral History
Subject Interests: Local hist
Wireless access
Function: Ref serv available, Res libr
Publications: Newsletter
Open Tues-Sat 11-4, Sun 12-4 (Sept-June)
Restriction: Authorized patrons

P PINAL COUNTY LIBRARY DISTRICT*, 92 W Butte Ave, 85132. (Mail add: PO Box 2974, 85132), SAN 300-3183. Tel: 520-866-6457. Reference Tel: 520-866-6473. Web Site: www.pinalcountyaz.gov/Departments/Library. *Dir,* Denise Keller; *Dep Libr Dir,* Alexander Conrad; E-mail: alexander.conrad@pinal.gov; Staff 9 (MLS 5, Non-MLS 4)
Founded 1960. Pop 320,000
Jul 2012-Jun 2013 Income $2,339,583, State $23,000, Federal $36,880, County $2,279,703. Mats Exp $3,445,385, Books $534,362, Electronic Ref Mat (Incl. Access Fees) $94,828. Sal $470,895 (Prof $46,945)
Library Holdings: e-journals 180; Electronic Media & Resources 16; Bk Titles 1,269; Bk Vols 1,341; Per Subs 16
Subject Interests: Prof
Automation Activity & Vendor Info: (Acquisitions) Innovative Interfaces, Inc; (Cataloging) Innovative Interfaces, Inc; (Circulation) Innovative Interfaces, Inc; (ILL) Innovative Interfaces, Inc; (OPAC) Innovative Interfaces, Inc; (Serials) Innovative Interfaces, Inc
Wireless access
Publications: PCLD (Newsletter)
Member Libraries: Apache Junction Public Library; Arizona City Community Library; Casa Grande Public Library; Coolidge Public Library; Eloy Santa Cruz Library; Florence Community Library; Kearny Public Library; Mammoth Public Library; Maricopa Public Library; Oracle Public Library; San Manuel Public Library; Superior Public Library
Special Services for the Deaf - Bks on deafness & sign lang; High interest/low vocabulary bks
Special Services for the Blind - Accessible computers; Audio mat; Bks on CD; Copier with enlargement capabilities; Digital talking bk; Extensive large print coll; Large print & cassettes; Large print bks; Playaways (bks on MP3)
Open Mon-Fri 8-5

FREDONIA

P FREDONIA PUBLIC LIBRARY*, 130 N Main, 86022. (Mail add: PO Box 218, 86022-0218), SAN 300-3205. Tel: 928-643-7137. FAX: 928-643-7137. E-mail: flibrary3@gmail.com. Web Site: fredoniaaz.net/services/publiclibrary.aspx, www.fredoniapubliclibraryaz.org. *Librn,* Lisa Findlay; Staff 1.5 (Non-MLS 1.5)
Founded 1958. Pop 1,335
Library Holdings: Bk Titles 21,929; Per Subs 13
Special Collections: Jonreed Lauritzen Books & Jensen Memorial Coll
Automation Activity & Vendor Info: (Cataloging) Follett Software; (Circulation) Follett Software
Mem of Flagstaff City-Coconino County Public Library System
Open Mon-Thurs 8-6, Fri 10-2

P KAIBAB PAIUTE PUBLIC LIBRARY, 250 N Pipe Springs Rd, 86022. (Mail add: HC 65, Box 2, 86022), SAN 376-317X. Tel: 928-643-6004. FAX: 928-643-7260. *Dir,* Amanda Bundy; E-mail: abundy@kaibabpaiute-nsn.gov
Library Holdings: Bk Titles 10,000; Bk Vols 11,000; Per Subs 12
Open Mon-Thurs 9-6, Fri 8-5

GLENDALE

CR ARIZONA CHRISTIAN UNIVERSITY*, R S Beal Sr Library, One W Firestorm Way, 85306. SAN 300-3949. Tel: 602-386-4117. Toll Free Tel: 800-247-2697, Ext 117. FAX: 602-404-2159. Web Site: arizonachristian.edu/library. *Head Librn,* Rob Oliverio; Tel: 602-489-5300, Ext 1110, E-mail: robert.oliverio@arizonachristian.edu; *Libr Tech,* Janelle Breedveld; E-mail: janelle.breedveld@arizonachristian.edu; Staff 2 (MLS 2)
Founded 1960. Enrl 804; Fac 32; Highest Degree: Bachelor
Library Holdings: AV Mats 2,334; CDs 78; DVDs 21; e-books 19,300; e-journals 2,047; Music Scores 41; Bk Titles 22,343; Bk Vols 27,332; Per Subs 130; Videos 745
Subject Interests: Biblical studies, Theol
Automation Activity & Vendor Info: (Cataloging) OPALS (Open-source Automated Library System); (Circulation) OPALS (Open-source Automated Library System); (ILL) OCLC WorldShare Interlibrary Loan; (OPAC) OPALS (Open-source Automated Library System)
Wireless access
Partic in OCLC Online Computer Library Center, Inc

J GLENDALE COMMUNITY COLLEGE - MAIN*, John F Prince Library Media Center, 6000 W Olive Ave, 85302. SAN 300-3256. Tel: 623-845-3109. Interlibrary Loan Service Tel: 623-845-3107. Reference Tel: 623-845-3112. Administration Tel: 623-845-3101. FAX: 623-845-3102. Web Site: lib.gccaz.edu/lmc. *Dept Chair,* Frank Torres; Tel: 623-845-3904, E-mail: frank.torres@gccaz.edu; *Media/Instruction Librn,* Renee Smith; Tel: 623-845-3110, E-mail: renee.smith@gccaz.edu; *Instruction Coordr, Ref & Coll Develop Librn,* Dede Elrobeh; Tel: 623-845-3108, E-mail: dorothy.elrobeh@gccaz.edu; *Ref & Instruction Librn,* Ed McKennon; Tel:

623-845-3195, E-mail: edward.mckennon@gccaz.edu; *Supvr, Access Serv,* Judy Fleming; Tel: 623-845-3117, E-mail: j.fleming@gccaz.edu; Staff 21 (MLS 9, Non-MLS 12)
Founded 1965. Enrl 21,300; Fac 30; Highest Degree: Associate
Library Holdings: Bk Titles 173,244; Bk Vols 173,244; Per Subs 34,276
Automation Activity & Vendor Info: (Acquisitions) SirsiDynix; (Cataloging) SirsiDynix; (Circulation) SirsiDynix; (Course Reserve) SirsiDynix; (ILL) OCLC ILLiad; (Media Booking) SirsiDynix; (OPAC) SirsiDynix; (Serials) SirsiDynix
Wireless access
Open Mon-Thurs 7am-10pm, Fri 7-6, Sat 9-5, Sun 1-6
Friends of the Library Group

J GLENDALE COMMUNITY COLLEGE - NORTH*, Library Computer Center, Bldg GCN B (Beshbito), 5727 W Happy Valley Rd, 85310. Circulation Tel: 623-888-7109. Reference Tel: 623-888-7112. FAX: 623-845-4041. Web Site: lib.gccaz.edu/lmc/aboutus/gccnlibrary.html. *Libr Tech,* Dennis Topel; E-mail: dennis.topel@gccaz.edu
Library Holdings: Bk Vols 20,000
Wireless access
Open Mon-Thurs (Fall-Spring) 8-8, Fri 8-3, Sat 8-1; Mon-Thurs (Summer) 8-8

P GLENDALE PUBLIC LIBRARY*, 5959 W Brown St, 85302-1248. SAN 300-3264. Tel: 623-930-3530. Interlibrary Loan Service Tel: 623-930-3558. Reference Tel: 623-930-3531. Administration Tel: 623-930-3546. Automation Services Tel: 623-930-3586. FAX: 623-842-2161. Reference FAX: 623-842-4227. Web Site: www.glendaleaz.com/library. *Chief Librn,* Michael Beck; E-mail: MBeck@GLENDALEAZ.COM; Staff 77 (MLS 19, Non-MLS 58)
Founded 1895. Pop 237,723; Circ 1,554,972
Jul 2016-Jun 2017 Income (Main & Associated Libraries) $4,783,767. Mats Exp $722,815, Books $365,292, AV Mat $189,291, Electronic Ref Mat (Incl. Access Fees) $168,232
Library Holdings: AV Mats 26,909; DVDs 41,781; Bk Vols 387,965; Per Subs 349
Special Collections: Southwest Coll
Automation Activity & Vendor Info: (Acquisitions) Horizon; (Cataloging) Horizon; (Circulation) Horizon; (ILL) OCLC Connexion; (OPAC) Horizon; (Serials) Horizon
Wireless access
Function: 24/7 Electronic res, 24/7 Online cat, 3D Printer, Activity rm, Adult bk club, Adult literacy prog, Audiobks via web, Bilingual assistance for Spanish patrons, Bk club(s), Bks on CD, Butterfly Garden, Children's prog, Computers for patron use, Digital talking bks, Electronic databases & coll, Family literacy, For res purposes, Free DVD rentals, Holiday prog, ILL available, Internet access, Life-long learning prog for all ages, Literacy & newcomer serv, Magazines, Meeting rooms, Microfiche/film & reading machines, Movies, Museum passes, Music CDs, Online cat, Online info literacy tutorials on the web & in blackboard, Online ref, Outside serv via phone, mail, e-mail & web, OverDrive digital audio bks, Photocopying/Printing, Preschool reading prog, Printer for laptops & handheld devices, Prog for adults, Prog for children & young adult, Ref & res, Ref serv available, Spanish lang bks, Story hour, Summer reading prog, Tax forms, Teen prog, Telephone ref, Wheelchair accessible, Workshops, Writing prog
Open Mon & Wed 12-8, Tues & Thurs 10-8, Sat 12-5, Sun 1-5
Friends of the Library Group
Branches: 2
FOOTHILLS, 19055 N 57th Ave, 85308. Tel: 623-930-3830. Reference Tel: 623-930-3831. FAX: 623-930-3855. Reference FAX: 623-930-3866. *Admin Librn,* Kristin Fletcher-Spear; E-mail: KFletcher-Spear@GLENDALEAZ.com
Founded 1999
Function: 24/7 Electronic res, 24/7 Online cat, Activity rm, Adult bk club, Adult literacy prog, Bk club(s), Bks on CD, Children's prog, Computers for patron use, Digital talking bks, Electronic databases & coll, Family literacy, Free DVD rentals, Holiday prog, ILL available, Internet access, Life-long learning prog for all ages, Literacy & newcomer serv, Magazines, Meeting rooms, Movies, Museum passes, Music CDs, Online cat, Online info literacy tutorials on the web & in blackboard, Online ref, Photocopying/Printing, Preschool reading prog, Printer for laptops & handheld devices, Prog for adults, Prog for children & young adult, Ref & res, Ref serv available, Spanish lang bks, Spoken cassettes & CDs, Spoken cassettes & DVDs, Story hour, Study rm, Summer reading prog, Tax forms, Teen prog, Telephone ref, Wheelchair accessible, Workshops, Writing prog
Open Mon 12-8, Tues & Wed 10-8, Fri 1-5, Sat 12-5
Friends of the Library Group
VELMA TEAGUE BRANCH, 7010 N 58th Ave, 85301, SAN 376-8821. Tel: 623-930-3430. Reference Tel: 623-930-3431. FAX: 602-937-8798. *Admin Librn,* Greg Kinder; E-mail: GKinder@glendaleaz.com
Founded 1971
Function: 24/7 Electronic res, 24/7 Online cat, Activity rm, Adult bk club, Adult literacy prog, After school storytime, Audiobks via web, Bilingual assistance for Spanish patrons, Bk club(s), Bks on CD, Children's prog, Citizenship assistance, Computers for patron use, Digital talking bks, Electronic databases & coll, Family literacy, Free DVD rentals, Holiday prog, ILL available, Internet access, Life-long learning prog for all ages, Literacy & newcomer serv, Magazines, Movies, Museum passes, Music CDs, Online cat, Online info literacy tutorials on the web & in blackboard, Online ref, Outreach serv, OverDrive digital audio bks, Photocopying/Printing, Preschool reading prog, Printer for laptops & handheld devices, Prog for adults, Prog for children & young adult, Ref & res, Ref serv available, Spanish lang bks, Spoken cassettes & CDs, Spoken cassettes & DVDs, Story hour, Summer reading prog, Tax forms, Teen prog, Telephone ref, Wheelchair accessible, Workshops
Open Mon & Thurs 12-8, Tues & Wed 10-6, Sat 12-5
Friends of the Library Group

C THUNDERBIRD SCHOOL OF GLOBAL MANAGEMENT*, Merle A Hinrichs International Business Information Centre, One Global Pl, 85306. SAN 300-3248. Tel: 602-978-7232. Interlibrary Loan Service Tel: 602-978-7236. Reference Tel: 602-978-7306. FAX: 602-978-7762. Web Site: lib.asu.edu/ibic, thunderbird.asu.edu/students/campus-life/library. *Mgr,* Shane Hunt; E-mail: Shane.Hunt@thunderbird.asu.edu; Staff 14 (MLS 5, Non-MLS 9)
Founded 1946. Enrl 1,200; Fac 110; Highest Degree: Master
Library Holdings: AV Mats 4,000; Bk Titles 70,000; Per Subs 1,400
Special Collections: Foreign Language Feature Films, video; Foreign Language Newspapers & Periodicals
Subject Interests: Acctg, Finance, Intl, Mkt, Polit sci
Automation Activity & Vendor Info: (Acquisitions) SirsiDynix; (Cataloging) SirsiDynix; (Circulation) SirsiDynix; (Course Reserve) SirsiDynix; (ILL) SirsiDynix; (Media Booking) SirsiDynix; (OPAC) SirsiDynix; (Serials) SirsiDynix
Wireless access
Publications: Library Guides
Partic in OCLC Online Computer Library Center, Inc
Open Tues-Thurs 9am-10pm, Fri 9-6, Sat & Sun 2-10
Restriction: Open to students, fac & staff

GLOBE

S ARIZONA DEPARTMENT OF CORRECTIONS - ADULT INSTITUTIONS*, Arizona State Prison Complex - Globe Library, PO Box 2799, 85502-2799. Tel: 928-425-8141. FAX: 928-425-2408. *Library Contact,* Audrey Taylor
Library Holdings: Bk Vols 2,930
Restriction: Not open to pub

S GILA COUNTY HISTORICAL MUSEUM LIBRARY*, 1330 N Broad St, 85501. (Mail add: PO Box 2891, 85502-2891), SAN 374-8251. Tel: 928-425-7385. E-mail: museum@gilahistoricalmuseum.org. Web Site: gilahistoricalmuseum.org. *Mus Dir,* Sheldon Miller
Founded 1972
Library Holdings: Bk Vols 250; Spec Interest Per Sub 1
Subject Interests: Local hist
Open Tues-Fri 10-4, Sat 11-3
Restriction: Not a lending libr

GL GILA COUNTY LAW LIBRARY*, 1400 E Ash St, 85501. SAN 300-3272. Tel: 928-425-3231.
Founded 1908
Library Holdings: Bk Vols 1,000; Per Subs 10
Restriction: Prof mat only, Pub use on premises

P GILA COUNTY LIBRARY DISTRICT*, 1400 E Ash St, 85501-1414. SAN 375-3182. Tel: 928-402-8768, 928-402-8770. Toll Free Tel: 800-304-4452, Ext 8768. FAX: 928-425-3462. Web Site: gcldaz.org/gila/. *Dir,* Jacque Sanders; E-mail: jsanders@gilacountyaz.gov; *Pub Serv Librn,* Elaine Votruba; Tel: 928-402-8768, E-mail: evotruba@gilacountyaz.gov; *Syst Programmer, Syst Coordr,* Yodona Pennell; Tel: 928-402-8769; Staff 3 (MLS 2, Non-MLS 1)
Founded 1971. Pop 54,060
Library Holdings: AV Mats 19,306; CDs 4,476; DVDs 10,380; e-books 1,200; Large Print Bks 6,316; Bk Titles 270,790; Per Subs 150; Videos 850
Automation Activity & Vendor Info: (Cataloging) Innovative Interfaces, Inc; (Circulation) Innovative Interfaces, Inc; (ILL) OCLC FirstSearch; (OPAC) Innovative Interfaces, Inc
Wireless access
Function: 24/7 Electronic res, 24/7 Online cat, Adult bk club, Adult literacy prog, Art exhibits, Audiobks via web, AV serv, Bilingual assistance for Spanish patrons, Bk club(s), Bks on CD, CD-ROM, Children's prog, Citizenship assistance, Computer training, Computers for patron use, Digital talking bks, Distance learning, Doc delivery serv, E-Readers, E-Reserves, Electronic databases & coll, Family literacy, For res purposes, Free DVD rentals, Games & aids for people with disabilities, Govt ref serv, Health sci info serv, Holiday prog, Homebound delivery serv, ILL

available, Internet access, Large print keyboards, Life-long learning prog for all ages, Literacy & newcomer serv, Magazines, Mail & tel request accepted, Mango lang, Meeting rooms, Movies, Music CDs, Notary serv, Online cat, Online info literacy tutorials on the web & in blackboard, Online ref, Outreach serv, Outside serv via phone, mail, e-mail & web, OverDrive digital audio bks, Photocopying/Printing, Preschool outreach, Preschool reading prog, Prog for adults, Prog for children & young adult, Ref & res, Ref serv available, Res libr, Scanner, Senior computer classes, Senior outreach, Serves people with intellectual disabilities, Spanish lang bks, Spoken cassettes & CDs, Spoken cassettes & DVDs, Story hour, Study rm, Summer & winter reading prog, Summer reading prog, Tax forms, Teen prog, Telephone ref, Wheelchair accessible, Workshops
Member Libraries: Globe Public Library; Hayden Public Library; Isabelle Hunt Memorial Public Library; Payson Public Library; San Carlos Public Library; Tonto Basin Public Library; Young Public Library
Special Services for the Deaf - TDD equip
Open Mon-Fri 8-5

P GLOBE PUBLIC LIBRARY*, 339 S Broad St, 85501. SAN 300-3299. Tel: 928-425-6111. FAX: 928-425-3357. Web Site: www.gcldaz.org/globepubliclibrary.asp. *Libr Mgr,* Adrea Ricke; E-mail: aricke@gcldaz.org; *Dep Librn,* Mary Helen Avalos; E-mail: mavalos@gcldaz.org; Staff 1 (Non-MLS 1)
Pop 7,495; Circ 44,649
Library Holdings: AV Mats 2,294; Bks on Deafness & Sign Lang 21; CDs 144; DVDs 848; High Interest/Low Vocabulary Bk Vols 11; Large Print Bks 364; Bk Titles 19,951; Bk Vols 20,239; Per Subs 67; Talking Bks 655; Videos 185
Special Collections: Arizona Southwest
Automation Activity & Vendor Info: (Cataloging) Innovative Interfaces, Inc; (Circulation) Innovative Interfaces, Inc; (ILL) OCLC FirstSearch; (OPAC) Innovative Interfaces, Inc
Wireless access
Mem of Gila County Library District
Open Mon, Tues, Fri & Sat 10-5:30, Wed & Thurs 10:30-6
Friends of the Library Group

GOODYEAR

S ARIZONA DEPARTMENT OF CORRECTIONS - ADULT INSTITUTIONS*, Arizona State Prison Complex - Perryville Library, 2015 N Citrus Rd, 85338. (Mail add: PO Box 3000, 85338-3000). Tel: 623-853-0304.
Library Holdings: Bk Vols 16,000

GRAND CANYON

G GRAND CANYON NATIONAL PARK RESEARCH LIBRARY*, Park Headquarters Bldg, 20 S Entrance Rd, 86023. (Mail add: PO Box 129, 86023-0129), SAN 300-3329. Tel: 928-638-7768. FAX: 928-638-7776. Web Site: www.nps.gov/grca/learn/historyculture/reslib.htm. *Librn,* Edward McClure; E-mail: edward.mcclure@nps.gov; Staff 1 (MLS 1)
Founded 1922
Library Holdings: AV Mats 500; Bk Titles 8,000; Bk Vols 12,000; Per Subs 15
Special Collections: Rare Books
Subject Interests: Anthrop, Astronomy, Biology, Environ, Geol, Native Am, SW states hist
Automation Activity & Vendor Info: (Acquisitions) EOS International; (Cataloging) OCLC Connexion; (Circulation) EOS International; (ILL) OCLC; (OPAC) EOS International; (Serials) EOS International
Wireless access
Function: 24/7 Online cat, Archival coll, Computers for patron use, Doc delivery serv, For res purposes, Govt ref serv, ILL available, Online cat, Ref serv available, Res libr
Partic in Amigos Library Services, Inc; OCLC-LVIS
Open Mon-Thurs 8-4:30
Restriction: Lending to staff only, Non-circulating of rare bks, Open to pub with supv only

HAYDEN

P HAYDEN PUBLIC LIBRARY*, 520 Velasco Ave, 85135. (Mail add: PO Box 99, 85135-0099), SAN 300-3337. Tel: 520-356-7801, Ext 501. FAX: 520-357-0763. Web Site: www.gcldaz.org/haydenpubliclibrary.asp. *Libr Mgr,* Mary Helen Lopez; E-mail: mlopez@gcldaz.org
Founded 1966. Pop 3,000; Circ 21,116
Library Holdings: Bk Titles 12,000; Bk Vols 14,000
Special Collections: Spanish, bks & records
Wireless access
Mem of Gila County Library District
Open Mon-Thurs 9-4
Friends of the Library Group

HEBER

P RIM COMMUNITY LIBRARY*, 3404 Mustang Ave, 85928. (Mail add: PO Box 305, 85928-0305). Tel: 928-535-5749. FAX: 928-535-6409. E-mail: rimcommunitylibrary@gmail.com. Web Site: www.navajocountylibraries.org/members.asp. *Librn,* Paula Grigsby
Founded 1985. Pop 4,800; Circ 13,500
Library Holdings: AV Mats 200; Bks on Deafness & Sign Lang 10; Large Print Bks 300; Bk Titles 13,300
Wireless access
Mem of Navajo County Library System
Special Services for the Blind - Talking bks
Open Tues-Thurs 11-5, Fri 11-2
Friends of the Library Group

HOLBROOK

P HOLBROOK PUBLIC LIBRARY*, 403 Park St, 86025. SAN 300-3345. Tel: 928-524-3732. FAX: 928-524-2159. E-mail: holbrookpl@gmail.com. Web Site: www.holbrooklibrary.org. *Dir,* Wendy Skevington; Staff 2 (MLS 1, Non-MLS 1)
Founded 1958. Pop 5,300; Circ 65,000
Library Holdings: Bk Titles 45,000; Per Subs 52
Automation Activity & Vendor Info: (Cataloging) SirsiDynix; (Circulation) SirsiDynix; (OPAC) SirsiDynix
Wireless access
Mem of Navajo County Library System
Partic in Ariz Resources Consortium; Navajo County Libr District
Open Tues 10-5, Wed & Thurs 12-7, Fri 12-5, Sat 10-3
Friends of the Library Group

P NAVAJO COUNTY LIBRARY SYSTEM, 121 W Buffalo, 86025. (Mail add: PO Box 668, 86025). Tel: 928-524-4745. Toll Free Tel: 866-928-5244. FAX: 928-524-4747. Web Site: navajocountylibraries.org. *Libr District Dir,* David Ehrensperger; Tel: 928-524-4749, E-mail: david.ehrensperger@navajocountyaz.gov; *Coordr,* Jennifer Volkert; E-mail: jennifer.volkert@navajocountyaz.gov; *Library District, Tribal Community Outreach Specialist, Courier,* Triva Dickson; E-mail: triva.dickson@navajocountyaz.gov; *Libr Tech,* Alonna Larson; E-mail: alonna.larson@navajocountyaz.gov
Member Libraries: Cibecue Community Library; Clay Springs Public Library; Holbrook Public Library; Hopi Public Library; Kayenta Community Library; McNary Community Library; Pinedale Public Library; Pinetop-Lakeside Public Library; Rim Community Library; Show Low Public Library; Snowflake-Taylor Public Library; Whiteriver Public Library; Winslow Public Library; Woodruff Community Library

J NORTHLAND PIONEER COLLEGE LIBRARIES*, PO Box 610, 86025. SAN 376-8791. Administration Tel: 928-524-7320. Web Site: www.npc.edu/library. *Assoc Librn,* Luann Crosby; Tel: 928-536-6222, E-mail: luann.crosby@npc.edu; *Libr Spec III,* Daphne Brimhall; Tel: 928-532-6123, E-mail: daphne.brimhall@npc.edu; *Libr Spec III,* Denise Rominger; Tel: 928-532-6122, E-mail: denise.rominger@npc.edu; Staff 3 (MLS 2, Non-MLS 1)
Founded 1975. Enrl 2,100; Fac 210; Highest Degree: Associate
Library Holdings: Audiobooks 469; Bks on Deafness & Sign Lang 164; Braille Volumes 39; CDs 299; DVDs 774; e-books 399; e-journals 2; Electronic Media & Resources 10,426; Large Print Bks 28; Microforms 18,345; Bk Titles 72,509; Bk Vols 83,830; Per Subs 25; Videos 1,235
Special Collections: US Document Depository
Automation Activity & Vendor Info: (Acquisitions) EOS International; (Cataloging) EOS International; (Circulation) EOS International; (ILL) OCLC; (Media Booking) EOS International; (OPAC) EOS International; (Serials) EOS International
Wireless access
Open Mon-Thurs 7:45am-9pm, Fri 7:45-4

HUACHUCA CITY

P HUACHUCA CITY PUBLIC LIBRARY*, 506 N Gonzales Blvd, 85616-9610. SAN 300-3361. Tel: 520-456-1063. FAX: 520-456-8852. Web Site: huachucacityaz.gov/town-departments/library. *Dir,* Suzanne Harvey; E-mail: sharvey@huachucacityaz.gov; *Circ,* Jann Frampton; Staff 3 (Non-MLS 3)
Founded 1958. Pop 12,000
Library Holdings: AV Mats 695; CDs 100; DVDs 95; High Interest/Low Vocabulary Bk Vols 5,335; Large Print Bks 400; Music Scores 160; Bk Titles 15,000; Bk Vols 20,144; Per Subs 26; Talking Bks 875; Videos 958
Special Collections: Cochise County History & Tourism Coll
Subject Interests: Arizona, Literacy, Local hist, Music, SW, Tourism, Video
Automation Activity & Vendor Info: (Cataloging) SirsiDynix; (Circulation) SirsiDynix; (ILL) SirsiDynix; (OPAC) SirsiDynix
Function: After school storytime, AV serv, Homework prog, ILL available, Music CDs, Photocopying/Printing, Prog for children & young adult, Ref

serv available, Spoken cassettes & CDs, Spoken cassettes & DVDs, Summer reading prog, VHS videos, Wheelchair accessible
Publications: LC's Bookmark (Newsletter)
Mem of Cochise County Library District
Special Services for the Deaf - Bks on deafness & sign lang; Closed caption videos; High interest/low vocabulary bks
Special Services for the Blind - Home delivery serv; Large print bks; Ref serv; Videos on blindness & physical disabilties
Open Tues & Wed 9-5, Thurs & Fri 9-6, Sat 10-5
Restriction: Authorized patrons, Circ to mem only, In-house use for visitors, Open to pub for ref & circ; with some limitations
Friends of the Library Group

JEROME

P JEROME PUBLIC LIBRARY*, 600 Clark St, 86331. (Mail add: PO Drawer I, 86331-0247), SAN 300-337X. Tel: 928-639-0574. FAX: 928-639-0574. Web Site: www.jerome.az.gov/jerome-public-library. *Librn,* Kathleen Jarvis; E-mail: jeromelibrary.jarvis@gmail.com; Staff 1 (Non-MLS 1)
Founded 1919. Pop 500; Circ 12,000
Library Holdings: Bk Titles 9,500; Bk Vols 10,000
Special Collections: Arizona & the Southwest (National Geographic 1949-1976, Arizona Highways 1953-1977)
Automation Activity & Vendor Info: (Cataloging) SirsiDynix; (Circulation) SirsiDynix; (OPAC) SirsiDynix
Wireless access
Open Mon-Fri 9-5, Sat & Sun 12-4

KAYENTA

§P KAYENTA COMMUNITY LIBRARY, 1/4 Mile N US Hwy 163, 86033. (Mail add: PO Box 2670, 86033). Tel: 928-697-5563. FAX: 928-697-5564. *Libr Asst,* Trina Lipscomb; E-mail: trinalipscomb@nndode.org; Staff 1 (MLS 1)
Wireless access
Mem of Navajo County Library System
Open Mon-Fri 8-5

KEARNY

P KEARNY PUBLIC LIBRARY*, 912-A Tilbury Rd, 85237. (Mail add: PO Box 220, 85237-0220), SAN 300-3388. Tel: 520-363-5861. FAX: 520-363-5214. Web Site: kearnylibrary.wordpress.com. *Head Librn,* Janet Danilow; E-mail: Janet.Danilow@pinalcountyaz.gov
Founded 1958. Pop 2,000; Circ 39,399
Library Holdings: Audiobooks 680; DVDs 1,957; e-books 420; Bk Vols 18,400; Per Subs 10
Special Collections: History (Southwestern Coll)
Subject Interests: Local hist
Automation Activity & Vendor Info: (Cataloging) Innovative Interfaces, Inc; (Circulation) Innovative Interfaces, Inc; (OPAC) Innovative Interfaces, Inc
Wireless access
Publications: Booklist; Library Journal; School Library Journal
Mem of Pinal County Library District
Partic in LibraryLinkNJ, The New Jersey Library Cooperative
Open Mon-Thurs 10-5

KINGMAN

J MOHAVE COMMUNITY COLLEGE LIBRARY*, 1971 Jagerson Ave, 86409-1238. SAN 330-6186. Tel: 928-757-0856. FAX: 928-757-0896. Web Site: mohave.libguides.com. *Libr Operations Spec,* Amber Tacey; Tel: 928-692-3008, E-mail: ATACEY@mohave.edu; Staff 12 (MLS 3, Non-MLS 9)
Founded 1971. Enrl 7,887; Fac 52; Highest Degree: Associate
Library Holdings: CDs 53; DVDs 33; Bk Titles 76,789; Bk Vols 65,651; Per Subs 415; Talking Bks 1,375; Videos 1,393
Automation Activity & Vendor Info: (Acquisitions) Innovative Interfaces, Inc; (Cataloging) SirsiDynix; (Circulation) Innovative Interfaces, Inc; (Course Reserve) Innovative Interfaces, Inc; (ILL) Innovative Interfaces, Inc; (Media Booking) Innovative Interfaces, Inc; (OPAC) Innovative Interfaces, Inc; (Serials) EBSCO Online
Wireless access
Open Mon-Thurs (Winter) 8-7, Fri 8-5; Mon-Thurs (Summer) 8-6
Departmental Libraries:
BULLHEAD CITY CAMPUS, 3400 Hwy 95, Bullhead City, 86442-8204. Tel: 928-758-2420. FAX: 928-758-4436. *Campus Librn,* Sara Brandel; E-mail: sbrandel@mohave.edu; Staff 3 (MLS 1, Non-MLS 2)
Library Holdings: Per Subs 219
KINGMAN CAMPUS, 1971 Jagerson Ave, 86401. Tel: 928-757-0856. FAX: 928-757-0871. *Campus Librn,* Adele Maxson; Tel: 928-757-0802; Staff 3 (MLS 1, Non-MLS 2)
Library Holdings: Bk Vols 30,000; Per Subs 420
LAKE HAVASU CITY CAMPUS, 1977 W Acoma Blvd, Lake Havasu City, 86403-2999. Tel: 928-453-5809. Interlibrary Loan Service Tel: 928-505-3311. Administration Tel: 928-505-3337. FAX: 928-453-8335. *Campus Librn,* Wendi Birkhead; E-mail: wbirkhead@mohave.edu; *ILL/Doc Delivery Serv,* Mary Jo Powell; E-mail: mpowell@mohave.edu; Staff 3 (MLS 1, Non-MLS 2)
Founded 1971. Highest Degree: Associate
Library Holdings: Bk Vols 40,000; Per Subs 88
NORTH MOHAVE CAMPUS, 480 S Central, Colorado City, 86021. (Mail add: PO Box 980, Colorado City, 86021-0980). Tel: 928-875-2799, Ext 2224. FAX: 928-875-2831. *Librn,* Kim Naylor; E-mail: knaylor@mohave.edu
Library Holdings: Bk Vols 2,000; Per Subs 10

S MOHAVE COUNTY HISTORICAL SOCIETY, Mohave Museum of History & Arts Library, 400 W Beale St, 86401. SAN 300-3396. Tel: 928-753-3195. FAX: 928-718-1562. E-mail: library@mohavemuseum.org. Web Site: www.mohavemuseum.org/mohave-museum.html. *Dir,* Shannon Rossiter; E-mail: director@mohavemuseum.org; *Curator, Research Librn,* Mickey Chace
Founded 1966
Library Holdings: Bk Titles 4,000
Special Collections: Camp Beale's Springs Coll, bks, ms, micro; Genealogical Coll; Maps; Photographs from 1880 Related to Mohave County. Oral History
Subject Interests: Arizona, Indians, Mining, Ranching
Wireless access
Function: Archival coll, Computers for patron use, Electronic databases & coll, For res purposes, Genealogy discussion group, Internet access, Magazines, Microfiche/film & reading machines, Ref serv available, Res assist avail, Res libr, Res performed for a fee
Open Wed & Thurs 9-3
Restriction: Access at librarian's discretion, Authorized patrons, By permission only, Open to pub for ref & circ; with some limitations

P MOHAVE COUNTY LIBRARY DISTRICT*, 3269 N Burbank St, 86402. (Mail add: PO Box 7000, 86402-7000), SAN 330-6038. Administration Tel: 928-692-5717. Toll Free Tel: 800-525-8987 (AZ only). Administration FAX: 928-692-5762. Web Site: www.mohavecountylibrary.us. *Libr Dir,* Kathryn Pennell; E-mail: kathy.pennell@mohavecounty.us; Staff 9 (MLS 6, Non-MLS 3)
Founded 1926. Pop 205,000; Circ 660,182
Library Holdings: AV Mats 36,502; Bk Vols 209,633; Per Subs 564
Subject Interests: Arizona
Automation Activity & Vendor Info: (Acquisitions) SirsiDynix-Unicorn; (Cataloging) SirsiDynix-Unicorn; (Circulation) SirsiDynix-Unicorn; (ILL) OCLC; (OPAC) SirsiDynix-iBistro
Wireless access
Function: Bks on cassette, Bks on CD, Children's prog, Computer training, Computers for patron use, Digital talking bks, Free DVD rentals, Holiday prog, Home delivery & serv to seniorr ctr & nursing homes, Homebound delivery serv, Homework prog, ILL available, Internet access, Music CDs, Online cat, Photocopying/Printing, Prog for adults, Prog for children & young adult, Story hour, Summer reading prog, Tax forms, Teen prog, Telephone ref, VHS videos, Wheelchair accessible
Partic in Amigos Library Services, Inc; OCLC Online Computer Library Center, Inc
Special Services for the Deaf - Bks on deafness & sign lang; Closed caption videos; High interest/low vocabulary bks
Special Services for the Blind - Bks on cassette; Bks on CD; Copier with enlargement capabilities; Large print & cassettes; Large print bks; Large print bks & talking machines; Playaways (bks on MP3); Recorded bks; Ref serv; Sound rec; Talking bks; VisualTek equip
Friends of the Library Group
Branches: 10
BULLHEAD CITY BRANCH, 1170 Hancock Rd, Bullhead City, 86442, SAN 330-6062. Tel: 928-758-0714. FAX: 928-758-0720. Web Site: www.mohavecountylibrary.us/bullhead-city-branch-3. *Br Mgr,* Cathy McMahon; E-mail: cathy.mcmahon@mohavecounty.us; Staff 2 (MLS 2)
Founded 1942. Circ 187,143
Library Holdings: Audiobooks 2,604; AV Mats 7,087; Bks-By-Mail 502; Bks on Deafness & Sign Lang 31; Braille Volumes 3; CDs 3,864; DVDs 2,843; e-books 3,988; e-journals 4,031; Electronic Media & Resources 134; High Interest/Low Vocabulary Bk Vols 36; Large Print Bks 2,575; Music Scores 37; Bk Titles 44,377; Bk Vols 46,798; Per Subs 102; Videos 130
Special Collections: Arizona Region
Function: Audiobks via web, Bks on CD, Computers for patron use, Electronic databases & coll, Free DVD rentals, Home delivery & serv to seniorr ctr & nursing homes, ILL available, Online cat, OverDrive digital audio bks, Photocopying/Printing, Prog for adults, Prog for children & young adult, Spanish lang bks, Wheelchair accessible
Special Services for the Blind - Bks on CD; Large print bks; Playaways (bks on MP3); Talking bk serv referral

Open Mon & Wed 9-6, Tues & Thurs 9-8, Fri & Sat 9-5
Friends of the Library Group

CHLORIDE COMMUNITY LIBRARY, 4901 Pay Roll Ave, Chloride, 86431. (Mail add: PO Box 111, Chloride, 86431-0111). Tel: 928-565-2200. FAX: 928-565-2200. Web Site: www.mohavecountylibrary.us/chloride. *Commun Libr Rep,* Janice Garoutte; E-mail: janice.garoutte@mohavecounty.us
Founded 1994. Circ 9,577
Library Holdings: Audiobooks 139; AV Mats 1,218; Bks on Deafness & Sign Lang 2; CDs 130; DVDs 1,051; e-books 3,988; e-journals 4,031; Electronic Media & Resources 16; High Interest/Low Vocabulary Bk Vols 4; Large Print Bks 29; Bk Titles 2,680; Bk Vols 2,782; Per Subs 17; Videos 5
Special Collections: Arizona Region
Function: Audiobks via web, Bks on CD, Computers for patron use, Electronic databases & coll, Free DVD rentals, Home delivery & serv to seniorr ctr & nursing homes, ILL available, Online cat, OverDrive digital audio bks, Photocopying/Printing, Prog for adults, Prog for children & young adult, Wheelchair accessible
Special Services for the Blind - Bks on CD; Large print bks; Playaways (bks on MP3); Talking bk serv referral
Open Tues & Thurs 9am-12:30pm, Wed 2-6, Sat 10-2

DOLAN SPRINGS COMMUNITY LIBRARY, 16140 Pierce Ferry Rd, Dolan Springs, 86441. (Mail add: PO Box 427, Dolan Springs, 86441-0427). Tel: 928-767-4292. FAX: 928-767-4292. Web Site: www.mohavecountylibrary.us/dolan-springs. *Commun Libr Rep,* Robin Wynn; E-mail: robin.wynn@mohavecounty.us
Founded 1975. Circ 17,528
Library Holdings: Audiobooks 396; AV Mats 1,746; CDs 448; DVDs 1,189; e-books 3,988; e-journals 4,031; Electronic Media & Resources 30; High Interest/Low Vocabulary Bk Vols 4; Large Print Bks 341; Music Scores 1; Bk Titles 5,297; Bk Vols 5,340; Per Subs 18; Videos 68
Special Collections: Arizona Region
Function: Audiobks via web, Bks on CD, Computers for patron use, Electronic databases & coll, Free DVD rentals, Home delivery & serv to seniorr ctr & nursing homes, ILL available, Online cat, OverDrive digital audio bks, Photocopying/Printing, Prog for adults, Prog for children & young adult, Wheelchair accessible
Special Services for the Blind - Bks on CD; Large print bks; Playaways (bks on MP3); Talking bk serv referral
Open Tues 8-1, Thurs 12-6, Sat 9-1
Friends of the Library Group

GOLDEN SHORES COMMUNITY LIBRARY, 13136 S Gplden Shores Pkwy, Topock, 86436. Tel: 928-768-2235. FAX: 928-768-2235. Web Site: www.mohavecountylibrary.us/golden-shorestopock. *Commun Libr Rep,* Dick Gebhart; E-mail: dick.gebhart@mohavecounty.us
Founded 1991. Circ 11,801
Library Holdings: Audiobooks 247; AV Mats 1,223; Bks on Deafness & Sign Lang 2; CDs 235; DVDs 923; e-books 3,988; e-journals 4,031; Electronic Media & Resources 24; High Interest/Low Vocabulary Bk Vols 3; Large Print Bks 233; Bk Titles 4,875; Bk Vols 4,958; Per Subs 9; Videos 7
Special Collections: Arizona Region
Function: Audiobks via web, Bks on CD, Computers for patron use, Electronic databases & coll, Free DVD rentals, Home delivery & serv to seniorr ctr & nursing homes, ILL available, Online cat, OverDrive digital audio bks, Photocopying/Printing, Prog for adults, Prog for children & young adult, Wheelchair accessible
Special Services for the Blind - Bks on CD; Large print bks; Playaways (bks on MP3); Talking bk serv referral
Open Tues, Thurs & Sat 9-1, Wed 2-5
Friends of the Library Group

GOLDEN VALLEY COMMUNITY LIBRARY, 3417 N Verde Rd, Golden Valley, 86413-0671. Tel: 928-565-2989. FAX: 928-565-2989. Web Site: www.mohavecountylibrary.us/golden-valley. *Commun Libr Rep,* Roxana Berry; E-mail: roxana.berry@mohavecounty.us
Founded 2005. Circ 13,037
Library Holdings: Audiobooks 452; AV Mats 1,439; Bks on Deafness & Sign Lang 1; CDs 416; DVDs 816; e-books 3,988; e-journals 4,031; Electronic Media & Resources 15; High Interest/Low Vocabulary Bk Vols 6; Large Print Bks 252; Bk Titles 4,625; Bk Vols 4,749; Per Subs 8; Videos 7
Special Collections: Arizona Region
Function: Audiobks via web, Bks on CD, Computers for patron use, Electronic databases & coll, Free DVD rentals, Home delivery & serv to seniorr ctr & nursing homes, ILL available, Online cat, OverDrive digital audio bks, Photocopying/Printing, Prog for adults, Prog for children & young adult, Wheelchair accessible
Special Services for the Blind - Bks on CD; Large print bks; Playaways (bks on MP3); Talking bk serv referral
Open Tues 9-3, Thurs 12-6, Sat 10-1
Friends of the Library Group

KINGMAN LIBRARY, 3269 N Burbank St, 86401. (Mail add: PO Box 7000, 86402-7000). Tel: 928-692-2665. FAX: 928-692-5788. Web Site: www.mohavecountylibrary.us/kingman-branch-library. *Br Mgr,* Beverly Clouse; E-mail: bev.clouse@mohavecounty.us; Staff 2 (MLS 2)
Founded 1926. Circ 251,535
Library Holdings: Audiobooks 2,680; AV Mats 8,240; Bks-By-Mail 502; Bks on Deafness & Sign Lang 34; Braille Volumes 109; CDs 3,583; DVDs 1,436; e-books 3,988; e-journals 4,031; Electronic Media & Resources 132; High Interest/Low Vocabulary Bk Vols 99; Large Print Bks 3,385; Music Scores 12; Bk Titles 50,548; Bk Vols 52,067; Per Subs 135; Videos 148
Special Collections: Arizona Region
Function: Audiobks via web, Bks on CD, Computers for patron use, Electronic databases & coll, Free DVD rentals, Home delivery & serv to seniorr ctr & nursing homes, ILL available, Magnifiers for reading, Online cat, OverDrive digital audio bks, Photocopying/Printing, Prog for adults, Prog for children & young adult, Spanish lang bks, Wheelchair accessible
Special Services for the Blind - Assistive/Adapted tech devices, equip & products; Bks on CD; Braille equip; Children's Braille; Copier with enlargement capabilities; Large print bks; Photo duplicator for making large print; Playaways (bks on MP3); Talking bk serv referral
Open Mon & Wed 9-6, Tues & Thurs 9-8, Fri & Sat 9-5
Friends of the Library Group

LAKE HAVASU CITY BRANCH LIBRARY, 1770 N McCulloch Blvd, Lake Havasu City, 86403-8847, SAN 330-6097. Tel: 928-453-0718. FAX: 928-453-0720. Web Site: www.mohavecountylibrary.us/lake-havasu-city. *Br Mgr,* Wendy Wagner; E-mail: wendy.wagner@mohavecounty.us; Staff 2 (MLS 2)
Founded 1968. Circ 2,254,427
Library Holdings: Audiobooks 2,900; AV Mats 8,332; Bks-By-Mail 502; Bks on Deafness & Sign Lang 40; Braille Volumes 2; CDs 3,556; DVDs 3,839; e-books 3,988; e-journals 4,031; Electronic Media & Resources 292; High Interest/Low Vocabulary Bk Vols 740; Large Print Bks 3,226; Music Scores 11; Bk Titles 45,471; Bk Vols 48,288; Per Subs 183; Videos 99
Special Collections: Arizona Region; Health
Subject Interests: Adult literacy, Graphic novels, Spanish
Function: Audiobks via web, Bk club(s), Bks on CD, Computers for patron use, Electronic databases & coll, Free DVD rentals, Home delivery & serv to seniorr ctr & nursing homes, ILL available, Online cat, OverDrive digital audio bks, Photocopying/Printing, Prog for adults, Prog for children & young adult, Spanish lang bks, Wheelchair accessible
Special Services for the Blind - Bks on CD; Large print bks; Magnifiers; Playaways (bks on MP3); Talking bk serv referral
Open Mon & Wed 9-6, Tues & Thurs 9-8, Fri & Sat 9-5
Friends of the Library Group

MEADVIEW COMMUNITY LIBRARY, 149 E Meadview Blvd, Meadview, 86444. (Mail add: PO Box 187, Meadview, 86444-0187), SAN 370-906X. Tel: 928-564-2535. FAX: 928-564-2535. Web Site: www.mohavecountylibrary.us/meadview. *Commun Libr Rep,* Tonia Turner; E-mail: tonia.turner@mohavecounty.us
Founded 1990. Circ 4,100
Library Holdings: Audiobooks 435; AV Mats 1,427; CDs 377; DVDs 918; e-books 3,988; e-journals 4,031; Electronic Media & Resources 9; High Interest/Low Vocabulary Bk Vols 2; Large Print Bks 151; Bk Titles 4,575; Bk Vols 4,706; Per Subs 7; Videos 1
Special Collections: Arizona Region
Function: Audiobks via web, Bks on CD, Computers for patron use, Electronic databases & coll, Free DVD rentals, Home delivery & serv to seniorr ctr & nursing homes, ILL available, Online cat, OverDrive digital audio bks, Photocopying/Printing, Prog for adults, Prog for children & young adult, Wheelchair accessible
Special Services for the Blind - Bks on CD; Large print bks; Playaways (bks on MP3); Talking bk serv referral
Open Tues, Thurs & Sat 10-3
Friends of the Library Group

SOUTH MOHAVE VALLEY COMMUNITY LIBRARY, 5744 S Hwy 95, Ste 102, Fort Mohave, 86426, SAN 373-191X. Tel: 928-768-1151. FAX: 928-768-1151. Web Site: www.mohavecountylibrary.us/south-mohave-valley. *Commun Libr Rep,* Kim Stoddard; E-mail: kim.stoddard@mohavecounty.us
Founded 1992. Circ 21,791
Library Holdings: Audiobooks 322; AV Mats 1,326; Bks on Deafness & Sign Lang 2; CDs 318; DVDs 933; e-books 3,988; e-journals 4,031; Electronic Media & Resources 37; High Interest/Low Vocabulary Bk Vols 3; Large Print Bks 222; Bk Titles 5,239; Bk Vols 5,314; Per Subs 10; Videos 1
Special Collections: Arizona Region
Function: Audiobks via web, Bks on CD, Computers for patron use, Electronic databases & coll, Free DVD rentals, Home delivery & serv to seniorr ctr & nursing homes, ILL available, Online cat, OverDrive digital audio bks, Photocopying/Printing, Prog for adults, Prog for children & young adult, Wheelchair accessible

Special Services for the Blind - Bks on CD; Large print bks; Playaways (bks on MP3); Talking bk serv referral
Open Tues & Thurs 10-6, Wed 11-7, Fri & Sat 9-5
Friends of the Library Group

VALLE VISTA COMMUNITY LIBRARY, 7264 E Concho Dr, Ste B, 86401-9466, SAN 378-1666. Tel: 928-692-7662. FAX: 928-692-7662. Web Site: www.mohavecountylibrary.us/valle-vista. *Commun Libr Rep,* Position Currently Open
Founded 1998. Circ 10,786
Library Holdings: Audiobooks 225; AV Mats 1,497; Bks on Deafness & Sign Lang 1; Braille Volumes 1; CDs 258; DVDs 1,123; e-books 3,988; e-journals 4,031; Electronic Media & Resources 30; High Interest/Low Vocabulary Bk Vols 2; Large Print Bks 295; Bk Titles 4,924; Bk Vols 4,994; Per Subs 10; Videos 71
Special Collections: Arizona Region
Function: Audiobks via web, Bks on CD, Computers for patron use, Electronic databases & coll, Free DVD rentals, Home delivery & serv to seniorr ctr & nursing homes, ILL available, Online cat, OverDrive digital audio bks, Photocopying/Printing, Prog for adults, Prog for children & young adult, Wheelchair accessible
Special Services for the Blind - Bks on CD; Large print bks; Playaways (bks on MP3); Talking bk serv referral
Open Tues & Thurs 2:30-6, Wed & Sat 10-2
Friends of the Library Group
Bookmobiles: 2. Contact, Rob Walker. Bk titles 9,106

KYKOTSMOVI VILLAGE

P HOPI PUBLIC LIBRARY*, c/o Hopi Educ Dept, One Main St, 86039. (Mail add: PO Box 123, 86039-0123), SAN 377-5488. Tel: 928-734-4500. FAX: 928-734-4545. E-mail: hopi@navajocountylibraries.org. *Dir,* Dr Noreen E Sakiestewa; Tel: 928-734-3501, E-mail: nsakiestewa@hopi.nsn.us; *Libr Asst,* Dinah Pongyesva; Staff 1 (Non-MLS 1)
Founded 1974
Library Holdings: Bk Titles 1,100
Wireless access
Mem of Navajo County Library System
Open Mon-Thurs 8-5, Fri 9-4
Bookmobiles: 1

LAKESIDE

P PINETOP-LAKESIDE PUBLIC LIBRARY*, 1595 Johnson Dr, 85929. SAN 300-340X. Tel: 928-368-6688. FAX: 928-368-8963. E-mail: info@pinetoplakesidelibrary.org. Web Site: www.pinetoplakesidelibrary.org. *Libr Mgr,* Betsy Peck; Tel: 928-368-6688, Ext 4, E-mail: bpeck@pinetoplakesideaz.gov; Staff 5 (MLS 1, Non-MLS 4)
Founded 1930. Pop 20,000; Circ 80,000
Library Holdings: CDs 40; DVDs 200; Large Print Bks 13,000; Bk Titles 31,000; Bk Vols 32,000; Per Subs 70
Special Collections: National Geographic Coll
Subject Interests: Arizona, Indians
Automation Activity & Vendor Info: (Acquisitions) SirsiDynix; (Cataloging) SirsiDynix; (Circulation) SirsiDynix; (OPAC) SirsiDynix
Wireless access
Function: ILL available, Photocopying/Printing, Prog for children & young adult, Summer reading prog, Telephone ref
Mem of Navajo County Library System
Partic in Navajo County Libr District
Special Services for the Blind - Talking bks
Open Mon-Fri 9:30-6, Sat 10-2

LUKE AFB

A UNITED STATES AIR FORCE*, Luke Air Force Base Library, Bldg 219, 7424 N Homer Dr, 56 SVS/SVMG FL 4887, 85309. SAN 330-6216. Tel: 623-856-7191. FAX: 623-935-2023. Web Site: www.lukeevents.com/library. *Dir,* Todd Simonson; Staff 2 (MLS 2)
Founded 1951
Library Holdings: AV Mats 4,000; e-books 450; Large Print Bks 1,000; Bk Vols 49,500; Per Subs 225; Talking Bks 4,500
Special Collections: Arizona, Mission Support. Oral History
Subject Interests: Aeronaut, Mil hist
Automation Activity & Vendor Info: (Cataloging) SirsiDynix; (Circulation) SirsiDynix; (ILL) OCLC
Wireless access
Publications: Bibliographies; Library Links (Newsletter)
Partic in OCLC Online Computer Library Center, Inc; Proquest Dialog
Restriction: Mem only

MAMMOTH

P MAMMOTH PUBLIC LIBRARY*, 125 N Clark St, 85618. (Mail add: PO Box 549, 85618-0549), SAN 300-3434. Tel: 520-487-2026. FAX: 520-487-2364. Web Site: library.townofmammoth.us. *Librn,* Sharon Christiansen; E-mail: sharon.christiansen@pinalcountyaz.gov
Founded 1962. Pop 1,850; Circ 7,833
Library Holdings: Audiobooks 1,500; CDs 30; DVDs 4,000; Bk Titles 8,000; Bk Vols 8,500; Per Subs 40
Automation Activity & Vendor Info: (Cataloging) SirsiDynix; (Circulation) SirsiDynix; (OPAC) SirsiDynix
Wireless access
Mem of Pinal County Library District
Open Tues, Wed, Fri & Sat 12-6, Thurs 10-6

MARICOPA

P MARICOPA PUBLIC LIBRARY*, 41600 W Smith-Enke Rd, Bldg 10, 85138. Tel: 520-568-2926. FAX: 520-568-2680. *Libr Dir,* Erik Surber; E-mail: erik.surber@pinalcountyaz.gov; *Senior Coord,* Ann Marie Creegan; Staff 10.5 (MLS 3, Non-MLS 7.5)
Founded 1958. Pop 48,000
Library Holdings: Audiobooks 5,500; CDs 2,000; DVDs 15,000; Large Print Bks 3,500; Bk Vols 23,000; Per Subs 52
Special Collections: Arizona Coll
Automation Activity & Vendor Info: (Cataloging) Horizon; (Circulation) Horizon
Wireless access
Function: 24/7 Electronic res, 24/7 Online cat, 3D Printer, Activity rm, Adult bk club, After school storytime, Archival coll, Art exhibits, Audiobks via web, Bilingual assistance for Spanish patrons, Bk club(s), Bks on CD, Chess club, Children's prog, Citizenship assistance, Computer training, Computers for patron use, Digital talking bks, Doc delivery serv, E-Reserves, Electronic databases & coll, Equip loans & repairs, Free DVD rentals, Govt ref serv, Health sci info serv, Holiday prog, Home delivery & serv to seniorr ctr & nursing homes, Homebound delivery serv, ILL available, Instruction & testing, Internet access, Life-long learning prog for all ages, Magazines, Meeting rooms, Movies, Museum passes, Music CDs, Online cat, Outreach serv, Photocopying/Printing, Preschool outreach, Preschool reading prog, Prog for adults, Prog for children & young adult, Ref serv available, Senior computer classes, Serves people with intellectual disabilities, Spanish lang bks, Story hour, Study rm, Summer & winter reading prog, Summer reading prog, Tax forms, Teen prog, Telephone ref, Visual arts prog, Wheelchair accessible, Winter reading prog, Workshops
Mem of Pinal County Library District
Open Mon-Thurs 9-7, Fri & Sat 9-6
Friends of the Library Group

MESA

CM A T STILL UNIVERSITY*, Arizona Campus Library, 5850 E Still Circle, 85206-6091. Tel: 480-219-6090. FAX: 480-219-6100. E-mail: libaz@atsu.edu. Web Site: www.atsu.edu/atsmlib. *Dir of the Univ Libr,* Hal Bright; Tel: 480-219-6036, E-mail: hbright@atsu.edu; *Communications Librn, Web Librn,* Samantha Maley; Tel: 480-219-6259, E-mail: samanthamaley@atsu.edu; *Electronic Res Librn,* Lora Hanson; Tel: 480-219-6091, E-mail: lorahanson@atsu.edu; *Liaison Librn,* Adrienne Brodie; Tel: 480-218-6192, E-mail: abrodie@atsu.edu; Staff 5 (MLS 4, Non-MLS 1)
Founded 2002. Enrl 4,074; Highest Degree: Doctorate
Library Holdings: e-books 150,000; e-journals 25,000; Bk Vols 800; Per Subs 90
Special Collections: Osteopathic Medicine
Automation Activity & Vendor Info: (Acquisitions) CyberTools for Libraries; (Cataloging) OCLC; (Discovery) EBSCO Discovery Service; (OPAC) CyberTools for Libraries; (Serials) EBSCO Online
Wireless access
Partic in Arizona Health Information Network; MOBIUS
Open Mon-Sun 8am-11pm

M BANNER DESERT MEDICAL CENTER*, Health Science Library, 1400 S Dobson Rd, 85202. Tel: 480-512-3024. FAX: 480-512-8720. Web Site: www.bannerhealth.com/health-professionals/medical-libraries/arizona/contact-us. *Librn,* Kathy Bilko; E-mail: kathy.bilko@bannerhealth.com
Library Holdings: Bk Titles 700
Wireless access
Open Mon-Fri 7-4

S IDEA MUSEUM LIBRARY*, 150 W Pepper Pl, 85201. SAN 375-7161. Tel: 480-644-2468. FAX: 480-644-2466. E-mail: ideaMuseum@MesaAz.gov. Web Site: www.ideamuseum.org. *Curator,* Jeffory Morris; Tel: 480-644-5769, E-mail: Jeffory.Morris@MesaAZ.gov
Library Holdings: Bk Titles 1,000
Open Tues-Sat 9-4, Sun 12-4

J MESA COMMUNITY COLLEGE LIBRARY*, Paul A Elsner Library, 1833 W Southern Ave, 85202. SAN 300-3469. Tel: 480-461-7671. Circulation Tel: 480-461-7680. Reference Tel: 480-461-7682. FAX: 480-461-7681. TDD: 480-969-5387. Web Site: www.mesacc.edu/library/. *Chair,* Ann Tolzman; *Libr Mgr,* Jennifer Hunt; E-mail: jennifer.hunt@mesacc.edu; Staff 29 (MLS 10, Non-MLS 19)
Founded 1963. Enrl 24,470; Fac 350; Highest Degree: Associate
Library Holdings: AV Mats 679; e-books 28,752; Bk Vols 85,184; Per Subs 528
Automation Activity & Vendor Info: (Acquisitions) SirsiDynix; (Cataloging) SirsiDynix; (Circulation) SirsiDynix; (Course Reserve) SirsiDynix; (ILL) SirsiDynix; (Media Booking) SirsiDynix; (OPAC) SirsiDynix; (Serials) EBSCO Online
Wireless access
Function: Electronic databases & coll, ILL available, Online ref, Ref serv available, Tax forms, Wheelchair accessible
Special Services for the Blind - Computer with voice synthesizer for visually impaired persons
Open Mon-Thurs 6am-Midnight, Fri 6-5, Sat 8-5, Sun Noon-10
Departmental Libraries:
RED MOUNTAIN, 7110 E McKellips Rd, 85207. Tel: 480-654-7741. Reference Tel: 480-654-7740. FAX: 480-654-7401. *Dir,* Marie C Brown; E-mail: marie.brown@mesacc.edu
Library Holdings: Per Subs 85
Open Mon-Thurs (Fall & Spring) 7am-8:30pm, Fri 7-4, Sat 10-2

P MESA PUBLIC LIBRARY*, 64 E First St, 85201-6768. (Mail add: PO Box 1466, 85211), SAN 300-3477. Tel: 480-644-3100. Interlibrary Loan Service Tel: 480-644-2732. FAX: 480-644-2991. E-mail: library.info@mesaaz.gov. Web Site: www.mesalibrary.org. *Dir,* Heather Wolf; E-mail: heather.wolf@mesaaz.gov; *Br Coordr,* Polly Bonnett; E-mail: Polly.Bonnett@MesaAZ.gov; *Coll Develop,* Liz Costanzo-Lee; E-mail: liz.costanzo-lee@mesaaz.gov; *Tech Adminr,* Brandon Williams; E-mail: brandon.williams@mesaaz.gov; Staff 74.9 (MLS 24, Non-MLS 50.9)
Founded 1926. Pop 481,275; Circ 2,890,835
Jul 2017-Jun 2018 Income (Main & Associated Libraries) $6,702,944, State $22,539, City $6,205,888, Federal $152,970, Other $321,547
Library Holdings: Audiobooks 18,021; AV Mats 33,507; Braille Volumes 50; DVDs 5,913; e-books 76; Large Print Bks 15,864; Bk Titles 285,527; Bk Vols 585,127; Per Subs 280
Special Collections: Oral History
Subject Interests: Local hist, Spanish (Lang)
Automation Activity & Vendor Info: (Acquisitions) Innovative Interfaces, Inc; (Cataloging) Innovative Interfaces, Inc; (Circulation) Innovative Interfaces, Inc; (ILL) OCLC ILLiad; (OPAC) Innovative Interfaces, Inc; (Serials) Innovative Interfaces, Inc
Wireless access
Partic in OCLC Online Computer Library Center, Inc
Special Services for the Deaf - ADA equip; Bks on deafness & sign lang; Closed caption videos; TTY equip
Special Services for the Blind - Braille bks; Copier with enlargement capabilities; Large print bks
Open Mon-Thurs 10-8, Fri & Sat 10-5
Branches: 3
DOBSON RANCH BRANCH, 2425 S Dobson Rd, 85202, SAN 328-6800. Tel: 480-644-3444. FAX: 602-644-3445. *Br Coordr,* Anna Matthews; E-mail: anna.matthews@mesaaz.gov; Staff 9 (MLS 3, Non-MLS 6)
Founded 1987
Function: Bks on CD, Children's prog, Computers for patron use, Electronic databases & coll, Free DVD rentals, ILL available, OverDrive digital audio bks, Photocopying/Printing, Prog for adults, Prog for children & young adult, Story hour, Summer reading prog
Open Mon-Thurs 9-8, Fri & Sat 10-5
MESA EXPRESS LIBRARY, 2055 S Power Rd, Ste 1031, 85209. Tel: 480-644-3300. *Librn II,* Margie Trzcinski; E-mail: margie.trzcinski@mesaaz.gov
Founded 2011
Function: Bks on CD, Computers for patron use, Electronic databases & coll, Free DVD rentals, ILL available, Online cat, OverDrive digital audio bks, Photocopying/Printing, Summer reading prog, Wheelchair accessible
Open Mon-Thurs 10-5, Fri & Sat 10-5
RED MOUNTAIN BRANCH, 635 N Power Rd, 85205, SAN 325-3791. Tel: 480-644-3183. Circulation Tel: 480-644-3182. FAX: 480-644-3559. *Br Coordr,* Joyce Abbott; E-mail: Joyce.Abbott@mesaaz.gov; Staff 21 (MLS 6, Non-MLS 15)
Founded 1985
Function: Art exhibits, Bks on CD, Children's prog, Computers for patron use, Electronic databases & coll, Free DVD rentals, ILL available, Large print keyboards, Magnifiers for reading, Museum passes, Music CDs, Online cat, Photocopying/Printing, Prog for adults, Prog for children & young adult, Ref & res, Ref serv available, Story hour, Summer reading prog, Teen prog, Telephone ref
Open Mon-Thurs 10-8, Fri & Sat 10-5

MIAMI

P MIAMI MEMORIAL LIBRARY*, 282 S Adonis Ave, 85539. SAN 300-3493. Tel: 928-473-2621. FAX: 928-473-2567. E-mail: mmlibsp@gmail.com. *Libr Mgr,* Sue Pontel
Pop 37,098
Library Holdings: Bk Vols 70,000; Per Subs 10
Wireless access
Open Tues-Fri 10-6, Sat 9-1
Friends of the Library Group

MORENCI

P MORENCI COMMUNITY LIBRARY*, 346 Plaza Dr, 85540. SAN 376-3269. Tel: 928-865-7042. Web Site: www.morencitown.com/residents/library. *Dir,* Kia Gaethje
Library Holdings: Bk Titles 18,050; Bk Vols 19,127; Per Subs 58
Subject Interests: Arizona, Mining
Wireless access
Open Mon-Thurs 10-8, Fri 10-6
Friends of the Library Group

NOGALES

P NOGALES-SANTA CRUZ COUNTY PUBLIC LIBRARY*, Nogales-Rochlin Public Library, 518 N Grand Ave, 85621. SAN 300-3507. Tel: 520-285-5717. Web Site: www.nogalesaz.gov/library-department. *Libr Dir,* Danitza Lopez; E-mail: dalopez@nogalesaz.gov; *ILL,* Sandra Mascareñas; Tel: 520-285-5717, Ext 0241, E-mail: smascareñas@nogalesaz.gov; Staff 6 (MLS 1, Non-MLS 5)
Founded 1923. Pop 44,575; Circ 143,748
Jul 2015-Jun 2016 Income (Main & Associated Libraries) $509,989, City $248,647, Federal $9,700, County $248,647, Locally Generated Income $2,995. Mats Exp $41,482, Books $32,942, AV Mat $8,540. Sal $269,990
Library Holdings: CDs 1,590; DVDs 2,163; Bk Vols 56,000; Per Subs 92; Videos 2,163
Special Collections: Arizona & Southwest History Coll; Spanish Language Coll
Automation Activity & Vendor Info: (Cataloging) Innovative Interfaces, Inc; (Circulation) Innovative Interfaces, Inc
Function: Adult bk club, Bilingual assistance for Spanish patrons, Bks on cassette, Bks on CD, Chess club, Children's prog, Computer training, Computers for patron use, Homework prog, ILL available, Internet access, Music CDs, Online cat, Photocopying/Printing, Senior computer classes, Spoken cassettes & CDs, Spoken cassettes & DVDs, Story hour, Summer reading prog, Tax forms, Wheelchair accessible
Partic in OCLC Online Computer Library Center, Inc
Special Services for the Deaf - TDD equip
Open Mon & Wed 9:30-6, Tues & Thurs 9:30-7, Fri 9-5, Sat 9-4
Restriction: Borrowing requests are handled by ILL
Friends of the Library Group
Branches: 3
RIO RICO LIBRARY, 275 Rio Rico Dr, Rio Rico, 85648, SAN 320-9520. Tel: 520-281-8067. *Libr Asst,* Clarissa Martinez; Staff 1 (Non-MLS 1)
Founded 1982
Friends of the Library Group
SONOITA COMMUNITY LIBRARY, County Complex Bldg, 3147 State Rte 83, Sonoita, 85637, SAN 373-1820. Tel: 520-455-5517. *Library Contact,* Valerie Hing; *Library Contact,* Jennifer Riehl
Open Mon-Fri 10-2
Friends of the Library Group
TUBAC COMMUNITY LIBRARY, 50 Bridge Rd, Tubac, 85646, SAN 326-7911. Tel: 520-398-9814. *Library Contact,* Bethany Lamb-Garcia
Open Mon-Thurs 9-2, Fri 9-1
Friends of the Library Group

S PIMERIA ALTA HISTORICAL SOCIETY*, Alma D Ready Research Library, 136 N Grand Ave, 85621. (Mail add: PO Box 2281, 85628-2281), SAN 326-5609. Tel: 520-287-4621. E-mail: pimeriaaltamuseum@gmail.com. Web Site: www.pimeriaaltamuseum.org. *Pres,* Jose Ramon Garcia
Founded 1942
Library Holdings: Bk Titles 1,500; Bk Vols 1,600; Per Subs 10
Special Collections: Municipal Document Depository; Oral History; US Document Depository
Wireless access
Open Tues-Sat 11-3:30

ORACLE

P ORACLE PUBLIC LIBRARY*, 565 E American Ave, 85623. (Mail add: PO Box 960, 85623), SAN 300-3515. Tel: 520-896-2121. FAX: 520-896-2149. Web Site: oraclepubliclibrary.wordpress.com, www.pinalcountyaz.gov/Departments/Library/Locations/Pages/Oracle.aspx. *Dir & Librn,* Pauline Skiba
Founded 1920. Pop 5,500; Circ 12,000

Library Holdings: Bk Titles 12,000; Per Subs 20
Special Collections: Southwest Coll
Automation Activity & Vendor Info: (Cataloging) Horizon; (Circulation) Horizon; (OPAC) Horizon
Wireless access
Mem of Pinal County Library District

PAGE

P PAGE PUBLIC LIBRARY, 479 S Lake Powell Blvd, 86040. (Mail add: PO Box 1776, 86040-1776), SAN 300-354X. Tel: 928-645-4270. Administration Tel: 928-645-4272, 928-645-5803. FAX: 928-645-5804. TDD: 928-645-4133. Web Site: pagepubliclibrary.org. *Libr Mgr,* Debbie Winlock; E-mail: dwinlock@pageaz.gov; *Children's Coordr,* Seairah Combest; Tel: 928-645-5802, E-mail: scombest@pageaz.gov; *Adult Serv, Ref,* Mikalah Clark; E-mail: mclark@pageaz.gov; Staff 8 (MLS 1, Non-MLS 7)
Founded 1959. Pop 8,000
Library Holdings: CDs 3,788; DVDs 3,132; Bk Titles 55,697; Bk Vols 58,585; Per Subs 50
Subject Interests: Arizona, Native Am
Automation Activity & Vendor Info: (Acquisitions) Koha; (Cataloging) Koha; (Circulation) Koha; (OPAC) Koha
Wireless access
Function: 24/7 Electronic res, 24/7 Online cat, Activity rm, Adult bk club, Adult literacy prog, After school storytime, Archival coll, Audio & video playback equip for onsite use, Audiobks on Playaways & MP3, Audiobks via web, Bk club(s), Bks on CD, CD-ROM, Children's prog, Computer training, Computers for patron use, Digital talking bks, Distance learning, Doc delivery serv, E-Readers, Electronic databases & coll, Equip loans & repairs, Family literacy, For res purposes, Free DVD rentals, Games & aids for people with disabilities, Govt ref serv, Holiday prog, Homebound delivery serv, Homework prog, ILL available, Instruction & testing, Internet access, Laminating, Life-long learning prog for all ages, Magazines, Magnifiers for reading, Mail & tel request accepted, Meeting rooms, Microfiche/film & reading machines, Movies, Notary serv, Online cat, Online info literacy tutorials on the web & in blackboard, Online ref, Outreach serv, Outside serv via phone, mail, e-mail & web, OverDrive digital audio bks, Photocopying/Printing, Preschool outreach, Preschool reading prog, Prof lending libr, Prog for adults, Prog for children & young adult, Ref & res, Ref serv available, Scanner, Senior computer classes, Senior outreach, Spanish lang bks, Story hour, Summer & winter reading prog, Summer reading prog, Tax forms, Teen prog, Telephone ref, Wheelchair accessible, Winter reading prog, Workshops
Publications: Annual Report; Library Board Policy Manual
Mem of Flagstaff City-Coconino County Public Library System
Open Mon-Fri 10-6
Restriction: Access at librarian's discretion
Friends of the Library Group

PARKER

P COLORADO RIVER INDIAN TRIBES PUBLIC LIBRARY/ARCHIVES*, Second Ave & Mohave Rd, Rte 1, Box 23-B, 85344. SAN 300-3558. Tel: 928-669-1332. FAX: 928-669-8262. E-mail: crit.library@crit-nsn.gov. Web Site: www.crit-nsn.gov/critlibrary. *Dir,* Gilford Harper
Founded 1958. Circ 4,376
Library Holdings: Bks on Deafness & Sign Lang 16; Bk Titles 12,000; Bk Vols 22,000
Special Collections: Archival documents, History & Culture (Indian Coll), micro, photo
Automation Activity & Vendor Info: (Acquisitions) Follett Software; (Cataloging) Follett Software; (Circulation) Follett Software
Open Mon-Fri 8-5, Sat 9-1

P PARKER PUBLIC LIBRARY*, 1001 S Navajo Ave, 85344. SAN 300-3566. Tel: 928-669-2622. FAX: 928-669-8668. Web Site: www.parkerpubliclibrary.com. *Libr Mgr,* Ruthie Davis; E-mail: libmgr@townofparkeraz.us; *Adult, Children & Teen Serv,* Tracy McConnell; E-mail: tmcconnell@townofparkeraz.us; Staff 4 (Non-MLS 4)
Founded 1957. Pop 3,500; Circ 43,000
Library Holdings: Bk Vols 22,000
Subject Interests: Arizona
Automation Activity & Vendor Info: (Cataloging) Book Systems; (Circulation) Book Systems; (OPAC) Book Systems
Wireless access
Function: 24/7 Electronic res, 24/7 Online cat, After school storytime, Art exhibits, Audiobks on Playaways & MP3, Audiobks via web, AV serv, Bk club(s), Bks on CD, Children's prog, Computers for patron use, Digital talking bks, Distance learning, Electronic databases & coll, Free DVD rentals, Holiday prog, Home delivery & serv to seniorr ctr & nursing homes, Homebound delivery serv, ILL available, Instruction & testing, Internet access, Large print keyboards, Life-long learning prog for all ages, Magazines, Makerspace, Meeting rooms, Microfiche/film & reading machines, Movies, Music CDs, Notary serv, Online cat, OverDrive digital audio bks, Photocopying/Printing, Preschool outreach, Preschool reading prog, Printer for laptops & handheld devices, Prof lending libr, Prog for adults, Prog for children & young adult, Scanner, Senior outreach, Spanish lang bks, Spoken cassettes & CDs, STEM programs, Story hour, Study rm, Summer & winter reading prog, Summer reading prog, Tax forms, Teen prog, VHS videos, Wheelchair accessible, Winter reading prog
Special Services for the Deaf - Bks on deafness & sign lang; High interest/low vocabulary bks
Special Services for the Blind - Aids for in-house use; Bks available with recordings; Bks on cassette; Cassette playback machines; Digital talking bk machines; Large print bks; Playaways (bks on MP3); Talking bk & rec for the blind cat; Talking bk serv referral; Talking bks; Talking bks & player equip
Open Mon-Thurs 10-7
Friends of the Library Group

PATAGONIA

P PATAGONIA PUBLIC LIBRARY*, 346 Duquesne, 85624. (Mail add: PO Box 415, 85624), SAN 320-2054. Tel: 520-394-2010. FAX: 520-394-2113. E-mail: info@patagoniapubliclibrary.org. Web Site: www.patagoniapubliclibrary.org. *Libr Dir,* Laura Wenzel; E-mail: lwenzel@patagoniapubliclibrary.org; Staff 1.8 (MLS 1, Non-MLS 0.8)
Founded 1957. Pop 3,200; Circ 22,500. Sal $35,000 (Prof $28,750)
Library Holdings: Audiobooks 785; Braille Volumes 1; CDs 317; DVDs 1,234; Electronic Media & Resources 40; Large Print Bks 558; Bk Titles 12,433; Bk Vols 12,487; Per Subs 52; Videos 211
Special Collections: Foreign Language Video & DVD Coll; Library of Congress Classic DVD & Video Coll; Southwest & Local History Coll
Automation Activity & Vendor Info: (OPAC) Biblionix
Wireless access
Function: Adult bk club, Computer training, Electronic databases & coll, Homebound delivery serv, ILL available, Internet access, Mail & tel request accepted, Music CDs, Online ref, Photocopying/Printing, Preschool outreach, Prog for adults, Prog for children & young adult, Spoken cassettes & CDs, Spoken cassettes & DVDs, Summer reading prog, Tax forms, VHS videos, Wheelchair accessible
Open Mon-Fri 10-5, Sat 10-2
Friends of the Library Group

PAYSON

P PAYSON PUBLIC LIBRARY*, 328 N McLane Rd, 85541. SAN 300-3574. Tel: 928-474-9260. FAX: 928-474-2679. Web Site: www.paysonaz.gov/Departments/Library/LibraryHome.html. *Dir,* Emily Linkey; E-mail: elinkey@gcldaz.org; *Asst Libr Mgr,* David Grasse; *Ch,* Sarah English
Founded 1923. Pop 13,000; Circ 101,000
Library Holdings: Bk Vols 85,000; Per Subs 90
Special Collections: History (Southwest Coll); Native Americans
Automation Activity & Vendor Info: (Cataloging) Innovative Interfaces, Inc; (Circulation) Innovative Interfaces, Inc; (OPAC) Innovative Interfaces, Inc
Mem of Gila County Library District
Open Mon, Tues, Thurs & Fri 10-6, Wed 10-8, Sat 10-5
Friends of the Library Group

PEACH SPRINGS

P EDWARD MCELWAIN MEMORIAL LIBRARY*, 460 Hualapai Way, 86434. (Mail add: PO Box 179, 86434-0179). Tel: 928-769-2200. E-mail: HualapaiEducationDepartment@gmail.com. Web Site: hualapai-nsn.gov/services/education. *Head Librn,* Misty Watahomigie
Library Holdings: Bk Vols 10,000
Open Mon-Fri 8-5

PEORIA

P PEORIA PUBLIC LIBRARY*, 8463 W Monroe St, 85345. (Mail add: 8401 W Monroe St, 85345), SAN 300-3590. Tel: 623-773-7555. Reference Tel: 623-773-7556. FAX: 623-773-7567. Web Site: library.peoriaaz.gov. *Libr Syst Adminr,* Kathleen Wade; *Libr Serv Coordr,* Jill Thomsen; Tel: 623-773-7566, E-mail: jill.thomsen@peoriaaz.gov; Staff 8 (MLS 4, Non-MLS 4)
Founded 1920. Circ 111,819
Library Holdings: Bk Titles 198,050; Per Subs 105
Subject Interests: Spanish (Lang)
Automation Activity & Vendor Info: (Acquisitions) Innovative Interfaces, Inc; (Cataloging) Innovative Interfaces, Inc; (Circulation) Innovative Interfaces, Inc; (OPAC) Innovative Interfaces, Inc; (Serials) Innovative Interfaces, Inc
Wireless access
Function: Art exhibits, Bks on CD, Children's prog, Computers for patron use, E-Readers, Electronic databases & coll, Free DVD rentals, ILL available, Internet access, Jazz prog, Magazines, Movies, Music CDs,

Online ref, Photocopying/Printing, Story hour, Study rm, Teen prog, Telephone ref, Wheelchair accessible
Open Mon-Thurs 9-8, Fri & Sat 9-6, Sun 1-5
Restriction: Borrowing requests are handled by ILL
Friends of the Library Group
Branches: 1
SUNRISE MOUNTAIN, 21109 N 98th Ave, 85382, SAN 377-7553. Tel: 623-773-8650. FAX: 623-773-8670. *Librn III,* Pattie Fransen; Staff 5 (MLS 5)
Founded 1996
Library Holdings: Bk Titles 75,000
Open Mon-Thurs 9-8, Fri & Sat 9-6, Sun 1-5
Friends of the Library Group

PHOENIX

CR AMERICAN INDIAN COLLEGE*, Dorothy Cummings Library, 10020 N 15th Ave, 85021-2199. SAN 300-3639. Tel: 602-944-3335. E-mail: library@sagu.edu. Web Site: www.aicag.edu/services/library. *Librn,* Denise Baldetti; Tel: 602-944-3335, Ext 217, E-mail: dbaldetti@sagu.edu; Staff 1 (MLS 0.5, Non-MLS 0.5)
Founded 1965. Enrl 68; Fac 15; Highest Degree: Bachelor
Library Holdings: Bk Vols 25,000; Per Subs 50; Videos 670
Special Collections: Native American Coll; Religion, Bible
Subject Interests: Relig, Theol
Automation Activity & Vendor Info: (Cataloging) OPALS (Open-source Automated Library System); (Circulation) OPALS (Open-source Automated Library System); (Course Reserve) OPALS (Open-source Automated Library System); (OPAC) OPALS (Open-source Automated Library System)
Wireless access
Function: Computers for patron use, Internet access, Online cat, Online ref, Orientations, Photocopying/Printing, Scanner, VHS videos
Partic in Theological Library Cooperative of Arizona
Open Mon-Thurs 9-8, Fri 9-5, Sat 1-4
Restriction: Open to students, fac, staff & alumni

ARIZONA DEPARTMENT OF CORRECTIONS - ADULT INSTITUTIONS
S ARIZONA STATE PRISON COMPLEX - PHOENIX LIBRARY*, 2500 E Van Buren St, 85008. (Mail add: PO Box 52109, 85072-2109). Tel: 602-685-3100. FAX: 602-685-3129. *Educ Supvr,* Ron Brugman; Tel: 602-685-3100, Ext 3758
Library Holdings: Bk Vols 15,000
S ARIZONA STATE PRISON PHOENIX-WEST*, 3402 W Cocopah St, 85009. Tel: 602-352-0350, Ext 109. FAX: 602-352-0357. Web Site: www.librarything.com/profile/PrisonLib. *Librn,* Alexandra Rowland; Staff 1 (MLS 1). Sal $32,000
Library Holdings: Audiobooks 204; Bk Vols 6,116; Per Subs 8
Automation Activity & Vendor Info: (Cataloging) DEMCO; (Circulation) DEMCO
Function: Accelerated reader prog, Adult bk club, Adult literacy prog, BA reader (adult literacy), Bilingual assistance for Spanish patrons, Distance learning, ILL available, Legal assistance to inmates, Literacy & newcomer serv, Notary serv, Orientations, Photocopying/Printing, Wheelchair accessible
Restriction: Internal circ only

G ARIZONA DEPARTMENT OF EDUCATION LIBRARY*, 1535 W Jefferson St, Bin 6, 85007. SAN 300-3647. Tel: 602-542-5416. *Dir,* Linda Edgington; E-mail: linda.edgington@azed.gov; Staff 1 (MLS 1)
Library Holdings: Bk Titles 700; Per Subs 8
Subject Interests: Educ

M ARIZONA STATE HOSPITAL LIBRARY*, 2500 E Van Buren St, 85008. SAN 330-6240. Tel: 602-220-6045. FAX: 602-629-7285. Web Site: www.azdhs.gov/azsh/library.htm. *Library Contact,* Tory Bellavance; E-mail: tory.bellavance@azdhs.gov; Staff 1 (MLS 1)
Founded 1965
Library Holdings: AV Mats 500; DVDs 200; Large Print Bks 50; Bk Titles 10,000; Bk Vols 850; Per Subs 20; Talking Bks 80; Videos 300
Special Collections: State Document Depository
Subject Interests: Drug abuse, Mental health, Nursing, Psychiat, Psychol, Psychotherapy, Soc serv (soc work)
Automation Activity & Vendor Info: (Cataloging) CyberTools for Libraries; (Circulation) CyberTools for Libraries; (ILL) OCLC FirstSearch; (OPAC) CyberTools for Libraries; (Serials) CyberTools for Libraries
Function: ILL available, Ref serv available, Res libr
Partic in Association of Mental Health Libraries; Cent Ariz Biomed Librns; Pacific Southwest Regional Medical Library
Open Mon-Fri 8-12 & 1-3
Restriction: Non-circulating to the pub

G ARIZONA STATE LAW LIBRARY, ARCHIVES & PUBLIC RECORDS, 1700 W Washington, Rm 300, 85007. Tel: 602-926-3948. FAX: 602-256-7984. E-mail: research@azlibrary.gov. Web Site: www.azlibrary.gov/sla. *Adminr,* Malavika Muralidharan; *State Librn,* Holly Henley; Tel: 602-542-6200
Library Holdings: Bk Vols 150,000; Per Subs 380
Special Collections: Arizona Revised Statutes
Automation Activity & Vendor Info: (Acquisitions) SirsiDynix; (Cataloging) SirsiDynix; (Circulation) SirsiDynix; (OPAC) SirsiDynix; (Serials) SirsiDynix
Wireless access
Function: ILL available
Partic in OCLC Online Computer Library Center, Inc
Open Mon-Fri 9-4
Restriction: Circ limited

P ARIZONA STATE LIBRARY, ARCHIVES & PUBLIC RECORDS*, 1901 W Madison St, 85009. SAN 300-3701. Tel: 602-926-3870. Toll Free Tel: 800-228-4710 (AZ only). FAX: 602-256-7982. E-mail: research@azlibrary.gov. Web Site: azlibrary.gov. *Dir, Libr Serv, State Librn,* Holly Henley; Tel: 602-542-6181, E-mail: hhenley@azlibrary.gov; *Dir, Archives & Rec Mgt, State Archivist,* Dennis Preisler, PhD; Tel: 602-926-4035, E-mail: dpreisler@azlibrary.gov; *Adminr, Libr Develop,* Janet Ball; Tel: 602-542-6200, E-mail: jball@azlibrary.gov; *Adminr, Talking Bks,* Janet Fisher; Tel: 602-255-5578, E-mail: jfisher@azlibrary.gov; *Res Libr Adminr,* Megan Hammond; Tel: 602-926-3469, E-mail: mhammond@azlibrary.gov; *E-rate Coord for Public Libraries,* Malavika Muralidharan; Tel: 602-364-4855, E-mail: mala@azlibrary.gov; Staff 22 (MLS 20, Non-MLS 2)
Founded 1864
Jul 2015-Jun 2016 Income $11,390,220, State $7,665,797, Federal $3,449,913. Mats Exp $117,200. Sal $5,259,656
Library Holdings: Bk Vols 519,686; Per Subs 1,821; Talking Bks 10,423; Videos 1,521
Subject Interests: Arizona, Genealogy, Law
Automation Activity & Vendor Info: (Acquisitions) SirsiDynix; (Cataloging) SirsiDynix; (Circulation) SirsiDynix; (ILL) SirsiDynix; (OPAC) SirsiDynix; (Serials) SirsiDynix
Wireless access
Function: ILL available
Publications: Arizona Public Library Statistics; Arizona Reading Program Manual; Capitol Stacks (Bimonthly); Library Services Newsletter; Talking Book News
Partic in OCLC Online Computer Library Center, Inc
Open Mon-Fri 8-5
Restriction: Circ limited

CL ARIZONA SUMMIT LAW SCHOOL*, Law Library, One N Central Ave, 85004. Tel: 602-682-6897, 602-682-6898. FAX: 602-682-6996. E-mail: research@azsummitlaw.edu. Circulation E-mail: circdept@azsummitlaw.edu. Web Site: www.azsummitlaw.edu. *Assoc Dean of Libr,* Christy Ryan; E-mail: cryan@azsummitlaw.edu; *Ref Librn,* Alison Ewing; E-mail: aewing@azsummitlaw.edu; *Tech Serv Librn,* Brady Peneton; E-mail: bpeneton@azsummitlaw.edu; Staff 12 (MLS 5, Non-MLS 7)
Founded 2005. Enrl 200; Fac 22; Highest Degree: Doctorate
Automation Activity & Vendor Info: (Acquisitions) Innovative Interfaces, Inc; (Cataloging) Innovative Interfaces, Inc; (Circulation) Innovative Interfaces, Inc; (Course Reserve) Innovative Interfaces, Inc; (ILL) OCLC; (OPAC) Innovative Interfaces, Inc; (Serials) Innovative Interfaces, Inc
Wireless access
Partic in Amigos Library Services, Inc
Open Mon-Thurs 7:30am-9pm, Fri 7:30-6, Sat & Sun 10-6
Restriction: Open to students, fac & staff

P ARIZONA TALKING BOOK LIBRARY, 1030 N 32nd St, 85008. SAN 300-368X. Tel: 602-255-5578. Toll Free Tel: 800-255-5578. FAX: 602-286-0444. Web Site: www.azlibrary.gov/talkingbooks. *Adminr,* Janet L Fisher; E-mail: jfisher@azlibrary.gov; *Asst Admin,* Erin Pawlus; *Tech Serv,* Antonio Bucci; Staff 8 (MLS 6, Non-MLS 2)
Founded 1970
Jul 2020-Jun 2021 Income $986,228, State $899,080, Federal $87,148
Library Holdings: Braille Volumes 521; DVDs 913; Per Subs 14; Talking Bks 272,280; Videos 471
Special Collections: Arizona & Spanish Language audio, locally produced; Reference Materials on Blindness & Disablities, print
Automation Activity & Vendor Info: (Cataloging) Keystone Systems, Inc (KLAS); (Circulation) Keystone Systems, Inc (KLAS); (Discovery) Keystone Systems, Inc (KLAS); (OPAC) Keystone Systems, Inc (KLAS)
Wireless access
Function: Audiobks via web, Digital talking bks, Summer reading prog
Publications: Talking Book News (Newsletter)
Special Services for the Blind - Bks on flash-memory cartridges; Braille equip; Descriptive video serv (DVS); Digital talking bk; Digital talking bk machines; Home delivery serv; Info on spec aids & appliances; Local mags

& bks recorded; Machine repair; Newsletter (in large print, Braille or on cassette); Newsline for the Blind; Production of talking bks; Volunteer serv
Open Mon-Fri 8-5
Restriction: Authorized patrons, Restricted pub use
Friends of the Library Group

M BANNER - UNIVERSITY MEDICAL CENTER - PHOENIX*, Health Sciences Library, 1111 E McDowell Rd, 85006. SAN 300-3736. Tel: 602-839-4353. FAX: 602-839-3493. Web Site: www.bannerhealth.com. *Libr Serv Dir,* Bryan Nugent; E-mail: bryan.nugent@bannerhealth.com; *Sr Mgr,* Nancy Showalter; Staff 6 (MLS 3, Non-MLS 3)
Founded 1965
Library Holdings: Bk Vols 10,000; Per Subs 750
Special Collections: GSRMC Heritage Coll
Subject Interests: Clinical med, Consumer health, Hospital admin, Nursing
Wireless access
Function: ILL available
Partic in Arizona Health Information Network; Cent Ariz Biomed Librns; Medical Library Group of Southern California & Arizona
Special Services for the Blind - Reader equip
Open Mon-Fri 7:30-5

L BURCH & CRACCHIOLO PA*, Law Library, 702 E Osborn Rd, Ste 200, 85014. SAN 323-6854. Tel: 602-234-8704. FAX: 602-344-3704. E-mail: info@bcattorneys.com. Web Site: www.bcattorneys.com. *Tech Adminr,* Diane Husband; E-mail: dhusband@bcattorneys.com; Staff 1 (MLS 1)
Library Holdings: Bk Vols 12,000
Restriction: Staff use only

S DESERT BOTANICAL GARDEN LIBRARY*, Schilling Library, 1201 N Galvin Pkwy, 85008. SAN 321-0324. Tel: 480-481-8133. FAX: 480-481-8124. E-mail: library@dbg.org. Web Site: www.dbg.org/schilling-library. *Librn,* Beth Brand; Staff 1 (Non-MLS 1)
Founded 1939
Library Holdings: Bk Vols 8,000; Per Subs 50
Special Collections: Cactaceae; Desert Landscape Design
Subject Interests: Agavaceae, Agro-ecology, Arid land plants, Cactaceae, Endangered, Ethnobotany, Rare plants
Automation Activity & Vendor Info: (Cataloging) OCLC Connexion; (OPAC) EOS International
Wireless access
Function: Adult bk club, Archival coll, Online cat, Photocopying/Printing
Publications: Index Seminum; Sonoran Quarterly (Newsletter)
Partic in Council on Botanical & Horticultural Libraries, Inc
Open Mon-Fri 12-4
Restriction: In-house use for visitors, Not a lending libr, Ref only to non-staff

L FENNEMORE CRAIG*, Law Library, 2394 E Camelback Rd, 85016. SAN 372-3712. Tel: 602-916-5280. FAX: 602-916-5964. *Knowledge Mgr,* Nataly Cardona; E-mail: ncardona@fclaw.com
Library Holdings: Per Subs 250
Automation Activity & Vendor Info: (Acquisitions) EOS International; (Cataloging) EOS International; (Circulation) EOS International; (Course Reserve) EOS International; (ILL) EOS International; (Media Booking) EOS International; (OPAC) EOS International; (Serials) EOS International
Restriction: Not open to pub

S FOUNDATION FOR BLIND CHILDREN LIBRARY & MEDIA CENTER, Arizona Instructional Resource Center, 1234 E Northern Ave, 85020. SAN 300-4163. Tel: 602-678-5810, 602-678-5816. Toll Free Tel: 800-322-4870. FAX: 602-678-5811. Web Site: www.seeitourway.org. *Dir,* Jared Leslie; E-mail: jleslie@seeitourway.org; Staff 8 (Non-MLS 8)
Founded 1952
Library Holdings: Braille Volumes 5,000; e-books 100; High Interest/Low Vocabulary Bk Vols 100; Large Print Bks 8,000; Bk Titles 26,000; Bk Vols 130,000; Per Subs 25; Videos 40
Special Collections: Braille, Large Print, Print/Braille & Electronic Files for Blind & Visually Impaired Students
Wireless access
Special Services for the Blind - Braille bks; Descriptive video serv (DVS); Large print bks
Open Mon-Fri 8-4:30

C GRAND CANYON UNIVERSITY LIBRARY, 3300 W Camelback Rd, 85017-3030. SAN 300-3744. Tel: 602-639-6641. Toll Free Tel: 800-800-9776. FAX: 602-639-7835. E-mail: library@gcu.edu. Web Site: library.gcu.edu. *Dir, Libr Serv,* Nita Mailander; Staff 32 (MLS 22, Non-MLS 10)
Founded 1949. Highest Degree: Doctorate
Automation Activity & Vendor Info: (Circulation) Innovative Interfaces, Inc - Sierra; (ILL) OCLC Tipasa; (OPAC) Innovative Interfaces, Inc - Sierra
Wireless access

S HALL OF FLAME*, Richard S Fowler Memorial Library, 6101 E Van Buren, 85008. SAN 300-3752. Tel: 602-275-3473. FAX: 602-275-0896. E-mail: info@hallofflame.org. Web Site: www.hallofflame.org. *Dir,* Peter Molloy; *Librn,* Leslie Marshall
Founded 1968
Library Holdings: Bk Vols 6,000; Per Subs 12
Special Collections: History of Firefighting in the US & Europe
Wireless access
Restriction: Staff use only

S HEARD MUSEUM, Billie Jane Baguley Library & Archives, 2301 N Central Ave, 85004-1323. SAN 300-3760. Tel: 602-252-8840. FAX: 602-252-9757. Web Site: heard.org/library. *Dir,* Mario Nick Klimiades; E-mail: mario@heard.org; *Chief Curator,* Diana Pardue; E-mail: dpardue@heard.org; Staff 2 (MLS 2)
Founded 1929
Library Holdings: AV Mats 1,500; CDs 1,000; DVDs 300; e-journals 1,100; Electronic Media & Resources 5; Bk Titles 45,000; Per Subs 240; Videos 700
Special Collections: Atlatl Coll; Barry Goldwater Color Photography Coll; Fred Harvey Company Papers & Photographs; Indian Arts & Crafts Association Coll; Native American Art Studies Association Coll; Native American Artists Resource Coll; Native American Boarding School Coll; North American Indian (Curtis Coll); Pablita Velarde Coll; Phoenix Indian School Coll; R Brownell McCrew Papers & Photographs
Subject Interests: Anthrop, Archaeology, Native Am art
Automation Activity & Vendor Info: (Cataloging) OCLC; (OPAC) OCLC Connexion
Wireless access
Function: 24/7 Electronic res, Archival coll, Art exhibits, Computers for patron use, Internet access, Magazines, Movies, Online cat, Online ref, Outreach serv, Outside serv via phone, mail, e-mail & web, Photocopying/Printing, Ref serv available, VHS videos, Wheelchair accessible
Publications: Archival Collections Guide; Native American Artist Directory
Open Mon-Fri 10-4:45
Restriction: Circulates for staff only, Free to mem, Non-circulating, Open to pub for ref only

M HONORHEALTH JOHN C LINCOLN MEDICAL CENTER*, Grigg Medical Library, 250 E Dunlap Ave, 85020. Tel: 602-870-6328. FAX: 602-997-9325. Web Site: www.honorhealth.com/academic-affairs/honorhealth-library-services. *Med Librn,* Kelly Howell; E-mail: khowell@honorhealth.com; Staff 2 (MLS 2)
Founded 1983
Library Holdings: Bk Titles 5,000; Per Subs 300
Special Collections: Medical Libraries
Wireless access
Open Mon-Fri 8-4:30

M INDIAN HEALTH SERVICES*, Phoenix Indian Medical Center Library, 4212 N 16th St, 85016. SAN 320-9075. Tel: 602-263-1676. FAX: 602-263-1577. *Dir, Med Libr,* Kelly Akin; E-mail: kelly.akin@ihs.gov; Staff 1 (MLS 1)
Founded 1950
Special Collections: Diseases of Native Americans Coll
Subject Interests: Endocrinology
Partic in Arizona Health Information Network; Cent Ariz Biomed Librns
Restriction: Not open to pub

L JENNINGS, STROUSS & SALMON*, Law Library, One E Washington St, Ste 1900, 85004-2554. SAN 372-3739. Tel: 602-262-5911. FAX: 602-495-2676. Web Site: www.jsslaw.com. *Librn,* Renee Stanbery; E-mail: rstanbery@jsslaw.com
Library Holdings: Bk Vols 20,000

GL JUDICIAL BRANCH OF ARIZONA, MARICOPA COUNTY*, Superior Court Law Library Resource Center, 101 W Jefferson St, 85003. SAN 300-3795. Tel: 602-506-7353. FAX: 602-506-3677. E-mail: services@scll.maricopa.gov. Web Site: superiorcourt.maricopa.gov/llrc/law-library. *Adminr,* Shawn Haught; *Asst Dir,* Jennifer Murray; Fax: 602-506-2940, E-mail: murrayj006@scll.maricopa.gov; *Acq, Coll Develop,* Valerie Lerma; Tel: 602-506-1647, E-mail: vlerma@scll.maricopa.gov; Staff 15 (MLS 7, Non-MLS 8)
Founded 1913
Library Holdings: Bk Titles 20,000; Bk Vols 140,000
Subject Interests: Law

Wireless access
Publications: Court Informer; En Banc (Newsletter)
Partic in Proquest Dialog
Open Mon-Fri 8-5

CR KINO INSTITUTE DIOCESAN LIBRARY*, 400 E Monroe St, 85004-2336. SAN 325-268X. Tel: 602-354-2311. Web Site: kinoinstitute.org/library. *Librn,* Darcy Peletich; E-mail: dpeletich@diocesephoenix.org
Founded 1978. Enrl 130; Fac 7
Library Holdings: AV Mats 3,850; CDs 60; DVDs 60; Bk Titles 26,000; Per Subs 120; Videos 1,800
Subject Interests: Sacred scripture, Spirituality, Theol
Automation Activity & Vendor Info: (Circulation) Book Systems
Function: ILL available
Open Tues, Wed & Thurs 12:30-6:30

L LEWIS ROCA ROTHGERBER CHRISTIE LLP LIBRARY*, 201 E Washington, Ste 1200, 85004. SAN 326-5641. Tel: 602-262-5311. FAX: 602-734-3739. Web Site: www.lrrc.com. *Dir, Knowledge & Res Serv,* Genevieve Nicholson; Staff 4 (MLS 2, Non-MLS 2)
Library Holdings: Bk Titles 5,500; Bk Vols 40,000; Per Subs 100
Subject Interests: Corporate law, Real estate
Partic in Proquest Dialog
Restriction: Staff use only

P MARICOPA COUNTY LIBRARY DISTRICT*, Central Express Branch & Administrative Offices, 2700 N Central Ave, Ste 700, 85004. SAN 300-3809. Tel: 602-652-3000. FAX: 602-652-3071. Web Site: www.mcldaz.org. *Chief Tech Officer,* Matt Miller; E-mail: mattmiller@mcldaz.org; *Dir,* Jeremy Reeder; E-mail: jeremyreeder@mcldaz.org; *Br Operations Adminr,* Alicia Snarr; E-mail: aliciasnarr@mcldaz.org; *Communications Adminr, Libr Develop,* Lena Beecher-Sherman; E-mail: lenabeechersherman@mcldaz.org; *Customer Experience Adminr,* Erin MacFarlane; E-mail: erinmacfarlane@mcldaz.org; *Coll Mgr,* Laura Jamison; E-mail: laurajamison@mcldaz.org; *Electronic Res Mgr,* Michael Porter; E-mail: michaelporter@mcldaz.org; *Finance Mgr,* John Werbach; E-mail: johnwerbach@mcldaz.org; Staff 258 (MLS 57, Non-MLS 201)
Founded 1986. Pop 797,840; Circ 7,454,130
Jul 2012-Jun 2013 Income (Main & Associated Libraries) $21,477,596. Mats Exp $4,782,000
Automation Activity & Vendor Info: (Acquisitions) Innovative Interfaces, Inc; (Cataloging) Innovative Interfaces, Inc; (Circulation) Innovative Interfaces, Inc; (ILL) OCLC WorldShare Interlibrary Loan; (OPAC) Innovative Interfaces, Inc
Wireless access
Open Mon-Fri 8-5
Friends of the Library Group
Branches: 18
AGUILA BRANCH, 51300 W US Hwy 60, Aguila, 85320, SAN 378-2328. Tel: 928-685-2214.
Library Holdings: Bk Titles 6,312
Open Mon 10-7, Tues-Thurs 10-6, Fri & Sat 10-5
ASANTE LIBRARY, 16755 W Vereda Solana Dr, Surprise, 85387. Tel: 602-652-3000.
Open Mon, Tues & Wed 10-7, Thurs, Fri & Sat 10–5
EL MIRAGE BRANCH, 14011 N First Ave, El Mirage, 85335, SAN 378-2344.
Library Holdings: Bk Titles 12,526
Open Mon-Wed, Fri & Sat 9-5, Thurs 9-7
FAIRWAY BRANCH, 10600 W Peoria Ave, Rm 144, Sun City, 85351, SAN 330-7026.
Library Holdings: Bk Titles 10,444
Open Mon-Fri 8-4, Sat 8-Noon
Friends of the Library Group
FOUNTAIN HILLS BRANCH, 12901 N La Montana Dr, Fountain Hills, 85268, SAN 376-8422.
Library Holdings: Bk Titles 43,520
Open Mon-Thurs 9-8, Fri & Sat 9-5
Friends of the Library Group
GILA BEND BRANCH, 202 N Euclid Ave, Gila Bend, 85337. (Mail add: PO Box B, Gila Bend, 85337), SAN 378-2387.
Library Holdings: Bk Titles 9,064
Open Mon 10-7, Tues-Thurs 10-6, Fri 10-5
GOODYEAR BRANCH LIBRARY, 14415 W Van Buren St, Ste C101, Goodyear, 85338.
Library Holdings: Bk Titles 18,031
Open Mon-Wed 10-7, Thurs-Sat 10-5, Sun 1-5
Friends of the Library Group
GUADALUPE BRANCH, 9241 S Avenida del Yaqui, Guadalupe, 85283, SAN 376-8449.
Library Holdings: Bk Titles 9,676
Open Mon 10-7, Tues-Thurs 10-6, Fri 10-5
HOLLYHOCK BRANCH, 15844 N Hollyhock St, Surprise, 85374, SAN 376-849X.
Library Holdings: Bk Titles 3,526
Open Tues & Thurs 1-7, Sat 9-3
LITCHFIELD PARK BRANCH, 101 W Wigwam Blvd, Litchfield, 85340, SAN 378-2360.
Library Holdings: Bk Titles 36,289
Open Mon-Wed 10-8, Thurs-Sat 10-5
Friends of the Library Group
NORTH VALLEY REGIONAL, 40410 N Gavilan Peak Pkwy, Anthem, 85086.
Library Holdings: Bk Titles 69,286
Open Mon-Thurs 9-8, Fri & Sat 9-5
Friends of the Library Group
NORTHWEST REGIONAL, 16089 N Bullard Ave, Surprise, 85374.
Library Holdings: Bk Titles 96,639
Open Mon-Thurs 9-8, Fri & Sat 9-5
PERRY BRANCH, 1965 E Queen Creek Rd, Gilbert, 85297.
Library Holdings: Bk Titles 45,132
Open Mon-Thurs 10-7, Fri & Sat 10-4
Friends of the Library Group
QUEEN CREEK BRANCH, 21802 S Ellsworth Rd, Queen Creek, 85242, SAN 376-8465.
Library Holdings: Bk Titles 75,182
Open Mon-Thurs 9-8, Fri & Sat 9-5
Friends of the Library Group
ED ROBSON BRANCH, 9330 E Riggs Rd, Sun Lakes, 85248, SAN 376-8481.
Library Holdings: Bk Titles 14,346
Open Mon-Sat 9-5
Friends of the Library Group
SOUTHEAST REGIONAL, 775 N Greenfield Rd, Gilbert, 85234.
Library Holdings: Bk Titles 143,399
Open Mon-Thurs 10-9, Fri & Sat 10-5, Sun 1-5
Friends of the Library Group
SUN CITY BRANCH, 16828 N 99th Ave, Sun City, 85351.
Library Holdings: Bk Titles 32,998
Open Mon 9-7, Tues-Sat 9-5
Friends of the Library Group
WHITE TANK BRANCH, 20304 W White Tank Mountain Rd, Waddell, 85355.
Open Mon-Wed 10-7, Thurs-Sat 10-5
Friends of the Library Group

S MARICOPA COUNTY SHERIFF'S OFFICE INMATE LIBRARY, 3150 W Lower Buckeye Rd, Ste C, 85009. Tel: 602-876-5633, 602-876-5638. *Libr Mgr,* Lisa Poulin; E-mail: l_poulin@mcso.maricopa.gov; Staff 4 (MLS 1, Non-MLS 3)
Jan 2019-Dec 2019. Mats Exp $78,000, Books $52,000, Per/Ser (Incl. Access Fees) $26,000
Library Holdings: Braille Volumes 5; Large Print Bks 200; Bk Titles 200,000; Per Subs 12
Restriction: Staff & inmates only

J PARADISE VALLEY COMMUNITY COLLEGE, Buxton Library, 18401 N 32nd St, 85032-1200. Tel: 602-787-7200. Reference Tel: 602-787-7215. FAX: 602-787-7205. Web Site: www.paradisevalley.edu/library. *Dept Chair, Librn,* Paula Crossman; Tel: 602-787-7203, E-mail: paula.crossman@paradisevalley.edu; *Librn,* John U Chavez; Tel: 602-787-7222, E-mail: j.chavez@paradisevalley.edu; *Librn,* Lili Kang; Tel: 602-787-7209, E-mail: li.kang@paradisevalley.edu; *Librn,* Samantha Lange; Tel: 602-787-6692, E-mail: samantha.lange@paradisevalley.edu; *Coordr,* Alexis Romo; Tel: 602-787-7259, E-mail: alexis.romo@paradisevalley.edu; *Libr Spec Supvr,* Gretchen Lebron; Tel: 602-787-7207, E-mail: gretchen.lebron@paradisevalley.edu; *Circ, Libr Asst,* Whitley Abrams; Tel: 602-787-7238, E-mail: whitley.abrams@paradisevalley.edu; *Circ, Libr Asst,* Jerice Eckels; E-mail: jerice.eckels@pvmail.maricopa.edu; Staff 8 (MLS 4, Non-MLS 4)
Founded 1987. Enrl 7,800; Highest Degree: Associate
Library Holdings: Audiobooks 164; AV Mats 7,572; Bks on Deafness & Sign Lang 60; CDs 1,636; DVDs 2,546; e-books 157,680; High Interest/Low Vocabulary Bk Vols 203; Music Scores 67; Bk Vols 33,414; Per Subs 121
Special Collections: Caldecott & Newbury Coll; Career & College Resources Coll; Children's Fiction/Nonfiction/Picture Books Coll; General Coll; Leisure Reading Coll; Literacy Coll; Music CDs Coll; Periodicals - Current Coll; Popular Movies Coll; Young Adults Coll
Automation Activity & Vendor Info: (ILL) OCLC ILLiad
Wireless access
Function: 24/7 Electronic res, 24/7 Online cat, Archival coll, Art exhibits, Audio & video playback equip for onsite use, Bilingual assistance for Spanish patrons, Bks on CD, Computers for patron use, Electronic databases & coll, Free DVD rentals, ILL available, Internet access, Magazines, Music CDs, Online cat, Online ref, Photocopying/Printing, Ref

serv available, Scanner, Spanish lang bks, Tax forms, Telephone ref, Wheelchair accessible
Special Services for the Deaf - Assistive tech; Closed caption videos; High interest/low vocabulary bks
Special Services for the Blind - Accessible computers; Audio mat; Bks on CD; Closed circuit TV magnifier; Computer with voice synthesizer for visually impaired persons; Copier with enlargement capabilities; Dragon Naturally Speaking software; Internet workstation with adaptive software; Radio reading serv; Reader equip; Ref serv; Screen reader software
Open Mon-Thurs 7-7, Fri 7-2, Sat 10-2
Restriction: Open to pub for ref & circ; with some limitations, Open to students, fac & staff
Friends of the Library Group

L PERKINS COIE LIBRARY*, 2901 N Central Ave, Ste 2000, 85012. SAN 329-8191. Tel: 602-351-8213. Web Site: www.perkinscoie.com. *Librn,* Karen Anderson; Staff 1 (MLS 1)
Library Holdings: Bk Vols 20,000; Per Subs 150
Subject Interests: Law
Wireless access
Restriction: Not open to pub, Private libr

S PHOENIX ART MUSEUM, Gene & Cathie Lemon Art Research Library, 1625 N Central Ave, 85004-1685. SAN 300-3868. Tel: 602-257-2136. FAX: 602-253-8662. E-mail: library@phxart.org. Web Site: www.phxart.org. *Librn,* Jesse Lopez; Staff 2 (MLS 1, Non-MLS 1)
Founded 1959
Library Holdings: Electronic Media & Resources 6; Bk Vols 40,000; Per Subs 65
Special Collections: American Art Coll; Auction Records Coll; Latin American Art Coll; One-Person Exhibition Coll; Rembrandt Print Catalogs from 1751 (Orme Lewis Coll); Vertical Files (Subject Artist Museum)
Subject Interests: Art & archit, Decorative art, European art, Fashion, Graphic arts, Sculpture, Western Am art
Automation Activity & Vendor Info: (Cataloging) Innovative Interfaces, Inc
Wireless access
Function: Adult bk club, Archival coll, Online cat, Ref serv available
Restriction: Not a lending libr, Open by appt only, Pub use on premises

M PHOENIX CHILDREN'S HOSPITAL, Emily Center Library, 1919 E Thomas Rd, 85016. SAN 373-3386. Tel: 602-933-1400. Toll Free Tel: 866-933-6459. FAX: 602-933-1409. E-mail: emilycenter@phoenixchildrens.com. Web Site: www.phoenixchildrens.org/centers-programs/emily-center-health-library. *Dir,* Andrea Aken'Ova; E-mail: aakenova@phoeixchildrens.com; Staff 4 (Non-MLS 4)
Founded 1990
Library Holdings: AV Mats 200; Bk Titles 6,000
Special Collections: Spanish Information about Child Health & Illness Issues
Subject Interests: Pediatrics
Automation Activity & Vendor Info: (Cataloging) Innovative Interfaces, Inc; (Circulation) Innovative Interfaces, Inc
Wireless access
Function: Bilingual assistance for Spanish patrons, Computers for patron use, Internet access, Mail & tel request accepted, Notary serv, OverDrive digital audio bks, Photocopying/Printing, Spanish lang bks, Wheelchair accessible
Open Mon-Fri 9-7, Sat & Sun 10-4

J PHOENIX COLLEGE*, Fannin Library, 1202 W Thomas Rd, 85013. SAN 300-3876. Tel: 602-285-7457. Circulation Tel: 602-285-7473. Reference Tel: 602-285-7470. FAX: 602-285-7368. E-mail: library@phoenixcollege.edu. Web Site: www.phoenixcollege.edu/academics/library. *Chair,* Christine Moore; E-mail: christine.moore@phoenixcollege.edu; *Fac Librn,* Mercedes Miramontes; E-mail: mercedes.miramontes@phoenixcollege.edu; *Fac Librn,* Ann Roselle; E-mail: ann.roselle@phoenixcollege.edu; *Libr Supvr,* Linda Frakes; E-mail: linda.frakes@phoenixcollege.edu; Staff 6 (MLS 5, Non-MLS 1)
Founded 1925. Fac 153; Highest Degree: Associate
Library Holdings: Bk Vols 60,000; Per Subs 55
Subject Interests: Arizona
Wireless access

P PHOENIX PUBLIC LIBRARY*, Burton Barr Central Library, 1221 N Central Ave, 85004. SAN 330-6429. Tel: 602-262-4636. Administration Tel: 602-262-6157. FAX: 602-261-8836. TDD: 602-254-8205. Web Site: www.phoenixpubliclibrary.org. *City Librn,* Rita Hamilton; E-mail: rita.hamilton@phoenix.gov; *Dep Dir, Coll & Prog,* Karl Kendall; E-mail: karl.kendall@phoenix.gov; *Dep Dir, Info Tech & Digital Initiatives,* Maria Dominguez; *Dep Dir, Mgt Serv,* Martin Whitfield; E-mail: martin.whitfield@phoenix.gov; *Dep Dir, Pub Serv,* Paula Fortier; E-mail: paula.fortier@phoenix.gov; Staff 85.7 (MLS 83.7, Non-MLS 2)
Founded 1898. Pop 1,488,750; Circ 10,427,548
Jul 2013-Jun 2014 Income (Main & Associated Libraries) $1,079,884. Mats Exp $4,606,967
Special Collections: Arizona History Coll; Art of Book Coll; Center for Children's Literature; Map Room; Rare Book Room. US Document Depository
Automation Activity & Vendor Info: (Acquisitions) Innovative Interfaces, Inc; (Cataloging) Innovative Interfaces, Inc; (Circulation) Innovative Interfaces, Inc; (OPAC) Innovative Interfaces, Inc; (Serials) Innovative Interfaces, Inc
Wireless access
Special Services for the Deaf - TDD equip; TTY equip
Special Services for the Blind - Assistive/Adapted tech devices, equip & products; Braille bks; Descriptive video serv (DVS); Talking bks
Open Mon, Fri & Sat 9-5, Tues-Thurs 9-9, Sun 1-5
Friends of the Library Group
Branches: 16
ACACIA LIBRARY, 750 E Townley Ave, 85020, SAN 330-6453. *Br Mgr,* Dawn Porfirio-Milton
Founded 1969
Special Services for the Deaf - TDD equip
Open Tues-Thurs 11-7, Fri & Sat 9-5, Sun 1-5
Friends of the Library Group
AGAVE LIBRARY, 23550 N 36th Ave, 85310. *Br Mgr,* Yvonne Murphy
Open Tues-Thurs 10-8, Fri & Sat 9-5, Sun 1-5
CENTURY LIBRARY, 1750 E Highland Ave, 85016-4648, SAN 330-6488. *Br Mgr,* Eric Rueda
Founded 1973
Open Tues-Thurs 11-7, Fri & Sat 9-5, Sun 1-5
Friends of the Library Group
CESAR CHAVEZ LIBRARY, 3635 W Baseline Rd, Laveen, 85339. *Br Mgr,* Nikki Ney
Founded 2007
Special Services for the Deaf - TDD equip
Open Mon & Sat 9-5, Tues-Thurs 10-8, Sun 1-5
CHOLLA LIBRARY, 10050 Metro Pkwy E, 85051, SAN 330-6518. *Br Mgr,* Terry Lawler
Founded 1975
Special Services for the Deaf - TDD equip
Open Mon & Sat 9-5, Tues-Thurs 10-8, Sun 1-5
Friends of the Library Group
DESERT BROOM LIBRARY, 29710 N Cave Creek Rd, Cave Creek, 85331. *Br Mgr,* Jen Masiello
Founded 2005
Special Services for the Deaf - TDD equip
Open Tues-Thurs 11-7, Fri & Sat 9-5, Sun 1-5
Friends of the Library Group
DESERT SAGE LIBRARY, 7602 W Encanto Blvd, 85035, SAN 377-7960. *Br Mgr,* Claudia Leon
Founded 1997
Special Services for the Deaf - TDD equip
Open Tues-Thurs 11-7, Fri & Sat 9-5, Sun 1-5
Friends of the Library Group
HARMON LIBRARY, 1325 S Fifth Ave, 85003, SAN 330-6542. *Br Mgr,* Keith Feldt
Founded 1950
Special Services for the Deaf - TDD equip
Open Tues-Thurs 11-7, Fri & Sat 9-5, Sun 1-5
Friends of the Library Group
IRONWOOD LIBRARY, 4333 E Chandler Blvd, 85048, SAN 372-0195. *Br Mgr,* Karen Idehara
Founded 1991
Special Services for the Deaf - TDD equip
Open Mon & Sat 9-5, Tues-Thurs 10-8, Sun 1-5
Friends of the Library Group
JUNIPER LIBRARY, 1825 W Union Hills Dr, 85027, SAN 370-8098. *Br Mgr,* Alicia Martin
Founded 1996
Open Mon & Sat 9-5, Tues-Thurs 10-8, Sun 1-5
Friends of the Library Group
MESQUITE LIBRARY, 4525 E Paradise Village Pkwy N, 85032, SAN 330-6577. *Br Mgr,* Stephanie Martinez
Founded 1982
Special Services for the Deaf - TDD equip
Open Mon & Sat 9-5, Tues-Thurs 10-8, Sun 1-5
Friends of the Library Group
OCOTILLO LIBRARY & WORKFORCE LITERACY CENTER, 102 W Southern Ave, 85041, SAN 330-6607. *Br Mgr,* Mary Mitchell
Founded 1967
Special Services for the Deaf - TDD equip
Open Tues-Thurs 11-7, Fri & Sat 9-5, Sun 1-5
Friends of the Library Group

PALO VERDE LIBRARY, 4402 N 51st Ave, 85031, SAN 330-6631. *Br Mgr,* Sabrena Adams
Founded 1966
Special Services for the Deaf - TDD equip
Open Mon & Sat 9-5, Tues-Thurs 10-8, Sun 1-5
Friends of the Library Group

SAGUARO LIBRARY, 2808 N 46th St, 85008, SAN 330-6666. *Br Mgr,* Lee Payne
Founded 1964
Special Services for the Deaf - TDD equip
Open Mon & Sat 9-5, Tues-Thurs 10-8, Sun 1-5
Friends of the Library Group

SOUTH MOUNTAIN COMMUNITY LIBRARY, 7050 S 24th St, 85042. Tel: 602-243-8187. *Br Mgr,* Robb Barr
Open Mon-Thurs 7:30am-9pm, Fri & Sat 7:30-5, Sun 1-5
Friends of the Library Group

YUCCA LIBRARY, 5648 N 15th Ave, 85015, SAN 330-6690. *Br Mgr,* Pam Brown
Founded 1969
Special Services for the Deaf - TDD equip
Open Tues-Thurs 10-8, Fri & Sat 9-5, Sun 1-5
Friends of the Library Group

GM PHOENIX VA HEALTH CARE SYSTEM, Medical Library, 650 E Indian School Rd, 85012. SAN 300-4023. Tel: 602-222-6411. *Librn,* Mark Simmons; E-mail: mark.simmons@va.gov; *Libr Tech,* Robin Ferguson; E-mail: robin.ferguson@va.gov; Staff 3 (MLS 1, Non-MLS 2)
Founded 1951
Library Holdings: e-journals 190; Bk Titles 115; Bk Vols 125; Per Subs 23
Subject Interests: Consumer health, Med, Nursing
Automation Activity & Vendor Info: (Cataloging) LibraryWorld, Inc; (Circulation) LibraryWorld, Inc; (OPAC) LibraryWorld, Inc
Partic in Cent Ariz Biomed Librns; Dept of Vet Affairs Libr Network; Medical Library Group of Southern California & Arizona
Open Mon-Fri 7-4:30

S PUEBLO GRANDE MUSEUM & ARCHAEOLOGICAL PARK, Research Library, 4619 E Washington St, 85034-1909. SAN 372-7629. Tel: 602-495-0901. E-mail: pgm.collections@phoenix.gov. Web Site: www.phoenix.gov/parks/arts-culture-history/pueblo-grande/collections/research-access. *Curator,* Lindsey Vogel-Teeter; E-mail: lindsey.vogel-teeter@phoenix.gov
Library Holdings: Bk Titles 5,000; Spec Interest Per Sub 75
Special Collections: Halseth Coll; Hayden Coll; Hohokam Coll, bks, ms; Pueblo Grande Museum Archives; Schroeder Coll
Subject Interests: Archaeology
Function: Archival coll, ILL available, Photocopying/Printing, Telephone ref
Restriction: Non-circulating to the pub, Open by appt only

M SAINT JOSEPH'S HOSPITAL & MEDICAL CENTER*, Health Sciences Library, 350 W Thomas Rd, 85013. (Mail add: PO Box 2071, 85013-2071), SAN 300-3906. Tel: 602-406-3299. FAX: 602-406-4171. *Mgr,* Molly Harrington; molly.harrington@dignityhealth.org; Staff 2 (MLS 2)
Founded 1942
Library Holdings: Bk Vols 5,000; Per Subs 320
Special Collections: Neurological Sciences (Barrow Neurological Institute of Neurological Sciences Coll)
Subject Interests: Med, Nursing
Partic in Arizona Health Information Network; Cent Ariz Biomed Librns
Open Mon-Fri 8-5

J SOUTH MOUNTAIN COMMUNITY COLLEGE LIBRARY*, 7050 S 24th St, 85042-5806. SAN 320-9989. Reference Tel: 602-243-8194. FAX: 602-243-8180. Web Site: www.southmountaincc.edu/library. *Div Chair, Libr & Teaching & Learning Ctr,* Lydia Johnson; E-mail: lydia.johnson@southmountaincc.edu; *Instruction Librn,* Lora Largo; Tel: 602-243-8345, E-mail: lora.largo@southmountaincc.edu; Staff 8 (MLS 3, Non-MLS 5)
Founded 1980. Enrl 3,937; Highest Degree: Associate
Library Holdings: Bk Titles 38,000; Bk Vols 40,000
Automation Activity & Vendor Info: (Cataloging) SirsiDynix; (Circulation) SirsiDynix
Wireless access
Partic in Amigos Library Services, Inc
Open Mon-Thurs 7:30am-9pm, Fri & Sat 7:30-5, Sun 1-5
Friends of the Library Group

GL UNITED STATES COURTS LIBRARY*, Sandra Day O'Connor United States Courthouse, Ste 410, 401 W Washington St, SPC16, 85003-2135. SAN 321-8023. Tel: 602-322-7295. FAX: 602-322-7299. Web Site: www.ca9.uscourts.gov/library. *Satellite Librn,* Stefanie Vartabedian; E-mail: stefanie_vartabedian@lb9.uscourts.gov; *Asst Satellite Librn,* Margaret A Ackroyd; Staff 3 (MLS 2, Non-MLS 1)
Founded 1980
Library Holdings: Bk Titles 3,951; Bk Vols 33,764
Wireless access
Function: Archival coll, Ref & res, Ref serv available, Res libr, Tax forms
Publications: Library Guide; Library Newsletter (Monthly)
Partic in OCLC Online Computer Library Center, Inc
Open Mon-Fri 8-4:30
Restriction: Open to staff only, Prof mat only, Restricted pub use

PIMA

P PIMA PUBLIC LIBRARY, 50 S 200 West, 85543. (Mail add: PO Box 487, 85543-0489), SAN 300-404X. Tel: 928-485-2822. FAX: 928-485-0701. E-mail: librarian@pimalibrary.org. Web Site: www.pimalibrary.org. *Dir,* Rane Jones; *Asst Dir,* Natalie McCray; Staff 2 (Non-MLS 2)
Founded 1960. Pop 2,458; Circ 20,000
Jul 2020-Jun 2021 Income $80,700, State $4,000, City $74,000, Locally Generated Income $2,700. Mats Exp $14,500, Books $8,000, Other Print Mats $800, Electronic Ref Mat (Incl. Access Fees) $5,700. Sal $42,000
Library Holdings: Audiobooks 289; DVDs 2,057; Bk Titles 12,277
Special Collections: Arizona (Nonfiction)
Automation Activity & Vendor Info: (Acquisitions) Baker & Taylor; (Cataloging) Book Systems; (Circulation) Book Systems; (OPAC) Book Systems
Wireless access
Function: Activity rm, Bks on CD, Children's prog, Computers for patron use, Free DVD rentals, Internet access, Laminating, Movies, Online cat, Outreach serv, Photocopying/Printing, Preschool outreach, Preschool reading prog, Prog for children & young adult, Scanner, Spanish lang bks, Story hour, Summer reading prog, Wheelchair accessible
Open Mon-Thurs 9-6, Fri 9-2
Restriction: ID required to use computers (Ltd hrs), Ref only
Friends of the Library Group

PINE

P ISABELLE HUNT MEMORIAL PUBLIC LIBRARY*, 6124 N Randall Pl, 85544. (Mail add: PO Box 229, 85544-0229), SAN 300-4058. Tel: 928-476-3678. FAX: 928-476-2914. Web Site: www.pinepubliclibrary.com. *Dir,* Becky L Waer; E-mail: pinepubliclibrary@gmail.com; Staff 2 (Non-MLS 2)
Founded 1974. Pop 3,000; Circ 27,513
Jul 2016-Jun 2017 Income (Main Library Only) $118,400, County $108,400, Locally Generated Income $10,000
Library Holdings: Bk Vols 16,000
Special Collections: Arizona Coll, bks, pamphlets
Automation Activity & Vendor Info: (ILL) OCLC FirstSearch
Wireless access
Function: Homebound delivery serv, ILL available, Photocopying/Printing, Prog for children & young adult, Summer reading prog, Wheelchair accessible
Mem of Gila County Library District
Open Tues & Fri 10-5, Wed 10-4, Thurs 10-6, Sat 9-2
Restriction: Open to pub for ref & circ; with some limitations
Friends of the Library Group

PINEDALE

§P PINEDALE PUBLIC LIBRARY, 1264 Pinedale Rd, 85934. (Mail add: PO Box 1166, 85934). Tel: 928-535-7144. FAX: 928-535-7145. E-mail: pinedalelibrary@gmail.com. Web Site: www.facebook.com/PinedalePublicLibrary.
Mem of Navajo County Library System
Open Mon-Fri 1:30-4:30

PRESCOTT

C EMBRY-RIDDLE AERONAUTICAL UNIVERSITY, Christine & Steven F Udvar-Hazy Library & Learning Center, 3700 Willow Creek Rd, 86301-3720. SAN 323-7621. Tel: 928-777-3811. Reference Tel: 928-777-3761. Administration FAX: 928-777-6987. E-mail: prlib@erau.edu. Web Site: hazylibrary.erau.edu. *Libr Dir,* Sarah K Thomas; Tel: 928-777-3812, E-mail: sarah@erau.edu; *Assoc Dir, Access Serv,* Laura Pope Robbins; Tel: 928-777-6686, E-mail: Laura.PopeRobbins@erau.edu; *Assoc Dir, Res & Instruction,* Position Currently Open; *Assoc Dir, Technologies & Info Resources,* Joanne Evanoff; Tel: 928-777-3802, E-mail: joanne.evanoff@erau.edu; *Coll Mgt, Research Librn,* Robin Vickery; Tel: 928-777-3915, E-mail: vickeryr@erau.edu; *Res & Instruction Librn,* Dani Carmack; Tel: 928-777-3858, E-mail: dani.carmack@erau.edu; *Res & Instruction Librn,* Jessica Quarles; Tel: 928-777-6658, E-mail: jessica.quarles@erau.edu; *Scholarly Communications & Res Serv Librn,* Position Currently Open; Staff 14 (MLS 8, Non-MLS 6)
Founded 1978. Enrl 3,004; Fac 133; Highest Degree: Master

Jul 2020-Jun 2021 Income $1,183,939. Mats Exp $274,104, Books $37,897, Per/Ser (Incl. Access Fees) $31,902, AV Mat $60, Electronic Ref Mat (Incl. Access Fees) $204,245. Sal $587,853
Library Holdings: DVDs 2,830; e-books 531,277; e-journals 105,318; Bk Titles 24,128; Per Subs 135
Special Collections: Kalusa Miniature Aircraft Coll
Subject Interests: Aeronaut sci, Aerospace engr, Aviation safety, Cyber security, Global security & intelligence studies, Mechanical engr, Space physics
Automation Activity & Vendor Info: (Acquisitions) SirsiDynix; (Cataloging) SirsiDynix; (Circulation) SirsiDynix; (ILL) Clio; (OPAC) SirsiDynix
Wireless access
Publications: Annual Report; Annual Student Survey Results; Assessment Plan
Partic in Yavapai Libr Network
Open Mon-Thurs 7am-1am, Fri 7am-9pm, Sat 9-9, Sun 9am-1am

S MUSEUM OF INDIGENOUS PEOPLE*, 147 N Arizona St, 86301. SAN 375-3913. Tel: 928-445-1230. FAX: 928-777-0573. Web Site: www.museumofindigenouspeople.org. *Exec Dir,* Manuel Lucero, IV; E-mail: manuel.lucero@museumofindigenouspeople.org
Founded 1995
Library Holdings: Bk Vols 1,000
Special Collections: E S Curtis Coll, photogravures; Kate T Cory Coll, diary, dictionary of Hopi words, paintings, photos
Subject Interests: Anthrop, Archaeology, SW
Open Mon-Sat 10-4, Sun 1-4

C PRESCOTT COLLEGE LIBRARY, 220 Grove Ave, 86301. SAN 321-4656. Tel: 928-350-1300. Toll Free Tel: 877-350-2100, Ext 1300. FAX: 928-776-5224. E-mail: library@prescott.edu. Web Site: library.prescott.edu. *Libr Dir,* Richard Lewis; E-mail: rlewis@prescott.edu; *Dir, Res,* Gretchen Gano; E-mail: gretchen.gano@prescott.edu; Staff 4 (MLS 2, Non-MLS 2)
Founded 1966. Enrl 800; Fac 75; Highest Degree: Doctorate
Library Holdings: e-books 150,000; e-journals 35,000; Bk Titles 29,844; Bk Vols 33,500; Per Subs 150; Videos 1,700
Subject Interests: Adventure educ, Arts & letters, Counseling psychol, Environ studies, Experiential educ, Peace studies, Sustainability studies
Automation Activity & Vendor Info: (Cataloging) SirsiDynix-Enterprise; (ILL) Clio
Wireless access
Partic in Yavapai Libr Network

P PRESCOTT PUBLIC LIBRARY*, 215 E Goodwin St, 86303. SAN 330-6720. Tel: 928-777-1500. Circulation Tel: 928-777-1524. Interlibrary Loan Service Tel: 928-777-1510. Reference Tel: 928-777-1526. FAX: 928-771-5829. Web Site: www.prescottlibrary.info. *Dir,* Roger Saft; Tel: 928-777-1523, E-mail: roger.saft@prescott-az.gov; *Circ Librn,* Cindy Campbell; Tel: 928-777-1508, E-mail: cindy.campbell@prescott-az.gov; *Pub Serv Mgr,* Martha Baden; Tel: 928-777-1519, E-mail: martha.baden@prescott-az.gov; *Mgr, Support Serv,* Toni Johnson; Tel: 928-777-1504, E-mail: toni.johnson@prescott-az.gov; *Adult Serv,* Shannon Schinagl; Tel: 928-777-1509, E-mail: shannon.schinagl@prescott-az.gov; *Tech Serv,* Lisa Zierke; Tel: 928-777-1507, E-mail: lisa.zierke@prescott-az.gov; *Youth Serv,* Jennifer Kendall; Tel: 928-777-1506, E-mail: jennifer.kendall@prescott-az.gov; Staff 11.5 (MLS 6.5, Non-MLS 5)
Founded 1903. Pop 40,731; Circ 731,830
Jul 2014-Jun 2015 Income $2,316,955, City $1,720,744, County $596,211. Mats Exp $244,907, Books $159,445, Per/Ser (Incl. Access Fees) $16,000, AV Mat $36,462, Electronic Ref Mat (Incl. Access Fees) $33,000. Sal $1,388,795 (Prof $807,611)
Library Holdings: Audiobooks 6,576; AV Mats 22,261; CDs 6,391; DVDs 15,875; e-books 9,785; Large Print Bks 5,361; Bk Vols 154,220; Per Subs 285
Automation Activity & Vendor Info: (Cataloging) OCLC; (Circulation) SirsiDynix; (ILL) OCLC WorldShare Interlibrary Loan; (OPAC) SirsiDynix-Enterprise
Wireless access
Function: 24/7 Electronic res, 24/7 Online cat, Adult bk club, Audiobks on Playaways & MP3, Audiobks via web, Bk club(s), Bks on CD, Children's prog, Computer training, Computers for patron use, Electronic databases & coll, Free DVD rentals, Homebound delivery serv, ILL available, Life-long learning prog for all ages, Mail & tel request accepted, Mango lang, Music CDs, Online cat, Outside serv via phone, mail, e-mail & web, OverDrive digital audio bks, Photocopying/Printing, Preschool outreach, Printer for laptops & handheld devices, Prog for adults, Prog for children & young adult, Ref serv available, Spanish lang bks, Study rm, Summer reading prog, Tax forms, Teen prog, Telephone ref, Wheelchair accessible, Writing prog
Partic in Yavapai Libr Network
Special Services for the Deaf - Assistive tech; Bks on deafness & sign lang; Sign lang interpreter upon request for prog
Special Services for the Blind - Accessible computers; Bks on CD; Closed circuit TV magnifier; Computer access aids; Large print bks; Low vision equip; Magnifiers; Screen reader software
Open Mon, Fri & Sat 9-5, Tues, Wed & Thurs 9-8, Sun 1-5
Friends of the Library Group

S SHARLOT HALL MUSEUM LIBRARY & ARCHIVES*, Granite Creek Ctr, 115 S McCormick St, 86301. Tel: 928-277-2003, 928-445-3122. FAX: 928-776-9053. E-mail: archivesrequest@sharlothallmuseum.org. Web Site: www.sharlothallmuseum.org/historic_buildings/the-sharlot-hall-museum-library-and-archives. *Archivist, Librn,* Brenda Taylor
Founded 1928
Library Holdings: Bk Titles 10,000
Special Collections: Archives Coll; Arizona History Coll, newspaper, ms; Early Arizona & Indian Coll, photog. Oral History
Wireless access
Open Wed-Fri 12-4, Sat 10-2

C YAVAPAI COLLEGE LIBRARY*, Bldg 19, 1100 E Sheldon St, 86301. SAN 300-4104. Tel: 928-776-2260. Interlibrary Loan Service Tel: 928-776-2059. Reference Tel: 928-776-2261. FAX: 928-776-2275. E-mail: library@yc.edu. Web Site: www.yc.edu/v5content/library. *Dir,* Mike Byrnes; Tel: 928-771-6124, E-mail: mike.byrnes@yc.edu; *Tech Serv Mgr,* Ustadza White; Tel: 928-776-2264, E-mail: ustadza.white@yc.edu; Staff 6 (MLS 4, Non-MLS 2)
Founded 1969. Enrl 9,063; Fac 427; Highest Degree: Associate
Library Holdings: AV Mats 15,464; CDs 804; Electronic Media & Resources 34; Bk Vols 114,125; Per Subs 557
Special Collections: College Archives
Subject Interests: SW
Automation Activity & Vendor Info: (Acquisitions) SirsiDynix; (Cataloging) SirsiDynix; (Circulation) SirsiDynix; (Course Reserve) SirsiDynix; (OPAC) SirsiDynix
Wireless access
Function: Archival coll, Audio & video playback equip for onsite use, AV serv, Govt ref serv, ILL available, Internet access, Photocopying/Printing, Ref serv available, Wheelchair accessible, Workshops
Partic in Yavapai Libr Network
Open Mon-Thurs 8-8, Fri 8-4, Sat 12-4

Departmental Libraries:

VERDE VALLEY CAMPUS, 601 Black Hills Dr, Clarkdale, 86324, SAN 370-0224. Tel: 928-634-6541. Interlibrary Loan Service Tel: 928-634-6539. Reference Tel: 928-634-6540. FAX: 928-634-6543. *Libr Mgr,* Sheri Kinney; Tel: 928-634-6542, E-mail: sheri.kinney@yc.edu; Staff 5 (MLS 1, Non-MLS 4)
Library Holdings: CDs 534; DVDs 584; Electronic Media & Resources 51; Bk Titles 33,990; Per Subs 149; Videos 6,272
Open Mon-Thurs 8-7, Fri 8-4, Sat 11-3

P YAVAPAI COUNTY FREE LIBRARY DISTRICT*, 1971 Commerce Ctr Circle, Ste D, 86301. SAN 323-8091. Tel: 928-771-3191. FAX: 928-771-3113. E-mail: web.library.district@yavapai.us. Web Site: www.yavapai.us/library, yavapailibrary.org. *Dir,* Corey Christians; E-mail: corey.christians@yavapai.us; *Asst Dir,* Susan Lapis; *Cat Librn,* Karen Straube; *Acq, ILL Spec,* Jill Redmer; *Libr Spec,* Kelly Roberge; Staff 41 (MLS 6, Non-MLS 35)
Founded 1987. Pop 228,168
Library Holdings: Bk Titles 3,500
Automation Activity & Vendor Info: (Acquisitions) SirsiDynix; (Cataloging) SirsiDynix; (Circulation) SirsiDynix; (Course Reserve) SirsiDynix; (ILL) OCLC; (OPAC) SirsiDynix; (Serials) SirsiDynix
Wireless access
Partic in Yavapai Libr Network
Friends of the Library Group

Branches: 15

ASH FORK PUBLIC LIBRARY, 450 W Lewis Ave, Ash Fork, 86320. (Mail add: PO Box 295, Ash Fork, 86320-0295), SAN 323-7796. Tel: 928-637-2442. FAX: 928-637-9986. Web Site: www.yavapailibrary.org. *Libr Coord,* Mary Rigby; *Libr Coord,* Marilyn Wallace
Library Holdings: Bk Vols 8,000
Automation Activity & Vendor Info: (Cataloging) SirsiDynix; (OPAC) SirsiDynix
Open Mon-Fri 9:30-4:30

BAGDAD PUBLIC LIBRARY, 700 Palo Verde, Bldg C, Bagdad, 86321. (Mail add: PO Box 95, Bagdad, 86321-0095), SAN 323-7818. Tel: 928-633-2325. FAX: 928-633-2054. E-mail: bagdadyfl@gmail.com. Web Site: www.yavapailibrary.org/bagdad. *Coordr,* Trina Keil; *Coordr,* Julie Peterson
Library Holdings: Bk Titles 10,000
Automation Activity & Vendor Info: (Cataloging) SirsiDynix; (Circulation) SirsiDynix; (OPAC) SirsiDynix
Open Mon, Tues & Thurs 10-4, Wed 10-5

BEAVER CREEK PUBLIC LIBRARY, 4810 E Beaver Creek Rd, Rimrock, 86335. Tel: 928-567-4034. FAX: 928-567-4971. Web Site: www.yavapailibrary.org/beavercreek.
Open Mon-Thurs 10:30-6, Fri & Sat 9-3

BLACK CANYON CITY COMMUNITY LIBRARY, 34701 S Old Black Canyon Hwy, Black Canyon City, 85324. (Mail add: PO Box 87, Black Canyon City, 85324-0087), SAN 323-7834. Tel: 623-374-5866. FAX: 623-374-0465. E-mail: blackcanyoncitylibrary@gmail.com. Web Site: yavapailibrary.org/blackcanyon. *Libr Coord,* Christina Cooper; E-mail: christina.cooper@yavapai.us; *Libr Coord,* Charles Goulding; E-mail: charles.goulding@yavapai.us
Library Holdings: Audiobooks 200; Bks on Deafness & Sign Lang 5; DVDs 1,000; Large Print Bks 200; Bk Titles 19,000; Per Subs 10; Videos 200
Automation Activity & Vendor Info: (Cataloging) SirsiDynix; (Circulation) SirsiDynix; (OPAC) SirsiDynix
Open Tues-Thurs 9-7, Fri & Sat 9-5

CLARK MEMORIAL LIBRARY, 39 N Ninth St, Clarkdale, 86324. (Mail add: PO Box 308, Clarkdale, 86324-0308), SAN 323-7893. Tel: 928-634-5423. FAX: 928-649-3730. E-mail: library@clarkdale.az.gov. Web Site: www.yavapailibrary.org/clarkdale. *Commun Serv Supvr,* Joni Westcott; E-mail: Joni.Westcott@clarkdale.az.gov
Pop 3,824
Library Holdings: Bk Vols 10,000; Per Subs 32
Automation Activity & Vendor Info: (Cataloging) SirsiDynix; (Circulation) SirsiDynix; (OPAC) SirsiDynix
Function: Accelerated reader prog, Adult bk club, Archival coll, Art exhibits, Audio & video playback equip for onsite use, Audiobks via web, AV serv, Bk club(s), Bks on CD, CD-ROM, Children's prog, Computer training, Computers for patron use, Distance learning, E-Reserves, Electronic databases & coll, Free DVD rentals, Homework prog, ILL available, Internet access, Notary serv, Online cat, Online ref, OverDrive digital audio bks, Photocopying/Printing, Printer for laptops & handheld devices, Prog for adults, Prog for children & young adult, Spoken cassettes & CDs, Story hour, Summer reading prog, Wheelchair accessible
Open Mon-Thurs 1-5:30, Fri 8-Noon
Friends of the Library Group

CONGRESS PUBLIC LIBRARY, 26750 Santa Fe Rd, Congress, 85332. (Mail add: PO Box 280, Congress, 85332-0280), SAN 323-7915. Tel: 928-427-3945. FAX: 928-427-6497. Web Site: www.yavapailibrary.org/congress. *Libr Coord,* Dorothy Dalton; E-mail: dorothy.dalton@yavapai.us; *Libr Coord,* Mary Ann Paulic; E-mail: mary.paulic@yavapai.us; Staff 2 (Non-MLS 2)
Founded 1984. Pop 1,700; Circ 16,468
Jul 2016-Jun 2017 Income $4,814. Mats Exp $4,814, Books $4,114, AV Mat $700. Sal $27,000
Library Holdings: Audiobooks 50; DVDs 600; Large Print Bks 150; Bk Titles 7,000; Videos 200
Automation Activity & Vendor Info: (Circulation) SirsiDynix
Function: 24/7 Electronic res, 24/7 Online cat, Audiobks via web, Bks on cassette, Bks on CD, Computer training, Computers for patron use, Free DVD rentals, ILL available, Internet access, Life-long learning prog for all ages, Magazines, Mango lang, Online cat, OverDrive digital audio bks, Photocopying/Printing, Prog for adults, Scanner, Senior computer classes, Summer reading prog, Tax forms, VHS videos, Wheelchair accessible
Special Services for the Blind - Bks on cassette; Bks on CD; Large print bks; Magnifiers
Open Wed, Thurs & Fri 10-4, Sat 9-1

CORDES LAKES PUBLIC LIBRARY, 15989 S Cordes Lake Dr, Cordes Lakes, 86333, SAN 323-7931. Tel: 928-632-5492. FAX: 928-632-5903. Web Site: www.yavapailibrary.org/cordes. *Libr Coord,* Melody Emmett; E-mail: melody.emmett@yavapai.us
Library Holdings: Bk Vols 5,079
Automation Activity & Vendor Info: (Cataloging) SirsiDynix; (Circulation) SirsiDynix; (OPAC) SirsiDynix
Open Mon-Thurs 10:30-6, Fri & Sat 9-4

CROWN KING PUBLIC LIBRARY, 23550 S Towers Mountain Rd, Crown King, 86343. Tel: 928-632-5986. FAX: 928-632-5986. Web Site: www.yavapailibrary.org/crownking.
Open Tues-Thurs 10-4

DEWEY-HUMBOLDT TOWN LIBRARY, 2735 S Corral St, Humboldt, 86329. Tel: 928-632-5049. FAX: 928-632-5356. Web Site: www.yavapailibrary.org/dewey.
Open Tues, Wed & Fri 10-noon & 12:30-5, Thurs 12:30-7, Sat 10-2

MAYER PUBLIC LIBRARY, 10004 Wicks Ave, Mayer, 86333, SAN 323-7974. Tel: 928-632-7370. FAX: 928-632-4022. Web Site: yavapailibrary.org/mayer. *Libr Coord,* Victoria Hungerford; E-mail: victoria.hungerford@yavapai.us; *Libr Coord,* Rebecca Zuniga; E-mail: rebecca.zuniga@yavapai.us
Founded 1965
Library Holdings: Bk Vols 14,000
Subject Interests: SW
Automation Activity & Vendor Info: (Cataloging) SirsiDynix; (Circulation) SirsiDynix; (OPAC) SirsiDynix
Open Tues-Sat 9-5
Friends of the Library Group

PAULDEN PUBLIC LIBRARY, 16 W Big Chino Rd, Paulden, 86334. Tel: 928-636-1202. FAX: 928-636-1201. Web Site: www.yavapailibrary.org/paulden.
Open Tues-Thurs 10-6, Fri & Sat 10-4

SELIGMAN PUBLIC LIBRARY, 54170 N Floyd St, Seligman, 86337, SAN 323-8016. Tel: 928-422-3633. FAX: 928-422-4399. Web Site: www.yavapailibrary.org/seligman. *Libr Coord,* Amy Appoloni; E-mail: amy.appoloni@yavapai.us
Library Holdings: Bk Vols 4,500
Automation Activity & Vendor Info: (Cataloging) SirsiDynix; (Circulation) SirsiDynix; (OPAC) SirsiDynix
Open Mon-Fri 9:30-5

SPRING VALLEY LIBRARY, 17320 E Mule Deer Dr, Mayer, 86333. Tel: 928-171-8118. FAX: 928-717-8119. Web Site: www.yavapailibrary.org/springvalley.
Open Mon-Thurs-10-5:30, Fri 8-3

WILHOIT PUBLIC LIBRARY, 9325 Donegal Dr, Ste B, Wilhoit, 86332. Tel: 928-442-3611. FAX: 928-442-2407. Web Site: yavapailibrary.org/wilhoit.
Library Holdings: Bk Vols 3,600
Automation Activity & Vendor Info: (Cataloging) SirsiDynix; (Circulation) SirsiDynix; (OPAC) SirsiDynix
Open Tues-Sat 11-4

YARNELL PUBLIC LIBRARY, 22278 N Hwy 89, Yarnell, 85362. (Mail add: PO Box 808, Yarnell, 85362), SAN 323-8032. Tel: 928-427-3191. FAX: 928-427-6341. Web Site: www.yavapailibrary.org/yarnell. *Libr Coord,* Priscilla Phelps; E-mail: priscilla.phelps@yavapai.us; *Libr Coord,* Patti Rutherford; E-mail: patti.rutherford@yavapai.us
Library Holdings: AV Mats 800; Bk Vols 7,000; Per Subs 20; Talking Bks 1,000
Special Collections: Local Archives
Automation Activity & Vendor Info: (Cataloging) SirsiDynix; (Circulation) SirsiDynix; (OPAC) SirsiDynix
Open Mon-Fri 9-4, Sat 9-2

GL YAVAPAI COUNTY LAW LIBRARY*, Yavapai County Courthouse, 120 S Cortez St, Rm 112, 86303. SAN 300-4090. Tel: 928-771-3309. E-mail: YavLawLib@courts.az.gov. Web Site: courts.yavapai.us/superiorcourt/law-library. *Librn,* Daniel Furlong; E-mail: yavlawlib@courts.az.gov; Staff 1 (Non-MLS 1)
Function: Res libr
Open Mon-Fri 8-5

S YAVAPAI-PRESCOTT TRIBAL LIBRARY, 530 E Merritt, 86301-2038. SAN 375-1813. Tel: 928-515-7321.
Library Holdings: AV Mats 40; Bk Titles 5,000; Per Subs 21; Talking Bks 20
Wireless access
Function: After school storytime, Audio & video playback equip for onsite use, Bks on cassette, Children's prog, Computer training, Computers for patron use, Family literacy, Homework prog, Internet access, Photocopying/Printing, Preschool outreach, Ref serv available, Senior outreach, Story hour, Summer & winter reading prog, VHS videos
Restriction: Open to tribal commun mem only

PRESCOTT VALLEY

P PRESCOTT VALLEY PUBLIC LIBRARY*, 7401 E Skoog Blvd, 86314. SAN 323-7990. Tel: 928-759-3040. FAX: 928-759-3121. Web Site: www.pvlib.net. *Libr Dir,* Casey Van Haren; E-mail: cvanharen@pvaz.net; *Dep Dir,* Robert Kieren; E-mail: rkieren@pvaz.net; *Libr Mgr,* Joslyn Joseph; E-mail: jjoseph@pvaz.net; Staff 28 (MLS 7, Non-MLS 21)
Library Holdings: Per Subs 81
Automation Activity & Vendor Info: (Cataloging) SirsiDynix; (Circulation) SirsiDynix; (OPAC) SirsiDynix
Function: 24/7 Electronic res, 24/7 Online cat, 3D Printer, Activity rm, Adult bk club, Adult literacy prog, Art exhibits, Art programs, Audiobks via web, BA reader (adult literacy), Bk club(s), Bks on CD, Children's prog, Citizenship assistance, Computer training, Computers for patron use, Digital talking bks, E-Readers, Electronic databases & coll, Equip loans & repairs, For res purposes, Free DVD rentals, Holiday prog, Home delivery & serv to seniorr ctr & nursing homes, Homebound delivery serv, ILL available, Instruction & testing, Internet access, Large print keyboards, Life-long learning prog for all ages, Magazines, Mail & tel request accepted, Makerspace, Mango lang, Meeting rooms, Movies, Music CDs, Notary serv, Online cat, Online ref, Outreach serv, Outside serv via phone, mail, e-mail & web, OverDrive digital audio bks, Photocopying/Printing, Preschool outreach, Preschool reading prog, Printer for laptops & handheld devices, Prof lending libr, Prog for adults, Prog for children & young adult, Ref & res, Ref serv available, Res assist avail, Scanner, Senior computer classes, Senior outreach, Serves people with intellectual disabilities,

Spanish lang bks, STEM programs, Story hour, Study rm, Summer & winter reading prog, Summer reading prog, Teen prog, Telephone ref, Wheelchair accessible, Winter reading prog, Workshops
Partic in Yavapai Libr Network
Open Mon-Thurs 9-7, Fri 9-5, Sat 9-3, Sun 1-5
Friends of the Library Group

QUARTZSITE

P QUARTZSITE PUBLIC LIBRARY*, 465 N Plymouth Ave, 85346. (Mail add: PO Box 2812, 85346-2812), SAN 377-032X. Tel: 928-927-4333, Ext 4. FAX: 928-927-3593. E-mail: qsitelib@hotmail.com. Web Site: ci.quartzsite.az.us. *Libr Mgr,* Billie Fowler; Staff 4 (MLS 1, Non-MLS 3)
Founded 1968. Pop 3,600; Circ 55,000
Library Holdings: Audiobooks 1,200; CDs 666; DVDs 2,496; High Interest/Low Vocabulary Bk Vols 100; Large Print Bks 2,350; Bk Titles 38,851; Per Subs 30; Talking Bks 3; Videos 3,500
Special Collections: Arizona Coll; Arizona Western College Coll; Caregiver Resource Zone Coll
Automation Activity & Vendor Info: (Acquisitions) Book Systems; (Cataloging) Book Systems; (Circulation) Book Systems; (ILL) OCLC CatExpress; (OPAC) Book Systems; (Serials) Book Systems
Wireless access
Function: Accelerated reader prog, Children's prog, Computers for patron use, Distance learning, Electronic databases & coll, Free DVD rentals, Games & aids for people with disabilities, ILL available, Internet access, Music CDs, Online cat, Photocopying/Printing, Prog for adults, Prog for children & young adult, Senior outreach, Spoken cassettes & CDs, Spoken cassettes & DVDs, Story hour, Summer reading prog, Tax forms, VHS videos, Wheelchair accessible
Special Services for the Blind - Talking bks
Open Mon-Fri 8-5; Mon-Thurs (Summer) 7-6
Friends of the Library Group

SACATON

P IRA H HAYES MEMORIAL LIBRARY*, 94 N Church St, 85147. (Mail add: PO Box 97, 85147-0097), SAN 376-3188. Tel: 520-562-3225. FAX: 520-562-3903. *Head Librn,* Ramona Tecumseh; E-mail: ramona.tecumseh1@gric.nsn.us
Library Holdings: Bk Titles 15,000
Open Mon-Fri 9-6

SAFFORD

S ARIZONA DEPARTMENT OF CORRECTIONS - ADULT INSTITUTIONS*, Arizona State Prison Complex - Safford Resource Library, 896 S Cook Rd, 85546. Tel: 928-428-4698, Ext 75508. Web Site: corrections.az.gov/location/102/safford. *Librn II,* Matt Angleton; E-mail: mangleton@azcorrections.gov
Library Holdings: Bk Vols 9,000
Restriction: Not open to pub

S ARIZONA DEPARTMENT OF CORRECTIONS, ARIZONA STATE PRISON COMPLEX-SAFFORD*, Fort Grant Library, 15500 S Fort Grant Rd, 85643. (Mail add: Fort Grant Unit, 896 S Cook Rd, 85546). Tel: 928-828-3393, Ext 94508. *Librn,* Diane Alvarez; E-mail: dalvarez3@azcorrections.gov; Staff 1 (Non-MLS 1)
Founded 1881
Jul 2012-Jun 2013 Income $4,824. Mats Exp $4,824, Books $3,500, Per/Ser (Incl. Access Fees) $324, Presv $1,000. Sal $39,000
Library Holdings: Audiobooks 6; Bks on Deafness & Sign Lang 4; High Interest/Low Vocabulary Bk Vols 1,000; Large Print Bks 60; Bk Titles 7,600; Bk Vols 8,000; Per Subs 30
Special Collections: Addiction & Recovery Coll; Adult Basic Education Coll; African American Coll; Distance Learning Reference Coll; General Equivalency Diploma Coll; Hispanic Coll; Lewis vs Casey Legal Reference Coll; Man-Woman Relationships Coll; Marriage Coll; Methamphetamine Addiction & Recovery Coll; Native American Coll; Parenting Coll; Southwestern States History Coll; Spanish Language Coll; Transition/Life Skills Coll
Subject Interests: Fantasy, Mystery, SW hist, Western
Automation Activity & Vendor Info: (Cataloging) MC2 Systems; (Circulation) MC2 Systems
Function: Bilingual assistance for Spanish patrons, Distance learning, Govt ref serv, Learning ctr, Literacy & newcomer serv, Notary serv, Orientations, Outreach serv, Photocopying/Printing, Prog for adults, Ref serv available
Restriction: Not open to pub, Secured area only open to authorized personnel, Staff & inmates only

P SAFFORD CITY-GRAHAM COUNTY LIBRARY, 808 S Seventh Ave, 85546. SAN 300-4112. Tel: 928-432-4165. Web Site: www.saffordlibrary.org. *Libr Dir,* Victoria Silva; Tel: 928-432-4151, E-mail: vsilva@saffordaz.gov; *Libr Operations Supvr,* Lesley Talley; Tel: 928-432-4169, E-mail: ltalley@saffordaz.gov; Staff 9 (MLS 1, Non-MLS 8)
Founded 1916. Pop 37,000; Circ 110,000
Special Collections: Arizona Coll
Automation Activity & Vendor Info: (Cataloging) Book Systems; (Circulation) Book Systems; (Course Reserve) Book Systems; (ILL) OCLC; (OPAC) Book Systems
Wireless access
Function: 24/7 Online cat, Archival coll, Art exhibits, Audiobks via web, Bilingual assistance for Spanish patrons, Bks on CD, Children's prog, Computers for patron use, Digital talking bks, Electronic databases & coll, Family literacy, Free DVD rentals, Holiday prog, ILL available, Internet access, Life-long learning prog for all ages, Mango lang, Meeting rooms, Microfiche/film & reading machines, Movies, Notary serv, Online cat, Online ref, Outreach serv, Photocopying/Printing, Preschool outreach, Preschool reading prog, Prof lending libr, Prog for adults, Prog for children & young adult, Ref & res, Ref serv available, Res assist avail, Scanner, Senior outreach, Spanish lang bks, STEM programs, Summer reading prog, Tax forms, Teen prog, Telephone ref, Wheelchair accessible
Special Services for the Blind - Bks on CD; Large print bks; Talking bk serv referral
Open Mon-Thurs 10-7
Restriction: ID required to use computers (Ltd hrs)
Friends of the Library Group

SAINT DAVID

SR HOLY TRINITY MONASTERY LIBRARY*, 1605 S St Mary's Way, 85630. (Mail add: PO Box 298, 85630-0298), SAN 375-3832. Tel: 520-720-4642. FAX: 520-720-4202. E-mail: guestmaster@theriver.com. Web Site: www.holytrinitymonasterycenter.com/?page_id=92. *Librn,* Sister Jeanne Hill; Staff 1 (Non-MLS 1)
Founded 1974
Library Holdings: Bk Titles 47,300; Bk Vols 49,300; Per Subs 40
Special Collections: Great Books; Monastic Coll; Southwest/Native American Coll, bks, mags. Oral History
Wireless access

SAINT JOHNS

P APACHE COUNTY LIBRARY DISTRICT*, 30 S Second W, 85936. (Mail add: PO Box 2760, 85936-2760), SAN 300-4120. Tel: 928-337-4923. FAX: 928-337-3960. Web Site: www.apachecountylibraries.com. *Dir,* SueAn Stradling-Collins; E-mail: scollis@co.apache.az.us; *Head, Pub Serv,* Jaymie Lewis-Smith; *Head, Tech Serv,* Alice Webb; Staff 1 (MLS 1)
Founded 1986. Pop 71,686; Circ 179,985
Jul 2014-Jun 2015 Income (Main & Associated Libraries) $1,713,504, State $25,000, Federal $33,314, County $1,617,563, Other $37,627. Sal $679,140
Library Holdings: Audiobooks 4,693; DVDs 11,569; e-books 4,479; Bk Vols 64,037; Per Subs 132
Special Collections: Southwest Coll
Automation Activity & Vendor Info: (Cataloging) Innovative Interfaces, Inc; (Circulation) Innovative Interfaces, Inc; (ILL) OCLC; (OPAC) Innovative Interfaces, Inc
Wireless access
Function: Adult bk club, Art exhibits, Bks on CD, Children's prog, Computers for patron use, Free DVD rentals, ILL available, Online cat, Photocopying/Printing, Prog for adults, Scanner, Story hour, Summer reading prog, Teen prog, Workshops
Open Mon-Thurs 8-5
Restriction: Lending limited to county residents
Branches: 7
ALPINE PUBLIC, 17 County Rd 2061, Alpine, 85920. (Mail add: PO Box 528, Alpine, 85920-0528), SAN 328-0314. Tel: 928-339-4925. FAX: 928-339-4925. *Libr Mgr,* Anne MacGregor; E-mail: amacgregor@co.apache.az.us; Staff 1 (Non-MLS 1)
Open Mon-Fri 10-5
Friends of the Library Group
CONCHO PUBLIC, 18 County Rd 5101, Concho, 85924. (Mail add: PO Box 339, Concho, 85924-0339), SAN 371-3490. Tel: 928-337-2167. FAX: 928-337-2167. *Libr Mgr,* Carol Roberts; E-mail: croberts@co.apache.az.us; Staff 1 (Non-MLS 1)
Open Mon-Thurs 12-6
GREER MEMORIAL, 74A County Rd 1120 / Main St, Greer, 85927. (Mail add: PO Box 144, Greer, 85927-0144), SAN 371-3520. Tel: 928-735-7710. *Libr Mgr,* Fely Earl; E-mail: fearl@co.apache.az.us; Staff 1 (Non-MLS 1)
Open Sat 9-2
Friends of the Library Group
ROUND VALLEY PUBLIC, 179 S Main St, Eagar, 85925. (Mail add: PO Box 1180, Eagar, 85925-1180), SAN 371-3482. Tel: 928-333-4694. FAX: 928-333-5682. *Libr Mgr,* Fely Earl; E-mail: fearl@co.apache.az.us; Staff 1 (Non-MLS 1)
Open Mon-Fri 10-5

SAINT JOHNS PUBLIC, 35 S Third W, 85936. (Mail add: PO Box 766, 85936-0766), SAN 371-3547. Tel: 928-337-4405. FAX: 928-337-2224. *Libr Mgr,* Ryan Barker; Staff 1 (Non-MLS 1)
Open Mon-Fri 10-5

SANDERS PUBLIC, I-40, Exit 339, 191 N Frontage Rd E, Sanders, 86512. (Mail add: PO Box 1000, Sanders, 86512-1000), SAN 371-3539. Tel: 928-688-2677. FAX: 928-688-3077. *Libr Mgr,* Lucinda Baloo; Staff 1 (Non-MLS 1)
Open Mon-Thurs 10-5

VERNON PUBLIC, Ten County Rd 3142, Vernon, 85940. (Mail add: PO Box 600, Vernon, 85940-0600). Tel: 928-532-5005. *Libr Mgr,* Tamara Applegate; E-mail: tapplegate@co.apache.az.us; Staff 1 (Non-MLS 1)
Open Mon, Tues & Thurs 10-12 & 1-5, Fri 9-3

SALOME

P CENTENNIAL PUBLIC LIBRARY*, 69725 Centennial Rd, 85348. (Mail add: PO Box 309, 85348), SAN 377-0303. Tel: 928-859-4271. FAX: 928-859-4364. E-mail: cplsalome@yahoo.com. Web Site: www.centennialpubliclibrary.com, www.parkerpubliclibrary.com/centennial.html. *Mgr,* Sharon Hillhouse; Staff 1 (Non-MLS 1)
Library Holdings: Bk Titles 4,500
Automation Activity & Vendor Info: (Cataloging) Follett Software; (Circulation) Follett Software; (ILL) OCLC CatExpress; (OPAC) Follett Software
Wireless access
Function: 24/7 Electronic res, 24/7 Online cat, Activity rm, Adult bk club, Adult literacy prog, Bk club(s), Bks on cassette, Bks on CD, Children's prog, Computers for patron use, Electronic databases & coll, Free DVD rentals, Holiday prog, ILL available, Internet access, Life-long learning prog for all ages, Literacy & newcomer serv, Magazines, Meeting rooms, Movies, Online cat, Prog for adults, Prog for children & young adult, Summer reading prog, Tax forms, VHS videos, Wheelchair accessible, Winter reading prog
Open Mon-Wed 9-3:30, Thurs 8-4:30

SAN CARLOS

P SAN CARLOS PUBLIC LIBRARY, 89 San Carlos Ave, 85550. (Mail add: PO Box 545, 85550), SAN 300-4139. Tel: 928-475-2611. FAX: 928-475-2614. Web Site: www.gcldaz.org/san-carlos-public-library. *Libr Mgr,* Emma Victor; E-mail: emma.victor@scat-nsn.gov
Founded 1971. Pop 7,000
Library Holdings: Bk Vols 10,000; Per Subs 18
Special Collections: Arizona Indian Coll
Wireless access
Mem of Gila County Library District
Open Mon-Fri 8-12 & 1-4

SAN LUIS

S ARIZONA DEPARTMENT OF CORRECTIONS - ADULT INSTITUTIONS*, Arizona State Prison Complex - Yuma Library, 7125 E Juan Sanchez Blvd, 85349. (Mail add: PO Box 8909, Yuma, 85366). Tel: 928-627-8871. Web Site: corrections.az.gov/location/99/yuma. *Librn,* Maria Carkuff
Library Holdings: Bk Vols 12,000
Restriction: Not open to pub

SAN MANUEL

P SAN MANUEL PUBLIC LIBRARY*, 108 Fifth Ave, 85631. SAN 300-4147. Tel: 520-385-4470. FAX: 520-385-2910. Web Site: www.pinalcountyaz.gov/Departments/Library/Locations/Pages/SanManuel.aspx. *Dir,* Kathy Smith; E-mail: kathy.smith@pinalcountyaz.gov
Founded 1959. Pop 4,300; Circ 18,112
Library Holdings: Bk Vols 12,000
Automation Activity & Vendor Info: (Cataloging) Innovative Interfaces, Inc; (Circulation) Innovative Interfaces, Inc; (OPAC) Innovative Interfaces, Inc
Wireless access
Mem of Pinal County Library District
Open Mon-Fri 9-5:30, Sat 10-Noon

SCOTTSDALE

R CONGREGATION BETH ISRAEL*, Marian & Ralph Feffer Library, 10460 N 56th St, 85253. SAN 300-3973. Tel: 480-951-0323. FAX: 480-951-7150. E-mail: library@cbiaz.org. Web Site: www.cbiaz.org/library. *Libr Dir,* Carol Reynolds; Tel: 480-951-0323, Ext 121
Founded 1958
Library Holdings: Bk Titles 12,000; Bk Vols 14,000
Special Collections: Holocaust Books; Judaica Coll
Restriction: Open by appt only

S THE FRANK LLOYD WRIGHT FOUNDATION*, William Wesley Peters Library, 12621 N Frank Lloyd Wright Blvd, Taliesin West, 85259. SAN 374-8243. Tel: 480-391-4011. FAX: 480-860-8472. E-mail: edawsari@franklloydwright.org. Web Site: franklloydwright.org. *Librn,* Elizabeth Dawsari; E-mail: edawsari@franklloydwright.org
Special Collections: Frank Lloyd Wright Coll
Subject Interests: Archit
Automation Activity & Vendor Info: (ILL) Surpass
Wireless access
Publications: Subject Bibliographies (Architecture)
Restriction: Open by appt only

M MAYO CLINIC SCOTTSDALE LIBRARIES*, 13400 E Shea Blvd, 85259. SAN 370-5366. Tel: 480-301-8443. FAX: 480-301-7005. E-mail: library.clinic@mayo.edu. Web Site: libraryguides.mayo.edu/arizona. *Dir,* Lisa Marks; E-mail: marks.lisa@mayo.edu; *Libr Asst,* Cindy Heltne; E-mail: Heltne.cynthia@mayo.edu; Staff 7 (MLS 2, Non-MLS 5)
Founded 1987
Library Holdings: Bk Titles 2,000; Per Subs 320
Subject Interests: Clinical med, Molecular biol
Function: ILL available
Restriction: Staff use only

R PHOENIX SEMINARY LIBRARY, 7901 E Shea Blvd, 85260. Tel: 602-429-4974. FAX: 602-850-8085. E-mail: library@ps.edu. Web Site: ps.edu/ps-students/library-overview. *Dir, Libr Serv,* Doug Olbert; E-mail: dolbert@ps.edu; *Tech Serv Librn,* Jim Santeford; E-mail: jsanteford@ps.edu
Library Holdings: CDs 334; DVDs 405; Microforms 7,391; Music Scores 208; Bk Titles 52,098; Per Subs 3,082
Automation Activity & Vendor Info: (Cataloging) OPALS (Open-source Automated Library System)
Wireless access
Partic in Theological Library Cooperative of Arizona
Open Mon-Thurs 8:30am-10pm, Fri 8:30-5, Sat 9:30-5

P SALT RIVER TRIBAL LIBRARY*, 11725 E Indian School Rd, 85256. (Mail add: 10005 E Osborn Rd, 85256), SAN 300-4198. Tel: 480-362-2557. FAX: 480-362-6969. Web Site: www.srpmic-nsn.gov/government/recreation/library. *Librn,* Melissa Rave; E-mail: melissa.rave@srpmic-nsn.gov
Founded 1969. Pop 4,000; Circ 4,500
Library Holdings: Bk Vols 8,600; Per Subs 45
Automation Activity & Vendor Info: (Cataloging) Follett Software; (Circulation) Follett Software
Wireless access
Open Mon-Thurs 7:30-7, Fri 7:30-6

J SCOTTSDALE COMMUNITY COLLEGE LIBRARY*, 9000 E Chaparral Rd, 85256. SAN 300-4201. Tel: 480-423-6651. Reference Tel: 480-423-6650. Web Site: library.scottsdalecc.edu. *Dir,* Dr Lisa Young; Tel: 480-423-6222, E-mail: lisa.young@scottsdalecc.edu; *Tech Serv Librn,* Marsha Ballard; Tel: 480-423-6638, E-mail: marsha.ballard@sccmail.maricopa.edu; Staff 9.5 (MLS 6, Non-MLS 3.5)
Founded 1971. Enrl 10,000; Fac 160; Highest Degree: Associate
Library Holdings: AV Mats 1,724; Bks on Deafness & Sign Lang 32; CDs 170; DVDs 686; e-books 31,110; e-journals 72; Electronic Media & Resources 12; High Interest/Low Vocabulary Bk Vols 20; Large Print Bks 20; Music Scores 26; Bk Titles 40,000; Bk Vols 36,796; Per Subs 319; Talking Bks 37; Videos 693
Special Collections: Colleges and Careers; Indians of the Southwest Coll; Language
Automation Activity & Vendor Info: (Acquisitions) SirsiDynix; (Cataloging) SirsiDynix; (Circulation) SirsiDynix; (Course Reserve) SirsiDynix; (ILL) OCLC ILLiad; (Media Booking) SirsiDynix; (OPAC) SirsiDynix; (Serials) SirsiDynix
Wireless access
Open Mon-Thurs 7:30am-9:30pm, Fri 7:30-3

SCOTTSDALE HEALTHCARE

M DR ROBERT C FOREMAN HEALTH SCIENCES LIBRARY*, Scottsdale Healthcare Osborn, 7400 E Osborn Rd, 85251, SAN 300-421X. Tel: 480-882-4870. FAX: 480-882-4200. E-mail: olibrary@shc.org. *Supvr,* Evonda Copeland; E-mail: ecopeland@shc.org; Staff 3 (MLS 2, Non-MLS 1)
Founded 1968
Library Holdings: Bk Titles 2,000; Per Subs 250
Special Collections: Family Practice; Obstetrics, Gynecology & Urology
Subject Interests: Internal med, Nursing, Obstetrics & gynecology, Orthopedics, Pediatrics, Radiology, Surgery
Automation Activity & Vendor Info: (Cataloging) CyberTools for Libraries; (OPAC) CyberTools for Libraries; (Serials) CyberTools for Libraries

Partic in Arizona Health Information Network; Cent Ariz Biomed Librns; Medical Library Group of Southern California & Arizona
Open Mon-Fri 7:30-5:30

M HEALTH SCIENCES LIBRARY*, 9003 E Shea Blvd, 85260, SAN 375-2836. Tel: 480-323-3870. FAX: 480-323-3864. E-mail: slibrary@shc.org. Web Site: www.shc.org. *Supvr,* Evonda Copeland; Staff 4 (MLS 2, Non-MLS 2)
Library Holdings: Bk Vols 1,200; Per Subs 150
Automation Activity & Vendor Info: (Cataloging) CyberTools for Libraries; (OPAC) CyberTools for Libraries; (Serials) CyberTools for Libraries
Partic in Arizona Health Information Network; Cent Ariz Biomed Librns; Medical Library Group of Southern California & Arizona
Open Mon-Fri 7:30-5:30

P SCOTTSDALE PUBLIC LIBRARY*, 3839 N Drinkwater Blvd, 85251-4467. (Mail add: PO Box 1000, 85252-1000), SAN 300-4228. Tel: 480-312-7323. FAX: 480-312-7993. Web Site: www.scottsdalelibrary.org. *Libr Dir,* Kira Peters; E-mail: KCPeters@ScottsdaleAZ.gov; *Br Mgr,* Erin Jones; Tel: 480-312-6225, E-mail: EJones@ScottsdaleAZ.gov; *Adult Serv Coordr,* Erin Krause Riley; E-mail: ERiley@ScottsdaleAZ.gov; *Youth/Teen Serv Coordr,* Mariko Whelan; E-mail: MWhelan@ScottsdaleAZ.gov; Staff 24 (MLS 24)
Founded 1968. Pop 217,379; Circ 1,518,000. Sal $6,750,231
Library Holdings: Audiobooks 11,952; CDs 25,409; DVDs 64,303; e-books 113,766; Bk Vols 419,647
Special Collections: Scottsdale Coll. Oral History
Subject Interests: Hist of Scottsdale
Automation Activity & Vendor Info: (Acquisitions) Innovative Interfaces, Inc - Millennium; (Cataloging) Innovative Interfaces, Inc - Millennium; (Circulation) Innovative Interfaces, Inc - Millennium; (Course Reserve) Innovative Interfaces, Inc - Millennium; (ILL) Innovative Interfaces, Inc - Millennium; (OPAC) Innovative Interfaces, Inc - Millennium; (Serials) Innovative Interfaces, Inc - Millennium
Wireless access
Function: Homebound delivery serv, ILL available, Magnifiers for reading, Prog for children & young adult, Summer reading prog, Wheelchair accessible
Partic in Amigos Library Services, Inc; OCLC Online Computer Library Center, Inc
Special Services for the Deaf - TDD equip
Special Services for the Blind - Home delivery serv
Open Mon-Thurs 9-8, Fri & Sat 10-6, Sun 1-5
Friends of the Library Group
Branches: 3
ARABIAN LIBRARY, 10215 E McDowell Mountain Ranch Rd, 85255. (Mail add: PO Box 1000, 85252-1000), SAN 376-8945. *Br Mgr,* Alyssa Black; E-mail: ABlack@scottsdaleaz.gov
Founded 2007
Open Mon-Thurs 9-8, Fri & Sat 10-6, Sun 1-5
Friends of the Library Group
MUSTANG LIBRARY, 10101 N 90th St, 85258-4404. (Mail add: PO Box 1000, 85252-1000), SAN 374-4493. *Br Mgr,* Medina Zick; Tel: 480-312-6031, E-mail: MZick@scottsdaleaz.gov
Special Services for the Deaf - TTY equip
Open Mon-Thurs 9-8, Fri & Sat 10-6, Sun 1-5
Friends of the Library Group
PALOMINO LIBRARY, 12575 E Via Linda, Ste 102, 85259. (Mail add: PO Box 1000, 85252-1000), SAN 376-8953. *Lead Librn,* Louise Aikin; Tel: 480-312-6011, E-mail: LAikin@scottsdaleaz.gov
Founded 1995
Open Mon-Wed 9-5:30, Thurs 9-7, Fri 10-5:30, Sun 1-5
Friends of the Library Group

SEDONA

P SEDONA PUBLIC LIBRARY, 3250 White Bear Rd, 86336. SAN 300-4252. Tel: 928-282-7714. Reference Tel: 928-282-7714, Ext 3. FAX: 928-282-5789. E-mail: reference@sedonalibrary.org. Web Site: www.sedonalibrary.org. *Dir,* Judy Poe; E-mail: director@sedonalibrary.org; Staff 12 (MLS 4, Non-MLS 8)
Founded 1958. Pop 15,000; Circ 123,702
Library Holdings: Bk Vols 80,000; Per Subs 230
Special Collections: Arizona Coll
Automation Activity & Vendor Info: (Acquisitions) SirsiDynix; (Cataloging) SirsiDynix; (Circulation) SirsiDynix; (OPAC) SirsiDynix
Wireless access
Mem of Flagstaff City-Coconino County Public Library System
Partic in Yavapai Libr Network
Open Mon-Thurs 10-6, Fri & Sat 10-5
Friends of the Library Group

S WORLD RESEARCH FOUNDATION LIBRARY*, 41 Bell Rock Plaza, 86351. (Mail add: PO Box 20828, 86341), SAN 373-1030. Tel: 928-284-3300. FAX: 928-284-3530. E-mail: info@wrf.org. Web Site: www.wrf.org/wrf-library.php. *Chief Exec Officer,* Steve Ross
Library Holdings: Bk Vols 30,000
Restriction: Open by appt only

SELLS

P VENITO GARCIA PUBLIC LIBRARY & ARCHIVES*, PO Box 837, 85634-0837. Tel: 520-383-5756. FAX: 520-383-2429. E-mail: asklibrary@tonation-nsn.gov. Web Site: www1.youseemore.com/venitogarcia. *Interim Librn,* Althea M Salvicio; Tel: 520-383-5756, E-mail: althea.salvicio@tonation-nsn.gov
Pop 1,300; Circ 9,000
Library Holdings: Bk Vols 6,000; Per Subs 20
Open Mon-Fri 8-5
Friends of the Library Group
Branches: 1
SAN LUCY DISTRICT, 1125 C St, Gila Bend, 85337. (Mail add: PO Box GG, Gila Bend, 85337-0479). Tel: 928-683-2012, 928-683-2796. FAX: 928-683-2802. Reference FAX: 928-683-6956. *Librn,* E Frances Venegas; E-mail: fecv5@yahoo.com
Open Mon-Fri 8-5
Friends of the Library Group

J TOHONO O'ODHAM COMMUNITY COLLEGE LIBRARY*, Hwy 86 Milepost 111 W, 85634. (Mail add: PO 3129, 85634-3129). Tel: 520-383-0032. FAX: 520-383-8403. Web Site: www.youseemore.com/tocc. *Col Librn,* Ofelia Zepeda; E-mail: ozepeda@tccc.edu; *Libr Asst,* Wendi Cline; E-mail: wcline@tccc.edu; *Libr Asst,* Carmella Pablo; E-mail: cpablo@tocc.edu
Founded 2001. Enrl 200; Fac 18; Highest Degree: Associate
Library Holdings: CDs 122; DVDs 1,498; e-books 10; Large Print Bks 20; Bk Titles 9,600; Bk Vols 10,000; Per Subs 28; Talking Bks 15; Videos 725
Special Collections: O'odham Materials Coll; Rare Materials; Tohono O'odham Community College Special Colls
Subject Interests: Agr, Bus, Early childhood educ, Educ, Environ studies, Native American
Automation Activity & Vendor Info: (Acquisitions) TLC (The Library Corporation); (Cataloging) TLC (The Library Corporation); (Circulation) TLC (The Library Corporation); (Course Reserve) TLC (The Library Corporation); (ILL) TLC (The Library Corporation); (OPAC) TLC (The Library Corporation)
Wireless access
Function: Archival coll, Audio & video playback equip for onsite use, Bks on cassette, Bks on CD, CD-ROM, Computer training, Computers for patron use, Electronic databases & coll, Equip loans & repairs, Govt ref serv, Health sci info serv, Internet access, Jail serv, Learning ctr, Magnifiers for reading, Music CDs, Online cat, Online ref, Orientations, Outreach serv, Photocopying/Printing, Ref & res, Scanner, Spoken cassettes & CDs, Spoken cassettes & DVDs, Telephone ref, VHS videos, Wheelchair accessible
Open Mon & Thurs 8-6, Tues & Wed 8-7, Fri 8-5
Restriction: Non-circulating of rare bks, Open to fac, students & qualified researchers, Open to pub for ref & circ; with some limitations, Open to students, fac, staff & alumni
Friends of the Library Group

SHOW LOW

P SHOW LOW PUBLIC LIBRARY, 181 N Ninth St, 85901. SAN 300-4287. Tel: 928-532-4070. FAX: 928-532-4079. E-mail: library@showlowaz.gov. Web Site: www.showlowaz.gov/library. *Libr Serv Mgr,* Lisa Lewis; Tel: 928-532-4073, E-mail: llewis@showlowaz.gov; *Info Spec,* Don Fogle; Tel: 928-532-4065, E-mail: dfogle@showlowaz.gov; *Info Spec,* Heather Hatcher; Tel: 928-532-4075, E-mail: hhatcher@showlowaz.gov; Staff 9 (MLS 1, Non-MLS 8)
Pop 15,000; Circ 129,000
Library Holdings: CDs 1,460; DVDs 2,245; Electronic Media & Resources 40; High Interest/Low Vocabulary Bk Vols 200; Bk Titles 40,324; Per Subs 90
Special Collections: Adult Basic Education Coll
Subject Interests: Arizona
Automation Activity & Vendor Info: (Cataloging) SirsiDynix; (Circulation) SirsiDynix; (ILL) OCLC Connexion; (OPAC) SirsiDynix; (Serials) DEMCO
Wireless access
Mem of Navajo County Library System
Open Mon, Tues, Thurs & Fri 9-6, Wed 9-4, Sat 10-5
Friends of the Library Group

SIERRA VISTA

P SIERRA VISTA PUBLIC LIBRARY*, 2600 E Tacoma, 85635. SAN 300-4309. Tel: 520-458-4225. Administration Tel: 520-458-4239. FAX: 520-458-5377. E-mail: library@sierravistaaz.gov. Web Site: www.sierravistaaz.gov/city-departments/Library. *Libr Mgr,* Emily Scherrer; E-mail: Emily.Scherrer@SierraVistaAZ.gov; *Librn,* Susan Abend; E-mail: Susan.Abend@sierravistaaz.gov; *Spec,* Debra Chatham; E-mail: Debra.Chatham@SierraVistaAZ.gov; *Youth Serv Librn,* Sierra Baril-Lash; E-mail: Sierra.Baril@sierravistaaz.gov; Staff 4 (MLS 4)
Founded 1959. Pop 45,000; Circ 310,000
Library Holdings: Bk Vols 105,000; Per Subs 180
Special Collections: Arizona Coll. Oral History
Automation Activity & Vendor Info: (Cataloging) OCLC; (Circulation) SirsiDynix-WorkFlows; (ILL) OCLC; (OPAC) SirsiDynix-iBistro
Wireless access
Mem of Cochise County Library District
Special Services for the Blind - Talking bks
Open Mon-Thurs 10-7, Fri 10-6, Sat 10-4
Friends of the Library Group

SNOWFLAKE

P SNOWFLAKE-TAYLOR PUBLIC LIBRARY*, 418 S Fourth W, 85937. SAN 321-7779. Tel: 928-536-7103, Ext 245. FAX: 928-536-3057. E-mail: library@ci.snowflake.az.us. Web Site: www.ci.snowflake.az.us/departments/library. *Librn,* Cathryn McDowell; E-mail: librarian@ci.snowflake.az.us; Staff 3 (Non-MLS 3)
Founded 1965. Pop 8,000; Circ 60,000
Library Holdings: Audiobooks 1,450; Bk Vols 39,000; Per Subs 36
Special Collections: Snowflake Herald, 1903-1914
Automation Activity & Vendor Info: (Cataloging) SirsiDynix; (Circulation) SirsiDynix; (ILL) OCLC Online; (OPAC) SirsiDynix
Wireless access
Mem of Navajo County Library System
Partic in Navajo County Libr District
Special Services for the Deaf - Closed caption videos
Special Services for the Blind - Assistive/Adapted tech devices, equip & products
Open Tues-Thurs 10-6, Fri 11-5, Sat 10-2
Friends of the Library Group

SOMERTON

P COCOPAH TRIBAL LIBRARY*, 14250 S Ave 1, 85350. (Mail add: 14515 S Veterans Dr, 85350), SAN 376-3196. Tel: 928-627-8026. FAX: 928-627-2510. E-mail: cococvt@cocopah.com. Web Site: www.cocopah.com. *Dir,* Diana Navarro; E-mail: navarrod@cocopah.com
Library Holdings: Bk Titles 6,300; Per Subs 14
Open Mon-Fri 8-5

SUN CITY WEST

S R H JOHNSON LIBRARY, 13801 W Meeker Blvd, 85375. SAN 321-110X. Tel: 623-544-6130. Administration Tel: 623-544-6160. FAX: 623-544-6131. Web Site: suncitywest.com/library. *Dir,* Tracy Skousen; E-mail: tracy.skousen@suncitywest.com; Staff 6 (Non-MLS 6)
Founded 1979
Library Holdings: Audiobooks 1,600; AV Mats 12,900; DVDs 11,569; Large Print Bks 8,900; Bk Titles 39,000; Bk Vols 42,000; Per Subs 100
Special Collections: Southwest Coll
Subject Interests: Arizona
Automation Activity & Vendor Info: (Circulation) Follett Software
Wireless access
Restriction: Residents only
Friends of the Library Group

SUPERIOR

P SUPERIOR PUBLIC LIBRARY*, 99 Kellner Ave, 85273. SAN 300-435X. Tel: 520-689-2327. FAX: 520-689-5809. Web Site: superiorpublib.wordpress.com. *Dir,* Josie Campos; E-mail: josie.campos@pinalcountyaz.gov
Founded 1952. Pop 3,400; Circ 24,000
Library Holdings: Bk Titles 12,000; Bk Vols 12,300; Per Subs 35
Automation Activity & Vendor Info: (Acquisitions) Horizon
Wireless access
Publications: Library News (Monthly newsletter)
Mem of Pinal County Library District
Open Mon-Thurs 12-6
Friends of the Library Group

TEMPE

S AMERICAN FEDERATION OF ASTROLOGERS, INC LIBRARY, 6535 S Rural Rd, 85283-3746. SAN 300-4368. Tel: 480-838-1751. Toll Free Tel: 888-301-7630. E-mail: info@astrologers.com. Web Site: www.astrologers.com/about/afa-library. *Exec Secy,* Celeste Nash-Weninger
Founded 1938
Library Holdings: Bk Vols 3,000
Special Collections: Various Out-of-Print Publications (1600-1800)
Publications: Today's Astrologer (Monthly)
Restriction: Private libr

S ARIZONA HISTORICAL SOCIETY MUSEUM LIBRARY & ARCHIVES, 1300 N College Ave, 85281. SAN 321-8813. Tel: 480-387-5355. E-mail: ahsreference@azhs.gov. Web Site: arizonahistoricalsociety.org/research/library-archives. *VPres, Archives & Libr,* Rebekah Tabah-Percival; E-mail: rtabah@azhs.gov; Staff 3 (MLS 1, Non-MLS 2)
Founded 1973
Library Holdings: Bk Titles 3,500
Special Collections: A J Bayless Coll; Arizona Homebuilders Association Coll; Arizona Quilt Project; Betty Puckle Photo Coll; Charles A Stauffer Coll; Elton Kunselman Photo Coll; George M Aurelius Theater Coll; Laura Danieli Coll; LeForgee Photo Coll; Lescher-Mahoney Architectural Drawing Coll; Orpheus Men's Choir Coll; Papago Park German POW Camp Photo Coll; Phoenix History Project Coll; Phoenix Streetcar Company; Photograph Coll; Robert Isbell Coll; Smarthwaite Family Coll; Snell Family Papers. Oral History
Subject Interests: Cent Ariz in 20th Century, Phoenix
Wireless access
Restriction: Non-circulating to the pub, Open by appt only

CL ARIZONA STATE UNIVERSITY, COLLEGE OF LAW*, Ross-Blakley Law Library, 1102 S McAllister Ave, 85281. (Mail add: PO Box 877806, 85287-7806), SAN 330-714X. Tel: 480-965-6144. Reference Tel: 480-965-7161. FAX: 480-965-4283. Web Site: lawlib.asu.edu. *Asst Dean, Libr Dir,* Beth DiFelice; Tel: 480-965-4871, E-mail: beth.difelice@asu.edu; *Ref Librn,* Andrea Gass; Tel: 480-965-2521, E-mail: algass@asu.edu; *Digital Serv Librn,* Leslie Pardo; Tel: 480-965-3579, E-mail: leslie.pardo@asu.edu. Subject Specialists: *Legal res,* Beth DiFelice; Staff 16 (MLS 5, Non-MLS 11)
Founded 1966. Enrl 600; Fac 50; Highest Degree: Doctorate
Library Holdings: AV Mats 651; Bk Vols 406,853; Per Subs 3,901
Special Collections: State Document Depository; US Document Depository
Automation Activity & Vendor Info: (Course Reserve) Innovative Interfaces, Inc; (ILL) OCLC Online; (OPAC) Innovative Interfaces, Inc
Wireless access
Partic in OCLC Online Computer Library Center, Inc
Restriction: 24-hr pass syst for students only, Access at librarian's discretion, Access for corporate affiliates, Authorized patrons, Authorized personnel only, Authorized scholars by appt, Badge access after hrs, Borrowing privileges limited to anthropology fac & libr staff, Borrowing privileges limited to fac & registered students, Borrowing requests are handled by ILL, By permission only, Circ limited, Circ privileges for students & alumni only, Circ to mem only, Circ to mil employees only, Circulates for staff only, Clients only, Closed stack, Co libr, Employee & client use only, Teacher & adminr only

C ARIZONA STATE UNIVERSITY LIBRARIES, Hayden Library, 300 E Orange Mall Dr, 85287. (Mail add: PO Box 871006, 85287-1006), SAN 330-7050. Tel: 480-965-3417. Circulation Tel: 480-965-3605. Interlibrary Loan Service Tel: 480-965-3282. FAX: 480-965-9169. Web Site: lib.asu.edu. *Univ Librn,* James J O'Donnell; E-mail: jod@asu.edu; *Asst Dir, Learning Services,* Daphne Gill; Tel: 480-965-2653, E-mail: daphne.gill@asu.edu; Staff 197.5 (MLS 68, Non-MLS 129.5)
Founded 1891. Enrl 72,254; Fac 2,513; Highest Degree: Doctorate
Library Holdings: e-books 1,641,439; e-journals 180,918; Microforms 7,700,000; Bk Vols 3,584,693; Per Subs 65,586
Special Collections: Alberto Pradeau Archives; American Indian, Arizona & Southwest History; Barry Goldwater Archives; Carl Hayden Archives; Jimmy Starr Archives; John R Rhodes Archives; Mexican Numismatics; Solar Energy Archives; Spain; Theatre for Youth Coll; Victorian Literature including Pre-Raphaelites & New; William Burroughs Archives. US Document Depository
Automation Activity & Vendor Info: (Acquisitions) Innovative Interfaces, Inc; (Circulation) Innovative Interfaces, Inc; (Serials) Innovative Interfaces, Inc
Wireless access
Function: Res libr
Publications: Bibliographies (Newsletter)
Partic in Amigos Library Services, Inc; Association of Research Libraries; Center for Research Libraries; Greater Western Library Alliance
Friends of the Library Group

Departmental Libraries:

BIBLIOGRAPHIC & METADATA SERVICES, PO Box 871006, 85287-1006. *Head, Bibliog & Metadata Serv,* Position Currently Open
Automation Activity & Vendor Info: (Acquisitions) Innovative Interfaces, Inc; (Cataloging) Innovative Interfaces, Inc; (OPAC) Innovative Interfaces, Inc; (Serials) Innovative Interfaces, Inc

COLLECTIONS & SCHOLARLY COMMUNICATION, PO Box 871006, 85287-1006. Tel: 480-727-6301. *Chief Officer, Coll Serv, Scholarly Communications Officer,* Jeanne Richardson; Tel: 480-965-5345, E-mail: jeanne.richardson@asu.edu; Staff 10.5 (MLS 7, Non-MLS 3.5)
Library Holdings: Audiobooks 67,179; e-books 325,320; Microforms 7,614,192; Bk Vols 4,393,156; Per Subs 95,515
Open Mon-Fri 8-5

DESIGN & FINE ARTS, 810 S Forest Mall, CDN 153, 85287. (Mail add: PO Box 871006, 85287-1006). Tel: 480-965-6400. FAX: 480-727-6965. Web Site: lib.asu.edu/locations/design. *Mgr, Access Serv,* Karina Wilhem; Tel: 480-727-4808, E-mail: karina.welhelm@asu.edu; Staff 3 (MLS 1, Non-MLS 2)
Library Holdings: Bk Vols 50,000
Subject Interests: Archit, Indust design, Interior design, Landscape archit, Urban planning

DOWNTOWN PHOENIX CAMPUS, UCENT Lower Level, Ste L1-61, 411 N Central Ave, Phoenix, 85004-2115. Tel: 602-496-0300. FAX: 602-496-0312. Web Site: lib.asu.edu/downtown. *Mgr, Learning Serv,* Kathleen M Kennedy; Tel: 602-496-0318, E-mail: kathleen.m.kennedy@asu.edu; Staff 10 (MLS 4, Non-MLS 6)
Jul 2012-Jun 2013. Mats Exp $135,000, Books $35,000, Electronic Ref Mat (Incl. Access Fees) $100,000
Library Holdings: e-journals 50,000; Bk Titles 25,000
Automation Activity & Vendor Info: (Acquisitions) Innovative Interfaces, Inc; (Cataloging) Innovative Interfaces, Inc; (Circulation) Innovative Interfaces, Inc
Open Mon-Thurs 7am-10pm, Fri 7-7, Sat 10-6, Sun Noon-8
Friends of the Library Group

FLETCHER LIBRARY, 4701 W Thunderbird Rd, Glendale, 85306. (Mail add: PO Box 37100, Phoenix, 85069-7100), SAN 323-7788. Tel: 602-543-8502. Web Site: lib.asu.edu/fletcher. *Mgr, Learning Serv,* Shane Hunt; Tel: 602-543-8553, E-mail: shane.hunt@asu.edu; Staff 11 (MLS 3, Non-MLS 8)
Founded 1984. Enrl 13,504; Fac 221; Highest Degree: Doctorate
Library Holdings: Bk Vols 400,000
Automation Activity & Vendor Info: (Acquisitions) Innovative Interfaces, Inc; (Circulation) Innovative Interfaces, Inc; (Course Reserve) Innovative Interfaces, Inc; (ILL) Innovative Interfaces, Inc; (Media Booking) Innovative Interfaces, Inc; (OPAC) Innovative Interfaces, Inc; (Serials) Innovative Interfaces, Inc
Partic in Ariz Univ Librs Coun; Greater Western Library Alliance
Open Mon-Thurs 7:30am-11pm, Fri 7:30am-8pm, Sat & Sun Noon-8

MUSIC, Music Bldg, 50 E Gammage Pk, 85287. (Mail add: PO Box 870505, 85287-0505), SAN 330-7174. Tel: 480-965-3513. Web Site: lib.asu.edu/music. *Mgr, Learning Serv,* Linda Elsasser; Tel: 480-965-9596, E-mail: linda.elsasser@asu.edu; Staff 3 (MLS 1, Non-MLS 2)
Highest Degree: Doctorate
Library Holdings: CDs 11,871; DVDs 863; Microforms 1,620; Music Scores 75,039; Bk Vols 30,648; Per Subs 244; Videos 937
Open Mon-Thurs 8-8, Fri 8-5, Sat 1-5, Sun 1-8

DANIEL E NOBLE SCIENCE & ENGINEERING LIBRARY, 601 E Tyler Mall, 85287. (Mail add: PO Box 871006, 85287-1006), SAN 330-7123. Tel: 480-965-2600. Web Site: lib.asu.edu/noble. *Mgr, Learning Serv,* Stephen Arougheti; Tel: 480-965-7564, E-mail: stephen.arougheti@asu.edu; Staff 20 (MLS 8, Non-MLS 12)
Library Holdings: Bk Vols 425,000
Special Collections: Map Coll, aerial photos, sheet maps
Open Mon-Thurs 7am-Midnight, Fri 7am-9pm, Sat 10-9, Sun 10am-Midnight

POLYTECHNIC CAMPUS, Academic Ctr, Lower Level, 5988 S Backus Mall, Mesa, 85212. Tel: 480-727-1037. FAX: 480-727-1077. Web Site: lib.asu.edu/polytechnic. *Mgr, Learning Serv,* Laura Cox; Tel: 480-727-1330, E-mail: laura.m.cox.1@asu.edu; *Librn,* Jeanette Mueller-Alexander; Tel: 480-965-3084, E-mail: jenny.muller-alexander@asu.edu; Staff 8.5 (MLS 3, Non-MLS 5.5)
Founded 1996. Enrl 4,877; Highest Degree: Doctorate
Automation Activity & Vendor Info: (Cataloging) Innovative Interfaces, Inc; (Circulation) Innovative Interfaces, Inc; (OPAC) Innovative Interfaces, Inc
Open Mon-Thurs 8am-Midnight, Fri 8am-9pm, Sat 11-7, Sun Noon-Midnight

J RIO SALADO COLLEGE*, 2323 W 14th St, 85281. SAN 321-4745. Tel: 480-517-8424. Toll Free Tel: 866-670-8420. FAX: 480-517-8449. Web Site: www.riosalado.edu/library. *Fac Chair, Libr Serv,* Karen Docherty; Tel: 480-517-8432, E-mail: karen.docherty@riosalado.edu; *Instruction Librn,* Sarah Stohr; Tel: 480-517-8281, E-mail: sarah.stohr@riosalado.edu; *Supvr, Libr Access Serv,* Kim Watson; Tel: 480-517-8428, E-mail: kimberly.watson@riosalado.edu; *Instrul Coordr, Libr Serv,* Kirstin Thomas; Tel: 480-517-8423, E-mail: kirstin.thomas@riosalado.edu; Staff 7 (MLS 5, Non-MLS 2)
Founded 1982. Enrl 51,840; Fac 1,000; Highest Degree: Associate
Automation Activity & Vendor Info: (Acquisitions) SirsiDynix; (Cataloging) SirsiDynix; (Circulation) SirsiDynix; (Course Reserve) SirsiDynix; (OPAC) SirsiDynix; (Serials) SirsiDynix
Wireless access
Function: 24/7 Electronic res, 24/7 Online cat
Open Mon-Thurs 8-5, Fri 9-2

S SALT RIVER PROJECT LIBRARY*, ISB/PAB Library, 1600 N Priest Dr, 85281-1213. Tel: 602-236-5676. FAX: 602-629-8585. E-mail: isblib@srpnet.com. *Librn,* Cathy Large; Tel: 602-236-2259, Fax: 602-236-2664, E-mail: cathy.large@srpnet.com; Staff 2 (MLS 1, Non-MLS 1)
Founded 1958
Library Holdings: Bk Titles 22,000; Per Subs 115
Special Collections: Career Resources
Subject Interests: Bus & mgt, Computers, Electric utilities, Engr, Info tech, Utilities industry, Water
Automation Activity & Vendor Info: (Acquisitions) SydneyPlus; (Cataloging) SydneyPlus; (Circulation) SydneyPlus; (ILL) OCLC; (OPAC) SydneyPlus; (Serials) SydneyPlus
Wireless access
Function: For res purposes, ILL available, Photocopying/Printing, Telephone ref
Restriction: Co libr

CM SOUTHWEST COLLEGE OF NATUROPATHIC MEDICINE & HEALTH SCIENCES LIBRARY, 2140 E Broadway Rd, 85282-1751. Tel: 480-222-9247. Administration Tel: 480-222-9278. FAX: 480-222-9447. E-mail: library@scnm.edu. Web Site: my.scnm.edu/ICS/Library.
Founded 1996. Enrl 530; Fac 50; Highest Degree: Doctorate
Library Holdings: Bk Titles 6,500; Per Subs 40
Special Collections: Randolph Environmental Medicine Coll
Subject Interests: Alternative med, Health, Wellness
Automation Activity & Vendor Info: (Cataloging) EOS International; (Circulation) EOS International; (OPAC) EOS International; (Serials) EOS International
Wireless access
Function: 24/7 Electronic res, 24/7 Online cat
Partic in Arizona Health Information Network; Cent Ariz Biomed Librns; Medical Library Group of Southern California & Arizona
Open Mon-Fri 8-5
Friends of the Library Group

P TEMPE PUBLIC LIBRARY*, 3500 S Rural Rd, 85282. SAN 300-4406. Tel: 480-350-5500. FAX: 480-350-5544. Web Site: www.tempe.gov/library. *Libr Dir,* Katherine Husser; Tel: 480-350-5237, E-mail: katherine_husser@tempe.gov; *Tech Serv Mgr,* Kathy Schoepe; Tel: 480-350-5540; *Libr Supvr,* Micah Corporaal; Tel: 480-350-5554, E-mail: micah_corporaal@tempe.gov; *Adult Serv, Libr Supvr,* Katie O'Connor; Tel: 480-350-5557, E-mail: kathleen_oconnor@tempe.gov; *Coll Supvr,* McKay Wellikson; Tel: 480-350-5508, E-mail: mckay_wellikson@gmail.com; Staff 15 (MLS 15)
Founded 1935. Pop 169,712; Circ 175,578
Jul 2016-Jun 2017 Income $3,560,664, City $3,560,664. Mats Exp $418,800
Automation Activity & Vendor Info: (Acquisitions) Innovative Interfaces, Inc; (Cataloging) Innovative Interfaces, Inc; (Circulation) Innovative Interfaces, Inc; (OPAC) Innovative Interfaces, Inc; (Serials) Innovative Interfaces, Inc
Wireless access
Function: 24/7 Electronic res, 24/7 Online cat, Activity rm, Adult bk club, Adult literacy prog, After school storytime, Art exhibits, Audiobks on Playaways & MP3, Audiobks via web, AV serv, Bilingual assistance for Spanish patrons, Bk club(s), Bks on CD, Children's prog, Citizenship assistance, Computer training, Computers for patron use, Digital talking bks, Distance learning, Electronic databases & coll, Family literacy, Free DVD rentals, Homebound delivery serv, Homework prog, ILL available, Internet access, Life-long learning prog for all ages, Literacy & newcomer serv, Magazines, Meeting rooms, Museum passes, Music CDs, Online cat, Online info literacy tutorials on the web & in blackboard, Outreach serv, OverDrive digital audio bks, Photocopying/Printing, Prog for adults, Prog for children & young adult, Ref & res, Ref serv available, Spanish lang bks, Story hour, Study rm, Summer & winter reading prog, Summer reading prog, Teen prog, Telephone ref, Wheelchair accessible, Writing prog
Open Mon, Tues & Wed 9-8, Thurs, Fri & Sat 9-5, Sun 12-5
Friends of the Library Group

THATCHER

J EASTERN ARIZONA COLLEGE*, Alumni Library, 615 N Stadium Ave, 85552. SAN 300-4414. Tel: 928-428-8304. E-mail: library@eac.edu. Web Site: eac.libguides.com/libraryhome. *Dir, Libr Serv,* Kristen Becker; Tel: 928-428-8308, E-mail: kristen.becker@eac.edu; Staff 10 (MLS 1, Non-MLS 9)
Founded 1888. Enrl 5,710; Fac 237; Highest Degree: Associate
Library Holdings: AV Mats 391; e-books 253; Bk Titles 47,244; Bk Vols 51,063; Per Subs 64
Automation Activity & Vendor Info: (Acquisitions) Innovative Interfaces, Inc; (Cataloging) Innovative Interfaces, Inc; (Circulation) Innovative Interfaces, Inc; (Discovery) EBSCO Discovery Service; (OPAC) Innovative Interfaces, Inc
Wireless access
Open Mon-Thurs 7am-10pm, Fri 7-5, Sat 10-4, Sun 6pm-10pm; Mon-Thurs (Summer) 7-7, Fri 7-5

TOLLESON

P TOLLESON PUBLIC LIBRARY*, 9555 W Van Buren St, 85353. SAN 300-4422. Tel: 623-936-7111, Ext 2746. FAX: 623-936-9793. Web Site: www.tollesonaz.org. *Libr Mgr,* Kim Eckhoff; Tel: 623-936-2746, E-mail: keckhoff@tollesonaz.org; *Libr Coord,* Mark Robles; E-mail: mrobles@tollesonaz.org; *Libr Asst,* Lisa Gallegos; E-mail: lgallegos@tollesonaz.org; Staff 4 (Non-MLS 4)
Founded 1949. Pop 5,445; Circ 29,556
Library Holdings: Bks on Deafness & Sign Lang 10; CDs 100; DVDs 1,200; Bk Vols 23,000; Per Subs 40; Talking Bks 269
Special Collections: Prehistoric Arizona Indian Pottery, Kachinas & Artifacts; Spanish Language Materials; Young Adult Coll
Automation Activity & Vendor Info: (Acquisitions) Innovative Interfaces, Inc; (Cataloging) OCLC CatExpress; (Circulation) Innovative Interfaces, Inc; (OPAC) Innovative Interfaces, Inc
Wireless access
Function: 24/7 Electronic res, 24/7 Online cat, Adult bk club, Bilingual assistance for Spanish patrons, Bks on CD, Children's prog, Computers for patron use, Electronic databases & coll, Free DVD rentals, Internet access, Music CDs, Online cat, Photocopying/Printing, Preschool outreach, Prog for adults, Prog for children & young adult, Ref serv available, Spoken cassettes & CDs, Story hour, Summer reading prog, Tax forms, Telephone ref
Partic in OCLC Online Computer Library Center, Inc
Open Mon-Wed 9-7, Thurs & Fri 9-5, Sat 9-1

TOMBSTONE

P TOMBSTONE CITY LIBRARY*, 210 S Fourth St, 85638. (Mail add: PO Box 218, 85638-0218), SAN 300-4430. Tel: 520-457-3612. FAX: 520-457-3612. Web Site: cochiselibrary.org/client/en_US/tombstone#. *Libr Dir,* Mary Buchanan; E-mail: mary.buchanan@cityoftombstoneaz.gov; Staff 2 (Non-MLS 2)
Founded 1961
Library Holdings: Bk Vols 15,000
Subject Interests: Arizona
Mem of Cochise County Library District
Open Mon-Fri 8-12 & 1-5
Friends of the Library Group

TONTO BASIN

P TONTO BASIN PUBLIC LIBRARY*, 415 Old Hwy 188, 85553. (Mail add: PO Box 368, 85553-0368), SAN 376-7280. Tel: 928-479-2355. FAX: 928-479-2355. E-mail: tontobasinlibrary@gmail.com. Web Site: www.tontobasinlibrary.com. *Libr Mgr,* Kathy Womack
Founded 1983. Pop 1,424; Circ 38,000
Library Holdings: Bk Titles 15,000; Per Subs 2
Automation Activity & Vendor Info: (Cataloging) Innovative Interfaces, Inc; (Circulation) Innovative Interfaces, Inc; (OPAC) Innovative Interfaces, Inc
Wireless access
Mem of Gila County Library District
Open Mon-Fri 8-4

TSAILE

C DINE COLLEGE*, Kinyaa'aanii Charlie Benally Library, One Circle Dr, Rte 12, 86556. (Mail add: PO Box C26, 86556), SAN 300-4457. Tel: 928-724-6757. E-mail: library@dinecollege.edu. Web Site: library.dinecollege.edu. *Col Librn,* Herman Peterson; Tel: 928-724-6764; *Cat Librn,* Rosita Klee; *AV Tech, Per,* Mary Norcross; *Circ Tech,* Ruby Johnson
Founded 1969. Enrl 2,000; Fac 51
Library Holdings: Bk Vols 55,000; Per Subs 260
Special Collections: North American Indians (Moses Donner Coll), bks & film; RC German Coll
Wireless access
Open Mon-Thurs (Fall-Spring) 8am-9pm, Fri 8-4, Sun 5pm-9pm; Mon-Thurs (Summer) 8-7, Fri 8-4

TUCSON

S ARIZONA DEPARTMENT OF CORRECTIONS - ADULT INSTITUTIONS*, Arizona State Prison Complex - Tucson Library, 10000 S Wilmot Rd, 85734. (Mail add: PO Box 24400, 85734-4400). Tel: 520-574-0024, Ext 37919. Web Site: corrections.az.gov/location/101/tucson. *Head Librn,* Lisa Klukosky; E-mail: lklukosky@azadc.gov; *Librn,* Renee Hermsen; *Librn,* Jon Meade; *Librn,* Jeffery St Clair
Library Holdings: Bk Vols 46,225
Open Tues, Wed & Fri 7-3

S ARIZONA GEOLOGICAL SURVEY AT UNIVERSITY OF ARIZONA, Reference Library, 1955 E Sixth St, 85721. (Mail add: PO Box 210284, 85721), SAN 370-338X. Web Site: repository.azgs.az.gov, www.azgs.arizona.edu. *Library Contact,* Michael Conway; Tel: 520-621-2352, E-mail: fmconway@arizona.edu
Library Holdings: Bk Titles 500; Bk Vols 1,000
Special Collections: Arizona Theses & Dissertations; Mine Coll. US Document Depository
Subject Interests: Geol
Wireless access
Open Mon-Fri 8-5
Restriction: Open to pub for ref only

S ARIZONA HISTORICAL SOCIETY*, Library Archives-Southern Arizona Division, 949 E Second St, 85719. SAN 300-449X. Tel: 520-617-1157. FAX: 520-629-8966. E-mail: ahsreference@azhs.gov. Web Site: arizonahistoricalsociety.org/research/library-archives. *Coll, VPres, Archives & Libr,* Rebekah Tabah-Percival; E-mail: rtabah@azhs.gov; *Archivist, Librn,* Rachel Black; Tel: 520-617-1152, E-mail: rblack@azhs.gov; *Archivist, Librn,* Perri Pyle; Tel: 520-617-1147, E-mail: ppyle@azhs.gov; *Colls Mgr,* Trish Norman; Tel: 520-617-1179, E-mail: pnorman@azhs.gov; Staff 3 (MLS 3)
Founded 1884
Library Holdings: Microforms 9,000; Bk Titles 50,000; Per Subs 40
Subject Interests: Arizona, Mexico
Automation Activity & Vendor Info: (Acquisitions) Ex Libris Group; (Cataloging) Ex Libris Group; (Media Booking) Ex Libris Group; (OPAC) Ex Libris Group
Wireless access
Function: For res purposes, Mail & tel request accepted, Online cat, Online ref, Outreach serv, Ref & res, Ref serv available, Res libr, Res performed for a fee
Open Mon-Fri 9-4
Restriction: Non-circulating

S ARIZONA-SONORA DESERT MUSEUM LIBRARY*, 2021 N Kinney Rd, 85743. SAN 330-7204. Tel: 520-883-1380. FAX: 520-883-2500. E-mail: info@desertmuseum.org. Web Site: www.desertmuseum.org/about/archives. *Archivist, Librn,* Peggy Larson; E-mail: plarson@desertmuseum.org; Staff 1 (MLS 1)
Founded 1952
Library Holdings: AV Mats 200; Bk Titles 7,000; Per Subs 58
Special Collections: Natural History Coll, slides
Subject Interests: Botany, Ecology, Geol, Natural hist, SW region, Zoology
Automation Activity & Vendor Info: (Cataloging) LibraryWorld, Inc; (Circulation) LibraryWorld, Inc; (Course Reserve) LibraryWorld, Inc; (ILL) LibraryWorld, Inc; (Media Booking) LibraryWorld, Inc; (OPAC) LibraryWorld, Inc
Function: Res libr
Publications: ASDM News; Sonorensis
Restriction: Open by appt only

S ARIZONA STATE MUSEUM LIBRARY, University of Arizona, 1013 E University Blvd, 85721-0026. (Mail add: PO Box 210026, 85721-0026), SAN 300-4678. Tel: 520-621-4695. FAX: 520-621-2976. Web Site: www.statemuseum.arizona.edu. *Head Librn,* Molly Stothert-Maurer; E-mail: stothert@email.arizona.edu; Staff 2 (MLS 2)
Founded 1957
Library Holdings: Bk Vols 50,000; Per Subs 30
Subject Interests: Anthrop, Archaeology, Museology, SW
Automation Activity & Vendor Info: (Acquisitions) Ex Libris Group; (Cataloging) Ex Libris Group; (Circulation) Ex Libris Group; (OPAC) Ex Libris Group
Wireless access
Open Tues-Thurs 11-4
Restriction: Non-circulating

S ARIZONA STATE SCHOOLS FOR THE DEAF & THE BLIND LIBRARY*, 1200 W Speedway, 85745. (Mail add: PO Box 85000, 85754-5000), SAN 300-4503. Tel: 520-770-3671. Web Site: asdb.az.gov/services/campus-services/library. *Librn,* Dennis Cobb; E-mail: dennis.cobb@asdb.az.gov; Staff 2 (MLS 1, Non-MLS 1)
Library Holdings: Bk Vols 30,000; Per Subs 25
Special Collections: Braille; Deaf & Visually Impaired (Professional Coll); Deaf Studies; Described & Captioned Media Accessible Learning Center; Descriptive Videos; Parent Lending Library, Shared Reading Project
Subject Interests: Regional
Automation Activity & Vendor Info: (Cataloging) Follett Software; (Circulation) Follett Software; (OPAC) Follett Software
Wireless access
Special Services for the Deaf - Am sign lang & deaf culture; Bks on deafness & sign lang; Closed caption videos; Coll on deaf educ; Deaf publ; Interpreter on staff; Staff with knowledge of sign lang; Video relay services
Special Services for the Blind - Descriptive video serv (DVS); Digital talking bk machines; Large print bks; ZoomText magnification & reading software

M CARONDELET HEALTH NETWORK MEDICAL LIBRARIES*, Bruce Cole Memorial Library, Saint Joseph's Hospital, 350 N Wilmot Rd, 1st Flr Admin Hallway, 85711. SAN 328-588X. Tel: 520-873-3925. FAX: 520-873-6554. E-mail: CHNMedicalLibrary@carondelet.org. Web Site: www.carondelet.org/our-locations/st-josephs. *Med Librn,* Lindsey Miller; E-mail: lindsey.miller@carondelet.org
Library Holdings: Bk Vols 800
Subject Interests: Ophthalmology
Wireless access
Partic in Arizona Health Information Network; Pacific Southwest Regional Medical Library
Restriction: Not open to pub

Branches:

RALPH HENRY FULLER MEDICAL LIBRARY, St Mary's Hospital, 1601 W St Mary's Rd, 2nd Flr Central, 85745, SAN 300-4600. Tel: 520-872-4974. FAX: 520-872-4936. *Med Librn,* Michelle Bureau
Founded 1937
Library Holdings: e-books 240; e-journals 900; Bk Titles 340; Per Subs 25
Subject Interests: Allied health, Med, Nursing
Publications: Serials list (annual)
Restriction: Not open to pub

DEPARTMENT OF VETERANS AFFAIRS

GM PATIENT EDUCATION RESOURCE CENTER*, 3601 S Sixth Ave, 7-14A, 85723. Tel: 520-792-1450, Ext 6516. FAX: 520-629-4638. *Librn,* Sharon Hammond
Library Holdings: Bk Vols 250
Open Mon-Fri 8-4:30

GM SOUTHERN ARIZONA VA HEALTHCARE SYSTEM*, 3601 S Sixth Ave, 85723, SAN 300-4686. Tel: 520-629-1836. FAX: 520-629-4638. E-mail: tucson.library@va.gov. *Librn,* Lynn Flance; Staff 1 (MLS 1)
Library Holdings: Bk Vols 1,400; Per Subs 200
Subject Interests: Med, Nursing, Psychiat, Psychol
Partic in Pacific Southwest Regional Medical Library
Open Mon-Fri 8-4:30

S NATIONAL PARK SERVICE*, Western Archeological & Conservation Center Library, 255 N Commerce Park Loop, 85745. SAN 300-4570. Tel: 520-791-6416. FAX: 520-791-6465. Web Site: www.nps.gov/orgs/1260/library.htm. *Prog Mgr,* Tef Rodeffer; E-mail: tef_rodeffer@nps.gov
Founded 1952
Library Holdings: Bk Titles 14,000; Per Subs 40
Special Collections: Archives of Archeological Records of Southwestern US; Stabilization & Environmental Impact Statements; Unpublished Reports & Manuscripts on Archaeological Excavations
Subject Interests: Anthrop, Natural res
Automation Activity & Vendor Info: (Cataloging) Ex Libris Group; (Serials) EBSCO Online
Partic in OCLC Online Computer Library Center, Inc
Restriction: Open by appt only, Staff use only

J PIMA COMMUNITY COLLEGE*, West Campus Library, 2202 W Anklam Rd, 85709-0001. SAN 330-7328. Tel: 520-206-6821. FAX: 520-206-3059. Web Site: www.pima.edu/current-students/library. *Fac Librn,* Sandra Ley; E-mail: sjley@pima.edu; Staff 4 (MLS 3, Non-MLS 1)
Founded 1970. Enrl 12,500; Fac 203; Highest Degree: Associate
Library Holdings: Bk Vols 165,000; Per Subs 550
Automation Activity & Vendor Info: (Acquisitions) Innovative Interfaces, Inc; (Circulation) Innovative Interfaces, Inc; (Serials) Innovative Interfaces, Inc
Wireless access
Special Services for the Deaf - Closed caption videos; Deaf publ; Videos & decoder
Special Services for the Blind - Assistive/Adapted tech devices, equip & products; Computer with voice synthesizer for visually impaired persons
Open Mon-Thurs 8-8, Fri 8-5, Sat 9-1

Departmental Libraries:

DESERT VISTA, 5901 S Calle Santa Cruz, 85709-6055, SAN 373-0069. Tel: 520-206-5095. FAX: 520-206-5090. *Dir,* Antonio Arroyo; Tel: 520-206-5068, E-mail: antonio.arroyo@pima.edu
Library Holdings: Bk Titles 18,017; Per Subs 145
Open Mon-Thurs 8am-9pm, Fri 8-5, Sat 9-3

DISTRICT LIBRARY SERVICES, 4905B E Broadway Blvd, 85709-1010, SAN 374-8189. Tel: 520-206-4607. FAX: 520-206-4890. *Dir,* Michael Hanson; Tel: 520-206-4608, E-mail: mhanson6@pima.edu; Staff 9 (MLS 2, Non-MLS 7)
Founded 1969. Enrl 20,000; Fac 363; Highest Degree: Associate
Function: Doc delivery serv, ILL available
Partic in OCLC Online Computer Library Center, Inc
Restriction: Open to pub for ref & circ; with some limitations, Open to students, fac & staff, Residents only

DOWNTOWN, 1255 N Stone Ave, 85709-3035, SAN 330-7352. Tel: 520-206-7267. FAX: 520-206-7217. *Dir,* Theresa Stanley; Tel: 520-206-7245; Staff 8 (MLS 4, Non-MLS 4)
Founded 1978. Enrl 4,000; Fac 88; Highest Degree: Associate
Library Holdings: Bk Titles 22,829; Bk Vols 24,764; Per Subs 162
Subject Interests: Automotive engr, Graphic arts
Open Mon-Thurs 8am-9pm, Fri 8-5, Sat 9-3

EAST, 8181 E Irvington Rd, 85709-4000, SAN 330-7387. Tel: 520-206-7693. FAX: 520-206-7690. *Dir,* Charles Becker; E-mail: cbecker@pima.edu; *Librn,* Becky Moore; Staff 4 (MLS 2, Non-MLS 2)
Founded 1976. Enrl 2,070; Fac 40
Library Holdings: Bk Vols 29,000; Per Subs 63
Open Mon-Thurs 8am-9pm, Fri 8-5, Sat 9-3

G PIMA COUNTY JUVENILE COURT CENTER LIBRARY, 2225 E Ajo Way, 85713-6295. SAN 326-3266. Tel: 520-724-2082. *Librn,* Gwen Reid; E-mail: greid@sc.pima.gov; Staff 2 (MLS 1, Non-MLS 1)
Founded 1976
Jul 2020-Jun 2021. Mats Exp $2,012, Books $2,000, Per/Ser (Incl. Access Fees) $12
Library Holdings: CDs 5; DVDs 40; Bk Titles 1,500; Per Subs 19; Spec Interest Per Sub 10
Subject Interests: Child abuse, Juv delinquency, Juv justice, Mental disorders of children, Sexual abuse, Trauma
Function: Prof lending libr
Restriction: Staff use only

GL PIMA COUNTY LAW LIBRARY*, Superior Court Bldg, 110 W Congress, Rm 256, 85701-1317. SAN 300-4597. Tel: 520-724-8456. FAX: 520-724-9122. E-mail: lawlibrary@sc.pima.gov. Web Site: www.sc.pima.gov/Default.aspx?tabid=60. *Dir,* Leanne Yoder; Staff 4 (MLS 1, Non-MLS 3)
Founded 1915
Library Holdings: Bk Titles 2,252; Bk Vols 35,000
Subject Interests: Law
Automation Activity & Vendor Info: (Cataloging) LibraryWorld, Inc; (Circulation) LibraryWorld, Inc; (OPAC) LibraryWorld, Inc; (Serials) LibraryWorld, Inc
Open Mon-Fri 8-5

P PIMA COUNTY PUBLIC LIBRARY*, 101 N Stone Ave, 85701. SAN 330-7417. Tel: 520-594-5600. FAX: 520-594-5621. Web Site: www.library.pima.gov. *Dir,* Amber Mathewson; E-mail: amber.mathewson@pima.gov; *Dep Dir, Pub Serv,* Karyn Prechtel; *Dep Dir, Support Serv,* Michelle Simon; *Coll Develop Mgr,* Richard DiRusso; Staff 104 (MLS 104)
Founded 1883. Pop 100,162; Circ 6,573,085
Library Holdings: CDs 43,222; DVDs 18,311; Bk Vols 1,427,983; Per Subs 3,403; Talking Bks 35,641; Videos 38,212
Special Collections: Arizona Coll; Business Coll; Southwestern Literature for Children; Spanish Language Coll. US Document Depository
Subject Interests: Arizona, Bus & mgt, Govt
Automation Activity & Vendor Info: (Acquisitions) Innovative Interfaces, Inc; (Cataloging) Innovative Interfaces, Inc; (Circulation) Innovative Interfaces, Inc; (OPAC) Innovative Interfaces, Inc
Wireless access
Partic in Association for Rural & Small Libraries; OCLC Online Computer Library Center, Inc
Special Services for the Deaf - Closed caption videos; TTY equip
Special Services for the Blind - Assistive/Adapted tech devices, equip & products; Computer with voice synthesizer for visually impaired persons
Open Mon-Fri 8-5
Friends of the Library Group

Branches: 26
WHEELER TAFT ABBETT SR LIBRARY, 7800 N Schisler Dr, 85743. Tel: 520-594-5200. Web Site: www.library.pima.gov/locations/ABB. *Br Mgr,* Em Lane
Library Holdings: Bk Vols 60,000
Open Mon-Thurs 10-8, Fri 10-5, Sat 9-5, Sun 1-5
CAVIGLIA-ARIVACA, 17050 W Arivaca Rd, Arivaca, 85601. (Mail add: PO Box 668, Arivaca, 85601), SAN 371-9685. Tel: 520-594-5235. FAX: 520-594-5236. Web Site: www.library.pima.gov/locations/ARI. *Br Mgr,* Jodi Ohlson
Library Holdings: Bk Vols 15,939
Open Tues 12-8, Wed-Sat 10-6
Friends of the Library Group
MARTHA COOPER LIBRARY, 1377 N Catalina Ave, 85712. Tel: 520-594-5315. Web Site: www.library.pima.gov/locations/MID. *Br Mgr,* Tara Foxx-Lupo
Library Holdings: Bk Vols 20,000
Open Mon-Thurs 10-8, Fri 10-5, Sat 9-5, Sun 1-5
DEWHIRST-CATALINA, 15631 N Oracle Rd, No 199, Catalina, 85739, SAN 371-9693. Tel: 520-594-5240. FAX: 520-594-5241. Web Site: www.library.pima.gov/locations/CAT. *Br Mgr,* Christine Dykgraaf
Library Holdings: Bk Vols 15,746
Open Mon, Wed & Thurs 10-6, Tues 9-6, Fri 10-5, Sat 9-5
QUINCIE DOUGLAS, 1585 E 36th St, 85713. Tel: 520-594-5335. FAX: 520-594-5336. Web Site: www.library.pima.gov/locations/QUI. *Br Mgr,* Marissa Alcorta
Open Mon-Thurs 10-8, Fri 10-5, Sat 9-5, Sun 1-5
DUSENBERRY-RIVER BRANCH, 5605 E River Rd, Ste 105, 85750, SAN 371-9707. Tel: 520-594-5345. FAX: 520-594-5346. Web Site: www.library.pima.gov/locations/RIV. *Br Mgr,* Dianna Thor
Library Holdings: Bk Vols 85,201
Open Mon-Thurs 10-8, Fri 10-5, Sat 9-5, Sun 1-5
ECKSTROM-COLUMBUS, 4350 E 22nd St, 85711, SAN 330-7476. Tel: 520-594-5285. FAX: 520-770-4102. Web Site: www.library.pima.gov/locations/COl. *Br Mgr,* Mary Sanchez
Library Holdings: Bk Vols 76,166
Open Mon-Thurs 10-8, Fri 10-5, Sat 9-5, Sun 1-5
EL PUEBLO, 101 W Irvington Rd, 85714, SAN 330-7743. Tel: 520-594-5250. FAX: 520-594-5251. Web Site: www.library.pima.gov/locations/ELP. *Br Mgr,* Anna Sanchez
Library Holdings: Bk Vols 18,524
Open Mon & Tues 9-6, Wed & Thurs 10-6, Fri 10-5
EL RIO, 1390 W Speedway Blvd, 85745, SAN 330-7778. Tel: 520-594-5245. FAX: 520-594-5246. Web Site: www.library.pima.gov/locations/ELR. *Br Mgr,* Emily Hunt
Library Holdings: Bk Vols 7,738
Open Mon & Tues 9-6, Wed & Thurs 10-6, Fri 10-5
FLOWING WELLS BRANCH, 1730 W Wetmore Rd, 85705. Tel: 520-594-5225. Web Site: www.library.pima.gov/locations/FLW. *Br Mgr,* Ingrid Trebisky
Library Holdings: Bk Vols 13,000
Open Mon-Thurs 10-8, Fri 10-5, Sat 9-5, Sun 1-5
HIMMEL PARK, 1035 N Treat Ave, 85716, SAN 330-7565. Tel: 520-594-5305. FAX: 520-594-5306. Web Site: www.library.pima.gov/locations/HIM. *Br Mgr,* Heather Ross
Library Holdings: Bk Vols 49,199
Open Mon-Thurs 10-8, Fri 10-5, Sat 9-5, Sun 1-5
JOYNER-GREEN VALLEY, 601 N La Canada Dr, Green Valley, 85614, SAN 330-7530. Tel: 520-594-5295. FAX: 520-770-4113. Web Site: www.library.pima.gov/locations/gvy. *Br Mgr,* Kathy Konecny
Library Holdings: Bk Vols 70,968
Open Mon-Thurs 9-7, Fri 10-5, Sat 9-5, Sun 1-5
Friends of the Library Group
KIRK-BEAR CANYON, 8959 E Tanque Verde Rd, 85749, SAN 371-9715. Tel: 520-594-5275. FAX: 520-594-5276. Web Site: www.library.pima.gov/locations/BCN. *Br Mgr,* Coni Weatherford
Library Holdings: Bk Vols 77,066
Open Mon-Thurs 10-8, Fri 10-5, Sat 9-5, Sun 1-5
Friends of the Library Group
SAM LENA-SOUTH TUCSON, 1607 S Sixth Ave, 85713, SAN 330-7867. Tel: 520-594-5265. FAX: 520-594-5266. Web Site: www.library.pima.gov/locations/STU. *Br Mgr,* Kelly Wilson
Library Holdings: Bk Vols 20,548
Open Mon-Thurs 9-6, Fri 10-5, Sat 9-5
MILLER-GOLF LINKS, 9640 E Golf Links Rd, 85730. Tel: 520-594-5355. FAX: 520-770-4104. Web Site: www.library.pima.gov/locations/GLF. *Br Mgr,* Mary McKinney
Library Holdings: Bk Vols 82,444
Open Mon-Thurs 10-8, Fri 10-5, Sat 9-5, Sun 1-5
MISSION, 3770 S Mission Rd, 85713, SAN 330-762X. Tel: 520-594-5325. FAX: 520-770-4106. Web Site: www.library.pima.gov/locations/MIS. *Br Mgr,* Margaret Wilkie
Library Holdings: Bk Vols 65,786
Open Mon-Thurs 10-8, Fri 10-5, Sat 9-5, Sun 1-5
MURPHY-WILMOT, 530 N Wilmot Rd, 85711, SAN 330-7719. Tel: 520-594-5420. FAX: 520-770-4110. Web Site: www.library.pima.gov/locations/WIL. *Br Mgr,* Daphne Daly
Library Holdings: Bk Vols 123,253
Open Mon-Thurs 10-8, Fri 10-5, Sat 9-5, Sun 1-5
NANINI, 7300 N Shannon Rd, 85741, SAN 330-7654. Tel: 520-594-5365. FAX: 520-594-5366. Web Site: www.library.pima.gov/locations/NAN. *Br Mgr,* Kristi Bradford
Library Holdings: Bk Vols 118,187
Open Mon-Thurs 10-8, Fri 10-5, Sat 9-5, Sun 1-5
ORO VALLEY PUBLIC LIBRARY, 1305 W Naranja Dr, Oro Valley, 85737. Tel: 520-594-5580. Web Site: www.library.pima.gov/locations/ORO. *Br Mgr,* Ruth Grant; Staff 28.5 (MLS 5.5, Non-MLS 23)
Founded 2002. Pop 41,000; Circ 305,766
Library Holdings: AV Mats 9,944; CDs 2,794; DVDs 1,792; Large Print Bks 1,849; Bk Vols 76,765; Per Subs 227; Talking Bks 2,751; Videos 2,607
Function: Adult bk club, Adult literacy prog, Chess club, Computer training, Digital talking bks, Electronic databases & coll, Homework prog, ILL available, Music CDs, Online ref, Photocopying/Printing, Prog for adults, Prog for children & young adult, Ref serv available, Senior computer classes, Spoken cassettes & CDs, Summer reading prog, Telephone ref, VHS videos, Wheelchair accessible
Open Mon-Thurs 9-7, Fri 10-5, Sat 9-5, Sun 1-5
Friends of the Library Group
SAHUARITA, 725 W Via Rancho Sahuarita, Sahuarita, 85629. Tel: 520-594-5490. Web Site: www.library.pima.gov/locations/SAH. *Br Mgr,* Tenecia Phillips
Open Tues-Thurs 10-6, Fri 10-5, Sat 9-5
Friends of the Library Group
SALAZAR-AJO BRANCH, 15 W Plaza St, Ste 179, Ajo, 85321, SAN 330-7441. Tel: 520-387-6075. FAX: 520-387-5345. Web Site: www.library.pima.gov/locations/AJO. *Br Mgr,* Richard Guinn
Library Holdings: Bk Vols 21,935
Open Mon-Thurs 10-6, Fri & Sat 9-5
SANTA ROSA BRANCH, 1075 S Tenth Ave, 85701. Tel: 520-594-5260. Web Site: www.library.pima.gov/locations/SRO. *Libr Serv Mgr,* Kate DeMeester
Open Mon 11-8, Tues 9-7, Wed & Thurs 9-6, Fri 10-5
SOUTHWEST, 6855 S Mark Rd, 85757. Tel: 520-594-5270. Web Site: www.library.pima.gov/locations/SWE. *Br Mgr,* Maureen Kearney
Library Holdings: Bk Vols 21,071
Open Mon & Tues 10-6, Wed & Thurs 10-7, Fri 10-5, Sat 9-5
JOEL D VALDEZ, 101 N Stone Ave, 85701, SAN 330-759X. Tel: 520-594-5500. FAX: 520-594-5501. Web Site: www.library.pima.gov/locations/mai. *Br Mgr,* Kate DeMeester
Library Holdings: Bk Vols 186,219
Open Mon-Thurs 9-6, Fri 9-5, Sat 10-5, Sun 1-5
Friends of the Library Group
VALENCIA, 202 W Valencia Rd, 85706, SAN 330-7689. Tel: 520-594-5390. FAX: 520-594-5391. Web Site: www.library.pima.gov/locations/VAL. *Br Mgr,* Paulina Aguirre-Clinch
Library Holdings: Bk Vols 83,633
Open Mon-Thurs 10-8, Fri 10-5, Sat 9-5, Sun 1-5
WOODS MEMORIAL BRANCH, 3455 N First Ave, 85719, SAN 330-7506. Tel: 520-594-5445. FAX: 520-770-4111. Web Site: www.library.pima.gov/locations/WDS. *Br Mgr,* Alina Rowe
Library Holdings: Bk Vols 99,013
Open Mon-Thurs 10-8, Fri 10-5, Sat 9-5, Sun 1-5
Bookmobiles: 1

SR SAINT MARK'S PRESBYTERIAN CHURCH LIBRARY, 3809 E Third St, 85716. SAN 373-3890. Tel: 520-325-1001. FAX: 520-327-4599. E-mail: stmarksaz@gmail.com. Web Site: stmarksaz.org.
Library Holdings: AV Mats 100; Bk Titles 2,500; Bk Vols 4,000
Subject Interests: Border studies, Counseling, Marriage, Philos, Relig, Theol
Open Sun 8-Noon

SR ST THOMAS MORE CATHOLIC NEWMAN CENTER*, 1615 E Second St, 85719. SAN 300-4589. Tel: 520-327-4665. FAX: 520-327-6559. E-mail: newman@uacatholic.org. Web Site: www.uacatholic.org. *Library Contact,* Sister Angelica Velez
Founded 1952
Library Holdings: Bk Vols 4,100; Per Subs 15
Subject Interests: Catholicism, Philos, Psychol, Theol
Wireless access
Open Mon-Fri 9am-11am

S SAN XAVIER LEARNING CENTER LIBRARY, 2018 W San Xavier Rd, 85746. SAN 377-0761. Tel: 520-807-8621. FAX: 520-807-8689. *Dir,* Victoria Hobbs; *Coordr,* Gertie Lopez; E-mail: glopez@waknet.org
Library Holdings: Bk Vols 2,000
Open Mon-Fri 8-5

R TEMPLE EMANUEL LIBRARY*, 225 N Country Club Rd, 85716. SAN 300-4619. Tel: 520-327-4501. FAX: 520-327-4504. Web Site: www.templeemanueltucson.org. *Exec Dir,* Donna Beyer; E-mail: dbeyer@tetucson.org
Founded 1910
Library Holdings: Bk Titles 9,500; Per Subs 10
Subject Interests: Fiction, Judaica (lit or hist of Jews), Relig orders

S TOHONO CHUL PARK LIBRARY, 7366 N Paseo del Norte, 85704. SAN 375-6572. Tel: 520-742-6455, Ext 228. FAX: 520-797-1213. Web Site: tohonochulpark.org. *Dir of Educ,* James Schubb; E-mail: jschaub@tohonochul.org
Founded 1985
Library Holdings: Bk Titles 600
Special Collections: Desert Plants (Boyce Thompson Arboretum); Journal of Arizona Archaeological & Historical Society; Journal of Arizona History
Function: Ref serv available, Res libr

S TUCSON ELECTRIC POWER CO LIBRARY*, 3950 E Irvington, 85714-2114. (Mail add: PO Box 711, 85702-0711), SAN 300-4635. Tel: 520-745-3318. FAX: 520-571-4019.
Founded 1974
Library Holdings: Bk Vols 1,100; Per Subs 325
Restriction: Staff use only

S TUCSON MUSEUM OF ART*, Research Library, 140 N Main Ave, 85701. SAN 300-466X. Tel: 520-624-2333. FAX: 520-624-7202. E-mail: library@tucsonmuseumofart.org. Web Site: www.tucsonmuseumofart.org/adults. *Chief Exec Officer,* Jeremy Mikolajczak; Staff 13 (MLS 1, Non-MLS 12)
Founded 1974
Library Holdings: AV Mats 25; DVDs 20; Bk Titles 13,000; Bk Vols 13,500; Per Subs 18; Videos 150
Special Collections: American Art (Lee & Pam Parry Coll); Archival Papers of Arizona Artists, including John Maul, Charles Clement & Ray Strang; Artists Biography Files; Dorcas Worsley Contemporary & Latin American Coll; Extensive Print & Slide Colls of Pre-Columbian, Art of the Americas, Art of the West, 20th Century European & American Art, Folk Art, Contemporary Art, Arts & Crafts Movement, African & Oceanic Art; Folk Art (Berta Wright Coll); Pre-Columbian Art (Frederick Pleasant Coll)
Subject Interests: Art hist, Art of the Americas, Contemporary art, Folk art, Modern art, Pre-Columbian art, Spanish colonial art
Automation Activity & Vendor Info: (OPAC) Innovative Interfaces, Inc; (Serials) EBSCO Online
Function: Archival coll, Outside serv via phone, mail, e-mail & web, Photocopying/Printing, Ref serv available, Res libr, Telephone ref
Open Tues-Thurs 10-3
Restriction: Circ limited
Friends of the Library Group

C UNIVERSITY OF ARIZONA LIBRARIES, Main Library, 1510 E University Blvd, 85721. (Mail add: PO Box 210055, 85721-0055), SAN 330-7891. Tel: 520-621-6442. Administration Tel: 520-621-5079. Administration FAX: 520-621-9733. E-mail: library@arizona.edu. Web Site: www.library.arizona.edu. *Dean, Univ Libr,* Shan C Sutton; Tel: 520-621-0717, E-mail: ssutton@arizona.edu; *Vice Dean,* Sarah Shreeves; E-mail: sshreeves@arizona.edu; *Assoc Dean,* Gerald Perry; Tel: 520-621-8132, E-mail: jerryperry@arizona.edu; *Asst Dean, Finance & Admin,* Octavio Fuentes; Tel: 520-621-2668, E-mail: octaviofuentes@arizona.edu; *Senior Info Resources Officer,* Michael Brewer; Tel: 520-307-2771, E-mail: brewerm@arizona.edu
Founded 1891. Enrl 46,932; Fac 3,266; Highest Degree: Doctorate
Library Holdings: e-books 2,300,000; e-journals 375,000; Electronic Media & Resources 900
Special Collections: American Vaudeville Museum Coll; Andrew Ellicott Douglass Papers; Arizona, Southwestern & Borderlands Photograph Coll; Bart Bok Coll; Charles Bukowski Papers; Documented Border Coll; Edward Abbey Papers; Edwin Francis Carpenter Papers; Historic Mexican & Mexican American Press; Levi Stewart Udall Papers; Morris K Udall Papers; Peter Wexler Papers; Raul Castro Papers; University of Arizona Campus Repository; University of Arizona History Coll, photog, rec, yearbks; University of Arizona Research Data Repository; University of Arizona Theses & Dissertations; Up with People Archive; Women Mystery Writers Coll
Subject Interests: Arizona, Hist of sci, Lit, Performing arts, Political issues, SW
Wireless access
Function: Doc delivery serv, ILL available, Online cat, Ref serv available, Wheelchair accessible
Partic in Association of Research Libraries; OCLC Research Library Partnership
Special Services for the Deaf - Assistive tech

Departmental Libraries:

CL DANIEL F CRACCHIOLO LAW LIBRARY, James E Rogers College of Law, 1201 E Speedway, 85721. (Mail add: PO Box 210176, 85721-0176). Circulation Tel: 520-626-8023. FAX: 520-621-5455. Web Site: lawlibrary.arizona.edu. *Assoc Dean, Legal Info Innovation, Dir,* Teresa Miguel-Stearns; Tel: 520-621-5477, E-mail: tmiguelstearns@arizona.edu; *Head, Faculty & Access Servs,* Cynthia Condit; E-mail: cbcondit@email.arizona.edu; *Head, Library Tech & Admin Services,* Travis Spence; E-mail: tspence@email.arizona.edu; *Head, Research, Data & Instruction,* Cas Laskowski; E-mail: claskowski@arizona.edu; Staff 10 (MLS 9, Non-MLS 1)
Founded 1915. Enrl 395; Fac 57; Highest Degree: Doctorate
Library Holdings: Bk Titles 453,711
Special Collections: US Document Depository
Subject Interests: Constitutional law, Criminal law, Family law, Indigenous people, Intl bus law, Intl trade law, Natural res
Function: ILL available, Photocopying/Printing, Res assist avail, Scanner
Partic in Legal Information Preservation Alliance; NELLCO Law Library Consortium, Inc.; OCLC Online Computer Library Center, Inc
Restriction: Open to fac, students & qualified researchers

CM HEALTH SCIENCES LIBRARY, 1501 N Campbell Ave, 85724. (Mail add: PO Box 245079, 85724-5079), SAN 330-7921. Tel: 520-626-6125. Administration Tel: 520-626-6121. FAX: 520-626-2922. Web Site: ahsl.arizona.edu. *Dir,* Janet Crum; Tel: 520-626-6178, E-mail: janetcrum@arizona.edu; *Assoc Dir,* Annabelle Nunez; Tel: 520-626-3660, E-mail: anunez@arizona.edu; *Librn,* Jennifer Martin; Tel: 520-626-3381, E-mail: jenmartin@arizona.edu; *Assoc Librn,* Yamila El-Khayat; Tel: 520-626-6770, E-mail: yme@arizona.edu; *Assoc Librn,* Jeanne Pfander; Tel: 520-621-6375, E-mail: jpfander@arizona.edu; *Assoc Librn,* Dr Ahlam Saleh; Tel: 520-626-5450, E-mail: saleh1@arizona.edu; *Assoc Librn,* Maribeth Slebodnik; Tel: 520-626-7431, E-mail: slebodnik@arizona.edu; *Asst Librn,* Jean McClelland; Tel: 520-626-7508, E-mail: jmcc@arizona.edu; *Coord, Operations & Facilities,* Jerry Flanary; E-mail: flanary@arizona.edu; *Program Coord, Sr,* Mikel Bates; Tel: 520-626-2921, E-mail: batesm@arizona.edu; *Info Assoc,* Philip Brown; Tel: 520-626-6707, E-mail: philipbrown@arizona.edu; *Info Assoc,* Pipei Guo; Tel: 520-626-7172, E-mail: guo1@arizona.edu; *Info Assoc,* Kathy Lowers; Tel: 520-626-6142, E-mail: lowersk@arizona.edu; Staff 11.8 (MLS 7.8, Non-MLS 4)
Founded 1965. Enrl 49,471; Fac 3,266; Highest Degree: Doctorate
Library Holdings: e-journals 28,952; Electronic Media & Resources 175; Bk Titles 91,796
Special Collections: Arts, Wellness & Health Humanities Coll; Merlin Kearfott Duval Jr Papers; Pima County Medical Society Minutes; Space Technology Applied to Rural Papago Advanced Health Care Archive (STARPAHC also known as the Telemedicine Coll); University of Arizona College of Medicine Scrapbooks
Subject Interests: Med, Nursing, Pharm, Pub health, Veterinary med
Automation Activity & Vendor Info: (Acquisitions) Ex Libris Group; (Cataloging) Ex Libris Group; (Circulation) Ex Libris Group; (OPAC) Ex Libris Group; (Serials) Ex Libris Group
Partic in Arizona Health Information Network; Greater Western Library Alliance; National Network of Libraries of Medicine Region 4
Restriction: Borrowing privileges limited to fac & registered students

SPACE IMAGERY CENTER, 1629 E University Blvd, 85721-0092, SAN 321-6721. Tel: 520-621-0407. E-mail: sic@lpl.arizona.edu. Web Site: www.lpl.arizona.edu/sic. *Dir,* Shane Byrne; E-mail: shane@lpl.arizona.edu
Founded 1977
Special Collections: Apollo Prints; Clementine CDs; Earth Atlases; Jupiter, Saturn, Uranus & Neptune (Voyager 1 & 2 Prints); Lunar Atlases; Lunar Orbiter Prints; Mariner 6, 7, 9, 10 Coll; Mars (Viking 1 & 2 Orbiter & Lander Prints); Mars Atlases; Mars Global Surveyor; Pioneer 10 & 11 Coll; Space Probes - Gemini Coll; Venus (Magellan Coll), CDs, maps
Subject Interests: Planetary sci
Open Mon, Wed & Fri 8-12 & 1-5, Tues & Thurs 10:30-5

ALBERT B WEAVER SCIENCE-ENGINEERING LIBRARY, 744 N Highland, Bldg 54, 85721. (Mail add: PO Box 210055, 85721-0055). Tel: 520-621-6384. *Assoc Librn,* Jim Martin; E-mail: djmartin@email.arizona.edu

WHITERIVER

P WHITERIVER PUBLIC LIBRARY*, 100 E Walnut St, 85941. (Mail add: PO Box 370, 85941-0370), SAN 300-4716. Tel: 928-594-3164. FAX: 928-338-4470. Web Site: www.navajocountylibraries.org/Pages/Index/91129/whiteriver-public-library. *Librn,* Darryl Quesada; E-mail: darrylquesada@wmat.us
Founded 1934. Pop 10,000
Library Holdings: Bk Titles 12,000; Per Subs 25
Special Collections: Arizona Coll
Automation Activity & Vendor Info: (Cataloging) SirsiDynix; (Circulation) SirsiDynix; (OPAC) SirsiDynix

Mem of Navajo County Library System
Open Mon-Fri 10-5

WICKENBURG

S DESERT CABALLEROS WESTERN MUSEUM*, Blossom Memorial Library, 21 N Frontier St, 85390. SAN 375-7579. Tel: 928-684-2272. FAX: 928-684-5794. E-mail: info@westernmuseum.org, Web Site: westernmuseum.org. *Exec Dir,* Daniel M Finley; *Curator, Dep Dir,* Mary Ann Igna; E-mail: maigna@westernmuseum.org
Founded 1960
Library Holdings: Bk Titles 1,500
Open Mon-Fri 10-5

P WICKENBURG PUBLIC LIBRARY & LEARNING CENTER*, 164 E Apache St, 85390. SAN 300-4724. Tel: 928-684-2665, 928-684-5451, Ext 1541. E-mail: library@wickenburgaz.org. Web Site: ci.wickenburg.az.us/library. *Librn,* Jane Horsefield; Staff 4 (MLS 1, Non-MLS 3)
Founded 1942. Pop 11,000; Circ 134,687
Library Holdings: Audiobooks 506; CDs 874; DVDs 1,206; Large Print Bks 1,484; Bk Titles 40,000; Bk Vols 41,110; Per Subs 32; Talking Bks 822; Videos 1,671
Special Collections: History (Southwest Coll)
Automation Activity & Vendor Info: (Cataloging) Innovative Interfaces, Inc; (Circulation) Innovative Interfaces, Inc
Wireless access
Function: Adult bk club, Bks on cassette, Bks on CD, Children's prog, Computers for patron use, Free DVD rentals, Music CDs, Online cat, Summer reading prog, Tax forms, VHS videos, Wheelchair accessible
Open Mon-Fri 8:30-5, Sat 8:30-12:30
Friends of the Library Group

WILLCOX

P ELSIE S HOGAN COMMUNITY LIBRARY*, 100 N Curtis Ave, 85643. SAN 330-5376. Tel: 520-766-4250. FAX: 520-384-0126. Web Site: cochiselibrary.org/client/en_US/willcox, willcoxlibrary.com. *Libr Mgr,* Michelle Cooley; E-mail: mcooley@willcoxcity.org; Staff 1 (Non-MLS 1)
Founded 1923. Pop 7,350; Circ 24,569
Library Holdings: Bk Titles 30,016; Per Subs 30
Automation Activity & Vendor Info: (Acquisitions) Baker & Taylor; (Cataloging) SirsiDynix; (Circulation) SirsiDynix; (ILL) SirsiDynix; (OPAC) SirsiDynix
Wireless access
Function: 24/7 Electronic res, 24/7 Online cat, Adult bk club, Art exhibits, Audio & video playback equip for onsite use, Audiobks on Playaways & MP3, Audiobks via web, Bi-weekly Writer's Group, Bk club(s), Bks on cassette, Bks on CD, Children's prog, Computers for patron use, E-Reserves, Electronic databases & coll, Equip loans & repairs, Free DVD rentals, Games & aids for people with disabilities, Genealogy discussion group, Holiday prog, Homework prog, ILL available, Instruction & testing, Internet access, Life-long learning prog for all ages, Literacy & newcomer serv, Magazines, Magnifiers for reading, Mail & tel request accepted, Meeting rooms, Movies, Music CDs, Online cat, Orientations, Outreach serv, Outside serv via phone, mail, e-mail & web, OverDrive digital audio bks, Photocopying/Printing, Preschool outreach, Preschool reading prog, Printer for laptops & handheld devices, Prog for adults, Prog for children & young adult, Ref & res, Ref serv available, Scanner, Senior computer classes, Senior outreach, Serves people with intellectual disabilities, Spanish lang bks, Spoken cassettes & CDs, Spoken cassettes & DVDs, Story hour, Study rm, Summer reading prog, Tax forms, Teen prog, Wheelchair accessible, Workshops
Mem of Cochise County Library District
Special Services for the Blind - Aids for in-house use; Assistive/Adapted tech devices, equip & products; Audio mat; Bks & mags in Braille, on rec, tape & cassette; Bks available with recordings
Open Mon-Thurs 10-6, Fri 9-5
Friends of the Library Group

G UNITED STATES NATIONAL PARK SERVICE*, Chiricahua National Monument Library, 13063 E Bonita Canyon Rd, 85643-9737. SAN 375-2259. Tel: 520-824-3560, Ext 9307. FAX: 520-824-3421. Web Site: www.nps.gov/chir. *Library Contact,* Libby Schaaf; E-mail: libby_schaaf@nps.gov
Founded 1924
Library Holdings: Bk Titles 4,000
Function: For res purposes
Restriction: Access at librarian's discretion

WILLIAMS

P WILLIAMS PUBLIC LIBRARY*, 113 S First St, 86046. SAN 300-4740. Tel: 928-635-2263. FAX: 928-635-4495. Web Site: www.williamsaz.gov/visitors/library, www.williamspubliclibrary.org. *Libr Dir,* Mary Corcoran; E-mail: mcorcoran@williamsaz.gov; Staff 1 (Non-MLS 1)
Founded 1895. Pop 2,800; Circ 14,450
Library Holdings: Bk Titles 10,000; Bk Vols 11,000; Per Subs 20
Subject Interests: Arizona
Wireless access
Mem of Flagstaff City-Coconino County Public Library System
Open Tues-Thurs 9-5 & 6-8, Fri 9-5:30, Sat 9-1

WINDOW ROCK

S OFFICE OF NAVAJO NATION LIBRARY*, Hwy 264, Post Office Loop Rd, 86515. (Mail add: PO Box 9040, 86515-9040), SAN 321-0693. Tel: 928-871-6526. FAX: 928-871-7304. Web Site: navajonationlibrary.org. *Supvr,* Irving Nelson; Tel: 928-871-7303, E-mail: inelson979@yahoo.com; Staff 14 (MLS 6, Non-MLS 8)
Founded 1941
Library Holdings: Bk Titles 90,000; Per Subs 135
Special Collections: Navajo History & Culture; 17000 books on Native American History
Subject Interests: Archaeology
Wireless access
Open Mon-Fri 8-5

WINSLOW

S ARIZONA DEPARTMENT OF CORRECTIONS - ADULT INSTITUTIONS*, Arizona State Prison Complex - Winslow Library, 2100 S Hwy 87, 86047. Tel: 928-289-9551, Ext 6538. *Librn II,* Casey Ubben
Library Holdings: Bk Vols 15,000
Open Mon-Fri 7-3:30
Restriction: Staff & inmates only

S ARIZONA STATE PARKS*, Homolovi State Park Library, HCR63, Box 5, 86047. SAN 371-2788. Tel: 928-289-4106. FAX: 928-289-2021. E-mail: ctm2@azstateparks.gov. Web Site: azstateparks.com/homolovi. *Librn,* Chad Meunler
Library Holdings: Bk Vols 3,000
Special Collections: Indian Culture Archeolology
Wireless access
Restriction: Ref only

P WINSLOW PUBLIC LIBRARY*, 420 W Gilmore St, 86047. SAN 300-4767. Tel: 928-289-4982. E-mail: library@winslowaz.gov. Web Site: www.navajocountylibraries.org. *Dir,* Brandee Leary; *Prog Coordr,* Mervine Nelson; *Libr Asst,* Dawnna Ybarra; Staff 5 (MLS 2, Non-MLS 3)
Founded 1969. Pop 15,000; Circ 31,000
Library Holdings: Bk Titles 27,000; Bk Vols 29,250; Per Subs 12
Special Collections: Arizona History
Subject Interests: Indians
Automation Activity & Vendor Info: (Cataloging) SirsiDynix; (Circulation) SirsiDynix; (OPAC) SirsiDynix
Wireless access
Mem of Navajo County Library System
Partic in Channeled Ariz Info Network; Navajo County Libr District
Special Services for the Deaf - TDD equip
Special Services for the Blind - Talking bks
Open Mon-Fri 9:30-5:30
Friends of the Library Group

WOODRUFF

P WOODRUFF COMMUNITY LIBRARY*, 6414 W First St, 85942. (Mail add: PO Box 77, 85942-0077). Tel: 928-524-3885. FAX: 928-524-3885. E-mail: woodrufflibrary0@gmail.com. Web Site: azlibrary.gov/location/woodruff-community-library, www.navajocountylibraries.org/navajo/members.asp. *Dir,* Darlynn Mobley
Library Holdings: Bk Vols 4,500
Automation Activity & Vendor Info: (Cataloging) SirsiDynix; (Circulation) SirsiDynix
Wireless access
Mem of Navajo County Library System
Open Tues & Thurs 10-1:30, Sat 9-5

YOUNG

P YOUNG PUBLIC LIBRARY*, 124 S Midway Ave, 85554. (Mail add: PO Box 150, 85554), SAN 300-4783. Tel: 928-462-3588. FAX: 928-462-3599.
Founded 1984. Pop 850; Circ 3,790
Library Holdings: AV Mats 250; Bks on Deafness & Sign Lang 25; CDs 150; Large Print Bks 350; Bk Vols 18,000; Per Subs 4; Talking Bks 120; Videos 800
Special Collections: Southwest Nonfiction; Western Fiction
Wireless access
Function: Adult literacy prog, ILL available, Photocopying/Printing, Prog for children & young adult, Summer reading prog, Wheelchair accessible

Mem of Gila County Library District
Open Tues-Fri 12-5, Sat 10-2

YOUNGTOWN

P YOUNGTOWN PUBLIC LIBRARY*, 12035 Clubhouse Sq, 85363. SAN 300-4791. Tel: 623-974-3401. Web Site: youngtownaz.org/index.aspx?NID=379. *Libr Mgr,* Heidi Speed; E-mail: hspeed@youngtownaz.org
Founded 1956. Pop 2,500; Circ 14,000
Library Holdings: Bk Titles 8,500
Special Collections: Arizona & Southwestern
Automation Activity & Vendor Info: (Cataloging) Follett Software; (Circulation) Follett Software
Wireless access
Open Mon-Wed & Fri 9-4, Thurs 9-7, Sat 9-1

YUMA

S ARIZONA HISTORICAL SOCIETY*, Sanguinetti House Museum & Gardens Library, 240 Madison Ave, 85364. SAN 300-4821. Tel: 928-782-1841. Web Site: arizonahistoricalsociety.org/museums/yuma. *Mus Dir,* Yanna Kruse; Tel: 928-782-1842, E-mail: ykruse@azhs.gov
Founded 1963
Library Holdings: Bk Titles 500
Special Collections: Lower Colorado River Area Historical Photographs; Military Oral History Tapes-WWII Period. Oral History
Restriction: Non-circulating, Open by appt only

J ARIZONA WESTERN COLLEGE*, Academic Library, 2020 S Ave 8E, 85366. (Mail add: PO Box 929, 85366-0929), SAN 300-4805. Tel: 928-344-7777. FAX: 928-344-7751. E-mail: library@azwestern.edu. Web Site: www.azwestern.edu/library. *Dir, Libr Serv,* Angela Creel; Tel: 928-344-7776, E-mail: angie.creel@azwestern.edu; *Distance Learning Librn,* Tymmi A Woods; Tel: 928-317-6434, E-mail: tymmi.woods@azwestern.edu; *IT Librn,* Wendy Hoag; Tel: 928-344-7718, E-mail: wendy.hoag@azwestern.edu; *Tech Serv Librn,* Carrie E Dawson; Tel: 928-317-6491, E-mail: elizabeth.dawson@azwestern.edu; *Circ Mgr,* Lupi Rojas; Tel: 928-344-7768, E-mail: lupi.rojas@azwestern.edu; *Circ,* Julia Williamson; Tel: 928-317-5884, E-mail: julia.williamson@azwestern.edu; Staff 8 (MLS 5, Non-MLS 3)
Founded 1963. Enrl 5,000; Fac 150; Highest Degree: Associate
Library Holdings: Bk Titles 84,000; Bk Vols 90,000; Per Subs 463
Special Collections: SouthWest Border Coll
Automation Activity & Vendor Info: (Acquisitions) SirsiDynix; (Cataloging) SirsiDynix; (Circulation) SirsiDynix; (Course Reserve) SirsiDynix; (OPAC) SirsiDynix; (Serials) SirsiDynix
Wireless access
Function: Audio & video playback equip for onsite use, Audiobks on Playaways & MP3, Bilingual assistance for Spanish patrons, Bks on CD, Computers for patron use, Distance learning, Doc delivery serv, Electronic databases & coll, Equip loans & repairs, For res purposes, Free DVD rentals, Govt ref serv, ILL available, Magazines, Magnifiers for reading, Makerspace, Microfiche/film & reading machines, Movies, Music CDs, Online cat, Online info literacy tutorials on the web & in blackboard, Online ref, Orientations, Outreach serv, Outside serv via phone, mail, e-mail & web, OverDrive digital audio bks, Photocopying/Printing, Prog for adults, Ref & res, Ref serv available, Res assist avail, Scanner, Spanish lang bks, Study rm, Tax forms, VHS videos
Partic in OCLC Online Computer Library Center, Inc
Open Mon-Thurs 8am-9pm, Fri 10-5, Sat 12-5

A UNITED STATES ARMY*, Yuma Proving Ground Post Library, Bldg 300, 301 C St, 85365-9848. SAN 330-8286. Tel: 928-328-2558. Interlibrary Loan Service Tel: 928-328-3068. FAX: 928-328-3055. E-mail: YPGlibrary@gmail.com. Web Site: www.yumamwr.com/library.html. *Libr Tech,* Melissa Donato; Staff 2 (Non-MLS 2)
Founded 1953
Library Holdings: AV Mats 1,774; Bk Vols 43,256; Per Subs 24; Talking Bks 704
Subject Interests: Arizona
Automation Activity & Vendor Info: (Acquisitions) Bibliomation Inc; (Cataloging) OCLC; (Circulation) Horizon; (ILL) OCLC; (OPAC) Horizon
Wireless access
Partic in OCLC Online Computer Library Center, Inc
Open Tues-Thurs 10-7, Fri 10-6, Sat 10-2

A UNITED STATES MARINE CORPS*, Station Library, Bldg 633, 85369. (Mail add: PO Box 99119, 85369-9119), SAN 330-8340. Tel: 928-269-2785. FAX: 928-269-2795. E-mail: yumacirc@usmc-mccs.org. Web Site: www.mccsyuma.org/index.cfm/military-family/library. *Mgr,* Bonnie Miller
Founded 1948
Library Holdings: Bk Vols 20,500; Per Subs 93
Subject Interests: Aviation
Wireless access
Restriction: Non-circulating to the pub

P YUMA COUNTY FREE LIBRARY DISTRICT*, Main Library, 2951 S 21st Dr, 85364. SAN 330-8375. Tel: 928-782-1871. Circulation Tel: 928-373-6492. Interlibrary Loan Service Tel: 928-373-6504. Reference Tel: 928-373-6482. Administration Tel: 928-373-6460, 928-373-6462. Automation Services Tel: 928-373-6467. Information Services Tel: 928-373-6482, 928-373-6513. FAX: 928-782-9420. Administration FAX: 928-782-9420. E-mail: admin_staff@yumalibrary.org. Web Site: yumalibrary.org. *Dir,* Lisa J Mendez; Tel: 928-373-6462, E-mail: lisa.mendez@yumalibrary.org; *Bus Off Adminr,* Arthur S Duran; Tel: 928-373-6463, E-mail: sduran@yumalibrary.org; *Bus Librn,* Andrew Zollman; E-mail: andrew.zollman@yumalibrary.org; *Info Serv Librn,* Julieta Calderon; Tel: 928-373-6498, E-mail: julieta.calderon@yumalibrary.org; *Spec Coll Librn,* Laurie Boone; Tel: 928-373-6517, E-mail: lboone@yumalibrary.org; *Spec Serv Librn,* James Patrick; Tel: 928-373-6484, E-mail: jpatrick@yumalibrary.org; *Adminr, Mgr, Grants & Spec Project,* Maria Gnagy; Tel: 928-373-6465, E-mail: Maria.gnagy@yumalibrary.org; *Coll Serv Mgr,* Position Currently Open; *Commun Relations Mgr,* Sarah Wisdom; Tel: 928-373-6483, E-mail: swisdom@yumalibrary.org; *IT Mgr,* Daniel Paz; Tel: 928-373-6467, E-mail: daniel.paz@yumalibrary.org; *Teen Serv Mgr,* Elia Juarez; Tel: 928-373-6487, E-mail: elia.juarez@yumalibrary.org; *Youth Serv Librn,* Position Currently Open; *Circ Supvr,* Sandra Nicasio; Tel: 928-373-6491, E-mail: snicasio@yumalibrary.org; *Computer Lab/Per Supvr,* Jerry Mendez; Tel: 928-314-2456, E-mail: jmendez@yumalibrary.org; *Adul Prog Coordr/LAII,* Lourdes Rose; E-mail: lourdes.rose@yumalibrary.org; *LAII Teen/Spanish Outreach Coordr,* Alex Garcia; Tel: 928-373-6481, E-mail: agarcia@yumalibrary.org; *Admin Serv, Libr Spec,* Sandra Gutierrez; Tel: 928-373-6495, Fax: 928-782-9420, E-mail: sgutierrez@yumalibrary.org; *Homebound Serv/Computer Access,* David Monypeny; E-mail: dmonypeny@yumalibrary.org; *ILL,* Sylvia Moore; Tel: 928-373-6488, E-mail: smoore@yumalibrary.org; Staff 17 (MLS 17)
Founded 2009. Pop 225,212; Circ 418,455
Jul 2018-Jun 2019 Income (Main & Associated Libraries) $8,644,897, State $27,879, Federal $40,648, County $7,936,214, Other $640,156. Mats Exp $1,214,121, Books $465,716, Other Print Mats $85,924, AV Mat $662,481. Sal $3,599,089
Special Collections: Arizona Room (Arizona & Local History); Rio Colorado Coll (Yuma History Coll). Oral History
Subject Interests: Arizona, Local hist
Automation Activity & Vendor Info: (Acquisitions) SirsiDynix; (Circulation) SirsiDynix; (ILL) OCLC ILLiad; (OPAC) SirsiDynix; (Serials) SirsiDynix
Wireless access
Function: 24/7 Electronic res, 24/7 Online cat, 3D Printer, Activity rm, Adult bk club, Adult literacy prog, After school storytime, Archival coll, Art exhibits, Art programs, Audiobks via web, Bilingual assistance for Spanish patrons, Bk club(s), Bk reviews (Group), Bks on CD, Chess club, Children's prog, Citizenship assistance, Computer training, Computers for patron use, Electronic databases & coll, Family literacy, Free DVD rentals, Games & aids for people with disabilities, Genealogy discussion group, Holiday prog, Home delivery & serv to seniorr ctr & nursing homes, Homebound delivery serv, Homework prog, ILL available, Internet access, Life-long learning prog for all ages, Literacy & newcomer serv, Magazines, Magnifiers for reading, Mango lang, Meeting rooms, Microfiche/film & reading machines, Movies, Music CDs, Notary serv, Online cat, Online ref, Outreach serv, Outside serv via phone, mail, e-mail & web, OverDrive digital audio bks, Photocopying/Printing, Preschool outreach, Preschool reading prog, Printer for laptops & handheld devices, Prog for adults, Prog for children & young adult, Ref serv available, Scanner, Senior computer classes, Senior outreach, Spanish lang bks, Spoken cassettes & DVDs, STEM programs, Story hour, Study rm, Summer & winter reading prog, Summer reading prog, Tax forms, Teen prog, Telephone ref, Wheelchair accessible, Winter reading prog, Words travel prog, Workshops, Writing prog
Special Services for the Deaf - Assisted listening device; Assistive tech; Bks on deafness & sign lang; TDD equip; TTY equip
Special Services for the Blind - Assistive/Adapted tech devices, equip & products; Audio mat; BiFolkal kits; Bks on cassette; Bks on CD; Computer with voice synthesizer for visually impaired persons; Copier with enlargement capabilities; Home delivery serv; Large print bks; Lending of low vision aids; Magnifiers
Open Mon-Thurs 9-9, Fri & Sat 9-5
Friends of the Library Group
Branches: 7
DATELAND BRANCH, Ave 64E & Interstate 8, Dateland, 85333. (Mail add: PO Box 3000, Dateland, 85333). Tel: 928-454-2242. FAX: 928-454-2217. *Br Assoc,* Lucy Shaw; E-mail: lshaw@yumalibrary.org
Function: 24/7 Electronic res, 24/7 Online cat, Children's prog, Computers for patron use, Electronic databases & coll, Free DVD rentals, Holiday prog, Life-long learning prog for all ages, Mango lang, Online cat, Prog for adults, Prog for children & young adult, Spanish

lang bks, Story hour, Summer & winter reading prog, Summer reading prog
Open Mon-Wed & Fri 9-3
Friends of the Library Group
FOOTHILLS BRANCH, 13226 E South Frontage Rd, 85367, SAN 328-6827. Tel: 928-342-1640. Circulation Tel: 928-373-6522. Information Services Tel: 928-314-2444. FAX: 928-305-0497. *Br Mgr,* Brian Franssen; Tel: 928-373-6509, Fax: 928-305-0497, E-mail: bfranssen@yumalibrary.org; *Br Librn,* Monica Colorado; Tel: 928-373-6524, Fax: 928-305-0497, E-mail: monica.colorado@yumalibrary.org; Staff 2 (MLS 2)
Library Holdings: Audiobooks 1,662; Bk Vols 47,647; Videos 3,168
Function: 24/7 Electronic res, 24/7 Online cat, Activity rm, Adult bk club, Adult literacy prog, After school storytime, Art exhibits, Audiobks via web, Bi-weekly Writer's Group, Bilingual assistance for Spanish patrons, Bk club(s), Bks on CD, Children's prog, Computer training, Computers for patron use, Family literacy, Free DVD rentals, Genealogy discussion group, Holiday prog, Homework prog, ILL available, Internet access, Life-long learning prog for all ages, Magazines, Mango lang, Meeting rooms, Movies, Music CDs, Online cat, Online ref, Outreach serv, Photocopying/Printing, Preschool outreach, Preschool reading prog, Prog for adults, Prog for children & young adult, Ref serv available, Scanner, Senior computer classes, Senior outreach, Spanish lang bks, Story hour, Study rm, Summer & winter reading prog, Summer reading prog, Tax forms, Teen prog, Telephone ref, Wheelchair accessible, Winter reading prog, Writing prog
Open Tues-Thurs 10-7, Fri & Sat 10-5
Friends of the Library Group
HERITAGE BRANCH, 350 Third Ave, 85364. Tel: 928-783-5415. Circulation Tel: 928-373-6515. Information Services Tel: 928-373-6516. FAX: 928-783-5840. *Br Mgr,* Ashley Jackman; Tel: 928-373-6531, E-mail: ashley.jackman@yumalibrary.org; *Br Librn,* Valerie Weber; Tel: 928-373-6507, Fax: 928-783-5840, E-mail: valerie.weber@yumalibrary.org; *Spec Coll Librn,* Laurie Boone; Tel: 928-373-6486, E-mail: lboone@yumalibrary.org; Staff 3 (MLS 3)
Circ 23,785
Special Collections: Arizona Historical Society Rio Colorado Coll
Function: 24/7 Electronic res, 24/7 Online cat, Activity rm, Adult bk club, Adult literacy prog, After school storytime, Archival coll, Art exhibits, Audiobks via web, Bilingual assistance for Spanish patrons, Bk club(s), Chess club, Children's prog, Computer training, Computers for patron use, Electronic databases & coll, Family literacy, Genealogy discussion group, Holiday prog, Homework prog, ILL available, Internet access, Life-long learning prog for all ages, Magazines, Mango lang, Meeting rooms, Online cat, Online ref, Outreach serv, OverDrive digital audio bks, Photocopying/Printing, Preschool outreach, Preschool reading prog, Printer for laptops & handheld devices, Prog for adults, Prog for children & young adult, Ref serv available, Scanner, Senior computer classes, Senior outreach, Spanish lang bks, Story hour, Study rm, Summer & winter reading prog, Summer reading prog, Tax forms, Teen prog, Telephone ref, Wheelchair accessible, Winter reading prog, Workshops, Writing prog
Open Tues-Thurs 10-7, Fri & Sat 10-5
Friends of the Library Group
ROLL BRANCH, 5151 S Ave 39E, Roll, 85347. Tel: 928-785-3701. FAX: 928-785-3701. *Br Assoc,* Lucy Shaw; Tel: 928-785-9575, E-mail: lshaw@yumalibrary.org
Pop 846; Circ 3,254
Function: 24/7 Electronic res, 24/7 Online cat, After school storytime, Bilingual assistance for Spanish patrons, Children's prog, Computers for patron use, Holiday prog, Homework prog, Internet access, Mango lang, Online cat, Outreach serv, OverDrive digital audio bks, Preschool outreach, Preschool reading prog, Prog for adults, Prog for children & young adult, Spanish lang bks, Story hour, Summer reading prog, Teen prog
Open Mon, Tues & Thurs 10-3, Wed & Fri 9-5
Friends of the Library Group
SAN LUIS BRANCH, 1075 N Sixth Ave, San Luis, 85349. (Mail add: PO Box 1630, San Luis, 85349-1630), SAN 328-8900. Tel: 928-627-8344. FAX: 928-627-8296. *Br Mgr,* Megan Baird; Tel: 928-317-2447, E-mail: megan.baird@yumalibrary.org; Staff 2 (MLS 2)
Pop 29,377; Circ 25,977
Function: 24/7 Electronic res, 24/7 Online cat, Activity rm, Adult bk club, Adult literacy prog, After school storytime, Art exhibits, Audiobks via web, Bi-weekly Writer's Group, Bilingual assistance for Spanish patrons, Bk club(s), Children's prog, Citizenship assistance, Computer training, Computers for patron use, Electronic databases & coll, Family literacy, Free DVD rentals, Genealogy discussion group, Holiday prog, Homework prog, ILL available, Internet access, Learning ctr, Life-long learning prog for all ages, Magazines, Mango lang, Meeting rooms, Online cat, Online ref, Outreach serv, OverDrive digital audio bks, Photocopying/Printing, Preschool outreach, Preschool reading prog, Printer for laptops & handheld devices, Prog for adults, Prog for children & young adult, Ref serv available, Scanner, Senior computer classes, Senior outreach, Spanish lang bks, Story hour, Study rm, Summer & winter reading prog, Summer reading prog, Tax forms, Teen prog, Telephone ref, Wheelchair accessible
Open Tues & Wed 9-7, Thurs 9-8, Fri & Sat 9-5
Friends of the Library Group
WELLTON BRANCH, 28790 San Jose Ave, Wellton, 85356. (Mail add: PO Box 577, Wellton, 85356-0577), SAN 330-8499. Tel: 928-785-9575. FAX: 928-785-4410. *Br Supvr,* Lee Irwin; Tel: 928-373-6552, Fax: 928-785-4410
Pop 2,938; Circ 17,915
Function: 24/7 Electronic res, 24/7 Online cat, Activity rm, Adult bk club, Adult literacy prog, After school storytime, Audiobks via web, Bilingual assistance for Spanish patrons, Bk club(s), Bks on cassette, Bks on CD, Children's prog, Computer training, Computers for patron use, Electronic databases & coll, Free DVD rentals, Holiday prog, Homework prog, ILL available, Internet access, Mango lang, Meeting rooms, Music CDs, Online cat, Online ref, Outreach serv, OverDrive digital audio bks, Photocopying/Printing, Preschool outreach, Preschool reading prog, Printer for laptops & handheld devices, Prog for adults, Prog for children & young adult, Ref serv available, Scanner, Senior computer classes, Senior outreach, Spanish lang bks, Story hour, Study rm, Summer & winter reading prog, Teen prog, Telephone ref, Wheelchair accessible, Writing prog
Open Tues-Thurs 10-7, Fri & Sat 10-5
Restriction: Registered patrons only
Friends of the Library Group
SOMERTON BRANCH, 240 Canal St, Somerton, 85350. (Mail add: PO Box 460, Somerton, 85350-0460), SAN 330-8464. Tel: 928-627-2149. FAX: 928-627-8345. *Br Supvr,* Frances Murrietta; Tel: 928-373-6543, E-mail: fmurrietta@yumalibrary.org
Pop 22,726; Circ 14,233
Function: 24/7 Electronic res, 24/7 Online cat, Activity rm, Adult bk club, After school storytime, Art exhibits, Bilingual assistance for Spanish patrons, Bk club(s), Children's prog, Computer training, Computers for patron use, Electronic databases & coll, Family literacy, Free DVD rentals, Holiday prog, ILL available, Internet access, Life-long learning prog for all ages, Magazines, Mango lang, Meeting rooms, Movies, Online cat, Online ref, Outreach serv, OverDrive digital audio bks, Photocopying/Printing, Preschool outreach, Preschool reading prog, Printer for laptops & handheld devices, Prog for adults, Prog for children & young adult, Ref serv available, Scanner, Senior computer classes, Senior outreach, Spanish lang bks, Story hour, Study rm, Summer & winter reading prog, Summer reading prog, Teen prog, Wheelchair accessible
Open Tues-Thurs 10-7, Fri & Sat 10-5
Friends of the Library Group

GL YUMA COUNTY LAW LIBRARY, 250 W Second St, 85364. SAN 300-483X. Tel: 928-817-4165. E-mail: YumaSCLawLibrary@courts.az.gov. Web Site: www.yumacountyaz.gov/government/courts/superior-court/law-library. *Law Librn,* Maria Beltran
Library Holdings: Bk Vols 16,000
Subject Interests: Law
Open Mon-Fri 8-5

ARKANSAS

Date of Statistics: FY 2020
Population, 2020 U.S. Census: 3,042,231
Population Served by Public Libraries: 2,935,531
Unserved: 106,708
Total Volumes in Public Libraries: 5,597,328
Volumes Per Capita: 1.84
Total Public Library Circulation: 9,817,810
Circulation Per Capita: 3.24
Digital Resources
Total e-books: 5,512,939
Total audio items (physical and downloadable units): 3,713,392
Total video items (physical and downloadable units): 789,870
Total computers for use by the public: 2,841
Total annual wireless sessions: 638,310
Income and Expenditures:
Total Public Library Income (including federal and state funds): $93,057,242
Expenditures Per Capita: $30.59
Number of County or Multi-County (Regional) Libraries: 44
City Public Libraries: 16
Single County Systems: 27
Multi-county Systems: 17
Number of Bookmobiles in State: 5
Federal (Title I LSTA in 2020): $1,994,233
Total State Aid in 2020: $5,254,117
Information provided courtesy of: Michael Strickland, Manager of Information Services; Arkansas State Library

ALMA

P ALMA PUBLIC LIBRARY*, 624 Fayetteville Ave, 72921. SAN 330-9878. Tel: 479-632-4140. FAX: 479-632-6099. E-mail: alma@crawfordcountylib.org. Web Site: www2.youseemore.com/crawfordcls. *Br Dir,* Marla Cantrell; E-mail: mcantrell@crawfordcountylib.org
Library Holdings: Bk Vols 45,626
Wireless access
Mem of Crawford County Library System
Open Mon-Fri 9-4, Sat 10-2
Friends of the Library Group

ARKADELPHIA

P CLARK COUNTY LIBRARY*, 609 Caddo St, 71923. SAN 330-8553. Tel: 870-246-2271. FAX: 870-246-4189. E-mail: library22@yahoo.com. Web Site: www.clark-library.com. *Dir,* Ashley Graves
Founded 1897. Pop 24,932; Circ 118,000
Library Holdings: Bk Titles 90,000; Per Subs 80
Special Collections: Genealogy (Daughters of the American Revolution); History of Arkansas
Automation Activity & Vendor Info: (Cataloging) Follett Software; (Circulation) Follett Software; (OPAC) Follett Software
Wireless access
Open Tues-Fri 8:30-5, Sat 9-1
Branches: 1
GURDON PUBLIC, 204 E Walnut, Gurdon, 71743, SAN 330-8618. Tel: 870-353-2911. *Dir,* Judy Golden
Library Holdings: Bk Vols 20,000
Open Tues-Fri 9:30-5

C HENDERSON STATE UNIVERSITY*, Huie Library, 1100 Henderson St, 71999-0001. SAN 300-4848. Tel: 870-230-5258. Reference Tel: 870-230-5292. Administration Tel: 870-230-5305. FAX: 870-230-5365. E-mail: refdesk@hsu.edu. Web Site: library.hsu.edu. *Assoc Libn, Dir,* Lea Ann Alexander; E-mail: alexande@hsu.edu; *Assoc Libn,* Linda Evans; E-mail: evansl@hsu.edu; *Asst Libn,* Brian George; E-mail: georgeb@hsu.edu; Staff 18 (MLS 6, Non-MLS 12)
Founded 1890. Enrl 3,500; Highest Degree: Master
Library Holdings: Bk Titles 212,825; Bk Vols 255,567; Per Subs 1,478
Special Collections: Graphic novels; History of comics
Automation Activity & Vendor Info: (Acquisitions) Innovative Interfaces, Inc; (Cataloging) Innovative Interfaces, Inc; (Circulation) Innovative Interfaces, Inc; (OPAC) Innovative Interfaces, Inc; (Serials) Innovative Interfaces, Inc
Wireless access
Friends of the Library Group

C OUACHITA BAPTIST UNIVERSITY, Riley-Hickingbotham Library, 410 Ouachita St, OBU Box 3742, 71998-0001. SAN 330-8677. Tel: 870-245-5119. FAX: 870-245-5245. Web Site: www.obu.edu/library. *Interim Dir, Syst Librn,* Dr Anping Wu; Tel: 870-245-5115, E-mail: awu@obu.edu; *Circ, Head, Ref,* Kristi Smith; E-mail: smithk@obu.edu; *Per Librn,* Margaret Reed; Tel: 870-245-5125, E-mail: reedm@obu.edu; *Circ, Ref Librn,* Autumn Mortenson; Tel: 870-245-5123, E-mail: mortensona@obu.edu; *Archivist,* Lisa Speer; Tel: 870-245-5332, E-mail: speerl@obu.edu; *Govt Info Librn, Resources Librn,* Janice Ford; Tel: 870-245-5122, E-mail: fordj@obu.edu; Staff 7 (MLS 7)
Founded 1886. Enrl 1,639; Highest Degree: Bachelor
Jun 2013-May 2014. Mats Exp $253,262, Books $90,000, Manu Arch $34,264, Micro $93,700, AV Mat $1,098, Electronic Ref Mat (Incl. Access Fees) $34,200
Library Holdings: Bk Vols 70,000; Per Subs 200
Special Collections: Associational Minutes of the Arkansas Baptist State Convention; Papers of Governor Mike Huckabee; Papers of Representative Mike Ross; Papers of Senator John L McClellan 1940-1977. Oral History; State Document Depository; US Document Depository
Subject Interests: Educ, Humanities, Music
Automation Activity & Vendor Info: (Acquisitions) Innovative Interfaces, Inc - Millennium; (Cataloging) Innovative Interfaces, Inc - Millennium; (Circulation) Innovative Interfaces, Inc - Millennium; (Course Reserve) Innovative Interfaces, Inc - Millennium; (Media Booking) Innovative Interfaces, Inc - Millennium; (OPAC) Innovative Interfaces, Inc - Millennium; (Serials) Innovative Interfaces, Inc - Millennium
Wireless access
Open Mon-Thurs 7:45am-11pm, Fri 7:45-5, Sat Noon-5, Sun 6pm-11pm

BATESVILLE

P INDEPENDENCE COUNTY LIBRARY*, 267 E Main St, 72501. SAN 300-4864. Tel: 870-793-8814. FAX: 870-793-8896. E-mail: info@indcolib.com. Web Site: www.indcolib.com. *Dir,* Vanessa Adams; E-mail: vanessa@indcolib.com; Staff 2 (MLS 2)
Founded 1948. Pop 91,428; Circ 394,482
Library Holdings: Bk Vols 151,905; Per Subs 462
Special Collections: Arkansas History (Vela Jernigan Memorial)
Automation Activity & Vendor Info: (Acquisitions) Follett Software; (Cataloging) Follett Software
Wireless access
Open Mon-Thurs 10-6, Fri & Sat 9-5
Friends of the Library Group

CR LYON COLLEGE, Mabee-Simpson Library, 2300 Highland Rd, 72501-3699. SAN 300-4856. Tel: 870-307-7205. FAX: 870-307-7279. E-mail: ill@lyon.edu. Web Site: libguides.lyon.edu, library.lyon.edu. *Libr Dir,* Robert Krapohl; Tel: 870-307-7206, E-mail: robert.krapohl@lyon.edu; *Asst Dir,* Camille Beary; Tel: 870-307-7444, E-mail: camille.beary@lyon.edu; Staff 2 (MLS 2)
Founded 1975. Enrl 601; Fac 42; Highest Degree: Bachelor
Jul 2021-Jun 2022. Mats Exp $187,000, Books $10,000, Per/Ser (Incl. Access Fees) $24,000, Electronic Ref Mat (Incl. Access Fees) $153,000

Library Holdings: Audiobooks 60; CDs 1,197; DVDs 1,894; e-books 23,753; e-journals 42,817; Microforms 2,928; Bk Vols 148,059; Per Subs 329; Videos 1,107
Special Collections: Arkansas & Ozark History & Culture; John Quincy Wolf Folk Music/Folklore Coll. State Document Depository
Automation Activity & Vendor Info: (Acquisitions) OCLC Worldshare Management Services; (Cataloging) OCLC Worldshare Management Services; (Circulation) OCLC Worldshare Management Services; (Course Reserve) OCLC Worldshare Management Services; (ILL) OCLC WorldShare Interlibrary Loan; (OPAC) OCLC Worldshare Management Services; (Serials) OCLC Worldshare Management Services
Wireless access
Function: 24/7 Online cat
Partic in ARKLink
Open Mon-Fri 8-5
Restriction: Authorized patrons

J ROY ROW, SR & IMOGENE ROW JOHNS LIBRARY*, 2005 White Dr, 72501. (Mail add: PO Box 3350, 72503-3350). Tel: 870-612-2020. Reference Tel: 870-612-2019. Web Site: www.uaccb.edu/library. *Dir,* Jay Strickland; E-mail: jay.strickland@uaccb.edu; *Libr Coord,* Sharon Gage; E-mail: sharon.gage@uaccb.edu; Staff 4 (MLS 1, Non-MLS 3)
Founded 1998. Enrl 1,300; Fac 50; Highest Degree: Associate
Library Holdings: e-books 9,000; Bk Titles 15,000; Bk Vols 18,000; Per Subs 150
Special Collections: Independence County Law Library
Automation Activity & Vendor Info: (Cataloging) Innovative Interfaces, Inc; (Circulation) Innovative Interfaces, Inc; (Course Reserve) Innovative Interfaces, Inc; (ILL) OCLC; (OPAC) Innovative Interfaces, Inc; (Serials) EBSCO Online
Wireless access
Function: ILL available, Internet access, Online cat, Orientations, Ref serv available, VHS videos
Open Mon-Thurs 7:30am-9pm, Fri 7:30-5, Sat 10-2, Sun 2-7
Restriction: Authorized patrons, Open to students, Open to students, fac & staff, Pub use on premises

BEEBE

J ARKANSAS STATE UNIVERSITY*, Abington Memorial Library, 1000 W Iowa St, 72012. (Mail add: PO Box 1000, 72012), SAN 300-4872. Tel: 501-882-8976. Interlibrary Loan Service Tel: 501-882-8991. Administration Tel: 501-882-8807. FAX: 501-882-8833. TDD: 501-882-8969. Circulation E-mail: circ@asub.edu. Web Site: www.asub.edu/abington-library. *Libr Dir,* Tracy D Smith; Tel: 501-882-8806, E-mail: tdsmith@asub.edu; Staff 8 (MLS 2, Non-MLS 6)
Founded 1929. Enrl 2,640; Fac 150; Highest Degree: Associate
Library Holdings: AV Mats 3,600; e-books 38,000; e-journals 32,000; Bk Vols 76,000; Per Subs 251; Talking Bks 70
Subject Interests: Arkansas
Automation Activity & Vendor Info: (Cataloging) TLC (The Library Corporation); (Circulation) TLC (The Library Corporation); (Serials) TLC (The Library Corporation)
Wireless access
Function: Audio & video playback equip for onsite use, CD-ROM, Digital talking bks, Distance learning, Health sci info serv, ILL available, Internet access, Mail loans to mem, Music CDs, Orientations, Outside serv via phone, mail, e-mail & web, Photocopying/Printing, Ref serv available, Spoken cassettes & CDs, Telephone ref, VHS videos, Wheelchair accessible, Workshops
Partic in ARKLink
Special Services for the Deaf - Closed caption videos; TDD equip; TTY equip
Special Services for the Blind - Assistive/Adapted tech devices, equip & products; Audio mat; Bks on cassette; Bks on CD; Cassette playback machines; Computer with voice synthesizer for visually impaired persons; HP Scan Jet with photo-finish software; Large print bks; PC for people with disabilities; Rec; Ref serv; Talking bks; Videos on blindness & physical disabilties
Open Mon-Thurs (Fall-Spring) 7:30am-9pm, Fri 7:30-4:30, Sat 10-3, Sun 1-5; Mon-Thurs (Summer) 7:30–6, Fri 7:30-4:30, Sun 1-5
Restriction: Open to pub for ref & circ; with some limitations, Restricted borrowing privileges

BELLA VISTA

S BELLA VISTA HISTORICAL SOCIETY MUSEUM, 1885 Bella Vista Way, 72714. SAN 371-7100. Tel: 479-855-2335. E-mail: BellaVistaMuseum@gmail.com. Web Site: www.bellavistamuseum.org.
Founded 1976
Library Holdings: DVDs 30; Bk Titles 50
Special Collections: 100 year history of Bella Vista. Oral History
Wireless access
Function: Res libr
Open Wed-Sun 1-5
Restriction: Non-circulating

P BELLA VISTA PUBLIC LIBRARY*, 11 Dickens Pl, 72714-4603. Tel: 479-855-1753. FAX: 479-855-4475. E-mail: library@bellavistaar.gov. Web Site: www.bvpl.org. *Libr Dir,* Suzanne Adams; E-mail: sadams@bellavistaar.gov; *Asst Dir,* Argie Willis; E-mail: awillis@bellavistaar.gov; *Children & Youth Serv Librn,* Ellen Farwell; E-mail: efarwell@bellavistaar.gov; Staff 7 (MLS 3, Non-MLS 4)
Founded 1981. Pop 26,000; Circ 73,678
Jan 2016-Dec 2016 Income $295,332, Locally Generated Income $284,832, Other $10,500. Mats Exp $42,583, Books $31,063, Per/Ser (Incl. Access Fees) $5,463, Other Print Mats $250, AV Mat $5,807. Sal $156,114 (Prof $156,114)
Library Holdings: Audiobooks 930; Bks on Deafness & Sign Lang 10; CDs 330; DVDs 3,336; High Interest/Low Vocabulary Bk Vols 3,024; Large Print Bks 3,673; Bk Vols 55,000; Per Subs 40; Talking Bks 930
Automation Activity & Vendor Info: (Cataloging) Innovative Interfaces, Inc; (Circulation) Innovative Interfaces, Inc; (OPAC) Innovative Interfaces, Inc
Wireless access
Function: 24/7 Electronic res, 24/7 Online cat, Adult bk club
Special Services for the Blind - Free checkout of audio mat
Open Mon-Thurs 9-8, Fri & Sat 9-5
Friends of the Library Group

BENTON

P SALINE COUNTY PUBLIC LIBRARY*, Bob Herzfeld Memorial Library, 1800 Smithers Dr, 72015. SAN 330-8855. Tel: 501-778-4766. Toll Free Tel: 800-476-4466. FAX: 501-778-0536. E-mail: administrator@salinecountylibrary.org. Web Site: www.salinecountylibrary.org. *Dir,* Patricia Hector; E-mail: pattyh@salinecountylibrary.org; *Libr Mgr,* Janine Miller; E-mail: janinem@salinecountylibrary.org; *Colls Mgr,* Stacy Childress; E-mail: stacyc@salinecountylibrary.org; *Adult Serv Mgr,* Alissa Turner; E-mail: aturner@salinecountylibrary.org; *IT Mgr,* William Picking; E-mail: williamp@salinecountylibrary.org; *Pub Serv Mgr,* Rick Johnson; E-mail: rickj@salinecountylibrary.org; *Youth Serv Mgr,* SaraBeth Lesko; E-mail: sarabethl@salinecountylibrary.org; *Human Res Coordr,* Erin Loy; E-mail: erinl@salinecountylibrary.org; *Mkt Coordr,* Kari Beesley; Staff 32 (MLS 10, Non-MLS 22)
Founded 1931
Library Holdings: DVDs 11,550; e-books 5,201; Bk Titles 138,435; Per Subs 175; Talking Bks 9,888
Subject Interests: Arkansas
Automation Activity & Vendor Info: (Acquisitions) Innovative Interfaces, Inc; (Cataloging) Innovative Interfaces, Inc; (Circulation) Innovative Interfaces, Inc; (OPAC) Innovative Interfaces, Inc
Wireless access
Function: 24/7 Electronic res, 24/7 Online cat, Accelerated reader prog, Activity rm, Adult bk club, Archival coll, Audiobks on Playaways & MP3, Audiobks via web, Bk club(s), Bks on CD, Children's prog, Computers for patron use, E-Readers, Electronic databases & coll, Free DVD rentals, Home delivery & serv to seniorr ctr & nursing homes, Homebound delivery serv, Homework prog, ILL available, Internet access, Meeting rooms, Microfiche/film & reading machines, Music CDs, Notary serv, Online cat, Online ref, Outreach serv, OverDrive digital audio bks, Passport agency, Photocopying/Printing, Preschool outreach, Prog for adults, Prog for children & young adult, Ref serv available, Scanner, Story hour, Summer reading prog, Tax forms, Teen prog, Telephone ref, Wheelchair accessible, Writing prog
Open Mon, Tues & Thurs 9-8, Wed & Fri 9-5:30, Sat 9-4
Friends of the Library Group
Branches: 1
MABEL BOSWELL MEMORIAL LIBRARY - BRYANT, 201 Pricket Rd, Bryant, 72022, SAN 330-888X. Tel: 501-847-2166. FAX: 501-847-4524. *Br Mgr,* Leigh Espey; E-mail: leighe@salinecountylibrary.org; Staff 4 (Non-MLS 4)
Library Holdings: Bk Vols 43,234
Open Mon, Wed & Fri 9-5:30, Tues & Thurs 9-8, Sat 9-4

BENTONVILLE

P BENTONVILLE PUBLIC LIBRARY*, 405 S Main St, 72712. SAN 300-4880. Tel: 479-271-3192. Reference Tel: 479-271-6815. FAX: 479-271-6775. E-mail: library@bentonvillear.com. Web Site: www.bentonvillelibrary.org. *Dir,* Hadi Dudley; Tel: 479-271-3194, E-mail: hdudley@bentonvillear.com; *Ch,* Sue Ann Pekel; Tel: 479-271-6816, E-mail: spekel@bentonvillear.com; *Ref Librn,* Heather Hays; Tel: 479-271-5976, E-mail: hhays@bentonvillear.com; Staff 12 (MLS 1, Non-MLS 11)
Founded 1947. Pop 19,730; Circ 92,500
Library Holdings: AV Mats 2,335; Large Print Bks 4,000; Bk Vols 62,000; Per Subs 205; Talking Bks 3,500

Special Collections: Arkansas History, bk & microfilm; Benton County Daily Record, large print, micro
Automation Activity & Vendor Info: (Cataloging) TLC (The Library Corporation); (Circulation) TLC (The Library Corporation); (OPAC) TLC (The Library Corporation)
Wireless access
Open Mon-Thurs 9-8, Fri & Sat 9-5
Friends of the Library Group

J NORTHWEST ARKANSAS COMMUNITY COLLEGE*, Pauline Whitaker Library, One College Dr, 72712. Tel: 479-619-4244. E-mail: library@nwacc.edu. Web Site: library.nwacc.edu. *Libr Dir,* Gwen Dobbs; E-mail: gdobbs@nwacc.edu; *Ref Librn,* Allison Floyd; E-mail: afloyd6@nwacc.edu; *Ref Librn,* Erin Galbraith; E-mail: egalbraith@nwacc.edu
Highest Degree: Associate
Library Holdings: Bk Vols 30,000; Per Subs 100
Automation Activity & Vendor Info: (Cataloging) LibLime; (Circulation) LibLime; (OPAC) LibLime
Wireless access
Function: ILL available, Photocopying/Printing
Open Mon-Thurs (Winter) 8-8, Fri & Sat 9-3; Mon & Tues (Summer) 8-8, Wed & Thurs 8-6, Fri 9-3

BERRYVILLE

P BERRYVILLE PUBLIC LIBRARY*, 104 Spring St, 72616. SAN 331-0922. Tel: 870-423-2323. FAX: 870-423-2432. E-mail: info@berryvillelibrary.org. Web Site: berryvillelibrary.org. *Dir,* Julie Hall
Founded 1978
Library Holdings: Bks on Deafness & Sign Lang 10; High Interest/Low Vocabulary Bk Vols 150; Bk Vols 26,000; Per Subs 80
Wireless access
Mem of Carroll & Madison Library System
Open Mon-Fri 9-6, Sat 9-1
Friends of the Library Group

P CARROLL & MADISON LIBRARY SYSTEM, 106 Spring St, 72616. Tel: 870-423-5300. FAX: 870-423-7117. Administration E-mail: admin@camals.org. Web Site: www.carrollmadisonlibraries.org. *Regional Adminr,* Johnice Glisson; *Tech Serv Mgr,* Kris Burks; Staff 3 (MLS 2, Non-MLS 1)
Founded 2000
Member Libraries: Berryville Public Library; Green Forest Public Library; Kingston Community Library; Madison Public Library; St Paul Public Library
Open Mon-Fri 9-5

BLYTHEVILLE

J ARKANSAS NORTHEASTERN COLLEGE*, Adams-Vines Library, 2501 S Division St, 72315-5111. Tel: 870-762-3189. FAX: 870-762-5534. Web Site: www.anc.edu/facstaff/staff_library.htm. *Dir, AV, Dir, Libr Serv,* Karen Ellis; Tel: 870-762-1020, Ext 1234, E-mail: kellis@smail.anc.edu; Staff 3 (MLS 1, Non-MLS 2)
Founded 1993. Enrl 1,200; Fac 75; Highest Degree: Associate
Library Holdings: DVDs 125; High Interest/Low Vocabulary Bk Vols 100; Bk Vols 21,000; Per Subs 225; Videos 1,500
Special Collections: Arkansas Coll
Automation Activity & Vendor Info: (Cataloging) Innovative Interfaces, Inc; (Circulation) Innovative Interfaces, Inc; (ILL) OCLC; (OPAC) Innovative Interfaces, Inc
Wireless access
Partic in Amigos Library Services, Inc
Open Mon-Thurs 8-8, Fri 9-4, Sat 9-Noon

P MISSISSIPPI COUNTY LIBRARY SYSTEM*, 200 N Fifth St, 72315-2709. SAN 330-891X. Tel: 870-762-2431. FAX: 870-762-2242. E-mail: info@mclibrary.net. Web Site: www.mclibrary.net. *Dir,* Lowell Walters; E-mail: lwalters@mclibrary.net; Staff 19 (MLS 1, Non-MLS 18)
Founded 1921. Pop 42,000; Circ 24,750
Jul 2018-Jun 2019 Income (Main & Associated Libraries) $938,057, State $95,000, County $798,307, Other $20,000. Mats Exp $97,680, Books $77,370, Per/Ser (Incl. Access Fees) $3,711. Sal $125,504 (Prof $305,421)
Library Holdings: Audiobooks 5,905; e-books 6,517; Bk Vols 110,322; Per Subs 117; Videos 1,095
Wireless access
Function: 24/7 Electronic res, 24/7 Online cat, Activity rm, Adult bk club, Adult literacy prog, Audiobks via web, Bks on CD, Children's prog, Electronic databases & coll, Free DVD rentals, ILL available, Internet access, Laminating, Life-long learning prog for all ages, Magazines, Microfiche/film & reading machines, Notary serv, Online cat, OverDrive digital audio bks, Photocopying/Printing, Preschool outreach, Prog for children & young adult, Summer reading prog, Tax forms, Wheelchair accessible
Partic in OCLC Online Computer Library Center, Inc
Open Mon & Thurs 9-8, Tues, Wed & Fri 9-5, Sat 10-5, Sun 1-4
Restriction: ID required to use computers (Ltd hrs), In-house use for visitors, Internal use only
Branches: 6
BLYTHEVILLE PUBLIC, 200 N Fifth St, 72315. Tel: 870-762-2431. FAX: 870-762-2242. *Br Mgr,* Mary Razor; E-mail: mrazor@mclibrary.net; Staff 1 (MLS 1)
Founded 1921. Pop 15,620; Circ 100,000
Library Holdings: Bk Vols 150,000; Per Subs 100; Talking Bks 250
Function: After school storytime, ILL available, Photocopying/Printing, Prog for children & young adult, Spoken cassettes & CDs, Summer reading prog, Tax forms, VHS videos, Wheelchair accessible
Open Mon & Thurs 9-8, Tues & Wed 9-5, Sat 10-5, Sun 1-4
KEISER PUBLIC, 112 E Main St, Keiser, 72351, SAN 330-8944. Tel: 870-526-2073. *Br Mgr,* Karen Harrison; E-mail: kharrison@mclibrary.net
Pop 759; Circ 20,000
Library Holdings: Bk Titles 4,000; Per Subs 15; Talking Bks 20
Function: Prog for children & young adult, Summer reading prog, Tax forms
LEACHVILLE PUBLIC, 105 S Main St, Leachville, 72438. (Mail add: PO Box 686, Leachville, 72438-0686), SAN 330-8979. Tel: 870-539-6485. *Br Mgr,* Donna Austin; E-mail: daustin@mclibrary.net
Pop 1,993; Circ 20,000
Library Holdings: Bk Vols 4,000; Per Subs 15; Talking Bks 20
Function: Prog for children & young adult, Spoken cassettes & CDs, Summer reading prog, Tax forms, Wheelchair accessible
Open Mon 1:30-5:30, Wed & Fri 1-5
MANILA PUBLIC, 103 N Dewey Ave, Manila, 72442. (Mail add: PO Box 569, Manila, 72442-0559), SAN 330-9002. Tel: 870-561-3525. FAX: 870-561-3525. *Br Mgr,* Mary Alice Ketchum; E-mail: mketchum@mclibrary.net
Pop 3,324; Circ 30,000
Library Holdings: Bk Vols 4,000; Per Subs 15; Talking Bks 20
Function: After school storytime, Prog for children & young adult, Summer reading prog, Tax forms, Wheelchair accessible
Open Mon 2-6, Wed & Fri 1-5, Sat 1-4
OSCEOLA PUBLIC, 320 West Hale Ave, Osceola, 72370-2530, SAN 330-9037. Tel: 870-563-2721. FAX: 870-563-6550. *Br Mgr,* Denise Hester; E-mail: dhester@mclibrary.net; Staff 2 (MLS 1, Non-MLS 1)
Founded 1948. Pop 7,757; Circ 50,000
Library Holdings: Large Print Bks 300; Bk Titles 30,000; Per Subs 75; Talking Bks 200
Special Collections: Arkansas genealogy
Subject Interests: Local genealogy
Function: Computer training, ILL available, Internet access, Photocopying/Printing, Prog for adults, Prog for children & young adult, Ref serv available, Senior computer classes, Spoken cassettes & CDs, Summer reading prog, Tax forms, Telephone ref, VHS videos, Wheelchair accessible
Special Services for the Deaf - Bks on deafness & sign lang
Open Mon, Wed & Fri 9-5, Tues 12-8, Sat 10-5, Sun 1-4
WILSON PUBLIC, One Park St, Wilson, 72395, SAN 330-9061. Tel: 870-655-8414. FAX: 870-655-8414. *Br Mgr,* Linda Dawson; E-mail: ldawson@mclibrary.net
Pop 903; Circ 20,000
Library Holdings: Bk Vols 4,000; Per Subs 15; Talking Bks 20
Function: After school storytime, Prog for children & young adult, Spoken cassettes & CDs, Summer reading prog, Tax forms, Wheelchair accessible
Open Mon 1:30-5:30, Wed & Fri 12:30-4:30

BULL SHOALS

P BULL SHOALS LIBRARY*, 1218 Central Blvd, 72619. (Mail add: PO Box 406, 72619-0406), SAN 329-5419. Tel: 870-445-4265. E-mail: bullslibrary@hotmail.com. Web Site: bullshoalslibrary.mystrikingly.com. *Pres,* Michelle Skinner
Pop 3,000
Library Holdings: DVDs 30; Bk Vols 20,000; Per Subs 50; Talking Bks 403; Videos 705
Automation Activity & Vendor Info: (Cataloging) LiBRARYSOFT; (Circulation) LiBRARYSOFT; (OPAC) LiBRARYSOFT
Wireless access
Function: Computers for patron use, Free DVD rentals, Magazines, Movies, Printer for laptops & handheld devices, Wheelchair accessible
Open Tues & Thurs 10-6, Wed, Fri & Sat 10-3
Friends of the Library Group

CALICO ROCK

P IZARD COUNTY LIBRARY*, Calico Rock Public Library, 301 Second St, 72519. Tel: 870-297-3785. FAX: 870-297-2385. E-mail: calicorocklibrary@yahoo.com. *Librn,* Aimee Watts; Staff 2 (Non-MLS 2)
Founded 1959. Circ 16,000

Library Holdings: Audiobooks 226; DVDs 1,335; Large Print Bks 826; Bk Titles 15,296; Bk Vols 16,166; Per Subs 7
Special Collections: Genealogy Coll
Wireless access
Function: Bks on CD, Computers for patron use, Free DVD rentals, ILL available, Internet access, Magazines, Microfiche/film & reading machines, Online cat, Summer reading prog, Tax forms, Wheelchair accessible
Mem of White River Regional Library
Open Mon, Tues, Thurs & Fri 10:30-5, Wed & Sat 10-2

CAMDEN

P OUACHITA COUNTY LIBRARIES*, Public Library of Camden & Ouachita County, 405 Cash Rd SW, 71701-3735. SAN 331-2631. Tel: 870-836-5083. FAX: 870-836-0163. *Mgr,* Lisa Pickett; E-mail: lrpickett@hotmail.com
Pop 13,154
Library Holdings: Bk Titles 43,000
Wireless access
Open Mon-Fri 9:30-5:30, Sat 9-12
Branches: 2
BEARDEN PUBLIC LIBRARY, 210 N Cedar, Bearden, 71720. (Mail add: PO Box 136, Bearden, 71720-0136), SAN 331-2577. Tel: 870-687-2634. *Mgr,* Lucy Shurtleff
Pop 1,125
Open Mon-Thurs 2-5
STEPHENS PUBLIC LIBRARY, 108 W Ruby St, Stephens, 71764. (Mail add: PO Box 104, Stephens, 71764-0104), SAN 331-278X. Tel: 870-786-5231. *Mgr,* Rita Waller
Open Mon-Thurs 1-4

J SOUTHERN ARKANSAS UNIVERSITY TECH*, Rocket Success Center/Library, 6415 Spellman Rd, 71701. (Mail add: PO Box 3499, 71711-1599), SAN 300-4961. Tel: 870-574-4518, 870-574-4544. FAX: 870-574-4568. Web Site: library.sautech.edu. *Dir,* Kyra Jerry; Staff 2 (MLS 1, Non-MLS 1)
Founded 1967
Automation Activity & Vendor Info: (Cataloging) SirsiDynix; (Circulation) SirsiDynix; (Course Reserve) SirsiDynix; (ILL) OCLC WorldShare Interlibrary Loan; (OPAC) SirsiDynix; (Serials) EBSCO Online
Wireless access
Partic in ARKLink
Open Mon-Thurs 8-5, Fri 8-Noon

CEDARVILLE

P CEDARVILLE PUBLIC LIBRARY*, 737 Pirates Way, 72932. (Mail add: PO Box 95, 72932-0095), SAN 330-9908. Tel: 479-410-1853. FAX: 479-410-1853. E-mail: cedarville@crawfordcountylib.org. Web Site: www.youseemore.com/crawfordcls/location.asp?SchoolType=0&sID=19. *Br Dir,* Michele Belk; E-mail: mbelk@crawfordcountylib.org
Library Holdings: Bk Vols 11,334
Mem of Crawford County Library System
Open Mon-Fri 9:30-5:30, Sat 10-2
Friends of the Library Group

CLARKSVILLE

C UNIVERSITY OF THE OZARKS, Robson Library, 415 N College Ave, 72830. SAN 300-4899. Tel: 479-979-1382. Web Site: robson.ozarks.edu. *Dir,* Stuart P Stelzer; E-mail: sstelzer@ozarks.edu; *Resource Librn,* Douglas Denne; E-mail: ddenne@ozarks.edu; Staff 2 (MLS 2)
Founded 1891. Enrl 850; Fac 70; Highest Degree: Bachelor
Library Holdings: e-books 250,000; e-journals 60,000; Bk Vols 100,000; Per Subs 100
Automation Activity & Vendor Info: (Acquisitions) Insignia Software; (Cataloging) Insignia Software; (Circulation) Insignia Software; (Course Reserve) Insignia Software; (Discovery) EBSCO Discovery Service; (ILL) OCLC; (OPAC) Insignia Software; (Serials) OCLC
Wireless access
Partic in Amigos Library Services, Inc; ARKLink; OCLC Online Computer Library Center, Inc; Statewide California Electronic Library Consortium
Open Mon-Thurs 8am-Midnight, Fri 8-4:30, Sat 1-5, Sun 3-10

CONWAY

CR CENTRAL BAPTIST COLLEGE*, Story Library, 1501 College Ave, 72034. SAN 300-4902. Tel: 501-205-8878. E-mail: library@cbc.edu. Web Site: library.cbc.edu. *Libr Dir,* Rachel Whittingham; E-mail: rwhittingham@cbc.edu; Staff 4 (MLS 2, Non-MLS 2)
Founded 1952. Enrl 385; Highest Degree: Bachelor
Library Holdings: AV Mats 1,658; Bks on Deafness & Sign Lang 15; Bk Titles 48,135; Bk Vols 54,236; Per Subs 310
Special Collections: Baptist Missionary Association of Arkansas History
Automation Activity & Vendor Info: (Cataloging) TLC (The Library Corporation); (Circulation) TLC (The Library Corporation); (Discovery) EBSCO Discovery Service; (ILL) TLC (The Library Corporation); (OPAC) TLC (The Library Corporation)
Wireless access
Function: 24/7 Online cat, Internet access, Meeting rooms
Partic in ARKLink
Special Services for the Blind - Assistive/Adapted tech devices, equip & products
Open Mon-Thurs 7:30am-11:30pm, Fri 7:30-4, Sun 5pm-11:30pm
Restriction: Badge access after hrs, Limited access for the pub, Non-circulating coll, Non-circulating of rare bks

P FAULKNER-VAN BUREN REGIONAL LIBRARY SYSTEM*, 1900 Tyler St, 72034. SAN 330-9126. Tel: 501-327-7482. Administration Tel: 501-450-4981. FAX: 501-327-9098. E-mail: fcl@fcl.org. Web Site: www.fcl.org. *Dir,* John McGraw; E-mail: john@fcl.org; Staff 20.5 (MLS 2.5, Non-MLS 18)
Founded 1938. Pop 112,206; Circ 436,411
Library Holdings: AV Mats 15,162; Large Print Bks 100; Bk Titles 120,000; Bk Vols 183,005; Per Subs 309
Special Collections: Arkansas Coll; Genealogy Coll
Automation Activity & Vendor Info: (Acquisitions) LibraryWorld, Inc; (Cataloging) LibraryWorld, Inc; (Circulation) LibraryWorld, Inc; (ILL) OCLC; (OPAC) LibraryWorld, Inc; (Serials) EBSCO Online
Wireless access
Publications: Newsletter
Special Services for the Deaf - Assistive tech
Open Mon-Thurs 9-7, Fri & Sat 9-5, Sun 1-5
Restriction: Open to pub for ref & circ; with some limitations
Friends of the Library Group
Branches: 6
GREENBRIER BRANCH, 13 Wilson Farm Rd, Greenbrier, 72058, SAN 377-7723. Tel: 501-679-6344. FAX: 501-679-6934. *Librn,* Gail Polak; E-mail: gail@fcl.org
Open Mon-Thurs 9-6, Fri 9-5
MAYFLOWER BRANCH, Six Ashmore Dr, Mayflower, 72106, SAN 377-774X. Tel: 501-470-9678. FAX: 501-470-9039. *Librn,* Jean Smith; E-mail: jean@fcl.org
Open Mon-Thurs 9-6, Fri 9-5
MT VERNON BRANCH, 1371 Hwy 36, Mount Vernon, 72111. *Librn,* Kathy Blackwell; E-mail: kathy@fcl.org
Open Mon-Fri 11-6
TWIN GROVES BRANCH, Ten Twin Groves Lane, Twin Groves, 72039. Tel: 501-335-8088. FAX: 501-335-8088. *Librn,* Trudy Smith; E-mail: trudy@fcl.org
Library Holdings: Bk Vols 3,000
Open Mon-Fri Noon-6
VAN BUREN COUNTY, 289 Factory Rd, Clinton, 72031, SAN 330-9215. Tel: 501-745-2100. FAX: 501-745-5860. *Librn,* Karla Fultz; E-mail: karla@fcl.org
Library Holdings: Bk Vols 22,000
Open Mon 9-7, Tues-Thurs 9-5, Sat 10-1
Friends of the Library Group
VILONIA BRANCH, Three Bise St, Vilonia, 72173, SAN 374-4388. Tel: 501-796-8520. FAX: 501-796-8753. *Librn,* Shelia Finch; E-mail: sheila@fcl.org
Open Mon-Thurs 9-6, Fri 9-5
Friends of the Library Group

C HENDRIX COLLEGE, Olin C Bailey Library, 1600 Washington Ave, 72032. SAN 300-4910. Tel: 501-450-1303. FAX: 501-450-3800. Reference E-mail: libraryreference@hendrix.edu. Web Site: www.hendrix.edu/baileylibrary. *Dir & Librn,* Britt Anne Murphy; Tel: 501-450-1288, E-mail: murphyb@hendrix.edu; *Asst Librn, Pub Serv, Head, Instruction & Outreach,* Janice Weddle; Tel: 501-450-4560, E-mail: weddle@hendrix.edu; *Circ Mgr,* Amy DeVooght; E-mail: devooght@hendrix.edu; *Libr Spec,* Tina Murdock; Tel: 501-450-1302, E-mail: murdock@hendrix.edu; Staff 10 (MLS 4, Non-MLS 6)
Founded 1876. Enrl 1,375; Fac 108; Highest Degree: Master
Library Holdings: CDs 1,096; DVDs 3,101; e-books 35,000; e-journals 65,518; Microforms 74,279; Bk Titles 245,013; Bk Vols 275,500; Per Subs 350
Special Collections: Arkansas Methodist Archives; Arkansasiana; Hendrix College Archives; Stebbins Coll of Arkansiana; Wilbur D Mills Archives. State Document Depository
Automation Activity & Vendor Info: (Acquisitions) Innovative Interfaces, Inc; (Cataloging) Innovative Interfaces, Inc; (Circulation) Innovative Interfaces, Inc; (Course Reserve) Innovative Interfaces, Inc; (OPAC) Innovative Interfaces, Inc; (Serials) Innovative Interfaces, Inc
Wireless access
Partic in Amigos Library Services, Inc; ARKLink; Associated Colleges of the South

C UNIVERSITY OF CENTRAL ARKANSAS, Torreyson Library, 201 Donaghey Ave, 72035. SAN 300-4929. Tel: 501-450-3174. Interlibrary Loan Service Tel: 501-450-5205. Reference Tel: 501-450-5224.

Administration Tel: 501-450-5201. FAX: 501-450-5208. Web Site: www.uca.edu/library. *Libr Dir,* Dean Covington; E-mail: dcovington@uca.edu; Staff 35 (MLS 9, Non-MLS 26)
Founded 1907. Enrl 11,000; Highest Degree: Doctorate
Subject Interests: Arkansas
Automation Activity & Vendor Info: (Acquisitions) OCLC Worldshare Management Services; (Cataloging) OCLC Worldshare Management Services; (Circulation) OCLC Worldshare Management Services; (Course Reserve) OCLC Worldshare Management Services; (Discovery) OCLC Worldshare Management Services; (ILL) OCLC Tipasa; (OPAC) OCLC Worldshare Management Services; (Serials) OCLC Worldshare Management Services
Wireless access
Partic in ARKLink; OCLC Online Computer Library Center, Inc; OCLC-LVIS

CORNING

P CORNING PUBLIC LIBRARY*, 613 Pine St, 72422. SAN 331-3239. Tel: 870-857-3453. FAX: 870-857-3453. E-mail: corning@mylibrarynow.org. Web Site: www.mylibrarynow.org/corning. *Dir & Librn,* Kathy Butler; *Asst Dir, Cataloger,* Peggy Renee Bliss; *Circ,* Whitney Leonard; *Circ,* Chelsa Whitworth; Staff 4 (Non-MLS 4)
Founded 1926. Pop 6,000; Circ 36,000
Library Holdings: Bk Titles 32,000; Per Subs 10
Subject Interests: Genealogy
Automation Activity & Vendor Info: (Cataloging) Book Systems; (Circulation) Book Systems; (OPAC) Book Systems
Wireless access
Function: 24/7 Electronic res, 24/7 Online cat, After school storytime, Audiobks via web, Bks on cassette, Bks on CD, Children's prog, Computers for patron use, Free DVD rentals, ILL available, Internet access, Magazines, Mail & tel request accepted, Mango lang, Microfiche/film & reading machines, OverDrive digital audio bks, Photocopying/Printing, Summer reading prog, Tax forms, VHS videos
Mem of Northeast Arkansas Regional Library System
Open Mon, Tues & Thurs 8:30-5:30, Wed 8:30-5, Fri 8:30-4, Sat 9-1
Restriction: Borrowing requests are handled by ILL, Circ limited, Non-resident fee

CROSSETT

P CROSSETT PUBLIC LIBRARY*, 1700 Main St, 71635. SAN 300-4937. Tel: 870-364-2230. FAX: 870-364-2231. E-mail: mail@crossett.lib.ar.us. Web Site: crossettlibrary.com. *Dir,* David Anderson; E-mail: david@crossett.lib.ar.us; Staff 2 (MLS 2)
Founded 1938. Pop 14,000; Circ 103,789
Library Holdings: Bk Vols 44,000; Per Subs 65
Special Collections: Arkansas Coll
Wireless access
Open Mon, Tues, Thurs & Fri 9-6:30, Wed 9-5:30, Sat 9-3
Friends of the Library Group

C UNIVERSITY OF ARKANSAS AT MONTICELLO*, College of Technology-Crossett Library, 1326 Hwy 52 W, 71635. Tel: 870-364-6414. FAX: 870-364-5707. Web Site: www.uamont.edu. *Dir,* Daniel Boice; E-mail: Boice@uamont.edu
Enrl 3,000
Library Holdings: AV Mats 500; Bk Vols 6,500; Per Subs 12
Automation Activity & Vendor Info: (Cataloging) Follett Software; (Circulation) Follett Software; (Course Reserve) Follett Software; (ILL) Follett Software
Wireless access
Special Services for the Deaf - Adult & family literacy prog; Assistive tech; Bks on deafness & sign lang; High interest/low vocabulary bks
Special Services for the Blind - Assistive/Adapted tech devices, equip & products
Open Mon-Thurs 8-4, Fri 8-Noon

DAMASCUS

FAULKNER-VAN BUREN REGIONAL LIBRARY SYSTEM*, Damascus Branch, 17379 US 65, 72039. Tel: 501-335-8142. FAX: 501-335-8142. *Librn,* Karen Martin; E-mail: karen.martin@fcl.org
Open Tues, Thurs & Fri 10:30-5

DARDANELLE

P ARKANSAS RIVER VALLEY REGIONAL LIBRARY SYSTEM*, Headquarters, 501 N Front St, 72834. SAN 330-924X. Tel: 479-229-4418. FAX: 479-229-2595. E-mail: arvrls@centurytel.net. Web Site: www.arvrls.com. *Dir,* Donna McDonald
Founded 1959. Pop 71,434; Circ 358,759
Library Holdings: Bk Vols 146,132; Per Subs 200
Special Collections: Arkansas; Local History Coll
Automation Activity & Vendor Info: (Cataloging) SirsiDynix; (Circulation) SirsiDynix; (OPAC) SirsiDynix
Wireless access
Open Mon 12-7, Tues-Fri 9-5
Branches: 6
CHARLESTON BRANCH, 12 S School St, Charleston, 72933-0338, SAN 330-9304. Tel: 479-965-2605. FAX: 479-965-2755. E-mail: chpublibrary@yahoo.com. *Librn,* Misty Hawkins
Open Mon 12-7, Tues-Fri 9-5, Sat 10-Noon
FRANKLIN COUNTY, 407 W Market St, Ozark, 72949-2727, SAN 330-9363. Tel: 479-667-2724. FAX: 479-667-9021. E-mail: ozlib@centurytel.net. *Librn,* Nancy Smith
Open Mon 12-7, Tues-Fri 9-5, Sat 10-Noon
BOYD T & MOLLIE GATTIS-LOGAN COUNTY, 100 E Academy, Paris, 72855-4432, SAN 330-9452. Tel: 479-963-2371. FAX: 479-963-9243. E-mail: parlib@centurytel.net. *Librn,* Rita Eckart
Open Mon 11-7, Tues-Fri 9-5, Sat 9-1
Friends of the Library Group
JOHNSON COUNTY, Two Taylor Circle, Clarksville, 72830-3653, SAN 330-9398. Tel: 479-754-3135. FAX: 479-754-6343. E-mail: jclib@centurytel.net. *Librn,* Kathy Jones
Library Holdings: Bk Titles 30,000
Open Mon 12-7, Tues-Fri 9:30-5, Sat 9:30-12
LOGAN COUNTY, 419 N Kennedy, Booneville, 72927-3630, SAN 330-9428. Tel: 479-675-2735. E-mail: bblog@centurytel.net. *Librn,* Bridget Williams
Open Mon 11-7, Tues-Fri 9-5, Sat 9-1
Friends of the Library Group
YELL COUNTY, 904 Atlanta St, Danville, 72833. (Mail add: PO Box 850, Danville, 72833-0850), SAN 330-9517. Tel: 479-495-2911. FAX: 479-495-2822. E-mail: ycl@arkwest.com. *Librn,* Stacey Laurie
Open Mon 9-6, Tues-Fri 9-5

DE QUEEN

J COSSATOT COMMUNITY COLLEGE OF THE UNIVERSITY OF ARKANSAS*, Kimball Library, 195 College Dr, 71832. Tel: 870-584-4471. FAX: 870-642-3320. Web Site: www2.youseemore.com/cccua. *Dir, Educ Res,* Relinda Ruth; E-mail: rruth@cccua.edu; *Educ Res Assoc,* Beverly Foreman; E-mail: bforeman@cccua.edu
Library Holdings: Bk Vols 10,000; Per Subs 50
Wireless access
Open Mon-Thurs 7:30-7, Fri 7:30-4

P SEVIER COUNTY LIBRARY*, De Queen Branch, 200 W Stillwell Ave, 71832. SAN 331-1287. Tel: 870-584-4364. FAX: 870-642-8319. E-mail: seviercountylibrary@yahoo.com. Web Site: seviercountylibrary.com. *Head Librn,* Johnye Fisher
Founded 1906
Wireless access
Function: Children's prog, Computers for patron use, Free DVD rentals, Internet access, Photocopying/Printing
Open Mon-Fri 9-5, Sat 9-Noon
Branches: 3
GILLHAM BRANCH, 202 N Second St, Gillham, 71841-9511. (Mail add: PO Box 173, Gillham, 71842-0173), SAN 331-1376. Tel: 870-386-5665. FAX: 870-386-5665. E-mail: libgillham@yahoo.com. *Librn,* Brenda Tollett
Open Tues & Thurs 9-5, Sat 9-12
HORATIO BRANCH, 108 Main St, Horatio, 71842, SAN 331-1430. Tel: 870-832-6882. FAX: 870-832-6882. E-mail: horatiolibrary@yahoo.com. *Librn,* Amy Zuniga
Open Tues & Thurs 9:30-5, Wed 1-5, Sat 9-12

DECATUR

P IVA JANE PEEK PUBLIC LIBRARY*, 121 N Main St, 72722. (Mail add: PO Box 247, 72722-0247). Tel: 479-752-7323. FAX: 479-752-7323. E-mail: ijppublib121@yahoo.com. *Librn,* Karen Jones; Staff 1 (Non-MLS 1)
Founded 2001. Pop 1,699; Circ 2,222
Library Holdings: Audiobooks 31; Bks on Deafness & Sign Lang 3; CDs 77; DVDs 70; High Interest/Low Vocabulary Bk Vols 70; Large Print Bks 211; Bk Vols 9,236; Per Subs 2; Videos 399
Automation Activity & Vendor Info: (Cataloging) Book Systems; (Circulation) Book Systems; (OPAC) Book Systems
Wireless access
Function: Bks on CD, CD-ROM, Children's prog, Computers for patron use, Free DVD rentals, ILL available, Internet access, Learning ctr, Magazines, Microfiche/film & reading machines, Music CDs, Photocopying/Printing, Scanner, Spanish lang bks, Spoken cassettes & CDs, Summer reading prog, Tax forms, VHS videos
Open Mon-Fri 3:30-7, Wed 10:30-1
Restriction: Circ to mem only

DEWITT

P DEWITT PUBLIC LIBRARY*, 205 W Maxwell St, 72042. SAN 300-4945. Tel: 870-946-1151. FAX: 870-946-1151. E-mail: dewittpl@yahoo.com. Web Site: www.facebook.com/DeWittPublicLibrary. *Mgr,* Sarah Cole
Founded 1926. Pop 4,000; Circ 14,000
Library Holdings: Bk Vols 43,000
Wireless access
Open Mon-Fri 9-5, Sat 9-1
Branches: 1
CLEON COLLIER MEMORIAL LIBRARY, 211 Main St, Gillett, 72055, SAN 320-0817. Tel: 870-548-2821. FAX: 870-548-2821. *Mgr,* Stacey Clawson
Founded 1976. Circ 4,388
Library Holdings: Bk Titles 3,928
Open Mon-Wed & Fri 12:30-5:30

J PHILLIPS COMMUNITY COLLEGE OF THE UNIVERSITY OF ARKANSAS*, DeWitt Campus Library, 1210 Ricebelt Ave, 72042. (Mail add: PO Box 427, 72042-0427). Tel: 870-946-3506, Ext 1621. FAX: 870-946-2644. Web Site: www.pccua.edu/students/resources/library/dewitt. *Libr Tech,* Cornelya Jackson; E-mail: cjackson@pccua.edu
Library Holdings: Bk Vols 6,500; Per Subs 50
Automation Activity & Vendor Info: (Cataloging) Innovative Interfaces, Inc; (Circulation) Innovative Interfaces, Inc; (OPAC) Innovative Interfaces, Inc
Wireless access
Open Mon (Fall & Spring) 9:30-6:30, Tues-Thurs 7:30-4:30, Fri 7:30-1:30; Mon-Thurs (Summer) 7:30-5:30

EL DORADO

P BARTON PUBLIC LIBRARY*, 200 E Fifth St, 71730-3897. SAN 330-9541. Tel: 870-863-5447. FAX: 870-862-3944. E-mail: inquiries@bartonlibrary.org. Web Site: www.bartonlibrary.org. *Interim Dir,* Nancy L Arn; Tel: 870-863-5447, E-mail: narn@bartonlibrary.org; Staff 1 (MLS 1)
Founded 1958
Jan 2018-Dec 2018 Income (Main & Associated Libraries) $512,954, State $65,795, City $256,323, County $158,849, Locally Generated Income $32,987. Mats Exp $31,700, Books $22,000, Per/Ser (Incl. Access Fees) $1,700, Manu Arch $500, AV Mat $3,500, Electronic Ref Mat (Incl. Access Fees) $4,000. Sal $237,698 (Prof $52,000)
Library Holdings: Audiobooks 2,016; Bks on Deafness & Sign Lang 7; DVDs 1,613; Electronic Media & Resources 87; Microforms 618; Bk Titles 75,872; Per Subs 107
Special Collections: Arkansas Coll, monographs & periodicals; Genealogy Coll, micro, monographs; Large Print Coll
Automation Activity & Vendor Info: (Cataloging) TLC (The Library Corporation); (Circulation) TLC (The Library Corporation); (Course Reserve) TLC (The Library Corporation); (ILL) TLC (The Library Corporation); (Media Booking) TLC (The Library Corporation); (OPAC) TLC (The Library Corporation)
Wireless access
Function: 24/7 Electronic res, 24/7 Online cat, Accelerated reader prog, Archival coll, Bk club(s), Bks on CD, Children's prog, Computers for patron use, Genealogy discussion group, Holiday prog, Homebound delivery serv, Homework prog, ILL available, Mail & tel request accepted, Notary serv, Online cat, Outreach serv, Photocopying/Printing, Preschool outreach, Prog for adults, Prog for children & young adult, Ref serv available, Story hour, Summer reading prog, Tax forms, Teen prog, Wheelchair accessible
Publications: Tracks and Traces/ Genealogy (Quarterly newsletter)
Partic in OCLC Online Computer Library Center, Inc
Special Services for the Deaf - Bks on deafness & sign lang
Special Services for the Blind - Bks on CD; Large print bks; Ref serv
Open Mon-Fri 10-7, Sat 1-5
Friends of the Library Group
Branches: 5
HARPER MEMORIAL, 301 N Myrtle, Junction City, 71749. (Mail add: PO Box 730, Junction City, 71749-0730), SAN 330-9606. Tel: 870-924-5556. FAX: 870-924-5556. *Librn,* Position Currently Open
Library Holdings: Bk Vols 5,255
Open Mon, Tues, Thurs & Fri 12-5 (1-6 Summer)
Friends of the Library Group
HUTTIG BRANCH, Frost St, Huttig, 71747. (Mail add: PO Box 396, Huttig, 71747-0458), SAN 330-9576. Tel: 870-943-3411. FAX: 870-943-3411. *Librn,* Linda Miller
Library Holdings: Bk Vols 7,000
Open Mon, Tues, Thurs & Fri 12-5
NORPHLET PUBLIC, City Hall Bldg, 101 E Padgett St, Norphlet, 71759. (Mail add: PO Box 44, Norphlet, 71759-0044), SAN 330-9630. Tel: 870-546-2274. FAX: 870-546-2274. *Br Mgr,* Mrs Rose Ables; Tel: 870-546-2274, E-mail: norphlet@bartonlibrary.org
Open Mon & Fri 8-1, Tue & Thurs 1:30-6:30
SMACKOVER PUBLIC, 700 N Broadway, Smackover, 71762, SAN 330-969X. Tel: 870-725-3741. FAX: 870-725-3798. *Librn,* Melba Bussell
Library Holdings: Bk Vols 8,230
Subject Interests: Genealogy, Local hist
Open Mon, Tues, Thurs & Fri 8:30-4:45
Friends of the Library Group
STRONG PUBLIC, 246 Second Ave, Strong, 71765. (Mail add: PO Box 157, Strong, 71765-0157), SAN 330-972X. Tel: 870-797-2165. FAX: 870-797-2165. *Librn,* Nelia Jones
Pop 626; Circ 6,000
Library Holdings: Audiobooks 10; Bks on Deafness & Sign Lang 3; CDs 20; Large Print Bks 1,000; Bk Vols 5,400; Per Subs 10; Spec Interest Per Sub 3
Function: Summer reading prog
Open Mon, Tues, Thurs & Fri 11-4

J SOUTH ARKANSAS COMMUNITY COLLEGE*, SouthArk Library, 300 S West Ave, 71730. (Mail add: PO Box 7010, 71731), SAN 321-1754. Tel: 870-864-7115. FAX: 870-864-7134. E-mail: LibraryStaff@southark.edu. Web Site: southark.libguides.com. *Dir,* Philip Shackelford; E-mail: pshackelford@southark.edu; *Tech Serv Spec,* Lauri Wilson; E-mail: ltwilson@shouthark.edu; Staff 2 (MLS 1, Non-MLS 1)
Founded 1976. Enrl 1,250; Fac 75; Highest Degree: Associate
Library Holdings: Bk Titles 22,000; Bk Vols 24,000; Per Subs 98
Automation Activity & Vendor Info: (Acquisitions) LS 2000; (Cataloging) LS 2000; (Circulation) LS 2000; (Course Reserve) LS 2000; (OPAC) LS 2000; (Serials) LS 2000
Function: AV serv
Partic in Ark Libr Asn

ELKINS

P ELKINS PUBLIC LIBRARY*, 352 N Center St, 72727. SAN 328-6843. Tel: 479-643-2904. E-mail: elkinspubliclibrary@gmail.com. Web Site: elkinspubliclibrary.com. *Libr Dir,* Audra Bell
Library Holdings: DVDs 1,000; Bk Vols 13,000
Automation Activity & Vendor Info: (Acquisitions) Innovative Interfaces, Inc; (Cataloging) Innovative Interfaces, Inc; (Circulation) Innovative Interfaces, Inc; (OPAC) Innovative Interfaces, Inc
Wireless access
Mem of Washington County Library System
Open Mon-Fri 10-6, Sat 10-2
Friends of the Library Group

EUREKA SPRINGS

P EUREKA SPRINGS CARNEGIE PUBLIC LIBRARY*, 194 Spring St, 72632. SAN 331-0957. Tel: 479-253-8754. FAX: 479-253-7807. E-mail: info@eurekalibrary.org. Web Site: carrollmadisonlibraries.org/library.aspx?lib=eureka. *Dir,* April Griffith; *Asst Dir,* Kate Zakar; Staff 3 (MLS 1, Non-MLS 2)
Founded 1910. Pop 8,500; Circ 65,000
Library Holdings: Bks on Deafness & Sign Lang 20; High Interest/Low Vocabulary Bk Vols 75; Bk Vols 38,000; Per Subs 55
Special Collections: Local History Coll
Wireless access
Open Mon-Thurs 9-7, Fri & Sat 9-5, Sun 1-5
Friends of the Library Group

FAIRFIELD BAY

P FAIRFIELD BAY LIBRARY, INC, 369 Dave Creek Pkwy, 72088. SAN 330-9150. Tel: 501-884-4930. E-mail: ffbaylibrary@yahoo.com. Web Site: www.fairfieldbaylibrary.com. *Dir,* Karen Tangen
Wireless access
Special Services for the Deaf - Adult & family literacy prog; Bks on deafness & sign lang; Closed caption videos
Open Mon, Tues & Thurs 1-4, Wed & Fri 10-5, Sat 10-12:30
Friends of the Library Group

FARMINGTON

P FARMINGTON PUBLIC LIBRARY*, 175 W Cimarron Pl, 72730. Tel: 479-267-2674. FAX: 479-267-2641. E-mail: library@farmpl.org. Web Site: farmpl.org. *Librn,* Rachel Sawyer
Open Mon, Wed & Fri 9-5, Tues & Thurs 9-6, Sat 10-4

FAYETTEVILLE

P FAYETTEVILLE PUBLIC LIBRARY*, Blair Library, 401 W Mountain St, 72701. SAN 330-9932. Tel: 479-856-7000. FAX: 479-571-0222. E-mail: questions@faylib.org. Web Site: www.faylib.org. *Exec Dir,* David Johnson; Tel: 479-856-7100, E-mail: djohnson@faylib.org; *Dir, Info Tech,* Lynn Yandell; E-mail: lyandell@faylib.org; *Dir, Libr Serv,* Willow Fitzgibbon; E-mail: wfitzgibbon@faylib.org; *Mgr, Circ Serv,* Gwyneth Jelinek; E-mail: gjelinek@faylib.org; *Mgr, Tech Serv,* Sarah Houk; E-mail: shouk@faylib.org; Staff 23 (MLS 10, Non-MLS 13)
Founded 1916. Pop 68,980; Circ 951,872
Library Holdings: Bk Vols 270,000; Per Subs 357
Subject Interests: Genealogy
Automation Activity & Vendor Info: (Acquisitions) Innovative Interfaces, Inc; (Cataloging) Innovative Interfaces, Inc; (Circulation) Innovative Interfaces, Inc; (OPAC) Innovative Interfaces, Inc; (Serials) Innovative Interfaces, Inc
Wireless access
Function: After school storytime, Audio & video playback equip for onsite use, Bi-weekly Writer's Group, Games & aids for people with disabilities, Homebound delivery serv, ILL available, Music CDs, Prog for adults, Prog for children & young adult, Ref serv available, Spoken cassettes & CDs, Summer reading prog, Wheelchair accessible, Workshops
Special Services for the Blind - Assistive/Adapted tech devices, equip & products
Open Mon-Thurs 9-8, Fri & Sat 9-5, Sun 1-5
Restriction: Non-resident fee
Friends of the Library Group

C UNIVERSITY OF ARKANSAS LIBRARIES*, 365 N McIlroy Ave, 72701-4002. SAN 331-0264. Tel: 479-575-4101. Circulation Tel: 479-575-4104. Interlibrary Loan Service Tel: 479-575-6424. Reference Tel: 479-575-6645. Administration Tel: 479-575-6702. FAX: 479-575-6656. Interlibrary Loan Service FAX: 479-575-5558. Reference FAX: 479-575-4592. Web Site: libinfo.uark.edu. *Dean,* Carolyn Henderson Allen; E-mail: challen@uark.edu; *Dir, Admin Serv,* Marco DeProsperis; Tel: 479-575-3079, E-mail: mdeprosp@uark.edu; *Dir, Acad Res & Serv,* Lora Lennertz; Tel: 479-575-5545, E-mail: lennertz@uark.edu; *Dir, Coll Mgt & IT Serv,* ; *Dir, Law Libr,* Randy Thompson; Tel: 479-575-5831, E-mail: rjthomps@uark.edu; *Develop Dir,* Ben Carter; Tel: 479-575-4663, E-mail: bcarter@uark.edu; *Asst Dir, Human Res,* Jeff Banks; Tel: 479-575-4769, E-mail: jbbanks@uark.edu; *Head, Chemistry & Biochemistry Library,* Lutishoor Salisbury; Tel: 479-575-8418, E-mail: lsalisbu@uark.edu; *Head, Fine Arts Library,* Philip J Jones; Tel: 479-575-3081, E-mail: pjj01@uark.edu; *Head, ILL,* Tess Gibson; Tel: 479-575-2925, E-mail: tmgibso@uark.edu; *Head, Instruction Serv,* Joel Thornton; Tel: 479-575-4133, E-mail: jbt012@uark.edu; *Head, Monographs,* Mary Gilbertson; Tel: 479-575-5417, E-mail: mag@uark.edu; *Head, Performing Arts & Media,* Tim Zou; Tel: 479-575-5514, E-mail: tzou@uark.edu; *Head, Scholarly Communications,* Dr Melody Herr; *Head, Spec Coll,* Position Currently Open; *Head, Spec Coll Cat,* Mikey King; Tel: 479-575-4657, E-mail: mikey@uark.edu; *Head, Tech Serv,* Deb Kulczak; Tel: 479-575-4811, E-mail: dkulczak@uark.edu; *Bus Librn,* Position Currently Open; *Communications Librn,* Michelle Gibeault; Tel: 479-575-3362, E-mail: gibeault@uark.edu; *Digital Serv Librn,* Martha Parker; Tel: 479-575-2032, E-mail: map012@uark.edu; *Distance Educ Librn,* Elaine Thornton; Tel: 479-575-4856, E-mail: met022@uark.edu; *Educ Librn,* Position Currently Open; *Eng & Math Librn,* Patricia Kirkwood; Tel: 479-575-2480, E-mail: pkirkwo@uark.edu; *Geoscience Librn,* Dr Jozef Laincz; Tel: 479-575-2241, E-mail: jlaincz@uark.edu; *Life Sci Librn,* Tony Stankus; Tel: 479-575-4031, E-mail: tstankus@uark.edu; *Ref Librn,* Norma Johnson; Tel: 479-575-3498, E-mail: njohns@uark.edu; *Ref Librn,* Sarah Spiegel; Tel: 479-575-8415, E-mail: sspiegel@uark.edu; *Sci Librn,* Necia Parker-Gibson; Tel: 479-575-8421, E-mail: neciap@uark.edu; *Spec Coll Res & Outreach Serv Librn,* Joshua Youngblood; Tel: 479-575-7251, E-mail: jcyoungb@uark.edu; *User Experience Librn,* Kathleen Lehman; Tel: 479-575-7048, E-mail: kalehman@uark.edu; *Web Serv Librn,* Beth Juhl; Tel: 479-575-4665, E-mail: bjuhl@uark.edu; *Librn in Residence,* Position Currently Open; *Govt Doc & Soc Sci Serv,* Donna Daniels; Tel: 479-575-8417, E-mail: donnad@uark.edu; *Univ Archivist,* Amy Allen; Tel: 479-575-6370, E-mail: ala005@uark.edu. Subject Specialists: *Asian studies, Chinese lang & lit, Japanese lang & lit,* Lora Lennertz; *Art & archit, Interior design, Lang,* Philip J Jones; *Asian studies, Chinese lang & lit, Japanese lang & lit,* Tim Zou; *Composition, English, Lit,* Michelle Gibeault; *Engr, Math, Transportation,* Patricia Kirkwood; *Anthrop, Archaeology, Geog,* Dr Jozef Laincz; Staff 50 (MLS 32, Non-MLS 18)
Founded 1872. Enrl 26,237; Fac 1,108; Highest Degree: Doctorate
Jul 2014-Jun 2015. Mats Exp $6,994,251, Books $776,103, Per/Ser (Incl. Access Fees) $5,446,911, Other Print Mats $419,834, Micro $309,161. Sal $5,934,314 (Prof $3,520,905)
Library Holdings: CDs 33,212; DVDs 8,611; e-books 295,971; Electronic Media & Resources 9,013; Microforms 5,590,687; Bk Vols 2,393,346
Special Collections: Arkansas Coll; William J Fulbright Coll. Oral History; US Document Depository
Subject Interests: Agr, Archit, Creative writing, Intl relations
Automation Activity & Vendor Info: (Acquisitions) Innovative Interfaces, Inc; (Cataloging) Innovative Interfaces, Inc; (Circulation) Innovative Interfaces, Inc; (Course Reserve) Innovative Interfaces, Inc; (ILL) Innovative Interfaces, Inc; (Media Booking) Innovative Interfaces, Inc; (OPAC) Innovative Interfaces, Inc; (Serials) Innovative Interfaces, Inc
Wireless access
Publications: Arkansauce (Journal); Arkansian (Special Collections) (Newsletter); Retrospective (Annual report)
Partic in Amigos Library Services, Inc; Arkansas Academic & Research Network; Center for Research Libraries; Council of University of Arkansas Research Libraries; EPSCoR Science Information Group; Greater Western Library Alliance
Special Services for the Blind - Assistive/Adapted tech devices, equip & products
Open Mon-Thurs 7am-2am, Fri 7-6, Sat 10-6, Sun Noon-2am

Departmental Libraries:

CHEMISTRY & BIOCHEMISTRY, University of Arkansas, 225 CHEM, 72701-4002. Tel: 479-575-2557. Administration Tel: 479-575-8418. Web Site: libinfo.uark.edu/chemistry. *Head of Libr,* Lutishoor Salisbury; Fax: 479-575-6656, E-mail: lsalisbu@uark.edu. Subject Specialists: *Biochem, Chem,* Lutishoor Salisbury; Staff 2 (MLS 1, Non-MLS 1)
Enrl 330; Fac 23; Highest Degree: Doctorate

FINE ARTS, 104 Fine Arts Bldg, 72701. (Mail add: 365 N McIlroy Ave, 72701-4002). Tel: 479-575-4708. Web Site: libinfo.uark.edu/fal. *Head of Libr,* Phillip J Jones; Tel: 479-575-3081, E-mail: pjj01@uark.edu. Subject Specialists: *Archit, Art, Interior design,* Phillip J Jones; Staff 3 (MLS 1, Non-MLS 2)
Enrl 876; Fac 48; Highest Degree: Bachelor
Library Holdings: Bk Vols 36,231
Automation Activity & Vendor Info: (Circulation) Innovative Interfaces, Inc; (OPAC) Innovative Interfaces, Inc
Open Mon-Thurs 8am-11pm, Fri 8-6, Sat 1-6, Sun 2-11
Friends of the Library Group

PHYSICS, 221 Physics, 72701. (Mail add: 365 N McIlroy Ave, 72701-4002). Tel: 479-575-2505. E-mail: physlib@uark.edu. Web Site: libinfo.uark.edu/physics. *Head of Libr,* Stephanie Pierce; Tel: 479-575-4483, E-mail: sjpierce@uark.edu
Library Holdings: Bk Vols 19,407

CL ROBERT A & VIVIAN YOUNG LAW LIBRARY, School of Law, Waterman Hall 107, 72701-1201, SAN 331-0353. Tel: 479-575-5601. FAX: 479-575-2053. Web Site: law.uark.edu/library/research. *Dir,* Randall Thompson; Tel: 479-575-5831, E-mail: rjthomps@uark.edu; *Assoc Dir,* Monika Szakasits; Tel: 479-575-2839, E-mail: mszakas@uark.edu; *Bus Mgr,* Jackie Dunn; Tel: 479-575-5310, E-mail: jmd03@uark.edu; *Cat Supvr,* Nancy Phillips; Tel: 479-575-5984, E-mail: nphillips@uark.edu; *Circ,* Jo Anna Collins; Tel: 479-575-5051, E-mail: jcollins@uark.edu; *Ref (Info Servs),* Cathy Chick; Tel: 479-575-5835, E-mail: cchick@uark.edu; Staff 13 (MLS 6, Non-MLS 7)
Founded 1924. Enrl 400; Fac 35; Highest Degree: Doctorate
Library Holdings: Bk Titles 89,462; Bk Vols 158,353; Per Subs 545
Special Collections: State Document Depository; UN Document Depository; US Document Depository
Subject Interests: Law
Automation Activity & Vendor Info: (Acquisitions) Innovative Interfaces, Inc; (Cataloging) Innovative Interfaces, Inc; (Circulation) Innovative Interfaces, Inc; (Course Reserve) Innovative Interfaces, Inc; (ILL) Innovative Interfaces, Inc; (Media Booking) Innovative Interfaces, Inc; (OPAC) Innovative Interfaces, Inc; (Serials) Innovative Interfaces, Inc
Partic in Mid-America Law Library Consortium; OCLC Online Computer Library Center, Inc
Publications: Young in a Nutshell (Newsletter)

P WASHINGTON COUNTY LIBRARY SYSTEM*, 1080 W Clydesdale Dr, 72701. Tel: 479-442-6253. FAX: 479-442-6812. E-mail: info@wcls.lib.ar.us. Web Site: www.co.washington.ar.us/government/departments-f-z/library. *Dir,* Glenda Audrain; E-mail: glendaa@wcls.lib.ar.us; Staff 2 (MLS 2)
Founded 2000. Pop 199,060; Circ 1,051,830
Library Holdings: Bk Vols 350,000
Function: ILL available
Member Libraries: Elkins Public Library; Lincoln Public Library; Prairie Grove Public Library; Springdale Public Library; West Fork Municipal Library
Open Mon-Fri 8-5
Friends of the Library Group

Branches: 2

GREENLAND BRANCH LIBRARY, 8 E Ross St, Greenland, 72737, SAN 330-9967. Tel: 479-582-5992. E-mail: greenlandbranch@wcls.lib.ar.us. *Librn,* Scott Baker
Library Holdings: Bk Vols 7,500
Open Mon, Tues, Thurs & Fri 12-5

WINSLOW BRANCH LIBRARY, 351 South Hwy 71, Winslow, 72959, SAN 331-023X. Tel: 479-634-5405. E-mail: winslowbranch@wcls.lib.ar.us. *Br Mgr,* Jean Cosgrove
Library Holdings: Bk Titles 6,000
Open Tues-Thurs & Sat 9-5

FORREST CITY

J EAST ARKANSAS COMMUNITY COLLEGE*, Learning Resources Center, 1700 Newcastle Rd, 72335. SAN 320-1201. Tel: 870-633-4480, Ext 322. FAX: 870-633-7222. Web Site: www.eacc.edu/EACC-library. *Dir,* Paige Laws; E-mail: plaws@eacc.edu; Staff 4 (MLS 1, Non-MLS 3)
Founded 1974. Enrl 972
Library Holdings: Bk Vols 30,000; Per Subs 100
Automation Activity & Vendor Info: (Cataloging) TLC (The Library Corporation); (Circulation) TLC (The Library Corporation); (OPAC) TLC (The Library Corporation)
Open Mon & Tues 7:30-6:30, Wed & Thurs 7:30-4:30, Fri 8-Noon

P FORREST CITY PUBLIC LIBRARY*, 421 S Washington St, 72335-3839. SAN 300-502X. Tel: 870-633-5646. FAX: 870-633-5647. E-mail: fcpl@forrestcitylibrary.org. Web Site: www.forrestcitylibrary.org. *Dir,* Arlisa Harris; E-mail: Arlisa@forrestcitylibrary.org; Staff 4 (MLS 1, Non-MLS 3)
Founded 1921. Pop 15,000; Circ 34,019
Library Holdings: Bk Titles 29,156; Per Subs 31
Subject Interests: Arkansas
Wireless access
Function: Adult bk club, Bks on CD, Children's prog, Computers for patron use, Free DVD rentals, Laminating, Magazines, Online cat, OverDrive digital audio bks, Photocopying/Printing, Prog for adults, STEM programs, Summer reading prog, Tax forms
Open Mon-Wed 9-6, Thurs 9-5, Fri 9-4, Sat 9-Noon

FORT SMITH

M BAPTIST HEALTH - FORT SMITH*, Regional Health Sciences Library/UAMS West, 1001 Towson Ave, 72902. (Mail add: PO Box 2406, 72902-2406), SAN 300-5054. Tel: 479-441-5337. FAX: 479-441-5339.
Founded 1972
Library Holdings: Bk Titles 3,000; Per Subs 20
Automation Activity & Vendor Info: (Cataloging) Koha
Wireless access
Function: ILL available
Partic in OCLC Online Computer Library Center, Inc
Open Mon-Fri 8-4:30

S WILLIAM O DARBY RANGER MEMORIAL FOUNDATION INC*, Museum & Heritage Centre, 311 General Darby St, 72902. (Mail add: PO Box 1625, 72902-1625), SAN 375-3514. Tel: 479-782-3388. E-mail: GenDarby@yahoo.com. Web Site: www.darbyrangerfoundation.com. *Dir,* Emory S Dockery, Jr; E-mail: esdockery34@gmail.com
Founded 1977
Library Holdings: Bk Vols 5,000
Special Collections: Victor L Cary Civil War Book Coll; World War II Coll
Wireless access
Open Mon-Fri 8-1

P FORT SMITH PUBLIC LIBRARY*, 3201 Rogers Ave, 72903. SAN 331-0507. Tel: 479-783-0229. Circulation Tel: 479-783-0229, Ext 1101. Reference Tel: 479-783-0229, Ext 1171. Information Services Tel: 479-783-0229, Ext 1100. FAX: 479-783-5129. E-mail: information@fortsmithlibrary.org. Web Site: www.fortsmithlibrary.org. *Libr Dir,* Jennifer Goodson; E-mail: jgoodson@fortsmithlibrary.org; *Asst Dir,* Diane Holwick; E-mail: dholwick@fortsmithlibrary.org; *Ref Librn,* Galen Webb; E-mail: gwebb@fortsmithlibrary.org; *Spec Projects Librn,* Ashley Hagan; E-mail: ahagan@fortsmithlibrary.org; *Tech Serv Librn,* Jennie Ballinger; E-mail: jballinger@fortsmithlibrary.org; *Youth Serv Librn,* Robin Benham; E-mail: rbenham@fortsmithlibrary.org; *Circ Supvr,* Ronny Phengsouvanna Vong; E-mail: rphengsouvan@fortsmithlibrary.org; *Info Spec,* Diana Curry; E-mail: dcurry@fortsmithlibrary.org. Subject Specialists: *Genealogy,* Diana Curry; Staff 14 (MLS 6, Non-MLS 8)
Founded 1906. Pop 80,268; Circ 686,013
Library Holdings: AV Mats 12,477; Bk Titles 169,249; Bk Vols 252,952; Per Subs 475
Special Collections: Local, State History & Genealogy (Arkansas Coll), bks & micro; Mathew C Clark American Sign Language Coll; Vietnamese Coll
Subject Interests: Spanish
Automation Activity & Vendor Info: (Cataloging) Innovative Interfaces, Inc; (Circulation) Innovative Interfaces, Inc; (OPAC) Innovative Interfaces, Inc
Wireless access
Partic in OCLC Online Computer Library Center, Inc
Open Mon-Thurs 9-9, Fri 9-6, Sat 10-5, Sun 1-5
Friends of the Library Group
Branches: 3
DALLAS STREET, 8100 Dallas St, 72903. Tel: 479-484-5650. FAX: 479-484-5658. E-mail: dallas@fortsmithlibrary.org. Web Site: www.fortsmithlibrary.org/about-the-library/dallas-street-branch. *Br Mgr,* Mark Raymond; E-mail: mraymond@fortsmithlibrary.org; Staff 2 (MLS 1, Non-MLS 1)
Library Holdings: Bk Vols 24,730
Open Mon 9-9, Tues-Fri 9-6, Sat 12-5
MILLER, 8701 S 28th St, 72908. Tel: 479-646-3945. FAX: 479-646-3965. E-mail: miller@fortsmithlibrary.org. Web Site: www.fortsmithlibrary.org/about-the-library/miller-branch. *Br Mgr,* Tiffany DeVries; E-mail: tdevries@fortsmithlibrary.org; Staff 1 (Non-MLS 1)
Library Holdings: Bk Vols 26,786
Open Mon & Wed-Fri 9-6, Tues 9-9, Sat 12-5
WINDSOR DRIVE, 4701 Windsor Dr, 72904. Tel: 479-785-0405. FAX: 479-785-0431. E-mail: windsor@fortsmithlibrary.org. Web Site: www.fortsmithlibrary.org/about-the-library/windsor-drive-branch. *Br Mgr,* Rachel Smith; E-mail: rsmith@fortsmithlibrary.org; Staff 1 (Non-MLS 1)
Library Holdings: Bk Vols 24,829
Open Mon-Wed & Fri 9-6, Thurs 9-9, Sat 12-5

M SAINT EDWARD MERCY MEDICAL CENTER LIBRARY*, 7301 Rogers Ave, 72917. (Mail add: PO Box 17000, 72917-7000), SAN 300-5038. Tel: 479-314-6520. FAX: 479-314-5646. Web Site: www.mercy.net/medical-library. *Med Librn,* Pat Morris; E-mail: Pat.morris@mercy.net
Library Holdings: Bk Vols 1,600; Per Subs 52
Subject Interests: Med, Nursing
Wireless access
Open Mon-Fri 7:30-4

GL SEBASTIAN COUNTY LAW LIBRARY*, 623 Garrison Ave, Ste 418, 72901. SAN 300-5046. Tel: 479-783-4730. FAX: 479-783-4730. E-mail: sebcoll76@gmail.com. *Librn,* Jennifer Dunn
Library Holdings: Bk Vols 18,000
Wireless access
Open Mon-Thurs 9-12:30 & 1:30-5

C UNIVERSITY OF ARKANSAS FORT SMITH*, Boreham Library, 5210 Grand Ave, 72903. (Mail add: PO Box 3649, 72913-3649), SAN 300-5062. Tel: 479-788-7200. FAX: 479-788-7209. E-mail: Library@UAFS.edu. Web Site: library.uafs.edu. *Dir, Libr Serv,* Anne Liebst; Tel: 479-788-7205, E-mail: anne.liebst@uafs.edu; *Libr Tech,* Dianne Werthmuller; E-mail: dianne.werthmuller@uafs.edu; Staff 6 (MLS 6)
Founded 1928. Enrl 5,400; Fac 240; Highest Degree: Bachelor
Library Holdings: CDs 354; DVDs 2,316; e-books 163,000; e-journals 56,000; Music Scores 500; Bk Titles 62,408; Bk Vols 66,646; Per Subs 240
Special Collections: Grantsmanship Coll; Olive, Kathleen & Rosa Belle A Pebley Historical & Cultural Center; Wilder Historical Coll
Automation Activity & Vendor Info: (Cataloging) Innovative Interfaces, Inc; (Circulation) Innovative Interfaces, Inc; (Course Reserve) Innovative Interfaces, Inc; (ILL) OCLC ILLiad; (OPAC) Innovative Interfaces, Inc; (Serials) Innovative Interfaces, Inc
Wireless access
Function: Online cat
Partic in Amigos Library Services, Inc; ARKLink; OCLC Online Computer Library Center, Inc
Open Mon-Thurs (Fall & Spring) 7am-Midnight, Fri 7-5, Sat 11-5, Sun 1-Midnight

GARFIELD

S US NATIONAL PARK SERVICE*, Pea Ridge Military Park Library, 15930 Hyw 62, 72732. SAN 370-2855. Tel: 479-451-8122. FAX: 479-451-8639. Web Site: www.nps.gov/peri. *Library Contact,* Troy Banzhaf; E-mail: troy_banzhaf@nps.gov
Library Holdings: Bk Vols 500
Special Collections: Battle of Pea Ridge, microfilm, rpts
Wireless access
Restriction: Open to pub by appt only, Open to pub for ref only

GENTRY

P GENTRY PUBLIC LIBRARY*, 105 E Main St, 72734. Tel: 479-736-2054. FAX: 479-736-8567. E-mail: bookmark@gentrylibrary.us. Web Site: www.gentrylibrary.us. *Interim Dir,* Linda Crume; E-mail: lcrume@gentrylibrary.us; Staff 3 (Non-MLS 3)
Founded 1975. Pop 15,359; Circ 25,397
Jan 2017-Dec 2017 Income $134,650, City $3,425, Locally Generated Income $4,600, Other $126,625. Mats Exp $6,400, Books $6,000, Per/Ser (Incl. Access Fees) $400. Sal $41,794
Library Holdings: Audiobooks 983; Bks on Deafness & Sign Lang 14; DVDs 1,702; Large Print Bks 72; Bk Titles 19,961; Per Subs 25

Special Collections: American Civil War (Quantrill Special Coll Research)
Automation Activity & Vendor Info: (Acquisitions) Book Systems; (Cataloging) Book Systems; (Circulation) Book Systems
Wireless access
Function: 24/7 Electronic res, 24/7 Online cat, Activity rm, Adult bk club, Archival coll, Audio & video playback equip for onsite use, Audiobks on Playaways & MP3, Bks on CD, Children's prog, Computers for patron use, Free DVD rentals, Internet access, Magazines, Meeting rooms, Movies, Notary serv, OverDrive digital audio bks, Photocopying/Printing, Summer reading prog, Wheelchair accessible
Open Mon-Thurs 9-6, Fri 9-5, Sat 9-Noon
Friends of the Library Group

GLENWOOD

P BAINUM LIBRARY, Pike County / Glenwood Branch Library, 128 E Broadway, 71943. (Mail add: PO Box 1980, 71943), SAN 331-1406. Tel: 870-356-5193. E-mail: bainumlibrary@gmail.com. Web Site: 16566.rmwebopac.com. *Head Librn,* Shelly Skelton
Founded 1972. Pop 800
Library Holdings: Audiobooks 171; Bks on Deafness & Sign Lang 2; CDs 6; DVDs 2,005; Large Print Bks 1,089; Bk Vols 18,346
Automation Activity & Vendor Info: (Cataloging) ResourceMATE; (Circulation) ResourceMATE; (OPAC) ResourceMATE
Wireless access
Function: Accelerated reader prog, Bks on CD, Children's prog, Computers for patron use, Holiday prog, Internet access, Laminating, Photocopying/Printing, Scanner, Wheelchair accessible
Open Tues-Fri 10-5

GRAVETTE

P GRAVETTE PUBLIC LIBRARY*, 119 Main St SE, 72736-9363. Tel: 479-787-6955. FAX: 479-250-3726. E-mail: librarystaff@gravettear.com. Web Site: www.gravettelibrary.org. *Libr Dir,* Karen Benson; Staff 3 (Non-MLS 3)
Founded 1976. Pop 4,000; Circ 11,655
Library Holdings: Bk Vols 20,000; Per Subs 10
Automation Activity & Vendor Info: (Cataloging) Book Systems; (Circulation) Book Systems; (OPAC) Book Systems
Wireless access
Function: 24/7 Online cat, After school storytime
Special Services for the Blind - Accessible computers; Audio mat
Open Mon-Fri 10-6, Sat 10-1
Friends of the Library Group

GREEN FOREST

P GREEN FOREST PUBLIC LIBRARY*, 206 E Main St, 72638-2627. (Mail add: PO Box 746, 72638-0746), SAN 331-0981. Tel: 870-438-6700. FAX: 870-438-4586. E-mail: info@greenforestlibrary.org. Web Site: www.carrollmadisonlibraries.org/library.aspx?lib=greenforest. *Libr Dir,* Tiffany Newton; E-mail: tnewton@greenforestlibrary.org; *Asst Librn,* LeAnn Stark; *Libr Asst,* Tammy Martin; Staff 4 (MLS 1, Non-MLS 3)
Founded 1935
Library Holdings: Audiobooks 1,174; Bks on Deafness & Sign Lang 29; Braille Volumes 2; CDs 10; DVDs 2,099; High Interest/Low Vocabulary Bk Vols 150; Large Print Bks 300; Bk Vols 23,973; Per Subs 50; Videos 175
Automation Activity & Vendor Info: (Acquisitions) Innovative Interfaces, Inc; (Cataloging) Innovative Interfaces, Inc; (Circulation) Innovative Interfaces, Inc; (OPAC) Innovative Interfaces, Inc; (Serials) Innovative Interfaces, Inc
Wireless access
Mem of Carroll & Madison Library System
Open Mon-Thurs 9-6, Fri & Sat 9-5
Friends of the Library Group

GREENWOOD

P SCOTT-SEBASTIAN REGIONAL LIBRARY*, 18 N Adair, 72936. (Mail add: PO Box 400, 72936-0400), SAN 331-0566. Tel: 479-996-2856. FAX: 479-996-2236. *Dir,* Judy Beth Clevenger; E-mail: judybc111@yahoo.com; Staff 9 (MLS 1, Non-MLS 8)
Founded 1954. Pop 42,000
Library Holdings: Bk Vols 92,000; Per Subs 150
Special Collections: Arkansas History Coll
Automation Activity & Vendor Info: (Cataloging) Follett Software; (Circulation) Follett Software
Open Mon 9-7:30, Tues-Fri 9-5, Sat 9-12
Friends of the Library Group
Branches: 5
HARTFORD LIBRARY, 22 Broadway, Hartford, 72938. (Mail add: PO Box 236, Hartford, 72938-0236), SAN 331-0655. *Br Mgr,* Jacqueline Hoopengarner
Library Holdings: Bk Vols 4,000
Open Tues & Thurs 10:30-11:30 & 12:30-4:30
Friends of the Library Group
LAVACA LIBRARY, 100 S Davis, Lavaca, 72941, SAN 331-071X. *Br Mgr,* Sara McCormick
Library Holdings: Bk Vols 4,000
Open Tues 1-5
Friends of the Library Group
MANSFIELD LIBRARY, 200 N Sebascott Ave, Mansfield, 72944. (Mail add: PO Box 476, Mansfield, 72944-0476), SAN 331-0744. *Br Mgr,* Anna Carter
Library Holdings: Bk Vols 3,700
Open Mon 10-12 & 1-4, Thurs 9-1 & 1-4
Friends of the Library Group
SCOTT COUNTY LIBRARY, 149 Second St, Waldron, 72958. (Mail add: PO Box 957, Waldron, 72958-0957), SAN 331-0809. Tel: 479-637-3516. FAX: 479-637-3516. *Librn,* Patsy Vaughn
Library Holdings: Bk Vols 34,000
Special Collections: Arkansas History
Open Tues-Fri 9-5, Sat 10-1
Friends of the Library Group
SEBASTIAN COUNTY LIBRARY, 18 N Adair, 72936. (Mail add: PO Box 400, 72936), Tel: 479-996-2856. *Librn,* Marla Hicks
Library Holdings: AV Mats 925; Bk Vols 78,000; Per Subs 145; Videos 1,881
Special Collections: Arkansas History; Gifted & Talented Children; Large Print; Reference
Open Mon 9-7:30, Tues-Fri 9-5, Sat 9-12
Friends of the Library Group

HAMBURG

P ASHLEY COUNTY LIBRARY*, 211 E Lincoln St, 71646. SAN 300-5070. Tel: 870-853-2078. E-mail: ashcolib@gmail.com. Web Site: ashcolib.com. *Dir,* Holly Gillum
Founded 1935. Pop 24,319; Circ 69,500
Library Holdings: Large Print Bks 350; Bk Titles 53,830; Per Subs 64; Talking Bks 1,088
Subject Interests: Genealogy
Publications: Weekly newspaper column
Open Mon & Wed-Fri 9-5:30, Tues 10-5:30

HAMPTON

P CALHOUN COUNTY LIBRARY*, 115 S 2nd St, 71744. (Mail add: PO Box 1162, 71744-1162), SAN 373-1863. Tel: 870-798-4492. FAX: 870-798-4492. E-mail: calcolib@gmail.com. *Dir,* Allie Stevens; Staff 2 (MLS 1, Non-MLS 1)
Founded 1959. Pop 5,000
Library Holdings: Bk Vols 15,000
Wireless access
Function: Audio & video playback equip for onsite use, Audiobks via web, Children's prog, Computer training, Computers for patron use, Electronic databases & coll, Family literacy, ILL available, Internet access, Life-long learning prog for all ages, Magazines, Magnifiers for reading, Online cat, Outside serv via phone, mail, e-mail & web, OverDrive digital audio bks, Photocopying/Printing, Prog for adults, Prog for children & young adult, Ref serv available, Res assist avail, Scanner, Serves people with intellectual disabilities, Summer reading prog, Tax forms, Teen prog, Telephone ref, Wheelchair accessible
Open Mon-Wed & Fri 12-5
Branches: 1
THORNTON PUBLIC LIBRARY, 220 Second St, Rte 1, Thornton, 71766. (Mail add: PO Box 40, Thornton, 71766), SAN 331-2844. Tel: 870-352-5990. *Librn,* Venita Ann Ables
Open Mon, Tues, Thurs & Fri 2-5

HARDY

P SHARP COUNTY LIBRARY*, 201 Church St, 72542. Tel: 870-856-3934. FAX: 870-856-3934. E-mail: hardylib@hotmail.com. Web Site: www.library.arkansas.gov/facilities/details/sharp-county-library. *Mgr,* Cecilia Mullins
Founded 1934. Pop 578
Library Holdings: Bk Vols 28,500; Per Subs 49
Wireless access
Mem of White River Regional Library
Open Mon-Fri 8:30-5, Sat 9-1
Friends of the Library Group
Branches: 3
CAVE CITY BRANCH, 120 Spring St, Cave City, 72521. (Mail add: PO Box 240, Cave City, 72521-0240). Tel: 870-283-6947. *Mgr,* Vera Anderson
Library Holdings: Bk Vols 4,000; Per Subs 21
Open Mon & Wed 10-5, Fri 10:30-5:30
Friends of the Library Group

EVENING SHADE BRANCH, 222 Main St, Evening Shade, 72532. (Mail add: PO Box 118, Evening Shade, 72532-0118). Tel: 870-266-3873. *Mgr,* Angela Haley
Library Holdings: Bk Vols 4,500
Open Tues, Thurs & Fri 10-5
Friends of the Library Group
WILLIFORD BRANCH, 232 Main St, Williford, 72482. (Mail add: PO Box 94, Williford, 72482-0094). Tel: 870-966-4227. *Mgr,* Lisa Duncan
Library Holdings: Bk Vols 4,000
Open Mon & Fri 10:30-4:30

HARRISON

P BOONE COUNTY LIBRARY*, 221 W Stephenson, 72601-4225. SAN 331-0892. Tel: 870-741-5913. FAX: 870-741-5946. Web Site: www.boonecountylibrary.org. *Dir,* Ginger Schoenenberger; E-mail: ginger@boonecountylibrary.org; Staff 9 (MLS 1, Non-MLS 8)
Founded 1903. Pop 33,000; Circ 170,363
Library Holdings: Bk Vols 81,000
Automation Activity & Vendor Info: (Cataloging) TLC (The Library Corporation); (Circulation) TLC (The Library Corporation); (Course Reserve) TLC (The Library Corporation); (ILL) OCLC WorldShare Interlibrary Loan; (OPAC) TLC (The Library Corporation); (Serials) TLC (The Library Corporation)
Wireless access
Function: Accelerated reader prog, Art exhibits, Bk reviews (Group), CD-ROM, Children's prog, Computers for patron use, E-Reserves, Electronic databases & coll, Genealogy discussion group, Homebound delivery serv, ILL available, Internet access, Music CDs, Online cat, Online ref, Photocopying/Printing, Preschool outreach, Prog for children & young adult, Scanner, Summer reading prog, Tax forms, Teen prog, Telephone ref, VHS videos, Wheelchair accessible
Special Services for the Deaf - Bks on deafness & sign lang; Closed caption videos; High interest/low vocabulary bks
Special Services for the Blind - Aids for in-house use; Bks & mags in Braille, on rec, tape & cassette; Bks available with recordings; Bks on cassette; Bks on CD; Braille & cassettes; Braille bks; Children's Braille; Copier with enlargement capabilities; Home delivery serv; Large print & cassettes; Large print bks; Magnifiers; Talking bks
Open Mon, Wed, Fri & Sat 9-5, Tues & Thurs 9-7
Restriction: Sub libr
Friends of the Library Group

C NORTH ARKANSAS COLLEGE LIBRARY*, South Campus, 1515 Pioneer Dr, 72601. SAN 378-391X. Tel: 870-391-3355. Reference Tel: 870-391-3358. FAX: 870-391-3245. Web Site: www.northark.edu/campus-life/library. *Interim Dir,* Michelle Palmer; Tel: 870-391-3356, E-mail: mpalmer@northark.edu; *Cat,* Lacey Vanderpool; E-mail: lvanderpool@northark.edu; Staff 5 (MLS 2, Non-MLS 3)
Founded 1974. Enrl 1,500; Fac 121; Highest Degree: Bachelor
Library Holdings: AV Mats 2,800; Bk Titles 22,500; Bk Vols 25,200; Per Subs 212
Subject Interests: Arkansas
Automation Activity & Vendor Info: (Cataloging) TLC (The Library Corporation); (Circulation) TLC (The Library Corporation); (ILL) OCLC; (OPAC) TLC (The Library Corporation); (Serials) TLC (The Library Corporation)
Wireless access
Function: For res purposes
Partic in OCLC Online Computer Library Center, Inc
Open Mon-Thurs 8-7, Fri 8-5
Friends of the Library Group

HAZEN

P PRAIRIE COUNTY LIBRARY SYSTEM*, Hazen Public Library (Headquarters), 201 US Hwy 70 E, 72064. (Mail add: PO Box 428, 72064), SAN 324-8070. Tel: 870-255-3576. FAX: 870-255-1212. Web Site: www1.youseemore.com/prairiecountyrl. *Dir,* April Highfill; E-mail: ahighfill.prairiecountylibrary@gmail.com
Wireless access
Open Mon-Fri 9:30-5
Branches: 2
DES ARC PUBLIC, 408 Curran St, Des Arc, 72040, SAN 373-5036. Tel: 870-256-3003. FAX: 870-256-3003.
Open Mon-Thurs 9:30-5
Friends of the Library Group
DEVALLS BLUFF PUBLIC, 173 Market St, Devalls Bluff, 72041. (Mail add: PO Box 504, Devalls Bluff, 72041), SAN 373-5044. Tel: 870-998-7010. FAX: 870-998-7010.
Open Thurs 9:30-1 & 1:30-4

HEBER SPRINGS

P CLEBURNE COUNTY LIBRARY*, Mary I Wold Library, 1009 W Main St, 72543. SAN 377-8592. Tel: 501-362-2477. FAX: 501-362-2606. Web Site: www.cleburnecountylibrary.com. *Dir,* Zac Cothren; E-mail: director@cleburnecountylibrary.com; Staff 5 (Non-MLS 5)
Founded 1935
Library Holdings: Bk Vols 42,000; Per Subs 95
Automation Activity & Vendor Info: (Cataloging) Follett Software; (Circulation) Follett Software; (Course Reserve) Follett Software; (OPAC) Follett Software; (Serials) Follett Software
Mem of White River Regional Library
Open Mon 12-8, Tues, Wed & Fri 9-5, Thurs 9-8, Sat 9-4
Friends of the Library Group
Branches: 2
GREERS FERRY BRANCH, Greers Ferry Lake Plaza, 8249 Edgemont Rd, Ste 9, Greers Ferry, 72067, SAN 372-5138. Tel: 501-825-8677. *Librn,* Constance Jean Cothren; E-mail: constancecothren@yahoo.com; Staff 1 (Non-MLS 1)
Founded 1974
Library Holdings: Bk Vols 9,000
Function: Art exhibits
Open Mon, Wed & Fri 12-4:30, Sat 9-12
Restriction: 24-hr pass syst for students only, Access at librarian's discretion, Access for corporate affiliates, Authorized personnel only, Authorized scholars by appt, Badge access after hrs
Friends of the Library Group
QUITMAN BRANCH, 5904 Hebner Springs Rd W, Quitman, 72131. (Mail add: PO Box 32, Quitman, 72131-0032). Tel: 501-589-2332. *Mgr,* Melissa Reynolds

HELENA

J PHILLIPS COMMUNITY COLLEGE OF THE UNIVERSITY OF ARKANSAS*, Helena - West Helena Campus Library, 1000 Campus Dr, 72342. (Mail add: PO Box 785, 72342-0785), SAN 300-5097. Tel: 870-338-6474. FAX: 870-338-7542. Web Site: www.pccua.edu/students/resources/library. *Interim Libr Dir,* Ruthie Pride; Tel: 870-338-6474, Ext 1145, E-mail: rpride@pccua.edu; *Libr Tech,* Dorie Tate; Tel: 870-338-6474, Ext 1167, E-mail: dtate@pccua.edu; *Libr Tech,* Linda Washington; E-mail: lwashington@pccua.edu; Staff 4 (MLS 1, Non-MLS 3)
Founded 1966. Enrl 1,486
Library Holdings: Bk Titles 43,550; Per Subs 351
Wireless access
Partic in Library & Information Resources Network
Open Mon-Thurs (Fall & Spring) 7:45am-8pm, Fri 7:45-4:30; Mon-Thurs (Summer) 7-5:30

P PHILLIPS-LEE-MONROE REGIONAL LIBRARY*, Phillips County Library, 702 Porter St, 72342-3142. SAN 331-1139. Tel: 870-338-7732. FAX: 870-338-8855. E-mail: ral72342@yahoo.com. *Dir,* Linda Bennett; Staff 1 (Non-MLS 1)
Founded 1961. Pop 50,000; Circ 53,302
Library Holdings: Bk Vols 219,786; Per Subs 121
Subject Interests: Arkansas, Genealogy, Local hist
Wireless access
Open Mon-Fri 7-5, Sat 9-1
Branches: 5
ELAINE LIBRARY, 126 Main St, Elaine, 72333. (Mail add: PO Box 328, Elaine, 72333), SAN 331-1147. Tel: 870-827-6628. *Librn,* Wanda Fowler
Founded 1974
Open Mon-Wed 9-4
JACOBS MEMORIAL LIBRARY, 270 Madison St, Clarendon, 72029-2792, SAN 331-1155. Tel: 870-747-5593. FAX: 870-747-5593. *Br Librn,* Jim Rogers
Open Mon-Fri 9-4
LEE COUNTY LIBRARY, 77 W Main St, Marianna, 72360-2297, SAN 321-8511. Tel: 870-295-2688. FAX: 870-295-2688. *Librn,* Betsy Bowman
Open Mon-Wed & Fri 9-4
MARVELL LIBRARY, 806 Carruth St, Marvell, 72366. (Mail add: PO Box 625, Marvell, 72366-0625), SAN 331-1163. Tel: 870-829-3183. *Librn,* Edwynne Story
Founded 1924
Open Tues-Thurs 9-4:30
WEST HELENA LIBRARY, 721 Plaza St, West Helena, 72390-2698, SAN 331-118X. Tel: 870-572-2861. *Br Coordr,* Jean Smith
Founded 1916
Open Mon-Fri 10-5

HOPE

P HEMPSTEAD COUNTY LIBRARY, 500 S Elm St, 71801. Tel: 870-777-4564. FAX: 870-777-2915. E-mail: hempcolib@gmail.com. Web Site: www.hempcolib.org. *Dir,* Courtney McNiel; Staff 3 (MLS 1, Non-MLS 2)
Founded 1948. Pop 22,500; Circ 28,200
Library Holdings: Audiobooks 586; DVDs 341; e-books 701; Large Print Bks 1,427; Bk Vols 43,897; Per Subs 15
Wireless access
Open Mon 12-8, Tues-Thurs 9-5:30
Friends of the Library Group

J UNIVERSITY OF ARKANSAS AT HOPE-TEXARKANA*, 2500 S Main St, 71801. (Mail add: PO Box 140, 71801), SAN 375-4197. Tel: 870-722-8250. FAX: 870-777-8254. Web Site: www.uacch.edu. *Dir, Libr & Info Serv,* Marielle McFarland; Tel: 870-722-8251, E-mail: marielle.mcfarland@uacch.edu; Staff 3 (MLS 1, Non-MLS 2)
Founded 1992. Enrl 1,485; Fac 45; Highest Degree: Associate
Library Holdings: AV Mats 1,100; e-books 30,000; Bk Vols 11,500
Automation Activity & Vendor Info: (Course Reserve) Follett Software
Function: CD-ROM, Computers for patron use, Electronic databases & coll, ILL available, Online cat, Online ref, Photocopying/Printing, Ref serv available, VHS videos, Wheelchair accessible
Open Mon-Thurs 7-7, Fri 7-3

HORSESHOE BEND

P IZARD COUNTY LIBRARY, Horseshoe Bend Public Library, Nine Club Rd, 72512-2717. Tel: 870-670-4318. E-mail: horseshoebendlib@gmail.com. Web Site: horseshoebendpubliclibrary.weebly.com/. *Librn,* Megan L Crouch
Founded 1974. Pop 2,500
Library Holdings: Bk Titles 12,000
Wireless access
Function: Adult bk club, Bk club(s), Bks on CD, Computers for patron use, Free DVD rentals, Internet access, Magazines, Meeting rooms, Movies, Photocopying/Printing, Prog for adults, Prog for children & young adult, Ref & res, Ref serv available, Res assist avail, Scanner, Spoken cassettes & CDs, Study rm, Summer reading prog, Wheelchair accessible
Mem of White River Regional Library
Special Services for the Deaf - Bks on deafness & sign lang
Special Services for the Blind - Bks on cassette; Bks on CD; Closed circuit TV magnifier; Large print bks; Low vision equip
Open Mon-Fri 11-5, Sat 10-2:30
Restriction: Circ to mem only, Open to pub for ref & circ; with some limitations
Friends of the Library Group

HOT SPRINGS

P GARLAND COUNTY LIBRARY*, 1427 Malvern Ave, 71901. SAN 372-767X. Tel: 501-623-4161. FAX: 501-623-5647. E-mail: gcl@gclibrary.com. Web Site: www.gclibrary.com. *Dir,* Adam A Webb; E-mail: awebb@gclibrary.com; Staff 7 (MLS 7)
Founded 1833. Pop 97,322; Circ 873,247
Library Holdings: Bk Vols 110,000; Per Subs 450
Automation Activity & Vendor Info: (Acquisitions) SirsiDynix-WorkFlows; (Cataloging) SirsiDynix-WorkFlows; (Circulation) SirsiDynix-WorkFlows; (Discovery) SirsiDynix-Enterprise; (ILL) OCLC WorldShare Interlibrary Loan; (OPAC) SirsiDynix
Wireless access
Function: 24/7 Electronic res, 24/7 Online cat, Accelerated reader prog, Adult bk club, After school storytime, Art exhibits, Audiobks on Playaways & MP3, Audiobks via web, Bk club(s), Bks on CD, Children's prog, Computer training, Computers for patron use, E-Readers, Electronic databases & coll, Family literacy, Free DVD rentals, Holiday prog, Homebound delivery serv, ILL available, Internet access, Jazz prog, Life-long learning prog for all ages, Magazines, Meeting rooms, Microfiche/film & reading machines, Movies, Music CDs, Online cat, Online ref, Outreach serv, OverDrive digital audio bks, Photocopying/Printing, Preschool outreach, Preschool reading prog, Printer for laptops & handheld devices, Prog for adults, Prog for children & young adult, Ref & res, Ref serv available, Res performed for a fee, Senior computer classes, Spanish lang bks, Story hour, Study rm, Summer & winter reading prog, Summer reading prog, Tax forms, Teen prog, Wheelchair accessible, Winter reading prog, Workshops
Open Mon, Fri & Sat 9-5, Tues, Wed & Thurs 9-8, Sun 12:30-5:30
Friends of the Library Group

J NATIONAL PARK COLLEGE LIBRARY*, 101 College Dr, 71913. SAN 300-5100. Tel: 501-760-4101, 501-760-4110. Interlibrary Loan Service Tel: 501-760-4105. FAX: 501-760-4106. Web Site: www1.youseemore.com/npc. *Dir,* Lynn Valetutti; E-mail: lynn.valetutti@np.edu; *Librn,* Kristen Quintanilla; E-mail: kquintanilla@np.edu; Staff 6 (MLS 2, Non-MLS 4)
Founded 1973. Enrl 3,500; Fac 150; Highest Degree: Associate
Jul 2016-Jun 2017 Income $414,273. Mats Exp $81,600, Books $39,000, Per/Ser (Incl. Access Fees) $10,000, AV Equip $2,000, AV Mat $5,000, Electronic Ref Mat (Incl. Access Fees) $25,600. Sal $13,000 (Prof $175,462)
Library Holdings: Audiobooks 54; CDs 203; DVDs 1,899; e-books 62,557; Electronic Media & Resources 87; Bk Titles 25,234; Per Subs 80
Special Collections: Arkansas Coll
Subject Interests: Art, Hist, Lit, Nursing, Sciences
Automation Activity & Vendor Info: (Acquisitions) TLC (The Library Corporation); (Cataloging) TLC (The Library Corporation); (Circulation) TLC (The Library Corporation); (Course Reserve) TLC (The Library Corporation); (ILL) OCLC FirstSearch; (OPAC) TLC (The Library Corporation); (Serials) EBSCO Online
Wireless access
Partic in Amigos Library Services, Inc; Arkansas Academic & Research Network; ARKLink; OCLC Online Computer Library Center, Inc
Special Services for the Deaf - Bks on deafness & sign lang; Closed caption videos
Special Services for the Blind - Bks on CD; Copier with enlargement capabilities; Low vision equip
Open Mon-Thurs 7am-7:30 pm, Fri 7-3:30

HUNTSVILLE

P MADISON PUBLIC LIBRARY*, 827 N College Ave, 72740. (Mail add: PO Box 745, 72740-0745), SAN 331-1015. Tel: 479-738-2754. FAX: 479-738-5542. E-mail: info@madisoncountylibraries.org. Web Site: www.carrollmadisonlibraries.org/library.aspx?lib=huntsville. *Libr Dir,* Staci Evans; *Asst Librn,* Rose Fowler; *Libr Asst,* Johna Cornett
Founded 1953
Library Holdings: Bk Vols 15,000; Per Subs 20
Wireless access
Mem of Carroll & Madison Library System
Partic in Morris Automated Information Network; Northeast Ohio Regional Library System
Open Mon & Tues 8-6, Wed-Fri 8-4:30, Sat 9-1
Friends of the Library Group

JASPER

P NEWTON COUNTY PUBLIC LIBRARY*, Hwy 7 S, 72641. (Mail add: HC31, Box 8, 72641), SAN 331-1074. Tel: 870-446-2983. FAX: 870-446-2986. E-mail: newtonark@yahoo.com, outreach@newtoncountylibrary.org. Web Site: www.newtoncountylibrary.com. *Librn,* Teresa Hayes
Library Holdings: Bk Vols 15,000
Partic in Evergreen Indiana Consortium
Open Mon-Fri 9:30-5:30, Sat 10-2
Friends of the Library Group

JONESBORO

P CROWLEY RIDGE REGIONAL LIBRARY, 315 W Oak Ave, 72401. SAN 331-1821. Tel: 870-935-5133. FAX: 870-935-7987. Web Site: www.libraryinjonesboro.org. *Dir,* David Eckert; E-mail: david@libraryinjonesboro.org; Staff 18 (MLS 7, Non-MLS 11)
Founded 1966. Pop 97,018; Circ 398,655
Automation Activity & Vendor Info: (Acquisitions) Innovative Interfaces, Inc - Millennium; (Cataloging) Innovative Interfaces, Inc - Millennium; (Circulation) Innovative Interfaces, Inc - Millennium; (OPAC) Innovative Interfaces, Inc - Millennium
Wireless access
Function: Adult bk club, Adult literacy prog, Art exhibits, Audio & video playback equip for onsite use, Bk club(s), CD-ROM, Digital talking bks, Games & aids for people with disabilities, ILL available, Internet access, Magnifiers for reading, Music CDs, Photocopying/Printing, Prog for adults, Prog for children & young adult, Satellite serv, Summer reading prog, VHS videos, Wheelchair accessible, Workshops
Open Mon-Fri 9-7, Sat 9-5, Sun 1-5
Friends of the Library Group

CM UNIVERSITY OF ARKANSAS FOR MEDICAL SCIENCES*, Regional Center Northeast Medical Library, 223 E Jackson, 72401. (Mail add: 311 E Matthews, 72401), SAN 300-5135. Tel: 870-972-1290. FAX: 870-931-0839. Web Site: www.uark.edu. *Dir, Libr Serv,* Donna Petrus; E-mail: dpetrus@uams.edu
Founded 1974
Library Holdings: Bk Vols 2,015; Per Subs 145
Subject Interests: Family practice
Publications: Updates (NE Arkansas Hosp Libr Consortium)
Partic in Northeast Arkansas Hospital Library Consortium; OCLC Online Computer Library Center, Inc; Univ of Ark for Med Sci
Open Mon-Fri 8-5

KINGSTON

P KINGSTON COMMUNITY LIBRARY*, 120 Madison 2605, 72742-0006. (Mail add: PO Box 6, 72624). Tel: 479-665-2745. FAX: 479-665-2745. E-mail: klibrary@madisoncounty.net. Web Site: www.klibrary.org. *Librn,* Linda Davidson
Library Holdings: Bk Vols 5,000
Wireless access
Mem of Carroll & Madison Library System
Open Mon 10-1 & 2-6, Tues-Fri 2-6, Sat 9-1
Friends of the Library Group

LEWISVILLE

P LAFAYETTE COUNTY LIBRARY*, 219 E Third St, 71845. SAN 331-2720. Tel: 870-921-4757. FAX: 870-921-4756. E-mail: lewisvillelibrary2004@yahoo.com. Web Site: www.youseemore.com/Columbia/default.asp?xID=26. *Library Contact,* Rosey Byrd
Library Holdings: Bk Titles 9,651
Open Mon-Fri 12-6

LINCOLN

P LINCOLN PUBLIC LIBRARY, 107 W Bean St, 72744. (Mail add: PO Box 555, 72744-0555), SAN 330-9991. Tel: 479-824-3294. E-mail: library@lincolnarkansas.com. Web Site: lincolnarlibrary.com. *Dir,* Dianna Payne
Pop 1,752
Library Holdings: Bk Vols 30,000; Per Subs 3
Automation Activity & Vendor Info: (Cataloging) Innovative Interfaces, Inc. - Polaris; (Circulation) Innovative Interfaces, Inc. - Polaris; (OPAC) Innovative Interfaces, Inc. - Polaris
Wireless access
Mem of Washington County Library System
Open Mon-Thurs 9-5, Fri 10-5, Sat 9-1

LITTLE ROCK

S THE ARKANSAS ARTS CENTER*, Elizabeth Prewitt Taylor Memorial Library, MacArthur Park, 501 E Ninth St, 72202. (Mail add: PO Box 2137, 72203-2137), SAN 300-5151. Tel: 501-372-4000. FAX: 501-375-8053. E-mail: library@arkansasartscenter.org. Web Site: www.arkansasartscenter.org.
Founded 1963
Library Holdings: Bk Vols 7,000; Per Subs 25
Special Collections: George Fisher Political Cartoons
Subject Interests: Art, Decorative art
Automation Activity & Vendor Info: (Acquisitions) Innovative Interfaces, Inc; (Cataloging) Innovative Interfaces, Inc; (Circulation) Innovative Interfaces, Inc; (Course Reserve) Innovative Interfaces, Inc; (ILL) Innovative Interfaces, Inc; (Media Booking) Innovative Interfaces, Inc; (OPAC) Innovative Interfaces, Inc; (Serials) Innovative Interfaces, Inc
Wireless access
Restriction: Non-circulating

C ARKANSAS BAPTIST COLLEGE, J C Oliver Library, 1600 Martin Luther King Dr, 72202. SAN 300-516X. Tel: 501-420-1252. Circulation Tel: 501-420-1254. FAX: 501-244-5102. Web Site: www.arkansasbaptist.edu/library. *Libr Dir,* Jacqueline McGehee; E-mail: jacqueline.mcgehee@arkansasbaptist.edu
Library Holdings: Bk Titles 20,000; Bk Vols 30,000; Per Subs 98
Automation Activity & Vendor Info: (Cataloging) Follett Software; (ILL) Follett Software
Wireless access
Open Mon-Thurs 8:30-6:30, Fri 8:30-5

G ARKANSAS GEOLOGICAL SURVEY LIBRARY*, 3815 W Roosevelt Rd, 72204-6369. SAN 300-5208. Tel: 501-296-1877. FAX: 501-663-7360. E-mail: ags@arkansas.gov. Web Site: www.geology.arkansas.gov. *Librn,* Natalie Birdsong; Tel: 501-683-0120; *Library Contact,* Celeste Haner; E-mail: celeste.haner@arkansas.gov
Founded 1923
Library Holdings: Bk Titles 10,000; Per Subs 11
Publications: Bulletins; Guidebooks; Information Circulars, Miscellaneous Publications; Water Resources Circulars & Summaries
Open Mon-Fri 8-4:30

S ARKANSAS HISTORY COMMISSION LIBRARY*, One Capitol Mall, 2nd Flr, 72201. SAN 326-7008. Tel: 501-682-6900. FAX: 501-682-6916. E-mail: state.archives@arkansas.gov. Web Site: archives.arkansas.gov. *Librn,* Sheila Bevill; E-mail: sheila.bevill@arkansas.gov; *Managing Archivist,* Mary Dunn; E-mail: mary.e.dunn@arkansas.gov; *Curator,* Julienne Crawford; E-mail: julienne.crawford@arkansas.gov; Staff 6 (MLS 2, Non-MLS 4)
Library Holdings: Microforms 53,000; Bk Vols 20,000; Per Subs 1,000
Subject Interests: Arkansas, State hist
Open Mon-Sat 8-4:30

S ARKANSAS SCHOOL FOR THE DEAF LIBRARY*, 2400 W Markham St, 72205. (Mail add: PO Box 3811, 72203-3811), SAN 300-5240. Tel: 501-324-9515. FAX: 501-324-9553. TDD: 501-324-9506. Web Site: arschoolforthedeaf.org. *Librn,* Regina Dettra; E-mail: reginad@asd.k12.ar.us
Library Holdings: Bks on Deafness & Sign Lang 600; Bk Vols 10,000; Per Subs 75
Automation Activity & Vendor Info: (Cataloging) Follett Software; (Circulation) Follett Software
Special Services for the Deaf - Bks on deafness & sign lang; Captioned film dep; Staff with knowledge of sign lang; TTY equip
Open Mon-Fri 9-5

P ARKANSAS STATE LIBRARY, 900 W Capitol, Ste 100, 72201-3108. SAN 331-2097. Tel: 501-682-2053. Interlibrary Loan Service Tel: 501-682-2866. Administration Tel: 501-682-1527. Automation Services Tel: 501-682-1849. FAX: 501-682-1899. Interlibrary Loan Service FAX: 501-682-1529. Administration FAX: 501-682-1533. TDD: 501-682-1002. E-mail: ASLIB.REF@ade.arkansas.gov. Web Site: www.library.arkansas.gov. *State Librn,* Jennifer Chilcoat; Tel: 501-682-1526, E-mail: jennifer.chilcoat@ade.arkansas.gov; *Dep Dir,* Kristen Cooke; Tel: 501-682-2863, E-mail: kristen.cooke@ade.arkansas.gov; *Admin Serv Mgr,* Brooke Crawford; E-mail: brooke.crawford@ade.arkansas.gov; *Div Mgr, Coll Develop,* Sarah Lipsey; Tel: 501-682-2840, E-mail: sarah.lipsey@ade.arkansas.gov; *Mgr, Grants & Spec Project,* Deborah Hall; Tel: 501-682-2836, E-mail: debbie.hall@ade.arkansas.gov; *Digital Serv, Mgr,* Danielle Butler; Tel: 501-682-2840, E-mail: danielle.butler@ade.arkansas.gov; *ILL, Mgr, Info Serv, Ref,* Michael Strickland; Tel: 501-682-2864, E-mail: michael.strickland@ade.arkansas.gov; *Mgr, Libr Develop,* Jennifer Wann; Tel: 501-682-5288, E-mail: jenn.wann@ade.arkansas.gov; *Acq, Mgr,* Katie Walton; Tel: 501-682-2266, E-mail: katie.walton@ade.arkansas.gov; *Info Tech, IT Mgr,* Kenneth Giesbrecht; Tel: 501-682-1849, E-mail: ken.giesbrecht@ade.arkansas.gov; *Pub Info Spec,* Danny Koonce; Tel: 501-682-2837, E-mail: danny.koonce@ade.arkansas.gov. Subject Specialists: *Admin,* Jennifer Chilcoat; *Admin,* Kristen Cooke; *Financial,* Brooke Crawford; *Digitization,* Sarah Lipsey; Staff 52 (MLS 22, Non-MLS 30)
Founded 1935. Pop 2,988,248
Jul 2015-Jun 2016 Income $4,994,774, State $3,591,373, Federal $1,403,401
Library Holdings: Audiobooks 39; Bk Vols 32,057; Per Subs 167; Videos 248
Special Collections: Arkansiana; Blind & Print Disabled Coll; CIS Coll, microfiche; Library & Information Science (Professional Coll); Patent Depository. State Document Depository; US Document Depository
Subject Interests: Bus & mgt, Computer sci, US industries
Automation Activity & Vendor Info: (Acquisitions) SirsiDynix; (Circulation) SirsiDynix; (OPAC) SirsiDynix; (Serials) SirsiDynix
Wireless access
Function: Electronic databases & coll, Govt ref serv, Tax forms
Publications: Arkansas Documents; directories; indexes
Partic in OCLC Online Computer Library Center, Inc
Open Mon-Fri 8-4:30

P ARKANSAS STATE LIBRARY FOR THE BLIND & PRINT DISABLED, (Formerly Arkansas Regional Library for the Blind & Physically Handicapped), 900 W Capitol Ave, Ste 100, 72201-3108. SAN 300-5224. Tel: 501-682-1155. Toll Free Tel: 866-660-0885. FAX: 501-682-1529. E-mail: nlsbooks@ade.arkansas.gov. Web Site: www.library.arkansas.gov/services/lbpd. *Libr Mgr,* Kristina Hancock; E-mail: kristina.hancock@ade.arkansas.gov; *Readers' Advisory,* Jeff Kersey; Tel: 501-682-2856, E-mail: Jeff@Library.Arkansas.gov; *Readers' Advisory,* Kelly Smith; Tel: 501-682-2871, E-mail: Kelly@Library.Arkansas.gov; *Patron Serv, Reader Serv,* Kristina Waltermire; Tel: 501-682-2858, E-mail: Kristina@Library.Arkansas.gov. Subject Specialists: *Ch,* Kelly Smith; Staff 8.5 (MLS 4, Non-MLS 4.5)
Founded 1969. Pop 3,500; Circ 200,225
Library Holdings: Audiobooks 72,176; Braille Volumes 37,172; Bk Titles 88,387
Special Collections: Duplication on Demand for digital audio books
Subject Interests: Bks, Braille
Wireless access
Function: Mail loans to mem, Summer reading prog, Wheelchair accessible
Special Services for the Blind - Accessible computers; Bks on flash-memory cartridges; Braille bks; Digital talking bk; Digital talking bk machines; Free checkout of audio mat; Talking bks; Web-Braille
Open Mon-Fri 8-4:30
Restriction: Authorized patrons, Free to mem, Lending libr only via mail

GL ARKANSAS SUPREME COURT LIBRARY*, 625 Marshall St, Ste 1500, 72201. SAN 300-5267. Tel: 501-682-2147. FAX: 501-682-6877. Web Site: courts.arkansas.gov/courts/supreme-court/library. *Dir,* Ava M Hicks; Tel: 501-682-2041, E-mail: ava.hicks@arcourts.gov; *Pub Serv Coordr,* Rod Miller; E-mail: rod.miller@arcourts.gov; *Tech Asst,* Carol Hampton; E-mail: carol.hampton@arcourts.gov; Staff 3 (MLS 2, Non-MLS 1)
Founded 1851
Library Holdings: Bk Vols 90,000
Special Collections: State Document Depository; US Document Depository
Subject Interests: Law
Automation Activity & Vendor Info: (Acquisitions) Innovative Interfaces, Inc; (Cataloging) Innovative Interfaces, Inc; (Circulation) Innovative Interfaces, Inc; (OPAC) Innovative Interfaces, Inc; (Serials) Innovative Interfaces, Inc
Partic in OCLC Online Computer Library Center, Inc
Open Mon-Fri 8-5

P CENTRAL ARKANSAS LIBRARY SYSTEM*, 100 Rock St, 72201-4698. SAN 331-2216. Tel: 501-918-3000. Circulation Tel: 501-918-3041. Interlibrary Loan Service Tel: 501-918-3014. Reference Tel: 501-918-3003. Administration Tel: 501-918-3030. Administration FAX: 501-375-7451. E-mail: calsinfo@cals.org. Web Site: cals.org. *Exec Dir,* Nate Coulter; Tel: 501-918-3037, E-mail: ncoulter@cals.org; *Dep Exec Dir, Libr Operations,* Lisa Donovan; Tel: 501-918-3053, E-mail: ldonovan@cals.org; *Dep Dir, Bus Operations,* Ms Jo Spencer; *Dir of Libr Operations,* Lance Ivy; *Dir, Libr Res,* Carol Coffey; Tel: 501-918-3008, E-mail: ccoffey@cals.org; *Communications Dir, Pub Relations,* Ms Tameka Lee; *Dir, Spec Coll,* Dr David Stricklin; *ILL,* Lee Razer; *Ref (Info Servs),* Aldo Botti; Staff 342 (MLS 35, Non-MLS 307)
Founded 1910. Pop 337,104; Circ 2,701,123
Library Holdings: Audiobooks 35,064; CDs 6,896; DVDs 99,170; e-books 39,163; Bk Titles 488,351; Bk Vols 1,060,302
Special Collections: Charlie May Simon Awards Coll; Clinton Gubernatorial Papers; Foundation Center Regional Coll. Oral History; State Document Depository
Subject Interests: Genealogy, Local hist, State hist
Automation Activity & Vendor Info: (Acquisitions) Innovative Interfaces, Inc; (Cataloging) Innovative Interfaces, Inc; (Circulation) Innovative Interfaces, Inc; (ILL) OCLC; (OPAC) BiblioCommons; (Serials) Innovative Interfaces, Inc
Wireless access
Function: 24/7 Online cat, Adult bk club, After school storytime, Archival coll, Art exhibits, Audiobks via web, Bk club(s), Bks on CD, Children's prog, Computer training, Computers for patron use, Electronic databases & coll, Free DVD rentals, Homebound delivery serv, ILL available, Internet access, Magazines, Magnifiers for reading, Mail & tel request accepted, Meeting rooms, Microfiche/film & reading machines, Music CDs, Notary serv, Online cat, Online ref, OverDrive digital audio bks, Photocopying/Printing, Preschool outreach, Prog for adults, Prog for children & young adult, Ref serv available, Spanish lang bks, Spoken cassettes & CDs, Story hour, Summer reading prog, Tax forms, Teen prog, Telephone ref, Wheelchair accessible
Partic in OCLC Online Computer Library Center, Inc
Special Services for the Deaf - Closed caption videos; TDD equip
Special Services for the Blind - Audio mat; Bks on CD
Open Mon-Thurs 9-8, Fri & Sat 9-6, Sun 1-5
Friends of the Library Group
Branches: 13
DEE BROWN LIBRARY, 6325 Baseline Rd, 72209-4810, SAN 331-2364. Tel: 501-568-7494. Web Site: cals.org/dee-brown-library. *Libr Mgr,* Brian Martin
Open Mon, Tues & Thurs 10-8, Wed, Fri & Sat 10-6, Sun 1-5
Friends of the Library Group
HILLARY RODHAM CLINTON CHILDREN'S LIBRARY & LEARNING CENTER, 4800 W Tenth St, 72204. Tel: 501-978-3870. Web Site: cals.org/childrens-library. *Libr Mgr,* Rettina Hill
Open Mon-Sat 9-6, Sun 1-5
JOHN GOULD FLETCHER LIBRARY, 823 N Buchanan St, 72205-3211, SAN 331-2240. Tel: 501-663-5457. Web Site: cals.org/fletcher-library. *Libr Mgr,* Liz Wooley
Open Mon-Wed 9-8, Thurs-Sat 9-6
MAUMELLE BRANCH, Ten Lake Pointe Dr, Maumelle, 72113-6230, SAN 378-2492. Tel: 501-851-2551. Web Site: cals.org/maumelle-library. *Libr Mgr,* Marilyn Cash
Open Mon, Tues & Thurs 10-8, Wed, Fri & Sat 10-6
SIDNEY S MCMATH BRANCH, 2100 John Barrow Rd, 72204. Tel: 501-225-0066. Web Site: cals.org/mcmath-library. *Libr Mgr,* Laura Hodo
Open Mon-Wed 10-8, Thurs-Sat 10-6
MAX MILAM BRANCH, 609 Aplin Ave, Perryville, 72126, SAN 331-2305. Tel: 501-889-2554. Web Site: cals.org/milam-library. *Libr Mgr,* Allen Jarvis
Open Mon, Wed-Sat 10-6, Tues 10-8
ESTHER DEWITT NIXON BRANCH, 703 W Main St, Jacksonville, 72076, SAN 331-2275. Tel: 501-457-5038. Web Site: cals.org/nixon-library. *Libr Mgr,* Shya N Washington
Open Mon, Wed, Fri & Sat 9:30-6, Tues & Thurs 9:30-8
OLEY E ROOKER LIBRARY, 11 Otter Creek Ct, 72210. Tel: 501-907-5991. Web Site: cals.org/rooker-library. *Libr Mgr,* Audrey Taylor
Open Mon, Wed & Thurs 10-8, Tues, Fri & Sat 10-6
AMY SANDERS BRANCH, 10200 Johnson Dr, Sherwood, 72120, SAN 331-233X. Tel: 501-835-7756. Web Site: cals.org/sanders-library. *Libr Mgr,* Ginann Swindle
Open Mon, Wed, Fri & Sat 9:30-6, Tues & Thurs 9:30-8
ADOLPHINE FLETCHER TERRY BRANCH, 2015 Napa Valley Dr, 72212, SAN 370-5773. Tel: 501-228-0129. Web Site: cals.org/terry-library. *Libr Mgr,* Jennifer Cordell
Open Mon, Wed & Thurs 9-8, Tues, Fri & Sat 9-6
ROOSEVELT THOMPSON BRANCH, 38 Rahling Circle, 72223. Tel: 501-821-3060. Web Site: cals.org/thompson-library. *Libr Mgr,* Delphine Durst
Open Mon, Tues & Thurs 10-8, Wed, Fri & Sat 10-6
SUE COWAN WILLIAMS BRANCH, 1800 Chester St, 72206-1010, SAN 378-2514. Tel: 501-376-4282. Web Site: cals.org/williams-library. *Libr Mgr,* Latina Sheard
Open Mon, Wed, Fri & Sat 10-6, Tues & Thurs 10-8

G CENTRAL ARKANSAS VETERANS HEALTHCARE SYSTEM, Health Sciences Library, 4300 W Seventh St, 72205-5484. SAN 300-5321. Tel: 501-257-5620. Administration Tel: 501-257-5622. FAX: 501-257-5626. *Chief Librn,* Edward Poletti; E-mail: edward.poletti@va.gov; Staff 4 (MLS 2, Non-MLS 2)
Founded 1950
Library Holdings: AV Mats 1,247; e-books 100; Bk Titles 2,959; Per Subs 34
Automation Activity & Vendor Info: (Cataloging) Follett Software; (Circulation) Follett Software; (OPAC) Follett Software
Wireless access
Function: Health sci info serv
Partic in OCLC-LVIS; Veterans Affairs Library Network
Open Mon- Fri 7:30-4

M CHI SAINT VINCENT INFIRMARY LIBRARY*, Frank T Padberg Medical Library, Two Saint Vincent Circle, 72205. SAN 300-5305. Tel: 501-552-3000. FAX: 501-552-4311. Web Site: chistvincent.com/hospitals-locations/chi-st-vincent-infirmary. *Dir of Educ,* Nisa Trenthem
Founded 1900
Library Holdings: Bk Vols 4,048; Per Subs 142
Subject Interests: Health sci, Med
Wireless access
Open Mon-Fri 8-4:30

S HISTORIC ARKANSAS MUSEUM LIBRARY*, LeFevre Research Library, 200 E Third St, 72201-1608. SAN 370-3355. Tel: 501-324-9351. FAX: 501-324-9345. Web Site: www.historicarkansas.org. *Exec Dir,* Swannee Bennett; Tel: 501-324-9395; *Dep Dir,* Donna Uptigrove; Tel: 501-324-9701; *Curator,* Carey Voss; E-mail: carey.voss@arkansas.gov. Subject Specialists: *State hist,* Swannee Bennett; Staff 1 (Non-MLS 1)
Founded 1941. Pop 25
Library Holdings: Bk Vols 4,250
Subject Interests: State hist
Wireless access
Function: 24/7 Online cat, Art exhibits, Audio & video playback equip for onsite use, Bks on CD, Computers for patron use, Digital talking bks, Electronic databases & coll, For res purposes, Internet access, Magazines, Magnifiers for reading, Microfiche/film & reading machines, Movies, Music CDs, Ref & res, Res libr, Spoken cassettes & DVDs, VHS videos, Wheelchair accessible
Restriction: Authorized personnel only, Authorized scholars by appt, Circ limited, Circulates for staff only, Employees only, Lending to staff only, Non-circulating, Not a lending libr, Not open to pub, Open to employees & special libr, Secured area only open to authorized personnel, Staff use only

S NATIONAL ARCHIVES & RECORDS ADMINISTRATION, William J Clinton Presidential Library & Museum, 1200 President Clinton Ave, 72201. Tel: 501-374-4242, 501-748-0419. FAX: 501-244-2883. E-mail: clinton.library@nara.gov. Web Site: www.clintonlibrary.gov. *Curator,* Christine Mouw; E-mail: christine.mouw@nara.gov
Special Collections: Music Exhibit; Presidential Archives, official recs, papers, photogs, v-tapes
Open Mon-Sat 9-5, Sun 1-5

C PHILANDER SMITH COLLEGE*, Donald W Reynolds Library, 900 Daisy Bates Dr, 72202. SAN 300-5291. Tel: 501-370-5262. FAX: 501-370-5307. E-mail: library@philander.edu. Web Site:

www.philander.edu/library-services. *Dir,* Teresa I Ojezua; Tel: 501-370-5306, E-mail: Tojezua@philander.edu; *Archivist, Digital Serv Librn,* LeTisha Stacey; Tel: 501-370-5263, E-mail: lstacey@philander.edu; *Ref & Instruction Librn,* Joyce Campbell; Tel: 501-370-5366, E-mail: jcampbell@philander.edu. Subject Specialists: *Sci,* Teresa I Ojezua; *Digital humanities, Humanities,* LeTisha Stacey; *Bus admin, Educ, Tech,* Joyce Campbell; Staff 6.5 (MLS 3, Non-MLS 3.5)
Founded 1920. Enrl 870; Fac 42; Highest Degree: Bachelor
Library Holdings: CDs 340; DVDs 490; e-journals 14,878; Microforms 2,375; Bk Titles 72,910; Bk Vols 74,500; Per Subs 209; Videos 935
Special Collections: African American/Black History; PSC Archives
Subject Interests: African-Am (ethnic), Arkansas, Bus & mgt, Ethnic studies, Soc justice
Automation Activity & Vendor Info: (Acquisitions) EOS International; (Cataloging) EOS International; (Circulation) EOS International; (Discovery) EBSCO Discovery Service; (ILL) OCLC WorldShare Interlibrary Loan; (OPAC) EOS International; (Serials) EBSCO Online
Wireless access
Function: Computers for patron use, Internet access, Microfiche/film & reading machines, Movies, Music CDs, Online cat, Online info literacy tutorials on the web & in blackboard, Orientations, Outreach serv, Outside serv via phone, mail, e-mail & web, Photocopying/Printing, Scanner, Serves people with intellectual disabilities, Workshops
Publications: Knowledge is Freedom (Newsletter)
Partic in Amigos Library Services, Inc; ARKLink; HBCU Library Alliance; OCLC Online Computer Library Center, Inc
Special Services for the Blind - Accessible computers; Assistive/Adapted tech devices, equip & products; Computer with voice synthesizer for visually impaired persons; Low vision equip; PC for people with disabilities
Open Mon-Thurs 7:30am-10pm, Fri 7:30-5, Sat 12-5, Sun 1-10
Restriction: Borrowing privileges limited to fac & registered students

J PULASKI TECHNICAL COLLEGE*, Ottenheimer-South Library, 13000 Interstate 30, 72210. Tel: 501-812-2878. Web Site: www.pulaskitech.edu/library. *Librn,* Carita Alexander; E-mail: calexander@uaptc.edu; *Libr Tech,* Vanessa White; E-mail: vwhite@uaptc.edu
Wireless access
Open Mon-Thurs 7:30-6, Fri 7:30-3

G UNITED STATES COURT OF APPEALS*, Branch Library, 600 W Capitol Ave, Rm 224, 72201. SAN 324-6701. Tel: 501-604-5215. FAX: 501-604-5217. Web Site: www.ca8.uscourts.gov. *Librn,* Crata Castleberry; E-mail: crata_castleberry@ca8.uscourts.gov; Staff 2 (MLS 1, Non-MLS 1)
Founded 1981
Library Holdings: Bk Titles 5,000; Bk Vols 16,000; Per Subs 65
Subject Interests: Fed law
Automation Activity & Vendor Info: (Acquisitions) SirsiDynix; (Cataloging) SirsiDynix; (Circulation) SirsiDynix; (Course Reserve) SirsiDynix; (ILL) SirsiDynix; (Media Booking) SirsiDynix; (OPAC) SirsiDynix
Partic in OCLC Online Computer Library Center, Inc
Open Mon-Fri 8:30-5

C UNIVERSITY OF ARKANSAS AT LITTLE ROCK, Ottenheimer Library, 2801 S University Ave, 72204. SAN 331-2429. Tel: 501-916-3123. Interlibrary Loan Service Tel: 501-916-6188. Toll Free Tel: 800-340-9367. E-mail: library@ualr.edu. Web Site: ualr.edu/library. *Exec Dir, Libr Serv,* J B Hill; Tel: 501-916-6186, E-mail: jbhill@ualr.edu; *Instruction & Engagement Librn,* Chelsea Young; Tel: 501-916-6190, E-mail: kcyoung2@ualr.edu; *Metadata Lead Librn,* Donna Rose; Tel: 501-916-6182, E-mail: dkrose@ualr.edu; *Information Technology Coord,* Ben Fisher; Tel: 501-916-6195, E-mail: btfisher1@ualr.edu; *Research & Scholarly Communication Coord,* Carol Macheak; Tel: 501-916-6181, E-mail: cimacheak@ualr.edu; *Collections Management Coord,* Maureen James; Tel: 501-916-6180, E-mail: mejames@ualr.edu; Staff 17 (MLS 13, Non-MLS 4)
Founded 1927. Enrl 13,167; Fac 442; Highest Degree: Doctorate
Library Holdings: AV Mats 5,963; e-books 31,057; e-journals 62,682; Microforms 233,938; Music Scores 2,182; Bk Vols 512,661; Per Subs 49,134; Talking Bks 273; Videos 4,778
Special Collections: US Document Depository
Subject Interests: Bus & mgt, Educ, Govt, Humanities, Psychol
Automation Activity & Vendor Info: (Acquisitions) Innovative Interfaces, Inc; (Cataloging) Innovative Interfaces, Inc; (Circulation) Innovative Interfaces, Inc; (Course Reserve) Innovative Interfaces, Inc; (OPAC) Innovative Interfaces, Inc; (Serials) Innovative Interfaces, Inc
Wireless access
Function: Computers for patron use, Doc delivery serv, E-Reserves, Electronic databases & coll, Music CDs, Online cat, Online ref, Orientations, Photocopying/Printing, Telephone ref
Publications: Ottenheimer News (Newsletter)
Partic in ARKLink
Special Services for the Deaf - TDD equip
Open Mon-Thurs 7:30am-8pm, Fri 7:30-5, Sun 12-8
Restriction: Access at librarian's discretion
Departmental Libraries:

CL WILLIAM H BOWEN SCHOOL OF LAW / PULASKI COUNTY LAW LIBRARY, 1201 McMath Ave, 72202, SAN 331-2453. Tel: 501-916-5453. Reference Tel: 501-916-5496. FAX: 501-916-3971. Web Site: ualr.edu/lawlibrary. *Assoc Dean Information & Tech Services, Dir, Law Libr,* Ms Jessie Burchfield; Tel: 501-916-5407, E-mail: jwburchfield@ualr.edu; *Research Support & Reference Librn,* Jeff Woodmansee; Tel: 501-916-5470, E-mail: jbwoodmansee@ualr.edu; *Acq & Ser Librn,* Harry Lah; Tel: 501-916-5505, E-mail: ehlah@ualr.edu; *Systems & Metadata Librn,* Sherrie C Noorwood; Tel: 501-916-5446, E-mail: scnorwood@ualr.edu; *Electronic Res & Ref Librn,* Melissa Serfass; Tel: 501-916-5459, E-mail: mmserfass@ualr.edu; Staff 16 (MLS 6, Non-MLS 10)
Founded 1965. Enrl 400; Fac 22; Highest Degree: Doctorate
Library Holdings: Bk Titles 36,877; Bk Vols 277,950; Per Subs 3,252
Special Collections: Arkansas Supreme Court Briefs & Records (Civil 1836-1926, Criminal 1836-1963). State Document Depository; US Document Depository
Automation Activity & Vendor Info: (Acquisitions) Innovative Interfaces, Inc; (Cataloging) Innovative Interfaces, Inc; (Circulation) Innovative Interfaces, Inc; (ILL) Innovative Interfaces, Inc; (OPAC) Innovative Interfaces, Inc; (Serials) Innovative Interfaces, Inc
Partic in Mid-America Law Library Consortium
Publications: Law Library Guide; Legal Reader (Newsletter)
Open Mon-Thurs 8am-11pm, Fri 8-6, Sat 9-6, Sun 11am-11pm
Friends of the Library Group

CM UNIVERSITY OF ARKANSAS FOR MEDICAL SCIENCES LIBRARY*, 4301 W Markham St, Library No 586, 72205. SAN 331-2488. Tel: 501-686-5980. Interlibrary Loan Service Tel: 501-686-6744. Reference Tel: 501-686-6734. FAX: 501-686-6745. E-mail: LibraryReferenceDesk@uams.edu. Circulation E-mail: LibraryCircDesk@uams.edu. Interlibrary Loan Service E-mail: LibraryInterlibraryLoan@uams.edu. Web Site: www.library.uams.edu. *Libr Dir,* Lisa Smith; Tel: 501-686-6751, Fax: 501-296-1423, E-mail: SmithLisaM@uams.edu; *Asst Dir, Libr Operations,* Nancy Clark; Tel: 501-686-6731, E-mail: naclark@uams.edu; Staff 13 (MLS 12, Non-MLS 1)
Founded 1879. Enrl 2,820; Fac 1,354; Highest Degree: Doctorate
Library Holdings: AV Mats 468; e-books 883; e-journals 4,509; Electronic Media & Resources 250; Bk Titles 34,056; Bk Vols 40,956; Per Subs 3,618
Special Collections: History of Medicine in Arkansas; Pathology (Schlumberger Coll)
Automation Activity & Vendor Info: (Acquisitions) Innovative Interfaces, Inc; (Cataloging) Innovative Interfaces, Inc; (Circulation) Innovative Interfaces, Inc; (Course Reserve) Innovative Interfaces, Inc; (ILL) Innovative Interfaces, Inc; (OPAC) Innovative Interfaces, Inc; (Serials) Innovative Interfaces, Inc
Wireless access
Publications: UAMS Library (Newsletter)
Partic in ARKLink; OCLC Online Computer Library Center, Inc; South Central Academic Medical Libraries Consortium
Open Mon-Thurs 7:30am-10pm, Fri 7:30-6, Sat 9-6, Sun 1-10
Friends of the Library Group

LITTLE ROCK AFB

A UNITED STATES AIR FORCE, Little Rock Air Force Base Library, Walters Community Support Ctr, 940 Arnold Dr, 72099-4927. SAN 331-2518. Tel: 501-987-6979. E-mail: library2@us.af.mil. Web Site: lrafblibrary.sirsi.net.
Founded 1956
Library Holdings: Audiobooks 1,500; CDs 150; DVDs 4,700; Bk Vols 21,000; Per Subs 70
Subject Interests: Aeronaut, Bus & mgt
Wireless access

LONOKE

P LONOKE COUNTY LIBRARY SYSTEM*, Marjorie Walker McCrary Memorial Library (Headquarters), 204 E Second St, 72086-2858. SAN 324-041X. Toll Free Tel: 855-572-6657, Ext 03. FAX: 501-676-7687. Web Site: www.youseemore.com/lonoke. *County Libr Dir,* Deborah Moore; E-mail: dmoore@lonokecountylibrary.org; *Br Mgr,* Ashlee Minson; E-mail: aminson@lonokecountylibrary.org; Staff 8 (MLS 1, Non-MLS 7)
Founded 1937. Pop 70,000; Circ 165,000
Library Holdings: Bk Titles 80,000; Bk Vols 131,000; Per Subs 240
Special Collections: Genealogy Coll; Local History Coll
Wireless access
Open Mon-Fri 9-5, Sat 9-1
Friends of the Library Group

Branches: 3
CABOT PUBLIC, 909 W Main St, Cabot, 72023, SAN 324-0649. Toll Free Tel: 855-572-6657, Ext 01. FAX: 501-843-6316. *Br Mgr,* Kathleen Ashmore; E-mail: kashmore@lonokecountylibrary.org
Open Mon-Thurs 8:30-7, Fri 8:30-5, Sat 9-1
Friends of the Library Group
CARLISLE PUBLIC, 105 E Fifth St, Carlisle, 72024, SAN 324-0665. Toll Free Tel: 855-572-6657, Ext 02. FAX: 870-552-9306. *Br Mgr,* Mrs Sherri Rollins; E-mail: srollins@lonokecountylibrary.org
Founded 1972. Pop 2,304
Function: Bks on CD, Children's prog, Computers for patron use, Electronic databases & coll, Free DVD rentals, Holiday prog, ILL available, Music CDs, Photocopying/Printing, Preschool outreach, Prog for children & young adult, Senior outreach, Story hour, Summer reading prog, Tax forms, Teen prog
Open Mon-Fri 9-5
Friends of the Library Group
WILLIAM F FOSTER LIBRARY, 100 E Taylor St, England, 72046-2181, SAN 324-0673. Toll Free Tel: 855-572-6657, Ext 04. FAX: 501-842-0203. *Br Mgr,* Nanette Palmer; E-mail: npalmer@lonokecountylibrary.org
Open Mon-Fri 9-5
Friends of the Library Group

MAGNOLIA

P COLUMBIA COUNTY LIBRARY*, 2057 N Jackson St, 71753. SAN 331-2542. Tel: 870-234-1991. FAX: 870-234-5077. E-mail: library@cocolib.org. Web Site: www2.youseemore.com/columbia. *Dir,* Rhonda Rolen; E-mail: rhonda@cocolib.org; *Asst Dir,* Ms Morgan Chance; E-mail: morgan@cocolib.org; Staff 1 (MLS 1)
Founded 1929. Pop 71,734
Library Holdings: Bk Vols 125,000; Per Subs 58
Special Collections: Arkansas Coll; Genealogy Coll
Automation Activity & Vendor Info: (Cataloging) TLC (The Library Corporation); (Circulation) TLC (The Library Corporation); (OPAC) TLC (The Library Corporation)
Wireless access
Function: Bks on cassette, Bks on CD, CD-ROM, Children's prog, Computers for patron use, Homebound delivery serv, ILL available, Online cat, Online ref, Photocopying/Printing, Prog for adults, Prog for children & young adult, Summer reading prog, Tax forms, Teen prog, VHS videos
Open Mon & Thurs 12-8, Tues, Wed & Fri 9-6, Sat 9-Noon
Restriction: Circ to mem only, Non-circulating coll, Registered patrons only
Branches: 1
TAYLOR PUBLIC LIBRARY, 101 W Pope, Taylor, 71861. (Mail add: PO Box 307, Taylor, 71861), SAN 331-281X. Tel: 870-694-2051. FAX: 870-694-7190. *Mgr,* Betty Ann Jackson; E-mail: bj.cityhall@centurytel.net; Staff 1 (MLS 1)
Pop 524
Open Mon-Fri 2-5

C SOUTHERN ARKANSAS UNIVERSITY, Magale Library, 100 E University, 71753-5000. (Mail add: SAU Box 9401, 71753-9401), SAN 300-533X. Tel: 870-235-4170. FAX: 870-235-5018. Web Site: web.saumag.edu/library. *Libr Dir,* Dr Del Duke; Tel: 870-235-4171, E-mail: dgduke@saumag.edu; *Asst Libr Dir, Assoc Librn, Tech Serv,* Margo Pierson; Tel: 870-235-4177, E-mail: mmpierson@saumag.edu; *Asst Librn, Bus Librn, Pub Serv Librn,* Kayla Rasberry; Tel: 870-235-4175, E-mail: KaylaRasberry@saumag.edu; *Coll Develop Librn,* Julie Metro; Tel: 870-235-4181, E-mail: jmetro@saumag.edu; *Asst Librn, Ref (Info Servs),* Donna McCloy; Tel: 870-235-4178, E-mail: dmmccloy@saumag.edu. Subject Specialists: *Engr, Sciences,* Margo Pierson; *Performing arts,* Julie Metro; Staff 6 (MLS 5, Non-MLS 1)
Founded 1909. Enrl 3,500; Fac 180; Highest Degree: Doctorate
Library Holdings: AV Mats 12,693; e-books 6,141; Bk Titles 140,237; Bk Vols 155,038; Per Subs 83
Special Collections: Arkansiana. State Document Depository; US Document Depository
Automation Activity & Vendor Info: (Acquisitions) SirsiDynix; (Cataloging) SirsiDynix; (Circulation) SirsiDynix; (Course Reserve) SirsiDynix; (OPAC) SirsiDynix; (Serials) SirsiDynix
Wireless access
Partic in Amigos Library Services, Inc; ARKLink; OCLC Online Computer Library Center, Inc
Restriction: Authorized patrons, In-house use for visitors
Friends of the Library Group

CM UNIVERSITY OF ARKANSAS FOR MEDICAL SCIENCES SOUTH ARKANSAS LIBRARY*, Carroll Medical Library, 1617 N. Washington, 71753. SAN 300-4996. Tel: 870-234-7676, 870-562-2587. Web Site: regionalprograms.uams.edu/regional-centers/uams-south/carroll-medical-library. *Dir,* Jana Terry
Founded 1974
Library Holdings: Bk Vols 1,000; Per Subs 100
Special Collections: Consumer Health Information Coll
Wireless access
Partic in OCLC Online Computer Library Center, Inc; S Cent Regional Med Libr Program

MALVERN

J COLLEGE OF THE OUACHITAS*, Library/Learning Resource Center, One College Circle, 72104. Tel: 501-337-5000. Interlibrary Loan Service Tel: 501-332-0208. Information Services Tel: 501-332-0210. FAX: 501-337-9382. Web Site: library.coto.edu. *Dir,* Irene Girgente; E-mail: igirgente@asutr.edu; Staff 2 (MLS 1, Non-MLS 1)
Founded 1991. Enrl 1,692; Fac 116; Highest Degree: Associate
Library Holdings: Bk Vols 25,000
Special Collections: Paper of Senator John L. McClellan
Automation Activity & Vendor Info: (Acquisitions) TLC (The Library Corporation); (Cataloging) TLC (The Library Corporation); (Circulation) TLC (The Library Corporation); (OPAC) TLC (The Library Corporation)
Wireless access
Function: Adult bk club, Art exhibits, Audio & video playback equip for onsite use, Bk club(s), Bks on cassette, Bks on CD, CD-ROM, Computer training, Computers for patron use, E-Reserves, Electronic databases & coll, Free DVD rentals, ILL available, Instruction & testing, Internet access, Magnifiers for reading, Mail & tel request accepted, Mail loans to mem, Music CDs, Online cat, Online ref, Orientations, Outside serv via phone, mail, e-mail & web, Photocopying/Printing, Ref & res, Ref serv available, Res libr, Scanner, Spoken cassettes & CDs, Spoken cassettes & DVDs, Telephone ref, VHS videos, Wheelchair accessible
Partic in ARKLink
Open Mon-Thurs (Winter) 8-7, Fri 8-4:30; Mon-Thurs (Summer) 7:30-5, Fri 8-Noon
Restriction: Authorized patrons, Circ limited, In-house use for visitors, Lending libr only via mail, Non-circulating coll, Open to pub for ref & circ; with some limitations, Open to students, fac & staff, Photo ID required for access

P MID ARKANSAS REGIONAL LIBRARY*, Malvern Hot Spring County Library Headquarters, 202 E Third St, 72104. SAN 300-5348. Tel: 501-332-5441. FAX: 501-332-6679. Web Site: www.hsclibrary.arkansas.gov. *Chair,* John Allan Funk; *Libr Dir,* Clare Graham; E-mail: clare.graham@arkansas.gov; *Libr Mgr,* Charlotte Smith; E-mail: charlotte.m.smith@arkansas.gov; *Libr Serv Mgr,* Jan Lambert; E-mail: jan.lambert@arkansas.gov; *Circ Mgr,* Arnescia Lee; Staff 1 (Non-MLS 1)
Founded 1928. Pop 29,000; Circ 120,000
Library Holdings: Bk Vols 74,000; Per Subs 70
Subject Interests: Arkansas, Genealogy
Automation Activity & Vendor Info: (Cataloging) Innovative Interfaces, Inc; (Circulation) Innovative Interfaces, Inc; (OPAC) Innovative Interfaces, Inc
Wireless access
Open Mon, Wed & Fri 9-5, Tues 9-7, Thurs 12-7, Sat 9-1
Friends of the Library Group
Branches: 4
DALLAS COUNTY LIBRARY, 501 E Fourth St, Fordyce, 71742. (Mail add: PO Box 584, Fordyce, 71742-0584), SAN 331-0418. Tel: 870-352-3592. FAX: 870-352-3508. *Libr Mgr,* Kena Trammel
Founded 1934. Pop 9,168; Circ 32,000
Library Holdings: Large Print Bks 75; Bk Vols 34,295
Automation Activity & Vendor Info: (Cataloging) Follett Software; (Circulation) Follett Software; (OPAC) Follett Software
Open Mon-Wed & Fri 9-4:30
FOHRELL PUBLIC LIBRARY, 186 Dallas 208, Sparkman, 71763, SAN 331-0477. Tel: 870-678-2561. FAX: 870-352-3598. *Librn,* Amy Ketzer
Open Tues & Wed 2-4
GRANT COUNTY LIBRARY, 210 N Oak St, Sheridan, 72150-2495, SAN 300-5496. Tel: 870-942-4436. FAX: 870-942-7500. *Librn,* Jessica Reeves; Staff 4 (MLS 1, Non-MLS 3)
Library Holdings: Bk Vols 34,000
Automation Activity & Vendor Info: (Cataloging) Innovative Interfaces, Inc; (Circulation) Innovative Interfaces, Inc; (OPAC) Innovative Interfaces, Inc
Open Mon 9-8, Tues, Wed & Fri 9-5, Sat 10-2
ROY & CHRISTINE STURGIS LIBRARY OF CLEVELAND COUNTY, 203 W Magnolia St, Rison, 71665. (Mail add: PO Box 388, Rison, 71665-0388), SAN 300-5461. Tel: 870-325-7270. FAX: 870-325-7008. *Librn,* Hilda Terry
Pop 7,781; Circ 14,160
Library Holdings: Bk Vols 29,153; Per Subs 36
Open Mon & Thurs 8:30-6, Tues, Wed & Fri 8:30-4:30, Sat 9-12
Friends of the Library Group
Bookmobiles: 1. Coordr, Barry Honold

MAMMOTH SPRING

P FULTON COUNTY LIBRARY*, Mammoth Spring Library, 325 Main St, 72554. (Mail add: PO Box 256, 72554-3205). Tel: 870-625-3205. *Mgr,* Carole Howell
Library Holdings: Audiobooks 100; Bks on Deafness & Sign Lang 5; CDs 100; DVDs 20; Large Print Bks 200; Bk Vols 10,000; Per Subs 5; Videos 500
Wireless access
Mem of White River Regional Library
Open Mon & Wed-Fri 9:30-4:30, Sat 9-3
Friends of the Library Group

MARION

P CRITTENDEN COUNTY LIBRARY*, Margaret Woolfolk Library, 100 N Currie St, 72364. SAN 300-5364. Tel: 870-739-3238. FAX: 870-739-4624. E-mail: Woolfolklibrary@yahoo.com. Web Site: marionar.org/relocation/woolfolk-library, www.crittendencountylibrary.org. *Librn,* Cassey Clayman; Staff 4 (Non-MLS 4)
Pop 22,140; Circ 24,000
Library Holdings: Bk Vols 41,000; Per Subs 75
Special Collections: Arkansas Coll
Wireless access
Open Mon-Fri 9-6, Sat 9-12; Mon-Fri (Summer) 9-5
Friends of the Library Group
Branches: 6
CRAWFORDSVILLE BRANCH, 5444 Main St, Crawfordsville, 72327. (Mail add: PO Box 102, Crawfordsville, 72327-0102), SAN 321-9143. Tel: 870-823-5204. *Librn,* Patty Jenkins
Founded 1963. Pop 514
Function: Summer reading prog
Open Mon & Wed 11-6, Thurs 11:30-5:30
Friends of the Library Group
EARLE BRANCH, 703 Commerce St, Earle, 72331, SAN 321-9135. Tel: 870-792-8500. *Librn,* Myra Arquitt
Open Tues-Thurs 9-4:30
Friends of the Library Group
EDMONDSON BRANCH, 61 Waterford St, Edmondson, 72332. (Mail add: PO Box 300, Edmondson, 72332-0300). Tel: 870-732-9532. FAX: 870-735-6988. *Mgr,* Bonnie Ellis
Library Holdings: Bk Vols 2,400
Open Mon-Fri 1-5
GILMORE BRANCH, 87 Front St, Gilmore, 72339. (Mail add: PO Box 253, Gilmore, 72339), SAN 321-916X. Tel: 870-343-2697. FAX: 870-343-2601. *Librn,* Position Currently Open
Open Mon-Fri 2-5
Friends of the Library Group
HORSESHOE BRANCH, 3181 Horseshoe Circle, Hughes, 72348, SAN 321-9178. Tel: 870-339-3862. E-mail: horseshoelakelibrary@gmail.com. *Librn,* Harris Lentz; *Librn,* Nikki Walker
Pop 2,000; Circ 5,000
Function: Homebound delivery serv
Open Mon, Wed & Fri 12-5
Friends of the Library Group
TURRELL BRANCH, 52 Flippo St, Turrell, 72384. Tel: 870-343-4005. *Librn,* Jennifer Carr
Open Mon & Wed 4-6

MARSHALL

P SEARCY COUNTY LIBRARY, Jim G Ferguson Memorial, 202 E Main St, 72650. SAN 331-1104. Tel: 870-448-2420. FAX: 870-448-5453. Web Site: searcycountylibrary.com. *Librn,* Pat Halsted
Library Holdings: Bk Vols 35,000
Wireless access
Open Mon-Fri 10-5
Friends of the Library Group

MCCRORY

EAST CENTRAL ARKANSAS REGIONAL LIBRARY, McCrory Branch Library, 115 N Edmonds Ave, 72396. Tel: 870-731-0150. Web Site: www.ecarls.org.
Founded 2014
Wireless access
Function: 24/7 Electronic res, 24/7 Online cat, Accelerated reader prog, After school storytime
Mem of East Central Arkansas Regional Library
Open Mon-Thurs 12:30-5

MELBOURNE

P IZARD COUNTY LIBRARY*, Melbourne Public Library, 1007 E Main St, 72556. (Mail add: PO Box 343, 72556-0343), SAN 326-7121. Tel: 870-368-7467. FAX: 870-368-3242. Web Site: www.melbournelibrary.webs.com. *Library Contact,* Mino Diaz
Founded 1957. Pop 1,673
Library Holdings: Bk Titles 10,000; Per Subs 10
Mem of White River Regional Library
Open Mon-Sat 11-5

J OZARKA COLLEGE*, Paul Weaver Library, 218 College Dr, 72556-8708. (Mail add: PO Box 10, 72556). Tel: 870-368-7371. Circulation Tel: 870-368-2054. Interlibrary Loan Service Tel: 870-368-2055. Toll Free Tel: 800-821-4335. FAX: 870-368-2092. Web Site: www.ozarka.edu/library.cfm. *Libr Dir,* Mary Ellen Hawkins; E-mail: mhawkins@ozarka.edu; Staff 2 (MLS 2)
Founded 1991. Enrl 1,500; Fac 50; Highest Degree: Associate
Library Holdings: Bks on Deafness & Sign Lang 12; DVDs 550; e-books 1,200; e-journals 6,500; Large Print Bks 10; Bk Vols 17,000; Per Subs 45; Videos 1,530
Automation Activity & Vendor Info: (Acquisitions) OpenBiblio; (Cataloging) OpenBiblio; (Circulation) OpenBiblio; (Course Reserve) OCLC; (ILL) OpenBiblio; (Media Booking) OpenBiblio; (OPAC) OpenBiblio; (Serials) OpenBiblio
Wireless access
Function: 24/7 Electronic res, 24/7 Online cat, Activity rm, Free DVD rentals
Partic in ARKLink
Open Mon-Thurs 8-7:30, Fri 8-4:30
Restriction: Authorized patrons, Badge access after hrs
Friends of the Library Group

MENA

P POLK COUNTY LIBRARY*, 410 Eighth St, 71953. SAN 331-1589. Tel: 479-394-2314. FAX: 479-394-2314. E-mail: polkcountylibrary@yahoo.com. Web Site: menapolkcountylibrary.org. *Librn,* Mary Renick
Founded 1897
Wireless access
Function: Computers for patron use, ILL available, Photocopying/Printing, Story hour
Mem of Ouachita Mountains Regional Library
Open Mon-Wed & Fri 9-5, Thurs 9-6, Sat 9-2
Friends of the Library Group

J RICH MOUNTAIN COMMUNITY COLLEGE*, Saint John Library, 1100 College Dr, 71953-2503. Tel: 479-394-7622. FAX: 479-394-2828. Web Site: www.rmcc.edu/index.php?option=com_content&view=article&id=35-library. *Dir,* Brenda Miner; Tel: 501-394-7622, Ext 1370, E-mail: bminer@uarichmountain.edu
Founded 1983
Library Holdings: Bk Vols 15,000; Per Subs 90
Automation Activity & Vendor Info: (Cataloging) Mandarin Library Automation; (Circulation) Mandarin Library Automation; (OPAC) Mandarin Library Automation
Function: ILL available, Ref serv available
Open Mon-Thurs 7am-8pm, Fri 7-3:30

MONTICELLO

P SOUTHEAST ARKANSAS REGIONAL LIBRARY*, 114 E Jackson St, 71655. SAN 331-2879. Tel: 870-367-8584. FAX: 870-367-1658. Web Site: www1.youseemore.com/seark. *Regional Dir,* Judy Calhoun; Tel: 870-367-8584, Ext 222, E-mail: director.searl@gmail.com; *Cat,* Jennifer Knight; Tel: 870-367-8584, Ext 224, E-mail: cataloging.searl@gmail.com; *Coll Develop,* Melissa Benefield; Tel: 870-367-8584, Ext 223, E-mail: collection.searl@gmail.com; Staff 44 (MLS 1, Non-MLS 43)
Founded 1947. Pop 75,000; Circ 203,204
Library Holdings: Bk Titles 80,000; Bk Vols 183,000; Per Subs 495
Subject Interests: Arkansas
Automation Activity & Vendor Info: (Cataloging) TLC (The Library Corporation); (Circulation) TLC (The Library Corporation)
Wireless access
Open Mon-Fri 8-4:30
Branches: 9
DERMOTT BRANCH, 117 S Freeman St, Dermott, 71638, SAN 321-9518. Tel: 870-538-3514. FAX: 870-538-3514. E-mail: dermott.searl@gmail.com. *Br Mgr,* Kellie Washington
Open Mon & Wed 9-12 & 12:30-5:30, Tues, Thurs & Fri 12:30-5:30
Friends of the Library Group

DUMAS BRANCH, 120 E Choctow, Dumas, 71639, SAN 331-2968. Tel: 870-382-5763. FAX: 870-382-5763. E-mail: dumas.searl@gmail.com. *Br Mgr,* Hunter Bennett
Open Mon-Fri 9-6, Sat 10-2
Friends of the Library Group

EUDORA BRANCH, 161 N Cherry St, Eudora, 71640, SAN 321-9526. Tel: 870-355-2450. FAX: 870-355-2450. E-mail: eudora.searl@gmail.com. *Br Mgr,* Mary Bates
Open Mon, Wed & Fri 9-12:30 & 1-5:30, Tues & Thurs 1-5:30

HERMITAGE BRANCH, First State Bank Bldg, 122 S Main, Hermitage, 71647. (Mail add: PO Box 98, Hermitage, 71647-0098), SAN 331-3034. Tel: 870-463-8962. FAX: 870-463-8962. E-mail: hermitage.searl@gmail.com. *Br Mgr,* Jamie Thomas
Open Mon, Wed & Fri 12-5

LAKE VILLAGE BRANCH, 108 Church St, Lake Village, 71653, SAN 300-5143. Tel: 870-265-6116. FAX: 870-265-6116. E-mail: lakevillage.searl@gmail.com. *Br Mgr,* Sandra McAllister
Open Mon-Fri 9-6
Friends of the Library Group

MCGEHEE BRANCH, 211 N Fourth St, McGehee, 71654, SAN 331-3050. Tel: 870-222-4097. FAX: 870-222-4097. E-mail: mcgehee.searl@gmail.com. *Br Mgr,* Sarah Hardin
Open Mon-Fri 9-5:30, Sat 10-2
Friends of the Library Group

MONTICELLO BRANCH, 114 W Jefferson Ave, 71655, SAN 331-3069. Tel: 870-367-8583. FAX: 870-367-4392. E-mail: monticello.searl@gmail.com. *Br Mgr,* Elizabeth Newman
Open Mon-Fri 9-5:30, Sat 10-2
Friends of the Library Group

STAR CITY BRANCH, 200 E Wiley, Star City, 71667, SAN 331-3085. Tel: 870-628-4711. FAX: 870-628-4711. E-mail: starcity.searl@gmail.com. *Br Mgr,* Simone Kirk
Open Mon 1-5:30, Tues-Fri 9-5:30, Sat 10-2
Friends of the Library Group

WARREN BRANCH, 115 W Cypress, Warren, 71671, SAN 331-3131. Tel: 870-226-2536. FAX: 870-226-2536. E-mail: warrenlibrary.searl@gmail.com. *Br Mgr,* Sandy Doss
Open Mon-Fri 9-5:30, Sat 10-2
Friends of the Library Group

C UNIVERSITY OF ARKANSAS-MONTICELLO LIBRARY*, Taylor Library & Technology Center, 514 University Dr, 71656. (Mail add: PO Box 3599, 71656-3599), SAN 300-5372. Tel: 870-460-1080. FAX: 870-460-1980. Web Site: www.uamont.edu/academics/library. *Dir, Libr Serv,* Daniel Boice; Tel: 870-460-1480, E-mail: Boice@uamont.edu; *Asst Librn, Chair, Spec Coll & Archives, Ref Serv,* A Blake Denton; Tel: 870-460-1581, E-mail: dentona@uamont.edu; *Asst Librn,* Elizabeth K Parish; Tel: 870-460-1280, E-mail: parishe@uamont.edu; *Asst Librn,* Renee Cherie Clark; Tel: 870-460-1481, E-mail: clarkr@uamont.edu; *Circ Mgr, Coordr,* Annette Vincent; *ILL, Libr Tech,* Dana Weast; E-mail: weastd@uamont.edu; *Libr Tech, Ser,* Amber Schober; Staff 9 (MLS 4, Non-MLS 5)
Founded 1909. Enrl 2,942; Fac 150; Highest Degree: Master
Library Holdings: Bk Vols 151,176; Per Subs 1,000
Special Collections: State Document Depository; US Document Depository
Subject Interests: Arkansas, Forestry
Automation Activity & Vendor Info: (Acquisitions) Innovative Interfaces, Inc; (Cataloging) Innovative Interfaces, Inc; (Circulation) Innovative Interfaces, Inc; (Course Reserve) Innovative Interfaces, Inc; (OPAC) Innovative Interfaces, Inc; (Serials) Innovative Interfaces, Inc
Function: 24/7 Electronic res, 24/7 Online cat
Publications: Annual Report
Partic in ARKLink
Open Mon-Thurs 7:30am-10pm, Fri 7:30-4:30, Sun 2-10 (Aug-May); Mon-Thurs 7-5:30 (June-July)

MORRILTON

P CONWAY COUNTY LIBRARY HEADQUARTERS*, 101 W Church St, 72110. SAN 300-5380. Tel: 501-354-5204. FAX: 501-354-5206. Web Site: conwaycountylibrary.org. *Libr Dir,* Jay Carter; E-mail: jay.carter@conwaycountylibrary.org; *Dir of Outreach, Dir, Youth Serv,* Linda Green; E-mail: linda.green@conwaycountylibrary.org; *Asst Dir,* Denise Burton; E-mail: denise.burton@conwaycountylibrary.org; *Coordr, ILL, Libr Asst,* Mary Bell; E-mail: mary.bell@conwaycountylibrary.org; *Cataloger, Tech Asst,* Cassie Beall; E-mail: cassie.beall@conwaycountylibrary.org; Staff 4 (MLS 1, Non-MLS 3)
Founded 1916. Pop 21,273; Circ 64,840
Library Holdings: Bk Titles 35,000; Per Subs 34
Automation Activity & Vendor Info: (Cataloging) TLC (The Library Corporation); (Circulation) TLC (The Library Corporation); (ILL) OCLC FirstSearch; (OPAC) TLC (The Library Corporation)
Wireless access
Function: Bk club(s), Computers for patron use, ILL available, Online cat, Preschool outreach, Prog for adults, Prog for children & young adult, Spoken cassettes & CDs, Spoken cassettes & DVDs, Story hour, Summer reading prog, Teen prog
Open Tues-Fri 9-6:30, Sat 9-1
Friends of the Library Group

JR UNIVERSITY OF ARKANSAS COMMUNITY COLLEGE AT MORRILTON*, Gordon Library, 1537 University Blvd, 72110. Tel: 501-977-2092. FAX: 501-354-7560. E-mail: library@uaccm.edu. Web Site: www1.youseemore.com/uaccm. *Dir,* Justin Lillard; E-mail: jlillard@uaccm.edu
Founded 1961. Highest Degree: Associate
Library Holdings: Bk Titles 13,440; Bk Vols 16,469; Per Subs 44
Automation Activity & Vendor Info: (Cataloging) SirsiDynix; (Circulation) SirsiDynix
Open Mon-Fri 8-4:30

MOUNT IDA

P MONTGOMERY COUNTY LIBRARY, 145A Whittington St, 71957-9404. (Mail add: PO Box 189, 71957-0189), SAN 300-5399. Tel: 870-867-3812. FAX: 870-867-3812. E-mail: montlibrary@hotmail.com. Web Site: www.montgomerycountyarlibrary.org. *County Librn,* Joann Whisenhunt
Founded 1958. Pop 9,245; Circ 25,168
Library Holdings: Bk Titles 14,000
Special Collections: Montgomery County Genealogy Coll
Wireless access
Function: Computers for patron use, ILL available, Photocopying/Printing
Mem of Ouachita Mountains Regional Library
Open Mon-Fri 9:30-4:30, Sat 9:30-1
Friends of the Library Group

P OUACHITA MOUNTAINS REGIONAL LIBRARY*, 145 A Whittington St, 71957. (Mail add: PO Box 307, 71957). E-mail: omreglibrary@hotmail.com. Web Site: ouachitamountainsregionallibrary.com. *Regional Librn,* Brenda Miner
Wireless access
Member Libraries: Montgomery County Library; Polk County Library
Open Mon-Fri 9:30-4:30, Sat 9:30-1

MOUNTAIN HOME

C ARKANSAS STATE UNIVERSITY*, Norma Wood Library, 1600 S College St, 72653-5326. Tel: 870-508-6112. FAX: 870-508-6291. Web Site: asumh.edu/pages/main/426/asumh-library. *Libr Dir,* Tina Bradley; E-mail: tbradley@asumh.edu; Staff 3 (MLS 1, Non-MLS 2)
Library Holdings: Bk Vols 17,000; Per Subs 167
Automation Activity & Vendor Info: (Acquisitions) Ex Libris Group; (Cataloging) Ex Libris Group; (Circulation) Ex Libris Group; (Course Reserve) Ex Libris Group; (ILL) Ex Libris Group; (OPAC) Ex Libris Group
Wireless access
Function: 24/7 Online cat, Archival coll, Audiobks on Playaways & MP3, ILL available, Internet access, Photocopying/Printing, Ref serv available, Telephone ref
Open Mon-Wed 8-8, Thurs & Fri 8-5
Restriction: Open to students, fac & staff, Pub use on premises

P BAXTER COUNTY LIBRARY*, Donald W Reynolds Library, 300 Library Hill, 72653. Tel: 870-580-0987. Administration Tel: 870-580-0979. FAX: 870-580-0935. Web Site: www.baxtercountylibrary.org. *Libr Dir,* Kim Crow Sheaner; E-mail: kim.c@baxlib.org; Staff 19 (MLS 2, Non-MLS 17)
Founded 1952. Pop 42,000; Circ 340,605
Library Holdings: Bk Vols 73,000
Automation Activity & Vendor Info: (Cataloging) TLC (The Library Corporation); (Circulation) TLC (The Library Corporation); (OPAC) TLC (The Library Corporation)
Wireless access
Open Mon & Wed-Fri 10-6:30, Tues 10-8, Sat 10-5, Sun 1-5
Friends of the Library Group

MOUNTAIN VIEW

P STONE COUNTY LIBRARY*, Bessie Boehm Moore Library, 326 W Washington St, 72560. Tel: 870-269-3100. E-mail: stonecolibrary@mvtel.net. *Mgr,* Lenora Duncan
Library Holdings: Bk Vols 25,000; Per Subs 45
Automation Activity & Vendor Info: (Cataloging) Follett Software; (Circulation) Follett Software
Wireless access
Mem of White River Regional Library
Open Mon, Wed & Fri 9:30-5, Tues 9:30-6, Thurs 9:30-7, Sat 9:30-1
Friends of the Library Group

P WHITE RIVER REGIONAL LIBRARY*, Headquarters, PO Box 1107, 72560. Tel: 870-269-4682. E-mail: wrrlibrary@yahoo.com. *Regional Librn,* Debra Sutterfield
Member Libraries: Cleburne County Library; Fulton County Library; Izard County Library; Sharp County Library; Stone County Library
Open Mon-Fri 9-5

MOUNTAINBURG

P MOUNTAINBURG PUBLIC LIBRARY*, 225 Hwy 71 NW, 72946. SAN 331-0027. Tel: 479-369-1600. FAX: 479-369-1600. E-mail: mountainburg@crawfordcountylib.org. Web Site: www2.youseemore.com/crawfordcls. *Br Dir,* Margaux Burleson; Tel: 479-369-1600, E-mail: mburleson@crawfordcountylib.org
Library Holdings: Bk Vols 18,889
Automation Activity & Vendor Info: (Cataloging) TLC (The Library Corporation); (Circulation) TLC (The Library Corporation); (ILL) OCLC; (OPAC) TLC (The Library Corporation)
Wireless access
Open Mon-Fri 8:30-5:30, Sat 10-3
Friends of the Library Group

MULBERRY

P MULBERRY PUBLIC LIBRARY*, 220 N Main St, 72947. (Mail add: PO Box 589, 72947-0589), SAN 331-0051. Tel: 479-997-1226. FAX: 479-997-1226. E-mail: mulberry@crawfordcountylib.org. Web Site: www.youseemore.com/crawfordcls/location.asp?SchoolType=0&sID=18. *Br Dir,* Robin Egerton; E-mail: regerton@crawfordcountylib.org
Founded 1950. Pop 1,600
Library Holdings: Bk Vols 16,553
Automation Activity & Vendor Info: (Cataloging) TLC (The Library Corporation); (Circulation) TLC (The Library Corporation); (OPAC) TLC (The Library Corporation)
Wireless access
Mem of Crawford County Library System
Partic in Association for Rural & Small Libraries
Open Mon-Fri 8:30-5, Sat 10-2
Friends of the Library Group

MURFREESBORO

P PIKE COUNTY LIBRARY*, 210 Second Ave, 71958. (Mail add: PO Box 153, 71958-0153), SAN 331-149X. Tel: 870-285-2575. E-mail: murfreesboropubliclibrary@gmail.com. Web Site: pikecountylibrary.weebly.com. *Librn,* Mona Swihart
Library Holdings: Bk Titles 4,700
Wireless access
Open Tues-Fri 10-12:30 & 1:30-5
Branches: 1
DELIGHT BRANCH LIBRARY, 401 E Antioch St, Delight, 71940. (Mail add: PO Box 88, Delight, 71940-0142), SAN 331-1252. Tel: 870-379-2456. E-mail: delightlib1@hotmail.com. Web Site: delightbranchlibrary.weebly.com. *Librn,* Carrie Tidwell
Open Tues-Fri 10-5

NASHVILLE

P TRI-COUNTY REGIONAL LIBRARY*, Howard County Library, 426 N Main St, Ste 5, 71852-2009. SAN 331-1643. Tel: 870-845-2566. FAX: 870-845-7533. E-mail: hcpubliclibrary@yahoo.com. Web Site: www.facebook.com/howardcountylibrary. *Mgr,* Janice Curry
Pop 6,000; Circ 34,000
Subject Interests: Arkansas
Wireless access
Open Mon 11-7, Tues-Sat 10-5
Branches: 7
ASHDOWN COMMUNITY LIBRARY, 160 E Commerce St, Ashdown, 71822, SAN 331-1228. Tel: 870-898-3233. FAX: 870-898-3233. E-mail: ashcomlib@yahoo.com. *Mgr,* Maureen Nations
Pop 2,944
Open Mon 12-7, Tues-Fri 9-6
DIERKS PUBLIC LIBRARY, 202 W Third St, Dierks, 71833. (Mail add: PO Box 10, Dierks, 71833-0010), SAN 331-1317. Tel: 870-286-3228. FAX: 870-286-2570. E-mail: dierkslib@yahoo.com. *Mgr,* Ruth White
Open Tues-Thurs 8:30-4:30
FOREMAN PUBLIC LIBRARY, 216 Schumann St, Foreman, 71836. (Mail add: PO Box 7, Foreman, 71836-0007), SAN 331-1341. Tel: 870-542-7409. FAX: 870-542-7409. E-mail: foremanpublib@yahoo.com. *Mgr,* Tammy Whitlow
Open Mon-Fri 8:30-5
LOCKESBURG PUBLIC LIBRARY, 112 E Main St, Lockesburg, 71846. (Mail add: PO Box 46, Lockesburg, 71846). Tel: 870-289-2233. FAX: 870-289-2233. E-mail: loxlib@hotmail.com. *Mgr,* Wendy Clay
Open Wed & Thurs 8:30-5, Sat 8:30-12:30
MINERAL SPRINGS PUBLIC LIBRARY, 310 E Runnels, Mineral Springs, 71851. (Mail add: PO Box 309, Mineral Springs, 71851-0309), SAN 331-152X. Tel: 870-287-7162. E-mail: mineralspringspubliclibrary@gmail.com. *Mgr,* Nicole McGilberry
Open Tues 11-6, Wed & Thurs 10-5
TOLLETTE PUBLIC LIBRARY, 205 Town Hall Dr, Tollette, 71851. (Mail add: PO Box 418, Tollette, 71851-0418), SAN 331-1651. Tel: 870-287-7166. E-mail: tollettebranchlibrary@yahoo.com. *Librn,* Wilma Lafferty
Library Holdings: Bk Vols 5,000
Open Mon-Wed 9-3
WINTHROP PUBLIC LIBRARY, 720 High St, Winthrop, 71866. (Mail add: PO Box 193, Winthrop, 71866-0193), SAN 331-1554. Tel: 870-381-7580. FAX: 870-381-7580. E-mail: chunbug@yahoo.com. *Mgr,* Susan Lansdell
Open Mon-Fri 10-5
Friends of the Library Group

NEWPORT

C ARKANSAS STATE UNIVERSITY*, Newport Library, 7648 Victory Blvd, 72112-8912. Tel: 870-512-7861. FAX: 870-512-7870. Web Site: www.asun.edu/library. *Librn,* Jennifer Ballard; E-mail: jennifer_ballard@asun.edu; *Libr Tech,* Debbie Jewell; Tel: 870-512-7862, E-mail: deborah_jewell@asun.edu
Library Holdings: Bk Titles 6,400; Bk Vols 8,000; Per Subs 76
Automation Activity & Vendor Info: (Acquisitions) Ex Libris Group; (Cataloging) Ex Libris Group; (Circulation) Ex Libris Group; (ILL) OCLC FirstSearch; (OPAC) Ex Libris Group
Wireless access
Open Mon-Thurs 8-6, Fri 8-4:30

P JACKSON COUNTY LIBRARY*, W A Billingsley Memorial Library, 213 Walnut St, 72112. SAN 300-5402. Tel: 870-523-2952. FAX: 870-523-5218. Web Site: jacksoncolib.wordpress.com. *Dir & Librn,* Jennifer Ballard; E-mail: director@jacksoncolibrary.net; *Ref Librn,* Ellen Crain; *Children's Prog, Circ,* Sally Dunkin
Founded 1930. Pop 18,944
Library Holdings: Large Print Bks 2,750; Bk Titles 53,000; Per Subs 70
Subject Interests: Arkansas, Genealogy
Automation Activity & Vendor Info: (Cataloging) Book Systems; (Circulation) Book Systems; (ILL) OCLC
Wireless access
Open Mon-Fri 9-5, Sat 9-Noon
Branches: 1
TUCKERMAN BRANCH, 200 W Main St, Tuckerman, 72473. (Mail add: PO Box 1117, Tuckerman, 72473-1117). Tel: 870-349-5336. FAX: 870-349-5336. *Librn,* Margaret Campbell
Pop 1,741
Library Holdings: Bk Vols 59,750
Open Mon-Fri 8-12 & 12:30-4:30

NORTH LITTLE ROCK

P WILLIAM F LAMAN PUBLIC LIBRARY*, 2801 Orange St, 72114-2296. SAN 300-5429. Tel: 501-758-1720. Web Site: www.laman.net. *Dir,* Crystal Gates; E-mail: crystal.gates@lamanlibrary.org; Staff 22 (MLS 4, Non-MLS 18)
Founded 1945. Pop 61,741; Circ 206,078
Library Holdings: e-books 25; Bk Titles 165,057; Per Subs 252
Special Collections: Ark History; Genealogy Coll
Automation Activity & Vendor Info: (OPAC) Innovative Interfaces, Inc
Wireless access
Partic in OCLC Online Computer Library Center, Inc
Open Mon-Thurs 9-8, Fri & Sat 9-5

J UNIVERSITY OF ARKANSAS - PULASKI TECHNICAL COLLEGE*, Ottenheimer - North Library, 3000 W Scenic Dr, 72118. Tel: 501-812-2272. FAX: 501-812-2315. Web Site: www.uaptc.edu/library. *Dir,* Wendy Davis; E-mail: wdavis@uaptc.edu; Staff 7 (MLS 4, Non-MLS 3)
Enrl 8,500; Highest Degree: Associate
Library Holdings: AV Mats 2,228; Bk Titles 28,633; Bk Vols 32,530; Per Subs 275
Automation Activity & Vendor Info: (Acquisitions) Ex Libris Group; (Cataloging) Ex Libris Group; (Circulation) Ex Libris Group; (Course Reserve) Ex Libris Group; (OPAC) Ex Libris Group; (Serials) Ex Libris Group
Wireless access
Function: Distance learning, ILL available, Photocopying/Printing, Ref serv available
Partic in ARKLink
Open Mon-Thurs 7:30-6, Fri 7:30-3

PARAGOULD

M ARKANSAS METHODIST HOSPITAL, Doctors' Memorial Library, 900 W Kingshighway, 72450. (Mail add: PO Box 339, 72451-0339), SAN 320-1236. Tel: 870-239-7165. FAX: 870-239-7484. *Librn*, Nancy Ryan; E-mail: nancy.ryan@arkansasmethodist.org
Founded 1970
Library Holdings: Bk Titles 800; Per Subs 10
Subject Interests: Med, Nursing
Wireless access
Restriction: Staff use only

J CROWLEY'S RIDGE COLLEGE LIBRARY & LEARNING CENTER*, 100 College Dr, 72450. SAN 300-5445. Tel: 870-236-6901. FAX: 870-236-7748. Web Site: crc.insigniails.com/library. *Dir, Libr Serv*, Darah Watson; Tel: 870-236-6901, Ext 145, E-mail: dwatson@crc.edu
Founded 1964. Enrl 100; Fac 8
Library Holdings: Bk Vols 15,400; Per Subs 60
Subject Interests: Relig
Wireless access
Open Mon, Tues & Thurs 8am-9pm, Wed & Fri 9-5

P GREENE COUNTY PUBLIC LIBRARY*, 120 N 12th St, 72450. Tel: 870-236-8711. FAX: 870-236-1442. E-mail: greene@mylibrarynow.org. Web Site: www.mylibrarynow.org/greene. *County Librn, Regional Dir*, Mike Rogers; E-mail: mike@mylibrarynow.org; *Asst Dir*, Connie Whitman; *ILL/Ref Librn*, Cathy Howard; E-mail: cathy@mylibrarynow.org; *Cat & Proc Mgr*, Kelly Cole; E-mail: kelly@mylibrarynow.org; *Children's Prog*, Sonya Nelson; E-mail: sonya@mylibrarynow.org; *Ch Serv, Circ*, Sherry Crafton; E-mail: sherryc@mylibrarynow.org; *Circ*, Ronda Griffin; E-mail: ronda@mylibrarynow.org; *Circ*, Christy Martin; *Circ*, Virginia Tate; *Circ*, Connie Willetts; E-mail: connie@mylibrarynow.org; Staff 7 (Non-MLS 7)
Founded 1965. Pop 68,194; Circ 274,503
Subject Interests: Arkansas, Genealogy
Automation Activity & Vendor Info: (Acquisitions) Follett Software; (Cataloging) Follett Software; (Circulation) Follett Software; (Course Reserve) Follett Software; (ILL) Follett Software; (Serials) EBSCO Online
Wireless access
Mem of Northeast Arkansas Regional Library System
Open Mon-Thurs 8-6, Fri 8-4, Sat 8-1
Friends of the Library Group

P NORTHEAST ARKANSAS REGIONAL LIBRARY SYSTEM*, 120 N 12th St, 72450. SAN 331-3204. Tel: 870-236-8711. FAX: 870-236-1442. Web Site: mylibrarynow.org. *Dir*, Mike E Rogers; E-mail: mike@mylibrarynow.org; Staff 1 (MLS 1)
Founded 1965. Pop 71,000
Automation Activity & Vendor Info: (Circulation) Book Systems; (ILL) Book Systems; (OPAC) Book Systems
Wireless access
Function: Adult bk club, Bk club(s), Computer training, Electronic databases & coll, ILL available, Internet access, Magnifiers for reading, Music CDs, Online ref, Photocopying/Printing, Prog for adults, Prog for children & young adult, Ref & res, Senior computer classes, Serves people with intellectual disabilities, Spoken cassettes & CDs, Spoken cassettes & DVDs, Summer reading prog, Tax forms, VHS videos, Wheelchair accessible
Member Libraries: Corning Public Library; Greene County Public Library; Piggott Public Library; Randolph County Library; Rector Public Library
Open Mon-Thurs 8-6, Fri 8-4, Sat 8-1

PEA RIDGE

P PEA RIDGE COMMUNITY LIBRARY*, 801 N Curtis Ave, 72751-2306. (Mail add: PO Box 9, 72751-0009). Tel: 479-451-8442. E-mail: library@cityofpearidge.com. Web Site: pearidgecommunitylibrary.org. *Librn*, Megan Bryant
Founded 1974. Pop 5,500; Circ 3,000
Library Holdings: High Interest/Low Vocabulary Bk Vols 900; Large Print Bks 55; Bk Vols 13,100; Talking Bks 58
Special Collections: Arkansas History Coll
Wireless access
Function: Accelerated reader prog
Open Mon-Fri 10-6, Sat 10-2
Restriction: ID required to use computers (Ltd hrs)

PIGGOTT

P PIGGOTT PUBLIC LIBRARY, 361 W Main, 72454. SAN 331-3263. Tel: 870-598-3666. FAX: 870-598-3669. E-mail: piggott@mylibrarynow.org. Web Site: mylibrarynow.org/index.php/piggott. *Dir*, Gay Johnson; E-mail: gay@mylibrarynow.org; Staff 4 (Non-MLS 4)
Founded 1935
Library Holdings: AV Mats 122; CDs 803; DVDs 730; Large Print Bks 1,255; Microforms 122; Bk Titles 26,721; Per Subs 12; Videos 295
Automation Activity & Vendor Info: (Cataloging) Book Systems; (Circulation) Book Systems; (OPAC) Book Systems
Wireless access
Mem of Northeast Arkansas Regional Library System
Open Mon, Tues & Thurs 8:30-5:30, Wed 8:30-5, Fri 8:30-4, Sat 9-1

PINE BLUFF

ARKANSAS DEPARTMENT OF CORRECTION
S DIAGNOSTIC UNIT LIBRARY*, 7500 Correction Circle, 71603-1498. Tel: 870-267-6410. FAX: 870-267-6721. *Supvr*, Cathy Herring
Library Holdings: Bk Vols 1,297; Per Subs 16
Open Mon-Fri 8-11, 1-4 & 6-8
S PINE BLUFF WORK COMPLEX CHAPEL LIBRARY*, 890 Freeline Dr, 71603-1498. Tel: 870-267-6510. FAX: 870-267-6529. *Library Contact*, John Mark Wheeler; E-mail: john.wheeler@arkansas.gov
Library Holdings: Bk Vols 6,000; Per Subs 40
Open Tues-Fri 8-10 & 2-4

P PINE BLUFF & JEFFERSON COUNTY LIBRARY SYSTEM*, Main Library, 600 S Main St, 71601. SAN 300-5453. Tel: 870-534-4802. Circulation Tel: 870-534-4818. Reference Tel: 870-534-2159. FAX: 870-534-8707. E-mail: info@pinebluffibrary.org. Web Site: www.pinebluffibrary.org. *Libr Dir*, Barbara Morgan; E-mail: bmorgan@pinebluffibrary.org; *Asst Dir*, Ricky Williams; E-mail: rwilliams@pinebluffibrary.org; *Circ Mgr*, Trisha Rodenberg; *Ref Mgr*, Jana Mitchell; *Tech Serv*, Sylvia Washington; Staff 17 (MLS 1, Non-MLS 16)
Founded 1913. Pop 47,000; Circ 78,481
Jan 2014-Dec 2014 Income (Main & Associated Libraries) $1,304,500, State $134,000, City $585,000, County $560,000, Locally Generated Income $25,500. Mats Exp $205,186, Books $127,000, Per/Ser (Incl. Access Fees) $10,000, AV Mat $30,000, Electronic Ref Mat (Incl. Access Fees) $38,186
Library Holdings: Audiobooks 1,005; DVDs 3,079; Microforms 5,686; Bk Titles 57,172; Bk Vols 64,771; Per Subs 62
Special Collections: Arkansas Coll; Genealogy with Emphasis on Arkansas, North Carolina, South Carolina, Tennessee & Virginia; Index to Deaths for Pine Bluff & Jefferson County Newspapers; Regional History of Arkansas & Mississippi Valley, bks, maps, micro
Automation Activity & Vendor Info: (Acquisitions) TLC (The Library Corporation); (Cataloging) TLC (The Library Corporation); (Circulation) TLC (The Library Corporation); (OPAC) TLC (The Library Corporation); (Serials) TLC (The Library Corporation)
Wireless access
Function: AV serv, ILL available, Photocopying/Printing, Prog for children & young adult, Ref serv available, Summer reading prog, Telephone ref, Wheelchair accessible
Partic in OCLC Online Computer Library Center, Inc
Open Mon-Thurs 9-6, Fri 9-4:30, Sat 9-2
Restriction: Open to pub for ref & circ; with some limitations
Friends of the Library Group
Branches: 4
ALTHEIMER PUBLIC LIBRARY, 222 S Edline, Altheimer, 72004. Tel: 870-766-8499. FAX: 870-766-8499. *Br Mgr*, Melony Darrough; Staff 1 (Non-MLS 1)
Founded 2001. Pop 5,000
Library Holdings: Audiobooks 38; DVDs 384; Bk Titles 13,831; Per Subs 11
Open Mon 12-6, Tues 12-7, Wed 10-5:30, Thurs & Fri 12-4
REDFIELD PUBLIC LIBRARY, 310 Brodie St, Redfield, 72132. Tel: 501-397-5070. *Br Mgr*, Cathy Ackerman; Staff 1.3 (Non-MLS 1.3)
Founded 1999. Pop 2,500; Circ 15,418
Library Holdings: Audiobooks 238; DVDs 701; Bk Titles 20,468; Per Subs 10
Open Mon-Thurs 9:30-5:30, Fri 9:30-4
Friends of the Library Group
WATSON CHAPEL PUBLIC LIBRARY, 4120 Camden Rd, 71603, SAN 322-6204. Tel: 870-879-3406. *Br Mgr*, Shay Green; Staff 1.5 (Non-MLS 1.5)
Founded 1985. Pop 2,500; Circ 44,461
Library Holdings: Audiobooks 521; DVDs 1,306; Bk Titles 31,457; Per Subs 24
Open Mon-Thurs 9:30-5:30, Fri 9:30-4
WHITE HALL PUBLIC LIBRARY, 300 Anderson Ave, White Hall, 71602, SAN 320-0825. Tel: 870-247-5064. E-mail: whitehalllibrary@pinebluffibrary.org. *Br Mgr*, Ellen Bauer; Staff 2.5 (Non-MLS 2.5)
Founded 1978. Pop 5,000; Circ 68,297
Library Holdings: Audiobooks 812; DVDs 1,588; Bk Titles 41,532; Per Subs 26
Open Mon-Thurs 9-6, Fri 9-4:30, Sat 9-2
Friends of the Library Group

C SOUTHEAST ARKANSAS COLLEGE*, SEARK Library & Center for E-Learning, 1900 Hazel St, 71603. Tel: 870-543-5936. Interlibrary Loan Service Tel: 870-850-4814. FAX: 870-850-5937. E-mail: library@seark.edu. Web Site: www.seark.edu/academic-support/library. *Librn,* Kimberly Williams; Tel: 870-850-4815, E-mail: kwilliams@seark.edu; *Libr Tech,* TiKeecha Spikes; Tel: 870-850-4840, Fax: 870-850-4840, E-mail: tspikes@seark.edu; Staff 4.5 (MLS 2, Non-MLS 2.5)
Founded 1993. Highest Degree: Associate
Library Holdings: Bk Titles 11,000; Bk Vols 14,000; Per Subs 120
Special Collections: Early Childhood Paraprofessional Coll
Automation Activity & Vendor Info: (Cataloging) TLC (The Library Corporation); (Circulation) TLC (The Library Corporation); (ILL) OCLC FirstSearch; (OPAC) TLC (The Library Corporation)
Wireless access
Function: AV serv, Distance learning, ILL available, Photocopying/Printing, Ref serv available
Partic in ARKLink
Open Mon-Thurs 7:30am-8pm, Fri 7:30-5

C UNIVERSITY OF ARKANSAS-PINE BLUFF, Watson Memorial Library-Learning & Instructional Resources Centers, 1200 N University Dr, 71601. SAN 331-3352. Tel: 870-575-8411. Circulation Tel: 870-575-8848. Reference Tel: 870-575-8896. FAX: 870-575-4651. Web Site: www.uapb.edu/administration/academic_affairs/john_brown_watson_memorial_library.aspx. *Dir,* Edward J Fontenette; Tel: 870-575-8410, E-mail: fontenettee@uapb.edu; *Assoc Dir,* Maplean Donaldson; E-mail: donaldsonm@uapb.edu; *Assoc Librn, Coordr, Spec Serv,* Evelyn Yates; E-mail: yatese@uapb.edu; Staff 7 (MLS 7)
Founded 1938. Enrl 2,917; Fac 140; Highest Degree: Bachelor
Library Holdings: AV Mats 35,000; e-books 270,000; Bk Titles 48,000; Bk Vols 750,000; Videos 5,500
Special Collections: Afro American Coll; Arkansas (Raley Coll); Literature (Rare Books Coll); State Government (Knox Nelson Coll). State Document Depository; UN Document Depository; US Document Depository
Subject Interests: Agr, Educ, Indust arts, Nursing
Automation Activity & Vendor Info: (Acquisitions) Innovative Interfaces, Inc; (Cataloging) Innovative Interfaces, Inc; (Circulation) Innovative Interfaces, Inc; (Course Reserve) Innovative Interfaces, Inc; (ILL) Innovative Interfaces, Inc; (Media Booking) Innovative Interfaces, Inc; (OPAC) Innovative Interfaces, Inc; (Serials) Innovative Interfaces, Inc
Wireless access
Publications: Acquisitions List (Monthly)
Open Mon-Thurs 7:30am-11pm, Fri 7:30-5, Sat 8:30-4:30, Sun 3:30-11
Departmental Libraries:
FINE ARTS, Art Department, Mail Slot 4925, 71601. Tel: 870-575-8896. FAX: 870-575-4642. *Librn,* Shenise McGhee; E-mail: mcghees@uapb.edu
Open Mon-Fri 8:30-4:30
HUMAN SCIENCES, Mail Slot 4971, 71601. Tel: 870-575-8423. FAX: 870-570-7623. *Librn,* Sonya Lockett; E-mail: locketts@uapb.edu
MUSIC LAB, 1200 N University Dr, Mail Stop 4956, 71601. Tel: 870-575-7036. FAX: 870-575-4631. *Music Librn,* James Mincy; E-mail: mincyj@uapb.edu
NURSING LAB, 1200 University Dr, Mail Slot 4973, 71611. Tel: 870-575-8896. FAX: 870-575-4642. *Librn,* Shenise McGhee; E-mail: mcghees@uapb.edu
Library Holdings: Bk Vols 100
Open Mon-Fri 8-5

POCAHONTAS

J BLACK RIVER TECHNICAL COLLEGE LIBRARY*, 1410 Hwy 304 E, 72455. (Mail add: PO Box 468, 72455-0468). Tel: 870-248-4060. FAX: 870-248-4100. Web Site: www.blackrivertech.org/black-river-technical-college-library. *Libr Tech,* Brittany Obregon; E-mail: brittany.obregon@blackrivertech.edu
Library Holdings: Bk Vols 25,000; Per Subs 200
Automation Activity & Vendor Info: (Cataloging) SirsiDynix; (Circulation) SirsiDynix
Wireless access
Function: Ref serv available
Open Mon-Thurs (Fall & Spring) 7:30-6, Fri 7:30-3:30; Mon-Thurs (Summer) 7-5

P RANDOLPH COUNTY LIBRARY, 111 W Everett St, 72455. SAN 331-3298. Tel: 870-892-5617. E-mail: randolph@mylibrarynow.org. Web Site: www.mylibrarynow.org/index.php/randolph. *Dir,* Jackie Salyards; E-mail: jackie@mylibrarynow.org
Founded 1939. Circ 12,000
Jan 2016-Dec 2016 Income $322,000. Mats Exp $322,000. Sal $112,000
Library Holdings: AV Mats 2,500; Bks on Deafness & Sign Lang 25; Braille Volumes 1; CDs 1,700; DVDs 1,500; Large Print Bks 6,500; Bk Titles 65,000; Per Subs 45; Talking Bks 1,246; Videos 500
Special Collections: Arkansas Reference, microfilm, newsp, family histories; Genealogy Coll; History Coll
Automation Activity & Vendor Info: (Cataloging) Book Systems; (Circulation) Book Systems; (OPAC) Book Systems
Wireless access
Mem of Northeast Arkansas Regional Library System
Special Services for the Deaf - Bks on deafness & sign lang
Open Mon-Fri 9-5, Sat 9-12
Friends of the Library Group
Bookmobiles: 1

PRAIRIE GROVE

P PRAIRIE GROVE PUBLIC LIBRARY*, 123 S Neal St, 72753. (Mail add: PO Box 10, 72753-0010), SAN 331-0086. Tel: 479-846-3782. FAX: 479-846-3428. E-mail: prairiegrove@wcls.lib.ar.us. Web Site: www.library.arkansasusa.com/prairie_grove. *Libr Dir,* Iva Sorrell; *Children's Coordr,* Megan Wood; Tel: 479-846-3782, E-mail: prairiegrove@wcls.lib.ar.us
Library Holdings: Bk Vols 25,000
Wireless access
Mem of Washington County Library System
Open Mon-Sat 9:30-5:30
Friends of the Library Group

PRESCOTT

P PRESCOTT/NEVADA COUNTY LIBRARY & EDUCATIONAL FACILITY*, 121 W Main St, 71857. SAN 331-1619. Tel: 870-887-5846. FAX: 870-887-8226. E-mail: nevcolib@yahoo.com. Web Site: nevadacountylibrary.wordpress.com. *Librn,* Theresa Tyree; *Asst Librn,* Susan Wright
Wireless access
Open Tues-Fri 9:30-5:30
Friends of the Library Group

RECTOR

P RECTOR PUBLIC LIBRARY*, 121 W Fourth St, 72461. SAN 331-3328. Tel: 870-595-2410. FAX: 870-595-1052. E-mail: rector@mylibrarynow.org. Web Site: www.mylibrarynow.org/rector. *Dir,* Deana Mills; E-mail: deana@mylibrarynow.org; *Asst Dir,* Virginia Shipley; E-mail: rectorlibrary@yahoo.com; Staff 4 (Non-MLS 4)
Founded 1934. Pop 3,000
Automation Activity & Vendor Info: (Acquisitions) Book Systems
Wireless access
Mem of Northeast Arkansas Regional Library System
Open Mon, Tues & Thurs 8:30-5:30, Wed 8:30-5, Fri 8:30-4, Sat 9-1

ROGERS

P ROGERS PUBLIC LIBRARY*, 711 S Dixieland Rd, 72758. SAN 331-0116. Tel: 479-621-1152. FAX: 479-621-1165. Information Services E-mail: rplaskalibrarian@rogersar.gov. Web Site: rogerspubliclibrary.org. *Dir,* Judy F Casey; E-mail: jcasey@rogersar.gov; *Asst Dir,* Robert Finch; E-mail: rfinch@rogersar.gov; *Syst Mgr,* Hisham Makki; E-mail: hmakki@rogersar.gov; Staff 34 (MLS 7, Non-MLS 27)
Founded 1904. Pop 48,666; Circ 456,115
Library Holdings: Audiobooks 4,633; AV Mats 5,269; CDs 2,486; DVDs 3,900; e-books 4,134; Electronic Media & Resources 28; High Interest/Low Vocabulary Bk Vols 177; Large Print Bks 5,176; Bk Titles 96,755; Bk Vols 118,518; Per Subs 314; Videos 3,909
Automation Activity & Vendor Info: (Acquisitions) Innovative Interfaces, Inc; (Cataloging) Innovative Interfaces, Inc; (Circulation) Innovative Interfaces, Inc; (ILL) OCLC; (OPAC) Innovative Interfaces, Inc
Wireless access
Function: Homebound delivery serv, ILL available, Internet access, Magnifiers for reading, Photocopying/Printing, Prog for children & young adult, Ref serv available, Summer reading prog, Telephone ref, Wheelchair accessible
Open Mon-Thurs 9-9, Fri & Sat 9-5, Sun 1-5
Friends of the Library Group

RUSSELLVILLE

C ARKANSAS TECH UNIVERSITY*, Ross Pendergraft Library & Technology Center, 305 West Q St, 72801-2222. SAN 300-547X. Tel: 479-964-0569. Interlibrary Loan Service Tel: 479-968-0416. Reference Tel: 479-964-0570. Toll Free Tel: 855-761-0006. FAX: 479-964-0559. Interlibrary Loan Service FAX: 479-968-2185. Web Site: libguides.atu.edu/research. *Dir,* Brent Etzel; Tel: 479-968-0417, E-mail: betzel@atu.edu; *Acq Librn,* Frances Hager; Tel: 479-964-0561, E-mail: fhager@atu.edu; *Electronic Res Librn,* Carol Hanan; Tel: 479-968-0288, E-mail: chanan@atu.edu; *Music & Media Librn,* Dr Lowell Lybarger; Tel: 479-964-0584, E-mail: llybarger@atu.edu; *Pub Serv Librn,* Sherry Tinerella; Tel: 479-964-0571, E-mail: stinerella@atu.edu; *Syst Librn,*

Philippe Van Houtte; Tel: 479-498-6042, E-mail: pvanhoutte@atu.edu; *Tech Serv Librn,* Angela Black; Tel: 479-964-0558, E-mail: ablack9@atu.edu. Subject Specialists: *Ethnomusicology,* Dr Lowell Lybarger; Staff 7 (MLS 7)
Founded 1999. Enrl 11,350; Fac 330; Highest Degree: Master
Jul 2012-Jun 2013 Income $1,638,956, Federal $18,460, Parent Institution $1,620,496. Mats Exp $559,811, Books $64,173, Per/Ser (Incl. Access Fees) $145,263, Micro $23,357, AV Mat $22,374, Electronic Ref Mat (Incl. Access Fees) $298,457, Presv $6,187. Sal $765,201 (Prof $367,089)
Library Holdings: Audiobooks 200; AV Mats 15,500; e-books 20,000; e-journals 40,000; Microforms 902,200; Music Scores 4,000; Bk Vols 174,600; Per Subs 756
Special Collections: Parks & Recreation Administration, bk & micro. State Document Depository; US Document Depository
Subject Interests: Engr, Humanities, Music, Nursing
Automation Activity & Vendor Info: (Acquisitions) Ex Libris Group; (Cataloging) Ex Libris Group; (Circulation) Ex Libris Group; (Course Reserve) Ex Libris Group; (ILL) OCLC WorldShare Interlibrary Loan; (Media Booking) Ex Libris Group; (OPAC) Ex Libris Group; (Serials) Ex Libris Group
Wireless access
Function: ILL available
Publications: Arkansas Gazette Newspapers Index
Partic in ARKLink
Open Mon-Thurs 7am-1am, Fri 7am-8pm, Sat 10-8, Sun 1pm-1am

P POPE COUNTY LIBRARY SYSTEM*, Russellville Headquarters Branch, 116 E Third St, 72801. SAN 371-7992. Tel: 479-968-4368. FAX: 479-968-3222. Web Site: www.popelibrary.org. *Syst Dir,* Sherry Simpson; E-mail: director@popelibrary.org; *Br Mgr,* Kevin Massey; E-mail: kmassey@popelibrary.org; Staff 8 (MLS 2, Non-MLS 6)
Founded 1920. Pop 52,063; Circ 391,425
Library Holdings: AV Mats 4,200; Bks on Deafness & Sign Lang 45; High Interest/Low Vocabulary Bk Vols 3,000; Large Print Bks 2,362; Bk Titles 76,493; Bk Vols 115,125; Per Subs 142
Special Collections: Arkansas Hist, films; Genealogy (Katie Murdoch Coll), bks, docs; Local Hist Coll
Automation Activity & Vendor Info: (Cataloging) Innovative Interfaces, Inc; (Circulation) Innovative Interfaces, Inc; (OPAC) Innovative Interfaces, Inc
Wireless access
Special Services for the Deaf - Bks on deafness & sign lang; High interest/low vocabulary bks; Staff with knowledge of sign lang
Open Mon-Fri 8:30-5:30
Friends of the Library Group
Branches: 3
ATKINS CENTENNIAL BRANCH, 216 NE First St, Atkins, 72823, SAN 371-800X. Tel: 479-641-7904. FAX: 479-641-1169. Web Site: atkins.popelibrary.org. *Br Mgr,* Ms Riley Taurone; E-mail: atkins.branchmgr@popelibrary.org
Founded 1933
Library Holdings: Bk Vols 10,000
Open Mon-Fri 8:30-5:30
DOVER BRANCH, 80 Library Rd, Dover, 72837, SAN 371-8018. Tel: 479-331-2173. FAX: 479-331-4151. Web Site: dover.popelibrary.org. *Br Mgr,* Melissa Sanders; E-mail: dover.branchmgr@popelibrary.org
Library Holdings: Bk Vols 9,000
Open Mon-Fri 8:30-5:30
Friends of the Library Group
HECTOR BRANCH, 11600 State Rd 27, Hector, 72843, SAN 377-5925. Tel: 479-284-0907. FAX: 479-284-0907. Web Site: hector.popelibrary.org. *Br Mgr,* Ruth Mason; E-mail: rmason@popelibrary.org
Founded 1996
Library Holdings: Bk Vols 4,000
Open Mon, Wed & Fri 1-5, Tues 9-1, Thurs 2-6
Bookmobiles: 1

SAINT PAUL

P ST PAUL PUBLIC LIBRARY, 145 Fifth St, 72760. (Mail add: PO Box 123, 72760-0123). Tel: 479-677-2907. FAX: 479-677-2907. E-mail: library72760@gmail.com. Web Site: www.carrollmadisonlibraries.org/library.aspx?lib=stpaul. *Libr Dir,* Sabine Schmidt; *Asst Librn,* Denise Bednar; Staff 1 (Non-MLS 1)
Wireless access
Function: 24/7 Electronic res, 24/7 Online cat, Activity rm, Adult bk club
Mem of Carroll & Madison Library System
Open Mon-Wed 9-2, Thurs & Fri 9-6, Sat 9-1
Friends of the Library Group

SALEM

P FULTON COUNTY LIBRARY*, Salem Public Library, 131 Pickren St, 72576. (Mail add: PO Box 277, 72576-0277). Tel: 870-895-2014. FAX: 870-895-2014. *Mgr,* Betty J Roork
Pop 12,000; Circ 14,000
Library Holdings: Bk Vols 20,260; Per Subs 19; Talking Bks 100
Mem of White River Regional Library
Open Mon-Fri 8:30-4:30

SEARCY

J ARKANSAS STATE UNIVERSITY-SEARCY*, Media Center, 1800 E Moore, 72143-4710. (Mail add: PO Box 909, 72145-0909). Tel: 501-207-6231. FAX: 501-268-6263. *Learning Coordr, Media Spec,* Cheryl Cherry; E-mail: cdcherry@asub.edu
Founded 1988. Enrl 700; Fac 92; Highest Degree: Associate
Library Holdings: Bk Vols 4,500
Automation Activity & Vendor Info: (Circulation) TLC (The Library Corporation)
Wireless access
Open Mon-Fri 8-4:30

CR HARDING UNIVERSITY, Brackett Library, 915 E Market St, 72149-5615. (Mail add: PO Box 12267, 72149-0001), SAN 300-5488. Tel: 501-279-4354. Circulation Tel: 501-279-4279. Interlibrary Loan Service Tel: 501-279-4238. Reference Tel: 501-279-4775. Interlibrary Loan Service FAX: 501-279-4268. Web Site: library.harding.edu. *Libr Dir,* Jean Waldrop; Tel: 501-279-4011, E-mail: jwaldrop@harding.edu; *Archives & Spec Coll Librn,* Hannah Wood; Tel: 501-279-4205, E-mail: hwood@harding.edu; *Electronic Res Librn,* Amy McGohan; Tel: 501-279-5334, E-mail: amcgohan@harding.edu; *Health Sciences & Graduate Studies Librn,* John Boone; Tel: 501-279-4376, E-mail: jboone@harding.edu; *Instruction & Outreach Librn,* Whitney Hammes; Tel: 501-279-4228, E-mail: khammes1@harding.edu; *Syst Librn,* Brenda Breezeel; Tel: 501-279-5387; *Tech Serv Librn,* Alyssa Eller; Tel: 501-279-4349, E-mail: aeller1@harding.edu. Subject Specialists: *Biology, Family & consumer sci, Intl studies,* Jean Waldrop; *Communication, Hist, Theatre,* Hannah Wood; *Communication, Undergrad educ,* Amy McGohan; *Nursing, Phys therapy, Sciences,* John Boone; *Bible, Music, Theol,* Whitney Hammes; *Computer sci,* Brenda Breezeel; *Art, Math, Prints,* Alyssa Eller; Staff 13 (MLS 8, Non-MLS 5)
Founded 1924. Enrl 4,144; Fac 316; Highest Degree: Doctorate
Library Holdings: Audiobooks 2,684; AV Mats 12,286; Bks on Deafness & Sign Lang 337; CDs 793; DVDs 1,681; e-books 377,891; e-journals 81,461; Microforms 237,770; Music Scores 1,434; Per Subs 164; Videos 227
Special Collections: Harding History; LAC; Williams-Miles Science History Coll. Oral History
Automation Activity & Vendor Info: (Acquisitions) OCLC Worldshare Management Services; (Cataloging) OCLC Worldshare Management Services; (Circulation) OCLC Worldshare Management Services; (Course Reserve) OCLC Worldshare Management Services; (Discovery) OCLC; (ILL) OCLC Tipasa; (OPAC) OCLC Worldshare Management Services; (Serials) OCLC Worldshare Management Services
Wireless access
Function: Archival coll, Distance learning, Doc delivery serv, E-Reserves, Electronic databases & coll, ILL available, Music CDs, Online cat, Online ref, Outside serv via phone, mail, e-mail & web, Photocopying/Printing, Ref serv available, Telephone ref, VHS videos
Partic in Amigos Library Services, Inc; ARKLink; Christian Library Consortium; OCLC Online Computer Library Center, Inc
Open Mon-Thurs 7:45am-11pm, Fri 7:45-5, Sat 12-6, Sun 1-11
Restriction: Authorized patrons, ID required to use computers (Ltd hrs), In-house use for visitors, Non-circulating of rare bks

P WHITE COUNTY REGIONAL LIBRARY SYSTEM*, 113 E Pleasure Ave, 72143. SAN 331-3417. Tel: 501-268-2449, 501-279-2870. Circulation Tel: 501-269-2449, Ext 22. Interlibrary Loan Service Tel: 501-279-2870, Ext 21. Administration Tel: 501-279-2870, Ext 24. FAX: 501-268-2215. Web Site: www.whitecountylibraries.org. *Dir,* Darla Ino; E-mail: darla.ino@arkansas.gov; Staff 1 (MLS 1)
Founded 1896. Pop 72,560; Circ 289,686
Library Holdings: AV Mats 6,722; Bks on Deafness & Sign Lang 30; CDs 1,610; DVDs 12; High Interest/Low Vocabulary Bk Vols 89; Large Print Bks 1,200; Bk Titles 11,380; Bk Vols 113,795; Per Subs 720; Talking Bks 1,200; Videos 1,774
Special Collections: Mental Illness
Subject Interests: Arkansas
Automation Activity & Vendor Info: (Acquisitions) SirsiDynix-iBistro; (Cataloging) OCLC; (Circulation) SirsiDynix; (ILL) OCLC; (OPAC) SirsiDynix
Wireless access
Function: Accelerated reader prog, After school storytime, AV serv, Bks on cassette, Bks on CD, Children's prog, Computers for patron use, Doc delivery serv, E-Reserves, Electronic databases & coll, Free DVD rentals, ILL available, Internet access, Mail & tel request accepted, Online cat, Online ref, Outside serv via phone, mail, e-mail & web, Photocopying/Printing, Preschool outreach, Prog for children & young adult, Ref serv available, Serves people with intellectual disabilities,

Summer reading prog, Tax forms, Telephone ref, VHS videos, Wheelchair accessible
Open Mon-Fri 8-5
Friends of the Library Group
Branches: 8
BALDWIN-KITTLER MEMORIAL, 612 Van Buren, Judsonia, 72081. (Mail add: PO Box 577, Judsonia, 72081-0577), SAN 331-3476. Tel: 501-729-3995. FAX: 501-729-5994. *Br Mgr,* Travis Allen
Library Holdings: AV Mats 574; Bk Vols 15,569
Open Mon-Thurs 10-5, Fri 12-4, Sat 10-2
BRADFORD BRANCH, 302 W Walnut St, Bradford, 72020, SAN 377-7707. Tel: 501-344-2558. FAX: 501-344-2558. *Br Mgr,* Gail Tucker
Library Holdings: AV Mats 410; Bk Vols 3,704
Open Mon, Wed & Thurs 12-6, Tues 10-6, Sat 10-2
EL PASO COMMUNITY LIBRARY, 1607 Ridge Rd, El Paso, 72045. Tel: 501-796-5974. FAX: 501-796-5974. *Br Mgr,* Janet Blansett
Open Tues 10-6, Wed 10-5, Thurs & Fri 12-5, Sat 10-2
GOFF PUBLIC, 323 N Elm, Beebe, 72012-3245, SAN 331-3506. Tel: 501-882-3235. FAX: 501-882-6439. *Br Mgr,* Ramona Howell
Circ 17,141
Library Holdings: AV Mats 488; Bk Vols 10,247
Open Mon 10-8, Tues-Thurs 10-6, Sat 10-2
LYDA MILLER PUBLIC, 2609 Hwy 367 N, Bald Knob, 72010. (Mail add: PO Box 287, Bald Knob, 72010-0287), SAN 331-3441. Tel: 501-724-5452. *Br Mgr,* Patty Jean Corbit
Library Holdings: AV Mats 514; Bk Vols 8,268
Open Mon & Tues 10-6, Wed & Thurs 1-6, Sat 10-2
PANGBURN PUBLIC, 914 Main St, Pangburn, 72121, SAN 331-3530. Tel: 501-728-4612. FAX: 501-728-4612. *Br Mgr,* Lisa Hambrick
Library Holdings: AV Mats 310; Bk Vols 6,686
Open Mon & Tues 10-5, Thurs & Fri 10-6
ROSE BUD PUBLIC, 548A Hwy 5, Rose Bud, 71237. (Mail add: PO Box 327, Rose Bud, 72137-0327). Tel: 501-556-4447. FAX: 501-556-4447. *Br Mgr,* Gina Anderson
Library Holdings: AV Mats 225; Bk Vols 5,848
Open Mon & Wed 10-5, Tues & Thurs 10-6, Sat 10-2
Friends of the Library Group
SEARCY PUBLIC, 113 E Pleasure Ave, 72143, SAN 331-3565. FAX: 501-268-5682. *Br Mgr,* Teresa Scritchfield
Library Holdings: AV Mats 4,201; Bk Vols 59,236
Open Mon & Thurs 9-8, Tues & Wed 9-6, Fri 9-5, Sat 10-5 (10-1 Summer)

SILOAM SPRINGS

C JOHN BROWN UNIVERSITY LIBRARY*, Arutunoff Learning Resource Center, 2000 W University, 72761. SAN 300-550X. Tel: 479-524-7202. Interlibrary Loan Service Tel: 479-524-7276. Reference Tel: 479-524-7153. Administration Tel: 479-524-7203. FAX: 479-524-7335. E-mail: library@jbu.edu. Web Site: www.jbu.edu/library. *Libr Serv Dir,* Brent Swearingen; *ILL Librn,* Simone Schroder; E-mail: simones@jbu.edu; *Liaison & Instruction Librn,* Rachel Maxson; E-mail: Rmaxson@jbu.edu; *Ref Serv,* Mary E Habermas; E-mail: mhaberma@jbu.edu; Staff 11 (MLS 4, Non-MLS 7)
Founded 1919. Enrl 1,900; Fac 80; Highest Degree: Master
Library Holdings: AV Mats 3,751; e-books 10,000; e-journals 12,000; Bk Titles 87,958; Bk Vols 107,055; Per Subs 450
Special Collections: J Vernon McGee Coll; Oliver Coll; Romig Coll
Automation Activity & Vendor Info: (Cataloging) TLC (The Library Corporation); (Circulation) TLC (The Library Corporation); (Course Reserve) TLC (The Library Corporation); (ILL) OCLC; (OPAC) TLC (The Library Corporation)
Wireless access
Function: 24/7 Electronic res, 24/7 Online cat, Archival coll, Audio & video playback equip for onsite use, Computers for patron use, Electronic databases & coll, For res purposes, ILL available, Internet access, Magazines, Meeting rooms, Microfiche/film & reading machines, Online cat, Online ref, Photocopying/Printing, Prof lending libr, Ref & res, Ref serv available, Scanner, Study rm, VHS videos
Partic in ARKLink; Westchester Academic Library Directors Organization
Open Mon-Thurs 7:30am-Midnight, Fri 7:30-5, Sat 11-4, Sun 3-Midnight

P SILOAM SPRINGS PUBLIC LIBRARY*, 205 E Jefferson, 72761. (Mail add: PO Box 80, 72761), SAN 300-5518. Tel: 479-524-4236. FAX: 479-373-6306. E-mail: Library@siloamsprings.com. Web Site: siloamsprings.com/155/Library. *Libr Mgr,* Dolores Deuel; E-mail: ddeuel@siloamsprings.com; *Asst Libr Mgr,* Stephanie Reed; *Prog Coordr,* Delilah Williamson; E-mail: dwilliamson@siloamsprings.com; Staff 1 (MLS 1)
Founded 1966. Pop 25,000; Circ 112,562
Library Holdings: Audiobooks 1,380; CDs 986; DVDs 3,256; e-books 9,701; Large Print Bks 1,612; Bk Titles 41,596; Per Subs 23
Automation Activity & Vendor Info: (Cataloging) Innovative Interfaces, Inc; (Circulation) Innovative Interfaces, Inc; (ILL) OCLC
Wireless access
Function: Adult bk club, After school storytime, Audiobks via web, Bk club(s), Bks on CD, Children's prog, Computers for patron use, E-Reserves, Free DVD rentals, Holiday prog, Laminating, Magazines, Magnifiers for reading, Movies, Music CDs, Online cat, Photocopying/Printing, Prog for adults, Prog for children & young adult, Story hour, Summer reading prog, Tax forms, Teen prog
Open Mon-Fri 9-7, Sat 9-4
Friends of the Library Group

SPRINGDALE

J NORTHWEST TECHNICAL INSTITUTE*, Walter Turnbow Learning Resource Center, 709 S Old Missouri Rd, 72764. Tel: 479-751-8824, Ext 140. FAX: 479-756-8744. E-mail: NTILibrary@nwti.edu. Web Site: www.nwti.edu/learning-resource-center.html. *Learning Res Coordr,* Becky Echols; Staff 2 (Non-MLS 2)
Highest Degree: Certificate
Library Holdings: Bk Vols 300; Per Subs 20
Wireless access
Function: Photocopying/Printing
Open Mon-Fri 7:30-4

S SHILOH MUSEUM OF OZARK HISTORY LIBRARY*, 118 W Johnson Ave, 72764. SAN 373-3947. Tel: 479-750-8165. FAX: 479-750-8693. E-mail: shiloh@springdalear.gov. Web Site: shilohmuseum.org. *Archivist, Librn,* Marie Demeroukas; E-mail: mdemeroukas@springdalear.gov. Subject Specialists: *Arkansas Ozarks,* Marie Demeroukas; Staff 1.8 (Non-MLS 1.8)
Founded 1968
Library Holdings: Bk Vols 900
Special Collections: Photos of Arkansas Ozarks
Open Mon-Sat 10-5
Restriction: In-house use for visitors, Internal use only, Not a lending libr, Open to researchers by request
Friends of the Library Group

P SPRINGDALE PUBLIC LIBRARY*, 405 S Pleasant St, 72764. SAN 331-0140. Tel: 479-750-8180. FAX: 479-750-8182. Web Site: www.springdalelibrary.org. *Dir,* Marcia Ransom; E-mail: mransom@springdalelibrary.org; *Asst Dir,* Anne Gresham; E-mail: agresham@springdalelibrary.org; *Ch,* Nathalie DeFelice; E-mail: ndefelice@springdalelibrary.org; *Ch,* Elizabeth Hurtado; E-mail: ehurtado@springdalelibrary.org; *Multicultural Librn,* Tanya Evans; E-mail: tevans@springdalelibrary.org; *Ref Librn,* Claudia Driver; E-mail: cdriver@springdalelibrary.org; *Ref Librn,* Jennifer Johnson; E-mail: jjohnson@springdalelibrary.org; *YA Librn,* Sarah Loch; E-mail: sloch@springdalelibrary.org; *Circ Supvr,* Kim Jones; E-mail: kjones@springdalelibrary.org; *Ref Coordr,* Jessica Reed; E-mail: jreed@springdalelibrary.org; *Children's Serv Coordr,* Caitlyn Spaulding; E-mail: cspaulding@springdalelibrary.org. Subject Specialists: *Multicultural,* Elizabeth Hurtado; Staff 10 (MLS 8, Non-MLS 2)
Founded 1923
Library Holdings: AV Mats 18,732; Bk Vols 140,753; Per Subs 277
Automation Activity & Vendor Info: (Acquisitions) Innovative Interfaces, Inc; (Cataloging) Innovative Interfaces, Inc; (Circulation) Innovative Interfaces, Inc; (OPAC) Innovative Interfaces, Inc
Wireless access
Function: 24/7 Electronic res, 24/7 Online cat, 3D Printer, Activity rm, Adult bk club, After school storytime, Art exhibits, Art programs, Audiobks on Playaways & MP3, Audiobks via web, AV serv, Bi-weekly Writer's Group, Bilingual assistance for Spanish patrons, Bk club(s), Bks on CD, Children's prog, Citizenship assistance, Computer training, Computers for patron use, Digital talking bks, Doc delivery serv, E-Readers, Electronic databases & coll, Equip loans & repairs, Free DVD rentals, Games & aids for people with disabilities, Holiday prog, Home delivery & serv to seniorr ctr & nursing homes, Homebound delivery serv, Homework prog, ILL available, Internet access, Life-long learning prog for all ages, Literacy & newcomer serv, Magazines, Magnifiers for reading, Mail & tel request accepted, Mango lang, Meeting rooms, Microfiche/film & reading machines, Movies, Music CDs, Notary serv, Online cat, Online info literacy tutorials on the web & in blackboard, Online ref, Outreach serv, Outside serv via phone, mail, e-mail & web, OverDrive digital audio bks, Photocopying/Printing, Preschool outreach, Preschool reading prog, Printer for laptops & handheld devices, Prof lending libr, Prog for adults, Prog for children & young adult, Ref & res, Ref serv available, Scanner, Spanish lang bks, STEM programs, Story hour, Study rm, Summer & winter reading prog, Summer reading prog, Tax forms, Teen prog, Telephone ref, Visual arts prog, Wheelchair accessible, Winter reading prog, Workshops, Writing prog
Publications: Newsletter (Quarterly)
Mem of Washington County Library System
Open Mon-Thurs 9-8, Fri & Sat 9-6, Sun 1-5
Friends of the Library Group

STATE UNIVERSITY

C ARKANSAS STATE UNIVERSITY*, Dean B Ellis Library, 322 University Loop Circle, 72401. (Mail add: PO Box 2040, 72467-2040), SAN 331-1678. Tel: 870-972-3077. Reference Tel: 870-972-3208. Administration Tel: 870-972-3099. FAX: 870-972-3199. Interlibrary Loan Service FAX: 870-972-3846. E-mail: refdesk@astate.edu. Web Site: www.library.astate.edu. *Libr Dir,* Jeff Bailey; E-mail: jbailey@astate.edu; *Asst Libr Dir,* April Sheppard; E-mail: asheppard@astate.edu; *Govt Doc Librn,* Dominique Hallett; E-mail: dhallett@astate.edu; Staff 31 (MLS 13, Non-MLS 18)
Founded 1909. Enrl 13,079; Fac 13; Highest Degree: Doctorate
Jul 2019-Jun 2020 Income Parent Institution $3,598,627. Mats Exp $1,845,000. Sal $1,362,058 (Prof $776,720)
Special Collections: Arkansas Coll; Cass Hough Aeronautica Coll; Governor Mike Beebe Coll; Ira F. Twist Coll; Judd Hill Plantation Records; Lois Lenski Coll; Midsouth Center for Oral History; Saint Francis Levee District Tax Coll Records; US Representative Bill Alexander Coll; US Representative E C "Took" Gathings Coll; US Representative Marion Berry Coll. US Document Depository
Automation Activity & Vendor Info: (Acquisitions) Ex Libris Group; (Cataloging) Ex Libris Group; (Circulation) Ex Libris Group; (Course Reserve) Ex Libris Group; (Discovery) EBSCO Discovery Service; (ILL) OCLC Tipasa; (OPAC) Ex Libris Group; (Serials) Ex Libris Group
Wireless access
Partic in ARKLink; LYRASIS
Open Mon-Thurs (Fall & Spring) 7am-1am, Fri 7-6, Sat Noon-6, Sun Noon-1am; Mon-Thurs (Summer) 7:30am-10pm, Fri 7:30-5, Sat Noon-6, Sun 2pm-9pm

STUTTGART

J PHILLIPS COMMUNITY COLLEGE OF THE UNIVERSITY OF ARKANSAS*, Stuttgart Campus Library, 2807 Hwy 165 S, 72160. Tel: 870-673-4201, Ext 1819. FAX: 870-673-8166. Web Site: www.pccua.edu/students/resources/library/stuttgart-library-information. *Dir,* Jerrie Townsend; Tel: 870-673-4201, Ext 1818; *Libr Tech,* Jamie Milliken; E-mail: jmilliken@pccua.edu
Library Holdings: Bk Vols 3,000
Wireless access
Open Mon & Tues (Fall & Spring) 9:30-6:30, Wed &Thurs 8-5, Fri 8-2; Mon-Thurs (Summer) 7-5

P STUTTGART PUBLIC LIBRARY, Arkansas County Library Headquarters, 2002 S Buerkle St, 72160-6508. SAN 300-5526. Tel: 870-673-1966. FAX: 870-673-4295. E-mail: stuttgartpubliclibrary@gmail.com. Web Site: www.stuttgartpubliclibrary.org. *Dir,* Clara Timmerman; *Mgr,* Estella Dudman
Founded 1922. Pop 19,019; Circ 92,465
Library Holdings: AV Mats 891; Bks on Deafness & Sign Lang 12; Braille Volumes 10; CDs 288; DVDs 70; High Interest/Low Vocabulary Bk Vols 300; Large Print Bks 1,284; Music Scores 192; Bk Titles 62,675; Bk Vols 83,650; Per Subs 135; Spec Interest Per Sub 14; Talking Bks 27; Videos 495
Special Collections: Arkansas Coll; Rare Books (Queeny Coll)
Subject Interests: Agr, Antiques, Genealogy
Wireless access
Function: 24/7 Electronic res, 24/7 Online cat, 3D Printer, Accelerated reader prog, Activity rm, Adult bk club, Adult literacy prog, Audiobks via web, Bk club(s)
Open Mon-Fri 10-3

G US DEPARTMENT OF AGRICULTURE, Agricultural Research, 2955 Hwy 130 E, 72160. (Mail add: PO Box 1050, 72160-1050), SAN 325-5271. Tel: 870-673-4483. FAX: 870-673-7710. *Library Contact,* Teresa Lazenby; E-mail: teresa.lazenby@ars.usda.gov
Library Holdings: Bk Titles 985; Per Subs 125
Special Collections: Reprint Coll - Cross indexed & filed numerically (subject & author)
Subject Interests: Aquaculture, Fish culture, Water quality
Partic in OCLC Online Computer Library Center, Inc
Restriction: Open by appt only

SULPHUR SPRINGS

P SULPHUR SPRINGS PUBLIC LIBRARY*, 512 S Black Ave, 72768. (Mail add: PO Box 275, 72768-0275). Tel: 479-298-3753. FAX: 479-298-3963. E-mail: sspringslib@yahoo.com. *Librn,* Position Currently Open
Library Holdings: Audiobooks 20; CDs 100; DVDs 20; Large Print Bks 96; Bk Vols 20,000; Videos 143
Open Mon 8-5, Tues & Wed 8-2:30
Friends of the Library Group

TEXARKANA

CM UNIVERSITY OF ARKANSAS FOR MEDICAL SCIENCES*, Southwest Medical Library, 300 E Sixth St, 71854. SAN 300-5534. Tel: 870-779-6053. FAX: 870-779-6050. Web Site: regionalprograms.uams.edu/regional-centers/uams-southwest/medical-library. *Libr Dir,* Destiny Carter; E-mail: dncarter@uams.edu; Staff 2 (Non-MLS 2)
Founded 1976
Library Holdings: AV Mats 600; Bk Titles 2,000; Per Subs 200
Special Collections: Consumer Health, bks, AV mats, brochures & pamphlets
Automation Activity & Vendor Info: (Circulation) Innovative Interfaces, Inc
Publications: Union Catalog of Monographs; Union Catalog of Serials
Open Mon-Fri 8-5

TRUMANN

P TRUMANN PUBLIC LIBRARY*, 1200 W Main St, 72472. (Mail add: PO Box 73, 72472-0073), SAN 371-8379. Tel: 870-483-7744. FAX: 870-483-7744. Web Site: cityoftrumann.org/departments/public-library. *Librn,* Janie Teague; E-mail: teaguejanie@hotmail.com; Staff 1 (Non-MLS 1)
Founded 1975. Pop 6,000
Library Holdings: Bks on Deafness & Sign Lang 2; CDs 25; DVDs 70; Large Print Bks 425; Bk Titles 11,565; Bk Vols 12,000; Per Subs 6; Talking Bks 410; Videos 79
Automation Activity & Vendor Info: (Cataloging) Follett Software; (Circulation) Follett Software
Wireless access
Special Services for the Blind - Bks on cassette
Open Mon-Fri 11:30-5:30

VAN BUREN

P CRAWFORD COUNTY LIBRARY SYSTEM*, 1409 Main St, 72956. Tel: 479-471-3226. FAX: 479-471-3227. E-mail: ccls@crawfordcountylib.org. Web Site: www2.youseemore.com/crawfordcls. *Dir,* Eva White; E-mail: ewhite@crawfordcountylib.org; *Tech Serv Asst,* Amy Gunn; E-mail: agunn@crawfordcountylib.org; Staff 8 (MLS 1, Non-MLS 7)
Founded 1999
Function: 24/7 Electronic res, 24/7 Online cat, 3D Printer, Accelerated reader prog, Adult bk club, After school storytime, Art programs, Audio & video playback equip for onsite use, Audiobks on Playaways & MP3, Audiobks via web, Bk club(s), Bks on CD, Chess club, Children's prog, Computer training, Computers for patron use, Digital talking bks, Doc delivery serv, Electronic databases & coll, Free DVD rentals, Genealogy discussion group, Holiday prog, ILL available, Instruction & testing, Internet access, Magazines, Magnifiers for reading, Mail & tel request accepted, Makerspace, Mango lang, Meeting rooms, Microfiche/film & reading machines, Movies, Music CDs, Online cat, Outreach serv, Outside serv via phone, mail, e-mail & web, OverDrive digital audio bks, Photocopying/Printing, Preschool outreach, Preschool reading prog, Printer for laptops & handheld devices, Prof lending libr, Prog for adults, Prog for children & young adult, Ref & res, Ref serv available, Res assist avail, Scanner, Senior outreach, Serves people with intellectual disabilities, STEM programs, Story hour, Study rm, Summer reading prog, Tax forms, Teen prog, Telephone ref, Visual arts prog, Wheelchair accessible, Writing prog
Member Libraries: Alma Public Library; Cedarville Public Library; Mulberry Public Library; Van Buren Public Library
Open Mon-Fri 8:30-5
Restriction: ID required to use computers (Ltd hrs), Lending limited to county residents

P VAN BUREN PUBLIC LIBRARY, 1409 Main St, 72956. SAN 331-0175. Tel: 479-474-6045. E-mail: vanburen@crawfordcountylib.org. Web Site: www.youseemore.com/crawfordcls/directory.asp. *Libr Dir,* Dr George Fowler; E-mail: gfowler@crawfordcountylib.org; *Ch,* Yuvonka Tapp; E-mail: ytapp@crawfordcountylib.org; *Adult Programming, Librn,* Bridgette Waid; E-mail: bwaid@crawfordcountylib.org; Staff 5 (Non-MLS 5)
Founded 1899. Pop 24,000
Library Holdings: Bk Vols 60,000; Per Subs 20
Subject Interests: Genealogy, State hist
Automation Activity & Vendor Info: (Acquisitions) TLC (The Library Corporation); (Cataloging) TLC (The Library Corporation); (Circulation) TLC (The Library Corporation); (ILL) OCLC; (OPAC) TLC (The Library Corporation)
Wireless access
Mem of Crawford County Library System
Open Mon-Thurs 8:30-7, Fri & Sat 8:30-5:30, Sun 1-4
Friends of the Library Group

VIOLA

P FULTON COUNTY LIBRARY*, Viola Public Library, 199 Hwy 223, 72583. (Mail add: PO Box 258, 72583-0258). Tel: 870-458-3070 (library.arkansas.gov/facilities/details/fulton-county-library-viola-branch). Web Site: library.arkansas.gov/facilities/details/fulton-county-library-viola-branch. *Mgr,* Terry Wineland
Library Holdings: Bk Vols 4,000
Wireless access
Mem of White River Regional Library
Open Mon 9:30-1, Tues 9:30-5:30, Wed-Fri 9:30-4:30

WALNUT RIDGE

P LAWRENCE COUNTY LIBRARY*, 115 W Walnut St, 72476. SAN 331-359X. Tel: 870-886-3222. FAX: 870-886-9520. E-mail: lawcolibrary@yahoo.com. Web Site: lawrencecountylibrary.com. *Dir,* Ashley Burris
Founded 1942. Pop 17,457; Circ 111,708
Library Holdings: Bk Vols 62,285; Per Subs 92
Automation Activity & Vendor Info: (Cataloging) Follett Software; (Circulation) Follett Software; (ILL) OCLC
Wireless access
Open Mon-Fri 8-6, Sat 9-1
Friends of the Library Group
Branches: 2
BOBBI JEAN MEMORIAL, 102 Hendrix St, Imboden, 72434, SAN 331-362X. Tel: 870-869-2093. FAX: 870-869-2093. E-mail: imbodenlibrarian@yahoo.com. Web Site: imbodenlibrary.wordpress.com. *Br Mgr,* Vicky Mitchell
Founded 1942
Library Holdings: Bk Vols 10,000
Open Mon 10-5, Tues, Thurs & Fri 12-5, Sat 9-12
Friends of the Library Group
DRIFTWOOD BRANCH, 28 S Hwy 25, Lynn, 72440. (Mail add: PO Box 7, Lynn, 72440-0007), SAN 372-7866. Tel: 870-528-3506. FAX: 870-528-3506. *Br Mgr,* Kathy Bates; E-mail: thekathybates@yahoo.com
Founded 1991
Library Holdings: Audiobooks 389; CDs 223; DVDs 151; Large Print Bks 250; Bk Titles 13,097; Per Subs 10; Videos 87
Open Mon-Thurs 12-5, Sat 9-12

CR WILLIAMS BAPTIST UNIVERSITY*, Felix Goodson Library, 60 W Fulbright, 72476. SAN 300-5542. Tel: 870-759-4139. Web Site: williamsbu.edu/library. *Dir, Libr Serv,* Pamela Meridith; E-mail: pmeridith@williamsbu.edu; *Supvr, Pub Serv,* Joel D Olive; E-mail: jolive@williamsbu.edu; *Libr Tech,* Peggy Chadwick; E-mail: pchadwick@williamsbu.edu; Staff 3 (MLS 1, Non-MLS 2)
Founded 1941. Enrl 480; Fac 35; Highest Degree: Bachelor
Library Holdings: Audiobooks 7; AV Mats 233; CDs 29; DVDs 185; e-books 196; Bk Vols 59,964; Per Subs 35; Videos 14
Special Collections: Digital Archive; Harrison Coll
Automation Activity & Vendor Info: (Cataloging) OCLC CatExpress; (Circulation) Koha; (Course Reserve) Koha; (ILL) OCLC FirstSearch; (OPAC) Koha
Wireless access
Function: 24/7 Electronic res, Art exhibits, Bks on CD, Computers for patron use, Doc delivery serv, E-Readers, E-Reserves, Electronic databases & coll, Free DVD rentals, ILL available, Instruction & testing, Internet access, Magazines, Microfiche/film & reading machines, Online cat, Online info literacy tutorials on the web & in blackboard, Orientations, Outreach serv, Photocopying/Printing, Prof lending libr, Ref & res, Ref serv available, Scanner, Spanish lang bks, Study rm, Wheelchair accessible, Workshops
Partic in Amigos Library Services, Inc; ARKLink; OCLC Online Computer Library Center, Inc
Special Services for the Deaf - Bks on deafness & sign lang
Special Services for the Blind - Bks on cassette; Bks on CD
Open Mon-Thurs 8am-11:30pm, Fri 8-4, Sat 12-4, Sun 1-5 & 7-Midnight; Mon-Fri 9-12 & 1-4 (Summer)
Restriction: Limited access for the pub, Open to students, fac & staff

WASHINGTON

S SOUTHWEST ARKANSAS REGIONAL ARCHIVES, 201 Hwy 195, 71862. (Mail add: PO Box 134, 71862). Tel: 870-983-2633. FAX: 870-983-2636. E-mail: southwest.archives@arkansas.gov. Web Site: www.arkansasheritage.com/arkansasstatearchives/home. *Archives Mgr,* Melissa Nesbitt; E-mail: melissa.nesbitt@arkansas.gov; *Archives Asst,* Joshua Fischer; E-mail: joshua.fischer@arkansas.gov; Staff 2 (Non-MLS 2)
Founded 1978
Library Holdings: Bk Vols 1,100
Special Collections: Cemetery Records; Census Coll, microfilm & print; Genealogical Research Materials & Family Histories; Land Records; Marriage Records; Newspaper Coll, microfilm; Obituaries; Tax Lists. Oral History; State Document Depository
Subject Interests: Civil War, Hist SW Arkansas
Wireless access
Function: Archival coll, Computers for patron use, For res purposes, Genealogy discussion group, Internet access, Microfiche/film & reading machines, Online cat, Outreach serv, Photocopying/Printing, Ref & res, Ref serv available, Res libr, Wheelchair accessible
Open Tues-Sat 8-4:30
Restriction: In-house use for visitors, Non-circulating, Not a lending libr, Open to pub for ref only, Photo ID required for access, Pub use on premises, Registered patrons only, Restricted pub use
Friends of the Library Group

WEST FORK

P WEST FORK MUNICIPAL LIBRARY*, 198 Main St, 72774. (Mail add: PO Box 304, 72774-0304), SAN 331-0205. Tel: 479-839-2626. FAX: 479-839-2626. E-mail: westfork@wcls.lib.ar.us. Web Site: www.westforklibrary.com. *Head Libn,* John Riley
Library Holdings: Audiobooks 690; DVDs 5,000; Large Print Bks 1,800; Bk Vols 35,000
Wireless access
Mem of Washington County Library System
Open Mon & Wed 9:30-6, Tues, Thurs & Fri 9:30-5, Sat 9:30-2:30
Friends of the Library Group

WEST MEMPHIS

J ARKANSAS STATE UNIVERSITY MID-SOUTH*, Sandra C Goldsby Library, Donald W Reynolds Ctr, 2000 W Broadway, 72301-3829. Tel: 870-733-6768. FAX: 870-733-6719. E-mail: library@asumidsouth.edu. Web Site: www.asumidsouth.edu/students/library/. *Dir,* Claire Jones; E-mail: rjones@asumidsouth.edu; *Libr Tech,* Patricia McGarrity; Staff 2.5 (MLS 1, Non-MLS 1.5)
Library Holdings: Audiobooks 709; AV Mats 3,385; CDs 389; DVDs 531; Large Print Bks 664; Bk Titles 20,468; Bk Vols 22,772; Per Subs 45; Videos 1,947
Automation Activity & Vendor Info: (Cataloging) TLC (The Library Corporation); (Circulation) TLC (The Library Corporation); (ILL) OCLC WorldShare Interlibrary Loan; (OPAC) TLC (The Library Corporation)
Wireless access
Function: 24/7 Electronic res, Audio & video playback equip for onsite use, Bks on cassette, Bks on CD, Computers for patron use, Electronic databases & coll, ILL available, Magazines, Online cat, Orientations, Photocopying/Printing, Ref & res, Wheelchair accessible
Open Mon-Thurs 7:30-7, Fri 7:30-4:30

P WEST MEMPHIS PUBLIC LIBRARY*, 213 N Avalon St, 72301. SAN 331-3654. Tel: 870-732-7590. FAX: 870-732-7636. E-mail: wmplexec@gmail.com. Web Site: westmemphislibrary.org. *Dir,* Rebecca Bledsoe
Pop 29,800; Circ 50,000
Library Holdings: Bk Vols 50,000; Per Subs 47
Wireless access
Open Mon-Thurs 10-7, Fri 10-5, Sat 9-3
Friends of the Library Group

WYNNE

P EAST CENTRAL ARKANSAS REGIONAL LIBRARY*, 410 E Merriman Ave, 72396. SAN 324-0797. Tel: 870-238-3850. FAX: 870-238-5434. Web Site: www.ecarls.org. *Exec Dir, Regional Librn,* John Paul Myrick; E-mail: jpaul@crosscountylibrary.org; *Operations Mgr,* Karen Golden; *Operations Mgr,* Asti Ogletree; Staff 7 (MLS 1, Non-MLS 6)
Founded 1951. Pop 28,267; Circ 101,535
Library Holdings: Bk Vols 39,405; Per Subs 136
Automation Activity & Vendor Info: (Cataloging) Follett Software; (Circulation) Follett Software; (OPAC) Follett Software
Wireless access
Member Libraries: East Central Arkansas Regional Library
Partic in Association for Rural & Small Libraries; National Network of Libraries of Medicine Region 3
Open Mon & Thurs 9-8, Tues, Wed & Fri 9-5
Friends of the Library Group
Branches: 4
COTTON PLANT BRANCH LIBRARY, 124 Main St, Cotton Plant, 72036. Tel: 870-459-1063.
Special Collections: Children's Coll
Function: Computers for patron use, Story hour
Open Mon 11-5, Tues-Thurs 11-3:30
CROSS COUNTY, 410 E Merriman Ave, 72396, SAN 300-5569. Tel: 870-238-3850. FAX: 870-238-5434.
Founded 1951
Library Holdings: Bk Titles 25,000; Bk Vols 30,000
Open Mon & Thurs 9-8, Tues, Wed & Fri 9-5

PARKIN BRANCH LIBRARY, Parkin Municipal Complex, 122 Wilson St, Parkin, 72373. Tel: 870-755-5499.
Open Tues & Thurs 1:30-6:30, Wed 11:30-4:30, Fri Noon-4:30
Friends of the Library Group

WOODRUFF COUNTY, 201 Mulberry St, Augusta, 72006, SAN 330-8766. Tel: 870-347-5331. FAX: 870-347-5331.
Library Holdings: Bk Titles 15,000; Bk Vols 20,000
Open Mon 12-7, Tues-Fri 10-5

YELLVILLE

P MARION COUNTY LIBRARY*, 308 Old Main, 72687. (Mail add: PO Box 554, 72687-0554). Tel: 870-449-6015. E-mail: contact.librarystaff@gmail.com. Web Site: www.marcolibrary.org. *Dir of Libr Operations,* Dana E Scott; E-mail: dana.librarydirector@gmail.com; Staff 3 (Non-MLS 3)
Library Holdings: Bk Vols 21,000
Function: ILL available, Photocopying/Printing, Summer reading prog, Wheelchair accessible
Open Mon-Fri 9-5, Sat 10-2
Restriction: Open to pub for ref & circ; with some limitations

CALIFORNIA

Date of Statistics: FY 2018-2019
Population 2020 U.S. Census: 39,368,078
Staffing & Facilities:
- **Jurisdictions:** 186
- **Libraries:** 1,128
- **Staff:** 17,355
- **Volunteer FTE per week:** 1,486

Collections & Circulation:
- **Total Collection Items (physical & digital):** 98,600,000
- **Total Collection Use:** 256,000,000
- **Total Collection Expenditures:** $150,100,000
- **Physical Item Circulation:** 181,900,000
- **Children's Books Held:** 21,800,000
- **Young Adult Books Held:** 3,100,000
- **Interlibrary Loans Made:** 3,500,000

Public Use:
- **Library Visits:** 138,000,000
- **Reference Transactions:** 14,500,000
- **Adult Programs:** 139,959
- **Young Adult Programs:** 43,718
- **Children's Programs:** 251,481
- **Total Program Attendance:** 10,600,000
- **Annual Use of Public Internet Computers:** 24,100,000
- **Virtual Visits to Library Websites:** 113,700,000

Information derived from public sources.

ALAMEDA

P ALAMEDA FREE LIBRARY*, 1550 Oak St, 94501. SAN 331-3719. Tel: 510-747-7777. Circulation Tel: 510-747-7740. Interlibrary Loan Service Tel: 510-747-7743. Reference Tel: 510-747-7713. Administration Tel: 510-747-7720. Administration FAX: 510-865-1230. Web Site: alamedaca.gov/library. *Dir,* Jane Chisaki; E-mail: jchisaki@alamedaca.gov; *Supv Librn,* Cosette Ratliff; Tel: 510-747-7716, E-mail: cratliff@alamedaca.gov; *Supvr, Ch Serv,* Eva Volin; Tel: 510-747-7707, E-mail: evolin@alamedaca.gov; *Tech Serv Supvr,* David Hall; Tel: 510-747-7730, E-mail: dhall@alamedaca.gov. Subject Specialists: *Graphic novels,* Eva Volin; Staff 33 (MLS 12, Non-MLS 21)
Founded 1877. Pop 74,000; Circ 516,814
Library Holdings: Bks on Deafness & Sign Lang 60; High Interest/Low Vocabulary Bk Vols 90; Large Print Bks 1,719; Bk Titles 120,000; Bk Vols 178,573; Per Subs 322
Special Collections: Asian Languages Coll (Chinese, Japanese & Tagalog); Audio Book Coll; City, County & State History Coll; Large Print Coll; Leap Frog Coll (bk/cassette kits & reading machines); Media Coll, DVDs & videocassettes; Spanish Language Coll
Automation Activity & Vendor Info: (Acquisitions) Horizon; (Cataloging) Horizon; (Circulation) Horizon; (ILL) OCLC FirstSearch; (OPAC) Horizon
Wireless access
Mem of Pacific Library Partnership (PLP)
Partic in Califa
Special Services for the Deaf - Bks on deafness & sign lang; High interest/low vocabulary bks; Staff with knowledge of sign lang
Special Services for the Blind - Closed circuit TV; Reader equip
Open Mon & Tues Noon-8, Wed 10-8, Thurs-Sat 10-5, Sun 1-5
Friends of the Library Group
Branches: 2
BAY FARM ISLAND, 3221 Mecartney Rd, 94502, SAN 331-3727. Tel: 510-747-7787. FAX: 510-337-1426. *Sr Librn,* Lynda Williams; E-mail: lwilliam@ci.alameda.ca.us; Staff 2 (MLS 1, Non-MLS 1)
Founded 1980. Pop 12,039; Circ 99,636
Library Holdings: Bk Vols 23,862
Open Mon & Thurs 10-6, Tues 12-8, Sat 10-5
WEST END, 788 Santa Clara Ave, 94501-3334, SAN 331-3743. Tel: 510-747-7767. FAX: 510-337-0877. *Sr Librn,* Karin Lundstrom; Tel: 510-747-7780, E-mail: klunstr@ci.alameda.ca.us; *Libr Tech,* Valerie Levitt; Staff 3 (MLS 1, Non-MLS 2)
Founded 1933. Pop 25,078; Circ 64,407
Library Holdings: Bk Vols 32,131
Open Mon 12-8, Wed & Thurs 10-6, Sat 10-5

J COLLEGE OF ALAMEDA*, Library & Learning Resources Center, 555 Ralph Appezzato Memorial Pkwy, 94501. SAN 300-5577. Tel: 510-748-2120, 510-748-2398. Reference Tel: 510-748-2122. Web Site: alameda.peralta.edu/library. *Head Librn,* Jane McKenna; Tel: 510-748-2366, E-mail: jmckenna@peralta.edu; *Syst Librn, Tech Serv Librn,* Ann Buchalter; Tel: 510-748-2253, E-mail: abuchalter@peralata.edu; Staff 7 (MLS 3, Non-MLS 4)
Founded 1970
Library Holdings: Electronic Media & Resources 13; Bk Vols 34,000; Per Subs 30
Automation Activity & Vendor Info: (Acquisitions) Innovative Interfaces, Inc - Millennium; (Cataloging) Innovative Interfaces, Inc - Millennium; (Circulation) Innovative Interfaces, Inc - Millennium; (Course Reserve) Innovative Interfaces, Inc - Millennium; (Media Booking) Innovative Interfaces, Inc - Millennium; (OPAC) Innovative Interfaces, Inc - Millennium; (Serials) Innovative Interfaces, Inc - Millennium
Wireless access
Open Mon-Thurs 7:50-7:50, Fri 7:50-3:50

ALHAMBRA

P ALHAMBRA CIVIC CENTER LIBRARY*, 101 S First St, 91801-3432. SAN 331-3832. Tel: 626-570-5008. Circulation Tel: 626-570-5028. Reference Tel: 626-570-3212. FAX: 626-457-1104. E-mail: refstaff@alhambralibrary.org. Web Site: alhambralibrary.org, www.cityofalhambra.org/207/Library. *Dir,* Hilda LohGuan; E-mail: hildal@alhambralibrary.org; *ILL,* Estella Reyes; *Ref (Info Servs),* Connie Chan; *Ref (Info Servs),* Robert Herberg; *Ref (Info Servs),* Patricia Todd; *Ref Serv,* Lori Kremer; *Tech Serv,* David Brown; *Libr Spec,* Shannen Dang; Staff 8 (MLS 8)
Founded 1906. Pop 89,700; Circ 550,000
Library Holdings: AV Mats 7,933; Bk Vols 158,047; Per Subs 213
Automation Activity & Vendor Info: (Acquisitions) SirsiDynix; (Cataloging) SirsiDynix; (Circulation) SirsiDynix; (OPAC) SirsiDynix; (Serials) SirsiDynix
Wireless access
Partic in Califa; Southern California Library Cooperative
Open Mon 11-9, Tues & Wed 10-9, Thurs-Sat 10-5, Sun 1-5
Friends of the Library Group

C ALLIANT INTERNATIONAL UNIVERSITY*, Los Angeles Campus Library, 1000 S Fremont Ave, Unit 5, 91803. SAN 300-9009. Tel: 626-270-3270. Administration Tel: 626-270-3275. FAX: 626-284-1682. E-mail: library@alliant.edu. Web Site: library.alliant.edu. *Univ Librn,* Scott Zimmer; E-mail: szimmer@alliant.edu; Staff 3 (MLS 2, Non-MLS 1)
Founded 1969. Enrl 607; Fac 60; Highest Degree: Doctorate
Library Holdings: AV Mats 627; DVDs 222; Bk Vols 22,580; Per Subs 41; Videos 534
Special Collections: Psychology Assessement Coll (Restricted access)
Subject Interests: Multiculturalism, Psychol
Automation Activity & Vendor Info: (Acquisitions) Innovative Interfaces, Inc - Millennium; (Cataloging) Innovative Interfaces, Inc - Millennium; (Circulation) Innovative Interfaces, Inc - Millennium; (Course Reserve) Innovative Interfaces, Inc - Millennium; (ILL) Innovative Interfaces, Inc - Millennium; (Media Booking) Innovative Interfaces, Inc - Millennium; (OPAC) Innovative Interfaces, Inc - Millennium; (Serials) Innovative Interfaces, Inc - Millennium

Wireless access
Partic in Link+; Pacific Southwest Regional Medical Library
Open Mon-Thurs 8:30-8, Fri 8:30-6, Sat & Sun 12-5
Restriction: Borrowing privileges limited to fac & registered students, In-house use for visitors

R FIRST UNITED METHODIST CHURCH*, Dorothy Hooper Memorial Library, Nine N Almansor St, 91801-2699. SAN 300-5615. Tel: 626-289-4258. FAX: 626-289-4316. E-mail: firstumcalhambra@sbcglobal.net. *Librn,* Marge Brann
Founded 1940
Library Holdings: Bk Titles 5,500

ALTADENA

P ALTADENA LIBRARY DISTRICT*, 600 E Mariposa St, 91001. SAN 300-5631. Tel: 626-798-0833. FAX: 626-798-5351. E-mail: Hello@Altadenalibrary.org. Web Site: altadenalibrary.org. *District Dir,* Nikki Winslow; E-mail: nwinslow@altadenalibrary.org; *Pub Serv Dir,* Estella Terrazas; *Adult Serv Mgr,* Jesse Lopez; *Ch Mgr,* Mylinh Hamlington; *IT Mgr,* Christopher Kellermeyer; *Acq,* Victoria Escobar; *Tech Serv,* Carlene Chiu; *YA Serv,* Isabelle Briggs; Staff 7 (MLS 7)
Founded 1908. Pop 53,445; Circ 218,494
Library Holdings: AV Mats 11,719; Bk Vols 64,618; Per Subs 220
Special Collections: Altadena History Coll
Automation Activity & Vendor Info: (OPAC) Koha
Wireless access
Publications: Connect (Monthly newsletter); Poetry & Cookies (Annual)
Partic in Southern California Library Cooperative
Open Mon & Tues 10-9, Wed-Sat 10-6
Friends of the Library Group
Branches: 1
BOB LUCAS MEMORIAL LIBRARY & LITERACY CENTER, 2659 N Lincoln Ave, 91001-4963, SAN 375-524X. Tel: 626-798-8338. FAX: 626-798-3968. *Librn,* Erica Buss; Staff 2 (MLS 1, Non-MLS 1)
Open Mon, Tues & Fri 10-6, Wed & Thurs 10-8
Friends of the Library Group

S THEOSOPHICAL LIBRARY CENTER*, 2416 N Lake Ave, 91001. (Mail add: PO Box C, Pasadena, 91109-7107), SAN 300-5666. Tel: 626-798-8020. FAX: 626-791-0319. E-mail: tslibrary@theosociety.org. Web Site: www.theosociety.org/pasadena/ts/h_tlc.htm. *Head of Libr,* James T Belderis; *Ref (Info Servs),* I Belderis
Founded 1919
Library Holdings: Bk Titles 40,000; Bk Vols 45,000; Per Subs 30
Special Collections: Theosophy Coll, bks, per
Subject Interests: Art, Philos, World relig

ALTURAS

P MODOC COUNTY LIBRARY*, 212 W Third St, 96101. SAN 331-3891. Tel: 530-233-6340. E-mail: library@co.modoc.ca.us. Web Site: www.modoccountylibrary.org. *County Librn,* Cheryl Baker; *Libr Assoc,* Kris Anderson
Founded 1906. Pop 9,825
Library Holdings: Bk Vols 62,733; Per Subs 65
Special Collections: California Indian Library Coll; Modoc County History Coll
Mem of NorthNet Library System
Open Mon & Fri 10-5, Tues 12-6, Thurs 12-7
Friends of the Library Group
Branches: 3
ADIN BRANCH, Adin Community Hall, Hwy 299, Adin, 96006, SAN 331-3921. Tel: 530-299-3502. *Br Assoc,* Kathie Nelson
Library Holdings: Bk Vols 5,000
Open Tues 1-6
CEDARVILLE BRANCH, 460 Main St, Cedarville, 96104. (Mail add: PO Box 573, Cedarville, 96104-0573), SAN 331-4073. Tel: 530-279-2614. *Br Assoc,* Sue Becker; *Br Assoc,* Jan Farschon
Library Holdings: Bk Vols 5,000
Open Tues 12-6
LOOKOUT BRANCH, Lookout Park, Lookout, 96054, SAN 331-4049. Tel: 530-294-5776. *Br Assoc,* Betty Hallberg
Library Holdings: Bk Vols 1,000
Open Wed 12-5

ANAHEIM

P ANAHEIM PUBLIC LIBRARY*, 500 W Broadway, 92805-3699. SAN 331-4103. Tel: 714-765-1880. Administration Tel: 714-765-1810. Administration FAX: 714-765-1730. E-mail: tedelblute@anaheim.net. Web Site: anaheim.net/902/Library. *City Librn,* Audrey Lujan; E-mail: alujan@anaheim.net; *Acq of New Ser/Per,* Chan Harris; Tel: 714-765-1840; Staff 44 (MLS 44)
Founded 1901
Library Holdings: Bk Vols 209,083
Special Collections: Anaheim History Coll (Anaheim History Room), bks, pamphlets, pictures
Subject Interests: Bus & mgt, Local hist
Automation Activity & Vendor Info: (Acquisitions) SirsiDynix; (Cataloging) SirsiDynix; (Circulation) SirsiDynix; (OPAC) SirsiDynix
Wireless access
Mem of Santiago Library System
Partic in Southern California Library Cooperative
Open Mon-Fri 10-8, Sat 10-6
Friends of the Library Group
Branches: 6
CANYON HILLS, 400 Scout Trail, 92807-4763, SAN 331-412X. Tel: 714-765-6444. *Mgr, Libr Serv,* Cynthia Hicks
Library Holdings: Bk Vols 83,154
Open Mon-Thurs 11-8, Fri 10-6, Sat 10-5
Friends of the Library Group
EAST ANAHEIM LIBRARY, 8201 E Santa Ana Canyon Rd, 92808. Tel: 714-765-3887. *Br Mgr,* Cynthia Hicks
Library Holdings: Bk Vols 44,594
Open Mon-Wed 11-7, Thurs 11-6, Sat 10-5
EUCLID, 1340 S Euclid St, 92802-2008, SAN 331-4138. Tel: 714-765-3625. FAX: 714-765-3624. *Br Mgr,* Tasneem Watts
Library Holdings: Bk Vols 48,709
Open Mon-Thurs 12-8, Fri 12-6
Friends of the Library Group
ELVA L HASKETT BRANCH, 2650 W Broadway, 92804, SAN 331-4162. Tel: 714-765-5075. FAX: 714-765-5076. *Br Mgr,* Guadalupe Gomez
Library Holdings: Bk Vols 74,413
Open Mon-Thurs 11-8, Fri & Sat 12-6
Friends of the Library Group
PONDEROSA JOINT USE LIBRARY, 240 E Orangewood Ave, 92802. Tel: 714-740-0202.
Library Holdings: Bk Vols 22,512
Open Mon-Thurs 4:30-8, Sat 11-4
SUNKIST, 901 S Sunkist St, 92806-4739, SAN 331-4197. Tel: 714-765-3576. FAX: 714-765-3574.
Library Holdings: Bk Vols 54,438
Open Mon-Thurs 12-8, Fri 12-6
Friends of the Library Group
Bookmobiles: 1. Principal Librn. Keely Hall

M ANAHEIM REGIONAL MEDICAL CENTER*, Medical Library, 1111 W La Palma Ave, 92801. SAN 300-5674. Tel: 714-999-6020. FAX: 714-999-3907. *Librn,* Carol Schechter
Founded 1975
Library Holdings: Bk Titles 411; Bk Vols 451; Per Subs 50
Wireless access
Function: ILL available
Restriction: Staff use only

CM SOUTH BAYLO UNIVERSITY LIBRARY*, Main Campus, 1126 N Brookhurst St, 92801-1704. SAN 300-6581. Tel: 714-533-1495. FAX: 714-533-6040. Web Site: www.southbaylo.edu/ca/library. *Univ Librn,* Vanja K Anderson; E-mail: vanderson@southbaylo.edu; Staff 2 (MLS 1, Non-MLS 1)
Founded 1978. Enrl 681; Fac 45; Highest Degree: Doctorate
Library Holdings: Bk Vols 10,000
Special Collections: Traditional Chinese Medicine
Wireless access
Function: Archival coll, Health sci info serv, Internet access, Photocopying/Printing, Ref serv available, Res libr, Satellite serv
Open Mon-Sat 9-9

ANGWIN

C PACIFIC UNION COLLEGE*, W E Nelson Memorial Library, One Angwin Ave, 94508-9705. Tel: 707-965-6241. Reference Tel: 707-965-6639. FAX: 707-965-6504. Web Site: www.library.puc.edu. *Dept Chair, Dir, Syst Librn,* Patrick Benner; Tel: 707-965-6641, E-mail: pbenner@puc.edu; *Dir, Media Serv,* Junn Artigas; Tel: 707-965-7221, E-mail: jrartigas@puc.edu; *Spec Coll Librn,* Katharine Van Arsdale; Tel: 707-965-6244, E-mail: kvanarsdale@puc.edu; *Cat,* Jason St Clair; Tel: 707-965-6640, E-mail: jstclair@puc.edu; Staff 9 (MLS 5, Non-MLS 4)
Founded 1882. Enrl 1,662; Fac 104; Highest Degree: Master
Library Holdings: CDs 768; e-books 2,297; Music Scores 3,861; Bk Titles 119,118; Bk Vols 142,407; Per Subs 812; Videos 3,001
Special Collections: Ellen G White Study Center; Pitcairn Islands Study Center; Seventh-Day Adventist Study Center
Automation Activity & Vendor Info: (Cataloging) TLC (The Library Corporation); (Circulation) TLC (The Library Corporation); (ILL) OCLC Connexion; (OPAC) TLC (The Library Corporation)
Wireless access

Publications: Special Collection Bibliographies (Reference guide)
Partic in Adventist Librs Info Coop; OCLC Online Computer Library Center, Inc; Statewide California Electronic Library Consortium

APTOS

J CABRILLO COLLEGE, Robert E Swenson Library, 6500 Soquel Dr, 95003-3198. SAN 300-578X. Tel: 831-479-6473. FAX: 831-479-6500. Web Site: www.cabrillo.edu/library. *Dir, Prog & Serv,* Joanna Messer Kimmit; E-mail: jokimmit@cabrillo.edu; *Instruction Librn,* Michelle Morton; E-mail: mimorton@cabrillo.edu; *Outreach Librn,* Betsy Vaca; E-mail: bevaca@cabrillo.edu; *Tech Serv Librn,* Aloha Sargent; E-mail: alsargen@cabrillo.edu; Staff 12.5 (MLS 8, Non-MLS 4.5)
Founded 1959. Enrl 12,000; Fac 250; Highest Degree: Associate
Library Holdings: Bk Vols 55,000
Automation Activity & Vendor Info: (Acquisitions) Ex Libris Group; (Cataloging) Ex Libris Group; (Circulation) Ex Libris Group; (Course Reserve) Ex Libris Group; (Discovery) Ex Libris Group; (ILL) OCLC; (OPAC) Ex Libris Group; (Serials) Ex Libris Group
Wireless access
Partic in Monterey Bay Area Cooperative Library System
Open Mon-Thurs 8:45-4

S SPACES - SAVING + PRESERVING ARTS + CULTURAL ENVIRONMENTS*, Library & Archives, 9053 Soquel Dr, Ste 203, 95003. SAN 328-2139. Tel: 831-531-7154. FAX: 831-662-2918. E-mail: archivist@spacesarchives.org, info@spacesarchives.org. Web Site: www.spacesarchives.org. *Dir,* Jo Farb Hernández; Tel: 531-662-2907
Founded 1978
Special Collections: Art Environments Coll; Popular Culture Coll; Self-taught Artists
Subject Interests: Archit, Art

ARCADIA

P ARCADIA PUBLIC LIBRARY*, 20 W Duarte Rd, 91006. SAN 300-5798. Tel: 626-821-5567. Circulation Tel: 626-821-5571. Interlibrary Loan Service Tel: 626-294-4806. Reference Tel: 626-821-5569. Administration Tel: 626-821-5573. Information Services Tel: 626-821-4326. FAX: 626-447-8050. Interlibrary Loan Service FAX: 626-447-9753. E-mail: ref247@ci.arcadia.ca.us. Web Site: www.arcadiaca.gov/government/city-departments/library. *Dir, Libr & Mus Serv,* Darlene Bradley; Tel: 626-821-4364, E-mail: dbradley@arcadiaca.gov; *Head, Adult/Teen Serv,* David Dolim; Tel: 626-821-4327, E-mail: ddolim@arcadiaca.gov; *Head, Children's Servx,* Petra Morris; Tel: 626-821-5568, E-mail: pmorris@arcadiaca.gov; *Head, Circ,* Samantha Alba; Tel: 626-294-4804, E-mail: salba@arcadiaca.gov; *Head, Info Syst,* Peter Mercado; E-mail: pmercado@arcadiaca.gov; *Head, Tech Serv,* Kathy Meacham; Tel: 626-821-5574, E-mail: kmeacham@arcadiaca.gov; *Mgr, Libr Serv,* Roger Hiles; Tel: 626-821-5565, E-mail: rhiles@arcadiaca.gov; *Acq, ILL,* Christina Vallejo; E-mail: cvallejo@arcadiaca.gov; Staff 11.5 (MLS 11.5)
Founded 1920. Pop 57,761; Circ 685,362
Jul 2014-Jun 2015 Income $3,341,950, State $24,000, City $3,246,600, Locally Generated Income $71,350. Mats Exp $299,283, Books $168,445, Per/Ser (Incl. Access Fees) $15,070, Micro $6,000, Electronic Ref Mat (Incl. Access Fees) $81,726, Presv $2,000. Sal $1,573,100
Library Holdings: Audiobooks 11,086; e-books 13,860; Bk Vols 177,624
Special Collections: US Document Depository
Subject Interests: Local hist
Automation Activity & Vendor Info: (Acquisitions) Baker & Taylor; (Cataloging) ByWater Solutions; (Circulation) ByWater Solutions; (ILL) OCLC; (OPAC) ByWater Solutions; (Serials) ByWater Solutions
Wireless access
Function: 24/7 Electronic res, Accelerated reader prog, Adult bk club, Archival coll, Art exhibits, Audiobks via web, Bilingual assistance for Spanish patrons, Bks on CD, Children's prog, Computer training, Computers for patron use, Digital talking bks, Electronic databases & coll, Free DVD rentals, Govt ref serv, Homebound delivery serv, Homework prog, ILL available, Internet access, Life-long learning prog for all ages, Magazines, Mail & tel request accepted, Microfiche/film & reading machines, Movies, Music CDs, Online cat, Outside serv via phone, mail, e-mail & web, OverDrive digital audio bks, Photocopying/Printing, Prog for adults, Prog for children & young adult, Scanner, Spanish lang bks, Study rm, Summer reading prog, Tax forms, Teen prog, Telephone ref, Wheelchair accessible, Workshops, Writing prog
Partic in Southern California Library Cooperative
Special Services for the Deaf - ADA equip; Bks on deafness & sign lang
Special Services for the Blind - Assistive/Adapted tech devices, equip & products; Audio mat; Bks & mags in Braille, on rec, tape & cassette; Braille bks; Magnifiers
Open Mon-Thurs 10-9, Fri & Sat 10-6
Friends of the Library Group

S CALIFORNIA THOROUGHBRED BREEDERS ASSOCIATION*, Carleton F Burke Memorial Library, 201 Colorado Pl, 91007. SAN 300-5801. Tel: 626-445-7800. Toll Free Tel: 800-573-2822. Web Site: www.ctba.com. *Librn,* Vivian Montoya; E-mail: vivian@ctba.com
Founded 1964
Library Holdings: Bk Titles 3,000; Bk Vols 10,000; Per Subs 20
Special Collections: American Breeding (C C Moseley Coll), bks & flm; Foreign Racing & Breeding (Edward Lasker Coll); Kent Cochran Coll
Open Mon-Fri 9-4 by appointment
Restriction: Open to pub for ref only

S LOS ANGELES COUNTY ARBORETUM & BOTANIC GARDEN, Arboretum Library, 301 N Baldwin Ave, 91007-2697. SAN 300-581X. Tel: 626-821-3213. FAX: 626-445-1217. Web Site: www.arboretum.org/learn/library. *Plant Sci Librn,* Susan C Eubank; E-mail: susan.eubank@arboretum.org. Subject Specialists: *Botany, Gardening,* Susan C Eubank; Staff 1 (MLS 1)
Founded 1948
Jul 2019-Jun 2020 Income $120,000, County $85,000, Locally Generated Income $35,000. Mats Exp $20,000, Books $5,500, Per/Ser (Incl. Access Fees) $13,000, Electronic Ref Mat (Incl. Access Fees) $1,500. Sal $84,000
Library Holdings: DVDs 4; e-books 7,285; High Interest/Low Vocabulary Bk Vols 10; Bk Titles 30,000; Bk Vols 35,000; Per Subs 10; Spec Interest Per Sub 10
Special Collections: Plants, Gardens & Travel in California (William Aplin Slide Coll), 1940-1980
Subject Interests: Botany, Gardening, Hort, Local hist
Automation Activity & Vendor Info: (Cataloging) OCLC Connexion; (Circulation) EOS International; (Discovery) EOS International; (ILL) EOS International; (OPAC) EOS International
Wireless access
Function: Art exhibits, Bk club(s), Children's prog, ILL available, Internet access, Mail loans to mem, Online ref, Orientations, Photocopying/Printing, Prog for adults, Ref & res, Ref serv available, Story hour
Partic in Council on Botanical & Horticultural Libraries, Inc
Open Tues-Fri 8:30-5:30 by appointment
Restriction: Circ to mem only, Non-circulating of rare bks

M METHODIST HOSPITAL OF SOUTHERN CALIFORNIA*, Medical Library, 300 W Huntington Dr, 91007. SAN 300-5828. Tel: 626-898-8000, Ext 3681. FAX: 626-574-3712. *Coordr,* Joyce Ogle; E-mail: joyce.ogle@methodisthospital.org
Founded 1957
Library Holdings: Bk Vols 100; Per Subs 5
Wireless access
Restriction: Staff use only

ARCATA

C HUMBOLDT STATE UNIVERSITY LIBRARY, One Harpst St, 95521-8299. SAN 300-5836. Circulation Tel: 707-826-3431. Interlibrary Loan Service Tel: 707-826-4889. Reference Tel: 707-826-3418. Administration Tel: 707-826-3441. FAX: 707-826-3440. Web Site: library.humboldt.edu. *Dean of Libr,* Cyril Oberlander; E-mail: co522@humboldt.edu; *Head, Info Res Mgt,* George Wrenn; Tel: 707-826-3412, E-mail: glw11@humboldt.edu; *Spec Coll & Archives Librn,* Carly Marino; Tel: 707-826-4955, E-mail: cm2816@humboldt.edu; Staff 39 (MLS 14, Non-MLS 25)
Founded 1913. Enrl 8,046; Fac 517; Highest Degree: Master
Library Holdings: e-books 22,561; Bk Vols 595,208; Per Subs 1,714
Special Collections: Regional History (Humboldt County Coll, Humboldt State University Archives). State Document Depository; US Document Depository
Automation Activity & Vendor Info: (Acquisitions) Ex Libris Group; (Cataloging) Ex Libris Group; (Circulation) Ex Libris Group; (Course Reserve) Ex Libris Group; (ILL) OCLC ILLiad; (OPAC) Ex Libris Group; (Serials) Ex Libris Group
Wireless access
Mem of NorthNet Library System
Partic in OCLC Online Computer Library Center, Inc

ARMONA

P ARMONA COMMUNITY LIBRARY, 11115 C St, 93202. (Mail add: PO Box 368, 93202-0368). Tel: 559-583-5005. FAX: 559-583-5004. E-mail: askus@kingscountylibrary.org. Web Site: www.auesd.com/District/5062-Library-Hours.html, www.kingscountylibrary.org/armona-community-branch. *Library Contact,* Laura Amos; Tel: 559-583-5020, Ext 5005, E-mail: lamos@auesd.org
Library Holdings: Bk Vols 14,000
Automation Activity & Vendor Info: (Acquisitions) Horizon; (Cataloging) Horizon; (Circulation) Horizon; (OPAC) Horizon
Wireless access
Open Mon-Thurs 8-4:45, Fri 8-3:45
Friends of the Library Group

ARROYO GRANDE

P BLACK GOLD COOPERATIVE LIBRARY SYSTEM*, 580 Camino Mercado, 93420. SAN 301-5114. Tel: 805-543-6082. Administration FAX: 805-543-9487. Web Site: www.blackgold.org. *Dir, Operations,* Glynis Fitzgerald; E-mail: gfitzgerald@blackgold.org; Staff 6 (MLS 2, Non-MLS 4)
Founded 1963
Automation Activity & Vendor Info: (Acquisitions) Innovative Interfaces, Inc; (Cataloging) Innovative Interfaces, Inc; (Circulation) Innovative Interfaces, Inc; (ILL) Innovative Interfaces, Inc; (OPAC) Innovative Interfaces, Inc; (Serials) Innovative Interfaces, Inc
Member Libraries: Blanchard-Santa Paula Library District; Goleta Valley Library; Lompoc Public Library; Paso Robles City Library; San Luis Obispo County Library; Santa Barbara Public Library; Santa Maria Public Library
Open Mon-Fri 8-5

ATASCADERO

S ATASCADERO HISTORICAL SOCIETY MUSEUM LIBRARY*, 6600 Lewis Ave, 93422. (Mail add: PO Box 1047, 93423-1047), SAN 370-341X. Tel: 805-466-8341. E-mail: atascaderocolonymuseum@gmail.com. Web Site: www.atascaderohistoricalsociety.org. *Archivist, Dir,* Jim Blaes
Founded 1965
Library Holdings: Bk Vols 300
Special Collections: Atascadero High School Yearbooks; Atascadero Newspapers; E G Lewis Photograph Coll
Open Wed & Sat 1-4

ATASCADERO STATE HOSPITAL

M LOGAN PATIENT'S LIBRARY*, 10333 El Camino Real, 93422. (Mail add: PO Box 7003, 93423-7003), SAN 331-4227. Tel: 805-468-2520. FAX: 805-468-3027. *Librn,* Nancy Gulliver; *Law Librn,* Veronica Gutierrez; Tel: 805-468-3343. Subject Specialists: *Med,* Nancy Gulliver; Staff 3 (MLS 1, Non-MLS 2)
Founded 1957
Library Holdings: AV Mats 400; High Interest/Low Vocabulary Bk Vols 500; Bk Titles 9,000; Bk Vols 15,000; Per Subs 29
Special Collections: Law (California & Federal Laws & Codes)
Partic in Gold Coast Library Network
Special Services for the Deaf - Bks on deafness & sign lang; High interest/low vocabulary bks
Special Services for the Blind - Audio mat; Bks on cassette; Cassette playback machines; Cassettes; Large print bks; Magnifiers
Restriction: Not open to pub, Staff & patient use

M LOGAN PROFESSIONAL LIBRARY*, 10333 El Camino Real, 93422. (Mail add: PO Box 7003, 93423-7003), SAN 331-4251. Tel: 805-468-2491. FAX: 805-468-3027. *Librn,* Nancy Gulliver; E-mail: ngullive@ashdsh.ca.gov; Staff 2 (MLS 1, Non-MLS 1)
Founded 1957
Library Holdings: Bk Titles 8,500; Bk Vols 9,000; Videos 200
Special Collections: Treatment Enhancement Coll
Subject Interests: Med, Nursing, Psychiat, Psychotherapy, Rehabilitation
Function: ILL available
Partic in Gold Coast Library Network; Medical Library Group of Southern California & Arizona; National Network of Libraries of Medicine Region 5
Restriction: Not open to pub

ATHERTON

C MENLO COLLEGE, Bowman Library, 1000 El Camino Real, 94027. SAN 301-0511. Tel: 650-543-3826. Circulation Tel: 650-543-3825. E-mail: libraryhelp@menlo.edu. Web Site: menlocollege.libguides.com/home. *Interim Dean, Libr Serv,* Anne Linvill; E-mail: alinvill@menlo.edu; *Access & Info Serv Librn,* Destiny Rivera; E-mail: destiny.rivera@menlo.edu; *Info Serv Librn,* Tricia Soto; E-mail: tricia.soto@menlo.edu; *Info Res Librn,* Randi Proescholdt; E-mail: randi.proescholdt@menlo.edu; Staff 4 (MLS 4)
Founded 1927. Enrl 795; Fac 95; Highest Degree: Bachelor
Library Holdings: Bk Vols 60,000; Per Subs 40,000
Subject Interests: Bus, Soc sci
Automation Activity & Vendor Info: (Acquisitions) OCLC; (Cataloging) OCLC; (Circulation) Innovative Interfaces, Inc; (Course Reserve) OCLC; (ILL) OCLC; (Media Booking) OCLC; (OPAC) OCLC; (Serials) OCLC
Wireless access
Function: Archival coll, Audio & video playback equip for onsite use, Computers for patron use, E-Reserves, Electronic databases & coll, ILL available, Internet access, Magnifiers for reading, Online cat, Photocopying/Printing, Ref serv available, Telephone ref, Workshops
Partic in MLC; Northern & Central California Psychology Libraries; San Francisco Bay Area Library & Information Network; Statewide California Electronic Library Consortium
Special Services for the Blind - Assistive/Adapted tech devices, equip & products
Open Mon-Thurs 8am-11pm, Fri 9-5, Sat 12-5, Sun 1pm-11:45pm
Restriction: Open to pub for ref & circ; with some limitations, Open to students, fac, staff & alumni

AUBURN

L PLACER COUNTY LAW LIBRARY*, 1523 Lincoln Way, 95603. SAN 377-7766. Tel: 530-557-2078. E-mail: ref.placerlawlib@outlook.com. Web Site: www.placer.ca.gov/1841/Placer-County-Law-Library. *Dir, Libr Serv,* Mary George; E-mail: mgeorge@placer.ca.gov
Library Holdings: Bk Vols 7,800
Open Mon, Wed & Fri 9-5, Tues & Thurs 9-8, Sat 10-4

P PLACER COUNTY LIBRARY*, Headquarters, 145 Fulweiler Ave, Ste 150, 95603. Tel: 530-886-4550. Reference Tel: 530-886-4510. FAX: 530-886-4555. E-mail: library@placer.ca.gov. Web Site: www.placer.ca.gov/Facilities/Facility/Details/Auburn-Library-10, www.placer.ca.gov/library. *Dir, Libr Serv,* Mary L George; E-mail: mgeorge@placer.ca.gov; *Asst Dir,* Sophie Bruno; E-mail: sbruno@placer.ca.gov; *Admin Officer,* Kelly Heikila; E-mail: kheikila@placer.ca.gov
Founded 1937. Pop 145,500; Circ 732,106
Library Holdings: Bk Vols 115,300
Special Collections: State Document Depository
Wireless access
Open Tues-Thurs 10-7, Fri & Sat 10-5
Friends of the Library Group
Branches: 9
APPLEGATE BRANCH, 18018 Applegate Rd, Applegate, 95703, SAN 331-4316. Tel: 530-878-2721. FAX: 530-878-2721. Web Site: www.placer.ca.gov/Facilities/Facility/Details/Applegate-Library-9. *Libr Supvr,* Mollie Hawkins
Library Holdings: Bk Vols 15,300
Open Wed 10-1 & 1:30-6, Fri 10-1 & 1:30-5, Sat 1-5
Friends of the Library Group
AUBURN BRANCH, 350 Nevada St, 95603-3789, SAN 331-4286. Tel: 530-886-4500. *Sr Librn,* Suzanne Payne; *Librn,* Felicia Black
COLFAX BRANCH, Ten W Church St, Colfax, 95713, SAN 331-4340. Tel: 530-346-8211. FAX: 530-346-8211. Web Site: www.placer.ca.gov/Facilities/Facility/Details/Colfax-Library-12. *Librn,* Kathryn Cantwell-Cole
Open Tues-Thurs 10-6, Fri & Sat 10-5
Friends of the Library Group
FORESTHILL BRANCH, 24580 Main St, Foresthill, 95631, SAN 331-4405. Tel: 530-367-2785. FAX: 530-367-4721. Web Site: www.placer.ca.gov/Facilities/Facility/Details/Foresthill-Library-13. *Libr Supvr,* Janice Christian-Whitney
Library Holdings: Bk Vols 14,400
Open Tues & Wed 12-6, Thurs 10-2, Fri & Sat 1-5
Friends of the Library Group
GRANITE BAY BRANCH, 6475 Douglas Blvd, Granite Bay, 95746, SAN 373-5737. Tel: 916-791-5590. FAX: 916-791-1837. Web Site: www.placer.ca.gov/Facilities/Facility/Details/Granite-Bay-Library-14. *Librn,* Scott Noblitt
Library Holdings: Bk Titles 44,900
Open Tues-Thurs 10-7, Fri & Sat 10-5
Friends of the Library Group
KINGS BEACH BRANCH, 301 Secline St, Kings Beach, 96143. (Mail add: PO Box 246, Kings Beach, 96143), SAN 331-443X. Tel: 530-546-2021. FAX: 530-546-2126. Web Site: www.placer.ca.gov/Facilities/Facility/Details/Kings-Beach-16. *Libr Supvr,* Anne Greenwood
Library Holdings: Bk Vols 14,500
Open Tues & Thurs 10-4, Wed 12-6, Fri 12-5, Sat 1-5
Friends of the Library Group
PENRYN BRANCH, 2215 Rippey Rd, Penryn, 95663. (Mail add: PO Box 405, Penryn, 95663-0405), SAN 331-4499. Tel: 916-663-3621. FAX: 916-663-3621. Web Site: www.placer.ca.gov/Facilities/Facility/Details/Penryn-Library-17. *Libr Supvr,* Mollie Hawkins
Library Holdings: Bk Vols 8,500
Open Tues & Thurs 9-12 & 12:30-4:30, Sat 8-Noon
Friends of the Library Group
ROCKLIN BRANCH, 4890 Granite Dr, Rocklin, 95677, SAN 331-4529. Tel: 916-624-3133. FAX: 916-632-9152. Web Site: www.placer.ca.gov/Facilities/Facility/Details/Rocklin-Library-18. *Sr Librn,* Tony Carmack
Library Holdings: Bk Vols 57,300
Open Tues-Thurs 10-7, Fri & Sat 10-5
Friends of the Library Group
TAHOE CITY BRANCH, 740 N Lake Blvd, Tahoe City, 96145. (Mail add: PO Box 6570, Tahoe City, 96145-6570), SAN 331-4553. Tel: 530-583-3382. FAX: 530-583-5805. Web Site:

www.placer.ca.gov/Facilities/Facility/Details/Tahoe-City-Library-19. *Libr Supvr,* Livia Lewin
Library Holdings: Bk Vols 20,900
Open Tues & Thurs 10-4, Wed 12-6, Fri 12-5, Sat 1-5
Friends of the Library Group
Bookmobiles: 1. Mgr, Michael McCurdy. Bk vols 5,300

AZUSA

P AZUSA CITY LIBRARY*, 729 N Dalton Ave, 91702. SAN 300-5844. Tel: 626-812-5232. Circulation Tel: 626-812-5477. Reference Tel: 626-812-5268. FAX: 626-334-4868. Web Site: www.ci.azusa.ca.us/191/Library. *Libr Serv Mgr,* Leila Hassen; Tel: 626-812-5279, E-mail: lhassen@ci.azusa.ca.us; Staff 22 (MLS 3, Non-MLS 19)
Founded 1898. Pop 44,712; Circ 126,600
Library Holdings: Bk Vols 100,000; Per Subs 163
Special Collections: Indians of North America Coll; Spanish Language Coll
Subject Interests: Local hist
Automation Activity & Vendor Info: (Cataloging) SirsiDynix; (Circulation) SirsiDynix; (OPAC) SirsiDynix
Wireless access
Partic in Southern California Library Cooperative
Open Mon-Wed 10-9, Thurs 10-6, Fri & Sat 10-5
Friends of the Library Group

BAKER

C CALIFORNIA STATE UNIVERSITY*, Desert Studies Center Library, PO Box 490, 92309. SAN 373-4935. Tel: 714-936-0461. Web Site: nsm.fullerton.edu/dsc. *Mgr,* Jason Wallace; E-mail: jwallace@fullerton.edu
Library Holdings: Bk Vols 1,800
Wireless access
Restriction: Open by appt only, Open to pub for ref only

BAKERSFIELD

J BAKERSFIELD COLLEGE*, Grace Van Dyke Bird Library, 1801 Panorama Dr, 93305-1298. SAN 300-5879. Tel: 661-395-4461. Reference Tel: 661-395-4466. FAX: 661-395-4397. Web Site: www.bakersfieldcollege.edu/library. *Chair,* Kirk Russell; E-mail: krussell@bakersfieldcollege.edu; *Ref Librn,* Laura Luiz; E-mail: laura.luiz@bakersfieldcollege.edu; *Libr Tech 1,* Dora Hare; E-mail: thare@bakersfieldcollege.edu; Staff 10 (MLS 5, Non-MLS 5)
Founded 1913. Enrl 16,000; Fac 236
Library Holdings: Bk Vols 80,000; Per Subs 145
Special Collections: Bell British Plays, 1776-1795; Grove Plays of the Bohemian Club of San Francisco, 1911-1958
Subject Interests: Calif
Automation Activity & Vendor Info: (Acquisitions) Horizon; (Cataloging) Horizon; (Circulation) Horizon; (Course Reserve) Horizon; (ILL) Horizon; (OPAC) Horizon; (Serials) Horizon
Wireless access
Publications: Bulletin
Mem of Kern Community College District
Open Mon-Thurs 8-8, Fri 8-2, Sat 11-3

C CALIFORNIA STATE UNIVERSITY*, Walter W Stiern Library, 9001 Stockdale Hwy, 60 LIB, 93311. SAN 300-5895. Tel: 661-654-3172. Interlibrary Loan Service Tel: 661-654-2159. Reference Tel: 661-654-3231. Administration Tel: 661-654-3042. FAX: 661-654-3238. Interlibrary Loan Service FAX: 661-654-2259. E-mail: csub_library@csub.edu. Web Site: csub.libguides.com/library. *Dean of Libr,* Curt Asher; E-mail: casher@csub.edu; *Distance Serv Librn,* Kristine Holloway; Tel: 661-654-5072, E-mail: kholloway2@csub.edu; *Distance Serv Librn,* Jamie Jacks; Tel: 661-654-3372, E-mail: jjacks@csub.edu; *First Year Experience Librn, Instrul Tech Librn,* Sandra Bozarth; E-mail: sbozarth2@csub.edu; *Web Serv Librn,* Ying Zhong; Tel: 661-654-3119, E-mail: yzhong@csub.edu; *Libr Serv Mgr,* Sherry Bennett; Tel: 661-654-3254, E-mail: sbennett@csub.edu; *Admin Support Coordr,* Eileen Montoya; E-mail: emontoya@csub.edu; *Ref Serv Coordr,* Johanna Alexander; Tel: 661-664-3256, E-mail: jalexander@csub.edu; *Acq,* monica Ibarra; Tel: 661-654-3249, E-mail: mibarra3@csub.edu; *Circ,* Kristi Chavez; E-mail: kchavez4@csub.edu; *Circ,* F Javier Llamas; Tel: 661-654-3233, E-mail: fllamas@csub.edu; *Circ,* Aide Zaragoza; Tel: 661-654-3234, E-mail: azaragoza@csub.edu; *ILL,* Janet Gonzales; Tel: 661-654-2129, E-mail: jgonzales@csub.edu; *ILL,* Ariel Lauricio; Tel: 661-664-3189, E-mail: alauricio@csub.edu; *Syst Analyst,* Frank Aguirre; Tel: 661-664-2274, E-mail: faguirre@csub.edu. Subject Specialists: *Educ, Multicultural studies,* Sandra Bozarth; *Computer sci, Math, Nursing,* Ying Zhong; *Bus, Econ,* Johanna Alexander
Founded 1970. Enrl 8,002; Fac 366; Highest Degree: Master
Library Holdings: AV Mats 10,097; Bk Titles 358,808; Bk Vols 461,829; Per Subs 1,208
Special Collections: Oral History; State Document Depository; US Document Depository
Automation Activity & Vendor Info: (Acquisitions) Ex Libris Group; (Cataloging) Ex Libris Group; (Circulation) Ex Libris Group; (ILL) Ex Libris Group; (Serials) Ex Libris Group
Wireless access
Partic in OCLC Online Computer Library Center, Inc; Proquest Dialog; SDC Search Serv; Southern Calif Answering Network
Open Mon-Thurs 8am-1am, Fri 8-5, Sat 9-5 Sun 11am-1am
Friends of the Library Group

P KERN COMMUNITY COLLEGE DISTRICT*, 2100 Chester Ave, 93301. Tel: 661-336-5100. E-mail: web@kccd.edu. Web Site: www.kccd.edu.
Member Libraries: Bakersfield College; Cerro Coso Community College Library; Porterville College Library

GL KERN COUNTY LAW LIBRARY*, 1415 Truxtun Ave, Rm 301, 93301. SAN 300-5917. Tel: 661-868-5320. FAX: 661-868-5368. E-mail: lawlibrary@co.kern.ca.us. Web Site: www.kclawlib.org. *Librn,* Annette Heath; E-mail: aheath@kclawlib.org; Staff 5 (Non-MLS 5)
Founded 1891
Library Holdings: CDs 28; Bk Vols 18,261; Videos 5
Special Collections: State Document Depository
Subject Interests: Legal
Open Mon-Fri 8-4

P KERN COUNTY LIBRARY*, Headquarters, 701 Truxtun Ave, 93301. SAN 331-4588. Tel: 661-868-0700. FAX: 661-868-0799. E-mail: info@kernlibrary.org. Web Site: www.kerncountylibrary.org. *Dir of Libr,* Ms Andie Sullivan; E-mail: andie.sullivan@kernlibrary.org; *Bus Mgr,* Mark Lewis; E-mail: mark.lewis@kernlibrary.org; Staff 28.5 (MLS 27.5, Non-MLS 1)
Founded 1900. Pop 857,882; Circ 1,350,507
Library Holdings: AV Mats 65,000; e-books 1,000; Bk Vols 1,810,000; Per Subs 191
Special Collections: California Geology-Mining-Petroleum Coll, bks & micro; Kern County Historical Coll, bks & micro. State Document Depository; US Document Depository
Subject Interests: Hist, Natural sci
Wireless access
Mem of San Joaquin Valley Library System
Open Mon-Thurs 11-7, Fri & Sat 10-6
Friends of the Library Group
Branches: 24

ARVIN BRANCH, 201 Campus Dr, Arvin, 93203, SAN 331-4596. Tel: 661-854-5934. FAX: 661-584-3744. *Br Supvr,* Candace Sluder; E-mail: Candace.Sluder@kernlibrary.org
Founded 1914. Pop 17,147; Circ 21,123
Library Holdings: Bk Vols 29,542
Open Mon-Thurs 11-7
Friends of the Library Group

BAKER BRANCH, 1400 Baker St, 93305-3731, SAN 331-4618. Tel: 661-861-2390. *Br Supvr,* Jason Casper; E-mail: Jason.Casper@kernlibrary.org
Founded 1910. Pop 29,878
Library Holdings: Bk Vols 17,430
Open Mon & Wed 10-7, Sat 10-6
Friends of the Library Group

BEALE MEMORIAL, 701 Truxtun Ave, 93301-4816, SAN 331-4816. Tel: 661-868-0701. FAX: 661-868-0831. *Libr Supvr,* Sherry Wade; E-mail: sherry.wade@kernlibrary.org
Founded 1900. Pop 36,728; Circ 362,692
Library Holdings: Bk Vols 292,354
Special Collections: Genealogy Coll; Geology Mining & Petroleum Coll; Kern County History Coll
Open Mon-Thurs 11-7, Fri & Sat 10-6
Friends of the Library Group

BORON BRANCH, 26967 20 Mule Team Rd, Boron, 93516-1550, SAN 331-460X. Tel: 760-762-5606. *Br Supvr,* Andrea Mason; E-mail: Andrea.Mason@kernlibrary.org
Founded 1955. Pop 2,314; Circ 6,744
Library Holdings: Bk Vols 12,232
Open Mon, Wed & Fri 10-6
Friends of the Library Group

BUTTONWILLOW BRANCH, 101 Main St, Buttonwillow, 93206, SAN 331-4626. Tel: 661-764-5337. FAX: 661-764-5337. *Br Supvr,* Adrian Evers; E-mail: Adrian.Evers@kernlibrary.org
Founded 1913. Pop 3,238
Library Holdings: Bk Vols 9,268
Open Mon, Wed & Fri 11-6
Friends of the Library Group

CALIFORNIA CITY BRANCH, 9507 California City Blvd, California City, 93505-2280, SAN 331-2280. Tel: 760-373-4757. FAX: 760-373-4757. *Br Supvr,* Veronica Wilson; E-mail: Veronica.Wilson@kernlibrary.org

Founded 1963. Pop 13,595; Circ 33,298
Library Holdings: Bk Vols 21,129
Open Tues & Thurs 11-7, Fri & Sat 9-5
Friends of the Library Group
DELANO BRANCH, 925 Tenth Ave, Delano, 93215-2229, SAN 331-4677. Tel: 661-725-1078. *Br Supvr,* Fahra Noorani; E-mail: Fahra.Noorani@kernlibrary.org
Founded 1919. Pop 52,509; Circ 61,758
Library Holdings: Bk Vols 34,000
Open Tues-Thurs 11-7, Sat 9-5
Friends of the Library Group
FRAZIER PARK BRANCH, 3732 Park Dr, Frazier Park, 93225, SAN 321-8686. Tel: 661-245-1267. *Br Supvr,* Susan Templeton; E-mail: Susan.Templeton@kernlibrary.org
Founded 1982. Pop 8,480; Circ 20,434
Library Holdings: Bk Vols 15,963
Open Tues-Thurs 11-7, Fri & Sat 9-5
Friends of the Library Group
HOLLOWAY-GONZALES BRANCH, 506 E Brundage Lane, 93307-3337, SAN 331-4707. Tel: 661-861-2083. *Br Supvr,* Rachelle Ehteshami; E-mail: Rachelle.Ehteshami@kernlibrary.org
Founded 1975. Pop 21,930
Library Holdings: Bk Vols 21,670
Open Wed & Fri 9-5
Friends of the Library Group
KERN RIVER VALLEY BRANCH, 7054 Lake Isabella Blvd, Lake Isabella, 93240-9205, SAN 331-4685. Tel: 760-549-2083. *Br Supvr,* Elizabeth Duvall; E-mail: Elizabeth.Duvall@kerncountylibrary.org
Founded 1914. Pop 13,519; Circ 63,590
Library Holdings: Bk Vols 37,377
Open Tues & Thurs 11-7, Fri & Sat 9-5
Friends of the Library Group
LAMONT BRANCH, 8304 Segrue Rd, Lamont, 93241-2123, SAN 331-4715. Tel: 661-845-3471. FAX: 661-845-7701. *Br Supvr,* Candace Sluder; E-mail: Candace.Sluder@kernlibrary.org
Founded 1911. Pop 21,031; Circ 24,781
Library Holdings: Bk Vols 35,444
Open Wed & Thurs 12-8, Fri & Sat 9-5
Friends of the Library Group
MCFARLAND BRANCH, 500 W Kern Ave, McFarland, 93250-1355, SAN 377-6662. Tel: 661-792-2318. FAX: 661-792-6588. *Br Supvr,* Jazmin Navarro-Ayala; E-mail: Jazmin.Navarro-Ayala@kernlibrary.org
Founded 1913. Pop 12,146
Library Holdings: Bk Vols 20,000
Open Wed-Fri 10-6
Friends of the Library Group
MOJAVE BRANCH, 15555 O St, Mojave, 93501, SAN 331-474X. Tel: 661-824-2243. *Br Supvr,* Lisa Redmond; E-mail: Lisa.Redmond@kernlibrary.org; Staff 2 (MLS 1, Non-MLS 1)
Founded 1914. Pop 7,104; Circ 7,213
Library Holdings: Bk Vols 12,000
Function: Bks on cassette, Bks on CD, CD-ROM, Computers for patron use, Electronic databases & coll, Holiday prog, Internet access, Music CDs, OverDrive digital audio bks, Photocopying/Printing, Ref serv available, Summer reading prog, Tax forms, VHS videos
Open Mon, Wed & Fri 10-6
Friends of the Library Group
NORTHEAST BRANCH, 2671 Oswell St, Ste B, 93306, SAN 331-4847. Tel: 661-871-9017. *Br Supvr,* Amy Schmidt; E-mail: Amy.Schmidt@kernlibrary.org
Founded 1982. Pop 81,649; Circ 92,182
Library Holdings: Bk Vols 52,000
Open Tues & Thurs 11-7, Sat 9-5
Friends of the Library Group
BRYCE C RATHBUN BRANCH, 200 W China Grade Loop, 93308-1709, SAN 331-4731. Tel: 661-393-6431. FAX: 661-393-6432. *Br Supvr,* Adrienne Myers; E-mail: Adrienne.Myers@kernlibrary.org
Founded 1917. Pop 33,753; Circ 42,414
Library Holdings: Bk Vols 38,702
Open Tues & Thurs 11-7, Sat 9-5
Friends of the Library Group
RIDGECREST BRANCH, 131 E Las Flores Ave, Ridgecrest, 93555-3648, SAN 331-4766. Tel: 760-384-5870. FAX: 760-384-3211. *Br Supvr,* Charissa Wagner; E-mail: Charissa.Wagner@kerncountylibrary.org; Staff 3 (MLS 1, Non-MLS 2)
Founded 1941. Pop 37,012; Circ 119,787
Library Holdings: Audiobooks 200; Bks on Deafness & Sign Lang 20; CDs 500; DVDs 250; e-books 100; High Interest/Low Vocabulary Bk Vols 30; Large Print Bks 500; Bk Vols 54,098; Per Subs 100; Talking Bks 20
Special Collections: Flora & Fauna of Indian Wells Valley; Local History Coll; Petroglyphs
Automation Activity & Vendor Info: (Circulation) SirsiDynix
Open Tues-Thurs 11-7, Fri & Sat 9-5
Friends of the Library Group
ROSAMOND BRANCH, 3611 Rosamond Blvd, Rosamond, 93560-7653, SAN 378-2093. Tel: 661-256-3236. FAX: 661-256-2906. *Br Supvr,* Andrea Mason; E-mail: Andrea.Mason@kernlibrary.org
Founded 1914. Pop 25,455; Circ 61,211
Library Holdings: Bk Vols 45,000
Open Tues & Thurs 11-7, Fri & Sat 9-5
Friends of the Library Group
SHAFTER BRANCH, 236 James St, Ste 2, Shafter, 93263-2031, SAN 331-4774. Tel: 661-746-2156. *Br Supvr,* Ethan Picman; E-mail: Ethan.Picman@kernlibrary.org
Founded 1915. Pop 26,468
Library Holdings: Bk Vols 25,412
Open Mon-Thurs 11-7
Friends of the Library Group
SOUTHWEST BRANCH, 8301 Ming Ave, 93311-2020, SAN 331-4839. Tel: 661-664-7716. FAX: 661-664-7717. *Br Supvr,* Rafael Moreno; E-mail: Rafael.Moreno@kernlibrary.org
Founded 1981. Pop 169,671; Circ 317,917
Library Holdings: Bk Vols 79,939
Open Tues-Thurs 11-7, Fri & Sat 9-5
Friends of the Library Group
TAFT BRANCH, 27 Cougar Ct, Taft, 93268-2327, SAN 331-4820. Tel: 661-763-3294. FAX: 661-763-1237. *Br Supvr,* David Squires; E-mail: David.Squires@kernlibrary.org
Founded 1912. Pop 23,542; Circ 31,510
Library Holdings: Bk Vols 34,846
Open Tues-Thurs 11-7, Sat 9-5
Friends of the Library Group
TEHACHAPI BRANCH, 212 S Green St, Tehachapi, 93561, SAN 331-4782. Tel: 661-822-4938. FAX: 661-823-8406. *Br Supvr,* Veronica Wilson; E-mail: Veronica.Wilson@kernlibrary.org
Founded 1912. Pop 34,142; Circ 121,421
Library Holdings: Bk Vols 37,000
Open Mon & Wed 11-7, Fri & Sat 9-5
Friends of the Library Group
WASCO BRANCH, 1102 Seventh St, Wasco, 93280-1801, SAN 331-4804. Tel: 661-758-2114. *Br Supvr,* Ernestina Garcia; E-mail: Ernestina.Garcia@kernlibrary.org
Founded 1912. Pop 29,931
Library Holdings: Bk Vols 26,289
Open Mon, Wed & Fri 10-6, Tues & Thurs 4-7
Friends of the Library Group
ELEANOR N WILSON BRANCH, 1901 Wilson Rd, 93304-5612, SAN 331-4790. Tel: 661-834-4044. *Br Supvr,* David Squires; E-mail: David.Squires@kernlibrary.org
Founded 1970. Pop 94,010
Library Holdings: Bk Vols 35,424
Open Mon & Wed 11-7, Fri 9-5
Friends of the Library Group
WOFFORD HEIGHTS BRANCH, 6400-B Wofford Blvd, Wofford Heights, 93285, SAN 331-4812. Tel: 760-376-6160. *Br Supvr,* Nancy Moore; E-mail: Nancy.Moore@kernlibrary.org
Founded 1953. Pop 2,721; Circ 17,927
Library Holdings: Bk Vols 8,101
Open Mon & Wed 10-6, Fri 9-5
Friends of the Library Group
Bookmobiles: 2. In Charge, Sandra Gordon & Elizabeth Duvall. Bk vols 7,844

S KERN COUNTY MUSEUM*, Historical Reference Library, 3801 Chester Ave, 93301-1395. SAN 300-5925. Tel: 661-437-3330. FAX: 661-633-9829. Web Site: www.kcmuseum.org. *Curator of Coll,* Lori Wear; Tel: 661-437-3330,Ext 213, E-mail: lwear@kerncountymuseum.org; Staff 1 (Non-MLS 1)
Founded 1941
Library Holdings: CDs 15; DVDs 10; Music Scores 2,100; Bk Titles 3,000
Special Collections: Archives; City Directories; Photographs; Product Catalogs; Reference Books
Subject Interests: Archaeology, Calif hist, Local hist, Museology
Wireless access
Restriction: Not a lending libr, Open by appt only, Open to researchers by request

M KERN MEDICAL CENTER*, Health Sciences Library, 1700 Mt Vernon Ave, 93306. SAN 300-5933. Tel: 661-326-2227. E-mail: kmclibrary@kernmedical.com. Staff 1 (Non-MLS 1)
Founded 1945
Library Holdings: Bk Vols 200; Per Subs 31
Wireless access
Partic in Medical Library Association; Medical Library Group of Southern California & Arizona; National Network of Libraries of Medicine Region 5
Open Mon-Fri 7-3:30

BANNING

P BANNING LIBRARY DISTRICT*, 21 W Nicolet St, 92220. Tel: 951-849-3192. E-mail: bld@banninglibrarydistrict.org. Web Site: www.banninglibrarydistrict.org. *Dir,* Kevin Lee; E-mail: kevin@banninglibrarydistrict.org; *Libr Adminr,* Erika Aguila; E-mail: erika@banninglibrarydistrict.org; *Circ Mgr,* Fernando Morales; E-mail: fernandom@banninglibrarydistrict.org
Pop 26,400; Circ 116,088
Library Holdings: AV Mats 5,420; Bk Vols 72,292; Per Subs 138
Wireless access
Mem of Inland Library System
Open Mon-Fri 10-5
Friends of the Library Group

M SAN GORGONIO MEMORIAL HOSPITAL*, Medical Library, 600 N Highland Springs Ave, 92220. SAN 327-5930. Tel: 951-845-1121. FAX: 951-845-2836. *Librn,* Position Currently Open
Library Holdings: Bk Vols 151
Restriction: Staff use only

BARSTOW

J BARSTOW COMMUNITY COLLEGE, Thomas Kimball Library, 2700 Barstow Rd, 92311. SAN 300-595X. Tel: 760-252-2411, Ext 7270. FAX: 760-252-6725. E-mail: library@barstow.edu. Reference E-mail: kfreeman@barstow.edu. Web Site: www.barstow.edu/Library.html. *Interim Dir,* Bryan Asdel; E-mail: basdel@barstow.edu; *Librn,* Kyri Freeman; E-mail: kfreeman@barstow.edu; Staff 4 (MLS 2, Non-MLS 2)
Founded 1960. Fac 1; Highest Degree: Associate
Library Holdings: Bk Vols 41,000
Subject Interests: Desert ecology
Automation Activity & Vendor Info: (Acquisitions) Ex Libris Group; (Cataloging) Ex Libris Group; (Course Reserve) Ex Libris Group; (OPAC) Ex Libris Group; (Serials) Ex Libris Group
Wireless access
Function: 24/7 Electronic res, Archival coll, Art exhibits, Audio & video playback equip for onsite use, AV serv, Distance learning, Electronic databases & coll, For res purposes, Free DVD rentals, Instruction & testing, Internet access, Magazines, Mail & tel request accepted, Meeting rooms, Microfiche/film & reading machines, Online cat, Online info literacy tutorials on the web & in blackboard, Online ref, Orientations, Outside serv via phone, mail, e-mail & web, Photocopying/Printing, Ref & res, Ref serv available, Res assist avail, Res libr, Spanish lang bks, Telephone ref, Wheelchair accessible
Open Mon-Thurs 8-5 (Summer); Mon-Thurs 8-8, Fri 8-4 (Winter)
Restriction: Open to students, fac, staff & alumni

BEALE AFB

A UNITED STATES AIR FORCE*, Hub Zemke Library, Nine SVS/SVMG, 17849 16th St, Bldg 25219, 95903-1611. SAN 331-4944. Tel: 530-634-2314. FAX: 530-634-2032. E-mail: hzlstaff@gmail.com. Web Site: www.bealefss.com/hub-zemke-library. *Dir,* Sally Morral
Library Holdings: Bk Vols 44,000; Per Subs 150
Special Collections: Aeronautics & California Coll
Open Mon-Thurs 10-8, Fri 10-3, Sat & Sun 12-5

BEAUMONT

P BEAUMONT LIBRARY DISTRICT, 125 E Eighth St, 92223-2194. SAN 300-5968. Tel: 951-845-1357. E-mail: info@bld.lib.ca.us. Web Site: bld.lib.ca.us. *Dir,* Luren Dickinson; Staff 8 (MLS 7, Non-MLS 1)
Founded 1911. Pop 60,000; Circ 215,000
Library Holdings: Audiobooks 525; DVDs 7,570; Large Print Bks 3,840; Bk Vols 51,954; Per Subs 28
Automation Activity & Vendor Info: (Cataloging) TLC (The Library Corporation); (Circulation) TLC (The Library Corporation); (OPAC) TLC (The Library Corporation)
Wireless access
Mem of Inland Library System
Partic in OCLC Online Computer Library Center, Inc
Open Mon, Fri & Sat 10-6, Tues & Thurs 10-8, Sun 1-6
Friends of the Library Group

BELMONT

C NOTRE DAME DE NAMUR UNIVERSITY LIBRARY*, The Carl Gellert & Celia Berta Gellert Library, 1500 Ralston Ave, 94002-1908. SAN 300-5992. Tel: 650-508-3748. Administration Tel: 650-508-3746. E-mail: library@ndnu.edu. Web Site: library.ndnu.edu. *Interim Dir,* Carmen Martinez; E-mail: clmartinez@ndnu.edu; *Ref Librn,* Nora Mercer; Tel: 650-508-3748, E-mail: cmercer@ndnu.edu; *Libr Asst, Tech Serv,* Hai Huynh; Tel: 650-508-3486, E-mail: hhuynh@ndnu.edu; Staff 8 (MLS 4.5, Non-MLS 3.5)
Founded 1922. Enrl 1,600; Fac 104; Highest Degree: Master
Library Holdings: e-journals 10,000; Bk Vols 90,702; Per Subs 500; Videos 1,461
Special Collections: California Coll
Automation Activity & Vendor Info: (Cataloging) Auto-Graphics, Inc; (Circulation) Auto-Graphics, Inc; (OPAC) Auto-Graphics, Inc
Wireless access
Partic in CAL/PALS; Statewide California Electronic Library Consortium
Open Mon-Thurs 8am-11pm, Fri 8-4, Sat 10-6, Sun 12-9

BENICIA

P BENICIA PUBLIC LIBRARY*, 150 East L St, 94510-3281. SAN 300-6018. Tel: 707-746-4343. FAX: 707-747-8122. Web Site: www.BeniciaLibrary.org. *Dir,* David Dodd; E-mail: DDodd@ci.benicia.ca.us; *Head, Children's Servx,* Allison Angell; E-mail: aangell@ci.benicia.ca.us; *Head, Pub Serv,* Fran Martinez-Coyne; E-mail: fmartinezcoyne@ci.benicia.ca.us; *Head, Tech Serv,* Anita Falltrick; Tel: 707-746-4357, E-mail: afalltrick@ci.benicia.ca.us; Staff 52 (MLS 6, Non-MLS 46)
Founded 1911. Pop 28,086; Circ 384,056
Library Holdings: AV Mats 7,783; DVDs 5,068; e-books 11,988; Electronic Media & Resources 25; Bk Titles 89,803; Bk Vols 95,888; Per Subs 159
Special Collections: California Coll; Local Newspaper (1899-present). Oral History
Subject Interests: Local hist
Automation Activity & Vendor Info: (Cataloging) CARL.Solution (TLC); (Circulation) CARL.Solution (TLC); (ILL) OCLC Online; (OPAC) CARL.Solution (TLC)
Wireless access
Function: Adult bk club, Adult literacy prog, Art exhibits, Audiobks on Playaways & MP3, Audiobks via web, Children's prog, Computers for patron use, E-Readers, Electronic databases & coll, Homebound delivery serv, ILL available, Internet access, Magazines, Meeting rooms, Museum passes, Music CDs, Online ref, OverDrive digital audio bks, Preschool outreach, Printer for laptops & handheld devices, Scanner
Mem of NorthNet Library System
Partic in Solano Partner Libraries & St Helena
Open Mon-Thurs 10-9, Fri-Sun 12-6
Restriction: Access for corporate affiliates
Friends of the Library Group

BERKELEY

J BERKELEY CITY COLLEGE LIBRARY*, 2050 Center St, Rm 131, 94704. SAN 323-5726. Circulation Tel: 510-981-2824. Reference Tel: 510-981-2821. Web Site: berkeleycitycollege.edu/wp/library. *Dept Chair, Librn,* Joshua Boatright; Tel: 510-981-2991, E-mail: jboatright@peralta.edu; *Librn,* Heather Dodge; E-mail: hdodge@peralta.edu; *Librn,* Jenny Yap; E-mail: jyap@peralta.edu; Staff 2 (MLS 2)
Enrl 5,000
Library Holdings: Bk Vols 7,000; Per Subs 33
Wireless access
Open Mon-Thurs (Sept-May) 8:30-7:30, Fri 8:30-4; Mon-Fri (June-Aug) 8:45-5

P BERKELEY PUBLIC LIBRARY*, 2090 Kittredge St, 94704-1427. (Mail add: 2031 Bancroft Way, 94704), SAN 331-5428. Tel: 510-981-6100. Reference Tel: 510-981-6148. Administration Tel: 510-981-6195. FAX: 510-981-6111. Reference FAX: 510-981-6219. TDD: 510-548-1240. Web Site: www.berkeleypubliclibrary.org. *Dir, Libr Serv,* Elliot Warren; E-mail: ewarren@cityofberkeley.info; Staff 71 (MLS 71)
Founded 1893. Pop 102,743; Circ 1,541,221
Library Holdings: Bk Vols 446,703; Per Subs 1,524
Special Collections: Swingle Coll of Berkeley History, bks, maps, oral hist, pamphlets, photog, misc; World War I & World War II Poster Coll
Subject Interests: Art & archit, Civil rights, Ethnic studies, Feminism, Music
Automation Activity & Vendor Info: (Circulation) Innovative Interfaces, Inc; (OPAC) Innovative Interfaces, Inc
Wireless access
Special Services for the Deaf - TDD equip
Special Services for the Blind - Reader equip
Open Mon 12-8, Tues 10-8, Wed-Sat 10-6, Sun 1-5
Friends of the Library Group
Branches: 2
CLAREMONT BRANCH, 2940 Benvenue Ave, 94705, SAN 331-5452. Tel: 510-981-6280. FAX: 510-843-1603. *Br Supvr,* Shani Leonards
Founded 1924. Circ 139,672
Library Holdings: Bk Vols 49,236
Open Mon, Tues, Fri & Sat 10-6, Wed & Thurs 12-8
Friends of the Library Group

NORTH BRANCH, 1170 The Alameda, 94707, SAN 331-5487. Tel: 510-981-6250. FAX: 510-528-8975. *Br Mgr,* Marge Sussman; Staff 17 (MLS 4, Non-MLS 13)
Founded 1936. Circ 235,556
Library Holdings: Bk Vols 45,807
Open Mon, Tues, Fri & Sat 10-6, Wed & Thurs 12-8
Friends of the Library Group

CR GRADUATE THEOLOGICAL UNION LIBRARY*, Flora Lamson Hewlett Library, 2400 Ridge Rd, 94709-1212. SAN 331-5630. Tel: 510-649-2500. Interlibrary Loan Service Tel: 510-649-2502. Reference Tel: 510-649-2501. E-mail: library@gtu.edu. Web Site: www.gtu.edu/library. *Dir, Libr Serv,* Clay-Edward Dixon; Tel: 510-649-2540, E-mail: cedixon@gtu.edu; *Head, Ref Serv,* Beth Kumar; Tel: 510-649-2504, E-mail: bkumar@gtu.edu; *Spec Coll Librn,* David Stiver; Tel: 510-649-2523, E-mail: dstiver@gtu.edu; *Conservator,* Gillian Boal; Tel: 510-649-2527, E-mail: gboal@gtu.edu; Staff 16 (MLS 7, Non-MLS 9)
Founded 1969. Enrl 1,100; Fac 110; Highest Degree: Doctorate
Library Holdings: AV Mats 294,910; CDs 1,000; DVDs 637; Electronic Media & Resources 54; Bk Vols 494,364; Per Subs 1,512; Videos 1,237
Special Collections: Ecumenical & Inter-Religious Activity in the Western United States & Pacific Rim (Archival Coll); Institutional Record of the Graduate Theological Union; Manuscript Coll; New Religious Movements Research Coll; Rare Book Coll, bks, pamphlets
Subject Interests: Biblical studies, Christianity, Relig, Theol, World relig
Automation Activity & Vendor Info: (Acquisitions) Innovative Interfaces, Inc; (Cataloging) Innovative Interfaces, Inc; (Circulation) Innovative Interfaces, Inc; (Course Reserve) Innovative Interfaces, Inc; (ILL) OCLC Connexion; (OPAC) Innovative Interfaces, Inc; (Serials) Innovative Interfaces, Inc
Wireless access
Function: Art exhibits, Computers for patron use, Electronic databases & coll, Free DVD rentals, ILL available, Instruction & testing, Music CDs, Online cat, Online ref, Orientations, Outside serv via phone, mail, e-mail & web, Photocopying/Printing, Ref serv available, Telephone ref, VHS videos, Wheelchair accessible, Workshops
Partic in Statewide California Electronic Library Consortium
Special Services for the Blind - Reader equip
Open Mon-Thurs 8:30am-9pm, Fri 8:30-5, Sat 11-6, Sun 1-7; Mon-Thurs (Summer) 8:30-5
Friends of the Library Group

C INSTITUTE OF TRANSPORTATION STUDIES LIBRARY*, Harmer E Davis Transportation Library, 412 McLaughlin Hall, MC 1720, 94720-1720. SAN 331-7013. Tel: 510-642-3604. FAX: 510-642-9180. E-mail: itslib@berkeley.edu. Web Site: library.its.berkeley.edu. *Libr Dir,* Kendra Levine; Tel: 510-643-3348, E-mail: kklevine@berkeley.edu; *Libr Asst,* Marissa Young; E-mail: marissay@berkeley.edu
Founded 1948
Library Holdings: Bk Vols 149,426
Automation Activity & Vendor Info: (Acquisitions) Innovative Interfaces, Inc - Millennium; (Cataloging) OCLC Connexion; (Circulation) Innovative Interfaces, Inc - Millennium; (Course Reserve) Innovative Interfaces, Inc - Millennium; (OPAC) Innovative Interfaces, Inc
Wireless access
Partic in OCLC Online Computer Library Center, Inc
Open Mon-Fri 1-5

S PESTICIDE ACTION NETWORK NORTH AMERICAN, International Information Program, (Formerly Pesticide Action Network North American Regional Center), 2029 University Ave, Ste 200, 94704. SAN 372-6827. Tel: 590-788-9020, Ext 332. E-mail: info@panna.org. Web Site: www.panna.org. *Adminr,* Tiffany Seals; E-mail: tiffany@panna.org
Founded 1988
Library Holdings: Bk Titles 4,000; Per Subs 250
Special Collections: Pesticides, Agriculture & International Development Coll; US Environmental Protection Agency, reports & bd doc
Subject Interests: Agr, Pesticides
Wireless access
Restriction: Open by appt only

SR SWEDENBORGIAN LIBRARY & ARCHIVES*, 1798 Scenic Ave, 94709. SAN 307-5672. Tel: 510-849-8228, 510-849-8248. FAX: 510-849-8296. E-mail: cssinfo@gtu.edu. Web Site: css.gtu.edu/swedenborgian-library-and-archives. *Librn,* Michael Yockey
Founded 1866
Library Holdings: Bk Vols 25,000; Per Subs 12
Special Collections: Emanuel Swedenborg Coll; New Church Coll; New Jerusalem Church Coll; Swedenborgian Church Coll
Subject Interests: New Church hist
Function: Archival coll, Ref serv available
Restriction: Non-circulating to the pub, Open by appt only

C UNIVERSITY OF CALIFORNIA, BERKELEY*, Doe Library, South Hall Rd, 94704. SAN 331-6025. Tel: 510-642-6657. Circulation Tel: 510-643-4331. Administration Tel: 510-642-3773. FAX: 510-643-8179. Web Site: www.lib.berkeley.edu, www.lib.berkeley.edu/libraries/doe-library. *Univ Librn,* Jeffrey MacKie-Mason; E-mail: jmmason@berkeley.edu; *Sr Assoc Univ Librn,* Elizabeth Dupuis; E-mail: edupuis@berkeley.edu
Founded 1871. Enrl 32,000; Fac 1,482; Highest Degree: Doctorate
Library Holdings: Bk Vols 10,000,000; Per Subs 89,750
Special Collections: Letters, Literary Manuscripts & Scrapbooks of Samuel Clemens (Mark Twain Coll); Music History, bks, ms, scores; Persons Who Have Contributed to the Development of the West Coll (Regional Oral History Office) oral hist, memoirs, compilatiions; Radio Carbon Date Cards, Photographic Plates, Rubbings, University Archive Photographs, Aerial Photographs, VF mat. State Document Depository; UN Document Depository; US Document Depository
Wireless access
Publications: A Program for the Conservation & Preservation of Library Materials in the General Library; Bene Legere Newsletter for Library Associates; Bibliographic Guides to Research Resources in Selected Subjects; Collection Development Policy Statement; Faculty Newsletter (Quarterly); Orientation Leaflets; Titles Classified by the Library of Congress Classification: National Shelflist Count
Partic in Association of Research Libraries; OCLC Online Computer Library Center, Inc; Proquest Dialog; Research Libraries Information Network; Wilsonline
Special Services for the Deaf - TDD equip
Special Services for the Blind - Blind students ctr; Reader equip; Rental typewriters & computers
Open Mon-Fri 8-9, Sat 9-5, Sun 1-9
Friends of the Library Group

Departmental Libraries:

ART HISTORY/CLASSICS, 308 Doe Library, 94720-6000, SAN 331-684X. Tel: 510-642-7361. FAX: 510-643-2185. E-mail: ahc-library@berkeley.edu. Web Site: www.lib.berkeley.edu/libraries/art-history-classics-library. *Art Librn,* Lynn Cunningham; E-mail: lynncunningham@berkeley.edu
Open Mon-Thurs 9-9, Fri 9-7, Sat 1-5, Sun 1-9

BANCROFT LIBRARY, 94720-6000. Tel: 510-642-6481. Administration Tel: 510-642-3781. FAX: 510-642-7589. Administration FAX: 510-643-4313. E-mail: bancroft@library.berkeley.edu. Reference E-mail: bancref@library.berkeley.edu. Web Site: www.lib.berkeley.edu/libraries/bancroft-library. *Dep Dir,* Peter Hanff; E-mail: phanff@library.berkeley.edu
Library Holdings: Bk Vols 600,000
Special Collections: Fine Printing Coll; History of Science & Technology (Rare Books Coll); History of Western North America, especially California & Mexico (Bancroft Coll), bks, ms; Humanities Coll; Mark Twain Coll, bks, ms; Modern Poetry Coll; North & Central America Coll; Rare Imprints of Western Europe; University Archives. Oral History
Open Mon-Fri 10-5
Friends of the Library Group

CHEMISTRY & CHEMICAL ENGINEERING, 100 Hildebrand Hall, 94720-6000, SAN 331-6718. Tel: 510-642-3753. E-mail: chem@library.berkeley.edu. Web Site: www.lib.berkeley.edu/libraries/chemistry-library. *Circ & Reserves Supvr,* Agnes Concepcion; Tel: 510-643-4477, E-mail: aconcepc@library.berkeley.edu
Library Holdings: e-journals 700; Bk Vols 88,000; Per Subs 2,300
Open Mon-Thurs 9-7, Fri 9-5, Sat 1-5

EARTH SCIENCES & MAPS, 50 McCone Hall, 94720-6000, SAN 331-6742. Tel: 510-642-2997. E-mail: eart@library.berkeley.edu. Web Site: www.lib.berkeley.edu/libraries/earth-sciences-library. *Sci Librn,* Samantha Teplitzky; E-mail: steplitz@library.berkeley.edu; *Maps Librn,* Susan Powell; E-mail: spowell@library.berkeley.edu; Staff 6 (MLS 1, Non-MLS 5)
Library Holdings: Bk Vols 140,000; Per Subs 1,500
Automation Activity & Vendor Info: (Acquisitions) Innovative Interfaces, Inc; (Serials) Innovative Interfaces, Inc
Open Mon-Thurs 9-7, Fri 9-5

ENVIRONMENTAL DESIGN LIBRARY, 210 Wurster Hall, 94720-6000, SAN 331-6238. Tel: 510-642-4818. Reference Tel: 510-643-7421. E-mail: envi@library.berkely.edu. Web Site: www.lib.berkeley.edu/libraries/environmental-design-library. *Librn,* David Eifler; Tel: 510-643-7422, E-mail: deifler@library.berkeley.edu; Staff 5.3 (MLS 2.3, Non-MLS 3)
Founded 1903. Enrl 1,010; Fac 84; Highest Degree: Doctorate
Library Holdings: Bk Vols 210,000; Per Subs 500; Spec Interest Per Sub 750
Special Collections: Beatrix Farrand Rare Books
Subject Interests: Archit, City planning, Landscape archit
Function: Doc delivery serv, Electronic databases & coll, ILL available, Online cat, Online info literacy tutorials on the web & in blackboard, Photocopying/Printing, Ref serv available, Wheelchair accessible

Open Mon-Thurs 9am-10pm, Fri 9-5, Sat 11-5, Sun 11-10
Restriction: Borrowing privileges limited to fac & registered students, In-house use for visitors, Non-circulating of rare bks, Off-site coll in storage - retrieval as requested

ETHNIC STUDIES, 30 Stephens Hall, 94720-2360, SAN 376-9518. Tel: 510-643-1234. FAX: 510-643-8433. E-mail: esl@library.berkeley.edu. Web Site: eslibrary.berkeley.edu, www.lib.berkeley.edu/libraries/ethnic-studies-library. *Head Librn,* Lillian Castillo-Speed; Tel: 510-642-3947, E-mail: csl@library.berkeley.edu; Staff 5 (MLS 3, Non-MLS 2)
Special Collections: AAS Archives; AAS Special Coll; Asian American Studies; CS A/V; CS Archives; CS Locked Case; NAS California Coll & NAS A/V Coll
Subject Interests: Chicano studies, Ethnic studies, Native Am studies
Open Mon-Fri 9-6, Sat 1-6

GEORGE & MARY FOSTER ANTHROPOLOGY LIBRARY, 230 Kroeber Hall, 94720-6000, SAN 331-6173. Tel: 510-642-2400. FAX: 510-643-9293. Web Site: www.lib.berkeley.edu/libraries/anthropology-library. *Div Head,* Susan Edwards; Tel: 510-643-6224, E-mail: sedwards@library.berkeley.edu; *Circ Supvr,* Lillian Lee; Tel: 510-642-2419, E-mail: llee@library.berkeley.edu. Subject Specialists: *Soc serv,* Susan Edwards
Library Holdings: Bk Vols 59,000
Open Mon-Thurs 9-8, Fri 9-5, Sat & Sun 1-5

JEAN GRAY HARGROVE MUSIC LIBRARY, 94720-6000, SAN 331-6297. Tel: 510-642-2623. Reference Tel: 510-642-2624. FAX: 510-642-8237. E-mail: music_reference@berkeley.edu. Web Site: www.lib.berkeley.edu/libraries/music-library. *Archivist, Music Librn, Ref,* Manuel Erviti; Tel: 510-642-6197, E-mail: merviti@library.berkeley.edu; *Circ Supvr,* Angela Arnold; Tel: 510-643-6196, E-mail: musicirc@library.berkeley.edu; *Curator of Coll,* John Shepard; Tel: 510-642-2428, E-mail: jshepard@library.berkeley.edu
Library Holdings: Bk Vols 165,326
Open Mon-Thurs 9-8, Fri 9-5, Sat 1-5, Sun 1-5

HOWISON PHILOSOPHY LIBRARY, Moses Hall, 3rd Flr, 94720, SAN 331-7021. Tel: 510-642-2722. Web Site: philosophy.berkeley.edu/facilities, www.lib.berkeley.edu/libraries/philosophy-library. *Library Contact,* Jan Carter; Tel: 510-643-2281, E-mail: jcarter@library.berkeley.edu
Library Holdings: Bk Vols 10,000; Per Subs 60
Restriction: Non-circulating coll

INSTITUTE FOR RESEARCH ON LABOR & EMPLOYMENT LIBRARY, 2521 Channing Way, MC 5555, 94720-5555, SAN 331-6955. Tel: 510-642-1705. FAX: 510-642-6432. Web Site: irle.berkeley.edu/library. *Operations Mgr,* Janice Kimball; E-mail: jankim@berkeley.edu
Founded 1945. Enrl 30,000; Fac 65; Highest Degree: Doctorate
Library Holdings: Bk Vols 45,000
Restriction: Open by appt only

INSTITUTE OF GOVERNMENTAL STUDIES, 109 Moses Hall, Ground Flr, 94720-2370, SAN 331-6920. Tel: 510-642-1472. FAX: 510-642-3020. E-mail: igsl@berkeley.edu. Web Site: www.igs.berkeley.edu, www.lib.berkeley.edu/libraries/igs-library. *Dir,* Julie Lefevre; Tel: 510-643-6445, E-mail: jlefevre@library.berkeley.edu
Library Holdings: Bk Vols 400,000
Open Mon-Fri 10-5

MARIAN KOSHLAND BIOSCIENCE, NATURAL RESOURCES & PUBLIC HEALTH LIBRARY, 2101 Valley Life Science Bldg, No 6500, 94720-6500, SAN 331-6475. Tel: 510-642-2531. Reference Tel: 510-642-0456. E-mail: bios@library.berkeley.edu. Web Site: www.lib.berkeley.edu/bios. *Librn,* Michael Sholinbeck; Tel: 510-642-2532, E-mail: msholinb@library.berkeley.edu; *Emerging Tech Librn,* Elliott Smith; Tel: 510-643-6482, E-mail: esmith@library.berkeley.edu; *Health Sci Librn,* Deborah Jan; Tel: 510-643-7254, E-mail: djan@library.berkeley.edu; *Natural Res Librn,* Rebecca Miller; Tel: 510-643-6475, E-mail: rcmiller@berkeley.edu; *Circ Supvr,* Michele Buchman; E-mail: mbuchman@library.berkeley.edu. Subject Specialists: *Pub health,* Michael Sholinbeck; *Optometry,* Deborah Jan; Staff 4 (MLS 4)
Library Holdings: Bk Vols 500,000; Per Subs 6,500
Open Mon-Thurs 9am-10pm, Fri 9-5, Sat 1-5

KRESGE ENGINEERING LIBRARY, 110 Bechtel Engineering Ctr, 94720-6000, SAN 331-6777. Tel: 510-642-3366. FAX: 510-643-6771. E-mail: engi@library.berkeley.edu. Web Site: www.lib.berkeley.edu/libraries/engineering-library. *Eng Librn,* Lisa Ngo; Tel: 510-643-4299, E-mail: lngo@library.berkeley.edu; *Sci/Eng Librn,* Anna Sackmann; Tel: 510-642-9478, E-mail: asackmann@berkeley.edu; Staff 3 (MLS 3)
Library Holdings: Bk Vols 236,257; Per Subs 1,804
Subject Interests: Engr
Open Mon-Thurs 9am-Midnight, Fri 9-7, Sat 1-7

CL LAW, Berkley Law South Addition, 2nd Flr, 2778 Bancroft Way, 94720, SAN 331-7072. Tel: 510-642-0621. Reference Tel: 510-642-0900. FAX: 510-643-5039. Web Site: www.law.berkeley.edu/law-library, www.lib.berkeley.edu/libraries/law-library. *Dir,* Kathleen Vanden Heuvel; E-mail: kvandenh@law.berkeley.edu; *Assoc Dir,* Marci Hoffman; E-mail: mhoffman@law.berkeley.edu; *Assoc Dir,* Michael Levy; E-mail: mlevy@law.berkeley.edu
Founded 1912. Highest Degree: Doctorate
Special Collections: Anglo-American, Foreign & International Law Research Coll; Canon, Medieval & Roman Law Coll
Partic in Research Libraries Information Network
Publications: Acquisitions list
Open Mon-Fri 8am-Midnight, Sat 10am-10pm, Sun 10am-Midnight

THOMAS J LONG BUSINESS LIBRARY, Haas School of Business, Rm S350, 2220 Piedmont Ave, 94720-6000, SAN 331-6327. Tel: 510-642-0370. FAX: 510-643-5277. E-mail: haasref-library@berkeley.edu. Web Site: www.lib.berkeley.edu/libraries/business-library. *Bus Librn,* Hilary Schiraldi; E-mail: hschiral@library.berkeley.edu; *Bus Librn, Evening Librn,* Monica Singh; E-mail: msingh@library.berkeley.edu
Library Holdings: Bk Vols 159,000
Subject Interests: Bus admin, Econ
Open Mon-Thurs 9am-10pm, Fri 9-5, Sat & Sun 12-5

MATHEMATICS-STATISTICS, 100 Evans Hall, No 6000, 94720-6000, SAN 331-6688. Tel: 510-642-3381. FAX: 510-642-8257. E-mail: math@library.berkeley.edu. Web Site: www.lib.berkeley.edu/libraries/math-library. *Math Librn, Statistics Librn,* Brian Quigley; E-mail: bquigley@berkeley.edu; *Evening/Weekend Supvr,* Mr Blake Lindsey; E-mail: blindsey@berkeley.edu
Library Holdings: Bk Vols 85,205
Open Mon-Thurs 9-7, Fri 9-5

OPTOMETRY & HEALTH SCIENCES LIBRARY, 490 Minor Hall, 94720-6000, SAN 331-6599. Tel: 510-642-1020. FAX: 510-643-8600. E-mail: opto@library.berkeley.edu. Web Site: www.lib.berkeley.edu/libraries/optometry-library. *Health Sci Librn,* Deborah Jan; E-mail: djan@library.berkeley.edu; *Circ Supvr,* Michele Buchman; E-mail: mbuchman@library.berkeley.edu. Subject Specialists: *Optometry,* Deborah Jan; Staff 4 (MLS 1, Non-MLS 3)
Founded 1949. Highest Degree: Doctorate
Library Holdings: Bk Vols 15,000
Subject Interests: Med, Ophthalmology, Optometry, Vision sci
Partic in Association of Vision Science Librarians
Open Mon-Fri 9-5
Restriction: Badge access after hrs

PACIFIC EARTHQUAKE ENGINEERING RESEARCH (PEER) CENTER LIBRARY - NISEE, Bldg 453, 1301 S 46th St, Richmond, 94804, SAN 331-6912. Tel: 510-665-3419. E-mail: nisee@berkeley.edu. Web Site: peer.berkeley.edu/library, www.lib.berkeley.edu/libraries/earthquake-engineering-library. *Libr Coord,* Christina Bodnar-Anderson; E-mail: cbodnarand@berkeley.edu
Founded 1972
Library Holdings: Bk Vols 56,000
Special Collections: Godden International Structural Slide Library; Kovak Historical Image Coll; Steinbrugge Image Coll
Subject Interests: Earthquakes, Engr, Geotech engr, Seismology, Structural engr
Open Mon-Fri 9-5

PHYSICS-ASTRONOMY LIBRARY, 351 LeConte Hall, 94720-6000, SAN 331-6807. Tel: 510-642-3122. FAX: 510-642-8350. E-mail: phys@library.berkeley.edu. Web Site: www.lib.berkeley.edu/libraries/physics-library. *Circ & Reserves Supvr,* Agnes Conception; E-mail: aconcepc@library.berkeley.edu
Library Holdings: Bk Vols 48,321
Open Mon-Thurs 9-7, Fri 9-5

SOCIAL RESEARCH LIBRARY, 227 Haviland Hall, 94720-6000, SAN 331-6351. Tel: 510-642-4432. FAX: 510-643-1476. E-mail: socwcirc@berkeley.edu. Web Site: www.lib.berkeley.edu/libraries/social-research-library. *Div Head,* Susan Edwards; E-mail: sedwards@library.berkeley.edu; *Circ/Reserves,* Craig Alderson; E-mail: calderso@library.berkeley.edu
Library Holdings: Bk Vols 33,000; Per Subs 200
Open Mon-Thurs 9-6, Fri 9-5

SOUTH-SOUTHEAST ASIA LIBRARY, 120 Doe Library, 94720-6000, SAN 331-6831. Tel: 510-642-3095. FAX: 510-643-8817. E-mail: ssea@library.berkeley.edu. Web Site: www.lib.berkeley.edu/libraries/ssea-library. *Curator,* Virginia Shih; Tel: 510-643-0850, E-mail: vshih@library.berkeley.edu
Library Holdings: Bk Vols 400,000
Open Mon-Thurs 9-6, Fri 9-5

C V STARR EAST ASIAN LIBRARY, 94720-6000, SAN 331-6084. Tel: 510-642-2556. FAX: 510-642-3817. E-mail: eal@library.berkeley.edu. Web Site: lib.berkeley.edu/libraries/east-asian-library. *Electronic Res Librn, Head, Info Serv, Head, Pub Serv,* Susan Xue; E-mail: sxue@library.berkeley.edu
Library Holdings: Bk Vols 900,000
Open Mon-Thurs 9am-10pm, Fri 9-5, Sat 10-5, Sun 12-8

S WRIGHT INSTITUTE LIBRARY*, 2728 Durant Ave, 94704. SAN 323-4649. Tel: 510-841-9230, Ext 140. FAX: 510-841-0167. E-mail: library@wi.edu. Web Site: www.wi.edu/library. *Libr Dir,* Jason Strauss; E-mail: jstrauss@wi.edu
Library Holdings: Bk Titles 10,000; Per Subs 115
Subject Interests: Psychol
Wireless access
Partic in Northern & Central California Psychology Libraries
Open Mon-Fri 8:30-5, Sat 9-4:30

BEVERLY HILLS

S ACADEMY OF MOTION PICTURE ARTS & SCIENCES*, Margaret Herrick Library, 333 S La Cienega Blvd, 90211. SAN 300-6212. Tel: 310-247-3000. Reference Tel: 310-247-3020. FAX: 310-657-5193. Web Site: www.oscars.org. *Libr Dir,* Linda Harris Mehr; Tel: 310-247-3000, Ext 2201, E-mail: lmehr@oscars.org; *Graphic Arts Librn,* Anne Coco; Tel: 310-247-3000, Ext 2274; *Librn/Acad Files,* Libby Wertin; Tel: 310-247-3000, Ext 2208; *Librn/Scripts/Festivals & Awards,* Greg Walsh; Tel: 310-247-3000, Ext 2209; *Syst Librn,* Zoe Friedlander; Tel: 310-247-3000, Ext 2239; *Photographic Serv Adminr,* Matthew Severson; Tel: 310-247-3000, Ext 2227; *Acq Archivist,* Howard Prouty; Tel: 310-247-3000, Ext 2225; *Coll Archivist,* Val Almendarez; Tel: 310-247-3000, Ext 2224; *Ser,* Lea Whittington; Tel: 310-247-3000, Ext 2223. Subject Specialists: *Graphic arts,* Anne Coco; Staff 62 (MLS 10, Non-MLS 52)
Founded 1927
Library Holdings: Bk Vols 50,013; Per Subs 200
Special Collections: Adolph Zukor Coll; Alfred Hitchcock Coll; Andrew Marton Coll; Arthur Hiller Coll; Barry Lyndon Coll; Cary Grant Coll; Cecil B DeMille Coll, stills; Charlton Heston Coll; Colleen Moore Coll, scrapbks, stills; David Niven Coll; Edith Head Coll, sketches & stills; Elmer-Dyer Coll; Endre Bohem Coll; Fred Renaldo Coll; Fred Zinnemann Coll; George Cukor Coll, correspondence & scripts; George Steven Coll, correspondence, financial rec, production files, scripts & stills; Gregory Peck Coll; Hal B Wallis Coll; Hedda Hopper Coll; J Roy Hunt Coll, correspondence, scripts & stills; Jackie Coogan Coll; James Wong Howe Coll; Jean Hersholt Coll; John Engstead Coll; John Paxton Coll; John Sturges Coll; Joseph Biroc Coll; Jules White Coll; Kay Van Pipper Coll; Leo Kuter Coll; Leonard Goldstein Coll; Lewis Milestone, Mary Pickford, Martin Ritt, Paul Mazursky, William Friedkin, Hal Ashby, George Roy Hill & Bryan Forbes (Hollywood Museum Coll), papers & stills; Louella Parsons Coll; Mack Sennett Coll, contracts, financial rec, scripts & stills; Merle Oberon Coll; Metro-Goldwyn-Mayer Inc Coll, stills; MGM Scripts Coll; Milton Krims Coll; MPAA Production Code, case files; Paramount Pictures Coll, scripts, still bks & stills; Paul Ivano Coll; Pete Smith Coll; Ring Lardner Jr Coll; RKO Radio Pictures Coll, stills; Robert Lees Coll; Sam Peckinpah Coll; Saul Bass Coll; Selig Coll, copyrights, scripts & stills; Sid Avery Coll, stills; Sidney Skolsky Coll; Steve McQueen Coll; Thomas Ince Coll; Valentine Davies Coll; Vaudeville (Buster Keaton Coll); William Beaudine Coll. Oral History
Automation Activity & Vendor Info: (Acquisitions) Ex Libris Group; (Cataloging) Ex Libris Group; (OPAC) Ex Libris Group
Wireless access
Open Mon, Thurs & Fri 10-6, Tues 10-8

P BEVERLY HILLS PUBLIC LIBRARY*, 444 N Rexford Dr, 90210-4877. SAN 300-6239. Tel: 310-288-2220. Circulation Tel: 310-288-2222. Interlibrary Loan Service Tel: 310-288-2240. Reference Tel: 310-288-2244. FAX: 310-278-3387. E-mail: library@beverlyhills.org. Web Site: www.bhpl.org. *City Librn, Dir, Commun Serv,* Nancy Hunt-Coffey; E-mail: NHuntCoffey@beverlyhills.org; *Libr Serv Mgr/Access Serv,* Karen Buth; E-mail: KButh@beverlyhills.org; *Libr Serv Mgr/Pub Serv,* Marilyn Taniguchi; E-mail: MTaniguchi@beverlyhills.org; Staff 26 (MLS 26)
Founded 1929. Pop 34,000; Circ 682,000
Library Holdings: Bk Titles 233,382; Per Subs 236
Special Collections: 19th & 20th Century Art & Artists; Beverly Hills Coll
Subject Interests: Art, Dance
Automation Activity & Vendor Info: (Acquisitions) Innovative Interfaces, Inc; (Cataloging) Innovative Interfaces, Inc; (Circulation) Innovative Interfaces, Inc; (ILL) OCLC; (OPAC) Innovative Interfaces, Inc; (Serials) Innovative Interfaces, Inc
Wireless access
Partic in Southern California Library Cooperative
Open Mon-Thurs 9:30-9:30, Fri & Sat 10-6, Sun Noon-6
Friends of the Library Group
Branches: 1
ROXBURY BOOK NOOK, 471 S Roxbury Dr, 90212. Tel: 310-285-6849. *Libr Serv Mgr,* Karen Buth; E-mail: KButh@beverlyhills.org
Founded 1982. Pop 4,800; Circ 9,900
Library Holdings: Bk Vols 1,800; Per Subs 50
Automation Activity & Vendor Info: (Acquisitions) Innovative Interfaces, Inc - Sierra; (Cataloging) Innovative Interfaces, Inc - Sierra; (Circulation) Innovative Interfaces, Inc - Sierra; (ILL) OCLC WorldShare Interlibrary Loan; (Serials) Innovative Interfaces, Inc - Sierra
Open Mon-Fri 10-2 & 3-5

BISHOP

S LAWS RAILROAD MUSEUM & HISTORICAL SITE LIBRARY, Library & Arts Bldg, Silver Canyon Rd, 93515. (Mail add: PO Box 363, 93515-0363), SAN 375-4685. Tel: 760-873-5950. E-mail: lawsrailroadmuseum@gmail.com. Web Site: www.lawsmuseum.org.
Founded 1966
Library Holdings: Bk Vols 500
Restriction: Non-circulating, Not a lending libr, Open by appt only

BLYTHE

J PALO VERDE COLLEGE LIBRARY, Harry A Faull Library, One College Dr, 92225. SAN 300-628X. Tel: 760-921-5518. Administration Tel: 760-921-5558. E-mail: pvc-library@paloverde.edu. Web Site: library.paloverde.edu. *Librn,* June Turner; E-mail: jturner@paloverde.edu; *Libr Tech,* Danya Estrada -Mendez; E-mail: danya.estrada@paloverde.edu; Staff 2 (MLS 1, Non-MLS 1)
Founded 1947. Enrl 4,500; Fac 40; Highest Degree: Associate
Library Holdings: AV Mats 988; Bk Titles 16,978; Bk Vols 17,665; Per Subs 1
Automation Activity & Vendor Info: (Cataloging) Ex Libris Group; (Circulation) Ex Libris Group; (Discovery) Ex Libris Group; (OPAC) Ex Libris Group
Wireless access
Function: 24/7 Online cat, Computers for patron use, Internet access
Open Mon-Thurs 8-6, Fri 8-4:30

P PALO VERDE VALLEY LIBRARY DISTRICT*, 125 W Chanslorway, 92225. SAN 300-6298. Tel: 760-922-5371. FAX: 760-922-5334. Web Site: blythelibrary.org. *Libr Dir,* Kime Williams; E-mail: kwilliams@blythelibrary.org; Staff 4 (Non-MLS 4)
Founded 1959. Pop 40,700; Circ 39,378
Library Holdings: AV Mats 324; Bks on Deafness & Sign Lang 16; Bk Titles 44,105; Bk Vols 51,588; Per Subs 79
Special Collections: Palo Verde Times (local) 1911 to present (microfilm); Palo Verde Valley Local History (complete set)
Automation Activity & Vendor Info: (Cataloging) Brodart; (Circulation) SirsiDynix
Wireless access
Mem of Inland Library System
Open Mon-Fri 10-5:30
Friends of the Library Group

BRAWLEY

P BRAWLEY PUBLIC LIBRARY*, 400 Main St, 92227-2491. SAN 300-631X. Tel: 760-344-1891. FAX: 760-344-0212. Web Site: www.brawley-ca.gov/section/Library. *Dir,* Marjo Mello; E-mail: mmello@brawley-ca.gov; Staff 1 (MLS 1)
Founded 1921. Pop 25,000; Circ 72,000
Library Holdings: Audiobooks 1,200; Large Print Bks 800; Bk Titles 58,000; Per Subs 35
Automation Activity & Vendor Info: (Acquisitions) Biblionix/Apollo; (Cataloging) Biblionix/Apollo; (Circulation) Biblionix/Apollo; (OPAC) Biblionix/Apollo
Wireless access
Function: 24/7 Online cat, Adult literacy prog, Bilingual assistance for Spanish patrons, Bks on CD, Children's prog, Computer training, Computers for patron use, Family literacy, Holiday prog, Internet access, Large print keyboards, Magazines, Online cat, OverDrive digital audio bks, Photocopying/Printing, Preschool reading prog, Scanner, Senior computer classes, Spanish lang bks, Story hour, Summer reading prog, Wheelchair accessible
Partic in Serra Cooperative Library System
Open Wed & Thurs 10-7, Fri & Sat 9-5
Friends of the Library Group

BRENTWOOD

J LOS MEDANOS COLLEGE LIBRARY*, Brentwood Campus Library, 101A Sandcreek Rd, Rm 13, 94513. Tel: 925-513-1625. *Librn,* Roseann Erwin; Tel: 925-473-7572, E-mail: rerwin@losmedanos.edu
Automation Activity & Vendor Info: (Cataloging) Innovative Interfaces, Inc
Wireless access
Open Tues 10-1, Wed 1-4, Thurs 2-5

BUENA PARK

P BUENA PARK LIBRARY DISTRICT*, 7150 La Palma Ave, 90620-2547. SAN 300-6352. Tel: 714-826-4100. FAX: 714-826-5052. E-mail: library@buenapark.lib.ca.us. Web Site: www.buenaparklibrary.org. *Libr Dir,* Mary McCasland; E-mail: marymac@buenapark.lib.ca.us; Staff 11 (MLS 8, Non-MLS 3)
Founded 1919. Pop 83,995
Library Holdings: Audiobooks 3,135; CDs 3,630; DVDs 7,786; e-books 21,819; e-journals 138; Large Print Bks 1,757; Bk Titles 111,549; Bk Vols 119,676; Per Subs 125
Automation Activity & Vendor Info: (Acquisitions) Innovative Interfaces, Inc; (Cataloging) Innovative Interfaces, Inc; (Circulation) Innovative Interfaces, Inc; (ILL) OCLC Online; (OPAC) Innovative Interfaces, Inc; (Serials) Innovative Interfaces, Inc
Wireless access
Function: 24/7 Electronic res, 24/7 Online cat, 3D Printer, Accelerated reader prog, Activity rm, Adult bk club, Audiobks via web, Bilingual assistance for Spanish patrons, Bks on CD, Children's prog, Computers for patron use, Electronic databases & coll, Family literacy, Free DVD rentals, Homework prog, ILL available, Internet access, Magazines, Mango lang, Meeting rooms, Music CDs, Online cat, Outreach serv, OverDrive digital audio bks, Passport agency, Photocopying/Printing, Preschool outreach, Preschool reading prog, Prog for adults, Prog for children & young adult, Ref serv available, Scanner, Spanish lang bks, Summer reading prog, Tax forms, Teen prog, Telephone ref, Wheelchair accessible
Mem of Santiago Library System
Special Services for the Deaf - Bks on deafness & sign lang
Special Services for the Blind - Bks available with recordings; Bks on CD; Copier with enlargement capabilities; Large print bks; Ref serv; Talking bks
Open Mon-Thurs 10-8, Fri & Sat 10-5
Friends of the Library Group

BURBANK

P BURBANK PUBLIC LIBRARY*, 110 N Glenoaks Blvd, 91502-1203. SAN 331-7161. Tel: 818-238-5600. Reference Tel: 818-238-5580. Administration Tel: 818-238-5551. FAX: 818-238-5553. TDD: 818-238-5575. E-mail: library@ci.burbank.ca.us. Web Site: www.burbankLibrary.com. *Libr Serv Dir,* Elizabeth Goldman; E-mail: egoldman@burbankca.gov; *Asst Libr Serv Dir,* Melissa Potter; E-mail: mmpotter@burbankca.gov; Staff 64.6 (MLS 25.3, Non-MLS 39.3)
Founded 1913
Library Holdings: AV Mats 76,998; Large Print Bks 6,630; Bk Titles 457,520; Per Subs 466
Automation Activity & Vendor Info: (Cataloging) SirsiDynix; (Circulation) SirsiDynix; (OPAC) SirsiDynix
Wireless access
Function: 24/7 Electronic res, 24/7 Online cat, Accelerated reader prog, Activity rm, Adult bk club, Adult literacy prog, Archival coll, Art exhibits, Audio & video playback equip for onsite use, Audiobks via web, AV serv, Bilingual assistance for Spanish patrons, Bk club(s), Bk reviews (Group), Bks on CD, Children's prog, Computer training, Computers for patron use, Electronic databases & coll, Family literacy, Free DVD rentals, Govt ref serv, Health sci info serv, Holiday prog, Homebound delivery serv, Homework prog, ILL available, Instruction & testing, Internet access, Life-long learning prog for all ages, Literacy & newcomer serv, Magazines, Magnifiers for reading, Mail & tel request accepted, Mango lang, Meeting rooms, Microfiche/film & reading machines, Movies, Music CDs, Online cat, Online ref, Orientations, Outreach serv, OverDrive digital audio bks, Photocopying/Printing, Preschool outreach, Preschool reading prog, Printer for laptops & handheld devices, Prog for adults, Prog for children & young adult, Ref & res, Ref serv available, Res assist avail, Senior computer classes, Senior outreach, Serves people with intellectual disabilities, Spanish lang bks, Story hour, Study rm, Summer reading prog, Tax forms, Teen prog, Telephone ref, Visual arts prog, Wheelchair accessible, Workshops, Writing prog
Partic in Califa; OCLC Online Computer Library Center, Inc; Southern California Library Cooperative
Special Services for the Blind - Braille bks; Talking bks; Web-Braille
Open Mon-Thurs 9:30-9, Fri 9:30-6, Sat 10-6, Sun 1-5
Friends of the Library Group
Branches: 2
BUENA VISTA, 300 N Buena Vista St, 91505-3208, SAN 331-7196. Tel: 818-238-5620. Reference Tel: 818-238-5625. FAX: 818-238-5623. *Supv Librn,* Christine Rodriguez
Pop 30,600; Circ 655,959
Library Holdings: Bk Vols 179,281
Automation Activity & Vendor Info: (Course Reserve) SirsiDynix
Open Mon-Thurs 10-9, Fri 10-6, Sat 10-5, Sun 1-5
Friends of the Library Group
NORTHWEST, 3323 W Victory Blvd, 91505-1543, SAN 331-7226. Tel: 818-238-5640. FAX: 818-238-5642. *Supv Librn,* Melissa Gwynne
Pop 16,000; Circ 72,562
Library Holdings: Bk Vols 61,107
Open Mon-Fri 12-6
Friends of the Library Group

M PROVIDENCE SAINT JOSEPH MEDICAL CENTER*, Health Science Library, 501 S Buena Vista St, 91505-4866. SAN 300-6425. Tel: 818-847-3822. FAX: 818-847-3823. E-mail: librarian@providence.org. *Regional Librn,* Carrie Grinstead; Tel: 818-847-3881, E-mail: carrie.grinstead@providence.org; Staff 1 (MLS 1)
Founded 1943
Library Holdings: Bk Vols 7,314; Per Subs 150
Subject Interests: Cardiology, Mgt, Nursing, Oncology
Automation Activity & Vendor Info: (Cataloging) LibraryWorld, Inc; (Circulation) LibraryWorld, Inc; (OPAC) LibraryWorld, Inc
Function: 24/7 Electronic res, Internet access, Orientations, Photocopying/Printing, Ref serv available
Partic in Medical Library Group of Southern California & Arizona; Pacific Southwest Regional Medical Library
Open Mon-Thurs 7:30-3:30, Fri 8-Noon
Restriction: Circulates for staff only, In-house use for visitors

S SOUTHERN CALIFORNIA GENEALOGICAL SOCIETY*, Family Research Library, 417 Irving Dr, 91504-2408. SAN 324-5675. Tel: 818-843-7247. FAX: 818-843-7262. E-mail: scgs@scgsgenealogy.com. Web Site: www.scgsgenealogy.com. *Pres,* Alice Fairhurst; *Libr Operations,* Linda Golovko; *Acq,* Sally Emerson; *Per,* Beverly Truesdale
Founded 1964
Library Holdings: Microforms 1,000; Bk Titles 40,000; Per Subs 1,200
Special Collections: Cornwall, England (Ross Coll); French Canadian Heritage Society of California; German Genealogical Society of America Coll; Hispanic-America
Subject Interests: Calif, Fr Can, Genealogy, Hispanic, Tex
Publications: The Searcher (Online only)
Partic in Genealogical Alliance
Restriction: Open to pub for ref only

C WOODBURY UNIVERSITY LIBRARY*, 7500 Glenoaks Blvd, 91510. SAN 301-0236. Tel: 818-252-5200. Interlibrary Loan Service Tel: 818-252-5211. Reference Tel: 818-252-5201. E-mail: reference@woodbury.edu. Web Site: library.woodbury.edu. *Univ Librn,* Nedra Peterson; E-mail: nedra.peterson@woodbury.edu; *Access Serv Librn,* Solomon Blaylock; E-mail: solomon.blaylock@woodbury.edu; *DEI Librn,* Ayanna Gaines; E-mail: ayanna.gaines@woodbury.edu; *Syst Librn,* Jared Cowing; E-mail: jared.cowing@woodbury.edu; *Coordr, Libr Instruction,* Karla Bluestone; E-mail: karla.bluestone@woodbury.edu. Subject Specialists: *Archit,* Solomon Blaylock; Staff 12 (MLS 5, Non-MLS 7)
Founded 1884. Enrl 1,180; Fac 240; Highest Degree: Master
Library Holdings: e-books 2,575; Bk Vols 66,654; Per Subs 307; Videos 1,896
Subject Interests: Archit, Bus, Design, Fashion, Interior archit
Automation Activity & Vendor Info: (Cataloging) OCLC; (Circulation) OCLC; (ILL) OCLC WorldShare Interlibrary Loan; (OPAC) OCLC; (Serials) EBSCO Online
Wireless access
Partic in Statewide California Electronic Library Consortium
Open Mon-Thurs 8am-10pm, Fri 8-6, Sun 10-6
Friends of the Library Group
Departmental Libraries:
SAN DIEGO CAMPUS, 2212 Main St, San Diego, 92113. Tel: 619-235-2900. E-mail: san.diego@woodbury.edu. *Libr Coord,* Brenda Hernandez; E-mail: brenda.hernandez@woodbury.edu; *Ref & Instruction Librn,* Kelly Fortmann; Tel: 619-693-4422, E-mail: kelly.fortmann@woodbury.edu
Library Holdings: Bk Vols 6,500; Per Subs 30
Subject Interests: Archit, Real estate
Automation Activity & Vendor Info: (Acquisitions) ProQuest; (Cataloging) OCLC Worldshare Management Services; (Circulation) OCLC Worldshare Management Services; (Course Reserve) OCLC Worldshare Management Services; (Discovery) OCLC Worldshare Management Services; (ILL) OCLC Worldshare Management Services; (OPAC) OCLC Worldshare Management Services; (Serials) OCLC Worldshare Management Services
Open Mon 10-7, Tues & Fri 9-6, Wed 9-7, Thurs 9-9

BURLINGAME

P BURLINGAME PUBLIC LIBRARY*, 480 Primrose Rd, 94010. SAN 331-7315. Tel: 650-558-7400. FAX: 650-342-1948. Reference E-mail: bplref@plsinfo.org. Web Site: www.burlingame.org/library. *City Librn,* Brad McCulley; E-mail: mcculley@plsinfo.org; *Br Mgr,* Kathy von Mayrhauser; E-mail: vonmayrhauser@plsinfo.org; Staff 22 (MLS 10, Non-MLS 12)
Founded 1909. Pop 35,602; Circ 624,000
Library Holdings: Audiobooks 4,046; AV Mats 14,782; CDs 3,191; DVDs 7,545; Bk Vols 182,926; Per Subs 200

Automation Activity & Vendor Info: (Acquisitions) Innovative Interfaces, Inc; (Cataloging) Innovative Interfaces, Inc; (Circulation) Innovative Interfaces, Inc; (ILL) OCLC; (OPAC) Innovative Interfaces, Inc; (Serials) EBSCO Online
Wireless access
Mem of Peninsula Library System
Open Mon-Thurs 10-9, Fri & Sat 10-5, Sun 1-5
Friends of the Library Group
Branches: 1
EASTON DRIVE BRANCH, 1800 Easton Dr, 94010. Tel: 650-340-6180. FAX: 650-340-6184. *Br Mgr,* Sue Reiterman; E-mail: reiterman@plsinfo.org; Staff 2 (MLS 1, Non-MLS 1)
Pop 5,000; Circ 60,000
Library Holdings: Audiobooks 591; AV Mats 1,649; DVDs 1,058; Bk Vols 14,557
Open Mon-Thurs 2-8, Fri & Sat 2-5
Friends of the Library Group

CALABASAS

P CITY OF CALABASAS LIBRARY*, 200 Civic Center Way, 91302. Tel: 818-225-7616. Web Site: www.cityofcalabasas.com/library.html. *City Librn,* Barbara Lockwood; E-mail: blockwood@calabasaslibrary.org; *Principal Librn,* Karilyn Steward; E-mail: ksteward@cityofcalabasas.com; *Supvr, Circ,* Anita Torres; E-mail: atorres@cityofcalabasas.com; *Tech Serv Coordr,* Suchandra Ghosh; E-mail: sghosh@cityofcalabasas.com; *Children's Spec,* Jill Nevins; E-mail: jnevins@cityofcalabasas.com; Staff 9 (MLS 4, Non-MLS 5)
Founded 1998. Pop 24,212; Circ 144,912
Jul 2015-Jun 2016 Income (Main Library Only) $1,832,203, Federal $18,000, Locally Generated Income $1,814,203. Mats Exp $139,778, Books $40,000, Per/Ser (Incl. Access Fees) $7,000, AV Mat $12,500, Electronic Ref Mat (Incl. Access Fees) $78,978, Presv $1,300. Sal $769,216
Library Holdings: Audiobooks 3,850; AV Mats 2,650; Bks on Deafness & Sign Lang 76; CDs 757; DVDs 4,104; e-books 3,552; Large Print Bks 493; Music Scores 41; Bk Vols 66,921; Per Subs 70; Talking Bks 1,964
Subject Interests: Local hist
Automation Activity & Vendor Info: (Acquisitions) Innovative Interfaces, Inc; (Cataloging) Innovative Interfaces, Inc; (Circulation) Innovative Interfaces, Inc; (ILL) OCLC; (OPAC) Innovative Interfaces, Inc; (Serials) Innovative Interfaces, Inc
Wireless access
Function: 24/7 Electronic res, 24/7 Online cat, 3D Printer, Accelerated reader prog, Activity rm, Adult bk club, Archival coll, Audiobks via web, Bk club(s), Bks on CD, Children's prog, Computer training, Computers for patron use, Digital talking bks, Electronic databases & coll, Free DVD rentals, Health sci info serv, Holiday prog, Homework prog, ILL available, Internet access, Life-long learning prog for all ages, Magazines, Mail & tel request accepted, Mango lang, Meeting rooms, Movies, Music CDs, Online cat, Photocopying/Printing, Preschool outreach, Preschool reading prog, Prog for adults, Prog for children & young adult, Ref & res, Ref serv available, Senior outreach, Serves people with intellectual disabilities, Spanish lang bks, Story hour, Study rm, Summer & winter reading prog, Summer reading prog, Teen prog, Telephone ref, Wheelchair accessible, Writing prog
Partic in Southern California Library Cooperative
Open Tues-Thurs 11-8, Fri & Sat 11-5, Sun 12-5
Friends of the Library Group

CALEXICO

P CAMARENA MEMORIAL LIBRARY, 850 Encinas Ave, 92231. SAN 300-6441. Tel: 760-768-2170. FAX: 760-357-0404. E-mail: library@calexico.ca.gov. Web Site: www.calexicolibrary.org. *Libr Mgr,* Lizeth Legaspi; E-mail: llegaspi@calexico.ca.gov; *Libr Tech,* Julio Manriquez; Staff 3 (MLS 1, Non-MLS 2)
Founded 1919. Pop 37,000; Circ 106,455
Library Holdings: Audiobooks 602; AV Mats 1,502; High Interest/Low Vocabulary Bk Vols 150; Large Print Bks 600; Bk Titles 68,750; Bk Vols 75,000; Per Subs 104; Talking Bks 100
Special Collections: History of Imperial Valley
Automation Activity & Vendor Info: (Cataloging) Innovative Interfaces, Inc; (Circulation) Innovative Interfaces, Inc; (OPAC) Innovative Interfaces, Inc
Wireless access
Partic in Serra Cooperative Library System
Open Mon-Thurs 10-8, Fri 10-6
Friends of the Library Group

C SAN DIEGO STATE UNIVERSITY, Imperial Valley Campus Library, 720 Heber Ave, 92231-0550. SAN 331-7374. Tel: 760-768-5585. Reference Tel: 760-768-5633. FAX: 760-768-5525. Web Site: imperialvalley.sdsu.edu/academics/library. *Ref Librn,* Mara Cota; E-mail: mccota@sdsu.edu; Staff 3 (MLS 1, Non-MLS 2)
Founded 1959. Highest Degree: Master
Library Holdings: Bk Titles 60,000; Bk Vols 115,000; Per Subs 150
Special Collections: US-Mexico Borderlands (Border Coll)
Subject Interests: Criminal justice, Liberal studies, Psychol, Pub admin, Spanish, Teacher educ
Automation Activity & Vendor Info: (Cataloging) Innovative Interfaces, Inc; (Circulation) Innovative Interfaces, Inc
Wireless access
Partic in OCLC Online Computer Library Center, Inc; San Diego Greater Metro Area Libr & Info Agency Coun
Open Mon-Thurs 8:30am-9pm, Fri 8:30-6

CAMARILLO

P CAMARILLO PUBLIC LIBRARY*, 4101 Las Posas Rd, 93010. SAN 335-2269. Tel: 805-388-5222. Reference Tel: 805-388-5811. E-mail: askus@camarillolibrary.org. Web Site: www.camarillolibrary.org. *Libr Dir,* Jo Rolfe; Staff 43 (MLS 6, Non-MLS 37)
Wireless access
Partic in Southern California Library Cooperative
Open Mon-Thurs 10-9, Fri-Sun 10-5
Friends of the Library Group

G DIVISION OF JUVENILE JUSTICE OF DEPARTMENT OF CORRECTIONS*, Ventura Youth Correctional Facility Library, 3100 Wright Rd, 93010-8307. SAN 322-8681. Tel: 805-485-7951. FAX: 805-485-2801. *Sr Librn,* Position Currently Open
Founded 1962
Library Holdings: Bk Titles 6,000; Per Subs 20
Special Collections: Law Coll
Subject Interests: Law, Sociol
Open Mon-Fri 7-3

CAMERON PARK

M MARSHALL COMMUNITY HEALTH LIBRARY*, 3581 Palmer Dr, Ste 101, 95682. Tel: 530-626-2778. FAX: 530-626-2779. Web Site: www.marshallmedical.org/library. *Librn,* Jennifer Fiterre; Tel: 530-344-5459, E-mail: jfiterre@marshallmedical.org; Staff 2 (MLS 1, Non-MLS 1)
Library Holdings: Bks on Deafness & Sign Lang 10; CDs 30; DVDs 30; Large Print Bks 10; Bk Vols 4,000; Per Subs 10
Special Collections: Children's Picture Books on Health & Wellness
Automation Activity & Vendor Info: (Cataloging) SirsiDynix; (Circulation) SirsiDynix; (OPAC) SirsiDynix
Wireless access
Function: Computers for patron use, Internet access, Ref & res, Ref serv available, Telephone ref, Wheelchair accessible
Open Mon-Thurs 9-4

CAMP PENDLETON

UNITED STATES MARINE CORPS
A LIBRARY SERVICES*, Bldg 1146, 92055. (Mail add: PO Box 555005, 92055-5005), SAN 331-7528. Tel: 760-725-5104, 760-725-5669. FAX: 760-725-6569. Web Site: library.usmc-mccs.org. *Dir,* Sandra Jensen; *Asst Librn,* Ariel Gasper; Staff 19 (MLS 4, Non-MLS 15)
Founded 1950
Library Holdings: Bk Vols 16,000
Subject Interests: Mil hist
Partic in San Diego Greater Metro Area Libr & Info Agency Coun
Open Mon-Thurs 9-8, Fri-Sun 9-5
A SEASIDE SQUARE LIBRARY*, San Onofre, Bldg 51093, 92055. Tel: 760-725-7325. FAX: 760-763-1360. *Tech Serv,* Geraldine Hagen
Library Holdings: Bk Vols 10,124; Per Subs 70
Open Mon-Thurs 12-8, Fri-Sun 12-5

UNITED STATES NAVY
A CREW'S LIBRARY*, Naval Hospital, 200 Mercy Circle, 92055-5191. (Mail add: Box 555191, 92055-5191), SAN 331-7587. Tel: 760-719-3463, 760-719-4636. FAX: 760-725-4156. *Libr Dir,* Kathleen Dunning-Torbett; E-mail: kathleen.dunning-torbett@med.navy.mil
Founded 1943
Library Holdings: Audiobooks 500; DVDs 2,500; Bk Vols 500; Per Subs 200
Automation Activity & Vendor Info: (Cataloging) EOS International
Function: Bks on CD, Computers for patron use, Free DVD rentals, ILL available, Internet access, Magazines, Online cat, Ref serv available, Wheelchair accessible
Restriction: Not open to pub
AM MEDICAL LIBRARY*, Naval Hospital, Box 555191, 92055-5191, SAN 331-7617. Tel: 760-725-1322. FAX: 760-725-4156. *Libr Dir,* Kathleen Dunning-Torbett; Tel: 760-725-1229, E-mail: kathleen.dunning-torbett@med.navy.mil; Staff 2 (MLS 1, Non-MLS 1)
Founded 1947

Library Holdings: AV Mats 300; CDs 600; DVDs 130; e-books 350; e-journals 150; Bk Titles 2,000; Per Subs 235
Subject Interests: Dentistry, Med, Nursing
Automation Activity & Vendor Info: (Acquisitions) Baker & Taylor; (Cataloging) EOS International; (OPAC) EOS International; (Serials) EOS International
Partic in Consortium of Naval Libraries; OCLC Online Computer Library Center, Inc; Pacific Southwest Regional Medical Library
Publications: Newsletter
Open Mon-Fri 6:30-3:45

CAMPBELL

P SANTA CLARA COUNTY LIBRARY DISTRICT*, 1370 Dell Ave, 95032. SAN 334-7281. Tel: 408-293-2326. Web Site: www.sccld.org. *County Librn,* Jennifer Weeks; E-mail: jweeks@sccl.org; *Dep County Librn,* Chris Brown; E-mail: cbrown@sccl.org; *Info Syst Mgr,* Michael Krueer; Tel: 408-293-2326, Ext 3051, E-mail: mkrueer@sccl.org; *Serv Mgr, Coll Develop & Reading Serv,* Gail Mason; E-mail: gmason@sccl.org; Staff 82 (MLS 75, Non-MLS 7)
Founded 1912. Pop 424,918; Circ 11,319,133
Library Holdings: High Interest/Low Vocabulary Bk Vols 3,871; Large Print Bks 34,518; Bk Titles 386,308; Bk Vols 1,700,000; Per Subs 2,831; Talking Bks 30,498
Special Collections: California Western Americana. State Document Depository; US Document Depository
Automation Activity & Vendor Info: (Acquisitions) SirsiDynix; (Cataloging) SirsiDynix; (Circulation) SirsiDynix; (ILL) OCLC WorldShare Interlibrary Loan; (OPAC) SirsiDynix; (Serials) SirsiDynix
Wireless access
Function: Accelerated reader prog, Adult bk club, Adult literacy prog, After school storytime, Archival coll, Art exhibits, Audio & video playback equip for onsite use, Audiobks via web, AV serv, BA reader (adult literacy), Bi-weekly Writer's Group, Bilingual assistance for Spanish patrons, Bk club(s), Bk reviews (Group), Bks on cassette, Bks on CD, CD-ROM, Chess club, Children's prog, Citizenship assistance, Computer training, Computers for patron use, Digital talking bks, E-Reserves, Electronic databases & coll, Family literacy, For res purposes, Free DVD rentals, Games & aids for people with disabilities, Genealogy discussion group, Govt ref serv, Health sci info serv, Holiday prog, Home delivery & serv to seniorr ctr & nursing homes, Homebound delivery serv, Homework prog, ILL available, Internet access, Jail serv, Large print keyboards, Learning ctr, Legal assistance to inmates, Literacy & newcomer serv, Magnifiers for reading, Mail & tel request accepted, Mail loans to mem, Museum passes, Music CDs, Online cat, Online info literacy tutorials on the web & in blackboard, Online ref, Orientations, Outreach serv, Outside serv via phone, mail, e-mail & web, OverDrive digital audio bks, Photocopying/Printing, Preschool outreach, Prof lending libr, Prog for adults, Prog for children & young adult, Ref & res, Ref serv available, Res libr, Senior computer classes, Senior outreach, Serves people with intellectual disabilities, Spoken cassettes & CDs, Spoken cassettes & DVDs, Story hour, Summer reading prog, Tax forms, Teen prog, Telephone ref, VHS videos, Wheelchair accessible
Partic in Califa
Friends of the Library Group
Branches: 8
CAMPBELL PUBLIC, 77 Harrison Ave, 95008-1409, SAN 334-7370. Tel: 408-866-1991. FAX: 408-866-1433. *Commun Librn,* Cheryl Houts; *Dep County Librn,* Chris Brown; Staff 10 (MLS 9, Non-MLS 1)
Pop 49,733; Circ 912,112
Library Holdings: Bk Vols 189,662
Friends of the Library Group
CUPERTINO LIBRARY, 10800 Torre Ave, Cupertino, 95014, SAN 334-7435. Tel: 408-446-1677. FAX: 408-252-8749. Web Site: www.sccl.org/locations/CU. *Commun Librn,* Clare Varesio; E-mail: cupertino_manager@sccl.org; Staff 15 (MLS 15)
Pop 58,302; Circ 2,800,000
Library Holdings: Bk Vols 370,000
Special Collections: Local History (California Western Americana Coll)
Open Mon, Tues, Fri & Sat 1-5, Wed & Thurs 3-7
Friends of the Library Group
GILROY LIBRARY, 350 W Sixth St, Gilroy, 95020, SAN 334-746X. Tel: 408-842-8207. Web Site: sccld.org/locations/GI. *Commun Librn,* Cassandra Wong; E-mail: gilroy_manager@sccl.org; Staff 6 (MLS 6)
Pop 54,848; Circ 428,347
Library Holdings: Bk Titles 111,282; Bk Vols 142,468
Open Mon & Tues 3-7, Wed-Sat 1-5
Friends of the Library Group
LOS ALTOS MAIN LIBRARY, 13 S San Antonio Rd, Los Altos, 94022, SAN 334-7494. Tel: 650-948-7683. Web Site: sccld.org/locations/la. *Commun Librn,* Bryant Bao; E-mail: los_altos_manager@sccl.org; Staff 11 (MLS 11)
Pop 41,348; Circ 1,515,157
Library Holdings: Bk Vols 262,826
Function: Adult bk club, Adult literacy prog, Art exhibits, Audio & video playback equip for onsite use, Audiobks via web, Bk club(s), Bks on CD, CD-ROM, Children's prog, Computers for patron use, Digital talking bks, Electronic databases & coll, Family literacy, Free DVD rentals, Health sci info serv, Homebound delivery serv, ILL available, Internet access, Large print keyboards, Magnifiers for reading, Microfiche/film & reading machines, Music CDs, Online cat, Online ref, Outreach serv, OverDrive digital audio bks, Photocopying/Printing, Preschool outreach, Prog for adults, Prog for children & young adult, Ref serv available, Scanner, Senior computer classes, Senior outreach, Spanish lang bks, Spoken cassettes & CDs, Spoken cassettes & DVDs, Story hour, Summer reading prog, Tax forms, Teen prog, Telephone ref, Wheelchair accessible
Open Mon & Tues 3-7, Wed-Sat 1-5
Friends of the Library Group
MILPITAS PUBLIC, 160 N Main St, Milpitas, 95035, SAN 334-7346. Tel: 408-262-1171. Web Site: sccld.org/locations/mi. *Commun Librn,* Kelly McKean; E-mail: milpitas_manager@sccl.org; Staff 10 (MLS 8, Non-MLS 2)
Pop 70,000; Circ 1,960,000
Library Holdings: Bk Vols 300,000
Open Mon & Tues 3-7, Wed-Sat 1-5
Friends of the Library Group
MORGAN HILL BRANCH, 660 W Main Ave, Morgan Hill, 95037, SAN 334-7524. Tel: 408-779-3196. Web Site: sccld.org/locations/MH. *Commun Librn,* Heather Geddes; E-mail: morgan_hill_manager@sccl.org; Staff 22 (MLS 8, Non-MLS 14)
Pop 45,763; Circ 841,673
Library Holdings: Bk Titles 125,771; Bk Vols 160,689
Automation Activity & Vendor Info: (Circulation) Horizon; (Serials) EBSCO Online
Function: Adult bk club, Adult literacy prog, Audio & video playback equip for onsite use, Audiobks via web, Bilingual assistance for Spanish patrons, Bks on CD, CD-ROM, Children's prog, Computers for patron use, Digital talking bks, Electronic databases & coll, Free DVD rentals, Holiday prog, Home delivery & serv to seniorr ctr & nursing homes, Homebound delivery serv, ILL available, Internet access, Large print keyboards, Magnifiers for reading, Microfiche/film & reading machines, Museum passes, Music CDs, Online cat, Online ref, Outreach serv, OverDrive digital audio bks, Photocopying/Printing, Preschool outreach, Preschool reading prog, Printer for laptops & handheld devices, Prog for adults, Prog for children & young adult, Ref serv available, Scanner, Senior outreach, Spanish lang bks, Story hour, Summer reading prog, Tax forms, Teen prog, Telephone ref, Wheelchair accessible, Workshops
Special Services for the Deaf - ADA equip; Adult & family literacy prog; Bks on deafness & sign lang; Closed caption videos; High interest/low vocabulary bks; TTY equip
Special Services for the Blind - Children's Braille; Computer access aids; Computer with voice synthesizer for visually impaired persons; Extensive large print coll; Free checkout of audio mat; Home delivery serv; Large print bks; Magnifiers; PC for people with disabilities; Talking bks
Open Mon & Tues 3-7, Wed-Sat 1-5
Restriction: Non-resident fee
Friends of the Library Group
SARATOGA COMMUNITY LIBRARY, 13650 Saratoga Ave, Saratoga, 95070, SAN 334-7559. Tel: 408-867-6126. Web Site: sccld.org/locations/sa. *Commun Librn,* Annapurna Dandu; E-mail: saratoga_manager@sccl.org; Staff 8 (MLS 8)
Pop 35,558; Circ 1,359,483
Library Holdings: Bk Titles 149,953; Bk Vols 204,583
Open Mon & Tues 3-7, Wed-Sat 1-5
Friends of the Library Group
WOODLAND BRANCH, 1975 Grant Rd, Los Altos, 94024, SAN 334-7672. Tel: 650-969-6030. Web Site: sccld.org/locations/wo. *Interim Librn,* Bryant Bao
Circ 229,542
Library Holdings: Bk Titles 40,177; Bk Vols 46,582
Friends of the Library Group
Bookmobiles: 2

CANYON LAKE

R CANYON LAKE COMMUNITY CHURCH LIBRARY*, 30515 Railroad Canyon Rd, 92587. Tel: 951-244-1877. E-mail: library@canyonlakechurch.org. *Libr Mgr,* Bob Haskins; E-mail: library@canyonlakechurch.org
Jul 2017-Jun 2018 Income $700, Parent Institution $400, Other $300. Mats Exp $1,000, Books $800, AV Mat $200
Library Holdings: Audiobooks 45; CDs 323; DVDs 464; Electronic Media & Resources 85; Large Print Bks 40; Bk Titles 6,479
Automation Activity & Vendor Info: (Cataloging) LibraryWorld, Inc; (Circulation) LibraryWorld, Inc; (OPAC) LibraryWorld, Inc
Wireless access
Function: Bks on CD, E-Readers, Free DVD rentals, Music CDs, Online cat, Story hour, Summer reading prog

Open Tues 6pm-8:30pm, Sun 7-12:30
Restriction: Lending limited to county residents

CARLSBAD

P CARLSBAD CITY LIBRARY*, Dove Library, 1775 Dove Lane, 92011. SAN 300-6492. Tel: 760-602-2049. Administration Tel: 760-602-2011. FAX: 760-602-7942. E-mail: librarian@carlsbadca.gov. Web Site: www.carlsbadca.gov/services/depts/library. *Libr Dir,* Heather Pizzuto; E-mail: heather.pizzuto@carlsbadca.gov; *Dep Libr Dir,* Diane Bednarski; Tel: 760-602-2010, E-mail: Diane.Bednarski@carlsbadca.gov; *Dep Libr Dir,* Suzanne Smithson; Tel: 760-434-2876, E-mail: suzanne.smithson@carlsbadca.gov; *Commun Relations Mgr,* Jessica Padilla Bowen; Tel: 760-602-2024, E-mail: jessica.padillabowen@carlsbadca.gov; *Sr Bus Mgr, Syst Spec,* Devin Castel; Tel: 760-602-2065, E-mail: devin.castel@carlsbadca.gov; *Coll, Tech Serv Supvr,* Kristi Bell; Tel: 760-602-2029, E-mail: kristi.bell@carlsbadca.gov; *ILL,* Kamling Tsang; Tel: 760-602-2031, E-mail: kamling.tsang@carlsbadca.gov; Staff 101.8 (MLS 25.8, Non-MLS 76)
Founded 1956. Pop 114,622; Circ 1,235,364
Library Holdings: Audiobooks 14,255; Bks on Deafness & Sign Lang 74; Braille Volumes 1; CDs 28,683; DVDs 15,704; e-books 9,949; Electronic Media & Resources 29; High Interest/Low Vocabulary Bk Vols 3,238; Large Print Bks 5,678; Microforms 174,262; Bk Titles 212,150; Bk Titles 212,150; Bk Titles 212,150; Bk Vols 267,666; Per Subs 443
Subject Interests: Genealogy, Local hist
Automation Activity & Vendor Info: (Acquisitions) SirsiDynix; (Cataloging) SirsiDynix; (Circulation) SirsiDynix; (Discovery) SirsiDynix-Enterprise; (ILL) OCLC ILLiad; (Media Booking) SirsiDynix; (OPAC) SirsiDynix; (Serials) SirsiDynix
Wireless access
Function: 24/7 Electronic res, 24/7 Online cat, 3D Printer, Activity rm, Adult bk club, Adult literacy prog, After school storytime, Archival coll, Art exhibits, Art programs, Audio & video playback equip for onsite use, Audiobks on Playaways & MP3, Audiobks via web, AV serv, Bilingual assistance for Spanish patrons, Bk club(s), Bks on CD, Children's prog, Computer training, Computers for patron use, Electronic databases & coll, Free DVD rentals, Genealogy discussion group, Holiday prog, Homebound delivery serv, Homework prog, ILL available, Internet access, Learning ctr, Life-long learning prog for all ages, Literacy & newcomer serv, Magazines, Makerspace, Mango lang, Meeting rooms, Microfiche/film & reading machines, Movies, Music CDs, Online cat, Online ref, Outreach serv, Outside serv via phone, mail, e-mail & web, OverDrive digital audio bks, Photocopying/Printing, Preschool outreach, Preschool reading prog, Printer for laptops & handheld devices, Prog for adults, Prog for children & young adult, Ref & res, Ref serv available, Res assist avail, Scanner, Spanish lang bks, Spoken cassettes & CDs, STEM programs, Story hour, Study rm, Summer & winter reading prog, Summer reading prog, Tax forms, Teen prog, Telephone ref, Visual arts prog, Wheelchair accessible, Winter reading prog, Workshops
Publications: Carlsbad: A Village by the Sea; Carlsbad: An Unabashed History of the Village by the Sea; Seekers of the Spring: A History of Carlsbad
Partic in OCLC Online Computer Library Center, Inc; Serra Cooperative Library System
Special Services for the Deaf - Assisted listening device; Bks on deafness & sign lang; Closed caption videos
Special Services for the Blind - Accessible computers; Aids for in-house use; Assistive/Adapted tech devices, equip & products; Large print bks; Playaways (bks on MP3)
Open Mon-Thurs 9-9, Fri & Sat 9-5, Sun 1-5
Friends of the Library Group
Branches: 2
GEORGINA COLE LIBRARY, 1250 Carlsbad Village Dr, 92008, SAN 322-5550. Tel: 760-434-2870. FAX: 760-434-9975. *Dep Libr Dir,* Suzanne Smithson; Tel: 760-434-2876, E-mail: suzanne.smithson@carlsbadca.gov
Open Mon-Thurs 9-9, Fri 9-5, Sun 1-5
Friends of the Library Group
LIBRARY LEARNING CENTER, 3368 Eureka Pl, 92008, SAN 375-5428. Tel: 760-931-4500. FAX: 760-729-8335. *Principal Librn,* Viktor Sjöberg; Tel: 760-931-4520, E-mail: viktor.sjoberg@carlsbadca.gov; *Commun Outreach Supvr-Bilingual,* Lizeth Simonson; Tel: 760-931-4509, E-mail: lizeth.simonson@carlsbadca.gov; *Commun Outreach Supvr-Literacy,* Carrie Scott; Tel: 760-931-4515, E-mail: carrie.scott@carlsbadca.gov
Open Mon-Thurs 9-8, Fri 9-5
Friends of the Library Group

S RICHARD T LIDDICOAT GEMOLOGICAL LIBRARY & INFORMATION CENTER*, GIA Library, 5345 Armada Dr, 92008. SAN 301-5866. Tel: 760-603-4046, 760-603-4068. Toll Free Tel: 800-421-7250, Ext 4046, 800-421-7250, Ext 4068. FAX: 760-603-4256. E-mail: library@gia.edu. Web Site: www.gia.edu/library. *Dir,* Robert Weldon; E-mail: rweldon@gia.edu; *Sr Librn,* Rosemary Tozer; E-mail: rtozer@gia.edu; *Mgr,* Judy Colbert; E-mail: jcolbert@gia.edu; *Mgr,* Paula Jean Rucinski; E-mail: paula.rucinski@gia.edu. Subject Specialists: *Rare bks,* Rosemary Tozer; *Digital asset mgt, Gemology, Visual res,* Judy Colbert; *Bus, Gemology,* Paula Jean Rucinski; Staff 18 (MLS 4, Non-MLS 14)
Founded 1931
Library Holdings: CDs 250; DVDs 333; Bk Vols 57,000; Per Subs 230; Videos 1,103
Special Collections: Auction Catalogs; Gemology & Mineralogy (Joseph A Freilich Library, John & Marjorie Jane Sinkankas Coll & Henry Polissack Library); Jewelry & Jewelry History (Theodore Horovitz Library); Science & Mineralogy (Clifford J Awald Library). Oral History
Subject Interests: Gemology, Geol, Jewelry hist, Jewelry manufacturing, Mineralogy
Automation Activity & Vendor Info: (Acquisitions) EOS International; (Cataloging) EOS International; (Circulation) EOS International; (ILL) OCLC Online; (OPAC) EOS International; (Serials) EOS International
Wireless access
Function: For res purposes
Partic in Library & Information Resources Network
Open Mon-Fri 7:30-5
Restriction: Circ limited, Closed stack, Co libr, Non-circulating coll, Non-circulating to the pub, Open to pub for ref only, Photo ID required for access, Pub use on premises

CARMEL

P HARRISON MEMORIAL LIBRARY*, Carmel Public Library, Ocean Ave & Lincoln St, 93921. (Mail add: PO Box 800, 93921-0800), SAN 300-6514. Tel: 831-624-4629. Reference Tel: 831-624-7323. Administration Tel: 831-624-1366. FAX: 831-624-0407. Reference E-mail: hml.reference@gmail.com. Web Site: www.hm-lib.org. *Libr Dir,* Ashlee Wright; Tel: 831-624-1366, E-mail: awright@ci.carmel.ca.us; *Head Archivist,* Katie O'Connell; Tel: 831-624-1615, E-mail: koconnell@ci.carmel.ca.us; *Head, Ref,* Jean Chapin; E-mail: jchapin@ci.carmel.ca.us; *Head, Youth Serv,* Grace Melady; Tel: 831-624-4664, E-mail: gmelady@ci.carmel.ca.us; *Circ Supvr,* Amy Rector; E-mail: arector@ci.carmel.ca.us; *ILL/Doc Delivery Serv,* Jeanette Campbell; E-mail: jcampbell@ci.carmel.ca.us; Staff 12 (MLS 5, Non-MLS 7)
Founded 1906. Pop 3,738; Circ 140,848
Jul 2015-Jun 2016 Income $1,392,489, City $1,061,489, Locally Generated Income $331,000. Mats Exp $206,776, Books $102,081, Per/Ser (Incl. Access Fees) $12,450, Manu Arch $2,500, AV Equip $34,987, AV Mat $26,900, Electronic Ref Mat (Incl. Access Fees) $32,880, Presv $2,500. Sal $660,389
Library Holdings: Audiobooks 3,311; AV Mats 8,500; DVDs 5,177; e-books 60,963; Electronic Media & Resources 30; Large Print Bks 2,022; Bk Titles 63,419; Bk Vols 68,944; Per Subs 110; Talking Bks 3,311; Videos 13
Special Collections: Carmel History Coll, photog; Carmel Pine Cone Local Newspaper Coll, 1915-present; Edward Weston Photographs; Robinson Jeffers Coll
Automation Activity & Vendor Info: (Acquisitions) Baker & Taylor; (Cataloging) OCLC Connexion; (Circulation) ByWater Solutions; (ILL) OCLC FirstSearch; (OPAC) ByWater Solutions; (Serials) EBSCO Online
Wireless access
Function: 24/7 Electronic res, 24/7 Online cat, Adult literacy prog, Audiobks via web, Bks on CD, Children's prog, Computer training, Computers for patron use, Digital talking bks, E-Readers, Electronic databases & coll, Free DVD rentals, Homebound delivery serv, ILL available, Internet access, Magazines, Magnifiers for reading, Mail & tel request accepted, Mango lang, Microfiche/film & reading machines, Movies, Online cat, Outreach serv, Outside serv via phone, mail, e-mail & web, OverDrive digital audio bks, Photocopying/Printing, Preschool outreach, Preschool reading prog, Printer for laptops & handheld devices, Prog for adults, Prog for children & young adult, Ref & res, Ref serv available, Scanner, Spanish lang bks, Story hour, Summer reading prog, Tax forms, Teen prog, Telephone ref
Partic in Monterey Bay Area Cooperative Library System
Open Mon & Sat 1-5, Tues & Wed 11-8, Thurs & Fri 10-6
Friends of the Library Group

CARPINTERIA

§C PACIFICA GRADUATE INSTITUTE, Graduate Research Library, 249 Lambert Rd, 93013. Tel: 805-969-3626, Ext 115. Reference Tel: 805-969-3626, Ext 144. E-mail: circulation@pacifica.edu, ill@pacifica.edu, reference@pacifica.edu. Web Site: www.pacifica.edu/student-services/graduate-research-library. *Asst Dir, Libr Serv,* Diana Zakhour; Tel: 805-969-3626, Ext 169, E-mail: dzakhour@pacifica.edu; *Lead Reference Services Librn,* Mark Kelly; *Special Colls & Reference Librn,* Richard Buchen; Tel: 805-969-3626, Ext 133, E-mail: rbuchen@pacifica.edu; *Circ,* Amanda Brown
Special Collections: OPUS Archives & Research Center

Subject Interests: Cross-cultural studies, Mythology, Psychol, Relig studies, Research methodology
Partic in Northern & Central California Psychology Libraries

CARSON

C CALIFORNIA STATE UNIVERSITY DOMINGUEZ HILLS*, University Library, 1000 E Victoria St, 90747. SAN 300-6549. Tel: 310-243-3700. Circulation Tel: 310-243-3712. Interlibrary Loan Service Tel: 310-243-3716. Reference Tel: 310-243-3586. Information Services Tel: 310-243-3715. FAX: 310-516-4219. Web Site: www.csudh.edu/library. *Dean of Libr,* Stephanie Brasley; E-mail: sbrasley@csudh.edu; *Assoc Dean,* Marwin Britto; Tel: 310-243-2207, E-mail: mbritto@csudh.edu; *Dir, Archives & Spec Coll,* Gregory Williams; Tel: 310-243-3013, E-mail: gwilliams@csudh.edu; *Electronic Res Librn,* Wei Ma; Tel: 310-243-2085, E-mail: wma@csudh.edu; *Open Education Librn,* Cristina Springfield; Tel: 310-243-2062, E-mail: cspringfield@csudh.edu; *ILL Coordr,* Karla Salinas; Tel: 310-243-3758, E-mail: ksalinas@csudh.edu; *Ref Coordr,* Maggie Clarke; Tel: 310-243-2084, E-mail: mclarke@csudh.edu; *Coordr, User Serv,* Joanna Messer Kimmitt; Tel: 310-243-2088, E-mail: jkimmitt@csudh.edu; *Libr Syst Spec,* Robert Downs; Tel: 310-243-2404, E-mail: rdowns@csudh.edu; *Archivist, Cataloger,* Thomas Philo; Tel: 310-243-3361, E-mail: tphilo@csudh.edu; *Acq Asst,* Shilo Moreno; Tel: 310-243-2850, E-mail: smoreno@csudh.edu; *Asst to the Dean of Libraries,* Alyse Freeman; Tel: 310-243-2305, E-mail: afreeman@csudh.edu. Subject Specialists: *Develop, Grants,* Gregory Williams; Staff 12 (MLS 10, Non-MLS 2)
Founded 1965. Enrl 9,038; Fac 680; Highest Degree: Master
Library Holdings: AV Mats 10,438; Bk Vols 434,328; Per Subs 669
Special Collections: American Best Sellers (Claudia Buckner Coll); Archives of California State Univ Syst. State Document Depository; US Document Depository
Automation Activity & Vendor Info: (Acquisitions) Innovative Interfaces, Inc; (Cataloging) Innovative Interfaces, Inc; (Circulation) Innovative Interfaces, Inc; (Course Reserve) Innovative Interfaces, Inc; (ILL) Innovative Interfaces, Inc; (Serials) Innovative Interfaces, Inc
Wireless access
Function: Distance learning, Electronic databases & coll, Govt ref serv, ILL available, Online cat, Ref serv available, Telephone ref
Partic in OCLC Online Computer Library Center, Inc
Open Mon-Thurs 8-7, Fri 8-5, Sat 10-5
Friends of the Library Group

CERRITOS

P CERRITOS LIBRARY*, 18025 Bloomfield Ave, 90703. SAN 300-6611. Tel: 562-916-1350. Circulation Tel: 562-916-1340. Reference Tel: 562-916-1342. Administration Tel: 562-916-1378. FAX: 562-916-1375. E-mail: library@cerritos.us. Web Site: menu.ci.cerritos.ca.us. *City Librn,* Annie Hylton; E-mail: ahylton@cerritos.us; *Head, Adult Serv,* Marie Furrows; E-mail: marie_furrows@ci.cerritos.ca.us; *Syst Librn,* Steve Henderson; E-mail: steve_henderson@ci.cerritos.ca.us; Staff 11 (MLS 9.5, Non-MLS 1.5)
Founded 1973. Pop 54,834; Circ 971,057
Library Holdings: AV Mats 23,992; CDs 4,296; DVDs 6,442; e-books 2,700; Bk Titles 266,133; Bk Vols 237,797; Per Subs 243; Talking Bks 2,053; Videos 12,715
Special Collections: Art of the Book: the Book as Art (Artists' Books); First Ladies' Coll; Performing Arts Coll
Automation Activity & Vendor Info: (Acquisitions) BiblioMondo; (Cataloging) BiblioMondo; (Circulation) BiblioMondo; (ILL) OCLC; (OPAC) BiblioMondo
Wireless access
Function: Archival coll, Art exhibits, Bk club(s), CD-ROM, Computer training, Electronic databases & coll, Games & aids for people with disabilities, ILL available, Internet access, Large print keyboards, Magnifiers for reading, Mail & tel request accepted, Music CDs, Online ref, Orientations, Photocopying/Printing, Prog for adults, Prog for children & young adult, Ref & res, Ref serv available, Senior computer classes, Spoken cassettes & CDs, Spoken cassettes & DVDs, Summer reading prog, Tax forms, Telephone ref, VHS videos, Wheelchair accessible, Workshops
Partic in OCLC Online Computer Library Center, Inc
Special Services for the Deaf - Assisted listening device; Assistive tech; Bks on deafness & sign lang; Closed caption videos
Special Services for the Blind - Assistive/Adapted tech devices, equip & products; Audio mat; Bks on cassette; Bks on CD; Closed circuit TV magnifier; Computer with voice synthesizer for visually impaired persons; Copier with enlargement capabilities; Large print & cassettes; Large print bks; Low vision equip; Magnifiers; Networked computers with assistive software; PC for people with disabilities; Scanner for conversion & translation of mats; Screen enlargement software for people with visual disabilities; Screen reader software; Text reader; ZoomText magnification & reading software
Open Mon-Fri 10-9, Sat 9-5, Sun 1-5
Friends of the Library Group

CHATSWORTH

S CHATSWORTH HISTORICAL SOCIETY*, Frank H Schepler Jr & William F Schepler Memorial Library, 10385 Shadow Oak Dr, 91311. SAN 371-2435. Tel: 818-882-5614. FAX: 818-882-5614. E-mail: chatsworthhistory@gmail.com. Web Site: www.chatsworthhistory.com. *Co-Pres,* Andre van der Valk; *Co-Pres,* Linda van der Valk
Library Holdings: Bk Titles 500
Special Collections: Photographs of San Fernando Valley History; San Fernando Valley & California History (Lila & Bill Schepler Book Coll); Slide Coll
Subject Interests: Geog, Local authors
Function: Res libr
Restriction: Open by appt only

C PHILLIPS GRADUATE UNIVERSITY LIBRARY, 19900 Plummer St, 91311. SAN 300-8908. Tel: 818-386-5640. FAX: 818-386-5696. E-mail: library@pgu.edu. Web Site: www.pgu.edu. *Dir, Libr Serv,* Caroline Sisneros; Tel: 818-386-5642, E-mail: csisneros@pgu.edu; *Circ,* Linda Folse; Staff 3 (MLS 1, Non-MLS 2)
Founded 1981. Highest Degree: Doctorate
Library Holdings: Audiobooks 1,200; AV Mats 1,800; CDs 800; e-books 1,000; e-journals 31; Bk Vols 9,800; Per Subs 75
Subject Interests: Family therapy, Marriage, Organizational behavior, Psychol, Sch counseling
Automation Activity & Vendor Info: (Acquisitions) EOS International; (Cataloging) EOS International; (Circulation) EOS International; (OPAC) EOS International; (Serials) EOS International
Wireless access
Function: Res libr
Partic in Medical Library Group of Southern California & Arizona; OCLC Online Computer Library Center, Inc
Special Services for the Deaf - Coll on deaf educ

CHICO

C CALIFORNIA STATE UNIVERSITY, CHICO*, Meriam Library, 400 W First St, 95929-0295. SAN 300-6646. Tel: 530-898-6501. FAX: 530-898-4443. Web Site: library.csuchico.edu. *Dean of Libr,* Patrick Newell; E-mail: pnewell@csuchico.edu; *Vice Provost & CIO, Info Res,* Michael Schilling; Tel: 530-898-6209, E-mail: mlschilling@csuchico.edu; *Head, Acq & Coll Serv,* Jodi Shepherd; Tel: 530-898-5499, E-mail: jrshepherd@csuchico.edu; *Head, Coll Mgt & Tech Serv,* Marc Langston; Tel: 530-898-4587, E-mail: mlangston@csuchico.edu; *Head, Spec Coll & Archives,* George Thompson; Tel: 530-898-6603, E-mail: ghthompson@csuchico.edu; *Res, Instruction & Outreach Librn,* Sarah Blakeslee; Tel: 530-898-4244, E-mail: sblakeslee@csuchico.edu; Staff 35.3 (MLS 11, Non-MLS 24.3)
Founded 1887. Enrl 16,470; Fac 862; Highest Degree: Master. Sal $2,185,244 (Prof $842,663)
Library Holdings: Bk Vols 930,321; Per Subs 534
Special Collections: Northeast California Coll, photog & print. Oral History; US Document Depository
Automation Activity & Vendor Info: (Acquisitions) Innovative Interfaces, Inc; (Cataloging) Innovative Interfaces, Inc; (Circulation) Innovative Interfaces, Inc; (Course Reserve) Innovative Interfaces, Inc; (ILL) OCLC ILLiad; (OPAC) Innovative Interfaces, Inc; (Serials) Innovative Interfaces, Inc
Wireless access
Mem of NorthNet Library System
Open Mon-Thurs 7:30am-11:45pm, Fri 7:30-5:45, Sat Noon-4:45, Sun Noon-11:45

CHINA LAKE

A UNITED STATES NAVY*, Naval Air Warfare Center Weapons Division Technical Library, One Administration Circle, Stop 6203, 93555-6100. Tel: 760-939-3389. Interlibrary Loan Service Tel: 760-939-4132. FAX: 760-939-2431. E-mail: nwtechlib@navy.mil. *Dir,* Sang Park; Staff 7 (MLS 4, Non-MLS 3)
Founded 1946
Library Holdings: Bk Vols 40,000; Per Subs 400
Subject Interests: Aerospace, Chem, Computer sci, Electronics, Engr, Math, Naval sci, Physics, Weapons
Automation Activity & Vendor Info: (Acquisitions) SirsiDynix; (Cataloging) SirsiDynix; (Circulation) SirsiDynix; (OPAC) SirsiDynix; (Serials) SirsiDynix
Partic in Consortium of Naval Libraries
Restriction: Authorized personnel only, Not open to pub, Restricted access

CHULA VISTA

P CHULA VISTA PUBLIC LIBRARY*, Civic Center, 365 F St, 91910-2697. SAN 300-6662. Tel: 619-691-5069. Administration Tel: 619-585-5689. FAX: 619-427-4246. Web Site: www.chulavistalibrary.com.

Libr Dir, Joy Whatley; Tel: 619-691-5170, E-mail: jwhatley@chulavistaca.gov; Staff 12 (MLS 10, Non-MLS 2)
Founded 1891. Pop 246,496; Circ 952,847
Library Holdings: CDs 15,041; DVDs 16,701; Electronic Media & Resources 750; Bk Vols 412,649
Subject Interests: Genealogy, Local hist
Automation Activity & Vendor Info: (Acquisitions) Baker & Taylor; (Cataloging) Innovative Interfaces, Inc - Millennium; (Circulation) Innovative Interfaces, Inc - Millennium; (OPAC) Innovative Interfaces, Inc - Millennium; (Serials) Innovative Interfaces, Inc - Millennium
Wireless access
Function: Art exhibits, Audiobks via web, Bilingual assistance for Spanish patrons, Bk club(s), Bks on CD, Children's prog, Computers for patron use, Digital talking bks, E-Reserves, Electronic databases & coll, Genealogy discussion group, Holiday prog, ILL available, Music CDs, Online cat, OverDrive digital audio bks, Passport agency, Photocopying/Printing, Prog for adults, Prog for children & young adult, Story hour, Summer & winter reading prog, Tax forms, Telephone ref, Wheelchair accessible
Publications: Calendar of Events (Monthly); Library Brochure; Library Buzz (Newsletter)
Partic in OCLC Online Computer Library Center, Inc; Serra Cooperative Library System
Open Mon-Thurs 10-8, Fri & Sat 10-5, Sun 1-5
Friends of the Library Group
Branches: 2
SOUTH CHULA VISTA, 389 Orange Ave, 91911-4116, SAN 370-2952. Tel: 619-585-5750. FAX: 619-420-1591. *Br Mgr,* Joy Whatley; Tel: 619-585-5786, E-mail: jwhatley@chulavista.lib.ca.us; Staff 4 (MLS 4)
Founded 1995. Pop 21,727; Circ 350,084
Library Holdings: Bk Vols 160,395
Function: Adult literacy prog, After school storytime, Art exhibits, Bilingual assistance for Spanish patrons, Bks on CD, Children's prog, Citizenship assistance, Computer training, Computers for patron use, E-Reserves, Electronic databases & coll, Holiday prog, Homework prog, ILL available, Literacy & newcomer serv, Mail & tel request accepted, Music CDs, Online cat, Outreach serv, Photocopying/Printing, Preschool outreach, Prog for adults, Prog for children & young adult, Ref & res, Story hour, Summer reading prog, Tax forms, Teen prog, Telephone ref
Open Mon-Wed 11-8, Thurs & Fri 10-6, Sat 10-2
Friends of the Library Group

J SOUTHWESTERN COLLEGE LIBRARY*, 900 Otay Lakes Rd, Bldg 64, 91910-7299. SAN 300-6689. Circulation Tel: 619-482-6397. Information Services Tel: 619-421-6700, Ext 5381. E-mail: library@swccd.edu. Web Site: www.swccd.edu/student-support/library/index.aspx. *Dean,* Mink Stavenga; Tel: 619-482-6569, E-mail: mstavenga@swccd.edu; *Librn,* Naomi Trapp Davis; E-mail: ntrapp@swccd.edu; Staff 11 (MLS 6, Non-MLS 5)
Founded 1961. Enrl 18,597; Fac 752; Highest Degree: Associate
Library Holdings: High Interest/Low Vocabulary Bk Vols 487; Bk Titles 79,946; Bk Vols 86,539; Per Subs 240
Automation Activity & Vendor Info: (Cataloging) SirsiDynix; (Circulation) SirsiDynix; (OPAC) SirsiDynix
Wireless access
Partic in OCLC Online Computer Library Center, Inc
Special Services for the Deaf - TDD equip
Friends of the Library Group

CITY OF INDUSTRY

S WORKMAN & TEMPLE FAMILY HOMESTEAD MUSEUM LIBRARY, 15415 E Don Julian Rd, 91745-1029. SAN 374-793X. Tel: 626-968-8492. E-mail: info@homesteadmuseum.org. Web Site: www.homesteadmuseum.org/research-collection. *Dir,* Paul R Spitzzeri; E-mail: p.spitzzeri@homesteadmuseum.org
Founded 1981
Library Holdings: Bk Vols 2,500; Per Subs 40
Special Collections: Pre-1930 Imprints; Southern California & California History, 1830-1930
Subject Interests: Archit, Decorative art, Interior design, Mus admin
Function: Photocopying/Printing
Restriction: Non-circulating, Open by appt only

CLAREMONT

S CALIFORNIA BOTANIC GARDEN LIBRARY*, 1500 N College Ave, 91711. SAN 300-6751. Tel: 909-625-8767, Ext 210. FAX: 909-626-7670. Web Site: www.calbg.org/collections/library-archives. *Libr Spec,* Irene Holiman; E-mail: iholiman@calbg.org; Staff 2 (MLS 1, Non-MLS 1)
Founded 1927
Library Holdings: e-journals 1,000; Bk Vols 56,000; Per Subs 600
Special Collections: Californiana; Marcus E Jones Archival Materials
Subject Interests: Biology, Botany, Conserv, Evolution, Hort
Automation Activity & Vendor Info: (Cataloging) OCLC
Partic in OCLC Online Computer Library Center, Inc
Restriction: Non-circulating, Open by appt only

C CLAREMONT COLLEGES LIBRARY*, Honnold-Mudd Library, 800 Dartmouth Ave, 91711. SAN 331-7765. Tel: 909-621-8014. E-mail: library@claremont.edu. Web Site: library.claremont.edu. *Dean of Libr,* Janet Bishop; E-mail: janet.bishop@claremont.edu; Staff 26.5 (MLS 24, Non-MLS 2.5)
Founded 1887. Enrl 7,574; Fac 723; Highest Degree: Doctorate
Jul 2016-Jun 2017 Income $12,398,373. Mats Exp $5,233,178. Sal $3,345,590 (Prof $1,932,078)
Library Holdings: e-books 881,347; e-journals 133,046; Electronic Media & Resources 91,223; Bk Titles 995,122; Bk Vols 1,023,687; Per Subs 22,335
Special Collections: Cartography of the Pacific Coast; Claremont Colleges Archives; Honnold Library: Calif & Western Americana; Irving Wallace; Northern Europe & Scandinavia; Oxford & its Colleges; Philbrick Library of Dramatic Arts; Renaissance; Water Resources of Southern Calif, bk, ms. Oral History; State Document Depository; US Document Depository
Subject Interests: Art, Bus & mgt, Econ, Educ, Environ studies, Hist, Law, Lit, Music, Natural sci, Relig, Soc sci & issues, Women's studies
Automation Activity & Vendor Info: (Acquisitions) OCLC Worldshare Management Services; (Cataloging) OCLC Worldshare Management Services; (Circulation) OCLC Worldshare Management Services; (Course Reserve) OCLC Worldshare Management Services; (Discovery) OCLC Worldshare Management Services; (ILL) OCLC ILLiad; (OPAC) OCLC Worldshare Management Services; (Serials) OCLC Worldshare Management Services
Wireless access
Partic in Center for Research Libraries; Coalition for Networked Information; Digital Libr Fedn; Greater Western Library Alliance; Oberlin Group; Statewide California Electronic Library Consortium
Restriction: Restricted access
Departmental Libraries:
ELLA STRONG DENISON LIBRARY, Scripps College, 1090 N Columbia Ave, 91711. (Mail add: Scripps College, 1030 N Columbia Ave, No 2031, 91711), SAN 331-779X. Tel: 909-607-3941. FAX: 909-607-1548. Web Site: scrippscollege.edu/denison. *Dir & Librn,* Jennifer Martinez Wormser; Tel: 909-621-8973, E-mail: JMWormse@scrippscollege.edu; Staff 4 (MLS 2, Non-MLS 2)
Library Holdings: Bk Vols 55,000; Per Subs 40
Special Collections: Bookplates; Ellen Browning Scripps; Gertrude Stein Coll; History of Book & Book Arts; Juvenilia; Latin America Coll; Macpherson Coll on Women; Melville Coll; Robert & Elizabeth Browning Coll; Southwest Coll
Subject Interests: Art & archit, Humanities, Women's studies
Open Mon-Thurs 10am-Midnight, Fri 10-5, Sat 12-5, Sun Noon-Midnight

CR CLAREMONT SCHOOL OF THEOLOGY LIBRARY*, 1325 N College Ave, 91711. SAN 300-676X. Tel: 909-447-2589. Reference Tel: 909-447-2511. Interlibrary Loan Service E-mail: ILL@cst.edu. Reference E-mail: reference@cst.libanswers.com. Web Site: www.cst.edu/library. *Dean, Libr & Info Tech,* Dr Tom Phillips; Tel: 909-447-2512, E-mail: tphillips@cst.edu; *Asst Libr Dir, Head, Tech Serv,* Drew Baker; Tel: 909-447-2513, E-mail: dbaker@cst.edu; *Acq Librn,* Fiona McMillan; Tel: 909-447-2518, E-mail: fmcmillan@cst.edu; *Circ Librn,* Koala Jones; Tel: 909-447-2510, E-mail: kjones@cst.edu; *Ref Librn,* Maggie Froelich; Tel: 909-447-2516, E-mail: mfroelich@cst.edu; Staff 7 (MLS 4, Non-MLS 3)
Founded 1957. Enrl 395; Fac 33; Highest Degree: Doctorate
Library Holdings: Bk Vols 192,000; Per Subs 641
Special Collections: James C Baker Manuscripts; Kirby Page Manuscripts; Robert H Mitchell Hymnology Coll
Subject Interests: Biblical studies
Wireless access
Partic in OCLC Online Computer Library Center, Inc
Open Mon & Fri 9-7, Tues-Thurs 9am-10pm, Sat 9-5
Departmental Libraries:
CENTER FOR PROCESS STUDIES, 1325 N College Ave, 91711-3154. Tel: 909-447-2533, 909-621-5330. Circulation Tel: 909-447-2589. FAX: 909-621-2760. E-mail: process@ctr4process.org. Circulation E-mail: cstlibcirc@cst.edu. Web Site: cst.edu/library, www.ctr4process.org. *Dean of Libr, Info Res,* Dr Thomas Phillips; Tel: 909-447-2512, E-mail: tphillips@cst.edu; *Dir,* Andrew Schwartz; Tel: 909-447-2559, E-mail: andrew@ctr4process.org; *Asst Libr Dir,* Dr Drew Baker; E-mail: dbaker@cst.edu; *Acq Librn,* Dr Ann Hidalgo; E-mail: ahidalgo@cst.edu; *Circ Librn,* Koala Jones; E-mail: kjones@cst.edu; Staff 5 (MLS 3, Non-MLS 2)
Founded 1957
Library Holdings: e-books 126,000; e-journals 21,000; Bk Titles 156,000
Subject Interests: Philos, Relig, Theol
Publications: Claremont Press Classic Reprints; Claremont Studies in Hebrew Bible & Septuagint; Claremont Studies in Methodism & Wesleyanism; Claremont Studies in New Testament & Christian Origins;

Claremont Studies in Science and Religion; Process Perspectives (Newsletter); Process Studies (Biannually)
Open Mon-Fri 9-5

CLOVIS

CL SAN JOAQUIN COLLEGE OF LAW LIBRARY, 901 Fifth St, 93612. SAN 300-7669. Tel: 559-323-2100, Ext 121. FAX: 559-323-5566. Web Site: www.sjcl.edu/index.php/library. *Dir,* Mark Masters; Tel: 559-326-1476, E-mail: mmasters@sjcl.edu; *Head, Pub Serv,* Kerry Hanson; E-mail: khanson@sjcl.edu; *Tech Serv Librn,* Cyndee Robinson; E-mail: crobinson@sjcl.edu
Founded 1969
Library Holdings: Bk Vols 80,000; Per Subs 300
Automation Activity & Vendor Info: (Acquisitions) EOS International; (Cataloging) EOS International; (Circulation) EOS International; (OPAC) EOS International; (Serials) EOS International
Wireless access
Open Mon-Thurs 9am-10pm, Fri 9-5, Sat & Sun 10-6

COALINGA

P COALINGA-HURON LIBRARY DISTRICT*, Coalinga District Library, 305 N Fourth St, 93210. SAN 331-8060. Tel: 559-935-1676. FAX: 559-935-1058. Web Site: chld.org. *Dir, Libr Serv,* Mary Leal; E-mail: mary.leal@coalingahuronlibrary.org; *Circ,* Hilda Crawford; *Tech Serv,* Yvonne Galvan; Staff 1 (Non-MLS 1)
Founded 1912. Pop 30,274; Circ 58,058
Jul 2014-Jun 2015 Income (Main & Associated Libraries) $10,127,000, State $10,643, County $943,063, Other $1,406,685. Mats Exp $112,500, Books $91,000, Other Print Mats $6,500, Electronic Ref Mat (Incl. Access Fees) $8,000. Sal $69,568
Library Holdings: Audiobooks 979; AV Mats 3,614; CDs 109; Large Print Bks 1,060; Bk Titles 78,130; Bk Vols 78,276; Per Subs 125; Talking Bks 1,833; Videos 4,260
Subject Interests: Calif, Genealogy, Local hist, Native Am
Automation Activity & Vendor Info: (Acquisitions) Horizon; (Cataloging) Horizon
Wireless access
Mem of San Joaquin Valley Library System
Open Mon-Thurs 10-8, Fri & Sat 10-5
Branches: 1
HURON BRANCH, 36050 O St, Huron, 93234. (Mail add: PO Box 190, Huron, 93234-0190), SAN 331-8095. Tel: 559-945-2284. FAX: 559-945-2855. *Br Spec,* Melba McHaney
Library Holdings: Bk Vols 18,000; Per Subs 45
Open Mon-Thurs 10-7

J WEST HILLS COMMUNITY COLLEGE*, Fitch Library, 300 Cherry Lane, 93210. SAN 331-8125. Tel: 559-934-2420. Web Site: www.westhillscollege.com. *Librn,* Matthew Magnuson; Tel: 559-934-2403, E-mail: MatthewMagnuson@whccd.edu; Staff 3 (MLS 1, Non-MLS 2)
Founded 1956. Enrl 2,100; Fac 41
Library Holdings: High Interest/Low Vocabulary Bk Vols 2,000; Bk Vols 44,000; Per Subs 112
Subject Interests: Chicano studies, Corrections, English as a second lang, Graphic novels, Studio art
Automation Activity & Vendor Info: (Cataloging) SirsiDynix; (Circulation) SirsiDynix; (Course Reserve) SirsiDynix
Wireless access
Partic in Heartland Regional Library Network of the Library of California
Open Mon-Thurs (Fall & Spring) 7:30am-8pm, Fri 7:30-4

COLTON

M ARROWHEAD REGIONAL MEDICAL CENTER*, Health Sciences Library, 400 N Pepper Ave, 92324-1819. SAN 301-3014. Tel: 909-580-1300. FAX: 909-580-1310. *Dir, Libr Serv,* ; *ILL, Libr Asst,* Marisa Luna; Tel: 909-580-1308, E-mail: lunam@armc.sbcounty.gov; Staff 2 (MLS 1, Non-MLS 1)
Library Holdings: e-books 1,704; e-journals 7,503; Bk Titles 2,800; Per Subs 313
Subject Interests: Med
Automation Activity & Vendor Info: (Acquisitions) EOS International; (Cataloging) EOS International; (Circulation) EOS International; (OPAC) EOS International; (Serials) EOS International
Wireless access
Function: ILL available, Res libr
Publications: San Bernardino County Medical Center Library Brochure
Partic in Inland Empire Med Libr Coop; Medical Library Group of Southern California & Arizona; Pacific Southwest Regional Medical Library; San Bernardino, Inyo, Riverside Counties United Library Services
Restriction: Med staff only

P COLTON PUBLIC LIBRARY*, 656 N Ninth St, 92324. SAN 300-6778. Tel: 909-370-5083. Web Site: www.ci.colton.ca.us/index.aspx?NID=134. *Libr Supvr,* Edward Pedroza; Tel: 909-370-5189, E-mail: epedroza@ci.colton.ca.us; Staff 14 (MLS 1, Non-MLS 13)
Founded 1906. Pop 49,100; Circ 353,365
Library Holdings: Bk Titles 88,060; Bk Vols 99,826; Per Subs 300
Automation Activity & Vendor Info: (Cataloging) SirsiDynix; (Circulation) SirsiDynix; (OPAC) SirsiDynix
Wireless access
Mem of Inland Library System
Open Mon, Fri & Sat 10-6, Wed 12-8
Friends of the Library Group
Branches: 1
LUQUE BRANCH, 294 East O St, 92324, SAN 329-2673. Tel: 909-370-5182. FAX: 909-370-5182. *Br Supvr,* Edward Pedroza; Tel: 909-370-5189, E-mail: epedroza@ci.colton.ca.us; Staff 1 (Non-MLS 1)

COLUSA

P COLUSA COUNTY FREE LIBRARY*, 738 Market St, 95932. SAN 376-3722. Tel: 530-458-7671. FAX: 530-458-7358. Web Site: www.countyofcolusa.org/library. *County Librn,* Stacy Zwald Costello; E-mail: scostello@countyofcolusa.org; Staff 6 (MLS 1, Non-MLS 5)
Founded 1915. Pop 21,951; Circ 39,651
Library Holdings: AV Mats 4,700; Bk Vols 96,835; Per Subs 77; Videos 5,814
Special Collections: California Indian Library Coll (Colusa County); Colusa County History Coll
Automation Activity & Vendor Info: (Cataloging) Innovative Interfaces, Inc; (Circulation) Innovative Interfaces, Inc; (ILL) Innovative Interfaces, Inc; (OPAC) Innovative Interfaces, Inc
Wireless access
Function: Adult literacy prog, Bilingual assistance for Spanish patrons, Bks on cassette, Bks on CD, Children's prog, Computers for patron use, Family literacy, ILL available, Online cat, Photocopying/Printing, Ref serv available, Story hour, Summer reading prog, Telephone ref, VHS videos, Wheelchair accessible
Mem of NorthNet Library System
Open Mon 9-2, Tues & Thurs 10-8, Wed & Fri 10-5, Sat 10-2
Friends of the Library Group
Branches: 6
ARBUCKLE BRANCH, 610 King St, Arbuckle, 95912. Tel: 530-476-2526. FAX: 530-476-2526. E-mail: arbucklelibrary@countyofcolusa.org. *Library Contact,* Penny Walgenbach
Library Holdings: Bk Vols 2,500
Open Mon & Wed 1-6, Tues 10-3
Friends of the Library Group
GRIMES BRANCH, 240 Main St, Grimes, 95950. Tel: 530-437-2428. FAX: 530-437-2428. E-mail: grimeslibrary@countyofcolusa.org. *Library Contact,* Juana Rodriguez
Library Holdings: Bk Vols 7,600
Open Tues & Thurs 2-7
Friends of the Library Group
MAXWELL BRANCH, 34 Oak St, Maxwell, 95955. Tel: 530-438-2250. FAX: 530-438-2250. E-mail: maxwelllibrary@countyofcolusa.org. *Library Contact,* Maria Iniguez
Library Holdings: Bk Vols 7,000
Open Tues-Thurs 1:30-6
Friends of the Library Group
PRINCETON BRANCH, 232 Prince St, Princeton, 95970. Tel: 530-439-2235. FAX: 530-439-2235. E-mail: princetonlibrary@countyofcolusa.org. *Library Contact,* Mary Beth Massa; E-mail: mbmassa2002@yahoo.com; *Library Contact,* Melissa Roach
Library Holdings: Bk Vols 10,000
Open Tues 8-1, Wed 8-5
Friends of the Library Group
STONYFORD BRANCH, 5080 Stonyford-Lodoga Rd, Stonyford, 95979. Tel: 530-963-3722. E-mail: stonyfordlibrary@countyofcolusa.org. *Library Contact,* Jeff Applegate; *Library Contact,* Ms Rashell Sachez
Library Holdings: Bk Vols 3,000
Open Wed 11-5:30, Thurs 12-6, Sat 10-2
Friends of the Library Group
WILLIAMS BRANCH, 901 E St, Williams, 95987. (Mail add: PO Box 517, Williams, 95987-0517). Tel: 530-473-5955. FAX: 530-473-5955. E-mail: williamslibrary@countyofcolusa.org. *Library Contact,* Perla Tineda Ramirez
Library Holdings: Bk Vols 8,500
Open Tues & Thurs 12-5, Wed 1-6
Friends of the Library Group

COMMERCE

P CITY OF COMMERCE PUBLIC LIBRARY*, Rosewood Library, 5655 Jillson St, 90040. SAN 331-8338. Tel: 323-722-6660. Reference Tel: 323-722-6660, Ext 2275. FAX: 323-724-1978. E-mail: reference1@ci.commerce.ca.us. Web Site: www.cityofcommercepubliclibrary.org. *Dir, Libr Serv,* Beatriz Sarmiento; E-mail: director.library@ci.commerce.ca.us; *Social Servs Coord,* Ed Saucedo; Staff 70 (MLS 8, Non-MLS 62)
Founded 1961. Pop 13,504; Circ 161,880
Library Holdings: AV Mats 11,994; CDs 4,053; DVDs 3,446; High Interest/Low Vocabulary Bk Vols 600; Large Print Bks 884; Bk Titles 80,098; Bk Vols 131,796; Per Subs 399; Talking Bks 978; Videos 5,540
Automation Activity & Vendor Info: (Cataloging) SirsiDynix; (Circulation) SirsiDynix; (ILL) OCLC Online; (OPAC) SirsiDynix; (Serials) SirsiDynix
Wireless access
Function: Art exhibits, BA reader (adult literacy), Home delivery & serv to seniorr ctr & nursing homes, ILL available, Magnifiers for reading, Music CDs, Photocopying/Printing, Prog for adults, Prog for children & young adult, Ref serv available, Spoken cassettes & CDs, Summer reading prog, VHS videos, Workshops
Partic in Southern California Library Cooperative
Open Mon-Thurs 10-8, Fri 10-6, Sat 10-2
Branches: 3
BANDINI LIBRARY, 2269 S Atlantic Blvd, 90040, SAN 377-5712. Tel: 323-887-4494. *Libr Supvr,* Cris Muniz; Staff 7 (Non-MLS 7)
Founded 1996. Circ 32,289
Library Holdings: CDs 857; DVDs 558; Bk Titles 12,532; Bk Vols 13,909; Per Subs 46; Videos 544
Function: Photocopying/Printing, Prog for children & young adult, Ref serv available, Summer reading prog
Open Mon-Thurs 1-8, Fri 10-5, Sat 10-3
BRISTOW LIBRARY, 1466 S McDonnell Ave, 90040, SAN 378-1852. Tel: 323-887-4492. *Libr Supvr,* Luis Martinez; Staff 7 (Non-MLS 7)
Founded 1988. Circ 37,783
Library Holdings: CDs 475; DVDs 662; Bk Titles 14,214; Bk Vols 16,386; Per Subs 71; Videos 882
Function: Photocopying/Printing, Prog for children & young adult, Ref serv available, Summer reading prog
Open Mon-Thurs 1-8, Fri 10-5, Sat 10-3
VETERANS LIBRARY, 6134 Greenwood Ave, 90040, SAN 378-1879. Tel: 562-887-4493. *Libr Supvr,* Victoria Perez; Staff 7 (Non-MLS 7)
Founded 1966. Circ 39,834
Library Holdings: CDs 512; DVDs 633; Bk Titles 14,017; Bk Vols 15,514; Per Subs 59; Videos 791
Function: Adult bk club, After school storytime, Bilingual assistance for Spanish patrons, Bks on CD, Children's prog, Computer training, Computers for patron use, Free DVD rentals, Holiday prog, Homebound delivery serv, Homework prog, ILL available, Internet access, Learning ctr, Mail & tel request accepted, Music CDs, Online cat, Online info literacy tutorials on the web & in blackboard, Orientations, Photocopying/Printing, Preschool outreach, Prog for children & young adult, Summer reading prog, Tax forms, Teen prog, VHS videos, Wheelchair accessible, Workshops
Open Mon-Thurs 1-8, Fri 10-5, Sat 10-3

COMPTON

J COMPTON COMMUNITY COLLEGE LIBRARY*, Emily B Hart-Holifield Library, 1111 E Artesia Blvd, 90221. SAN 300-6816. Tel: 310-900-1600, Ext 2175. FAX: 310-900-1693. E-mail: library@compton.edu. Web Site: www.compton.edu/library. *Adjunct Librn,* Estina Pratt; E-mail: epratt@compton.edu; *Acq, Ref Librn,* Andree Valdry; E-mail: avaldry@compton.edu
Founded 1927. Highest Degree: Associate
Library Holdings: AV Mats 384; CDs 100; High Interest/Low Vocabulary Bk Vols 804; Bk Titles 32,391; Bk Vols 39,277; Per Subs 139
Automation Activity & Vendor Info: (Acquisitions) Ex Libris Group; (Cataloging) Ex Libris Group; (Circulation) Ex Libris Group; (OPAC) Ex Libris Group
Wireless access
Function: For res purposes
Open Mon-Thurs 8-8, Fri & Sat 8-4 (Winter); Mon-Thurs 8-6 (Summer)

CONCORD

S CALRECOVERY INC LIBRARY*, 2454 Stanwell Dr, 94520. SAN 373-4951. Tel: 925-356-3700. FAX: 925-356-7956. E-mail: mail@calrecovery.com. Web Site: www.calrecovery.com. *Librn,* Cheryl Henry
Founded 1975
Library Holdings: Bk Vols 7,000; Per Subs 20
Open Mon-Fri 8-4

CORONA

P CORONA PUBLIC LIBRARY, 650 S Main St, 92882. SAN 300-6824. Tel: 951-736-2381. Circulation Tel: 951-279-3737. Administration Tel: 951-736-2384. FAX: 951-736-2499. Web Site: coronaca.gov/government/departments/library. *Asst Dir,* Abigail Lenning; Tel: 951-279-3728, E-mail: Abigail.Lenning@CoronaCA.gov; *Libr Supvr,* Betty Luscher; Tel: 951-736-2389, E-mail: bettyl@CoronaCA.gov; *Libr Supvr,* Chris-Tina Smith; Tel: 951-739-4860, E-mail: chris-tinas@CoronaCA.gov; Staff 7 (MLS 7)
Founded 1899. Pop 165,000; Circ 370,002
Library Holdings: Bk Vols 116,000; Per Subs 100
Special Collections: Calif; Corona Newspaper Archives, photographs. Oral History
Subject Interests: Local hist
Automation Activity & Vendor Info: (Acquisitions) Koha; (Cataloging) Koha; (Circulation) Koha; (OPAC) Koha; (Serials) Koha
Wireless access
Function: 24/7 Electronic res, 24/7 Online cat, Adult bk club, Adult literacy prog
Mem of Inland Library System
Open Mon-Wed 10-9, Thurs & Fri 10-5, Sat 12-5
Friends of the Library Group

CORONA DEL MAR

S SHERMAN LIBRARY & GARDENS*, 2647 E Pacific Coast Hwy, 92625. SAN 300-6832. Tel: 949-673-1880. FAX: 949-675-5458. Web Site: www.slgardens.org/library. *Libr Dir,* Paul Wormser; E-mail: paul@slgardens.org; *Librn,* Jill Thrasher; E-mail: jill@slgardens.org; Staff 3 (MLS 1, Non-MLS 2)
Founded 1966
Library Holdings: Bk Vols 25,000
Subject Interests: Hist of the Pacific Southwest
Open Mon-Fri 10:30-4
Restriction: Non-circulating, Not a lending libr

CORONADO

P CORONADO PUBLIC LIBRARY*, 640 Orange Ave, 92118-1526. SAN 300-6840. Tel: 619-522-7390. Administration Tel: 619-522-2475. FAX: 619-435-4205. Web Site: www.coronado.ca.us/government/departments_divisions/library_services. *Dir,* Shaun R Briley; E-mail: sbriley@coronado.ca.us; *Head, Circ,* Christopher Morris; Tel: 619-522-2472, E-mail: cmorris@coronado.lib.ca.us; *Sr Librn, Tech Serv,* Vy Tu; Tel: 619-522-2473, E-mail: vtu@coronado.lib.ca.us; *Principal Librn,* Glenn Risolo; Tel: 619-522-2470, E-mail: grisolo@coronado.lib.ca.us; Staff 9 (MLS 9)
Founded 1890. Pop 23,916; Circ 357,841
Library Holdings: Audiobooks 3,357; AV Mats 21,168; CDs 6,908; DVDs 12,260; Large Print Bks 2,910; Microforms 86; Bk Titles 137,040; Bk Vols 161,048; Per Subs 339; Videos 727
Special Collections: Coronado Government Documents; Coronado Local History Photograph & Map Coll
Subject Interests: Gardening, Local hist, Spec operations, World War II
Automation Activity & Vendor Info: (Acquisitions) Innovative Interfaces, Inc - Millennium; (Cataloging) Innovative Interfaces, Inc; (Circulation) Innovative Interfaces, Inc; (OPAC) Innovative Interfaces, Inc - Millennium
Wireless access
Function: Online cat
Publications: Calendar of Events; Summer Reading Brochure; The Story of the Ramos Martinez Murals & the La Avenida Cafe
Partic in OCLC Online Computer Library Center, Inc; Serra Cooperative Library System
Open Mon-Thurs 10-9, Fri & Sat 10-6, Sun 1-5
Friends of the Library Group

COSTA MESA

J ORANGE COAST COLLEGE LIBRARY*, 2701 Fairview Rd, 92626. (Mail add: PO Box 5005, 92626-5005), SAN 300-6905. Tel: 714-432-5885. Circulation Tel: 714-432-5705. Reference Tel: 714-432-5900. FAX: 714-432-6850. Web Site: www.orangecoastcollege.edu/academics/library/Pages/default.aspx. *Dean, Libr & Learning Support,* John Taylor; E-mail: jtaylor174@occ.cccd.edu; *Acq Librn,* Carl Morgan; E-mail: cmorgan@occ.cccd.edu; *Archives Librn, Cat & Per Librn,* Jodi Della Marna; E-mail: jdellamarna@occ.cccd.edu; *Instrul Design Librn,* Lori Cassidy; E-mail: lcassidy@occ.cccd.edu; *Instrul Serv Librn,* Erin Gratz; E-mail: egratz@occ.cccd.edu; *Pub Serv Librn,* John Dale; E-mail: jdale@occ.cccd.edu; *Syst Librn,* Ward Smith; E-mail: wsmith30@occ.cccd.edu; Staff 15 (MLS 9, Non-MLS 6)
Founded 1948. Highest Degree: Associate
Library Holdings: AV Mats 3,462; e-books 18,747; Bk Titles 93,529; Bk Vols 95,000; Per Subs 212

Automation Activity & Vendor Info: (Cataloging) Ex Libris Group; (Circulation) Ex Libris Group; (Course Reserve) Ex Libris Group; (OPAC) Ex Libris Group; (Serials) Ex Libris Group
Wireless access
Partic in OCLC Online Computer Library Center, Inc
Open Mon-Thurs 7:30am-9pm, Fri 7:30-3, Sat 10-3
Friends of the Library Group

C VANGUARD UNIVERSITY OF SOUTHERN CALIFORNIA*, O Cope Budge Library, 55 Fair Dr, 92626. SAN 300-6913. Tel: 714-966-6381. E-mail: librarystaff@vanguard.edu. Web Site: www.vanguard.edu/academics/library. *Head of Libr,* Pam Crenshaw; Tel: 714-966-6377, E-mail: pcrenshaw@vanguard.edu; *Ref & Instruction Librn,* Elena Nipper; Tel: 714-966-6378, E-mail: enipper@vanguard.edu; *Circ Supvr,* William Morgan; Tel: 714-966-6380, E-mail: jack.morgan@vanguard.edu; Staff 6 (MLS 4, Non-MLS 2)
Founded 1920. Enrl 1,900; Fac 100; Highest Degree: Master
Library Holdings: e-books 37,000; Bk Titles 75,000; Bk Vols 180,000; Per Subs 800
Special Collections: Christian Religion & Judaic Coll; Drama Coll; Nursing Coll; Pentecostal Coll; Spanish Coll
Automation Activity & Vendor Info: (Cataloging) Follett Software; (Circulation) Follett Software; (ILL) OCLC; (OPAC) Follett Software
Wireless access
Partic in OCLC Online Computer Library Center, Inc; Statewide California Electronic Library Consortium
Open Mon-Thurs 7:30am-11pm, Fri 7:30-5, Sat 10-5, Sun 2-8
Friends of the Library Group

L WOODRUFF, SPRADLIN & SMART LIBRARY*, 555 Anton Blvd, Ste 1200, 92626. SAN 301-5416. Tel: 714-558-7000. FAX: 714-835-7787. Web Site: wss-law.com. *Librn,* Christi Anne Kirk; E-mail: christiannekirk@aol.com
Library Holdings: Bk Vols 5,000
Subject Interests: Law
Restriction: Not open to pub

COVINA

C AMERICAN GRADUATE UNIVERSITY LIBRARY, 733 N Dodsworth Ave, 91724. SAN 373-0239. Tel: 626-966-4576, Ext 1001. FAX: 626-915-1709. E-mail: info@agu.edu. Web Site: www.agu.edu. *Library Contact,* Debbie McDonald; E-mail: debbiemcdonald@agu.edu
Library Holdings: Bk Titles 3,500; Per Subs 30
Restriction: Staff use only

P COVINA PUBLIC LIBRARY*, 234 N Second Ave, 91723-2198. SAN 300-6921. Tel: 626-384-5303. Reference Tel: 626-384-5303. Administration Tel: 626-384-5276. E-mail: parksandrecreation@covinaca.gov. Web Site: www.covinaca.gov. *Dir, Libr Serv,* Lisa Evans; *Ch,* Monica Roman; Tel: 626-384-5312, E-mail: mroman@covinaca.gov; *Libr Serv Supvr,* Krizia Virbia; E-mail: kvirbia@covinaca.gov; Staff 9.5 (MLS 1, Non-MLS 8.5)
Founded 1897. Pop 49,541; Circ 162,855
Library Holdings: CDs 4,443; DVDs 4,014; Bk Vols 94,295; Per Subs 161
Automation Activity & Vendor Info: (Cataloging) SirsiDynix; (Circulation) SirsiDynix; (OPAC) SirsiDynix
Wireless access
Function: Accelerated reader prog, Adult bk club, Adult literacy prog, After school storytime, Bks on CD, Children's prog, Computers for patron use, Electronic databases & coll, Family literacy, Holiday prog, Homework prog, ILL available, Large print keyboards, Literacy & newcomer serv, Music CDs, Photocopying/Printing, Preschool reading prog, Prog for adults, Prog for children & young adult, Ref serv available, Scanner, Senior computer classes, Story hour, Telephone ref
Partic in Southern California Library Cooperative
Open Tues & Wed 12-8, Thurs & Fri 11-6, Sat 10-5
Restriction: Non-circulating of rare bks
Friends of the Library Group

CRESCENT CITY

S DEL NORTE COUNTY HISTORICAL SOCIETY MUSEUM LIBRARY*, 577 H St, 95531. SAN 327-3202. Tel: 707-464-3922. FAX: 707-464-7186. E-mail: manager@delnortehistory.org. Web Site: www.delnortehistory.org/museum. *Coordr,* Karen Betlejewski
Founded 1951
Library Holdings: Bk Vols 1,000
Special Collections: Historical Files of Settlement of Del Norte County Area (circa 1800-1900)
Subject Interests: Local hist
Open Mon-Sat (May-Sept)10-4; Mon & Sat (Oct-April) 10-4
Friends of the Library Group

P DEL NORTE COUNTY LIBRARY DISTRICT, 190 Price Mall, 95531-4395. SAN 300-693X. Tel: 707-464-9793. FAX: 707-464-6726. Web Site: www.delnortecountylibrary.org. *Libr Mgr,* Beth Austen; E-mail: bausten@delnortecountylibrary.org; Staff 7 (MLS 1, Non-MLS 6)
Founded 1978. Pop 27,850
Library Holdings: Bk Vols 60,000; Per Subs 48
Special Collections: California Indian Library Coll - Del Norte; Del Norte County History
Automation Activity & Vendor Info: (Cataloging) ByWater Solutions; (Circulation) ByWater Solutions; (OPAC) ByWater Solutions
Wireless access
Function: Family literacy, ILL available, Summer reading prog, Telephone ref
Mem of NorthNet Library System
Open Mon-Sat 10-6
Friends of the Library Group
Branches: 2
DEL NORTE READS, 1080 Mason Mall, No 9, 95531. Tel: 707-464-7072. *Literacy Coordr,* Phoebe Lenhart
Open Mon-Thurs 10-2
SMITH RIVER BRANCH, 241 First St, Smith River, 95567. Tel: 707-487-8048. *Library Contact,* Linda Kaufmann
Bookmobiles: 1

CULVER CITY

S MAYME A CLAYTON LIBRARY & MUSEUM, 4130 Overland Ave, 90230-3734. Tel: 310-202-1647. FAX: 310-202-1617. E-mail: info@claytonmuseum.org. Web Site: www.claytonmuseum.org/visit/library-. *Exec Dir,* Lloyd Clayton; E-mail: MaymeClaytonPR@gmail.com
Library Holdings: AV Mats 1,700; Bk Vols 30,000
Subject Interests: African-Am hist & culture
Wireless access
Restriction: Non-circulating, Researchers by appt only

J WEST LOS ANGELES COLLEGE LIBRARY*, Heldman Learning Resource Center, 9000 Overland Ave, 90230. SAN 309-4618. Tel: 310-287-4408. Reference Tel: 310-287-4269. Administration Tel: 310-287-4401. FAX: 310-287-4366. Web Site: www.wlac.edu/library. *Librn,* Judy Chow; E-mail: chowjc@wlac.edu; *Librn,* Ken Lee; Tel: 310-287-4402, E-mail: leeken@wlac.edu; *Librn,* Susan Trujillo; Tel: 310-287-4406, E-mail: trujls@wlac.edu; Staff 7 (MLS 3, Non-MLS 4)
Founded 1969. Enrl 12,000; Fac 199; Highest Degree: Associate
Library Holdings: AV Mats 150; DVDs 25; e-books 15,000; e-journals 10,500; Bk Titles 69,000; Bk Vols 70,500; Per Subs 95; Videos 350
Special Collections: Law Coll
Automation Activity & Vendor Info: (Acquisitions) Baker & Taylor; (Cataloging) SirsiDynix-WorkFlows; (Circulation) SirsiDynix-Unicorn; (Course Reserve) SirsiDynix-Unicorn; (OPAC) SirsiDynix-Unicorn; (Serials) EBSCO Online
Wireless access
Special Services for the Blind - Low vision equip
Open Mon-Thurs 7:30am-8pm, Fri 9-1, Sat 11-3

CUPERTINO

J DE ANZA COLLEGE*, A Robert DeHart Learning Center, 21250 Stevens Creek Blvd, 95014-5793. SAN 300-6999. Circulation Tel: 408-864-8761. Reference Tel: 408-864-8479. FAX: 408-864-8603. Web Site: www.deanza.edu/library. *Dir,* Tom Dolen; Tel: 408-864-8764, E-mail: dolentom@deanza.edu; *Head, Ref,* Lena Chang; Tel: 408-864-8728, E-mail: changlena@deanza.edu; *Librn,* Pauline Yeckley; Tel: 408-864-8303, E-mail: yeckleypauline@deanza.edu; *Access Serv Librn,* Alex Swanner; Tel: 408-864-8486, E-mail: swanneralex@deanza.edu; *Syst Librn,* Cecilia Hui; Tel: 408-864-8383, E-mail: huicecilia@deanza.edu; *Syst Coordr,* Trung Thai; Tel: 408-846-8438, E-mail: trungthai@deanza.edu; *Syst Coordr,* Quang Thanh; Tel: 408-864-8494, E-mail: thanhquang@deanza.edu; *Acq,* Tracy Lam; Tel: 408-864-8439; *Cat,* Lisa Hatt; Tel: 408-864-8459, E-mail: hattlisa@deanza.edu; *Circ,* Irene Niazov; Tel: 408-864-8763, E-mail: niazovirene@deanza.edu; *Circ/Reserves,* David Byars; Tel: 408-864-8759, E-mail: byarsdavid@deanza.edu; *ILL,* Kathy Munson; Tel: 408-864-8335, E-mail: munsonkathy@deanza.edu; *Media Spec,* Sandy Cardoza; Tel: 408-864-8771, E-mail: cardozasandy@deanza.edu; *Media Spec,* Keri Kirkpatrick; Tel: 408-864-8581, E-mail: kirkpatrickkeri@deanza.edu; Staff 15 (MLS 5, Non-MLS 10)
Founded 1967. Enrl 22,000; Fac 935; Highest Degree: Associate
Library Holdings: Bk Titles 87,000; Bk Vols 110,000; Per Subs 300
Special Collections: Vietnam Conflict (De Cillis Coll). Oral History
Subject Interests: Art & archit, Hist, Spec educ
Automation Activity & Vendor Info: (Acquisitions) SirsiDynix; (Cataloging) SirsiDynix; (OPAC) SirsiDynix
Wireless access
Function: Ref serv available
Special Services for the Deaf - TDD equip
Open Mon-Thurs 8am-9pm, Fri 8-4

CYPRESS

J CYPRESS COLLEGE LIBRARY*, 9200 Valley View St, 90630-5897. SAN 300-7049. Tel: 714-484-7125. Circulation Tel: 714-484-8381. Reference Tel: 714-484-7069. FAX: 714-826-6723. E-mail: librarian@cypresscollege.edu. Web Site: library.cypresscollege.edu/. *Dean, Libr & Learning Res,* Dr Treisa Cassens; Tel: 714-484-7302; *Ref,* Joyce Peacock; Tel: 714-484-7068, E-mail: jpeacock@cypresscollege.edu; *Acq & Per Mgr,* Peggy Austin; Tel: 714-484-7066, E-mail: paustin@cypresscollege.edu; *Cat, Syst,* Monica Doman; Tel: 714-484-7067, E-mail: mdoman@cypresscollege.edu; *Coordr, Instruction & Outreach,* Billy Pashaie; Tel: 714-484-7418, E-mail: wpashaie@cypresscollege.edu; Staff 9 (MLS 4, Non-MLS 5)
Founded 1966. Enrl 16,500; Fac 4; Highest Degree: Associate
Library Holdings: CDs 572; DVDs 2,085; e-books 5,100; Bk Titles 53,948; Bk Vols 62,089; Per Subs 40
Automation Activity & Vendor Info: (Acquisitions) Ex Libris Group; (Cataloging) Ex Libris Group; (Circulation) Ex Libris Group; (Course Reserve) Ex Libris Group; (ILL) OCLC; (OPAC) Ex Libris Group; (Serials) Ex Libris Group
Wireless access
Open Mon-Thurs (Winter) 8am-9pm, Fri 8-1; Mon-Thurs (Summer) 11-7

DALY CITY

P DALY CITY PUBLIC LIBRARY*, Serramonte Main Library, 40 Wembley Dr, 94015-4399. SAN 331-8664. Tel: 650-991-8023. FAX: 650-991-8225. Reference E-mail: library@dalycity.org. Web Site: www.dalycity.org/211/library. *Libr Serv Mgr,* Chela Anderson; Staff 25 (MLS 7, Non-MLS 18)
Founded 1925. Circ 259,703
Special Collections: Philippine History, Culture & Arts (Filipiana)
Automation Activity & Vendor Info: (Acquisitions) Innovative Interfaces, Inc; (Cataloging) Innovative Interfaces, Inc; (Circulation) Innovative Interfaces, Inc; (ILL) OCLC Online; (OPAC) BiblioCommons
Wireless access
Function: 24/7 Electronic res, 24/7 Online cat, Adult bk club, After school storytime, ILL available
Mem of Pacific Library Partnership (PLP)
Partic in Peninsula Libraries Automated Network
Special Services for the Blind - Screen reader software
Open Mon & Tues 10-8, Wed & Fri 10-6
Branches: 3
BAYSHORE, 460 Martin St, 94014, SAN 331-8699. Tel: 650-991-8074. FAX: 415-508-0860. *Librn,* Karen Engle; Staff 2 (MLS 1, Non-MLS 1)
Circ 22,648
Library Holdings: DVDs 1,809; Bk Vols 20,173; Per Subs 41; Talking Bks 335; Videos 460
Open Tues & Thurs 10-6
JOHN D DALY BRANCH, 134 Hillside Blvd, 94014, SAN 331-8729. Tel: 650-991-8073. FAX: 650-757-6547. *Librn,* Joshua Rees
Circ 86,857
Library Holdings: DVDs 2,583; Bk Vols 27,769; Per Subs 60; Talking Bks 469; Videos 281
Open Mon 10-6, Wed 12-8, Fri 12-6
WESTLAKE, 275 Southgate Ave, 94015-3471, SAN 331-8753. Tel: 650-991-8071. FAX: 650-997-3460. *Librn,* Sarah Spence; Staff 4 (MLS 1, Non-MLS 3)
Circ 184,932
Library Holdings: DVDs 3,087; Bk Vols 52,982; Per Subs 40; Talking Bks 972; Videos 1,011
Open Tues 12-8, Wed & Thurs 10-6, Fri 12-6, Sat 10-5

M SETON MEDICAL CENTER*, Health Sciences Library, 1900 Sullivan Ave, Ground Flr Hospital, 94015. SAN 300-7057. Tel: 650-991-6315, 650-991-6700. FAX: 650-991-6638. E-mail: smclibrary@dochs.org. Web Site: www.smc-connect.org/locations/health-sciences-library-at-seton. *Librn,* Jeanie Fraser
Library Holdings: Bk Vols 1,300; Per Subs 128
Subject Interests: Cardiology, Infectious diseases, Med, Orthopedics
Wireless access
Partic in Northern California & Nevada Medical Library Group

DAVIS

R DAVIS COMMUNITY CHURCH LIBRARY*, 412 C St, 95616. SAN 300-7073. Tel: 530-753-2894. FAX: 530-753-0182. E-mail: office@dccpres.org. Web Site: www.dccpres.org.
Library Holdings: Bk Vols 3,015
Automation Activity & Vendor Info: (Cataloging) Follett Software
Open Mon-Thurs 9-2

SR DAVIS FRIENDS MEETING LIBRARY*, 345 L St, 95616. (Mail add: PO Box 4477, 95617-4477), SAN 371-6562. Tel: 530-758-8492. E-mail: info@davisfriendsmeeting.org. Web Site: www.fgcquaker.org/cloud/davis-friends-meeting.
Library Holdings: Bk Titles 1,700; Per Subs 20
Special Collections: Quaker History Coll
Subject Interests: Quaker info
Publications: Annual Report (cumulative 1986-1993); Subject Headings with Supplements

C UNIVERSITY OF CALIFORNIA, DAVIS*, Peter J Shields Library, 100 NW Quad, 95616. SAN 331-8788. Tel: 530-752-8792. Interlibrary Loan Service Tel: 530-752-2251. Reference Tel: 530-752-1126. Administration Tel: 530-752-2110. Automation Services Tel: 530-752-1202. FAX: 530-752-3148. Web Site: www.library.ucdavis.edu/library/peter-j-shields. *Univ Librn,* MacKenzie Smith; E-mail: macsmith@ucdavis.edu; *Chief of Staff, Dep Univ Librn,* William Garrity; E-mail: wgarrity@ucdavis.edu; *Head, Res Support Serv, Interim Assoc Univ Librn,* Beth Callahan; E-mail: bcallahan@ucdavis.edu; *Dir, Admin Serv,* Helen Zaccari; E-mail: hhenry@ucdavis.edu; *Head, Access & Delivery Serv,* Robin Gustafson; E-mail: rlgustafson@ucdavis.edu; *Interim Head, Spec Coll, Univ Archivist,* Kevin Miller; E-mail: kcmiller@ucdavis.edu; *Head, Coll Strategies,* Bob Heyer-Gray; E-mail: rheyer@ucdavis.edu; *Head, Content Support Servs,* Ms Xiaoli Li; E-mail: xlli@ucdavis.edu; *Mgr of Computing,* Dale Snapp; E-mail: dfsnapp@ucdavis.edu; Staff 109 (MLS 36, Non-MLS 73)
Founded 1908. Enrl 34,175; Fac 1,596; Highest Degree: Doctorate
Special Collections: 16th-20th Century British Coll, bks, pamphlets; 18th-Early 20th Century American History & Literature; Agricultural Technology, advertising mat, archives, bks, manufacturer's cat, ms pamphlets, per, photog, repair manuals; Apiculture, bks, cat, ms, pamphlets, per, photog; Asian History, bks, ms, pamphlets; Botany, bks, ms, per, photog; California Agricultural & Northern California History, bks, ms, oral hist, pamphlets, per, photog, promotional mats; California Artists & Architecture, bibliographies, cat, drawings & paintings, ms, photog; Chicano History, bks, ms, oral history, pamphlets; Civil Rights, bks, broadsides, ms, pamphlets; Ecology, archives, bks, ms, pamphlets; Enology & Viticulture, bks, ms, oral hist, pamphlets, per, photog, posters, promotional mats; Fine Printing, bks, broadsides, pamphlets; Food Industry & Technology, archives, bks, ms, menus, pamphlets, photog; French Revolution, doc, engravings, ms; German Literature, bks, clippings, ms; Horticulture & Pomology, advertising mat, archives, bks, cats, drawings, ms, paintings, pamphlets, photog, posters; Michael & Margaret B Harrison Western Research Center; Native American History, bks, broadsides, ms, pamphlets; Performing Arts, archives, bks, clippings, engravings, ms, photog, playbills, posters, programs, scripts, stage & lighting designs; Poetry (US Avant Garde & British 1789-1972), bks, broadsides, ms, pamphlets, per; Russian History, engravings, ms, photog; Water & Irrigation, archives, bks, ms, pamphlets, photog; Western American History & Thought, bks, clippings, ethnographic reports, pamphlets, photog, pictures; World War I & II, bks, ms, pamphlets, posters. Oral History
Subject Interests: Agr, Agr econ, Art & archit, Biochem, Biology, Botany, Bus & mgt, Chem, Econ, Educ, Entomology, Ethnic studies, Genetics, Geol, Hist, Hort, Law, Lit, Math, Med, Music, Natural sci, Nutrition, Philos, Physics, Physiology, Toxicology, Veterinary med, Women's studies
Automation Activity & Vendor Info: (Acquisitions) Ex Libris Group; (Cataloging) Ex Libris Group; (Circulation) Ex Libris Group; (Course Reserve) Ex Libris Group; (Serials) Ex Libris Group
Wireless access
Partic in Association of Research Libraries; OCLC Online Computer Library Center, Inc; Pacific Southwest Regional Medical Library; Univ of Calif Librs
Open Mon-Thurs 7:30am-Midnight, Fri 7:30-6, Sat Noon-6, Sun Noon-Midnight
Friends of the Library Group
Departmental Libraries:
AGRICULTURAL & RESOURCE ECONOMICS LIBRARY, Social Sciences & Humanities Bldg, Rm 4101, One Shields Ave, 95616, SAN 331-8966. Tel: 530-752-1540. E-mail: arel@primal.ucdavis.edu. Web Site: are.ucdavis.edu/department/library.
Founded 1950. Highest Degree: Doctorate
Library Holdings: Bk Vols 9,284; Per Subs 763
Subject Interests: Agr econ, Develop economics, Environ econ, Natural res econ
Restriction: Non-circulating coll
CM LOREN D CARLSON HEALTH SCIENCES LIBRARY, Med Sci 1B, One Shields Ave, 95616, SAN 331-8990. Tel: 530-752-8041. Interlibrary Loan Service Tel: 530-752-6379. Reference Tel: 530-752-7042. FAX: 530-752-4718. Circulation E-mail: hslcirc@ucdavis.edu. Reference E-mail: hslref@ucdavis.edu. Web Site: www.library.ucdavis.edu/library/carlson-health-sciences. *Librn,* Deanna Johnson; E-mail: deejohnson@ucdavis.edu
Founded 1966. Highest Degree: Doctorate
Special Collections: Veterinary Historical Coll
Open Mon-Thurs 8am-10pm, Fri 8-6, Sat 12-6, Sun 10-6
CL MABIE LAW LIBRARY, King Hall, 400 Mrak Hall Dr, 95616. Tel: 530-752-3327. Reference Tel: 530-752-0210. FAX: 530-752-8766. Reference E-mail: lawlibref@ucdavis.edu. Web Site:

law.ucdavis.edu/library. *Dir,* Judy Janes; Tel: 530-752-3328, E-mail: jcjanes@ucdavis.edu; Staff 23 (MLS 7, Non-MLS 16)
Founded 1964. Enrl 610; Fac 60; Highest Degree: Doctorate
Library Holdings: Bk Titles 112,139; Bk Vols 307,988; Per Subs 5,436
Special Collections: State Document Depository; US Document Depository
Automation Activity & Vendor Info: (Acquisitions) Innovative Interfaces, Inc; (Cataloging) Innovative Interfaces, Inc; (Circulation) Innovative Interfaces, Inc; (Course Reserve) Innovative Interfaces, Inc; (ILL) Innovative Interfaces, Inc; (OPAC) Innovative Interfaces, Inc; (Serials) Innovative Interfaces, Inc
Open Mon-Thurs 8-8, Fri 8-5, Sat 11-5, Sun Noon-5

PHYSICAL SCIENCES & ENGINEERING LIBRARY, One Shields Ave, 95616, SAN 331-9059. Tel: 530-752-5507. FAX: 530-752-4719. E-mail: pse@ucdavis.edu. Circulation E-mail: psecirc@ucdavis.edu. Web Site: www.library.ucdavis.edu/library/physical-sciences-engineering. *Librn,* Ms Cory Craig; Tel: 530-752-0347, E-mail: cjcraig@ucdavis.edu
Subject Interests: Astrophysics, Atmospheric sci, Chem, Engr, Geol, Meteorology, Physics
Open Mon-Thurs 8am-10pm, Fri 8-6, Sat Noon-6, Sun Noon-10

DIXON

P DIXON PUBLIC LIBRARY*, 230 N First St, 95620-3028. SAN 300-712X. Tel: 707-678-5447. FAX: 707-678-3515. Web Site: solanolibrary.com/dixon. *Supv Librn,* Catherine Wesenfeld; Staff 16 (MLS 3, Non-MLS 13)
Founded 1911. Pop 19,100; Circ 45,115. Sal $614,202 (Prof $416,109)
Library Holdings: Bk Titles 45,000; Per Subs 150
Special Collections: Local History Photograph & Scrapbook Coll. Oral History
Automation Activity & Vendor Info: (Acquisitions) CARL.Solution (TLC); (Cataloging) CARL.Solution (TLC); (Circulation) CARL.Solution (TLC); (ILL) CARL.Solution (TLC); (OPAC) CARL.Solution (TLC); (Serials) CARL.Solution (TLC)
Wireless access
Function: Adult bk club, After school storytime, Archival coll, Bk club(s), Bks on CD, Digital talking bks, Doc delivery serv, Electronic databases & coll, Homebound delivery serv, ILL available, Internet access, Music CDs, Photocopying/Printing, Preschool outreach, Prog for adults, Prog for children & young adult, Ref serv available, Summer reading prog, Telephone ref, Wheelchair accessible, Workshops
Publications: Dixon Public Library News (Newsletter)
Mem of NorthNet Library System
Partic in Solano Napa & Partners Library Consortium
Friends of the Library Group

DOWNEY

P COUNTY OF LOS ANGELES PUBLIC LIBRARY*, 7400 E Imperial Hwy, 90242-3375. (Mail add: PO Box 7011, 90241-7011), SAN 332-3765. Tel: 562-940-8462. Interlibrary Loan Service Tel: 562-940-8561. FAX: 562-803-3032. TDD: 562-940-8477. Web Site: lacountylibrary.org. *County Librn,* Skye Patrick; Tel: 562-940-8400, E-mail: LibraryDirector@library.lacounty.gov; *Asst Dir, Admin Serv, Chief Dep,* Yolanda De Ramus; Tel: 562-940-8406, E-mail: yderamus@library.lacounty.gov; *Asst Dir, Cap Projects & Fac Serv,* Pat McGee; Tel: 562-940-4145, E-mail: pmcgee@library.lacounty.gov; *Asst Direc, Community Engagement & Education,* Debbie Anderson; Tel: 562-940-4187, E-mail: danderson@library.lacounty.gov; *Asst Dir, Pub Serv,* Jesse Walker-Lanz; Tel: 562-940-8409, E-mail: jlanz@library.lacounty.gov; *Asst Dir, Info Syst,* Binh Le; Tel: 562-940-8418, E-mail: ble@library.lacounty.gov; *Adult Serv, Digital Serv, Libr Adminr,* Kelly Hulbert; Tel: 562-940-8521, E-mail: khulbert@library.lacounty.gov; *Youth Serv Adminr,* Heather Firchow; Tel: 562-940-8522, E-mail: hfirchow@library.lacounty.gov; *Coll Develop Coordr, Head, Tech Serv,* Wendy Crutcher; Tel: 562-940-8571, E-mail: wcrutcher@library.lacounty.gov; Staff 371 (MLS 275, Non-MLS 96)
Founded 1912. Pop 3,337,360; Circ 10,864,274
Jul 2017-Jun 2018 Income (Main & Associated Libraries) $296,576,493, State $190,102, County $139,238,875, Locally Generated Income $157,147,516. Mats Exp $16,973,105, Books $7,759,856, Per/Ser (Incl. Access Fees) $5,387, AV Mat $3,558,569, Electronic Ref Mat (Incl. Access Fees) $5,642,287, Presv $7,006. Sal $57,312,326
Library Holdings: AV Mats 676,886; CDs 129,154; DVDs 529,281; Large Print Bks 28,485; Bk Titles 791,792; Bk Vols 4,729,753; Per Subs 5,387; Talking Bks 91,380
Special Collections: American Indian Resource Center; Arkel Erb Memorial Mountaineering Coll; Asian Pacific Resource Center; Black Resource Center; Californiana; Chicano Resource Center; HIV Information Center; Nautical Coll. Oral History; State Document Depository; US Document Depository
Automation Activity & Vendor Info: (Acquisitions) SirsiDynix; (Cataloging) SirsiDynix; (Circulation) SirsiDynix; (OPAC) SirsiDynix
Wireless access
Publications: Annual Report
Partic in Consumer Health Information Program & Services; OCLC Online Computer Library Center, Inc; Southern California Library Cooperative
Special Services for the Deaf - Assistive tech; High interest/low vocabulary bks; Staff with knowledge of sign lang; TDD equip
Special Services for the Blind - Magnifiers; Screen enlargement software for people with visual disabilities
Restriction: Access at librarian's discretion
Friends of the Library Group
Branches: 85

ACTON AGUA DULCE LIBRARY, 33792 Crown Valley Rd, Acton, 93510. Tel: 661-269-7101. FAX: 661-269-7101. Web Site: lacountylibrary.org/acton-agua-dulce-library. *Mgr,* Jim Wall
Founded 2010. Pop 15,423; Circ 70,415
Library Holdings: Bk Vols 46,647
Open Mon & Tues 10-8, Wed & Thurs 10-6, Fri & Sat 9-5
Friends of the Library Group

AGOURA HILLS LIBRARY, 29901 Ladyface Ct, Agoura Hills, 91301, SAN 332-5598. Tel: 818-889-2278. FAX: 818-991-5019. Web Site: lacountylibrary.org/agoura-hills-library. *Mgr,* Nina Hull
Founded 2001. Pop 23,044; Circ 191,022
Library Holdings: Bk Vols 87,673
Open Mon-Wed 10-8, Thurs-Sat 9-5
Friends of the Library Group

ALONDRA LIBRARY, 11949 Alondra Blvd, Norwalk, 90650-7108, SAN 332-4303. Tel: 562-868-7771. FAX: 562-863-8620. Web Site: lacountylibrary.org/alondra-library. *Mgr,* Sue Kane
Founded 1970. Pop 44,949; Circ 45,574
Library Holdings: Bk Vols 29,472
Open Tues & Wed 12-8, Thurs & Fri 10-6, Sat 9-5
Friends of the Library Group

ARTESIA LIBRARY, 18801 Elaine Ave, Artesia, 90701, SAN 332-4338. Tel: 562-865-6614. FAX: 562-924-4644. Web Site: lacountylibrary.org/artesia-library. *Mgr,* Robert Gardner
Founded 1968. Pop 16,815; Circ 86,321
Library Holdings: Bk Vols 43,162
Open Tues & Wed 12-8, Thurs 10-6, Fri & Sat 9-5
Friends of the Library Group

AVALON LIBRARY, 210 Metropole Ave, Avalon, 90704. (Mail add: PO Box 585, Avalon, 90704), SAN 332-4362. Tel: 310-510-1050. FAX: 310-510-1645. Web Site: lacountylibrary.org/avalon-library. *Mgr,* Paul Birchall
Founded 1961. Pop 4,051; Circ 24,093
Library Holdings: Bk Vols 14,504
Open Tues-Sat 10-6
Friends of the Library Group

BALDWIN PARK LIBRARY, 4181 Baldwin Park Blvd, Baldwin Park, 91706-3203, SAN 332-4397. Tel: 626-962-6947. FAX: 626-337-6631. Web Site: lacountylibrary.org/baldwin-park-library. *Mgr,* Christina Larios
Founded 1969. Pop 75,615; Circ 128,923
Library Holdings: Bk Vols 46,106
Open Tues, Wed & Thurs 11-8, Fri & Sat 9-5
Friends of the Library Group

BELL GARDENS LIBRARY, 7110 S Garfield Ave, Bell Gardens, 90201-3244, SAN 332-4451. Tel: 562-927-1309. FAX: 562-928-4512. Web Site: lacountylibrary.org/bell-gardens-library. *Mgr,* Soledad Castillo
Founded 1968. Pop 36,420; Circ 52,239
Library Holdings: Bk Vols 25,635
Open Tues, Wed & Thurs 10-7, Fri 10-6, Sat 9-5

BELL LIBRARY, 4411 E Gage Ave, Bell, 90201-1216, SAN 332-4427. Tel: 323-560-2149. FAX: 323-773-7557. Web Site: lacountylibrary.org/bell-library. *Mgr,* Diane Zaher
Founded 1960. Pop 42,842; Circ 42,186
Library Holdings: Bk Vols 25,837
Open Tues 10-8, Wed & Thurs 10-6, Fri & Sat 9-5

A C BILBREW LIBRARY, 150 E El Segundo Blvd, Los Angeles, 90061, SAN 332-4516. Tel: 310-538-3350. FAX: 562-327-0824. Web Site: lacountylibrary.org/a-c-bilbrew-library. *Mgr,* Jeffrey Sichaleune
Founded 1974. Pop 18,793; Circ 82,651
Library Holdings: Bk Vols 78,243
Special Collections: Black Resource Center
Open Mon-Thurs 10-8, Fri 10-6, Sat 9-5
Friends of the Library Group

CLIFTON M BRAKENSIEK LIBRARY, 9945 E Flower St, Bellflower, 90706-5486, SAN 332-4575. Tel: 562-925-5543. FAX: 562-920-9249. Web Site: lacountylibrary.org/clifton-m-brakensiek-library. *Mgr,* Josh Murray
Founded 1975. Pop 76,667; Circ 182,893
Library Holdings: Bk Vols 76,635
Open Mon-Wed 10-8, Thurs 10-6, Fri & Sat 9-5
Friends of the Library Group

CARSON LIBRARY, 151 E Carson St, Carson, 90745-2797, SAN 332-463X. Tel: 310-830-0901. FAX: 310-830-6181. Web Site: lacountylibrary.org/carson-library. *Mgr,* Leticia Tan
Founded 1972. Pop 102,635; Circ 180,201

Library Holdings: Bk Vols 91,428
Open Mon-Thurs 10-8, Fri 10-6, Sat 9-5, Sun 1-5
Friends of the Library Group
CASTAIC LIBRARY, 27971 Sloan Canyon Rd, Castaic, 91384. Tel: 661-257-7410. FAX: 661-257-5959. Web Site: lacountylibrary.org/castaic-library. *Mgr,* Victoria Vallejos
Founded 2008. Pop 30,609; Circ 88,835
Library Holdings: Bk Vols 47,733
Open Mon & Tues 10-8, Wed & Thurs 10-6, Fri & Sat 10-5
Friends of the Library Group
CHARTER OAK LIBRARY, 20540 E Arrow Hwy, Ste K, Covina, 91724-1238, SAN 332-4664. Tel: 626-339-2151. FAX: 626-339-2799. Web Site: lacountylibrary.org/charter-oak-library. *Mgr,* Dina Malakoff
Founded 1990. Pop 30,631; Circ 94,986
Library Holdings: Bk Vols 29,551
Open Mon-Wed 11-8, Thurs & Fri 10-6, Sat 9-5
CITY TERRACE LIBRARY, 4025 E City Terrace Dr, Los Angeles, 90063-1297, SAN 332-4699. Tel: 323-261-0295. FAX: 323-261-1790. Web Site: lacountylibrary.org/city-terrace-library. *Mgr,* Gabriela Torres
Founded 1979. Pop 19,501; Circ 52,082
Library Holdings: Bk Vols 44,854
Open Mon & Tues 10-6, Wed & Thurs 11-8, Fri & Sat 9-5
Friends of the Library Group
COMPTON LIBRARY, 240 W Compton Blvd, Compton, 90220-3109, SAN 332-4753. Tel: 310-637-0202. FAX: 310-537-1141. Web Site: lacountylibrary.org/compton-library. *Mgr,* Crystal Hodges
Founded 1975. Pop 101,134; Circ 54,766
Library Holdings: Bk Vols 57,525
Open Tues-Thurs 10-8, Fri 10-6, Sat 9-5
Friends of the Library Group
CUDAHY LIBRARY, 5218 Santa Ana St, Cudahy, 90201-6098, SAN 332-4788. Tel: 323-771-1345. FAX: 323-771-6973. Web Site: lacountylibrary.org/cudahy-library. *Mgr,* Jose Rivera
Founded 1968. Pop 24,412; Circ 30,966
Library Holdings: Bk Vols 22,742
Open Tues-Thurs 10-8, Fri & Sat 8-6
DIAMOND BAR LIBRARY, 21800 Copley Dr, Diamond Bar, 91765-2299, SAN 332-4877. Tel: 909-861-4978. FAX: 909-860-3054. Web Site: lacountylibrary.org/diamond-bar-library. *Mgr,* Pui-Ching Ho
Founded 1977. Pop 57,241; Circ 435,030
Library Holdings: Bk Vols 70,901
Open Mon-Thurs 10-8, Fri & Sat 9-5
Friends of the Library Group
CULVER CITY JULIAN DIXON LIBRARY, 4975 Overland Ave, Culver City, 90230-4299, SAN 332-4818. Tel: 310-559-1676. FAX: 310-559-2994. Web Site: lacountylibrary.org/culver-city-julian-dixon-library. *Mgr,* Laura Frakes
Founded 1970. Pop 41,366; Circ 341,849
Library Holdings: Bk Vols 103,303
Special Collections: Judaica Coll
Open Mon-Thurs 10-8, Fri & Sat 10-6
Friends of the Library Group
DUARTE LIBRARY, 1301 Buena Vista St, Duarte, 91010-2410, SAN 332-4931. Tel: 626-358-1865. FAX: 626-303-4917. Web Site: lacountylibrary.org/duarte-library. *Mgr,* Joanna Gee
Founded 1966. Pop 23,383; Circ 95,659
Library Holdings: Bk Vols 51,828
Open Mon-Thurs 11-8, Fri 10-6, Sat 9-5
Friends of the Library Group
EAST LOS ANGELES LIBRARY, 4837 E Third St, Los Angeles, 90022-1601, SAN 332-4990. Tel: 323-264-0155. FAX: 323-264-5465. Web Site: lacountylibrary.org/east-los-angeles-library. *Mgr,* Martin Delgado
Founded 1965. Pop 61,841; Circ 2,016,089
Library Holdings: Bk Vols 124,158
Special Collections: Chicano Resource Center
Open Mon-Thurs 10-9, Fri 10-6, Sat 9-5, Sun 1-5
Friends of the Library Group
EAST RANCHO DOMINGUEZ LIBRARY, 4420 E Rose St, East Rancho Dominguez, 90221-3664, SAN 332-4966. Tel: 310-632-6193. FAX: 310-608-0294. Web Site: lacountylibrary.org/east-rancho-dominguez-library. *Mgr,* Alejandra Garcia
Founded 1966. Pop 15,813; Circ 60,005
Library Holdings: Bk Vols 24,785
Open Mon, Wed & Thurs 10-6, Tues 10-8, Fri & Sat 9-5
EL CAMINO REAL LIBRARY, 4264 E Whittier Blvd, Los Angeles, 90023-2036, SAN 332-5059. Tel: 323-269-8102. FAX: 323-268-5186. Web Site: lacountylibrary.org/el-camino-real-library. *Mgr,* Kathy Teague
Founded 1971. Pop 24,010; Circ 47,308
Library Holdings: Bk Vols 28,059
Open Mon & Tues 11-7, Wed & Thurs 10-6, Fri & Sat 9-5
Friends of the Library Group
EL MONTE LIBRARY, 3224 Tyler Ave, El Monte, 91731-3356, SAN 332-5083. Tel: 626-444-9506. FAX: 626-443-5864. Web Site: lacountylibrary.org/el-monte-library. *Mgr,* Cheryl Gilera
Founded 1961. Pop 54,952; Circ 115,227
Library Holdings: Bk Vols 40,686
Open Mon-Thurs 10-8, Fri & Sat 9-5, Sun 1-5
Friends of the Library Group
FLORENCE EXPRESS LIBRARY, 7600 Graham Ave, Los Angeles, 90001. Tel: 323-581-8028. FAX: 323-587-3240. Web Site: lacountylibrary.org/florence-library. *Mgr,* Julian Zamora
Founded 1970. Pop 48,934; Circ 71,363
Library Holdings: Bk Vols 38,929
This is the library's temporary location as of 2/2019. The old location at 1610 E Florence Ave is under construction.
Open Mon & Thurs 10-6, Tues & Wed 12-8, Fri & Sat 9-5
Friends of the Library Group
GARDENA MAYME DEAR LIBRARY, 1731 W Gardena Blvd, Gardena, 90247-4726, SAN 332-5148. Tel: 310-323-6363. FAX: 310-327-0992. Web Site: lacountylibrary.org/gardena-mayme-dear-library. *Mgr,* Wendy Lee
Founded 1964. Pop 60,821; Circ 118,658
Library Holdings: Bk Vols 80,533
Open Tues-Thurs 10-8, Fri & Sat 10-6
Friends of the Library Group
GRAHAM LIBRARY, 1900 E Firestone Blvd, Los Angeles, 90001-4126, SAN 332-5172. Tel: 323-582-2903. FAX: 323-581-8478. Web Site: lacountylibrary.org/graham-library. *Mgr,* Leticia Napoles
Founded 1969. Pop 32,279; Circ 50,916
Library Holdings: Bk Vols 37,696
Open Mon & Tues 12-8, Wed & Thurs 10-6, Fri & Sat 9-5
HACIENDA HEIGHTS LIBRARY, 16010 La Monde St, Hacienda Heights, 91745, SAN 332-5202. Tel: 626-968-9356. FAX: 626-336-3126. Web Site: lacountylibrary.org/hacienda-heights-library. *Mgr,* Christina Cabrera-Labrador
Founded 1972. Pop 65,417; Circ 280,476
Library Holdings: Bk Vols 56,166
Open Mon-Thurs 9-9, Fri 9-6, Sat 9-5, Sun 1-5
Friends of the Library Group
HAWAIIAN GARDENS LIBRARY, 11940 Carson St, Hawaiian Gardens, 90716-1137, SAN 332-5229. Tel: 562-496-1212. FAX: 562-425-0410. Web Site: lacountylibrary.org/hawaiian-gardens-library. *Mgr,* Carolyn Reed
Founded 1972. Pop 14,547; Circ 40,561
Library Holdings: Bk Vols 32,961
Open Tues & Wed 12-8, Thurs 10-6, Fri & Sat 9-5
Friends of the Library Group
HAWTHORNE LIBRARY, 12700 S Grevillea Ave, Hawthorne, 90250-4396, SAN 332-5237. Tel: 310-679-8193. FAX: 310-679-4846. Web Site: lacountylibrary.org/hawthorne-library. *Mgr,* Daniel Granados
Founded 1961. Pop 85,990; Circ 97,071
Library Holdings: Bk Vols 69,025
Open Tues-Thurs 10-8, Fri & Sat 9-5
Friends of the Library Group
HERMOSA BEACH LIBRARY, 550 Pier Ave, Hermosa Beach, 90254-3892, SAN 332-5261. Tel: 310-379-8475. FAX: 310-374-0746. Web Site: lacountylibrary.org/hermosa-beach-library. *Mgr,* Sarah Mae Harper
Founded 1962. Pop 19,570; Circ 114,390
Library Holdings: Bk Vols 36,685
Open Tues-Thurs 11-7, Fri 10-6, Sat 9-5
Friends of the Library Group
CHET HOLIFIELD LIBRARY, 1060 S Greenwood Ave, Montebello, 90640-6030, SAN 332-5296. Tel: 323-728-0421. FAX: 323-888-6053. Web Site: lacountylibrary.org/chet-holifield-library. *Mgr,* Charmetria Marshall
Founded 1969. Pop 16,699; Circ 21,313
Library Holdings: Bk Vols 29,244
Open Mon & Tues 11-7, Wed & Thurs 10-6
Friends of the Library Group
HOLLYDALE LIBRARY, 12000 S Garfield Ave, South Gate, 90280-7894, SAN 332-5326. Tel: 562-634-0156. FAX: 562-531-9530. Web Site: lacountylibrary.org/hollydale-library. *Mgr,* Julie Hernandez-Chan
Founded 1966. Pop 11,798; Circ 29,813
Library Holdings: Bk Vols 42,909
Open Tues & Wed 12-8, Thurs 10-6, Fri & Sat 12-5
Friends of the Library Group
HUNTINGTON PARK LIBRARY, 6518 Miles Ave, Huntington Park, 90255-4388, SAN 332-5385. Tel: 323-583-1461. FAX: 323-587-2061. Web Site: lacountylibrary.org/huntington-park-library. *Mgr,* Catherine Bueno-Granados
Founded 1970. Pop 59,391; Circ 85,816
Library Holdings: Bk Vols 76,386
Special Collections: American Indian Resource Center
Subject Interests: Native North American Indians

Open Mon & Tues 12-8, Wed & Thurs 10-6, Sat 9-5
Friends of the Library Group

ANGELO M IACOBONI LIBRARY, 4990 Clark Ave, Lakewood, 90712-2676, SAN 332-5415. Tel: 562-866-1777. FAX: 562-866-1217. Web Site: lacountylibrary.org/angelo-m-iacoboni-library. *Mgr,* Sarah Comfort
Founded 1972. Pop 52,404; Circ 307,384
Library Holdings: Bk Vols 112,645
Open Mon-Thurs 10-8, Fri 10-6, Sat 9-5, Sun 1-5
Friends of the Library Group

DR MARTIN LUTHER KING, JR LIBRARY, 17906 S Avalon Blvd, Carson, 90746-1598, SAN 332-6705. Tel: 310-327-4830. FAX: 310-327-3630. Web Site: lacountylibrary.org/dr-martin-luther-king-jr-library. *Mgr,* Mercedes Santos
Founded 1973. Pop 15,720; Circ 23,167
Library Holdings: Bk Vols 17,419
Open Tues & Wed 12-8, Thurs & Fri 10-6, Sat 9-5
Friends of the Library Group

LA CANADA FLINTRIDGE LIBRARY, 4545 N Oakwood Ave, La Canada Flintridge, 91011-3358, SAN 332-544X. Tel: 818-790-3330. FAX: 818-952-1754. Web Site: lacountylibrary.org/la-canada-flintridge-library. *Mgr,* Mark Totten
Founded 1971. Pop 22,082; Circ 211,705
Library Holdings: Bk Vols 66,074
Open Mon, Tues & Wed 10-8, Thurs 10-6, Fri & Sat 9-5
Friends of the Library Group

LA CRESCENTA LIBRARY, 2809 Foothill Blvd, La Crescenta, 91214-2999, SAN 332-5474. Tel: 818-248-5313. FAX: 818-248-1289. Web Site: lacountylibrary.org/la-crescenta-library. *Mgr,* Marta Wiggins
Founded 1963. Pop 19,762; Circ 314,612
Library Holdings: Bk Vols 66,352
Open Mon, Tues & Wed 10-8, Thurs 10-6, Fri & Sat 9-5, Sun 1-5
Friends of the Library Group

LA MIRADA LIBRARY, 13800 La Mirada Blvd, La Mirada, 90638, SAN 332-5504. Tel: 562-943-0277. FAX: 562-943-3920. Web Site: lacountylibrary.org/la-mirada-library. *Mgr,* Allison Ortiz
Founded 1969. Pop 49,438; Circ 186,429
Library Holdings: Bk Vols 58,047
Open Tues, Wed & Thurs 10-8, Fri & Sat 9-5
Friends of the Library Group

LA PUENTE LIBRARY, 15920 E Central Ave, La Puente, 91744-5499, SAN 332-5563. Tel: 626-968-4613. FAX: 626-369-0294. Web Site: lacountylibrary.org/la-puente-library. *Mgr,* Jeanette Freels
Founded 1968. Pop 67,057; Circ 83,663
Library Holdings: Bk Vols 50,257
Open Tues & Wed 11-8, Thurs, Fri & Sat 9-5
Friends of the Library Group

LA VERNE LIBRARY, 3640 D St, La Verne, 91750-3572, SAN 332-5628. Tel: 909-596-1934. FAX: 909-596-7303. Web Site: lacountylibrary.org/la-verne-library. *Mgr,* George May
Founded 1985. Pop 34,136; Circ 153,919
Library Holdings: Bk Vols 45,903
Open Mon & Tues 10-6, Wed & Thurs 11-8, Fri & Sat 9-5
Friends of the Library Group

LAKE LOS ANGELES LIBRARY, 16921 E Ave O, Ste A, Palmdale, 93591, SAN 373-563X. Tel: 661-264-0593. FAX: 661-264-0859. Web Site: lacountylibrary.org/lake-los-angeles-library. *Mgr,* Mary MacTaggart
Founded 1991. Pop 14,475; Circ 53,652
Library Holdings: Bk Vols 31,358
Open Mon & Tues 11-7, Wed, Thurs & Fri 10-6, Sat 9-5
Friends of the Library Group

LANCASTER LIBRARY, 601 W Lancaster Blvd, Lancaster, 93534, SAN 332-5539. Tel: 661-948-5029. FAX: 661-945-0480. Web Site: lacountylibrary.org/lancaster-library. *Mgr,* John Elford
Founded 1997. Pop 156,993; Circ 397,607
Library Holdings: Bk Vols 158,695
Open Mon, Tues & Wed 10-8,Thurs-Sat 9-5, Sun 1-5
Friends of the Library Group

LAWNDALE LIBRARY, 14615 Burin Ave, Lawndale, 90260-1431, SAN 332-5652. Tel: 310-676-0177. FAX: 310-973-0498. Web Site: lacountylibrary.org/lawndale-library. *Mgr,* Jessica Romero
Founded 1955. Pop 33,374; Circ 126,883
Library Holdings: Bk Vols 57,756
Open Tues, Wed & Thurs 10-8, Fri & Sat 10-6
Friends of the Library Group

LENNOX LIBRARY, 4359 Lennox Blvd, Lennox, 90304, SAN 332-5687. Tel: 310-674-0385. FAX: 310-673-6508. Web Site: lacountylibrary.org/lennox-library. *Mgr,* Carina Castellanos
Founded 1949. Pop 23,352; Circ 72,612
Library Holdings: Bk Vols 39,031
Open Mon-Thurs 11-7, Fri 11-6, Sat 11-5
Friends of the Library Group

LITTLEROCK LIBRARY, 35119 80th St E, Littlerock, 93543, SAN 332-5717. Tel: 661-944-4138. FAX: 661-944-4150. Web Site: lacountylibrary.org/littlerock-library. *Mgr,* Trisha Pritchard
Founded 1998. Pop 23,937; Circ 65,275
Library Holdings: Bk Vols 30,609
Open Mon & Tues 11-7, Wed-Sat 9-5
Friends of the Library Group

LIVE OAK LIBRARY, 4153 E Live Oak Ave, Arcadia, 91006-5895, SAN 332-5741. Tel: 626-446-8803. FAX: 626-446-9418. Web Site: lacountylibrary.org/live-oak-library. *Mgr,* Denise Dilley
Founded 1966. Pop 16,442; Circ 67,165
Library Holdings: Bk Vols 37,581
Open Mon, Tues & Wed 11-8, Thurs 10-6, Fri & Sat 9-5
Friends of the Library Group

LOMITA LIBRARY, 24200 Narbonne Ave, Lomita, 90717-1188, SAN 332-5776. Tel: 310-539-4515. FAX: 310-534-8649. Web Site: lacountylibrary.org/lomita-library. *Mgr,* Michael Mackavoy
Founded 1976. Pop 22,381; Circ 94,036
Library Holdings: Bk Vols 26,421
Open Mon, Tues & Wed 10-8, Thurs & Fri 10-6, Sat 9-5
Friends of the Library Group

LOS NIETOS LIBRARY, 8511 Duchess Dr, Whittier, 90606, SAN 332-5806. Tel: 562-695-0708. FAX: 562-699-3876. Web Site: lacountylibrary.org/los-nietos. *Mgr,* Theresa Cazares
Founded 1979. Pop 7,597; Circ 37,670
Library Holdings: Bk Vols 32,598
Open Mon & Tues 11-7, Wed & Thurs 10-6, Fri & Sat 9-5

LYNWOOD LIBRARY, 11320 Bullis Rd, Lynwood, 90262-3661, SAN 332-5830. Tel: 310-635-7121. FAX: 310-635-4967. Web Site: lacountylibrary.org/lynwood-library. *Mgr,* Angel Nicolas
Founded 1977. Pop 71,408; Circ 128,970
Library Holdings: Bk Vols 76,334
Open Mon-Thurs 10-8, Fri 10-6, Sat 9-5

MALIBU LIBRARY, 23519 W Civic Center Way, Malibu, 90265-4804, SAN 332-5865. Tel: 310-456-6438. FAX: 310-456-8681. Web Site: lacountylibrary.org/malibu-library. *Mgr,* Melissa Stallings
Founded 1970. Pop 18,616; Circ 79,438
Library Holdings: Bk Vols 48,583
Special Collections: Arkel Erb Memorial Mountaineering Coll
Open Mon, Tues & Wed 10-8, Thurs 10-6, Fri & Sat 9-5, Sun 1-5
Friends of the Library Group

MANHATTAN BEACH LIBRARY, 1320 Highland Ave, Manhattan Beach, 90266-4789, SAN 332-589X. Tel: 310-545-8595. FAX: 310-545-5394. Web Site: lacountylibrary.org/manhattan-beach-library. *Mgr,* Maria Manigbas
Founded 1975. Pop 35,572; Circ 244,347
Library Holdings: Bk Vols 54,341; Per Subs 93
Open Mon, Tues & Wed 10-9, Thurs 10-6, Fri 12-6, Sat 10-5, Sun 1-5
Friends of the Library Group

MAYWOOD CESAR CHAVEZ LIBRARY, 4323 E Slauson Ave, Maywood, 90270-2837, SAN 332-5989. Tel: 323-771-8600. FAX: 323-560-0515. Web Site: lacountylibrary.org/maywood-cesar-chavez-library. *Mgr,* Edmond Osborn
Founded 1949. Pop 28,016; Circ 45,627
Library Holdings: Bk Vols 25,385
Open Mon & Tues 12-8, Wed & Thurs 10-6, Fri & Sat 9-5
Friends of the Library Group

MONTEBELLO LIBRARY, 1550 W Beverly Blvd, Montebello, 90640-3993, SAN 332-6012. Tel: 323-722-6551. FAX: 323-722-3018. Web Site: lacountylibrary.org/montebello-library. *Mgr,* Rosemary Gurrola
Founded 1966. Pop 47,237; Circ 124,387
Library Holdings: Bk Vols 107,687
Special Collections: Asian-Pacific Resource Center
Open Mon & Tues 10-8, Wed, Thurs & Fri 10-6, Sat 9-5
Friends of the Library Group

NORWALK LIBRARY, 12350 Imperial Hwy, Norwalk, 90650-3199, SAN 332-6071. Tel: 562-868-0775. FAX: 562-929-1130. Web Site: lacountylibrary.org/norwalk-library. *Mgr,* Sue Kane
Founded 1969. Pop 61,188; Circ 179,988
Library Holdings: Bk Vols 159,761
Special Collections: Business Subject Specialty Center; Edelman Public Policy Coll
Subject Interests: Bus
Open Mon-Thurs 10-8, Fri 10-6, Sat 9-5
Friends of the Library Group

NORWOOD LIBRARY, 4550 N Peck Rd, El Monte, 91732-1998, SAN 332-6101. Tel: 626-443-3147. FAX: 626-350-6099. Web Site: lacountylibrary.org/norwood-library. *Mgr,* Stephen Trumble
Founded 1977. Pop 59,370; Circ 92,789
Library Holdings: Bk Vols 51,781
Open Mon-Thurs 10-8, Fri & Sat 9-5
Friends of the Library Group

GEORGE NYE JR LIBRARY, 6600 Del Amo Blvd, Lakewood, 90713-2206, SAN 332-6136. Tel: 562-421-8497. FAX: 562-496-3943. Web Site: lacountylibrary.org/george-nye-jr-library. *Mgr,* Carol Burke
Founded 1972. Pop 28,769; Circ 55,443
Library Holdings: Bk Vols 40,605
Open Tues, Wed & Thurs 10-8, Fri & Sat 8-6
Friends of the Library Group

PARAMOUNT LIBRARY, 16254 Colorado Ave, Paramount, 90723-5085, SAN 332-6160. Tel: 562-630-3171. FAX: 562-630-3968. Web Site: lacountylibrary.org/paramount-library. *Mgr,* Andrea Crow
Founded 1967. Pop 55,959; Circ 74,476
Library Holdings: Bk Vols 44,158
Open Tues & Wed 10-8, Thurs & Fri 10-6, Sat 9-5
Friends of the Library Group

PICO RIVERA LIBRARY, 9001 Mines Ave, Pico Rivera, 90660-3098, SAN 332-6195. Tel: 562-942-7394. FAX: 562-942-7779. Web Site: lacountylibrary.org/pico-rivera-library. *Mgr,* Lauren Talbott
Founded 1961. Pop 40,933; Circ 103,172
Library Holdings: Bk Vols 57,793
Open Mon & Tues 10-8, Wed 10-6, Sat 9-5
Friends of the Library Group

QUARTZ HILL LIBRARY, 5040 West Ave M-2, Quartz Hill, 93536-3509, SAN 332-6225. Tel: 661-943-2454. FAX: 661-943-6337. Web Site: lacountylibrary.org/quartz-hill-library. *Mgr,* Daria Bounds
Founded 1959. Pop 19,892; Circ 271,858
Library Holdings: Bk Vols 41,042
Open Mon & Thurs-Sat 9-5, Tues & Wed 10-8
Friends of the Library Group

ANTHONY QUINN LIBRARY, 3965 Cesar E Chavez Ave, Los Angeles, 90063, SAN 332-4486. Tel: 323-264-7715. FAX: 323-262-7121. Web Site: lacountylibrary.org/anthony-quinn-library. *Mgr,* Mariko Farinacci-Gonzalez
Founded 1973. Pop 19,193; Circ 49,744
Library Holdings: Bk Vols 38,382
Open Mon & Tues 11-8, Wed-Fri 10-6, Sat 9-5
Friends of the Library Group

HELEN RENWICK LIBRARY - CLAREMONT BRANCH, 208 N Harvard Ave, Claremont, 91711, SAN 332-4729. Tel: 909-621-4902. FAX: 909-621-2366. Web Site: lacountylibrary.org/claremont-library. *Mgr,* Amy Crow
Founded 1971. Pop 37,288; Circ 255,852
Library Holdings: Bk Vols 89,420
Open Mon-Thurs 10-7, Fri & Sat 9-5, Sun 1-5
Friends of the Library Group

RIVERA LIBRARY, 7828 S Serapis Ave, Pico Rivera, 90660-4600, SAN 332-625X. Tel: 562-949-5485. FAX: 562-948-3455. Web Site: lacountylibrary.org/rivera-library. *Mgr,* Lauren Talbott
Founded 1969. Pop 24,470; Circ 40,135
Library Holdings: Bk Vols 30,397
Open Mon & Thurs 10-6, Tues & Wed 12-8
Friends of the Library Group

ROSEMEAD LIBRARY, 8800 Valley Blvd, Rosemead, 91770-1788, SAN 332-6284. Tel: 626-573-5220. FAX: 626-280-8523. Web Site: lacountylibrary.org/rosemead-library. *Mgr,* Sue Yamamoto
Founded 1965. Pop 63,888; Circ 233,941
Library Holdings: Bk Vols 108,997
Open Tues & Wed 10-8, Thurs & Fri 10-6, Sat 9-5
Friends of the Library Group

ROWLAND HEIGHTS LIBRARY, 1850 Nogales St, Rowland Heights, 91748, SAN 332-6314. Tel: 626-912-5348. FAX: 626-810-3538. Web Site: lacountylibrary.org/rowland-heights-library. *Mgr,* Desiree Lee
Founded 1979. Pop 50,801; Circ 194,457
Library Holdings: Bk Vols 73,309
Open Mon-Thurs 9-9, Fri 9-6, Sat 9-5, Sun 1-5
Friends of the Library Group

SAN DIMAS LIBRARY, 145 N Walnut Ave, San Dimas, 91773-2603, SAN 332-6349. Tel: 909-599-6738. FAX: 909-592-4490. Web Site: lacountylibrary.org/san-dimas-library. *Mgr,* Nora Chen
Founded 1971. Pop 36,231; Circ 141,964
Library Holdings: Bk Vols 56,481
Open Mon & Tues 11-8, Wed & Thurs 10-6, Fri & Sat 9-5
Friends of the Library Group

SAN FERNANDO LIBRARY, 217 N Maclay Ave, San Fernando, 91340-2433, SAN 332-6373. Tel: 818-365-6928. FAX: 818-365-3820. Web Site: lacountylibrary.org/san-fernando-library. *Mgr,* Liana Stepanyan
Founded 2001. Pop 25,871; Circ 83,051
Library Holdings: Bk Vols 46,174
Open Mon, Tues & Wed 11-7, Thurs 10-6, Fri & Sat 9-5
Friends of the Library Group

SAN GABRIEL LIBRARY, 500 S Del Mar Ave, San Gabriel, 91776-2408, SAN 332-6403. Tel: 626-287-0761. FAX: 626-285-2610. Web Site: lacountylibrary.org/san-gabriel-library. *Mgr,* Julie Sorensen
Founded 1967. Pop 52,371; Circ 180,315
Library Holdings: Bk Vols 54,623
Open Mon,Tues & Wed 10-8, Thurs & Fri 10-6, Sat 9-5
Friends of the Library Group

MASAO W SATOW LIBRARY, 14433 S Crenshaw Blvd, Gardena, 90249-3142, SAN 332-6462. Tel: 310-679-0638. FAX: 310-970-0275. Web Site: lacountylibrary.org/masao-w-satow-library. *Mgr,* Elaine Fukumoto
Founded 1977. Pop 8,785; Circ 70,967
Library Holdings: Bk Vols 47,275
Open Mon, Tues & Wed 12-8, Thurs 10-6, Fri & Sat 9-5
Friends of the Library Group

SORENSEN LIBRARY, 6934 Broadway Ave, Whittier, 90606-1994, SAN 377-6549. Tel: 562-695-3979. FAX: 562-695-8925. Web Site: lacountylibrary.org/sorensen-library. *Mgr,* Charmaine Sello
Founded 1956. Pop 19,055; Circ 106,093
Library Holdings: Bk Vols 41,561
Open Mon & Tues 10-8, Wed, Thurs & Fri 10-6, Sat 9-5
Friends of the Library Group

SOUTH EL MONTE LIBRARY, 1430 N Central Ave, South El Monte, 91733-3302, SAN 332-6527. Tel: 626-443-4158. FAX: 626-575-7450. Web Site: lacountylibrary.org/south-el-monte-library. *Mgr,* Angie Macias-Mendez
Founded 1966. Pop 23,706; Circ 46,147
Library Holdings: Bk Vols 28,816
Open Tues & Wed 12-8, Thurs 10-6, Fri & Sat 9-5

SOUTH WHITTIER LIBRARY, 11543 Colima Rd, Whittier, 90604-2966, SAN 332-6551. Tel: 562-946-4415. FAX: 562-941-6138. Web Site: lacountylibrary.org/south-whittier-library. *Mgr,* Oscar Villagomez
Founded 1988. Pop 69,321; Circ 138,725
Library Holdings: Bk Vols 59,077
Open Mon, Tues & Wed 10-8, Thurs 10-6, Fri & Sat 9-5
Friends of the Library Group

STEVENSON RANCH LIBRARY, 25950 The Old Road, Stevenson Ranch, 91381. Tel: 661-255-2707. FAX: 661-257-5959. Web Site: lacountylibrary.org/stevenson-ranch-library. *Mgr,* Arpine Eloyan
Pop 69,321; Circ 138,725
Library Holdings: Bk Vols 49,916
Open Mon, Tues & Wed 10-8, Thurs 10-6, Fri & Sat 9-5
Friends of the Library Group

SUNKIST LIBRARY, 840 N Puente Ave, La Puente, 91746-1316, SAN 332-6586. Tel: 626-960-2707. FAX: 626-338-5141. Web Site: lacountylibrary.org/sunkist-library. *Mgr,* Grace Yang
Founded 1977. Pop 42,328; Circ 108,089
Library Holdings: Bk Vols 40,662
Open Mon-Thurs 10-8, Fri 10-6, Sat 9-5

LLOYD TABER-MARINA DEL REY LIBRARY, 4533 Admiralty Way, Marina del Rey, 90292-5416, SAN 332-5954. Tel: 310-821-3415. FAX: 310-306-3372. Web Site: lacountylibrary.org/lloyd-taber-marina-del-rey-library. *Mgr,* Winona Phillabaum
Founded 1975. Pop 9,443; Circ 140,099
Library Holdings: Bk Vols 43,679
Special Collections: Nautical Coll
Open Mon 11-7, Tues, Wed & Thurs 10-8, Fri 10-6, Sat 9-5
Friends of the Library Group

TEMPLE CITY LIBRARY, 5939 Golden West Ave, Temple City, 91780-2292, SAN 332-6640. Tel: 626-285-2136. FAX: 626-285-2314. Web Site: lacountylibrary.org/temple-city-library. *Mgr,* Jing Li
Founded 1962. Pop 57,646; Circ 213,165
Library Holdings: Bk Vols 47,622
Open Mon, Tues & Wed 10-8, Thurs & Fri 10-6, Sat 9-5
Friends of the Library Group

TOPANGA LIBRARY, 122 N Topanga Canyon Blvd, Topanga, 90290. Tel: 310-455-3480. FAX: 310-455-3491. Web Site: lacountylibrary.org/topanga-library. *Mgr,* Ashley Abrams
Pop 12,100; Circ 90,315
Library Holdings: Bk Vols 55,157
Open Mon, Tues & Wed 10-8, Thurs & Fri 10-6, Sat 9-5, Sun 1-5
Friends of the Library Group

VIEW PARK BEBE MOORE CAMPBELL LIBRARY, 3854 W 54th St, Los Angeles, 90043-2297, SAN 332-673X. Tel: 323-293-5371. FAX: 323-292-4330. Web Site: lacountylibrary.org/view-park-library. *Mgr,* Camille Ray
Founded 1977. Pop 18,598; Circ 49,929
Library Holdings: Bk Vols 34,037
Open Mon, Tues & Wed 11-7, Thurs 10-6, Fri & Sat 9-5
Friends of the Library Group

WALNUT LIBRARY, 21155 La Puente Rd, Walnut, 91789-2017, SAN 332-6829. Tel: 909-595-0757. FAX: 909-595-7553. Web Site: lacountylibrary.org/walnut-library. *Mgr,* Jenny Cheng
Founded 1985. Pop 31,613; Circ 214,716
Library Holdings: Bk Vols 44,031
Open Tues, Wed & Thurs 10-8, Fri & Sat 9-5
Friends of the Library Group

LELAND R WEAVER LIBRARY, 4035 Tweedy Blvd, South Gate, 90280-6199, SAN 332-6853. Tel: 323-567-8853. FAX: 323-563-1046. Web Site: lacountylibrary.org/leland-r-weaver-library. *Mgr,* Iris Ilagan
Founded 1973. Pop 86,873; Circ 87,202
Library Holdings: Bk Vols 75,169
Open Tues & Wed 10-8, Thurs 10-6, Fri & Sat 9-5, Sun 1-5
Friends of the Library Group

WEST COVINA LIBRARY, 1601 W Covina Pkwy, West Covina, 91790-2786, SAN 332-6888. Tel: 626-962-3541. FAX: 626-962-1507. Web Site: lacountylibrary.org/west-covina-library. *Mgr,* Wen Wen Zhang
Founded 1960. Pop 139,069; Circ 313,515
Library Holdings: Bk Vols 114,588
Open Mon-Thurs 10-8, Fri & Sat 9-5
Friends of the Library Group

WEST HOLLYWOOD LIBRARY, 625 N San Vicente Blvd, West Hollywood, 90069-5020, SAN 332-6438. Tel: 310-652-5340. FAX: 310-652-2580. Web Site: lacountylibrary.org/west-hollywood-library. *Mgr,* Matt Gill
Founded 1962. Pop 35,949; Circ 237,067
Library Holdings: Bk Vols 79,151
Special Collections: Ron Shipton HIV Information Center
Open Mon-Thurs 11-7, Fri & Sat 10-6, Sun 1-5
Friends of the Library Group

WESTLAKE VILLAGE LIBRARY, 31220 Oak Crest Dr, Westlake Village, 91361, SAN 373-5648. Tel: 818-865-9230. FAX: 818-865-0724. Web Site: lacountylibrary.org/westlake-village-library. *Mgr,* Julie Frieze
Founded 2001. Pop 10,274; Circ 140,277
Library Holdings: Bk Vols 47,161
Open Tues & Wed 10-8, Thurs & Fri 10-6, Sat 9-5, Sun 1-5
Friends of the Library Group

WILLOWBROOK LIBRARY, 11737 Wilmington Ave, Los Angeles, 90059, SAN 332-6918. Tel: 323-564-5698. FAX: 323-564-7709. Web Site: lacountylibrary.org/willowbrook-library. *Mgr,* Amy Luu
Founded 1988. Pop 26,796; Circ 38,286
Library Holdings: Bk Vols 20,881
Open Mon & Tues 12-8, Wed & Thurs 10-6, Fri & Sat 9-5
Friends of the Library Group

WISEBURN LIBRARY, 5335 W 135th St, Hawthorne, 90250-4948, SAN 332-6942. Tel: 310-643-8880. FAX: 310-536-0749. Web Site: lacountylibrary.org/wiseburn-library. *Mgr,* Samantha Kline
Founded 1966. Pop 14,546; Circ 72,125
Library Holdings: Bk Vols 30,720
Open Tues, Wed & Thurs 12-8, Fri & Sat 9-5
Friends of the Library Group

WOODCREST LIBRARY, 1340 W 106th St, Los Angeles, 90044-1626, SAN 332-6977. Tel: 323-757-9373. FAX: 323-756-4907. Web Site: lacountylibrary.org/woodcrest-library. *Mgr,* Lyda Truick
Founded 1967. Pop 41,961; Circ 50,434
Library Holdings: Bk Vols 34,404
Open Mon-Fri 10-6, Sat 9-5

Bookmobiles: 3

P DOWNEY CITY LIBRARY*, 11121 Brookshire Ave, Caller Box 7015, 90241. SAN 300-7146. Tel: 562-904-7360. Circulation Tel: 562-904-7360, Ext 7366. Reference Tel: 562-904-7360, Ext 7364. FAX: 562-923-3763. Web Site: www.downeyca.org/residents/library. *Dir,* Ben Dickow; E-mail: bdickow@downeyspacecenter.org; Staff 7 (MLS 7)
Founded 1958. Pop 110,000; Circ 491,355
Library Holdings: Audiobooks 1,800; AV Mats 6,000; CDs 1,300; DVDs 2,900; Large Print Bks 891; Bk Titles 96,345; Bk Vols 137,219; Per Subs 240
Special Collections: US Document Depository
Automation Activity & Vendor Info: (Cataloging) Innovative Interfaces, Inc; (ILL) OCLC FirstSearch; (OPAC) Innovative Interfaces, Inc
Wireless access
Function: Accelerated reader prog, Adult bk club, Adult literacy prog, Art exhibits, AV serv, Bilingual assistance for Spanish patrons, Bks on CD, Children's prog, Computer training, Computers for patron use, Electronic databases & coll, Family literacy, Govt ref serv, Home delivery & serv to seniorr ctr & nursing homes, ILL available, Internet access, Magnifiers for reading, Music CDs, Online cat, Online ref, Outside serv via phone, mail, e-mail & web, Photocopying/Printing, Preschool outreach, Prog for adults, Prog for children & young adult, Ref serv available, Story hour, Summer reading prog, Tax forms, Teen prog, Telephone ref, Wheelchair accessible
Partic in Southern California Library Cooperative
Open Mon-Thurs 10-8, Fri & Sat 10-5
Friends of the Library Group

S DOWNEY HISTORICAL SOCIETY*, Downey History Center Library, 12540 Rives Ave, 90242-3444. (Mail add: PO Box 554, 90241-0554), SAN 328-2406. Tel: 562-862-2777. E-mail: downeyhistorycenter@gmail.com. Web Site: www.downeyhistoricalsociety.org. *Pres,* John Vincent
Founded 1965
Library Holdings: Bk Titles 800
Special Collections: Aerospace; Clipping File; Downey Court Dockets (1871-1957); Local Newspapers (1888-present); Los Angeles County District Attorney's Records of Arrests (1883- 1919); Photographs; School, Insurance & Agriculture Records
Subject Interests: Aerospace, Governor Downey, Local hist, Los Nietos Valley pioneers
Open Wed & Thus 10-2

S LOS ANGELES COUNTY OFFICE OF EDUCATION*, eLibrary Services, 9300 Imperial Hwy, 90242-2813. Tel: 562-922-6359. FAX: 562-940-1699. E-mail: prc_reference_desk@lacoe.edu. Web Site: www.lacoe.edu. *Coordr,* Tess Icasas; E-mail: icasas_tess@lacoe.edu; Staff 2 (MLS 2)
Founded 1974
Library Holdings: Per Subs 300
Subject Interests: Curric, Educ
Wireless access
Open Mon-Fri 8-5

DUARTE

M CITY OF HOPE*, Lee Graff Medical & Scientific Library, 1500 E Duarte Rd, 91010. SAN 300-7170. Tel: 626-301-8497. FAX: 909-357-1929. E-mail: library@coh.org. Web Site: www.cityofhope.org/education/graff-library. *Dir, Libr Serv,* Mr Keir Reavie; E-mail: kreavie@coh.org; *Clinical Librn,* Laura Brown; E-mail: laurabrown@coh.org; *Scholarly Communications Librn,* Andrea Lynch; E-mail: alynch@coh.org; Staff 6.5 (MLS 3, Non-MLS 3.5)
Founded 1954
Library Holdings: e-journals 12,000; Bk Titles 20,000; Per Subs 73
Subject Interests: Biology, Cancer, Endocrinology, Genetics, Hematology, Immunology, Pathology, Respiratory diseases
Automation Activity & Vendor Info: (Cataloging) Innovative Interfaces, Inc - Millennium; (Circulation) Innovative Interfaces, Inc - Millennium; (ILL) OCLC ILLiad; (OPAC) Innovative Interfaces, Inc - Millennium; (Serials) Innovative Interfaces, Inc - Millennium
Wireless access
Partic in OCLC Online Computer Library Center, Inc; Statewide California Electronic Library Consortium
Open Mon-Fri 8-6

EDWARDS AFB

UNITED STATES AIR FORCE

A AIR FORCE FLIGHT TEST CENTER TECHNICAL RESEARCH LIBRARY*, 812 TSS/ENTL, 307 E Popson Ave, Bldg 1400, Rm 106, 93524-6630, SAN 331-9113. Tel: 661-277-3606. FAX: 661-277-6451. *Chief Librn,* Marie L Nelson; *Librn,* Jennie Paton; Tel: 661-275-5516, Fax: 661-275-6070; *Asst Librn,* Darrell Shiplett; Staff 5 (MLS 3, Non-MLS 2)
Founded 1955
Library Holdings: Bk Vols 32,000
Subject Interests: Aeronaut, Chem, Engr, Math, Physics
Automation Activity & Vendor Info: (Cataloging) OCLC Connexion; (Circulation) SirsiDynix; (ILL) OCLC; (OPAC) SirsiDynix; (Serials) SirsiDynix
Partic in OCLC Online Computer Library Center, Inc
Restriction: Authorized patrons

A EDWARDS AIR FORCE BASE LIBRARY*, Five W Yeager Blvd, 93524-1295, SAN 331-9083. Tel: 661-275-2665. FAX: 661-277-6100. *Dir,* Alison Vasquez; Staff 1 (MLS 1)
Founded 1942
Library Holdings: Bk Vols 28,000; Per Subs 54
Subject Interests: Educ, Recreation
Partic in OCLC Online Computer Library Center, Inc
Special Services for the Blind - Web-Braille
Restriction: Access at librarian's discretion

EL CAJON

J CUYAMACA COLLEGE LIBRARY*, 900 Rancho San Diego Pkwy, 92019. SAN 322-872X. Tel: 619-660-4416. Circulation Tel: 619-660-4446. Interlibrary Loan Service Tel: 619-660-4499. Reference Tel: 619-660-4421. Administration Tel: 619-660-4400. FAX: 619-660-4493. TDD: 619-660-4418. Circulation E-mail: cuyamaca.circulation@gcccd.edu. Web Site: www.cuyamaca.edu/academics/support/library/default.aspx. *Dean, Info Tech & Learning Res,* Kerry Kilber Rebman; Tel: 619-660-4400; *Librn,* Jeri Edelen; Tel: 619-660-4423, E-mail: jeri.edelen@gcccd.edu; *Librn,* Angela Nesta; Tel: 619-660-4403, E-mail: angela.nesta@gcccd.edu; *Librn,* Kari Wergeland; Tel: 619-660-4412, E-mail: kari.wergeland@gcccd.edu; Staff 9 (MLS 4, Non-MLS 5)
Founded 1978. Enrl 8,000; Fac 89; Highest Degree: Associate
Library Holdings: AV Mats 2,029; Bks on Deafness & Sign Lang 59; CDs 44; DVDs 155; e-books 1,810; Large Print Bks 22; Bk Vols 32,052; Per Subs 109; Videos 1,649

Automation Activity & Vendor Info: (Cataloging) SirsiDynix; (Circulation) SirsiDynix; (Course Reserve) SirsiDynix; (ILL) OCLC Online; (OPAC) SirsiDynix; (Serials) SirsiDynix
Wireless access
Open Mon-Thurs 7:30am-9pm, Fri 7:30-1, Sat 9-3; Mon-Thurs (Summer) 11-5

SR FIRST PRESBYTERIAN CHURCH OF EL CAJON LIBRARY, 500 Farragut Circle, 92020. SAN 374-8448. Tel: 619-442-2583. E-mail: office@firstpres-elcajon.org. Web Site: www.firstpres-elcajon.org/resources.
Founded 1981
Library Holdings: AV Mats 57; CDs 5; DVDs 30; Large Print Bks 20; Bk Vols 3,140; Per Subs 1; Videos 193
Subject Interests: Christian fiction
Automation Activity & Vendor Info: (Cataloging) ResourceMATE; (OPAC) ResourceMATE

J GROSSMONT COLLEGE LIBRARY*, Learning & Technology Resource Center, 8800 Grossmont College Dr, 92020-1799. SAN 300-7200. Tel: 619-644-7356. Circulation Tel: 619-644-7356. Interlibrary Loan Service Tel: 619-644-7472. Reference Tel: 619-644-7361. FAX: 619-644-7054, 619-644-7921. Web Site: www.grossmont.edu/library. *Dean, Learning Res,* Dr Eric Klein; E-mail: eric.klein@gcccd.edu; *Colls Librn, Dept Chair,* Julie Middlemas; Tel: 619-644-7371, E-mail: julie.middlemas@gcccd.edu; *Cat Librn, Outreach Serv,* Nadra Farina-Hess; E-mail: nadra.farina-hess@gcccd.edu; *Syst Librn,* Jessica Owens; E-mail: jessica.owens@gcccd.edu; *Libr Mgr,* Melissa Takagi; Tel: 619-644-7359, E-mail: melissa.takagi@gcccd.edu; *Libr Instruction,* Felicia Kalker; Tel: 619-644-7553, E-mail: felicia.kalker@gcccd.edu; Staff 5 (MLS 5)
Founded 1961. Enrl 16,660; Fac 1,393
Library Holdings: Bk Vols 106,149; Per Subs 431
Special Collections: Career Information; Reference Resources. Oral History
Automation Activity & Vendor Info: (Acquisitions) SirsiDynix
Wireless access

EL CENTRO

P EL CENTRO PUBLIC LIBRARY*, 1140 N Imperial Ave, 92243. SAN 331-9202. Tel: 760-337-4565. FAX: 760-352-1384. Web Site: www.cityofelcentro.org/library. *Libr Dir,* Roland Banks; E-mail: rbanks@ci.el-centro.ca.us; *Libr Operations Supvr,* Lois Shelton; E-mail: lshelton@eclib.org; Staff 5 (MLS 1, Non-MLS 4)
Founded 1909. Pop 42,000; Circ 147,000
Library Holdings: Bk Titles 95,000; Per Subs 45
Special Collections: Imperial Valley California Coll, bks & pamphlets. State Document Depository
Automation Activity & Vendor Info: (Acquisitions) Innovative Interfaces, Inc; (Cataloging) Innovative Interfaces, Inc; (Circulation) Innovative Interfaces, Inc; (ILL) Innovative Interfaces, Inc; (Media Booking) Innovative Interfaces, Inc; (OPAC) Innovative Interfaces, Inc; (Serials) Innovative Interfaces, Inc
Wireless access
Function: Prog for children & young adult
Partic in Serra Cooperative Library System
Open Mon-Thurs 9-7, Fri 9-5, Sat 9-1
Friends of the Library Group
Branches: 1
EL CENTRO COMMUNITY CENTER, 375 S First St, 92243, SAN 331-9237. Tel: 760-336-8977. *Librn,* Michelle Aris
Library Holdings: Bk Vols 1,500
Open Thurs 9-6, Fri 9-5

P IMPERIAL COUNTY FREE LIBRARY*, Headquarters, 1331 S Clark Rd, Bldg 24, 92243. (Mail add: 1125 Main St, 92243-2748), SAN 332-1606. Tel: 760-339-7100. FAX: 760-339-6465. E-mail: imperialcountylibrary@co.imperial.ca.us. Web Site: www.co.imperial.ca.us/library. *County Librn,* Crystal Duran; E-mail: crystalduran@co.imperial.ca.us; Staff 6.5 (MLS 1, Non-MLS 5.5)
Founded 1912. Pop 55,740
Library Holdings: Audiobooks 1,490; AV Mats 1,974; Bks on Deafness & Sign Lang 25; Electronic Media & Resources 1; Large Print Bks 1,000; Bk Titles 47,631; Bk Vols 53,378; Per Subs 45; Videos 1,974
Special Collections: Local History (Holtville & Imperial Valley Coll); Spanish Language Coll, audios, bks, pers, videos
Wireless access
Function: Adult literacy prog, CD-ROM, Computer training, Electronic databases & coll, Family literacy, Homework prog, ILL available, Music CDs, Photocopying/Printing, Prog for adults, Prog for children & young adult, Ref serv available, Spoken cassettes & CDs, Spoken cassettes & DVDs, Summer reading prog, Tax forms, VHS videos
Partic in Serra Cooperative Library System
Special Services for the Blind - Assistive/Adapted tech devices, equip & products; Audio mat; Bks available with recordings; Bks on cassette; Bks on CD; Cassette playback machines; Cassettes; Large print bks; Screen enlargement software for people with visual disabilities
Friends of the Library Group
Branches: 4
CALIPATRIA BRANCH, 105 S Lake, Calipatria, 92233. (Mail add: PO Box 707, Calipatria, 92233-0707), SAN 332-1630. Tel: 760-348-2630. FAX: 760-348-5575. *Library Contact,* Linda Hoff
Function: Audio & video playback equip for onsite use, CD-ROM, Computer training, Electronic databases & coll, Family literacy, ILL available, Photocopying/Printing, Prog for adults, Prog for children & young adult, Ref serv available, Spoken cassettes & CDs, Spoken cassettes & DVDs, Summer reading prog, Tax forms, Telephone ref, VHS videos
Open Mon-Wed 9-6, Thurs 10-7, Fri 9-5
Friends of the Library Group
HEBER BRANCH, 1132 Heber Ave, Heber, 92249. Tel: 442-265-7131. *Libr Asst,* Rebecca Mendoza
Pop 5,000; Circ 14,084
Open Mon & Thurs 9-6, Tues 10-7
HOLTVILLE BRANCH, 101 E Sixth St, Holtville, 92250. (Mail add: PO Box 755, Holtville, 92250-0755), SAN 332-1665. Tel: 760-356-2385. FAX: 760-356-2437. *Libr Asst,* Lorenza Carpenter
Pop 7,000
Special Collections: Local History (Holtville & Imperial County History Coll); Spanish Language Coll
Function: Adult literacy prog, CD-ROM, Computer training, Electronic databases & coll, Family literacy, Homework prog, ILL available, Online info literacy tutorials on the web & in blackboard, Orientations, Photocopying/Printing, Prog for adults, Prog for children & young adult, Ref serv available, Spoken cassettes & CDs, Summer reading prog, Tax forms, VHS videos, Wheelchair accessible
Open Mon, Tues & Thurs 9-6, Wed 9-7, Fri 9-5
Friends of the Library Group
SALTON CITY BRANCH, 1209 Van Buren Rd, Ste 2, Salton City, 92275. (Mail add: PO Box 5340, Salton City, 92275-5340). Tel: 760-604-6956. E-mail: saltoncity.icfl@gmail.com. *Libr Asst,* Maudie Baca
Library Holdings: Bk Vols 3,500
Open Tues 9-5, Wed 3-7, Thurs 9-1

GL IMPERIAL COUNTY LAW LIBRARY*, El Centro Courthouse Lower Level, 939 W Main St, 92243. SAN 300-7227. Tel: 760-482-2271. FAX: 760-482-4530. E-mail: iclawlib@imperial.courts.ca.gov. Web Site: imperial.courts.ca.gov/LawLibrary. *Librn,* Elizabeth Lopez; E-mail: elizabeth.lopez@imperial.courts.ca.gov
Library Holdings: Bk Vols 4,000
Wireless access
Open Mon-Fri 8-12 & 1-5

EL MONTE

S EL MONTE MUSEUM OF HISTORY LIBRARY*, Museum Library, 3150 N Tyler Ave, 91731. SAN 327-3148. Tel: 626-580-2232. E-mail: museum@elmonteca.gov. Web Site: www.ci.el-monte.ca.us/455/El-Monte-Historical-Museum. *Curator,* Sheila Crippen; E-mail: scrippen@elmonteca.gov
Library Holdings: Bk Titles 1,700; Bk Vols 3,000; Per Subs 20
Open Mon-Wed 10-4, Thurs 12:30-4

EL SEGUNDO

S AEROSPACE CORP, Charles C Lauritsen Library, 2360 E El Segundo Blvd, 90245. (Mail add: PO Box 80966, Mail Sta M1/199, Los Angeles, 90009-0966), SAN 300-7251. Tel: 310-336-5000. FAX: 310-563-7922. *Dir, Libr & Info Mgt,* Patricia W Green; E-mail: patricia.w.green@aero.org; *Knowledge Mgr,* Caroline Smith; E-mail: caroline.smith@aero.org; Staff 13 (MLS 10, Non-MLS 3)
Founded 1960
Library Holdings: e-books 230,000; e-journals 8,300; Bk Titles 73,000; Bk Vols 140,000; Per Subs 100
Special Collections: Aerospace Corporation Authors
Subject Interests: Aeronaut, Aerospace sci, Astronautics, Engr
Automation Activity & Vendor Info: (Acquisitions) Ex Libris Group; (Cataloging) Ex Libris Group; (Circulation) Ex Libris Group; (OPAC) Ex Libris Group; (Serials) Ex Libris Group
Wireless access
Function: Archival coll, Res libr
Publications: Professional Papers
Partic in Statewide California Electronic Library Consortium
Restriction: Authorized personnel only

P EL SEGUNDO PUBLIC LIBRARY*, 111 W Mariposa Ave, 90245. SAN 300-7286. Tel: 310-524-2722. Reference Tel: 310-524-2728. Administration Tel: 310-524-2770. Web Site: www.elsegundo.org/library. *Libr Dir,* Debra F Brighton; Tel: 310-524-2730, E-mail: brighton@elsegundo.org; *Sr Librn, Ad Serv,* Julie Todd; Tel: 310-524-2729, E-mail: jtodd@elsegundo.org; *Sr*

Librn, Support Serv, Mark Herbert; Tel: 310-524-2732, E-mail: mherbert@elsegundo.org; *Librn II/Youth Serv, Sch Serv,* Sindee Pickens; Tel: 310-524-2771, E-mail: spickens@elsegundo.org; Staff 16.5 (MLS 4.5, Non-MLS 12)
Founded 1948. Pop 16,654; Circ 220,000
Library Holdings: Audiobooks 5,500; AV Mats 6,000; Bks on Deafness & Sign Lang 20; CDs 5,600; DVDs 7,350; e-books 6,150; Electronic Media & Resources 10; High Interest/Low Vocabulary Bk Vols 500; Large Print Bks 5,000; Microforms 400; Bk Titles 149,880; Bk Vols 159,000; Per Subs 112; Spec Interest Per Sub 20; Videos 1,000
Special Collections: Adult Literacy; Archival Photos Online; El Segundo Local History Coll
Subject Interests: Art, Biographies, Cooking, Job search, Local hist, Popular fiction, Sci fict, Spanish lang, Travel
Automation Activity & Vendor Info: (Acquisitions) Baker & Taylor; (Cataloging) Innovative Interfaces, Inc; (Circulation) Innovative Interfaces, Inc; (ILL) Innovative Interfaces, Inc; (OPAC) Innovative Interfaces, Inc; (Serials) Innovative Interfaces, Inc
Wireless access
Publications: El Segundo Public Library News (Online only)
Partic in Southern California Library Cooperative
Open Mon-Thurs 9-9, Fri & Sat 10-5
Friends of the Library Group

S LOS ANGELES TIMES*, Editorial Library, 2300 E Imperial Hwy, 90245. SAN 300-9599. Tel: 213-237-5000. Web Site: www.latimes.com. *Dir,* Cary Schneider; E-mail: cary.schneider@latimes.com; *Librn,* Scott Wilson; E-mail: scott.wilson@latimes.com; Staff 5 (MLS 5)
Founded 1905
Library Holdings: Bk Titles 10,000
Special Collections: Core Reference Coll; Los Angeles Times, clippings, flm, photogs
Subject Interests: Current events
Publications: Library Information Notes; Library Updates
Partic in OCLC Online Computer Library Center, Inc; Southern California Library Cooperative

EMERYVILLE

S ALCOHOL RESEARCH GROUP LIBRARY*, 6001 Shellmound St, Ste 450, 94608. SAN 329-8272. Tel: 510-898-5800. FAX: 510-985-6459. E-mail: library@arg.org. Web Site: arg.org/about-us/library. *Adminr,* Dustin Khebzou; E-mail: dkhebzou@arg.org; *Libr Tech,* Eric Rosen; E-mail: erosen@arg.org; Staff 1 (Non-MLS 1)
Founded 1959
Library Holdings: Bk Vols 6,300; Per Subs 249
Subject Interests: Alcohol abuse, Drug abuse, Smoking, Socio-cultural aspects of alcohol, Tobacco
Automation Activity & Vendor Info: (Acquisitions) Inmagic, Inc.; (Cataloging) Inmagic, Inc.; (Serials) Inmagic, Inc.
Restriction: Authorized scholars by appt, Circulates for staff only, Open by appt only

ENCINITAS

S SAN DIEGO BOTANIC GARDENS LIBRARY*, 230 Quail Gardens Dr, 92024-0005. (Mail add: PO Box 230005, 92024), SAN 373-3998. Tel: 760-436-3036, Ext 210. FAX: 760-632-0917. E-mail: info@SDBGarden.org. Web Site: www.sdbgarden.org. *Librn,* Position Currently Open
Library Holdings: Bk Vols 2,000
Special Collections: Out-of-Print Botanical Coll, bks, slides & videos
Subject Interests: Botany, Gardening, Hort
Restriction: Open by appt only

ESCONDIDO

S ESCONDIDO HISTORY CENTER, 321 N Broadway, 92025. (Mail add: PO Box 263, 92033-0263), SAN 373-4013. Tel: 760-743-8207. FAX: 760-743-8267. E-mail: ehc@escondidohistory.org. Web Site: www.escondidohistory.org. *Educ Coordr, Exec Dir,* Robin Fox; E-mail: fox@escondidohistory.org
Library Holdings: Bk Vols 1,000
Subject Interests: Calif, Furniture, Local hist, State hist
Wireless access
Open Tues-Sat 10-4
Restriction: Open to pub for ref only

P ESCONDIDO PUBLIC LIBRARY*, 239 S Kalmia St, 92025. SAN 300-7340. Tel: 760-839-4683. Circulation Tel: 760-839-4684. Reference Tel: 760-839-4840. Administration Tel: 760-839-4601. FAX: 760-741-4255. Web Site: library.escondido.org. *City Librn, Libr Dir,* Dara Bradds; E-mail: dara.bradds@escondidolibrary.org; *Adult Serv, Principal Librn,* Azar Katouzian; Tel: 760-839-4839, E-mail: azar.katouzian@escondido.org; *Principal Librn, Youth Serv,* Dan Wood; Tel: 760-839-5456, E-mail: dan.wood@escondido.org; Staff 27 (MLS 12, Non-MLS 15)
Founded 1898. Pop 138,015; Circ 753,415
Library Holdings: AV Mats 32,472; e-books 2,000; Bk Titles 160,259; Per Subs 200
Special Collections: Local & Family History (Pioneer Room)
Subject Interests: Bus & mgt, Local hist
Automation Activity & Vendor Info: (Circulation) Horizon; (ILL) OCLC
Wireless access
Function: Adult literacy prog, Art exhibits, Bilingual assistance for Spanish patrons, Bk club(s), Bks on CD, Chess club, Children's prog, Computer training, Computers for patron use, E-Reserves, Electronic databases & coll, Family literacy, Home delivery & serv to seniorr ctr & nursing homes, Homework prog, Music CDs, Online cat, Online ref, Outreach serv, Photocopying/Printing, Prog for adults, Prog for children & young adult, Senior computer classes, Story hour, Summer reading prog, Tax forms, Teen prog, Telephone ref, VHS videos, Wheelchair accessible
Publications: 100 Years of Library History in Escondido
Partic in Califa
Open Mon-Fri 9:30-7, Sat 9:30-6, Sun 1-5
Friends of the Library Group
Bookmobiles: 1

S SAN DIEGO ZOO GLOBAL LIBRARY*, Beckman Ctr, 15600 San Pasqual Valley Rd, 92027. Tel: 760-747-8702, Ext 5736. Web Site: library.sandiegozoo.org. *Assoc Dir, Libr Serv,* Beth Autin; Tel: 760-291-5479, E-mail: bautin@sandiegozoo.org; *Asst Librn,* Kathy Elliott; E-mail: kelliott@sandiegozoo.org; *Libr Res Spec,* Kate Jirik; Tel: 760-747-8702, Ext 5735, E-mail: kjirik@sandiegozoo.org; Staff 2.5 (MLS 2, Non-MLS 0.5)
Founded 1916
Library Holdings: Bk Vols 11,000; Per Subs 680
Special Collections: Ernst Schwarz Coll, reprints; Herpetology (Charles E Shaw Coll), bks, reprints; Zoo Publications (annual reports, guidebooks, newsletters)
Subject Interests: Conserv sci, Ecology, Hort, Veterinary med, Zoology
Publications: Accessions list (Monthly)
Partic in International Environment Library Consortium; OCLC Online Computer Library Center, Inc; Statewide California Electronic Library Consortium
Restriction: Staff use only

R WESTMINSTER SEMINARY CALIFORNIA LIBRARY*, 1725 Bear Valley Pkwy, 92027. SAN 321-236X. Tel: 760-480-8474. FAX: 760-480-0252. Web Site: www.wscal.edu/resources/wsc-library. *Dir, Libr Serv,* James Lund; E-mail: jlund@wscal.edu; *Ref Librn,* Katherine VanDrunen; E-mail: kvandrunen@wscal.edu; Staff 6 (MLS 1, Non-MLS 5)
Founded 1980. Enrl 147; Fac 13; Highest Degree: Master
Library Holdings: Bk Vols 63,420; Per Subs 260
Special Collections: 16th/17th Century Reformation & Puritanism, micro
Subject Interests: Biblical studies, Theol
Automation Activity & Vendor Info: (Cataloging) Follett Software; (Circulation) Follett Software; (OPAC) Follett Software
Wireless access
Partic in Statewide California Electronic Library Consortium
Open Mon-Fri (Winter) 7:45am-10pm, Sat 9-5; Mon-Fri (Summer) 8-4:30

EUREKA

J COLLEGE OF THE REDWOODS*, 7351 Tompkins Hill Rd, 95501. SAN 300-7375. Tel: 707-476-4260. Reference Tel: 707-476-4263. FAX: 707-476-4432. Web Site: www.redwoods.edu/library. *Dir,* Catherine Cox; E-mail: catherine-cox@redwoods.edu; *Librn,* Ruth Moon; E-mail: ruth-moon@redwoods.edu; Staff 2 (MLS 2)
Founded 1965. Enrl 6,673; Highest Degree: Associate
Library Holdings: Bk Titles 57,000; Bk Vols 66,313
Subject Interests: Nursing
Automation Activity & Vendor Info: (Cataloging) ByWater Solutions; (Circulation) ByWater Solutions; (Course Reserve) ByWater Solutions; (ILL) ByWater Solutions; (OPAC) ByWater Solutions
Wireless access
Mem of NorthNet Library System
Partic in Community College League of California; OCLC Online Computer Library Center, Inc
Open Mon-Thurs (Fall/Spring) 7:45am-8pm, Fri 7:45-5

GL HUMBOLDT COUNTY LAW LIBRARY*, Courthouse, 825 Fourth St, RM G04, 95501. (Mail add: PO Box 331, 95502), SAN 300-7383. Tel: 707-476-2356, 707-497-8727. FAX: 707-268-0690. E-mail: publiclawlibrary95501@outlook.com. Web Site: publiclawlibrary95.wixsite.com/publiclawlibrary. *Dir, Law Librn,* Stephanie Richter
Founded 1907
Library Holdings: Bk Vols 18,000

Wireless access
Open Mon-Fri 9-4:30

P HUMBOLDT COUNTY LIBRARY*, Library Administration, 1313 Third St, 95501-0553. SAN 331-9415. Tel: 707-269-1918. Web Site: humboldtgov.org/1346/Public-Library. *Dir, Libr Serv,* Nick Wilczek; E-mail: nwilczek@co.humboldt.ca.us; *Libr Operations Mgr,* Ronda Wittenberg; E-mail: rwittenberg@co.humboldt.ca.us; Staff 12 (MLS 12)
Founded 1878. Pop 121,000
Library Holdings: Bk Titles 148,308; Bk Vols 239,625; Per Subs 332
Special Collections: American Indians Coll, especially California Indians; Humboldt County History Coll; NRC Nuclear Power Plants LDR
Automation Activity & Vendor Info: (Circulation) Innovative Interfaces, Inc
Wireless access
Mem of NorthNet Library System
Special Services for the Deaf - TDD equip
Open Tues-Sat 8-5
Friends of the Library Group
Branches: 11
ARCATA BRANCH, 500 Seventh St, Arcata, 95521-6315, SAN 331-944X. Tel: 707-822-5954.
Library Holdings: Bk Vols 12,000
Open Tues & Fri 12-5, Wed & Sat 10-5, Thurs 12-8
Friends of the Library Group
BLUE LAKE BRANCH, 111 Greenwood Ave, Blue Lake, 95525. (Mail add: PO Box 236, Blue Lake, 95525-0236), SAN 331-9474. Tel: 707-668-4207.
Library Holdings: Bk Vols 3,000
Open Wed 2-7, Sat 11-4
Friends of the Library Group
EUREKA (MAIN LIBRARY), 1313 Third St, 95501, SAN 331-9490. Tel: 707-269-1915. Reference Tel: 707-269-1905.
Library Holdings: Bk Vols 161,860
Open Tues & Thurs 12-5, Wed 12-8, Fri 10-5, Sat 11-4
Friends of the Library Group
FERNDALE BRANCH, 807 Main St, Ferndale, 95536. (Mail add: PO Box 397, Ferndale, 95536-0397), SAN 331-9504. Tel: 707-786-9559.
Library Holdings: Bk Vols 10,000
Open Tues & Thurs 12-5 & 7-9, Wed & Sat 12-5, Fri 12-4
Friends of the Library Group
FORTUNA BRANCH, 753 14th St, Fortuna, 95540-2113, SAN 331-9539. Tel: 707-725-3460.
Library Holdings: Bk Vols 7,000
Open Tues 12-5, Wed 12-9, Thurs-Sat 10-5
Friends of the Library Group
GARBERVILLE BRANCH, 715 Cedar St, Garberville, 95542-3201, SAN 331-9563. Tel: 707-923-2230. FAX: 707-923-2230.
Library Holdings: Bk Vols 7,000
Open Wed 12-7, Thurs & Fri 12-6, Sat 12-4
Friends of the Library Group
MCKINLEYVILLE BRANCH, 1606 Pickett Rd, McKinleyville, 95519, SAN 331-9652. Tel: 707-839-4459.
Library Holdings: Bk Vols 2,500
Open Tues & Fri 12-5, Wed 12-8, Thurs & Sat 10-5
Friends of the Library Group
RIO DELL BRANCH, 715 Wildwood Ave, Rio Dell, 95562-1321, SAN 331-9687. Tel: 707-764-3333.
Library Holdings: Bk Vols 3,600
Open Tues & Sat 11-4, Wed 1-6
Friends of the Library Group
TRINIDAD BRANCH, 380 Janis Ct, Trinidad, 95570. (Mail add: PO Box 856, Trinidad, 95570), SAN 331-9717. Tel: 707-677-0227.
Library Holdings: Bk Vols 2,500
Open Tues Noon-3:30, Thurs 11-1 & 2-7, Sat Noon-4
Friends of the Library Group
WILLOW CREEK BRANCH, Hwy 299 & Hwy 96, Willow Creek, 95573-0466. (Mail add: PO Box 466, Willow Creek, 95573), SAN 331-9628. Tel: 530-629-2146.
Library Holdings: Bk Vols 5,458
Open Wed & Thurs 12-5, Fri & Sat 12-4
Friends of the Library Group
KIM YERTON MEMORIAL BRANCH, 370 Loop Rd, Hoopa, 95546. (Mail add: PO Box 1407, Hoopa, 95546). Tel: 530-625-5082. FAX: 530-625-5022.
Open Tues, Thurs, Fri & Sat 10-1 & 2-5, Wed 10-1 & 2-8
Friends of the Library Group
Bookmobiles: 1

S KIM YERTON INDIAN ACTION LIBRARY*, 2905 Hubbard Ln, Ste C, 95501. SAN 324-2773. Tel: 707-443-8401. E-mail: indianaction@att.net. *Dir,* Coleen Bruno
Founded 1974
Library Holdings: Bk Titles 3,000
Special Collections: American Indians; California Northwest Coast Tribes (Yurok, Hupa, Karok Coll), bks, flms, photogs, tapes; Photographs (Ericson, Curtis, Boyle, Roberts Coll), bd vols
Wireless access
Open Mon-Thurs 9-1

FAIRFIELD

J SOLANO COMMUNITY COLLEGE LIBRARY*, 4000 Suisun Valley Rd, 94534. SAN 301-6838. Tel: 707-864-7000, Ext 4519, 707-864-7132. E-mail: scclibrary@solano.edu. Web Site: www.solano.edu/library. *Librn,* Erin Duane; Tel: 707-864-7000, Ext 4706, E-mail: Erin.Duane@solano.edu; Staff 8 (MLS 4, Non-MLS 4)
Founded 1965. Enrl 10,377; Fac 146; Highest Degree: Associate
Library Holdings: High Interest/Low Vocabulary Bk Vols 200; Bk Titles 30,550; Bk Vols 36,500; Per Subs 165
Automation Activity & Vendor Info: (Circulation) TLC (The Library Corporation); (OPAC) TLC (The Library Corporation)
Wireless access
Mem of NorthNet Library System
Partic in Coop Libr Agency for Syst & Servs; OCLC Online Computer Library Center, Inc; Solano Napa & Partners Library Consortium
Open Mon-Thurs 7:45am-7:50pm, Fri (Aug-May) 7:45-2:50

P SOLANO COUNTY LIBRARY*, 1150 Kentucky St, 94533. SAN 331-9741. Toll Free Tel: 866-572-7587. FAX: 707-421-7474. Web Site: www.solanolibrary.com. *Dir, Libr Serv,* Bonnie A Katz; E-mail: bkatz@solanocounty.com; *Dep Dir,* Nancy Wilson; E-mail: njwilson@solanocounty.com; *Asst Dir,* Suzanne Olawski; E-mail: seolawski@solanocounty.com; Staff 111 (MLS 33, Non-MLS 78)
Founded 1914. Pop 360,023; Circ 3,700,433
Library Holdings: Audiobooks 50,000; AV Mats 160,316; e-books 24,831; Electronic Media & Resources 4,352; Bk Vols 534,219; Per Subs 1,119
Special Collections: Printing (Donovan J McCune Coll), rare bks, specimens; Solano County History Coll; Vallejo History Coll
Automation Activity & Vendor Info: (Acquisitions) TLC (The Library Corporation); (Cataloging) OCLC; (Circulation) TLC (The Library Corporation); (Course Reserve) TLC (The Library Corporation); (ILL) OCLC; (OPAC) TLC (The Library Corporation); (Serials) TLC (The Library Corporation)
Wireless access
Mem of NorthNet Library System
Partic in Solano Napa & Partners Library Consortium; Solano Partner Libraries & St Helena
Friends of the Library Group
Branches: 9
FAIRFIELD CIVIC CENTER, 1150 Kentucky St, 94533, SAN 331-9776. Toll Free Tel: 866-572-7587. FAX: 707-421-7207.
Pop 106,379; Circ 576,462
Friends of the Library Group
FAIRFIELD CORDELIA LIBRARY, 5050 Business Ctr Dr, 94534. FAX: 707-863-7311. Toll Free FAX: 866-572-7587.
Pop 26,959; Circ 282,916
Friends of the Library Group
JOHN F KENNEDY BRANCH, 505 Santa Clara St, Vallejo, 94590, SAN 331-9806. Toll Free Tel: 866-572-7587. FAX: 707-553-5667.
Pop 115,928; Circ 485,549
Friends of the Library Group

L LAW LIBRARY, Hall of Justice, 600 Union Ave, 94533, SAN 300-7405. Tel: 707-421-6520. FAX: 707-421-6516. *Librn,* Jonathan Watson; Staff 2 (MLS 1, Non-MLS 1)
Founded 1911
Special Collections: California Statutes; Codes of Solano Co & Cities therein
Open Mon-Fri 8-4:30
RIO VISTA LIBRARY, 44 S Second St, Rio Vista, 94571, SAN 331-9830. Toll Free Tel: 866-572-7587. FAX: 707-374-2919.
Pop 7,418; Circ 86,506
Friends of the Library Group
SPRINGSTOWNE LIBRARY, 1003 Oakwood Ave, Vallejo, 94591, SAN 331-9865. Toll Free Tel: 866-572-7587. FAX: 707-553-5656.
Pop 46,371; Circ 190,246
Friends of the Library Group
SUISUN CITY LIBRARY, 601 Pintail Dr, Suisun City, 94585, SAN 373-8760. Toll Free Tel: 866-572-7587. FAX: 707-784-1426.
Pop 27,978; Circ 200,757
Friends of the Library Group
VACAVILLE PUBLIC LIBRARY-CULTURAL CENTER, 1020 Ulatis Dr, Vacaville, 95687, SAN 331-989X. Toll Free Tel: 866-572-7587. FAX: 707-451-0987.
Pop 92,092; Circ 554,430
Open Mon-Thurs 10-9, Fri & Sat 10-5, Sun 1-5
Friends of the Library Group

VACAVILLE PUBLIC LIBRARY-TOWN SQUARE, One Town Square Pl, Vacaville, 95688. Toll Free Tel: 866-572-7587. FAX: 707-455-7509. Pop 36,837; Circ 305,696
Friends of the Library Group

FOLSOM

C FOLSOM LAKE COLLEGE LIBRARY*, Ten College Pkwy, 95630. Tel: 916-608-6613. Reference Tel: 916-608-6612. FAX: 916-608-6533. E-mail: FLC-Librarian@flc.losrios.edu. Web Site: www.flc.losrios.edu/academics/library, www.flc.losrios.edu/libraries.htm. *Librn,* Rebecca Mendell; Tel: 916-608-6708, E-mail: mendelr@flc.losrios.edu; *Librn,* Lorilie Roundtree; Tel: 916-608-6818, E-mail: roundtl@flc.losrios.edu; *Librn,* James Telles; Tel: 916-608-6528, E-mail: tellesj@flc.losrios.edu; *Librn,* Stacia S Thiessen; Tel: 916-608-6557, E-mail: thiesss@flc.losrios.edu; Staff 4 (MLS 4)
Automation Activity & Vendor Info: (Cataloging) Innovative Interfaces, Inc; (Circulation) Innovative Interfaces, Inc; (OPAC) Innovative Interfaces, Inc
Wireless access
Open Mon-Thurs 8-8, Fri 8-5

P FOLSOM PUBLIC LIBRARY*, George Murray Bldg, 411 Stafford St, 95630. SAN 375-4987. Tel: 916-461-6130. E-mail: libcirc@folsom.ca.us. Web Site: www.folsom.ca.us/city_hall/depts/library. *Libr Dir,* Lori Easterwood; E-mail: leasterwood@folsom.ca.us
Founded 1993. Pop 72,000; Circ 610,000
Automation Activity & Vendor Info: (Cataloging) Innovative Interfaces, Inc; (Circulation) Innovative Interfaces, Inc
Wireless access
Open Tues & Wed 10-8, Thurs-Sat 10-5, Sun 12-5
Friends of the Library Group

FONTANA

M KAISER-PERMANENTE MEDICAL CENTER*, Health Sciences Library, 17234 Valley Rd, 92335. SAN 300-743X. Tel: 909-427-5086. FAX: 909-427-6288. *Librn,* Grace Johnston; Staff 1 (Non-MLS 1)
Founded 1950
Library Holdings: Audiobooks 10; AV Mats 50; DVDs 50; e-books 250; e-journals 5,566; Electronic Media & Resources 52; Bk Vols 1,704; Per Subs 15
Subject Interests: Dermatology, Family med, Internal med, Neurology, Obstetrics & gynecology, Orthopedics, Pediatrics, Radiology, Sports med, Surgery, Urology
Automation Activity & Vendor Info: (Cataloging) Innovative Interfaces, Inc - Millennium; (Circulation) Innovative Interfaces, Inc - Millennium; (Serials) Innovative Interfaces, Inc - Millennium
Wireless access
Partic in Inland Empire Med Libr Coop
Open Mon-Fri 8-4:30
Restriction: Access for corporate affiliates, Authorized personnel only, Authorized scholars by appt, Circulates for staff only, Employees only, External users must contact libr, Hospital employees & physicians only, Hospital staff & commun, ID required to use computers (Ltd hrs), Lending limited to county residents, Lending to staff only, Med staff & students, Med staff only, Open to hospital affiliates only, Staff use only

FORT IRWIN

UNITED STATES ARMY

A FORT IRWIN POST LIBRARY*, National Training Ctr, Bldg 331, Second St & F Ave, 92310. (Mail add: PO Box 105091, 92310-5091), SAN 321-8716. Tel: 760-380-3462. FAX: 760-380-5071. Web Site: www.fortirwinmwr.com/recreation-2/the-post-library. *Librn,* Cara Bates; Staff 4.5 (MLS 1, Non-MLS 3.5)
Founded 1981
Library Holdings: CDs 812; DVDs 1,146; Bk Vols 30,916; Per Subs 94; Talking Bks 859; Videos 1,464
Subject Interests: Calif, Mil hist, Mil sci
Automation Activity & Vendor Info: (Acquisitions) Horizon; (Cataloging) Horizon; (Circulation) Horizon; (OPAC) Horizon
Function: Adult bk club, Bilingual assistance for Spanish patrons, Bks on cassette, Bks on CD, Children's prog, Computers for patron use, Family literacy, Free DVD rentals, Holiday prog, ILL available, Internet access, Music CDs, Online cat, Photocopying/Printing, Prog for adults, Prog for children & young adult, Ref serv available, Story hour, Telephone ref, VHS videos, Wheelchair accessible, Workshops
Partic in OCLC Online Computer Library Center, Inc
Special Services for the Deaf - Bks on deafness & sign lang
Special Services for the Blind - Aids for in-house use; Bks on cassette; Bks on CD; Cassette playback machines; Cassettes; Copier with enlargement capabilities; Large print bks; Magnifiers; Recorded bks; Sound rec
Open Mon-Fri 10-7, Sat 10-2
Restriction: Authorized patrons, Circ to mil employees only, Photo ID required for access

AM WEED ARMY COMMUNITY HOSPITAL, MEDICAL LIBRARY*, PO Box 105109, 92310-5109, SAN 324-153X. Tel: 760-380-6889. FAX: 760-380-5734. *Tech Info Spec,* Peggy Makie; Staff 1 (MLS 1)
Library Holdings: Bk Titles 326; Per Subs 35
Subject Interests: Dentistry, Emergency room, Nursing, Pharm, Preventive med

FREMONT

P ALAMEDA COUNTY LIBRARY*, 2450 Stevenson Blvd, 94538-2326. SAN 332-091X. Tel: 510-745-1500. FAX: 510-793-2987. TDD: 888-663-0660. Web Site: www.aclibrary.org/home. *County Librn,* Cindy Chadwick; Tel: 510-745-1504, E-mail: cchadwick@aclibrary.org; *Dep County Librn,* Deb Sica; E-mail: dsica@aclibrary.org; *Head, Br Libr,* Ben Gomberg; E-mail: bgomberg@aclibrary.org; *Principal Librn,* Erin Berman; Staff 56 (MLS 43, Non-MLS 13)
Founded 1910. Pop 540,620; Circ 6,056,555
Library Holdings: Bk Vols 1,051,767; Per Subs 2,201
Special Collections: Extension Services. State Document Depository
Subject Interests: Bus & mgt, Local hist, Spanish (Lang)
Automation Activity & Vendor Info: (Acquisitions) Innovative Interfaces, Inc; (Cataloging) Innovative Interfaces, Inc; (Circulation) Innovative Interfaces, Inc; (OPAC) Innovative Interfaces, Inc; (Serials) Innovative Interfaces, Inc
Wireless access
Open Mon-Fri 8:30-5
Friends of the Library Group
Branches: 10
ALBANY LIBRARY, 1247 Marin Ave, Albany, 94706-2043, SAN 332-0944. Tel: 510-526-3720. Web Site: guides.aclibrary.org/albany. *Libr Mgr,* Rachel Sher
Library Holdings: Bk Vols 80,000; Per Subs 125
Special Services for the Deaf - TDD equip
Open Mon 12-6, Tues & Wed 12-8, Thurs 10-6, Sat 10-5, Sun 1-5
Friends of the Library Group
CASTRO VALLEY LIBRARY, 3600 Norbridge Ave, Castro Valley, 94546-5878, SAN 332-1002. Tel: 510-667-7900. Web Site: guides.aclibrary.org/castro-valley. *Libr Mgr,* Dawn Balestreri
Library Holdings: Bk Vols 96,296; Per Subs 190
Special Services for the Deaf - TDD equip
Open Mon & Tues 12-8, Wed & Thurs 10-6, Sat 10-5, Sun 1-5
Friends of the Library Group
CENTERVILLE LIBRARY, 3801 Nicolet Ave, 94536-3409, SAN 332-1037. Tel: 510-795-2629. Web Site: guides.aclibrary.org/centerville. *Libr Mgr,* Becky Machetta
Library Holdings: Bk Vols 44,000; Per Subs 100
Open Tues 1-8, Thurs 11-6, Sat 10-5
Friends of the Library Group
DUBLIN LIBRARY, 200 Civic Plaza, Dublin, 94568, SAN 332-1061. Tel: 925-803-7252. Web Site: guides.aclibrary.org/dublin. *Libr Mgr,* Shammi Gill
Library Holdings: Bk Vols 145,700; Per Subs 448
Special Services for the Deaf - TDD equip
Open Mon-Thurs 10-8, Sat 10-5, Sun 1-5
Friends of the Library Group
FREMONT LIBRARY, 2400 Stevenson Blvd, 94538-2326, SAN 332-1096. Tel: 510-745-1400. Web Site: guides.aclibrary.org/fremont. *Libr Mgr,* Brian Edwards
Library Holdings: Bk Vols 286,209; Per Subs 531
Special Services for the Deaf - Bks on deafness & sign lang; Staff with knowledge of sign lang; TDD equip
Open Mon & Tues 1-9, Wed 12-6, Thurs & Fri 11-6, Sat 10-5, Sun 1-5
Friends of the Library Group
IRVINGTON LIBRARY, 41825 Greenpark Dr, 94538-4084, SAN 332-1150. Tel: 510-608-1170. Web Site: guides.aclibrary.org/irvington. *Libr Mgr,* Becky Machetta
Library Holdings: Bk Vols 37,500; Per Subs 44
Open Wed 10-5
NEWARK LIBRARY, 6300 Civic Terrace Ave, Newark, 94560-3766, SAN 332-1185. Tel: 510-284-0675. Web Site: guides.aclibrary.org/newark. *Libr Mgr,* Joe Stoner
Library Holdings: Bk Vols 73,297; Per Subs 158
Open Mon & Tues 12-8, Wed & Thurs 10-6, Sat 10-5, Sun 1-5
NILES LIBRARY, 150 I St, 94538, SAN 332-1215. Tel: 510-284-0695. Web Site: guides.aclibrary.org/niles. *Libr Mgr,* Becky Machetta
Library Holdings: Bk Vols 11,000; Per Subs 34
Open Fri 10-5
SAN LORENZO LIBRARY, 395 Paseo Grande, San Lorenzo, 94580-2453, SAN 332-1274. Tel: 510-284-0640. Web Site: guides.aclibrary.org/san-lorenzo. *Libr Mgr,* Danielle Wilson
Library Holdings: Bk Vols 83,646; Per Subs 251

Open Mon & Tues 12-8, Wed & Thurs 10-6, Sat 10-5, Sun 1-5
Friends of the Library Group
UNION CITY LIBRARY, 34007 Alvarado-Niles Rd, Union City, 94587-4498, SAN 332-1304. Tel: 510-745-1464. Web Site: guides.aclibrary.org/union-city. *Libr Mgr,* Blaine Wentworth
Library Holdings: Bk Vols 100,000
Subject Interests: Spanish (Lang)
Open Mon & Wed 10-6, Tues & Thurs 1-8, Fri 2-6, Sat 10-5, Sun 1-5
Friends of the Library Group
Bookmobiles: 1. Mgr, Christina Grove

P CALIFORNIA SCHOOL FOR THE BLIND LIBRARY*, 500 Walnut Ave, 94536. SAN 300-6069. Tel: 510-794-3800, Ext 259, 510-936-5575. FAX: 510-794-3813. Web Site: www.csb-cde.ca.gov/instruction/library. *Libr Tech,* Elizabeth Hart; E-mail: ehart@csb-cde.ca.gov; Staff 1 (Non-MLS 1)
Founded 1860
Library Holdings: Audiobooks 3,900; Braille Volumes 5,000; CDs 1,000; DVDs 110; e-journals 1; High Interest/Low Vocabulary Bk Vols 280; Large Print Bks 2,400; Per Subs 27; Talking Bks 88; Videos 150
Special Collections: Audio Books, Fiction & Non-Fiction; Braille Fiction & Non-Fiction; Large Print Fiction & Non-Fiction; Manipulative & Tactile Items for Students; Print/Braille Books, Fiction & Non-Fiction; Professional Coll; Reading/Language Arts, Science, Mathematic & Social Studies Textbooks, audio, braille, large print, print
Automation Activity & Vendor Info: (Cataloging) Book Systems; (Circulation) Book Systems; (OPAC) Book Systems
Function: 24/7 Online cat, Audio & video playback equip for onsite use, Audiobks on Playaways & MP3, Bks on cassette, Bks on CD, Computers for patron use, Digital talking bks, Free DVD rentals, Games & aids for people with disabilities, ILL available, Online cat, Photocopying/Printing, Spoken cassettes & CDs, VHS videos
Special Services for the Blind - Accessible computers; Assistive/Adapted tech devices, equip & products; Bks & mags in Braille, on rec, tape & cassette; Bks available with recordings; Bks on cassette; Bks on CD; Bks on flash-memory cartridges; Braille bks; Braille equip; Cassette playback machines; Cassettes; Children's Braille; Closed circuit TV magnifier; Computer with voice synthesizer for visually impaired persons; Copier with enlargement capabilities; Daisy reader; Descriptive video serv (DVS); Digital talking bk; Digital talking bk machines; Extensive large print coll; Large print bks; Large type calculator; Merlin electronic magnifier reader; Playaways (bks on MP3); Recorded bks; Screen enlargement software for people with visual disabilities; Screen reader software; Sound rec; Talking calculator
Open Mon-Thurs 8-5, Fri 8-2:30
Restriction: Access at librarian's discretion, Open to students, fac & staff, Use of others with permission of librn

J OHLONE COLLEGE*, Blanchard Learning Resources Center, 43600 Mission Blvd, 94539. SAN 300-7480. Tel: 510-659-6160. Interlibrary Loan Service Tel: 510-659-6171. Administration Tel: 510-659-6166. Automation Services Tel: 510-659-6164. FAX: 510-659-6265. E-mail: librarians@ohlone.edu. Web Site: www.ohlone.edu/library. *Librn,* Barbara Duggal; E-mail: bduggal@ohlone.edu; *Librn,* Jim Landavazo; Tel: 510-659-6163, E-mail: jlandavazo@ohlone.edu; *Librn,* Elizabeth Silva; Tel: 510-659-6000, Ext 7484, E-mail: esilva@ohlone.edu; *Tech Serv,* Kathy Sparling; E-mail: ksparling@ohlone.edu; Staff 9 (MLS 4, Non-MLS 5)
Founded 1967. Enrl 10,442; Fac 650; Highest Degree: Associate
Library Holdings: CDs 13,100; Bk Titles 69,116; Per Subs 194; Videos 3,290
Automation Activity & Vendor Info: (Acquisitions) Ex Libris Group; (Cataloging) Ex Libris Group; (Circulation) Ex Libris Group; (OPAC) Ex Libris Group; (Serials) Ex Libris Group
Function: AV serv, ILL available, Photocopying/Printing, Ref serv available
Partic in San Francisco Bay Area Library & Information Network
Special Services for the Blind - Assistive/Adapted tech devices, equip & products
Restriction: Non-circulating to the pub

R QUEEN OF THE HOLY ROSARY CENTER LIBRARY, 43326 Mission Circle, 94539. SAN 321-4265. Tel: 510-657-2468. Web Site: qhrc.follettdestiny.com. *Librn,* Mary Ellen D Parker; E-mail: qhrcparker@msjdominicans.org; *Libr Asst,* Sister Rosaleen Stoiber; Staff 2 (MLS 1, Non-MLS 1)
Founded 1908
Library Holdings: Bk Titles 15,000
Subject Interests: Philos, Relig, Theol
Automation Activity & Vendor Info: (Cataloging) Follett Software; (Circulation) Follett Software; (OPAC) Follett Software
Wireless access
Function: 24/7 Online cat, Adult bk club, Bk club(s), Workshops
Partic in Califa

M WASHINGTON HOSPITAL HEALTHCARE SYSTEM*, Community Health Resource Library, 2500 Mowry Ave, 94538. Tel: 510-494-7030. FAX: 510-608-1373. TDD: 510-494-7050. Web Site: www.whhs.com/About/Community-Connection/Community-Health-Resource-Library.aspx. *Commun Outreach Mgr, Project Mgr,* Lucy Hernandez; E-mail: lucy_hernandez@whhs.com; Staff 1 (MLS 1)
Library Holdings: AV Mats 400; Bk Vols 7,000; Per Subs 30
Automation Activity & Vendor Info: (Cataloging) Follett Software; (Circulation) Follett Software; (OPAC) Follett Software
Open Mon, Tues, Thurs & Fri 10-2, Wed 10-5

FRESNO

C ALLIANT INTERNATIONAL UNIVERSITY*, Kauffman Library - Fresno Campus, 5130 E Clinton Way, 93727. SAN 300-7510. Tel: 559-253-2265. FAX: 559-253-2223. Web Site: library.alliant.edu. *Libr Dir,* Scott Zimmer; E-mail: szimmer@alliant.edu; *Ref & Instruction Librn,* Kristen Bahler; Tel: 916-561-3202, E-mail: kristen.bahler@alliant.edu; Staff 5 (MLS 2, Non-MLS 3)
Founded 1973. Enrl 547; Fac 51; Highest Degree: Doctorate
Library Holdings: Audiobooks 176; DVDs 142; Bk Vols 10,609; Per Subs 47; Videos 738
Special Collections: Children's Therapy Coll; Psychological Testing Materials
Subject Interests: Clinical psychol, Forensic psychol, Psychol
Automation Activity & Vendor Info: (Acquisitions) Innovative Interfaces, Inc - Millennium; (Cataloging) Innovative Interfaces, Inc - Millennium; (Circulation) Innovative Interfaces, Inc - Millennium; (Course Reserve) Innovative Interfaces, Inc - Millennium; (ILL) Innovative Interfaces, Inc - Millennium; (Media Booking) Innovative Interfaces, Inc - Millennium; (OPAC) Innovative Interfaces, Inc - Millennium; (Serials) Innovative Interfaces, Inc - Millennium
Wireless access
Partic in Association of Mental Health Libraries; Link+
Open Mon-Thurs 8-9, Fri 8-6, Sat & Sun 10-4
Restriction: Borrowing privileges limited to fac & registered students

L BAKER, MANOCK & JENSEN LIBRARY*, Fig Garden Financial Ctr, 5260 N Palm Ave, Ste 421, 93704. SAN 372-266X. Tel: 559-432-5400. FAX: 559-432-5620. *Librn,* Lori Sanders; Tel: 559-436-2086
Library Holdings: Bk Vols 20,000
Restriction: Non-circulating, Staff use only

C CALIFORNIA CHRISTIAN COLLEGE, Cortese Library, 5364 E Belmont Ave, 93727. SAN 300-7502. Tel: 559-302-9653, Ext 1008. FAX: 559-251-4231. E-mail: library@calchristiancollege.edu. Web Site: www.calchristiancollege.edu/library. *Librn,* Nanne Singh
Founded 1955. Highest Degree: Bachelor
Library Holdings: Bk Vols 22,000; Per Subs 15
Special Collections: California Free Will Baptist History; Free Will Baptist Denominational History
Subject Interests: Relig
Automation Activity & Vendor Info: (OPAC) LibraryWorld, Inc
Open Mon-Thurs 7:45-9:30 & 10-5
Friends of the Library Group

L CALIFORNIA COURT OF APPEAL*, Fifth Appellate District Library, 2424 Ventura St, 93721. SAN 372-2678. Tel: 559-445-5686. FAX: 559-445-6684. Web Site: www.courts.ca.gov/5dca.htm. *Librn,* Tara Crabtree
Library Holdings: Bk Vols 10,000; Per Subs 50
Restriction: Staff use only

CALIFORNIA STATE UNIVERSITY, FRESNO
C HENRY MADDEN LIBRARY*, 5200 N Barton Ave, Mail Stop ML-34, 93740-8014, SAN 300-7529. Tel: 559-278-2403. Circulation Tel: 559-278-2551. Interlibrary Loan Service Tel: 559-278-3032. Reference Tel: 559-278-2174. Information Services Tel: 559-278-2596. FAX: 559-278-6952. Web Site: www.csufresno.edu/library. *Assoc Univ Librn,* Dave Tyckoson; Tel: 559-278-5678, E-mail: davety@csufresno.edu; *Asst Univ Librn, Coll Develop,* Kimberley Smith; Tel: 559-278-4578, E-mail: kimberle@csufresno.edu; *Dean, Libr Serv,* Delritta Hornbuckle; *Dir, Libr Develop,* Marcia Morrison; Tel: 559-278-7177, E-mail: marciamo@csufresno.edu; *Head, Admin Serv,* Glenda Harada; Tel: 559-278-2142, E-mail: gharada@csufresno.edu; *Head, Circ Serv,* Christine Evans; E-mail: chevans@csufresno.edu; *Head, Info & Outreach Serv,* Monica Fusich; Tel: 559-278-7673, E-mail: monicaf@csufresno.edu; *Head, Libr Info Tech,* Patrick Newell; Tel: 559-278-6528, E-mail: pnewell@csufresno.edu; *Head, Pub Serv,* Paula Popma; Tel: 559-278-5794, E-mail: ppopma@csufresno.edu; *Head, Ref,* Allison Cowgill; Tel: 559-278-1022, E-mail: acowgill@csufresno.edu; *Head, Resource Sharing,* Gretchen Higginbottom; Tel: 559-278-3032, E-mail: ghigginbottom@csufresno.edu; *Maps & Govt Info Librn,* Carol Doyle; Tel: 559-278-2335, E-mail: caroldo@csufresno.edu; *Spec Coll Librn,* Tammy Lau; Tel: 559-278-2595, E-mail: tammyl@csufresno.edu;

Teacher Res Ctr Librn, Mike Tillman; Tel: 559-278-2054, E-mail: miket@csufresno.edu; *Coordr, Bldg Mgt,* Susan Christensen; Tel: 559-278-5792, E-mail: susanm@csufresno.edu; *Cataloger,* Janet Bochin; Tel: 559-278-2158, E-mail: janetbo@csufresno.edu. Subject Specialists: *Engr,* Dave Tyckoson; *Educ,* Patrick Newell; *Soc sci,* Allison Cowgill; *Agr, Sciences,* Carol Doyle; *Engr,* Mike Tillman; *Music,* Janet Bochin; Staff 61.9 (MLS 23.1, Non-MLS 38.8)
Founded 1911. Enrl 18,229; Fac 1,142; Highest Degree: Doctorate
Library Holdings: AV Mats 92,426; CDs 83,321; DVDs 9,105; e-books 89,192; e-journals 12,581; Microforms 1,430,346; Bk Titles 1,044,948; Bk Vols 1,151,598; Per Subs 42,585
Special Collections: Arne Nixon Center for the Study of Children's Literature; Central Valley Political Archives; Credit Foncier Colony, Topolobampo, Sinaloa (Mexico Coll); Enology; History (Roy J Woodward Memorial Library of California); International Exhibitions; Literature (William Saroyan Coll). State Document Depository; US Document Depository
Automation Activity & Vendor Info: (Acquisitions) Innovative Interfaces, Inc - Millennium; (Cataloging) Innovative Interfaces, Inc - Millennium; (Circulation) Innovative Interfaces, Inc - Millennium; (ILL) OCLC ILLiad; (Media Booking) Innovative Interfaces, Inc - Millennium; (OPAC) Innovative Interfaces, Inc - Millennium; (Serials) Innovative Interfaces, Inc - Millennium
Function: Art exhibits, CD-ROM, Computers for patron use, Electronic databases & coll, Free DVD rentals, ILL available, Learning ctr, Mail & tel request accepted, Microfiche/film & reading machines, Music CDs, Online cat, Online info literacy tutorials on the web & in blackboard, Online ref, Orientations, Photocopying/Printing, Printer for laptops & handheld devices, Ref & res, Ref serv available, Scanner, Spanish lang bks, Tax forms, Telephone ref, VHS videos, Wheelchair accessible, Workshops
Partic in Link+; OCLC Online Computer Library Center, Inc
Publications: Madden Library Update & Friendscript (Newsletter); The Magic Mirror (Newsletter)
Special Services for the Deaf - Am sign lang & deaf culture; Assistive tech; Bks on deafness & sign lang; Closed caption videos; Coll on deaf educ
Special Services for the Blind - Accessible computers; Assistive/Adapted tech devices, equip & products; Cassette playback machines; Copier with enlargement capabilities; Internet workstation with adaptive software; Networked computers with assistive software
Open Mon-Thurs 7:45am-11pm, Fri 7:45-5, Sat 10-6, Sun 2-10
Friends of the Library Group

C SAHATDJIAN LIBRARY*, Armenian Studies Program, 5245 N Backer Ave PB4, 93740-8001. Tel: 559-278-2669. FAX: 559-278-2129. Web Site: armenianstudies.csufresno.edu. *Dir,* Dr Barlow Der Mugrdechian; E-mail: barlowd@csufresno.edu
Founded 1988. Enrl 225; Fac 2; Highest Degree: Master
Library Holdings: Bk Titles 2,000; Per Subs 30
Special Collections: Armenian Film Archive; Elbrecht Historic Churches Archive; Index of Armenian Art; William Saroyan Coll
Subject Interests: Archives
Open Mon-Fri 8-4

S FRESNO CITY & COUNTY HISTORICAL SOCIETY ARCHIVES*, 7160 W Kearney Blvd, 93706. SAN 300-7553. Tel: 559-441-0862. FAX: 559-441-1372. E-mail: info@valleyhistory.org. Web Site: www.valleyhistory.org. *Archivist,* Kathy Hogue
Founded 1919
Library Holdings: Bk Titles 3,000
Special Collections: Agriculture, Fresno City & County, Ethnic & Cultural Groups, Logging (Photograph Colls); Ben R Walker History Files, 1850-1953, newsp clippings; Ephemera Coll, ad mats, calendars, invitations, paper currency, postcards, posters, programs, trade cats; Municipal & County Records; Personal, Family, Organization & Business Records, ms; Vertical Files, ann reports, brochures, church & organization anniversary publs, newsp clippings, pamphlets. Oral History
Subject Interests: Calif Cent Valley, Fresno City, Fresno County
Wireless access
Restriction: Researchers by appt only

J FRESNO CITY COLLEGE LIBRARY*, 1101 E University Ave, 93741. SAN 300-7561. Tel: 559-442-8204. Circulation Tel: 559-442-8205. Reference Tel: 559-442-4600, Ext 8764. Web Site: www.fresnocitycollege.edu/academics/library. *Librn,* Paula Demanett; Tel: 559-442-4600, Ext 8048, E-mail: paula.demanett@fresnocitycollege.edu; *Librn,* Laurel Doud; Tel: 559-442-4600, Ext 8920, E-mail: laurel.doud@fresnocitycollege.edu; *Librn,* Mai Yang; Tel: 559-442-4600, Ext 8918, E-mail: mai.yang@fresnocitycollege.edu; *Bibliog Instruction Librn,* Donna Chandler; Tel: 559-442-4600, Ext 8150, E-mail: donna.chandler@fresnocitycollege.edu; Staff 7 (MLS 7)
Founded 1910. Enrl 25,000; Fac 530; Highest Degree: Associate
Library Holdings: AV Mats 1,000; e-books 24,000; Electronic Media & Resources 15; Bk Titles 90,000; Per Subs 150
Automation Activity & Vendor Info: (Cataloging) Innovative Interfaces, Inc - Millennium; (Circulation) Innovative Interfaces, Inc - Millennium; (Course Reserve) Innovative Interfaces, Inc - Millennium; (ILL) OCLC; (OPAC) Innovative Interfaces, Inc - Millennium
Wireless access
Publications: Library News (Newsletter)
Partic in Community College League of California
Special Services for the Deaf - ADA equip; Closed caption videos; Sign lang interpreter upon request for prog
Special Services for the Blind - Assistive/Adapted tech devices, equip & products; Copier with enlargement capabilities; Dragon Naturally Speaking software; Magnifiers; Screen enlargement software for people with visual disabilities
Open Mon-Thurs 7:30-7:30, Fri 7:30-2, Sat 10-3
Friends of the Library Group

S FRESNO COUNTY GENEALOGICAL SOCIETY LIBRARY*, San Joaquin Valley Heritage & Genealogy Center, Fresno Public Library, 2420 Mariposa St, 93721-2285. (Mail add: PO Box 1429, 93716-1429), SAN 370-6834. Tel: 559-600-6230. E-mail: infofcgs@gmail.com. Web Site: fresnogenealogy.org, www.fresnolibrary.org/heritage. *Librn,* Kathleen Coleman
Founded 1965
Library Holdings: CDs 568; Microforms 2,079; Bk Titles 12,508; Per Subs 87; Videos 29
Subject Interests: Genealogy, State hist
Automation Activity & Vendor Info: (Cataloging) SirsiDynix; (Circulation) SirsiDynix; (OPAC) SirsiDynix
Wireless access
Publications: Ash Tree Echo; The Jotted Line (Newsletter)
Open Mon-Thurs 10-7, Fri & Sat 10-5, Sun 12-5
Restriction: Non-circulating
Friends of the Library Group

GL FRESNO COUNTY PUBLIC LAW LIBRARY*, Fresno County Courthouse, Ste 600, 1100 Van Ness Ave, 93724. SAN 300-7626. Tel: 559-600-2227. E-mail: lawlibrary@co.fresno.ca.us. Web Site: www.fresnolawlibrary.org. *Dir,* Pete Rooney; E-mail: prooney@co.fresno.ca.us; *Acq/ILL Librn, Ref Librn,* Mark Masters; E-mail: mmasters@co.fresno.ca.us; *Circ Serv,* Karina conchas
Founded 1891
Library Holdings: Bk Titles 3,300; Bk Vols 44,000
Automation Activity & Vendor Info: (Cataloging) EOS International; (Circulation) EOS International; (OPAC) EOS International; (Serials) EOS International
Wireless access
Open Mon-Fri 8-5

P FRESNO COUNTY PUBLIC LIBRARY*, 2420 Mariposa St, 93721. SAN 331-9989. Tel: 559-600-7323. Administration Tel: 559-600-6237. Web Site: www.fresnolibrary.org. *County Librn,* Raman Bath; E-mail: raman.bath@fresnolibrary.org; *Assoc County Librn,* Sally Gomez; E-mail: sally.gomez@fresnolibrary.org; *Financial Mgr,* Jeannie Christiansen; E-mail: jeannie.christiansen@fresnolibrary.org; *Ad,* James Tyner; *Pub Serv Mgr,* Lisa Lindsay; E-mail: lisa.lindsay@fresnolibrary.org; *Support Serv Mgr,* Deborah Janzen; E-mail: deborah.janzen@fresnolibrary.org; *Branch Cluster Supvr,* Mark Berner; Tel: 559-225-0140, E-mail: mark.berner@fresnolibrary.org; *Branch Cluster Supvr,* Jennifer Bethel; E-mail: jennifer.bethel@fresnolibrary.org; *Branch Cluster Supvr,* Wendy Eisenberg; E-mail: wendy.eisenberg@fresnolibrary.org; *Branch Cluster Supvr,* Penny Hill; E-mail: penny.hill@fresnolibrary.org; *Branch Cluster Supvr,* Joy Sentman-Paz; E-mail: joy.sentman-paz@fresnolibrary.org; *Branch Cluster Supvr,* Nicole Settle; E-mail: nicole.settle@fresnolibrary.org; *Facilities Coordr,* Aaron Smith; E-mail: aaron.smith@fresnolibrary.org; *Literacy Coordr,* Deborah Bernal; E-mail: deborah.bernal@fresnolibrary.org; *Vols Serv Coordr,* Elizabeth Finkle; E-mail: elizabeth.finkle@fresnolibrary.org; *Develop Officer,* Susan Renfro; E-mail: susan.renfro@fresnolibrary.org; *Spec Coll,* Mike Drake; E-mail: mike.drake@fresnolibrary.org; Staff 300 (MLS 51, Non-MLS 249)
Founded 1910. Pop 946,252
Library Holdings: Audiobooks 104,866; CDs 50,011; DVDs 88,377; e-books 6,647; Large Print Bks 17,258; Microforms 11,611; Bk Vols 981,536; Talking Bks 27,751
Special Collections: Gary Soto Coll; Leo Politi Coll; Manly Australia (Sister City) Coll; Miwok & Yokut Native American Coll; Mother Goose Coll; Oral History Coll (Japanese & Fresno County); William Saroyan Coll. Oral History; State Document Depository; US Document Depository
Subject Interests: Calif, City hist, Genealogy, Local hist, Punjabi (Lang), Spanish (Lang)
Automation Activity & Vendor Info: (Acquisitions) SirsiDynix; (Cataloging) SirsiDynix; (Circulation) SirsiDynix; (ILL) OCLC; (OPAC) SirsiDynix; (Serials) SirsiDynix
Wireless access
Function: 24/7 Electronic res, Activity rm, Adult bk club, Adult literacy prog, After school storytime, Archival coll, Art exhibits, Audio & video

playback equip for onsite use, Audiobks on Playaways & MP3, Audiobks via web, AV serv, Bilingual assistance for Spanish patrons, Bk club(s), Bks on CD, Children's prog, Citizenship assistance, Computer training, Computers for patron use, Digital talking bks, Electronic databases & coll, Family literacy, Free DVD rentals, Games & aids for people with disabilities, Genealogy discussion group, Govt ref serv, Holiday prog, Home delivery & serv to seniorr ctr & nursing homes, Homebound delivery serv, Homework prog, ILL available, Internet access, Jazz prog, Learning ctr, Life-long learning prog for all ages, Literacy & newcomer serv, Magazines, Meeting rooms, Microfiche/film & reading machines, Movies, Music CDs, Online cat, Online ref, Orientations, Outreach serv, Outside serv via phone, mail, e-mail & web, OverDrive digital audio bks, Photocopying/Printing, Preschool outreach, Preschool reading prog, Printer for laptops & handheld devices, Prog for adults, Prog for children & young adult, Ref & res, Ref serv available, Res performed for a fee, Scanner, Senior computer classes, Senior outreach, Spanish lang bks, Spoken cassettes & CDs, Spoken cassettes & DVDs, Story hour, Study rm, Summer & winter reading prog, Summer reading prog, Tax forms, Teen prog, Telephone ref, Wheelchair accessible, Workshops

Publications: Book Notes & Footnotes (Newsletter); Talking Book Library (Newsletter)

Mem of San Joaquin Valley Library System

Partic in Califa; CLA; OCLC Online Computer Library Center, Inc

Special Services for the Deaf - Closed caption videos; Staff with knowledge of sign lang

Special Services for the Blind - Bks on CD; Digital talking bk; Digital talking bk machines; Home delivery serv; Large print bks; Playaways (bks on MP3); Talking bks & player equip; Tel Pioneers equip repair group

Open Mon-Thurs 10-7, Fri & Sat 10-5, Sun 12-5

Friends of the Library Group

Branches: 36

AUBERRY BRANCH, 33049 Auberry Rd, Auberry, 93602. (Mail add: PO Box 279, Auberry, 93602-0279), SAN 374-4094. Tel: 559-855-8523. FAX: 559-855-8523. Web Site: www.fresnolibrary.org/branch/aub.html.
Founded 1918. Pop 9,704; Circ 59,192
Special Collections: Miwok & Yokut Native American Coll
Open Mon-Wed 10-6, Thurs 11-8, Sat 10-5
Friends of the Library Group

BEAR MOUNTAIN BRANCH, 30733 E Kings Canyon Rd, Squaw Valley, 93675, SAN 378-2239. Tel: 559-332-2528. Web Site: www.fresnolibrary.org/branch/bear.html.
Founded 1981. Pop 6,304; Circ 35,467
Open Mon-Thurs 10-6, Sat 10-2
Friends of the Library Group

BIG CREEK BRANCH, 55185 Point Rd, Big Creek, 93605. (Mail add: PO Box 25, Big Creek, 93605-0025), SAN 378-2255. Tel: 559-893-6614. Web Site: www.fresnolibrary.org/branch/bcr.html.
Founded 1917. Pop 2,973; Circ 2,977
Open Mon, Tues, Thurs & Fri 1-5
Friends of the Library Group

BIOLA BRANCH, 4885 N Biola Ave, 93723. Tel: 559-843-2001. Web Site: www.fresnolibrary.org/branch/bio.html.
Pop 3,306; Circ 6,737
Open Mon & Thurs 3-7, Sat 10-2

CARUTHERS BRANCH, 13382 S Henderson Rd, Caruthers, 93609. (Mail add: PO Box 95, Caruthers, 93609-0095), SAN 378-2271. Tel: 559-864-8766. Web Site: www.fresnolibrary.org/branch/car.html.
Founded 1998. Pop 10,093; Circ 37,603
Open Mon-Wed 10-6, Thurs 11-8, Sat 10-5
Friends of the Library Group

CLOVIS REGIONAL, 1155 Fifth St, Clovis, 93612, SAN 332-0103. Tel: 559-600-9531. Web Site: www.fresnolibrary.org/branch/clo.html.
Founded 1915
Open Mon-Thurs 9-9, Fri & Sat 9-5, Sun 12-5
Friends of the Library Group

EASTON BRANCH, 25 E Fantz Ave, Easton, 93706, SAN 378-231X. Tel: 559-237-3929. Web Site: www.fresnolibrary.org/branch/east.html.
Founded 1910. Pop 4,615; Circ 19,783
Open Mon-Thurs 10-6, Sat 10-2

FIG GARDEN REGIONAL, 3071 W Bullard Ave, 93711, SAN 332-0162. Tel: 559-600-4071. Web Site: www.fresnolibrary.org/branch/fig.html.
Founded 1962. Pop 72,441; Circ 351,273
Open Mon-Thurs 9-9, Fri & Sat 9-5, Sun 12-5
Friends of the Library Group

FIREBAUGH BRANCH, 1315 O St, Firebaugh, 93622, SAN 378-2336. Tel: 559-600-9274. Web Site: www.fresnolibrary.org/branch/frb.html.
Founded 1923. Pop 9,143; Circ 17,966
Open Mon-Thurs 10-6, Sat 10-2
Friends of the Library Group

FOWLER BRANCH, 306 S Seventh St, Fowler, 93625, SAN 377-6387. Tel: 559-600-9281. Web Site: www.fresnolibrary.org/branch/fowl.html.
Founded 1913. Pop 13,006; Circ 36,115
Open Mon-Wed 10-6, Thurs 12-8, Fri 1-5, Sat 10-2
Friends of the Library Group

GILLIS BRANCH, 629 W Dakota Ave, 93705, SAN 377-6425. Tel: 559-225-0140. Web Site: www.fresnolibrary.org/branch/gil.html.
Founded 1940. Pop 61,770; Circ 214,668
Open Mon-Thurs 10-8, Fri & Sat 10-5
Friends of the Library Group

KERMAN BRANCH, 15081 W Kearney Plaza, Kerman, 93630, SAN 377-6093. Tel: 559-846-8804. Web Site: www.fresnolibrary.org/branch/kman.html.
Founded 1907. Pop 23,487; Circ 72,075
Special Collections: Panjabi Language Materials
Open Mon-Wed 10-6, Thurs 12-8, Fri 1-5, Sat 10-2
Friends of the Library Group

KINGSBURG BRANCH, 1399 Draper St, Kingsburg, 93631, SAN 377-6115. Tel: 559-897-3710. Web Site: www.fresnolibrary.org/branch/kbrg.html.
Founded 1910. Pop 12,780; Circ 76,397
Open Mon-Wed 10-6, Thurs 12-8, Fri 1-5, Sat 10-2
Friends of the Library Group

LATON STATION, 6313 DeWoody St, Laton, 93242. (Mail add: PO Box 389, Laton, 93242-0389), SAN 377-6131. Tel: 559-923-4554. Web Site: www.fresnolibrary.org/branch/lat.html.
Founded 1904. Pop 3,548; Circ 11,349
Open Mon, Tues & Thurs 2-6, Sat 10-2

LITERACY SERVICES CENTER, 2420 Mariposa St, 93721. Tel: 559-600-9243. Web Site: fresnolibrary.org/literacy. *Literacy Coordr,* Deborah Bernal
Subject Interests: Adult literacy, Early childhood literacy & learning, Parenting
Function: Adult literacy prog
Open Tues-Thurs 10-7, Fri & Sat 10-5

MENDOTA BRANCH, 1246 Belmont Ave, Mendota, 93640, SAN 378-2352. Tel: 559-600-9291. Web Site: www.fresnolibrary.org/branch/men.html.
Founded 1919. Pop 12,551; Circ 17,307
Open Mon-Wed 10-6, Thurs 11-8, Sat 10-5

MOSQUEDA BRANCH, 4670 E Butler Ave, 93702, SAN 377-6174. Tel: 559-600-4072. Web Site: www.fresnolibrary.org/branch/mosq.html.
Founded 1976. Pop 38,109
Special Collections: Gary Soto Coll
Open Mon-Thurs 10-6, Sat 10-2

ORANGE COVE BRANCH, 815 Park Blvd, Orange Cove, 93646, SAN 378-2379. Tel: 559-600-9292. Web Site: www.fresnolibrary.org/branch/orco.html.
Founded 1915. Pop 10,821; Circ 39,491
Open Mon-Wed 10-6, Thurs 12-8, Fri 1-5, Sat 10-2
Friends of the Library Group

PARLIER BRANCH, 1130 E Parlier Ave, Parlier, 93648, SAN 377-6190. Tel: 559-646-3835. Web Site: www.fresnolibrary.org/branch/parl.html.
Founded 1910. Pop 16,533; Circ 19,707
Open Mon-Thurs 10-6, Sat 10-2
Friends of the Library Group

PIEDRA BRANCH, 25385 Trimmer Springs Rd, Piedra, 93657. (Mail add: PO Box 389, Piedra, 93649-0389), SAN 377-6212. Tel: 559-787-3266. Web Site: www.fresnolibrary.org/branch/pdra.html.
Founded 1982. Pop 6,304
Open Mon, Tues & Thurs 2-6, Sat 10-2

PINEDALE BRANCH, 7170 N San Pablo Ave, Pinedale, 93650, SAN 377-6239. Tel: 559-439-0486. Web Site: www.fresnolibrary.org/branch/pine.html.
Founded 1948. Pop 3,556; Circ 21,220
Open Mon-Thurs 10-6, Sat 10-2

LEO POLITI BRANCH, 5771 N First St, 93710, SAN 378-2395. Tel: 559-431-6450. Web Site: www.fresnolibrary.org/branch/pol.html.
Founded 1974. Pop 63,534; Circ 202,038
Special Collections: Leo Politi Coll
Open Mon-Thurs 10-8, Fri & Sat 10-5
Friends of the Library Group

REEDLEY BRANCH, 1027 E St, Reedley, 93654, SAN 332-0227. Tel: 559-638-2818. Web Site: www.fresnolibrary.org/branch/reed.html.
Founded 1910. Pop 29,161; Circ 116,605
Open Mon-Thurs 10-8, Fri & Sat 10-5
Friends of the Library Group

RIVERDALE NEIGHBORHOOD, 20975 Malsbary Ave, Riverdale, 93656. (Mail add: PO Box 757, Riverdale, 93656-0757), SAN 377-6255. Tel: 559-867-3381. Web Site: www.fresnolibrary.org/branch/rivd.html.
Founded 1913. Pop 6,304; Circ 19,777
Open Mon-Thurs 10-6, Sat 10-2
Friends of the Library Group

BETTY RODRIGUEZ REGIONAL LIBRARY, 3040 N Cedar Ave, 93703. Tel: 559-600-9245. Web Site: www.fresnolibrary.org/branch/betty.html.
Founded 2016. Pop 79,346; Circ 205,606
Open Mon-Thurs 9-9, Fri & Sat 9-5, Sun Noon-5
Friends of the Library Group

SAN JOAQUIN BRANCH, 8781 Main St, San Joaquin, 93660. (Mail add: PO Box 948, San Joaquin, 93660-0948), SAN 377-6271. Tel: 559-693-2171. Web Site: www.fresnolibrary.org/branch/joaq.html.
Founded 1916. Pop 6,978; Circ 22,470
Open Mon 12-8, Tues-Thurs 10-6, Fri 1-5, Sat 10-2

SANGER BRANCH, 1812 Seventh St, Sanger, 93657, SAN 332-0251. Tel: 559-875-2435. Web Site: www.fresnolibrary.org/branch/sang.html.
Founded 1913. Pop 38,065; Circ 106,179
Open Mon-Thurs 10-8, Fri & Sat 10-5
Friends of the Library Group

SELMA BRANCH, 2200 Selma St, Selma, 93662, SAN 332-0286. Tel: 559-896-3393. Web Site: www.fresnolibrary.org/branch/sel.html.
Founded 1910. Pop 30,557; Circ 82,503
Special Collections: Sister City Coll (Sister City with Manly, Australia)
Open Mon-Thurs 10-8, Fri & Sat 10-5

SENIOR RESOURCE CENTER, 2025 E Dakota Ave, 93726, SAN 378-2433. Tel: 559-600-6767. Web Site: www.fresnolibrary.org/seniors. *Br Supvr,* Penny Hill
Founded 2005. Circ 11,161
Special Collections: Large Print & Nonprint Colls; Programs to Seniors & Caregivers
Open Mon-Fri 10-2

SHAVER LAKE BRANCH, 41344 Tollhouse Rd, Shaver Lake, 93664. (Mail add: PO Box 169, Shaver Lake, 93664-0169), SAN 378-2417. Tel: 559-841-3330. Web Site: www.fresnolibrary.org/branch/shlk.html.
Founded 1934. Pop 2,973; Circ 6,422
Open Mon, Tues & Thurs 2-6, Sat 10-2

SUNNYSIDE REGIONAL, 5566 E Kings Canyon Rd, 93727. Tel: 559-600-6594. Web Site: www.fresnolibrary.org/branch/sun.html.
Founded 1965. Pop 62,020; Circ 212,935
Open Mon-Thurs 9-9, Fri & Sat 9-5, Sun 12-5
Friends of the Library Group

P TALKING BOOK LIBRARY FOR THE BLIND, Ted C Wills Community Center, 770 N San Pablo Ave, 93728, SAN 332-0014. Tel: 559-600-3217. Toll Free Tel: 800-742-1011, Ext 3217. E-mail: tblb@fresnolibrary.org. Web Site: www.fresnolibrary.org/tblb. *Br Supvr,* Penny Hill
Founded 1975. Circ 71,491
Special Services for the Blind - Assistive/Adapted tech devices, equip & products; Digital talking bk; Digital talking bk machines; Talking bks & player equip; Tel Pioneers equip repair group
Open Mon-Fri 9-5
Friends of the Library Group

TEAQUE BRANCH, 4718 N Polk Ave, 93722. Tel: 559-970-0045. Web Site: www.fresnolibrary.org/branch/tea.html.
Open Tues-Thurs 2-6, Sat 10-2

TRANQUILLITY BRANCH, 25561 Williams St, Tranquillity, 93668. (Mail add: PO Box 246, Tranquillity, 93668-0246), SAN 377-6298. Tel: 559-698-5158. Web Site: www.fresnolibrary.org/branch/tran.html.
Founded 1977. Circ 71,491
Open Mon, Tues & Thurs 2-6, Sat 10-2

WEST FRESNO BRANCH, 188 E California Ave, 93706. Tel: 559-600-9277. Web Site: www.fresnolibrary.org/branch/wfr.html.
Founded 1973. Pop 30,258; Circ 56,493
Open Mon-Wed 10-6, Thurs 10-7, Sat 10-5

WOODWARD PARK REGIONAL, 944 E Perrin Ave, 93720. Tel: 559-600-3135. Information Services Tel: 559-600-9236. FAX: 559-600-1348. Web Site: www.fresnolibrary.org/branch/wdwd.html.
Founded 2004. Pop 60,147; Circ 520,746
Special Collections: Chinese Language Materials
Open Mon-Thurs 9-9, Fri & Sat 9-5, Sun 12-5
Friends of the Library Group

Bookmobiles: 2. Supvr, Deborah Bernal

C FRESNO PACIFIC UNIVERSITY*, Hiebert Library, 1717 S Chestnut Ave, 93702. SAN 300-7642. Tel: 559-453-2090. FAX: 559-453-2124. Web Site: www.fresno.edu/library. *Libr Dir,* Kevin Enns-Rempel; Tel: 559-453-2225, E-mail: kevin.enns-rempel@fresno.edu; *Instrul Librn,* Erin Wahl; Tel: 559-453-2121, E-mail: erin.wahl@fresno.edu; *Archivist,* Hannah Keeney; Tel: 559-453-3437, E-mail: hannah.keeney@fresno.edu; *Acq,* Hope Nisly; Tel: 559-453-2223, E-mail: hope.nisly@fresno.edu; *Cat, Tech Serv,* Vern Carter; Tel: 559-453-7124, E-mail: vern.carter@fresno.edu; *Ref,* Ernest Carrere; Tel: 559-453-2131, E-mail: ernest.carrere@fresno.edu; Staff 6 (MLS 5, Non-MLS 1)
Founded 1944. Enrl 3,800; Fac 150; Highest Degree: Master
Library Holdings: AV Mats 5,500; e-books 171,026; Bk Titles 124,893; Bk Vols 139,532; Per Subs 414
Special Collections: Mennonite Library & Archives
Subject Interests: Hist, Relig
Automation Activity & Vendor Info: (Acquisitions) Innovative Interfaces, Inc - Sierra; (Cataloging) Innovative Interfaces, Inc - Sierra; (Circulation) Innovative Interfaces, Inc - Sierra; (Course Reserve) Innovative Interfaces, Inc - Sierra; (ILL) OCLC WorldShare Interlibrary Loan; (OPAC) Innovative Interfaces, Inc - Sierra; (Serials) Innovative Interfaces, Inc - Sierra
Wireless access
Function: 24/7 Electronic res, 24/7 Online cat, Archival coll, Art exhibits, Audio & video playback equip for onsite use, Electronic databases & coll, Online cat, Photocopying/Printing
Partic in Link+; OCLC Online Computer Library Center, Inc; Statewide California Electronic Library Consortium
Open Mon-Thurs 8am-10pm, Fri 8-5, Sat 9-5

L MCCORMICK BARSTOW, LLP*, Law Library, 7647 N Freso St, 93720. SAN 373-7446. Tel: 559-433-1300. FAX: 559-433-2300. Web Site: www.mccormickbarstow.com. *Librn,* Pat Sullivan; E-mail: pat.sullivan@mccormickbarstow.com
Library Holdings: Bk Titles 1,300; Bk Vols 12,000

M WILLIAM O OWEN MEDICAL LIBRARY*, Saint Agnes Medical Ctr, 1303 E Herndon Ave, 93720. SAN 320-5592. Tel: 559-450-3322. Reference Tel: 559-450-3325. FAX: 559-450-3315. E-mail: medlib@samc.com. Web Site: www.samc.com/medical-library. *Libr Mgr,* Judith Kammerer; Staff 1 (MLS 1)
Founded 1974
Library Holdings: Bk Vols 900; Per Subs 30
Subject Interests: Cardiology, Gen surgery, Med, Nursing
Automation Activity & Vendor Info: (Cataloging) Marcive, Inc; (Circulation) CyberTools for Libraries; (OPAC) CyberTools for Libraries
Wireless access
Function: Health sci info serv, ILL available, Internet access, Orientations, Photocopying/Printing, Ref serv available
Partic in Medical Library Group of Southern California & Arizona; Northern California & Nevada Medical Library Group
Open Mon-Fri 8:30-5:30
Restriction: Circulates for staff only

SR ROMAN CATHOLIC DIOCESE OF FRESNO LIBRARY*, 1550 N Fresno St, 93703-3788. SAN 300-7537. Tel: 559-488-7400. FAX: 559-493-2845. E-mail: archives@dioceseoffresno.org. Web Site: www.dioceseoffresno.org. *Archivist,* James Culleton
Founded 1934
Library Holdings: Bk Vols 20,000
Subject Interests: Relig, Western Americana
Restriction: Open by appt only

P SAN JOAQUIN VALLEY LIBRARY SYSTEM*, 2420 Mariposa St, 93721-2285. SAN 300-7677. Tel: 559-600-6283. FAX: 559-600-6295. E-mail: info@sjvls.org. Web Site: www.sjvls.org. *Libr Prog Mgr,* Mary Ellen Tyckoson; E-mail: Mary.Tyckoson@sjvls.org; Staff 7.5 (MLS 4, Non-MLS 3.5)
Founded 1960. Pop 2,884,045; Circ 6,982,552
Jul 2015-Jun 2016. Mats Exp $134,000. Sal $1,076,136 (Prof $1,024,112)
Automation Activity & Vendor Info: (Acquisitions) SirsiDynix; (Cataloging) SirsiDynix; (Circulation) SirsiDynix; (ILL) SirsiDynix; (OPAC) SirsiDynix; (Serials) SirsiDynix
Member Libraries: Coalinga-Huron Library District; Fresno County Public Library; Kern County Library; Kings County Library; Madera County Library; Mariposa County Library; Merced County Library; Porterville Public Library; Tulare County Library; Tulare Public Library
Special Services for the Blind - Talking bks
Restriction: Circ to mem only

SR TEMPLE BETH ISRAEL LIBRARY*, 6622 N Maroa Ave, 93704. SAN 320-5606. Tel: 559-432-3600. FAX: 559-432-3685. Web Site: www.tbifresno.org. *Pres,* Steve Negin
Library Holdings: Bk Titles 2,000
Special Collections: Holocaust Coll
Automation Activity & Vendor Info: (Cataloging) JayWil Software Development, Inc
Wireless access

L UNITED STATES COURTS LIBRARY*, 2500 Tulare St, Ste 2401, 93721. SAN 372-2686. Tel: 559-499-5615. FAX: 559-499-5698. *Librn,* Daniella Garcia; E-mail: daniella_garcia@lb9.uscourts.gov; Staff 1 (MLS 1)
Library Holdings: Bk Titles 884; Bk Vols 17,000
Automation Activity & Vendor Info: (Acquisitions) SirsiDynix-WorkFlows; (Cataloging) SirsiDynix-WorkFlows; (OPAC) SirsiDynix; (Serials) SirsiDynix-WorkFlows
Wireless access
Open Mon-Fri 9-12 & 1-4

FULLERTON

C CALIFORNIA STATE UNIVERSITY, FULLERTON*, Paulina June & George Pollak Library, 800 N State College Blvd, 92834. (Mail add: PO Box 4150, 92834-4150), SAN 300-774X. Tel: 657-278-2633. FAX: 657-278-2439. E-mail: libadmin@fullerton.edu, libraryanswers@fullerton.edu. Web Site: www.library.fullerton.edu. *Dean of*

Libr, Emily Bonney; Tel: 657-278-2715, E-mail: ebonney@fullerton.edu; *Librn*, Barbara Miller; Tel: 657-278-4460, E-mail: bmiller@fullerton.edu; *Ref & Instruction Librn*, Adolfo Prieto; Tel: 657-278-5238, E-mail: aprieto@fullerton.edu; *Ref Librn*, Susan Tschabrun; Tel: 657-278-7556, E-mail: stschabrun@fullerton.edu; Staff 62 (MLS 25, Non-MLS 37)
Founded 1959. Enrl 37,000; Fac 2,100; Highest Degree: Master
Library Holdings: Bk Titles 743,945; Bk Vols 1,111,419; Per Subs 2,476
Special Collections: State Document Depository; US Document Depository
Automation Activity & Vendor Info: (Cataloging) Innovative Interfaces, Inc; (Circulation) Innovative Interfaces, Inc
Wireless access
Publications: Exhibition Catalogue for Maps Illustrating the History of Cartography; Reference Department Bibliographies & Guides
Partic in Dow Jones News Retrieval; OCLC Online Computer Library Center, Inc; SDC Info Servs
Friends of the Library Group

J FULLERTON COLLEGE*, William T Boyce Library, 321 E Chapman Ave, 92832-2095. SAN 300-7758. Tel: 714-992-7039. Interlibrary Loan Service Tel: 714-992-5682. Administration Tel: 714-732-5680. FAX: 714-992-9961. Interlibrary Loan Service FAX: 714-992-9960. E-mail: librarian@fullcoll.edu. Web Site: library.fullcoll.edu. *Dean, Libr & Learning Res*, Dani Wilson; Tel: 714-992-7040, E-mail: dwilson@fullcoll.edu; *Acq Librn*, Monique Delatte Starkey; Tel: 714-992-7379, E-mail: mdelatte@fullcoll.edu; *Cat Librn*, Dave Brown; Tel: 714-992-7376, E-mail: dbrown@fullcoll.edu; *Circ Librn*, Jane Ishibashi; Tel: 714-992-7378, E-mail: jishibashi@fullcoll.edu; *Syst Librn*, Erica Bennett; Tel: 714-992-7375, E-mail: ebennett@fullcoll.edu; *Instruction Librn*, Jill Okamura; Tel: 714-992-7380, E-mail: jokamura@fullcoll.edu; *Online Learning Librn, Outreach Librn*, Alberto Romero; Tel: 714-992-7377, E-mail: aromero@fullcoll.edu; Staff 18 (MLS 6, Non-MLS 12)
Founded 1913. Enrl 25,254; Fac 6; Highest Degree: Associate
Library Holdings: Audiobooks 6; AV Mats 2,408; Bks on Deafness & Sign Lang 129; CDs 467; DVDs 121; e-books 153,632; e-journals 22; Electronic Media & Resources 10; High Interest/Low Vocabulary Bk Vols 797; Large Print Bks 21; Microforms 7,036; Bk Titles 77,814; Bk Vols 88,220; Per Subs 120
Special Collections: Topographic Maps of California (United States Geological Survey Coll). Oral History
Subject Interests: Calif, Libr & info sci, Literary criticism, Local hist, Music, Women's studies
Automation Activity & Vendor Info: (Acquisitions) Ex Libris Group; (Cataloging) Ex Libris Group; (Circulation) Ex Libris Group; (Course Reserve) Ex Libris Group; (OPAC) Ex Libris Group; (Serials) Ex Libris Group
Wireless access
Function: Archival coll, Audio & video playback equip for onsite use, Computers for patron use, Electronic databases & coll, ILL available, Internet access, Magazines, Microfiche/film & reading machines, Music CDs, Online cat, Orientations, Photocopying/Printing, Printer for laptops & handheld devices, Ref serv available, Wheelchair accessible
Partic in OCLC Online Computer Library Center, Inc
Special Services for the Blind - Closed circuit TV magnifier
Open Mon-Thurs 7:30am-9pm, Fri 7:30-4, Sat 10-2
Friends of the Library Group

P FULLERTON PUBLIC LIBRARY*, 353 W Commonwealth Ave, 92832. SAN 332-0340. Tel: 714-738-6333. Circulation Tel: 714-738-6334. Reference Tel: 714-738-6326. Administration Tel: 714-738-6380. FAX: 714-447-3280. Reference E-mail: reference@fullertonlibrary.org. Web Site: www.fullertonlibrary.org. *Libr Dir*, Judy Booth; E-mail: judyb@cityoffullerton.com; *Sr Librn, Tech Serv*, Carol Wright; E-mail: carolwr@cityoffullerton.com; *Adult Serv Mgr*, Tim Mountain; E-mail: timm@cityoffullerton.com; *Ch Mgr*, Janine Jacobs; E-mail: janinej@cityoffullerton.com; Staff 30 (MLS 15, Non-MLS 15)
Founded 1906. Pop 134,100; Circ 997,013
Library Holdings: Bk Titles 250,000; Per Subs 400
Special Collections: Local History Room; Mary Campbell Children's Coll
Subject Interests: Chinese lang, Korean (Lang), Spanish (Lang)
Automation Activity & Vendor Info: (Acquisitions) SirsiDynix; (Cataloging) SirsiDynix; (Circulation) SirsiDynix; (ILL) SirsiDynix; (Media Booking) SirsiDynix; (OPAC) SirsiDynix; (Serials) SirsiDynix
Wireless access
Mem of Santiago Library System
Open Mon-Thurs 10-9, Fri & Sat 10-5, Sun 1-5
Friends of the Library Group
Branches: 1
HUNT BRANCH, 201 S Basque Ave, 92833-3372, SAN 332-0375. Tel: 714-738-3122. *Sr Librn*, Judy Booth; Tel: 714-738-5364, E-mail: judyb@ci.fullerton.ca.us
Library Holdings: Bk Vols 30,024
Open Tues 10-6, Thurs 12-8
Friends of the Library Group

C HOPE INTERNATIONAL UNIVERSITY*, Hugh & Hazel Darling Library, 2500 E Nutwood Ave, 92831. SAN 300-7782. Tel: 714-879-3901, Ext 1234. E-mail: darlinglibrary@hiu.edu. Web Site: library.hiu.edu. *Dir, Libr Serv*, Robin R Hartman; Tel: 714-879-3901, Ext 1212, E-mail: rhartman@hiu.edu; *Syst & Tech Serv Librn*, Jennifer Rich; Tel: 714-879-3901, Ext 1218, E-mail: jarich@hiu.edu; Staff 2.3 (MLS 2, Non-MLS 0.3)
Founded 1928. Enrl 1,200; Fac 75; Highest Degree: Master
Jun 2014-May 2015 Income $489,250, Parent Institution $486,250, Other $3,000. Mats Exp $130,500, Books $25,000, Per/Ser (Incl. Access Fees) $45,000, Electronic Ref Mat (Incl. Access Fees) $60,500. Sal $163,064 (Prof $115,640)
Library Holdings: AV Mats 2,287; e-books 124,635; Bk Vols 68,763; Per Subs 164
Special Collections: George P Taubman Coll; Restoration Movement (Rare Book Coll)
Subject Interests: Restoration movement
Automation Activity & Vendor Info: (Acquisitions) OCLC; (Cataloging) OCLC; (Circulation) OCLC; (Course Reserve) OCLC; (ILL) OCLC; (OPAC) OCLC; (Serials) OCLC
Wireless access
Partic in OCLC Online Computer Library Center, Inc; Statewide California Electronic Library Consortium
Open Mon & Wed 8am-11pm, Tues & Thurs 8-9:30 & 10:30am-11pm, Fri 8-3, Sun 5-11

C MARSHALL B KETCHUM UNIVERSITY*, M B Ketchum Memorial Library, 2575 Yorba Linda Blvd, 92831-1699. SAN 300-7790. Tel: 714-449-7440. FAX: 714-879-0481. E-mail: library@ketchum.edu. Web Site: ketchum.ent.sirsi.net. *Dir, Libr Serv*, Scott Johnson; E-mail: scottjohnson@ketchum.edu; *Ser Librn*, Diana Jacobson; E-mail: djacobson@ketchum.edu; Staff 3 (MLS 2, Non-MLS 1)
Founded 1950. Enrl 475; Fac 60; Highest Degree: Doctorate
Library Holdings: Bk Titles 13,000; Per Subs 130
Special Collections: Historical Vision Coll
Subject Interests: Ophthalmology, Optics, Optometry
Publications: Faculty Publications; Library's Latest Additions (Bimonthly); Student Research Papers (Annual)
Partic in Coop Libr Agency for Syst & Servs; OCLC Online Computer Library Center, Inc
Restriction: Open to students, fac & staff, Pub use on premises

M ST JUDE MEDICAL CENTER*, Medical Library, 101 E Valencia Mesa Dr, 92835. SAN 327-4098. Tel: 714-992-3000, Ext 3708. FAX: 714-447-6481. *Librn*, Carol Schechter; Staff 1 (MLS 1)
Library Holdings: Bk Vols 1,000; Per Subs 70
Special Collections: Consumer Health Coll
Subject Interests: Med, Nursing
Automation Activity & Vendor Info: (Cataloging) Surpass; (OPAC) Surpass
Partic in Medical Library Group of Southern California & Arizona

GILROY

J GAVILAN COLLEGE LIBRARY*, 5055 Santa Teresa Blvd, 95020. SAN 300-7839. Circulation Tel: 408-848-4810. Reference Tel: 408-848-4806. FAX: 408-846-4927. E-mail: reference@gavilan.edu. Web Site: www.gavilan.edu/library. *Head Librn*, Douglas Achterman; Tel: 408-848-4809, E-mail: dachterman@gavilan.edu; *Tech & Instruction Librn*, Dana Young; E-mail: dyoung@gavilan.edu; *Libr Office Mgr*, Tara Myers; E-mail: tmyers@gavilan.edu; Staff 2 (MLS 2)
Founded 1963. Enrl 4,838; Fac 70
Library Holdings: e-books 9,332; Bk Titles 56,500; Bk Vols 65,227
Automation Activity & Vendor Info: (Acquisitions) Ex Libris Group; (Cataloging) Ex Libris Group; (Circulation) Ex Libris Group; (Course Reserve) Ex Libris Group; (OPAC) Ex Libris Group; (Serials) Ex Libris Group
Wireless access
Publications: Bibliographies; Handouts
Mem of Pacific Library Partnership (PLP)
Partic in Monterey Bay Area Cooperative Library System; OCLC Online Computer Library Center, Inc
Open Mon-Thurs 8-8, Fri 8-3

GLENDALE

M ADVENTIST HEALTH GLENDALE*, Medical Library, 1509 Wilson Terrace, 91206. SAN 300-7855. Tel: 818-409-8034. FAX: 818-546-5633. Web Site: www.adventisthealth.org/glendale/health-wellness/the-medical-library-at-ahgl. *Dir*, June Levy; E-mail: june.levy@ah.org; *Sr Librn*, Zahra Fotovat; E-mail: fotovazh@ah.org; Staff 1 (MLS 1)
Founded 1957
Library Holdings: AV Mats 700; Bk Titles 8,500; Per Subs 650
Subject Interests: Allied health, Med, Nursing

Automation Activity & Vendor Info: (Cataloging) SydneyPlus; (Circulation) SydneyPlus; (OPAC) SydneyPlus
Partic in CinaHL; Medical Library Group of Southern California & Arizona; Proquest Dialog
Restriction: Mem only

S AMERICAN HERITAGE LIBRARY & MUSEUM*, 600 S Central Ave, 91204-2009. SAN 300-7928. Tel: 818-240-1775. E-mail: library@srcalifornia.com. Web Site: www.srcalifornia.com. *Libr Dir,* Richard H Breithaupt, Jr; E-mail: rick@srcalifornia.com
Founded 1893
Library Holdings: AV Mats 2,000; CDs 500; Electronic Media & Resources 1,000; Bk Titles 23,000; Bk Vols 25,000; Spec Interest Per Sub 5,000
Special Collections: Family Histories; Photographic; Vital Records
Subject Interests: 17th-20th Century Am, Am colonial hist, English genealogy, English hist, Genealogy, Mil hist (US)
Automation Activity & Vendor Info: (Acquisitions) Inmagic, Inc.; (Cataloging) OCLC WorldShare Interlibrary Loan
Wireless access
Function: Ref serv available
Partic in OCLC Online Computer Library Center, Inc
Open Tues-Thurs 10-4
Restriction: Not a lending libr
Friends of the Library Group

J GLENDALE COMMUNITY COLLEGE LIBRARY*, 1500 N Verdugo Rd, 91208-2894. SAN 300-7863. Tel: 818-240-1000, Ext 5581, 818-240-1000, Ext 5586. Reference Tel: 818-240-1000, Ext 5577. E-mail: library@glendale.edu. Web Site: gcc.glendale.edu/gcclibrary. *Dean, Libr & Learning Support Serv,* Eric Hanson; E-mail: ehanson@glendale.edu; *Coll Develop Librn,* Shelley Aronoff; E-mail: saronoff@glendale.edu; *Instrul Serv Librn,* Susie Chin; E-mail: schin@glendale.edu; *Ref Serv Librn,* Brenda Jones; E-mail: bjones@glendale.edu; *Tech Serv Librn,* Becka Cooling; E-mail: rcooling@glendale.edu; *Circ, Libr Tech,* Angela Khachikian; E-mail: angelak@glendale.edu; Staff 17.6 (MLS 6.2, Non-MLS 11.4)
Founded 1927. Enrl 22,593; Fac 752; Highest Degree: Associate. Sal $1,335,469 (Prof $693,973)
Library Holdings: e-books 24,000; Bk Titles 92,170; Bk Vols 113,000; Per Subs 166
Automation Activity & Vendor Info: (Acquisitions) Ex Libris Group; (Cataloging) Ex Libris Group; (Circulation) Ex Libris Group; (Course Reserve) Ex Libris Group; (OPAC) Ex Libris Group; (Serials) Ex Libris Group
Wireless access
Partic in Council of Chief Librarian; OCLC Online Computer Library Center, Inc
Open Mon-Thurs 8am-9pm, Fri & Sat 10-2

P GLENDALE LIBRARY, ARTS & CULTURE*, Downtown Central Library, 222 E Harvard St, 91205. SAN 332-043X. Tel: 818-548-2021. Interlibrary Loan Service Tel: 818-548-6430. Reference Tel: 818-548-2027. Administration Tel: 818-548-2030. FAX: 818-548-7225. TDD: 818-543-0368. E-mail: libraryinfo@glendaleca.gov. Web Site: www.glendaleca.gov/government/departments/library-arts-culture. *Dir, Libr, Arts & Culture,* Gary Schaffer; E-mail: gschaffer@glendaleca.gov; *Asst Dir,* Nikki Winslow; E-mail: nwinslow@glendaleca.gov; Staff 94 (MLS 31, Non-MLS 63)
Founded 1906. Pop 191,719; Circ 1,097,061
Jul 2013-Jun 2014 Income (Main & Associated Libraries) $8,246,769, City $8,062,909, Federal $5,000, Locally Generated Income $178,860. Mats Exp $716,308, Books $453,346, Per/Ser (Incl. Access Fees) $4,700, Micro $14,100, AV Mat $61,718, Electronic Ref Mat (Incl. Access Fees) $182,444. Sal $4,002,047 (Prof $2,108,985)
Library Holdings: Bk Vols 571,942
Special Collections: Domestic Cat Genealogy; Original Art Coll; Piano Roll Coll; Sheet Music Coll
Subject Interests: Art, Calif, Local hist, Music
Automation Activity & Vendor Info: (Acquisitions) SirsiDynix; (Cataloging) SirsiDynix; (Circulation) SirsiDynix; (ILL) SirsiDynix; (OPAC) SirsiDynix
Wireless access
Partic in OCLC Online Computer Library Center, Inc; Proquest Dialog
Special Services for the Deaf - TDD equip
Special Services for the Blind - Cassettes; Computer with voice synthesizer for visually impaired persons; Large print bks; Magnifiers; Rec; Talking bks
Open Mon-Thurs 9am-10pm, Fri & Sat 9-6, Sun 12-6
Friends of the Library Group
Branches: 7
BRAND LIBRARY & ART CENTER, 1601 W Mountain St, 91201, SAN 332-0464. Tel: 818-548-2051. FAX: 818-548-5079. E-mail: info@brandlibrary.org. Web Site: www.glendaleca.gov/government/departments/library-arts-culture/brand-library-art-center. *Sr Libr Supvr,* Caley Cannon; Tel: 818-548-2010, E-mail: ccannon@glendaleca.gov; *Librn Spec,* Blair Whittington; Tel: 818-548-2050, E-mail: bwhittington@glendaleca.gov. Subject Specialists: *Art,* Caley Cannon; *Music,* Blair Whittington; Staff 3 (MLS 3)
Circ 150,000
Library Holdings: CDs 32,337; DVDs 1,515; Bk Vols 78,069
Subject Interests: Art, Music
Function: Art exhibits, Computers for patron use, Music CDs, Photocopying/Printing, Prog for adults
Open Tues-Thurs 11-8, Fri-Sun 10-5
Friends of the Library Group
CASA VERDUGO, 1151 N Brand Blvd, 91202, SAN 332-0499. Tel: 818-548-2047. FAX: 818-548-8052. Web Site: www.glendaleca.gov/government/departments/library-arts-culture/locations-hours/casa-verdugo-library. *Supvr,* Thomas Eiden; E-mail: teiden@glendaleca.gov; Staff 2 (MLS 2)
Founded 1951. Pop 26,526; Circ 50,000
Library Holdings: Bk Vols 55,000
Open Mon-Thurs 11-8, Fri & Sat 1-6
Friends of the Library Group
CHEVY CHASE, 3301 E Chevy Chase Dr, 91206, SAN 332-0529. Tel: 818-548-2046. FAX: 818-548-7713. Web Site: www.glendaleca.gov/government/departments/library-arts-culture/locations-hours/chevy-chase-library. *Supvr,* Tiffany Barrios; E-mail: tbarrios@glendaleca.gov
Founded 1972. Circ 6,000
Library Holdings: Bk Vols 30,895
Open Wed 2-8, Sat 12-5
GRANDVIEW, 1535 Fifth St, 91201, SAN 332-0553. Tel: 818-548-2049. FAX: 818-549-0678. Web Site: www.glendaleca.gov/government/departments/library-arts-culture/locations-hours/grandview-library. *Supvr,* Thomas Eiden; E-mail: teiden@glendaleca.gov
Circ 44,253
Library Holdings: Bk Vols 44,115
Open Mon-Fri 1:30-6
Friends of the Library Group
LIBRARY CONNECTION @ ADAMS SQUARE, 1100 E Chevy Chase Dr, 91205. Tel: 818-548-3833. FAX: 818-500-1039. Web Site: www.glendaleca.gov/government/departments/library-arts-culture/locations-hours. *Supvr,* Kristine Markosyan; E-mail: kmarkosyan@glendaleca.gov
Open Mon 11-8, Tues-Thurs & Sat 11-6
MONTROSE LIBRARY, 2465 Honolulu Ave, Montrose, 91020, SAN 332-0588. Tel: 818-548-2048. FAX: 818-248-6987. Web Site; www.glendaleca.gov/government/departments/library-arts-culture/locations-hours/montrose-library. *Supvr,* Tiffany Barrios; E-mail: tbarrios@glendaleca.gov
Pop 35,016; Circ 134,428
Library Holdings: Bk Vols 66,033
Special Services for the Deaf - TDD equip
Open Mon- Thurs 11-7, Fri & Sat 12-5
Friends of the Library Group
PACIFIC PARK, 501 S Pacific Ave, 91204. Tel: 818-548-3760. FAX: 818-409-7154. Web Site: www.glendaleca.gov/government/departments/library-arts-culture/locations-hours/pacific-park-library. *Supvr,* Kristine Markosyan; E-mail: kmarkosyan@glendaleca.gov; *Ch Serv,* Arpine Eloyan; E-mail: aeloyan@ci.glendale.ca.us
Open Mon-Wed 2-8, Thurs 10-6, Fri 2-5, Sat 10-5
Bookmobiles: 1. Librn, Mindy Liberman. Bk vols 7,777

CL GLENDALE UNIVERSITY, College of Law Library, 220 N Glendale Ave, 91206. SAN 300-7871. Tel: 818-247-0770. FAX: 559-323-5566. Web Site: www.glendalelaw.edu. *Dean,* Darrin Greitzer
Founded 1967
Library Holdings: Bk Vols 50,000; Per Subs 125
Special Collections: English Common Law Coll; Rare Law Books
Open Mon-Thurs 9-6:30, Fri 9-5
Friends of the Library Group

L KNAPP, PETERSEN & CLARKE*, Law Library, 550 N Brand Blvd, Ste 1500, 91203-1922. SAN 372-3194. Tel: 818-547-5000. FAX: 818-547-5329. Web Site: www.kpclegal.com. *Librn,* Kim Kramer; E-mail: kmg@kpclegal.com
Library Holdings: Bk Vols 14,250; Per Subs 28

S WALT DISNEY IMAGINEERING*, Information Research Center, 1401 Flower St, 91201. (Mail add: PO Box 25020, 91221-5020), SAN 300-7952. Tel: 818-544-6594. FAX: 818-544-7845. *Chief Librn,* Aileen Kutaka; Staff 1 (MLS 1)
Founded 1962
Library Holdings: Bk Vols 50,000; Per Subs 500
Subject Interests: Art & archit, Bus & mgt, Costume design, Engr, Hist, Interior design, Travel

Special Services for the Deaf - Staff with knowledge of sign lang
Open Mon-Fri 9-5

GLENDORA

J CITRUS COLLEGE*, Hayden Memorial Library, 1000 W Foothill Blvd, 91741-1899. SAN 300-5860. Tel: 626-914-8640. Reference Tel: 626-914-8644. FAX: 626-963-2531. E-mail: library@citruscollege.edu. Web Site: libguides.citruscollege.edu/library. *Dean,* Dr Gina Hogan; E-mail: ghogan@citruscollege.edu; *Pub Serv Librn,* Sarah Bosler; E-mail: sbosler@citruscollege.edu; *Libr Supvr,* Lari Kirby; E-mail: lkirby@citruscollege.edu; Staff 11 (MLS 7, Non-MLS 4)
Founded 1915. Enrl 11,000; Fac 170; Highest Degree: Associate
Library Holdings: e-books 20,000; Bk Titles 38,607; Bk Vols 50,000; Per Subs 140
Special Collections: Astronomy (Schlesinger Coll); Hayden Coll
Subject Interests: Art & archit, Educ, Music, Soc sci & issues
Automation Activity & Vendor Info: (Circulation) Innovative Interfaces, Inc - Millennium
Wireless access
Function: Archival coll, Art exhibits, Audio & video playback equip for onsite use, AV serv, ILL available, Music CDs, Orientations, Photocopying/Printing, Ref & res, VHS videos, Wheelchair accessible
Partic in Community College League of California; Inland Empire Acad Libr Coop; OCLC Online Computer Library Center, Inc
Open Mon-Thurs 7:30am-8pm, Fri 7:30-4
Restriction: Borrowing privileges limited to fac & registered students, In-house use for visitors, Open to students, fac & staff

P GLENDORA PUBLIC LIBRARY & CULTURAL CENTER*, 140 S Glendora Ave, 91741. SAN 300-7979. Tel: 626-852-4891. FAX: 626-852-4899. E-mail: library@glendoralibrary.org. Web Site: www.cityofglendora.org/departments-services/library. *Libr Dir,* Janet Stone; Tel: 626-852-4896, E-mail: jstone@glendoralibrary.org; *Sr Librn,* Cindy Romero; Tel: 626-852-4813, E-mail: cromero@glendoralibrary.org; *Libr Serv Mgr,* Margaret Hatanaka; Tel: 626-852-4862, E-mail: mhatanaka@glendoralibrary.org; *Mgt Analyst,* Elke Cathel; Tel: 626-852-4827, E-mail: ecathel@glendoralibrary.org; Staff 9 (MLS 7, Non-MLS 2)
Founded 1911. Pop 51,000; Circ 370,341
Jul 2014-Jun 2015 Income $1,906,436, City $1,800,342, Federal $12,582, Locally Generated Income $93,512. Mats Exp $131,820, Books $50,634, Per/Ser (Incl. Access Fees) $12,600, AV Mat $13,479, Electronic Ref Mat (Incl. Access Fees) $55,107
Library Holdings: AV Mats 18,896; DVDs 9,297; e-books 23,627; Electronic Media & Resources 31; Bk Vols 93,670; Per Subs 231
Automation Activity & Vendor Info: (Acquisitions) Innovative Interfaces, Inc; (Cataloging) Innovative Interfaces, Inc; (Circulation) Innovative Interfaces, Inc; (ILL) OCLC; (OPAC) Innovative Interfaces, Inc
Wireless access
Function: 24/7 Electronic res, 24/7 Online cat, Adult bk club, Adult literacy prog, After school storytime, Audiobks via web, AV serv, Bk club(s), Bks on cassette, Bks on CD, Children's prog, Computers for patron use, Digital talking bks, Doc delivery serv, E-Reserves, Electronic databases & coll, Home delivery & serv to seniorr ctr & nursing homes, Homebound delivery serv, ILL available, Magnifiers for reading, Music CDs, Online cat, Online ref, Outreach serv, Outside serv via phone, mail, e-mail & web, OverDrive digital audio bks, Photocopying/Printing, Preschool outreach, Prog for adults, Prog for children & young adult, Ref & res, Ref serv available, Scanner, Spoken cassettes & CDs, Spoken cassettes & DVDs, Story hour, Summer reading prog, Tax forms, Teen prog, Telephone ref, VHS videos, Wheelchair accessible, Workshops
Partic in Southern California Library Cooperative
Special Services for the Deaf - ADA equip; Adult & family literacy prog; Bks on deafness & sign lang; Closed caption videos; High interest/low vocabulary bks; TDD equip
Special Services for the Blind - ZoomText magnification & reading software
Open Mon, Tues & Wed 10-8, Thurs, Fri & Sat 10-5
Friends of the Library Group

GOLETA

P GOLETA VALLEY LIBRARY*, 500 N Fairview Ave, 93117. SAN 334-9292. Tel: 805-964-7878. E-mail: GoletaValleyLibrary@cityofgoleta.org. Web Site: www.cityofgoleta.org/city-hall/goleta-valley-library. *Dir,* B Allison Gray; Tel: 805-562-5502, E-mail: agray@cityofgoleta.org; Staff 11 (MLS 2, Non-MLS 9)
Wireless access
Mem of Black Gold Cooperative Library System
Open Mon-Thurs 10-7, Fri & Sat 10-5:30, Sun 1-5
Friends of the Library Group
Branches: 4
BUELLTON BRANCH, 140 W Hwy 246, Buellton, 93427. (Mail add: PO Box 187, Buellton, 93427), SAN 332-2386. Tel: 805-688-3115. FAX: 805-688-3115. E-mail: buelltonlibrary@cityofgoleta.org. ; Staff 4.5 (Non-MLS 4.5)
Founded 1923. Pop 5,382
Open Mon, Tues & Wed 11-7, Fri & Sat Noon-5:30
Friends of the Library Group
LOS OLIVOS BRANCH, Los Olivos Community Hall, 2374 Alamo Pintado Ave, Los Olivos, 93441, SAN 377-7790.
Open Sat 10-1
SANTA YNEZ BRANCH, 3598 Sagunto St, Santa Ynez, 93460.
Open Sat 1-4
SOLVANG BRANCH, 1745 Mission Dr, Solvang, 93463, SAN 334-9411. Tel: 805-688-4214. E-mail: solvanglibrary@cityofgoleta.org.
Open Tues & Fri 10-5, Wed & Thurs 10-7, Sat 10-4
Friends of the Library Group

GRASS VALLEY

J SIERRA COLLEGE LIBRARY*, Nevada County Campus, 250 Sierra College Dr, 95945. SAN 375-4243. Tel: 530-274-5304. FAX: 530-274-5333. Web Site: www.sierracollege.edu. *Dean of Libr,* Sabrina Pape; E-mail: spape@sierracollege.edu; *Librn,* Halley Little; E-mail: hlittle1@sierracollege.edu; *Librn,* Tina Sixt; E-mail: tsixt@sierracollege.edu
Library Holdings: Bk Titles 16,000; Bk Vols 17,000; Per Subs 100
Automation Activity & Vendor Info: (Cataloging) Ex Libris Group; (Circulation) Ex Libris Group; (ILL) OCLC; (OPAC) Ex Libris Group
Open Mon-Thurs (Winter) 9-8, Fri 9-1; Mon-Thurs (Summer) 10-7

HANFORD

GL KINGS COUNTY LAW LIBRARY*, Kings County Govt Ctr, Bldg 4, 1400 W Lacey Blvd, 93230. SAN 320-5649. Tel: 559-852-4430. Web Site: www.countyofkings.com/services/law-library. *Librn,* Ms Dale Lefkowitz
Founded 1898
Library Holdings: Bk Vols 8,500
Wireless access
Open Mon-Fri 8-5

P KINGS COUNTY LIBRARY*, 401 N Douty St, 93230. SAN 332-0618. Tel: 559-582-0261. Circulation Tel: 559-582-0261, Ext 4001. FAX: 559-583-6163. Web Site: www.kingscountylibrary.org. *Dir,* Natalie Rencher; E-mail: natalie.rencher@kingscountylibrary.org; *Ref Librn,* Sherman Lee; *Ch Serv,* Position Currently Open; Staff 3 (MLS 3)
Founded 1911. Pop 144,000; Circ 110,829
Library Holdings: AV Mats 1,373; Bk Titles 120,000; Bk Vols 191,747; Per Subs 249; Spec Interest Per Sub 10
Special Collections: Kings County and California History; The Jewish Holocaust
Automation Activity & Vendor Info: (Acquisitions) SirsiDynix; (Cataloging) SirsiDynix; (Circulation) SirsiDynix; (ILL) OCLC
Wireless access
Mem of San Joaquin Valley Library System
Open Mon-Wed 10-8, Thurs 10-6, Fri & Sat 12-5
Friends of the Library Group
Branches: 6
AVENAL BRANCH, 501 E King St, Avenal, 93204, SAN 332-0677. Tel: 559-386-5741. FAX: 559-386-1418. *Supvr,* Sherman Lee; E-mail: sherman.lee@kingscountylibrary.org
Circ 7,051
Library Holdings: Large Print Bks 150; Bk Titles 12,000; Bk Vols 14,850; Per Subs 30
Open Mon-Wed 11-7, Thurs & Fri 12-5
Friends of the Library Group
CORCORAN BRANCH, 1001-A Chittenden Ave, Corcoran, 93212, SAN 332-0731. Tel: 559-992-3314. FAX: 559-992-3364. *Supvr,* Sherman Lee
Pop 21,554; Circ 9,335
Library Holdings: Large Print Bks 500; Bk Titles 16,240; Bk Vols 24,541; Per Subs 40
Open Mon-Wed 11-8, Thurs 10-6, Fri & Sat 12-5
HANFORD BRANCH, 401 N Douty St, 93230, SAN 332-0790. Tel: 559-582-0261. FAX: 559-583-6163. *Supvr,* Tonya Russell
Pop 54,686; Circ 131,413
Library Holdings: Bk Vols 76,000
Open Mon-Wed 10-8, Thurs 10-6, Fri & Sat 12-5
Friends of the Library Group
KETTLEMAN CITY BRANCH, 104 Becky Pease St, Kettleman City, 93239, SAN 332-0820. Tel: 559-386-9804. *Supvr,* Sherman Lee
Library Holdings: Bk Titles 11,807; Bk Vols 9,356; Per Subs 45
Open Tues-Thurs 1-6
Friends of the Library Group
LEMOORE BRANCH, 457 C St, Lemoore, 93245, SAN 332-0855. Tel: 559-924-2188. FAX: 559-924-1521. *Supvr,* Tamara Evans
Pop 20,850; Circ 31,543

Library Holdings: Bk Titles 17,500; Bk Vols 20,850; Per Subs 100
Open Mon-Wed 10-8, Thurs 10-6, Fri & Sat 12-5
STRATFORD BRANCH, 20300 Main St, Stratford, 93266. (Mail add: 401 N Douty St, 93230), SAN 332-088X. Tel: 559-947-3003. *Supvr,* Tamara Evans
Pop 1,264; Circ 1,744
Library Holdings: Large Print Bks 200; Bk Titles 10,640; Bk Vols 12,504; Per Subs 25
Open Tues-Thurs 1-6

HAYWARD

C CALIFORNIA STATE UNIVERSITY, EAST BAY LIBRARY*, CSU East Bay Library, 25800 Carlos Bee Blvd, 94542-3052. SAN 300-8142. Tel: 510-885-3664. Circulation Tel: 510-885-3612. Interlibrary Loan Service Tel: 510-885-2986. Reference Tel: 510-885-3765. FAX: 510-885-2049. E-mail: libhelp@csueastbay.edu. Circulation E-mail: circservices@csueastbay.edu. Web Site: library.csueastbay.edu. *Dean of Libr,* John E Wenzler; E-mail: john.wenzler@csueastbay.edu; *Dir, Student Ctr for Academic Achievement,* Jen Nguyen; Tel: 510-885-4759; *Librn,* Doug Highsmith; Tel: 510-885-3610, E-mail: doug.highsmith@csueastbay.edu; *Librn,* Aline Soules; Tel: 510-885-4596, E-mail: aline.soules@csueastbay.edu; *Librn/Concord Campus Libr,* Liz Ginno; Tel: 510-885-2969, Fax: 510-885-2969, E-mail: liz.ginno@csueastbay.edu; *Assoc Librn,* Stephanie Alexander; Tel: 510-885-7674, E-mail: stephanie.alexander@csueastbay.edu; *Assoc Librn,* Tom Bickley; Tel: 510-885-7554, E-mail: tom.bickley@csueastbay.edu; *Assoc Librn,* Dana Edwards; Tel: 510-885-3632, E-mail: dana.edwards@csueastbay.edu; *Assoc Librn,* Kyzyl Fenno-Smith; Tel: 510-885-2974, E-mail: kyzyl.fenno-smith@csueastbay.edu; *Assoc Librn,* Sharon Radcliff; Tel: 510-885-7452, E-mail: sharon.radcliff@csueastbay.edu; *Assoc Librn,* Diana Wakimoto; Tel: 510-885-4287, E-mail: diana.wakimoto@csueastbay.edu; *Assoc Librn, Syst,* Jiannan Wang; Tel: 510-885-2973, E-mail: jiannan.wang@csueastbay.edu; *Sr Asst Librn,* Jeffra Bussmann; Tel: 510-885-3780, E-mail: jeffra.bussmann@csueastbay.edu; *Sr Asst Librn,* Andrew Carlos; Tel: 510-885-2303, E-mail: andrew.carlos@csueastbay.edu; *Sr Asst Librn,* Gretchen Keer; Tel: 510-885-2968, E-mail: gretchen.keer@csueastbay.edu; *Access Serv Mgr,* Paula Kapteyn; Tel: 510-885-4905; *Bibliog Control Mgr,* Tom Holt; Tel: 510-885-2429, E-mail: tom.holt@csueastbay.edu; *Learning Commons Mgr,* Paulette Washington; Tel: 510-885-2651, E-mail: paulette.washington@csueastbay.edu; *Media Res & Reserves Mgr,* Jason Chavez; Tel: 510-885-2299, E-mail: jason.chavez@csueastbay.edu; *Acq,* Shaunt Hamstra; E-mail: shaunt.hamstra@csueastbay.edu; Staff 33 (MLS 16, Non-MLS 17)
Founded 1957. Enrl 14,000; Fac 752; Highest Degree: Master
Jul 2013-Jun 2014 Income $3,486,995, State $3,178,057, Federal $8,938. Mats Exp $1,070,309, Books $298,204, Per/Ser (Incl. Access Fees) $261,965, Micro $850, AV Mat $12,415, Electronic Ref Mat (Incl. Access Fees) $494,516, Presv $2,359. Sal $2,111,502 (Prof $1,086,718)
Library Holdings: AV Mats 36,610; CDs 4,562; DVDs 1,294; e-books 189,228; e-journals 103,000; Electronic Media & Resources 310,000; Microforms 12,803; Music Scores 21,219; Bk Titles 684,571; Bk Vols 922,749; Per Subs 390; Videos 22,434
Special Collections: Artists Book Coll; Bay Area Poetry Coll; Early Voyages & Travels Coll; Marco Polo Coll. State Document Depository; US Document Depository
Automation Activity & Vendor Info: (Acquisitions) Innovative Interfaces, Inc; (Cataloging) Innovative Interfaces, Inc; (Circulation) Innovative Interfaces, Inc; (Course Reserve) Innovative Interfaces, Inc; (ILL) OCLC ILLiad; (Media Booking) Innovative Interfaces, Inc; (OPAC) Innovative Interfaces, Inc; (Serials) Innovative Interfaces, Inc
Wireless access
Function: Doc delivery serv, E-Reserves, Electronic databases & coll, ILL available, Orientations, Photocopying/Printing, Ref & res, Ref serv available, Spoken cassettes & CDs, Spoken cassettes & DVDs, Telephone ref, VHS videos, Wheelchair accessible
Partic in OCLC Online Computer Library Center, Inc; San Francisco Bay Area Library & Information Network
Special Services for the Deaf - TTY equip
Open Mon-Thurs 8am-10pm, Fri 8-5, Sat 11-5, Sun 12-7
Restriction: In-house use for visitors, Open to fac, students & qualified researchers

J CHABOT COLLEGE LIBRARY, 25555 Hesperian Blvd, 94545. SAN 332-1339. Circulation Tel: 510-723-7513. Reference Tel: 510-723-6764, 510-723-7006. Information Services Tel: 510-723-6765. Administration FAX: 510-723-7005. Reference E-mail: chabotref@clpccd.cc.ca.us. Web Site: www.chabotcollege.edu/library. *Info Literacy, Libr Coord,* Dr Kim Morrison; Tel: 510-723-6762, E-mail: kmorrison@chabotcollege.edu; *Librn,* Paul Maclennan; E-mail: pmaclennan@chabotcollege.edu; *Coll Develop, Online Learning Librn,* John Chan; Tel: 510-723-6778, E-mail: jchan@chabotcollege.edu; *Libr Serv Spec,* Heather Hernandez; Tel: 510-723-6763, E-mail: hhernandez@chabotcollege.edu; *Info Tech,* Norman Buchwald; Tel: 510-723-6993, E-mail: nbuchwald@chabotcollege.edu; *Cat, Circ, Libr Tech,* Blake Lewis; Tel: 510-723-7113, E-mail: blewis@chabotcollege.edu; *Instruction & Outreach,* Pedro Reynoso; Tel: 510-723-6767, E-mail: preynoso@chabotcollege.edu; Staff 10 (MLS 5, Non-MLS 5)
Founded 1961. Enrl 15,000; Fac 264; Highest Degree: Associate
Library Holdings: AV Mats 11,855; Bk Titles 65,460; Per Subs 201
Special Collections: California History Coll
Subject Interests: Fire sci, Nursing
Automation Activity & Vendor Info: (Cataloging) OCLC Online; (Circulation) SirsiDynix; (OPAC) SirsiDynix
Wireless access
Partic in California Community College Library Consortium
Open Mon-Thurs 7:30am-8pm, Fri 8-2, Sat 8:30-3

P HAYWARD PUBLIC LIBRARY*, 835 C St, 94541. SAN 332-1363. Tel: 510-293-8685. Administration Tel: 510-881-7954. Administration FAX: 510-733-6669. E-mail: library@hayward-ca.gov. Web Site: www.hayward-ca.gov/public-library. *Dir, Libr & Commun Serv,* Sean Reinhart; Tel: 510-881-7956, E-mail: sean.reinhart@hayward-ca.gov; *Operations Mgr,* Vince Ang; Tel: 510-881-7987, E-mail: vince.ang@hayward-ca.gov; *Supv Librn,* Clio Hathaway; Tel: 510-881-7948, E-mail: clio.hathaway@hayward-ca.gov; *Supv Librn,* Sally Thomas; E-mail: sally.thomas@hayward-ca.gov; Staff 12.5 (MLS 9, Non-MLS 3.5)
Founded 1897. Pop 148,756; Circ 1,087,737
Library Holdings: Audiobooks 3,664; AV Mats 36,762; Bks on Deafness & Sign Lang 75; CDs 8,870; DVDs 24,855; e-books 8,074; Large Print Bks 844; Bk Vols 124,928; Per Subs 159
Automation Activity & Vendor Info: (Acquisitions) Innovative Interfaces, Inc; (Cataloging) Innovative Interfaces, Inc; (Circulation) Innovative Interfaces, Inc; (ILL) Innovative Interfaces, Inc; (OPAC) Innovative Interfaces, Inc
Wireless access
Function: Adult bk club, Adult literacy prog, After school storytime, Audiobks via web, Bilingual assistance for Spanish patrons, Bk club(s), Bks on CD, Children's prog, Computers for patron use, Electronic databases & coll, Family literacy, Free DVD rentals, Home delivery & serv to seniorr ctr & nursing homes, Homebound delivery serv, Homework prog, Internet access, Literacy & newcomer serv, Museum passes, Music CDs, Online cat, OverDrive digital audio bks, Photocopying/Printing, Preschool outreach, Printer for laptops & handheld devices, Prog for adults, Prog for children & young adult, Ref serv available, Satellite serv, Senior outreach, Spanish lang bks, Spoken cassettes & CDs, Story hour, Summer reading prog, Tax forms, Teen prog, Wheelchair accessible, Workshops, Writing prog
Partic in Califa; Link+
Special Services for the Deaf - TDD equip
Special Services for the Blind - Large print bks
Open Mon-Wed 11-8, Thurs-Sat 10-5
Friends of the Library Group
Branches: 1
WEEKES BRANCH, 27300 Patrick Ave, 94544, SAN 332-1398. Tel: 510-782-2155. FAX: 510-259-0429. *Supv Librn,* Melesha Owen; Tel: 510-293-5239, E-mail: melesha.owen@hayward-ca.gov; Staff 7 (MLS 3, Non-MLS 4)
Circ 353,910
Function: After school storytime, Audiobks via web, Bilingual assistance for Spanish patrons, Bks on CD, Children's prog, Computers for patron use, Electronic databases & coll, Family literacy, Free DVD rentals, Homebound delivery serv, ILL available, Music CDs, Online cat, OverDrive digital audio bks, Photocopying/Printing, Printer for laptops & handheld devices, Prog for adults, Prog for children & young adult, Ref serv available, Senior outreach, Spoken cassettes & CDs, Story hour, Summer reading prog, Teen prog, Telephone ref, Wheelchair accessible
Open Mon-Wed 11-8, Thurs-Sat 10-5
Friends of the Library Group

M LIFE CHIROPRACTIC COLLEGE-WEST LIBRARY*, 25001 Industrial Blvd, 94545. SAN 327-9162. Tel: 510-780-4507. Reference Tel: 510-780-4500, Ext 2730. FAX: 510-780-4590. E-mail: library@lifewest.edu. Web Site: www.lifewest.edu/academics/library. *Dir,* Barbara Delli-Gatti; E-mail: bdelligatti@lifewest.edu; Staff 4 (MLS 2, Non-MLS 2)
Founded 1981. Enrl 350; Highest Degree: Doctorate
Library Holdings: AV Mats 5,300; e-journals 116; Bk Titles 8,500; Bk Vols 10,300; Per Subs 200
Special Collections: Chiropractic Rare Book Coll; College Archives
Automation Activity & Vendor Info: (Cataloging) SirsiDynix; (Circulation) SirsiDynix; (OPAC) SirsiDynix
Wireless access
Function: Audio & video playback equip for onsite use, AV serv, CD-ROM, Computers for patron use, Distance learning, Doc delivery serv, E-Reserves, Electronic databases & coll, Health sci info serv, ILL available, Internet access, Online cat, Photocopying/Printing, Ref serv available, Res performed for a fee, Telephone ref

Publications: New Materials (Acquisition list)
Partic in Chiropractic Libr Consortium; National Network of Libraries of Medicine Region 5; Northern California & Nevada Medical Library Group; OCLC Online Computer Library Center, Inc
Open Mon-Thurs 7am-8pm, Fri 7-5, Sat 12-5
Restriction: Borrowing privileges limited to fac & registered students, Borrowing requests are handled by ILL, Circ to mem only, In-house use for visitors

HEMET

P HEMET PUBLIC LIBRARY*, 300 E Latham Ave, 92543. SAN 300-8177. Tel: 951-765-2440. FAX: 951-765-2446. Web Site: www.cityofhemet.org/index.aspx?nid=94. *Libr Mgr,* Katherine Caines; E-mail: kcaines@cityofhemet.org; Staff 7 (MLS 3, Non-MLS 4)
Founded 1907. Pop 72,000; Circ 470,000
Library Holdings: CDs 1,457; DVDs 7,000; Bk Vols 105,000; Per Subs 192; Talking Bks 2,520; Videos 1,000
Subject Interests: Local hist
Automation Activity & Vendor Info: (Circulation) Horizon
Wireless access
Function: Adult literacy prog, Homebound delivery serv, ILL available, Music CDs, Photocopying/Printing, Prog for adults, Prog for children & young adult, Ref serv available, Spoken cassettes & CDs, Summer reading prog, Telephone ref, VHS videos, Wheelchair accessible
Mem of Inland Library System
Partic in San Bernardino, Inyo, Riverside Counties United Library Services
Special Services for the Deaf - Closed caption videos
Special Services for the Blind - Talking bks; Talking bks & player equip
Open Wed & Thurs 9-7, Fri & Sat 9-6
Friends of the Library Group

HOLLISTER

P SAN BENITO COUNTY FREE LIBRARY*, 470 Fifth St, 95023-3885. SAN 300-8185. Tel: 831-636-4107. FAX: 831-636-4099. E-mail: library@cosb.us. Web Site: sbcfl.org. *County Librn,* Nora S Conte; Tel: 831-636-4097, E-mail: nconte@cosb.us; *Literacy Coordr, Ref & Ad Serv Librn,* Betty J Mason; E-mail: bmason@cosb.us. Subject Specialists: *Early childhood educ, Mgt, Pub relations,* Nora S Conte; *Adult literacy, Native American,* Betty J Mason; Staff 8.5 (MLS 2.5, Non-MLS 6)
Founded 1918. Pop 56,414; Circ 93,667
Jul 2014-Jun 2015 Income $823,136, State $16,037, City $15,000, Federal $45,000, County $692,181. Mats Exp $223,298, Books $17,830, Per/Ser (Incl. Access Fees) $3,545, Other Print Mats $4,180, AV Mat $785, Electronic Ref Mat (Incl. Access Fees) $15,154, Presv $964. Sal $581,401 (Prof $60,000)
Library Holdings: Audiobooks 1,052; Bk Titles 91,065; Bk Vols 91,385; Per Subs 36; Spec Interest Per Sub 2; Videos 3,556
Special Collections: American Indian Coll; Automotive Coll; Goverment Documents; Japanese Language Coll; Large Print Coll; Local & State (California Coll); Mysteries Coll; Science Fiction Coll; Spanish Language Coll
Automation Activity & Vendor Info: (Acquisitions) Koha; (ILL) OCLC WorldShare Interlibrary Loan; (OPAC) ByWater Solutions
Wireless access
Function: Children's prog, Citizenship assistance, Computer training, Computers for patron use, Photocopying/Printing
Mem of Pacific Library Partnership (PLP)
Partic in Monterey Bay Area Cooperative Library System
Special Services for the Deaf - Assistive tech; Bks on deafness & sign lang; High interest/low vocabulary bks
Special Services for the Blind - Accessible computers; Bks & mags in Braille, on rec, tape & cassette; Bks available with recordings; Bks on cassette; Bks on CD; Cassette playback machines; Cassettes; Computer with voice synthesizer for visually impaired persons; Copier with enlargement capabilities; Digital talking bk; Extensive large print coll; Large print & cassettes; Large print bks; Magnifiers; PC for people with disabilities; Ref serv; Talking bks; Talking bks & player equip; Videos on blindness & physical disabilties
Open Mon & Wed 10-6, Tues & Thurs 12-8, Fri 2-6
Friends of the Library Group
Bookmobiles: 2. Mobile Servs Coordr, Carlos Munoz. Bk titles 3,000

GL SAN BENITO COUNTY LAW LIBRARY*, Courthouse, 440 Fifth St, 95023. SAN 320-5665. Tel: 831-637-0071. *Library Contact,* Amy Freitos
Library Holdings: Bk Titles 5,200; Bk Vols 12,537
Special Collections: Federal & California Case Law & Statutes

HOPLAND

S HOPLAND RESEARCH & EXTENSION CENTER LIBRARY*, 4070 University Rd, 95449. SAN 373-4943. Tel: 707-744-1424. FAX: 707-744-1040. Web Site: hrec.ucanr.edu. *Dir,* Kimberly A Rodrigues; Tel: 707-744-1424, Ext 115, E-mail: karodrigues@ucanr.edu
Library Holdings: Bk Vols 200
Wireless access
Open Mon-Fri 12-6

HUNTINGTON BEACH

S AMERICAN AVIATION HISTORICAL SOCIETY*, Reference Library, 15211 Springdale St, 92649-1156. (Mail add: PO Box 3023, 92649-1156), SAN 371-2834. Tel: 714-549-4818. E-mail: aahs2333@aahs-online.org. Web Site: aahs-online.org. *Pres,* Jerri Bergen; *Librn,* Robert Palazzola
Founded 1956
Library Holdings: Bk Vols 15,000; Per Subs 300; Spec Interest Per Sub 300
Wireless access
Open Wed 10-5
Restriction: Mem only

J GOLDEN WEST COLLEGE*, R Dudley Boyce Library & Learning Center, 15744 Golden West St, 92647. SAN 300-8215. Tel: 714-895-8741. Reference Tel: 714-895-8741, Ext 55184. FAX: 714-895-8926. Web Site: www.goldenwestcollege.edu/library. *Dean of Libr,* Dr Carla Martinez; E-mail: cmartinez@gwc.cccd.edu; *Co-Chair, Online Serv, Syst,* Gonzalo Garcia; Tel: 714-895-8741, Ext 55250, E-mail: ggarcia@gwc.cccd.edu; *Acq, Cat,* Julie Terrazas; Tel: 714-895-8741, Ext 55207, E-mail: jadavis@gwc.cccd.edu; *Pub Serv,* Vanessa Aguirre; Tel: 714-895-8741, Ext 51243, E-mail: vgarcia@gwc.cccd.edu; Staff 11 (MLS 5, Non-MLS 6)
Founded 1966. Highest Degree: Associate
Subject Interests: Art, Nursing, Soc sci & issues
Automation Activity & Vendor Info: (Acquisitions) Baker & Taylor; (Cataloging) Baker & Taylor; (Circulation) Baker & Taylor; (Course Reserve) Baker & Taylor; (OPAC) Baker & Taylor
Wireless access
Function: ILL available, Instruction & testing, Ref & res, Wheelchair accessible
Special Services for the Deaf - Bks on deafness & sign lang; Closed caption videos; High interest/low vocabulary bks; TDD equip; TTY equip
Special Services for the Blind - Computer with voice synthesizer for visually impaired persons
Open Mon-Thurs 8am-8:45pm, Fri 8-3

P HUNTINGTON BEACH PUBLIC LIBRARY SYSTEM*, Information & Cultural Resource Center, 7111 Talbert Ave, 92648. SAN 332-1428. Tel: 714-842-4481. FAX: 714-375-5180. E-mail: library@hbpl.org. Web Site: www.hbpl.org, www.huntingtonbeachca.gov/government/departments/library. *Dir, Libr Serv,* Stephanie Beverage; E-mail: stephanie.beverage@surfcity-hb.org; *Principal Librn,* Steven Park; E-mail: steven.park@surfcity-hb.org; *ILL,* Bonnie Nowak; Staff 28.3 (MLS 10, Non-MLS 18.3)
Founded 1909. Pop 190,377; Circ 1,001,000
Jul 2018-Jun 2019 Income (Main & Associated Libraries) $5,176,920, City $5,004,995, Federal $56,000, Other $115,965. Mats Exp $398,267, Books $257,457, Per/Ser (Incl. Access Fees) $21,490, AV Mat $35,000, Electronic Ref Mat (Incl. Access Fees) $84,320. Sal $2,719,453
Library Holdings: Audiobooks 796; AV Mats 20,334; Bks on Deafness & Sign Lang 124; CDs 7,854; DVDs 8,075; e-books 1,891; Electronic Media & Resources 18; Large Print Bks 5,297; Bk Titles 302,266; Bk Vols 388,588; Per Subs 277
Special Collections: Genealogy (Orange County, CA, Genealogical Society Coll)
Automation Activity & Vendor Info: (Cataloging) Horizon; (Circulation) Horizon; (OPAC) Horizon
Wireless access
Function: 24/7 Electronic res, 24/7 Online cat, 3D Printer, Adult bk club, Adult literacy prog, After school storytime, Art exhibits, Audiobks via web, Bk club(s), Bks on cassette, Bks on CD, Children's prog, Computer training, Computers for patron use, Digital talking bks, E-Reserves, Electronic databases & coll, Family literacy, Free DVD rentals, Genealogy discussion group, Holiday prog, Homework prog, ILL available, Internet access, Life-long learning prog for all ages, Literacy & newcomer serv, Magazines, Meeting rooms, Microfiche/film & reading machines, Music CDs, Online cat, Photocopying/Printing, Prog for adults, Prog for children & young adult, Ref serv available, Scanner, Story hour, Study rm, Summer & winter reading prog, Summer reading prog, Teen prog, Wheelchair accessible, Winter reading prog, Workshops
Mem of Santiago Library System
Open Mon 1-9, Tues-Thurs 9-9, Fri & Sat 9-5, Sun 1-5
Friends of the Library Group
Branches: 4
BANNING, 9281 Banning Ave, 92646-8302, SAN 332-1517. Tel: 714-375-5005. FAX: 714-375-5091. *Br Mgr, Libr Spec,* Robin Ott; E-mail: rott@surfcity-hb.org
Open Wed & Thurs 10-7, Fri & Sat 9-5
Friends of the Library Group

MAIN STREET BRANCH, 525 Main St, 92648-5133, SAN 332-1452. Tel: 714-375-5071. FAX: 714-375-5072. *Br Mgr, Librn,* Susan Foster; E-mail: susan.foster@surfcity-hb.org
Open Tues-Thurs 10-7, Fri & Sat 9-5
Friends of the Library Group

HELEN MURPHY BRANCH, 15882 Graham St, 92649-1724, SAN 332-1487. Tel: 714-375-5006. FAX: 714-373-3088.
Open Tues-Thurs 10-7
Friends of the Library Group

OAK VIEW, 17251 Oak Lane, 92648, SAN 377-0265. Tel: 714-375-5068. FAX: 714-375-5073. *Br Mgr, Libr Spec,* Claudia Locke
Open Mon-Thurs 10-7, Fri 9-5
Friends of the Library Group

IMPERIAL

P IMPERIAL PUBLIC LIBRARY*, 200 W Ninth St, 92251. SAN 300-8231. Tel: 760-355-1332. FAX: 760-355-4857. Web Site: imperial.polarislibrary.com, www.cityofimperial.org/public-library. *Dir, Commun Serv,* Amber Haller; E-mail: ehaller@cityofimperial.org
Founded 1909. Pop 14,758; Circ 39,523
Library Holdings: Bk Vols 34,600
Wireless access
Partic in Serra Cooperative Library System
Open Mon-Thurs 10-8, Fri 10-5, Sat 11-3

J IMPERIAL VALLEY COLLEGE*, Spencer Library Media Center, 380 E Ira Aten Rd, 92251. SAN 300-824X. Tel: 760-355-6382. Circulation Tel: 760-355-6409. Reference Tel: 760-355-6445. FAX: 760-355-1090. Web Site: www.imperial.edu/courses-and-programs/divisions/arts-and-letters/library-department. *Librn,* Mary J Guerrero; E-mail: mary.guerrero@imperial.edu; *Sr Libr Tech,* Mary Ann Smith; Tel: 760-355-6380, E-mail: maryann.smith@imperial.edu; Staff 9 (MLS 3, Non-MLS 6)
Founded 1922. Enrl 7,633; Fac 119; Highest Degree: Associate
Library Holdings: AV Mats 778; Bk Titles 55,789; Bk Vols 59,571; Per Subs 463
Subject Interests: Local hist
Automation Activity & Vendor Info: (Cataloging) OCLC Online; (Circulation) SirsiDynix; (ILL) OCLC; (OPAC) SirsiDynix
Wireless access
Open Mon-Thurs 8-8, Fri 8-3

INDEPENDENCE

P INYO COUNTY FREE LIBRARY*, 168 N Edwards St, 93526. (Mail add: PO Drawer K, 93526-0610), SAN 332-169X. Tel: 760-878-0260. FAX: 760-878-0360. E-mail: inyocolib@inyocounty.us. Web Site: www.inyocounty.us/library. *Libr Dir,* Nancy Masters; E-mail: nmasters@inyocounty.us; *Librn,* Jayne Hall
Founded 1913. Pop 18,400; Circ 130,000
Library Holdings: Bk Vols 101,500; Per Subs 129
Special Collections: Mary Hunter Austin Coll
Subject Interests: Inyo County
Wireless access
Mem of Inland Library System
Partic in San Bernardino, Inyo, Riverside Counties United Library Services
Open Tues & Fri 12-5, Wed 12-8, Sat 10-1
Branches: 5

BIG PINE BRANCH, 500 S Main St, Big Pine, 93513. (Mail add: PO Box 760, Big Pine, 93513-0760), SAN 377-6018. Tel: 760-938-2420. E-mail: bplibrary@inyocounty.us. *Libr Spec,* Elizabeth Porter
Library Holdings: Bk Vols 16,000; Per Subs 11
Open Tues, Thurs & Fri 12-5, Wed 2-7, Sat 10-4
Friends of the Library Group

BISHOP BRANCH, 210 Academy Ave, Bishop, 93514-2693, SAN 375-5509. Tel: 760-873-5115. FAX: 760-873-5356. E-mail: bishoplib@inyocounty.us. *Librn,* Joe Frankel; *Librn,* Emily Lanphear
Library Holdings: Bk Vols 30,200; Per Subs 33
Open Tues & Thurs 12-8, Wed & Fri 10-6, Sat 10-4
Friends of the Library Group

FURNACE CREEK, 201 Nevares, Death Valley, 92328. (Mail add: PO Box 568, Death Valley, 92328). Tel: 760-786-2408. *Librn,* Mark Gatlin
Library Holdings: Bk Vols 2,450; Per Subs 6
Open Wed 4:30-8:30, Sat 9-Noon

LONE PINE BRANCH, 127 Bush St, Lone Pine, 93545. (Mail add: PO Box 745, Lone Pine, 93545-0745), SAN 377-6034. Tel: 760-876-5031. E-mail: lplibrary@inyocounty.us. *Librn,* Kathy Chambers
Library Holdings: Bk Vols 12,500; Per Subs 33
Open Tues & Thurs 2-7, Wed & Fri 10-12 & 1-5, Sat 10-4
Friends of the Library Group

TECOPA BRANCH, 408 Tecopa Hot Springs Rd, Tecopa, 92389. (Mail add: PO Box 218, Tecopa, 92389). Tel: 760-852-4171. *Librn,* Johnnie Lutze
Library Holdings: Bk Vols 4,500; Per Subs 6
Open Tues-Thurs 10-3, Sat 10-2

GL INYO COUNTY LAW LIBRARY*, 168 N Edwards St, 93526. (Mail add: PO Box K, 93526-0610), SAN 320-1562. Tel: 760-878-0260. FAX: 760-878-0360. E-mail: inyocolib@inyocounty.us. Web Site: www.inyocounty.us/services/library. *Libr Dir,* Nancy Masters; E-mail: nmasters@inyocounty.us
Library Holdings: Bk Vols 3,700
Subject Interests: Calif
Open Tues, Thurs & Fri 12-5, Wed 12-8, Sat 10-1

INDIO

GL RIVERSIDE COUNTY LAW LIBRARY*, Indio Branch, 82-995 Hwy 111, Ste 102, 92201. SAN 300-8258. Tel: 760-848-7151. FAX: 760-863-2022. E-mail: lawlibrary.indio@rclawlibrary.org. Web Site: rclawlibrary.org. *Libr Asst,* Theresa Schwake; E-mail: theresa.schwake@rclawlibrary.org
Library Holdings: Electronic Media & Resources 9; Bk Vols 12,000; Per Subs 14
Subject Interests: Law
Wireless access
Open Mon-Fri 8-5

INGLEWOOD

P INGLEWOOD PUBLIC LIBRARY*, 101 W Manchester Blvd, 90301-1771. SAN 332-172X. Tel: 310-412-5397. FAX: 310-412-8848. Web Site: www.cityofinglewood.org/787/Inglewood-Public-Library. *Head, Tech Serv, Libr Mgr,* Frances Tracht; E-mail: ftracht@cityofinglewood.org; *Head, Children's/Youth Serv,* Angela Citizen; E-mail: acitizen@cityofinglewood.org; *Ch Serv Librn,* Dawn Fechter; E-mail: dfite@cityofinglewood.org; *Supvr, Ad Serv,* Frank Francis; E-mail: ffrancis@cityofinglewood.org; *Br Serv Supvr,* Lori Williams; E-mail: lwilliams@cityofinglewood.org; Staff 10 (MLS 9, Non-MLS 1)
Founded 1971. Pop 112,333; Circ 112,758
Oct 2014-Sept 2015 Income (Main & Associated Libraries) $2,643,541. Mats Exp $2,643,541. Sal $1,349,814
Library Holdings: AV Mats 6,971; DVDs 4,228; e-books 553; Bk Vols 311,456; Per Subs 306
Special Collections: Inglewood (Local History Coll); Large Print; Military History (Special Coll of Local); Rare Books (Includes some rare books published in Southern California); Spanish. Municipal Document Depository; State Document Depository; US Document Depository
Automation Activity & Vendor Info: (Acquisitions) Innovative Interfaces, Inc; (Cataloging) Innovative Interfaces, Inc; (Circulation) Innovative Interfaces, Inc; (ILL) Innovative Interfaces, Inc; (OPAC) Innovative Interfaces, Inc; (Serials) Innovative Interfaces, Inc
Wireless access
Function: 24/7 Electronic res, Activity rm, After school storytime, Archival coll, Art exhibits, Audio & video playback equip for onsite use, Audiobks via web, AV serv, Bilingual assistance for Spanish patrons, Bks on cassette, Bks on CD, CD-ROM, Children's prog, Citizenship assistance, Computer training, Computers for patron use, Electronic databases & coll, Free DVD rentals, Govt ref serv, Holiday prog, ILL available, Internet access, Life-long learning prog for all ages, Magazines, Mail & tel request accepted, Microfiche/film & reading machines, Movies, Music CDs, Online cat, Online ref, Orientations, Passport agency, Photocopying/Printing, Prog for adults, Prog for children & young adult, Ref serv available, Senior computer classes, Spanish lang bks, Spoken cassettes & CDs, Spoken cassettes & DVDs, Story hour, Study rm, Summer reading prog, Tax forms, Teen prog, Telephone ref, VHS videos, Wheelchair accessible
Partic in Califa; Southern California Library Cooperative
Open Mon-Wed 11-8, Thurs 11-6, Sat 10-2
Restriction: Circ to mem only, Closed stack, Free to mem, ID required to use computers (Ltd hrs), In-house use for visitors, Non-circulating coll, Non-circulating of rare bks
Friends of the Library Group
Branches: 1

CRENSHAW-IMPERIAL BRANCH LIBRARY, 11141 Crenshaw Blvd, 90303-2338, SAN 332-1754. *Br Mgr,* Kerri Arroyo; E-mail: karroyo@cityofinglewood.org
Library Holdings: Bk Vols 43,841
Open Mon, Tues & Thurs 11-6

CL UNIVERSITY OF WEST LOS ANGELES*, Law School Library, 9800 S LaCienega Blvd, 90301. SAN 331-863X. Tel: 310-342-5253. Web Site: uwla.edu. *Libr Asst,* Nohemi Rodriquez; Tel: 310-342-5253
Founded 1968. Enrl 400
Library Holdings: Bk Vols 31,000; Per Subs 100
Open Mon, Tues & Wed 12:30-8:30, Thurs & Fri 1:30-8:30, Sat 9:30-1:30

IRVINE

CR CONCORDIA UNIVERSITY LIBRARY*, 1530 Concordia W, 92612. SAN 322-7065. Tel: 949-214-3090, 949-854-8002, Ext 1500. E-mail: librarian@cui.edu. Web Site: www.cui.edu/library. *Ref & Instruction Librn,* Laura Guzman; E-mail: laura.guzman@cui.edu; Staff 3 (MLS 2, Non-MLS 1)
Founded 1976. Enrl 2,100; Fac 72; Highest Degree: Master
Library Holdings: CDs 250; Bk Titles 85,000; Bk Vols 90,000; Per Subs 850
Special Collections: Dale Hartmann Curriculum Coll; Gehrke Reformation Coll; Robert C Baden Memorial Children's Coll
Subject Interests: Lutheran theol, Reformation hist
Automation Activity & Vendor Info: (Acquisitions) TLC (The Library Corporation); (Cataloging) TLC (The Library Corporation); (Circulation) TLC (The Library Corporation); (Course Reserve) TLC (The Library Corporation); (OPAC) TLC (The Library Corporation); (Serials) TLC (The Library Corporation)
Wireless access
Function: Music CDs, Orientations, Photocopying/Printing, Spoken cassettes & CDs, VHS videos, Wheelchair accessible
Partic in Concordia Univ Syst; Southern Calif Area Theol Librns Asn
Open Mon-Thurs 7:30am-11pm, Fri 7:30-4:30, Sun 2-10
Restriction: Fee for pub use, Open to students, fac & staff

S FASHION INSTITUTE OF DESIGN & MERCHANDISING LIBRARY*, 17590 Gillette Ave, 92614. SAN 328-6622. Tel: 949-851-6200. Circulation Tel: 949-851-6200, Ext 1737. Reference Tel: 949-851-6200, Ext 1738. FAX: 949-851-6808. Web Site: fidm.edu/en/student+life/fidm+library. *Librn,* Rebecca Markman; E-mail: rmarkman@fidm.edu; Staff 3 (MLS 1, Non-MLS 2)
Library Holdings: AV Mats 1,200; Bk Vols 2,100; Per Subs 65
Wireless access
Restriction: Open by appt only

J IRVINE VALLEY COLLEGE LIBRARY*, 5500 Irvine Center Dr, 92618-4399. SAN 324-7333. Tel: 949-451-5761. Information Services Tel: 949-451-5266. FAX: 949-451-5796. E-mail: library@ivc.edu. Web Site: www.ivc.edu/library. *Librn,* Cheryl Bailey; E-mail: cbailey@ivc.edu; *Librn,* Tony Lin; E-mail: alin@ivc.edu; Staff 4 (MLS 4)
Founded 1979. Enrl 14,768; Fac 70
Library Holdings: Bk Vols 45,000; Per Subs 120
Wireless access
Partic in OCLC Online Computer Library Center, Inc; Proquest Dialog
Open Mon-Thurs 8am-9pm, Fri 8-4, Sat 10-2

S MUTUAL UFO NETWORK, INC*, MUFON Library, 18023 Sky Park Circle, F2, 92614. SAN 329-1626. Tel: 949-476-8366. E-mail: hq@mufon.com. Web Site: www.mufon.com. *Exec Dir,* Jan C Harzan; Staff 1 (Non-MLS 1)
Founded 1969
Library Holdings: Bk Titles 300; Per Subs 65
Special Collections: Unidentified Flying Objects, bks, flms
Publications: MUFON UFO Journal (Monthly)
Restriction: Open by appt only

L RUTAN & TUCKER LIBRARY, 18575 Jamboree Rd, 9th Flr, 92612. SAN 301-5424. Tel: 714-641-5100. FAX: 714-546-9035. *Dir, Libr Serv,* Arlen Bristol; E-mail: abristol@rutan.com
Library Holdings: Bk Vols 30,000; Per Subs 150

C UNIVERSITY OF CALIFORNIA IRVINE LIBRARIES*, Langson Library, PO Box 19557, 92623-9557. SAN 300-8355. Tel: 949-824-6836. Administration Tel: 949-824-5212. Web Site: www.lib.uci.edu. *Univ Librn,* Lorelei Tanji; E-mail: ltanji@uci.edu; *Admin Serv, Assoc Univ Librn,* Kevin Ruminson; Tel: 949-824-4440, E-mail: ruminson@uci.edu; *Assoc Univ Librn, Pub Serv,* Alison Regan; Tel: 949-824-9753, E-mail: aeregan@uci.edu; *Assoc University Librn, Resources, Res,* John Renaud; Tel: 949-824-5216, E-mail: jrenaud@uci.edu
Founded 1965. Highest Degree: Doctorate
Special Collections: Bibliotheca Neurologica Courville Coll, artifacts, bks; Book Art Coll; British Naval History Coll; Contemporary Small Press Poetry Coll; Dance Coll; History of Literary Criticism (Wellek Coll); Neurology, Neuropathology (Courville Coll); Orchids & Horticulture (Menninger Coll); Regional California History Coll; Southeast Asian Archive; Thomas Mann (Waldmuller Coll). State Document Depository; US Document Depository
Wireless access
Publications: Library Update (Newsletter); UCI Libraries for Library Partners & Friends (Newsletter)
Partic in Association of Research Libraries; Center for Research Libraries; OCLC Online Computer Library Center, Inc; OCLC Research Library Partnership; Univ of Calif Librs
Special Services for the Deaf - Assistive tech
Friends of the Library Group
Departmental Libraries:
CM GRUNIGEN MEDICAL LIBRARY, Bldg 22A Rt 81, 101 The City Dr S, Orange, 92868, SAN 326-713X. Tel: 714-456-5585. Web Site: grunigen.lib.uci.edu/.
SCIENCE LIBRARY, PO Box 19557, 92623-9557, SAN 326-7091. Tel: 949-824-3692. Web Site: www.lib.uci.edu/science.

CL WESTCLIFF UNIVERSITY, Western State College of Law Library, 16735 Von Karman, Ste 100, 92606. SAN 300-7804. Tel: 714-459-1111. FAX: 714-871-4806. Web Site: www.wsulaw.edu/library. *Dir,* John O'Donnell; Tel: 714-459-1110, E-mail: jodonnell@wsulaw.edu; *Ref Librn,* Christopher Boatman; Tel: 714-459-1171, E-mail: cboatman@wsulaw.edu; *Ref Librn,* Christine Han; Tel: 714-459-1177, E-mail: christinehan@wsulaw.edu; *Tech Serv Librn,* Margot McLaren; Tel: 714-459-1178, E-mail: mmclaren@wsulaw.edu; Staff 4 (MLS 4)
Enrl 226; Fac 19; Highest Degree: Doctorate
Library Holdings: Bk Titles 1,625; Bk Vols 2,132
Subject Interests: Anglo-Am law
Wireless access
Partic in OCLC Online Computer Library Center, Inc
Open Mon-Fri 8am-11pm, Sat & Sun 8-6

IRWINDALE

P IRWINDALE PUBLIC LIBRARY*, 5050 N Irwindale Ave, 91706. SAN 300-8363. Tel: 626-430-2229. E-mail: librarystaff@ci.irwindale.ca.us. Web Site: ci.irwindale.ca.us/121/Library. *City Librn,* Shayna Balli; E-mail: sballi@irwindaleca.gov; Staff 4 (MLS 1, Non-MLS 3)
Founded 1961. Pop 1,445; Circ 23,440
Library Holdings: Bk Vols 16,055; Per Subs 45
Special Collections: Irwindale City History Coll
Wireless access
Function: After school storytime, Archival coll, Homebound delivery serv, Online cat, Photocopying/Printing, Tax forms
Partic in Southern California Library Cooperative
Open Mon-Thurs 9-6

JACKSON

GL AMADOR COUNTY LAW LIBRARY*, Amador County Main Library, 530 Sutter St, 95642. Interlibrary Loan Service Tel: 209-223-6400. Web Site: www.amadorgov.org/library. *County Librn,* Laura Einstadter
Founded 1918
Library Holdings: Bk Vols 1,000
Wireless access
Open Mon-Wed 10-6, Thurs & Fri 10-5

P AMADOR COUNTY LIBRARY*, Main Library, 530 Sutter St, 95642. SAN 300-8371. Tel: 209-223-6400. E-mail: library@amadorgov.org. Web Site: www.amadorgov.org/library. *County Librn,* Laura Einstadter; E-mail: leinstadter@amadorgov.org; Staff 5 (MLS 1, Non-MLS 4)
Library Holdings: Audiobooks 3,792; DVDs 5,919; e-books 3,976; Electronic Media & Resources 3,608; Microforms 1,037; Bk Titles 75,896; Bk Vols 98,212; Per Subs 44
Special Collections: Amador County History Coll (local mining, history, genealogy); Index of Amador County Newspapers (microfilm); Mines & Mineral Research Coll
Automation Activity & Vendor Info: (Acquisitions) SirsiDynix; (Cataloging) SirsiDynix-WorkFlows; (Circulation) SirsiDynix-WorkFlows; (OPAC) SirsiDynix-Enterprise
Wireless access
Function: 24/7 Electronic res, 24/7 Online cat, Adult bk club, Adult literacy prog
Publications: Friends of Library Newsletter (Quarterly)
Partic in 49-99 Cooperative Library System
Open Mon-Wed 10-6, Thurs & Fri 10-5
Friends of the Library Group
Branches: 4
IONE BRANCH, 25 E Main St, Ione, 95640. Tel: 209-274-2560. ; Staff 1 (Non-MLS 1)
Pop 7,500
Open Mon & Wed 10-1, Tues 2-7, Thurs 1-5, Fri 1-4
Friends of the Library Group
PINE GROVE BRANCH, 19889 Hwy 88, Pine Grove, 95665. Tel: 209-296-3111. *County Librn,* Laura Einstadter; Staff 1 (Non-MLS 1)
Library Holdings: Bk Vols 6,502
Open Tues & Wed 12-5
Friends of the Library Group
PIONEER BRANCH, 25070 Buckhorn Ridge Rd, Pioneer, 95666. (Mail add: PO Box 821, Pioneer, 95666-0821). Tel: 209-295-7330. ; Staff 1 (Non-MLS 1)
Library Holdings: Bk Vols 5,586

Open Thurs & Fri 12-5
Friends of the Library Group
PLYMOUTH BRANCH, 9375 Main St, Plymouth, 95669. (Mail add: PO Box 61, Plymouth, 95669-0061). Tel: 209-245-6476. *Library Contact,* ; Staff 1 (Non-MLS 1)
Library Holdings: Bk Vols 6,561
Open Tues 1:30-5, Wed 10-12 & 1-5, Thurs & Fri 1:30-5
Friends of the Library Group

JOLON

A UNITED STATES ARMY*, Fort Hunter Liggett Cybrary, Bldg 291, 93928. Tel: 831-386-2719. FAX: 831-386-2002. E-mail: cybrary@fhlfmwr.com. Web Site: hunterliggett.armymwr.com/programs/cybrary.
Library Holdings: Bk Vols 10,000
Wireless access
Function: Wheelchair accessible
Open Mon-Fri 7:30am-8pm
Restriction: Mil only

JOSHUA TREE

J COPPER MOUNTAIN COLLEGE*, Greenleaf Library, 6162 Rotary Way, 92252. (Mail add: PO Box 1398, 92251-0879), SAN 301-6722. Tel: 760-366-3791. FAX: 760-366-5256. Web Site: library.cmccd.edu. *Librn,* Ingrid Johnson; Tel: 760-366-3791, Ext 5904, E-mail: ijohnson@cmccd.edu; *Coordr, Libr Serv,* Carolyn Hopkins; Tel: 760-366-5293, E-mail: chopkins@cmccd.edu; *Libr Spec,* Barbara Griswold; Tel: 760-366-3791, Ext 5906, E-mail: bgriswold@cmccd.edu; *Libr Spec,* Cathy Inscore; Tel: 760-366-3791, Ext 5901; *Libr Spec,* Katherine Roberts; Tel: 760-366-3794, Ext 5902, E-mail: kroberts@cmccd.edu; Staff 5 (MLS 2, Non-MLS 3)
Enrl 2,400; Fac 39; Highest Degree: Associate
Library Holdings: CDs 20; DVDs 194; e-books 64,439; Bk Titles 13,606; Bk Vols 15,615; Per Subs 46; Videos 278
Special Collections: Desert Studies
Automation Activity & Vendor Info: (Cataloging) TLC (The Library Corporation); (Circulation) TLC (The Library Corporation); (OPAC) TLC (The Library Corporation)
Wireless access
Function: 24/7 Electronic res, 24/7 Online cat, Distance learning, Electronic databases & coll, For res purposes, Online cat, Online ref, Orientations, Photocopying/Printing, Ref serv available, Study rm, Workshops
Open Mon-Thurs 8am-8:30pm, Fri 8-6, Sat 8-3:30
Restriction: Open to students, fac & staff, Restricted pub use

KENTFIELD

J COLLEGE OF MARIN LIBRARY*, 835 College Ave, 94904. SAN 300-8398. Tel: 415-485-9656. Reference Tel: 415-845-0536. FAX: 415-457-5395. Web Site: library.marin.edu. *Dept Chair, Librn,* Sarah Frye; E-mail: SFrye@marin.edu; *Librn,* John Erdmann; E-mail: JErdmann@marin.edu; Staff 5 (MLS 5)
Founded 1926
Library Holdings: Bk Titles 92,100; Bk Vols 137,000; Per Subs 331
Wireless access
Open Mon-Thurs 8am-9pm, Fri 8-4 (Winter); Mon-Thurs 8-4 (Summer)
Friends of the Library Group

LA JOLLA

S LIBRARY ASSOCIATION OF LA JOLLA*, Athenaeum Music & Arts Library, 1008 Wall St, 92037. SAN 300-8479. Tel: 858-454-5872. FAX: 858-454-5835. E-mail: info@ljathenaeum.org. Web Site: www.ljathenaeum.org. *Exec Dir,* Erika Torri; *Librn,* Kathi Bower Peterson; E-mail: kpeterson@ljathenaeum.org; Staff 15 (MLS 2, Non-MLS 13)
Founded 1899
Library Holdings: AV Mats 17,300; Bk Titles 19,000; Per Subs 71
Special Collections: Artists Books; Music (Bach Gesellschaft Coll)
Subject Interests: Art, Music
Automation Activity & Vendor Info: (Cataloging) EOS International; (Circulation) EOS International; (OPAC) EOS International; (Serials) EOS International
Wireless access
Publications: Annual Report; Art Exhibition Catalogues; Newsletter (Bimonthly); School Brochures (Quarterly)
Open Tues & Thurs-Sat 10-5:30, Wed 10-8:30
Restriction: Non-circulating to the pub

S SALK INSTITUTE FOR BIOLOGICAL STUDIES*, Salk Institute Library, 10010 N Torrey Pines Rd, 92037. SAN 300-8495. Tel: 858-453-4100, Ext 1235. FAX: 858-452-7472. E-mail: library@salk.edu. Web Site: jonas.salk.edu, www.salk.edu. *Libr Mgr,* Carol Bodas; E-mail: bodas@salk.edu; *Libr Asst,* Rosa Lopez; E-mail: lopez@salk.edu; Staff 2 (Non-MLS 2)
Founded 1962. Enrl 119; Fac 60
Library Holdings: DVDs 1,600; e-books 1,000; e-journals 500; Bk Vols 2,000; Per Subs 10
Subject Interests: Biochem, Genetics, Immunology, Molecular biol, Neuroscience, Plant biol, Proteomics, Virology
Wireless access
Function: Res libr
Partic in Statewide California Electronic Library Consortium
Restriction: Limited access for the pub

M THE SCRIPPS RESEARCH INSTITUTE*, Kresge Library, 10550 N Torrey Pines Rd, 92037. SAN 300-8509. Tel: 858-784-8705. FAX: 858-784-2035. E-mail: helplib@scripps.edu. Web Site: www.scripps.edu/research/resources/library.html. *Dir,* Rachelle Georger; Staff 8 (MLS 5, Non-MLS 3)
Founded 1962
Library Holdings: Bk Vols 4,400; Per Subs 720
Subject Interests: Biochem, Chem, Immunology, Med, Molecular biol, Neurobiology
Automation Activity & Vendor Info: (OPAC) OCLC WorldShare Interlibrary Loan
Wireless access
Function: For res purposes, ILL available
Partic in National Network of Libraries of Medicine Region 5; OCLC Online Computer Library Center, Inc; Statewide California Electronic Library Consortium
Restriction: Authorized personnel only, Not open to pub

G UNITED STATES DEPARTMENT OF COMMERCE, NOAA FISHERIES*, Southwest Fisheries Science Center La Jolla Laboratory Library, 8901 La Jolla Shores Dr, 92037-1509. (Mail add: SWFSC La Jolla Laboratory LIBRARY, 8901 La Jolla Shores Dr, 92037), SAN 300-8487. Tel: 858-546-7196. FAX: 858-546-7003. *Librn,* Debra A Losey; E-mail: debra.losey@noaa.gov; Staff 1 (MLS 1)
Founded 1965
Special Collections: Inter-American Tropical Tuna Commission
Subject Interests: Fisheries, Fisheries econ, Marine biol, Marine mammals, Oceanography
Automation Activity & Vendor Info: (Cataloging) OCLC; (ILL) OCLC; (OPAC) SirsiDynix-WorkFlows
Wireless access
Function: 24/7 Electronic res, 24/7 Online cat
Partic in Federal Library & Information Network; NOAA Libraries Network; OCLC Online Computer Library Center, Inc
Restriction: Open to others by appt, Restricted access

C UNIVERSITY OF CALIFORNIA, SAN DIEGO, University Libraries, 9500 Gilman Dr, Mail Code 0175G, 92093-0175. SAN 332-1878. Tel: 858-534-0134. Interlibrary Loan Service Tel: 858-534-2528. Administration Tel: 858-534-3061. FAX: 858-534-4970. Interlibrary Loan Service FAX: 858-534-1256. Web Site: library.ucsd.edu. *Univ Librn,* Erik Mitchell; Tel: 858-534-3060, E-mail: etm@ucsd.edu; *Assoc Univ Libn, Learning & User Experience,* Dani Cook; Tel: 858-534-1278, E-mail: danicook@ucsd.edu; *Assoc Univ Librn, Scholarly Resources & Serv,* Roger Smith; Tel: 858-534-1235, E-mail: ros001@ucsd.edu; *Dir for Spaces, Lending & Access,* Kymberly Anne Goodson; Tel: 858-534-1271, E-mail: kgoodson@ucsd.edu; *Dir of Develop,* Jennifer Brown; Tel: 858-822-4554, E-mail: jgbrown@ucsd.edu; *Program Dir, Comms & Engagement,* Nikki Kolupailo; Tel: 858-534-0667, E-mail: nkolupailo@ucsd.edu; *Head, Tech Serv,* Declan Fleming; Tel: 858-534-1287, E-mail: dfleming@uscd.edu; *ILL,* Judea D'Arnaud; Tel: 858-534-3011, E-mail: jdarnaud@ucsd.edu; Staff 286 (MLS 61, Non-MLS 225)
Founded 1959. Enrl 27,682; Fac 7,126; Highest Degree: Doctorate
Library Holdings: AV Mats 144,225; CDs 53,399; e-books 231,216; Microforms 3,309,102; Music Scores 44,157; Bk Vols 3,372,785; Per Subs 7,861
Special Collections: Baja, CA; Contemporary American Poetry (Archive for New Poetry); Contemporary Music; European Communities Common Market Publications; Melanesian Ethnography; Pacific Voyages; Renaissance; Science & Public Policy; Spanish Civil War. State Document Depository; US Document Depository
Automation Activity & Vendor Info: (Acquisitions) Innovative Interfaces, Inc; (Circulation) Innovative Interfaces, Inc; (OPAC) Innovative Interfaces, Inc; (Serials) Innovative Interfaces, Inc
Wireless access
Publications: Faculty/Friends (Newsletter); Melanesian Acquisition; Pacific Voyages Collection Bibliography; Renaissance Collection Bibliography
Partic in Am Asn of Health Sci Librs; Center for Research Libraries; Coalition for Networked Information; Coun of Libr Info Resources; Medical Library Association; National Initiative for a Networked Cultural Heritage; OCLC Online Computer Library Center, Inc; OCLC Research

Library Partnership; Pacific Southwest Regional Medical Library; Proquest Dialog; Scholarly Publ & Acad Resources Coalition; SDC Search Serv
Friends of the Library Group

Departmental Libraries:

SPECIAL COLLECTIONS & ARCHIVES, UCSD Libraries 0175S, 9500 Gilman Dr, 92093-0175. Tel: 858-534-2533. E-mail: spcoll@ucsd.edu. Web Site: libraries.ucsd.edu/collections/sca. *Dir,* Lynda C Claassen; E-mail: lclaassen@ucsd.edu
Open Mon-Fri 9-5
Friends of the Library Group

LA MIRADA

C BIOLA UNIVERSITY LIBRARY*, 13800 Biola Ave, 90639. SAN 300-8525. Tel: 562-903-4834. Circulation Tel: 562-903-4835. Interlibrary Loan Service Tel: 562-903-4833. FAX: 562-903-4840. Web Site: library.biola.edu. *Dean of Libr,* Dr Gregg Geary; Tel: 562-944-0351, Ext 5605, E-mail: gregg.geary@biola.edu; *Assoc Dean of Libr,* Jeremy Labosier; Tel: 562-906-4532, E-mail: jeremy.labosier@biola.edu; *Asst Dean of Libr, Electronic Res Librn,* John Tiffin; Tel: 562-944-0351, Ext 4837, E-mail: john.s.tiffin@biola.edu; *Head, Pub Serv,* Juliana Morley; Tel: 562-944-0351, Ext 5620, E-mail: juliana.morley@biola.edu; *Head, Tech Serv,* Eileen Walraven; Tel: 562-944-0351, Ext 3653, E-mail: eileen.walraven@biola.edu; *Instruction & Outreach Librn,* Ruth Cho; Tel: 562-944-0351 Ext 5625, E-mail: ruth.cho@biola.edu; *Ref & Instruction Librn,* Stacie Schmidt; Tel: 562-944-0351, Ext 5154, E-mail: stacie.schmidt@biola.edu; *Music, Spec Projects Librn,* John Redford; Tel: 562-944-0351, Ext 5613, E-mail: john.redford@biola.edu; *Syst Librn,* Chuck Koontz; Tel: 562-944-0351 Ext 5611, E-mail: chuck.koontz@biola.edu; *Mgr, Libr Info Tech,* Simon Heres; Tel: 562-944-0351, Ext 5612, E-mail: simon.heres@biola.edu; Staff 20 (MLS 10, Non-MLS 10)
Founded 1908. Enrl 6,103; Fac 525; Highest Degree: Doctorate
Jul 2019-Jun 2020 Income $2,804,600, Parent Institution $2,804,600. Mats Exp $1,298,275, Books $222,491, Per/Ser (Incl. Access Fees) $53,249, AV Mat $3,766, Electronic Ref Mat (Incl. Access Fees) $1,016,318, Presv $11,535. Sal $1,310,583 (Prof $739,978)
Library Holdings: Audiobooks 407; AV Mats 13,218; Bks on Deafness & Sign Lang 112; Braille Volumes 55; CDs 4,923; DVDs 6,276; e-books 548,384; e-journals 132,556; Electronic Media & Resources 61,880; Large Print Bks 12; Microforms 172,331; Music Scores 7,489; Bk Titles 268,788; Bk Vols 270,459; Per Subs 203
Special Collections: Bible Versions & Translations Coll; Biola University Archives
Subject Interests: Nursing, Relig
Automation Activity & Vendor Info: (Acquisitions) Innovative Interfaces, Inc; (Cataloging) Innovative Interfaces, Inc; (Circulation) Innovative Interfaces, Inc; (Course Reserve) Innovative Interfaces, Inc; (Discovery) EBSCO Discovery Service; (ILL) Innovative Interfaces, Inc; (Media Booking) Innovative Interfaces, Inc; (OPAC) Innovative Interfaces, Inc; (Serials) Innovative Interfaces, Inc
Wireless access
Partic in American Theological Library Association; Association of Christian Librarians; Christian Library Consortium; OCLC Online Computer Library Center, Inc; Southern California Theological Library Association; Statewide California Electronic Library Consortium
Special Services for the Deaf - Assistive tech; Bks on deafness & sign lang
Special Services for the Blind - Assistive/Adapted tech devices, equip & products; Braille bks
Open Mon-Thurs 7:30am-1am, Fri 7:30-7, Sat 10-8, Sun Noon-1am

LA VERNE

C UNIVERSITY OF LA VERNE*, Elvin & Betty Wilson Library, 2040 Third St, 91750. SAN 332-205X. Tel: 909-593-3511, Ext 4305. Circulation Tel: 909-593-3511, Ext 4301. Interlibrary Loan Service Tel: 909-593-3511, Ext 4309. Administration Tel: 909-593-3511, Ext 4304. Automation Services Tel: 909-593-3511, Ext 4307. FAX: 909-392-2733. Reference E-mail: reference@ulv.edu. Web Site: www.ulv.edu/library. *Prof, Univ Librn,* Vinaya Tripuraneni; *Prof, User Serv Librn,* Dona Bentley; *Prof, Res & Instruction Librn,* Linda Gordon; *Asst Prof, Res & Instruction Librn,* Andre Ambrus; *Asst Prof, Instrul Tech Librn, Web Librn,* Erin Gratz; *Asst Prof, Info Literacy Librn,* Shelley Urbizagastegui; *Assessment Librn, Asst Prof,* Darryl Swarm; *Evening/Weekend Librn,* Alex Valdivia; Staff 18 (MLS 9, Non-MLS 9)
Founded 1891. Enrl 5,947; Fac 263; Highest Degree: Doctorate
Library Holdings: e-books 2,476; e-journals 11,400; Bk Vols 148,790; Per Subs 11,585; Videos 2,462
Automation Activity & Vendor Info: (Acquisitions) Innovative Interfaces, Inc; (Cataloging) Innovative Interfaces, Inc; (Circulation) Innovative Interfaces, Inc; (ILL) OCLC; (OPAC) Innovative Interfaces, Inc; (Serials) Innovative Interfaces, Inc
Function: Archival coll, ILL available
Partic in Inland Empire Acad Libr Coop; NELLCO Law Library Consortium, Inc.; Statewide California Electronic Library Consortium
Friends of the Library Group

LAFAYETTE

R LAFAYETTE-ORINDA PRESBYTERIAN CHURCH LIBRARY*, 49 Knox Dr, 94549. SAN 300-855X. Tel: 925-283-8722. FAX: 925-283-0138. E-mail: info@lopc.org. Web Site: www.lopc.org.
Library Holdings: Bk Vols 1,957
Open Mon-Fri 9-5, Sun 9-11

S SOYINFO CENTER LIBRARY*, 1021 Dolores Dr, 94549-2907. SAN 325-4925. Tel: 925-283-2991. E-mail: info@soyinfocenter.com. Web Site: www.soyinfocenter.com/soylibrary.php. *Head Librn,* William Shurtleff; Staff 1 (MLS 1)
Founded 1976
Library Holdings: e-books 156; Bk Titles 2,832; Per Subs 12
Special Collections: Soybeans & Soyfoods Coll, archives, bks, databases (1100 BC-present), reprints. Oral History
Subject Interests: Soybeans, Soyfoods, Vegetarianism
Publications: Digital Bibliography of Soy Series; Digital History of Soy Series; History of Soybeans & Soyfoods Series Free on Google Books; Soyfoods Industry & Market Directory & Databook; Thesaurus for Soya
Open Mon-Sun 9-6
Restriction: Open to pub by appt only
Friends of the Library Group

R TEMPLE ISAIAH, Cantor Ted Cotler Memorial Library, 945 Risa Rd, 94549. Tel: 925-283-8575. FAX: 925-283-8355. Web Site: temple-isaiah.org/education/library. *Dir,* Deb Kirsch; E-mail: debk@temple-isaiah.org; Staff 2 (MLS 1, Non-MLS 1)
Pop 900; Circ 3,500
Library Holdings: AV Mats 665; Bk Vols 6,886; Per Subs 26; Spec Interest Per Sub 26; Talking Bks 30; Videos 455
Special Collections: Children's Coll; Jewish Music Coll; Jewish Parenting Coll; Jewish Videos & Audios; Multicultural Judaism Coll
Subject Interests: Judaica
Automation Activity & Vendor Info: (Cataloging) Follett Software; (Circulation) Follett Software; (OPAC) Follett Software
Wireless access
Function: CD-ROM, ILL available, Internet access, Music CDs, Photocopying/Printing, Prog for adults, Prog for children & young adult, Ref serv available, Spoken cassettes & CDs, Telephone ref, VHS videos, Wheelchair accessible
Publications: Ruach/Library Column (Monthly bulletin)
Special Services for the Deaf - Closed caption videos
Open Mon-Fri 8:30-5
Restriction: In-house use for visitors, Non-circulating to the pub, Open to fac, students & qualified researchers, Pub use on premises
Friends of the Library Group

LAKEPORT

S HISTORIC COURTHOUSE MUSEUM LIBRARY, 255 N Main St, 95453. (Mail add: 255 N Forbes St, 95453), SAN 329-966X. Tel: 707-262-4552. FAX: 707-263-7918. E-mail: museums@lakecountyca.gov. Web Site: www.lakecountyca.gov/Government/Directory/Museums.htm. *Curator,* J Clark McAbee; E-mail: jclark.mcabee@lakecountyca.gov
Library Holdings: Bk Vols 500
Special Collections: Historic County Court Records; Lake County, California History Coll
Wireless access
Open Wed-Sat 10-4, Sun 12-4
Friends of the Library Group

GL LAKE COUNTY LAW LIBRARY*, 175 Third St, 95453. (Mail add: 255 N Forbes St, 95453), SAN 320-5673. Tel: 707-263-2205. FAX: 707-263-2207. Web Site: www.lakecountyca.gov/Government/Directory/LawLibrary.htm. *Law Librn,* Kelly Kobetsky; E-mail: Kelly.Kobetsky@lakecountyca.gov
Library Holdings: Bk Vols 7,500
Special Collections: Federal Cases, micro; Local Ordinances
Function: Computers for patron use, ILL available, Photocopying/Printing
Open Mon-Fri 9:30-1:15 & 1:30-3
Restriction: Circ limited, Lending limited to county residents

P LAKE COUNTY LIBRARY*, Lakeport Library, 1425 N High St, 95453-3800. SAN 332-2114. Tel: 707-263-8817. E-mail: Library@lakecountyca.gov. Web Site: library.lakecountyca.gov. *Dir,* Christopher Veach; E-mail: christopher.veach@lakecountyca.gov; *Circ,* Barbara Green; *Circ, Tech Serv,* Amy Patton; *ILL, Tech Serv,* Jan Cook; Staff 1 (MLS 1)
Founded 1974. Pop 63,000; Circ 207,000
Library Holdings: Bk Vols 145,000; Per Subs 174

Special Collections: Geothermal Resources; Lake County History; Pomo Indians
Automation Activity & Vendor Info: (Cataloging) SirsiDynix; (Circulation) SirsiDynix; (OPAC) SirsiDynix
Wireless access
Mem of NorthNet Library System
Open Tues & Thurs-Sat 10-5, Wed 10-7
Friends of the Library Group
Branches: 3
MIDDLETOWN BRANCH, 21256 Washington St, Middletown, 95461. (Mail add: PO Box 578, Middletown, 95461-0578), SAN 332-2149. Tel: 707-987-3674. FAX: 707-987-3674. *Br Coordr,* Yesenia Lopez
Library Holdings: Bk Vols 10,238
Open Tues-Fri 12-5, Sat 10-3
Friends of the Library Group
REDBUD BRANCH, 14785 Burns Valley Rd, Clearlake, 95422-0600, SAN 332-2173. Tel: 707-994-5115. FAX: 707-995-6012.
Library Holdings: Bk Vols 35,129
Open Tues & Thurs-Sat 10-5, Wed 12-7
Friends of the Library Group
UPPER LAKE BRANCH, 310 Second St, Upper Lake, 95485. (Mail add: PO Box 486, Upper Lake, 95485-0486), SAN 332-2203. Tel: 707-275-2049. *Br Coordr,* Gina Rankin
Library Holdings: Bk Vols 10,478
Open Tues-Fri 12-5, Sat 10-3
Friends of the Library Group

LANCASTER

J ANTELOPE VALLEY COLLEGE LIBRARY*, 3041 W Ave K, 93536. SAN 300-8584. Tel: 661-722-6300, Ext 6276. Web Site: www.avc.edu/studentservices/library. *Dean, Institutional Effectiveness, Res & Planning,* Meeta Goel; E-mail: mgoel@avc.edu; *Info Competency Librn,* Scott Lee; E-mail: slee@avc.edu; *Ref & Instrul Serv Librn,* Van Rider; E-mail: vrider@avc.edu; *Ref/Electronic Res Librn,* Carolyn Burrell; E-mail: cburrell@avc.edu; Staff 3 (MLS 3)
Founded 1962. Enrl 8,800; Fac 320
Library Holdings: Bk Vols 50,000
Automation Activity & Vendor Info: (Acquisitions) SirsiDynix; (Cataloging) SirsiDynix; (Circulation) SirsiDynix; (Course Reserve) SirsiDynix; (ILL) OCLC; (OPAC) SirsiDynix; (Serials) SirsiDynix
Wireless access
Open Mon-Thurs 7:30am-8pm, Fri 7:30am-11:30am, Sat 10-2

LARKSPUR

P LARKSPUR PUBLIC LIBRARY*, 400 Magnolia Ave, 94939. SAN 300-8592. Tel: 415-927-5005. FAX: 415-927-5136. E-mail: library@cityoflarkspur.org. Web Site: www.ci.larkspur.ca.us/296/Larkspur-Library. *Dir,* Franklin Escobedo; E-mail: fescobedo@cityoflarkspur.org
Pop 12,000; Circ 98,000
Library Holdings: Bk Titles 55,000; Per Subs 100
Wireless access
Open Mon-Thurs 10-7, Fri & Sat 10-5
Friends of the Library Group

LEMON GROVE

S PRICE-POTTENGER NUTRITION FOUNDATION LIBRARY*, 7890 Broadway, 91945. SAN 371-4268. Tel: 619-462-7600. Toll Free Tel: 800-366-3748. FAX: 619-433-3136. E-mail: info@price-pottenger.org. Web Site: price-pottenger.org.
Founded 1965
Library Holdings: CDs 1,273; DVDs 385; Bk Titles 7,014; Per Subs 20; Videos 385
Special Collections: Bernard Jensen Coll; Dr Emmanuel Cheraskin Coll; Dr Francis M Pottenger Jr Coll; Dr George E Meinig, DDS Coll; Dr Granville Knight, MD Coll; Dr Henry Bieler Coll; Dr John Myers Coll; Dr Martha Jones, PhD Coll; Dr Melvin Page Coll; Dr Royal Lee Coll, Lee Foundation; Dr Weston A Price, DDS Coll; Dr William Albrecht Coll; Edgar Cayce Coll; Edward Rosenow Coll; George Chapman Coll; Lee Foundation Coll
Subject Interests: Dental, Ecology, Gardening, Health, Nutrition
Function: Res libr
Publications: Journal of Health and Healing (Quarterly)
Restriction: Mem only, Not a lending libr, Open by appt only

LEMOORE

J WEST HILLS COLLEGE LEMOORE LIBRARY*, 555 College Ave, 93245. SAN 300-7421. Tel: 559-925-3403. Circulation Tel: 559-925-3420. Web Site: www.westhillscollege.com/lemoore/resources/library. *Librn,* Ron Oxford; E-mail: ronoxford@whccd.edu; *Adjunct Librn,* Danielle Rapue; E-mail: daniellerapue@whccd.edu; Staff 3 (MLS 1, Non-MLS 2)
Founded 2002. Enrl 2,000; Highest Degree: Associate
Library Holdings: CDs 1,500; DVDs 1,004; e-books 11,400; Bk Vols 35,000; Per Subs 97
Automation Activity & Vendor Info: (Acquisitions) SirsiDynix; (Cataloging) SirsiDynix; (Circulation) SirsiDynix; (Course Reserve) SirsiDynix; (ILL) SirsiDynix; (Media Booking) SirsiDynix; (OPAC) SirsiDynix; (Serials) SirsiDynix
Wireless access
Function: Archival coll, AV serv, Distance learning, Homework prog, Internet access, Learning ctr, Orientations, Photocopying/Printing, Ref & res, Ref serv available, VHS videos, Wheelchair accessible
Partic in Community College League of California
Special Services for the Blind - Computer with voice synthesizer for visually impaired persons; Reader equip
Open Mon-Thurs 7:30am-8pm, Fri 7:30-4
Restriction: Borrowing privileges limited to fac & registered students, Circ to mem only, In-house use for visitors, Open to students, fac & staff

LINCOLN

P LINCOLN PUBLIC LIBRARY*, 485 Twelve Bridges Dr, 95648. SAN 300-8622. Tel: 916-434-2410. Administration Tel: 916-434-2409. E-mail: library@lincolnca.gov. Web Site: lincolnca.gov/city-hall/departments-divisions/library. *Libr Mgr,* Kathryn Hunt; E-mail: Kathryn.Hunt@lincolnca.gov; *Libr Coord,* Renae Hart; E-mail: Renae.Hart@lincolnca.gov; Staff 2.9 (MLS 0.5, Non-MLS 2.4)
Founded 1906. Pop 40,000; Circ 328,768
Library Holdings: Bk Vols 101,387
Automation Activity & Vendor Info: (Acquisitions) Ex Libris Group; (Cataloging) Ex Libris Group; (Circulation) Ex Libris Group; (ILL) OCLC; (OPAC) Ex Libris Group; (Serials) Ex Libris Group
Wireless access
Function: Adult bk club, Art exhibits, Audio & video playback equip for onsite use, Bks on CD, Children's prog, Computer training, Computers for patron use, Free DVD rentals, Genealogy discussion group, Holiday prog, Homework prog, ILL available, Music CDs, Online cat, Photocopying/Printing, Prog for adults, Prog for children & young adult, Ref serv available, Story hour, Summer reading prog, Teen prog, Telephone ref, Wheelchair accessible
Special Services for the Deaf - Bks on deafness & sign lang; Closed caption videos; Staff with knowledge of sign lang
Special Services for the Blind - Bks on cassette; Bks on CD; Large print bks; Low vision equip
Friends of the Library Group

LIVERMORE

J LAS POSITAS COLLEGE LIBRARY*, 3000 Campus Hill Dr, 94551. SAN 300-8630. Tel: 925-424-1150. Circulation Tel: 925-424-1151. FAX: 925-606-7249. E-mail: lpclibrarian@laspositascollege.edu. Web Site: www.laspositascollege.edu/library. *Dean,* Stuart McElderry; E-mail: smcelderry@laspositascollege.edu; *Librn,* Angela Amaya; E-mail: aamaya@laspositascollege.edu; *Librn,* Tina Inzerilla; E-mail: tinzerilla@laspositascollege.edu; *Librn,* Kali Rippel; E-mail: krippel@laspositascollege.edu; *Librn,* Collin Thormoto; E-mail: cthormoto@laspositascollege.edu; Staff 4 (MLS 4)
Founded 1975. Enrl 4,665
Library Holdings: Bk Titles 34,000; Per Subs 100
Automation Activity & Vendor Info: (Acquisitions) SirsiDynix; (Cataloging) SirsiDynix; (Circulation) SirsiDynix; (Course Reserve) SirsiDynix; (OPAC) SirsiDynix; (Serials) SirsiDynix
Wireless access
Partic in California Community College Library Consortium; OCLC Online Computer Library Center, Inc; San Francisco Bay Area Library & Information Network
Open Mon-Thurs 8-7, Fri 8-2

S LAWRENCE LIVERMORE NATIONAL LABORATORY LIBRARY*, 7000 East Ave, 94550. (Mail add: PO Box 808, L-611, 94550), SAN 300-8665. Tel: 925-424-4922. Circulation Tel: 925-422-5277. Interlibrary Loan Service Tel: 925-422-7563. FAX: 925-424-2921. Reference E-mail: library-reference@llnl.gov. Web Site: library-ext.llnl.gov. *Libr Mgr,* Mary Allen; Tel: 925-423-8386; Staff 8 (MLS 5, Non-MLS 3)
Founded 1952
Library Holdings: Bk Vols 335,000; Per Subs 7,179
Automation Activity & Vendor Info: (Acquisitions) SirsiDynix; (Cataloging) SirsiDynix; (Circulation) SirsiDynix; (Course Reserve) SirsiDynix; (ILL) Relais International; (Media Booking) SirsiDynix; (OPAC) SirsiDynix; (Serials) SirsiDynix
Wireless access
Publications: New Titles
Partic in Proquest Dialog; Research Libraries Information Network
Restriction: Authorized patrons, Authorized personnel only, Restricted loan policy

P LIVERMORE PUBLIC LIBRARY*, 1188 S Livermore Ave, 94550. SAN 300-8649. Tel: 925-373-5500. Circulation Tel: 925-373-5502. Reference Tel: 925-373-5505. Administration Tel: 925-373-5509. Automation Services Tel: 925-373-5512. FAX: 925-373-5503. E-mail: lib@livermore.lib.ca.us. Web Site: www.livermorelibrary.net. *Dir, Libr Serv,* Tamera LeBeau; E-mail: tklebeau@livermore.lib.ca.us; Staff 27 (MLS 12.5, Non-MLS 14.5)
Founded 1896. Pop 89,648; Circ 753,072
Jul 2017-Jun 2018 Income (Main & Associated Libraries) $5,639,115, State $39,622, City $5,535,992, Locally Generated Income $63,501. Mats Exp $334,789, Books $185,129, Per/Ser (Incl. Access Fees) $13,404, Micro $2,500, AV Mat $42,892, Electronic Ref Mat (Incl. Access Fees) $130,000. Sal $4,276,787 (Prof $2,396,428)
Library Holdings: Audiobooks 5,465; DVDs 11,910; e-books 124,190; e-journals 28; Microforms 3,076; Bk Vols 210,259; Per Subs 202
Subject Interests: Local hist
Automation Activity & Vendor Info: (Acquisitions) Innovative Interfaces, Inc; (Cataloging) Innovative Interfaces, Inc; (Circulation) Innovative Interfaces, Inc; (OPAC) Innovative Interfaces, Inc; (Serials) Innovative Interfaces, Inc
Wireless access
Function: 24/7 Electronic res, 24/7 Online cat, Adult bk club, Adult literacy prog, Art exhibits, Audiobks via web, Bilingual assistance for Spanish patrons, Bk club(s), Bks on CD, Children's prog, Computer training, Computers for patron use, Digital talking bks, E-Reserves, Electronic databases & coll, Free DVD rentals, Homework prog, ILL available, Internet access, Jazz prog, Life-long learning prog for all ages, Literacy & newcomer serv, Magazines, Mail & tel request accepted, Meeting rooms, Microfiche/film & reading machines, Museum passes, Music CDs, Online cat, Online ref, Outside serv via phone, mail, e-mail & web, OverDrive digital audio bks, Photocopying/Printing, Preschool outreach, Preschool reading prog, Prog for adults, Prog for children & young adult, Ref serv available, Scanner, Senior computer classes, Spanish lang bks, Spoken cassettes & CDs, STEM programs, Story hour, Study rm, Summer reading prog, Tax forms, Teen prog, Telephone ref, Wheelchair accessible, Workshops, Writing prog
Publications: Annual Report; Strategic Services Plan; Technology Plan
Mem of Pacific Library Partnership (PLP)
Partic in Link+
Open Mon-Thurs 10-9, Fri 10-6, Sat 10-5, Sun 12-6
Friends of the Library Group
Branches: 2
RINCON, 725 Rincon Ave, 94550, SAN 377-5933. Tel: 925-373-5540. ; Staff 2 (MLS 1, Non-MLS 1)
Founded 1996. Pop 13,250; Circ 34,846
Library Holdings: DVDs 1,869; Large Print Bks 139; Bk Vols 20,496; Per Subs 25
Function: Bilingual assistance for Spanish patrons, Bks on CD, Children's prog, Computers for patron use, Digital talking bks, Electronic databases & coll, Free DVD rentals, Homework prog, ILL available, Online cat, OverDrive digital audio bks, Photocopying/Printing, Preschool reading prog, Prog for children & young adult, Story hour, Summer reading prog, Wheelchair accessible
Open Mon 12-8, Wed 10-6, Fri 10-5
SPRINGTOWN, 998 Bluebell Dr, 94550, SAN 377-595X. Tel: 925-373-5518.
Founded 1986. Pop 9,750; Circ 31,223
Library Holdings: Audiobooks 224; DVDs 1,147; Large Print Bks 102; Bk Vols 18,957; Per Subs 10
Function: STEM programs, Story hour
Open Tues 12-8, Thurs 10-1
Friends of the Library Group

S SANDIA NATIONAL LABORATORIES, CA Technical Library, 7011 East Ave, 94550. (Mail add: PO Box 969, MS 9960, 94551-0969), SAN 300-8657. Tel: 925-294-1085. E-mail: cateclib@sandia.gov. Web Site: www.sandia.gov/resources/employees/technical_library. *Tech Librn,* Greta Lopez
Founded 1956
Library Holdings: Bk Titles 16,000; Per Subs 23
Subject Interests: Chem, Computer sci, Energy, Engr, Math, Nuclear sci, Physics
Automation Activity & Vendor Info: (Acquisitions) SirsiDynix; (Cataloging) SirsiDynix; (Circulation) SirsiDynix; (Serials) SirsiDynix
Wireless access
Function: Res libr
Restriction: Not open to pub

LODI

P LODI PUBLIC LIBRARY*, 201 W Locust St, 95240. SAN 300-8681. Tel: 209-333-5566. Reference Tel: 209-333-5503. Administration Tel: 209-333-5534. E-mail: library@lodi.gov. Web Site: library.lodi.gov. *Libr Dir,* Anwan Baker; E-mail: abaker@lodi.gov; *Vols Mgr,* Yvette Herrera; E-mail: literacy@lodi.gov; Staff 5 (MLS 5)
Founded 1907. Pop 63,000; Circ 260,000
Library Holdings: Bk Titles 130,000; Per Subs 150; Videos 2,000
Special Collections: Lodi History & Californiana, micro, photog
Automation Activity & Vendor Info: (Acquisitions) SirsiDynix; (Cataloging) SirsiDynix; (Circulation) SirsiDynix; (ILL) SirsiDynix; (OPAC) SirsiDynix; (Serials) SirsiDynix
Wireless access
Function: Adult bk club, Adult literacy prog, Art exhibits, Computer training, Computers for patron use, Homework prog, ILL available, Magnifiers for reading, Prog for children & young adult, Summer reading prog, Teen prog, VHS videos, Wheelchair accessible
Partic in 49-99 Cooperative Library System
Open Mon-Thurs 9-8, Sat & Sun 10-5
Friends of the Library Group

S SAN JOAQUIN COUNTY HISTORICAL MUSEUM*, Gerald D Kennedy Reference Library, 11793 N Micke Grove Rd, 95241. (Mail add: PO Box 30, 95241-0030), SAN 327-8905. Tel: 209-331-2055. FAX: 209-331-2057. E-mail: info@sanjoaquinhistory.org. Web Site: www.sanjoaquinhistory.org. *Librn & Archivist,* Ignacio Sanchez-Alonso; Staff 1 (MLS 0.5, Non-MLS 0.5)
Founded 1986
Library Holdings: Bk Vols 3,000; Per Subs 12
Special Collections: Agricultural Technology Manuals; City of Lodi Records; City of Stockton Records; San Joaquin County Records; UC Cooperative Agricultural Extension Records, San Joaquin County; Weber Family Papers. Oral History
Subject Interests: Local county hist
Function: Archival coll, Photocopying/Printing, Ref serv available, Res libr
Restriction: In-house use for visitors, Not a lending libr, Open by appt only

LOMA LINDA

GM DEPARTMENT OF VETERANS AFFAIRS*, Medical Center Library Service, 11201 Benton St, 92357. SAN 300-869X. Tel: 909-422-3000, Ext 2970. *Chief, Libr Serv,* Erica Bass; E-mail: erica.bass@va.gov; Staff 2 (MLS 1, Non-MLS 1)
Founded 1977
Library Holdings: Bk Titles 2,000; Per Subs 201
Subject Interests: Med
Automation Activity & Vendor Info: (Cataloging) Innovative Interfaces, Inc; (Circulation) Innovative Interfaces, Inc
Wireless access
Open Mon-Fri 7:30-4:30

C LOMA LINDA UNIVERSITY*, Del E Webb Memorial Library, 11072 Anderson St, 92350-0001. SAN 332-2297. Tel: 909-558-4581. Circulation Tel: 909-558-4550. Interlibrary Loan Service Tel: 909-558-4925. Reference Tel: 909-558-4588. FAX: 909-558-4121. Interlibrary Loan Service FAX: 909-558-4188. E-mail: libwebeditor@llu.edu. Web Site: library.llu.edu. *Dir,* Shanalee Tamares; E-mail: stamares@llu.edu; *Cat Librn,* Warren Johns; *Access Serv,* Elisa Cortez; *Per,* Shirley Rais; *Ref (Info Servs),* Gurmeet Sehgal; *Ref (Info Servs),* Shan Tamares; *Spec Coll & Archives Librn,* Lori Curtis; *Tech Serv,* Nelia Wurangian; Staff 30 (MLS 8, Non-MLS 22)
Founded 1907. Enrl 4,026; Highest Degree: Doctorate
Library Holdings: e-journals 11,299; Bk Titles 212,712; Bk Vols 385,015
Special Collections: Archival Coll; Medicine (Peter C Remondino Coll), bks, Archives of American Dental Society of Anesthesiology; Seventh-Day Adventist Church (Heritage Coll). Oral History
Subject Interests: Health sci, Med, Relig
Automation Activity & Vendor Info: (Acquisitions) Innovative Interfaces, Inc; (Cataloging) Innovative Interfaces, Inc; (Circulation) Innovative Interfaces, Inc; (Course Reserve) Innovative Interfaces, Inc; (ILL) Innovative Interfaces, Inc; (Media Booking) Innovative Interfaces, Inc; (OPAC) Innovative Interfaces, Inc; (Serials) Innovative Interfaces, Inc
Wireless access
Partic in Adventist Librs Info Coop; Inland Empire Acad Libr Coop; National Network of Libraries of Medicine Region 5; Statewide California Electronic Library Consortium
Open Mon-Thurs 7:30am-11pm, Fri 7:30-2, Sun 10am-11pm

LOMPOC

P LOMPOC PUBLIC LIBRARY*, 501 E North Ave, 93436. SAN 332-2351. Tel: 805-875-8775. Administration Tel: 805-875-8787. Web Site: www.cityoflompoc.com/library. *Libr Dir,* Sarah J Bleyl; Tel: 805-875-8785, E-mail: s_bleyl@ci.lompoc.ca.us; *Libr Mgr,* Christine J Bolivar; *Youth Serv,* Xochitl Rocha; Tel: 805-875-8788, E-mail: x_rocha@ci.lompoc.ca; Staff 27 (MLS 2, Non-MLS 25)
Founded 1907. Pop 66,000
Special Collections: Local History Coll
Subject Interests: Gardening, Hort
Automation Activity & Vendor Info: (Acquisitions) Innovative Interfaces, Inc; (Cataloging) Innovative Interfaces, Inc; (Circulation) Innovative

Interfaces, Inc; (OPAC) Innovative Interfaces, Inc; (Serials) Innovative Interfaces, Inc
Wireless access
Mem of Black Gold Cooperative Library System
Open Mon-Thurs 10-7, Fri & Sat 1-5
Friends of the Library Group
Branches: 1
VILLAGE, 3755 Constellation Rd, 93436, SAN 332-2416. Tel: 805-733-3323. FAX: 805-733-3323. *Br Mgr,* Alexandra Newman; Staff 2.5 (Non-MLS 2.5)
Founded 1976
Open Tues & Wed 11-5, Thurs & Fri 12-6, Sat 1-5
Friends of the Library Group

LONG BEACH

R ARBOR ROAD CHURCH*, 5336 E Arbor Rd, 90808. SAN 300-872X. Tel: 562-420-1471. E-mail: info@ArborRoad.com. Web Site: arborroad.com. *Librn,* David Riseley
Founded 1950
Library Holdings: Bk Vols 9,500
Subject Interests: Biblical studies, Children's lit, Marriage, Missions & missionaries
Wireless access
Restriction: Not open to pub

C CALIFORNIA STATE UNIVERSITY, LONG BEACH*, University Library, 1250 N Bellflower Blvd, 90840. SAN 300-8711. Tel: 562-985-8472. Circulation Tel: 562-985-5512. Interlibrary Loan Service Tel: 562-985-4629. Administration Tel: 562-985-4047. FAX: 562-985-8131. Web Site: www.csulb.edu/university-library. *Dean & Dir, Libr Serv,* Roman V Kochan; *Dir of Develop,* Mary Ann Solic; E-mail: solic@csulb.edu; Staff 21 (MLS 19, Non-MLS 2)
Founded 1949. Enrl 32,686; Fac 2,001; Highest Degree: Doctorate
Jul 2012-Jun 2013. Mats Exp $1,817,152, Books $149,475, Per/Ser (Incl. Access Fees) $601,013, Other Print Mats $43,412, AV Mat $10,640, Electronic Ref Mat (Incl. Access Fees) $1,011,759, Presv $853. Sal $3,571,488 (Prof $1,726,114)
Library Holdings: Audiobooks 1,866; CDs 8,920; DVDs 4,834; e-books 378,254; e-journals 74,790; Microforms 1,502,855; Bk Titles 663,099; Bk Vols 1,102,003; Per Subs 1,956
Special Collections: Abolition Movement (Dumond Coll); Art Prints & Photography Coll; Arts in Southern California Archive; California History (Bekeart Coll); Radical Politics in California (Dorothy Healey Coll); Theater History (Pasadena Playhouse Coll), playscripts; United States Revolutionary War; University Archives. Oral History; State Document Depository; US Document Depository
Automation Activity & Vendor Info: (Acquisitions) Innovative Interfaces, Inc; (Cataloging) Innovative Interfaces, Inc; (Circulation) Innovative Interfaces, Inc; (Course Reserve) Innovative Interfaces, Inc; (ILL) OCLC ILLiad; (OPAC) Innovative Interfaces, Inc; (Serials) Innovative Interfaces, Inc
Wireless access
Publications: Library Skills
Partic in Statewide California Electronic Library Consortium
Open Mon-Thurs 7am-Midnight, Fri 7-5, Sat 10-5, Sun 12:30pm-Midnight
Friends of the Library Group

M COLLEGE MEDICAL CENTER*, Harris Memorial Library, 2776 Pacific Ave, 90806. SAN 300-8800. Tel: 562-997-2181. FAX: 562-595-0271. *Coordr,* Kenny Jones; E-mail: kjones@collegemedicalcenter.com; Staff 1 (MLS 1)
Founded 1964
Library Holdings: Bk Titles 722; Per Subs 145
Subject Interests: Acupuncture, Med, Nursing, Osteopathology, Osteopathy, Podiatry
Function: Bks on cassette, ILL available, Internet access, Ref serv available
Partic in Medical Library Group of Southern California & Arizona
Open Mon-Fri 8-5

S HISTORICAL SOCIETY OF LONG BEACH, 4260 Atlantic Ave, 90807. SAN 326-4807. Tel: 562-424-2220. E-mail: archives@hslb.org. Web Site: hslb.org. *Exec Dir,* Julie Bartolotto; E-mail: julieb@hslb.org; *Project Archivist,* Tristan Willenburg; Staff 3 (MLS 1, Non-MLS 2)
Founded 1962
Library Holdings: Bk Titles 400
Special Collections: Documents; Historical Newspaper Coll; Pamphlets; Photograph Coll; Scrapbooks. Oral History
Subject Interests: Artifacts, Local hist, Maps
Function: Ref serv available
Publications: Photograph Journals
Open Tues, Wed & Fri 1-5, Thurs 1-7, Sat 11-5
Restriction: Non-circulating

J LONG BEACH CITY COLLEGE*, Liberal Arts Campus & Pacific Coast Campus Libraries, 4901 E Carson St, 90808. SAN 332-2475. Tel: 562-938-3028 (PCC Campus), 562-938-4232 (LAC Campus). Circulation Tel: 562-928-4231 (LAC Campus). Interlibrary Loan Service Tel: 562-938-4576, 562-938-4809. FAX: 562-938-3062, 562-938-4777. E-mail: pcclibrary@lbcc.edu. *Dept Head,* Dr Ramachandran Sethuraman; E-mail: rsethuraman@lbcc.edu; *Access Serv & Electronic Res Librn,* Nenita Buenaventura; E-mail: nbuenaventura@lbcc.edu; *Cat Librn,* Dele Ukwu; Tel: 562-938-4581, E-mail: dukwu@lbcc.edu; *Coll Develop Librn, Outreach Librn,* Shamika Simpson; E-mail: ssimpson@lbcc.edu; *Syst Librn,* Dena Laney; Tel: 562-938-4714, E-mail: dlaney@lbcc.edu. Subject Specialists: *Allied health, Med, Sci,* Nenita Buenaventura; *Soc sci,* Dena Laney; Staff 28 (MLS 19, Non-MLS 9)
Founded 1927. Enrl 24,828; Highest Degree: Associate
Library Holdings: Bk Vols 145,639; Per Subs 466
Automation Activity & Vendor Info: (Cataloging) OCLC; (Circulation) OCLC; (ILL) OCLC FirstSearch; (OPAC) OCLC; (Serials) EBSCO Online
Wireless access
Open Mon-Thurs (LAC Campus) 7am-10pm, Fri 7-4, Sat 10-4; Mon-Thurs (PCC Campus) 8am-9pm, Fri 9-2:30, Sat 10-2
Friends of the Library Group

S LONG BEACH JEWISH COMMUNITY CENTER - THE ALPERT JCC*, Stanley S Zack Library, 3801 E Willow St, 90815. SAN 300-8762. Tel: 562-426-7601. FAX: 562-424-3915. E-mail: info@alpert.jcc.org. Web Site: www.jewishlongbeach.org. *Exec Dir,* Jeffrey Rips; Tel: 562-426-7601, Ext 1011, E-mail: jrips@alpertjcc.org
Founded 1961
Library Holdings: Bk Titles 3,500; Per Subs 20
Subject Interests: Judaica (lit or hist of Jews)
Wireless access
Open Mon-Thurs 6am-10pm, Fri 6-6, Sat & Sun 7-6

M LONG BEACH MEMORIAL/MILLER CHILDREN'S HOSPITAL LONG BEACH*, Memorial Care Health Sciences Library, 2801 Atlantic Ave, 90806. SAN 300-8797. Tel: 562-933-3841. FAX: 562-933-3888. E-mail: MHSMedicalLibrary@memorialcare.org. Web Site: millerchildrenshospitallb.org. *Libr Tech,* Elizabeth Mason; E-mail: emrenteria@memorialcare.org; Staff 2 (MLS 1, Non-MLS 1)
Founded 1927
Library Holdings: Bk Titles 1,000; Bk Vols 2,100; Per Subs 600
Subject Interests: Allied health, Bus, Med, Nursing
Automation Activity & Vendor Info: (Acquisitions) SirsiDynix; (Cataloging) SirsiDynix; (Circulation) SirsiDynix; (OPAC) SirsiDynix; (Serials) SirsiDynix
Wireless access
Function: Audio & video playback equip for onsite use, Computers for patron use, Doc delivery serv, E-Reserves, Electronic databases & coll, Health sci info serv, ILL available, Internet access, Online cat, Online ref, Orientations, Outreach serv, Outside serv via phone, mail, e-mail & web, Photocopying/Printing, Prof lending libr, Ref & res, Ref serv available, Telephone ref, Wheelchair accessible, Workshops
Publications: Fact Sheet (Documents)
Partic in Medical Library Group of Southern California & Arizona; Statewide California Electronic Library Consortium
Restriction: Authorized personnel only

S LONG BEACH MUSEUM OF ART LIBRARY*, 2300 E Ocean Blvd, 90803. SAN 300-8770. Tel: 562-439-2119, Ext 226. FAX: 562-439-3587. Web Site: www.lbma.org. *Exec Dir,* Ronald C Nelson; E-mail: ronn@lbma.org; *Executive Asst,* Laurie Webb; E-mail: lauriew@lbma.org
Founded 1957
Library Holdings: Bk Titles 2,000; Bk Vols 2,600
Wireless access
Open Thurs 11-8, Fri-Sun 11-5

P LONG BEACH PUBLIC LIBRARY*, 200 W Broadway, 90802. SAN 332-2564. Tel: 562-570-7500. Circulation Tel: 562-570-6901. FAX: 562-570-7408. E-mail: lbpl_reference@lbpl.org. Web Site: www.longbeach.gov/library. *Dir,* Glenda Williams; E-mail: glenda.williams@lbpl.org; *Mgr, Main Libr,* Susan Jones; E-mail: susan.jones@lbpl.org; *Mgr, Br Serv,* Cathy De Leon; Staff 187 (MLS 47, Non-MLS 140)
Founded 1896. Pop 460,000; Circ 1,644,125. Sal $9,778,290
Library Holdings: Audiobooks 6,233; AV Mats 28,644; CDs 8,030; DVDs 14,381; e-books 79; e-journals 5,846; Electronic Media & Resources 17; Large Print Bks 8,967; Bk Titles 403,293; Bk Vols 794,828
Special Collections: Bertrand L Smith Rare Book; Long Beach History; Marilyn Horne Archives, pictures, press clippings, rec. State Document Depository; US Document Depository
Subject Interests: Petroleum
Automation Activity & Vendor Info: (Acquisitions) Innovative Interfaces, Inc - Millennium; (Cataloging) Innovative Interfaces, Inc - Millennium; (Circulation) Innovative Interfaces, Inc - Millennium; (ILL) Innovative

Interfaces, Inc - Millennium; (OPAC) Innovative Interfaces, Inc - Millennium; (Serials) Innovative Interfaces, Inc - Millennium
Wireless access
Function: Adult bk club, Adult literacy prog, Audiobks via web, Bks on cassette, Bks on CD, Computer training, Computers for patron use, Electronic databases & coll, Family literacy, Homework prog, ILL available, Magnifiers for reading, Music CDs, Online cat, Online ref, OverDrive digital audio bks, Photocopying/Printing, Prog for children & young adult, Ref & res, Ref serv available, Story hour, Summer reading prog, Tax forms, Telephone ref, Wheelchair accessible
Partic in Coop Libr Agency for Syst & Servs; Southern Calif Interlibr Loan Network
Special Services for the Deaf - Assistive tech; Closed caption videos; TTY equip
Special Services for the Blind - Bks on cassette; Bks on CD; Reader equip; Screen reader software
Open Tues 12-8, Wed 12-6, Thurs 12-7, Fri & Sat 10-5
Friends of the Library Group
Branches: 11
ALAMITOS, 1836 E Third St, 90802, SAN 332-2599. Tel: 562-570-1037. *Sr Librn,* Cyndi Effrain
Library Holdings: Bk Vols 34,520
Open Tues & Thurs 12-7, Wed 12-6, Fri & Sat 10-5
Friends of the Library Group
BAY SHORE, 195 Bay Shore Ave, 90803, SAN 332-2653. Tel: 562-570-1039. *Sr Librn,* Debi Vilander
Library Holdings: Bk Vols 45,676
Open Tues & Thurs 12-7, Wed 12-6, Fri & Sat 10-5, Sun 12-4
Friends of the Library Group
BREWITT, 4036 E Anaheim St, 90804, SAN 332-2688. Tel: 562-570-1040. *Sr Librn,* Elizabeth Rogers
Library Holdings: Bk Vols 34,563
Open Tues & Thurs 12-7, Wed 12-6, Fri & Sat 10-5
Friends of the Library Group
BURNETT, 560 E Hill St, 90806, SAN 332-2718. Tel: 562-570-1041. *Sr Librn,* Erica Lansdown
Library Holdings: Bk Vols 40,719
Open Tues & Thurs 12-7, Wed 12-7, Fri & Sat 10-5
Friends of the Library Group
DANA, 3680 Atlantic Ave, 90807, SAN 332-2742. Tel: 562-570-1042. *Sr Librn,* Josephine Caron
Library Holdings: Bk Vols 41,566
Open Tues & Thurs 12-7, Wed 12-6, Fri & Sat 10-5
Friends of the Library Group
EL DORADO, 2900 Studebaker Rd, 90815, SAN 332-2777. Tel: 562-570-3136. *Sr Librn,* Gail Tweedt
Library Holdings: Bk Vols 62,444
Open Tues & Thurs 12-7, Wed 12-6, Fri & Sat 10-5
Friends of the Library Group
BRET HARTE BRANCH, 1595 W Willow St, 90810, SAN 332-2807. Tel: 562-570-1044. *Sr Librn,* Silke Kinoshita
Library Holdings: Bk Vols 40,900
Open Tues & Thurs 12-7, Wed 12-6, Fri & Sat 10-5
Friends of the Library Group
LOS ALTOS, 5614 Britton Dr, 90815, SAN 332-2831. Tel: 562-570-1045. *Sr Librn,* Position Currently Open; Staff 2 (MLS 2)
Founded 1957. Pop 41,286; Circ 141,286
Library Holdings: Bk Vols 41,287
Open Tues & Thurs 12-7, Wed 12-6, Fri & Sat 10-5
Friends of the Library Group
MICHELLE OBAMA BRANCH, 5870 Atlantic Ave, 90805. Tel: 562-570-1047. *Sr Librn,* Ketzie Diaz
Library Holdings: Bk Vols 57,008
Open Tues & Thurs 12-7, Wed 12-6, Fri & Sat 10-5, Sun 12-4
Friends of the Library Group
RUTH BACH BRANCH, 4055 N Bellflower Blvd, 90808, SAN 332-2629. Tel: 562-570-1038. *Sr Librn,* Cynthia Bautista
Library Holdings: Bk Vols 45,208
Open Tues & Thurs 12-7, Wed 12-6, Fri & Sat 10-5
Friends of the Library Group
MARK TWAIN BRANCH, 1401 E Anaheim St, 90813, SAN 332-2890. Tel: 562-570-1046. *Sr Librn,* Jennifer Songster
Library Holdings: Bk Vols 65,578
Open Tues & Thurs 12-7, Wed 12-6, Fri & Sat 10-5
Friends of the Library Group

M ST MARY MEDICAL CENTER, Bellis Medical Library, 1050 Linden Ave, 90813. SAN 300-8819. Tel: 562-491-9295, 714-886-9067. FAX: 562-491-9293. Web Site: libguides.dignityhealth.org/SMLB. *Med Librn,* Judy Kraemer; E-mail: judy.kraemer@commonspirit.org. Subject Specialists: *Bus, Health sci, Law,* Judy Kraemer; Staff 0.8 (MLS 0.8)
Founded 1955
Jul 2020-Jun 2021 Income $48,594. Mats Exp $32,205, Per/Ser (Incl. Access Fees) $15,786, Electronic Ref Mat (Incl. Access Fees) $16,419. Sal $80,512
Library Holdings: Bk Vols 1,500; Per Subs 10
Subject Interests: Hist of med, Hospital admin, Nursing
Automation Activity & Vendor Info: (Cataloging) CyberTools for Libraries; (Circulation) CyberTools for Libraries; (Discovery) EBSCO Discovery Service; (OPAC) CyberTools for Libraries
Wireless access
Function: 24/7 Electronic res, 24/7 Online cat, Archival coll, Computers for patron use, Doc delivery serv, Electronic databases & coll, For res purposes, Health sci info serv, ILL available, Internet access, Mail & tel request accepted, Online cat, Online info literacy tutorials on the web & in blackboard, Online ref, Orientations, Outreach serv, Outside serv via phone, mail, e-mail & web, Photocopying/Printing, Prof lending libr, Ref & res, Ref serv available, Res assist avail, Res libr, Scanner, Study rm, Telephone ref, Wheelchair accessible
Partic in Medical Library Group of Southern California & Arizona; National Network of Libraries of Medicine Region 5
Restriction: Authorized personnel only, Badge access after hrs, Circ limited, Circulates for staff only, Co libr, Hospital employees & physicians only, ID required to use computers (Ltd hrs), In-house use for visitors, Internal circ only, Lending to staff only, Med & nursing staff, patients & families, Non-circulating of rare bks, Non-circulating to the pub, Not open to pub, Open to hospital affiliates only, Open to staff, patients & family mem, Photo ID required for access, Private libr, Restricted access, Restricted borrowing privileges, Restricted loan policy, Secured area only open to authorized personnel, Staff & patient use

GM VA LONG BEACH HEALTH CARE SYSTEM*, Health Care Sciences Library, 5901 E Seventh St, Bldg 2, Rm 345, 90822-5201. SAN 300-8835. Tel: 562-826-8000, ext 5463. FAX: 562-826-5447. Web Site: www.longbeach.va.gov. *Libr Mgr,* Marie Carter; E-mail: marie.carter@va.gov; Staff 2 (MLS 1, Non-MLS 1)
Founded 1946
Library Holdings: Bk Titles 3,000; Per Subs 7,000
Special Collections: Management Coll
Subject Interests: Clinical med
Open Mon-Fri 8-4:30

LOS ALTOS HILLS

R CONGREGATION BETH AM LIBRARY*, 26790 Arastradero Rd, 94022. SAN 300-8878. Tel: 650-493-4661. FAX: 650-494-8248. E-mail: library@betham.org. Web Site: www.betham.org/library.html. *Exec Dir,* Rachel Tasch; E-mail: rtasch@betham.org; *Librn,* Diane Rauchwerger
Library Holdings: Bk Vols 10,000
Special Collections: Judaica

J FOOTHILL COLLEGE*, Hubert H Semans Library, 12345 El Monte Rd, 94022-4599. SAN 300-8894. Circulation Tel: 650-949-7611. Interlibrary Loan Service Tel: 650-949-7029. Reference Tel: 650-949-7608. FAX: 650-949-7123. Web Site: www.foothill.edu/library. *Dean,* Valerie Fong; E-mail: fongvalerie@fhda.edu; *Coll Develop Librn,* Mary Thomas; *Instruction Librn,* Micaela Agyare; *Tech Serv Librn,* Kay Jones; Tel: 650-949-7602, E-mail: joneskay@foothill.edu; *Tech & Syst Librn,* Pawel Szponar; E-mail: szponarpaul@foothill.edu; Staff 10 (MLS 4, Non-MLS 6)
Founded 1958. Enrl 14,976; Fac 334; Highest Degree: Associate
Library Holdings: Bk Titles 80,193; Bk Vols 89,022; Per Subs 250
Subject Interests: Art, Lit, Philos, Relig
Automation Activity & Vendor Info: (Acquisitions) SirsiDynix; (Cataloging) SirsiDynix; (Circulation) SirsiDynix; (ILL) SirsiDynix; (Serials) SirsiDynix
Wireless access
Publications: Student Handbook
Partic in OCLC Online Computer Library Center, Inc
Special Services for the Deaf - Closed caption videos
Special Services for the Blind - Assistive/Adapted tech devices, equip & products
Open Mon-Thurs 8-7, Fri 8-4
Restriction: Open to pub for ref only
Friends of the Library Group

LOS ANGELES

S AMERICAN FILM INSTITUTE, Louis B Mayer Library, 2021 N Western Ave, 90027. SAN 300-6220. Tel: 323-856-7654. FAX: 323-856-7803. E-mail: library@afi.com. Web Site: www.afi.com. *Archives Mgr, Interim Dir,* Emily Wittenberg; Staff 8 (MLS 2, Non-MLS 6)
Founded 1969. Enrl 280; Fac 40; Highest Degree: Master
Library Holdings: AV Mats 25,000; DVDs 8,000; Bk Vols 9,000; Per Subs 10; Videos 11,000
Special Collections: Charles K. Feldman Coll; Fritz Lang Coll; Manuscript Coll; Martin Scorsese Coll; Motion Picture & Television Scripts Coll; Oral History Transcripts Coll; RKO Radio Flash Coll (1932-1955); Seminar Transcripts & Tape Coll. Oral History
Subject Interests: Am film production
Automation Activity & Vendor Info: (Circulation) LibraryWorld, Inc

Wireless access
Function: Archival coll, Res libr
Open Mon-Thurs 9-9, Fri 9-7, Sat & Sun 10-6
Restriction: Access at librarian's discretion, By permission only, Circ privileges for students & alumni only, Circ to mem only, Circulates for staff only, Non-circulating to the pub, Open to others by appt, Open to pub by appt only, Open to researchers by request

R AMERICAN JEWISH UNIVERSITY*, Ostrow Library, 15600 Mulholland Dr, 90077. SAN 301-0155. Tel: 310-476-9777, Ext 238. E-mail: library@aju.edu. Web Site: library.aju.edu. *Dir, Libr Serv,* Paul Miller; E-mail: pmiller@aju.edu
Library Holdings: Bk Vols 115,000; Per Subs 150
Special Collections: Judaica & Hebraica Coll
Subject Interests: Educ, Humanities, Judaica (lit or hist of Jews)
Automation Activity & Vendor Info: (Cataloging) OCLC; (Circulation) OCLC; (OPAC) OCLC; (Serials) OCLC
Open Mon-Thurs 8-8, Fri 8-2:30, Sun 1-5

L ANDERSON, MCPHARLIN & CONNERS LLP LIBRARY*, 707 Wilshire Blvd #4000, 90017. Tel: 213-236-1677. FAX: 213-622-7594. E-mail: sml@amclaw.com. Web Site: www.amclaw.com. *Librn,* Diane Garrity; E-mail: dlg@amclaw.com; Staff 1 (MLS 1)
Founded 1947
Library Holdings: High Interest/Low Vocabulary Bk Vols 30; Bk Titles 1,000; Bk Vols 5,000; Per Subs 20
Function: For res purposes
Publications: Collection Catalog

L ARNOLD & PORTER KAYE SCHOLAR LLP*, Law Library, 777 S Figueroa St, 90017-5844. SAN 372-2694. Tel: 310-788-1000. Web Site: www.arnoldporter.com. *Library Contact,* Mary Ann Donaldson
Library Holdings: Bk Vols 12,000
Restriction: Private libr

AUTRY NATIONAL CENTER

S AUTRY LIBRARY*, 4700 Western Heritage Way, 90027-1462, SAN 372-6606. Tel: 323-667-2000, Ext 349. FAX: 323-660-5721. E-mail: rroom@theautry.org. Web Site: theautry.org/research/autry-library. *Dir,* Marva Felchlin; *Sr Mgr, Tech Serv,* Cheryl Miller; Staff 5 (MLS 4, Non-MLS 1)
Founded 1988
Library Holdings: Bk Vols 25,000; Per Subs 100
Special Collections: Dime Novels; Dude Ranch Brochures; Gene Autry Archive; Nudie's Rodeo Tailor Coll, customer files, photog; Postcards; Saddle & Western Wear Trade Catalogs; Western Americana (Fred Rosenstock Coll), archival coll, bks, maps, photog, postcards; Western Character Comic Books; Western Film Posters & Stills; Western Music Coll, rec, sheet music, WLS radio family yearbks; Western TV Scripts & Photographic Stills; Women of the West Museum Coll
Subject Interests: Bus of western entertainment, Hist & mythology of Am W
Automation Activity & Vendor Info: (Cataloging) Innovative Interfaces, Inc; (OPAC) Innovative Interfaces, Inc; (Serials) EBSCO Online
Partic in OCLC Online Computer Library Center, Inc; Proquest Dialog
Restriction: Circulates for staff only, In-house use for visitors, Non-circulating to the pub, Open to others by appt

S BRAUN RESEARCH LIBRARY*, 234 Museum Dr, 90065. Tel: 323-221-2164. FAX: 322-221-8223. E-mail: rroom@theautry.org. Web Site: theautry.org/research/braun-research-library. *Dir,* Kim Walters; Tel: 323-221-2164, Ext 255; *Ref Librn,* Liza Posas; Tel: 323-221-2164, Ext 256, E-mail: lposas@theautry.org; Staff 3 (MLS 2, Non-MLS 1)
Library Holdings: Bk Vols 50,000
Special Collections: Manuscript Coll (History & Founding of Archaeology & Anthropology in the US); Photo Archives (Primarily Native Americans 1890s-1940s); Sound Recording Archives (California Hispanic Folk Songs, 1900-1908 & Native American Recordings), wax cylinder recs
Automation Activity & Vendor Info: (Cataloging) Innovative Interfaces, Inc; (OPAC) Innovative Interfaces, Inc; (Serials) EBSCO Online
Partic in OCLC Online Computer Library Center, Inc
Open Mon-Fri 9-5
Restriction: Non-circulating to the pub

P BRAILLE INSTITUTE LIBRARY SERVICES*, 741 N Vermont Ave, 90029-3514. SAN 300-8975. Tel: 323-660-3880. Toll Free Tel: 800-808-2555 (Southern California only). FAX: 323-662-2440. E-mail: bils@brailleinstitute.org. Reference E-mail: reference@braillelibrary.org. Web Site: www.brailleinstitute.org/library. *Dir, Libr Serv,* Reed Strege; Tel: 323-906-3185, E-mail: rwstrege@brailleinstitute.org; *Info Res Librn,* Kathryn Hayes; Tel: 323-663-1111, Ext 1283, E-mail: khayes@braillelibrary.org; *Circ Serv Mgr,* Hung-Ming Cheng; Tel: 323-663-1111, Ext 1317, E-mail: ming@brailleinstitute.org; *Reader Serv Mgr,* Tina Herbison; Tel: 323-663-1111, Ext 1382, E-mail: tina@braillelibrary.org; *Support Serv Mgr,* Edith Gavino; Tel: 323-663-1111, Ext 1284, E-mail: edith@braillelibrary.org; *Mat Develop Coordr,* Ivan G Johnson; Tel: 323-663-1111, Ext 1388, E-mail: igjohnson@braillelibrary.org; Staff 27 (MLS 3, Non-MLS 24)
Founded 1919
Jul 2016-Jun 2017 Income (Main & Associated Libraries) $3,209,000, State $409,000, Parent Institution $2,800,000. Mats Exp $35,000, Books $30,000, Per/Ser (Incl. Access Fees) $5,000. Sal $1,700,000
Library Holdings: Audiobooks 90,000; Braille Volumes 50,000; Large Print Bks 1,000; Bk Titles 100,000; Per Subs 50; Videos 3,000
Special Collections: Blindness & Other Handicap Reference Material; Southern California Coll
Subject Interests: Blindness, Physically handicapped
Automation Activity & Vendor Info: (Cataloging) Keystone Systems, Inc (KLAS); (Circulation) Keystone Systems, Inc (KLAS); (OPAC) Keystone Systems, Inc (KLAS); (Serials) Keystone Systems, Inc (KLAS)
Wireless access
Function: Audiobks via web, Bk club(s), Bks on cassette, Computers for patron use, Digital talking bks, ILL available, Online cat, Wheelchair accessible
Publications: Fiction Classics Catalog; Librarian Newsletter; Record Books on Tapes about California; Subject Bibliographies; Transcribe Books into Braille
Special Services for the Blind - Accessible computers; Bks on cassette; Cassette playback machines; Computer with voice synthesizer for visually impaired persons; Digital talking bk; Digital talking bk machines; Large print bks; Newsletter (in large print, Braille or on cassette); Newsp reading serv; Volunteer serv; Web-Braille
Open Mon-Fri 8:30-5
Restriction: Authorized patrons, Limited access based on advanced application, Limited access for the pub, Registered patrons only, Restricted borrowing privileges
Branches: 4
DESERT CENTER, 70-251 Ramon Rd, Rancho Mirage, 92270, SAN 372-7637. Tel: 760-321-1111. FAX: 760-321-9715. *Coordr,* Gayle Wormell; E-mail: gpwormell@brailleinstitute.org; Staff 1 (Non-MLS 1)
Library Holdings: Audiobooks 8,417; Braille Volumes 20; Bk Titles 6,156; Videos 47
Special Services for the Blind - Bks on cassette; Digital talking bk; Digital talking bk machines
Open Mon-Fri 8:30-5
ORANGE COUNTY CENTER, 527 N Dale Ave, Anaheim, 92801, SAN 372-7645. Tel: 714-821-5000. FAX: 714-527-7621. *Coordr,* Benjamin Gabriel; Tel: 714-821-5000, Ext 2126, E-mail: BGabriel@brailleinstitute.org; Staff 2 (Non-MLS 2)
Library Holdings: Audiobooks 8,344; Braille Volumes 163; Bk Titles 6,236; Videos 126
Special Services for the Blind - Bks on cassette; Cassette playback machines; Digital talking bk; Digital talking bk machines
Open Mon-Fri 8:30-5
Friends of the Library Group
SAN DIEGO CENTER, 4555 Executive Dr, San Diego, 92121-3021, SAN 372-7653. Tel: 858-452-1111. FAX: 858-452-1688. *Coordr,* Louise Zuckerman; Tel: 858-452-1111, Ext 5011, E-mail: lmzuckerman@brailleinstitute.org; Staff 1 (MLS 1)
Library Holdings: Audiobooks 9,611; Braille Volumes 193; Bk Titles 7,020; Videos 237
Special Services for the Blind - Bks on cassette; Cassette playback machines; Digital talking bk; Digital talking bk machines
Open Mon-Fri 8:30-5
Friends of the Library Group
SANTA BARBARA CENTER, 2031 De La Vina St, Santa Barbara, 93105, SAN 372-7661. Tel: 805-682-6222. FAX: 805-687-6141. *Coordr,* Nate Streeper; E-mail: nkstreeper@brailleinstitute.org; Staff 1 (Non-MLS 1)
Library Holdings: Audiobooks 7,709; Braille Volumes 68; Bk Titles 7,626; Videos 172
Special Services for the Blind - Digital talking bk; Digital talking bk machines

L BUCHALTER NEMER*, Law Library, 1000 Wilshire Blvd, Ste 1500, 90017. SAN 372-2740. Tel: 213-891-0700. Administration Tel: 213-891-5655. FAX: 213-896-0400. Web Site: www.buchalter.com. *Dir, Libr Serv,* Michelle Kuczma; E-mail: mkuczma@buchalter.com
Library Holdings: Bk Vols 20,000
Restriction: Staff use only

M CALIFORNIA HOSPITAL MEDICAL CENTER LOS ANGELES*, Medical Library, 1401 S Grand Ave, 90015. SAN 320-4448. Tel: 213-742-5872. FAX: 213-765-4046. *Library Contact,* Derilyn Clark; E-mail: derilyn.clark@dignityhealth.org; Staff 2 (MLS 1, Non-MLS 1)
Founded 1964
Library Holdings: Bk Vols 1,200; Per Subs 9
Subject Interests: Clinical med, Nursing, Oncology
Wireless access
Restriction: Not open to pub

L CALIFORNIA SECOND DISTRICT COURT OF APPEALS*, 300 S Spring St, Rm 3547, 90013. SAN 300-9114. Tel: 213-830-7241. FAX: 213-897-2429. Web Site: courts.ca.gov/2dca. *Head Librn*, Position Currently Open
Founded 1967
Library Holdings: Bk Vols 65,000
Subject Interests: Calif
Restriction: Not open to pub

C CALIFORNIA STATE UNIVERSITY, LOS ANGELES*, John F Kennedy Memorial Library, 5151 State University Dr, 90032-8300. SAN 300-9017. Tel: 323-343-3950. Circulation Tel: 323-343-3987. Interlibrary Loan Service Tel: 323-343-3983, 323-343-4983. Reference Tel: 323-343-4927, 323-343-4928. Administration Tel: 323-343-3929, 323-343-3953. Information Services Tel: 323-343-3994. FAX: 323-343-5600. Interlibrary Loan Service FAX: 323-343-6401. Web Site: www.calstatela.edu/library. *Dean*, Carlos Rodriguez; E-mail: Carlos.Rodriguez@calstatela.edu; *Assoc Dean*, Marla Peppers; E-mail: mpepper@calstatela.edu; Staff 35 (MLS 14, Non-MLS 21)
Founded 1947. Enrl 23,258; Fac 12; Highest Degree: Master
Jul 2016-Jun 2017. Mats Exp $1,425,650. Sal $2,597,875 (Prof $2,390,234)
Library Holdings: CDs 5,918; DVDs 4,001; e-books 168,920; e-journals 67,700; Electronic Media & Resources 15,562; Microforms 808,960; Bk Vols 983,229; Per Subs 63,861
Special Collections: Carlos Montes Papers & Gloria Arellanes Papers; East LA Archives; Film Scripts (Anthony Quinn Coll); Joseph Wambaugh Manuscript Coll; Mexican American Baseball: From the Barrios to the Big Leagues; Musical Scores (Eugene List & Carol Glenn Coll); Musical Scores (Otto Klemperer Coll); Printing Books (Perry R Long Coll); Public Officials Papers: Mervyn Dymally, Julian Nava, Julian Dixon, Richard Alatorre; Roy Harris & Stan Kenton Music Archives; Theatre Arts (Arthur M Applebaum Coll). State Document Depository; US Document Depository
Automation Activity & Vendor Info: (Acquisitions) Innovative Interfaces, Inc; (Cataloging) Innovative Interfaces, Inc; (Circulation) Innovative Interfaces, Inc; (Course Reserve) Docutek; (Media Booking) Innovative Interfaces, Inc; (OPAC) Innovative Interfaces, Inc; (Serials) Innovative Interfaces, Inc
Wireless access
Partic in Metronet; OCLC Online Computer Library Center, Inc
Friends of the Library Group

M CDU HEALTH SCIENCES LIBRARY*, 1731 E 120th St, 90059. SAN 300-9424. Tel: 323-563-4869. FAX: 323-563-4861. E-mail: library2@cdrewu.edu. Web Site: www.cdrewu.edu. *Dir*, Darlene Parker Kelly; Tel: 323-563-9340, E-mail: darleneparkerkelly@cdrewu.edu; Staff 10 (MLS 3, Non-MLS 7)
Founded 1972
Library Holdings: Bk Titles 14,000; Bk Vols 48,000; Per Subs 760
Special Collections: Clinical Medicine
Automation Activity & Vendor Info: (Cataloging) EOS International; (Circulation) EOS International
Wireless access
Open Mon-Thurs 8am-9pm, Fri 8-7, Sat & Sun 11-4:45

M CEDARS-SINAI MEDICAL CENTER, Medical Library, South Tower Plaza, Rm 2815, 8700 Beverly Blvd, 90048. SAN 300-9033. Tel: 310-423-3751. Interlibrary Loan Service Tel: 310-423-3647. FAX: 310-423-4017. E-mail: library@cshs.org. Web Site: www.cedars-sinai.edu/Education/Medical-Library. *Assoc Dir*, Elizabeth McGaughey; E-mail: elizabeth.mcgaughey@cshs.org; Staff 7 (MLS 5, Non-MLS 2)
Library Holdings: e-books 23,760; e-journals 34,107; Bk Vols 7,500
Special Collections: Cedars-Sinai Authors; History of Medicine; Judaica; Medical Ethics
Automation Activity & Vendor Info: (Acquisitions) SirsiDynix; (Cataloging) SirsiDynix; (Circulation) SirsiDynix; (Course Reserve) SirsiDynix; (Serials) SirsiDynix
Wireless access
Function: 24/7 Electronic res, 24/7 Online cat, Archival coll, Computers for patron use, Doc delivery serv, Electronic databases & coll, For res purposes, Govt ref serv, ILL available, Photocopying/Printing, Prof lending libr, Ref serv available
Restriction: Med staff only

M CHILDREN'S HOSPITAL LOS ANGELES*, Health Sciences Library, 4650 Sunset Blvd, MS41, 90027. SAN 300-9068. Tel: 323-361-2254, 323-361-2428. Web Site: www.chla.org/health-sciences-library. *Librn*, Lynn Kysh; E-mail: lkysh@chla.usc.edu; Staff 2 (MLS 1, Non-MLS 1)
Founded 1928
Library Holdings: Per Subs 7
Subject Interests: Pediatrics
Open Mon-Thurs 8-6, Fri 8-5

C COLUMBIA COLLEGE HOLLYWOOD, Library & Learning Resource Center, 18618 Oxnard St, 91356-1411. SAN 328-2449. Tel: 818-345-8414. Toll Free Tel: 800-785-0585. Web Site: www.columbiacollege.edu/academics/library-learning-resources. *Dir, Learning Res Ctr*, April Cheverette; Tel: 818-401-1027, E-mail: april.cheverette@columbiacollege.edu; Staff 1 (MLS 1)
Founded 1952. Enrl 350; Fac 70; Highest Degree: Bachelor
Library Holdings: Bk Titles 12,000; Per Subs 100
Special Collections: Hollywood Museum Coll; Motion Picture & Revision Script Coll, scripts; Society of Motion Picture & Television Engineers, jrnls, 1910-present
Open Mon-Thurs 8:45am-9:15pm, Fri 8:45-6, Sat 9-2
Friends of the Library Group

L COX, CASTLE & NICHOLSON LLP LIBRARY*, 2029 Century Park E, 21st Flr, 90067. SAN 300-9122. Tel: 310-277-4222, Ext 2444. FAX: 310-277-7889. *Law Librn*, Janet Kasabian
Library Holdings: Bk Vols 17,000; Per Subs 500

M DOHENY EYE INSTITUTE LIBRARY*, 1355 San Pablo St, 90033. SAN 321-6128. Tel: 323-342-6600. Web Site: deilibrary.wordpress.com. *Library Contact*, Darlene Villegas; E-mail: dvillegas@doheny.org; Staff 1 (MLS 1)
Founded 1976
Library Holdings: Bk Vols 1,975
Subject Interests: Ophthalmology
Automation Activity & Vendor Info: (Cataloging) LibraryWorld, Inc; (OPAC) LibraryWorld, Inc
Wireless access
Function: Computers for patron use, ILL available, Online cat, Scanner
Partic in Medical Library Group of Southern California & Arizona; Pacific Southwest Regional Medical Library
Open Mon-Fri 8:30-5
Restriction: Badge access after hrs

S EDUCATIONAL COMMUNICATIONS, INC*, Environmental Resources Library, PO Box 351419, 90035-9119. SAN 326-1654. Tel: 310-559-9160. E-mail: ECNP@aol.com. Web Site: www.ecoprojects.org. *Exec Dir*, Nancy Pearlman; Tel: 213-705-4992
Founded 1958
Library Holdings: AV Mats 3,000; CDs 2,300; DVDs 150; e-journals 36; Electronic Media & Resources 600; Bk Titles 2,500; Per Subs 20; Spec Interest Per Sub 25; Videos 650
Special Collections: Autographed Books by Authors on Environmental Topics; Compendium Newsletter Coll; Ecology & Ecotourism (ECONEWS Television Series & Environmental Directions Radio Series Coll); Environment
Subject Interests: Conserv, Ecology, Environ, Land use, Natural res, Sustainability, Wildlife
Publications: The Compendium (Newsletter)
Restriction: Open by appt only

S FASHION INSTITUTE OF DESIGN & MERCHANDISING LIBRARY*, 919 S Grand Ave, 90015. SAN 375-4774. Tel: 213-486-2009. E-mail: library@fidm.edu. Web Site: fidm.edu/en/student+life/fidm+library. *Colls Mgr, Head Librn*, Robin Dodge; Staff 32 (MLS 7, Non-MLS 25)
Founded 1969
Library Holdings: Per Subs 200
Wireless access
Open Mon-Thurs 7am-10pm, Fri 7-7, Sat 8-6

L FOLEY & LARDNER LLP*, Los Angeles Library, 555 S Flower St, Ste 3500, 90071-2418. SAN 371-6007. Tel: 213-972-4500. Reference Tel: 213-972-4657. FAX: 213-486-0065. Web Site: foley.com. *Dir*, Stefanie Frame; E-mail: sframe@foley.com; Staff 2 (MLS 1, Non-MLS 1)
Library Holdings: Bk Titles 800; Bk Vols 8,000; Per Subs 142
Subject Interests: Health law, Intellectual property, Litigation, Securities law
Automation Activity & Vendor Info: (Acquisitions) Inmagic, Inc.; (Cataloging) Inmagic, Inc.; (Circulation) Inmagic, Inc.; (OPAC) Inmagic, Inc.; (Serials) Inmagic, Inc.
Wireless access
Restriction: Staff use only

S GETTY RESEARCH INSTITUTE*, Research Library, 1200 Getty Center Dr, Ste 1100, 90049-1688. SAN 301-0325. Tel: 310-440-7390. Interlibrary Loan Service Tel: 310-440-7395. FAX: 310-440-7780. E-mail: reference@getty.edu. Web Site: www.getty.edu/research/library. *Assoc Dir*, Marcia Reed; E-mail: mreed@getty.edu; *Assoc Dir*, Kathleen Salomon; E-mail: ksalomon@getty.edu; Staff 120 (MLS 30, Non-MLS 90)
Founded 1983
Library Holdings: AV Mats 17,343; Microforms 10,725; Bk Titles 731,277; Bk Vols 1,006,148; Per Subs 2,981

Special Collections: Collecting, Display & Visual Resources for the Study of Art History; Historiography of Art; Modern Period
Subject Interests: Archaeology, Archit, Archives, Drawings, Manuscripts, Prints, Rare bks
Automation Activity & Vendor Info: (Acquisitions) Ex Libris Group; (Cataloging) Ex Libris Group; (Circulation) Ex Libris Group; (ILL) Ex Libris Group; (OPAC) Ex Libris Group; (Serials) Ex Libris Group
Wireless access
Function: Res libr
Publications: Getty Research Journal (Annual); Getty Thesaurus of Geographic Names (Online only); Getty Vocabularies: Art & Architecture (Online only); Issues & Debates Series; Text & Document Series; Union List of Artists Names (Online only)
Partic in Independent Res Libr Asn; OCLC Online Computer Library Center, Inc; OCLC Research Library Partnership; Statewide California Electronic Library Consortium
Open Mon-Fri 9:30-5

L GIBSON DUNN & CRUTCHER*, Law Library, 333 S Grand Ave, 90071-3197. SAN 300-9238. Tel: 213-229-7000. FAX: 213-229-7520. *Sr Res Libr Mgr,* Reed Nelson; E-mail: rnelson@gibsondunn.com; Staff 12 (MLS 6, Non-MLS 6)
Library Holdings: Bk Vols 50,000
Wireless access
Restriction: Private libr

M GOOD SAMARITAN HOSPITAL*, Medical Library, 637 S Lucas Ave, 90017. SAN 300-9300. Tel: 213-977-2047, 213-977-2323. FAX: 213-977-2325. E-mail: library@goodsam.org. Web Site: www.goodsam.org/Our-Services/Support-Services/Medical-Library. *Managing Dir,* Andrea Harrow; Staff 1 (MLS 1)
Founded 1941
Sept 2015-Aug 2016. Mats Exp $80,000, Other Print Mats $2,000, Electronic Ref Mat (Incl. Access Fees) $60,000. Sal Prof $70,000
Automation Activity & Vendor Info: (Serials) OVID Technologies
Wireless access
Partic in Basic Health Sciences Library Network; Medical Library Group of Southern California & Arizona; National Network of Libraries of Medicine Region 5; Southern Calif Electronic Libr Consortium
Open Mon-Fri 8:30-4:30
Restriction: Non-circulating to the pub

L GREENBERG GLUSKER LLP LIBRARY*, 1900 Avenue of the Stars, Ste 2100, 90067. SAN 300-9246. Tel: 310-553-3610. FAX: 310-201-1781. Web Site: www.greenbergglusker.com. *Dir, Libr & Res Serv,* Marjorie Jay; Tel: 310-785-6853, E-mail: MJay@ggfirm.com; Staff 1 (MLS 1)
Library Holdings: CDs 70; DVDs 5; Bk Titles 2,050; Bk Vols 14,290; Per Subs 275
Subject Interests: Law
Wireless access
Restriction: Not open to pub

S GRIFFITH OBSERVATORY LIBRARY*, 2800 E Observatory Rd, 90027. SAN 300-9254. Tel: 213-473-0800. FAX: 213-473-0816. Web Site: www.griffithobservatory.org. *Dir,* Dr Edwin C Krupp; E-mail: edwin.c.krupp@lacity.org
Founded 1935
Library Holdings: Bk Vols 10,130; Per Subs 20
Subject Interests: Astronomy
Publications: Griffith Observer
Restriction: Non-circulating to the pub

CR HEBREW UNION COLLEGE-JEWISH INSTITUTE OF RELIGION*, Frances-Henry Library, 3077 University Ave, 90007. SAN 300-9262. Tel: 213-765-2125. Toll Free Tel: 800-899-0925. FAX: 213-749-1937. Web Site: www.huc.edu/libraries/la. *Dir of Libr,* Yoram Bitton; E-mail: ybitton@huc.edu; *Libr Dir,* Sheryl F Stahl; E-mail: sstahl@huc.edu; *Asst Librn,* Taylor Dwyer; E-mail: tdwyer@huc.edu. Subject Specialists: *Bible, Hebrew, Judaica,* Sheryl F Stahl; *Judaica,* Taylor Dwyer; Staff 3 (MLS 2, Non-MLS 1)
Founded 1958. Enrl 300; Fac 30; Highest Degree: Doctorate
Library Holdings: Bks on Deafness & Sign Lang 25; Bk Vols 112,000; Per Subs 100
Special Collections: American Jewish Archives, West Coast Microfilm Branch; American Jewish Periodical Center, West Coast Microfilm Branch
Subject Interests: Art, Culture, Hist, Judaica (lit or hist of Jews), Music, Practice, Relig
Automation Activity & Vendor Info: (Cataloging) OCLC Worldshare Management Services; (Circulation) OCLC Worldshare Management Services; (Course Reserve) OCLC Worldshare Management Services; (Discovery) OCLC Worldshare Management Services; (ILL) OCLC WorldShare Interlibrary Loan; (OPAC) OCLC; (Serials) OCLC Worldshare Management Services
Wireless access
Function: 24/7 Electronic res, 24/7 Online cat, Electronic databases & coll, For res purposes, ILL available, Internet access, Mail loans to mem, Meeting rooms, Microfiche/film & reading machines, Music CDs, Online cat, Orientations, Photocopying/Printing, Ref & res, Ref serv available, Res assist avail, Res libr, Scanner, Spoken cassettes & CDs, Spoken cassettes & DVDs, Study rm, Telephone ref, Wheelchair accessible
Partic in Asn of Jewish Librs; Southern Calif Area Theol Librns Asn
Special Services for the Blind - Audio mat; Braille bks
Open Mon-Thurs 8:30-5, Fri 8:30-2:30
Restriction: Fee for pub use, Non-circulating of rare bks, Open to pub for ref & circ; with some limitations, Open to students, fac & staff, Open to students, fac, staff & alumni

L JONES DAY*, Law Library, 555 S Flower St, 50th Flr, 90071. SAN 329-9953. Tel: 213-489-3939. FAX: 213-243-2539. Web Site: www.jonesday.com. *Law Librn,* Patrick Sullivan; E-mail: psullivan@jonesday.com
Library Holdings: Bk Vols 3,000
Automation Activity & Vendor Info: (Acquisitions) Innovative Interfaces, Inc - Millennium; (Cataloging) Innovative Interfaces, Inc - Millennium; (Circulation) Innovative Interfaces, Inc - Millennium; (OPAC) Innovative Interfaces, Inc - Millennium; (Serials) Innovative Interfaces, Inc - Millennium
Wireless access
Open Mon-Fri 9-5:30

S C G JUNG INSTITUTE OF LOS ANGELES*, Max & Lore Zeller Library, 10349 W Pico Blvd, 90064. SAN 300-9378. Tel: 310-556-1193, Ext 229. FAX: 310-556-2290. E-mail: library@junginla.org. Web Site: www.junginla.org/words&images/zeller_library. *Librn,* Stephanie Dolph
Founded 1948
Library Holdings: Bk Vols 6,500; Per Subs 15
Special Collections: Analytical Psychology Club of Los Angeles, lectures 1944-76; ARAS (Archive for Research in Archetypal Symbolism), cat sheets, photog, slides
Subject Interests: Analytical psychol
Wireless access
Function: Ref serv available, Res libr, Spoken cassettes & CDs, Spoken cassettes & DVDs, Telephone ref, VHS videos
Restriction: Mem only
Friends of the Library Group

M KAISER-PERMANENTE MEDICAL CENTER*, Irving P Ackerman MD Health Sciences Library, 4733 Sunset Blvd, 1st Flr, 90027. SAN 300-9394. Tel: 323-783-8568. Administration Tel: 323-783-4687. FAX: 323-783-4192. *Mgr, Libr Serv,* Thomas E Shreves; E-mail: thomas.e.shreves@kp.org; Staff 5 (MLS 2, Non-MLS 3)
Founded 1953
Library Holdings: e-books 200; Bk Titles 1,200
Subject Interests: Clinical med, Nursing, Psychiat, Psychol
Open Mon-Fri 8-5

S KOREAN CULTURAL CENTER LIBRARY*, 5505 Wilshire Blvd, 90036. SAN 327-5795. Tel: 323-936-7141. FAX: 323-936-5712. E-mail: librarian@kccla.org. Web Site: library.kccla.org. *Librn,* Daniel Kim; Staff 2 (MLS 1, Non-MLS 1)
Founded 1980
Library Holdings: Bk Vols 25,000; Per Subs 52
Wireless access
Publications: Korean Culture (Quarterly)
Open Mon-Fri 9-5, Sat 10-1

S LA84 FOUNDATION*, Sports Library, 2141 W Adams Blvd, 90018. SAN 300-9076. Tel: 323-730-4646. FAX: 323-730-0546. E-mail: library@la84.org. Web Site: www.la84.org. *AV Coordr, Librn, Ref (Info Servs),* Michael W Salmon; E-mail: msalmon@la84.org; Staff 3.5 (MLS 3, Non-MLS 0.5)
Founded 1988
Library Holdings: Bk Titles 30,000; Bk Vols 35,000; Per Subs 350; Videos 5,000
Special Collections: Digital Archive; National Track & Field Research Coll; Olympic Games Coll; Ralph Miller Golf Coll; Sport Films; Sport Photographs
Subject Interests: Coaches educ, Olympic games, Sports
Automation Activity & Vendor Info: (Cataloging) EOS International; (Circulation) EOS International; (OPAC) EOS International; (Serials) EOS International
Function: Ref & res
Partic in OCLC Online Computer Library Center, Inc

L LEGAL AID FOUNDATION OF LOS ANGELES*, Law Library, 1550 W Eight St, 90017. SAN 372-2937, *Librn,* Andre E Caceres; Staff 1 (MLS 1)
Library Holdings: Bk Vols 1,100

Subject Interests: Consumer, Domestic violence, Employment, Evictions, Family law, Govt benefits, Housing, Human trafficking, Immigration
Function: Res libr
Restriction: Not open to pub

L LEWIS, BRISBOIS, BISGAARD & SMITH*, Law Library, 633 W Fifth St, Ste 4000, 90071. SAN 372-2708. Tel: 213-250-1800. FAX: 213-250-7900. Web Site: www.lewisbrisbois.com. *Dir,* Jill Robins; Staff 2 (MLS 1, Non-MLS 1)
Founded 1978
Library Holdings: Bk Titles 1,550
Subject Interests: Environ law
Wireless access
Restriction: Staff use only

J LOS ANGELES CITY COLLEGE LIBRARY*, Martin Luther King Jr Library, 855 N Vermont Ave, 90029. SAN 300-9491. Tel: 323-953-4000. Circulation Tel: 323-953-4000, Ext 2395. Reference Tel: 323-953-4000, Ext 2406. FAX: 323-953-4013. Web Site: lacitycollege.edu/Resources/Library/MLK-Library-Home. *Chair,* Barbara J Vasquez; Tel: 323-953-4000, Ext 2407, E-mail: vasquebj@lacitycollege.edu; *Acq, Cat, Ref,* Dorothy Fuhrmann; Tel: 323-953-4000, Ext 2401, E-mail: fuhrmadm@lacitycollege.edu; *Bibliog Instruction/Ref,* Katherine Coon Hamilton; Tel: 323-953-4000, Ext 1396, E-mail: hamiltke@lacitycollege.edu; *Bibliog Instruction/Ref,* Andy Mezynski; Tel: 323-953-4000, Ext 2403, E-mail: mezynsa@lacitycollege.edu; Staff 11 (MLS 4, Non-MLS 7)
Founded 1929. Enrl 16,268; Fac 1,212; Highest Degree: Associate
Library Holdings: Bk Titles 115,880; Bk Vols 146,900; Per Subs 85
Automation Activity & Vendor Info: (Acquisitions) Ex Libris Group; (Cataloging) Ex Libris Group; (Circulation) Ex Libris Group; (Course Reserve) Ex Libris Group; (Discovery) Ex Libris Group; (OPAC) Ex Libris Group; (Serials) Ex Libris Group
Wireless access
Partic in California Community College Library Consortium
Special Services for the Blind - Accessible computers; Closed circuit TV; Magnifiers; Screen enlargement software for people with visual disabilities; Screen reader software; ZoomText magnification & reading software
Restriction: Open to students, fac & staff, Photo ID required for access

L LOS ANGELES COUNTY COUNSEL LAW LIBRARY*, Kenneth Hahn Hall of Administration, 500 W Temple St, 90012. SAN 372-3704. Tel: 213-974-1982. FAX: 213-626-7446. Web Site: counsel.lacounty.gov. *Librn,* Karen Sanchez; E-mail: ksanchez@counsel.lacounty.gov
Library Holdings: Bk Vols 15,000
Automation Activity & Vendor Info: (Cataloging) Inmagic, Inc.
Restriction: Staff use only

L LOS ANGELES COUNTY LAW LIBRARY*, Mildred L Lillie Bldg, 301 W First St, 90012-3100. SAN 332-334X. Tel: 213-785-2529. Reference Tel: 213-785-2513. FAX: 213-613-1329. Web Site: www.lalawlibrary.org. *Exec Dir,* Sandra J Levin; *Chief Tech Officer, Sr Dir,* Jaye Steinbrick; *Dir, Coll Mgt,* Meilling Li; *Circ, Sr Librn,* Linda J Heichman; *Res & Ref Serv, Sr Librn,* Austin Toub; Staff 66 (MLS 12, Non-MLS 54)
Founded 1891
Library Holdings: Bk Titles 189,150; Bk Vols 992,060; Per Subs 11,876
Special Collections: State Document Depository; US Document Depository
Subject Interests: Comparative law, Fed law, Foreign law, Intl law, State law
Automation Activity & Vendor Info: (Cataloging) Ex Libris Group; (Circulation) Ex Libris Group; (OPAC) Ex Libris Group; (Serials) Ex Libris Group
Wireless access
Open Mon, Wed, Thurs & Fri 8:30-6, Tues 8:30-8, Sat 9-5
Friends of the Library Group
Branches:
LONG BEACH, Governor George Deukmejian Courthouse, 3rd Flr, 275 Magnolia Ave, Long Beach, 90802, SAN 332-3439. Tel: 562-508-4882. *Br Asst,* Position Currently Open
Subject Interests: Fed law, State law
Open Mon-Fri 8:30-4:30
Friends of the Library Group
NORWALK, SE Superior Courts Bldg, Rm 714, 12720 Norwalk Blvd, Norwalk, 90650, SAN 332-3463. Tel: 562-807-7310. FAX: 562-868-8936.
Subject Interests: Fed law, State law
Open Mon-Fri 8:30-4:30
Friends of the Library Group
SANTA MONICA, County Bldg, 1725 Main St, Rm 219, Santa Monica, 90401, SAN 332-3552. Tel: 310-260-3644. FAX: 310-917-9230.
Subject Interests: Fed law, State law
Open Mon-Fri 8:30-1:30
Friends of the Library Group
TORRANCE, Torrance Superior Court, Rm 110, 825 Maple Ave, Torrance, 90503, SAN 332-3587. Tel: 424-201-0748.
Subject Interests: Fed law, State law
Open Mon-Fri 8:30-4:30
Friends of the Library Group

G LOS ANGELES COUNTY METROPOLITAN TRANSPORTATION AUTHORITY*, Dorothy Peyton Gray Transportation Library & Archive, One Gateway Plaza, 15th Flr, Mail Stop 99-15-1, 90012-2952. SAN 325-4933. Tel: 213-922-4859. E-mail: library@metro.net. Web Site: www.metro.net/about/metrolibrary. *Dir, Libr Serv, Dir, Rec Mgt,* Matthew Barrett; E-mail: barrettm@metro.net; Staff 2 (MLS 2)
Founded 1971
Library Holdings: CDs 300; Bk Titles 48,000; Bk Vols 200,000; Per Subs 165; Videos 1,000
Special Collections: Deeds; Local Transit; Photographs 1871 to present; Urban Transportation & Urban Planning
Subject Interests: Transportation
Automation Activity & Vendor Info: (Circulation) CyberTools for Libraries; (ILL) OCLC; (OPAC) CyberTools for Libraries; (Serials) EBSCO Online
Wireless access
Function: ILL available
Publications: Acquisitions List
Partic in OCLC Online Computer Library Center, Inc
Special Services for the Deaf - TDD equip
Open Mon & Thurs 9-4
Restriction: Circ limited, Employees & their associates, In-house use for visitors

S LOS ANGELES COUNTY MUSEUM OF ART*, Mr & Mrs Allan C Balch Art Research Library, 5905 Wilshire Blvd, 90036-4597. SAN 332-3641. Tel: 323-857-6118. FAX: 323-857-4790. E-mail: library@lacma.org. Web Site: www.lacma.org. *Head Librn,* Alexis Curry; Tel: 323-857-6122, E-mail: acurry@lacma.org; *Sr Librn,* Pauline Wolstencroft; Tel: 323-857-6121, E-mail: pwolsten@lacma.org; *Ser & Electronic Res Librn,* Douglas Cordell; Tel: 323-857-6531, E-mail: dcordell@lacma.org; *Archivist,* Jessica Gambling; E-mail: jgambling@lacma.org; Staff 8 (MLS 4, Non-MLS 4)
Founded 1965
Library Holdings: Bk Titles 175,000; Bk Vols 176,000; Per Subs 400
Special Collections: Costume & Textiles Rare Books (Doris Stearns Coll); Rifkind Center for German Expressionist Studies (Library & Print Coll)
Subject Interests: Art hist
Automation Activity & Vendor Info: (Acquisitions) OCLC; (Cataloging) OCLC; (Circulation) OCLC; (OPAC) OCLC; (Serials) OCLC
Function: For res purposes, ILL available, Photocopying/Printing, Ref serv available, Res libr, Telephone ref, Wheelchair accessible
Partic in OCLC Online Computer Library Center, Inc; Statewide California Electronic Library Consortium
Restriction: Circulates for staff only, In-house use for visitors, Open to pub by appt only
Friends of the Library Group
Branches:
ROBERT GORE RIFKIND CENTER FOR GERMAN EXPRESSIONIST STUDIES, 5905 Wilshire Blvd, 90036, SAN 320-3646. Tel: 323-857-4752, 323-857-6165. FAX: 323-857-4790. E-mail: library@lacma.org. *Librn,* Julia Kim; E-mail: jkim@lacma.org
Founded 1979
Library Holdings: Bk Titles 6,000; Bk Vols 6,500
Special Collections: German Expressionist Graphics Coll
Publications: Bibliography of German Expressionism: Catalog of the Robert Gore Rifkind Center for German Expressionist Studies at the Los Angeles County Museum of Art (G K Hall, 1990)
Restriction: Open by appt only
Friends of the Library Group

M LOS ANGELES COUNTY-UNIVERSITY OF SOUTHERN CALIFORNIA MEDICAL CENTER*, Medical Library, Medical Center, Inpatient Tower -3K111, 2053 Marengo St, 90033. SAN 332-7000. Tel: 323-409-7006. FAX: 323-441-8291. E-mail: iptmedicallibrary@dhs.lacounty.gov. Web Site: libraries.usc.edu/locations/wilson-dental-library/affiliated-libraries. *Med Librn,* Bella Kwong; E-mail: bkwong@dhs.lacounty.gov; Staff 3.5 (MLS 1, Non-MLS 2.5)
Library Holdings: e-journals 350; Bk Vols 6,300; Per Subs 80
Subject Interests: Clinical med
Open Mon-Fri 8:30-6

P LOS ANGELES PUBLIC LIBRARY SYSTEM*, Central Library, 630 W Fifth St, 90071. SAN 332-7124. Tel: 213-228-7000. FAX: 213-228-7069. Web Site: www.lapl.org. *City Librn,* John F Szabo; Tel: 213-228-7515, E-mail: jszabo@lapl.org; *Asst City Librn,* Susan Broman; Tel: 213-228-7461, E-mail: sbroman@lapl.org; *Dir, Br,* Chad Helton; Tel:

213-228-7570, E-mail: chelton@lapl.org; *Dir, Libr Serv,* Kren Malone; Tel: 213-228-7470, E-mail: kmalone@lapl.org; *Dir, Pub Relations,* Peter Persic; Tel: 213-228-7556, E-mail: ppersic@lapl.org; *Dir, Engagement & Learning,* Eva Mitnick; Tel: 213-228-7527, E-mail: emitnick@lapl.org; *Colls Serv Mgr,* Peggy Murphy; Tel: 213-228-7191, E-mail: pmurphy@lapl.org; Staff 443.5 (MLS 443.5)
Founded 1872. Pop 4,390,379; Circ 15,574,773
Library Holdings: Bk Vols 6,433,567
Special Collections: Automotive Repair Manuals; California History Coll; California in Fiction; Catholicism of Early Spanish Southwest; Children's Literature Coll; Cookery; Corporation Records; Dobinson Coll of Drama & Theatre, bks, programs; Fiction by & about Blacks; Film Study; Genealogy Coll; Government Specifications & Standards; Japanese Prints; Language Study; Large Type Books; Menus Coll; Orchestral Scores & Parts; Rare Books Coll; United States Patents. State Document Depository; UN Document Depository; US Document Depository
Wireless access
Partic in OCLC Online Computer Library Center, Inc; Southern California Library Cooperative
Special Services for the Deaf - Staff with knowledge of sign lang; TDD equip
Open Mon-Thurs 10-8, Fri & Sat 9:30-5:30, Sun 1-5
Friends of the Library Group

Branches: 72

ANGELES MESA BRANCH LIBRARY, 2700 W 52nd St, 90043-1953, SAN 332-7272. Tel: 323-292-4328. FAX: 323-296-3508. Web Site: www.lapl.org/branches/angeles-mesa. *Sr Librn,* Matthew Rodriguez
Library Holdings: Bk Vols 27,511
Open Mon & Wed 10-8, Tues & Thurs 12-8, Fri & Sat 9:30-5:30
Friends of the Library Group

ARROYO SECO REGIONAL LIBRARY, 6145 N Figueroa St, 90042-3565, SAN 332-7302. Tel: 323-255-0537. FAX: 323-255-1710. Web Site: www.lapl.org/branches/arroyo-seco. *Sr Librn,* Dora Suarez
Library Holdings: Bk Vols 46,758
Open Mon-Thurs 10-8, Fri & Sat 9:30-5:30, Sun 1-5

ASCOT BRANCH LIBRARY, 120 W Florence Ave, 90003, SAN 332-7337. Tel: 323-759-4817. FAX: 323-758-6578. Web Site: www.lapl.org/branches/ascot. *Sr Librn,* Frances Jaffe
Library Holdings: Bk Vols 34,751
Open Mon & Wed 10-8, Tues & Thurs 12-8, Fri & Sat 9:30-5:30

ATWATER VILLAGE BRANCH LIBRARY, 3379 Glendale Blvd, 90039-1825, SAN 332-7361. Tel: 323-664-1353. FAX: 323-913-4765. Web Site: www.lapl.org/branches/atwater-village. *Sr Librn,* Stella Nahapetian
Library Holdings: Bk Vols 37,343
Open Mon & Wed 10-8, Tues & Thurs 12-8, Fri & Sat 9:30-5:30
Friends of the Library Group

BALDWIN HILLS BRANCH LIBRARY, 2906 S La Brea Ave, 90016-3902, SAN 332-7396. Tel: 323-733-1196. FAX: 323 733-0774. Web Site: www.lapl.org/branches/baldwin-hills. *Sr Librn,* Sada Mozer
Library Holdings: Bk Vols 46,297
Open Mon & Wed 10-8, Tues & Thurs 12-8, Fri & Sat 9:30-5:30

BENJAMIN FRANKLIN BRANCH LIBRARY, 2200 E First St, 90033, SAN 332-7426. Tel: 323-263-6901. FAX: 323-526-3043. Web Site: www.lapl.org/branches/benjamin-franklin. *Sr Librn,* Connie Topete; Staff 9 (MLS 4, Non-MLS 5)
Founded 1916
Library Holdings: Bk Vols 39,246
Open Mon & Wed 10-8, Tues & Thurs 12-8, Fri & Sat 9:30-5:30
Friends of the Library Group

CAHUENGA BRANCH LIBRARY, 4591 Santa Monica Blvd, 90029-1937, SAN 332-7485. Tel: 323-664-6418. FAX: 323-664-6200. Web Site: www.lapl.org/branches/cahuenga. *Sr Librn,* Hillary St George
Library Holdings: Bk Vols 34,203
Open Mon & Wed 10-8, Tues & Thurs 12-8, Fri & Sat 9:30-5:30
Friends of the Library Group

CANOGA PARK BRANCH LIBRARY, 20939 Sherman Way, Canoga Park, 91303, SAN 332-7515. Tel: 818-887-0320. FAX: 818-346-1074. Web Site: www.lapl.org/branches/canoga-park. *Sr Librn,* Holly Rutan
Library Holdings: Bk Vols 61,866
Open Mon & Wed 10-8, Tues & Thurs 12-8, Fri & Sat 9:30-5:30
Friends of the Library Group

CHATSWORTH BRANCH LIBRARY, 21052 Devonshire St, Chatsworth, 91311, SAN 332-754X. Tel: 818-341-4276. FAX: 818-341-7905. Web Site: www.lapl.org/branches/chatsworth. *Sr Librn,* Janet Metzler
Library Holdings: Bk Vols 50,382
Open Mon & Wed 10-8, Tues & Thurs 12-8, Fri & Sat 9:30-5:30
Friends of the Library Group

CHINATOWN BRANCH LIBRARY, 639 N Hill St, 90012-2317, SAN 332-7574. Tel: 213-620-0925. FAX: 213-620-9956. Web Site: www.lapl.org/branches/chinatown. *Sr Librn,* Shan Liang
Library Holdings: Bk Vols 69,165
Open Mon & Wed 10-8, Tues & Thurs 12-8, Fri & Sat 9:30-5:30

CYPRESS PARK BRANCH LIBRARY, 1150 Cypress Ave, 90065-1144, SAN 332-7604. Tel: 323-224-0039. FAX: 323-224-0454. Web Site: www.lapl.org/branches/cypress-park. *Sr Librn,* Patrick Xavier
Library Holdings: Bk Vols 36,013
Open Mon & Wed 10-8, Tues & Thurs 12-8, Fri & Sat 9:30-5:30
Friends of the Library Group

WILL & ARIEL DURANT BRANCH LIBRARY, 7140 W Sunset Blvd, 90046, SAN 332-8899. Tel: 323-876-2741. FAX: 323-876-0485. Web Site: www.lapl.org/branches/durant. *Sr Librn,* John Frank
Library Holdings: Bk Vols 55,475
Open Mon & Wed 10-8, Tues & Thurs 12-8, Fri & Sat 9:30-5:30
Friends of the Library Group

EAGLE ROCK BRANCH LIBRARY, 5027 Caspar Ave, 90041-1901, SAN 332-7639. Tel: 323-258-8078. FAX: 323-478-9530. Web Site: www.lapl.org/branches/eagle-rock. *Sr Librn,* Sonja Hannah
Library Holdings: Bk Vols 52,160
Open Mon & Wed 10-8, Tues & Thurs 12-8, Fri & Sat 9:30-5:30
Friends of the Library Group

ECHO PARK BRANCH LIBRARY, 1410 W Temple St, 90026-5605, SAN 332-7663. Tel: 213-250-7808. FAX: 213-580-3744. Web Site: www.lapl.org/branches/echo-park. *Sr Librn,* Victoria Sikora
Library Holdings: Bk Vols 45,414
Open Mon & Wed 10-8, Tues & Thurs 12-8, Fri & Sat 9:30-5:30
Friends of the Library Group

EDENDALE BRANCH LIBRARY, 2011 W Sunset Blvd, 90026. Tel: 213-207-3000. FAX: 213-207-3097. Web Site: www.lapl.org/branches/edendale. *Sr Librn,* Niels Bartels
Open Mon & Wed 10-8, Tues & Thurs 12-8, Fri & Sat 9:30-5:30
Friends of the Library Group

EL SERENO BRANCH LIBRARY, 5226 S Huntington Dr, 90032, SAN 332-7698. Tel: 323-225-9201. FAX: 323-441-0112. Web Site: www.lapl.org/branches/el-sereno. *Sr Librn,* Eugene Estrada
Library Holdings: Bk Vols 56,742
Open Mon & Wed 10-8, Tues & Thurs 12-8, Fri & Sat 9:30-5:30

ENCINO-TARZANA BRANCH LIBRARY, 18231 Ventura Blvd, Tarzana, 91356-3620, SAN 332-7728. Tel: 818-343-1983. FAX: 818-343-7867. Web Site: www.lapl.org/branches/encino-tarzana. *Sr Librn,* Lawrence Nash
Library Holdings: Bk Vols 62,724
Open Mon & Wed 10-8, Tues & Thurs 12-8, Fri & Sat 9:30-5:30
Friends of the Library Group

EXPOSITION PARK - DR MARY MCLEOD BETHUNE REGIONAL LIBRARY, 3900 S Western Ave, 90062, SAN 332-7752. Tel: 323-290-3113. FAX: 323-290-3153. Web Site: www.lapl.org/branches/exposition-park. *Sr Librn,* Alberto Alvarez
Library Holdings: Bk Vols 44,556
Open Mon-Thurs 10-8, Fri & Sat 9:30-5:30, Sun 1-5
Friends of the Library Group

FAIRFAX BRANCH LIBRARY, 161 S Gardner St, 90036-2717, SAN 332-7787. Tel: 323-936-6191. FAX: 323-934-2675. Web Site: www.lapl.org/branches/fairfax. *Actg Sr Librn,* Jennifer Hamm
Library Holdings: Bk Vols 50,379
Open Mon & Wed 10-8, Tues & Thurs 12-8, Fri & Sat 9:30-5:30
Friends of the Library Group

FELIPE DE NEVE BRANCH LIBRARY, 2820 W Sixth St, 90057-3114, SAN 332-7817. Tel: 213-384-7676. FAX: 213-368-7667. Web Site: www.lapl.org/branches/felipe-de-neve. *Sr Librn,* Cathie Ehle
Library Holdings: Bk Vols 34,122
Open Mon & Wed 10-8, Tues & Thurs 12-8, Fri & Sat 9:30-5:30

JOHN C FREMONT BRANCH LIBRARY, 6121 Melrose Ave, 90038-3501, SAN 332-7841. Tel: 323-962-3521. FAX: 323-962-4553. Web Site: www.lapl.org/branches/john-c-fremont. *Sr Librn,* Annie Cipolla; Staff 10 (MLS 4, Non-MLS 6)
Library Holdings: Bk Vols 38,847
Open Mon & Wed 10-8, Tues & Thurs 12-8, Fri & Sat 9:30-5:30
Friends of the Library Group

FRANCES HOWARD GOLDWYN-HOLLYWOOD REGIONAL LIBRARY, 1623 Ivar Ave, 90028-6304, SAN 332-7906. Tel: 323-856-8260. FAX: 323-467-5707. Web Site: www.lapl.org/branches/hollywood. *Sr Librn,* Jeff Sargeant
Library Holdings: Bk Vols 87,279
Subject Interests: Motion pictures
Open Mon-Thurs 10-8, Fri & Sat 9:30-5:30, Sun 1-5

GRANADA HILLS BRANCH LIBRARY, 10640 Petit Ave, Granada Hills, 91344-6452, SAN 332-7876. Tel: 818-368-5687. FAX: 818-756-9286. Web Site: www.lapl.org/branches/granada-hills. *Sr Librn,* Pamela Rhodes
Library Holdings: Bk Vols 63,670
Open Mon & Wed 10-8, Tues & Thurs 12-8, Fri & Sat 9:30-5:30
Friends of the Library Group

HARBOR CITY-HARBOR GATEWAY BRANCH LIBRARY, 24000 S Western Ave, 90710, SAN 377-6492. Tel: 310-534-9520. FAX: 310-534-9532. Web Site: www.lapl.org/branches/harbor-city-harbor-gateway. *Sr Librn,* John Pham
Library Holdings: Bk Vols 50,882

Open Mon & Wed 10-8, Tues & Thurs 12-8, Fri & Sat 9:30-5:30
Friends of the Library Group
HYDE PARK MIRIAM MATTHEWS BRANCH LIBRARY, 2205 W Florence Ave, 90043, SAN 332-7930. Tel: 323-750-7241. Web Site: www.lapl.org/branches/hyde-park. *Sr Librn,* Justin Sugiyama
Library Holdings: Bk Vols 32,880
Open Mon & Wed 10-8, Tues & Thurs 12-8, Fri & Sat 9:30-5:30
Friends of the Library Group
JEFFERSON-VASSIE D WRIGHT MEMORIAL BRANCH LIBRARY, 2211 W Jefferson Blvd, 90018-3741, SAN 332-799X. Tel: 323-734-8573. FAX: 323-737-2885. Web Site: www.lapl.org/branches/jefferson. *Sr Librn,* Karla Valdez
Library Holdings: Bk Vols 29,369
Open Mon & Wed 10-8, Tues & Thurs 12-8, Fri & Sat 9:30-5:30
Friends of the Library Group
JUNIPERO SERRA BRANCH LIBRARY, 4607 S Main St, 90037-2735, SAN 332-8023. Tel: 323-234-1685. FAX: 323-846-5389. Web Site: www.lapl.org/branches/junipero-serra. *Sr Librn,* Celia Avila
Library Holdings: Bk Vols 42,901
Open Mon & Wed 10-8, Tues & Thurs 12-8, Fri & Sat 9:30-5:30
DONALD BRUCE KAUFMAN-BRENTWOOD BRANCH LIBRARY, 11820 San Vicente Blvd, 90049-5002, SAN 332-7450. Tel: 310-575-8273. FAX: 310-575-8276. Web Site: www.lapl.org/branches/brentwood. *Sr Librn,* Henry Gambill
Library Holdings: Bk Vols 44,357
Open Mon & Wed 10-8, Tues & Thurs 12-8, Fri & Sat 9:30-5:30
Friends of the Library Group
LAKE VIEW TERRACE BRANCH LIBRARY, 12002 Osborne St, 91342, SAN 332-8112. Tel: 818-890-7404. FAX: 818-897-2738. Web Site: www.lapl.org/branches/lake-view-terrace. *Sr Librn,* Constance Dosch
Library Holdings: Bk Vols 53,032
Open Mon & Wed 10-8, Tues & Thurs 12-8, Fri & Sat 9:30-5:30
LINCOLN HEIGHTS BRANCH LIBRARY, 2530 Workman St, 90031-2322, SAN 332-8058. Tel: 323-226-1692. FAX: 323-226-1691. Web Site: www.lapl.org/branches/lincoln-heights. *Sr Librn,* Steven Cheng
Library Holdings: Bk Vols 37,273
Open Mon & Wed 10-8, Tues & Thurs 12-8, Fri & Sat 9:30-5:30
LITTLE TOKYO BRANCH LIBRARY, 203 S Los Angeles St, 90012, SAN 329-658X. Tel: 213-612-0525. FAX: 213-612-0424. Web Site: www.lapl.org/branches/little-tokyo. *Sr Librn,* James Sherod
Library Holdings: Bk Vols 67,900
Open Mon & Wed 10-8, Tues & Thurs 12-8, Fri & Sat 9:30-5:30
Friends of the Library Group
LOS FELIZ BRANCH LIBRARY, 1874 Hillhurst Ave, 90027-4427, SAN 332-8082. Tel: 323-913-4710. FAX: 323-913-4714. Web Site: www.lapl.org/branches/los-feliz. *Sr Librn,* Pearl Yonezawa
Library Holdings: Bk Vols 54,325
Open Mon & Wed 10-8, Tues & Thurs 12-8, Fri & Sat 9:30-5:30
Friends of the Library Group
MALABAR BRANCH LIBRARY, 2801 Wabash Ave, 90033-2604, SAN 332-8147. Tel: 323-263-1497. FAX: 323-612-0416. Web Site: www.lapl.org/branches/malabar. *Sr Librn,* Yan Wen
Library Holdings: Bk Vols 34,328
Open Mon & Wed 10-8, Tues & Thurs 12-8, Fri & Sat 9:30-5:30
Friends of the Library Group
MAR VISTA BRANCH LIBRARY, 12006 Venice Blvd, 90066-3810, SAN 332-8171. Tel: 310-390-3454. FAX: 310-391-0531. Web Site: www.lapl.org/branches/mar-vista. *Sr Librn,* Carole Kealoha
Library Holdings: Bk Vols 44,910
Open Mon & Wed 10-8, Tues & Thurs 12-8, Fri & Sat 9:30-5:30
Friends of the Library Group
MEMORIAL BRANCH LIBRARY, 4625 W Olympic Blvd, 90019-1832, SAN 332-8201. Tel: 323-938-2732. FAX: 323-938-3378. Web Site: www.lapl.org/branches/memorial. *Sr Librn,* Jane Dobija
Library Holdings: Bk Vols 38,116
Open Mon & Wed 10-8, Tues & Thurs 12-8, Fri & Sat 9:30-5:30
Friends of the Library Group
MID-VALLEY REGIONAL LIBRARY, 16244 Nordhoff St, North Hills, 91343, SAN 377-6476. Tel: 818-895-3650. FAX: 818-895-3657. Web Site: www.lapl.org/branches/mid-valley. *Sr Librn,* Victoria Magaw
Library Holdings: Bk Vols 133,455
Open Mon-Thurs 10-8, Fri & Sat 9:30-5:30, Sun 1-5
Friends of the Library Group
JOHN MUIR BRANCH LIBRARY, 1005 W 64th St, 90044-3605, SAN 332-8236. Tel: 323-789-4800. FAX: 323-789-5758. Web Site: www.lapl.org/branches/john-muir. *Actg Sr Librn,* Kristy Moldrem
Library Holdings: Bk Vols 27,329
Open Mon & Wed 10-8, Tues & Thurs 12-8, Fri & Sat 9:30-5:30
Friends of the Library Group
NORTH HOLLYWOOD AMELIA EARHART REGIONAL LIBRARY, 5211 Tujunga Ave, 91601, SAN 332-7159. Tel: 818-766-7185. FAX: 818-755-7671. Web Site: www.lapl.org/branches/north-hollywood. *Sr Librn,* Ann Bowman
Library Holdings: Bk Vols 51,036
Open Mon-Thurs 10-8, Fri & Sat 9:30-5:30, Sun 1-5
Friends of the Library Group
NORTHRIDGE BRANCH LIBRARY, 9051 Darby Ave, Northridge, 91325-2743, SAN 332-8295. Tel: 818-886-3640. FAX: 818-886-6850. Web Site: www.lapl.org/branches/northridge. *Sr Librn,* Mandy Nasr
Library Holdings: Bk Vols 61,323
Open Mon & Wed 10-8, Tues & Thurs 12-8, Fri & Sat 9:30-5:30
Friends of the Library Group
PACOIMA BRANCH LIBRARY, 13605 Van Nuys Blvd, Pacoima, 91331-3613, SAN 332-8325. Tel: 818-899-5203. FAX: 818-899-5336. Web Site: www.lapl.org/branches/pacoima. *Sr Librn,* Laura Contin
Library Holdings: Bk Vols 51,293
Open Mon & Wed 10-8, Tues & Thurs 12-8, Fri & Sat 9:30-5:30
Friends of the Library Group
PALISADES BRANCH LIBRARY, 861 Alma Real Dr, Pacific Palisades, 90272-3730, SAN 332-835X. Tel: 310-459-2754. FAX: 310-454-3198. Web Site: www.lapl.org/branches/palisades. *Sr Librn,* Mary Hopf
Library Holdings: Bk Vols 44,984
Open Mon & Wed 10-8, Tues & Thurs 12-8, Fri & Sat 9:30-5:30
Friends of the Library Group
PALMS-RANCHO PARK BRANCH LIBRARY, 2920 Overland Ave, 90064-4220, SAN 332-8384. Tel: 310-840-2142. Web Site: belleplaine.scklslibrary.info, www.bpks.org/library. *Sr Librn,* Rachel Bindman
Library Holdings: Bk Vols 50,853
Open Mon & Wed 10-8, Tues & Thurs 12-8, Fri & Sat 9:30-5:30
Friends of the Library Group
PANORAMA CITY BRANCH LIBRARY, 14345 Roscoe Blvd, Panorama City, 91402-4222, SAN 332-8414. Tel: 818-894-4071. FAX: 818-895-6482. Web Site: www.lapl.org/branches/panorama-city. *Sr Librn,* Roman Antonio
Library Holdings: Bk Vols 46,076
Open Mon & Wed 10-8, Tues & Thurs 12-8, Fri & Sat 9:30-5:30
Friends of the Library Group
PICO UNION BRANCH LIBRARY, 1030 S Alvarado St, 90006. Tel: 213-368-7545. FAX: 213-368-7543. Web Site: www.lapl.org/branches/pico-union. *Actg Sr Librn,* Kim Hughes
Open Mon & Wed 10-8, Tues & Thurs 12-8, Fri & Sat 9:30-5:30
PIO PICO-KOREATOWN BRANCH LIBRARY, 694 S Oxford Ave, 90005-2872, SAN 332-8449. Tel: 213-368-7647. FAX: 213-639-1653. Web Site: www.lapl.org/branches/pio-pico. *Sr Librn,* Beth Feinberg
Library Holdings: Bk Vols 88,184
Open Mon & Wed 10-8, Tues & Thurs 12-8, Fri & Sat 9:30-5:30
Friends of the Library Group
PLATT BRANCH LIBRARY, 23600 Victory Blvd, Woodland Hills, 91367, SAN 377-0117. Tel: 818-340-9386. FAX: 818-340-9645. Web Site: www.lapl.org/branches/platt. *Sr Librn,* David Hagopian
Library Holdings: Bk Vols 61,612
Open Mon & Wed 10-8, Tues & Thurs 12-8, Fri & Sat 9:30-5:30
Friends of the Library Group
PLAYA VISTA BRANCH LIBRARY, 6400 Playa Vista Dr, 90094. Tel: 310-437-6680. FAX: 310-437-6690. Web Site: www.lapl.org/branches/playa-vista. *Actg Sr Librn,* Hillary Perelyubskiy
Open Mon & Wed 10-8, Tues & Thurs 12-8, Fri & Sat 9:30-5:30
Friends of the Library Group
PORTER RANCH BRANCH LIBRARY, 11371 Tampa Ave, Porter Ranch, 91326, SAN 377-0095. Tel: 818-360-5706. FAX: 818-360-3106. Web Site: www.lapl.org/branches/porter-ranch. *Sr Librn,* Shayeri Tangri
Library Holdings: Bk Vols 58,427
Open Mon & Wed 10-8, Tues & Thurs 12-8, Fri & Sat 9:30-5:30
Friends of the Library Group
ROBERTSON BRANCH LIBRARY, 1719 S Robertson Blvd, 90035-4315, SAN 332-8473. Tel: 310-840-2147. FAX: 310-840-2156. Web Site: www.lapl.org/branches/robertson. *Sr Librn,* Laura Barnes
Library Holdings: Bk Vols 39,584
Open Mon & Wed 10-8, Tues & Thurs 12-8, Fri 9:30-5:30, Sun 1-5
Friends of the Library Group
SAN PEDRO REGIONAL LIBRARY, 931 S Gaffey St, San Pedro, 90731-3606, SAN 332-8503. Tel: 310-548-7779. FAX: 310-548-7453. Web Site: www.lapl.org/branches/san-pedro. *Sr Librn,* David Ellis
Library Holdings: Bk Vols 71,553
Open Mon-Thurs 10-8, Fri & Sat 9:30-5:30, Sun 1-5
Friends of the Library Group
SHERMAN OAKS MARTIN POLLARD BRANCH LIBRARY, 14245 Moorpark St, Sherman Oaks, 91423-2722, SAN 332-8538. Tel: 818-205-9716. FAX: 818-205-9866. Web Site: www.lapl.org/branches/sherman-oaks. *Actg Sr Librn,* Meredith McGowan
Library Holdings: Bk Vols 62,855
Open Mon & Wed 10-8, Tues & Thurs 12-8, Fri & Sat 9:30-5:30
SILVER LAKE BRANCH LIBRARY, 2411 Glendale Blvd, 90039. Tel: 323-913-7451. FAX: 323-913-7460. Web Site: www.lapl.org/branches/silver-lake. *Sr Librn,* Lisa Palombi
Open Mon & Wed 10-8, Tues & Thurs 12-8, Fri & Sat 9:30-5:30
Friends of the Library Group

ROBERT LOUIS STEVENSON BRANCH LIBRARY, 803 Spence St, 90023-1727, SAN 332-8562. Tel: 323-268-4710. FAX: 213-268-7622. Web Site: www.lapl.org/branches/robert-louis-stevenson. *Sr Librn,* Lupita Leyva
Library Holdings: Bk Vols 31,341
Open Mon & Wed 10-8, Tues & Thurs 12-8, Fri & Sat 9:30-5:30
Friends of the Library Group

STUDIO CITY BRANCH LIBRARY, 12511 Moorpark St, Studio City, 91604-1372, SAN 332-8597. Tel: 818-755-7873. FAX: 818-755-7878. Web Site: www.lapl.org/branches/studio-city. *Sr Librn,* Veronica Majd
Library Holdings: Bk Vols 60,988
Open Mon & Wed 10-8, Tues & Thurs 12-8, Fri & Sat 9:30-5:30
Friends of the Library Group

SUN VALLEY BRANCH LIBRARY, 7935 Vineland Ave, Sun Valley, 91352-4477, SAN 332-8627. Tel: 818-764-1338. FAX: 818-764-2245. Web Site: www.lapl.org/branches/sun-valley. *Sr Librn,* Christopher Barreiro
Library Holdings: Bk Vols 47,183
Open Mon & Wed 10-8, Tues & Thurs 12-8, Fri & Sat 9:30-5:30

SUNLAND-TUJUNGA BRANCH LIBRARY, 7771 Foothill Blvd, Tujunga, 91042-2137, SAN 332-8651. Tel: 818-352-4481. FAX: 818-352-2501. Web Site: www.lapl.org/branches/sunland-tujunga. *Sr Librn,* Ardem Tajerian
Library Holdings: Bk Vols 47,281
Open Mon & Wed 10-8, Tues & Thurs 12-8, Fri & Sat 9:30-5:30
Friends of the Library Group

SYLMAR BRANCH LIBRARY, 14561 Polk St, Sylmar, 91342-4055, SAN 332-8686. Tel: 818-367-6102. FAX: 818-367-5872. Web Site: www.lapl.org/branches/sylmar. *Sr Librn,* Chukwuji Onianwa
Library Holdings: Bk Vols 47,162
Open Mon & Wed 10-8, Tues & Thurs 12-8, Fri & Sat 9:30-5:30

MARK TWAIN BRANCH LIBRARY, 9621 S Figueroa St, 90003, SAN 332-8716. Tel: 323-755-4088. FAX: 323-755-3185. Web Site: www.lapl.org/branches/mark-twain. *Sr Librn,* Senele Rios; Staff 8 (MLS 2, Non-MLS 6)
Library Holdings: Bk Vols 41,888
Open Mon & Wed 10-8, Tues & Thurs 12-8, Fri & Sat 9:30-5:30
Friends of the Library Group

VALLEY PLAZA BRANCH LIBRARY, 12311 Vanowen St, North Hollywood, 91605, SAN 332-9100. Tel: 818-765-9251. FAX: 818-765-9260. Web Site: www.lapl.org/branches/valley-plaza. *Sr Librn,* Patricia Rostomian
Library Holdings: Bk Vols 45,937
Open Mon & Wed 10-8, Tues & Thurs 12-8, Fri & Sat 9:30-5:30
Friends of the Library Group

VAN NUYS BRANCH LIBRARY, 6250 Sylmar Ave, Van Nuys, 91401, SAN 332-8740. Tel: 818-756-8453. Web Site: www.lapl.org/branches/van-nuys.
Library Holdings: Bk Vols 63,478
Closed for renovations until Summer of 2020
Friends of the Library Group

VENICE-ABBOT KINNEY MEMORIAL BRANCH LIBRARY, 501 S Venice Blvd, Venice, 90291-4201, SAN 332-9070. Tel: 310-821-1769. Web Site: www.lapl.org/branches/venice. *Actg Sr Librn,* Ramin Naderi
Library Holdings: Bk Vols 47,358
Open Mon & Wed 10-8, Tues & Thurs 12-8, Fri & Sat 9:30-5:30

VERMONT SQUARE BRANCH LIBRARY, 1201 W 48th St, 90037-2838, SAN 332-8864. Tel: 323-290-7405. FAX: 323-290-7408. Web Site: www.lapl.org/branches/vermont-square. *Sr Librn,* Martha Sherod; Staff 8 (MLS 3, Non-MLS 5)
Library Holdings: Bk Vols 29,199
Subject Interests: African-Am hist
Open Mon & Wed 10-8, Tues & Thurs 12-8, Fri & Sat 9:30-5:30
Friends of the Library Group

WASHINGTON IRVING BRANCH LIBRARY, 4117 W Washington Blvd, 90018-1053, SAN 332-7965. Tel: 323-734-6303. FAX: 323-731-2416. Web Site: www.lapl.org/branches/washington-irving. *Sr Librn,* Marcie Jones
Library Holdings: Bk Vols 41,265
Open Mon & Wed 10-8, Tues & Thurs 12-8, Fri & Sat 9:30-5:30
Friends of the Library Group

LEON H WASHINGTON JR MEMORIAL-VERNON BRANCH LIBRARY, 4504 S Central Ave, 90011-3632, SAN 332-8953. Tel: 213-234-9106. FAX: 213-231-4291. Web Site: www.lapl.org/branches/vernon. *Sr Librn,* Daisy Pulido
Library Holdings: Bk Vols 41,126
Open Mon & Wed 10-8, Tues & Thurs 12-8, Fri & Sat 9:30-5:30

WEST LOS ANGELES REGIONAL LIBRARY, 11360 Santa Monica Blvd, 90025-3152, SAN 332-9046. Tel: 310-575-8323. FAX: 310-575-8475. Web Site: www.lapl.org/branches/west-los-angeles. *Sr Librn,* Kathryn Ross
Library Holdings: Bk Vols 43,805
Open Mon-Thurs 10-8, Fri & Sat 9:30-5:30, Sun 1-5
Friends of the Library Group

WEST VALLEY REGIONAL BRANCH LIBRARY, 19036 Vanowen St, Reseda, 91335, SAN 332-7213. Tel: 818-345-9806. FAX: 818-345-4288. Web Site: www.lapl.org/branches/west-valley. *Sr Librn,* Kevin Hasely
Open Mon-Thurs 10-8, Fri & Sat 9:30-5:30, Sun 1-5
Friends of the Library Group

WESTCHESTER-LOYOLA VILLAGE BRANCH LIBRARY, 7114 W Manchester Ave, 90045-3509. Tel: 310-348-1096. FAX: 310-348-1082. Web Site: www.lapl.org/branches/westchester. *Sr Librn,* Claudia Martinez
Library Holdings: Bk Vols 34,374
Open Mon & Wed 10-8, Tues & Thurs 12-8, Fri & Sat 9:30-5:30
Friends of the Library Group

WESTWOOD BRANCH LIBRARY, 1246 Glendon Ave, 90024, SAN 332-7221. Tel: 310-474-1739. FAX: 310-470-3892. Web Site: www.lapl.org/branches/westwood. *Sr Librn,* Jennifer Noble
Open Mon & Wed 10-8, Tues & Thurs 12-8, Fri & Sat 9:30-5:30
Friends of the Library Group

WILMINGTON BRANCH LIBRARY, 1300 N Avalon Blvd, Wilmington, 90744, SAN 332-883X. Tel: 310-834-1082. FAX: 310-548-7418. Web Site: www.lapl.org/branches/wilmington. *Sr Librn,* Denise Nossett
Library Holdings: Bk Vols 56,745
Open Mon & Wed 10-8, Tues & Thurs 12-8, Fri & Sat 9:30-5:30
Friends of the Library Group

WILSHIRE BRANCH LIBRARY, 149 N Saint Andrew Pl, 90004, SAN 332-8805. Tel: 323-957-4550. FAX: 323-957-4555. Web Site: www.lapl.org/branches/wilshire. *Actg Sr Librn,* Eric Kennedy
Library Holdings: Bk Vols 38,172
Open Mon & Wed 10-8, Tues & Thurs 12-8, Fri & Sat 9:30-5:30
Friends of the Library Group

WOODLAND HILLS BRANCH LIBRARY, 22200 Ventura Blvd, Woodland Hills, 91364-1517, SAN 332-8988. Tel: 818-226-0017. FAX: 818-226-9056. Web Site: www.lapl.org/branches/woodland-hills. *Sr Librn,* Barbara Metzenbaum
Library Holdings: Bk Vols 53,346
Open Mon & Wed 10-8, Tues & Thurs 12-8, Fri & Sat 9:30-5:30

ALMA REAVES WOODS-WATTS BRANCH LIBRARY, 10205 Compton Ave, 90002-2804, SAN 332-8775. Tel: 323-789-2850. FAX: 323-789-2859. Web Site: www.lapl.org/branches/watts. *Sr Librn,* Jasmine Slaughter
Library Holdings: Bk Vols 46,116
Open Mon & Wed 10-8, Tues & Thurs 12-8, Fri & Sat 9:30-5:30
Friends of the Library Group

J LOS ANGELES SOUTHWEST COLLEGE*, Founders Library, Cox Bldg, 1600 W Imperial Hwy, 90047-4899. SAN 300-9580. Tel: 323-241-5235. FAX: 323-241-5221. E-mail: lasclibrary@lasc.edu. Web Site: www.lasc.edu. *Dept Chair, Librn,* Parisa Samaie; E-mail: samaiep@lasc.edu; *Head of Libr,* Shelley Werts; *Cat,* Gabrielle Arvig; E-mail: Arvigg@lasc.edu; Staff 8 (MLS 4, Non-MLS 4)
Founded 1967. Enrl 7,169; Fac 250; Highest Degree: Associate
Library Holdings: AV Mats 700; Bk Vols 48,970; Per Subs 265
Subject Interests: African-Am, Hispanic
Automation Activity & Vendor Info: (Cataloging) SirsiDynix; (Circulation) SirsiDynix; (OPAC) SirsiDynix
Publications: Library Brochure; Los Angeles Southwest College - A Selected List of New Books; Periodicals Holding List
Partic in LYRASIS
Special Services for the Blind - Reader equip
Open Mon-Thurs 7:45am-8pm, Fri 7:45-1

J LOS ANGELES TRADE TECHNICAL COLLEGE LIBRARY*, 400 W Washington Blvd, 90015. SAN 300-9602. Tel: 213-763-3958. Circulation Tel: 213-763-3950. Administration Tel: 213-763-3978. FAX: 213-763-5393. Web Site: college.lattc.edu/library. *Dept Chair,* Gabriella Lopez; E-mail: lopezGM@lattc.edu; *Librn,* Robert King; E-mail: kingrm@lattc.edu; Staff 2 (MLS 2)
Founded 1927. Enrl 6,440; Fac 500
Library Holdings: e-books 5,312; Microforms 114; Bk Titles 84,963; Bk Vols 85,487; Per Subs 193
Special Collections: Blanche Gottlieb Culinary Arts Coll
Subject Interests: Culinary arts, Fashion
Automation Activity & Vendor Info: (Cataloging) SirsiDynix-WorkFlows; (Circulation) SirsiDynix-WorkFlows; (Course Reserve) SirsiDynix-WorkFlows; (ILL) SirsiDynix-WorkFlows; (OPAC) SirsiDynix
Wireless access
Open Mon-Thurs 9-6, Fri 8-Noon

CL LOYOLA LAW SCHOOL, William M Rains Library, 919 S Albany St, 90015-1211. SAN 332-916X. Tel: 213-736-1117. Interlibrary Loan Service Tel: 213-736-8119. Reference Tel: 213-736-1177. E-mail: circdesk@lls.edu, ill@lls.edu, reference@lls.edu. Web Site: www.lls.edu/library. *Dir,* Cheryl Kelly Fischer; Tel: 213-736-1197, E-mail: cheryl.fischer@lls.edu; *Head, Access & Collection Mgmt Services,* Suzie Shatarevyan; Tel: 213-736-1147, E-mail: suzie.shatarevyan@lls.edu; *Head, Ref,* Laura Cadra; Tel: 213-736-1141, E-mail: laura.cadra@lls.edu; *Acq Librn,* Annie Mellott; Tel:

213-736-1174, E-mail: anne.mellott@lls.edu; *Cat Librn,* Sofia Vazquez-Duran; Tel: 213-736-1419, E-mail: sofia.vazquez-duran@lls.edu; *Ref Librn,* Jacob Samuelson; Tel: 213-736-1413, E-mail: jacob.samuelson@lls.edu; *Ref Librn,* Lisa Schultz; Tel: 213-736-1132, E-mail: lisa.schultz@lls.edu; *Ref Librn,* Victoria Tokar; Tel: 213-736-8132, E-mail: victoria.tokar@lls.edu; *Service Desk Support Tech,* Edwin Majano; Tel: 213-736-1417, E-mail: edwin.majano@lls.edu. Subject Specialists: *Foreign law, Intl law,* Laura Cadra; Staff 24 (MLS 11, Non-MLS 13)
Founded 1920. Highest Degree: Doctorate
Special Collections: Loyola Law School Archive Coll; Rare Books on Law
Wireless access
Restriction: Not open to pub

C LOYOLA MARYMOUNT UNIVERSITY*, William H Hannon Library, One LMU Dr, MS 8200, 90045-2659. SAN 332-9135. Tel: 310-338-2788. Circulation Tel: 310-338-5709. Interlibrary Loan Service Tel: 310-338-5705. Reference Tel: 310-338-2790. Administration Tel: 310-338-4593. FAX: 310-338-4366. Circulation FAX: 310-338-3006. Administration FAX: 310-338-4484. E-mail: library@lmu.edu. Web Site: library.lmu.edu. *Dean of Libr,* Kristine R Brancolini; *Head, Acq & Coll Develop,* Glenn Johnson-Grau; Tel: 310-338-6063, E-mail: gjohnson@lmu.edu; *Head, Archives & Spec Coll,* Cynthia Becht; Tel: 310-338-2780, E-mail: cbecht@lmu.edu; *Head, Cat,* Walt Walker; Tel: 310-338-7687, E-mail: wwalker@lmu.edu; *Head, Ref & Instruction,* Susan Gardner Archambault; Tel: 310-338-7680, E-mail: susan.gardner@lmu.edu; *Circ Serv Librn,* Rhonda Rosen; Tel: 310-338-4584, E-mail: rrosen@lmu.edu; *Communications Librn, Outreach Librn,* John Jackson; Tel: 310-338-5234, E-mail: john.jackson@lmu.edu; *Digital Prog Librn,* Shilpa Rele; Tel: 310-338-2792, E-mail: shilpa.rele@lmu.edu; *Ref & Instruction Librn,* Jennifer Masunaga; *Syst Librn,* Meghan Weeks; Tel: 310-338-5929; *Instruction Coordr, Ref & Instruction,* Elisa Slater Acosta; Tel: 310-338-7679, E-mail: eslater@lmu.edu; *Ref Asst,* Kathryn Ryan; Staff 26 (MLS 24, Non-MLS 2)
Founded 1929. Enrl 8,307; Fac 521; Highest Degree: Doctorate
Library Holdings: AV Mats 29,632; e-books 73,615; e-journals 43,751; Bk Vols 554,025; Per Subs 964
Special Collections: 20th Century Theater & Film Coll; Arthur P Jacobs Coll; Oliver Goldsmith Coll; Rare Books; Saint Thomas Moore Coll; Werner von Boltenstern Postcard Coll
Automation Activity & Vendor Info: (Acquisitions) Innovative Interfaces, Inc; (Cataloging) Innovative Interfaces, Inc; (Circulation) Innovative Interfaces, Inc; (Course Reserve) Blackboard Inc; (ILL) OCLC ILLiad; (Media Booking) Innovative Interfaces, Inc; (OPAC) Innovative Interfaces, Inc; (Serials) Innovative Interfaces, Inc
Wireless access
Partic in Association of Jesuit Colleges & Universities; Link+; OCLC Online Computer Library Center, Inc; Statewide California Electronic Library Consortium
Open Mon-Thurs 8am-2am, Fri 8-8, Sat 11-8, Sun 11-2
Restriction: Open to students, fac & staff, Restricted pub use

L MESERVE, MUMPER & HUGHES*, Law Library, 800 Wilshire Blvd, Ste 500, 90017-2611. SAN 328-4093. Tel: 213-620-0300. FAX: 213-625-1930. Web Site: www.mmhllp.com. *Adminr,* Kirk Simons; E-mail: ksimons@mmhllp.com
Library Holdings: Bk Vols 10,000
Subject Interests: Labor
Restriction: Not open to pub

L MILBANK, TWEED, HADLEY & MCCLOY*, Law Library, 2029 Century Park E, 33rd Flr, 90067-3019. SAN 372-3046. Tel: 213-892-4468. FAX: 213-892-4798. Web Site: www.milbank.com.
Library Holdings: Bk Titles 1,000; Bk Vols 2,000; Per Subs 218
Partic in OCLC Online Computer Library Center, Inc
Restriction: Not a lending libr, Not open to pub

L MITCHELL SILBERBERG & KNUPP LLP*, Law Library, 11377 W Olympic Blvd, 90064-1683. SAN 300-9696. Tel: 310-312-2000. FAX: 310-312-3100. E-mail: library@msk.com. Web Site: www.msk.com. *Librn,* Carolyn A Pratt; *Asst Librn,* Sunan Xing; Staff 3 (MLS 2, Non-MLS 1)
Library Holdings: Bk Vols 35,000
Automation Activity & Vendor Info: (Cataloging) EOS International; (OPAC) EOS International; (Serials) EOS International
Wireless access
Restriction: Staff use only

S MORRISON & FOERSTER LLP LIBRARY*, 707 Wilshire Blvd, 90017-3543. SAN 370-1662. Tel: 213-892-5359. Web Site: www.mofo.com. *Librn,* Jeff Schoerner; E-mail: jschoerner@mofo.com
Library Holdings: Bk Titles 20,000; Per Subs 500
Special Collections: California City Charters; California Municipal Planning & Zoning Ordinances
Subject Interests: Labor, Law, Real estate
Partic in CDB Infotek; CourtLink; Dun & Bradstreet Info Servs; Proquest Dialog
Restriction: Staff use only

C MOUNT SAINT MARY'S UNIVERSITY, Charles Willard Coe Memorial Library, 12001 Chalon Rd, 90049-1599. SAN 332-9194. Tel: 310-954-4370. FAX: 310-954-4379. E-mail: circdesk@msmu.edu. Web Site: www.msmu.edu/libraries. *Dir of Libr,* Danielle Salomon; Tel: 310-954-4371, E-mail: dsalomon@msmu.edu; *Asst Dir, Coll,* Cheryl Ocampo; Tel: 310-954-4372, E-mail: cocampo@msmu.edu; *Asst Dir of User Experience & Digital Initiatives,* Amy Sonnichsen; Tel: 310-954-4389, E-mail: asonnichsen@msmu.edu; *Cat & Tech Serv Librn,* Terry Fresquez; E-mail: tfresquez@msmu.edu; *Instruction & Outreach Librn,* Rebekah Tweed Fox; Tel: 310-954-4087, E-mail: rtweedfox@msmu.edu; Staff 6 (MLS 6)
Founded 1925. Enrl 1,200; Fac 89; Highest Degree: Master
Library Holdings: CDs 643; DVDs 3,562; e-books 305,300; Microforms 2,005; Bk Titles 151,641; Bk Vols 202,364; Per Subs 563; Videos 1,066
Special Collections: Cardinal Newman Coll; Lasallian Studies Coll
Subject Interests: Humanities, Nursing, Phys therapy
Automation Activity & Vendor Info: (Cataloging) Innovative Interfaces, Inc; (Circulation) Innovative Interfaces, Inc
Wireless access
Partic in National Network of Libraries of Medicine Region 5; OCLC Online Computer Library Center, Inc; Proquest Dialog
Open Mon-Thurs 9am-10pm, Fri 9-4, Sat 9-5

Departmental Libraries:

J THOMAS MCCARTHY LIBRARY, Doheny Campus, Ten Chester Pl, 90007, SAN 332-9224. Tel: 213-477-2750. *Assoc Dir, Res & Instruction,* Marjorie Acevedo; Tel: 213-477-275, E-mail: macevedo@msmu.edu; *Asst Dir, Access Services & Spaces,* Abbey Thompson; Tel: 213-477-2720, E-mail: athompson@msmu.edu; *Electronic Res Librn,* Samantha Silver; Tel: 213-477-2754, E-mail: ssilver@msmu.edu; *Health Sci Librn,* Dylan Smith; Tel: 213-234-9834, E-mail: dsmith1@msmu.edu; *Coordr, Acq,* Claudia Alvarado; E-mail: calvarado@msmu.edu; *Circ Coordr,* Monica Johnson; Tel: 213-477-2752, E-mail: mjohnson@msmu.edu
Open Mon-Sat 10-6

L MUNGER, TOLLES & OLSON LLP*, Law Library, 350 S Grand Ave, 50th Flr, 90071-1560. SAN 300-970X. Tel: 213-683-9100. Reference Tel: 213-593-2400. FAX: 213-683-5173. Web Site: www.mto.com. *Libr Dir,* Charles Frey; E-mail: charles.frey@mto.com; Staff 3 (MLS 3)
Founded 1963
Library Holdings: Bk Vols 10,000
Subject Interests: Am law

L MUSICK, PEELER & GARRETT LIBRARY*, One Wilshire Bldg, 624 S Grand Ave, Ste 2000, 90017. SAN 300-9718. Tel: 213-629-7600. FAX: 213-624-1376. Web Site: www.musickpeeler.com. *Librn,* Barry Kelley; E-mail: bkelley@mpglaw.com
Library Holdings: Bk Vols 20,000; Per Subs 400
Subject Interests: Corporate, Labor, Law, Litigation, Real estate, Tax
Automation Activity & Vendor Info: (Cataloging) Inmagic, Inc.; (OPAC) Inmagic, Inc.
Restriction: Staff use only

S NEW CENTER FOR PSYCHOANALYSIS LIBRARY*, 2014 Sawtelle Blvd, 90025. SAN 300-6271. Tel: 310-478-6541. FAX: 310-477-5968. E-mail: info@n-c-p.org. Web Site: www.n-c-p.org/Archival_Collections.html. *Archivist, Historian,* Vladimir Melamed; E-mail: vladimirm@n-c-p.org
Founded 1958
Library Holdings: Bk Titles 3,200; Bk Vols 4,500; Per Subs 20
Subject Interests: Humanities, Psychiat, Psychoanalysis, Psychol, Soc sci
Partic in Pacific Southwest Regional Medical Library

L NORTON ROSE FULBRIGHT*, Law Library, 555 S Flower St, 41st Flr, 90071. SAN 372-2805. Tel: 213-892-9200. FAX: 213-892-9494. Web Site: www.fulbright.com. *Librn,* Position Currently Open
Library Holdings: Bk Vols 25,000
Automation Activity & Vendor Info: (Cataloging) Inmagic, Inc.; (Serials) Inmagic, Inc.
Restriction: Not open to pub

L NOSSAMAN LLP LIBRARY*, 777 S Figueroa St, Ste 3400, 90017. SAN 300-9742. Tel: 213-312-8355. FAX: 213-612-7801. E-mail: library@nossaman.com. Web Site: www.nossaman.com.
Library Holdings: Bk Vols 12,000; Per Subs 350
Automation Activity & Vendor Info: (Cataloging) EOS International; (Circulation) EOS International; (OPAC) EOS International; (Serials) EOS International
Wireless access
Restriction: Authorized personnel only

Branches:
ORANGE COUNTY, 18101 Von Karman Ave, Ste 1800, Irvine, 92612.
Restriction: Authorized personnel only
SACRAMENTO, 621 Capitol Mall, 25th Fl, Sacramento, 95814.
Restriction: Authorized personnel only
SAN FRANCISCO, 50 California St, 34th Fl, San Francisco, 94111.
Automation Activity & Vendor Info: (Cataloging) EOS International
Restriction: Authorized personnel only

C OCCIDENTAL COLLEGE LIBRARY*, Mary Norton Clapp Library, 1600 Campus Rd, 90041. SAN 300-9750. Circulation Tel: 323-259-2640. Interlibrary Loan Service Tel: 323-259-2628. Administration Tel: 323-259-2832. FAX: 323-341-4991. Interlibrary Loan Service FAX: 323-259-2815. E-mail: library@oxy.edu. Web Site: www.oxy.edu/academics/library. *Col Librn,* Kevin Mulroy, PhD; *Librn, Data Mgt & Integrity,* John De La Fontaine; Tel: 323-259-2914, E-mail: delafo@oxy.edu; *Col Archivist & Spec Coll Librn,* Dale Stieber; Tel: 323-259-2852, E-mail: dstieber@oxy.edu; *Circ & Reserves Mgr,* Hoda Abdelghani; E-mail: habdelghani@oxy.edu; *Asst Archivist,* Anne Mar; E-mail: amar@oxy.edu; Staff 5 (MLS 4, Non-MLS 1)
Founded 1887. Highest Degree: Master
Automation Activity & Vendor Info: (Acquisitions) Innovative Interfaces, Inc; (Cataloging) Innovative Interfaces, Inc; (Circulation) Innovative Interfaces, Inc; (Course Reserve) Innovative Interfaces, Inc; (ILL) Innovative Interfaces, Inc; (Media Booking) Innovative Interfaces, Inc; (OPAC) Innovative Interfaces, Inc; (Serials) Innovative Interfaces, Inc
Wireless access
Partic in Link+; OCLC Online Computer Library Center, Inc; Statewide California Electronic Library Consortium

L O'MELVENY & MYERS LLP*, Law Library, 400 S Hope St, 90071-2899. SAN 300-9769. Tel: 213-430-6000. FAX: 213-430-6407. *Dir,* Cheryl Smith; E-mail: csmith@omm.com; *Head Librn,* Gail Okazaki; E-mail: gokazaki@omm.com; *Head, Ref,* Cindy Spadoni; Staff 14 (MLS 8, Non-MLS 6)
Founded 1885
Library Holdings: Bk Vols 45,000; Per Subs 500
Automation Activity & Vendor Info: (Cataloging) Horizon
Partic in Dow Jones News Retrieval; OCLC Online Computer Library Center, Inc; Proquest Dialog
Restriction: Staff use only

S ONE NATIONAL GAY & LESBIAN ARCHIVES AT THE USC LIBRARIES*, 909 W Adams Blvd, 90007. SAN 300-9297. Tel: 213-741-2771. FAX: 213-741-0220. E-mail: askone@usc.edu. Web Site: one.usc.edu. *Dir,* Joseph Hawkins, PhD; *Libr Supvr, Operations Mgr,* Bud Thomas; E-mail: bud.thomas@usc.edu; *Archivist,* Michael Oliveira; E-mail: michael.c.oliveira@usc.edu; *Archivist,* Loni Shibuyama; Fax: shibuyam@usc.edu
Founded 1952
Library Holdings: Bk Vols 25,000
Special Collections: Homophile & Gay Liberation Movements, 1948-present
Subject Interests: Gay & lesbian, Lesbian culture & hist
Wireless access
Function: Archival coll, For res purposes, Photocopying/Printing, Res libr
Restriction: Open by appt only

C PACIFIC STATES UNIVERSITY LIBRARY*, 3424 Wilshire Blvd, Ste 1200, 90010. SAN 300-9807. Tel: 323-731-2383. FAX: 323-731-7276. E-mail: library@psuca.edu. Web Site: www.psuca.edu/facilities. *Library Contact,* Tai-Wei Tseng; Staff 1 (MLS 1)
Founded 1928. Enrl 300; Fac 30; Highest Degree: Master
Library Holdings: DVDs 20; Electronic Media & Resources 1; Bk Titles 900; Bk Vols 1,000; Per Subs 1; Spec Interest Per Sub 1
Wireless access
Open Mon-Fri 8:30am-10pm
Restriction: Borrowing privileges limited to fac & registered students

L PAUL HASTINGS LLP*, Law Library, 515 S Flower, 25th Flr, 90071. SAN 329-9333. Tel: 213-683-6000. FAX: 213-627-0705. Web Site: www.paulhastings.com. *Info Res Mgr,* Liana Juliano; E-mail: lianajuliano@paulhastings.com
Library Holdings: Bk Vols 10,000; Per Subs 400
Subject Interests: Labor law
Wireless access
Restriction: Open to staff only

S PHILOSOPHICAL RESEARCH SOCIETY LIBRARY*, 3910 Los Feliz Blvd, 90027. SAN 300-9831. Tel: 323-663-2167. FAX: 323-663-9443. E-mail: library@uprs.edu. Web Site: www.uprs.edu/philosophical-research-library. *Librn,* Cathy Willis; Staff 2 (Non-MLS 2)
Founded 1934
Library Holdings: Bk Titles 50,000
Special Collections: Bohn Coll; E T Seton Coll; Edwin Parker Coll; Le Plongeon Coll; Manly P Hall Coll; Max Muller Coll; Oliver L Reiser Coll
Subject Interests: Ancient philos, Art, Astrology, Comparative relig, Egypt, Metaphysics, Modern philos, Mythology, Psychol
Wireless access
Open Mon-Thurs 10:30-3:30 by appointment; Tues 5pm-7pm, Fri 10:30-3:30
Friends of the Library Group

L PROSKAUER ROSE LLP*, Law Library, 2049 Century Park E, Ste 2400, 90067. SAN 372-3054. Tel: 310-284-5683, 310-557-2900. FAX: 310-557-2193. Web Site: www.proskauer.com. *Library Contact,* Sheila Williams; E-mail: swilliams@proskauer.com; Staff 2 (MLS 1, Non-MLS 1)
Founded 1875
Library Holdings: Bk Vols 15,000; Per Subs 100
Restriction: Private libr

L REED SMITH LLP, Law Library, 355 S Grand Ave, Ste 2900, 90017. SAN 370-7571. Tel: 213-457-8000. FAX: 213-457-8080. Web Site: www.reedsmith.com. *Librn,* Linda Rauhauser; Staff 2 (MLS 1, Non-MLS 1)
Library Holdings: Bk Titles 200; Bk Vols 5,000; Per Subs 24
Open Mon-Fri 8-5

S REISS-DAVIS CHILD STUDY CENTER, Research Library, Vista Del Mar, 3200 Motor Ave, 90034. SAN 300-9874. Tel: 310-204-1666, Ext 359. E-mail: rdlibrarian@reissdavis.edu. Web Site: reissdavis.edu/library.html. *Librn,* Simran Khalsa; Staff 1 (MLS 1)
Founded 1950
Library Holdings: Bk Titles 9,000; Bk Vols 16,000; Per Subs 5
Special Collections: Freud Coll
Wireless access
Partic in National Network of Libraries of Medicine Region 5
Open Fri 1-5 & by appointment

L SEYFARTH SHAW LIBRARY*, 2029 Century Park E, Ste 3300, 90067. SAN 325-7614. Tel: 310-277-7200. FAX: 310-201-5219. *Librn,* Beth Bernstein
Library Holdings: Bk Vols 10,000
Wireless access
Restriction: Staff use only

L SHEPPARD, MULLIN, RICHTER & HAMPTON LIBRARY*, 333 S Hope, 43rd Flr, 90071. SAN 300-9912. Tel: 213-620-1780. FAX: 213-620-1398. Web Site: www.sheppardmullin.com/los-angeles. *Dir, Res,* Martin Korn; E-mail: mkorn@sheppardmullin.com; Staff 5 (MLS 2, Non-MLS 3)
Library Holdings: e-books 250; e-journals 150; Bk Titles 7,000; Bk Vols 50,000; Per Subs 225
Subject Interests: Antitrust law, Banking, Intellectual property, Labor, Litigation, Real estate, Securities
Restriction: Staff use only

L SIDLEY AUSTIN LLP LIBRARY*, 555 W Fifth St, Ste 4000, 90013. SAN 371-6309. Tel: 213-896-6000. FAX: 213-896-6600. *Dir, Libr Serv,* John DiGilio; E-mail: jdigilio@sidley.com; Staff 4 (MLS 2, Non-MLS 2)
Founded 1980
Subject Interests: Bankruptcy, Corporate law, Entertainment, Ins, Intellectual property, Labor, Litigation, Real estate, Tax
Automation Activity & Vendor Info: (OPAC) EOS International; (Serials) EOS International
Wireless access
Restriction: Not open to pub

C SIMON WIESENTHAL CENTER & MUSEUM OF TOLERANCE*, Library & Archives, 1399 S Roxbury Dr, 3rd Flr, 90035-4709. SAN 320-5681. Tel: 310-772-7605. FAX: 310-772-7628. E-mail: library@wiesenthal.net. Web Site: www.wiesenthal.com/library. *Dir,* Adaire Klein; *Ref (Info Servs),* Nancy Saul; *Tech Serv,* Margo Gutstein
Founded 1978
Library Holdings: Bk Vols 50,000; Per Subs 200
Special Collections: Books by & about Simon Wiesenthal; Primary Anti-Semitica & Holocaust Denial
Subject Interests: Holocaust, Judaica (lit or hist of Jews), Racism
Open Mon-Thurs 9-5

SR SINAI TEMPLE*, Blumenthal Library, 10400 Wilshire Blvd, 90024. SAN 300-9920. Tel: 310-474-1518, 310-481-3218. FAX: 310-474-6801. E-mail: info@sinaitemple.org. Web Site: www.sinaitemple.org/learn/library. *Head Librn,* Martha McMahon; E-mail: mmcmahon@sinaiakiba.org; *Librn,* Alex Quay; E-mail: aquay@sinaiakiba.org
Founded 1969

Library Holdings: Bk Titles 20,899; Bk Vols 30,000; Per Subs 38
Special Collections: Haggadot Coll; Parenting Coll; Sinai Akiba Day School Coll for General Studies; William R Blumenthal Rare Book Coll
Subject Interests: Children's lit, Judaica (lit or hist of Jews), Lit
Publications: Articles for Association of Jewish Libraries (bulletins); Articles on children's literature with Jewish themes; Central Cataloging Service for Libraries of Judaica; Reform Judaism
Partic in Metronet
Open Mon-Thurs 7:45-5, Fri 7:45-4

C SOUTHERN CALIFORNIA INSTITUTE OF ARCHITECTURE, Kappe Library, 960 E Third St, 90013. SAN 301-5947. Tel: 213-613-5323. FAX: 213-613-2260. Web Site: www.sciarc.edu/institution/facility/kappe-library. *Mgr,* Kevin McMahon; E-mail: kevin@sciarc.edu
Founded 1972. Enrl 380; Fac 50; Highest Degree: Master
Library Holdings: Bk Titles 20,000; Per Subs 100
Subject Interests: Art & archit, Urban planning
Wireless access

S SOUTHERN CALIFORNIA LIBRARY FOR SOCIAL STUDIES & RESEARCH*, 6120 S Vermont Ave, 90044. SAN 300-9955. Tel: 323-759-6063. E-mail: archives@socallib.org. Web Site: www.socallib.org. *Dir,* Yusef Omowale; E-mail: omowale@socallib.org; *Dir, Communications,* Michele Welsing; E-mail: mwelsing@socallib.org; Staff 7 (MLS 2, Non-MLS 5)
Founded 1963
Special Collections: Calif Democratic Council Records; Chicano & Black Liberation, newsp files; Civil Rights Congress Records; Committee for the Protection of Foreign Born Files; Folk Music (Earl Robinson & William Wolff Colls); Harry Bridges Deportation Case Records; Morris Kominsky Coll (American Right); Organization History (Peace, Civil Rights, Political & Social Action Groups as well as Civil Rights & Civil Liberties Ad Hoc Committees), files from turn of century to present; Smith Act Case Records
Subject Interests: African-Am hist, Civil liberties, Civil rights, Labor, Latino hist
Wireless access
Function: Archival coll, Art exhibits, Computers for patron use, Electronic databases & coll, For res purposes, Photocopying/Printing, Prog for adults, Prog for children & young adult, Ref & res, Ref serv available, Res libr, Telephone ref, VHS videos, Wheelchair accessible, Workshops
Publications: Heritage (Newsletter)
Open Tues-Sat 11-5

CL SOUTHWESTERN LAW SCHOOL*, Leigh H Taylor Law Library, Bullock Wilshire Bldg, 1st Flr, 3050 Wilshire Blvd, 90010. Tel: 213-738-5771. Interlibrary Loan Service Tel: 213-738-6728. Reference Tel: 213-738-6725. FAX: 213-738-5792. E-mail: library@swlaw.edu. Web Site: www.swlaw.edu/bullocks-wilshire-campus/law-library. *Assoc Dean, Libr Serv,* Linda A Whisman; E-mail: LWhisman@SWLaw.edu; *Assoc Dir,* Margaret Hall; E-mail: mhall@swlaw.edu; *Head, Circ Serv,* Aaron Brown; E-mail: akbrown@swlaw.edu; *Head, Ser,* Lorena Sanchez; E-mail: lsanchez@swlaw.edu; *Sr Ref Librn,* David McFadden; E-mail: dmcfadden@swlaw.edu; *Cat Librn,* Connie Deng; E-mail: cdeng@swlaw.edu; *Syst Librn,* Tracy Tsui; E-mail: ttsui@swlaw.edu; Staff 10 (MLS 7, Non-MLS 3)
Founded 1911. Enrl 875; Fac 55; Highest Degree: Doctorate
Library Holdings: e-books 22,000; Bk Titles 135,800; Bk Vols 492,400; Per Subs 4,000
Special Collections: State Document Depository; US Document Depository
Automation Activity & Vendor Info: (Acquisitions) Innovative Interfaces, Inc; (Cataloging) Innovative Interfaces, Inc; (Circulation) Innovative Interfaces, Inc; (Course Reserve) Innovative Interfaces, Inc; (ILL) OCLC; (OPAC) Innovative Interfaces, Inc; (Serials) Innovative Interfaces, Inc
Wireless access
Function: ILL available
Restriction: Not open to pub

L STROOCK & LAVAN*, Law Library, 2029 Century Park E, Ste 1800, 90067. SAN 372-3747. Tel: 310-556-5800. FAX: 310-556-5959. *Head Librn,* Debra Hogan
Library Holdings: Bk Vols 12,000
Restriction: Staff use only

L TRANSAMERICA OCCIDENTAL LIFE INSURANCE*, Law Library, 1150 S Olive St, Ste T-2700, 90015-2211. SAN 370-4106. Tel: 213-742-3129. FAX: 213-741-6623. *Library Contact,* Maggie Velasquez
Library Holdings: Bk Vols 1,000; Per Subs 5
Restriction: Employees only

L TROYGOULD*, Law Library, 1801 Century Park E, Ste 1600, 90067. SAN 372-3755. Tel: 310-553-4441. FAX: 310-201-4746. E-mail: library@troygould.com. Web Site: www.troygould.com.
Library Holdings: Bk Vols 5,000; Per Subs 12
Wireless access
Restriction: Employees only

GL UNITED STATES COURTS LIBRARY*, 255 E Temple St, Rm 680, 90012. SAN 301-0104. Tel: 213-894-8900. FAX: 213-894-8906. *Librn,* Jane Kim
Library Holdings: Bk Vols 30,000
Subject Interests: Law
Automation Activity & Vendor Info: (Acquisitions) SirsiDynix; (Cataloging) SirsiDynix; (Circulation) SirsiDynix; (Serials) SirsiDynix
Partic in OCLC Online Computer Library Center, Inc
Open Mon-Fri 9-4

UNIVERSITY OF CALIFORNIA, LOS ANGELES

C RALPH J BUNCHE CENTER FOR AFRICAN-AMERICAN STUDIES LIBRARY & MEDIA CENTER*, 135 Haines Hall, Box 951545, 90095-1545, SAN 332-9550. Tel: 310-825-6060. FAX: 310-825-5019. Web Site: www.bunchecenter.ucla.edu. *Librn,* Dalena E Hunter. Subject Specialists: *African-Am studies,* Dalena E Hunter; Staff 1 (MLS 1)
Founded 1969
Library Holdings: Audiobooks 10; CDs 50; DVDs 250; Bk Vols 8,479; Per Subs 21; Videos 205
Special Collections: African Student Union (ASU) Archive; Carlos Moore Archive; Kenny Burrell Archive
Subject Interests: African-Am studies
Function: Electronic databases & coll, Orientations, Ref serv available, Scanner, VHS videos
Partic in Association of Research Libraries
Open Mon-Thurs 9-6, Fri 9-3
Restriction: In-house use for visitors, Non-circulating

C INSTRUCTIONAL MEDIA LIBRARY*, Powell Library, Rm 46, 90095-1517, SAN 332-9585. Tel: 310-825-0755. FAX: 310-206-5392. E-mail: imlib@ucla.edu. Web Site: www.oid.ucla.edu/lmlib. *Mgr,* Kathleen Ford
Founded 1963
Subject Interests: Bus & mgt, Ethnic studies, Hist, Performing arts, Soc sci & issues
Publications: Video periodicals & directories

C UNIVERSITY OF CALIFORNIA LOS ANGELES LIBRARY*, PO Box 951575, 90095-1575. Tel: 310-825-1201. Circulation Tel: 310-825-4732. Interlibrary Loan Service Tel: 310-825-1733. Reference Tel: 310-825-1323. Web Site: www.library.ucla.edu. *Univ Librn,* Virginia Steel; E-mail: vsteel@library.ucla.edu
Founded 1919. Enrl 44,947; Fac 13,740; Highest Degree: Doctorate
Library Holdings: Bk Vols 12,420,000; Per Subs 110,000
Special Collections: 19th & 20th Century British & American Literature; 19th Century British Fiction (Michael Sadleir Coll); British Commonwealth History, especially Australia & New Zealand; British History; California History; Contemporary Western Writers Coll; Early English Children's Books; Early Italian Printing (Ahmanson-Murphy Coll); Elmer Belt Library of Vinciana; Folklore; History of Medicine; Latin American Studies; Mazarinades; Mountaineering Literature (Farquhar Coll); National Parks & Conservation (Albright Coll); Organizational; Southern California Imprints, pamphlets; Spinoza Coll; Western Americana. Oral History; UN Document Depository; US Document Depository
Automation Activity & Vendor Info: (Acquisitions) Ex Libris Group; (Cataloging) Ex Libris Group; (Circulation) Ex Libris Group; (Course Reserve) Ex Libris Group; (OPAC) Ex Libris Group
Wireless access
Publications: Library News for the Faculty (Newsletter); UCLA Library News (Newsletter)
Partic in Association of Research Libraries; Metronet; OCLC Research Library Partnership
Friends of the Library Group

Departmental Libraries:

ARTS LIBRARY, 1400 Public Affairs Bldg, 90095. (Mail add: Box 951392, 90095-1392), SAN 332-9704. Tel: 310-206-5425. Reference E-mail: arts-ref@library.ucla.edu. Web Site: www.library.ucla.edu/arts, www.library.ucla.edu/location/arts-library. *Dir,* Allison R Benedetti; Tel: 310-206-8746, E-mail: abenedetti@library.ucla.edu; *Librn,* Diana King; Tel: 310-206-4823, E-mail: diking@library.ucla.edu; *Archit Librn,* Janine Henri; Tel: 310-206-4587, E-mail: jhenri@library.ucla.edu; *Visual Arts Librn,* Robert Gore; Tel: 310-206-5426, E-mail: rjcgore@library.ucla.edu; Staff 4 (MLS 4)
Library Holdings: Bk Vols 285,680; Per Subs 1,987
Special Collections: Bookworks & Artist Publications (Hoffberg Coll); Leonardo da Vinci (Elmer Belt Library of Vinciana)
Subject Interests: Archit, Art, Ceramics, Film, Photog, Television, Textiles
Partic in OCLC Online Computer Library Center, Inc
Publications: Art Catalogs
Open Mon-Thurs 8am-9pm, Fri 8-5, Sat & Sun 1-5

CHICANO STUDIES RESEARCH CENTER LIBRARY & ARCHIVE, 144 Haines Hall, 90095-1544. Tel: 310-206-6052. FAX: 310-206-1784. E-mail: librarian@chicano.ucla.edu. Web Site: www.chicano.ucla.edu/library. *Librn & Archivist,* Xaviera Flores; E-mail: floresx@ucla.edu; *Archive Spec,* Doug Johnson; E-mail: dejohnson@chicano.ucla.edu
Founded 1969
Library Holdings: AV Mats 1,030; Bk Titles 1,500; Bk Vols 16,536
Special Collections: Microfilm reels, digital objects, posters & archival coll
Subject Interests: Chicano hist & culture
Automation Activity & Vendor Info: (Cataloging) Ex Libris Group; (OPAC) Ex Libris Group
Open Mon-Fri 10-5 or by appointment
Restriction: Non-circulating, Researchers only

WILLIAM ANDREWS CLARK MEMORIAL LIBRARY, 2520 Cimarron St, 90018, SAN 332-9798. Tel: 310-794-5155. FAX: 323-731-8617. Web Site: clarklibrary.ucla.edu. *Dir,* Helen Deutsch; E-mail: hdeutsch@humnet.ucla.edu; *Head Librn,* Anna Chen; E-mail: achen@humnet.ucla.edu; Staff 6 (MLS 5, Non-MLS 1)
Founded 1934
Library Holdings: Per Subs 97,259; Spec Interest Per Sub 678
Special Collections: 17th & early 18th Century English & European Civilization; Eric Gill Coll; John Dryden Coll; Modern Fine Printing; Montana History Coll; Oscar Wilde & the Nineties; Robert Boyle Coll; Robert Gibbings Coll
Open Mon-Fri 9-4:45
Friends of the Library Group

CL HUGH & HAZEL DARLING LAW LIBRARY, 1112 Law Bldg, 385 Charles E Young Dr E, 90095-1458, SAN 332-9941. Tel: 310-825-7826. Circulation Tel: 310-825-4743. Reference Tel: 310-825-6414. FAX: 310-825-1372. Web Site: www.law.ucla.edu/library. *Dir, Law Libr,* Kevin Gerson; E-mail: gerson@law.ucla.edu; *Dir, Ref, Dir, Res Serv,* Jodi Kruger; *Dir, Access Serv, Dir, Info Serv,* Donna Gulnac; *Dir, Bibliog Serv, Dir, Coll Mgt,* Cindy Spadoni; *E-Res Mgt, Head, Acq,* Jennifer Friedman; *Head, Cat,* Melissa Beck; *Head, Coll, Ref Librn,* Jennifer Lentz; *Head, Instruction Serv, Ref Librn,* Cheryl Kelly Fischer; *Ref Librn,* Lynn McClelland
Library Holdings: Bk Vols 592,266; Per Subs 8,258
Special Collections: David Bernard Memorial Aviation Law Library. State Document Depository; US Document Depository
Subject Interests: E Asia, Islam, Latin Am
Partic in Legal Lexis; OCLC Online Computer Library Center, Inc
Open Mon-Thurs 8am-11:30pm, Fri 8am-8:30pm, Sat 9-5:30, Sun 1pm-11:30pm

CM LOUISE M DARLING BIOMEDICAL LIBRARY, 12-077 Ctr for the Health Sciences, 90095. (Mail add: PO Box 951798, 90095-1798), SAN 332-9739. Tel: 310-825-4904. Interlibrary Loan Service Tel: 310-825-4055. FAX: 310-825-0465. Interlibrary Loan Service FAX: 310-206-8675. E-mail: biomed-ref@library.ucla.edu. Web Site: library.ucla.edu/location/biomedical-library-louise-m-darling, www.library.ucla.edu/biomed. *Dir,* Judith C Consales; Tel: 310-825-1201, E-mail: consales@library.ucla.edu; *Assoc Dir,* Alan F Carr; Tel: 310-825-7263, E-mail: acarr@library.ucla.edu
Library Holdings: Bk Vols 651,167; Per Subs 3,471
Special Collections: Dr M N Beigelman Coll (opthalmology); Florence Nightingale Coll; History of the Health Sciences; History of the Life Sciences; Japanese Medical Books & Prints, 17th-19th Centuries; S Weir Mitchell Coll; Slide, Portrait, Realia & Print Coll
Subject Interests: Dentistry, Med, Neurology, Nursing, Pub health
Partic in Cap Area Libr Network Inc; Coop Libr Agency for Syst & Servs
Open Mon-Fri 7:30am-Midnight, Sat 9am-Midnight, Sun 1-10

GRACE M HUNT MEMORIAL ENGLISH READING ROOM, 235 Humanities Bldg, 415 Portola Plaza, 90095, SAN 332-9887. Tel: 310-825-4511. FAX: 310-267-4339. Web Site: library.ucla.edu/location/english-reading-room, www.library.ucla.edu/err. *Librn,* Lynda Tolly; E-mail: tolly@english.ucla.edu
Library Holdings: Bk Vols 34,396; Per Subs 167
Special Collections: Josephine Miles Poetry Coll; Modern Contemporary Poetry (1500 vols)
Subject Interests: Am lit, English lit, Literary criticism

POWELL LIBRARY, Powell Library Bldg, 90095. (Mail add: Box 951450, 90095-1450), SAN 332-964X. Tel: 310-825-1938. FAX: 310-206-9312. E-mail: ask.powell@library.ucla.edu. Web Site: library.ucla.edu/location/powell-library, www.library.ucla.edu/powell. *Dir,* Allison R Benedetti; E-mail: abenedetti@library.ucla.edu; *Librn,* Miki Goral; E-mail: miki@library.ucla.edu
Friends of the Library Group

EUGENE & MAXINE ROSENFELD MANAGEMENT LIBRARY, UCLA Anderson School of Management, 110 Westwood Plaza, E-301, 90095, SAN 332-9976. Tel: 310-825-3138. FAX: 310-825-6632. E-mail: RosenfeldLibrary@anderson.ucla.edu. Web Site: www.anderson.ucla.edu/rosenfeld-library. *Dir,* Angela Horne; Tel: 310-875-3047, E-mail: ahorne@library.ucla.edu; *Bus Res Librn, Colls Librn,* Michael Oppenheim; Tel: 310-825-0769, E-mail: moppenhe@library.ucla.edu; Staff 8 (MLS 4, Non-MLS 4)
Founded 1961. Enrl 1,700; Highest Degree: Doctorate
Library Holdings: Microforms 548,495; Bk Vols 182,663
Special Collections: Corporate History Coll; Goldsmiths-Kress Library of Economic Literature Microfilm Coll (Pre-1850); New York Stock Exchange Listing Applications (1957-1999); Rare Books in Business & Economics, 16th-18th Centuries (Robert E Gross Coll)
Subject Interests: Bus, Mgt
Open Mon-Fri 8am-11pm, Sat 9am-11pm, Sun 1-11

RICHARD C RUDOLPH EAST ASIAN LIBRARY, 21617 Research Library YRL, 90095, SAN 333-0060. Tel: 310-825-4836. FAX: 310-206-4960. Web Site: www.library.ucla.edu/location/east-asian-library-richard-c-rudolph. *Head Librn,* Su Chen; Tel: 310-825-1401, E-mail: suchen11@library.ucla.edu; *Librn,* Hong Cheng; Tel: 310-206-9606, E-mail: chengh@library.ucla.edu; *Librn,* Sanghun Cho; Tel: 310-825-9535, E-mail: sanghuncho@library.library.ucla.edu. Subject Specialists: *Chinese,* Hong Cheng; *Korea,* Sanghun Cho; Staff 12 (MLS 5, Non-MLS 7)
Founded 1948
Library Holdings: Bk Vols 673,215; Per Subs 3,124
Special Collections: Chinese Archeology Coll; Fine Arts Coll; Japanese Buddhism Coll; Korean Literature Coll - Classical & Modern; Religion Coll
Subject Interests: E Asia
Partic in OCLC Online Computer Library Center, Inc
Publications: Richard C Rudolph East Asian Library Bibliographic Series

SCIENCE & ENGINEERING LIBRARIES, 8270 Boelter Hall, 90095, SAN 332-9852. Tel: 310-825-4951. E-mail: sel-ref@library.ucla.edu. Web Site: library.ucla.edu/location/sel, www.library.ucla.edu/sel. *Dir,* Rikke S Ogawa; Tel: 310-825-5781, E-mail: rikke.ogawa@library.ucla.edu; *Librn,* Courtney Hoffner; Tel: 310-825-0190, E-mail: choffner@library.ucla.edu
Library Holdings: Bk Vols 602,152; Per Subs 4,461
Special Collections: Technical Reports Coll (including depository items from DOE, NASA, NTIS, Rand Corp)
Subject Interests: Astronomy
Partic in Proquest Dialog

C UNIVERSITY OF SOUTHERN CALIFORNIA LIBRARIES*, University Park Campus, 3550 Trousdale Pkwy, 90089. SAN 333-0184. Tel: 213-740-2543. Interlibrary Loan Service Tel: 213-740-4020. Reference Tel: 213-740-4039. Administration Tel: 213-821-2344. FAX: 213-740-9962. Web Site: libraries.usc.edu. *Dean of Libr,* Catherine Quinlan; E-mail: cquinlan@usc.edu
Founded 1880. Enrl 38,000; Fac 3,440; Highest Degree: Doctorate
Library Holdings: e-books 721,441; Bk Vols 3,978,705
Special Collections: American Literature Coll (1850-); Cinematic Arts Coll; East Asian Coll; German Literature in Exile Coll; Latin American (Boeckmann Coll); Natural History Coll (Hancock); Philosophy (Gomperz Coll); Southern California Regional History. Canadian and Provincial; State Document Depository; UN Document Depository; US Document Depository
Automation Activity & Vendor Info: (Acquisitions) SirsiDynix; (Cataloging) SirsiDynix; (Circulation) SirsiDynix; (Course Reserve) SirsiDynix; (ILL) OCLC ILLiad; (OPAC) SirsiDynix; (Serials) SirsiDynix
Wireless access
Function: Res libr
Partic in Association of Research Libraries; Center for Research Libraries; Greater Western Library Alliance; National Network of Libraries of Medicine Region 5; OCLC Online Computer Library Center, Inc; OCLC Research Library Partnership; Pacific Rim Digital Library Alliance; Southern Calif Electronic Libr Consortium; Statewide California Electronic Library Consortium
Friends of the Library Group

Departmental Libraries:

CL ASA V CALL LAW LIBRARY, 699 Exposition Blvd, LAW 202, MC 0072, 90089-0072, SAN 333-0753. Tel: 213-740-6482. FAX: 213-740-7179. Web Site: law.usc.edu. *Dir, Law Libr, Assoc Dean & Chief Info Officer,* Pauline Aranas; E-mail: paranas@law.usc.edu; *Assoc Dir, Law Libr for Coll & Admin Serv,* Leonette Williams; E-mail: lwilliams@law.usc.edu; *Asst Dir, Pub Serv,* Brian Raphael; E-mail: braphael@law.usc.edu; *Bus Coordr,* Steven Benson; E-mail: sbenson@law.usc.edu
Special Collections: State Document Depository; US Document Depository
Publications: Asa V Call Law Guide to Legal Secondary Source in the Law Library

HOOSE LIBRARY OF PHILOSOPHY, Mudd Memorial Hall of Philos, 3709 Trousdale Pkwy, 90089-0182, SAN 333-0397. Tel: 213-740-7434. Web Site: www.usc.edu/library/phil/. *Head Librn,* Dr Ross Scimeca; E-mail: scimeca@calvin.usc.edu; *Libr Supvr,* Melissa Miller; E-mail: millerm@usc.edu

Library Holdings: Bk Vols 55,000; Per Subs 150
Special Collections: Western European Philosophers, First & Early Editions, 1700-1850

CM NORRIS MEDICAL LIBRARY, 2003 Zonal Ave, 90089-9130, SAN 333-0788. Tel: 323-442-1116. Reference Tel: 323-442-1111. Administration Tel: 323-442-1130. FAX: 323-221-1235. E-mail: medlib@usc.edu. Web Site: www.usc.edu/nml. *Assoc Dean/Dir,* Cynthia Henderson; E-mail: cynthia.henderson@usc.edu; *Asst Dir, Info Syst,* Janice Brown; *Asst Dir, Info Syst,* Janice Brown; E-mail: jbrown@usc.edu; *Assoc Dir, Coll Serv,* Megan Rosenbloom; E-mail: megan.rosenbloom@usc.edu; Staff 36 (MLS 12, Non-MLS 24)
Founded 1928. Enrl 3,849; Fac 1,365; Highest Degree: Doctorate
Library Holdings: AV Mats 13,741; DVDs 57; e-books 545; e-journals 2,425; Bk Titles 43,672; Bk Vols 48,099; Per Subs 2,219
Special Collections: American Indian Ethnopharmacology Coll; Far West Medicine Coll; Salerni Collegium History of Medicine Coll
Subject Interests: Med, Nursing, Occupational therapy, Pharm, Phys therapy
Automation Activity & Vendor Info: (Acquisitions) Horizon; (Cataloging) Horizon; (Circulation) Horizon; (Course Reserve) Docutek; (ILL) OCLC ILLiad; (OPAC) Horizon; (Serials) SerialsSolutions
Function: Health sci info serv
Open Mon-Thurs 7am-Midnight, Fri 7am-8pm, Sat 9-5, Sun 9am-10pm
Friends of the Library Group

SCIENCE & ENGINEERING, Seaver Science Ctr, 920 W 37th Pl, 90089-0481, SAN 333-0540. Tel: 213-740-4419, 213-740-8507. Reference Tel: 213-740-4416. FAX: 213-740-0558. Web Site: www.usc.edu/isd/locations/science/sci. *Head, Sci & Eng,* Linda Weber; E-mail: lindaweb@usc.edu; *Mgr,* Suzanne Henderson; Tel: 213-740-8285, E-mail: sueh@usc.edu; *Librn,* Najwa Hanel; E-mail: nhanel@usc.edu; Staff 9 (MLS 4, Non-MLS 5)
Library Holdings: Bk Vols 250,000; Per Subs 2,500
Automation Activity & Vendor Info: (Cataloging) SirsiDynix

HELEN TOPPING ARCHITECTURE & FINE ARTS LIBRARY, Watt Hall Rm 4, 90089-0182, SAN 333-0214. Tel: 213-740-1956. FAX: 213-749-1221. E-mail: afalib@usc.edu. Web Site: www.usc.edu/library/afa. *Head of Libr,* Ruth Wallach; Tel: 213-740-6917, E-mail: rwallach@usc.edu; Staff 5 (MLS 3, Non-MLS 2)
Library Holdings: Bk Vols 78,000
Special Collections: Art & Architecture Ephemera; Artist's Books
Partic in OCLC Online Computer Library Center, Inc

VON KLEINSMID CENTER LIBRARY, Von KleinSmid Ctr, 3518 Trousdale Pkwy, 90089-0182, SAN 333-0605. Tel: 213-740-1768. Circulation Tel: 213-740-1769. FAX: 213-821-1993. E-mail: vkc@usc.edu. Web Site: www.usc.edu/isd/locations/international/vkc. *Head of Libr,* Sherry Mosley; E-mail: smosley@usc.edu; *Libr Supvr,* Lourina Agnew; Tel: 213-821-3965, E-mail: lagnew@usc.edu; *Ref Serv,* Anthony Anderson; Tel: 213-740-1190, E-mail: anthonya@usc.edu; *Govt Doc, Ref Serv,* Julia Johnson; Tel: 213-740-9377, E-mail: juliajoh@usc.edu; *Circ,* Tanya Zarotsky; Tel: 213-740-8227, E-mail: zarotsky@usc.edu; *Ser,* Joy Collins; Tel: 213-740-1770, E-mail: joycolli@usc.edu
Library Holdings: Bk Vols 195,000; Per Subs 450
Special Collections: International Documents; Planning Documents
Subject Interests: Intl relations, Polit sci, Urban planning
Automation Activity & Vendor Info: (Cataloging) SirsiDynix

CM JENNIFER ANN WILSON DENTAL LIBRARY & LEARNING CENTER, 925 W 34th St, DEN 21, University Park - MC 0641, 90089-0641, SAN 333-0729. Tel: 213-740-6476. Circulation Tel: 213-740-0008. Interlibrary Loan Service Tel: 213-740-8578. Reference Tel: 213-740-1441. FAX: 213-748-8565. E-mail: wdl@usc.edu. Web Site: wdl.usc.edu. *Dir,* John P Glueckert; E-mail: gluecker@usc.edu; *Info Serv Librn,* Annie Hughes; E-mail: amhughes@usc.edu; Staff 8 (MLS 2, Non-MLS 6)
Founded 1897. Enrl 928; Fac 116; Highest Degree: Doctorate
Library Holdings: Audiobooks 248; AV Mats 5,296; DVDs 40; e-books 283; e-journals 237; Bk Titles 17,408; Bk Vols 20,257; Per Subs 317; Videos 229
Special Collections: Dentistry Rare Books Coll
Automation Activity & Vendor Info: (Acquisitions) Horizon; (Cataloging) Horizon; (Circulation) Horizon; (Course Reserve) Horizon; (OPAC) Horizon; (Serials) Horizon
Function: Doc delivery serv, ILL available, Photocopying/Printing
Partic in National Network of Libraries of Medicine Region 5; Pacific Southwest Regional Medical Library
Restriction: Access at librarian's discretion, Access for corporate affiliates, Authorized patrons, Authorized scholars by appt, Borrowing privileges limited to fac & registered students, Circ limited, In-house use for visitors, Non-circulating of rare bks, Non-circulating to the pub, Open to fac, students & qualified researchers, Open to qualified scholars, Open to researchers by request, Restricted loan policy, Restricted pub use

GM VA GREATER LOS ANGELES HEALTH CARE SYSTEM*, West Los Angeles Health Care Center, 11301 Wilshire Blvd, W142D, 90073. SAN 333-0842, Staff 1 (MLS 1)
Founded 1936
Subject Interests: Med, Psychiat, Psychol
Open Mon-Fri 8-4:30

M WHITE MEMORIAL MEDICAL CENTER*, Courville-Abbott Memorial Library, North Bldg, Basement, 1720 Cesar E Chavez Ave, 90033. SAN 301-0198. Tel: 323-260-5715. FAX: 323-260-5748. *Libr Dir,* June Levy; E-mail: June.Levy@ah.org; *Med Librn,* Zahra Fotovat; E-mail: FotovatZH@ah.org; *Med Librn,* Myrna Y Uyengco-Harooch; E-mail: Myrna.Uyengco-Harooch@ah.org; Staff 2 (MLS 1, Non-MLS 1)
Founded 1920
Library Holdings: e-books 1,000; Bk Vols 43,000; Per Subs 350
Special Collections: History & Religion (Percy T Magan Coll); History Coll; History of Medicine (Margaret & H James Hara Memorial Coll)
Subject Interests: Med, Nursing
Automation Activity & Vendor Info: (Cataloging) SydneyPlus; (Circulation) SydneyPlus
Partic in National Network of Libraries of Medicine Region 5
Restriction: Staff & mem only, Staff & patient use
Friends of the Library Group

R WILSHIRE BOULEVARD TEMPLE, Brawerman Elementary School Temple - Libraries, 3663 Wilshire Blvd (Mid-Wilshire)), 90010. (Mail add: 11661 W Olympic Blvd (Westside), 90064), SAN 301-021X, *Libr Spec,* Karen Morgenstern; Tel: 424-208-8945, E-mail: kmorgenstern@brawerman.org; *Libr Spec,* Gail Robillard; E-mail: grobillard@brawerman.org; Staff 2 (MLS 1, Non-MLS 1)
Founded 1929
Library Holdings: Bk Vols 17,050
Special Collections: Judaica
Wireless access
Function: 24/7 Electronic res, 24/7 Online cat, 3D Printer, Children's prog, Distance learning, E-Reserves, Electronic databases & coll, Online cat, Online info literacy tutorials on the web & in blackboard, Prog for children & young adult, Ref & res, Ref serv available, Res assist avail, Res libr
Restriction: Authorized patrons, Borrowing privileges limited to fac & registered students, Private libr

R STEPHEN S WISE TEMPLE LIBRARY, 15500 Stephen S Wise Dr, 90077. SAN 301-0228. Tel: 310-889-2241. FAX: 310-476-2353. E-mail: letsconnect@wisela.org. *Librn,* Esme McTighe; E-mail: emctighe@wise-school.org; Staff 1 (Non-MLS 1)
Founded 1967
Subject Interests: Judaica (lit or hist of Jews)
Wireless access
Open Mon-Wed 7:45-3:45

LOS GATOS

M EL CAMINO LOS GATOS HEALTH LIBRARY*, 815 Pollard Rd, 95032. SAN 370-5676. Tel: 408-866-4044. FAX: 408-866-3829. *Sr Librn,* Michael Liddicoat; E-mail: Mike_Li@elcaminohospital.org; Staff 5 (MLS 1, Non-MLS 4)
Founded 1989
Library Holdings: DVDs 40; e-books 104; e-journals 16; Bk Titles 1,500; Per Subs 50
Subject Interests: Consumer health, Med, Nursing
Automation Activity & Vendor Info: (Cataloging) EOS International; (Circulation) EOS International; (Serials) Prenax, Inc
Wireless access
Partic in Coop Libr Agency for Syst & Servs
Open Mon-Thurs 9-3:30

P LOS GATOS PUBLIC LIBRARY*, 100 Villa Ave, 95030-6981. SAN 301-0260. Tel: 408-354-6891. Interlibrary Loan Service Tel: 408-399-5784. Reference Tel: 408-354-6896. Administration Tel: 408-354-6898. FAX: 408-399-6008. E-mail: library@losgatosca.gov. Web Site: library.losgatosca.gov. *Libr Dir,* Ryan Baker; E-mail: rbaker@losgatosca.gov; Staff 5 (MLS 5)
Founded 1898. Pop 29,500; Circ 450,000
Jul 2012-Jun 2013 Income $2,192,690
Library Holdings: Large Print Bks 1,077; Bk Titles 130,000; Per Subs 150
Subject Interests: Local hist
Automation Activity & Vendor Info: (Acquisitions) ByWater Solutions; (Cataloging) ByWater Solutions; (Circulation) ByWater Solutions; (ILL) OCLC CatExpress; (OPAC) ByWater Solutions; (Serials) ByWater Solutions
Wireless access
Open Mon & Tues 11-8, Wed-Fri 10-6, Sat 10-5, Sun 12-5
Friends of the Library Group

MADERA

S MADERA COUNTY HISTORICAL SOCIETY*, Museum-Library, 210 W Yosemite Ave, 93637-3533. (Mail add: PO Box 150, 93639-0150), SAN 371-7267. Tel: 559-673-0291. E-mail: mchs210@gmail.com. *Curator,* Karen Elmore
Library Holdings: Bk Vols 130
Special Collections: County
Wireless access
Restriction: Open by appt only

L MADERA COUNTY LAW LIBRARY*, County Government Ctr, 209 W Yosemite Ave, 93637. SAN 301-0309. Tel: 559-673-0378. FAX: 559-673-0378. E-mail: frontdesk@maderalawlibrary.com. Web Site: www.maderacountylibrary.org/madera-county-law-library. *Law Libr Dir/Law Librn,* Trudy J Burke; E-mail: director@maderalawlibrary.com
Founded 1909
Subject Interests: Legal ref mat
Wireless access
Open Mon-Fri 10am-1pm

P MADERA COUNTY LIBRARY*, 121 North G St, 93637-3592. SAN 333-0966. Tel: 559-675-7871. FAX: 559-675-7998. E-mail: madera@maderacountylibrary.org. Web Site: www.maderacounty.com/government/madera-county-library. *Libr Dir,* Krista Riggs; E-mail: krista.riggs@maderacountylibrary.org
Founded 1910
Library Holdings: DVDs 7,321; e-books 523; Bk Vols 241,458; Per Subs 210
Subject Interests: Calif, Civil War, Genealogy
Automation Activity & Vendor Info: (Acquisitions) Horizon; (Cataloging) Horizon; (Circulation) Horizon; (Course Reserve) Horizon; (ILL) Horizon; (OPAC) Horizon; (Serials) Horizon
Wireless access
Mem of San Joaquin Valley Library System
Open Mon-Thurs 11-6, Fri & Sat 11-3
Friends of the Library Group
Branches: 4
CHOWCHILLA BRANCH, 300 Kings Ave, Chowchilla, 93610-2059, SAN 333-0990. Tel: 559-665-2630. FAX: 559-665-4216. *Br Mgr,* Nellie Serna
Library Holdings: Bk Vols 34,523
Open Tues 11-6, Wed & Thurs 11-5, Fri & Sat 11-3
Friends of the Library Group
MADERA RANCHOS BRANCH, 37398 Berkshire Dr, 93636, SAN 371-9537. Tel: 559-645-1214. *Br Mgr,* Amanda Jude
Founded 1990
Library Holdings: Bk Vols 18,000
Open Tues 11-6, Wed & Thurs 11-5, Fri & Sat 11-3
Friends of the Library Group
NORTH FORK BRANCH, 32908 Rd 222, North Fork, 93643, SAN 333-1024. Tel: 559-877-2387. FAX: 559-877-3527. *Br Mgr,* Sarah Koehler
Library Holdings: Bk Vols 21,328
Open Tues 11-6, Wed & Thurs 11-5, Fri & Sat 11-3
Friends of the Library Group
OAKHURST BRANCH, 49044 Civic Circle, Oakhurst, 93644-0484, SAN 333-1059. Tel: 559-683-4838. FAX: 559-642-4591. *Br Mgr,* Dale Rushing
Library Holdings: Bk Vols 42,000
Open Mon-Thurs 10-5, Fri & Sat 10-2
Friends of the Library Group

M VALLEY CHILDREN'S HEALTHCARE, Nathalie Wolfe Pediatric Sciences Library, 9300 Valley Children's Pl, 93638-8762. SAN 320-5614. Tel: 559-353-6178. Web Site: valleychildrens.org/medical-education/medical-library. *Library Services, Prog Mgr,* Brian Baker; E-mail: bbaker@valleychildrens.org; Staff 2 (MLS 1, Non-MLS 1)
Founded 1989
Library Holdings: Bk Vols 1,500; Per Subs 200
Subject Interests: Pediatrics
Automation Activity & Vendor Info: (Cataloging) CyberTools for Libraries; (Circulation) CyberTools for Libraries; (OPAC) CyberTools for Libraries; (Serials) CyberTools for Libraries
Wireless access
Function: Computers for patron use, Doc delivery serv, Electronic databases & coll, Health sci info serv, Internet access, Online cat, Photocopying/Printing, Wheelchair accessible
Partic in Northern California & Nevada Medical Library Group
Restriction: Circulates for staff only, Hospital staff & commun, Med staff & students, Pub use on premises

MALIBU

C PEPPERDINE UNIVERSITY LIBRARIES*, Payson Library, 24255 Pacific Coast Hwy, 90263. SAN 333-1083. Tel: 310-506-4252. Circulation Tel: 310-506-7273. Web Site: library.pepperdine.edu. *Dean of Libr,* Mark Roosa; E-mail: mark.roosa@pepperdine.edu; *Dir of Libr Advan,* Jeanette Woodburn; *Assoc Univ Librn, Info Res,* Lynne Jacobsen; E-mail: lynne.jacobsen@pepperdine.edu; *Assoc Univ Librn, Pub Serv,* Melinda Raine; E-mail: melinda.raine@pepperdine.edu; *Assoc Univ Librn, Spec Coll & Univ Archives,* Melissa Nykanen; E-mail: melissa.nykanen@pepperdine.edu; *Access Serv Librn,* Sally Bryant; *Bus Liaison Librn, Ref Librn,* Marc Vinyard; *Data Librn,* Cory Aitchison; *Librn for Digital Publishing, Curation & Conversion,* Josias Bartram; *Digital Syst Librn,* Grace Ye; *Instrul Design Librn,* Paul Stenis; *Res & Ref Librn,* Jaimie Beth Colvin; *Res & Ref Librn,* Mary Ann Naumann; *Res & Instruction Librn,* Elizabeth Parang; *Scholarly Resources Librn,* Jeremy Whitt; *Archivist, Spec Coll & Univ Archives,* Kelsey Knox; *ILL,* Melissa Pichette; Staff 25 (MLS 14, Non-MLS 11)
Founded 1937. Enrl 6,388; Fac 478; Highest Degree: Doctorate
Library Holdings: Music Scores 3,827; Bk Vols 350,467; Per Subs 249
Special Collections: French Coll on 19th Century Paris (Mlynarsky Coll); Malibu Historical Coll; Religious History (Churches of Christ). US Document Depository
Automation Activity & Vendor Info: (Acquisitions) OCLC Worldshare Management Services; (Circulation) OCLC Worldshare Management Services; (OPAC) OCLC Worldshare Management Services
Wireless access
Partic in OCLC Online Computer Library Center, Inc; Statewide California Electronic Library Consortium
Open Mon-Thurs 7:30am-3am, Fri 7:30-6, Sat 9-5, Sun Noon-3am
Friends of the Library Group
Departmental Libraries:
DRESCHER GRADUATE CAMPUS LIBRARY, 24255 Pacific Coast Hwy, 90263. Tel: 310-506-8568. Circulation Tel: 310-506-8566. Web Site: library.pepperdine.edu/locations/drescher. *Campus Librn,* Jacquie Kowalczyk; E-mail: jacquie.kowalczyk@pepperdine.edu; Staff 1 (MLS 1)
Subject Interests: Bus & mgt, Psychol, Pub policy
Open Mon-Thurs 8am-Midnight, Fri 8am-9pm, Sat 10-6, Sun 1-Midnight
ENCINO GRADUATE CAMPUS LIBRARY, 16830 Ventura Blvd, Ste 200, Encino, 91436, SAN 373-5567. Tel: 818-501-1615. *Libr Asst,* Dana Robinson; E-mail: dana.robinson@pepperdine.edu; Staff 1 (Non-MLS 1)
Subject Interests: Bus & mgt, Educ, Psychol
Open Mon-Thurs 2:30-10:30, Fri 11-7, Sat 9-5

CL SCHOOL OF LAW-JERENE APPLEBY HARNISH LAW LIBRARY, 24255 Pacific Coast Hwy, 90263. Tel: 310-506-4643. Web Site: www.law.pepperdine.edu. *Asst Dean,* Katie Kerr Dobbs; E-mail: katie.dodds@pepperdine.edu; *Assoc Dir, Pub Serv, Coll,* Joy Humphrey; E-mail: joy.humphrey@pepperdine.edu; *Assoc Dir, Ref Serv,* Jodi Kruger; E-mail: jodi.kruger@pepperdine.edu; *Sr Serv, Student Serv Librn,* Don Buffaloe; E-mail: donald.buffaloe@pepperdine.edu; *Pub Serv,* Jessica Drewitz
Library Holdings: Bk Titles 125,000; Bk Vols 400,000; Per Subs 3,603
Special Collections: American Arbitration Association Library & Information Center Coll
Automation Activity & Vendor Info: (Course Reserve) Ex Libris Group; (ILL) Ex Libris Group; (Media Booking) Ex Libris Group; (OPAC) Ex Libris Group; (Serials) Ex Libris Group
IRVINE CENTER LIBRARY, Lakeshore Towers III, 18111 Von Karman Ave, Irvine, 92612, SAN 321-4044. Tel: 949-223-2520. *Info Serv Librn,* Toby Berger; E-mail: tberger@pepperdine.edu
Subject Interests: Bus & mgt, Educ, Psychol
Function: ILL available
Open Mon-Thurs 12-10:30, Fri 12-6, Sat 9-5
WEST LOS ANGELES GRADUATE CAMPUS LIBRARY, Howard Hughes Ctr, 6100 Center Dr, Los Angeles, 90045, SAN 332-9402. Tel: 310-568-5670. Circulation Tel: 310-568-5685. *Head Librn,* Maria Brahme; E-mail: mbrahme@pepperdine.edu
Subject Interests: Bus & mgt, Educ, Psychol
Open Mon-Thurs 9am-10:30pm, Fri 9-7, Sat 9-5, Sun 1-7
WESTLAKE VILLAGE GRADUATE CAMPUS LIBRARY, Westlake Ctr, 2829 Townsgate Rd, Ste 180, Westlake Village, 91361. Tel: 805-379-5801.
Open Mon-Thurs 9am-10:30pm, Fri 9am-9:30pm, Sat 8-5

MAMMOTH LAKES

P MONO COUNTY FREE LIBRARY*, Mammoth Lakes, 400 Sierra Park Rd, 93546. (Mail add: PO Box 1120, 93546-1120), SAN 377-8576. Tel: 760-934-4777. FAX: 760-934-6268. Web Site: www.monocolibraries.org/branches/mammoth-lakes. *County Libr Dir,* Christopher Platt; E-mail: cplatt@monocoe.org; *Librn,* Doug Oldham; E-mail: doldham@monocoe.org
Founded 1947. Pop 14,500; Circ 100,000

Library Holdings: Audiobooks 4,794; AV Mats 364; CDs 5,220; DVDs 8,627; e-books 66,832; Large Print Bks 600; Bk Titles 50,000; Bk Vols 73,000; Per Subs 120
Automation Activity & Vendor Info: (Circulation) Koha; (ILL) OCLC; (OPAC) Koha
Wireless access
Function: 24/7 Electronic res, 24/7 Online cat, Activity rm, Adult bk club, Art exhibits, Audio & video playback equip for onsite use, Audiobks via web, Bilingual assistance for Spanish patrons, Bk club(s), Bks on cassette, Bks on CD, CD-ROM, Children's prog, Citizenship assistance, Computers for patron use, Digital talking bks, Electronic databases & coll, Family literacy, Free DVD rentals, Govt ref serv, Holiday prog, Homework prog, ILL available, Instruction & testing, Internet access, Learning ctr, Life-long learning prog for all ages, Magazines, Mango lang, Meeting rooms, Movies, Music CDs, Online cat, Online ref, OverDrive digital audio bks, Photocopying/Printing, Preschool outreach, Preschool reading prog, Prog for adults, Prog for children & young adult, Ref & res, Scanner, Spanish lang bks, Spoken cassettes & CDs, Spoken cassettes & DVDs, Story hour, Study rm, Summer reading prog, Tax forms, Teen prog, VHS videos
Mem of NorthNet Library System
Open Mon-Fri 10-7, Sat 10-5:30
Friends of the Library Group
Branches: 4
BRIDGEPORT, 94 N School St, Bridgeport, 93517. (Mail add: PO Box 398, Bridgeport, 93517-0398), SAN 300-6344. Tel: 760-932-7482. FAX: 760-932-7539. Web Site: www.monocolibraries.org/branches/bridgeport. *Librn,* Abbie Bridges; E-mail: abridges@monocoe.org
Founded 1965. Pop 11,200; Circ 63,391
Library Holdings: Bk Vols 26,000; Per Subs 19
Special Collections: Native American Coll
Publications: Bibliographies
Open Tues-Fri 10-5, Sat 10-1 & 2-5
Friends of the Library Group
COLEVILLE, 111591 Hwy 395, Coleville, 96107, SAN 377-8428. Tel: 530-495-2788. FAX: 530-495-2295. Web Site: www.monocolibraries.org/branches/coleville. *Library Contact,* S Domanski; E-mail: sdomanski@monocoe.org
Library Holdings: Bk Vols 30,000
Automation Activity & Vendor Info: (Cataloging) SirsiDynix; (Circulation) SirsiDynix
Open Tues-Thurs 12:30-5:30, Sat 8:30-1:30
Friends of the Library Group
CROWLEY LAKE, 3627 Crowley Lake Dr, Crowley Lake, 93546. Tel: 760-935-4505. FAX: 760-935-4560. Web Site: www.monocolibraries.org/branches/crowley-lake. *Sr Librn,* Diane Thoman; E-mail: dthoman@monocoe.org
Open Tues & Thurs 1-6, Fri & Sat 10-3
Friends of the Library Group
JUNE LAKE, 90 W Granite Ave, June Lake, 93529. (Mail add: PO Box 145, June Lake, 93529-0145), SAN 377-8444. Tel: 760-648-7284. FAX: 760-648-7284. Web Site: www.monocolibraries.org/branches/june-lake. *Library Contact,* C Lester; E-mail: clester@monocoe.org
Library Holdings: Bk Vols 14,000; Per Subs 3
Open Tues & Thurs 1-6, Wed & Sat 11-4
Friends of the Library Group

MARINA

P MONTEREY COUNTY FREE LIBRARIES*, 188 Seaside Ctr, 93933-2500. SAN 334-0953. Tel: 831-883-7573. Web Site: www.co.monterey.ca.us/government/departments-i-z/library. *County Librn,* Hillary Theyer; E-mail: TheyerHA@co.monterey.ca.us; Staff 25 (MLS 11, Non-MLS 14)
Founded 1912. Pop 220,825; Circ 649,117
Jul 2012-Jun 2013 Income (Main & Associated Libraries) $7,445,942, County $6,881,904, Locally Generated Income $564,038. Mats Exp $7,272,407, Books $337,822. Sal $2,887,221
Library Holdings: Audiobooks 7,763; AV Mats 26,202; CDs 7,763; DVDs 14,551; e-books 6,005; Large Print Bks 4,379; Microforms 2,846; Bk Titles 186,602; Bk Vols 389,074; Per Subs 440; Talking Bks 7,763; Videos 2,497
Special Collections: Californiana Coll
Automation Activity & Vendor Info: (Acquisitions) Innovative Interfaces, Inc; (Cataloging) Innovative Interfaces, Inc; (Circulation) Innovative Interfaces, Inc; (OPAC) Innovative Interfaces, Inc
Wireless access
Function: Adult bk club, Adult literacy prog, Archival coll, Art exhibits, Audiobks via web, Bilingual assistance for Spanish patrons, Bk club(s), Bks on cassette, Bks on CD, Children's prog, Computer training, Computers for patron use, Digital talking bks, Electronic databases & coll, Family literacy, Free DVD rentals, Homebound delivery serv, Homework prog, ILL available, Internet access, Magnifiers for reading, Microfiche/film & reading machines, Online cat, Online ref, OverDrive digital audio bks, Photocopying/Printing, Prog for adults, Prog for children & young adult, Spanish lang bks, Story hour, Summer reading prog, Tax forms, VHS videos, Wheelchair accessible, Workshops
Partic in Monterey Bay Area Cooperative Library System
Special Services for the Deaf - Bks on deafness & sign lang; Closed caption videos
Special Services for the Blind - Bks on cassette; Bks on CD; Extensive large print coll; Free checkout of audio mat; Home delivery serv; Large print bks; Magnifiers; Recorded bks; Talking bks
Open Mon-Fri 8-5
Friends of the Library Group
Branches: 17
AROMAS BRANCH, 387 Blohm Ave, Aromas, 95004. (Mail add: PO Box 298, Aromas, 95004-0298), SAN 334-0988. Tel: 831-726-3240. FAX: 831-726-0102. *Br Head,* Monica Guaracha-Martinez
Pop 2,797; Circ 9,711
Library Holdings: Bk Vols 8,852
Function: Prog for adults, Prog for children & young adult, Summer reading prog
Open Wed & Thurs 1-6, Fri 1-5, Sat 12-4
Friends of the Library Group
BIG SUR BRANCH, Hwy 1 at Ripplewood Resort, Big Sur, 93920. (Mail add: PO Box 217, Big Sur, 93920-0217), SAN 334-1135. Tel: 831-667-2537. FAX: 831-667-0708. *Br Head,* Tammy DelConte
Pop 1,336; Circ 9,956
Library Holdings: Bk Vols 10,647
Function: Prog for children & young adult
Open Wed & Thurs 2-6, Fri & Sat 10-3
Friends of the Library Group
BRADLEY BRANCH, Dixie St, Bradley, 93426. (Mail add: PO Box 330, Bradley, 93426-0330), SAN 334-1046. Tel: 805-472-9407. FAX: 805-472-9565.
Pop 450; Circ 4,814
Library Holdings: Bk Vols 3,476
Function: Prog for children & young adult, Summer reading prog
Closed due to construction of new library 2021-
BUENA VISTA, 18250 Tara Dr, Salinas, 93908, SAN 378-0376. Tel: 831-455-9699. FAX: 831-455-0369. *Libr Mgr,* Dana Armstrong; Staff 1 (Non-MLS 1)
Pop 16,069; Circ 38,298
Library Holdings: Bk Vols 18,139
Function: Prog for children & young adult, Summer reading prog
Open Tues 10-7, Wed 10-6, Thurs & Sat 10-5, Fri 10-4
CARMEL VALLEY BRANCH, 65 W Carmel Valley Rd, Carmel Valley, 93924, SAN 334-1070. Tel: 831-659-2377. FAX: 831-659-0589. *Br Mgr,* Eddy Hamelin; Staff 1 (MLS 1)
Pop 6,819; Circ 50,776
Library Holdings: Bk Vols 30,725
Function: Prog for adults, Prog for children & young adult, Summer reading prog
Open Tues & Thurs 11-7, Wed 10-6, Fri & Sat 10-5
Friends of the Library Group
CASTROVILLE BRANCH, 11160 Speegle St, Castroville, 95012, SAN 334-1100. Tel: 831-769-8724. FAX: 831-633-6315. *Br Mgr,* David Tavares; Staff 1 (MLS 1)
Pop 9,525; Circ 36,019
Library Holdings: Bk Vols 31,322
Function: Prog for children & young adult, Summer reading prog
Open Tues-Thurs 11-7, Fri & Sat 10-5
GONZALES BRANCH, 851 Fifth St, Ste T, Gonzales, 93926, SAN 334-116X. Tel: 831-675-2209. FAX: 831-675-9525. *Br Mgr,* Christopher Gallegos; Staff 1 (MLS 1)
Pop 8,364; Circ 19,612
Library Holdings: Bk Vols 20,616
Function: Bilingual assistance for Spanish patrons, Computers for patron use, Homework prog, Photocopying/Printing, Prog for children & young adult, Spanish lang bks, Story hour, Summer reading prog
Open Tues-Thurs 11-7, Fri & Sat 10-5
GREENFIELD BRANCH, 315 El Camino Real, Greenfield, 93927, SAN 334-1194. Tel: 831-674-2614. FAX: 831-674-2688. *Br Mgr,* Dawn Vest; Staff 1 (Non-MLS 1)
Pop 16,629; Circ 599,886
Library Holdings: Bk Vols 25,352
Function: Prog for children & young adult, Summer reading prog
Open Tues & Wed 11-7, Thurs 10-6, Fri & Sat 10-5
Friends of the Library Group
KING CITY BRANCH, 402 Broadway St, King City, 93930, SAN 370-7946. Tel: 831-385-3677. FAX: 831-385-0918. *Br Mgr,* Robin Cauntay; Staff 1 (MLS 1)
Pop 11,518; Circ 60,249
Library Holdings: Bk Vols 36,075
Function: Prog for children & young adult, Summer reading prog
Open Tues-Thurs 11-7, Fri & Sat 10-5
Friends of the Library Group
MARINA BRANCH, 190 Seaside Circle, 93933, SAN 334-1224. Tel: 831-883-7507. FAX: 831-883-9473. *Br Mgr,* Melissa Meija
Pop 21,750; Circ 85,761
Library Holdings: Bk Vols 26,677

Function: Prog for children & young adult, Summer reading prog
Open Tues & Wed 11-7, Thurs 10-6, Fri & Sat 10-5
Friends of the Library Group
PAJARO BRANCH, 29 Bishop St, Pajaro, 95076, SAN 376-9186. Tel: 831-761-2545. FAX: 831-768-7782. *Br Head,* Joseantonio Gonzalez
Pop 3,600; Circ 4,916
Library Holdings: Bk Vols 8,517
Function: Prog for children & young adult, Summer reading prog
Open Tues & Wed 2-7, Fri & Sat 1-5
PARKFIELD, 70643 Parkfield-Coalinga Rd, San Miguel, 93451, SAN 334-1283. Tel: 805-463-2347. FAX: 805-463-2347.
Library Holdings: Bk Vols 6,039
Function: Prog for children & young adult, Summer reading prog
Temporarily closed, remodeling 2020-
PRUNEDALE, 17822 Moro Rd, Salinas, 93907, SAN 334-1313. Tel: 831-663-2292. FAX: 831-663-0203. *Br Mgr,* Tammy DelConte; Staff 1 (Non-MLS 1)
Pop 16,432; Circ 69,255
Library Holdings: Bk Vols 41,488
Function: Prog for children & young adult, Summer reading prog
Open Tues & Wed 11-7, Thurs 10-6, Fri & Sat 10-5
Friends of the Library Group
SAN ARDO BRANCH, 62350 College St, San Ardo, 93450. (Mail add: PO Box 127, San Ardo, 93450-0127), SAN 334-1348. Tel: 831-627-2503. FAX: 831-627-4229. *Br Head,* Martin Zuniga
Pop 873; Circ 8,806
Library Holdings: Bk Vols 8,111
Function: Prog for children & young adult, Summer reading prog
Open Wed 1-6, Thurs 2-6, Fri 2-5, Sat 11-5
SAN LUCAS BRANCH, 54692 Teresa St, San Lucas, 93954. (Mail add: PO Box 28, San Lucas, 93954-0028), SAN 334-1372. Tel: 831-382-0414. FAX: 831-382-0554. *Br Head,* Liz Bednar
Library Holdings: Bk Vols 7,290
Function: Prog for children & young adult, Summer reading prog
Open Wed & Sat 11-4, Thurs 2-6, Fri 1-5
SEASIDE BRANCH, 550 Harcourt Ave, Seaside, 93955, SAN 334-1402. Tel: 831-899-2055. FAX: 831-899-2735. *Br Mgr,* Beata Obydzinski; Staff 3 (MLS 1, Non-MLS 2)
Pop 36,568; Circ 113,217
Library Holdings: Bk Vols 69,049
Function: Adult literacy prog, Prog for children & young adult, Summer reading prog
Open Mon 10-6, Tues-Thurs 11-7, Fri & Sat 10-5
Friends of the Library Group
SOLEDAD BRANCH, 401 Gabilan Dr, Soledad, 93960, SAN 334-1437. Tel: 831-678-2430. FAX: 831-678-3087. *Br Mgr,* Denise Campos; Staff 1 (Non-MLS 1)
Pop 24,502; Circ 42,191
Library Holdings: Bk Vols 33,570
Function: Prog for children & young adult, Summer reading prog
Open Tues & Wed 11-7, Thurs 10-6, Fri & Sat 10-5
Bookmobiles: 2. Head, Kameta Harrington. Bk titles 10,125

S MONTEREY INSTITUTE FOR RESEARCH & ASTRONOMY*, Priscilla Fairfield Bok Library, 200 Eighth St, 93933. SAN 327-7119. Tel: 831-883-1000. FAX: 831-883-1031. E-mail: mira@mira.org. Web Site: www.mira.org. *Libra,* Joanna Sorci
Library Holdings: Bk Vols 3,000
Restriction: Open by appt only
Friends of the Library Group

MARIPOSA

L MARIPOSA COUNTY LAW LIBRARY*, 4978 Tenth St, 95338. (Mail add: PO Box 106, 95338), SAN 324-3532. Tel: 209-966-2140. Web Site: mariposalibrary.org. *Head Libra,* Janet Chase-Williams; E-mail: janet.chase-williams@sjvls.org; *Asst Libra II,* Isa Rodrigues
Library Holdings: Bk Vols 1,993
Wireless access

P MARIPOSA COUNTY LIBRARY*, 4978 Tenth St, 95338. (Mail add: PO Box 109, 95338), SAN 374-6291. Tel: 209-966-2140. FAX: 209-742-7527. Web Site: www.mariposalibrary.org. *Dir,* Janet Chase-Williams; E-mail: jchase-williams@sjvls.org; Staff 9 (MLS 1, Non-MLS 8)
Founded 1926. Pop 16,000; Circ 81,133
Library Holdings: Bk Vols 33,000; Per Subs 75
Wireless access
Mem of San Joaquin Valley Library System
Special Services for the Deaf - Bks on deafness & sign lang; Captioned film dep; High interest/low vocabulary bks
Open Mon & Sat 8:30-4, Tues -Fri 8:30-6
Friends of the Library Group

Branches: 4
BASSETT MEMORIAL, 7971 Chilnualna Falls Rd, Wawona, 95389. (Mail add: PO Box 2008, Wawona, 95389-2008), SAN 374-6321. Tel: 209-375-6510. *Br Head,* Diane Mello; Staff 3 (Non-MLS 3)
Open Wed & Fri (Winter) 12-5, Sat 10-3; Mon-Fri (Summer) 1-5, Sat 10-2
Friends of the Library Group
EL PORTAL BRANCH, 9670 Rancheria Flat Rd, 1st Flr, El Portal, 95318. (Mail add: PO Box 160, El Portal, 95318-0160), SAN 374-6305. Tel: 209-379-2401. *Br Head,* Andrea Canapary; Staff 3 (Non-MLS 3)
Open Mon & Thurs 10-6:30, Sun & Mon (Summer) 12-7
RED CLOUD, 10332-C Fiske Rd, Coulterville, 95311, SAN 374-6313. Tel: 209-878-3692. *Br Libra,* Pam Lagomarsino; Staff 3 (Non-MLS 3)
Open Tues, Wed & Fri 11-3, Sat (Winter) 12-4
Friends of the Library Group
YOSEMITE NATIONAL PARK BRANCH, Girls Club Bldg, 58 Cedar Ct, Yosemite National Park, 95389. (Mail add: PO Box 395, Yosemite National Park, 95389-0395), SAN 374-633X. Tel: 209-372-4552. *Br Head,* Alice Rosenfeld; Staff 3 (Non-MLS 3)
Open Mon 12-3, Tues & Wed 10-2, Thurs 3-6

MARKLEEVILLE

S ALPINE COUNTY HISTORICAL SOCIETY*, Alpine County Museum Library, One School St, 96120. (Mail add: PO Box 517, 96120-0517), SAN 371-7038. Tel: 530-694-2317. FAX: 530-694-1087. E-mail: alpinemuseum@yahoo.com. Web Site: alpinecounty.com/alpine-county-museum, www.alpinecountymuseum.org. *Curator,* Jim Boyd
Founded 1964
Library Holdings: Bk Titles 600; Per Subs 16
Special Collections: Alpine County First Familes Coll; Spicer Archealogical Coll. Oral History
Wireless access
Function: Res libr
Publications: Alpine Review (Quarterly)
Open Thurs-Sun (June-Oct) 10-4
Restriction: Not a lending libr

P ALPINE COUNTY LIBRARY*, 270 Laramie St, 96120. (Mail add: PO Box 187, 96120-0187), SAN 301-0406. Tel: 530-694-2120. FAX: 530-694-2408. E-mail: library@alpinecountyca.gov. Web Site: www.alpinecountyca.gov. *County Libra,* Rita Lovell; E-mail: rlovell@alpinecountyca.gov; Staff 3 (MLS 1, Non-MLS 2)
Founded 1969. Pop 1,200; Circ 1,265
Library Holdings: CDs 192; Large Print Bks 47; Bk Titles 14,044; Bk Vols 15,832; Per Subs 70; Talking Bks 474; Videos 1,532
Special Collections: Local History Coll
Subject Interests: Local hist
Automation Activity & Vendor Info: (Cataloging) TLC (The Library Corporation); (Circulation) TLC (The Library Corporation); (OPAC) TLC (The Library Corporation)
Wireless access
Function: Archival coll, ILL available, Photocopying/Printing, Prog for adults, Prog for children & young adult, Ref serv available, Summer reading prog, Wheelchair accessible
Publications: Library Newsletter (Bimonthly)
Open Tues-Sat 10-5
Friends of the Library Group
Branches: 1
BEAR VALLEY BRANCH, 367 Creekside Dr, Bear Valley, 95223. (Mail add: PO Box 5237, Bear Valley, 95223-5237), SAN 370-4904. Tel: 209-753-6219. FAX: 209-753-2219. *Libr Asst III,* Thea Schoettgen; E-mail: tschoettgen@alpinecountyca.gov
Circ 5,011
Library Holdings: Bk Titles 4,776; Bk Vols 4,808; Per Subs 44; Talking Bks 262; Videos 662
Function: AV serv, ILL available, Photocopying/Printing, Prog for adults, Prog for children & young adult, Ref serv available, Summer reading prog, Wheelchair accessible
Open Wed-Sat 12:30-5:30
Friends of the Library Group
Bookmobiles: 1

MARTINEZ

P CONTRA COSTA COUNTY LIBRARY*, Library Administration, 777 Arnold Dr, Ste 210, 94553. SAN 333-6662. Tel: 925-608-7700. Interlibrary Loan Service Tel: 925-608-7756. Toll Free Tel: 800-984-4636. FAX: 925-608-7761. Reference FAX: 925-646-6030. E-mail: libadmin@ccclib.org. Web Site: www.ccclib.org. *County Libra,* Melinda Cervantes; *Dep County Libra, Pub Serv,* Nancy Kreiser; *Dep County Libra, Pub Serv,* Gail McPartland; *Dep County Libra, Support Serv,* Alison McKee; Staff 165 (MLS 58, Non-MLS 107)
Founded 1913. Pop 902,200; Circ 4,736,101

Library Holdings: AV Mats 158,971; Bk Vols 1,291,051; Per Subs 1,981
Special Collections: California Hist Coll; Contra Costa Hist Coll; Food Technology (Vincent Davi Coll). State Document Depository; US Document Depository
Automation Activity & Vendor Info: (Acquisitions) TLC (The Library Corporation); (Cataloging) TLC (The Library Corporation); (Circulation) TLC (The Library Corporation); (OPAC) TLC (The Library Corporation); (Serials) TLC (The Library Corporation)
Wireless access
Function: Adult literacy prog, Govt ref serv, Homebound delivery serv, ILL available, Photocopying/Printing, Prog for adults, Prog for children & young adult, Ref serv available, Summer reading prog, Wheelchair accessible
Special Services for the Blind - Closed circuit radio for broadcast serv; Talking bks & player equip
Open Mon-Fri 8-5
Friends of the Library Group
Branches: 26
ANTIOCH COMMUNITY LIBRARY, 501 W 18th St, Antioch, 94509, SAN 333-6697. Tel: 925-757-9224. Web Site: ccclib.org/locations/1. *Commun Libr Mgr,* Geneva Moss; E-mail: gmoss@ccclib.org
Pop 102,113; Circ 214,591
Library Holdings: Bk Vols 64,333
Open Mon & Tues 12-8, Wed & Thurs 11-6, Sat 12-5
Friends of the Library Group
BAY POINT LIBRARY, 205 Pacifica Ave, Bay Point, 94565, SAN 377-6654. Tel: 925-458-9597. Web Site: ccclib.org/locations/2. *Commun Libr Mgr,* Ginny Golden; E-mail: ggolden@ccclib.org
Pop 22,074; Circ 11,976
Library Holdings: Bk Vols 8,706
Open Mon & Fri 2:30-6, Tues & Thurs 2:30-8
Friends of the Library Group
BRENTWOOD LIBRARY, 104 Oak St, Brentwood, 94513, SAN 333-6727. Tel: 925-516-5290. Web Site: ccclib.org/locations/4. *Sr Commun Libr Mgr,* Liz Fuller; E-mail: lfuller@ccclib.org
Pop 56,492; Circ 161,593
Library Holdings: Bk Vols 45,996
Open Mon-Thurs 10-8, Fri & Sat 10-6
Friends of the Library Group
CLAYTON LIBRARY, 6125 Clayton Rd, Clayton, 94517, SAN 377-6670. Tel: 925-673-0659. Web Site: ccclib.org/locations/6. *Commun Libr Mgr,* Karen Hansen-Smith; E-mail: khansen@ccclib.org; Staff 4 (MLS 2, Non-MLS 2)
Pop 11,398; Circ 222,073
Library Holdings: Bk Vols 63,457
Open Mon & Wed 1-9, Tues, Thurs & Sat 10-6, Sun 1-5
Friends of the Library Group
CONCORD LIBRARY, 2900 Salvio St, Concord, 94519, SAN 333-6786. Tel: 925-646-5455. Web Site: ccclib.org/locations/7. *Sr Commun Libr Mgr,* Kimberli Buckley; E-mail: kbuckley@ccclib.org
Circ 289,307
Library Holdings: Bk Vols 79,858
Open Mon & Thurs 12-9, Tues & Wed 10-6, Fri & Sat 10-5, Sun 1-5
Friends of the Library Group
CROCKETT LIBRARY, 991 Loring Ave, Crockett, 94525, SAN 333-6816. Tel: 510-787-2345. Web Site: ccclib.org/locations/8. *Commun Libr Mgr,* Lynne Noone; E-mail: lnoone@ccclib.org
Pop 3,443; Circ 7,240
Library Holdings: Bk Vols 5,449
Open Mon 2-8, Wed & Fri 11-5, Sat 10-4
Friends of the Library Group
DANVILLE LIBRARY, 400 Front St, Danville, 94526, SAN 333-7235. Tel: 925-314-3750. Web Site: ccclib.org/locations/9. *Sr Commun Libr Mgr,* Seng Lovan; E-mail: slovan@ccclib.org
Library Holdings: Bk Vols 81,690
Open Mon-Thurs 10-8, Fri & Sat 10-6, Sun 1-5
Friends of the Library Group
DOUGHERTY STATION LIBRARY, 17017 Bollinger Canyon Rd, San Ramon, 94582. Tel: 925-973-3380. Web Site: ccclib.org/locations/60. *Sr Commun Libr Mgr,* Dena Hollowood; E-mail: dhollowo@ccclib.org
Library Holdings: Bk Vols 57,349
Open Mon & Thurs-Sat 10-8, Tues & Wed 12-8, Sat 10-5
Friends of the Library Group
EL CERRITO LIBRARY, 6510 Stockton Ave, El Cerrito, 94530, SAN 333-6840. Tel: 510-526-7512. Web Site: ccclib.org/locations/11. *Commun Libr Mgr,* Heidi Goldstein; E-mail: hgoldste@ccclib.org
Pop 26,751; Circ 110,645
Library Holdings: Bk Vols 33,476
Open Mon & Tues 12-8, Wed & Thurs 10-6, Fri & Sat 10-5
Friends of the Library Group
EL SOBRANTE LIBRARY, 4191 Appian Way, El Sobrante, 94803, SAN 333-6875. Tel: 510-374-3991. Web Site: ccclib.org/locations/12. *Sr Commun Libr Mgr,* Dr Francis Adebola-Wilson; E-mail: fadebola@ccclib.org
Founded 1961
Library Holdings: Bk Vols 30,037
Function: Adult bk club, Children's prog, Computers for patron use, Electronic databases & coll, Free DVD rentals, Large print keyboards, Magnifiers for reading, Photocopying/Printing
Open Mon & Thurs 12-8, Tues 10-6, Fri 1-5, Sat 10-5
Friends of the Library Group
HERCULES LIBRARY, 109 Civic Dr, Hercules, 94547. Tel: 510-245-2420. Web Site: ccclib.org/locations/55. *Sr Commun Libr Mgr,* Lynne Noone; E-mail: lnoone@ccclib.org
Library Holdings: Bk Vols 56,277
Open Mon & Tues 12-8, Wed & Thurs 10-6, Fri 1-5, Sat 10-5
Friends of the Library Group
KENSINGTON LIBRARY, 61 Arlington Ave, Kensington, 94707, SAN 333-6905. Tel: 510-524-3043. Web Site: ccclib.org/locations/13. *Commun Libr Mgr,* Steven DeFrank; E-mail: sdefrank@ccclib.org
Pop 4,975; Circ 75,780
Library Holdings: Bk Vols 25,934
Open Mon & Tues 12-8, Thurs 10-6, Fri 1-5, Sat 10-5
Friends of the Library Group
LAFAYETTE LIBRARY, 3491 Mount Diablo Blvd, Lafayette, 94549, SAN 333-693X. Tel: 925-385-2280. Web Site: ccclib.org/locations/14. *Sr Commun Libr Mgr,* Vickie Sciacca; E-mail: vsciacca@ccclib.org
Library Holdings: Bk Vols 72,461
Open Mon-Thurs 10-8, Fri & Sat 10-5, Sun 1-5
Friends of the Library Group
MARTINEZ LIBRARY, 740 Court St, 94553, SAN 333-6964. Tel: 925-646-9900. Web Site: ccclib.org/locations/16. *Commun Libr Mgr,* Noelle Burch; E-mail: nburch@ccclib.org; Staff 2.5 (MLS 2, Non-MLS 0.5)
Founded 1941
Library Holdings: Bk Vols 29,485
Special Collections: John Muir Coll; Shell Community Environmental Impact Reports
Function: Bi-weekly Writer's Group
Open Mon 12-8, Tues 10-8, Wed & Fri 12-5, Sat 10-5
Restriction: Access for corporate affiliates
Friends of the Library Group
MORAGA LIBRARY, 1500 Saint Mary's Rd, Moraga, 94556, SAN 333-6999. Tel: 925-376-6852. Web Site: ccclib.org/locations/15. *Commun Libr Mgr,* Jenna Skinner; E-mail: jskinner@ccclib.org
Library Holdings: Bk Vols 50,216
Open Tues & Thurs 12-8, Wed 10-6, Fri & Sun 1-5, Sat 10-5
Friends of the Library Group
OAKLEY BRANCH, 1050 Neroly Rd, Oakley, 94561, SAN 333-7022. Tel: 925-625-2400. Web Site: ccclib.org/locations/17. *Commun Libr Mgr,* Andrea Freyler; E-mail: afreyler@ccclib.org
Library Holdings: Bk Vols 31,665
Open Tues & Wed 10-9, Thurs-Sat 10-6
Friends of the Library Group
ORINDA LIBRARY, 26 Orinda Way, Orinda, 94563, SAN 333-7057. Tel: 925-254-2184. Web Site: ccclib.org/locations/19. *Sr Commun Libr Mgr,* Michael Beller; E-mail: mbeller@ccclib.org
Library Holdings: Bk Vols 67,988
Open Mon-Thurs 10-8, Fri & Sat 10-6, Sun 1-5
Friends of the Library Group
PINOLE LIBRARY, 2935 Pinole Valley Rd, Pinole, 94564, SAN 333-7111. Tel: 510-758-2741. Web Site: ccclib.org/locations/20. *Sr Commun Libr Mgr,* Francis Adebola-Wilson; E-mail: fadebola@ccclib.org
Library Holdings: Bk Vols 36,826
Open Tues 10-6, Wed & Thurs 12-8, Fri 1-5, Sat 10-5
Friends of the Library Group
PITTSBURG LIBRARY, 80 Power Ave, Pittsburg, 94565, SAN 333-7146. Tel: 925-427-8390. Web Site: ccclib.org/locations/21. *Commun Libr Mgr,* Ginny Golden; E-mail: ggolden@ccclib.org
Library Holdings: Bk Vols 39,226
Open Tues 12-8, Wed 10-6, Thurs 1-8, Fri & Sat 11-5
Friends of the Library Group
PLEASANT HILL LIBRARY, 1750 Oak Park Blvd, Pleasant Hill, 94523, SAN 333-6751. Tel: 925-646-6434. Web Site: ccclib.org/locations/43. *Commun Libr Mgr,* Patrick Remer; E-mail: premer@ccclib.org
Pop 39,650; Circ 518,646
Library Holdings: Bk Vols 153,449
Open Mon 12-8, Tues 1-8, Wed & Thurs 11-6, Fri & Sat 10-5
Friends of the Library Group
PREWETT LIBRARY, 4703 Lone Tree Way, Antioch, 94531. Tel: 925-776-3060. Web Site: ccclib.org/locations/94. *Commun Libr Mgr,* Geneva Moss; E-mail: gmoss@ccclib.org
Library Holdings: Bk Vols 5,958
Open Tues 10-7, Wed & Thurs 12-8, Fri & Sat 12-5
Friends of the Library Group
RODEO COMMUNITY LIBRARY, 220 Pacific Ave, Rodeo, 94572, SAN 333-7170. Tel: 510-799-2606. Web Site: ccclib.org/locations/23. *Commun Libr Mgr,* Heidi Goldstein; E-mail: hgoldste@ccclib.org
Library Holdings: Bk Vols 7,873

Open Mon 11-5, Tues & Thurs 1-7, Sat 12-5
Friends of the Library Group
SAN PABLO LIBRARY, 13751 San Pablo Ave, San Pablo, 94806, SAN 371-3350. Tel: 510-374-3998. Web Site: ccclib.org/locations/24. *Commun Libr Mgr,* Gia Paolini; E-mail: gpaolini@ccclib.org
Library Holdings: Bk Vols 30,011
Open Mon & Tues 12-8, Wed & Thurs 10-6, Fri & Sun 1-5, Sat 10-5
Friends of the Library Group
SAN RAMON LIBRARY, 100 Montgomery St, San Ramon, 94583, SAN 333-7200. Tel: 925-973-2850. Web Site: ccclib.org/locations/25. *Commun Libr Mgr,* Dena Hollowood; E-mail: dhollowo@ccclib.org
Library Holdings: Bk Vols 73,843
Open Mon-Thurs 10-8, Fri & Sat 10-5, Sun 1-5
Friends of the Library Group
WALNUT CREEK LIBRARY, 1644 N Broadway, Walnut Creek, 94596, SAN 333-726X. Tel: 925-977-3340. Web Site: ccclib.org/locations/26. *Sr Commun Libr Mgr,* Rob Tygett; E-mail: rtygett@ccclib.org
Library Holdings: Bk Vols 72,160
Open Mon-Thurs 10-8, Fri & Sat 10-6
Friends of the Library Group
YGNACIO VALLEY LIBRARY, 2661 Oak Grove Rd, Walnut Creek, 94598, SAN 333-7294. Tel: 925-938-1481. Web Site: ccclib.org/locations/27. *Commun Libr Mgr,* Karen Hansen-Smith; E-mail: khansen@ccclib.org
Pop 23,338; Circ 348,680
Library Holdings: Bk Vols 65,634
Function: Adult bk club, Art exhibits, Audiobks via web, Bks on CD, Children's prog, Computers for patron use, Free DVD rentals, ILL available, Music CDs, Photocopying/Printing, Prog for adults, Prog for children & young adult, Story hour, Summer reading prog, Wheelchair accessible
Open Mon-Thurs 10-8, Fri & Sat 10-6
Friends of the Library Group

GL CONTRA COSTA COUNTY PUBLIC LAW LIBRARY, 1020 Ward St, 1st Flr, 94553-1360. SAN 301-0414. Tel: 925-646-2783. FAX: 925-646-2438. Web Site: www.cccpllib.org. *Dir,* Carey Rowan; E-mail: carey.rowan@ll.cccounty.us; *Admin Serv,* Kathy Meany
Founded 1893
Library Holdings: Bk Vols 36,450; Per Subs 15
Automation Activity & Vendor Info: (Cataloging) Koha; (OPAC) Koha; (Serials) Koha
Wireless access
Open Mon-Fri 8-5
Restriction: Non-circulating
Branches:
SIMONE DEL DAVID MEMORIAL LAW LIBRARY, George D Carroll Courthouse, Rm 237, 100 37th St, Richmond, 94805. Tel: 510-374-3019.

MARYSVILLE

J YUBA COMMUNITY COLLEGE*, Learning Resources Center, 2088 N Beale Rd, 95901. SAN 301-0449. Tel: 530-741-6762. Circulation Tel: 530-741-6755. Reference Tel: 530-741-6756. FAX: 530-741-6824. Web Site: www.yccd.edu. *Dean,* Carla Tweed; *Librn,* Elena Heilman; Staff 1.3 (MLS 1.3)
Founded 1927. Enrl 2,600; Fac 83; Highest Degree: Associate
Library Holdings: Bk Titles 40,000; Per Subs 125
Automation Activity & Vendor Info: (Circulation) Innovative Interfaces, Inc; (Course Reserve) Innovative Interfaces, Inc; (OPAC) Innovative Interfaces, Inc; (Serials) EBSCO Online
Wireless access
Open Mon-Thurs 7:45am-8pm, Fri 7:45-4:30

P YUBA COUNTY LIBRARY*, 303 Second St, 95901-6099. SAN 301-0430. Tel: 530-749-7380. Interlibrary Loan Service Tel: 530-749-7323. Reference Tel: 530-749-7386. FAX: 530-741-3098. E-mail: library@co.yuba.ca.us. Web Site: library.yuba.org. *Interim Libr Dir,* Kevin Mallen; E-mail: library@co.yuba.ca.us; Staff 6 (MLS 1, Non-MLS 5)
Founded 1858. Pop 72,615; Circ 156,382. Sal $311,057
Library Holdings: Bk Vols 123,229; Per Subs 45
Special Collections: California History
Automation Activity & Vendor Info: (Cataloging) SirsiDynix; (Circulation) SirsiDynix; (Course Reserve) SirsiDynix; (ILL) OCLC; (OPAC) SirsiDynix-iBistro
Wireless access
Function: Archival coll, Art exhibits, Audio & video playback equip for onsite use, Bilingual assistance for Spanish patrons, Bks on cassette, Bks on CD, CD-ROM, Children's prog, Computer training, Computers for patron use, E-Reserves, Electronic databases & coll, Free DVD rentals, Holiday prog, Homebound delivery serv, ILL available, Instruction & testing, Internet access, Mail & tel request accepted, Music CDs, Online cat, Online ref, Outreach serv, Photocopying/Printing, Preschool outreach, Prog for adults, Prog for children & young adult, Ref & res, Ref serv available, Scanner, Senior computer classes, Spoken cassettes & CDs, Story hour, Summer reading prog, Tax forms, Teen prog, Telephone ref, VHS videos, Wheelchair accessible, Workshops, Writing prog
Mem of NorthNet Library System
Open Tues, Wed, Fri 12-6, Thurs 12-8
Friends of the Library Group

MENDOCINO

S KELLEY HOUSE MUSEUM, INC, 45007 Albion St, 95460. (Mail add: PO Box 922, 95460-0922), SAN 373-4102. Tel: 707-937-5791. E-mail: curator@kelleyhousemuseum.org. Web Site: www.kelleyhousemuseum.org. *Curator,* Karen McGrath; Staff 1 (Non-MLS 1)
Founded 1973
Library Holdings: DVDs 90; Electronic Media & Resources 11,165; Bk Vols 492
Special Collections: Emery Escola Coll; Kelley House Coll (photographs, documents, archival materials pertaining to the Town of Mendocino); Mae Johnson Coll (images from the town of Casper). Oral History
Wireless access
Function: Archival coll, Electronic databases & coll, Internet access, Online cat, Res libr, Res performed for a fee
Restriction: In-house use for visitors, Non-circulating, Open by appt only, Open to pub for ref only, Open to pub with supv only, Open to researchers by request, Visitors must make appt to use bks in the libr

S MENDOCINO ART CENTER LIBRARY*, Visual Arts, 45200 Little Lake St, 95460. (Mail add: PO Box 765, 95460-0765), SAN 333-1202. Tel: 707-937-5818. Toll Free Tel: 800-653-3328. FAX: 707-937-4625. E-mail: register@mendocinoartcenter.org. Web Site: www.mendocinoartcenter.org. *Communications Dir,* Mike McDonald; E-mail: marketing@mendocinoartcenter.org
Founded 1962
Library Holdings: Bk Titles 500
Subject Interests: Visual arts
Wireless access
Restriction: Mem only

MENLO PARK

S EXPONENT*, Information Resources, 149 Commonwealth Dr, 94025. SAN 371-7453. Tel: 650-688-7155, 650-688-7163. FAX: 650-329-9526. Web Site: www.exponent.com. *Mgr,* Judith Theodori; Tel: 650-688-7184, E-mail: jtheodori@exponent.com; *Info Spec,* Kathi Lohmann; E-mail: klohmann@exponent.com; *Info Spec,* Carlos Medina; E-mail: cmedina@exponent.com; Staff 3 (MLS 2, Non-MLS 1)
Founded 1984
Library Holdings: Bk Titles 1,500; Bk Vols 2,000; Per Subs 3
Subject Interests: Electronics, Engr
Automation Activity & Vendor Info: (Cataloging) Cuadra Associates, Inc
Restriction: Private libr

P MENLO PARK PUBLIC LIBRARY*, 800 Alma St, Alma & Ravenswood, 94025-3455. SAN 301-052X. Tel: 650-330-2500. Circulation Tel: 650-330-2501. Reference Tel: 650-330-2520. FAX: 650-327-7030. Web Site: menlopark.org/389/Library. *Libr Serv Dir,* Sean Reinhart; E-mail: ssreinhart@menlopark.org; Staff 16.6 (MLS 6.8, Non-MLS 9.8)
Founded 1916. Pop 32,513; Circ 624,669
Library Holdings: Bk Vols 149,927
Automation Activity & Vendor Info: (Acquisitions) Innovative Interfaces, Inc; (Cataloging) Innovative Interfaces, Inc; (Circulation) Innovative Interfaces, Inc; (OPAC) Innovative Interfaces, Inc
Wireless access
Mem of Pacific Library Partnership (PLP)
Partic in Peninsula Libraries Automated Network
Open Mon & Wed 10-9, Tues 12-9, Thurs & Fri 10-6, Sat 10-5, Sun 12-5
Friends of the Library Group
Branches: 1
BELLE HAVEN, 413 Ivy Dr, 94025. Tel: 650-330-2540. *Libr Serv Dir,* Sean Reinhart; E-mail: ssreinhart@menlopark.org
Library Holdings: Bk Vols 10,000; Per Subs 30
Open Mon-Wed Noon-9, Thurs & Fri 10-6, Sat 10-5, Sun Noon-5

R SAINT PATRICK'S SEMINARY*, Carl Gellert & Celia Berta Gellert Foundation Memorial Library, 320 Middlefield Rd, 94025. SAN 301-0546. Tel: 650-321-5655. FAX: 650-323-5447. E-mail: library@stpsu.edu. Web Site: stpsu.edu/library-home. *Libr Dir,* Matthew Horwitz; Tel: 650-289-3327, E-mail: matthew.horwitz@stpsu.edu; *Tech Asst,* Sharon Hamrick; Tel: 650-289-3359, E-mail: sharon.hamrick@stpsu.edu; Staff 4 (MLS 4)
Founded 1898. Enrl 96; Fac 20; Highest Degree: Master
Library Holdings: AV Mats 2,484; Bk Vols 109,716; Per Subs 300; Videos 770
Special Collections: Californiana & Western Americana (C Albert Shumate MD Coll); Library of Archbishop Alemany (First Archbishop of San Francisco Coll)

Subject Interests: Scripture, Theol
Automation Activity & Vendor Info: (Cataloging) OCLC Connexion; (ILL) OCLC; (OPAC) Cassidy Cataloguing Services, Inc
Wireless access
Function: Computers for patron use, ILL available, Online cat, Photocopying/Printing, Ref serv available, Wheelchair accessible
Partic in Califa; OCLC Online Computer Library Center, Inc; Statewide California Electronic Library Consortium
Open Mon-Sat 9-12- & 1-6
Restriction: Restricted borrowing privileges

S SRI INTERNATIONAL*, Research Information Services, 333 Ravenswood Ave, 94025. SAN 333-1261. Tel: 650-859-5506. FAX: 650-859-2757. E-mail: library@sri.com. Web Site: www.sri.com. *Mgr,* Lisa Beffa; E-mail: lisa.beffa@sri.com; Staff 2 (MLS 1, Non-MLS 1)
Founded 1948
Library Holdings: Bk Titles 25,000; Per Subs 2,200
Restriction: Staff use only
Branches:
LIFE SCIENCES LIBRARY, 333 Ravenswood Ave, 94025, SAN 333-1296. Tel: 650-859-3549. *Circ Asst,* Jim Johnson

G UNITED STATES GEOLOGICAL SURVEY LIBRARY*, 345 Middlefield Rd, Bldg 15 (MS-955), 94025-3591. SAN 301-0554. Tel: 650-329-5027. FAX: 650-329-5132. E-mail: men_lib@usgs.gov. Web Site: library.usgs.gov/menlib.html. *Br Mgr,* Keith Van Cleave; Tel: 303-236-1004, E-mail: kvancleave@usgs.gov; *ILL/Tech Serv Librn,* Mike Moore; Tel: 650-329-5009, E-mail: mmmoore@usgs.gov; *Ref Librn,* Ronald Rodrigues Wenger; Tel: 650-329-5427, E-mail: men_lib@usgs.gov; Staff 2 (MLS 1, Non-MLS 1)
Founded 1953
Special Collections: Aerial Photo Coll; California History Coll
Subject Interests: Calif, Earth sci, Hist, Maps, Natural hazards, Water res
Automation Activity & Vendor Info: (Acquisitions) SirsiDynix; (Cataloging) SirsiDynix; (Circulation) SirsiDynix; (ILL) OCLC GovDoc; (OPAC) SirsiDynix; (Serials) SirsiDynix
Wireless access
Function: Govt ref serv, ILL available, Online cat, Photocopying/Printing, Wheelchair accessible
Open Mon-Fri 8:30-4:30
Restriction: Borrowing requests are handled by ILL

MERCED

J MERCED COLLEGE, Learning Resources Center, 3600 M St, 95348. SAN 333-1326. Tel: 209-384-6080. Circulation Tel: 209-384-6081. Reference Tel: 209-384-6083. FAX: 209-384-6084. E-mail: refdesk@mccd.edu. Web Site: www.mccd.edu/lrc/index.html. *Dean of Learning Resource Ctr, Distance Educ,* Dr Marie Bruley; Tel: 209-384-6082, E-mail: bruley.m@mccd.edu; *Assessment & Planning, Librn,* Joey Merritt; Tel: 209-384-6283, E-mail: joey.merritt@mccd.edu; *Ref Librn,* Wayne Altenberg; Tel: 209-381-6431, E-mail: wayne.altenberg@mccd.edu; *Ref Librn,* Karrie Bullock; Tel: 209-386-6703, E-mail: Karrie.bullock@mccd.edu; *Ref Librn,* Lindsay Davis; Tel: 209-384-6086, E-mail: lindsay.davis@mccd.edu; *Ref Librn,* Nancy Golz; Tel: 209-386-6725, E-mail: nancy.golz@mccd.edu. Subject Specialists: *Distance learning, Educ, Prisons,* Dr Marie Bruley; Staff 12 (MLS 5, Non-MLS 7)
Founded 1972. Enrl 10,004; Fac 310; Highest Degree: Associate
Library Holdings: Bk Vols 44,272; Per Subs 235
Automation Activity & Vendor Info: (Circulation) Ex Libris Group; (Course Reserve) Ex Libris Group; (OPAC) Ex Libris Group; (Serials) Ex Libris Group
Wireless access
Partic in 49-99 Cooperative Library System
Open Mon-Thurs 8-8:30, Fri 8-2; Mon & Tues (Summer) 12-8, Wed & Thurs (Summer) 8-5
Friends of the Library Group

GL MERCED COUNTY LAW LIBRARY, 670 W 22nd St, 95340-3780. SAN 301-0570. Tel: 209-385-7332. FAX: 209-385-7448. E-mail: lawlibrary@countyofmerced.com. Web Site: www.co.merced.ca.us/1402/About-Us. *Law Librn,* Samantha Thompson; Staff 1 (Non-MLS 1)
Library Holdings: Bk Titles 10,000

P MERCED COUNTY LIBRARY*, 2100 O St, 95340-3637. SAN 333-1350. Circulation Tel: 209-385-7484. FAX: 209-726-7912. E-mail: info@mercedcountylibrary.org. Web Site: www.mercedcountylibrary.org. *County Librn,* Amy Taylor; E-mail: Amy.Taylor@countyofmerced.com; Staff 17 (MLS 5, Non-MLS 12)
Founded 1910. Pop 255,793; Circ 264,427
Special Collections: California History; Genealogy & Local History
Automation Activity & Vendor Info: (Acquisitions) Horizon; (Cataloging) Horizon; (Circulation) Horizon; (OPAC) Horizon; (Serials) Horizon
Wireless access
Function: 24/7 Electronic res, 24/7 Online cat, Adult bk club, Adult literacy prog, Archival coll, Bk club(s), Bks on CD, Children's prog, Computers for patron use, Electronic databases & coll, Family literacy, Internet access, Magazines, Meeting rooms, Microfiche/film & reading machines, Movies, Online cat, OverDrive digital audio bks, Photocopying/Printing, Preschool reading prog, Prog for children & young adult, Story hour, Summer reading prog, Teen prog
Mem of San Joaquin Valley Library System
Open Mon-Thurs 10-6, Fri & Sat 10-5
Friends of the Library Group
Branches: 11
ATWATER BRANCH, 1600 Third St, Atwater, 95301-3607, SAN 333-1415. Tel: 209-358-6651.
Open Tues-Thurs 10-6, Fri & Sat 10-5
Friends of the Library Group
DELHI EDUCATIONAL PARK COMMUNITY, 16881 Schendel Rd, Delhi, 95315, SAN 333-1539. Tel: 209-656-2049.
Open Mon-Thurs 10-6, Fri 10-5, Sat 10-3
DOS PALOS BRANCH, 2002 Almond St, Dos Palos, 93620-2304, SAN 333-1563. Tel: 209-392-2155.
Open Wed 10-6, Fri 10-5, Sat 10-3
Friends of the Library Group
GUSTINE BRANCH, 205 Sixth St, Gustine, 95322-1112, SAN 333-1687. Tel: 209-854-3013.
Open Tues & Thurs 10-6, Sat 10-5
Friends of the Library Group
IRWIN-HILMAR BRANCH, 20041 W Falke St, Hilmar, 95324-9778, SAN 333-1717. Tel: 209-632-0746.
Open Wed 10-6, Fri 10-5, Sat 10-3
Friends of the Library Group
LE GRAND BRANCH, 12949 Le Grand Rd, Le Grand, 95333, SAN 333-1741. Tel: 209-389-4541.
Founded 1910
Open Mon-Thurs 10-6, Fri 10-5, Sat 10-3
LIVINGSTON BRANCH, 1212 Main St, Livingston, 95334-1215, SAN 333-1776. Tel: 209-394-7330.
Open Tues & Thurs 10-6, Sat 10-5
Friends of the Library Group
LOS BANOS BRANCH, 1312 Seventh St, Los Banos, 93635-4757, SAN 333-1806. Tel: 209-826-5254.
Open Tues-Thurs 10-6, Fri & Sat 10-5
Friends of the Library Group
SANTA NELLA BRANCH, 29188 W Centinella Ave, Santa Nella, 95322-9625, SAN 333-1911. Tel: 209-826-6059.
Open Tues & Thurs 1-6
SNELLING BRANCH, 15916 N Hwy 59, Snelling, 95369, SAN 333-192X. Tel: 209-563-6616.
Founded 1932
Open Tues & Thurs 1-6
WINTON BRANCH, 7057 W Walnut, Winton, 95388, SAN 333-2012. Tel: 209-358-3651.
Open Wed 1-6, Fri 12-5

C UNIVERSITY OF CALIFORNIA, MERCED LIBRARY*, 5200 N Lake Rd, 95343. Tel: 209-228-4444. FAX: 209-228-4271. E-mail: library@ucmerced.edu. Web Site: library.ucmerced.edu. *Univ Librn,* Haipeng Li; Tel: 209-201-7632, E-mail: haipengli@ucmerced.edu; *Dep Univ Librn,* Donald Barclay; Tel: 209-201-9724, E-mail: dbarclay@ucmerced.edu; *Dir, Libr Tech,* Tom Bustos; Tel: 209-337-8710, E-mail: tbustos@ucmerced.edu; *Assoc Univ Librn, Libr Operations,* Eric Scott; Tel: 209-675-8040, E-mail: escott@ucmerced.edu; *Head, Access Serv,* Joe Ameen; Tel: 209-761-4512, E-mail: sameen@ucmerced.edu; *Head, Coll Serv,* Jim Dooley; Tel: 209-658-7161, E-mail: jdooley@ucmerced.edu; *Head, Digital Assets,* Emily S Lin; Tel: 209-658-7146, E-mail: elin@ucmerced.edu; *Head, Learning Serv, Head, Res Serv,* Sara Davidson Squibb; Tel: 209-205-8237, E-mail: sdavidson2@ucmerced.edu; *Instruction & Res Serv Librn,* Elizabeth McMunn-Tetangco; Tel: 209-631-8359, E-mail: emcmunn@ucmerced.edu; *Research Servs Librn,* Elizabeth Salmon; Tel: 209-631-6954, E-mail: esalmon@ucmerced.edu; *Spec Coll Librn, Univ Archivist,* Jerrold Shiroma; Tel: 209-756-0237, E-mail: jshiroma@ucmerced.edu; *Libr Serv Mgr,* Ross Anastos; Tel: 209-201-6485, E-mail: ranastos@ucmerced.edu; *Digitization Coordr,* Heather Wagner; Tel: 209-205-0794, E-mail: hwagner3@ucmerced.edu; *Electronic Res Coordr,* Sarah Sheets; Tel: 209-228-4422, E-mail: ssheets@ucmerced.edu; *Interlibrary Serv Coordr,* Nathan Garcia; Tel: 209-291-9394, E-mail: ngarcia8@ucmerced.edu; *Night/Weekend Serv Coordr,* Fabiola Chavez; Tel: 209-201-5013, E-mail: fchavez4@ucmerced.edu; *Night/Weekend Serv Coordr,* Sunni Nelson; Tel: 209-382-4263, E-mail: snelson4@ucmerced.edu; *Tech Serv Coordr,* Latasha Means; Tel: 209-631-8042, E-mail: lmeans@ucmerced.edu; *Tech Serv*

Coordr, Samantha Fort; Tel: 209-631-0953, E-mail: sfort@ucmerced.edu; Staff 24 (MLS 9, Non-MLS 15)
Founded 2005. Enrl 6,685; Fac 375; Highest Degree: Doctorate
Library Holdings: DVDs 1,182; e-books 33,965,000; e-journals 70,000; Electronic Media & Resources 635; Bk Vols 120,000
Special Collections: US Document Depository
Automation Activity & Vendor Info: (Acquisitions) Innovative Interfaces, Inc - Millennium; (Cataloging) Innovative Interfaces, Inc - Millennium; (Circulation) Innovative Interfaces, Inc - Millennium; (ILL) Innovative Interfaces, Inc; (OPAC) Innovative Interfaces, Inc - Millennium; (Serials) Innovative Interfaces, Inc - Millennium
Wireless access
Function: Archival coll, Art exhibits, Computers for patron use, Doc delivery serv, E-Reserves, Electronic databases & coll, Govt ref serv, ILL available, Mail & tel request accepted, Music CDs, Online cat, Online ref, Photocopying/Printing, Ref serv available, Telephone ref, Wheelchair accessible
Open Mon-Thurs 7am-Midnight, Fri 7-6, Sat 12-6, Sun Noon-Midnight

MILL VALLEY

P MILL VALLEY PUBLIC LIBRARY*, 375 Throckmorton Ave, 94941. SAN 301-0597. Tel: 415-389-4292. FAX: 415-388-8929. E-mail: reference@cityofmillvalley.org. Web Site: millvalleylibrary.org. *City Librn,* Anji Brenner; Tel: 415-389-4292, Ext 4742, E-mail: abrenner@cityofmillvalley.org; *Ref Librn,* Andrew Murphy; Tel: 415-389-4292, Ext 4729; *Operations Mgr,* Kristen Clark; Tel: 415-389-4292, Ext 4730, E-mail: kclark@cityofmillvalley.org; *Circ Supvr,* Shannon Jones; Tel: 415-389-4292, Ext 4737, E-mail: sjones@cityofmillvalley.org; Staff 20 (MLS 7, Non-MLS 13)
Founded 1908. Pop 13,686; Circ 317,694
Library Holdings: Bk Titles 102,117; Per Subs 359
Special Collections: Local History Room; Lucretia Little History Room, bks, clippings, pamphlets, photog; Miwok Indians. Oral History
Automation Activity & Vendor Info: (Acquisitions) Innovative Interfaces, Inc; (Cataloging) Innovative Interfaces, Inc; (Circulation) Innovative Interfaces, Inc; (ILL) OCLC; (OPAC) Innovative Interfaces, Inc; (Serials) Innovative Interfaces, Inc
Wireless access
Function: Archival coll, Art exhibits, Audio & video playback equip for onsite use, Homebound delivery serv, ILL available, Internet access, Music CDs, Photocopying/Printing, Prog for adults, Prog for children & young adult, Summer reading prog, Wheelchair accessible
Mem of NorthNet Library System
Partic in Califa; Marin Automated Resources & Information Network
Special Services for the Blind - Bks on cassette; Bks on CD
Open Mon-Thurs 10-9, Fri 12-6, Sat 10-5, Sun 1-5
Friends of the Library Group

MINERAL

S NATIONAL PARK SERVICE, Lassen Volcanic National Park Library, PO Box 100, 96063-0100. SAN 301-0619. E-mail: lavo_information@nps.gov. Web Site: www.nps.gov/lavo.
Library Holdings: Bk Vols 800
Subject Interests: Natural hist
Restriction: Staff use only

MISSION HILLS

M PROVIDENCE HOLY CROSS MEDICAL CENTER*, Strazzeri Medical Library, 15031 Rinaldi St, 91345. (Mail add: PO Box 9600, 91346-9600), SAN 329-3963. Tel: 818-496-4545. FAX: 818-496-4481. E-mail: phcmc.library@providence.org. Web Site: nnlm.gov/members/directory/12096. *Libr Spec,* Pamela Gay; E-mail: pamela.gay@providence.org; Staff 2 (MLS 1, Non-MLS 1)
Library Holdings: Bk Titles 2,400; Bk Vols 2,500; Per Subs 171
Subject Interests: Allied health, Nursing
Automation Activity & Vendor Info: (Cataloging) EOS International; (Circulation) EOS International; (OPAC) EOS International; (Serials) EOS International
Wireless access
Function: Health sci info serv, ILL available, Photocopying/Printing
Partic in Medical Library Group of Southern California & Arizona
Restriction: In-house use for visitors, Lending to staff only, Non-circulating to the pub, Restricted pub use

SR ROMAN CATHOLIC ARCHDIOCESE OF LOS ANGELES, Archival Center Library & Historical Museum, 15151 San Fernando Mission Blvd, 91345. SAN 371-1099. Tel: 818-365-1501. FAX: 818-361-3276. E-mail: info@archivalcenter.org. Web Site: lacatholics.org/departments-ministries/archival-center. *Archivist,* Kevin Feeney; E-mail: kevin@archivalcenter.org
Library Holdings: Bk Vols 15,000
Open Mon & Thurs 8:30-12 & 1-4:30
Friends of the Library Group

MISSION VIEJO

P MISSION VIEJO LIBRARY*, 100 Civic Ctr, 92691. SAN 375-4227. Tel: 949-830-7100. Circulation Tel: 949-830-7100, Ext 5101. Interlibrary Loan Service Tel: 949-830-7100, Ext 5119. Reference Tel: 949-830-7100, Ext 5105. Administration Tel: 949-830-7100, Ext 5128. FAX: 949-586-8447. Reference E-mail: generalreference@cityofmissionviejo.org. Web Site: cityofmissionviejo.org/departments/library. *Dir, Libr & Cultural Serv,* Genesis Hansen; Tel: 949-470-3076, E-mail: ghansen@cityofmissionviejo.org; *Circ Serv Mgr,* Kathleen Kelton; Tel: 949-830-7100, Ext 5130, E-mail: kkelton@cityofmissionviejo.org; *Mgr, Pub Serv,* Sarah Stimson; Tel: 949-830-7100, Ext 5132; *Mgr, Support Serv,* Tony Dillehunt; Tel: 949-830-7100, Ext 5123, E-mail: tdillehunt@cityofmissionviejo.org; Staff 34 (MLS 10, Non-MLS 24)
Founded 1997. Pop 98,000; Circ 939,734
Library Holdings: e-books 895; Bk Titles 130,000; Bk Vols 155,406; Per Subs 169
Subject Interests: Genealogy, Local hist
Automation Activity & Vendor Info: (Acquisitions) SirsiDynix; (Cataloging) SirsiDynix; (Circulation) SirsiDynix; (ILL) OCLC FirstSearch; (OPAC) SirsiDynix; (Serials) EBSCO Online
Wireless access
Function: Archival coll, Art exhibits, Audiobks via web, Bk club(s), Bks on CD, Children's prog, Computers for patron use, Electronic databases & coll, Free DVD rentals, ILL available, Magnifiers for reading, Music CDs, Online cat, OverDrive digital audio bks, Passport agency, Photocopying/Printing, Prog for adults, Prog for children & young adult, Summer reading prog, Teen prog
Mem of Santiago Library System
Partic in Southern California Library Cooperative
Special Services for the Blind - Large print bks; Low vision equip; Magnifiers
Open Mon-Thurs 10-9, Fri 1-5, Sat 10-5, Sun 12-5
Friends of the Library Group

J SADDLEBACK COLLEGE*, James B Utt Library, 28000 Marguerite Pkwy, 92692. SAN 301-0635. Tel: 949-582-4314. Circulation Tel: 949-582-4526. Reference Tel: 949-582-4525. FAX: 949-364-0284. E-mail: sclibrary@saddleback.edu. Web Site: www.saddleback.edu/library. *Dean,* Marina Aminy; Tel: 949-582-4365; *Libr Tech,* James Locke; Tel: 949-582-4241, E-mail: jlocke@saddleback.edu; *Libr Asst II,* Vannie Pham; Tel: 949-582-4285, E-mail: vpham@saddleback.edu; *Libr Asst II,* Lucila Soria; E-mail: lsoria@saddleback.edu; Staff 14 (MLS 6, Non-MLS 8)
Founded 1968. Enrl 25,000; Fac 270; Highest Degree: Associate
Library Holdings: AV Mats 9,000; Bks on Deafness & Sign Lang 65; Bk Titles 87,611; Bk Vols 101,438; Per Subs 283
Automation Activity & Vendor Info: (Circulation) SirsiDynix; (OPAC) SirsiDynix
Wireless access
Function: AV serv, Distance learning, ILL available, Photocopying/Printing, Ref serv available, Telephone ref
Publications: Library Skills Workbook
Partic in Coop Libr Agency for Syst & Servs; OCLC Online Computer Library Center, Inc
Friends of the Library Group

MODESTO

M DOCTORS MEDICAL CENTER*, Professional Library, 1441 Florida Ave, 95352. (Mail add: PO Box 4138, 95352-4138), SAN 321-5628. Tel: 209-576-3782. FAX: 209-576-3595. E-mail: dmc.library@tenethealth.com. Web Site: library.dmc-modesto.com. *Med Librn,* Sherri Husman; E-mail: sherri.husman@tenethealth.com; Staff 1 (MLS 1)
Founded 1966
Library Holdings: Bk Titles 586; Bk Vols 625; Per Subs 166
Subject Interests: Med, Nursing
Partic in National Network of Libraries of Medicine Region 5
Open Mon-Fri 7:30-3

GL STANISLAUS COUNTY LAW LIBRARY*, 1101 13th St, 95354. SAN 301-0716. Tel: 209-558-7759. FAX: 209-558-8284. E-mail: library@stanlaw.org. Web Site: stanlaw.org. *Dir,* Janice Schmidt; E-mail: schmidtja@stancounty.com; *Asst Librn,* Alex Kern; E-mail: kern@arrival.net
Library Holdings: CDs 139; DVDs 10; Bk Vols 18,689; Per Subs 51
Special Collections: Local Municipal & County Codes
Automation Activity & Vendor Info: (Cataloging) LibraryWorld, Inc; (Serials) LibraryWorld, Inc
Wireless access
Open Mon-Fri 8-5

P STANISLAUS COUNTY LIBRARY*, 1500 I St, 95354-1166. SAN 333-2101. Tel: 209-558-7800. Circulation Tel: 209-558-7808. Reference Tel: 209-558-7814. Administration Tel: 209-558-7801. FAX: 209-529-4779. Web Site: www.stanislauslibrary.org. *County Librn,* Sarah Dentan; E-mail: sdentan@stanlibrary.org; *Br Operations Mgr,* Bryan Sontag; *Operations Mgr,* Thomas Kaps; *Acq,* Stacey Chen; Staff 16 (MLS 16)
Founded 1912. Pop 519,940; Circ 1,719,393. Sal $5,711,621
Library Holdings: Bk Vols 639,948; Per Subs 184
Special Collections: Californiana; Selections in Spanish & Vietnamese; Song File; Stanislaus County Hist Coll
Subject Interests: Genealogy
Automation Activity & Vendor Info: (Cataloging) Horizon; (Circulation) SirsiDynix; (OPAC) SirsiDynix; (Serials) EBSCO Online
Wireless access
Partic in 49-99 Cooperative Library System
Special Services for the Deaf - Closed caption videos; TDD equip
Special Services for the Blind - Bks on cassette; Bks on CD; Computer with voice synthesizer for visually impaired persons; Reader equip
Open Mon-Thurs 10-8, Fri & Sat 10-5
Friends of the Library Group
Branches: 12
NORA BALLARD LIBRARY (WATERFORD BRANCH), 324 E St, Waterford, 95386-9005, SAN 333-2497. Tel: 209-874-2191. FAX: 209-874-2191. *Br Mgr,* Position Currently Open
Pop 8,763; Circ 60,782
Library Holdings: Bk Vols 21,756
Special Collections: Oral History
Subject Interests: Relig
Open Mon & Tues 10-6, Wed 10-8, Thurs & Fri 10-5, Sat 12-5
Friends of the Library Group
DAVID F BUSH LIBRARY (OAKDALE BRANCH), 151 S First Ave, Oakdale, 95361-3902, SAN 333-2314. Tel: 209-847-4204. FAX: 209-847-4205. *Br Mgr,* Karina Mendoza
Pop 17,440; Circ 134,989
Library Holdings: Bk Vols 45,883
Open Mon & Wed 10-6, Tues & Thurs 10-8, Fri & Sat 10-5
Friends of the Library Group
DENAIR BRANCH, 4801 Kersey Rd, Denair, 95316-9350, SAN 333-2160. Tel: 209-634-1283. FAX: 209-634-1283. *Br Mgr,* Paden Hardy
Pop 3,719; Circ 26,181
Library Holdings: Bk Vols 15,117
Open Tues-Thurs 12-6, Fri & Sat 11-5
Friends of the Library Group
EMPIRE BRANCH, 18 S Abbie St, Empire, 95319, SAN 333-2195. Tel: 209-524-5505. FAX: 209-524-5505. *Br Mgr,* Diane Ramirez
Pop 4,203; Circ 18,362
Library Holdings: Bk Vols 11,180
Open Tues-Thurs 12-6, Fri & Sat 11-5
Friends of the Library Group
FLORENCE L GONDRING LIBRARY, 2250 Magnolia, Ceres, 95307-3209, SAN 333-2136. Tel: 209-537-8938. FAX: 209-537-8939. *Br Mgr,* Position Currently Open
Pop 45,854; Circ 114,464
Library Holdings: Bk Vols 36,817
Open Mon 10-8, Tues-Thurs 10-6, Fri & Sat 10-5
Friends of the Library Group
HUGHSON BRANCH, 2412 Third St, Ste A, Hughson, 95326, SAN 333-2225. Tel: 209-883-2293. FAX: 209-883-2293. *Br Mgr,* Hardy Paden
Pop 6,187; Circ 25,183
Library Holdings: Bk Vols 12,888
Open Tues-Thurs 12-6, Fri & Sat 11-5
Friends of the Library Group
KEYES BRANCH, 4420 Maud Ave, Keyes, 95328-0367, SAN 333-225X. Tel: 209-664-8006. FAX: 209-664-8006. *Br Mgr,* Christine Ryu
Pop 4,928; Circ 18,742
Library Holdings: Bk Vols 14,436
Open Mon-Wed 9-5:30, Thurs 9-7:30, Fri 9-5
Friends of the Library Group
NEWMAN BRANCH, 1305 Kern St, Newman, 95360-1603, SAN 333-2284. Tel: 209-862-2010. FAX: 209-862-2010. *Br Mgr,* Sophia Petrakis
Founded 1909. Pop 10,586; Circ 34,309
Library Holdings: Bk Vols 17,657
Open Tues 12-8, Wed-Sat 10-5
Friends of the Library Group
PATTERSON BRANCH, 46 N Salado, Patterson, 95363-2587, SAN 333-2349. Tel: 209-892-6473. FAX: 209-892-5100. *Br Mgr,* Xia Thao
Founded 1976. Pop 19,337; Circ 124,350
Library Holdings: Bk Vols 25,764
Automation Activity & Vendor Info: (OPAC) SirsiDynix
Open Mon & Tues 10-6, Wed 10-8, Thurs & Fri 10-5, Sat 12-5
Friends of the Library Group
RIVERBANK BRANCH, 3442 Santa Fe St, Riverbank, 95367-2319, SAN 333-2373. Tel: 209-869-7008. FAX: 209-869-7008. *Br Mgr,* Vicky Holt
Pop 21,757; Circ 66,142
Library Holdings: Bk Vols 25,763
Open Mon & Fri 10-5, Tues & Thurs 10-6, Wed 10-8, Sat 12-5
Friends of the Library Group
SALIDA BRANCH, 4835 Sisk Rd, Salida, 95368-9445, SAN 333-2403. Tel: 209-543-7353. Information Services Tel: 209-543-7315. FAX: 209-543-7318. *Br Mgr,* Wayne Philbrook
Pop 16,000; Circ 302,753
Library Holdings: Bk Vols 77,547
Open Mon & Tues 10-8, Wed & Thurs 10-6, Fri & Sat 10-5
Friends of the Library Group
TURLOCK BRANCH, 550 Minaret Ave, Turlock, 95380-4198, SAN 333-2438. Tel: 209-664-8100. FAX: 209-664-8101. *Br Mgr,* Diane Bartlett
Pop 70,158; Circ 316,098
Library Holdings: Bk Vols 88,744
Open Mon-Wed 10-8, Thurs-Sat 10-5
Friends of the Library Group

M SUTTER HEALTH MEMORIAL MEDICAL CENTER*, Health Sciences Library, 1800 Coffee Rd, Ste 43, 95355-2700. SAN 328-4344. Web Site: www.memorialmedicalcenter.org. *Health Educ Asst,* Andrea Perez Shelton; E-mail: pereza11@sutterhealth.org; Staff 1 (MLS 1)
Library Holdings: DVDs 100; e-books 1,500; e-journals 2,000; Bk Titles 1,000; Per Subs 50; Videos 100
Subject Interests: Med, Nursing, Pharmacology
Wireless access
Partic in Medical Library Association; Northern California & Nevada Medical Library Group
Restriction: Staff use only

MOFFETT FIELD

NASA AMES RESEARCH CENTER
S LIFE SCIENCES LIBRARY*, Mail Stop 239-13, 94035-1000, SAN 333-2527. Tel: 650-604-5387. FAX: 650-604-7741. E-mail: arc-dl-library@mail.nasa.gov. Web Site: www.library.arc.nasa.gov. *Librn,* Lisa Sewell; Staff 2 (MLS 1, Non-MLS 1)
Founded 1965
Library Holdings: e-journals 2,000; Bk Titles 18,500; Bk Vols 20,000; Per Subs 112
Special Collections: Aerospace Biology & Medicine; Biochemistry (Origin of Life Coll); Biogenesis Coll; Evolution Genetics
Subject Interests: Aerospace med, Aviation med, Biochem, Human factors, Physiology, Planetary sci
Automation Activity & Vendor Info: (Cataloging) SirsiDynix; (Circulation) SirsiDynix
Partic in Proquest Dialog
S TECHNICAL LIBRARY*, Bldg 202, Mail Stop 202-3, 94035-1000, SAN 333-2551. Tel: 650-604-6325. FAX: 650-604-4988. E-mail: arc-dl-library@mail.nasa.gov. Web Site: www.ameslib.arc.nasa.gov. *Head, Ref,* Dan Pappas; *Mgr,* Evelyn Warren; Tel: 650-604-5681; *Acq Librn,* Donna Kleiner; Staff 4 (MLS 3, Non-MLS 1)
Founded 1940
Library Holdings: e-books 400; e-journals 1,000; Bk Titles 39,000; Per Subs 250
Special Collections: NASA & NACA Reports
Subject Interests: Aeronaut, Astronomy, Astrophysics, Chem, Computer sci, Engr, Life sci, Math
Automation Activity & Vendor Info: (Acquisitions) SirsiDynix; (Cataloging) SirsiDynix; (Circulation) SirsiDynix; (OPAC) SirsiDynix; (Serials) SirsiDynix
Partic in NASA Library Network

MONROVIA

R FIRST PRESBYTERIAN CHURCH LIBRARY*, 101 E Foothill Blvd, 91016. SAN 374-843X. Tel: 626-358-3297. FAX: 626-358-5997. E-mail: church@fpcmonrovia.org. Web Site: fpcmonrovia.org.
Library Holdings: Bk Vols 100; Per Subs 20
Open Mon-Fri 9-4

P MONROVIA PUBLIC LIBRARY*, 321 S Myrtle Ave, 91016-2848. SAN 301-0732. Tel: 626-256-8274. Reference Tel: 626-256-8259. Administration Tel: 626-256-8250. FAX: 626-256-8255. *Dir, Commun Serv,* Tina Cherry; Tel: 626-256-8246, E-mail: tcherry@ci.monrovia.ca.us; *Libr Mgr,* Carey Vance; Tel: 626-256-8229, E-mail: cvance@ci.monrovia.ca.us; Staff 9.6 (MLS 7.5, Non-MLS 2.1)
Founded 1895. Pop 39,006; Circ 110,203
Library Holdings: Bk Vols 120,000; Per Subs 161
Automation Activity & Vendor Info: (Acquisitions) SirsiDynix; (Cataloging) SirsiDynix; (Circulation) SirsiDynix; (OPAC) SirsiDynix; (Serials) SirsiDynix
Wireless access
Function: Adult literacy prog, Home delivery & serv to seniorr ctr & nursing homes, ILL available, Photocopying/Printing, Prog for children &

young adult, Ref serv available, Summer reading prog, Wheelchair accessible
Special Services for the Deaf - Assistive tech; TDD equip; TTY equip
Open Mon-Wed 10-8, Thurs-Sat Noon-5
Restriction: Open to pub for ref & circ; with some limitations
Friends of the Library Group

MONTEBELLO

M BEVERLY HOSPITAL*, Breitman Memorial Library, 309 W Beverly Blvd, 90640. SAN 373-4129. Tel: 323-725-4305. FAX: 323-889-2424. *Librn,* Irene Bogner; E-mail: ibogner@beverly.org
Founded 1978
Library Holdings: e-books 2,118; Bk Vols 500; Per Subs 25
Subject Interests: Med, Nutrition, Pharmacology
Wireless access
Restriction: Not open to pub

MONTEREY

G AISO LIBRARY*, 543 Lawton Rd, Ste 617A, 93944-3214. SAN 301-2212. Reference Tel: 831-242-6948. E-mail: aiso_library@dliflc.edu. Web Site: dliflc.edu/resources/libraries. *Libr Tech,* Rebecca Ramos; Staff 14 (MLS 7, Non-MLS 7)
Founded 1943
Library Holdings: Bk Titles 110,000; Bk Vols 115,000; Per Subs 800
Special Collections: Foreign Language Coll
Subject Interests: Foreign lang
Automation Activity & Vendor Info: (Cataloging) TLC (The Library Corporation); (Circulation) TLC (The Library Corporation); (ILL) OCLC; (OPAC) TLC (The Library Corporation); (Serials) TLC (The Library Corporation)
Function: ILL available, Ref serv available
Partic in Federal Library & Information Network
Open Mon-Thurs 8-8, Fri 8-5, Sun 12-5
Restriction: Open to pub for ref only

S COLTON HALL MUSEUM LIBRARY*, 570 Pacific St, 93940. SAN 327-8158. Tel: 831-646-5640, 831-646-5648. FAX: 831-646-3917. E-mail: libraryinfo@monterey.org. Web Site: www.monterey.org/museums/City-Museums/Colton-Hall-Museum.
Library Holdings: Bk Vols 2,500; Per Subs 15
Special Collections: Monterey History American Period, 1846-present. Oral History
Open Sun-Sat 10-4

S MONTEREY HISTORY & ART ASSOCIATION, Mayo Hayes O'Donnell Library, 155 Van Buren St, 93940. SAN 301-0775. Tel: 831-747-1027. Web Site: www.mayohayeslibrary.org. *Librn,* Gary Spradlin; E-mail: gary_spradlin@sbcglobal.net
Founded 1970
Library Holdings: Bk Vols 3,000
Special Collections: Californiana; Western United States, especially Monterey. Oral History
Subject Interests: Calif
Function: Res libr
Open Wed-Sun 1:30-3:45

C MONTEREY INSTITUTE OF INTERNATIONAL STUDIES*, William Tell Coleman Library, 425 Van Buren St, 93940. (Mail add: 460 Pierce St, 93940), SAN 301-0783. Tel: 831-647-4136. Administration Tel: 831-647-4135. E-mail: library@miis.edu. Web Site: middlebury.edu/institute/academics/library, monti.miis.edu. *Asst Dir,* Ann Flower; E-mail: aflower@miis.edu; *Acq, Ser Librn,* Pamela Jungerberg; E-mail: pjungerberg@middlebury.edu; *Res & Instruction Librn,* Joelle Mellon; E-mail: jmellon@middlebury.edu; Staff 9 (MLS 4, Non-MLS 5)
Founded 1955. Enrl 700; Fac 70; Highest Degree: Master
Library Holdings: e-books 3,050; Bk Vols 92,000; Per Subs 600
Special Collections: Foreign Language; General & Technical Dictionaries (English & Foreign Languages); International Business; MIIS Theses; Monterey Institute of International Studies Archives
Subject Interests: Econ, Humanities, Intl, Lit, Trade
Automation Activity & Vendor Info: (Acquisitions) Innovative Interfaces, Inc; (Cataloging) Innovative Interfaces, Inc; (Circulation) Innovative Interfaces, Inc; (Course Reserve) Innovative Interfaces, Inc; (OPAC) Innovative Interfaces, Inc; (Serials) Innovative Interfaces, Inc
Wireless access
Publications: MIIS/List of Periodicals
Partic in Monterey Bay Area Cooperative Library System; Statewide California Electronic Library Consortium
Open Mon-Thurs 8:30am-11pm, Fri 8:30-8, Sat 10-8, Sun 10am-11pm

J MONTEREY PENINSULA COLLEGE LIBRARY*, 980 Fremont St, 93940. SAN 301-0791. Tel: 831-646-4095. Circulation Tel: 831-646-3098. Reference Tel: 831-646-4262. FAX: 831-645-1308. E-mail: library@mpc.edu. Web Site: www.mpc.edu/academics/library-learning-centers/library. *Libr Dir,* Jeffery Sundquist; Tel: 831-646-4036, E-mail: jsundquist@mpc.edu; *Instruction & Ref Librn,* Bill Easton; Tel: 831-645-1382, E-mail: weaston@mpc.edu; *Instruction & Ref Librn,* Deborah Ruiz; Tel: 831-646-1309, E-mail: druiz@mpc.edu
Founded 1947. Enrl 12,500; Highest Degree: Associate
Library Holdings: Bk Vols 60,000; Per Subs 225
Automation Activity & Vendor Info: (Acquisitions) Ex Libris Group; (Cataloging) Ex Libris Group; (Circulation) Ex Libris Group; (Course Reserve) Ex Libris Group; (ILL) Ex Libris Group; (OPAC) Ex Libris Group; (Serials) Ex Libris Group
Wireless access
Partic in Monterey Bay Area Cooperative Library System; OCLC Online Computer Library Center, Inc
Open Mon-Thurs 8am-9pm, Fri 8-2, Sun 1-5

P MONTEREY PUBLIC LIBRARY*, 625 Pacific St, 93940. SAN 301-0805. Tel: 831-646-3933. Circulation Tel: 831-646-3930. Administration Tel: 831-646-5602. E-mail: refdesk@monterey.org. Web Site: www.monterey.org/library. *Libr Dir,* Inga Waite; E-mail: waite@monterey.org; *Librn,* Kim Smith; E-mail: ksmith@monterey.org; Staff 11 (MLS 11)
Founded 1849. Pop 30,000; Circ 418,989
Library Holdings: AV Mats 9,182; Bk Titles 114,612; Per Subs 340
Special Collections: Monterey History
Automation Activity & Vendor Info: (Acquisitions) Innovative Interfaces, Inc; (Cataloging) Innovative Interfaces, Inc; (Circulation) Innovative Interfaces, Inc; (OPAC) Innovative Interfaces, Inc; (Serials) Innovative Interfaces, Inc
Wireless access
Publications: Annual Report; Calendar of Events
Partic in Monterey Bay Area Cooperative Library System
Friends of the Library Group
Bookmobiles: 1

C NAVAL POSTGRADUATE SCHOOL*, Dudley Knox Library, 411 Dyer Rd, 93943. SAN 301-0813. Tel: 831-656-2947. Interlibrary Loan Service Tel: 831-656-7735. Administration Tel: 831-656-2343. Interlibrary Loan Service FAX: 831-656-2842. E-mail: circdesk@nps.edu. Web Site: www.nps.edu/library. *Univ Librn,* Tom Rosko; E-mail: thomas.rosko@nps.edu; *Outreach & Coll Develop Mgr,* Greta Marlatt; Tel: 831-656-3500, E-mail: gmarlatt@nps.edu; Staff 27 (MLS 16, Non-MLS 11)
Founded 1946. Enrl 2,870; Fac 323; Highest Degree: Doctorate
Oct 2014-Sept 2015 Income $5,620,764. Sal $1,773,390 (Prof $1,081,440)
Library Holdings: Audiobooks 224; DVDs 1,469; e-books 345,504; Microforms 20,417; Bk Titles 538,167; Bk Vols 638,961
Special Collections: Hotel Del Monte, Naval Postgraduate School Special Coll & Archives; Intelligence Coll; Military & Naval History (Buckley Coll). US Document Depository
Subject Interests: Bus, Computer sci, Econ, Engr, Finance, Hist, Math, Mgt, Nat security, Physics, Polit sci
Automation Activity & Vendor Info: (Acquisitions) SirsiDynix; (Cataloging) SirsiDynix; (Circulation) SirsiDynix; (ILL) OCLC ILLiad; (OPAC) SirsiDynix; (Serials) SirsiDynix
Wireless access
Function: ILL available
Publications: Periodical Holdings
Mem of Pacific Library Partnership (PLP)
Partic in Califa; Consortium of Naval Libraries; Federal Library & Information Center Committee; Military Education Coordination Conference; Nat Res Libr Alliance
Restriction: Open by appt only

MONTEREY PARK

C EAST LOS ANGELES COLLEGE*, Helen Miller Bailey Library, Bldg F3, 1301 Avenida Cesar Chaves, 91754. SAN 301-083X. Tel: 323-265-8758. FAX: 323-267-3714. Web Site: www.elac.edu/library. *Cat Librn, Chairperson,* Unjoo Lee; E-mail: leeu@elac.edu; Staff 15 (MLS 7, Non-MLS 8)
Founded 1946. Enrl 20,000; Fac 350; Highest Degree: Associate
Library Holdings: Bk Titles 100,000; Bk Vols 110,000; Per Subs 150
Automation Activity & Vendor Info: (Cataloging) SirsiDynix; (Circulation) SirsiDynix; (OPAC) SirsiDynix
Wireless access
Publications: Bibliographic Instructional Handouts; Library handbook
Open Mon-Thurs 7am-10pm, Fri 8-5, Sat 9-5, Sun Noon-5

P MONTEREY PARK BRUGGEMEYER LIBRARY*, Monterey Park Public Library, 318 S Ramona Ave, 91754-3399. SAN 301-0821. Tel: 626-307-1368. Circulation Tel: 626-307-1366. Interlibrary Loan Service Tel: 626-307-1399. Administration Tel: 626-307-1269. Automation Services

Tel: 626-307-1379. FAX: 626-288-4251. TDD: 626-307-2540. E-mail: library@montereypark.ca.gov. Web Site: montereypark.ca.gov/238/Library. *City Librn,* Diana Garcia; Tel: 626-307-1418, E-mail: dgarcia@montereypark.ca.gov; *Adult & Teen Serv Mgr, Sr Librn,* Cindy Costales; Tel: 626-307-1398, E-mail: ccostales@montereypark.ca.gov; *Mgr, Tech Serv, Sr Librn,* Evena Shu; E-mail: eshu@montereypark.ca.gov; *Teen Serv Librn,* Darren Braden; E-mail: dbraden@montereypark.ca.gov; *Circ Supvr,* Julie Villanueva; E-mail: jvillanueva@montereypark.ca.gov; *Adult Ref, AV,* Maggie Wang; E-mail: mwang@montereypark.ca.gov; *Actg Literacy Contact,* Jose Garcia; Tel: 626-307-1251, E-mail: jgarcia@montereypark.ca.gov. Subject Specialists: *Adult prog, Fiction,* Cindy Costales; *Teen lit, Young adult lit,* Darren Braden; *Adult literacy, Citizen prep,* Julie Villanueva; *Chinese lang & lit,* Maggie Wang; Staff 7 (MLS 6, Non-MLS 1)
Founded 1929. Pop 63,300; Circ 460,000
Jul 2017-Jun 2018 Income $2,528,241, State $35,385, City $1,914,556, Federal $78,300, Locally Generated Income $500,000. Mats Exp $152,390, Books $103,218, Per/Ser (Incl. Access Fees) $4,910, Micro $4,322, AV Mat $27,089, Electronic Ref Mat (Incl. Access Fees) $10,551, Presv $2,300. Sal $728,953 (Prof $463,582)
Library Holdings: Audiobooks 1,362; AV Mats 10,548; CDs 2,744; DVDs 3,572; e-books 1; Large Print Bks 728; Microforms 661; Bk Titles 135,666; Bk Vols 148,586; Per Subs 93; Videos 2,860
Special Collections: Chinese, Japanese, Korean, Spanish & Vietnamese Languages Coll. US Document Depository
Subject Interests: Calif, Local hist
Automation Activity & Vendor Info: (Cataloging) Innovative Interfaces, Inc; (Circulation) Innovative Interfaces, Inc; (ILL) OCLC Online; (OPAC) Innovative Interfaces, Inc
Wireless access
Function: 24/7 Electronic res, 24/7 Online cat, 3D Printer, Adult bk club, Adult literacy prog, Art exhibits, Computer training, Computers for patron use, Electronic databases & coll, Family literacy, Govt ref serv, Holiday prog, Homework prog, ILL available, Internet access, Literacy & newcomer serv, Mail & tel request accepted, Music CDs, Online cat, Online ref, Outreach serv, Photocopying/Printing, Preschool outreach, Prof lending libr, Prog for adults, Prog for children & young adult, Ref serv available, Res libr, Senior computer classes, Senior outreach, Spoken cassettes & CDs, Story hour, Summer & winter reading prog, Summer reading prog, Teen prog, Telephone ref, Wheelchair accessible, Winter reading prog, Workshops, Writing prog
Publications: Message from the City Librarian (Online only)
Partic in Califa; Southern California Library Cooperative
Special Services for the Deaf - Adult & family literacy prog; Closed caption videos; TDD equip
Special Services for the Blind - Bks available with recordings; Bks on cassette; Bks on CD; Large print bks
Open Mon & Tues 12-9, Wed & Thurs 10-6, Fri & Sat 10-1, Sun 1-5
Restriction: Access at librarian's discretion, Authorized personnel only, Badge access after hrs, Borrowing requests are handled by ILL, Circ to mem only, ID required to use computers (Ltd hrs), Mem only
Friends of the Library Group

MOORPARK

P MOORPARK CITY LIBRARY, 699 Moorpark Ave, 93021. SAN 335-2471. Tel: 805-517-6370. FAX: 805-523-2736. E-mail: AskUs@MoorparkLibrary.org. Web Site: moorparkca.gov/355/Library. *City Librn,* Christine Conwell; Tel: 805-517-6371, E-mail: christine.conwell@lsslibraries.com
Wireless access
Open Mon-Thurs 10-8, Fri & Sat 10-5, Sun 1-5
Friends of the Library Group

J MOORPARK COLLEGE LIBRARY*, 7075 Campus Rd, 93021-1695. SAN 301-0848. Tel: 805-378-1450. Reference Tel: 805-378-1472. E-mail: mcreference@vcccd.edu. Web Site: www.moorparkcollege.edu/departments/student-services/library. *Dean,* Dr Carol Higashida; E-mail: chigashida@vcccd.edu; *Librn,* Mary LaBarge; Tel: 805-553-4857, E-mail: mlabarge@vcccd.edu; *Ref Librn,* Mrs Faten Habib; Tel: 805-553-1472, E-mail: fhabib@vcccd.edu; *Libr Tech,* Penny Hahn; Tel: 805-553-1422, E-mail: phahn@vcccd.edu; Staff 3 (MLS 3)
Founded 1967. Enrl 13,704; Fac 621
Library Holdings: Bk Vols 100,000; Per Subs 293
Automation Activity & Vendor Info: (Acquisitions) Ex Libris Group; (Cataloging) Ex Libris Group; (Circulation) Ex Libris Group; (Course Reserve) Ex Libris Group; (ILL) Ex Libris Group; (OPAC) Ex Libris Group; (Serials) Ex Libris Group
Wireless access
Open Mon-Thurs 8-8, Fri 8-Noon

MORAGA

S MORAGA HISTORICAL SOCIETY ARCHIVES*, 1500 Saint Mary's Rd, 94556-2037. (Mail add: PO Box 103, 94556-0103), SAN 372-7343. Tel: 925-377-8734. E-mail: info@moragahistory.org. Web Site: www.moragahistory.org/archives. *Archivist,* Margaret DePriester; Staff 1 (MLS 1)
Library Holdings: Bk Titles 600
Special Collections: Rancho Land Case No 590 (1852). Oral History
Subject Interests: Genealogy
Wireless access
Publications: El Rancho (historical journal); Newsletter
Open Mon, Wed & Fri 1-3 or by appointment
Restriction: Open to pub for ref only
Friends of the Library Group

C SAINT MARY'S COLLEGE LIBRARY*, Saint Albert Hall Library, 1928 Saint Mary's Rd, 94575. (Mail add: PO Box 4290, 94575-4290), SAN 301-0856. Tel: 925-631-4229. Administration Tel: 925-631-4525. FAX: 925-376-6097. Web Site: library.stmarys-ca.edu. *Dean of Libr,* Lauren MacDonald; E-mail: lmm24@stmarys-ca.edu; *Head, Access Serv, Institutional Repository Mgr,* Shannon Meaney-Ryer; *Head, Cat & Coll,* Hannah Thomas; *Head, Coll Mgt,* Lauren MacDonald; *Cat Librn, Institutional Repository Mgr,* Elise Wong; *Archivist, Instruction Librn,* Position Currently Open; *Ref & Instruction Librn, Web Serv Coordr,* Susan Birkenseer; *Ref & Instruction Librn,* Sarah Vital; *Ref & Instruction Librn,* Joshua Rose; *Mgr, Electronic Res,* Mike Jung; *Mgr, Per,* Bruce Engelfried; *Circ Supvr, ILL Mgr,* Position Currently Open; *Circ Supvr, Head, Student Serv,* Norm Patridge; *Circ Supvr, Reserves Mgr,* Steve Stonewell; *Coordr, Instrul Serv, Ref Librn,* Gina Kessler Lee; *Ref & Instruction Librn, Ref Serv Coordr,* Patricia Wade; *Circ Supvr,* Position Currently Open; *Circ Supvr, Publ Librn,* Fred Schlichting; *Circ Supvr,* Alyson Runke; *Budget Officer, Mgr, Acad Res,* Tania Fernandez Rodriguez. Subject Specialists: *Prints,* Steve Stonewell; Staff 21.7 (MLS 12.3, Non-MLS 9.4)
Founded 1863. Enrl 3,908; Fac 219; Highest Degree: Doctorate
Library Holdings: AV Mats 10,729; e-books 179,777; e-journals 150,000; Electronic Media & Resources 477,148; Microforms 2,164; Bk Titles 179,912; Bk Vols 201,656; Per Subs 926; Videos 4,500
Special Collections: Byron Bryant Film Coll; California Mathematical Society Archives; College Archives; Oxford Movement (Newman Coll); Spirituality of 17th & 18th Century (Lasallian Research Center). Oral History
Subject Interests: Bus, Educ, Liberal arts, Sciences
Automation Activity & Vendor Info: (Acquisitions) Innovative Interfaces, Inc; (Cataloging) Innovative Interfaces, Inc; (Circulation) Innovative Interfaces, Inc; (Course Reserve) Innovative Interfaces, Inc; (ILL) OCLC ILLiad; (OPAC) Innovative Interfaces, Inc; (Serials) Innovative Interfaces, Inc
Wireless access
Partic in Northern & Central California Psychology Libraries; OCLC Online Computer Library Center, Inc; Research Libraries Information Network; Statewide California Electronic Library Consortium

MORENO VALLEY

P MORENO VALLEY PUBLIC LIBRARY*, 25480 Alessandro Blvd, 92553. SAN 378-2565. Tel: 951-413-3880. FAX: 951-413-3895. E-mail: citylibrary@moval-library.org. Web Site: www.moval.org. *Libr Dir,* Maria Sunio; E-mail: maria.sunio@lsslibraries.com; *Circ,* Karen Morales; Staff 22 (MLS 4, Non-MLS 18)
Founded 1987. Pop 195,000; Circ 429,072
Library Holdings: Bk Vols 146,948; Per Subs 77
Automation Activity & Vendor Info: (Acquisitions) SirsiDynix; (Cataloging) SirsiDynix; (Circulation) SirsiDynix; (Serials) SirsiDynix
Wireless access
Function: 24/7 Electronic res, 24/7 Online cat, Activity rm, Adult bk club, After school storytime, Bilingual assistance for Spanish patrons, Bks on CD, Computers for patron use, Digital talking bks, Electronic databases & coll, Free DVD rentals, ILL available, Internet access, Magnifiers for reading, Music CDs, Online cat, Online ref, Photocopying/Printing, Ref serv available, Spanish lang bks, Story hour, Summer reading prog, Wheelchair accessible, Workshops, Writing prog
Mem of Inland Library System
Open Mon-Thurs 9-8, Sat 9-6
Friends of the Library Group

J RIVERSIDE COMMUNITY COLLEGE DISTRICT*, Moreno Valley College Library, 16130 Lasselle St, 92551. SAN 371-9626. Tel: 951-571-6356. Circulation Tel: 951-571-6111. Reference Tel: 951-571-6109. FAX: 951-571-6191. Web Site: mvc.edu/library. *Dean of Instruction, Libr Mgr,* Anna Marie Amezquita; E-mail: annamarie.amezquita@mvc.edu; *Pub Serv Librn,* Debbie Renfrow; E-mail: debbi.renfrow@mvc.edu; *Libr Operations Asst,* Mark Robinson; Staff 4 (MLS 2, Non-MLS 2)
Founded 1991. Enrl 7,000; Fac 55; Highest Degree: Associate

Library Holdings: Bk Titles 20,000; Bk Vols 22,000; Per Subs 150
Wireless access
Open Mon-Thurs 7:30am-8pm, Fri 7:30-5, Sat 8-3:30

M RIVERSIDE UNIVERSITY HEALTH SYSTEM MEDICAL LIBRARY*, 26520 Cactus Ave, 92555. SAN 301-2557. Tel: 951-486-5101. FAX: 951-486-5045. *Libr Mgr,* Denise Adams; E-mail: d.adams@ruhealth.org
Founded 1957
Library Holdings: Bk Titles 995; Bk Vols 1,025; Per Subs 209
Subject Interests: Bacteriology, Dermatology, Internal med, Mental health, Neurology, Nursing, Obstetrics & gynecology, Ophthalmology, Otolaryngology, Pediatrics, Radiology, Surgery
Wireless access
Open Mon-Fri 8-4:30

MOSS LANDING

CM CALIFORNIA STATE UNIVERSITY*, MLML/MBARI Research Library, 8272 Moss Landing Rd, 95039. SAN 301-0864. Tel: 831-771-4414. E-mail: library@mlml.calstate.edu. Web Site: www.mlml.calstate.edu/library. *Head Librn,* Katie Lage; E-mail: klage@mlml.calstate.edu; Staff 1 (MLS 1)
Founded 1966. Enrl 150; Fac 9; Highest Degree: Master
Library Holdings: e-journals 1,000; Bk Vols 25,000
Special Collections: Elkhorn Slough Coll
Subject Interests: Calif, Mammals, Marine biol, Oceanography
Wireless access
Open Mon-Fri 8:30-5
Friends of the Library Group

S SHAKESPEARE SOCIETY OF AMERICA, New Shakespeare Sanctuary Library, 7981 Moss Landing Rd, 95039. SAN 371-134X. Tel: 831-633-2989. Administration E-mail: admin@shakespearesocietyofamerica.org. Web Site: www.shakespearesocietyofamerica.org. *Pres & Dir,* Terry Taylor
Founded 1968
Library Holdings: Bk Vols 3,000
Subject Interests: Elizabethan studies, Shakespeare studies
Restriction: Open by appt only

MOUNTAIN VIEW

M EL CAMINO HOSPITAL LIBRARY & INFORMATION CENTER*, 2500 Grant Rd, 94039. SAN 370-2006. Tel: 650-940-7210. FAX: 650-940-7299. E-mail: healthlib@elcaminohospital.org. Web Site: www.elcaminohospital.org. *Mgr,* Joy Tobin
Library Holdings: Bk Vols 4,460; Per Subs 200
Subject Interests: Ethics, Med, Nursing
Automation Activity & Vendor Info: (Acquisitions) EOS International; (Cataloging) EOS International; (Circulation) EOS International; (OPAC) EOS International; (Serials) EOS International
Publications: Holdings Lists; Special Selected Bibliographies
Partic in Northern California & Nevada Medical Library Group

L FENWICK & WEST LLP, LIBRARY*, Silicon Valley Ctr, 801 California St, 94041. SAN 373-739X. Tel: 650-335-7575. FAX: 650-938-5200. E-mail: library@fenwick.com. Web Site: www.fenwick.com. *Libr Mgr,* Cathy Hardy; Tel: 650-335-7518, E-mail: chardy@fenwick.com; Staff 5 (MLS 3, Non-MLS 2)
Founded 1975
Automation Activity & Vendor Info: (Cataloging) EOS International; (OPAC) EOS International; (Serials) EOS International
Wireless access
Restriction: Not open to pub

P MOUNTAIN VIEW PUBLIC LIBRARY, 585 Franklin St, 94041-1998. SAN 301-0899. Tel: 650-903-6887. E-mail: librarycustomerservice@mountainview.gov. Web Site: www.mountainview.gov/library. *Dir,* Tracy Gray
Founded 1905
Special Collections: Mountain View History Center
Wireless access
Function: 24/7 Electronic res, 24/7 Online cat, Adult literacy prog, Audiobks via web, Bks on CD, Children's prog, Computers for patron use, Electronic databases & coll, Free DVD rentals, Homebound delivery serv, Internet access, Magazines, Mango lang, Music CDs, Online cat, OverDrive digital audio bks, Photocopying/Printing, Prog for adults, Prog for children & young adult, Ref & res, Ref serv available, Spanish lang bks, Study rm, Summer reading prog, Teen prog, Wheelchair accessible
Open Mon-Thurs 10-9, Fri & Sat 10-6, Sun 1-5
Friends of the Library Group

S PACIFIC STUDIES CENTER*, 2423B Old Middlefield Way, 94043. SAN 320-1597. Tel: 650-961-8918. FAX: 650-961-8918. *Dir,* Lenny Siegel; E-mail: lsiegel@cpeo.org
Founded 1969
Library Holdings: Bk Titles 1,000; Per Subs 10
Special Collections: Alternative Magazines; Newspaper Clippings, vf
Restriction: Open by appt only

MURRIETA

P MURRIETA PUBLIC LIBRARY, 8 Town Sq, 92562. Tel: 951-304-2665. FAX: 951-696-0165. Web Site: murrietaca.gov/261/library. *Actg Libr Mgr,* Gretchen Sedlacek; Fax: gsedlacek@murrietaca.gov; *Supv Librn, Adult Serv,* Agnes Rita; Tel: 951-461-6130, E-mail: arita@murrietaca.gov; *Circ Supvr,* JoLene Vert; Tel: 951-461-6142, E-mail: jvert@murrietaca.gov; Staff 17.5 (MLS 5.5, Non-MLS 12)
Founded 1999. Pop 115,000; Circ 439,694
Library Holdings: Bk Vols 85,000; Per Subs 75
Automation Activity & Vendor Info: (Cataloging) Innovative Interfaces, Inc. - Polaris; (Circulation) Innovative Interfaces, Inc. - Polaris; (OPAC) Innovative Interfaces, Inc. - Polaris; (Serials) Innovative Interfaces, Inc. - Polaris
Wireless access
Mem of Inland Library System
Open Mon-Thurs 10-6, Fri & Sat 12-5
Friends of the Library Group

NAPA

S NAPA COUNTY HISTORICAL SOCIETY*, Goodman Library Bldg, 1219 First St, 94559. SAN 326-6338. Tel: 707-224-1739. E-mail: info@napahistory.org. Web Site: www.napahistory.org. *Mgr,* Liz Alessio; Staff 14 (MLS 1, Non-MLS 13)
Founded 1948
Library Holdings: Bk Titles 3,686; Bk Vols 7,000
Special Collections: City & Co of Napa
Function: Archival coll
Restriction: Non-circulating to the pub, Open by appt only

GL NAPA COUNTY LAW LIBRARY*, Historic Courthouse, 825 Brown St, Rm 138, 94559. Tel: 707-299-1201. FAX: 707-253-4229. Web Site: www.napalawlibrary.com. *Librn,* Michael Blend; E-mail: michael.blend@napacourts.ca.gov
Library Holdings: Bk Vols 14,696
Open Mon-Fri 8-4

P NAPA COUNTY LIBRARY*, Napa Main Library, 580 Coombs St, 94559-3396. SAN 301-0929. Tel: 707-253-4241. Circulation Tel: 707-253-4243. Reference Tel: 707-253-4235. Administration Tel: 707-253-4242. FAX: 707-253-4615. TDD: 707-253-6088. E-mail: Library@countyofnapa.org. Web Site: www.countyofnapa.org/Library. *Libr Dir,* Anthony Halstead; E-mail: anthony.halstead@countyofnapa.org; *Head, Circ,* Tina Jolley; Tel: 707-253-4072, E-mail: tina.jolley@countyofnapa.org; *Supvr, Ch Serv,* Ann Davis; Tel: 707-253-4079, E-mail: adavis2@co.napa.ca.us; *Coll Serv Supvr,* Nancy Bradford; Tel: 707-253-4281, E-mail: nancy.bradford@countyofnapa.org; *Supvr, Extn Serv,* Nicole Shields; Tel: 707-259-8391, E-mail: nicole.shields@countyofnapa.org; *Literacy Supvr,* Robin Rafael; Tel: 707-253-4283, E-mail: robin.rafael@countyofnapa.org; *Ref Supvr,* Breanna Feliciano; Tel: 707-265-2787, E-mail: breanna.feliciano@countyofnapa.org. Subject Specialists: *Literacy,* Robin Rafael; Staff 24.1 (MLS 9.8, Non-MLS 14.3)
Founded 1916. Pop 105,353; Circ 615,089
Special Collections: Local Newspaper Index
Subject Interests: County hist
Automation Activity & Vendor Info: (Acquisitions) Innovative Interfaces, Inc; (Cataloging) Innovative Interfaces, Inc; (Circulation) Innovative Interfaces, Inc; (OPAC) Innovative Interfaces, Inc
Wireless access
Function: 24/7 Electronic res, 24/7 Online cat, Activity rm, Adult bk club, Adult literacy prog, Art exhibits, Audiobks on Playaways & MP3, Audiobks via web, Bilingual assistance for Spanish patrons, Bk club(s), Bks on CD, Children's prog, Computer training, Computers for patron use, Electronic databases & coll, Family literacy, Free DVD rentals, Homebound delivery serv, Homework prog, ILL available, Internet access, Jail serv, Life-long learning prog for all ages, Magazines, Magnifiers for reading, Mango lang, Meeting rooms, Movies, Museum passes, Music CDs, Online cat, OverDrive digital audio bks, Photocopying/Printing, Preschool outreach, Prog for adults, Prog for children & young adult, Ref & res, Ref serv available, Senior computer classes, Spanish lang bks, Spoken cassettes & CDs, Spoken cassettes & DVDs, Story hour, Study rm, Summer & winter reading prog, Summer reading prog, Tax forms, Teen prog, Telephone ref, Wheelchair accessible
Publications: Local History Indexer's Manual
Mem of NorthNet Library System

Special Services for the Deaf - TDD equip
Open Mon-Thurs 10-9, Fri 10-6, Sat 10-6
Friends of the Library Group
Branches: 3
AMERICAN CANYON BRANCH, 300 Crawford Way, American Canyon, 94503. Tel: 707-644-1136. *Libr Assoc,* Caren Cucco; E-mail: caren.cucco@countyofnapa.org
Pop 16,031; Circ 76,090
Friends of the Library Group
CALISTOGA BRANCH, 1108 Myrtle, Calistoga, 94515-1730, SAN 321-7353. Tel: 707-942-4833. FAX: 707-942-0941. *Libr Assoc,* Daniel Cottrell; E-mail: daniel.cottrell@countyofnapa.org
Pop 5,302; Circ 35,001
Subject Interests: Local hist
Friends of the Library Group
YOUNTVILLE BRANCH, 6516 Washington St, Yountville, 94599-1271, SAN 328-7769. Tel: 707-944-1888. *Libr Assoc,* Ruth Barney
Pop 3,290; Circ 14,950
Friends of the Library Group

M NAPA STATE HOSPITAL*, John Stewart Richie Patients' Library, 2100 Napa-Vallejo Hwy, 94558-6293. Tel: 707-253-5000. *Libr Supvr,* Bliss Ezike; *Actg Librn,* Lindsey Segura
Library Holdings: Bk Vols 6,500; Per Subs 40
Wireless access
Open Mon-Fri 9-4:30

J NAPA VALLEY COLLEGE*, McCarthy Library, 1700 Bldg, 2277 Napa-Vallejo Hwy, 94558. SAN 301-0937. Tel: 707-256-7400. Reference Tel: 707-256-7430. Web Site: www.napavalley.edu/library. *Dean, Libr & Learning Res,* Rebecca Scott; Tel: 707-256-7438, E-mail: rscott@napavalley.edu; *Librn,* Stephanie Grohs; E-mail: sgrohs@napavalley.edu; *Disability Serv Librn,* Jan Schardt; Tel: 707-256-7412, E-mail: jschardt@napavalley.edu; *Librn,* Nancy McEnery; Tel: 707-256-7430, E-mail: nmcenery@napavalley.edu; *Learning Res Tech,* Amy Guan; E-mail: aguan@napavalley.edu
Founded 1942. Enrl 10,000; Fac 200; Highest Degree: Associate
Jul 2013-Jun 2014 Income $492,874. Mats Exp $74,500, Books $5,000, Per/Ser (Incl. Access Fees) $13,000, Other Print Mats $5,000, AV Mat $6,500, Electronic Ref Mat (Incl. Access Fees) $45,000. Sal $357,803
Library Holdings: AV Mats 5,120; CDs 100; Bk Titles 57,000; Bk Vols 59,000; Per Subs 295
Special Collections: Cookbook Coll; Copia Coll; Jessamyn West Coll; Napa History Coll; Winery & Viticulture Technology Coll
Automation Activity & Vendor Info: (Acquisitions) CARL.Solution (TLC); (Cataloging) OCLC; (Circulation) CARL.Solution (TLC); (Course Reserve) CARL.Solution (TLC); (ILL) OCLC; (OPAC) CARL.Solution (TLC); (Serials) CARL.Solution (TLC)
Wireless access
Mem of NorthNet Library System
Partic in Solano Napa & Partners Library Consortium
Open Mon-Thurs 7:30am-8pm, Fri 7:30-Noon

NATIONAL CITY

S BEAUCHAMP BOTANICAL LIBRARY*, 1434 E 24th St, 91950-6010. (Mail add: PO Box 985, 91951-0985), SAN 324-7325. Tel: 619-477-5333. FAX: 619-477-5380. E-mail: bio@psbs.com. Web Site: psbs.com. *Librn,* R Mitchel Beauchamp; E-mail: mitch@psbs.com
Founded 1970
Jan 2014-Dec 2014. Mats Exp $1,500, Books $1,000, Per/Ser (Incl. Access Fees) $500
Library Holdings: Bk Titles 7,200; Per Subs 60
Special Collections: Floristic Monographs
Subject Interests: Petaloid monocots (esp amaryllidaceae), Vascular floras of the world

P NATIONAL CITY PUBLIC LIBRARY*, 1401 National City Blvd, 91950-4401. SAN 301-0953. Tel: 619-470-5800. FAX: 619-470-5880. E-mail: library@nationalcityca.gov. Web Site: nationalcityca.gov/government/library. *City Librn,* Joyce Ryan; E-mail: jryan@nationalcityca.gov; Staff 11 (MLS 9, Non-MLS 2)
Founded 1896. Pop 55,600; Circ 103,740
Jul 2015-Jun 2016 Income $19,999,197, City $1,909,734, Other $89,463. Mats Exp $83,000, Books $45,000, Per/Ser (Incl. Access Fees) $6,000, AV Mat $10,000, Electronic Ref Mat (Incl. Access Fees) $22,000. Sal $803,874
Library Holdings: AV Mats 27,738; DVDs 22,040; e-books 4,697; e-journals 63; Bk Vols 205,370; Per Subs 110
Special Collections: Local History, bks, tapes; Spanish bks, per
Subject Interests: Ethnic studies, Hist
Automation Activity & Vendor Info: (Acquisitions) Horizon; (Cataloging) Horizon; (Circulation) Horizon; (OPAC) Horizon
Wireless access
Function: 24/7 Electronic res, 24/7 Online cat, Adult literacy prog, Archival coll, Audiobks on Playaways & MP3, BA reader (adult literacy), Bilingual assistance for Spanish patrons, Children's prog, Computer training, Computers for patron use, Electronic databases & coll, Free DVD rentals, Homework prog, Internet access, Magazines, Movies, Online cat, OverDrive digital audio bks, Photocopying/Printing, Prog for adults, Prog for children & young adult, Ref & res, Scanner, Senior computer classes, Spanish lang bks, Spoken cassettes & CDs, Spoken cassettes & DVDs, Story hour, Study rm, Summer reading prog, Teen prog
Open Mon-Thurs 10-8, Sat & Sun 1-5
Friends of the Library Group

NEVADA CITY

S AMERICAN HERB ASSOCIATION LIBRARY*, PO Box 1673, 95959. SAN 370-9914. Tel: 530-274-3140. Web Site: www.ahaherb.com. *Dir,* Kathi Keville; E-mail: kathikeville@yahoo.com
Library Holdings: Bk Vols 6,000; Per Subs 40

P NEVADA COUNTY COMMUNITY LIBRARY*, Headquarters, 980 Helling Way, 95959. SAN 991-4978. Tel: 530-265-7050. Interlibrary Loan Service Tel: 530-470-2773. FAX: 530-265-9863. E-mail: library.reference@co.nevada.ca.us. Web Site: www.mynevadacounty.com/290/Library. *County Librn,* Nick Wilczek
Founded 1972
Wireless access
Branches: 6
BEAR RIVER STATION, 11130 Magnolia Rd, Grass Valley, 95949, SAN 333-2640. Circulation Tel: 530-271-4147. Web Site: www.mynevadacounty.com/377/Bear-River-Library. *Br Mgr,* Cindy Pawlowski; E-mail: cindy.pawlowski@co.nevada.ca.us
Founded 2002
Function: Adult bk club, Adult literacy prog, Bks on cassette, Bks on CD, Children's prog, Computers for patron use, Electronic databases & coll, Home delivery & serv to seniorr ctr & nursing homes, Homebound delivery serv, ILL available, Music CDs, Online cat, Online ref, Photocopying/Printing, Prog for adults, Prog for children & young adult, Ref serv available, Summer reading prog, Tax forms, Telephone ref, VHS videos, Wheelchair accessible
Open Mon, Wed & Fri 12-3
Friends of the Library Group
DORIS FOLEY LIBRARY FOR HISTORICAL RESEARCH, 211 N Pine St, 95959, SAN 333-2705. Tel: 530-265-4606. E-mail: foleyhistorylibrary@co.nevada.ca.us. Web Site: www.mynevadacounty.com/337/Doris-Foley-Library-for-Historical-Resea. *Br Mgr,* Laura Pappani; E-mail: laura.pappani@co.nevada.ca.us
Founded 1907
Special Collections: Nevada County Court Records
Subject Interests: Local hist, Mining
Friends of the Library Group
GRASS VALLEY LIBRARY - ROYCE BRANCH, 207 Mill St, Grass Valley, 95945, SAN 333-2675. Tel: 530-273-4117. Web Site: www.mynevadacounty.com/307/Grass-Valley-Library—Royce-Branch. *Br Mgr,* Rachel Tucker; E-mail: rachel.tucker@co.nevada.ca.us; *Youth Serv Librn,* Mellisa Hannum; E-mail: mellisa.hunnum@co.nevada.ca.us
Founded 1916
Open Mon-Fri 12-5
Friends of the Library Group
MADELYN HELLING LIBRARY, 980 Helling Way, 95959, SAN 373-5931. Tel: 530-265-7078. Web Site: www.mynevadacounty.com/300/Madelyn-Helling-Library. *Br Mgr,* Cindy Pawlowski; E-mail: cindy.pawlowski@co.nevada.ca.us; *Youth Serv Librn,* Jill Davidson; E-mail: jillene.davidson@co.nevada.ca.us
Founded 1991. Pop 97,182; Circ 634,488
Library Holdings: Audiobooks 15,347; e-books 4,959; Bk Titles 184,205; Per Subs 302; Videos 17,083
Automation Activity & Vendor Info: (Acquisitions) SirsiDynix; (Cataloging) SirsiDynix; (Circulation) SirsiDynix; (ILL) OCLC; (OPAC) SirsiDynix
Function: Adult literacy prog, After school storytime, Audiobks via web, Bks on cassette, Bks on CD, Children's prog, Computers for patron use, Electronic databases & coll, Free DVD rentals, Home delivery & serv to seniorr ctr & nursing homes, Homebound delivery serv, ILL available, Literacy & newcomer serv, Music CDs, Online cat, OverDrive digital audio bks, Photocopying/Printing, Prog for adults, Prog for children & young adult, Story hour, Summer reading prog, Tax forms, VHS videos, Wheelchair accessible
Special Services for the Blind - Audio mat; Bks on cassette; Bks on CD; Extensive large print coll; Magnifiers; Talking bk serv referral
Open Mon-Fri 11-3
Friends of the Library Group
PENN VALLEY STATION, 11336 Pleasant Valley Rd, Penn Valley, 95946. Tel: 530-432-5764. Web Site: www.mynevadacounty.com/367/Penn-Valley-Library. *Br Mgr,* Cindy Pawlowski; E-mail: cindy.pawlowski@co.nevada.ca.us

Founded 2002
Open Mon-Fri 12-3
Friends of the Library Group
TRUCKEE LIBRARY, 10031 Levon Ave, Truckee, 96161, SAN 333-273X. Tel: 530-582-7846. Web Site: www.mynevadacounty.com/336/Truckee-Library. *Br Mgr,* Bobbi Luster; E-mail: bobbi.luster@co.nevada.ca.us
Founded 1976
Open Mon-Fri 11-3
Friends of the Library Group

S NEVADA COUNTY HISTORICAL SOCIETY*, Searls Historical Library, 161 Nevada City Hwy, 95959. SAN 301-0961. Tel: 530-265-5910. Web Site: nevadacountyhistory.org/searls-historical-library. *Dir,* Patricia J Chesnut; E-mail: pchesnut@hughes.net
Founded 1972
Library Holdings: CDs 250; Bk Titles 3,500
Special Collections: Nevada County Photographs. Oral History
Subject Interests: Local hist, State hist
Open Mon-Sat 1-4 or by appointment
Restriction: Open to pub for ref only

NEWPORT BEACH

P NEWPORT BEACH PUBLIC LIBRARY*, 1000 Avocado Ave, 92660-6301. SAN 333-2764. Tel: 949-717-3800. FAX: 949-640-5681. Web Site: www.newportbeachlibrary.org. *Libr Serv Dir,* Tim Hetherton; E-mail: thetherton@newportbeachca.gov; Staff 65.5 (MLS 19.5, Non-MLS 46)
Founded 1920. Pop 83,120; Circ 1,622,573
Library Holdings: Bk Titles 282,874; Bk Vols 325,890; Per Subs 708
Special Collections: Nautical Coll; Newport Beach History Coll
Automation Activity & Vendor Info: (Acquisitions) Innovative Interfaces, Inc; (Cataloging) Innovative Interfaces, Inc; (Circulation) Innovative Interfaces, Inc; (OPAC) Innovative Interfaces, Inc; (Serials) Innovative Interfaces, Inc
Wireless access
Publications: Bookends (Newsletter); Lighthouse (Newsletter)
Mem of Santiago Library System
Partic in Califa; Metro Coop Libr Syst; Southern California Library Cooperative
Open Mon-Thurs 9-9, Fri & Sat 9-6, Sun 12-5
Friends of the Library Group
Branches: 4
BALBOA BRANCH, 100 E Balboa Blvd, Balboa, 92661, SAN 333-2799. Tel: 949-644-3076. FAX: 949-675-8524. *Br Librn,* Evelyn Rogers; E-mail: erogers@newportbeachca.gov
Library Holdings: Bk Vols 50,353
Open Mon & Wed 9-9, Tues & Thurs-Sat 9-6
Friends of the Library Group
CENTRAL LIBRARY, 1000 Avocado Ave, 92660-6301, SAN 333-2888. *Libr Serv Dir,* Tim Hetherton; Staff 24 (MLS 22, Non-MLS 2)
Founded 1920. Pop 75,662; Circ 1,002,877
Library Holdings: Bk Vols 226,811
Subject Interests: Am hist, Art, Bus
Open Mon-Thurs 9-9, Fri & Sat 9-6, Sun 12-5
Friends of the Library Group
CORONA DEL MAR BRANCH, 410 Marigold Ave, Corona del Mar, 92625, SAN 333-2829. Tel: 949-644-3075. FAX: 949-673-4917. *Br Librn,* Annika Helmuth; E-mail: ahelmuth@newportbeachca.gov; Staff 1 (MLS 1)
Library Holdings: Bk Vols 32,653
Open Tues & Thurs 9-9, Wed, Fri & Sat 9-6
Friends of the Library Group
MARINERS BRANCH, 1300 Irvine Ave, 92660, SAN 333-2853. Tel: 949-717-3838. *Br Librn,* Rebecca Lightfoot; E-mail: rlightfoot@newportbeachca.gov; Staff 2 (MLS 2)
Founded 1950
Library Holdings: Bk Vols 64,582
Open Mon-Thurs 9-9, Fri & Sat 9-6, Sun 12-5
Friends of the Library Group

L O'MELVENY & MYERS LLP*, Law Library, 610 Newport Center Dr, 17th Flr, 92660-6429. SAN 372-3801. Tel: 949-760-9600. FAX: 949-823-6994. Web Site: www.omm.com. *Library Contact,* Kelsey Weber
Founded 1979
Library Holdings: Bk Vols 5,000
Restriction: Staff use only

S STRADLING, YOCCA, CARLSON & RAUTH*, Law Library, 660 Newport Ctr, Ste 1600, 92660. SAN 373-9007. Tel: 949-725-4000. FAX: 949-725-4100. Web Site: www.sycr.com. *Chief Tech Officer,* Peter Baran; E-mail: pbaran@sycr.com; Staff 2 (MLS 1, Non-MLS 1)
Founded 1975
Library Holdings: Bk Titles 1,100; Bk Vols 9,000; Per Subs 250
Restriction: Not open to pub

NORCO

GL CALIFORNIA DEPARTMENT OF CORRECTIONS*, California Rehabilitation Center Library, Fifth St & Western, 92860. (Mail add: PO Box 1841, 92860), SAN 300-838X. Tel: 951-737-2683, Ext 4202. FAX: 951-273-2380. Web Site: www.cdcr.ca.gov/Facilities_Locator/CRC.html. *Sr Librn,* William Swafford; E-mail: william.swafford@cdcr.ca.gov; *Librn,* Mitchell Lindenbaum; E-mail: mitch.lindenbaum@cdcr.ca.gov; Staff 3 (MLS 2, Non-MLS 1)
Founded 1966
Library Holdings: Bk Vols 43,077
Special Collections: Federal & California Law, cases & statutes
Restriction: Not open to pub

NORTH HOLLYWOOD

S PACIFICA FOUNDATION*, Pacifica Radio Archives, 3729 Cahuenga Blvd W, 91604. SAN 326-0577. Tel: 818-506-1077. Toll Free Tel: 800-735-0230. FAX: 818-506-1084. Web Site: www.pacificaradioarchives.org. *Interim Dir,* Mark Torres; Tel: 818-506-1077, Ext 266, E-mail: mark@pacificaradioarchives.org; *Adminr, Outreach Coordr,* Shawn Dellis; Tel: 818-506-1077, Ext 261, E-mail: shawn@pacificaradioarchives.org; Staff 2 (MLS 1, Non-MLS 1)
Founded 1970
Library Holdings: Bk Titles 40,000
Subject Interests: Polit sci, Pub affairs
Automation Activity & Vendor Info: (Cataloging) Inmagic, Inc.
Function: Archival coll
Publications: Annual Cassette & Reel to Reel Catalogues (print)
Partic in OCLC Online Computer Library Center, Inc
Restriction: Open by appt only

S WESTERN COSTUME CO*, Research Library, 11041 Vanowen St, 91605. SAN 326-3800. Tel: 818-508-2148. E-mail: research@westerncostume.com. Web Site: www.westerncostumeresearch.com. *Dir,* Leighton Bowers; Staff 1 (MLS 1)
Founded 1915
Library Holdings: Bk Titles 12,500; Bk Vols 13,500; Per Subs 60
Special Collections: Godey, Peterson & Vogue, mags; Sears & Montgomery Ward Catalogs (1895 to present); Twentieth Century Fox Costume Still Coll
Subject Interests: Costume, Fashion
Open Mon-Fri 9-6

NORTHRIDGE

C CALIFORNIA STATE UNIVERSITY, NORTHRIDGE, Delmar T Oviatt Library, 18111 Nordhoff St, 91330. SAN 333-2918. Tel: 818-677-2285. Circulation Tel: 818-677-2274. Interlibrary Loan Service Tel: 818-677-2294. Reference Tel: 818-538-7814. Administration Tel: 818-677-2271. FAX: 818-677-2676. TDD: 818-677-6519. Web Site: library.csun.edu. *Dean,* Mark Stover, PhD; E-mail: mark.stover@csun.edu; *Assoc Dean,* Katherine S Dabbour; Tel: 818-677-2272, E-mail: kathy.dabbour@csun.edu; *Dir, Library Administrative Operations,* Jamie Skeggs; Tel: 818-677-2205, E-mail: jamie.skeggs@csun.edu; *Dir, Libr Info Tech,* Justin Kovalcik; Tel: 818-677-4549, E-mail: justin.kovalcik@csun.edu; Staff 89 (MLS 32, Non-MLS 57)
Founded 1958. Enrl 35,000; Fac 1,929; Highest Degree: Doctorate
Library Holdings: e-books 570,000; e-journals 53,000; Electronic Media & Resources 200; Microforms 3,170,000; Bk Vols 1,500,000; Videos 45,000
Special Collections: 19th Century English & American Playbills (Theater Program Coll, 1809-1930); 19th Century English Theatre Playbills Coll; California & Local History Coll; California Tourism & Promotional Literature Coll; Carl Sandburg Coll, bks, news clippings, pamphlets; Catherine Mulholland Coll; Chinese Antiquities (Tseng Coll); Contemporary 20th Century American Writers (McDermott Coll); Edwin Booth Coll; Francis Gilbert Webb Correspondence, 1898-1934; Gwen Driston Papers; Haldeman-Julius Publications, Big & Little Blue Books, etc; History of Printing (Lynton Kistler-Merle Armitage Coll); Human Sexuality (Vern & Bonnie Bullough Coll); International Guitar Research Archives; Japanese-American World War II Relocation Camps, doc, newsp; Migrant Farm Labor Camp Newsletters, 1930s; Milton Geiger Papers; Old China Hands Coll; Radio & Film Scripts, NBC Radio Plays, 1935-1943; Ray Martin Coll, music scores; Revolutionary & Political Movements in Russia, 1875-1937 (Patrick Coll); San Fernando Valley Digital History Library; Slaves & Slavery (American Plantation Documents, 1756-1869); Urban Archives Coll; Vern & Bonnie Bullough Coll; Voluntary Labor & Civic Associations Papers; Women Music Composers (Aaron Cohen Coll, Ruth Shaw Wylie Scores, Ardis O Higgin Coll). State Document Depository; US Document Depository
Subject Interests: Local hist, Music
Automation Activity & Vendor Info: (Acquisitions) Innovative Interfaces, Inc; (Cataloging) Innovative Interfaces, Inc; (Circulation) Innovative

Interfaces, Inc; (Course Reserve) Innovative Interfaces, Inc; (ILL) OCLC; (OPAC) Innovative Interfaces, Inc; (Serials) Innovative Interfaces, Inc
Wireless access
Function: Archival coll, Art exhibits, Audio & video playback equip for onsite use, Bks on cassette, Bks on CD, Computers for patron use, Doc delivery serv, E-Reserves, Electronic databases & coll, Equip loans & repairs, Govt ref serv, ILL available, Internet access, Large print keyboards, Online cat, Online info literacy tutorials on the web & in blackboard, Online ref, Orientations, Outreach serv, Outside serv via phone, mail, e-mail & web, Photocopying/Printing, Ref & res, Ref serv available, Wheelchair accessible
Publications: Faculty Guide to the Oviatt Library; Library eNews (Quarterly newsletter); Oviatt Friends (Newsletter); Student Guide to the Oviatt Library; University Library (Annual report)
Partic in OCLC Online Computer Library Center, Inc
Special Services for the Deaf - Assistive tech; Bks on deafness & sign lang; Closed caption videos; Staff with knowledge of sign lang; TTY equip
Special Services for the Blind - Assistive/Adapted tech devices, equip & products; Audio mat; Bks on cassette; Bks on CD; Braille equip; Talking bks; Talking calculator
Open Mon-Thurs 7:45am-10:45pm, Fri 7:45-6:45, Sat Noon-4:45, Sun Noon-7:45
Restriction: Authorized patrons, Borrowing privileges limited to fac & registered students, Borrowing requests are handled by ILL, External users must contact libr, ID required to use computers (Ltd hrs), Open to students, fac, staff & alumni
Friends of the Library Group
Departmental Libraries:
MAP COLLECTION, University Library, Rm 26, 18111 Nordhoff St, 91330, SAN 333-2977. Tel: 818-677-3465. E-mail: librarymaps@csun.edu. Web Site: library.csun.edu/map-collection. *Curator, Maps,* Chris Salvano; E-mail: chris.salvano@csun.edu; *Asst Map Curator,* Emilie Docourneau; E-mail: emilie.ducourneau@csun.edu; Staff 2 (MLS 1, Non-MLS 1)
Library Holdings: Bk Vols 2,000
Special Collections: Automobile Club Road & Touring Maps (1920s-1990s); California State University, Northridge Campus Maps; Dibblee Geologic Maps of the San Fernando Valley (1991-1996); Los Angeles City Street Atlases (1940s-2008); Los Angeles County Topographic Maps (1925-1948); San Fernando Valley Neighborhood, Transportation & City Maps; San Fernando Valley Plat Book (1953); Spencer Air Photo Coll (1921-1941); Teledyn Geotronics Air Photo Coll (1976); Thomas Brothers Road Maps of The San Fernando Valley (1940s-1990s); US Geological Survey Geologic & Soil Maps of the San Fernando Valley; Whitehurst Air Photo Coll (1955)
Open Mon-Fri 9-5

M NORTHRIDGE HOSPITAL*, Medical Library, 18300 Roscoe Blvd, 91328. SAN 321-5601. Tel: 818-885-8500, Ext 4610. FAX: 818-885-0372. *Librn,* Kathy Jeschke
Founded 1975
Library Holdings: Bk Titles 2,000; Per Subs 100
Open Mon-Fri 7:30-5:30
Restriction: Staff use only

NORWALK

J CERRITOS COLLEGE LIBRARY*, 11110 Alondra Blvd, 90650. SAN 301-1127. Tel: 562-860-2451, Ext 2430. Circulation Tel: 562-860-2451, Ext 2424. Reference Tel: 562-860-2451, Ext 2425. Administration Tel: 562-860-2451, Ext 2413. Web Site: cert.ent.sirsi.net/client/cerritos. *Dean of Libr,* Shawna Baskette; E-mail: sbaskette@cerritos.edu; *Coll Develop & Acq Librn,* Monica Lopez; Tel: 562-860-2451, Ext 2434, E-mail: mmlopez@cerritos.edu; *Adjunct Ref Librn,* Valencia Mitchell; E-mail: vmitchell@cerritos.edu; *Adjunct Ref Librn,* Lynda Sampson; *Syst & Tech Serv Librn,* Debra Moore; Tel: 562-860-2451, Ext 2418, E-mail: dmoore@cerritos.edu; *Libr Instruction Coordr, Ref Coordr,* Lorraine Gersitz; Tel: 562-860-2451, Ext 2414, E-mail: lgersitz@cerritos.edu; Staff 14 (MLS 7, Non-MLS 7)
Founded 1956. Enrl 24,000; Highest Degree: Associate
Library Holdings: Bk Titles 110,000; Per Subs 200
Automation Activity & Vendor Info: (Acquisitions) SirsiDynix; (Cataloging) SirsiDynix; (Circulation) SirsiDynix; (Course Reserve) SirsiDynix; (ILL) OCLC; (OPAC) SirsiDynix; (Serials) SirsiDynix
Wireless access
Function: Distance learning, ILL available, Orientations, Photocopying/Printing
Partic in California Community College Library Consortium; OCLC Online Computer Library Center, Inc
Special Services for the Deaf - Bks on deafness & sign lang
Special Services for the Blind - Text reader; ZoomText magnification & reading software
Open Mon-Thurs 7:30am-9pm, Fri 7:30-3

M METROPOLITAN STATE HOSPITAL*, Staff Library, 11401 Bloomfield Ave, 90650. SAN 333-306X. Tel: 562-651-2295, 562-863-7011 (Main Hospital). FAX: 562-651-4439. Web Site: www.dsh.ca.gov/Metropolitan. *Sr Librn,* James Church; Staff 1 (MLS 1)
Founded 1950
Library Holdings: CDs 200; Large Print Bks 100; Bk Vols 3,600; Talking Bks 200; Videos 1,000
Subject Interests: Psychiat, Psychol, Sociol
Partic in Docline
Open Mon-Fri 8-4

NOVATO

S MARIN HISTORY MUSEUM LIBRARY*, Craemer Family Collection & Research Facility, 45 Leveroni Ct, 94949. (Mail add: PO Box 150727, San Rafael, 94915), SAN 327-6546. Tel: 415-382-1182. FAX: 415-454-6137. E-mail: research@marinhistory.org. Reference E-mail: info@marinhistory.org. Web Site: www.marinhistory.org. *Dir,* Michelle Sarjeant Kaufman; E-mail: michelle@marinhistory.org
Founded 1935
Library Holdings: Bk Vols 1,000
Special Collections: Bound Newspapers (1868-present); Land Grants Coll. Oral History
Subject Interests: Genealogy, Local hist
Function: Archival coll, Photocopying/Printing, Ref serv available
Publications: Marin People (3 vols)
Open Tues 10-Noon, Wed & Thurs 10-2 or by appointment

S MUSEUM OF THE AMERICAN INDIAN LIBRARY*, Miwok Park, 2200 Novato Blvd, 94947. (Mail add; PO Box 864, 94948-0864), SAN 329-0662. Tel: 415-897-4064. Web Site: www.marinindian.com. *Dir,* Teresa Saltzman
Founded 1967
Library Holdings: Bk Vols 600
Function: Ref serv available
Restriction: Non-circulating to the pub, Open by appt only

OAKLAND

M ALAMEDA HEALTH SYSTEM MEDICAL LIBRARY*, 1411 E 31st St, 94602. SAN 301-1135. Tel: 510-437-4701. Web Site: www.alamedahealthsystem.org. *Supv Librn,* Laurie Bagley; E-mail: labagley@alamedahealthsystem.org; Staff 1 (MLS 1)
Founded 1917
Library Holdings: CDs 300; e-books 50; e-journals 180; Bk Vols 4,000; Per Subs 200
Subject Interests: Clinical med
Automation Activity & Vendor Info: (Acquisitions) EOS International; (Cataloging) EOS International; (Circulation) EOS International; (OPAC) EOS International; (Serials) EOS International
Wireless access
Function: ILL available, Res libr
Partic in National Network of Libraries of Medicine Region 5; Northern California & Nevada Medical Library Group
Restriction: Circ limited, Circulates for staff only, Employees & their associates, Internal circ only, Lending to staff only, Mem organizations only, Not a lending libr, Not open to pub, Prof mat only, Restricted access, Restricted loan policy, Secured area only open to authorized personnel, Staff use only

C CALIFORNIA COLLEGE OF THE ARTS LIBRARIES*, Meyer Library, 5212 Broadway, 94618. SAN 301-1186. Circulation Tel: 510-594-3658. E-mail: refdesk@cca.edu. Web Site: libraries.cca.edu. *Dir of Libr,* Annemarie Haar; Tel: 510-594-3657, E-mail: ahaar@cca.edu; *Assoc Dir of Libr,* Teri Dowling; Tel: 415-703-9559, E-mail: tdowling@cca.edu; Staff 3 (MLS 3)
Founded 1926. Enrl 1,800; Fac 250; Highest Degree: Master
Library Holdings: Bk Titles 35,000; Bk Vols 38,000; Per Subs 125; Videos 2,200
Special Collections: Capp Street Project Archives; College Archives; Hamaguchi Study Print Coll
Subject Interests: Fine arts
Automation Activity & Vendor Info: (OPAC) Innovative Interfaces, Inc
Wireless access
Partic in BayNet Library Association; Statewide California Electronic Library Consortium
Restriction: Open to others by appt, Open to students, fac & staff
Departmental Libraries:
SIMPSON LIBRARY, 1111 Eighth St, San Francisco, 94107. Administration Tel: 415-703-9574. Information Services Tel: 415-703-9558. *Assoc Dir of Libr,* Teri Dowling; E-mail: tdowling@cca.edu; *Pub Serv Mgr,* Donald Smith; E-mail: dsmith@cca.edu; Staff 2 (MLS 2)
Founded 1986

Library Holdings: Bk Titles 17,000; Bk Vols 19,000; Per Subs 130; Videos 600
Special Collections: Joseph Sinel Coll; Small Press Traffic Archives
Subject Interests: Archit, Design
Automation Activity & Vendor Info: (OPAC) Innovative Interfaces, Inc
Partic in Southern Calif Electronic Libr Consortium
Restriction: Open to others by appt, Open to students, fac & staff

G CALIFORNIA STATE DEPARTMENT OF HEALTH SERVICES*, Office of Environmental Health Hazard Assessment, 1515 Clay St, 16th Flr, 94612. Tel: 510-622-2928, 510-622-3200. FAX: 510-622-3197. Web Site: oehha.ca.gov. *Librn*, Nancy Firchow; E-mail: nancy.firchow@oehha.ca.gov
Library Holdings: Bk Vols 10,000
Automation Activity & Vendor Info: (Cataloging) Inmagic, Inc.
Open Mon-Fri 9-5
Restriction: Staff use only

M CHILDREN'S HOSPITAL & RESEARCH CENTER OAKLAND*, Gordon Health Sciences Library, 747 52nd St, 4th Flr, 94609. SAN 301-1208. Tel: 510-428-3448. Web Site: childrenshospitaloakland.org. *Librn*, Mina Davenport; E-mail: mina.davenport@ucsf.edu; Staff 1 (MLS 1)
Founded 1938
Jul 2015-Jun 2016 Income $448,530, Locally Generated Income $5,000, Parent Institution $442,130, Other $700. Mats Exp $449,130, Books $2,000, Per/Ser (Incl. Access Fees) $118,218, Electronic Ref Mat (Incl. Access Fees) $328,912. Sal $63,000
Library Holdings: CDs 47; DVDs 181; e-books 1,011; e-journals 350; Electronic Media & Resources 3; Bk Titles 3,100; Bk Vols 3,600; Per Subs 127
Subject Interests: Pediatrics
Automation Activity & Vendor Info: (Acquisitions) EOS International; (Cataloging) EOS International; (Circulation) EOS International; (OPAC) EOS International; (Serials) EOS International
Wireless access
Function: ILL available, Internet access, Photocopying/Printing, Ref serv available
Publications: Online Acquisitions List; Online Newsletter; Serials Holdings
Partic in Northern California & Nevada Medical Library Group; OCLC Online Computer Library Center, Inc
Restriction: Circulates for staff only, Not open to pub

C HOLY NAMES UNIVERSITY*, Paul J Cushing Library, 3500 Mountain Blvd, 94619. SAN 301-1267. Tel: 510-436-1332. FAX: 510-436-1260. E-mail: hnulibrary@hnu.edu. Web Site: www.hnu.edu/library. *Univ Librn*, Sylvia Contreras; Tel: 510-436-1160, E-mail: scontreras@hnu.edu; *Assoc Dir, Access Serv*, Eugenia Chan; E-mail: chan@hnu.edu; Staff 3 (MLS 2, Non-MLS 1)
Founded 1880. Enrl 930; Fac 90; Highest Degree: Master
Library Holdings: AV Mats 4,975; e-books 25,000; Bk Titles 75,000; Bk Vols 111,174; Talking Bks 85
Subject Interests: Music, Nursing, Relig
Wireless access
Function: For res purposes, ILL available, Res libr
Partic in Northern & Central California Psychology Libraries
Open Mon-Thurs 9am-10pm, Fri 9-5, Sat 10-5, Sun 12-8
Restriction: Non-circulating to the pub

S INDEPENDENT INSTITUTE LIBRARY*, 100 Swan Way, 94621-1428. SAN 371-7410. Tel: 510-632-1366. FAX: 510-568-6040. E-mail: info@independent.org. Web Site: www.independent.org. *Librn*, Mr Sanjeev Saini; Tel: 510-632-1366, Ext 143; Staff 1 (MLS 1)
Founded 1986
Library Holdings: Bk Titles 6,500; Per Subs 85
Subject Interests: Econ, Hist, Law, Polit sci, Sociol
Wireless access
Open Mon-Fri 8:30-5:30

J LANEY COLLEGE*, Library-Learning Resources Center, 900 Fallon St, 94607. SAN 301-1291. Tel: 510-464-3495. FAX: 510-464-3264. Web Site: laney.edu/library. *Head Librn*, Evelyn Lord; E-mail: elord@peralta.edu; *Media/Instruction Librn*, YiPing Wang; E-mail: yipingwang@peralta.edu; *Pub Serv*, Reginald Constant; E-mail: rconstant@peralta.edu; Staff 5 (MLS 5)
Founded 1956. Enrl 10,508; Fac 177
Library Holdings: DVDs 600; Bk Titles 80,634; Bk Vols 89,000; Per Subs 108
Automation Activity & Vendor Info: (Cataloging) Innovative Interfaces, Inc - Millennium; (Circulation) Innovative Interfaces, Inc - Millennium
Wireless access
Open Mon-Thurs 8-8, Fri 8-6, Sat 9-2

C LINCOLN UNIVERSITY LIBRARY*, 401 15th St, 94612. SAN 321-9380. Tel: 510-379-4048. FAX: 510-628-8012. E-mail: library@lincolnuca.edu. Web Site: www.lincolnuca.edu/studentlife/library#%2Fstudentlife%2Flibrary. *Head Librn*, Nicole Y Marsh; E-mail: nmarsh@lincolnuca.edu; Staff 3 (MLS 1, Non-MLS 2)
Founded 1962. Enrl 600; Fac 35; Highest Degree: Doctorate
Library Holdings: DVDs 400; e-books 90,000; e-journals 4,000; Electronic Media & Resources 20; Bk Titles 19,500; Bk Vols 21,500; Per Subs 40; Spec Interest Per Sub 20; Videos 2,000
Automation Activity & Vendor Info: (Acquisitions) LibraryWorld, Inc
Wireless access
Partic in Statewide California Electronic Library Consortium
Open Mon-Thurs 8:45-6:30, Fri & Sat 8:45-3:30 (Fall & Spring); Mon-Thurs 8:45-6:30, Fri 8:45-3:30 (Summer)
Restriction: Access at librarian's discretion, Authorized personnel only

J MERRITT COLLEGE LIBRARY*, 12500 Campus Dr, 94619. SAN 301-1305. Tel: 510-436-2461. Circulation Tel: 510-436-2457. Reference Tel: 510-436-2557. FAX: 510-531-4960. Web Site: www.merritt.edu/wp/library. *Interim Dean*, Dr Chriss Warren Foster; E-mail: cfoster@peralta.edu; *Tech Serv Librn*, Eva Ng-Chin; E-mail: engchin@peralta.edu; Staff 6 (MLS 3, Non-MLS 3)
Founded 1954. Enrl 2,500; Fac 128; Highest Degree: Associate
Library Holdings: Bk Titles 55,000; Per Subs 100
Special Collections: Black Panthers Archive Coll
Automation Activity & Vendor Info: (Acquisitions) Innovative Interfaces, Inc; (Cataloging) Innovative Interfaces, Inc; (Circulation) Innovative Interfaces, Inc; (Course Reserve) Innovative Interfaces, Inc; (OPAC) Innovative Interfaces, Inc
Wireless access
Special Services for the Blind - Computer with voice synthesizer for visually impaired persons; Reader equip
Open Mon-Thurs 8-8, Fri 8-4, Sat 10-4 (Fall & Spring); Mon-Thurs 9-4 (Summer)

C MILLS COLLEGE*, F W Olin Library, 5000 MacArthur Blvd, 94613. SAN 333-3159. Tel: 510-430-2385. Circulation Tel: 510-430-2196. FAX: 510-430-2278. E-mail: library@mills.edu. Web Site: inside.mills.edu/academics/library, www.mills.edu/academics/library.php. *Libr Dir, Spec Coll & Archives Librn*, Janice Braun; Tel: 510-430-2047, E-mail: jbraun@mills.edu; *Head, Tech Serv, Syst Librn*, John Winsor; Tel: 510-430-2066, E-mail: jwinsor@mills.edu; Staff 14 (MLS 7, Non-MLS 7)
Founded 1852. Enrl 1,256; Fac 155; Highest Degree: Doctorate
Library Holdings: Bk Titles 183,674; Bk Vols 224,059; Per Subs 920
Special Collections: 19th & 20th Century English & American Dance (Jane Bourne Parton Coll); Fine Press Books; Music (Darius Milhaud Archive); Rare Americana
Subject Interests: Art, Bk arts, Dance, Lit, Shakespeare
Automation Activity & Vendor Info: (Acquisitions) Innovative Interfaces, Inc; (Cataloging) Innovative Interfaces, Inc; (Circulation) Innovative Interfaces, Inc; (Course Reserve) Innovative Interfaces, Inc; (ILL) Innovative Interfaces, Inc; (Media Booking) Innovative Interfaces, Inc; (OPAC) Innovative Interfaces, Inc; (Serials) Innovative Interfaces, Inc
Wireless access
Function: Res libr
Publications: Literary & Cultural Journeys: Selected Letters to Arturo Torres-Rioseco; Salon at Larkmead; The Flying Cloud & Her First Passengers
Partic in Statewide California Electronic Library Consortium
Open Mon-Thurs 8:30am-Midnight, Fri 8:30-6, Sat Noon-6, Sun Noon-11

P OAKLAND PUBLIC LIBRARY*, 125 14th St, 94612. SAN 333-3213. Tel: 510-238-3282. Circulation Tel: 510-238-3144. Administration Tel: 510-238-3281. Information Services Tel: 510-238-3134. FAX: 510-238-2232. TDD: 510-834-7446. E-mail: eanswers@oaklandlibrary.org. Web Site: www.oaklandlibrary.org. *Dir, Libr Serv*, Jamie Turbak; Tel: 510-238-6610, E-mail: jturbak@oaklandlibrary.org; *Assoc Dir*, Nina Lindsay; Tel: 510-228-6706, E-mail: nlindsay@oaklandlibrary.org; *Pub Info Officer*, Matt Berson; Tel: 510-238-6932, E-mail: mberson@oaklandlibrary.org; *Chief Curator*, Bamidele Agbasegbe-Demerson; Tel: 510-637-0200, Fax: 510-637-0204, E-mail: bagbasegbe-Demerson@oaklandlibrary.org; *Libr Mgr*, Mana Tominaga; Tel: 510-238-6611, E-mail: mtominaga@oaklandlibrary.org; *Tech Serv Mgr*, Jiao Han; Tel: 510-238-2217, E-mail: jhan@oaklandlibrary.org; *Br Coordr*, Jenera Burton; Tel: 510-238-3670, E-mail: jburton@oaklandlibrary.org; *Br Coordr*, Derrick DeMay; Tel: 510-238-3479, E-mail: ddemay@oaklandlibrary.org; Staff 79.6 (MLS 79.6)
Founded 1878. Pop 431,291; Circ 2,317,505
Library Holdings: AV Mats 76,021; e-books 7,457; Electronic Media & Resources 37; Large Print Bks 4,881; Music Scores 27,000; Bk Titles 526,574; Bk Vols 1,148,809; Per Subs 3,359; Videos 38,581
Special Collections: African-American Museum & Library (Archival Coll); Asian Coll; Local History Coll; Oakland History Room; Tool

Lending Library; USGS Topographical Maps. State Document Depository; US Document Depository
Subject Interests: Art, Asia, Bus, Local hist, Music
Automation Activity & Vendor Info: (Acquisitions) Innovative Interfaces, Inc; (Cataloging) Innovative Interfaces, Inc; (Circulation) Innovative Interfaces, Inc; (ILL) Innovative Interfaces, Inc; (OPAC) Innovative Interfaces, Inc
Wireless access
Function: Adult literacy prog, Archival coll, AV serv, CD-ROM, E-Reserves, Electronic databases & coll, Family literacy, Govt ref serv, ILL available, Internet access, Magnifiers for reading, Photocopying/Printing, Prog for adults, Prog for children & young adult, Ref serv available, Summer reading prog, Tax forms, Wheelchair accessible
Publications: Annual Reports; Calendar of Events; Staff Newsletter
Partic in Bergen County Cooperative Library System, Inc
Special Services for the Deaf - Assistive tech; Bks on deafness & sign lang; TTY equip
Special Services for the Blind - ABE/GED & braille classes for the visually impaired; Aids for in-house use; Assistive/Adapted tech devices, equip & products; Audio mat; Computer with voice synthesizer for visually impaired persons; Reader equip
Open Mon-Thurs 10-8, Fri 12-5:30, Sat & Sun 10-5:30
Friends of the Library Group
Branches: 16
ASIAN, 388 Ninth St, Ste 190, 94612, SAN 333-3248. Tel: 510-238-3400. FAX: 510-238-4732.
Founded 1975. Pop 12,200; Circ 335,797
Library Holdings: Bk Vols 75,334
Special Collections: Asian American Coll, English; Asian Materials in Asian Languages (Chinese, Japanese, Korean, Vietnamese, Thai, Cambodian, Tagalog & Laotian) gen subj titles, major ref titles; Asian Studies Coll
Open Mon, Thurs & Sat 10-5:30, Tues & Wed 10-8, Fri 12-5:30
Friends of the Library Group
BROOKFIELD, 9255 Edes Ave, 94603, SAN 333-3272. Tel: 510-615-5725. FAX: 510-615-5862.
Founded 1992. Pop 11,347; Circ 27,494
Library Holdings: Bk Vols 34,534
Function: Computers for patron use, Digital talking bks, E-Reserves, Electronic databases & coll, Free DVD rentals, Internet access, Music CDs, Online cat, OverDrive digital audio bks, Photocopying/Printing, Preschool outreach, Prog for adults, Prog for children & young adult, Ref serv available, Spanish lang bks, Story hour, Summer reading prog, Tax forms, Teen prog, Telephone ref, VHS videos, Wheelchair accessible
Open Mon, Thurs & Sat 10-5:30, Tues & Wed 10-8, Fri 12-5:30
Restriction: 24-hr pass syst for students only
Friends of the Library Group
CESAR E CHAVEZ BRANCH, 3301 E 12th St, Ste 271, 94601, SAN 333-3515. Tel: 510-535-5620. FAX: 510-535-5622.
Founded 1966. Pop 32,889; Circ 108,874
Library Holdings: Bk Vols 49,668
Special Collections: Spanish Language Coll
Open Mon, Thurs & Sat 10-5:30, Tues & Wed 10-8, Fri 12-5:30
Friends of the Library Group
DIMOND, 3565 Fruitvale Ave, 94602, SAN 333-3302. Tel: 510-482-7844. FAX: 510-482-7824.
Founded 1915. Pop 45,319; Circ 221,079
Library Holdings: Bk Vols 75,532
Special Collections: American Indian Coll
Function: Adult literacy prog, Prog for adults, Prog for children & young adult, Summer reading prog
Open Mon, Thurs & Sat 10-5:30, Tues & Wed 10-8, Fri 12-5:30
Friends of the Library Group
EASTMONT, Eastmont Town Ctr, Ste 211, 7200 Bancroft Ave, 94605, SAN 333-3337. Tel: 510-615-5726. FAX: 510-615-5863.
Founded 1945. Pop 31,716; Circ 35,375
Library Holdings: Bk Vols 41,786
Open Mon 9-7, Tues-Thurs 9-5:30, Fri 12-5:30
Friends of the Library Group
ELMHURST, 1427 88th Ave, 94621, SAN 333-3361. Tel: 510-615-5727. FAX: 510-615-5869.
Founded 1911. Pop 31,811; Circ 26,643
Library Holdings: Bk Vols 29,063
Open Mon, Thurs & Sat 10-5:30, Tues & Wed 10-8, Fri 12-5:30
GOLDEN GATE, 5606 San Pablo Ave, 94608, SAN 333-3426. Tel: 510-597-5023. FAX: 510-597-5030.
Pop 22,866; Circ 49,071
Library Holdings: Bk Vols 32,978
Special Collections: Materials in Hindi & Punjabi (East Indian Coll)
Function: Adult bk club, Chess club, Homework prog, Jazz prog, Prog for adults, Prog for children & young adult, Summer reading prog
Open Mon, Thurs & Sat 10-5:30, Tues & Wed 10-8, Fri 12-5:30
Friends of the Library Group
MARTIN LUTHER KING BRANCH, 6833 International Blvd, 94621, SAN 333-3450. Tel: 510-615-5728. FAX: 510-615-5739.
Founded 1916. Pop 20,188; Circ 23,308
Library Holdings: Bk Vols 29,123
Open Mon, Thurs & Sat 10-5:30, Tues & Wed 10-8, Fri 12-5:30
LAKEVIEW, 550 El Embarcadero, 94610, SAN 333-3485. Tel: 510-238-7344. FAX: 510-238-6760.
Founded 1949. Pop 39,768; Circ 110,651
Library Holdings: Bk Vols 40,966
Function: Prog for adults, Prog for children & young adult, Summer reading prog
Open Mon, Thurs & Sat 10-5:30, Tues & Wed 10-8, Fri 12-5:30
MAIN LIBRARY, 125 14th St, 94612, SAN 333-3221. Tel: 510-238-3134. FAX: 510-238-2232. *Libr Mgr,* Mana Tominaga; E-mail: mtominaga@oaklandlibrary.org; Staff 20.7 (MLS 20.7)
Founded 1878. Pop 432,291; Circ 588,835
Library Holdings: Bk Vols 355,257
Function: Archival coll, ILL available, Photocopying/Printing, Prog for adults, Prog for children & young adult, Ref serv available, Summer reading prog, VHS videos
Special Services for the Deaf - Assistive tech; Closed caption videos; TTY equip
Special Services for the Blind - Descriptive video serv (DVS); Reader equip; ZoomText magnification & reading software
Open Mon-Thurs 10-8, Fri 12-5:30, Sat & Sun 10-5:30
MELROSE, 4805 Foothill Blvd, 94601, SAN 333-3574. Tel: 510-535-5623. Interlibrary Loan Service FAX: 510-535-5641.
Founded 1916. Pop 39,822; Circ 34,704
Library Holdings: Bk Vols 31,951
Open Mon, Thurs & Sat 10-5:30, Tues & Wed 10-8, Fri 12-5:30
Friends of the Library Group
MONTCLAIR, 1687 Mountain Blvd, 94611, SAN 333-3604. Tel: 510-482-7810. FAX: 510-482-7865.
Founded 1930. Pop 21,112; Circ 159,148
Library Holdings: Bk Vols 47,840
Open Mon, Thurs & Sat 10-5:30, Tues & Wed 10-8, Fri 12-5:30
PIEDMONT AVENUE, 80 Echo Ave, 94611, SAN 333-3663. Tel: 510-597-5011. FAX: 510-597-5078.
Founded 1912. Pop 19,174; Circ 182,599
Library Holdings: Bk Vols 39,930
Open Mon, Thurs & Sat 10-5:30, Tues & Wed 10-8, Fri 12-5:30
Friends of the Library Group
ROCKRIDGE, 5366 College Ave, 94618, SAN 333-3698. Tel: 510-597-5017. FAX: 510-597-5067.
Founded 1919. Pop 9,026; Circ 261,723
Library Holdings: Bk Vols 84,218
Open Mon, Thurs & Sat 10-5:30, Tues & Wed 10-8, Fri 12-5:30
Friends of the Library Group
TEMESCAL, 5205 Telegraph Ave, 94609, SAN 333-3728. Tel: 510-597-5049. FAX: 510-597-5062.
Founded 1918. Pop 17,657; Circ 58,107
Library Holdings: Bk Vols 29,000
Special Collections: Amharic & Tigrinya Language Coll; Tool Lending Library, bks, tools, videos
Open Mon, Thurs & Sat 10-5:30, Tues & Wed 10-8, Fri 12-5:30
Friends of the Library Group
WEST OAKLAND, 1801 Adeline St, 94607, SAN 333-3752. Tel: 510-238-7352. FAX: 510-238-7551.
Founded 1878. Circ 27,106
Library Holdings: Bk Vols 51,519
Open Mon, Thurs & Sat 10-5:30, Tues & Wed 10-8, Fri 12-5:30
Bookmobiles: 1. Sr Librn, Christine Saed. Bk titles 2,500

S PACIFIC INSTITUTE FOR RESEARCH & EVALUATION*, Prevention Research Center Library, 180 Grand Ave, Ste 1200, 94612. SAN 374-8553. Tel: 510-486-1111, 510-883-5746. FAX: 510-644-0594. E-mail: center@prev.org. Web Site: www.prev.org. *Dir, Libr Serv,* Julie Murphy; E-mail: jmurphy@prev.org; Staff 1 (MLS 1)
Founded 1984
Library Holdings: Bk Titles 3,500; Per Subs 28
Subject Interests: Alcohol, drug & tobacco prevention
Wireless access
Restriction: Open by appt only

CM SAMUEL MERRITT UNIVERSITY*, John A Graziano Memorial Library, Health Education Center, 400 Hawthorne Ave, 94609. SAN 301-1313. Tel: 510-879-9290. FAX: 510-457-4404. Web Site: www.samuelmerritt.edu/library. *Libr Dir,* Hai-Thom Sota; Tel: 510-879-9264, E-mail: ttran@samuelmerritt.edu; Staff 2 (MLS 2)
Founded 1909. Enrl 600; Fac 102; Highest Degree: Doctorate
Library Holdings: Bk Vols 15,548; Per Subs 437
Subject Interests: Health sci, Nursing, Occupational therapy, Phys therapy, Podiatric med

Automation Activity & Vendor Info: (Acquisitions) Koha; (Cataloging) Koha; (Circulation) Koha; (Course Reserve) Koha; (OPAC) Koha; (Serials) Koha
Wireless access
Partic in National Network of Libraries of Medicine Region 5; Northern & Central California Psychology Libraries; Northern California & Nevada Medical Library Group; Pacific Southwest Regional Medical Library
Open Mon-Thurs 7:30am-10pm, Fri 7:30-5, Sat 8-4, Sun 12-10
Restriction: Non-circulating to the pub

C SAYBROOK UNIVERSITY LIBRARY*, 475 14th St, 9th Flr, 94612. SAN 378-2212. Tel: 425-278-9318. FAX: 425-278-9305. E-mail: library@saybrook.edu. Web Site: www.saybrook.edu. *Dir, Libr Serv,* Noah Lowenstein; E-mail: nlowenstein@saybrook.edu. Subject Specialists: *Philos, Psychol, Sociol,* Noah Lowenstein; Staff 1 (MLS 1)
Founded 1970. Enrl 600; Fac 40; Highest Degree: Doctorate
Library Holdings: e-books 250,000; e-journals 36,000; Electronic Media & Resources 34,000
Special Collections: Rollo May Library Coll
Subject Interests: Psychol
Automation Activity & Vendor Info: (Cataloging) Koha; (Circulation) Koha; (ILL) OCLC WorldShare Interlibrary Loan; (OPAC) Koha
Wireless access
Partic in Northern & Central California Psychology Libraries; Statewide California Electronic Library Consortium

S SIERRA CLUB*, William E Colby Memorial Library, 2101 Webster St, Ste 1300, 94612. SAN 301-4657. Tel: 415-977-5506. E-mail: colby.library@sierraclub.org. Web Site: www.sierraclub.org/library. *Librn,* Therese Dunn; *Digital Archivist,* Joanna Black. Subject Specialists: *Organizational hist,* Therese Dunn; *Archives, Digital asset mgt,* Joanna Black; Staff 2 (MLS 2)
Founded 1892
Library Holdings: Bk Vols 8,000
Special Collections: Film Coll (early films by and about the Sierra Club); Historic Photographs (late 19th- & early 20th-century photographs about the Sierra Club and it's members); Legacy Book Coll (antiquarian books about early Club history, mountaineering, and parks)
Subject Interests: Climate change, Conserv, Natural hist, Pollution
Automation Activity & Vendor Info: (OPAC) SirsiDynix
Wireless access
Function: 24/7 Online cat, Art exhibits, Ref & res
Partic in OCLC Online Computer Library Center, Inc
Open Mon-Fri 9-4
Restriction: Non-circulating

GL BERNARD E WITKIN ALAMEDA COUNTY LAW LIBRARY*, 125 Twelfth St, 94607-4912. SAN 301-1143. Tel: 510-208-4800. Circulation Tel: 510-208-4835. Reference Tel: 510-208-4832. Administration Tel: 510-272-6483. FAX: 510-208-4823. E-mail: lawlib@acgov.org. Web Site: www.acgov.org/law. *Dir,* Mark E Estes; Tel: 510-272-6481; *Ref Librn,* Emily Bergfeld; Tel: 510-272-6486, E-mail: emily.bergfeld@acgov.org; *Ref Serv,* Nancy McEnroe; Tel: 510-208-4830, E-mail: nancy.mcenroe@acgov.org; Staff 4 (MLS 4)
Founded 1891
Jul 2017-Jun 2018 Income $1,375,500. Mats Exp $138,000, Books $75,700, Electronic Ref Mat (Incl. Access Fees) $62,300. Sal $680,000 (Prof $372,000)
Library Holdings: AV Mats 524; CDs 95; DVDs 4; Electronic Media & Resources 351; Microforms 551,872; Bk Titles 13,177; Bk Vols 74,637; Per Subs 1,898; Videos 38
Special Collections: Alameda County Ordinance Code, Administrative Code, Budgets & Other Special Publications; California Supreme Court & Appellate Briefs, microfiche; Federal & State Statutes, Indexes & Digests; Legal Periodical Coll, California & US Law Schools; Legal Practice Material, California & Federal; Local Municipal Codes. Municipal Document Depository; State Document Depository; US Document Depository
Automation Activity & Vendor Info: (Acquisitions) ByWater Solutions; (Cataloging) ByWater Solutions; (Circulation) ByWater Solutions; (OPAC) ByWater Solutions
Wireless access
Function: 24/7 Online cat, Art exhibits, Audio & video playback equip for onsite use, CD-ROM, Computers for patron use, Doc delivery serv, Electronic databases & coll, ILL available, Internet access, Magnifiers for reading, Mail & tel request accepted, Meeting rooms, Microfiche/film & reading machines, Online cat, Outreach serv, Outside serv via phone, mail, e-mail & web, Photocopying/Printing, Printer for laptops & handheld devices, Ref & res, Ref serv available, Res libr, Res performed for a fee, Scanner, Spanish lang bks, Telephone ref, Wheelchair accessible
Publications: ACLL (Newsletter); MCLE Titles (Acquisition list); Recent Acquisitions List
Open Mon, Wed & Fri 8:30-4:30, Tues & Thurs 8:30am-9pm, Sat 9-3

OCEANSIDE

J MIRACOSTA COLLEGE LIBRARY*, Oceanside Campus, One Barnard Dr, 92056-3899. SAN 301-1372. Circulation Tel: 760-795-6715. Reference Tel: 760-795-6716. FAX: 760-795-6723. Web Site: library.miracosta.edu. *Dean,* Mario Valente; Tel: 760-795-6720, E-mail: mvalente@miracosta.edu; *Coll Develop Librn, Tech Serv,* Glorian Sipman; Tel: 760-795-6722, E-mail: gsipman@miracosta.edu; *Electronic Res Librn,* Jennifer Paris; Tel: 760-634-7814, E-mail: jparis@miracosta.edu; *Online Serv Librn,* Pamela Perry; Tel: 760-795-6719, E-mail: pperry@miracosta.edu; Staff 12 (MLS 6, Non-MLS 6)
Founded 1934. Enrl 10,840; Fac 875; Highest Degree: Associate
Library Holdings: AV Mats 7,186; e-books 16,508; Bk Titles 61,292; Bk Vols 72,743; Per Subs 214
Automation Activity & Vendor Info: (Cataloging) SirsiDynix; (Circulation) SirsiDynix; (Course Reserve) SirsiDynix; (ILL) OCLC; (OPAC) SirsiDynix; (Serials) SirsiDynix
Wireless access
Function: AV serv, Distance learning, For res purposes, ILL available, Photocopying/Printing, Ref serv available, Telephone ref, Wheelchair accessible
Publications: Citation Guides (Reference guide)
Partic in N County Higher Educ Alliance; OCLC Online Computer Library Center, Inc
Special Services for the Deaf - Closed caption videos
Special Services for the Blind - Braille bks; Computer with voice synthesizer for visually impaired persons
Open Mon-Thurs 7:30-7, Fri 9-3
Friends of the Library Group
Departmental Libraries:
SAN ELIJO CAMPUS, 3333 Manchester Ave, Cardiff, 92007-1516. Circulation Tel: 760-634-7850. Reference Tel: 760-634-7864. FAX: 760-634-7890. *Librn,* Myla Stokes Kelly; Tel: 760-634-7836, E-mail: mkelly@miracosta.edu
Open Mon-Thurs 8am-9:30pm, Fri 8-3, Sat 10-5

P OCEANSIDE PUBLIC LIBRARY*, Civic Center Library, 330 N Coast Hwy, 92054. SAN 301-1380. Tel: 760-435-5600. E-mail: public.library@ci.oceanside.ca.us. Web Site: www.ci.oceanside.ca.us/gov/lib. *Libr Dir,* Sherri Cosby; Tel: 760-435-5609, E-mail: scosby@ci.oceanside.ca.us; *Adult Serv, Principal Librn,* Monica Chapa-Domercq; Tel: 760-435-5586, E-mail: mcdomercq@ci.oceanside.ca.us; *Principal Librn, Youth Serv,* Marie Town; Tel: 760-435-5597, E-mail: mtown@ci.oceanside.ca.us; *Libr Div Mgr/Pub Serv,* Bradley Penner; Tel: 760-435-5575, E-mail: bpenner@ci.oceanside.ca.us; *Commun Outreach Coordr,* Kristine Moralez; Tel: 760-435-5571, E-mail: kmoralez@ci.oceanside.ca.us; *Tech Analyst,* Samuel Liston; Tel: 760-435-5628, E-mail: sliston@ci.oceanside.ca.us; Staff 21.4 (MLS 15, Non-MLS 6.4)
Founded 1904. Pop 179,681; Circ 553,323
Library Holdings: Audiobooks 2,991; CDs 7,348; DVDs 9,265; e-books 3,500; Microforms 3,815; Bk Titles 189,929; Bk Vols 255,115; Per Subs 493; Videos 4,628
Special Collections: Caldecott-Newberry Memorial Coll; Martin Luther King Jr Coll; Parents Resource Coll; Samoan Culture Coll; Teachers Resource Center
Subject Interests: Bus & mgt, Children's lit, Employment, Parent
Automation Activity & Vendor Info: (Acquisitions) SirsiDynix; (Cataloging) SirsiDynix; (Circulation) SirsiDynix; (ILL) SirsiDynix; (OPAC) SirsiDynix; (Serials) SirsiDynix
Wireless access
Partic in Serra Cooperative Library System
Open Mon-Thurs 10-8, Fri & Sat 10-6
Friends of the Library Group
Branches: 2
MISSION BRANCH, 3861 B Mission Ave, 92058, SAN 370-3819. Tel: 760-435-5600. FAX: 760-433-6850. *Principal Librn,* CJ Di Mento; Tel: 760-435-5614, E-mail: cdimento@ci.oceanside.ca.us; *Librn I,* Hilary Holley; Tel: 760-435-5577, E-mail: hholley@ci.oceanside.ca.us; *Circ Supvr,* Israel Marroquin; Tel: 760-435-5633, E-mail: imarroquin@ci.oceanside.ca.us; Staff 2 (MLS 2)
Open Mon-Thurs 10-8, Fri & Sat 10-6, Sun 1-5
Friends of the Library Group
OCEANSIDE READS LITERACY CENTER, 321 N Nevada St, 92054, SAN 378-1240. Tel: 760-435-5680. *Literacy Coordr,* Corrie Miles; Tel: 760-435-5682, E-mail: cmiles@ci.oceanside.ca.us; Staff 2 (Non-MLS 2)
Open Mon-Wed, 10-7, Fri 10-2
Friends of the Library Group
Bookmobiles: 2

OJAI

S KRISHNAMURTI FOUNDATION OF AMERICA*, Krishnamurti Library & Study Center, 1098 McAndrew Rd, 93023. (Mail add: PO Box 1560, 93024), SAN 374-4817. Tel: 805-646-2726, Ext 816. Web Site:

kfa.org/krishnamurti-educational-center. *Librn,* Michael Krohnen; Tel: 805-746-2171, E-mail: michaelk@kfa.org
Founded 1984
Library Holdings: Bk Vols 2,000
Special Collections: J Krishnamurti, bks & teachings
Open Wed-Fri 1-5, Sat & Sun 10-5

SR KROTONA INSTITUTE OF THEOSOPHY LIBRARY*, Two Krotona Hill, 93023. SAN 301-1399. Tel: 805-646-2653. E-mail: library@krotonainstitute.org. Web Site: www.krotonainstitute.org/library. *Librn,* Lakshmi Narayan; *Co-Librn,* Pablo Sender
Founded 1912
Library Holdings: DVDs 250; Bk Titles 15,000; Videos 200
Subject Interests: Astrology, Eastern philosophy, Philos, Psychol, Relig, Theosophy
Wireless access
Open Wed-Sat 12-5, Sun 1-5

ONTARIO

R GATEWAY SEMINARY LIBRARY, 3210 E Gausti Rd, 91761-8642. SAN 301-0589. Tel: 909-687-1800. Web Site: library.gs.edu. *Dir, Libr Serv,* Dr Jonathan McCormick; Tel: 909-687-1482, E-mail: JonathanMcCormick@gs.edu; *Ref & Instruction Librn,* Dr Kenneth Litwak; E-mail: kennethlitwak@gs.edu. Subject Specialists: *New Testament,* Dr Kenneth Litwak; Staff 7 (MLS 4, Non-MLS 3)
Founded 1944. Enrl 1,307; Fac 30; Highest Degree: Doctorate
Library Holdings: Bks on Deafness & Sign Lang 40; Per Subs 256
Special Collections: Baptist History; Music Coll; Rare Book Coll; William O Crews Leadership Coll
Subject Interests: Music, Relig, Theol
Automation Activity & Vendor Info: (Acquisitions) OCLC Worldshare Management Services; (Cataloging) OCLC Worldshare Management Services; (Circulation) OCLC Worldshare Management Services; (Course Reserve) OCLC Worldshare Management Services; (Discovery) EBSCO Discovery Service; (ILL) OCLC WorldShare Interlibrary Loan; (OPAC) OCLC Worldshare Management Services; (Serials) OCLC Worldshare Management Services
Wireless access
Partic in American Theological Library Association; Southern California Theological Library Association; Statewide California Electronic Library Consortium
Open Mon, Tues & Thurs 8-7, Wed & Fri 8-5

P ONTARIO CITY LIBRARY*, Ovitt Family Community Library, 215 East C St, 91764. SAN 301-1429. Tel: 909-395-2004. Circulation Tel: 909-395-2521. Reference Tel: 909-395-2205. FAX: 909-395-2043. E-mail: reference@ontarioca.gov. Web Site: www.ontarioca.gov/library. *Libr Dir,* Shawn Thrasher; E-mail: sthrasher@ontarioca.gov; Staff 71 (MLS 13, Non-MLS 58)
Founded 1885. Pop 173,690
Library Holdings: AV Mats 28,658; CDs 16,378; DVDs 8,552; Bk Titles 145,245; Bk Vols 208,912; Per Subs 686; Videos 10,902
Special Collections: Oral History; State Document Depository; US Document Depository
Subject Interests: Local hist
Automation Activity & Vendor Info: (Acquisitions) SirsiDynix; (Cataloging) SirsiDynix; (Circulation) SirsiDynix; (OPAC) SirsiDynix; (Serials) SirsiDynix
Wireless access
Function: Accelerated reader prog, Adult bk club, Adult literacy prog, After school storytime, Archival coll, AV serv, BA reader (adult literacy), Bk club(s), Bks on cassette, Bks on CD, CD-ROM, Children's prog, Computer training, Computers for patron use, E-Reserves, Electronic databases & coll, Family literacy, Free DVD rentals, Govt ref serv, Holiday prog, Home delivery & serv to seniorr ctr & nursing homes, Homebound delivery serv, Homework prog, ILL available, Internet access, Learning ctr, Literacy & newcomer serv, Mail & tel request accepted, Online cat, Online ref, Outreach serv, Photocopying/Printing, Preschool outreach, Prog for adults, Prog for children & young adult, Ref & res, Ref serv available, Senior computer classes, Spoken cassettes & CDs, Spoken cassettes & DVDs, Story hour, Summer reading prog, Tax forms, Telephone ref, VHS videos, Wheelchair accessible
Mem of Inland Library System
Open Mon-Thurs 10-9, Fri & Sat 10-6, Sun 1-4
Friends of the Library Group
Branches: 1
LEWIS FAMILY BRANCH, 3850 E Riverside Dr, 91761-2603. Tel: 909-395-2014. FAX: 909-930-0836. *Br Mgr,* Heather Withrow; E-mail: hwithrow@ci.ontario.ca.us; Staff 13 (MLS 2, Non-MLS 11)
Library Holdings: AV Mats 5,200; CDs 1,500; DVDs 1,000; Bk Titles 54,085; Bk Vols 55,849; Per Subs 57; Videos 875
Open Mon-Wed 12-8, Thurs-Sat 10-6

CL UNIVERSITY OF LA VERNE*, College of Law Library, 320 E D St, 91764. SAN 329-6679. Tel: 909-460-2070. FAX: 909-460-2083. E-mail: lawadm@laverne.edu, lawlibrary@laverne.edu. Web Site: law.laverne.edu/library. *Dir,* Kenneth Rudolf; Tel: 909-460-2065, E-mail: krudolf@laverne.edu; *Asst Dir, Coll Mgt,* Jennifer Argueta; Tel: 909-460-2064, E-mail: jargueta@laverne.edu; *Ref Librn,* William Ketchum; Tel: 909-460-2063, E-mail: wketchum@laverne.edu; *Tech Serv Mgr,* Isaac Ramirez; E-mail: iramirez@laverne.edu; *Coll Mgt, Libr Asst,* Kristen Jacobson; Tel: 909-460-2066, E-mail: kjacobson@laverne.edu; Staff 5 (MLS 5)
Founded 1970. Enrl 350; Fac 20; Highest Degree: Doctorate
Library Holdings: Microforms 217,000; Bk Titles 28,000; Bk Vols 80,000; Per Subs 475; Videos 75
Special Collections: State Document Depository; US Document Depository
Automation Activity & Vendor Info: (Acquisitions) Innovative Interfaces, Inc - Millennium; (Cataloging) Innovative Interfaces, Inc; (Circulation) Innovative Interfaces, Inc - Millennium; (ILL) OCLC; (OPAC) Innovative Interfaces, Inc - Millennium; (Serials) Innovative Interfaces, Inc - Millennium
Wireless access
Partic in Inland Empire Acad Libr Coop; OCLC Online Computer Library Center, Inc
Open Mon-Thurs 8am-11pm, Fri 8-7, Sat 10-7, Sun 12-7
Restriction: Prof mat only

ORANGE

C CHAPMAN UNIVERSITY*, Leatherby Libraries, One University Dr, 92866. SAN 301-1437. Tel: 714-532-7756. Circulation Tel: 714-532-7723. Interlibrary Loan Service Tel: 714-532-6025. Reference Tel: 714-532-7732. FAX: 714-532-7743. E-mail: libweb@chapman.edu. Web Site: www.chapman.edu/library. *Dean, Leatherby Libr,* Charlene Baldwin; E-mail: baldwin@chapman.edu; *Interim Dean,* Kevin Ross; E-mail: kross@chapman.edu; *Chair, Coll Mgt,* Julie Artman; E-mail: artman@chapman.edu; *Chair, Libr Syst & Tech,* Brett Fisher; E-mail: bfisher@chapman.edu; *Head, Acq,* Theresa Paulsrud; E-mail: paulsrud@chapman.edu; *Head, Circ,* Eduardo Sauceda; E-mail: sauceda@chapman.edu; *Head, Ser,* Andrew Valbuena; E-mail: valbuen@chapman.edu; *Spec Coll Librn,* Rand Boyd; E-mail: rboyd@chapman.edu; *Coordr, Cat & Gifts,* Shahrzad Khasrowpour; E-mail: shahrzad@chapman.edu; *Coordr, Scholarly Communications & Electronic Res,* Kristin Laughtin-Dunker; E-mail: laughtin@chapman.edu; *Libr Develop Coordr,* Essraa Nawar; E-mail: nawar@chapman.edu
Founded 1923. Enrl 13,376; Fac 879; Highest Degree: Doctorate
Library Holdings: AV Mats 26,242; CDs 5,517; DVDs 10,791; e-books 160,897; e-journals 75,655; Bk Vols 333,162; Per Subs 743
Special Collections: Center for American War Letters; Charles C Chapman Rare Book Coll; Disciple of Christ Church History; Huell Howser Archive
Subject Interests: Orange County hist
Automation Activity & Vendor Info: (Acquisitions) Innovative Interfaces, Inc; (Cataloging) Innovative Interfaces, Inc; (Circulation) Innovative Interfaces, Inc; (Course Reserve) Innovative Interfaces, Inc; (Discovery) EBSCO Discovery Service; (ILL) OCLC ILLiad; (OPAC) Innovative Interfaces, Inc; (Serials) Innovative Interfaces, Inc
Wireless access
Function: ILL available, Ref serv available
Partic in OCLC Online Computer Library Center, Inc; Statewide California Electronic Library Consortium
Open Mon-Fri 7-2, Sat & Sun 10-2

CL CHAPMAN UNIVERSITY FOWLER SCHOOL OF LAW*, Hugh & Hazel Darling Law Library, One University Dr, 92866. SAN 378-438X. Tel: 714-628-2537. Circulation Tel: 714-628-2552. Reference Tel: 714-628-2548. Web Site: www.chapman.edu/LAW/student-resources/library/. *Libr Dir,* Linda Kawaguchi; Tel: 714-628-2538, E-mail: kawaguch@chapman.edu; *Assoc Dir, Libr Serv,* Brendan Starkey; Tel: 714-628-2681, E-mail: starkey@chapman.edu; *Coll Mgt Librn,* Rachel Decker; Tel: 714-628-2544, E-mail: rdecker@chapman.edu; *Tech & Syst Librn,* Seong Heon Lee; Tel: 714-628-2598, E-mail: selee@chapman.edu; Staff 14 (MLS 8, Non-MLS 6)
Wireless access
Open Mon-Thurs 8am-Midnight, Fri 8am-10pm, Sat 9am-10pm, Sun 9am-Midnight

P ORANGE PUBLIC LIBRARY & HISTORY CENTER*, 407 E Chapman Ave, 92866-1509. SAN 333-483X. Tel: 714-288-2400. Interlibrary Loan Service Tel: 714-288-2575. Reference Tel: 714-288-2413. Administration Tel: 714-288-2471. FAX: 714-771-6126. E-mail: LibraryManagementTeam@cityoforange.org. Web Site: www.cityoforange.org/244/library. *Libr Dir,* Dave Curtis; Tel: 214-288-2474, E-mail: dcurtis@cityoforange.org; *Asst Dir,* Amy Harpster; Tel: 714-288-2425; Staff 48 (MLS 12, Non-MLS 36)
Founded 1885. Pop 139,279; Circ 636,846; Fac 48

Library Holdings: Audiobooks 14,824; e-books 48,343; Bk Vols 189,803; Per Subs 100; Videos 16,696
Special Collections: Local History Coll
Automation Activity & Vendor Info: (Acquisitions) SirsiDynix; (Cataloging) SirsiDynix; (Circulation) SirsiDynix; (OPAC) SirsiDynix
Wireless access
Function: Adult bk club, Art exhibits, Audiobks on Playaways & MP3, Audiobks via web, Bilingual assistance for Spanish patrons, Bk club(s), Bks on CD, CD-ROM, Children's prog, Computer training, Computers for patron use, Digital talking bks, Electronic databases & coll, Free DVD rentals, Games & aids for people with disabilities, Holiday prog, Homebound delivery serv, Homework prog, ILL available, Internet access, Magazines, Meeting rooms, Microfiche/film & reading machines, Movies, Music CDs, Online cat, Outreach serv, Photocopying/Printing, Prog for adults, Prog for children & young adult, Scanner, Spanish lang bks, Spoken cassettes & CDs, Spoken cassettes & DVDs, Story hour, Study rm, Summer reading prog, Tax forms, Teen prog, Wheelchair accessible, Workshops
Mem of Santiago Library System
Open Mon-Wed 10-9, Thurs-Sat 10-6
Friends of the Library Group
Branches: 2
EL MODENA BRANCH, 380 S Hewes Ave, 92869, SAN 333-4864. Tel: 714-288-2450. FAX: 714-771-6126. *Librn I,* Jean Ong; Tel: 714-288-2445
Founded 1978. Pop 138,792; Circ 646,807
Open Mon-Wed 2-7, Thurs-Sat 1-6
TAFT BRANCH, 740 E Taft Ave, 92865-4406, SAN 333-4899. Tel: 714-288-2430. FAX: 714-282-8663. *Librn I,* Ryan Gan; Tel: 714-288-2440; Staff 4 (MLS 1, Non-MLS 3)
Founded 1969. Pop 40,644; Circ 218,235
Open Mon-Wed 2-7, Thurs-Sat 1-6
Friends of the Library Group

M SAINT JOSEPH HOSPITAL & CHILDRENS HOSPITAL OF ORANGE COUNTY*, Burlew Medical Library, 1100 W Stewart Dr, 92868. SAN 301-147X. Tel: 714-771-8291. E-mail: burlewmedicallibrary@stjoe.org. Web Site: www.providence.org/locations/st-joseph-hospital-orange. *Libr Mgr,* Danielle Linden; E-mail: Danielle.Linden@stjoe.org; Staff 3 (MLS 1, Non-MLS 2)
Founded 1955
Library Holdings: e-books 10; e-journals 400; Bk Titles 6,000; Per Subs 400
Subject Interests: Cardiology, Ethics, Internal med, Nursing, Orthopedics, Pediatrics, Surgery
Automation Activity & Vendor Info: (Cataloging) Sydney; (Serials) Sydney
Wireless access
Function: Doc delivery serv, ILL available, Ref serv available, Res libr
Partic in Coop Libr Agency for Syst & Servs; National Network of Libraries of Medicine Region 5; SDC
Open Mon-Fri 8:30-5
Restriction: In-house use for visitors, Lending to staff only

R SAINT JOSEPH LIBRARY*, 480 S Batavia St, 92868-3907. SAN 333-3965. Tel: 714-633-8121, Ext 7765. E-mail: sjlibrary@csjorange.org. *Libr Coord,* Margaret Catahan; E-mail: mcatahan@csjorange.org; Staff 2 (Non-MLS 2)
Founded 1953
Library Holdings: CDs 400; DVDs 450; Bk Titles 12,000; Per Subs 6
Subject Interests: Art, Christian, Relig, Roman Catholic relig, Spirituality, Theol
Automation Activity & Vendor Info: (Acquisitions) Follett Software; (Cataloging) Follett Software
Wireless access
Open Tues, Thurs & Sat 9-5, Wed & Fri 1-5
Friends of the Library Group

C SANTIAGO CANYON COLLEGE LIBRARY*, 8045 E Chapman Ave, 92869. SAN 329-3017. Tel: 714-628-5001. Reference Tel: 714-628-5005, 714-628-5006. FAX: 714-633-2842. Web Site: www.sccollege.edu/library. *Dean, Libr & Learning Support Serv,* Dr Aaron Voelcker; E-mail: voelcker_aaron@sccollege.edu
Founded 1978. Enrl 26,672; Fac 158
Library Holdings: High Interest/Low Vocabulary Bk Vols 354; Bk Titles 65,000
Wireless access
Open Mon, Wed & Thurs 7:30-7:30, Tues 7:30am-9pm
Restriction: Open to students, fac & staff
Friends of the Library Group

ORLAND

P ORLAND FREE LIBRARY*, 333 Mill St, 95963. SAN 333-4929. Tel: 530-865-1640. E-mail: orlandfreelibrary@yahoo.com. Web Site: www.orlandfreelibrary.wordpress.com. *City Librn,* Jody Halsey Meza; Staff 6 (MLS 2, Non-MLS 4)
Founded 1909. Pop 14,616; Circ 51,040
Library Holdings: Bk Vols 62,000; Per Subs 80
Automation Activity & Vendor Info: (Cataloging) TLC (The Library Corporation); (Circulation) TLC (The Library Corporation); (ILL) OCLC WorldShare Interlibrary Loan; (OPAC) TLC (The Library Corporation)
Wireless access
Function: Adult literacy prog, Computer training, Family literacy, ILL available, Magnifiers for reading, Photocopying/Printing, Prog for children & young adult, Summer reading prog, Telephone ref, Wheelchair accessible
Mem of NorthNet Library System
Open Mon, Wed & Fri 11-6, Tues & Thurs 11-7, Sat 11-3
Friends of the Library Group

OROVILLE

J BUTTE COLLEGE LIBRARY*, Frederick S Montgomery Library, 3536 Butte Campus Dr, 95965. SAN 301-1518. Tel: 530-879-4017. Interlibrary Loan Service Tel: 530-879-4026. Reference Tel: 530-879-4024. Administration Tel: 530-879-4050. Administration FAX: 530-879-6164. E-mail: referenceli@butte.edu. Web Site: www.butte.edu/library. *Dean of Libr & Instrul Serv,* Carrie L Monlux, PhD; E-mail: monluxca@butte.edu; *Ref & Instruction Librn,* Tia Germar; Tel: 530-879-4067, E-mail: germarti@butte.edu; *Ref & Instruction Librn,* Michael Smith; Tel: 530-879-4066, E-mail: smithmic@butte.edu; *Circ & Reserves Supvr,* Jennifer Lasell; Tel: 530-879-4060, E-mail: lasellje@butte.edu; *Acq & Cat, Tech Serv,* Tiyebeh Jodari; Tel: 530-879-4022, E-mail: jodariti@butte.edu; Staff 8 (MLS 4, Non-MLS 4)
Founded 1967. Enrl 13,700; Highest Degree: Associate
Library Holdings: e-books 610,000; e-journals 28,000; High Interest/Low Vocabulary Bk Vols 600; Bk Titles 72,000; Bk Vols 80,000; Per Subs 165
Automation Activity & Vendor Info: (Acquisitions) OCLC; (Cataloging) OCLC; (Circulation) OCLC; (Course Reserve) OCLC; (ILL) OCLC WorldShare Interlibrary Loan; (Media Booking) OCLC; (OPAC) OCLC; (Serials) EBSCO Online
Wireless access
Function: Computers for patron use, ILL available, Instruction & testing, Internet access, Online cat, Online info literacy tutorials on the web & in blackboard, Online ref, Orientations, Outreach serv, Outside serv via phone, mail, e-mail & web, Ref & res, Ref serv available, Workshops
Mem of NorthNet Library System
Partic in Commun Col Libr Automation Consortium; OCLC Online Computer Library Center, Inc
Open Mon-Thurs 7:30-5:50, Fri 7:30am-11:50pm
Restriction: Open to students, fac, staff & alumni, Pub use on premises
Departmental Libraries:
CHICO CENTER, 2320 Forest Ave, Rm 219, Chico, 95928. Tel: 530-879-4366. Web Site: www.butte.edu/services/library/about/chc.html. *Ref & Instruction Librn,* Louise Lee; Tel: 530-879-4398, E-mail: leelo@butte.edu; *Reserves,* Ian Allen; E-mail: allenia@butte.edu; *Reserves,* Dan Buzan; E-mail: buzanda@butte.edu
Open Mon-Thurs 7:30am-9pm, Fri 7:30am-Noon

P BUTTE COUNTY LIBRARY*, 1820 Mitchell Ave, 95966-5387. SAN 333-4988. Tel: 530-538-7525, 530-552-5652. Reference Tel: 530-538-7642. Information Services Tel: 855-379-4097. E-mail: OrovilleBCLibrary@ButteCounty.net. Web Site: www.buttecounty.net/bclibrary. *County Librn,* Melanie Lightbody; *Asst Dir,* Narinder Sufi; Tel: 530-538-7196; *Librn,* Misty Wright; Staff 6 (MLS 5, Non-MLS 1)
Founded 1913. Pop 221,000; Circ 826,821
Library Holdings: AV Mats 17,043; e-books 4; Bk Vols 276,528; Per Subs 526
Special Collections: Butte County History Coll. State Document Depository
Subject Interests: County hist
Automation Activity & Vendor Info: (Cataloging) TLC (The Library Corporation); (Circulation) TLC (The Library Corporation); (OPAC) TLC (The Library Corporation)
Wireless access
Function: Adult literacy prog, ILL available, Magnifiers for reading, Photocopying/Printing, Prog for children & young adult, Summer reading prog, Wheelchair accessible
Mem of NorthNet Library System
Partic in OCLC Online Computer Library Center, Inc
Special Services for the Deaf - Bks on deafness & sign lang
Special Services for the Blind - Assistive/Adapted tech devices, equip & products; Bks on cassette; Bks on CD; Braille bks; Extensive large print coll; Large print bks; Low vision equip; Reader equip

Open Mon-Sat 10-5, Sun 1-5
Friends of the Library Group
Branches: 5
BIGGS BRANCH, 464A B St, Biggs, 95917-9796. (Mail add: PO Box 516, Biggs, 95917-0516), SAN 370-7938. Tel: 530-868-5724. E-mail: BiggsBCLibrary@ButteCounty.net. *Librn,* Cynthia Pustejovsky
Open Tues 12-6, Sat 10-4
CHICO BRANCH, 1108 Sherman Ave, Chico, 95926-3575, SAN 333-5046. Tel: 530-891-2762. E-mail: ChicoBCLibrary@ButteCounty.net. *Librn,* Janae Kambestad; Staff 1 (MLS 1)
Function: Photocopying/Printing, Prog for adults, Prog for children & young adult, Ref serv available, Summer reading prog, Telephone ref, VHS videos
Open Tues-Thurs 10-6, Fri & Sat 10-5, Sun 1-5
Friends of the Library Group
DURHAM BRANCH, 2545 Durham-Dayton Hwy, Durham, 95938-9615, SAN 333-5100. Tel: 530-879-3835. E-mail: DurhamBCLibrary@ButteCounty.net. *Librn,* Cynthia Pustejovsky
Open Tues & Wed 12-6, Thurs & Fri 10-5
Friends of the Library Group
GRIDLEY BRANCH, 299 Spruce St, Gridley, 95948-0397, SAN 333-516X. Tel: 530-846-3323. E-mail: GridleyBCLibrary@ButteCounty.net. *Librn,* Cynthia Pustejovsky; Staff 1 (MLS 1)
Open Tues & Wed 12-6, Thurs-Sat 10-4
Friends of the Library Group
PARADISE BRANCH, 5922 Clark Rd, Paradise, 95969-4896, SAN 333-5194. Tel: 530-872-6320. E-mail: ParadiseBCLibrary@ButteCounty.net. *Librn,* Cynthia Pustejovsky; Staff 1 (MLS 1)
Function: Art exhibits, ILL available, Photocopying/Printing, Prog for adults, Prog for children & young adult, Ref serv available, Summer reading prog, Telephone ref, VHS videos, Wheelchair accessible
Open Tues & Thurs 1-6, Sat 11-4
Friends of the Library Group
Bookmobiles: 1

GL BUTTE COUNTY PUBLIC LAW LIBRARY*, 1675 Montgomery St, 95965. SAN 301-1526. Tel: 530-538-7122. Administration Tel: 530-538-4349. FAX: 530-534-1499. E-mail: publiclawlibrarian@gmail.com. Web Site: www.buttecountylawlibrary.org. *Dir,* John A Zorbas; E-mail: jzorbas@sbcglobal.net; *Librn,* Joyce Monday; Staff 1.8 (MLS 1, Non-MLS 0.8)
Founded 1907
Jul 2015-Jun 2016 Income $147,800, Locally Generated Income $15,800, Other $132,000. Mats Exp $27,750, Books $15,750, Electronic Ref Mat (Incl. Access Fees) $12,000. Sal $134,500
Library Holdings: Bk Titles 600; Bk Vols 5,000; Per Subs 15
Subject Interests: Law
Wireless access
Function: Citizenship assistance, Computers for patron use, Doc delivery serv, Electronic databases & coll, Govt ref serv, Internet access, Photocopying/Printing, Ref & res, Ref serv available, Tax forms
Open Mon-Fri 8:30-4:30
Restriction: Restricted borrowing privileges

M OROVILLE HOSPITAL*, Goddard Memorial Library, 2767 Olive Hwy, 95966. SAN 301-1534. Tel: 530-554-1309. *Dir,* Roger Brudno; E-mail: rbrudno@orohosp.com; Staff 1 (MLS 1)
Founded 1968
Library Holdings: e-books 40; e-journals 80; Electronic Media & Resources 4
Partic in National Network of Libraries of Medicine Region 5; Northern California & Nevada Medical Library Group; Pacific Southwest Regional Medical Library
Restriction: Hospital employees & physicians only, Med & nursing staff, patients & families, Not a lending libr, Not open to pub

OXNARD

J OXNARD COLLEGE LIBRARY*, 4000 S Rose Ave, 93033-6699. SAN 321-4788. Tel: 805-986-5819. Reference Tel: 805-986-5820. Administration Tel: 805-986-5818. E-mail: ocreference@vccd.edu. Web Site: www.oxnardcollege.edu. *Dean of Libr,* Louis Gonzalez; Tel: 805-986-5949, E-mail: lgonzalez@vccd.edu; *Librn,* Tom Stough; E-mail: tstough@vcccd.edu; *Libr Tech,* Ray Acosta; Tel: 805-986-5150, E-mail: racosta@vcccd.edu; Staff 1 (MLS 1)
Founded 1975. Enrl 7,233; Fac 88
Library Holdings: e-books 19,000; Bk Titles 36,630; Bk Vols 43,384; Per Subs 70
Subject Interests: Soc sci
Automation Activity & Vendor Info: (Cataloging) Ex Libris Group; (Circulation) Ex Libris Group; (OPAC) Ex Libris Group; (Serials) Ex Libris Group
Wireless access
Open Mon-Thurs 8am-9pm, Fri & Sat 8-5

P OXNARD PUBLIC LIBRARY*, 251 South A St, 93030. SAN 301-1542. Tel: 805-385-7500. Circulation Tel: 805-385-7507. Reference Tel: 805-385-7532. Administration Tel: 805-385-7528. FAX: 805-385-7526. E-mail: Library@oxnard.org. Web Site: www.oxnardlibrary.net. *Interim Dir,* Sofia Kimsey; Tel: 805-385-7529, E-mail: sofia.kimsey@oxnard.org; *Circ Supvr,* Yvonne Harper; Tel: 805-385-7512, E-mail: yvonne.harper@oxnard.org; *Librn I,* Robert Franks; Tel: 805-385-7530, E-mail: Robert.Franks@oxnard.org; *Librn I,* Vanesa Chua; Tel: 805-240-7339, E-mail: vanesa.chua@oxnard.org; *Librn I,* Laura Duncan; Tel: 805-385-7504, E-mail: laura.duncan@oxnard.org; *Librn II,* Karen Schatz; Tel: 805-240-7344, E-mail: karen.schatz@oxnard.org; Staff 44 (MLS 11, Non-MLS 33)
Founded 1907. Pop 203,645; Circ 470,992
Jul 2014-Jun 2015 Income (Main & Associated Libraries) $4,763,542, City $4,372,581, Other $390,961. Mats Exp $212,919, Books $131,091, Other Print Mats $36,127, AV Mat $13,373, Electronic Ref Mat (Incl. Access Fees) $31,700, Presv $628. Sal $2,981,705
Library Holdings: AV Mats 15,129; e-books 703; Bk Vols 331,061; Per Subs 235
Subject Interests: Local govt, Local hist, Spanish (Lang)
Automation Activity & Vendor Info: (Acquisitions) Innovative Interfaces, Inc; (Cataloging) Innovative Interfaces, Inc; (Circulation) Innovative Interfaces, Inc; (OPAC) Innovative Interfaces, Inc; (Serials) Innovative Interfaces, Inc
Wireless access
Function: Activity rm, Adult literacy prog, After school storytime, Art exhibits, Audiobks via web, AV serv, Bilingual assistance for Spanish patrons, Bks on cassette, Bks on CD, Children's prog, Computers for patron use, Electronic databases & coll, Free DVD rentals, Holiday prog, Homebound delivery serv, ILL available, Internet access, Large print keyboards, Life-long learning prog for all ages, Literacy & newcomer serv, Magazines, Magnifiers for reading, Mail & tel request accepted, Meeting rooms, Microfiche/film & reading machines, Movies, Music CDs, Online cat, Orientations, Outreach serv, Outside serv via phone, mail, e-mail & web, Passport agency, Photocopying/Printing, Preschool outreach, Preschool reading prog, Prof lending libr, Prog for adults, Prog for children & young adult, Ref & res, Ref serv available, Res libr, Spanish lang bks, Spoken cassettes & CDs, Spoken cassettes & DVDs, Story hour, Study rm, Summer & winter reading prog, Summer reading prog, Teen prog, Telephone ref, VHS videos, Wheelchair accessible, Winter reading prog
Partic in Southern California Library Cooperative
Special Services for the Deaf - Bks on deafness & sign lang; Staff with knowledge of sign lang
Special Services for the Blind - Cassettes; Internet workstation with adaptive software; Large print bks; Magnifiers; Reader equip; ZoomText magnification & reading software
Open Mon-Thurs 9-8, Sat 9-5:30, Sun 1-5
Friends of the Library Group
Branches: 2
COLONIA, 1500 Camino del Sol, No 26, 93030, SAN 377-5917. Tel: 805-385-8108. FAX: 805-385-8323. *Librn,* Pamela Wood; Tel: 805-385-7984, E-mail: pamela.wood@oxnard.org; Staff 2 (MLS 1, Non-MLS 1)
Founded 1978. Circ 10,455
Jul 2014-Jun 2015 Income $4,805,987, Federal $42,445, Locally Generated Income $4,372,581, Other $390,961. Mats Exp AV Mat $2,000
Library Holdings: Bk Vols 11,207; Per Subs 20
Function: 24/7 Electronic res, 24/7 Online cat, Bilingual assistance for Spanish patrons, Bks on cassette, Bks on CD, Children's prog, Computers for patron use, E-Reserves, Electronic databases & coll, Free DVD rentals, ILL available, Internet access, Magazines, Mail & tel request accepted, Movies, Online cat, Orientations, Outreach serv, Outside serv via phone, mail, e-mail & web, Prog for children & young adult, Ref & res, Ref serv available, Spanish lang bks, Spoken cassettes & CDs, Spoken cassettes & DVDs, Story hour, Summer reading prog, Teen prog, Telephone ref, VHS videos, Wheelchair accessible
Open Mon-Thurs 12-6
Friends of the Library Group
SOUTH OXNARD, 4300 Saviers Rd, 93033, SAN 377-8401. Tel: 805-385-8129. FAX: 805-488-1336. *Br Librn,* Alan Neal; Tel: 805-247-8951, E-mail: alan.neal@ci.oxnard.ca.us; Staff 5 (MLS 3, Non-MLS 2)
Founded 2007. Pop 91,641; Circ 413,897
Library Holdings: Bk Vols 329,628
Open Mon-Thurs 9-8, Sat 9-5:30
Friends of the Library Group

PACIFIC GROVE

P PACIFIC GROVE PUBLIC LIBRARY*, 550 Central Ave, 93950-2789. SAN 301-1585. Tel: 831-648-5760. Reference Tel: 831-648-5762. FAX: 831-373-3268. Web Site: www.pacificgrovelibrary.org. *Libr Dir,* Diana Godwin; E-mail: dgodwin@cityofpacificgrove.org; Staff 16 (MLS 7, Non-MLS 9)
Founded 1908. Pop 15,431; Circ 278,171
Jul 2016-Jun 2017 Income $1,888,585, City $1,088,585, Locally Generated Income $80,000. Mats Exp $80,000, Books $50,500, Per/Ser (Incl. Access Fees) $6,000, Other Print Mats $14,000, AV Mat $3,500, Electronic Ref Mat (Incl. Access Fees) $6,000
Library Holdings: Audiobooks 4,301; AV Mats 5,782; CDs 1,574; DVDs 3,581; e-books 3,355; Large Print Bks 3,613; Bk Titles 97,498; Bk Vols 98,094; Per Subs 206; Talking Bks 1,461; Videos 1,035
Automation Activity & Vendor Info: (Acquisitions) Koha; (Cataloging) Koha; (Circulation) Koha; (OPAC) Koha; (Serials) Koha
Wireless access
Function: 24/7 Electronic res, After school storytime, Art exhibits, Bilingual assistance for Spanish patrons, Bks on CD, Children's prog, Computers for patron use, Electronic databases & coll, Free DVD rentals, Home delivery & serv to seniorr ctr & nursing homes, Magnifiers for reading, Music CDs, Online cat, Outside serv via phone, mail, e-mail & web, OverDrive digital audio bks, Photocopying/Printing, Prog for adults, Prog for children & young adult, Ref serv available, Story hour, Summer reading prog, Tax forms, Teen prog, Telephone ref, VHS videos, Wheelchair accessible
Partic in Califa; Monterey Bay Area Cooperative Library System
Special Services for the Deaf - Assistive tech; Bks on deafness & sign lang; Closed caption videos; TTY equip
Special Services for the Blind - Bks on cassette; Bks on CD; Large print bks; Magnifiers; Reader equip; VisualTek equip
Open Mon-Thurs 10-7, Fri & Sat 10-5
Friends of the Library Group

PACIFIC PALISADES

R KEHILLAT ISRAEL RECONSTRUCTIONIST CONGREGATION OF PACIFIC PALISADES LIBRARY*, 16019 W Sunset Blvd, 90272. SAN 301-1607. Tel: 310-459-2328. Web Site: www.ourki.org/ki-library. *Interim Exec Dir,* Jerry Scharlin; E-mail: jscharlin@ourki.org
Founded 1968
Library Holdings: Bk Titles 2,500; Per Subs 25
Special Collections: Reconstructionist Judaism
Subject Interests: Judaica (lit or hist of Jews)
Restriction: Mem only

PALM DESERT

C COLLEGE OF THE DESERT LIBRARY*, 43-500 Monterey Ave, 92260. SAN 301-1615. Tel: 760-773-2563. FAX: 760-568-5955. Web Site: www.collegeofthedesert.edu/students/library. *Librn,* Joshua Kunkle; *Electronic Res Librn,* Jonathan Fernald; Tel: 760-679-3775, E-mail: jfernald@collegeofthedesert.edu; *Ref Librn,* Claudia Derum; Tel: 760-776-7258, E-mail: cderum@collegeofthedesert.edu; Staff 3 (Non-MLS 3)
Founded 1962. Enrl 8,360; Fac 417; Highest Degree: Doctorate
Library Holdings: AV Mats 929; Bks on Deafness & Sign Lang 35; e-books 4,700; High Interest/Low Vocabulary Bk Vols 14; Bk Vols 51,602; Per Subs 200
Special Collections: Desert Coll, rare books; Winston S Churchill Coll, bks, pamphlets, rare bks
Subject Interests: Rare bks
Automation Activity & Vendor Info: (Cataloging) OCLC; (Circulation) SirsiDynix; (ILL) OCLC; (OPAC) SirsiDynix
Wireless access
Partic in Coop Libr Agency for Syst & Servs; Inland Empire Acad Libr Coop; San Bernardino, Inyo, Riverside Counties United Library Services
Open Mon-Thurs 8-8, Fri 8-5
Friends of the Library Group

PALM SPRINGS

S PALM SPRINGS ART MUSEUM LIBRARY*, 101 Museum Dr, 92262. (Mail add: PO Box 2310, 92263-2310), SAN 301-1631. Tel: 760-325-7186. FAX: 760-327-5069. Web Site: www.psmuseum.org. *Chief Curator,* Rochelle Steiner; E-mail: rsteiner@psmuseum.org; Staff 1 (MLS 1)
Founded 1938
Library Holdings: Bk Titles 11,000; Bk Vols 12,000; Per Subs 20
Special Collections: Albert Frey, Hugh Kaptur, E. Stewart Williams, Patrick McGrew, Arthur Elrod Assoc/Harold Broderick, Stephen Willard
Subject Interests: Archit, Art, Design, Glass, Native Am, Photog
Automation Activity & Vendor Info: (Cataloging) LibraryWorld, Inc; (Circulation) LibraryWorld, Inc; (OPAC) LibraryWorld, Inc
Restriction: Non-circulating to the pub, Open by appt only

P PALM SPRINGS PUBLIC LIBRARY*, 300 S Sunrise Way, 92262-7699. SAN 333-5224. Tel: 760-322-7323. Administration Tel: 760-322-8375. FAX: 760-320-9834. E-mail: library.info@palmspringsca.gov. Web Site: www.ci.palm-springs.ca.us/government/departments/library. *Dir, Libr Serv,* Jeannie Kays; E-mail: jeannie.kays@palmspringsca.gov; *Libr Operation & Coll Mgr,* Lisa Brock; Tel: 760-322-8387, E-mail: lisa.brock@palmspringsca.gov; *Libr Serv & Pub Relations Mgr,* Julie Warren; Tel: 760-416-6731, E-mail: julie.warren@palmspringsca.gov; Staff 7 (MLS 6, Non-MLS 1)
Founded 1919. Pop 47,601; Circ 429,910
Special Collections: Spanish Language Coll. Oral History
Subject Interests: Genealogy, Hist, Local hist
Automation Activity & Vendor Info: (Acquisitions) Brodart; (Cataloging) OCLC; (Circulation) Innovative Interfaces, Inc; (ILL) OCLC WorldShare Interlibrary Loan; (OPAC) Innovative Interfaces, Inc; (Serials) Innovative Interfaces, Inc
Wireless access
Function: 24/7 Electronic res, 24/7 Online cat, 3D Printer, Activity rm, Adult bk club, Archival coll, Art exhibits, Audiobks via web, Bilingual assistance for Spanish patrons, Bk club(s), Bks on CD, Children's prog, Computer training, Computers for patron use, Electronic databases & coll, Free DVD rentals, Genealogy discussion group, Holiday prog, ILL available, Internet access, Life-long learning prog for all ages, Magazines, Mail & tel request accepted, Mango lang, Microfiche/film & reading machines, Movies, Music CDs, Online cat, Online info literacy tutorials on the web & in blackboard, Online ref, Orientations, OverDrive digital audio bks, Photocopying/Printing, Preschool outreach, Printer for laptops & handheld devices, Prog for adults, Prog for children & young adult, Ref serv available, Res performed for a fee, Spanish lang bks, Story hour, Summer reading prog, Teen prog, Wheelchair accessible, Workshops
Mem of Inland Library System
Partic in Califa
Special Services for the Blind - Audio mat; Bks on CD
Open Mon & Thurs 10-6, Tues & Wed 10-8, Fri & Sat 10-5
Restriction: Ref only
Friends of the Library Group

PALMDALE

P PALMDALE CITY LIBRARY*, 700 E Palmdale Blvd, 93550. SAN 324-2781. Tel: 661-267-5600. E-mail: pcl@cityofpalmdale.org. Web Site: www.cityofpalmdale.org/Library. *Dir,* Robert Shupe; Staff 7 (MLS 6, Non-MLS 1)
Founded 1977. Pop 136,734; Circ 431,290
Library Holdings: AV Mats 8,200; Bk Vols 127,760; Per Subs 453
Special Collections: Local History Coll
Automation Activity & Vendor Info: (Acquisitions) SirsiDynix; (Cataloging) SirsiDynix; (Circulation) SirsiDynix; (OPAC) SirsiDynix
Wireless access
Partic in Southern California Library Cooperative
Open Mon-Thurs 10-8, Fri & Sat 10-5, Sun 1-5
Friends of the Library Group
Bookmobiles: 1

PALO ALTO

P CITY OF PALO ALTO LIBRARY*, 270 Forest Ave, 94301. (Mail add: PO Box 10250, 94303-0250), SAN 333-5348. Tel: 650-329-2436. FAX: 650-327-2033. TDD: 650-856-6839. E-mail: pa.library@cityofpaloalto.org. Web Site: www.cityofpaloalto.org/gov/depts/lib. *Interim Dir,* Mrs Gayathri Kanth; Tel: 650-329-2668, E-mail: gayathri.kanth@cityofpaloalto.org; *Coll, Div Head, Info & Tech Serv,* Diane Lai; Tel: 650-329-2517, E-mail: diane.lai@cityofpaloalto.org; *Br Mgr,* RuthAnn Garcia; Tel: 650-329-2562, E-mail: ruthann.garcia@cityofpaloalto.org; *Br Mgr,* Alex Perez; Tel: 650-838-2981, E-mail: alex.perez@cityofpaloalto.org; Staff 24 (MLS 20, Non-MLS 4)
Founded 1904. Pop 62,600; Circ 1,414,509
Library Holdings: AV Mats 30,657; Bk Titles 167,008; Bk Vols 240,098; Per Subs 681
Special Collections: Palo Alto Historical Association Files
Subject Interests: Local hist
Automation Activity & Vendor Info: (Acquisitions) SirsiDynix; (Cataloging) SirsiDynix; (Circulation) SirsiDynix; (ILL) SirsiDynix; (OPAC) SirsiDynix; (Serials) SirsiDynix
Publications: Hot Off the Shelf (Newsletter)
Open Mon & Thurs 12-8, Tues & Wed 10-8, Fri & Sat 10-6, Sun 1-5
Restriction: Circ limited
Friends of the Library Group
Branches: 5
CHILDREN'S, 1276 Harriet St, 94301, SAN 333-5372. Administration Tel: 650-329-2501. FAX: 650-463-4964. Administration FAX: 650-327-7568. E-mail: librarychildrensservices@cityofpaloalto.org. *Br Mgr,* Alex Perez; Tel: 650-838-2981, E-mail: alex.perez@cityofpaloalto.org; *Sr Librn,* Elizabeth Stewart; Tel: 650-838-2975, E-mail: elizabeth.stewart@cityofpaloalto.org; *Supv Librn,*

Alison de Geus; Tel: 650-838-2960, E-mail: alison.degeus@cityofpaloalto.org; Staff 7.4 (MLS 3.4, Non-MLS 4)
Founded 1940. Pop 4,000; Circ 371,997
Library Holdings: AV Mats 6,428; Bk Vols 40,223
Function: After school storytime, Children's prog, Computers for patron use, E-Reserves, Electronic databases & coll, Free DVD rentals, Holiday prog, Homebound delivery serv, Internet access, Music CDs, Online cat, Online ref, Outreach serv, Photocopying/Printing, Prog for children & young adult, Ref serv available, Story hour, Summer reading prog, Telephone ref
Open Mon & Thurs 12-6, Tues & Wed 10-6, Fri & Sat 10-5, Sun 1-5
Friends of the Library Group

COLLEGE TERRACE, 2300 Wellesley St, 94306, SAN 333-5402. *Mgr, Libr Serv,* Alex Perez; Tel: 650-838-2981, E-mail: alex.perez@cityofpaloalto.org; *Libr Assoc,* Sue Chang; Tel: 650-838-2965, E-mail: sue.chang@cityofpaloalto.org; Staff 2.4 (Non-MLS 2.4)
Founded 1936. Pop 7,000; Circ 67,227
Library Holdings: AV Mats 2,147; Bk Vols 11,728
Function: Bks on CD, Children's prog, Computers for patron use, E-Reserves, Electronic databases & coll, Free DVD rentals, Internet access, Music CDs, Online cat, Online ref, Story hour, Summer reading prog, Wheelchair accessible
Open Tues, Wed, Fri & Sat 10-6
Friends of the Library Group

DOWNTOWN, 270 Forest Ave, 94301, SAN 333-5437. FAX: 650-327-7568. *Mgr, Libr Serv,* Alex Perez; Tel: 650-838-2981, E-mail: alex.perez@cityofpaloalto.org; *Admin Assoc,* Josh Martinez; Tel: 650-329-2501, E-mail: josh.martinez@cityofpaloalto.org; *Libr Assoc,* David Sigua; Tel: 650-838-2964, E-mail: david.sigua@cityofpaloalto.org; Staff 3 (Non-MLS 3)
Founded 1971. Pop 8,000; Circ 67,227
Library Holdings: AV Mats 4,091; Bk Vols 11,218
Function: Bks on CD, Children's prog, Computers for patron use, Electronic databases & coll, Free DVD rentals, Internet access, Music CDs, Online cat, Online ref, Photocopying/Printing, Prog for adults, Wheelchair accessible
Open Tues, Wed & Sat 10-6, Thurs 12-6
Friends of the Library Group

MITCHELL PARK, 3700 Middlefield Rd, 94303, SAN 333-5461. FAX: 650-856-7925. *Br Mgr,* RuthAnn Garcia; E-mail: ruthann.garcia@cityofpaloalto.org; *Supv Librn,* Valeh Dabiri Alaee; Tel: 650-838-2976, E-mail: Valeh.Dabiri@CityofPaloAlto.org
Founded 1958. Circ 507,531
Library Holdings: AV Mats 16,096; Bk Vols 70,793
Function: After school storytime, Bks on CD, Children's prog, Computers for patron use, Electronic databases & coll, Free DVD rentals, Internet access, Music CDs, Online cat, Online ref, Photocopying/Printing, Prog for children & young adult, Story hour, Summer reading prog, Teen prog, Wheelchair accessible
Special Services for the Deaf - TDD equip
Open Mon & Thurs 12-8, Tues & Wed 10-8, Fri & Sat 10-6, Sun 1-5
Friends of the Library Group

RINCONDA LIBRARY, 1213 Newell Rd, 94303. *Mgr, Libr Serv,* Alex Perez; Tel: 650-383-2981, E-mail: alex.perez@cityofpaloalto.org; *Sr Librn,* Rebecca Kohn; Tel: 650-838-2951, E-mail: rebecca.kohn@cityofpaloalto.org; *Sr Librn,* Melody Tehrani; Tel: 650-329-2426, E-mail: melody.tehrani@cityofpaloalto.org

R FIRST CONGREGATIONAL CHURCH LIBRARY*, 1985 Louis Rd, 94303-3499. SAN 301-1720. Tel: 650-856-6662. FAX: 650-856-6664. E-mail: office@fccpa.org. Web Site: www.fccpa.org.
Library Holdings: Bk Titles 2,100
Subject Interests: Fiction
Open Mon-Fri 9-3

SR FIRST UNITED METHODIST CHURCH LIBRARY*, 625 Hamilton Ave, 94301. SAN 301-1739. Tel: 650-323-6167. FAX: 650-323-3923. Web Site: www.firstpaloalto.com. *Librn,* Joseph Heim; Tel: 650-654-1930, E-mail: joeheim@aol.com
Founded 1964
Jan 2017-Dec 2017. Mats Exp $4,100, Books $3,500, Per/Ser (Incl. Access Fees) $100, AV Mat $500
Library Holdings: AV Mats 200; CDs 10; DVDs 50; High Interest/Low Vocabulary Bk Vols 400; Large Print Bks 20; Bk Titles 4,000; Bk Vols 5,000; Per Subs 10
Subject Interests: Relig
Wireless access
Partic in Church & Synagogue Libr Asn
Friends of the Library Group

C PALO ALTO UNIVERSITY*, Omar Seddiqui Research Library, 1791 Arastradero Rd, 94304. SAN 371-8425. Tel: 650-433-3808. Interlibrary Loan Service Tel: 650-433-3848. Reference Tel: 650-433-3855. FAX: 650-433-3888. Circulation E-mail: library-circ@paloaltou.edu. Web Site: www.paloaltou.edu/about/departments-and-offices/library. *Dir, Acad Tech, Univ Librn,* Scott Hines; E-mail: shines@paloaltou.edu; *Head, Tech Serv, ILL & Circ,* Mary Anderson; Tel: 650-433-3816, E-mail: manderson@paloaltou.edu; Staff 4 (MLS 2, Non-MLS 2)
Founded 1975. Enrl 1,000; Fac 100; Highest Degree: Doctorate
Library Holdings: DVDs 500; e-books 150,000; e-journals 19,500; Bk Titles 155,000; Bk Vols 5,000; Per Subs 19,500; Videos 2,500
Subject Interests: Psychiat, Psychol
Automation Activity & Vendor Info: (Acquisitions) OCLC WorldShare Interlibrary Loan; (Cataloging) OCLC WorldShare Interlibrary Loan; (Circulation) OCLC WorldShare Interlibrary Loan; (Course Reserve) Docutek; (ILL) OCLC ILLiad; (OPAC) OCLC WorldShare Interlibrary Loan; (Serials) OCLC WorldShare Interlibrary Loan
Wireless access
Function: ILL available, Res libr
Partic in Association of Mental Health Libraries; Northern & Central California Psychology Libraries; Northern California & Nevada Medical Library Group; Statewide California Electronic Library Consortium
Restriction: Private libr

C SOFIA UNIVERSITY LIBRARY*, 1069 E Meadow Circle, 94303. SAN 326-4483. Tel: 650-493-4430, Ext 223. FAX: 650-852-9780. E-mail: refdesk@sofia.edu. Web Site: sofia.libguides.com/homepage. *Librn,* Lisa Sammon; E-mail: lisa.sammon@sofia.edu; Staff 1 (MLS 1)
Founded 1981. Enrl 500; Fac 150; Highest Degree: Doctorate
Library Holdings: AV Mats 1,000; CDs 240; DVDs 500; e-books 100,000; e-journals 7,000; Bk Titles 17,000; Per Subs 169
Special Collections: Collected Works of C G Jung; Complete Psychological Works of Sigmund Freud; Deepak Chopra Coll; Spirituality (Classics of Western Spirituality Coll)
Subject Interests: Psychol, Relig
Automation Activity & Vendor Info: (Cataloging) EOS International; (Circulation) EOS International; (ILL) OCLC; (OPAC) EOS International; (Serials) EBSCO Online
Wireless access
Partic in Califa; Northern & Central California Psychology Libraries; Northern California & Nevada Medical Library Group; Statewide California Electronic Library Consortium
Open Mon-Fri 10-6
Restriction: Pub use on premises
Friends of the Library Group

M STANFORD HEALTH LIBRARY*, 211 Quarry Rd, Ste 201, 94304. SAN 374-5376. Tel: 650-725-8400. Toll Free Tel: 800-295-5177. FAX: 650-725-1444. E-mail: healthlibrary@stanfordhealthcare.org. Web Site: healthlibrary.stanford.edu. *Librn,* Jean Johnson; E-mail: jeanjohnson@stanfordhealthcare.org; Staff 5 (MLS 3, Non-MLS 2)
Founded 1989
Library Holdings: AV Mats 1,000; e-books 1,000; Bk Titles 8,000; Per Subs 40
Subject Interests: Consumer health, Med
Automation Activity & Vendor Info: (Cataloging) OCLC Connexion; (Circulation) OCLC Worldshare Management Services; (OPAC) OCLC Worldshare Management Services
Wireless access
Open Mon-Fri 9-5
Branches:

CANCER CENTER SOUTH BAY, 2589 Samaritan Dr, Rm 3302, San Jose, 95124. Tel: 408-353-0197. *Librn,* Michele Benitez; *Librn,* Sandra Erickson; Staff 1 (MLS 1)
Founded 2015

STANFORD COMPREHENSIVE CANCER CENTER, 875 Blake Wilbur Dr, Stanford, 94305. Tel: 650-736-1960. FAX: 650-736-7157. *Librn,* Gillian Kumagai; E-mail: gkumagai@stanfordmed.org; Staff 1 (MLS 1)
Library Holdings: Bk Titles 1,000
Subject Interests: Cancer, Surgery
Open Mon-Fri 9-5

STANFORD HOSPITAL, Stanford Hospital, 500 Pasteur Dr, 94305. Tel: 650-725-8100. FAX: 650-725-8102. *Librn,* James Liu; Staff 1 (MLS 1)
Library Holdings: Bk Titles 1,100
Open Mon-Fri 9-5

L WILSON, SONSINI, GOODRICH & ROSATI*, Library, 650 Page Mill Rd, 94304. SAN 372-2988. Tel: 650-493-9300. FAX: 650-493-6811. Web Site: www.wsgr.com. *Info Serv Mgr,* Julie Watters; E-mail: jwatters@wsgr.com
Library Holdings: Bk Vols 40,000; Per Subs 300
Open Mon-Fri 9-5

PASADENA

C ART CENTER COLLEGE OF DESIGN*, James Lemont Fogg Memorial Library, 1700 Lida St, 91103. SAN 301-1895. Tel: 626-396-2233. FAX: 626-568-0428. E-mail: library@artcenter.edu. Web Site:

library.artcenter.edu, www.artcenter.edu/about/campus/hillside-campus/facilities/james-lemont-fogg-memorial-library.html. *Col Librn,* Mario Ascencio; E-mail: mario.ascencio@artcenter.edu; *Liaison Librn,* Claudia Michelle Betty; E-mail: claudia.betty@artcenter.edu; *Liaison Librn,* Simone Fujita; E-mail: simone.fujita@artcenter.edu; *Liaison Librn,* Rachel Julius; E-mail: rachel.julius@artcenter.edu; *Liaison Librn,* Robert Lundquist; E-mail: robert.lundquist@artcenter.edu; Staff 11 (MLS 5, Non-MLS 6)
Founded 1930. Enrl 1,700; Fac 300; Highest Degree: Master
Library Holdings: DVDs 2,000; Electronic Media & Resources 14; Bk Titles 86,000; Bk Vols 100,000; Per Subs 400; Spec Interest Per Sub 400; Videos 6,000
Special Collections: College Archives; Melinda Fassett Welles, PhD, Children's Illustrated Books
Subject Interests: Advertising, Art, Films & filmmaking, Graphic design, Photog, Product design, Transportation
Automation Activity & Vendor Info: (Cataloging) Innovative Interfaces, Inc; (Circulation) Innovative Interfaces, Inc; (Course Reserve) Innovative Interfaces, Inc; (OPAC) Innovative Interfaces, Inc; (Serials) Innovative Interfaces, Inc
Wireless access
Partic in OCLC Online Computer Library Center, Inc
Restriction: Not open to pub, Open to students, fac & staff

C CALIFORNIA INSTITUTE OF TECHNOLOGY*, Caltech Library System 1-32, 1200 E California Blvd, M/C 1-43, 91125-4300. SAN 333-5704. Tel: 626-395-3405. FAX: 626-792-7540. E-mail: library@caltech.edu. Web Site: www.library.caltech.edu. *Univ Librn,* Kara Whatley; Tel: 626-395-3805, E-mail: kwhatley@caltech.edu; *Libr Bus Adminr,* Catherine Geard; Tel: 626-395-6834, E-mail: cgeard@library.caltech.edu; *Head, Digital Libr Develop & Syst,* Stephen Davison; Tel: 626-395-6149, E-mail: sdavison@library.caltech.edu; *Spec Coll, Univ Archivist,* Peter Collopy; Tel: 626-395-2702, E-mail: pcollopy@caltech.edu; Staff 18 (MLS 12, Non-MLS 6)
Founded 1891. Enrl 2,100; Fac 400; Highest Degree: Doctorate
Library Holdings: Bk Vols 548,752; Per Subs 3,144
Special Collections: NACA/NASA Technical Reports. Oral History; State Document Depository; US Document Depository
Subject Interests: Engr, Hist of sci, Soc sci & issues
Automation Activity & Vendor Info: (Acquisitions) Innovative Interfaces, Inc; (Cataloging) Innovative Interfaces, Inc; (Circulation) Innovative Interfaces, Inc; (Serials) Innovative Interfaces, Inc
Publications: CLS Guide to SciSearch Services; CLS Online Resources; CLS Rules of Access
Open Mon-Fri 8-5
Friends of the Library Group

Departmental Libraries:

ASTROPHYSICS, 1201 E California Blvd, M/C 11-17, 91125, SAN 333-5763. Tel: 626-395-2290. *Librn,* Joy Painter; E-mail: joy@library.caltech.edu
Library Holdings: Bk Vols 12,000; Per Subs 35
Automation Activity & Vendor Info: (Cataloging) Innovative Interfaces, Inc; (Circulation) Innovative Interfaces, Inc; (OPAC) Innovative Interfaces, Inc
Open Mon-Fri 8-5

EARTHQUAKE ENGINEERING RESEARCH, Sherman Fairchild Library, 200 E California Blvd, M/C 1-43, 91125, SAN 333-5852. Tel: 626-395-3409. FAX: 626-568-2719. Web Site: libguides.caltech.edu/EarthquakeEngineering. *Librn,* George Porter; E-mail: george@library.caltech.edu
Library Holdings: Bk Vols 15,000; Per Subs 25
Publications: Earthquake Engineering Abstracts; Quakeline
Open Mon-Fri 1:30-4

SHERMAN FAIRCHILD LIBRARY OF ENGINEERING & APPLIED SCIENCE, Fairchild Library I-43, 91125, SAN 376-8961. Tel: 626-395-3409. FAX: 626-431-2681. *Eng Librn,* George Porter; E-mail: george@library.caltech.edu
Founded 1997
Library Holdings: Bk Vols 75,000
Open Mon-Fri 8-5, Sat 9am-1am

S CALIFORNIA INSTITUTE OF TECHNOLOGY*, Jet Propulsion Laboratory Library, Archives & Records Section, 4800 Oak Grove Dr, MS 111-113, 91109-8099. SAN 301-195X. Reference Tel: 818-354-4200. E-mail: library@jpl.nasa.gov. Web Site: jpl-nasa.libguides.com/beacon. *Mgr, Knowledge Mgt,* Camille Mathieu; E-mail: camille.e.mathieu@jpl.nasa.gov; Staff 21 (MLS 11, Non-MLS 10)
Founded 1948
Library Holdings: Bk Titles 40,977; Bk Vols 84,827; Per Subs 1,030
Special Collections: JPL Archives. Oral History
Subject Interests: Aerospace, Astronomy, Astrophysics, Bus & mgt, Engr, Phys sci
Automation Activity & Vendor Info: (Acquisitions) OCLC; (Cataloging) OCLC; (Circulation) OCLC; (OPAC) OCLC; (Serials) OCLC
Function: Archival coll, ILL available, Online cat, Ref & res
Partic in OCLC Online Computer Library Center, Inc
Restriction: Not open to pub

SR FIRST UNITED METHODIST CHURCH LIBRARY*, 500 E Colorado Blvd, 91101. SAN 373-0344. Tel: 626-796-0157. FAX: 626-568-1615. E-mail: library@fumcpasadena.org. Web Site: www.fumcpasadena.org. *Librn,* Ruth McPherson
Library Holdings: Bk Vols 5,000
Subject Interests: Relig
Restriction: Mem only

CR FULLER THEOLOGICAL SEMINARY, David Allan Hubbard Library, 135 N Oakland Ave, 91182. SAN 301-1933. Tel: 626-584-5218. Circulation Tel: 626-584-5618. Interlibrary Loan Service Tel: 626-304-3739. Reference Tel: 626-584-5624. Administration Tel: 626-584-5219. FAX: 626-584-5613. E-mail: lib-info@fuller.edu. Web Site: library.fuller.edu. *Exec Dir,* Mariea Daniell Whittington; E-mail: daniellwhittington@fuller.edu
Founded 1948. Enrl 1,704; Fac 93; Highest Degree: Doctorate
Library Holdings: Bk Vols 227,000; Per Subs 960
Subject Interests: Biblical studies, Church hist, Feminism, Philos, Psychol, Relig, Theol
Wireless access
Partic in Metronet; OCLC Online Computer Library Center, Inc
Open Mon-Thurs 9-5, Fri 9-Noon, Sat 1-4
Friends of the Library Group

M HUNTINGTON HOSPITAL*, Center for Health Evidence, 100 W California Blvd, 91105-3010. SAN 301-1941. Tel: 626-397-5161. FAX: 626-397-2908. E-mail: che@huntingtonhospital.com. Web Site: www.huntingtonhospital.com. *Ref Serv,* Louisa Verma; Staff 4 (MLS 4)
Library Holdings: Bk Vols 800; Per Subs 8
Special Collections: Medical & Paramedical Texts, bks, journals
Subject Interests: Allied health, Nursing
Automation Activity & Vendor Info: (Acquisitions) Marcive, Inc; (Cataloging) EOS International; (Circulation) EOS International; (OPAC) EOS International; (Serials) EBSCO Online
Wireless access
Function: 24/7 Electronic res, 24/7 Online cat, Bus archives, Electronic databases & coll, For res purposes, Health sci info serv, Online cat, Online ref, Photocopying/Printing, Printer for laptops & handheld devices, Ref & res, Ref serv available, Res assist avail
Partic in National Network of Libraries of Medicine Region 5; Statewide California Electronic Library Consortium
Open Mon-Fri 8-4
Restriction: Authorized personnel only, Badge access after hrs, By permission only, Circulates for staff only, Hospital staff & commun, Mem only, Open to hospital affiliates only, Open to others by appt

P INLAND LIBRARY SYSTEM*, 254 N Lake Ave, No 874, 91101. SAN 301-231X. Tel: 626-283-5949. E-mail: ils@inlandlib.org. Web Site: www.inlandlib.org. *Exec Dir,* Diane Zinser Bednarski; E-mail: dbednarski@socallibraries.org
Founded 1966
Library Holdings: Bk Titles 375
Wireless access
Member Libraries: Banning Library District; Beaumont Library District; City of San Bernardino Library Services; Colton Public Library; Corona Public Library; Hemet Public Library; Inyo County Free Library; Moreno Valley Public Library; Murrieta Public Library; Ontario City Library; Palm Springs Public Library; Palo Verde Valley Library District; Rancho Cucamonga Public Library; Rancho Mirage Library; Riverside County Library System; Riverside Public Library; San Bernardino County Library; Upland Public Library; Victorville City Library
Partic in OCLC Online Computer Library Center, Inc
Restriction: Mem organizations only

S OBSERVATORIES OF THE CARNEGIE INSTITUTION, Hale Library, 813 Santa Barbara St, 91101. SAN 371-0297. Tel: 626-304-0228. FAX: 626-795-8136. Web Site: obs.carnegiescience.edu. *Archivist, Libr Asst,* Ms Kit Whitten; E-mail: swhitten@carnegiescience.edu; Staff 1 (MLS 1)
Founded 1904
Library Holdings: Bk Titles 4,660; Bk Vols 31,498; Per Subs 40
Subject Interests: Astronomy, Astrophysics
Automation Activity & Vendor Info: (Cataloging) Koha; (Circulation) Koha
Function: Res libr
Restriction: Open by appt only, Restricted access

C PACIFIC OAKS COLLEGE*, Andrew Norman Library, 55 Eureka St, Ste 145, 91103. SAN 301-1976. Tel: 626-529-8451. Toll Free Tel: 800-645-8603. E-mail: library@pacificoaks.edu. Web Site: tcsedsystem.libguides.com/POC_Library, www.pacificoaks.edu/student-resources/andrew-norman-library. *Campus*

Librn, Ms Kelsey Vukic; Tel: 626-529-8453. Subject Specialists: *Info sci,* Ms Kelsey Vukic
Founded 1946. Enrl 1,100; Fac 40; Highest Degree: Master
Library Holdings: AV Mats 420; e-books 100; Electronic Media & Resources 250; Bk Titles 5,000; Videos 300
Automation Activity & Vendor Info: (Cataloging) EOS International; (Circulation) EOS International; (ILL) OCLC; (OPAC) EOS International
Wireless access
Open Mon-Thurs 11-7, Fri 8:30-4:30, Sat 9-1
Restriction: Access at librarian's discretion

J PASADENA CITY COLLEGE LIBRARY, Shatford Library, 1570 E Colorado Blvd, 91106-2003. SAN 301-1992. Tel: 626-585-7221. Circulation Tel: 626-585-7174. Interlibrary Loan Service Tel: 626-585-3309. Reference Tel: 626-585-7360. FAX: 626-585-7913. Web Site: www.pasadena.edu/library.
Founded 1924. Enrl 28,000; Fac 1,102; Highest Degree: Associate
Library Holdings: Bk Vols 120,000
Subject Interests: Educ, Hist, Local hist
Automation Activity & Vendor Info: (Cataloging) Ex Libris Group; (Circulation) Ex Libris Group; (Course Reserve) Ex Libris Group
Wireless access
Function: Archival coll, AV serv, ILL available, Internet access, Magnifiers for reading, Photocopying/Printing, Ref serv available, Telephone ref, Wheelchair accessible
Restriction: Open to students, fac & staff, Residents only

S PASADENA MUSEUM OF HISTORY*, Research Library & Archives, 470 W Walnut St, 91103-3594. SAN 301-200X. Tel: 626-577-1660. FAX: 626-577-1662. E-mail: research@pasadenahistory.org. Web Site: www.pasadenahistory.org. *Archivist,* Anuja Navare; Tel: 626-577-1660,Ext 13, E-mail: anavare@pasadenahistory.org
Founded 1924
Library Holdings: Bk Titles 1,800; Bk Vols 2,000
Special Collections: Fenyes-Curtin-Paloheimo Family Archives; Giddings-Hollingsworth Family Coll; J Allen Hawkins Photo Coll; Pasadena Star-News Photo Archive; Sylvanus Marston Coll; Tournament of Roses. Oral History
Subject Interests: African-Am hist, Archit, Local hist, Maps, Real estate
Function: Archival coll, Photocopying/Printing, Res libr
Publications: A Southern California Paradise; Historic Pasadena (Lund); Pasadena Photographs & Photographers 1880-1920; Pasadena's Super Athletes; Walter Raymond, A Gentleman of the Old School
Open Thurs-Sun 1-4
Restriction: Non-circulating, Open to pub for ref only

P PASADENA PUBLIC LIBRARY*, 285 E Walnut St, 91101. SAN 333-6212. Tel: 626-744-4066. FAX: 626-585-8396. Web Site: ww5.cityofpasadena.net/library. *Dir of Libr, Info Serv,* Michelle Perera; E-mail: mperera@cityofpasadena.net; *Dep Dir,* Tim McDonald; E-mail: timmcdonald@cityofpasadena.net; *Principal Librn,* Carlos Baffigo; E-mail: CBaffigo@cityofpasadena.net; *Principal Librn,* Michael Pierce; E-mail: mpierce@cityofpasadena.net
Founded 1882. Pop 146,166; Circ 1,589,247
Library Holdings: Bk Vols 710,566; Per Subs 1,145
Special Collections: US Document Depository
Automation Activity & Vendor Info: (Acquisitions) SirsiDynix-WorkFlows; (Cataloging) SirsiDynix-WorkFlows; (Circulation) SirsiDynix-WorkFlows; (ILL) OCLC WorldShare Interlibrary Loan; (OPAC) SirsiDynix-Enterprise
Wireless access
Function: 24/7 Electronic res, 24/7 Online cat, 3D Printer, Adult bk club, Archival coll, Bk club(s), Bks on CD, Children's prog, Citizenship assistance, Computers for patron use, Digital talking bks, ILL available, Magazines, Microfiche/film & reading machines, Music CDs, Online cat, Outreach serv, OverDrive digital audio bks, Photocopying/Printing, Printer for laptops & handheld devices, Prog for adults, Prog for children & young adult, Ref serv available, Res assist avail, Scanner, Spanish lang bks, STEM programs, Summer reading prog, Tax forms, Teen prog, Telephone ref
Partic in Southern California Library Cooperative
Open Mon-Thurs 9-9, Fri & Sat 9-6, Sun 1-5
Friends of the Library Group
Branches: 9
ALLENDALE, 1130 S Marengo Ave, 91106, SAN 333-6247. Tel: 626-744-7260. *Br Mgr,* Veronica Bernal; E-mail: vbernal@cityofpasadena.net
Pop 8,760; Circ 65,289
Library Holdings: Bk Vols 41,418
Open Mon-Thurs & Sat 10-6
HASTINGS, 3325 E Orange Grove Blvd, 91107, SAN 333-6271. Tel: 626-744-7262. FAX: 626-440-0222.
Pop 19,860; Circ 210,275
Library Holdings: Bk Vols 64,069
Open Mon-Thurs 10-9, Fri 10-6
HILL AVENUE, 55 S Hill Ave, 91106, SAN 333-6301. Tel: 626-744-7264. FAX: 626-440-0183.
Pop 22,572; Circ 83,514
Library Holdings: Bk Vols 41,859
Open Mon-Thurs & Sat 10-6
LA PINTORESCA, 1355 N Raymond Ave, 91103, SAN 333-6360. Tel: 626-744-7268.
Pop 33,291; Circ 77,010
Library Holdings: Bk Vols 56,861
Open Mon-Thurs 10-7, Fri 10-6
LAMANDA PARK, 140 S Altadena Dr, 91107, SAN 333-6336. Tel: 626-744-7266.
Founded 1967. Pop 5,621; Circ 77,264
Library Holdings: Bk Vols 51,846
Open Mon-Thurs & Sat 10-6
LINDA VISTA, 1281 Bryant St, 91103, SAN 333-6395. Tel: 626-744-7278.
Founded 1957. Pop 5,447; Circ 48,957
Library Holdings: Bk Vols 28,976
Open Mon-Thurs & Sat 10-6
Friends of the Library Group
SAN RAFAEL, 1240 Nithsdale Rd, 91105, SAN 333-6425. Tel: 626-744-7270. FAX: 626-440-0160.
Founded 1957. Pop 5,201; Circ 58,101
Library Holdings: Bk Vols 37,555
Open Mon-Thurs & Sat 10-6
SANTA CATALINA, 999 E Washington Blvd, 91104, SAN 333-645X. Tel: 626-744-7272.
Founded 1930. Pop 20,270; Circ 95,128
Library Holdings: Bk Vols 48,589
Open Mon-Thurs & Sat 10-6
VILLA PARKE COMMUNITY CENTER, 363 E Villa St, 91101, SAN 374-8103. Tel: 626-744-6510.
Founded 1992. Circ 24,353
Open Mon-Fri 10-6

S RIGHT TO LIFE LEAGUE OF SOUTHERN CALIFORNIA LIBRARY*, 1028 N Lake Ave, Ste 207, 91104. SAN 370-4327. Tel: 626-398-6100. FAX: 626-398-6101. Web Site: rtllsc.org.
Founded 1969
Subject Interests: Abortion, Abstinence educ, Euthanasia, Genetic engr, Human experimentation, Infanticide, Pop control, Pre-natal develop, Sex educ
Function: AV serv, Res libr
Open Mon-Fri 9-5

P SANTIAGO LIBRARY SYSTEM, c/o Southern California Library Cooperative, 254 N Lake Ave, No 874, 91101. Tel: 626-359-6111. E-mail: sclcadmin@socallibraries.org.
Member Libraries: Anaheim Public Library; Buena Park Library District; Fullerton Public Library; Huntington Beach Public Library System; Mission Viejo Library; Newport Beach Public Library; Orange Public Library & History Center; Yorba Linda Public Library

L US COURT OF APPEALS, NINTH CIRCUIT LIBRARY*, 125 S Grand Ave, 91105. SAN 323-7680. Tel: 626-229-7190. FAX: 626-229-7460. Web Site: www.ca9.uscourts.gov/library. *Librn,* Joy M Shoemaker; Staff 3 (MLS 2, Non-MLS 1)
Founded 1985
Library Holdings: Bk Titles 2,020; Bk Vols 26,000; Per Subs 30
Subject Interests: Law
Wireless access
Open Mon-Fri 8:30-5

PASO ROBLES

P PASO ROBLES CITY LIBRARY*, 1000 Spring St, 93446-2207. SAN 301-2069. Tel: 805-237-3870. FAX: 805-238-3665. Web Site: www.prcity.com. *City Librn,* Angelica Fortin; E-mail: afortin@prcity.com; *Ad,* Karen Christiansen; E-mail: kchristiansen@prcity.com; *Youth Serv,* Melissa Bailey; E-mail: mbailey@prcity.com; *Vols Coordr,* Suzanne Robitaille; E-mail: srobitaille@prcity.com
Founded 1903. Pop 29,793; Circ 286,735
Library Holdings: Audiobooks 5,086; AV Mats 12,630; DVDs 7,544; e-books 2,160,205; Bk Vols 60,225
Special Collections: Paso Robles Newspapers from 1892, micro
Automation Activity & Vendor Info: (Cataloging) Innovative Interfaces, Inc; (Circulation) Innovative Interfaces, Inc; (ILL) OCLC WorldShare Interlibrary Loan; (OPAC) Innovative Interfaces, Inc
Wireless access
Function: 24/7 Electronic res, 24/7 Online cat, Adult bk club, Adult literacy prog
Mem of Black Gold Cooperative Library System

Open Mon-Fri 10-8, Sat 10-5
Friends of the Library Group

PATTON

PATTON STATE HOSPITAL

M PATIENTS LIBRARY*, 3102 E Highland Ave, 92369, SAN 320-1600. Tel: 909-425-6039. FAX: 909-425-6162. *Sr Librn,* Frederick Brenion; Staff 1 (MLS 1)
Library Holdings: Bk Titles 10,300; Bk Vols 13,000; Per Subs 50

M STAFF LIBRARY*, 3102 E Highland Ave, 92369, SAN 320-1619. Tel: 909-425-7484. FAX: 909-425-6053. *Librn,* Angela Stoner; Staff 1 (MLS 1)
Founded 1941
Library Holdings: Bk Titles 3,300; Per Subs 130
Subject Interests: Psychiat
Automation Activity & Vendor Info: (Acquisitions) Sydney; (Cataloging) Sydney; (Circulation) Sydney; (Course Reserve) Sydney; (ILL) Sydney; (Media Booking) Sydney; (OPAC) Sydney; (Serials) Sydney
Function: Ref serv available
Partic in Medical Library Group of Southern California & Arizona; San Bernardino, Inyo, Riverside Counties United Library Services
Restriction: Open by appt only

PITTSBURG

J LOS MEDANOS COLLEGE LIBRARY*, 2700 E Leland Rd, 94565. Tel: 925-439-2181. Circulation Tel: 925-473-7570. Reference Tel: 925-473-7575. Web Site: www.losmedanos.edu/lmc_library/default.htm. *Dir, Instruction Librn,* Christina Goff; Tel: 925-473-7571, E-mail: cgoff@losmedanos.edu; *Electronic Res Librn,* Kim Wentworth; Tel: 925-473-7573; *Tech Serv Librn,* Leila Swisher; Tel: 925-473-7576, E-mail: lswisher@losmedanos.edu
Library Holdings: Bk Vols 17,000
Wireless access
Open Mon-Thurs 8am-9:45pm, Fri 8-2:45, Sat 10-2

PLACENTIA

P PLACENTIA LIBRARY DISTRICT*, 411 E Chapman Ave, 92870. SAN 301-1488. Tel: 714-528-1906. FAX: 714-528-8236. Reference E-mail: reference@placentialibrary.org. Web Site: www.placentialibrary.org. *Dir,* Jeanette Contreras; Tel: 714-528-1925, Ext 200, Fax: 714-579-1082, E-mail: jcontreras@placentialibrary.org; *Bus Mgr,* Timothy Hino; Tel: 714-528-1906, Ext 216, E-mail: thino@placentialibrary.org; *Pub Serv Mgr,* Yesenia Baltierra; Tel: 714-528-1906, Ext 201, E-mail: ybaltierra@placentialibrary.org; Staff 14.6 (MLS 6.3, Non-MLS 8.3)
Founded 1919. Pop 54,980; Circ 263,400
Library Holdings: Audiobooks 2,424; CDs 2,029; DVDs 5,056; Large Print Bks 1,280; Bk Vols 84,903; Per Subs 100
Special Collections: Placentia Local History Coll
Automation Activity & Vendor Info: (Circulation) SirsiDynix
Wireless access
Function: Adult bk club, Adult literacy prog, Art exhibits, AV serv, Bilingual assistance for Spanish patrons, Bk club(s), Bks on CD, Children's prog, Citizenship assistance, Computer training, Computers for patron use, Digital talking bks, Electronic databases & coll, Free DVD rentals, Holiday prog, Homework prog, ILL available, Internet access, Life-long learning prog for all ages, Magazines, Music CDs, Online cat, Online ref, Outside serv via phone, mail, e-mail & web, Passport agency, Photocopying/Printing, Preschool outreach, Prog for adults, Prog for children & young adult, Ref serv available, Story hour, Summer reading prog, Teen prog, Telephone ref, Wheelchair accessible, Workshops
Open Mon-Thurs 9-8, Fri & Sat 9-5, Sun 1-5
Friends of the Library Group

PLACERVILLE

GL EL DORADO COUNTY LAW LIBRARY*, 550 Main St, Ste A, 95667. SAN 301-2123. Tel: 530-626-1932. E-mail: edlawlibrary@gmail.com. Web Site: eldoradocountylawlibrary.org. *Adminr,* Cathy McMillan. Subject Specialists: *Legal res,* Cathy McMillan; Staff 4 (Non-MLS 4)
Pop 183,087
Jul 2014-Jun 2015 Income $137,858, State $99,672, County $33,855, Locally Generated Income $3,666, Other $665. Mats Exp $62,111, Books $33,133, Electronic Ref Mat (Incl. Access Fees) $28,978. Sal $38,077 (Prof $32,924)
Library Holdings: CDs 31; Bk Vols 9,123; Videos 7
Special Collections: CA & FED Legal Materials
Subject Interests: Legal
Wireless access
Function: Computers for patron use, Electronic databases & coll, Internet access, Photocopying/Printing, Ref serv available, Scanner, Workshops
Restriction: Non-circulating, Open by appt only

P EL DORADO COUNTY LIBRARY*, 345 Fair Lane, 95667. SAN 333-6484. Tel: 530-621-5540. FAX: 530-622-3911. E-mail: library@eldoradolibrary.org. Web Site: www.eldoradolibrary.org. *Libr Dir,* Jeanne Amos; Tel: 530-621-5546, E-mail: jeanne.amos@eldoradolibrary.org; Staff 14.1 (MLS 3.5, Non-MLS 10.6)
Founded 1906. Pop 62,448; Circ 291,731
Jul 2012-Jun 2013 Income (Main & Associated Libraries) $3,222,553, State $205,610, Federal $14,736, County $2,698,135, Other $304,072. Mats Exp $286,187, Books $158,941, Per/Ser (Incl. Access Fees) $18,546, Other Print Mats $47,588, Electronic Ref Mat (Incl. Access Fees) $61,112. Sal $1,641,237
Library Holdings: Audiobooks 5,262; DVDs 4,277; e-books 2,952; Bk Titles 210,114; Bk Vols 123,062; Per Subs 454
Subject Interests: Calif
Automation Activity & Vendor Info: (Acquisitions) SirsiDynix; (Cataloging) SirsiDynix; (Circulation) SirsiDynix; (OPAC) SirsiDynix
Wireless access
Function: ILL available
Mem of NorthNet Library System
Open Tues & Wed 12-7, Thurs-Sat 10-5
Friends of the Library Group
Branches: 5
CAMERON PARK BRANCH, 2500 Country Club Dr, Cameron Park, 95682, SAN 374-6852. Tel: 530-621-5500. FAX: 530-672-1346. E-mail: lib-cp@eldoradolibrary.org. *Br Mgr,* Nancy Owen-Hazard; Staff 4.8 (Non-MLS 4.8)
Pop 31,092; Circ 153,987
Library Holdings: Audiobooks 3,038; DVDs 2,780; Bk Vols 57,209
Open Mon, Wed & Fri 10-5, Tues & Thurs 12-7
Friends of the Library Group
EL DORADO HILLS BRANCH, 7455 Silva Valley Pkwy, El Dorado Hills, 95762, SAN 333-6514. Tel: 916-358-3500. FAX: 916-933-7089. E-mail: lib-edh@eldoradolibrary.org. *Br Mgr,* Jan Robbins; Staff 6.6 (MLS 1.8, Non-MLS 4.8)
Pop 28,735; Circ 213,465
Library Holdings: Audiobooks 3,592; DVDs 3,802; Bk Vols 63,153
Open Mon, Wed & Fri 10-5, Tues & Thurs 10-7, Sat 1-5
Friends of the Library Group
GEORGETOWN BRANCH, 6680 Orleans St, Georgetown, 95634. (Mail add: PO Box 55, Georgetown, 95634-0055), SAN 333-6549. Tel: 530-333-4724. FAX: 530-333-4724. E-mail: lib-gt@eldoradolibrary.org. *Br Mgr,* Angela Bernoudy; Staff 1.5 (Non-MLS 1.5)
Pop 8,188; Circ 32,135
Library Holdings: Audiobooks 1,085; DVDs 2,470; Bk Vols 18,411
Open Tues & Wed Noon-7, Thurs 10-5, Fri 1-5, Sat 10-3
Friends of the Library Group
POLLOCK PINES BRANCH, 6210 Pony Express Trail, Pollock Pines, 95726. (Mail add: PO Box 757, Pollock Pines, 95726-0757), SAN 333-6603. Tel: 530-644-2498. FAX: 530-644-2498. E-mail: lib-pp@eldoradolibrary.org. *Br Mgr,* Krystal Owens; Staff 1 (Non-MLS 1)
Pop 19,037; Circ 23,001
Library Holdings: Audiobooks 869; DVDs 962; Bk Vols 15,896
Special Services for the Blind - Audio mat; Bks & mags in Braille, on rec, tape & cassette; Bks available with recordings; Bks on cassette; Bks on CD; Large print bks; Lending of low vision aids; Magnifiers
Open Tues & Wed 10-6, Thurs 12-5
Friends of the Library Group
SOUTH LAKE TAHOE BRANCH, 1000 Rufus Allen Blvd, South Lake Tahoe, 96150, SAN 333-6573. Tel: 530-573-3185. FAX: 530-544-8954. E-mail: lib-slt@eldoradolibrary.org. *Br Mgr,* Katharine Miller; E-mail: katharine.miller@eldoradolibrary.org; Staff 6.3 (MLS 1, Non-MLS 5.3)
Library Holdings: Audiobooks 3,008; DVDs 3,187; Bk Vols 56,928
Open Tues & Wed 10-8, Thurs-Sat 10-5
Friends of the Library Group
Bookmobiles: 1. Bk titles 2,500

PLEASANT HILL

J DIABLO VALLEY COLLEGE LIBRARY*, 321 Golf Club Rd, 94523-1576. SAN 301-2131. Tel: 925-969-2610. Reference Tel: 925-969-2595. Web Site: www.dvc.edu/library. *Dean of Libr,* Richard Robison; E-mail: rrobison@dvc.edu; *Dept Chair,* Daniel Kiely; Tel: 925-969-2583, E-mail: dkiely@dvc.edu; *Instrul Serv Librn,* Emily Moss; Tel: 925-969-2587, E-mail: emmoss@dvc.edu; *Tech Serv Librn,* Florence Espiritu; Tel: 925-969-2584, E-mail: fespiritu@dvc.edu; Staff 13 (MLS 6, Non-MLS 7)
Founded 1950. Enrl 22,022; Fac 767; Highest Degree: Associate
Library Holdings: CDs 367; e-books 18,005; Bk Titles 97,159; Bk Vols 106,517; Per Subs 250
Special Collections: Californiana
Automation Activity & Vendor Info: (Acquisitions) Innovative Interfaces, Inc; (Cataloging) Innovative Interfaces, Inc; (Circulation) Innovative Interfaces, Inc; (Course Reserve) Innovative Interfaces, Inc; (OPAC) Innovative Interfaces, Inc; (Serials) Innovative Interfaces, Inc

Wireless access
Partic in Community College League of California; San Francisco Bay Area Library & Information Network
Special Services for the Blind - Assistive/Adapted tech devices, equip & products
Open Mon-Thurs 7:45am-9pm, Fri 10-3, Sat 12-4
Friends of the Library Group

C JOHN F KENNEDY UNIVERSITY LIBRARIES*, Robert M Fisher Library, 100 Ellinwood Way, 94523. SAN 301-150X. Tel: 925-969-3100. Reference Tel: 925-969-3109. FAX: 925-969-3101. E-mail: reference@jfku.edu. Web Site: library2.jfku.edu/about/contact. *Head Librn,* Jamie Diermier; E-mail: jdiermier@jfku.edu; *Libr Asst,* Shawn Laramie; E-mail: slaramier@jfku.edu; Staff 8.7 (MLS 5, Non-MLS 3.7)
Founded 1964. Enrl 1,494; Fac 518; Highest Degree: Doctorate
Jul 2012-Jun 2013 Income (Main Library Only) $483,865. Mats Exp $203,298, Books $45,308, Per/Ser (Incl. Access Fees) $62,402, AV Mat $4,794, Electronic Ref Mat (Incl. Access Fees) $90,794. Sal $383,486 (Prof $279,692)
Library Holdings: AV Mats 2,570; e-books 72,879; e-journals 47,608; Bk Titles 39,749; Bk Vols 60,283; Videos 1,679
Subject Interests: Bus & mgt, Holistic studies, Psychol
Automation Activity & Vendor Info: (Acquisitions) Innovative Interfaces, Inc; (Cataloging) Innovative Interfaces, Inc; (Circulation) Innovative Interfaces, Inc; (Course Reserve) Innovative Interfaces, Inc; (ILL) Innovative Interfaces, Inc; (OPAC) Innovative Interfaces, Inc; (Serials) Innovative Interfaces, Inc
Wireless access
Function: Audio & video playback equip for onsite use, Computers for patron use, Distance learning, Doc delivery serv, Electronic databases & coll, Free DVD rentals, ILL available, Mail loans to mem, Online cat, Online ref, Orientations, Photocopying/Printing, Ref serv available, Spoken cassettes & CDs, Spoken cassettes & DVDs, VHS videos, Wheelchair accessible
Partic in BayNet Library Association; Califa; Northern & Central California Psychology Libraries; OCLC Online Computer Library Center, Inc
Special Services for the Deaf - Bks on deafness & sign lang; Closed caption videos
Special Services for the Blind - Audio mat; Cassette playback machines; Cassettes; Sound rec
Open Mon-Thurs 10-8, Fri & Sat 10-5
Restriction: Borrowing requests are handled by ILL, Fee for pub use, In-house use for visitors, Open to students, fac, staff & alumni
Departmental Libraries:
CL LAW LIBRARY, 100 Ellinwood Way, 94523-4817, SAN 321-4400. Tel: 925-969-3120. *Head Librn,* Jamie Diermier; E-mail: jdiermier@jfku.edu
Highest Degree: Doctorate
Library Holdings: Bk Vols 24,000; Per Subs 50
Open Mon-Thurs 9:30-9, Fri 9:30-5, Sat 10-5, Sun 1-6

PLEASANTON

P PLEASANTON PUBLIC LIBRARY*, 400 Old Bernal Ave, 94566. SAN 332-124X. Tel: 925-931-3400. FAX: 925-846-8517. E-mail: circadm@cityofpleasantonca.gov. Web Site: www.cityofpleasantonca.gov/gov/depts/lib. *Dir,* Heidi Murphy; E-mail: hmurphy@cityofpleasantonca.gov; Staff 11 (MLS 9, Non-MLS 2)
Founded 1999. Pop 71,300; Circ 1,385,211
Library Holdings: AV Mats 1,260; Bk Titles 105,000; Bk Vols 168,000; Per Subs 329
Special Collections: Pleasanton History Coll. Municipal Document Depository
Automation Activity & Vendor Info: (Acquisitions) Innovative Interfaces, Inc; (Cataloging) Innovative Interfaces, Inc; (Circulation) Innovative Interfaces, Inc; (ILL) Innovative Interfaces, Inc; (OPAC) Innovative Interfaces, Inc; (Serials) Innovative Interfaces, Inc
Wireless access
Function: Adult bk club, Adult literacy prog, Audiobks via web, AV serv, Bk club(s), Bks on cassette, Bks on CD, Children's prog, Computer training, Computers for patron use, Digital talking bks, E-Reserves, Electronic databases & coll, Free DVD rentals, Genealogy discussion group, Homebound delivery serv, Internet access, Jazz prog, Magnifiers for reading, Music CDs, Online cat, Online ref, Outside serv via phone, mail, e-mail & web, Photocopying/Printing, Prog for adults, Prog for children & young adult, Ref & res, Ref serv available, Senior computer classes, Senior outreach, Story hour, Summer reading prog, Telephone ref, Wheelchair accessible
Special Services for the Deaf - TDD equip
Open Mon-Thurs 10-9, Fri & Sat 10-5, Sun 1-5
Friends of the Library Group

POINT REYES STATION

G US NATIONAL PARK SERVICE, Point Reyes National Seashore Library & Archives, One Bear Valley Rd, 94956. SAN 323-7168. Tel: 415-464-5125. FAX: 415-464-5229. Web Site: www.nps.gov/pore. *Archivist,* Deborah Morgan; E-mail: deborah_morgan@nps.gov
Library Holdings: Bk Vols 1,350
Restriction: Open by appt only

POMONA

C CALIFORNIA STATE POLYTECHNIC UNIVERSITY LIBRARY*, 3801 W Temple Ave, Bldg 15, 91768. SAN 301-2158. Tel: 909-869-3074. Circulation Tel: 909-869-3075. FAX: 909-869-6922. E-mail: library@cpp.edu. Web Site: www.cpp.edu/~library. *Interim Dean,* Emma C Gibson; E-mail: ecgibson@cpp.edu; *Asst Univ Librn, Tech Serv,* Yvonne Zhang; E-mail: ywzhang@cpp.edu; *Libr Serv Spec,* Isela Gomez; E-mail: iigomez@cpp.edu; Staff 47 (MLS 12, Non-MLS 35)
Founded 1938. Enrl 19,804; Fac 672; Highest Degree: Master
Library Holdings: AV Mats 10,574; e-books 12,436; e-journals 3,460; Electronic Media & Resources 6,377; Bk Titles 492,551; Bk Vols 760,350; Per Subs 2,384
Special Collections: Poetry Coll; Twentieth Century English & American Literature (First Editions); Wine Coll
Automation Activity & Vendor Info: (Acquisitions) Innovative Interfaces, Inc; (Cataloging) Innovative Interfaces, Inc; (Circulation) Innovative Interfaces, Inc; (Course Reserve) Innovative Interfaces, Inc; (OPAC) Innovative Interfaces, Inc; (Serials) Innovative Interfaces, Inc
Wireless access
Partic in OCLC Online Computer Library Center, Inc
Open Mon-Thurs 7:30am-11:30pm, Fri 7:30-5, Sat 10-7, Sun 12-9
Friends of the Library Group
Departmental Libraries:
COLLEGE OF ENVIRONMENTAL DESIGN LIBRARY, Bldg 7, 3801 W Temple Ave, 91768, SAN 329-0352. Tel: 909-869-2665. Information Services Tel: 909-869-7659. *Library Contact,* Christine Johnson
Founded 1975. Enrl 1,150; Highest Degree: Master
Library Holdings: Bk Titles 18,000; Per Subs 152
Special Collections: Architect Craig Elwood Coll, letters, papers, photographs; Architect Raphael Soriano, drawings, letters, papers; Richard Nentra sketches, papers
Open Mon-Fri 8-4

P POMONA PUBLIC LIBRARY*, 625 S Garey Ave, 91766-3322. (Mail add: PO Box 2271, 91769), SAN 301-2174. Tel: 909-620-2043. Circulation Tel: 909-620-2043, Ext 2720, 909-620-2043, Ext 2722. Reference Tel: 909-620-2043, Ext 2701, 909-620-2043, Ext 2702. Administration Tel: 909-620-2473. Automation Services Tel: 909-620-3709. TDD: 909-620-3690. E-mail: library@ci.pomona.ca.us. Web Site: www.pomonalibrary.org. Staff 9 (MLS 7, Non-MLS 2)
Founded 1887. Pop 163,683; Circ 182,812
Library Holdings: Audiobooks 9,339; AV Mats 870; Large Print Bks 4,025; Microforms 11,837; Bk Titles 239,388; Bk Vols 287,231; Per Subs 207; Videos 300
Special Collections: Citrus Crate Labels; Cooper Photo Coll; Frasher Coll, photos & postcards; Laura Ingalls Wilder Coll, bks, dolls, ms & papers; Pomona Valley History Coll. Oral History
Subject Interests: Local hist, Photog
Automation Activity & Vendor Info: (Acquisitions) TLC (The Library Corporation); (Cataloging) TLC (The Library Corporation); (Circulation) TLC (The Library Corporation); (ILL) OCLC; (OPAC) TLC (The Library Corporation); (Serials) TLC (The Library Corporation)
Wireless access
Function: 24/7 Online cat, Activity rm, After school storytime, Archival coll, Art exhibits, Bilingual assistance for Spanish patrons, Bks on cassette, Bks on CD, Children's prog, Computers for patron use, Electronic databases & coll, Genealogy discussion group, Homework prog, Magazines, Meeting rooms, Microfiche/film & reading machines, Online cat, Orientations, Photocopying/Printing, Prog for children & young adult, Ref serv available, Spoken cassettes & CDs, Story hour, Summer reading prog, Tax forms, Teen prog, Telephone ref, Wheelchair accessible
Partic in OCLC Online Computer Library Center, Inc; Southern California Library Cooperative
Special Services for the Deaf - TDD equip
Special Services for the Blind - Bks on cassette; Bks on CD; Large print bks
Open Mon-Thurs 1-7, Sat Noon-5
Restriction: Non-resident fee
Friends of the Library Group

CM WESTERN UNIVERSITY OF HEALTH SCIENCES, Harriet K & Philip Pumerantz Library, 287 E Third St, 91766. (Mail add: 309 E Second St, 91766-1854), SAN 322-8894. Tel: 909-469-5323. FAX: 909-469-5486. Reference E-mail: reference@westernu.edu. Web Site:

www.westernu.edu/library. *Libr Dir,* Karoline G Almanzar; E-mail: kalmanzar@westernu.edu; Staff 16 (MLS 4, Non-MLS 12)
Founded 1977. Enrl 1,923; Highest Degree: Doctorate
Library Holdings: Bk Titles 13,411; Bk Vols 13,541; Per Subs 374
Special Collections: Osteopathic Medicine, bks, journals
Subject Interests: Allied health, Nursing, Osteopathic med, Veterinary med
Automation Activity & Vendor Info: (Cataloging) SirsiDynix; (Circulation) SirsiDynix; (Course Reserve) SirsiDynix; (OPAC) SirsiDynix; (Serials) SirsiDynix
Wireless access
Function: ILL available
Partic in Inland Empire Acad Libr Coop
Open Mon 8am-9pm, Tues-Thurs 7am-9pm, Fri 7-6, Sat & Sun 11-7
Restriction: In-house use for visitors, Open to students, fac & staff, Photo ID required for access

PORTERVILLE

J PORTERVILLE COLLEGE LIBRARY*, 100 E College Ave, 93257. SAN 301-2182. Tel: 559-791-2271, 559-791-2318. Circulation Tel: 559-791-8123. Reference Tel: 559-372-9662. FAX: 559-791-2289. E-mail: pclibrary@portervillecollege.edu. Web Site: www.portervillecollege.edu/about-pc/library. *Dir,* Jeff Spalsbury; Staff 5 (MLS 2, Non-MLS 3)
Founded 1927. Highest Degree: Associate
Special Collections: Anthropology Library; Valley Writers Coll
Automation Activity & Vendor Info: (Cataloging) Follett Software; (Circulation) Follett Software
Wireless access
Publications: Library Handbook
Mem of Kern Community College District
Open Mon-Thurs 7am-9pm, Fri 8-Noon

P PORTERVILLE PUBLIC LIBRARY*, 15 E Thurman Ave, 2nd Flr, Ste B, 93257. SAN 301-2190. Tel: 559-782-7493, 559-784-0177. FAX: 559-781-4396. E-mail: library@ci.porterville.ca.us. Web Site: www.ci.porterville.ca.us/depts/library. *City Librn,* Vikki Cervantes; Staff 6 (Non-MLS 6)
Founded 1904. Pop 34,450
Library Holdings: AV Mats 788; Bk Titles 68,889; Bk Vols 70,000; Per Subs 151
Special Collections: Local History, bks, photos
Wireless access
Mem of San Joaquin Valley Library System
Open Mon-Thurs 9-8, Fri & Sat 9-6
Friends of the Library Group

QUINCY

C FEATHER RIVER COLLEGE LIBRARY, 570 Golden Eagle Ave, 95971-9124. SAN 301-2220. Tel: 530-283-0202, Ext 236. FAX: 530-283-4097. E-mail: library@frc.edu. Web Site: frc.libguides.com. *Libr Dir,* Darryl Swarm; E-mail: dswarm@frc.edu; Staff 2 (Non-MLS 2)
Founded 1969. Enrl 1,102; Fac 85; Highest Degree: Associate
Library Holdings: Bks on Deafness & Sign Lang 32; DVDs 47,000; e-books 250,000; Bk Vols 23,500; Per Subs 400; Spec Interest Per Sub 13
Special Collections: Oral History
Subject Interests: Bus & mgt, Environ studies, Equine studies, Forestry, Natural sci, Nursing, Rodeos
Automation Activity & Vendor Info: (Cataloging) TLC (The Library Corporation); (Circulation) TLC (The Library Corporation); (OPAC) TLC (The Library Corporation)
Wireless access
Special Services for the Deaf - Bks on deafness & sign lang; Closed caption videos; Deaf publ
Special Services for the Blind - Assistive/Adapted tech devices, equip & products; Computer with voice synthesizer for visually impaired persons
Open Mon-Thurs 8am-9pm, Fri 8-4:30

P PLUMAS COUNTY LIBRARY*, 445 Jackson St, 95971. SAN 301-2247. Tel: 530-283-6310. FAX: 530-283-3242. Web Site: www.plumascounty.us/index.aspx?nid=546. *County Librn,* Lynn Sheehy; E-mail: lynnsheehy@countyofplumas.com; *Tech Serv,* Jeannette Legg; Staff 1.8 (MLS 0.8, Non-MLS 1)
Founded 1916. Pop 24,440; Circ 90,612
Library Holdings: Bk Vols 73,324; Per Subs 220; Talking Bks 805
Special Collections: Local History & Local Mining Colls
Subject Interests: Botany
Automation Activity & Vendor Info: (Cataloging) LibLime; (Circulation) LibLime; (OPAC) LibLime
Wireless access
Function: Bks on cassette, Bks on CD, Computers for patron use, Electronic databases & coll, Family literacy, Free DVD rentals, ILL available, Jail serv, Literacy & newcomer serv, Music CDs, Online cat, OverDrive digital audio bks, Photocopying/Printing, Summer reading prog, Wheelchair accessible
Mem of NorthNet Library System
Partic in Association for Rural & Small Libraries
Special Services for the Blind - Assistive/Adapted tech devices, equip & products; Bks on cassette; Bks on CD; Closed circuit TV; Computer with voice synthesizer for visually impaired persons; Large print bks; Magnifiers; Talking bks; Talking bks & player equip
Open Mon-Wed 10-6, Thurs 12-8, Fri 10-4
Friends of the Library Group
Branches: 3
CHESTER BRANCH, 210 First Ave, Chester, 96020-0429. (Mail add: PO Box 429, Chester, 96020-0429), SAN 377-8142. Tel: 530-258-2742. FAX: 530-258-3725. *Br Mgr,* Wanda Heath-Grunder
Library Holdings: Bk Vols 9,000; Per Subs 32
Automation Activity & Vendor Info: (OPAC) TLC (The Library Corporation)
Open Mon-Wed & Fri 10-1 & 1:30-5:30, Thurs 12-5 & 6-8
Friends of the Library Group
GREENVILLE BRANCH, 204 Ann St, Greenville, 95947. (Mail add: PO Box 635, Greenville, 95947-0635). Tel: 530-284-7416. *Br Mgr,* Andrea Wilson; Staff 1 (Non-MLS 1)
Library Holdings: Bk Vols 10,000; Per Subs 20
Open Mon-Wed 10-1 & 1:30-5:30, Thurs 12-4 & 4:30-7
Friends of the Library Group
PORTOLA BRANCH, 34 Third Ave, Portola, 96122. Tel: 530-832-4241. FAX: 530-832-4241. *Br Mgr,* Linda Hale; Staff 1 (Non-MLS 1)
Library Holdings: Bk Vols 10,000; Per Subs 30
Open Mon-Wed 10-1 & 2-6, Thurs 12-4 & 5-7
Friends of the Library Group

RANCHO CUCAMONGA

J CHAFFEY COLLEGE LIBRARY*, 5885 Haven Ave, 91737-3002. SAN 300-5623. Tel: 909-652-6800. Circulation Tel: 909-652-6807. Reference Tel: 909-652-6808. E-mail: library@chaffey.edu. Web Site: www.chaffey.edu/library. *Interim Dean, Support Serv,* Robert Rundquist; E-mail: robert.rundquist@chaffey.edu; *Ref Librn,* William Araiza; Tel: 909-652-8119, E-mail: william.araiza@chaffey.edu; *Ref Librn,* Carol Hutte; E-mail: carol.hutte@chaffey.edu; *Ref Librn,* Shelley Marcus; Tel: 909-652-7451, E-mail: shelley.marcus@chaffey.edu; Staff 5 (MLS 5)
Founded 1916. Enrl 20,500; Fac 270; Highest Degree: Associate
Library Holdings: e-books 20,000; Electronic Media & Resources 20; Bk Vols 80,350; Per Subs 89
Automation Activity & Vendor Info: (Acquisitions) Auto-Graphics, Inc; (Cataloging) Auto-Graphics, Inc; (Circulation) Auto-Graphics, Inc; (Course Reserve) Auto-Graphics, Inc; (OPAC) Auto-Graphics, Inc; (Serials) Auto-Graphics, Inc
Wireless access
Function: Distance learning, E-Reserves, Internet access, Online cat, Online info literacy tutorials on the web & in blackboard, Online ref, Orientations, Photocopying/Printing, Study rm, Wheelchair accessible
Partic in California Community College Library Consortium
Open Mon-Thurs 7:30am-8pm, Fri 8-4, Sat & Sun 10-3
Restriction: Open to students, fac & staff

P RANCHO CUCAMONGA PUBLIC LIBRARY, Paul A Biane Library, 12505 Cultural Center Dr, 91739. SAN 376-6756. Tel: 909-477-2720. Circulation Tel: 909-477-2720, Ext 5000. Reference Tel: 909-477-2720, Ext 5008. FAX: 909-477-2721. E-mail: library.reference@cityofrc.us. Web Site: www.cityofrc.us/library. *Libr Dir,* Julie A Sowles; E-mail: julie.sowles@cityofrc.us; *Dep Libr Dir,* Wess Garcia; *Head of Children's & Family Services,* Angelica Trummell; *Libr Serv Mgr,* Cara Vera; Staff 64 (MLS 14, Non-MLS 50)
Founded 1994. Pop 179,000; Circ 860,000
Library Holdings: AV Mats 39,110; Bks on Deafness & Sign Lang 82; e-books 622,953; High Interest/Low Vocabulary Bk Vols 2,464; Large Print Bks 1,734; Bk Vols 100,335; Per Subs 160; Talking Bks 4,446
Automation Activity & Vendor Info: (Cataloging) SirsiDynix; (Circulation) SirsiDynix; (OPAC) SirsiDynix
Wireless access
Mem of Inland Library System
Partic in Link+
Open Tues-Fri 10-6
Friends of the Library Group
Branches: 1
ARCHIBALD PUBLIC LIBRARY, 7368 Archibald Ave, 91730.
Library Holdings: Bk Titles 113,517; Bk Vols 123,809
Open Tues-Sat 10-6
Bookmobiles: 1. Bk vols 4,126

RANCHO MIRAGE

M EISENHOWER MEDICAL CENTER, Medical Library, 39000 Bob Hope Dr, 92270. SAN 301-2255. Tel: 760-340-3911. Administration E-mail: lbennett@eisenhowerhealth.org. Web Site: eisenhowerhealth.org. *Library Contact,* Dixon Bennett; E-mail: lbennett@eisenhowerhealth.org; Staff 1 (Non-MLS 1)
Founded 1973
Library Holdings: Per Subs 140
Subject Interests: Clinical med
Function: 24/7 Electronic res
Restriction: Hospital employees & physicians only, Staff use only

P RANCHO MIRAGE LIBRARY*, 71-100 Hwy 111, 92270. SAN 375-3549. Tel: 760-341-7323. FAX: 760-341-5213. E-mail: info@ranchomiragelibrary.org. Web Site: www.ranchomiragelibrary.org. *Dir,* Aaron Espinosa; E-mail: aarone@ranchomiragelibrary.org; *Libr Operations Mgr,* Robert Rekuc; E-mail: robertr@ranchomiragelibrary.org; *Ch,* Valentine Llort; E-mail: valentinel@ranchomiragelibrary.org; Staff 12.9 (MLS 9.3, Non-MLS 3.6)
Founded 1994. Pop 21,886; Circ 491,604
Library Holdings: AV Mats 14,000; CDs 10,600; DVDs 14,000; e-books 68; Bk Vols 84,918; Per Subs 35
Special Collections: Oral History
Subject Interests: Golf, Local authors
Automation Activity & Vendor Info: (Acquisitions) Auto-Graphics, Inc; (Cataloging) Auto-Graphics, Inc; (Circulation) Auto-Graphics, Inc; (ILL) Auto-Graphics, Inc; (OPAC) Auto-Graphics, Inc
Wireless access
Function: Art exhibits, Audiobks via web, AV serv, Bks on cassette, Bks on CD, Children's prog, Computer training, Computers for patron use, E-Reserves, Electronic databases & coll, Holiday prog, ILL available, Internet access, Jazz prog, Mail & tel request accepted, Music CDs, Online cat, Outside serv via phone, mail, e-mail & web, OverDrive digital audio bks, Photocopying/Printing, Preschool outreach, Prog for adults, Prog for children & young adult, Ref & res, Ref serv available, Spoken cassettes & CDs, Summer reading prog, Tax forms, Telephone ref, VHS videos, Wheelchair accessible
Publications: Bi-Monthly Program & Exhibits Calendar; The Bookworm (Newsletter)
Mem of Inland Library System
Partic in OCLC Online Computer Library Center, Inc; Southern California Library Cooperative
Special Services for the Blind - Bks on cassette; Bks on CD; Cassettes; Large print bks
Open Mon, Tues & Thurs-Sat 9-6, Wed 9-8
Friends of the Library Group

RANCHO PALOS VERDES

CR MARYMOUNT CALIFORNIA UNIVERSITY LIBRARY*, 30800 Palos Verdes Dr E, 90275-6299. SAN 301-2263. Tel: 310-303-7260. FAX: 310-377-6223. E-mail: library@marymountcalifornia.edu. Web Site: www.marymountcalifornia.edu/academics/academic-resources/library. *Dir, Libr Serv,* Jose Rincon; Tel: 310-303-7205, E-mail: jrincon@marymountcalifornia.edu; Staff 1 (MLS 1)
Founded 1932. Enrl 550; Fac 48; Highest Degree: Master
Library Holdings: DVDs 1,077; e-books 75,842; Electronic Media & Resources 20,221; Bk Vols 24,034; Per Subs 107
Automation Activity & Vendor Info: (Cataloging) OCLC; (Circulation) OCLC; (Course Reserve) OCLC; (ILL) OCLC; (OPAC) OCLC
Wireless access
Function: 24/7 Electronic res, 24/7 Online cat, Adult literacy prog, Electronic databases & coll, Magazines, Online cat, Online ref, Outreach serv, Photocopying/Printing, Ref & res, Res assist avail, Scanner
Publications: Library Guides; Library Newsletter
Partic in Statewide California Electronic Library Consortium
Open Mon-Thurs (Fall & Spring) 8-7, Fri 8-5; Mon-Fri (Summer & Winter) 9-4

S THE SALVATION ARMY COLLEGE FOR OFFICER TRAINING AT CRESTMONT*, Library Services, 30840 Hawthorne Blvd, 90275. SAN 301-2271. Tel: 310-265-6129, 310-377-0481. Web Site: www.crestmont.edu/crestmont/library-and-museum-services. *Dir, Libr & Archives,* Andrea Anaya; E-mail: Andrea.Anaya@usw.salvationarmy.org; Staff 3 (MLS 1, Non-MLS 2)
Founded 1923. Enrl 92; Fac 20; Highest Degree: Associate
Library Holdings: e-journals 1,500; Bk Titles 40,000; Per Subs 100; Spec Interest Per Sub 50
Special Collections: Salvation Army Publications
Subject Interests: Relig
Automation Activity & Vendor Info: (Cataloging) LibraryWorld, Inc; (Circulation) LibraryWorld, Inc
Wireless access
Partic in Christian Library Consortium
Open Mon-Fri (Winter) 8:15am-9pm, Sat 1-5; Mon-Fri (Summer) 8:15-4:15

RED BLUFF

GL TEHAMA COUNTY LAW LIBRARY*, 955 Main St, Ste C, 96080. Tel: 530-529-5033. E-mail: lawlibrary@tehamacountylibrary.org. *Law Librn,* Sarah Cegan
Library Holdings: Bk Vols 10,500
Special Collections: City & County Charter & Code Coll
Subject Interests: Fed law, Local law, State law
Open Mon-Fri 10-1

P TEHAMA COUNTY LIBRARY*, 545 Diamond Ave, 96080. SAN 333-7804. Tel: 530-527-0604. FAX: 530-527-1562. E-mail: reference@tehamacountylibrary.org. Web Site: www.tehamacountylibrary.org. *County Librn,* Sally Ainsworth; E-mail: sally@tehamacountylibrary.org; Staff 2 (MLS 1, Non-MLS 1)
Founded 1916. Pop 61,774; Circ 103,000
Library Holdings: Bk Titles 114,640; Bk Vols 122,336; Per Subs 45
Special Collections: Tehama County History
Wireless access
Mem of NorthNet Library System
Open Mon, Wed & Thurs 12-6, Tues 2-8, Fri 2-6, Sat 10-2
Friends of the Library Group
Branches: 2
CORNING BRANCH, 740 Third St, Corning, 96021-2517, SAN 333-7839. Tel: 530-824-7050. FAX: 530-824-7051. *County Librn,* Sally Ainsworth; Staff 2 (MLS 1, Non-MLS 1)
Open Mon, Thurs & Fri 2-6, Tues 9-1, Wed 4-8
Friends of the Library Group
LOS MOLINOS BRANCH, 7881 Hwy 99E, Los Molinos, 96055-9701. (Mail add: 645 Madison St, 96080), SAN 329-6598. Tel: 530-384-2772. FAX: 530-384-9826. *Librn,* Caryn Brown
Pop 63,100
Open Mon-Thurs 9-1 & 2-6

REDDING

J SHASTA COLLEGE LIBRARY*, 11555 Old Oregon Trail, 96003-7692. (Mail add: PO Box 496006, 96049-6006), SAN 301-2298. Tel: 530-242-7550. Interlibrary Loan Service Tel: 530-242-2343. Reference Tel: 530-242-7551. Web Site: www.shastacollege.edu/library. *Dean, Libr Serv & Educ Tech,* Will Breitbach; E-mail: wbreitbach@shastacollege.edu; *Syst/Tech Proc Librn,* Cheryl Cruse; Tel: 530-242-2348, E-mail: ccruse@shastacollege.edu; *Info & Instruction Librn,* Carolyn Singh; Tel: 530-242-2347, E-mail: csingh@shastacollege.edu; Staff 9.2 (MLS 2.7, Non-MLS 6.5)
Founded 1948. Enrl 7,253; Fac 4; Highest Degree: Associate
Library Holdings: Audiobooks 760; AV Mats 3,232; e-books 27,013; Bk Titles 70,903; Bk Vols 78,750; Per Subs 71
Subject Interests: Local hist
Automation Activity & Vendor Info: (Acquisitions) SirsiDynix; (Cataloging) SirsiDynix; (Circulation) SirsiDynix; (Course Reserve) SirsiDynix; (ILL) SirsiDynix; (Media Booking) SirsiDynix; (OPAC) SirsiDynix; (Serials) SirsiDynix
Wireless access
Mem of NorthNet Library System
Partic in Community College League of California; OCLC Online Computer Library Center, Inc
Open Mon-Thurs 7:45-6:45, Fri 7:45-3:45

GL SHASTA COUNTY PUBLIC LAW LIBRARY*, 1500 Court St, Rm B-7, 96001. SAN 370-4246. Tel: 530-245-6243. FAX: 530-229-8140. Web Site: www.shastalibraries.org/604. *Librn,* Laura Hernandez
Founded 1968
Library Holdings: Bk Titles 7,600
Subject Interests: Legal res
Wireless access
Open Mon-Thurs 8-4:30, Fri 8:30-2

S SHASTA HISTORICAL SOCIETY*, Research Library, 1449 Market St, 96001. SAN 375-1945. Tel: 530-243-3720. FAX: 530-246-3708. E-mail: shs@shastahistorical.org. Web Site: www.shastahistorical.org. *Curator,* Jay Thompson
Founded 1930
Library Holdings: Microforms 30; Bk Vols 2,000; Spec Interest Per Sub 5; Videos 20
Automation Activity & Vendor Info: (Cataloging) ByWater Solutions; (OPAC) ByWater Solutions
Function: Archival coll, Art exhibits, Electronic databases & coll, Magnifiers for reading, Online cat, Photocopying/Printing, Prog for adults, VHS videos

Open Mon-Fri 10-4
Restriction: Non-circulating

P SHASTA PUBLIC LIBRARIES*, 1100 Parkview Ave, 96001. SAN 333-8010. Tel: 530-245-7250. Reference Tel: 530-245-7252. E-mail: askus@shastalibraries.org. Web Site: www.shastalibraries.org. *Interim Libr Dir,* Elizabeth Kelley; E-mail: elizabethk@shastalibraries.org; Staff 16 (MLS 6, Non-MLS 10)
Founded 1949. Pop 181,483; Circ 262,253
Library Holdings: AV Mats 7,363; Bk Vols 204,681; Per Subs 249
Special Collections: Californiana Coll. State Document Depository; US Document Depository
Subject Interests: Calif, County hist, Forestry, Parenting, Shasta County Indians
Automation Activity & Vendor Info: (Acquisitions) SirsiDynix; (Circulation) SirsiDynix; (OPAC) SirsiDynix
Wireless access
Function: 24/7 Online cat, 3D Printer, Activity rm, Adult bk club, Adult literacy prog, After school storytime, Art exhibits, Audio & video playback equip for onsite use, Audiobks on Playaways & MP3, Audiobks via web, Bk club(s), Bks on CD, Children's prog, Citizenship assistance, Computer training, Computers for patron use, Digital talking bks, Free DVD rentals, Holiday prog, Internet access, Large print keyboards, Magazines, Magnifiers for reading, Makerspace, Meeting rooms, Microfiche/film & reading machines, Movies, Museum passes, Music CDs, Online cat, Outreach serv, Outside serv via phone, mail, e-mail & web, OverDrive digital audio bks, Photocopying/Printing, Preschool outreach, Preschool reading prog, Prog for adults, Prog for children & young adult, Serves people with intellectual disabilities, Spanish lang bks, STEM programs, Story hour, Study rm, Summer reading prog, Tax forms, Teen prog, Visual arts prog, Wheelchair accessible, Workshops
Mem of NorthNet Library System
Partic in Research Libraries Information Network
Special Services for the Deaf - Bks on deafness & sign lang
Special Services for the Blind - Bks on cassette; Bks on CD; Copier with enlargement capabilities; Large print bks; Magnifiers
Open Mon-Thurs 10-8, Fri & Sat 10-6, Sun 1-5
Friends of the Library Group
Branches: 2
ANDERSON BRANCH, 3200 W Center St, Anderson, 96007, SAN 333-8045. Tel: 530-365-7685. FAX: 530-365-7685. *Br Mgr,* Christy Windle; E-mail: christyw@shastalibraries.org
Founded 1950
Open Tues-Thurs 11-7, Fri & Sat 9-5
Friends of the Library Group
BURNEY LIBRARY, 37038 Siskiyou St, Burney, 96013, SAN 333-807X. Tel: 530-335-4317. FAX: 530-335-4317. *Br Head,* Deborah Dean
Founded 1949
Automation Activity & Vendor Info: (Circulation) SirsiDynix; (OPAC) SirsiDynix
Open Mon-Thurs 10-1 & 2-6
Friends of the Library Group

CR SIMPSON UNIVERSITY*, Start-Kilgour Memorial Library, 2211 College View Dr, 96003. SAN 301-4665. Tel: 530-226-4117. Interlibrary Loan Service Tel: 530-226-4944. Reference Tel: 530-226-4943. FAX: 530-226-4858. E-mail: library@simpsonu.edu. Web Site: www.simpsonulibrary.org. *Dir, Libr Serv,* Larry L Haight; Tel: 530-226-4110, E-mail: lhaight@simpsonu.edu; *Reader & Digital Serv Librn,* Eric Wheeler; E-mail: ewheeler@simpsonu.edu; Staff 3 (MLS 2, Non-MLS 1)
Founded 1921. Enrl 1,267; Fac 221; Highest Degree: Master
May 2013-Apr 2014 Income $371,530. Mats Exp $122,343, Books $26,139, Per/Ser (Incl. Access Fees) $12,332, AV Mat $1,653, Electronic Ref Mat (Incl. Access Fees) $82,219. Sal $163,151 (Prof $114,288)
Library Holdings: CDs 571; DVDs 2,239; e-books 292,000; Microforms 242,910; Bk Vols 103,800; Per Subs 85
Special Collections: A W Tozer Coll; Christian & Missionary Alliance Denominational History (A B Simpson Coll)
Automation Activity & Vendor Info: (Acquisitions) OCLC; (Cataloging) OCLC; (Circulation) OCLC; (Course Reserve) OCLC; (ILL) OCLC; (OPAC) OCLC WorldShare Interlibrary Loan; (Serials) OCLC
Wireless access
Function: Archival coll, Computers for patron use, Distance learning, E-Reserves, Electronic databases & coll, ILL available, Internet access, Microfiche/film & reading machines, Music CDs, Online cat, Online ref, Orientations, Photocopying/Printing, Ref & res, Tax forms, Wheelchair accessible
Partic in Christian Library Consortium; Statewide California Electronic Library Consortium
Open Mon-Thurs (Fall & Spring) 7:45am-Midnight, Fri 7:45-6, Sun 2-10; Mon-Fri (Summer) 9:30-8, Fri 9:30-6
Restriction: Borrowing privileges limited to fac & registered students, In-house use for visitors, Open to students, fac, staff & alumni, Pub use on premises

REDLANDS

P A K SMILEY PUBLIC LIBRARY, 125 W Vine St, 92373. SAN 301-2344. Tel: 909-798-7565. FAX: 909-798-7566. Administration E-mail: admin@akspl.org. Web Site: www.akspl.org. *Libr Dir,* Don McCue; Staff 5 (MLS 2, Non-MLS 3)
Founded 1894. Pop 71,926; Circ 264,663
Library Holdings: AV Mats 9,246; DVDs 3,171; e-books 1,540; Large Print Bks 2,480; Bk Titles 113,096; Bk Vols 136,466; Per Subs 237
Special Collections: Californiana, Redlands Heritage, bks & pamphlets, ms, maps, photog; Encountering the Lincoln Scholarly Zareba; Horace Greely, Lincoln & the War for the Union; Lincoln (Watchorn Memorial Shrine), bks, pamphlets, photog, tapes & ephemera; Lincoln Shrine, bks, pamphlets, photos, tapes & ephemera; Powderly, Lincoln & the Shrine; Smiley Family Letters, papers; The Archives of the A K Smiley Public Library; The Lincoln Memorial Shrine Golden Jubilee; The Lincoln Memorial Shrine, Redlands, California; What is Patron Saint's Day?. Oral History; State Document Depository
Subject Interests: Art & archit, Civil War
Automation Activity & Vendor Info: (Cataloging) SirsiDynix; (Circulation) SirsiDynix; (OPAC) SirsiDynix
Wireless access
Publications: A K Smiley Public Library, A Brief History; A Lost Letter Found
Special Services for the Blind - Assistive/Adapted tech devices, equip & products
Open Mon-Thurs 10-6, Fri & Sat 10-5, Sun 1-5
Friends of the Library Group

C UNIVERSITY OF REDLANDS*, George & Verda Armacost Library, 1249 E Colton Ave, 92374-3755. SAN 301-2352. Tel: 909-748-8022. Circulation Tel: 909-748-8876. FAX: 909-335-5392. E-mail: library@redlands.edu. Web Site: library.redlands.edu. *Librn,* Les Canterbury; *Librn,* Lua Gregory; *Librn,* Shana Higgins; *Librn,* Janelle Julagay; *Librn,* William Kennedy; *Librn,* Paige Mann; *Librn,* Sanjeet Mann; Staff 18 (MLS 9, Non-MLS 9)
Founded 1907. Enrl 5,215; Fac 206; Highest Degree: Doctorate. Sal $941,028 (Prof $506,507)
Library Holdings: AV Mats 11,550; Bks on Deafness & Sign Lang 312; Braille Volumes 27; CDs 4,489; DVDs 1,657; e-books 16,844; e-journals 68,040; Microforms 748,962; Music Scores 9,656; Bk Vols 516,398; Per Subs 55,230; Videos 3,439
Special Collections: Barney Childs Coll & Papers; Californiana & the Great Southwest (Vernon & Helen Farquhar Coll); Harley Farnsworth & Florence Ayscough McNair Far Eastern Library; Harry Pottle Coll; James Irvine Foundation Map Coll. US Document Depository
Automation Activity & Vendor Info: (Acquisitions) Innovative Interfaces, Inc; (Cataloging) Innovative Interfaces, Inc; (Circulation) Innovative Interfaces, Inc; (Course Reserve) Innovative Interfaces, Inc; (ILL) OCLC ILLiad; (OPAC) Innovative Interfaces, Inc; (Serials) Innovative Interfaces, Inc
Wireless access
Partic in Inland Empire Acad Libr Coop; Link+; OCLC Online Computer Library Center, Inc; San Bernardino, Inyo, Riverside Counties United Library Services; Statewide California Electronic Library Consortium

REDONDO BEACH

P REDONDO BEACH PUBLIC LIBRARY*, 303 N Pacific Coast Hwy, 90277. SAN 333-8525. Tel: 310-318-0675. FAX: 310-318-3809. E-mail: rbplweb@redondo.org. Web Site: www.redondo.org/library. *Dir,* Susan Anderson; E-mail: susan.anderson@redondo.org; *Sr Librn,* Erin Schoonover; E-mail: erin.schoonover@redondo.org; *Youth Serv,* Donia Sichler; Staff 11 (MLS 3, Non-MLS 8)
Founded 1908. Pop 67,488; Circ 347,474
Jul 2019-Jun 2020 Income (Main & Associated Libraries) $4,819,279, City $4,740,605, Other $78,674. Mats Exp $332,244, Books $134,634, Per/Ser (Incl. Access Fees) $12,637, AV Mat $47,488, Electronic Ref Mat (Incl. Access Fees) $137,489. Sal $1,471,680
Library Holdings: Audiobooks 9,819; AV Mats 37,655; CDs 10,012; DVDs 17,824; Electronic Media & Resources 15; Large Print Bks 3,999; Microforms 13,488; Bk Titles 113,964; Bk Vols 122,011; Per Subs 164; Videos 54
Automation Activity & Vendor Info: (Acquisitions) SirsiDynix; (Cataloging) SirsiDynix; (Circulation) SirsiDynix; (ILL) OCLC; (OPAC) SirsiDynix
Wireless access
Function: 24/7 Electronic res, 24/7 Online cat, Activity rm, Adult bk club, Audiobks via web, AV serv, Bks on CD, Children's prog, Computer training, Computers for patron use, Electronic databases & coll, Free DVD rentals, Holiday prog, ILL available, Internet access, Life-long learning prog for all ages, Magazines, Music CDs, Online cat, Photocopying/Printing, Story hour, Study rm, Teen prog, Telephone ref, Writing prog

Partic in Califa; Southern California Library Cooperative
Special Services for the Blind - Reader equip
Open Mon 3-7, Tues, Wed & Thurs 11-7, Fri 2-6, Sat 9-5
Friends of the Library Group
Branches: 1
NORTH BRANCH, 2000 Artesia Blvd, 90278, SAN 333-855X. Tel: 310-318-0677. FAX: 310-374-3768.
Circ 100,492
Library Holdings: Audiobooks 1,468; AV Mats 7,647; CDs 2,118; DVDs 4,061; Large Print Bks 700; Bk Vols 34,860; Per Subs 51
Function: 24/7 Electronic res, 24/7 Online cat, Activity rm, After school storytime, Audiobks via web, AV serv, Bks on CD, Children's prog, Computers for patron use, Digital talking bks, Electronic databases & coll, Free DVD rentals, ILL available, Internet access, Magazines, Mail & tel request accepted, Meeting rooms, Movies, Music CDs, Online cat, Online ref, OverDrive digital audio bks, Photocopying/Printing, Printer for laptops & handheld devices, Prog for adults, Prog for children & young adult, Ref serv available, Scanner, Story hour, Study rm, Summer reading prog, Tax forms, Telephone ref
Open Mon-Thurs 1-7, Sat 9-5
Friends of the Library Group

REDWOOD CITY

J CANADA COLLEGE LIBRARY*, Bldg 9, 3rd Flr, 4200 Farm Hill Blvd, 94061-1099. SAN 301-2395. Circulation Tel: 650-306-3485. Reference Tel: 650-306-3480. FAX: 650-306-3434. Web Site: canadacollege.edu/library. *Dean,* David Reed; E-mail: reedd@smccd.edu; *Librn,* Valeria Estrada; E-mail: estradav@smccd.edu; *Circ,* Paul Gaskins; E-mail: gaskins@smccd.net; Staff 5 (MLS 3, Non-MLS 2)
Founded 1968. Enrl 3,000; Fac 100; Highest Degree: Associate
Library Holdings: Bk Vols 60,000; Per Subs 110
Special Collections: Center for the American Musical Library, Archives
Subject Interests: Early childhood educ, Fashion design, Interior design, Radiologic tech
Wireless access
Partic in Coop Libr Agency for Syst & Servs
Open Mon-Thurs 8-9, Fri 8-3, Sat 10-2

M KAISER-PERMANENTE MEDICAL CENTER*, Health Sciences Library, 1150 Veterans Blvd, 94063. SAN 301-2409. Tel: 650-299-2437. FAX: 650-299-2488. *Librn,* Chadrika Kanungo
Library Holdings: Bk Vols 1,500
Open Mon-Fri 8:30-5

P REDWOOD CITY PUBLIC LIBRARY*, 1044 Middlefield Rd, 94063-1868. SAN 333-8584. Tel: 650-780-7018. Circulation Tel: 650-780-7020. Administration Tel: 650-780-7061. FAX: 650-780-7069. E-mail: rclinfo@redwoodcity.org. Web Site: www.redwoodcity.org/library. *Libr Dir,* Derek Wolfgram; *Div Mgr,* Maria Kramer; *Mgr, Br,* Elizabeth Meeks; Tel: 650-780-5740
Founded 1865. Pop 80,768
Special Collections: State Document Depository; US Document Depository
Automation Activity & Vendor Info: (Circulation) Innovative Interfaces, Inc
Wireless access
Partic in Coop Libr Agency for Syst & Servs
Open Mon-Thurs 10-9, Fri & Sat 10-5, Sun 12-5
Friends of the Library Group
Branches: 3
FAIR OAKS, 2510 Middlefield Rd, 94063-3402, SAN 333-8614. Tel: 650-780-7261. FAX: 650-568-3371.
Open Mon-Thurs 10-7, Fri-Sat 10-5
Friends of the Library Group
REDWOOD SHORES, 399 Marine Pkwy, 94065. Tel: 650-780-5740.
Founded 2007
Open Mon-Thurs 10-8, Sat 10-5, Sun 12-5
SCHABERG BRANCH, 2140 Euclid Ave, 94061-1327, SAN 333-8649. Tel: 650-780-7010. FAX: 650-568-1702.
Open Mon-Thurs 10-7, Sat 10-5
Friends of the Library Group

L ROPERS MAJESKI*, Law Library, 1001 Marshall St, Ste 500, 94063. SAN 323-6919. Tel: 650-364-8200. FAX: 650-780-1701. Web Site: www.ropers.com. *Library Contact,* Raja Bakshi
Library Holdings: Bk Titles 1,800; Bk Vols 10,000; Per Subs 12
Automation Activity & Vendor Info: (Acquisitions) Inmagic, Inc.
Open Mon-Fri 8-6

S SAN MATEO COUNTY HISTORICAL ASSOCIATION, 2200 Broadway St, 94063. SAN 301-522X. Tel: 650-299-0104. FAX: 650-299-0141. E-mail: archives@historysmc.org. Web Site: historysmc.org/smcha-archives. *Archivist,* Debra Peterson; E-mail: debra@historysmc.org
Founded 1935
Library Holdings: Bk Vols 1,500
Subject Interests: County hist
Wireless access
Publications: Historical Happenings (Newsletter); La Peninsula (Journal)
Open Tues-Thurs 10-12 & 1-4, Sun 12-4
Restriction: Non-circulating to the pub
Friends of the Library Group

GL SAN MATEO COUNTY LAW LIBRARY*, 710 Hamilton St, 94063. SAN 301-2417. Tel: 650-363-4913. FAX: 650-367-8040. Web Site: smclawlibrary.org/. *Dir,* Andrew Gurthet; *Asst Dir,* Caroline Bracco; E-mail: cbracco@smclawlibrary.org; *Libr Asst,* Antonella Conventini; Staff 3 (MLS 2, Non-MLS 1)
Founded 1916
Library Holdings: Bk Titles 1,944; Bk Vols 32,524; Per Subs 3
Special Collections: State Document Depository
Wireless access
Function: 24/7 Online cat, Art exhibits, Computers for patron use, Electronic databases & coll, Govt ref serv, Internet access, Meeting rooms, Photocopying/Printing, Ref & res, Ref serv available
Open Mon-Fri 8-5
Friends of the Library Group

S WESTERN PHILATELIC LIBRARY*, 3004 Spring St, 94063. (Mail add: PO Box 7063, 94063-7063), SAN 324-3524. Tel: 650-306-9150. E-mail: info@fwpl.org. Web Site: www.fwpl.org. *Chairperson,* Stuart Leven; E-mail: sleven@fwpl.org; *Dir,* Edward Jarvis; E-mail: edjarvis@fwpl.org; *Dir,* Roy Teixeria; E-mail: rteixeria@fwpl.org
Library Holdings: Bk Titles 8,000; Per Subs 50
Subject Interests: Stamp collecting
Automation Activity & Vendor Info: (Cataloging) Inmagic, Inc.
Publications: The Bay Phil
Open Tues & Sat 12-5, Fri 9-5

REEDLEY

R FIRST MENNONITE CHURCH LIBRARY*, 1208 L St, 93654. (Mail add: PO Box 111, 93654-0111), SAN 301-2433. Tel: 559-638-2917. FAX: 559-637-8826. E-mail: fmcreedley@gmail.com. Web Site: www.fmcreedley.org.
Library Holdings: Bk Vols 2,000
Subject Interests: Bible, Mennonite-Anabaptist theol
Wireless access

J REEDLEY COLLEGE LIBRARY*, 995 N Reed Ave, 93654. SAN 301-2441. Tel: 559-638-0352. FAX: 559-638-0384. E-mail: library@reedleycollege.edu. Web Site: www.reedleycollege.edu/campus-life/library. *Librn,* Shivon Hess; E-mail: shivon.hess@reedleycollege.edu; Staff 6 (MLS 2, Non-MLS 4)
Founded 1956. Enrl 6,000; Fac 91
Library Holdings: e-books 4,000; Large Print Bks 100; Bk Titles 3,800; Per Subs 100
Automation Activity & Vendor Info: (Cataloging) OCLC WorldShare Interlibrary Loan; (Circulation) OCLC WorldShare Interlibrary Loan
Wireless access
Function: ILL available, Photocopying/Printing, Wheelchair accessible
Open Mon-Thurs 7:30-8, Fri 7:30-3

RICHMOND

S CHEVRON INFORMATION TECHNOLOGY COMPANY, DIVISION OF CHEVRON USA, INC*, Chevron Global Library, 100 Chevron Way, Bldg 50, Rm 1212, 94802. SAN 301-2468. Tel: 510-242-4755. FAX: 510-242-5621. E-mail: infomgmt@chevron.com. *Libr Mgr,* Nan M Dubbelde; E-mail: ndubbelde@chevron.com; Staff 12 (MLS 10, Non-MLS 2)
Founded 1908
Subject Interests: Chem, Chem engr, Fuels, Patents, Petroleum
Publications: Library bulletin
Restriction: By permission only, Co libr, Employees only, External users must contact libr

P RICHMOND PUBLIC LIBRARY, 325 Civic Center Plaza, 94804-9991. SAN 333-8673. Tel: 510-620-6561. Circulation Tel: 510-620-6559. FAX: 510-620-6850. E-mail: rpl_reference@ci.richmond.ca.us. Web Site: www.ci.richmond.ca.us/105/library. *Dir,* Jane Pratt; Staff 17 (MLS 17)
Founded 1907. Pop 89,300; Circ 421,979
Library Holdings: AV Mats 1,788; Bk Titles 176,322; Bk Vols 312,030; Per Subs 558
Special Collections: Afro-American History & Literature; California History Coll; Richmond History Coll. Oral History; State Document Depository; US Document Depository
Automation Activity & Vendor Info: (Circulation) Innovative Interfaces, Inc

Publications: Monthly Booklist
Partic in Coop Libr Agency for Syst & Servs; OCLC Online Computer Library Center, Inc
Special Services for the Deaf - TDD equip; TTY equip; Videos & decoder
Open Mon & Tues 12-7, Wed 10-7, Thurs 10-5, Fri & Sat 12-5
Friends of the Library Group
Bookmobiles: 1

RIDGECREST

J CERRO COSO COMMUNITY COLLEGE LIBRARY*, 3000 College Heights Blvd, 93555-9571. SAN 333-8827. Tel: 760-384-6131. FAX: 760-384-6270. Reference E-mail: reference@cerrocoso.edu. Web Site: www.cerrocoso.edu/library. *Librn,* Julie Cornett; Tel: 760-384-6132, E-mail: jcornett@cerrocoso.edu; *Librn,* Sharlene Paxton; Tel: 760-384-6216, E-mail: sharlene.paxton@cerrocoso.edu; Staff 4.3 (MLS 2, Non-MLS 2.3)
Founded 1973. Enrl 4,994; Fac 163; Highest Degree: Associate
Library Holdings: AV Mats 2,180; CDs 54; DVDs 100; e-books 27,400; Bk Titles 25,000; Bk Vols 32,901; Per Subs 1
Automation Activity & Vendor Info: (Acquisitions) SirsiDynix; (Cataloging) SirsiDynix; (Circulation) SirsiDynix; (Course Reserve) SirsiDynix; (OPAC) SirsiDynix
Wireless access
Mem of Kern Community College District
Special Services for the Blind - Braille bks
Open Mon-Thurs 8am-9pm, Fri 8-Noon

S MATURANGO MUSEUM*, Resource Library, 100 E Las Flores Ave, 93555. SAN 375-8184. Tel: 760-375-6900. FAX: 760-375-0479. E-mail: info@maturango.org. Web Site: maturango.org. *Exec Dir,* Debbie Benson; E-mail: debbie@maturango.org; *Curator,* Sherry Brubaker; E-mail: sherry@maturango.org; *Curator,* Alexander Rogers; E-mail: sandy@maturango.org; *Curator,* Elaine Wiley; E-mail: elaine@maturango.org. Subject Specialists: *Natural hist,* Sherry Brubaker; *Archaeology,* Alexander Rogers; *Hist,* Elaine Wiley
Library Holdings: Bk Titles 2,500
Wireless access
Open Mon-Sun 10-5
Restriction: Non-circulating

RIVERSIDE

CR CALIFORNIA BAPTIST UNIVERSITY, Annie Gabriel Library, 8432 Magnolia Ave, 92504. SAN 301-2492. Tel: 951-343-4228. Reference Tel: 951-343-4333. E-mail: library@calbaptist.edu. Web Site: www.calbaptist.edu/library. *Libr Dir,* Dr Steve Emerson; E-mail: semerson@calbaptist.edu; *Coll Develop Librn,* Elizabeth Flater; Tel: 951-552-8624, E-mail: eflater@calbaptist.edu; *Instrul Serv Librn,* Carolyn Heine; E-mail: cheine@calbaptist.edu; *Access Serv Mgr,* Rob Diaz; Tel: 951-343-8490, E-mail: rdiaz@calbaptist.edu; *Cat,* Helen Xu; Tel: 951-343-4354, E-mail: hxu@calbaptist.edu; *Circ,* Keri Murcray; E-mail: kmurcray@calbaptist.edu; *Digital Serv,* Katie Zeeb; Tel: 951-343-4365, E-mail: kzeeb@calbaptist.edu; *Ser,* Dr Barry Parker; E-mail: bparker@calbaptist.edu; *Tech Serv,* Rachel Murrell; Tel: 951-343-4353, E-mail: rmurrell@calbaptist.edu; Staff 9 (MLS 6, Non-MLS 3)
Founded 1950. Enrl 11,814; Fac 353; Highest Degree: Doctorate
Library Holdings: Bk Vols 436,495; Per Subs 220
Special Collections: Hymnology (P Boyd Smith Coll); Nie Wieder Coll; Virginia Hyatt Baptist Coll; Wallace Coll
Subject Interests: Evangelism, Holocaust studies, Hymnology, Relig
Automation Activity & Vendor Info: (Acquisitions) SirsiDynix; (Cataloging) SirsiDynix; (Circulation) SirsiDynix; (Discovery) EBSCO Discovery Service; (ILL) OCLC; (OPAC) SirsiDynix; (Serials) SerialsSolutions
Wireless access
Function: ILL available, Ref serv available, Wheelchair accessible
Partic in Christian Library Consortium; Inland Empire Acad Libr Coop; OCLC Online Computer Library Center, Inc; Statewide California Electronic Library Consortium
Open Mon-Thurs 7am-1am, Fri 7-5, Sat 10-6, Sun 2pm-1am

S CALIFORNIA SCHOOL FOR THE DEAF LIBRARY*, 3044 Horace St, 92506. SAN 320-5746. Tel: 951-248-7700. E-mail: info@csdr-cde.ca.gov. Web Site: www.csdr-cde.ca.gov. *Libr Supvr,* Erik Lasiewski; Tel: 951-248-7700, Ext 4138
Library Holdings: Bk Vols 13,000
Special Collections: American Annals for the Deaf; Volta Review
Subject Interests: Deaf, Spec educ
Automation Activity & Vendor Info: (Acquisitions) Follett Software
Partic in San Bernardino, Inyo, Riverside Counties United Library Services
Special Services for the Deaf - TTY equip
Restriction: Mem only

G CALIFORNIA STATE COURT OF APPEAL*, Fourth Appellate District, Division Two Library, 3389 12th St, 92501. SAN 327-1587. Tel: 951-782-2485. FAX: 909-248-0235. Web Site: www.courts.ca.gov/4dca.htm. *Librn,* Terry R Lynch; E-mail: terry.lynch@jud.ca.gov
Library Holdings: Bk Vols 30,000
Restriction: Not open to pub

R CALVARY PRESBYTERIAN CHURCH USA LIBRARY*, 4495 Magnolia Ave, 92501. SAN 301-2506. Tel: 951-686-0761. FAX: 951-686-1488. E-mail: church@calvarypresch.com. Web Site: www.calvarypresch.org.
Library Holdings: Bk Vols 2,000
Open Mon-Thurs 9-5, Fri 9-1:30
Restriction: Mem only

M KAISER-PERMANENTE MEDICAL CENTER*, Health Sciences Library, 10800 Magnolia Ave, 92505. SAN 377-5208. Tel: 951-353-3658. FAX: 951-353-3262. *Libr Serv Mgr,* Katherine Staab; E-mail: katherine.e.staab@kp.org
Library Holdings: Bk Vols 500
Wireless access

C LA SIERRA UNIVERSITY LIBRARY*, 4500 Riverwalk Pkwy, 92505-3344. SAN 333-8851. Tel: 951-785-2397. Circulation Tel: 951-785-2044. Interlibrary Loan Service Tel: 951-785-2403. Reference Tel: 951-785-2396. FAX: 951-785-2445. Web Site: www.lasierra.edu/library. *Dir,* Kitty Simmons; E-mail: ksimmons@lasierra.edu; *Ref Librn,* Jeffrey De Vries; E-mail: jdevries@lasierra.edu; *Ref Librn,* Hilda Smith; E-mail: hsmith@lasierra.edu; *Ref, Spec Coll Librn,* Michelle Rojas; E-mail: mrojas@lasierra.edu; *Tech Serv Librn,* Christina Viramontes; E-mail: cviramon@lasierra.edu; Staff 11 (MLS 5, Non-MLS 6)
Founded 1927. Enrl 2,000; Fac 100; Highest Degree: Doctorate
Jul 2016-Jun 2017. Mats Exp $422,413, Books $82,648, Per/Ser (Incl. Access Fees) $115,774, Electronic Ref Mat (Incl. Access Fees) $214,991, Presv $9,000
Library Holdings: e-books 139,619; e-journals 72,723; Bk Vols 218,855; Per Subs 742
Special Collections: Far Eastern Coll; History (W A Scharffenberg Coll); Library of American Civilization, micro; Library of English Literature, micro; Reformation History (William M Landeen Coll); Seventh Day Adventist Coll
Automation Activity & Vendor Info: (Acquisitions) Innovative Interfaces, Inc; (Cataloging) Innovative Interfaces, Inc; (Circulation) Innovative Interfaces, Inc; (ILL) Innovative Interfaces, Inc; (OPAC) Innovative Interfaces, Inc; (Serials) Innovative Interfaces, Inc
Wireless access
Partic in OCLC Online Computer Library Center, Inc; Statewide California Electronic Library Consortium
Open Mon-Thurs 8am-Midnight, Fri 8am-1pm, Sun 1pm-Midnight

J RIVERSIDE COMMUNITY COLLEGE DISTRICT*, Digital Library & Learning Resource Center, 4800 Magnolia Ave, 92506-1299. SAN 301-2530. Reference Tel: 951-222-8652. FAX: 951-328-3679. Web Site: library.rcc.edu. *Per/Ref Librn,* Linda Braiman; E-mail: linda.braiman@rcc.edu; *Network Serv,* Hayley Ashby; E-mail: hayley.ashby@rcc.edu; *Tech Serv,* Shannon Hammock; E-mail: shannon.hammock@rcc.edu; Staff 8 (MLS 8)
Founded 1919. Enrl 35,170; Fac 830; Highest Degree: Associate
Library Holdings: AV Mats 7,733; Bks on Deafness & Sign Lang 183; Bk Titles 121,346; Bk Vols 153,865; Per Subs 888; Talking Bks 30
Automation Activity & Vendor Info: (Acquisitions) Innovative Interfaces, Inc; (Cataloging) Innovative Interfaces, Inc; (Circulation) Innovative Interfaces, Inc; (Course Reserve) Innovative Interfaces, Inc; (ILL) Innovative Interfaces, Inc; (Media Booking) Innovative Interfaces, Inc; (OPAC) Innovative Interfaces, Inc; (Serials) Innovative Interfaces, Inc
Wireless access
Open Mon-Thurs 7:30am-9pm, Fri 7:30-4
Departmental Libraries:
MORENO VALLEY CAMPUS LIBRARY
See Separate Entry in Moreno Valley

GL RIVERSIDE COUNTY LAW LIBRARY*, Victor Miceli Law Library, 3989 Lemon St, 92501-4203. SAN 301-2549. Tel: 951-368-0368. Administration Tel: 951-368-0360. FAX: 951-368-0185. E-mail: lawlibrary.riverside@rclawlibrary.org. Web Site: www.rclawlibrary.org. *Dir,* Victoria Williamson; E-mail: victoria.williamson@rclawlibrary.org; *Admin Officer,* Lauren Patterson; Tel: 951-368-0361, E-mail: lauren.patterson@rclawlibrary.org; *Pub Serv Librn,* Vanessa Christman; Tel: 951-368-0365, E-mail: vanessa.christman@rclawlibrary.org; *Tech Serv Librn,* Margot McLaren; Tel: 951-368-0362, E-mail: techservices@rclawlibrary.org; Staff 5 (MLS 4, Non-MLS 1)
Founded 1941
Library Holdings: Bk Titles 6,043; Bk Vols 102,782
Special Collections: Municipal Codes. State Document Depository

Automation Activity & Vendor Info: (Acquisitions) SirsiDynix; (Cataloging) SirsiDynix; (Circulation) SirsiDynix; (OPAC) SirsiDynix; (Serials) SirsiDynix
Wireless access
Function: Ref & res
Publications: Bookmark; Brochure; The ABC's of the RCLL (CD)
Partic in SIRCULS
Open Mon-Thurs 8-7, Fri 8-5, Sat 9-1
Restriction: Non-circulating

P RIVERSIDE COUNTY LIBRARY SYSTEM*, 5840 Mission Blvd, 92509. Tel: 951-369-3003. FAX: 951-369-6801. TDD: 760-342-0185. Web Site: www.rivlib.info. *County Librn,* Barbara Howison; Staff 65.3 (MLS 33.7, Non-MLS 31.6)
Founded 1911. Pop 1,084,811; Circ 3,280,929
Library Holdings: Bk Vols 1,034,429; Per Subs 875
Automation Activity & Vendor Info: (Acquisitions) SirsiDynix; (Cataloging) SirsiDynix; (Circulation) SirsiDynix; (ILL) SirsiDynix; (OPAC) SirsiDynix; (Serials) SirsiDynix
Wireless access
Function: Adult bk club, Adult literacy prog, Art exhibits, Audiobks via web, Bilingual assistance for Spanish patrons, Bk club(s), Bks on cassette, Bks on CD, CD-ROM, Children's prog, Computer training, Computers for patron use, Electronic databases & coll, Family literacy, Free DVD rentals, Games & aids for people with disabilities, Holiday prog, Homebound delivery serv, Homework prog, ILL available, Internet access, Learning ctr, Magnifiers for reading, Mail & tel request accepted, Music CDs, Online cat, Online info literacy tutorials on the web & in blackboard, Online ref, Orientations, Outreach serv, Outside serv via phone, mail, e-mail & web, Photocopying/Printing, Preschool outreach, Prog for adults, Prog for children & young adult, Ref serv available, Senior computer classes, Senior outreach, Spoken cassettes & CDs, Spoken cassettes & DVDs, Story hour, Summer reading prog, Tax forms, Teen prog, Telephone ref, VHS videos, Wheelchair accessible, Workshops, Writing prog
Mem of Inland Library System
Open Mon-Fri 8-5

Branches: 35

ANZA LIBRARY, 57430 Mitchell Rd, Anza, 92539. Tel: 951-763-4216. FAX: 951-763-0657. Web Site: www.rivlib.info/website/branch-page-829/location/Anza. *Br Mgr,* Doreen Nagel
Open Mon & Fri 9-3, Tues-Thurs 9-7, Sat 10-2

CABAZON BRANCH, 50425 Carmen Ave, Cabazon, 92230, SAN 331-488X. Tel: 951-849-8234. FAX: 951-849-8237. Web Site: www.rivlib.info/website/branch-page-829/location/Cabazon. *Br Mgr,* Ted Conable
Library Holdings: Bk Vols 8,000
Open Mon, Tues & Thurs 10-6, Wed 10-8, Sat 10-4

CALIMESA LIBRARY, 974 Calimesa Blvd, Calimesa, 92320. Tel: 909-795-9807. FAX: 909-795-3198. Web Site: www.rivlib.info/website/branch-page-829/location/Calimesa. *Br Mgr,* Alyson Hamlin
Open Tues, Thurs & Fri 10-6, Wed 12-8, Sat 9-5

CANYON LAKE LIBRARY, 31516 Railroad Canyon Rd, Canyon Lake, 92587. Tel: 951-244-9181. FAX: 951-244-7382. Web Site: www.rivlib.info/website/branch-page-829/location/CanyonLake. *Br Mgr,* Amanda McLaughlin
Open Mon 10-7, Wed & Fri 10-6, Sat 10-3

CATHEDRAL CITY LIBRARY, 33520 Date Palm Dr, Cathedral City, 92234. Tel: 760-328-4262. FAX: 760-770-9828. Web Site: www.rivlib.info/website/branch-page-829/location/CathedralCity. *Br Mgr,* Kristin Lehigh
Open Mon, Tues, Thurs & Sat 10-6, Wed 12-8, Sun 1-5
Friends of the Library Group

COACHELLA LIBRARY, 1500 Sixth St, Coachella, 92236. Tel: 760-398-5148. FAX: 760-398-1068. Web Site: www.rivlib.info/website/branch-page-829/location/Coachella. *Br Mgr,* Veronica C Evans
Open Mon, Tues & Thurs 10-6, Wed 12-8, Sat 10-6

DESERT HOT SPRINGS LIBRARY, 11691 West Dr, Desert Hot Springs, 92240. Tel: 760-329-5926. FAX: 760-329-3593. Web Site: www.rivlib.info/website/branch-page-829/location/DesertHotSprings. *Br Mgr,* Alexis Brodie
Open Mon-Wed 10-6, Thurs 12-8, Sat 9-3

EASTVALE LIBRARY, 7447 Scholar Way, Corona, 92880-4019. Tel: 951-273-2025. FAX: 951-273-9442. Web Site: www.rivlib.info/website/branch-page-829/location/Eastvale. *Br Mgr,* Felicia Chien
Open Mon-Thurs 3-8, Fri 3-6, Sat 10-5

EL CERRITO LIBRARY, 7581 Rudell Rd, Corona, 92881. Tel: 951-270-5012. FAX: 951-270-5018. Web Site: www.rivlib.info/website/branch-page-829/location/ElCerrito. *Br Mgr,* Elizabeth Ram
Open Mon-Thurs 3-7, Sat 10-2

GLEN AVON LIBRARY, 9244 Galena St, Jurupa Valley, 92509. Tel: 951-685-8121. FAX: 951-685-7158. Web Site: www.rivlib.info/website/branch-page-829/location/GlenAvon. *Br Mgr,* Tracie Randolph
Open Mon, Tues & Thurs 10-6, Wed 12-8, Fri 1-5, Sat 10-2

HIGHGROVE LIBRARY, 530 W Center St, Highgrove, 92507. Tel: 951-682-1507. FAX: 951-321-4107. Web Site: www.rivlib.info/website/branch-page-829/location/Highgrove. *Br Mgr,* Louise Gutierrez
Open Tues-Thurs 10-6, Fri 12-6, Sat 10-3

HOME GARDENS LIBRARY, 3785 Neece St, Corona, 92879. Tel: 951-279-2148. FAX: 951-734-3170. Web Site: www.rivlib.info/website/branch-page-829/location/HomeGardens. *Br Mgr,* Nancy Reiter
Open Mon & Tues 12-8, Wed & Thurs 10-6, Fri & Sat 10-5, Sun 1-5

IDYLLWILD LIBRARY, 54401 Village Center Dr, Idyllwild, 92549. Tel: 951-659-2300. FAX: 951-659-2453. Web Site: www.rivlib.info/website/branch-page-829/location/Idyllwild. *Br Mgr,* Shannon Houlihan Ng
Open Mon & Wed 10-6, Tues 12-8, Thurs & Fri 12-5, Sat 10-4

INDIO LIBRARY, 200 Civic Ctr Mall, Indio, 92201. Tel: 760-347-2383. FAX: 760-347-3159. Web Site: www.rivlib.info/website/branch-page-829/location/Indio. *Br Mgr,* Casey Bowen
Open Mon 12-8, Tues-Thurs & Sat 10-6

LA QUINTA LIBRARY, 78-275 Calle Tampico, La Quinta, 92253. Tel: 760-564-4767. FAX: 760-771-0237. Web Site: www.rivlib.info/website/branch-page-829/location/LaQuinta. *Br Mgr,* Melissa Lundell
Open Mon-Thurs 10-7, Fri & Sat 10-6, Sun 12-4

LAKE ELSINORE LIBRARY, 600 W Graham, Lake Elsinore, 92530. Tel: 951-674-4517. FAX: 951-245-7715. Web Site: www.rivlib.info/website/branch-page-829/location/LakeElsinore. *Br Mgr,* Krystal Van Eyk
Open Mon, Wed & Thurs 10-6, Tues 11-7, Fri 10-5, Sat 10-2

LAKE TAMARISK LIBRARY, 43-880 Lake Tamarisk Dr, Desert Center, 92239. (Mail add: PO Box 260, Desert Center, 92239-0260). Tel: 760-227-3273. FAX: 760-227-0043. Web Site: www.rivlib.info/website/branch-page-829/location/LakeTamarisk. *Br Mgr,* Andrayah Jackson
Open Tues & Thurs 9-5, Sat 10-2

LAKESIDE LIBRARY, 32593 Riverside Dr, Lake Elsinore, 92530. Tel: 951-678-7083. FAX: 951-678-7018. Web Site: www.rivlib.info/website/branch-page-829/location/Lakeside. *Br Mgr,* Jennifer Hyde
Open Mon-Thurs 3-8, Sat 10-6, Sun 12-5

MEAD VALLEY, 21580 Oakwood St, Mead Valley, 92570. Tel: 951-943-4727. FAX: 951-943-4064. Web Site: www.rivlib.info/website/branch-page-829/location/MeadValley. *Br Mgr,* Karen Snider
Open Mon-Wed 10-6, Thurs 12-8, Fri 1-5, Sat 10-2

MECCA LIBRARY, 91-260 Ave 66, Mecca, 92254. Tel: 760-396-2363. FAX: 760-396-1503. Web Site: www.rivlib.info/website/branch-page-829/location/Mecca. *Br Mgr,* Miguel Guitron-Rodriguez
Open Mon-Thurs & Sat 10-6

NORCO LIBRARY, 3240 Hamner Ave, Ste 101B, Norco, 92860. Tel: 951-735-5329. FAX: 951-735-0263. Web Site: www.rivlib.info/website/branch-page-829/location/Norco. *Br Mgr,* Luz Wood
Open Mon-Thurs 10-8, Sat 10-4
Friends of the Library Group

NUVIEW LIBRARY, 29990 Lakeview Ave, Nuevo, 92567. Tel: 951-928-0769. FAX: 951-928-3360. Web Site: www.rivlib.info/website/branch-page-829/location/Nuview. *Br Mgr,* Eden Ovando
Open Mon & Tues 1-7, Wed 10-6, Thurs & Fri 1-6

PALM DESERT LIBRARY, 73-300 Fred Waring Dr, Palm Desert, 92260. Tel: 760-346-6552. Web Site: www.rivlib.info/website/branch-page-829/location/PalmDesert. *Br Mgr,* Julia Schumacher
Open Mon-Thurs 10-8, Fri & Sat 10-5, Sun 1-5

PALOMA VALLEY LIBRARY, 31375 Bradley Rd, Menifee, 92584. Tel: 951-301-3682. FAX: 951-301-8423. Web Site: www.rivlib.info/website/branch-page-829/location/PalomaValley. *Br Mgr,* Eden Ovando
Open Mon-Wed 12-7, Thurs 12-5, Sat 10-2

PERRIS LIBRARY, 163 E San Jacinto, Perris, 92570. Tel: 951-657-2358. FAX: 951-657-9849. Web Site: www.rivlib.info/website/branch-page-829/location/Perris. *Br Mgr,* Tyler Klaas
Open Mon & Thurs-Sat 10-6, Tues & Wed 12-8, Sun 1-5

LOUIS ROBIDOUX LIBRARY, 5840 Mission Blvd, Jurupa Valley, 92509. Tel: 951-682-5485. FAX: 951-682-8641. Web Site: www.rivlib.info/website/branch-page-829/location/Robidoux. *Br Mgr,* Joan Tyler; Staff 3.7 (MLS 1, Non-MLS 2.7)
Founded 1948
Function: Adult bk club, Bilingual assistance for Spanish patrons, Bks on CD, Children's prog, Computer training, Computers for patron use, Electronic databases & coll, Free DVD rentals, ILL available, Music CDs, Online cat, Online ref, OverDrive digital audio bks, Photocopying/Printing, Prog for children & young adult, Ref serv available, Story hour, Summer reading prog, Tax forms, Teen prog, Telephone ref, Wheelchair accessible
Open Mon-Wed, Fri & Sat 10-6, Thurs 12-8, Sun 1-5
Restriction: ID required to use computers (Ltd hrs), In-house use for visitors
Friends of the Library Group

ROMOLAND LIBRARY, 26001 Briggs Rd, Menifee, 92585. Tel: 951-325-2090. FAX: 951-926-7989. Web Site: www.rivlib.info/website/branch-page-829/location/Romoland. *Br Mgr,* Armando Nantanapibul
Open Mon-Thurs 3-7, Sat 10-2

SAN JACINTO LIBRARY, 595 S San Jacinto Ave, Ste B, San Jacinto, 92583. Tel: 951-654-8635. Web Site: www.rivlib.info/website/branch-page-829/location/SanJacinto. *Site Supvr,* Trevor Drown; Staff 1 (MLS 1)
Open Mon & Fri 10-6, Tues-Thurs 10-7, Sat 9-2
Friends of the Library Group

SUN CITY LIBRARY, 26982 Cherry Hills Blvd, Menifee, 92586. Tel: 951-679-3534. FAX: 951-672-8293. Web Site: www.rivlib.info/website/branch-page-829/location/SunCity. *Br Mgr,* Elizabeth Baiz
Open Mon, Wed & Fri 10-6, Tues & Thurs 11-7, Sat 9-3, Sun 12-4

TEMECULA - GRACE MELLMAN LIBRARY, 41000 County Center Dr, Temecula, 92591. Tel: 951-296-3893. FAX: 951-296-0229. Web Site: www.rivlib.info/website/branch-page-829/location/TemeculaGraceMellman. *Br Mgr,* Kim Christofferson
Open Mon & Tues 11-7, Wed & Thurs 10-6, Fri & Sat 1-5

TEMECULA PUBLIC LIBRARY, 30600 Pauba Rd, Temecula, 92592. Tel: 951-693-8900. FAX: 951-693-8997. Web Site: www.rivlib.info/website/branch-page-829/location/TemeculaPublicLibrary. *Br Mgr,* Rosie Vanderhaak
Open Mon-Thurs 10-9, Fri 10-6, Sat 10-5, Sun 1-5

THOUSAND PALMS LIBRARY, 31189 Robert Rd, Thousand Palms, 92276. Tel: 760-343-1556. FAX: 760-343-0957. Web Site: www.rivlib.info/website/branch-page-829/location/ThousandPalms. *Br Mgr,* Lara Reyes
Open Mon, Tues & Thurs 10-6, Wed 10-8, Sat 10-4

VALLE VISTA LIBRARY, 25757 Fairview Ave, Hemet, 92544. Tel: 951-927-2611. FAX: 951-927-7902. Web Site: www.rivlib.info/website/branch-page-829/location/ValleVista. *Br Mgr,* Ashley Horton
Open Mon & Wed 10-7, Tues & Thurs 10-6, Fri 10-5, Sat 10-2

WILDOMAR LIBRARY, 34303 Mission Trail, Wildomar, 92595. Tel: 951-471-3855. FAX: 951-471-0188. Web Site: www.rivlib.info/website/branch-page-829/location/Wildomar. *Br Mgr,* Sandra Brautigam
Open Mon 12-8, Tues-Fri 10-6, Sat 10-3
Friends of the Library Group

WOODCREST LIBRARY, 16625 Krameria, 92504. Tel: 951-789-7324. FAX: 951-789-2812. Web Site: www.rivlib.info/website/branch-page-829/location/Woodcrest. *Br Mgr,* Connie Rynning
Closed for renovations from Aug 2019 until Spring of 2020

Bookmobiles: 2

RIVERSIDE PUBLIC LIBRARY*, Orange Terrace Branch, 20010-B Orange Terrace Pkwy, 92508. Tel: 951-826-2184. *Br Supvr,* Hayden Birkett; E-mail: hbirkett@riversideca.gov
Wireless access
Open Tues-Thurs 12-6, Fri & Sat 11-5

RIVERSIDE PUBLIC LIBRARY*, Arlanza Branch, 8267 Philbin Ave, 92503. Tel: 951-826-2217. *Br Supvr,* Joseph Garcia; E-mail: jagarcia@riversideca.gov
Wireless access
Open Tues-Thurs 12-6, Fri & Sat 11-5

P RIVERSIDE PUBLIC LIBRARY*, 3900 Mission Inn Ave, 92501. (Mail add: PO Box 468, 92502-0468), SAN 333-8886. Tel: 951-826-5201. Administration Tel: 951-826-5213. FAX: 951-788-1528. Administration FAX: 951-826-5407. E-mail: RPLLibrary@riversideca.gov. Web Site: www.riversideca.gov/library. *Libr Dir,* Erin Christmas; E-mail: Echristmas@riversideca.gov; *Admin Serv Mgr,* George Guzman; E-mail: gguzman@riversideca.gov; *Libr Supvr,* Jessica Herdina; E-mail: jherdina@riversideca.gov; Staff 73 (MLS 17, Non-MLS 56)
Founded 1888. Pop 291,398; Circ 1,060,244
Library Holdings: AV Mats 36,500; Bk Vols 522,459; Per Subs 997
Special Collections: Black History Coll; Genealogy Coll; Historical Children's Books (Dorothy Daniels Memorial Coll); Local History Coll; Mexican American Coll; Sight Handicapped Coll, bks, cassettes, per
Automation Activity & Vendor Info: (Cataloging) Innovative Interfaces, Inc; (Circulation) Innovative Interfaces, Inc; (ILL) Innovative Interfaces, Inc; (OPAC) Innovative Interfaces, Inc
Wireless access
Function: Adult literacy prog, Archival coll, Bks on cassette, Bks on CD, Children's prog, Computers for patron use, Digital talking bks, Electronic databases & coll, Home delivery & serv to seniorr ctr & nursing homes, Homebound delivery serv, ILL available, Magnifiers for reading, Music CDs, Online cat, Photocopying/Printing, Prog for adults, Prog for children & young adult, Spoken cassettes & CDs, Spoken cassettes & DVDs, Story hour, Summer reading prog, Teen prog, VHS videos, Wheelchair accessible
Mem of Inland Library System
Special Services for the Deaf - Bks on deafness & sign lang; Closed caption videos; Coll on deaf educ; Staff with knowledge of sign lang; TDD equip; TTY equip
Special Services for the Blind - Home delivery serv; Large print bks
Open Mon-Thurs 10-9, Fri & Sat 10-6, Sun 12-5
Friends of the Library Group

Branches: 5

ARLINGTON, 9556 Magnolia Ave, 92503-3698, SAN 333-8916. Tel: 951-826-2291. FAX: 951-689-6612. *Br Supvr,* Nancy Walker; E-mail: nwalker@riversideca.gov; Staff 1 (MLS 1)
Library Holdings: Bk Vols 50,815
Open Tues-Thurs 12-6, Fri & Sat 11-5
Friends of the Library Group

SPC JESUS D DURAN EASTSIDE LIBRARY, 4033-C Chicago Ave, 92507. Tel: 951-826-2235. *Libr Supvr,* Yesenia Littlefield; E-mail: ylittlefield@riversideca.gov; Staff 1 (MLS 1)
Library Holdings: Bk Vols 9,920
Open Tues-Thurs 12-6, Fri & Sat 11-5

LA SIERRA, 4600 La Sierra Ave, 92505-2722, SAN 333-9181. Tel: 951-826-2461. *Br Supvr,* Isabel Guzman; E-mail: iguzman@riversideca.gov; Staff 1 (MLS 1)
Library Holdings: Bk Vols 77,925
Open Mon-Thurs 11-7, Fri & Sat 10-6
Friends of the Library Group

SSGT SALVADOR J LARA CASA BLANCA LIBRARY, 2985 Madison St, 92504-4480, SAN 333-8940. Tel: 951-826-2120. FAX: 951-826-2120. *Supvr,* Jon Andersen; E-mail: jandersen@riversideca.gov
Library Holdings: Bk Vols 45,681
Open Tues-Thurs 12-6, Fri & Sat 11-5
Friends of the Library Group

MARCY BRANCH, 6927 Magnolia Ave, 92506, SAN 333-9270. Tel: 951-826-2078. *Br Supvr,* Position Currently Open
Library Holdings: Bk Vols 42,451
Open Tues-Thurs 12-6, Fri & Sat 11-5
Friends of the Library Group

C UNIVERSITY OF CALIFORNIA, RIVERSIDE, Tomas Rivera Library, 900 University Ave, 92521. (Mail add: PO Box 5900, 92517-5900). Tel: 951-827-3220. Web Site: library.ucr.edu/libraries/tomas-rivera-library. *Univ Librn,* Steven Mandeville-Gamble; *Assoc Dir, Develop,* Jernine McBride; *Assoc UniveLibrn for Content & Discovery,* Tiffany Moxham; *Assoc Univ Librn for the Digital Library,* Kevin Comerford; *Head, Access Serv,* Vincent Novoa; *Innovative Media Librn,* Alvaro Alvarez; *Metadata & Discovery Librn,* Jessica Kruppa; *Metadata & Media Cataloging Librn,* Yoko Kudo; *Univ Programs Teaching Librn,* Judy Lee; *Circ & Reserves Mgr,* Sahra Missaghieh Klawitter; *Collection Maintenance Mgr,* Michelle Gipson; *Collection Strategies Services Coord,* Pam Sun; *Course Reserves Coord,* Joanne Austin; *ILL Coordr,* Bernice Ridgeway; *ILL Coordr,* Sabrina Simmons; *Reserves Streaming Coord,* Philip Chiu
Founded 1954
Library Holdings: Bk Vols 2,000,000
Special Collections: African American Life & Culture Coll; Chicano/Latino Studies Coll; Children's & Young Adult Literature; Chinese & Asian Studies Coll; Chinese Literature & History (Prof Paul Chou Coll); Coll of Citrus Labels Coll; Greek Onomastics & Epigraphy Coll; Higher Education Administration & Policy Coll, abstracts, journals; History of Inland Southern California Coll; Japanese Hip Hop (Dexter Thomas Jr Coll); Latin American & Iberian Music Coll, bks, pers, rec, scores; Latin American & Iberian Studies Coll; Music Coll, bks, journals, media, rec, scores; Native American Studies Coll, archival mats, art objects, audio rec, pamphlets, slides; Photography Coll, bks, exhibition cats, negatives, pers, prints, reproductions; Science Fiction & Fantasy (Eaton Coll); Sikh Studies (W H McLeod Coll); Vietnam & Southeast Asian Studies Coll
Subject Interests: Arts, Humanities, Soc sci
Wireless access
Partic in California Digital Library; OCLC Online Computer Library Center, Inc

Departmental Libraries:
RAYMOND L ORBACH SCIENCE LIBRARY, 900 University Ave, 92521. (Mail add: PO Box 5900, 92517-5900). Tel: 951-827-3701. Web Site: library.ucr.edu/libraries/orbach-science-library. *Circulation/Reserves Services Mgr,* Sahra Missaghieh Klawitter; *Circ Serv Coordr,* Elisha Hankins; *Access Serv Asst,* Lori Alaniz; *Circulation/Course Reserves Asst,* Peter Reyna; Staff 20 (MLS 15, Non-MLS 5)
Founded 1998
Subject Interests: Agr, Engr, Life sci, Med, Phys sci
Open Mon-Thurs 7:30am-10pm, Fri 8-5, Sat 7:30-5, Sun 1pm-9pm
SPECIAL COLLECTIONS & UNIVERSITY ARCHIVES, 900 University Ave, 92521. (Mail add: PO Box 5900, 92517-5900). Tel: 951-827-3233. Web Site: library.ucr.edu/libraries/special-collections-university-archives. *Director, Distinctive Collections,* Cherry Williams; *Coll Mgt Librn,* Jessica Geiser; *Commun Engagement Librn, Special Colls Public Services,* Sandy Enriquez; *Special Collections Public Services Coord,* Karen Raines; *Univ Archivist,* Andrea Hoff; *Special Colls Processing Archivist,* Andrew Lippert
Special Collections: Manuscript Coll, artifacts, correspondence, diaries, doc, maps, photog, rec; Rare Books Coll; Science Fiction & Fantasy (Eaton Coll); University Archives; Water Resources Coll & Archives, bks, maps, photog, tech reports
Open Mon-Fri 10-4

ROCKLIN

J SIERRA JOINT COMMUNITY COLLEGE DISTRICT*, Learning Resource Center, 5100 Sierra College Blvd, 95677. SAN 301-2565. Tel: 916-660-7230. Reference Tel: 916-660-7232. FAX: 916-630-4539. E-mail: library@sierracollege.libanswers.com. Web Site: sierracollege.edu/library/. *Dean,* Sabrina Pape; Tel: 916-660-7201; *Coll Develop, Ref Serv,* Tina Sixt; *Librn,* Kacey Bullock
Founded 1914
Library Holdings: Bk Titles 90,000; Per Subs 189
Subject Interests: Calif, Mining
Automation Activity & Vendor Info: (Cataloging) Ex Libris Group; (Circulation) Ex Libris Group; (Course Reserve) Ex Libris Group; (OPAC) Ex Libris Group
Wireless access
Friends of the Library Group

ROHNERT PARK

P SONOMA COUNTY LIBRARY*, 6135 State Farm Dr, 94928. SAN 335-0401. Tel: 707-545-0831. Web Site: www.sonomalibrary.org. *Libr Dir,* Ann Hammond; E-mail: director@sonomalibrary.org; *Asst to the Dir,* Jaylene Demapan; E-mail: jdemapan@sonomalibrary.org; Staff 128.3 (MLS 54.5, Non-MLS 73.8)
Founded 1965. Pop 481,785; Circ 263,554
Library Holdings: AV Mats 21,347; Bk Vols 721,629; Per Subs 1,758
Special Collections: Sonoma County History; Sonoma County Wine Library. State Document Depository; US Document Depository
Automation Activity & Vendor Info: (Acquisitions) Horizon; (Cataloging) Horizon; (Circulation) Horizon; (ILL) SirsiDynix; (OPAC) SirsiDynix; (Serials) Horizon
Wireless access
Function: Adult bk club, Adult literacy prog, After school storytime, Art exhibits, Audiobks via web, Children's prog, E-Reserves, Family literacy, ILL available, Photocopying/Printing, Prog for adults, Prog for children & young adult, Summer reading prog, Tax forms
Mem of NorthNet Library System
Special Services for the Deaf - TDD equip
Open Mon-Fri 8-5
Friends of the Library Group
Branches: 15
CENTRAL SANTA ROSA LIBRARY, 211 E St, Santa Rosa, 95404, SAN 376-8988. Tel: 707-308-3020. E-mail: central@sonomalibrary.org. Web Site: sonomalibrary.org/locations/central-santa-rosa-library. *Br Mgr,* Kate Keaton
Library Holdings: Bk Vols 173,919
Open Mon & Wed 10-9, Tues & Thurs-Sat 10-6, Sun 2-6
Friends of the Library Group
CLOVERDALE REGIONAL LIBRARY, 401 N Cloverdale Blvd, Cloverdale, 95425, SAN 376-8996. Tel: 707-894-5271. E-mail: cloverdale@sonomalibrary.org. Web Site: sonomalibrary.org/locations/cloverdale-regional-library. *Br Mgr,* Donna Romeo; Staff 5 (MLS 2, Non-MLS 3)
Library Holdings: Bk Titles 21,603
Open Mon & Wed 10-9, Tues & Thurs-Sat 10-6
Friends of the Library Group
FORESTVILLE LIBRARY, 7050 Covey Rd, Forestville, 95436, SAN 376-9097. Tel: 707-887-7654. E-mail: forestville@sonomalibrary.org. Web Site: sonomalibrary.org/locations/forestville-library. *Interim Br Mgr,* Ana Dawe; Staff 1 (Non-MLS 1)
Library Holdings: Bk Titles 4,152
Open Mon-Fri 3-6:30
Friends of the Library Group
GUERNEVILLE REGIONAL LIBRARY, 14107 Armstrong Woods Rd, Guerneville, 95446, SAN 376-9003. Tel: 707-869-9004. E-mail: guerneville@sonomalibrary.org. Web Site: sonomalibrary.org/locations/guerneville-regional-library. *Interim Br Mgr,* Ana Dawe
Library Holdings: Bk Titles 23,063
Open Mon & Wed 10-9, Tues & Thurs-Sat 10-6
Friends of the Library Group
HEALDSBURG REGIONAL LIBRARY, 139 Piper St, Healdsburg, 95448, SAN 376-9011. Tel: 707-433-3772. E-mail: healdsburg@sonomalibrary.org. Web Site: sonomalibrary.org/locations/healdsburg-regional-library. *Br Mgr,* John Haupt; E-mail: jhaupt@sonomalibrary.org; Staff 7 (MLS 4, Non-MLS 3)
Library Holdings: Bk Titles 44,377
Special Collections: Sonoma County Wine Library
Open Mon & Wed 10-9, Tues & Thurs-Sat 10-6
Friends of the Library Group
NORTHWEST SANTA ROSA LIBRARY, 150 Coddingtown Ctr, Santa Rosa, 95401, SAN 376-9046. Tel: 707-546-2265. E-mail: northwest@sonomalibrary.org. Web Site: sonomalibrary.org/locations/northwest-santa-rosa-library. *Br Mgr,* Lara Mayelian
Library Holdings: Bk Titles 36,918
Open Mon & Wed 10-9, Tues & Thurs-Sat 10-6
Friends of the Library Group
OCCIDENTAL LIBRARY, 73 Main St, Occidental, 95465, SAN 376-9100. Tel: 707-874-3080. E-mail: occidental@sonomalibrary.org. Web Site: sonomalibrary.org/locations/occidental-library. *Interim Br Mgr,* Ana Dawe
Library Holdings: Bk Titles 2,394
Open Mon-Wed & Sat 12-5
Friends of the Library Group
PETALUMA REGIONAL LIBRARY, 100 Fairgrounds Dr, Petaluma, 94952, SAN 376-902X. Tel: 707-763-9801. E-mail: petaluma@sonomalibrary.org. Web Site: sonomalibrary.org/locations/petaluma-regional-library. *Br Mgr,* Joe Cochrane
Library Holdings: Bk Titles 87,809
Special Collections: Petaluma History Room
Open Mon & Wed 10-9, Tues & Thurs-Sat 10-6
Friends of the Library Group
RINCON VALLEY LIBRARY, 6959 Montecito Blvd, Santa Rosa, 95409, SAN 376-9054. Tel: 707-537-0162. E-mail: rinconvalley@sonomalibrary.org. Web Site: sonomalibrary.org/locations/rincon-valley-library. *Br Mgr,* Bill Coolidge
Library Holdings: Bk Titles 48,229
Open Mon & Wed 10-9, Tues & Thurs-Sat 10-6
Friends of the Library Group
ROHNERT PARK-COTATI REGIONAL LIBRARY, 6250 Lynne Conde Way, 94928, SAN 376-9038. Tel: 707-584-9121. E-mail: rohnertpark@sonomalibrary.org. Web Site: sonomalibrary.org/locations/rohnert-park-cotati-regional-library. *Interim Br Mgr,* Phil Lynn Hoeft
Library Holdings: Bk Titles 80,595
Open Mon & Wed 10-9, Tues & Thurs-Sat 10-6
Friends of the Library Group
ROSELAND COMMUNITY LIBRARY, 470 Sebastopol Rd, Santa Rosa, 95407. Tel: 707-755-2029. E-mail: roseland@sonomalibrary.org. *Br Mgr,* Kate Keaton
Open Mon, Tues, Thurs & Fri 10-2, Wed 6pm-9pm, Sat 10-6
Friends of the Library Group
SEBASTOPOL REGIONAL LIBRARY, 7140 Bodega Ave, Sebastopol, 95472, SAN 376-9062. Tel: 707-823-7691. E-mail: sebastopol@sonomalibrary.org. Web Site: sonomalibrary.org/locations/sebastopol-regional-library. *Br Mgr,* Matthew Rose; Staff 7 (MLS 3, Non-MLS 4)
Library Holdings: Bk Titles 49,346
Special Collections: Municipal Document Depository
Open Mon & Wed 10-9, Tues & Thurs-Sat 10-6
Friends of the Library Group
SONOMA COUNTY HISTORY & GENEALOGY LIBRARY, 725 Third St, Santa Rosa, 95404. Tel: 707-308-3212. E-mail: history@sonomalibrary.org. *Br Mgr,* Katherine J Rinehart
Open Mon-Sat 10-6
SONOMA VALLEY REGIONAL LIBRARY, 755 W Napa St, Sonoma, 95476, SAN 376-9070. Tel: 707-996-5217. E-mail: sonomavalley@sonomalibrary.org. Web Site: sonomalibrary.org/locations/sonoma-valley-regional-library. *Interim Br Mgr,* Diana Spaulding; Staff 3 (MLS 3)
Library Holdings: Bk Titles 39,091
Open Mon & Wed 10-9, Tues & Thurs-Sat 10-6
Friends of the Library Group

WINDSOR REGIONAL LIBRARY, Bldg 100, 9291 Old Redwood Hwy, Windsor, 95492, SAN 376-9089. Tel: 707-838-1020. E-mail: windsor@sonomalibrary.org. Web Site: sonomalibrary.org/locations/windsor-regional-library. *Br Mgr,* Aleta Dimas; Staff 6 (MLS 2, Non-MLS 4)
Founded 1996
Library Holdings: Bk Titles 33,374
Open Mon & Wed 10-9, Tues & Thurs-Sat 10-6
Friends of the Library Group

C SONOMA STATE UNIVERSITY LIBRARY*, Jean & Charles Schulz Information Center, 1801 E Cotati Ave, 94928. SAN 301-2573. Tel: 707-664-2375. Administration Tel: 707-664-2397. FAX: 707-664-2090. Web Site: library.sonoma.edu. *Dean,* Karen Schneider; E-mail: karen.schneider@sonoma.edu; *Access Serv, Interim Asst Dean, Tech Serv,* Jonathan Smith; E-mail: jonathan.smith@sonoma.edu; *Coll Develop Librn,* Mary Wegmann; Tel: 707-664-3983, E-mail: mary.wegmann@sonoma.edu; *Mgr Digital Initiatives,* Julie Dinkins; Tel: 707-664-4077, E-mail: dinkins@sonoma.edu; *Coordr, ILL,* Dawnelle Lynn Ricciardi; Tel: 707-664-2877, E-mail: dawnell.ricciardi@sonoma.edu; Staff 11 (MLS 11)
Founded 1961. Enrl 7,500; Fac 300; Highest Degree: Master
Library Holdings: Bk Vols 560,000
Special Collections: Celtic Coll; North Bay Regional Information Center; Small California Press
Automation Activity & Vendor Info: (Acquisitions) Innovative Interfaces, Inc; (Cataloging) Innovative Interfaces, Inc; (Circulation) Innovative Interfaces, Inc; (OPAC) OCLC
Wireless access
Friends of the Library Group

ROLLING HILLS ESTATES

P PALOS VERDES LIBRARY DISTRICT*, Peninsula Center Library, 701 Silver Spur Rd, 90274. SAN 333-5550. Tel: 310-377-9584. Circulation Tel: 310-377-9584, Ext 602. Interlibrary Loan Service Tel: 310-377-9584, Ext 239. Reference Tel: 310-377-9584, Ext 601. Administration Tel: 310-377-9584, Ext 245. Automation Services Tel: 310-377-9584, Ext 258. FAX: 310-541-6807. E-mail: info@pvld.org. Web Site: www.pvld.org. *Dir,* Jennifer Addington; E-mail: jaddington@pvld.org; *Mgr, Ad Serv,* Sylvia Richardson; Tel: 310-377-9584, Ext 210, E-mail: srichardson@pvld.org; *Mgr, Circ & Customer Serv,* Eve Wittenmyer; Tel: 310-377-9584, Ext 263, E-mail: ewittenmyer@pvld.org; *Mgr, Digital Serv & Mkt,* David Campbell; Tel: 310-377-9584, Ext 284, E-mail: dcampbell@pvld.org; *Mgr, Tech Serv,* Mary Cohen; Tel: 310-377-9584, Ext 242, E-mail: mcohen@pvld.org; *Mgr, Young Readers,* Laura Henry; Tel: 310-377-9584, Ext 206, E-mail: lhenry@pvld.org; Staff 38 (MLS 29, Non-MLS 9)
Founded 1928. Pop 67,500; Circ 988,452
Jul 2014-Jun 2015 Income (Main & Associated Libraries) $7,445,100, State $20,000, Locally Generated Income $6,728,400, Other $696,700. Mats Exp $520,300, Books $219,400, Per/Ser (Incl. Access Fees) $36,200, Other Print Mats $17,500, Micro $4,500, AV Mat $72,700, Electronic Ref Mat (Incl. Access Fees) $170,000. Sal $5,717,900
Library Holdings: Audiobooks 8,302; CDs 7,335; DVDs 12,275; e-books 14,000; e-journals 13,780; Electronic Media & Resources 3,410; Large Print Bks 6,013; Music Scores 1,118; Bk Vols 224,000; Per Subs 650; Talking Bks 8,302; Videos 12,275
Special Collections: Oral History
Subject Interests: Art, Genealogy, Investing, Local hist, Travel
Automation Activity & Vendor Info: (Acquisitions) Innovative Interfaces, Inc - Millennium; (Cataloging) Innovative Interfaces, Inc - Millennium; (Circulation) Innovative Interfaces, Inc - Millennium; (ILL) Innovative Interfaces, Inc - Millennium; (OPAC) Innovative Interfaces, Inc - Millennium; (Serials) Innovative Interfaces, Inc - Millennium
Wireless access
Function: Adult bk club, Art exhibits, Bk club(s), Bks on CD, Chess club, Children's prog, Computers for patron use, Digital talking bks, Electronic databases & coll, Holiday prog, Homebound delivery serv, ILL available, Internet access, Notary serv, Online cat, Outside serv via phone, mail, e-mail & web, OverDrive digital audio bks, Passport agency, Photocopying/Printing, Preschool outreach, Prog for adults, Prog for children & young adult, Ref serv available, Summer reading prog, Tax forms, Telephone ref, Wheelchair accessible, Workshops
Publications: Friends of the Library Newsletter (Quarterly); Library Update
Partic in Southern California Library Cooperative
Special Services for the Deaf - ADA equip
Special Services for the Blind - Audio mat; Bks on cassette; Bks on CD; Free checkout of audio mat; Home delivery serv; Large print bks; Ref serv; Talking bks; Videos on blindness & physical disabilties
Open Mon-Thurs 9-8, Fri 9-6, Sat 10-5, Sun 1-5
Restriction: Vols & interns use only
Friends of the Library Group
Branches: 2
MALAGA COVE, 2400 Via Campesina, Palos Verdes Estates, 90274-3662, SAN 333-5585. Tel: 310-377-9584, Ext 551. FAX: 310-373-7594. *Br Mgr,* Eve Wittenmyer; Tel: 310-377-9584, Ext 263, E-mail: ewittenmyer@pvld.org; Staff 5 (MLS 1, Non-MLS 4)
Automation Activity & Vendor Info: (ILL) OCLC ILLiad
Open Mon-Sat 10-5
Friends of the Library Group
MIRALESTE, 29089 Palos Verdes Dr E, Rancho Palos Verdes, 90275, SAN 333-5615. Tel: 310-377-9584, Ext 452. FAX: 310-547-4067. *Br Mgr,* Eve Wittenmyer; E-mail: ewittenmyer@pvld.org; Staff 2 (MLS 2)
Library Holdings: Bk Titles 38,500; Bk Vols 40,687
Open Mon-Fri 11-6, Sat 10-5
Friends of the Library Group

ROSEMEAD

J DON BOSCO TECHNICAL INSTITUTE*, Lee Memorial Library, 1151 San Gabriel Blvd, 91770. SAN 301-2581. Tel: 626-940-2000. FAX: 626-940-2001. E-mail: generalinfo@boscotech.edu. Web Site: www.boscotech.edu.
Founded 1957
Library Holdings: Bk Titles 7,500; Bk Vols 9,500; Per Subs 30
Subject Interests: Art, Relig
Automation Activity & Vendor Info: (Cataloging) Follett Software; (Circulation) Follett Software
Open Mon-Fri 7:30-5
Friends of the Library Group

ROSEVILLE

P ROSEVILLE PUBLIC LIBRARY*, 225 Taylor St, 95678-2681. SAN 333-9815. Tel: 916-774-5221. FAX: 916-773-5594. E-mail: library@roseville.ca.us. Web Site: www.roseville.ca.us. *City Librn,* Natasha Martin; *Librn II,* Karen Holt; Staff 24 (MLS 6, Non-MLS 18)
Founded 1912. Pop 95,000
Library Holdings: Bk Titles 109,000; Bk Vols 159,000; Per Subs 474
Special Collections: Local History, photogs. Oral History
Subject Interests: Railroads
Automation Activity & Vendor Info: (Acquisitions) SirsiDynix; (Cataloging) SirsiDynix; (Circulation) SirsiDynix; (OPAC) SirsiDynix
Wireless access
Partic in Suburban Library Cooperative
Open Mon-Wed 10-7, Thurs & Sat 10-5
Friends of the Library Group
Branches: 2
MAIDU, 1530 Maidu Dr, 95661, SAN 333-984X. Tel: 916-774-5900. FAX: 916-773-0972.
Founded 1990. Pop 11,000
Library Holdings: Bk Vols 48,365; Per Subs 116
Open Mon-Thurs 10-8 (10-7 Summer), Fri & Sat 10-5
Friends of the Library Group
MARTHA RILEY COMMUNITY LIBRARY, Mahany Park, 1501 Pleasant Grove Blvd, 95747.
Open Mon-Wed 10-7, Thurs & Sat 10-5
Bookmobiles: 1

M SUTTER ROSEVILLE MEDICAL CENTER LIBRARY*, One Medical Plaza, 95661-3037. SAN 301-2603. Tel: 916-781-1580. *Med Librn,* Heidi J Mortensen-Torres; E-mail: mortenh@sutterhealth.org; Staff 1 (MLS 1)
Founded 1968
Library Holdings: Bk Titles 1,000; Per Subs 140
Special Collections: Medical Coll
Subject Interests: Surgery
Function: Health sci info serv, ILL available, Internet access, Photocopying/Printing, Ref serv available, Telephone ref, Wheelchair accessible
Publications: Book Lists; Library Brochure
Partic in Medical Library Association; Northern California & Nevada Medical Library Group
Restriction: Circulates for staff only, In-house use for visitors, Non-circulating coll, Open to pub for ref only, Pub use on premises

SACRAMENTO

J AMERICAN RIVER COLLEGE LIBRARY*, 4700 College Oak Dr, 95841. SAN 333-9874. Tel: 916-484-8455. Reference Tel: 916-484-8458. Administration Tel: 916-484-8460. FAX: 916-484-8657. Web Site: www.arc.losrios.edu/student-resources/library. *Admin Serv, VPres,* Kuldeep Kaur; E-mail: kaurk@arc.losrios.edu; *Pub Serv Librn,* Dan Crump; E-mail: CrumpD@arc.losrios.edu; *Pub Serv Librn,* Sarah Lehmann; E-mail: LehmannS@arc.losrios.edu; *Pub Serv Librn,* David McCusker; E-mail: McCuskD@arc.losrios.edu; *Pub Serv Librn,* Deborah Ondricka; E-mail: OndricD@arc.losrios.edu; *Ref Serv,* Connie Ferrara; Staff 14 (MLS 7, Non-MLS 7)

Founded 1955. Enrl 31,675; Highest Degree: Associate
Library Holdings: AV Mats 6,409; Bk Titles 66,078; Bk Vols 75,976; Per Subs 411
Automation Activity & Vendor Info: (Acquisitions) Innovative Interfaces, Inc; (Cataloging) Innovative Interfaces, Inc; (Circulation) Innovative Interfaces, Inc; (Course Reserve) Innovative Interfaces, Inc; (ILL) Innovative Interfaces, Inc; (Media Booking) Innovative Interfaces, Inc; (OPAC) Innovative Interfaces, Inc; (Serials) Innovative Interfaces, Inc
Wireless access
Partic in OCLC Online Computer Library Center, Inc
Open Mon-Thurs 7:30am-10pm, Fri 7:30-5, Sat 9-3

SR BETHANY PRESBYTERIAN CHURCH LIBRARY*, 5624 24th St, 95822. SAN 301-262X. Tel: 916-428-5281. FAX: 916-428-3716. E-mail: office@bethpres.com. Web Site: www.bethpres.com.
Library Holdings: Bk Vols 1,000
Open Mon-Fri 9-3:30
Restriction: Mem only

GL CALIFORNIA COURT OF APPEAL*, Third Appellate District-Robert K Puglia Library, Mosk Library & Courts Bldg, Ste 501A, 914 Capitol Mall, 95814. SAN 301-2700. Tel: 916-654-0209. Administration Tel: 916-653-0207. Web Site: www.courts.ca.gov/3dca.htm. *Librn,* Holly Lakatos; E-mail: holly.lakatos@jud.ca.gov; Staff 2 (MLS 1, Non-MLS 1)
Founded 1906. Pop 150
Library Holdings: Bk Titles 1,500; Bk Vols 25,000; Per Subs 50
Special Collections: Court Archives; Robert K Puglia Papers
Subject Interests: Judiciary, Law, Legal hist
Automation Activity & Vendor Info: (Acquisitions) LibraryWorld, Inc; (Cataloging) LibraryWorld, Inc; (Circulation) LibraryWorld, Inc; (Discovery) LibraryWorld, Inc; (OPAC) LibraryWorld, Inc
Wireless access
Function: 24/7 Online cat, AV serv, Equip loans & repairs, Govt ref serv, ILL available, Mail & tel request accepted
Restriction: Authorized personnel only, By permission only, In-house use for visitors, Non-circulating to the pub, Open to pub by appt only, Open to researchers by request

S CALIFORNIA DEPARTMENT OF CONSERVATION, California Geological Survey Library, 801 K St, MS 14-34, 95814-3532. SAN 323-553X. Tel: 916-327-1850. FAX: 916-327-1853. E-mail: cgslibrary@conservation.ca.gov. Web Site: www.conservation.ca.gov/cgs/library. *Head Librn,* Amy Loseth; Staff 2 (MLS 1, Non-MLS 1)
Founded 1880
Library Holdings: Bk Vols 100,000; Per Subs 130
Special Collections: California Fieldtrip Guidebooks; Historic Mine Files & Maps; United States Bureau of Mines Publications; United States Geological Survey Publications
Automation Activity & Vendor Info: (Acquisitions) SirsiDynix-WorkFlows; (Cataloging) SirsiDynix-WorkFlows; (Circulation) SirsiDynix-WorkFlows; (Discovery) SirsiDynix-Enterprise; (ILL) OCLC WorldShare Interlibrary Loan; (OPAC) SirsiDynix-Enterprise; (Serials) SirsiDynix-WorkFlows
Open Mon-Thurs 9-12 & 1-4

S CALIFORNIA DEPARTMENT OF CORRECTIONS LIBRARY SYSTEM*, c/o The Office of Correctional Education, 1515 S St, 95814-7243. SAN 371-8026. FAX: 916-324-1416. Web Site: www.cdcr.ca.gov. *Libr Serv Adminr,* Brandy Buenafe; Tel: 916-322-2803, E-mail: brandy.buenafe@cdcr.ca.gov; Staff 141 (MLS 74, Non-MLS 67)
Library Holdings: Bk Vols 469,838; Per Subs 1,660
Partic in 49-99 Cooperative Library System

Branches:

AVENAL STATE PRISON, One Kings Way, Avenal, 93204. (Mail add: PO Box 8, Avenal, 93204-0008), SAN 371-8034. Tel: 559-386-0587. *Sr Librn,* Erin Farrell; E-mail: Erin.Farrell@cdcr.ca.gov
Library Holdings: Bk Vols 30,000
Restriction: Staff & inmates only

CALIFORNIA CORRECTIONAL CENTER, 711-045 Center Rd, Susanville, 96127. (Mail add: PO Box 790, Susanville, 96130-0790), SAN 371-8042. Tel: 530-257-2181. FAX: 530-252-3020. *Sr Librn,* Gabrielle Smith; Tel: 530-257-2181, Ext 4370, E-mail: gabrielle.smith@cdcr.ca.gov; *Librn,* Fawn Russell; E-mail: Fawn.Russell@cdcr.ca.gov; Staff 3 (MLS 3)
Library Holdings: Bk Vols 11,218
Restriction: Staff & inmates only

CALIFORNIA CORRECTIONAL INSTITUTION, 24900 Hwy 202, Tehachapi, 93561. (Mail add: PO Box 1031, Tehachapi, 93581-1031), SAN 301-6544. Tel: 661-822-4402. FAX: 661-823-3358, 661-823-5016. *Sr Librn,* Jewel Ludwigsen; Tel: 916-985-2561, Ext 4236, E-mail: Jewel.Lewigsen@cdcr.ca.gov; *Librn,* Kim Thomas; Tel: 681-822-4402, Ext 4447, E-mail: Kimberly.Thomas1@cdcr.ca.gov; Staff 6 (MLS 1, Non-MLS 5)
Library Holdings: Bk Vols 5,500; Per Subs 15
Subject Interests: Law
Restriction: Staff & inmates only

CALIFORNIA INSTITUTION FOR MEN, 14901 Central Ave, Chino, 91710. (Mail add: PO Box 128, Chino, 91708-0128), SAN 300-6654. Tel: 909-597-1821, Ext 4368. FAX: 909-606-7012. *Sr Librn,* Christina Tejada; E-mail: Christina.Tejada@cdcr.ca.gov; *Librn,* Nermine Hanna; E-mail: Nermine.Hanna@cdcr.ca.gov
Library Holdings: Bk Vols 15,000
Restriction: Staff & inmates only

CALIFORNIA INSTITUTION FOR WOMEN, 16756 Chino-Corona Rd, Corona, 92880, SAN 300-7723. Tel: 909-597-1771. FAX: 909-606-4936. *Sr Librn,* Laurie McConnell; Tel: 909-597-1771, Ext 6488, E-mail: Laurie.McConnell@cdcr.ca.gov; *Librn,* Clifford Bushin; Tel: 909-597-1771, Ext 7303, E-mail: Cliff.Bushin@cdcr.ca.gov
Founded 1952
Library Holdings: Bk Titles 30,000; Per Subs 24
Subject Interests: Women studies
Restriction: Staff & inmates only

CALIFORNIA MEDICAL FACILITY, 1600 California Dr, Vacaville, 95696. (Mail add: PO Box 2237, Vacaville, 95696-2237), SAN 335-2056. Tel: 707-448-6841. FAX: 707-449-6541. *Sr Librn,* Suzanna Marshak; E-mail: Elizabeth.Marshak@cdcr.ca.gov; *Librn,* Leovigildo Sanchez; Tel: 707-448-6841, Ext 2585, E-mail: Leovigildo.Sanchez@cdcr.ca.gov; Staff 2 (MLS 2)
Founded 1955
Restriction: Staff & inmates only

CALIFORNIA MEN'S COLONY-EAST, Colony Dr, Hwy 1, San Luis Obispo, 93409. (Mail add: PO Box 8101, San Luis Obispo, 93409), SAN 301-5122. Tel: 805-547-7185. FAX: 805-547-7517. *Sr Librn,* Patrick Maloney; E-mail: Patrick.Maloney@cdcr.ca.gov; *Librn,* Sharaya Olemida; Tel: 805-547-7900, Ext 4721, E-mail: Sharaya.Olemida@cdcr.ca.gov; *Librn,* Steven Sallberg; E-mail: Steven.Sallberg@cdcr.ca.gov; Staff 1 (MLS 1)
Founded 1961
Library Holdings: Bk Vols 25,000; Per Subs 125
Subject Interests: Law

CALIFORNIA MEN'S COLONY-WEST, Colony Dr, Hwy 1, San Luis Obispo, 93409. Tel: 805-547-7900, Ext 7185. FAX: 805-547-7792. *Sr Librn,* Patrick Moloney; E-mail: Patrick.Maloney@cdcr.ca.gov
Library Holdings: Bk Vols 25,000; Per Subs 65
Automation Activity & Vendor Info: (Cataloging) Winnebago Software Co; (Circulation) Winnebago Software Co; (OPAC) Winnebago Software Co
Open Mon-Fri 8-8, Sat & Sun 8-4

CALIFORNIA STATE PRISON, CORCORAN, 4001 King Ave, Corcoran, 93212. (Mail add: PO Box 8800, Corcoran, 93212-8800), SAN 371-8050. Tel: 559-992-8800, Ext 5888. FAX: 559-992-7354. *Sr Librn,* Margaret Lirones; E-mail: Margaret.Lirones@cdcr.ca.gov; *Librn,* Francis Hebert; E-mail: Frances.Hebert@cdcr.ca.gov
Restriction: Staff & inmates only

CALIFORNIA STATE PRISON, LOS ANGELES COUNTY, 44750 60th St W, Lancaster, 93536-7620. (Mail add: PO Box 8487, Lancaster, 93539-8487), SAN 375-5819. Tel: 661-729-2000. FAX: 661-729-6993. *Sr Librn,* Position Currently Open; *Librn,* Marva Augustus; Tel: 661-729-2000, Ext 6148, E-mail: Marva.Augustus@cdcr.ca.gov; Staff 1 (MLS 1)
Library Holdings: Bk Vols 27,000
Function: Legal assistance to inmates
Restriction: Staff & inmates only

CALIFORNIA STATE PRISON, SACRAMENTO, 100 Prison Rd, Represa, 95671. (Mail add: PO Box 290001, Represa, 95671), SAN 371-8069. Tel: 916-985-8610. FAX: 916-294-3128. *Sr Law Librn,* Andrea Hubbard; E-mail: andrea.hubbard@cdcr.ca.gov; *Librn,* Tanya Lindquist; Tel: 916-985-8610, Ext 6605, E-mail: Tanya.Lindquist@cdcr.ca.gov; *Librn,* Adrienna Turner; Tel: 916-985-8610, Ext 7781, E-mail: andrienna.Turner@cdcr.ca.gov. Subject Specialists: *Criminal law,* Andrea Hubbard; Staff 4 (MLS 3, Non-MLS 1)
Library Holdings: Bk Vols 28,000
Function: Adult bk club, Adult literacy prog, Doc delivery serv, Govt ref serv, ILL available, Legal assistance to inmates, Literacy & newcomer serv, Magazines, Magnifiers for reading, Photocopying/Printing, Ref serv available, Serves people with intellectual disabilities, Wheelchair accessible
Restriction: Staff & inmates only

CALIFORNIA STATE PRISON, SOLANO, 2100 Peabody Rd, Vacaville, 95696. (Mail add: PO Box 4000, Vacaville, 95696-4000), SAN 375-5789. Tel: 707-451-0182. FAX: 707-454-3244. *Sr Librn,* Position Currently Open; *Librn,* Christine Brown-Kitamura; Tel: 704-451-0182, Ext 3435, E-mail: Chris.Brown2@cdcr.ca.gov
Restriction: Staff & inmates only

CALIPATRIA STATE PRISON, 7018 Blair Rd, Calipatria, 92233. (Mail add: PO Box 5001, Calipatria, 92233-5001), SAN 371-8085. Tel: 760-348-7000. FAX: 760-348-6041. *Sr Librn,* Position Currently Open
Library Holdings: Bk Vols 20,000
Restriction: Staff & inmates only

CENTINELA STATE PRISON, 2302 Brown Rd, Imperial, 92251. (Mail add: PO Box 731, Imperial, 92251-0731), SAN 375-5827. Tel: 760-337-7900. FAX: 760-337-7631. *Sr Librn,* Position Currently Open; *Librn,* Joel Eanes; Tel: 760-337-7900, Ext 6158, E-mail: Joel.Eanes@cdcr.ca.gov
Library Holdings: Bk Vols 35,000
Restriction: Staff & inmates only

CENTRAL CALIFORNIA WOMEN'S FACILITY, 23370 Rd 22, Chowchilla, 93610. (Mail add: PO Box 1501, Chowchilla, 93610-1501), SAN 371-8093. Tel: 559-665-5531. FAX: 559-665-6037. *Sr Librn,* Robert Oldfield; Tel: 559-665-5531, Ext 7210, E-mail: Robert.Oldfield@cdcr.ca.gov; *Librn,* Garin A Gonzales; E-mail: Garin.Gonzales@cdcr.ca.gov; *Librn,* Clarke Jett; E-mail: Clarke.Jett@cdcr.ca.gov
Library Holdings: Bk Vols 25,000
Restriction: Staff & inmates only

CORRECTIONAL TRAINING FACILITY, Soledad Prison Rd, Hwy 101 N, Soledad, 93960. (Mail add: PO Box 686, Soledad, 93960-0686), SAN 301-6137. Tel: 831-678-3951. FAX: 831-678-5910. *Sr Librn,* Position Currently Open; *Librn,* Annissa Madison; E-mail: Annissa.Madison@cdcr.ca.gov; *Librn,* Marisa Martinez; Tel: 831-678-3951, Ext 5872, E-mail: Marisa.Martinez@cdcr.ca.gov
Restriction: Staff & inmates only

RICHARD J DONOVAN CORRECTIONAL FACILITY AT ROCK MOUNTAIN, 480 Alta Rd, San Diego, 92179, SAN 371-814X. Tel: 619-661-6500. FAX: 619-661-7875. *Sr Librn,* Ralph Blahnik; Tel: 619-661-6500, Ext 5590, E-mail: Ralph.Blahnik@cdcr.ca.gov; *Librn,* Victoria Crim; E-mail: Victoria.Crim@cdcr.ca.gov; *Librn,* Dorothy Nowroozian; E-mail: Dorothy.Nowroozian@cdcr.ca.gov; Staff 6 (MLS 3, Non-MLS 3)
Library Holdings: Bk Titles 40,000; Per Subs 30
Function: Adult literacy prog, Audio & video playback equip for onsite use, BA reader (adult literacy), Bilingual assistance for Spanish patrons, Bks on cassette, Bks on CD, Computers for patron use, Digital talking bks, Distance learning, Electronic databases & coll, Internet access, Learning ctr, Legal assistance to inmates, Life-long learning prog for all ages, Literacy & newcomer serv, Magazines, Magnifiers for reading, Microfiche/film & reading machines, Notary serv, Online ref, Photocopying/Printing, Prog for adults, Ref serv available, Satellite serv, Scanner, Serves people with intellectual disabilities, Spanish lang bks, Wheelchair accessible
Restriction: Staff & inmates only

FOLSOM STATE PRISON, 300 Prison Rd, Represa, 95671. (Mail add: PO Box 715071, Represa, 95671), SAN 371-8077. Tel: 916-985-2561. FAX: 916-608-3130. *Sr Librn,* Matthew Colvin; Tel: 831-678-3951, Ext 4549, E-mail: Matthew.Colvin@cdcr.ca.gov; *Librn,* Leslie Purdie; Tel: 916-985-2561, Ext 4236, E-mail: Leslie.Purdie@cdcr.ca.gov
Library Holdings: Bk Vols 28,000
Subject Interests: African-Am, Law, Literacy, Mental health, Spanish lang
Restriction: Staff & inmates only

HIGH DESERT STATE PRISON, 475-750 Rice Canyon Rd, Susanville, 96127. (Mail add: PO Box 750, Susanville, 96127-0750), SAN 375-5835. Tel: 530-251-5100. FAX: 530-251-5036. *Sr Librn,* Cristi Jenkins; Tel: 530-251-5100, Ext 6449, E-mail: Cristi.Jenkins@cdcr.ca.gov
Founded 1995
Library Holdings: Bk Vols 3,000
Function: Legal assistance to inmates
Restriction: Staff & inmates only

IRONWOOD STATE PRISON LIBRARY-CENTRAL LIBRARY, 19005 Wiley's Well Rd, Blythe, 92225. (Mail add: PO Box 2229, Blythe, 92226-2229), SAN 375-5843. Tel: 760-921-3000. FAX: 760-921-7526. *Sr Librn,* Lois Hightshoe; Tel: 760-921-3000, Ext 5623, E-mail: Lois.Hightshoe@cdcr.ca.gov; Staff 6 (MLS 2, Non-MLS 4)
Founded 1994
Jul 2013-Jun 2014. Mats Exp $13,800, Books $10,000, Per/Ser (Incl. Access Fees) $3,800
Library Holdings: Audiobooks 54; Bks on Deafness & Sign Lang 7; CDs 57; High Interest/Low Vocabulary Bk Vols 1,760; Large Print Bks 975; Bk Titles 52,000; Bk Vols 54,000; Per Subs 4; Videos 284
Function: Adult literacy prog, Bilingual assistance for Spanish patrons, Bks on cassette, Computers for patron use, Digital talking bks, Distance learning, Homework prog, ILL available, Jail serv, Literacy & newcomer serv, Magnifiers for reading, Notary serv, Photocopying/Printing, Wheelchair accessible
Restriction: Staff & inmates only

MULE CREEK STATE PRISON, 4001 Hwy 104, Ione, 95640. (Mail add: PO Box 409099, Ione, 95640-9099), SAN 371-8115. Tel: 209-274-4911. FAX: 209-274-5904. *Sr Librn,* Stephanie Gyles; Tel: 209-274-4911, Ext 6510, E-mail: Stephanie.Gyles@cdcr.ca.gov; *Librn,* Brian Heath; E-mail: Brian.Heath@cdcr.ca.gov; *Librn,* Ryan Szichak; Tel: 209-274-4911, Ext 6409, E-mail: Ryan.Szichak@cdcr.ca.gov; Staff 4 (MLS 1, Non-MLS 3)
Library Holdings: Bk Titles 14,000; Per Subs 11
Restriction: Staff & inmates only

NORTH KERN STATE PRISON, 2737 W Cecil Ave, Delano, 93215. (Mail add: PO Box 567, Delano, 93216-0567), SAN 375-5851. Tel: 661-721-2345. *Sr Librn,* Josephine Kamau; Tel: 661-721-2345, Ext 5260, E-mail: Josephine.Kamau@cdcr.ca.gov; *Librn,* William Cooper; Tel: 661-721-2345, Ext 5224, E-mail: William.Cooper@cdcr.ca.gov
Founded 1993
Library Holdings: High Interest/Low Vocabulary Bk Vols 500; Bk Vols 24,000; Per Subs 22
Subject Interests: Fed law, State law
Function: For res purposes
Special Services for the Blind - Bks on cassette; Closed circuit TV magnifier
Restriction: Staff & inmates only

PELICAN BAY STATE PRISON, 5905 Lake Earl Dr, Crescent City, 95532. (Mail add: PO Box 7000, Crescent City, 95531-7000), SAN 371-8131. Tel: 707-465-1000, Ext 7995. FAX: 707-465-9120. *Sr Librn,* Denise Rusk; E-mail: Denise.Rusk@cdcr.ca.gov; *Librn,* Charlotte Roi; E-mail: CHARLOTTE.ROI@cdcr.ca.gov
Library Holdings: Bk Vols 10,000
Restriction: Staff & inmates only

PLEASANT VALLEY STATE PRISON, 24863 W Jayne Ave, Coalinga, 93210. (Mail add: PO Box 8500, Coalinga, 93210-8500), SAN 375-586X. Tel: 559-935-4900. *Sr Librn,* Daniel Brunk; Tel: 559-935-4900, Ext 6165, E-mail: Daniel.Brunk@cdcr.ca.gov; Staff 2 (MLS 2)
Library Holdings: Bk Vols 44,244; Per Subs 54
Special Services for the Blind - Reader equip
Restriction: Staff & inmates only

SALINAS VALLEY STATE PRISON, 31625 Hwy 101, Soledad, 93960. (Mail add: PO Box 1020, Soledad, 93960-1020), SAN 375-5878. Tel: 831-678-5500. FAX: 831-678-5569. *Sr Librn,* Shelley Tomilson; Tel: 831-678-5500, Ext 6232, E-mail: Shelley.Tomilson@cdcr.ca.gov
Restriction: Staff & inmates only

SAN QUENTIN STATE PRISON LIBRARY, Main St, San Quentin, 94964, SAN 334-8695. Tel: 415-454-1460. FAX: 415-455-5049. *Sr Librn,* Douglas Jeffrey; Tel: 415-454-1460, Ext 6135, E-mail: Douglas.Jeffery@cdcr.ca.gov; *Librn,* John Cornell; Tel: 415-454-4160, Ext 3384, E-mail: John.Cornell@cdcr.ca.gov; *Librn,* Isaiah Hurtado; E-mail: ISAIAH.HURTADO@cdcr.ca.gov; *Librn,* Gabriel Loiederman; E-mail: Gabriel.Loiederman@cdcr.ca.gov; Staff 3 (MLS 3)
Library Holdings: Bk Vols 40,000; Per Subs 50
Restriction: Staff & inmates only

SUBSTANCE ABUSE TREATMENT FACLITY & STATE PRISON, CORCORAN, 900 Quebec Ave, Corcoran, 93212. (Mail add: PO Box 7100, Corcoran, 93212-7100), SAN 377-8002. Tel: 559-992-7100. FAX: 559-992-7182. *Sr Librn,* Velva Hampson; Tel: 559-992-7100, Ext 5066, E-mail: Velva.Hampson@cdcr.ca.gov; *Librn,* Gabe Burke; E-mail: Gabe.Burke@cdcr.ca.gov; Staff 5 (MLS 1, Non-MLS 4)
Library Holdings: Bk Titles 40,000; Bk Vols 50,000; Per Subs 72
Subject Interests: Law ref bks
Special Services for the Blind - Extensive large print coll; Talking bks
Restriction: Staff & inmates only

VALLEY STATE PRISON, 21633 Ave 24, Chowchilla, 93610. (Mail add: PO Box 99, Chowchilla, 93610-0099), SAN 375-5886. Tel: 559-665-6100. *Sr Librn,* Diane Johnson; Tel: 559-665-6100, Ext 6066, E-mail: Diane.Johnson@cdcr.ca.gov; *Librn,* Darin Garr; E-mail: Darin.Garr@cdcr.ca.gov
Library Holdings: Bk Vols 48,000
Restriction: Staff & inmates only

WASCO STATE PRISON, 701 Scofield Ave, Wasco, 93280. (Mail add: PO Box 8800, Wasco, 93280-8800), SAN 371-8158. Tel: 661-758-8400. FAX: 661-758-7049. *Sr Librn,* Joel Bowlin; Tel: 661-758-8400, Ext 5477, E-mail: Joel.Bowlin@cdcr.ca.gov
Library Holdings: Bk Vols 44,000
Restriction: Staff & inmates only

CALIFORNIA DEPARTMENT OF JUSTICE

GL ATTORNEY GENERAL'S LAW LIBRARY*, 1300 I St, 95814. (Mail add: PO Box 944255, 94244-2550), SAN 309-8184. Tel: 916-324-5312. FAX: 916-323-5342. *Principal Librn,* Marguerite Beveridge; E-mail: marguerite.beveridge@doj.ca.gov; Staff 7 (MLS 7)
Library Holdings: Bk Vols 25,000
Subject Interests: Calif law
Automation Activity & Vendor Info: (Cataloging) Inmagic, Inc.

G CCI FORENSIC LIBRARY*, 4949 Broadway, Rm A-107, 95820, SAN 371-6554. Tel: 916-227-3575. FAX: 916-454-5433. *Supv Librn,* Jawadi Waheed; E-mail: waheed.jawadi@doj.ca.gov; Staff 2 (MLS 1, Non-MLS 1)
Founded 1987
Library Holdings: Bk Vols 8,000; Per Subs 13
Subject Interests: Criminal justice, Forensic sci

Partic in Northern California & Nevada Medical Library Group
Restriction: Not open to pub, Staff use only

G CALIFORNIA ENERGY COMMISSION LIBRARY, 1516 Ninth St, MS10, 95814-5512. SAN 320-5754. Tel: 916-654-4292. FAX: 916-654-4046. E-mail: library@energy.ca.gov. Web Site: ww2.energy.ca.gov/. Staff 2 (MLS 2)
Founded 1975
Library Holdings: Bk Vols 18,000; Per Subs 100
Special Collections: California Energy Commission Publications
Subject Interests: Energy, Environ
Automation Activity & Vendor Info: (Acquisitions) SydneyPlus; (Cataloging) SydneyPlus; (Circulation) SydneyPlus; (ILL) OCLC; (OPAC) SydneyPlus; (Serials) SydneyPlus
Wireless access
Function: Doc delivery serv, Electronic databases & coll, Govt ref serv, Online cat
Partic in OCLC Online Computer Library Center, Inc
Open Mon-Fri 8:30-4:30
Restriction: Circulates for staff only

S CALIFORNIA ENVIRONMENTAL PROTECTION AGENCY PUBLIC LIBRARY*, 1001 I St, 2nd Flr, 95814. SAN 320-1627. Tel: 916-327-0635. E-mail: CalEPALibrary@arb.ca.gov. Web Site: www.calepa.ca.gov/library. *Librn,* Adrienne Richey; Tel: 916-323-9591, E-mail: Adrienne.Richey@arb.ca.gov; Staff 3 (MLS 1, Non-MLS 2)
Founded 1976
Library Holdings: Bk Titles 13,500; Per Subs 600
Special Collections: Air Pollution Technical Information Center, rpts & micro
Subject Interests: Air pollution
Wireless access
Open Mon-Fri 8:30-4:30
Branches:
DEPARTMENT OF TOXIC SUBSTANCES CONTROL - TECHNICAL REFERENCE, 1001 I St, 95814-2828. (Mail add: PO Box 806, 95812-0806), SAN 372-3038. Tel: 916-324-5898. FAX: 916-327-4494. *Sr Librn,* Gwen Chen; E-mail: gchen@dtsc.ca.gov
Library Holdings: Bk Vols 7,000; Per Subs 76
Subject Interests: Hazardous waste
Automation Activity & Vendor Info: (Cataloging) EOS International; (Circulation) EOS International; (Serials) EOS International
Open Mon-Fri 8-4

S CALIFORNIA HIGHWAY PATROL*, Headquarters Library, 601 N Seventh St, 95811. (Mail add: PO Box 942898, 94298-0001), SAN 320-5762. Tel: 916-843-3000. Web Site: www.chp.ca.gov.
Library Holdings: Bk Vols 2,525; Per Subs 75
Special Collections: Codes, Federal Register, Reports & Studies
Open Tues & Thurs 9-11:30 or by appointment

G CALIFORNIA STATE ARCHIVES, 1020 O St, 95814. SAN 326-5706. Tel: 916-653-7715. Reference Tel: 916-653-2246. FAX: 916-653-7363. Administration FAX: 916-653-7134. E-mail: archivesweb@sos.ca.gov. Web Site: www.sos.ca.gov/archives. *State Archivist,* Tamara Martin; Staff 25 (MLS 13, Non-MLS 12)
Founded 1850
Special Collections: California State History & Government. Oral History
Wireless access
Function: Archival coll, Art exhibits, Computers for patron use, Mail & tel request accepted, Online cat, Photocopying/Printing, Ref & res, Ref serv available, Telephone ref
Open Mon-Fri 9:30-4
Restriction: Closed stack, Non-circulating, Not a lending libr
Friends of the Library Group

GL CALIFORNIA STATE BOARD OF EQUALIZATION*, Law Library, 450 N St, 95814. SAN 301-2697. Tel: 916-445-7356. FAX: 916-323-3387. *Librn,* Lisa Ben-Reuven; E-mail: lisa.ben-reuven@cdtfa.ca.gov
Library Holdings: Bk Titles 2,000
Special Collections: State Taxation
Restriction: Open by appt only

GL CALIFORNIA STATE DEPARTMENT OF TRANSPORTATION*, Law Library, 1120 N St, Rm 1315, 95812. (Mail add: PO Box 1438, MS 57, 95812-1438), SAN 333-9998. Tel: 916-654-2630. FAX: 916-654-6128. *Librn,* Steven Arozena; E-mail: steven.arozena@dot.ca.gov; Staff 2 (MLS 1, Non-MLS 1)
Library Holdings: Bk Vols 15,000; Per Subs 179
Restriction: Not open to pub

GL CALIFORNIA STATE DEPARTMENT OF WATER RESOURCES*, Law Library, 1416 Ninth St, Rm 1118-13, 95814. (Mail add: PO Box 942836, 94236-0001), SAN 371-5590. Tel: 916-651-0822. FAX: 916-653-0952. Web Site: water.ca.gov. *Librn,* Eric Bender; E-mail: eric.bender@water.ca.gov; *Tech Asst,* Roslind Moses; Tel: 916-653-0474; Staff 2 (MLS 1, Non-MLS 1)
Founded 1966
Library Holdings: Bk Vols 20,000; Per Subs 30
Subject Interests: Law
Restriction: Not open to pub, Staff use only

P CALIFORNIA STATE LIBRARY*, 900 N St, 95814. (Mail add: PO Box 942837, 94237-0001), SAN 334-0058. Tel: 916-323-9843. FAX: 916-323-9768. TDD: 916-653-0692. E-mail: cslinfo@library.ca.gov. Web Site: www.library.ca.gov. *State Librn,* Greg Lucas; E-mail: Greg.Lucas@library.ca.gov; *Dep State Librn,* Narinder Sufi; E-mail: Narinder.Sufi@library.ca.gov
Founded 1850
Special Collections: State Document Depository; US Document Depository
Subject Interests: Calif, Educ, Genealogy, Govt publ, Hist, Law
Automation Activity & Vendor Info: (Cataloging) Ex Libris Group; (Circulation) Ex Libris Group; (ILL) OCLC; (OPAC) Ex Libris Group; (Serials) Ex Libris Group
Wireless access
Publications: BTBL News (Newsletter); California Library Directory; California Library Laws; California Library Statistics; California State Publications; Studies in the News
Partic in Association for Rural & Small Libraries; Califa; OCLC Online Computer Library Center, Inc
Special Services for the Deaf - TDD equip
Special Services for the Blind - Assistive/Adapted tech devices, equip & products; Bks & mags in Braille, on rec, tape & cassette; Cassette playback machines; Closed circuit TV
Open Mon-Fri 9:30-5
Friends of the Library Group
Branches: 1
P BRAILLE & TALKING BOOK LIBRARY, 900 N St, 95814. (Mail add: PO Box 942837, 94237-0001), SAN 301-2735. Tel: 916-654-0640. Toll Free Tel: 800-952-5666. FAX: 916-654-1119. E-mail: btbl@library.ca.gov. Web Site: www.btbl.ca.gov. *Dir,* Mike Marlin; E-mail: mmarlin@library.ca.gov; *Librn,* Mary Jane Kayes; Staff 18 (MLS 2, Non-MLS 16)
Founded 1904
Library Holdings: Audiobooks 73,000; Braille Volumes 7,000; Bk Titles 100,000; Per Subs 70
Special Collections: Blindness & Other Disabilities Reference Material
Automation Activity & Vendor Info: (Circulation) SirsiDynix
Publications: Borrower's Handbook; BTBL Recorded Books on California
Special Services for the Blind - Braille bks
Open Mon-Fri 9:30-4

S CALIFORNIA STATE RAILROAD MUSEUM LIBRARY*, Big Four Bldg, 111 I St, 2nd Flr, 95814. (Mail add: 125 I St, 95814), SAN 321-6470. Tel: 916-323-8073. FAX: 916-327-5655. E-mail: library.CSRM@parks.ca.gov. Web Site: www.californiarailroad.museum/visit/library. *Archivist,* Kathryn Santos; Tel: 916-322-0375, E-mail: kathryn.santos@parks.ca.gov; Staff 3 (MLS 3)
Founded 1981
Library Holdings: Bk Vols 10,000; Per Subs 80
Special Collections: Baldwin Locomotive Works Engine Specification Books, 1869-1938, micro; Corporate Records (Central Pacific, Southern Pacific & Western Pacific Railroads), ms; Correspondence & Business Records (Collis P Huntington Papers, 1856-1901), micro; Drawings & Specifications (Lima Locomotive Works); Railroad Equipment (Pullman Company), glass plate negatives; Railroad History (Gerald M Best, Grahame H Hardy, Gilbert H Kneiss, Stanley F Merritt & Louis L Stein Jr Colls), artifacts, bks, ephemera, ms; Railroad History (Railway & Locomotive Historical Society), artifacts, bks, ms; Railroad History, negatives, photog
Automation Activity & Vendor Info: (Cataloging) Inmagic, Inc.; (OPAC) Inmagic, Inc.
Function: Archival coll, Ref serv available
Publications: Pullman Company Negative Collection Guide; Research & Restoration Reports for CSRM Locomotive & Cars
Open Tues-Sat 1-5
Restriction: Non-circulating coll, Not a lending libr, Open to pub for ref only

C CALIFORNIA STATE UNIVERSITY, SACRAMENTO*, University Library, 2000 State University Dr E, 95819-6039. SAN 301-2751. Tel: 916-278-6708. Reference Tel: 916-278-5673. Web Site: library.csus.edu. *Dean, Univ Libr,* Amy Kautzman; E-mail: kautzman@csus.edu; *Assoc Dean, Acad,* Nicole Lawson; E-mail: nicole.lawson@csus.edu; *Digital Tech Librn, Interim Assoc Dean, Resource Management,* David Gibbs; E-mail: david.gibbs@csus.edu; *Head, Libr Syst, Info Tech,* Erik Beck; E-mail:

beck@csus.edu; *Head, Res & Instruction,* Jian-zhong Zhou; E-mail: zhou@csus.edu; *Head, Spec Coll & Archives,* James Fox; E-mail: james.fox@csus.edu; *Head, User Serv,* Lesley Brown; E-mail: brown@csus.edu; Staff 59 (MLS 32, Non-MLS 27)
Founded 1947. Enrl 30,661; Fac 1,729; Highest Degree: Doctorate
Special Collections: Archives & Special Colls; Congressman John Moss Papers; Dissent & Social Change Coll; Florin Japanese American Citizens League Oral History Project; Japanese American Archival Coll; K-12 Curriculum (Learning Resource Display Center); Rock & Roll Poster Coll; Royal Chicano Air Force Poster Coll; Tsakopoulos Hellenic Coll. Oral History; State Document Depository; US Document Depository
Subject Interests: Bus, Criminal justice, Educ, Engr, Humanities
Automation Activity & Vendor Info: (Acquisitions) Ex Libris Group; (Cataloging) Ex Libris Group; (Circulation) Ex Libris Group; (Course Reserve) Ex Libris Group; (Discovery) Ex Libris Group; (OPAC) Ex Libris Group; (Serials) Ex Libris Group
Wireless access
Friends of the Library Group

J COSUMNES RIVER COLLEGE LIBRARY*, Library & Learning Resources Center, 8401 Center Pkwy, 95823. SAN 301-2778. Tel: 916-691-7266. Reference Tel: 916-691-7265. FAX: 916-691-7349. Web Site: crc.losrios.edu/Student-Resources/Library. *Dean of Libr,* Stephen McGloughlin; Tel: 916-691-7589, E-mail: mcglous@crc.losrios.edu; *Pub Serv Librn,* Andi Adkins Pogue; Tel: 916-691-7904, E-mail: adkinsa@crc.losrios.edu; *Instruction & Outreach, Pub Serv,* Emily Bond; Tel: 916-691-7249, E-mail: bonde@crc.losrios.edu; *Instruction & Outreach, Pub Serv,* Dr Rochelle Perez; Tel: 916-691-7629, E-mail: perezr@crc.losrios.edu; Staff 10.6 (MLS 5.6, Non-MLS 5)
Founded 1970. Enrl 16,124; Fac 670; Highest Degree: Associate
Library Holdings: Bks on Deafness & Sign Lang 100; e-books 15,141; High Interest/Low Vocabulary Bk Vols 300; Bk Titles 59,157; Bk Vols 72,856; Per Subs 123; Spec Interest Per Sub 25; Videos 1,705
Special Collections: California History, examples of fine printing; Campus Oral History
Automation Activity & Vendor Info: (Acquisitions) Innovative Interfaces, Inc; (Cataloging) Innovative Interfaces, Inc; (Circulation) Innovative Interfaces, Inc; (Course Reserve) Innovative Interfaces, Inc; (ILL) OCLC Connexion; (OPAC) Innovative Interfaces, Inc; (Serials) Innovative Interfaces, Inc
Wireless access
Publications: Library Lines & the Learning Resources (Newsletter)
Mem of NorthNet Library System
Partic in Coop Libr Agency for Syst & Servs; OCLC Online Computer Library Center, Inc
Special Services for the Blind - Braille equip
Open Mon-Thurs 7:30am-8pm, Fri 7:30-4, Sat 10-4
Restriction: Open to students, fac & staff

M KAISER-PERMANENTE MEDICAL CENTER*, Health Sciences Library, 2025 Morse Ave, 95825. SAN 324-508X. Tel: 916-973-6944. FAX: 916-973-6999.
Founded 1965
Library Holdings: Bk Titles 700; Per Subs 25
Subject Interests: Clinical med
Partic in National Network of Libraries of Medicine Region 5

GL OFFICE OF LEGISLATIVE COUNSEL, STATE OF CALIFORNIA*, Law Library, 925 L St, Lower Level, 95814-3772. SAN 301-2727. Tel: 916-341-8036. E-mail: lcb.library@lc.ca.gov. *Supv Librn,* Lindsay Pealer; Staff 4 (MLS 2, Non-MLS 2)
Founded 1951
Library Holdings: Bk Vols 45,000; Per Subs 152
Special Collections: Legal Coll
Subject Interests: Legislation
Automation Activity & Vendor Info: (Cataloging) Inmagic, Inc.
Wireless access
Open Mon-Fri 8:30-5

S SACRAMENTO AREA COUNCIL OF GOVERNMENTS LIBRARY*, 1415 L St, Ste 300, 95814. SAN 327-1684. Tel: 916-321-9000. FAX: 916-321-9551. E-mail: infocenter@sacog.org. Web Site: www.sacog.org. *Demographer,* Tina Glover; Staff 1 (Non-MLS 1)
Library Holdings: Bk Titles 1,076; Per Subs 35
Special Collections: Census Data
Subject Interests: Transportation planning
Publications: New Library Acquisitions (Monthly); SACOG Publications
Open Mon-Fri 8-12 & 1-4

J SACRAMENTO CITY COLLEGE*, Learning Resources Division Library, 3835 Freeport Blvd, 95822. SAN 301-2824. Tel: 916-558-2253. FAX: 916-558-2114. Web Site: www.scc.losrios.edu/~library. *Dean,* Kevin Flash; E-mail: FlashK@scc.losrios.edu; *Librn,* Catherine Chenu-Campbell
Founded 1916. Enrl 24,000
Library Holdings: Bk Vols 68,894; Per Subs 410
Partic in OCLC Online Computer Library Center, Inc
Open Mon-Thurs (Summer) 8-6; Mon-Thurs (Winter) 7:30am-9:30pm, Fri 7:30-5, Sat 9-3
Friends of the Library Group

GL SACRAMENTO COUNTY PUBLIC LAW LIBRARY*, 609 Ninth St, 95814. SAN 301-2832. Tel: 916-874-6012. Circulation Tel: 916-874-8541. FAX: 916-244-0699. Circulation FAX: 916-874-7050. Automation Services FAX: 916-874-7053. E-mail: reference@saclaw.org. Web Site: saclaw.org. *Dir,* Coral Henning; Tel: 916-874-6013, E-mail: CHenning@saclaw.org; *Asst Dir, Support Serv,* Jean Willis; E-mail: JWillis@saclaw.org; Staff 18 (MLS 9, Non-MLS 9)
Founded 1891
Library Holdings: AV Mats 576; Bk Titles 6,450; Bk Vols 53,000; Per Subs 2,250
Automation Activity & Vendor Info: (Acquisitions) SirsiDynix; (Cataloging) SirsiDynix; (Circulation) SirsiDynix; (OPAC) SirsiDynix; (Serials) SirsiDynix
Wireless access
Function: AV serv, Govt ref serv, ILL available, Magnifiers for reading, Photocopying/Printing, Wheelchair accessible
Publications: Annual Report; Pathfinders (Reference guide)
Partic in Research Libraries Information Network
Special Services for the Blind - Computer with voice synthesizer for visually impaired persons
Open Mon 8-8, Tues-Thurs 8-7, Fri 8-5

P SACRAMENTO PUBLIC LIBRARY*, 828 I St, 95814. SAN 334-0112. Tel: 916-264-2700, 916-264-2920. Circulation Tel: 916-264-2789. Toll Free Tel: 800-561-4636. Web Site: www.saclibrary.org. *Libr Dir,* Ms Rivkah K Sass; E-mail: director@saclibrary.org; *Dep Dir, Pub Serv,* Kathy Middleton; E-mail: deputydirector@saclibrary.org; *Dep Dir, Tech Serv,* Jarrid Keller
Founded 1857. Pop 1,335,969; Circ 6,806,754
Library Holdings: Bk Titles 485,921; Bk Vols 2,100,251
Special Collections: Art; Californiana; City & County; City Planning & Urban Development; Genealogical; History of Printing. State Document Depository; US Document Depository
Subject Interests: Art & archit, Bus & mgt, Genealogy, Music
Automation Activity & Vendor Info: (Acquisitions) Innovative Interfaces, Inc; (Cataloging) Innovative Interfaces, Inc; (Circulation) Innovative Interfaces, Inc; (OPAC) Innovative Interfaces, Inc; (Serials) Innovative Interfaces, Inc
Wireless access
Publications: Library News
Mem of NorthNet Library System
Special Services for the Deaf - TDD equip
Open Tues-Thurs 10-6, Fri-Sun 10-5
Friends of the Library Group
Branches: 28

ARCADE LIBRARY, 2443 Marconi Ave, 95821, SAN 334-0147. Web Site: www.saclibrary.org/Locations/Arcade.
Founded 1941
Open Mon-Thurs 10-7, Fri & Sat 10-5
Friends of the Library Group

ARDEN-DIMICK LIBRARY, 891 Watt Ave, 95864, SAN 334-0171. Web Site: www.saclibrary.org/Locations/Arden-Dimick.
Founded 1949
Open Mon-Thurs 10-7, Fri & Sat 10-5, Sun 12-5
Friends of the Library Group

BELLE COOLEDGE LIBRARY, 5600 S Land Park Dr, 95822, SAN 334-0260. Web Site: www.saclibrary.org/Locations/Belle-Cooledge.
Founded 1958
Open Mon-Fri 10-7, Fri 12-5, Sat 10-5
Friends of the Library Group

CARMICHAEL LIBRARY, 5605 Marconi Ave, Carmichael, 95608, SAN 334-0201. Web Site: www.saclibrary.org/Locations/Carmichael.
Special Collections: California
Open Mon-Thurs 10-7, Fri & Sat 10-5, Sun 12-5
Friends of the Library Group

COLONIAL HEIGHTS LIBRARY, 4799 Stockton Blvd, 95820, SAN 329-5958. Web Site: www.saclibrary.org/Locations/Colonial-Heights.
Founded 1989
Open Tues-Thurs 10-7, Fri 12-5, Sat 10-5
Friends of the Library Group

DEL PASO HEIGHTS LIBRARY, 920 Grand Ave, 95838, SAN 334-0325. Web Site: www.saclibrary.org/Locations/Del-Paso-Heights.
Founded 1913
Special Collections: African-American Coll
Open Tues-Thurs 10-6, Fri 1-6, Sat 10-5
Friends of the Library Group

ELK GROVE LIBRARY, 8900 Elk Grove Blvd, Elk Grove, 95624, SAN 334-035X. Web Site: www.saclibrary.org/Locations/Elk-Grove.
Founded 1908. Pop 64,000

Library Holdings: Bk Titles 21,000
Open Mon-Thurs 10-7, Fri & Sat 10-5
Friends of the Library Group
FAIR OAKS LIBRARY, 11601 Fair Oaks Blvd, Fair Oaks, 95628, SAN 334-0384. Web Site: www.saclibrary.org/Locations/Fair-Oaks.
Founded 1909
Open Mon-Thurs 10-7, Fri & Sat 10-5, Sun 12-5
Friends of the Library Group
FRANKLIN LIBRARY, 10055 Franklin High Rd, Elk Grove, 95757. Web Site: www.saclibrary.org/Locations/Franklin.
Founded 2002
Open Mon, Wed & Fri 10-6, Tues 10-8, Sat 10-5
Friends of the Library Group
ISLETON LIBRARY, 412 Union St, Isleton, 95641. (Mail add: PO Box 517, Isleton, 95641-0517), SAN 374-7158. Web Site: www.saclibrary.org/Locations/Isleton.
Founded 1915
Open Tues-Fri 1-6, Sat 1-5
Friends of the Library Group
MARTIN LUTHER KING JR LIBRARY, 7340 24th St Bypass, 95822, SAN 334-0597. Web Site: www.saclibrary.org/Locations/Martin-Luther-King,-Jr.
Founded 1970
Special Collections: Martin Luther King Jr Coll; Samuel C Pannell African-American Coll
Open Tues-Thurs 10-7, Fri 12-5, Sat 10-5
Friends of the Library Group
MARIAN O LAWRENCE LIBRARY, 1000 Caroline Ave, Galt, 95632, SAN 334-0473. Web Site: www.saclibrary.org/Locations/Galt-Marian-O-Lawrence.
Founded 1908
Open Tues-Thurs 10-7, Fri 12-5, Sat 10-5
Friends of the Library Group
ELLA K MCCLATCHY LIBRARY, 2112 22nd St, 95818, SAN 334-0627. Web Site: www.saclibrary.org/Locations/Ella-K-McClatchy.
Founded 1940
Open Tues & Thurs 10-6, Wed 12-8, Fri 1-6, Sat 10-5
Friends of the Library Group
MCKINLEY LIBRARY, 601 Alhambra Blvd, 95816, SAN 334-0651. Web Site: www.saclibrary.org/Locations/McKinley.
Founded 1936
Open Tues-Thurs 10-7, Fri 12-5, Sat 10-5
Friends of the Library Group
NORTH HIGHLANDS/ANTELOPE LIBRARY, 4235 Antelope Rd, Antelope, 95843, SAN 334-0686. Web Site: www.saclibrary.org/Locations/North-Highlands-Antelope.
Founded 2000
Open Mon-Thurs 10-7, Fri & Sat 10-5, Sun 12-5
Friends of the Library Group
NORTH NATOMAS LIBRARY, 4660 Via Ingoglia, 95835. Web Site: www.saclibrary.org/Locations/North-Natomas.
Founded 2004
Open Tues-Thurs 10-7, Fri 12-5, Sat 10-5
Friends of the Library Group
NORTH SACRAMENTO-HAGGINWOOD LIBRARY, 2109 Del Paso Blvd, 95815, SAN 334-0716. Web Site: www.saclibrary.org/Locations/North-Sacramento-Hagginwood.
Founded 1987
Open Tues-Thurs 11-7, Fri 12-5, Sat 11-5
Friends of the Library Group
ORANGEVALE LIBRARY, 8820 Greenback Lane, Ste L, Orangevale, 95662, SAN 374-7166. Web Site: www.saclibrary.org/Locations/Sacramento.
Founded 1912
Open Tues 12-8, Wed & Thurs 10-6, Fri 1-6, Sat 10-5
Friends of the Library Group
RANCHO CORDOVA LIBRARY, 9845 Folsom Blvd, 95827, SAN 334-0775. Web Site: www.saclibrary.org/Locations/Rancho-Cordova.
Founded 1959
Open Mon-Thurs 10-7, Fri & Sat 10-5, Sun 12-5
Friends of the Library Group
RIO LINDA LIBRARY, 6724 Sixth St, Rio Linda, 95673, SAN 334-0805. Web Site: www.saclibrary.org/Locations/Rio-Linda.
Founded 1968
Function: Adult literacy prog, Audiobks via web, Bks on cassette, Bks on CD, CD-ROM, Children's prog, Computers for patron use, Digital talking bks, Electronic databases & coll, Free DVD rentals, ILL available, Internet access, Music CDs, Online cat, Online ref, OverDrive digital audio bks, Photocopying/Printing, Prog for children & young adult, Spoken cassettes & CDs, Spoken cassettes & DVDs, Story hour, Summer reading prog, Tax forms, Teen prog, VHS videos, Wheelchair accessible
Open Tues 12-8, Wed & Thurs 10-6, Fri 1-6, Sat 10-5
Friends of the Library Group
SACRAMENTO ROOM, 828 I St, 2nd Flr, 95814, SAN 334-0236. Web Site: www.saclibrary.org/Locations/Sacramento-Room.
Founded 1857
Special Collections: Sacramento Authors & Printing History. State Document Depository
Subject Interests: Art, Local hist, Music
Open Tues-Thurs 10-6, Sat & Sun 12-5
Friends of the Library Group
SOUTH NATOMAS LIBRARY, 2901 Truxel Rd, 95833, SAN 374-7174. Web Site: www.saclibrary.org/Locations/South-Natomas.
Founded 2001
Open Tues-Thurs 10-7, Fri 12-5, Sat 10-5
Friends of the Library Group
SOUTHGATE LIBRARY, 6132 66th Ave, 95823, SAN 334-083X. Web Site: www.saclibrary.org/Locations/Southgate.
Founded 1975. Pop 75,000
Open Mon-Thurs 10-7, Fri & Sat 10-5, Sun 12-5
Friends of the Library Group
SYLVAN OAKS LIBRARY, 6700 Auburn Blvd, Citrus Heights, 95621, SAN 334-0864. Web Site: www.saclibrary.org/Locations/Sylvan-Oaks.
Founded 1919
Open Mon-Thurs 10-7, Fri & Sat 10-5
Friends of the Library Group
VALLEY HI-NORTH LAGUNA LIBRARY, 7400 Imagination Pkwy, 95823. Web Site: www.saclibrary.org/Locations/Valley-Hi-North-Laguna.
Founded 2001
Open Tues-Thurs 10-7, Fri 12-5, Sat 10-5
Friends of the Library Group
WALNUT GROVE LIBRARY, 14177 Market St, Walnut Grove, 95690. (Mail add: PO Box 40, Walnut Grove, 95690-0040), SAN 334-0899. Web Site: www.saclibrary.org/Locations/Walnut-Grove.
Founded 1919
Open Tues-Fri 1-6, Sat 1-5
Friends of the Library Group
ROBBIE WATERS POCKET-GREENHAVEN, 7335 Gloria Dr, 95831. Web Site: www.saclibrary.org/Locations/Robbie-Waters-Pocket-Greenhaven.
Library Holdings: Bk Vols 52,000
Open Tues-Thurs 10-7, Fri 12-5, Sat 10-5
Friends of the Library Group
NONIE WETZEL COURTLAND LIBRARY, 170 Primasing Ave, Courtland, 95615. (Mail add: PO Box 536, Courtland, 95615), SAN 374-714X. Web Site: www.saclibrary.org/Locations/Nonie-Wetzel-Courtland.
Founded 1993
Open Tues, Thurs & Fri 1-6, Wed 1-7, Sat 1-5
Friends of the Library Group
Bookmobiles: 3

S SEARCH GROUP, INC LIBRARY, 1900 Point West Way, Ste 161, 95815. SAN 370-4262. Tel: 916-392-2550. FAX: 916-392-8440. Web Site: www.search.org. *Communications Spec,* Twyla R Putt; E-mail: twyla@search.org. Subject Specialists: *Criminal justice, Policy, Statistics,* Twyla R Putt
Library Holdings: Bk Titles 250; Per Subs 24
Subject Interests: Criminal justice, Law enforcement

G US DEPARTMENT OF THE INTERIOR, BUREAU OF RECLAMATION*, Mid-Pacific Regional Library, 2800 Cottage Way, Rm W-1825, 95825-1898. SAN 301-2867. Tel: 916-978-5594. FAX: 916-978-5599. *Library Contact,* Patricia Stuart; *Tech Info Spec,* Geoffrey McDonald; Tel: 916-978-5593, E-mail: gmcdonald@usbr.gov; Staff 2 (MLS 2)
Founded 1946
Library Holdings: Bk Titles 18,000; Bk Vols 21,000; Per Subs 120
Special Collections: Project Histories - Mid-Pacific Region BOR; San Joaquin Valley Drainage Program
Subject Interests: Water res

CM UNIVERSITY OF CALIFORNIA, DAVIS*, F William Blaisdell Medical Library, 4610 X St, 95817. SAN 301-2875. Tel: 916-734-3529. Interlibrary Loan Service Tel: 530-752-1978. FAX: 916-734-7418. E-mail: bmlcir@ucdavis.edu. Reference E-mail: bmlref@ucdavis.edu. Web Site: www.library.ucdavis.edu/library/blaisdell-medical/. *Head of Libr,* Nicole Capdarest-Arest; E-mail: ncapdarest@ucdavis.edu
Founded 1929
Special Collections: Bioethics Coll; Birth Defects Coll; Civil War Medicine
Subject Interests: Clinical med, Nursing
Wireless access
Partic in National Network of Libraries of Medicine Region 5
Open Mon-Thurs 7-7, Fri 7-6, Sat & Sun 10-6

CL UNIVERSITY OF THE PACIFIC - MCGEORGE SCHOOL OF LAW, Gordon D Schaber Law Library, 3282 Fifth Ave, 95817. SAN 301-2883. Tel: 916-739-7131. Interlibrary Loan Service Tel: 916-739-7240. Reference Tel: 916-739-7164. E-mail: refdesk@pacific.edu. Web Site: law.pacific.edu/sacramento-library. *Asst Dean, Libr Serv,* James Wirrell; Tel: 916-739-7076, E-mail: jwirrel@pacific.edu
Founded 1924. Enrl 1,091; Fac 85; Highest Degree: Doctorate
Library Holdings: Bk Titles 119,470; Bk Vols 497,000; Per Subs 4,492
Special Collections: State Document Depository; US Document Depository
Automation Activity & Vendor Info: (Acquisitions) Innovative Interfaces, Inc; (Cataloging) Innovative Interfaces, Inc; (Circulation) Innovative Interfaces, Inc; (Course Reserve) Innovative Interfaces, Inc; (OPAC) Innovative Interfaces, Inc; (Serials) Innovative Interfaces, Inc
Wireless access
Partic in Research Libraries Information Network
Open Mon-Thurs 7:30am-Midnight, Fri 7:30am-10pm, Sat 8am-10pm, Sun 8am-Midnight

L WEINTRAUB TOBIN*, Law Library, 400 Capitol Mall, Ste 1100, 95814. SAN 372-302X. Tel: 916-558-6000. FAX: 916-446-1611. Web Site: www.weintraub.com. *Librn,* Jeannie Powell
Library Holdings: Bk Vols 10,000; Per Subs 52
Wireless access
Open Mon-Fri 8:30-5
Restriction: Staff use only

SAINT HELENA

P SAINT HELENA PUBLIC LIBRARY, George & Elsie Wood Public Library, 1492 Library Lane, 94574-1143. SAN 301-2891. Tel: 707-963-5244. Administration E-mail: admin@shpl.org. Web Site: www.shpl.org. *Libr Dir,* Chris Kreiden; E-mail: chris@shpl.org; *Ch Serv, Outreach Serv Librn,* Mariah McGuire; E-mail: mariah@shpl.org; *Adult Serv, Circ Supvr,* Cecilia Raffo; E-mail: cecilia@shpl.org; *Tech Serv,* Lynne Albrecht; E-mail: lynne@shpl.org; Staff 5 (MLS 2, Non-MLS 3)
Founded 1892. Pop 6,225; Circ 254,247
Library Holdings: AV Mats 35,390; CDs 2,241; DVDs 2,279; e-books 4,600; Large Print Bks 1,877; Bk Vols 92,499; Per Subs 132; Spec Interest Per Sub 50
Special Collections: Napa Valley Wine Library
Subject Interests: Wine, Wine hist
Automation Activity & Vendor Info: (Acquisitions) TLC (The Library Corporation); (Circulation) TLC (The Library Corporation); (OPAC) TLC (The Library Corporation)
Wireless access
Function: 24/7 Electronic res, 24/7 Online cat, Art exhibits, Audiobks via web, Bilingual assistance for Spanish patrons, Bks on CD, Children's prog, Computers for patron use, Free DVD rentals, Internet access, Life-long learning prog for all ages, Magazines, Meeting rooms, Microfiche/film & reading machines, Museum passes, Music CDs, Online cat, OverDrive digital audio bks, Photocopying/Printing, Prog for adults, Prog for children & young adult, Spanish lang bks, Story hour, Summer reading prog
Mem of NorthNet Library System
Partic in Solano Partner Libraries & St Helena
Open Mon 10-6, Tues & Wed 10-7, Thurs 10-9, Fri & Sat 2-6
Friends of the Library Group

SALINAS

J HARTNELL COLLEGE LIBRARY*, 411 Central Ave, 93901. SAN 301-2913. Reference Tel: 831-759-6078. FAX: 831-759-6084. E-mail: circ@hartnell.edu, reference@hartnell.edu. Web Site: www.hartnell.edu/library. *Head Librn,* Peggy Mayfield; Tel: 831-755-6898, E-mail: mmayfield@hartnell.edu; Staff 11 (MLS 3, Non-MLS 8)
Founded 1936. Fac 147
Library Holdings: Bk Titles 60,000; Per Subs 257
Special Collections: Ornithology (O P Silliman Memorial Library of Natural History), bks, ser
Automation Activity & Vendor Info: (Acquisitions) Ex Libris Group; (Media Booking) Ex Libris Group; (OPAC) Ex Libris Group; (Serials) Ex Libris Group
Wireless access
Partic in Monterey Bay Area Cooperative Library System; OCLC Online Computer Library Center, Inc
Open Mon-Thurs 8am-9pm, Fri 8-4, Sat 10-2

GL MONTEREY COUNTY LAW LIBRARY*, Bldg 1, 230 Church St, 93901. SAN 301-293X. Tel: 831-755-5046. FAX: 831-422-9593. Web Site: www.co.monterey.ca.us/government/government-links/law-library. *Libr Dir,* Christopher Cobb; E-mail: christophercobb11@gmail.com; *Asst Librn,* Melissa Foster
Library Holdings: Bk Vols 15,058
Special Collections: California Legal
Wireless access
Function: For res purposes
Open Mon-Thurs 8:30-4:30
Branches:
MONTEREY BRANCH, Monterey County Courthouse, 1200 Aguajito Rd, Rm 202, Monterey, 93940, SAN 377-015X. Tel: 831-264-4207. FAX: 831-372-6036. *Libr Dir,* Christopher Cobb; *Asst Librn,* Melissa Foster
Library Holdings: Bk Vols 15,536
Function: For res purposes
Open Mon-Fri 8:30-4:30

P SALINAS PUBLIC LIBRARY*, John Steinbeck Library, 350 Lincoln Ave, 93901. SAN 334-1496. Tel: 831-758-7311. Web Site: www.salinaspubliclibrary.org/about/john-steinbeck-library. *Libr Dir,* Kristan Ann Lundquist; E-mail: kristanl@ci.salinas.ca.us; Staff 6 (MLS 5, Non-MLS 1)
Founded 1909. Pop 152,677
Library Holdings: AV Mats 14,902; Bk Vols 204,665; Per Subs 271
Special Collections: John Steinbeck Coll
Automation Activity & Vendor Info: (Acquisitions) SirsiDynix; (Cataloging) SirsiDynix; (Circulation) SirsiDynix; (OPAC) SirsiDynix; (Serials) SirsiDynix
Wireless access
Function: Adult literacy prog, Audio & video playback equip for onsite use, CD-ROM, Digital talking bks, Homework prog, Internet access, Magnifiers for reading, Music CDs, Outside serv via phone, mail, e-mail & web, Photocopying/Printing, Spoken cassettes & CDs, Spoken cassettes & DVDs, Telephone ref, VHS videos
Partic in Monterey Bay Area Cooperative Library System
Open Mon, Fri & Sat 10-6, Tues & Thurs 12-8, Wed 12-6, Sun 1-6
Friends of the Library Group
Branches: 2
CESAR CHAVEZ LIBRARY, 615 Williams Rd, 93905, SAN 334-1526. Tel: 831-758-7345. FAX: 831-758-9172. Web Site: salinaspubliclibrary.org/about/cesar-chavez-library. *Librn,* Don Gardner; Staff 2 (MLS 2)
Pop 52,000; Circ 75,000
Library Holdings: Bk Vols 55,000; Per Subs 86
Special Collections: Chicano Cultural Resource Center
Open Mon, Fri & Sat 10-6, Tues & Thurs 12-8, Wed 12-6, Sun 1-6
Friends of the Library Group
EL GABILAN, 1400 N Main St, 93906, SAN 334-1550. Tel: 831-758-7302. FAX: 831-442-0817. *Br Mgr,* Position Currently Open
Pop 55,000; Circ 124,000
Library Holdings: Bk Vols 54,000; Per Subs 55
Open Mon, Fri & Sat 10-6, Tues & Thurs 12-8, Wed 12-6, Sun 1-6
Friends of the Library Group

SAN ANDREAS

L CALAVERAS COUNTY LAW LIBRARY*, Government Ctr, 891 Mountain Ranch Rd, 95249. SAN 326-0526. Tel: 209-754-6314. *Library Contact,* Sarah Dekay
Jul 2015-Jun 2016. Mats Exp $22,670, Books $22,670. Sal $1,771
Library Holdings: Bk Vols 9,050
Wireless access
Open Mon-Fri 8-5
Restriction: Restricted borrowing privileges

P CALAVERAS COUNTY LIBRARY*, San Andreas Central (Headquarters), 891 Mountain Ranch Rd, 95249. (Mail add: 1299 Gold Hunter Rd, 95249), SAN 301-2956. Tel: 209-754-6510. FAX: 209-754-6512. E-mail: publiclibrary@co.calaveras.ca.us. Web Site: library.calaverasgov.us. *County Librn,* Nancy Giddens; E-mail: ngiddens@co.calaveras.ca.us; *Br Mgr,* Position Currently Open
Founded 1939. Pop 43,350; Circ 50,797
Library Holdings: Bk Vols 50,418; Per Subs 90
Subject Interests: Local hist, Mining
Automation Activity & Vendor Info: (Cataloging) SirsiDynix; (Circulation) SirsiDynix; (ILL) OCLC FirstSearch; (OPAC) SirsiDynix
Wireless access
Partic in 49-99 Cooperative Library System; Association for Rural & Small Libraries; OCLC Online Computer Library Center, Inc
Open Mon 1-5, Tues, Wed & Fri 9-5, Thurs 12-8
Friends of the Library Group
Branches: 7
ANGELS CAMP BRANCH, 426 N Main St, Angels Camp, 95222. (Mail add: PO Box 456, Angels Camp, 95222-0456), SAN 324-2382. Tel: 209-736-2198. E-mail: aclib@co.calaveras.ca.us. *Br Mgr,* Pat Smalling
Circ 12,401
Library Holdings: Bk Vols 9,464
Open Tues & Fri 10-2, Wed & Thurs 10-5
Friends of the Library Group

ARNOLD BRANCH, 1065 Blagen Rd, Arnold, 95223. (Mail add: PO Box 788, Arnold, 95223-0788), SAN 324-2390. Tel: 209-795-1009. E-mail: arlib@co.calaveras.ca.us. *Br Mgr,* Fran Devlin
Circ 17,883
Library Holdings: Bk Vols 6,897
Special Collections: Verna Johnston Nature Coll
Subject Interests: Ecology, Environ, Geol, Global warming, Indigenous people, Nature, Plants
Open Tues-Sat 10-4
Friends of the Library Group

COPPEROPOLIS BRANCH, Lake Tulloch Plaza, 3505 Spangler Lane, Ste 106, Copperopolis, 95228. Tel: 209-785-0920. E-mail: cplib@co.calaveras.ca.us. *Br Mgr,* Shannon Jewel
Founded 1998. Pop 2,363; Circ 9,574
Library Holdings: Bk Vols 5,530
Open Tues-Thurs 11-5:30, Fri 10-1
Friends of the Library Group

MOKELUMNE HILL BRANCH, 8328 Main St, Mokelumne Hill, 95245. (Mail add: PO Box 282, Mokelumne Hill, 95245-0282). Tel: 209-286-0507. E-mail: mhlib@co.calaveras.ca.us. *Br Mgr,* Judy Galli
Founded 1999. Pop 1,557; Circ 3,371
Library Holdings: Bk Vols 4,855
Open Tues-Thurs 1:30-6, Fri 9-1:30
Friends of the Library Group

MURPHYS BRANCH, 480 Park Lane, Murphys, 95247. (Mail add: PO Box 702, Murphys, 95247-0702), SAN 324-2412. Tel: 209-728-3036. E-mail: mrlib@co.calaveras.ca.us. *Br Mgr,* Kris Loving
Circ 8,605
Library Holdings: Bk Vols 5,878
Open Tues-Sat 11-4:30
Friends of the Library Group

VALLEY SPRINGS BRANCH, 240 Pine St, Valley Springs, 95252, SAN 324-2447. Tel: 209-772-1318. E-mail: vslib@co.calaveras.ca.us. *Br Mgr,* Ray Bettinger
Circ 22,576
Library Holdings: Bk Vols 17,091
Open Mon-Thurs 1-5:30, Fri 1-4
Friends of the Library Group

WEST POINT BRANCH, 54 Bald Mountain Rd, West Point, 95255. (Mail add: PO Box 195, West Point, 95255-0195), SAN 324-2455. Tel: 209-293-7020. E-mail: wplib@co.calaveras.ca.us. *Br Mgr,* Joan Jessup
Circ 2,493
Library Holdings: Bk Vols 4,292
Open Wed & Thurs 11-5:30, Fri 10-3
Friends of the Library Group

SAN ANSELMO

P SAN ANSELMO PUBLIC LIBRARY*, 110 Tunstead Ave, 94960-2617. SAN 301-2972. Tel: 415-258-4656. FAX: 415-258-4666. Web Site: sananselmolibrary.org. *Town Librn,* Linda M Kenton; E-mail: lkenton@townofsananselmo.org; Staff 6 (MLS 3, Non-MLS 3)
Founded 1915. Pop 12,450; Circ 117,996
Library Holdings: AV Mats 2,500; e-books 3,939; Bk Vols 47,525; Per Subs 100
Special Collections: San Anselmo Historical Museum Coll
Wireless access
Mem of NorthNet Library System
Partic in Marin Automated Resources & Information Network
Open Mon-Wed 10-8, Thurs-Sat 10-5
Friends of the Library Group

SAN BERNARDINO

C CALIFORNIA STATE UNIVERSITY, SAN BERNARDINO*, John M Pfau Library, 5500 University Pkwy, 92407-2318. SAN 301-2980. Tel: 909-537-5090. Interlibrary Loan Service Tel: 909-537-5093. Reference Tel: 909-537-5091. Administration Tel: 909-537-5102. Automation Services Tel: 909-537-5116. FAX: 909-537-7048. Web Site: library.csusb.edu. *Dean & Univ Librn,* Cesar Caballero; E-mail: ccaballe@csusb.edu; *Head, Circ,* Denise Gipson-Perry; E-mail: dgipson@csusb.edu; *Head, ILL,* Juvette McNew; E-mail: jmcnew@csusb.edu; *Ref Librn,* Bonnie Petry; Tel: 909-537-5114, E-mail: bpetry@csusb.edu; *Ref Librn,* Xiwen Zhang; Tel: 909-537-5106, E-mail: xzhang@csusb.edu; *Coord, Coll Develop,* Lisa Bartle; Tel: 909-537-7552, E-mail: lbartle@csusb.edu; *Coordr of Ref Serv,* Brent Singleton; Tel: 909-537-5083, E-mail: bsinglet@csusb.edu; *Coordr, Cat,* Eva Sorrell; Tel: 909-537-7392, E-mail: esorrell@csusb.edu; *Coordr, Electronic Res, Ser,* Stacy Magedaz; Tel: 909-537-5103, E-mail: magedanz@csusb.edu; *Coordr, Instruction,* Barbara Quarton; Tel: 909-537-7553, E-mail: bquarton@csusb.edu; *Coordr, Spec Coll, Govt Doc,* Jill Vassilakos-Long; Tel: 909-537-7541, E-mail: jvlong@csusb.edu; *Coordr, Multimedia,* Les Kong; Tel: 909-537-5111, E-mail: lkong@csusb.edu; Staff 12 (MLS 12)
Founded 1963. Enrl 14,000; Fac 400; Highest Degree: Master
Library Holdings: CDs 1,563; DVDs 1,001; e-books 10,000; e-journals 21,000; Bk Titles 750,000
Wireless access
Publications: Pfau Library (Newsletter)
Partic in Info Globe; Inland Empire Acad Libr Coop; San Bernardino, Inyo, Riverside Counties United Library Services
Open Mon-Thurs 7:30am-Midnight, Fri 7:30-5, Sat 9-2
Friends of the Library Group

P CITY OF SAN BERNARDINO LIBRARY SERVICES*, Norman F Feldheym Central Library, 555 W Sixth St, 92410-3001. SAN 334-2425. Tel: 909-381-8215. Circulation Tel: 909-381-8201. Reference Tel: 909-381-8221. FAX: 909-381-8229. E-mail: lmt@sbpl.org. Web Site: www.sbcity.org/cityhall/library/default.asp. *Dir,* Edward Erjavek; *Ch Serv, ILL,* Angela Encinas; Staff 11 (MLS 4, Non-MLS 7)
Founded 1891. Pop 189,800; Circ 569,867
Library Holdings: Bk Vols 219,367; Per Subs 489
Special Collections: California History (California Coll)
Automation Activity & Vendor Info: (Circulation) TLC (The Library Corporation); (OPAC) TLC (The Library Corporation)
Wireless access
Mem of Inland Library System
Partic in OCLC Online Computer Library Center, Inc; San Bernardino, Inyo, Riverside Counties United Library Services
Friends of the Library Group
Branches: 3

DOROTHY INGHRAM BRANCH, 1505 W Highland Ave, 92411, SAN 334-2484. Tel: 909-887-4494. FAX: 909-887-6594. *Br Mgr,* Yvette Freeman; E-mail: freeman.yve@sbpl.org
Pop 15,000; Circ 54,020
Library Holdings: Bk Vols 15,000
Special Collections: Black History Coll
Open Mon-Wed 10-8, Thurs-Sat 10-6
Friends of the Library Group

HOWARD M ROWE BRANCH, 108 E Marshall Blvd, 92404, SAN 334-2514. Tel: 909-883-3411. FAX: 909-882-4941. *Br Mgr,* Andrea Zuniga; E-mail: zuniga.and@sbpl.org
Pop 60,000; Circ 165,103
Library Holdings: Bk Vols 41,080
Open Mon & Tues 3-8, Wed & Thurs 10-3
Friends of the Library Group

PAUL VILLASENOR BRANCH, 525 N Mount Vernon Ave, 90411, SAN 334-2549. Tel: 909-383-5156. FAX: 909-381-1766. *Br Mgr,* Rosemary Dubois; E-mail: duboisrose@sbpl.org
Pop 12,500; Circ 36,085
Library Holdings: Bk Vols 22,299
Special Collections: Bilingual Material; Spanish language material
Open Mon & Tues 3-8, Wed & Thurs 10-3

M COMMUNITY HOSPITAL OF SAN BERNARDINO*, Medical Library, 1805 Medical Center Dr, 92411-1288. SAN 324-5071. Tel: 909-887-6333, Ext 1488. FAX: 909-806-1062. *Library Contact,* Janice Castro
Library Holdings: Bk Titles 700; Per Subs 80
Partic in Nat Libr of Med, Coop Libr Agency for Systems & Servs; Proquest Dialog
Restriction: Staff use only

GL LAW LIBRARY FOR SAN BERNARDINO COUNTY*, 402 North D St, 92401. SAN 334-1585. Tel: 909-885-3020. Web Site: www.sblawlibrary.org. *Dir,* Lawrence R Meyer; E-mail: larrym@sblawlibrary.org; Staff 9 (MLS 2, Non-MLS 7)
Founded 1891
Library Holdings: Bk Vols 140,000
Special Collections: American Law & Foreign Law. State Document Depository; US Document Depository
Wireless access
Open Mon-Fri 8:30-5
Restriction: Non-circulating coll
Branches:

HIGH DESERT, 15455 Seneca Rd, Victorville, 92392-2226, SAN 373-8477. Tel: 760-243-2044.
Open Mon-Fri 9-1:30 & 2-5
Restriction: Non-circulating

WEST END BRANCH, 8409 Utica Ave, Rancho Cucamonga, 91730-3893, SAN 328-2899. Tel: 909-944-5106.
Special Collections: California Legal Materials, Primary Authority & Treatises. State Document Depository
Open Mon-Fri 8:30-5
Restriction: Non-circulating

P SAN BERNARDINO COUNTY LIBRARY*, Administration, 777 E Rialto Ave, 92415-0035. SAN 334-164X. Tel: 909-387-2220. FAX: 909-387-2288. Web Site: www.sbclib.org. *County Librn,* Michael Jimenez; E-mail: michael.jimenez@lib.sbcounty.gov; *Libr Adminr, Regional Mgr,* Melanie

Orosco; Tel: 909-520-2352, E-mail: melanie.orosco@lib.sbcounty.gov; *Regional Mgr,* Kristen Stevens; Tel: 909-771-9265, E-mail: kristen.stevens@lib.sbcounty.gov; *Regional Mgr,* Melanee Stovall; Tel: 909-665-0296, E-mail: melanee.stovall@lib.sbcounty.gov; *Regional Mgr,* Patty Turley; Tel: 909-855-5486, E-mail: patty.turley@lib.sbcounty.gov
Founded 1914. Pop 1,207,667; Circ 2,460,991
Wireless access
Mem of Inland Library System
Open Mon-Fri 8-5
Friends of the Library Group
Branches: 32

ADELANTO BRANCH, 11497 Bartlett, Adelanto, 92301. (Mail add: PO Box 37, Adelanto, 92301-0037), SAN 334-1674. Tel: 760-246-5661. FAX: 760-246-4157. Web Site: www.sbclib.org/LibraryLocations/AdelantoBranchLibrary.aspx. *Br Mgr,* Liza Hazen
Founded 1921
Library Holdings: Bk Vols 21,630
Open Mon-Wed 11-7, Thurs 10-6, Sat 9-5
Friends of the Library Group

BAKER FAMILY LEARNING CENTER, 2818 N Macy St, Muscoy, 92407. Tel: 909-887-5167. Web Site: www.sbclib.org/LibraryLocations/MuscoyBakerFamilyLearningCenter.aspx. *Supvr,* Victoria Elias
Founded 2013
Open Mon-Wed 11-7, Thurs 10-6, Sat 9-5

BARSTOW BRANCH, 304 E Buena Vista St, Barstow, 92311-2806, SAN 334-1739. Tel: 760-256-4850. FAX: 760-256-4852. Web Site: www.sbclib.org/LibraryLocations/BarstowBranchLibrary.aspx. *Br Mgr,* Amy Zillner
Founded 1914
Library Holdings: Bk Vols 34,882
Open Mon-Wed 11-7, Thurs 10-6, Sat 9-5
Friends of the Library Group

NEWTON T BASS BRANCH, 14901 Dale Evans Pkwy, Apple Valley, 92307, SAN 334-1704. Tel: 760-247-2022. FAX: 760-247-7099. Web Site: www.sbclib.org/LibraryLocations/AppleValleyNewtonTBassBranchLibrary.aspx. *Br Mgr,* Jake Zylman
Founded 1949
Library Holdings: Bk Vols 71,286
Open Mon-Wed 11-7, Thurs 10-6, Sat 9-5
Friends of the Library Group

BIG BEAR LAKE BRANCH, 41930 Garstin Dr, Big Bear Lake, 92315. (Mail add: PO Box 1809, Big Bear Lake, 92315-1809), SAN 334-1763. Tel: 909-866-5571. FAX: 909-866-4382. Web Site: www.sbclib.org/LibraryLocations/BigBearLakeBranch.aspx. *Br Mgr,* Ina Feeney
Founded 1915
Library Holdings: Bk Vols 40,011
Open Mon-Wed 11-7, Thurs 10-6, Sat 9-5
Friends of the Library Group

BLOOMINGTON BRANCH, 18028 Valley Blvd, Bloomington, 92316, SAN 334-1798. Tel: 909-820-0533. Web Site: www.sbclib.org/LibraryLocations/BloomingtonBranchLibrary.aspx. *Br Mgr,* Charlene Wade
Founded 1914
Library Holdings: Bk Vols 17,678
Open Mon-Wed 11-7, Thurs 10-6, Sat 9-5

CAL AERO PRESERVE ACADEMY BRANCH, 15850 Main St, Chino, 91708. Tel: 909-606-2173. Web Site: www.sbclib.org/LibraryLocations/CalAeroPreserveAcademyBranchLibrary.aspx. *Br Mgr,* Melanee Stovall
Open Mon-Thurs 3:30-8, Sat 10-5
Friends of the Library Group

CARTER BRANCH, 2630 N Linden Ave, Rialto, 92377. Tel: 909-854-4100, Ext 28148. Web Site: www.sbclib.org/LibraryLocations/CarterBranchLibrary.aspx. *Br Mgr,* Melanie Orosco
Open Mon-Thurs 3-8, Sat 9-5

CHINO BRANCH, 13180 Central Ave, Chino, 91710, SAN 334-1828. Tel: 909-465-5280. FAX: 909-465-5240. Web Site: www.sbclib.org/LibraryLocations/ChinoBranchLibrary.aspx. *Br Mgr,* Melanee Stovall
Founded 1915
Library Holdings: Bk Vols 59,475
Open Mon-Wed 11-7, Thurs & Fri 10-6, Sat 9-5

CRESTLINE BRANCH, 24105 Lake Gregory Dr, Crestline, 92325-1087, SAN 334-1852. Tel: 909-338-3294. FAX: 909-338-0964. Web Site: www.sbclib.org/LibraryLocations/CrestlineBranchLibrary.aspx. *Br Mgr,* Lauren Lane
Founded 1919
Library Holdings: Bk Vols 18,458
Open Mon-Wed 11-7, Thurs 10-6, Sat 9-5
Friends of the Library Group

GRAND TERRACE BRANCH, 22795 Barton Rd, Grand Terrace, 92313, SAN 325-4453. Tel: 909-783-0147. FAX: 909-783-1913. Web Site: www.sbclib.org/LibraryLocations/GrandTerraceBranchLibrary.aspx. *Br Mgr,* Lisa Llewellyn
Founded 1985
Library Holdings: Bk Vols 24,771
Open Mon-Wed 11-7, Thurs & Fri 10-6, Sat 9-5
Friends of the Library Group

HESPERIA BRANCH, 9650 Seventh Ave, Hesperia, 92345, SAN 334-1976. Tel: 760-244-4898. FAX: 760-244-1530. Web Site: www.sbclib.org/LibraryLocations/HesperiaBranchLibrary.aspx. *Br Mgr,* Robin Hawley
Founded 1970
Library Holdings: Bk Vols 78,553
Open Mon-Thurs 10-8, Fri 10-6, Sat 9-5, Sun 1-5
Friends of the Library Group

JANICE HORST BRANCH, 33103 Old Woman Springs Rd, Lucerne Valley, 92356, SAN 334-2093. Tel: 760-248-7521. FAX: 760-248-1131. Web Site: www.sbclib.org/LibraryLocations/LucerneValleyJaniceHorstBranchLibrary.aspx. *Br Mgr,* Kristen Stevens
Founded 1914
Library Holdings: Bk Vols 20,620
Open Mon-Wed 11-7, Thurs 10-6, Sat 9-5

JOSHUA TREE BRANCH, 6465 Park Blvd, Joshua Tree, 92252, SAN 334-200X. Tel: 760-366-8615. FAX: 760-366-8615. Web Site: www.sbclib.org/LibraryLocations/JoshuaTreeBranchLibrary.aspx. *Br Mgr,* Sarah Correa
Founded 1945
Library Holdings: Bk Vols 17,560
Open Mon-Wed 11-7, Thurs 10-6, Sat 9-5
Friends of the Library Group

KAISER BRANCH, 11155 Almond Ave, Fontana, 92337. Tel: 909-357-5900, Ext 14174. FAX: 909-428-8494. Web Site: www.sbclib.org/LibraryLocations/KaiserBranchLibrary.aspx. *Br Mgr,* Melanie Orosco
Founded 2000
Library Holdings: Bk Vols 29,123
Open Mon-Thurs 3-8, Sat 9-5
Friends of the Library Group

LAKE ARROWHEAD, 27235 Hwy 189, Blue Jay, 92317, SAN 334-2034. Tel: 909-337-3118. FAX: 909-337-2287. Web Site: www.sbclib.org/LibraryLocations/LakeArrowheadBranch.aspx. *Br Mgr,* Frederick Malcomb
Founded 1924
Library Holdings: Bk Vols 26,284
Open Mon-Wed 11-7, Thurs 10-6, Sat 9-5
Friends of the Library Group

LEWIS LIBRARY & TECHNOLOGY CENTER, 8437 Sierra Ave, Fontana, 92335-3892. Tel: 909-574-4500. Web Site: www.sbclib.org/LibraryLocations/FontanaLewisLibraryTechnologyCenter.aspx. *Br Mgr,* Beth Djonne
Open Mon-Thurs 10-9, Fri & Sat 10-6, Sun 12-5
Friends of the Library Group

LOMA LINDA BRANCH, 25581 Barton Rd, Loma Linda, 92354-3125, SAN 334-2069. Tel: 909-796-8621. FAX: 909-796-4221. Web Site: www.sbclib.org/LibraryLocations/LomaLindaBranchLibrary.aspx. *Br Mgr,* Latoya Courtney
Founded 1967
Library Holdings: Bk Vols 42,866
Open Mon-Wed 11-7, Thurs 10-6, Sun 9-5

MENTONE SENIOR CENTER & LIBRARY, 1331 Opal Ave, Mentone, 92359, SAN 334-2123. Tel: 909-794-0327. FAX: 909-794-8394. Web Site: www.sbclib.org/LibraryLocations/MentoneSeniorCenterandLibrary.aspx. *Br Mgr,* Sonam Devi
Founded 1939
Library Holdings: Bk Vols 15,965
Open Mon-Wed 11-7, Thurs 10-6, Sat 9-5

MONTCLAIR BRANCH, 9955 Fremont Ave, Montclair, 91763, SAN 334-2158. Tel: 909-624-4671. FAX: 909-621-1261. Web Site: www.sbclib.org/LibraryLocations/MontclairBranchLibrary.aspx. *Br Mgr,* Griselda Flores
Founded 1952
Library Holdings: Bk Vols 37,347
Open Mon-Wed 11-7, Thurs & Fri 10-6, Sat 9-5

NEEDLES BRANCH, 1111 Bailey Ave, Needles, 92363, SAN 334-2182. Tel: 760-326-9255. FAX: 760-326-9238. Web Site: www.sbclib.org/LibraryLocations/NeedlesBranchLibrary.aspx. *Br Mgr,* Joan Meis Wilson
Founded 1917
Library Holdings: Bk Vols 20,951
Open Mon-Wed 11-7, Thurs 10-6, Sat 9-5

PHELAN MEMORIAL LIBRARY, 9800 Clovis Rd, Phelan, 92371. (Mail add: PO Box 292688, Phelan, 92329). Tel: 760-868-3053. FAX: 760-868-1386. Web Site:

www.sbclib.org/LibraryLocations/PhelanMemorialLibrary.aspx. *Br Mgr,* Tim Johnson
Founded 2002
Library Holdings: Bk Vols 27,174
Open Mon-Wed 11-7, Thurs 10-6, Sat 9-5
Friends of the Library Group

SAM J RACADIO LIBRARY & ENVIRONMENTAL LEARNING CENTER, 7863 Central Ave, Highland, 92346-4107, SAN 334-1917. Tel: 909-425-4700. FAX: 909-425-4710. Web Site: www.sbclib.org/LibraryLocations/HighlandSamJRacadioLibrary.aspx. *Interim Br Mgr,* Latoya Courtney
Founded 1914
Library Holdings: Bk Vols 68,593
Open Mon-Wed 10-8, Thurs & Fri 10-6, Sat 9-5
Friends of the Library Group

RIALTO BRANCH, 251 W First St, Rialto, 92376, SAN 334-2212. Tel: 909-875-0144. FAX: 909-875-2801. Web Site: www.sbclib.org/LibraryLocations/RialtoBranchLibrary.aspx. *Br Mgr,* Stacey Ramos
Founded 1914
Library Holdings: Bk Vols 46,880
Open Mon-Wed 11-7, Thurs & Fri 10-6, Sat 9-5
Friends of the Library Group

RUNNING SPRINGS BRANCH, 2677 Whispering Pines Dr, Running Springs, 92382, SAN 334-2247. Tel: 909-867-3604. Web Site: www.sbclib.org/LibraryLocations/RunningSpringsBranchLibrary.aspx. *Br Mgr,* Jessica Harp
Founded 1938
Library Holdings: Bk Vols 9,337
Open Mon-Wed 11-7, Thurs 10-6, Sat 9-5

SUMMIT BRANCH LIBRARY, 15551 Summit Ave, Fontana, 92336, SAN 334-1941. Tel: 909-357-5950, Ext 15113. Web Site: www.sbclib.org/LibraryLocations/SummitBranchLibrary.aspx. *Br Mgr,* Melanie Orosco
Founded 1914
Library Holdings: Bk Vols 27,395
Open Mon-Thurs 3-8, Sat 9-5

JAMES S THALMAN BRANCH, 14020 City Center Dr, Chino Hills, 91709-5442, SAN 373-5885. Tel: 909-590-5380. FAX: 909-591-5267. Web Site: www.sbclib.org/LibraryLocations/JamesSThalmanChinoHillsBranchLibrary.aspx. *Br Mgr,* Leslie Tepe
Founded 1992
Library Holdings: Bk Vols 75,161
Open Mon-Thurs 10-8, Fri 10-6, Sat 9-5, Sun 1-5
Friends of the Library Group

TRONA BRANCH, 82805 Mountain View St, Trona, 93562, SAN 334-2271. Tel: 760-372-5847. FAX: 760-372-5847. Web Site: www.sbclib.org/LibraryLocations/TronaBranchLibrary.aspx. *Br Mgr,* Stacy Cliff
Founded 1915
Library Holdings: Bk Vols 9,356
Open Mon-Wed 11-7, Thurs 10-6, Sat 9-5

TWENTYNINE PALMS BRANCH, 6078 Adobe Rd, Twentynine Palms, 92277, SAN 334-2301. Tel: 760-367-9519. FAX: 760-361-0703. Web Site: www.sbclib.org/LibraryLocations/TwentyninePalmsBranchLibrary.aspx. *Br Mgr,* Sarah Bartlett
Founded 1928
Library Holdings: Bk Vols 27,299
Open Mon-Wed 11-7, Thurs 10-6, Sat 9-5
Friends of the Library Group

WRIGHTWOOD BRANCH, 6011 Pine St, Wrightwood, 92397-1962, SAN 334-2344. Tel: 760-249-4577. FAX: 760-249-3263. Web Site: www.sbclib.org/LibraryLocations/WrightwoodBranchLibrary.aspx. *Br Mgr,* Robin Cornett
Founded 1981
Library Holdings: Bk Vols 14,752
Open Mon-Wed 11-7, Thurs 10-6, Sat 9-5
Friends of the Library Group

YUCAIPA BRANCH, 12040 Fifth St, Yucaipa, 92399, SAN 334-2360. Tel: 909-790-3146. FAX: 909-790-3151. Web Site: www.sbclib.org/LibraryLocations/YucaipaBranchLibrary.aspx. *Br Mgr,* Elizabeth Williams
Founded 1914
Library Holdings: Bk Vols 44,830
Open Mon-Wed 11-7, Thurs & Fri 10-6, Sat 9-5
Friends of the Library Group

YUCCA VALLEY BRANCH, 57098 Twentynine Palms Hwy, Yucca Valley, 92284, SAN 334-2395. Tel: 760-228-5455. FAX: 760-228-5459. Web Site: www.sbclib.org/LibraryLocations/YuccaValleyBranch.aspx. *Br Mgr,* Michael Jacome
Founded 1946
Library Holdings: Bk Vols 44,432
Open Mon-Wed 11-7, Thurs 10-6, Sat 9-5
Friends of the Library Group

J SAN BERNARDINO VALLEY COLLEGE LIBRARY*, 701 S Mount Vernon Ave, 92410. SAN 301-3022. Tel: 909-384-4448. Reference Tel: 909-384-8289. Administration Tel: 909-384-8542. Web Site: library.valleycollege.edu. *Libr Dir,* Ron Hastings; E-mail: rhastings@valleycollege.edu; *Librn,* Virginia Evans-Perry; Tel: 909-384-8699, E-mail: gperry@valleycollege.edu; *Librn,* Dr Celia Huston; Tel: 909-384-8574, E-mail: cmckinl@valleycollege.edu; *Librn,* Dr Marie D Mestas; Tel: 909-384-8576, E-mail: mmestas@valleycollege.edu; *Librn,* Patricia A Wall; Tel: 909-384-8577, E-mail: pwall@valleycollege.edu; *Circ Supvr,* Angelita Gideon; Tel: 909-384-8567, E-mail: agideon@valleycollege.edu. Subject Specialists: *Theatre arts,* Ron Hastings; *English lit, Hist, Libr sci,* Dr Marie D Mestas; Staff 7 (MLS 4, Non-MLS 3)
Founded 1928. Highest Degree: Associate
Library Holdings: Bk Vols 101,043; Per Subs 305
Special Collections: Local History, California & The West. State Document Depository; US Document Depository
Subject Interests: Humanities, Native Am culture, Native Am hist
Automation Activity & Vendor Info: (Acquisitions) OCLC; (Cataloging) OCLC; (Circulation) OCLC; (Course Reserve) OCLC; (OPAC) OCLC; (Serials) OCLC
Wireless access
Special Services for the Deaf - ADA equip; Assisted listening device; Assistive tech
Special Services for the Blind - Assistive/Adapted tech devices, equip & products
Open Mon-Thurs 7:30am-8pm, Fri 7:30-5, Sat 9-2

SAN BRUNO

G THE NATIONAL ARCHIVES AT SAN FRANCISCO*, 1000 Commodore Dr, 94066-2350. SAN 301-3030. Tel: 650-238-3501. FAX: 650-238-3510. E-mail: sanbruno.archives@nara.gov. Web Site: www.archives.gov/san-francisco. *Dir,* Stephanie Bayless; E-mail: stephanie.bayless@nara.gov; Staff 11 (MLS 1, Non-MLS 10)
Founded 1969
Library Holdings: Microforms 60,000
Special Collections: Archival Holdings, 1850-1980, architectural drawings, maps, photos, textual doc; Bureau of Indian Affairs, California & Nevada, 1859-1960, doc, micro; Bureau of Land Management, 1853-1960, doc, micro; Chinese Immigration Records, 1882-1955, doc; Department of Energy, 1915-1970, doc; Government of American Samoa, 1900-1966, doc; National Park Service, 1910-1969, doc; San Francisco Mint, 1853-1960, doc; United States Army Corps of Engineers, 1853-1976, doc; United States Attorneys (San Francisco), 1913-1971, doc; United States Census, 1790-1930, micro; United States Committee on Fair Employment Practice, 1941-1946, doc; United States Court of Appeals for Ninth Circuit, 1891-1969, doc; United States District Court, Eastern District of California, 1900-1973, doc; United States District Court, Hawaii, 1900-1968, doc; United States District Court, Nevada (Reno/Carson City), 1865-1963, doc, micro; United States District Courts for Northern District of California, 1851-1972, doc, micro; United States Forest Service, 1870-1970, doc; United States National War Labor Board, 1942-1947; United States Naval Shipyards (Mare Island, Pearl Harbor & San Francisco), 1854-1965, doc; United States Penitentiary at Alcatraz, 1934-1964, doc
Subject Interests: Asian-Am studies, Genealogy, Immigration, Labor, Land, Maritime, Native Am, Natural res, Naturalization, Naval hist, World War II
Function: Archival coll, For res purposes, Govt ref serv, Magnifiers for reading, Photocopying/Printing, Telephone ref, Wheelchair accessible, Workshops
Publications: A Guide to Records of Asian Americans & Pacific Islanders at NARA's Pacific Region (San Francisco); Chinese Immigration & Chinese in the United States: Records in the Regional Archives of the National Archives & Records Administration; Guide to Records in the National Archives-Pacific Sierra Region; Records in the National Archives-Pacific Sierra Region for Study of Science, Technology, Natural Resources & the Environment; Records in the National Archives-Pacific Sierra Region for the Study of Ethnic History; Records in the National Archives-Pacific Sierra Region for the Study of Labor & Business History
Partic in Cooperative Information Network
Open Mon-Fri 7:30-4
Restriction: Non-circulating coll, Not a lending libr, Open to pub for ref only, Pub ref by request, Pub use on premises

P SAN BRUNO PUBLIC LIBRARY, 701 Angus Ave W, 94066-3490. SAN 301-3049. Tel: 650-616-7078. FAX: 650-876-0848. E-mail: sbpl@plsinfo.org. Web Site: www.sanbrunolibrary.org. *Community Servs Superintendent, Library Servs,* Tim Wallace; E-mail: twallace@sanbruno.ca.gov; Staff 7 (MLS 5, Non-MLS 2)
Founded 1916. Pop 42,850; Circ 337,498
Library Holdings: Bk Vols 94,000
Special Collections: San Bruno Historical Pictures. Oral History

Automation Activity & Vendor Info: (OPAC) Innovative Interfaces, Inc - Millennium
Wireless access
Function: 24/7 Electronic res, 24/7 Online cat, 3D Printer, Archival coll, Art exhibits, Audiobks via web, Bilingual assistance for Spanish patrons, Bks on CD, Children's prog, Computer training, Computers for patron use, Digital talking bks, E-Reserves, Electronic databases & coll, Free DVD rentals, Homebound delivery serv, Homework prog, ILL available, Internet access, Magazines, Museum passes, Music CDs, Online cat, Online ref, OverDrive digital audio bks, Photocopying/Printing, Printer for laptops & handheld devices, Prog for adults, Prog for children & young adult, Ref serv available, Scanner, Spanish lang bks, Spoken cassettes & CDs, Story hour, Summer & winter reading prog, Summer reading prog, Tax forms, Teen prog, Telephone ref
Mem of Peninsula Library System
Open Mon 12-8, Tues-Fri 12-6, Sat 10-5
Friends of the Library Group

J SKYLINE COLLEGE LIBRARY*, 3300 College Dr, 94066-1698. SAN 301-3057. Tel: 650-738-4311. FAX: 650-738-4149. E-mail: skylibrary@smccd.edu. Web Site: www.skylinecollege.edu/library. *Interim Dir,* Anya Arnold; E-mail: arnolda@smccd.edu; *Librn,* Eric Brenner; E-mail: brenner@smccd.edu; Staff 3 (MLS 3)
Founded 1969. Enrl 6,455; Fac 156
Library Holdings: Bk Titles 50,000; Per Subs 240
Subject Interests: Feminism
Partic in OCLC Online Computer Library Center, Inc
Open Mon-Thurs 8am-10pm, Fri 8-4, Sat (Sept-May) 10-2

SAN DIEGO

C ALLIANT INTERNATIONAL UNIVERSITY*, Walter Library - San Diego Campus, 10455 Pomerado Rd, 92131-1799. SAN 301-357X. Tel: 858-635-4511. Interlibrary Loan Service Tel: 858-635-4605. Reference Tel: 858-635-4510. FAX: 858-635-4599. E-mail: library@alliant.edu, wlibrary@alliant.edu. Web Site: library.alliant.edu. *Dir, Libr Serv, Univ Librn,* Scott Zimmer; Tel: 858-635-4553, E-mail: szimmer@alliant.edu; *Ref & Instruction Librn,* Irina Clark; Tel: 858-635-4552, E-mail: iclark@alliant.edu; *ILL Tech,* Kanjana Boes; E-mail: kboes@alliant.edu; Staff 9 (MLS 5, Non-MLS 4)
Founded 1952. Enrl 1,521; Fac 75; Highest Degree: Doctorate
Library Holdings: DVDs 225; e-books 148,595; Bk Vols 68,108; Per Subs 123; Videos 598
Subject Interests: Bus, Educ, Intl relations, Psychol
Automation Activity & Vendor Info: (Acquisitions) Innovative Interfaces, Inc - Millennium; (Cataloging) Innovative Interfaces, Inc - Millennium; (Circulation) Innovative Interfaces, Inc - Millennium; (Course Reserve) Innovative Interfaces, Inc - Millennium; (ILL) Innovative Interfaces, Inc - Millennium; (Media Booking) Innovative Interfaces, Inc - Millennium; (OPAC) Innovative Interfaces, Inc - Millennium; (Serials) Innovative Interfaces, Inc - Millennium
Wireless access
Partic in Link+
Open Mon-Thurs 8am-10pm, Fri 8-6, Sat 10-6, Sun 12-8
Restriction: Borrowing privileges limited to fac & registered students
Friends of the Library Group

GL CALIFORNIA COURT OF APPEAL*, Fourth Appellate District-Division One Law Library, 750 B St, Ste 300, 92101. SAN 301-312X. Tel: 619-744-0760. Web Site: www.courts.ca.gov/4dca. *Librn,* Ruth Gervais; E-mail: ruth.gervais@jud.ca.gov; Staff 1 (MLS 1)
Founded 1929
Library Holdings: Bk Vols 45,000
Subject Interests: State law
Automation Activity & Vendor Info: (Cataloging) Innovative Interfaces, Inc - Sierra
Wireless access
Restriction: Staff use only

GL CALIFORNIA DEPARTMENT OF JUSTICE LIBRARY*, 600 W Broadway, Ste 1800, 92101. SAN 301-3138. Tel: 619-738-9000. *Libr Tech,* Norma Santa Cruz; E-mail: norma.santacruz@doj.ca.gov; Staff 2 (MLS 1, Non-MLS 1)
Founded 1972
Library Holdings: Bk Titles 26,000; Per Subs 50
Automation Activity & Vendor Info: (Cataloging) Inmagic, Inc.; (Serials) Inmagic, Inc.
Publications: Newsletter
Restriction: Staff use only

CL CALIFORNIA WESTERN SCHOOL OF LAW LIBRARY*, 290 Cedar St, 92101. (Mail add: 225 Cedar St, 92101), SAN 301-3162. Tel: 619-525-1418. Reference Tel: 619-525-1419. FAX: 619-685-2918. Web Site: www.cwsl.edu/library. *Assoc Dean, Libr & Info Serv,* Phyllis Gragg; Tel: 619-525-1420, E-mail: pgragg@cwsl.edu; *Asst Dir, Tech & Admin Serv,* Amy Moberly; Tel: 619-525-1421, E-mail: alm@cwsl.edu; *Assoc Dir, Educational Tech & Strategic Initiatives,* Barbara Glennan; Tel: 619-525-1499, E-mail: bag@cwsl.edu; *Acq & Budget Control Librn,* Ian R Kipnes; Tel: 619-515-1512, E-mail: ikipnes@cwsl.edu; *Foreign & Intl Law Ref Librn,* Bobbi Weaver; Tel: 619-525-1497, E-mail: baw@cwsl.edu; *Ref Librn, Stacks Mgr,* Ms Brandon Baker; Tel: 619-525-1425, E-mail: blb@cwsl.edu; *Ref Librn,* Robert O'Leary; Tel: 619-515-1584, E-mail: ROLeary@cwsl.edu. Subject Specialists: *Foreign law, Intl law,* Bobbi Weaver; Staff 8 (MLS 8)
Founded 1958. Fac 52; Highest Degree: Doctorate
Aug 2012-Jul 2013 Income $1,553,192. Mats Exp $1,020,767, Books $63,937, Per/Ser (Incl. Access Fees) $605,467, Micro $1,007, AV Mat $1,148, Electronic Ref Mat (Incl. Access Fees) $334,451, Presv $14,757
Library Holdings: AV Mats 751; CDs 151; DVDs 568; Bk Titles 60,178; Bk Vols 355,814; Per Subs 5,771
Special Collections: Congressional Information Service (US Congress Coll), micro; US Supreme Court Records & Briefs, micro. State Document Depository
Subject Interests: Law
Automation Activity & Vendor Info: (Acquisitions) Innovative Interfaces, Inc; (Cataloging) Innovative Interfaces, Inc; (Circulation) Innovative Interfaces, Inc; (Course Reserve) Innovative Interfaces, Inc; (ILL) OCLC; (OPAC) Innovative Interfaces, Inc; (Serials) Innovative Interfaces, Inc
Wireless access
Function: Computers for patron use, Electronic databases & coll, Free DVD rentals, ILL available, Online cat, Photocopying/Printing, VHS videos, Wheelchair accessible
Partic in Law Library Microform Consortium; NELLCO Law Library Consortium, Inc.; OCLC Online Computer Library Center, Inc; Statewide California Electronic Library Consortium
Restriction: Borrowing privileges limited to fac & registered students, Circ privileges for students & alumni only, Not open to pub

J FASHION INSTITUTE OF DESIGN & MERCHANDISING*, Resource & Research Center, 350 Tenth Ave, 3rd Flr, 92101. SAN 370-2197. Tel: 619-235-2049. Toll Free Tel: 800-243-3436. Web Site: www.fidm.com. *Dir,* Kathy Bailon; E-mail: kbailon@fidm.com; Staff 3 (MLS 1, Non-MLS 2)
Founded 1969. Enrl 3,000; Highest Degree: Bachelor
Library Holdings: Bk Vols 7,000; Per Subs 120
Automation Activity & Vendor Info: (Acquisitions) Gateway; (Cataloging) Gateway; (Circulation) Gateway; (Course Reserve) Gateway; (ILL) Gateway; (OPAC) Gateway; (Serials) Gateway
Function: For res purposes, ILL available, Ref serv available
Restriction: Not open to pub, Open to students, fac & staff

R FIRST PRESBYTERIAN CHURCH OF SAN DIEGO LIBRARY*, 320 Date St, 92101. SAN 301-3219. Tel: 619-232-7513. FAX: 619-232-8469. Web Site: www.fpcsd.org. *Library Contact,* Ginny Van Tassel
Founded 1940
Library Holdings: Bk Titles 2,000; Per Subs 6
Open Mon-Fri 8:30-12:15 & 1-4

L HIGGS, FLETCHER & MACK LLP*, Law Library, 401 West A St, Ste 2600, 92101-7913. SAN 301-3243. Tel: 619-236-1551. FAX: 619-696-1410. Web Site: www.higgslaw.com.
Founded 1939
Library Holdings: Bk Vols 12,000
Partic in American Association of Law Libraries
Restriction: Staff use only

S HUBBS-SEA WORLD RESEARCH INSTITUTE*, 2595 Ingraham St, 92109. SAN 326-4084. Tel: 619-226-3870. FAX: 619-226-3944. Web Site: hswri.org. *Library Contact,* Dena Leon
Library Holdings: Bk Vols 620; Per Subs 30
Restriction: Not open to pub

L LATHAM & WATKINS*, Law Library, 12670 High Bluff Dr, 92130. SAN 371-1021. Tel: 858-523-5400. Web Site: lw.com/offices/sandiego. *Ref Librn,* Kara Gelman; E-mail: kara.gelman@lw.com; Staff 4 (MLS 4)
Founded 1982
Library Holdings: Bk Titles 1,000; Bk Vols 2,700
Open Mon-Fri 8-5

A MARINE CORPS RECRUIT DEPOT LIBRARY*, 3800 Chosin Ave, Bldg 7 W, 92140-5196. Tel: 619-524-1849. *Supvry Librn,* Holland Kessenger; *Head, Program Dev,* Jennifer Leubbert; E-mail: jennifer.leubbert@usmc-mccs.org; Staff 6 (MLS 1, Non-MLS 5)
Founded 1927
Library Holdings: CDs 1,245; DVDs 2,638; Bk Vols 31,173; Per Subs 72
Special Collections: Marine Corps Professional Reading Program
Subject Interests: Marine Corps
Automation Activity & Vendor Info: (Circulation) SirsiDynix-WorkFlows
Wireless access

Function: Audiobks via web, Bks on CD, Children's prog, Computers for patron use, Distance learning, Electronic databases & coll, Holiday prog, Internet access, Literacy & newcomer serv, Online cat, Orientations, Outreach serv, Photocopying/Printing, Prog for adults, Prog for children & young adult, Ref & res, Ref serv available, Scanner, Spoken cassettes & CDs, Story hour, Summer reading prog, Tax forms
Restriction: Mil, family mem, retirees, Civil Serv personnel NAF only

S MARITIME MUSEUM OF SAN DIEGO, The MacMullen Library & Research Archives, 1492 N Harbor Dr, 92101. SAN 371-5604. Tel: 619-234-9153, Ext 118. FAX: 619-234-8345. E-mail: librarian@sdmaritime.org. Web Site: www.sdmaritime.org/library-and-research. *Colls Mgr,* Dr Kevin Sheehan; Staff 1 (Non-MLS 1)
Founded 1977
Library Holdings: Bk Titles 7,500; Bk Vols 7,800; Per Subs 68
Special Collections: Maritime Historical Technical & Commercial Magazines; Maritime History Coll, ephemera, flms, hist docs, photos, postcards, scrapbks, videos; Museum Ship Archives (Star of India, Berkeley, Medea, Pilot, Butcher Boy & Californian); Passenger Ship Memorabilia; Ship & Boat Plans & Blueprints; Ships' Logs. Oral History
Subject Interests: Nautical, Pacific Ocean
Function: For res purposes
Open Mon-Fri 9-Noon
Restriction: Pub use on premises
Friends of the Library Group

S MINGEI INTERNATIONAL MUSEUM, Frances Hamilton White Art Reference Library, 1439 El Prado, 92101-1617. SAN 373-1359. Tel: 619-239-0003, Ext 132. FAX: 619-239-0605. E-mail: library@mingei.org. Web Site: www.mingei.org/. *Libr Mgr,* Kristi Ehrig-Burgess; *Libr Asst,* Casey Prado; Tel: 619-331-3569
Library Holdings: Bk Vols 12,000; Videos 200
Special Collections: Chinese Textiles; Florence Temko Paper Coll; Indonesian Coll; Japanese Ceramics; Meiers Mexico Coll; V'Ann Cornelius Origami Book Coll
Subject Interests: Baskets, Ceramics, Clay, Folk art, Glass, Metals, Sculpture, Textiles, Wood
Open Tues-Sun 10-5
Restriction: Mem only, Not a lending libr, Open to others by appt

S NATIONAL STEEL & SHIPBUILDING CO*, Engineering Library, 7470 Mission Valley Rd, 92108. SAN 301-3383. Tel: 619-544-3400. FAX: 619-544-3543. Web Site: www.nassco.com. *Tech Serv Librn,* Kathy M Baker
Library Holdings: Bk Vols 3,000
Restriction: Staff use only

C NATIONAL UNIVERSITY LIBRARY*, 9393 Lightwave Ave, 92123-1447. SAN 301-3391. Tel: 858-541-7900. Toll Free Tel: 800-628-8648, Ext 7900. FAX: 858-541-7994. E-mail: refdesk@nu.edu. Web Site: library.nu.edu, nu.libguides.com/about. *Interim Dir, Libr Serv,* Phil Oels; Tel: 858-541-7942, E-mail: poels@nu.edu; *Assoc Dir, Assessment & Tech Serv,* Ed Jones; Tel: 858-541-7920, E-mail: ejones@nu.edu; *Assoc Dir, Coll, Assoc Dir, User Experience,* Betty Kellogg; Tel: 858-541-7944, E-mail: bkellogg@nu.edu; *Access Serv Supvr,* Patrick Pemberton; Tel: 858-541-7909, E-mail: ppembert@nu.edu; Staff 17 (MLS 13, Non-MLS 4)
Founded 1975. Enrl 18,207; Fac 1,046; Highest Degree: Master
Jul 2014-Jun 2015. Mats Exp $2,289,592, Books $376,543, Per/Ser (Incl. Access Fees) $226,052, Other Print Mats $295,246, Micro $9,319, AV Equip $2,772, AV Mat $58,183, Electronic Ref Mat (Incl. Access Fees) $1,103,186. Sal $1,619,153
Library Holdings: AV Mats 24,449; Bks on Deafness & Sign Lang 373; CDs 658; DVDs 4,079; e-books 242,163; e-journals 106,145; Electronic Media & Resources 24,449; Microforms 1,250; Bk Titles 158,163; Bk Vols 198,789; Per Subs 1,035; Videos 5,595
Special Collections: Adult Learners
Automation Activity & Vendor Info: (Acquisitions) Ex Libris Group; (Cataloging) Ex Libris Group; (Circulation) Ex Libris Group; (Course Reserve) Ex Libris Group; (ILL) OCLC; (Media Booking) Dymaxion; (OPAC) Ex Libris Group; (Serials) Ex Libris Group
Wireless access
Function: Art exhibits, Computers for patron use, Doc delivery serv, Electronic databases & coll, ILL available, Mail & tel request accepted, Online cat, Online info literacy tutorials on the web & in blackboard, Online ref, Outreach serv, Outside serv via phone, mail, e-mail & web, Ref serv available
Partic in Statewide California Electronic Library Consortium
Special Services for the Deaf - Assisted listening device; Assistive tech; Bks on deafness & sign lang; Closed caption videos; Coll on deaf educ
Special Services for the Blind - Ednalite Hi-Vision scope
Open Mon-Thurs 10-10, Fri 10-6, Sat 8:30-5, Sun 10-5
Restriction: Circ privileges for students & alumni only, Open to pub for ref only, Open to students, fac & staff, Pub use on premises

C POINT LOMA NAZARENE UNIVERSITY*, Ryan Library, 3900 Lomaland Dr, 92106-2899. SAN 301-3405. Tel: 619-849-2312. Circulation Tel: 619-849-2312. Interlibrary Loan Service Tel: 619-849-2262. Reference Tel: 619-849-2337. Administration Tel: 619-849-2335. FAX: 619-222-0711. E-mail: reflib@pointloma.edu. Web Site: libguides.pointloma.edu/ryanlibrary. *Libr Dir,* Denise Nelson; E-mail: denisenelson@pointloma.edu; *Head, Tech Serv & Syst,* Anne-Elizabeth Powell; *Instrul Serv Librn,* Phyllis Fox; *Instrul Serv Librn,* Robin Lang; *Instrul Serv Librn,* Julie Sweeney; Staff 9 (MLS 5, Non-MLS 4)
Founded 1902. Enrl 3,445; Highest Degree: Master
Library Holdings: Bk Vols 170,000; Per Subs 613
Special Collections: Armenian-Wesleyan Theological Library; Religion (Holiness Authors)
Subject Interests: Relig
Automation Activity & Vendor Info: (OPAC) OCLC
Wireless access
Partic in Coop Libr Agency for Syst & Servs; OCLC Online Computer Library Center, Inc; Southern California Theological Library Association; Statewide California Electronic Library Consortium

M RADY CHILDREN'S HOSPITAL - SAN DIEGO*, Health Sciences Library, 3020 Children's Way, Mailcode 5043, 92123-4282. SAN 325-0369. Tel: 858-966-7474. FAX: 858-966-4934. Web Site: www.rchsd.org. *Librn,* Lisa Naidoo; Staff 1 (MLS 1)
Founded 1955
Library Holdings: AV Mats 291; CDs 54; Bk Titles 2,744; Bk Vols 1,379; Per Subs 237
Subject Interests: Pediatrics
Automation Activity & Vendor Info: (Cataloging) Innovative Interfaces, Inc; (Circulation) Innovative Interfaces, Inc; (OPAC) Innovative Interfaces, Inc; (Serials) Innovative Interfaces, Inc
Partic in Medical Library Association; Medical Library Group of Southern California & Arizona; National Network of Libraries of Medicine Region 5

S SAN DIEGO AIR & SPACE MUSEUM, INC, N Paul Whittier Historical Aviation Library, 2001 Pan American Plaza, Balboa Park, 92101-1636. SAN 321-2653. Tel: 619-234-8291, Ext 125. FAX: 619-233-4526. E-mail: dseracini@sdasm.org. Web Site: www.sandiegoairandspace.org. *Libr Dir,* Katrina Pescador; Tel: 619-234-8291, Ext 123, E-mail: kpescador@sdasm.org; *Librn,* Pamela Gay; Tel: 619-234-8291, Ext 126, E-mail: pgay@sdasm.org; *Archivist,* Alan Renga; Staff 2 (MLS 2)
Founded 1978
Library Holdings: Bk Titles 24,000; Bk Vols 24,500; Per Subs 18
Special Collections: Air Mail Pioneers (Edwin Cooper Coll); Convair Corporate Files; Ed Heinemann Coll; FH Fleet Coll (Consolidated); Flying Cars (T P Hall Coll); Flying Wings Engineering (Wilhelm F Schult Coll); Frank T Courtney, Early Birds; George E A Hallett, Adm Marc Mitscher, John J Montgomery, Waldo D Waterman; Gliding & Soaring (Waldo Waterman Coll); John & Helen Sloan (Fokker); Ray Fife & Tex LaGrone Coll; Ryan Aeronautical Libr Coll
Subject Interests: Aerospace, Aviation, Mil aircraft
Function: Archival coll, For res purposes, Photocopying/Printing, Res libr, Telephone ref
Open Tues-Fri 10-4 by appointment only
Restriction: Non-circulating to the pub, Open to researchers by request, Restricted borrowing privileges, Staff & prof res

J SAN DIEGO CITY COLLEGE*, Learning Resource Center, 1313 Park Blvd, 92101. SAN 301-3421. Tel: 619-388-3421. FAX: 619-388-3410. E-mail: citylib@sdccd.edu. Web Site: library.sdcity.edu. *Dean, Info & Learning Tech,* Robbi Ewell; Tel: 619-388-3870, E-mail: rewell@sdccd.edu; *Chair, Librn,* Barbara Ring; Tel: 619-388-3319, E-mail: bring@sdccd.edu; *Librn,* Carol Withers; Tel: 619-388-3871, E-mail: cwithers@sdccd.edu; Staff 6 (MLS 6)
Founded 1916. Enrl 13,280; Fac 295
Library Holdings: Bk Vols 70,000; Per Subs 225
Automation Activity & Vendor Info: (Cataloging) SirsiDynix; (Circulation) SirsiDynix
Wireless access
Open Mon-Thurs 8am-9:50pm, Fri 8-4:20, Sat 10-2
Friends of the Library Group

P SAN DIEGO COUNTY LIBRARY*, MS 070, 5560 Overland Ave, Ste 110, 92123. Tel: 858-694-2415. Circulation Tel: 858-505-6353. FAX: 858-495-5981. Web Site: www.sdcl.org. *Dir,* Migell Acosta; Tel: 858-694-2389, E-mail: migell.acosta@sdcounty.ca.gov; *Dep Dir,* Susan Moore; Tel: 858-694-2448, E-mail: susan.moore@sdcounty.ca.gov; *Dep Dir,* Donna Ohr; Tel: 858-694-3786, E-mail: donna.ohr@sdcounty.ca.gov; Staff 316 (MLS 75, Non-MLS 241)
Founded 1913. Pop 1,091,536; Circ 10,788,181
Library Holdings: Audiobooks 46,807; AV Mats 303,463; CDs 50,150; DVDs 149,459; e-books 3,611; Large Print Bks 30,647; Microforms 9,234; Bk Titles 369,365; Bk Vols 1,270,103; Per Subs 2,969; Videos 8,478

Special Collections: African Languages; Arabic; Armenian; Cantonese; French; German; Greek; Hebrew; Hindi; Hmong; Italian; Japanese; Korean; Laotian; Mandarin; Miao; Mon-Khmer, Cambodian; Pashto; Persian; Portuguese; Punjabi; Russian; Scandinavian Languages; Spanish; Tagalog; Thai; Urdu; Vietnamese
Automation Activity & Vendor Info: (Acquisitions) Innovative Interfaces, Inc - Millennium; (Cataloging) Innovative Interfaces, Inc - Millennium; (Circulation) Innovative Interfaces, Inc - Millennium; (ILL) Innovative Interfaces, Inc - Millennium; (Media Booking) Innovative Interfaces, Inc - Millennium; (OPAC) Innovative Interfaces, Inc - Millennium
Wireless access
Publications: Library Calendar of Events (Monthly); Library Services Brochures; Library User's Guide
Partic in Serra Cooperative Library System
Special Services for the Blind - Assistive/Adapted tech devices, equip & products
Friends of the Library Group
Branches: 33
4S RANCH BRANCH, 10433 Reserve Dr, 92127. Tel: 858-673-4697. FAX: 858-673-1629. *Br Mgr,* June Zhou; E-mail: june.zhou@sdcounty.ca.gov
Pop 13,309; Circ 365,513
Library Holdings: Bk Vols 46,955
Open Mon & Thurs 9:30-6, Tues & Wed 9:30-8, Fri & Sat 9:30-5, Sun 12-5
Friends of the Library Group
ALPINE BRANCH, 1752 Alpine Blvd, Alpine, 91901, SAN 334-2603. Tel: 619-445-4221. FAX: 619-445-4856. *Br Mgr,* Jenne Bergstrom; E-mail: jenne.bergstrom@sdcounty.ca.gov
Pop 15,588; Circ 112,999
Library Holdings: Bk Vols 22,554
Open Mon & Wed 9:30-6, Tues & Thurs 9:30-8, Fri & Sat 9:30-5
Friends of the Library Group
BONITA-SUNNYSIDE BRANCH, 4375 Bonita Rd, Bonita, 91902-2698, SAN 334-2638. Tel: 619-475-4642. FAX: 619-475-4366. *Br Mgr,* Christopher Curley; Tel: 619-475-3867, E-mail: christopher.curley@sdcounty.ca.gov
Pop 14,294; Circ 294,010
Library Holdings: Bk Vols 44,103
Open Mon & Tues 9:30-8, Wed & Thurs 9:30-6, Fri & Sat 9:30-5, Sun 12-5
Friends of the Library Group
BORREGO SPRINGS BRANCH, 2580 Country Club Rd, Borrego Springs, 92004, SAN 334-2662. Tel: 760-767-5761. FAX: 760-767-3619. *Br Mgr,* Cynthia Thompson; E-mail: cynthia.thompson@sdcounty.ca.gov
Pop 4,971; Circ 47,777
Library Holdings: Bk Vols 13,876
Open Tues 9:30-6, Wed & Thurs 9:30-8, Fri & Sat 9-5, Sun 12-5
Friends of the Library Group
CAMPO-MORENA VILLAGE BRANCH, 31356 Hwy 94, Campo, 91906-3112, SAN 334-2697. Tel: 619-478-5945. FAX: 619-478-2446. *Br Mgr,* Keith Davis; E-mail: Keith.Davis@sdcounty.ca.gov
Pop 3,710; Circ 46,700
Library Holdings: Bk Vols 13,819
Open Tues & Wed 9-6, Thurs 12-8, Fri 9-5, Sat 9-4
Friends of the Library Group
CARDIFF-BY-THE-SEA BRANCH, 2081 Newcastle Ave, Cardiff, 92007-1724, SAN 334-3480. Tel: 760-753-4027. FAX: 760-753-4267. *Br Mgr,* Gabriel Aguirre; E-mail: gabriel.aguirre@sdcounty.ca.gov
Pop 17,291; Circ 123,972
Library Holdings: Bk Vols 31,231
Open Mon & Tues 9:30-6, Wed & Thurs 9:30-8, Fri & Sat 9:30-5
Friends of the Library Group
CASA DE ORO BRANCH, 9805 Campo Rd, No 180, Spring Valley, 91977-1477, SAN 334-2727. Tel: 619-463-3236. FAX: 619-463-8670. *Br Mgr,* Jefferson Baker; E-mail: jefferson.baker@sdcounty.ca.gov
Pop 23,634; Circ 136,056
Library Holdings: Bk Vols 36,374
Open Mon & Wed 9:30-6, Tues & Thurs 9:30-8, Fri & Sat 9:30-5
Friends of the Library Group
CREST BRANCH, 105 Juanita Lane, El Cajon, 92021-4399, SAN 334-2786. Tel: 619-442-7083. FAX: 619-442-4972. *Br Mgr,* Shannon Foster; E-mail: shannon.foster@sdcounty.ca.gov
Pop 7,954; Circ 30,653
Library Holdings: Bk Vols 12,998
Open Tues 12-8, Wed & Thurs 9:30-6, Fri 9:30-5, Sat 9:30-3
Friends of the Library Group
DEL MAR BRANCH, 1309 Camino del Mar, Del Mar, 92014-2693, SAN 334-2816. Tel: 858-755-1666. FAX: 858-755-8734. *Br Mgr,* Polly Cipparrone; E-mail: Polly.Cipparrone@sdcounty.ca.gov
Pop 4,780; Circ 140,089
Library Holdings: Bk Vols 32,184
Open Tues 9:30-6, Wed & Thurs 9:30-8, Fri & Sat 9:30-5, Sun 12-5
Friends of the Library Group
DESCANSO BRANCH, 9545 River Dr, Descanso, 91916, SAN 334-2840. Tel: 619-445-5279. FAX: 619-445-4891. *Br Mgr,* Christine Buckmaster; E-mail: Christine.Buckmaster@sdcounty.ca.gov
Pop 2,877; Circ 38,917
Library Holdings: Bk Vols 11,715
Open Tues & Wed 9-6, Thurs 12-8, Fri 9-5, Sat 9-4
Friends of the Library Group
EL CAJON BRANCH, 201 E Douglas, El Cajon, 92020, SAN 334-2875. Tel: 619-588-3718. FAX: 619-588-3701. *Br Mgr,* Elizabeth Vagani; Tel: 619-588-3708, E-mail: Elizabeth.Vagani@sdcounty.ca.gov
Pop 103,860; Circ 713,517
Library Holdings: Bk Vols 127,495
Open Mon-Thurs 9:30-8, Fri & Sat 9:30-5, Sun 12-5
Friends of the Library Group
ENCINITAS BRANCH, 540 Cornish Dr, Encinitas, 92024-4599, SAN 334-2905. Tel: 760-753-7376. FAX: 760-753-0582. *Br Mgr,* Jayne Henn; Tel: 760-634-6451, E-mail: jayne.henn@sdcounty.ca.gov
Pop 47,093; Circ 632,659
Library Holdings: Bk Vols 90,272
Open Mon-Thurs 9:30-8, Fri & Sat 9:30-5, Sun 12-5
Friends of the Library Group
FALLBROOK BRANCH, 124 S Mission Rd, Fallbrook, 92028, SAN 334-293X. Tel: 760-731-4650. FAX: 760-728-4731. *Br Mgr,* Kristopher Jorgensen; E-mail: kristopher.jorgensen@sdcounty.ca.gov
Pop 49,961; Circ 404,064
Library Holdings: Bk Vols 53,208
Open Mon & Wed 9:30-6, Tues & Thurs 9:30-8, Fri & Sat 9:30-5, Sun 12-5
Friends of the Library Group
FLETCHER HILLS BRANCH, 576 Garfield Ave, El Cajon, 92020-2792, SAN 334-2964. Tel: 619-466-1132. FAX: 619-466-4682. *Br Mgr,* Rebekah Sanders; E-mail: Rebekah.Sanders@sdcounty.ca.gov
Pop 16,364; Circ 102,427
Library Holdings: Bk Vols 24,457
Open Tues & Thurs 9:30-6, Wed 12-8, Fri & Sat 9:30-5
Friends of the Library Group
IMPERIAL BEACH BRANCH, 810 Imperial Beach Blvd, Imperial Beach, 91932-2798, SAN 334-2999. Tel: 619-424-6981. FAX: 619-424-8749. *Br Mgr,* June Frost; E-mail: june.frost@sdcounty.ca.gov
Pop 28,351; Circ 180,560
Library Holdings: Bk Vols 34,767
Open Mon & Thurs 9:30-6, Tues & Wed 9:30-8, Fri & Sat 9:30-5
Friends of the Library Group
JACUMBA BRANCH, 44605 Old Hwy 80, Jacumba, 91934, SAN 334-3022. Tel: 619-766-4608. FAX: 619-766-9206. *Br Mgr,* Sarah Misquez; E-mail: Sarah.Misquez@sdcounty.ca.gov
Pop 2,053; Circ 40,879
Library Holdings: Bk Vols 10,867
Open Tues 12-8, Wed & Thurs 9-6, Fri 9-5, Sat 9-4
Friends of the Library Group
JULIAN BRANCH, 1850 Hwy 78, Julian, 92036, SAN 334-3057. Tel: 760-765-0370. FAX: 760-765-2748. *Br Mgr,* Joshua Mitchell; E-mail: joshua.mitchell@sdcounty.ca.gov
Pop 4,275; Circ 99,942
Library Holdings: Bk Vols 28,474
Open Tues 9-8, Wed & Thurs 9-6, Fri & Sat 9-5
Friends of the Library Group
LA MESA BRANCH, 8074 Allison Ave, La Mesa, 91941-5001, SAN 334-3111. Tel: 619-469-2151. FAX: 619-697-3751. *Br Mgr,* Chelsie Harris; E-mail: Chelsie.Harris@sdcounty.ca.gov
Pop 59,544; Circ 711,643
Library Holdings: Bk Vols 90,918
Open Mon-Thurs 9:30-8, Fri & Sat 9:30-5, Sun 12-5
Friends of the Library Group
LAKESIDE BRANCH, 9839 Vine St, Lakeside, 92040-3199, SAN 334-3081. Tel: 619-443-1811. FAX: 619-443-8002. *Br Mgr,* Doris Adam; E-mail: doris.adam@sdcounty.ca.gov
Pop 54,906; Circ 215,872
Library Holdings: Bk Vols 47,377
Open Mon & Thurs 9:30-6, Tues & Wed 9:30-8, Fri & Sat 9:30-5
Friends of the Library Group
LEMON GROVE BRANCH, 3001 School Lane, Lemon Grove, 91945, SAN 334-3146. Tel: 619-463-9819. FAX: 619-463-8069. *Br Mgr,* Charlotte King-Mills; E-mail: Charlotte.King-Mills@sdcounty.ca.gov
Pop 30,691; Circ 157,754
Library Holdings: Bk Vols 49,134
Open Mon & Thurs 9:30-6, Tues & Wed 9:30-8, Fri & Sat 9:30-5
Friends of the Library Group
LINCOLN ACRES BRANCH, 2725 Granger Ave, National City, 91950-0168, SAN 334-3170. Tel: 619-475-9880. FAX: 619-475-4382. *Br Mgr,* Jose Ocadiz; E-mail: Jose.Ocadiz@sdcounty.ca.gov
Pop 2,097; Circ 28,652
Library Holdings: Bk Vols 10,068
Open Tues 12-8, Wed & Thurs 9:30-6, Fri & Sat 9:30-5
Friends of the Library Group

PINE VALLEY BRANCH, 28804 Old Hwy 80, Pine Valley, 91962, SAN 334-3200. Tel: 619-473-8022. FAX: 619-473-9638. *Br Mgr,* Naomi Ince; E-mail: Naomi.Ince@sdcounty.ca.gov
Pop 2,797; Circ 50,856
Library Holdings: Bk Vols 11,222
Open Tues 12-8, Wed & Thurs 9-6, Fri 9-5, Sat 9-4
Friends of the Library Group

POTRERO BRANCH, 24883 Potrero Valley Rd, Potrero, 91963-0051, SAN 334-3235. Tel: 619-478-5978. FAX: 619-478-2695. *Br Mgr,* Veronica Ortiz; E-mail: veronica.ortiz@sdcounty.ca.gov
Pop 228; Circ 61,098
Library Holdings: Bk Vols 16,795
Open Tues & Thurs 9-6, Wed 12-8, Fri 9-5, Sat 9-4
Friends of the Library Group

POWAY BRANCH, 13137 Poway Rd, Poway, 92064-4687, SAN 334-326X. Tel: 858-513-2900. FAX: 858-513-2922. *Br Mgr,* Marisa Lowe; E-mail: marisa.lowe@sdcounty.ca.gov
Pop 51,391; Circ 638,494
Library Holdings: Bk Vols 121,457
Open Mon-Thurs 9:30-8, Fri & Sat 9:30-5, Sun 12-5
Friends of the Library Group

RAMONA BRANCH, 1275 Main St, Ramona, 92065, SAN 334-3294. Tel: 760-788-5270. FAX: 760-738-2475. *Br Mgr,* Colleen Baker; E-mail: colleen.baker@sdcounty.ca.gov
Pop 35,904; Circ 178,060
Library Holdings: Bk Vols 42,116
Open Mon & Wed 9:30-6, Tues & Thurs 9:30-8, Fri & Sat 9:30-5, Sun 12-5
Friends of the Library Group

RANCHO SAN DIEGO BRANCH, 11555 Via Rancho San Diego, El Cajon, 92019. Tel: 619-660-5370. FAX: 619-660-6327. *Br Mgr,* Brenna Ring; E-mail: Brenna.Ring@sdcounty.ca.gov
Founded 2002. Pop 47,956; Circ 390,868
Library Holdings: Bk Vols 68,984
Open Mon & Wed 9:30-6, Tues & Thurs 9:30-8, Fri & Sat 9:30-5, Sun 12-5
Friends of the Library Group

RANCHO SANTA FE BRANCH, 17040 Avenida de Acacias, Rancho Santa Fe, 92067, SAN 334-3324. Tel: 858-756-2512. FAX: 858-756-3485. *Br Mgr,* Kathy Jung; E-mail: kathy.jung@sdcounty.ca.gov
Pop 13,424; Circ 85,187
Library Holdings: Bk Vols 39,623
Open Mon-Sat 9-5
Friends of the Library Group

SAN MARCOS BRANCH, Two Civic Center Dr, San Marcos, 92069-2949, SAN 334-3359. Tel: 760-891-3000. FAX: 760-891-3015. *Br Mgr,* Rebecca Lynn; E-mail: rebecca.lynn@sdcounty.ca.gov
Pop 113,292; Circ 667,137
Library Holdings: Bk Vols 92,576
Open Mon-Thurs 9:30-8, Fri & Sat 9:30-5, Sun 12-5
Friends of the Library Group

SANTEE BRANCH, 9225 Carlton Hills Blvd, No 17, Santee, 92071-3192, SAN 334-3383. Tel: 619-448-1863. FAX: 619-448-1497. *Br Mgr,* Cheryl Cosart; E-mail: Cheryl.Cosart@sdcounty.ca.gov
Pop 58,909; Circ 403,073
Library Holdings: Bk Vols 66,941
Open Mon-Thurs 9:30-8, Fri & Sat 9:30-5, Sun 12-5
Friends of the Library Group

SOLANA BEACH BRANCH, Earl Warren Middle School, 157 Stevens Ave, Solana Beach, 92075-1873, SAN 334-3413. Tel: 858-755-1404. FAX: 858-755-9327. *Br Mgr,* Pat Tirona; E-mail: Pat.Tirona@sdcounty.ca.gov
Pop 14,546; Circ 276,309
Library Holdings: Bk Vols 67,472
Open Mon & Thurs 8-6, Tues & Wed 8-8, Fri 8-5, Sat 9:30-5
Friends of the Library Group

SPRING VALLEY BRANCH, 836 Kempton St, Spring Valley, 91977, SAN 334-3448. Tel: 619-463-3006. FAX: 619-463-8917. *Br Mgr,* Jodi Delapena; E-mail: jodi.delapena@sdcounty.ca.gov
Pop 36,810; Circ 183,904
Library Holdings: Bk Vols 45,036
Open Mon & Thurs 9:30-6, Tues & Wed 9:30-8, Fri & Sat 9:30-5
Friends of the Library Group

VALLEY CENTER BRANCH, 29200 Cole Grade Rd, Valley Center, 92082-5880, SAN 334-3472. Tel: 760-749-1305. FAX: 760-749-1764. *Br Mgr,* Laura Zuckerman; E-mail: laura.zuckerman@sdcounty.ca.gov
Pop 15,236; Circ 176,570
Library Holdings: Bk Vols 49,437
Open Mon-Thurs 9:30-8, Fri & Sat 9:30-5
Friends of the Library Group

VISTA BRANCH, 700 Eucalyptus Ave, Vista, 92084-6245, SAN 334-3502. Tel: 760-643-5100. FAX: 760-643-5127. *Br Mgr,* Orquidia Contreras; E-mail: orquidia.contreras@sdcounty.ca.gov
Pop 109,618; Circ 792,750
Library Holdings: Bk Vols 152,495
Open Mon-Thurs 9:30-8, Fri & Sat 9:30-5, Sun 12-5
Friends of the Library Group
Bookmobiles: 2. Supvr, William Sannwald. Bk titles 7,500

S SAN DIEGO FAMILYSEARCH LIBRARY (FAMILY HISTORY CENTER), 4195 Camino Del Rio S, 92108. SAN 329-2118. Tel: 619-584-7668. Web Site: familysearch.org/wiki/en/San_Diego_California_FamilySearch_Center. *Dir,* David Kressin; *Dir,* Patricia Kressin
Founded 1966
Library Holdings: Bk Vols 13,000
Wireless access
Function: Genealogy discussion group, Res assist avail, Scanner
Special Services for the Deaf - Staff with knowledge of sign lang
Open Wed 11-8, Thurs & Fri 11-5, Sat 10-3

S SAN DIEGO HISTORY CENTER*, Balboa Park, 1649 El Prado, Ste 3, 92101. SAN 301-3448. Tel: 619-232-6203. FAX: 619-232-1059. E-mail: info@sandiegohistory.org. Web Site: www.sandiegohistory.org. *Coll Spec,* Natalie Fiocre; Tel: 616-232-6203, Ext 120, E-mail: nfiocre@sandiegohistory.org. Subject Specialists: *Photog,* Natalie Fiocre; Staff 3 (Non-MLS 3)
Founded 1929
Library Holdings: Bk Titles 10,000; Per Subs 30
Special Collections: Architectural Drawings; Booth Historical Photograph Coll; City, County & Superior Court Public Records; Ephemera Coll; Institute of History Coll; Manuscript Coll; Map Coll; Oral History Coll; Scrapbook Coll. Oral History
Subject Interests: Local hist
Automation Activity & Vendor Info: (Cataloging) Sydney; (OPAC) Sydney
Wireless access
Function: Photocopying/Printing, Ref serv available, Res libr, Wheelchair accessible
Publications: Guide to the Architectural Records Collection (2003) (Research guide); Guide to the Photograph Collection (1998) (Research guide); Guide to the Public Records Collection (Research guide); Journal of San Diego History
Open Wed-Fri 9:30-1 or by appointment
Restriction: Non-circulating, Not a lending libr, Open to pub for ref only, Photo ID required for access

GL SAN DIEGO LAW LIBRARY*, 1105 Front St, 92101-3904. SAN 301-343X. Tel: 619-531-3900. FAX: 619-238-7716. Web Site: sandiegolawlibrary.org. *Dir of Libr,* John Adkins; Tel: 619-531-3904, E-mail: jadkins@sdlawlibrary.org; Staff 30 (MLS 8, Non-MLS 22)
Founded 1891
Library Holdings: Bk Vols 221,975; Per Subs 298
Special Collections: California Appellate Court Briefs since 1895; California Supreme Court Briefs 1895; Local Legal History
Automation Activity & Vendor Info: (Cataloging) Innovative Interfaces, Inc; (Circulation) Innovative Interfaces, Inc
Wireless access
Publications: Guide to Collections & Services; Newsletters
Partic in Coop Libr Agency for Syst & Servs; Lexis, OCLC Online Computer Libr Ctr, Inc; Proquest Dialog
Open Mon-Thurs 8-6, Fri 8-5, Sat 9-1
Branches:
EAST COUNTY, 250 E Main St, El Cajon, 92020-3941, SAN 321-9364. Tel: 619-441-4451. FAX: 619-441-0235.
Library Holdings: Bk Vols 10,754
Open Wed 9-4
NORTH COUNTY, 325 S Melrose, Ste 300, Vista, 92081-6697, SAN 321-4117. Tel: 760-940-4386. FAX: 760-724-7694.
Library Holdings: Bk Vols 20,176
Open Mon-Thurs 9-4, Fri 9-1
Friends of the Library Group
SOUTH BAY, 500 Third Ave, Chula Vista, 91910-5617, SAN 321-4109. Tel: 619-691-4929. FAX: 619-427-7521.
Library Holdings: Bk Vols 16,071
Open Mon-Thurs 9-1

J SAN DIEGO MESA COLLEGE LIBRARY*, 7250 Mesa College Dr, 92111-4998. SAN 301-3456. Tel: 619-388-2695. Circulation Tel: 619-388-2696. Reference Tel: 619-388-2660. Administration Tel: 619-388-2799. Web Site: www.sdmesa.edu/library. *Chair, Instrul Serv Librn, Online Serv,* Alison Steinberg Gurganus; E-mail: asteinbe@sdccd.edu; *Coll Develop, Librn,* Lisa Burgert; E-mail: lburgert@sdccd.edu; Staff 7 (MLS 7)
Founded 1963. Enrl 23,000; Fac 774; Highest Degree: Associate
Library Holdings: e-books 20,000; Bk Titles 112,000; Per Subs 250
Special Collections: Career Coll; ESL; Oversize Books
Automation Activity & Vendor Info: (Cataloging) SirsiDynix; (Circulation) SirsiDynix; (Course Reserve) SirsiDynix; (ILL) OCLC; (OPAC) SirsiDynix; (Serials) SirsiDynix

Wireless access
Function: Art exhibits, Audio & video playback equip for onsite use, Computer training, Computers for patron use, Electronic databases & coll, Internet access, Learning ctr, Online cat, Online info literacy tutorials on the web & in blackboard, Online ref, Orientations, Photocopying/Printing, Tax forms, Telephone ref, Wheelchair accessible
Partic in San Diego Greater Metro Area Libr & Info Agency Coun
Open Mon-Thurs 7am-10pm, Fri 7-5, Sat 8-3
Restriction: Borrowing privileges limited to fac & registered students

J SAN DIEGO MIRAMAR COLLEGE*, Learning Resource Center, 10440 Black Mountain Rd, 92126-2999. SAN 301-3359. Tel: 619-388-7310. Reference Tel: 619-388-7316. FAX: 619-388-7918. Web Site: www.sdmiramar.edu/library/. *Librn,* Mary K Hart; Tel: 619-388-7614, E-mail: mhart@sdccd.edu; *Librn,* Eric M Mosier; Tel: 619-388-7622, E-mail: emosier@sdccd.net; Staff 13 (MLS 5, Non-MLS 8)
Founded 1973. Enrl 11,105; Highest Degree: Associate
Library Holdings: e-books 8,437; Bk Vols 23,295; Per Subs 65
Special Collections: Law Library
Subject Interests: Automotive, Diesel, Emergency med, Fire sci, Law, Transportation
Automation Activity & Vendor Info: (Acquisitions) SirsiDynix; (Cataloging) SirsiDynix; (Circulation) SirsiDynix; (Course Reserve) SirsiDynix; (OPAC) SirsiDynix; (Serials) SirsiDynix
Partic in OCLC Online Computer Library Center, Inc

S SAN DIEGO MODEL RAILROAD MUSEUM*, Erwin Welsch Memorial Research Library, 1649 El Prado, 92101. SAN 374-5651. Tel: 619-696-0199. FAX: 619-696-0239. E-mail: library@sdmrm.org. Web Site: sdmrm.org. *Exec Dir,* Anthony Ridenour; *Librn,* James F Helt; Staff 5 (Non-MLS 5)
Founded 1992
Library Holdings: Audiobooks 10; AV Mats 24,000; CDs 49; DVDs 500; Electronic Media & Resources 160; Bk Titles 7,000; Spec Interest Per Sub 1,257; Talking Bks 10; Videos 1,907
Special Collections: Railroads Coll
Subject Interests: Railroads
Automation Activity & Vendor Info: (Cataloging) LibraryWorld, Inc; (Serials) LibraryWorld, Inc
Wireless access
Function: Archival coll, Audio & video playback equip for onsite use, CD-ROM, Electronic databases & coll, For res purposes, Free DVD rentals, Internet access, Mail & tel request accepted, Online cat, Online ref, Photocopying/Printing, Res libr, Scanner, VHS videos
Open Tues-Fri 10-3:30, Sat & Sun 11-4:30
Restriction: Non-circulating, Not a lending libr, Open to pub for ref only, Ref only
Friends of the Library Group

S SAN DIEGO MUSEUM OF ART LIBRARY*, 1450 El Prado, 92101. (Mail add: PO Box 122107, 92112-2107), SAN 301-3464. Tel: 619-696-1959. FAX: 619-232-9367. E-mail: library@sdmart.org. Web Site: www.sdmart.org. *Libr Serv Coordr,* April Smitley; E-mail: asmitley@sdmart.org; Staff 1 (MLS 1)
Founded 1926
Library Holdings: Bk Vols 30,000; Per Subs 20
Special Collections: Books & Catalogues in Subject Area of Indian Miniature Painting (Binney Coll); Exhibition & Auction Catalogues Coll; Rare Books; San Diego Museum of Art Archive
Subject Interests: Art
Automation Activity & Vendor Info: (Cataloging) EOS International; (Circulation) EOS International; (ILL) OCLC WorldShare Interlibrary Loan; (Media Booking) EOS International; (OPAC) EOS International; (Serials) EOS International
Function: 24/7 Electronic res, 24/7 Online cat, Adult bk club, Archival coll, Art exhibits, AV serv, Bk club(s), Computers for patron use, Electronic databases & coll, For res purposes, Free DVD rentals, ILL available, Internet access, Magazines, Mail & tel request accepted, Movies, Online cat, Orientations, Outreach serv, Outside serv via phone, mail, e-mail & web, Photocopying/Printing, Printer for laptops & handheld devices, Prof lending libr, Ref & res, Ref serv available, Res libr, Scanner, Spanish lang bks, Telephone ref, VHS videos, Visual arts prog
Partic in OCLC Online Computer Library Center, Inc
Open Mon & Wed 9-4:30, Fri 9-3:30
Restriction: Access at librarian's discretion, Authorized scholars by appt, Badge access after hrs, By permission only, Circ limited, Circulates for staff only, Clients only, Employees & their associates, External users must contact libr, Free to mem, In-house use for visitors, Limited access for the pub, Non-circulating of rare bks, Non-circulating to the pub, Open to authorized patrons, Open to others by appt, Open to pub by appt only, Restricted borrowing privileges, Restricted loan policy, Secured area only open to authorized personnel, Staff use, pub by appt, Visitors must make appt to use bks in the libr

S SAN DIEGO NATURAL HISTORY MUSEUM*, Research Library, Balboa Park, 1788 El Prado, 92101. (Mail add: PO Box 121390, 92112-1390), SAN 301-3480. Tel: 619-232-3821. FAX: 619-232-0248. E-mail: library@sdnhm.org. Web Site: www.sdnhm.org/science/research-library. *Dir,* Margaret Dykens; Staff 1 (MLS 1)
Founded 1874
Library Holdings: Bk Vols 56,000
Special Collections: Bird Paintings (Sutton & Brooks Coll); Geology & Paleontology (Anthony W Vodges Coll); Herpetology (Laurence Klauber Coll); Photo Archives; Wild Flower Paintings (Valentien Coll)
Subject Interests: Botany, Entomology, Herpetology, Mammals, Ornithology, Paleontology
Automation Activity & Vendor Info: (OPAC) LibraryWorld, Inc
Publications: Occasional Papers; Proceedings; Transactions & Memoirs superseded by Proceedings of the San Diego Society of Natural History 1990
Restriction: Open by appt only

P SAN DIEGO PUBLIC LIBRARY*, Central Library, 330 Park Blvd, MS 17, 92101. SAN 334-3650. Tel: 619-236-5800. E-mail: weblibrary@sandiego.gov. Web Site: www.sandiego.gov/public-library. *Libr Dir,* Misty Jones; Tel: 619-236-5870, E-mail: LibraryDirector@sandiego.gov; *Dep Dir, Pub Serv,* Bob Cronk; E-mail: rcronk@sandiego.gov; *Dep Dir, Support Serv,* Sheila Burnett; E-mail: sburnett@sandiego.gov
Founded 1882. Pop 1,066,571; Circ 654,802
Library Holdings: Audiobooks 6,898; AV Mats 61,183; Bks on Deafness & Sign Lang 342; Braille Volumes 172; CDs 35,794; DVDs 18,998; e-books 56,052; Electronic Media & Resources 53; Large Print Bks 5,743; Microforms 214; Music Scores 23,693; Bk Titles 837,121; Bk Vols 1,049,909; Per Subs 2,463; Talking Bks 2; Videos 23,624
Special Collections: Society for American Baseball Research Coll. State Document Depository; US Document Depository
Automation Activity & Vendor Info: (Acquisitions) SirsiDynix; (Cataloging) SirsiDynix; (Circulation) SirsiDynix; (OPAC) SirsiDynix
Wireless access
Function: Adult literacy prog, Art exhibits, Audiobks via web, Bilingual assistance for Spanish patrons, Bks on cassette, Bks on CD, Bus archives, CD-ROM, Children's prog, Citizenship assistance, Computer training, Computers for patron use, Digital talking bks, E-Reserves, Electronic databases & coll, Family literacy, Free DVD rentals, Games & aids for people with disabilities, Govt ref serv, Homebound delivery serv, Homework prog, ILL available, Internet access, Large print keyboards, Magnifiers for reading, Music CDs, Online cat, Online info literacy tutorials on the web & in blackboard, OverDrive digital audio bks, Photocopying/Printing, Prog for adults, Prog for children & young adult, Ref serv available, Spoken cassettes & CDs, Spoken cassettes & DVDs, Summer reading prog, Tax forms, Teen prog, Telephone ref, VHS videos, Wheelchair accessible
Partic in Serra Cooperative Library System
Open Mon, Wed & Thurs 9:30-7, Tues, Fri & Sat 9:30-6, Sun 12-6
Friends of the Library Group
Branches: 35
ALLIED GARDENS/BENJAMIN, 5188 Zion Ave, 92120, SAN 334-374X. Tel: 619-533-3970. E-mail: bjstaff@sandiego.gov. Web Site: www.sandiego.gov/public-library/locations/allied-gardens-benjamin-library. *Br Mgr,* Kathryn Johnson
Founded 1965. Pop 86,661
Library Holdings: Audiobooks 1,624; AV Mats 6,510; Bks on Deafness & Sign Lang 25; CDs 2,911; DVDs 3,069; Large Print Bks 598; Music Scores 15; Bk Titles 27,262; Bk Vols 28,614; Per Subs 91; Videos 3,340
Automation Activity & Vendor Info: (Course Reserve) SirsiDynix; (ILL) SirsiDynix; (Media Booking) SirsiDynix; (Serials) SirsiDynix
Open Mon-Sat 9:30-6
Friends of the Library Group
BALBOA, 4255 Mt Abernathy Ave, 92117, SAN 334-3685. Tel: 858-573-1390. E-mail: bastaff@sandiego.gov. Web Site: www.sandiego.gov/public-library/locations/balboa-library. *Br Mgr,* Ann Gomez
Founded 1971. Circ 110,503
Library Holdings: Audiobooks 1,676; AV Mats 8,843; Bks on Deafness & Sign Lang 71; CDs 3,273; DVDs 4,100; Large Print Bks 394; Music Scores 30; Bk Titles 37,716; Bk Vols 41,110; Per Subs 91; Videos 5,264
Open Mon-Sat 9:30-6
Friends of the Library Group
CARMEL MOUNTAIN RANCH, 12095 World Trade Dr, 92128, SAN 377-6808. Tel: 858-538-8181. E-mail: cmstaff@sandiego.gov. Web Site: www.sandiego.gov/public-library/locations/carmel-mountain-ranch-library. *Br Mgr,* Janet Yeager
Founded 1997. Pop 153,773; Circ 174,789
Library Holdings: Audiobooks 2,130; AV Mats 12,323; Bks on Deafness & Sign Lang 46; CDs 5,060; DVDs 6,070; Large Print Bks 407; Music Scores 29; Bk Titles 44,276; Bk Vols 50,605; Per Subs 73; Videos 6,856

Open Mon-Sat 9:30-6
Friends of the Library Group
CARMEL VALLEY, 3919 Townsgate Dr, 92130, SAN 373-9228. Tel: 858-552-1668. E-mail: vastaff@sandiego.gov. Web Site: www.sandiego.gov/public-library/locations/carmel-valley-library. *Br Mgr,* Brenda Wegener
Founded 1993. Pop 239,722; Circ 357,067
Library Holdings: Audiobooks 4,420; AV Mats 18,281; Bks on Deafness & Sign Lang 55; CDs 7,986; DVDs 8,332; Large Print Bks 847; Music Scores 96; Bk Titles 70,476; Bk Vols 80,249; Per Subs 167; Videos 9,503
Open Mon-Sat 9:30-6, Sun 12:30-5
Restriction: Authorized patrons
Friends of the Library Group
CITY HEIGHTS/WEINGART, 3795 Fairmount Ave, 92105, SAN 334-3839. Tel: 619-641-6100. E-mail: ctstaff@sandiego.gov. Web Site: www.sandiego.gov/public-library/locations/city-heights-weingart-library-and-performance-annex. *Br Mgr,* Jennifer Geran
Founded 1998. Pop 255,739
Library Holdings: Audiobooks 1,368; AV Mats 15,626; Bks on Deafness & Sign Lang 40; CDs 2,665; DVDs 9,719; Large Print Bks 54; Music Scores 20; Bk Titles 48,450; Bk Vols 55,502; Per Subs 118; Talking Bks 1; Videos 12,410
Special Services for the Deaf - TDD equip
Open Mon-Sat 9:30-6, Sun 12:30-5
Friends of the Library Group
CLAIREMONT, 2920 Burgener Blvd, 92110-1027, SAN 334-3774. Tel: 858-581-9935. E-mail: clstaff@sandiego.gov. Web Site: www.sandiego.gov/public-library/locations/clairemont-library. *Br Mgr,* William Mallory
Founded 1958. Pop 91,625; Circ 95,276
Library Holdings: Audiobooks 1,745; AV Mats 8,049; Bks on Deafness & Sign Lang 31; CDs 3,445; DVDs 3,985; Large Print Bks 609; Music Scores 8; Bk Titles 31,514; Bk Vols 33,281; Per Subs 106; Videos 4,396
Open Mon-Sat 9:30-6
Friends of the Library Group
COLLEGE-ROLANDO, 6600 Montezuma Rd, 92115-2828, SAN 334-3804. Tel: 619-533-3902. E-mail: chstaff@sandiego.gov. Web Site: www.sandiego.gov/public-library/locations/college-rolando-library. *Br Mgr,* Sara King
Founded 1955. Pop 176,884
Library Holdings: Audiobooks 1,948; AV Mats 12,435; Bks on Deafness & Sign Lang 43; CDs 4,253; DVDs 7,262; Large Print Bks 735; Music Scores 44; Bk Titles 44,942; Bk Vols 48,013; Per Subs 114; Videos 7,964
Open Mon-Sat 9:30-6
Friends of the Library Group
KENSINGTON-NORMAL HEIGHTS, 4121 Adams Ave, 92116, SAN 334-4010. Tel: 619-533-3974. E-mail: knstaff@sandiego.gov. Web Site: www.sandiego.gov/public-library/locations/kensington-normal-heights-library. *Br Mgr,* Lynne Russo
Founded 1954. Circ 73,651
Library Holdings: Audiobooks 1,111; AV Mats 7,315; Bks on Deafness & Sign Lang 23; CDs 2,619; DVDs 3,876; Large Print Bks 174; Music Scores 38; Bk Titles 21,909; Bk Vols 23,565; Per Subs 65; Videos 4,498
Open Mon-Sat 9:30-6
Friends of the Library Group
LA JOLLA/RIFORD, 7555 Draper Ave, La Jolla, 92037-4802, SAN 334-3863. Tel: 858-552-1657. E-mail: ljstaff@sandiego.gov. Web Site: www.sandiego.gov/public-library/locations/la-jolla-riford-library. *Br Mgr,* Position Currently Open
Founded 1989. Circ 177,334
Library Holdings: Audiobooks 3,756; AV Mats 18,116; Bks on Deafness & Sign Lang 64; CDs 7,823; DVDs 7,396; Large Print Bks 819; Music Scores 74; Bk Titles 89,135; Bk Vols 96,129; Per Subs 257; Videos 8,931
Special Services for the Deaf - TDD equip
Open Mon-Sat 9:30-6, Sun 12:30-5
Friends of the Library Group
LINDA VISTA, 2160 Ulric St, 92111-6628, SAN 334-3898. Tel: 858-573-1399. E-mail: lvstaff@sandiego.gov. Web Site: www.sandiego.gov/public-library/locations/linda-vista-library. *Br Mgr,* Jeffrey Davis
Founded 1987. Circ 118,139
Library Holdings: Audiobooks 1,662; AV Mats 16,036; Bks on Deafness & Sign Lang 30; CDs 5,093; DVDs 7,500; Large Print Bks 370; Music Scores 47; Bk Titles 43,357; Bk Vols 47,964; Per Subs 199; Videos 10,396
Open Mon-Sat 9:30-6
Friends of the Library Group
LOGAN HEIGHTS, 567 S 28th St, 92113-2498, SAN 334-3928. Tel: 619-533-3968. E-mail: lostaff@sandiego.gov. Web Site: www.sandiego.gov/public-library/locations/logan-heights-library. *Br Mgr,* Stephen Wheeler
Founded 1927. Circ 65,920
Library Holdings: Audiobooks 1,447; AV Mats 12,138; Bks on Deafness & Sign Lang 48; CDs 4,374; DVDs 7,048; Large Print Bks 511; Music Scores 47; Bk Titles 58,591; Bk Vols 68,104; Per Subs 136; Videos 7,631
Open Mon-Sat 9:30-6, Sun 12:30-5
Friends of the Library Group
MIRA MESA, 8405 New Salem St, 92126-2398, SAN 334-3952. Tel: 858-538-8165. E-mail: mmstaff@sandiego.gov. Web Site: www.sandiego.gov/public-library/locations/mira-mesa-library. *Br Mgr,* Ina Gibson
Founded 1994. Circ 260,296
Library Holdings: Audiobooks 2,479; AV Mats 18,280; Bks on Deafness & Sign Lang 71; CDs 6,043; DVDs 9,618; Large Print Bks 1,079; Music Scores 115; Bk Titles 71,153; Bk Vols 83,375; Per Subs 199; Videos 11,739
Special Services for the Deaf - TDD equip
Open Mon-Sat 9:30-6, Sun 12:30-5
Friends of the Library Group
MISSION HILLS-HILLCREST/KNOX, 215 W Washington St, 92103, SAN 334-3987. Tel: 619-692-4910. E-mail: mhstaff@sandiego.gov. Web Site: www.sandiego.gov/public-library/locations/mission-hills-library. *Br Mgr,* Gina Bravo
Founded 1961. Pop 115,987; Circ 122,024
Library Holdings: Audiobooks 1,986; AV Mats 9,855; Bks on Deafness & Sign Lang 36; CDs 4,298; DVDs 4,879; Large Print Bks 404; Music Scores 16; Bk Titles 33,992; Bk Vols 35,723; Per Subs 99; Talking Bks 1; Videos 5,098
Open Mon-Sat 9:30-6
Friends of the Library Group
MISSION VALLEY, 2123 Fenton Pkwy, 92108. Tel: 858-573-5007. E-mail: mvstaff@sandiego.gov. Web Site: www.sandiego.gov/public-library/locations/mission-valley-library. *Br Mgr,* Karen Reilly
Founded 2002. Circ 158,028
Library Holdings: Audiobooks 3,339; AV Mats 16,749; Bks on Deafness & Sign Lang 59; CDs 6,522; DVDs 6,390; Large Print Bks 1,178; Music Scores 102; Bk Titles 62,454; Bk Vols 68,914; Per Subs 112; Videos 8,711
Special Services for the Deaf - TDD equip
Open Mon-Sat 9:30-6, Sun 12:30-5
Friends of the Library Group
MOUNTAIN VIEW-BECKWOURTH, 721 San Pasqual St, 92113-1839, SAN 334-3715. Tel: 619-527-3404. E-mail: bwstaff@sandiego.gov. Web Site: www.sandiego.gov/public-library/locations/mountain-view-beckwourth-library. *Br Mgr,* Anne Defazio
Founded 1976. Circ 57,312
Library Holdings: Audiobooks 491; AV Mats 5,828; Bks on Deafness & Sign Lang 39; CDs 1,586; DVDs 3,312; Large Print Bks 22; Music Scores 36; Bk Titles 39,226; Bk Vols 43,906; Per Subs 129; Videos 4,100
Open Mon-Sat 9:30-6
Friends of the Library Group
NORTH CLAIREMONT, 4616 Clairemont Dr, 92117, SAN 334-4045. Tel: 858-581-9931. E-mail: ncstaff@sandiego.gov. Web Site: www.sandiego.gov/public-library/locations/north-clairemont-library. *Br Mgr,* Arianne Leigh
Founded 1962. Circ 104,535
Library Holdings: Audiobooks 1,708; AV Mats 9,368; Bks on Deafness & Sign Lang 42; CDs 3,869; DVDs 4,818; Large Print Bks 775; Music Scores 17; Bk Titles 31,003; Bk Vols 32,899; Per Subs 99; Videos 5,279
Open Mon-Sat 9:30-6
Friends of the Library Group
NORTH PARK, 3795 31st St, 92104, SAN 334-407X. Tel: 619-533-3972. E-mail: npstaff@sandiego.gov. Web Site: www.sandiego.gov/public-library/locations/north-park-library. *Br Mgr,* Zar Shain
Founded 1959. Circ 140,855
Library Holdings: Audiobooks 2,210; AV Mats 14,874; Bks on Deafness & Sign Lang 38; CDs 4,936; DVDs 7,966; Large Print Bks 713; Music Scores 49; Bk Titles 48,206; Bk Vols 51,801; Per Subs 173; Talking Bks 1; Videos 9,540
Special Services for the Deaf - TDD equip
Open Mon-Sat 9:30-6
Friends of the Library Group
NORTH UNIVERSITY COMMUNITY, 8820 Judicial Dr, 92122. Tel: 858-581-9637. E-mail: nustaff@sandiego.gov. Web Site: www.sandiego.gov/public-library/locations/north-university-community-library. *Br Mgr,* Michelle Ruiz
Founded 2007. Pop 194,564; Circ 239,219
Library Holdings: Audiobooks 2,032; AV Mats 12,069; Bks on Deafness & Sign Lang 45; CDs 4,776; DVDs 7,140; Large Print Bks 892; Music Scores 75; Bk Titles 54,901; Bk Vols 64,068; Per Subs 147; Talking Bks 1; Videos 7,212
Special Services for the Deaf - TDD equip

Open Mon-Sat 9:30-6, Sun 12:30-5
Friends of the Library Group
OAK PARK, 2802 54th St, 92105, SAN 334-410X. Tel: 619-527-3406. E-mail: okstaff@sandiego.gov. Web Site: www.sandiego.gov/public-library/locations/oak-park-library. *Br Mgr,* Mark Davis
Founded 1969. Circ 45,838
Library Holdings: Audiobooks 1,044; AV Mats 8,019; Bks on Deafness & Sign Lang 18; CDs 2,681; DVDs 4,414; Large Print Bks 366; Music Scores 30; Bk Titles 31,177; Bk Vols 34,041; Per Subs 93; Videos 5,093
Open Mon-Sat 9:30-6
Friends of the Library Group
OCEAN BEACH, 4801 Santa Monica Ave, 92107, SAN 334-4134. Tel: 619-531-1532. E-mail: obstaff@sandiego.gov. Web Site: www.sandiego.gov/public-library/locations/ocean-beach-library. *Br Mgr,* Matt Beatty
Founded 1927. Circ 65,529
Library Holdings: Audiobooks 1,546; AV Mats 9,907; Bks on Deafness & Sign Lang 37; CDs 3,621; DVDs 5,216; Large Print Bks 460; Music Scores 45; Bk Titles 32,678; Bk Vols 34,592; Per Subs 105; Videos 6,021
Open Mon-Sat 9:30-6
Friends of the Library Group
OTAY MESA-NESTOR, 3003 Coronado Ave, 92154, SAN 334-4169. Tel: 619-424-0474. E-mail: otstaff@sandiego.gov. Web Site: www.sandiego.gov/public-library/locations/otay-mesa-nestor-library. *Br Mgr,* Coco Rios Fidel
Founded 1986. Circ 97,696
Library Holdings: Audiobooks 1,559; AV Mats 13,996; Bks on Deafness & Sign Lang 45; CDs 3,432; DVDs 8,604; Large Print Bks 454; Music Scores 27; Bk Titles 51,160; Bk Vols 57,363; Per Subs 148; Talking Bks 1; Videos 9,992
Special Services for the Deaf - TDD equip
Open Mon-Sat 9:30-6, Sun 12:30-5
Friends of the Library Group
PACIFIC BEACH/TAYLOR, 4275 Cass St, 92109, SAN 334-4193. Tel: 858-581-9934. E-mail: pbstaff@sandiego.gov. Web Site: www.sandiego.gov/public-library/locations/pacific-beach-taylor-library. *Br Mgr,* Christina Wainwright
Founded 1997. Pop 155,888; Circ 166,830
Library Holdings: Audiobooks 3,323; AV Mats 17,123; Bks on Deafness & Sign Lang 53; CDs 6,610; DVDs 8,357; Large Print Bks 1,307; Music Scores 53; Bk Titles 60,440; Bk Vols 65,148; Per Subs 148; Talking Bks 1; Videos 9,843
Open Mon-Sat 9:30-6, Sun 12:30-5
Friends of the Library Group
PARADISE HILLS, 5922 Rancho Hills Dr, 92139-3137, SAN 334-4223. Tel: 619-527-3461. E-mail: phstaff@sandiego.gov. Web Site: www.sandiego.gov/public-library/locations/paradise-hills-library. *Br Mgr,* Karina Balinda
Founded 1964. Circ 45,321
Library Holdings: Audiobooks 975; AV Mats 6,490; Bks on Deafness & Sign Lang 24; CDs 1,938; DVDs 3,634; Large Print Bks 225; Music Scores 27; Bk Titles 25,675; Bk Vols 27,386; Per Subs 87; Videos 4,243
Open Mon-Sat 9:30-6
Friends of the Library Group
POINT LOMA/HERVEY, 3701 Voltaire St, 92107, SAN 334-4258. Tel: 619-531-1539. E-mail: postaff@sandiego.gov. Web Site: www.sandiego.gov/public-library/locations/point-loma-hervey-library. *Br Mgr,* Christine Gonzalez
Founded 1959. Circ 203,757
Library Holdings: Audiobooks 3,420; AV Mats 12,891; Bks on Deafness & Sign Lang 45; CDs 4,270; DVDs 5,906; Large Print Bks 3,388; Music Scores 53; Bk Titles 61,954; Bk Vols 68,533; Per Subs 189; Videos 7,372
Special Services for the Deaf - TDD equip
Open Mon-Sat 9:30-6, Sun 12:30-5
Friends of the Library Group
RANCHO BERNARDO, 17110 Bernardo Center Dr, 92128, SAN 334-4282. Tel: 858-538-8163. E-mail: rbstaff@sandiego.gov. Web Site: www.sandiego.gov/public-library/locations/rancho-bernardo-library. *Br Mgr,* Trish Jenkins
Founded 1996. Pop 268,132; Circ 296,617
Library Holdings: Audiobooks 4,177; AV Mats 15,813; Bks on Deafness & Sign Lang 65; CDs 7,255; DVDs 5,737; Large Print Bks 3,211; Music Scores 87; Bk Titles 71,341; Bk Vols 79,000; Per Subs 206; Videos 7,502
Special Services for the Deaf - TDD equip
Open Mon-Sat 9:30-6, Sun 12:30-5
Friends of the Library Group
RANCHO PENASQUITOS, 13330 Salmon River Rd, 92129-2640, SAN 322-5577. Tel: 858-538-8159. E-mail: rpstaff@sandiego.gov. Web Site: www.sandiego.gov/public-library/locations/rancho-peñasquitos-library. *Br Mgr,* Adrianne Peterson; E-mail: AKPeterson@sandiego.gov
Founded 1992. Pop 81,110; Circ 265,049
Library Holdings: Audiobooks 3,506; AV Mats 16,408; Bks on Deafness & Sign Lang 63; Braille Volumes 1; CDs 6,585; DVDs 7,787; Large Print Bks 589; Music Scores 67; Bk Titles 60,262; Bk Vols 67,680; Per Subs 131; Videos 9,166
Open Mon-Sat 9:30-6
Friends of the Library Group
SAN CARLOS, 7265 Jackson Dr, 92119, SAN 334-4312. Tel: 619-527-3430. E-mail: scstaff@sandiego.gov. Web Site: www.sandiego.gov/public-library/locations/san-carlos-library. *Br Mgr,* David Ege
Founded 1972. Circ 134,063
Library Holdings: Audiobooks 2,527; AV Mats 10,464; Bks on Deafness & Sign Lang 34; CDs 4,637; DVDs 5,086; Large Print Bks 795; Music Scores 54; Bk Titles 46,174; Bk Vols 49,590; Per Subs 102; Talking Bks 1; Videos 5,432
Open Mon-Sat 9:30-6
Friends of the Library Group
SAN YSIDRO, 4235 Beyer Blvd, 92173, SAN 334-4347. Tel: 619-424-0475. E-mail: systaff@sandiego.gov. Web Site: www.sandiego.gov/public-library/locations/san-ysidro-library. *Br Mgr,* Adolfo R Ocampo
Founded 1924. Circ 42,938
Library Holdings: Audiobooks 646; AV Mats 6,836; Bks on Deafness & Sign Lang 29; CDs 1,628; DVDs 3,848; Large Print Bks 24; Music Scores 23; Bk Titles 32,135; Bk Vols 35,734; Per Subs 193; Videos 4,941
Open Mon-Sat 9:30-6
Friends of the Library Group
SCRIPPS MIRAMAR RANCH, 10301 Scripps Lake Dr, 92131-1026, SAN 328-7904. Tel: 858-538-8158. E-mail: srstaff@sandiego.gov. Web Site: www.sandiego.gov/public-library/locations/scripps-miramar-ranch-library. *Br Mgr,* Trevor Jones
Founded 1986. Circ 195,826
Library Holdings: Audiobooks 2,566; AV Mats 10,319; Bks on Deafness & Sign Lang 49; CDs 4,791; DVDs 4,238; Large Print Bks 321; Music Scores 76; Bk Titles 72,701; Bk Vols 79,302; Per Subs 158; Videos 4,997
Open Mon-Sat 9:30-6
Friends of the Library Group
SERRA MESA-KEARNY MESA, 9005 Aero Dr, 92123, SAN 334-4371. Tel: 858-573-1396. E-mail: smstaff@sandiego.gov. Web Site: www.sandiego.gov/public-library/locations/serra-mesa-kearny-mesa-library. *Br Mgr,* Rosa Kwon
Founded 2006. Circ 153,632
Library Holdings: Audiobooks 1,892; AV Mats 10,658; Bks on Deafness & Sign Lang 49; CDs 4,201; DVDs 4,356; Large Print Bks 780; Music Scores 30; Bk Titles 48,331; Bk Vols 53,724; Per Subs 141; Videos 5,966
Special Services for the Deaf - TDD equip
Open Mon-Sat 9:30-6, Sun 12:30-5
Friends of the Library Group
SKYLINE HILLS, 7900 Paradise Valley Rd, 92139, SAN 334-4401. Tel: 619-527-3485. E-mail: skstaff@sandiego.gov. Web Site: www.sandiego.gov/public-library/locations/skyline-hills-library. *Br Mgr,* Glenn Risolo
Founded 1969. Circ 34,765
Library Holdings: Audiobooks 1,004; AV Mats 8,130; Bks on Deafness & Sign Lang 37; CDs 2,874; DVDs 4,032; Large Print Bks 222; Music Scores 29; Bk Titles 34,267; Bk Vols 36,612; Per Subs 79; Videos 4,889
Open Mon-Sat 9:30-6
Friends of the Library Group
TIERRASANTA, 4985 La Cuenta Dr, 92124, SAN 334-4428. Tel: 858-573-1384. E-mail: tsstaff@sandiego.gov. Web Site: www.sandiego.gov/public-library/locations/tierrasanta-library. *Br Mgr,* Judy Cunninghum
Founded 1984. Circ 114,728
Library Holdings: Audiobooks 2,740; AV Mats 9,705; Bks on Deafness & Sign Lang 55; CDs 4,172; DVDs 4,019; Large Print Bks 323; Music Scores 30; Bk Titles 44,717; Bk Vols 49,473; Per Subs 134; Talking Bks 1; Videos 4,979
Open Mon-Sat 9:30-6
Friends of the Library Group
UNIVERSITY COMMUNITY, 4155 Governor Dr, 92122, SAN 334-4460. Tel: 858-552-1655. E-mail: ucstaff@sandiego.gov. Web Site: www.sandiego.gov/public-library/locations/university-community-library. *Br Mgr,* Melissa Martin
Founded 1978. Circ 146,131
Library Holdings: Audiobooks 2,803; AV Mats 12,250; Bks on Deafness & Sign Lang 40; CDs 4,927; DVDs 6,009; Large Print Bks 750; Music Scores 47; Bk Titles 51,247; Bk Vols 55,809; Per Subs 213; Videos 6,795
Open Mon-Sat 9:30-6
Friends of the Library Group

UNIVERSITY HEIGHTS, 4193 Park Blvd, 92103, SAN 334-4436. Tel: 619-692-4912. E-mail: uhstaff@sandiego.gov. Web Site: www.sandiego.gov/public-library/locations/university-heights-library. *Br Mgr,* Elaine Sinsuan
Founded 1966. Circ 107,698
Library Holdings: Audiobooks 1,529; AV Mats 10,532; Bks on Deafness & Sign Lang 31; CDs 4,750; DVDs 4,824; Large Print Bks 497; Music Scores 18; Bk Titles 27,218; Bk Vols 28,684; Per Subs 114; Videos 5,553
Open Mon-Sat 9:30-6

VALENCIA PARK/MALCOLM X, 5148 Market St, 92114, SAN 334-4495. Tel: 619-527-3405. E-mail: mxstaff@sandiego.gov. Web Site: www.sandiego.gov/public-library/locations/valencia-park-malcolm-x-library. *Br Mgr,* Alan Bugg
Founded 1996. Circ 65,193
Library Holdings: Audiobooks 1,133; AV Mats 11,640; Bks on Deafness & Sign Lang 51; CDs 2,959; DVDs 7,281; Large Print Bks 243; Music Scores 53; Bk Titles 59,687; Bk Vols 68,095; Per Subs 130; Videos 8,411
Open Mon-Sat 9:30-6, Sun 12:30-5
Friends of the Library Group

C SAN DIEGO STATE UNIVERSITY, Library & Information Access, 5500 Campanile Dr, 92182-8050. SAN 334-4525. Tel: 619-594-6728. Circulation Tel: 619-594-6793. Administration Tel: 619-594-6014. FAX: 619-594-3270. Administration FAX: 619-594-2700. E-mail: eref@sdsu.edu. Web Site: library.sdsu.edu. *Dean, Univ Libr Serv,* Scott Walter, PhD; E-mail: slwalter@sdsu.edu; *Assoc Dean,* Patrick McCarthy; E-mail: pmmcarthy@sdsu.edu; *Dir, Budget & Fiscal Operations,* Sallee Spearman; Tel: 619-594-4921, E-mail: sspearman@sdsu.edu; *Dir, Libr Info Technologies & Digital Initiatives,* Mark Figueroa; Tel: 619-594-2945, E-mail: mfigueroa@sdsu.edu; *Admin Operations Specialist, Facilities Coordr,* Maureen Dotson; Tel: 619-594-4472, E-mail: mdotson@sdsu.edu; *Circ Serv Dept Head,* Troy Compton; Tel: 619-594-2184, E-mail: tcompton@sdsu.edu; *Head, Coll Mgt,* Wil Weston; Tel: 619-594-6988, E-mail: wweston@sdsu.edu; *Head, Ref Serv,* Linda Salem; Tel: 619-594-5148, E-mail: lsalem@sdsu.edu; *Head, Ser,* Julie Su; Tel: 619-594-0904, E-mail: jsu@sdsu.edu; *Head, Spec Coll & Univ Archives,* Rob Ray; Tel: 619-594-4303, E-mail: rray@rohan.sdsu.edu; *Outreach Librn,* Gloria L Rhodes; Tel: 619-594-1169, E-mail: grhodes@sdsu.edu; *Info Literacy,* Pamela Jackson; Tel: 619-594-3809, E-mail: pamela.jackson@sdsu.edu. Subject Specialists: *Chemistry, LGBTQ Studies, Urban studies,* Wil Weston; *Children's lit, Comparative lit, Educ,* Linda Salem; *Asian studies,* Julie Su; *Africana studies,* Gloria L Rhodes; *Television, Theatre,* Pamela Jackson; Staff 76 (MLS 28, Non-MLS 48)
Founded 1897. Enrl 32,936; Fac 2,163; Highest Degree: Doctorate
Library Holdings: AV Mats 12,060; e-books 108,647; e-journals 12,365; Bk Titles 1,102,167; Bk Vols 1,649,455; Per Subs 4,177
Special Collections: 20th Century San Diego History; Adams Postcard Coll; Astronomy & History of Astronomy (Ernst Zinner Coll); Bookbinding (Wallace A Pearce Coll); Chesterfield Coll; Early Botanical Works Coll; H L Mencken Coll; History of Biology (Norland Coll); JFK Coll; Jiddu Krishnamurti Coll; Modern Rare Editions (Paul L Pfaff Coll); Music Scores (Vincent Meads Coll); Orchidology (Reginald S Davies Coll); San Diego State University Archives; Science Fiction (Chater Coll). Oral History; State Document Depository; US Document Depository
Automation Activity & Vendor Info: (Course Reserve) Docutek; (OPAC) Innovative Interfaces, Inc
Wireless access
Open Mon-Thurs 7am-10pm, Fri 7-6, Sat Noon-6, Sun Noon-10
Friends of the Library Group

M SCRIPPS MERCY HOSPITAL MEDICAL LIBRARY*, Melisa Reasner McGuire Health Sciences Library, 4077 Fifth Ave, MER-36, 92103-2180. SAN 301-3340. Tel: 619-260-7024. FAX: 619-260-7262. E-mail: library.mercy@scrippshealth.org. Web Site: mercy.scripps.libguides.com. *Libr Mgr,* Sunny McGowan; E-mail: mcgowan.sunny@scrippshealth.org; *Med Librn,* Lee Luniewski; E-mail: Luniewski.Lee@scrippshealth.org; *Med Libr Tech,* Mindy Kelly; E-mail: kelley.melinda@scrippshealth.org; Staff 3 (MLS 2, Non-MLS 1)
Founded 1937
Library Holdings: AV Mats 250; e-books 150; e-journals 500; Bk Titles 4,000; Bk Vols 4,300; Per Subs 150
Subject Interests: Archives, Clinical med, Nursing, Psychiat
Automation Activity & Vendor Info: (Cataloging) EOS International; (Circulation) EOS International; (OPAC) EOS International; (Serials) EOS International
Wireless access
Function: Archival coll, Computers for patron use, ILL available, Internet access, Online cat, Photocopying/Printing
Partic in Medical Library Group of Southern California & Arizona; National Network of Libraries of Medicine Region 5; OCLC Online Computer Library Center, Inc
Open Mon-Fri 8-5
Restriction: Badge access after hrs, In-house use for visitors, Open to staff, patients & family mem

L SELTZER, CAPLAN, MCMAHON, VITEK*, Law Library, 750 B St, Ste 2100, 92101. SAN 372-3011. Tel: 619-685-3009. Web Site: www.scmv.com. *Dir, Libr Serv,* Patricia Rusheen
Library Holdings: CDs 50; Electronic Media & Resources 15; Bk Vols 2,500; Per Subs 20
Wireless access
Restriction: Staff use only

M SHARP HEALTHCARE*, Sharp Memorial Hospital Medical Library, 7901 Frost St, 92123. SAN 301-3529. Tel: 858-939-3242. FAX: 858-939-3248. E-mail: library@sharp.com. Web Site: www.sharp.com/hospitals/memorial. *Coll Develop, Head of Libr,* Laura Stubblefield; *Asst Librn,* Heather Mire; *Asst Librn,* Amy Sharpe
Founded 1970
Library Holdings: Bk Vols 1,100; Per Subs 250
Subject Interests: Health sci, Med, Nursing
Automation Activity & Vendor Info: (Cataloging) EOS International; (Circulation) EOS International; (OPAC) EOS International; (Serials) EOS International
Wireless access
Partic in Proquest Dialog

S UNION-TRIBUNE PUBLISHING CO LIBRARY*, 600 B St, Ste 1201, 92101. SAN 301-3561. Tel: 619-299-3131. Web Site: www.uniontrib.com. *Researcher,* Merrie Monteagudo; Tel: 619-718-5431, E-mail: merrie.monteagudo@sduniontribune.com; Staff 15 (MLS 3, Non-MLS 12)
Founded 1945
Library Holdings: Bk Vols 2,000; Per Subs 7
Subject Interests: Current events, Hist
Open Mon-Fri 8:30-5

GL UNITED STATES COURTS LIBRARY*, 221 W Broadway, Rm 3185, 92101. SAN 372-3003. Tel: 619-557-5066. Web Site: www.casd.uscourts.gov/Court%20Info/Locations/SitePages/Home.aspx. *Librn,* Valerie A Railey; *Libr Tech,* Cynthia Kokocinski; Tel: 619-557-5387; Staff 2 (MLS 1, Non-MLS 1)
Library Holdings: Bk Vols 52,000
Special Collections: Law Library
Subject Interests: Conflicts, Fed procedure, Foreign law, Immigration, Intl law
Wireless access
Function: Ref & res
Partic in OCLC Online Computer Library Center, Inc
Open Mon-Fri 8:30-4:30
Restriction: Authorized patrons

S US NATIONAL PARK SERVICE*, Cabrillo National Monument Library, 1800 Cabrillo Memorial Dr, 92106-3601. Tel: 619-557-5450. FAX: 619-226-6311. TDD: 619-222-8211. Web Site: www.nps.gov/cabr. *Colls Mgr,* Robert Munson; Tel: 619-523-4574, E-mail: robert_munson@nps.gov. Subject Specialists: *Hist,* Robert Munson
Founded 1913
Library Holdings: Bk Vols 2,700; Per Subs 20
Special Collections: Archives-Park Records & Manuscripts
Function: Archival coll, Bus archives, For res purposes, Ref serv available, Res libr
Special Services for the Deaf - TDD equip
Open Mon-Sun 9-5
Restriction: Circulates for staff only, In-house use for visitors, Open to pub with supv only, Ref only to non-staff

UNITED STATES NAVY

A THE COMMAND LIBRARY*, Fleet Anti-Sub Warfare Training Ctr, 32444 Echo Lane, Ste 100, 92147-5199, SAN 334-4703. Tel: 619-524-1908. FAX: 619-524-6875.
Founded 1967
Library Holdings: Bk Titles 3,100; Bk Vols 18,000; Per Subs 30
Open Mon-Fri 7-4

A NAVAL BASE CORONADO LIBRARY*, MWR Base Library, 2478 Munda Rd, 92155-5396, SAN 334-4797. Tel: 619-437-3026. FAX: 619-437-3891. *Mgr,* Barbara Siemer
Founded 1944
Library Holdings: AV Mats 1,000; Bk Vols 22,000; Per Subs 124; Talking Bks 900
Special Collections: Special Warfare Coll
Automation Activity & Vendor Info: (Cataloging) EOS International; (Circulation) EOS International; (OPAC) EOS International

AM NAVAL MEDICAL CENTER*, Library Bldg 5-2, Naval Medical Ctr, 92134-5200, SAN 334-4940. Tel: 619-532-7950. FAX: 619-532-9293. Web Site: library.hosted.exlibrisgroup.com/medical.html. *Dir, Libr Serv,* Kathy Parker; Staff 7 (MLS 3, Non-MLS 4)

Founded 1922
Library Holdings: e-books 8,000; e-journals 12,000; Bk Vols 20,000; Per Subs 350
Special Collections: Layman Health Information
Subject Interests: Dentistry, Med, Nursing
Automation Activity & Vendor Info: (Acquisitions) Ex Libris Group; (Cataloging) Ex Libris Group; (Circulation) Ex Libris Group; (OPAC) Ex Libris Group; (Serials) Ex Libris Group
Partic in Consortium of Naval Libraries; Medical Library Group of Southern California & Arizona; National Network of Libraries of Medicine Region 5; OCLC Online Computer Library Center, Inc

AM NAVAL HEALTH RESEARCH CENTER, WILKINS BIOMEDICAL LIBRARY*, Gate 4, Barracks Bldg 333, Rm 101, McClelland & Patterson Rds, 92152. (Mail add: 140 Sylvester Rd, 92106-3521), SAN 334-4916. Tel: 619-553-8426. FAX: 619-553-0213. *Librn,* Donna Dutton; Tel: 619-767-4614, E-mail: donna.dutton.ctr@med.navy.mil; *Libr Tech,* Betty Croft; E-mail: betty.croft@med.navy.mil; Staff 3 (MLS 1, Non-MLS 2)
Founded 1959
Library Holdings: Bk Titles 5,550; Per Subs 230
Special Collections: Prisoner of War Studies Publications; United States Naval Medical Bulletin, 1907-1949
Subject Interests: Biochem, Immunology, Med, Mil hist, Psychiat, Psychol, Sociol, Statistics
Automation Activity & Vendor Info: (Acquisitions) SirsiDynix; (Cataloging) SirsiDynix; (Circulation) SirsiDynix; (OPAC) SirsiDynix; (Serials) SirsiDynix
Partic in Medical Library Group of Southern California & Arizona
Publications: Journal Holdings List; New Acquisitions List
Restriction: Not open to pub, Staff use only

A SPAWAR SYSTEMS CENTER SAN DIEGO TECHNICAL LIBRARY*, Code 84300, 53560 Hull St, 92152-5001, SAN 334-4851. Tel: 619-553-4890. FAX: 619-553-4893. E-mail: ssc_pac_library@navy.mil. *Dir,* Barbara Busch; E-mail: bbusch@spawar.navy.mil. Subject Specialists: *Engr, Phys sci,* Barbara Busch; Staff 6 (MLS 1, Non-MLS 5)
Founded 1949
Library Holdings: Bk Titles 60,000; Bk Vols 225,000; Per Subs 700
Special Collections: National Defense Research Committee Coll, University of California Division of War Research; Navy Radio & Sound Laboratory Reports
Subject Interests: Computer sci, Electronics, Engr, Marine biol, Math, Ocean engr, Physics
Automation Activity & Vendor Info: (OPAC) SirsiDynix
Function: Govt ref serv
Partic in OCLC Online Computer Library Center, Inc
Publications: Periodical Holdings
Restriction: Not open to pub, Open to govt employees only, Open to researchers by request, Photo ID required for access, Restricted access

UNIVERSITY OF SAN DIEGO

C HELEN K & JAMES S COPLEY LIBRARY*, 5998 Alcala Park, 92110, SAN 334-5181. Circulation Tel: 619-260-4799. Interlibrary Loan Service Tel: 619-260-2364. Reference Tel: 619-260-4765. Administration Tel: 619-260-2370. FAX: 619-260-4617. Web Site: marian.sandiego.edu. *Univ Librn,* Edward D Starkey; E-mail: estarkey@sandiego.edu; *Assoc Univ Librn,* Steve Staninger; E-mail: sstan@sandiego.edu; *Outreach Librn,* Jade Winn; *Head, Access Serv,* Bill Hall; E-mail: billhall@sandiego.edu; *Head, Acq,* Jacqueline Sabanos; *Head, Cat,* Margit Smith; E-mail: mjps@sandiego.edu; *Electronic Res,* Michael Epstein; E-mail: epstein@sandiego.edu; *ILL,* Alex Moran; E-mail: moran1@sandiego.edu; *Ref Serv,* Alma Ortega; E-mail: alma@sandiego.edu; *Ref Serv,* Tamara Shaw; *Sci,* Amy Besnoy; E-mail: abesnoy@sandiego.edu; *Spec Coll & Archives Librn,* Diane Maher; E-mail: diane@sandiego.edu; *Syst Coordr,* Michael O'Brien; E-mail: michaelo@sandiego.edu. Subject Specialists: *Humanities, Philos, Relig,* Edward D Starkey; *Bus, Polit sci,* Steve Staninger; *Educ, Nursing, Psychol,* Jade Winn; *Ethnic studies,* Alma Ortega; *Communications, Lit,* Tamara Shaw; *Sciences,* Amy Besnoy; *Arts,* Diane Maher; Staff 12 (MLS 10, Non-MLS 2)
Founded 1949. Enrl 7,200; Fac 300; Highest Degree: Doctorate
Library Holdings: Bk Titles 325,000; Bk Vols 500,000; Per Subs 2,200
Subject Interests: Catholicism, Hist, Lit, Philos, Relig
Automation Activity & Vendor Info: (Acquisitions) Innovative Interfaces, Inc; (Cataloging) Innovative Interfaces, Inc; (Circulation) Innovative Interfaces, Inc; (ILL) Innovative Interfaces, Inc; (Media Booking) Innovative Interfaces, Inc; (OPAC) Innovative Interfaces, Inc; (Serials) Innovative Interfaces, Inc
Partic in San Diego Library Circuit; Statewide California Electronic Library Consortium
Friends of the Library Group

CL KATHERINE M & GEORGE M PARDEE JR LEGAL RESEARCH CENTER*, 5998 Alcala Park, 92110-2492, SAN 334-5211. Tel: 619-260-4542. Reference Tel: 619-260-4612. Administration Tel: 619-260-4600, Ext 4337. Automation Services Tel: 619-260-4759. FAX: 619-260-4616. Web Site: www.sandiego.edu/law/lrc. *Assoc Dean, Libr & Info Serv,* Karl Gruben; Tel: 619-260-6846; *Assoc Dir,* L Ruth Levor; Tel: 619-260-4604, E-mail: rlevor@sandiego.edu; *Head, Circ,* Inna Muradyan; Tel: 619-260-7479, E-mail: innam@sandiego.edu; *Head, Pub Serv,* Lihosit Judith; Tel: 619-260-4766, E-mail: jlihosit@sandiego.edu; *Head, Tech Serv,* Harry Loren Stamper; Tel: 619-260-4543, E-mail: stamper@sandiego.edu; *Acq Librn,* Jason Curtis; Tel: 619-260-2875; *Coll Develop Librn,* Brent Bernau; Tel: 619-260-7557, E-mail: bbernau@sandiego.edu; *Electronic Serv Librn,* Anna Russell; E-mail: russell@sandiego.edu; *Fac Serv & Outreach Librn, Law Ref Librn,* Jane Larrington; Tel: 619-260-4752, E-mail: jlarrington@sandiego.edu; *Law Ref Librn,* Michele Knapp; Tel: 619-260-4532; *Law Ref Librn/Foreign & Intl Spec,* Melissa Fung; Tel: 619-260-4734. Subject Specialists: *Oral hist,* L Ruth Levor; *Linguistics,* Harry Loren Stamper; *Govt doc, Tax,* Michele Knapp; *Foreign law, Intl law,* Melissa Fung; Staff 11 (MLS 10, Non-MLS 1)
Founded 1954. Enrl 992; Fac 60; Highest Degree: Doctorate
Library Holdings: DVDs 94; Bk Titles 1,128,920; Per Subs 4,760; Videos 379
Special Collections: State Document Depository; UN Document Depository; US Document Depository
Automation Activity & Vendor Info: (Acquisitions) Innovative Interfaces, Inc; (Cataloging) Innovative Interfaces, Inc; (Circulation) Innovative Interfaces, Inc; (Course Reserve) Innovative Interfaces, Inc; (ILL) Innovative Interfaces, Inc; (OPAC) Innovative Interfaces, Inc; (Serials) Innovative Interfaces, Inc
Function: Archival coll, CD-ROM, Computer training, Computers for patron use, Doc delivery serv, E-Reserves, Free DVD rentals, Govt ref serv, ILL available, Internet access, Online cat, Photocopying/Printing, Ref serv available, Scanner, Tax forms, Telephone ref, Wheelchair accessible
Partic in San Diego Circuit
Publications: Guide Series (Research guide); Information Series; Patron Guide (Library handbook)
Open Mon-Thurs 7am-Midnight, Fri & Sat 8am-10pm, Sun 8am-Midnight
Restriction: Circ limited
Friends of the Library Group

SAN DIMAS

CR LIFE PACIFIC COLLEGE LIBRARY*, 1100 W Covina Blvd, 91773. SAN 300-9467. Tel: 909-706-3009. FAX: 909-599-6690. E-mail: library@lifepacific.edu. Web Site: lifepacific.libguides.com/library. *Head Librn,* Gary Merriman; Tel: 909-706-3008, E-mail: gmerriman@lifepacific.edu. Subject Specialists: *Bible, Theol,* Gary Merriman; Staff 2 (MLS 1, Non-MLS 1)
Founded 1923. Enrl 500; Fac 24; Highest Degree: Master
Library Holdings: e-books 1,500; Bk Vols 40,000; Per Subs 130
Special Collections: Archive of International Church of the Foursquare Gospel
Subject Interests: Educ, Relig
Automation Activity & Vendor Info: (Cataloging) Follett Software; (Circulation) Follett Software; (OPAC) Follett Software
Wireless access
Open Mon-Thurs 7:20am-10:30pm, Fri 7:20-5, Sun 3-9; Mon-Fri (Summer) 8-12 & 1-5

SAN FRANCISCO

C ACADEMY OF ART UNIVERSITY LIBRARY*, 180 New Montogomery, 6th Flr, 94105. (Mail add: 79 New Montgomery St, 94105), SAN 372-6452. Tel: 415-274-2270. Circulation Tel: 415-618-3842. E-mail: library@academyart.edu. Web Site: library.academyart.edu. *Libr Dir,* Debra Sampson; E-mail: dsampson@academyart.edu; Staff 7 (MLS 4, Non-MLS 3)
Founded 1977. Enrl 8,500; Fac 1,000; Highest Degree: Master
Jan 2017-Dec 2017 Income $1,083,714. Mats Exp $296,756, Books $17,171, Per/Ser (Incl. Access Fees) $24,009, Manu Arch $100,000, AV Mat $979, Electronic Ref Mat (Incl. Access Fees) $150,613, Presv $3,984. Sal $562,951 (Prof $446,070)
Library Holdings: CDs 115; DVDs 2,500; e-books 9,313; Electronic Media & Resources 21; Music Scores 28; Bk Titles 38,000; Bk Vols 48,000; Per Subs 200; Videos 1,000
Special Collections: Art & Applied Art, bks, slides, videos, cd-rom
Subject Interests: Visual arts
Automation Activity & Vendor Info: (Acquisitions) Innovative Interfaces, Inc - Sierra; (Cataloging) Innovative Interfaces, Inc - Sierra; (Circulation) Innovative Interfaces, Inc - Sierra; (Course Reserve) Innovative Interfaces, Inc - Sierra; (Discovery) Innovative Interfaces, Inc - Sierra; (ILL) Innovative Interfaces, Inc; (OPAC) Innovative Interfaces, Inc - Sierra; (Serials) Innovative Interfaces, Inc - Sierra
Wireless access
Open Mon-Thurs 8am-10pm, Fri 8-7, Sat & Sun 10-6
Restriction: Researchers by appt only

C ALLIANT INTERNATIONAL UNIVERSITY, Hurwich Library, San Francisco Campus, San Francisco Law School, One Beach St, Ste 100, 94133-2221. SAN 300-6085. Tel: 415-955-2131. Interlibrary Loan Service Tel: 415-955-2158. Reference Tel: 415-955-2068. E-mail: library@alliant.edu. Web Site: alliant.libguides.com. *Dir, Libr Serv,* Joe Tally; Tel: 415-955-2157, E-mail: jtally@alliant.edu; Staff 5 (MLS 3, Non-MLS 2)
Founded 1969. Enrl 1,040; Fac 69; Highest Degree: Doctorate
Library Holdings: e-books 70,000; e-journals 16,000; Bk Vols 140,000; Per Subs 300; Videos 1,500
Special Collections: Education Coll; Psychological Assessment Coll
Subject Interests: Clinical psych, Cross cultural subjects, Forensic psychol, Neuropsychology, Organizational behavior, Psychopharmacology
Automation Activity & Vendor Info: (Acquisitions) Innovative Interfaces, Inc - Sierra; (Cataloging) Innovative Interfaces, Inc - Sierra; (Circulation) Innovative Interfaces, Inc - Sierra; (Course Reserve) Innovative Interfaces, Inc - Sierra; (ILL) Innovative Interfaces, Inc - Sierra; (Media Booking) Innovative Interfaces, Inc - Sierra; (OPAC) Innovative Interfaces, Inc - Sierra; (Serials) Innovative Interfaces, Inc - Sierra
Wireless access
Partic in LexisNexis; Link+; Statewide California Electronic Library Consortium
Open Mon-Thurs 9-8, Fri 9-5
Restriction: Borrowing privileges limited to fac & registered students

M AMERICAN ACADEMY OF OPHTHALMOLOGY LIBRARY*, 655 Beach St, 94109. (Mail add: PO Box 7424, 94120-7424), SAN 374-8995. Tel: 415-561-8500. FAX: 415-561-8533.
Restriction: Staff use only

L ARNOLD & PORTER RESEARCH SERVICES*, Three Embarcadero Ctr, 10th Flr, 94111-4024. SAN 327-5760. Tel: 415-434-1600. FAX: 415-217-5910. Web Site: www.arnoldporter.com.
Library Holdings: Bk Vols 13,000
Subject Interests: Law

S ASTRONOMICAL SOCIETY OF THE PACIFIC LIBRARY*, 390 Ashton Ave, 94112. SAN 325-6677. Tel: 415-337-1100. FAX: 415-337-5205. E-mail: membership@astrosociety.org. Web Site: www.astrosociety.org. *Chief Exec Officer,* Linda Shore; E-mail: lshore@astrosociety.org; *Coordr,* Pablo Nelson; E-mail: pnelson@astrosociety.org
Founded 1889
Library Holdings: Bk Titles 1,600; Per Subs 20
Special Collections: People & Objects in Astronomy, Photo Archive
Subject Interests: Astronomy, Hist of sci, Space sci
Publications: Publications of the Astronomical Society of the Pacific (Journal)
Restriction: Open by appt only

S THE BOOK CLUB OF CALIFORNIA, Albert Sperisen Library, 312 Sutter St, Ste 500, 94108-4320. SAN 326-6249. Tel: 415-781-7532, Ext 4. E-mail: library@bccbooks.org. Web Site: www.bccbooks.org/library. *Librn,* Elizabeth Newsom; E-mail: elizabeth@bccbooks.org
Founded 1912
Library Holdings: Bk Vols 8,500
Special Collections: Printing History
Subject Interests: Bk arts, Western hist
Automation Activity & Vendor Info: (Cataloging) OCLC
Publications: Fine Press Books (Annual); Keepsake (Annual); Newsletter (Quarterly)
Restriction: Open by appt only

S CALIFORNIA ACADEMY OF SCIENCES LIBRARY*, Golden Gate Park, 55 Music Concourse Dr, 94118. SAN 301-3774. Tel: 415-379-5487. E-mail: library@calacademy.org. Web Site: www.calacademy.org/scientists/library. *Head Librn,* Rebekah Kim; E-mail: rkim@calacademy.org; *Libr & Archives Asst,* Seth Cotterell; E-mail: scotterell@calacademy.org; Staff 4.7 (MLS 3.4, Non-MLS 1.3)
Founded 1853
Library Holdings: CDs 100; DVDs 300; e-journals 900; Bk Vols 250,000; Per Subs 1,400; Videos 500
Special Collections: Academy Archives; Natural History Image Clippings Files; Natural History Photography Coll. Oral History
Subject Interests: Anthrop, Astronomy, Botany, Entomology, Geog, Geol, Herpetology, Ichthyology, Marine biol, Museology, Natural hist, Ornithology, Paleontology, Zoology
Automation Activity & Vendor Info: (Acquisitions) Ex Libris Group; (Cataloging) Ex Libris Group; (Circulation) Ex Libris Group; (ILL) OCLC Online; (OPAC) Ex Libris Group; (Serials) Ex Libris Group
Function: Ref serv available, Res libr, Telephone ref
Publications: Accessions List (Quarterly)
Partic in OCLC Online Computer Library Center, Inc; San Francisco Bay Area Library & Information Network
Restriction: Non-circulating to the pub, Open by appt only

S CALIFORNIA HISTORICAL SOCIETY*, North Baker Research Library, 678 Mission St, 94105. SAN 320-1635. Tel: 415-357-1848, Ext 220. FAX: 415-357-1850. E-mail: reference@calhistory.org. Web Site: www.californiahistoricalsociety.org. *Ref Librn,* Frances Kaplan; E-mail: fkaplan@calhist.org; *Metadata Librn, Syst Librn,* Al Bersch; Staff 6 (MLS 6)
Founded 1922
Library Holdings: Bk Titles 36,000; Bk Vols 57,000; Spec Interest Per Sub 80
Special Collections: Ephemera Coll; Manuscript & Archival Coll; Photograph Coll; Taylor & Taylor (S F) Archives; Western Printing & Publishing (Edward C Kemble Coll)
Subject Interests: Calif, Hist, Maps, Rare bks
Function: Ref serv available, Res libr
Partic in Melvyl; Research Libraries Information Network
Open Wed-Fri 1-5
Restriction: Not a lending libr

C CALIFORNIA INSTITUTE OF INTEGRAL STUDIES*, Laurance S Rockefeller Library, 1453 Mission St, 2nd Flr, 94103. SAN 320-6025. Tel: 415-575-6180. Interlibrary Loan Service Tel: 415-575-6193. Reference Tel: 415-575-6186. FAX: 415-575-1264. E-mail: library@ciis.edu. Web Site: www.ciis.edu/campus-resources/library. *Assoc Libr Dir,* Kelly Sundin; *Ref Librn,* Joan Eahr; Tel: 415-575-6182, E-mail: ejoan@ciis.edu; *Ref/Syst Librn,* Salina Lee; Tel: 415-575-6183, E-mail: slee@ciis.edu; Staff 8 (MLS 3, Non-MLS 5)
Founded 1968. Enrl 1,000; Fac 76; Highest Degree: Doctorate
Library Holdings: AV Mats 600; e-books 22,000; Bk Vols 35,000; Per Subs 200
Special Collections: Heritage Coll (Alan Watts, Frederic Spiegelberg, Haridas Chaudhuri); Institute Authors Coll; Langley-Porter Psychology Coll
Subject Interests: Comparative relig, Cultural studies, E-W relations, Philos, Psychol, Spirituality, Women
Automation Activity & Vendor Info: (Cataloging) ByWater Solutions; (Circulation) ByWater Solutions; (Course Reserve) Docutek; (ILL) OCLC ILLiad; (OPAC) ByWater Solutions
Wireless access
Function: Archival coll, Audio & video playback equip for onsite use, ILL available, Online cat, Online ref, Ref serv available
Partic in Northern & Central California Psychology Libraries; Statewide California Electronic Library Consortium
Open Mon-Fri 10-6, Sat & Sun 11-5
Restriction: Circ privileges for students & alumni only

M CALIFORNIA PACIFIC MEDICAL CENTER*, Health Sciences Library, 1375 Sutter St, Ste 100, 94109. (Mail add: PO Box 7999, 94120-7999), SAN 301-4851. Tel: 415-600-0540. FAX: 415-600-2397. E-mail: cpmclib@sutterhealth.org. Web Site: www.cpmc.org/professionals/hslibrary. *Dir,* Anne Shew; E-mail: shewa@sutterhealth.org; Staff 2 (MLS 1.3, Non-MLS 0.7)
Founded 1912
Library Holdings: e-books 100; e-journals 1,400; Bk Titles 1,700; Per Subs 2
Subject Interests: Med, Ophthalmology
Automation Activity & Vendor Info: (Cataloging) LibraryWorld, Inc; (Circulation) LibraryWorld, Inc; (OPAC) LibraryWorld, Inc; (Serials) LibraryWorld, Inc
Wireless access
Function: 24/7 Electronic res, 24/7 Online cat, Electronic databases & coll, ILL available, Ref serv available, Res assist avail
Partic in Asn for Vision Sci Librns; Northern California & Nevada Medical Library Group
Restriction: Authorized patrons, By permission only, Hospital employees & physicians only, Open by appt only, Private libr

G CALIFORNIA STATE LIBRARY*, Sutro Library, J Paul Leonard Library-Sutro Library, 1630 Holloway Ave, 5th Flr, 94132-4030. SAN 301-4754. Tel: 415-469-6100. FAX: 415-469-6172. E-mail: sutro@library.ca.gov. Web Site: www.library.ca.gov/sutro. *Dir,* Mattie Taormina
Founded 1913
Library Holdings: Bk Vols 250,000
Special Collections: Adolph Sutro Coll, ms; Art Coll (Japanese & Chinese); British Pamphlets; German Reformation Pamphlets; Hebraica Coll; Incunabula Coll; Italian Coll, ms; James O. Halliwell-Phillipps Coll; John Murray Coll; Mexican Coll (1540-1889), mats; Pieter van den Keere Coll, maps; Rivers & Harbors Coll; Sir Joseph Banks Coll, ms, letters & papers; William Shakespeare Coll (1623-1685), folios 1st, 2nd, 3rd & 4th
Subject Interests: Genealogy & family histories for 49 states
Automation Activity & Vendor Info: (Circulation) SirsiDynix
Wireless access

Open Mon-Fri 10-4
Restriction: Non-circulating of rare bks

J CITY COLLEGE OF SAN FRANCISCO*, Rosenberg Library, 50 Frida Kahlo Way, 4th Flr, 94112. SAN 301-388X. Tel: 415-452-5433. Reference Tel: 415-452-5541. FAX: 415-452-5588. Web Site: library.ccsf.edu. *Dean, Learning & Libr Serv,* Dr Donna Reed; Tel: 415-452-5455, E-mail: dreed@ccsf.edu; *Dept Chair,* Anthony Costa; E-mail: acosta@ccsf.edu; *Fac Librn,* Michele Alaniz; E-mail: malaniz@ccsf.edu; *Fac Librn,* Maggie Frankel; E-mail: mfrankel@ccsf.edu; *Fac Librn,* Megan Kinney; E-mail: mkinney@ccsf.edu; *Fac Librn,* Michele McKenzie; E-mail: mmmkenzie@ccsf.edu; *Fac Librn,* Wendy Owens; E-mail: wowens@ccsf.edu; *Fac Librn,* Julian Prentice; E-mail: jprentice@ccsf.edu; *Fac Librn,* Katrina Rahn; E-mail: krahn@ccsf.edu; Staff 23 (MLS 23)
Founded 1935. Fac 1,500; Highest Degree: Associate
Library Holdings: CDs 127; DVDs 85; e-books 512; Bk Titles 140,868; Bk Vols 178,811; Per Subs 677; Videos 138
Special Collections: Hotel-Restaurant (Alice Statler Coll)
Automation Activity & Vendor Info: (Acquisitions) Ex Libris Group; (Cataloging) Ex Libris Group; (Circulation) Ex Libris Group; (Course Reserve) Ex Libris Group; (Discovery) Ex Libris Group; (Media Booking) Ex Libris Group; (OPAC) Ex Libris Group; (Serials) Ex Libris Group
Wireless access
Function: 24/7 Electronic res, 24/7 Online cat, 3D Printer, Activity rm, Art exhibits
Partic in Coop Libr Agency for Syst & Servs; OCLC Online Computer Library Center, Inc; San Francisco Bay Area Library & Information Network
Friends of the Library Group

S THE HENRY WILSON COIL LIBRARY & MUSEUM OF FREEMASONRY*, 1111 California St, 94108. SAN 301-4088, *Colls Mgr,* Joe Evans; Tel: 415-292-9141, E-mail: jevans@freemason.org; Staff 1 (Non-MLS 1)
Founded 1949
Library Holdings: Bk Vols 7,000; Per Subs 6
Special Collections: Annual Proceedings of Masonic Grand Lodge, California 1850-present; Archives of California Masonic Lodges; Archives of the Grand Lodge of California
Subject Interests: Calif, Freemasonry
Wireless access
Restriction: Open by appt only

S THE COMMONWEALTH CLUB OF CALIFORNIA LIBRARY*, 110 The Embarcadero, 94105. (Mail add: PO Box 194210, 94119), SAN 301-3901. Tel: 415-597-6700. FAX: 415-597-6729. E-mail: club@commonwealthclub.org, info@commonwealthclub.org. Web Site: www.commonwealthclub.org. *Library Contact,* Greg Dalton; Tel: 415-597-6710, E-mail: gdalton@commonwealthclub.org
Founded 1903
Library Holdings: Bk Titles 1,000
Wireless access
Restriction: Mem only

L COOPER, WHITE & COOPER*, Law Library, 201 California St, 17th Flr, 94111-5002. SAN 372-3917. Tel: 415-433-1900. Interlibrary Loan Service Tel: 415-433-1900, Ext 6269. FAX: 415-433-5530. Web Site: www.cwclaw.com. *Mgr, Libr Serv,* Cindy Beck Weller; E-mail: cweller@cwclaw.com. Subject Specialists: *Legal,* Cindy Beck Weller; Staff 1 (MLS 1)
Founded 1896
Library Holdings: Bk Vols 5,000; Per Subs 200
Special Collections: Law
Subject Interests: Construction, Corporate law, Employment, Labor, Litigation, Telecommunications law
Wireless access
Function: Computers for patron use, ILL available, Internet access, Online cat, Ref & res
Partic in Northern Calif Asn of Law Librs
Restriction: Co libr, Employee & client use only

S DEGENKOLB ENGINEERS LIBRARY*, 375 Beale St, Ste 500, 94105. SAN 327-6864. Tel: 415-392-6952. Web Site: degenkolb.com. *Coop Librn,* Kristiana Rockne; Staff 1 (MLS 1)
Library Holdings: Bk Vols 6,000
Special Collections: EERC Reports; Technical Papers; Earthquake engineering; California & Worldwide Seismicity
Subject Interests: Earthquake engr, Seismology, Structural engr
Wireless access
Restriction: Employees only, Not open to pub

GM DEPARTMENT OF VETERANS AFFAIRS*, Marvin Siperstein Medical Library, Medical Library 142D, 4150 Clement St, 94121. SAN 301-4878. Tel: 415-221-4810, Ext 3302. Interlibrary Loan Service Tel: 415-221-4810, Ext 3304. FAX: 415-750-6919. *Librn,* Nadine Walas; E-mail: nadine.walas@va.gov
Founded 1949
Library Holdings: Bk Titles 3,500; Bk Vols 3,700; Per Subs 20
Subject Interests: Patient educ
Automation Activity & Vendor Info: (Cataloging) EOS International; (OPAC) EOS International; (Serials) EOS International
Open Mon-Fri 8-4:30

S DOLBY LABORATORIES, INC, Technical Library, 1275 Market St, 94103. SAN 370-2286. Tel: 415-558-0268. FAX: 415-863-1373. E-mail: technicallibrary@dolby.com. Web Site: www.dolby.com. *Res Serv, Sr Mgr,* Tamara Horacek; E-mail: tlh@dolby.com; *Info Res Mgr,* E Azinheira; E-mail: ema@dolby.com; Staff 2 (MLS 2)
Founded 1986
Restriction: Open to pub upon request

S FARALLONES MARINE SANCTUARY ASSOCIATION*, Resource Library, Bldg 991, Old Coast Guard Sta, Marine Dr, 94129. SAN 375-2453. Tel: 415-561-6625. FAX: 415-561-6616. Web Site: www.farallones.org. *Exec Dir,* Deb Self; E-mail: dself@farallones.org
Founded 1998
Library Holdings: Bk Vols 1,000
Open Wed-Sun 10-4

L FARELLA, BRAUN & MARTEL*, Law Library, 235 Montgomery St, 17th Flr, 94104. SAN 372-297X. Tel: 415-954-4714. FAX: 415-954-4480. Web Site: www.fbm.com. *Librn,* Judy Heier; E-mail: jheier@fbm.com
Library Holdings: Bk Titles 2,500; Bk Vols 15,000
Wireless access

J FASHION INSTITUTE OF DESIGN & MERCHANDISING LIBRARY*, 55 Stockton St, 5th Flr, 94108. SAN 326-8918. Tel: 415-675-5200. Toll Free Tel: 800-422-3436. FAX: 415-989-5312. Web Site: www.fidm.edu. *Libr Dir,* Kathy Bailon; E-mail: kbailon@fidm.edu; Staff 5 (MLS 1, Non-MLS 4)
Enrl 540
Library Holdings: AV Mats 800; Bk Titles 4,500; Per Subs 150
Special Collections: Costume Study Coll, 1860s to present
Subject Interests: Apparel, Communications, Fashion design, Graphic design, Interior design, Manufacturing, Mkt
Automation Activity & Vendor Info: (Acquisitions) Gateway; (Cataloging) Gateway; (Circulation) Gateway; (Course Reserve) Gateway; (OPAC) Gateway
Function: For res purposes
Open Mon-Thurs 8-8, Fri 8-5, Sat 9-3
Restriction: Open to students, fac & staff

S FEDERAL RESERVE BANK OF SAN FRANCISCO*, Research Library, 101 Market St, 94105-1579. (Mail add: PO Box 7702, 94120-7702), SAN 301-4029. Tel: 415-974-3216. FAX: 415-974-3429. E-mail: reference.library@sf.frb.org. *Mgr,* Cindy Hill; *Ref/Archives Librn,* Anne Hall
Library Holdings: Bk Titles 18,000; Bk Vols 35,000; Per Subs 350
Automation Activity & Vendor Info: (Cataloging) Inmagic, Inc.; (Circulation) Inmagic, Inc.
Restriction: Open by appt only

S FINE ARTS MUSEUMS OF SAN FRANCISCO RESEARCH LIBRARY*, M H de Young Memorial Museum, Golden Gate Park, 50 Hagiwara Tea Garden Dr, 94118. SAN 301-4045. Tel: 415-750-3600. FAX: 415-750-7692. Web Site: deyoung.famsf.org. *Librn,* Abigail Dansiger; E-mail: adansiger@famsf.org
Founded 1955
Library Holdings: Bk Titles 42,000; Per Subs 150
Special Collections: Bothin American Art Library Coll - Achenbach Foundation for Graphic Arts Library

C GOLDEN GATE UNIVERSITY*, University Library, 536 Mission St, 94105-2967. SAN 334-5300. Tel: 415-442-7242. Interlibrary Loan Service Tel: 415-442-7256. Reference Tel: 415-442-7244. FAX: 415-543-6779. Web Site: www.ggu.edu/libraries/university-library. *Dir, Head, Teaching & Learning Serv,* James Krusling; Tel: 415-442-7248, E-mail: jkrusling@ggu.edu; *E-Resources Librn, Syst Librn,* Allegra Porter; Tel: 415-442-7247, E-mail: aporter@ggu.edu; *Ref Librn,* Larry Burg; Tel: 415-442-7250, E-mail: lburg@ggu.edu; *Ref Librn,* Jason De Castro; Tel: 415-442-7249, E-mail: jdecastro@ggu.edu; *Web Serv Librn,* Jennifer Weiser; Tel: 415-442-7258, E-mail: jweiser@ggu.edu; *Pub Serv Spec,* Curtis Guy; Tel: 415-442-7256, E-mail: cguy@ggu.edu; *Tech Serv Spec,* Deborah Sanborn; Tel: 415-442-5215, E-mail: dsanborn@ggu.edu
Founded 1901. Enrl 1,161; Fac 100; Highest Degree: Doctorate
Library Holdings: Per Subs 370
Wireless access

Partic in Statewide California Electronic Library Consortium
Open Mon-Thurs 7:30am-10:30pm, Fri 7:30am-9pm, Sat 10-7, Sun 11-6

Departmental Libraries:

CL SCHOOL OF LAW LIBRARY, 536 Mission St, 94105, SAN 334-5335. Tel: 415-442-6680. FAX: 415-512-9395. Web Site: www.law.ggu.edu/law-library. *Dir,* Michael Daw; Staff 8 (MLS 7, Non-MLS 1)
Founded 1901. Enrl 750; Fac 38
Library Holdings: Bk Vols 275,000; Per Subs 3,424
Special Collections: State Document Depository; US Document Depository
Subject Interests: Anglo-Am law, Calif, Law
Automation Activity & Vendor Info: (Acquisitions) Innovative Interfaces, Inc; (Cataloging) Innovative Interfaces, Inc; (Circulation) Innovative Interfaces, Inc; (Course Reserve) Innovative Interfaces, Inc; (ILL) Innovative Interfaces, Inc; (Media Booking) Innovative Interfaces, Inc; (OPAC) Innovative Interfaces, Inc; (Serials) Innovative Interfaces, Inc
Publications: Guide Series; Information Series
Open Mon-Thurs (Winter) 7:30am-10:30pm, Fri 7:30am-9pm, Sat 10-7, Sun 10am-10:30pm; Mon-Thurs (Summer) 7:30am-10pm, Fri 7:30-7, Sat & Sun 10-6
Restriction: Private libr

L GORDON & REES SCULLY MANSUKHANI*, Law Library, 275 Battery St, Ste 2000, 94111. SAN 372-3143. Tel: 415-986-5900. FAX: 415-986-8054. Web Site: www.gordonrees.com. *Librn,* Joanne Dumapay; E-mail: jdumapay@grsm.com
Library Holdings: Bk Vols 20,000
Subject Interests: Med
Open Mon-Fri 7:45-6

L HANSON BRIDGETT LLP*, Law Library, 425 Market St, 26th Flr, 94105. SAN 372-3429. Tel: 415-995-5855. FAX: 415-541-9366. Web Site: www.hansonbridgett.com. *Mgr, Libr Serv,* Leslie Hesdorfer
Library Holdings: Bk Vols 24,000
Wireless access
Restriction: Staff use only

L HASSARD BONNINGTON LLP*, Law Library, Two Embarcadero Ctr, Ste 1800, 94111. SAN 324-1335. Tel: 415-288-9800. FAX: 415-288-9801. Web Site: www.hassard.com. *Librn,* Stacy McKenzie
Library Holdings: Bk Titles 3,000; Bk Vols 14,000; Per Subs 100
Subject Interests: Med
Restriction: Staff use only

S INSTITUTE FOR CHILDHOOD RESOURCES*, Family Information Center, 268 Bush St, 94104. SAN 324-5128. Tel: 510-540-0111. FAX: 510-540-0171. Web Site: www.drtoy.com. *Dir,* Dr Stevanne Auerbach; E-mail: drtoy@drtoy.com; Staff 4 (MLS 2, Non-MLS 2)
Library Holdings: Bk Titles 5,000; Per Subs 10
Special Collections: Toys
Subject Interests: Child care, Early childhood, Parenting educ
Publications: Choosing Childcare: A Guide for Parents; Dr Toy's Smart Play: Raising a Child with a High PQ (Play Quotient); Toychest: A Sourcebook; Whole Child: A Sourcebook
Restriction: Not open to pub

S INTERNATIONAL LONGSHORE & WAREHOUSE UNION*, Anne Rand Research Library, 1188 Franklin St, 4th Flr, 94109. SAN 301-4177. Tel: 415-775-0533. FAX: 415-775-1302. Web Site: www.ilwu.org. *Dir, Educ Serv, Librn & Archivist,* Robin Walker; E-mail: robin.walker@ilwu.org
Founded 1942
Library Holdings: Bk Titles 3,000; Per Subs 125
Open Mon-Fri 9-5

S JAPANESE AMERICAN NATIONAL LIBRARY, 1619 Sutter St, 94109. SAN 374-7751. Tel: 415-567-5006. E-mail: info@janlibrary.org. Web Site: www.janlibrary.org. *Dir,* Karl K Matsushita
Founded 1969
Library Holdings: Bk Vols 50,000; Per Subs 75
Special Collections: Japanese American Redress, Japanese American Citizens League-National, Japanese American Vernacular Newspapers
Subject Interests: Japanese, Japanese in Am
Function: Archival coll, Ref serv available, Res libr
Restriction: Open by appt only, Open to pub for ref only

R JEWISH COMMUNITY LIBRARY*, 1835 Ellis St, 94115. SAN 301-3766. Tel: 415-567-3327. E-mail: library@jewishlearningworks.org. Web Site: www.jewishcommunitylibrary.org. *Dir,* Howard Freedman; Tel: 415-567-3327, Ext 705, E-mail: hfreedman@jewishlearningworks.org; *Reader Serv Librn,* Rose Katz; Tel: 415-567-3327, Ext 706, E-mail: rkatz@jewishlearningworks.org
Library Holdings: DVDs 2,100; Bk Vols 35,000; Per Subs 9
Special Collections: Havas Children's Library
Subject Interests: Culture, Jewish hist, Jewish philos, Judaism (religion)
Open Mon & Wed 10-4, Tues 12-6, Thurs 12-8, Sun 12-4
Friends of the Library Group

S JFCS HOLOCAUST CENTER*, Tauber Holocaust Library, 2245 Post St, 94115. (Mail add: PO Box 159004, 94115), SAN 326-064X. Tel: 415-449-3717, 415-449-3748. FAX: 415-449-3720. E-mail: HolocaustCenter@jfcs.org. Web Site: holocaustcenter.jfcs.org/library-archives. *Dir,* Morgan Blum Schneider; Staff 2 (MLS 1, Non-MLS 1)
Founded 1979
Library Holdings: Bk Vols 13,500
Special Collections: Archives; Historical Pamphlet Coll; Periodicals Coll; Rare Books; Yizkor Book Coll. Oral History
Subject Interests: Genocide, Holocaust, World War II
Wireless access
Function: Ref serv available
Restriction: Non-circulating, Open by appt only

S C G JUNG INSTITUTE OF SAN FRANCISCO*, Virginia Allan Detloff Library, 2040 Gough St, 94109. SAN 372-5928. Tel: 415-771-8055, Ext 207. FAX: 415-771-8926. E-mail: library@sfjung.org. Web Site: www.sfjung.org. *Admin Dir,* Steve Hargis-Bullen; E-mail: shargis-bullen@sfjung.org; *Librn,* Marianne Morgan; E-mail: mmorgan@sfjung.org; *Libr Asst,* Brian Carr; Staff 2 (MLS 1, Non-MLS 1)
Founded 1965
Jul 2018-Jun 2019. Mats Exp $8,700, Books $3,000, Per/Ser (Incl. Access Fees) $4,500, Manu Arch $600, AV Mat $300, Presv $300. Sal $52,000 (Prof $52,000)
Library Holdings: AV Mats 1,500; CDs 60; DVDs 131; e-books 110; e-journals 10; Bk Titles 17,000; Bk Vols 18,000; Per Subs 25; Videos 160
Special Collections: Archive of Historical Jungiana, Audio & Video. Oral History
Subject Interests: Analytical psychol, Art, Jungian psychol, Mythology, Psychol
Automation Activity & Vendor Info: (Acquisitions) Inmagic, Inc.; (Cataloging) ByWater Solutions; (Circulation) ByWater Solutions; (Course Reserve) ByWater Solutions; (OPAC) ByWater Solutions; (Serials) Inmagic, Inc.
Wireless access
Function: ILL available, Ref serv available
Partic in National Network of Libraries of Medicine Region 5; Northern & Central California Psychology Libraries
Open Mon-Fri 9-5 or by appointment
Restriction: Sub libr
Friends of the Library Group

M KAISER-PERMANENTE MEDICAL CENTER*, Health Sciences Library, 2425 Geary Blvd, Mezzanine M150, 94115. SAN 301-4207. Tel: 415-833-2000. Administration Tel: 415-833-4755. FAX: 415-833-2307. E-mail: ask@kplibraries.libanswers.com. Web Site: healthy.kaiserpermanente.org. *Librn,* Scott Boothe; E-mail: scott.boothe@kp.org; Staff 1 (MLS 1)
Founded 1954
Library Holdings: Bk Titles 3,700; Per Subs 190
Wireless access
Open Mon-Fri 8-6

S KMD ARCHITECTS LIBRARY*, 222 Vallejo St, 94111. SAN 327-5809. Tel: 415-398-5191. FAX: 415-394-7158. Web Site: www.kmdarchitects.com. *Librn,* Mr Dima Torres; E-mail: torres@kmd-arch.com; Staff 1 (MLS 1)
Library Holdings: Bk Titles 500; Spec Interest Per Sub 25
Special Collections: Architectural Library
Subject Interests: Archit, Design, Planning
Automation Activity & Vendor Info: (Cataloging) Inmagic, Inc.; (Circulation) Inmagic, Inc.; (OPAC) Inmagic, Inc.; (Serials) Inmagic, Inc.
Restriction: Open by appt only

S LIGHTHOUSE FOR THE BLIND & VISUALLY IMPAIRED*, Free Lending-Browsing Braille Library, 1155 Market St, 10th Flr, 94103. SAN 301-4606. Tel: 415-431-1481. FAX: 415-863-7568. E-mail: info@lighthouse-sf.org. Web Site: lighthouse-sf.org. *Prog Coordr,* Serena Olsen; E-mail: solsen@lighthouse-sf.org
Founded 1949
Library Holdings: Bk Titles 300; Bk Vols 1,200
Special Collections: Braille Codes, Thesaurus, Unabridged Dictionary, World Book
Subject Interests: Fiction, Philos, Relig
Special Services for the Deaf - TTY equip
Open Mon-Fri 8:30-5

S MECHANICS' INSTITUTE LIBRARY*, 57 Post St, Ste 504, 94104-5003. SAN 301-4304. Tel: 415-393-0101. Reference Tel: 415-393-0102. Administration Tel: 415-393-0113. Reference E-mail: reference@milibrary.org. Web Site: www.milibrary.org. *Libr Dir,* Deborah Hunt; E-mail: dhunt@milibrary.org; *Head, Tech Serv,* Steven Dunlap; E-mail: sdunlap@milibrary.org; *Coll Mgt Librn,* Craig Jackson; E-mail: acjackson@milibrary.org; *Librn, Strategic Partnerships Mgr,* Taryn Edwards; E-mail: tedwards@milibrary.org; *Programming Librn,* Myles Cooper; E-mail: mcooper@milibrary.org; *Libr Supvr,* Celeste Steward; Tel: 415-393-0118, E-mail: csteward@milibrary.org; *Archivist,* Diane Lai; E-mail: dlai@milibrary.org; Staff 13 (MLS 7, Non-MLS 6)
Founded 1854. Pop 3,109
Library Holdings: Audiobooks 8,284; CDs 2,192; DVDs 5,041; e-books 2,183; e-journals 38; Large Print Bks 482; Bk Vols 171,000; Per Subs 399; Videos 10
Special Collections: Californiana; Chess Books & Journals; Industrial Expositions & World's Fairs; Local Authors; Mechanics' Institute Archives; Membership Libraries & Mechanics' Institutes; San Francisco; Western Americana
Automation Activity & Vendor Info: (Cataloging) Innovative Interfaces, Inc - Sierra; (Circulation) Innovative Interfaces, Inc - Sierra; (Discovery) Innovative Interfaces, Inc - Sierra; (ILL) OCLC WorldShare Interlibrary Loan; (OPAC) Innovative Interfaces, Inc - Sierra; (Serials) Innovative Interfaces, Inc - Sierra
Wireless access
Function: 24/7 Electronic res, 24/7 Online cat, Adult bk club, Archival coll, Art exhibits, Audiobks via web, Bk club(s), Bks on CD, Chess club, Computers for patron use, Digital talking bks, Electronic databases & coll, Free DVD rentals, Homebound delivery serv, ILL available, Instruction & testing, Internet access, Large print keyboards, Magazines, Music CDs, Online cat, Orientations, Outreach serv, Photocopying/Printing, Printer for laptops & handheld devices, Prog for adults, Ref & res, Ref serv available, Res assist avail, Res libr, Telephone ref, Wheelchair accessible, Writing prog
Publications: Annual Report; Mechanics' Quarterly (Quarterly newsletter); This Week at the Mechanics' Institute (Online only)
Partic in Califa
Open Mon-Thurs 9-8, Fri 9-6, Sat 10-5, Sun 1-5
Restriction: Circ to mem only, Free to mem, Open to pub upon request, Sub libr

G METROPOLITAN TRANSPORTATION COMMISSION*, MTC-ABAG Library, 375 Beale St, Ste 800, 94105. SAN 331-5363. Tel: 415-778-5236. E-mail: library@bayareametro.gov. Web Site: mtc.ca.gov/tools-resources/mtc-abag-library-information-asking. *Head Librn,* Julie Tunnell; Staff 3 (MLS 2, Non-MLS 1)
Founded 1972
Library Holdings: Bk Vols 25,000; Per Subs 1,000
Special Collections: Environmental Impact Reports; San Francisco Bay Region Planning & Transportation History
Subject Interests: Census, City planning, Regional planning, Transportation
Wireless access
Partic in OCLC Online Computer Library Center, Inc
Open Mon-Fri 8:30-5

S MUSEUM OF RUSSIAN CULTURE, INC LIBRARY*, 2450 Sutter St, 94115. SAN 320-605X. Tel: 415-921-4082. FAX: 415-921-4082. E-mail: contact@mrcsf.org. Web Site: mrcsf.org. *Pres,* Dr Alex Gansa; *VPres,* Yves Franquin
Founded 1949
Library Holdings: Bk Vols 20,000

S NATIONAL PARK SERVICE, Golden Gate National Recreation Area Park Archives, Park Archives & Records Ctr, Bldg 667, Presidio of San Francisco, 94129. (Mail add: Fort Mason Bldg 201, 94123-0022), SAN 333-7758. Tel: 415-561-2808. Web Site: www.nps.gov/goga. *Curator,* Amanda Williford; E-mail: amanda_williford@nps.gov; Staff 3 (MLS 3)
Founded 1974
Library Holdings: Bk Titles 1,000
Special Collections: Alcatraz; History of San Francisco; History of the West; Indian Wars; Korea; Presidio History of San Francisco; US Army History; Vietnam; Women of War; World War I & II. Oral History
Restriction: Open by appt only

L ORRICK, HERRINGTON & SUTCLIFFE LLP*, Law Library, The Orrick Bldg, 405 Howard St, 94105-2669. SAN 301-4398. Tel: 415-773-5700. FAX: 415-773-5759. Web Site: www.orrick.com.
Founded 1884
Library Holdings: Bk Titles 7,000; Bk Vols 30,000; Per Subs 350
Subject Interests: Calif, Corporate law
Partic in Northern Calif Asn of Law Librs
Restriction: Staff use only

L PILLSBURY WINTHROP SHAW PITTMAN LLP*, Law Library, Four Embarcadero Ctr, 22nd Flr, 94111. SAN 301-4460. Tel: 415-983-1000. FAX: 415-983-1200. Web Site: www.pillsburywinthrop.com. *Research Coordr,* Tracy Helser; E-mail: tracy.helser@pillsburylaw.com; *Res Spec,* Karen Guiden; E-mail: karen.guiden@pillsburylaw.com; Staff 2 (MLS 1, Non-MLS 1)
Library Holdings: Bk Vols 30,000; Per Subs 500
Open Mon-Fri 8:30-5:30

S SAN FRANCISCO AFRICAN-AMERICAN HISTORICAL & CULTURAL SOCIETY*, Library of San Francisco, 762 Fulton St, 2nd Flr, 94102. SAN 301-3618. Tel: 415-292-6172. FAX: 415-440-4231. E-mail: info@sfaahcs.org. Web Site: www.sfaahcs.org. *Pres,* Al Williams; E-mail: awilliams@sfaahcs.org
Founded 1955
Library Holdings: Bk Vols 35,892; Per Subs 10
Publications: A Walking Tour of Black Presence in California during the 19th Century; Ascension - Literary Anthology
Partic in San Francisco Bay Area Library & Information Network
Open Tues-Sat 1-5
Friends of the Library Group

C SAN FRANCISCO ART INSTITUTE*, Anne Bremer Memorial Library, 800 Chestnut St, 94133. SAN 301-4533. Tel: 415-749-4562. E-mail: library@sfai.edu. Web Site: sfai.edu/current-students/anne-bremer-memorial-library. *Librn,* Jeff Gunderson; E-mail: jgunderson@sfai.edu; *Tech Serv Librn,* Claudia Marlowe; E-mail: cmarlowe@sfai.edu; *Access Serv, Visual Res Mgr,* Rebecca Alexander; E-mail: ralexander@sfai.edu; Staff 2 (MLS 1, Non-MLS 1)
Founded 1871. Enrl 550; Fac 60; Highest Degree: Master
Library Holdings: Bk Titles 31,000; Bk Vols 34,000; Per Subs 220
Special Collections: California Art, 1871-; History (San Francisco Art Institute), archives, bks, doc, photogs
Subject Interests: Art, Films & filmmaking, Photog
Automation Activity & Vendor Info: (Cataloging) LibraryWorld, Inc; (Circulation) LibraryWorld, Inc; (ILL) OCLC; (OPAC) LibraryWorld, Inc
Wireless access
Publications: Hey You!; Read This First (Quarterly)
Open Mon-Thurs 8:30-7:30, Fri 8:30-6, Sat 1-5; Mon-Fri (Winter-Summer) 9-5
Restriction: Open to fac, students & qualified researchers

S SAN FRANCISCO BOTANICAL GARDEN SOCIETY AT STRYBING ARBORETUM, Helen Crocker Russell Library of Horticulture, 1199 Ninth Ave, 94122-2384. SAN 301-4738. Tel: 415-661-1316, Ext 403. FAX: 415-661-3539. E-mail: library@sfbg.org. Web Site: www.sfbotanicalgarden.org/library. *Libr Dir,* Brandy Kuhl; E-mail: bkuhl@sfbg.org. Subject Specialists: *Botany, Hort,* Brandy Kuhl; Staff 1 (MLS 1)
Founded 1972
Library Holdings: Bk Vols 27,000; Per Subs 250
Special Collections: Nursery & Seed Catalogs
Subject Interests: Botany, Hort
Automation Activity & Vendor Info: (Cataloging) OCLC; (OPAC) Innovative Interfaces, Inc; (Serials) EBSCO Online
Wireless access
Function: Archival coll, Art exhibits, Art programs, Bk club(s), Children's prog, For res purposes, Internet access, Online cat, Orientations, Outside serv via phone, mail, e-mail & web, Photocopying/Printing, Prog for adults, Prog for children & young adult, Ref & res, Ref serv available, Res libr, Story hour, Summer reading prog, Telephone ref, Wheelchair accessible
Publications: Bibliography Series (Acquisition list)
Partic in CDB-S; Council on Botanical & Horticultural Libraries, Inc; OCLC Online Computer Library Center, Inc
Restriction: In-house use for visitors, Non-circulating, Open to pub for ref only

S SAN FRANCISCO CAMERAWORK*, Reference Library, 1011 Market St, 2nd Flr, 94103. SAN 328-1140. Tel: 415-487-1011. E-mail: info@sfcamerawork.org, sfcamera@sfcamerawork.org. Web Site: www.sfcamerawork.org. *Mgr,* Kristina Graber; *Prog Mgr,* Joseph De Mario
Founded 1974
Library Holdings: Bk Vols 100
Special Collections: Artist's bks; Exhibition Catalogues
Subject Interests: Criticism, Hist, Photog
Publications: Camerawork: A Journal of Photographic Arts
Open Tues-Fri 2-6, Sat 12-5

S SAN FRANCISCO CENTER FOR PSYCHOANALYSIS*, Erik Erikson Library, 2340 Jackson St, 4th Flr, 94115. SAN 301-4622. Tel: 415-563-4477. FAX: 415-563-8406. E-mail: library@sf-cp.org. Web Site: www.sf-cp.org/Library/library.htm. *Libr Dir, Tech Serv,* Eric Rosen; Tel:

203-524-5173, E-mail: jones10@sonic.net. Subject Specialists: *Mgt,* Eric Rosen; Staff 1 (Non-MLS 1)
Founded 1950
Library Holdings: AV Mats 582; Electronic Media & Resources 2; Bk Titles 5,600; Per Subs 50
Special Collections: Bernice S Engle Coll; Emmanuel Windholz Coll
Subject Interests: Psychoanalysis
Automation Activity & Vendor Info: (Cataloging) LibraryWorld, Inc; (OPAC) LibraryWorld, Inc; (Serials) LibraryWorld, Inc
Publications: Dialogue
Partic in BayNet Library Association; Northern & Central California Psychology Libraries; Pacific Southwest Regional Medical Library
Friends of the Library Group

S SAN FRANCISCO CHRONICLE LIBRARY*, 901 Mission St, 94103. SAN 301-4541. Tel: 415-777-7843. Web Site: www.sfchronicle.com. *Libr Dir,* Bill Van Niekerken; Staff 6 (MLS 5, Non-MLS 1)
Founded 1879
Library Holdings: Bk Vols 400
Subject Interests: Local hist

S SAN FRANCISCO CONSERVATORY OF MUSIC LIBRARY*, 50 Oak St, 94102. SAN 301-4568. Tel: 415-503-6213, 415-503-6253. FAX: 415-503-6299. Web Site: sfcm.edu/library. *Head Librn,* Jeong Lee; E-mail: library@sfcm.edu; *Libr Supvr,* Andrew Barnhart; E-mail: libsuper@sfcm.edu; Staff 2 (MLS 1, Non-MLS 1)
Founded 1917. Enrl 400; Highest Degree: Master
Library Holdings: AV Mats 13,000; Bk Titles 44,000; Bk Vols 75,000; Per Subs 73
Subject Interests: Humanities, Music
Automation Activity & Vendor Info: (Acquisitions) OCLC; (Cataloging) OCLC WorldShare Interlibrary Loan; (Circulation) OCLC WorldShare Interlibrary Loan; (ILL) OCLC WorldShare Interlibrary Loan
Wireless access
Open Mon-Thurs 8:30am-9pm, Fri 8:30-5, Sat 9-3, Sun 12-7
Restriction: Non-circulating to the pub, Open to fac, students & qualified researchers, Open to pub by appt only, Open to pub upon request

GL SAN FRANCISCO LAW LIBRARY*, 1145 Market St, 4th Flr, 94103. SAN 334-5424. Tel: 415-554-1772. Reference Tel: 415-554-1797. FAX: 415-863-4022. E-mail: sflawlibrary@sfgov.org. Reference E-mail: sfll.reference@sfgov.org. Web Site: www.sflawlibrary.org. *Dir,* Marcia R Bell; E-mail: marcia.bell@sfgov.org; *Asst Dir,* Diane M Rodriguez
Founded 1870
Special Collections: Archived Coll (California chapter statutes 1850-present); California Administrative Registers Archive (1945-present); Law Practice Management Coll; Rare Legal Book Coll; San Francisco Municipal Code Archive (SF Charters & previous codes, SF Bldg codes; Self Help Legal Coll; Statutes for all 50 States
Automation Activity & Vendor Info: (Acquisitions) Innovative Interfaces, Inc - Millennium; (Cataloging) Innovative Interfaces, Inc - Millennium; (Circulation) Innovative Interfaces, Inc - Millennium; (ILL) Innovative Interfaces, Inc - Millennium; (OPAC) Innovative Interfaces, Inc - Millennium
Wireless access
Function: Computers for patron use, Doc delivery serv, Electronic databases & coll, Online cat, Photocopying/Printing, Ref serv available, Wheelchair accessible
Open Mon-Thurs 8:30-6, Fri 8:30-5, Sat 10-4
Restriction: ID required to use computers (Ltd hrs), Non-circulating to the pub, Pub access for legal res only

S SAN FRANCISCO MARITIME LIBRARY*, Bldg E, 2nd Flr, Two Marina Blvd, 94123. SAN 301-4363. Tel: 415-561-7030. FAX: 415-556-1624. Web Site: www.nps.gov/safr. *Ref Librn,* Gina Bardi; E-mail: gina_bardi@nps.gov; Staff 5 (MLS 2, Non-MLS 3)
Founded 1959
Library Holdings: Bk Vols 75,000; Per Subs 120
Special Collections: Alaska Packers Asn Coll; Barbara Johnson Whaling Coll; Bethlehem Shipbuilding Coll; David W Dickie Coll; Hester Coll; John Lyman Coll; John W Proctor Coll; Mawdeley Coll; Plummer Beaton Coll; Proctor Coll; Reardon Coll. Oral History
Partic in Federal Library & Information Network; OCLC Online Computer Library Center, Inc
Restriction: Borrowing requests are handled by ILL, Circulates for staff only, Closed stack, Non-circulating of rare bks, Non-circulating to the pub, Off-site coll in storage - retrieval as requested, Open to pub by appt only
Friends of the Library Group

S SAN FRANCISCO MUSEUM OF MODERN ART*, Research Library, Archives & Records Management, 151 Third St, 94103-3107. SAN 301-4614. E-mail: library@sfmoma.org. *Head of Libr & Archives,* David Senior; Tel: 415-357-4121; Staff 7 (MLS 5, Non-MLS 2)
Founded 1935
Library Holdings: Bk Titles 80,000; Per Subs 2,000
Special Collections: Kurenboh Japanese Photography Book Coll; Margery Mann Photography Book Coll; Sidney Tillim Photography Book Coll
Subject Interests: Contemporary art, Modern art
Wireless access
Function: Online cat
Restriction: Circulates for staff only, Closed stack, Off-site coll in storage - retrieval as requested, Open to pub by appt only

P SAN FRANCISCO PUBLIC LIBRARY*, 100 Larkin St, 94102. SAN 334-5483. Tel: 415-557-4400. Interlibrary Loan Service Tel: 415-557-4406. Administration Tel: 415-557-4236. E-mail: info@sfpl.org. Web Site: sfpl.org. *City Librn,* Michael Lambert; E-mail: citylibrarian@sfpl.org; *Chief Operating Officer,* Maureen Singleton; E-mail: citylibrarian@sfpl.org; *Chief of Main Libr,* Thomas Fortin; Tel: 415-557-4200, E-mail: chiefofmain@sfpl.org; *Chief, Coll & Tech Serv,* Shellie Cocking; Tel: 415-557-4369, E-mail: shellie.cocking@sfpl.org; *Chief Financial Officer,* Heather Green; Tel: 415-347-4209, E-mail: Finance@sfpl.org; *Chief Info Officer,* Michael Liang; Tel: 415-347-3179, E-mail: InfoTech@sfpl.org; *Chief, Community Partnerships,* Michelle Jeffers; Tel: 415-557-4277, E-mail: publicaffairs@sfpl.org; *Chief Officer, Libr Syst Analyst,* Randle McClure; Tel: 415-509-1514, E-mail: analytics@sfpl.org; *Dir, Human Res,* Lori Regler; Tel: 415-557-4585, E-mail: humanresources@sfpl.org; *Dir, Facilities,* Roberto Lombardi; Tel: 415-557-4245, E-mail: facilities@spfl.org; *Br Mgr,* Catherine Delneo; Tel: 415-557-4353, E-mail: chiefofbranches@sfpl.org. Subject Specialists: *Programs,* Michelle Jeffers; Staff 670 (MLS 203, Non-MLS 467)
Founded 1878. Pop 897,806; Circ 10,866,519
Jul 2019-Jun 2020 Income (Main & Associated Libraries) $129,670,334, State $59,872, City $128,246,732, Other $1,363,730. Mats Exp $14,826,304, Books $3,240,800, Per/Ser (Incl. Access Fees) $854,563, AV Mat $1,844,708, Electronic Ref Mat (Incl. Access Fees) $8,886,233. Sal $61,473,229
Library Holdings: Audiobooks 18,580; AV Mats 299,717; CDs 45,634; DVDs 224,320; e-books 393,871; Electronic Media & Resources 277,494; Music Scores 66,183; Bk Vols 2,305,721; Per Subs 5,562; Videos 2,421
Special Collections: Calligraphy (Richard Harrison Coll); Chinese Language & Interest (Chinatown Branch); Eric Hoffer Manuscripts; Fine Printing & Binding (Kuhl); Gay & Lesbian Archives; History of Printing & Development of the Book (Robert Grabhorn Coll); San Francisco Coll; San Francisco Newspaper Morgues; Science Fiction & Fantasy (McComas Coll); Spanish Language & Interest (Mission Branch); Wit & Humor (Schmulowitz Coll). State Document Depository; US Document Depository
Automation Activity & Vendor Info: (Acquisitions) Innovative Interfaces, Inc; (Cataloging) Innovative Interfaces, Inc; (Circulation) Innovative Interfaces, Inc; (OPAC) BiblioCommons; (Serials) Innovative Interfaces, Inc
Wireless access
Function: 24/7 Electronic res, 24/7 Online cat, Adult bk club, Adult literacy prog, Archival coll, Art exhibits, Audiobks via web, Bilingual assistance for Spanish patrons, Bk club(s), Bks on CD, Children's prog, Computers for patron use, Digital talking bks, Distance learning, Electronic databases & coll, For res purposes, Free DVD rentals, Govt ref serv, Holiday prog, Homebound delivery serv, Homework prog, ILL available, Internet access, Jail serv, Life-long learning prog for all ages, Magazines, Meeting rooms, Microfiche/film & reading machines, Movies, Museum passes, Music CDs, Online cat, Online ref, Outreach serv, Outside serv via phone, mail, e-mail & web, OverDrive digital audio bks, Photocopying/Printing, Preschool outreach, Printer for laptops & handheld devices, Prog for adults, Prog for children & young adult, Ref serv available, Scanner, Senior outreach, Spanish lang bks, Spoken cassettes & CDs, Spoken cassettes & DVDs, STEM programs, Story hour, Study rm, Summer reading prog, Teen prog, Telephone ref, Wheelchair accessible
Mem of Pacific Library Partnership (PLP)
Special Services for the Deaf - ADA equip; Am sign lang & deaf culture; Assistive tech; Bks on deafness & sign lang; Closed caption videos; Coll on deaf educ; Deaf publ; Spec interest per; Staff with knowledge of sign lang; TTY equip; Videos & decoder
Special Services for the Blind - Accessible computers; Assistive/Adapted tech devices, equip & products; Audio mat; Bks & mags in Braille, on rec, tape & cassette; Braille bks; Braille equip; Closed circuit TV; Closed circuit TV magnifier; Digital talking bk; Digital talking bk machines; Extensive large print coll; Free checkout of audio mat; Home delivery serv; Info on spec aids & appliances; Internet workstation with adaptive software; Large print bks; Large screen computer & software; PC for people with disabilities; Recorded bks; Ref serv; Scanner for conversion & translation of mats; Screen enlargement software for people with visual disabilities; Spec prog; Talking bk & rec for the blind cat; Talking bks & player equip; Text reader; ZoomText magnification & reading software
Open Mon 9-6, Tues-Thurs 9-8, Fri & Sun 12-6, Sat 10-6
Friends of the Library Group

Branches: 27
ANZA BRANCH LIBRARY, 550 37th Ave, 94121-2691, SAN 334-5548. Tel: 415-355-5717. *Br Mgr,* Regan Gong
Open Mon 12-6, Tues 10-9, Wed 1-9, Thurs & Sat 10-6, Fri 1-6, Sun 1-5
Friends of the Library Group
BAYVIEW-LINDA BROOKS-BURTON, 5075 Third St, 94124-2311, SAN 334-6269. Tel: 415-557-5757. FAX: 415-822-1001. *Br Mgr,* Annie Tang
Open Mon & Sat 10-6, Tues-Thurs 10-8, Fri 1-6, Sun 1-5
Friends of the Library Group
BERNAL HEIGHTS BRANCH LIBRARY, 500 Cortland Ave, 94110-5612, SAN 334-5572. Tel: 415-355-2810. FAX: 415-642-9951. *Br Mgr,* Rebecca Gonzales
Open Mon & Thurs 10-6, Tues 10-9, Wed 1-9, Fri & Sat 1-6, Sun 1-5
Friends of the Library Group
EXCELSIOR BRANCH LIBRARY, 4400 Mission St (at Cotter), 94112-1927, SAN 334-5696. Tel: 415-355-2868. FAX: 415-337-4738. *Br Mgr,* Ramses Escobedo
Open Mon & Fri 1-6, Tues, Wed & Thurs 10-9, Thurs & Sat 10-6, Sun 1-5
GLEN PARK BRANCH LIBRARY, 2825 Diamond St, 94131-3033, SAN 334-5726. Tel: 415-355-2858. FAX: 415-469-8557. *Br Mgr,* Michelle Waddy
Open Mon, Tues & Sat 10-6, Wed 12-8, Thurs 10-7, Fri 1-6, Sun 1-5
GOLDEN GATE VALLEY BRANCH LIBRARY, 1801 Green St, 94123-4921, SAN 334-5750. Tel: 415-355-5666. FAX: 415-561-0153. *Br Mgr,* Chela Lucas
Open Mon, Tues & Sat 10-6, Wed 12-9, Thurs 12-8, Fri 1-6, Sun 1-5
Friends of the Library Group
INGLESIDE BRANCH LIBRARY, 1298 Ocean Ave, 94112-1717, SAN 334-5785. Tel: 415-355-2898. FAX: 415-469-7390. *Br Mgr,* Nina Pogosyan
Open Mon, Tues, Fri & Sat 10-6, Wed 10-8, Thurs 12-7, Sun 1-5
Friends of the Library Group
CHINATOWN/HIM MARK LAI BRANCH LIBRARY, 1135 Powell St, 94108, SAN 334-5637. Tel: 415-355-2888. FAX: 415-274-0277. *Br Mgr,* Chao Qun Huang
Founded 1921
Open Mon & Fri 1-6, Tues, Wed & Thurs 10-9, Sat 10-6, Sun 1-5
Friends of the Library Group
MARINA BRANCH LIBRARY, 1890 Chestnut St, 94123-2804, SAN 334-5815. Tel: 415-355-2823. FAX: 415-447-9308. *Br Mgr,* Chieko Wealand
Open Mon, Tues & Sat 10-6, Wed 1-8, Thurs 10-8, Fri 1-6, Sun 1-5
Friends of the Library Group
MERCED BRANCH LIBRARY, 155 Winston Dr, 94132-2032, SAN 334-584X. Tel: 415-355-2825. FAX: 415-337-8350. *Br Mgr,* Elizabeth Thacker
Open Mon & Sat 10-6, Tues & Thurs 10-9, Wed 1-9, Fri 1-6, Sun 1-5
Friends of the Library Group
EUREKA VALLEY-HARVEY MILK MEMORIAL BRANCH LIBRARY, One Jose Sarria Ct, 94114-1621, SAN 334-5661. Tel: 415-355-5616. FAX: 415-552-2584. *Interim Br Mgr,* Anne Vannuchi
Open Mon, Thurs & Sat 10-6, Tues & Wed 10-9, Fri 1-6, Sun 1-5
Friends of the Library Group
MISSION BAY BRANCH LIBRARY, 960 Fourth St, 94158-1628. Tel: 415-355-2838. FAX: 415-947-0723. *Br Mgr,* Melanie McCallum
Open Mon, Tues, Thurs & Sat 10-6, Wed 11-8, Fri 1-6, Sun 1-5
Friends of the Library Group
MISSION BRANCH LIBRARY, 300 Bartlett St, 94110, SAN 334-5874. Tel: 415-355-2800. FAX: 415-648-6566. *Br Mgr,* Ramon Hernandez
Open Mon & Fri 1-6, Tues-Thurs 10-9, Sat 10-6, Sun 1-5
Friends of the Library Group
NOE VALLEY/SALLY BRUNN BRANCH LIBRARY, 451 Jersey St, 94114-3632, SAN 334-5904. Tel: 415-355-5707. FAX: 415-282-8736. *Br Mgr,* Denise Sanderson
Open Mon 12-6, Tues 10-9, Wed 1-9, Thurs & Sat 10-6, Fri 1-6, Sun 1-5
Friends of the Library Group
NORTH BEACH BRANCH LIBRARY, 2000 Mason St, 94133-2337, SAN 334-5939. Tel: 415-355-5626. FAX: 415-772-8251. *Br Mgr,* Richard Le
Open Mon & Fri 1-6, Tues 10-9, Wed 12-9, Thurs & Sat 10-6, Sun 1-5
Friends of the Library Group
OCEAN VIEW BRANCH LIBRARY, 345 Randolph St, 94132-3119, SAN 334-5963. Tel: 415-355-5615. FAX: 415-452-8584. *Br Mgr,* Lynne Maes
Open Mon, Tues & Sat 10-6, Wed 12-8, Thurs 10-7, Fri 1-6, Sun 1-5
Friends of the Library Group
ORTEGA BRANCH LIBRARY, 3223 Ortega St, 94122-4053, SAN 334-5998. Tel: 415-355-5700. FAX: 415-665-5942. *Br Mgr,* Tiffany Lac
Open Mon, Tues & Sat 10-6, Wed 1-9, Thurs 12-9, Fri 1-6, Sun 1-5
Friends of the Library Group
PARK BRANCH LIBRARY, 1833 Page St, 94117-1909, SAN 334-6021. Tel: 415-355-5656. FAX: 415-752-2290. *Br Mgr,* Darice Murray-McKay
Open Mon 12-6, Tues 10-9, Wed 1-9, Thurs & Sat 10-6, Fri 1-6, Sun 1-5
Friends of the Library Group
PARKSIDE BRANCH LIBRARY, 1200 Taraval St, 94116-2452, SAN 334-6056. Tel: 415-355-5770. FAX: 415-566-8014. *Br Mgr,* Ana Elisa de Campos Salles
Open Mon & Fri 1-6, Tues 10-9, Wed 12-9, Thurs & Sat 10-6, Sun 1-5
Friends of the Library Group
PORTOLA BRANCH LIBRARY, 380 Bacon St (at Goettingen), 94134-1526, SAN 334-6080. Tel: 415-355-5660. FAX: 415-468-1644. *Br Mgr,* Nicole Termini Germain
Open Mon, Tues & Sat 10-6, Wed 12-8, Thurs 10-7, Fri 1-6, Sun 1-5
Friends of the Library Group
POTRERO BRANCH LIBRARY, 1616 20th St, 94107-2811, SAN 334-6110. Tel: 415-355-2822. FAX: 415-401-8147. *Br Mgr,* Genevieve Feldman
Open Mon & Fri 1-6, Tues & Thurs 10-8, Wed 12-8, Sat 10-6, Sun 1-5
Friends of the Library Group
PRESIDIO BRANCH LIBRARY, 3150 Sacramento St, 94115-2006, SAN 334-5513. Tel: 415-355-2880. FAX: 415-563-3299. *Br Mgr,* Robert Carlson
Open Mon & Fri 1-6, Tues 10-9, Wed 12-9, Thurs & Sat 10-6, Sun 1-5
Friends of the Library Group
RICHMOND/SENATOR MILTON MARKS BRANCH LIBRARY, 351 Ninth Ave, 94118-2210, SAN 334-617X. Tel: 415-355-5600. FAX: 415-752-7785. *Ch Mgr,* Benjamin Cohen
Open Mon & Fri 1-6, Tues-Thurs 10-9, Sat 10-6, Sun 1-5
Friends of the Library Group
SUNSET BRANCH LIBRARY, 1305 18th Ave, 94122-1807, SAN 334-620X. Tel: 415-355-2808. FAX: 415-665-2461. *Br Mgr,* Wing Chan
Open Mon & Fri 1-6, Tues-Thurs 10-9, Sat 10-6, Sun 1-5
Friends of the Library Group
VISITACION VALLEY BRANCH LIBRARY, 201 Leland Ave, 94134-2829, SAN 334-6234. Tel: 415-355-2848. FAX: 415-333-1027. *Br Mgr,* Barbara Maes
Open Mon & Sat 10-6, Tues-Thurs 10-8, Fri 1-6, Sun 1-5
Friends of the Library Group
WEST PORTAL BRANCH LIBRARY, 190 Lenox Way, 94127-1113, SAN 334-6293. Tel: 415-355-2886. FAX: 415-731-3269. *Br Mgr,* Jessica Jaramillo
Founded 1936
Open Mon & Fri 1-6, Tues-Thurs 10-9, Sat 10-6, Sun 1-5
Friends of the Library Group
WESTERN ADDITION BRANCH LIBRARY, 1550 Scott St, 94115-3512, SAN 334-6323. Tel: 415-355-5727. FAX: 415-440-4527. *Br Mgr,* Naima Dean
Open Mon, Tues & Sat 10-6, Wed 1-8, Thurs 10-8, Fri 1-6, Sun 1-5
Friends of the Library Group
Bookmobiles: 4. Mgr Mobile Outreach Servs, Suzanne Beattie. Bk vols 23,741

C SAN FRANCISCO STATE UNIVERSITY*, J Paul Leonard Library, 1630 Holloway Ave, 94132-4030. SAN 301-4630. Tel: 415-338-1854. Circulation Tel: 415-338-1552. Interlibrary Loan Service Tel: 415-338-1727. Reference Tel: 415-338-1974. Administration Tel: 415-338-1681. Interlibrary Loan Service FAX: 415-338-6199. Administration FAX: 415-338-1504. Reference E-mail: libref@sfsu.edu. Web Site: www.library.sfsu.edu. *Dept Chair, Head, Coll Mgt Serv,* Ya Wang; Tel: 415-405-2680, E-mail: wangy@sfsu.edu; *Univ Librn,* Deborah C Masters; Tel: 415-338-1681, E-mail: dmasters@sfsu.edu; *Dept Chair, Spec Coll, Head, Res & Instrul Serv,* Jeff Rosen; Tel: 415-338-1811, E-mail: jrosen@sfsu.edu; *Access Serv, Head, Info Tech,* Thoreau Lovell; Tel: 415-338-2285, E-mail: tlovell@sfsu.edu. Subject Specialists: *Chinese, Computer sci, Info syst, Japanese,* Ya Wang; *Gerontology, Labor studies, Parks, Recreation, Tourism,* Jeff Rosen; Staff 74 (MLS 25, Non-MLS 49)
Founded 1899. Enrl 30,256; Fac 1,728; Highest Degree: Doctorate
Jul 2015-Jun 2016 Income $7,880,401. Mats Exp $2,829,599. Sal $4,111,448 (Prof $1,601,540)
Library Holdings: e-books 168,880; e-journals 54,697; Microforms 1,613,021; Bk Titles 1,580,912; Per Subs 460
Special Collections: Archer Children's Book Coll; Bay Area TV Archives; Frank V deBellis Coll; Labor Archives & Research Center. State Document Depository; US Document Depository
Subject Interests: Art & archit, Bus & mgt, Econ, Educ, Hist
Automation Activity & Vendor Info: (Acquisitions) Innovative Interfaces, Inc; (Cataloging) Innovative Interfaces, Inc; (Circulation) Innovative Interfaces, Inc; (Course Reserve) Innovative Interfaces, Inc; (Discovery) Ex Libris Group; (ILL) Innovative Interfaces, Inc; (OPAC) Innovative Interfaces, Inc; (Serials) Innovative Interfaces, Inc
Wireless access
Publications: Labor Archives and Research Center (Newsletter); Research Guides

Partic in Consortium of Western Univ & Col; Link+; OCLC Online Computer Library Center, Inc
Open Mon-Thurs 8am-10pm, Fri 8-5, Sat 10-6, Sun noon-9
Friends of the Library Group

L SHEARMAN & STERLING LLP*, 535 Mission St, 25th Flr, 94105-2997. SAN 373-1006. Tel: 415-616-1100. FAX: 415-616-1199. Web Site: www.shearman.com. *Res Spec,* Catherine Deane
Library Holdings: Bk Vols 10,000; Per Subs 50

S SMITH-KETTLEWELL EYE RESEARCH INSTITUTE LIBRARY*, 2318 Fillmore St, 94115. SAN 327-7038. Tel: 415-345-2000. FAX: 415-345-8455. Web Site: www.ski.org.
Library Holdings: Bk Vols 400
Restriction: Not open to pub

L SQUIRE PATTON BOGGS*, Law Library, 275 Battery St, Ste 2600, 94111. SAN 372-2996. Tel: 415-945-0200. FAX: 415-393-9887. Web Site: www.squirepattonboggs.com/en/locations/san-francisco. *Head Librn,* Nancy Castor
Library Holdings: Bk Vols 10,000
Automation Activity & Vendor Info: (Cataloging) TLC (The Library Corporation); (Circulation) TLC (The Library Corporation)
Partic in OCLC Online Computer Library Center, Inc
Restriction: Staff use only

S STANTEC ARCHITECTURE INC LIBRARY*, 100 California St, Ste 1000, 94111-4575. SAN 325-6375. Tel: 415-882-9500. FAX: 415-882-9523. Web Site: www.stantec.com. *Librn,* Rachel Ginsberg.
Subject Specialists: *Archit, Phys environment,* Rachel Ginsberg
Library Holdings: Bk Vols 1,000
Restriction: Staff use only

GL UNITED STATES COURT OF APPEALS FOR THE NINTH CIRCUIT - LIBRARY*, James R Browning Courthouse, 95 Seventh St, 94103. (Mail add: PO Box 193728, 94119-3728), SAN 301-4789. Tel: 415-355-8650. FAX: 415-355-8696. Web Site: www.ca9.uscourts.gov/library. *Circuit Librn,* Eric D Wade; *Dep Circuit Librn,* Edward Hosey; *HQ Librn,* Julie Horst; E-mail: julie_horst@lb9.uscourts.gov; *Ref (Info Servs),* Fil Govea; *Ref (Info Servs),* Christina Luini; *Acq,* Lisa Larribeau; Staff 16 (MLS 9, Non-MLS 7)
Founded 1891
Library Holdings: Per Subs 1,600
Subject Interests: Law
Automation Activity & Vendor Info: (Acquisitions) SirsiDynix; (Cataloging) SirsiDynix; (OPAC) SirsiDynix; (Serials) SirsiDynix
Wireless access
Function: Res libr
Partic in OCLC Online Computer Library Center, Inc
Open Mon-Fri 9-5
Restriction: Authorized patrons, Closed stack, Limited access for the pub, Not a lending libr, Open to pub for ref only, Restricted pub use

GL UNITED STATES DISTRICT COURT, Law Library, Phillip Burton Federal Bldg, 450 Golden Gate Ave, 94102. SAN 301-4800. Tel: 415-436-8130. FAX: 415-436-8134. *Librn,* Susan Wong Caulder; E-mail: susan_wong_caulder@lb9.uscourts.gov; *Asst Librn,* Christina Luini; E-mail: christina_luini@lb9.uscourts.gov; *Tech Serv,* Loan Le; E-mail: loan_le@lb9.uscourts.gov; Staff 3 (MLS 2, Non-MLS 1)
Founded 1960
Library Holdings: Bk Titles 2,463; Bk Vols 36,773
Automation Activity & Vendor Info: (Acquisitions) SirsiDynix; (Cataloging) SirsiDynix; (OPAC) SirsiDynix; (Serials) SirsiDynix
Wireless access
Restriction: Staff use only

CL UNIVERSITY OF CALIFORNIA*, Hastings College of the Law Library, 200 McAllister St, 94102-4978. SAN 301-4835. Tel: 415-565-4757. Web Site: www.uchastings.edu/academics/library. *Assoc Dean for Libr & Tech Serv,* Camilla Tubbs; E-mail: tubbsc@uchastings.edu; *Dep Dir,* Hilary Hardcastle; E-mail: hardcast@uchastings.edu; *Head, Tech Serv,* Stephanie Schmitt; E-mail: schmitt@uchastings.edu; *Access Serv Librn,* Justin Edgar; E-mail: edgarj@uchastings.edu; *Fac Serv Librn,* Charles Marcus; E-mail: marcusc@uchastings.edu; *Instrul Serv Librn,* Tony Pelczynski; E-mail: pelczyns@uchastings.edu; *Res & Instruction Librn,* Holly Herndon; E-mail: herndonholly@uchastings.edu; Staff 20 (MLS 11, Non-MLS 9)
Founded 1878. Enrl 1,290; Fac 50; Highest Degree: Doctorate
Library Holdings: Bk Titles 146,442; Bk Vols 438,121; Per Subs 7,857
Special Collections: State Document Depository; US Document Depository
Subject Interests: Criminal law & justice, Law
Automation Activity & Vendor Info: (Acquisitions) Innovative Interfaces, Inc; (Cataloging) Innovative Interfaces, Inc; (Circulation) Innovative Interfaces, Inc; (ILL) OCLC; (OPAC) Innovative Interfaces, Inc; (Serials) Innovative Interfaces, Inc
Wireless access
Open Mon-Thurs 8am-11pm, Fri 8am-9pm, Sat 8-8, Sun 10am-11pm
Restriction: Circ limited, Open to students, fac & staff

CM UNIVERSITY OF CALIFORNIA SAN FRANCISCO*, Parnassus Library, 530 Parnassus Ave, 94143. SAN 301-4843. Tel: 415-476-2336. Web Site: www.library.ucsf.edu. *Asst Vice Chancellor, Univ Librn,* Chris Shaffer; Tel: 415-476-5557, E-mail: chris.shaffer@ucsf.edu; *Coll, Dir, Res Serv, Educ Dir,* Julia Kochi; Tel: 415-502-7539, E-mail: julia.kochi@ucsf.edu; *Dir, Finance & Operations,* Jim Munson; Tel: 415-476-8060, E-mail: jim.munson@ucsf.edu; *Dir, Learning Tech & Educ Serv,* Gail Persily; Tel: 415-476-3766, E-mail: gail.persily@ucsf.edu; *Asst Dir, Scholarly Communications & Coll,* Anneliese Taylor; Tel: 415-476-8415, E-mail: anneliese.taylor@ucsf.edu; *Copyright Librn, Research Librn,* Peggy Tahir; Tel: 415-476-5765, E-mail: peggy.tahir@ucsf.edu; Staff 68 (MLS 14, Non-MLS 54)
Founded 1873. Enrl 3,664; Fac 4,278; Highest Degree: Doctorate
Library Holdings: e-books 14,987; e-journals 13,068; Bk Vols 817,724; Per Subs 570
Special Collections: California Medicine (special concentration in communicable diseases, high altitude physiology, industrial/organizational medicine); East Asian Medicine; History of Health Sciences; Japanese Woodblock Print Coll; Legacy Tobacco Documents Library; University Archives
Subject Interests: Health sci, Life sci, Tobacco
Automation Activity & Vendor Info: (Acquisitions) Innovative Interfaces, Inc - Millennium; (Cataloging) Innovative Interfaces, Inc - Millennium; (Circulation) Innovative Interfaces, Inc - Millennium; (OPAC) Innovative Interfaces, Inc - Millennium; (Serials) Innovative Interfaces, Inc - Millennium
Wireless access
Function: Archival coll, Distance learning, Doc delivery serv, For res purposes, ILL available, Photocopying/Printing, Prof lending libr, Ref serv available, Res libr, Telephone ref
Partic in California Digital Library; National Network of Libraries of Medicine Region 5; OCLC Online Computer Library Center, Inc
Open Mon-Thurs 7:45am-10pm, Fri 7:45am-8pm, Sat 10-6, Sun Noon-10
Friends of the Library Group

Departmental Libraries:

MISSION BAY FAMRI LIBRARY, William J Rutter Conference Ctr, Rm 150, 1675 Owens St, 94143-2119. Tel: 415-514-4060. Web Site: www.library.ucsf.edu/locations/missionbay. *Access Serv Mgr,* Andy Panado; Tel: 415-502-4178, E-mail: andres.panado@ucsf.edu
Highest Degree: Doctorate
Library Holdings: Bk Vols 1,400; Per Subs 18
Subject Interests: Health sci, Life sci
Function: Distance learning, Doc delivery serv, For res purposes, ILL available, Photocopying/Printing, Prof lending libr, Ref serv available, Res libr, Telephone ref

C UNIVERSITY OF SAN FRANCISCO, Richard A Gleeson Library-Charles & Nancy Geschke Resource Center, 2130 Fulton St, 94117-1080. SAN 334-6471. Tel: 415-422-2039. Interlibrary Loan Service Tel: 415-422-2662. Administration Tel: 415-422-6167. Web Site: www.usfca.edu/library. *Dean,* Tyrone Cannon; E-mail: cannont@usfca.edu; *Actg Dean,* Shawn Calhoun; Tel: 415-422-2048, E-mail: calhouns@usfca.edu; *Asst Dean, Bus Mgr,* Carmen Fernandez-Baybay; Tel: 415-422-2035, E-mail: fernandezc@usfca.edu; *Associate Dean, Collection Services,* Erika Johnson; Tel: 415-422-6417, E-mail: eljohnson5@usfca.edu; *Head, Electronic Resources & Systems,* Sherise Kimura; Tel: 415-422-5379, E-mail: kimura@usfca.edu; *Head, Instruction & Outreach,* Annie Pho; Tel: 415-422-2759, E-mail: apho2@usfca.edu; *Head, Reference & Access Servs,* Randy Souther; Tel: 412-422-5388, E-mail: southerr@usfca.edu; *Head, Spec Coll & Archives,* John Hawk; Tel: 415-422-2036, E-mail: hawkj@usfca.edu; *Digital Coll Librn,* Gina Solares; Tel: 415-422-5361, E-mail: gsolares@usfca.edu; *Reference & Government Info Librn,* Carol Spector; Tel: 415-422-2040, E-mail: csspector@usfca.edu; *Ref Librn,* Penny Scott; Tel: 415-422-5389, E-mail: plscott@usfca.edu; *Tech Serv Librn,* Deborah Benrubi; Tel: 415-422-5672, E-mail: benrubi@usfca.edu; *Univ Archivist,* Annie Reid; Tel: 415-422-5352, E-mail: areid1@usfca.edu; *Outreach Library Asst,* Reimi Akin; Tel: 415-422-5387, E-mail: rakin@usfca.edu; Staff 42 (MLS 20, Non-MLS 22)
Founded 1855. Enrl 8,568; Fac 861; Highest Degree: Doctorate
Library Holdings: AV Mats 1,754; Bks on Deafness & Sign Lang 364; CDs 1,000; DVDs 600; e-books 35,000; e-journals 15,000; Bk Titles 501,022; Bk Vols 607,020; Per Subs 1,905; Talking Bks 445; Videos 1,600
Special Collections: 1890's English Literature; A E & Lawrence Housman; Book Club of California; Carrollton; Charles Carroll; Eric Gill; Fine Printing; Grabhorn Press; John Henry Nash; Recusant Literature; Richard Le Gallienne; Robert Graves; Sir Thomas More & Contemporaries; Victor Hammer. State Document Depository; US Document Depository

Automation Activity & Vendor Info: (Acquisitions) Innovative Interfaces, Inc; (Cataloging) Innovative Interfaces, Inc; (Circulation) Innovative Interfaces, Inc; (ILL) Innovative Interfaces, Inc; (OPAC) Innovative Interfaces, Inc; (Serials) Innovative Interfaces, Inc
Wireless access
Function: Archival coll, Art exhibits, Distance learning, Doc delivery serv, Govt ref serv, ILL available, Internet access, Music CDs, Orientations, Photocopying/Printing, Ref serv available, Workshops
Partic in Association of Jesuit Colleges & Universities; Association of Research Libraries; Coop Libr Agency for Syst & Servs; OCLC Online Computer Library Center, Inc; Southern Calif Electronic Libr Consortium
Open Mon-Thurs 8am-Midnight, Fri 8-8, Sat 10-8, Sun Noon-Midnight
Restriction: Limited access for the pub, Private libr
Friends of the Library Group

Departmental Libraries:

CL ZIEF LAW LIBRARY, 2101 Fulton St, 94117-1004. (Mail add: 2130 Fulton St, 94117-1080), SAN 334-6536. Tel: 415-422-6679. FAX: 415-422-2345. Web Site: www.usfca.edu/law/library. *Interim Dir,* Suzanne Mawhinney; E-mail: skmawhinney@usfca.edu; *Head, Coll Serv,* Shannon S Burchard; E-mail: burchards@usfca.edu; *Research Librn,* April Ham; E-mail: ahham@usfca.edu; *Research Librn,* John Shafer; E-mail: shafer@usfca.edu; Staff 6 (MLS 6)
Founded 1912. Enrl 640; Fac 30; Highest Degree: Master
Library Holdings: Bk Titles 36,379; Bk Vols 354,849; Per Subs 3,293
Restriction: Restricted access

G US ENVIRONMENTAL PROTECTION AGENCY LIBRARY*, Pacific Southwest, Region 9, 75 Hawthorne St, 94105. SAN 301-3979. Tel: 415-947-4406. Toll Free Tel: 866-372-9378. E-mail: library-reg9@epa.gov. Web Site: www.epa.gov/libraries/region-9-environmental-information-centerlibrary-services. *Libr Dir,* Deborra Cohen; Tel: 415-972-3655, E-mail: cohen.deborra@epa.gov; *Supvry Librn,* Lisa Wheeler; Tel: 415-972-3695, E-mail: wheeler.lisa@epa.gov; *Librn,* Helga Holoubek; Tel: 415-972-3657, E-mail: holoubek.helga@epa.gov; Staff 3 (MLS 3)
Founded 1970
Library Holdings: Bk Titles 8,000; Per Subs 10
Subject Interests: Air pollution, Environ justice, Environ law, Hazardous waste, Pesticides, Sustainability, Water pollution
Automation Activity & Vendor Info: (Cataloging) OCLC; (ILL) OCLC
Function: Doc delivery serv, For res purposes, Govt ref serv, Health sci info serv, ILL available, Internet access, Outside serv via phone, mail, e-mail & web, Photocopying/Printing, Ref serv available, Res libr
Partic in OCLC Online Computer Library Center, Inc
Open Mon-Thurs 9-12 & 1-4
Restriction: External users must contact libr, Limited access for the pub, Open to pub by appt only, Photo ID required for access, Restricted access, Restricted borrowing privileges

S WELLS FARGO BANK LIBRARY*, Historical Research Library, MAC-A0101-022, 420 Montgomery St, 94163. SAN 334-6595. Tel: 415-396-2619. E-mail: wfmuseum.sf@wellsfargo.com.
Library Holdings: Bk Vols 8,000; Per Subs 15
Special Collections: California Gold Rush & Mining; Californiana; History of Banking & Finance; San Francisco History; Staging & Western Transportation; Wells Fargo & Co History
Restriction: Open by appt only, Researchers by appt only

S ALAN WOFSY FINE ARTS REFERENCE LIBRARY, Wittenborn Art Books Library, 1109 Geary Blvd, 94109. SAN 374-8979. Tel: 415-292-6500. FAX: 415-292-6594. E-mail: art-books.com@jps.net. Web Site: www.art-books.com. *Dir,* Mark Hyman; E-mail: editeur@earthlink.net; *Coll Develop,* Buzzard Cohen; *Curator,* Adior Butler
Founded 1969
Library Holdings: Bk Titles 1,000
Subject Interests: Art
Wireless access
Restriction: Open by appt only

M ZUCKERBERG SAN FRANCISCO GENERAL HOSPITAL*, ZSFG Library, 1001 Potrero Ave, Bldg 30, 94110. SAN 301-4584. Tel: 415-206-3114. Web Site: library.ucsf.edu/zsfg. *Clinical Librn,* Jill Barr-Walker; Tel: 628-206-6638, E-mail: jill.barr-walker@ucsf.edu
Founded 1966
Library Holdings: Bk Titles 18,120; Per Subs 420
Wireless access
Partic in Coop Libr Agency for Syst & Servs; Northern California & Nevada Medical Library Group; Pacific Southwest Regional Medical Library
Open Mon-Fri 8-5

SAN JACINTO

J MOUNT SAN JACINTO COLLEGE*, Milo P Johnson Library, 300 Bldg, 1499 N State St, 92583-2399. SAN 301-4924. Tel: 951-487-3455. Reference Tel: 951-487-3452. FAX: 951-654-8387. Web Site: libguides.msjc.edu/msjclibraries. *Librn,* Adrienne Walker; Tel: 951-487-3450, E-mail: awalker@msjc.edu; *Assoc Librn,* Ross Valenzuela; E-mail: rvalenzuela@msjc.edu; *Tech Serv Coordr,* Robert Pipes; Tel: 951-487-3453, E-mail: rpipes@msjc.edu
Founded 1963. Enrl 2,930; Highest Degree: Associate
Library Holdings: Bk Titles 34,202; Per Subs 325
Automation Activity & Vendor Info: (Cataloging) SirsiDynix; (Circulation) SirsiDynix; (OPAC) SirsiDynix
Wireless access
Partic in Inland Empire Acad Libr Coop; San Bernardino, Inyo, Riverside Counties United Library Services
Open Mon-Thurs 8-8, Fri 8-Noon

Departmental Libraries:

MENIFEE VALLEY, 800/LRC Bldg, 2nd Flr, 28237 La Piedra Rd, Menifee Valley, 92584, SAN 378-2085. Tel: 951-639-5455. Reference Tel: 951-639-5450. FAX: 951-672-0874. Web Site: libguides.msjc.edu/c.php?g=122985&p=831539. *Librn,* Carrie Consalvi; Tel: 951-639-5456, E-mail: cconsalvi@msjc.edu; *Librn,* Sherri Moore; Tel: 951-639-5451, E-mail: smoore@msjc.edu; Staff 7 (MLS 2, Non-MLS 5)
Founded 1991. Enrl 10,000; Fac 2; Highest Degree: Associate
Jul 2012-Jun 2013. Mats Exp $89,290, Books $31,422, Per/Ser (Incl. Access Fees) $6,147, AV Mat $3,700, Electronic Ref Mat (Incl. Access Fees) $48,021
Library Holdings: Audiobooks 61; AV Mats 4,926; CDs 326; DVDs 1,127; e-books 54,116; Bk Titles 19,069; Per Subs 101; Videos 1,109
Automation Activity & Vendor Info: (Cataloging) OCLC; (Circulation) OCLC; (Course Reserve) OCLC; (ILL) OCLC; (OPAC) OCLC WorldShare Interlibrary Loan; (Serials) EBSCO Online
Partic in Inland Empire Acad Libr Coop
Open Mon-Thurs 8-8, Fri 8-4, Sat 9-2

SAN JOSE

C COGSWELL COLLEGE LIBRARY*, 191 Baypointe Pkwy, 95134. SAN 301-3898. Tel: 408-498-5158. E-mail: library@cogswell.edu. Web Site: cogswell.edu/student-life/library.
Founded 1887. Enrl 300; Fac 50; Highest Degree: Bachelor
Library Holdings: Bk Titles 13,000; Per Subs 80
Automation Activity & Vendor Info: (Cataloging) LibraryWorld, Inc; (Circulation) LibraryWorld, Inc
Wireless access
Open Mon-Thurs 9-7:30, Fri 9-5

J EVERGREEN VALLEY COLLEGE LIBRARY*, 3095 Yerba Buena Rd, 95135. SAN 320-166X. Tel: 408-270-6433. Reference Tel: 408-274-7900, Ext 6661. FAX: 408-532-1925. E-mail: librarian@evc.edu. Web Site: www.evc.edu/library. *Dean,* Merryl Kravitz; E-mail: merryl.kravitz@evc.edu; *Librn,* Lorena Mata; Tel: 408-274-7900, Ext 6743, E-mail: lorena.mata@evc.edu; Staff 8 (MLS 2, Non-MLS 6)
Founded 1975. Fac 282; Highest Degree: Associate
Library Holdings: Bk Titles 49,187; Bk Vols 53,568; Per Subs 58
Special Collections: Oral History
Automation Activity & Vendor Info: (Acquisitions) Innovative Interfaces, Inc; (Circulation) Innovative Interfaces, Inc; (OPAC) Innovative Interfaces, Inc
Wireless access
Function: Ref serv available
Special Services for the Deaf - TDD equip
Special Services for the Blind - Reader equip
Open Mon-Thurs 8-8, Fri 9-3, Sat 10-2 (Winter); Mon-Thurs 10-3 (Summer)
Restriction: Open to students, fac & staff

S HISTORY SAN JOSE RESEARCH LIBRARY & ARCHIVES, 1661 Senter Rd, 95112. (Mail add: 1650 Senter Rd, 95112), SAN 323-9519. Tel: 408-521-5025. E-mail: research@historysanjose.org. Web Site: www.historysanjose.org. *Curator, Archives & Libr,* Catherine Mills; E-mail: research@historysanjose.org; Staff 1 (MLS 1)
Founded 1970
Library Holdings: AV Mats 5,000; CDs 32; DVDs 96; Music Scores 217; Bk Titles 5,800; Videos 249
Special Collections: Early Electronics (Perham Coll); KNTV Channel 11 News Archive; New Almaden Mines Coll; San Jose Pueblo Records, early local govt rec, maps; Santa Clara Valley Historical Photos; Sempervirens Club Coll
Subject Interests: Local hist, San Jose, Santa Clara Valley
Wireless access
Function: Archival coll, Online cat
Restriction: Non-circulating, Open by appt only

L HOPKINS & CARLEY LIBRARY*, 70 S First St, 95113. (Mail add: PO Box 1469, 95109-1469), SAN 329-4919. Tel: 408-286-9800. FAX: 408-998-4790. E-mail: info@hopkinscarley.com. Web Site:

www.hopkinscarley.com. *Librn,* Paul Reavis; E-mail: preavis@hopkinscarley.com
Library Holdings: Bk Vols 3,000; Per Subs 75
Restriction: Not open to pub

CL LINCOLN LAW SCHOOL OF SAN JOSE, James F Boccardo Law Library, 384 S Second St, 95113. SAN 301-424X. Tel: 408-977-7227. FAX: 408-977-7228.
Founded 1919. Enrl 150; Fac 25; Highest Degree: Doctorate
Library Holdings: Bk Vols 24,000; Per Subs 70
Automation Activity & Vendor Info: (OPAC) LibraryWorld, Inc
Wireless access
Open Mon-Thurs 10-10, Sat 10-5

CM PALMER COLLEGE OF CHIROPRACTIC*, West Campus Library, 90 E Tasman Dr, 95134. SAN 326-4602. Tel: 408-944-6014. FAX: 408-944-6181. Web Site: www.palmer.edu/academics/library. *Br Mgr,* Denise Ulett; E-mail: denise.ulett@palmer.edu; Staff 4 (MLS 1, Non-MLS 3)
Founded 1978. Enrl 600; Fac 52; Highest Degree: Doctorate
Library Holdings: Bk Titles 14,000; Bk Vols 15,000; Per Subs 140
Special Collections: Chiropractic Archives, bks
Subject Interests: Chiropractic med
Automation Activity & Vendor Info: (Acquisitions) EOS International; (Cataloging) EOS International; (Circulation) EOS International
Publications: Newsletter
Partic in Coop Libr Agency for Syst & Servs; OCLC Online Computer Library Center, Inc
Open Mon-Thurs 7:30am-11pm, Fri 7:30-5, Sat 10-5, Sun 12-5

S ROSICRUCIAN ORDER, AMORC*, Rosicrucian Research Library, Rosicrucian Park, 1660 Park Ave, 95191. (Mail add: 1342 Naglee Ave, 95126), SAN 301-4983. Tel: 408-947-3600. FAX: 408-947-3677. E-mail: librarian@rosicrucian.org. Web Site: rosicrucianpark.org/researach-library, www.rosicrucian.org. *Exec Dir,* Julie Scott; E-mail: gmo@rosicrucian.org
Founded 1939
Library Holdings: Bk Vols 16,000; Per Subs 21
Subject Interests: Alchemy, Egypt, Esoteric studies, Mysticism, Rosicrucians, Spirituality
Function: For res purposes, Ref serv available, Res libr
Publications: Rosicrucian Indexes
Restriction: Non-circulating, Open to pub for ref only
Friends of the Library Group

J SAN JOSE CITY COLLEGE LIBRARY*, Cesar E Chavez Library, LRC Bldg, 2nd & 3rd Flrs, 2100 Moorpark Ave, 95128-2799. SAN 301-5009. Tel: 408-288-3775. Reference Tel: 408-298-2181, Ext 3899. FAX: 408-293-4728. TDD: 408-993-0354. E-mail: sjcc.library@sjcc.edu. Web Site: www.sjcc.edu/library. *Dean, Libr & Learning Res,* Susan Hines; Tel: 408-288-3115, E-mail: Susan.Hines@scjcc.edu; *Librn,* Mary Nino; E-mail: Mary.Nino@scjcc.edu; *Librn,* Robert Wing; E-mail: Robert.Wing@scjcc.edu; Staff 3 (MLS 3)
Founded 1921. Enrl 12,100; Fac 350; Highest Degree: Associate
Library Holdings: Bk Titles 66,090; Per Subs 90
Automation Activity & Vendor Info: (Acquisitions) Innovative Interfaces, Inc; (Cataloging) Innovative Interfaces, Inc; (Circulation) Innovative Interfaces, Inc; (Course Reserve) Innovative Interfaces, Inc; (ILL) OCLC; (Media Booking) Innovative Interfaces, Inc; (OPAC) Innovative Interfaces, Inc; (Serials) Innovative Interfaces, Inc
Wireless access
Publications: Information Sheets; Resource Guides

S SAN JOSE MUSEUM OF ART LIBRARY*, 110 S Market St, 95113. SAN 321-6454. Tel: 408-271-6840. FAX: 408-294-2977. E-mail: info@sjmusart.org. Web Site: sjmusart.org. *Library Contact,* Kathryn Wade; Staff 1 (MLS 1)
Founded 1978
Library Holdings: Bk Vols 3,200; Per Subs 12
Special Collections: Children's Art Books Coll
Subject Interests: Art
Restriction: Staff use only

P SAN JOSE PUBLIC LIBRARY, Dr Martin Luther King Jr Library, 150 E San Fernando St, 95112-3580. SAN 334-6773. Tel: 408-808-2000. Reference Tel: 408-808-2100. Administration Tel: 408-808-2355. Administration FAX: 408-808-2133. Administration E-mail: admin.sjpl@sjlibrary.org. Web Site: www.sjpl.org. *Dir,* Jill Bourne; Tel: 408-808-2150, E-mail: jill.bourne@sjlibrary.org; *Dep Dir, Pub Serv,* Michelle Ornat; Tel: 408-808-2112, E-mail: michelle.ornat@sjlibrary.org; *Dep Dir, Operations,* Jenny Choi; Tel: 408-808-2152, E-mail: jenny.choi@sjlibrary.org; *Div Mgr,* Michelle Amores; Tel: 408-808-2186, E-mail: michelle.amores@sjlibrary.org; *Div Mgr,* Jean Herriges; Tel: 408-808-2188, E-mail: jean.herriges@sjlibrary.org; *Admin Officer,* Andrea Maestre; Tel: 408-808-2192, E-mail: andrea.maestre@sjlibrary.org; *Access Serv,* Jennifer Luayon; Tel: 408-808-2325, E-mail: jennifer.luayon@sjlibrary.org; *Coll, Tech Serv,* Sharon Fung; Tel: 408-808-2468, E-mail: sharon.fung@sjlibrary.org; *IT Serv,* Howard Yeilding; Tel: 408-808-2420, E-mail: howard.yeilding@sjlibrary.org; Staff 86.6 (MLS 86.1, Non-MLS 0.5)
Founded 1872. Pop 984,299; Circ 10,702,251
Jul 2012-Jun 2013 Income (Main & Associated Libraries) $37,576,020, City $28,929,488, Federal $107,838, Locally Generated Income $8,113,436, Other $425,258. Mats Exp $5,472,508, Books $3,394,164, Per/Ser (Incl. Access Fees) $178,417, Micro $8,156, AV Mat $1,421,628, Electronic Ref Mat (Incl. Access Fees) $470,143. Sal $26,011,231 (Prof $6,467,541)
Library Holdings: AV Mats 364,356; CDs 65,497; DVDs 255,745; e-books 41,041; Bk Titles 390,862; Bk Vols 1,700,765; Per Subs 578; Talking Bks 42,281; Videos 515
Special Collections: Aging-Handicapped; California Room; Mexican-American Literature & Spanish Language; Vietnamese Language Coll
Subject Interests: Bus & mgt, Chinese lang, Music
Automation Activity & Vendor Info: (Acquisitions) Innovative Interfaces, Inc; (Cataloging) Innovative Interfaces, Inc; (Circulation) Innovative Interfaces, Inc; (OPAC) Innovative Interfaces, Inc; (Serials) Innovative Interfaces, Inc
Wireless access
Friends of the Library Group
Branches: 23
ALMADEN, 6445 Camden Ave, 95120. Tel: 408-808-3040. FAX: 408-997-1212. E-mail: ab.sjpl@sjlibrary.org. *Mgr,* Rachel Gaither; E-mail: rachel.gaither@sjlibrary.org
Pop 228,121; Circ 672,528
Library Holdings: Bk Vols 98,408
Open Wed 11-8, Thurs-Sat 10-6
Friends of the Library Group
ALVISO BRANCH, 5050 N First St, Alviso, 95002, SAN 334-6838. Tel: 408-263-3626. FAX: 408-956-9435. E-mail: al.sjpl@sjlibrary.org. *Mgr,* Mark Giannuzzi; E-mail: mark.giannuzzi@sjlibrary.org
Pop 62,598; Circ 189,123
Library Holdings: Bk Vols 33,094
Open Wed 11-8, Thurs-Sat 10-6
Friends of the Library Group
BASCOM LIBRARY, 1000 S Bascom Ave, 95128. Tel: 408-808-3077. FAX: 408-286-3951. E-mail: bamail@sjlibrary.org. *Mgr,* Trina Richbourg; E-mail: trina.richbourg@sjlibrary.org
Pop 49,660; Circ 132,847
Library Holdings: Bk Vols 63,351
Open Mon 1-7, Tues & Thurs 10-7, Fri 12-6, Sat 10-6
Friends of the Library Group
BERRYESSA, 3355 Noble Ave, 95132-3198, SAN 334-6862. Tel: 408-808-3050. FAX: 408-923-3222. E-mail: bb.sjpl@sjlibrary.org. *Mgr,* Candice Tran; E-mail: candice.tran@sjlibrary.org
Pop 320,741; Circ 1,067,070
Library Holdings: Bk Vols 123,512
Open Wed 11-8, Thurs-Sat 10-6
Friends of the Library Group
BIBLIOTECA LATINOAMERICANA BRANCH, 921 S First St, 95110-2939, SAN 334-6897. Tel: 408-294-1237. FAX: 408-297-4278. E-mail: bla.sjpl@sjlibrary.org. *Mgr,* Oscar Hernandez; E-mail: oscar.hernandez@sjlibrary.org
Pop 90,749; Circ 102,476
Library Holdings: Bk Vols 52,790
Subject Interests: Spanish (Lang)
Open Mon & Thurs 10-6, Tues & Wed 11-8
Friends of the Library Group
CALABAZAS, 1230 S Blaney Ave, 95129-3799, SAN 334-6927. Tel: 408-808-3066. FAX: 408-297-4278. E-mail: cz.sjpl@sjlibrary.org. *Mgr,* Emily Lowell; E-mail: emily.lowell@sjlibrary.org
Pop 16,257; Circ 30,461
Library Holdings: Bk Vols 65,282
Open Mon & Thurs 10-6, Tues & Wed 11-8
Friends of the Library Group
CAMBRIAN, 1780 Hillsdale Ave, 95124-3199, SAN 334-6951. Tel: 408-808-3080. FAX: 408-264-1894. E-mail: cb.sjpl@sjlibrary.org. *Mgr,* Rebekah Bonzalez Gonzalez; E-mail: rebekah.gonzalez@sjlibrary.org
Pop 221,359; Circ 613,407
Library Holdings: Bk Vols 113,427
Open Mon & Thurs 10-6, Tues & Wed 11-8
Friends of the Library Group
DR ROBERTO CRUZ - ALUM ROCK, 3090 Alum Rock Ave, 95127. Tel: 408-808-3090. FAX: 408-928-5628. E-mail: ar.sjpl@sjlibrary.org. *Mgr,* Kyle Burkett; E-mail: kyle.burkett@sjlibrary.org
Pop 243,256; Circ 327,023
Library Holdings: Bk Vols 81,098
Open Mon & Thurs 10-6, Tues & Wed 11-8
Friends of the Library Group

EAST SAN JOSE CARNEGIE, 1102 E Santa Clara St, 95116-2246, SAN 334-6986. Tel: 408-808-3075. FAX: 408-288-9750. E-mail: eb.sjpl@sjlibrary.org. *Mgr,* Oscar Hernandez; E-mail: oscar.hernandez@sjlibrary.org
Pop 81,804; Circ 125,172
Library Holdings: Bk Vols 37,634
Open Wed 11-8, Thurs-Sat 10-6
Friends of the Library Group

EDENVALE, 101 Branham Lane E, 95111. Tel: 408-808-3036. FAX: 408-224-9836. E-mail: en.sjpl@sjlibrary.org. *Mgr,* Joan Bowlby; E-mail: joan.bowlby@sjlibrary.org
Pop 189,266; Circ 455,451
Library Holdings: Bk Vols 69,086
Open Mon & Thurs 10-6, Tues & Wed 11-8
Friends of the Library Group

EDUCATIONAL PARK, 1772 Educational Park Dr, 95133-1703, SAN 334-701X. Tel: 408-808-3073. FAX: 408-254-4278. E-mail: ekmail@sjlibrary.org. *Mgr,* Mark Giannuzzi
Pop 22,531; Circ 56,334
Library Holdings: Bk Vols 69,086
Friends of the Library Group

JOYCE ELLINGTON BRANCH, 491 E Empire St, 95112-3308, SAN 334-7044. Tel: 408-808-3043. FAX: 408-286-0664. E-mail: je.sjpl@sjlibrary.org. *Mgr,* Trina Richbourg
Pop 107,489; Circ 159,654
Library Holdings: Bk Vols 53,035
Open Mon & Thurs 10-6, Tues & Wed 11-8
Friends of the Library Group

EVERGREEN, 2635 Aborn Rd, 95121-1294, SAN 334-7079. Tel: 408-808-3060. FAX: 408-238-0584. E-mail: ev.sjpl@sjlibrary.org. *Mgr,* Margaret Yamasaki; E-mail: margaret.yamasaki@sjlibrary.org
Pop 278,251; Circ 1,026,066
Library Holdings: Bk Vols 118,611
Open Mon, Thurs & Sat 10-6, Tues & Wed 11-8
Friends of the Library Group

HILLVIEW, 1600 Hopkins Dr, 95122-1199, SAN 334-7109. Tel: 408-808-3033. FAX: 408-729-9518. E-mail: hb.sjpl@sjlibrary.org. *Mgr,* Kyle Burkett; E-mail: kyle.burkett@sjlibrary.org
Pop 158,523; Circ 268,868
Library Holdings: Bk Vols 58,779
Open Wed 11-8, Thurs-Sat 10-6
Friends of the Library Group

PEARL AVENUE, 4270 Pearl Ave, 95136-1899, SAN 334-7133. Tel: 408-808-3053. FAX: 408-723-6930. E-mail: pa.sjpl@sjlibrary.org. *Mgr,* Rebekah Gonzalez
Pop 151,040; Circ 377,164
Library Holdings: Bk Vols 65,841
Open Wed 11-8, Thurs-Sat 10-6
Friends of the Library Group

ROSE GARDEN, 1580 Naglee Ave, 95126-2094, SAN 334-7168. Tel: 408-808-3070. FAX: 408-999-0909. E-mail: rg.sjpl@sjlibrary.org. *Mgr,* Nancy Donnell; E-mail: nancy.donnell@sjlibrary.org
Founded 1960. Pop 149,440; Circ 249,795
Library Holdings: Bk Vols 64,115
Open Mon & Thurs 10-6, Tues & Wed 11-8
Friends of the Library Group

SANTA TERESA, 290 International Circle, 95119-1132, SAN 334-7176. Tel: 408-808-3068. FAX: 408-365-5787. E-mail: sa.sjpl@sjlibrary.org. *Mgr,* Joan Bowlby
Pop 205,861; Circ 764,155
Library Holdings: Bk Vols 104,301
Open Wed 11-8, Thurs-Sat 10-6
Friends of the Library Group

SEVEN TREES, 3590 Cas Dr, 95111-2499, SAN 334-7192. Tel: 408-808-3056. FAX: 408-629-3394. E-mail: stmail@sjlibrary.org. *Mgr,* Chieu Nguyen; E-mail: chieu.nguyen@sjlibrary.org
Pop 73,357; Circ 167,033
Library Holdings: Bk Vols 57,076
Open Wed 11-8, Thurs-Sat 10-6
Friends of the Library Group

TULLY COMMUNITY, 880 Tully Rd, 95111. Tel: 408-808-3030. FAX: 408-977-3113. E-mail: tumail@sjlibrary.org. *Mgr,* Chieu Nguyen
Pop 293,735; Circ 704,947
Library Holdings: Bk Vols 89,181
Open Mon & Thurs 10-6, Tues & Wed 11-8
Friends of the Library Group

VILLAGE SQUARE BRANCH LIBRARY, 4001 Evergreen Village Sq, 95135. Tel: 408-808-3093. E-mail: vs.sjpl@sjlibrary.org. *Mgr,* Margaret Yamasaki
Friends of the Library Group

VINELAND, 1450 Blossom Hill Rd, 95118, SAN 334-6803. Tel: 408-808-3000. FAX: 408-978-1080. E-mail: vl.sjpl@sjlibrary.org. *Mgr,* Rachel Gaither; E-mail: rachel.gaither@sjlibrary.org
Pop 157,208; Circ 421,823
Library Holdings: Bk Vols 96,309
Open Mon & Thurs 10-6, Tues & Wed 11-8
Friends of the Library Group

WEST VALLEY, 1243 San Tomas Aquino Rd, 95117-3399, SAN 334-7222. Tel: 408-244-4747. FAX: 408-984-3736. E-mail: wv.sjpl@sjlibrary.org. *Mgr,* Emily Lowell
Pop 220,254; Circ 740,849
Library Holdings: Bk Vols 103,192
Open Wed 11-8, Thurs-Sat 10-6
Friends of the Library Group

WILLOW GLEN, 1157 Minnesota Ave, 95125-3324, SAN 334-7257. Tel: 408-808-3045. FAX: 408-947-8901. E-mail: wg.sjpl@sjlibrary.org. *Mgr,* Nancy Donnell
Pop 136,020; Circ 328,149
Library Holdings: Bk Vols 61,803
Open Wed 11-8, Thurs-Sat 10-6
Friends of the Library Group

C SAN JOSE STATE UNIVERSITY*, Dr Martin Luther King Jr Library, One Washington Sq, 95192-0028. SAN 301-5033. Tel: 408-808-2000. Circulation Tel: 408-808-2304. Interlibrary Loan Service Tel: 408-808-2076. FAX: 408-808-2141. TDD: 408-808-2130. Web Site: www.sjlibrary.org. *Dean, Univ Libr,* Tracy Elliott; Tel: 404-808-2419, E-mail: tracy.elliott@sjsu.edu; *Assoc Dean, Innovation & Resource Mgmt,* Christina Mune; E-mail: christina.mune@sjsu.edu; *Assoc Dean, Research & Scholarship,* Emily Chan; Tel: 408-808-2044, E-mail: emily.chan@sjsu.edu; *Faculty Dir,* Kathryn Blackmer Reyes; Tel: 408-808-2097; *Head of Doc Delivery,* Danny Soares; Tel: 408-808-2078, E-mail: danny.soares@sjsu.edu; *Academic Liaison, Librn,* Marci Hunsaker; Tel: 408-808-2114, E-mail: marci.hunsaker@sjsu.edu; *User Experience Librn,* Sharesly Rodriguez; E-mail: sharesly.rodriguez@sjsu.edu; *Communications Coordr, Events Coord,* Mariah Ramsour; Tel: 408-808-2050, E-mail: mariah.ramsour@sjsu.edu; Staff 78 (MLS 33, Non-MLS 45)
Founded 1857. Enrl 32,100; Fac 2,224; Highest Degree: Master
Library Holdings: CDs 24,489; DVDs 11,901; e-books 54,535; e-journals 77,092; Bk Titles 1,020,297; Bk Vols 1,351,494; Per Subs 448
Special Collections: Beethoven Studies; Gay/Lesbian Community in San Jose 1975-2000 (Ted Sahl Archives); John C Gordon Coll of Photography (Santa Clara Valley/San Jose Area 1920-1940); John Steinbeck Coll; World War II Diplomatic & Military History. State Document Depository; US Document Depository
Automation Activity & Vendor Info: (Acquisitions) Innovative Interfaces, Inc; (Cataloging) Innovative Interfaces, Inc; (Circulation) Innovative Interfaces, Inc; (Course Reserve) Innovative Interfaces, Inc; (ILL) Innovative Interfaces, Inc; (Media Booking) Innovative Interfaces, Inc; (OPAC) Innovative Interfaces, Inc; (Serials) Innovative Interfaces, Inc
Wireless access
Partic in OCLC Online Computer Library Center, Inc

GL SANTA CLARA COUNTY LAW LIBRARY, 360 N First St, 95113. SAN 301-505X. Tel: 408-299-3568. FAX: 408-286-9283. E-mail: circdesk@sccll.org. Web Site: www.sccll.org. *Libr Dir,* Roger Huynh; E-mail: roger@sccll.org; Staff 3 (MLS 1, Non-MLS 2)
Founded 1874
Library Holdings: Bk Vols 70,000; Per Subs 200
Special Collections: State Document Depository
Wireless access
Open Mon-Thurs 8-7, Fri 8-5
Friends of the Library Group

S SANTA CLARA COUNTY OFFICE OF EDUCATION*, Learning Multimedia Center, 1290 Ridder Park Dr, 95131-2304. SAN 329-8140. Tel: 408-453-6800. FAX: 408-453-6815. E-mail: professional_library@sccoe.org. Web Site: www.sccoe.org/depts/library. *Supvr,* Beth Olshewsky; Staff 5 (MLS 2, Non-MLS 3)
Library Holdings: Bk Vols 15,000; Per Subs 152
Subject Interests: Educ mat for professionals
Automation Activity & Vendor Info: (OPAC) SirsiDynix
Wireless access
Open Tues (Sept-May) 8-5, Thurs 10-7; Mon-Fri (June-Aug) 10-5

M SANTA CLARA VALLEY MEDICAL CENTER, Milton J Chatton Medical Library, 751 S Bascom Ave, Rm 2E063, 95128. SAN 334-7702. Tel: 408-885-5650. FAX: 408-885-5655. E-mail: medical.library@hhs.sccgov.org. Web Site: www.scvmc.org/education-and-training/Medical-Library/Pages/Overview.aspx. *Med Librn,* Hella Bluhm-Stieber; Tel: 408-885-5654; *Med Librn,* Judith Mills; Tel: 408-885-5651, E-mail: judith.mills@hhs.sccgov.org; *Libr Asst,* Vaughn Flaming; Tel: 408-885-5652, E-mail: vaughn.flaming@hhs.sccgov.org; Staff 1.5 (MLS 1, Non-MLS 0.5)
Founded 1930
Library Holdings: AV Mats 250; DVDs 50; e-books 4,000; e-journals 1,000; Microforms 2,800; Bk Titles 5,500; Per Subs 100; Spec Interest Per Sub 16; Talking Bks 100; Videos 200

Subject Interests: Head injury, Med, Nursing, Pub health, Spinal cord injury
Automation Activity & Vendor Info: (Acquisitions) SirsiDynix; (Cataloging) SirsiDynix-WorkFlows; (Circulation) SirsiDynix-WorkFlows; (Discovery) EBSCO Discovery Service; (ILL) SERHOLD; (OPAC) SirsiDynix; (Serials) SirsiDynix-WorkFlows
Wireless access
Function: 24/7 Electronic res, 24/7 Online cat, Audio & video playback equip for onsite use, Bks on CD, Computers for patron use, Doc delivery serv, Electronic databases & coll, ILL available, Internet access, Magazines, Microfiche/film & reading machines, Online cat, Photocopying/Printing, Ref serv available, Scanner, Wheelchair accessible
Partic in Med Libr Consortium of Santa Clara County; US National Library of Medicine
Open Mon, Wed, Thurs & Fri 8-1, Tues 8-5
Restriction: Badge access after hrs, Circulates for staff only, Hospital staff & commun, In-house use for visitors, Med & nursing staff, patients & families, Med staff & students, Open to pub for ref & circ; with some limitations, Open to staff, patients & family mem

G SANTA CLARA VALLEY WATER DISTRICT LIBRARY, 1020 Blossom Hill Rd, 95123. (Mail add: 5750 Almaden Expressway, 95118), SAN 375-5533. Tel: 408-630-2360, 408-630-3748. FAX: 408-979-5693. Web Site: www.valleywater.org. *Librn,* Robert J Teeter; E-mail: bteeter@valleywater.org; Staff 1 (MLS 1)
Library Holdings: Bk Titles 20,000; Per Subs 200
Subject Interests: Engr, Environ, Pub admin, Water
Automation Activity & Vendor Info: (Cataloging) Cuadra Associates, Inc; (Circulation) Cuadra Associates, Inc; (ILL) OCLC WorldShare Interlibrary Loan; (OPAC) Cuadra Associates, Inc; (Serials) Cuadra Associates, Inc
Wireless access
Partic in OCLC Online Computer Library Center, Inc
Restriction: Circ limited, In-house use for visitors

L UNITED STATES DISTRICT COURT LIBRARY*, 280 S First St, 95113. SAN 372-3127. Tel: 669-272-1629. FAX: 408-535-5322. Web Site: www.cand.uscourts.gov/libraries. *Librn,* Stefanie Vartabedian
Library Holdings: Bk Vols 20,000; Per Subs 20
Wireless access
Partic in OCLC Online Computer Library Center, Inc
Restriction: Not open to pub

SAN JUAN BAUTISTA

P SAN JUAN BAUTISTA CITY LIBRARY, Carl Martin Luck Memorial Library, 801 Second St, 95045. (Mail add: PO Box 1420, 95045-1420), SAN 301-5068. Tel: 831-623-4687. FAX: 831-623-4701. E-mail: library@san-juan-bautista.ca.us. Web Site: www.san-juan-bautista.ca.us/community/library.php. *Lead Libr Tech,* Rochelle Eagen; *Libr Tech,* Dilia Blanco; Staff 2 (Non-MLS 2)
Founded 1896. Pop 1,796; Circ 4,800
Library Holdings: CDs 100; DVDs 150; Large Print Bks 200; Music Scores 100; Bk Vols 9,716; Videos 400
Automation Activity & Vendor Info: (Cataloging) Follett Software
Wireless access
Partic in Monterey Bay Area Cooperative Library System
Open Mon, Wed & Fri 1-5, Tues & Thurs 1-7, Sat 9-1
Friends of the Library Group

SAN LEANDRO

S PORTUGUESE SOCIETY OF AMERICA*, J A Freitas Library, 1120 E 14th St, 94577. SAN 301-5092. Tel: 510-351-4972. Administration Tel: 510-483-7676. FAX: 510-483-5015. E-mail: mypfsa@mypfsa.org. Web Site: www.mypfsa.org/library. *Dir,* Carla Cardoso; E-mail: carla.cardoso@mypfsa.org
Founded 1967
Library Holdings: Bk Titles 12,000
Special Collections: Portuguese Newspapers of California 1880s
Open Mon-Fri 9-4:30

P SAN LEANDRO PUBLIC LIBRARY*, 300 Estudillo Ave, 94577. SAN 334-7761. Tel: 510-577-3970. Reference Tel: 510-577-3971. Administration Tel: 510-577-3980. Automation Services Tel: 510-577-3977. FAX: 510-577-3987. E-mail: LibraryInfo@sanleandro.org. Web Site: www.sanleandro.org/depts/library. *Dir,* Theresa Mallon; Tel: 510-577-3942, E-mail: tmallon@sanleandro.org; Staff 80 (MLS 16, Non-MLS 64)
Founded 1906. Pop 83,183; Circ 961,462
Library Holdings: AV Mats 26,536; e-books 5; Bk Vols 306,395; Per Subs 473
Special Collections: Californiana. US Document Depository
Automation Activity & Vendor Info: (Acquisitions) Horizon; (Cataloging) Horizon; (Circulation) Horizon; (OPAC) Horizon; (Serials) Horizon
Wireless access
Function: Adult literacy prog, Archival coll, Bks on CD, Children's prog, Computers for patron use, Digital talking bks, Electronic databases & coll, Govt ref serv, Holiday prog, Internet access, Large print keyboards, Magnifiers for reading, Music CDs, Photocopying/Printing, Prog for adults, Prog for children & young adult, Ref serv available, Story hour, Summer reading prog, Teen prog, Wheelchair accessible, Workshops
Special Services for the Deaf - TTY equip
Special Services for the Blind - Computer with voice synthesizer for visually impaired persons
Friends of the Library Group
Branches: 3
MANOR, 1241 Manor Blvd, 94579, SAN 334-7850. Tel: 510-577-7970. Reference Tel: 510-577-7971. *Sr Librn,* William Sherwood; E-mail: bsherwood@ci.san-leandro.ca.us; Staff 2 (MLS 1, Non-MLS 1)
Founded 1971. Pop 15,038; Circ 91,933
Library Holdings: Bk Vols 42,873
Function: Bk club(s), Bks on CD, Children's prog, Computers for patron use, Free DVD rentals, Holiday prog, Music CDs, Photocopying/Printing, Prog for children & young adult, Story hour, Summer reading prog
MULFORD-MARINA, 13699 Aurora Dr, 94577-4036, SAN 334-7885. Tel: 510-577-7976. *Sr Librn,* Lori Hitchcock; E-mail: lhitchcock@sanleandro.org
Founded 1975
Library Holdings: Bk Vols 17,881
Open Mon 2-6, Wed 10-12 & 2-6, Fri 2-5:30
Friends of the Library Group
SOUTH, 14799 E 14th St, 94578-2818, SAN 334-7915. Tel: 510-577-7980. *Sr Librn,* Loanne Hill; E-mail: lhill@sanleandro.org
Founded 1966
Library Holdings: Bk Vols 15,050
Open Tues 2-6, Thurs 10-12 & 2-6, Sat 10-12 & 1-5

SAN LUIS OBISPO

C CALIFORNIA POLYTECHNIC STATE UNIVERSITY*, Robert E Kennedy Library, One Grand Ave, 93407. SAN 301-5130. Tel: 805-756-5760. Interlibrary Loan Service Tel: 805-756-1222. Reference Tel: 805-756-2649. FAX: 805-756-2346. Circulation E-mail: library@calpoly.edu. Web Site: lib.calpoly.edu. *Dean, Libr Serv,* Adriana Popescu; Tel: 805-756-2345, E-mail: popescu@calpoly.edu; *Coll, Dir,* Tim Strawn; Tel: 805-756-1485, E-mail: tstrawn@calpoly.edu; Staff 43 (MLS 11.5, Non-MLS 31.5)
Founded 1901. Enrl 20,000; Fac 1,294; Highest Degree: Master
Jul 2017-Jun 2018 Income $8,005,000. Mats Exp $1,949,000. Sal $6,352,000
Library Holdings: e-books 604,694; e-journals 60,000; Bk Titles 267,353; Bk Vols 290,115; Per Subs 150
Special Collections: California Promotional & Travel Literature; Fairs & Expositions; Healy Newspaper Coll; Hearst Castle Architectural Drawings; John Henry Nash Coll; Julia Morgan Coll; Local History; Upton Sinclair Coll; William F Cody Coll; William McDill Railroad Coll. US Document Depository
Subject Interests: Agr, Archit, Graphic arts
Automation Activity & Vendor Info: (Acquisitions) Ex Libris Group; (Cataloging) Ex Libris Group; (Circulation) Ex Libris Group; (Course Reserve) Ex Libris Group; (Discovery) Ex Libris Group; (ILL) OCLC ILLiad; (OPAC) Ex Libris Group; (Serials) Ex Libris Group
Wireless access
Function: 24/7 Electronic res, 24/7 Online cat, Art exhibits, Computers for patron use, E-Reserves, Electronic databases & coll, ILL available, Online info literacy tutorials on the web & in blackboard, Photocopying/Printing, Ref serv available, Telephone ref, Wheelchair accessible
Partic in Coalition for Networked Information; OCLC Online Computer Library Center, Inc
Special Services for the Deaf - Assistive tech; Closed caption videos
Special Services for the Blind - Accessible computers; Assistive/Adapted tech devices, equip & products; Audio mat; Dragon Naturally Speaking software
Open Mon-Sun (Winter) 8am-2am
Restriction: 24-hr pass syst for students only, Borrowing privileges limited to fac & registered students, Borrowing requests are handled by ILL, Open to pub for ref & circ; with some limitations, Open to students, fac & staff

J CUESTA COLLEGE LIBRARY*, Hwy 1, 93401. (Mail add: PO Box 8106, 93403-8106), SAN 301-5149. Tel: 805-546-3155. Interlibrary Loan Service Tel: 805-546-3100, Ext 2469. Reference Tel: 805-546-3157. FAX: 805-546-3109. Web Site: www.cuesta.edu/library. *Div Chair, Tech Serv Librn,* Carina Love; Tel: 805-546-3159, E-mail: clove@cuesta.edu; *Ref Librn,* Kevin Bontenbal; Tel: 805-546-3117, E-mail: kbontenb@cuesta.edu; Staff 14.4 (MLS 6, Non-MLS 8.4)
Founded 1965. Enrl 9,061; Fac 558; Highest Degree: Associate
Library Holdings: Audiobooks 113; AV Mats 1,848; Bks on Deafness & Sign Lang 182; CDs 399; DVDs 226; e-books 12,915; e-journals 38; Electronic Media & Resources 9; High Interest/Low Vocabulary Bk Vols

906; Large Print Bks 14; Microforms 6,541; Bk Titles 60,386; Bk Vols 73,318; Per Subs 255; Videos 1,331
Special Collections: Blythe History Coll; Health Coll; Morro Bay Coll; Professional Development Coll
Automation Activity & Vendor Info: (Cataloging) SirsiDynix; (Circulation) SirsiDynix; (Course Reserve) SirsiDynix; (OPAC) SirsiDynix; (Serials) SirsiDynix
Wireless access
Function: ILL available
Publications: Library Research Workbook
Partic in Amigos Library Services, Inc; Gold Coast Library Network; OCLC Online Computer Library Center, Inc
Open Mon-Thurs 7:30am-8pm, Fri 7:30-4, Sat 12-4
Friends of the Library Group

GL SAN LUIS OBISPO COUNTY LAW LIBRARY*, County Government Ctr, Rm 125, 1050 Monterey St, 93408. SAN 301-5157. Tel: 805-781-5855. FAX: 805-781-4172. E-mail: lawlibrarian@slocll.org. Web Site: www.slocll.org. *Librn,* Joseph Kalet; Staff 1 (MLS 1)
Founded 1896
Library Holdings: Bk Vols 14,076; Per Subs 60
Special Collections: State Document Depository
Subject Interests: Calif
Publications: WestLaw Next - CEB-OnLaw
Open Mon-Fri 9-4
Restriction: Non-circulating

P SAN LUIS OBISPO COUNTY LIBRARY*, 995 Palm St, 93403. (Mail add: PO Box 8107, 94303-8107), SAN 334-794X. Tel: 805-781-5991. Reference Tel: 805-781-5989. FAX: 805-781-1106. E-mail: oostaff@slolibrary.org. Web Site: www.slolibrary.org. *Dir,* Christopher Barnickel; Tel: 805-781-5785, E-mail: cbarnickel@slolibrary.org; *Asst Dir,* Chase McMunn; Tel: 805-781-5990, E-mail: cmcmunn@slolibrary.org; *Br Mgr,* Aracelli Astorga; Tel: 805-781-5783, E-mail: aastorga@slolibrary.org; Staff 80 (MLS 16, Non-MLS 64)
Founded 1919. Pop 240,480; Circ 2,432,510
Library Holdings: AV Mats 78,094; e-books 3,058; Electronic Media & Resources 14; Bk Vols 348,954; Per Subs 709
Special Collections: History of San Luis Obispo County (especially Hearst Family)
Subject Interests: Local hist
Automation Activity & Vendor Info: (Acquisitions) Innovative Interfaces, Inc; (Cataloging) Innovative Interfaces, Inc; (Circulation) Innovative Interfaces, Inc; (ILL) Innovative Interfaces, Inc; (OPAC) Innovative Interfaces, Inc
Wireless access
Function: 24/7 Electronic res, 24/7 Online cat, Activity rm, Adult bk club, Adult literacy prog, After school storytime, Archival coll, Art exhibits, Art programs, Audiobks on Playaways & MP3, Audiobks via web, AV serv, Bilingual assistance for Spanish patrons, Bk club(s), Bks on CD, Children's prog, Citizenship assistance, Computer training, Computers for patron use, Free DVD rentals, Genealogy discussion group, Holiday prog, Homebound delivery serv, Homework prog, Internet access, Jail serv, Large print keyboards, Life-long learning prog for all ages, Magazines, Magnifiers for reading, Makerspace, Meeting rooms, Microfiche/film & reading machines, Music CDs, Online cat, Online ref, Outreach serv, OverDrive digital audio bks, Passport agency, Photocopying/Printing, Preschool outreach, Printer for laptops & handheld devices, Prog for adults, Prog for children & young adult, Ref & res, Spanish lang bks, STEM programs, Study rm, Summer reading prog, Teen prog, Wheelchair accessible, Writing prog
Mem of Black Gold Cooperative Library System
Partic in Association for Rural & Small Libraries
Open Mon-Thurs 10-6, Fri & Sat 10-5, Sun 12-4
Friends of the Library Group
Branches: 13
ARROYO GRANDE LIBRARY, 800 W Branch St, Arroyo Grande, 93420, SAN 334-7974. Tel: 805-473-7161. Reference Tel: 805-473-7164. FAX: 805-473-7173. E-mail: osstaff@slolibrary.org. Web Site: www.slolibrary.org/index.php/about/locations/arroyo-grande-library. *Br Mgr,* Rosalyn Pierini; E-mail: rpierini@slolibrary.org; Staff 11 (MLS 3, Non-MLS 8)
Open Mon-Thurs 10-6, Fri & Sat 10-5
Friends of the Library Group
ATASCADERO LIBRARY, 6555 Capistrano Ave, Atascadero, 93422, SAN 334-8008. Tel: 805-461-6161. Reference Tel: 805-461-6162. FAX: 805-461-6045. E-mail: oastaff@slolibrary.org. Web Site: www.slolibrary.org/index.php/about/locations/atascadero-library. *Br Mgr,* Jackie Kinsey; Tel: 805-461-6164, E-mail: jkinsey@slolibrary.org; Staff 9.2 (MLS 3, Non-MLS 6.2)
Open Mon-Thurs 10-6, Fri & Sat 10-5
Friends of the Library Group
CAMBRIA LIBRARY, 1043 Main St, Cambria, 93428, SAN 334-8032. Tel: 805-927-4336. FAX: 805-927-3524. E-mail: ocstaff@slolibrary.org. Web Site: www.slolibrary.org/index.php/about/locations/cambria-library. *Br Mgr,* Destiny Johnson; E-mail: djohnson@slolibrary.org; Staff 4 (MLS 1, Non-MLS 3)
Open Tues & Wed 9-5, Thurs 10-6, Fri & Sat 10-5
Friends of the Library Group
CAYUCOS LIBRARY, 310 B St, Cayucos, 93430, SAN 334-8067. Tel: 805-995-3312. FAX: 805-995-0573. E-mail: oustaff@slolibrary.org. Web Site: www.slolibrary.org/index.php/about/locations/cayucos-library. *Br Mgr,* Bonnie Richan; E-mail: brichan@slolibrary.org
Open Mon-Wed 10-6, Fri 10-5
Friends of the Library Group
CRESTON LIBRARY, 6290 Adams, Creston, 93432. (Mail add: PO Box 1, Creston, 93432), SAN 334-8091. Tel: 805-237-3010. FAX: 805-237-3021. E-mail: otstaff@slolibrary.org. Web Site: www.slolibrary.org/index.php/about/locations/creston-library. *Br Mgr,* Kathleen Saffell; E-mail: ksaffell@slolibrary.org
Open Tues 1-7, Thurs 12-6, Fri 10-4
Friends of the Library Group
LOS OSOS LIBRARY, 2075 Palisades Ave, Los Osos, 93402, SAN 334-8423. Tel: 805-528-1862. FAX: 805-528-7835. E-mail: oystaff@slolibrary.org. Web Site: www.slolibrary.org/index.php/about/locations/los-osos-library. *Br Mgr,* Mary Blair; Tel: 805-582-5989, E-mail: mblair@slolibrary.org; Staff 6.8 (MLS 1, Non-MLS 5.8)
Open Tues & Wed 10-6, Thurs-Sat 10-5
Friends of the Library Group
MORRO BAY LIBRARY, 625 Harbor St, Morro Bay, 93442. Tel: 805-772-6394. FAX: 805-772-6396. E-mail: omstaff@slolibrary.org. Web Site: www.slolibrary.org/index.php/about/locations/morro-bay-library. *Br Mgr,* Kristin Nibbe; E-mail: knibbe@slolibrary.org; Staff 7 (MLS 1, Non-MLS 6)
Open Tues & Wed 10-6, Thurs-Sat 10-5
Friends of the Library Group
NIPOMO LIBRARY, 918 W Tefft, Nipomo, 93444, SAN 334-8210. Tel: 805-929-3994. FAX: 805-929-5476. E-mail: onstaff@slolibrary.org. Web Site: www.slolibrary.org/index.php/about/locations/nipomo-library. *Br Mgr,* Heidi LoCascio; E-mail: hlocascio@slolibrary.org
Open Tues-Thurs 10-6, Fri & Sat 10-5
Friends of the Library Group
OCEANO LIBRARY, 1551 17th St, Oceano, 93445. Tel: 805-474-7478. FAX: 805-474-7479. E-mail: oceano@slolibrary.org. Web Site: www.slolibrary.org/index.php/about/locations/oceano-library. *Br Mgr,* Kate McMillen; E-mail: kmcmillen@slolibrary.org
Open Tues-Thurs 11-6, Fri 11-5
Friends of the Library Group
SAN MIGUEL LIBRARY, 254 13th St, San Miguel, 93451, SAN 334-827X. Tel: 805-467-3224. FAX: 805-467-3224. E-mail: ogstaff@slolibrary.org. Web Site: www.slolibrary.org/index.php/about/locations/san-miguel-library. *Br Mgr,* Judy Brown; E-mail: jbrown@slolibrary.org
Open Wed 11-5, Thurs 12-6, Sat 10-4
SANTA MARGARITA LIBRARY, 9630 Murphy Ave, Santa Margarita, 93453. (Mail add: PO Box 960, Santa Margarita, 93453), SAN 334-830X. Tel: 805-438-5622. FAX: 805-438-4879. E-mail: orstaff@slolibrary.org. Web Site: www.slolibrary.org/index.php/about/locations/santa-margarita-library. *Br Mgr,* Shawnita Onwuma; E-mail: sonwuma@slolibrary.org; Staff 1 (MLS 1)
Open Wed & Thurs 12-6, Fri & Sat 10-5
Friends of the Library Group
SHANDON LIBRARY, 240 E Centre St, Shandon, 93461, SAN 334-8334. Tel: 805-237-3009. FAX: 805-237-3022. E-mail: shandon@slolibrary.org. Web Site: www.slolibrary.org/index.php/about/locations/shandon-library. *Br Mgr,* Tracey Montelongo; E-mail: tmontelongo@slolibrary.org
Open Tues-Thurs 11-6, Fri 11-5
SHELL BEACH LIBRARY, 230 Leeward Ave, Shell Beach, 93449, SAN 334-8369. Tel: 805-773-2263. FAX: 805-773-2891. E-mail: olstaff@slolibrary.org. Web Site: www.slolibrary.org/index.php/about/locations/shell-beach-library. *Br Mgr,* Vicki Cyr; E-mail: vcyr@slolibrary.org
Open Tues & Fri 11-5, Wed 12-6
Friends of the Library Group

SAN MARCOS

C CALIFORNIA STATE UNIVERSITY, San Marcos Library, 333 S Twin Oaks Valley Rd, 92096. SAN 323-911X. Tel: 760-750-4348. Interlibrary Loan Service Tel: 760-750-4345. Reference Tel: 760-750-4391. TDD: 760-750-3163. Web Site: biblio.csusm.edu. *Dean of Libr,* Jennifer Fabbi; Tel: 760-750-4330, E-mail: jfabbi@csusm.edu; *Dir, Learning & Tech Res,* Yvonne N Meulemans; E-mail: ymeulema@csusm.edu; *Academic Transitions Librn,* Allison Carr; E-mail: acarr@csusm.edu; *Assoc Librn, Coordr,* Susan M Thompson; Tel: 760-750-4373, E-mail: sthompsn@csusm.edu; *Bus Librn,* Ann M Fiegen; E-mail: afiegen@csusm.edu; *Coll Mgt Librn,* Hua Yi; Tel: 760-750-4368, E-mail: hyi@csusm.edu; *Educ Librn,* Antonia Olivas; E-mail: tolivas@csusm.edu;

Spec Coll Librn, Judith A Downie; E-mail: jdownie@csusm.edu. Subject Specialists: *Nursing, Sci,* Yvonne N Meulemans; *Soc sci,* Allison Carr; *Bus, Econ,* Ann M Fiegen; *Educ,* Antonia Olivas; *Hist,* Judith A Downie; Staff 43 (MLS 15, Non-MLS 28)
Founded 1989. Enrl 7,900; Fac 302; Highest Degree: Master
Library Holdings: AV Mats 10,290; CDs 3,132; e-books 28,832; e-journals 19,515; Bk Titles 192,450; Bk Vols 268,952; Per Subs 665
Special Collections: Barahona Center for Books in Spanish, bks for children & young adults. State Document Depository; US Document Depository
Automation Activity & Vendor Info: (Acquisitions) Innovative Interfaces, Inc; (Cataloging) Innovative Interfaces, Inc; (Circulation) Innovative Interfaces, Inc; (Course Reserve) Docutek; (ILL) OCLC ILLiad; (Media Booking) Innovative Interfaces, Inc; (OPAC) Innovative Interfaces, Inc; (Serials) Innovative Interfaces, Inc
Wireless access
Partic in San Diego Circuit
Special Services for the Deaf - Assistive tech
Special Services for the Blind - Assistive/Adapted tech devices, equip & products
Open Mon-Thurs 6am-Midnight, Fri 7-5, Sat 9-5, Sun 10-8

J PALOMAR COLLEGE LIBRARY, 1140 W Mission Rd, 92069-1487. SAN 334-8482. Tel: 760-744-1150, Ext 2612. FAX: 760-761-3500. TDD: 760-736-0246. E-mail: library@palomar.edu. Web Site: www2.palomar.edu/pages/library. *Dean,* Dr Fabienne Chauderlot; Tel: 760-744-1150, Ext 2251, E-mail: fchauderlot@palomar.edu; *Co-Chair,* Alexandra E Doyle Bauer; Tel: 760-744-1150, Ext 2669, E-mail: adoylebauer@palomar.edu; *Co-Chair,* Benhui Zou; Tel: 760-744-1150, Ext 2618, E-mail: bzou@palomar.edu; Staff 25 (MLS 13, Non-MLS 12)
Founded 1946. Enrl 18,946; Fac 260
Library Holdings: Bk Titles 169,306; Per Subs 900
Special Collections: California History Coll; Early California & Iowa Frontier, newsp on microfilm; Iceland; Indians of North America; World War I Posters. Oral History
Subject Interests: Art & archit, Career educ, Ethnic studies, Tech educ
Automation Activity & Vendor Info: (Acquisitions) OCLC Worldshare Management Services; (Cataloging) OCLC Worldshare Management Services; (Circulation) OCLC Worldshare Management Services; (Serials) OCLC Worldshare Management Services
Wireless access
Function: 24/7 Electronic res, 24/7 Online cat, Wheelchair accessible
Publications: A Guide to the Palomar College Library; Aging in the 1980s; Controversial Issues; Faculty in Print; Grants Bibliog; Library Self Help Bulletins
Partic in Community College League of California; Coop Libr Agency for Syst & Servs; OCLC Online Computer Library Center, Inc; San Diego Greater Metro Area Libr & Info Agency Coun
Special Services for the Deaf - TDD equip; Videos & decoder

§CM UNIVERSITY OF ST AUGUSTINE FOR HEALTH SCIENCES, San Marcos Campus Library, 700 Windy Point Dr, 92069. Tel: 760-410-5398. E-mail: library@usa.edu. Web Site: library.usa.edu. *Librn,* Matthew Chase; E-mail: mchase@usa.edu; *Circ Mgr,* Reynaldo Farfan; E-mail: rfarfan@usa.edu
Wireless access
Function: ILL available, Photocopying/Printing, Scanner, Study rm
Open Mon-Sun 7am-10pm

SAN MARINO

P CROWELL PUBLIC LIBRARY, 1890 Huntington Dr, 91108-2595. SAN 301-5173. Tel: 626-300-0777. FAX: 626-300-0121. E-mail: CrowellPL@CityofSanMarino.org. Web Site: www.cityofsanmarino.org/government/departments/community_services_/library. *City Librn,* Irene McDermott; Tel: 626-300-0775, E-mail: imcdermott@cityofsanmarino.org; *Circ Mgr, Librn,* Jeff Plumley; E-mail: jplumley@cityofsanmarino.org; *Ad,* Rebecca Russell; E-mail: rrussell@cityofsanmarino.org; *Youth Serv Librn,* Tera Forrest; E-mail: tforrest@cityofsanmarino.org; Staff 5 (MLS 5)
Founded 1933
Library Holdings: Bk Vols 90,000; Per Subs 200
Subject Interests: Art & archit, Calif, Travel
Automation Activity & Vendor Info: (Acquisitions) LibLime; (Cataloging) LibLime; (Circulation) LibLime; (ILL) OCLC FirstSearch; (OPAC) LibLime; (Serials) LibLime
Wireless access
Partic in Southern California Library Cooperative
Open Mon-Thurs 10-9, Sat 10-5, Sun 1-5
Friends of the Library Group

S HENRY E HUNTINGTON LIBRARY & ART GALLERY, 1151 Oxford Rd, 91108. SAN 301-5165. Tel: 626-405-2100. FAX: 626-449-5720. E-mail: publicInfo@huntington.org. Web Site: www.huntington.org. *Libr Dir,* Sandra L Brooke; Tel: 626-405-2244, E-mail: sbrooke@huntington.org; *Dep Dir,* Laura Stalker; E-mail: lstalker@huntington.org; Staff 65 (MLS 31, Non-MLS 34)
Founded 1919
Library Holdings: Bk Titles 686,154; Per Subs 600
Special Collections: 19th Century Americana; 19th Century England Coll; 20th Century American Literature & Letters; 20th Century British Literature; American Photography, History, Prints, Printmaking & Design; American Sheet Music; Colonial & Early Federal Americana; Early Hispanic Americana; Early Modern England Coll; Incunabula; Medieval Manuscript Coll; Restoration & 18th Century England Coll; Western Americana
Automation Activity & Vendor Info: (Acquisitions) Innovative Interfaces, Inc; (Cataloging) Innovative Interfaces, Inc; (OPAC) Innovative Interfaces, Inc; (Serials) Innovative Interfaces, Inc
Wireless access
Function: Res libr
Publications: Guide to American Historical Manuscripts in the Huntington Library; Guide to British Historical Manuscripts in the Huntington Library; Guide to Literary Manuscripts in the Huntington Library; Guide to Medieval & Renaissance Manuscripts; The Huntington Library (Quarterly)
Partic in OCLC Research Library Partnership
Restriction: Not open to pub, Restricted access

SAN MATEO

J COLLEGE OF SAN MATEO LIBRARY*, Bldg 9, 1700 W Hillsdale Blvd, 94402-3795. SAN 301-5181. Tel: 650-574-6100. Circulation Tel: 650-574-6548. Reference Tel: 650-574-6232. FAX: 650-574-6497. E-mail: csmlibrary@smccd.edu. Web Site: collegeofsanmateo.edu/library. *Dean, Acad Support, Learning Technologies Coordr,* Jennifer E Taylor-Mendoza; Tel: 650-574-6572, E-mail: mendozaj@smccd.edu; *Ref & Instrul Serv Librn,* Teresa M Morris; Tel: 650-574-6579, E-mail: morrist@smccd.edu; *Ref & Instruction Librn,* Teresa Morris; Tel: 650-574-6579, E-mail: morrist@smccd.edu; *Adjunct Librn,* Annie Costa; Tel: 650-574-6232, E-mail: costaa@smccd.edu; Staff 8 (MLS 3, Non-MLS 5)
Founded 1923. Enrl 13,800; Fac 300
Library Holdings: Bk Titles 74,150; Bk Vols 79,340; Per Subs 112
Special Collections: American History (LAC, Library of American Civilization)
Subject Interests: Art & archit, Ethnic studies, Feminism, Music, Natural sci, Nursing, Soc sci & issues
Automation Activity & Vendor Info: (Acquisitions) Innovative Interfaces, Inc; (Cataloging) Innovative Interfaces, Inc; (Circulation) Innovative Interfaces, Inc; (Course Reserve) Innovative Interfaces, Inc; (ILL) OCLC Connexion; (OPAC) Innovative Interfaces, Inc
Wireless access
Partic in Califa
Special Services for the Deaf - Assistive tech; TTY equip
Special Services for the Blind - Assistive/Adapted tech devices, equip & products; Closed circuit TV; Computer with voice synthesizer for visually impaired persons; Reader equip; ZoomText magnification & reading software
Open Mon-Thurs (Winter) 7:45-7, Fri 7:45-3, Sat 10-2; Mon-Thurs (Summer) 9-7

S INTERNATIONAL DATA CORP LIBRARY*, 155 Bovet Rd, Ste 800, 94402. SAN 329-0581. Tel: 650-653-7000. FAX: 650-653-7077. Web Site: www.idc.com. *Library Contact,* Position Currently Open
Library Holdings: Bk Vols 2,400; Per Subs 250
Subject Interests: Computer sci, Finance
Publications: Happenings; Industry News; Library News; Quote Alert; Reference Highlights
Partic in Dow Jones News Retrieval; OCLC Online Computer Library Center, Inc; Proquest Dialog
Restriction: Employee & client use only

P NORTHNET LIBRARY SYSTEM*, 2471 Flores St, 94403. Tel: 650-349-5538. FAX: 650-349-5089. Web Site: northnetlibs.org. *Exec Dir,* Susan Hildreth; *Adminr,* Wendy Cao; E-mail: caow@plsinfo.org; *Coordr,* Jacquelyn Brinkley; E-mail: brinkley@plpinfo.org
Member Libraries: Belvedere Tiburon Library; Benicia Public Library; Butte College Library; Butte County Library; California State University, Chico; College of the Redwoods; Colusa County Free Library; Cosumnes River College Library; Del Norte County Library District; Dixon Public Library; El Dorado County Library; Humboldt County Library; Humboldt State University Library; Lake County Library; Lassen Community College Library; Lassen Library District; Marin County Free Library; Mendocino County Library District; Mill Valley Public Library; Modoc County Library; Mono County Free Library; Napa County Library; Napa Valley College; Orland Free Library; Plumas County Library; Sacramento Public Library; Saint Helena Public Library; San Anselmo Public Library; San Rafael Public Library; Santa Rosa Junior College; Sausalito Public Library; Shasta College Library; Shasta Public Libraries; Siskiyou County Library; Solano Community College Library; Solano County Library; Sonoma

County Library; Sutter County Library; Tehama County Library; Trinity County Library; Willows Public Library; Yolo County Library; Yuba County Library

P PACIFIC LIBRARY PARTNERSHIP (PLP)*, 2471 Flores St, 94403-2273. Tel: 650-349-5538. FAX: 650-349-5089. E-mail: info@plpinfo.org. Web Site: www.plpinfo.org. *Asst Dir,* Carol Frost; E-mail: frost@plpinfo.org
Member Libraries: Alameda Free Library; Daly City Public Library; Gavilan College Library; Livermore Public Library; Menlo Park Public Library; Naval Postgraduate School; San Benito County Free Library; San Francisco Public Library; South San Francisco Public Library; Sunnyvale Public Library

R PENINSULA TEMPLE BETH EL LIBRARY*, 1700 Alameda de Las Pulgas, 94403. SAN 301-5203. Tel: 650-341-7701. FAX: 650-570-7183. E-mail: mail@ptbe.org. Web Site: www.ptbe.org. *Exec Dir,* Kate Lauzar; E-mail: klauzar@ptbe.org
Library Holdings: Bk Vols 5,500
Subject Interests: Judaica (lit or hist of Jews)

P SAN MATEO COUNTY LIBRARY*, Library Administration, 125 Lessingia Ct, 94402-4000. SAN 331-4979. Tel: 650-312-5258. FAX: 650-312-5382. Web Site: smcl.org. *Dir, Libr Serv,* Anne-Marie Despain; Tel: 650-312-5245, E-mail: despain@smcl.org; *Dep Dir, Libr Serv,* Nicole Pasini; Tel: 650-312-5251, E-mail: pasini@smcl.org; *Dep Dir, Libr Serv,* Carine Risley; Tel: 650-312-5312, E-mail: risley@smcl.org; *Access Serv Mgr,* Sandy Wee; Tel: 650-312-5276, E-mail: wee@smcl.org; *Communications Mgr,* Katie Woods; Tel: 650-312-5274, E-mail: woodsk@smcl.org; *Financial Serv, Mgr,* Danae Ramirez; Tel: 650-312-5236, E-mail: ramirezd@smcl.org; *IT Mgr,* Silvia Urena; Tel: 650-312-5524, E-mail: urena@smcl.org
Founded 1915. Pop 276,000; Circ 3,211,000
Wireless access
Partic in OCLC Online Computer Library Center, Inc; Peninsula Libraries Automated Network
Friends of the Library Group
Branches: 12
ATHERTON LIBRARY, Two Dinkelspiel Station Lane, Atherton, 94027, SAN 331-5002. Tel: 650-328-2422. FAX: 650-328-4138. E-mail: atherton@smcl.org. Web Site: www.smcl.org/locations/1A. *Libr Mgr,* Ally Garcia; Tel: 650-328-2422, Ext 227, E-mail: garciaa@smcl.org
Circ 84,140
Open Mon-Wed 10-8, Thurs & Fri 10-6, Sat 10-5, Sun 1-5
Friends of the Library Group
BELMONT LIBRARY, 1110 Alameda de las Pulgas, Belmont, 94002. Tel: 650-591-8286. FAX: 650-591-2763. E-mail: belmont@smcl.org. Web Site: www.smcl.org/locations/1B. *Libr Mgr,* Kathleen Beasley; Tel: 650-591-8286, Ext 227, E-mail: beasley@smcl.org
Circ 501,200
Open Mon-Wed 10-9, Thurs & Fri 10-6, Sat 10-5, Sun 1-5
Friends of the Library Group
BRISBANE LIBRARY, 250 Visitacion Ave, Brisbane, 94005, SAN 331-5061. Tel: 415-467-2060. FAX: 415-467-4824. E-mail: brisbane@smcl.org. Web Site: www.smcl.org/locations/1R. *Actg Br Mgr,* Elizabeth Karr; Tel: 415-467-2060, Ext 227, E-mail: karr@smcl.org
Circ 61,050
Open Mon-Wed 10-7, Thurs & Fri 12-5, Sat 11-5
Friends of the Library Group
EAST PALO ALTO LIBRARY, 2415 University Ave, East Palo Alto, 94303, SAN 331-5096. Tel: 650-321-7712. FAX: 650-326-8961. E-mail: eastpaloalto@smcl.org. Web Site: www.smcl.org/locations/1E. *Libr Mgr,* Adina Aguirre; Tel: 650-321-7712, Ext 227, E-mail: aguirre@smcl.org
Circ 98,240
Open Mon-Thurs 10-8, Fri 10-6, Sat 9-5, Sun 1-5
Friends of the Library Group
FOSTER CITY LIBRARY, 1000 E Hillsdale Blvd, Foster City, 94404, SAN 331-5126. Tel: 650-574-4842. FAX: 650-572-1875. E-mail: fostercity@smcl.org. Web Site: www.smcl.org/locations/1F. *Libr Mgr,* Anna Koch; Tel: 650-574-4842, Ext 227, E-mail: koch@smcl.org
Circ 785,820
Open Mon-Wed 10-9, Thurs & Fri 10-6, Sat 10-5, Sun 1-5
Friends of the Library Group
HALF MOON BAY LIBRARY, 620 Correas St, Half Moon Bay, 94019, SAN 331-5150. Tel: 650-726-2316. FAX: 650-726-9282. E-mail: halfmoonbay@smcl.org. Web Site: smcl.org/locations/1H. *Libr Mgr,* Annie Malley; Tel: 650-726-2316, Ext 227, E-mail: malley@smcl.org
Circ 296,430
Open Mon-Thurs 10-8, Fri 10-6, Sat 9-5, Sun 1-5
Friends of the Library Group
MILLBRAE LIBRARY, One Library Ave, Millbrae, 94030, SAN 331-5185. Tel: 650-697-7607. FAX: 650-692-4747. E-mail: millbrae@smcl.org. Web Site: www.smcl.org/locations/1M. *Libr Mgr,* Elizabeth Karr; Tel: 650-697-7607, Ext 227
Circ 501,350
Open Mon-Thurs 10-8, Fri 10-6, Sat 9-5, Sun 1-5
Friends of the Library Group
PACIFICA SANCHEZ LIBRARY, 1111 Terra Nova Blvd, Pacifica, 94044, SAN 331-5304. Tel: 650-359-3397. FAX: 650-359-3808. E-mail: pacifica@smcl.org. Web Site: www.smcl.org/locations/1Z. *Libr Mgr,* Julie Finklang; Tel: 650-359-3397, Ext 227, E-mail: finklang@smcl.org
Circ 293,200
Open Mon 12-8, Wed 10-6, Fri & Sat 10-5
Friends of the Library Group
PACIFICA SHARP PARK LIBRARY, 104 Hilton Way, Pacifica, 94044, SAN 331-5215. Tel: 650-355-5196. FAX: 650-355-6658. E-mail: pacifica@smcl.org. Web Site: www.smcl.org/locations/1P. *Libr Mgr,* Julie Finklang; Tel: 650-355-5196, Ext 227
Circ 293,200
Open Tues & Wed 12-8, Thurs & Sat 10-5
Friends of the Library Group
PORTOLA VALLEY LIBRARY, 765 Portola Rd, Portola Valley, 94028, SAN 331-524X. Tel: 650-851-0560. FAX: 650-851-8365. E-mail: portolavalley@smcl.org. Web Site: www.smcl.org/locations/1V. *Libr Mgr,* Garrett Kuramoto; Tel: 650-851-0560, Ext 227, E-mail: kuramoto@smcl.org
Circ 86,100
Open Mon-Thurs 11-7, Fri & Sat 11-5
Friends of the Library Group
SAN CARLOS LIBRARY, 610 Elm St, San Carlos, 94070, SAN 331-5274. Tel: 650-591-0341. E-mail: sancarlos@smcl.org. Web Site: www.smcl.org/locations/1S. *Libr Mgr,* Ally Garcia; Tel: 650-591-0341, Ext 227
Circ 341,680
Open Mon-Wed 10-9, Thurs & Fri 10-6, Sat 10-5, Sun 1-5
Friends of the Library Group
WOODSIDE LIBRARY, 3140 Woodside Rd, Woodside, 94062, SAN 331-5339. Tel: 650-851-0147. FAX: 650-851-2695. E-mail: woodside@smcl.org. Web Site: www.smcl.org/locations/1W. *Libr Mgr,* Garrett Kuramoto; Tel: 650-851-0147, Ext 227
Circ 101,990
Open Mon-Thurs 11-7, Fri & Sat 11-5
Friends of the Library Group
Bookmobiles: 1

P SAN MATEO PUBLIC LIBRARY*, 55 W Third Ave, 94402. SAN 334-8571. Tel: 650-522-7802. Circulation Tel: 650-522-7833. Reference Tel: 650-522-7818. FAX: 650-522-7801. E-mail: smplref@plsinfo.org. Web Site: www.cityofsanmateo.org/507/Library. *City Librn,* James Moore; E-mail: jmoore@cityofsanmateo.org; Staff 12 (MLS 12)
Founded 1899. Pop 94,200; Circ 642,498
Library Holdings: Bk Vols 280,000; Per Subs 794
Special Collections: Californiana, maps. State Document Depository
Subject Interests: Calif, Music
Automation Activity & Vendor Info: (Circulation) SirsiDynix
Wireless access
Publications: Annual Report; Business Reference (Bibliographies)
Partic in Coop Libr Agency for Syst & Servs
Open Mon-Thurs 10-9, Fri & Sat 10-5, Sun 1-5
Friends of the Library Group
Branches: 2
HILLSDALE, 205 W Hillsdale Blvd, 94403-4217, SAN 334-8601. Tel: 650-522-7882. FAX: 650-522-7881.
Library Holdings: Bk Vols 46,903
Open Mon, Wed, Thurs & Sat 10-5, Tues 1-8, Fri 12-5
Friends of the Library Group
MARINA, 1530 Susan Ct, 94403-1193, SAN 334-8660. Tel: 650-522-7892. FAX: 650-522-7891.
Founded 1966
Library Holdings: Large Print Bks 200; Bk Vols 32,431; Videos 8,000
Open Mon 1-8, Tues-Thurs & Sat 10-5, Fri 12-5
Friends of the Library Group

SAN PABLO

J CONTRA COSTA COLLEGE LIBRARY*, 2600 Mission Bell Dr, 94806. SAN 301-5262. Tel: 510-215-4921. Reference Tel: 510-215-4897. FAX: 510-234-8161. Web Site: www.contracosta.edu/library. *Bibliog Instruction Librn, Libr Coord,* Judith Flum; Tel: 510-215-4996, E-mail: jflum@contracosta.edu; *Circ Serv Librn, Libr Coord,* Andrew Kuo; Tel: 510-215-4997, E-mail: akuo@contracosta.edu; Staff 6.9 (MLS 3.1, Non-MLS 3.8)
Founded 1950. Enrl 7,277; Fac 176; Highest Degree: Associate
Library Holdings: Audiobooks 143; Bks on Deafness & Sign Lang 28; CDs 198; DVDs 323; e-books 51,941; High Interest/Low Vocabulary Bk Vols 636; Microforms 6,881; Bk Titles 50,000; Bk Vols 51,285; Per Subs 90; Videos 1,215
Special Collections: Ethnic Studies Coll

Automation Activity & Vendor Info: (Cataloging) Innovative Interfaces, Inc; (Circulation) Innovative Interfaces, Inc; (Course Reserve) Innovative Interfaces, Inc; (OPAC) Innovative Interfaces, Inc
Wireless access
Partic in California Community College Library Consortium
Special Services for the Deaf - Bks on deafness & sign lang; Closed caption videos; High interest/low vocabulary bks; Videos & decoder
Special Services for the Blind - Internet workstation with adaptive software; ZoomText magnification & reading software
Open Mon-Thurs 8:30-7:45, Fri & Sat 10am-1:45pm
Friends of the Library Group

SAN PEDRO

S CABRILLO MARINE AQUARIUM, Virginia Reid Moore Marine Research Library, 3720 Stephen White Dr, 90731. SAN 301-5270. Tel: 310-548-7562. Web Site: www.cabrillomarineaquarium.org/research/marine-research-library.asp.
Founded 1935
Library Holdings: Bk Titles 2,500; Per Subs 25; Spec Interest Per Sub 20
Subject Interests: Calif, Ecology, Marine biol
Function: Internet access, Orientations, Outside serv via phone, mail, e-mail & web, Photocopying/Printing, Prog for adults, Ref & res, Res libr, VHS videos, Wheelchair accessible
Restriction: Circulates for staff only, Non-circulating coll, Not open to pub

SAN RAFAEL

SR DOMINICAN SISTERS OF SAN RAFAEL, 1520 Grand Ave, 94901-2236. SAN 370-2057. Tel: 415-453-8303, Ext 110. FAX: 415-453-8367. Web Site: www.sanrafaelop.org. *Archivist,* Jack Doran; E-mail: archivist@sanrafaelop.org
Library Holdings: Bk Vols 400
Subject Interests: Hist of the congregation
Open Mon-Thurs 10-4

CR DOMINICAN UNIVERSITY OF CALIFORNIA, Archbishop Alemany Library, 50 Acacia Ave, 94901-2298. SAN 301-5319. Tel: 415-485-3251. Reference Tel: 415-485-3252. FAX: 415-459-2309. E-mail: circdesk@dominican.edu, ref@dominican.edu. Web Site: www.dominican.edu/academics/archbishop-alemany-library. *Univ Librn,* Gary Gorka; Tel: 415-247-1301, E-mail: gary.gorka@dominican.edu; *Assoc Dir, Librn,* Amy Gilbert; Tel: 415-257-1329, E-mail: amy.gilbert@dominican.edu; *Head, Access & Technical Services, Librn,* Ethan Annis; Tel: 415-482-1837, E-mail: ethan.annis@dominican.edu; *Head, Acq,* A J Real; Tel: 415-257-0104, E-mail: adolfo.real@dominican.edu; *Ref & Instruction Librn, Univ Archivist,* Louis Knecht; Tel: 415-458-3728, E-mail: louis.knecht@dominican.edu; *Ref & Instruction Librn,* Aaron Richardson; E-mail: aaron.richardson@dominican.edu; *Scholarly Communications Librn,* Michael Pujals; Tel: 415-485-3254, E-mail: michael.pujals@dominican.edu; *Coordr, Access Serv,* Diana Duran; Tel: 415-257-0168, E-mail: diana.duran@dominican.edu; *Coord, Interlibrary & Consortia Lending,* Kenneth Fish; Tel: 415-257-1340, E-mail: kenneth.fish@dominican.edu; Staff 10 (MLS 7, Non-MLS 3)
Founded 1890. Enrl 1,900; Fac 70; Highest Degree: Master
Library Holdings: AV Mats 396; e-books 50,000; Electronic Media & Resources 40,000; Bk Titles 91,799; Per Subs 100
Special Collections: Ansel Adams Photographic Coll
Automation Activity & Vendor Info: (Acquisitions) Baker & Taylor; (Cataloging) Innovative Interfaces, Inc; (Circulation) Innovative Interfaces, Inc; (Discovery) EBSCO Discovery Service; (ILL) OCLC FirstSearch; (OPAC) Innovative Interfaces, Inc
Wireless access
Partic in Northern & Central California Psychology Libraries; Statewide California Electronic Library Consortium
Open Mon-Thurs 8am-Midnight, Fri 8-5, Sat 9-5, Sun 2-10

M KAISER-PERMANENTE MEDICAL CENTER*, Health Sciences Library, Medical Office One, 1st Flr, 99 Montecillo Rd, 94903. Tel: 415-444-2058. FAX: 415-444-2492. *Librn,* Dawn Melberg; Tel: 707-393-4526, E-mail: dawn.m.melberg@kp.org; Staff 2 (MLS 1, Non-MLS 1)
Library Holdings: Bk Titles 1,200
Open Mon-Thurs 8:30-5

P MARIN COUNTY FREE LIBRARY*, 3501 Civic Center Dr, Ste 414, 94903-4177. SAN 334-8784. Tel: 415-473-3222. Administration Tel: 415-499-3220. FAX: 415-499-3726. Web Site: www.marinlibrary.org. *Dir,* Sara Jones; E-mail: sfjones@marincounty.org; Staff 89 (MLS 31, Non-MLS 58)
Founded 1927. Pop 1,045,756; Circ 1,986,529
Library Holdings: AV Mats 51,885; e-books 9,043; Bk Vols 416,127
Special Collections: CA Indian Library Coll; Frank Lloyd Wright Coll; San Quentin Prison Coll. Oral History
Wireless access
Function: Adult literacy prog, Archival coll, Art exhibits, Home delivery & serv to seniorr ctr & nursing homes, Homebound delivery serv, ILL available, Magnifiers for reading, Music CDs, Prog for adults, Prog for children & young adult, Ref serv available, Spoken cassettes & CDs, Summer reading prog, Telephone ref, VHS videos, Wheelchair accessible
Mem of NorthNet Library System
Partic in Marin Automated Resources & Information Network
Friends of the Library Group
Branches: 10
BOLINAS LIBRARY, 14 Wharf Rd, Bolinas, 94924. (Mail add: PO Box 508, Bolinas, 94924), SAN 334-8806. Tel: 415-868-1171. Web Site: www.marinlibrary.org/bolinas. *Br Mgr,* Raemona Little Taylor
Pop 1,630; Circ 24,492
Library Holdings: Bk Vols 9,982
Open Mon & Wed 10-6, Thurs 1-9, Sat 10-5
Friends of the Library Group
CIVIC CENTER LIBRARY, 3501 Civic Center Dr, Rm 427, 94903-4177, SAN 334-8814. Tel: 415-473-6057, 415-499-6056. Reference Tel: 415-499-6058. Web Site: www.marinlibrary.org/civic-center. *Br Mgr,* Eva Patterson
Pop 20,999; Circ 198,638
Library Holdings: Bk Vols 100,096
Special Collections: Oral History
Subject Interests: Archit, Calif, Local hist
Open Mon, Wed & Fri 10-6, Tues & Thurs 10-9, Sat 10-5
Friends of the Library Group
CORTE MADERA LIBRARY, 707 Meadowsweet Dr, Corte Madera, 94925-1717, SAN 334-8849. Tel: 415-924-3515, 415-924-4844. Web Site: www.marinlibrary.org/corte-madera. *Br Mgr,* Julie Magnus
Pop 18,895; Circ 334,530
Library Holdings: Bk Vols 88,813
Open Mon-Thurs 10-9, Sat 10-5, Sun 12-5
Friends of the Library Group
FAIRFAX LIBRARY, 2097 Sir Francis Drake Blvd, Fairfax, 94930-1198, SAN 334-8873. Tel: 415-453-8151. Web Site: www.marinlibrary.org/fairfax. *Br Mgr,* Margaret Miles
Pop 9,619; Circ 250,051
Library Holdings: Bk Vols 81,632
Open Mon-Thurs 10-9, Fri 12-5, Sat 10-6
Friends of the Library Group
INVERNESS LIBRARY, 15 Park Ave, Inverness, 94937. (Mail add: PO Box 160, Inverness, 94937-0160), SAN 334-8822. Tel: 415-669-1288. Web Site: www.marinlibrary.org/inverness. *Br Mgr,* Raemona Little Taylor
Pop 1,596; Circ 14,654
Library Holdings: Bk Vols 7,527
Open Mon 3-9, Tues & Wed 10-6, Fri 3-6, Sat 10-1
Friends of the Library Group
MARIN CITY LIBRARY, 164 Donahue St, Marin City, 94965, SAN 334-8830. Tel: 415-332-6158, 415-332-6159. Reference Tel: 415-332-6157. Web Site: www.marinlibrary.org/marin-city. *Br Mgr,* Diana Lopez
Pop 15,186; Circ 41,002
Library Holdings: Bk Vols 22,824
Open Mon & Tues 1-9, Wed & Thurs 10-6, Fri & Sun 12-5, Sat 10-5
Friends of the Library Group
NOVATO LIBRARY, 1720 Novato Blvd, Novato, 94947, SAN 334-8903. Tel: 415-473-2050. Web Site: www.marinlibrary.org/novato. *Br Mgr,* Janet Doerge
Pop 39,205; Circ 405,538
Library Holdings: Bk Vols 106,342
Open Mon-Thurs 10-9, Sat 10-5, Sun 12-5
Friends of the Library Group
POINT REYES LIBRARY, 11431 State Rte 1, Point Reyes Station, 94956. (Mail add: PO Box 1330, Point Reyes Station, 94956-1330), SAN 334-8857. Tel: 415-663-8375. Web Site: www.marinlibrary.org/point-reyes. *Br Mgr,* Raemona Little Taylor
Pop 4,681; Circ 30,570
Library Holdings: Bk Vols 15,809
Open Mon 10-6, Tues & Thurs 2-9, Fri & Sat 10-2
Friends of the Library Group
SOUTH NOVATO LIBRARY, 931 C St, Novato, 94949. Tel: 415-506-3165. Web Site: www.marinlibrary.org/south-novato. *Br Mgr,* Amy Sonnie
Pop 21,966; Circ 62,972
Library Holdings: Bk Vols 18,222
Open Tues & Thurs 12-8, Wed & Sat 10-5, Fri 12-5
Friends of the Library Group
STINSON BEACH LIBRARY, 3521 Shoreline Hwy, Stinson Beach, 94970. (Mail add: PO Box 578, Stinson Beach, 94970-0578), SAN 334-8881. Tel: 415-868-0252. Web Site: www.marinlibrary.org/stinson-beach. *Br Mgr,* Raemona Little Taylor
Pop 1,295; Circ 13,000
Library Holdings: Bk Vols 13,241
Open Mon & Fri 10-6, Tues 1-9, Sat 10-5

Friends of the Library Group
Bookmobiles: 1

GL MARIN COUNTY LAW LIBRARY*, 20 N San Pedro Rd, Ste 2007, 94903. SAN 301-5327. Tel: 415-472-3733. FAX: 415-472-3729. E-mail: lawlibsb@sonic.net. Web Site: marincountylawlibrary.org. *Dir,* Laurie Vaala-Olsen; Staff 3 (Non-MLS 3)
Founded 1891
Library Holdings: Bk Vols 28,700; Per Subs 66
Special Collections: Continuing Education of the Bar Coll
Wireless access
Open Mon & Thurs 8:30-7, Fri 8:30-Noon

P SAN RAFAEL PUBLIC LIBRARY*, 1100 E St, 94901. SAN 301-5335. Tel: 415-485-3323. Reference Tel: 415-485-3321. Administration Tel: 415-485-3319. FAX: 415-485-3112. Reference FAX: 415-485-3403. E-mail: library@cityofsanrafael.org. Web Site: srpubliclibrary.org. *Dir,* Position Currently Open; *Asst Dir,* Henry Bankhead; *Adult Serv Supvr,* Pam Klein; *Children's Serv Supvr,* Jill Harris; *Circ Supvr,* Lashalle Lyons; Staff 22 (MLS 10, Non-MLS 12)
Founded 1887. Pop 60,000; Circ 400,000
Library Holdings: AV Mats 2,811; Large Print Bks 2,646; Bk Titles 120,000; Bk Vols 128,000; Per Subs 302; Talking Bks 2,039
Special Collections: California Coll
Subject Interests: Art & archit
Automation Activity & Vendor Info: (Cataloging) Innovative Interfaces, Inc; (Circulation) Innovative Interfaces, Inc; (OPAC) Innovative Interfaces, Inc; (Serials) Innovative Interfaces, Inc
Wireless access
Function: After school storytime, Archival coll, Audiobks via web, Bilingual assistance for Spanish patrons, Bk club(s), Bks on CD, Children's prog, Computer training, Computers for patron use, Digital talking bks, Electronic databases & coll, Free DVD rentals, Holiday prog, Home delivery & serv to seniorr ctr & nursing homes, Homebound delivery serv, Homework prog, ILL available, Internet access, Mail & tel request accepted, Music CDs, Online cat, Online info literacy tutorials on the web & in blackboard, Outreach serv, Outside serv via phone, mail, e-mail & web, OverDrive digital audio bks, Photocopying/Printing, Preschool outreach, Preschool reading prog, Prog for adults, Prog for children & young adult, Ref & res, Ref serv available, Scanner, Senior outreach, Spanish lang bks, Story hour, Summer reading prog, Tax forms, Teen prog, Telephone ref, Wheelchair accessible, Workshops
Mem of NorthNet Library System
Partic in Marin Automated Resources & Information Network
Open Mon 1-8, Tues-Thurs 10-8, Fri & Sat 10-5, Sun 1-5
Friends of the Library Group
Branches: 1
PICKLEWEED LIBRARY, 50 Canal St, 94901. Tel: 415-485-3483. *Libr Supvr,* Joshua Alperin
Open Tues & Wed 1-8, Thurs 11-8, Fri & Sat 11-5

SAN SIMEON

S HEARST SAN SIMEON STATE HISTORICAL MONUMENT*, Hearst Castle Staff Library, 750 Hearst Castle Rd, 93452-9741. Tel: 805-927-2076. Toll Free Tel: 800-444-4445. FAX: 805-927-2117. TDD: 800-274-7275. Web Site: hearstcastle.org. *Staff Librn,* Jill Urquhart
Library Holdings: AV Mats 17; CDs 300; DVDs 200; Bk Vols 3,579; Spec Interest Per Sub 6; Videos 427
Special Collections: Oral History
Wireless access
Restriction: Not open to pub, Staff use only

SANTA ANA

P OC PUBLIC LIBRARIES*, Administrative Headquarters, 1501 E St Andrew Pl, 92705. SAN 333-4023. Tel: 714-566-3000. FAX: 714-566-3042. Web Site: www.ocpl.org. *County Librn,* Helen Fried; E-mail: LibraryAdmin@occr.ocgov.com; *Asst County Librn,* Paula Bruce; Staff 206 (MLS 126, Non-MLS 80)
Founded 1921. Pop 1,426,100
Library Holdings: AV Mats 4,689; Bk Vols 2,500,000; Per Subs 5,070; Talking Bks 2,860
Subject Interests: Bus, Chinese lang, Japanese (Lang), Korean (Lang), Popular music, Spanish (Lang)
Automation Activity & Vendor Info: (Acquisitions) SirsiDynix; (Cataloging) SirsiDynix; (Circulation) SirsiDynix; (OPAC) SirsiDynix; (Serials) SirsiDynix
Wireless access
Open Mon-Fri 8-5
Friends of the Library Group
Branches: 32
ALISO VIEJO LIBRARY, One Journey, Aliso Viejo, 92656-3333, SAN 378-2506. Tel: 949-360-1730. E-mail: ocpl.alisoviejo@occr.ocgov.com.
Library Holdings: AV Mats 830; Bk Vols 61,112; Per Subs 57
Special Services for the Blind - Low vision equip; Optolec clearview video magnifier
Open Mon-Thurs 10-7, Fri & Sat 9-5
Friends of the Library Group
BREA LIBRARY, One Civic Center Circle, Brea, 92821-5784, SAN 333-4058. Tel: 714-671-1722. E-mail: ocpl.brea@occr.ocgov.com.
Library Holdings: AV Mats 652; Bk Titles 72,422; Bk Vols 75,153; Per Subs 78
Subject Interests: Spanish (Lang)
Open Mon-Thurs 10-7, Fri & Sat 9-5
Friends of the Library Group
CHAPMAN LIBRARY, 9182 Chapman Ave, Garden Grove, 92841-2590, SAN 333-4082. Tel: 714-539-2115. E-mail: ocpl.chapman@occr.ocgov.com.
Library Holdings: AV Mats 380; Bk Titles 51,017; Bk Vols 53,147; Per Subs 61
Open Mon-Thurs 10-7, Sat 9-5
COSTA MESA/DONALD DUNGAN LIBRARY, 1855 Park Ave, Costa Mesa, 92627-2778, SAN 333-4112. Tel: 949-646-8845. E-mail: ocpl.costamesadd@occr.ocgov.com.
Library Holdings: AV Mats 302; Bk Titles 62,060; Bk Vols 63,001; Per Subs 79
Subject Interests: Spanish (Lang)
Open Mon-Thurs 10-9, Fri-Sun 9-5
Friends of the Library Group
COSTA MESA/MESA VERDE LIBRARY, 2969 Mesa Verde Dr E, Costa Mesa, 92626-3699, SAN 333-4473. Tel: 714-546-5274. E-mail: ocpl.mesaverde@occr.ocgov.com.
Library Holdings: AV Mats 640; Bk Titles 54,630; Bk Vols 59,204; Per Subs 92
Open Mon-Thurs 10-7, Fri-Sun 9-5
Friends of the Library Group
CYPRESS LIBRARY, 5331 Orange Ave, Cypress, 90630-2985, SAN 333-4147. Tel: 714-826-0350. E-mail: ocpl.cypress@occr.ocgov.com.
Library Holdings: AV Mats 1,141; Bk Titles 97,001; Bk Vols 104,088; Per Subs 93
Subject Interests: Adult lit, Music
Open Mon-Thurs 10-7, Sat & Sun 9-5
DANA POINT LIBRARY, 33841 Niguel Rd, Dana Point, 92629-4010, SAN 333-4171. Tel: 949-496-5517. E-mail: ocpl.danapoint@occr.ocgov.com.
Library Holdings: AV Mats 780; Bk Titles 76,209; Bk Vols 81,758; Per Subs 92
Open Mon-Thurs 10-7, Fri-Sun 9-5
EL TORO LIBRARY, 24672 Raymond Way, Lake Forest, 92630-4489, SAN 333-4228. Tel: 949-855-8173. E-mail: ocpl.eltoro@occr.ocgov.com.
Library Holdings: Bk Titles 111,500; Bk Vols 112,488; Per Subs 101
Special Services for the Blind - Braille & cassettes
Open Mon-Thurs 10-7, Fri & Sat 9-5
FOOTHILL RANCH LIBRARY, 27002 Cabriole Way, Foothill Ranch, 92610. Tel: 949-855-8072. E-mail: ocpl.fhr@occr.ocgov.com.
Open Mon-Thurs 10-7, Sat 9-5
FOUNTAIN VALLEY LIBRARY, 17635 Los Alamos, Fountain Valley, 92708-5299, SAN 333-4236. Tel: 714-962-1324. E-mail: ocpl.fountainvalley@occr.ocgov.com.
Library Holdings: AV Mats 560; Bk Titles 82,137; Bk Vols 84,321; Per Subs 88
Special Services for the Blind - Merlin electronic magnifier reader
Open Mon-Thurs 10-7, Fri & Sat 9-5
GARDEN GROVE MAIN LIBRARY, 11200 Stanford Ave, Garden Grove, 92840-5398, SAN 333-4260. Tel: 714-530-0711. E-mail: ocpl.ggr@occr.ocgov.com.
Library Holdings: AV Mats 1,280; Bk Titles 154,772; Bk Vols 162,258; Per Subs 133
Subject Interests: Calif, Consumer health, Korean (Lang)
Open Mon-Thurs 10-7, Fri-Sun 9-5
HERITAGE PARK LIBRARY, 14361 Yale Ave, Irvine, 92604-1901, SAN 328-9788. Tel: 949-936-4040. E-mail: ocpl.heritage@occr.ocgov.com.
Founded 1988. Pop 150,000; Circ 500,000
Library Holdings: AV Mats 2,100; Bk Titles 131,156; Bk Vols 133,000; Per Subs 350
Special Services for the Blind - Optolec clearview video magnifier
Open Mon-Thurs 10-8, Fri-Sun 9-5
Friends of the Library Group
LA HABRA LIBRARY, 221 E La Habra Blvd, La Habra, 90631-5437, SAN 333-4325. Tel: 562-694-0078, 714-526-7728. E-mail: ocpl.lahabra@occr.ocgov.com.
Library Holdings: Bk Titles 86,261; Bk Vols 87,473; Per Subs 98
Subject Interests: Spanish (Lang)
Open Mon-Thurs 10-7, Sat & Sun 9-5
LA PALMA LIBRARY, 7842 Walker St, La Palma, 90623-1721, SAN 333-435X. Tel: 714-523-8585. E-mail: ocpl.lapalma@occr.ocgov.com.
Library Holdings: Bk Titles 54,832; Bk Vols 59,951; Per Subs 77
Subject Interests: Japanese (Lang)
Open Mon-Thurs 10-7, Sat 9-5

LADERA RANCH LIBRARY, 29551 Sienna Pkwy, Ladera Ranch, 92694. Tel: 949-234-5940. E-mail: ocpl.laderaranch@occr.ocgov.com.
Founded 2003
Function: Adult literacy prog, After school storytime, Audiobks via web, Bi-weekly Writer's Group, Bks on cassette, Bks on CD, CD-ROM, Children's prog, Computers for patron use, Digital talking bks, E-Reserves, Electronic databases & coll, Free DVD rentals, ILL available, Internet access, Music CDs, Online cat, Online ref, OverDrive digital audio bks, Photocopying/Printing, Prog for children & young adult, Ref & res, Ref serv available, Spoken cassettes & CDs, Story hour, Summer reading prog, VHS videos, Wheelchair accessible
Open Mon-Thurs 9-6, Sat 9-5
Restriction: Open to pub for ref & circ; with some limitations
Friends of the Library Group

LAGUNA BEACH LIBRARY, 363 Glenneyre St, Laguna Beach, 92651-2310, SAN 333-4295. Tel: 949-497-1733. E-mail: ocpl.lagunabeach@occr.ocgov.com.
Library Holdings: Bk Titles 72,687; Bk Vols 75,496; Per Subs 78
Subject Interests: Art
Open Mon-Thurs 10-7, Fri & Sat 9-5
Friends of the Library Group

LAGUNA HILLS TECHNOLOGY LIBRARY, Laguna Hills Community Ctr, 25555 Alicia Pkwy, Laguna Hills, 92653. Tel: 949-707-2699. E-mail: ocpl.ltk@occr.ocgov.com.
Open Mon-Thurs 10-7, Sat 9-5

LAGUNA NIGUEL LIBRARY, 30341 Crown Valley Pkwy, Laguna Niguel, 92677, SAN 328-9745. Tel: 949-249-5252. E-mail: ocpl.lagunaniguel@occr.ocgov.com.
Library Holdings: AV Mats 680; Bk Titles 72,425; Bk Vols 77,190; Per Subs 82
Open Mon-Thurs 10-7, Fri-Sun 9-5

LAGUNA WOODS LIBRARY, Laguna Woods City Hall, 24264 El Toro Rd, Laguna Woods, 92637. Tel: 949-639-0500. E-mail: ocpl.lagunawoods@occr.ocgov.com.
Open Mon-Fri 10-4:30

LIBRARY OF THE CANYONS, 7531 E Santiago Canyons Rd, Silverado, 92676, SAN 333-4597. Tel: 714-649-2216. E-mail: ocpl.lotc@occr.ocgov.com.
Library Holdings: Bk Titles 14,657; Bk Vols 15,386; Per Subs 35
Open Mon-Thurs 10-7, Sat 9-5

LOS ALAMITOS-ROSSMOOR LIBRARY, 12700 Montecito Rd, Seal Beach, 90740-2745, SAN 333-4414. Tel: 562-430-1048. E-mail: ocpl.lar@occr.ocgov.com.
Library Holdings: Bk Titles 74,298; Bk Vols 79,333; Per Subs 91
Open Mon-Thurs 10-7, Sat 10-5
Friends of the Library Group

RANCHO SANTA MARGARITA LIBRARY, 30902 La Promesa, Rancho Santa Margarita, 92688-2821, SAN 376-2440. Tel: 949-459-6094. E-mail: ocpl.rsm@occr.ocgov.com.
Library Holdings: AV Mats 1,100; Bk Titles 90,270; Bk Vols 102,937; Per Subs 130
Open Mon-Thurs 10-7, Fri & Sat 9-5
Friends of the Library Group

TIBOR RUBIN LIBRARY, 11962 Bailey St, Garden Grove, 92845-1104, SAN 333-4775. Tel: 714-897-2594. E-mail: ocpl.ggtr@occr.ocgov.com.
Library Holdings: Bk Titles 51,542; Bk Vols 53,452; Per Subs 63
Open Mon-Thurs 10-7, Sat 9-5

SAN CLEMENTE LIBRARY, 242 Avenida Del Mar, San Clemente, 92672-4005, SAN 333-4538. Tel: 949-492-3493. E-mail: ocpl.sanclemente@occr.ocgov.com.
Library Holdings: Bks on Deafness & Sign Lang 80; Bk Titles 69,981; Bk Vols 72,590; Per Subs 112
Open Mon-Thurs 10-7, Fri-Sun 9-5
Friends of the Library Group

SAN JUAN CAPISTRANO LIBRARY, 31495 El Camino Real, San Juan Capistrano, 92675-2600, SAN 333-4562. Tel: 949-493-1752. E-mail: ocpl.sjc@occr.ocgov.com.
Library Holdings: Bk Titles 79,165; Bk Vols 81,996; Per Subs 103
Subject Interests: Archit, Calif, Spanish (Lang)
Open Mon-Thurs 10-7, Sat & Sun 9-5
Friends of the Library Group

SEAL BEACH-MARY WILSON LIBRARY, 707 Electric Ave, Seal Beach, 90740-6196, SAN 333-4449. Tel: 562-431-3585. E-mail: ocpl.sealbeach@occr.ocgov.com.
Library Holdings: Bk Titles 50,871; Bk Vols 54,904; Per Subs 80
Open Mon-Thurs 10-7, Sat 9-5

STANTON LIBRARY, 7850 Katella Ave, Stanton, 90680-3195, SAN 333-4651. Tel: 714-898-3302. E-mail: ocpl.stanton@occr.ocgov.com.
Library Holdings: Bk Titles 59,381; Bk Vols 62,040; Per Subs 79
Subject Interests: Spanish (Lang)
Open Mon-Thurs 10-7, Sat 9-5
Friends of the Library Group

TUSTIN LIBRARY, 345 E Main St, Tustin, 92780-4491, SAN 333-4686. Tel: 714-544-7725. E-mail: ocpl.tustin@occr.ocgov.com.
Library Holdings: Bk Titles 116,511; Bk Vols 117,004
Open Mon-Thurs 10-7, Fri-Sun 9-5

UNIVERSITY PARK LIBRARY, 4512 Sandburg Way, Irvine, 92612-2794, SAN 333-4716. Tel: 949-786-4001. E-mail: ocpl.universitypark@occr.ocgov.com.
Library Holdings: AV Mats 500; Bk Titles 91,399; Bk Vols 91,464; Per Subs 115
Open Mon-Thurs 10-8, Fri-Sun 9-5
Friends of the Library Group

VILLA PARK LIBRARY, 17865 Santiago Blvd, Villa Park, 92861-4105, SAN 333-4740. Tel: 714-998-0861. E-mail: ocpl.villapark@occr.ocgov.com.
Library Holdings: Bk Titles 19,880; Bk Vols 24,744; Per Subs 42
Open Mon-Thurs 10-7, Sat 9-5

WESTMINSTER LIBRARY, 8180 13th St, Westminster, 92683-8118, SAN 333-4805. Tel: 714-893-5057. E-mail: ocpl.westminster@occr.ocgov.com.
Library Holdings: AV Mats 1,200; Bk Titles 134,707; Bk Vols 140,614; Per Subs 127
Special Collections: Vietnamese Language Coll
Open Mon-Thurs 10-7, Fri & Sat 9-5
Friends of the Library Group

KATIE WHEELER LIBRARY, 13109 Old Myford Rd, Irvine, 92602. Tel: 714-669-8753. E-mail: ocpl.katiewheeler@occr.ocgov.com.
Open Mon-Thurs 10-8, Fri-Sun 9-5

M ORANGE COUNTY GLOBAL MEDICAL CENTER*, Medical Library, 1001 N Tustin Ave, 92705. SAN 301-5440. Tel: 714-953-3500. Web Site: orangecounty-gmc.com.
Founded 1968
Library Holdings: Bk Titles 40; Per Subs 160
Subject Interests: Dentistry, Med, Nursing, Surgery
Wireless access
Restriction: Staff use only

S ORANGE COUNTY MUSEUM OF ART LIBRARY*, South Coast Plaza Village, 1661 W Sunflower Ave, 92704. SAN 301-1046. Tel: 949-759-1122. FAX: 949-759-5623. Web Site: www.ocma.net. *Colls Mgr, Exhibitions Mgr,* Amanda Seadler; E-mail: aseadler@ocma.net; *Asst Curator,* Alyssa Cordova; E-mail: acordova@ocma.net
Founded 1965
Library Holdings: Bk Titles 200
Subject Interests: Calif, Contemporary art
Restriction: Staff use only

GL ORANGE COUNTY PUBLIC LAW LIBRARY*, 515 N Flower St, 92703-2354. SAN 334-8997. Tel: 714-338-6790. FAX: 714-338-6814. Web Site: www.ocpll.org. *Dir,* Brendan E Starkey; E-mail: bstarkey@ocpll.org; Staff 15 (MLS 5, Non-MLS 10)
Founded 1891
Library Holdings: CDs 1,781; DVDs 39; Bk Vols 378,778; Per Subs 928
Special Collections: California SC (Records & Briefs), 1960-64, 1969-, fiche; USSC (Records & Briefs), 1950, fiche. State Document Depository; US Document Depository
Automation Activity & Vendor Info: (Acquisitions) Innovative Interfaces, Inc; (Cataloging) Innovative Interfaces, Inc; (Circulation) Innovative Interfaces, Inc; (OPAC) Innovative Interfaces, Inc; (Serials) Innovative Interfaces, Inc
Wireless access
Publications: Acquisition List; Bibliographies; Newsletter
Partic in Law Library Microform Consortium
Open Mon-Thurs 8-5:55, Fri 8-4:55

J SANTA ANA COLLEGE*, Nealley Library, 1530 W 17th St, 92706-3398. SAN 301-5432. Tel: 714-564-6700. Reference Tel: 714-564-6708. FAX: 714-564-6729. Web Site: www.sac.edu/library. *Dean,* Eve Kikawa; Tel: 714-564-5600, E-mail: kikawa_eve@sac.edu; Staff 8 (MLS 8)
Founded 1915. Enrl 24,035; Fac 329
Library Holdings: Bk Vols 99,500; Per Subs 405
Automation Activity & Vendor Info: (Cataloging) SirsiDynix
Partic in Cooperative Library Association Shared System
Open Mon-Thurs 8-8, Fri 8-4, Sat (Fall & Spring) 9-2
Friends of the Library Group

P SANTA ANA PUBLIC LIBRARY*, 26 Civic Ctr Plaza, 92701-4010. SAN 334-9055. Tel: 714-647-5250. Interlibrary Loan Service Tel: 714-647-5267. FAX: 714-647-5291. Web Site: www.santa-ana.org/library. *Interim Dir,* Yolonda Moreno; E-mail: ymoreno@santa-ana.org; *Sr Librn,* David Lopez; E-mail: dlopez@santa-ana.org; *Principal Librn, Adult Serv,* Patricia Lopez; Tel: 714-647-5325, E-mail: plopez@santa-ana.org; *Principal Librn, Tech & Support,* Lynn Nguyen; Tel: 714-647-5259, E-mail: lnguyen@santa-ana.org; *Principal Librn, YA,* Cheryl Eberly; Tel: 714-647-5288, E-mail:

ceberly@santa-ana.org; *Principal Libn, Youth Serv,* Lupita Arroyo; Tel: 714-647-5283, E-mail: larroyo@santa-ana.org; Staff 14 (MLS 14)
Founded 1891
Jul 2016-Jun 2017. Mats Exp $499,728
Library Holdings: Audiobooks 9,099; e-journals 69; Electronic Media & Resources 38; Per Subs 46
Special Collections: California History Coll; Hispanic & Asian American Heritage Coll; Santa Ana & Orange County History Coll; Spanish Language Coll, AV, bks; Vietnamese Language Coll, AV. Oral History
Automation Activity & Vendor Info: (Acquisitions) Brodart; (Cataloging) Brodart; (Circulation) TLC (The Library Corporation); (OPAC) TLC (The Library Corporation); (Serials) TLC (The Library Corporation)
Wireless access
Function: 24/7 Electronic res, 24/7 Online cat, 3D Printer, Accelerated reader prog, Activity rm, Adult bk club, After school storytime, Archival coll, Art exhibits, Audiobks on Playaways & MP3, Audiobks via web, Bilingual assistance for Spanish patrons, Bks on CD, Children's prog, Citizenship assistance, Computer training, Computers for patron use, Digital talking bks, E-Readers, E-Reserves, Electronic databases & coll, Equip loans & repairs, Holiday prog, Homework prog, ILL available, Internet access, Learning ctr, Life-long learning prog for all ages, Literacy & newcomer serv, Magazines, Magnifiers for reading, Mail & tel request accepted, Microfiche/film & reading machines, Movies, Music CDs, Online cat, Online info literacy tutorials on the web & in blackboard, Orientations, OverDrive digital audio bks, Photocopying/Printing, Preschool outreach, Preschool reading prog, Printer for laptops & handheld devices, Prog for adults, Prog for children & young adult, Ref & res, Ref serv available, Res performed for a fee, Satellite serv, Serves people with intellectual disabilities, Spanish lang bks, Spoken cassettes & CDs, Spoken cassettes & DVDs, Story hour, Summer & winter reading prog, Summer reading prog, Teen prog, Telephone ref, Wheelchair accessible, Winter reading prog, Workshops, Writing prog
Open Mon-Thurs 10-9, Fri & Sat 10-6, Sun 12-4
Restriction: Authorized patrons, Circ to mem only, Free to mem, In-house use for visitors, Non-circulating of rare bks, Non-resident fee, Restricted borrowing privileges
Friends of the Library Group
Branches: 1
NEWHOPE LIBRARY LEARNING CENTER, 122 N Newhope, 92703, SAN 334-9098. Tel: 714-647-6992. FAX: 714-554-9633.
Library Holdings: Bk Vols 67,457; Per Subs 15
Automation Activity & Vendor Info: (Acquisitions) TLC (The Library Corporation); (Cataloging) TLC (The Library Corporation)
Open Mon-Thurs 2-7, Sat 10-5

CL TRINITY INTERNATIONAL UNIVERSITY, Trinity Law School Library & Information Center, 2200 N Grand Ave, 92705. SAN 326-5412. Toll Free Tel: 800-922-4748. Web Site: tls.edu/library.
Founded 1980. Enrl 250; Fac 6; Highest Degree: Doctorate
Library Holdings: Bk Vols 50,000; Per Subs 56
Special Collections: European Commission and Court of Human Rights; International Law & Human Rights (Arthur Henry Robertson Coll), bks, ms; Rarisma (15th-18th century classical, legal & apologetic books, including numerous English Reporters)
Subject Interests: Human rights
Automation Activity & Vendor Info: (Acquisitions) ComPanion Corp; (Cataloging) ComPanion Corp; (Circulation) ComPanion Corp; (OPAC) ComPanion Corp; (Serials) ComPanion Corp
Partic in LIBRAS, Inc
Open Mon-Thurs 8am-9:30pm, Fri 8-5
Restriction: Non-circulating
Friends of the Library Group

SR TRINITY UNITED PRESBYTERIAN CHURCH LIBRARY, 13922 Prospect Ave, 92705. SAN 301-5459. Tel: 714-544-7850. Web Site: trinityconnection.com.
Founded 1955
Library Holdings: Bk Vols 7,000; Per Subs 20
Subject Interests: Theol
Wireless access

SANTA BARBARA

M COTTAGE HEALTH SYSTEM*, SAGE Medical Library, 401 W Pueblo St, 93105. SAN 301-5548. Tel: 805-569-7240. Web Site: www.cottagehealth.org/patients-visitors/sage-medical-library. *Mgr, Libr Serv,* Brittney Haliani; E-mail: bhaliani@sbch.org; Staff 2.5 (MLS 1, Non-MLS 1.5)
Founded 1941
Library Holdings: CDs 100; DVDs 50; e-books 200; e-journals 1,500; Bk Titles 300; Per Subs 50; Videos 20
Special Collections: Shared Governance
Subject Interests: Consumer health, Internal med, Med, Surgery
Automation Activity & Vendor Info: (Cataloging) Marcive, Inc; (Circulation) CyberTools for Libraries; (OPAC) CyberTools for Libraries; (Serials) CyberTools for Libraries
Wireless access
Partic in National Network of Libraries of Medicine Region 5; Pacific Southwest Regional Medical Library
Open Mon-Fri 8-5
Restriction: Circ limited
Friends of the Library Group

C FIELDING GRADUATE UNIVERSITY*, Library Services, 2020 De La Vina St, 93105. SAN 375-6874. Tel: 805-690-4373. Reference Tel: 805-898-2920. E-mail: library@fielding.edu. Web Site: web.fielding.edu/library. *Dir, Libr Serv,* Abby Rae; E-mail: arae@fielding.edu; Staff 2 (MLS 2)
Founded 1974. Enrl 972; Fac 90; Highest Degree: Doctorate
Jul 2016-Jun 2017. Mats Exp $192,850. Sal $121,380 (Prof $121,380)
Library Holdings: e-books 203,789; e-journals 49,750; Videos 450
Subject Interests: Educ leadership, Human develop, Media psychol, Organizational develop, Psychol
Automation Activity & Vendor Info: (Discovery) SerialsSolutions; (Serials) SerialsSolutions
Wireless access
Function: Distance learning, Doc delivery serv, Electronic databases & coll, ILL available, Instruction & testing, Internet access, Online info literacy tutorials on the web & in blackboard, Online ref, Orientations, Outreach serv, Outside serv via phone, mail, e-mail & web, Ref & res
Partic in Northern & Central California Psychology Libraries; Statewide California Electronic Library Consortium
Open Mon-Fri 9-5, Sun 11-1
Restriction: Authorized patrons

GL MCMAHON LAW LIBRARY OF SANTA BARBARA COUNTY*, County Court House, 1100 Anacapa St, 2nd Flr, 93101. SAN 301-5572. Tel: 805-568-2296. FAX: 805-568-2299. E-mail: info@countylawlibrary.org. Web Site: www.countylawlibrary.com. *Dir,* Raymond MacGregor
Founded 1891
Library Holdings: Bk Titles 35,403; Per Subs 20
Wireless access
Open Mon-Fri 8-4:30

S SANTA BARBARA BOTANIC GARDEN*, Blaksley Library, 1212 Mission Canyon Rd, 93105-2199. SAN 301-5556. Tel: 805-682-4726, Ext 107. FAX: 805-563-0352. Web Site: www.sbbg.org. *Info Res,* Randy Wright; Tel: 805-682-4726, E-mail: rwright@sbbg.org
Founded 1942
Library Holdings: Bk Vols 15,000; Per Subs 200
Special Collections: Oral History
Subject Interests: Botany, Calif, Hort, Manuscripts
Automation Activity & Vendor Info: (Cataloging) Koha; (Circulation) Koha; (OPAC) Koha
Wireless access
Partic in Gold Coast Library Network
Restriction: Non-circulating to the pub, Open by appt only

J SANTA BARBARA CITY COLLEGE*, Eli Luria Library, 721 Cliff Dr, 93109-2394. SAN 301-5564. Tel: 805-730-4430. Reference Tel: 805-730-4444. FAX: 805-965-0771. TDD: 805-965-8853. E-mail: library@sbcc.edu. Web Site: library.sbcc.edu. *Libr Dir,* Elizabeth Bowman; Tel: 805-965-0581, Ext 2633; *Librn,* Corrie Bott; E-mail: cabott@pipeline.sbcc.edu; *Cat & Ref Librn, Syst,* Sally Chuah; Tel: 805-965-0581, Ext 2643, E-mail: sschuah@pipeline.sbcc.edu; Staff 10 (MLS 5, Non-MLS 5)
Founded 1909. Enrl 19,000; Fac 450; Highest Degree: Associate
Library Holdings: e-books 22,000; Bk Titles 118,846; Bk Vols 123,522; Per Subs 324
Automation Activity & Vendor Info: (Cataloging) SirsiDynix; (Circulation) SirsiDynix; (Course Reserve) SirsiDynix; (OPAC) SirsiDynix; (Serials) SirsiDynix
Wireless access
Partic in OCLC Online Computer Library Center, Inc
Special Services for the Blind - Assistive/Adapted tech devices, equip & products; Computer with voice synthesizer for visually impaired persons; Magnifiers
Open Mon-Thurs 7:30am-10pm, Fri 7:30-4, Sat 12-5, Sun 11-10; Mon & Thurs (Summer) 8-3, Tues & Wed 8-7
Friends of the Library Group

S SANTA BARBARA COUNTY GENEALOGICAL SOCIETY, Sahyun Library, 316 Castillo St, 93101-3814. SAN 376-0790. Tel: 805-884-9909. E-mail: sahyunlibrary@sbgen.org. Web Site: sbgen.org. *Libr Dir,* Kathie Morgan. Subject Specialists: *Genealogy,* Kathie Morgan
Founded 1972

Library Holdings: AV Mats 6,601; Electronic Media & Resources 504; Bk Titles 8,800; Per Subs 100
Subject Interests: Europe, Genealogy, US
Automation Activity & Vendor Info: (Cataloging) LibraryWorld, Inc
Wireless access
Function: Photocopying/Printing, Res libr
Publications: Ancestors West (Quarterly); Tree Tips (Monthly)
Open Tues, Thurs & Fri 10-4, Sun 1-4
Restriction: Pub use on premises

S SANTA BARBARA HISTORICAL MUSEUM*, Gledhill Library, 136 E De La Guerra St, 93101. SAN 301-5599. Tel: 805-966-1601, Ext 105. FAX: 805-966-1603. E-mail: archivist@sbhistorical.org. Web Site: www.sbhistorical.org/gledhill-library. *Head Archivist,* Chris Ervin; Staff 1 (Non-MLS 1)
Founded 1967
Library Holdings: DVDs 96; Microforms 176; Bk Vols 5,000; Per Subs 20
Special Collections: Oral History
Subject Interests: Genealogy, Local hist
Automation Activity & Vendor Info: (Cataloging) TLC (The Library Corporation)
Function: Telephone ref
Publications: Noticias (Research guide)
Open Tues-Fri 10-4
Restriction: Non-circulating to the pub

S SANTA BARBARA MISSION*, Archive-Library, 2201 Laguna St, 93105. SAN 301-5602. Tel: 805-682-4713. E-mail: research@sbmal.org. Web Site: www.sbmal.org. *Dir,* Monica Orozco, PhD; E-mail: director@sbmal.org; *Colls Mgr, Prog Mgr,* Bryan Stevenson
Founded 1786
Library Holdings: Bk Vols 23,000
Special Collections: California Missions (Father Junipero Serra Coll, covers all 21 California missions), docs; Early California (Webb Coll, Smilie Coll, Baer Coll & Wilson Coll), ms, papers, bks & docs; Original Spanish & Mexican Missionary Coll, bks; Spanish & Hispanic American Coll, bks; Spanish & Latin Coll, docs
Wireless access
Publications: Spanish California Revisited (Francis Guest, OFM); The Voyage of the Princesa to Southern California in 1782
Special Services for the Deaf - Bks on deafness & sign lang
Restriction: Open by appt only

S SANTA BARBARA MUSEUM OF NATURAL HISTORY LIBRARY*, 2559 Puesta del Sol Rd, 93105. SAN 301-5610. Tel: 805-682-4711. FAX: 805-682-3170. Web Site: www.sbnature.org/collections-research/library. *Mus Librn,* Terri Sheridan; Tel: 805-682-4711, Ext 134, E-mail: tsheridan@sbnature2.org; *Libr Asst,* Peggy Dahl; Tel: 805-682-4711, Ext 135, E-mail: pdahl@sbnature2.org; Staff 2 (Non-MLS 2)
Founded 1929
Library Holdings: Bk Titles 22,000; Bk Vols 40,000; Per Subs 420
Special Collections: Channel Islands Archive
Subject Interests: Exploration, Gas, Native Americans, Natural hist, Systematics, Zoology
Automation Activity & Vendor Info: (Cataloging) TLC (The Library Corporation); (Circulation) TLC (The Library Corporation); (ILL) OCLC; (OPAC) TLC (The Library Corporation)
Wireless access
Function: 24/7 Online cat, Archival coll, ILL available, Online cat, Photocopying/Printing, Ref serv available, Res libr
Partic in Central Coast Museum Consortium; Gold Coast Library Network; OCLC Online Computer Library Center, Inc
Open Mon-Fri 10-5; Sat-Sun 11-5
Restriction: Circ limited, Circulates for staff only, In-house use for visitors, Non-circulating of rare bks, Open to pub for ref only, Pub use on premises
Friends of the Library Group

S SANTA BARBARA NEWS PRESS LIBRARY, 715 Anacapa St, 93101. (Mail add: PO Box 1359, 93102-1359), SAN 327-6104. Tel: 805-564-5200, Ext 0. FAX: 805-966-6258. Web Site: www.newspress.com. *Research Librn,* Violet Barroso; E-mail: vbarroso@newspress.com; Staff 1 (Non-MLS 1)
Special Collections: New Press Back Issues, 1855-present, micro
Open Mon-Fri 1-5

P SANTA BARBARA PUBLIC LIBRARY*, 40 E Anapamu St, 93101-2722. (Mail add: PO Box 1019, 93102-1019), SAN 334-9179. Tel: 805-962-7623. Circulation Tel: 805-962-7653. Interlibrary Loan Service Tel: 805-564-5610. Reference Tel: 805-564-5604. Administration Tel: 805-564-5608. Interlibrary Loan Service FAX: 805-564-5626. Reference FAX: 805-564-5661. Administration FAX: 805-564-5660. E-mail: LibraryAdmin@SantaBarbaraCA.gov. Web Site: www.sbplibrary.org. *Dir,* Jessica Cadiente; *Mgr, Libr Serv,* Margaret Esther; Staff 115 (MLS 15, Non-MLS 100)
Pop 224,500; Circ 1,585,000. Sal $2,670,539
Library Holdings: AV Mats 15,200; Bk Vols 183,000; Per Subs 405
Subject Interests: Local hist
Automation Activity & Vendor Info: (Acquisitions) Innovative Interfaces, Inc; (Circulation) Innovative Interfaces, Inc; (ILL) Innovative Interfaces, Inc; (OPAC) Innovative Interfaces, Inc; (Serials) LS 2000
Mem of Black Gold Cooperative Library System
Partic in OCLC Online Computer Library Center, Inc; Proquest Dialog
Friends of the Library Group
Branches: 4
CARPINTERIA BRANCH, 5141 Carpinteria Ave, Carpinteria, 93013, SAN 334-9209. Tel: 805-684-4314. E-mail: CarpinteriaLibrary@SantaBarbaraCA.gov. *Br Supvr,* Tara O'Reilly; Staff 3 (Non-MLS 3)
Friends of the Library Group
CENTRAL LIBRARY, 40 E Anapamu St, 93101-2722. (Mail add: PO Box 1019, 93102-1019). Tel: 805-962-7653. FAX: 805-564-5660. *Dir,* Irene Macias; Staff 63.5 (MLS 9, Non-MLS 54.5)
Founded 1870. Pop 218,613; Circ 1,585,643
Library Holdings: e-books 7,551; Bk Vols 287,489; Videos 22,430
Friends of the Library Group
EASTSIDE, 1102 E Montecito St, 93103, SAN 334-9268. Tel: 805-963-3727. *Librn,* Marivel Zambrano-Esparza; Staff 5 (MLS 1, Non-MLS 4)
Friends of the Library Group
MONTECITO, 1469 E Valley Rd, 93108, SAN 334-9357. Tel: 805-969-5063. *Library Contact,* Jody Thomas
Friends of the Library Group
Bookmobiles: 1

R TRINITY EPISCOPAL CHURCH LIBRARY, 1500 State St, 93101. SAN 301-5645. Tel: 805-965-7419. FAX: 805-965-8840. E-mail: office@trinitysb.org. Web Site: www.trinitysb.org.
Library Holdings: Bk Vols 2,500

C UNIVERSITY OF CALIFORNIA, SANTA BARBARA, Davidson Library, UCEN Rd, Bldg 525, 93106-9010. SAN 301-5653. Tel: 805-893-2478. Circulation Tel: 805-893-3491. Interlibrary Loan Service Tel: 805-893-3436. FAX: 805-893-7010. Interlibrary Loan Service FAX: 805-893-5290. Web Site: www.library.ucsb.edu. *Univ Librn,* Kristin Antelman; Tel: 805-893-3256, E-mail: kantelman@ucsb.edu; *Dep Univ Librn, Human Res,* Alan Grosenheider; Tel: 805-893-4098, E-mail: alang@ucsb.edu; Staff 172 (MLS 41, Non-MLS 131)
Founded 1909. Enrl 22,417; Fac 963; Highest Degree: Doctorate
Library Holdings: e-books 34,500; e-journals 30,000; Bk Vols 3,000,000; Per Subs 23,218
Special Collections: 20th Century American & British Writers Coll; American Religions Coll; Art Exhibition Catalog Coll; Balkan History (Nikic Coll); California Ethnic & Multicultural Archive; Conservation in Southern California (Pearl Chase Coll); Evolution (Darwin Coll); Historic Sound Recordings (Todd Coll); History of Printing 19th & 20th Century (Skofield Coll); Humanistic Psychology Archive; Late 19th & 20th Century Trade Catalogs (Romaine Coll); Lincoln, Civil War & American Westward Expansion (Wyles Coll); Lotte Lehmann Archives Coll; Rare Bibles Coll. Oral History; State Document Depository; US Document Depository
Automation Activity & Vendor Info: (Acquisitions) Ex Libris Group; (Cataloging) Ex Libris Group; (Circulation) Ex Libris Group; (Course Reserve) Docutek; (ILL) Fretwell-Downing; (OPAC) Ex Libris Group; (Serials) Ex Libris Group
Wireless access
Partic in Association of Research Libraries; Center for Research Libraries; OCLC Online Computer Library Center, Inc
Departmental Libraries:
ARTS LIBRARY, UCSB Library, 93106-9010. Tel: 805-893-2850. FAX: 805-893-5879. Web Site: library.ucsb.edu/art/art-architecture-collection. *Head of Libr, Music Librn,* Kyra Folk-Farber; Tel: 805-893-2244, E-mail: kfolkfarber@ucsb.edu; *Art Librn,* Chizu Morihara; Tel: 805-893-2766, E-mail: cmorihara@ucsb.edu. Subject Specialists: *Arts,* Chizu Morihara; Staff 10 (MLS 3, Non-MLS 7)
Enrl 21,685; Fac 1,050; Highest Degree: Doctorate
Library Holdings: CDs 13,216; DVDs 1,352; Microforms 16,750; Music Scores 44,213; Bk Vols 320,000; Per Subs 534; Videos 500
Automation Activity & Vendor Info: (OPAC) Ex Libris Group

C WESTMONT COLLEGE*, Roger John Voskuyl Library, 955 La Paz Rd, 93108. SAN 301-5661. Tel: 805-565-6000, 805-565-6147. Interlibrary Loan Service Tel: 805-565-6142. FAX: 805-565-6220. Web Site: www.westmont.edu/library. *Interim Co-Dir,* Jana Mayfield Mullen; E-mail: jmayfield@westmont.edu; *Interim Co-Dir,* Diane Ziliotto; E-mail: dziliott@westmont.edu; *ILL Mgr,* Richard Burnweit; E-mail: burnweit@westmont.edu; *Circ Coordr,* Ruth Angelos; E-mail: rangel@westmont.edu; Staff 7 (MLS 6, Non-MLS 1)

Founded 1940. Enrl 1,200; Fac 64; Highest Degree: Bachelor
Library Holdings: Audiobooks 9,983; DVDs 1,764; e-books 50,000; e-journals 2,529; Electronic Media & Resources 143,263; Microforms 15,590; Bk Titles 106,411; Bk Vols 226,657; Per Subs 270
Automation Activity & Vendor Info: (Acquisitions) OCLC; (Cataloging) OCLC; (Circulation) OCLC; (Course Reserve) OCLC; (ILL) OCLC; (OPAC) OCLC; (Serials) OCLC
Wireless access
Partic in OCLC Online Computer Library Center, Inc; Statewide California Electronic Library Consortium
Open Mon-Thurs 7:30am-1am, Fri 7:30-6, Sat 10-6, Sun Noon-1am

SANTA CLARA

J MISSION COLLEGE LIBRARY, 3000 Mission College Blvd, 95054-1897. SAN 301-5742. Tel: 408-855-5150. Reference Tel: 408-855-5151. Web Site: missioncollege.edu/lib. *Dean of Libr,* Valerie Jensen; Tel: 408-855-5464, E-mail: valerie.jensen@missioncollege.edu; *Coll Develop Librn,* Melissa Destefano; Tel: 408-855-5167, E-mail: melissa.destefano@missioncollege.edu; *Electronic Res Librn,* Michele Speck; Tel: 408-855-5169, E-mail: michele.speck@wvm.edu; *Access Serv,* Tina Boghozian; Tel: 408-855-5165, E-mail: tina.boghozian@wvm.edu; *Ref & Instruction,* Elaine Wong; Tel: 408-855-5162, E-mail: elaine.wong@wvm.edu; Staff 8 (MLS 4, Non-MLS 4)
Founded 1975. Enrl 10,500; Fac 325; Highest Degree: Associate
Library Holdings: Audiobooks 794; AV Mats 2,682; e-books 12,617; Microforms 55,000; Bk Titles 48,975; Bk Vols 69,144; Per Subs 160
Special Collections: Asian American Coll
Subject Interests: Allied health, Fire sci
Automation Activity & Vendor Info: (Acquisitions) Ex Libris Group; (Cataloging) OCLC Connexion; (Circulation) Ex Libris Group; (Course Reserve) Ex Libris Group; (OPAC) Ex Libris Group
Wireless access
Partic in California Community College Library Consortium
Special Services for the Deaf - Assistive tech; Bks on deafness & sign lang; Closed caption videos
Special Services for the Blind - Assistive/Adapted tech devices, equip & products; Computer with voice synthesizer for visually impaired persons
Open Mon-Thurs 8:30-8, Fri 10:30-3:30, Sat 10-2

S NIELSEN ENGINEERING & RESEARCH, INC*, Division of Analytical Mechanics Associates, Inc Library, 900 Lafayette St, Ste 600, 95050. SAN 301-0902. Tel: 408-454-5246. E-mail: lib@nearinc.com. Web Site: www.nearinc.com. *Pres & Chief Exec Officer,* Michael R Mendenhall; E-mail: mrm@nearinc.com; *Library Contact,* Gloria L Mertl; E-mail: gloria.mertl@nearinc.com. Subject Specialists: *Knowledge mgt,* Michael R Mendenhall; Staff 1 (MLS 1)
Founded 1966
Library Holdings: Bk Vols 1,202; Per Subs 10
Automation Activity & Vendor Info: (Cataloging) Inmagic, Inc.; (Circulation) Inmagic, Inc.
Function: For res purposes, ILL available, Res libr
Publications: New in the Library (Acquisition list)
Restriction: Circ limited, Open by appt only

P SANTA CLARA CITY LIBRARY*, 2635 Homestead Rd, 95051. SAN 301-5750. Tel: 408-615-2900. Circulation Tel: 408-615-2970. Administration Tel: 408-615-2930. FAX: 408-247-9657. TDD: 408-246-2507. E-mail: librarian@santaclaraca.gov. Web Site: www.sclibrary.org. *City Librn,* Hilary Keith; *Asst City Librn,* Julie Passalacqua; E-mail: jpassalacqua@santaclaraca.gov; Staff 18.4 (MLS 15.4, Non-MLS 3)
Founded 1904. Pop 117,242; Circ 2,647,837
Library Holdings: AV Mats 50,586; e-books 2,951; Bk Titles 373,226; Per Subs 610
Special Collections: Adult New Reader Coll; Audiovisual Coll, bks on tape, CDs, DVDs, music CDs; Business Reference Coll; Children's Picture Books; Consumer Health Information (Kaiser Permanente Health & Wellness Coll); Large Print Coll; Local History/Genealogy Coll
Subject Interests: Bus, Local hist
Automation Activity & Vendor Info: (Acquisitions) Innovative Interfaces, Inc; (Cataloging) OCLC; (Circulation) Innovative Interfaces, Inc; (OPAC) Innovative Interfaces, Inc; (Serials) Innovative Interfaces, Inc
Wireless access
Function: Audiobks via web, BA reader (adult literacy), Bks on cassette, Bks on CD, CD-ROM, Children's prog, Computer training, Computers for patron use, Digital talking bks, Electronic databases & coll, Family literacy, Free DVD rentals, Health sci info serv, Homebound delivery serv, Internet access, Magnifiers for reading, Music CDs, Online cat, OverDrive digital audio bks, Photocopying/Printing, Preschool outreach, Prog for adults, Prog for children & young adult, Ref serv available, Senior outreach, Story hour, Summer reading prog, Teen prog, Telephone ref, VHS videos, Wheelchair accessible
Special Services for the Deaf - Assisted listening device; Assistive tech; Bks on deafness & sign lang; Closed caption videos; High interest/low vocabulary bks; TDD equip
Special Services for the Blind - Audio mat; Bks on cassette; Bks on CD; Closed circuit TV; Computer with voice synthesizer for visually impaired persons; Home delivery serv; Large print bks; Magnifiers; PC for people with disabilities; Reader equip; Screen enlargement software for people with visual disabilities
Open Mon-Thurs 10-9, Fri & Sat 10-6, Sun 1-5
Friends of the Library Group
Branches: 2
MISSION BRANCH LIBRARY, 1098 Lexington St, 95050, SAN 371-358X. Tel: 408-615-2964. FAX: 408-249-2486. E-mail: missionlibrary@santaclaraca.gov. *Br Mgr,* Justin Wasterlain; Tel: 408-615-2957; Staff 1 (Non-MLS 1)
Library Holdings: Bk Vols 20,868
Open Mon & Tues 10-6, Wed & Thurs 11-8, Fri & Sat 10-6
Friends of the Library Group
NORTHSIDE BRANCH, 695 Moreland Way, 95054. Tel: 408-615-5500. E-mail: NorthsideLibrary@santaclaraca.gov. *Br Mgr,* Cheryl Lee
Open Mon & Tues 10-9, Wed-Sat 10-6, Sun 1-5
Bookmobiles: 1. Librn, Cody Christians

C SANTA CLARA UNIVERSITY LIBRARY*, 500 El Camino Real, 95053-0500. SAN 334-9470. Tel: 408-554-5020. Interlibrary Loan Service Tel: 408-554-5428. Reference Tel: 408-551-1753. Administration Tel: 408-554-6830. FAX: 408-554-6827. E-mail: librarycirc@scu.edu. Web Site: www.scu.edu/library. *Univ Librn,* Jennifer Nutefall; E-mail: jnutefall@scu.edu; *Assoc Univ Librn, Learning & Engagement,* Nicole Branch; E-mail: nbranch@scu.edu; Staff 36 (MLS 13, Non-MLS 23)
Founded 1851. Enrl 7,359; Highest Degree: Doctorate
Library Holdings: Bk Vols 3,787; Per Subs 2,630
Special Collections: California: Denise Levertov & Jose Antonio Villareal; Labor Relations in California. State Document Depository
Automation Activity & Vendor Info: (Acquisitions) Innovative Interfaces, Inc; (Cataloging) Innovative Interfaces, Inc; (Circulation) Innovative Interfaces, Inc; (ILL) OCLC ILLiad; (OPAC) Innovative Interfaces, Inc; (Serials) Innovative Interfaces, Inc
Wireless access
Partic in OCLC Online Computer Library Center, Inc; Southern Calif Electronic Libr Consortium; Statewide California Electronic Library Consortium
Departmental Libraries:
ARCHIVES, 500 El Camino Real, 95053-0500. Tel: 408-554-5530. FAX: 408-554-5179. E-mail: specialcollections@scu.edu. Web Site: www.scu.edu/library/asc. *Head, Archives & Spec Coll,* Nadia Nasr; E-mail: nnasr@scu.edu; Staff 1 (Non-MLS 1)
Special Collections: Alaska (Bernard R Hubbard, S J Coll), ms, photog, Botany (George Schoener Coll); Early Aviation (John J Montgomery), ms, photog; Local History
CL EDWIN A HEAFEY LAW LIBRARY, School of Law, 500 El Camino Real, 95053-0430, SAN 334-9500. Tel: 408-554-4072. Interlibrary Loan Service Tel: 408-554-5133. Reference Tel: 408-554-4452. FAX: 408-554-5318. E-mail: lawref@scu.edu. Web Site: law.scu.edu/library. *Dir, Law Libr,* Whitney Alexander; Tel: 408-554-2733, E-mail: walexander@scu.edu; *Fac Serv Librn, Research Librn,* Ellen Platt; Tel: 408-554-5139, E-mail: eplatt@scu.edu; *Research Librn, Student Serv Librn,* Thomas Deguzman; Tel: 408-554-5327, E-mail: tdeguzman@scu.edu; Staff 22 (MLS 9, Non-MLS 13)
Founded 1912. Enrl 926; Fac 37; Highest Degree: Master
Library Holdings: AV Mats 5,135; Bk Titles 38,247; Bk Vols 169,192; Per Subs 4,153
Special Collections: Proceedings of the House Judiciary Committee on the Watergate Hearings
Partic in Jesuit Law Libr Consortium; Research Libraries Information Network; S Bay Area Ref Network
Publications: Heafey Headnotes (Newsletter)
Open Mon-Thurs 8am-11pm, Fri 8am-9pm, Sat 9am-11pm, Sun 10-9

SANTA CLARITA

J COLLEGE OF THE CANYONS LIBRARY*, 26455 Rockwell Canyon Rd, 91355-1899. SAN 301-6811. Tel: 661-362-3854. Circulation Tel: 661-362-3361. Web Site: www.canyons.edu/academics/library. *Head Librn,* Peter Hepburn; E-mail: peter.hepburn@canyons.edu; *Bibliog Instr, Electronic Res,* Ron Karlin; Tel: 661-362-3358, E-mail: ron.karlin@canyons.edu; *Coll Develop, Tech Serv,* Erin Barnthouse; E-mail: erin.barnthouse@canyons.edu; Staff 9 (MLS 3, Non-MLS 6)
Founded 1969. Enrl 14,233; Fac 161; Highest Degree: Associate
Library Holdings: Bk Titles 46,211; Bk Vols 54,783; Per Subs 229
Automation Activity & Vendor Info: (Acquisitions) Ex Libris Group; (Cataloging) Ex Libris Group; (Circulation) Ex Libris Group; (Course Reserve) Ex Libris Group; (ILL) OCLC; (OPAC) Ex Libris Group; (Serials) Ex Libris Group
Wireless access

Function: AV serv, ILL available, Photocopying/Printing, Ref serv available
Partic in Gold Coast Library Network; Santa Clarita Interlibrary Network
Special Services for the Deaf - Closed caption videos; TTY equip
Special Services for the Blind - Computer with voice synthesizer for visually impaired persons
Open Mon-Thurs 8-8, Fri 8-4:30, Sat 9-1
Restriction: Open to fac, students & qualified researchers
Friends of the Library Group

CR THE MASTER'S UNIVERSITY, Robert L Powell Library, 21726 W Placerita Canyon Rd, 91321-1200. SAN 301-0996. Tel: 661-259-3540. Circulation Tel: 661-362-2278. Reference Tel: 661-362-2201. Toll Free Tel: 800-568-6248. FAX: 661-362-2719. E-mail: libcircdesk@masters.edu. Web Site: www.masters.edu/library. *Libr Dir,* John W Stone; Tel: 661-362-2271, E-mail: jstone@masters.edu; *Acq Librn, ILL Librn,* Grace Kamffer; E-mail: gkamffer@masters.edu; *Ref Librn, Ser Librn,* Janet L Tillman; E-mail: jtillman@masters.edu; *Cat Mgr,* Peg Westphalen; Tel: 661-362-2277, E-mail: pwestphalen@masters.edu; *Circ Mgr,* Rachel Miller; Tel: 661-362-2272, E-mail: rmiller@masters.edu. Subject Specialists: *Theol,* John W Stone; *Liberal arts,* Janet L Tillman; Staff 7 (MLS 4, Non-MLS 3)
Founded 1927. Enrl 1,000; Fac 134; Highest Degree: Master
Library Holdings: e-books 60,000; e-journals 30,000; Bk Titles 133,000; Bk Vols 161,000; Per Subs 123
Subject Interests: Biblical studies
Automation Activity & Vendor Info: (Acquisitions) Ex Libris Group; (Cataloging) Ex Libris Group; (Circulation) Ex Libris Group; (Course Reserve) Ex Libris Group; (OPAC) Ex Libris Group; (Serials) Ex Libris Group
Wireless access
Function: ILL available
Partic in Southern Calif Electronic Libr Consortium; Southern Calif Interlibr Loan Network
Open Mon-Thurs 8am-11pm, Fri 8-5, Sat Noon-5, Sun 6pm-11pm

P SANTA CLARITA PUBLIC LIBRARY*, Canyon Country Jo Anne Darcy Library, 18601 Soledad Canyon Rd, 91351. SAN 991-0727. Tel: 661-259-0750. E-mail: info@santaclaritalibrary.com. Web Site: www.santaclaritalibrary.com. *City Librn,* Shannon Vonnegut; *Br Mgr,* Yanira Sidon; E-mail: ysidon@santaclaritalibrary.com
Founded 2001. Circ 381,424
Library Holdings: Bk Vols 91,530; Per Subs 75
Wireless access
Open Mon-Thurs 9-8, Fri 10-6, Sat 10-5, Sun 1-5
Friends of the Library Group
Branches: 2
OLD TOWN NEWHALL LIBRARY, 24500 Main St, 91321, SAN 332-6047. *Br Mgr,* Gina Roberson; E-mail: groberson@santaclaritalibrary.com
Founded 1957. Pop 36,393; Circ 385,404
Library Holdings: Bk Vols 50,854; Per Subs 35
Open Mon-Thurs 9-8, Fri 10-6, Sat 10-5, Sun 1-5
Friends of the Library Group
VALENCIA LIBRARY, 23743 W Valencia Blvd, 91355, SAN 991-0735. *Br Mgr,* Kim Christofferson
Founded 1972. Circ 713,699
Open Mon-Thurs 10-9, Fri 10-6, Sat 10-5, Sun 1-5
Friends of the Library Group

SANTA CRUZ

S MUSEUM OF ART & HISTORY LIBRARY, 705 Front St, 95060-4508. SAN 371-7860. Tel: 831-429-1964, Ext 7019. FAX: 831-429-1954. E-mail: archives@santacruzmah.org. Web Site: www.santacruzmah.org/history-collection. *Archives, Libr Coord,* Jessie Durant; E-mail: jessie@santacruzmah.org; Staff 1 (MLS 1)
Library Holdings: Bk Titles 2,500
Special Collections: Evergreen Cemetery Records. Oral History
Subject Interests: Local hist
Publications: Santa Cruz County History (Journal)
Restriction: Open by appt only

G NATIONAL MARINE FISHERIES SERVICE*, SWFSC Santa Cruz Library, 110 McAllister Way, 95060. SAN 301-6617. Tel: 831-420-3962. FAX: 831-420-3980. Web Site: swfsc.noaa.gov/textblock.aspx?ParentMenuld=121&id=1128. *Librn,* Kit Johnston; E-mail: kit.johnston@noaa.gov; Staff 1 (MLS 1)
Founded 1962
Library Holdings: Per Subs 120; Videos 15
Subject Interests: Fisheries
Function: For res purposes, ILL available
Partic in NOAA Libraries Network; OCLC Online Computer Library Center, Inc; OCLC-LVIS
Restriction: Open to others by appt, Staff use only

P SANTA CRUZ CITY-COUNTY LIBRARY SYSTEM*, Headquarters, 117 Union St, 95060-3873. SAN 334-9659. Tel: 831-427-7706. Interlibrary Loan Service Tel: 831-427-7726. Reference Tel: 831-427-7713. FAX: 831-427-7720. Web Site: www.santacruzpl.org. *Libr Dir,* Susan Nemitz; Tel: 831-427-7706, Ext 7611, E-mail: nemitzs@santacruzpl.org; *Asst Dir,* Eric Howard; Tel: 831-427-7706, Ext 7670, E-mail: howarde@santacruzpl.org; *Regional Mgr,* Jessica Goodman; Tel: 831-721-7706, Ext 7612, E-mail: goodmanj@santacruzpl.org; *Regional Mgr,* Heather Norquist; Tel: 831-427-7706, Ext 7698, E-mail: norquisthc@santacruzpl.org; *Regional Mgr,* Laura Whaley; Tel: 831-427-7706, Ext 7734, E-mail: whaleyl@santacruzpl.org; *Mgr, Coll Mgt,* Sarah Harbison; Tel: 831-427-7706, Ext 7616, E-mail: harbisons@santacruzpl.org
Wireless access
Partic in Monterey Bay Area Cooperative Library System
Special Services for the Deaf - TTY equip
Friends of the Library Group
Branches: 10
APTOS BRANCH, 7695 Soquel Dr, Aptos, 95003-3899, SAN 334-9683. Tel: 831-427-7702. Web Site: www.santacruzpl.org/branches/4. *Br Mgr,* Heather Pereira; E-mail: pereirah@santacruzpl.org
Open Mon-Thurs 10-8, Fri & Sat 10-5
Friends of the Library Group
BOULDER CREEK BRANCH, 13390 W Park Ave, Boulder Creek, 95006-9301, SAN 334-9772. Tel: 831-427-7703. Web Site: www.santacruzpl.org/branches/5. *Br Mgr,* Essy Barroso-Ramirez
Open Tues-Thurs 10-6, Fri & Sat 10-5
Friends of the Library Group
CAPITOLA BRANCH, 2005 Wharf Rd, Capitola, 95010-2002, SAN 378-0694. Tel: 831-427-7705. FAX: 831-427-7725. *Library Contact,* Melanee Barash; Tel: 831-427-7706, Ext 7672
Closed for renovation 2019-
DOWNTOWN, 224 Church St, 95060-3873, SAN 322-5666. Tel: 831-427-7707. Web Site: www.santacruzpl.org/branches/7. *Br Mgr,* James Lee; E-mail: leej@santacruzpl.org
Open Mon-Thurs 10-8, Fri & Sat 10-5, Sun 1-5
FELTON BRANCH, 6299 Gushee St, Felton, 95018-9140. (Mail add: PO Box 56, Felton, 95018-0056), SAN 334-9861. Tel: 831-427-7708. Web Site: www.santacruzpl.org/branches/8. *Interim Br Mgr,* Melanie Barash; Tel: 831-427-7700, Ext 5800, E-mail: barashm@santacruzpl.org
Friends of the Library Group
GARFIELD PARK, 705 Woodrow Ave, 95060, SAN 334-9926. Tel: 831-427-7709. Web Site: www.santacruzpl.org/branches/9. *Br Mgr,* Catherine Workman; E-mail: workmanc@santacruzpl.org
Open Mon 10-5, Tues-Thurs 11-6, Fri 1-5, Sat 10-2
LA SELVA BEACH BRANCH, 316 Estrella Ave, La Selva Beach, 95076, SAN 334-9950. Tel: 831-427-7710. Web Site: www.santacruzpl.org/branches/10.
Under construction to re-open June 2020
Friends of the Library Group
LIVE OAK, 2380 Portola Dr, 95062. Tel: 831-427-7711. Web Site: www.santacruzpl.org/branches/11. *Br Mgr, Libr Asst III,* Laura VanDerslice; E-mail: vanderslicel@santacruzpl.org
Library Holdings: Bk Vols 53,535
Open Mon-Thurs 10-7, Fri & Sat 10-5, Sun 1-5
SCOTTS VALLEY BRANCH, 251 Kings Valley Rd, Scotts Valley, 95066, SAN 334-9985. Tel: 831-427-7712. Web Site: www.santacruzpl.org/branches/12. *Br Mgr,* Linda Gault; Tel: 831-427-7700, Ext 7678, E-mail: gaultl@santacruzpl.org
Open Mon-Thurs 10-7, Fri & Sat 10-5
Friends of the Library Group
BRANCIFORTE, 230 Gault St, 95062-2599, SAN 334-9802. Tel: 831-427-7704. Web Site: www.santacruzpl.org/branches/3. *Br Mgr,* Diane Cowen; E-mail: cowend@santacruzpl.org
Library Holdings: Bk Vols 52,950
Open Tues-Thurs 10-6, Fri & Sat 11-5
Bookmobiles: 1

L SANTA CRUZ COUNTY LAW LIBRARY*, 701 Ocean St, Rm 070, 95060. SAN 301-5815. Tel: 831-420-2205. FAX: 831-457-2255. E-mail: scclawlib@yahoo.com. Web Site: www.lawlibrary.org. *Librn,* Renee J Fleming; Staff 2 (MLS 1, Non-MLS 1)
Founded 1896. Sal $176,411 (Prof $72,779)
Library Holdings: CDs 132; Bk Vols 12,000
Subject Interests: Law
Wireless access
Function: ILL available, Mail & tel request accepted, Wheelchair accessible
Partic in Pacer
Open Mon-Thurs 8-3, Fri 8-Noon
Restriction: Circ limited

C UNIVERSITY OF CALIFORNIA*, University Library, 1156 High St, 95064. SAN 335-0045. Tel: 831-459-2076. Interlibrary Loan Service Tel: 831-459-2234. FAX: 831-459-8206. Web Site: library.ucsc.edu. *Univ Librn,*

Elizabeth Cowell; E-mail: mcowell@ucsc.edu; *Head, Assessment & Planning,* Greg Careaga; Tel: 831-459-3687, E-mail: gcareaga@ucsc.edu; *Head, Digital Initiatives,* Sue Chesley Perry; Tel: 831-459-5590, E-mail: chesley@ucsc.edu; *Head, Metadata Serv,* Marcia Barrett; Tel: 831-459-5166, E-mail: barrett@ucsc.edu; *Head, Res Support Serv,* Kerry Scott; Tel: 831-459-2802, E-mail: scottk@ucsc.edu; *Head, Spec Coll,* Elizabeth Remak-Honnef; Tel: 831-459-2459, E-mail: remak@ucsc.edu; *Head User Serv & Resource Sharing,* Sarah Troy; Tel: 831-459-3878, E-mail: saraht@ucsc.edu; *Librn,* Christine Caldwell; Tel: 831-459-1287, E-mail: caldwell@ucsc.edu; *Librn,* Frank Gravier; Tel: 831-459-3319, E-mail: gravier@ucsc.edu; *Librn,* Christy Hightower; Tel: 831-459-4708, E-mail: christyh@ucsc.edu; *Librn,* Ann Hubble; Tel: 831-459-4974, E-mail: ahubble@ucsc.edu; *Librn,* Annette Marines; Tel: 831-459-3255, E-mail: amarines@ucsc.edu; *Librn,* Deborah Murphy; Tel: 831-459-3253, E-mail: damurphy@ucsc.edu; *Asst Librn,* Mary deVries; Tel: 831-459-3815, E-mail: mdevries@ucsc.edu; *Asst Librn,* Kate Dundon; Tel: 831-459-4425, E-mail: dundon@ucsc.edu; *Assoc Librn,* Rachel Jaffe; Tel: 831-502-7291, E-mail: jaffer@ucsc.edu; *Assoc Librn,* Ken Lyons; Tel: 831-459-2593, E-mail: kbplyons@ucsc.edu; *Asst Librn,* Alix Norton; Tel: 831-459-5113, E-mail: abnorton@ucsc.edu; *Assoc Librn,* Lucia Orlando; Tel: 831-459-1279, E-mail: luciao@ucsc.edu; *Digital Projects Librn, User Experience Librn,* Jessica Waggoner; Tel: 831-459-5654, E-mail: jspencer@ucsc.edu. Subject Specialists: *Arts, Humanities,* Kerry Scott; *Engr, Sci,* Christine Caldwell; *Arts, Humanities,* Frank Gravier; *Engr, Sci,* Christy Hightower; *Engr, Sci,* Ann Hubble; *Soc sci,* Annette Marines; *Arts, Humanities,* Deborah Murphy; *Spec coll,* Mary deVries; *Spec coll,* Kate Dundon; *Arts, Humanities,* Ken Lyons; *Spec coll,* Alix Norton; *Soc sci,* Lucia Orlando; Staff 80 (MLS 25, Non-MLS 55)
Founded 1965. Enrl 17,276; Fac 685; Highest Degree: Doctorate
Jul 2015-Jun 2016 Income $8,395,453, State $8,335,160, Other $60,293. Mats Exp $3,067,262, Books $369,216, Per/Ser (Incl. Access Fees) $469,088, Other Print Mats $6,613, Electronic Ref Mat (Incl. Access Fees) $2,184,461, Presv $37,884. Sal $4,623,094 (Prof $4,189,925)
Library Holdings: Bk Vols 2,365,077; Per Subs 56,506
Special Collections: Grateful Dead Archive; Gregory Bateson Coll; Kenneth Patchen Archive; Lime Kiln Press Archive; Mary Lea Shane Archives of the Lick Observatory; Pirkle Jones & Ruth Marion Baruch Photography Archive; Robert Heinlein Archive; Santa Cruz County History Coll; Strouse Coll of Thomas Carlyle; Trianon Press Archive; Turtle Island Press Archive. Oral History; US Document Depository
Automation Activity & Vendor Info: (Acquisitions) Innovative Interfaces, Inc; (Cataloging) Innovative Interfaces, Inc; (Circulation) Innovative Interfaces, Inc; (ILL) OCLC; (Media Booking) Innovative Interfaces, Inc; (OPAC) Innovative Interfaces, Inc; (Serials) Innovative Interfaces, Inc
Wireless access
Function: Archival coll, AV serv, Doc delivery serv, For res purposes, Govt ref serv, Homebound delivery serv, ILL available, Large print keyboards, Photocopying/Printing, Ref serv available, Res libr, Telephone ref, Wheelchair accessible
Publications: Catalog of South Pacific Collection (1978); Catalog of the Carlyle Coll (1980); Norman & Charlotte Strouse Lectures on Carlyle & His Era (Series)
Partic in Monterey Bay Area Cooperative Library System
Special Services for the Deaf - TTY equip
Open Mon-Thurs 8am-Midnight, Fri 8-8, Sat 11-7, Sun 10am-Midnight
Restriction: Circ limited, In-house use for visitors, Open to students, fac & staff, Restricted borrowing privileges, Restricted loan policy
Friends of the Library Group

SANTA FE SPRINGS

P SANTA FE SPRINGS CITY LIBRARY*, 11700 E Telegraph Rd, 90670-3600. SAN 301-5831. Tel: 562-868-7738. FAX: 562-929-3680. E-mail: library@santafesprings.org. Web Site: www.santafesprings.org/library. *Dir, Libr Serv,* Joyce Ryan; E-mail: joyceryan@santafesprings.org; *Librn I,* Maricelia Camona; E-mail: marieliacarmona@santafesprings.org; *Librn II,* Shannon Dailey; E-mail: shannondailey@santafesprings.org; *Librn II,* Deborah Raia; E-mail: deborahraia@santafesprings.org; Staff 29 (MLS 4, Non-MLS 25)
Founded 1961. Pop 18,000; Circ 146,000
Library Holdings: Bk Vols 87,500; Per Subs 225
Automation Activity & Vendor Info: (Acquisitions) SirsiDynix; (Cataloging) SirsiDynix; (Circulation) SirsiDynix; (ILL) OCLC; (OPAC) SirsiDynix; (Serials) SirsiDynix
Wireless access
Partic in Southern California Library Cooperative
Open Mon-Thurs 10-8, Fri 10-6, Sat 10-5
Friends of the Library Group
Branches: 1
WILLIAM C GORDON LEARNING CENTER, Gus Velasco Neighborhood Center, 9255 Pioneer Blvd, 90670. Tel: 562-692-0261.
Library Holdings: Bk Vols 500; Per Subs 15

SANTA MARIA

J ALLAN HANCOCK COLLEGE*, Library & Learning Resources, 800 S College Dr, 93455. SAN 301-584X. Tel: 805-922-6966, Ext 3224. Reference Tel: 805-922-6966, Ext 3322. Administration Tel: 805-922-6966, Ext 3215. E-mail: library@hancockcollege.edu. Web Site: www.hancockcollege.edu. *Dean,* Mary Patrick; Tel: 805-922-6966, Ext 3475, E-mail: mary.patrick@hancockcollege.edu; *Fac Librn,* Susannah Kopecky; Tel: 805-922-6966, Ext 3453, E-mail: susannah.kopecky@hancockcollege.edu; *Lead Multi-Media Tech,* Mildred Carpenter; Tel: 805-922-6966, Ext 3637, E-mail: mcarpenter@hancockcollege.edu; Staff 3 (MLS 3)
Founded 1920. Enrl 10,000; Fac 141; Highest Degree: Associate
Library Holdings: Bk Titles 50,000; Bk Vols 70,000; Per Subs 334
Special Collections: Theatre
Automation Activity & Vendor Info: (Cataloging) Ex Libris Group; (Circulation) Ex Libris Group; (OPAC) Ex Libris Group
Wireless access
Partic in Gold Coast Library Network
Friends of the Library Group

GL SANTA BARBARA COUNTY LAW LIBRARY, Santa Maria Branch, 312 E Cook St, 93454. SAN 301-5858. Tel: 805-346-7548. FAX: 805-346-7692. E-mail: info@countylawlibrary.org. Web Site: www.countylawlibrary.org/. *Dir,* Ray MacGregor; Staff 8 (Non-MLS 8)
Library Holdings: Bk Titles 48,963
Subject Interests: Fed law, State law
Wireless access
Open Mon-Fri 8-12 & 1-4
Restriction: Access at librarian's discretion, Circ limited

P SANTA MARIA PUBLIC LIBRARY*, 421 S McClelland St, 93454-5116. SAN 335-0134. Tel: 805-925-0994. FAX: 805-922-2330. Reference E-mail: libraryreference@cityofsantamaria.org. Web Site: www.cityofsantamaria.org/library. *City Librn,* Mary Housel; Tel: 805 925-0994, Ext 2322, E-mail: mhousel@cityofsantamaria.org; Staff 12 (MLS 7, Non-MLS 5)
Founded 1907. Pop 146,488; Circ 505,754
Jul 2015-Jun 2016 Income (Main & Associated Libraries) $3,141,699, State $32,661, City $1,753,000, County $1,144,437, Locally Generated Income $99,837, Other $111,764. Mats Exp $194,859, Books $94,086, Per/Ser (Incl. Access Fees) $13,645, AV Mat $33,577, Electronic Ref Mat (Incl. Access Fees) $53,551
Library Holdings: AV Mats 13,721; DVDs 18,490; e-books 144,721; Bk Vols 197,538; Per Subs 256
Special Collections: State Document Depository
Subject Interests: Genealogy, Local hist
Automation Activity & Vendor Info: (Acquisitions) Innovative Interfaces, Inc; (Cataloging) Innovative Interfaces, Inc; (Circulation) Innovative Interfaces, Inc; (ILL) Innovative Interfaces, Inc; (OPAC) Innovative Interfaces, Inc
Wireless access
Function: 24/7 Electronic res, 24/7 Online cat, Adult bk club, Adult literacy prog, After school storytime, Art exhibits, Audiobks via web, Bilingual assistance for Spanish patrons, Bks on CD, Children's prog, Computer training, Computers for patron use, Digital talking bks, E-Readers, Electronic databases & coll, For res purposes, Free DVD rentals, Games & aids for people with disabilities, Genealogy discussion group, Govt ref serv, Health sci info serv, Holiday prog, Homework prog, ILL available, Internet access, Large print keyboards, Learning ctr, Life-long learning prog for all ages, Magazines, Magnifiers for reading, Mail & tel request accepted, Meeting rooms, Microfiche/film & reading machines, Movies, Music CDs, Online cat, Outreach serv, OverDrive digital audio bks, Photocopying/Printing, Preschool outreach, Preschool reading prog, Printer for laptops & handheld devices, Prog for adults, Prog for children & young adult, Ref & res, Ref serv available, Scanner, Senior outreach, Serves people with intellectual disabilities, Spanish lang bks, Spoken cassettes & CDs, Spoken cassettes & DVDs, Story hour, Study rm, Summer reading prog, Teen prog, Telephone ref, VHS videos, Visual arts prog, Wheelchair accessible
Mem of Black Gold Cooperative Library System
Partic in Gold Coast Library Network
Special Services for the Deaf - ADA equip; Interpreter on staff; Sign lang interpreter upon request for prog; Staff with knowledge of sign lang; Video relay services
Special Services for the Blind - Bks & mags in Braille, on rec, tape & cassette; Bks on CD; Digital talking bk; Digital talking bk machines; Extensive large print coll; Large print bks; Magnifiers; Merlin electronic magnifier reader; Talking bks & player equip; Talking bks from Braille Inst
Open Mon-Thurs 10-8, Fri & Sat 10-6
Friends of the Library Group
Branches: 4
CUYAMA BRANCH, 4689 Hwy 166, Cuyama, 93254, SAN 335-0169. Tel: 661-766-2490.
Founded 1970. Pop 1,328; Circ 5,608

Library Holdings: Bk Vols 7,184
Subject Interests: Local hist
Function: 24/7 Electronic res, 24/7 Online cat, Bks on CD, Computers for patron use, Electronic databases & coll, Free DVD rentals, Online cat
Open Mon 2-6, Wed 3-7, Fri 3-6
GUADALUPE BRANCH, 4719 W Main St, Unit D, Guadalupe, 93434, SAN 335-0193. Tel: 805-343-1405.
Founded 1911. Pop 7,205; Circ 8,878
Library Holdings: Bk Vols 9,959
Function: 24/7 Electronic res, 24/7 Online cat, Bks on CD, Computers for patron use, Free DVD rentals, Internet access, Magazines, OverDrive digital audio bks, Photocopying/Printing
Open Mon-Fri 12:30-6, Sat 11-3:30
Friends of the Library Group
ORCUTT BRANCH, 175 S Broadway, Orcutt, 93455, SAN 335-0258. Tel: 805-937-6483.
Founded 1910. Pop 33,978; Circ 89,527
Library Holdings: Bk Vols 27,640
Function: 24/7 Electronic res, 24/7 Online cat, Bks on CD, Children's prog, Computers for patron use, Electronic databases & coll, Free DVD rentals, Internet access, Magazines, Magnifiers for reading, Online cat, Photocopying/Printing, Story hour, Wheelchair accessible
Open Mon-Thurs 11-6, Fri 2-6, Sat 10-2
Friends of the Library Group

SANTA MONICA

L BRYAN CAVE LEIGHTON PAISNER LLP*, Law Library, 120 Broadway, Ste 300, 90401-2386. SAN 327-6287. Tel: 310-576-2100. FAX: 310-576-2200. *Mgr, Libr Serv,* Karen Lasnick
Library Holdings: Bk Vols 60,000
Subject Interests: Corporate law, Intellectual property, Intl trade, Labor, Litigation, Real estate, Securities law
Restriction: Private libr

M PROVIDENCE - SAINT JOHN'S HEALTH CENTER*, John Wayne Cancer Institute Library, 2200 Santa Monica Blvd, 90404. SAN 301-5920. Tel: 310-582-7141. FAX: 310-582-7353. Web Site: california.providence.org/john-wayne. *Librn,* Gina Worthington; E-mail: worthingtong@jwci.org; Staff 1 (Non-MLS 1)
Founded 1952
Library Holdings: Bk Vols 300; Per Subs 200
Subject Interests: Allied health, Med, Nursing
Restriction: Staff use only

S RAND CORPORATION LIBRARY*, 1776 Main St, M1LIB, 90407. SAN 301-5912. Tel: 310-393-0411, Ext 7788. FAX: 310-451-7029. E-mail: library@rand.org. Web Site: www.rand.org. *Dir,* Lucy S Wegner; Tel: 310-393-0411, Ext 6940, E-mail: lwegner@rand.org; *Assoc Dir,* Susan Scheiberg; E-mail: susanls@rand.org; Staff 21 (MLS 14, Non-MLS 7)
Founded 1948
Special Collections: RAND Corporate Archives; RAND Publications Archive
Subject Interests: Behav sci, Civil justice, Criminal justice, Econ, Educ, Environ, Intl relations, Labor, Mil sci, Pub safety, Sci tech, Terrorism, Transportation
Automation Activity & Vendor Info: (Cataloging) EOS International; (Circulation) EOS International; (Course Reserve) EOS International; (ILL) OCLC ILLiad; (OPAC) EOS International; (Serials) EOS International
Wireless access
Function: Bus archives
Partic in OCLC Online Computer Library Center, Inc; Statewide California Electronic Library Consortium
Restriction: Authorized personnel only, Authorized scholars by appt, Circulates for staff only, Employees only, In-house use for visitors, Internal use only, Not open to pub

J SANTA MONICA COLLEGE LIBRARY, 1900 Pico Blvd, 90405-1628. SAN 301-5939. Tel: 310-434-4334. Reference Tel: 310-434-4254. Web Site: www.smc.edu/student-support/academic-support/library. *Interim Dir, Libr & Info Serv,* Steve Hunt; E-mail: hunt_steve@smc.edu; *Ref (Info Servs),* Brenda Antrim; E-mail: antrim_brenda@smc.edu; Staff 11 (MLS 4, Non-MLS 7)
Founded 1929. Enrl 12,000; Fac 300; Highest Degree: Associate
Library Holdings: Bk Titles 98,000; Bk Vols 105,000; Per Subs 30
Automation Activity & Vendor Info: (Acquisitions) Ex Libris Group; (Cataloging) Ex Libris Group; (Circulation) Ex Libris Group; (Course Reserve) Ex Libris Group; (OPAC) Ex Libris Group
Wireless access
Partic in California Community College Library Consortium; OCLC Online Computer Library Center, Inc
Open Mon-Thurs 8am-9:45pm, Fri 8-3:45, Sat 11-4:45

P SANTA MONICA PUBLIC LIBRARY*, 601 Santa Monica Blvd, 90401. SAN 335-0282. Tel: 310-458-8600. Circulation Tel: 310-458-8614. Reference Tel: 310-434-2608. Administration Tel: 310-458-8606. TDD: 310-395-8499. Web Site: www.smpl.org. *Dir, Libr Serv,* Patricia Wong; E-mail: patty.wong@smgov.net; *Asst City Librn,* Erica Cuyugan; E-mail: erica.cuyugan@smgov.net; *Principal Librn, Pub & Br Serv,* Cecilia Tovar; E-mail: cecilia.tovar@smgov.net; *Principal Librn, Ref,* Susan Lamb; E-mail: susan.lamb@smgov.net; Staff 41 (MLS 39, Non-MLS 2)
Founded 1890. Pop 92,185; Circ 1,757,971
Jul 2012-Jun 2013 Income (Main & Associated Libraries) $11,966,621, City $11,451,906, Federal $19,000, Locally Generated Income $488,054, Other $7,661. Mats Exp $1,101,000, Books $558,420, Per/Ser (Incl. Access Fees) $104,600, AV Mat $276,240, Electronic Ref Mat (Incl. Access Fees) $155,740, Presv $6,000. Sal $6,483,619
Library Holdings: AV Mats 73,000; e-books 4,485; Electronic Media & Resources 29; Bk Titles 279,000; Bk Vols 348,000; Per Subs 774
Special Collections: Santa Monica History & Biography Coll, card file & photog
Automation Activity & Vendor Info: (Acquisitions) Innovative Interfaces, Inc; (Cataloging) Innovative Interfaces, Inc; (Circulation) Innovative Interfaces, Inc; (ILL) OCLC WorldShare Interlibrary Loan; (OPAC) BiblioCommons; (Serials) Innovative Interfaces, Inc
Wireless access
Function: Adult bk club, Audiobks via web, Bilingual assistance for Spanish patrons, Bk club(s), Bks on CD, Children's prog, Computer training, Computers for patron use, Electronic databases & coll, Free DVD rentals, Homebound delivery serv, ILL available, Internet access, Large print keyboards, Magazines, Mango lang, Microfiche/film & reading machines, Music CDs, Online cat, OverDrive digital audio bks, Photocopying/Printing, Prog for adults, Prog for children & young adult, Ref serv available, Senior computer classes, Spanish lang bks, Story hour, Study rm, Summer reading prog, Teen prog, Telephone ref, Wheelchair accessible
Partic in Southern California Library Cooperative
Special Services for the Deaf - Assisted listening device
Special Services for the Blind - Magnifiers
Open Mon-Thurs 10-9, Fri & Sat 10-5:30, Sun 1-5
Restriction: Non-resident fee
Friends of the Library Group
Branches: 4
FAIRVIEW, 2101 Ocean Park Blvd, 90405-5013, SAN 335-0312. Tel: 310-458-8681. FAX: 310-450-5749. *Br Mgr,* Robert Graves; E-mail: robert.graves@smgov.net
Library Holdings: Bk Vols 54,916
Open Mon-Thurs Noon-9, Fri Noon-5:30, Sat 10-5:30
Friends of the Library Group
MONTANA AVENUE, 1704 Montana Ave, 90403, SAN 335-0347. Tel: 310-458-8682. FAX: 310-829-6391. *Br Mgr,* Stephanie Archer; E-mail: stephanie.archer@smgov.net; Staff 2 (MLS 2)
Library Holdings: Bk Vols 46,870
Open Mon-Thurs Noon-9, Fri Noon-5:30, Sat 10-5:30
Friends of the Library Group
OCEAN PARK, 2601 Main St, 90405, SAN 335-0371. Tel: 310-458-8683. FAX: 310-399-6739. *Br Mgr,* Karen Reitz; E-mail: karen.reitz@smgov.net; Staff 2 (MLS 2)
Library Holdings: Bk Vols 33,237
Open Mon-Thurs Noon-9, Fri Noon-5:30, Sat 10-5:30
Friends of the Library Group
PICO BRANCH LIBRARY, 2201 Pico Blvd, 90404. Tel: 310-458-8684. FAX: 424-280-7830. *Br Mgr,* Silvia Cisneros; E-mail: silvia.cisneros@smgov.net
Library Holdings: Bk Titles 27,140
Open Mon-Thurs 12-9, Fri 12-5:30, Sat 10-5:30

SANTA PAULA

P BLANCHARD-SANTA PAULA LIBRARY DISTRICT, Blanchard Community Library, 119 N Eighth St, 93060-2709. SAN 301-5963. Tel: 805-525-3615. FAX: 805-933-2324. Web Site: www.blanchardlibrary.org. *District Dir,* Ned Branch; E-mail: ned.branch@blanchardlibrary.org; Staff 3 (MLS 2, Non-MLS 1)
Founded 1909. Pop 34,000; Circ 79,000
Library Holdings: AV Mats 1,873; Bks on Deafness & Sign Lang 12; CDs 520; DVDs 500; Large Print Bks 1,276; Music Scores 37; Bk Vols 88,000; Per Subs 75; Videos 1,400
Special Collections: Spanish/Bilingual (Preciado Coll)
Subject Interests: Local authors, Local hist
Automation Activity & Vendor Info: (Acquisitions) Innovative Interfaces, Inc; (Cataloging) Innovative Interfaces, Inc; (Circulation) Innovative Interfaces, Inc; (ILL) Innovative Interfaces, Inc; (OPAC) Innovative Interfaces, Inc; (Serials) Innovative Interfaces, Inc
Wireless access
Function: 24/7 Electronic res, 24/7 Online cat, Accelerated reader prog, Adult bk club, Adult literacy prog, Art exhibits, Audiobks via web, BA reader (adult literacy), Bilingual assistance for Spanish patrons, Bk club(s),

Bks on CD, Children's prog, Computer training, Computers for patron use, Digital talking bks, Electronic databases & coll, Family literacy, Free DVD rentals, Holiday prog, Homebound delivery serv, Homework prog, ILL available, Internet access, Literacy & newcomer serv, Magazines, Magnifiers for reading, Mail & tel request accepted, Meeting rooms, Movies, Online cat, Online ref, OverDrive digital audio bks, Photocopying/Printing, Prof lending libr, Prog for adults, Prog for children & young adult, Ref & res, Ref serv available, Spanish lang bks, Story hour, Summer reading prog, Tax forms, Teen prog, Telephone ref, Wheelchair accessible
Mem of Black Gold Cooperative Library System
Open Mon, Tues & Thurs 12-8, Wed 10-6, Sat 10-2
Restriction: Open to pub for ref & circ; with some limitations, Open to students, Pub ref by request, Pub use on premises
Friends of the Library Group

C THOMAS AQUINAS COLLEGE*, Saint Bernardine of Siena Library, 10000 N Ojai Rd, 93060-9980. SAN 321-4621. Tel: 805-525-4417. Circulation Tel: 805-525-4419, Ext 5948. FAX: 805-525-9342. Web Site: www.thomasaquinas.edu. *Librn Emeritus,* Viltis A Jatulis; E-mail: vjatulis@thomasaquinas.edu; *Librn,* Richena Curphey; E-mail: rcurphey@thomasaquinas.edu; Staff 1 (MLS 1)
Founded 1971. Enrl 375; Fac 50; Highest Degree: Bachelor
Library Holdings: AV Mats 5,540; Bk Vols 69,000; Per Subs 69; Talking Bks 400
Subject Interests: Humanities, Philos, Theol
Automation Activity & Vendor Info: (Serials) EBSCO Online
Wireless access
Open Mon-Thurs 8am-10:45pm, Fri 8-7, Sat 1-5, Sun 1-10:45
Restriction: Open to fac, students & qualified researchers

SANTA ROSA

J SANTA ROSA JUNIOR COLLEGE*, Frank P Doyle Library, 1501 Mendocino Ave, 95401. SAN 301-6005. Circulation Tel: 707-527-4550. Interlibrary Loan Service Tel: 707-527-4554. Reference Tel: 707-527-4548. Interlibrary Loan Service FAX: 707-521-6070. Web Site: libraries.santarosa.edu. *Dean, Learning Res,* Mary-Catherine Oxford; Tel: 707-527-4392, E-mail: moxford@santarosa.edu; *Electronic Serv Librn,* Erin Daniels; Tel: 707-527-4773, E-mail: edaniels@santarosa.edu; *Librn,* Smita Avasthi; Tel: 707-524-1839, E-mail: savasthi@santarosa.edu; *Librn,* Canon Crawford; Tel: 707-527-4904, E-mail: ccrawford@santarosa.edu; *Librn,* Jessica Harris; Tel: 707-778-2425, E-mail: jharris@santarosa.edu; *Librn,* Samantha Lange; Tel: 707-778-3972; *Librn,* Molly Matheson; Tel: 707-778-4162, E-mail: mmatheson@santarosa.edu; *Librn,* Nancy Persons; Tel: 707-521-6902, E-mail: npersons@santarosa.edu; *Librn,* Phyllis Usina; Tel: 707-527-4547, E-mail: pusina@santarosa.edu; *Tech Serv Librn,* Eve-Marie Miller; Tel: 707-527-4544; Staff 9 (MLS 9)
Founded 1918
Library Holdings: Bk Vols 129,197; Per Subs 356
Automation Activity & Vendor Info: (Acquisitions) Ex Libris Group; (Cataloging) Ex Libris Group; (Circulation) Ex Libris Group; (Course Reserve) Ex Libris Group; (ILL) Ex Libris Group; (Media Booking) Ex Libris Group; (OPAC) Ex Libris Group; (Serials) Ex Libris Group
Wireless access
Mem of NorthNet Library System
Partic in Coop Libr Agency for Syst & Servs; OCLC Online Computer Library Center, Inc
Restriction: Borrowing privileges limited to fac & registered students
Friends of the Library Group

S SANTA ROSA PRESS DEMOCRAT*, News Research Center, 427 Mendocino Ave, 95401. (Mail add: PO Box 910, 95402-0910), SAN 325-0512. Tel: 707-526-8520. FAX: 707-521-5330. Web Site: www.pressdemocrat.com. *Res,* Janet Balicki; E-mail: janet.balicki@pressdemocrat.com; Staff 5 (MLS 2, Non-MLS 3)
Founded 1950
Special Collections: Glossy Photographs (In-house Photography Coll); Newspaper Clippings (Subject & Biographical Info Coll); Rare Local Photographs
Subject Interests: Local hist

GL SONOMA COUNTY PUBLIC LAW LIBRARY*, 2604 Ventura Ave, 95403. SAN 301-6013. Tel: 707-565-2668. FAX: 707-565-1126. Web Site: www.sonomacountylawlibrary.org. *Libr Mgr,* Nikolaos Pelekis; E-mail: nikolaos.pelekis@sonoma-county.org; *Libr Tech,* Douglas Sutro
Founded 1891
Library Holdings: Bk Vols 29,000
Wireless access
Function: Audio & video playback equip for onsite use, CD-ROM, Computers for patron use, Electronic databases & coll, For res purposes, Meeting rooms, Microfiche/film & reading machines, Scanner, Study rm, Wheelchair accessible
Publications: List of Holdings; Union List of Legal Periodicals in Sonoma County
Open Mon-Fri 8-4, Sat 10-4
Friends of the Library Group

SANTA YNEZ

S SANTA YNEZ VALLEY HISTORICAL SOCIETY*, Ellen Gleason Library, 3596 Sagunto St, 93460. (Mail add: PO Box 181, 93460), SAN 328-3364. Tel: 805-688-7889. FAX: 805-688-1109. E-mail: syvm@verizon.net. Web Site: www.santaynezmuseum.org. *Exec Dir,* Brian Stenforf
Library Holdings: Bk Titles 1,500
Subject Interests: Calif, Chumash Indian, Local hist, Santa Ynez Valley
Wireless access
Function: Res libr

SANTEE

CR SAN DIEGO CHRISTIAN COLLEGE & SOUTHERN CALIFORNIA SEMINARY LIBRARY, c/o San Diego Christian College, 200 Riverview Pkwy, 92071. SAN 331-9148. Tel: 619-201-8680. Circulation Tel: 619-201-8966. Interlibrary Loan Service Tel: 619-201-8778. Reference Tel: 619-201 8683. E-mail: library@sdcc.edu. Web Site: library.sdcc.edu. *College Library Director, Syst Librn,* Matt Owen; E-mail: mowen@sdcc.edu; *Seminary Library Director,* Jennifer Ewing; Tel: 619-201-8967, E-mail: jewing@socalsem.edu; *Operations Librn,* Mona Hsu; E-mail: mhsu@sdcc.edu; *Libr Asst,* Kathie Russell; E-mail: krussell@socalsem.edu; Staff 4 (MLS 3, Non-MLS 1)
Founded 1970. Enrl 790; Highest Degree: Master
Jul 2019-Jun 2020. Mats Exp $139,905. Sal $273,989
Library Holdings: Audiobooks 1,029; AV Mats 1,357; e-books 639,328; e-journals 39,906; Electronic Media & Resources 89; Bk Titles 75,573; Per Subs 68; Videos 26,871
Subject Interests: Biblical studies, Psychol
Automation Activity & Vendor Info: (Acquisitions) OCLC; (Cataloging) OCLC; (Circulation) OCLC; (Discovery) OCLC; (ILL) OCLC; (OPAC) OCLC
Wireless access
Partic in Association of Christian Librarians; Christian Library Consortium; OCLC Online Computer Library Center, Inc; Statewide California Electronic Library Consortium
Open Mon-Thurs 7:30am-10:30pm, Fri 7:30-5, Sat 11-5

SARATOGA

J WEST VALLEY COMMUNITY COLLEGE LIBRARY*, 14000 Fruitvale Ave, 95070-5698. SAN 301-6021. Tel: 408-741-2021. Interlibrary Loan Service Tel: 408-741-2028. Reference Tel: 408-741-2029. Web Site: www.westvalley.edu/library. *Acq Librn,* Yanghee Kim; Tel: 408-741-2484, E-mail: yanghee.kim@westvalley.edu; *Outreach & Instruction Librn,* Maryanne Mills; Tel: 408-741-4661, E-mail: maryanne.mills@westvalley.edu; *Syst Librn,* Rachel Sandoval; Tel: 408-741-2479, E-mail: rachel.sandoval@wvm.edu; *Tech Serv Librn,* Betsy Sandford; Tel: 408-741-2478, E-mail: betsy.sandford@westvalley.edu; Staff 15 (MLS 6, Non-MLS 9)
Founded 1964. Enrl 10,505; Fac 443; Highest Degree: Associate
Library Holdings: AV Mats 18,268; CDs 200; e-books 400; Bk Titles 81,500; Bk Vols 101,000; Per Subs 164; Talking Bks 2,200
Automation Activity & Vendor Info: (Acquisitions) Innovative Interfaces, Inc; (Cataloging) Innovative Interfaces, Inc; (Circulation) Innovative Interfaces, Inc; (Course Reserve) Innovative Interfaces, Inc; (ILL) Innovative Interfaces, Inc; (OPAC) Innovative Interfaces, Inc
Wireless access
Partic in OCLC Online Computer Library Center, Inc
Special Services for the Deaf - Bks on deafness & sign lang; Closed caption videos; Videos & decoder
Special Services for the Blind - Aids for in-house use; Audio mat; Bks on cassette; Bks on CD; Cassette playback machines; Closed circuit TV; Closed circuit TV magnifier; Computer with voice synthesizer for visually impaired persons; Low vision equip; Magnifiers; PC for people with disabilities; Screen enlargement software for people with visual disabilities; Screen reader software; Talking bks; ZoomText magnification & reading software
Open Mon-Thurs 8-7:30, Fri 8-Noon, Sat Noon-4

SAUSALITO

P SAUSALITO PUBLIC LIBRARY*, 420 Litho St, 94965. SAN 301-603X. Tel: 415-289-4121. Administration Tel: 415-289-4123. Reference E-mail: reference@sausalito.gov. Web Site: www.ci.sausalito.ca.us/library, www.sausalitolibrary.org. *City Librn,* Mr Abbot Chambers; E-mail: achambers@sausalito.gov; *Asst City Librn,* Augie Webb; E-mail: awebb@sausalito.gov; *Librn I,* Julieanne Randolph; E-mail: jrandolph@sausalito.gov; *Sr Libr Asst,* Rebecca Burgan; E-mail: rburgan@sausalito.gov; Staff 3 (MLS 3)
Founded 1906. Pop 7,325; Circ 89,000
Library Holdings: CDs 950; DVDs 611; Bk Vols 61,000; Per Subs 185

Subject Interests: Boating, Boats, Local hist
Automation Activity & Vendor Info: (Acquisitions) Innovative Interfaces, Inc; (Cataloging) Brodart; (Circulation) Innovative Interfaces, Inc; (OPAC) Innovative Interfaces, Inc
Wireless access
Mem of NorthNet Library System
Partic in Marin Automated Resources & Information Network
Open Mon-Thurs 10-9, Fri & Sat 10-5, Sun 12-5
Friends of the Library Group

SEASIDE

C CALIFORNIA STATE UNIVERSITY - MONTEREY BAY*, Tanimura & Antle Family Memorial Library, 3054 Divarty St, 93955. SAN 378-2530. Tel: 831-582-3733. Interlibrary Loan Service Tel: 831-582-3870. Reference Tel: 831-582-3872. FAX: 831-582-3875. E-mail: library_reference@csumb.edu. Web Site: csumb.edu/library. *Interim Dean of Libr,* Jacqueline Grallo; Tel: 831-582-3142, E-mail: jgrallo@csumb.edu; *Assoc Librn,* Sarah Dahlen; Tel: 831-582-4432, E-mail: sdahlen@csumb.edu; *Assoc Librn,* Jacqueline Grallo; Tel: 831-582-3142, E-mail: jgrallo@csumb.edu; *Assoc Librn,* Kathlene Hanson; Tel: 831-582-3883, E-mail: khanson@csumb.edu; *Librn,* Pam Baker; Tel: 831-582-3887, E-mail: pbaker@csumb.edu; Staff 15.2 (MLS 8.2, Non-MLS 7)
Founded 1995. Enrl 6,000; Fac 7; Highest Degree: Master. Sal $1,027,432 (Prof $661,626)
Library Holdings: AV Mats 3,085; e-books 73,595; e-journals 50,386; Microforms 175; Bk Vols 87,595; Per Subs 50,542; Videos 2,828
Special Collections: Environmental Clean-up (Ford Ord Reuse Coll)
Automation Activity & Vendor Info: (Acquisitions) Ex Libris Group; (Cataloging) Ex Libris Group; (Circulation) Ex Libris Group; (Course Reserve) Ex Libris Group; (ILL) OCLC ILLiad; (OPAC) Ex Libris Group; (Serials) Ex Libris Group
Wireless access
Function: Distance learning, Doc delivery serv, Electronic databases & coll, Learning ctr, Microfiche/film & reading machines, Online cat, Online info literacy tutorials on the web & in blackboard, Online ref, Telephone ref, Wheelchair accessible
Partic in Monterey Bay Area Cooperative Library System
Open Mon-Thurs 8am-Midnight, Fri 8-5, Sat 10-5, Sun 2-Midnight

SIERRA MADRE

P SIERRA MADRE PUBLIC LIBRARY*, 440 W Sierra Madre Blvd, 91024-2399. SAN 301-6102. Tel: 626-355-7186. E-mail: ref@cityofsierramadre.com. Web Site: www.cityofsierramadre.com/services/library. *City Librn,* Christine Smart; Staff 9 (MLS 4, Non-MLS 5)
Founded 1887. Pop 10,850
Library Holdings: Bk Vols 59,500; Per Subs 99; Videos 1,612
Special Collections: Sierra Madre Historical Archives
Automation Activity & Vendor Info: (Acquisitions) Biblionix/Apollo; (Cataloging) Biblionix/Apollo; (Circulation) Biblionix/Apollo; (OPAC) Biblionix/Apollo
Wireless access
Function: 24/7 Electronic res, 24/7 Online cat, Adult bk club, Archival coll, Audiobks on Playaways & MP3, Audiobks via web, Bk club(s), Bks on CD, Children's prog, Computers for patron use, Electronic databases & coll, ILL available, Internet access, Life-long learning prog for all ages, Magazines, Magnifiers for reading, Microfiche/film & reading machines, Music CDs, Online cat, Online ref, OverDrive digital audio bks, Photocopying/Printing, Preschool outreach, Prog for adults, Prog for children & young adult, Ref & res, Ref serv available, Scanner, Senior outreach, Spanish lang bks, Story hour, Summer reading prog, Tax forms, Teen prog, Telephone ref
Partic in Southern California Library Cooperative
Special Services for the Blind - Bks on CD; Copier with enlargement capabilities; Large print bks; Magnifiers; Playaways (bks on MP3)
Open Mon-Wed 11-8, Thurs & Sat 10-6
Friends of the Library Group

SIGNAL HILL

P SIGNAL HILL PUBLIC LIBRARY*, 1800 E Hill St, 90755. SAN 301-6110. Tel: 562-989-7323. Administration Tel: 562-989-7324. FAX: 562-989-7392. E-mail: Library2@cityofsignalhill.org. Web Site: cityofsignalhill.org/119/Signal-Hill-Public-Library. *Librn,* Charles Hughes; E-mail: chughes@cityofsignalhill.org; Staff 1 (Non-MLS 1)
Founded 1928. Pop 11,089; Circ 44,024
Library Holdings: AV Mats 1,093; DVDs 300; Large Print Bks 200; Bk Titles 24,052; Bk Vols 24,400; Per Subs 60; Talking Bks 121; Videos 400
Subject Interests: Local hist
Automation Activity & Vendor Info: (Cataloging) Follett Software; (Circulation) Follett Software; (OPAC) Follett Software
Wireless access
Partic in Califa; Southern California Library Cooperative
Open Mon, Tues & Thurs 12-8, Wed, Fri & Sat 10-5
Friends of the Library Group

SIMI VALLEY

S NATIONAL ARCHIVES & RECORDS ADMINISTRATION, Ronald Reagan Presidential Library & Museum, 40 Presidential Dr, 93065. SAN 373-0956. Tel: 805-577-4000. Toll Free Tel: 800-410-8354. FAX: 805-577-4074. E-mail: reagan.library@nara.gov. Web Site: www.reaganlibrary.gov. *Dir,* Duke Blackwood; Tel: 805-577-4014, E-mail: duke.blackwood@nara.gov; *Actg Dep Dir,* Ira Pemstein; Tel: 805-577-4073, E-mail: ira.pemstein@nara.gov; Staff 13 (MLS 4, Non-MLS 9)
Founded 1991
Library Holdings: Bk Titles 5,000; Per Subs 12
Special Collections: American Presidency, Ronald Reagan; Politics & Government, 1964-1989
Subject Interests: Am hist
Automation Activity & Vendor Info: (Cataloging) Inmagic, Inc.
Wireless access
Function: Archival coll
Restriction: Closed stack, Non-circulating, Not a lending libr, Secured area only open to authorized personnel

S SIMI VALLEY HISTORICAL SOCIETY & MUSEUM*, 137 Strathearn Pl, 93065-1605. SAN 370-4238. Tel: 805-526-6453. FAX: 805-526-6462. E-mail: simimuseum@sbcglobal.net. Web Site: www.simihistory.com. *City Historian, Dir,* Patricia Havens
Publications: Simi Valley, A Journey Through Time (Local historical information)
Open Tues-Fri 9-3, Sat & Sun 1-4
Restriction: Non-circulating

P SIMI VALLEY LIBRARY*, 2969 Tapo Canyon Rd, 93063. SAN 335-265X. Tel: 805-526-1735. FAX: 805-526-1738. Web Site: www.simivalleylibrary.org. *Dir,* Kelly Behle; E-mail: kelly.behle@simivalleylibrary.org; *Ad,* Jeremy Scarlet; *Teen Serv Librn,* Michael Whitehead; *Youth Serv Librn,* Katey Dager; *Mkt Coordr, Vols Coordr,* Lyssa Dueker; Staff 13 (MLS 2, Non-MLS 11)
Founded 1916. Pop 152,437; Circ 413,525
Library Holdings: Bk Vols 142,479
Wireless access
Open Mon-Thurs 10-8, Fri & Sun 1-5, Sat 10-5
Friends of the Library Group

SONORA

J COLUMBIA COLLEGE LIBRARY*, 11600 Columbia College Dr, 95370-8581. SAN 300-6794. Tel: 209-588-5119. FAX: 209-588-5121. Web Site: www.gocolumbia.edu/library. *Librn,* Brian Green; Tel: 209-588-5179, E-mail: greeneb@yosemite.edu; *Circ/Reserves,* Luisa Adams; E-mail: adams@yosemite.edu; Staff 1 (MLS 1)
Founded 1968. Enrl 3,656; Fac 168
Special Collections: History of the Mother Lode, ephemera, bk, maps, micro, per. Oral History
Subject Interests: Forestry
Wireless access
Publications: Mother Lode History (Bibliography)
Partic in 49-99 Cooperative Library System; OCLC Online Computer Library Center, Inc
Open Mon-Thurs 7:30-5:30, Fri 7:30-4 (Summer); Mon-Fri 7:30-7:45, Fri 7:30-4:30 (Fall-Spring)

S TUOLUMNE COUNTY GENEALOGICAL SOCIETY LIBRARY*, 158 Bradford St, 95370. (Mail add: PO Box 3956, 95370-3956), SAN 322-6956. Tel: 209-532-1317. E-mail: info@tcgen.org. Web Site: www.tcgen.org/library.html. *Libr Dir,* Lori East; *Asst Libr Dir,* Lin Gookin; *Asst Libr Dir,* Betty Sparagna; *Asst Libr Dir,* Susan Strope
Founded 1979
Library Holdings: Bk Vols 1,200; Per Subs 10
Special Collections: Books & Periodicals for Most States; Records for Some Surrounding Counties; Tuolumne County, California Records: Cemetery, Census, Church, Family Histories, Obituaries, School, Vital Records, Voter Registers
Subject Interests: Local family hist
Function: Res libr
Publications: 1890 Great Register, Tuolumne Country (Index to educational materials); CH Burden Undertaking Co Records, 1890-1943 (Index to educational materials); Gold Digger Golden Roots of the Mother Lode (Newsletter); Gold Rush Tales; Index to the History of Tuolumne County (Index to educational materials); Index to the Miners' & Business Mens' Directory (Index to educational materials); Tuolumne County Marriages, 1850-1900 (Index to educational materials)
Open Tues & Thurs 10-4, Sat 10-3:30
Restriction: Pub use on premises, Restricted borrowing privileges

P TUOLUMNE COUNTY PUBLIC LIBRARY*, 480 Greenley Rd, 95370-5956. SAN 301-6145. Tel: 209-533-5507. FAX: 209-533-0936. E-mail: libref@co.tuolumne.ca.us. Web Site: www.tuolumnecounty.ca.gov/library. *Dir, Libr Serv,* Deborah Samson; E-mail: dsamson@co.tuolumne.ca.us; *Ch,* Lynn McCormick; E-mail: lmccormick@co.tuolumne.ca.us; *Libr Operations Supvr,* Anita Simpson; E-mail: asimpson@co.tuolumne.ca.us; *Literacy Coordr,* Gail Sorensen; E-mail: gsorensen@co.tuolumne.ca.us; Staff 8 (MLS 2, Non-MLS 6)
Founded 1917. Pop 55,400; Circ 185,949
Library Holdings: Bk Titles 71,000; Bk Vols 83,000; Per Subs 214
Automation Activity & Vendor Info: (Acquisitions) SirsiDynix; (Cataloging) SirsiDynix; (Circulation) SirsiDynix; (OPAC) SirsiDynix
Wireless access
Partic in 49-99 Cooperative Library System; OCLC Online Computer Library Center, Inc
Open Tues-Sat 10-6
Friends of the Library Group
Branches: 3
GROVELAND BRANCH, 18990 Hwy 120, Groveland, 95321. Tel: 209-962-6144. FAX: 209-962-5178. E-mail: grovlib@co.tuolume.ca.us. *Br Mgr,* Michalene Martin; E-mail: mmartin@co.tuolumne.ca.us
Library Holdings: Large Print Bks 200; Bk Vols 7,000; Per Subs 50; Talking Bks 380; Videos 450
Open Tues-Thurs 1-6, Fri & Sat 10-2
Friends of the Library Group
TUOLUMNE CITY BRANCH, 18636 Main St, Tuolumne, 95379. Tel: 209-928-3612. E-mail: tulib@co.tuolumne.ca.us. *Br Mgr,* Gail Sorensen; E-mail: gsorensen@co.tuolumne.ca.us
Library Holdings: Bk Vols 4,400
Open Tues-Thurs 2-6, Fri & Sat 10-2
TWAIN HARTE BRANCH, 18701 Tiffeni Rd, Ste 1F, Twain Harte, 95383. Tel: 209-586-4501. E-mail: thlib@co.tuolumne.ca.us. *Br Mgr,* Sharyn Alomia; E-mail: salomia@co.tuolumne.ca.us
Library Holdings: Bk Vols 3,800; Per Subs 10
Open Tues-Thurs 1-5, Fri & Sat 10-2
Bookmobiles: 1. Contact, Terry Hoffman. Bk titles 1,000

SOUTH EL MONTE

S AMERICAN SOCIETY OF MILITARY HISTORY MUSEUM*, Tankland Library, 1918 Rosemead Blvd, 91733. SAN 328-039X. Tel: 626-442-1776. E-mail: tankland@aol.com. Web Site: www.tankland.com. *Library Contact,* Craig Michelson; Staff 5 (MLS 2, Non-MLS 3)
Founded 1962
Library Holdings: Bk Titles 40,000
Special Collections: Tankland Coll
Subject Interests: Hist, Mil, Presv
Automation Activity & Vendor Info: (Acquisitions) Koha; (Cataloging) Koha; (Circulation) Koha; (OPAC) Koha; (Serials) Koha
Wireless access
Restriction: Non-circulating, Researchers by appt only, Restricted access

SOUTH LAKE TAHOE

J LAKE TAHOE COMMUNITY COLLEGE*, Roberta Mason Library, One College Dr, 96150. SAN 301-617X. Tel: 530-541-4660, Ext 232. FAX: 530-541-7852. E-mail: library@ltcc.edu. Web Site: ltcc.edu/campusresources/library. *Dir,* Melanie Chu; E-mail: mchu@ltcc.edu; Staff 2 (MLS 2)
Founded 1976
Library Holdings: Bk Titles 43,000; Per Subs 25
Automation Activity & Vendor Info: (Circulation) OCLC; (OPAC) OCLC
Wireless access
Open Mon-Thurs 8-7, Fri 11-4

SOUTH PASADENA

P SOUTH PASADENA PUBLIC LIBRARY*, 1100 Oxley St, 91030. SAN 301-6188. Tel: 626-403-7350. Circulation Tel: 626-403-7340. Administration Tel: 626-403-7330. FAX: 626-403-7331. E-mail: library@southpasadenaca.gov. Web Site: southpasadenaca.gov/government/departments/library. *Libr Dir,* Cathy Warren Billings; E-mail: cbillings@southpasadenaca.gov; Staff 20.5 (MLS 6.5, Non-MLS 14)
Founded 1895. Pop 25,800; Circ 450,000
Jul 2014-Jun 2015 Income $1,537,832. Mats Exp $138,000. Sal $1,157,232 (Prof $550,000)
Library Holdings: AV Mats 4,784; CDs 5,000; DVDs 2,000; High Interest/Low Vocabulary Bk Vols 300; Large Print Bks 1,000; Bk Vols 125,000; Per Subs 400
Special Collections: Plays
Subject Interests: Art, Drama, Local hist
Automation Activity & Vendor Info: (Acquisitions) SirsiDynix; (Cataloging) SirsiDynix; (Circulation) SirsiDynix; (OPAC) SirsiDynix
Wireless access
Function: Bilingual assistance for Spanish patrons, Bks on cassette, Bks on CD, CD-ROM, Children's prog, Computers for patron use, E-Reserves, Electronic databases & coll, Free DVD rentals, Holiday prog, Homebound delivery serv, Homework prog, ILL available, Music CDs, Online ref, Photocopying/Printing, Preschool outreach, Prog for adults, Prog for children & young adult, Ref serv available, Spoken cassettes & CDs, Spoken cassettes & DVDs, Tax forms, Telephone ref, VHS videos, Wheelchair accessible
Publications: South Pasadena: A Centennial History, 1888-1988; Stories from Home: South Pasadena, CA; The South Pasadena Public Library: A History 1895-1982
Partic in OCLC Online Computer Library Center, Inc
Open Mon-Wed 11-9, Thurs & Fri 10-6, Sat 10-5, Sun 1-5
Restriction: Circ to mem only
Friends of the Library Group

SOUTH SAN FRANCISCO

M KAISER PERMANENTE HEALTH SCIENCES LIBRARY*, 1200 El Camino Real, 94080. SAN 320-1708. Tel: 650-742-2540. FAX: 650-742-2239. *Mgr, Libr Serv,* Rebecca Bayrer; Staff 1 (MLS 1)
Founded 1973
Library Holdings: e-books 100; e-journals 4,000; Bk Titles 700
Subject Interests: Health sci, Med, Nursing
Wireless access
Open Mon-Fri 9-5

P SOUTH SAN FRANCISCO PUBLIC LIBRARY*, 840 W Orange Ave, 94080-3125. SAN 335-0495. Tel: 650-829-3860. Administration Tel: 650-829-3863. FAX: 650-829-3866. E-mail: ssfpladm@plsinfo.org. Web Site: www.ssf.net/library. *Dir,* Valerie Sommer; Tel: 650-829-3872, E-mail: sommer@plsinfo.org; *Libr Serv Mgr,* Barbara Bruxvoort; E-mail: bruxvoort@plsinfo.org; Staff 20 (MLS 12, Non-MLS 8)
Founded 1916. Pop 64,067; Circ 723,592
Library Holdings: Audiobooks 13,105; AV Mats 20,852; DVDs 20,314; e-books 7,945; e-journals 6,431; Electronic Media & Resources 25; Bk Vols 172,755; Per Subs 223
Special Collections: South San Francisco Coll. Oral History
Subject Interests: Local hist
Automation Activity & Vendor Info: (Cataloging) Innovative Interfaces, Inc; (Circulation) Innovative Interfaces, Inc; (ILL) OCLC; (OPAC) Innovative Interfaces, Inc
Wireless access
Function: Computers for patron use, Homebound delivery serv, Homework prog, ILL available, Large print keyboards, Learning ctr, Magnifiers for reading, Music CDs, Online cat, OverDrive digital audio bks, Photocopying/Printing, Preschool outreach, Prog for adults, Prog for children & young adult, Ref & res, Ref serv available, Spoken cassettes & CDs, Story hour, Summer reading prog, Tax forms, Teen prog, Telephone ref, Wheelchair accessible, Workshops
Mem of Pacific Library Partnership (PLP)
Special Services for the Deaf - Video relay services
Special Services for the Blind - Reader equip
Open Mon & Tues 10-8, Wed & Fri 10-6, Thurs 12-8, Sat 10-5, Sun 2-5
Friends of the Library Group
Branches: 1
GRAND AVENUE, 306 Walnut Ave, 94080-2700, SAN 335-0525. Tel: 650-877-8530. FAX: 650-829-6615.
Founded 1916
Library Holdings: Bk Vols 48,040
Special Collections: Local History Coll; Spanish Language Coll, bks, DVDs, mags, music CDs
Function: Bilingual assistance for Spanish patrons, Bks on cassette, Bks on CD, Children's prog, Computers for patron use, Electronic databases & coll, Free DVD rentals, ILL available, Music CDs, Online cat, Online ref, Outside serv via phone, mail, e-mail & web, Photocopying/Printing, Prog for adults, Prog for children & young adult, Ref & res, Ref serv available, Spoken cassettes & CDs, Spoken cassettes & DVDs, Story hour, Summer reading prog, Tax forms, Teen prog, Telephone ref, VHS videos, Wheelchair accessible
Open Mon, Tues, Thurs & Fri 10-6, Wed 12-8, Sat 10-5
Friends of the Library Group

STANFORD

S CENTER FOR ADVANCED STUDY IN THE BEHAVIORAL SCIENCES LIBRARY*, 75 Alta Rd, 94305. SAN 301-6196. Tel: 650-736-0100. E-mail: casbs-library@stanford.edu. Web Site: www.casbs.org. *Info Mgr,* Jason Gonzales
Founded 1954
Library Holdings: e-journals 50; Bk Vols 3,500; Per Subs 35
Special Collections: Ralph Tyler Coll
Subject Interests: Anthrop, Hist, Philos, Polit sci, Psychiat, Sociol
Publications: Annual Reports; The Ralph W Tyler Collection, 1954-1979 & 1954-1994

Partic in Proquest Dialog; Research Libraries Information Network
Open Mon-Fri 8-5

C STANFORD UNIVERSITY LIBRARIES*, Cecil H Green Library, 557 Escondido Mall, 94305-6063. SAN 335-055X. Tel: 650-725-1064. Circulation Tel: 650-723-1493. Interlibrary Loan Service Tel: 650-725-1278. Circulation E-mail: greencirc@stanford.edu. Information Services E-mail: infocenter@stanford.edu. Web Site: library.stanford.edu/green. *Univ Librn,* Michael A Keller; Tel: 650-723-5553, E-mail: Michael.Keller@stanford.edu; *Assoc Univ Librn,* Tom Cramer; E-mail: tcramer@stanford.edu; *Assoc Univ Librn, Eng & Sci,* Robert Schwarzwalder; E-mail: rns@stanford.edu; *Dir, Communications & Develop,* Gabrielle Karampelas; E-mail: gkaram@stanford.edu; *Dir, Human Res,* Catalina Rodriguez; E-mail: cjara@stanford.edu
Founded 1919. Enrl 15,666; Fac 1,903; Highest Degree: Doctorate
Library Holdings: e-books 1,130,723; Music Scores 92,484; Bk Vols 6,474,233; Per Subs 436,966; Videos 58,505
Special Collections: American (Joyce Carol Thomas Coll); Archives & Professional Papers (Lourdes Portillo & Lynn Hershmann Coll); Artwork & Documentation Related to the Execution of the Stanford Memorial Church Mosaics by the Venetian Company A Salviati & Co; California (Borel Coll); Chicano (Ester M Hernandez Coll & Rolando Hinojosa-Smith Coll), ms; Children's Literature (Schofield Coll); Doug Menuez & Ira Nowinski Colls, photog; Engineering Mechanics (Timoshenko Coll); English & American Literature of the 19th & 20th Centuries (Felton Coll); Gunst Memorial Library (Book Arts), bks, ms; Hebraica & Judaica (Taube/Baron Coll & Samson Copenhagen Coll), bks, ms; History (Elmer E Robinson Coll); History of Science (Barchas, Brasch & Dudley Coll); Hopkins Transportation Library; Irish Literature (Healy Coll), bks, ms; Latin America (Jose Guadalupe Posada, Taller de Grafica Popular & Felipe Ehernberg Coll); Memorial Library of Music, bks, ms; Oscar I Norwich Coll, maps; Slavic (Andrei Voznesenskii Coll); Stanford Professor Emeritus Marjorie Perloff Papers; Tel Aviv (Eliasaf Robison Coll), 1909-1948; Theatre Coll. State Document Depository; UN Document Depository; US Document Depository
Subject Interests: Archit, Art, Bus & mgt, Computer sci, Educ, Hist, Law, Lit, Marine biol, Math, Med, Music, Natural sci, Physics, Soc sci & issues
Wireless access
Publications: A Vast & Useful Art: The Gustave Gimon Collection on French Political Economy; Catching the Light: Remembering Wallace Stegner; Contemporary Polish Book Art; Felipe Ehrenberg: A Neologist's Art & Archive; First Drafts, Last Drafts: Forty Years of the Creative Writing Program at Stanford; Ira Nowinski: The Photographer as Witness; Johannes Lebek: The Artist as a Witness of His Time; John Steinbeck: From Salinas to Stockholm; Jose Guadalupe Posada & the Taller de Gafica Popular: Mexican Popular Prints; Matt Phillips: The Magic in His Prints; Momentary Bliss: An American Memoir; Ordeal by Piton: Writings from the Golden Age of Yosemite Climbing; The Barchas Collection at Stanford University, History of Science & Ideas; The Heart Unguarded: William Abrahams; The Rediscovery of Africa 1400-1900: Antique Maps & Rare Images; The William Saroyan Collection at Stanford
Partic in Coop Libr Agency for Syst & Servs; Northeast Research Libraries Consortium; OCLC Online Computer Library Center, Inc; Pacific Neighborhood Consortium; Pacific Rim Digital Library Alliance

Departmental Libraries:

BOWES ART & ARCHITECTURE LIBRARY, McMurtry Bldg, 2nd Flr, 355 Roth Way, 94305, SAN 335-0614. Tel: 650-723-3408. FAX: 650-725-0140. E-mail: artlibrary@stanford.edu. Web Site: library.stanford.edu/art. *Head Librn,* Vanessa Kam; E-mail: dvkam@stanford.edu; *Operations Mgr,* Roy C Viado; E-mail: rcviado@stanford.edu
Library Holdings: Bk Vols 181,864; Per Subs 457

BRANNER EARTH SCIENCES & MAP COLLECTIONS, Mitchell Bldg, 2nd Flr, 397 Panama Mall, 94305-2174. Tel: 650-723-2746. FAX: 650-725-2534. E-mail: brannerlibrary@stanford.edu. Web Site: library.stanford.edu/branner. *Head Librn,* Julie Sweetkind-Singer; Tel: 650-725-1102, E-mail: sweetkind@stanford.edu
Library Holdings: Bk Vols 143,115; Per Subs 1,892
Special Collections: Geothermal Engineering Coll; GIS Maps; State Geological Survey, open-file rpts
Subject Interests: Geochemistry, Geol, Petroleum engr

CHEMISTRY & CHEMICAL ENGINEERING LIBRARY, Robin Li & Melissa Ma Science Library, 376 Lomita Dr, 94305. Tel: 650-725-1039. FAX: 650-725-2274. Web Site: library.stanford.edu/subjects/chemistry. *Chem Librn, Head Librn,* Grace Baysinger; E-mail: graceb@stanford.edu
Library Holdings: Bk Vols 40,000; Per Subs 300

CL ROBERT CROWN LAW LIBRARY, Crown Quadrangle, 559 Nathan Abbott Way, 94305-8610, SAN 335-1068. Tel: 650-723-2477. Interlibrary Loan Service Tel: 650-723-1932. Reference Tel: 650-725-0800. FAX: 650-723-1933. Reference E-mail: reference@law.stanford.edu. Web Site: law.stanford.edu/robert-crown-law-library, library.stanford.edu/libraries/law/about. *Libr Dir,* Beth Williams; Tel: 650-725-0804, E-mail: Beth.Williams@stanford.edu; *Dep Libr Dir,* Sergio Stone; Tel: 650-721-2199, E-mail: sstone2@law.stanford.edu
Founded 1897. Highest Degree: Doctorate
Library Holdings: Bk Vols 429,662; Per Subs 6,922
Subject Interests: Law
Partic in OCLC Research Library Partnership

CUBBERLEY EDUCATION LIBRARY, Education Bldg, Rm 202-205, 485 Lasuen Mall, 94305-3097. Tel: 650-723-2121. FAX: 650-736-0536. E-mail: cubberley@stanford.edu. Web Site: library.stanford.edu/cubberley. *Curator, Educ Res, Head of Libr,* Kathy Kerns; Tel: 650-996-0592, E-mail: kkerns@stanford.edu
Library Holdings: Bk Vols 92,293; Per Subs 1,077

EAST ASIA LIBRARY, Lathrop Library Bldg, 518 Memorial Way, 94305. Tel: 650-725-3435. FAX: 650-724-2028. E-mail: eastasialibrary@stanford.edu. Web Site: library.stanford.edu/eal. *Head Librn,* Jidong Yang; Tel: 650-644-8657, E-mail: jdyang@stanford.edu
Library Holdings: Bk Vols 686,905; Per Subs 4,883
Special Collections: Chinese Coll, bks, govt doc (pre-1949), microfilm reels, per, ser, statistical rpts; East Asia Library (EAL), Stanford's Primary East Asian-Language Coll; Japanese Coll, 1920's-1940's, ser; Korean Coll, bks, ser
Subject Interests: Chinese, Defense, Econ, Educ, Humanities, Japanese, Korean (Lang), Lang, Law, Lit, Politics, Pub finance, Sci tech, Soc sci, Sociol, Statistics

GRADUATE SCHOOL OF BUSINESS LIBRARY, Knight Management Ctr, 655 Knight Way, 94305-7298, SAN 335-1009. Tel: 650-725-2055. FAX: 650-723-0281. E-mail: library@gsb.stanford.edu. Web Site: www.gsb.stanford.edu/library. *Libr Dir,* Julie Williamson; Tel: 650-725-2002, E-mail: juliejw@stanford.edu
Founded 1933. Highest Degree: Doctorate
Subject Interests: Bus & mgt, Econ

HOOVER INSTITUTION LIBRARY & ARCHIVES, 434 Galvez Mall, 94305. Tel: 650-723-3563. E-mail: hoover-library-archives@stanford.edu. Web Site: library.stanford.edu/libraries/hila/about, www.hoover.org/library-archives. *Dep Dir,* Eric Wakin; Tel: 650-725-7750, E-mail: wakin@stanford.edu; *Deputy Archivist,* Linda Bernard; Tel: 650-723-0141, E-mail: linda.bernard@stanford.edu
Founded 1919
Library Holdings: Bk Vols 916,036; Per Subs 13
Special Collections: Hoover Institution Archives; Western Language Coll
Publications: Guide to Hoover Institution Archives (Hoover Institution Press, 1980); The Library Catalogs of the Hoover Institution on War, Revolution & Peace (G K Hall, 1969-77); The Library of the Hoover Institution on War, Revolution & Peace (Hoover Institution Press, 1985)

CM LANE MEDICAL LIBRARY, Stanford University Medical Ctr, 300 Pasteur Dr, Rm L109, 94305, SAN 335-1033. Tel: 650-723-6831. Interlibrary Loan Service Tel: 650-725-4584. FAX: 650-725-7471. E-mail: laneaskus@stanford.edu. Web Site: lane.stanford.edu, library.stanford.edu/libraries/lane/about. *Assoc Dean, Knowledge Mgt, Dir,* Heidi Heilemann; Tel: 650-723-7196, E-mail: heilemann@stanford.edu
Founded 1906. Highest Degree: Doctorate
Library Holdings: e-books 14,356; e-journals 9,003; Bk Vols 381,368; Per Subs 16,547
Special Collections: Fleischmann Learning Coll; History of Medicine Coll
Subject Interests: Biomed sci, Med, Nursing, Pub health
Automation Activity & Vendor Info: (Acquisitions) Ex Libris Group; (Cataloging) Ex Libris Group; (Circulation) Ex Libris Group; (Course Reserve) Ex Libris Group; (OPAC) Ex Libris Group; (Serials) Ex Libris Group

CM ROBIN LI & MELISSA MA SCIENCE LIBRARY, Sapp Ctr for Science Teaching & Learning, Rm 315, 376 Lomita Dr, 94305. Tel: 650-723-1528. FAX: 650-725-7712. E-mail: sciencelibrary@stanford.edu. Web Site: library.stanford.edu/science. *Life Sci Librn,* Michael L Newman; Tel: 650-723-1110, E-mail: mnewman@stanford.edu. Subject Specialists: *Biology,* Michael L Newman
Library Holdings: Bk Vols 108,575; Per Subs 439
Subject Interests: Biochem, Biophysics, Cell biol, Developmental biol, Genetics, Molecular biol, Neurobiology, Pop biol
Partic in National Network of Libraries of Medicine Region 5

MATHEMATICS & STATISTICS, Robin Li & Melissa Ma Science Library, 376 Lomita Dr, 94305. Tel: 650-206-0878. Web Site: library.stanford.edu/science/collections/mathematics-and-statistics-collection. *Asst Dir,* Ashley L Jester; E-mail: ajester@stanford.edu
Library Holdings: Bk Vols 108,979; Per Subs 209
Special Collections: Collected Works of Prominent Mathematicians; Computer Books Online; Electronic Journals; Online Reference Coll, MathSciNet (Mathematical Reviews), INSPEC (incl Computer & Control Abstracts) & Current Index to Statistics; Stanford Theses; Technical Reports in Computer Science
Subject Interests: Computer sci, Math, Statistics

HAROLD A MILLER MARINE BIOLOGY LIBRARY, Hopkins Marine Sta, 120 Ocean View Blvd, Pacific Grove, 93950-3094, SAN 371-1501. Tel: 831-655-6228, 831-655-6229. FAX: 831-373-7859. E-mail: HMS-Library@lists.stanford.edu. Web Site: library.stanford.edu/hopkins.

Bibliographer, Head Librn, Amanda L Whitmire; E-mail: thalassa@stanford.edu
Library Holdings: Bk Vols 44,266
Subject Interests: Marine biol

MUSIC LIBRARY, Braun Music Ctr, 541 Lasuen Mall, 94305-3076. Tel: 650-723-1211. FAX: 650-725-1145. Circulation E-mail: muslibcirc@stanford.edu. Web Site: library.stanford.edu/music. *Head Librn,* Jerry L McBride; Tel: 650-725-1146, E-mail: jerry.mcbride@stanford.edu
Library Holdings: Bk Vols 136,081
Special Collections: Kronos Quartet Coll; Lully Archive, a Repository of Primary Sources on Microfilm of the Music of Jean-Baptiste Lully; Women's Philharmonic Coll
Subject Interests: Historical musicology, Western art music

SLAC NATIONAL ACCELERATOR LABORATORY RESEARCH LIBRARY, Computer Bldg 50, 2575 Sand Hill Rd, MS82, Menlo Park, 94025-7090, SAN 335-1092. Tel: 650-926-2411. E-mail: library@slac.stanford.edu. Web Site: library.stanford.edu/libraries/slac/about, www-group.slac.stanford.edu/library. *Archivist, Mgr, Res Libr Serv,* Dorothy Leung; E-mail: dmleung@SLAC.Stanford.EDU; Staff 2 (MLS 2)
Founded 1962
Library Holdings: Bk Vols 18,509
Special Collections: High-energy Physics Archives; SLAC Archives & History Office; SPIRES-HEP Databases
Function: Res libr
Partic in Unix-Spires

TERMAN ENGINEERING LIBRARY, Jen-Hsun Huang Engineering Ctr, Rm 201, 475 Via Ortega, 94305-4121. Tel: 650-723-0001. FAX: 650-725-1096. E-mail: englibrary@stanford.edu. Web Site: library.stanford.edu/englib. *Digital Serv, Eng Librn,* Alexandra Krogman; Tel: 650-521-1811, E-mail: akrogman@stanford.edu; *Eng Librn, Res,* Zac Painter; Tel: 650-885-1793, E-mail: zwp@stanford.edu
Library Holdings: Bk Vols 16,458; Per Subs 91
Special Collections: Timoshenko Coll

STANFORD AUXILIARY LIBRARY, 691 Pampas Lane, 94305. Tel: 650-723-9201. E-mail: salcirculation@stanford.edu. Web Site: library.stanford.edu/libraries/sal/about. *Head, Access Serv, Librn,* Rebecca Ione Pernell; Tel: 650-725-1277, E-mail: pernell@stanford.edu
Library Holdings: Bk Vols 2,100,833

STOCKTON

CALIFORNIA YOUTH AUTHORITY

S N A CHADERJIAN YOUTH CORRECTIONAL FACILITY LIBRARY*, 7650 S Newcastle Rd, 95213. (Mail add: PO Box 213014, 95213-9014). Tel: 209-944-6444, Ext 6755. FAX: 209-944-6167. *Head Librn,* Tammy Fishman
Library Holdings: Bk Vols 5,837
Open Mon-Fri 8-4

S O H CLOSE YOUTH CORRECTIONAL FACILITY LIBRARY*, 7650 S Newcastle Rd, 95213-9001. (Mail add: PO Box 213001, 95213-9001). Tel: 209-944-6346. FAX: 209-944-6136. *Sr Librn,* Jonathan Frye
Library Holdings: Bk Vols 10,000
Open Mon-Fri 8-3

R CHRISTIAN LIFE COLLEGE LIBRARY*, Hogue Library, 9023 West Lane, 95210. SAN 301-6323. Tel: 209-476-7840. Toll Free Tel: 800-326-9495. FAX: 209-476-7868. Web Site: clc.edu/academics/learning-resource-center. *Dir,* Regina Lopez; E-mail: rlopez@clc.edu
Founded 1955
Library Holdings: Bk Vols 18,000; Per Subs 50
Open Mon & Tues 8-12 & 1:30-9:30, Wed 8-12 & 1:30-5, Thurs & Fri 8-12 & 1:30-8, Sat 10-1:30

S HAGGIN MUSEUM*, Library & Archives, 1201 N Pershing Ave, 95203-1699. SAN 301-6234. Tel: 209-940-6314. FAX: 209-940-6304. Web Site: www.hagginmuseum.org/library-and-archives. *Chief Exec Officer, Curator,* Tod Ruhstaller; E-mail: truhstaller@hagginmuseum.org
Founded 1949
Library Holdings: Bk Titles 7,000; Per Subs 15
Special Collections: California History Coll; Holt Manufacturing Company History Coll; James Ben Ali Haggin Family Records; Joseph Christian Leyendecker Coll; Ralph Yardley Drawings; San Joaquin Society of California Pioneers Coll; Stephens Bros Boat Builders Archive; Stockton Industrial Archive; Stockton/San Joaquin County History Coll; Valentines Coll
Subject Interests: Art Ref, Local hist
Wireless access
Function: Archival coll, Ref serv available
Restriction: Authorized scholars by appt, Non-circulating

C HUMPHREYS UNIVERSITY LIBRARY*, 6650 Inglewood Ave, 95207. SAN 301-6226. Tel: 209-478-0800. FAX: 209-478-8721. Web Site: www.humphreys.edu/student-support/library-and-learning-center. *Assoc Dean,* Donna Roberts; Tel: 209-235-2933, E-mail: droberts@humphreys.edu; Staff 1 (MLS 1)
Founded 1896
Library Holdings: Bk Vols 24,922; Per Subs 113
Subject Interests: Bus, Criminal justice, Educ, Law
Wireless access
Partic in Statewide California Electronic Library Consortium
Open Mon-Fri 8am-10pm, Sat 8-5, Sun 8-3

S THE RECORD LIBRARY*, 530 E Market St, 95202. SAN 301-6285. Tel: 209-546-8271. FAX: 209-547-8186. Web Site: www.recordnet.com. *Admin Supvr,* Paula Allard; E-mail: pallard@recordnet.com; Staff 1 (Non-MLS 1)
Founded 1960
Restriction: Not open to pub

M SAINT JOSEPH'S MEDICAL CENTER LIBRARY*, 1800 N California St, 95204. SAN 320-6076. Tel: 209-467-6332. FAX: 209-461-6882. Web Site: www.dignityhealth.org/stjosephs-stockton/for-physicians-residents-and-students/medical-library. *Librn,* Helen Chang; E-mail: Helen.Chang@DignityHealth.org; Staff 1 (MLS 1)
Founded 1990
Library Holdings: Bk Titles 1,200; Per Subs 140
Subject Interests: Human relations, Med, Nursing
Wireless access
Partic in National Network of Libraries of Medicine Region 5; Northern California & Nevada Medical Library Group
Open Mon-Fri 8-4:30

GL SAN JOAQUIN COUNTY LAW LIBRARY*, Kress Legal Ctr, 20 N Sutter St, 95202. SAN 301-6242. Tel: 209-468-3920. FAX: 209-468-9968. E-mail: sjcllstaff@gmail.com. Web Site: sjclawlibrary.org. *Dir,* Brenda Schultz; Staff 3 (MLS 1, Non-MLS 2)
Library Holdings: Bk Vols 30,000
Special Collections: State Document Depository
Automation Activity & Vendor Info: (Acquisitions) LibraryWorld, Inc; (Cataloging) LibraryWorld, Inc; (OPAC) LibraryWorld, Inc; (Serials) LibraryWorld, Inc
Wireless access
Open Mon-Fri 8-4:30

J SAN JOAQUIN DELTA COLLEGE*, Goleman Library, 5151 Pacific Ave, 95207. SAN 301-6250. Tel: 209-954-5139. Circulation Tel: 209-954-5143. Reference Tel: 209-954-5145. FAX: 209-954-5691. E-mail: library@deltacollege.edu. Web Site: www.deltacollege.edu/dept/library. *Dean, Libr Serv,* Joe Gonzales; E-mail: jgonzales@deltacollege.edu; *Syst Librn, Tech Serv,* Steve Schermerhorn; Tel: 209-954-5152, E-mail: sschermerhorn@deltacollege.edu; *Bibliog Instr,* Dr Jun Wang; Tel: 209-954-5146, E-mail: jwang@deltacollege.edu; *Coll Develop,* Josefina Gomez; Tel: 209-954-5862, E-mail: jgomez@deltacollege.edu; *Pub Serv,* Mary Weppler; Tel: 209-954-5147, E-mail: mweppler@deltacollege.edu; Staff 16 (MLS 6, Non-MLS 10)
Founded 1948. Enrl 18,836; Fac 565; Highest Degree: Associate
Library Holdings: AV Mats 6,696; Bks on Deafness & Sign Lang 136; e-books 7,212; High Interest/Low Vocabulary Bk Vols 61; Large Print Bks 14; Bk Titles 82,999; Bk Vols 95,966; Per Subs 528; Talking Bks 1,607
Automation Activity & Vendor Info: (Acquisitions) SirsiDynix; (Cataloging) SirsiDynix; (Circulation) SirsiDynix; (Course Reserve) SirsiDynix; (ILL) SirsiDynix; (OPAC) SirsiDynix
Wireless access
Publications: Handbook for Instructors; Instructor of Record Handbook; Library Handbook; Library Research Workbook; Library Skills Workbook
Partic in Coop Libr Agency for Syst & Servs; OCLC Online Computer Library Center, Inc
Open Mon-Thurs 7:30am-8:30pm, Fri 7:30-3:30
Friends of the Library Group

P STOCKTON-SAN JOAQUIN COUNTY PUBLIC LIBRARY*, Cesar Chavez Central Library Headquarters, 605 N El Dorado St, 95202. SAN 335-1122. Tel: 209-937-8221. Circulation Tel: 209-937-8416. Administration Tel: 209-937-8362. Automation Services Tel: 209-937-7388. Toll Free Tel: 866-805-7323 (San Joaquin). FAX: 209-937-8683. E-mail: reference@stocktonca.gov. Web Site: www.ssjcpl.org. *Dir, Commun Serv,* John Alita; E-mail: john.alita@stocktonca.gov; *City Librn, Deputy Dir, Community Serv,* Suzanne M Daveluy; E-mail: suzy.daveluy@stocktonca.gov; *Ref Librn,* Gretchen Louden
Founded 1880. Circ 1,497,430
Special Collections: Career Center; Local History; Online Community Info Database; Picture Book Subject Index; Southeast Asian Languages; Spanish Language; Stockton & San Joaquin County History; Stockton Record Index. US Document Depository

Automation Activity & Vendor Info: (Acquisitions) SirsiDynix; (Cataloging) SirsiDynix; (Circulation) SirsiDynix; (ILL) SirsiDynix; (OPAC) SirsiDynix; (Serials) SirsiDynix
Wireless access
Function: Adult bk club, Adult literacy prog, Audiobks via web, Bilingual assistance for Spanish patrons, Bk club(s), Bks on cassette, Bks on CD, Children's prog, Computer training, Computers for patron use, Electronic databases & coll, Free DVD rentals, Homebound delivery serv, Homework prog, ILL available, Music CDs, Outreach serv, OverDrive digital audio bks, Photocopying/Printing, Prog for adults, Prog for children & young adult, Ref serv available, Story hour, Summer reading prog, Tax forms, Teen prog, Telephone ref, VHS videos, Wheelchair accessible
Partic in 49-99 Cooperative Library System
Special Services for the Deaf - Closed caption videos
Special Services for the Blind - Assistive/Adapted tech devices, equip & products; BiFolkal kits; Bks on cassette; Bks on CD; Large print bks; Magnifiers
Open Mon, Tues & Thurs 10-8, Wed 1-8, Fri & Sat 10-5
Restriction: ID required to use computers (Ltd hrs)
Friends of the Library Group
Branches: 15
MAYA ANGELOU BRANCH, 2324 Pock Lane, 95205, SAN 335-1270. Web Site: www.ssjcpl.org/locations/stockton/angelou. *Br Librn,* Bill Walker; Staff 2 (MLS 1, Non-MLS 1)
Pop 19,165; Circ 61,380
Library Holdings: Bk Vols 56,913
Open Mon 10-8, Tues & Thurs 10-6, Wed 1-6, Fri 10-5, Sat 12-5
Friends of the Library Group
ARNOLD RUE BRANCH, 5758 Lorraine Ave, 95210. Web Site: www.ssjcpl.org/locations/stockton/rue.html. *Br Librn,* Amanda Luna
Open Tues-Thurs 1-5, Fri & Sat 10-2
Friends of the Library Group
ESCALON BRANCH, 1540 Second St, Escalon, 95320, SAN 335-1157. Web Site: www.ssjcpl.org/locations/county/escalon. *Br Librn,* Brianna Anderson; Staff 2 (MLS 1, Non-MLS 1)
Pop 13,320; Circ 43,570
Library Holdings: Bk Vols 53,785
Open Mon & Wed 1-6, Tues 2-7, Thurs 10-12 & 2-6, Fri 12-5, Sat 11-4
Friends of the Library Group
FAIR OAKS BRANCH, 2370 E Main St, 95205. Web Site: www.ssjcpl.org/locations/stockton/fairOaks.html. *Br Librn,* Milo S Rook
Open Mon & Tues 10-6, Wed 1-6, Thurs 10-8, Fri 10-5, Sat 12-5
Friends of the Library Group
LATHROP BRANCH, 450 Spartan Way, Lathrop, 95330. Web Site: www.ssjcpl.org/locations/stockton/lathrop. *Br Librn,* Nels Clarke; Staff 1 (MLS 1)
Pop 14,702; Circ 21,531
Library Holdings: Bk Titles 2,500
Open Mon-Thurs 1-6, Fri & Sat 12-5
LINDEN BRANCH, 19059 E Main St, Hwy 26, Linden, 95236, SAN 335-136X. Web Site: www.ssjcpl.org/locations/stockton/linden. *Br Librn,* Nazli R Ali; Staff 1 (MLS 1)
Pop 16,783; Circ 24,238
Library Holdings: Bk Vols 14,743
Open Mon, Tues & Thurs 12-5, Wed 1-6, Fri & Sat 10-3
Friends of the Library Group
MANTECA BRANCH, 320 W Center St, Manteca, 95336, SAN 335-1211. Web Site: www.ssjcpl.org/locations/stockton/manteca. *Br Librn,* Anne Stevens; Staff 6 (MLS 3, Non-MLS 3)
Pop 75,172; Circ 221,096
Library Holdings: Bk Vols 136,000
Open Mon 12-8, Tues & Thurs 10-6, Wed 1-6, Fri & Sat 10-5, Sun 12-5
Friends of the Library Group
MOUNTAIN HOUSE BRANCH, 250 E Main St, Mountain House, 95391. Web Site: www.ssjcpl.org/locations/county/mhouse.html. *Br Librn,* Kathleen Buffleben; Staff 3 (MLS 1, Non-MLS 2)
Pop 16,787; Circ 83,614
Function: 24/7 Electronic res, 24/7 Online cat
Friends of the Library Group
RIPON BRANCH, 333 W Main St, Ripon, 95336, SAN 335-1246. Web Site: www.ssjcpl.org/locations/county/ripon. *Br Librn,* Melinda Kopp; Staff 3 (MLS 1, Non-MLS 2)
Pop 16,688; Circ 77,990
Library Holdings: Bk Vols 60,034
Open Mon 10-8, Tues & Thurs 10-6, Wed 1-6, Fri & Sat 10-5
Friends of the Library Group
STRIBLEY MICRO BRANCH, 1760 E Sonora St, 95205. Web Site: www.ssjcpl.org/locations/stockton/stribley.html. *Br Mgr,* Amanda Luna
Open Tues & Sat 10-2, Wed-Fri 2-6
THORNTON BRANCH, 26341 N Thornton Rd, Thornton, 95686, SAN 335-1394. Web Site: www.ssjcpl.org/locations/county/thornton. *Br Librn,* Mark Rodriguez; Staff 1 (MLS 1)
Pop 10,313; Circ 10,652
Library Holdings: Bk Vols 18,481
Open Tues & Thurs 12-6, Wed 1-7, Fri & Sat 10-4
TRACY BRANCH, 20 E Eaton Ave, Tracy, 95376, SAN 335-1335. Web Site: www.ssjcpl.org/locations/county/tracy. *Br Librn,* Jamie Turner; Staff 5 (MLS 1, Non-MLS 4)
Pop 89,466; Circ 296,392
Library Holdings: Bk Vols 162,890
Function: Activity rm, Adult bk club, Bks on CD, Computers for patron use, Electronic databases & coll, Free DVD rentals, Internet access, Microfiche/film & reading machines, Music CDs, Online cat, OverDrive digital audio bks, Prog for adults, Prog for children & young adult, Spanish lang bks, Story hour, Summer reading prog, Teen prog, Wheelchair accessible
Open Mon & Thurs 10-8, Tues 10-7, Wed 1-6, Fri & Sat 10-5, Sun 12-5
Friends of the Library Group
MARGARET K TROKE BRANCH, 502 W Benjamin Holt Dr, 95207, SAN 335-1300. Web Site: www.ssjcpl.org/locations/stockton/troke. *Br Librn,* Alex Bailey; Staff 8 (MLS 3, Non-MLS 5)
Pop 182,009; Circ 376,139
Library Holdings: Bk Vols 183,941
Open Mon, Tues & Thurs 10-8, Wed 1-8, Fri & Sat 10-5
Friends of the Library Group
VAN BUSKIRK MIRO BRANCH, Van Buskirk Community Ctr, 734 Houston Ave, 95206. Web Site: www.ssjcpl.org/locations/stockton/vanBuskirk.html. *Br Librn,* Amanda Luna
Open Tues, Wed & Fri 2-6,Thurs & Sat 10-2
WESTON RANCH BRANCH, 1453 W French Camp Rd, 95206. Web Site: www.ssjcpl.org/locations/stockton/wranch.html. *Br Librn,* Jackie Rea; Staff 2 (MLS 1, Non-MLS 1)
Library Holdings: Bk Vols 30,691
Open Mon & Thurs 10-6, Tues 10-8, Wed 1-6, Fri 10-5, Sat 12-5
Friends of the Library Group
Bookmobiles: 1. Libr Asst, Oswaldo Vera

C UNIVERSITY OF THE PACIFIC LIBRARY*, 3601 Pacific Ave, 95211. SAN 335-1459. Tel: 209-946-2434. FAX: 209-946-2805. Web Site: www.pacific.edu/university-libraries.html. *Univ Librn,* Mary Somerville; E-mail: msomerville@pacific.edu; Staff 23 (MLS 11, Non-MLS 12)
Founded 1851. Enrl 6,128; Fac 429; Highest Degree: Doctorate
Jul 2018-Jun 2019 Income (Main Library Only) $4,336,020. Mats Exp $1,805,732. Sal $2,366,236
Special Collections: Japanese American Internment Colls; John Muir Papers; Western Americana
Subject Interests: Calif hist
Automation Activity & Vendor Info: (Acquisitions) Innovative Interfaces, Inc - Sierra; (Cataloging) Innovative Interfaces, Inc - Sierra; (Circulation) Innovative Interfaces, Inc - Sierra; (Discovery) Innovative Interfaces, Inc - Sierra; (ILL) OCLC ILLiad; (OPAC) Innovative Interfaces, Inc - Sierra; (Serials) Innovative Interfaces, Inc - Sierra
Wireless access
Function: 3D Printer
Partic in Statewide California Electronic Library Consortium
Departmental Libraries:
HOLT-ATHERTON DEPARTMENT OF SPECIAL COLLECTIONS, 3601 Pacific Ave, 95211. Tel: 209-946-2404.
Subject Interests: Calif, Western Americana
CM RITE AID INFORMATION COMMONS, School of Pharmacy Bldg, 3601 Pacific Ave, 95211. (Mail add: 751 Brookside Rd, 95211), SAN 335-1602. Tel: 209-946-2940. FAX: 209-946-2041. *Health Sci Librn,* Mickel A Paris; Tel: 209-946-3207, E-mail: mparis@pacific.edu
Subject Interests: Chem, Phys therapy

SUN VALLEY

SR THE MASTER'S SEMINARY LIBRARY, 13248 Roscoe Blvd, 91352. SAN 323-620X. Tel: 818-909-5545. Administration Tel: 818-909-5651. E-mail: library@tms.edu. Web Site: masters.libguides.com, www.tms.edu/students/library. *Libr Dir,* John Stone; E-mail: jstone@masters.edu; *Database Adminr,* Janet Tillman; E-mail: jtillman@masters.edu; *Circ Supvr,* Renaldo Barbosa; *Circ Supvr,* Morgan Maycumber; Staff 3 (MLS 1, Non-MLS 2)
Founded 1986. Enrl 440; Fac 14; Highest Degree: Doctorate
Library Holdings: CDs 75; DVDs 400; e-journals 40; Bk Titles 125,000; Bk Vols 175,000; Per Subs 510
Subject Interests: Archaeology, Biblical studies, Church hist, Theol
Automation Activity & Vendor Info: (Acquisitions) Ex Libris Group; (Cataloging) Ex Libris Group; (Circulation) Ex Libris Group; (ILL) OCLC; (OPAC) Ex Libris Group; (Serials) EBSCO Online
Wireless access
Function: Art exhibits, Doc delivery serv, E-Reserves, Electronic databases & coll, ILL available, Internet access, Photocopying/Printing
Partic in OCLC Online Computer Library Center, Inc
Open Mon-Thurs 8am-9pm, Fri 10-5, Sat 8-5
Restriction: Authorized patrons

SUNNYVALE

R ST THOMAS EPISCOPAL CHURCH LIBRARY, 231 Sunset Ave, 94086-5938. SAN 328-1884. Tel: 408-736-4155. FAX: 408-736-8655. E-mail: Library@stthomas-svale.us. Web Site: www.stthomas-svale.org. *Librn,* Carol Campbell; Staff 5 (MLS 1, Non-MLS 4)
Founded 1979
Library Holdings: DVDs 500; Large Print Bks 100; Bk Titles 7,000; Per Subs 33
Special Collections: Oral History
Subject Interests: Relig
Automation Activity & Vendor Info: (Acquisitions) OPALS (Open-source Automated Library System); (Cataloging) OPALS (Open-source Automated Library System); (Circulation) OPALS (Open-source Automated Library System); (OPAC) OPALS (Open-source Automated Library System)
Wireless access
Open Tues-Fri 10-4

P SUNNYVALE PUBLIC LIBRARY*, 665 W Olive Ave, 94086-7622. (Mail add: PO Box 3714, 94088-3714), SAN 301-6455. Tel: 408-730-7300. Administration Tel: 408-730-7314. FAX: 408-735-8767. E-mail: library@sunnyvale.ca.gov. Web Site: www.sunnyvalelibrary.org. *Dir,* Cynthia Bojorquez; *Head, Cat,* Liz Hickok; *Head, Children's Servx,* Sue Kaplan; *Head, Circ,* Ellen Giarrizzo; *Head, Coll Develop,* Christine Mendoza; *Admin Librn,* Steve Sloan; Staff 20 (MLS 19, Non-MLS 1)
Founded 1908. Pop 148,028; Circ 2,396,689
Jul 2015-Jun 2016 Income City $8,225,704. Mats Exp $851,430. Sal $2,641,134
Library Holdings: e-books 76,480; Bk Vols 224,410; Per Subs 253
Special Collections: Sunnyvale Local History Coll
Automation Activity & Vendor Info: (Acquisitions) Innovative Interfaces, Inc; (Cataloging) Innovative Interfaces, Inc; (Circulation) Innovative Interfaces, Inc; (Discovery) Innovative Interfaces, Inc; (ILL) Innovative Interfaces, Inc; (OPAC) Innovative Interfaces, Inc; (Serials) Innovative Interfaces, Inc
Wireless access
Function: 24/7 Electronic res, 24/7 Online cat, Adult bk club, After school storytime, Audiobks via web, Bk club(s), Bks on CD, Children's prog, Computer training, Computers for patron use, E-Readers, Electronic databases & coll, For res purposes, Free DVD rentals, Health sci info serv, Holiday prog, Homebound delivery serv, Homework prog, ILL available, Internet access, Life-long learning prog for all ages, Magazines, Mail & tel request accepted, Mango lang, Museum passes, Music CDs, Online cat, Outreach serv, Photocopying/Printing, Preschool outreach, Printer for laptops & handheld devices, Prog for adults, Prog for children & young adult, Ref & res, Ref serv available, Scanner, Senior outreach, Spanish lang bks, Story hour, Summer reading prog, Teen prog, Telephone ref, Wheelchair accessible, Workshops
Mem of Pacific Library Partnership (PLP)
Partic in Califa; OCLC Online Computer Library Center, Inc
Friends of the Library Group

SUSANVILLE

J LASSEN COMMUNITY COLLEGE LIBRARY*, 478-200 Hwy 139, 96130. (Mail add: PO Box 3000, 96130-3000), SAN 301-6498. Tel: 530-251-8830. FAX: 530-257-8964. Web Site: lassencollege.libguides.com/ARChome. *Dir,* Shar Murphy; E-mail: smurphy@lassencollege.edu; Staff 2 (MLS 1, Non-MLS 1)
Founded 1926. Fac 49; Highest Degree: Associate
Library Holdings: DVDs 200; e-books 150,000; e-journals 5,000; Per Subs 35
Special Collections: Gunsmithing
Automation Activity & Vendor Info: (Cataloging) Ex Libris Group; (Circulation) Ex Libris Group; (Course Reserve) Ex Libris Group; (OPAC) Ex Libris Group
Wireless access
Mem of NorthNet Library System
Partic in California Community College Library Consortium; Council of Chief Librarian
Open Mon-Fri 8-4:30

P LASSEN LIBRARY DISTRICT, 1618 Main St, 96130-4515. SAN 301-6501. Tel: 530-251-8127. Administration Tel: 530-257-8113. FAX: 530-257-8115. E-mail: lassenlibrary@citlink.net. Web Site: www.lassenlibrary.org. *Dir,* Heather Blevins; *IT Tech,* Jeffrey Hawkins; Staff 10 (MLS 1, Non-MLS 9)
Founded 1995. Pop 36,000; Circ 36,300
Library Holdings: CDs 476; DVDs 218; Large Print Bks 874; Bk Titles 40,000; Bk Vols 43,000; Per Subs 101; Talking Bks 725; Videos 2,189
Special Collections: California History Coll. Oral History
Subject Interests: Indians, Local hist
Automation Activity & Vendor Info: (Cataloging) Follett Software; (Circulation) Follett Software; (ILL) OCLC FirstSearch
Wireless access
Mem of NorthNet Library System
Open Tues-Thurs 11-4:30, Sat 11-2:30
Friends of the Library Group

SYLMAR

J LOS ANGELES MISSION COLLEGE LIBRARY*, 13356 Eldridge Ave, 91342. SAN 301-360X. Tel: 818-639-2221. E-mail: library@lamission.edu. Web Site: www.lamission.edu/library. *Actg Dean,* Kelly William Enos; E-mail: enoskw@lamission.edu; *Librn,* David Garza; E-mail: garzadp@lamission.edu; *Librn,* Sheila A MacDowell; E-mail: macdowsa@laccd.edu; *Librn,* Esmeralda Montes; E-mail: montese2@lamission.edu; *Librn,* Ashley Sparks-Jamal; Tel: 818-364-7750, E-mail: sparksa@lamission.edu; Staff 4 (MLS 4)
Founded 1975. Enrl 11,000; Fac 87
Library Holdings: Bk Vols 80,000; Per Subs 200
Special Collections: Los Angeles Mission College Archives
Wireless access
Publications: Bibliographies & Study Aids
Partic in Metronet

S ST JUDE MEDICAL LIBRARY & RESOURCE CENTER*, Information & Innovation Research Center, Library & Resource Ctr, 15900 Valley View Ct, 91342. SAN 373-286X. Tel: 818-362-6822, 818-493-3101. E-mail: library@sjm.com. *Mgr,* Sandra Crumlish; E-mail: scrumlish@sjm.com; Staff 1 (Non-MLS 1)
Founded 1990
Library Holdings: Bk Titles 1,000; Per Subs 110
Subject Interests: Cardiology, Neurology
Automation Activity & Vendor Info: (Cataloging) SirsiDynix; (Circulation) SirsiDynix; (OPAC) SirsiDynix
Wireless access
Partic in Medical Library Association; Medical Library Group of Southern California & Arizona
Restriction: Access for corporate affiliates, Employees & their associates, In-house use for visitors, Internal circ only, Internal use only, Not open to pub

TAFT

J TAFT COLLEGE LIBRARY*, 29 Cougar Ct, 93268. SAN 301-6536. Tel: 661-763-7707. Reference Tel: 661-763-7817. FAX: 661-763-7778. Web Site: www.taftcollege.edu/library. *Res & Instruction Librn,* Terri Smith; E-mail: tsmith@taftcollege.edu; Staff 1 (MLS 1)
Founded 1952. Fac 1; Highest Degree: Associate
Library Holdings: DVDs 1,600; e-books 140,000; Bk Vols 13,000; Per Subs 40
Automation Activity & Vendor Info: (Cataloging) OCLC; (Circulation) Ex Libris Group; (Course Reserve) OCLC; (ILL) OCLC WorldShare Interlibrary Loan; (OPAC) OCLC; (Serials) OCLC
Wireless access
Mem of West Kern Community College District
Partic in California Community College Library Consortium
Open Mon-Thurs (Fall & Spring) 8-8, Fri 8-5; Mon-Thurs (Summer) 8-8

THOUSAND OAKS

C CALIFORNIA LUTHERAN UNIVERSITY*, Pearson Library, 60 W Olsen Rd, No 5100, 91360. SAN 301-6560. Tel: 805-493-3250, 805-493-3937. Reference Tel: 805-493-3255. FAX: 805-493-3842. E-mail: clulibrary@callutheran.edu. Circulation E-mail: libcirc@callutheran.edu. Web Site: www.callutheran.edu/library. *Asst Dir,* Lala Badal; E-mail: lbadal@callutheran.edu; *Cat Spec,* Patricia Hilker; E-mail: philker@callutheran.edu; Staff 9 (MLS 4, Non-MLS 5)
Founded 1961. Enrl 2,766; Fac 111; Highest Degree: Master
Library Holdings: Bk Vols 300,000; Per Subs 425
Special Collections: Scandinavian
Subject Interests: Counseling, Marriage, Pacific Islands
Automation Activity & Vendor Info: (Acquisitions) SirsiDynix; (Cataloging) SirsiDynix; (Circulation) SirsiDynix; (OPAC) SirsiDynix; (Serials) SirsiDynix
Wireless access
Partic in Pac Net
Open Mon-Fri 8:15am-11:45pm, Sat & Sun 10:15am-11:45pm

P THOUSAND OAKS LIBRARY*, Grant R Brimhall Library, 1401 E Janss Rd, 91362-2199. SAN 335-2323. Tel: 805-449-2660. FAX: 805-373-6858. Web Site: www.toaks.org/library. *Libr Serv Dir,* Heather R Cousin; Tel: 805-449-2660, Ext 7316, E-mail: hcousin@tolibrary.org; *Dep Libr Serv Dir,* Darren Jeffery; Tel: 805-449-2660, Ext 7225, E-mail: djeffery@tolibrary.org; *Div Mgr,* Samantha Yeung; Tel: 805-449-2660, Ext 7332, E-mail: syeung@tolibrary.org; *Children's Serv Supvr,* Charlotte Burrows; Tel: 805-449-2660, Ext 7338, E-mail: cburrows@tolibrary.org; *Circ Serv Supvr,* Eamon McSweeney; Tel: 805-449-2660, Ext 7330, E-mail: emcsween@tolibrary.org; *Supvr, Pub Serv,* Dayna Canada; Tel:

805-449-2660, Ext 7347, E-mail: dcanada@tolibrary.org; Staff 20 (MLS 17, Non-MLS 3)
Founded 1982. Pop 128,000; Circ 1,559,385
Library Holdings: Audiobooks 19,980; AV Mats 32,728; e-books 13,613; Electronic Media & Resources 62; Bk Vols 458,677; Per Subs 614
Special Collections: American Radio Archives; Book Arts; Local History Coll
Subject Interests: Genealogy, Hist of radio, Local hist, TV broadcasting
Automation Activity & Vendor Info: (Acquisitions) Innovative Interfaces, Inc - Millennium; (Cataloging) Innovative Interfaces, Inc - Millennium; (Circulation) Innovative Interfaces, Inc - Millennium; (ILL) OCLC FirstSearch; (OPAC) Innovative Interfaces, Inc; (Serials) Innovative Interfaces, Inc
Wireless access
Function: Adult bk club, Archival coll, Audio & video playback equip for onsite use, Audiobks via web, AV serv, Bk club(s), Bks on cassette, Bks on CD, Children's prog, Computer training, Computers for patron use, Digital talking bks, Electronic databases & coll, Genealogy discussion group, Homebound delivery serv, Homework prog, ILL available, Magnifiers for reading, Microfiche/film & reading machines, Music CDs, Online cat, Online ref, Orientations, OverDrive digital audio bks, Photocopying/Printing, Prog for adults, Prog for children & young adult, Ref serv available, Senior computer classes, Serves people with intellectual disabilities, Spanish lang bks, Spoken cassettes & CDs, Spoken cassettes & DVDs, Story hour, Summer reading prog, Teen prog, Telephone ref, VHS videos, Wheelchair accessible
Publications: Bibliographies; Brochures; Fliers; Pathfinders; Programs
Partic in Southern California Library Cooperative
Open Mon-Thurs 10-8, Fri 10-6, Sat 10-5, Sun 12-5
Friends of the Library Group
Branches: 1
NEWBURY PARK BRANCH, 2331 Borchard Rd, Newbury Park, 91320-3206, SAN 372-5626. Tel: 805-498-2139. FAX: 805-498-7034. *Libr Serv Dir,* Heather Cousin; E-mail: hcousin@tolibrary.org; Staff 3.5 (MLS 3.5)
Library Holdings: Bk Vols 87,418
Function: Audiobks via web, Bks on cassette, Bks on CD, Children's prog, Computers for patron use, Digital talking bks, Electronic databases & coll, Free DVD rentals, ILL available, Music CDs, Online cat, Online ref, OverDrive digital audio bks, Photocopying/Printing, Prog for adults, Prog for children & young adult, Ref serv available, Spanish lang bks, Spoken cassettes & CDs, Spoken cassettes & DVDs, Summer reading prog, Teen prog, Telephone ref, VHS videos, Wheelchair accessible
Open Mon-Wed 12-8, Thurs & Fri 10-6, Sat 10-5
Friends of the Library Group

TIBURON

P BELVEDERE TIBURON LIBRARY*, 1501 Tiburon Blvd, 94920. Tel: 415-789-2665. Reference Tel: 415-789-2661. Administration Tel: 415-789-2660. FAX: 415-789-2650. E-mail: refdesk@beltiblibrary.org. Web Site: beltiblibrary.org/. *Dir,* Deborah Mazzolini; Tel: 415-789-2656, E-mail: dmazzolini@beltiblibrary.org; *Asst Dir,* Jacki Dunn; E-mail: jdunn@beltiblibrary.org; *Ch,* Alicia Bell; E-mail: abell@beltiblibrary.org; *Ref Librn,* Joey Della Santina; E-mail: jdellasantina@beltiblibrary.org; *Ref Librn, Web Serv,* Ivan Silva; E-mail: isilva@beltiblibrary.org; *Teen Librn,* Rebecca Jung; E-mail: rjung@beltiblibrary.org; *Adult Serv,* Linda Bennett; E-mail: lbennett@beltiblibrary.org; *Circ,* Jason Duran; E-mail: jduran@beltiblibrary.org; *Tech Serv,* Patty McDonough; E-mail: pmcdonough@beltiblibrary.org; Staff 18 (MLS 9, Non-MLS 9)
Founded 1997. Pop 13,048; Circ 266,500
Library Holdings: Audiobooks 2,050; AV Mats 12,700; CDs 6,100; DVDs 6,200; e-books 136,600; e-journals 500; Large Print Bks 1,420; Bk Titles 57,000; Per Subs 400
Automation Activity & Vendor Info: (Acquisitions) Innovative Interfaces, Inc; (Cataloging) Innovative Interfaces, Inc; (Circulation) Innovative Interfaces, Inc; (OPAC) BiblioCommons; (Serials) Innovative Interfaces, Inc
Wireless access
Function: 24/7 Electronic res, 24/7 Online cat, 3D Printer, Accelerated reader prog, After school storytime, Art exhibits, Audiobks via web, Bk club(s), Bks on CD, Chess club, Children's prog, Computer training, Computers for patron use, Digital talking bks, E-Readers, Electronic databases & coll, Free DVD rentals, Holiday prog, Homebound delivery serv, Homework prog, ILL available, Internet access, Life-long learning prog for all ages, Magazines, Mail & tel request accepted, Mango lang, Movies, Museum passes, Music CDs, Notary serv, Online cat, Outside serv via phone, mail, e-mail & web, OverDrive digital audio bks, Photocopying/Printing, Preschool outreach, Printer for laptops & handheld devices, Prog for adults, Prog for children & young adult, Ref & res, Ref serv available, Scanner, Spanish lang bks, Story hour, Summer reading prog, Tax forms, Teen prog, Telephone ref, Visual arts prog, Wheelchair accessible, Workshops
Mem of NorthNet Library System
Partic in Marin Automated Resources & Information Network
Open Mon 10-6, Tues-Thurs 10-9, Fri & Sat 10-5, Sun 12-5
Friends of the Library Group

TORRANCE

J EL CAMINO COLLEGE, Schauerman Library, 16007 S Crenshaw Blvd, 90506. SAN 301-6625. Tel: 310-660-3525. Circulation Tel: 310-660-3519. Reference Tel: 310-660-6483. FAX: 310-660-3513. E-mail: library@elcamino.edu. Web Site: elcamino.edu/library/division.aspx. *Dean of Libr,* Dr Crystle Martin; E-mail: cmartin@elcamino.edu; *Digital Res Librn,* Mary McMillan; E-mail: mmcmillan@elcamino.edu; *Outreach Librn,* Camila Jenkin; E-mail: cjenkin@elcamino.edu; *Pub Access Librn,* Gary Medina; E-mail: gmedina@elcamino.edu; *Ref & Instruction Librn,* Analu Josephides; E-mail: ajosephides@elcamino.edu; *Syst Librn,* Ryan Gan; E-mail: rgan@elcamino.edu; Staff 19 (MLS 6, Non-MLS 13)
Founded 1948. Enrl 24,756; Fac 321; Highest Degree: Associate
Library Holdings: Bks on Deafness & Sign Lang 64; High Interest/Low Vocabulary Bk Vols 193; Bk Titles 112,020; Bk Vols 122,063; Per Subs 220
Subject Interests: Japanese (Lang), Music
Automation Activity & Vendor Info: (Acquisitions) Innovative Interfaces, Inc; (Cataloging) Innovative Interfaces, Inc; (Circulation) Innovative Interfaces, Inc; (Course Reserve) Innovative Interfaces, Inc; (ILL) OCLC; (OPAC) Innovative Interfaces, Inc; (Serials) Innovative Interfaces, Inc
Wireless access
Function: 24/7 Electronic res, 24/7 Online cat, AV serv, Computers for patron use, Distance learning, Electronic databases & coll, Equip loans & repairs, For res purposes, Free DVD rentals, ILL available, Instruction & testing, Internet access, Learning ctr, Magazines, Mango lang, Meeting rooms, Online cat, Online info literacy tutorials on the web & in blackboard, Online ref, Orientations, Outreach serv, Ref & res, Ref serv available, Res assist avail
Publications: Bibliographies; Lamppost (Quarterly newsletter)

M LOS ANGELES COUNTY HARBOR UCLA MEDICAL CENTER*, A F Parlow Library of Health Sciences, 1000 W Carson St, 90509-2910. SAN 335-1637. Tel: 424-306-6100. Reference E-mail: libref@labiomed.org. Web Site: library.harbor-ucla.org. *Dir,* Jenna Kim
Founded 1964
Library Holdings: Bk Titles 37,201; Per Subs 515
Subject Interests: Hospital admin, Med, Nursing, Soc serv (soc work)
Automation Activity & Vendor Info: (OPAC) CyberTools for Libraries; (Serials) CyberTools for Libraries
Wireless access
Function: Prof lending libr
Partic in National Network of Libraries of Medicine Region 5
Open Mon-Fri 8-5:30
Restriction: Circulates for staff only, Lending to staff only, Non-circulating to the pub

M TORRANCE MEMORIAL MEDICAL CENTER*, Medical Library, West Tower, 1st Flr, 3330 W Lomita Blvd, 90505. SAN 301-6668. Tel: 310-517-4720. Web Site: www.torrancememorial.org. *Health Sci Librn,* Linda Russell; E-mail: linda.russell@tmmc.com; Staff 1 (MLS 1)
Founded 1972
Library Holdings: Bk Titles 500; Per Subs 110
Subject Interests: Med, Nursing
Publications: Serials Holding List
Partic in National Network of Libraries of Medicine Region 5
Restriction: Employees only, Staff use only

P TORRANCE PUBLIC LIBRARY*, Katy Geissert Civic Center, 3301 Torrance Blvd, 90503. SAN 335-1696. Tel: 310-618-5950. Circulation Tel: 310-618-5969. Reference Tel: 310-781-7599. FAX: 310-618-5952. Web Site: www.library.torranceca.gov. *City Librn,* Hillary Theyer; E-mail: htheyer@torranceca.gov; *Principal Librn,* Dana Vinke; Tel: 310-618-5974, E-mail: dvinke@torranceca.gov; *Principal Librn, Pub Serv,* Jan Wierzbicki; E-mail: jwierzbicki@torranceca.gov; *Sr Librn, Youth Serv Supvr,* Heather Firchow; Tel: 310-618-5964; Staff 20 (MLS 20)
Founded 1967. Pop 149,111; Circ 1,698,431
Library Holdings: AV Mats 36,068; Electronic Media & Resources 16; Microforms 147,840; Bk Vols 512,699; Per Subs 886; Videos 34,738
Special Collections: Oral History; State Document Depository; US Document Depository
Subject Interests: Art & archit, Hist, Radio
Automation Activity & Vendor Info: (Acquisitions) SirsiDynix; (Cataloging) SirsiDynix; (Circulation) SirsiDynix; (OPAC) SirsiDynix; (Serials) SirsiDynix
Wireless access
Function: 24/7 Electronic res, 24/7 Online cat, Adult bk club, After school storytime, Art exhibits, Art programs, Audiobks on Playaways & MP3, Audiobks via web, AV serv, Bk club(s), Bks on CD, Bus archives, Children's prog, Computer training, Computers for patron use, Digital talking bks, Electronic databases & coll, Family literacy, Free DVD rentals, Games & aids for people with disabilities, Holiday prog, Home delivery &

serv to seniorr ctr & nursing homes, Homebound delivery serv, Homework prog, ILL available, Internet access, Large print keyboards, Life-long learning prog for all ages, Magazines, Magnifiers for reading, Mango lang, Meeting rooms, Microfiche/film & reading machines, Movies, Music CDs, Online cat, Online ref, Orientations, Outreach serv, Photocopying/Printing, Preschool outreach, Preschool reading prog, Printer for laptops & handheld devices, Prof lending libr, Prog for adults, Prog for children & young adult, Ref & res, Ref serv available, Res assist avail, Scanner, Senior computer classes, Senior outreach, Serves people with intellectual disabilities, STEM programs, Story hour, Study rm, Summer reading prog, Teen prog, Telephone ref, Visual arts prog, Wheelchair accessible, Workshops
Partic in Southern California Library Cooperative
Special Services for the Deaf - ADA equip; Assistive tech; Bks on deafness & sign lang
Special Services for the Blind - Accessible computers; Assistive/Adapted tech devices, equip & products; Audio mat; BiFolkal kits; Bks & mags in Braille, on rec, tape & cassette; Bks available with recordings; Bks on CD; Bks on flash-memory cartridges; Braille bks; Braille equip; Computer access aids; Descriptive video serv (DVS); Digital talking bk; Digital talking bk machines; Disability awareness prog; Home delivery serv; Large print bks; Low vision equip; Magnifiers; PC for people with disabilities; Playaways (bks on MP3); Rental typewriters & computers; Talking bks; Talking bks & player equip; Talking bks from Braille Inst; Text reader; Videos on blindness & physical disabilties
Open Mon-Thurs 10-9, Fri 10-6, Sat 10-5:30, Sun (Sept-June) 1-5
Friends of the Library Group

Branches: 5

EL RETIRO, 126 Vista Del Parque, Redondo Beach, 90277, SAN 335-1726. Tel: 310-375-0922. *Supv Librn,* Kay Ujimori; E-mail: kujimori@torranceca.gov; Staff 7 (MLS 2, Non-MLS 5)
Library Holdings: Bk Vols 44,000
Open Mon-Thurs 11-8, Sat 10-5
Friends of the Library Group

ISABEL HENDERSON BRANCH, 4805 Emerald St, 90503-2899, SAN 335-1750. Tel: 310-371-2075. FAX: 310-371-5025. *Sr Librn,* Janice Wierzbicki; E-mail: jwierzbicki@torranceca.gov
Library Holdings: Bk Vols 38,931
Open Mon-Thurs 11-8, Sat 10-5
Friends of the Library Group

NORTH TORRANCE, 3604 Artesia Blvd, 90504-3315, SAN 335-1785. Tel: 310-323-7200. FAX: 310-323-9687. *Sr Librn,* Steve Frame; E-mail: sframe@torranceca.gov
Library Holdings: Bk Vols 45,281
Open Mon-Thurs 11-8, Sat 10-5
Friends of the Library Group

SOUTHEAST, 23115 S Arlington Ave, 90501-5816, SAN 335-1815. Tel: 310-530-5044. FAX: 310-530-5181. *Sr Librn,* Patrice Deleget; E-mail: pdeleget@torranceca.gov
Library Holdings: Bk Vols 46,044
Open Mon-Thurs 11-8, Sat 10-5
Friends of the Library Group

WALTERIA, 3815 W 242nd St, 90505-6410, SAN 335-184X. Tel: 310-375-8418. FAX: 310-375-8325. *Sr Librn,* Philip Ross; E-mail: pross@torranceca.gov
Library Holdings: Bk Vols 40,364
Open Mon-Thurs 11-8, Sat 10-5
Friends of the Library Group

TRAVIS AFB

UNITED STATES AIR FORCE

AM DAVID GRANT USAF MEDICAL CENTER LEARNING RESOURCE CENTER*, 101 Bodin Circle, 94535-1800, SAN 335-1874. Tel: 707-423-5344. FAX: 707-423-7965. *Info Spec,* Regina Ann Rowell; E-mail: regina.rowell@us.af.mil; Staff 1 (MLS 1)
Library Holdings: AV Mats 645; e-journals 51; Bk Vols 3,000; Per Subs 76
Subject Interests: Dentistry, Hospital admin, Med, Nursing
Automation Activity & Vendor Info: (Cataloging) Horizon; (Circulation) Horizon; (OPAC) Horizon; (Serials) Horizon
Function: Computers for patron use, Electronic databases & coll, ILL available, Internet access, Online cat, Orientations, Photocopying/Printing, Ref serv available
Partic in National Network of Libraries of Medicine Region 5; Sacramento Area Health Sciences Librs
Restriction: Badge access after hrs, Circulates for staff only, In-house use for visitors, Open to staff, patients & family mem

A MITCHELL MEMORIAL LIBRARY-TRAVIS AIR FORCE BASE LIBRARY*, 60 FSS/FSDL, 510 Travis Ave, 94535-2168, SAN 335-1904. Tel: 707-424-3279. Reference Tel: 707-424-5255. FAX: 707-424-3809. Web Site: www.mitchellmemoriallibrary.org. *Dir,* Marie Ludwig; Tel: 707-424-4940; Staff 2 (MLS 2)
Founded 1943
Automation Activity & Vendor Info: (Circulation) SirsiDynix-WorkFlows

TULARE

P TULARE PUBLIC LIBRARY*, 475 North M St, 93274. SAN 301-6684. Tel: 559-685-4500. Circulation Tel: 559-685-4501. Reference Tel: 559-685-4503. FAX: 559-685-2345. E-mail: info@tularepubliclibrary.org. Web Site: www.tularepubliclibrary.org. *Libr Mgr,* Heidi Clark; Tel: 559-685-4505, E-mail: heidi.clark@tularepubliclibrary.org; *Youth Serv Librn,* Melissa Emerson; Tel: 559-685-4507, E-mail: melissa.emerson@tularepubliclibrary.org; Staff 3 (MLS 3)
Founded 1878. Pop 59,535; Circ 298,547
Library Holdings: AV Mats 6,914; CDs 7,408; DVDs 4,205; e-books 279; Bk Vols 82,664; Per Subs 131
Special Collections: Genealogy & Local History Coll
Subject Interests: Art, Hist, Music, Relig
Automation Activity & Vendor Info: (Acquisitions) Horizon; (Cataloging) Horizon; (Circulation) Horizon
Wireless access
Mem of San Joaquin Valley Library System
Open Tues-Thurs 11-7, Fri & Sat 11-4
Friends of the Library Group

TULELAKE

S NATIONAL PARK SERVICE*, Lava Beds National Monument Research Library, One Indian Well Headquarters, 96134. (Mail add: PO Box 1240, 96134), SAN 370-0046. Tel: 530-667-8113, 530-667-8119. Web Site: www.nps.gov/labe. *Coordr,* Angela Sutton; E-mail: angela_sutton@nps.gov
Library Holdings: Bk Titles 2,500; Bk Vols 2,550
Restriction: Open by appt only

TURLOCK

C CALIFORNIA STATE UNIVERSITY, STANISLAUS*, University Library, One University Circle, 95382. SAN 301-6692. Circulation Tel: 209-667-3234. Interlibrary Loan Service Tel: 209-667-3236. Reference Tel: 209-664-6558. Administration Tel: 209-667-3232. Information Services Tel: 209-667-3761. Administration FAX: 209-664-7081. E-mail: library@library.csustan.edu. Web Site: library.csustan.edu. *Dean, Libr Serv,* Ronald Rodriguez; Tel: 209-667-3607, E-mail: rrodriguez36@csustan.edu; *Acq Librn,* Annie Hor; Tel: 209-667-3709, E-mail: ahor@csustan.edu; *Archives & Spec Coll Librn,* Laura French; Tel: 209-664-6557, E-mail: lfrench@csustan.edu; *Electronic Res Librn,* John Brandt; Tel: 209-664-6563, E-mail: jbrandt@csustan.edu; *Ref & Instruction Librn,* Tim Held; Tel: 209-667-6555, E-mail: theld@csustan.edu; *Ref & Instruction Librn,* Maryann Hight; Tel: 209-664-6553, E-mail: mhight@csustan.edu; *Ref & Instruction Librn,* Warren Jacobs; Tel: 209-664-6565, E-mail: wjacobs@csustan.edu; *Web Serv Librn,* Paul Park; Tel: 209-664-6556, E-mail: jpark5@csustan.edu; *Syst Supvr,* Rick Dietz; Tel: 209-667-3605, E-mail: rdietz@csustan.edu; *Admin Support Coordr,* Loretta Blakeley; E-mail: lblakeley@csustan.edu; *ILL Coordr,* Julie Reuben; E-mail: jreuben@csustan.edu; Staff 22 (MLS 9, Non-MLS 13)
Founded 1960. Enrl 9,282; Fac 294; Highest Degree: Doctorate
Jul 2015-Jun 2016 Income $2,437,651, Locally Generated Income $16,731, Parent Institution $2,067,845, Other $353,075. Mats Exp $813,624, Books $85,143, Electronic Ref Mat (Incl. Access Fees) $724,130, Presv $4,351. Sal $1,368,633 (Prof $716,798)
Library Holdings: AV Mats 16,934; e-books 8,002; Bk Titles 336,442; Bk Vols 514,045; Per Subs 634
Special Collections: Californiana Coll; Historical Regional Newspaper Coll; Portuguese Culture Photographs; Religious Assyriana Coll; Stanislaus County History Coll; Stanislaus County Photographs; Western US Fine Printing Coll. Oral History; State Document Depository; US Document Depository
Subject Interests: Bus, Liberal arts, Sci, Teacher educ
Automation Activity & Vendor Info: (Acquisitions) Innovative Interfaces, Inc; (Cataloging) Innovative Interfaces, Inc; (Circulation) Innovative Interfaces, Inc; (Course Reserve) Innovative Interfaces, Inc; (ILL) OCLC; (OPAC) Innovative Interfaces, Inc; (Serials) Innovative Interfaces, Inc
Wireless access
Partic in OCLC Online Computer Library Center, Inc
Special Services for the Deaf - Assistive tech
Special Services for the Blind - Assistive/Adapted tech devices, equip & products; Closed circuit TV magnifier; Computer with voice synthesizer for visually impaired persons
Open Mon-Thurs 7:45am-Midnight, Fri 7:45-5, Sat 9-5, Sun 11-7

M EMANUEL MEDICAL CENTER LIBRARY*, 825 Delbon Ave, 95382. (Mail add: PO Box 819005, 95381-9005), SAN 301-6706. Tel: 209-667-4200, Ext 2899. FAX: 209-664-5657. *Dir,* Tracey Lopez; E-mail: tracey.lopez@tenethealth.com
Founded 1971
Library Holdings: Bk Vols 106; Per Subs 21
Partic in N San Joaquin Health Sci Libr Consortium
Restriction: Staff use only

TWENTYNINE PALMS

A UNITED STATES MARINE CORPS*, Combat Center Library, 1524 Sixth St, MCAGCC Box 788150, 92278-8150. SAN 335-1939. Tel: 760-830-6875. FAX: 760-830-4497. Web Site: mccs29palms.com/index.cfm/marine-family-programs/ppd/combat-center-library. *Librn,* Kelley Lostis; Staff 1 (MLS 1)
Founded 1957
Library Holdings: DVDs 4,038; Bk Vols 30,535; Per Subs 50
Subject Interests: Mil hist
Automation Activity & Vendor Info: (Acquisitions) SirsiDynix; (Cataloging) SirsiDynix; (Circulation) SirsiDynix; (ILL) SirsiDynix
Wireless access
Open Mon-Fri 8-7:30, Sat & Sun 10-4
Restriction: Mil, family mem, retirees, Civil Serv personnel NAF only

S UNITED STATES NATIONAL PARK SERVICE*, Joshua Tree National Park Research Library, 74485 National Park Dr, 92277-3597. SAN 371-7879. Tel: 760-367-5571. FAX: 760-367-5588. Web Site: www.nps.gov/jotr/learn/historyculture/collections.htm. *Curator, Library Contact,* Melanie Spoo; E-mail: Melanie_Spoo@nps.gov
Founded 1994
Library Holdings: Bk Vols 4,000
Special Collections: Early Archeology/Anthropology volumes, William H Campbell Library
Subject Interests: Local hist, Local natural hist, Planning doc
Function: Ref serv available
Restriction: Not a lending libr

UKIAH

S THE HISTORICAL SOCIETY OF MENDOCINO COUNTY ARCHIVES, (Formerly Mendocino County Historical Society), Held-Poage Memorial Home, 603 W Perkins St, 95482-4726. SAN 301-6757. Tel: 707-462-6969. E-mail: mchs@pacific.net. Web Site: mendocinocountyhistory.org. *Archivist,* Alyssa Ballard
Founded 1976
Library Holdings: Bk Vols 5,300; Per Subs 200
Special Collections: Americana (Estelle Beard Coll); California Indians; Civil War (William P Held Coll); Mendocino County
Subject Interests: Genealogy
Publications: Newsletter (Quarterly)

J MENDOCINO COLLEGE LIBRARY*, 1000 Hensley Creek Rd, 95482. SAN 301-6749. Tel: 707-468-3245. Circulation Tel: 707-468-3158. FAX: 707-468-3056. E-mail: librarian@mendocino.edu, libraryhelp@mendocino.edu. Web Site: mclib.mendocino.edu. *Head Librn,* Robert Parmenter; E-mail: rparmenter@mendocino.edu; *Ref Librn,* Alison Finch; E-mail: afinch@mendocino.edu; *Circ,* Maricela Gallardo; E-mail: mgallardo@mendocino.edu; *Circ,* Diana Ratliff; E-mail: dratliff@mendocino.edu; Staff 3 (Non-MLS 3)
Founded 1973. Fac 200; Highest Degree: Associate
Library Holdings: Bk Vols 30,000; Per Subs 177
Automation Activity & Vendor Info: (Circulation) Follett Software; (OPAC) Follett Software
Wireless access
Partic in OCLC Online Computer Library Center, Inc
Restriction: Non-circulating to the pub
Friends of the Library Group

GL MENDOCINO COUNTY LAW LIBRARY*, Courthouse, Rm 307, 100 N State St, 95482. SAN 301-6765. Tel: 707-463-4201. FAX: 707-468-3459. E-mail: lawlib@pacific.net. Web Site: www.co.mendocino.ca.us/lawlib/. *Law Librn,* Daniel J Helsel
Library Holdings: Bk Vols 8,000
Wireless access
Open Mon-Fri 9-4

P MENDOCINO COUNTY LIBRARY DISTRICT*, 880 N Bush St, 95482. SAN 335-1963. Tel: 707-24-2872. Web Site: www.mendolibrary.org. *County Librn,* Position Currently Open; *Actg Asst Librn,* Nicole Bird; E-mail: birdn@co.mendocino.ca.us; Staff 11 (MLS 4, Non-MLS 7)
Founded 1964. Pop 90,000; Circ 398,794
Library Holdings: Bk Titles 93,000; Bk Vols 159,500; Per Subs 110
Special Collections: Native Americans of Mendocino County
Subject Interests: Art, Fishing, Forestry, Genealogy, Indians, Logging, Wines
Automation Activity & Vendor Info: (Cataloging) Horizon; (Circulation) Horizon; (ILL) OCLC; (OPAC) Horizon
Wireless access
Mem of NorthNet Library System
Partic in OCLC Online Computer Library Center, Inc
Open Tues & Thurs 10-6, Wed 12-8, Sat 10-5
Friends of the Library Group
Branches: 5
COAST COMMUNITY, 225 Main St, Point Arena, 95468. (Mail add: PO Box 294, Point Arena, 95468), SAN 376-8139. Tel: 707-882-3114. FAX: 707-882-3114. *Br Librn,* Julia Larke; E-mail: larkej@co.mendocino.ca.us; Staff 1 (Non-MLS 1)
Founded 1985. Pop 7,000; Circ 9,557
Library Holdings: Bk Vols 12,999
Publications: Redwood Coast Review
Open Mon & Fri 12-6, Tues 10-6, Wed 10-8, Thurs 12-8, Sat 12-3
Friends of the Library Group
FORT BRAGG BRANCH, 499 E Laurel St, Fort Bragg, 95437, SAN 335-1998. Tel: 707-964-2020. FAX: 707-961-2623. *Br Librn,* Dan Hess; E-mail: hessd@co.mendocino.ca.us
Pop 18,000; Circ 93,869
Library Holdings: Bk Titles 34,669; Per Subs 70
Open Tues & Sat 10-5, Wed 12-8
Friends of the Library Group
ROUND VALLEY, 23925 Howard St, Covelo, 95428, SAN 372-7858. Tel: 707-983-6736. *Br Librn,* Josh Bennett; E-mail: bennettj@co.mendocino.ca.us; Staff 1 (Non-MLS 1)
Founded 1990. Pop 2,300; Circ 10,560
Library Holdings: Bk Vols 10,782
Open Mon-Fri 10-5
Friends of the Library Group
UKIAH MAIN LIBRARY, 105 N Main St, 95482. Tel: 707-463-4490. FAX: 707-463-5472. *Br Librn,* Melissa Carr; E-mail: carrm@co.mendocino.ca.us; Staff 1 (MLS 1)
Friends of the Library Group
WILLITS BRANCH, 390 E Commercial St, Willits, 95490, SAN 335-2021. Tel: 707-459-5908. FAX: 707-459-7819. *Actg Asst Librn,* Nicole Bird; Staff 1 (MLS 1)
Founded 1972
Library Holdings: Bk Vols 34,000
Special Collections: Calif History Coll; Western Americana Coll
Automation Activity & Vendor Info: (Circulation) Horizon
Open Tues 10-8, Wed & Thurs 10-6, Fri & Sat 10-5
Friends of the Library Group
Bookmobiles: 1. Libr Assoc, David Frick

UPLAND

R FIRST PRESBYTERIAN CHURCH LIBRARY*, 869 N Euclid Ave, 91786. SAN 301-6781. Tel: 909-982-8811. FAX: 909-985-8014. *Librn,* Annette Davidson
Library Holdings: Bk Vols 500
Wireless access
Restriction: Mem only

P UPLAND PUBLIC LIBRARY*, 450 N Euclid Ave, 91786-4732. SAN 301-679X. Tel: 909-931-4200. Interlibrary Loan Service Tel: 909-931-4225. Administration Tel: 909-931-4201. Information Services Tel: 909-931-4205. FAX: 909-931-4209. Reference E-mail: reference@uplandlibrary.org. Web Site: uplandca.gov/library. *Dir,* Yuri Hurtado; E-mail: yhurtado@uplandlibrary.org; *Ch,* Christina Glass; Tel: 909-931-4216, E-mail: childrens@uplandlibrary.org; *Ref & Local Hist Librn,* Lorene Broersma; *Teen Serv Coordr,* Katie Laird; Tel: 909-931-4214, E-mail: teens@uplandlibrary.org; Staff 20 (MLS 4, Non-MLS 16)
Founded 1913. Pop 75,035; Circ 309,471
Library Holdings: AV Mats 7,241; CDs 1,916; DVDs 1,680; e-books 2,125; Large Print Bks 1,514; Bk Titles 157,390; Bk Vols 159,927; Per Subs 220; Talking Bks 1,941; Videos 1,626
Special Collections: Local History Coll. Oral History
Automation Activity & Vendor Info: (Acquisitions) SirsiDynix; (Cataloging) SirsiDynix; (Circulation) SirsiDynix; (ILL) OCLC; (OPAC) SirsiDynix
Wireless access
Function: Adult literacy prog, Homebound delivery serv, ILL available, Magnifiers for reading, Photocopying/Printing, Prog for adults, Prog for children & young adult, Ref serv available, Summer reading prog, Wheelchair accessible
Mem of Inland Library System
Partic in Califa; San Bernardino, Inyo, Riverside Counties United Library Services
Special Services for the Blind - Talking bks
Open Mon & Thurs 10-7, Tues & Wed 10-8, Fri & Sun 1-5, Sat 10-4
Friends of the Library Group
Bookmobiles: 1. Libr Clerk, Jamie Murray. Bk vols 2,212

VALENCIA

S CALIFORNIA INSTITUTE OF THE ARTS*, Division of Library & Information Resources, 24700 McBean Pkwy, 91355. SAN 301-6803. Tel: 661-253-7885. Reference Tel: 661-291-3024. Automation Services Tel: 661-253-7888. E-mail: libref@calarts.edu. Web Site: library.calarts.edu.

Interim Dean, Susan Lowenberg; E-mail: susan@calarts.edu; *Access Serv Librn,* Lavinia Busch; E-mail: lbusch@calarts.edu; *Ref & Instruction Librn,* Marisa Mendez-Brady; Tel: 661-291-3024, E-mail: mmendezbrady@calarts.edu; *Visual Arts Librn,* Karen Baxter; Tel: 661-253-7880, E-mail: kbaxter@calarts.edu; Staff 13 (MLS 6, Non-MLS 7)
Founded 1968. Enrl 1,459; Fac 358; Highest Degree: Doctorate
Jul 2019-Jun 2020. Mats Exp $244,664, Books $104,834, Per/Ser (Incl. Access Fees) $31,022, AV Mat $23,290, Electronic Ref Mat (Incl. Access Fees) $85,088, Presv $430. Sal $825,673
Library Holdings: AV Mats 37,902; e-books 157,009; e-journals 11,203; Microforms 5,632; Music Scores 26,798; Bk Vols 142,128; Per Subs 244
Special Collections: Artists Books; Film History Coll; MCA Coll; Viola Hegyi Swisher Dance Coll
Subject Interests: Art, Dance, Film, Music, Theatre, Writing
Automation Activity & Vendor Info: (Acquisitions) OCLC Worldshare Management Services; (Cataloging) OCLC Worldshare Management Services; (Circulation) OCLC Worldshare Management Services; (Course Reserve) OCLC Worldshare Management Services; (Discovery) OCLC Worldshare Management Services; (ILL) OCLC WorldShare Interlibrary Loan; (OPAC) OCLC Worldshare Management Services; (Serials) OCLC Worldshare Management Services
Wireless access
Function: Archival coll, Audio & video playback equip for onsite use, AV serv, Electronic databases & coll, ILL available, Music CDs, Online cat, Photocopying/Printing, Ref serv available, Scanner, VHS videos
Partic in Statewide California Electronic Library Consortium
Open Mon-Thurs 9am-Midnight, Fri 9-9, Sat 1-5, Sun 1-Midnight
Restriction: Borrowing requests are handled by ILL, Circ limited, In-house use for visitors

VALLEJO

C THE CALIFORNIA MARITIME ACADEMY LIBRARY*, 200 Maritime Academy Dr, 94590. SAN 301-682X. Tel: 707-654-1090, 707-654-1091. Administration Tel: 707-654-1093. Automation Services Tel: 707-654-1092. Information Services Tel: 707-654-1098. FAX: 707-654-1094. E-mail: library@csum.edu. Web Site: library.csum.edu. *Dean of Libr, Librn,* Michele Van Hoeck; Tel: 707-654-1097, E-mail: MVanHoeck@csum.edu; *Instruction & Outreach Librn,* Margot Hanson; E-mail: mhanson@csum.edu; *Library Technologist,* Mark Stackpole; E-mail: mstackpole@csum.edu; *Libr & Archives Asst,* Larry Stevens; Tel: 707-654-1089, E-mail: lstevens@csum.edu; *Circ Supvr, Student Asst Supvr,* Jennifer Haupt; E-mail: jhaupt@csum.edu. Subject Specialists: *Maritime, Music, Theatre,* Mark Stackpole; Staff 6 (MLS 4, Non-MLS 2)
Founded 1929. Enrl 1,025; Fac 82; Highest Degree: Master
Library Holdings: Bk Titles 38,000; Bk Vols 40,000; Per Subs 276; Spec Interest Per Sub 112
Special Collections: Cal Maritime Academy Historical Archives; Cal Maritime Academy Oral History Project. Oral History
Subject Interests: Electrical engr, Intl studies, Logistics, Marine engr, Marine tech, Marine transportation, Maritime law
Automation Activity & Vendor Info: (Cataloging) Innovative Interfaces, Inc; (Circulation) Innovative Interfaces, Inc; (Course Reserve) Innovative Interfaces, Inc; (ILL) OCLC; (OPAC) Innovative Interfaces, Inc
Wireless access
Function: Archival coll, For res purposes, ILL available, Photocopying/Printing, Ref serv available, Res libr
Partic in Link+; OCLC Online Computer Library Center, Inc
Open Mon-Thurs 7:30am-10pm, Fri 7:30-4:30, Sat 10:30-4:30, Sun 2-10
Restriction: Circ limited, Open to students, fac & staff, Pub use on premises

S VALLEJO NAVAL & HISTORICAL MUSEUM*, 734 Marin St, 94590. SAN 326-5048. Tel: 707-643-0077. FAX: 707-643-2443. E-mail: valmuse@pacbell.net. Web Site: www.vallejomuseum.org. *Librn,* Arlene Valdez
Founded 1974
Library Holdings: AV Mats 100; Bk Titles 5,200; Per Subs 10
Special Collections: Municipal Document Depository; Oral History
Subject Interests: Archives, Local hist, Maritime hist
Function: Res libr
Open Tues 12-4 or by appointment
Restriction: Non-circulating

VALLEY GLEN

J LOS ANGELES VALLEY COLLEGE LIBRARY*, 5800 Fulton Ave, 91401-4096. SAN 301-6900. Tel: 818-947-2425. Circulation Tel: 818-947-7264. Reference Tel: 818-947-2763, 818-947-2764. FAX: 818-947-2751. Web Site: lavc.edu/library/home.aspx. *Dept Chair,* Dora Esten; Tel: 818-947-2761, E-mail: estende@lavc.edu; *Librn,* Xiaoyang Liu Behlendorf; Tel: 818-947-2762, E-mail: behlenxl@lavc.edu; *Librn,* Meghan Gaynor Cason; Tel: 818-778-7261, E-mail: gaynorms@lavc.edu; *Librn,* Cynthia Cohen; Tel: 818-947-2766, E-mail: cohencm@lavc.edu; *Librn,* Mike FitzGerald; Tel: 818-778-5783, E-mail: fitzgemj@lavc.edu. Subject Specialists: *Info literacy,* Cynthia Cohen; Staff 10 (MLS 5, Non-MLS 5)
Founded 1949. Enrl 18,300; Fac 320; Highest Degree: Associate
Library Holdings: Bks on Deafness & Sign Lang 830; CDs 167; DVDs 205; e-books 18,075; Music Scores 164; Bk Titles 105,926; Bk Vols 129,083; Per Subs 106
Subject Interests: Art & archit, Ethnic studies, Humanities, Relig, Soc sci
Automation Activity & Vendor Info: (Cataloging) SirsiDynix-WorkFlows; (Circulation) SirsiDynix; (Course Reserve) SirsiDynix; (Discovery) EBSCO Discovery Service; (ILL) SirsiDynix; (OPAC) SirsiDynix
Wireless access
Function: 24/7 Electronic res, 24/7 Online cat, Electronic databases & coll, Free DVD rentals, Internet access, Magazines, Online cat, Online info literacy tutorials on the web & in blackboard, Online ref, Orientations, Photocopying/Printing, Ref serv available, Scanner, Study rm
Special Services for the Deaf - Accessible learning ctr; ADA equip; Assisted listening device; Assistive tech; Bks on deafness & sign lang; Captioned film dep
Special Services for the Blind - Accessible computers; Assistive/Adapted tech devices, equip & products
Open Mon-Thurs 8-8:45, Fri 9-1, Sat 9-3
Restriction: Circ privileges for students & alumni only

VENTURA

S THE CHURCH OF JESUS CHRIST OF LATTER-DAY SAINTS*, Family History Center Ventura Stake, 3501 Loma Vista, 93003. SAN 329-1790. Tel: 805-643-5607. E-mail: vfhlibrary@gmail.com. *Dir,* Amily Houlberg; Staff 6 (MLS 1, Non-MLS 5)
Founded 1978
Library Holdings: Bk Vols 1,400
Special Collections: IGI Ancestral File; Social Security Death Index
Open Tues & Thurs 10-5, Wed 6:30pm-8:30pm

S MUSEUM OF VENTURA COUNTY, Research Library, 100 E Main St, 93001. SAN 301-6994. Tel: 805-653-0323, Ext 320. FAX: 805-653-5267. E-mail: library@venturamuseum.org. Web Site: venturamuseum.org/library. *Dir, Research Library & Archives,* Deya Terrafranca; E-mail: dterrafranca@venturamuseum.org; Staff 1 (MLS 1)
Founded 1913
Library Holdings: Bk Vols 7,000; Per Subs 16
Special Collections: Architectural Plans & Drawings Coll; Biographical, Newspaper Clipping & Ephemera Vertical Files; California Ventura County History, 1864-present, bks, maps, newsp, photos; Ventura County Historical Society Quarterlies, 1955-Present. Oral History
Function: Archival coll, Mail & tel request accepted, Photocopying/Printing, Ref & res, Res libr, Res performed for a fee, Scanner
Publications: Journal of Ventura County History; Ventura County Historical Society (Quarterly)
Restriction: Non-circulating, Open by appt only

J VENTURA COLLEGE*, Evelyn & Howard Boroughs Library, 4667 Telegraph Rd, 93003. SAN 301-6986. Tel: 805-654-6482. FAX: 805-648-8900. E-mail: vclibrary@vcccd.edu. Web Site: www.venturacollege.edu/library. *Chair, Librn,* Peter H Sezzi; Tel: 805-289-6189, E-mail: psezzi@vcccd.edu; *Librn,* Kaela Casey; Tel: 805-289-6563, E-mail: kcasey@vcccd.edu; *Librn,* Linda Kennedy; Tel: 805-289-6399, E-mail: linda_kennedy@vcccd.edu; Staff 6 (MLS 2, Non-MLS 4)
Founded 1925. Enrl 10,500; Fac 625; Highest Degree: Associate
Library Holdings: Bk Vols 63,529; Per Subs 341
Subject Interests: Art, Costume, Ethnic studies, Feminism
Automation Activity & Vendor Info: (Cataloging) TLC (The Library Corporation); (Circulation) TLC (The Library Corporation); (OPAC) TLC (The Library Corporation)
Wireless access
Function: ILL available
Partic in Coop Libr Agency for Syst & Servs
Open Mon-Thurs 7:30am-9pm, Fri 7:30-3:30, Sat 9-Noon
Friends of the Library Group

GL VENTURA COUNTY LAW LIBRARY, 800 S Victoria Ave, 93009-2020. SAN 301-7001. Tel: 805-642-8982. Web Site: www.vencolawlib.org. *Dir,* Katie Drow; E-mail: katied@vencolawlib.org; Staff 6 (MLS 2, Non-MLS 4)
Founded 1891
Library Holdings: Bk Vols 81,292; Per Subs 328
Special Collections: Law Coll
Wireless access
Function: 24/7 Online cat, Computers for patron use, Electronic databases & coll, Govt ref serv, Internet access, Mail & tel request accepted, Meeting rooms, Microfiche/film & reading machines, Online cat, Online ref, Photocopying/Printing, Res libr, Tax forms

Open Mon-Fri 8-4
Restriction: Circ limited

P VENTURA COUNTY LIBRARY*, 5600 Everglades St, Ste A, 93003. SAN 335-220X. Tel: 805-677-7150. Interlibrary Loan Service Tel: 805-677-7169. Reference Tel: 805-648-2716. Automation Services Tel: 805 701-1317. FAX: 805-677-7173. Interlibrary Loan Service FAX: 805-677-7169. Web Site: www.vencolibrary.org. *Dir,* Nancy Schram; E-mail: nancy.schram@ventura.org; *Dep Libr Dir,* Dana Vinke; E-mail: Dana.Vinke@ventura.org; *Fiscal Officer,* Sarah Clancy; E-mail: Sarah.Clancy@ventura.org; *Regional Mgr, Sr City Librn,* Irma Morales; E-mail: Irma.Morales@ventura.org; *City Librn, Senior Mgr, East Region,* Position Currently Open; *City Librn, Regional Mgr, West Region,* Ron Solorzano; E-mail: Ron.Solorzano@ventura.org; *Support Serv Mgr,* Mark Lager; E-mail: mark.lager@ventura.org; *Coll, Tech Serv Mgr,* Derek Stalcup; E-mail: Derek.Stalcup@ventura.org; *Youth Serv Mgr,* Molly Krill; E-mail: molly.krill@ventura.org; *Adult Literacy Coordr,* Carol Chapman; Tel: 805-677-7159, E-mail: carol.chapman@ventura.org; *ILL,* Liz Romero; E-mail: liz.romero@ventura.org; *Webmaster,* Barbara Eales; Tel: 805-218-5360, E-mail: barbara.eales@ventura.org
Founded 1916
Special Collections: Local History (Ventura County)
Automation Activity & Vendor Info: (Acquisitions) Baker & Taylor; (Cataloging) SirsiDynix; (Circulation) SirsiDynix; (ILL) OCLC; (OPAC) SirsiDynix; (Serials) SirsiDynix
Wireless access
Partic in Southern California Library Cooperative
Friends of the Library Group
Branches: 12
AVENUE LIBRARY, 606 N Ventura Ave, 93001, SAN 335-2234. Tel: 805-643-6393. FAX: 805-648-3791. *Supvr,* Laura Paine; Staff 1.4 (Non-MLS 1.4)
Founded 1963. Pop 14,659; Circ 16,882
Library Holdings: Bk Vols 20,710
Open Mon 11-1 & 2-6, Tues & Thurs 2-6, Wed 12-6, Sat 10-3
Friends of the Library Group
FILLMORE LIBRARY, 502 Second St, Fillmore, 93015, SAN 335-2382. Tel: 805-524-3355. FAX: 808-524-4636. *Supvr,* Cathy Krushell; Staff 2 (Non-MLS 2)
Founded 1916. Pop 16,666; Circ 38,198
Library Holdings: Bk Vols 30,195
Open Mon & Tues 2-7, Wed 10-5, Thurs-Sat 12-5
Friends of the Library Group
E P FOSTER LIBRARY, 651 E Main St, 93001, SAN 335-2412. Tel: 805-648-2715. FAX: 805-648-3696. *Sr City Librn,* Mary Stewart; Tel: 805-641-4414; Staff 14 (MLS 2, Non-MLS 12)
Founded 1921. Pop 83,493; Circ 277,823
Library Holdings: Bk Vols 179,606
Open Mon-Thurs 10-8, Fri & Sat 10-5, Sun 1-5
Friends of the Library Group
HILL ROAD LIBRARY, 1070 S Hill Rd, 93003.
Friends of the Library Group
MEINERS OAKS LIBRARY, 114 N Padre Juan Ave, Meiners Oaks, 93023, SAN 335-2447. Tel: 805-646-4804. FAX: 805-646-8007. *Supvr,* Deborah Fletcher; Staff 1 (Non-MLS 1)
Founded 1958. Pop 6,834; Circ 11,518
Library Holdings: Bk Vols 16,749
Open Mon & Tues 10-1 & 2-6, Wed & Thurs 1-6
Friends of the Library Group
OAK PARK LIBRARY, 899 N Kanan Rd, Oak Park, 91377, SAN 335-2528. Tel: 818-889-2239. FAX: 818-706-9746. *Librn Spec,* Laurie Dunning; Staff 3.5 (MLS 1, Non-MLS 2.5)
Founded 1981. Pop 14,111; Circ 50,748
Library Holdings: Bk Vols 32,291
Open Mon & Tues 2-8, Wed & Thurs 10-6, Fri & Sat 10-5
Friends of the Library Group
OAK VIEW LIBRARY, 555 Mahoney Ave, Oak View, 93022, SAN 335-2536. Tel: 805-649-1523. FAX: 805-649-5591. *Supvr,* Sharon Dykstra; Staff 1 (Non-MLS 1)
Founded 1945. Pop 10,518; Circ 10,669
Library Holdings: Bk Vols 18,762
Open Mon-Thurs 1-6, Sat 10-2
Friends of the Library Group
OJAI LIBRARY, 111 E Ojai Ave, Ojai, 93023, SAN 335-2560. Tel: 805-646-1639. FAX: 805-646-4693. *City Librn,* Mary Lynch; *Youth Serv,* Julie Albright; Staff 7 (MLS 4, Non-MLS 3)
Founded 1916. Pop 11,251; Circ 115,252
Library Holdings: Bk Vols 39,429
Open Mon-Thurs 10-8, Fri-Sun 12-5
Friends of the Library Group
PIRU LIBRARY, 3811 Center St, Piru, 93040, SAN 329-7527. Tel: 805-521-1753. FAX: 805-521-0729. *Supvr,* Cindy Escoto
Founded 1916. Pop 2,822; Circ 13,691
Library Holdings: Bk Vols 14,627
Open Mon-Wed & Fri 3-7, Thurs 1-5, Sat 10-2
RAY D PRUETER LIBRARY, 510 Park Ave, Port Hueneme, 93041, SAN 335-2595. Tel: 805-486-5460. FAX: 805-487-9190. *City Librn,* Bernadette McDowell; *Youth Serv,* Susan Mikula; Staff 5.2 (MLS 2, Non-MLS 3.2)
Founded 1936. Pop 26,674; Circ 75,711
Library Holdings: Bk Vols 66,255
Open Mon 10-7, Tues & Wed 10-6, Thurs-Sat 12-5
Friends of the Library Group
SATICOY LIBRARY, 11426 Violeta St, Saticoy, 93004, SAN 376-2084. Tel: 805-647-5736. FAX: 805-672-0406. *Supvr,* Russell Stevens; Staff 1 (Non-MLS 1)
Founded 1919. Pop 17,505; Circ 23,918
Library Holdings: Bk Vols 17,424
Open Mon-Thurs 1-6, Sat 10-2
Friends of the Library Group
ALBERT H SOLIZ LIBRARY, 2820 Jourdan St, Oxnard, 93036, SAN 335-2358. Tel: 805-485-4515. FAX: 805-604-7966. *Supvr,* Humberto Tello; Staff 1.3 (Non-MLS 1.3)
Founded 1962. Pop 14,063; Circ 14,209
Library Holdings: Bk Vols 14,902
Open Mon, Tues & Fri 2-6, Wed 10-1 & 2-6, Thurs 2-7
Friends of the Library Group
Bookmobiles: 1

S VENTURA COUNTY MEDICAL CENTER*, Lillian Smolt Memorial Library, 3291 Loma Vista Rd, 93003. SAN 301-6978. Tel: 805-652-6030. Web Site: hospitals.vchca.org. *Library Contact,* Victoria Yuschenkoff; E-mail: victoria.yuschenkoff@ventura.org
Library Holdings: Bk Vols 1,200; Per Subs 150
Restriction: Med staff only

VICTORVILLE

J VICTOR VALLEY COLLEGE LIBRARY, 18422 Bear Valley Rd, 92395-5850. SAN 301-7028. Tel: 760-245-4271, Ext 2262. FAX: 760-245-4373. Web Site: www.vvc.edu/library. *Dean of Business, Law, & Academic Resources,* Dr Patricia Ellerson; *Dept Chair,* Leslie Huiner; E-mail: leslie.huiner@vvc.edu; *Syst Librn,* Yvonne Reed; E-mail: yvonne.reed@vvc.edu
Founded 1961
Library Holdings: Bk Titles 50,000; Bk Vols 54,000
Special Collections: Mojave Desert
Wireless access
Partic in Community College League of California; Inland Empire Acad Libr Coop; OCLC Online Computer Library Center, Inc
Open Mon-Thurs 8-6 (Summer-Winter); Mon-Thurs 8am-9pm, Fri 8-4, Sat 10-3 (Fall-Spring)
Friends of the Library Group

P VICTORVILLE CITY LIBRARY*, 15011 Circle Dr, 92395. Tel: 760-245-4222. Web Site: www.victorvilleca.gov/government/city-departments/community-services/library. *Librn,* George Carter
Library Holdings: Bk Vols 71,278
Wireless access
Mem of Inland Library System
Partic in Association for Rural & Small Libraries
Open Mon-Thurs 9-8, Fri 9-6, Sat 9-5
Friends of the Library Group

VISALIA

J COLLEGE OF THE SEQUOIAS LIBRARY*, 915 S Mooney Blvd, 93277. SAN 301-7036. Tel: 559-730-3824. Circulation Tel: 559-730-3825. FAX: 559-737-4835. Web Site: www.cos.edu/en-us/library. *Dir, Learning Res,* Mary-Catherine Oxford; E-mail: marycat@cos.edu; *Librn,* Linda Yamakawa; E-mail: linday@cos.edu; Staff 5 (MLS 5)
Founded 1926. Enrl 10,000; Fac 384
Library Holdings: Bk Vols 84,000; Per Subs 300
Automation Activity & Vendor Info: (Cataloging) Innovative Interfaces, Inc - Millennium; (Circulation) Innovative Interfaces, Inc - Millennium; (OPAC) Innovative Interfaces, Inc - Millennium
Wireless access
Open Mon-Thurs 7:30am-8pm, Fri 7:30-Noon

M KAWEAH DELTA HEALTH CARE DISTRICT LIBRARY*, 400 W Mineral King Ave, 93291-6263. SAN 320-6084. Tel: 559-624-2000. FAX: 559-635-4051. *Librn,* Karen Bontekoe
Subject Interests: Clinical med, Hospital admin, Nursing
Partic in National Network of Libraries of Medicine Region 5

P TULARE COUNTY LIBRARY*, Main Library, 200 W Oak Ave, 93291-4993. SAN 335-2749. Tel: 559-713-2700. Circulation Tel: 559-713-2711, 559-713-2712. Reference Tel: 559-713-2703. FAX: 559-737-4586. E-mail: questions@tularecountylibrary.org. Web Site: www.tularecountylibrary.org. *County Librn,* Darla Wegener; E-mail:

dwegener@co.tulare.ca.us; *Dep County Librn,* Florencia Wright; E-mail: florencia.wright@tularecountylibrary.org; Staff 38 (MLS 5, Non-MLS 33)
Founded 1910. Pop 146,023; Circ 391,030. Sal $1,318,200
Library Holdings: AV Mats 8,000; DVDs 4,500; e-books 6,893; Electronic Media & Resources 12; Bk Titles 154,356; Bk Vols 285,915; Per Subs 448; Talking Bks 3,500; Videos 4,500
Special Collections: History of Sequoia & Kings National Parks (George W Stewart Coll); Los Angeles Times 1989-2003, micro; The Years 1941-1946 in Tulare County; Tulare County Directory 1888-1950, micro; Tulare County History Coll; Visalia Times Delta: 1859-present, micro (weekly & daily). Oral History
Automation Activity & Vendor Info: (Acquisitions) Horizon; (Cataloging) Horizon; (Circulation) Horizon; (OPAC) Horizon
Wireless access
Function: Adult literacy prog, Archival coll, BA reader (adult literacy), Bilingual assistance for Spanish patrons, Computer training, Electronic databases & coll, ILL available, Music CDs, Online cat, Prog for children & young adult, Ref serv available, Spoken cassettes & CDs, Spoken cassettes & DVDs, Summer reading prog, Tax forms, VHS videos
Mem of San Joaquin Valley Library System
Partic in Association for Rural & Small Libraries; AWLNET; OCLC Online Computer Library Center, Inc
Special Services for the Deaf - ADA equip; Assisted listening device; Bks on deafness & sign lang; Sorenson video relay syst
Special Services for the Blind - Talking bk & rec for the blind cat; Talking bks; Talking bks & player equip
Open Tues-Thurs 9-8, Fri 12-6, Sat 9-5
Friends of the Library Group
Branches: 16
ALPAUGH BRANCH, 3816 Ave 54, Alpaugh, 93201, SAN 335-2773. Tel: 559-949-8355. FAX: 559-949-8225. Web Site: www.tularecountylibrary.org/locations-alpaugh.
Founded 1910. Pop 800
Library Holdings: Bk Vols 8,187
Open Tues & Wed 9-1 & 2-5
DINUBA BRANCH, 150 South I St, Dinuba, 93618, SAN 335-2838. Tel: 559-591-5829. FAX: 559-591-5886. Web Site: www.tularecountylibrary.org/locations-dinuba.
Founded 1910. Pop 19,297
Library Holdings: Bk Vols 31,931
Open Tues-Fri 9-1 & 2-6
Friends of the Library Group
EARLIMART BRANCH, 780 E Washington Ave, Earlimart, 93219, SAN 335-2897. Tel: 661-849-2525. FAX: 661-849-1517. Web Site: www.tularecountylibrary.org/locations-earlimart.
Founded 1914. Pop 7,020
Library Holdings: Bk Vols 10,603
Open Tues-Fri 9-1 & 2-5
EXETER BRANCH, 230 E Chestnut Ave, Exeter, 93221, SAN 335-2927. Tel: 559-592-5361. FAX: 559-592-4452. Web Site: www.tularecountylibrary.org/locations-exeter.
Founded 1910. Pop 10,160
Library Holdings: Bk Vols 25,305
Open Tues & Wed 11-5 & 6-8, Thurs & Fri 9-1 & 2-6
Friends of the Library Group
FAMERSVILLE BRANCH, 623 N Avery Ave, Farmersville, 93223. Tel: 559-592-0001. Web Site: www.tularecountylibrary.org/locations-farmersville.
Open Tues-Thurs 9-1 & 2-6
IVANHOE BRANCH, 15964 Heather Ave, Ivanhoe, 93235, SAN 335-3044. Tel: 559-798-1264. FAX: 559-798-5634. Web Site: www.tularecountylibrary.org/locations-ivanhoe.
Founded 1925. Pop 4,474
Library Holdings: Bk Vols 8,495
Open Tues & Fri 9-1 & 2-6
LINDSAY BRANCH, 157 N Mirage St, Lindsay, 93247, SAN 335-3079. Tel: 559-562-3021. FAX: 559-562-5066. Web Site: www.tularecountylibrary.org/locations-lindsay.
Founded 1910. Pop 10,860
Library Holdings: Bk Vols 22,888
Open Tues & Thurs 11-5 & 6-8, Wed & Fri 9-1 & 2-6
Friends of the Library Group
LONDON BRANCH, 5711 Ave 378, Dinuba, 93618. Tel: 559-591-1017. Web Site: www.tularecountylibrary.org/locations-london.
Open Wed & Thurs 9-1 & 2-6
OROSI BRANCH, 12646 Ave 416, Orosi, 93647, SAN 335-3133. Tel: 559-519-5830. FAX: 559-528-9156. Web Site: www.tularecountylibrary.org/locations-orosi.
Founded 1911. Pop 7,744
Library Holdings: Bk Vols 10,751
Open Wed-Fri 9-1 & 2-6
Friends of the Library Group
PIXLEY BRANCH, 927 S Center St, No B, Pixley, 93256, SAN 335-3192. Tel: 559-757-1010. Web Site: www.tularecountylibrary.org/locations-pixley.
Founded 1913. Pop 2,586
Library Holdings: Bk Vols 16,340
Open Tues-Fri 9-1 & 2-6
SPRINGVILLE BRANCH, 35800 Hwy 190, Springville, 93265, SAN 335-3257. Tel: 559-539-2624. FAX: 559-539-6307. Web Site: www.tularecountylibrary.org/locations-springville.
Founded 1928. Pop 1,109
Library Holdings: Bk Vols 8,509
Open Thurs & Fri 9-1 & 2-6, Sat 9-1 & 2-5
Friends of the Library Group
STRATHMORE BRANCH, 19646 Rd 230, Strathmore, 93267-9608, SAN 335-3281. Tel: 559-568-1087. FAX: 559-568-0633. Web Site: www.tularecountylibrary.org/locations-strathmore.
Founded 1911. Pop 2,584
Library Holdings: Bk Vols 12,635
Open Tues & Wed 9-1 & 2-6
Friends of the Library Group
TERRA BELLA BRANCH, 23825 Ave 92, Terra Bella, 93270-9756, SAN 335-3311. Tel: 559-535-5583. Web Site: www.tularecountylibrary.org/locations-terrabella.
Founded 1912. Pop 3,780
Library Holdings: Bk Vols 8,947
Open Mon-Thurs 8-Noon
THREE RIVERS BRANCH, 42052 Eggers Dr, Three Rivers, 93271-9774, SAN 335-3346. Tel: 559-561-4564. FAX: 559-561-7318. Web Site: www.tularecountylibrary.org/locations-threerivers.
Founded 1910. Pop 2,248
Library Holdings: Bk Vols 17,055
Open Tues & Thurs 12-5 & 6-8, Wed & Fri 10-1 & 2-6, Sat 10-1 & 2-5
Friends of the Library Group
TIPTON BRANCH, 301 E Woods, Tipton, 93272, SAN 335-3370. Tel: 559-752-4236. FAX: 559-752-7307. Web Site: www.tularecountylibrary.org/locations-tipton.
Founded 1912. Pop 1,790
Library Holdings: Bk Vols 8,023
Open Thurs & Fri 9-12 & 1-5
WOODLAKE BRANCH, 400 W Whitney Ave, Woodlake, 93286, SAN 335-346X. Tel: 559-564-8424. FAX: 559-564-6725. Web Site: www.tularecountylibrary.org/locations-woodlake.
Founded 1911. Pop 7,336
Library Holdings: Bk Vols 11,797
Open Tues-Fri 9-1 & 2-5

S TULARE COUNTY OFFICE OF EDUCATION*, Educational Resource Services Library, 7000 Doe Ave, Ste A, 93291. SAN 301-7044. Tel: 559-651-3031. FAX: 559-651-1012. Web Site: www.erslibrary.org. *Prog Mgr,* Debra Lockwood; Tel: 559-651-3042, E-mail: debra.lockwood@tcoe.org; Staff 7 (MLS 1, Non-MLS 6)
Founded 1927
Library Holdings: Bk Titles 100,000; Bk Vols 250,000; Per Subs 50
Special Collections: Instructional Materials Display Center of Textbooks & Media
Open Mon-Fri 8-5

GL TULARE COUNTY PUBLIC LAW LIBRARY*, County Courthouse, Rm 1, 221 S Mooney Blvd, 93291-4544. SAN 301-7052. Tel: 559-636-4600. E-mail: lawlibrary@co.tulare.ca.us. Web Site: tularecounty.ca.gov/lawlibrary. *Dir,* Anne R Bernardo; E-mail: abernard@co.tulare.ca.us; Staff 2 (Non-MLS 2)
Founded 1891
Jul 2015-Jun 2016 Income $307,488, Locally Generated Income $32,329, Other $275,159. Mats Exp $311,144, Books $109,681, Per/Ser (Incl. Access Fees) $1,442, Electronic Ref Mat (Incl. Access Fees) $42,304. Sal $106,031
Library Holdings: CDs 166; Electronic Media & Resources 20,000; Bk Titles 1,699; Bk Vols 17,025; Per Subs 73
Subject Interests: Legal
Automation Activity & Vendor Info: (Cataloging) ComPanion Corp; (OPAC) ComPanion Corp
Wireless access
Function: 24/7 Online cat, Computers for patron use, Electronic databases & coll, For res purposes, Govt ref serv, Mail & tel request accepted, Online cat, Online ref, Outside serv via phone, mail, e-mail & web, Photocopying/Printing, Ref & res, Ref serv available, Res libr, Wheelchair accessible
Open Mon-Fri 8-5
Restriction: Badge access after hrs, Non-circulating, Not a lending libr, Pub use on premises

WALNUT

J MT SAN ANTONIO COLLEGE LIBRARY*, 1100 N Grand Ave, 91789. SAN 301-7079. Tel: 909-274-4260. Administration Tel: 909-274-6600. Information Services Tel: 909-274-4289. FAX: 909-468-4011. Web Site: mtsac.edu/library. *Dept Chair, Librn,* Pauline Swartz; E-mail: pswartz@mtsac.edu; *Librn,* Jared Burton; E-mail: jburton6@mtsac.edu; *Electronic Res Librn,* Esteban Aguilar; E-mail: eaguilar100@mtsac.edu; *Ref Librn,* Emily Woolery; E-mail: ewoolery@mtsac.edu; Staff 16 (MLS 6, Non-MLS 10)
Founded 1946. Highest Degree: Associate
Library Holdings: e-books 8,500; Bk Titles 68,985; Per Subs 342
Automation Activity & Vendor Info: (Acquisitions) SirsiDynix; (Cataloging) SirsiDynix; (Circulation) SirsiDynix; (Course Reserve) SirsiDynix; (Media Booking) SirsiDynix; (OPAC) SirsiDynix; (Serials) SirsiDynix
Wireless access
Partic in Inland Empire Acad Libr Coop
Open Mon-Thurs 7:30am-9:30pm, Fri 7:30-4:30, Sat 9-4, Sun 1-9:30
Restriction: Staff use only, Students only

WALNUT CREEK

M JOHN MUIR HEALTH MEDICAL LIBRARY*, 1601 Ygnacio Valley Rd, 94598. SAN 326. Tel: 925-947-5231. FAX: 925-947-3237. Web Site: www.johnmuirhealth.com/locations/john-muir-medical-center-walnut-creek.html. *Librn,* Helen M Doughty; E-mail: helen.doughty@johnmuirhealth.com; Staff 1 (MLS 1)
Library Holdings: Bk Vols 3,750
Subject Interests: Hist of med
Function: Res libr
Partic in National Network of Libraries of Medicine Region 5
Restriction: Not open to pub

S WALNUT CREEK HISTORICAL SOCIETY, Shadelands Ranch Museum Library, 2660 Ygnacio Valley Rd, 94598. SAN 301-7117. Tel: 925-935-7871. E-mail: wchs@wchistory.org. Web Site: wchistory.org/museum. *Libr Office Mgr,* Jackie Byrd; *Archivist, Historian,* Moira Anwar
Founded 1972
Library Holdings: Bk Titles 500
Special Collections: Albert Johnson Business Papers; Hutchinson Family Photos; James P Howe Coll, papers; Joseph Reddeford Walker & Family, photog; Local Newspaper Coll: Walnut Creek Independent, Walnut Creek Sentinel, Walnut Kernel Newspaper 1932-1967; Rogers Hotel, photog; Seely Family Letters; Seely-Hodges Family Letters; Shadelands Ranch Business Documents; Walnut Creek (Robert Thain Coll), photog; Walnut Creek City Documents. Oral History
Subject Interests: Calif, Local hist
Wireless access
Restriction: Open by appt only

WATSONVILLE

P WATSONVILLE PUBLIC LIBRARY*, 275 Main St, Ste 100, 95076. SAN 301-7133. Tel: 831-768-3400. FAX: 831-763-4015. TDD: 831-763-4076. Web Site: www.watsonvillelibrary.org. *Dir,* Carol Heitzig; Tel: 831-768-3409, E-mail: Carol.heitzig@cityofwatsonville.org; *Principal Librn, Pub Serv,* Watonka Addison; E-mail: Watonka.addison@cityofwatsonville.org; *Principal Librn, Tech Serv,* Alicia Martinez; E-mail: Alicia.martinez@cityofwatsonville.org; *Circ Mgr,* Alex Chavez; E-mail: Alex.chavez@cityofwatsonville.org; *Ch Serv,* Position Currently Open; *YA Serv,* Hannah Clement; E-mail: hannah.clement@cityofwatsonville.org; Staff 9 (MLS 8, Non-MLS 1)
Founded 1895
Library Holdings: Bk Titles 132,922; Per Subs 189
Subject Interests: Spanish (Lang)
Automation Activity & Vendor Info: (Acquisitions) Innovative Interfaces, Inc; (Cataloging) Innovative Interfaces, Inc; (Circulation) Innovative Interfaces, Inc; (ILL) Innovative Interfaces, Inc; (Media Booking) Innovative Interfaces, Inc; (OPAC) Innovative Interfaces, Inc; (Serials) Innovative Interfaces, Inc
Wireless access
Function: 24/7 Online cat, Adult bk club, Adult literacy prog, After school storytime, Art exhibits, Audiobks on Playaways & MP3, Audiobks via web, Bilingual assistance for Spanish patrons, Bk club(s), Bks on cassette, Bks on CD, CD-ROM, Children's prog, Citizenship assistance, Computer training, Computers for patron use, Electronic databases & coll, Family literacy, Holiday prog, Homebound delivery serv, Homework prog, ILL available, Internet access, Large print keyboards, Magazines, Magnifiers for reading, Mail & tel request accepted, Meeting rooms, Microfiche/film & reading machines, Movies, Museum passes, Music CDs, Online cat, Online info literacy tutorials on the web & in blackboard, Online ref, Outreach serv, OverDrive digital audio bks, Photocopying/Printing, Preschool outreach, Printer for laptops & handheld devices, Prog for adults, Prog for children & young adult, Ref serv available, Senior computer classes, Spanish lang bks, Spoken cassettes & CDs, Story hour, Study rm, Summer reading prog, Tax forms, Teen prog, Telephone ref, VHS videos, Wheelchair accessible, Workshops, Writing prog
Partic in Monterey Bay Area Cooperative Library System
Special Services for the Deaf - TDD equip
Open Mon-Thurs 10-8, Fri-10-6, Sat 12-4
Friends of the Library Group
Branches: 1
FREEDOM BRANCH, 2021 Freedom Blvd, Freedom, 95019. Tel: 831-768-3420. FAX: 831-763-4143.
Pop 6,524; Circ 62,128
Function: 24/7 Online cat
Open Mon 12-6, Tues-Thurs 10-8, Fri 10-6, Sat 12-4
Friends of the Library Group

WEAVERVILLE

P TRINITY COUNTY LIBRARY*, 351 Main St, 96093. (Mail add: PO Box 1226, 96093-1226), SAN 301-7141. Tel: 530-623-1373. FAX: 530-623-4427. E-mail: request_trinity@trinitycounty.org. Web Site: trinitycounty.org/Library. *County Librn,* Kacy Guill; E-mail: kguill@trinitycounty.org; Staff 1 (MLS 1)
Founded 1916. Pop 13,020; Circ 50,483
Library Holdings: Per Subs 50
Special Collections: Trinity County History; Trinity River Basin Coll
Automation Activity & Vendor Info: (Cataloging) Koha
Wireless access
Mem of NorthNet Library System
Open Mon, Wed & Fri 1-6, Tues & Thurs 10-6
Friends of the Library Group
Branches: 2
HAYFORK BRANCH, 6641A State Hwy 3, Hayfork, 96041. (Mail add: PO Box 700, Hayfork, 96041-0700), SAN 329-3599. Tel: 530-628-5427. FAX: 530-628-5304. *Libr Asst,* Nancy Ferguson; Staff 2 (Non-MLS 2)
Open Mon & Wed 11-4, Tues & Thurs 10-2
Friends of the Library Group
TRINITY CENTER BRANCH, Scott Museum Bldg, 540-B Airport Rd, Trinity Center, 96091. (Mail add: PO Box 27, Trinity Center, 96091), SAN 370-4386. Tel: 530-266-3242. *Libr Asst,* Marianne Keesee
Open Wed 12-4
Friends of the Library Group

WEED

J COLLEGE OF THE SISKIYOUS LIBRARY*, 800 College Ave, 96094. SAN 301-715X. Tel: 530-938-5331. Toll Free Tel: 888-397-4339, Ext 5331. FAX: 530-938-5226. E-mail: library@siskiyous.edu. Web Site: www.siskiyous.edu/library. *Fac Librn,* Jude Baldwin; Tel: 530-938-5330, E-mail: jbaldwin2@siskiyous.edu; Staff 3 (MLS 1, Non-MLS 2)
Founded 1957. Enrl 1,084; Highest Degree: Associate
Special Collections: Mount Shasta California Coll
Subject Interests: Local hist
Automation Activity & Vendor Info: (Cataloging) OCLC Connexion; (Circulation) Ex Libris Group; (Course Reserve) Ex Libris Group; (Discovery) Ex Libris Group; (ILL) OCLC WorldShare Interlibrary Loan; (OPAC) Ex Libris Group
Wireless access
Partic in Community College League of California

WEST HOLLYWOOD

S CENTER FOR EARLY EDUCATION LIBRARY, 563 N Alfred St, 90048-2512. SAN 300-9041. Tel: 323-651-0707. FAX: 323-651-0860. Web Site: www.centerforearlyeducation.org. *Libr Dir,* Lucy Rafael; E-mail: rafaell@cee-school.org; *Early Childhood Librn,* Stephanie Steelman; Staff 3 (MLS 2, Non-MLS 1)
Founded 1965
Library Holdings: Bk Titles 22,093; Bk Vols 22,282; Per Subs 22
Subject Interests: Child develop, Children's lit, Educ, Parenting
Automation Activity & Vendor Info: (Acquisitions) Follett Software; (Cataloging) Follett Software; (Circulation) Follett Software; (Media Booking) Follett Software; (OPAC) Follett Software
Function: 24/7 Electronic res, 24/7 Online cat, Audiobks via web, Children's prog, Digital talking bks, E-Readers, Electronic databases & coll, Homework prog, Laminating, Magazines, Online cat, Online ref, Prog for children & young adult, Ref serv available
Restriction: Open to students, fac & staff, Private libr

WESTCHESTER

C OTIS COLLEGE OF ART & DESIGN LIBRARY*, Millard Sheets Library, 9045 Lincoln Blvd, 90045. SAN 300-9793. Tel: 310-665-6800, Ext 6930. Web Site: www.otis.edu/library. *Interim Dir,* Heather Cleary; Tel: 310-665-6925, E-mail: hcleary@otis.edu; *Cat Librn,* Cathy Chambers; E-mail: cathcham@otis.edu; *Circ Mgr,* Sheldon Forbes; E-mail:

sforbes@otis.edu; *Mgr, Per,* Ian Henderson; *Coordr,* Kathleen Forrest; Staff 3 (MLS 2, Non-MLS 1)
Founded 1917. Enrl 1,100; Fac 400; Highest Degree: Master
Library Holdings: Bk Vols 40,000; Per Subs 200
Special Collections: Artists bks
Subject Interests: Fashion, Fine arts, Photog
Wireless access
Partic in Statewide California Electronic Library Consortium
Restriction: Open by appt only

WHITTIER

J RIO HONDO COLLEGE LIBRARY*, 3600 Workman Mill Rd, 2nd Flr, 90601. SAN 301-7192. Tel: 562-908-3484. Circulation Tel: 562-908-3416. FAX: 562-463-4642. E-mail: library@riohondo.edu. Web Site: www.riohondo.edu/library. *Dean of Libr,* Position Currently Open; *Librn,* Robin Babou; E-mail: rbabou@riohondo.edu; *Librn,* Adele Enright; E-mail: aenright@riohondo.edu; *Librn,* Judy Sevilla-Marzona; E-mail: jsevilla@riohondo.edu; *Librn,* Irene Truong; E-mail: itruoung@riohondo.edu; *Librn,* Stephanie Wells; E-mail: swells@riohondo.edu; Staff 27 (MLS 14, Non-MLS 13)
Founded 1965. Enrl 18,497; Fac 559; Highest Degree: Bachelor
Library Holdings: AV Mats 2,498; DVDs 95; Music Scores 183; Bk Titles 74,856; Bk Vols 83,844; Per Subs 176; Videos 1,120
Subject Interests: Archit, Fire tech, Theatre arts
Automation Activity & Vendor Info: (Acquisitions) SirsiDynix; (Cataloging) SirsiDynix; (Circulation) SirsiDynix; (Course Reserve) SirsiDynix; (Media Booking) SirsiDynix; (OPAC) SirsiDynix; (Serials) SirsiDynix
Function: ILL available, Ref serv available
Partic in Southern California Library Cooperative
Special Services for the Deaf - Assistive tech; Closed caption videos
Special Services for the Blind - Closed circuit TV; Ref serv; Scanner for conversion & translation of mats
Open Mon-Thurs 7am-9pm, Fri 7am-3pm, Sat 9am-1pm
Restriction: Borrowing privileges limited to fac & registered students

CM SOUTHERN CALIFORNIA UNIVERSITY OF HEALTH SCIENCES*, Seabury Learning Resource Center, 16200 E Amber Valley Dr, 90604-4098. (Mail add: PO Box 1166, 90609-1166), SAN 300-7898. Tel: 562-902-3368. Toll Free Tel: 800-221-5222. FAX: 562-902-3323. E-mail: scuhslibrary@scuhs.edu. Web Site: scuhs.libguides.com/. *Exec Dir,* Kathleen Smith; *Circ,* Linda Horat; E-mail: lindahorat@scuhs.edu
Founded 1911. Enrl 1,000
Library Holdings: Bk Vols 140,000; Per Subs 222
Special Collections: Chiropractic History; Nutrition & Natural Therapeutics
Subject Interests: Anatomy, Chiropractic med, Herbals, Massage therapy, Neurology, Nutrition, Osteopathology, Phys therapy, Physiology, Sports, Traditional Chinese med, Yoga
Automation Activity & Vendor Info: (Acquisitions) Ex Libris Group; (Cataloging) Ex Libris Group; (Circulation) Ex Libris Group; (Serials) Ex Libris Group
Wireless access
Partic in Chiropractic Libr Consortium; CLS; Medical Library Group of Southern California & Arizona

WHITTIER COLLEGE

C FAIRCHILD AERIAL PHOTOGRAPHY COLLECTION*, Fairchild Collection, Whittier College, 90608. Tel: 562-907-4220. FAX: 562-693-6117. E-mail: fairchild@whittier.edu. Web Site: web.whittier.edu/fairchild/home.html. *Dir,* Stephanie Breaux
Founded 1965
Special Collections: Aerial Photography Coll 1927-1966
Function: Archival coll
Partic in Nat Cartographic Info Ctr
Restriction: Non-circulating, Not a lending libr, Open by appt only

C MEDIA CENTER*, 13406 Philadelphia St, 90601-4413. (Mail add: PO Box 634, 90608-0634), SAN 335-3559. Tel: 562-907-4267. FAX: 562-907-4922. Web Site: www.whittier.edu. *Dir,* Richard Cheatham; Tel: 562-907-4846, E-mail: rcheatham@whittier.edu
Founded 1971
Subject Interests: Educ, Environ studies, Ethnic studies, Feminism, Hist
Open Mon-Fri 8-5

C BONNIE BELL WARDMAN LIBRARY*, 7031 Founders Hill Rd, 90608-9984, SAN 335-3524. Tel: 562-907-4247. Circulation Tel: 562-907-4693. Reference Tel: 562-907-4692. Administration Tel: 562-907-4245. Automation Services Tel: 562-907-4235. FAX: 562-698-7168. Web Site: web.whittier.edu/academic/library. *Interim Dir,* Mary Ellen Vick; E-mail: mvick@whittier.edu; *Syst Mgr,* Paul Hong; *Media Coordr,* Terry McGonagle; *Cat Librn,* Mike Garabedian; *Ser Librn,* Joe Dmohowski; Tel: 562-907-4246, E-mail: jdmohowski@whittier.edu; *Acq,* Steven Musser; *Instructional Technologist,* Kathy Filatreau; *Tech Serv,* Cindy Bessler; Staff 4 (MLS 4)
Founded 1901. Enrl 1,330; Fac 103; Highest Degree: Master
Library Holdings: AV Mats 43; CDs 194; e-books 2,294; e-journals 10,239; Bk Vols 302,490; Per Subs 715; Talking Bks 12; Videos 44
Special Collections: Jan de Hartog Coll, bks, mss; Jessamyn West Coll, bks, mss; John Greenleaf Whittier Coll; Richard M Nixon Coll; Society of Friends (Clifford & Susan Johnson Library of Quaker Literature), bks, micro, pamphlets. State Document Depository; US Document Depository
Automation Activity & Vendor Info: (Acquisitions) Innovative Interfaces, Inc; (Cataloging) Innovative Interfaces, Inc; (Circulation) Innovative Interfaces, Inc; (Course Reserve) Innovative Interfaces, Inc; (ILL) Innovative Interfaces, Inc; (Media Booking) Innovative Interfaces, Inc; (OPAC) Innovative Interfaces, Inc; (Serials) Innovative Interfaces, Inc
Function: Govt ref serv, Photocopying/Printing, Ref serv available, Wheelchair accessible
Partic in OCLC Online Computer Library Center, Inc
Open Mon-Thurs 8am-11pm, Fri 8-5, Sat 10-5, Sun Noon-11pm

P WHITTIER PUBLIC LIBRARY*, 7333 Greenleaf Ave, 90602. SAN 335-3583. Tel: 562-567-9900. FAX: 562-567-2880. E-mail: lib@whittierpl.org. Web Site: www.whittierlibrary.org. *Dir,* Paymaneh Maghsoudi; E-mail: pmghsoudi@cityofwhittier.org; Staff 14 (MLS 14)
Founded 1900. Pop 83,000; Circ 636,930
Library Holdings: Bk Vols 251,991
Special Collections: Margaret Fulmer Peace Coll; Whittier Hills Archives; Whittier History. State Document Depository
Automation Activity & Vendor Info: (Circulation) SirsiDynix
Wireless access
Partic in Southern California Library Cooperative
Open Mon-Wed 10-9, Thurs & Fri 10-6, Sat 10-5
Friends of the Library Group
Branches: 1
WHITTWOOD BRANCH, 10537 Santa Gertrudes Ave, 90603-2760, SAN 335-3613. Tel: 562-567-9950. FAX: 562-567-2881.
Circ 192,148
Library Holdings: Bk Titles 47,196; Bk Vols 66,413; Per Subs 90
Open Mon & Tues 12-9, Wed-Fri 10-6, Sat 10-5
Friends of the Library Group

WILLOWS

P WILLOWS PUBLIC LIBRARY*, 201 N Lassen St, 95988-3010. SAN 301-7214. Tel: 530-934-5156. FAX: 530-934-2225. Web Site: www.cityofwillows.org/dept/library. *Libr Dir,* Jody Meza; E-mail: jodymeza@gmail.com; Staff 2 (Non-MLS 2)
Founded 1906. Pop 14,152; Circ 51,781
Library Holdings: Bk Vols 62,276; Per Subs 100; Talking Bks 1,387
Special Collections: Californiana Coll
Subject Interests: Local hist
Automation Activity & Vendor Info: (Acquisitions) TLC (The Library Corporation); (Cataloging) TLC (The Library Corporation); (Circulation) TLC (The Library Corporation)
Wireless access
Mem of NorthNet Library System
Partic in Cooperative Library Association Shared System; Research Libraries Information Network
Open Tues-Thurs 11-7, Fri & Sat 11-5
Friends of the Library Group
Branches: 2
BAYLISS, 7830 Rd 39, Glenn, 95943, SAN 376-2599. Tel: 530-934-2287.
Founded 1914. Pop 1,020
Library Holdings: Bk Vols 3,581; Per Subs 15
Open Tues 10-6
Friends of the Library Group
ELK CREEK BRANCH, 3432 County Rd 309, Elk Creek, 95939. Tel: 530-968-5238.
Pop 1,515
Library Holdings: Bk Vols 2,603; Per Subs 11
Open Tues & Thurs 1-5
Friends of the Library Group

WILMINGTON

J LOS ANGELES HARBOR COLLEGE*, Camille L Baxter Learning Resource Center, 1111 Figueroa Pl, 90744. SAN 301-7222. Tel: 310-233-4482. Reference Tel: 310-233-4478. FAX: 310-233-4689. Web Site: libguides.lahc.edu/library. *Cat, Chair, Ref Serv,* Jonathon Lee; Tel: 310-233-4475, E-mail: leeja@lahc.edu; *Librn, Ref,* Tamar Khajadourian; E-mail: khajadtr@lahc.edu; Staff 3 (MLS 3)
Founded 1949. Enrl 10,192; Fac 381; Highest Degree: Associate
Library Holdings: e-books 14,920; Bk Vols 86,989; Per Subs 168
Special Collections: Los Angeles Harbor Area History (Los Angeles Harbor College Historical Project), clippings, photogs. Oral History
Automation Activity & Vendor Info: (Acquisitions) EOS International; (Cataloging) SirsiDynix; (Circulation) SirsiDynix; (Course Reserve) SirsiDynix; (ILL) SirsiDynix; (OPAC) SirsiDynix

Wireless access
Function: ILL available, Photocopying/Printing, Ref serv available
Partic in California Community College Library Consortium
Special Services for the Blind - Assistive/Adapted tech devices, equip & products; Computer with voice synthesizer for visually impaired persons
Open Mon-Thurs 8am-8:30pm, Fri 8-2, Sat 10-2

WOODLAND

P WOODLAND PUBLIC LIBRARY*, 250 First St, 95695. SAN 301-7249. Tel: 530-661-5980. Circulation Tel: 530-661-5981. FAX: 530-666-5408. E-mail: library@cityofwoodland.org. Web Site: woodlandpubliclibrary.com. *Libr Serv Dir,* Greta Galindo; E-mail: greta.galindo@cityofwoodland.org; Staff 5 (MLS 5)
Founded 1892. Pop 53,000; Circ 217,527
Library Holdings: AV Mats 6,200; CDs 2,343; DVDs 1,952; Large Print Bks 2,482; Bk Vols 82,000; Per Subs 189; Talking Bks 2,508; Videos 1,331
Automation Activity & Vendor Info: (Cataloging) Innovative Interfaces, Inc; (Circulation) Innovative Interfaces, Inc; (ILL) OCLC; (OPAC) Innovative Interfaces, Inc
Wireless access
Partic in OCLC Online Computer Library Center, Inc
Open Mon-Thurs 1-6, Sat 9-1
Friends of the Library Group

GL YOLO COUNTY LAW LIBRARY*, 204 Fourth St, Ste A, 95695. SAN 301-7257. Tel: 530-666-8918. FAX: 530-666-8618. E-mail: law.library@yolocounty.org. Web Site: www.yolocounty.org/government/general-government-departments/county-counsel/law-library. *Law Librn,* Janet Coles; E-mail: janet.coles@yolocounty.org
Founded 1895
Library Holdings: CDs 35; Bk Vols 15,500
Function: Computers for patron use, Electronic databases & coll, Online cat, Photocopying/Printing
Open Mon-Thurs 10-4

P YOLO COUNTY LIBRARY*, 226 Buckeye St, 95695-2600. SAN 335-3648. Tel: 530-666-8005. Web Site: www.yolocountylibrary.org. *Chief Archivist, County Librn,* Mark Fink; Tel: 530-666-8002, E-mail: mark.fink@yolocounty.org; *Asst County Librn,* Elizabeth Gray; Tel: 530-666-8084, E-mail: elizabeth.gray@yolocounty.org; Staff 33.9 (MLS 14.8, Non-MLS 19.1)
Founded 1910. Pop 146,487; Circ 1,145,645. Sal $1,744,824 (Prof $929,662)
Library Holdings: Audiobooks 20,406; AV Mats 33,251; CDs 9,825; DVDs 23,119; Bk Vols 334,644; Per Subs 282; Talking Bks 8,401
Special Collections: Geography (Beulah Hughes Coll); Russian Language Coll; Spanish Language Coll; Yolo County History Coll
Automation Activity & Vendor Info: (Acquisitions) Innovative Interfaces, Inc - Millennium; (Cataloging) Innovative Interfaces, Inc; (Circulation) Innovative Interfaces, Inc; (ILL) Innovative Interfaces, Inc; (OPAC) Innovative Interfaces, Inc
Wireless access
Mem of NorthNet Library System
Open Mon-Fri 8-5
Friends of the Library Group
Branches: 7
CLARKSBURG BRANCH, 52915 Netherlands Ave, Clarksburg, 95612-5007, SAN 335-3672. Tel: 916-744-1755. FAX: 916-744-1072. *Br Supvr,* Cristina Ruiz; E-mail: cristina.ruiz@yolocounty.org
Founded 1911
Library Holdings: Audiobooks 79; AV Mats 900; CDs 391; Bk Vols 16,308; Per Subs 40
Open Tues & Thurs 9:30-12 & 1-7:30, Wed 5:30-7:30, Sat 9:30-1
Friends of the Library Group
ESPARTO BRANCH, 17065 Yolo Ave, Esparto, 95627, SAN 335-3737. Tel: 530-787-3426. E-mail: espartolibrary@yolocounty.org. *Br Supvr,* Malinda Baker; E-mail: malinda.baker@yolocounty.org
Library Holdings: Audiobooks 256; CDs 732; DVDs 1,805; Bk Vols 22,284; Per Subs 80
Open Mon 12-8, Tues & Wed 8:30-8, Thurs 10-8, Fri 12-5, Sat 10-2
Friends of the Library Group
KNIGHTS LANDING BRANCH, 42351 Third St, Knights Landing, 95645. (Mail add: PO Box 517, Knights Landing, 95645-0517), SAN 335-3761. Tel: 530-735-6593. E-mail: knightslandinglibrary@yolocounty.org. *Libr Assoc,* Hope Saldivar; E-mail: hope.saldivar@yolocounty.org
Library Holdings: Audiobooks 166; CDs 362; DVDs 1,299; Bk Vols 9,449; Per Subs 46
Open Mon 1-6, Tues 3-8, Wed 10-12 & 1-6, Sat 1-5
Friends of the Library Group
MARY L STEPHENS-DAVIS BRANCH LIBRARY, 315 E 14th St, Davis, 95616, SAN 335-3702. Tel: 530-757-5593. Circulation Tel: 530-757-5592. E-mail: davislibrary@yolocounty.org. *Regional Mgr,* Scott Love; E-mail: scott.love@yolocounty.org
Library Holdings: Audiobooks 2,458; CDs 5,701; DVDs 11,243; Bk Vols 144,351; Per Subs 239
Open Mon 1-9, Tues-Thurs 10-9, Fri & Sat 10-5:30, Sun 1-5
Friends of the Library Group
ARTHUR F TURNER COMMUNITY LIBRARY, 1212 Merkley Ave, West Sacramento, 95691, SAN 335-3796. Tel: 916-375-6465. E-mail: westaclibrary@yolocounty.org. *Regional Mgr,* Dana Christy; Tel: 916-375-6464
Library Holdings: Audiobooks 994; CDs 1,523; DVDs 4,461; Bk Vols 45,313; Per Subs 101
Open Mon 12-8, Tues-Thurs 11-8, Fri & Sat 10-5:30, Sun 1-5
Friends of the Library Group
WINTERS BRANCH, 708 Railroad Ave, Winters, 95694, SAN 335-3826. Tel: 530-795-4955. E-mail: winterslibrary@yolocounty.org. *Br Supvr,* Toni Mendieta; Tel: 530-795-3177, E-mail: toni.mendieta@yolocounty.org
Library Holdings: Audiobooks 520; CDs 914; DVDs 2,361; Bk Vols 21,086; Per Subs 137
Open Mon & Wed 8-6, Tues & Thurs 8-8, Fri 8-3:30, Sat 1-5 (Winter); Mon 12-6, Tues 10-8, Wed 10-6, Thurs 12-8, Sat 1-5 (Summer)
Friends of the Library Group
YOLO BRANCH, 37750 Sacramento St, Yolo, 95697. (Mail add: PO Box 447, Yolo, 95697-0447), SAN 335-3850. Tel: 530-662-2363. FAX: 530-662-1464. E-mail: yololibrary@yolocounty.org. *Libr Assoc,* Sue Billing; E-mail: sue.billing@yolocounty.org
Library Holdings: Audiobooks 29; CDs 202; DVDs 777; Bk Vols 4,565; Per Subs 12
Open Tues 1-5:30, Wed 3-8, Thurs 10-12 & 1-5:30, Sat 12-5
Friends of the Library Group

WOODLAND HILLS

J PIERCE COLLEGE LIBRARY*, 6201 Winnetka Ave, 91371. SAN 301-7281. Tel: 818-719-6409. Reference Tel: 818-710-2833. E-mail: library@piercecollege.edu. Web Site: library.piercecollege.edu. *Dept Chair,* Paula Paggi; Tel: 818-710-2843, E-mail: paggipm@piercecollege.edu; *Cat Librn,* Michael Habata; Tel: 818-710-2834, E-mail: habatamh@piercecollege.edu; *Info Literacy Librn,* Marisa Diehl; Tel: 818-710-4267; E-mail: diehlme@piercecollege.edu; *Syst Librn,* Lauren Saslow; Tel: 818-710-4442, E-mail: saslowle@piercecollege.edu; *Tech Librn,* Clay Gediman; Tel: 818-710-4268, E-mail: gedimac@piercecollege.edu; Staff 10 (MLS 5, Non-MLS 5)
Founded 1947. Enrl 20,000; Fac 350; Highest Degree: Associate
Library Holdings: e-books 70,000; e-journals 20,000; Bk Titles 80,000; Bk Vols 100,000; Per Subs 30
Subject Interests: Agr
Automation Activity & Vendor Info: (Cataloging) SirsiDynix; (Circulation) SirsiDynix; (Course Reserve) SirsiDynix; (ILL) SirsiDynix; (OPAC) SirsiDynix
Wireless access
Open Mon-Thurs 8:30-7:30

YORBA LINDA

S NATIONAL ARCHIVES & RECORDS ADMINISTRATION, Nixon Presidential Library & Museum, 18001 Yorba Linda Blvd, 92886. SAN 375-9636. Tel: 714-983-9120, 714-983-9320. E-mail: nixonreference@nara.gov. Web Site: www.nixonlibrary.gov. *Dir,* Michael D Ellzey; *Mus Historian,* Gregory Cumming; E-mail: gregory.cumming@nara.gov
Library Holdings: Bk Titles 3,000; Per Subs 150
Special Collections: American Political History 1946-1994; Richard Nixon
Function: Archival coll
Open Mon-Sat 10-5, Sun 11-5
Restriction: Non-circulating

P YORBA LINDA PUBLIC LIBRARY*, 18181 Imperial Hwy, 92886-3437. SAN 301-7303. Tel: 714-777-2873. FAX: 714-777-0640. TDD: 714-777-4812. E-mail: ylpl@ylpl.org. Web Site: www.ylpl.org. *Dir,* Carrie Lixey; Tel: 714-777-2466, E-mail: carrie.lixey@ylpl.org; *Adult Serv Mgr,* Julie Zeoli; E-mail: julie.zeoli@ylpl.org; *Circ & Tech Serv Mgr,* Diane Standefer; E-mail: diane.standefer@ylpl.org; *Info & Tech Serv Mgr,* Jon Legree; E-mail: jon.legree@ylpl.org; *Mgr, Ch Serv,* Lucy Salvado; E-mail: lucy.salvado@ylpl.org; Staff 10 (MLS 8, Non-MLS 2)
Founded 1913. Circ 845,592
Library Holdings: AV Mats 24,076; Bk Vols 137,160; Per Subs 177
Special Collections: Oral History
Subject Interests: Local hist
Automation Activity & Vendor Info: (Acquisitions) SirsiDynix; (Cataloging) Brodart; (Circulation) SirsiDynix; (OPAC) SirsiDynix; (Serials) SirsiDynix

Wireless access
Publications: California Missions; Yorba Legacy
Mem of Santiago Library System
Special Services for the Deaf - TDD equip
Open Mon-Thurs 9-9, Fri & Sat 9-5
Friends of the Library Group

YOSEMITE NATIONAL PARK

G YOSEMITE NATIONAL PARK SERVICE*, Research Library, 9037 Village Dr, 95389. SAN 301-7311. Tel: 209-372-0280. FAX: 209-372-0255. E-mail: YOSE_library@nps.gov. Web Site: www.nps.gov/yose/learn/historyculture/yrl.htm. Staff 1 (Non-MLS 1)
Founded 1923
Library Holdings: Bk Titles 12,000; Per Subs 60
Subject Interests: Hist
Open Mon-Thurs 10-12 & 12:30-4

YOUNTVILLE

S LINCOLN MEMORIAL LIBRARY*, 240 California Dr, 94599-1445. SAN 335-3885. Tel: 707-944-4915. Circulation Tel: 707-944-4916. *Sr Librn,* Jennifer Allen; Tel: 707-944-4792; *Asst Librn,* Barbara Morgan; Staff 2 (MLS 1, Non-MLS 1)
Founded 1886
Library Holdings: Large Print Bks 10,000; Bk Titles 35,000; Per Subs 62; Talking Bks 970
Subject Interests: World War I, World War II
Wireless access
Open Mon-Sun 9-8

M VETERANS HOME OF CALIFORNIA*, William K Murphy Health Sciences Memorial Library, 250 California Dr, 94599-1446. (Mail add: PO Box 1200, 94599-1297), SAN 335-394X. Tel: 707-944-4600. Reference Tel: 707-944-4792. *Sr Librn,* Jennifer Allen; E-mail: jennifer.allen@calvet.ca.gov; Staff 1 (MLS 1)
Library Holdings: Bk Titles 400; Per Subs 125
Subject Interests: Geriatrics & gerontology
Restriction: Not open to pub

YREKA

P SISKIYOU COUNTY LIBRARY*, Technical Services, 719 Fourth St, 96097. SAN 335-3974. Tel: 530-812-8807, 530-841-4175. FAX: 530-842-7001. E-mail: library@co.siskiyou.ca.us. Web Site: www.co.siskiyou.ca.us/library. *County Librn,* Michael Perry; Tel: 530-842-8805, E-mail: mperry@co.siskiyou.ca.us; Staff 4 (MLS 1, Non-MLS 3)
Founded 1915. Pop 45,000; Circ 130,000
Library Holdings: Bk Titles 110,000; Bk Vols 140,000; Per Subs 260
Subject Interests: Calif, Genealogy, Local Native Am, Mining
Automation Activity & Vendor Info: (Acquisitions) ByWater Solutions; (Cataloging) ByWater Solutions; (Circulation) ByWater Solutions; (ILL) OCLC FirstSearch; (OPAC) ByWater Solutions
Wireless access
Function: Adult literacy prog, Bks on CD, Computers for patron use, ILL available, Music CDs, Online cat, Photocopying/Printing, Summer reading prog, Tax forms
Mem of NorthNet Library System
Special Services for the Blind - Bks on CD; Extensive large print coll; Large print bks
Open Mon-Sat 12-5
Friends of the Library Group
Branches: 11
BUTTE VALLEY BRANCH, 800 W Third St, Dorris, 96023, SAN 335-4008. Tel: 530-397-4932.
Founded 2006
Library Holdings: Bk Titles 4,977
Open Tues-Thurs 10-4
Friends of the Library Group
DUNSMUIR BRANCH, 5714 Dunsmuir Ave, Dunsmuir, 96025, SAN 335-4032. Tel: 530-235-2035.
Library Holdings: Bk Titles 11,628
Open Tues & Thurs 1-6, Wed 1-8, Fri 1-5, Sat 10-2
Friends of the Library Group
ETNA BRANCH, 115 Collier Way, Etna, 96027, SAN 335-4067. Tel: 530-467-3661.
Library Holdings: Bk Titles 10,423
Open Mon, Tues & Thurs 1-5, Wed & Fri 10-5
Friends of the Library Group
FORT JONES BRANCH, 11960 East St, Fort Jones, 96032, SAN 335-4091. Tel: 530-468-2383.
Library Holdings: Bk Titles 7,236
Open Mon-Thurs 12-5
Friends of the Library Group
HAPPY CAMP BRANCH, 143 Buckhorn Rd, Happy Camp, 96039, SAN 335-4121. Tel: 530-493-2964.
Library Holdings: Bk Titles 7,878
Open Tues 12-5
Friends of the Library Group
MCCLOUD BRANCH, 300 E Columbero Dr, McCloud, 96057, SAN 335-4156. Tel: 530-964-2169.
Founded 1974
Library Holdings: Bk Titles 8,927
Open Mon-Thurs 12-4
Friends of the Library Group
MONTAGUE BRANCH, City Hall, 230 S 13th St, Montague, 96064, SAN 335-4164. Tel: 530-459-5473.
Library Holdings: Bk Titles 3,912
Special Services for the Deaf - Bks on deafness & sign lang
Special Services for the Blind - Bks on cassette; Bks on CD; Large print bks
Open Mon, Wed & Fri 1-5
Friends of the Library Group
MT SHASTA BRANCH, 515 E Alma St, Mount Shasta, 96067, SAN 335-4180. Tel: 530-926-2031. E-mail: mtshastalibrary@gmail.com. Web Site: www.mtshastalibrary.org.
Founded 1969
Library Holdings: Bk Titles 17,251
Open Mon-Sat 12-6
Friends of the Library Group
SCOTT BAR BRANCH, Post Office, 27233 Scott River Rd, Scott Bar, 96085. Tel: 530-496-3248.
Library Holdings: Bk Vols 400
Open Mon-Fri 3-5, Sat 11-1
Friends of the Library Group
TULELAKE BRANCH, 452 Main St, Tulelake, 96134, SAN 335-4199. Tel: 530-667-2291.
Library Holdings: Bk Titles 8,968
Open Mon-Wed 12-5
Friends of the Library Group
WEED BRANCH, 150 Alamo Ave, Weed, 96094, SAN 335-4210. Tel: 530-938-4769.
Library Holdings: Bk Titles 8,984
Open Mon-Fri 12-6, Sat 10-4
Friends of the Library Group

S SISKIYOU COUNTY MUSEUM LIBRARY, 910 S Main St, 96097. SAN 328-3658. Tel: 530-842-3836. E-mail: scmuseum@co.siskiyou.ca.us. Web Site: co.siskiyou.ca.us/museum. *Dir,* Position Currently Open
Founded 1951
Library Holdings: Bk Vols 2,000; Per Subs 12
Special Collections: Local newspapers 1917-1980
Subject Interests: Local hist
Wireless access
Open Tues-Sat 10-3
Friends of the Library Group

YUBA CITY

P SUTTER COUNTY LIBRARY*, 750 Forbes Ave, 95991. SAN 335-4245. Tel: 530-822-7137. FAX: 530-671-6539. E-mail: suttlibr@yahoo.com. Web Site: www.suttercounty.org/doc/government/depts/library. *Dir, Libr Serv,* James Ochsner; E-mail: jochsner@co.sutter.ca.us; Staff 3 (MLS 3)
Founded 1917. Pop 95,065; Circ 370,179
Library Holdings: Bk Vols 112,085; Per Subs 200
Special Collections: Sutter County History Coll
Wireless access
Mem of NorthNet Library System
Open Mon-Thurs 10-7, Fri & Sat 10-5
Friends of the Library Group
Branches: 2
BARBER, 10321 Live Oak Blvd, Live Oak, 95953, SAN 335-427X. Tel: 530-822-3223. *Librn,* Ellen English
Circ 6,358
Library Holdings: Bk Vols 15,000
Open Mon-Thurs 1-5, Fri 9-1
Friends of the Library Group
SUTTER BRANCH, 2147 California St, Sutter, 95982. (Mail add: PO Box 747, Sutter, 95982-0747), SAN 335-4393. Tel: 530-755-0485. *Librn,* Ellen English
Circ 6,045
Library Holdings: Bk Vols 8,717
Open Mon-Fri 1-5

YUCAIPA

J CRAFTON HILLS COLLEGE LIBRARY*, 11711 Sand Canyon Rd, 92399. SAN 301-7338. Tel: 909-389-3323, 909-794-2161. FAX: 909-794-9524. Web Site: www.craftonhills.edu. *Chief Librn,* Dr Sherrie

Loewen; E-mail: sloewen@craftonhills.edu; *Librn*, Catherine Hendrickson; E-mail: chendric@craftonhills.edu; *Librn*, Sam Job; Tel: 909-389-3322, E-mail: sejob@craftonhills.edu; Staff 6 (MLS 3, Non-MLS 3)
Founded 1972. Enrl 5,500; Fac 76; Highest Degree: Associate
Library Holdings: Bk Vols 50,000; Per Subs 500
Automation Activity & Vendor Info: (Cataloging) Innovative Interfaces, Inc; (Circulation) Innovative Interfaces, Inc; (Course Reserve) Innovative Interfaces, Inc; (ILL) Innovative Interfaces, Inc; (Media Booking) Innovative Interfaces, Inc; (OPAC) Innovative Interfaces, Inc; (Serials) Innovative Interfaces, Inc
Partic in Inland Empire Acad Libr Coop; San Bernardino, Inyo, Riverside Counties United Library Services
Open Mon-Thurs 8am-9pm, Fri 8-4

COLORADO

Date of Statistics: 2020
Population, 2020 U.S. Census: 5,773,714
Population Served by Public Libraries: 5,745,367
Total Print Volumes: 9,298,203
  Volumes Per Capita: 1.62
Digital Resources:
  Total e-books in Public Libraries: 6,367,061
  Total audio items (physical & downloadable units): 5,674,701
  Total video items (physical & downloadable units): 2,362,308
Total Public Library Circulation: 43,515,095
  Circulation Per Capita: 7.57

Income and Expenditures:
Total Public Library Income: $394,780,405 (local operating income)
  Source of Income: Mainly public funds from property tax
  2020 Regional Library Service Systems: $1,000,000
  2020 Federal Library Services & Technology Act: $3,479,967
Total Public Library Expenditures: $324,723,674 (operating expenditures)
  Expenditure Per Capita: $56.52
Information provided courtesy of: Melissa Carlson, Program Assistant; Colorado State Library

AGUILAR

P AGUILAR PUBLIC LIBRARY*, 146 W Main St, 81020. (Mail add: PO Box 578, 81020-0578), SAN 301-7346. Tel: 719-941-4426. Web Site: aguilarco.com/aguilar-public-library. *Libr Dir,* Linn G Baker; E-mail: aglibaker12@gmail.com; Staff 2 (Non-MLS 2)
Founded 1942. Pop 700; Circ 1,400
Library Holdings: Audiobooks 45; DVDs 125; Large Print Bks 250; Bk Vols 6,000; Talking Bks 200
Special Collections: Colorado Coll; Southwest Coll
Wireless access
Function: Audio & video playback equip for onsite use, Bks on CD, Children's prog, Computer training, Computers for patron use, Free DVD rentals, Internet access, Magnifiers for reading, Microfiche/film & reading machines, Photocopying/Printing, Summer reading prog, Wheelchair accessible
Partic in Colorado Library Consortium
Open Tues, Thurs-Sat 10-2, Wed 2-6
Friends of the Library Group

AKRON

P AKRON PUBLIC LIBRARY*, 302 Main Ave, 80720-1437. SAN 301-7354. Tel: 970-345-6818. E-mail: akronlibrary@centurytel.net. Web Site: akron.colibraries.org. *Dir,* Jan McCracken
Founded 1921. Pop 4,800; Circ 8,339
Library Holdings: Bk Vols 7,000; Talking Bks 300; Videos 300
Special Collections: Washington County History. Oral History
Automation Activity & Vendor Info: (Cataloging) SirsiDynix; (Circulation) SirsiDynix; (OPAC) SirsiDynix
Wireless access
Open Tues-Fri 9-5:30, Sat 9-1
Friends of the Library Group

S USDA AGRICULTURAL RESEARCH SERVICE*, Central Great Plains Research Station Library, 40335 County Rd GG, 80720. SAN 370-2499. Tel: 970-345-2259. FAX: 970-345-2088. Web Site: www.akron.ars.usda.gov. *Res,* Merle F Vigil; E-mail: merle.vigil@ars.usda.gov. Subject Specialists: *Agronomy,* Merle F Vigil
Founded 1949
Library Holdings: Bk Vols 300; Per Subs 10
Open Mon-Fri 7:30-4:15
Restriction: Open to pub for ref only

ALAMOSA

C ADAMS STATE UNIVERSITY*, Nielsen Library, 208 Edgemont Blvd, 81101-2373. SAN 301-7362. Tel: 719-587-7781. Interlibrary Loan Service Tel: 719-587-7173. Reference Tel: 719-587-7879. Administration Tel: 719-587-7820. FAX: 719-587-7590. E-mail: libreference@adams.edu. Web Site: www.adams.edu/library. *Libr Dir,* Jeffrey Bullington; E-mail: jsbullington@adams.edu; *Access Serv Librn, Distance Educ Librn,* Amanda Langdon; E-mail: anlangdon@adams.edu; *Circ Supvr,* Ronnie Medina; E-mail: rmedina@adams.edu; Staff 8 (MLS 6, Non-MLS 2)
Founded 1925. Enrl 93; Fac 102; Highest Degree: Master
Jul 2012-Jun 2013. Mats Exp $267,500, Books $48,000, Per/Ser (Incl. Access Fees) $106,000, AV Mat $2,000, Electronic Ref Mat (Incl. Access Fees) $97,500, Presv $2,200. Sal $425,952 (Prof $392,652)
Library Holdings: AV Mats 2,602; DVDs 2,683; e-journals 19,000; Microforms 25,056; Bk Titles 110,041; Bk Vols 125,288; Per Subs 362
Special Collections: Colorado Room. US Document Depository
Automation Activity & Vendor Info: (Acquisitions) Baker & Taylor; (Cataloging) OCLC Online; (Circulation) Innovative Interfaces, Inc; (ILL) OCLC; (OPAC) Innovative Interfaces, Inc; (Serials) Innovative Interfaces, Inc
Wireless access
Function: Archival coll, Distance learning, For res purposes, Homebound delivery serv, ILL available, Internet access, Photocopying/Printing, Ref serv available, Telephone ref, Wheelchair accessible
Partic in Marmot Library Network
Special Services for the Deaf - TDD equip; TTY equip
Open Mon-Thurs 8am-11pm, Fri 8-5, Sat 1-6, Sun 1-11
Restriction: Use of others with permission of librn

P ALAMOSA PUBLIC LIBRARY, 300 Hunt Ave, 81101. SAN 301-7370. Tel: 719-589-6592. FAX: 719-589-3786. Web Site: www.alamosalibrary.org. *Dir,* Andrew Rice; Tel: 719-587-2529, E-mail: arice@ci.alamosa.co.us; *Libr Mgr,* Salai Taylor; Tel: 719-587-2543, E-mail: staylor@ci.alamosa.co.us; *Ch,* Holly Van Hoy; Tel: 719-587-2550; *Support Librn,* Melissa Martinson; Tel: 719-587-2541; *Cat Tech,* Rose Strand; Tel: 719-587-2539; *Libr Tech - ILL,* Cathy Zverez; Tel: 719-587-2538; *Libr Tech-Mats,* Patty Martinez; Tel: 719-587-2542, E-mail: pmartinez@ci.alamosa.co.us. Subject Specialists: *Juv,* Holly Van Hoy; Staff 2.6 (Non-MLS 2.6)
Founded 1902. Pop 9,285; Circ 136,055
Jan 2020-Dec 2020 Income $429,472, State $5,500, City $404,260, Federal $8,000, Locally Generated Income $11,712. Mats Exp $72,523, Books $38,127, Per/Ser (Incl. Access Fees) $3,251, AV Mat $15,801, Electronic Ref Mat (Incl. Access Fees) $15,344. Sal $249,194
Library Holdings: Audiobooks 2,306; CDs 1,081; DVDs 6,283; e-books 50,693; Electronic Media & Resources 7; Large Print Bks 1,623; Bk Vols 32,962; Per Subs 65; Videos 5,734
Subject Interests: Colorado, Genealogy, Parenting, Spanish (Lang)
Automation Activity & Vendor Info: (Acquisitions) LibLime Koha; (Cataloging) LibLime Koha; (Circulation) LibLime Koha; (ILL) Fretwell-Downing; (OPAC) LibLime Koha
Wireless access
Function: 24/7 Electronic res, 24/7 Online cat, 3D Printer, Audiobks via web, Bks on CD, Children's prog, Computers for patron use, Electronic databases & coll, ILL available, Internet access, Large print keyboards, Magazines, Magnifiers for reading, Mail & tel request accepted, Mango lang, Movies, Music CDs, Online cat, Outreach serv, Photocopying/Printing, Preschool reading prog, Prog for children & young

adult, Ref serv available, Scanner, Spanish lang bks, Story hour, Study rm, Summer reading prog, Tax forms, Wheelchair accessible
Partic in Colorado Library Consortium
Special Services for the Deaf - ADA equip; Assistive tech; Closed caption videos; Sign lang interpreter upon request for prog; Staff with knowledge of sign lang
Special Services for the Blind - Accessible computers; Audio mat; Bks on CD; Braille bks; Computer access aids; Computer with voice synthesizer for visually impaired persons; Dragon Naturally Speaking software; Internet workstation with adaptive software; Large print bks; Large screen computer & software; Magnifiers; PC for people with disabilities; Talking bk serv referral
Open Mon-Thurs 9-6, Fri & Sat 10-2
Restriction: Non-circulating coll
Friends of the Library Group

ASPEN

S ASPEN HISTORICAL SOCIETY ARCHIVES*, 620 W Bleeker St, 81611. SAN 328-5073. Tel: 970-925-3721. FAX: 970-925-5347. E-mail: info@aspenhistory.org. Web Site: www.aspenhistory.org. *Dir,* Kelly Murphy; Tel: 970-925-3721, Ext 101, E-mail: director@aspenhistory.org; *Curator of Coll,* Lisa Hancock; Tel: 970-925-3721, Ext 110, E-mail: curator@aspenhistory.org
Library Holdings: AV Mats 300; DVDs 100; Bk Titles 1,000
Special Collections: Oral History
Wireless access
Open Mon-Fri 9-4:30

S THE ASPEN INSTITUTE, Paepcke Building Library, 1000 N Third St, 81611-1361. SAN 301-7397. Tel: 970-925-7010. FAX: 970-925-4188. Web Site: www.aspeninstitute.org. *Library Contact,* Katherine Seward; E-mail: katherine.seward@aspeninstitute.org
Founded 1963
Library Holdings: Bk Vols 4,000
Open Mon-Fri 9-5
Restriction: Not a lending libr

P PITKIN COUNTY LIBRARY*, 120 N Mill St, 81611. SAN 301-7400. Tel: 970-429-1900. FAX: 970-449-0793. E-mail: libraryinfo@pitkincounty.com. Web Site: www.pitcolib.org. *County Librn,* Kathleen Chandler; Tel: 970-429-1910, E-mail: kathy.chandler@pitkincounty.com; *Asst Dir, Pub Serv Librn,* Susan S Keenan; *Asst Dir, Tech Serv Librn,* Carol McArdell; *Librn,* Tammy Benninger; *Librn,* Jeffrey Bradley; *Librn,* Nathalie Crick; *Librn,* Martha Durgy; *Librn,* David V Gollon; *Librn,* Collins Kelly; *Librn,* Genevieve Smith; *ILL,* Molly Ireland; Staff 10 (MLS 7, Non-MLS 3)
Founded 1940. Circ 156,681
Library Holdings: Large Print Bks 300; Bk Titles 120,000; Per Subs 250
Special Collections: Aspen Newspapers, 1888-present, microfilm; Music, rec & scores
Automation Activity & Vendor Info: (Circulation) Innovative Interfaces, Inc
Wireless access
Function: 24/7 Electronic res, 24/7 Online cat, 3D Printer, Archival coll, Audio & video playback equip for onsite use, Audiobks on Playaways & MP3, Audiobks via web, Bk club(s), Bks on CD, Children's prog, Computers for patron use, Electronic databases & coll, Free DVD rentals, ILL available, Internet access, Magazines, Mango lang, Meeting rooms, Microfiche/film & reading machines, Movies, Music CDs, Photocopying/Printing, Printer for laptops & handheld devices, Prog for adults, Prog for children & young adult, Ref serv available, Scanner, Spanish lang bks, Story hour, Summer reading prog, Tax forms, Teen prog, Telephone ref, Wheelchair accessible, Workshops
Partic in Marmot Library Network
Open Mon-Thurs 9-8, Fri & Sat 9-6, Sun 12-6
Friends of the Library Group

AULT

P NORTHERN PLAINS PUBLIC LIBRARY*, 216 W Second St, 80610. (Mail add: PO Box 147, 80610-0147), SAN 301-7419. Tel: 970-834-1259. FAX: 970-834-1259. E-mail: northernplainspl@gmail.com. Web Site: northernplainspl.org. *Dir, Programs,* Terri K Hicks
Founded 1926. Pop 4,800; Circ 34,403
Library Holdings: DVDs 242; Large Print Bks 728; Bk Vols 34,790; Per Subs 70; Talking Bks 124; Videos 1,400
Special Collections: Oral History
Automation Activity & Vendor Info: (Cataloging) SirsiDynix; (Circulation) SirsiDynix; (OPAC) SirsiDynix
Wireless access
Mem of High Plains Library District
Open Mon-Fri 9-7, Sat 10-2
Friends of the Library Group

AURORA

S AURORA HISTORY MUSEUM LIBRARY*, 15051 E Alameda Pkwy, 80012. Tel: 303-739-6660. FAX: 303-739-6657. E-mail: museum@auroragov.org. Web Site: www.auroragov.org/things_to_do/aurora_history_museum/aurora_history/research. *Library Contact,* Elizabeth Ricci; E-mail: ericci@auroragov.org
Founded 1979
Library Holdings: Bk Vols 750
Special Collections: Local Directories (1930-1960); Local Newspapers (Aurora Democrat, Advocate, Sun & Sentinel on microfilm); Newspaper Photos (Aurora Sun & Aurora Advocate, 1950-Present)
Subject Interests: Area hist
Function: Ref serv available, Res libr
Restriction: Open by appt only

P AURORA PUBLIC LIBRARY*, Administration - Department of Library & Cultural Services, 14949 E Alameda Pkwy, 80012. SAN 335-4458. Tel: 303-739-6600. Circulation Tel: 303-739-6628. Reference Tel: 303-739-6630. Administration Tel: 303-739-6640. FAX: 303-739-6579. E-mail: library@auroragov.org. Web Site: www.auroragov.org/things_to_do/aurora_public_library. *Dir, Libr & Cultural Serv,* Patti Bateman; Tel: 303-739-6594, E-mail: pbateman@auroragov.org; *Br Mgr,* Phillip Challis; E-mail: pchallis@auroragov.org; *Libr Operations Mgr,* Steve Wasiecko; E-mail: swasieck@auroragov.org; Staff 61 (MLS 14, Non-MLS 47)
Founded 1929. Pop 335,000; Circ 801,649
Library Holdings: Bk Vols 269,986
Subject Interests: Spanish (Lang)
Automation Activity & Vendor Info: (Acquisitions) Innovative Interfaces, Inc; (Cataloging) Innovative Interfaces, Inc; (Circulation) Innovative Interfaces, Inc; (ILL) Innovative Interfaces, Inc; (OPAC) Innovative Interfaces, Inc; (Serials) Innovative Interfaces, Inc
Wireless access
Function: Adult bk club, Adult literacy prog, Bilingual assistance for Spanish patrons, Bk club(s), Bks on CD, Computer training, Computers for patron use, Digital talking bks, Electronic databases & coll, Free DVD rentals, Genealogy discussion group, ILL available, Internet access, Life-long learning prog for all ages, Magazines, Mango lang, Microfiche/film & reading machines, Movies, Museum passes, Music CDs, Online cat, Online ref, Outreach serv, OverDrive digital audio bks, Photocopying/Printing, Preschool outreach, Prog for adults, Prog for children & young adult, Ref serv available, Scanner, Spanish lang bks, Story hour, Study rm, Summer & winter reading prog, Telephone ref, Wheelchair accessible
Publications: Annual Report; Aurora Public Library "Five Year Strategic Plan"; Aurora Public Library Qtrly brochure: "The Resource"; Library News Online
Special Services for the Blind - Bks on CD; Large print & cassettes; Talking bk serv referral
Open Mon-Thurs 8am-10pm, Fri 8-8, Sat 8-6, Sun 10-6
Friends of the Library Group
Branches: 7
CENTRAL LIBRARY-MAIN BRANCH, 14949 E Alameda Pkwy, 80012. Tel: 303-739-6000. *Br Mgr,* Phillip Challis; Tel: 303-739-6625, E-mail: pchallis@auroragov.org; *Br Supvr,* Dustin Goforth
Automation Activity & Vendor Info: (Acquisitions) Innovative Interfaces, Inc - Sierra; (Cataloging) Innovative Interfaces, Inc - Sierra; (Circulation) Innovative Interfaces, Inc - Sierra; (OPAC) Innovative Interfaces, Inc - Sierra
Open Mon-Thurs 8am-10pm, Fri 8-8, Sat 8-6, Sun 10-6
Friends of the Library Group
COLFAX & CHAMBERS PC CENTER, 15200 E Colfax Ave, 80012. Tel: 303-739-1959. ; Staff 1 (Non-MLS 1)
Automation Activity & Vendor Info: (Acquisitions) Innovative Interfaces, Inc - Sierra; (Cataloging) Innovative Interfaces, Inc - Sierra; (Circulation) Innovative Interfaces, Inc - Sierra; (OPAC) Innovative Interfaces, Inc - Sierra
Function: 24/7 Online cat, Computer training, Computers for patron use, Online cat, OverDrive digital audio bks, Ref serv available, Scanner, Story hour, Summer & winter reading prog
Temporarily closed due to relocation 2021-
Friends of the Library Group
HOFFMAN LIBRARY, 1298 Peoria St, 80011. Tel: 303-739-1572. *Br Supvr,* Christine Johnson; E-mail: cjohnson@auroragov.org; *Libr Asst,* Tyler Walton; Staff 4 (Non-MLS 4)
Automation Activity & Vendor Info: (Acquisitions) Innovative Interfaces, Inc - Sierra; (Cataloging) Innovative Interfaces, Inc - Sierra; (Circulation) Innovative Interfaces, Inc - Sierra; (OPAC) Innovative Interfaces, Inc - Sierra
Function: 24/7 Electronic res, 24/7 Online cat, Activity rm, Adult literacy prog, Audiobks via web, Bilingual assistance for Spanish patrons, Bks on CD, Children's prog, Computer training, Computers for patron use, Electronic databases & coll, ILL available, Learning ctr, Magazines, Online cat, OverDrive digital audio bks,

Photocopying/Printing, Prog for children & young adult, Spanish lang bks, Story hour, Study rm, Summer & winter reading prog, Teen prog, Telephone ref, Wheelchair accessible
Open Mon 11-7, Tues-Sat 10-6
Friends of the Library Group

MARTIN LUTHER KING JR LIBRARY, 9898 E Colfax Ave, 80010, SAN 335-4547. Tel: 303-739-1940. FAX: 303-739-1944. *Supvr, N Region Libr,* Christine Johnson; E-mail: cajohnso@auroragov.org; Staff 7 (MLS 1, Non-MLS 6)
Automation Activity & Vendor Info: (Acquisitions) Innovative Interfaces, Inc - Sierra; (Cataloging) Innovative Interfaces, Inc - Sierra; (Circulation) Innovative Interfaces, Inc - Sierra; (OPAC) Innovative Interfaces, Inc - Sierra
Function: 24/7 Electronic res, Audiobks via web, Bilingual assistance for Spanish patrons, Bks on cassette, Bks on CD, CD-ROM, Children's prog, Citizenship assistance, Computer training, Computers for patron use, Digital talking bks, E-Reserves, Electronic databases & coll, Free DVD rentals, Games & aids for people with disabilities, Homework prog, ILL available, Internet access, Learning ctr, Life-long learning prog for all ages, Literacy & newcomer serv, Magazines, Mail & tel request accepted, Meeting rooms, Movies, Museum passes, Music CDs, Online cat, Orientations, Outreach serv, OverDrive digital audio bks, Photocopying/Printing, Preschool outreach, Preschool reading prog, Prog for adults, Prog for children & young adult, Ref & res, Ref serv available, Scanner, Senior computer classes, Spanish lang bks, Spoken cassettes & CDs, Spoken cassettes & DVDs, STEM programs, Story hour, Study rm, Summer & winter reading prog, Summer reading prog, Teen prog, Telephone ref, Wheelchair accessible, Winter reading prog
Open Mon & Wed-Sat 10-6
Friends of the Library Group

MISSION VIEJO BRANCH, 15324 E Hampden Circle, 80015, SAN 335-4571. Tel: 303-326-8600. *Libr Coord,* Erin Todd; Tel: 303-326-8604, E-mail: etodd@auroragov.org; Staff 8 (MLS 1, Non-MLS 7)
Automation Activity & Vendor Info: (Acquisitions) Innovative Interfaces, Inc - Sierra; (Cataloging) Innovative Interfaces, Inc - Sierra; (Circulation) Innovative Interfaces, Inc - Sierra; (OPAC) Innovative Interfaces, Inc - Sierra
Function: 24/7 Electronic res, 24/7 Online cat, Activity rm, Adult literacy prog, After school storytime, Audio & video playback equip for onsite use, AV serv, BA reader (adult literacy), Bilingual assistance for Spanish patrons, Bks on CD, CD-ROM, Children's prog, Citizenship assistance, Computer training, Computers for patron use, Digital talking bks, Electronic databases & coll, Free DVD rentals, Homework prog, Internet access, Learning ctr, Life-long learning prog for all ages, Literacy & newcomer serv, Magazines, Meeting rooms, Movies, Museum passes, Music CDs, Online cat, Orientations, Outreach serv, OverDrive digital audio bks, Photocopying/Printing, Prog for adults, Prog for children & young adult, Ref & res, Scanner, Senior outreach, Spanish lang bks, Spoken cassettes & CDs, STEM programs, Story hour, Study rm, Summer & winter reading prog, Summer reading prog, Teen prog, Telephone ref, Wheelchair accessible, Winter reading prog
Open Mon & Wed-Sat 10-6, Tues 11-7
Friends of the Library Group

TALLYNS REACH, 23911 E Arapahoe Rd, 80016. Tel: 303-627-3050. FAX: 303-627-3060. *Supvr, S Region Libr,* Erin Todd; Tel: 303-326-8604, E-mail: etodd@auroragov.org; Staff 6 (Non-MLS 6)
Automation Activity & Vendor Info: (Acquisitions) Innovative Interfaces, Inc - Sierra; (Cataloging) Innovative Interfaces, Inc - Sierra; (Circulation) Innovative Interfaces, Inc - Sierra; (OPAC) Innovative Interfaces, Inc - Sierra
Function: 24/7 Electronic res, 24/7 Online cat, Activity rm, After school storytime, Audiobks on Playaways & MP3, Audiobks via web, AV serv, Bilingual assistance for Spanish patrons, Bks on CD, CD-ROM, Children's prog, Computers for patron use, Digital talking bks, Electronic databases & coll, Free DVD rentals, Homework prog, ILL available, Internet access, Life-long learning prog for all ages, Magazines, Meeting rooms, Movies, Museum passes, Music CDs, Online cat, Orientations, Outreach serv, OverDrive digital audio bks, Photocopying/Printing, Preschool outreach, Prog for adults, Prog for children & young adult, Ref & res, Ref serv available, Res assist avail, Scanner, Senior outreach, Spanish lang bks, Spoken cassettes & DVDs, STEM programs, Story hour, Study rm, Summer & winter reading prog, Summer reading prog, Teen prog, Telephone ref, Winter reading prog
Open Mon 11-7, Tues-Sat 10-6
Friends of the Library Group

J COMMUNITY COLLEGE OF AURORA, 16000 E Centretech Pkwy, 80011. Tel: 303-360-4736. E-mail: library@ccaurora.edu. Web Site: www.ccaurora.edu/library. *Dir, Libr Serv,* Dan Lawrence; E-mail: dan.lawrence@ccaurora.edu; Staff 2 (MLS 1, Non-MLS 1)
Founded 1983. Enrl 8,000; Fac 61; Highest Degree: Associate
Library Holdings: Bk Vols 7,206; Videos 1,000
Automation Activity & Vendor Info: (Cataloging) ByWater Solutions; (Circulation) ByWater Solutions; (Course Reserve) ByWater Solutions; (Discovery) EBSCO Discovery Service; (OPAC) ByWater Solutions
Wireless access
Open Mon-Thurs 7:30am-8pm, Fri 7:30-5, Sat 9-1

G UNITED STATES DEPARTMENT OF JUSTICE*, The Robert J Kutak Memorial Library, National Institute of Corrections Information Ctr, 11900 E Cornell Ave, Unit C, 80014. SAN 323-6579. Tel: 303-338-6648. Toll Free Tel: 800-877-1461. *Prog Mgr,* Eric Bauer; Tel: 303-338-6643, Fax: 303-338-6601
Library Holdings: Bk Titles 20,000; Per Subs 200
Subject Interests: Corrections, Prisons
Wireless access
Special Services for the Deaf - TDD equip
Open Mon-Fri 7:30-5

CM UNIVERSITY OF COLORADO DENVER/ ANSCHUTZ MEDICAL CAMPUS*, Strauss Health Sciences Library, Anschutz Medical Campus, 12950 E Montview Blvd, 80045. (Mail add: Campus Box A003, 12950 E Montview Blvd, 80045), SAN 335-7600. Tel: 303-724-2152. FAX: 303-724-2166. Web Site: hslibrary.ucdenver.edu. *Dir,* Melissa De Santis; E-mail: melissa.desantis@ucdenver.edu; *Dep Dir,* Lisa Traditi; E-mail: lisa.traditi@ucdenver.edu; *Head Librn,* Douglas Stehle; E-mail: douglas.stehle@ucdenver.edu; *Cat Librn,* Emily Epstein; E-mail: emily.epstein@ucdenver.edu; Staff 28 (MLS 15, Non-MLS 13)
Founded 1924. Enrl 5,000; Fac 15; Highest Degree: Doctorate
Library Holdings: e-journals 14,092; Bk Vols 117,295; Per Subs 14,092
Special Collections: Indigenous Medicine Coll
Subject Interests: Med
Automation Activity & Vendor Info: (Acquisitions) Ex Libris Group; (Cataloging) Ex Libris Group; (Circulation) Ex Libris Group; (Course Reserve) Ex Libris Group; (Discovery) Ex Libris Group; (OPAC) Ex Libris Group
Wireless access
Partic in Colorado Alliance of Research Libraries; National Network of Libraries of Medicine Region 4; OCLC Online Computer Library Center, Inc
Open Mon-Thurs 7-7, Fri 7-5, Sat & Sun 9-5
Restriction: 24-hr pass syst for students only, Open to students, fac & staff

BAILEY

P PARK COUNTY PUBLIC LIBRARIES*, Bailey Public Library, 350 Bulldogger Rd, 80421. Tel: 303-838-5539. E-mail: baileylib@parkco.us. Web Site: parkcounty.colibraries.org/bailey. *Br Mgr,* Erna Taylor
Founded 1966
Automation Activity & Vendor Info: (Acquisitions) SirsiDynix; (Cataloging) SirsiDynix; (Circulation) SirsiDynix; (Course Reserve) SirsiDynix; (ILL) SirsiDynix; (Media Booking) SirsiDynix; (OPAC) SirsiDynix; (Serials) SirsiDynix
Wireless access
Friends of the Library Group
Branches: 3

FAIRPLAY BRANCH, 400 Front St, Fairplay, 80440. (Mail add: PO Box 592, Fairplay, 80440-0592). Tel: 719-836-4297. FAX: 719-836-0863. E-mail: fairplaylib@parkco.us. Web Site: parkcounty.colibraries.org/fairplay. *Libraries Mgr,* Patricia Shepard; E-mail: pshepard@parkco.us; *Br Mgr,* Nancy Wood; Staff 2 (MLS 1, Non-MLS 1)
Open Mon-Sat 11-5
Friends of the Library Group

GUFFEY BRANCH, 1625B Park County Rd 102, Guffey, 80820. (Mail add: PO Box 33, Guffey, 80820-0033). Tel: 719-689-9280. FAX: 719-689-9280. E-mail: guffeylib@parkco.us. Web Site: parkcounty.colibraries.org/libraries/guffey. *Br Mgr,* Rita Mick
Friends of the Library Group

LAKE GEORGE BRANCH, 37900 Hwy 24, Lake George, 80827. Tel: 719-748-3812. FAX: 719-748-3812. E-mail: lakegeorgelib@parkco.us. Web Site: parkcounty.colibraries.org/libraries/lake-george. *Br Mgr,* Cassandra Noftz
Friends of the Library Group

BASALT

P BASALT REGIONAL LIBRARY DISTRICT, 14 Midland Ave, 81621-8305. SAN 320-1724. Tel: 970-927-4311. FAX: 970-927-1351. Web Site: basaltlibrary.org. *Interim Dir,* Barbara Milnor; E-mail: bmilnor@basaltlibrary.org; *Asst Dir,* Berenice Forrest; E-mail: bforrest@basaltlibrary.org
Founded 1976. Pop 10,900; Circ 45,126
Library Holdings: Bk Vols 34,134; Per Subs 61
Special Collections: Oral History
Subject Interests: Colorado
Automation Activity & Vendor Info: (Circulation) Innovative Interfaces, Inc; (OPAC) Innovative Interfaces, Inc
Wireless access
Partic in Marmot Library Network

Open Mon-Thurs 10-7, Fri & Sat 10-5, Sun 12-5
Friends of the Library Group

BAYFIELD

P PINE RIVER PUBLIC LIBRARY DISTRICT*, 395 Bayfield Center Dr, 81122. (Mail add: PO Box 227, 81122-0227), SAN 301-746X. Tel: 970-884-2222. FAX: 970-884-7155. Web Site: www.prlibrary.org. *Dir,* Shelley Walchak; E-mail: shelley@prlibrary.org; *Asst Dir,* Brenda Marshall; E-mail: Brenda@prlibrary.org; *Programming Librn, Pub Relations Librn,* Darcy Harp; E-mail: darcy@prlibrary.org; *Acq & Cat Mgr,* Wendi Weinstein; E-mail: Wendi@prlibrary.org; *Ch Mgr,* Elizabeth VonTauffkirchen; E-mail: elizabeth@prlibrary.org; *Teen Serv Mgr,* Becky Van Den Berg; E-mail: becky@prlibrary.org; *IT Spec,* Tim Lovejoy; E-mail: tim@prlibrary.org; Staff 9 (MLS 2, Non-MLS 7)
Founded 1934. Pop 8,500
Library Holdings: Bk Titles 28,000; Bk Vols 30,000
Automation Activity & Vendor Info: (Cataloging) Innovative Interfaces, Inc - Sierra; (Circulation) Innovative Interfaces, Inc - Sierra; (OPAC) Innovative Interfaces, Inc - Sierra
Wireless access
Function: 24/7 Electronic res, 24/7 Online cat, 3D Printer, Activity rm, Adult bk club, Adult literacy prog, After school storytime, Art exhibits, Audio & video playback equip for onsite use, Audiobks via web, AV serv, Bilingual assistance for Spanish patrons, Bk club(s), Bks on CD, Children's prog, Computer training, Computers for patron use, E-Readers, Electronic databases & coll, Equip loans & repairs, Free DVD rentals, Holiday prog, ILL available, Instruction & testing, Internet access, Life-long learning prog for all ages, Magazines, Mail & tel request accepted, Mango lang, Meeting rooms, Movies, Music CDs, Notary serv, Online cat, Orientations, Outside serv via phone, mail, e-mail & web, OverDrive digital audio bks, Passport agency, Photocopying/Printing, Preschool outreach, Preschool reading prog, Printer for laptops & handheld devices, Prog for adults, Prog for children & young adult, Ref & res, Ref serv available, Scanner, Senior computer classes, Senior outreach, Spanish lang bks, Story hour, Study rm, Summer & winter reading prog, Summer reading prog, Tax forms, Teen prog, Telephone ref, Wheelchair accessible, Winter reading prog, Workshops, Writing prog
Partic in Marmot Library Network
Open Mon-Fri 9-7, Sat 9-5, Sun 1-5
Friends of the Library Group

BERTHOUD

P BERTHOUD PUBLIC LIBRARY, 236 Welch Ave, 80513. SAN 301-7478. Tel: 970-532-2757. FAX: 970-532-4372. E-mail: berthoudcommunitylibrary@gmail.com. Web Site: berthoud.colibraries.org. *Dir,* Amie Pilla; E-mail: director.bpl@gmail.com; Staff 4 (MLS 1, Non-MLS 3)
Founded 1931. Pop 11,000; Circ 50,834
Library Holdings: AV Mats 1,000; High Interest/Low Vocabulary Bk Vols 100; Large Print Bks 500; Bk Titles 28,000; Bk Vols 28,400; Per Subs 30; Talking Bks 529
Special Collections: Berthoud Bulletin, microfilm; Xeriscape Materials
Automation Activity & Vendor Info: (Cataloging) Follett Software; (Circulation) Follett Software; (OPAC) Follett Software
Wireless access
Partic in Colorado Library Consortium
Open Mon & Tues 9-8, Wed-Fri 9-6, Sat 9-5
Friends of the Library Group

BLACK HAWK

P GILPIN COUNTY PUBLIC LIBRARY DISTRICT, 15131 Hwy 119, 80422. SAN 378-0163. Tel: 303-582-5777. Administration Tel: 303-582-0161. FAX: 303-582-3938. E-mail: gilpinlib@gilpincounty.org. Web Site: www.gilpinlibrary.org. *Dir,* Michael Carlson; E-mail: mcarlson@gilpincounty.org; *Adult Serv,* Jeffrey Eggleston; E-mail: jeggleston@gilpincounty.org; *Ch Serv,* Debra Benitez; E-mail: dbenitez@gilpincounty.org; *Circ,* George Blevins; *Circ,* Jo Anne Carlin; *Circ,* Linda Craig; Staff 6 (MLS 2, Non-MLS 4)
Founded 1978. Pop 6,200; Circ 25,000
Library Holdings: CDs 560; DVDs 3,212; Large Print Bks 420; Bk Vols 17,950; Per Subs 23; Videos 1,479
Subject Interests: Colorado, County hist, State hist
Automation Activity & Vendor Info: (Cataloging) Koha; (Circulation) Koha; (OPAC) Koha
Wireless access
Function: Adult bk club, Adult literacy prog, Archival coll, Art exhibits, Audio & video playback equip for onsite use, Bk club(s), Bks on cassette, Bks on CD, CD-ROM, Children's prog, Computer training, Computers for patron use, E-Reserves, Free DVD rentals, Holiday prog, Homebound delivery serv, ILL available, Internet access, Notary serv, Online cat, Online ref, Orientations, Photocopying/Printing, Wheelchair accessible
Partic in Colorado Library Consortium
Open Mon, Wed & Fri 9-6, Tues & Thurs 9-8, Sat & Sun 10-2
Friends of the Library Group

BOULDER

M BOULDER COMMUNITY HOSPITAL*, Medical Library, 1100 Balsam Ave, 80304. (Mail add: PO Box 9019, 80301-9019), SAN 301-7508. Tel: 303-415-7496. FAX: 303-938-3483. Web Site: www.bch.org/Locations/Boulder-Community-Hospital.aspx. *Librn,* Joyce Moore; Staff 2 (MLS 1, Non-MLS 1)
Founded 1922
Library Holdings: e-journals 659; Bk Vols 425; Per Subs 30
Subject Interests: Med, Nursing
Wireless access
Partic in Colorado Council of Medical Librarians; Medical Library Association; Mid Continental Med Libr Asn
Open Mon, Wed & Fri 8-Noon, Tues & Thurs 12-4

S BOULDER COUNTY CORRECTIONS LIBRARY*, 3200 Airport Rd, 80301. SAN 377-0788. Tel: 303-441-4686. Web Site: www.co.boulder.co.us/sheriff. *Dir,* Erin E Miller; E-mail: emiller@bouldercounty.org; Staff 1 (MLS 1)
Library Holdings: Bk Titles 4,500; Bk Vols 5,000; Per Subs 15
Open Mon-Fri 7-3

P BOULDER PUBLIC LIBRARY*, 1001 Arapahoe Rd, 80302. SAN 335-4695. Tel: 303-441-3100. FAX: 720-564-2178. Web Site: boulderlibrary.org. *Libr & Arts Dir,* David Farnan; E-mail: farnand@boulderlibrary.org; *Dep Libr Dir,* Jennifer Phares; E-mail: pharesj@boulderlibrary.org; *Commun Engagement Mgr,* Aspen Walker; E-mail: walkera@boulderlibrary.org; *Mgr, E-Serv,* Aimee Schumm; E-mail: schumma@boulderlibrary.org; *Pub Serv Mgr,* Antonia Gaona; E-mail: gaonaa@boulderlibrary.org; *Resource Serv Mgr,* Terri Lewis; E-mail: lewiste@boulderlibrary.org; *Ch Serv, Teen Serv,* Anne Ledford; E-mail: ledforda@boulderlibrary.org
Pop 103,600; Circ 1,040,413
Jan 2015-Dec 2015 Income (Main & Associated Libraries) $7,690,028, State $26,156, City $6,586,733, Locally Generated Income $860,659, Other $216,480. Mats Exp $972,581, Books $488,426, Electronic Ref Mat (Incl. Access Fees) $484,155. Sal $5,120,018
Library Holdings: Audiobooks 8,184; CDs 8,838; DVDs 18,361; e-books 154,040; Electronic Media & Resources 6,602; Bk Vols 277,133; Per Subs 281
Special Collections: Local History; Municipal Government. Oral History
Automation Activity & Vendor Info: (Acquisitions) Innovative Interfaces, Inc; (Cataloging) Innovative Interfaces, Inc; (Circulation) Innovative Interfaces, Inc; (OPAC) Innovative Interfaces, Inc
Wireless access
Function: 24/7 Electronic res, Adult bk club, Adult literacy prog, Archival coll, Art exhibits, Audiobks via web, Bk club(s), Bks on CD, Bus archives, Children's prog, Citizenship assistance, Computers for patron use, Digital talking bks, E-Reserves, Electronic databases & coll, Family literacy, Free DVD rentals, Home delivery & serv to seniorr ctr & nursing homes, Homebound delivery serv, Homework prog, ILL available, Instruction & testing, Internet access, Jail serv, Life-long learning prog for all ages, Literacy & newcomer serv, Magazines, Mango lang, Meeting rooms, Movies, Music CDs, Notary serv, Online cat, Online ref, Outreach serv, OverDrive digital audio bks, Photocopying/Printing, Printer for laptops & handheld devices, Prog for adults, Prog for children & young adult, Ref serv available, Story hour, Summer reading prog, Teen prog, Wheelchair accessible
Publications: Boulder Municipal Government 1871-1946, 1965-1974, 1975-1979 & 1980-1984
Partic in Flatirons Library Consortium
Open Mon-Thurs 9-8, Fri & Sat 10-6, Sun 12-6
Branches: 4
CARNEGIE BRANCH FOR LOCAL HISTORY, 1125 Pine St, 80302-4024, SAN 335-4709. Tel: 303-441-3110. FAX: 720-406-7452. Web Site: boulderlibrary.org/locations/carnegie. *Br Mgr,* Wendy Hall; Tel: 303-441-4096, E-mail: hallw@boulderlibrary.org; Staff 4 (MLS 1, Non-MLS 3)
Founded 1983. Pop 90,000
Special Collections: Boulder Historical Society Photograph Coll; Digitized OPAC Images; Maria Rogers Oral History Program. Oral History
Subject Interests: Boulder County & Boulder
Function: Archival coll, Audio & video playback equip for onsite use, Computers for patron use, Genealogy discussion group, Internet access, Outside serv via phone, mail, e-mail & web, Ref serv available
Open Mon-Fri 1-5, Sat 10-3
Friends of the Library Group
MEADOWS BRANCH, 4800 Baseline Rd, Ste C112, 80303-2678, SAN 323-9381. Tel: 303-441-4390. Administration Tel: 303-441-4169. Web Site: boulderlibrary.org/locations/meadows. *Br Mgr,* Monnie Nilsson; E-mail: nilssonm@boulderlibrary.org

Function: Art exhibits, Children's prog, Citizenship assistance, Computer training, Computers for patron use, Electronic databases & coll, Free DVD rentals, Home delivery & serv to seniorr ctr & nursing homes, Homebound delivery serv, ILL available, Internet access, Literacy & newcomer serv, Music CDs, Online cat, Online ref, OverDrive digital audio bks, Photocopying/Printing, Prog for adults, Prog for children & young adult, Ref serv available, Serves people with intellectual disabilities, Story hour, Wheelchair accessible
Open Mon & Wed 9-8, Thurs-Sat 10-6, Sun 12-6
NORTH BOULDER CORNER LIBRARY, 4600 Broadway, 80304. Web Site: boulderlibrary.org/locations/nobo. *Br Mgr,* Leanne Slater; E-mail: slaterl@boulderlibrary.org
Open Mon, Tues & Sat 10-6, Wed 10-8, Sun 12-6
GEORGE F REYNOLDS BRANCH, 3595 Table Mesa Dr, 80305, SAN 335-4725. Tel: 303-441-3120. FAX: 303-441-4094. Web Site: boulderlibrary.org/locations/reynolds. *Br Mgr,* Linda Cumming; E-mail: cummingl@boulderlibrary.org
Open Mon-Thurs 9-8, Fri & Sat 10-6, Sun 12-6

R FIRST UNITED METHODIST CHURCH LIBRARY, 1421 Spruce St, 80302. SAN 301-7516. Tel: 303-442-3770. E-mail: office@fumcboulder.org. Web Site: www.fumcboulder.org.
Founded 1952
Library Holdings: Bk Vols 2,940
Subject Interests: Educ, Psychol, Relig, Soc sci & issues
Wireless access

C NAROPA UNIVERSITY LIBRARY*, Allen Ginsberg Library, 2130 Arapahoe Ave, 80302. SAN 320-443X. Tel: 303-546-3507. E-mail: library@naropa.edu. Web Site: www.naropa.edu/academics/ginsberg-library. *Dir,* Amanda Rybin Koob; E-mail: arybinkoob@naropa.edu; *Admin Coordr,* Nile Leach; E-mail: lleach@naropa.edu; Staff 4 (MLS 2, Non-MLS 2)
Founded 1974. Enrl 1,100; Highest Degree: Master
Library Holdings: AV Mats 2,300; e-books 1,676; Bk Vols 27,500; Per Subs 131
Special Collections: Naropa University Recordings; Small Press & Chapbook Coll; Tibetan Coll
Subject Interests: Buddhism, Poetry, Psychol, Tibetan (Lang), Traditional Eastern arts
Wireless access
Function: Archival coll, Audio & video playback equip for onsite use, AV serv, Distance learning, For res purposes, ILL available, Internet access, Music CDs, Orientations, Photocopying/Printing, Ref serv available, Spoken cassettes & CDs, Telephone ref, VHS videos, Wheelchair accessible
Partic in OCLC Online Computer Library Center, Inc
Open Mon-Thurs 8am-7pm, Fri 8-5, Sat & Sun 1-5; Mon-Fri (Summer) 10-4

G NATIONAL CENTER FOR ATMOSPHERIC RESEARCH LIBRARY*, Mesa Lab Campus, 1850 Table Mesa Dr, 80305. (Mail add: PO Box 3000, 80307-3000), SAN 335-4784. Tel: 303-497-1180. FAX: 303-497-1170. Reference E-mail: ncarref@ucar.edu. Web Site: library.ucar.edu. *Interim Dir,* Jennifer Phillips; Tel: 303-497-1173
Founded 1962
Library Holdings: e-journals 400; Per Subs 563
Special Collections: Meteorological Atlases; Meteorological Data
Subject Interests: Chem, Computer sci, Electrical engr, Electronics, Math, Mechanical engr, Meteorology, Oceanography, Physics
Automation Activity & Vendor Info: (Cataloging) OCLC CatExpress; (ILL) OCLC WorldShare Interlibrary Loan
Wireless access
Partic in OCLC Online Computer Library Center, Inc
Open Mon-Fri 8-12 & 1-5

Departmental Libraries:

FOOTHILLS LAB CAMPUS, Bldg 2, 3450 Mitchell Lane, 80301. Tel: 303-497-8505. FAX: 303-497-8503.
Restriction: Open to pub by appt only

L NATIONAL INDIAN LAW LIBRARY*, Native Americans Rights Fund, 1506 Broadway, 80302-6217. SAN 321-8007. Tel: 303-447-8760. FAX: 303-443-7776. Web Site: narf.org/nill. Staff 2 (MLS 1, Non-MLS 1)
Founded 1972
Oct 2017-Sept 2018 Income $340,000. Mats Exp $51,000, Books $5,000, Per/Ser (Incl. Access Fees) $40,000, Electronic Ref Mat (Incl. Access Fees) $6,000. Sal $195,000
Library Holdings: AV Mats 60; Bk Titles 8,000; Per Subs 80
Special Collections: Federal Indian Law (National Indian Law Repository), legal briefs, pleadings, legal opinions, rulings, treatises, studies, articles, reports & legislative mat; Tribal Codes & Constitutions; Tribal Pronunciation Guide
Automation Activity & Vendor Info: (Cataloging) Softlink America; (Circulation) Softlink America; (OPAC) Softlink America; (Serials) Softlink America

Function: 24/7 Electronic res, 24/7 Online cat, Doc delivery serv, Electronic databases & coll, For res purposes, Mail & tel request accepted, Online cat, Online ref, Res libr
Partic in Colorado Association of Law Libraries
Restriction: Access at librarian's discretion, Circulates for staff only, Closed stack, Employees & their associates, External users must contact libr, Limited access for the pub, Non-circulating coll, Open by appt only, Open to researchers by request, Pub by appt only, Ref only to non-staff, Researchers only, Visitors must make appt to use bks in the libr
Friends of the Library Group

S NATIONAL SOLAR OBSERVATORY*, Technical Library, 3665 Discovery Dr, 3rd Flr, 80303. SAN 310-7361. Tel: 303-735-7356. Web Site: www.nso.edu.
Founded 1953
Library Holdings: Bk Titles 3,900; Bk Vols 4,500; Per Subs 60
Special Collections: Publications of National Solar Observatory & Other Foreign & US Observatories; Solar Spectral Atlases
Subject Interests: Astronomy, Computer sci, Optics, Solar physics
Partic in OCLC Online Computer Library Center, Inc
Restriction: Not open to pub

G US DEPARTMENT OF COMMERCE, Boulder Laboratories Library, 325 Broadway, R/ESRL5, 80305-3328. SAN 335-4814. Tel: 303-497-3271. Interlibrary Loan Service Tel: 303-497-5569. FAX: 303-497-3890. E-mail: boulderlabs.ref@noaa.gov. Web Site: library.bldrdoc.gov. *Dir,* Stacy Bruss; E-mail: stacy.bruss@noaa.gov; *Ref & ILL Librn,* Mike Robinson; E-mail: mike.robinson@noaa.gov; *Ref Librn,* Daniel Draper; E-mail: daniel.draper@noaa.gov; *Mkt, Ref/Outreach Librn,* Marcus Elmore; E-mail: marcus.elmore@noaa.gov; *Coordr, Coll Serv,* Aurelia Mandani; E-mail: aurelia.mandani@noaa.gov; *ILL Tech, Pub Serv,* Laura Kistner. Subject Specialists: *Analysis, Tech,* Aurelia Mandani; Staff 6 (MLS 5, Non-MLS 1)
Founded 1954
Library Holdings: e-books 20,000; e-journals 10,000; Bk Titles 42,910; Per Subs 575
Special Collections: Boulder Laboratory Research Agencies Technical Reports; NOAA, NIST & NTIA Scientific Publications
Subject Interests: Astrophysics, Atmospheric sci, Chem, Chem engr, Engr, Geophysics, Mat sci, Math, Measurement sci, Optics, Physics, Solar physics, Statistics, Telecommunications sci
Automation Activity & Vendor Info: (Cataloging) OCLC Worldshare Management Services; (Circulation) OCLC Worldshare Management Services; (Discovery) OCLC Worldshare Management Services; (ILL) OCLC Tipasa; (OPAC) OCLC Worldshare Management Services
Wireless access
Function: 24/7 Electronic res, 24/7 Online cat, Archival coll, Doc delivery serv, Electronic databases & coll, For res purposes, ILL available, Internet access, Mail & tel request accepted, Online cat, Ref & res, Res libr, Scanner, Wheelchair accessible
Publications: Library Brochure; Library News
Partic in Colorado Library Consortium; Federal Library & Information Network; NOAA Libraries Network; OCLC Online Computer Library Center, Inc
Open Mon-Fri 8-4:30
Restriction: Authorized personnel only, Authorized scholars by appt, Badge access after hrs, Borrowing requests are handled by ILL, By permission only, Circulates for staff only, External users must contact libr, In-house use for visitors, Open to pub upon request, Photo ID required for access, Pub use on premises

C UNIVERSITY OF COLORADO BOULDER*, University Libraries, 1720 Pleasant St, 80309. (Mail add: Norlin Library, 184 UCB, 80309-0184), SAN 335-4903. Tel: 303-492-8705. Interlibrary Loan Service Tel: 303-492-1617. Reference Tel: 720-897-3333. E-mail: libraries@colorado.edu. Web Site: www.colorado.edu/libraries. *Dean, Univ Libr, Senior Vice Provost Online Ed,* Robert H McDonald; E-mail: rhmcdonald@colorado.edu; *Sr Assoc Dean,* Leslie Reynolds; E-mail: leslie.reynolds@colorado.edu; *Assoc Dean,* Jennie Gerke; E-mail: jennifer.gerke@colorado.edu; *Asst Dean,* Jamie Wittenberg; E-mail: jamie.wittenberg@colorado.edu; *Exec Dir, Ctr for Research Data & Digital Schol (CRDDS),* Thea Lindquist; E-mail: thea.lindquist@colorado.edu; *Team Lead, Branches & Servs,* Rebecca Kuglitsch; E-mail: rebecca.kuglitsch@colorado.edu; *Team Lead, Colls of Distinction Team,* Heather Bowden; E-mail: heather.bowden@colorado.edu; *Team Lead, Collection Mgmt Team,* Gabrielle Wiersma; E-mail: gabrielle.wiersma@colorado.edu; *Team Lead, Comms Team,* Carolyn Moreau; E-mail: carolyn.moreau@colorado.edu; *Team Lead, Core Tech & Apps Team,* Fred Schumacher; E-mail: fred.schumacher@colorado.edu; *Team Lead, Digital Asset Mgmt, Team Lead, Discovery Servs Team, Team Lead, Metadata Ops,* Paul Moeller; E-mail: paul.moeller@colorado.edu; *Team Lead, Finance,* Shelley Joy; E-mail: shelley.joy@colorado.edu; *Team Lead, Learning & Engagement Team,* Caroline Sinkinson; E-mail: caroline.sinkinson@colorado.edu; *Team Lead, Researcher & Colls Engagement Team,* Jennifer Knievel; E-mail:

jennifer.knievel@colorado.edu; *Team Lead, Resource Description Servs Team,* Chris Long; E-mail: chris.long@colorado.edu; Staff 114 (MLS 57, Non-MLS 57)
Founded 1876. Highest Degree: Doctorate
Special Collections: Colorado & Western Water, docs; David H. Tippit Photobook coll; Harry W. Mazal Holocaust coll; Innovation in Jewish Life; Ira Wolff Photographic History coll; Stan Brakhage coll; U.S. Congressional Publications; Women Poets of the Romantic Period. State Document Depository; UN Document Depository; US Document Depository
Subject Interests: Am music, Artists bks, Atlases, Atomic energy, Children's lit, Educ, Environ, Experimental media, Govt info, Hist of sci, Hist rec, Labor, Maps, travel & exploration, Medieval mss, Mountaineering, Natural sci, Old photos, Photog hist, Politicians, Politics, Rocky mountains, Soc change
Automation Activity & Vendor Info: (Acquisitions) Innovative Interfaces, Inc; (Cataloging) Innovative Interfaces, Inc; (Circulation) Innovative Interfaces, Inc; (Course Reserve) Innovative Interfaces, Inc; (OPAC) Innovative Interfaces, Inc; (Serials) Innovative Interfaces, Inc
Wireless access
Function: Art exhibits, Computers for patron use, E-Reserves, Electronic databases & coll, Govt ref serv, ILL available, Mail & tel request accepted, Online cat, Online ref, Outreach serv, Photocopying/Printing, Ref & res, Tax forms, Telephone ref
Partic in Association of Research Libraries; Center for Research Libraries; Colorado Alliance of Research Libraries; Colorado Library Consortium; Greater Western Library Alliance; OCLC Online Computer Library Center, Inc
Friends of the Library Group

Departmental Libraries:

GEMMILL LIBRARY OF ENGINEERING, MATHEMATICS & PHYSICS, Mathematics Bldg, Rm 135, 2300 Colorado Ave, 80309, SAN 335-5020. Tel: 303-492-5396. FAX: 303-492-6488. Reference E-mail: gemmill@colorado.edu. Web Site: www.colorado.edu/libraries/libraries/engineering-math-and-physics-library. *Sci/Eng Librn,* Emily Dommermuth; Tel: 303-735-8365, E-mail: emily.dommermuth@colorado.edu; Staff 5 (MLS 2, Non-MLS 3)
Special Collections: Engineering Societies Coll, conference, journal & rpt publs; Standards Coll, incl ANSI & ASTM
Subject Interests: Applied sci, Computer sci, Engr, Math, Physics
Friends of the Library Group

INSTITUTE OF ARCTIC & ALPINE RESEARCH INFORMATION CENTER, 4001 Discovery Dr, 80303. (Mail add: Campus Box 450, 80309-0450), SAN 335-5144. Tel: 303-492-1867, 303-492-6387. FAX: 303-492-6388. Web Site: instaar.colorado.edu/resources/library. *Dir, Info Outreach,* Shelly Sommer; E-mail: shelly.sommer@colorado.edu
Library Holdings: Bk Vols 6,700; Per Subs 240
Subject Interests: Climate, Environ sci, Geophysics, Polar regions
Automation Activity & Vendor Info: (Cataloging) Inmagic, Inc.
Publications: Arctic & Alpine Research (Quarterly); Occasional Papers
Restriction: In-house use for visitors, Internal circ only

JERRY CRAIL JOHNSON EARTH SCIENCES & MAP LIBRARY, Benson Earth Sciences, 2200 Colorado Ave, 80309, SAN 335-4997. Tel: 303-492-6133, 303-492-7578. FAX: 303-735-4879. E-mail: maplib@colorado.edu. Web Site: www.colorado.edu/libraries/libraries/earth-sciences-and-map-library. *Br Operations Mgr,* Brittany Reed; Tel: 303-492-4488, E-mail: brittany.reed@colorado.edu; Staff 7 (MLS 4, Non-MLS 3)
Founded 1998. Highest Degree: Doctorate
Library Holdings: Bk Vols 47,000; Per Subs 350
Special Collections: US Document Depository
Subject Interests: Atmospheric sci, Cartography, Geochemistry, Geog, Geographic Info Syst, Geol, Geophysics, Maps, Mineral, Mineralogy, Oceanography, Paleontology, Phys geog
Friends of the Library Group

HOWARD B WALTZ MUSIC LIBRARY, Imig Music Bldg, 2nd Flr N, 1020 18th St, 80302, SAN 335-5098. Tel: 303-492-8093. FAX: 303-735-0100. E-mail: mus@colorado.edu. Web Site: www.colorado.edu/libraries/libraries/howard-b-waltz-music-library. *Head Music Libr,* Stephanie Bonjack; Tel: 303-492-9895, E-mail: stephanie.bonjack@colorado.edu; Staff 6 (MLS 2, Non-MLS 4)
Library Holdings: AV Mats 55,000; DVDs 800; Music Scores 60,407; Bk Vols 74,033; Per Subs 300; Videos 811
Special Collections: 18th Century Comic Opera; American Music Research Center; California Mission Music; Early New England Singing Schools; Limpkin Folk Song; Moravian Music; Music of Colorado Composers; Popular Sheet Music
Friends of the Library Group

WILLIAM M WHITE BUSINESS LIBRARY, Koelbel Bldg, 995 Regent Dr, 80309, SAN 335-4962. Tel: 303-492-8367. FAX: 303-735-0333. E-mail: buslib@colorado.edu. Web Site: www.colorado.edu/libraries/libraries/william-m-white-business-library. *Head of Libr,* Juliann Couture; Tel: 303-492-9716, E-mail: juliann.couture@colorado.edu; *Bus Ref & Instruction Librn,* Natalia Tingle; Tel: 303-492-3034, E-mail: natalia.tingle@colorado.edu; Staff 6 (MLS 3, Non-MLS 3)
Founded 1970
Library Holdings: CDs 200; DVDs 25; Bk Vols 80,000; Per Subs 660
Subject Interests: Acctg, Finance, Mgt, Mkt, Real estate, Tax, Transportation
Friends of the Library Group

CL WILLIAM A WISE LAW LIBRARY, Wolf Law Bldg, 2nd Flr, 2450 Kittredge Loop Dr, 80309-0402, SAN 335-5055. Tel: 303-492-7534. Reference Tel: 303-492-3522. FAX: 303-492-2707. E-mail: lawref@colorado.edu. Web Site: lawlibrary.colorado.edu. *Dir,* Susan Nevelow Mart; Tel: 303-492-1233, E-mail: susan.nevelow.mart@colorado.edu; *Assoc Dir, Head, Pub Serv,* Robert Linz; Tel: 303-492-2504, E-mail: robert.linz@colorado.edu; *Assoc Dir, Faculty Servs,* Jane Thompson; Tel: 303-492-2705, E-mail: jane.thompson@colorado.edu; *Metadata Librn,* Karen Selden; Tel: 303-492-7535, E-mail: karen.selden@colorado.edu; Staff 20 (MLS 8, Non-MLS 12)
Founded 1892. Enrl 535; Fac 44; Highest Degree: Doctorate
Library Holdings: Bk Titles 210,000; Bk Vols 700,000
Special Collections: Commonwealth & Foreign Law. US Document Depository
Subject Interests: Constitutional law, Environ law, Intl law, Native Am law
Automation Activity & Vendor Info: (Acquisitions) Innovative Interfaces, Inc; (Cataloging) Innovative Interfaces, Inc; (Circulation) Innovative Interfaces, Inc; (Course Reserve) Innovative Interfaces, Inc; (ILL) Innovative Interfaces, Inc; (OPAC) Innovative Interfaces, Inc; (Serials) Innovative Interfaces, Inc
Partic in Colorado Association of Law Libraries; OCLC Online Computer Library Center, Inc
Special Services for the Deaf - Assistive tech
Special Services for the Blind - Assistive/Adapted tech devices, equip & products

BROOMFIELD

P MAMIE DOUD EISENHOWER PUBLIC LIBRARY, Three Community Park Rd, 80020. SAN 301-7575. Tel: 720-887-2300. Circulation Tel: 720-887-2301. Reference Tel: 720-887-2350. Information Services Tel: 720-887-2360. FAX: 720-887-1384. E-mail: library@broomfield.org. Web Site: broomfield.org/library. *Libr Dir,* Kathryn Lynip; Tel: 720-887-2368, E-mail: klynip@broomfield.org; *Bus Mgr,* Wendy Norris; Tel: 720-887-2356, E-mail: wnorris@broomfield.org; *Operations Mgr,* Esther Knox-Stutsman; Tel: 720-887-2328, E-mail: knox-stutsman@broomfield.org; *Circ Serv,* Danni Steiner; Tel: 720-887-2306, E-mail: dsteiner@broomfield.org; Staff 10 (MLS 9, Non-MLS 1)
Founded 1960. Pop 47,378; Circ 502,390
Library Holdings: AV Mats 13,000; Bk Vols 144,250; Per Subs 248
Special Collections: Mamie Doud Eisenhower Coll. US Document Depository
Automation Activity & Vendor Info: (Cataloging) Innovative Interfaces, Inc; (Circulation) Innovative Interfaces, Inc; (Course Reserve) Innovative Interfaces, Inc; (ILL) Innovative Interfaces, Inc; (Media Booking) Innovative Interfaces, Inc; (OPAC) Innovative Interfaces, Inc; (Serials) Innovative Interfaces, Inc
Wireless access
Function: Adult bk club, Adult literacy prog, Electronic databases & coll, Govt ref serv, Homebound delivery serv, ILL available, Magnifiers for reading, Online ref, Photocopying/Printing, Prog for adults, Prog for children & young adult, Ref serv available, Spoken cassettes & CDs, Summer reading prog, Telephone ref, VHS videos, Wheelchair accessible
Partic in Colorado Library Consortium
Special Services for the Deaf - Staff with knowledge of sign lang; TTY equip
Special Services for the Blind - Large print bks; Talking bks
Open Mon-Thurs 9-9, Fri & Sat 9-5, Sun 1-5
Friends of the Library Group

G NATIONAL ARCHIVES & RECORDS ADMINISTRATION*, National Archives at Denver, 17101 Huron St, 80023. Tel: 303-604-4740. FAX: 303-604-4750. E-mail: denver.archives@nara.gov. Web Site: www.archives.gov/denver. *Regional Archives Dir,* Eileen Bolger; E-mail: eileen.bolger@nara.gov
Special Collections: Colorado Naturalizations, microfilm; Federal Population Censuses for All States, 1790-1930, microfilm; Indian Censuses, microfilm; Pension & Bounty Land Warrant Applications, microfilm; Revolutionary War Records, microfilm; Utah Polygamy Prosecution Case Files, microfilm
Subject Interests: Indian hist, Land reclamation econ, Mining
Wireless access
Open Mon-Fri 8:30-4

BRUSH

P EAST MORGAN COUNTY LIBRARY DISTRICT*, 500 Clayton St, 80723-2110. SAN 301-7583. Tel: 970-842-4596. FAX: 970-842-2450. E-mail: emclcontact@gmail.com. Web Site: emcld.org. *Dir,* Laura McConnell; E-mail: director@emcl.info; *Asst Dir,* Elizabeth Jarrell; *Ch,* Christy Bellis; *Teen Librn,* Tammy Bass; Staff 11 (MLS 1, Non-MLS 10)
Founded 1915. Pop 7,985; Circ 87,529
Library Holdings: Audiobooks 900; Bks on Deafness & Sign Lang 23; Braille Volumes 2; CDs 175; DVDs 100; High Interest/Low Vocabulary Bk Vols 266; Large Print Bks 1,150; Bk Titles 27,000; Bk Vols 28,800; Per Subs 60; Videos 2,500
Special Collections: HOSPES. Oral History
Subject Interests: Colorado, Gen, Local hist
Automation Activity & Vendor Info: (Acquisitions) Innovative Interfaces, Inc; (Cataloging) Innovative Interfaces, Inc; (Circulation) Innovative Interfaces, Inc; (ILL) Innovative Interfaces, Inc; (OPAC) Innovative Interfaces, Inc
Wireless access
Function: After school storytime, Bks on CD, Children's prog, Computer training, Computers for patron use, E-Readers, Electronic databases & coll, Family literacy, Free DVD rentals, Genealogy discussion group, Home delivery & serv to seniorr ctr & nursing homes, Homebound delivery serv, ILL available, Large print keyboards, Magazines, Online cat, Photocopying/Printing, Preschool outreach, Preschool reading prog, Prog for adults, Prog for children & young adult, Scanner, Story hour, Study rm, Summer & winter reading prog, Summer reading prog, Tax forms, Teen prog, Wheelchair accessible, Winter reading prog
Publications: Friends (Quarterly newsletter); Friends Brochure (Annual); Newspaper Column
Special Services for the Deaf - ADA equip; Bks on deafness & sign lang
Special Services for the Blind - Audio mat; Recorded bks
Open Mon-Thurs 9-8, Fri & Sat 10-5
Friends of the Library Group

BUENA VISTA

S BUENA VISTA CORRECTIONAL COMPLEX LIBRARY*, Minimum Center Library, 15125 Hwys 24 & 285, 81211. (Mail add: PO Box 2005, 81211-2017), SAN 301-7605. Tel: 719-395-7363. *Libr Tech,* Debra James; E-mail: debra.james@state.co.us; Staff 4 (MLS 1, Non-MLS 3)
Library Holdings: Bk Titles 10,050; Bk Vols 10,097
Special Collections: Law Coll
Automation Activity & Vendor Info: (Cataloging) EOS International; (Circulation) EOS International
Function: AV serv, ILL available, Magnifiers for reading, Photocopying/Printing, Ref serv available
Restriction: Not open to pub, Residents only

P BUENA VISTA PUBLIC LIBRARY*, 131 Linderman Ave, 81211. (Mail add: PO Box 2019, 81211-2019), SAN 301-7591. Tel: 719-395-8700. FAX: 719-395-6426. E-mail: info@buenavistalibrary.org. Web Site: buenavistalibrary.org. *Dir,* Cecilia LaFrance; E-mail: clafrance@buenavistalibrary.org
Founded 1898
Library Holdings: AV Mats 1,243; Large Print Bks 585; Bk Titles 20,500; Bk Vols 21,000; Per Subs 85; Talking Bks 929
Wireless access
Special Services for the Blind - Bks on cassette; Bks on CD; Descriptive video serv (DVS); Large print bks; Magnifiers; Talking bks
Open Mon-Fri 9-7, Sat 9-4
Friends of the Library Group

S COLORADO DEPARTMENT OF CORRECTIONS*, Buena Vista Minimum Center Library, 5125 Hwy 24 & 285, 81211. (Mail add: PO Box 2005, 81211-2005). Tel: 719-395-2404, Ext 7354. FAX: 719-395-7362. *Library Contact,* Debra James; E-mail: debra.james@state.co.us
Library Holdings: Bk Vols 5,820; Per Subs 25
Automation Activity & Vendor Info: (Cataloging) EOS International; (Circulation) EOS International

BURLINGTON

P BURLINGTON PUBLIC LIBRARY*, 321 14th St, 80807. SAN 301-7613. Tel: 719-346-8109. FAX: 719-346-8672. Web Site: www.burlingtoncolo.com/burlington-public-library.htm. *Dir,* Nick McCarty; E-mail: nick.mccarty-daniels@burlingtoncolo.com
Founded 1921. Pop 4,000; Circ 10,000
Library Holdings: Bk Vols 15,000; Per Subs 35
Automation Activity & Vendor Info: (Cataloging) Koha; (Circulation) Koha; (OPAC) Koha
Wireless access
Partic in Colorado Library Consortium
Open Mon-Fri 10-6

CANON CITY

P CANON CITY PUBLIC LIBRARY*, 516 Macon Ave, 81212-3380. SAN 301-7621. Tel: 719-269-9020. FAX: 719-269-9031. E-mail: ccpl@canoncity.org. Web Site: ccpl.lib.co.us. *Dir,* Suzanne Lasha; Staff 3 (MLS 3)
Founded 1886
Library Holdings: Bk Titles 68,900; Bk Vols 69,300; Per Subs 130
Special Collections: Local History Coll
Automation Activity & Vendor Info: (Cataloging) Koha; (Circulation) Koha; (OPAC) Koha
Wireless access
Function: 24/7 Electronic res, 24/7 Online cat, 3D Printer, Activity rm, After school storytime
Partic in Colorado Library Consortium
Open Mon-Thurs 10-6, Fri & Sat 10-5
Friends of the Library Group

COLORADO DEPARTMENT OF CORRECTIONS

S ARROWHEAD CORRECTIONAL CENTER LIBRARY*, US Hwy 50, Evans Blvd, 81215. (Mail add: CMC, PO Box 300, 81215-0300), SAN 373-6369. Tel: 719-269-5601, Ext 3923. FAX: 719-269-5650. Web Site: www.doc.state.co.us. *Libr Tech,* Kristi Lloyd; Staff 1 (MLS 1)
Founded 1991
Library Holdings: Bk Titles 10,000; Per Subs 35
Automation Activity & Vendor Info: (Cataloging) EOS International; (Circulation) EOS International; (OPAC) EOS International
Special Services for the Deaf - Bks on deafness & sign lang; High interest/low vocabulary bks
Open Mon 5:30pm-7:30pm, Tues & Thurs 1-3:30 & 5:30-7:30, Wed 8:30am-10:30am, Fri 1-3:30, Sat 2:30-3:30

S CENTENNIAL CORRECTIONAL FACILITY LIBRARY*, PO Box 600, 81215-0600, SAN 301-763X. Tel: 719-269-5546. FAX: 719-269-5545. *Librn,* Jean Frost; E-mail: jean.frost@doc.state.co.us; *Tech Serv,* Diana Reese; Staff 8 (MLS 8)
Library Holdings: Bk Vols 8,000; Per Subs 28
Automation Activity & Vendor Info: (Acquisitions) EOS International; (Cataloging) EOS International; (Circulation) EOS International; (Course Reserve) EOS International; (ILL) EOS International; (OPAC) EOS International; (Serials) EOS International
Open Mon & Wed-Fri 7-4, Tues 7-9

S COLORADO STATE PENITENTIARY LIBRARY*, PO Box 777, 81215-0777, SAN 377-080X. Tel: 719-269-5268. FAX: 719-269-5125. Web Site: www.doc.state.co.us. *Librn,* Wendy Rowlands
Library Holdings: Bk Vols 11,500
Automation Activity & Vendor Info: (Cataloging) EOS International; (Circulation) EOS International; (OPAC) EOS International
Open Mon-Sun 7-4

S FOUR MILE CORRECTIONAL CENTER LIBRARY*, CMC - FMCC, PO Box 300, 81215. Tel: 719-269-5601, Ext 3339. FAX: 719-269-5364. Web Site: www.doc.state.co.us. *Libr Tech II,* Nancy Pettit
Library Holdings: Bk Vols 10,000; Per Subs 25
Automation Activity & Vendor Info: (Cataloging) EOS International; (Circulation) EOS International; (OPAC) EOS International
Open Tues, Sat & Sun 1-3:30, Mon, Wed & Fri 5:30-7:30pm, Thurs 9:30-10:30am

S FREMONT CORRECTIONAL FACILITY LIBRARY*, US Hwy 50, Evans Blvd, 81215. (Mail add: PO Box 999, 81215-0999), SAN 322-7316. Tel: 719-269-5002, Ext 3566. FAX: 719-269-5048. Web Site: www.doc.state.co.us. *Mgr,* Linda Lewis; Staff 3 (MLS 1, Non-MLS 2)
Founded 1957
Library Holdings: Bk Vols 18,000; Per Subs 52
Automation Activity & Vendor Info: (Cataloging) EOS International; (Circulation) EOS International; (OPAC) EOS International
Function: ILL available
Open Mon-Thurs 8am-8:30pm, Fri-Sun 8-3:30

S SKYLINE CORRECTIONAL CENTER LIBRARY*, PO Box 300, 81215, SAN 325-3635. Tel: 719-269-5420, Ext 3351. FAX: 719-269-5404. Web Site: www.doc.state.co.us. *Libr Tech II,* Nina Aldrich; E-mail: nina.aldrich@doc.state.co.us
Library Holdings: Bk Vols 3,500; Per Subs 23
Automation Activity & Vendor Info: (Cataloging) EOS International; (Circulation) EOS International; (OPAC) EOS International
Open Mon & Fri 7-4, Tues-Thurs 1-8, Sat & Sun 1-2

S COLORADO TERRITORIAL CORRECTIONAL FACILITY LIBRARY*, PO Box 1010, 81215-1010. SAN 370-7660. Tel: 719-275-4181, Ext 3167. FAX: 719-269-4115. *Librn,* LaDelle Williams
Founded 1985
Library Holdings: Bk Titles 11,000; Bk Vols 12,971; Per Subs 42
Subject Interests: Poetry

CASTLE ROCK

P DOUGLAS COUNTY LIBRARIES, 100 S Wilcox, 80104. SAN 335-5268. Tel: 303-791-7323. Web Site: www.dcl.org. *Exec Dir,* Bob Pasicznyuk; Tel: 303-688-7654, E-mail: rpasicznyuk@dclibraries.org; *Dir, Commun Engagement,* Amber DeBerry; Tel: 303-688-7641, E-mail: adeberry@dclibraries.org; *Customer Experience Dir,* Julianne Griffin; Tel: 303-688-7657, E-mail: jgriffin@dclibraries.org; *Dir, Enabling Infrastructure,* Jill Corrente; Tel: 303-688-7631, E-mail: jcorrente@dclibraries.org; *Dir of Finance,* Dave Anderson; Tel: 303-688-7623, E-mail: danderson@dclibraries.org; Staff 199 (MLS 49, Non-MLS 150)
Founded 1966. Pop 358,000; Circ 6,000,000
Library Holdings: AV Mats 51,741; e-books 550; Bk Vols 540,455; Per Subs 1,203; Talking Bks 41,457
Special Collections: Local History; Newspapers of Douglas County 1881-1992, micro; Photographs. State Document Depository
Automation Activity & Vendor Info: (Cataloging) SirsiDynix; (Circulation) SirsiDynix; (OPAC) SirsiDynix
Wireless access
Function: Adult bk club, Adult literacy prog, Archival coll, Art exhibits, Audio & video playback equip for onsite use, AV serv, Bk club(s), Bks on CD, Bus archives, CD-ROM, Chess club, Children's prog, Citizenship assistance, Computers for patron use, Digital talking bks, Electronic databases & coll, Family literacy, Free DVD rentals, Homebound delivery serv, Homework prog, ILL available, Internet access, Literacy & newcomer serv, Magnifiers for reading, Music CDs, Online cat, Online ref, Outside serv via phone, mail, e-mail & web, OverDrive digital audio bks, Photocopying/Printing, Prog for adults, Prog for children & young adult, Ref serv available, Spoken cassettes & CDs, Spoken cassettes & DVDs, Story hour, Summer reading prog, Telephone ref, Wheelchair accessible, Workshops
Special Services for the Deaf - TTY equip
Open Mon-Thurs 8-8, Fri 8-6, Sat & Sun 10-4
Branches: 7
CASTLE PINES BRANCH, 360 Village Square Lane, Castle Pines, 80108. Tel: 303-791-7323. *Customer Experience Supervisor,* Andrew Roth
Founded 2009
Open Mon-Thurs 9-7, Fri & Sat 9-5, Sun Noon-5
CASTLE ROCK BRANCH, 100 S Wilcox St, 80104-2726, SAN 370-4955. Tel: 303-791-7323. *Customer Experience Supervisor,* Stacey Walker
Library Holdings: Bk Titles 150,000
Subject Interests: Local hist
Open Mon-Thurs 9-7, Fri & Sat 9-5, Sun 12-5
HIGHLANDS RANCH BRANCH, 9292 S Ridgeline Blvd, Highlands Ranch, 80129, SAN 371-9510. Tel: 303-791-7323. *Customer Experience Supervisor,* Michael King
Library Holdings: Bk Titles 100,000; Bk Vols 138,336; Per Subs 150
Open Mon-Thurs 8-8, Fri 8-6, Sat & Sun 10-4
LONE TREE BRANCH, 10055 Library Way, Lone Tree, 80124, SAN 335-5357. Tel: 303-791-7323. *Customer Experience Supervisor,* Robin Warnke
Library Holdings: Bk Vols 60,000
Open Mon-Thurs 8-8, Fri 8-6, Sat & Sun 10-4
LOUVIERS BRANCH, 7885 Louviers Blvd, Louviers, 80131. (Mail add: PO Box 282, Louviers, 80131-0282), SAN 335-5292. Tel: 303-791-7323. FAX: 303-791-7323. *Supvr, Youth & Family Serv,* Rebecca Spilver
Library Holdings: Bk Vols 5,949
Open Tues 3-8, Sat 10-4
PARKER BRANCH, 20105 E Main St, Parker, 80138, SAN 335-5322. Tel: 303-791-7323. FAX: 303-841-7892. *Customer Experience Supervisor,* Stefani Wiest
Library Holdings: Bk Titles 130,000; Per Subs 150
Open Mon-Thurs 8-8, Fri 8-6, Sat & Sun 10-4
ROXBOROUGH BRANCH, 8357 N Rampart Range Rd, Ste 200, Littleton, 80125. Tel: 303-791-7323. *Customer Experience Supervisor,* Rebecca Spilver
Library Holdings: Bk Vols 23,000
Open Mon-Thurs 8-8, Fri 8-6, Sat & Sun 10-4

CENTENNIAL

SR GATEWAY SEMINARY*, Rocky Mountain Campus, 7393 S Alton Way, 80112-2302. Tel: 303-779-6431, Ext 204. FAX: 303-779-6432. Web Site: www.gs.edu/academics/library. *Librn,* John Pappert; E-mail: johnpappert@gs.edu
Founded 1996
Library Holdings: Bk Vols 15,000
Wireless access
Open Mon-Thurs 9-5

CHEYENNE WELLS

P EAST CHEYENNE COUNTY LIBRARY DISTRICT, 151 S First St W, 80810. (Mail add: PO Box 939, 80810-0939). Tel: 719-767-5138. FAX: 719-767-5379. E-mail: eccldcw@centurylink.net, echeyennecountylibrary@yahoo.com. Web Site: www.eccld.org. *Dir,* Vicki Henderson; *Cat Spec,* Position Currently Open
Founded 1996. Pop 1,084; Circ 4,300
Library Holdings: Audiobooks 500; Bks on Deafness & Sign Lang 15; CDs 200; DVDs 2,100; e-books 900; Large Print Bks 1,100; Bk Titles 16,000; Per Subs 6
Automation Activity & Vendor Info: (Cataloging) Biblionix/Apollo; (Circulation) Follett Software; (OPAC) Follett Software
Wireless access
Function: 24/7 Online cat, Adult bk club
Open Mon 9-6, Tues-Thurs 9-2

COLORADO SPRINGS

S AMERICAN NUMISMATIC ASSOCIATION LIBRARY*, Dwight N Manley Numismatic Library, 818 N Cascade Ave, 80903-3279. SAN 301-7664. Tel: 719-482-9821. FAX: 719-634-4085. E-mail: library@money.org. Web Site: www.money.org. *Libr Dir,* David Sklow; E-mail: dsklow@money.org; Staff 3 (Non-MLS 3)
Founded 1891
Library Holdings: Bks-By-Mail 70,016; CDs 36; DVDs 464; Bk Titles 71,250; Bk Vols 108,386; Per Subs 100; Videos 371
Special Collections: Arthur Braddan Coole Library of Oriental Numismatics
Subject Interests: Numismatics
Publications: The Numismatist
Open Tues-Sat 10:30-5

C COLORADO COLLEGE*, Charles Leaming Tutt Library, 1021 N Cascade Ave, 80903-3252. (Mail add: 14 E Cache La Poudre, 80903), SAN 301-7680. Tel: 719-389-6662. Interlibrary Loan Service Tel: 719-389-6664. Administration Tel: 719-389-6670. Reference E-mail: tuttref@coloradocollege.edu. Web Site: www.coloradocollege.edu/library. *Interim Libr Dir,* Steve Lawson; E-mail: slawson@coloradocollege.edu; Staff 23 (MLS 10, Non-MLS 13)
Founded 1874. Enrl 2,050; Highest Degree: Bachelor
Library Holdings: AV Mats 22,712; e-journals 3,761; Bk Titles 501,234; Per Subs 1,346
Special Collections: Autographs of the British Poets (Alice Bemis Taylor Coll); Chess Books (Alfred R Justice Coll); Colorado College Archives, Colorado Springs, files of early newspapers, also bks, clippings & pamphlets & mss relating to development of Colorado Springs; Colorado Imprints; Dickens (Carruthers Coll); Edmund van Diest Papers; Helen Hunt Jackson Papers; Hendee Coll of Lincolniana; Rare Books (Coll of mss & early printed leaves, Incunabula, drawings & prints from the Romanesque period to the Renaissance); Southwestern United States; United States Relocation Center, Granada, Colorado; Western Americana. US Document Depository
Automation Activity & Vendor Info: (Acquisitions) ByWater Solutions; (Cataloging) ByWater Solutions; (Circulation) ByWater Solutions; (Discovery) EBSCO Discovery Service; (ILL) Atlas Systems; (OPAC) ByWater Solutions; (Serials) EBSCO Discovery Service
Wireless access
Partic in Colorado Alliance of Research Libraries; Oberlin Group

S COLORADO SPRINGS FINE ARTS CENTER LIBRARY*, 30 W Dale St, 80903. SAN 301-7702. Tel: 719-477-4323. FAX: 719-634-0570. E-mail: info@csfineartscenter.org. Web Site: fac.coloradocollege.edu. *Curator,* Polly Nordstrand; Tel: 719-477-4316, E-mail: pnordstrand@coloradocollege.edu
Founded 1936
Library Holdings: Bk Vols 31,000; Per Subs 20
Special Collections: 20th Century American Art; Anthropology & Art of the Southwest (Taylor Museum Coll), bks, series, pamphlets
Automation Activity & Vendor Info: (Cataloging) OCLC
Wireless access
Restriction: Circulates for staff only, Limited access for the pub

S COLORADO SPRINGS PIONEERS MUSEUM, Starsmore Center for Local History, 215 S Tejon St, 80903. SAN 301-7818. Tel: 719-385-5650. Web Site: cspm.org. *Archivist,* Hillary Mannion; E-mail: hillary.mannion@coloradosprings.gov; *Curator of Hist,* Leah Davis-Witherow; E-mail: leah.witherow@coloradosprings.gov
Founded 1938
Library Holdings: Bk Titles 12,000; Per Subs 4
Special Collections: Charles Banks Coll; Colorado Springs/Pikes Peak Region; Frederick Stehr Glass Plate Negative Coll; Harry L Standley Photograph Coll; Helen Hunt Jackson Coll; Nellie Burget Miller Coll; Southwest (Francis W Cragin Coll), mss; Virginia & Gilbert McClurg Coll, mss; Western US Coll, photogs; William J Palmer Coll; Winfield Scott Stratton Coll. Oral History
Subject Interests: Colorado
Wireless access
Open Tues-Sat 1-4
Restriction: Not a lending libr

C COLORADO TECHNICAL UNIVERSITY LIBRARY, 4435 N Chestnut, 80907. SAN 322-7456. Tel: 719-590-6708. E-mail: librarian@coloradotech.edu, library@coloradotech.edu. Web Site: careered.libguides.com/university_ctuonline/libraryindex. *Librn,* Tina Morrell; *Librn,* Jenna Obee; Staff 3 (MLS 1, Non-MLS 2)
Enrl 1,800; Highest Degree: Doctorate
Library Holdings: Bk Vols 7,000
Automation Activity & Vendor Info: (ILL) OCLC
Wireless access
Open Mon-Thurs 9-9, Fri 9-6, Sat 9-5

S DEPARTMENT OF HUMAN SERVICES-YOUTH CORRECTIONS*, Zebulon Pike Youth Service Center Library, 1427 W Rio Grande, 80906. Tel: 719-329-6931. FAX: 719-633-5302. Web Site: www.colorado.gov/pacific/cdhs/zebulon-pike-youth-services-center. *Principal,* Allison Hanson
Library Holdings: Bk Vols 1,200
Restriction: Not open to pub

R THE DIOCESE OF COLORADO SPRINGS*, Resource Center Library, 228 N Cascade Ave, 80903. Tel: 719-636-2345. FAX: 719-636-1216. E-mail: info@diocs.org. Web Site: www.diocs.org/Faith/Diocese-Resource-Library.
Library Holdings: AV Mats 1,500; DVDs 30; Bk Titles 6,000; Per Subs 20; Videos 1,500
Subject Interests: Catechism, Catholic Church
Automation Activity & Vendor Info: (Acquisitions) L4U Library Software; (Cataloging) L4U Library Software; (Circulation) L4U Library Software; (Course Reserve) L4U Library Software; (ILL) L4U Library Software; (Media Booking) L4U Library Software; (OPAC) L4U Library Software; (Serials) L4U Library Software

J EVEREST COLLEGE LIBRARY*, 1815 Jet Wing Dr, 80916. SAN 326-4394. Tel: 719-638-6580. FAX: 719-638-6818. Web Site: everestlibrary.pbwiki.com. *Librn,* Matthew McNulty; E-mail: matthew.mcnulty@zenith.org; Staff 1 (MLS 1)
Enrl 400; Highest Degree: Associate
Library Holdings: AV Mats 200; Bk Vols 1,200; Per Subs 15
Subject Interests: Bus & mgt, Computer sci, Criminal justice, Legal, Nat security
Automation Activity & Vendor Info: (Acquisitions) LibraryWorld, Inc; (Cataloging) LibraryWorld, Inc; (Circulation) LibraryWorld, Inc
Wireless access
Function: Distance learning, Ref serv available, Telephone ref
Partic in Library & Information Resources Network
Open Mon & Wed 9-8, Tues & Thurs 9-6, Fri 9-2

R FIRST PRESBYTERIAN CHURCH*, John C Gardner Memorial Library, 219 E Bijou St, 80903. SAN 301-7737. Tel: 719-884-6121. FAX: 719-884-6200. Web Site: www.first-pres.org/about-us/library. *Adminr,* Janet M Wilcox; Staff 32 (MLS 2, Non-MLS 30)
Founded 1945
Library Holdings: CDs 55; DVDs 53; Bk Titles 9,981; Bk Vols 17,000; Per Subs 17; Videos 317
Automation Activity & Vendor Info: (Acquisitions) Follett Software; (Cataloging) Follett Software; (Circulation) Follett Software; (OPAC) Follett Software
Wireless access
Open Mon-Fri 10-2, Sun 9:30-12:30

R HOLY APOSTLES CATHOLIC CHURCH LIBRARY*, 4925 N Carefree Circle, 80917. Tel: 719-597-4249. Web Site: www.holyapostlescc.org. *Libr Dir,* Elaine Tourville; Tel: 719-597-7571, E-mail: tourville.elaineann@gmail.com
Founded 1975
Library Holdings: CDs 55; DVDs 700; Bk Titles 3,000
Subject Interests: Hist, Spirituality
Wireless access
Open Sun 8-1:30

M MEMORIAL HOSPITAL CENTRAL*, Health Sciences Library, 1400 E Boulder, Rm 2406, 80909-5599. SAN 301-7761. Tel: 719-365-5182. Web Site: www.uchealth.org/locations/uchealth-memorial-hospital-central. *Mgr,* Char Longwell; E-mail: Char.Longwell@uchealth.org; Staff 1 (MLS 1)
Founded 1950
Library Holdings: Bk Titles 3,500; Bk Vols 4,000; Per Subs 200
Special Collections: Historical Medical Works Coll; Rare Book Coll
Subject Interests: Cardiology, Nursing, Obstetrics & gynecology, Pediatrics, Surgery
Automation Activity & Vendor Info: (Cataloging) EBSCO Online; (Circulation) EBSCO Online
Wireless access
Partic in Capital District Library Council; Midcontinental Regional Med Libr Program; OCLC Online Computer Library Center, Inc
Open Mon-Fri 8:30-5

S NATIONAL ARCHIVES OF THE CHRISTIAN & MISSIONARY ALLIANCE*, Albert B Simpson Historical Library, 8595 Explorer Dr, 80920. SAN 329-8671. Tel: 719-599-5999. FAX: 719-599-8234. E-mail: archives@cmalliance.org. Web Site: www.cmalliance.org/resources/archives. *Archivist,* Kristin Rollins; Staff 2 (Non-MLS 2)
Library Holdings: Bk Vols 3,000
Special Collections: The Christian & Missionary Alliance Magazine, 1880 to present (also on microfilm). Oral History
Wireless access
Open Mon-Thurs 8-4:30

J PIKES PEAK COMMUNITY COLLEGE LIBRARY*, 5675 S Academy Blvd, C7, 80906-5498. SAN 301-780X. Circulation Tel: 719-502-2400. Reference Tel: 719-502-3410. Web Site: www.ppcc.edu/library. *Dir of Libr,* Carole Olds; Tel: 719-502-3249, E-mail: carole.olds@ppcc.edu; *Head, Circ Serv,* Cindy Myers; Tel: 719-502-3386, E-mail: cindy.myers@ppcc.edu; *Head, Ref Serv,* Graydon Miller; Tel: 719-502-3389, E-mail: graydon.miller@ppcc.edu; *Head, Tech Serv,* Patricia Stockwell; Tel: 719-502-3238, E-mail: patricia.stockwell@ppcc.edu; Staff 11 (MLS 5, Non-MLS 6)
Founded 1969. Fac 600; Highest Degree: Associate
Library Holdings: Audiobooks 204; DVDs 1,324; e-books 4,808; Bk Titles 13,219; Per Subs 70
Special Collections: PPCC Archives
Automation Activity & Vendor Info: (Cataloging) Auto-Graphics, Inc; (Circulation) Auto-Graphics, Inc; (ILL) OCLC; (OPAC) Auto-Graphics, Inc; (Serials) SerialsSolutions
Wireless access
Open Mon-Thurs 7:30am-8pm, Fri 8-5, Sat 9-2
Departmental Libraries:
RAMPART RANGE CAMPUS, 11195 Hwy 83, Box R-7, 80921-3602. Tel: 719-502-2440. Reference Tel: 719-502-3430. FAX: 719-502-3431. *Managing Librn,* Helen Casias; E-mail: helen.casias@ppcc.edu
Founded 1998. Fac 600; Highest Degree: Associate
Library Holdings: Audiobooks 130; DVDs 887; e-books 4,808; Bk Vols 7,478; Per Subs 70
Automation Activity & Vendor Info: (Cataloging) Auto-Graphics, Inc; (Circulation) Auto-Graphics, Inc; (OPAC) Auto-Graphics, Inc
Open Mon-Thurs 7:30am-8pm, Fri 7:30-5

P PIKES PEAK LIBRARY DISTRICT*, 20 N Cascade Ave, 80903. (Mail add: PO Box 1579, 80901-1579), SAN 335-5381. Tel: 719-531-6333. Web Site: ppld.org. *Chief Librn, Exec Dir,* John Spears; Tel: 719-531-6333, Ext 6009, E-mail: jspears@ppld.org; *Chief Develop Officer,* Lance James; Tel: 719-531-6333, Ext 6890, E-mail: ljames@ppld.org; *Chief, Financial & Bus Officer,* Michael Varnet; E-mail: mvarnet@ppld.org; *Chief Public Services Officer,* Tim Blevins; E-mail: tblevins@ppld.org; Staff 41.7 (MLS 41.7)
Founded 1885. Pop 585,158; Circ 8,839,963. Sal $10,902,147
Library Holdings: AV Mats 208,204; CDs 41,442; DVDs 113,205; e-books 34,042; Bk Vols 841,364; Per Subs 2,513
Special Collections: Oral History
Subject Interests: Genealogy, Local hist
Automation Activity & Vendor Info: (Acquisitions) SirsiDynix-WorkFlows; (Cataloging) SirsiDynix-WorkFlows; (Circulation) SirsiDynix-WorkFlows; (OPAC) SirsiDynix-iBistro
Wireless access
Function: ILL available
Special Services for the Deaf - Bks on deafness & sign lang; High interest/low vocabulary bks; Spec interest per; Staff with knowledge of sign lang
Open Mon-Thurs 9-9, Fri 10-6
Friends of the Library Group
Branches: 15
CALHAN LIBRARY, 600 Bank St, Calhan, 80808. Web Site: ppld.org/calhan-library. *Libr Mgr,* Liz Willhoff
Open Mon & Tues 11-8, Wed & Sat 10-6
CHEYENNE MOUNTAIN LIBRARY, 1785 S Eighth St, Ste 100, 80905, SAN 335-5411. Tel: 719-531-6333, Ext 6023. Web Site: ppld.org/cheyenne-mountain-library. *Libr Mgr,* Tiffany Paisley; E-mail: tpaisley@ppld.org
Open Mon-Thurs 9-9, Fri & Sat 10-6
Friends of the Library Group
EAST LIBRARY, 5550 N Union Blvd, 80918, SAN 335-5446. Tel: 719-531-6333, Ext 6013. Web Site: ppld.org/east-library. *Libr Mgr,* Janina Goodwin; E-mail: jgoodwin@ppld.org
Open Mon-Thurs 9-9, Fri & Sat 10-6, Sun 1-5
Friends of the Library Group

FOUNTAIN LIBRARY, 230 S Main St, Fountain, 80817, SAN 335-5608. Tel: 719-531-6333, Ext 6332. Web Site: ppld.org/fountain-library. *Libr Mgr,* Alicia Gomori; E-mail: agomori@ppld.org
Open Mon-Thurs 9-9, Fri & Sat 10-6
Friends of the Library Group

HIGH PRAIRIE LIBRARY, 7035 Old Meridian Rd, Peyton, 80831. Tel: 719-531-6333, Ext 6316. Web Site: ppld.org/high-prairie-library. *Libr Mgr,* Liz Willhoff; E-mail: ewillhoff@ppld.org
Open Mon & Tues 9-8, Wed & Thurs 9-6, Fri & Sat 10-6
Friends of the Library Group

RUTH HOLLEY LIBRARY, 685 N Murray Blvd, 80915, SAN 329-6350. Tel: 719-531-6333, Ext 6101. Web Site: ppld.org/ruth-holley-library. *Libr Mgr,* Abby Simpson; E-mail: asimpson@ppld.org
Open Mon-Thurs 9-9, Fri & Sat 10-6
Friends of the Library Group

LIBRARY 21C, 1175 Chapel Hills Dr, 80920. Tel: 719-531-6333, Ext 6201. Web Site: ppld.org/library-21c. *Commun Engagement & Outreach Officer,* Catie Tierney; E-mail: ctierney@ppld.org
Open Mon-Thurs 9-9, Fri & Sat 10-6, Sun 1-5
Friends of the Library Group

MANITOU SPRINGS LIBRARY, 701 Manitou Ave, Manitou Springs, 80829-1887, SAN 301-9853. Tel: 719-531-6333, Ext 6041. Web Site: ppld.org/manitou-springs-library. *Libr Mgr,* Michael Doherty; E-mail: mdoherty@ppld.org; Staff 4 (MLS 2, Non-MLS 2)
Founded 1910. Pop 5,000; Circ 28,000
Special Collections: Colo History Coll, bks & clippings; Large Print Coll
Automation Activity & Vendor Info: (Acquisitions) SirsiDynix; (Cataloging) SirsiDynix; (Circulation) SirsiDynix; (OPAC) SirsiDynix
Open Mon-Thurs 10-7, Fri & Sat 10-6
Friends of the Library Group

MONUMENT LIBRARY, 1706 Lake Woodmoor Dr, Monument, 80132-9074, SAN 335-5535. Tel: 719-531-6333, Ext 6061. Web Site: ppld.org/monument-library. *Libr Mgr,* Andrew Hart; E-mail: ahart@ppld.org
Open Mon-Thurs 9-9, Fri & Sat 10-6, Sun 1-5
Friends of the Library Group

OLD COLORADO CITY LIBRARY, 2418 W Pikes Peak Ave, 80904, SAN 335-556X. Tel: 719-531-6333, Ext 6202. Web Site: ppld.org/old-colorado-city-library. *Libr Mgr,* Sandy Hancock; E-mail: shancock@ppld.org
Open Mon-Thurs 9-9, Fri & Sat 10-6
Friends of the Library Group

PALMER LAKE LIBRARY, 66 Lower Glenway, Palmer Lake, 80133, SAN 335-5594. Web Site: ppld.org/palmer-lake-library. *Libr Mgr,* Andrew Hart
Open Tues-Fri 10-6, Sat 10-2
Friends of the Library Group

PENROSE LIBRARY, 20 N Cascade Ave, 80903, SAN 329-6334. Tel: 719-531-6333, Ext 6350. Web Site: ppld.org/penrose-library. *Libr Mgr,* Antonia Krupicka-Smith; E-mail: akrupicka@ppld.org
Subject Interests: Genealogy, Local hist
Open Mon-Thurs 9-9, Fri & Sat 10-6, Sun 1-5
Friends of the Library Group

ROCKRIMMON LIBRARY, 832 Village Center Dr, 80919, SAN 370-4505. Tel: 719-531-6333, Ext 6027. Web Site: ppld.org/rockrimmon-library. *Libr Mgr,* Steve Abbott; E-mail: sabbott@ppld.org
Open Mon-Thurs 9-9, Fri & Sat 10-6
Friends of the Library Group

SAND CREEK LIBRARY, 1821 S Academy Blvd, 80916, SAN 329-6377. Tel: 719-531-6333, Ext 6374. Web Site: ppld.org/sand-creek-library. *Libr Mgr,* Jacob Rundle; E-mail: jrundle@ppld.org
Open Mon-Thurs 9-9, Fri & Sat 10-6, Sun 1-5
Friends of the Library Group

UTE PASS LIBRARY, 8010 Severy Rd, Cascade, 80809, SAN 335-5624. Tel: 719-531-6333, Ext 6084. Web Site: ppld.org/ute-pass-library. *Libr Mgr,* Margaret Morris; E-mail: mmorris@ppld.org
Open Mon & Tues 1-7, Thurs-Sat 10-4
Friends of the Library Group

Bookmobiles: 2

GL PIKES PEAK LIBRARY DISTRICT LAW LIBRARY, El Paso County Bar Association Law Library, Penrose Library, 20 N Cascade Ave, 80903. SAN 301-7710. Tel: 719-531-6333. Web Site: ppld.org/penrose-library. *Law Librn,* Deb Hamilton; Tel: 719-531-6333, Ext 6058, E-mail: dhamilton@ppld.org; Staff 2 (MLS 1, Non-MLS 1)
Founded 1955
Library Holdings: Bk Titles 461
Automation Activity & Vendor Info: (Circulation) SirsiDynix; (OPAC) SirsiDynix
Wireless access
Open Mon-Thurs 9-9, Fri & Sat 10-6, Sun 1-5
Friends of the Library Group

C UNIVERSITY OF COLORADO COLORADO SPRINGS*, Kraemer Family Library, 1420 Austin Bluffs Pkwy, 80918. SAN 301-7850. Tel: 719-255-3286. Circulation Tel: 719-255-3296. Interlibrary Loan Service Tel: 719-255-3285. Reference Tel: 719-255-3295. Administration Tel: 719-255-3060. FAX: 719-528-5227. E-mail: refdesk@uccs.edu. Web Site: www.uccs.edu/library. *Assoc Dean,* Christina Martinez; Tel: 719-255-3287, E-mail: cmartine@uccs.edu; *Dir, Cat, Metadata Serv,* Lynn Gates; Tel: 719-255-3289, E-mail: lgates@uccs.edu; *Dir, Access Serv,* Federico Martinez-Garcia; Tel: 719-255-3908, E-mail: fmartin3@uccs.edu; *Dir, Coll Mgt,* Rhonda Glazier; Tel: 719-255-3291, E-mail: rglazier@uccs.edu; *Dir, Res Serv, Instrul Serv,* Norah Mazel; Tel: 719-255-3175, E-mail: nmazel@uccs.edu; *Dir, Web Serv,* Tabatha Farney; Tel: 719-255-3079, E-mail: tfarney@uccs.edu; Staff 27.5 (MLS 14, Non-MLS 13.5)
Founded 1965. Enrl 12,422; Fac 794; Highest Degree: Doctorate
Jul 2019-Jun 2020. Mats Exp $1,859,443, Books $337,591, Per/Ser (Incl. Access Fees) $117,000, Electronic Ref Mat (Incl. Access Fees) $1,395,702, Presv $9,150. Sal $1,515,735
Library Holdings: AV Mats 9,011; e-books 49,526; e-journals 105,000; Electronic Media & Resources 256; Microforms 446,967; Bk Vols 412,715; Per Subs 149
Special Collections: UCCS Archives. State Document Depository; US Document Depository
Subject Interests: Bus, Educ, Electrical engr, Nursing, Psychol
Automation Activity & Vendor Info: (Acquisitions) Innovative Interfaces, Inc - Sierra; (Cataloging) Innovative Interfaces, Inc - Sierra; (Circulation) Innovative Interfaces, Inc - Sierra; (Course Reserve) Innovative Interfaces, Inc - Sierra; (ILL) OCLC ILLiad; (OPAC) Innovative Interfaces, Inc - Sierra; (Serials) Innovative Interfaces, Inc - Sierra
Wireless access
Partic in Colorado Alliance of Research Libraries; OCLC Online Computer Library Center, Inc
Open Mon-Thurs 7:30am-Midnight, Fri 7:30am-8pm, Sat 10-8, Sun 11am-Midnight

S WESTERN MUSEUM OF MINING & INDUSTRY LIBRARY, 225 N Gate Blvd, 80921. SAN 326-3371. Tel: 719-488-0880. FAX: 719-488-9261. Web Site: www.wmmi.org. *Curator,* Dr Richard A Sauers; E-mail: rsauers@wmmi.org
Founded 1994
Library Holdings: DVDs 15; Bk Titles 10,000; Per Subs 8
Special Collections: Archival Coll; Mining Equipment and Supply Catalogs (Mining equipment, supply, and sales catalogs from the 1890s to the present); Photograph Coll
Subject Interests: Mining
Wireless access
Function: Archival coll, ILL available, Internet access, Magazines, Online cat, Photocopying/Printing, Ref serv available, Wheelchair accessible
Publications: Annual Report; Newsletter (Quarterly)
Restriction: Non-circulating of rare bks, Open to others by appt, Restricted borrowing privileges

CORTEZ

P CORTEZ PUBLIC LIBRARY, 202 N Park, 81321-3300. SAN 301-7869. Tel: 970-565-8117. FAX: 970-565-8720. Web Site: www.cityofcortez.com/141/library. *Interim Dir, ILL Tech,* Isabella Sharpensteen; E-mail: isharpensteen@cityofcortez.com; Staff 5 (MLS 1, Non-MLS 4)
Founded 1932. Pop 22,000; Circ 143,000
Library Holdings: CDs 400; DVDs 100; Large Print Bks 2,000; Bk Titles 65,000; Per Subs 65; Videos 4,000
Special Collections: Oral History
Automation Activity & Vendor Info: (Cataloging) Follett Software; (Circulation) Follett Software
Wireless access
Function: ILL available, Photocopying/Printing
Partic in Colorado Library Consortium
Open Mon-Thurs 9-7, Fri 9-4, Sat 10-4
Friends of the Library Group

S CROW CANYON ARCHAEOLOGICAL CENTER, Florence C Lister Research Library, 23390 County Rd K, 81321. SAN 377-0958. Tel: 970-565-8975. Toll Free Tel: 800-422-8975. FAX: 970-565-4859. E-mail: info@crowcanyon.org. Web Site: www.crowcanyon.org. *Colls Mgr,* Ms Jamie Merewether
Library Holdings: Bk Titles 5,000
Function: Res libr
Restriction: Non-circulating, Not open to pub

CRAIG

P MOFFAT COUNTY LIBRARIES*, 570 Green St, 81625. SAN 301-7885. Tel: 970-824-5116. FAX: 970-824-2867. E-mail: moffatlib@moffat.lib.co.us. Web Site:

moffatcounty.colorado.gov/services/library. *Dir,* Keisha Bickford; E-mail: kbickford@moffat.lib.co.us; Staff 7 (MLS 1, Non-MLS 6)
Founded 1911. Pop 13,000
Special Collections: Local History Coll. Oral History
Automation Activity & Vendor Info: (Cataloging) Follett Software; (Circulation) Follett Software; (OPAC) Follett Software
Wireless access
Function: 24/7 Electronic res, 24/7 Online cat, Adult literacy prog, Audiobks on Playaways & MP3, Audiobks via web, Bks on cassette, Bks on CD, Children's prog, Computers for patron use, Electronic databases & coll, Free DVD rentals, ILL available, Internet access, Magazines, Microfiche/film & reading machines, Movies, Online cat, Outreach serv, Preschool reading prog, Prog for adults, Prog for children & young adult, Ref & res, Ref serv available, Res assist avail, Scanner, Spanish lang bks, Story hour, Summer & winter reading prog, Summer reading prog, Tax forms, Teen prog, VHS videos, Wheelchair accessible, Winter reading prog
Partic in Colorado Library Consortium
Open Mon & Tues 10:30-7, Wed-Fri 9:30-5:30, Sat 11-5:30
Friends of the Library Group
Branches: 2
DINOSAUR BRANCH, 400 W School St, Dinosaur, 81610. (Mail add: PO Box 57, Dinosaur, 81610). Tel: 970-374-2700. FAX: 970-374-2026. *Libr Asst,* Bryan Nielsen
Open Mon 11-7, Tues 11-5, Thurs 12-5, Sat 12-2
Friends of the Library Group
MAYBELL BRANCH, 202 Collom St, Maybell, 81640. (Mail add: PO Box 156, Maybell, 81640-0156). Tel: 970-272-9919. FAX: 970-272-9919. *Libr Tech,* Marla Stephenson
Open Mon, Wed & Fri 11-6
Friends of the Library Group

CREEDE

P MINERAL COUNTY REGIONAL LIBRARY, 450 Corfair Dr, 81130. (Mail add: PO Box 429, 81130-0429), SAN 376-2831. Tel: 719-300-1452. Web Site: mineralcounty.colorado.gov/services/mineral-county-library. *Librn,* Frances Kolisch; E-mail: frances@creedek12.net
Pop 952; Circ 14,000
Library Holdings: Bk Vols 6,000; Per Subs 7
Wireless access
Open Mon-Thurs 8:30-4:30, Fri 9-2

CRIPPLE CREEK

P FRANKLIN FERGUSON MEMORIAL LIBRARY*, 410 N B St, 80813. (Mail add: PO Box 975, 80813), SAN 301-7893. Tel: 719-689-2800. FAX: 719-689-3187. Web Site: www.ccvschools.com/community-library. *Dir,* Mike McDonald; *Asst Librn,* Judy Hess; Staff 1 (MLS 1)
Founded 1976. Pop 1,500; Circ 22,764
Library Holdings: DVDs 120; Bk Titles 22,528; Bk Vols 23,011; Per Subs 33; Talking Bks 165; Videos 1,654
Special Collections: Colorado History; Local history
Subject Interests: Hist
Wireless access
Open Mon-Thurs 9-6, Fri 9-3

CROOK

P CROOK COMMUNITY LIBRARY*, Fourth St, 80726. (Mail add: PO Box 205, 80726-0205), SAN 301-7907. Tel: 970-886-2833. *Librn,* Elna Hamilton
Founded 1928. Circ 3,055
Library Holdings: Bk Titles 9,000
Partic in Colorado Library Consortium
Open Mon 1:30-4
Bookmobiles: 1

CROWLEY

S COLORADO DEPARTMENT OF CORRECTIONS, Arkansas Valley Correctional Facility Library, 12750 Hwy 96, Lane 13, 81034. (Mail add: Arkansas Valley Correctional Facility, General Library, Ordway, 81034), SAN 376-5768. Tel: 719-267-3520, Ext 3251. FAX: 719-267-5024. *Regional Librn,* Diane Walden; Tel: 303-866-6341, E-mail: diane.walden@state.co.us; *Libr Tech III,* Linda Sue Hollis; E-mail: linda.hollis@state.co.us; Staff 3 (MLS 2, Non-MLS 1)
Library Holdings: Audiobooks 20; Bks on Deafness & Sign Lang 6; CDs 800; DVDs 10; High Interest/Low Vocabulary Bk Vols 20; Large Print Bks 70; Per Subs 51; Videos 10
Automation Activity & Vendor Info: (Cataloging) EOS International; (Circulation) EOS International; (OPAC) EOS International
Function: ILL available, Internet access, Music CDs, Ref serv available, VHS videos
Restriction: Authorized patrons

DEL NORTE

P DEL NORTE PUBLIC LIBRARY, 790 Grand Ave, 81132. SAN 301-7915. Tel: 719-657-2633. FAX: 719-657-2633. E-mail: delnortepubliclibrary@gmail.com. Web Site: dnpl.colibraries.org. *Dir,* Susan Williams; Staff 4 (Non-MLS 4)
Founded 1899. Pop 11,305
Library Holdings: Bk Vols 15,000; Per Subs 12
Automation Activity & Vendor Info: (Cataloging) Koha; (Circulation) Koha
Wireless access
Function: 24/7 Electronic res, 24/7 Online cat, Audiobks via web, Bks on CD, Computers for patron use, Electronic databases & coll, ILL available, Internet access, Magazines, Movies, Online cat, Photocopying/Printing, Preschool outreach, Scanner, Story hour, Tax forms, Wheelchair accessible
Partic in Colorado Library Consortium
Open Mon-Wed & Fri 12-5, Thurs 10-7

DELTA

S COLORADO DEPARTMENT OF CORRECTIONS, Delta Correctional Center Library, 11363 Lockhart Rd, 81416. SAN 376-5784. Tel: 970-874-7614, Ext 2955. Web Site: cdoc.colorado.gov/facilities/delta-correctional-center. *Libr Tech II,* Kay Marie Chadwick; E-mail: kaymarie.chadwick@state.co.us
Library Holdings: AV Mats 793; Bk Titles 4,913; Per Subs 33
Automation Activity & Vendor Info: (Cataloging) EOS International; (Circulation) EOS International
Restriction: Staff & inmates only

DENVER

M AORN CENTER FOR LIBRARY SERVICES & ARCHIVES*, 2170 S Parker Rd, Ste 400, 80231-5711. SAN 301-7982. Tel: 303-755-6304. Toll Free Tel: 800-755-2676, Ext 314. FAX: 303-368-4460. E-mail: library@aorn.org. Web Site: www.aorn.org.
Founded 1972
Library Holdings: AV Mats 300; Bk Titles 4,500; Bk Vols 5,000; Per Subs 400
Special Collections: AORN Publications; Archives; Thesis Coll
Subject Interests: Health sci, Med, Nursing
Automation Activity & Vendor Info: (Cataloging) Innovative Interfaces, Inc; (Circulation) Innovative Interfaces, Inc; (ILL) OCLC; (OPAC) Innovative Interfaces, Inc; (Serials) Innovative Interfaces, Inc
Partic in Colorado Council of Medical Librarians; National Network of Libraries of Medicine Region 4

R AUGUSTANA LUTHERAN CHURCH LIBRARY*, 5000 E Alameda Ave, 80246. SAN 301-7990. Tel: 303-388-4678. FAX: 303-388-1338. E-mail: info@augustanadenver.org. Web Site: www.augustanadenver.org. *Librn,* Linda Crowe
Founded 1963
Library Holdings: Bk Titles 5,000; Bk Vols 5,308

C AURARIA LIBRARY*, 1100 Lawrence St, 80204-2095. SAN 335-5802. Tel: 303-315-7763. Reference Tel: 303-303-7711. Web Site: library.auraria.edu. *Dir,* Cinthya Ippoliti; E-mail: cinthya.ippoliti@ucdenver.edu; *Assoc Dir, Digital & Scholarly Servs,* Cynthia Hashert; Tel: 303-315-7767, E-mail: cynthia.hashert@ucdenver.edu; *Assoc Dir, Educ Serv/Pub Serv,* Keith Teeter; Tel: 303-315-7732, E-mail: keith.teeter@ucdenver.edu; *Assoc Dir, Tech Serv,* Sommer Browning; Tel: 303-315-7728, E-mail: sommer.browning@ucdenver.edu; *E-Res Cat Librn,* Vera Gao; Tel: 303-315-7716, E-mail: vera.gao@ucdenver.edu; *Researcher, Support Librn,* Orlando Archibeque; Tel: 303-315-7741, E-mail: orlando.archibeque@ucdenver.edu; *Teaching & Learning Librn,* Thomas J Beck; Tel: 303-315-7742, E-mail: thomas.j.beck@ucdenver.edu; *Digital Coll Mgr,* Matthew Mariner; Tel: 303-315-7776, E-mail: matthew.mariner@ucdenver.edu; Staff 53 (MLS 24, Non-MLS 29)
Founded 1976. Enrl 44,616; Fac 2,214; Highest Degree: Doctorate
Library Holdings: AV Mats 17,735; e-books 170,915; e-journals 46,985; Bk Titles 825,191; Bk Vols 905,630; Per Subs 1,474; Talking Bks 918; Videos 12,562
Special Collections: Amache Japanese-American Internment Center; Civil Liberties in Colorado; Colorado Railroads; Higher Education (Auraria Higher Education Center Archives); Literature & Literary Criticism (Donald Sutherland Coll); State & Local Policy (Seasongood Library, National Municipal League, Conservative Think Tanks); Women's History Coll. State Document Depository; US Document Depository
Subject Interests: Archit
Automation Activity & Vendor Info: (Acquisitions) Innovative Interfaces, Inc; (Cataloging) Innovative Interfaces, Inc; (Circulation) Innovative Interfaces, Inc; (Course Reserve) Docutek; (Media Booking) Innovative Interfaces, Inc; (OPAC) Innovative Interfaces, Inc; (Serials) Innovative Interfaces, Inc
Wireless access

Partic in Colorado Alliance of Research Libraries; OCLC Online Computer Library Center, Inc
Special Services for the Deaf - TTY equip
Special Services for the Blind - VisualTek equip
Friends of the Library Group

G BUREAU OF LAND MANAGEMENT LIBRARY*, Denver Federal Ctr, Bldg 50, 80225. (Mail add: PO Box 25047, 80225-0047), SAN 335-5926. Tel: 303-236-6650. Administration Tel: 303-236-9456. FAX: 303-236-4810. E-mail: blm_library@blm.gov. Web Site: www.blm.gov/learn/blm-library. *Digital Serv Librn,* Malia Burton; *Ref Librn,* Deborah Harnke; Staff 1 (Non-MLS 1)
Founded 1970
Library Holdings: Bk Vols 40,000; Per Subs 250
Special Collections: Bureau of Land Management Publications; Cadastral Survey Plats & Field Notes, micro
Automation Activity & Vendor Info: (Cataloging) EOS International; (Circulation) EOS International; (OPAC) EOS International; (Serials) EOS International
Wireless access
Restriction: Open by appt only

SR CARDINAL STAFFORD LIBRARY*, St John Vianney Seminary Library, 1300 S Steele St, 80210-2526. SAN 301-8741. Tel: 303-715-3146. FAX: 303-715-2007. Web Site: sjvdenver.edu/library. *Libr Dir,* Stephen Sweeney; Tel: 303-715-3192, E-mail: stephen.sweeney@archden.org; *Ref Librn,* Tamara Conley; Tel: 303-715-3146, E-mail: tamara.conley@archden.org; *Cat, Libr Asst, Ser,* Jennifer Murphy; Tel: 303-715-3234, E-mail: jennifer.murphy@archden.org; *Circ/Ser, Libr Asst, ILL,* Joseph R McGrail; Tel: 303-715-3228, E-mail: joseph.mcgrail@archden.org; Staff 4 (MLS 3, Non-MLS 1)
Founded 1907. Enrl 120; Fac 27; Highest Degree: Master
Library Holdings: Bk Vols 165,000; Per Subs 300
Special Collections: Anglican Studies; Hispanic Pastoral Ministry
Subject Interests: Philos, Theol
Automation Activity & Vendor Info: (Acquisitions) OCLC Worldshare Management Services; (Cataloging) OCLC Worldshare Management Services; (Circulation) OCLC Worldshare Management Services; (Course Reserve) OCLC Worldshare Management Services; (Discovery) OCLC Worldshare Management Services; (ILL) OCLC WorldShare Interlibrary Loan; (OPAC) OCLC Worldshare Management Services; (Serials) OCLC Worldshare Management Services
Wireless access
Partic in Colorado Library Consortium; OCLC Online Computer Library Center, Inc
Open Mon-Fri 10-4
Friends of the Library Group
Branches:
ARCHIVES OF THE CATHOLIC ARCHDIOCESE OF DENVER, 1300 S Steele St, 80210. Tel: 303-715-3144. *Archivist,* Karyl Klein; E-mail: karyl.klein@archden.org; Staff 1 (Non-MLS 1)
Founded 2006
Special Collections: Catholic Church of Colorado, Archbishops papers, photogs, Sacramental recs; Denver Catholic Register, microfilm
Function: Archival coll
Restriction: By permission only, Open by appt only, Private libr

CHILDREN'S HOSPITAL COLORADO
M CLINICAL & RESEARCH LIBRARY*, 13123 E 16th Ave, B180, Aurora, 80045, SAN 326-3185. Tel: 720-777-6400. FAX: 720-777-7152. E-mail: library@childrenscolorado.org. *Mgr,* Kristen Desanto; Staff 2.5 (MLS 2, Non-MLS 0.5)
Automation Activity & Vendor Info: (Acquisitions) OCLC; (Cataloging) OCLC; (Circulation) OCLC; (ILL) OCLC; (OPAC) OCLC; (Serials) OCLC
Open Mon-Thurs 7:30-5:30, Fri 7:30-4
Restriction: Staff use only
M FAMILY HEALTH LIBRARY*, 13123 E 16th Ave, Aurora, 80045, SAN 378-1739. Tel: 720-777-6378. FAX: 720-777-7121. E-mail: familylibrary@childrenscolorado.org. *Librn,* Zelda Hawkins
Library Holdings: Bk Titles 3,000; Bk Vols 3,150; Per Subs 25
Automation Activity & Vendor Info: (Acquisitions) OCLC WorldShare Interlibrary Loan; (Cataloging) OCLC WorldShare Interlibrary Loan
Open Mon-Fri 9-3:30

S COLORADO DEPARTMENT OF CORRECTIONS, Denver Women's Correctional Facility Library, 3600 Havana St, 80239. Tel: 303-307-2500, Ext 2659, 303-307-2721. FAX: 303-307-2674. *Librn,* Molly Bassford; E-mail: rebecca.bassford@state.co.us; Staff 3 (MLS 1, Non-MLS 2)
Founded 1999
Library Holdings: Bk Vols 12,000; Per Subs 40

G COLORADO DEPARTMENT OF TRANSPORTATION LIBRARY*, Shumate Bldg, 4201 E Arkansas Ave, 80222. SAN 301-8164. Tel: 303-757-9972. E-mail: CDOTlibrary@state.co.us. Web Site: www.codot.gov/library/materials-from-our-library. *Research Librn,* Jessica Weatherby
Founded 1949
Library Holdings: AV Mats 170; Bk Titles 17,000; Per Subs 12; Talking Bks 40
Subject Interests: Environ documentation, Safety, Transportation
Open Mon-Thurs 9-5

G COLORADO DIVISION OF STATE ARCHIVES & PUBLIC RECORDS*, 1313 Sherman St, Ste 122, 80203. SAN 373-8175. Tel: 303-866-2358, 303-866-4900. Toll Free Tel: 800-305-3442 (CO only). FAX: 303-866-2229, 303-866-2257. E-mail: archivesrm@state.co.us. Web Site: www.colorado.gov/archives. *State Archivist,* Aly Jabrocki; E-mail: aly.jabrocki@state.co.us; Staff 13 (MLS 6, Non-MLS 7)
Founded 1943
Special Collections: Colorado Public Officials; Records of Territory & State of Colorado, flm original docs, vols. Oral History
Function: Archival coll, Computers for patron use, For res purposes, Govt ref serv, Internet access, Microfiche/film & reading machines, Outreach serv, Photocopying/Printing, Ref & res, Ref serv available, Res assist avail, Res libr, Res performed for a fee, Scanner, Wheelchair accessible
Restriction: Staff use only
Friends of the Library Group

G COLORADO JOINT LEGISLATIVE LIBRARY*, State Capitol Bldg, Rm 048, 200 E Colfax Ave, 80203-1784. SAN 375-4510. Tel: 303-866-4011. FAX: 303-866-2167. E-mail: lcs.library@state.co.us. Web Site: leg.colorado.gov. *Actg Libr Serv Mgr,* Susan Liddle; Tel: 303-866-3521, E-mail: lcs.library@state.co.us; *Librn,* Position Currently Open; Staff 2 (MLS 2)
Founded 1973
Library Holdings: CDs 379; DVDs 14; e-journals 7; Electronic Media & Resources 78; Bk Titles 7,650; Bk Vols 15,500; Per Subs 37; Videos 46
Special Collections: Bills; Colorado General Assembly Materials; Fiscal Notes; Interim Committee Reports
Automation Activity & Vendor Info: (Acquisitions) NOTEbookS Library Automation; (Cataloging) NOTEbookS Library Automation; (Circulation) NOTEbookS Library Automation; (Serials) NOTEbookS Library Automation
Partic in Colorado Library Consortium
Restriction: Non-circulating to the pub

M COLORADO MENTAL HEALTH INSTITUTE AT FORT LOGAN*, Medical Library, 3520 W Oxford Ave, 80236. SAN 301-8385. Tel: 303-866-7844. FAX: 303-866-7845. Web Site: www.colorado.gov/pacific/cdhs/colorado-mental-health-institute-fort-logan. *Dir, Libr Serv,* Kate Elder; E-mail: kate.elder@state.co.us; Staff 1 (MLS 1)
Founded 1961
Library Holdings: Bk Vols 1,000; Spec Interest Per Sub 25
Subject Interests: Mental health, Nursing, Psychiat, Psychol, Soc work
Automation Activity & Vendor Info: (OPAC) LibraryWorld, Inc; (Serials) Prenax, Inc
Wireless access
Function: ILL available
Publications: The Supplement (Newsletter)
Partic in Association of Mental Health Libraries; Colorado Council of Medical Librarians
Open Mon-Fri 8:30-4:30
Restriction: Circulates for staff only, In-house use for visitors

G COLORADO STATE DEPARTMENT OF NATURAL RESOURCES*, Colorado Water Conservation Board Library, 1580 Logan St, Ste 600, 80203. (Mail add: 1313 Sherman St, Rm 721, 80203), SAN 335-6043. Tel: 303-866-3441. FAX: 303-866-4474. Web Site: www.cwcb.state.co.us. *Library Contact,* Erik Skeie; E-mail: Erik.Skeie@state.co.us
Library Holdings: Bk Titles 5,000
Restriction: Staff use only

P COLORADO STATE LIBRARY, 201 E Colfax Ave, Rm 309, 80203-1799. SAN 335-6108. Tel: 303-866-6900. FAX: 303-866-6940. E-mail: csl.info@cde.state.co.us. Web Site: cde.state.co.us/cdelib. *Dir, Libr Develop,* Lori Special; Tel: 303-866-6730, E-mail: special_l@cde.state.co.us; *Dir, Networking & Res Sharing,* Regan Harper; Tel: 303-866-6907, E-mail: harper_r@cde.state.co.us; *Dir, Res Serv,* Charissa Brammer; Tel: 720-648-2948, E-mail: brammer_c@cde.state.co.us; *Interim Asst Commissioner,* Debbi MacLeod; Tel: 303-866-6994, E-mail: macleod_d@cde.state.co.us; *Dir, State Publ & Talking Bk Libr,* Nicolle Steffen; E-mail: steffen_n@cde.state.co.us; *Fiscal Officer, LSTA Coordr,* Jean Heilig; Tel: 303-866-6731, E-mail: heilig_j@cde.state.co.us; Staff 22 (MLS 21, Non-MLS 1)
Founded 1876
Jul 2014-Jun 2015 Income $4,056,527, State $1,419,614, Federal $2,636,913. Mats Exp $72,000, Books $28,000, Per/Ser (Incl. Access Fees)

$4,000, Other Print Mats $1,000, AV Equip $15,000, Electronic Ref Mat (Incl. Access Fees) $24,000
Library Holdings: Braille Volumes 2,900; Large Print Bks 11,500; Bk Vols 21,000; Per Subs 25; Talking Bks 48,600; Videos 240
Special Collections: Colorado Talking Book Library; State Publications Library. State Document Depository
Subject Interests: Educ, Libr & info sci
Automation Activity & Vendor Info: (Cataloging) OCLC; (ILL) OCLC; (OPAC) Innovative Interfaces, Inc; (Serials) Innovative Interfaces, Inc
Function: Digital talking bks, Electronic databases & coll
Publications: Annual Report; Fast Facts Research Summaries; Getting Ready for Kindergarten; Long Range Plan; Public Library Standards; Reading Tips for Parents; Standards for Adult Correctional Institutions; Statistical Summaries by Type of Library; The Impact of School Library Media Centers on Academic Achievement
Partic in Association for Rural & Small Libraries; Colorado Library Consortium; OCLC Online Computer Library Center, Inc
Special Services for the Blind - Aids for in-house use; Assistive/Adapted tech devices, equip & products; Audio mat; Bks & mags in Braille, on rec, tape & cassette; Bks available with recordings; Bks on cassette; Braille bks; Braille equip; Descriptive video serv (DVS)
Open Mon-Fri 8-5
Friends of the Library Group
Branches: 1
COLORADO TALKING BOOK LIBRARY
See Separate Entry

GL COLORADO SUPREME COURT LIBRARY*, Ralph L Carr Colorado Judicial Ctr, Two E 14th Ave, 80203. SAN 301-8180. Tel: 720-625-5100. FAX: 720-625-5110. E-mail: library@judicial.state.co.us. Web Site: cscl.colibraries.org. *Head Librn,* Dan Cordova; Staff 3 (MLS 3)
Founded 1874
Library Holdings: Bk Vols 80,000; Per Subs 300
Subject Interests: Law
Automation Activity & Vendor Info: (Acquisitions) SirsiDynix; (Cataloging) SirsiDynix; (Circulation) SirsiDynix; (ILL) SirsiDynix; (OPAC) SirsiDynix; (Serials) SirsiDynix
Partic in Colorado Association of Law Libraries; OCLC Online Computer Library Center, Inc
Open Mon-Fri 8-5

P COLORADO TALKING BOOK LIBRARY*, 180 Sheridan Blvd, 80226-8101. SAN 301-8172. Tel: 303-727-9277. Toll Free Tel: 800-685-2136 (Colo only). FAX: 303-727-9281. E-mail: ctbl.info@cde.state.co.us. Web Site: www.myctbl.org. *Dir,* Debbi MacLeod; E-mail: macleod_d@cde.state.co.us; Staff 13 (MLS 5, Non-MLS 8)
Founded 1931
Jul 2016-Jun 2017 Income $942,258
Library Holdings: Braille Volumes 23,911; DVDs 462; Electronic Media & Resources 8; Large Print Bks 30,917; Per Subs 3; Talking Bks 289,876; Videos 575
Special Collections: Blindness & Other Handicaps, ref mat; Descriptive Videos; Spanish Language; Volunteer Produced Books & Magazines
Automation Activity & Vendor Info: (Acquisitions) Keystone Systems, Inc (KLAS); (Cataloging) Keystone Systems, Inc (KLAS); (Circulation) Keystone Systems, Inc (KLAS); (OPAC) Keystone Systems, Inc (KLAS)
Wireless access
Function: 24/7 Electronic res, 24/7 Online cat, Adult bk club, Audiobks via web, Computers for patron use, Digital talking bks, Electronic databases & coll, Equip loans & repairs, Home delivery & serv to seniorr ctr & nursing homes, Jail serv, Large print keyboards, Magazines, Magnifiers for reading, Mail & tel request accepted, Online cat, Outreach serv, Summer reading prog, Wheelchair accessible
Publications: CTBL News (Newsletter)
Partic in Colorado Library Consortium
Special Services for the Blind - Accessible computers; Audio mat; Bks & mags in Braille, on rec, tape & cassette; Bks available with recordings; Bks on flash-memory cartridges; Braille alphabet card; Braille bks; Braille equip; Children's Braille; Closed circuit TV magnifier; Computer with voice synthesizer for visually impaired persons; Copier with enlargement capabilities; Descriptive video serv (DVS); Digital talking bk; Digital talking bk machines; Disability awareness prog; Extensive large print coll; Free checkout of audio mat; Home delivery serv; Info on spec aids & appliances; Large print bks; Large screen computer & software; Local mags & bks recorded; Machine repair; Magnifiers; Mags & bk reproduction/duplication; Networked computers with assistive software; Newsletter (in large print, Braille or on cassette); Newsline for the Blind; PC for people with disabilities; Production of talking bks; Recorded bks; Screen enlargement software for people with visual disabilities; Screen reader software; Soundproof reading booth; Spanish Braille mags & bks; Talking bks; Talking bks & player equip; Tel Pioneers equip repair group; Volunteer serv; Web-Braille; ZoomText magnification & reading software
Open Mon-Fri 8-5
Restriction: Circ to mem only, Free to mem
Friends of the Library Group

L DAVIS, GRAHAM & STUBBS*, Law Library, 1550 17th St, Ste 500, 80202. SAN 301-8229. Tel: 303-892-7306. FAX: 303-893-1379. Web Site: www.dgslaw.com. *Mgr,* Andrea Hamilton; E-mail: andrea.hamilton@dgslaw.com; Staff 4 (MLS 2, Non-MLS 2)
Library Holdings: e-journals 2,700; Bk Vols 24,000; Per Subs 100
Wireless access
Restriction: Staff use only

S DENVER ACADEMY LIBRARY, 4400 E Iliff Ave, 80222. SAN 377-9068. Tel: 303-777-5870. FAX: 303-777-5893. Web Site: sites.google.com/a/denveracademy.org/library, www.denveracademy.org/page/student-life/library. *Librn,* Jolene Gutiérrez; E-mail: jgutierrez@denveracademy.org; *Libr Asst,* Jacob Theis; E-mail: rtheis@denveracademy.org; Staff 2 (MLS 1, Non-MLS 1)
Founded 1972
Library Holdings: DVDs 100; e-books 100; High Interest/Low Vocabulary Bk Vols 2,000; Bk Titles 15,000; Talking Bks 100
Wireless access
Open Mon-Fri 8-3:30

S DENVER ART MUSEUM*, Frederick R Mayer Library, 100 W 14th Ave Pkwy, 80204. SAN 301-8245. Tel: 720-913-0100. FAX: 720-913-0001. E-mail: library@denverartmuseum.org. Web Site: www.denverartmuseum.org/en/research-and-reports. *Dir,* Andrea Hansen; Staff 1 (MLS 1)
Founded 1935
Library Holdings: Bk Titles 40,000
Special Collections: Douglas Coll of Native Arts
Subject Interests: Art
Automation Activity & Vendor Info: (Cataloging) EOS International; (Circulation) EOS International; (OPAC) EOS International
Wireless access
Partic in OCLC Online Computer Library Center, Inc
Restriction: Authorized patrons, Authorized personnel only, Authorized scholars by appt, Circ limited, In-house use for visitors, Internal circ only, Open to pub by appt only

S DENVER BOTANIC GARDENS*, Helen Fowler Library, 1007 York St, 80206. (Mail add: 909 York St, 80206). Tel: 720-865-3570. E-mail: library@botanicgardens.org. Web Site: www.botanicgardens.org/york-street/helen-fowler-library. *Cat Librn,* Rory O'Connor; E-mail: o'connor@botanicgardens.org; Staff 2 (MLS 2)
Founded 1947
Library Holdings: Bk Titles 24,000; Bk Vols 30,000; Per Subs 400
Special Collections: Waring House Book Room
Subject Interests: Botany, Hort
Automation Activity & Vendor Info: (Acquisitions) EOS International
Wireless access
Partic in Colorado Library Consortium
Open Mon-Thurs, Sat & Sun 10-5

P DENVER PUBLIC LIBRARY*, Ten W 14th Ave Pkwy, 80204-2731. SAN 335-6167. Tel: 720-865-1111. Circulation Tel: 720-865-1325. Interlibrary Loan Service Tel: 720-865-1718. Reference Tel: 720-865-1363. Web Site: www.denverlibrary.org. *City Librn,* Michelle Jeske; E-mail: citylib@denverlibrary.org; *Chief of Staff,* Denise Boothby; E-mail: dboothby@denverlibrary.org; *Dir, Commun Engagement, Dir, Communications,* Erika Martinez; E-mail: emartinez@denverlibrary.org; *Dir, Human Res,* Bria Ward; E-mail: bward@denverlibrary.org; *Dir, Coll & Tech,* Zeth Lietzau; E-mail: zlietzau@denverlibrary.org; *Dir, Finance & Fac,* Amber Lindberg; E-mail: alindberg@denverlibrary.org; *Dir, Neighborhood Servs,* Annie Kemmerling; E-mail: akemmer@denverlibrary.org; *Cent Libr Adminr,* Rachel Fewell; E-mail: rfewell@denverlibrary.org; *Br Cluster Mgr,* Nicanor Diaz; *Br Cluster Mgr,* Jenny LaPerriere; *Br Cluster Mgr,* James Vallejos; *Br Cluster Mgr,* Nikki Van Thiel
Founded 1889. Pop 686,932; Circ 9,076,572
Jan 2015-Dec 2015 Income (Main & Associated Libraries) $44,001,954, State $153,666, City $41,526,606, Federal $22,585, Other $2,299,097. Mats Exp $5,515,701, Books $2,017,191, Per/Ser (Incl. Access Fees) $282,645, AV Mat $1,838,078, Electronic Ref Mat (Incl. Access Fees) $1,377,787. Sal $24,661,230
Library Holdings: Audiobooks 46,174; CDs 72,966; DVDs 193,207; e-books 58,775; e-journals 169; Electronic Media & Resources 35,552; Bk Vols 1,228,459; Per Subs 4,909
Special Collections: Aeronautics (Ross-Barrett Historical Aeronautical); Conservation Coll; Eugene Field; Fine Printing (Douglas); Mountaineering Coll; Original Western Art Coll; Western History Coll; World War II 10th Mountain Division. US Document Depository
Subject Interests: Genealogy
Automation Activity & Vendor Info: (Acquisitions) Innovative Interfaces, Inc; (Cataloging) OCLC; (Circulation) Innovative Interfaces, Inc; (ILL)

OCLC; (OPAC) Innovative Interfaces, Inc; (Serials) Innovative Interfaces, Inc
Wireless access
Function: 24/7 Electronic res, 24/7 Online cat, Archival coll, Art exhibits, Audiobks via web, Bilingual assistance for Spanish patrons, Bk club(s), Bks on CD, Children's prog, Citizenship assistance, Computer training, Computers for patron use, Electronic databases & coll, Free DVD rentals, Genealogy discussion group, Homebound delivery serv, Homework prog, ILL available, Internet access, Life-long learning prog for all ages, Literacy & newcomer serv, Magazines, Mango lang, Meeting rooms, Microfiche/film & reading machines, Movies, Museum passes, Music CDs, Online cat, Online ref, Outside serv via phone, mail, e-mail & web, OverDrive digital audio bks, Photocopying/Printing, Preschool outreach, Preschool reading prog, Prog for adults, Prog for children & young adult, Ref & res, Ref serv available, Spanish lang bks, Study rm, Summer & winter reading prog, Teen prog, Telephone ref, Wheelchair accessible
Publications: Engage! (Monthly)
Partic in Colorado Alliance of Research Libraries
Special Services for the Deaf - TTY equip
Special Services for the Blind - Accessible computers; Assistive/Adapted tech devices, equip & products; Bks on CD; Internet workstation with adaptive software; Large print bks
Open Mon & Tues 10-8, Wed-Fri 10-6, Sat 9-5, Sun 1-5
Friends of the Library Group
Branches: 25
ATHMAR PARK, 1055 S Tejon St, 80223, SAN 335-6469. Tel: 720-865-0230.
Open Mon & Wed 12-8, Tues, Thurs & Fri 10-6, Sat 9-5
Friends of the Library Group
BEAR VALLEY, 5171 W Dartmouth Ave, 80236-2006, SAN 335-6493. Tel: 720-865-0975.
Open Mon, Wed & Fri 10-6, Tues & Thurs 10-8, Sat 9-5
Friends of the Library Group
BLAIR-CALDWELL AFRICAN AMERICAN RESEARCH LIBRARY, 2401 Welton St, 80205-3015, SAN 328-6908. Tel: 720-865-2401.
Founded 2003
Special Collections: African American History Coll. Oral History
Open Mon & Wed 12-8, Tues, Thurs & Fri 10-6, Sat 9-5
Friends of the Library Group
BYERS, 675 Santa Fe Dr, 80204-4426, SAN 335-6523. Tel: 720-865-0160.
Open Mon, Tues & Fri 10-6, Wed & Thurs 12-8, Sat 9-5
Friends of the Library Group
DECKER, 1501 S Logan St, 80210-2632, SAN 335-6612. Tel: 720-865-0220.
Open Mon & Tues 12-8, Wed-Fri 10-6, Sat 9-5
Friends of the Library Group
EUGENE FIELD, 810 S University Blvd, 80209-4725, SAN 335-6647. Tel: 720-865-0240.
Open Mon, Tues & Fri 10-6, Wed & Thurs 12-8, Sat 9-5
Friends of the Library Group
FORD-WARREN BRANCH, 2825 High St, 80205-4545, SAN 335-6671. Tel: 720-865-0920.
Open Mon, Wed & Fri 10-6, Tues & Thurs 12-8, Sat 9-5
Friends of the Library Group
SAM GARY BRANCH LIBRARY, 2961 Roslyn St, 80238. Tel: 720-865-0325.
Open Mon, Tues & Fri 10-6, Wed & Thurs 12-8, Sat 9-5, Sun 1-5
Friends of the Library Group
HADLEY, 1890 S Grove St, 80219-4618, SAN 335-6701. Tel: 720-865-0170.
Open Mon & Tues 12-8, Wed & Thurs 10-8, Fri 10-6, Sat 9-5
Friends of the Library Group
HAMPDEN, 9755 E Girard Ave, 80231-5003, SAN 335-6736. Tel: 720-865-0185.
Open Mon, Thurs & Fri 10-6, Tues & Wed 12-8, Sat 9-5, Sun 1-5
Friends of the Library Group
MONTBELLO, 12955 Albrook Dr, 80239-4704, SAN 335-6795. Tel: 720-865-0200.
Open Mon & Tues 12-8, Wed & Thurs 10-8, Fri 10-6, Sat 9-5
Friends of the Library Group
PARK HILL, 4705 Montview Blvd, 80207-3760, SAN 335-685X. Tel: 720-865-0250.
Open Mon, Thurs & Fri 10-6, Tues & Wed 12-8, Sat 9-5
Friends of the Library Group
VALDEZ PERRY BRANCH, 4690 Vine St, 80216-2823, SAN 376-1088. Tel: 720-865-0300.
Open Mon & Wed 12-8, Tues, Thurs & Fri 10-6, Sat 9-5
Friends of the Library Group
PAULINE ROBINSON BRANCH, 5575 E 33rd Ave, 80207-2027, SAN 376-107X. Tel: 720-865-0290.
Founded 1995
Open Mon & Thurs 12-7, Tues, Wed & Fri 10-6, Sat 9-5
Friends of the Library Group
RODOLFO (CORKY) GONZALES BRANCH LIBRARY, 1498 N Irving St, 80204. Tel: 720-865-2370.
Open Mon & Tues 12-8, Wed-Fri 10-6, Sat 9-5, Sun 1-5
Friends of the Library Group
ROSS-BARNUM BRANCH, 3570 W First Ave, 80219-1346, SAN 335-6884. Tel: 720-865-0145.
Open Mon, Tues & Fri 10-6, Wed & Thurs 12-8, Sat 9-5
Friends of the Library Group
ROSS-BROADWAY, 33 E Bayaud Ave, 80209-1503, SAN 335-6914. Tel: 720-865-0135.
Open Mon & Tues 12-8, Wed-Fri 10-6, Sat 9-5
Friends of the Library Group
ROSS-CHERRY CREEK, 305 Milwaukee St, 80206-4329, SAN 335-6949. Tel: 720-865-0120.
Open Mon, Thurs & Fri 10-6, Tues & Wed 12-8, Sat 9-5
Friends of the Library Group
ROSS-UNIVERSITY HILLS, 4310 E Amherst Ave, 80222-6703, SAN 335-6973. Tel: 720-865-0955.
Open Mon, Wed & Fri 10-6, Tues & Thurs 10-8, Sat 9-5
Friends of the Library Group
SCHLESSMAN FAMILY, 100 Poplar St, 80220-4522, SAN 335-6825. Tel: 720-865-0000.
Founded 2002
Open Mon & Wed 12-8, Tues, Thurs & Fri 10-6, Sat 9-5, Sun 1-5
Friends of the Library Group
SMILEY, 4501 W 46th Ave, 80212-2582, SAN 335-7007. Tel: 720-865-0260.
Open Mon & Wed 12-8, Tues, Thurs & Fri 10-6, Sat 9-5
Friends of the Library Group
VIRGINIA VILLAGE, 1500 S Dahlia St, 80222, SAN 335-7031. Tel: 720-865-0940.
Open Mon & Wed 12-8, Tues, Thurs & Fri 10-6, Sat 9-5
Friends of the Library Group
WESTWOOD, 1000 S Lowell Blvd, 80219-3339, SAN 328-6886. Tel: 720-865-0215.
Open Mon-Thurs 9-6, Fri 9-5, Sat 1-5
Friends of the Library Group
WOODBURY, 3265 Federal Blvd, 80211-3211, SAN 335-7066. Tel: 720-865-0930.
Open Mon, Wed & Fri 10-6, Tues & Thurs 12-8, Sat 9-5
Friends of the Library Group
Bookmobiles: 2. Mgr, Bks & Borrowing, Jennifer Hoffman. Bk titles 10,000

S DEPARTMENT OF HUMAN SERVICES-YOUTH CORRECTIONS, Gilliam Youth Services Center Library, 2844 Downing St, 80205. SAN 378-0570. Tel: 303-291-8951. FAX: 303-291-8995. Web Site: cdhs.colorado.gov/our-services/youth-services/dys-residential-youth-centers.
Library Holdings: Bk Titles 1,000
Open Mon-Fri 6am-2pm

S HISTORY COLORADO*, Stephen H Hart Library & Research Center, 1200 Broadway, 80203. SAN 301-8083. Tel: 303-866-2305. Administration Tel: 303-866-4600. FAX: 303-866-2796. E-mail: cosearch@state.co.us. Web Site: www.historycolorado.org. *Head, Res Ctr,* Melissa de Bie; E-mail: melissa.debie@state.co.us; Staff 4.6 (MLS 4, Non-MLS 0.6)
Founded 1879
Library Holdings: Microforms 25,000; Bk Vols 22,000; Per Subs 491
Special Collections: Aultman Studio Photo Coll; Colorado Newspapers; Colorado Photographs; Denver & Rio Grande Railroads; H A W Tabor Coll, ms; W H Jackson Coll, ms, photog
Subject Interests: Colorado, Hist, Mining, Railroads, Soc hist
Wireless access
Function: Online cat, Res libr, Workshops
Partic in OCLC Online Computer Library Center, Inc
Restriction: Closed stack, Non-circulating

L HOLLAND & HART*, Law Library, 555 17th St, Ste 3200, 80201-3950. (Mail add: PO Box 8749, 80201-8749), SAN 301-8458. Tel: 303-295-8485. Web Site: www.hollandhart.com. *Dir, Knowledge & Res Serv,* Holly Pinto; E-mail: hpinto@hollandhart.com; Staff 7 (MLS 5, Non-MLS 2)
Founded 1948
Library Holdings: Bk Titles 15,000
Automation Activity & Vendor Info: (Acquisitions) EOS International; (Circulation) EOS International
Wireless access
Partic in Colorado Association of Law Libraries
Restriction: Staff use only

CR ILIFF SCHOOL OF THEOLOGY*, Ira J Taylor Library, 2201 S University Blvd, 80210. SAN 301-8474. Tel: 303-765-3173. Circulation Tel: 303-765-3172. E-mail: support@iliff.edu. Web Site: library.iliff.edu. *Chief Info Officer,* Michael Hemenway; E-mail: mhemenway@iliff.edu; *Head Librn,* Micah Saxton; E-mail: msaxton@iliff.edu; *Librn,* Erin Shafer;

E-mail: eshafer@iliff.edu; *Cat/Metadata Librn,* Alice Runis; E-mail: arunis@iliff.edu; Staff 5.5 (MLS 4.5, Non-MLS 1)
Founded 1892. Enrl 267; Fac 24; Highest Degree: Doctorate
Library Holdings: Microforms 60,700; Bk Vols 211,000; Per Subs 300
Special Collections: Hymnody (Van Pelt Hymnal Coll); Local Methodism (Archives of Iliff School of Theology & Rocky Mountain Conference of the United Methodist Church); Methodistica
Subject Interests: Relig
Automation Activity & Vendor Info: (Acquisitions) SirsiDynix; (Cataloging) SirsiDynix; (Circulation) SirsiDynix; (Course Reserve) SirsiDynix; (ILL) OCLC; (OPAC) SirsiDynix; (Serials) SirsiDynix
Wireless access
Partic in OCLC Online Computer Library Center, Inc
Open Mon-Thurs 8-8, Fri 8-4:30, Sat 10-4

C JOHNSON & WALES UNIVERSITY*, Denver Campus Library, College of Business, 7150 Montview Blvd, 80220. Tel: 303-256-9345. Reference Tel: 303-256-9518. E-mail: denvercampuslibrary@jwu.edu. Web Site: www.jwu.edu/campuses/providence/life-on-campus/library.html. *Instruction & Ref Librn,* Victoria West-Pawl; Tel: 303-256-9378; *Tech Serv Librn,* Merrie Valliant; Tel: 303-256-9445; Staff 4 (MLS 4)
Founded 2000. Enrl 1,450; Highest Degree: Bachelor
Library Holdings: AV Mats 1,400; Bk Titles 33,600; Per Subs 186
Special Collections: Leadership Library
Subject Interests: Bus, Criminal justice, Culinary arts, Hospitality
Automation Activity & Vendor Info: (Acquisitions) Innovative Interfaces, Inc - Millennium; (Cataloging) Innovative Interfaces, Inc - Millennium; (Circulation) Innovative Interfaces, Inc - Millennium; (Course Reserve) Innovative Interfaces, Inc - Millennium; (OPAC) Innovative Interfaces, Inc - Millennium; (Serials) Innovative Interfaces, Inc
Wireless access
Open Mon-Thurs 8am-10pm, Fri 8-4:30

L LEWIS ROCA ROTHGERBER CHRISTIE LLP*, Law Library, One Tabor Ctr, Ste 3000, 1200 17th St, 80202. SAN 372-3240. Tel: 303-623-9000. FAX: 303-623-9222. Web Site: www.rothgerber.com. *Librn,* Dianne Kulesa; E-mail: dkulesa@rothgerber.com
Library Holdings: Bk Vols 6,000; Per Subs 50

L MORRISON & FOERSTER LLP*, Law Library, 4200 Republic Plaza, 370 17th St, 80202. SAN 328-5863. Tel: 303-592-1500. FAX: 303-592-1510. E-mail: research@mofo.com. Web Site: www.mofo.com. *Res Serv Mgr,* Tom Duggan; E-mail: tduggan@mofo.com; Staff 2 (MLS 1, Non-MLS 1)
Library Holdings: Bk Vols 4,700; Per Subs 25
Restriction: Not open to pub

M NATIONAL JEWISH HEALTH*, Gerald Tucker Memorial Medical Library, 1400 Jackson St, 80206. SAN 301-861X. Tel: 303-398-1482. FAX: 303-270-2149. E-mail: library@njhealth.org. Web Site: www.nationaljewish.org/research-science/support/library/overview. *Libr Dir,* Shandra Knight; Tel: 303-398-1483, E-mail: KnightS@NJHealth.org; *Biomedical Librn,* Liz Kellermeyer; E-mail: KellermeyerL@njhealth.org; Staff 4 (MLS 2, Non-MLS 2)
Founded 1935
Library Holdings: e-books 120; e-journals 4,000; Bk Titles 3,000; Per Subs 300
Special Collections: Patient & Consumer Health Information
Subject Interests: Allergies, Immunology, Molecular biol, Respiratory med
Automation Activity & Vendor Info: (Acquisitions) Innovative Interfaces, Inc; (Cataloging) Innovative Interfaces, Inc; (Circulation) Innovative Interfaces, Inc; (Course Reserve) Innovative Interfaces, Inc; (OPAC) Innovative Interfaces, Inc; (Serials) Innovative Interfaces, Inc
Partic in Colorado Council of Medical Librarians; Colorado Library Consortium
Open Mon-Fri 8-4:30

M PORTER ADVENTIST HOSPITAL*, Harley E Rice Memorial Medical Library, 2525 S Downing St, 80210. SAN 301-8636. Tel: 303-778-5656. E-mail: porterlibrary@centura.org. Web Site: www.centura.org. *Libr Supvr,* Christine Fleuriel; Staff 1.4 (MLS 1.4)
Founded 1980
Library Holdings: Bk Titles 2,500; Per Subs 250
Subject Interests: Med, Nursing
Partic in Colorado Council of Medical Librarians; OCLC Online Computer Library Center, Inc
Open Mon-Fri 8-4

C REGIS UNIVERSITY, Dayton Memorial Library, 3333 Regis Blvd, D20, 80221-1099. SAN 301-8660. Tel: 303-458-4030, 303-458-4031. Interlibrary Loan Service Tel: 303-458-4263. Toll Free Tel: 800-388-2366, Ext 4031. FAX: 303-964-5497. Web Site: libguides.regis.edu/library. *Dean of Libr,* Erin McCaffrey; E-mail: emccaffr@regis.edu; *Access Serv Librn,* Ali Gomez; E-mail: agomez012@regis.edu; *Digital Initiatives Librn,* Hannah Miller; E-mail: hmiller003@regis.edu; *Res & Instruction Librn,* Paul Betty; E-mail: pbetty@regis.edu; *Archivist,* Position Currently Open; Staff 31 (MLS 15, Non-MLS 16)
Founded 1877. Enrl 16,800; Fac 400; Highest Degree: Doctorate
Library Holdings: AV Mats 100,000; e-books 10,000; Bk Titles 250,000; Bk Vols 300,000; Per Subs 25,000
Special Collections: Archives of Loretto Heights College; Archives of Regis College; Early 18th Century Religious Coll, pamphlets (American); Political Campaign Memorabilia; Western Jesuitica Coll. US Document Depository
Subject Interests: Bus, Liberal arts, Mgt, Relig
Automation Activity & Vendor Info: (Acquisitions) Innovative Interfaces, Inc; (Cataloging) Innovative Interfaces, Inc; (Circulation) Innovative Interfaces, Inc; (Course Reserve) Innovative Interfaces, Inc; (ILL) OCLC ILLiad; (Media Booking) Innovative Interfaces, Inc; (OPAC) Innovative Interfaces, Inc; (Serials) SerialsSolutions
Wireless access
Publications: Check It Out!
Partic in Colorado Academic Library Consortium; Colorado Alliance of Research Libraries; OCLC Online Computer Library Center, Inc
Special Services for the Blind - Computer with voice synthesizer for visually impaired persons
Open Mon-Thurs 7am-Midnight, Fri 7-6, Sat 9-6, Sun 11am-Midnight

SR SAINT JOHN'S CATHEDRAL LIBRARY*, 1350 Washington St, 80203. SAN 375-3468. Tel: 303-831-7115, Ext 7728. FAX: 303-831-7119. E-mail: info@sjcathedral.org. Web Site: library.sjcathedral.org. *Adminr,* Sarah Dougherty; *Vols Librn,* Ann Jones; E-mail: annlindou@msn.com; Staff 4 (MLS 1, Non-MLS 3)
Founded 1950
Library Holdings: Large Print Bks 25; Bk Vols 4,800; Per Subs 28; Spec Interest Per Sub 23
Special Collections: Old Prayer Books (BCP)
Subject Interests: Church hist, Theol
Partic in OCLC Online Computer Library Center, Inc

M SCLHS SAINT JOSEPH HOSPITAL*, Clinical Research Library, 1375 E 19th Ave, 3rd Flr, 80218-1191. SAN 301-8733. Tel: 303-812-3625. Administration Tel: 303-812-3628. FAX: 303-812-4216. *Mgr, Libraries & Media Serv,* Karen Wells; E-mail: karen.wells@sclhealth.org; *Ref Librn,* Lynne Fox; E-mail: Lynne.Fox@sclhs.net; *Ref Librn,* Deb Weaver; E-mail: Deb.Weaver@sclhs.net; *Libr Tech 1,* Nell Able; E-mail: nell.able@sclhs.net; *Libr Tech 1,* Lavonne Griffie; E-mail: lavonne.griffie@sclhs.net; *Libr Tech 1,* Darian Ingram; E-mail: darian.ingram@sclhs.net; Staff 6 (MLS 3, Non-MLS 3)
Founded 1965
Subject Interests: Med, Nursing
Automation Activity & Vendor Info: (Cataloging) OCLC; (Circulation) OCLC; (ILL) OCLC; (OPAC) OCLC
Wireless access
Partic in Colorado Council of Medical Librarians
Restriction: Circulates for staff only, Lending to staff only, Med staff only, Open to employees & special libr, Open to hospital affiliates only, Open to staff only, Restricted access, Secured area only open to authorized personnel, Staff use only

Departmental Libraries:

GERVASINI HEALTH LIBRARY, 1375 E 19th Ave, 1st Flr, 80218. Tel: 303 812-3622. Administration Tel: 303 812-3628. Administration FAX: 303 812-4216. Web Site: sclhealth.org/locations/saint-joseph-hospital/patients-visitors/gervasini-collection. *Mgr, Libraries & Media Serv,* Karen Wells; E-mail: karen.wells@sclhealth.org; *Consumer Health Ref Librn,* Amy Six-Means
Open Mon-Fri 8-4:30

SR TEMPLE EMANUEL LIBRARY*, Brenner Library, 51 Grape St, 80220. SAN 378-3790. Tel: 303-388-4013. FAX: 303-388-6328. E-mail: shalom@emanueldenver.org. Web Site: www.emanueldenver.org/learning/library. *Librn,* Rita Dahlke; Staff 1 (Non-MLS 1)
Library Holdings: AV Mats 600; Large Print Bks 25; Bk Titles 7,000; Bk Vols 10,000; Per Subs 30; Talking Bks 40
Automation Activity & Vendor Info: (Cataloging) Follett Software; (Circulation) Follett Software
Open Mon 10-5, Tues & Thurs 10-6, Wed 10-8:30, Sat 9-1:30, Sun 8:30-2

GL US COURTS LIBRARY - TENTH CIRCUIT COURT OF APPEALS*, Byron Rogers Courthouse, 1929 Stout St, Rm 430, 80294. SAN 301-8822. Tel: 303-844-3591. E-mail: library@ca10.uscourts.gov. Web Site: www.ca10.uscourts.gov/library. *Circuit Librn,* Diane Bauersfeld; Tel: 303-335-2654, E-mail: diane_bauersfeld@ca10.uscourts.gov; *Br Mgr,* Meg Martin; *Br Mgr,* Gregory Townsend; *Br Tech,* Amber Bell; Staff 23 (MLS 10, Non-MLS 13)
Founded 1929
Library Holdings: Bk Vols 36,000

Subject Interests: Law
Automation Activity & Vendor Info: (Acquisitions) SirsiDynix; (Cataloging) SirsiDynix; (Circulation) SirsiDynix
Wireless access
Open Mon-Fri 8-4:30
Restriction: Circulates for staff only

G UNITED STATES DEPARTMENT OF THE INTERIOR*, Bureau of Reclamation Library, Denver Fed Ctr, Sixth Ave & Kipling St, Bldg 67, 80225. (Mail add: PO Box 25007, 80225-0007), SAN 335-7392. Tel: 303-445-2072. E-mail: library@usbr.gov. Web Site: www.usbr.gov/library. *Tech Info Spec,* Kristi Thompson; Tel: 303-445-2039, E-mail: kthompson@usbr.gov; Staff 1 (Non-MLS 1)
Founded 1945
Library Holdings: Bk Titles 8,000
Special Collections: Construction Specifications
Subject Interests: Construction
Automation Activity & Vendor Info: (Cataloging) EOS International; (Circulation) EOS International; (ILL) OCLC; (OPAC) EOS International; (Serials) EOS International
Function: Govt ref serv

G UNITED STATES ENVIRONMENTAL PROTECTION*, Region 8 Technical Library, 1595 Wynkoop St, 3rd Flr, 80202-1129. SAN 301-8334. Tel: 303-312-7226. Toll Free Tel: 800-227-8917. FAX: 303-312-6007. E-mail: library-reg8@epa.gov. Web Site: www.epa.gov/libraries/region-8-technical-library-services. *Supvry Librn,* Dedre Henderson; Tel: 303-312-6745, E-mail: henderson.dedre@epa.gov; Staff 1 (MLS 1)
Founded 1973
Subject Interests: Air pollution, Environ, Mining, Water pollution, Wetlands
Wireless access
Function: 24/7 Online cat, Doc delivery serv, Govt ref serv, ILL available, Mail & tel request accepted, Mail loans to mem, Online cat, Ref & res
Partic in EPA National Libr Network
Open Mon-Thurs 8-4
Restriction: Borrowing requests are handled by ILL, Photo ID required for access

G UNITED STATES ENVIRONMENTAL PROTECTION NATIONAL ENFORCEMENT INVESTIGATIONS CENTER*, One Denver Federal Ctr, Bldg 25, Door W-2, 80225. (Mail add: PO Box 25227, 80225-0227), SAN 329-0786. Administration Tel: 303-462-9350. FAX: 303-462-9354. E-mail: NEIC-Library@epamail.epa.gov. Web Site: www.epa.gov/enforcement/national-enforcement-investigations-center-neic. *Librn,* Nancy B Greer; Staff 1 (MLS 1)
Founded 1976
Library Holdings: Bk Titles 4,500; Per Subs 10
Special Collections: EPA Methods Coll
Subject Interests: Analytical chem, Environ law, Indust chem
Function: ILL available, Mail & tel request accepted, Online cat, Res libr
Partic in Federal Library & Information Network
Restriction: Open to pub by appt only

G UNITED STATES GEOLOGICAL SURVEY LIBRARY*, Bldg 41, Rm 145, Denver Federal Ctr, 80225. (Mail add: PO Box 25046, Stop 914, 80225-0046), SAN 320-1260. Tel: 303-236-1000. Circulation Tel: 303-236-1015. Circulation FAX: 303-236-1013. E-mail: den_lib@usgs.gov. Web Site: library.usgs.gov. *Supvr, Tech Info Spec,* Keith Van Cleave; E-mail: kvancleave@usgs.gov; Staff 4 (MLS 4)
Founded 1948
Library Holdings: CDs 2,200; e-books 800; e-journals 1,000; Bk Titles 230,000
Special Collections: USGS Geological Division Field Records; USGS Historical Photographs
Subject Interests: Earth sci, Geol
Wireless access
Partic in OCLC Online Computer Library Center, Inc
Open Mon-Fri 8-4

C UNIVERSITY OF DENVER, Penrose Library, 2150 E Evans Ave, 80208. SAN 335-766X. Tel: 303-871-3441. Circulation Tel: 303-871-3707. Interlibrary Loan Service Tel: 303-871-3150. Reference Tel: 303-871-2905. Administration Tel: 303-871-2007. FAX: 303-871-2290. Interlibrary Loan Service FAX: 303-871-3446. Web Site: library.du.edu. *Dean & Dir, Libr Serv,* Michael Levine-Clark; E-mail: michael.levine-clark@du.edu; *Associate Dean for Student & Scholar Services,* Carrie Forbes; *Business & Economics Reference Librn,* Esther Gil; *Arts & Humanities Reference Librn,* Peggy Keeran; *Rare Bks, Spec Coll Librn,* Kate Crowe; *Cat,* Karl Pettitt; *Ref (Info Servs),* Chris Brown; *Ref (Info Servs),* Bridget Farrell; Staff 19 (MLS 19)
Founded 1864. Enrl 7,390; Fac 424; Highest Degree: Doctorate
Library Holdings: Bk Vols 909,100; Per Subs 5,540
Special Collections: Ira M Beck Memorial Archives; Levette J Davidson Folklore Coll; Margaret Husted Culinary Coll; Papers of Congressman Wayne Aspinall; Papers of Senator Peter Dominick; The Dance Archive. US Document Depository
Automation Activity & Vendor Info: (Acquisitions) Ex Libris Group; (Cataloging) Ex Libris Group; (Circulation) Ex Libris Group; (Serials) Ex Libris Group
Wireless access
Partic in Colorado Alliance of Research Libraries; Greater Western Library Alliance; OCLC Online Computer Library Center, Inc
Friends of the Library Group

Departmental Libraries:

MUSIC LIBRARY, Lamont School of Music, Rm 440, 2344 E Iliff Ave, 80208, SAN 301-8199. Tel: 303-871-6421. E-mail: musiclibrary@du.edu. Web Site: library.du.edu/collections-library-materials/music-library. *Music & Performing Arts Librn,* Woody Colahan; Tel: 303-871-6427, E-mail: ellwood.colahan@du.edu
Founded 1985
Library Holdings: AV Mats 17,000; Music Scores 26,000; Bk Vols 18,000
Open Mon-Thurs 8:30am-10pm, Fri 8:30-6, Sat & Sun 11-5

CL WESTMINSTER LAW LIBRARY, Sturm College of Law, 2255 E Evans Ave, 80208, SAN 335-7694. Tel: 303-871-6188. Reference Tel: 303-871-6206. FAX: 303-871-6999. Web Site: lawlibrary.du.edu. *Assoc Dean,* Catherine Dunn; Tel: 303-871-6494, E-mail: cmdunn@law.du.edu; *Asst Dir,* Madeline Cohen; Tel: 303-871-6252, E-mail: mcohen@law.du.edu; *Head, Access Serv,* Lewis Zimmerman; Tel; 303-871-6364, E-mail: lzimmerman@law.du.edu; *Head, Tech Serv,* Andi Molinet; Tel: 303-871-6363, E-mail: amolinet@law.du.edu; *Fac Serv Librn,* Michelle Penn; Tel: 303-871-6827, E-mail: mpenn@law.du.edu; *Ref Librn,* Karina Condra; Tel: 303-871-6567, E-mail: kcondra@law.du.edu; *Ref Librn,* Michael Whitlow; Tel: 303-871-6206, E-mail: mwhitlow@law.du.edu; Staff 12.5 (MLS 7.5, Non-MLS 5)
Enrl 1,000
Library Holdings: Bk Vols 420,007
Special Collections: Colorado Legislative Council Reports; Howard Jenkins Coll; Hughes Rare Book Room; Sturm College of Law Coll. US Document Depository
Automation Activity & Vendor Info: (Acquisitions) Innovative Interfaces, Inc; (Cataloging) Innovative Interfaces, Inc; (Circulation) Innovative Interfaces, Inc
Partic in Colorado Association of Law Libraries; OCLC Online Computer Library Center, Inc
Publications: Hearsay Blog (Newsletter)
Restriction: Circ limited

DOLORES

S ANASAZI HERITAGE CENTER RESEARCH LIBRARY*, Canyons of the Ancients Visitor Center & Museum, 27501 Hwy 184, 81323. Tel: 970-882-5600. FAX: 970-882-7035. Web Site: www.blm.gov/visit/anasazi-heritage-center.
Library Holdings: AV Mats 60; CDs 6; DVDs 14; Bk Vols 6,000; Per Subs 9; Videos 210
Subject Interests: Anasazi, Archaeology, Four Corners tribes
Function: Wheelchair accessible
Open Mon-Sun (Winter) 10-4; Mon-Sun (Summer) 9-5
Friends of the Library Group

P DOLORES PUBLIC LIBRARY*, 1002 Railroad Ave, 81323. (Mail add: PO Box 847, 81323-0847), SAN 301-892X. Tel: 970-882-4127. FAX: 970-882-2224. E-mail: circ@doloreslibrary.org. Web Site: doloreslibrary.org. *Dir,* Diana Donohue; E-mail: diana@doloreslibrary.org; Staff 6 (Non-MLS 6)
Founded 1956. Pop 8,000; Circ 25,000
Library Holdings: Audiobooks 2,000; CDs 25; DVDs 230; e-books 1; Large Print Bks 220; Bk Titles 22,000; Per Subs 30
Special Collections: Archeology 200; Railroad Coll; Spanish (Children's Dual-Language Books). Oral History
Subject Interests: Colorado, Local hist
Automation Activity & Vendor Info: (Acquisitions) LibLime; (Cataloging) LibLime; (Circulation) LibLime; (Course Reserve) LibLime; (ILL) Fretwell-Downing; (Serials) Horizon
Wireless access
Function: Adult bk club, After school storytime, Art exhibits, Audiobks via web, Bks on cassette, Bks on CD, Children's prog, Computer training, Computers for patron use, Digital talking bks, Doc delivery serv, Electronic databases & coll, Holiday prog, ILL available, Internet access, Magnifiers for reading, Music CDs, Online cat, Online ref, Photocopying/Printing, Prog for adults, Prog for children & young adult, Scanner, Story hour, Summer reading prog, Tax forms, Teen prog, VHS videos, Wheelchair accessible
Publications: Book List
Partic in OCLC Online Computer Library Center, Inc
Special Services for the Blind - Talking bks

Open Mon-Thurs 9-6, Fri 9-5, Sat 9-3
Friends of the Library Group

DOVE CREEK

P DOLORES COUNTY PUBLIC LIBRARY*, 525 N Main St, 81324. (Mail add: PO Box 578, 81324-0578), SAN 376-2823. Tel: 970-677-2389. FAX: 970-677-2389. Web Site: www.dc2j.org/home/library. *Libr Dir,* Laurie Ernst; E-mail: lernst@dc2j.org; *Librn,* Linda Deremo
Founded 1970. Pop 1,700
Library Holdings: Audiobooks 3,327; CDs 303; DVDs 1,698; Large Print Bks 500; Bk Titles 31,726; Per Subs 12
Automation Activity & Vendor Info: (Cataloging) ByWater Solutions; (Circulation) ByWater Solutions; (ILL) Koha
Wireless access
Partic in Access Colo Libr Info Network; Colorado Library Consortium
Special Services for the Blind - Bks on cassette
Open Mon-Thurs 7:30-6, Fri 9-Noon; Mon & Wed (Summer) 9-5
Branches: 2
PIONEER READING CENTER, Pioneer Reading Ctr, 8540 Rd 7 2, 81324. Tel: 970-677-2787. *Librn,* Barbara Saunders
Library Holdings: Bk Titles 1,375
Open Tues & Thurs 11-1
RICO PUBLIC, Two N Commercial St, Rico, 81332. (Mail add: PO Box 69, Rico, 81332-0069). Tel: 970-967-2103. FAX: 970-967-2103. *Librn,* Susan Robertson
Library Holdings: Bk Titles 3,200
Open Wed & Fri 1-7
Friends of the Library Group

DURANGO

P DURANGO PUBLIC LIBRARY, 1900 E Third Ave, 81301. SAN 301-8938. Tel: 970-375-3380. Interlibrary Loan Service Tel: 970-375-3393. Administration Tel: 970-375-3381. FAX: 970-375-3398. Reference E-mail: reference@durangogov.org. Web Site: durango.ent.sirsi.net. *Libr Dir,* Sandy Irwin; Tel: 970-375-3389, E-mail: sandy.irwin@durangogov.org; *Asst Dir,* Colleen Galvin; Tel: 970-375-3384, E-mail: colleen.galvin@durangogov.org; *Adult Serv, Circ Serv Supvr,* Daisy Grice; Tel: 970-375-3387, E-mail: daisy.grice@durangogov.org; *Supvr, Coll Develop,* Donna Arment; Tel: 970-375-3386, E-mail: donna.arment@durangogov.org; *Youth Serv Supvr,* Callie Blackmer; Tel: 970-375-3385, E-mail: callie.blackmer@durangogov.org; Staff 17 (MLS 8, Non-MLS 9)
Founded 1889. Pop 56,221; Circ 395,797
Subject Interests: Patents trademarks
Automation Activity & Vendor Info: (Acquisitions) SirsiDynix; (Cataloging) SirsiDynix; (Circulation) SirsiDynix; (OPAC) SirsiDynix-Enterprise
Wireless access
Function: 24/7 Electronic res, 24/7 Online cat, Activity rm, After school storytime, Archival coll, Art exhibits, Art programs, Audio & video playback equip for onsite use, Audiobks on Playaways & MP3, Audiobks via web, AV serv, Bks on CD, Children's prog, Computer training, Computers for patron use, Electronic databases & coll, For res purposes, Free DVD rentals, Home delivery & serv to seniorr ctr & nursing homes, Homebound delivery serv, ILL available, Internet access, Large print keyboards, Life-long learning prog for all ages, Magazines, Mail & tel request accepted, Mango lang, Meeting rooms, Movies, Music CDs, Online cat, Outreach serv, OverDrive digital audio bks, Photocopying/Printing, Preschool outreach, Preschool reading prog, Printer for laptops & handheld devices, Prog for adults, Prog for children & young adult, Ref & res, Ref serv available, Res assist avail, Scanner, Senior outreach, Spanish lang bks, Spoken cassettes & CDs, Spoken cassettes & DVDs, STEM programs, Story hour, Study rm, Summer reading prog, Tax forms, Teen prog, Telephone ref, Visual arts prog, Wheelchair accessible
Friends of the Library Group

C FORT LEWIS COLLEGE*, John F Reed Library, 1000 Rim Dr, 81301-3999. SAN 301-8946. Tel: 970-247-7250. Circulation Tel: 970-247-7270. Reference Tel: 970-247-7551. FAX: 970-247-7149. E-mail: library@fortlewis.edu. Web Site: library.fortlewis.edu. *Dir, E-Resources Librn,* Astrid Oliver; E-mail: oliver_a@fortlewis.edu; Staff 15 (MLS 7, Non-MLS 8)
Founded 1911. Enrl 3,900; Fac 300; Highest Degree: Bachelor
Library Holdings: e-journals 17,151; Bk Titles 198,645; Per Subs 845
Automation Activity & Vendor Info: (Acquisitions) Innovative Interfaces, Inc; (Cataloging) Innovative Interfaces, Inc; (Circulation) Innovative Interfaces, Inc; (OPAC) Innovative Interfaces, Inc; (Serials) Innovative Interfaces, Inc
Wireless access
Partic in Access Colo Libr Info Network
Open Mon-Thurs 7:30am-10pm, Fri 7:30-5, Sat 1-5, Sun 1-10
Friends of the Library Group

P SOUTHWEST LA PLATA LIBRARY DISTRICT*, Sunnyside Public Library, 75 County Rd 218, 81303. Tel: 970-375-3816. *Br Mgr,* Tricia Winslow; E-mail: tricia.swlpld@gmail.com
Wireless access
Open Mon 1-7, Tues-Thurs 2-7
Branches: 1
FORT LEWIS MESA PUBLIC LIBRARY, 11274 Colorado State Hwy 140, Hesperus, 81326, SAN 321-9313. Tel: 970-588-3331. *Br Mgr,* Chris Conrad; E-mail: chris.conrad.swlpld@gmail.com
Library Holdings: Bk Vols 3,200
Open Mon-Thurs 2-7

EADS

P KIOWA COUNTY PUBLIC LIBRARY DISTRICT, 1305 Goff St, 81036. (Mail add: PO Box 790, 81036-0790), SAN 301-8962. Tel: 719-438-5581. FAX: 719-438-6581. E-mail: kcpld.eads@gmail.com. Web Site: kiowacounty.colibraries.org. *Dir,* Kemma Alfano; E-mail: kcpld.director@gmail.com; *Asst Dir,* Valorie Brigss; E-mail: kcpld.assistant@gmail.com; Staff 3 (Non-MLS 3)
Founded 1939. Pop 1,800; Circ 8,789
Library Holdings: Large Print Bks 75; Bk Vols 8,000; Per Subs 20; Talking Bks 100
Wireless access
Function: Computer training, Computers for patron use, Electronic databases & coll, ILL available, Internet access, Magazines, Microfiche/film & reading machines, Movies, Online cat, Photocopying/Printing, Summer reading prog, Tax forms
Special Services for the Blind - Cassettes; Copier with enlargement capabilities; Large print bks; PC for people with disabilities; Talking bks; Videos on blindness & physical disabilties
Open Tues-Fri 8-4:30

EAGLE

P EAGLE VALLEY LIBRARY DISTRICT*, 600 Broadway St, 81631. (Mail add: PO Box 240, 81631-0240), SAN 335-7724. Tel: 970-328-8800. FAX: 970-328-6901. Web Site: www.evld.org. *Dir,* Linda Tillson; E-mail: ltillson@evld.org; Staff 33 (MLS 13, Non-MLS 20)
Founded 1993. Pop 45,000; Circ 276,418
Library Holdings: AV Mats 5,508; CDs 816; DVDs 3,036; Bk Vols 44,901; Per Subs 228
Special Collections: Colorado Coll; Eagle County Hist Coll
Automation Activity & Vendor Info: (Cataloging) Innovative Interfaces, Inc; (Circulation) Innovative Interfaces, Inc; (ILL) OCLC; (OPAC) Innovative Interfaces, Inc; (Serials) Innovative Interfaces, Inc
Wireless access
Function: After school storytime
Partic in Marmot Library Network; OCLC Online Computer Library Center, Inc
Open Mon-Thurs 10-8, Fri & Sat 10-5, Sun 1-5
Friends of the Library Group
Branches: 2
AVON PUBLIC LIBRARY, 200 Benchmark Rd, Avon, 81620. (Mail add: PO Box 977, Avon, 81620-0977), SAN 335-7740. Tel: 970-949-6797. FAX: 970-949-0233. *Br Mgr,* Kim Saalfeld
Library Holdings: AV Mats 8,052; CDs 1,339; DVDs 4,297; Bk Vols 59,910; Per Subs 265
Open Mon-Thurs 10-8, Fri & Sat 10-5, Sun 1-5
Friends of the Library Group
GYPSUM PUBLIC LIBRARY, 48 Lundgren Blvd, Gypsum, 81637. (Mail add: PO Box 979, Gypsum, 81637-0979), SAN 377-7227. Tel: 970-524-5080. FAX: 970-524-5082. *Br Mgr,* Position Currently Open
Library Holdings: AV Mats 3,183; CDs 383; DVDs 891; Bk Vols 23,915; Per Subs 64; Videos 1,303
Open Mon 10-8, Tues-Thurs 10-6
Friends of the Library Group

EATON

P EATON PUBLIC LIBRARY*, 132 Maple Ave, 80615-3441. SAN 301-8970. Tel: 970-454-2189. FAX: 970-454-2958. Web Site: www.Colorado.gov/pacific/townofeaton/eaton-public-library. *Libr Dir,* Brenda Carns; E-mail: BCarns@highplains.us; Staff 6 (MLS 2, Non-MLS 4)
Founded 1901. Pop 10,343; Circ 94,539
Jan 2017-Dec 2017 Income $862,966, Locally Generated Income $862,966, Other $4,000. Mats Exp $58,666, Books $33,929, Per/Ser (Incl. Access Fees) $3,137, AV Mat $21,600. Sal $244,716 (Prof $64,377)
Library Holdings: Audiobooks 1,626; CDs 400; DVDs 2,493; Large Print Bks 630; Bk Vols 24,416; Per Subs 25; Videos 625
Automation Activity & Vendor Info: (Acquisitions) Innovative Interfaces, Inc - Sierra; (Cataloging) Innovative Interfaces, Inc - Sierra; (Circulation) Innovative Interfaces, Inc - Sierra; (ILL) OCLC ILLiad; (OPAC) Innovative Interfaces, Inc - Sierra
Wireless access

Function: 24/7 Electronic res, 24/7 Online cat, Activity rm, Adult bk club, After school storytime, Art exhibits, Audiobks on Playaways & MP3, Bks on CD, Children's prog, Computer training, Computers for patron use, Doc delivery serv, E-Reserves, Family literacy, Free DVD rentals, ILL available, Magazines, Mango lang, Online cat, OverDrive digital audio bks, Photocopying/Printing, Preschool reading prog, Scanner, Tax forms, Wheelchair accessible
Mem of High Plains Library District
Open Mon-Thurs 9-7, Fri 9-6, Sat 10-5
Friends of the Library Group

ELIZABETH

P PINES & PLAINS LIBRARIES*, 651 W Beverly St, 80107-7560. SAN 335-8534. Tel: 303-646-3416. FAX: 303-646-0315. E-mail: simla@pplibraries.org. Web Site: pplibraries.org. *Dir,* Tim Miller; Tel: 303-358-8820
Founded 1937. Pop 22,000
Subject Interests: Agr, Antiques, Local hist
Automation Activity & Vendor Info: (Cataloging) SirsiDynix; (Circulation) SirsiDynix
Open Mon-Thurs 9-8, Fri 9-5, Sat 10-5
Friends of the Library Group
Branches: 4
ELBERT BRANCH, 24489 Main St, Elbert, 80106. (Mail add: PO Box 38, Elbert, 80106-0038). Tel: 303-648-3533. FAX: 303-648-3853. *Br Mgr,* Sue Dischner
Open Mon 10-3, Tues-Thurs 4:30-7, Sat 10-3
ELIZABETH BRANCH, 651 W Beverly St, 80107. Tel: 303-646-3416. FAX: 303-646-9217. E-mail: elizabeth@elbertcountylibrary.org. *Br Mgr,* Jan Gabehart
Open Mon-Thurs 9-7, Fri & Sat 9-5
Friends of the Library Group
KIOWA BRANCH, 331 Comanche, Kiowa, 80117. (Mail add: PO Box 538, Kiowa, 80117-0538). Tel: 303-621-2111. FAX: 303-621-2754. *Br Mgr,* Sue Dischner; E-mail: sdischner@elbertcountylibrary.org
Open Mon-Thurs 10-6, Fri 9-5, Sat 9-2
SIMLA BRANCH, 504 Washington, Simla, 80835. (Mail add: PO Box 245, Simla, 80835), SAN 335-8593. Tel: 719-541-2573. FAX: 719-541-2152. *Br Mgr,* Shanna Engler
Open Mon-Fri 9-7, Sat 10-2
Friends of the Library Group

ENGLEWOOD

P ARAPAHOE LIBRARY DISTRICT*, 12855 E Adam Aircraft Circle, 80112. SAN 335-9042. Tel: 303-542-7279. FAX: 303-798-2485. Web Site: arapahoelibraries.org. *Exec Dir,* Oli Sanidas
Founded 1966. Pop 202,000; Circ 4,510,000
Library Holdings: AV Mats 79,281; Large Print Bks 6,802; Bk Titles 225,971; Bk Vols 477,298; Per Subs 1,691; Talking Bks 25,047
Wireless access
Open Mon-Thurs 9-9, Fri 9-7, Sat 9-5, Sun 12-6
Friends of the Library Group
Branches: 8
CASTLEWOOD LIBRARY, 6739 S Uinta St, Centennial, 80112, SAN 335-9190. *Libr Mgr,* Nicole Wilhelms; E-mail: nwilhelms@ald.lib.co.us
Open Mon-Thurs 9-9, Fri 9-7, Sat 9-5, Sun 12-6
Friends of the Library Group
DAVIES LIBRARY, 303 Third Ave, Deer Trail, 80105, SAN 335-9131. Tel: 303-769-4310. *Libr Mgr,* Cynthia Kiyotake; E-mail: ckiyotake@ald.lib.co.us
Open Mon & Wed 9-8, Tues, Thurs, Fri & Sat 9-5
Friends of the Library Group
KELVER PUBLIC LIBRARY, 404 E Front St, Byers, 80103, SAN 335-9077. Tel: 303-822-9392. *Libr Mgr,* Cynthia Kiyotake
Open Mon, Wed & Fri 8-5, Tues & Thurs 8-8, Sat 9-5
Friends of the Library Group
KOELBEL PUBLIC LIBRARY, 5955 S Holly St, Centennial, 80121, SAN 335-9107. *Libr Mgr,* Taliah Abdullah; E-mail: tabdullah@ald.lib.co.us
Open Mon-Thurs 9-9, Fri 9-7, Sat 9-5, Sun 12-6
Friends of the Library Group
ELOISE MAY LIBRARY, 1471 S Parker Rd, Denver, 80231. *Libr Mgr,* Holly Whelan
Open Mon-Thurs 9-9, Fri 9-7, Sat 9-5, Sun 12-6
Friends of the Library Group
SHERIDAN PUBLIC LIBRARY, 3425 W Oxford Ave, Sheridan, 80236, SAN 335-9166. *Libr Mgr,* Cynthia Kiyotake
Open Mon-Thurs 9-8, Fri 9-7, Sat 9-5, Sun 12-6
Friends of the Library Group
SMOKY HILL PUBLIC LIBRARY, 5430 S Biscay Circle, Centennial, 80015, SAN 335-9174. *Libr Mgr,* Holly Whelan; E-mail: hwhelan@ald.lib.co.us
Open Mon-Thurs 9-9, Fri 9-7, Sat 9-5, Sun 12-6
Friends of the Library Group
SOUTHGLENN PUBLIC LIBRARY, 6972 S Vine St, Centennial, 80122-3270, SAN 373-5753. *Libr Mgr,* Nicole Wilhelms
Open Mon-Thurs 9-9, Fri & Sat 9-7, Sun 12-6
Friends of the Library Group

S DEPARTMENT OF HUMAN SERVICES-YOUTH CORRECTIONS*, Marvin W Foote Youth Services Center Library, 13500 E Fremont Pl, 80112. Tel: 303-768-7529, 303-768-7566. FAX: 303-768-7525. *Head Librn,* Brian Smith; E-mail: brianz.smith@state.co.us
Library Holdings: Bk Vols 4,000; Per Subs 12
Wireless access

P ENGLEWOOD PUBLIC LIBRARY*, 1000 Englewood Pkwy, 80110. SAN 301-9012. Tel: 303-762-2550. FAX: 303-783-6890. Web Site: www.englewoodco.gov/government/city-departments/library. *Libr Dir,* Christina Underhill; E-mail: cunderhill@englewoodco.gov; *Libr Mgr,* Mark Mullis; Tel: 303-762-2566, E-mail: mmullis@englewoodco.gov; Staff 16 (MLS 8, Non-MLS 8)
Founded 1920. Pop 32,500; Circ 197,729
Library Holdings: AV Mats 7,505; Bk Vols 105,108; Per Subs 310
Special Collections: Englewood Local History Coll, docs, newsp & photogs
Automation Activity & Vendor Info: (Acquisitions) SirsiDynix; (Cataloging) SirsiDynix; (Circulation) SirsiDynix; (OPAC) SirsiDynix
Wireless access
Partic in Colorado Library Consortium
Open Mon-Sat 12-5
Friends of the Library Group

R FIRST PLYMOUTH CONGREGATIONAL CHURCH LIBRARY*, 3501 S Colorado Blvd, 80113. SAN 301-9020. Tel: 303-762-0616. FAX: 303-789-2783. E-mail: info@firstplymouthchurch.org. Web Site: www.firstplymouthchurch.org.
Library Holdings: Bk Vols 3,000
Open Mon-Fri 8:30-4:30, Sun 8-Noon

ESTES PARK

P ESTES VALLEY LIBRARY*, 335 E Elkhorn Ave, 80517. (Mail add: PO Box 1687, 80517-1687), SAN 301-9055. Tel: 970-586-8116. Circulation Tel: 970-586-8116, Ext 829. FAX: 970-586-0189. Web Site: www.estesvalleylibrary.org. *Dir,* Claudine Perrault; E-mail: cperrault@estesvalleylibrary.org; *Head, Circ,* Peggy Moore; E-mail: pmoore@estesvalleylibrary.org; *Adult Serv,* Cheryl Homan-Wendell; E-mail: chomanwendell@estesvalleylibrary.org; Staff 17 (MLS 1, Non-MLS 16)
Founded 1922. Pop 12,615; Circ 134,743
Library Holdings: AV Mats 4,000; Large Print Bks 1,000; Bk Titles 50,000; Bk Vols 61,000; Per Subs 200
Special Collections: Oral History
Subject Interests: Local hist
Automation Activity & Vendor Info: (Cataloging) TLC (The Library Corporation); (Circulation) TLC (The Library Corporation); (OPAC) TLC (The Library Corporation)
Wireless access
Special Services for the Blind - Bks on cassette; Bks on CD; Talking bks
Open Mon-Thurs (Fall & Winter) 10-9, Fri & Sat 10-5, Sun 1-5; Mon-Thurs (Summer) 9-9, Fri & Sat 9-5, Sun 1-5
Friends of the Library Group

FLAGLER

P FLAGLER COMMUNITY LIBRARY*, 311 Main Ave, 80815. (Mail add: PO Box 364, 80815-0364), SAN 301-9071. Tel: 719-765-4310. FAX: 719-765-4498. E-mail: flibrary@esrta.com, townflag@esrta.com. Web Site: flaglercolorado.com/library. *Library Contact,* Doris King
Founded 1920. Pop 2,325; Circ 5,013
Library Holdings: Bk Titles 9,961; Per Subs 5
Special Collections: Hal Borland Coll; Page History Room, American History
Wireless access
Open Mon-Fri 8-4
Bookmobiles: 1

FLEMING

P FLEMING COMMUNITY LIBRARY*, 506 N Fremont Ave, 80728. SAN 301-908X. Tel: 970-265-2022. Web Site: www.flemingschools.org/domain/18. *Libr Dir,* Sandy Kinzie; Staff 2 (MLS 1, Non-MLS 1)
Pop 500; Circ 12,998
Library Holdings: Audiobooks 688; Bk Titles 12,831; Per Subs 35
Automation Activity & Vendor Info: (Cataloging) Follett Software; (Circulation) Follett Software
Wireless access
Special Services for the Deaf - ADA equip; Closed caption videos

Special Services for the Blind - Accessible computers; PC for people with disabilities
Open Mon 10-2, Tues-Thurs 8-6, Fri 8-5
Friends of the Library Group

FLORENCE

P JOHN C FREMONT LIBRARY DISTRICT, 130 Church Ave, 81226. SAN 301-9098. Tel: 719-784-4649. FAX: 719-784-3764. Web Site: www.jcfld.org. *Dir,* Tabitha Selakovich; E-mail: Tabby.Selakovich@JCFLD.org; *Asst Dir,* Vicki Masar; E-mail: Vicki.Masar@JCFLD.org; *Youth Serv Prog Coordr,* Deborah Plonkey; E-mail: deborah.plonkey@jcfld.org; Staff 6 (Non-MLS 6)
Founded 1908. Pop 5,000; Circ 12,000
Library Holdings: Bks on Deafness & Sign Lang 10; CDs 150; DVDs 250; High Interest/Low Vocabulary Bk Vols 100; Large Print Bks 150; Bk Titles 12,000; Bk Vols 24,000; Per Subs 24; Talking Bks 200; Videos 150
Wireless access
Function: 24/7 Electronic res, 24/7 Online cat, Adult bk club, Art exhibits, Audiobks via web, Bi-weekly Writer's Group, Bk club(s), Bks on CD, Children's prog, Computers for patron use, Digital talking bks, Electronic databases & coll, Free DVD rentals, Home delivery & serv to seniorr ctr & nursing homes, Homebound delivery serv, ILL available, Internet access, Laminating, Large print keyboards, Magazines, Mail & tel request accepted, Movies, Music CDs, Online cat, Online ref, Outreach serv, Outside serv via phone, mail, e-mail & web, Photocopying/Printing, Preschool outreach, Prog for adults, Prog for children & young adult, Scanner, Serves people with intellectual disabilities, Spanish lang bks, Story hour, Summer reading prog, Tax forms, Teen prog, Wheelchair accessible
Partic in Colorado Library Consortium
Special Services for the Deaf - Bks on deafness & sign lang
Special Services for the Blind - Bks on CD; Digital talking bk; Home delivery serv; Large print bks; Large print bks & talking machines; Recorded bks; Talking bk & rec for the blind cat; Talking bks
Open Mon-Thurs 10-6, Fri 10-5, Sat 10-2
Friends of the Library Group

FORT CARSON

UNITED STATES ARMY

A GRANT LIBRARY*, 1637 Flint St, 80913-4105, SAN 335-7813. Tel: 719-526-2350. Circulation Tel: 719-526-2842. Interlibrary Loan Service Tel: 719-526-8142. FAX: 719-524-0070. Web Site: peregrine.usafa.af.mil/grant.html. *Actg Dir,* Kevin Patrick Bokay; Tel: 719-526-8144, E-mail: kevin.bokay@us.army.mil; *Circ Mgr,* Cassandra Osuji; E-mail: cassandra.osuji@carson.army.mil; *Libr Tech,* Marie Acfalle; E-mail: marie.acfalle@carson.army.mil; *Libr Tech,* Viviana Barron; E-mail: viviana.barron@carson.army.mil; *Tech Serv Mgr,* Nadine Salmons; Tel: 719-526-8140, E-mail: nadine.salmons@carson.army.mil; Staff 9 (MLS 2, Non-MLS 7)
Founded 1942
Library Holdings: AV Mats 4,849; Bk Titles 51,000; Per Subs 200
Special Collections: Colorado; Military Arts & Sciences
Function: Audio & video playback equip for onsite use, ILL available, Orientations, Outside serv via phone, mail, e-mail & web, Photocopying/Printing, Prog for children & young adult, Ref & res, Ref serv available, Res libr, Senior computer classes, Spoken cassettes & CDs, Spoken cassettes & DVDs, Summer reading prog, Tax forms, VHS videos, Wheelchair accessible
Open Mon-Thurs 11-8, Fri 11-5, Sat & Sun 10-6
Restriction: Circ to mil employees only

AM LANE MEDICAL LIBRARY - EVANS ARMY COMMUNITY HOSPITAL*, 1650 Cochrane Circle, 80913-4604, SAN 335-7848. Tel: 719-526-7285. FAX: 719-526-7113. E-mail: usarmy.carson.medcom-each.list.library@mail.mil. *Librn,* Janet Klieman; Staff 1 (MLS 1)
Founded 1952
Library Holdings: Bk Vols 2,400; Per Subs 120
Special Collections: Consumer's Coll
Subject Interests: Dentistry, Med, Mental health, Nursing, Orthopedics, Phys therapy, Veterinary med
Automation Activity & Vendor Info: (Acquisitions) Ex Libris Group; (Cataloging) Ex Libris Group; (Circulation) Ex Libris Group; (Course Reserve) Ex Libris Group; (ILL) Ex Libris Group; (Media Booking) Ex Libris Group; (OPAC) Ex Libris Group; (Serials) Ex Libris Group
Partic in OCLC Online Computer Library Center, Inc; Proquest Dialog
Publications: Patients Health
Open Mon-Fri 7-4

FORT COLLINS

S COLORADO PARKS & WILDLIFE, Research Library, 317 W Prospect Rd, 80526-2097. SAN 301-9101. Tel: 970-472-4353. FAX: 970-472-4457. Web Site: www.cpw.state.co.us/learn/pages/researchlibrary.aspx. *Research Librn,* Alexandria Austermann; E-mail: alexandria.austermann@state.co.us
Founded 1967
Subject Interests: Environ studies, Wildlife, Zoology
Publications: Division Reports; Special Reports; Technical Publications
Partic in Colorado Library Consortium
Restriction: Restricted access

C COLORADO STATE UNIVERSITY LIBRARIES, Morgan Library, 1201 Center Ave Mall, 80523. (Mail add: 1019 Campus Delivery, 80523-1019), SAN 335-7872. Tel: 970-491-1838. Circulation Tel: 970-491-1842. Interlibrary Loan Service Tel: 970-491-1868. Reference Tel: 970-491-1841. FAX: 970-491-1195. E-mail: library_help@colostate.edu. Web Site: lib.colostate.edu. *Dean of Libr,* Karen Estlund; E-mail: karen.estlund@colostate.edu; *Sr Assoc Dean for Collections & Discovery,* Dawn Paschal; E-mail: dawn.paschal@colostate.edu; *Assoc Dean, User Services & Assessment,* Amy Hoseth; E-mail: amy.hoseth@colostate.edu; *Interim Head, Research & Community Engagement,* Michelle Wilde; E-mail: michelle.wilde@colostate.edu; *Coordr, Acq/Metadata,* Nancy Hunter; E-mail: nancy.hunter@colostate.edu; *ILL & Reserves Coordr,* Cristi MacWaters; E-mail: cristi.macwaters@colostate.edu; Staff 23 (MLS 20, Non-MLS 3)
Founded 1870. Enrl 22,000; Fac 2,000; Highest Degree: Doctorate
Library Holdings: e-books 535,000; e-journals 48,896; Bk Vols 2,010,900; Per Subs 9,782
Special Collections: Agricultural and Natural Resources Archive; Germans From Russia; International Poster Coll; Vietnam War Fiction; Warren & Genevieve Garst Photographic Coll; Water Resources Archive, a-tapes, docs, maps, photos. State Document Depository; US Document Depository
Subject Interests: Agr, Engr, Natural res
Automation Activity & Vendor Info: (Acquisitions) Innovative Interfaces, Inc; (Cataloging) Innovative Interfaces, Inc; (Circulation) Innovative Interfaces, Inc; (Course Reserve) Atlas Systems; (ILL) OCLC; (OPAC) Innovative Interfaces, Inc; (Serials) Innovative Interfaces, Inc
Wireless access
Publications: Stay Connected
Partic in Association of Research Libraries; Coalition for Networked Information; Colorado Alliance of Research Libraries; Greater Western Library Alliance; LYRASIS; OCLC Online Computer Library Center, Inc
Friends of the Library Group

Departmental Libraries:

CM VETERINARY TEACHING HOSPITAL, 300 West Drake Rd, 80523-1620. Tel: 970-297-1213. FAX: 970-297-4141. E-mail: vetlib@mail.colostate.edu. Web Site: libguides.colostate.edu/c.php?g=835571. *Libr Tech,* Sherri McCaskill; E-mail: sherri.mccaskill@colostate.edu
Library Holdings: e-books 1,500; e-journals 115; Bk Titles 5,500; Bk Vols 12,000; Per Subs 162

J FRONT RANGE COMMUNITY COLLEGE*, Harmony Library, Larimer Campus, 4616 S Shields St, 80526. SAN 301-9144. Tel: 970-221-6740. Circulation Tel: 970-204-8401. FAX: 970-204-8444. E-mail: LCLibrarian@frontrange.edu. Web Site: www.frontrange.edu/campuses/libraries. *Sr Librn,* Molly Thompson; E-mail: molly.thompson@frontrange.edu; Staff 1 (MLS 1)
Founded 1989. Enrl 5,102; Fac 60; Highest Degree: Associate
Library Holdings: AV Mats 1,000; e-books 6,000; Bk Vols 11,000; Per Subs 100
Subject Interests: Nursing, Veterinary tech
Automation Activity & Vendor Info: (Cataloging) Innovative Interfaces, Inc; (Circulation) Innovative Interfaces, Inc; (Course Reserve) Innovative Interfaces, Inc; (OPAC) Innovative Interfaces, Inc
Wireless access
Partic in Colorado Library Consortium
Open Mon-Thurs 9-9, Fri 9-6, Sat 9-5, Sun 12-5
Friends of the Library Group

G NATIONAL FOREST SERVICE LIBRARY*, 240 W Prospect Rd, 80526. SAN 316-8964. Tel: 970-498-1207. Interlibrary Loan Service Tel: 970-498-1205. FAX: 970-498-1059. E-mail: SM.FS.FSLib@usda.gov. Web Site: www.fs.fed.us/library. *Librn,* Sarah Flick; Staff 11 (MLS 7, Non-MLS 4)
Founded 1966
Library Holdings: Bk Vols 375,000; Per Subs 200
Special Collections: Forest Service Reports
Subject Interests: Forestry, Hydrol, Range mgt, Recreation, Silviculture, Watershed, Wildlife
Automation Activity & Vendor Info: (Cataloging) Innovative Interfaces, Inc; (ILL) OCLC; (OPAC) Innovative Interfaces, Inc
Function: Computers for patron use, ILL available, Online cat
Publications: Monthly Alert
Open Mon-Fri 8-4:30
Restriction: Circ limited, Limited access for the pub, Non-circulating coll, Open to pub for ref & circ; with some limitations

P POUDRE RIVER PUBLIC LIBRARY DISTRICT*, Old Town Library, 201 Peterson St, 80524-2990. (Mail add: 301 E Olive St, 80524), SAN 301-9128. Tel: 970-221-6740. FAX: 970-221-6398. Web Site: www.poudrelibraries.org. *Dir,* David E Slivken; Tel: 970-221-6670, E-mail: dslivken@poudrelibraries.org; *Dep Dir,* Ken Draves; E-mail: kdraves@poudrelibraries.org; *Libr Mgr,* Eileen McCluskey; E-mail: emccluskey@poudrelibraries.org; *Communications Mgr,* Paula Watson-Lakamp; E-mail: library-pr@poudrelibraries.org; *Coll,* Tova Aragon; E-mail: tdaragon@poudrelibraries.org; Staff 68 (MLS 18, Non-MLS 50)
Founded 1900. Pop 190,000; Circ 3,000,000
Library Holdings: Audiobooks 13,981; AV Mats 628,760; e-books 60,534; Electronic Media & Resources 60; Bk Titles 1,404,497; Per Subs 632
Special Collections: Local History Archive. Municipal Document Depository; Oral History
Subject Interests: Historic maps, Local hist
Automation Activity & Vendor Info: (Acquisitions) Innovative Interfaces, Inc; (Cataloging) Innovative Interfaces, Inc; (Circulation) Innovative Interfaces, Inc; (Course Reserve) Innovative Interfaces, Inc; (ILL) Innovative Interfaces, Inc; (Media Booking) Innovative Interfaces, Inc; (OPAC) Innovative Interfaces, Inc; (Serials) Innovative Interfaces, Inc
Wireless access
Function: 24/7 Electronic res, 24/7 Online cat, 3D Printer, Adult bk club, Adult literacy prog, After school storytime, Audiobks via web, Bilingual assistance for Spanish patrons, Bk club(s), Bks on CD, Bus archives, Children's prog, Computer training, Computers for patron use, Digital talking bks, E-Readers, E-Reserves, Electronic databases & coll, Family literacy, Free DVD rentals, Genealogy discussion group, Govt ref serv, Health sci info serv, Holiday prog, Home delivery & serv to seniorr ctr & nursing homes, Homebound delivery serv, ILL available, Internet access, Life-long learning prog for all ages, Magazines, Meeting rooms, Microfiche/film & reading machines, Movies, Music CDs, Online cat, Online ref, Outreach serv, OverDrive digital audio bks, Photocopying/Printing, Preschool outreach, Prof lending libr, Prog for adults, Prog for children & young adult, Ref serv available, Res assist avail, Senior computer classes, Senior outreach, Serves people with intellectual disabilities, Spanish lang bks, Spoken cassettes & DVDs, Story hour, Study rm, Summer reading prog, Teen prog, Telephone ref, Wheelchair accessible, Workshops, Writing prog
Special Services for the Deaf - TDD equip; TTY equip
Special Services for the Blind - Accessible computers; Bks on CD; Bks on flash-memory cartridges; Copier with enlargement capabilities; Large print bks; Large screen computer & software; Playaways (bks on MP3)
Open Mon-Thurs 9-9, Fri 9-6, Sat 10-5, Sun Noon-5
Friends of the Library Group
Branches: 2
COUNCIL TREE LIBRARY, 2733 Council Tree Ave, Ste 200, 80525. Tel: 970-221-6740. *Mgr,* Currie Meyer; E-mail: cmeyer@poudrelibraries.org
Open Mon-Sat 9-9, Sun 12-6
Friends of the Library Group
HARMONY LIBRARY, 4616 S Shields St, 80526-3812. (Mail add: 301 E Olive St, 80524), SAN 378-1054. Tel: 970-221-6740. FAX: 970-204-8444. *Br Mgr,* Ken Draves; E-mail: kdraves@poudrelibraries.org
Open Mon-Thurs 9-9, Fri 9-6, Sat 9-5, Sun Noon-5
Friends of the Library Group

G UNITED STATES DEPARTMENT OF AGRICULTURE, National Wildlife Research Center Library, 4101 LaPorte Ave, 80521-2154. SAN 335-7422. Tel: 970-266-6023. Interlibrary Loan Service Tel: 970-266-6053. FAX: 970-266-6010. E-mail: NWRC.Library@aphis.usda.gov. Web Site: www.aphis.usda.gov/aphis/ourfocus/wildlifedamage/programs/nwrc/sa_information_services/ct_library. *Library Contact,* Jenna Edwards; E-mail: jennifer.m.edwards@aphis.usda.gov; Staff 1 (MLS 1)
Founded 1967
Library Holdings: Bk Titles 7,000; Per Subs 15; Spec Interest Per Sub 15
Special Collections: Human-Wildlife Conflicts; National Wildlife Research Center Authors Coll, reprints; Predator Management; US Fish & Wildlife Service Coll, publs; Wildlife Management Coll, dissertations & theses. Oral History
Subject Interests: Wildlife diseases
Automation Activity & Vendor Info: (Cataloging) EOS International; (Circulation) EOS International; (ILL) OCLC; (OPAC) EOS International; (Serials) EOS International
Wireless access
Function: ILL available, Mail & tel request accepted, Res libr
Publications: Annual Publications List

G US GEOLOGICAL SURVEY*, Fort Collins Science Center Library, 2150 Centre Ave, Bldg C, 80526. SAN 375-653X. Tel: 970-226-9403. FAX: 970-226-9230. Web Site: www.fort.usgs.gov. *Br Chief,* Tim Kern; E-mail: kernt@usgs.gov; Staff 1 (MLS 1)
Founded 1978
Library Holdings: Bk Titles 12,000; Bk Vols 14,000; Per Subs 89
Subject Interests: Biology, Ecology, Fisheries, Wildlife
Automation Activity & Vendor Info: (Cataloging) EOS International; (Circulation) EOS International; (OPAC) EOS International; (Serials) EOS International
Function: For res purposes
Partic in OCLC Online Computer Library Center, Inc
Open Mon-Fri 7:45-4:30

FORT LUPTON

P FORT LUPTON PUBLIC & SCHOOL LIBRARY*, 425 S Denver Ave, 80621. SAN 301-9187. Tel: 303-857-7180. FAX: 303-857-7190. Web Site: www.fortluptonlibrary.org. *Dir,* Sarah Frank; Staff 7 (MLS 3, Non-MLS 4)
Founded 1978
Library Holdings: Bk Titles 43,000; Bk Vols 45,500; Per Subs 108
Automation Activity & Vendor Info: (Cataloging) SirsiDynix; (Circulation) SirsiDynix; (OPAC) SirsiDynix
Wireless access
Mem of High Plains Library District
Open Mon-Thurs 7:30am-8pm, Fri 7:30-5, Sat 9-4

FORT MORGAN

P FORT MORGAN PUBLIC LIBRARY, 414 Main St, 80701. (Mail add: PO Box 100, 80701-0100), SAN 301-9209. Tel: 970-542-4000. FAX: 970-542-4013. Web Site: www.cityoffortmorgan.com/99/library. *Dir, Libr & Mus Serv,* Chandra McCoy; Tel: 970-542-4006, E-mail: chandra.mccoy@cityoffortmorgan.com; Staff 7 (MLS 1, Non-MLS 6)
Founded 1893
Special Collections: Cecil J Osborne Coll; Lute Johnson Coll; USGS Maps
Subject Interests: Western hist
Wireless access
Function: 24/7 Online cat, 3D Printer, Adult bk club, Archival coll, Audiobks on Playaways & MP3, Audiobks via web, Bilingual assistance for Spanish patrons, Bk club(s), Bks on CD, Children's prog, Computer training, Computers for patron use, Electronic databases & coll, Family literacy, For res purposes, Free DVD rentals, Homebound delivery serv, ILL available, Internet access, Magazines, Makerspace, Meeting rooms, Microfiche/film & reading machines, Movies, Museum passes, Online cat, Outreach serv, OverDrive digital audio bks, Photocopying/Printing, Preschool outreach, Prog for adults, Prog for children & young adult, Ref & res, Scanner, Senior outreach, Serves people with intellectual disabilities, STEM programs, Story hour, Study rm, Summer & winter reading prog, Summer reading prog, Tax forms, Teen prog, Wheelchair accessible, Winter reading prog
Publications: The LAMB (Newsletter)
Partic in Colorado Library Consortium
Special Services for the Deaf - Closed caption videos
Open Mon 9-6, Tues-Thurs 9-7, Fri & Sat 9-5

J MORGAN COMMUNITY COLLEGE LIBRARY*, 920 Barlow Rd, 80701-4399. SAN 301-9217. Tel: 970-542-3185. Interlibrary Loan Service Tel: 970-542-3186. Toll Free Tel: 800-622-0216. FAX: 970-542-3114. TDD: 970-542-3145. Web Site: www.morgancc.edu. *Dir,* April Amack; Tel: 970-542-3187, E-mail: april.amack@morgancc.edu; Staff 3 (MLS 2, Non-MLS 1)
Founded 1972. Fac 93
Library Holdings: Bk Vols 10,000
Automation Activity & Vendor Info: (Acquisitions) Auto-Graphics, Inc; (Cataloging) Auto-Graphics, Inc; (Circulation) Auto-Graphics, Inc; (Discovery) EBSCO Discovery Service; (OPAC) Auto-Graphics, Inc
Wireless access
Open Mon-Thurs 8-7, Fri 8-3

FOWLER

P FOWLER PUBLIC LIBRARY*, 411 Sixth St, 81039. (Mail add: 114 E Cranston, 81039), SAN 301-9225. Tel: 719-263-4472. FAX: 719-224-1101. E-mail: library@fowlercolorado.com. Web Site: www.fowlercolorado.com/library.html. *Librn,* Kris Gonzalez; *Asst Librn,* JoAnna Negron
Founded 1891. Pop 1,570; Circ 13,600
Library Holdings: Bk Titles 8,000; Bk Vols 8,500
Wireless access
Function: 24/7 Online cat, After school storytime, Bks on CD, Electronic databases & coll, ILL available, Internet access, Summer reading prog
Open Mon-Sat 12-6
Friends of the Library Group

FRISCO

P SUMMIT COUNTY LIBRARIES*, Main Library, 0037 Peak One Dr, 80443. (Mail add: PO Box 770, 80443-0770), SAN 335-7937. Tel: 970-668-5555. FAX: 970-668-5556. Web Site: summitcountylibraries.org, www.co.summit.co.us/Directory.aspx?did=36. *Libr Dir,* Stephanie Ralph; E-mail: stephanie.ralph@summitcountyco.gov; *Asst Libr Dir,* Sarah

Nordholm; Tel: 970-668-4131, E-mail: Sarah.Nordholm@SummitCountyCO.gov; *Children's Prog,* Becky Astuto; Tel: 970-668-4135, E-mail: Becky.Astuto@SummitCountyCO.gov; Staff 10.6 (MLS 3, Non-MLS 7.6)
Founded 1962. Pop 29,280; Circ 253,903. Sal $546,961 (Prof $221,176)
Library Holdings: Audiobooks 6,060; DVDs 7,576; e-books 4,765; Large Print Bks 1,160; Bk Vols 119,642; Per Subs 220; Videos 428
Special Collections: Colorado History (Summit County History); Skiing Coll
Automation Activity & Vendor Info: (Cataloging) Innovative Interfaces, Inc; (Circulation) Innovative Interfaces, Inc; (OPAC) Innovative Interfaces, Inc
Wireless access
Function: Audiobks via web, Bks on cassette, Bks on CD, Children's prog, Computers for patron use, Free DVD rentals, Homebound delivery serv, ILL available, Internet access, Microfiche/film & reading machines, Online cat, Online ref, OverDrive digital audio bks, Photocopying/Printing, Preschool reading prog, Prog for adults, Prog for children & young adult, Ref serv available, Spanish lang bks, Story hour, Summer reading prog, Tax forms, Telephone ref, VHS videos
Partic in Colorado Library Consortium; Marmot Library Network
Open Mon-Thurs 9-7, Fri & Sat 9-5, Sun 1-5
Friends of the Library Group
Branches: 2
NORTH BRANCH, PO Box 1248, Silverthorne, 80498-1248, SAN 335-7996. Tel: 970-468-5887. FAX: 970-513-0854. *Br Mgr,* Janet Good; Staff 1 (MLS 1)
Open Mon-Thurs 9-6, Fri 9-5, Sat 1-5
Friends of the Library Group
SOUTH BRANCH, 504 Airport Rd, Breckenridge, 80424. (Mail add: PO Box 96, Breckenridge, 80424). Tel: 970-453-6098. FAX: 970-547-9637. *Br Mgr,* Pat Hasenfus; E-mail: path@co.summit.co.us
Open Mon-Thurs 9-6, Fri 9-5, Sat 1-5
Friends of the Library Group

GLENWOOD SPRINGS

J COLORADO MOUNTAIN COLLEGE*, Quigley Library, 3000 County Rd 114, 81601. SAN 335-802X. Tel: 970-947-8271. Web Site: library.coloradomtn.edu/quigley. *Libr Dir,* Mindy White; E-mail: mwhite@coloradomtn.edu; *Instrul & Ref Librn,* Becky Kramer; E-mail: bkramer@coloradomtn.edu; *Libr Tech,* Amy Currier; E-mail: aecurrier@coloradomtn.edu; Staff 1 (MLS 1)
Founded 1968. Enrl 3,200; Fac 70
Library Holdings: CDs 153; DVDs 116; Bk Titles 27,000; Per Subs 150; Talking Bks 445; Videos 536
Special Collections: State Document Depository
Automation Activity & Vendor Info: (Cataloging) Innovative Interfaces, Inc; (Circulation) Innovative Interfaces, Inc; (Course Reserve) Innovative Interfaces, Inc; (OPAC) Innovative Interfaces, Inc; (Serials) Innovative Interfaces, Inc
Wireless access
Partic in Marmot Library Network
Open Mon-Wed 8am-10pm, Thurs 8am-9pm, Fri 8-5, Sat 12-5, Sun 10-10

GOLDEN

S AMERICAN ALPINE CLUB LIBRARY*, 710 Tenth St, Ste 15, 80401. SAN 311-5674. Tel: 303-384-0110, 303-384-0112. E-mail: library@americanalpineclub.org. Web Site: americanalpineclub.org/library. *Libr Dir,* Katie Sauter; E-mail: ksauter@americanalpineclub.org. Subject Specialists: *Conserv, Presv,* Katie Sauter; Staff 2 (MLS 2)
Founded 1916
Library Holdings: AV Mats 600; Bks-By-Mail 20,000; Bk Vols 60,000; Per Subs 150
Special Collections: Boyle Himalayan Library; Central Asia Library
Subject Interests: Alps, Antarctic, Archives, Arctic, Glaciology, Himalayas, Maps, Mountaineering, Rare bks
Wireless access
Publications: High Places: The Blog of the American Alpine Club Library (Online only)
Restriction: Mem only
Friends of the Library Group

S COLORADO DEPARTMENT OF CORRECTIONS*, Colorado Correctional Center Library, 5445 S Golden Rd, 80401. (Mail add: PO Box 4020, 80401-0020), SAN 377-2594. Tel: 303-273-1635. FAX: 303-279-4407. Web Site: www.doc.state.co.us. *Libr Tech II,* Don Dickenson; E-mail: donald.dickenson@state.co.us
Library Holdings: Bk Vols 4,980; Per Subs 42
Open Mon-Thurs & Sun 12-8:30

S COLORADO RAILROAD MUSEUM, Robert W Richardson Railroad Library, 17155 W 44th Ave, 80403-1621. (Mail add: PO Box 10, 80402-0010), SAN 301-925X. Tel: 303-279-4591. Toll Free Tel: 800-365-6263. E-mail: library@crrm.org. Web Site: www.coloradorailroadmuseum.org/library. *Exec Dir,* Paul Hammond; E-mail: Paul@crrm.org
Founded 1959
Library Holdings: CDs 500; Bk Titles 10,000; Spec Interest Per Sub 50; Videos 100
Special Collections: Photograph Coll; Railroad History; Railroad Mechanical & Operating Instructions; Railroadiana Coll, maps, drawings & blueprints
Subject Interests: Railroads, Colo & Am W
Wireless access
Function: Archival coll, Microfiche/film & reading machines, Ref & res
Publications: Journal of Colorado Railroad Museum Library
Open Tues-Sat 11-3
Restriction: Open to pub for ref only

C COLORADO SCHOOL OF MINES*, Arthur Lakes Library, 1400 Illinois St, 80401-1887. SAN 301-9268. Tel: 303-273-3698. Interlibrary Loan Service Tel: 303-273-3899. FAX: 303-273-3199. E-mail: libcirc@mines.edu. Web Site: library.mines.edu. *Univ Librn,* Carol V Smith; E-mail: cesmith@mines.edu; *Head, Res Serv, Head, Spec Coll,* Lisa Dunn; E-mail: ldunn@mines.edu; *Assoc Librn, Maps Librn,* Christopher J J Thiry; Tel: 303-273-3697, E-mail: cthiry@mines.edu; *Asst Librn, Metadata Librn,* Christine Baker; Tel: 303-273-3446, E-mail: chbaker@mines.edu; *Assessment Librn, User Experience Librn,* Patricia Andersen; Tel: 303-273-3652, E-mail: panderse@mines.edu; *Systems Discovery Librn,* Lisa Nickum; Tel: 303-273-3695, E-mail: lnickum@mines.edu; *Acq Mgr,* Emma Covelli; E-mail: ecovelli@mines.edu. Subject Specialists: *Geol,* Carol V Smith; *Geol,* Lisa Dunn; Staff 20 (MLS 10, Non-MLS 10)
Founded 1874. Enrl 4,488; Fac 191; Highest Degree: Doctorate
Library Holdings: AV Mats 306; e-books 12,000; e-journals 25,407; Microforms 273,444; Bk Titles 192,128; Per Subs 600
Special Collections: Colorado & Mining History Coll; Energy, Environmental & Public Policy Coll. State Document Depository; US Document Depository
Subject Interests: Chem, Energy, Engr, Environ studies, Geol, Geophysics, Metallurgy, Mining, Petroleum engr, Physics
Automation Activity & Vendor Info: (Cataloging) Ex Libris Group; (Circulation) Ex Libris Group; (Course Reserve) Ex Libris Group; (ILL) Clio; (Media Booking) Ex Libris Group; (OPAC) Ex Libris Group; (Serials) Ex Libris Group
Wireless access
Publications: Inside Arthur Lakes (Newsletter)
Partic in Colorado Alliance of Research Libraries; Colorado Library Consortium
Special Services for the Blind - Accessible computers
Open Mon-Thurs 7:30am-2am, Fri 7:30-6, Sat 9-5, Sun 11am-Midnight
Restriction: Badge access after hrs

S DEPARTMENT OF HUMAN SERVICES-YOUTH CORRECTIONS*, Lookout Mountain Youth Services Center Library, MSCD Lab School Library, 2901 Ford St, 80401. Tel: 303-273-2636. FAX: 303-273-2638. Web Site: www.colorado.gov/pacific/cdhs/lookout-mountain-youth-services-center.
Library Holdings: Bk Vols 8,000; Per Subs 15
Automation Activity & Vendor Info: (Cataloging) Follett Software; (Circulation) Follett Software
Restriction: Not open to pub

S FOOTHILLS ART CENTER*, Mary S Robinson Art Library, 809 15th St, 80401. SAN 301-9292. Tel: 303-279-3922. FAX: 303-279-3996. E-mail: info@foothillsartcenter.org. Web Site: www.foothillsartcenter.org. *Exec Dir,* Hassan Najjar; E-mail: hassan@foothillsartcenter.org; *Curator,* Maura McInerney; E-mail: maura@foothillsartcenter.org
Library Holdings: Bk Vols 1,130
Subject Interests: Art, Poetry
Open Tues-Sat 10-5, Sun 12-5

G NATIONAL RENEWABLE ENERGY LABORATORY LIBRARY*, 15013 Denver West Pkwy, 80401-3305. SAN 321-5644. Tel: 303-275-4215. FAX: 303-275-4222. E-mail: library@nrel.gov. Web Site: www.nrel.gov. *Mgr, Libr Serv,* Tami Sandberg; Tel: 303-275-4024, E-mail: tami.sandberg@nrel.gov; *Librn, Syst & Tech Planning,* Jason Youngstrom; Tel: 303-275-4026, E-mail: jason.youngstrom@nrel.gov; *Doc Delivery, ILL,* Suzette Cohn; Tel: 303-275-4134, E-mail: suzette.cohn@nrel.gov; Staff 7 (MLS 6, Non-MLS 1)
Founded 1977
Subject Interests: Alternative fuels, Biomass energy, Energy efficiency, Energy policy, Photovoltaic cells, Renewable energy, Solar energy, Wave energy, Wind energy
Automation Activity & Vendor Info: (ILL) OCLC ILLiad; (OPAC) SirsiDynix; (Serials) Ex Libris Group
Wireless access
Restriction: Private libr

GRANBY

P GRANBY COUNTY LIBRARY DISTRICT*, 225 E Jasper Ave, 80446. (Mail add: PO Box 1050, 80446-1050), SAN 335-8054. Tel: 970-887-9411. FAX: 970-887-3227. E-mail: adminoffice@gcld.org. Web Site: www.gcld.org. *Dir,* Stephanie Ralph; Staff 24 (MLS 2, Non-MLS 22)
Founded 1933. Circ 188,759
Library Holdings: AV Mats 7,773; Bk Vols 74,500; Per Subs 100
Subject Interests: Colorado
Automation Activity & Vendor Info: (Acquisitions) Innovative Interfaces, Inc; (Cataloging) Innovative Interfaces, Inc; (Circulation) Innovative Interfaces, Inc
Function: 24/7 Online cat, Activity rm, Adult bk club, After school storytime, Art exhibits, Audiobks via web, Bks on CD, Children's prog, Computer training, Computers for patron use, Family literacy, Home delivery & serv to seniorr ctr & nursing homes, Internet access, Mango lang, Meeting rooms, Movies, Museum passes, Music CDs, Online cat, Online info literacy tutorials on the web & in blackboard, OverDrive digital audio bks, Photocopying/Printing, Preschool reading prog, Prog for adults, Prog for children & young adult, Ref & res, Scanner, Senior outreach, Spanish lang bks, Story hour, Study rm, Summer reading prog, Wheelchair accessible, Workshops, Writing prog
Partic in Marmot Library Network
Open Mon-Wed & Fri 10-6, Thurs 12-8, Sat 10-4
Friends of the Library Group
Branches: 5
FRASER VALLEY BRANCH, 241 Norgren Rd, Fraser, 80442. (Mail add: PO Box 160, Fraser, 80442-0421), SAN 335-8089. Tel: 970-726-5689. FAX: 970-726-9226. E-mail: fvlib@gcld.org. Web Site: www.gcld.org/fraservalley.htm. *Br Mgr,* Jeanette McQuade; E-mail: jmcquade@gcld.org; Staff 5 (Non-MLS 5)
Pop 14,584; Circ 79,900
Library Holdings: AV Mats 2,895; Large Print Bks 39; Bk Titles 21,449; Per Subs 60
Special Collections: Foreign Language, Lithuanian Coll
Open Mon-Tues 10-6, Wed-Thurs 10-7, Fri-Sat 10-3
Friends of the Library Group
GRANBY BRANCH, 55 Zero St, 80446. (Mail add: PO Box 1049, 80446-1049), SAN 335-8119. Tel: 970-887-2149. FAX: 970-887-3851. *Br Librn,* Linda Cumming; Staff 4 (Non-MLS 4)
Pop 14,489; Circ 38,500
Library Holdings: AV Mats 1,434; Large Print Bks 70; Bk Titles 10,000; Bk Vols 10,500; Per Subs 30
Special Collections: Local Newspaper, micro
Open Mon-Fri 11-7, Sat 11-4
Friends of the Library Group
HOT SULPHUR SPRINGS BRANCH, 105 Moffat, Hot Sulphur Springs, 80451. (Mail add: PO Box 336, Hot Sulphur Springs, 80451-0336), SAN 335-8143. Tel: 970-725-3942. FAX: 970-725-0570. E-mail: hsslib@gcld.org. Web Site: www.gcld.org/hss.htm. *Librn,* Lynn Shirley; Staff 2 (Non-MLS 2)
Pop 13,509
Library Holdings: AV Mats 792; Bk Titles 10,000; Per Subs 50
Special Collections: Crafts Coll
Automation Activity & Vendor Info: (Acquisitions) Innovative Interfaces, Inc
Publications: Newsletter (Bimonthly)
Open Tues & Thurs-Sat 10-3, Wed 12-7
Friends of the Library Group
JUNIPER LIBRARY AT GRAND LAKE, 316 Garfield St, Grand Lake, 80447. (Mail add: PO Box 506, Grand Lake, 80447-0506), SAN 329-613X. Tel: 970-627-8353. FAX: 970-627-0929. E-mail: junilib@gcld.org. Web Site: www.gcld.org/juniper.htm. *Br Librn,* Sue Luton; Staff 2 (Non-MLS 2)
Pop 13,909; Circ 19,880
Library Holdings: AV Mats 1,454; Large Print Bks 50; Bk Titles 11,000; Per Subs 75
Subject Interests: Local hist
Open Tues & Fri 11-6, Wed & Thurs 11-7, Sat 11-5
Friends of the Library Group
KREMMLING BRANCH, 300 S Eighth St, Kremmling, 80459. (Mail add: PO Box 1240, Kremmling, 80459-1240), SAN 335-8178. Tel: 970-724-9228. FAX: 970-724-3419. E-mail: kremlib@gcld.org. Web Site: www.gcld.org/kremmling.htm. *Br Librn,* Emily Pedersen; E-mail: epedersen@gcld.org; Staff 3 (Non-MLS 3)
Pop 14,540; Circ 38,678
Library Holdings: AV Mats 1,207; Large Print Bks 65; Bk Titles 15,000; Bk Vols 15,017; Per Subs 30
Open Mon & Wed-Fri 10-6, Tues 10-8, Sat 10-2
Friends of the Library Group

GRAND JUNCTION

C COLORADO MESA UNIVERSITY*, Tomlinson Library, 1100 North Ave, 81501. (Mail add: 1200 North Ave, 81501), SAN 301-9365. Tel: 970-248-1862. Circulation Tel: 970-248-1244. Interlibrary Loan Service Tel: 970-248-1844. Reference Tel: 970-248-1860. Administration Tel: 970-248-1406. FAX: 970-248-1930. TDD: 970-248-1805. Reference E-mail: library@coloradomesa.edu. Web Site: www.coloradomesa.edu/library. *Libr Dir,* Sylvia Rael; Tel: 970-248-1029, E-mail: srael@coloradomesa.edu; *Head of Instruction,* Anne Knipe Bledsoe; Tel: 970-248-1805, E-mail: aknipe@coloradomesa.edu; *Head, Tech Serv,* Jamie Walker; Tel: 970-248-1863, E-mail: jwalker@coloradomesa.edu; *Acq Librn,* Lisa Hughes; Tel: 970-248-1436, E-mail: lahughes@coloradomesa.edu; *Archives & Spec Coll Librn,* Amber D'Ambrosio; Tel: 970-248-1864, E-mail: adambrosio@coloradomesa.edu; *Coll Develop Coordr,* Barbara Borst; Tel: 970-248-1872, E-mail: bborst@coloradomesa.edu; *ILL,* Becky Bernal; Tel: 970-248-1844, E-mail: bbernal@coloradomesa.edu; Staff 16 (MLS 8, Non-MLS 8)
Founded 1925. Enrl 8,844; Fac 402; Highest Degree: Master
Library Holdings: AV Mats 19,149; CDs 3,247; DVDs 608; e-books 31,085; e-journals 14,800; Microforms 190,600; Bk Vols 202,919; Per Subs 2,004
Special Collections: Ethridge Indian Pottery Coll; Mesa College Archives; Walter Walker Memorial Coll; Wayne Aspinall Coll
Automation Activity & Vendor Info: (Acquisitions) Innovative Interfaces, Inc; (Cataloging) Innovative Interfaces, Inc; (Circulation) Innovative Interfaces, Inc; (Course Reserve) Innovative Interfaces, Inc; (OPAC) Innovative Interfaces, Inc; (Serials) Innovative Interfaces, Inc
Wireless access
Partic in Colorado Alliance of Research Libraries
Special Services for the Deaf - Closed caption videos; TDD equip
Special Services for the Blind - Accessible computers; Assistive/Adapted tech devices, equip & products; Audio mat; Bks on cassette; Bks on CD; Computer with voice synthesizer for visually impaired persons; Dragon Naturally Speaking software; Internet workstation with adaptive software; Screen reader software; Sound rec; Sub-lending agent for Braille Inst Libr; VisualTek equip
Open Mon-Thurs 7:30am-Midnight, Fri 7:30-5, Sat 10-5, Sun 1-Midnight
Friends of the Library Group

M COMMUNITY HOSPITAL*, Medical Library, 2351 G Rd, 81505. Tel: 970-242-0920, 970-256-6209. FAX: 970-644-3498. E-mail: library@gjhosp.org. Web Site: yourcommunityhospital.com/Health_Resources_and_Library.cfm. *Med Librn,* Steve Rauch
Library Holdings: Bk Titles 1,000; Per Subs 60
Automation Activity & Vendor Info: (Cataloging) CyberTools for Libraries; (Circulation) CyberTools for Libraries; (OPAC) CyberTools for Libraries
Wireless access
Open Mon-Fri 8-5

GM DEPARTMENT OF VETERANS AFFAIRS*, Medical Center Libraries, 2121 North Ave, 81501-6428. SAN 301-9403. Tel: 970-242-0731. FAX: 970-244-1309. Web Site: www.grandjunction.va.gov. *Libr Tech,* Dan McLaughlin; E-mail: daniel.mclaughlin@va.gov; *Support Serv,* Mona Leonard; E-mail: mona.leonard@va.gov
Founded 1951
Library Holdings: AV Mats 550; Large Print Bks 100; Bk Vols 4,300; Per Subs 160
Subject Interests: Patient health educ
Open Mon-Fri 8-4:30
Restriction: Non-circulating to the pub

P MESA COUNTY PUBLIC LIBRARY DISTRICT*, 443 N Sixth St, 81501. SAN 335-8208. Tel: 970-243-4442. Administration Tel: 970-683-2434. Administration FAX: 970-243-4744. TDD: 970-241-0500. Web Site: mesacountylibraries.org. *Dir,* Michelle Boisvenue-Fox; E-mail: mboisvinuefox@mcpld.org; *Assoc Dir,* Shana Wade; E-mail: swade@mcpld.org; *Head of Br Serv,* Wynell Webster; Staff 75 (MLS 14, Non-MLS 61)
Founded 1967. Pop 151,900; Circ 1,281,568
Special Collections: Regional History Coll
Automation Activity & Vendor Info: (Acquisitions) Innovative Interfaces, Inc - Sierra; (Cataloging) Innovative Interfaces, Inc - Sierra; (Circulation) Innovative Interfaces, Inc - Sierra; (Serials) Innovative Interfaces, Inc - Sierra
Wireless access
Function: 24/7 Electronic res, 24/7 Online cat, Adult bk club, Adult literacy prog, Art exhibits, Art programs, Audio & video playback equip for onsite use, Audiobks on Playaways & MP3, Audiobks via web, Bilingual assistance for Spanish patrons, Bk club(s), Bks on CD, Children's prog, Citizenship assistance, Computer training, Computers for patron use, Electronic databases & coll, Free DVD rentals, Homebound delivery serv,

ILL available, Internet access, Large print keyboards, Life-long learning prog for all ages, Magazines, Magnifiers for reading, Mango lang, Meeting rooms, Microfiche/film & reading machines, Movies, Museum passes, Music CDs, Online cat, Online ref, Outreach serv, OverDrive digital audio bks, Photocopying/Printing, Printer for laptops & handheld devices, Prog for adults, Prog for children & young adult, Ref & res, Ref serv available, Scanner, Spanish lang bks, Story hour, Study rm, Summer reading prog, Tax forms, Teen prog, Telephone ref, Wheelchair accessible, Writing prog
Partic in Marmot Library Network
Special Services for the Deaf - ADA equip
Special Services for the Blind - Accessible computers
Open Mon-Thurs 9-8, Fri 9-6, Sat 9-5
Friends of the Library Group
Branches: 7
CLIFTON BRANCH, Mesa Point Shopping Ctr, Ste 6F, 590 32 Rd, Clifton, 81520, SAN 335-8232. Tel: 970-434-6936. *Br Mgr,* Wynell Webster
Library Holdings: Bk Vols 13,000
Open Mon & Wed-Fri 9-6, Tues 9-8, Sat 9-4
Friends of the Library Group
COLLBRAN BRANCH, 111 Main St, Collbran, 81624, SAN 335-8267. Tel: 970-487-3545. *Br Mgr,* Susan Crossed
Library Holdings: Bk Titles 7,000
Open Tues, Thurs & Fri 10-12 & 1-6, Sat 9-1
Friends of the Library Group
DEBEQUE JOINT BRANCH, 730 Minter Ave, DeBeque, 81630, SAN 335-8291. Tel: 970-283-8625. *Br Mgr,* Apple Barker
Library Holdings: Bk Titles 8,184; Bk Vols 8,424
Open Wed & Thurs 4pm-7pm, Fri 9-1 & 2-6, Sat 9-4
Friends of the Library Group
FRUITA BRANCH, 324 N Coulson, Fruita, 81521, SAN 335-8321. Tel: 970-858-7703. *Br Mgr,* Giselle Smith
Open Mon & Thurs 9-7, Fri 9-6, Sat 9-4
Friends of the Library Group
GATEWAY BRANCH, 42700 Hwy 141, Gateway, 81522, SAN 335-833X. Tel: 970-931-2428. *Br Mgr,* Linda Krumton
Library Holdings: Bk Titles 2,859
Open Tues 3pm-5pm, Thurs 11-5
ORCHARD MESA, 230 Lynwood St, 81503, SAN 375-0531. Tel: 970-243-0181. *Br Mgr,* Susie Robertson
Library Holdings: Bk Titles 14,000
Open Tues-Fri 9-6, Sat 9-4
PALISADE BRANCH, 119 W Third St, Palisade, 81526, SAN 335-8356. Tel: 970-464-7557. *Br Mgr,* Alice Forte
Library Holdings: Bk Titles 14,529
Open Tues-Fri 9-1 & 2-6, Sat 9-4
Friends of the Library Group

S MUSEUM OF WESTERN COLORADO, Loyd Files Research Library, 462 Ute Ave, 81501. (Mail add: PO Box 20000, 81502-5020), SAN 301-9381. Tel: 970-242-0971, Ext 209. FAX: 970-242-3960. E-mail: library@westcomuseum.org. Web Site: museumofwesternco.com/research-library.
Founded 1965
Library Holdings: Bk Titles 6,000
Special Collections: Al Look Papers; Grand Junction Fire Department Coll; Local History (Western Colorado, Mesa County, Grand Junction); Mesa County Genealogical Society; Mesa County Historical Society Coll; Mesa County Newspapers, hardcopy, micro; Mesa County Oral History Coll, tapes (2400 hrs); Quahada Chapter Colorado Archaeological Society; Warren Kiefer Railroad Coll (1940-present)
Subject Interests: Archaeology, Paleontology, Railroads
Function: Archival coll
Publications: Museum Times (Newsletter)
Restriction: Non-circulating, Open by appt only, Open to pub for ref only
Friends of the Library Group

M ST MARY'S HOSPITAL*, Dr E H Munro Library, 2635 N Seventh St, 81502. (Mail add: PO Box 1628, 81502-1628), SAN 301-9373. Tel: 970-298-2171. FAX: 970-298-7509. E-mail: library@sclhs.net.
Founded 1945
Library Holdings: Bk Titles 1,900; Per Subs 45
Automation Activity & Vendor Info: (Cataloging) EOS International; (Circulation) EOS International; (OPAC) EOS International; (Serials) EOS International
Wireless access
Partic in Capital District Library Council; Colorado Council of Medical Librarians; Medical Library Association; Midcontinental Regional Med Libr Program
Open Mon-Fri 8-4

GREELEY

J AIMS COMMUNITY COLLEGE*, Kiefer Library, College Ctr, 5401 W 20th St, 7501, 80634-3002. (Mail add: PO Box 69, 80632-0069), SAN 301-942X. Tel: 970-339-6458. Circulation Tel: 970-339-6541. Toll Free Tel: 800-301-5388, Ext 6458. Web Site: www.aims.edu/kieferlibrary. *Dir, Learning Commons,* Position Currently Open; *Asst Dir,* Laurel Waller; E-mail: laurel.waller@aims.edu; *Librn,* Catherine Glaser; E-mail: catherine.glaser@aims.edu; *Librn,* Carol Satersmoen; Tel: 970-339-6589, E-mail: carol.satersmoen@aims.edu; Staff 5 (MLS 2, Non-MLS 3)
Founded 1969. Enrl 7,000; Fac 326; Highest Degree: Associate
Special Collections: Aims Community College Archives
Automation Activity & Vendor Info: (Cataloging) TLC (The Library Corporation); (Circulation) TLC (The Library Corporation); (Discovery) EBSCO Discovery Service; (ILL) OCLC; (OPAC) TLC (The Library Corporation); (Serials) TLC (The Library Corporation)
Wireless access
Function: Computer training, Computers for patron use, E-Readers, Electronic databases & coll, For res purposes, Free DVD rentals, ILL available, Internet access, Magazines, Mail & tel request accepted, Mango lang, Music CDs, Online cat, Online ref, Orientations, Outside serv via phone, mail, e-mail & web, Photocopying/Printing, Ref & res, Ref serv available, Res libr, Satellite serv, Scanner, Study rm, Telephone ref, Wheelchair accessible, Writing prog
Partic in Colorado Library Consortium; OCLC Online Computer Library Center, Inc
Open Mon-Thurs 7:30am-8pm, Fri 7:30-5, Sun 12-5

S DEPARTMENT OF HUMAN SERVICES-YOUTH CORRECTIONS*, Platte Valley Youth Services Center Library, 2200 O St, 80631-9503. Tel: 970-304-6277. FAX: 970-304-6274. Web Site: cdhs.colorado.gov/our-services/youth-services/residential-youth-centers/platte-valley-youth-. *Librn,* Wendy Ginther; E-mail: wendy.ginther@state.co.us
Library Holdings: Bk Vols 6,000; Per Subs 22
Automation Activity & Vendor Info: (Cataloging) Mandarin Library Automation; (Circulation) Mandarin Library Automation
Wireless access
Open Mon-Fri 8:30-3

R FIRST CONGREGATIONAL CHURCH LIBRARY*, 2101 16th St, 80631. SAN 301-9438. Tel: 970-353-0828. FAX: 970-353-8447. Web Site: www.firstconggreeley.com. *Adult Serv,* Judy Smith; *Ch Serv,* Joyce Best
Library Holdings: Bk Vols 1,600
Subject Interests: Relig
Wireless access
Open Mon-Thurs 9-4, Fri 9-1

P HIGH PLAINS LIBRARY DISTRICT*, 2650 W 29th St, 80631. SAN 301-9489. Toll Free Tel: 888-861-7323. Web Site: www.mylibrary.us. *Exec Dir,* Matthew Hortt; E-mail: mhortt@highplains.us; *Assoc Dir, Pub Serv,* Marjorie Elwood; E-mail: melwood@highplains.us
Founded 1931
Special Collections: Small Business & Non-Profit
Subject Interests: Colorado, Genealogy
Automation Activity & Vendor Info: (Acquisitions) Innovative Interfaces, Inc; (Cataloging) Innovative Interfaces, Inc; (Circulation) Innovative Interfaces, Inc; (ILL) OCLC; (OPAC) Innovative Interfaces, Inc; (Serials) Innovative Interfaces, Inc
Wireless access
Member Libraries: Eaton Public Library; Fort Lupton Public & School Library; Glenn A Jones Memorial Library; Hudson Public Library; Northern Plains Public Library; Platteville Public Library
Partic in Colorado Library Consortium
Branches: 7
CARBON VALLEY REGIONAL LIBRARY, Seven Park Ave, Firestone, 80504, SAN 371-3601. *Br Mgr,* Becki Loughlin
Open Mon-Thurs 9-8, Fri & Sat 10-5, Sun 1-5
Friends of the Library Group
CENTENNIAL PARK LIBRARY, 2227 23rd Ave, 80634-6632, SAN 372-4891. *Br Mgr,* Mallory Pillard
Open Mon-Thurs 9-8, Fri & Sat 10-5, Sun 1-5
ERIE COMMUNITY LIBRARY, 400 Powers St, Erie, 80516. *Br Mgr,* Joanna McNeal
Open Mon-Thurs 9-8, Fri & Sat 10-5, Sun 1-5
FARR REGIONAL LIBRARY, 1939 61st Ave, 80634. *Br Mgr,* Charlene Parker
Open Mon-Thurs 9-8, Fri & Sat 10-5, Sun 1-5
KERSEY LIBRARY, 413 First St, Kersey, 80644. *Br Mgr,* Rosa Granado
Open Mon-Thurs & Sat 1-5
LINCOLN PARK LIBRARY, 1012 11th St, Ste B, 80631, SAN 301-9462. *Br Mgr,* Melissa Beavers
Open Mon-Thurs 9-8, Fri & Sat 10-5, Sun 1-5

RIVERSIDE LIBRARY & CULTURAL CENTER, 3700 Golden St, Evans, 80620. *Br Mgr,* Rita Kadavy
Open Mon-Thurs 9-8, Fri & Sat 10-5, Sun 1-5
Bookmobiles: 1. Mgr, Rosa Granado

C UNIVERSITY OF NORTHERN COLORADO LIBRARIES*, James A Michener Library, 1400 22nd Ave, 80631. (Mail add: Campus Box 48, 80639), SAN 335-8380. Tel: 970-351-2671. Administration Tel: 970-351-2601. FAX: 970-351-2540. E-mail: libraries@unco.edu. Web Site: library.unco.edu. *Dean of Libr,* Jennifer Nutefall; E-mail: jennifer.nutefall@unco.edu; *Assoc Dean of Libr,* Jayne Blodgett; E-mail: jayne.blogdett@unco.edu; *Head, Access Serv,* Sarah Vaughn; Tel: 970-351-1539, E-mail: sarah.vaughn@unco.edu; *Head, Archives & Spec Coll,* Jay Trask; Tel: 970-351-2322, E-mail: jay.trask@unco.edu; *Head, Res Serv,* Jen Mayer; Tel: 970-351-1531, E-mail: jen.mayer@unco.edu; *Tech Serv Mgr,* Jennifer Leffler; Tel: 970-351-1543, E-mail: jennifer.leffler@unco.edu; Staff 19.6 (MLS 19.6)
Founded 1889. Enrl 10,132; Fac 764; Highest Degree: Doctorate
Jul 2013-Jun 2014 Income $6,508,315, State $5,233,455, Locally Generated Income $89,741, Other $1,185,119. Mats Exp $2,762,653, Books $569,920, Per/Ser (Incl. Access Fees) $151,592, Other Print Mats $17,032, AV Mat $65,825, Electronic Ref Mat (Incl. Access Fees) $1,942,487, Presv $15,797. Sal $2,433,575 (Prof $1,332,400)
Library Holdings: CDs 31,140; DVDs 11,354; e-books 60,828; e-journals 56,901; Music Scores 58,288; Bk Vols 1,166,761; Per Subs 505; Videos 1,600
Special Collections: Connie Willis Coll; James A Michener Special Coll; University Archives. US Document Depository
Subject Interests: Bus, Educ, Music
Automation Activity & Vendor Info: (Acquisitions) Innovative Interfaces, Inc; (Cataloging) Innovative Interfaces, Inc; (Circulation) Innovative Interfaces, Inc; (Course Reserve) Innovative Interfaces, Inc; (Media Booking) Innovative Interfaces, Inc; (OPAC) Innovative Interfaces, Inc; (Serials) Innovative Interfaces, Inc
Wireless access
Publications: Library Letters (Newsletter)
Partic in Colorado Alliance of Research Libraries; Minitex; OCLC Online Computer Library Center, Inc
Open Mon-Thurs 7:30am-Midnight, Fri 7:30-6, Sat 10-6, Sun Noon-Midnight
Friends of the Library Group

C UNIVERSITY OF NORTHERN COLORADO LIBRARIES*, Skinner Music Library, 1636 Tenth Ave, 80639. (Mail add: Campus Box 68, 80639). Tel: 970-351-2439. E-mail: library.music@unco.edu. *Music Librn,* Anne Myers; Tel: 970-351-2327, E-mail: anne.myers@unco.edu
Wireless access
Open Mon-Fri 7:30-6, Sat 9-6, Sun 1-10
Friends of the Library Group

GUNNISON

P GUNNISON PUBLIC LIBRARY OF THE GUNNISON COUNTY LIBRARY DISTRICT*, Ann Zugelder Library, 307 N Wisconsin, 81230-2627. SAN 335-847X. Tel: 970-641-3485. Administration Tel: 970-641-7903. FAX: 970-641-4653. E-mail: gcpl@marmot.org. Web Site: www.gunnisoncountylibraries.org. *Dir,* Drew Brookhart; E-mail: drew@gunnisoncountylibraries.org; *Family Serv Librn, Youth Serv Librn,* Kym Mcnamara; *Bus & Human Res Mgr,* Amanda Brackett
Founded 1939. Pop 15,000
Library Holdings: Bk Titles 40,000; Per Subs 70
Special Collections: Western History Coll. Oral History
Automation Activity & Vendor Info: (Cataloging) Innovative Interfaces, Inc
Wireless access
Open Mon-Thurs 9-7, Fri 9-6, Sat 10-4, Sun 1-5
Friends of the Library Group
Branches: 1
CRESTED BUTTE LIBRARY, 504 Maroon Ave, Crested Butte, 81224. (Mail add: PO Box 489, Crested Butte, 81224-0489), SAN 335-850X. Tel: 970-349-6535. FAX: 970-349-0348. *Libr Operations Coordr,* Jane Thomas; Staff 3 (Non-MLS 3)
Library Holdings: Bk Titles 11,000; Per Subs 76
Open Mon-Thurs 9-7, Fri 9-6, Sat 11-4, Sun 1-5
Friends of the Library Group

C WESTERN STATE COLLEGE*, Leslie J Savage Library, 600 N Adams St, 81231. SAN 301-9497. Tel: 970-943-2103. Interlibrary Loan Service Tel: 970-943-2054. Web Site: library.western.edu. *Dir, Libr Serv,* Dustin Fife; Tel: 970-943-2278, E-mail: dfife@western.edu; *Assoc Dir, Libr Serv, Electronic Res Librn,* Wick Tiffanie; Tel: 970-943-2477, E-mail: twick@western.edu; *Head, Access Serv,* Tamara Spezze; Tel: 970-943-2107, E-mail: tspezze@western.edu; *Info Literacy Librn, Pub Serv,* Renee Barney; Tel: 970-943-2898, E-mail: rbarney@western.edu; Staff 7 (MLS 4, Non-MLS 3)
Founded 1901. Enrl 2,300; Fac 118; Highest Degree: Bachelor
Library Holdings: CDs 624; DVDs 291; Bk Titles 113,191; Per Subs 428; Videos 2,298
Special Collections: Colorado History (Western Americana); Western Colorado Newspapers, micro. State Document Depository; US Document Depository
Automation Activity & Vendor Info: (Acquisitions) Innovative Interfaces, Inc; (Cataloging) Innovative Interfaces, Inc; (Circulation) Innovative Interfaces, Inc; (Course Reserve) Innovative Interfaces, Inc; (ILL) OCLC; (OPAC) Innovative Interfaces, Inc; (Serials) Innovative Interfaces, Inc
Wireless access
Partic in Colorado Alliance of Research Libraries; OCLC Online Computer Library Center, Inc; Proquest Dialog
Open Mon-Thurs 7:30am-Midnight, Fri 7:30-6, Sat 12-6, Sun Noon-Midnight

HAXTUN

P HAXTUN PUBLIC LIBRARY*, 141 S Colorado Ave, 80731-2711. (Mail add: PO Box 446, 80731-0446), SAN 301-9500. Tel: 970-774-6106. FAX: 970-774-6106. E-mail: townlibr@pctelcom.coop. Web Site: haxtun.colibraries.org. *Dir,* Vickie Freemyer
Founded 1925. Pop 1,000; Circ 16,500
Library Holdings: AV Mats 150; Large Print Bks 250; Bk Titles 8,000; Bk Vols 8,500
Subject Interests: Agr, Art & archit, Bus & mgt, Econ, Educ
Partic in Colorado Library Consortium
Special Services for the Blind - Talking bks
Open Mon, Wed & Fri 9-1, Tues 3-7, Thurs 12-4
Friends of the Library Group

HAYDEN

P WEST ROUTT LIBRARY DISTRICT, Hayden Public Library, 201 E Jefferson Ave, 81639. (Mail add: PO Box 1813, 81639-1813), SAN 336-0008. Tel: 970-276-3777. FAX: 970-276-3778. Web Site: haydenpubliclibrary.org. *Dir,* Anna Lash; E-mail: alashhpl@gmail.com
Founded 1930. Pop 2,600
Library Holdings: Bks on Deafness & Sign Lang 15; Large Print Bks 200; Bk Titles 34,000; Per Subs 57; Talking Bks 2,000
Automation Activity & Vendor Info: (Acquisitions) Koha; (Cataloging) Koha; (Circulation) Koha; (OPAC) Koha
Wireless access
Open Mon-Fri 10-6, Sat 10-2
Friends of the Library Group

HOLLY

P HOLLY PUBLIC LIBRARY, 100 Tony Garcia Dr, 81047-9149. (Mail add: PO Box 706, 81047-0706), SAN 301-9527. Tel: 719-537-6520. FAX: 719-537-6621. E-mail: hpl1912@gmail.com. *Dir & Librn,* Elaine Anderson; Staff 1 (Non-MLS 1)
Founded 1911. Pop 993; Circ 4,715
Library Holdings: DVDs 36; Bk Titles 6,030; Bk Vols 6,530; Videos 306
Wireless access
Open Tues 2-5, Wed 12-5, Thurs 2-7, Fri 10-12 & 2-5, Sat 10-12

HOLYOKE

P HEGINBOTHAM LIBRARY*, 539 S Baxter St, 80734. SAN 301-9535. Tel: 970-854-2597. FAX: 970-854-2636. Web Site: heginbotham.colibraries.org. *Libr Dir,* Kathy Bornhoft
Founded 1920. Pop 2,000; Circ 25,004
Library Holdings: Bk Vols 12,500; Per Subs 40
Automation Activity & Vendor Info: (Cataloging) SirsiDynix; (Circulation) SirsiDynix; (OPAC) SirsiDynix
Partic in Colorado Library Consortium
Open Mon-Fri 9-6, Sat 9-1
Friends of the Library Group

HOT SULPHUR SPRINGS

S GRAND COUNTY HISTORICAL ASSOCIATION LIBRARY, 110 E Byers Ave, 80451. (Mail add: PO Box 165, 80451-0165), SAN 372-5731. Tel: 970-725-3939. E-mail: gcha@rkymtnhi.com. Web Site: grandcountyhistory.org. *Exec Dir,* Shanna Ganne; E-mail: shanna@grandcountyhistory.org; *Curator,* Erica Rodenback; E-mail: erica@grandcountyhistory.org
Library Holdings: Bk Vols 200
Special Collections: Manuscripts Coll; Photograph Coll. Oral History
Wireless access
Publications: Grand County Historical Association Journal
Open Tues-Sat 10-5
Restriction: Non-circulating of rare bks, Pub use on premises
Friends of the Library Group

HOTCHKISS

P DELTA COUNTY LIBRARIES*, Administrative Office, 149 E Main St, 81419. (Mail add: PO Box 540, Delta, 81416). Tel: 970-399-7876. E-mail: dcpld@deltalibraries.org. Web Site: www.deltalibraries.org. *District Dir,* Lea Hart; Tel: 970-399-7878, E-mail: lhart@deltalibraries.org
Open Mon-Fri 10-2
Branches: 5
CEDAREDGE PUBLIC, 180 SW Sixth Ave, Cedaredge, 81413. (Mail add: PO Box 548, Cedaredge, 81413-0548), SAN 335-5683. Tel: 970-399-7674. FAX: 970-856-3170. Web Site: deltalibraries.org/cedaredge. *Mgr,* Position Currently Open
Founded 1911
Library Holdings: AV Mats 2,195; Large Print Bks 1,052; Bk Vols 16,677; Per Subs 45
Special Services for the Deaf - ADA equip
Special Services for the Blind - Assistive/Adapted tech devices, equip & products
Open Tues, Thurs & Fri 10-6, Wed 12-7, Sat 10-2
Friends of the Library Group
CRAWFORD PUBLIC, 545 Hwy 92, Crawford, 81415, SAN 335-5713. Tel: 970-399-7783. FAX: 970-921-5339. Web Site: deltalibraries.org/crawford. *Mgr,* Kathy Little; E-mail: klittle@deltalibraries.org
Founded 1981
Library Holdings: AV Mats 2,181; Bk Vols 12,381
Subject Interests: Civil War, Quilting
Open Wed-Fri 10-6, Sat 12-4
Friends of the Library Group
DELTA PUBLIC LIBRARY, 211 W Sixth St, Delta, 81416, SAN 335-5659. Tel: 970-874-9630. FAX: 970-874-8605. Web Site: deltalibraries.org/delta. *Mgr,* Adriana Chavira; E-mail: achavira@deltalibraries.org; Staff 1 (MLS 1)
Founded 1911
Library Holdings: AV Mats 2,771; Large Print Bks 402; Bk Vols 25,595; Per Subs 185
Special Collections: Western Colorado History
Automation Activity & Vendor Info: (Acquisitions) SirsiDynix; (Cataloging) SirsiDynix; (Circulation) SirsiDynix; (ILL) ADLiB; (OPAC) SirsiDynix; (Serials) SirsiDynix
Special Services for the Deaf - ADA equip; Bks on deafness & sign lang
Special Services for the Blind - Accessible computers; Audio mat; Bks available with recordings; Bks on cassette; Bks on CD; Computer with voice synthesizer for visually impaired persons; Copier with enlargement capabilities; Internet workstation with adaptive software; Large print bks; Large screen computer & software; PC for people with disabilities; Talking bks
Open Mon 10-7, Tues-Thurs 10-6, Sat 10-3
Friends of the Library Group
HOTCHKISS PUBLIC, 149 E Main St, 81419. (Mail add: PO Box 540, 81419), SAN 335-5748. Tel: 970-399-7781. FAX: 970-872-3108. Web Site: deltalibraries.org/hotchkiss. *Mgr,* Terry Johns; E-mail: tjohns@deltalibraries.org
Founded 1909
Library Holdings: AV Mats 1,500; Large Print Bks 600; Bk Vols 15,356; Per Subs 40
Subject Interests: Art
Open Mon-Thurs 10-6
PAONIA PUBLIC, 80 Samuel Wade Rd, Paonia, 81428, SAN 335-5772. Tel: 970-399-7881. FAX: 970-527-3837. Web Site: deltalibraries.org/paonia. *Mgr,* Position Currently Open
Founded 1932
Library Holdings: AV Mats 1,995; Large Print Bks 603; Bk Vols 20,184; Per Subs 85
Subject Interests: Hist
Open Tues-Fri 10-6, Sat 10-2
Friends of the Library Group

HUDSON

P HUDSON PUBLIC LIBRARY*, 100 S Beech St, 80642. (Mail add: PO Box 188, 80642-0188), SAN 301-9543. Tel: 303-536-4550. FAX: 303-536-4404. *Dir,* Teresa Redden; E-mail: tredden@highplains.us
Founded 1951. Pop 3,200; Circ 5,925
Library Holdings: Bk Vols 10,000
Automation Activity & Vendor Info: (Cataloging) SirsiDynix; (Circulation) SirsiDynix; (OPAC) SirsiDynix
Mem of High Plains Library District
Open Mon, Tues, Thurs & Fri 10-6, Wed 10-7, Sat 9-12

HUGO

P HUGO PUBLIC LIBRARY, 522 Second Ave, 80821. (Mail add: PO Box 429, 80821-0429), SAN 301-9551. Tel: 719-743-2325. E-mail: hugolibrary@esrta.com. Web Site: townhugo.com/?page.id=300. *Dir,* Kristin Allen
Founded 1921. Pop 880; Circ 8,206
Library Holdings: Bk Vols 7,500
Wireless access
Open Mon-Thurs 2pm-6pm, Fri 11-3

IDAHO SPRINGS

P IDAHO SPRINGS PUBLIC LIBRARY*, 219 14th Ave, 80452. (Mail add: PO Box 1509, 80452-1509), SAN 301-956X. Tel: 303-567-2020. FAX: 303-567-2020. E-mail: ispl@clearcreeklibrary.org. *Dir,* Position Currently Open; Staff 5 (MLS 1, Non-MLS 4)
Founded 1904. Pop 4,500; Circ 7,000
Library Holdings: Bk Titles 25,000; Bk Vols 19,000; Per Subs 106
Special Collections: Local Newspaper (1888-present), micro
Subject Interests: Colorado, Mineralogy
Automation Activity & Vendor Info: (Cataloging) TLC (The Library Corporation); (Circulation) TLC (The Library Corporation); (OPAC) TLC (The Library Corporation)
Wireless access
Function: ILL available
Open Mon & Wed 10-7, Tues & Thurs 10-6, Fri & Sat 10-5
Restriction: Residents only
Friends of the Library Group

IGNACIO

P IGNACIO COMMUNITY LIBRARY*, 470 Goddard Ave, 81137. (Mail add: PO Box 886, 81137-0886), SAN 371-8522. Tel: 970-563-9287. FAX: 970-563-9296. E-mail: generaldelivery@ignaciolibrary.org. Web Site: ignaciolibrary.org. *Libr Dir,* Marcia Vining; E-mail: mvining@ignaciolibrary.org; *Fac Mgr, Network Coordr,* Dixie Cook; E-mail: dcook@ignaciolibrary.org; Staff 6.5 (MLS 2, Non-MLS 4.5)
Founded 1991. Pop 5,500
Library Holdings: Bk Titles 20,000; Per Subs 18
Special Collections: Native American Coll; Southwest Coll
Automation Activity & Vendor Info: (Cataloging) SirsiDynix; (Circulation) SirsiDynix
Wireless access
Function: Computer training, Computers for patron use, E-Reserves, Free DVD rentals, ILL available, Mail & tel request accepted, Online cat, Photocopying/Printing, Prog for adults, Prog for children & young adult, Ref serv available, Story hour, Summer reading prog, Tax forms, VHS videos, Wheelchair accessible
Open Mon-Thurs 9-7, Fri & Sat 9-5, Sun 11-5
Friends of the Library Group

JOHNSTOWN

P GLENN A JONES MEMORIAL LIBRARY*, 400 S Parish Ave, 80534. SAN 301-9578. Tel: 970-587-2459. FAX: 970-587-2352. *Dir,* Lois Brown; E-mail: lbrown@highplains.us; *Asst Dir,* Jill Schraeder; Staff 1 (MLS 1)
Founded 1965
Library Holdings: Bk Vols 25,000; Per Subs 25
Special Collections: MacArthur Foundation Video Coll. Oral History
Automation Activity & Vendor Info: (Cataloging) SirsiDynix; (Circulation) SirsiDynix; (OPAC) SirsiDynix
Wireless access
Function: 24/7 Electronic res, 24/7 Online cat, Accelerated reader prog, Activity rm, Adult bk club
Mem of High Plains Library District
Partic in Colorado Library Consortium
Open Mon & Fri 9-5, Tues-Thurs 9-8, Sat 9-1

JULESBURG

P JULESBURG PUBLIC LIBRARY*, 320 Cedar St, 80737-1545. SAN 301-9586. Tel: 970-474-2608. FAX: 970-474-2787. *Dir,* Tina Stone; E-mail: julesburglibrary@kci.net
Founded 1922. Pop 1,576; Circ 10,994
Library Holdings: Bk Titles 8,000
Subject Interests: Hist, Natural sci
Automation Activity & Vendor Info: (Acquisitions) ByWater Solutions; (Cataloging) ByWater Solutions; (Circulation) ByWater Solutions
Open Mon-Fri 9-12 & 1-5, Sat 9-12
Friends of the Library Group

LA JARA

P CONEJOS COUNTY LIBRARY*, 17703 Hwy 285, 81140. SAN 376-2815. Tel: 719-274-5858. Web Site: conejos.colibraries.org. *Dir,* Maria De Herrera
Library Holdings: Bk Titles 19,000; Bk Vols 19,500; Per Subs 37
Automation Activity & Vendor Info: (Acquisitions) Follett Software
Open Mon & Thurs 8:30-5, Tues & Wed 9-5:30, Fri 8:30-3:30, Sat 9:30-3:30
Friends of the Library Group

Branches: 2
ANTONITO BRANCH, 220 Main St, Antonito, 81120. (Mail add: PO Box 7, Antonito, 81120). Tel: 719-376-5904. *Br Mgr,* Alice Trujillo
Open Thurs, Fri & Sat 11-4
CAPULIN BRANCH, 8047 Hwy 15, Capulin, 81124. Tel: 719-274-0953. *Br Mgr,* Margie Wagnor
Open Wed 12:30-5:30, Fri & Sat 11-4

LA JUNTA

S KOSHARE INDIAN MUSEUM LIBRARY*, 115 W 18th St, 81050. (Mail add: PO Box 580, 81050-0580), SAN 321-2394. Tel: 719-384-4411. Web Site: www.kosharehistory.org. *Dir,* Jeremy Manyik; E-mail: jeremy.manyik@ojc.edu; Staff 2 (Non-MLS 2)
Founded 1950
Library Holdings: Bk Titles 4,000
Special Collections: Oral History
Open Mon-Sun 12-5
Restriction: Non-circulating

J OTERO JUNIOR COLLEGE*, Wheeler Library, 20 Pinon Ave, 81050. SAN 301-9594. Tel: 719-384-6882. Administration Tel: 719-384-6946. E-mail: WheelerLibrary@ojc.edu. Web Site: libguides.ojc.edu. *Dir,* Hailey Wold; E-mail: Hailey.Wold@ojc.edu; Staff 2 (MLS 1, Non-MLS 1)
Founded 1941. Enrl 463; Fac 38; Highest Degree: Associate
Jul 2015-Jun 2016 Income $60,839, State $4,000, Parent Institution $56,839. Mats Exp $331,963, Books $4,337, Per/Ser (Incl. Access Fees) $4,207, Electronic Ref Mat (Incl. Access Fees) $323,419. Sal $137,943 (Prof $81,887)
Library Holdings: AV Mats 1,312; Bks on Deafness & Sign Lang 3; CDs 439; DVDs 143; e-books 8,341; Electronic Media & Resources 7,825; Bk Titles 6,129; Bk Vols 71,338; Per Subs 62
Special Collections: Southwest Coll
Automation Activity & Vendor Info: (Acquisitions) Auto-Graphics, Inc; (Cataloging) Auto-Graphics, Inc; (Circulation) Auto-Graphics, Inc; (Course Reserve) Auto-Graphics, Inc; (OPAC) Auto-Graphics, Inc; (Serials) Auto-Graphics, Inc
Wireless access
Function: 24/7 Electronic res, Audio & video playback equip for onsite use, Bilingual assistance for Spanish patrons, Computers for patron use, E-Reserves, Electronic databases & coll, Free DVD rentals, ILL available, Internet access, Learning ctr, Magazines, Mail & tel request accepted, Online cat, Photocopying/Printing, Ref & res, Ref serv available, Scanner, Spanish lang bks, Study rm, Telephone ref, Wheelchair accessible
Partic in Colorado Library Consortium
Special Services for the Deaf - ADA equip; Assisted listening device; Assistive tech; Bks on deafness & sign lang; Closed caption videos
Special Services for the Blind - Assistive/Adapted tech devices, equip & products
Open Mon-Thurs 7:30-5, Fri 7:30-3

S UNITED STATES NATIONAL PARK SERVICE*, Bent's Old Fort National Historic Site Library, 35110 Hwy 194 E, 81050. SAN 374-7956. Tel: 719-383-5010. FAX: 719-383-2129. Web Site: www.nps.gov/beol. *Superintendent,* Alexa Roberts; E-mail: alexa.roberts@nps.gov
Library Holdings: Bk Vols 1,500
Open Mon-Sun (Summer) 8-5:30; Mon-Sun (Winter) 9-4

P WOODRUFF MEMORIAL LIBRARY*, City Library of La Junta, 522 Colorado Ave, 81050-2308. SAN 301-9608. Tel: 719-384-4612. FAX: 719-383-2514. *Dir, Libr Serv,* Heather Maes; E-mail: heather.maes@lajunta.lib.co.us; Staff 11 (Non-MLS 11)
Founded 1888. Pop 11,500; Circ 94,000
Library Holdings: Bk Titles 37,000; Bk Vols 45,000; Per Subs 69
Special Collections: Affiliate Dat Center-1990 Census; Area Newspaper Coll. Oral History
Subject Interests: Local hist
Automation Activity & Vendor Info: (Cataloging) Insignia Software; (Circulation) Insignia Software; (OPAC) Insignia Software
Wireless access
Function: 24/7 Electronic res, 24/7 Online cat, Computer training, Computers for patron use, Electronic databases & coll, ILL available, Internet access, Magazines, Magnifiers for reading, Microfiche/film & reading machines, OverDrive digital audio bks, Photocopying/Printing, Prog for adults, Prog for children & young adult, Ref serv available, Summer reading prog, Teen prog, Telephone ref, Wheelchair accessible
Publications: Centennial Brochure, 1988; Otero County Centennial Brochure, 1989
Open Mon-Thurs 9-7, Fri 9-6, Sat 9-4
Friends of the Library Group

LA VETA

P LA VETA REGIONAL LIBRARY DISTRICT*, La Veta Public Library, 310 S Main St, 81055. (Mail add: PO Box 28, 81055-0028), SAN 301-9616. Tel: 719-742-3572. E-mail: info@lvpl.org. Web Site: lvpl.org. *Libr Dir,* Anthony Masinton; E-mail: director@lavetalibrary.org; Staff 8 (MLS 1, Non-MLS 7)
Founded 1974. Pop 1,299; Circ 34,000
Library Holdings: Bk Vols 18,000
Special Collections: History (Colorado Coll), large print
Wireless access
Function: 24/7 Electronic res, 24/7 Online cat, Activity rm, Adult bk club, Archival coll, Art exhibits, Audio & video playback equip for onsite use, Audiobks via web, AV serv, Bks on CD, Children's prog, Computer training, Computers for patron use, Digital talking bks, E-Readers, Electronic databases & coll, Equip loans & repairs, Free DVD rentals, Holiday prog, Home delivery & serv to seniorr ctr & nursing homes, Homebound delivery serv, ILL available, Internet access, Life-long learning prog for all ages, Magazines, Mail & tel request accepted, Meeting rooms, Movies, Online cat, Orientations, Photocopying/Printing, Preschool outreach, Preschool reading prog, Printer for laptops & handheld devices, Prog for adults, Prog for children & young adult, Ref serv available, Scanner, Spoken cassettes & CDs, Story hour, Summer & winter reading prog, Summer reading prog, Tax forms, Teen prog, Telephone ref, Visual arts prog, Wheelchair accessible
Partic in Colorado Library Consortium
Open Mon-Thurs 10-7, Fri & Sat 10-5:30
Friends of the Library Group

LAFAYETTE

P LAFAYETTE PUBLIC LIBRARY, 775 W Baseline Rd, 80026. SAN 301-9624. Tel: 303-665-5200. FAX: 303-665-8936. E-mail: library@cityoflafayette.com. Web Site: www.cityoflafayette.com/945/library. *Libr Dir,* Melissa Hisel; E-mail: melissa.hisel@cityoflafayette.com; Staff 8 (MLS 6, Non-MLS 2)
Founded 1923. Pop 25,000; Circ 377,000
Library Holdings: Audiobooks 4,479; CDs 4,215; DVDs 3,777; e-books 1,537; Electronic Media & Resources 35; Bk Titles 96,739; Per Subs 228
Special Collections: Local History Coll; Spanish Language
Automation Activity & Vendor Info: (Acquisitions) SirsiDynix; (Cataloging) SirsiDynix; (Circulation) SirsiDynix; (OPAC) SirsiDynix
Wireless access
Function: Activity rm, Adult bk club, Archival coll, Art exhibits, Audiobks via web, Bilingual assistance for Spanish patrons, Bk club(s), Bks on CD, Children's prog, Computer training, Computers for patron use, E-Readers, E-Reserves, Electronic databases & coll, Family literacy, Free DVD rentals, Holiday prog, Homebound delivery serv, Homework prog, ILL available, Internet access, Jazz prog, Large print keyboards, Magazines, Magnifiers for reading, Mail & tel request accepted, Microfiche/film & reading machines, Music CDs, Online cat, Outreach serv, Outside serv via phone, mail, e-mail & web, OverDrive digital audio bks, Photocopying/Printing, Preschool outreach, Preschool reading prog, Prog for adults, Prog for children & young adult, Ref serv available, Scanner, Senior outreach, Serves people with intellectual disabilities, Spanish lang bks, Story hour, Study rm, Summer reading prog, Tax forms, Teen prog, Telephone ref, Wheelchair accessible, Workshops
Partic in Colorado Library Consortium
Open Mon-Thurs 10-8, Fri & Sat 10-5, Sun 1-5
Friends of the Library Group

LAKE CITY

P HINSDALE COUNTY LIBRARY DISTRICT, Lake City Public Library, 206 Silver St, 81235. (Mail add: PO Box 607, 81235-0607), SAN 376-284X. Tel: 970-944-2615. FAX: 970-944-4102. Web Site: www.lakecitypubliclibrary.com. *Dir,* Elaine Gray; E-mail: elaineg@lakecityschool.org
Circ 2,888
Library Holdings: Bk Vols 18,528; Per Subs 25; Talking Bks 527; Videos 1,497
Wireless access
Open Mon-Fri 12-4, Sat 10-1 (Summer); Mon-Fri 1-4 (Winter)
Friends of the Library Group

LAKEWOOD

C COLORADO CHRISTIAN UNIVERSITY*, Clifton Fowler Library, 180 S Garrison St, 80226. (Mail add: 8787 W Alameda Ave, 80226). Tel: 303-963-3250. FAX: 303-301-8252. E-mail: cculibrary@ccu.edu. Web Site: libguides.ccu.edu. *Dean of Libr,* Gayle Gunderson; E-mail: ggunderson@ccu.edu; Staff 4 (MLS 4)
Founded 1974. Fac 60; Highest Degree: Doctorate
Library Holdings: e-books 560,000; Bk Titles 40,804; Per Subs 95; Videos 58,000
Subject Interests: Educ, Humanities, Music, Relig

Automation Activity & Vendor Info: (Cataloging) Innovative Interfaces, Inc - Sierra; (Circulation) Innovative Interfaces, Inc - Sierra; (Course Reserve) Innovative Interfaces, Inc - Sierra; (ILL) OCLC FirstSearch
Wireless access
Partic in Marmot Library Network
Open Mon-Wed 7:30am-11 pm, Thurs 7:30-5, Fri 8-5, Sat 10-5, Sun 2-Midnight

P JEFFERSON COUNTY PUBLIC LIBRARY*, 10200 W 20th Ave, 80215. SAN 335-8623. Tel: 303-235-5275. Reference Tel: 303-232-9507. FAX: 303-275-2202. Web Site: jeffcolibrary.org. *Exec Dir,* Donna Walker; Tel: 303-275-2201, E-mail: ExecutiveDirector@jeffcolibrary.org; *Budget Dir, Dir of Finance,* Barbara Long; Tel: 303-275-6236, E-mail: barbara.long@jeffcolibrary.org; *Dir, IT,* Bernadette Berger; E-mail: ITDirector@jeffcolibrary.org; *Dir of Libr,* Julianne Rist; Tel: 303-275-2236, E-mail: julianne.rist@jeffcolibrary.org; *Dir, Facilities,* Steve Chestnut; Tel: 303-275-6236, E-mail: steve.chestnut@jeffcolibrary.org; *Dir, Staff Develop,* Sandie Coutts; Tel: 303-275-6160, E-mail: sandie.coutts@jeffcolibrary.org; *Asst Dir, Libr Experiences,* Lizzie Gall; Tel: 303-275-2204, E-mail: lizzie.gall@jeffcolibrary.org; *Asst Dir, Libr Experiences,* Padma Polepeddi; Tel: 303-275-2206, E-mail: padma.polepeddi@jeffcolibrary.org; Staff 226 (MLS 56, Non-MLS 170)
Founded 1952. Pop 515,200; Circ 3,137,585
Library Holdings: AV Mats 101,000; e-books 2,594; Bk Titles 329,881; Bk Vols 1,200,000; Per Subs 4,357
Special Collections: Jefferson County Archives Coll. State Document Depository; US Document Depository
Subject Interests: Art, Colorado, Consumer health, Folk music, Law, Railroads
Automation Activity & Vendor Info: (Cataloging) Innovative Interfaces, Inc; (Circulation) Innovative Interfaces, Inc; (OPAC) Innovative Interfaces, Inc
Wireless access
Publications: Exploring Your Library (Newsletter)
Special Services for the Deaf - TDD equip
Open Mon-Fri 8-5
Friends of the Library Group
Branches: 10
ARVADA LIBRARY, 7525 W 57th Ave, Arvada, 80002, SAN 335-8658. Web Site: jeffcolibrary.org/locations/AR. *Mgr,* Jennifer Reading; Tel: 303-403-5385, E-mail: jennifer.reading@JeffcoLibrary.org
Open Mon-Thurs 9-8, Fri & Sat 9-5, Sun 12-5
Friends of the Library Group
BELMAR, 555 S Alison Pkwy, 80226. Web Site: jeffcolibrary.org/locations/bl. *Mgr,* Joanna Stankiewicz; Tel: 303-403-5360, E-mail: joanna.stankiewicz@jeffcolibrary.org
Closed for renovations until Spring 2020
Friends of the Library Group
COLUMBINE, 7706 W Bowles Ave, Littleton, 80123, SAN 335-8682. Web Site: jeffcolibrary.org/locations/CL. *Mgr,* Rene Yaws; Tel: 303-403-5340, E-mail: rene.yaws@jeffcolibrary.org
Open Mon-Thurs 9-8, Fri & Sat 9-5, Sun 12-5
Friends of the Library Group
CONIFER PUBLIC, 10441 Hwy 73, Conifer, 80433, SAN 376-9119. Web Site: jeffcolibrary.org/locations/CF. *Mgr,* Jessica Paulsen; Tel: 303-403-5165, E-mail: jessica.paulsen@jeffcolibrary.org
Open Mon-Fri 2:30-8, Sat 9-5, Sun 12-5
Friends of the Library Group
EDGEWATER BRANCH, 1800 Harlan St, Edgewater, 80214, SAN 335-8771. Web Site: jeffcolibrary.org/locations/ED. *Mgr,* Nick Taylor; Tel: 303-403-5140, E-mail: nick.taylor@jeffcolibrary.org
Open Mon-Thurs 9-8, Fri & Sat 9-5, Sun 12-5
Friends of the Library Group
EVERGREEN BRANCH, 5000 Country Rd 73, Evergreen, 80439, SAN 335-8801. Web Site: jeffcolibrary.org/locations/EV. *Mgr,* Jessica Paulsen
Open Mon-Thurs 9-8, Fri & Sat 9-5, Sun 12-5
Friends of the Library Group
GOLDEN LIBRARY, 1019 Tenth St, Golden, 80401, SAN 335-8836. Web Site: jeffcolibrary.org/locations/GN. *Mgr,* Julianna Sipeki; Tel: 303-403-5120, E-mail: julianna.sipeki@jeffcolibrary.org
Founded 1914
Open Mon-Thurs 9-8, Fri & Sat 9-5, Sun 12-5
Friends of the Library Group
LAKEWOOD LIBRARY, 10200 W 20th Ave, 80215, SAN 335-8860. Web Site: jeffcolibrary.org/locations/LK. *Mgr,* Kelly Duran; Tel: 303-275-6180, E-mail: kelly.duran@jeffcolibrary.org
Open Mon-Thurs 9-8, Fri & Sat 9-5, Sun 12-5
Friends of the Library Group
STANDLEY LAKE LIBRARY, 8485 Kipling St, Arvada, 80005, SAN 371-4918. Web Site: jeffcolibrary.org/locations/SL. *Mgr,* Peg Hooper; Tel: 303-403-5100, E-mail: peg.hooper@jeffcolibrary.org
Founded 1992
Open Mon-Thurs 9-8, Fri & Sat 9-5, Sun 12-5
Friends of the Library Group
WHEAT RIDGE LIBRARY, 5475 W 32nd Ave, Wheat Ridge, 80212. Web Site: jeffcolibrary.org/locations/WR. *Mgr,* Nick Taylor; E-mail: nick.taylor@jeffcolibrary.org
Open Mon & Wed 10-8, Tues & Thurs 10-6, Sat 10-5, Sun 12-5
Friends of the Library Group
Bookmobiles: 1

G NATIONAL PARK SERVICE LIBRARY*, Denver Service Center, 12795 W Alameda Pkwy, 80228. (Mail add: PO Box 25287, Denver, 80225-0287), SAN 301-9667. Tel: 303-969-2133. FAX: 303-969-2557. Web Site: www.library.nps.gov. *Libr Mgr,* Alvin Sellmer; Tel: 303-969-2133, E-mail: Alvin_Sellmer@nps.gov; *Libr Tech,* Rory O'Connor; Tel: 303-969-2715; Staff 2 (MLS 2)
Founded 1971
Library Holdings: Bk Titles 30,000; Per Subs 120
Subject Interests: Architects, Construction, Ecology, Hist, Landscape archit, Planning
Automation Activity & Vendor Info: (Cataloging) OCLC; (OPAC) EOS International
Function: ILL available
Partic in OCLC Online Computer Library Center, Inc
Open Mon-Fri 8-4:30
Restriction: Open to pub for ref only

J RED ROCKS COMMUNITY COLLEGE*, Marvin Buckels Library, 13300 W Sixth Ave, 80228-1255. (Mail add: PO Box 14, 80228), SAN 301-9276. Tel: 303-914-6740. FAX: 303-914-6741. E-mail: library@rrcc.edu. Web Site: www.rrcc.edu/library-services. *Dir, Libr Serv,* Karen Neville; E-mail: karen.neville@rrcc.edu; *Coll Librn,* Pat Dunn; E-mail: pat.dunn@rrcc.edu
Founded 1969. Enrl 4,000; Fac 65; Highest Degree: Associate
Library Holdings: AV Mats 4,500; Bk Titles 38,000; Bk Vols 50,000; Per Subs 320
Automation Activity & Vendor Info: (Cataloging) TLC (The Library Corporation); (Circulation) TLC (The Library Corporation); (OPAC) TLC (The Library Corporation); (Serials) TLC (The Library Corporation)
Wireless access

C ROCKY MOUNTAIN COLLEGE OF ART & DESIGN LIBRARY*, 1600 Pierce St, 80214. SAN 377-9017. Tel: 303-753-6046, 303-753-6046, Ext 22405. FAX: 303-759-4970. Web Site: www.rmcad.edu. *Libr Dir,* Hugh Thurlow; E-mail: hthurlow@rmcad.edu; Staff 7 (MLS 2, Non-MLS 5)
Founded 1962. Enrl 700; Fac 150; Highest Degree: Master
Library Holdings: DVDs 3,200; e-books 323; e-journals 25; Electronic Media & Resources 10; Bk Titles 15,500; Per Subs 11
Automation Activity & Vendor Info: (Cataloging) Follett Software; (Circulation) Follett Software; (OPAC) Follett Software
Wireless access
Open Mon-Thurs 7:45am-8pm, Fri 7:45-6, Sat & Sun 11-3
Restriction: Private libr

LAMAR

J LAMAR COMMUNITY COLLEGE LIBRARY*, Bowman Bldg, 2401 S Main St, 81052-3999. SAN 301-9691. Tel: 719-336-1541. FAX: 719-336-2448. E-mail: library@lamarcc.edu. Web Site: www.lamarcc.edu/academics/library. *Libr Dir,* Jennifer Goodland; E-mail: jennifer.goodland@lamarcc.edu
Founded 1937. Enrl 609; Fac 44
Library Holdings: CDs 50; Bk Vols 15,000; Per Subs 60
Special Collections: Colorado Coll; Professional Instructor's Coll
Subject Interests: Cosmetology, Educ, Horse training mgt, Nursing
Automation Activity & Vendor Info: (Cataloging) Follett Software; (Circulation) Follett Software
Wireless access
Publications: Online media catalog
Open Mon-Thurs (Summer) 8-8, Fri 8-5; Mon-Thurs (Winter) 8-7

P LAMAR PUBLIC LIBRARY, 102 E Parmenter St, 81052-3239. SAN 301-9705. Tel: 719-336-4632. FAX: 719-336-1294. Web Site: lamarlibrary.colibraries.org. *Dir,* Sue Lathrop; Tel: 719-336-1293, E-mail: Sue.lathrop@ci.lamar.co.us; *Outreach Serv Librn,* Sheri Eirhart; Tel: 719-336-1291, E-mail: sheri.eirhart@ci.lamar.co.us; *Tech Coordr,* Sarah Ausmus; Tel: 719-336-1296, E-mail: saray.ausmus@ci.lamar.co.us; *Youth Serv Coordr,* Cheri Aguilera; Tel: 719-336-1297, E-mail: cheri.aguilera@ci.lamar.co.us; *Cat,* Hilah Gillespie; Tel: 719-336-1295, E-mail: hilah.gillespie@ci.lamar.co.us; *Cat, ILL,* Misty L Warren; Tel: 719-336-1292, E-mail: misty.warren@ci.lamar.co.us; Staff 6 (MLS 1, Non-MLS 5)
Founded 1906. Pop 7,400; Circ 90,000
Library Holdings: AV Mats 1,638; Bks on Deafness & Sign Lang 15; Large Print Bks 1,452; Bk Vols 45,200; Per Subs 70; Talking Bks 1,583
Special Collections: Colorado History Coll
Subject Interests: Spanish (Lang)
Wireless access
Special Services for the Blind - Talking bks

Open Mon-Thurs 9-6, Fri & Sat 9-5
Friends of the Library Group

LAS ANIMAS

P LAS ANIMAS - BENT COUNTY PUBLIC LIBRARY*, 306 Fifth St, 81054. SAN 301-9713. Tel: 719-456-0111. FAX: 719-456-0112. E-mail: bent.library@bentco.lib.co.us. Web Site: www.labclibrary.com. *Dir,* Karen Leck; Staff 1 (MLS 1)
Founded 1922. Pop 6,100; Circ 22,251
Library Holdings: Audiobooks 634; CDs 9; DVDs 19; Bk Titles 13,347; Per Subs 7; Videos 896
Special Collections: Bent County Coll & Llewellyn Thompson Coll
Automation Activity & Vendor Info: (Acquisitions) A-G Canada Ltd; (Cataloging) A-G Canada Ltd; (Circulation) A-G Canada Ltd; (Course Reserve) A-G Canada Ltd; (ILL) A-G Canada Ltd; (Media Booking) A-G Canada Ltd; (OPAC) A-G Canada Ltd; (Serials) A-G Canada Ltd
Wireless access
Function: CD-ROM, Govt ref serv, ILL available, Internet access, Photocopying/Printing, Prog for children & young adult, Ref serv available, Spoken cassettes & CDs, Summer reading prog, Telephone ref, VHS videos, Wheelchair accessible
Partic in Colorado Library Consortium
Open Mon-Fri 10-3
Restriction: Authorized patrons
Friends of the Library Group

LEADVILLE

J COLORADO MOUNTAIN COLLEGE*, Timberline Campus Library, 901 S US Hwy 24, 80461. SAN 378-4541. Tel: 719-486-4249. Interlibrary Loan Service Tel: 719-486-4283. Web Site: library.coloradomtn.edu/timberline. *Libr Dir,* Liz Miller; Tel: 719-486-4248, E-mail: esmiller@coloradomtn.edu; Staff 1 (MLS 1)
Founded 1967. Enrl 287; Highest Degree: Associate
Jul 2013-Jun 2014 Income $105,617. Mats Exp $13,600, Books $7,000, Per/Ser (Incl. Access Fees) $4,500, AV Mat $1,500, Presv $600. Sal $127,000 (Prof $61,044)
Library Holdings: AV Mats 763; Bks on Deafness & Sign Lang 20; Bk Titles 15,400; Bk Vols 17,000; Per Subs 61
Special Collections: Documents relating to EPA California Gulch Superfund Site (Lake County, Colorado)
Automation Activity & Vendor Info: (Circulation) Innovative Interfaces, Inc; (OPAC) Innovative Interfaces, Inc
Wireless access
Partic in Marmot Library Network
Open Mon-Thurs 8am-9pm, Fri 8-5, Sat 1-5, Sun 12-9

P LAKE COUNTY PUBLIC LIBRARY, 1115 Harrison Ave, 80461-3398. SAN 335-8984. Tel: 719-486-0569. FAX: 719-486-3544. E-mail: lcpl@lakecountypubliclibrary.org. Web Site: www.lakecountypubliclibrary.org. *Dir,* Brena Smith; E-mail: brena@lakecountypubliclibrary.org; *Children's Serv Coordr,* Position Currently Open; *Coordr, Youth Serv,* Sadie Rehm; *Circ,* Stacy Contreras; Staff 4 (MLS 1, Non-MLS 3)
Founded 1897. Pop 9,000; Circ 36,530
Library Holdings: AV Mats 769; Bk Titles 22,700; Bk Vols 23,235; Per Subs 95
Special Collections: Early Newspapers, micro, memorabilia; Local History (Colorado Mountain History Coll), bks, photos, pamphlets. Oral History
Automation Activity & Vendor Info: (Cataloging) Follett Software; (Circulation) Follett Software
Wireless access
Open Mon & Wed 10-8, Tues & Thurs 10-5, Fri & Sat 1-5, Sun (Sept-May) 1-5

LIMON

COLORADO DEPARTMENT OF CORRECTIONS

S LIMON CORRECTIONAL FACILITY-LAW LIBRARY*, 49030 State Hwy 71, 80826. Tel: 719-775-9221, Ext 3238. E-mail: lcflib@plains.net. *Librn,* Lanny Shelley
Library Holdings: Bk Vols 500
Open Mon-Fri 8-4

S LIMON CORRECTIONAL FACILITY LIBRARY-GENERAL*, 49030 State Hwy 71, 80826. Tel: 719-775-9221, Ext 3240. FAX: 719-775-7676. Web Site: www.doc.state.co.us. *Libr Tech,* Phyllis Wilson; E-mail: phyllis.wilson@state.co.us
Library Holdings: Bk Vols 12,000; Per Subs 55
Automation Activity & Vendor Info: (Cataloging) EOS International; (Circulation) EOS International

P LIMON MEMORIAL LIBRARY*, 205 E Ave, 80828. (Mail add: PO Box 236, 80828-0236), SAN 301-973X. Tel: 719-775-2163. FAX: 719-775-8808. E-mail: limonlibrary@yahoo.com. Web Site: lincolncounty.colibraries.org/limon_public_library. *Dir,* Lucille Reimer
Founded 1948. Circ 18,000
Library Holdings: Bk Vols 11,000; Per Subs 38
Special Collections: Eastern Colorado History Coll; Historical Picture Coll; Local Historical Audio Coll
Automation Activity & Vendor Info: (Acquisitions) LibLime Koha; (Cataloging) LibLime Koha; (Circulation) LibLime Koha; (ILL) LibLime Koha; (Media Booking) LibLime Koha
Wireless access
Special Services for the Deaf - Bks on deafness & sign lang; High interest/low vocabulary bks; Spec interest per
Open Mon-Thurs 10-8, Fri & Sat 10-2
Bookmobiles: 1. Dir, Katie Zipperer. Bk vols 2,500

LITTLETON

J ARAPAHOE COMMUNITY COLLEGE*, Library & Learning Commons, 5900 S Santa Fe Dr, 80160. SAN 301-9748. Circulation Tel: 303-797-5090. Reference Tel: 303-797-5726. E-mail: librarians@arapahoe.edu. Web Site: www.arapahoe.edu/student-resources/library. *Dir,* Lisa Chestnut; Tel: 303-797-5746, E-mail: lisa.chestnut@arapahoe.edu; *Head Ref Librn,* Lisa Blake; Tel: 303-797-5731, E-mail: lisa.blake@arapahoe.edu; *Archives Librn, Ref,* Courtney Johnston; E-mail: courtney.johnston@arapahoe.edu; *Libr Serv Coordr,* Shannon Basher; E-mail: shannon.basher@arapahoe.edu; Staff 6 (MLS 4, Non-MLS 2)
Founded 1966. Enrl 9,225; Fac 96; Highest Degree: Bachelor
Special Collections: Jim and Nan McKinnell Special Book Coll: Art and Ceramics
Subject Interests: Law, Nursing
Automation Activity & Vendor Info: (Cataloging) OCLC Worldshare Management Services; (Circulation) OCLC Worldshare Management Services; (Course Reserve) OCLC Worldshare Management Services; (Discovery) OCLC Worldshare Management Services; (OPAC) OCLC Worldshare Management Services
Wireless access
Partic in Colorado Library Consortium
Open Mon-Thurs 7:30am-9pm, Fri 7:30-5, Sat 9-2

P EDWIN A BEMIS PUBLIC LIBRARY*, Littleton Public Library, 6014 S Datura St, 80120-2636. SAN 301-9756. Tel: 303-795-3961. FAX: 303-795-3996. TDD: 303-795-3913. E-mail: bemislib@earthlink.net. Web Site: www.littletongov.org/bemis. *Dir,* Tim Nimz; E-mail: tnimz@littletongov.org; *Adult Serv Supvr,* Nancy Barnes Trimm; E-mail: ntrimm@littletongov.org; *Circ Supvr,* Rich Allen; E-mail: rallen@littletongov.org; *Ch Serv,* Val Fetters; E-mail: vfetters@littletongov.org; *ILL,* Barbara Stoelb; E-mail: bstoelb@littletongov.org; *Tech Serv,* Robin Trehaeven; E-mail: rtrehaeven@littletongov.org; *Teen Serv,* Emily McCabe; E-mail: emccabe@littletongov.org; Staff 19 (MLS 7, Non-MLS 12)
Founded 1897. Pop 48,000; Circ 529,146
Special Collections: Braille Books for Children, Adults, Teens; Colorado & Western History Coll
Subject Interests: Genealogy
Automation Activity & Vendor Info: (Acquisitions) SirsiDynix; (Cataloging) OCLC; (Circulation) SirsiDynix; (OPAC) SirsiDynix; (Serials) SirsiDynix
Wireless access
Special Services for the Deaf - High interest/low vocabulary bks; Sign lang interpreter upon request for prog; TTY equip
Special Services for the Blind - ZoomText magnification & reading software
Open Mon-Thurs 9-9, Fri & Sat 9-5, Sun 1-5
Friends of the Library Group

R DENVER SEMINARY*, Carey S Thomas Library, 6399 S Santa Fe Dr, 80120-2912. SAN 301-9004. Tel: 303-762-6962. Reference Tel: 303-762-6961. FAX: 303-762-6950. E-mail: library@denverseminary.edu. Web Site: www.denverseminary.edu/resources/our-library. *Libr Dir,* Keith Wells; Tel: 303-762-6963, E-mail: keith.wells@denverseminary.edu; *Dir of Libr Operations, Syst Tech,* Nadine Ginkel; Tel: 303-762-6955, E-mail: nadine.ginkel@denverseminary.edu; Staff 10 (MLS 4, Non-MLS 6)
Founded 1950. Enrl 875; Fac 25; Highest Degree: Doctorate
Library Holdings: Bk Titles 170,000; Per Subs 550
Subject Interests: Biblical studies, Theol
Automation Activity & Vendor Info: (Acquisitions) TLC (The Library Corporation); (Cataloging) TLC (The Library Corporation); (Circulation) TLC (The Library Corporation); (Course Reserve) TLC (The Library Corporation); (ILL) OCLC; (OPAC) TLC (The Library Corporation)
Wireless access
Function: Telephone ref
Partic in OCLC Online Computer Library Center, Inc
Open Mon-Thurs 7:30am-9:30pm, Fri 7:30-6, Sat 9:30-5
Restriction: Circ to mem only

S FEDERAL CORRECTIONAL INSTITUTION - ENGLEWOOD LIBRARY*, 9595 W Quincy Ave, 80123. SAN 377-8770. Tel: 303-985-1566. FAX: 303-763-2599. Web Site: www.bop.gov/locations/institutions/eng. *Educ Supvr,* Lowell McCormick
Library Holdings: Bk Titles 6,000; Per Subs 17
Open Mon-Fri 7-3:30

S LITTLETON MUSEUM RESEARCH CENTER*, 6028 S Gallup, 80120. SAN 301-9764. Tel: 303-795-3950. FAX: 303-730-9818. Web Site: www.littletongov.org/museum. *Dir,* Timothy Nimz; E-mail: mutn@littletongov.org; *Curator,* Jennifer Hankinson; E-mail: jhankinson@littletongov.org; Staff 1 (Non-MLS 1)
Founded 1969
Library Holdings: Bk Vols 800; Per Subs 10
Special Collections: Early Exploration Maps; Littleton History Coll, bks, doc, micro, photog
Wireless access
Restriction: Open by appt only
Friends of the Library Group

LONGMONT

J FRONT RANGE COMMUNITY COLLEGE*, Boulder County Campus Library, 2190 Miller Dr, 80501. Tel: 303-678-3721. *Campus Librn,* Che Gant; E-mail: che.gant@frontrange.edu
Wireless access
Open Mon-Thurs 9-5, Fri 9-4

P LONGMONT PUBLIC LIBRARY, 409 Fourth Ave, 80501-6006. SAN 301-9780. Tel: 303-651-8470. Circulation Tel: 303-651-8476. Interlibrary Loan Service Tel: 303-651-8772. Reference Tel: 303-651-8472. E-mail: longmont.library@longmontcolorado.gov. Web Site: www.longmontcolorado.gov/departments/departments-e-m/library. *Dir,* Nancy Kerr; E-mail: nancy.kerr@longmontcolorado.gov; *Head, Adult Serv,* Pennie Burris; *Circ Serv Mgr,* Jennifer Marks; *Ch Serv,* Elektra Greer; Staff 20 (MLS 12, Non-MLS 8)
Founded 1871. Pop 92,000; Circ 1,100,000
Library Holdings: Bk Titles 260,000; Bk Vols 360,000; Per Subs 400
Special Collections: Local Newspaper Coll, to 1878, index/microfilm
Subject Interests: Automotive, Bus, Career, Consumer, Spanish
Automation Activity & Vendor Info: (Acquisitions) Innovative Interfaces, Inc - Sierra; (Cataloging) Innovative Interfaces, Inc - Sierra; (Circulation) Innovative Interfaces, Inc - Sierra; (ILL) OCLC; (OPAC) Innovative Interfaces, Inc - Sierra; (Serials) Innovative Interfaces, Inc - Sierra
Wireless access
Function: 24/7 Electronic res, 24/7 Online cat, Adult bk club
Partic in Flatirons Library Consortium
Special Services for the Deaf - Video relay services
Special Services for the Blind - Aids for in-house use
Open Mon-Thurs (Winter) 10-9, Fri & Sat 9-5, Sun 1-5; Mon-Thurs (Summer) 9-9, Fri & Sat 9-5
Friends of the Library Group

LOUISVILLE

P LOUISVILLE PUBLIC LIBRARY, 951 Spruce St, 80027. SAN 301-9810. Tel: 303-335-4849. FAX: 303-335-4833. E-mail: libraryinfo@louisvilleco.gov. Web Site: www.louisville-library.org. *Dir,* Sharon Nemechek; E-mail: snemechek@louisvilleco.gov; *Circ Supvr,* Lisa Merly; E-mail: lisam@louisvillego.gov; *Youth Serv Supvr,* Kristen Bodine; E-mail: kbodine@louisvilleco.gov; *Adult Serv,* Peggy Norris; E-mail: pnorris@louisvilleco.gov; Staff 18 (MLS 9, Non-MLS 9)
Founded 1925. Pop 31,000; Circ 494,889
Jan 2015-Dec 2015 Income $1,453,437, State $9,707, Federal $250. Mats Exp $139,058, Books $62,737, Per/Ser (Incl. Access Fees) $9,570, AV Mat $20,866, Electronic Ref Mat (Incl. Access Fees) $45,885. Sal $895,114
Library Holdings: Audiobooks 2,848; CDs 6,901; DVDs 6,154; e-books 14,804; Electronic Media & Resources 6,766; Bk Vols 77,121; Per Subs 183
Special Collections: Louisville History
Automation Activity & Vendor Info: (Acquisitions) Innovative Interfaces, Inc - Sierra; (Cataloging) Innovative Interfaces, Inc - Sierra; (Circulation) Innovative Interfaces, Inc - Sierra; (ILL) Innovative Interfaces, Inc - Sierra; (OPAC) Innovative Interfaces, Inc - Sierra
Wireless access
Function: 24/7 Electronic res, 24/7 Online cat, Adult bk club, After school storytime, Art exhibits, Audiobks via web, Bks on CD, Children's prog, Computer training, Computers for patron use, Electronic databases & coll, Family literacy, Free DVD rentals, Holiday prog, Home delivery & serv to seniorr ctr & nursing homes, Homebound delivery serv, Homework prog, ILL available, Internet access, Learning ctr, Life-long learning prog for all ages, Magazines, Mail & tel request accepted, Mango lang, Meeting rooms, Music CDs, Online cat, Online ref, Outreach serv, OverDrive digital audio bks, Photocopying/Printing, Preschool outreach, Preschool reading prog, Prog for adults, Prog for children & young adult, Ref serv available, Scanner, Spanish lang bks, Story hour, Summer & winter reading prog, Summer reading prog, Teen prog, Wheelchair accessible, Winter reading prog, Workshops
Open Mon-Thurs 10-8, Fri & Sat 10-6, Sun 1-5

LOVELAND

P LOVELAND PUBLIC LIBRARY*, 300 N Adams Ave, 80537. SAN 301-9837. Tel: 970-962-2665. Circulation Tel: 970-962-2586. Reference Tel: 970-962-2402. FAX: 970-962-2905. TDD: 970-962-2407. E-mail: reference@cityofloveland.org. Web Site: www.lovelandpubliclibrary.org. *Dir,* Diane Lapierre; Tel: 970-962-2404, E-mail: diane.lapierre@cityofloveland.org; *Media Coordr,* Jesse Lopez; *Ch Serv,* Beth Gudmestad; Tel: 970-962-2448, E-mail: beth.gudmestad@cityofloveland.org; *Ref (Info Servs),* Amy Phillips; Tel: 970-962-2589; Staff 46 (MLS 7, Non-MLS 39)
Founded 1905. Pop 66,250; Circ 872,870
Library Holdings: AV Mats 23,403; High Interest/Low Vocabulary Bk Vols 1,500; Bk Titles 137,915; Bk Vols 150,000; Per Subs 304; Talking Bks 2,102
Special Collections: Loveland History Coll; Western Americana Books Coll. Oral History
Automation Activity & Vendor Info: (Acquisitions) Innovative Interfaces, Inc; (Cataloging) Innovative Interfaces, Inc; (Circulation) Innovative Interfaces, Inc; (ILL) Innovative Interfaces, Inc; (OPAC) Innovative Interfaces, Inc; (Serials) Innovative Interfaces, Inc
Wireless access
Function: Adult bk club, After school storytime, Archival coll, Art exhibits, Audio & video playback equip for onsite use, Audiobks via web, AV serv, Bk club(s), Bks on cassette, Bks on CD, Bus archives, Children's prog, Computer training, Computers for patron use, Digital talking bks, E-Reserves, Electronic databases & coll, Free DVD rentals, Genealogy discussion group, Holiday prog, Home delivery & serv to seniorr ctr & nursing homes, Homebound delivery serv, ILL available, Instruction & testing, Internet access, Magnifiers for reading, Music CDs, Notary serv, Online cat, Online info literacy tutorials on the web & in blackboard, Online ref, Outreach serv, Outside serv via phone, mail, e-mail & web, OverDrive digital audio bks, Photocopying/Printing, Prog for adults, Prog for children & young adult, Ref serv available, Scanner, Senior computer classes, Senior outreach, Spoken cassettes & CDs, Spoken cassettes & DVDs, Story hour, Summer reading prog, Tax forms, Teen prog, Telephone ref, VHS videos, Wheelchair accessible, Workshops, Writing prog
Publications: Through Zethyl's Eyes: A Loveland History (Local historical information)
Special Services for the Deaf - TDD equip
Special Services for the Blind - Descriptive video serv (DVS)
Open Mon-Thurs 9-8, Fri & Sat 9-6, Sun (Sept-May) 1-5
Restriction: Badge access after hrs, In-house use for visitors, Non-circulating coll
Friends of the Library Group

LYONS

P LYONS REGIONAL LIBRARY, 451 Fourth Ave, 80540. (Mail add: PO Box 619, 80540), SAN 377-9858. Tel: 303-823-5165. E-mail: info@lyonslibrary.com. Web Site: lyons.colibraries.org. *Dir,* Kara Bauman; Staff 6 (MLS 3, Non-MLS 3)
Founded 1977. Pop 5,500; Circ 19,620
Library Holdings: AV Mats 1,700; Per Subs 25
Special Collections: Local History Coll
Wireless access
Function: 24/7 Electronic res, 24/7 Online cat, Adult bk club, Art exhibits, Audiobks via web, Bk club(s), Bks on CD, Chess club, Children's prog, Computer training, Computers for patron use, Digital talking bks, Electronic databases & coll, Free DVD rentals, Games & aids for people with disabilities, ILL available, Instruction & testing, Internet access, Magazines, Movies, Museum passes, Music CDs, Notary serv, Online cat, Preschool outreach, Printer for laptops & handheld devices, Prog for adults, Prog for children & young adult, Ref & res, Ref serv available, Senior computer classes, Senior outreach, Story hour, Summer & winter reading prog, Summer reading prog, Teen prog, Wheelchair accessible, Winter reading prog, Writing prog
Partic in Colorado Library Consortium
Open Mon & Fri 10-5, Tues-Thurs 10-7:30, Sat 10-2
Friends of the Library Group

MANCOS

P MANCOS PUBLIC LIBRARY, 211 W First St, 81328. (Mail add: PO Box 158, 81328-0158), SAN 301-9845. Tel: 970-533-7600. FAX: 970-533-7289. E-mail: info@mancoslibrary.org. Web Site: www.mancoslibrary.org. *Dir,* Lee Hallberg; E-mail: lhallberg@mancostlibrary.org; Staff 3 (Non-MLS 3)
Founded 1946. Pop 3,500; Circ 22,336
Library Holdings: Bk Titles 12,000; Bk Vols 35,000; Per Subs 12
Special Collections: Southwest Coll

Automation Activity & Vendor Info: (Cataloging) Follett Software
Wireless access
Open Mon-Thurs 10-7, Fri 10-5, Sat 10-3
Friends of the Library Group

MEEKER

P MEEKER REGIONAL LIBRARY DISTRICT*, 490 Main St, 81641. SAN 301-987X. Tel: 970-878-5911. FAX: 970-878-5495. E-mail: meekerlibrary@yahoo.com. *Libr Dir,* Mike Bartlett; Staff 2 (MLS 1, Non-MLS 1)
Founded 1913. Pop 2,400; Circ 27,000
Automation Activity & Vendor Info: (Acquisitions) Book Systems; (Cataloging) Book Systems; (Circulation) Book Systems; (OPAC) Book Systems
Wireless access
Function: Adult bk club, Bks on cassette, Bks on CD, CD-ROM, Children's prog, Free DVD rentals, ILL available, Instruction & testing, Magnifiers for reading, Music CDs, Online cat, Photocopying/Printing, Prog for adults, Ref serv available, Scanner, Serves people with intellectual disabilities, Spoken cassettes & CDs, Story hour, Summer reading prog, Tax forms, Telephone ref, VHS videos
Open Mon, Wed & Fri 9:30-5:30, Tues & Thurs 9:30-9, Sat 9:30-2
Friends of the Library Group

MODEL

S COLORADO DEPARTMENT OF CORRECTIONS*, Trinidad Correctional Facility Library, 21000 Hwy 350, 81059. Tel: 719-845-3212. Administration FAX: 719-845-3237. Web Site: www.doc.state.co.us. *Libr Tech,* Position Currently Open
Founded 2002
Library Holdings: Bk Titles 6,200; Per Subs 35
Automation Activity & Vendor Info: (Cataloging) EOS International; (Circulation) EOS International; (OPAC) EOS International
Restriction: Not open to pub

MONTE VISTA

P CARNEGIE PUBLIC LIBRARY*, 120 Jefferson St, 81144-1797. SAN 301-9896. Tel: 719-852-3931. FAX: 719-852-0821. E-mail: rgclibrarydistrict@yahoo.com. Web Site: www.montevistalibrary.org. *Dir,* Carol Lee Dugan; E-mail: cldugan70@gmail.com
Founded 1918. Pop 9,400; Circ 110,000
Library Holdings: Audiobooks 400; CDs 200; DVDs 290; e-books 3,050; Large Print Bks 890; Bk Vols 69,011; Talking Bks 300; Videos 600
Special Collections: Colorado History Coll; County Newspapers, microflm
Automation Activity & Vendor Info: (Circulation) Book Systems
Wireless access
Partic in Colorado Library Consortium
Open Mon-Wed & Fri 10-5, Thurs 10-8, Sat 10-4
Friends of the Library Group
Branches: 1
SOUTH FORK BRANCH, 0031 Mall St, South Fork, 81154, SAN 320-0833. Tel: 719-873-5079. FAX: 719-873-5192. E-mail: sfbcarnegie@yahoo.com. *Br Librn,* Melanie Dawn Hart
Open Mon-Wed & Fri 10-5, Thurs 10-8, Sat 10-4
Friends of the Library Group

MONTROSE

P MONTROSE REGIONAL LIBRARY DISTRICT*, 320 S Second St, 81401. SAN 335-9255. Tel: 970-249-9656. FAX: 970-240-1901. Web Site: www.montroselibrary.org. *Dir,* Paul H Paladino; Tel: 970-249-9656, Ext 2550, E-mail: ppaladino@montroselibrary.org; *Head, Circ,* Kristen Seger; E-mail: kseger@montroselibrary.org; *Head, Youth Serv,* Jeri Gilham; E-mail: jgilham@montroselibrary.org; *Head, Adult Serv,* Lindsay Beckman; E-mail: lbeckman@montroselibrary.org; *Asst Dir,* Tania Hajjar; E-mail: thajjar@montroselibrary.org; Staff 14 (MLS 8, Non-MLS 6)
Founded 1969. Pop 40,536; Circ 284,569
Library Holdings: Audiobooks 4,744; DVDs 10,865; Bk Vols 109,240; Per Subs 123
Special Collections: Genealogy; Local History
Automation Activity & Vendor Info: (Cataloging) SirsiDynix; (Circulation) SirsiDynix; (ILL) SirsiDynix; (OPAC) SirsiDynix; (Serials) SirsiDynix
Wireless access
Function: 24/7 Electronic res, 24/7 Online cat, Adult bk club, Art exhibits, Audiobks via web, Bilingual assistance for Spanish patrons, Bk club(s), Bks on CD, Chess club, Children's prog, Computers for patron use, Electronic databases & coll, Free DVD rentals, Holiday prog, Home delivery & serv to seniorr ctr & nursing homes, ILL available, Instruction & testing, Internet access, Large print keyboards, Life-long learning prog for all ages, Magazines, Magnifiers for reading, Mail & tel request accepted, Mango lang, Meeting rooms, Microfiche/film & reading machines, Movies, Music CDs, Online cat, Orientations, Outreach serv, OverDrive digital audio bks, Passport agency, Photocopying/Printing, Preschool outreach, Preschool reading prog, Prof lending libr, Prog for adults, Prog for children & young adult, Ref & res, Scanner, Senior outreach, Spanish lang bks, STEM programs, Story hour, Study rm, Summer reading prog, Tax forms, Teen prog, Telephone ref, Wheelchair accessible
Open Mon-Thurs 10-7, Fri 10-6, Sat 10-5, Sun 1-5
Friends of the Library Group
Branches: 2
NATURITA BRANCH, 107 W First Ave, Naturita, 81422. (Mail add: PO Box 466, Naturita, 81422-0466), SAN 335-928X. Tel: 970-865-2848. FAX: 970-865-2157. *Coordr,* Susan Rice; E-mail: srice@montroselibrary.org; Staff 4 (Non-MLS 4)
Library Holdings: Bk Vols 8,000
Friends of the Library Group
PARADOX BRANCH, 21501 Six Mile Rd, Paradox, 81429. (Mail add: PO Box 419, Paradox, 81429-0419), SAN 335-9344. Tel: 970-859-7236. FAX: 970-859-7235. E-mail: library@paradoxvalleyschool.org. *Br Coordr,* Raquel Schultz; Staff 1 (Non-MLS 1)
Library Holdings: Bk Vols 8,823; Per Subs 8
Open Mon 12:30-7, Wed & Fri 12:30-5
Friends of the Library Group
Bookmobiles: 1. Head, Outreach Servs, Jeri Gilham

NEDERLAND

P NEDERLAND COMMUNITY LIBRARY*, 200 Hwy 72 N, 80466. (Mail add: PO Box 836, 80466-0836). Tel: 303-258-1101. E-mail: nederlandlibrary@gmail.com. Web Site: nederland.colibraries.org. *Dir,* Elektra Greer; E-mail: egreer.ncl@gmail.com; *Libr Asst,* Marni Siegal; E-mail: marnis.ncl@gmail.com
Library Holdings: Bk Titles 13,400; Per Subs 52
Automation Activity & Vendor Info: (Cataloging) Koha; (Circulation) Koha
Wireless access
Open Mon-Sat 10-2

NORWOOD

P LONE CONE LIBRARY, 1455 Pinion St, 81423. (Mail add: PO Box 127, 81423-0127), SAN 376-2858. Tel: 970-327-4833. FAX: 970-327-4129. Web Site: loneconelibrary.org. *Dir,* Carrie Andrew; E-mail: carrie@loneconelibrary.org
Founded 1978. Pop 2,000
Library Holdings: Audiobooks 6,736; AV Mats 1,258; DVDs 2,170; e-books 23,201; Large Print Bks 595; Bk Titles 11,752; Per Subs 24; Talking Bks 601
Special Collections: Charlie Fowler Coll
Automation Activity & Vendor Info: (Cataloging) Mandarin Library Automation; (Circulation) Mandarin Library Automation; (OPAC) Mandarin Library Automation
Wireless access
Function: 24/7 Electronic res, 24/7 Online cat, Accelerated reader prog, Audiobks via web, Bks on CD, Children's prog, Computers for patron use, E-Reserves, Electronic databases & coll, For res purposes, Holiday prog, Homebound delivery serv, ILL available, Instruction & testing, Internet access, Learning ctr, Life-long learning prog for all ages, Magazines, Magnifiers for reading, Mail & tel request accepted, Movies, Notary serv, Online cat, Online info literacy tutorials on the web & in blackboard, Online ref, Orientations, Outreach serv, Outside serv via phone, mail, e-mail & web, OverDrive digital audio bks, Photocopying/Printing, Preschool outreach, Preschool reading prog, Printer for laptops & handheld devices, Prog for children & young adult, Ref & res, Ref serv available, Res assist avail, Scanner, Senior outreach, Serves people with intellectual disabilities, Spanish lang bks, STEM programs, Story hour, Summer & winter reading prog, Summer reading prog, Tax forms, Teen prog, Wheelchair accessible
Partic in Colorado Library Consortium
Open Mon-Fri 10-5, Sat 11-4
Friends of the Library Group

NUCLA

P NUCLA PUBLIC LIBRARY, 544 Main St, 81424. (Mail add: PO Box 129, 81424-0129), SAN 301-9942. Tel: 970-864-2166. FAX: 970-864-2123. E-mail: library.nucla@gmail.com. Web Site: nuclapl.colibraries.org. *Dir,* Lori McKinney
Pop 750; Circ 6,500
Library Holdings: CDs 250; DVDs 250; Bk Vols 6,500; Per Subs 20; Talking Bks 400; Videos 150
Wireless access
Partic in Colorado Library Consortium
Open Tues & Thurs-Sat 10-6, Wed 10-7

OAK CREEK

P SOUTH ROUTT LIBRARY DISTRICT*, Oak Creek Public Library, 227 Dodge Ave, 80467. (Mail add: PO Box 896, 80467-0896), SAN 336-0032. Tel: 970-736-8371. FAX: 970-736-8371. E-mail: southrouttlibrarydistrict@gmail.com. Web Site: southroutt.colibraries.org. *Libr Mgr,* Deborah Curtis; *Librn,* Crystal Rodgers; Staff 4 (Non-MLS 4)
Library Holdings: Bk Titles 8,000; Per Subs 4
Automation Activity & Vendor Info: (Acquisitions) Koha; (Circulation) Koha; (OPAC) Koha
Wireless access
Function: 24/7 Online cat, Adult bk club
Open Mon, Wed & Fri 10-5, Tues 1-5, Sat 10-2
Branches: 1
YAMPA PUBLIC LIBRARY, 116 Main St, Yampa, 80483. (Mail add: PO Box 10, Yampa, 80483-0010), SAN 302-0398. Tel: 970-638-4654. FAX: 970-638-4654. *Libr Mgr,* Debbie Curtis; *Librn,* Crystal Rodgers; *Librn,* Judy Wyatt
Founded 1934
Library Holdings: Audiobooks 200; DVDs 520; Bk Titles 6,000
Special Collections: Local History Coll; Old Western Novels
Open Mon & Tues 10-5, Thurs 3-7, Fri 10-4

ORDWAY

P COMBINED COMMUNITY LIBRARY, 1007 Main St, 81063-1316. SAN 301-9969. Tel: 719-267-3823. E-mail: ordwaylibrary@gmail.com. Web Site: combinedcommunity.colibraries.org. *Dir,* Jody O'Leary
Circ 4,154
Library Holdings: Bk Titles 27,000
Open Mon & Sun 11-5, Thurs & Fri 4pm-6pm, Sat 11-5
Friends of the Library Group

PAGOSA SPRINGS

P RUBY M SISSON MEMORIAL LIBRARY*, 811 San Juan St, 81147. (Mail add: PO Box 849, 81147-0849), SAN 302-0002. Tel: 970-264-2209. FAX: 970-264-4764. E-mail: ruby@pagosalibrary.org. Web Site: pagosa.colibraries.org. *Dir,* Meg Wempe; Staff 9 (MLS 4, Non-MLS 5)
Founded 1985. Pop 12,000; Circ 90,000
Library Holdings: Bk Titles 29,600; Per Subs 70
Special Collections: Chimney Rock Coll; Hershey Coll (Southwest Literature); Southwest Coll
Automation Activity & Vendor Info: (Cataloging) SirsiDynix; (Circulation) SirsiDynix; (OPAC) SirsiDynix
Wireless access
Function: Adult bk club, Adult literacy prog, Bk club(s), Bks on CD, Children's prog, Computer training, E-Readers, Electronic databases & coll, Free DVD rentals, Holiday prog, ILL available, Internet access, Laminating, Life-long learning prog for all ages, Magazines, Meeting rooms, Online cat, Outreach serv, Preschool outreach, Prog for adults, Prog for children & young adult, Ref serv available, Scanner, Spanish lang bks, Story hour, Teen prog
Special Services for the Blind - Accessible computers; Bks on CD; Large print bks
Open Mon & Wed 9-6, Tues & Thurs 9-7, Fri & Sat 9-5
Friends of the Library Group

PENROSE

P PENROSE COMMUNITY LIBRARY DISTRICT*, 35 Seventh Ave, 81240-0318. SAN 376-4966. Tel: 719-372-6017. Administration Tel: 719-372-6017, Ext 20. FAX: 719-372-6018. Web Site: penrose.colibraries.org. *Dir,* Kristi Lindsey; E-mail: klindsey40@hotmail.com
Founded 1992. Pop 5,000
Library Holdings: Audiobooks 510; CDs 147; Bk Vols 15,127; Per Subs 27; Videos 2,592
Automation Activity & Vendor Info: (Cataloging) Follett Software; (Circulation) Follett Software; (OPAC) Follett Software
Wireless access
Partic in Colorado Library Consortium
Open Mon & Wed 10-8, Tues, Thurs & Fri 10-6, Sat 10-2
Friends of the Library Group

PETERSON AFB

A UNITED STATES AIR FORCE, Peterson Air Force Base Library FL2500, 21 FSS/FSDL, 201 W Stewart Ave, Bldg 1171, 80914-1600. SAN 335-976X. Tel: 719-556-7462. FAX: 719-556-6752. E-mail: peterson.base.library@gmail.com. Web Site: www.21fss.com/about/library. *Dir,* Rebecca Perkins; Tel: 719-556-7643, E-mail: rebecca.perkins.1@us.af.mil; Staff 6 (MLS 2, Non-MLS 4)
Founded 1950
Library Holdings: DVDs 2,000; Large Print Bks 50; Bk Titles 40,000; Per Subs 150
Subject Interests: Aeronaut, Bus & mgt, Mil hist, Space sci
Wireless access
Open Mon & Wed-Fri 9-5, Tues 9-7, Sat 9-2
Restriction: Open to govt employees only

PINE GROVE

P PINE PUBLIC LIBRARY*, 16720 Pine Valley Rd, 80470. SAN 378-018X. Tel: 303-838-6093. FAX: 303-838-6093. Web Site: pinelibrary.org.
Library Holdings: Bk Titles 10,000
Wireless access
Open Tues & Thurs 3-6, Sat 10-2

PLATTEVILLE

P PLATTEVILLE PUBLIC LIBRARY*, 504 Marion Ave, 80651. (Mail add: PO Box 567, 80651-0567), SAN 302-0010. Tel: 970-785-2231. FAX: 970-785-0708. E-mail: plattevillelibrary@yahoo.com. Web Site: www.coloradoplattevillelibrary.us. *Dir,* Dianne Norgren; Staff 3 (Non-MLS 3)
Founded 1932. Pop 2,500; Circ 30,000
Library Holdings: DVDs 100; Large Print Bks 500; Bk Titles 24,000; Per Subs 25; Talking Bks 1,100; Videos 400
Subject Interests: State hist, World War II
Automation Activity & Vendor Info: (Circulation) Horizon
Wireless access
Mem of High Plains Library District
Open Mon, Tues & Fri 10-6, Wed & Thurs 10-8, Sat 10-2

PUEBLO

COLORADO DEPARTMENT OF CORRECTIONS
S LAVISTA CORRECTIONAL FACILITY LIBRARY*, 1401 W 17th St, 81003. (Mail add: PO Box 3, 81002-0003). Tel: 719-544-4800, Ext 3721. FAX: 719-583-5909. *Libr Tech II,* Kristy Scott; E-mail: kristy.scott@doc.state.co.us; Staff 3 (MLS 1, Non-MLS 2)
Automation Activity & Vendor Info: (Cataloging) EOS International; (Circulation) EOS International
S SAN CARLOS CORRECTIONAL FACILITY LIBRARY*, 1410 W 13th St, 81003-1961, SAN 376-5792. Tel: 719-544-4800, Ext 3346. FAX: 719-583-5510. *Libr Tech,* Beth Masterson
Library Holdings: Bk Titles 4,500; Per Subs 28
Automation Activity & Vendor Info: (Cataloging) EOS International; (Circulation) EOS International; (OPAC) EOS International
S YOUTH OFFENDER SERVICES*, PO Box 35010, 81003. Tel: 719-544-4800, Ext 3507. FAX: 719-583-5909. *Librn,* Elina Shneyder; *Libr Tech,* Sue Lutz
Automation Activity & Vendor Info: (Cataloging) EOS International; (Circulation) EOS International; (OPAC) EOS International
Function: ILL available, Photocopying/Printing
Open Mon-Wed 7am-8pm, Thurs & Fri 7-4, Sat & Sun 7:30-4
Restriction: Private libr

GM COLORADO MENTAL HEALTH INSTITUTE OF PUEBLO*, Hospital Community Library, 1600 W 24th St, 81003. SAN 335-9794. Tel: 719-546-4197. FAX: 719-546-4484. E-mail: cdhs_cmhipinfo@state.co.us. Web Site: www.colorado.gov/pacific/cdhs/colorado-mental-health-institute-pueblo. *Librn,* Sharon Foote; Staff 2 (MLS 1, Non-MLS 1)
Library Holdings: Audiobooks 150; DVDs 400; Large Print Bks 124; Bk Titles 960; Bk Vols 10,945; Per Subs 52; Videos 300
Automation Activity & Vendor Info: (Cataloging) Follett Software; (Circulation) Follett Software
Open Mon-Thurs 8-3:30, Fri 8-12
Restriction: Staff & patient use

C COLORADO STATE UNIVERSITY - PUEBLO*, 2200 Bonforte Blvd, 81001-4901. SAN 302-0053. Tel: 719-549-2361. Circulation Tel: 719-549-2386. Interlibrary Loan Service Tel: 719-549-2362. Reference Tel: 719-549-2333. FAX: 719-549-2738. Web Site: library.csupueblo.edu. *Dean, Libr Serv,* Rhonda Gonzales; E-mail: rhonda.gonzales@csupueblo.edu; *Dept Chair, Univ Archivist,* Beverly Allen; Tel: 719-549-2475, E-mail: beverly.allen@csupueblo.edu; *Liaison Librn, Outreach Coordr, User Experience Coord,* Betsy Schippers; Tel: 719-549-2826, E-mail: betsy.schippers@csupueblo.edu; *Information Literacy Coord,* Alexis Wolstein; Tel: 719-549-2363, E-mail: alexis.wolstein@csupueblo.edu; Staff 12 (MLS 6, Non-MLS 6)
Founded 1933. Enrl 3,500; Fac 185; Highest Degree: Master
Special Collections: Colorado Chicano Movement Archives; University Archives; US Western History, pamphlets, bks. US Document Depository
Automation Activity & Vendor Info: (Acquisitions) Ex Libris Group; (Cataloging) Ex Libris Group; (Circulation) Ex Libris Group; (Course Reserve) Ex Libris Group; (Discovery) Ex Libris Group; (ILL) OCLC Tipasa; (OPAC) Ex Libris Group; (Serials) Ex Libris Group
Wireless access

Partic in Colorado Alliance of Research Libraries; Colorado Library Consortium
Open Mon-Thurs 7am-11pm, Fri 7-6, Sat 10-6, Sun 1-11

S DEPARTMENT OF HUMAN SERVICES-YOUTH CORRECTIONS*, Pueblo Youth Services Center Library, 1406 W 17th St, 81003. Tel: 719-546-4928. FAX: 719-546-4917. Web Site: youthlibraries.org/pueblo-youth-services-center. *Librn,* Mark Valdez; E-mail: mark.s.valdez@state.co.us
Library Holdings: Bk Vols 500; Per Subs 13
Restriction: Not open to pub

P PUEBLO CITY-COUNTY LIBRARY DISTRICT*, Robert Hoag Rawlings Public Library, 100 E Abriendo Ave, 81004-4290. SAN 335-9859. Tel: 719-562-5600. FAX: 719-562-5610. Web Site: www.pueblolibrary.org. *Exec Dir,* Jon Walker; Tel: 719-562-5625, E-mail: jon.walker@pueblolibrary.org; *Assoc Exec Dir,* Sherri Baca; Tel: 719-562-5652, E-mail: sherri.baca@pueblolibrary.org; *Dir, Commun Relations,* Nick Potter; Tel: 719-562-5605, E-mail: nick.potter@pueblolibrary.org; *IT Dir,* Robert Childress; Tel: 719-562-5622, E-mail: robert.childress@pueblolibrary.org; *Libr Mgr,* Amy Nelson; E-mail: amy.nelson@pueblolibrary.org; Staff 88 (MLS 21, Non-MLS 67)
Founded 1891. Pop 156,737; Circ 1,278,881
Library Holdings: AV Mats 9,285; CDs 3,019; DVDs 13,357; e-journals 19,286; Electronic Media & Resources 63; Large Print Bks 8,153; Bk Titles 189,839; Bk Vols 553,091
Special Collections: Business (Frank I Lamb Memorial Coll); Southeastern Colorado Coll, photogs; Western-American History (Western Research Coll). Oral History; State Document Depository; US Document Depository
Subject Interests: Genealogy, Hispanic studies, Local hist
Automation Activity & Vendor Info: (Acquisitions) SirsiDynix; (Cataloging) SirsiDynix; (Circulation) SirsiDynix; (ILL) OCLC WorldShare Interlibrary Loan; (OPAC) SirsiDynix; (Serials) SirsiDynix
Wireless access
Publications: Calendar of Events (Monthly); InfoZone (Newsletter)
Partic in Colorado Library Consortium
Special Services for the Deaf - Assisted listening device; TDD equip
Special Services for the Blind - Accessible computers; Assistive/Adapted tech devices, equip & products; Audio mat; BiFolkal kits; Bks on CD; Closed circuit TV magnifier; Dragon Naturally Speaking software; Large print bks; Playaways (bks on MP3); ZoomText magnification & reading software
Open Mon-Thurs 9-9, Fri & Sat 9-6, Sun 1-5
Friends of the Library Group
Branches: 6
FRANK & MARIE BARKMAN BRANCH, 1300 Jerry Murphy Rd, 81001, SAN 335-9883. Reference E-mail: bark.ref@pueblolibrary.org. *Br Mgr,* Alicia Grebel; E-mail: alicia.grebel@pueblolibrary.org; Staff 8 (MLS 2, Non-MLS 6)
Founded 1990
Library Holdings: Audiobooks 3,023; DVDs 3,449; Large Print Bks 1,501; Bk Titles 40,000; Bk Vols 63,729
Open Mon-Thurs 9-9, Fri & Sat 9-6
Friends of the Library Group
TOM L & ANNA MARIE GIODONE LIBRARY, 24655 US Hwy 50 E, 81006. *Br Mgr,* Kayci Barnett; E-mail: kayci.barnett@pueblolibrary.org
Open Mon-Thurs 10-7, Fri & Sat 10-6
GREENHORN VALLEY LIBRARY, 4801 Cibola Dr, Colorado City, 81019. *Br Mgr,* Position Currently Open
Open Mon-Thurs 10-7, Fri & Sat 10-6
FRANK I LAMB BRANCH, 2525 S Pueblo Blvd, 81005, SAN 322-5801. *Br Mgr,* Jennifer Tozer; E-mail: jennifer.tozer@pueblolibrary.org; Staff 6 (MLS 2, Non-MLS 4)
Founded 1984. Circ 186,135
Open Mon-Thurs 9-9, Fri & Sat 9-6
Friends of the Library Group
PUEBLO WEST LIBRARY, 298 S Joe Martinez Blvd, Pueblo West, 81007, SAN 377-6360. *Br Mgr,* Heather Wilder; E-mail: heather.wilder@pueblolibrary.org; Staff 9 (MLS 4, Non-MLS 5)
Founded 1997. Circ 186,135
Open Mon-Thurs 9-9, Fri & Sat 9-6
Friends of the Library Group
PATRICK A LUCERO LIBRARY, 1315 E Seven St, 81001. *Br Mgr,* Diann Logie; E-mail: diann.logie@pueblolibrary.org
Open Mon-Thurs 9-9, Fri & Sat 10-6

J PUEBLO COMMUNITY COLLEGE LIBRARY*, 900 W Orman Ave, 81004-1430. SAN 325-2264. Tel: 719-549-3305. E-mail: libraryservices@pueblocc.edu. Web Site: www.pueblocc.edu/Library/Information. *Dir,* Christina McGrath; Tel: 719-549-3308, E-mail: Christina.McGrath@pueblocc.edu; *Circ Serv,* Dawn Reitz; Tel: 719-549-3113, E-mail: Dawn.Reitz@pueblocc.edu; *Tech Serv,* Tracy Overton; Tel: 719-549-3307, E-mail: Tracy.Overton@pueblocc.edu; Staff 3 (Non-MLS 3)
Founded 1979. Enrl 12,876; Fac 112; Highest Degree: Associate
Jul 2014-Jun 2015 Income $63,471, State $63,471. Mats Exp $41,394, Books $2,678, Per/Ser (Incl. Access Fees) $20,170, Other Print Mats $7,800, AV Mat $648, Electronic Ref Mat (Incl. Access Fees) $2,296
Library Holdings: Audiobooks 2; AV Mats 5,921; Braille Volumes 1; CDs 693; DVDs 5,010; e-books 33,004; e-journals 8,908; Electronic Media & Resources 13; Microforms 115; Bk Titles 18,526; Bk Vols 19,162; Per Subs 40; Talking Bks 1; Videos 78
Special Collections: College Archives
Subject Interests: Criminal justice, Dental hygiene, Respiratory therapy
Automation Activity & Vendor Info: (Acquisitions) Auto-Graphics, Inc; (Cataloging) OCLC; (Circulation) Auto-Graphics, Inc; (Course Reserve) Auto-Graphics, Inc; (OPAC) Auto-Graphics, Inc; (Serials) Auto-Graphics, Inc
Wireless access
Function: Archival coll
Partic in Colorado Library Consortium; LYRASIS
Special Services for the Deaf - ADA equip; Bks on deafness & sign lang; Closed caption videos
Special Services for the Blind - Digital talking bk machines
Open Mon-Thurs 8-8, Fri 8-4, Sat 10-2

RANGELY

J COLORADO NORTHWESTERN COMMUNITY COLLEGE LIBRARY*, 500 Kennedy Dr, CNCC-Box 29, 81648. SAN 302-0061. Tel: 970-675-3334, 970-675-3576. Toll Free Tel: 800-562-1105, Ext 3334. FAX: 970-675-3590. Web Site: www.cncc.edu/library. *Interim Libr Dir,* Leana J Cox; E-mail: leana.cox@cncc.edu; Staff 1 (Non-MLS 1)
Founded 1962. Enrl 762; Fac 46; Highest Degree: Associate
Jul 2019-Jun 2020 Income $31,300, State $25,250, Federal $5,000, Locally Generated Income $50, Other $1,000. Mats Exp $36,300, Books $4,000, Per/Ser (Incl. Access Fees) $10,161, Other Print Mats $249, AV Equip $100, AV Mat $2,000, Electronic Ref Mat (Incl. Access Fees) $19,790. Sal $54,000 (Prof $54,000)
Library Holdings: AV Mats 360; Bks on Deafness & Sign Lang 22; CDs 220; DVDs 6,360; e-books 774; High Interest/Low Vocabulary Bk Vols 632; Large Print Bks 120; Microforms 5,515; Music Scores 99; Bk Titles 21,356; Bk Vols 27,935; Per Subs 109; Talking Bks 936; Videos 190
Special Collections: Colorado History Coll; Native American, Children's Section and Drama Theater
Subject Interests: Rare bks, Ref bks
Automation Activity & Vendor Info: (Cataloging) Follett Software; (Circulation) Follett Software; (Discovery) EBSCO Online; (ILL) OCLC FirstSearch; (OPAC) Follett Software; (Serials) Follett Software
Wireless access
Function: Bks on CD, Spoken cassettes & CDs, VHS videos, Wheelchair accessible, Workshops
Partic in Capitol Area Library Consortium; Colorado Library Consortium; Western Colorado Academic Library Consortium
Open Mon-Thurs 7:30am-9pm, Fri 7:30-4, Sun 1-9
Friends of the Library Group

P RANGELY REGIONAL LIBRARY*, 109 E Main St, 81648-2737. SAN 302-007X. Tel: 970-675-8811. FAX: 970-675-8844. *Dir,* Amorette Hawkins; Staff 4 (Non-MLS 4)
Founded 1960. Pop 2,400; Circ 17,700
Library Holdings: Bk Titles 20,000; Bk Vols 23,000; Per Subs 25
Automation Activity & Vendor Info: (Cataloging) Follett Software; (Circulation) Follett Software
Wireless access
Open Mon-Fri 10-6

RED FEATHER LAKES

P RED FEATHER LAKES COMMUNITY LIBRARY*, 71 Firehouse Lane, 80545. (Mail add: PO Box 123, 80545-0123). Tel: 970-881-2664. FAX: 970-881-2836. E-mail: help@redfeatherlibrary.org. Web Site: redfeather.colibraries.org. *Libr Dir,* Creed Kidd; E-mail: director@redfeatherlibrary.org; *Financial Serv, User Serv,* Jeanette Heath; E-mail: jeanette@redfeatherlibrary.org; *Programming Serv, User Serv,* Darlene Kilpatrick; E-mail: darlene@redfeatherlibrary.org; Staff 7 (MLS 1, Non-MLS 6)
Founded 1969. Pop 1,810
Automation Activity & Vendor Info: (Cataloging) ByWater Solutions; (Circulation) ByWater Solutions; (OPAC) ByWater Solutions
Wireless access
Function: 24/7 Electronic res, 24/7 Online cat, 3D Printer, Accelerated reader prog, Adult bk club, After school storytime, Art exhibits, Audiobks on Playaways & MP3, Audiobks via web, AV serv, Bi-weekly Writer's Group, Bk club(s), Bks on cassette, Bks on CD, Children's prog, Computer training, Computers for patron use, E-Readers, E-Reserves, Electronic databases & coll, Equip loans & repairs, Free DVD rentals, Holiday prog, ILL available, Internet access, Laminating, Magazines, Magnifiers for reading, Mail & tel request accepted, Makerspace, Meeting rooms, Movies,

Music CDs, Notary serv, Online cat, Online ref, Outreach serv, OverDrive digital audio bks, Photocopying/Printing, Printer for laptops & handheld devices, Prog for adults, Prog for children & young adult, Ref & res, Ref serv available, Scanner, Serves people with intellectual disabilities, Spoken cassettes & CDs, Spoken cassettes & DVDs, Story hour, Summer reading prog, Teen prog, Telephone ref, Wheelchair accessible, Workshops, Writing prog
Partic in Colorado Library Consortium
Open Mon-Sun 9-6
Friends of the Library Group

RIDGWAY

P RIDGWAY PUBLIC LIBRARY*, 300 Charles St, 81432. Tel: 970-626-5252. FAX: 970-626-5252. E-mail: library@ouraynet.com. Web Site: www1.youseemore.com/ridgwayPL. *Dir,* Kristen Moberg
Pop 2,350
Library Holdings: AV Mats 500; Bk Titles 15,000
Open Mon, Tues & Thurs 10-6, Wed 10-7, Fri 10-5, Sat & Sun 10-3
Friends of the Library Group

RIFLE

S COLORADO DEPARTMENT OF CORRECTIONS*, Rifle Correctional Center Library, 0200 County Rd 219, 81650. SAN 327-7666. Tel: 970-625-1700. FAX: 970-625-7565. Web Site: www.colorado.gov/cdoc. *Libr Tech,* Amanda Reigel
Library Holdings: AV Mats 300; Bk Titles 5,200; Per Subs 24
Automation Activity & Vendor Info: (Cataloging) EOS International; (Circulation) EOS International
Restriction: Staff & inmates only

P GARFIELD COUNTY PUBLIC LIBRARY DISTRICT*, 207 East Ave, 81650. (Mail add: PO Box 832, 81650), SAN 335-9433. Tel: 970-625-4270. FAX: 970-625-4472. Web Site: www.gcpld.org. *Asst Exec Dir,* Amy Shipley; E-mail: ashipley@gcpld.org; Staff 30 (MLS 2, Non-MLS 28)
Founded 1938. Pop 37,627; Circ 226,229
Library Holdings: Bk Vols 157,420; Per Subs 292
Special Collections: Oral History
Subject Interests: Agr, Alternative sources (energy), Art, Colorado
Automation Activity & Vendor Info: (Acquisitions) Innovative Interfaces, Inc; (Cataloging) Innovative Interfaces, Inc; (Circulation) Innovative Interfaces, Inc; (Course Reserve) Innovative Interfaces, Inc; (ILL) Innovative Interfaces, Inc; (Media Booking) Innovative Interfaces, Inc; (OPAC) Innovative Interfaces, Inc; (Serials) Innovative Interfaces, Inc
Open Mon-Fri 9-5
Friends of the Library Group
Branches: 6
CARBONDALE BRANCH, 320 Sopris Ave, Carbondale, 81623, SAN 335-9468. Tel: 970-963-2889. FAX: 970-963-8573. *Br Mgr,* Lacy Dunlavy
Library Holdings: Bk Titles 21,000
Friends of the Library Group
GLENWOOD SPRINGS BRANCH, 815 Cooper Ave, Glenwood Springs, 81601, SAN 335-9492. Tel: 970-945-5958. FAX: 970-945-7723. *Br Mgr,* Laurin Arnold
Library Holdings: Bk Vols 29,527
Friends of the Library Group
NEW CASTLE BRANCH, 402 W Main, New Castle, 81647. (Mail add: PO Box 320, New Castle, 81647-0320), SAN 373-5249. Tel: 970-984-2346. FAX: 970-984-2081. *Br Mgr,* Jenn Cook
Library Holdings: Bk Vols 53,173
Friends of the Library Group
PARACHUTE BRANCH, 244 Grand Valley Way, Parachute, 81635-9608, SAN 335-9506. Tel: 970-285-9870. FAX: 970-285-7477.
Library Holdings: Bk Vols 14,131
Friends of the Library Group
RIFLE BRANCH, 207 East Ave, 81650, SAN 335-9522. Tel: 970-625-3471. FAX: 970-625-3549. *Br Mgr,* Judy Martens
Library Holdings: Bk Vols 24,431
Friends of the Library Group
SILT BRANCH, 680 Home Ave, Silt, 81652, SAN 335-9530. Tel: 970-876-5500. FAX: 970-876-5921. *Br Mgr,* Linda Lewis
Library Holdings: Bk Vols 15,147
Friends of the Library Group

ROCKY FORD

P ROCKY FORD PUBLIC LIBRARY*, 400 S Tenth St, 81067. SAN 302-0096. Tel: 719-254-6641. FAX: 719-254-6647. E-mail: rflib@rockyford.lib.co.us. Web Site: rockyford.colibraries.org. *Dir,* Leeana Chavez; Staff 4 (MLS 1, Non-MLS 3)
Founded 1905. Pop 5,000; Circ 20,000
Library Holdings: CDs 531; Large Print Bks 1,272; Bk Titles 21,000; Bk Vols 18,000; Per Subs 4; Talking Bks 460; Videos 517
Automation Activity & Vendor Info: (Cataloging) Auto-Graphics, Inc; (Circulation) Auto-Graphics, Inc; (OPAC) Auto-Graphics, Inc
Wireless access
Function: Homebound delivery serv, ILL available, Magnifiers for reading, Music CDs, Online cat, Photocopying/Printing, Preschool outreach, Prog for adults, Prog for children & young adult, Scanner, Senior outreach, Story hour, Summer reading prog, Tax forms, VHS videos, Wheelchair accessible
Special Services for the Deaf - Assisted listening device; Closed caption videos; Video & TTY relay via computer
Special Services for the Blind - Audio mat; Bks available with recordings; Bks on cassette; Bks on CD; Cassette playback machines; Cassettes; Closed circuit TV; Copier with enlargement capabilities; Home delivery serv; Integrated libr/media serv; Large print & cassettes; Large print bks; Large screen computer & software; Large type calculator; Low vision equip; Magnifiers
Open Mon-Wed 10-6, Thurs & Fri 9-5, Sat 9-1
Friends of the Library Group

SAGUACHE

P SAGUACHE PUBLIC LIBRARY, 702 Pitkin Ave, 81149. (Mail add: PO Box 448, 81149-0448), SAN 335-9913. Tel: 719-655-2551. Web Site: nscld.colibraries.org. *Dir,* Sarah Koehn Frey; E-mail: librarydirector@nsclibrarydistrict.org
Founded 1953. Pop 600; Circ 16,000
Library Holdings: Bk Titles 20,000; Per Subs 52
Special Collections: American History & Memorials; Bicentennial History; Colorado & Southwest History; Cookbooks; Juvenile; Saguache & Saguache County; Southwest Fiction & Nonfiction
Subject Interests: Am hist, Colorado
Automation Activity & Vendor Info: (Cataloging) Koha; (Circulation) Koha; (Course Reserve) Koha; (ILL) Koha; (OPAC) Koha
Function: 24/7 Electronic res, 24/7 Online cat, Activity rm, Audiobks via web, Bks on CD, Children's prog, Computers for patron use, Electronic databases & coll, Free DVD rentals, Magazines, Mail & tel request accepted, Meeting rooms, Movies, Online cat, Online info literacy tutorials on the web & in blackboard, Photocopying/Printing, Printer for laptops & handheld devices, Prog for adults, Prog for children & young adult, Ref & res, Res assist avail, Scanner, Story hour, Summer reading prog, Telephone ref
Partic in Colorado Library Consortium
Open Mon-Fri 10-5, Sat 10-4
Friends of the Library Group

SALIDA

P SALIDA REGIONAL LIBRARY, 405 E St, 81201. SAN 302-010X. Tel: 719-539-4826. Web Site: www.salidalibrary.org. *Libr Dir,* Susan Matthews; E-mail: smatthews@salidalibrary.org; *Cat, Ch,* Becky Nelson; *Circ Mgr,* Amy Potts; Staff 13 (Non-MLS 13)
Founded 1908. Pop 9,000; Circ 196,372
Library Holdings: Audiobooks 3,514; Bk Vols 57,645; Per Subs 205; Videos 5,273
Special Collections: Local History Coll; Sheet Music Coll
Automation Activity & Vendor Info: (Acquisitions) SirsiDynix; (Cataloging) SirsiDynix; (Circulation) SirsiDynix; (OPAC) SirsiDynix; (Serials) SirsiDynix
Wireless access
Publications: Library Information (Brochure)
Open Mon-Fri 9-7, Sat 9-5, Sun 1-5

SAN LUIS

P COSTILLA COUNTY LIBRARY*, 418 Gasper St, 81152. (Mail add: PO Box 351, 81152-0351), SAN 302-0118. Tel: 719-672-3309. FAX: 719-672-3309. E-mail: ccplsanluis@yahoo.com. Web Site: www.colorado.gov/pacific/costillacounty/public-library-system. *Libr Dir,* Alice Sanchez
Founded 1972. Pop 3,660
Library Holdings: CDs 5; DVDs 5; Bk Titles 10,000; Per Subs 4; Videos 20
Special Collections: Bilingual (Children; Bilingual-Bicultural); Literature (Adult Spanish Book); Minority Studies (Southwest Chicano); Solar Energy Coll. Oral History
Partic in Colorado Library Consortium
Open Mon-Fri 9:30-4:30
Branches: 1
BLANCA-FT GARLAND BRANCH, Garland Community Ctr, 2nd Flr, 17591 E Hwy 160, Blanca, 81123. (Mail add: PO Box 310, Blanca, 81123-0310). Tel: 719-379-3945. FAX: 719-379-3945. E-mail: ccplnorth@fone.net. *Libr Dir,* Alice Sanchez
Founded 2007

Library Holdings: CDs 10; DVDs 10; Large Print Bks 20; Bk Titles 5,000; Videos 20
Open Mon-Wed (Summer) 10-5, Thurs 10-6; Mon & Tues (Fall-Spring) 10-5, Wed 12-5, Thurs 10-6

SECURITY

P SECURITY PUBLIC LIBRARY, 715 Aspen Dr, 80911-1807. SAN 302-0126. Tel: 719-391-3191. Circulation Tel: 719-391-3196. Reference Tel: 719-391-3195. FAX: 719-392-7641. Web Site: www.securitypubliclibrary.org. *Libr Dir,* Susan Schmitz-Garrett; Tel: 719-390-2814, E-mail: garretts@wsd3.org; *Head, Pub Serv,* Sarah Anspach; Tel: 719-391-3190; *Ref Librn,* Samantha Lacy; Tel: 719-391-3195; *Children's Mgr,* Molly Uffelman; Tel: 719-391-3197; Staff 8 (MLS 5, Non-MLS 3)
Founded 1961. Pop 50,000; Circ 100,000
Subject Interests: Colorado
Automation Activity & Vendor Info: (Cataloging) Koha; (Circulation) Koha; (OPAC) Koha
Wireless access
Publications: Newsletter (Quarterly)
Partic in Colorado Library Consortium
Open Mon-Thurs 9-7, Fri & Sat 9-5
Friends of the Library Group

SILVERTON

P SILVERTON PUBLIC LIBRARY*, 1117 Reese, 81433. (Mail add: PO Box 68, 81433-0068), SAN 302-0142. Tel: 970-387-5770. FAX: 970-387-0217. Web Site: silverton.colibraries.org. *Dir,* Jackie Kerwin; E-mail: jkerwin@silverton.co.us
Founded 1901. Pop 800; Circ 8,700
Library Holdings: AV Mats 60; Bk Titles 10,000; Per Subs 21
Subject Interests: Local hist
Automation Activity & Vendor Info: (Cataloging) LibLime Koha; (Circulation) LibLime Koha; (OPAC) LibLime Koha
Wireless access
Open Tues-Thurs 11-8, Fri & Sat 10-5
Friends of the Library Group

SPRINGFIELD

P BACA COUNTY LIBRARY*, 1260 Main St, 81073-1542. SAN 302-0169. Tel: 719-523-6962. E-mail: bacalibrary@bacacountyco.gov. *Dir,* Beulah Collins
Founded 1925. Pop 4,514; Circ 9,996
Library Holdings: AV Mats 252; Bk Vols 10,283; Per Subs 40
Wireless access
Open Mon-Fri 10-5
Friends of the Library Group
Branches: 2
TWO BUTTES BRANCH, Main St, Two Buttes, 81084. (Mail add: PO Box 52, Two Buttes, 81084-0052). *Dir,* Beaulah Collins
Pop 50
Library Holdings: Bk Vols 2,000
WALSH BRANCH, 400 N Colorado St, Walsh, 81090. (Mail add: PO Box 201, Walsh, 81090-0201). Tel: 719-324-5349. FAX: 719-324-5349. *Librn,* Hebbard Janice
Library Holdings: Bk Vols 5,000; Per Subs 16
Open Mon-Wed 1:30-5:30

STEAMBOAT SPRINGS

J COLORADO MOUNTAIN COLLEGE*, Steamboat Campus Library, 1275 Crawford Ave, 80487. SAN 324-654X. Tel: 970-870-4445. FAX: 970-870-4490. Web Site: library.coloradomtn.edu/steamboat. *Dir,* Kevin Williams; Tel: 970-870-4493, E-mail: kwilliams@coloradomtn.edu; *Ref & Instruction Librn,* Tracey Urbick; Tel: 970-870-4451, E-mail: turbick@coloradomtn.edu; *ILL, Libr Tech,* Jonathan Beam; Tel: 970-870-4449, E-mail: jlbeam@coloradomtn.edu; Staff 3 (MLS 2, Non-MLS 1)
Founded 1983. Highest Degree: Bachelor
Special Collections: Colorado State Documents. State Document Depository
Subject Interests: Bus, Resort mgt, Ski bus, Sustainability
Wireless access
Open Mon-Thurs 9-9, Fri 9-5, Sat 12-5, Sun 1-9 (Winter); Mon-Thurs 9-8, Fri 9-5, Sun 1-8 (Summer)

P BUD WERNER MEMORIAL LIBRARY*, 1289 Lincoln Ave, 80487. SAN 335-9972. Tel: 970-879-0240. Web Site: www.steamboatlibrary.org. *Dir,* Christine Painter; Tel: 970-879-0240, Ext 304, E-mail: cpainter@steamboatlibrary.org; *Adminr,* Carolyn Peters; Tel: 970-879-0240, Ext 316, E-mail: cpeters@steamboatlibrary.org; *Ref Librn,* John Major; Tel: 970-879-0240, Ext 305, E-mail: jmajor@steamboatlibrary.org; *Circ Mgr,* Michelle Dover; Tel: 970-879-0240, Ext 307, E-mail: mdover@steamboatlibrary.org; *Adult Serv Coordr,* Jennie Lay; Tel: 970-879-0240, Ext 317, E-mail: jlay@steamboatlibrary.org; *Youth Serv,* Sarah Kostin; Tel: 970-879-0240, Ext 314, E-mail: skostin@steamboatlibrary.org; Staff 15 (MLS 3, Non-MLS 12)
Founded 1967. Pop 15,040; Circ 234,260
Library Holdings: Large Print Bks 431; Bk Titles 62,500; Bk Vols 72,695; Per Subs 250; Talking Bks 4,321; Videos 3,542
Special Collections: Ski History Coll; Western Coll
Automation Activity & Vendor Info: (Cataloging) Innovative Interfaces, Inc; (Circulation) Innovative Interfaces, Inc; (OPAC) Innovative Interfaces, Inc
Wireless access
Partic in Marmot Library Network; OCLC Online Computer Library Center, Inc
Open Mon-Thurs 9-8, Fri 9-6, Sat 9-5, Sun 10-5

STERLING

S COLORADO DEPARTMENT OF CORRECTIONS*, Sterling Correctional Facility Library-West Side, 12101 Hwy 61, 80751. (Mail add: PO Box 6000, 80751-6000). Tel: 970-521-5010, Ext 3404. FAX: 970-521-8905. Web Site: www.doc.state.co.us. *Dir,* Dale Boardman; E-mail: dale.boardman@state.co.us; *Libr Tech II,* Edna Edelen; E-mail: edna.edelen@state.co.us; *Libr Tech II,* Ralph Gadbois; E-mail: ralph.gadbois@state.co.us; *Libr Tech II,* Michelle Youngblood; E-mail: michelle.l.youngblood@state.co.us
Library Holdings: Bk Vols 18,500; Per Subs 50
Automation Activity & Vendor Info: (Cataloging) EOS International; (Circulation) EOS International; (OPAC) EOS International
Open Mon-Fri 8-10:30, 1-3 & 7-8, Sat & Sun 8-10:30 & 1-3:30
Branches:
STERLING CORRECTIONAL FACILITY LIBRARY- WEST - EAST, 12101 Hwy 61, 80751. (Mail add: PO Box 6000, 80751). Tel: 970-521-5010, Ext 3827. FAX: 970-521-8905. *Librn II,* Dale Boardman; Tel: 970-521-5010, E-mail: dale.boardman@state.co.us; *Libr Tech II,* Jessica Stucky; E-mail: jessica.stucky@state.co.us; *Libr Tech II,* Amelia Wirth; E-mail: amelia.wirth@state.co.us
Library Holdings: Bk Vols 14,000; Per Subs 50

J NORTHEASTERN JUNIOR COLLEGE*, Monahan Library, 100 College Ave, 80751. SAN 302-0177. Tel: 970-521-6612. Automation Services Tel: 970-521-6613. FAX: 970-521-6759. Web Site: www.njc.edu/library. *Libr Tech,* Leslie Rosa; E-mail: leslie.rosa@njc.edu; Staff 6 (MLS 1, Non-MLS 5)
Founded 1941. Enrl 1,500; Fac 95; Highest Degree: Associate
Jul 2012-Jun 2013 Income $150,000. Mats Exp $75,090. Sal $241,198
Subject Interests: Colorado
Automation Activity & Vendor Info: (Cataloging) Auto-Graphics, Inc; (Circulation) Auto-Graphics, Inc; (OPAC) Auto-Graphics, Inc
Wireless access
Open Mon-Thurs 7:45am-10pm, Fri 7:45-5, Sun 4pm-9pm

P STERLING PUBLIC LIBRARY, 420 N Fifth St, 80751-3363. (Mail add: PO Box 4000, 80751-4000), SAN 302-0185. Tel: 970-522-2023. FAX: 970-522-2657. E-mail: library@sterlingcolo.com. Web Site: sterlingcolo.com/departments/parks_library_and_recreation/library.php. *Dir,* Wade Gandee; E-mail: gandee@sterlingcolo.com; *Librn, Superintendent,* Sandy VanDusen; E-mail: vandusen@sterlingcolo.com; Staff 1 (MLS 1)
Founded 1918. Pop 18,000; Circ 103,000
Library Holdings: Bk Titles 70,000; Per Subs 71
Special Collections: Aviation Coll; Western History (Otto C Unfug Coll & T M Rogers Coll). State Document Depository
Automation Activity & Vendor Info: (Cataloging) Innovative Interfaces, Inc; (Circulation) Innovative Interfaces, Inc; (Serials) Innovative Interfaces, Inc
Wireless access
Open Mon-Thurs 9-8, Fri & Sat 9-5, Sun 1-5
Friends of the Library Group

STRATTON

P STRATTON PUBLIC LIBRARY*, 331 New York Ave, 80836. SAN 302-0193. Tel: 719-348-5922. FAX: 719-348-5922. E-mail: strattonlibrary@yahoo.com. Web Site: stratton.colibraries.org. *Head Librn,* Janice Salmans
Pop 500; Circ 7,250
Library Holdings: Bk Vols 5,000
Automation Activity & Vendor Info: (Cataloging) Koha; (Circulation) Koha
Wireless access
Open Tues & Thurs 10-1

TELLURIDE

P WILKINSON PUBLIC LIBRARY*, 100 W Pacific Ave, 81435. (Mail add: PO Box 2189, 81435), SAN 302-0215. Tel: 970-728-4519. E-mail: askus@telluridelibrary.org. Web Site: www.telluridelibrary.org. *Dir,* Sarah Landeryou; *Tech Serv Librn,* Alison Farnham; *Tech Serv Mgr,* Amy Sieving; Staff 9 (MLS 7, Non-MLS 2)
Founded 1975. Pop 6,300; Circ 250,000
Library Holdings: Audiobooks 9,800; Bk Vols 45,000; Videos 10,000
Special Collections: Books about Film; Classic Movie Video Coll
Automation Activity & Vendor Info: (Acquisitions) Innovative Interfaces, Inc - Millennium; (Cataloging) Innovative Interfaces, Inc - Millennium; (Circulation) Innovative Interfaces, Inc - Millennium; (OPAC) Innovative Interfaces, Inc
Wireless access
Partic in Marmot Library Network
Open Mon-Thurs 10-8, Fri & Sat 10-6, Sun Noon-5
Friends of the Library Group

THORNTON

S ALTIERUS CAREER COLLEGE*, Thornton Campus Library, 9065 Grant St, 80229. SAN 377-466X. Tel: 303-457-2757. *Librn,* Anna Andrews; E-mail: anna.andrews@zenith.org; Staff 1 (MLS 1)
Enrl 100; Fac 12; Highest Degree: Associate
Library Holdings: Bk Vols 1,262; Per Subs 18
Automation Activity & Vendor Info: (OPAC) LibraryWorld, Inc
Wireless access
Restriction: Students only

P ANYTHINK LIBRARIES*, 5877 E 120th Ave, 80602. SAN 335-9557. Tel: 303-288-2001. FAX: 303-451-0190. E-mail: ithink@anythinklibraries.org. Web Site: www.anythinklibraries.org. *Dir,* Pam Sandlian Smith; E-mail: psmith@anythinklibraries.org; *Dir, Strategic Initiatives,* Stacie Ledden; *Dir, Technology,* Logan Macdonald; *Asst Dir,* Susan Dobbs; E-mail: sdobbs@anythinklibraries.org; *Fac Mgr,* Doug Squires; *Finance Mgr,* Nanette Fisher; Staff 139 (MLS 25, Non-MLS 114)
Founded 1953. Pop 416,083; Circ 2,232,038
Jan 2015-Dec 2015 Income (Main & Associated Libraries) $14,041,957, County $13,442,423. Mats Exp $1,942,591, Books $1,111,823, Per/Ser (Incl. Access Fees) $34,472, Other Print Mats $433,162, Electronic Ref Mat (Incl. Access Fees) $363,134. Sal $4,750,558
Library Holdings: Audiobooks 15,536; CDs 16,582; e-books 34,220; Bk Vols 275,670; Per Subs 127; Videos 54,885
Special Collections: Community Health Resource Center
Automation Activity & Vendor Info: (Acquisitions) Horizon; (Cataloging) Horizon; (Circulation) Horizon; (OPAC) SirsiDynix
Wireless access
Function: Adult bk club, Adult literacy prog, Audiobks on Playaways & MP3, Audiobks via web, AV serv, Bilingual assistance for Spanish patrons, Bk club(s), Bks on CD, CD-ROM, Children's prog, Computer training, Computers for patron use, Electronic databases & coll, Free DVD rentals, ILL available, Internet access, Magazines, Meeting rooms, Movies, Music CDs, Online cat, Outreach serv, OverDrive digital audio bks, Photocopying/Printing, Printer for laptops & handheld devices, Prog for adults, Prog for children & young adult, Ref serv available, Scanner, Serves people with intellectual disabilities, Spanish lang bks, Story hour, Study rm, Summer reading prog, Teen prog, Wheelchair accessible
Special Services for the Deaf - Adult & family literacy prog; Bks on deafness & sign lang; Closed caption videos; High interest/low vocabulary bks; TDD equip
Special Services for the Blind - Assistive/Adapted tech devices, equip & products; Audio mat; Bks on cassette; Bks on CD; Copier with enlargement capabilities; Extensive large print coll; Large print bks; Talking bks
Open Wed 9:30-4, Fri 12:30-4:30, Sat 9-2:30
Branches: 7
ANYTHINK BENNETT, 495 Seventh St, Bennett, 80102, SAN 335-9581. Tel: 303-405-3231. FAX: 303-644-5419. *Br Mgr,* Whitney Oakley; E-mail: woakley@anythinklibraries.org
Library Holdings: AV Mats 914; CDs 304; Large Print Bks 174; Bk Vols 21,449; Per Subs 44; Talking Bks 600; Videos 342
Open Tues & Thurs 10-7, Wed, Fri & Sat 10-5:30
ANYTHINK BRIGHTON, 327 E Bridge St, Brighton, 80601, SAN 335-9611. Tel: 303-405-3230. *Br Mgr,* Kelly Allen; E-mail: kallen@anythinklibraries.org
Library Holdings: AV Mats 4,878; CDs 1,288; DVDs 250; Large Print Bks 760; Bk Vols 56,801; Per Subs 107; Talking Bks 1,400; Videos 1,688
Open Mon-Thurs 9:30-8:30, Fri & Sat 9:30-5:30
ANYTHINK COMMERCE CITY, 7185 Monaco St, Commerce City, 80022, SAN 335-9646. Tel: 303-287-0063. FAX: 303-289-6313. *Br Mgr,* Ricardo Cardenas; E-mail: rcardenas@anythinklibraries.org
Library Holdings: AV Mats 3,555; CDs 1,081; DVDs 296; Large Print Bks 458; Bk Vols 37,023; Per Subs 79; Talking Bks 1,450; Videos 1,288
Open Tues & Thurs 11-7, Wed, Fri & Sat 9:30-5:30
ANYTHINK HURON STREET, 9417 Huron St, 80260, SAN 335-9670. Tel: 303-452-7534. FAX: 303-450-2578. *Br Mgr,* Genne Boggs; E-mail: gboggs@anythinklibraries.org
Library Holdings: AV Mats 4,523; CDs 1,418; DVDs 434; Large Print Bks 1,043; Bk Vols 68,940; Per Subs 177; Videos 1,213
Open Mon-Thurs 9:30-8:30, Fri & Sat 9:30-5:30
ANYTHINK PERL MACK, 7611 Hilltop Circle, Denver, 80221, SAN 335-9700. Tel: 303-428-3576. FAX: 303-428-1358. *Br Mgr,* Annette Martinez; E-mail: amartinez@anythinklibraries.org
Library Holdings: AV Mats 2,561; CDs 903; DVDs 178; Large Print Bks 765; Bk Vols 38,256; Per Subs 144; Talking Bks 1,050; Videos 831
Open Tues & Thurs 11-7, Wed, Fri & Sat 9:30-5:30
ANYTHINK WRIGHT FARMS, 5877 E 120th Ave, 80602. Tel: 303-405-3200. *Br Mgr,* Rebecca Bowman; E-mail: rbowman@anythinklibraries.org
Open Mon-Thurs 9:30-8:30, Fri & Sat 9:30-5:30
ANYTHINK YORK STREET, 8990 York St, Ste A, 80229, SAN 335-9735. Tel: 303-405-3234. *Br Mgr,* Juli Wald; E-mail: jwald@anythinklibraries.org
Library Holdings: AV Mats 2,829; CDs 1,101; DVDs 213; Large Print Bks 888; Bk Vols 42,415; Per Subs 100; Talking Bks 1,050; Videos 921
Subject Interests: Colorado
Open Tues & Thurs 11-7, Wed, Fri & Sat 9:30-5:30
Bookmobiles: 1

TRINIDAD

P CARNEGIE PUBLIC LIBRARY*, 202 N Animas St, 81082. SAN 302-0223. Tel: 719-846-6841. FAX: 719-846-0885. E-mail: trinidadpubliclibrary@gmail.com. Web Site: www.carnegiepubliclibrary.org. *Dir,* Ms Mallory Pillard; *ILL,* Shawna Nall; Staff 1 (Non-MLS 1)
Founded 1882. Pop 10,000; Circ 45,000
Library Holdings: Audiobooks 1,699; AV Mats 3; DVDs 520; Large Print Bks 1,148; Bk Vols 34,000; Videos 609
Special Collections: Genealogy; Local History
Automation Activity & Vendor Info: (Cataloging) Auto-Graphics, Inc; (Circulation) Auto-Graphics, Inc; (OPAC) Auto-Graphics, Inc
Wireless access
Function: Res performed for a fee
Special Services for the Blind - Digital talking bk machines
Open Mon-Fri 9-5, Sat 9-3
Restriction: ID required to use computers (Ltd hrs)
Friends of the Library Group

J TRINIDAD STATE JUNIOR COLLEGE*, Samuel Freudenthal Memorial Library, 600 Prospect St, 81082. SAN 302-0231. Tel: 719-846-5593. FAX: 719-846-5432. Web Site: www.trinidadstate.edu/library-ts. *Dean of Instruction,* Debbie Ulibarri; E-mail: debbie.ulibarri@trinidadstate.edu; *Mgr, Libr Serv,* Josephine Chacon; Tel: 719-846-5474, E-mail: Josephine.Chacon@trinidadstate.edu; *Libr Coord,* Calvin Smith; E-mail: AAA@trinidadstate.edu; Staff 1 (MLS 1)
Founded 1925. Enrl 2,009; Fac 127
Library Holdings: Bk Titles 52,000; Per Subs 154
Subject Interests: Gunsmithing, Law enforcement, Local hist, Nursing
Wireless access
Partic in Colo Libr Asn
Open Mon-Wed (Fall & Spring) 8-8, Thurs 8-5, Fri 8-3; Mon-Fri (Summer) 8-5

USAF ACADEMY

C UNITED STATES AIR FORCE ACADEMY LIBRARIES, McDermott Library, 2354 Fairchild Dr, Ste 3A15, 80840-6214. SAN 336-0067. Tel: 719-333-4406. Circulation Tel: 719-333-4664. Interlibrary Loan Service Tel: 719-333-2461. Administration Tel: 719-333-2590. Automation Services Tel: 719-333-3660. E-mail: libinfo@afacademy.af.edu, libinfo@usafa.edu. Web Site: usafa.libguides.com/homepage, www.usafa.edu/facilities/library. *Assoc Dean & Dir,* Diane Klare; E-mail: diane.klare@afacademy.af.edu; *Assoc Dir, Pub Serv,* Andrea Wright; E-mail: andrea.wright@afacademy.af.edu; *Assoc Dir, Tech Serv,* David A. Schaffter; E-mail: david.schaffter@afacademy.af.edu; *Acq Librn,* Kathleen Kucharski; E-mail: kathleen.kucharski@afacademy.af.edu; *Cat Librn, Spec Coll,* Lizbeth A Jones; E-mail: lizbeth.jones@afacademy.af.edu; *Research Servs Librn,* Joe Barry; E-mail: joseph.barry@afacademy.af.edu; *Research Servs Librn,* Brooke Troutman; E-mail: brooke.troutman@afacademy.af.edu; *Syst Librn,* Michael Crane; E-mail: michael.crane@afacademy.af.edu; *Syst Librn,* Jo Ann Soriano; E-mail: joann.soriano@afacademy.af.edu; *Archives, Tech,* Ruth Kindreich; E-mail: ruth.kindreich@afacademy.af.edu; Staff 16 (MLS 15, Non-MLS 1)

Founded 1955. Enrl 4,100; Fac 520; Highest Degree: Bachelor
Oct 2014-Sept 2015 Income (Main Library Only) $4,648,515. Mats Exp $1,312,211, Books $167,400, Per/Ser (Incl. Access Fees) $73,736, AV Mat $49,366, Electronic Ref Mat (Incl. Access Fees) $1,294,709. Sal $2,691,000
Library Holdings: AV Mats 4,942; DVDs 2,275; e-books 71,418; e-journals 116; Bk Vols 459,915; Per Subs 317
Special Collections: Colonel Richard Gimbel Aeronautical Coll, bks, engravings, lithographs, photog, prints; Stalag Luft III Coll, bks, ms, photog, realia; US Air Force Academy Archives. Oral History; US Document Depository
Subject Interests: Aviation, Mil hist
Automation Activity & Vendor Info: (Acquisitions) SirsiDynix; (Cataloging) SirsiDynix; (Circulation) SirsiDynix; (Course Reserve) SirsiDynix; (ILL) SirsiDynix; (OPAC) SirsiDynix; (Serials) SirsiDynix
Wireless access
Publications: Special Bibliography Series
Partic in Colorado Alliance of Research Libraries; Federal Library & Information Network; MECC/LWG
Restriction: Limited access based on advanced application, Secured area only open to authorized personnel
Friends of the Library Group
Departmental Libraries:
BASE LIBRARY (10SVS/SVMG), Community Ctr Bldg, 5136 Eagle Dr, 80840, SAN 336-0091. Tel: 719-333-3198, 719-333-4665. Interlibrary Loan Service Tel: 719-333-7316. E-mail: usafabaselibrary@usaf.edu. Web Site: usafasupport.com/base-library.
Founded 1955
Library Holdings: Bk Vols 31,000; Per Subs 102
Function: Internet access, Photocopying/Printing, Prog for children & young adult, Ref serv available, Summer reading prog
Restriction: Employees & their associates, Not open to pub, Restricted access

VAIL

P VAIL PUBLIC LIBRARY*, 292 W Meadow Dr, 81657. SAN 302-024X. Tel: 970-479-2184. Circulation Tel: 970-479-2191. Reference Tel: 970-479-2187. Administration Tel: 970-479-2194. FAX: 970-479-2192. E-mail: libinfo@vailgov.com. Web Site: vaillibrary.com. *Dir, Libr Serv,* Lori Ann Barnes; E-mail: lbarnes@vailgov.com; *Sr Librn, Tech Serv,* Jo Norris; Tel: 970-479-2195, E-mail: jnorris@vailgov.com; *Ch Serv, Libr Assoc II,* Cricket Pylman; Tel: 970-479-2179, E-mail: cpylman@vailgov.com; *Libr Assoc II, Tech Serv,* Liz Schramm; Tel: 970-479-2193, E-mail: lschramm@vailgov.com; Staff 8.6 (MLS 3, Non-MLS 5.6)
Founded 1983. Pop 5,500; Circ 61,360
Jan 2014-Dec 2014 Income $853,352, City $832,758, Locally Generated Income $20,594. Mats Exp $129,646, Books $44,593, Per/Ser (Incl. Access Fees) $14,416, AV Mat $38,678, Electronic Ref Mat (Incl. Access Fees) $31,959. Sal $407,494 (Prof $88,484)
Library Holdings: Audiobooks 3,519; CDs 1,139; DVDs 8,429; e-books 35,167; e-journals 172; Bk Titles 38,012; Bk Vols 52,000; Per Subs 288
Special Collections: Municipal Document Depository; Oral History
Automation Activity & Vendor Info: (Cataloging) Innovative Interfaces, Inc; (Circulation) Innovative Interfaces, Inc; (ILL) Innovative Interfaces, Inc; (OPAC) Innovative Interfaces, Inc
Wireless access
Partic in Marmot Library Network
Open Mon-Sun 11-6
Friends of the Library Group

VICTOR

P VICTOR PUBLIC LIBRARY*, 124 S Third St, 80860. (Mail add: PO Box 5, 80860-0005), SAN 302-0258. Tel: 719-689-2011. FAX: 719-689-3157. E-mail: victorlibrary@yahoo.com. *Asst Dir,* Belinda Brown
Library Holdings: Bk Vols 10,000
Special Collections: Colorado Local History Coll
Automation Activity & Vendor Info: (Cataloging) Koha; (Circulation) Koha
Function: 24/7 Online cat
Open Mon-Fri 12-4

WALDEN

P JACKSON COUNTY PUBLIC LIBRARY*, 412 Fourth St, 80480. (Mail add: PO Box 398, 80480-0398), SAN 302-0266. Tel: 970-723-4602. FAX: 970-723-4602. Web Site: jacksoncountycogov.com/library. *Dir,* Kathy McKay
Founded 1954. Pop 1,577; Circ 17,423
Library Holdings: AV Mats 766; Bk Titles 16,472; Bk Vols 17,077; Per Subs 51
Special Collections: Local History Coll
Automation Activity & Vendor Info: (Cataloging) Koha; (Circulation) Koha
Wireless access
Partic in Evergreen Indiana Consortium
Open Mon 1-9, Tues & Thurs 1-6, Wed 10-6, Fri 9:30-4:30
Friends of the Library Group

WALSENBURG

P SPANISH PEAKS LIBRARY DISTRICT, 415 Walsen Ave, 81089. SAN 302-0274. Tel: 719-738-2774. FAX: 719-738-2468. E-mail: spldlibrary@gmail.com. Web Site: www.spld.org. *Dir,* Elizabeth Bennhoff; E-mail: elizabethspld@gmail.com; *Ch,* Sherry Pearson; E-mail: sherry@spld.org; Staff 1.5 (MLS 1, Non-MLS 0.5)
Founded 1906. Pop 5,403; Circ 24,746
Library Holdings: Audiobooks 1,518; AV Mats 1,398; CDs 446; Electronic Media & Resources 44; Bk Vols 20,303; Per Subs 62
Automation Activity & Vendor Info: (Cataloging) Insignia Software; (Circulation) Insignia Software; (ILL) Insignia Software; (OPAC) Insignia Software; (Serials) Insignia Software
Wireless access
Function: Art exhibits, Audio & video playback equip for onsite use, Audiobks via web, Bilingual assistance for Spanish patrons, Bks on cassette, Bks on CD, CD-ROM, Chess club, Children's prog, Computer training, Computers for patron use, Digital talking bks, Electronic databases & coll, Free DVD rentals, Holiday prog, Homework prog, ILL available, Mail & tel request accepted, Music CDs, Online cat, Online ref, Orientations, Outside serv via phone, mail, e-mail & web, Photocopying/Printing, Preschool outreach, Prog for adults, Prog for children & young adult, Ref serv available, Scanner, Senior computer classes, Spoken cassettes & CDs, Spoken cassettes & DVDs, Story hour, Summer reading prog, Tax forms, Teen prog, Telephone ref, VHS videos, Wheelchair accessible
Partic in Colorado Library Consortium
Special Services for the Blind - Audio mat; Bks on cassette; Bks on CD; Cassettes; Copier with enlargement capabilities; Digital talking bk; Extensive large print coll; Large print & cassettes; Large print bks; Recorded bks; Ref serv; Sound rec; Talking bk serv referral
Open Mon, Wed & Fri 10-6, Tues & Thurs 10-7, Sat 10-4
Friends of the Library Group
Bookmobiles: 1

WELLINGTON

P WELLINGTON PUBLIC LIBRARY*, 3800 Wilson Ave, 80549. (Mail add: PO Box 416, 80549-0416), SAN 370-6710. Tel: 970-568-3040. FAX: 970-568-9713. E-mail: library@wellingtoncolorado.gov. Web Site: wellington.colibraries.org. *Libr Dir,* Ross LaGenesa; Staff 3 (MLS 1, Non-MLS 2)
Founded 1980. Pop 4,500; Circ 48,000
Library Holdings: Audiobooks 1,200; AV Mats 190; Bks on Deafness & Sign Lang 25; CDs 175; DVDs 600; Large Print Bks 150; Bk Titles 24,000; Per Subs 40; Videos 500
Special Collections: Local History Coll. Oral History
Wireless access
Function: Adult bk club, Bks on CD, Children's prog, Computers for patron use, E-Reserves, Electronic databases & coll, Free DVD rentals, ILL available, Mail & tel request accepted, Music CDs, Online cat, Photocopying/Printing, Prog for children & young adult, Story hour, Summer reading prog, VHS videos, Wheelchair accessible
Special Services for the Deaf - Closed caption videos
Special Services for the Blind - Bks on cassette; Bks on CD; Copier with enlargement capabilities; Large print bks
Open Mon, Tues & Thurs 10-6, Wed 10-8, Fri 10-3:30, Sat 10-1
Friends of the Library Group

WESTCLIFFE

P WEST CUSTER COUNTY LIBRARY DISTRICT*, 209 Main St, 81252. (Mail add: PO Box 689, 81252-0689), SAN 302-0290. Tel: 719-783-9138. FAX: 719-783-2155. E-mail: info@westcusterlibrary.org. Web Site: www.westcusterlibrary.org. *Dir,* Sean Beharry; Tel: 719-893-9138, Ext 2, E-mail: sean@westcusterlibrary.org; *Asst Dir,* Genna Calkins-Mushrush; Tel: 719-893-9138, Ext 3, E-mail: genna@westcusterlibrary.org; Staff 3.2 (Non-MLS 3.2)
Founded 1930. Pop 4,000; Circ 34,000
Library Holdings: DVDs 1,175; e-books 4,400; Bk Vols 9,000; Per Subs 29
Special Collections: Local History Coll
Automation Activity & Vendor Info: (Cataloging) Koha; (Circulation) Koha; (ILL) Koha
Wireless access
Function: Adult bk club, Archival coll, Audiobks via web, Bk club(s), Bks on cassette, Bks on CD, Children's prog, Computer training, Computers for patron use, Digital talking bks, E-Readers, Electronic databases & coll, Free DVD rentals, ILL available, Internet access, Life-long learning prog for all ages, Magazines, Microfiche/film & reading machines, Music CDs, Online cat, Orientations, Outside serv via phone, mail, e-mail & web,

Photocopying/Printing, Preschool outreach, Preschool reading prog, Printer for laptops & handheld devices, Prog for adults, Prog for children & young adult, Ref serv available, Scanner, Senior computer classes, Study rm, Summer & winter reading prog, Summer reading prog, Teen prog, VHS videos, Wheelchair accessible, Winter reading prog, Workshops
Partic in Colorado Library Consortium
Open Tues-Fri 10-5:30, Sat 10-2
Friends of the Library Group

WESTMINSTER

J FRONT RANGE COMMUNITY COLLEGE*, College Hill Library, 3645 W 112th Ave, 80031. SAN 302-0312. Circulation Tel: 303-404-5504. Web Site: frontrange.edu/campuses/libraries. *Libr Dir,* Nancy Maloney; Tel: 303-404-5505, E-mail: nancy.maloney@frontrange.edu; *Librn,* Jesse Elston; E-mail: jesse.elston@frontage.edu; *Librn,* Pamela Fisher; E-mail: pamela.fisher@frontage.edu; *Librn,* Alejandro Marquez; E-mail: alejandro.marquez@frontage.edu; Staff 6.8 (MLS 3.8, Non-MLS 3)
Founded 1968. Highest Degree: Associate
Library Holdings: Bk Titles 39,715; Bk Vols 44,764; Per Subs 57
Automation Activity & Vendor Info: (Acquisitions) SirsiDynix; (Cataloging) SirsiDynix; (Circulation) SirsiDynix; (Course Reserve) SirsiDynix; (ILL) OCLC; (OPAC) SirsiDynix; (Serials) SirsiDynix
Wireless access
Partic in OCLC Online Computer Library Center, Inc
Open Mon-Thurs 9-8, Fri 10-5, Sat & Sun 1-5

P WESTMINSTER PUBLIC LIBRARY, College Hill Library, 3705 W 112th Ave, 80031. SAN 375-409X. Circulation Tel: 303-658-2601. FAX: 303-404-5135. Web Site: www.cityofwestminster.us/Libraries. *Mgr, Libr Serv,* J R Clanton; Tel: 303-658-2640, E-mail: jclanton@cityofwestminster.us; *Teen Librn,* Kristen Helm; Tel: 303-658-2624, E-mail: khelm@cityofwestminster.us; *Supvr, Circ,* Christine Pancoast; Tel: 303-658-2610, E-mail: cpancoa@cityofwestminster.us; *Tech Coordr,* Veronica Smith; Tel: 303-658-2645, E-mail: vsmith@cityofwestminster.us; Staff 13.1 (MLS 13.1)
Founded 1951. Pop 109,353; Circ 1,100,848
Library Holdings: Bk Vols 221,000; Per Subs 300
Automation Activity & Vendor Info: (Acquisitions) SirsiDynix; (Cataloging) SirsiDynix; (Circulation) SirsiDynix; (Serials) SirsiDynix
Wireless access
Partic in Colorado Library Consortium
Open Mon-Thurs 9-8, Fri 9-5, Sat & Sun 1-5
Friends of the Library Group
Branches: 1
IRVING STREET, 7392 Irving St, 80030. Tel: 303-658-2301. *Libr Supvr,* Patty Gendill; Tel: 303-658-2325, E-mail: pgendill@cityofwestminster.us; *Libr Coord,* Kaela Delgado; Tel: 303-658-2309, E-mail: kdelgado@cityofwestminster.us
Function: Computers for patron use, Photocopying/Printing
Open Tues-Sat 12-5

WETMORE

P WETMORE COMMUNITY LIBRARY*, 95 County Rd 393, 81253. (Mail add: PO Box 18, 81253-0018). Tel: 719-784-6669. FAX: 719-784-2301. E-mail: wetmorecommunitylibrary@yahoo.com. Web Site: wetmore.colibraries.org. *Dir,* Nan Davenport; Staff 1 (Non-MLS 1)
Pop 900; Circ 5,200
Library Holdings: AV Mats 180; CDs 60; DVDs 80; Large Print Bks 60; Bk Vols 6,758; Talking Bks 164; Videos 626
Automation Activity & Vendor Info: (Cataloging) Follett Software; (Circulation) Follett Software; (OPAC) Follett Software
Wireless access
Function: Digital talking bks, ILL available, Internet access, Music CDs, Photocopying/Printing, Prog for adults, Prog for children & young adult, Spoken cassettes & CDs, Summer reading prog, VHS videos
Open Mon 4-8, Tues 4-7, Wed 2-6, Thurs 11-3, Sat 12-3
Restriction: By permission only

WHEAT RIDGE

S COLORADO SNOWSPORTS MUSEUM & HALL OF FAME*, Research & Artifact Collection Facility, 13401 W 43rd Ave, Ste 9, 80403. (Mail add: 231 S Frontage Rd E, Vail, 81657-3616). Tel: 970-476-1876. Information Services Tel: 303-273-5810. Web Site: www.snowsportsmuseum.org. *Curator, Dir of Coll,* Dana Mathios; E-mail: dana@snowsportsmuseum.org
Founded 1990
Library Holdings: DVDs 179; Bk Titles 1,498; Per Subs 300; Videos 698
Special Collections: Oral History; State Document Depository; US Document Depository
Wireless access
Open Mon-Fri 9-5 by appointment

S WHEAT RIDGE HISTORICAL SOCIETY LIBRARY*, 4610 Robb St, 80033. (Mail add: PO Box 1833, 80034-1833), SAN 371-8751. Tel: 303-421-9111. *Pres,* Dave Curtis; *Presv Spec,* Claudia Worth; E-mail: cworth1234@aol.com
Founded 1974
Library Holdings: CDs 150; Bk Titles 500; Bk Vols 1,000; Per Subs 300
Special Collections: Crochet Books 1880-1950; Early Agricultural Books (Carnations, Dahlias, Trees); Early Movie Magazine (1929-1940); Early News Papers (1913-1916); Maps of Co Denver Metro,etc; School Coll, ms, vf; Victorian Toys (Including Doll House); Wheat Ridge, Jefferson County & Colorado History Coll. Municipal Document Depository; Oral History
Function: Res libr
Publications: Guide to Collections
Open Tues-Fri 10-3

WINDSOR

P CLEARVIEW LIBRARY DISTRICT*, Windsor Severance Library, 720 Third St, 80550-5109. SAN 302-0355. Tel: 970-686-5603. FAX: 970-686-2502. Web Site: www.clearviewlibrary.org. *Libr Dir,* Ann Kling; Tel: 970-686-5603, Ext 302, E-mail: director@clearviewlibrary.org; *Pub Serv Mgr,* Casey Lansinger-Pierce; E-mail: casey@clearviewlibrary.org; *Tech Serv Mgr,* Bud Hunt; E-mail: bud@clearviewlibrary.org
Founded 1922. Circ 362,142
Library Holdings: Bk Vols 65,000; Per Subs 60
Automation Activity & Vendor Info: (Cataloging) TLC (The Library Corporation); (Circulation) TLC (The Library Corporation); (OPAC) TLC (The Library Corporation)
Wireless access
Function: 24/7 Online cat, 3D Printer, Adult bk club, Art exhibits, Audiobks on Playaways & MP3, Audiobks via web, Bk club(s), Bks on CD, Children's prog, Computers for patron use, Electronic databases & coll, Free DVD rentals, ILL available, Internet access, Magazines, Mango lang, Meeting rooms, Music CDs, Online cat, Outreach serv, Photocopying/Printing, Preschool outreach, Printer for laptops & handheld devices, Prog for adults, Prog for children & young adult, Scanner, Senior outreach, Story hour, Summer reading prog, Tax forms, Teen prog, Wheelchair accessible
Partic in Colorado Library Consortium
Open Mon-Fri 9-8, Sat 9-5, Sun 1-5
Friends of the Library Group
Bookmobiles: 1

WOODLAND PARK

P RAMPART LIBRARY DISTRICT*, Woodland Park Public Library, 218 E Midland Ave, 80863. (Mail add: PO Box 336, 80866-0336), SAN 302-0363. Tel: 719-687-9281. FAX: 719-687-6631. Web Site: rampart.colibraries.org. *Dir,* Michelle Dukette; E-mail: michelled@rampartlibrarydistrict.org
Founded 1966. Pop 18,000; Circ 160,000
Library Holdings: Bk Vols 56,000; Per Subs 140
Subject Interests: Local hist
Automation Activity & Vendor Info: (Cataloging) SirsiDynix; (Circulation) SirsiDynix; (OPAC) SirsiDynix
Wireless access
Open Tues-Thurs 10-7, Fri 10-6, Sat 10-4, Sun 1-4
Friends of the Library Group
Branches: 1
FLORISSANT PUBLIC LIBRARY, 334 Circle Dr, Florissant, 80816. (Mail add: PO Box 252, Florissant, 80816-0252), SAN 320-9687. Tel: 719-748-3939. FAX: 719-748-1237. *Br Mgr,* Polly Roberts; E-mail: pollyr@rampartlibrarydistrict.org
Open Mon & Wed-Fri 10-5, Sat 10-2
Friends of the Library Group

WRAY

P WRAY PUBLIC LIBRARY*, 621 Blake St, 80758. SAN 302-038X. Tel: 970-332-4744. FAX: 970-332-4784. E-mail: wraypl@gmail.com. Web Site: cityofwray.org/161/Wray-Public-Library. *Libr Dir,* Shara Berghuis; E-mail: sberghuis@wraypl.com
Founded 1913. Circ 31,000
Library Holdings: Bk Titles 16,000; Per Subs 46
Automation Activity & Vendor Info: (Cataloging) Follett Software; (Circulation) Follett Software
Open Mon & Wed-Fri 10-5, Tues 10-6, Sat 9-1

YUMA

P YUMA PUBLIC LIBRARY*, 910 S Main St, 80759-2402. SAN 302-0401. Tel: 970-848-2368. FAX: 970-848-0423. Web Site: www.yumacolo.org, yuma.colibraries.org. *Dir,* Jeanne Triplett; E-mail: j.triplett@yumacolo.org
Founded 1924. Pop 3,500; Circ 24,600
Library Holdings: CDs 114; DVDs 228; Bk Titles 15,220; Per Subs 26; Talking Bks 1,450

Automation Activity & Vendor Info: (Acquisitions) Koha; (Cataloging) Koha; (Circulation) Koha
Wireless access
Function: 24/7 Electronic res, 24/7 Online cat, Adult bk club, Adult literacy prog, Archival coll, Audiobks on Playaways & MP3, Audiobks via web, Bks on cassette, Bks on CD, CD-ROM, Children's prog, Digital talking bks, Electronic databases & coll, Free DVD rentals, Genealogy discussion group, Home delivery & serv to seniorr ctr & nursing homes, Homebound delivery serv, ILL available, Internet access, Laminating, Magazines, Microfiche/film & reading machines, Movies, Online cat, OverDrive digital audio bks, Photocopying/Printing, Preschool reading prog, Printer for laptops & handheld devices, Prog for children & young adult, Res performed for a fee, Scanner, Spanish lang bks, Spoken cassettes & CDs, Story hour, Summer & winter reading prog, Summer reading prog, Tax forms, VHS videos, Wheelchair accessible
Open Mon-Fri 9-6, Sat 9-1

CONNECTICUT

Date of Statistics: FY 2021
Population, 2020 U.S. Census: 3,557,006
Population Served by Public Libraries: 3,557,006
Attendance at Public Library Programs: 728,599
Program Attendance Per Capita: 0.20
Average Weekly Hours Open Per Public Library: 42.4
Total Volumes in Public Libraries: 11,554,144
Volumes Per Capita: 3.21
Total Public Library Circulation: 15,533,517
Circulation Per Capita: 4.31
Income and Expenditures:
Source of Income: Local taxes: 84.3%; Other: 15.7%
Grants-in-Aid to Public Libraries: none
Federal LSTA FY 2021: $2,142,520
State Grants Public Library Construction (FY 2021): $981,332
State aid: none
borrowIT: Half of total annual appropriation is distributed to all participating libraries on a transaction basis; other half distributed to libraries with net plus transactions $703,638
Total Public Library Expenditures: $204,171,553
Operating Expenditures Per Capita: $56.66
Number of Bookmobiles in State: 5
Information provided courtesy of: Maria Bernier, Statewide Data Coordinator; Division of Library Development

ABINGTON

P ABINGTON SOCIAL LIBRARY*, 536 Hampton Rd, 06230. (Mail add: PO Box 73, Pomfret Center, 06259), SAN 302-041X. Tel: 860-974-0415. FAX: 860-974-3950. E-mail: abingtonsocial@gmail.com. Web Site: www.abingtonsociallibrary.org. *Libr Dir,* Carrie Wolfe
Founded 1793. Pop 3,000
Library Holdings: Bk Titles 12,500
Special Collections: 1700 Mss coll; primary sermons
Wireless access
Partic in Connecticut Library Consortium
Open Mon, Wed & Thurs 2-6, Sat 10-12

ANDOVER

P ANDOVER PUBLIC LIBRARY*, 355 Rte 6, 06232. (Mail add: PO Box 117, 06232-0117), SAN 302-0428. Tel: 860-742-7428. FAX: 860-742-7428. E-mail: andoverctpubliclibrary@yahoo.com. *Dir, Librn,* Amy E Orlomoski; *Ch Serv,* Cathy Campen; Staff 1.8 (MLS 0.8, Non-MLS 1)
Founded 1896. Pop 2,700; Circ 21,000
Library Holdings: Bk Titles 18,355; Per Subs 15
Automation Activity & Vendor Info: (Cataloging) Auto-Graphics, Inc; (Circulation) Auto-Graphics, Inc; (OPAC) Auto-Graphics, Inc
Wireless access
Open Mon 10-1 & 3-8, Tues & Thurs 12-8, Wed 10-8, Fri 10-1 & 3-6, Sat 10-4
Friends of the Library Group

ANSONIA

P ANSONIA LIBRARY*, 53 S Cliff St, 06401. SAN 302-0436. Tel: 203-734-6275. FAX: 203-732-4551. E-mail: ansonialibrary@biblio.org. Web Site: www.ansonialibrary.org. *Dir,* Jennifer Lester; E-mail: jlester@biblio.org; *Ch,* Janet Fitol; *ILL Librn,* Mary Ann Capone; *Cataloger,* Maureen Levine; Staff 5 (MLS 1, Non-MLS 4)
Founded 1896. Pop 18,744; Circ 89,965
Library Holdings: AV Mats 3,337; CDs 892; e-books 115; Bk Vols 83,707; Per Subs 144; Talking Bks 592; Videos 1,826
Special Collections: Daughters of American Revolution
Subject Interests: Local hist
Automation Activity & Vendor Info: (Cataloging) SirsiDynix; (Circulation) SirsiDynix; (OPAC) SirsiDynix; (Serials) SirsiDynix
Wireless access
Partic in Bibliomation Inc; Connecticut Library Consortium
Open Mon-Fri 9-4
Friends of the Library Group

ASHFORD

P BABCOCK LIBRARY, 25 Pompey Hollow Rd, 06278. SAN 323-6455. Tel: 860-487-4420. FAX: 860-744-5531. Web Site: www.babcocklibrary.org. *Dir,* Carolann MacMaster; E-mail: cmacmaster@babcocklibrary.org; Staff 8 (Non-MLS 8)
Founded 1866. Pop 4,300; Circ 30,000
Jul 2014-Jun 2015 Income $187,242
Library Holdings: Bks on Deafness & Sign Lang 75; Large Print Bks 352; Bk Vols 25,000; Per Subs 65; Talking Bks 135
Subject Interests: Genealogy, Local hist
Automation Activity & Vendor Info: (Cataloging) Follett Software; (Circulation) Follett Software; (ILL) Auto-Graphics, Inc; (OPAC) Follett Software
Function: AV serv, Bk club(s), Computer training, Computers for patron use, Digital talking bks, Electronic databases & coll, For res purposes, Free DVD rentals, Govt ref serv, Holiday prog, Home delivery & serv to seniorr ctr & nursing homes, ILL available, Internet access, Life-long learning prog for all ages, Magazines, Magnifiers for reading, Movies, Music CDs, Photocopying/Printing, Preschool reading prog, Prog for adults, Prog for children & young adult, Scanner, Story hour, Summer & winter reading prog, Summer reading prog, Tax forms, Teen prog, Wheelchair accessible
Partic in Bibliomation Inc
Open Mon, Tues & Fri 9-4, Wed 9-6
Friends of the Library Group

AVON

P AVON FREE PUBLIC LIBRARY, 281 Country Club Rd, 06001. SAN 302-0452. Tel: 860-673-9712. Circulation Tel: 860-673-9712, Ext 201. FAX: 860-675-6364. Reference E-mail: avonref@avonctlibrary.info. Web Site: www.avonctlibrary.info. *Libr Dir,* Glenn Grube; E-mail: ggrube@avonctlibrary.info; *Tech & Technical Serv Librn,* Jessica Noble; E-mail: jnoble@avonctlibrary.info; *Mgr, Children's & YA,* Kari Ann St Jean; E-mail: kstjean@avonctlibrary.info; *Ref & Adult Serv Mgr,* Tina Panik; E-mail: tpanik@avonctlibrary.info; Staff 37 (MLS 14, Non-MLS 23)
Founded 1791. Pop 18,932; Circ 204,815
Jul 2016-Jun 2017 Income $1,701,176, State $8,387, City $1,586,279, Locally Generated Income $106,510. Mats Exp $155,515, Books $92,481, Per/Ser (Incl. Access Fees) $10,192, AV Mat $20,515, Electronic Ref Mat (Incl. Access Fees) $32,327. Sal $941,960
Library Holdings: AV Mats 50,977; Bk Titles 102,985; Per Subs 201
Subject Interests: Local hist
Automation Activity & Vendor Info: (Acquisitions) Innovative Interfaces, Inc - Sierra; (Cataloging) Innovative Interfaces, Inc - Sierra; (Circulation) Innovative Interfaces, Inc - Sierra; (Discovery) Innovative Interfaces, Inc; (ILL) Innovative Interfaces, Inc - Sierra; (OPAC) Innovative Interfaces, Inc; (Serials) Innovative Interfaces, Inc - Sierra
Wireless access
Function: 24/7 Electronic res, 24/7 Online cat, 3D Printer, Adult bk club, Archival coll, Art exhibits, Audiobks on Playaways & MP3, Audiobks via web, AV serv, Bk club(s), Bks on CD, Chess club, Children's prog,

Computer training, Computers for patron use, E-Readers, Electronic databases & coll, Free DVD rentals, Home delivery & serv to seniorr ctr & nursing homes, Homebound delivery serv, Internet access, Life-long learning prog for all ages, Magazines, Mango lang, Meeting rooms, Movies, Museum passes, Music CDs, Online cat, OverDrive digital audio bks, Photocopying/Printing, Prog for adults, Prog for children & young adult, Ref serv available, Scanner, Summer reading prog, Tax forms, Teen prog, Telephone ref, Wheelchair accessible
Publications: Beyond the Bookends (Newsletter)
Partic in Library Connection, Inc
Special Services for the Blind - ZoomText magnification & reading software
Friends of the Library Group

BALTIC

P SPRAGUE PUBLIC LIBRARY*, 76 Main St, 06330. SAN 376-5334. Tel: 860-822-3012. E-mail: spraguepublic.library@gmail.com. Web Site: sites.google.com/site/spraguepubliclibrary2, www.ctsprague.org. *Dir,* Christine Kolar; Staff 2 (MLS 1, Non-MLS 1)
Pop 2,975
Library Holdings: AV Mats 575; Bk Vols 90,000; Talking Bks 213
Subject Interests: Genealogy, Local hist, Native Am lit
Automation Activity & Vendor Info: (Cataloging) Follett Software; (Circulation) Follett Software; (OPAC) Follett Software
Wireless access
Function: Telephone ref
Publications: Our Town (Newsletter)
Partic in Bibliomation Inc
Open Open Tues 9-7, Wed & Thurs 9-6, Sat 9-12
Friends of the Library Group

BEACON FALLS

P BEACON FALLS PUBLIC LIBRARY*, Ten Maple Ave, 06403. SAN 302-0460. Tel: 203-729-1441. FAX: 203-729-4927. E-mail: beaconfallslibrary@yahoo.com. Web Site: mybflib.org. *Dir,* Sue Dowdell; E-mail: director@mybflib.org; Staff 2.1 (MLS 0.8, Non-MLS 1.3)
Founded 1957. Pop 6,052; Circ 31,000
Library Holdings: AV Mats 2,000; Bks on Deafness & Sign Lang 10; CDs 240; DVDs 600; Large Print Bks 90; Bk Vols 18,000; Talking Bks 300; Videos 564
Automation Activity & Vendor Info: (Acquisitions) Evergreen; (Cataloging) Evergreen; (Circulation) Evergreen; (ILL) Evergreen; (OPAC) Evergreen
Wireless access
Function: Adult bk club, Bks on cassette, Bks on CD, Children's prog, Computer training, Computers for patron use, Electronic databases & coll, Free DVD rentals, Holiday prog, Homebound delivery serv, ILL available, Mail & tel request accepted, Museum passes, Music CDs, Online cat, Online ref, Photocopying/Printing, Prog for adults, Prog for children & young adult, Scanner, Spoken cassettes & CDs, Spoken cassettes & DVDs, Story hour, Summer reading prog, Tax forms, Telephone ref, VHS videos, Wheelchair accessible, Workshops
Partic in Bibliomation Inc; Connecticut Library Consortium
Special Services for the Blind - Assistive/Adapted tech devices, equip & products; Bks on cassette; Bks on CD; Large print bks
Open Mon, Wed & Fri 10-5:30, Tues & Thurs 12:30-8, Sat (Sept-June) 9-1
Friends of the Library Group

BERLIN

P BERLIN FREE LIBRARY*, 834 Worthington Ridge, 06037-3203. (Mail add: PO Box 8187, 06037-8187), SAN 302-0479. Tel: 860-828-3344. *Librn,* Marcia Trotta; *Ch,* Martha Neault; *Asst Librn,* Jean Munson
Pop 17,800
Library Holdings: Bk Vols 17,500; Per Subs 15
Open Mon & Fri 2:30-5, Wed 9-11:30 & 7-8:30

P BERLIN-PECK MEMORIAL LIBRARY*, 234 Kensington Rd, 06037. SAN 302-2005. Tel: 860-828-7125. FAX: 860-829-1848. E-mail: library@berlinpeck.org. Web Site: berlinpeck.org. *Libr Dir,* Helen Malinka; Tel: 860-828-7131, E-mail: hmalinka@berlinpeck.org; *Head, Children's Servx,* Jennifer Needham; Tel: 860-828-7117, E-mail: jneedham@berlinpeck.org; *Head, Circ,* Jonathan Noyes; Tel: 860-828-7119, E-mail: jnoyes@berlinpeck.org; *Head, Ref & Adult Serv,* Carrie Tyszka; Tel: 860-828-7120, E-mail: ctyszka@berlinpeck.org; *Digital Serv Librn,* Andrea Raynor; Tel: 860-828-7118, E-mail: araynor@berlinpeck.org; Staff 11.5 (MLS 4.5, Non-MLS 7)
Founded 1829. Pop 20,450; Circ 217,000
Library Holdings: AV Mats 11,286; Bk Titles 106,000; Per Subs 135
Special Collections: Oral History
Subject Interests: Local hist
Automation Activity & Vendor Info: (Cataloging) Innovative Interfaces, Inc - Sierra; (Circulation) Innovative Interfaces, Inc - Sierra; (ILL) Innovative Interfaces, Inc - Sierra; (OPAC) Innovative Interfaces, Inc - Sierra
Wireless access
Partic in Library Connection, Inc
Open Mon-Thurs 10-8, Fri 10-5, Sat 10-4
Friends of the Library Group

BETHANY

P CLARK MEMORIAL LIBRARY*, 538 Amity Rd, 06524-3015. SAN 302-0495. Tel: 203-393-2103. Web Site: www.bethanylibrary.org. *Dir,* Melissa Canham-Clyne; *Librn,* Jean Johnson; *Ch,* Dorothy Esparo
Founded 1930. Pop 4,600; Circ 50,400
Library Holdings: Bk Vols 36,000
Automation Activity & Vendor Info: (Cataloging) Follett Software; (Circulation) Follett Software; (OPAC) Follett Software
Wireless access
Open Tues-Thurs 10-8, Fri 2-6, Sat 10-4
Friends of the Library Group

BETHEL

P BETHEL PUBLIC LIBRARY, 189 Greenwood Ave, 06801-2598. SAN 302-0509. Tel: 203-794-8756. Circulation Tel: 203-794-8756, Ext 3. Reference Tel: 203-794-8756, Ext 4. Administration Tel: 203-794-8756, Ext 6. FAX: 203-794-8761. E-mail: adult@bethellibrary.org. Web Site: www.bethellibrary.org. *Dir,* Megan Dean; *Head, Circ,* Elizabeth Alexander; *Ad,* Thomas J Borysiewicz; *Outreach Librn,* Amy Davenport; Staff 22 (MLS 4, Non-MLS 18)
Founded 1909. Pop 18,000; Circ 143,000
Library Holdings: AV Mats 4,146; High Interest/Low Vocabulary Bk Vols 75; Bk Vols 92,975; Per Subs 209; Talking Bks 2,155
Subject Interests: Local hist
Automation Activity & Vendor Info: (Acquisitions) Evergreen; (Cataloging) Evergreen; (Circulation) Evergreen; (OPAC) Evergreen; (Serials) Evergreen
Wireless access
Publications: Newsletter (Bimonthly)
Partic in Bibliomation Inc
Open Mon, Wed & Thurs 10-8, Tues, Fri & Sat 10-5
Friends of the Library Group

BETHLEHEM

SR ABBEY OF REGINA LAUDIS LIBRARY*, 273 Flanders Rd, 06751. SAN 302-0517. Tel: 203-266-7727. E-mail: rllibrary@sbcglobal.net. Web Site: www.abbeyofreginalaudis.com. *Librn,* Mother Lucia Kuppens; Staff 3 (MLS 1, Non-MLS 2)
Founded 1947
Library Holdings: Bk Vols 24,100; Per Subs 12
Special Collections: Art & Art History (Lauren Ford Coll); English Monastic History (Hope Emily Allen Coll); Gregorian Chant (Rev Thomas F Dennehy Coll); Literature (Heinrich Brunning & Lloyd B Holsapple Coll); Medieval Mystics; Patristics (Sources Chretiennes, Migne & Corpus Christianorum); Sacred Music (T F Dennehy Coll); Social Science (Sage Coll)
Subject Interests: Art & archit, Church hist, Ecumenism, Judaism (religion), Liturgy, Near East, Theol
Restriction: Not open to pub

P BETHLEHEM PUBLIC LIBRARY*, 32 Main St S, 06751. (Mail add: PO Box 99, 06751-0099), SAN 302-0525. Tel: 203-266-7510. FAX: 203-266-7510. Web Site: www.bethlehemlibraryct.org. *Dir,* Anne Small; E-mail: blib.bet6751@yahoo.com
Founded 1857. Pop 3,540
Library Holdings: Per Subs 10
Special Collections: Oral History
Subject Interests: Local hist
Automation Activity & Vendor Info: (Circulation) ByWater Solutions
Wireless access
Function: 24/7 Online cat, Activity rm, Adult bk club
Open Mon & Wed 10-8, Tues & Thurs 10-5, Fri & Sat 10-2
Friends of the Library Group

BLOOMFIELD

CR ARCHDIOCESE OF HARTFORD PASTORAL CENTER, Archbishop O'Brien Library, (Formerly St Thomas Seminary & Archdiocesan Center), 467 Bloomfield Ave, 06002. SAN 302-0576. Tel: 860-242-5573, Ext 2623. Administration Tel: 860-242-5573, Ext 2608. FAX: 860-242-4886. Web Site: archdioceseofhartford.org/archbishop-obrien-library. *Librn,* Rody Bazzano; E-mail: rody.bazzano@aohct.org; *Archival Librn,* Rebecca Empoliti; Tel: 860-242-5573, Ext 2609, E-mail: rempoliti@stseminary.org; Staff 2.5 (MLS 1.5, Non-MLS 1)
Founded 1928
Jul 2019-Jun 2020. Mats Exp $10,000. Sal $65,000

Library Holdings: AV Mats 2,500; Bk Titles 26,000; Bk Vols 30,000; Per Subs 87
Special Collections: 15th-18th Century Religious Coll, docs, ms, rare bks; 19th-20th Century Catholic Americana; Bibles
Subject Interests: Catholicism, Philos, Scripture, Spiritual life, Theol
Automation Activity & Vendor Info: (Cataloging) Follett Software; (Circulation) Follett Software; (Course Reserve) Follett Software; (ILL) Bibliomation Inc; (Media Booking) Follett Software; (OPAC) Follett Software; (Serials) Follett Software
Wireless access
Publications: Word & Spirit (Newsletter)
Partic in Connecticut Library Consortium
Special Services for the Deaf - Closed caption videos
Special Services for the Blind - Audio mat; Bks on cassette; Bks on CD; Copier with enlargement capabilities; Large print bks; Magnifiers; Recorded bks; Ref serv; Scanner for conversion & translation of mats
Open Mon & Wed-Fri 9:30-5, Tues 9:30-6:30 (Sept-May); Mon-Fri 9:30-5 (July-Aug)

P BLOOMFIELD PUBLIC LIBRARY*, Prosser Public Library, One Tunxis Ave, 06002. SAN 336-0245. Tel: 860-243-9721. FAX: 860-242-1629. E-mail: askbplct@gmail.com. Web Site: bplct.org. *Libr Dir,* Elizabeth Lane; E-mail: elane@libraryconnection.info; *Youth Serv Librn,* Nicole Dolat; E-mail: ndolat@libraryconnection.info; Staff 34 (MLS 14, Non-MLS 20)
Founded 1901. Pop 20,486
Automation Activity & Vendor Info: (Acquisitions) Innovative Interfaces, Inc - Sierra; (Cataloging) Innovative Interfaces, Inc - Sierra; (Circulation) Innovative Interfaces, Inc - Sierra; (ILL) Innovative Interfaces, Inc - Sierra; (OPAC) Innovative Interfaces, Inc - Sierra
Wireless access
Function: 24/7 Electronic res, 24/7 Online cat, Art exhibits, Audiobks via web, Bk club(s), Bks on CD, Children's prog, Computer training, Computers for patron use, Electronic databases & coll, Free DVD rentals, Homebound delivery serv, ILL available, Internet access, Life-long learning prog for all ages, Magazines, Mango lang, Meeting rooms, Movies, Museum passes, Music CDs, Notary serv, OverDrive digital audio bks, Photocopying/Printing, Preschool outreach, Printer for laptops & handheld devices, Prog for adults, Prog for children & young adult, Ref serv available, Scanner, Senior computer classes, Senior outreach, Story hour, Summer reading prog, Tax forms, Teen prog
Publications: Monthly Calendar
Partic in Connecticut Library Consortium; Library Connection, Inc
Open Mon, Tues, Thurs & Fri 11-6, Wed 11-8, Sat 11-3
Friends of the Library Group
Branches: 1
P FAITH MCMAHON WINTONBURY LIBRARY, 1015 Blue Hills Ave, 06002. Tel: 860-242-0041. *Ad, Youth Serv Librn,* Sheila McCallum; E-mail: smccallum@libraryconnection.info
Automation Activity & Vendor Info: (Acquisitions) Innovative Interfaces, Inc - Sierra; (Cataloging) Innovative Interfaces, Inc - Sierra; (Circulation) Innovative Interfaces, Inc - Sierra; (ILL) Innovative Interfaces, Inc - Sierra; (OPAC) Innovative Interfaces, Inc - Sierra
Open Mon, Tues, Thurs & Fri 11-6, Wed 11-8, Sat 11-3
Friends of the Library Group

BOLTON

P BENTLEY MEMORIAL LIBRARY*, 206 Bolton Center Rd, 06043. SAN 302-0584. Tel: 860-646-7349. FAX: 860-649-9059. E-mail: bentley@biblio.org. Web Site: town.boltonct.org/library. *Dir,* Elizabeth Thornton; Staff 5 (MLS 1, Non-MLS 4)
Founded 1915. Pop 5,000; Circ 45,562
Library Holdings: Bk Vols 49,000; Per Subs 85
Special Collections: Dolls from around the World (Private Coll)
Automation Activity & Vendor Info: (Cataloging) Bibliomation Inc; (Circulation) Bibliomation Inc
Wireless access
Partic in Bibliomation Inc
Open Mon-Thurs 10-8, Sat 10-3
Friends of the Library Group

BRANFORD

P JAMES BLACKSTONE MEMORIAL LIBRARY*, 758 Main St, 06405-3697. SAN 302-0592. Tel: 203-488-1441. FAX: 203-488-1260. E-mail: library@blackstone.lioninc.org. Web Site: www.blackstone.lioninc.org. *Dir,* Karen Jensen; Tel: 203-488-1441, Ext 312, E-mail: kjensen@blackstonelibrary.org; *Assoc Librn, Access Serv,* Deirdre Santora; Tel: 203-488-1441, Ext 311, E-mail: dsantora@blackstone.lioninc.org; *Assoc Librn, Youth Serv,* Carly Lemire; Tel: 203-488-1441, Ext 322, E-mail: clemire@blackstone.lioninc.org; *Assoc Librn, Development & Outreach,* Katy McNicol; Tel: 203-488-1441, Ext 313, E-mail: kmcnicol@blackstonelibrary.org; *Assoc Librn, Ref, Tech,* Deborah Trofatter; Tel: 203-488-1441, Ext 318, E-mail: dtrofatter@blackstonelibrary.org; *Assoc Librn, Tech Serv,* Gennett Grinnell; Tel: 203-488-1441, Ext 316, E-mail: ggrinnell@blackstonelibrary.org; *Coordr, Prog,* Whitney Gale; Tel: 203-488-1441, Ext 317, E-mail: wgale@blackstonelibrary.org; Staff 6 (MLS 6)
Founded 1896. Pop 28,683; Circ 202,957
Library Holdings: Audiobooks 1,563; AV Mats 203; CDs 1,176; DVDs 4,168; Electronic Media & Resources 63; Bk Vols 76,753; Per Subs 138; Videos 1,138
Subject Interests: Genealogy, Local hist
Automation Activity & Vendor Info: (Cataloging) Innovative Interfaces, Inc; (Circulation) Innovative Interfaces, Inc; (Course Reserve) Innovative Interfaces, Inc; (ILL) Innovative Interfaces, Inc; (OPAC) Innovative Interfaces, Inc
Wireless access
Publications: Constant Contact (Online only); Marble Columns (Newsletter)
Partic in Libraries Online, Inc
Special Services for the Deaf - Assistive tech
Special Services for the Blind - Assistive/Adapted tech devices, equip & products
Open Mon-Thurs 9-8, Fri & Sat 9-5, Sun (Sept-May) 1-4
Friends of the Library Group

BRIDGEPORT

M BRIDGEPORT HOSPITAL*, Reeves Health Sciences Library, 267 Grant St, 06610-2870. (Mail add: PO Box 5000, 06610-0120), SAN 302-0622. Tel: 203-384-3254. FAX: 203-384-3107. E-mail: library@bpthosp.org. Web Site: www.bridgeporthospital.org/medical-professionals/library/about.aspx. *Chief Librn,* Todd Allen Lane; Tel: 203-384-3615, E-mail: todd.lane@bpthosp.org
Library Holdings: e-books 84; Bk Titles 3,500; Bk Vols 4,400; Per Subs 300
Subject Interests: Health sci
Automation Activity & Vendor Info: (Cataloging) EOS International
Partic in Conn Asn of Health Scis Librs
Open Mon-Fri 8-4:30

P BRIDGEPORT PUBLIC LIBRARY*, 925 Broad St, 06604. SAN 336-0334. Tel: 203-576-7400. Circulation Tel: 203-576-7400, Ext 444. Administration Tel: 203-576-7400, Ext 8. Information Services Tel: 203-576-7400, Ext 5. FAX: 203-576-8255. Administration FAX: 203 333-0253. Information Services FAX: 203-576-7137. E-mail: questions@bridgeportpubliclibrary.org. Web Site: bportlibrary.org. *City Librn,* Elaine Braithwaite; E-mail: ebraithwaite@bridgeportpubliclibrary.org; *Asst City Librn,* John Soltis; E-mail: jsoltis@bridgeportpubliclibrary.org; Staff 87 (MLS 31, Non-MLS 56)
Founded 1881. Pop 139,529; Circ 443,010
Library Holdings: AV Mats 40,075; Bk Vols 514,960
Special Collections: P T Barnum Circus. Oral History; State Document Depository; US Document Depository
Subject Interests: Art & archit, Bus & mgt, Lit, Local hist
Automation Activity & Vendor Info: (Acquisitions) SirsiDynix; (Cataloging) SirsiDynix; (Circulation) SirsiDynix; (OPAC) SirsiDynix; (Serials) SirsiDynix
Wireless access
Partic in Bibliomation Inc
Special Services for the Deaf - TDD equip
Open Mon 10-6, Tues-Thurs 10-8, Fri & Sat 10-5, Sun 1-5
Friends of the Library Group
Branches: 4
BLACK ROCK, 2705 Fairfield Ave, 06605, SAN 336-0369. Tel: 203-576-7025. FAX: 203-576-7407. *Br Mgr,* Michele Jacobsen
Library Holdings: Bk Vols 17,897
Friends of the Library Group
EAST SIDE BRANCH, 1174 E Main St, 06608, SAN 336-0393. Tel: 203-576-7634. *Br Mgr,* Luis Rodriguez; Staff 4.5 (MLS 2, Non-MLS 2.5)
Library Holdings: Bk Vols 34,000
Subject Interests: Spanish lang
Open Mon 10-6, Tues-Thurs 10-8, Fri & Sat 10-5
Friends of the Library Group
NEWFIELD, 755 Central Ave, 06607, SAN 336-0423. Tel: 203-576-7828. *Br Mgr,* Nykia Eaddy
Library Holdings: Bk Vols 15,000
Open Mon & Fri 12-5, Tues & Thurs 10-6, Wed 12-8
Friends of the Library Group
NORTH, 3455 Madison Ave, 06606, SAN 336-0458. Tel: 203-576-7003. FAX: 203-576-7752. *Br Mgr,* Paula Keegan
Library Holdings: Bk Vols 50,000
Open Mon & Wed 1-9, Tues & Thurs 10-6, Sat 9-5
Friends of the Library Group

R CONGREGATION B'NAI ISRAEL LIBRARY, 2710 Park Ave, 06604. SAN 302-0649. Tel: 203-336-1858. FAX: 203-367-7889. E-mail: info@cbibpt.org. Web Site: cbibpt.org.
Founded 1960
Library Holdings: Bk Vols 2,000
Subject Interests: Judaica (lit or hist of Jews)
Wireless access
Open Mon-Fri 9:30-4

J HOUSATONIC COMMUNITY COLLEGE LIBRARY*, 900 Lafayette Blvd, 06604. SAN 302-0657. Tel: 203-332-5070. FAX: 203-332-5252. Web Site: www.hcc.commnet.edu/library. *Dir,* Shelley Strohm; Tel: 203-332-5072, E-mail: SStrohm@hcc.commnet.edu; *Librn,* Omaa Chukwurah; Tel: 203-332-5179, E-mail: ochukwurah@hcc.commnet.edu; *Media Serv Tech,* Doug Alton; Tel: 203-332-5077, E-mail: dalton@hcc.commnet.edu; *Media Serv Librn,* Lois McCracken; Tel: 203-332-5076, E-mail: lmccracken@hcc.commnet.edu; *Pub Serv Librn,* Peter Everett; Tel: 203-332-5074, E-mail: peverett@hcc.commnet.edu; *Syst Librn,* Qiming Han; Tel: 203-332-5073, E-mail: qhan@hcc.commnet.edu; *Libr Assoc,* Jennifer Falasco; Staff 8 (MLS 6, Non-MLS 2)
Founded 1967. Enrl 4,500; Fac 83; Highest Degree: Associate
Library Holdings: AV Mats 6,300; Bk Vols 42,500; Per Subs 170
Automation Activity & Vendor Info: (Cataloging) Ex Libris Group; (Circulation) Ex Libris Group; (Course Reserve) Ex Libris Group
Partic in LYRASIS; OCLC Online Computer Library Center, Inc
Special Services for the Blind - Magnifiers
Open Mon-Thurs 8:30am-9pm, Fri 8:30-4, Sat 8:30-2:30, Sun 1-5

C UNIVERSITY OF BRIDGEPORT*, Wahlstrom Library, 126 Park Ave, 06604-5620. SAN 302-0711. Tel: 203-576-4745. Interlibrary Loan Service Tel: 203-576-4745. Reference Tel: 203-576-4747. FAX: 203-576-4791. Reference E-mail: reference@bridgeport.edu. Web Site: library.bridgeport.edu. *Univ Librn,* Deborah Dulepski; Tel: 203-576-2388, E-mail: ddulepsk@bridgeport.edu; *Digital Content Librn,* Matthew Sherman; Tel: 203-576-4539, E-mail: msherman@bridgeport.edu; *Health Sci Librn,* Sahar Khan; E-mail: sahkhan@bridgeport.edu; *Instruction/Info Lit Librn,* Position Currently Open; *Syst Librn,* Zhimen Chen; Tel: 203-576-6648, E-mail: zhchen@bridgeport.edu; *Tech Serv Librn,* Dale Outhouse; Tel: 203-576-4528, E-mail: douthous@bridgeport.edu; Staff 8 (MLS 6, Non-MLS 2)
Founded 1927. Highest Degree: Doctorate
Jul 2013-Jun 2014. Mats Exp $1,248,556, Per/Ser (Incl. Access Fees) $446,737, AV Equip $80,000. Sal $671,693
Automation Activity & Vendor Info: (Cataloging) OCLC Connexion; (Circulation) Koha; (Course Reserve) Koha; (Discovery) EBSCO Discovery Service; (OPAC) Koha; (Serials) Koha
Wireless access
Function: Ref serv available
Partic in Chiropractic Libr Consortium; Council of Connecticut Academic Library Directors; OCLC Online Computer Library Center, Inc
Restriction: Badge access after hrs, Borrowing privileges limited to fac & registered students, Borrowing requests are handled by ILL, Restricted borrowing privileges

BRIDGEWATER

P BRIDGEWATER LIBRARY ASSOCIATION*, Burnham Library, 62 Main St S, 06752-9998. (Mail add: PO Box 430, 06752-0430), SAN 302-0738. Tel: 860-354-6937. FAX: 860-354-4583. E-mail: staff@burnhamlibrary.org. Web Site: www.burnhamlibrary.org. *Libr Dir,* Jean Kallay; E-mail: jkallay@burnhamlibrary.org; *Asst Dir,* Christopher Fisher; E-mail: cfisher@burnhamlibrary.org; Staff 2 (Non-MLS 2)
Founded 1926. Pop 1,895; Circ 25,619
Library Holdings: Audiobooks 877; CDs 61; DVDs 707; e-books 9,005; Large Print Bks 75; Bk Titles 31,146; Per Subs 33
Special Collections: Bridgewater Authors; Civil War Letters; Historical Scrapbooks from 1955-1994; Van Wyck Brooks
Automation Activity & Vendor Info: (Acquisitions) Bibliomation Inc; (Cataloging) Bibliomation Inc; (Circulation) Bibliomation Inc; (ILL) Bibliomation Inc; (OPAC) Bibliomation Inc; (Serials) Bibliomation Inc
Wireless access
Function: 24/7 Electronic res, 24/7 Online cat, Activity rm, Adult bk club, Archival coll, Art exhibits, Audio & video playback equip for onsite use, Audiobks via web, AV serv, Bks on CD, Chess club, Children's prog, Computer training, Computers for patron use, Electronic databases & coll, Equip loans & repairs, Free DVD rentals, Holiday prog, Homebound delivery serv, ILL available, Internet access, Life-long learning prog for all ages, Magazines, Museum passes, Music CDs, Online cat, Photocopying/Printing, Preschool reading prog, Prog for adults, Prog for children & young adult, Ref serv available, Scanner, Senior computer classes, Senior outreach, Story hour, Summer reading prog, Tax forms, Teen prog, VHS videos, Wheelchair accessible, Workshops
Publications: Friends of the Library Events Postcard (Quarterly newsletter); Library Gazette (Quarterly newsletter)
Partic in Bibliomation Inc
Special Services for the Blind - Extensive large print coll; Home delivery serv; Large print bks
Open Tues 1-5, Wed 9-6, Thurs 9-5, Sat 9-1
Friends of the Library Group

BRISTOL

S AMERICAN CLOCK & WATCH MUSEUM, INC, Edward Ingraham Library, 100 Maple St, 06010-5092. SAN 302-0746. Tel: 860-583-6070. FAX: 860-583-1862. Information Services E-mail: info@clockmuseum.org. Web Site: www.clockandwatchmuseum.org. *Exec Dir,* Patricia Philippon
Founded 1952
Library Holdings: Bk Vols 2,000
Subject Interests: Clock historical, Watch
Wireless access
Open Wed-Sun 10-5
Restriction: Non-circulating

M BRISTOL HOSPITAL & HEALTH CARE GROUP*, Library Services Department, 41 Brewster Rd, 06010. (Mail add: PO Box 977, 06011-0977). Tel: 860-585-3239. Web Site: www.bristolhospital.org. *Librn,* Position Currently Open
Library Holdings: Bk Titles 1,300; Per Subs 100
Partic in Basic Health Sciences Library Network; Conn Asn of Health Scis Librs; LYRASIS; National Network of Libraries of Medicine Region 7
Open Mon-Thurs 9-2

P BRISTOL PUBLIC LIBRARY*, Five High St, 06010. SAN 336-0571. Tel: 860-584-7787. FAX: 860-584-7696. Web Site: www.bristollib.com. *Dir,* Deborah Prozzo; E-mail: deborahprozzo@bristolct.gov; *Supvr, Ch Serv,* Valerie Toner; *Circ Supvr,* Floyd Wyche; *Ref Supvr,* Claire Strillacci
Founded 1892. Pop 60,790; Circ 296,315
Library Holdings: Bk Vols 142,000; Per Subs 328
Special Collections: Local & State History Coll
Subject Interests: Agr, Art & archit, Educ, Environ studies, Music
Automation Activity & Vendor Info: (Acquisitions) SirsiDynix; (Cataloging) SirsiDynix; (Circulation) SirsiDynix; (Course Reserve) SirsiDynix; (ILL) SirsiDynix; (Media Booking) SirsiDynix; (OPAC) SirsiDynix; (Serials) SirsiDynix
Wireless access
Special Services for the Blind - Bks on cassette; Bks on CD; Home delivery serv; Large print bks
Open Mon-Thurs 8:30-8, Fri & Sat 8:30-5, Sun (June-March) 1-5
Friends of the Library Group
Branches: 1
MANROSS MEMORIAL, 260 Central St, Forestville, 06010. SAN 336-0601. Tel: 860-584-7790. *Br Supvr,* Deborah Prozzo
Library Holdings: Bk Vols 45,000
Open Mon-Thurs 10-8, Fri & Sat 9-5
Friends of the Library Group

BROAD BROOK

P BROAD BROOK PUBLIC LIBRARY*, 78 Main St, 06016. Tel: 860-627-0493. *Librn,* Patricia Shary; E-mail: patricia.shary10@gmail.com
Founded 1919
Library Holdings: Bk Titles 9,000; Bk Vols 11,000
Open Wed 1-6, Sat 10-5

BROOKFIELD

P THE BROOKFIELD LIBRARY*, 182 Whisconier Rd, 06804. SAN 302-0762. Tel: 203-775-6241. FAX: 203-740-7723. E-mail: info@brookfieldlibrary.org. Web Site: www.brookfieldlibrary.org. *Dir,* Yvonne Cech; Tel: 203-775-6241, Ext 101; *Adult Serv, Asst Dir,* Katherine Van Leeuwen; Tel: 203-775-6241, Ext 108, E-mail: kvanlee@brookfieldlibrary.org; *Ref Librn,* Elizabeth Oedel; Tel: 203-775-6241, Ext 103, E-mail: eoedel@brookfieldlibrary.org; *Circ Supvr,* George Grumman; *Ch Serv, Commun Serv,* Mary Proudfoot; Tel: 203-775-6241, Ext 104, E-mail: mproud@brookfieldlibrary.org; *Tech Serv,* Dawn Cioffi; Staff 7.3 (MLS 3.3, Non-MLS 4)
Founded 1951. Pop 16,700; Circ 156,000
Jul 2012-Jun 2013 Income $613,019, State $2,500, City $589,519, Locally Generated Income $21,000. Mats Exp $75,000. Sal $449,369
Library Holdings: Bk Vols 64,000; Per Subs 60
Automation Activity & Vendor Info: (Acquisitions) Evergreen; (Cataloging) Evergreen; (Circulation) Evergreen; (ILL) Bibliomation Inc; (OPAC) Evergreen
Wireless access
Function: Adult bk club, Audiobks via web, AV serv, Bk club(s), Bks on CD, Children's prog, Computer training, Computers for patron use, Electronic databases & coll, Free DVD rentals, Holiday prog, Home delivery & serv to seniorr ctr & nursing homes, Homebound delivery serv, ILL available, Jazz prog, Mail & tel request accepted, Microfiche/film & reading machines, Museum passes, Music CDs, Notary serv, Online cat,

Outside serv via phone, mail, e-mail & web, OverDrive digital audio bks, Photocopying/Printing, Printer for laptops & handheld devices, Prog for adults, Prog for children & young adult, Ref & res, Scanner, Story hour, Summer & winter reading prog, Summer reading prog, Tax forms, Teen prog, Telephone ref, Wheelchair accessible, Workshops
Publications: The Brookfield Library E-Newsletter (Monthly)
Partic in Bibliomation Inc; Connecticut Library Consortium
Open Mon & Wed 10-6, Tues & Thurs 10-8, Fri & Sat 10-5, Sun 12-4
Friends of the Library Group

BROOKLYN

P BROOKLYN TOWN LIBRARY ASSOCIATION*, Ten Canterbury Rd, 06234. (Mail add: PO Box 357, 06234-0357), SAN 302-0770. Tel: 860-774-0649. FAX: 860-774-0649. E-mail: brooklyntownlibrary4@yahoo.com. Web Site: www.brooklyntownlibrary.org. *Librn,* Catherine Tucker
Pop 6,600; Circ 15,070
Library Holdings: Bk Vols 18,000
Subject Interests: Local hist
Partic in Connecticut Library Consortium
Open Mon & Wed 2-7, Tues & Sat 11-5, Thurs & Fri 2-5
Friends of the Library Group

BURLINGTON

P BURLINGTON PUBLIC LIBRARY*, 34 Library Lane, 06013. SAN 302-0789. Tel: 860-673-3331. FAX: 860-673-0897. E-mail: info@burlingtonctlibrary.org. Web Site: burlingtonctlibrary.org. *Libr Dir,* Marie Spratlin Hasskarl; E-mail: mshasskarl@burlingtonctlibrary.org; *Asst Dir,* Jodi Papazian; *Teen Librn,* Victoria Kiszka; *Circ Supvr,* Kaitlin Checovetes; *Children's Programmer,* April Jones; Staff 3 (MLS 3)
Founded 1896. Pop 9,200
Library Holdings: Bk Vols 57,000
Subject Interests: Local hist
Automation Activity & Vendor Info: (Circulation) Innovative Interfaces, Inc - Sierra; (OPAC) Innovative Interfaces, Inc - Sierra
Wireless access
Function: ILL available, Photocopying/Printing, Prog for children & young adult, Summer reading prog, Wheelchair accessible
Open Mon-Thurs 10-8, Fri & Sat 10-5
Friends of the Library Group

CANTERBURY

P CANTERBURY PUBLIC LIBRARY*, One Municipal Dr, 06331-1453. SAN 376-3234. Tel: 860-546-9022. FAX: 860-546-1142. E-mail: canterburypublic@yahoo.com. Web Site: canterburylibrary.org. *Libr Dir,* Kelsey Casey; *Ref & Ad Serv Librn,* Marilyn Kitlas; *Prog Coordr,* Kathleen Hart; *ILL,* Bobbi Ann Orlomoski; Staff 1 (Non-MLS 1)
Founded 1925. Pop 5,060; Circ 45,125
Jul 2012-Jun 2013 Income $149,271, State $3,455, City $117,559, Locally Generated Income $3,098. Mats Exp $37,540, Books $14,589. Sal $94,151 (Prof $36,400)
Library Holdings: AV Mats 683; DVDs 1,836; e-books 162; Bk Titles 16,781; Per Subs 26
Automation Activity & Vendor Info: (Acquisitions) Baker & Taylor; (Cataloging) Auto-Graphics, Inc; (Circulation) Auto-Graphics, Inc; (ILL) Auto-Graphics, Inc; (OPAC) Auto-Graphics, Inc
Wireless access
Function: Adult bk club, Audiobks via web, Bk club(s), Bks on CD, Children's prog, Computer training, Computers for patron use, E-Reserves, Electronic databases & coll, Free DVD rentals, Home delivery & serv to seniorr ctr & nursing homes, Homebound delivery serv, ILL available, Magnifiers for reading, Mail & tel request accepted, Museum passes, Music CDs, Online cat, Outside serv via phone, mail, e-mail & web, Photocopying/Printing, Preschool outreach, Preschool reading prog, Prog for adults, Prog for children & young adult, Ref serv available, Senior computer classes, Senior outreach, Serves people with intellectual disabilities, Spoken cassettes & CDs, Spoken cassettes & DVDs, Story hour, Summer reading prog, Tax forms, Teen prog, Telephone ref, Wheelchair accessible
Partic in Connecticut Library Consortium
Special Services for the Deaf - Pocket talkers
Special Services for the Blind - Closed circuit TV magnifier
Open Mon-Wed 9-7, Thurs 9-8, Sat 9-2
Friends of the Library Group

CANTON

P CANTON PUBLIC LIBRARY, 40 Dyer Ave, 06019. SAN 302-0878. Tel: 860-693-5800. FAX: 860-693-5804. Web Site: www.cantonpubliclibrary.org. *Libr Dir,* Sarah McCusker; E-mail: smccusker@townofcantonct.org; *Head, Tech Serv,* Mary Beth Morrill; E-mail: bmorrill@townofcantonct.org; *Ch,* Heather Baker; E-mail: hbaker@townofcantonct.org; *Circ Supvr,* Katie Bunn; E-mail: kbunn@townofcantonct.org; *Ref Serv,* Elizabeth Van Ness; E-mail: bvanness@townofcantonct.org; *Teen Serv,* Maghan Glasgow; E-mail: mglasgow@townofcantonct.org
Pop 8,453
Library Holdings: Bk Vols 60,000
Subject Interests: Connecticut, Local hist
Automation Activity & Vendor Info: (Cataloging) SirsiDynix; (Circulation) SirsiDynix; (OPAC) SirsiDynix
Wireless access
Partic in Metronet
Open Mon, Tues, Thurs & Fri 10-5, Wed 10-7, Sat 10-1
Friends of the Library Group

CHAPLIN

P CHAPLIN PUBLIC LIBRARY, 130 Chaplin St, 06235-2302. SAN 302-0819. Tel: 860-455-9424. FAX: 860-455-9424. Web Site: www.chaplinpubliclibrary.org. *Libr Dir,* Sandra Horning; E-mail: librarydirector@chaplinct.org
Founded 1911. Pop 1,900
Library Holdings: Bk Vols 12,000; Per Subs 40
Subject Interests: Local hist
Partic in Connecticut Library Consortium
Open Mon & Wed 10-6, Fri 2-6, Sat 10-1

CHESHIRE

S CHESHIRE CORRECTIONAL INSTITUTION LIBRARY, 900 Highland Ave, 06410. Tel: 203-651-6100, Ext 3124. FAX: 203-651-6069. *Librn,* Position Currently Open
Library Holdings: Bk Titles 1,800; Bk Vols 2,000
Restriction: Not open to pub

P CHESHIRE PUBLIC LIBRARY*, 104 Main St, 06410-2499. SAN 302-0827. Tel: 203-272-2245. Reference Tel: 203-272-2245, Ext 33007. FAX: 203-272-7714. Circulation E-mail: circ@cheshirelibrary.org. Interlibrary Loan Service E-mail: ill@cheshirelibrary.org. Web Site: cheshirelibrary.com. *Dir,* Position Currently Open; *Dep Dir,* Deborah Rutter; E-mail: drutter@cheshirelibrary.org; *Asst Libr Dir,* Mary Dattilo; E-mail: mdattilo@cheshirelibrary.org; *Head, Children's Servx,* Lucas Franklin; E-mail: lfranklin@cheshirelibrary.org; *Head, Circ, Tech Serv,* Sandra Hernandez; E-mail: shernandez@cheshirelibrary.org; *Head, Ref,* William Basel; E-mail: bbasel@cheshirelibrary.org; Staff 30 (MLS 12, Non-MLS 18)
Founded 1892. Pop 28,883; Circ 424,041
Jul 2015-Jun 2016 Income $1,782,704, State $14,873, City $1,721,387, Locally Generated Income $43,856. Mats Exp $201,726, Books $102,953, AV Mat $53,043, Electronic Ref Mat (Incl. Access Fees) $45,730. Sal $1,395,252
Library Holdings: AV Mats 25,155; Bk Vols 107,911; Per Subs 255
Subject Interests: Genealogy
Automation Activity & Vendor Info: (Cataloging) Innovative Interfaces, Inc; (Circulation) Innovative Interfaces, Inc; (OPAC) Innovative Interfaces, Inc; (Serials) Innovative Interfaces, Inc
Wireless access
Function: 24/7 Electronic res, 24/7 Online cat, Activity rm, Adult bk club, After school storytime, Art exhibits, Audiobks on Playaways & MP3, Audiobks via web, AV serv, Bilingual assistance for Spanish patrons, Bk club(s), Bk reviews (Group), Bks on CD, Children's prog, Computer training, Computers for patron use, Digital talking bks, E-Reserves, Electronic databases & coll, Equip loans & repairs, Family literacy, Free DVD rentals, Holiday prog, Home delivery & serv to seniorr ctr & nursing homes, Homebound delivery serv, ILL available, Internet access, Life-long learning prog for all ages, Literacy & newcomer serv, Magazines, Magnifiers for reading, Mail & tel request accepted, Mango lang, Meeting rooms, Microfiche/film & reading machines, Movies, Museum passes, Music CDs, Online cat, Online ref, Outreach serv, OverDrive digital audio bks, Photocopying/Printing, Preschool outreach, Preschool reading prog, Printer for laptops & handheld devices, Prog for adults, Prog for children & young adult, Ref & res, Ref serv available, Scanner, Senior computer classes, Senior outreach, Serves people with intellectual disabilities, Spoken cassettes & CDs, Spoken cassettes & DVDs, Story hour, Study rm, Summer & winter reading prog, Summer reading prog, Tax forms, Teen prog, Telephone ref, Wheelchair accessible, Workshops
Partic in Library Connection, Inc
Open Mon-Thurs 9-8:30, Fri & Sat 9-5 (9-1 Summer), Sun(Nov-March) 1-5
Friends of the Library Group

CHESTER

P CHESTER PUBLIC LIBRARY*, 21 W Main St, 06412. (Mail add: PO Box 310, 06412-0310), SAN 302-0843. Tel: 860-526-0018. E-mail: library@chesterct.org. Web Site: chesterct.org/library. *Libr Dir,* Stephanie Romano; E-mail: librarydirector@chesterct.org; *Asst Librn, ILL,* Pam

Larson; *Circ,* Patricia Petrus. Subject Specialists: *Children's prog,* Patricia Petrus
Founded 1789. Pop 3,700; Circ 32,120
Library Holdings: AV Mats 800; Large Print Bks 100; Bk Vols 17,700; Per Subs 63
Subject Interests: Local hist
Automation Activity & Vendor Info: (Cataloging) Auto-Graphics, Inc; (Circulation) Auto-Graphics, Inc; (OPAC) Auto-Graphics, Inc
Wireless access
Function: Ref serv available
Open Mon 10-8, Tues-Fri 10-6, Sat 10-3
Friends of the Library Group

CLINTON

P HENRY CARTER HULL LIBRARY, INC, Ten Killingworth Tpk, 06413. SAN 302-0851. Tel: 860-669-2342. FAX: 860-669-8318. E-mail: askus@hchlibrary.org. Web Site: www.hchlibrary.org. *Dir,* Maribeth Breen; E-mail: Maribeth@hchlibrary.org; *Head, Outreach Serv,* Sarah Borgnis-Tobin; E-mail: Sarah@hchlibrary.org; *Ref Librn, YA Librn,* Cathleen Cole; E-mail: cathleen@hchlibrary.org; *Ref Librn,* Kathleen Crea; E-mail: KC3@hchlibrary.org; *Ref & Tech Librn,* Kathleen Cartwright; E-mail: kathleen@hchlibrary.org; *Ch Serv,* Coralie Williams; E-mail: coralie@hchlibrary.org; *ILL,* Annette Viglione; E-mail: annette@hchlibrary.org; Staff 5 (MLS 5)
Founded 1925. Pop 13,500
Library Holdings: Bk Vols 84,000; Per Subs 130
Automation Activity & Vendor Info: (Acquisitions) Koha; (Cataloging) Koha; (Circulation) Koha
Wireless access
Publications: H C Hull Library News
Open Mon 12-8, Tues-Thurs 9-8, Fri 9-5, Sat 10-4
Friends of the Library Group

COLCHESTER

P CRAGIN MEMORIAL LIBRARY, Eight Linwood Ave, 06415. SAN 302-086X. Tel: 860-537-5752. FAX: 860-537-4559. E-mail: library@colchesterct.gov. Web Site: www.colchesterct.gov/cragin-memorial-library. *Libr Dir,* Kate Byroade; E-mail: kbyroade@colchesterct.gov; *Ad,* Sam Partney; E-mail: spartney@colchesterct.gov; *Ch, YA Librn,* Jennifer Rummel; E-mail: jrummel@colchesterct.gov; *Asst Librn,* Peter Ciparelli; *Asst Librn, Teen Serv,* Valerie Grabek; *Circ Supvr,* Alexis Turner; E-mail: aturner@colchesterct.gov; *Cataloger,* Joann Koch; E-mail: jkoch@colchesterct.gov; *Ch Asst,* Joann MacDonald; E-mail: jmacdonald@colchesterct.gov; *Libr Asst,* Kristan Gallucci; *Libr Asst,* Pamela Gonzalez; *Libr Asst,* Tracy Grigas; *Libr Asst,* Katrina Kirby; *Libr Asst,* Vickie Lynch; E-mail: vlynch@colchesterct.gov; *Libr Asst,* Liz Perez-Balesky; *Prog Asst,* Sara Perrin. Subject Specialists: *Adult fiction, Non-fiction,* Kate Byroade; *Adult fiction, Graphic novels, Non-fiction,* Sam Partney; *Sci fict,* Valerie Grabek; *Popular fiction,* Alexis Turner; *Fantasy, Mystery, Sci fict,* Joann Koch; *Picture bks,* Sara Perrin; Staff 6.3 (MLS 3, Non-MLS 3.3)
Founded 1905. Pop 16,000; Circ 115,000
Jul 2020-Jun 2021 Income $610,000. Mats Exp $53,000
Special Collections: Local History Coll
Automation Activity & Vendor Info: (Cataloging) Innovative Interfaces, Inc - Sierra; (Circulation) Innovative Interfaces, Inc - Sierra; (Discovery) Innovative Interfaces, Inc; (OPAC) Innovative Interfaces, Inc
Wireless access
Function: 24/7 Electronic res, 24/7 Online cat, Activity rm, Adult bk club, After school storytime, Art exhibits, Audiobks via web, Bi-weekly Writer's Group, Bk club(s), Bks on CD, Children's prog, Computers for patron use, Electronic databases & coll, Free DVD rentals, Homebound delivery serv, ILL available, Internet access, Magazines, Magnifiers for reading, Mango lang, Meeting rooms, Movies, Museum passes, Music CDs, Online cat, Outreach serv, OverDrive digital audio bks, Photocopying/Printing, Preschool outreach, Preschool reading prog, Prog for adults, Prog for children & young adult, Story hour, Summer reading prog, Tax forms, Teen prog, Wheelchair accessible
Partic in Connecticut Library Consortium; Library Connection, Inc
Special Services for the Blind - Home delivery serv
Open Mon, Wed & Thurs 10-8, Tues 10-5, Fri & Sat 10-4
Friends of the Library Group

COLLINSVILLE

S CANTON HISTORICAL SOCIETY LIBRARY*, 11 Front St, 06019. SAN 329-8418. Tel: 860-693-2793. E-mail: Library@CantonMuseum.org. Web Site: www.cantonmuseum.org. *Curator,* Kathleen Woolman; Tel: 860-693-8893
Library Holdings: Bk Vols 400
Special Collections: Local Census, 1790-1930; Samuel W Collins & the Collins Company Coll, 1826-1966. Oral History
Subject Interests: Local hist
Function: Res libr
Restriction: Open by appt only, Open to pub for ref only

COLUMBIA

P SAXTON B LITTLE FREE LIBRARY, INC, 319 Rte 87, 06237-1143. SAN 302-0886. Tel: 860-228-0350. FAX: 860-228-1569. E-mail: staff@columbiactlibrary.org. Web Site: www.columbiactlibrary.org. *Dir,* Su Epstein; *Ch,* Megan Quigley; *Adult Serv,* Caitlyn Orlomoski; Staff 10 (MLS 3, Non-MLS 7)
Founded 1883. Pop 5,406; Circ 63,352
Library Holdings: AV Mats 6,000; Bk Vols 55,000; Per Subs 100
Automation Activity & Vendor Info: (Acquisitions) Auto-Graphics, Inc; (Cataloging) Auto-Graphics, Inc; (Circulation) Auto-Graphics, Inc; (Course Reserve) Auto-Graphics, Inc; (ILL) Auto-Graphics, Inc; (Media Booking) Auto-Graphics, Inc; (OPAC) Auto-Graphics, Inc; (Serials) Auto-Graphics, Inc
Wireless access
Publications: SBL Newsletter
Special Services for the Deaf - Am sign lang & deaf culture
Open Mon, Fri & Sat 10-5, Tues-Thurs 10-8
Friends of the Library Group

CORNWALL

P CORNWALL LIBRARY, 30 Pine St, 06753. (Mail add: PO Box 126, 06753-0126), SAN 302-0908. Tel: 860-672-6874. FAX: 860-672-6398. Web Site: cornwalllibrary.org. *Dir,* Margaret Haske Hare; E-mail: Director@CornwallLibrary.org; *Libr Asst,* Raymonde Burke; Staff 2 (Non-MLS 2)
Pop 1,443; Circ 19,500
Library Holdings: Bk Vols 26,000; Per Subs 50
Automation Activity & Vendor Info: (Cataloging) SirsiDynix; (Circulation) SirsiDynix
Wireless access
Open Tues & Thurs 12-5, Wed 12-7, Fri 12-6, Sat 10-2
Friends of the Library Group

COS COB

S GREENWICH HISTORICAL SOCIETY*, Merck Stevenson Library & Archives, 47 Strickland Rd, 06807. SAN 302-0924. Tel: 203-869-6899. FAX: 203-861-9720. Web Site: greenwichhistory.org. *Curator, Archives & Libr,* Christopher Shields; Tel: 203-869-6899, Ext 23, E-mail: cshields@greenwichhistory.org; *Coll Curator,* Karen L Frederick; Tel: 203-869-6899, Ext 22, E-mail: curator@greenwichhistory.org; Staff 2 (MLS 1, Non-MLS 1)
Founded 1931
Library Holdings: Bk Vols 3,500
Special Collections: Anya Seton Papers; Greenwich Family History Coll; Holley/MacRae Family Papers; Photograph Coll; Postcard Coll; Real Estate Company Records
Subject Interests: Am Impressionism, Archit, Decorative art, Genealogy, Local hist, State hist
Function: Archival coll, For res purposes, Photocopying/Printing, Ref serv available, Telephone ref, Wheelchair accessible
Publications: Annual Report of the Historical Society of the Town of Greenwich; Building Greenwich: Architectural & Design, 1640 to the Present; Post (Newsletter)
Open Wed 10-4
Restriction: Non-circulating

COVENTRY

P BOOTH & DIMOCK MEMORIAL LIBRARY*, 1134 Main St, 06238. SAN 302-0932. Tel: 860-742-7606. FAX: 860-742-7491. E-mail: bdlibrary@coventryct.org. Web Site: www.CoventryPL.org. *Dir,* Position Currently Open; *Actg Dir, Head, Children's Servx,* Meg Schiebel; E-mail: mschiebel@coventryct.org; *Head, Teen Serv,* Kayla Fontaine; Staff 8 (MLS 5, Non-MLS 3)
Founded 1880. Pop 12,215; Circ 96,000
Library Holdings: Bk Titles 55,000; Per Subs 75; Talking Bks 2,400; Videos 2,300
Automation Activity & Vendor Info: (Cataloging) Auto-Graphics, Inc; (Circulation) Auto-Graphics, Inc; (ILL) Auto-Graphics, Inc; (OPAC) Auto-Graphics, Inc
Wireless access
Function: 24/7 Electronic res, 24/7 Online cat, Activity rm, Adult bk club, Adult literacy prog, Audiobks on Playaways & MP3, Audiobks via web, Bk club(s), Bks on CD, Children's prog, Computer training, Computers for patron use, Doc delivery serv, E-Readers, E-Reserves, Electronic databases & coll, Family literacy, Free DVD rentals, Home delivery & serv to seniorr ctr & nursing homes, Homebound delivery serv, ILL available, Internet access, Large print keyboards, Magazines, Movies, Museum passes, Music CDs, Online cat, Outreach serv, Photocopying/Printing, Preschool outreach, Prog for adults, Prog for children & young adult, Ref serv available,

Scanner, Story hour, Summer reading prog, Tax forms, Teen prog, Wheelchair accessible
Publications: Library Lingo (Newsletter)
Partic in Bibliomation Inc
Open Tues-Thurs 10-8, Fri 10-6, Sat 10-3

CROMWELL

P CROMWELL BELDEN PUBLIC LIBRARY*, 39 West St, 06416. SAN 302-0959. Tel: 860-632-3460. FAX: 860-632-3484. Web Site: www.cromwellct.com/library.html. *Dir,* Kara Canney; *Ad,* Emma Russo-Savage; *Ch,* Lois Meltzer
Founded 1888
Library Holdings: Electronic Media & Resources 15; Bk Vols 52,025; Per Subs 150; Talking Bks 2,375; Videos 3,250
Subject Interests: Local hist
Automation Activity & Vendor Info: (Cataloging) Innovative Interfaces, Inc; (Circulation) Innovative Interfaces, Inc
Wireless access
Partic in Connecticut Library Consortium; Library Connection, Inc
Open Mon, Tues & Thurs 10-8, Wed 12-8, Fri & Sat 10-5
Friends of the Library Group

C HOLY APOSTLES COLLEGE & SEMINARY LIBRARY*, 33 Prospect Hill Rd, 06416-2005. SAN 302-0967. Tel: 860-632-3009. FAX: 860-632-3090. E-mail: library@holyapostles.edu. Web Site: www.holyapostles.edu. *Dir, Libr Serv,* Clare Adamo; Staff 3 (MLS 1, Non-MLS 2)
Founded 1957. Enrl 450; Fac 29; Highest Degree: Master
Library Holdings: Bk Titles 60,000; Per Subs 220
Special Collections: Papal Documents; USCCB Documents
Subject Interests: Bioethics, Philos, Theol
Automation Activity & Vendor Info: (Cataloging) OCLC; (OPAC) Auto-Graphics, Inc
Wireless access
Partic in Connecticut Library Consortium; OCLC Online Computer Library Center, Inc
Friends of the Library Group

DANBURY

M DANBURY HOSPITAL, Health Sciences Library, 24 Hospital Ave, 06810. SAN 302-0991. Tel: 203-739-7035. Web Site: www.nuvancehealth.org/en/locations/danbury-hospital. *Mgr,* Amanda Pomeroy; *Med Librn,* Kristin Chapman; Staff 2 (MLS 2)
Founded 1956
Library Holdings: Bk Vols 3,000; Per Subs 300
Subject Interests: Allied health, Hospital admin, Med, Nursing
Automation Activity & Vendor Info: (Cataloging) CyberTools for Libraries
Wireless access
Open Mon-Fri 8-5
Restriction: Badge access after hrs

S DANBURY MUSEUM & HISTORICAL SOCIETY*, Research Library & Archives, 43 Main St, 06810. SAN 302-1025. Tel: 203-743-5200. FAX: 203-743-1131. Information Services E-mail: info@danburymuseum.org. Web Site: www.danburymuseum.org. *Exec Dir,* Brigid Guertin; E-mail: b.guertin@danbury-ct.gov; *Colls Mgr,* Michele Lee Amundsen; Staff 2 (Non-MLS 2)
Founded 1947
Library Holdings: Bk Vols 600
Special Collections: DAR Lineage Books; Hat Life Magazine Coll; Hatting Industry (Charles Ives Coll)
Subject Interests: Antiques, Genealogy, Local hist
Wireless access
Function: For res purposes
Open Tues-Sat 10-4
Restriction: Non-circulating to the pub
Friends of the Library Group

P DANBURY PUBLIC LIBRARY*, 170 Main St, 06810. SAN 302-1017. Tel: 203-797-4505. Information Services Tel: 203-797-4527. FAX: 203-797-4501. Web Site: danburylibrary.org. *Libr Dir,* Katie Pearson; E-mail: kpearson@danburylibrary.org; *Asst Dir,* Katharine Chung; E-mail: kchung@danburylibrary.org; Staff 30 (MLS 14, Non-MLS 16)
Founded 1869. Pop 79,226; Circ 622,356
Library Holdings: AV Mats 19,896; e-books 4,146; Bk Vols 99,912; Per Subs 336
Special Collections: State Document Depository
Subject Interests: Local hist
Automation Activity & Vendor Info: (Acquisitions) Innovative Interfaces, Inc; (Cataloging) Innovative Interfaces, Inc; (Circulation) Innovative Interfaces, Inc; (Course Reserve) Innovative Interfaces, Inc; (ILL) Innovative Interfaces, Inc; (Media Booking) Innovative Interfaces, Inc; (OPAC) Innovative Interfaces, Inc; (Serials) Innovative Interfaces, Inc
Wireless access
Open Mon, Tues & Thurs 10-7, Wed 1-7, Fri & Sat 10-5, Sun 1-5; Mon, Tues & Thurs (Summer) 10-7, Wed 1-7, Fri 10-5, Sat 10-2
Friends of the Library Group

S FEDERAL CORRECTIONAL INSTITUTION*, Department of Justice Centralized Library, 33 1/2 Pembroke Sta, 06811. SAN 302-1033. Tel: 203-743-6471. FAX: 203-312-5138. Web Site: www.bop.gov/locations/institutions/dan.
Founded 1979
Library Holdings: Bk Vols 2,000; Per Subs 25
Special Collections: World War I & II Coll
Open Mon-Fri 7:30-4

P LONG RIDGE LIBRARY, 191 Long Ridge Rd, 06810-8463. SAN 321-6578. Tel: 203-748-1011. E-mail: thelongridgelibrary@gmail.com. Web Site: longridgelibrary.org. *Librn,* Barbara Fulton; Tel: 203-748-7520
Founded 1919. Pop 78,000
Library Holdings: CDs 25; DVDs 50; Bk Titles 2,100; Bk Vols 2,300; Talking Bks 85; Videos 102
Special Collections: Oral History
Subject Interests: Historic bldg
Wireless access
Open Wed 5-7, Sat 10-4
Friends of the Library Group

C WESTERN CONNECTICUT STATE UNIVERSITY*, Ruth A Haas Library, 181 White St, 06810. SAN 302-1076. Tel: 203-837-9100. FAX: 203-837-9108. Web Site: library.wcsu.edu. *Assoc Dean, Libr Serv,* Veronica Kenausis; Tel: 203-837-9109, E-mail: kenausisv@wcsu.edu; *Access Serv Librn,* Position Currently Open; *Acq Librn,* Xiao Hua Yang; Tel: 203-837-9105, Fax: 203-837-9103, E-mail: yangx@wcsu.edu; *Archives & Spec Coll Librn,* Brian Stevens; E-mail: stevensb@wcsu.edu; *Bus Librn,* Xiaomei Gong; E-mail: gongx@wcsu.edu; *Digital Serv Librn,* Christina DiCarro; E-mail: dicarroc@wcsu.edu; *Educ Librn, Pub Serv,* Tom Schmiedel; E-mail: schmiedeltf@wcsu.edu; *Instruction Librn,* Joan Reitz; Tel: 203-837-8308, E-mail: reitzj@wcsu.edu; *Ser Librn,* Jennifer O'Brien; E-mail: obrienj@wcsu.edu; *Student Serv Librn,* Julie Hunter; E-mail: hunterj@wcsu.edu; *Resource Coordr, Tutoring Servs,* Lauren Eddy; E-mail: eddyl@wcsu.edu; *Doc Delivery, ILL,* Joanne Elpern; Tel: 203-837-9114, E-mail: elpernj@wcsu.edu; *Instrul Designer,* Aura Lippincott; E-mail: lippincotta@wcsu.edu; Staff 12 (MLS 9, Non-MLS 3)
Founded 1905. Enrl 5,080; Fac 220; Highest Degree: Doctorate
Library Holdings: AV Mats 8,315; Bk Titles 105,000; Bk Vols 200,000; Per Subs 700
Special Collections: Fairfield County & Connecticut History (Connecticut Room), bks, doc; Music Education, bks, rec; Teacher Educ (Curriculum Room). US Document Depository
Subject Interests: Local hist
Automation Activity & Vendor Info: (Acquisitions) Ex Libris Group; (Cataloging) Ex Libris Group; (Circulation) Ex Libris Group; (Course Reserve) Ex Libris Group; (Discovery) Ex Libris Group; (ILL) OCLC ILLiad; (OPAC) Ex Libris Group
Wireless access
Function: 24/7 Electronic res, 24/7 Online cat, Archival coll, Art exhibits, Computers for patron use, Distance learning, Doc delivery serv, E-Reserves, Electronic databases & coll, Govt ref serv, Health sci info serv, ILL available, Internet access, Meeting rooms, Online cat, Online info literacy tutorials on the web & in blackboard, Orientations, Outreach serv, Ref & res, Ref serv available, Res assist avail, Scanner, Telephone ref, Writing prog
Publications: Library Guide
Partic in Connecticut Library Consortium; Connecticut State University Library System; OCLC Online Computer Library Center, Inc
Open Mon-Thurs 8am-11pm, Fri 8-4, Sat 10-6, Sun 2-10

Departmental Libraries:

ROBERT S YOUNG BUSINESS LIBRARY, 181 White St, 06810-6885. Tel: 203-837-9139. FAX: 203-837-9135. *Bus Librn,* Xiaomei Gong; E-mail: gongx@wcsu.edu; *Libr Tech,* Teresa Saunders; E-mail: saunderst@wcsu.edu; Staff 2 (MLS 2)
Founded 1982
Library Holdings: Bk Vols 6,000; Per Subs 125
Open Mon-Thurs 9-9, Fri 9-4, Sat 11-4, Sun 2-7

DANIELSON

P KILLINGLY PUBLIC LIBRARY, 25 Westcott Rd, 06239. SAN 302-1092. Tel: 860-779-5383. E-mail: info@killinglypl.org. Web Site: www.killinglypl.org. *Dir,* Claudette Stockwell; E-mail: cstockwell@biblio.org; Staff 16 (MLS 2, Non-MLS 14)
Founded 1903. Pop 17,428; Circ 105,209
Special Collections: Local History (Windham County Coll)

Automation Activity & Vendor Info: (Cataloging) Evergreen; (Circulation) Evergreen; (OPAC) Evergreen; (Serials) Evergreen
Wireless access
Function: 24/7 Electronic res, 24/7 Online cat, Adult bk club, Archival coll, Audiobks via web, Bk club(s), Bk reviews (Group), Bks on CD, Children's prog, Computer training, Computers for patron use, Distance learning, Electronic databases & coll, Family literacy, Free DVD rentals, Genealogy discussion group, Holiday prog, ILL available, Internet access, Life-long learning prog for all ages, Magazines, Magnifiers for reading, Mango lang, Microfiche/film & reading machines, Movies, Museum passes, Music CDs, Online cat, Online info literacy tutorials on the web & in blackboard, Outreach serv, OverDrive digital audio bks, Photocopying/Printing, Preschool outreach, Prog for adults, Prog for children & young adult, Ref & res, Ref serv available, Scanner, Senior outreach, STEM programs, Story hour, Study rm, Summer reading prog, Tax forms, Teen prog, Telephone ref, Wheelchair accessible, Winter reading prog, Workshops
Partic in Bibliomation Inc; Connecticut Library Consortium; OPEN
Open Mon & Fri 9:30-5, Tues-Thurs 9:30-6:30, Sat 9:30-2
Friends of the Library Group

J QUINEBAUG VALLEY COMMUNITY COLLEGE LIBRARY*, 742 Upper Maple St, 06239. SAN 302-1106. Tel: 860-932-4007. FAX: 860-932-4308. E-mail: library@qvcc.edu. Web Site: qvcc.edu/library. *Dir, Libr Serv,* M'lyn Hines; Tel: 860-932-4131, E-mail: mhines@qvcc.edu; *Ref & Instruction Librn,* Fyiane Nsilo-Swai; Tel: 860-932-4056, E-mail: fnsilowai@qvcc.edu; *Libr Assoc II,* Cheryl White; Tel: 860-932-4171, E-mail: cwhite@qvcc.edu; Staff 4 (MLS 3, Non-MLS 1)
Founded 1971. Enrl 2,000; Highest Degree: Associate
Library Holdings: DVDs 2,500; e-books 250,000; e-journals 45,000; Bk Titles 28,000; Bk Vols 30,000; Per Subs 125
Automation Activity & Vendor Info: (Acquisitions) Ex Libris Group; (Cataloging) Ex Libris Group; (Circulation) Ex Libris Group; (Course Reserve) Ex Libris Group; (ILL) OCLC; (Media Booking) Ex Libris Group; (OPAC) Ex Libris Group; (Serials) EBSCO Online
Wireless access
Partic in Council of Connecticut Academic Library Directors; Westchester Academic Library Directors Organization
Open Mon & Tues 2-7, Wed & Thurs 9-2

DARIEN

P DARIEN LIBRARY*, 1441 Post Rd, 06820-5419. SAN 302-1122. Tel: 203-655-1234. Circulation Tel: 203-669-5239. Administration Tel: 203-669-5220. Information Services Tel: 203-669-5236. FAX: 203-655-1547. E-mail: askus@darienlibrary.org. Web Site: www.darienlibrary.org. *Dir,* Kiera Parrott; E-mail: kparrott@darienlibrary.org; *Asst Dir,* John Blyberg; Tel: 203-669-5222, E-mail: jblyberg@darienlibrary.org; Staff 29 (MLS 13, Non-MLS 16)
Founded 1894. Pop 20,732; Circ 638,957
Jul 2017-Jun 2018 Income $4,896,939, State $52,310, City $3,685,375, Locally Generated Income $1,159,254. Mats Exp $533,781, Books $318,208, Per/Ser (Incl. Access Fees) $25,362, Other Print Mats $4,549, AV Mat $54,025, Electronic Ref Mat (Incl. Access Fees) $108,800. Sal $2,313,096
Library Holdings: Audiobooks 6,046; AV Mats 416; DVDs 12,036; Electronic Media & Resources 60; Bk Vols 107,258; Per Subs 274
Subject Interests: Genealogy, Lit, Local hist, Travel
Automation Activity & Vendor Info: (Acquisitions) Baker & Taylor; (Cataloging) Baker & Taylor; (Circulation) Innovative Interfaces, Inc; (ILL) OCLC
Wireless access
Function: 24/7 Electronic res, 24/7 Online cat, Adult bk club, After school storytime, Art exhibits, Audio & video playback equip for onsite use, Audiobks via web, AV serv, Bk club(s), Bk reviews (Group), Bks on CD, CD-ROM, Children's prog, Computer training, Computers for patron use, E-Readers, E-Reserves, Electronic databases & coll, Equip loans & repairs, For res purposes, Free DVD rentals, Games & aids for people with disabilities, Genealogy discussion group, Govt ref serv, Health sci info serv, Holiday prog, Home delivery & serv to seniorr ctr & nursing homes, Homebound delivery serv, Homework prog, ILL available, Internet access, Large print keyboards, Life-long learning prog for all ages, Magazines, Magnifiers for reading, Mail & tel request accepted, Mango lang, Meeting rooms, Microfiche/film & reading machines, Movies, Museum passes, Music CDs, Notary serv, Online cat, Online info literacy tutorials on the web & in blackboard, Online ref, Outreach serv, Outside serv via phone, mail, e-mail & web, OverDrive digital audio bks, Photocopying/Printing, Preschool outreach, Printer for laptops & handheld devices, Prog for adults, Prog for children & young adult, Ref & res, Ref serv available, Res libr, Scanner, Senior computer classes, Senior outreach, Serves people with intellectual disabilities, Story hour, Study rm, Summer & winter reading prog, Summer reading prog, Tax forms, Teen prog, Telephone ref, Visual arts prog, Wheelchair accessible, Winter reading prog, Workshops, Writing prog
Partic in Connecticut Library Consortium
Open Mon-Thurs 9-9, Fri 9-6, Sat 9-5, Sun 1-5
Friends of the Library Group

S MUSEUM OF DARIEN LIBRARY, (Formerly Darien Historical Society, Inc Library), 45 Old Kings Hwy N, 06820. SAN 302-1114. Tel: 203-655-9233. E-mail: info@museumofdarien.org. Web Site: museumofdarien.org. *Libr Office Mgr, Spec Events Coordr,* Ulla Kremer; E-mail: ukremer@darienhistorical.org
Founded 1953
Library Holdings: Bk Vols 1,600
Subject Interests: Decorative art, Genealogy, Local hist, New England
Wireless access
Open Tues-Thurs 11-4

S ZOTOS INTERNATIONAL LIBRARY*, 100 Tokeneke Rd, 06820-1005. SAN 320-6149. Tel: 203-656-7700, 203-656-7805. FAX: 203-656-7963. *Research Librn,* Position Currently Open
Founded 1932
Library Holdings: Bk Titles 5,300; Per Subs 30
Subject Interests: Cosmetics industry, Toiletries
Publications: Newsletters
Partic in Proquest Dialog
Restriction: Staff use only

DEEP RIVER

P DEEP RIVER PUBLIC LIBRARY, 150 Main St, 06417. SAN 302-1157. Tel: 860-526-6039. FAX: 860-526-6040. E-mail: deepriverpubliclibrary@gmail.com. Web Site: deepriverlibrary.accountsupport.com. *Dir,* Susan J Rooney; Staff 4 (MLS 4)
Founded 1900. Pop 4,600; Circ 69,051
Library Holdings: Bk Titles 3,100; Per Subs 100
Automation Activity & Vendor Info: (Acquisitions) Baker & Taylor; (Cataloging) Bibliomation Inc; (Circulation) Bibliomation Inc; (OPAC) Bibliomation Inc; (Serials) Bibliomation Inc
Wireless access
Function: 24/7 Electronic res, 24/7 Online cat, Adult bk club, Art exhibits, Bk club(s), Computer training, Computers for patron use, Family literacy, Free DVD rentals, Holiday prog, Home delivery & serv to seniorr ctr & nursing homes, Homebound delivery serv, ILL available, Museum passes, Music CDs, Photocopying/Printing, Preschool reading prog, Prog for adults, Prog for children & young adult, Senior computer classes, Tax forms, Wheelchair accessible, Workshops
Partic in Bibliomation Inc; ReQuest OPAC Catalog
Open Mon & Wed 1-8, Tues, Thurs & Fri 10-6, Sat 10-2
Restriction: Authorized patrons
Friends of the Library Group

DERBY

P DERBY NECK LIBRARY*, 307 Hawthorne Ave, 06418. SAN 302-1165. Tel: 203-734-1492. FAX: 203-732-2913. E-mail: derbynecklibrary@yahoo.com. Web Site: derbynecklibrary.org. *Head Librn,* Ian Parsells; E-mail: headlibrarian@biblio.org; *Head, Circ,* Roberto Carmona; *Ch,* Kathleen Gordon; *Ref Librn,* Patricia Sweeney; Staff 4 (MLS 2, Non-MLS 2)
Founded 1897. Pop 12,500; Circ 49,581
Library Holdings: Audiobooks 1,511; CDs 1,065; DVDs 5,892; e-books 29; Large Print Bks 2,426; Bk Vols 54,466; Per Subs 95; Videos 276
Subject Interests: Cooking, Fiction, Irish, Local hist, Poetry, Urban affairs
Automation Activity & Vendor Info: (Acquisitions) Bibliomation Inc; (Cataloging) Evergreen; (Circulation) Evergreen; (ILL) Evergreen; (OPAC) Evergreen; (Serials) Evergreen
Wireless access
Function: Audio & video playback equip for onsite use, Audiobks via web, Bilingual assistance for Spanish patrons, Bk club(s), Bks on CD, Children's prog, Computer training, Computers for patron use, Electronic databases & coll, Free DVD rentals, Genealogy discussion group, Holiday prog, Mail & tel request accepted, Museum passes, Music CDs, Online cat, OverDrive digital audio bks, Photocopying/Printing, Preschool outreach, Prog for adults, Prog for children & young adult, Ref serv available, Res libr, Scanner, Senior computer classes, Spoken cassettes & CDs, Spoken cassettes & DVDs, Story hour, Summer reading prog, Tax forms, Teen prog, Telephone ref, VHS videos, Wheelchair accessible, Workshops, Writing prog
Partic in Bibliomation Inc
Open Mon-Thurs 10-8, Sat & Sun 1-5
Friends of the Library Group

P DERBY PUBLIC LIBRARY, Harcourt Wood Memorial Library, 313 Elizabeth St, 06418. SAN 302-1173. Tel: 203-736-1482. FAX: 203-736-1419. Web Site: www.derbypubliclibrary.org. *Dir,* Nicole Cignoli; E-mail: ncignoli@biblio.org; *Head, Circ,* Kathy Wilson; E-mail: kwilson@biblio.org; *Ch,* Susan Sherman; E-mail: ssherman@biblio.org; *Ref*

Librn, Tony DeLos; E-mail: tdelos@biblio.org; *Tech Librn,* Marc Weissman; E-mail: mweissman@biblio.org; Staff 4 (MLS 1, Non-MLS 3)
Founded 1902. Pop 12,520; Circ 45,000
Library Holdings: DVDs 1,975; Bk Vols 47,044; Per Subs 97; Talking Bks 1,040
Special Collections: Family Place; Parent's Place
Subject Interests: Career, Compact discs, Employment, Finance, Genealogy, Hist, Lit, Literacy, Local hist, Sheet music
Automation Activity & Vendor Info: (Acquisitions) Bibliomation Inc; (Cataloging) Bibliomation Inc; (Circulation) Bibliomation Inc; (Course Reserve) Bibliomation Inc; (ILL) Bibliomation Inc; (OPAC) Bibliomation Inc; (Serials) Bibliomation Inc
Wireless access
Publications: Derby Public Library Newsletter
Partic in Bibliomation Inc
Special Services for the Deaf - Closed caption videos; TDD equip
Special Services for the Blind - Bks on cassette; Large print bks; Magnifiers
Open Mon-Wed 9-8, Thurs 9-6, Fri 9-5, Sat (Sept-June) 9-2
Friends of the Library Group

M GRIFFIN HOSPITAL*, Health Resource Center, 130 Division St, 06418. SAN 371-5264. Tel: 203-732-7399. FAX: 203-732-1274. E-mail: griflib@griffinhealth.org. Web Site: www.griffinhealth.org/prevention-lifestyle/health-information/community-health-resource-center. *Coordr,* Kerry Dennigan; Staff 2 (MLS 1, Non-MLS 1)
Founded 1994
Library Holdings: Bk Titles 1,000; Per Subs 250
Subject Interests: Consumer health
Partic in Conn Asn of Health Scis Librs
Open Mon, Tues & Fri 9-5, Wed & Thurs 9-8, Sat 11-3

DURHAM

P DURHAM PUBLIC LIBRARY*, Seven Maple Ave, 06422. SAN 302-1181. Tel: 860-349-9544. FAX: 860-349-1897. Web Site: www.durhamlibrary.org. *Libr Dir,* Christine Michaud; E-mail: cmichaud@durhamlibrary.org; *Adult Serv, Asst Dir,* Kim McNally; E-mail: kmcnally@durhamlibrary.org; *Head, Youth Serv,* Lauren Redfield; E-mail: lredfield@durhamlibrary.org; *Youth Serv Librn,* Kristen Carpentier; E-mail: kcarpentier@durhamlibrary.org; Staff 8 (MLS 4, Non-MLS 4)
Founded 1894. Pop 7,200; Circ 210,000
Library Holdings: Audiobooks 600; CDs 590; DVDs 3,200; Large Print Bks 1,200; Bk Vols 58,989; Per Subs 75; Videos 500
Subject Interests: Local hist
Automation Activity & Vendor Info: (Acquisitions) Innovative Interfaces, Inc; (Cataloging) Innovative Interfaces, Inc; (Circulation) Innovative Interfaces, Inc; (ILL) Innovative Interfaces, Inc; (OPAC) Innovative Interfaces, Inc
Wireless access
Partic in Libraries Online, Inc
Open Mon-Thurs 12-8, Fri & Sat 12-5
Friends of the Library Group

EAST BERLIN

P EAST BERLIN LIBRARY ASSOCIATION, 80 Main St, 06023. (Mail add: PO Box 334, 06023-0334), SAN 302-119X. Tel: 860-828-3123. *Libr Dir,* Helen Malinka; E-mail: hmalinka@berlinpeck.org
Circ 6,000
Library Holdings: Bk Vols 6,900
Open Mon & Thurs 3-5 & 6:30-8:30

EAST GRANBY

P EAST GRANBY PUBLIC LIBRARY*, 24 Center St, 06026. SAN 302-1203. Tel: 860-653-3002. FAX: 860-653-3936. E-mail: eastgranbylibrary@egpl.org. Web Site: www.egpl.org. *Dir,* Doreen Jacius; E-mail: doreenj@egpl.org; *Ch,* Amy Thompson; E-mail: amyt@egpl.org; Staff 9 (MLS 1, Non-MLS 8)
Founded 1922. Pop 4,500; Circ 33,990
Library Holdings: Bk Vols 30,000; Per Subs 28
Subject Interests: Careers, Consumer info, Educ, Local hist
Automation Activity & Vendor Info: (Circulation) Follett Software
Wireless access
Publications: Literally Speaking
Partic in Connecticut Library Consortium
Open Mon-Thurs 10-7, Fri & Sat 10-2

EAST HADDAM

S GOODSPEED OPERA HOUSE FOUNDATION*, The Scherer Library of Musical Theatre, 20 Norwich Rd, 06423-1344. (Mail add: PO Box A, 06423-0281), SAN 370-6044. Tel: 860-873-8664, Ext 522. FAX: 860-873-2329. Web Site: www.goodspeed.org/education-library/library. *Educ Mgr, Outreach Mgr,* Erin Lafferty; Tel: 860-873-8664, Ext 521, E-mail: elafferty@goodspeed.org; Staff 2 (Non-MLS 2)
Founded 1979
Special Collections: 20th & 21st Century Musical Theatre (Crowley-Stoll Coll), memorabilia, audio & video recs; Carol & Frank Tuit Record Coll of George Gershwin, tape, vinyl & acetate, including rare recs; Goodspeed Opera House Archives, libretti, scores, videos, orchestrations & memorabilia; Irving Berlin & George Gershwin sheet music (Janice Grower Coll); Josef Weinberger Coll, libretti & scores; Judge David I Harfeld Coll, vinyl recs, cds, memorabilia, photogs, news clippings, reviews & videos; Michael Kuchwara Coll, plays, scores, libretti, playbills & bks; Music Theatre International Coll, libretti & scores; National Broadcasting Company (NBC) Sheet Music Library Coll; Patricia Hoag Simon Coll, interviews with associates of Joshua Logan, taped seminars 1987-2010 at Marymount Manhattan Col, includes seminars by Arthur Laurents, Harold Prince, Stephen Sondheim & Chita Rivera; Rodgers & Hammerstein Organization Coll, libretti & scores
Subject Interests: Musical theatre
Automation Activity & Vendor Info: (Acquisitions) ByWater Solutions; (Cataloging) ByWater Solutions; (Circulation) ByWater Solutions; (OPAC) ByWater Solutions
Wireless access
Function: 24/7 Online cat, Archival coll, Art exhibits, Audio & video playback equip for onsite use, Bus archives, Computers for patron use, Electronic databases & coll, For res purposes, Internet access, Magazines, Mail & tel request accepted, Movies, Music CDs, Online cat, Orientations, Outreach serv, Outside serv via phone, mail, e-mail & web, Photocopying/Printing, Prog for adults, Ref & res, Ref serv available, Res libr, Res performed for a fee, Scanner, Serves people with intellectual disabilities, Telephone ref, VHS videos, Wheelchair accessible, Workshops
Restriction: Access at librarian's discretion, Circ limited, Internal circ only, Open by appt only, Open to pub by appt only, Open to pub with supv only, Open to students, fac & staff, Private libr
Friends of the Library Group

EAST HAMPTON

P EAST HAMPTON PUBLIC LIBRARY, 105 Main St, 06424. SAN 302-1238. Tel: 860-267-6621. FAX: 860-267-4427. Web Site: easthamptonpubliclibrary.org. *Libr Dir,* Ellen Paul; E-mail: epaul@easthamptonct.gov; *Ch,* April Hannon; E-mail: ahannon@easthamptonnet.gov; Staff 13 (MLS 2, Non-MLS 11)
Founded 1898. Pop 12,300; Circ 118,958
Library Holdings: AV Mats 7,843; Bk Vols 53,439; Per Subs 85
Subject Interests: Local hist
Automation Activity & Vendor Info: (Cataloging) Auto-Graphics, Inc; (Circulation) Auto-Graphics, Inc; (ILL) Auto-Graphics, Inc; (OPAC) Auto-Graphics, Inc
Wireless access
Function: Bk club(s), Bks on cassette, Bks on CD, Children's prog, Computers for patron use, Digital talking bks, E-Reserves, Electronic databases & coll, Holiday prog, Home delivery & serv to seniorr ctr & nursing homes, ILL available, Museum passes, Music CDs, Photocopying/Printing, Preschool outreach, Prog for adults, Prog for children & young adult, Wheelchair accessible
Open Mon-Wed 10-8, Thurs-Sat 10-5
Friends of the Library Group

EAST HARTFORD

S CONNECTICUT SOCIETY OF GENEALOGISTS, INC LIBRARY, 175 Maple St, 06118-2364. (Mail add: PO Box 435, Glastonbury, 06033-0435), SAN 372-6525. Tel: 860-569-0002. FAX: 860-569-0339. E-mail: csginc@csginc.org. Web Site: www.csginc.org. *Libr Office Mgr,* Stephanie Hyland; Staff 1 (Non-MLS 1)
Founded 1968
Library Holdings: Bk Titles 5,000
Wireless access
Open Tues-Fri 11-4

P EAST HARTFORD PUBLIC LIBRARY*, Raymond Memorial Library, 840 Main St, 06108. SAN 336-0636. Tel: 860-289-4329. FAX: 860-291-9166. Web Site: www.easthartfordct.gov/library. *Dir,* Sarah Kline Morgan; Tel: 860-290-4340; *Asst Dir,* Katherine Beaudry; Tel: 860-290-4339
Founded 1879. Pop 59,000; Circ 250,000
Library Holdings: Bk Vols 290,000; Per Subs 400
Special Collections: Aviation Coll; Tobacco Coll
Automation Activity & Vendor Info: (Cataloging) Innovative Interfaces, Inc; (Circulation) Innovative Interfaces, Inc; (OPAC) Innovative Interfaces, Inc
Wireless access
Open Mon-Thurs 9-8, Fri & Sat 9-5
Friends of the Library Group

§C GOODWIN UNIVERSITY, Hoffman Family Library, One Riverside Dr, 06118. Tel: 860-528-4111, 860-913-2042. Web Site: goodwin.edu/library. *Dir of Libr,* Scott Hughes; Tel: 860-727-6782, E-mail: shughes@goodwin.edu; *Asst Dir,* Cynthia Hunt; Tel: 860-913-2066, E-mail: chunt@goodwin.edu
Library Holdings: Bk Vols 9,000; Per Subs 50
Wireless access
Function: ILL available, Photocopying/Printing, Study rm
Partic in Council of Connecticut Academic Library Directors
Open Mon-Thurs 9-6, Fri 8-3, Sat 8-4

EAST HAVEN

P HAGAMAN MEMORIAL LIBRARY*, 227 Main St, 06512. SAN 302-1262. Tel: 203-468-3890. FAX: 203-468-3892. Web Site: www.hagamanlibrary.org. *Libr Dir,* Bruce George; Tel: 203-468-3893, E-mail: bgeorge@hagamanlibrary.org; *Head, Tech Serv, Librn,* Wahid Nabiz; *Circ Librn,* Chrisropher Hemingway; E-mail: chemingway@hagamanlibrary.org; *Ch,* Sascha Gardiner; E-mail: sgardiner@hagamanlibrary.org; *Commun Serv Librn,* Cynthia Gwiazda; E-mail: cgwiazda@hagamanlibrary.org; *Ref Librn,* Fawn Gillespie; E-mail: fgillespie@hagamanlibrary.org; *Teen Serv Librn,* Emily Kalota; Staff 18 (MLS 7, Non-MLS 11)
Founded 1909. Pop 27,969; Circ 112,000
Jul 2014-Jun 2015 Income $828,868, State $4,380, City $739,124, Locally Generated Income $27,648, Other $57,716. Mats Exp $56,825, Books $44,000, Per/Ser (Incl. Access Fees) $3,000, AV Mat $7,500, Electronic Ref Mat (Incl. Access Fees) $2,325. Sal $632,820
Library Holdings: AV Mats 5,377; CDs 855; DVDs 1,216; Large Print Bks 3,096; Bk Vols 66,642; Per Subs 133; Talking Bks 2,040; Videos 3,213
Special Collections: Local History
Automation Activity & Vendor Info: (Cataloging) Evergreen; (Circulation) Evergreen; (OPAC) Evergreen
Wireless access
Function: Homebound delivery serv, ILL available, Magnifiers for reading
Partic in Bibliomation Inc; Connecticut Library Consortium
Special Services for the Blind - Closed circuit TV magnifier
Open Mon, Fri & Sat 10-5, Tues-Thurs 10-8
Friends of the Library Group

S THE SHORE LINE TROLLEY MUSEUM LIBRARY*, 17 River St, 06512. SAN 302-1254. Tel: 203-467-6927. FAX: 203-467-7635. E-mail: info@shorelinetrolley.org. Web Site: shorelinetrolley.org, www.bera.org. *Exec Dir,* John Proto; E-mail: director@shorelinetrolley.org
Library Holdings: Bk Vols 4,000
Special Collections: Technical & Social History of the Street Railway & Electric Railway Industry, equip, blueprints, doc, trade journals & photos
Open Wed & Sat 11-3

EAST WINDSOR

S CONNECTICUT ELECTRIC RAILWAY ASSOCIATION, INC*, Connecticut Trolley Museum Library, 58 North Rd, 06088. (Mail add: PO Box 360, 06088-0360), SAN 326-3983. Tel: 860-627-6540. FAX: 860-627-6510. E-mail: office@ct-trolley.org. Web Site: www.ct-trolley.org. *Pres,* Robert Brogle
Founded 1940
Library Holdings: Bk Vols 3,000; Spec Interest Per Sub 1,200
Special Collections: Historic Connecticut Trolley Companies; Historic Material Including Pictures, Book/Literature
Restriction: Open by appt only

P LIBRARY ASSOCIATION OF WAREHOUSE POINT*, 107 Main St, 06088. SAN 302-4091. Tel: 860-623-5482. Web Site: www.warehousepointlibrary.info. *Libr Dir,* Lois Hiller; E-mail: lhiller@libraryconnection.info; Staff 10 (MLS 1, Non-MLS 9)
Founded 1811. Pop 11,300; Circ 39,000
Library Holdings: Audiobooks 1,133; DVDs 2,602; Bk Titles 36,000; Per Subs 85
Automation Activity & Vendor Info: (Cataloging) Innovative Interfaces, Inc - Sierra; (Circulation) Innovative Interfaces, Inc - Sierra; (ILL) Innovative Interfaces, Inc - Sierra; (OPAC) Innovative Interfaces, Inc - Sierra
Wireless access
Function: 24/7 Electronic res, 24/7 Online cat, Activity rm, Adult bk club
Partic in Connecticut Library Consortium
Open Mon-Wed 10-8, Thurs-Sat 10-5
Friends of the Library Group

EAST WOODSTOCK

P EAST WOODSTOCK LIBRARY ASSOCIATION*, May Memorial Library, 15 Prospect St, 06244. (Mail add: PO Box 14, 06244-0014), SAN 323-7249. Tel: 860-928-0284. E-mail: maymemoriallibrary@sbcglobal.net. Web Site: www.townofwoodstock.com/services-40/libraries. *Librn,* Mary M Weaver; Staff 1 (Non-MLS 1)
Founded 1930. Pop 6,000; Circ 8,000
Library Holdings: Audiobooks 100; DVDs 100; Bk Titles 8,216
Wireless access
Partic in Connecticut Library Consortium
Open Wed & Fri 1-5, Sat 10-12

EASTFORD

P EASTFORD PUBLIC LIBRARY, Ivy Glenn Memorial Bldg, 179 Eastford Rd, 06242. (Mail add: PO Box 908, 06242), SAN 302-1270. Tel: 860-974-0125. E-mail: eastfordpublib@gmail.com. Web Site: www.eastfordct.org/domain/1133. *Librn,* Elizabeth Platt; Staff 1 (Non-MLS 1)
Founded 1896
Library Holdings: Bk Titles 14,000
Wireless access
Function: 24/7 Online cat, Adult bk club
Partic in Connecticut Library Consortium
Open Tues & Thurs 11-6:30, Wed 10-5, Sat 9-12

EASTON

P EASTON PUBLIC LIBRARY, 691 Morehouse Rd, 06612. (Mail add: PO Box 2, 06612-0002), SAN 302-1289. Tel: 203-261-0134. FAX: 203-261-0708. Web Site: www.eastonlibrary.org. *Libr Dir,* Lynn Zaffino; E-mail: lzaffino@eastonlibrary.org; Staff 8 (MLS 3, Non-MLS 5)
Founded 1934. Pop 7,500
Automation Activity & Vendor Info: (Acquisitions) Baker & Taylor; (Cataloging) Evergreen; (Circulation) Evergreen; (OPAC) Evergreen
Wireless access
Function: 24/7 Electronic res, 24/7 Online cat, Activity rm, Adult bk club, Archival coll, Art exhibits, Audiobks on Playaways & MP3, Audiobks via web, Bk club(s), Bks on CD, Butterfly Garden, Children's prog, Computer training, Computers for patron use, Digital talking bks, Electronic databases & coll, Free DVD rentals, Holiday prog, Homebound delivery serv, ILL available, Instruction & testing, Internet access, Magazines, Mail & tel request accepted, Makerspace, Meeting rooms, Movies, Museum passes, Music CDs, Online cat, Online info literacy tutorials on the web & in blackboard, Online ref, Outreach serv, OverDrive digital audio bks, Photocopying/Printing, Preschool outreach, Preschool reading prog, Prog for adults, Prog for children & young adult, Ref & res, Ref serv available, Res assist avail, Scanner, Spoken cassettes & CDs, STEM programs, Story hour, Summer & winter reading prog, Summer reading prog, Tax forms, Teen prog, Telephone ref, Visual arts prog, Wheelchair accessible, Workshops
Partic in Bibliomation Inc; Connecticut Library Consortium
Open Mon-Wed 10-6, Thurs 10-7, Fri 10-5, Sat 10-3
Friends of the Library Group

ELLINGTON

P HALL MEMORIAL LIBRARY*, 93 Main St, 06029. (Mail add: PO Box 280, 06029), SAN 302-1297. Tel: 860-870-3160. FAX: 860-870-3163. E-mail: hallmlib@ellington-ct.gov. Web Site: www.library.ellington-ct.gov. *Libr Dir,* Susan J Phillips; *Asst Dir, Children's Servs,* Patricia W Grundman; Staff 6 (MLS 5, Non-MLS 1)
Founded 1903. Pop 15,856; Circ 119,708
Jul 2016-Jun 2017 Income $802,284, State $1,899, City $756,018, Locally Generated Income $44,367
Library Holdings: Audiobooks 1,695; CDs 4,193; DVDs 4,873; e-books 1,000; e-journals 70; Large Print Bks 2,509; Bk Vols 63,001; Per Subs 66
Special Collections: Ellington History, docs, pamphlets
Automation Activity & Vendor Info: (Acquisitions) Evergreen; (Cataloging) Evergreen; (Circulation) Evergreen; (ILL) Evergreen; (OPAC) Evergreen; (Serials) Evergreen
Wireless access
Function: 24/7 Electronic res, 24/7 Online cat, Activity rm, Adult bk club, Archival coll, Art exhibits, Audio & video playback equip for onsite use, Audiobks on Playaways & MP3, Audiobks via web, AV serv, Bk club(s), Bks on cassette, Bks on CD, Chess club, Children's prog, Computer training, Computers for patron use, Digital talking bks, Distance learning, Doc delivery serv, E-Readers, E-Reserves, Electronic databases & coll, Equip loans & repairs, For res purposes, Free DVD rentals, Holiday prog, Home delivery & serv to seniorr ctr & nursing homes, Homebound delivery serv, ILL available, Internet access, Laminating, Life-long learning prog for all ages, Magazines, Magnifiers for reading, Mail & tel request accepted, Mail loans to mem, Meeting rooms, Microfiche/film & reading machines, Movies, Museum passes, Music CDs, Notary serv, Online cat, Outreach serv, Outside serv via phone, mail, e-mail & web, OverDrive digital audio bks, Passport agency, Photocopying/Printing, Preschool outreach, Preschool reading prog, Printer for laptops & handheld devices, Prog for adults, Prog for children & young adult, Ref & res, Ref serv available, Scanner, Senior outreach, Serves people with intellectual disabilities, Spoken cassettes & CDs, Spoken cassettes & DVDs, Story

hour, Study rm, Summer & winter reading prog, Summer reading prog, Tax forms, Teen prog, Telephone ref, Visual arts prog, Wheelchair accessible, Winter reading prog, Workshops
Partic in Bibliomation Inc; Connecticut Library Consortium
Open Mon-Thurs 10-8, Fri 10-5, Sat 10-5 (10-1 July-Aug), Sun (Oct-May) 1-5
Friends of the Library Group

ENFIELD

J ASNUNTUCK COMMUNITY COLLEGE LIBRARY*, 170 Elm St, 06082-0068. SAN 302-1300. Tel: 860-253-3174. Reference Tel: 860-253-3170. FAX: 860-253-3176. Reference E-mail: as-lrcref@acc.commnet.edu. Web Site: asnuntuck.edu/library. *Dir, Libr Serv,* Matthew Hall; Tel: 860-253-3171, E-mail: mhall@asnuntuck.edu; *Evening Librn,* Susanna Phillips; E-mail: sphillips@asnuntuck.edu; *Info Literacy Librn,* Angelina Hinojosa; E-mail: ahinojosa@asnuntuck.edu; *Syst Librn,* Qiong Zou; Tel: 860-253-3172, E-mail: qzou@asnuntuck.edu; Staff 4 (MLS 4)
Founded 1972. Enrl 1,000; Highest Degree: Associate
Library Holdings: CDs 100; DVDs 800; e-books 1,000; Bk Vols 28,000; Per Subs 100; Videos 700
Special Collections: Copernicus Coll (Polish History & Culture); Literacy Volunteers
Automation Activity & Vendor Info: (Cataloging) OCLC Connexion; (Circulation) Ex Libris Group; (Course Reserve) Ex Libris Group; (ILL) OCLC FirstSearch; (OPAC) Ex Libris Group; (Serials) OCLC Connexion
Wireless access
Partic in Connecticut Library Consortium
Special Services for the Deaf - TTY equip
Special Services for the Blind - Assistive/Adapted tech devices, equip & products; Internet workstation with adaptive software; Reader equip; Scanner for conversion & translation of mats
Open Mon-Thurs 8:30am-9pm, Fri 8:30-4:30, Sat 9-3

P ENFIELD PUBLIC LIBRARY*, Central Library, 104 Middle Rd, 06082. SAN 336-0784. Tel: 860-763-7510. Reference Tel: 860-763-7511. Web Site: www.enfieldpubliclibrary.org. *Dir of Libr,* Jason Neely; E-mail: jneely@enfield.org; *Dep Dir,* Katie Werth; E-mail: kwerth@enfield.org; *Head, Children's & Teen Serv,* Kristin Raiche; *Head, Ref Serv,* Samantha Lee; E-mail: slee@enfield.org; *Br Librn,* Kristen Massetti; *Pub Serv Librn,* Lisa Sprague; *ILL,* Roberta Merrigan; Staff 29 (MLS 5, Non-MLS 24)
Founded 1874
Special Collections: Local History/Shaker History (Enfield Centennial Coll), bks; Musical Instrument Lending Library
Automation Activity & Vendor Info: (Acquisitions) Baker & Taylor; (Cataloging) Innovative Interfaces, Inc - Sierra; (Circulation) Innovative Interfaces, Inc - Sierra; (OPAC) Innovative Interfaces, Inc - Sierra
Wireless access
Function: 24/7 Electronic res, 24/7 Online cat, Adult bk club, After school storytime, Archival coll, Art exhibits, Audio & video playback equip for onsite use, Audiobks via web, AV serv, Bk club(s), Bks on CD, Children's prog, Computer training, Computers for patron use, E-Readers, E-Reserves, Electronic databases & coll, Free DVD rentals, Holiday prog, Homebound delivery serv, ILL available, Internet access, Life-long learning prog for all ages, Magazines, Mango lang, Movies, Museum passes, Music CDs, Notary serv, Online cat, Online info literacy tutorials on the web & in blackboard, Online ref, Outreach serv, OverDrive digital audio bks, Photocopying/Printing, Preschool outreach, Preschool reading prog, Printer for laptops & handheld devices, Prog for adults, Prog for children & young adult, Ref & res, Ref serv available, Scanner, Senior computer classes, Spanish lang bks, Story hour, Summer reading prog, Tax forms, Teen prog, Telephone ref, Visual arts prog
Partic in Connecticut Library Consortium; Library Connection, Inc
Open Mon-Thurs 9-8, Fri & Sat 9-5
Friends of the Library Group
Branches: 1
PEARL STREET, 159 Pearl St, 06082. Tel: 860-253-6433. FAX: 860-253-6433. *Br Librn,* Kristen Massetti; Staff 2 (Non-MLS 2)
Open Mon-Thurs 10-8, Fri 12-6
Friends of the Library Group

S CARL ROBINSON CORRECTIONAL INSTITUTION LIBRARY*, 285 Shaker Rd, 06082. (Mail add: PO Box 1400, 06083-1400), SAN 324-4466. Tel: 860-253-8000. FAX: 860-253-8317.
Founded 1985
Library Holdings: Bk Vols 30,000; Per Subs 58
Restriction: Staff & inmates only

ESSEX

S CONNECTICUT RIVER MUSEUM, Stevens Library, 67 Main St, 06426. Tel: 860-767-8269, Ext 115. Web Site: www.ctrivermuseum.org. *Curator,* Amy Trout; E-mail: atrout@ctrivermuseum.org; Staff 1 (Non-MLS 1)
Library Holdings: Bk Vols 2,000
Special Collections: Manuscript Coll Relating to Connecticut River Maritime Individuals, corresp, personal papers; River Industries Business Records; River Related Vessels, accounts, journals & logs; West Indies Documents, Summary Registers & Enrollments from Middletown Customs District
Subject Interests: Local hist, Maritime hist
Wireless access
Function: Ref serv available
Restriction: Closed stack, Open by appt only

P ESSEX LIBRARY ASSOCIATION, INC*, 33 West Ave, 06426-1196. SAN 302-1327. Tel: 860-767-1560. FAX: 860-767-2500. Web Site: www.essexlib.org. *Exec Dir,* Deborah Smith; E-mail: dsmith@essexlib.org; *Head, Children's & Young Adult Serv,* Jessica Branciforte; E-mail: jbranciforte@essexlib.org; *Head, Adult Serv,* Ann Thompson; E-mail: athompson@essexlib.org; *Ref Librn, Tech Librn,* Anna Cierocki; E-mail: acierocki@essexlib.org; *Adult Serv,* Sue Bradley; E-mail: sbradley@essexlib.org; Staff 7 (MLS 4, Non-MLS 3)
Founded 1889. Pop 6,500; Circ 70,000
Library Holdings: Bk Titles 27,000
Subject Interests: Gardening, Sailing
Automation Activity & Vendor Info: (Cataloging) Innovative Interfaces, Inc; (Circulation) Innovative Interfaces, Inc; (ILL) Innovative Interfaces, Inc; (OPAC) Innovative Interfaces, Inc
Wireless access
Function: Adult bk club, Art exhibits, Audiobks via web, AV serv, Bk club(s), Bks on CD, Children's prog, Computer training, Computers for patron use, E-Reserves, Electronic databases & coll, Equip loans & repairs, Free DVD rentals, Govt ref serv, Home delivery & serv to seniorr ctr & nursing homes, Homebound delivery serv, ILL available, Museum passes, Music CDs, Online cat, Outreach serv, OverDrive digital audio bks, Photocopying/Printing, Prog for adults, Prog for children & young adult, Ref serv available, Senior computer classes, Senior outreach, Story hour, Summer reading prog, Tax forms, Teen prog, Telephone ref, Wheelchair accessible, Writing prog
Publications: Ex Libris (Newsletter)
Partic in Libraries Online, Inc
Open Mon & Wed 10-6, Tues & Thurs 10-7, Fri 10-5, Sat 10-4
Friends of the Library Group

FAIRFIELD

S FAIRFIELD MUSEUM & HISTORY CENTER*, Library & Special Collections, 370 Beach Rd, 06824. SAN 302-1335. Tel: 203-259-1598, Ext 106. FAX: 203-255-2716. E-mail: library@fairfieldhs.org. Web Site: www.fairfieldhistory.org. *Libr Dir,* Dr Elizabeth Rose; Staff 1 (MLS 1)
Founded 1903
Library Holdings: Bk Titles 10,000; Per Subs 18
Special Collections: Manuscript Coll, account bks, architectural rec, bus & family papers, city directories, diaries, ephemera, glass slides, local church & cemetery rec, local organization rec, photog, sch & town rec, scrapbks, shipping logs, VF. Municipal Document Depository; Oral History
Subject Interests: Decorative art, Genealogy, Local hist
Automation Activity & Vendor Info: (Cataloging) SirsiDynix-WorkFlows; (OPAC) SirsiDynix-WorkFlows
Wireless access
Function: Archival coll, Online cat, Photocopying/Printing, Ref serv available, Res libr
Open Tues-Fri 10-4, Sat 12-4
Restriction: Non-circulating

P FAIRFIELD PUBLIC LIBRARY*, 1080 Old Post Rd, 06824. SAN 336-0873. Tel: 203-256-3155. Reference Tel: 203-256-3160. Administration FAX: 203-256-3198. Web Site: www.fairfieldpubliclibrary.org. *Town Librn,* Helene Murtha; Tel: 203 256-3158, E-mail: hmurtha@fplct.org; *Dep Town Librn,* Jan Fisher; Tel: 203-256-3154, E-mail: jfisher@fplct.org; *Ch Serv Librn,* Tamara Lyhne; *IT Librn,* Jim Swift; *Ref Serv Librn,* Philip Bahr; *Tech Serv Librn,* Position Currently Open; *Teen Librn,* Jennifer Laseman; Staff 26 (MLS 14, Non-MLS 12)
Founded 1877. Pop 58,400; Circ 1,004,417
Automation Activity & Vendor Info: (Acquisitions) SirsiDynix; (Cataloging) SirsiDynix; (Circulation) SirsiDynix; (OPAC) SirsiDynix; (Serials) SirsiDynix
Wireless access
Function: 24/7 Electronic res, 24/7 Online cat, Adult bk club, Adult literacy prog, After school storytime, Art exhibits, Art programs, Audiobks on Playaways & MP3, Audiobks via web, Bi-weekly Writer's Group, Bk club(s), Bks on CD, Children's prog, Computer training, Computers for patron use, Digital talking bks, E-Readers, E-Reserves, Electronic databases & coll, Free DVD rentals, Home delivery & serv to seniorr ctr & nursing homes, Homebound delivery serv, Internet access, Large print keyboards, Life-long learning prog for all ages, Magazines, Magnifiers for reading, Mail & tel request accepted, Mango lang, Meeting rooms, Microfiche/film & reading machines, Movies, Museum passes, Music CDs, Online cat, Online ref, Outreach serv, Outside serv via phone, mail, e-mail

& web, OverDrive digital audio bks, Photocopying/Printing, Preschool outreach, Preschool reading prog, Printer for laptops & handheld devices, Prog for adults, Prog for children & young adult, Ref & res, Ref serv available, Scanner, Serves people with intellectual disabilities, Spanish lang bks, STEM programs, Story hour, Study rm, Summer reading prog, Tax forms, Teen prog, Telephone ref, Wheelchair accessible, Workshops, Writing prog
Open Mon-Thurs 9-9, Fri & Sat 9-5, Sun 1-5
Friends of the Library Group
Branches: 1
FAIRFIELD WOODS, 1147 Fairfield Woods Rd, 06825, SAN 336-0903. Tel: 203-255-7310. Reference Tel: 203-255-7308. FAX: 203-255-7311. *Actg Br Mgr,* Mary Coe; E-mail: mcoe@fplct.org
Open Mon-Thurs 9-8, Fri & Sat 9-5, Sun 1-5
Friends of the Library Group

C FAIRFIELD UNIVERSITY*, DiMenna-Nyselius Library, 1073 N Benson Rd, 06430-5195. SAN 302-1343. Tel: 203-254-4044. Circulation Tel: 203-254-4000, Ext 2188. Interlibrary Loan Service Tel: 203-254-4000, Ext 2135. Reference Tel: 203-254-4000, Ext 2178. FAX: 203-254-4135. Reference E-mail: reference@fairfield.edu. Staff 19 (MLS 13, Non-MLS 6)
Founded 1948. Enrl 4,524; Fac 370; Highest Degree: Doctorate
Jul 2015-Jun 2016. Mats Exp $3,214,980, Books $497,457, Per/Ser (Incl. Access Fees) $864,046, AV Mat $13,238, Electronic Ref Mat (Incl. Access Fees) $565,293. Sal $1,324,952 (Prof $942,571)
Library Holdings: AV Mats 22,725; e-books 898,580; e-journals 36,383; Microforms 110,693; Bk Vols 373,404
Subject Interests: Catholic studies, Celtic studies
Automation Activity & Vendor Info: (Acquisitions) Innovative Interfaces, Inc - Millennium; (Cataloging) Innovative Interfaces, Inc - Millennium; (Circulation) Innovative Interfaces, Inc - Millennium; (Course Reserve) Innovative Interfaces, Inc - Millennium; (ILL) Innovative Interfaces, Inc - Millennium; (OPAC) Innovative Interfaces, Inc - Millennium; (Serials) Innovative Interfaces, Inc - Millennium
Wireless access
Function: Art exhibits, Audio & video playback equip for onsite use, Computers for patron use, Doc delivery serv, E-Reserves, Electronic databases & coll, Online cat, Photocopying/Printing
Partic in Association of Jesuit Colleges & Universities; Coun of Conn Acad Libr Dirs; LYRASIS

C SACRED HEART UNIVERSITY, Ryan Matura Library, 5151 Park Ave, 06825-1000. SAN 302-069X. Tel: 203-371-7702. Interlibrary Loan Service Tel: 203-371-7705. Reference Tel: 203-371-7726. Administration Tel: 203-371-7700. Interlibrary Loan Service FAX: 203-396-8090. Web Site: library.sacredheart.edu. *Univ Librn,* P Gavin Ferriby, PhD; Tel: 203-396-8283, E-mail: ferribyp@sacredheart.edu; *Dir, Digital Serv,* Jeff Orrico; Tel: 203-365-4841, E-mail: orricoj@sacredheart.edu; *Dir of Library Data & Budget,* M Renata Cioffi; E-mail: cioffim@sacredheart.edu; *Dir, Health Sci Libr,* Geoffrey Staysniak; Tel: 203-396-6051, E-mail: staysniakg@sacredheart.edu; *Dir, Instrul Serv,* Elizabeth Knapik; Tel: 203-365-4816, E-mail: knapike@sacredheart.edu; *Assessment Librn, Develop,* Susan Lucharss; Tel: 203-371-7701, E-mail: lucharss@sacredheart.edu; *Research Librn,* Erin Thompson; Tel: 203-520-8196, E-mail: thompsone3@sacredheart.edu; *Educ Ref & User Services Librn,* Kimberly Macomber; Tel: 203-371-7746, E-mail: macomberk@sacredheart.edu; *Metadata & Discovery Librn,* Emily Komornik; Tel: 203-371-7749, E-mail: komornike@sacredheart.edu; *Metadata Librn,* Lysobey Beverly; Tel: 203-365-4855, E-mail: lysobeyb@sacredheart.edu; *Head Bldg Serv,* Shari Baron; E-mail: barons@sacredheart.edu; *Instrul Serv Mgr, Tech Serv,* Mark Denny; Tel: 203-396-8278, E-mail: dennym@sacredheart.edu. Subject Specialists: *Computer sci,* Jeff Orrico; *Bus,* Elizabeth Knapik; *Literacy,* Erin Thompson; *Hist,* Emily Komornik; *Scholarly literature,* Lysobey Beverly; *Data serv,* Shari Baron; Staff 14 (MLS 11, Non-MLS 3)
Founded 1967. Highest Degree: Doctorate
Jul 2019-Jun 2020. Mats Exp $702,054, Books $25,813, Per/Ser (Incl. Access Fees) $238,517, Other Print Mats $15,690, AV Mat $21,684, Electronic Ref Mat (Incl. Access Fees) $395,197, Presv $5,153
Library Holdings: DVDs 1,087; e-books 228,647; e-journals 62,094; Microforms 7,222; Bk Titles 89,846
Automation Activity & Vendor Info: (Acquisitions) ByWater Solutions; (Cataloging) ByWater Solutions; (Circulation) ByWater Solutions; (Course Reserve) EBSCO Discovery Service; (Discovery) EBSCO Discovery Service; (ILL) OCLC Tipasa; (OPAC) ByWater Solutions; (Serials) ByWater Solutions
Wireless access
Partic in OCLC Online Computer Library Center, Inc
Open Mon-Thurs 8:15am-3am, Fri 8:15am-9pm, Sat 10-9, Sun 10am-3am

FALLS VILLAGE

P DAVID M HUNT LIBRARY*, 63 Main St, 06031. (Mail add: PO Box 217, 06031-0217), SAN 324-5152. Tel: 860-824-7424. E-mail: dmhuntlibrary@gmail.com. Web Site: www.huntlibrary.org. *Dir,* Erica Joncyk; *Asst Dir,* Megan Sher; *Ch,* Rita Delgado; *Asst Librn,* Akke Jasmine deVlas
Founded 1891. Pop 1,080; Circ 24,067
Library Holdings: Audiobooks 297; CDs 154; DVDs 544; Large Print Bks 140; Bk Titles 23,333; Per Subs 48; Videos 175
Subject Interests: Local hist
Automation Activity & Vendor Info: (Circulation) Bibliomation Inc; (Course Reserve) Bibliomation Inc; (ILL) Best-Seller, Inc; (OPAC) Bibliomation Inc
Wireless access
Partic in Bibliomation Inc
Open Tues & Thurs 10-5, Fri 3-7, Sat 10-1
Friends of the Library Group

FARMINGTON

P THE FARMINGTON LIBRARY*, Six Monteith Dr, 06032. SAN 336-0938. Tel: 860-673-6791, Option 1. FAX: 860-675-7148. E-mail: flref@farmingtonlibraries.org. Web Site: farmingtonlibraries.org. *Libr Dir,* Jay Johnston; Tel: 860-673-6791, Ext 123, E-mail: johnston@farmingtonlibraries.org
Founded 1901. Pop 25,361; Circ 433,259
Library Holdings: Bk Vols 190,000; Per Subs 375
Special Collections: Oral History
Automation Activity & Vendor Info: (Circulation) SirsiDynix; (OPAC) SirsiDynix
Wireless access
Partic in Connecticut Library Consortium
Open Mon-Thurs 9-9, Fri & Sat 9-5, Sun (Jan-March) 1-4
Friends of the Library Group
Branches: 1
BARNEY BRANCH, 71 Main St, 06032, SAN 336-0962. Tel: 860-673-6791, Option 2. *Br Asst,* Susan Porter; E-mail: sporter@farmingtonlibraries.org; Staff 1 (MLS 1)
Library Holdings: Bk Vols 30,000
Open Mon-Thurs 9-5, Sat 9-5 (9-1 Summer)
Friends of the Library Group

S HARTFORD MEDICAL SOCIETY*, Historical Library, UConn Health, 263 Farmington Ave, 06030-4003. (Mail add: PO Box 4003, 06030-4003), SAN 302-1823. Tel: 860-679-3200. FAX: 860-679-1068. Web Site: lib.uconn.edu/health/research-assistance/hartford-medical-society-library/. *Librn,* Jennifer Miglus; E-mail: miglus@uchc.edu
Founded 1846
Library Holdings: Bk Titles 4,500; Bk Vols 5,000; Spec Interest Per Sub 200
Special Collections: Gershom Bulkeley manuscripts; Records of the CT Society of Social Hygiene; Records of the Hartford Medical Society; Steiner Pamphlet Coll
Subject Interests: Hist of med, Med hist
Wireless access
Restriction: Open by appt only

J TUNXIS COMMUNITY COLLEGE LIBRARY*, 271 Scott Swamp Rd, 06032. SAN 302-1416. Tel: 860-773-1550. Interlibrary Loan Service Tel: 860-773-1561. Reference Tel: 860-773-1556. Administration Tel: 860-773-1543. FAX: 860-606-9760. Web Site: www.tunxis.edu/library. *Dir, Libr Serv,* Dr Lisa Lavoie; Tel: 860-773-1543, E-mail: LLavoie@tunxis.edu; Staff 9 (MLS 6, Non-MLS 3)
Founded 1970. Enrl 4,740; Fac 305; Highest Degree: Associate
Automation Activity & Vendor Info: (Acquisitions) Ex Libris Group; (Cataloging) Ex Libris Group; (Circulation) Ex Libris Group; (Course Reserve) Ex Libris Group; (ILL) OCLC FirstSearch; (OPAC) Ex Libris Group; (Serials) Ex Libris Group
Wireless access
Function: Audio & video playback equip for onsite use, Bks on CD, Computers for patron use, Electronic databases & coll, ILL available, Internet access, Museum passes, Music CDs, Online cat, Online ref, Photocopying/Printing, Ref serv available, Tax forms, Wheelchair accessible
Partic in Connecticut Library Consortium; OCLC Online Computer Library Center, Inc
Open Mon-Thurs 8-8, Fri 8-3, Sat 9-2

CM UCONN HEALTH*, Lyman Maynard Stowe Library, 263 Farmington Ave, 06034-4003. SAN 302-1424. Tel: 860-679-3808. Interlibrary Loan Service Tel: 860-679-2940. Reference Tel: 860-679-2942. Administration Tel: 860-679-2840. Interlibrary Loan Service FAX: 860-679-4046. Reference FAX: 860-679-1068. E-mail: library@uchc.edu. Interlibrary Loan Service E-mail: ill@uchc.edu. Web Site: lib.uconn.edu/health. *Libr Dir,* Susan Fowler; Tel: 860-679-3323, E-mail: sfowler@uchc.edu; *Head, Libr Syst & Tech,* Sheryl Bai; Tel: 860-679-8371, E-mail: bai@uchc.edu; *Head, Res & Instrul Serv,* Hongjie Wang; Tel: 860-679-4053, E-mail: wang@uchc.edu; *Res & Instrul Serv Librn,* Teri Shiel; Tel: 860-679-4108, E-mail:

shiel@uchc.edu; *Mgr, Bus Serv,* Mary Petruzzi; E-mail: petruzzi@uchc.edu; Staff 19 (MLS 11, Non-MLS 8)
Founded 1965. Enrl 116; Fac 489; Highest Degree: Doctorate
Special Collections: Hartford Medical Society Library Coll; History of Medicine Coll
Subject Interests: Dentistry, Med, Nursing
Automation Activity & Vendor Info: (Acquisitions) Ex Libris Group; (Cataloging) Ex Libris Group; (Circulation) Ex Libris Group; (Course Reserve) Ex Libris Group; (Discovery) Ex Libris Group; (ILL) OCLC ILLiad; (OPAC) Ex Libris Group; (Serials) Ex Libris Group
Wireless access
Open Mon-Thurs 7am-11pm, Fri 7-7, Sat 9-5, Sun Noon-10

S THE STANLEY WHITMAN HOUSE LIBRARY, 37 High St, 06032. Tel: 860-677-9222. Web Site: www.stanleywhitman.org. *Exec Dir,* Andres Verzosa; Tel: 860-677-9222, Ext 305, E-mail: averzosa@stanleywhitman.org
Library Holdings: Bk Vols 1,500
Special Collections: 18th Century Farmington Coll, archival docs; Photographs & Slides, Early 1900s; Solomon Whitman, Esq Private Subscription Coll
Subject Interests: Bibles, Genealogy, Philos
Function: Ref serv available
Publications: Newsletter
Restriction: Open by appt only

FRANKLIN

§P JANET CARLSON CALVERT LIBRARY, One Tyler Dr, 06254. Tel: 860-642-6207. E-mail: janetcarlsoncalvertlibrary@yahoo.com. Web Site: www.calvertlibrary.org. *Libr Dir,* Christine Schulz
Automation Activity & Vendor Info: (Cataloging) Bibliomation Inc; (OPAC) Bibliomation Inc
Wireless access
Function: Adult bk club, Children's prog, Photocopying/Printing, Story hour
Partic in Bibliomation Inc
Open Tues & Wed 9-5, Thurs 9-7, Sat 9-1
Friends of the Library Group

GALES FERRY

SR ST DAVID'S EPISCOPAL CHURCH LIBRARY, 284 Stoddard's Wharf Rd, 06335. SAN 372-5162. Tel: 860-464-6516. FAX: 860-464-6446. E-mail: churchoffice@saintdavidsgf.org. Web Site: saintdavidsgf.org.
Founded 1968
Library Holdings: Bk Titles 2,700
Open Mon-Fri 10-2

GLASTONBURY

P EAST GLASTONBURY PUBLIC LIBRARY*, 1389 Neipsic Rd, 06033. SAN 324-279X. Tel: 860-633-5637.
Founded 1960. Pop 32,000; Circ 12,088
Library Holdings: Bk Vols 14,000; Per Subs 40
Wireless access
Open Mon 1-4 & 7-8:30, Tues 1-4, Thurs 9-4 & 7-8:30
Friends of the Library Group

P WELLES-TURNER MEMORIAL LIBRARY, 2407 Main St, 06033. SAN 302-1440. Tel: 860-652-7719. Reference Tel: 860-652-7720. Administration Tel: 860-652-7717. FAX: 860-652-7721. Web Site: www.wtmlib.com. *Dir,* Barbara J Bailey; E-mail: barbara.bailey@glastonbury-ct.gov; *Ad,* Meghan Withers-Tong; Tel: 860-652-7730, E-mail: meghan.withers-tong@glastonbury-ct.gov; *Ch Serv Librn,* Renee Pease; Tel: 860-652-7718, E-mail: renee.pease@glastonbury-ct.gov; Staff 23 (MLS 9, Non-MLS 14)
Founded 1865. Pop 32,575; Circ 552,403
Library Holdings: Bk Vols 136,525; Per Subs 312
Subject Interests: Gardening, Local hist, Parenting
Automation Activity & Vendor Info: (Cataloging) SirsiDynix; (Circulation) SirsiDynix; (OPAC) SirsiDynix; (Serials) SirsiDynix
Wireless access
Function: Homebound delivery serv, ILL available, Internet access, Prog for adults, Prog for children & young adult, Ref serv available, Spoken cassettes & CDs, Spoken cassettes & DVDs, Summer reading prog, Telephone ref, VHS videos, Wheelchair accessible
Partic in Cap Region Libr Coun
Special Services for the Deaf - Bks on deafness & sign lang; Closed caption videos
Special Services for the Blind - Videos on blindness & physical disabilties
Open Mon, Tues & Thurs 9-9, Wed 12-9, Fri 9-6, Sat 9-5, Sun (Sept-May) 1-5
Friends of the Library Group

GOSHEN

S GOSHEN HISTORICAL SOCIETY LIBRARY*, 21 Old Middle Rd, 06756-2001. (Mail add: PO Box 457, 06756-0457), SAN 302-1459. Tel: 860-491-9610. Administration Tel: 860-491-3129. Web Site: www.goshenhistoricalct.org. *Curator, Pres,* Henrietta C Horvay; *Asst Curator,* Walter M Horvay
Founded 1955
Library Holdings: Bk Vols 1,000
Special Collections: Furniture; Glass; Natural Science; Pewter; Tools; Toys. Oral History
Subject Interests: Local hist
Open Tues (April-Oct) 10-Noon or by appointment
Friends of the Library Group

P GOSHEN PUBLIC LIBRARY*, 42 North St, 06756. SAN 376-2726. Tel: 860-491-3234. FAX: 860-491-0100. E-mail: frontdesk@goshenpublib.org. Web Site: www.goshenpublib.org. *Libr Dir,* Lynn Barker Steinmayer; E-mail: director@goshenpublib.org; Staff 1 (MLS 1)
Founded 1901. Pop 3,000
Library Holdings: Bk Titles 25,921; Per Subs 29
Automation Activity & Vendor Info: (Acquisitions) Auto-Graphics, Inc; (Cataloging) Auto-Graphics, Inc; (Circulation) Auto-Graphics, Inc; (OPAC) Auto-Graphics, Inc; (Serials) Auto-Graphics, Inc
Wireless access
Open Mon & Wed-Fri 10-6, Tues 10-8, Sat (July-Aug) 9-Noon
Friends of the Library Group

GRANBY

P GRANBY PUBLIC LIBRARY*, 15 N Granby Rd, 06035. SAN 302-1467. Tel: 860-844-5275. FAX: 860-653-0241. Web Site: www.granby-ct.gov/granby-public-library-system. *Libr Dir,* Amy McCue; E-mail: amccue@granby-ct.gov; *Ch,* Joan Beatson; Tel: 860-844-5284, E-mail: jbeatson@granby-ct.gov; Staff 2 (MLS 2)
Founded 1869
Library Holdings: Bk Vols 53,353; Per Subs 106
Wireless access
Function: 24/7 Electronic res, Adult bk club, Art exhibits, Audiobks via web, Bk club(s), Bks on CD, Chess club, Children's prog, Computers for patron use, Electronic databases & coll, ILL available, Internet access, Life-long learning prog for all ages, Magazines, Meeting rooms, Movies, Museum passes, Music CDs, Online cat, OverDrive digital audio bks, Photocopying/Printing, Preschool reading prog, Printer for laptops & handheld devices, Prog for adults, Prog for children & young adult, Ref serv available, Scanner, Story hour, Summer reading prog, Tax forms, Teen prog, Telephone ref, Writing prog
Partic in Connecticut Library Consortium; Library Connection, Inc
Friends of the Library Group
Branches: 1
F H COSSITT LIBRARY, 388 N Granby Rd, North Granby, 06060. (Mail add: 15 N Granby Rd, 06035), SAN 374-3594. Tel: 860-653-8958. FAX: 860-653-8958. E-mail: cossittlib@granby-ct.gov. *Adult Programming, Br Mgr,* Holly Johnson; E-mail: hjohnson@granby-ct.gov
Founded 1890
Friends of the Library Group

S SALMON BROOK HISTORICAL SOCIETY*, Genealogy & Research Library, 208 Salmon Brook St, 06035-2402. (Mail add: PO Box 840, 06035-0840), SAN 302-1475. Tel: 860-653-9713. Web Site: www.salmonbrookhistorical.org. *Librn,* Carol Laun. Subject Specialists: *Archives, Genealogy, Local hist,* Carol Laun
Founded 1975
Library Holdings: Bk Titles 1,000
Special Collections: American History (State 19th Century Newspapers); Connecticut History, doc; Granby Town Records (1786-1853); Home Guard, doc; Local Document Colls, account bks, bus papers, deeds, letters
Subject Interests: Genealogy
Publications: Collections 1979, 1980, 1987, 1989, 1995, 1999
Open Tues & Thurs 9-12 or by appointment
Restriction: In-house use for visitors, Internal use only, Non-circulating, Not a lending libr, Open to pub with supv only, Pub use on premises

GREENWICH

M GREENWICH HOSPITAL*, Sackler Medical Library, Five Perryridge Rd, 06830. SAN 302-1521. Tel: 203-863-3285. Interlibrary Loan Service Tel: 203-863-3284. FAX: 203-863-4522. Web Site: www.greenwichhospital.org/medical-professionals/medical-resources/medical-library.aspx. *Managing Librn,* Donna Belcinski; Tel: 203-863-3293, E-mail: donna.belcinski@greenwichhospital.org; *Consumer Health Librn,* Carolyn English; Staff 3 (MLS 3)
Founded 1965
Library Holdings: e-books 2,500; e-journals 4,000; Bk Vols 2,000; Per Subs 25
Subject Interests: Nursing

Wireless access
Function: Ref serv available
Partic in Basic Health Sciences Library Network; Conn Asn of Health Scis Librs; North Atlantic Health Sciences Libraries, Inc
Open Mon-Fri 9-4:30
Restriction: Non-circulating to the pub, Staff use only

P GREENWICH LIBRARY*, 101 W Putnam Ave, 06830-5387. SAN 336-1144. Tel: 203-622-7956. Circulation Tel: 203-625-6524. Administration FAX: 203-625-6555. E-mail: info@greenwichlibrary.org. Web Site: www.greenwichlibrary.org. *Dir,* Barbara Ormerod-Glynn; E-mail: bglynn@greenwichlibrary.org; *Dep Dir,* Joseph Williams; E-mail: jwilliams@greenwichlibrary.org; Staff 66 (MLS 27, Non-MLS 39)
Founded 1878. Pop 61,871; Circ 1,484,619
Library Holdings: AV Mats 6,922; CDs 41,070; DVDs 14,287; e-books 8,228; Electronic Media & Resources 94; Bk Vols 361,227; Per Subs 739; Videos 14,078
Special Collections: Oral History
Subject Interests: Local hist
Automation Activity & Vendor Info: (Acquisitions) Innovative Interfaces, Inc; (Circulation) Innovative Interfaces, Inc; (ILL) OCLC; (OPAC) Innovative Interfaces, Inc; (Serials) Innovative Interfaces, Inc
Wireless access
Function: Adult bk club, Art exhibits, Audio & video playback equip for onsite use, Audiobks via web, Bk club(s), Bks on CD, Bus archives, Children's prog, Computer training, Computers for patron use, E-Reserves, Electronic databases & coll, Free DVD rentals, Home delivery & serv to seniorr ctr & nursing homes, ILL available, Instruction & testing, Jazz prog, Learning ctr, Magnifiers for reading, Music CDs, Online cat, OverDrive digital audio bks, Photocopying/Printing, Preschool outreach, Prog for adults, Prog for children & young adult, Ref & res, Ref serv available, Senior computer classes, Senior outreach, Spoken cassettes & CDs, Spoken cassettes & DVDs, Story hour, Summer reading prog, Tax forms, Teen prog, Telephone ref, Wheelchair accessible, Workshops
Partic in LYRASIS
Special Services for the Deaf - ADA equip; Bks on deafness & sign lang; Coll on deaf educ; Sign lang interpreter upon request for prog; Staff with knowledge of sign lang; TTY equip
Special Services for the Blind - Accessible computers; Aids for in-house use; Assistive/Adapted tech devices, equip & products; Audio mat; Bks available with recordings; Bks on cassette; Bks on CD; Braille bks; Children's Braille; Closed circuit TV magnifier; Computer access aids; Computer with voice synthesizer for visually impaired persons; Copier with enlargement capabilities; Disability awareness prog; Home delivery serv; Internet workstation with adaptive software; Large print & cassettes; Large print bks; Lending of low vision aids; Low vision equip; Magnifiers; Networked computers with assistive software; Talking bk serv referral; ZoomText magnification & reading software
Open Mon-Fri 9-9, Sat 9-5, Sun 1-5
Friends of the Library Group
Branches: 2
COS COB BRANCH, Five Sinawoy Rd, Cos Cob, 06807-2701, SAN 336-1209. Tel: 203-622-6883. FAX: 203-661-5315. *Br Mgr,* Laura Matthews; Staff 4 (MLS 1, Non-MLS 3)
Founded 1930
Library Holdings: Bk Vols 41,424
Special Services for the Deaf - TTY equip
Special Services for the Blind - Reader equip
Open Mon 12-8, Tues-Sat 9-5
Friends of the Library Group
BYRAM SHUBERT BRANCH, 21 Mead Ave, 06830-6812, SAN 336-1179. Tel: 203-531-0426. FAX: 203-531-0789. *Br Mgr,* Miguel Garcia-Colon; E-mail: mcolon@greenwichlibrary.org; Staff 4 (MLS 1, Non-MLS 3)
Library Holdings: Bk Vols 26,927
Special Collections: Byram Historical Vertical File. Oral History
Special Services for the Deaf - TTY equip
Special Services for the Blind - Reader equip
Open Mon, Wed, Fri & Sat 9-5, Tues 10-6, Thurs 12-8
Friends of the Library Group

GROTON

P BILL MEMORIAL LIBRARY, 240 Monument St, 06340. SAN 302-1556. Tel: 860-445-0392. FAX: 860-449-8971. E-mail: staff@billmemorial.org. Web Site: www.billmemorial.org. *Dir,* Wendy Connal; E-mail: wconnal@billmemorial.org; *Ch,* Mary-Jane Carle; E-mail: mcarle@billmemorial.org; Staff 5 (MLS 1, Non-MLS 4)
Founded 1890
Library Holdings: Bk Vols 21,000
Subject Interests: Genealogy, Local hist
Automation Activity & Vendor Info: (Cataloging) Auto-Graphics, Inc; (Circulation) Auto-Graphics, Inc; (ILL) Auto-Graphics, Inc; (OPAC) Auto-Graphics, Inc
Wireless access
Function: Homebound delivery serv, ILL available, Prog for adults, Prog for children & young adult, Summer reading prog, Wheelchair accessible
Partic in Connecticut Library Consortium
Open Mon & Thurs 10-9, Tues & Wed 10-5, Sat 10-3
Friends of the Library Group

P GROTON PUBLIC LIBRARY, 52 Newtown Rd, 06340. SAN 302-1572. Tel: 860-441-6750. FAX: 860-448-0363. Reference E-mail: reference@groton-ct.gov. Web Site: www.grotonpl.org. *Dir, Libr Serv,* Jennifer Miele; E-mail: jmiele@groton-ct.gov; *Asst Dir,* Michael Spellmon; E-mail: mspellmon@groton-ct.gov; *Commun Outreach Coordr, Librn II,* Kimmerle Balentine; E-mail: kbalentine@groton-ct.gov; *Digital Serv Coordr, Librn II,* Judy Kelmelis; E-mail: jkelmelis@groton-ct.gov; *Librn II, Programming & Partnerships Coord,* Anne Campbell; E-mail: acampbell@groton-ct.gov; *Librn II, Youth Serv Coordr,* Tracy Torres; E-mail: ttorres@groton-ct.gov; *Cat, Librn I,* Lindsey Mahn; E-mail: lmahn@groton-ct.gov; *Ch Serv, Librn I,* Position Currently Open; *Circ Supvr, Librn I,* Cathleen Clifford; E-mail: cclifford@groton-ct.gov; *Librn I, Pub Relations/Mkt Librn,* Kara Popinchalk; E-mail: kpopinchalk@groton-ct.gov; *Librn I, Teen Serv,* Jessica Franco; E-mail: jfranco@groton-ct.gov; *Municipal Video Spec,* Shawn Greeley; E-mail: sgreeley@groton-ct.gov. Subject Specialists: *Genealogy, Local hist,* Michael Spellmon; *Workforce develop,* Jessica Franco; Staff 18 (MLS 9, Non-MLS 9)
Founded 1959
Special Collections: Local History Room
Subject Interests: Genealogy, Local hist, Regional hist
Automation Activity & Vendor Info: (Acquisitions) Baker & Taylor; (Circulation) SirsiDynix-WorkFlows; (OPAC) SirsiDynix-Enterprise
Wireless access
Function: 24/7 Electronic res, 24/7 Online cat, Activity rm, Adult bk club, Adult literacy prog, Archival coll, Art exhibits, Art programs, Audio & video playback equip for onsite use, Audiobks on Playaways & MP3, Audiobks via web, AV serv, Bk club(s), Bks on CD, Butterfly Garden, Children's prog, Computer training, Computers for patron use, Digital talking bks, Doc delivery serv, E-Readers, E-Reserves, Electronic databases & coll, Equip loans & repairs, Family literacy, For res purposes, Free DVD rentals, Genealogy discussion group, Govt ref serv, Home delivery & serv to seniorr ctr & nursing homes, Homebound delivery serv, ILL available, Instruction & testing, Internet access, Life-long learning prog for all ages, Magazines, Magnifiers for reading, Meeting rooms, Microfiche/film & reading machines, Movies, Museum passes, Music CDs, Online cat, Online ref, Orientations, Outreach serv, OverDrive digital audio bks, Passport agency, Photocopying/Printing, Preschool outreach, Preschool reading prog, Printer for laptops & handheld devices, Prog for adults, Prog for children & young adult, Ref & res, Ref serv available, Res assist avail, Scanner, Senior outreach, Serves people with intellectual disabilities, Spanish lang bks, Spoken cassettes & CDs, Spoken cassettes & DVDs, STEM programs, Story hour, Study rm, Summer & winter reading prog, Summer reading prog, Tax forms, Teen prog, Telephone ref, Wheelchair accessible, Winter reading prog, Workshops, Writing prog
Open Mon-Thurs 9-9, Fri 9-5:30, Sat 9-5, Sun (Sept-May) 1-5
Friends of the Library Group

UNITED STATES NAVY
A BASE LIBRARY*, Naval Submarine Base New London, Bldg 164, 06349. (Mail add: PO Box 15, 06349-5015), SAN 336-1233. Tel: 860-694-2578, 860-694-3723. FAX: 860-694-2578. Web Site: www.navy.mil/nwr. *Dir,* Tammy-Jo Ferdula; E-mail: tammyjo.ferdula@navy.mil; *YA Serv,* Marie Jennings; E-mail: marie.jennings@navy.mil; Staff 2 (MLS 1, Non-MLS 1)
Founded 1942
Library Holdings: CDs 100; DVDs 300; Bk Titles 20,000; Per Subs 60; Talking Bks 100; Videos 700
Special Collections: CNO Suggested Navy Reading List Coll
Automation Activity & Vendor Info: (Cataloging) Follett Software; (Circulation) Follett Software; (OPAC) Follett Software
Partic in OCLC Online Computer Library Center, Inc
Open Mon-Thurs 11-6, Fri & Sat 10:30-5:30
A HISTORIC SHIP NAUTILUS-SUBMARINE FORCE LIBRARY & ARCHIVES*, One Crystal Lake Rd, 06340-2464. (Mail add: Naval Submarine Base NLON, 06349-5571), SAN 336-1292. Tel: 860-694-3558. FAX: 860-694-4150. *Librn,* Wendy S Gulley
Library Holdings: Bk Vols 7,600
Special Collections: Copies of World War II Patrol Reports-US; Histories of General Dynamics-Electric Boat (1915-1964) & Naval Submarine Base, Groton (1868-); John P Holland & Simon Lake Papers; Photograph Coll; Scrapbook Binders on all US Submarines; Submarines & Related Topics; Submarines & their Inventors Prior to 1900
Automation Activity & Vendor Info: (Cataloging) Surpass; (OPAC) Surpass
Function: Archival coll, For res purposes, Res libr
Restriction: Closed stack, Non-circulating, Not a lending libr, Open by appt only

GUILFORD

P GUILFORD FREE LIBRARY*, 67 Park St, 06437. SAN 302-1602. Tel: 203-453-8282. FAX: 203-453-8288. Web Site: www.guilfordfreelibrary.org. *Dir,* Sandra Ruoff; *Asst Dir,* Rob McCoole; E-mail: rmccoole@guilfordfreelibrary.org; *Ch Serv,* Suellen Heinrich; *Ref (Info Servs),* Patty Baldwin; Staff 7 (MLS 7)
Founded 1888. Pop 20,000; Circ 250,000
Library Holdings: Bk Titles 112,000; Bk Vols 117,000; Per Subs 209
Special Collections: Guilford History & Genealogy; Spanish Language Books. Oral History
Subject Interests: Poetry
Automation Activity & Vendor Info: (Acquisitions) Innovative Interfaces, Inc; (Cataloging) Innovative Interfaces, Inc; (Circulation) Innovative Interfaces, Inc; (Course Reserve) Innovative Interfaces, Inc; (ILL) Innovative Interfaces, Inc; (Media Booking) Innovative Interfaces, Inc; (OPAC) Innovative Interfaces, Inc; (Serials) Innovative Interfaces, Inc
Publications: Steiner's History of Guilford & Madison
Partic in Connecticut Library Consortium; Libraries Online, Inc
Open Mon-Thurs 9-8, Fri 9-6, Sat 9-5, Sun (Oct-April) 1-4
Friends of the Library Group

S HENRY WHITFIELD STATE MUSEUM RESEARCH LIBRARY*, 248 Old Whitfield St, 06437. Tel: 203-453-2457. FAX: 203-453-7544. E-mail: whitfieldmuseum@ct.gov. Web Site: portal.ct.gov/ECD-HenryWhitfieldStateMuseum. *Sr Curator,* Michelle Parrish; E-mail: michelle.parrish@ct.gov; *Curator,* Michael McBride; E-mail: michael.mcbride@ct.gov
Founded 1899
Library Holdings: Bk Vols 500
Special Collections: 17th-19th Century History Coll, incl ledgers, town records, Grand Army of the Republic mat & maps
Subject Interests: 17th Century hist, Genealogy, Local hist, State hist
Function: Ref serv available
Restriction: Non-circulating coll, Open by appt only

HADDAM

P BRAINERD MEMORIAL LIBRARY*, 920 Saybrook Rd, 06438. SAN 302-1610. Tel: 860-345-2204. FAX: 860-345-7735. E-mail: library@brainerdlibrary.lioninc.org. Web Site: www.brainerdlibrary.lioninc.org. *Dir,* Tom Piezzo; E-mail: tpiezzo@brainerdlibrary.org; Staff 12 (MLS 5, Non-MLS 7)
Founded 1908. Pop 8,346
Jul 2016-Jun 2017 Income $419,756, State $1,200, City $345,156, Locally Generated Income $73,400. Mats Exp $46,350, Books $26,141, AV Mat $20,209. Sal $233,701
Library Holdings: AV Mats 8,895; Bk Vols 38,421; Per Subs 58
Special Collections: Genealogy & Haddam History Coll
Automation Activity & Vendor Info: (Cataloging) Innovative Interfaces, Inc; (Circulation) Innovative Interfaces, Inc; (ILL) Auto-Graphics, Inc; (OPAC) Innovative Interfaces, Inc
Wireless access
Function: Bks on CD, Children's prog, Computer training, Computers for patron use, Free DVD rentals, Home delivery & serv to seniorr ctr & nursing homes, Homebound delivery serv, ILL available, Museum passes, Music CDs, Online cat, OverDrive digital audio bks, Photocopying/Printing, Preschool outreach, Prog for adults, Prog for children & young adult, Ref serv available, Story hour, Summer reading prog, Tax forms, Wheelchair accessible
Partic in Libraries Online, Inc
Open Mon 1-8, Tues, Wed & Thurs 10-8, Fri 10-6, Sat 10-3
Friends of the Library Group

HAMDEN

R CONGREGATION MISHKAN ISRAEL LIBRARY*, 785 Ridge Rd, 06517. SAN 302-1629. Tel: 203-288-3877. FAX: 203-248-2148. Web Site: cmihamden.org. *Librn,* Carrie Kerzner; E-mail: librarian@cmihamden.org
Founded 1840
Library Holdings: Bk Titles 4,000; Per Subs 6
Special Collections: Archives of Congregation (founded 1840); Rabbi Robert E Goldburg Coll
Subject Interests: Judaica (lit or hist of Jews)
Wireless access

P HAMDEN PUBLIC LIBRARY*, Miller Memorial Central Library, 2901 Dixwell Ave, 06518-3135. SAN 336-1357. Circulation Tel: 203-287-2682. Reference Tel: 203-287-2680. Administration Tel: 203-287-2686. FAX: 203-287-2685. E-mail: info@hamdenlibrary.org. Web Site: www.hamdenlibrary.org. *Dir,* Melissa ' Canham-Clyne; Tel: 203-287-2686, Ext 1, E-mail: mcanhamclyne@hamdenlibrary.org; *Assoc Dir,* Nancy McNicol; Tel: 203-287-2686, Ext 2, E-mail: nmcnicol@hamdenlibrary.org; *Head, Children's Servx,* Marcy Goldman; Tel: 203-230-3770, E-mail: marcy@hamdenlibrary.org; Staff 32 (MLS 13, Non-MLS 19)
Founded 1944. Pop 58,180; Circ 451,874
Jul 2015-Jun 2016 Income (Main & Associated Libraries) $1,783,544, State $7,840, City $1,762,704, Other $13,000. Mats Exp $240,000, Books $175,805, Per/Ser (Incl. Access Fees) $13,500, AV Mat $10,000, Electronic Ref Mat (Incl. Access Fees) $40,695. Sal $143,403
Library Holdings: AV Mats 21,101; Bk Vols 200,000; Per Subs 231
Special Collections: ADA Coll; Business Resource Center; Hamden History Coll; Job Resource Center; Literacy Coll
Automation Activity & Vendor Info: (Acquisitions) Innovative Interfaces, Inc - Sierra; (Cataloging) Innovative Interfaces, Inc - Sierra; (Circulation) Innovative Interfaces, Inc - Sierra; (OPAC) Innovative Interfaces, Inc - Sierra
Wireless access
Function: Adult bk club, Art exhibits, Bks on cassette, Bks on CD, Children's prog, Computers for patron use, E-Reserves, Electronic databases & coll, Free DVD rentals, Games & aids for people with disabilities, Holiday prog, Homebound delivery serv, ILL available, Magnifiers for reading, Mail & tel request accepted, Museum passes, Music CDs, Online cat, Online ref, Outreach serv, Outside serv via phone, mail, e-mail & web, Photocopying/Printing, Prog for adults, Prog for children & young adult, Spoken cassettes & CDs, Story hour, Summer reading prog, Tax forms, Telephone ref, VHS videos, Wheelchair accessible
Partic in Libraries Online, Inc
Open Mon-Wed 10-9, Thurs-Sat 10-5:30; Sun (Nov-May) 1-5
Friends of the Library Group
Branches: 2
BRUNDAGE COMMUNITY, 91 Circular Ave, 06514, SAN 336-1381. Tel: 203-287-2675. FAX: 203-287-2675. *Br Mgr,* Sandra Bartell; E-mail: sbartell@hamdenlibrary.org; Staff 2 (MLS 1, Non-MLS 1)
Special Collections: Spanish Language Coll
Open Mon, Tues, Thurs & Fri 10-12 & 1-5:30; Sat(Sept-June) 10-1
Friends of the Library Group
WHITNEYVILLE, 125 Carleton St, 06517, SAN 336-1446. Tel: 203-287-2677. FAX: 203-287-2677. *Br Mgr,* Maureen McKeon Armstrong; E-mail: marmstrong@hamdenlibrary.org; Staff 2 (MLS 1, Non-MLS 1)
Open Mon, Tues, Thurs & Fri 10-12:30 & 1-6; Sat 10-1 (Sept-June)
Friends of the Library Group

C PAIER COLLEGE OF ART, INC LIBRARY*, 20 Gorham Ave, 06514-3902. SAN 324-2803. Tel: 203-287-3023. FAX: 203-287-3021. E-mail: paierartlibrary@snet.net. Web Site: www.paierart.com. *Librn, Tech Serv,* Beth R Harris; Staff 1 (MLS 1)
Enrl 170; Fac 30; Highest Degree: Bachelor
Library Holdings: Bk Vols 13,000
Special Collections: Picture Reference File
Subject Interests: Fine arts, Lit, Photog, Tech arts
Automation Activity & Vendor Info: (OPAC) Follett Software
Wireless access
Publications: ARLIS (Newsletter)

C QUINNIPIAC UNIVERSITY, Arnold Bernhard Library, 275 Mount Carmel Ave, 06518. SAN 302-1645. Tel: 203-582-8634. FAX: 203-582-3451. E-mail: bernhardlibrary@quinnipiac.edu. Web Site: qu.edu/student-life/campuses-and-facilities/quinnipiac-libraries. *Univ Librn,* Robert Joven; E-mail: robert.joven@quinnipiac.edu; *Cat,* Susan O'Brien; E-mail: susan.pfister@quinnipiac.edu; *Coll Mgt,* Position Currently Open; Staff 24 (MLS 14, Non-MLS 10)
Founded 1929. Enrl 5,000; Fac 5; Highest Degree: Doctorate
Library Holdings: e-books 620,000; e-journals 117,000; Bk Titles 140,000; Bk Vols 167,000; Per Subs 900
Special Collections: Albert Schweitzer Related; Great Hunger (Irish Famine)
Subject Interests: Holocaust
Automation Activity & Vendor Info: (Acquisitions) Innovative Interfaces, Inc; (Cataloging) Innovative Interfaces, Inc; (Circulation) Innovative Interfaces, Inc; (OPAC) Innovative Interfaces, Inc
Wireless access
Function: ILL available
Partic in Coun of Conn Acad Libr Dirs; LYRASIS
Open Mon-Fri 8am-Midnight, Sat & Sun 9am-Midnight
Restriction: Circ limited

J SACRED HEART ACADEMY*, Mary & James Dimeo Library, c/o Sacred Heart Academy, 265 Benham St, 06514. SAN 302-1637. Tel: 203-288-2309. FAX: 203-230-9680. Web Site: www.sacredhearthamden.org/page/academics/library. *Dir,* Maureen Hayes; E-mail: mhayes@sacredhearthamden.org; *Asst Librn,* Karen Reidy; E-mail: kreidy@sacredhearthamden.org
Founded 1946. Enrl 480; Fac 46; Highest Degree: Doctorate
Library Holdings: Bk Vols 40,000; Per Subs 100
Automation Activity & Vendor Info: (Cataloging) Follett Software; (Circulation) Follett Software; (OPAC) Follett Software

Wireless access
Open Mon-Thurs 7:15-3:30, Fri 7:15-3

R TEMPLE BETH SHOLOM*, Rhoda & Aaron Cohen Library, 1809 Whitney Ave, 06517. SAN 302-1653. Tel: 203-288-7748. FAX: 203-288-0582. E-mail: library@tbshamden.com. Web Site: www.tbshamden.com. *Librn,* Michael Brooks
Founded 1960
Library Holdings: Bk Titles 1,500; Videos 75
Subject Interests: Holocaust

HAMPTON

P FLETCHER MEMORIAL LIBRARY, 257 Main St, 06247. (Mail add: PO Box 6, 06247), SAN 302-1661. Tel: 860-455-1086. E-mail: fletchermemoriallibrary@gmail.com. Web Site: www.fletchermemoriallibrary.org. *Librn,* Deb Andstrom; *Asst Librn,* Sonja Larsen
Pop 1,350; Circ 12,000
Library Holdings: Bk Vols 20,000
Wireless access
Partic in Connecticut Library Consortium
Open Mon 9-12, Tues 6-8, Wed 2-8, Thurs 9-12 & 6-8, Sat 10-5

HARTFORD

J CAPITAL COMMUNITY COLLEGE LIBRARY*, 950 Main St, 06103-1207. SAN 302-1777. Tel: 860-906-5020. FAX: 860-906-5255. Web Site: www.ccc.commnet.edu/library. *Dir,* Eileen Rhodes; E-mail: erhodes@ccc.commnet.edu; Staff 5 (MLS 4, Non-MLS 1)
Founded 1967
Library Holdings: AV Mats 4,500; e-books 130,000; Bk Vols 45,000; Per Subs 158
Automation Activity & Vendor Info: (Acquisitions) Ex Libris Group; (Cataloging) Ex Libris Group; (Circulation) Ex Libris Group; (Course Reserve) Ex Libris Group; (OPAC) Ex Libris Group
Wireless access
Publications: Guide to Research; Library Workbook
Partic in Connecticut Library Consortium; OCLC Online Computer Library Center, Inc
Open Mon-Thurs 9-5, Fri 9-4:30, Sat 10-2

GL CONNECTICUT JUDICIAL BRANCH LAW LIBRARIES*, Administrative Office, 90 Washington St, Third Flr, 06106. Tel: 860-706-5145. FAX: 860-706-5086. E-mail: lawlibrarians@jud.ct.go. Web Site: www.jud.ct.gov/lawlib. *Dep Dir,* Ann Doherty; E-mail: ann.doherty@jud.ct.gov; *Supv Law Librn,* Jeffrey Dowd; E-mail: jeffrey.dowd@jud.ct.gov; *Supv Law Librn,* Claudia Jalowka; E-mail: claudia.beth.jalowka@jud.ct.gov
Partic in NELLCO Law Library Consortium, Inc.
Open Mon-Fri 8-4:30

Branches:

BRIDGEPORT LAW LIBRARY, Bridgeport Courthouse, 1061 Main St, Bridgeport, 06604, SAN 336-1802. Tel: 203-579-7244. FAX: 203-579-7298. *Law Librn II,* Mary Ann Krivicky; E-mail: maryann.krivicky@jud.ct.gov
Library Holdings: Bk Vols 38,000; Per Subs 92
Automation Activity & Vendor Info: (Cataloging) Auto-Graphics, Inc; (Circulation) Auto-Graphics, Inc
Open Mon-Fri 9-5

DANBURY LAW LIBRARY, Danbury Courthouse, 146 White St, Danbury, 06810, SAN 302-1009. Tel: 203-207-8625. FAX: 203-207-8627. *Law Librn II,* George Booth; E-mail: george.booth@jud.ct.gov; Staff 2 (MLS 1, Non-MLS 1)
Library Holdings: Bk Titles 400; Bk Vols 28,000; Per Subs 30
Special Collections: Connecticut Legislative Histories; Historical Information (Connecticut Law)
Subject Interests: Connecticut, Law
Open Mon-Fri 9-5

HARTFORD LAW LIBRARY, Hartford Courthouse, 95 Washington St, 06106, SAN 336-1837. Tel: 860-548-2866. FAX: 860-548-2868. *Law Librn,* Sean Carey; E-mail: sean.carey@jud.ct.gov
Library Holdings: Bk Vols 40,000
Automation Activity & Vendor Info: (Cataloging) Auto-Graphics, Inc; (Circulation) Auto-Graphics, Inc
Open Mon-Thurs 9-5

MIDDLETOWN LAW LIBRARY, Middletown Courthouse, One Court St, Middletown, 06457. Tel: 860-343-6560. FAX: 860-343-6568. *Law Librn II,* Karen Townsend; E-mail: karen.townsend@jud.ct.go
Open Mon-Fri 9-5

NEW BRITAIN LAW LIBRARY, New Britain Courthouse, 20 Franklin Sq, New Britain, 06051. Tel: 860-515-5110. FAX: 860-515-5111. *Law Librn II,* Christopher Roy; E-mail: christopher.roy@jud.ct.gov
Open Mon-Fri 9-5

NEW HAVEN LAW LIBRARY, New Haven Courthouse, 235 Church St, New Haven, 06510, SAN 336-1926. Tel: 203-503-6828. FAX: 203-789-6499. *Law Librn II,* Michele Penn; E-mail: michele.penn@jud.ct.gov; *Law Librn II,* Astoria Ridley; E-mail: astoria.ridley@jud.ct.gov
Library Holdings: Bk Vols 55,000; Per Subs 75
Automation Activity & Vendor Info: (Cataloging) Auto-Graphics, Inc
Open Mon-Fri 9-5

NEW LONDON LAW LIBRARY, New London Courthouse, 70 Huntington St, New London, 06320. Tel: 860-442-7561. FAX: 860-442-9416. *Law Librn II,* Peter Jenkins; E-mail: peter.jenkins@jud.ct.gov
Open Mon-Fri 9-5

PUTNAM LAW LIBRARY, Putnam Courthouse, 155 Church St, Putnam, 06260, SAN 336-1985. Tel: 860-928-3716. FAX: 860-963-7531. *Law Librn,* Nicholas Beams; E-mail: nicholas.beams@jud.ct.gov; Staff 1 (MLS 1)
Library Holdings: Bk Vols 17,500
Open Mon-Fri 9-5

ROCKVILLE LAW LIBRARY, Rockville Courthouse, 69 Brooklyn St, Rockville, 06066, SAN 336-2019. Tel: 860-896-4955. FAX: 860-875-3213. *Law Librn,* Emily Oumano; E-mail: emily.oumano@jud.ct.gov
Library Holdings: Bk Vols 25,000
Automation Activity & Vendor Info: (Cataloging) Auto-Graphics, Inc; (OPAC) Auto-Graphics, Inc
Open Mon-Fri 9-5

STAMFORD LAW LIBRARY, Stamford Courthouse, 123 Hoyt St, Stamford, 06905, SAN 336-2043. Tel: 203-965-5250. FAX: 203-965-5784. *Law Librn II,* Michael Beetham; E-mail: michael.beetham@jud.ct.gov; *Law Librn II,* Pamela Kaufman; Tel: 203-965-5377, E-mail: pamela.kaufman@jud.ct.gov; Staff 2 (MLS 2)
Library Holdings: Microforms 129,806; Bk Vols 38,954; Per Subs 19
Automation Activity & Vendor Info: (Cataloging) Auto-Graphics, Inc; (OPAC) Auto-Graphics, Inc
Open Mon-Fri 9-5

TORRINGTON LAW LIBRARY, Torrington Courthouse, 50 Field St, Torrington, 06790. Tel: 860-626-2696. FAX: 860-626-2156. *Law Librn II,* Taryn Agati; E-mail: taryn.agati@jud.ct.gov
Founded 2017
Library Holdings: Bk Vols 21,710
Automation Activity & Vendor Info: (Cataloging) Auto-Graphics, Inc; (Circulation) Auto-Graphics, Inc
Open Mon-Fri 9-5

WATERBURY LAW LIBRARY, Waterbury Courthouse, 300 Grand St, Waterbury, 06702, SAN 375-7528. Tel: 203-591-3338. FAX: 203-596-4137. *Law Librn II,* Janet Zigadto; E-mail: janet.zigadto@jud.ct.gov; Staff 1 (MLS 1)
Library Holdings: Bk Vols 40,000; Per Subs 35
Automation Activity & Vendor Info: (Cataloging) Auto-Graphics, Inc; (OPAC) Auto-Graphics, Inc
Open Mon-Fri 9-5

S CONNECTICUT LEGISLATIVE LIBRARY*, Legislative Office Bldg, Rm 5400, 300 Capitol Ave, 06106-1591. SAN 372-3844. Tel: 860-240-8888. FAX: 860-240-8881. E-mail: library@cga.ct.gov. Web Site: www.cga.ct.gov/lib. *Co-Librn,* Jennifer Bernier; E-mail: jennifer.bernier@cga.ct.gov; *Co-Librn,* Carrie Rose; E-mail: carrie.rose@cga.ct.gov; Staff 4 (MLS 3, Non-MLS 1)
Library Holdings: Bk Vols 10,000
Wireless access
Open Mon-Fri 8:30-5
Restriction: Non-circulating

P CONNECTICUT STATE LIBRARY, 231 Capitol Ave, 06106. SAN 336-1594. Tel: 860-757-6500. Circulation Tel: 860-757-6530. Interlibrary Loan Service Tel: 860-757-6590. Administration Tel: 860-757-6510. Toll Free Tel: 866-886-4478. FAX: 860-757-6503. Interlibrary Loan Service FAX: 860-757-6559. Web Site: www.ctstatelibrary.org. *State Librn,* Deborah Schander; E-mail: Deborah.Schander@ct.gov; *Dir, Libr Develop,* Dawn La Valle; Tel: 860-757-6665, E-mail: Dawn.lavalle@ct.gov; *Head, Coll Serv,* Carol Trinchitella; Tel: 860-757-6561; *Cat Mgr,* Stephen Slovasky; Tel: 860-757-6546; *Digital Projects Mgr,* Anna Newman; Tel: 860-757-6525; *Ch Serv, YA Serv,* Kymberlee Powe; Tel: 860-704-2207, E-mail: Kymberlee.Powe@ct.gov; *Circ & ILL,* Judy Crooks; Tel: 860-704-2205, E-mail: Judy.Crooks@ct.gov; Staff 124 (MLS 48, Non-MLS 76)
Founded 1854
Jul 2013-Jun 2014 Income (Main & Associated Libraries) $17,603,154, State $13,248,004, Federal $1,931,653, Other $2,423,497. Mats Exp $825,954, Books $18,659, Per/Ser (Incl. Access Fees) $424,760, Manu Arch $1,005, Electronic Ref Mat (Incl. Access Fees) $342,168, Presv $39,362. Sal $6,173,239 (Prof $3,394,103)

Library Holdings: AV Mats 595; Bks on Deafness & Sign Lang 151; DVDs 1,213; e-journals 70,410; Electronic Media & Resources 86; Bk Vols 1,338,809; Per Subs 8,821; Videos 276
Special Collections: Archives & Historical Manuscripts; Cemetery Inscriptions; Census Records; Charter of 1662; Church, Town & Vital Records; Colt Firearms; Connecticut Aerial Photographic Surveys; Connecticut Shelf Clock Coll; Fraternal Orders; Governor's Portraits; Law Coll; Legislative Transcripts; Maps; Medals & Coins; Military Records & War Posters Coll; Newspapers; Old Houses of Connecticut Coll; State & Local History Coll; State Statutes. State Document Depository; US Document Depository
Subject Interests: Genealogy, Govt, Law, Legislation, Pub policy, State hist
Automation Activity & Vendor Info: (Acquisitions) Ex Libris Group; (Cataloging) Ex Libris Group; (Circulation) Ex Libris Group; (ILL) OCLC; (OPAC) Ex Libris Group; (Serials) Ex Libris Group
Wireless access
Function: Archival coll, Computers for patron use, Electronic databases & coll, Govt ref serv, Ref & res
Publications: Checklist of Connecticut State Documents; Connecticut Union List of Serials; The Connector; The CONNservator
Special Services for the Deaf - Bks on deafness & sign lang
Open Tues-Fri 9-5, Sat 9-2
Restriction: Circ limited
Branches: 2
LIBRARY FOR THE BLIND & PHYSICALLY HANDICAPPED
See Separate Entry in Rocky Hill
MIDDLETOWN LIBRARY SERVICE CENTER, 786 S Main St, Middletown, 06457, SAN 336-1683. Tel: 860-704-2200. FAX: 860-704-2228. *LSTA Coordr,* Maria Bernier; Tel: 860-704-2204, E-mail: maria.bernier@ct.gov; Staff 4 (MLS 2, Non-MLS 2)
Founded 1955
Library Holdings: Audiobooks 4,461; CDs 1,169; DVDs 35; Large Print Bks 14,408; Bk Vols 51,879; Per Subs 2
Subject Interests: Librarianship
Automation Activity & Vendor Info: (Circulation) Innovative Interfaces, Inc - Millennium; (OPAC) Innovative Interfaces, Inc - Millennium
Function: Workshops
Restriction: Open only to librarians

M HARTFORD HOSPITAL*, Robinson Health Sciences Library, Education & Resource Ctr, 3rd Flr, 560 Hudson St, 06102. (Mail add: PO Box 5037, 06102-5037), SAN 336-2108. Tel: 860-972-2230. Interlibrary Loan Service Tel: 860-972-5085. FAX: 860-545-2572. E-mail: hh.library@hhchealth.org. Web Site: www.harthosp.org/hsl. *Dir,* Lisa Carter; E-mail: lisa.carter@hhchealth.org; *Librn,* Katarzyna (Kathy) Woznica; Tel: 860-845-5096, E-mail: Katarzyna.Woznica@hhchealth.org; *Clinical Librn, Surgery,* Ellen MacNaughton; Tel: 860-545-2424, E-mail: Ellen.MacNaughton@hhchealth.org. Subject Specialists: *Surgery,* Ellen MacNaughton; Staff 11 (MLS 6, Non-MLS 5)
Founded 1855
Library Holdings: e-books 350; e-journals 2,000; Bk Titles 30,875; Per Subs 343
Special Collections: History of Nursing (Foley Coll), archives, bks
Subject Interests: Allied health, Clinical med, Hospital admin, Nursing
Automation Activity & Vendor Info: (Acquisitions) Ex Libris Group; (Cataloging) Ex Libris Group; (Circulation) EOS International; (OPAC) EOS International; (Serials) EOS International
Wireless access
Function: Computers for patron use, Doc delivery serv, Electronic databases & coll, ILL available, Online cat, Photocopying/Printing
Partic in Capital Area Health Consortium; Conn Asn of Health Scis Librs; Medical Library Association; National Network of Libraries of Medicine Region 7; North Atlantic Health Sciences Libraries, Inc; OCLC Online Computer Library Center, Inc
Restriction: Badge access after hrs, Borrowing requests are handled by ILL, Hospital employees & physicians only, Med & health res only, Med & nursing staff, patients & families, Not open to pub, Open to fac, students & qualified researchers, Open to hospital affiliates only, Private libr, Prof mat only
Branches:
INSTITUTE OF LIVING MEDICAL LIBRARY, Research/Burlingame Bldg, 3rd Flr, 200 Retreat Ave, 06106, SAN 302-1866. Tel: 860-545-7276. FAX: 860-545-7275. *Libr Asst,* Lori Hayes; E-mail: Lori.Hayes@hhchealth.org; Staff 1 (MLS 1)
Library Holdings: e-books 250; e-journals 2,000; Bk Titles 10,000; Per Subs 150
Subject Interests: Psychiat, Psychol
Automation Activity & Vendor Info: (Acquisitions) EOS International; (Cataloging) EOS International; (Circulation) EOS International; (OPAC) EOS International; (Serials) EOS International
Function: Computers for patron use, Doc delivery serv, ILL available, Online cat, Photocopying/Printing
Open Mon-Fri 7:30-4
Restriction: Hospital employees & physicians only, In-house use for visitors, Med & nursing staff, patients & families, Med staff & students, Open to hospital affiliates only, Private libr

P HARTFORD PUBLIC LIBRARY*, 500 Main St, 06103. SAN 336-2280. Tel: 860-695-6300. Circulation Tel: 860-695-6290. Reference Tel: 860-695-6295. Administration Tel: 860-695-6280. FAX: 860-722-6900. TDD: 860-722-6890. Reference E-mail: reference@hplct.org. Web Site: www.hplct.org. *Pres & Chief Exec Officer,* Bridget Quinn-Carey; Tel: 860-695-6285, E-mail: quinncarey@hplct.org; *Chief Admin Officer,* Mary T Tzambazakis; Tel: 860-695-6312, E-mail: mtzambazakis@hplct.org; *Customer Experience Officer,* Leticia Cotto; Tel: 860-695-6335, E-mail: lcotto@hplct.org; Staff 15 (MLS 15)
Founded 1774. Pop 124,775; Circ 305,830
Jul 2020-Jun 2021 Income (Main & Associated Libraries) $10,446,014, State $126,364, City $8,100,000, Federal $306,800, Locally Generated Income $1,430,360, Other $482,490. Mats Exp $450,094, Books $221,675, Per/Ser (Incl. Access Fees) $37,849, AV Mat $127,615, Electronic Ref Mat (Incl. Access Fees) $62,955. Sal $5,130,897
Special Collections: Anthony S. "Tony" DeBonee Image Coll; Boyd Hinds Coll; Butch Lewis Video Coll Documenting the Civil Rights Era, Hartford; Caroline M. Hewins Children's Book Coll; Foundation Center Cooperating Coll; Hartford Business Ephemera Coll; Hartford City Parks Coll; Hartford Coll/Photographs; Hartford Map Coll; Hartford Pamphlet Coll; Hartford Postcard Coll; Hartford Public Library's Institutional Archive; Hartford Town and City Clerk Coll; Hartford Voter Registration Records Coll; Helen Rice Memorial Chamber Music Coll; Richard Welling Coll; The Bob Steele Coll; The Elbert Weinberg Coll; The Gwen Reed Coll; The Hartford Business and Professional Women's Club Coll; The Hartford Hip Hop Coll; The Hartford Times Image Morgue 1955-1976; The Real Art Ways Coll. Oral History
Subject Interests: Art, Bus & mgt, Econ, Educ, Hist, Literary criticism, Music
Automation Activity & Vendor Info: (Acquisitions) Innovative Interfaces, Inc; (Cataloging) Innovative Interfaces, Inc; (Circulation) Innovative Interfaces, Inc; (OPAC) Innovative Interfaces, Inc; (Serials) Innovative Interfaces, Inc
Wireless access
Function: 24/7 Electronic res, 24/7 Online cat, 3D Printer, Activity rm, Adult bk club, Adult literacy prog, Archival coll, Art exhibits, Art programs, Audiobks via web, AV serv, Bilingual assistance for Spanish patrons, Bks on CD, Children's prog, Citizenship assistance, Computer training, Computers for patron use, E-Readers, Electronic databases & coll, Family literacy, For res purposes, Free DVD rentals, Health sci info serv, Holiday prog, Homework prog, ILL available, Instruction & testing, Internet access, Jazz prog, Large print keyboards, Learning ctr, Life-long learning prog for all ages, Literacy & newcomer serv, Magazines, Magnifiers for reading, Makerspace, Meeting rooms, Microfiche/film & reading machines, Movies, Museum passes, Music CDs, Notary serv, Online cat, Online info literacy tutorials on the web & in blackboard, Online ref, Outreach serv, Outside serv via phone, mail, e-mail & web, OverDrive digital audio bks, Passport agency, Photocopying/Printing, Preschool outreach, Preschool reading prog, Prog for adults, Prog for children & young adult, Ref & res, Ref serv available, Scanner, Senior outreach, Serves people with intellectual disabilities, Spanish lang bks, STEM programs, Story hour, Study rm, Summer & winter reading prog, Summer reading prog, Tax forms, Teen prog, Telephone ref, Visual arts prog, Wheelchair accessible, Workshops, Writing prog
Special Services for the Deaf - ADA equip; Assistive tech; Bks on deafness & sign lang; Sorenson video relay syst; TDD equip; TTY equip
Special Services for the Blind - Accessible computers; Assistive/Adapted tech devices, equip & products; Bks on CD; Computer with voice synthesizer for visually impaired persons; Copier with enlargement capabilities; HP Scan Jet with photo-finish software; Large print bks; Magnifiers; PC for people with disabilities; Screen enlargement software for people with visual disabilities; Screen reader software; ZoomText magnification & reading software
Open Mon-Thurs 9:30-8, Fri & Sat 9:30-5, Sun 1-5 (Winter)
Branches: 6
ALBANY, 1250 Albany Ave, 06112, SAN 336-2310. Tel: 860-695-7380. FAX: 860-722-6903. *Community Hub Mgr,* Christopher Brown; E-mail: cbrown@hplct.org; Staff 6 (Non-MLS 6)
Founded 1926. Circ 23,320
Open Mon & Wed 10-8, Tues & Thurs 10-6, Fri & Sat 10-5
BARBOUR, 261 Barbour St, 06120, SAN 336-2345. Tel: 860-695-7400. FAX: 860-722-6881. *Br Mgr,* Irene Blean; E-mail: iblean@hplct.org; Staff 5 (MLS 1, Non-MLS 4)
Founded 1927. Circ 15,701
Open Mon & Wed 10-6, Tues & Thurs 10-8, Fri 10-5
CAMP FIELD, 30 Campfield Ave, 06114, SAN 336-240X. Tel: 860-695-7440. FAX: 860-722-6874. *Br Mgr,* Patricia Knapp; E-mail: pknapp@hplct.org; Staff 5 (MLS 1, Non-MLS 4)
Founded 1916. Circ 18,581
Open Mon & Wed 10-6, Tues & Thurs 10-8, Fri 10-5

DWIGHT BRANCH, Seven New Park Ave, 06106, SAN 336-2434. Tel: 860-695-7460. FAX: 860-231-7443. *Br Mgr,* Lizandra Matias; E-mail: lmatias@hplct.org; Staff 5 (Non-MLS 5)
Founded 1907. Circ 18,658
Open Mon & Wed 10-6, Tues & Thurs 10-8, Fri 10-5

PARK, 744 Park St, 06106, SAN 336-2523. Tel: 860-695-7500. FAX: 860-722-6878. *Br Mgr,* Graciela Rivera; E-mail: grivera@hplct.org; Staff 6 (Non-MLS 6)
Founded 1928. Circ 20,857
Open Mon & Wed 10-8, Tues & Thurs 10-6, Fri & Sat 10-5

ROPKINS BRANCH, 1750 Main St, 06120, SAN 336-2558. Tel: 860-695-7520. FAX: 860-722-6906. *Coordr, Br Serv,* Bonnie Solberg; E-mail: bsolberg@hplct.org; Staff 2 (Non-MLS 2)
Founded 1995. Circ 11,279
Open Mon, Wed & Thurs 3-6, Tues 1:30-6

R HARTFORD SEMINARY LIBRARY*, 77 Sherman St, 06105-2260. SAN 302-1831. Tel: 860-509-9561. Interlibrary Loan Service Tel: 860-509-9500. Administration Tel: 860-509-9560. FAX: 860-509-9509. E-mail: library@hartsem.edu. Web Site: www.hartsem.edu/library. *Dir, Libr Serv,* Ann Crawford; E-mail: anncrawford@hartsem.edu; Staff 7 (MLS 3, Non-MLS 4)
Founded 1834. Enrl 100; Fac 18; Highest Degree: Doctorate
Library Holdings: CDs 60; DVDs 93; e-books 7,500; e-journals 73; Microforms 6,669; Bk Titles 76,869; Bk Vols 80,098; Per Subs 307; Videos 301
Special Collections: Arabian Nights (multiple languages); Macdonald Coll (Arabic/Islamic studies)
Automation Activity & Vendor Info: (Acquisitions) EOS International; (Cataloging) OCLC Connexion; (Circulation) EOS International; (Course Reserve) EOS International; (ILL) Clio; (OPAC) EOS International; (Serials) EOS International
Wireless access
Function: Archival coll, CD-ROM, Computers for patron use, Doc delivery serv, E-Reserves, Electronic databases & coll, Free DVD rentals, ILL available, Microfiche/film & reading machines, Online cat, Orientations, Photocopying/Printing, Printer for laptops & handheld devices, Ref serv available, Spanish lang bks, Spoken cassettes & CDs, Study rm, Telephone ref, VHS videos, Wheelchair accessible
Partic in Connecticut Library Consortium; LYRASIS; OCLC Online Computer Library Center, Inc
Open Mon-Thurs 9am-10pm, Fri 9-5, Sat 8:30-5
Restriction: Non-circulating of rare bks

L PULLMAN & COMLEY*, Law Library, 90 State House Sq, Flr 13, 06103-3711. SAN 372-3380. Tel: 860-424-4300. FAX: 860-424-4370. *Librn,* Dottie McCaughtry; E-mail: dmccaughtry@pullcom.com
Library Holdings: Bk Vols 5,000

S ROBINSON & COLE LLP*, Information Resource Center, 280 Trumbull St, 06103-3597. SAN 326-1557. Tel: 860-275-8200. *Info Res Mgr,* Christine Graesser; Staff 3 (MLS 2, Non-MLS 1)
Library Holdings: Bk Titles 5,000
Wireless access
Restriction: Staff use only

M SAINT FRANCIS HOSPITAL & MEDICAL CENTER*, Health Sciences Library, 114 Woodland St, 06105. SAN 336-2582. Tel: 860-714-4773. FAX: 860-714-8022. E-mail: sfhlibrary@trinityhealthofne.org. Web Site: trinityhealthofne.org/location/saint-francis-hospital. *Dir,* Joseph M Pallis; Tel: 860-714-4883, E-mail: jpallis@stfranciscare.org; Staff 3 (MLS 2, Non-MLS 1)
Library Holdings: Bk Vols 5,000; Per Subs 600
Special Collections: Hospital Archives
Automation Activity & Vendor Info: (Acquisitions) Ex Libris Group; (Cataloging) Ex Libris Group; (Circulation) Ex Libris Group; (OPAC) Ex Libris Group; (Serials) Ex Libris Group
Wireless access
Publications: Library Notes
Partic in Conn Asn of Health Scis Librs; LYRASIS; Medical Library Association; North Atlantic Health Sciences Libraries, Inc; OCLC Online Computer Library Center, Inc
Open Mon-Fri 7:30-5

S HARRIET BEECHER STOWE CENTER RESEARCH COLLECTIONS, 77 Forest St, 06105-3296. SAN 336-2647. Tel: 860-522-9258, Ext 313. FAX: 860-522-9259. E-mail: research@stowecenter.org. Web Site: www.harrietbeecherstowecenter.org/programs-learning/collections. *Director, Collections & Research,* Elizabeth Burgess; E-mail: bburgess@stowecenter.org; Staff 1 (Non-MLS 1)
Founded 1965
Library Holdings: Bk Vols 15,000; Per Subs 40
Special Collections: Birdoff Coll of Uncle Tom's Cabin stage and screen ephemera; E. Bruce Kirkham Coll of annotated Harriet Beecher Stowe Letters, 1822-1896; Foote Family Coll, photogs; George Keller Coll, architectural drawings; Hartford Architectural Conservancy photo survey & data sheets; Isabella Beecher Hooker Coll; Katharine Seymour Day Coll of personal correspondence and collected letters of Beecher/Stowe family; Lyman Beecher Family Coll, photogs; William H Gillette Coll, photogs
Subject Interests: 19th Century Am decorative arts, 19th Century women's hist
Wireless access
Function: Archival coll, Electronic databases & coll, For res purposes, Microfiche/film & reading machines, Res libr
Partic in OCLC Online Computer Library Center, Inc
Restriction: Closed stack, Non-circulating, Open by appt only, Photo ID required for access

C TRINITY COLLEGE LIBRARY*, 300 Summit St, 06106. SAN 336-2701. Information Services Tel: 860-297-2248. FAX: 860-297-2007. E-mail: library.feedback@trincoll.edu. Web Site: www.trincoll.edu/LITC/Library. *Chief Info Officer, VPres for Info Serv,* Suzanne Aber; Tel: 860-297-2525, E-mail: suzanne.aber@trincoll.edu; *Coll, Dir, Discovery & Access,* Kathleen Bauer; Tel: 860-297-2258, E-mail: kathleen.bauer@trincoll.edu; *Cat Librn,* Todd Falkowski; Tel: 860-297-2271, E-mail: todd.falkowski@trincoll.edu; Staff 30.5 (MLS 15, Non-MLS 15.5)
Founded 1823. Enrl 2,127; Fac 223; Highest Degree: Master
Jul 2013-Jun 2014. Mats Exp $4,232,151, Books $425,319, Per/Ser (Incl. Access Fees) $1,090,982, Presv $13,276. Sal $1,607,583
Library Holdings: CDs 8,495; DVDs 5,341; e-books 805,366; e-journals 87,292; Microforms 364,319; Bk Vols 936,704; Per Subs 434
Special Collections: American Indian Coll; Americana; Bibliography & History of Printing; Charles Dudley Warner Coll, mss; Charles Nodier Coll; Civil War Coll; Cruikshank Coll; Early American Education Textbooks (Henry Barnard Coll); Early American Sheet Music & Periodicals; Early Voyages & Discoveries; Edna St Vincent Millay Coll; Edwin Arlington Robinson Coll; Folklore Coll; Horology Coll; Incunabula (Trumbull-Prime Coll); Philology Coll; Private Press Books; Psalm & Hymn Books; Robert Frost Coll; Slavery Coll; Walter de la Mare Coll; Witchcraft Coll; World War I Coll. US Document Depository
Subject Interests: Educ, Hist, Music
Automation Activity & Vendor Info: (Acquisitions) Ex Libris Group; (Cataloging) Ex Libris Group; (Circulation) Ex Libris Group; (Course Reserve) Ex Libris Group; (ILL) Atlas Systems; (OPAC) Ex Libris Group; (Serials) Ex Libris Group
Wireless access
Partic in Connecticut Library Consortium; CTW Library Consortium; Greater Hartford Consortium for Higher Education; LYRASIS
Open Mon-Wed 8am-11pm, Thurs & Fri 8am-9pm, Sat Noon-9, Sun Noon-11
Friends of the Library Group

Departmental Libraries:

WATKINSON LIBRARY, 300 Summit St, 06106. Tel: 860-297-2268. Web Site: www.trincoll.edu/LITC/Watkinson. *Dir, Spec Coll & Archives,* Christina Bleyer, PhD; Tel: 860-297-2266, E-mail: christina.bleyer@trincoll.edu; Staff 4 (MLS 3, Non-MLS 1)
Open Mon-Fri 9-4
Restriction: Non-circulating

SR UNITED CHURCH OF CHRIST*, Connecticut Conference Archives, 125 Sherman St, 06105. SAN 325-7665. Tel: 860-233-5564. FAX: 860-231-8111. Web Site: ctucc.org. *Archivist,* John Van Epps; E-mail: johnve@ctucc.org
Library Holdings: Bk Vols 5,000
Special Collections: Church Records, doc; Early Americana; Missionary Papers

S WADSWORTH ATHENEUM MUSEUM OF ART, Auerbach Art Library, 600 Main St, 06103. SAN 302-1955. Tel: 860-838-4116. Web Site: www.thewadsworth.org/learn/research. *Head of Libr & Archives,* Amy Kilkenny; E-mail: amy.kilkenny@thewadsworth.org; Staff 1 (MLS 1)
Founded 1934
Library Holdings: Bk Vols 50,000; Per Subs 50
Special Collections: Art (Watkinson Coll); Artists' Books; Bookplates (Baker Coll)
Subject Interests: Costume design, Decorative art, Fine arts, Local hist, Mus studies, Painting, Photog
Automation Activity & Vendor Info: (Cataloging) TLC (The Library Corporation)
Wireless access
Open Wed & Thurs 11-5
Restriction: Non-circulating to the pub, Open to pub for ref only
Friends of the Library Group

HARWINTON

P HARWINTON PUBLIC LIBRARY, 80 Bentley Dr, 06791. SAN 302-198X. Tel: 860-485-9113. FAX: 860-485-2713. E-mail: staff@harwintonlibrary.org. Web Site: www.harwintonlibrary.org. *Libr Dir,*

Alice Freiler; E-mail: director@harwintonlibrary.org; *Ad,* Lydia Smith; *Children's Programmer,* Amanda Urcinas; Staff 5 (MLS 2, Non-MLS 3)
Founded 1909. Pop 5,000; Circ 21,000
Library Holdings: CDs 409; DVDs 119; Large Print Bks 300; Bk Vols 30,000; Per Subs 75; Talking Bks 1,270; Videos 1,294
Subject Interests: Local hist
Automation Activity & Vendor Info: (Acquisitions) Follett Software; (Cataloging) Follett Software; (Circulation) Follett Software
Wireless access
Open Mon & Wed 12:30-8:30, Tues, Thurs & Fri 9:30-5:30, Sat 9:30-3
Friends of the Library Group

HEBRON

P DOUGLAS LIBRARY OF HEBRON*, 22 Main St, 06248. SAN 302-1998. Tel: 860-228-9312. FAX: 860-228-4372. Web Site: douglaslibrary.org. *Libr Dir,* Kevin Sullivan; Tel: 860-228-9312, Ext 316, E-mail: ksullivan@hebronct.com; *Head, Circ,* Clare Betz; Tel: 860-228-9312, Ext 310, E-mail: clare@douglaslibrary.org; *Ch,* Cheri LaBombard; Tel: 860-228-9312, Ext 317, E-mail: cheri@douglaslibrary.org; Staff 7 (MLS 2, Non-MLS 5)
Founded 1899. Pop 9,500
Jul 2013-Jun 2014 Income $365,000. Mats Exp $40,000. Sal $202,000
Library Holdings: AV Mats 6,000; Bk Vols 39,000
Subject Interests: Genealogy
Automation Activity & Vendor Info: (Cataloging) OCLC; (Circulation) Evergreen; (OPAC) Evergreen
Wireless access
Function: ILL available, Photocopying/Printing, Prog for children & young adult, Summer reading prog, Wheelchair accessible
Publications: Our Town's Heritage (by John Sibun)
Partic in Bibliomation Inc
Open Mon & Wed 12-7:30, Sat 10-2:30
Friends of the Library Group

IVORYTON

P IVORYTON LIBRARY ASSOCIATION*, 106 Main St, 06442. (Mail add: PO Box 515, 06442-0515), SAN 324-2811. Tel: 860-767-1252. Web Site: www.ivoryton.com. *Dir,* Elizabeth Alvord; *Asst Dir, Ch Serv,* Elizabeth Bartlett; E-mail: ebartlett@ivoryton.com
Founded 1871. Pop 1,500; Circ 12,000
Library Holdings: Bk Titles 8,000; Per Subs 30
Special Collections: Oral History
Automation Activity & Vendor Info: (Cataloging) SirsiDynix; (Circulation) SirsiDynix; (OPAC) SirsiDynix
Wireless access
Open Tues & Thurs 10-6, Wed 10-8, Fri 2-6, Sat 9-Noon, Sun 1-4

JEWETT CITY

P SLATER LIBRARY & FANNING ANNEX, 26 Main St, 06351. SAN 376-2629. Tel: 860-376-0024. FAX: 860-376-0024. E-mail: slaterlibrary@yahoo.com. Web Site: sites.google.com/site/slaterlibrary. *Dir,* Rebecca Jusseaume; *Ch Serv,* Kathleen Brown; Staff 9 (Non-MLS 9)
Founded 1882. Pop 14,000; Circ 35,000
Library Holdings: AV Mats 1,000; CDs 437; DVDs 2,265; Large Print Bks 858; Bk Titles 27,000; Per Subs 40
Automation Activity & Vendor Info: (Serials) EBSCO Online
Wireless access
Function: 24/7 Electronic res, 24/7 Online cat, Adult bk club, Bk club(s), Bks on CD, Children's prog, Computers for patron use, Free DVD rentals, Govt ref serv, Holiday prog, ILL available, Internet access, Magazines, Magnifiers for reading, Meeting rooms, Movies, Museum passes, Music CDs, Online cat, Online ref, Photocopying/Printing, Prog for adults, Prog for children & young adult, Ref serv available, Scanner, Story hour, Summer reading prog, Tax forms, Teen prog, Wheelchair accessible
Partic in Bibliomation Inc; Connecticut Library Consortium; SLiMs
Open Mon-Wed 12-5:30, Thurs 12-6:30, Fri 11-5, Sat 10-2
Friends of the Library Group

KENT

P KENT LIBRARY ASSOCIATION*, Kent Memorial Library, 32 N Main St, 06757. (Mail add: PO Box 127, 06757-0127), SAN 302-2013. Tel: 860-927-3761. FAX: 860-927-1427. E-mail: kmlinfo@biblio.org. Web Site: www.kentmemoriallibrary.org. *Libr Dir,* Donna Miller; *Dir, Ch Serv,* Sarah Marshall; *Marketing & Special Events Dir,* Lucy C Pierpont; *Tech Serv & Circ Supvr,* Mary Ellen Casey; *Children's & Teen Serv,* Kim Seeger
Founded 1915. Pop 2,960; Circ 36,073
Library Holdings: Audiobooks 125; AV Mats 1,052; Bk Vols 25,548; Per Subs 15
Automation Activity & Vendor Info: (Cataloging) Evergreen; (Circulation) Evergreen
Wireless access
Partic in Bibliomation Inc; Connecticut Library Consortium
Open Mon-Fri 10-5:30, Sat 10-4

KILLINGWORTH

P KILLINGWORTH LIBRARY ASSOCIATION*, 301 Rte 81, 06419. (Mail add: PO Box 725, 06419-0725), SAN 302-2021. Tel: 860-663-2000. FAX: 860-663-2783. E-mail: mail@killingworthlibrary.org. Web Site: killingworthlibrary.org. *Head Librn,* Tammy Eustis; *Ch,* Gayle Byrne; *Circ, Tech Serv,* Janis Leird; Staff 5 (MLS 3, Non-MLS 2)
Founded 1964. Pop 6,381; Circ 69,053
Library Holdings: AV Mats 3,176; CDs 1,300; DVDs 2,000; Large Print Bks 738; Bk Titles 32,200; Bk Vols 33,600; Per Subs 94
Special Collections: Business Resource Center; Early Literacy Resource; Education Resources; Listening Center
Automation Activity & Vendor Info: (Acquisitions) Auto-Graphics, Inc; (Cataloging) Auto-Graphics, Inc; (Circulation) Auto-Graphics, Inc; (ILL) Auto-Graphics, Inc; (OPAC) Auto-Graphics, Inc; (Serials) Auto-Graphics, Inc
Wireless access
Function: Art exhibits, Bk club(s), Bks on CD, Children's prog, Computer training, Computers for patron use, E-Reserves, Electronic databases & coll, Free DVD rentals, ILL available, Internet access, Magnifiers for reading, Mail & tel request accepted, Museum passes, Music CDs, Online cat, Online ref, Photocopying/Printing, Preschool outreach, Prog for adults, Prog for children & young adult, Ref & res, Ref serv available, Senior computer classes, Spoken cassettes & CDs, Story hour, Summer & winter reading prog, Tax forms, Telephone ref, VHS videos, Wheelchair accessible
Partic in Bibliomation Inc
Open Mon, Wed, Fri & Sat 10-4:30, Tues & Thurs 10-8

LEBANON

P JONATHAN TRUMBULL LIBRARY*, 580 Exeter Rd, 06249. (Mail add: PO Box 145, 06249-0145), SAN 302-203X. Tel: 860-642-2020, 860-642-7763. FAX: 860-642-4880. E-mail: librarian@lebanonctlibrary.org. Web Site: www.lebanonctlibrary.org. *Dir,* Julie Culp; E-mail: jculp@lebanonctlibrary.org; *Ch Serv,* Linda Slate; E-mail: lslate@lebanonctlibrary.org; Staff 3 (MLS 1, Non-MLS 2)
Founded 1896. Pop 7,250; Circ 69,000
Library Holdings: Bk Vols 53,000
Automation Activity & Vendor Info: (Cataloging) Evergreen; (Circulation) Evergreen; (OPAC) Evergreen
Wireless access
Function: 24/7 Electronic res, 24/7 Online cat, Adult bk club, E-Reserves, Electronic databases & coll, Free DVD rentals, ILL available, Internet access, Life-long learning prog for all ages, Magazines, Museum passes, Music CDs, Online cat, OverDrive digital audio bks, Photocopying/Printing, Prog for adults, Prog for children & young adult, Ref serv available, Summer reading prog, Tax forms
Partic in Bibliomation Inc
Open Mon 9-5, Tues & Thurs 1-8, Wed 10-6, Sat 9-2
Friends of the Library Group

LEDYARD

P LEDYARD PUBLIC LIBRARIES*, Bill Library, 718 Colonel Ledyard Hwy, 06339. (Mail add: PO Box 225, 06339-0225), SAN 302-2048. Tel: 860-464-9912. Administration Tel: 860 464-9917. FAX: 860-464-9927. E-mail: bill-lib@ledyard.lioninc.org. Web Site: www.ledyard.lioninc.org. *Libr Dir,* Gale F Bradbury; E-mail: bradbury@ledyard.lioninc.org; *Head, Tech Serv,* Andrea Buka; E-mail: abuka@ledyard.lioninc.org; *Ch,* Nancy Brewer; E-mail: nbrewer@ledyard.lioninc.org; *Sr Asst Librn,* Marty Hubbard; E-mail: mhubbard@ledyard.lioninc.org
Founded 1863. Pop 15,149; Circ 159,701
Library Holdings: CDs 2,186; Bk Titles 72,876; Bk Vols 85,225; Per Subs 178; Videos 2,116
Special Collections: Oral History
Subject Interests: Local hist
Automation Activity & Vendor Info: (Acquisitions) Innovative Interfaces, Inc; (Cataloging) Innovative Interfaces, Inc; (Circulation) Innovative Interfaces, Inc; (OPAC) Innovative Interfaces, Inc
Wireless access
Publications: Books & Beyond (Newsletter)
Partic in Connecticut Library Consortium; Libraries Online, Inc
Open Mon-Wed 9-8, Fri & Sat 9-5, Sun 1-5
Friends of the Library Group
Branches: 1
GALES FERRY LIBRARY, 18 Hurlbutt Rd, Gales Ferry, 06335. (Mail add: PO Box 225, 06339). Tel: 860-464-6943. E-mail: gf-lib@ledyard.lioninc.org. *Asst Librn,* Mary Ellen Osborne; E-mail: mosborne@ledyard.lioninc.org
Open Mon & Tues 9-8, Wed & Thurs 9-5, Sat 9-5 (9-1 Summer)

LITCHFIELD

S LITCHFIELD HISTORICAL SOCIETY, H J Ingraham Memorial Research Library, Seven South St, 06759-0385. (Mail add: PO Box 385, 06759-0385), SAN 302-2056. Tel: 860-567-4501. FAX: 860-567-3565. E-mail: lhsoc@snet.net. Web Site: www.litchfieldhistoricalsociety.org/collection/library. *Archivist,* Linda Hocking; E-mail: archivist@litchfieldhistoricalsociety.org; *Curator,* Alex Dubois; E-mail: curator@litchfieldhistoricalsociety.org
Founded 1856
Library Holdings: Bk Titles 6,150; Bk Vols 8,000; Per Subs 5
Special Collections: American History; Litchfield Female Academy Coll (1792-1833); Litchfield Law Coll (1784-1833); Local Economic History (Account Bk (571) Coll); Local History (Litchfield Newspaper)
Subject Interests: Local hist
Wireless access
Partic in Bibliomation Inc
Open Tues-Fri 10-12 & 1-4 by appointment

P OLIVER WOLCOTT LIBRARY*, Litchfield Public Library, 160 South St, 06759-0187. (Mail add: PO Box 187, 06759-0187), SAN 302-2064. Tel: 860-567-8030. FAX: 860-567-4784. E-mail: owlibrary@owlibrary.org. Web Site: www.owlibrary.org. *Libr Dir,* Ann Marie White; E-mail: awhite@owlibrary.org; *Ad,* Patricia Moore; *Tech Librn,* Audra MacLaren; Staff 12 (MLS 6, Non-MLS 6)
Founded 1862. Pop 8,747
Library Holdings: Bk Vols 50,000; Per Subs 99
Special Collections: Oral History
Subject Interests: Local hist
Automation Activity & Vendor Info: (Cataloging) Evergreen; (Circulation) Evergreen
Wireless access
Function: 24/7 Electronic res, 24/7 Online cat, Activity rm, Adult bk club, Art exhibits, Bks on CD, Children's prog, Computer training, Computers for patron use, Free DVD rentals, Holiday prog, Home delivery & serv to seniorr ctr & nursing homes, Homebound delivery serv, ILL available, Internet access, Magazines, Magnifiers for reading, Mango lang, Museum passes, Music CDs, Online cat, Outreach serv, OverDrive digital audio bks, Preschool outreach, Preschool reading prog, Prog for adults, Prog for children & young adult, Senior outreach, Story hour, Summer reading prog, Tax forms
Publications: E_news (Online only); Owl News (Newsletter)
Partic in Bibliomation Inc; Connecticut Library Consortium
Open Mon 12-5, Tues & Thurs 10-9, Wed & Fri 10-5, Sat 9-2, Sun 11-3
Friends of the Library Group

LYME

P LYME PUBLIC LIBRARY*, 482 Hamburg Rd, 06371-3110. SAN 302-2072. Tel: 860-434-2272. FAX: 860-434-9972. E-mail: staff@lymepl.org. Web Site: www.lymepl.org. *Dir,* Theresa R Conley; E-mail: tconley@lymepl.org; *Ch Serv,* Barbara L Carlson; E-mail: bcarlson@lymepl.org; *Libr Asst,* LynnAnn Baldi; *Libr Asst,* Sarah Karpinski; *Libr Asst,* Judith Leonard; *Libr Asst,* Kathy Varady; Staff 6 (MLS 1, Non-MLS 5)
Founded 1913. Pop 2,099; Circ 15,287
Jul 2019-Jun 2020 Income $206,058, State $184, City $146,518, Locally Generated Income $59,356
Library Holdings: Audiobooks 1,251; DVDs 2,238; Bk Vols 23,281; Per Subs 65
Special Collections: Dominick Dunne Video Coll; Dot Orr Cookbook Coll; Tucky Jewett Garden Book Coll
Automation Activity & Vendor Info: (Cataloging) Auto-Graphics, Inc; (Circulation) Auto-Graphics, Inc; (ILL) Auto-Graphics, Inc; (OPAC) Auto-Graphics, Inc
Wireless access
Function: 24/7 Electronic res, 24/7 Online cat, Adult bk club, Bks on CD, Children's prog, Computers for patron use, E-Reserves, ILL available, Internet access, Mango lang, Meeting rooms, Museum passes, Music CDs, Online cat, OverDrive digital audio bks, Photocopying/Printing, Preschool reading prog, Prog for adults, Prog for children & young adult, Ref serv available, Story hour, Study rm, Summer reading prog, Tax forms, Telephone ref
Partic in Connecticut Library Consortium
Open Tues & Thurs 10-8, Wed & Fri 10-5, Sat 10-4
Friends of the Library Group

MADISON

P E C SCRANTON MEMORIAL LIBRARY*, 1250 Durham Rd, Ste F, 06443. SAN 302-2080. Tel: 203-245-7365. FAX: 203-245-7821. E-mail: info@scrantonlibrary.org. Web Site: www.scrantonlibrary.org. *Dir,* Sunnie Scarpa; E-mail: scarpas@scrantonlibrary.org; *Asst Dir,* Marcia Sokolnicki; E-mail: sokolnickim@scrantonlibrary.org; Staff 12 (MLS 6, Non-MLS 6)
Founded 1900. Pop 18,791; Circ 300,374
Library Holdings: AV Mats 13,679; Large Print Bks 1,740; Bk Vols 116,000; Per Subs 215
Automation Activity & Vendor Info: (Cataloging) Innovative Interfaces, Inc; (Circulation) Innovative Interfaces, Inc; (Course Reserve) Innovative Interfaces, Inc; (ILL) Innovative Interfaces, Inc; (OPAC) Innovative Interfaces, Inc; (Serials) Innovative Interfaces, Inc
Wireless access
Partic in Libraries Online, Inc
Open Mon-Thurs (Sept-June) 9-9, Fri 9-5:30, Sat 9-5, Sun 1-4; Mon-Thurs (June-Sept) 9-9, Fri 9-5:30, Sat 9-12
Friends of the Library Group

MANCHESTER

M EASTERN CONNECTICUT HEALTH NETWORK*, Medical Library, 71 Haynes St, 06040-4188. SAN 302-2110. Tel: 860-646-1222, Ext 2225. FAX: 860-647-6443. Web Site: echnlibrary.libguides.com. *Libr Coord,* Amanda Doughty; E-mail: adoughty@echn.org; Staff 1 (Non-MLS 1)
Founded 1948
Library Holdings: Bk Titles 1,000; Per Subs 300
Subject Interests: Allied health, Nursing
Automation Activity & Vendor Info: (Cataloging) CyberTools for Libraries
Open Mon-Fri 8-4
Friends of the Library Group

S FUSS & O'NEILL INC*, 146 Hartford Rd, 06040-5992. Tel: 860-646-2469, Ext 5367. FAX: 860-533-5143. Web Site: www.fando.com. *Librn,* Maggie Snape; Staff 1 (MLS 1)
Founded 1989
Library Holdings: Bk Titles 6,500; Bk Vols 7,000; Per Subs 170
Subject Interests: Civil engr, Environ engr
Automation Activity & Vendor Info: (OPAC) Inmagic, Inc.
Partic in Connecticut Library Consortium
Restriction: Not open to pub

J MANCHESTER COMMUNITY COLLEGE LIBRARY*, Great Path, 06040. (Mail add: MS No 15, PO Box 1046, 06045-1046), SAN 302-2102. Tel: 860-512-2880. Interlibrary Loan Service Tel: 860-512-2886. Reference Tel: 860-512-2883. FAX: 860-512-2871. Web Site: www.manchestercc.edu/library. *Dir, Libr Serv,* Debbie Herman; Tel: 860-512-2872, E-mail: dherman@manchestercc.edu; *Acq & Cat,* Zhijiang Zhang; Tel: 860-512-2875, E-mail: zzhang@mcc.commnet.edu; *Circ,* Donna Brice; Tel: 860-512-2878, E-mail: dbrice@mcc.commnet.edu; *Circ, ILL,* Christi Geisinger; E-mail: cgeisinger@mcc.commnet.edu; *Per,* Melissa Rivera; Tel: 860-512-2884, E-mail: mrivera@mcc.commnet.edu; *Ref Serv,* Evelyn Angry-Smith; Tel: 860-512-2874, E-mail: eangry-smith@mcc.commnet.edu; *Ref Serv,* Paula Pini; Tel: 860-512-2877, E-mail: ppini@mcc.commnet.edu; Staff 8 (MLS 4, Non-MLS 4)
Founded 1963. Enrl 6,780; Fac 496; Highest Degree: Associate
Automation Activity & Vendor Info: (Acquisitions) Ex Libris Group; (Cataloging) Ex Libris Group; (Circulation) Ex Libris Group; (Course Reserve) Ex Libris Group; (Discovery) Ex Libris Group; (ILL) OCLC; (OPAC) Ex Libris Group; (Serials) Ex Libris Group
Wireless access
Function: 24/7 Electronic res, 24/7 Online cat, Archival coll, Art exhibits, Bks on CD, Computers for patron use, Distance learning, E-Readers, Electronic databases & coll, Free DVD rentals, ILL available, Instruction & testing, Internet access, Magazines, Magnifiers for reading, Meeting rooms, Music CDs, Online cat, Online info literacy tutorials on the web & in blackboard, Online ref, Orientations, Photocopying/Printing, Printer for laptops & handheld devices, Ref & res, Ref serv available, Workshops
Partic in Connecticut Library Consortium; OCLC Online Computer Library Center, Inc; Westchester Academic Library Directors Organization
Open Mon-Thurs 8-8, Fri 8-3, Sat 10-2

P MANCHESTER PUBLIC LIBRARY*, Mary Cheney Library, 586 Main St, 06040. SAN 302-2129. Tel: 860-643-2471. Reference Tel: 860-645-0821. FAX: 860-643-9453. Web Site: library.townofmanchester.org. *Dir,* Douglas McDonough; E-mail: dmcdonough@manchesterct.gov; *Asst Dir, Head, Children's Servx,* Norma Nevers; E-mail: nnevers@manchesterct.gov; *Head, Cat & Circ,* Jessica Sweetland; E-mail: jsweetland@manchesterct.gov; *Head, Ref,* Jennifer Bartlett; E-mail: jbartlett@manchesterct.gov; *Br Mgr,* Hong Chen; Tel: 860-643-6892, E-mail: hchen@manchesterct.gov; Staff 13 (MLS 13)
Founded 1871. Pop 58,241; Circ 629,139
Jul 2019-Jun 2020 Income (Main & Associated Libraries) $3,319,497, State $24,000, City $3,206,497, Locally Generated Income $89,000. Mats Exp $330,000, Books $241,000, Per/Ser (Incl. Access Fees) $10,000, AV Mat $21,000, Electronic Ref Mat (Incl. Access Fees) $58,000. Sal $2,014,740 (Prof $988,200)
Library Holdings: Audiobooks 7,800; CDs 4,600; DVDs 17,000; e-books 22,200; e-journals 110; Large Print Bks 4,400; Bk Vols 178,000; Per Subs 255

Automation Activity & Vendor Info: (Cataloging) Innovative Interfaces, Inc; (Circulation) Innovative Interfaces, Inc; (OPAC) Innovative Interfaces, Inc
Wireless access
Function: 24/7 Electronic res, 24/7 Online cat, Adult bk club, After school storytime, Audiobks on Playaways & MP3, Audiobks via web, AV serv, Bk club(s), Bks on CD, Children's prog, Computer training, Computers for patron use, Digital talking bks, Electronic databases & coll, Family literacy, For res purposes, Free DVD rentals, Home delivery & serv to seniorr ctr & nursing homes, Homebound delivery serv, ILL available, Internet access, Magazines, Magnifiers for reading, Mail & tel request accepted, Microfiche/film & reading machines, Movies, Museum passes, Music CDs, Online cat, Online ref, Outreach serv, OverDrive digital audio bks, Photocopying/Printing, Preschool outreach, Printer for laptops & handheld devices, Prog for adults, Prog for children & young adult, Ref serv available, Scanner, Spanish lang bks, Story hour, Summer reading prog, Tax forms, Teen prog, Telephone ref
Partic in Library Connection, Inc
Open Mon-Thurs 9-9, Fri & Sat 9-5, Sun (Winter) 1-5
Friends of the Library Group
Branches: 1
WHITON BRANCH, 100 N Main St, 06040, SAN 371-3571. Tel: 860-643-6892. FAX: 860-533-1251. *Librn II,* Hong Chen; Staff 4 (MLS 2, Non-MLS 2)
Library Holdings: Audiobooks 600; CDs 800; DVDs 1,200; e-books 20,000; Large Print Bks 300; Bk Titles 30,000; Per Subs 68
Open Mon-Thurs 10-8:30, Fri & Sat 9-5
Bookmobiles: 1

MANSFIELD CENTER

P MANSFIELD PUBLIC LIBRARY*, 54 Warrenville Rd, 06250. SAN 302-2137. Tel: 860-423-2501. FAX: 860-423-9856. E-mail: MansfieldLibrary@MansfieldCT.org. Web Site: mansfieldpubliclibraryct.org. *Dir,* Leslie McDonough; E-mail: mcdonoughlb@mansfieldct.org; *Librn, Adult Serv,* Peggy McCarthy; E-mail: mccarthyml@mansfieldct.org; *Ch,* Judy Stoughton; E-mail: stoughtonj@mansfieldct.org; *YA Librn,* Emily Tinnel; E-mail: tinnelew@mansfieldct.org; Staff 3 (MLS 3)
Founded 1906. Pop 18,000; Circ 250,000
Library Holdings: Bk Vols 81,000
Automation Activity & Vendor Info: (Circulation) Horizon; (OPAC) Horizon; (Serials) Horizon
Partic in SAILS Library Network
Open Mon & Wed 10-5, Tues & Thurs 10-8, Fri & Sat 9-5
Friends of the Library Group

MARLBOROUGH

P RICHMOND MEMORIAL LIBRARY*, 15 School Dr, 06447-1582. SAN 302-2145. Tel: 860-295-6210. FAX: 860-295-6212. Web Site: richmondlibrary.info. *Libr Dir,* Nancy M Wood; E-mail: nwood@richmondlibrary.info; *Ch & Youth Librn,* Eileen Washburn; E-mail: ewashburn@richmondlibrary.info; Staff 10 (MLS 3, Non-MLS 7)
Founded 1924. Pop 6,400; Circ 86,685
Jul 2017-Jun 2018 Income $385,046, State $2,771, City $341,668, Locally Generated Income $40,607. Mats Exp $37,615, Books $33,179, Per/Ser (Incl. Access Fees) $3,293, AV Mat $9,026, Electronic Ref Mat (Incl. Access Fees) $45. Sal $214,793 (Prof $116,068)
Library Holdings: AV Mats 3,821; Bks on Deafness & Sign Lang 20; DVDs 4,687; e-books 8,036; Large Print Bks 175; Bk Vols 37,887; Per Subs 81
Automation Activity & Vendor Info: (Acquisitions) Innovative Interfaces, Inc - Sierra; (Cataloging) Innovative Interfaces, Inc - Sierra; (Circulation) Innovative Interfaces, Inc - Sierra; (ILL) Innovative Interfaces, Inc - Sierra; (OPAC) Innovative Interfaces, Inc - Sierra
Wireless access
Function: 24/7 Electronic res, 24/7 Online cat, Accelerated reader prog, Activity rm, Adult bk club, After school storytime, Archival coll, Art programs, Audio & video playback equip for onsite use, Audiobks via web, Bk club(s), Bks on CD, Children's prog, Computer training, Computers for patron use, Electronic databases & coll, Family literacy, For res purposes, Free DVD rentals, Homebound delivery serv, ILL available, Internet access, Magazines, Magnifiers for reading, Mail & tel request accepted, Meeting rooms, Museum passes, Music CDs, Online cat, Online info literacy tutorials on the web & in blackboard, Online ref, Photocopying/Printing, Preschool outreach, Preschool reading prog, Prog for children & young adult, Ref & res, Ref serv available, Scanner, STEM programs, Story hour, Summer & winter reading prog, Summer reading prog, Tax forms, Teen prog, Telephone ref, Winter reading prog, Workshops
Partic in Library Connection, Inc
Open Mon-Thurs 10-8, Fri 10-6, Sat 10-4 (10-1 Spring)
Friends of the Library Group

MERIDEN

SR EPISCOPAL CHURCH IN CONNECTICUT ARCHIVES, The Commons, 290 Pratt St, Box 52, 06450. SAN 325-7541. Tel: 203-639-3501, Ext 135. Administration Tel: 203-639-3501. FAX: 203-235-1008. Web Site: www.episcopalct.org, www.episcopalct.org/staff/archives. *Archivist,* Greg Farr; E-mail: gfarr@episcopalct.org. Subject Specialists: *Episcopal Church,* Greg Farr; Staff 1 (MLS 1)
Founded 1784
Special Collections: Bishop Samuel Seabury's Papers; Colonial Connecticut Church Records; Letters & papers of early Anglican missionaries in USA
Subject Interests: Relig
Function: Archival coll
Open Mon-Thurs 9-4:30
Restriction: Access at librarian's discretion, Non-circulating, Researchers by appt only

P MERIDEN PUBLIC LIBRARY*, 105 Miller St, 06450. SAN 302-217X. Tel: 203-238-2344. Circulation Tel: 203-238-2345. Administration Tel: 203-630-6353. Information Services Tel: 203-238-2346. FAX: 203-238-3647. Administration FAX: 203-238-6950. E-mail: communityservices@meriden.lioninc.org. Interlibrary Loan Service E-mail: meridenILL@hotmail.com. Web Site: www.meridenlibrary.org. *Dir,* Clevell Roseboro, II; E-mail: Croseboro@meridenct.gov; *Head, Bibliog Serv,* Lauren Thompson; *Head, Children's Servx,* Meagan Schiebel; *Head, Circ, Pub Serv Coordr,* Rebecca Starr; *Cat & Ref Librn,* Shelby Anderson; *Ref Librn,* Jerry Maust; E-mail: jmaust@meridenct.gov; *Ref Librn, Teen Serv,* Melissa Murphy; *Ch,* Michelle Farella; Staff 12.5 (MLS 12.5)
Founded 1903. Pop 60,868; Circ 232,000. Sal $1,560,285 (Prof $835,120)
Library Holdings: AV Mats 16,707; Bk Vols 234,635; Per Subs 137
Special Collections: Silver Industry Coll. Oral History
Subject Interests: Local hist
Automation Activity & Vendor Info: (Acquisitions) Innovative Interfaces, Inc; (Cataloging) Innovative Interfaces, Inc; (Circulation) Innovative Interfaces, Inc; (ILL) Innovative Interfaces, Inc; (OPAC) Innovative Interfaces, Inc
Wireless access
Function: Adult bk club, Art exhibits, Audiobks via web, Bi-weekly Writer's Group, Bks on CD, Chess club, Children's prog, Computer training, Computers for patron use, Doc delivery serv, E-Reserves, Free DVD rentals, Home delivery & serv to seniorr ctr & nursing homes, Homebound delivery serv, ILL available, Internet access, Large print keyboards, Magnifiers for reading, Microfiche/film & reading machines, Museum passes, Music CDs, Notary serv, Online cat, Online ref, Outreach serv, OverDrive digital audio bks, Photocopying/Printing, Preschool outreach, Preschool reading prog, Prog for adults, Prog for children & young adult, Scanner, Spanish lang bks, Wheelchair accessible
Publications: Friends of the Library Newsletter (Monthly); MPL Newsletter (Monthly)
Partic in Libraries Online, Inc
Special Services for the Deaf - ADA equip; Bks on deafness & sign lang; Closed caption videos
Special Services for the Blind - Accessible computers; Audio mat; Bks available with recordings; Bks on cassette; Bks on CD; Computer with voice synthesizer for visually impaired persons; Copier with enlargement capabilities; Internet workstation with adaptive software; Large print bks; Magnifiers; ZoomText magnification & reading software
Open Mon-Wed 9:30-6:30, Thurs & Fri 9-5
Restriction: Residents only
Friends of the Library Group
Bookmobiles: 1

MIDDLE HADDAM

P MIDDLE HADDAM PUBLIC LIBRARY, Two Knowles Landing, 06456. SAN 302-2196. Tel: 860-267-9093. E-mail: middlehaddamlibrary@gmail.com. Web Site: middlehaddamlibrary.com. *Librn,* Janet McDonald
Founded 1909. Pop 600; Circ 5,650
Library Holdings: Bk Vols 12,000
Subject Interests: Antiques, Gardening, Local hist
Publications: 80 Years of Progress
Open Tues, Thurs & Fri 3-7, Wed 10-2, Sat 12-4

MIDDLEBURY

P MIDDLEBURY PUBLIC LIBRARY*, 30 Crest Rd, 06762. SAN 302-220X. Tel: 203-758-2634. FAX: 203-577-4164. Web Site: www.middleburypubliclibrary.org. *Libr Dir,* Jo-Ann LoRusso; E-mail: jlorusso@middlebury-ct.org; Staff 8 (MLS 3, Non-MLS 5)
Founded 1794. Pop 7,400; Circ 106,000
Library Holdings: Bk Vols 65,000; Per Subs 90
Automation Activity & Vendor Info: (Acquisitions) Baker & Taylor; (Cataloging) Auto-Graphics, Inc; (Circulation) Auto-Graphics, Inc; (OPAC) Auto-Graphics, Inc

Wireless access
Publications: Newsletter (Monthly)
Open Mon, Wed & Fri 10-5, Tues & Thurs 10-8, Sat 10-2
Friends of the Library Group

MIDDLEFIELD

P LEVI E COE LIBRARY, 414 Main St, 06455-1207. SAN 302-2226. Tel: 860-349-3857. FAX: 860-349-2131. E-mail: levicoelibrary@gmail.com. Web Site: leviecoe.lioninc.org. *Dir,* Jessica Lobner; E-mail: levicoelibrary.Jess@gmail.com; *Asst Dir,* Susan Mizla; Staff 4 (MLS 1, Non-MLS 3)
Founded 1893. Pop 4,200; Circ 37,892
Library Holdings: AV Mats 1,000; Large Print Bks 200; Bk Vols 25,000; Per Subs 60; Talking Bks 225
Wireless access
Open Mon-Thurs 10-7, Sat (Sept-May) 10-2
Friends of the Library Group

MIDDLETOWN

CONNECTICUT VALLEY HOSPITAL
M HALLOCK MEDICAL LIBRARY*, Page Hall, Silver St, 06457. (Mail add: PO Box 351, 06457-7023), SAN 302-2234. Tel: 860-262-5059. FAX: 860-262-5049. *Librn,* Mary Conlon; E-mail: mary.conlon@po.state.ct.us; *Librn,* Pauline A Kruk; E-mail: pauline.kruk@po.state.ct.us; Staff 2 (MLS 2)
Founded 1950
Library Holdings: Bk Titles 10,000; Per Subs 75
Subject Interests: Mental health, Psychiat, Psychol
Function: ILL available
Partic in Basic Health Sciences Library Network; Conn Asn of Health Scis Librs; LYRASIS; OCLC Online Computer Library Center, Inc
Publications: Health Source; Psych Lit
Restriction: Open by appt only, Staff use only

M WILLIS ROYLE LIBRARY*, Silver St, 06457. (Mail add: PO Box 351, 06457), SAN 324-3303. Tel: 860-262-5520. FAX: 860-262-5049. *Med Librn,* Kandace Yuen; E-mail: kandace.yuen@ct.gov; Staff 2 (MLS 2)
Founded 1980
Library Holdings: AV Mats 1,000; Large Print Bks 50; Bk Titles 4,000; Bk Vols 5,000; Per Subs 40; Talking Bks 100
Special Collections: Daily Living Skills; Entertainment videos; High interest - low reading level materials; Large Print; Music Cassettes & CD's; Spanish Language
Subject Interests: Addictions, Commun living, Fiction, Mental health, Psychol, Soc sci
Automation Activity & Vendor Info: (Cataloging) Follett Software; (Circulation) Follett Software; (Serials) EBSCO Online
Function: ILL available
Restriction: Open by appt only, Residents only

S GODFREY MEMORIAL LIBRARY, 134 Newfield St, 06457-2534. SAN 302-2242. Tel: 860-346-4375. E-mail: refdesk@godfrey.org. Web Site: www.godfrey.org. *Libr Dir,* Carol Ansel; E-mail: carol.ansel@godfrey.org; *Asst Libr Dir,* Michael Steffman
Founded 1950
Library Holdings: Bk Vols 40,000
Subject Interests: Genealogy, Hist
Automation Activity & Vendor Info: (Acquisitions) Surpass; (Cataloging) Surpass
Wireless access
Function: Genealogy discussion group, Internet access, Online ref
Publications: The Godfrey Update (Newsletter)
Open Tues, Wed & Fri 9-4
Restriction: Not a lending libr, Pub use on premises

J MIDDLESEX COMMUNITY COLLEGE, Jean Burr Smith Library, 100 Training Hill Rd, 06457. SAN 302-2250. Tel: 860-343-5830. FAX: 860-343-5874. E-mail: mx-library@mxcc.commnet.edu. Web Site: mxcc.edu/library. *Dir, Libr & Learning Commons,* Melissa Behney; Tel: 860-343-5833, E-mail: mbehney@mxcc.commnet.edu; *Librn,* Wei Cen; Tel: 860-343-5834, E-mail: wcen@mxcc.commnet.edu; *Librn,* Donovan Reinwald; Tel: 860-343-5835, E-mail: dreinwald@mxcc.commnet.edu; *Digital Syst Librn,* Lisa Gugliotti; Tel: 860-343-5832, E-mail: lgugliotti@mxcc.commnet.edu; *Libr Asst,* Lisa Gangone; Tel: 860-343-5829, E-mail: lgangone@mxcc.commnet.edu; Staff 4.5 (MLS 4, Non-MLS 0.5)
Founded 1966. Enrl 1,263; Fac 46; Highest Degree: Associate
Library Holdings: CDs 258; DVDs 2,268; e-books 35,702; e-journals 13,873; Bk Titles 85,603; Bk Vols 88,187; Per Subs 103
Automation Activity & Vendor Info: (Acquisitions) Ex Libris Group; (Cataloging) Ex Libris Group; (Circulation) Ex Libris Group; (Course Reserve) Ex Libris Group; (ILL) OCLC; (OPAC) Ex Libris Group; (Serials) Ex Libris Group
Wireless access
Partic in Connecticut Library Consortium
Special Services for the Deaf - Accessible learning ctr; ADA equip; Assistive tech; Closed caption videos
Open Mon-Thurs 8-8, Fri 8-4; Mon-Fri 8-4 (Summer)

S MIDDLESEX COUNTY HISTORICAL SOCIETY LIBRARY*, 151 Main St, 06457-3423. SAN 326-159X. Tel: 860-346-0746. FAX: 860-346-0746. E-mail: middlesexhistory@wesleyan.edu. Web Site: mchsct.org. *Dir,* Deborah Shapiro; Staff 1 (Non-MLS 1)
Founded 1901
Special Collections: Genealogy (African-American Coll), bks, ms; Genealogy (Frank Farnsworth Starr Coll), bks, ms; Local History Coll; Town Coll
Wireless access
Open Mon-Thurs 10-2

M MIDDLESEX HOSPITAL*, Tremaine Library, 28 Crescent St, 06457-7005. SAN 302-2269. Tel: 860-358-6286. E-mail: library@midhosp.org. Web Site: www.midhosp.org. *Dir,* Jeannine Cyr Gluck; Tel: 860-358-6286; *Librn,* Janis Leird; Tel: 860-358-6286; Staff 2 (MLS 2)
Founded 1972
Subject Interests: Med, Nursing
Wireless access
Partic in Conn Asn of Health Scis Librs; Regional Med Libr Network

P RUSSELL LIBRARY, 123 Broad St, 06457. SAN 302-2277. Tel: 860-347-2528. Reference Tel: 860-347-2520. Administration Tel: 860-347-0196. Administration FAX: 860-347-6690. Web Site: www.russelllibrary.org. *Chief Exec Officer, Libr Dir,* Ramona Burkey; E-mail: rburkey@russelllibrary.org; *Asst Dir, Admin Serv,* Brandie Doyle; Tel: 860-347-2528, Ext 144, E-mail: bdoyle@russelllibrary.org; *Asst Dir, Pub Serv,* Mary Dattilo; Tel: 860-347-2528, Ext 175, E-mail: mdattilo@russelllibrary.org; *Head, Emerging Technologies & Digital Content,* Debra Barberi; Tel: 860-347-2528, Ext 151, E-mail: dbarberi@russelllibrary.org; *Head, Borrowing & Discovery,* Amy Slowik; Tel: 860-347-2528, Ext 155, E-mail: aslowik@russelllibrary.org; *Head, Info Servs & Adult Learning,* Catherine Ahern; Tel: 860-347-2528, Ext 123, E-mail: cahern@russelllibrary.org; *Head, Property Mgmt & Security,* Robb Prchal; Tel: 860-347-2528, Ext 130, E-mail: rprchal@russelllibrary.org; *Head, Youth & Family Learning,* Jennifer Billingsley; Tel: 860-347-2528, Ext 174; *Bus Mgr,* Lynn Harlow; Tel: 860-347-2528, Ext 145, E-mail: lharlow@russelllibrary.org; Staff 18 (MLS 17, Non-MLS 1)
Founded 1875. Pop 47,749; Circ 271,312
Jul 2021-Jun 2022 Income $3,385,053, State $11,000, City $3,225,419, Other $148,634
Library Holdings: Bk Vols 151,930
Special Collections: Adult Basic Education (ABE); Literacy Materials
Subject Interests: Genealogy, Local hist
Automation Activity & Vendor Info: (Acquisitions) Innovative Interfaces, Inc; (Cataloging) Innovative Interfaces, Inc; (Circulation) Innovative Interfaces, Inc; (OPAC) Innovative Interfaces, Inc
Wireless access
Function: 24/7 Electronic res, 24/7 Online cat, Activity rm, Adult bk club, After school storytime, Archival coll, Art exhibits, Audiobks on Playaways & MP3, Audiobks via web, AV serv, Bk club(s), Bks on CD, Children's prog, Computer training, Computers for patron use, Digital talking bks, Electronic databases & coll, Family literacy, Free DVD rentals, Holiday prog, Home delivery & serv to seniorr ctr & nursing homes, ILL available, Internet access, Life-long learning prog for all ages, Magazines, Magnifiers for reading, Mail & tel request accepted, Meeting rooms, Microfiche/film & reading machines, Movies, Museum passes, Music CDs, Online cat, Online ref, Outreach serv, OverDrive digital audio bks, Photocopying/Printing, Preschool outreach, Preschool reading prog, Printer for laptops & handheld devices, Prog for adults, Prog for children & young adult, Ref & res, Ref serv available, Res assist avail, Scanner, Senior outreach, Story hour, Study rm, Summer & winter reading prog, Summer reading prog, Tax forms, Teen prog, Telephone ref, Wheelchair accessible, Workshops, Writing prog
Publications: Russell Library (Newsletter)
Partic in Libraries Online, Inc
Special Services for the Deaf - Assistive tech
Special Services for the Blind - Accessible computers; Assistive/Adapted tech devices, equip & products; Bks on CD; Closed circuit TV magnifier; Computer with voice synthesizer for visually impaired persons; Copier with enlargement capabilities; Large print bks; Low vision equip; Magnifiers; Talking bks
Open Mon-Thurs 9-8, Fri 9-6, Sat 9-5, Sun (Oct-March) 1-5
Friends of the Library Group

S STATE EDUCATION RESOURCE CENTER LIBRARY, 100 Roscommon Dr, Ste 110, 06457. SAN 324-5497. Tel: 860-740-2102. E-mail: libraryhelp@ctserc.org. Web Site: www.ctserc.org/library. *Librn,* Elizabeth

Karr; E-mail: karr@ctserc.org; *Librn,* Position Currently Open; Staff 2 (MLS 2)
Founded 1969
Jan 2020-Dec 2020. Mats Exp $45,000, Books $5,000, Per/Ser (Incl. Access Fees) $40,000
Library Holdings: Bks on Deafness & Sign Lang 99; DVDs 200; Electronic Media & Resources 4; High Interest/Low Vocabulary Bk Vols 45; Bk Titles 10,000; Per Subs 200; Spec Interest Per Sub 200
Subject Interests: Disability, Soc justice
Automation Activity & Vendor Info: (Cataloging) Auto-Graphics, Inc; (Circulation) Auto-Graphics, Inc; (OPAC) Auto-Graphics, Inc; (Serials) EBSCO Discovery Service
Function: Res libr
Publications: Test List
Restriction: Circ to mem only, Free to mem, In-house use for visitors

C WESLEYAN UNIVERSITY, Olin Memorial Library, 252 Church St, 06459. SAN 336-2825. Tel: 860-685-3844. Circulation Tel: 860-685-2660. Interlibrary Loan Service Tel: 860-685-3876. FAX: 860-685-3910. E-mail: reference@wesleyan.edu. Web Site: www.wesleyan.edu/libr. *Univ Librn,* Andrew W White; Tel: 860-685-2570, E-mail: awhite02@wesleyan.edu; *Dir, Spec Coll & Archives,* Suzy Taraba; Tel: 860-685-3375, E-mail: staraba@wesleyan.edu; *Adminr, Micro,* Elizabeth S Mainella; Tel: 860-685-3827, E-mail: emainella@wesleyan.edu; *Coll Develop & Acq Librn,* Aaron Sandoval; Tel: 860-685-3834, E-mail: asandoval01@wesleyan.edu; Staff 17 (MLS 14, Non-MLS 3)
Founded 1831. Enrl 3,190; Fac 320; Highest Degree: Doctorate
Library Holdings: Bk Vols 1,230,750
Special Collections: US Document Depository
Automation Activity & Vendor Info: (Acquisitions) Ex Libris Group; (Cataloging) Ex Libris Group; (Circulation) Ex Libris Group; (Course Reserve) Ex Libris Group; (ILL) OCLC ILLiad; (OPAC) Ex Libris Group; (Serials) Ex Libris Group
Wireless access
Publications: Numerous Guides & Pathfinders
Partic in CTW Library Consortium; LYRASIS
Friends of the Library Group
Departmental Libraries:
ART LIBRARY, 252 Church St, 2nd Flr, 06459.
Library Holdings: Bk Vols 50,000
Subject Interests: Archit hist, Art, Art hist, Photog, Studio arts
MUSIC LIBRARY, 252 Church St, 06459. Tel: 860-685-3898. E-mail: musiclibrary@wesleyan.edu. Web Site: wesleyan.edu/libr/collections/music-library.html. *Dir, Music Librn,* Aaron Bittel; Tel: 860-685-3899, E-mail: abittel@wesleyan.edu
Special Collections: World Music Archives
SCIENCE LIBRARY, 265 Church St, 06459. Tel: 860-685-2860. *Library Assistant V,* Linda Hurteau; Tel: 860-685-3728, E-mail: lhurteau@wesleyan.edu
Enrl 3,247
Subject Interests: Astronomy, Biology, Chem, Geol, Math, Physics

G WHITING FORENSIC INSTITUTE LIBRARY*, 70 O'Brien Dr, 06457. SAN 326-0097. Tel: 860-262-6466. FAX: 860-262-5470. *Library Contact,* Daniel E Gribko; E-mail: daniel.gribko@ct.gov
Founded 1970
Library Holdings: Bk Vols 1,100; Per Subs 50
Automation Activity & Vendor Info: (ILL) OCLC
Partic in Conn Asn of Health Scis Librs; Inter-Conn Orgn
Open Mon-Fri 8:30-4

MILFORD

P MILFORD PUBLIC LIBRARY, 57 New Haven Ave, 06460. SAN 336-2973. Tel: 203-783-3290. Circulation Tel: 203-783-3304. Reference Tel: 203-783-3292. Administration Tel: 203-783-3291. Automation Services Tel: 203-783-3307. FAX: 203-877-1072. Web Site: www.ci.milford.ct.us/milford-public-library. *Libr Dir,* Christine Angeli; Tel: 203-783-3399, E-mail: cangeli@milfordct.gov; *Asst Dir, Head, Tech Serv,* Nancy Abbey; E-mail: nabbey@milfordct.gov; *Info Syst Librn,* Fred Danowski; Tel: 203-701-4553, E-mail: fdanowski@milfordct.gov; *YA Librn,* Danielle Valenzano; Tel: 203-701-4554, E-mail: dvalenzano@milfordct.gov; *Ch Serv,* Suzanne Harrison-Thomas; Tel: 203-783-3312, E-mail: sthomas@milfordct.gov; *Circ,* Maria Teresa Battad; E-mail: mbattad@milfordct.gov; *Ref Serv,* Diana Preece; E-mail: dpreece@milfordct.gov; Staff 6.8 (MLS 5.9, Non-MLS 0.9)
Founded 1895. Pop 53,600; Circ 284,215
Jul 2020-Jun 2021. Mats Exp $120,000. Sal $850,000
Library Holdings: AV Mats 10,591; CDs 2,665; DVDs 2,275; Large Print Bks 2,352; Bk Vols 101,777; Per Subs 216
Special Collections: Milford & Connecticut History & Genealogy
Automation Activity & Vendor Info: (Acquisitions) Evergreen; (Cataloging) Evergreen; (Circulation) Evergreen; (OPAC) Evergreen; (Serials) Evergreen
Wireless access
Partic in Bibliomation Inc
Open Mon & Sat 10-5, Tues-Thurs 10-8:30, Fri 1-5
Friends of the Library Group

G US DEPARTMENT OF COMMERCE, NATIONAL OCEANIC & ATMOSPHERIC ADMINISTRATION*, National Marine Fisheries Service, Milford Laboratory Library, 212 Rogers Ave, 06460. SAN 302-2307. Tel: 203-882-6509. Administration Tel: 203-882-6500. FAX: 203-882-6517. Administration FAX: 203-882-6570. Web Site: www.mi.nmfs.gov. *Head Librn,* Steven Pitchford; E-mail: Steven.Pitchford@noaa.gov; *Librn,* Sylvia Feeney; E-mail: Sylvia.Feeney@noaa.gov
Library Holdings: Bk Vols 2,800; Per Subs 15
Special Collections: Food & Agriculture Organization of the United Nations, fisheries items; NOAA Documents; United States Bureau of Fisheries
Function: Res libr
Partic in NOAA Libraries Network; Proquest Dialog
Open Mon-Fri 8-4:30

MONROE

P EDITH WHEELER MEMORIAL LIBRARY*, 733 Monroe Tpk, 06468. SAN 302-2315. Tel: 203-452-2850. FAX: 203-261-3359. Reference E-mail: reference@ewml.org. Web Site: www.ewml.org. *Dir,* Margaret Borchers; E-mail: mborchers@ewml.org; *Adult & Teen Serv,* Lorna Rhyins; E-mail: lrhyins@ewml.org; *Ch Serv,* Michelle Turbak; E-mail: mturbak@ewml.org; Staff 23 (MLS 4, Non-MLS 19)
Founded 1954. Pop 20,000; Circ 176,269
Special Collections: Environmental Resources Information Center; Loveland Newspaper Clippings of Monroe History
Automation Activity & Vendor Info: (Cataloging) SirsiDynix; (Circulation) SirsiDynix; (ILL) SirsiDynix; (OPAC) SirsiDynix; (Serials) SirsiDynix
Wireless access
Partic in Bibliomation Inc
Open Mon & Tues 10-8, Thurs 10-5, Fri 1-5, Sat 10-4
Friends of the Library Group

MOODUS

P EAST HADDAM LIBRARY SYSTEM*, East Haddam Free Public Library, 18 Plains Rd, 06469. (Mail add: PO Box 372, 06469-0372), SAN 302-1211. Tel: 860-873-8248. FAX: 860-873-1269. Web Site: easthaddamlibrarysystem.org. *Dir,* Michael Gilroy; E-mail: mgilroy@easthaddamlibrarysystem.org; Staff 6 (MLS 1, Non-MLS 5)
Founded 1888. Pop 8,880; Circ 2,153
Library Holdings: AV Mats 897; Large Print Bks 289; Bk Vols 18,785; Per Subs 67; Videos 1,214
Subject Interests: Genealogy
Automation Activity & Vendor Info: (Acquisitions) Auto-Graphics, Inc; (Cataloging) Auto-Graphics, Inc; (Circulation) Auto-Graphics, Inc; (Course Reserve) Auto-Graphics, Inc; (ILL) Auto-Graphics, Inc; (Media Booking) Auto-Graphics, Inc; (OPAC) Auto-Graphics, Inc; (Serials) Auto-Graphics, Inc
Wireless access
Function: Homebound delivery serv
Open Mon, Tues & Thurs 10-4, Wed & Fri 10-7, Sat 9-1
Restriction: Non-circulating coll
Friends of the Library Group
Branches: 1
RATHBUN FREE MEMORIAL LIBRARY, 36 Main St, East Haddam, 06423. (Mail add: PO Box G, East Haddam, 06423), SAN 302-122X. Tel: 860-873-8210. FAX: 860-873-3601. *Br Mgr,* Patricia Griswold; E-mail: pgriswold@Rathbun.lioninc.org
Founded 1935. Circ 59,604
Library Holdings: Bk Vols 23,000; Per Subs 68
Special Collections: East Haddam History Coll, clippings, micro
Open Mon, Wed & Fri 10-4, Tues & Thurs 10-7, Sat 9-1
Friends of the Library Group

MOOSUP

P ALDRICH FREE PUBLIC LIBRARY, 299 Main St, 06354. SAN 302-2331. Tel: 860-564-8760. FAX: 860-564-8491. E-mail: info@aldrichlibrary.org. Web Site: aldrichlibrary.org. *Dir,* Jean Jakoboski; *Asst Dir, ILL Librn,* Bonnie Theriault; *Asst Librn,* Arlene Sweet; Staff 5 (Non-MLS 5)
Founded 1896. Pop 15,000; Circ 20,439
Library Holdings: Bk Titles 26,500; Per Subs 32
Automation Activity & Vendor Info: (Circulation) Follett Software
Wireless access
Open Mon, Wed & Fri 2-7:30, Tues & Sat 9-12:30

MORRIS

P MORRIS PUBLIC LIBRARY, Four North St, 06763-1415. (Mail add: PO Box 85, 06763-0085), SAN 302-234X. Tel: 860-567-7440. FAX: 860-567-7432. E-mail: mplstaff@biblio.org. Web Site: www.morrispubliclibrary.net. *Dir,* Elena Granoth; E-mail: egranoth@biblio.org; Staff 4 (Non-MLS 4)
Founded 1900. Pop 2,000; Circ 21,251
Library Holdings: Bk Titles 13,975; Per Subs 30; Talking Bks 343; Videos 468
Automation Activity & Vendor Info: (Cataloging) Bibliomation Inc
Wireless access
Function: 24/7 Electronic res, 24/7 Online cat, Adult bk club, After school storytime, Art exhibits, Audiobks on Playaways & MP3, Audiobks via web, Bk club(s), Children's prog, Computer training, Computers for patron use, E-Readers, Electronic databases & coll, Free DVD rentals, Govt ref serv, Holiday prog, ILL available, Magazines, Museum passes, Music CDs, Online cat, OverDrive digital audio bks, Photocopying/Printing, Preschool outreach, Preschool reading prog, Prog for adults, Prog for children & young adult, Ref & res, Senior outreach, Spoken cassettes & CDs, Story hour, Summer & winter reading prog, Summer reading prog, Winter reading prog
Partic in Bibliomation Inc
Open Tues & Wed 10-8, Thurs & Fri 1-8, Sat 10-3
Friends of the Library Group

MYSTIC

P MYSTIC & NOANK LIBRARY, INC*, 40 Library St, 06355. SAN 302-2358. Tel: 860-536-7721. FAX: 860-536-2350. E-mail: info@mysticnoanklibrary.org. Web Site: www.mysticnoanklibrary.com. *Interim Dir,* Roberta Donahue; E-mail: rdonahue@mysticnoanklibrary.org; Staff 4 (MLS 3, Non-MLS 1)
Founded 1893. Pop 15,000; Circ 83,000
Library Holdings: Audiobooks 1,664; DVDs 1,016; e-books 2,715; Bk Vols 44,746; Per Subs 134; Videos 1,331
Subject Interests: Genealogy, Local hist
Automation Activity & Vendor Info: (Cataloging) SirsiDynix; (Circulation) SirsiDynix
Wireless access
Publications: Annual Report
Partic in Connecticut Library Consortium
Open Mon-Wed 10-9, Thurs-Sat 10-5
Friends of the Library Group

S MYSTIC SEAPORT MUSEUM*, G W Blunt White Library, 75 Greenmanville Ave, 06355-0990. (Mail add: PO Box 6000, 06355-6000), SAN 302-2366. Tel: 860-572-5367. E-mail: collections@mysticseaport.org. Web Site: research.mysticseaport.org. *Dir of Libr,* Paul J O'Pecko; E-mail: paul.opecko@mysticseaport.org; *Research Librn,* Position Currently Open
Founded 1929
Library Holdings: Bk Titles 40,000; Bk Vols 70,000; Per Subs 404
Special Collections: American Maritime Studies, ms. Oral History
Wireless access
Partic in Council of Connecticut Academic Library Directors
Open Wed 2-5, Thurs 10-5, Fri 10-3
Friends of the Library Group

NAUGATUCK

S LANXESS SOLUTIONS US INC*, Virtual Information Services-Library, 12 Spencer St, 06770. SAN 302-2218. Tel: 203-714-8692. Web Site: techcenter.lanxess.com/scp/americas/en/libscp/article.jsp?docId=86489. *Libr Mgr,* Patricia Ann Harmon; Staff 1 (MLS 1)
Founded 1914
Special Collections: ACS: American Chemical Society eJournals; Elsevier: Science Direct eJournals; Encyclopedia of Polymer Science & Engineering; Kirk-Othmer Encyclopedia of Chemical-Technology; Knovel, eBooks and database; Wiley eJournals
Subject Interests: Chem, Engr, Plastics
Wireless access
Partic in Connecticut Library Consortium
Restriction: Employees only

P HOWARD WHITTEMORE MEMORIAL LIBRARY*, 243 Church St, 06770-4198. SAN 336-3090. Tel: 203-729-4591. FAX: 203-723-1820. Web Site: www.whittemorelibrary.org. *Dir,* Jocelyn Miller; Staff 2 (MLS 2)
Founded 1894. Pop 31,862; Circ 83,696. Sal $414,443 (Prof $81,627)
Library Holdings: Audiobooks 615; CDs 300; DVDs 1,535; Electronic Media & Resources 31; Bk Vols 62,154; Per Subs 56; Videos 400
Subject Interests: Art & archit, Connecticut, Local hist
Automation Activity & Vendor Info: (Acquisitions) Bibliomation Inc; (Cataloging) Bibliomation Inc; (Circulation) Bibliomation Inc; (OPAC) Bibliomation Inc
Wireless access
Partic in Bibliomation Inc; Connecticut Library Consortium
Open Mon & Thurs 10-6, Tues & Wed 10-8, Fri & Sat 10-2
Friends of the Library Group

NEW BRITAIN

C CENTRAL CONNECTICUT STATE UNIVERSITY*, Elihu Burritt Library, 1615 Stanley St, 06050. SAN 302-2382. Tel: 860-832-2055. Circulation Tel: 860-832-3410. Interlibrary Loan Service Tel: 860-832-3408. Reference Tel: 860-832-2060. FAX: 860-832-2118. Web Site: library.ccsu.edu. *Dir, Libr Serv,* Carl Antonucci; Tel: 860-832-2099, E-mail: antonucci@ccsu.edu; *Head, Access Serv & ILL,* Kim Farrington; Tel: 860-832-3403, E-mail: farringtonk@ccsu.edu; *Head, Acq, Head, Ser,* Kristin D'Amato; Tel: 860-832-2074, E-mail: damatok@ccsu.edu; *Head, Info Syst,* Dana Hanford; Tel: 860-832-2058, E-mail: hanfordd@ccsu.edu; *Head, Ref & Instruction,* Susan Slaga-Metiver; Tel: 860-832-2095, E-mail: slagas@ccsu.edu; *Head, Spec Coll,* Ewa Wolynska; Tel: 860-832-2086, E-mail: wolynska@ccsu.edu; *Assessment Librn, Ref & Instruction,* Martha Kruy; Tel: 860-832-2063, E-mail: mkruy@ccsu.edu; *Digital Res Librn,* Sharon Clapp; Tel: 860-832-2059, E-mail: sclapp@ccsu.edu; *Outreach & Spec Coll Librn, Univ Archivist,* Renata Vickrey; Tel: 860-832-2085, E-mail: vickreyr@ccsu.edu; *Ref & Instruction Librn,* Jillian Maynard; Tel: 860-832-2068, E-mail: j.maynard@ccsu.edu; *Ref & Instruction Librn,* Briana McGuckin; E-mail: bmcguckin@ccsu.edu; *Assoc Cataloging Librn,* Steven Bernstein; Tel: 860-832-2079, E-mail: bernsteinstj@ccsu.edu. Subject Specialists: *Govt doc,* Martha Kruy; Staff 16 (MLS 16)
Founded 1849. Enrl 9,539; Fac 434; Highest Degree: Doctorate
Library Holdings: AV Mats 11,203; CDs 4,037; DVDs 1,854; e-books 433; e-journals 64,644; Bk Vols 733,377; Per Subs 1,592
Special Collections: Bruce Rogers Coll; Daniel Webster Coll; Elihu Burritt Coll, bks, ms; Frederic W Goudy Coll; GLBTQ Archives; John J Woodcock Lemon Law Archives; Polish Heritage Coll; Walter Hart Blumenthal Coll; William A O'Neill Gubernatorial Records & Oral History Interviews; World's Fairs Coll. US Document Depository
Subject Interests: Educ, Humanities
Automation Activity & Vendor Info: (Acquisitions) Innovative Interfaces, Inc; (Cataloging) Innovative Interfaces, Inc; (Circulation) Innovative Interfaces, Inc; (Course Reserve) Innovative Interfaces, Inc; (OPAC) Innovative Interfaces, Inc; (Serials) Innovative Interfaces, Inc
Wireless access
Publications: CCSU Library (Newsletter)
Partic in Connecticut Library Consortium; LYRASIS; OCLC Online Computer Library Center, Inc; Westchester Academic Library Directors Organization
Open Mon-Thurs 8-8, Fri 8-4, Sat 9-4, Sun 2-8

S NEW BRITAIN MUSEUM OF AMERICAN ART LIBRARY*, 56 Lexington St, 06052. SAN 371-232X. Tel: 860-229-0257. FAX: 860-229-3445. E-mail: nbmaa@nbmaa.org. Web Site: www.nbmaa.org. *Colls Mgr,* Keith Gervase; E-mail: collections@nbmaa.org
Founded 1903
Library Holdings: Bk Vols 4,000
Function: Ref serv available
Restriction: Open by appt only

P NEW BRITAIN PUBLIC LIBRARY*, 20 High St, 06051. SAN 336-3155. Tel: 860-224-3155. Web Site: www.nbpl.info. *Dir,* Patricia Rutkowski; Tel: 860-224-3155, Ext 113, E-mail: prutkowski@nbpl.info; *Asst Dir,* Marian D Farley; Tel: 860-224-3155, Ext 114, E-mail: mfarley@nbpl.info; *Head, Adult Serv,* Arnie Lemire; Tel: 860-224-3155, Ext 140, E-mail: alemire@nbpl.info; *Head, Children's Servx,* Amy Litke; Tel: 860-224-3155, Ext 117, E-mail: alitke@nbpl.info; *Head, Tech Serv,* Barbara Morse; Tel: 860-224-3155, Ext 126, E-mail: bmorse@nbpl.info; *Teen Librn,* Emily Mulvey; Tel: 860-224-3155, Ext 119, E-mail: emulvey@nbpl.info; Staff 47 (MLS 14, Non-MLS 33)
Founded 1858. Pop 71,832; Circ 406,067
Library Holdings: Bk Vols 229,245; Per Subs 297
Special Collections: Elihu Burritt, bks, ms, pamphlets; Materials in other Languages, Polish & Spanish
Subject Interests: Local hist
Automation Activity & Vendor Info: (Circulation) SirsiDynix
Wireless access
Publications: Monthly Calendar
Partic in Connecticut Library Consortium
Open Mon-Thurs 9-9, Fri 9-5, Sat 10-5
Friends of the Library Group
Branches: 1
JEFFERSON, 140 Horseplain Rd, 06053, SAN 336-321X. Tel: 860-225-4700. FAX: 860-832-9521. *Br Coordr,* Kathi Holly; E-mail: kholly@nbpl.info
Library Holdings: Bk Vols 16,500
Open Mon & Tues 9-6, Wed & Thurs 9-5, Fri 9-3
Friends of the Library Group

S POLISH GENEALOGICAL SOCIETY OF CONNECTICUT & THE NORTHWEST, INC, Archive & Resource Center, Eight Lyle Rd, 06053-2104. SAN 370-6974. Tel: 860-229-8873. E-mail: info@pgsctne.org. Web Site: www.pgsctne.org/resources-and-links. *Archivist, Pres,* Jonathan D Shea; Staff 1 (MLS 1)
Founded 1984
Library Holdings: Bk Vols 3,500; Per Subs 19
Special Collections: Cartography Coll; Cemetery Inscriptions; Marriage & Immigrant Origins Databases; Polish & Lithuanian Telephone Directories; Polish Diocesan Church Directories; Polish-American Church Histories
Friends of the Library Group

NEW CANAAN

P NEW CANAAN LIBRARY*, 151 Main St, 06840. SAN 302-2439. Tel: 203-594-5000. Circulation Tel: 203-594-5001. Information Services Tel: 203-594-5003. FAX: 203-594-5026. Toll Free FAX: 866-245-6033. Reference E-mail: onlineref@newcanaanlibrary.org. Web Site: newcanaanlibrary.org. *Exec Dir,* Lisa Oldham; Tel: 203-594-5005, E-mail: loldham@newcanaanlibrary.org; *Dir of Develop,* Ellen Crovatto; Tel: 203-594-5025, E-mail: ecrovatto@newcanaanlibrary.org; *Head, Children's Servx, Manager, Family Services,* Cheryl Capitani; Tel: 203-594-5011; *Head, Infrastructure & Content,* Jeff Zaino; Tel: 203-594-5010, E-mail: jzaino@newcanaanlibrary.org; *Mgr, Ad Serv, Programming,* Anthony Marrocolla; Tel: 203-594-5010, E-mail: amarrocolla@newcanaanlibrary.org; *Colls Mgr,* Lauren Phillips; Tel: 203-594-5070, E-mail: lphillips@newcanaanlibrary.org; Staff 23 (MLS 12, Non-MLS 11)
Founded 1877. Pop 19,395; Circ 478,791
Library Holdings: AV Mats 25,000; Bk Vols 157,200; Per Subs 345
Special Collections: Broadcast Journalism (Richard Salant Room with Eric Sevareid Coll); European Art, 476-1900 (Arturo Alfandari Coll); Gardening/Landscaping (Susan McDaniel Coll); Howard Schless Medieval Coll; Nature (Alice A & Helen C Bristow Coll); World War II (Chester Hansen Coll)
Subject Interests: Art & archit, Natural sci, Popular
Automation Activity & Vendor Info: (Acquisitions) Innovative Interfaces, Inc; (Cataloging) OCLC; (Circulation) Innovative Interfaces, Inc; (Course Reserve) Innovative Interfaces, Inc; (ILL) Innovative Interfaces, Inc; (Media Booking) Innovative Interfaces, Inc; (OPAC) Innovative Interfaces, Inc; (Serials) Innovative Interfaces, Inc
Wireless access
Publications: Beyond the Best Seller (Monthly bulletin); New Canaan Library News (Newsletter)
Special Services for the Blind - Closed circuit TV magnifier; Reader equip
Open Mon-Thurs 9-8, Fri & Sat 9-5, Sun 12-5

S NEW CANAAN MUSEUM & HISTORICAL SOCIETY LIBRARY*, 13 Oenoke Ridge, 06840. SAN 302-2420. Tel: 203-966-1776. E-mail: info@nchistory.org. Web Site: www.nchistory.org. *Exec Dir,* Nancy Geary; E-mail: ngeary@nchistory.org; *Asst Dir,* Donna Dearth; E-mail: ddearth@nchistory.org; *Librn & Archivist,* Michael Murphy; E-mail: mmurphy@nchistory.org
Founded 1889
Library Holdings: Bk Titles 6,000; Per Subs 30
Special Collections: Historical Society Biographical & Genealogical Index, 1640-present, filecards; Historical Society Newspaper File & Subject Index, 1868-present, bd vols, microfilm; Hoyt Nursery Coll; Noyes Family; Paul Prindle FASG (Weed Coll); Price & Lee New Canaan Darien Directories, original to 1903 & current; Silliman Coll
Subject Interests: Art & archit, Costume design, Genealogy
Wireless access
Publications: A Child's Walking Tour of New Canaan; A Guide to God's Acre; A New Canaan Private in the Civil War (Letters of Justus M Silliman, 17th Connecticut Volunteers); Annuals; John Rogers & the Rogers Groups; Mary J Kelley & the Little Red Schoolhouse; My Impressions of the Hour - The Diary of an Early New Canaan Teacher; New Canaan; New Canaan, Texture of a Community, 1950-2000; Philip Johnson in New Canaan; The Hanford Silliman House; The Merritt Parkway; Wampum to Wall Street
Open Tues-Fri 9:30-4:30, Sat 10-2
Restriction: Open to pub for ref only

M SILVER HILL HOSPITAL*, Charles P Neumann MD Medical & Patient Library, 208 Valley Rd, 06840. Tel: 203-966-3561, Ext 2270. FAX: 203-801-2388. Web Site: www.silverhillhospital.org. *Dir, Libr Serv,* Anne Romano; E-mail: aromano@silverhillhospital.org
Library Holdings: Bk Titles 1,110; Per Subs 157
Restriction: Not open to pub

NEW FAIRFIELD

P NEW FAIRFIELD FREE PUBLIC LIBRARY*, Two Brush Hill Rd, 06812. SAN 302-2463. Tel: 203-312-5679. FAX: 203-312-5685. E-mail: nfl@newfairfieldlibrary.org. Web Site: www.newfairfieldlibrary.org. *Libr Dir,* Linda Fox; E-mail: lfox@newfairfieldlibrary.org; Staff 4 (MLS 4)
Founded 1897. Pop 14,338
Library Holdings: Audiobooks 2,885; DVDs 5,568; Electronic Media & Resources 7; Large Print Bks 1,215; Bk Vols 38,959; Per Subs 76
Special Collections: Census Records
Subject Interests: Local hist
Automation Activity & Vendor Info: (Acquisitions) Auto-Graphics, Inc; (Cataloging) Auto-Graphics, Inc; (Circulation) Auto-Graphics, Inc; (ILL) Auto-Graphics, Inc; (OPAC) Auto-Graphics, Inc; (Serials) Auto-Graphics, Inc
Wireless access
Function: 24/7 Electronic res, 24/7 Online cat, Activity rm, Audiobks on Playaways & MP3, Audiobks via web, Bks on CD, Children's prog, Computers for patron use, Electronic databases & coll, Free DVD rentals, Genealogy discussion group, Holiday prog, Homebound delivery serv, ILL available, Internet access, Magazines, Mail & tel request accepted, Meeting rooms, Microfiche/film & reading machines, Movies, Museum passes, Music CDs, Online cat, Online ref, OverDrive digital audio bks, Photocopying/Printing, Preschool outreach, Printer for laptops & handheld devices, Prog for adults, Prog for children & young adult, Ref serv available, Scanner, Spoken cassettes & CDs, Story hour, Summer reading prog, Tax forms, Wheelchair accessible
Special Services for the Blind - Bks on CD; Home delivery serv; HP Scan Jet with photo-finish software; Large print bks; Playaways (bks on MP3)
Friends of the Library Group

NEW HARTFORD

P BAKERVILLE LIBRARY, Six Maple Hollow Rd, 06057. SAN 302-2471. Tel: 860-482-8806. FAX: 860-482-8806. E-mail: info@bakervillelibrary.org. Web Site: www.bakervillelibrary.org. *Librn,* Philip Armentrout
Founded 1949. Pop 5,810
Library Holdings: Bk Titles 14,500; Per Subs 39
Special Collections: Bicentennial of the Constitution Bookshelf
Subject Interests: Agr, Art, Gardening
Automation Activity & Vendor Info: (Cataloging) Follett Software; (Circulation) Follett Software
Publications: Friends of Bakerville Library (Newsletter)
Partic in Region I Coop Libr Servs Unit
Open Mon & Wed-Fri 2-6, Tues 10-8, Sat 9-2
Friends of the Library Group

P LICIA & MASON BEEKLEY COMMUNITY LIBRARY*, Ten Central Ave, 06057. (Mail add: PO Box 247, 06057), SAN 302-248X. Tel: 860-379-7235. FAX: 860-379-5806. E-mail: staff@beekleylibrary.org. Web Site: www.beekleylibrary.org. *Libr Dir,* David MacHenry; *Asst Dir,* Karin Schneider; *Ch,* Nicole Misko; *ILL Librn,* Valerie Berlin; *Libr Asst,* Peggy Grohs; Staff 4 (Non-MLS 4)
Founded 1906. Pop 6,700
Library Holdings: Audiobooks 799; CDs 2,181; DVDs 3,700; Large Print Bks 681; Bk Titles 48,225; Bk Vols 49,362; Per Subs 63; Videos 278
Automation Activity & Vendor Info: (Acquisitions) Follett Software; (Cataloging) Follett Software; (Circulation) Follett Software; (Serials) Follett Software
Wireless access
Function: Audio & video playback equip for onsite use, Bks on cassette, Bks on CD, Children's prog, Computers for patron use, Family literacy, For res purposes, Free DVD rentals, Home delivery & serv to seniorr ctr & nursing homes, Homebound delivery serv, ILL available, Instruction & testing, Internet access, Large print keyboards, Magnifiers for reading, Museum passes, Music CDs, Online cat, Photocopying/Printing, Prog for adults, Prog for children & young adult, Ref serv available, Spoken cassettes & CDs, Story hour, Summer reading prog, Tax forms, Telephone ref, VHS videos, Wheelchair accessible
Publications: Program Brochures (Library handbook)
Partic in Bibliomation Inc
Special Services for the Deaf - Closed caption videos
Special Services for the Blind - Assistive/Adapted tech devices, equip & products; Bks on cassette; Bks on CD; Cassette playback machines; Closed circuit TV magnifier; Large print bks; Magnifiers; Talking bks
Open Mon 12-6, Tues & Thurs 10-8, Wed & Fri 10-6, Sat 9-3 (9-12 Summer)
Friends of the Library Group

NEW HAVEN

CR ALBERTUS MAGNUS COLLEGE*, Rosary Hall Library, 700 Prospect St, 06511. SAN 302-2498. Tel: 203-773-8511. FAX: 203-773-8588. E-mail: library@albertus.edu. Reference E-mail: refdesk@albertus.edu. Web Site: albertus.libguides.com/home. *Dir,* Anne Leeney-Panagrossi; E-mail: apanagrossi@albertus.edu; *Asst Dir, Tech Serv Librn,* Joanne Day; E-mail: jday@albertus.edu; *Head, Ref,* John McCann; E-mail: jmccann@albertus.edu; *Emerging Tech Librn,* Eileen Bujalski; Tel: 203-773-8594, E-mail: ebujalski@albertus.edu; *ILL/Ser & Media Coordr,*

Patricia Dawson; Tel: 203-672-6650, E-mail: pdawson@albertus.edu; Staff 10 (MLS 5, Non-MLS 5)
Founded 1925. Enrl 2,157; Highest Degree: Master
Library Holdings: Bk Vols 103,994; Per Subs 588
Special Collections: Donald Grant Mitchell Coll; Louis Imogen Guiney Coll; Samuel Flagg Bemis Coll
Automation Activity & Vendor Info: (Acquisitions) Ex Libris Group; (Cataloging) Ex Libris Group; (Circulation) Ex Libris Group; (OPAC) Ex Libris Group; (Serials) Ex Libris Group
Wireless access
Partic in LYRASIS
Open Mon-Thurs 8am-11pm, Fri 8am-9pm, Sat 10-6, Sun 1-9

SR BLESSED MICHAEL MCGIVNEY PILGRIMAGE CENTER*, (Formerly Knights of Columbus Supreme Council Archives), One State St, 06511-6702. SAN 372-6126. Tel: 203-752-4578. Web Site: www.kofcmuseum.org, www.michaelmcgivneycenter.org/mmc/en/explore/archives.html. *Archivist,* VivianLea Solek; E-mail: vivianlea.solek@kofc.org; Staff 1 (MLS 1)
Founded 1981
Special Collections: Christopher Columbus Coll, archival mats, bks; Knights of Columbus Supreme Council Archives, archival mats, bks, recs
Restriction: Open by appt only

G THE CONNECTICUT AGRICULTURAL EXPERIMENT STATION*, Thomas B Osborne Library, 123 Huntington St, 06511-2000. (Mail add: PO Box 1106, 06504-1106), SAN 302-2528. Tel: 203-974-8447. Administration Tel: 203-974-8500. Toll Free Tel: 877-855-2237 (CT only). FAX: 203-974-8502. Web Site: portal.ct.gov/caes. *Info Officer,* Vickie Marie Bomba-Lewandoski; E-mail: Vickie.Bomba-Lewandoski@ct.gov
Founded 1875
Library Holdings: Bk Vols 11,000; Per Subs 500
Subject Interests: Analytical chem, Biochem, Climatology, Ecology, Entomology, Environ studies, Forestry, Genetics, Hort, Plant pathology, Tobacco
Automation Activity & Vendor Info: (OPAC) Follett Software
Wireless access

J GATEWAY COMMUNITY COLLEGE LIBRARY & LEARNING COMMONS*, 20 Church St, 06510. SAN 302-2617. Tel: 203-285-2057. FAX: 203-285-2055. E-mail: library@gatewayct.edu. Web Site: www.gatewayct.edu/library-home. *Dir, Libr Serv,* Dr Clara Ogbaa; Tel: 203-285-2058, E-mail: cogbaa@gwcc.commnet.edu; *Head, Ref,* Martha Lipowski; Tel: 203-285-2053, E-mail: mlipowski@gwcc.commnet.edu; *Cataloger/Ref Librn,* Michael Cifferelli; Tel: 203-285-2052, E-mail: mcifferelli@gwcc.commmnet.edu; *Emerging Tech Librn,* Jainxin Yang; Tel: 203-285-2158, E-mail: jyang@gwcc.commnet.edu; *Mkt Librn, Outreach Librn,* Shauna DeStefano; Tel: 203-285-2059, E-mail: sdestefano@gwcc.commnet.edu; *Coordr, Info Literacy,* Todd Hampton; Tel: 203-285-2615, E-mail: thampton@gwcc.commnet.edu; Staff 7 (MLS 6, Non-MLS 1)
Founded 1968. Enrl 3,690; Highest Degree: Associate
Library Holdings: Bk Vols 53,000; Per Subs 350
Automation Activity & Vendor Info: (Acquisitions) Ex Libris Group; (Cataloging) Ex Libris Group; (Circulation) Ex Libris Group; (Course Reserve) Ex Libris Group; (ILL) OCLC; (OPAC) Ex Libris Group; (Serials) Ex Libris Group
Wireless access
Partic in Connecticut Library Consortium
Open Mon-Thurs 8-8, Fri 8-5, Sat 8-Noon

Departmental Libraries:

NORTH HAVEN CAMPUS, 88 Bassett Rd, North Haven, 06473, SAN 377-7650. Tel: 203-285-2340. FAX: 203-285-2342. *Dir,* Michele Cone
Open Mon-Thurs 8-8, Fri 8-3

P NEW HAVEN FREE PUBLIC LIBRARY*, Ives Main, 133 Elm St, 06510. SAN 336-3244. Tel: 203-946-8130. Reference Tel: 203-946-8130, Ext 101. FAX: 203-946-8140. TDD: 203-946-6200. E-mail: refdesk@nhfpl.org. Web Site: nhfpl.org. *City Librn & Exec Dir,* John Jessen; Tel: 203-946-8124, E-mail: jjessen@nhfpl.org; *Dep Dir,* Luis Chavez-Brumell; Tel: 203-946-8130, Ext 318, E-mail: Lchavez-Brumell@nhfpl.org; *Pub Serv Adminr, Adult Serv,* Gina Bingham; Tel: 203-946-8130, Ext 216, E-mail: gbindham@nhfpl.org; *Pub Serv Adminr, Youth Serv,* Susan Totter; Tel: 203-946-8139, E-mail: stotter@nhfpl.org; *Pub Serv Adminr,* Sharon Lovett-Graff; Tel: 203-946-7091, E-mail: slovett-graff@nhfpl.org; Staff 75 (MLS 33, Non-MLS 42)
Founded 1887. Pop 130,850; Circ 200,000
Automation Activity & Vendor Info: (Cataloging) Innovative Interfaces, Inc; (Circulation) Innovative Interfaces, Inc
Wireless access
Function: 24/7 Electronic res, 24/7 Online cat, 3D Printer, Adult bk club, Adult literacy prog, Archival coll, Art exhibits, Audiobks on Playaways & MP3, Audiobks via web, AV serv, Bk club(s), Bks on CD, Computer training, Computers for patron use, Electronic databases & coll, Family literacy, For res purposes, Internet access, Makerspace, Meeting rooms, Microfiche/film & reading machines, Movies, Museum passes, Music CDs, Online cat, OverDrive digital audio bks, Photocopying/Printing, Prog for adults, Prog for children & young adult, Ref & res, Scanner, Senior computer classes, STEM programs, Story hour, Summer reading prog
Partic in Connecticut Library Consortium
Open Mon-Thurs 10-8, Fri & Sat 10-5

Branches: 4

FAIR HAVEN, 182 Grand Ave, 06513, SAN 336-3368. Tel: 203-946-8115. *Br Mgr,* Kirk Morrison; Tel: 203-946-8116, E-mail: kmorrison@nhfpl.org; Staff 5 (MLS 3, Non-MLS 2)
Library Holdings: Bk Vols 25,140
Open Mon, Tues & Thurs (Winter) 10-6, Wed 12-8, Sat 1-5; Mon, Tues & Thurs (Summer) 10-6, Wed 12-8, Fri 1-5
Friends of the Library Group

MITCHELL BRANCH, 37 Harrison St, 06515, SAN 336-3422. Tel: 203-946-8117. *Br Mgr,* Marian Huggins; Tel: 203-946-6514, E-mail: mhuggins@nhfpl.org; Staff 6 (MLS 2, Non-MLS 4)
Library Holdings: Bk Vols 51,000
Open Mon, Tues & Thurs (Winter) 10-6, Wed 12-8, Sat 1-5; Mon, Tues & Thurs (Summer) 10-6, Wed 12-8, Fri 1-5
Friends of the Library Group

STETSON BRANCH, 200 Dixwell Ave, 06511, SAN 336-3457. Tel: 203-946-8119. FAX: 203-946-6782. *Br Mgr,* Diane Brown; Tel: 203-946-6786, E-mail: dbrown@nhfpl.org; Staff 5 (MLS 2, Non-MLS 3)
Function: ILL available

WILSON BRANCH, 303 Washington St, 06511. Tel: 203-946-2228. FAX: 203-946-6540. *Library Contact,* Bill Armstrong; E-mail: warmstrong@nhfpl.org
Library Holdings: Bk Vols 30,000
Open Mon, Tues & Thurs (Winter) 10-6, Wed 12-8, Sat 1-5; Mon, Tues & Thurs (Summer) 10-6, Wed 12-8, Fri 1-5

Bookmobiles: 1

S NEW HAVEN MUSEUM & HISTORICAL SOCIETY*, Whitney Library, 114 Whitney Ave, 06510-1025. SAN 302-2579. Tel: 203-562-4183. FAX: 203-562-2002. E-mail: library@newhavenmuseum.org. Web Site: newhavenmuseum.org/the-whitney-library. *Librn,* Ed Surato; Tel: 203-562-4183, Ext 115; *Ref Librn,* Bonnie L Campbell; *Ref Librn,* Frances H Skelton; Staff 1 (MLS 1)
Founded 1863
Library Holdings: Bk Vols 30,000; Per Subs 20
Special Collections: Genealogy (Lewis, Sedgwick & Sperry Family Colls), ms; Local History (business, civic & religious organizations)
Subject Interests: Genealogy
Wireless access
Publications: A Guide to the Manuscripts & Archives in the Whitney Library of the New Haven Colony Historical Society; The Seton Guide to Business & Industrial Holdings in the Whitney Library
Open Tues-Fri 10-5, Sat 12-5
Friends of the Library Group

S PLANNED PARENTHOOD OF SOUTHERN NEW ENGLAND, 345 Whitney Ave, 06511. SAN 376-1932. Tel: 203-865-5158. FAX: 203-752-2914. E-mail: education@ppsne.org. Web Site: plannedparenthood.org. *Educ Mgr,* Sarah Gannon
Library Holdings: Bk Vols 4,600

C SOUTHERN CONNECTICUT STATE UNIVERSITY*, Hilton C Buley Library, 501 Crescent St, 06515. SAN 302-2625. Tel: 203-392-5750. Circulation Tel: 203-392-5756. Interlibrary Loan Service Tel: 203-392-7038. Reference Tel: 203-392-5732. Administration Tel: 203-392-5742. Automation Services Tel: 203-392-5734. FAX: 203-392-5775. Web Site: libguides.southernct.edu. *Dir,* Olga Ogbaa; E-mail: ogbaac1@southernct.edu; *Head, Access Serv,* Jamie Aschenbach; Tel: 203-392-5768, E-mail: aschenbachj1@southernct.edu; *Head, Ref,* Winnie Shyam; Tel: 203-392-5762, E-mail: shyamw1@southernct.edu; *Head, Tech Serv,* Cindy Schofield-Bodt; Tel: 203-392-5778, E-mail: schofieldbc1@southernct.edu; *Acq & Coll Develop Librn,* David Feinmark; Tel: 203-392-5731, E-mail: feinmarkd1@southernct.edu; *Archives Librn, Spec Coll Librn,* Paul Holmer; Tel: 203-392-5746, E-mail: holmerp1@southernct.edu; Staff 23 (MLS 20, Non-MLS 3)
Founded 1895. Enrl 12,143; Fac 541; Highest Degree: Doctorate
Library Holdings: Bk Titles 400,000; Bk Vols 600,000; Per Subs 1,450
Special Collections: Children's Books (Caroline Sherwin Bailey Historical Coll), early Am textbks; Connecticut books, pamphlets, photogs, maps (Connecticut Room). US Document Depository
Subject Interests: Educ, Info sci, Libr sci, Women's studies
Automation Activity & Vendor Info: (Acquisitions) Innovative Interfaces, Inc; (Cataloging) Innovative Interfaces, Inc; (Circulation) Innovative Interfaces, Inc; (ILL) Innovative Interfaces, Inc; (OPAC) Innovative Interfaces, Inc; (Serials) Innovative Interfaces, Inc
Wireless access
Publications: Buley Bulletin (Newsletter)
Partic in LYRASIS

C YALE UNIVERSITY LIBRARY*, 120 High St, 06511. (Mail add: PO Box 208240, 06520-8240), SAN 336-3546. Circulation Tel: 203-432-1775. Interlibrary Loan Service Tel: 203-432-1788. Administration Tel: 203-432-1810. Administration FAX: 203-432-1294. E-mail: askyalelibrary@yale.edu. Reference E-mail: askyale@gmail.com. Web Site: web.library.yale.edu. *Deputy Provost, Univ Librn,* Susan Gibbons; Tel: 203-432-1818, E-mail: susan.gibbons@yale.edu; Staff 233 (MLS 158, Non-MLS 75)
Founded 1701. Enrl 17,046; Fac 1,736; Highest Degree: Doctorate
Library Holdings: Bk Vols 12,025,695; Per Subs 76,022
Special Collections: Beinecke Rare Book & Manuscript Library; Manuscript & Archives, see also School & Department Libraries
Automation Activity & Vendor Info: (Acquisitions) Ex Libris Group; (Cataloging) Ex Libris Group; (Circulation) Ex Libris Group; (Course Reserve) Ex Libris Group; (OPAC) Ex Libris Group; (Serials) Ex Libris Group
Wireless access
Partic in Northeast Research Libraries Consortium; OCLC Online Computer Library Center, Inc; OCLC Research Library Partnership
Open Mon-Fri 8-5

Departmental Libraries:

AMERICAN ORIENTAL SOCIETY, Sterling Memorial Library, Rm 329, 120 High St, 06520, SAN 336-3635. Web Site: www.americanorientalsociety.org.
Library Holdings: Bk Vols 22,774; Per Subs 250
Subject Interests: Hist, Lang arts, Lit
Partic in Research Libraries Information Network
Publications: American Oriental Series (89 vols); Journal of the American Oriental Society
Open Mon-Thurs 8:30am -11:45pm, Fri 8:30-4:45, Sat 10-4:45, Sun Noon-11:45

ASTRONOMY, Steinbach Hall, 56 Hillhouse Ave, 06511. (Mail add: PO Box 208101, 06520-8101), SAN 336-4356. Tel: 203-432-3000. FAX: 203-432-5048. Web Site: astronomy.yale.edu. *Librn,* Kim Monocchi; E-mail: kim.monocchi@yale.edu. Subject Specialists: *Astronomy,* Kim Monocchi
Library Holdings: Bk Vols 38,000
Special Collections: Astronomy Slides; Domestic & Foreign Observatory Publications
Subject Interests: Astronomy, Astrophysics, Math, Physics

BABYLONIAN COLLECTION, Sterling Memorial Library, 3rd Flr, 120 High St, 06520. (Mail add: PO Box 208240, 06520-8240), SAN 336-3724. Tel: 203-432-1837. E-mail: babylonian.collection@yale.edu. Web Site: babylonian-collection.yale.edu. *Assoc Curator,* Agnete Wisti Lassen; E-mail: agnete.lassen@yale.edu; Staff 3 (MLS 1, Non-MLS 2)
Founded 1911
Library Holdings: AV Mats 10,000; Bk Titles 12,000; Bk Vols 20,000; Per Subs 42
Special Collections: Cuneiform Tablets & Cylinder Seals
Subject Interests: Ancient & Near Eastern studies, Ancient hist, Archaeology, Art hist, Lit
Function: Online cat
Partic in Research Libraries Information Network
Publications: Catalogue of the Babylonian Collections at Yale
Restriction: Non-circulating

BEINECKE RARE BOOK & MANUSCRIPT LIBRARY, 121 Wall St, 06511. (Mail add: PO Box 208330, 06520-8330), SAN 336-3759. Tel: 203-432-2972, 203-432-2977. FAX: 203-432-4047. E-mail: beinecke.library@yale.edu. Web Site: beinecke.library.yale.edu, web.library.yale.edu/building/beinecke-library. *Dir,* Edwin Schroeder; Tel: 203-432-2959, E-mail: edwin.schroeder@yale.edu; *Head, Access Serv,* Moira Fitzgerald; Tel: 203-432-2973, E-mail: moira.fitzgerald@yale.edu; *Head, Acq,* Eric Friede; Tel: 203-432-2975, E-mail: eric.friede@yale.edu; *Cataloger, Spec Projects,* Matthew Beacom; Tel: 202-432-4947, E-mail: matthew.beacom@yale.edu; Staff 52 (MLS 29, Non-MLS 23)
Founded 1963
Library Holdings: Bk Vols 575,092
Special Collections: Aldus Manutius; Arthus Davison Ficke; Asch; Barrett Clark; Barrie; Baskerville; Baskin; Boccaccio; Boswell; Browning; Bruce Rogers; Bryon; Buchan; Burney; Cabell; Carlyle; Coleridge; Conrad; Cooper; D H Lawrence; David Low; Defoe; Dickens; Dorothy Richardson; Dryden; Edith Wharton; Edmund Wilson; Eleanor Wylie; Erza Stiles; Ezra Pound; F T Marinetti; Fielding; Garrick; George Eliot; George MacDonald; George Moore; Gertrude Stein; Gissing; Goethe; Hardy; Herman Hagedorn; Hermann Broch; Hilda Doolittle; Hogg; Hutchins & Neith Boyce Hapgood; James Gates Percival; James Purdy; James Weldon Johnson; Jean Giono; Joel Barlow; John Gould Fletcher; John Hersey; Jonathan Edwards; Joseph Ireland; Joyce; Katherine Dreier; Kipling; Kurt & Helen Wolff; Landor; Langston Hughes; Leo Stein; Leonie Adams; Mabel Luhan; MacLeish; Maria Edgeworth; Marquand; Marsden Hartley; Masefield; Matthew Arnold; Mencken; Meredith; Milosz; Milton; Muriel Draper; Norman Douglas; Norman MacLeod; O'Neill; Paul Horgan; Paul Leicester Ford; Pope; Rachel Carson; Rebecca West; Richard Wright; Rilke; Robert Nathan; Robert Penn Warren; Robinson Jeffers; Ruskin; S V Benet; Samuel Johnson; Samuel Richardson; Shakespeare; Sheridan; Sinclair Lewis; Sir Thomas More; Sir Winston Churchill; Spenser; Spinelli Family; Stevenson; Stieglitz; Swinburne; Tennyson; Thackeray; Theatre Guild; Thomas Mann; Tocqueville; Toklas; Trollope; Van Vechten; Vardis Fisher; W R Benet; Walter Crane; Walton; Washington Irving; Whitman; Wilder; William Beckford; William Carlos Williams; William McFee; Wordsworth
Subject Interests: Alchemy, Children's lit, European hist, Hist of sci, Judaica (lit or hist of Jews), Latin Am, Lit, Music, Theol, Travel
Partic in Research Libraries Information Network
Publications: The Yale University Library Gazette
Open Mon 10-7, Tues-Thurs 9-7, Fri 9-5
Restriction: Open to students, fac & staff, Photo ID required for access

CENTER FOR SCIENCE & SOCIAL SCIENCE INFORMATION, Kline Biology Tower, Concourse Level, 219 Prospect St, 06520. (Mail add: PO Box 208111, 06520-8111), SAN 336-447X. Tel: 203-432-3300. Administration Tel: 203-432-3303, 203-432-3304. FAX: 203-432-8979. E-mail: csssi@yale.edu. Web Site: csssi.yale.edu, web.library.yale.edu/building/center-science-and-social-science-information. *Assoc Univ Librn,* Jill Parchuck; E-mail: jill.parchuck@yale.edu; Staff 16 (MLS 7, Non-MLS 9)
Highest Degree: Doctorate
Library Holdings: Bk Vols 150,000
Special Collections: Economic Growth Center Coll; Geology Coll; Roper Center Archive; Social Science Data Archive
Subject Interests: Econ, Finance, Intl relations, Polit sci, Psychol, Sociol
Automation Activity & Vendor Info: (ILL) Ex Libris Group
Function: Doc delivery serv, ILL available, Ref serv available, Res libr, Telephone ref
Open Mon-Thurs (Winter) 8:30am-11pm, Fri 8:30-7, Sat 12-8, Sun 1-11
Restriction: Open to fac, students & qualified researchers, Open to pub for ref only

CLASSICS, Phelps Hall, 344 College St, 5th Flr, 06511. (Mail add: PO Box 208266, 06520-8266), SAN 336-3813. Tel: 203-432-0854, 203-432-1079. Web Site: web.library.yale.edu/classics-library. *Classics Librn,* Colin McCaffrey; Tel: 203-432-8239, E-mail: colin.mccaffrey@yale.edu. Subject Specialists: *Ancient philos, Classics,* Colin McCaffrey; Staff 1 (MLS 1)
Founded 1892. Highest Degree: Doctorate
Library Holdings: Bk Vols 27,000
Subject Interests: Ancient hist, Classics, Greek, Latin, Philology
Function: Specialized serv in classical studies
Restriction: Open to students, fac & staff, Photo ID required for access

THE WILLIAM ROBERTSON COE ORNITHOLOGY LIBRARY, Environmental Science Ctr, Rm 151, 21 Sachem St, 06520. (Mail add: PO Box 208118, 06520-8118), SAN 336-4380. Tel: 203-436-4892. E-mail: ornithology.library@yale.edu. Web Site: peabody.yale.edu/collections/vertebrate-zoology/ornithology. *Librn,* Jorge De Leon; E-mail: jorge.deleon@yale.edu
Founded 1890
Library Holdings: Bk Vols 4,000; Per Subs 300
Open Tues 3-7, Fri 9-7
Restriction: Non-circulating

CM HARVEY CUSHING/JOHN HAY WHITNEY MEDICAL LIBRARY, Sterling Hall of Medicine, 333 Cedar St, 06510. (Mail add: PO Box 208014, 06520-8014), SAN 336-4291. Tel: 203-785-5352. Circulation Tel: 203-785-5354. Information Services Tel: 203-737-4065. FAX: 203-785-5636. E-mail: AskYaleMedicalLibrary@yale.edu. Web Site: library.medicine.yale.edu, web.library.yale.edu/building/medical-library. *Dir,* John Gallagher; Tel: 202-785-5356, E-mail: john.gallagher@yale.edu; *Asst Dir, Tech, Asst Dir, Innovation & User Experience,* Lei Wang; Tel: 203-785-6485, E-mail: lei.wang@yale.edu; *Asst Dir, Res & Educ,* Judy Spak; Tel: 203-737-2961, E-mail: judy.spak@yale.edu; *Coll Develop Librn,* Lindsay Barnett; Tel: 203-785-2883, E-mail: lindsay.barnett@yale.edu; *Web Serv Librn,* Dana Haugh; Tel: 203-785-3969, E-mail: dana.haugh@yale.edu; *Mgr, Libr Syst,* Arthur Belanger; Tel: 203-785-6928, E-mail: arthur.belanger@yale.edu; Staff 41 (MLS 17, Non-MLS 24)
Founded 1814. Enrl 975; Fac 1,304; Highest Degree: Doctorate
Library Holdings: Bk Vols 433,240; Per Subs 2,483
Special Collections: Early Ichthyology (George Milton Smith Coll), bks & per; History of Medicine, Medical Prints & Drawings (Clements C Fry Coll); Weights & Measures (Edward Clark Streeter Coll), artifacts
Subject Interests: Med, Nursing
Partic in National Network of Libraries of Medicine Region 7; Research Libraries Information Network
Publications: Connections
Open Mon-Thurs 7:30am-Midnight, Fri 7:30am-10pm, Sat 10-10, Sun 9:30am-Midnight

DIVINITY SCHOOL LIBRARY, 409 Prospect St, 06511, SAN 336-3902. Tel: 203-432-5274. FAX: 203-432-3906. E-mail: divinity.library@yale.edu. Web Site: web.library.yale.edu/building/divinity-library. *Dir,* Stephen D Crocco; Tel: 203-432-5292, E-mail: stephen.crocco@yale.edu; *Assoc Dir, Access Serv, Assoc Dir, Res & Coll,* Suzanne Estelle-Holmer; Tel: 203-432-6374,

E-mail: suzanne.estelle-holmer@yale.edu; *Spec Coll Librn/Curator, Day Missions Coll,* Christopher J Anderson; Tel: 203-432-5289, E-mail: christopher.j.anderson@yale.edu; Staff 8.5 (MLS 5, Non-MLS 3.5)
Founded 1932. Enrl 367; Fac 34; Highest Degree: Master
Library Holdings: Microforms 270,000; Bk Vols 550,000; Per Subs 1,700
Special Collections: American Home Missionary Society; China Missions; Day Historical Library of Foreign Missions; Ghana Archives of the Basel Mission; Historical Sermons Coll; International Missionary Council & Conference of British Missionary Societies; Jansenism; John R Mott Papers; Kenneth Scott Latourette Papers; Liston Pope Coll of Christian Social Ethics; Methodist Missionary Society; Mircofilm/Fiche Coll-Council for World Mission; Missions Pamphlets; Religious Education Association Archives; Student Volunteer Movement Archives; The United Board for Christian Higher Education in Asia Archives; World Student Christian Federation Archives
Automation Activity & Vendor Info: (Acquisitions) Ex Libris Group
Open Mon-Thurs 8:30am-10:50pm, Fri & Sat 8:30-4:50, Sun 2-10:50

GEOLOGY, 210 Whitney Ave, Rm 328, 06511, SAN 336-4054. Tel: 203-432-3157. Web Site: web.library.yale.edu/building/geology-library. *Libr Support Serv Asst,* Robert Heister; E-mail: robert.heister@yale.edu; Staff 2 (Non-MLS 2)
Library Holdings: Bk Vols 113,840; Per Subs 1,395
Subject Interests: Geochemistry, Geol, Geophysics, Meteorology, Oceanography, Paleontology
Open Mon-Fri 8:30-5

IRVING S GILMORE MUSIC LIBRARY, 120 High St, 06520. (Mail add: PO Box 208240, 06520-8240), SAN 336-4321. Tel: 203-432-0492. Circulation Tel: 203-432-0496. Reference Tel: 203-432-0497. FAX: 203-432-7339. E-mail: musiclibrary@yale.edu. Circulation E-mail: musiccirc@yale.edu. Web Site: web.library.yale.edu/music. *Dir,* Ruthann McTyre; Tel: 203-432-0495, E-mail: ruthann.mctyre@yale.edu; *Ref & Instruction Librn,* Suzanne Eggleston Lovejoy; E-mail: suzanne.lovejoy@yale.edu; *Tech Serv Librn,* Helen Bartlett; Tel: 203-432-0493, E-mail: helen.bartlett@yale.edu; Staff 11 (MLS 5, Non-MLS 6)
Founded 1917
Library Holdings: Bk Vols 139,606
Special Collections: 19th Century American Hymn Tunes Coll; Alec Templeton Papers; Benny Goodman Papers; Carl Ruggles Papers; Charles Ives Papers; David Kraehenbuehl Papers; David Stanley Smith Papers; Deems Taylor Papers; E Robert Schmitz/Pro Musica Society Papers; Franz Schreker Coll; German Theoretical Literature 16th-18th Centuries; Harold Rome Papers; Henry Gilbert Papers; Hershey Kay Papers; Horatio Parker Papers; J Rosamund Johnson Papers; John Kirkpatrick Papers; Karl Weigl Papers; Kay Swift Papers; Kurt Weill & Lotte Lenya Papers; Lehman Engel Papers; Leo Ornstein Coll; Leo Ornstein Papers; Leroy Anderson Papers; Lowell Mason Coll; Mel Powell Papers; Miscellaneous Manuscripts; Newell Jenkins/Clarion Society Papers; Paul Bekker Coll; Paul Hindemith Coll; Quincy Porter Papers; Ralph Kirkpatrick Coll; Robert Shaw Papers; Seymour Shifrin Papers; Stanley Dance Coll; Thomas de Hartmann Coll; Virgil Thomson Coll; Vladimir Horowitz Coll
Partic in OCLC Online Computer Library Center, Inc
Open Mon-Thurs 8:30am-8:45pm, Fri 8:30-4:45, Sat 10-4:45, Sun 1-8:45

CL LILLIAN GOLDMAN LIBRARY YALE LAW SCHOOL, 127 Wall St, 06511. (Mail add: PO Box 208215, 06520-8215), SAN 336-4232. Tel: 203-432-1606. Circulation Tel: 203-432-1608. E-mail: reference.law@yale.edu. Web Site: library.law.yale.edu, web.library.yale.edu/building/law-library. *Librn,* Teresa Miguel; Tel: 203-432-1601, E-mail: teresa.miguel@yale.edu; *Access & Fac Serv Librn,* Julian Aiken; Tel: 203-432-9616, E-mail: julian.aiken@yale.edu; *Emerging Tech Librn,* Jason Eiseman; Tel: 203-432-1600, E-mail: jason.eiseman@yale.edu; *Rare Bk Librn,* Mike Widener; Tel: 203-432-4494, E-mail: mike.widener@yale.edu; *Ref Librn,* Evelyn Ma; Tel: 203-432-7120, E-mail: evelyn.ma@yale.edu; *Ref Librn,* Michael VanderHeijden; Tel: 203-432-4367, E-mail: michael.vanderheijden@yale.edu; *Assoc Law Librn, Res & Instruction Librn,* Julie Krishnaswami; Tel: 203-432-7934, E-mail: julie.krishnaswami@yale.edu; *Assoc Law Librn,* John Nann; Tel: 203-432-1259, E-mail: john.nann@yale.edu; *Assoc Librn, Coll,* Fred Shapiro; Tel: 203-432-4840, E-mail: fred.shapiro@yale.edu; *Assoc Librn, Tech Serv,* Scott Matheson; Tel: 203-432-1603, E-mail: scott.matheson@yale.edu; *Libr Asst,* Alison Burke; Tel: 203-432-1640, E-mail: alison.burke@yale.edu; Staff 17 (MLS 17)
Founded 1834. Enrl 600; Fac 50; Highest Degree: Doctorate
Library Holdings: Bk Vols 1,000,000
Special Collections: American Statute Law (Cole Coll); Blackstone Coll; International Law; Italian Medieval Statutes; Roman Law (Wheeler Coll)
Automation Activity & Vendor Info: (Acquisitions) Innovative Interfaces, Inc; (Cataloging) Innovative Interfaces, Inc; (Circulation) Innovative Interfaces, Inc; (Course Reserve) Innovative Interfaces, Inc; (ILL) Innovative Interfaces, Inc; (Media Booking) Innovative Interfaces, Inc; (OPAC) Innovative Interfaces, Inc; (Serials) Innovative Interfaces, Inc
Partic in Northeast Foreign Law Libraries Cooperative Group; Research Libraries Information Network
Open Mon-Thurs 8am-Midnight, Fri 8am-10pm, Sat 9am-10pm, Sun 9am-Midnight

ROBERT B HAAS FAMILY ARTS LIBRARY, Loria Ctr, 180 York St, 06511. (Mail add: PO Box 208318, 06520-8318), SAN 336-3694. Tel: 203-432-2645. FAX: 203-432-8257. E-mail: art.library@yale.edu. Web Site: web.library.yale.edu/arts, web.library.yale.edu/building/arts-library. *Dir,* Heather Gendron; Tel: 203-432-2642, E-mail: heather.gendron@yale.edu; Staff 9 (MLS 3, Non-MLS 6)
Library Holdings: Bk Vols 500,000
Special Collections: Arts Library Locked Case Coll; Arts of the Book; Faber Birren Coll on Color
Subject Interests: Archit, Art hist, Graphic arts, Painting, Photog, Sculpture
Partic in Research Libraries Information Network
Open Mon-Thurs 8:30am-11pm, Fri 8:30-5, Sat 10-6, Sun 2-11

LIBRARY SHELVING FACILITY, 147 Leeder Hill Rd, Hamden, 06518. Tel: 203-436-9373. Web Site: web.library.yale.edu/departments/lcs. *Dir,* Michael DiMassa; Tel: 203-432-9140, E-mail: michael.dimassa@yale.edu; Staff 2 (Non-MLS 2)
Library Holdings: Bk Titles 2,500,000
Special Collections: Less frequently used research materials from all Yale University Library coll

MATHEMATICS, Leet Oliver Memorial Hall, 12 Hillhouse Ave, 06511, SAN 336-4267. Tel: 203-432-4179. E-mail: mathematics.library@yale.edu. Web Site: guides.library.yale.edu/math, web.library.yale.edu/building/math-library. *Libr Asst,* Christopher Kaminski; E-mail: christopher.kaminski@yale.edu
Library Holdings: Bk Vols 21,000; Per Subs 331
Subject Interests: Math
Open Mon-Fri 8:30-5

REFERENCE LIBRARY, YALE CENTER FOR BRITISH ART, 1080 Chapel St, 06520. (Mail add: PO Box 208280, 06520-8280), SAN 336-3783. Tel: 203-432-2818. FAX: 203-432-7180. Reference E-mail: ycba.reference@yale.edu. Web Site: britishart.yale.edu, web.library.yale.edu/building/yale-center-for-british-art. *Dir,* Courtney Martin; Tel: 203-432-2822, E-mail: ycba.director@yale.edu; *Chief Librn,* Kraig Binkowski; Tel: 203-432-2846, E-mail: kraig.binkowski@yale.edu; *Librn,* Elizabeth Morris; Tel: 203-432-2848, E-mail: elizabeth.morris@yale.edu; *Sr Archivist,* Rachel Chatalbash; Tel: 203-432-8395, E-mail: rachel.chatalbash@yale.edu; *Sr Libr Asst,* Lori Misura; Tel: 203-432-7689, E-mail: lori.misura@yale.edu; Staff 6 (MLS 3, Non-MLS 3)
Founded 1977
Library Holdings: Bk Vols 40,000; Per Subs 80
Special Collections: British Art Photograph Archive; Jennings Album of Historical English Portraits; Sotheby & Christie Catalogs on British Art
Subject Interests: Archit, Art, Hist, Lit, Performing arts
Function: Ref serv available, Res libr
Partic in OCLC Online Computer Library Center, Inc
Open Tues-Sat 10-5, Sun 12-5
Restriction: Non-circulating

STERLING MEMORIAL LIBRARY, 120 High St, 06520. (Mail add: PO Box 208240, 06520-8240), SAN 336-3600. Tel: 203-432-1775. Interlibrary Loan Service Tel: 203-432-1788. Administration Tel: 203-432-1810. FAX: 203-432-1294. Circulation FAX: 203-432-9486. E-mail: askyale@gmail.com. Web Site: web.library.yale.edu/building/sterling-library. *Deputy Provost, Univ Librn,* Susan Gibbons; Tel: 203-432-1818, E-mail: susan.gibbons@yale.edu
Founded 1932
Library Holdings: Bk Vols 3,000,000
Special Collections: American Musical Theater, Civic Repertory Theater & Theater Guild; Antebellum American South & Civil War; Arts of the Book; Babylonian Tablets; Bibliography; Bookplates; British Economic Tracts; Canadian History & Literature (including French Canadian literature); Classical Archaeology; Congregationalism; Connecticut & New England History; Contemporary Medical & Health Care Policy; Economic History; Ethnic (Black) Arts & Letters; Family History; Forestry & Ecology; Futurism; German Literature; Greek & Latin Classics; Historical Sound Recordings; Historiography; Individuals: Henry Ward Beecher Family, Berkeley, Chester Bowles, Edmund Burke, Aaron Burr Family, John Collier (1884-1968), Jerome Frank, Franklin, Gay, Goldsmith, Heine, Edward M House, Ellsworth Huntington, Josephus Flavius, Juvenal, Lafayette, Max Lerner, Lincoln, Lindbergh Family (restricted), Walter Lippman, Malinowski, Marcus Aurelius, O C Marsh, J S Mill, Jedediah & Samuel F B Morse Family, Napoleon, Ouspensky, Philo Judaeus, C Rhodes, Richelieu, Shaw, Silliman Family, Henry L Stimson, Anson Phelps Stokes, Harold Phelps Stokes, Rose Pastor Stokes, William Graham Sumner, Tacitus, Mabel Loomis Todd, Ernst Toller, John Trumbull, Twain, Eli Whitney. Subjects of Special Strength - American & English Literature & History; Italian Literature & Travel; Journalism & Political Writing, 20th Century; Judaica; Latin America; Legal Thought; Maps & Atlases; Modern African History; Naval History; Near East, including Arabic & Sanskrit; Newspapers;

Oxford; Printing History; Scandinavia; Science & Technology, 19th Century; Slavic; Social Sciences; Southeast Asia; Sporting Books; United States Colonial & Progressive Period, Religious History & Contemporary Reform Movements; Urban & Regional Planning; World War I & II Diplomacy; Yale University
Open Mon-Thurs 8:30am-11:45pm, Fri 8:30-4:45, Sat 10-4:45, Sun Noon-11:45

LEWIS WALPOLE LIBRARY, 154 Main St, Farmington, 06032. (Mail add: PO Box 1408, Farmington, 06034), SAN 336-4526. Tel: 860-677-2140. FAX: 860-677-6369. E-mail: walpole@yale.edu. Web Site: walpole.library.yale.edu, web.library.yale.edu/building/lewis-walpole-library. *Exec Dir/Librn,* Nicole Bouche; E-mail: nicole.bouche@yale.edu; *Head, Pub Serv,* Susan Walker; E-mail: susan.walker@yale.edu; *Head, Tech Serv,* Ellen Cordes; E-mail: ellen.cordes@yale.edu; *Curator,* Cynthia Roman; E-mail: cynthia.roman@yale.edu. Subject Specialists: *Drawings, Paintings, Prints,* Cynthia Roman; Staff 11.5 (MLS 5, Non-MLS 6.5)
Library Holdings: Bk Vols 35,000; Per Subs 32
Special Collections: British 18th Century Prints & Drawings; Charles Hanbury Williams (1708-1759) Coll, ms; Horace Walpole (1717-1797) Coll, bks, ms, prints & drawings, fine & decorative arts; William Hogarth (1696-1764) Coll, prints
Subject Interests: 18th Century Britain
Function: Archival coll, Res libr
Restriction: Non-circulating, Open by appt only

S YOUNG MEN'S INSTITUTE LIBRARY*, 847 Chapel St, 06510. SAN 302-2633. Tel: 203-562-4045. E-mail: home@institutelibrary.org. Web Site: institutelibrary.org. *Operations Mgr,* Eva Geertz; E-mail: eva@institutelibrary.org
Founded 1826
Library Holdings: Bk Vols 29,500
Wireless access
Restriction: Mem only, Private libr

NEW LONDON

S LYMAN ALLYN ART MUSEUM LIBRARY, 625 Williams St, 06320-4130. SAN 302-2641. Tel: 860-443-2545. FAX: 860-442-1280. E-mail: info@lymanallyn.org. Web Site: www.lymanallyn.org. *Dir,* D Samuel Quigley; Tel: 860-443-2545, Ext 113, E-mail: quigley@lymanallyn.org; *Registrar,* Jane LeGrow; Tel: 860-443-2545, Ext 126, E-mail: legrow@lymanallyn.org
Founded 1931
Library Holdings: Bk Vols 4,500; Per Subs 15
Special Collections: Art Exhibition Catalogs
Subject Interests: Art hist, Decorative art, Fine arts, Local hist
Function: Ref & res
Open Tues-Sat 10-5, Sun 1-5
Restriction: Not a lending libr

C CONNECTICUT COLLEGE, Charles E Shain Library, 270 Mohegan Ave, 06320-4196. SAN 336-4534. Tel: 860-439-2655. Circulation Tel: 860-439-3005. FAX: 860-439-2871. E-mail: refdesk@conncoll.edu. Reference E-mail: library@conncoll.edu. Web Site: www.conncoll.edu/information-services/libraries/libraries-locations/charles-e-shain-library. *Librn of the Col, VPres for Info Serv,* W Lee Hisle; E-mail: wlhis@conncoll.edu; *Dir, Info Res,* Beth Hansen; E-mail: beth.hansen@conncoll.edu; *Dir, Instrul Tech,* Chris Penniman; E-mail: chris.penniman@conncoll.edu; *Dir, Linda Lear Ctr for Spec Coll & Archives,* Benjamin Panciera; E-mail: bpancier@conncoll.edu; *Dir, Res Support & Instruction,* Jessica McCullough; E-mail: jmccull1@conncoll.edu; *Asst Dir, Media Serv Tech,* David Baratko; E-mail: dmbar@conncoll.edu; *E-Res & Ser Librn,* Kathleen Gehring; E-mail: kmgeh@conncoll.edu; *Res & Instruction Librn,* Ashley Hanson; E-mail: abpow@conncoll.edu; *Res & Instruction Librn,* W James MacDonald; E-mail: jim.macdonald@conncoll.edu; *Spec Coll Librn,* Jenifer Ishee; E-mail: jishee@conncoll.edu; *Ser & Electronic Res Librn,* Melodie Hamilton; E-mail: mhamil@conncoll.edu; *Tech Serv & Syst Librn,* Joseph Frawley; E-mail: jfrawley@conncoll.edu; *Visual Res Librn,* Mark Braunstein; E-mail: mmbra@conncoll.edu; *Mgr, Access Serv,* Emily Aylward; E-mail: eaylward@conncoll.edu; *Acq, Supvr,* Lorraine McKinney; E-mail: lmmck@conncoll.edu. Subject Specialists: *Govt doc,* W James MacDonald; Staff 27 (MLS 14, Non-MLS 13)
Founded 1911. Enrl 1,866; Fac 169; Highest Degree: Master
Library Holdings: e-journals 6,675; Bk Vols 525,944; Per Subs 1,325
Special Collections: 19th & 20th Century Children's Literature (Helen O Gildersleeve Coll); John Masefield (Charles H Simmons Coll); Linda Lear & Rachel Carson Coll; Louis Schaeffer-Eugene O'Neill Coll; New London County History Coll; Poetry (William Meredith Coll); Printing History (Carl & Alma Weiss Coll); Susanne K Langer Coll; William Meredith & Blanche McCrary Boyd Papers; Wyman Ballad Coll. State Document Depository; US Document Depository
Subject Interests: Art, Chinese lang, Dance, Hist, Humanities, Japanese (Lang), Judaica (lit or hist of Jews), Natural sci, Soc sci & issues
Automation Activity & Vendor Info: (Acquisitions) Ex Libris Group; (Cataloging) Ex Libris Group; (Circulation) Ex Libris Group; (Course Reserve) Ex Libris Group; (ILL) OCLC ILLiad; (OPAC) Ex Libris Group; (Serials) Ex Libris Group
Wireless access
Publications: Friends (Newsletter); Inside Information (Newsletter)
Partic in Connecticut Library Consortium; CTW Library Consortium; LYRASIS; OCLC Online Computer Library Center, Inc; Westchester Academic Library Directors Organization
Open Mon-Thurs 8am-2am, Fri & Sat 8am-10pm, Sun 10am-2am
Friends of the Library Group

Departmental Libraries:

GREER MUSIC LIBRARY, 270 Mohegan Ave, Box 5234, 06320-4196. Tel: 860-439-2711. FAX: 860-439-2871. Web Site: www.conncoll.edu/information-services/libraries/libraries-locations/greer-music-library. *Music Librn,* Carolyn A Johnson; E-mail: cajoh@conncoll.edu; *Research & Support Librn,* Andrew Lopez; E-mail: alopez6@conncoll.edu; Staff 2 (MLS 1, Non-MLS 1)
Highest Degree: Bachelor
Library Holdings: Bk Vols 12,000
Special Collections: Historic Sheet Music Coll, Mid-19th Century-1950; Jazz (Shelley Colls); LP Coll; Opera & Operetta (Hilliar Coll)
Publications: Greer Music Library (Informational brochure)
Restriction: Open by appt only
Friends of the Library Group

M LAWRENCE & MEMORIAL HOSPITAL*, Health Sciences Library, 365 Montauk Ave, 06320. SAN 302-265X. Tel: 860-442-0711, Ext 2238. *Mgr, Libr Serv,* Anne-Marie Kaminsky; E-mail: anne-marie.kaminsky@lmhosp.org
Founded 1972
Subject Interests: Nursing
Wireless access
Restriction: Not open to pub

C MITCHELL COLLEGE LIBRARY*, 437 Pequot Ave, 06320. SAN 302-2668. Tel: 860-701-5156. FAX: 860-701-5099. E-mail: asklis@mitchell.edu. Web Site: mitchell.libguides.com. *Instruction Librn,* Lauren Consolatore; Tel: 860-701-5486, E-mail: consolatore_l@mitchell.edu; *User Serv Librn,* Katie Nazarian; Tel: 860-701-7789, E-mail: nazarian_k@mitchell.edu; Staff 5 (MLS 1, Non-MLS 4)
Founded 1939. Enrl 750; Highest Degree: Bachelor
Library Holdings: Bk Vols 48,500; Per Subs 28
Special Collections: Robert Penn Warren Letters
Subject Interests: Art, Art hist
Automation Activity & Vendor Info: (Acquisitions) Innovative Interfaces, Inc; (Cataloging) Innovative Interfaces, Inc; (Circulation) Innovative Interfaces, Inc; (Course Reserve) Innovative Interfaces, Inc; (ILL) Innovative Interfaces, Inc; (OPAC) Innovative Interfaces, Inc
Wireless access
Function: Archival coll, Audiobks via web, AV serv, Bks on CD, CD-ROM, Computers for patron use, Doc delivery serv, E-Readers, E-Reserves, Electronic databases & coll, Equip loans & repairs, Free DVD rentals, ILL available, Internet access, Magazines, Movies, Music CDs, Online cat, Online info literacy tutorials on the web & in blackboard, Online ref, OverDrive digital audio bks, Photocopying/Printing, Ref & res, Ref serv available, Wheelchair accessible
Partic in Connecticut Library Consortium; Libraries Online, Inc
Open Mon-Thurs 8am-10pm, Fri 8-6, Sat 12-5

S NEW LONDON COUNTY HISTORICAL SOCIETY LIBRARY, 11 Blinman St, 06320. SAN 302-2676. Tel: 860-443-1209. FAX: 860-443-1209. E-mail: info@nlchs.org. Web Site: www.nlchs.org. *Exec Dir,* Steve Manuel; *Researcher,* Patricia M Schaefer; Staff 1 (MLS 1)
Founded 1870
Library Holdings: Bk Titles 5,000
Special Collections: Newspapers, 1758-present; Whaling Coll, journals, logs, registers. Oral History
Subject Interests: Genealogy, Local hist
Wireless access
Function: Archival coll, For res purposes, Photocopying/Printing, Ref serv available, Res libr, Res performed for a fee, Telephone ref
Publications: Amistad Incident in New London Gazette (Local historical information); Black Roots in Southeastern Connecticut (Reference guide); Diary of Joshua Hempsted (Local historical information); Greetings from New London (Local historical information); History of the Amistad Captives (Local historical information); Life of Venture (Local historical information); Newsletter (Bimonthly); Tapestry (Local historical information); View From the Sixties (Local historical information)
Restriction: Fee for pub use, Not a lending libr, Researchers by appt only, Visitors must make appt to use bks in the libr

§S NEW LONDON MARITIME SOCIETY-CUSTOM HOUSE MARITIME MUSEUM, Frank L McGuire Maritime Research Library, 150 Bank St, 06320. Tel: 860-447-2501. Web Site: nlmaritimesociety.org/library.html. *Exec Dir,* Susan Tamulevich; E-mail: nlmaritimedirector@gmail.com; *Librn,* Laurie Deredita; *Assoc Librn,* Brian Rogers
Special Collections: 18th & 19th Century Prints from Newspapers & Illustrated Magazines; Cone & Bachman Archives; Frank Racette Coll, glass plate negatives; Harold J Cone Coll, 1806-1919, newsp article excerpts & summaries; Long Island Sound & Eastern Connecticut Coast Charts; New London Custom House (Robert Mills Coll), photog; New London Customs Logs, 1818-1821; New London Postcards, 1920s-1940s; Robert Stewart Ship Model Coll
Subject Interests: Am hist, Boating, Commercial fishing, Connecticut, Maritime, Meteorology, Navigation, New England hist, Sailing, Seamanship, Shipbuilding, Submarines, Whaling, Yachting
Automation Activity & Vendor Info: (Cataloging) Bibliomation Inc; (OPAC) Bibliomation Inc
Function: Res assist avail, Res performed for a fee
Partic in Bibliomation Inc
Restriction: Not a lending libr, Open by appt only

P NEW LONDON PUBLIC LIBRARY*, 63 Huntington St, 06320. SAN 302-2684. Tel: 860-447-1411. FAX: 860-443-2083. Web Site: www.plnl.org. *Exec Dir,* Suzanne Maryeski; Tel: 860-447-1411, Ext 106, E-mail: smaryeski@plnl.org; *Asst Dir, Head, Tech Serv,* Fran Gibbs-Kail; Tel: 860-447-1411, Ext 107, E-mail: frangk@plnl.org; *Head, Circ, Outreach Coordr,* Maritza Vargas; Tel: 860-447-1411, Ext 3, E-mail: mvargas@plnl.org; Staff 18 (MLS 4, Non-MLS 14)
Founded 1891. Pop 26,583; Circ 167,880
Library Holdings: DVDs 450; Bk Vols 83,000; Per Subs 155; Videos 3,000
Subject Interests: Genealogy, Local hist
Automation Activity & Vendor Info: (Acquisitions) Innovative Interfaces, Inc; (Cataloging) Innovative Interfaces, Inc; (Circulation) Innovative Interfaces, Inc; (ILL) Innovative Interfaces, Inc; (OPAC) Innovative Interfaces, Inc; (Serials) Innovative Interfaces, Inc
Wireless access
Function: ILL available
Publications: Loomings (Quarterly newsletter)
Partic in Libraries Online, Inc; Ohio Public Library Information Network
Special Services for the Blind - Closed circuit TV magnifier
Open Mon, Tues & Thurs 9:30-7, Wed 1-7, Fri & Sat 9:30-5, Sun 1-5
Friends of the Library Group

C UNITED STATES COAST GUARD ACADEMY LIBRARY*, 35 Mohegan Ave, 06320. SAN 302-2692. Tel: 860-444-8510. Administration Tel: 860-444-8517. FAX: 860-444-8516. E-mail: libnotification@uscga.edu. Web Site: libguides.uscga.edu. *Libr Dir,* Lucy Maziar; E-mail: lucia.maziar@uscga.edu; *Head, Ref & Instruction,* Pam Dolin; Tel: 860-444-8515, E-mail: pamela.r.dolin@uscga.edu; *Ref & Instruction Librn,* Joan Clark; Tel: 860-444-6421, E-mail: joan.e.clark@uscga.edu; *Syst Librn,* Leigh Mihlrad; Tel: 860-444-8519, E-mail: leigh.m.mihlrad@uscga.edu; *Spec Coll Librn,* Elisa Graydon; Tel: 860-444-8553, E-mail: elisa.p.graydon@uscga.edu; *ILL Tech,* T J Crocco; Tel: 860-444-8513, E-mail: theodore.j.crocco@uscga.edu; Staff 9 (MLS 5, Non-MLS 4)
Founded 1876. Enrl 900; Fac 119; Highest Degree: Bachelor
Oct 2014-Sept 2015. Mats Exp $540,000
Subject Interests: Civil engr, Electrical engr, Hist, Leadership, Marine engr, Marine sci, Maritime, Mechanical engr, Naval archit
Automation Activity & Vendor Info: (Acquisitions) SirsiDynix; (Cataloging) SirsiDynix; (Circulation) SirsiDynix; (Course Reserve) SirsiDynix; (OPAC) SirsiDynix; (Serials) SirsiDynix
Wireless access
Partic in Federal Library & Information Network
Restriction: Not open to pub, Open to researchers by request

NEW MILFORD

P NEW MILFORD PUBLIC LIBRARY*, 24 Main St, 06776. SAN 302-2706. Tel: 860-355-1191. Circulation Tel: 860-355-1191, Ext 201. Interlibrary Loan Service Tel: 860-355-1191, Ext 206. Reference Tel: 860-355-1191, Ext 207. FAX: 860-350-9579. TDD: 860-350-3418. Web Site: www.newmilfordlibrary.org. *Dir,* Lorna Rhyins; E-mail: lrhyins@biblio.org; *Ch Serv Librn,* Sue Ford; Tel: 860-355-1191, Ext 205, E-mail: sford@biblio.org; *Pub Serv Librn,* Valerie Fisher; Tel: 860-355-1191, Ext 203, E-mail: vfisher@biblio.org; *YA Librn,* Meghan Morin; Tel: 860-355-1191, Ext 204, E-mail: mmorin@biblio.org; *Tech Coordr,* Peggy Ganong; Tel: 860-355-1191, Ext 211, E-mail: pganong@biblio.org; Staff 7 (MLS 5, Non-MLS 2)
Founded 1898. Pop 27,972; Circ 252,113
Jul 2013-Jun 2014 Income $1,085,523, State $4,770, City $977,100, Locally Generated Income $33,073, Other $70,580. Mats Exp $206,356, Books $117,763, Per/Ser (Incl. Access Fees) $10,129, Micro $1,080, AV Mat $36,798, Electronic Ref Mat (Incl. Access Fees) $40,586. Sal $599,878 (Prof $347,329)
Library Holdings: Audiobooks 766; CDs 4,973; DVDs 7,392; e-books 1,357; Large Print Bks 1,071; Microforms 338; Bk Vols 88,346; Per Subs 120; Videos 7,475
Special Collections: Connecticut, Local History
Automation Activity & Vendor Info: (Acquisitions) Baker & Taylor; (Cataloging) Evergreen; (Circulation) Evergreen; (ILL) Evergreen; (OPAC) Evergreen
Wireless access
Function: 24/7 Electronic res, Adult bk club, After school storytime, Art exhibits, Audiobks via web, Bks on CD, Children's prog, Computer training, Computers for patron use, Electronic databases & coll, Free DVD rentals, Health sci info serv, ILL available, Magazines, Mango lang, Microfiche/film & reading machines, Movies, Museum passes, Music CDs, Notary serv, Online cat, Photocopying/Printing, Preschool outreach, Printer for laptops & handheld devices, Prog for adults, Prog for children & young adult, Senior computer classes, Senior outreach, Story hour, Study rm, Summer & winter reading prog, Tax forms, Teen prog, Telephone ref, Wheelchair accessible
Publications: New Milford Public Library (Newsletter)
Partic in Bergen County Cooperative Library System, Inc; Bibliomation Inc
Special Services for the Deaf - Bks on deafness & sign lang
Special Services for the Blind - Bks on CD; Copier with enlargement capabilities; Large print bks; Playaways (bks on MP3)
Open Mon-Thurs 10-8, Fri 10-5, Sat 9-5, Sun (Oct-May) 1-5
Friends of the Library Group

NEWINGTON

G CONNDOT LIBRARY & INFORMATION CENTER*, 2800 Berlin Tpk, 06111. SAN 302-4474. Tel: 860-594-2000. *Librn,* Position Currently Open
Founded 1984
Library Holdings: Bk Vols 20,000
Subject Interests: Transportation
Automation Activity & Vendor Info: (Cataloging) OCLC; (ILL) OCLC
Restriction: Employees only

P LUCY ROBBINS WELLES LIBRARY, 95 Cedar St, 06111. SAN 302-2749. Tel: 860-665-8700. FAX: 860-667-1255. E-mail: refdept@newingtonct.gov. Web Site: www.newingtonct.gov/2428/library. *Libr Dir,* Lisa Masten; Tel: 860-665-8724; *Asst Dir,* Karen Benner; Tel: 860-665-8729, E-mail: kbenner@newingtonct.gov; *Head, Children's Servx,* Pat Pierce; Tel: 860-665-8783, E-mail: ppierce@newingtonct.gov; *Head, Coll Mgt,* Jeanette Francini; Tel: 860-665-8714, E-mail: jfrancini@newingtonct.gov; *Head, Commun Serv,* Michelle Royer; Tel: 860-665-8707, E-mail: mroyer@newingtonct.gov; *Head, Ref Serv,* Diane Durette; Tel: 860-665-8705, E-mail: ddurette@newingtonct.gov; *Bus Mgr,* Lynn Caley; Tel: 860-665-8728, E-mail: lcaley@newingtonct.gov; *YA Serv,* Bailey Francis; Tel: 860-665-8704, E-mail: bfrancis@newingtonct.gov; Staff 15.8 (MLS 11, Non-MLS 4.8)
Founded 1752. Pop 29,699; Circ 404,506
Library Holdings: Audiobooks 3,254; DVDs 9,214; Bk Vols 140,654; Per Subs 258
Special Collections: Index of Local Newspaper; Local History Coll
Automation Activity & Vendor Info: (Acquisitions) SirsiDynix; (Cataloging) SirsiDynix; (Circulation) SirsiDynix; (OPAC) SirsiDynix-iBistro
Wireless access
Publications: Index of Local Newspaper; Newington Business Directory; Newington Information Packet
Partic in Connecticut Library Consortium; OCLC Online Computer Library Center, Inc
Open Mon-Thurs 10-9, Fri & Sat 10-5
Friends of the Library Group

NEWTOWN

P CYRENIUS H BOOTH LIBRARY, 25 Main St, 06470. SAN 302-2757. Tel: 203-426-4533. FAX: 203-426-2196. Reference E-mail: reference@chboothlibrary.org. Web Site: www.chboothlibrary.org. *Dir,* Douglas C Lord; E-mail: dlord@chboothlibrary.org; *Asst Dir,* Jennifer Nash; E-mail: jnash@chboothlibrary.org; *Head, Ref,* Amy Schumann; *Ch,* Alana Bennison; *YA Librn,* Catherine Findorack; *Circ Supvr,* Anne Mastroianni; Staff 37 (MLS 7, Non-MLS 30)
Founded 1932. Pop 25,000; Circ 240,000
Library Holdings: Bks on Deafness & Sign Lang 30; High Interest/Low Vocabulary Bk Vols 25; Large Print Bks 400; Bk Vols 130,000; Per Subs 507; Spec Interest Per Sub 36
Special Collections: Antiques (Scudder Smith coll)); Arts (Jack Landau Coll); Genealogy (Julia Brush Coll); Sculpture (John Angel Coll)
Subject Interests: Art & archit, Genealogy, Hist
Automation Activity & Vendor Info: (Acquisitions) Evergreen; (Cataloging) Evergreen; (Circulation) Evergreen; (ILL) Evergreen; (OPAC) Evergreen
Wireless access

Function: Archival coll, Homebound delivery serv, ILL available, Large print keyboards, Magnifiers for reading, Photocopying/Printing, Prog for children & young adult, Ref serv available, Summer reading prog, Telephone ref, Wheelchair accessible
Partic in Bibliomation Inc
Special Services for the Blind - Home delivery serv; Videos on blindness & physical disabilties
Open Mon-Thurs 9:30-7, Fri & Sat 9:30-4
Restriction: Open to pub for ref & circ; with some limitations
Friends of the Library Group

S GARNER CORRECTIONAL INSTITUTION LIBRARY*, 50 Nunnawauk Rd, 06470. Tel: 203-270-2800. Web Site: portal.ct.gov/DOC/Facility/Garner-CI.
Library Holdings: Bk Vols 5,000; Per Subs 15
Automation Activity & Vendor Info: (Cataloging) Follett Software; (Circulation) Follett Software; (OPAC) Follett Software
Restriction: Not open to pub

NIANTIC

P EAST LYME PUBLIC LIBRARY, 39 Society Rd, 06357. SAN 302-279X. Tel: 860-739-6926. FAX: 860-691-0020. E-mail: elpl@ely.lioninc.org. Web Site: www.eastlymepubliclibrary.org. *Exec Dir,* Lisa Timothy; E-mail: ltimothy@ely.lioninc.org; *Asst Dir,* Tara Borden; E-mail: tborden@ely.lioninc.org; *Ch, YA Librn,* Rebecca Scotka; E-mail: rscotka@ely.lioninc.org; *Ref & ILL Librn,* Catherine Shields; *Circ,* Jean Lachance; E-mail: jlachance@ely.lioninc.org; *Tech Serv,* Tracey Willis; E-mail: twillis@ely.lioninc.org
Founded 1868. Pop 18,118; Circ 161,938
Library Holdings: CDs 671; DVDs 365; Bk Titles 100,000; Bk Vols 103,000; Per Subs 218; Talking Bks 1,224; Videos 2,322
Special Collections: East Lyme Manuscript Coll; The Chadwick Letters; The Comstock Letter; Victor Frank Ridder & Marie Thompson Ridder Music Coll
Subject Interests: Chinese lang, Fr lang, Gardening, Genealogy, Greek, Local hist, Native Americans
Automation Activity & Vendor Info: (Acquisitions) Innovative Interfaces, Inc; (Cataloging) Innovative Interfaces, Inc; (Circulation) Innovative Interfaces, Inc; (ILL) Innovative Interfaces, Inc; (OPAC) Innovative Interfaces, Inc; (Serials) Innovative Interfaces, Inc
Wireless access
Publications: Annual report; Bibliographic & Program Brochures; Dear & Affectionate Wife, the Letters of Charles & Mary Chadwick, 1828-1851
Partic in Connecticut Library Consortium; Libraries Online, Inc
Open Mon-Wed 9-9, Thurs 9-6, Fri 9-5, Sat 9-1
Friends of the Library Group

S YORK CORRECTIONAL INSTITUTION LIBRARY*, 201 W Main St, 06357. SAN 371-7984. Tel: 860-451-3001. FAX: 860-451-3200. *Media Spec,* Shamol Rozario
Library Holdings: Bk Vols 10,000; Per Subs 20
Special Collections: Law
Publications: The Niantic Voice (Newspaper)
Restriction: Not open to pub

NORFOLK

P NORFOLK LIBRARY*, Nine Greenwoods Rd E, 06058-1320. (Mail add: PO Box 605, 06058-0605), SAN 302-2811. Tel: 860-542-5075. FAX: 860-542-1795. E-mail: norfolklibrary@biblio.org. Web Site: www.norfolklibrary.org. *Dir,* Ann Havemeyer; E-mail: norfolkdirector@biblio.org; *Ch Serv, Prog Coordr,* Eileen Fitzgibbons; E-mail: efitzgibbons@biblio.org; *Circ Serv,* Chaya Berlstein; E-mail: cstone@biblio.org; *Circ Serv,* Laurie Foulke-Green; E-mail: lfoulke-green@biblio.org; *Circ Serv,* Christopher Keyes; E-mail: ckeyes@biblio.org; *Tech Serv,* MaryAnn Anderson; E-mail: manderson@biblio.org; Staff 5 (MLS 1, Non-MLS 4)
Founded 1889. Pop 1,800; Circ 27,000
Library Holdings: Bk Titles 30,000
Special Collections: Fishing & Hunting (Barbour Coll)
Wireless access
Publications: The Owl (Newsletter)
Partic in Bibliomation Inc
Open Mon & Thurs 10-7, Tues, Wed & Fri 10-5, Sat 10-2, Sun 1-4
Friends of the Library Group

NORTH BRANFORD

P NORTH BRANFORD LIBRARY DEPARTMENT*, Atwater Memorial, 1720 Foxon Rd, 06471. (Mail add: PO Box 258, 06471-0258), SAN 336-4623. Tel: 203-315-6020. FAX: 203-315-6021. Web Site: nbranfordlibraries.org. *Dir,* Lauren Davis; E-mail: director@nbranfordlibraries.org
Library Holdings: Bk Vols 60,000; Per Subs 210
Automation Activity & Vendor Info: (Cataloging) Innovative Interfaces, Inc; (Circulation) Innovative Interfaces, Inc; (OPAC) Innovative Interfaces, Inc
Wireless access
Open Mon-Thurs 10-8, Fri 9-6, Sat 9-3 (9-12 Summer); Sun 1-4 (Winter)
Friends of the Library Group
Branches: 1
EDWARD SMITH BRANCH, Three Old Post Rd, Northford, 06472. (Mail add: PO Box 130, Northford, 06472-0130), SAN 336-4682. Tel: 203-484-0469. FAX: 203-484-6024. *Ch,* Debra Verrillo
Open Mon-Thurs 10-8, Fri 9-6, Sat 9-3 (9-12 Summer), Sun 1-4 (Winter)
Friends of the Library Group

NORTH CANAAN

P DOUGLAS LIBRARY*, 108 Main St, 06018. (Mail add: PO Box 608, 06018), SAN 302-0797. Tel: 860-824-7863. FAX: 860-824-7863. E-mail: douglaslibrary@comcast.net. Web Site: douglaslibrarycanaan.org. *Libr Dir,* Norma DeMay; Staff 2 (Non-MLS 2)
Founded 1821. Pop 3,000; Circ 20,694
Library Holdings: Audiobooks 969; CDs 500; DVDs 726; Bk Vols 17,702; Per Subs 60
Automation Activity & Vendor Info: (Acquisitions) Follett Software; (Cataloging) Follett Software; (Circulation) Follett Software; (OPAC) Follett Software
Wireless access
Function: Adult bk club, Adult literacy prog, Art exhibits, Bk club(s), Bks on cassette, Bks on CD, Children's prog, Computers for patron use, Electronic databases & coll, Free DVD rentals, Holiday prog, Home delivery & serv to seniorr ctr & nursing homes, Homebound delivery serv, ILL available, Museum passes, Music CDs, Online ref, Outreach serv, Photocopying/Printing, Preschool outreach, Prog for adults, Prog for children & young adult, Spoken cassettes & CDs, Spoken cassettes & DVDs, Story hour, Summer reading prog, VHS videos, Wheelchair accessible, Workshops
Partic in Bibliomation Inc; Region I Coop Libr Servs Unit
Open Mon 1:30-8, Wed & Fri 10-8, Sat 10-1
Friends of the Library Group

NORTH GROSVENORDALE

P THOMPSON PUBLIC LIBRARY, 934 Riverside Dr, 06255. (Mail add: PO Box 855, 06255-0855), SAN 336-5131. Tel: 860-923-9779. Web Site: www.thompsonpubliclibrary.org. *Libr Dir,* Alison Boutaugh; E-mail: aboutaugh@thompsonpubliclibrary.org; Staff 9 (MLS 1, Non-MLS 8)
Founded 1902. Pop 9,324; Circ 85,400
Library Holdings: Bk Vols 55,000; Per Subs 97
Subject Interests: Local hist
Automation Activity & Vendor Info: (Acquisitions) Evergreen; (Cataloging) Bibliomation Inc; (Circulation) Evergreen; (OPAC) Evergreen
Wireless access
Function: Adult bk club, Art exhibits, Audiobks via web, Computers for patron use, Homebound delivery serv, Large print keyboards, Magnifiers for reading, Museum passes, Photocopying/Printing, Prog for adults, Prog for children & young adult, Scanner, Story hour, Summer reading prog, Tax forms, Wheelchair accessible
Partic in Bibliomation Inc
Open Mon-Thurs 10-8, Fri 10-5, Sat (Sept-June) 10-2
Friends of the Library Group

NORTH HAVEN

P NORTH HAVEN MEMORIAL LIBRARY, 17 Elm St, 06473. SAN 302-2838. Tel: 203-239-5803. FAX: 203-234-2130. Web Site: www.northhavenlibrary.net. *Dir, Libr Serv,* Susan Griffiths; E-mail: sgriffiths@northhavenlibrary.net; *Asst Dir, Libr Serv,* Shauna DeStefano; E-mail: sdestefano@northhavenlibrary.net; *Ch,* Emily Jenkins; *Ref (Info Servs),* Brittany Pearson; Staff 20 (MLS 7, Non-MLS 13)
Founded 1894
Library Holdings: AV Mats 7,752; Bk Vols 95,387; Per Subs 225
Special Collections: Cake Pan Coll; Rotary Coll
Automation Activity & Vendor Info: (Circulation) Innovative Interfaces, Inc; (OPAC) Innovative Interfaces, Inc
Wireless access
Function: Children's prog, ILL available, Prog for adults
Partic in Libraries Online, Inc
Special Services for the Blind - Large print bks; Reader equip
Open Mon-Thurs 10-8, Fri & Sat 10-5 (Sept-June); Mon-Thurs 10-8, Fri 10-5, Sat 10-1 (July-Aug)
Friends of the Library Group

NORTH STONINGTON

P WHEELER LIBRARY, 101 Main St, 06359. (Mail add: PO Box 217, 06359-0217), SAN 302-2862. Tel: 860-535-0383. E-mail: wheelerlibrarystaff@gmail.com. Web Site: www.wheelerlibrary.org. *Dir,* Amy Kennedy; E-mail: amykennedy@wheelerlibrary.org
Founded 1900. Pop 111,489
Library Holdings: Bk Vols 32,000; Per Subs 84
Subject Interests: Local hist, World War II
Automation Activity & Vendor Info: (Cataloging) Auto-Graphics, Inc; (Circulation) Auto-Graphics, Inc; (OPAC) Auto-Graphics, Inc
Open Mon, Wed & Fri 10-4, Tues & Thurs 10-8, Sat 10-1
Friends of the Library Group

NORTHFIELD

P GILBERT LIBRARY, INC*, 38 Main St, 06778. SAN 302-2870. Tel: 860-283-8176. E-mail: gilbert.library@snet.net. Web Site: www.gilbertlibrary.org. *Librn,* Nancy Gnitzcavich
Founded 1892. Pop 1,000; Circ 8,675
Library Holdings: Bk Titles 8,385; Per Subs 50
Special Collections: Local History, scrapbks
Open Mon, Wed & Fri 2-7

NORWALK

P EAST NORWALK IMPROVEMENT ASSOCIATION LIBRARY*, 51 Van Zant St, 06855. SAN 302-2900. Tel: 203-838-0408, Ext 100. FAX: 203-855-8382. E-mail: info@eastnorwalklibrary.org. Web Site: www.eastnorwalklibrary.org. *Exec Dir,* Sylvia Archibald; E-mail: sylvia@eastnorwalklibrary.org; *Tech Asst,* Daniel Cisek; E-mail: dan@eastnorwalklibrary.org
Pop 6,540; Circ 50,941
Library Holdings: Bk Vols 25,000; Per Subs 100
Automation Activity & Vendor Info: (Cataloging) Follett Software; (Circulation) Follett Software
Open Mon-Fri 12:30-5:30, Sat 9:30-5:30

S FINANCIAL ACCOUNTING FOUNDATION LIBRARY, Information Research Center, 401 Merritt 7, 06856. (Mail add: PO Box 5116, 06856-5116), SAN 320-619X. Tel: 203-847-0700. FAX: 203-849-9470. E-mail: informationresearch@f-a-f.org. Web Site: www.fasb.org. *Dir, Admin Serv, Dir, Info & Res,* Lisa Valentini-Ghosh
Founded 1973
Subject Interests: Acctg, Finance
Automation Activity & Vendor Info: (Acquisitions) EOS International; (Cataloging) EOS International; (OPAC) EOS International; (Serials) EOS International
Wireless access
Partic in Connecticut Library Consortium
Restriction: Not open to pub

J NORWALK COMMUNITY COLLEGE*, Baker Library, 188 Richards Ave, 06854-1655. SAN 302-2935. Tel: 203-857-7200. Reference Tel: 203-857-7379. FAX: 203-857-7380. Web Site: www.norwalk.edu/library. *Dir, Libr Serv,* Linda Lerman; *Electronic Res & Instruction Librn,* Alison Wang; Tel: 203-857-7207, E-mail: awong@ncc.commnet.edu; *Ref & Instruction Librn,* Position Currently Open; *Libr Assoc,* Kimberly Bryant-Smith; Tel: 203-857-6895, E-mail: KBryant-Smith@ncc.commnet.edu; *Libr Assoc,* Paula Podlaski; Tel: 203-857-7201, E-mail: ppodlaski@norwalk.edu; *Libr Asst,* Ilene Boyar; Tel: 203-857-3319, E-mail: IBoyar@ncc.commnet.edu; Staff 6 (MLS 3, Non-MLS 3)
Founded 1961. Fac 104; Highest Degree: Associate
Automation Activity & Vendor Info: (Acquisitions) Ex Libris Group; (Cataloging) Ex Libris Group; (Circulation) Ex Libris Group; (Course Reserve) Ex Libris Group; (ILL) Ex Libris Group; (OPAC) Ex Libris Group; (Serials) Ex Libris Group
Wireless access
Partic in Connecticut State University Library System; Council of Connecticut Academic Library Directors; OCLC Online Computer Library Center, Inc
Open Mon-Thurs 8:30-8, Fri & Sat 10-3

M NORWALK HOSPITAL*, Health Sciences Library, 24 Stevens St, 06856. SAN 336-4712. Tel: 203-852-2793. FAX: 203-855-3575. E-mail: library@wchn.org. *Med Librn,* Position Currently Open; Staff 1 (MLS 1)
Founded 1950
Library Holdings: e-books 1,000; e-journals 800; Bk Vols 200; Per Subs 3
Subject Interests: Med
Wireless access
Partic in Conn Asn of Health Scis Librs; Health Info Librs of Westchester
Restriction: Badge access after hrs, Circ limited

P NORWALK PUBLIC LIBRARY*, One Belden Ave, 06850. SAN 336-4771. Tel: 203-899-2780. FAX: 203-866-7982. E-mail: informationnpl@norwalkpubliclibrary.org. Web Site: norwalkpl.org. *Dir,* Christine Bradley; Tel: 203-899-2780, Ext 15126, E-mail: cbradley@norwalkpubliclibrary.org; *Dir, Ch Serv,* Vicki Oatis; Tel: 203-899-2780, Ext 15127, E-mail: voatis@norwalkpubliclibrary.org; *Dir, Info Serv,* Cynde Lahey; Tel: 203-899-2780, Ext 15133, E-mail: clahey@norwalkpubliclibrary.org; *Dir, Tech Serv,* Tom Schadlich; Tel: 203-899-2780, Ext 15124, E-mail: tschadlich@norwalkpubliclibrary.org; *Asst Dir,* Sherelle Harris; Tel: 203-899-2780, Ext 15123, E-mail: sharris@norwalkpubliclibrary.org; *Circ Mgr,* Sharon Daniel; Tel: 203-899-2780, Ext 15164, E-mail: sdaniel@norwalkpubliclibrary.org; Staff 60 (MLS 20, Non-MLS 40)
Founded 1895. Pop 82,000; Circ 450,000
Library Holdings: AV Mats 28,426; Bk Titles 140,000; Bk Vols 225,000; Per Subs 410
Automation Activity & Vendor Info: (Acquisitions) Innovative Interfaces, Inc; (Cataloging) Innovative Interfaces, Inc; (Circulation) Innovative Interfaces, Inc; (OPAC) Innovative Interfaces, Inc
Wireless access
Open Mon, Wed & Thurs 9-8:30, Tues, Fri & Sat 9-5:30
Friends of the Library Group
Branches: 1
SOUTH NORWALK BRANCH, Ten Washington St, South Norwalk, 06854, SAN 336-4801. Tel: 203-899-2790. FAX: 203-899-2788. *Libr Asst,* Kamille Claudio; Tel: 203-899-2790, Ext 15903, E-mail: kclaudio@norwalkpubliclibrary.org
Library Holdings: Bk Vols 71,654
Subject Interests: Gen interest
Open Mon & Wed-Sat 9-5:30, Tues 12-8:30, Sun 1-5

NORWICH

P OTIS LIBRARY, 261 Main St, 06360. SAN 302-3044. Tel: 860-889-2365. FAX: 860-889-2533. Web Site: www.otislibrarynorwich.org. *Exec Dir,* Bob Farwell; E-mail: bfarwell@otislibrarynorwich.org; *Asst Dir,* Cathy Special; E-mail: cspecial@otislibrarynorwich.org; *Tech Serv Librn,* Nancy Bruckner; E-mail: rlbrucker@otislibrarynorwich.org; Staff 30 (MLS 3, Non-MLS 27)
Founded 1850. Pop 39,500; Circ 200,000
Library Holdings: Bk Vols 99,000; Per Subs 158
Special Collections: Genealogy & Local Hist; Large Print
Subject Interests: Bus & mgt, Careers
Automation Activity & Vendor Info: (Acquisitions) Innovative Interfaces, Inc; (Cataloging) Innovative Interfaces, Inc; (Circulation) Innovative Interfaces, Inc; (Course Reserve) Innovative Interfaces, Inc; (ILL) Innovative Interfaces, Inc; (Media Booking) Innovative Interfaces, Inc; (OPAC) Innovative Interfaces, Inc; (Serials) Innovative Interfaces, Inc
Wireless access
Function: ILL available
Publications: Monthly Activities Calendar
Partic in Connecticut Library Consortium; Libraries Online, Inc
Special Services for the Blind - Bks on cassette; Large print bks
Open Mon & Wed 10-8, Tues, Thurs & Fri 10-5, Sat (Sept-June) 10-3
Friends of the Library Group

J THREE RIVERS COMMUNITY COLLEGE*, Donald R Welter Library, 574 New London Tpk, 06360-6598. SAN 302-3060. Tel: 860-215-9051. Reference Tel: 860-215-9052. FAX: 860-215-9911. Web Site: www.trcc.commnet.edu/div_it/library/library.shtml. *Dir, Libr Serv,* Mildred Hodge; Tel: 860-215-9252, E-mail: MHodge@trcc.commnet.edu; *Ref & Instruction Librn,* Pam Williams; E-mail: PWilliams@trcc.commnet.edu; Staff 7 (MLS 2, Non-MLS 5)
Founded 1964. Enrl 4,000; Fac 96; Highest Degree: Associate
Library Holdings: AV Mats 2,937; Bk Titles 51,186; Per Subs 420
Special Collections: Local Public Records Room; Nuclear Regulatory Commission Documents
Automation Activity & Vendor Info: (Acquisitions) Ex Libris Group; (Cataloging) Ex Libris Group; (Circulation) Ex Libris Group; (Course Reserve) Ex Libris Group; (ILL) OCLC; (OPAC) Ex Libris Group; (Serials) EBSCO Online
Wireless access
Open Mon-Thurs 8:30-8, Fri 8:30-3

OAKDALE

P RAYMOND LIBRARY, 832 Raymond Hill Rd, 06370. SAN 376-2637. Tel: 860-848-9943. FAX: 860-848-9933. E-mail: raymond.library@yahoo.com. Web Site: raymondlibraryblog.wordpress.com. *Dir,* Joanne Westkamper
Library Holdings: Bk Titles 21,000; Bk Vols 23,000; Per Subs 25
Wireless access
Function: Adult bk club, Online cat, Preschool reading prog, Story hour
Partic in Connecticut Library Consortium

Open Tues 12-8, Wed 10-7, Thurs 10-6, Sat 9-2. Winter Hours: Tues 12-7, Wed & Thurs 10-6, Sat 9-2
Friends of the Library Group

OLD GREENWICH

P PERROT MEMORIAL LIBRARY*, 90 Sound Beach Ave, 06870. SAN 302-3095. Tel: 203-637-1066. Reference Tel: 203-637-3870. FAX: 203-698-2620. Web Site: www.perrotlibrary.org. *Libr Dir,* Kevin McCarthy; E-mail: kevinm@perrotlibrary.org; *Dir, Youth Serv,* Kathy Jarombek; Tel: 203-637-8802; *Asst Dir, Ref (Info Servs),* Linda White; *Circ,* Judy Sgammato; *Tech Serv,* Mirja Johanson
Founded 1905. Pop 62,000; Circ 111,703
Jul 2019-Jun 2020 Income $1,813,026
Library Holdings: Bk Vols 70,000
Special Collections: Oral History
Subject Interests: Cooking, Gardening, Sailing
Automation Activity & Vendor Info: (Acquisitions) Innovative Interfaces, Inc; (Cataloging) Innovative Interfaces, Inc; (Circulation) Innovative Interfaces, Inc - Millennium; (OPAC) Innovative Interfaces, Inc
Wireless access
Function: 24/7 Electronic res, 24/7 Online cat, Adult bk club, After school storytime, Audiobks on Playaways & MP3, Audiobks via web, Bk club(s), Bks on CD, Children's prog, Computers for patron use, Digital talking bks, Distance learning, E-Readers, Electronic databases & coll, Free DVD rentals, Govt ref serv, Health sci info serv, ILL available, Internet access, Learning ctr, Life-long learning prog for all ages, Magazines, Magnifiers for reading, Mail & tel request accepted, Mango lang, Movies, Museum passes, Music CDs, Online cat, Online ref, Outside serv via phone, mail, e-mail & web, OverDrive digital audio bks, Photocopying/Printing, Preschool reading prog, Printer for laptops & handheld devices, Prog for adults, Prog for children & young adult, Ref & res, Ref serv available, Scanner, Spoken cassettes & CDs, Story hour, Study rm, Summer reading prog, Tax forms, Teen prog, Telephone ref, Wheelchair accessible
Partic in Connecticut Library Consortium; OCLC Online Computer Library Center, Inc
Special Services for the Blind - Accessible computers; Bks & mags in Braille, on rec, tape & cassette; Bks on CD; Magnifiers
Open Mon, Wed & Fri 9-6, Tues & Thurs 9-8, Sat 9-5, Sun 1-5

OLD LYME

C LYME ACADEMY COLLEGE OF FINE ARTS*, Krieble Library, 84 Lyme St, 06371-2333. Tel: 860-434-5232.
Founded 1991. Enrl 200; Fac 23; Highest Degree: Bachelor
Library Holdings: AV Mats 25,306; Electronic Media & Resources 20; Bk Titles 13,291; Per Subs 79
Subject Interests: Drawing, Fine arts, Painting, Sculpture
Automation Activity & Vendor Info: (Cataloging) Follett Software; (Circulation) Follett Software; (ILL) OCLC; (OPAC) Follett Software
Wireless access
Partic in Connecticut Library Consortium
Restriction: Open to pub for ref only, Open to students, fac & staff

S LYME HISTORICAL SOCIETY LIBRARY*, 96 Lyme St, 06371. SAN 302-3109. Tel: 860-434-5542. FAX: 860-434-9778. Web Site: www.florencegriswold.org. *Dir,* Jeff Andersen; *Archives Coordr,* Charlie Beal; E-mail: charlie@flogris.org
Founded 1956
Library Holdings: Bk Titles 700
Special Collections: Art Colony at Old Lyme Archives; History of Lyme & Old Lyme Conn; Papers of Local Families
Subject Interests: Connecticut, Genealogy, Local hist
Restriction: Open by appt only

P OLD LYME*, Phoebe Griffin Noyes Library, Two Library Lane, 06371. SAN 302-3117. Tel: 860-434-1684. FAX: 860-434-9547. Web Site: www.oldlyme.lioninc.org. *Dir,* Katie Huffman; E-mail: khuffman@oldlymelibrary.org; *Ch,* Julie Bartley; E-mail: jbartley@oldlymelibrary.org; *Ref & Tech Librn,* Jessica Steding; E-mail: jsteding@oldlymelibrary.org; *YA Librn,* Nike Desis; E-mail: ndesis@oldlymelibrary.org; *Access Serv Mgr,* Kristine Ferguson; E-mail: kferguson@oldlymelibrary.org; *Pub Serv Mgr,* Linda Alexander; E-mail: lalexander@oldlymelibrary.org; Staff 9 (MLS 5, Non-MLS 4)
Founded 1898. Pop 7,525; Circ 74,661
Library Holdings: AV Mats 4,190; Electronic Media & Resources 30; Bk Titles 42,155; Per Subs 30
Subject Interests: Genealogy, Local hist
Automation Activity & Vendor Info: (Acquisitions) Innovative Interfaces, Inc; (Cataloging) Innovative Interfaces, Inc; (Circulation) Innovative Interfaces, Inc; (ILL) Auto-Graphics, Inc; (OPAC) Innovative Interfaces, Inc; (Serials) Innovative Interfaces, Inc
Wireless access
Publications: More Than Just Books (Newsletter)
Partic in Libraries Online, Inc
Open Mon-Thurs 9-7, Fri & Sat 9-5
Friends of the Library Group

OLD MYSTIC

S INDIAN & COLONIAL RESEARCH CENTER, INC*, Butler Library, 39 Main St Rte 27, 06372. (Mail add: PO Box 525, 06372-0525), SAN 302-3125. Tel: 860-536-9771. E-mail: icrc06372@yahoo.com. Web Site: indianandcolonial.org.
Founded 1965
Library Holdings: Bk Vols 3,500
Special Collections: Glass Plate negatives & prints 1890-1920; Local Genealogy; Rare American School Books. Oral History
Subject Interests: Genealogy, Native Americans
Publications: Along Shore; Around the Pond; Two Little Navahos Dip Their Sheep; When the Frogs Begin to Peep
Open Tues & Thurs 10-4 & by appointment

OLD SAYBROOK

P ACTON PUBLIC LIBRARY*, 60 Old Boston Post Rd, 06475-2200. SAN 302-3133. Tel: 860-395-3184. FAX: 860-395-2462. E-mail: actonpubliclibrary@gmail.com. Web Site: www.actonlibrary.org. *Dir,* Amanda Brouwer; Tel: 860-388-8924, E-mail: abrouwer@actonlibrary.org; *Asst Dir, Ch,* Karen Giugno; Tel: 860-501-5060, E-mail: kgiugno@actonlibrary.org; *Head, Circ,* Virginia Clarke; Tel: 860-501-5066, E-mail: vclarke@actonlibrary.org; *Cataloger,* Norma Wright; Tel: 860-501-5065, E-mail: nwright@actonlibrary.org; Staff 17 (MLS 4, Non-MLS 13)
Founded 1872. Pop 10,535; Circ 244,218
Library Holdings: CDs 1,023; DVDs 402; Large Print Bks 3,200; Bk Vols 71,180; Per Subs 133; Talking Bks 1,520; Videos 1,440
Subject Interests: Local hist
Automation Activity & Vendor Info: (Cataloging) Follett Software
Wireless access
Function: Adult bk club, Adult literacy prog, Bk club(s), Digital talking bks, Homebound delivery serv, ILL available, Magnifiers for reading, Mail & tel request accepted, Online ref, Orientations, Photocopying/Printing, Preschool outreach, Prof lending libr, Prog for adults, Prog for children & young adult, Ref serv available, Satellite serv, Spoken cassettes & CDs, Summer reading prog, Tax forms, Telephone ref, VHS videos, Wheelchair accessible
Publications: Old Saybrook Events (Quarterly)
Open Mon-Thurs 10-8, Fri & Sat 10-5, Sun (Oct-May) 1-5
Friends of the Library Group

ONECO

P STERLING PUBLIC LIBRARY*, 1183 Plainfield Pike, 06373. (Mail add: PO Box 157, 06373-0157), SAN 323-6226. Tel: 860-564-2692. FAX: 860-564-0789. E-mail: sterlingpublib@atlanticbbn.net. Web Site: www.sterlingct.us/departments/library. *Librn,* Rachel Vincent
Founded 1928. Pop 3,400
Library Holdings: CDs 75; DVDs 375; Large Print Bks 150; Bk Titles 21,000; Per Subs 25
Wireless access
Function: ILL available, Photocopying/Printing
Open Tues 10-7, Thurs 1-7, Sat 9-Noon

ORANGE

P CASE MEMORIAL LIBRARY*, 176 Tyler City Rd, 06477-2498. SAN 302-315X. Tel: 203-891-2170. FAX: 203-891-2190. E-mail: caseref@lioninc.org. Web Site: orange.lioninc.org. *Dir,* Meryl P Farber; E-mail: mfarber@lioninc.org; *Head, Children's Servx,* Michelle DeSarbo; E-mail: mdesarbo@lioninc.org; *Head, Circ,* Samantha Macelis; E-mail: smacelis@lioninc.org; *Head, Ref & Adult Serv,* Rebecca Harlow; E-mail: rharlow@lioninc.org; *Head, Tech Serv,* Jonathan Wiener; E-mail: jwiener@lioninc.org; Staff 14 (MLS 5, Non-MLS 9)
Founded 1956. Pop 13,233; Circ 137,000
Library Holdings: AV Mats 12,056; Bk Vols 103,957; Per Subs 143
Subject Interests: Local hist
Automation Activity & Vendor Info: (Acquisitions) Innovative Interfaces, Inc; (Cataloging) Innovative Interfaces, Inc; (Circulation) Innovative Interfaces, Inc; (ILL) Innovative Interfaces, Inc - Millennium; (OPAC) Innovative Interfaces, Inc
Wireless access
Partic in Libraries Online, Inc
Open Mon & Thurs Noon-8, Tues, Wed & Fri 10-5, Sat 10-4
Friends of the Library Group

OXFORD

P OXFORD PUBLIC LIBRARY, 49 Great Oak Rd, 06478. SAN 302-3176. Tel: 203-888-6944. FAX: 203-888-2666. E-mail: staff@oxfordlib.org. Web Site: www.oxfordlib.org. *Director, Municipal Libr,* Ms Robbi Costigan; E-mail: robbi.costigan@oxford-ct.gov; Staff 5 (MLS 3, Non-MLS 2)
Founded 1883. Pop 13,100; Circ 52,000
Jul 2020-Jun 2021 Income $610,235, State $350, City $608,385, Locally Generated Income $1,500. Mats Exp $28,300, Books $20,000, Per/Ser (Incl. Access Fees) $4,500, Electronic Ref Mat (Incl. Access Fees) $3,800. Sal $285,491 (Prof $165,285)
Library Holdings: Bk Vols 30,000; Per Subs 40
Subject Interests: Hist
Automation Activity & Vendor Info: (Acquisitions) Bibliomation Inc; (Cataloging) Evergreen; (Circulation) Evergreen; (OPAC) Evergreen
Wireless access
Function: 24/7 Electronic res, 24/7 Online cat, Activity rm, Adult bk club, After school storytime, Art exhibits, Art programs, Audiobks via web, Bk club(s), Bks on CD, Children's prog, Computer training, Computers for patron use, Digital talking bks, E-Readers, Electronic databases & coll, Free DVD rentals, Holiday prog, ILL available, Internet access, Life-long learning prog for all ages, Magazines, Meeting rooms, Movies, Museum passes, Music CDs, Online cat, Online ref, Outside serv via phone, mail, e-mail & web, OverDrive digital audio bks, Photocopying/Printing, Preschool outreach, Preschool reading prog, Prog for adults, Prog for children & young adult, Ref & res, Ref serv available, Scanner, Senior computer classes, Serves people with intellectual disabilities, STEM programs, Story hour, Study rm, Summer & winter reading prog, Summer reading prog, Tax forms, Teen prog, Telephone ref, Wheelchair accessible, Winter reading prog, Workshops, Writing prog
Partic in Bibliomation Inc; CLA
Open Mon, Wed, Fri & Sat 9-4, Tues & Thurs 9-7
Friends of the Library Group

PLAINVILLE

S CONNECTICUT CLEARINGHOUSE LIBRARY*, 334 Farmington Ave, 06062. SAN 378-3723. Tel: 860-793-9791. Toll Free Tel: 800-232-4424. FAX: 860-793-9813. E-mail: info@ctclearinghouse.org. Web Site: www.ctclearinghouse.org.
Library Holdings: AV Mats 1,600; Bk Titles 3,600
Subject Interests: Mental health, Substance abuse, Wellness
Automation Activity & Vendor Info: (Cataloging) SirsiDynix; (OPAC) SirsiDynix
Open Mon-Wed & Fri 8:30-5, Thurs 8:30-7:30

P PLAINVILLE PUBLIC LIBRARY, 56 East Main St, 06062. SAN 302-3206. Tel: 860-793-1446. FAX: 860-793-2241. E-mail: plainvillepubliclibrary@gmail.com. Web Site: plainvillect.com/library. *Dir,* Trish Tomlinson; Staff 4 (MLS 3, Non-MLS 1)
Founded 1894. Pop 16,770; Circ 163,896
Library Holdings: Bk Vols 94,000; Per Subs 164
Automation Activity & Vendor Info: (Acquisitions) Baker & Taylor; (Cataloging) Innovative Interfaces, Inc - Sierra; (Circulation) Innovative Interfaces, Inc - Sierra; (OPAC) Innovative Interfaces, Inc; (Serials) Innovative Interfaces, Inc - Sierra
Wireless access
Function: 24/7 Electronic res, 24/7 Online cat, Activity rm, Adult bk club, Art exhibits, Bi-weekly Writer's Group, Bk club(s), Bks on CD, Children's prog, Computers for patron use, Electronic databases & coll, Free DVD rentals, ILL available, Internet access, Magazines, Mail & tel request accepted, Meeting rooms, Microfiche/film & reading machines, Movies, Museum passes, Music CDs, Online cat, OverDrive digital audio bks, Photocopying/Printing, Preschool outreach, Prog for adults, Prog for children & young adult, Ref serv available, Story hour, Study rm, Summer reading prog, Tax forms, Telephone ref, Wheelchair accessible
Partic in Library Connection, Inc
Open Mon-Thurs 9-8, Fri & Sat 9-4
Friends of the Library Group

PLYMOUTH

P PLYMOUTH LIBRARY ASSOCIATION*, 692 Main St, 06782. SAN 302-3222. Tel: 860-283-5977. E-mail: plymouth.library.ct@gmail.com. Web Site: www.plymouthlibraryct.org. *Head Librn,* Rebecca Schaffrick
Founded 1871. Pop 3,500
Library Holdings: Bk Titles 9,521; Per Subs 16
Special Collections: Local History (Plymouth Coll)
Wireless access
Partic in Region I Coop Libr Servs Unit
Open Mon & Fri 11-4, Wed 11-4 & 6-8, Sat 10-2

POMFRET

R CHRIST CHURCH LIBRARY*, 527 Pomfret St, 06258, (Mail add: PO Box 21, 06258-0021). Tel: 860-315-7780, 860-576-7907. E-mail: christchurchpomfret@gmail.com. Web Site: christchurchpomfret.org. *Librn,* Kristin Archambault; E-mail: sraarch7569@gmail.com; Staff 1 (MLS 1)
Founded 1988
Library Holdings: Bk Titles 2,000
Function: Prof lending libr
Friends of the Library Group

P POMFRET PUBLIC LIBRARY*, 449 Pomfret St, 06258. SAN 302-3230. Tel: 860-928-3475. E-mail: circdesk@pomfretlibrary.org. Web Site: pomfretlibrary.org. *Libr Dir,* Laurie M Bell; E-mail: lbell@pomfretlibrary.org; *Children's Prog Mgr,* Heather Reilly; *Libr Asst,* Kim Farragher; Staff 1.5 (MLS 0.5, Non-MLS 1)
Founded 1740. Pop 4,000; Circ 12,600
Library Holdings: Bk Vols 20,000; Per Subs 30
Special Collections: Pomfret & Windham County Historical Coll. Oral History
Wireless access
Function: Bk club(s), ILL available, Photocopying/Printing, Prog for children & young adult, Summer reading prog, Wheelchair accessible
Partic in Connecticut Library Consortium
Special Services for the Blind - Bks on cassette; Bks on CD; Large print bks; Lending of low vision aids
Open Tues-Thurs 10-6, Fri 2-6, Sat 10-2
Friends of the Library Group

PORTLAND

P PORTLAND LIBRARY, 20 Freestone Ave, 06480. SAN 302-3257. Tel: 860-342-6770. FAX: 860-342-6778. E-mail: PortlandLibrary@portlandct.org. Web Site: www.portlandlibraryct.org. *Dir,* Janet Nocek; E-mail: jnocek@portlandct.org; *Adult Serv,* Beth Kauczka; E-mail: bkauczka@portlandct.org
Founded 1895. Pop 9,052; Circ 145,000
Library Holdings: Bk Vols 60,000; Per Subs 256
Subject Interests: Local hist
Automation Activity & Vendor Info: (Cataloging) Innovative Interfaces, Inc; (Circulation) SirsiDynix; (OPAC) Innovative Interfaces, Inc
Wireless access
Function: Prog for children & young adult
Partic in Connecticut Library Consortium; Library Connection, Inc
Special Services for the Blind - Audio mat; Bks on cassette; Bks on CD; Large print bks; Magnifiers
Open Mon-Thurs 10-6, Fri 10-5, Sat 10-2
Friends of the Library Group

PRESTON

P PRESTON PUBLIC LIBRARY*, 389 Rt 2, 06365. SAN 376-3242. Tel: 860-886-1010. FAX: 860-886-4952. E-mail: library@prestonlibrary.org. Web Site: prestonlibrary.org. *Dir,* Susan Brosnan; *Asst Librn,* Marion Landi; Staff 7 (Non-MLS 7)
Founded 1898. Pop 5,500
Library Holdings: Bks on Deafness & Sign Lang 50; Large Print Bks 858; Bk Vols 27,000; Per Subs 40; Talking Bks 450; Videos 1,877
Special Collections: Preston Historical Society Coll
Subject Interests: Genealogy
Automation Activity & Vendor Info: (Cataloging) Auto-Graphics, Inc; (Circulation) Auto-Graphics, Inc; (ILL) Auto-Graphics, Inc; (OPAC) Auto-Graphics, Inc
Wireless access
Function: Adult bk club, Bks on cassette, Bks on CD, CD-ROM, Children's prog, Computer training, Computers for patron use, Digital talking bks, E-Reserves, Electronic databases & coll, Free DVD rentals, Homebound delivery serv, ILL available, Large print keyboards, Learning ctr, Magnifiers for reading, Museum passes, Music CDs, Online cat, Photocopying/Printing, Prog for adults, Prog for children & young adult, Ref serv available, Story hour, Summer reading prog, Tax forms, VHS videos, Wheelchair accessible
Special Services for the Deaf - Assistive tech; Bks on deafness & sign lang; Closed caption videos; TTY equip
Special Services for the Blind - Assistive/Adapted tech devices, equip & products; Closed circuit TV; Dragon Naturally Speaking software; Large print bks; Magnifiers; Reader equip; Talking bks
Open Mon 9-3, Tues-Thurs 9-8, Fri 9-5, Sat 9-1
Friends of the Library Group

PROSPECT

P PROSPECT PUBLIC LIBRARY*, 17 Center St, 06712. SAN 302-3273. Tel: 203-758-3001. FAX: 203-758-0080. E-mail: libraryprospect@yahoo.com. Web Site: www.prospectlibrary.com. *Dir,* John

Wiehn; *Asst Dir,* Kristina Garner; Tel: 203-758-0813; Staff 7 (MLS 2, Non-MLS 5)
Founded 1904. Pop 9,500; Circ 65,000
Library Holdings: DVDs 2,300; Bk Vols 45,000; Per Subs 42
Special Collections: Large Print-Mysteries
Automation Activity & Vendor Info: (Cataloging) Auto-Graphics, Inc; (Circulation) Auto-Graphics, Inc; (OPAC) Auto-Graphics, Inc
Wireless access
Function: 24/7 Electronic res, 24/7 Online cat, 3D Printer, Activity rm, Adult bk club, After school storytime, Art exhibits, Audiobks on Playaways & MP3, Audiobks via web, Bk club(s), Bks on CD, Chess club, Children's prog, Computers for patron use, Electronic databases & coll, Free DVD rentals, Genealogy discussion group, ILL available, Internet access, Magazines, Mail & tel request accepted, OverDrive digital audio bks, Photocopying/Printing, Prog for adults, Prog for children & young adult, Spoken cassettes & CDs, Story hour
Partic in Connecticut Library Consortium
Open Mon, Wed & Fri 10-5, Tues & Thurs 10-8, Sat 10-3
Friends of the Library Group

PUTNAM

P PUTNAM PUBLIC LIBRARY*, 225 Kennedy Dr, 06260-1691. SAN 302-3303. Tel: 860-963-6826. FAX: 860-963-6828. E-mail: ppl2252000@yahoo.com. *Dir,* Priscilla Colwell; E-mail: priscilla.colwell@putnamct.us; *Asst Dir, Ch,* Tina Aubin; *Ad,* Patricia Jensen; *Circ Supvr,* Mary Jo Abt; Staff 6.8 (MLS 1.8, Non-MLS 5)
Founded 1884. Pop 9,579; Circ 80,789
Library Holdings: Bk Vols 38,376; Per Subs 66
Special Collections: Genealogy Coll
Automation Activity & Vendor Info: (Cataloging) Bibliomation Inc; (Circulation) Bibliomation Inc; (ILL) Bibliomation Inc; (OPAC) Bibliomation Inc
Wireless access
Function: Adult bk club, Adult literacy prog, Audiobks via web, Bks on CD, Children's prog, Computers for patron use, Distance learning, Free DVD rentals, ILL available, Magazines, Microfiche/film & reading machines, Museum passes, Music CDs, Notary serv, Online cat, OverDrive digital audio bks, Photocopying/Printing, Preschool reading prog, Prog for adults, Prog for children & young adult, Summer reading prog, Tax forms, Teen prog
Partic in Bibliomation Inc
Special Services for the Blind - Bks on CD; Large print bks; Low vision equip; Magnifiers; Talking bk serv referral
Open Mon-Thurs 10-8, Fri 10-5, Sat 10-3
Friends of the Library Group

REDDING

P MARK TWAIN LIBRARY, 439 Redding Rd, 06896. (Mail add: PO Box 1009, 06875-1009), SAN 302-332X. Tel: 203-938-2545. FAX: 203-938-4026. Web Site: marktwainlibrary.org. *Dir,* Beth Dominianni; E-mail: Beth@marktwainlibrary.org; *Asst Dir, Head, Children's Servx, Head, Teen Serv,* Mary Hoskinson-Dean; E-mail: mhdean@marktwainlibrary.org; *Head, Adult Serv, Head, Circ,* Janet Ivaldi; E-mail: janet@marktwainlibrary.org; *Ch,* Lisa Cederbaum; E-mail: lisa@marktwainlibrary.org; Staff 5.3 (MLS 2.3, Non-MLS 3)
Founded 1908. Pop 8,572; Circ 96,978
Library Holdings: AV Mats 4,150; Bk Vols 45,162; Per Subs 122
Special Collections: Civil War (Massie Coll); Mark Twain Coll; Redding Land Trust; Religion & Mysticism (Hutchinson Coll)
Automation Activity & Vendor Info: (Cataloging) Follett Software; (Course Reserve) Follett Software; (ILL) Auto-Graphics, Inc; (Serials) Follett Software
Wireless access
Publications: Mark Twain Tatler (Newsletter)
Special Services for the Blind - Bks on CD
Open Mon-Fri 10-5, Sat 10-4

RIDGEFIELD

P RIDGEFIELD LIBRARY ASSOCIATION INC*, 472 Main St, 06877-4585. SAN 302-3346. Tel: 203-438-2282. FAX: 203-438-4558. Web Site: www.ridgefieldlibrary.org. *Dir,* Brenda B McKinley; E-mail: bjmckinley@ridgefieldlibrary.org; *Asst Dir,* Andy Forsyth; E-mail: aforsyth@ridgefieldlibrary.org; *Head, Adult Serv,* Dorothy Pawlowski; E-mail: dlpawl@ridgefieldlibrary.org; *Head, Children's Servx,* Kristina Lareau; E-mail: kjlareau@ridgefieldlibrary.org; *Ref Librn,* Victoria Carlquist; E-mail: vmcarlquist@ridgefieldlibrary.org; *ILL,* Karen Kazzi; E-mail: klkazzi@ridgefieldlibrary.org; Staff 7.5 (MLS 7.5)
Founded 1901. Pop 24,000; Circ 408,557
Library Holdings: Bk Titles 106,000; Bk Vols 130,000; Per Subs 240
Special Collections: Ridgefield History, bks, monographs
Subject Interests: Genealogy
Automation Activity & Vendor Info: (Acquisitions) SirsiDynix; (Cataloging) SirsiDynix; (Circulation) SirsiDynix; (OPAC) SirsiDynix; (Serials) SirsiDynix
Wireless access
Function: Adult bk club, Art exhibits, Audiobks via web, Bk club(s), Bks on CD, Children's prog, Computers for patron use, Electronic databases & coll, Homebound delivery serv, ILL available, Museum passes, Music CDs, Online cat, Online ref, Photocopying/Printing, Prog for adults, Prog for children & young adult, Story hour, Summer reading prog, Tax forms, Telephone ref
Publications: Newsletter
Partic in Bibliomation Inc
Special Services for the Blind - Reader equip
Open Mon-Thurs 10-8, Fri 10-6, Sat 9-5, Sun (Winter) 1-5
Friends of the Library Group

ROCKY HILL

P CORA J BELDEN LIBRARY, 33 Church St, 06067-1568. SAN 302-3370. Tel: 860-258-7621. Reference Tel: 860-258-7623. Web Site: www.rockyhillct.gov/library. *Dir,* Mary Hogan; E-mail: mhogan@rockyhillct.gov; *Asst Dir,* Michael Murphy; E-mail: mmurphy@rockyhillct.gov; Staff 14 (MLS 4, Non-MLS 10)
Founded 1794. Circ 235,280
Library Holdings: Per Subs 60
Automation Activity & Vendor Info: (Cataloging) Innovative Interfaces, Inc - Sierra; (Circulation) Innovative Interfaces, Inc; (ILL) OCLC; (OPAC) Innovative Interfaces, Inc
Wireless access
Function: 24/7 Electronic res, 24/7 Online cat, 3D Printer, Activity rm, Adult bk club, Adult literacy prog, After school storytime, Art exhibits, Audiobks via web, Bk club(s), Bks on CD, Children's prog, Computer training, Computers for patron use, Distance learning, E-Readers, Electronic databases & coll, Family literacy, Free DVD rentals, Holiday prog, ILL available, Life-long learning prog for all ages, Magazines, Magnifiers for reading, Meeting rooms, Movies, Museum passes, Music CDs, Online cat, Online info literacy tutorials on the web & in blackboard, OverDrive digital audio bks, Photocopying/Printing, Preschool outreach, Preschool reading prog, Prog for adults, Prog for children & young adult, Ref & res, Ref serv available, Scanner, Senior computer classes, Story hour, Summer & winter reading prog, Summer reading prog, Tax forms, Teen prog, Telephone ref, Wheelchair accessible, Winter reading prog, Workshops
Partic in Connecticut Library Consortium; Library Connection, Inc
Friends of the Library Group

S CONNECTICUT HORTICULTURAL SOCIETY LIBRARY*, 2433 Main St, 06067-2539. SAN 321-6748. Tel: 860-529-8713. E-mail: office@cthort.org. Web Site: cthort.org/library. *Library Contact,* Karen Bachand; Tel: 860-225-8852
Founded 1960
Library Holdings: Bk Titles 2,000
Subject Interests: Hort
Open Tues & Thurs 11-4

P CONNECTICUT STATE LIBRARY*, Library for the Blind & Physically Handicapped, 198 West St, 06067. SAN 302-1750. Tel: 860-721-2020. Toll Free Tel: 800-842-4516. FAX: 860-721-2056. E-mail: csl.lbph@ct.gov. *Dir,* Gordon Reddick; E-mail: gordon.reddick@ct.gov; Staff 8 (MLS 1, Non-MLS 7)
Founded 1968
Library Holdings: Bk Titles 92,834; Bk Vols 189,926
Special Collections: Connecticut Cassettes
Subject Interests: Connecticut, New England
Function: 24/7 Electronic res, 24/7 Online cat, Audiobks on Playaways & MP3, Audiobks via web, Bilingual assistance for Spanish patrons, Bk club(s), Computers for patron use, Digital talking bks, Equip loans & repairs, Homebound delivery serv, ILL available, Internet access, Magnifiers for reading, Mail & tel request accepted, Mail loans to mem, Online cat, Wheelchair accessible
Special Services for the Blind - Braille bks; Digital talking bk; Digital talking bk machines; Home delivery serv; Talking bks & player equip; Web-Braille
Open Mon-Fri 9-3
Restriction: Authorized patrons, Borrowing privileges limited to fac & registered students, Open to authorized patrons, Registered patrons only, Restricted loan policy
Friends of the Library Group

S ROCKY HILL HISTORICAL SOCIETY LIBRARY, Ethel Miner Cooke Historical & Genealogical Library, 785 Old Main St, 06067. (Mail add: PO Box 185, 06067-0185), SAN 302-3397. Tel: 860-563-6704. E-mail: inforhhistory@gmail.com. Web Site: www.rhhistory.org. *Librn,* Susan Karpuk; *Librn,* Lorrie Wallace

Founded 1969
Library Holdings: Bk Titles 310
Subject Interests: Genealogy, Local hist
Wireless access
Function: Res libr
Open Sat 12:30-3 or by appointment

ROWAYTON

P ROWAYTON LIBRARY*, The Association of the Free Library & Reading Room of Rowayton, Inc., 33 Highland Ave, 06853. SAN 302-3419. Tel: 203-838-5038. FAX: 203-523-0438, 928-437-5038. E-mail: library@rowayton.org. Web Site: www.rowayton.org, www.rowaytonlibrary.org. *Libr Dir,* Melissa Yurechko; E-mail: myurechko@rowayton.org; *Asst Dir,* Christina Anzalone; Staff 4 (MLS 1, Non-MLS 3)
Founded 1903. Pop 4,000; Circ 23,473
Library Holdings: Bk Vols 33,000; Per Subs 75
Automation Activity & Vendor Info: (Acquisitions) Bibliomation Inc; (Cataloging) Bibliomation Inc; (Circulation) Bibliomation Inc; (ILL) Auto-Graphics, Inc; (OPAC) Bibliomation Inc; (Serials) Bibliomation Inc
Wireless access
Function: Adult bk club, Bk club(s), Bk reviews (Group), Bks on CD, CD-ROM, Chess club, Children's prog, Computer training, Computers for patron use, Digital talking bks, Electronic databases & coll, Free DVD rentals, Holiday prog, Homework prog, ILL available, Instruction & testing, Internet access, Jazz prog, Museum passes, Music CDs, Online cat, Online info literacy tutorials on the web & in blackboard, Online ref, Orientations, OverDrive digital audio bks, Photocopying/Printing, Preschool outreach, Prog for adults, Prog for children & young adult, Ref & res, Ref serv available, Scanner, Senior outreach, Spoken cassettes & CDs, Spoken cassettes & DVDs, Story hour, Summer reading prog, Tax forms, Teen prog, Telephone ref, Wheelchair accessible, Workshops, Writing prog
Partic in Bibliomation Inc
Special Services for the Deaf - Assisted listening device
Open Mon, Tues, Thurs & Fri 10-5, Wed 10-7, Sat 10-5

ROXBURY

P MINOR MEMORIAL LIBRARY*, 23 South St, 06783. (Mail add: PO Box 249, 06783-0249), SAN 374-5791. Tel: 860-350-2181. FAX: 860-350-6882. E-mail: roxbury@biblio.org. Web Site: www.minormemoriallibrary.org. *Dir,* Teresa Roxburgh; *Librn,* Joan Temple; *Adult Prog Coordr,* Sarah Griswold; *Coord, Ad Serv,* Betty Synnestvedt; *Coordr, Ch Serv,* Paula Sapse; Staff 6 (MLS 1, Non-MLS 5)
Founded 1896. Pop 2,300; Circ 16,138
Library Holdings: AV Mats 5,792; Electronic Media & Resources 5,454; Large Print Bks 345; Bk Titles 35,737; Per Subs 20; Talking Bks 2,299; Videos 3,493
Special Collections: Hanson Baldwin Coll
Subject Interests: World War II
Automation Activity & Vendor Info: (Cataloging) Evergreen; (Circulation) Evergreen; (OPAC) Evergreen
Wireless access
Publications: Bookmark (Friends)
Partic in Bibliomation Inc
Special Services for the Blind - Assistive/Adapted tech devices, equip & products
Open Mon 12-7, Wed & Fri 10-5, Thurs 12-5, Sat 10-2
Friends of the Library Group

SALEM

P SALEM FREE PUBLIC LIBRARY*, 264 Hartford Rd, 06420. SAN 376-2645. Tel: 860-859-1130. FAX: 860-859-9961. Web Site: www.salemct.gov/library. *Libr Dir,* Vicky Coffin; E-mail: vicky.coffin@salemct.gov; Staff 3 (MLS 1, Non-MLS 2)
Founded 1915. Pop 6,500; Circ 71,500
Library Holdings: Audiobooks 2,065; CDs 620; DVDs 1,840; e-books 24; Large Print Bks 755; Bk Vols 26,000; Per Subs 40; Videos 1,450
Automation Activity & Vendor Info: (Cataloging) Bibliomation Inc; (Circulation) Horizon; (OPAC) Infor Library & Information Solutions
Wireless access
Partic in Bibliomation Inc
Open Mon & Thurs 10-6, Tues & Wed 12-8, Fri 10-4, Sat 10-2
Friends of the Library Group

SALISBURY

P SCOVILLE MEMORIAL LIBRARY*, 38 Main St, 06068. SAN 302-3443. Tel: 860-435-2838. FAX: 860-435-8136. Web Site: www.scovillelibrary.org. *Dir,* Claudia E Cayne; E-mail: ccayne@biblio.org
Pop 3,452; Circ 54,793
Library Holdings: Bk Vols 35,000; Per Subs 70
Special Collections: Local History (Smith & Bingham Coll)
Automation Activity & Vendor Info: (Acquisitions) Evergreen; (Cataloging) Evergreen; (Circulation) Evergreen; (OPAC) Evergreen
Wireless access
Function: 24/7 Electronic res, 24/7 Online cat, Activity rm, Adult bk club, Audiobks via web, AV serv, Bks on CD, Butterfly Garden, Children's prog, Computer training, Computers for patron use, E-Readers, E-Reserves, Free DVD rentals, Holiday prog, Home delivery & serv to seniorr ctr & nursing homes, Homebound delivery serv, ILL available, Internet access, Laminating, Life-long learning prog for all ages, Magazines, Magnifiers for reading, Mail & tel request accepted, Meeting rooms, Microfiche/film & reading machines, Movies, Museum passes, Music CDs, Online cat, Outreach serv, OverDrive digital audio bks, Photocopying/Printing, Preschool outreach, Printer for laptops & handheld devices, Prog for adults, Prog for children & young adult, Ref serv available, Scanner, Senior computer classes, Spoken cassettes & CDs, Story hour, Study rm, Summer reading prog, Tax forms, Writing prog
Partic in Bibliomation Inc
Open Tues, Wed & Fri 10-5, Thurs 10-7, Sat 10-4, Sun 1-4
Friends of the Library Group

SCOTLAND

P SCOTLAND PUBLIC LIBRARY*, 21 Brook Rd, 06264. (Mail add: PO Box 286, 06264-0286), SAN 302-3451. Tel: 860-423-1492. FAX: 860-423-1526. Web Site: scotlandpubliclibrary.org. *Dir,* Mary Geragotelis; E-mail: spldirector@scotlandpubliclibrary.org; Staff 2 (Non-MLS 2)
Pop 1,700; Circ 3,307
Library Holdings: AV Mats 575; Large Print Bks 200; Bk Vols 14,000; Per Subs 30; Videos 900
Wireless access
Partic in Connecticut Library Consortium
Open Tues, Wed & Fri 2-5, Thurs & Sat 9-12

SEYMOUR

P SEYMOUR PUBLIC LIBRARY*, 46 Church St, 06483. SAN 302-346X. Tel: 203-888-3903. FAX: 203-888-4099. Web Site: www.seymourpubliclibrary.org. *Dir,* Suzanne Garvey; E-mail: sgarvey@biblio.org; *Asst Librn,* Lisa Omlor; E-mail: lomlor@biblio.org; *Ref Librn,* Charlotte Rowell; E-mail: crowell@biblio.org; *Ch Serv,* Ann Szaley; E-mail: aszaley@biblio.org; Staff 6 (MLS 2, Non-MLS 4)
Founded 1892. Pop 15,700; Circ 87,556
Jul 2013-Jun 2014 Income $520,163, City $427,902, Locally Generated Income $92,261. Mats Exp $84,790. Sal $300,277
Library Holdings: AV Mats 2,374; e-books 5,000; Bk Vols 76,000; Per Subs 7,000; Talking Bks 1,194; Videos 4,000
Special Collections: Historical Reference Coll
Automation Activity & Vendor Info: (Circulation) Evergreen; (OPAC) Evergreen
Wireless access
Publications: Voices (Newsletter)
Partic in Bibliomation Inc; Connecticut Library Consortium
Open Tues & Wed 9-8, Thurs 9-5:30, Fri 9-5, Sat 9-4
Friends of the Library Group

SHARON

P HOTCHKISS LIBRARY OF SHARON, INC*, Ten Upper Main St, 06069. SAN 302-3478. Tel: 860-364-5041. FAX: 860-364-6060. E-mail: hotchkisslibrary@gmail.com. Web Site: www.hotchkisslibrary.org. *Exec Dir,* Gretchen Hachmeister; *Ch, Head, Libr Serv,* Robin Yuran
Founded 1893. Pop 2,700; Circ 29,645
Library Holdings: Audiobooks 800; DVDs 1,300; Per Subs 18
Special Collections: Connecticut Historical Room
Wireless access
Function: 24/7 Online cat, Adult bk club, Art exhibits, Audiobks via web, Bk club(s), Bks on CD, Chess club, Children's prog, Computer training, Computers for patron use, Free DVD rentals, Internet access, Life-long learning prog for all ages, Magazines, Magnifiers for reading, Movies, Online cat, Photocopying/Printing, Preschool outreach, Preschool reading prog, Prog for adults, Prog for children & young adult, Scanner, Senior computer classes, Senior outreach, Story hour, Summer reading prog, Tax forms
Partic in Bibliomation Inc; Region I Coop Libr Servs Unit
Open Mon & Fri 10-5, Tues 12-7, Wed & Thurs 12-5, Sat 10-4, Sun 12-3
Friends of the Library Group

E SHARON HOSPITAL*, Health Science Library, 50 Hospital Hill Rd, 06069. SAN 302-3486. Tel: 860-364-4008. *Library Contact,* Position Currently Open
Library Holdings: e-books 400; e-journals 90
Wireless access
Partic in Conn Asn of Health Scis Librs; North Atlantic Health Sciences Libraries, Inc; NW Conn Health Sci Libr
Restriction: Staff use only

SHELTON

P PLUMB MEMORIAL LIBRARY*, 65 Wooster St, 06484, SAN 302-3516. Tel: 203-924-1580. FAX: 203-924-8422. Web Site: www.sheltonlibrarysystem.org. *Dir, Libr Syst,* Joan Stokes; E-mail: jstokes@biblio.org; *Ch,* Maura Guartiere; E-mail: mguartiere@biblio.org; Staff 10 (MLS 4, Non-MLS 6)
Founded 1896. Pop 38,000; Circ 277,051
Jul 2015-Jun 2016. Mats Exp $163,883, Books $70,000, Per/Ser (Incl. Access Fees) $15,035, AV Mat $38,950, Electronic Ref Mat (Incl. Access Fees) $39,898. Sal $80,000
Library Holdings: Audiobooks 4,161; CDs 3,189; DVDs 14,390; e-books 2,503; Electronic Media & Resources 43; Large Print Bks 3,144; Bk Vols 127,311; Per Subs 387; Videos 567
Subject Interests: Connecticut, Local hist
Automation Activity & Vendor Info: (Cataloging) Evergreen; (Circulation) Evergreen; (ILL) Evergreen; (OPAC) Evergreen
Wireless access
Function: 24/7 Electronic res, 24/7 Online cat, Activity rm, Adult bk club, Audiobks on Playaways & MP3, Audiobks via web, Bks on CD, Children's prog, Computers for patron use, Electronic databases & coll, Free DVD rentals, Home delivery & serv to seniorr ctr & nursing homes, Homebound delivery serv, ILL available, Internet access, Magazines, Meeting rooms, Microfiche/film & reading machines, Museum passes, Music CDs, Online cat, OverDrive digital audio bks, Photocopying/Printing, Prog for adults, Prog for children & young adult, Story hour, Summer reading prog, Tax forms
Partic in Bibliomation Inc; Connecticut Library Consortium
Open Mon-Thurs 9-8:30, Fri & Sat 9-4:30
Friends of the Library Group
Branches: 1
HUNTINGTON BRANCH, 41 Church St, 06484-5804, SAN 375-5940. Tel: 203-926-0111. FAX: 203-926-0181. *Br Dir,* Marcia Austin; E-mail: director.hbl@sheltonlibrarysystem.org; Staff 4 (MLS 1, Non-MLS 3)
Founded 1991. Pop 40,000; Circ 54,037
Automation Activity & Vendor Info: (Circulation) Evergreen
Function: 24/7 Electronic res, 24/7 Online cat, Activity rm, Adult bk club, Audiobks on Playaways & MP3, Audiobks via web, Bks on CD, Children's prog, Computers for patron use, Electronic databases & coll, Free DVD rentals, Home delivery & serv to seniorr ctr & nursing homes, Homebound delivery serv, ILL available, Internet access, Magazines, Meeting rooms, Movies, Museum passes, Music CDs, Online cat, OverDrive digital audio bks, Photocopying/Printing, Preschool outreach, Prog for adults, Prog for children & young adult, Scanner, Story hour, Summer reading prog, Tax forms, Teen prog
Open Mon 12-8, Tues-Thurs 10-8, Fri 10-5, Sat 10-3
Friends of the Library Group

SHERMAN

P SHERMAN LIBRARY ASSOCIATION*, Rte 37 & 39, 06784. (Mail add: PO Box 40, 06784-0040), SAN 302-3524. Tel: 860-354-2455. FAX: 860-354-7215. E-mail: sl@biblio.org. Web Site: shermanlibrary.org. *Dir,* Ashleigh Blake; E-mail: ablake@biblio.org; Staff 4 (Non-MLS 4)
Founded 1926. Pop 3,827; Circ 60,000
Library Holdings: Bk Vols 25,000; Per Subs 40
Special Collections: Sherman Authors
Automation Activity & Vendor Info: (Cataloging) Bibliomation Inc; (Circulation) Bibliomation Inc; (ILL) Bibliomation Inc; (OPAC) Bibliomation Inc
Partic in Bibliomation Inc; Region I Coop Libr Servs Unit
Open Tues, Wed & Fri 11-6, Thurs 11-7, Sat 10-4

SIMSBURY

S SIMSBURY HISTORICAL SOCIETY ARCHIVES*, Phelps Tavern Museum, 800 Hopmeadow St, 06070. (Mail add: PO Box 2, 06070-0002), SAN 302-3532. Tel: 860-658-2500. FAX: 860-651-4354. E-mail: info@simsburyhistory.org. Web Site: www.simsburyhistory.org/research. *Archivist,* Stephen E Simon; E-mail: archives@simsburyhistory.org; Staff 3 (MLS 1, Non-MLS 2)
Founded 1911
Special Collections: Early Fuse Manufacturing Industry (Ensign Bickford Company Coll); Early Republic Period Documents Detailing the Barber Family of Connecticut (Lucius Israel Barber Coll); Family Papers of the Eno & Related Phelps Families (William P Eno Foundation Coll); Photographic Images in Various Media of People & Places Connected to Simsbury; Simsbury Area Persons Family Papers. Oral History
Subject Interests: Local hist
Wireless access
Function: Archival coll, Audio & video playback equip for onsite use, Bus archives, Computers for patron use, For res purposes, Mail & tel request accepted, Photocopying/Printing, Ref & res, VHS videos
Restriction: Closed stack, Non-circulating coll, Open by appt only, Photo ID required for access

P SIMSBURY PUBLIC LIBRARY*, 725 Hopmeadow St, 06070. SAN 302-3540. Tel: 860-658-7663. FAX: 860-658-6732. Web Site: www.simsburylibrary.info. *Dir,* Lisa Karim; E-mail: lkarim@simsburylibrary.info; *Head of Borrowing & Tech Services,* Rachel Gravel; E-mail: rgravel@simsburylibrary.info; *Head, Adult Serv,* Susan Ray; E-mail: sray@simsburylibrary.info; *Head, Children's Servx,* Stephanie C Prato; E-mail: sprato@simsburylibrary.info; *Bus Resource Ctr Coord,* Position Currently Open; Staff 27 (MLS 15, Non-MLS 12)
Founded 1890. Pop 23,985
Library Holdings: Bk Vols 175,000
Subject Interests: Genealogy
Automation Activity & Vendor Info: (Cataloging) Innovative Interfaces, Inc - Sierra; (Circulation) Innovative Interfaces, Inc - Sierra; (OPAC) Innovative Interfaces, Inc - Sierra
Wireless access
Partic in Connecticut Library Consortium; Library Connection, Inc
Open Mon-Thurs 9:30-8:30, Fri & Sat 9:30-5:30, Sun 1-5
Friends of the Library Group

SOMERS

S OSBORN CORRECTIONAL INSTITUTION*, Osborn CI Library, 335 Bilton Rd, 06071. (Mail add: PO Box 100, 06071-0100), SAN 302-3559. Tel: 860-814-4600. FAX: 860-814-4826. *Librn,* Position Currently Open
Library Holdings: Bk Vols 18,000
Subject Interests: Law
Open Mon-Fri 8-4 & 7-9

P SOMERS PUBLIC LIBRARY, Two Vision Blvd, 06071. SAN 302-3567. Tel: 860-763-3501. FAX: 860-763-1718. Web Site: www.somerspubliclibrary.org. *Libr Dir,* Jessica M Miller; E-mail: jmmiller@biblio.org; *Ch,* Marie Stromwall; E-mail: mstromwall@biblio.org; *Ref Librn, Tech Coordr,* Cecelia Becker; E-mail: cbecker@biblio.org; *Teen Librn,* Brooke Morrill, Jr; E-mail: som-teen@biblio.org; *Circ Supvr,* Frances Clark; E-mail: fclark@biblio.org; *Circ Asst, ILL,* Allison Rief; E-mail: som-ill@biblio.org; Staff 6 (MLS 3, Non-MLS 3)
Founded 1887. Pop 11,000; Circ 87,905
Subject Interests: Local hist
Automation Activity & Vendor Info: (Acquisitions) SirsiDynix; (Cataloging) SirsiDynix; (Circulation) SirsiDynix; (ILL) Auto-Graphics, Inc; (OPAC) SirsiDynix; (Serials) SirsiDynix
Wireless access
Function: 24/7 Electronic res, 24/7 Online cat, Activity rm, Adult bk club, Archival coll, Art exhibits, Art programs, Audiobks on Playaways & MP3, Audiobks via web, Bk club(s), Bks on CD, Children's prog, Computer training, Computers for patron use, E-Readers, Electronic databases & coll, Family literacy, For res purposes, Free DVD rentals, Govt ref serv, Holiday prog, Home delivery & serv to seniorr ctr & nursing homes, Homebound delivery serv, ILL available, Internet access, Life-long learning prog for all ages, Literacy & newcomer serv, Magazines, Magnifiers for reading, Mail & tel request accepted, Meeting rooms, Movies, Museum passes, Music CDs, Online cat, Outreach serv, Outside serv via phone, mail, e-mail & web, OverDrive digital audio bks, Photocopying/Printing, Preschool outreach, Preschool reading prog, Printer for laptops & handheld devices, Prog for adults, Prog for children & young adult, Ref & res, Ref serv available, Res assist avail, Scanner, Story hour, Study rm, Summer & winter reading prog, Summer reading prog, Tax forms, Teen prog, Telephone ref, Wheelchair accessible, Winter reading prog, Writing prog
Partic in Bibliomation Inc
Open Mon-Thurs 10-8, Fri 10-5, Sat 10-5 (10-1 Summer)
Friends of the Library Group

SOUTH WINDHAM

P GUILFORD SMITH MEMORIAL LIBRARY, 17 Main St, 06266-1121. (Mail add: PO Box 159, 06266-0159), SAN 302-3583. Tel: 860-423-5159. FAX: 860-423-5159. Web Site: www.guilfordsmith.blog. *Libr Dir,* Andrea Holbrook; E-mail: aholbrook@biblio.org; Staff 3 (Non-MLS 3)
Founded 1930. Pop 500; Circ 10,000
Library Holdings: Audiobooks 25; AV Mats 138; Bks on Deafness & Sign Lang 12; CDs 80; DVDs 100; e-books 201; High Interest/Low Vocabulary Bk Vols 225; Large Print Bks 130; Bk Titles 9,969; Per Subs 40
Special Collections: Connecticut History Coll; South Windham History Coll; Windham County History Coll. Oral History
Automation Activity & Vendor Info: (Acquisitions) Baker & Taylor; (Circulation) Bibliomation Inc; (Serials) EBSCO Online
Wireless access
Function: 24/7 Online cat, Adult bk club, After school storytime, Audiobks via web, Bk club(s), Bks on cassette, Bks on CD, CD-ROM, Children's prog, Computer training, Computers for patron use, Electronic databases & coll, Free DVD rentals, Genealogy discussion group, Holiday prog, Home delivery & serv to seniorr ctr & nursing homes, Homebound delivery serv, Homework prog, ILL available, Magazines, Magnifiers for

reading, Movies, Museum passes, Music CDs, Online cat, OverDrive digital audio bks, Photocopying/Printing, Prog for adults, Prog for children & young adult, Scanner, Serves people with intellectual disabilities, Story hour, Study rm, Summer & winter reading prog, Summer reading prog, Tax forms, Teen prog, Wheelchair accessible, Winter reading prog
Partic in Bibliomation Inc
Open Tues 10-8, Wed 10-1, Thurs 5-8, Fri 2-6, Sat 10-2
Friends of the Library Group

SOUTH WINDSOR

P SOUTH WINDSOR PUBLIC LIBRARY, 1550 Sullivan Ave, 06074. SAN 302-3605. Tel: 860-644-1541. FAX: 860-644-7645. Web Site: www.southwindsorlibrary.org. *Dir,* Mary J Etter; E-mail: metter@libraryconnection.info; *Ch Serv,* Michelle Kaminiski; *Circ,* Linda Clark; *Coll Develop,* Joseph Pava; *Ref,* Sandy Westbrook; Staff 29 (MLS 5, Non-MLS 24)
Founded 1898. Pop 25,000
Library Holdings: Bk Vols 124,000; Per Subs 350
Subject Interests: Local hist
Automation Activity & Vendor Info: (Cataloging) SirsiDynix; (Circulation) SirsiDynix; (ILL) SirsiDynix
Wireless access
Partic in Connecticut Library Consortium; Library Connection, Inc
Open Mon-Thurs 9-9, Fri & Sat 9-4:30, Sun 1-4:30
Friends of the Library Group

P WOOD MEMORIAL LIBRARY, 783 Main St, 06074. (Mail add: PO Box 131, 06074-0131), SAN 376-2807. Tel: 860-289-1783. Web Site: woodmemoriallibrary.org. *Exec Dir,* Carolyn Venne; E-mail: director@woodmemoriallibrary.org; *Archivist, Research Librn,* Leith Johnson; E-mail: archives@woodmemoriallibrary.org
Founded 1927
Library Holdings: Bk Titles 12,000; Bk Vols 15,000
Subject Interests: Birding, Birds, Local hist
Partic in Connecticut Library Consortium
Open Mon 10-5, Thurs 10-8
Friends of the Library Group

SOUTHBURY

P SOUTHBURY PUBLIC LIBRARY*, 100 Poverty Rd, 06488. SAN 302-3613. Tel: 203-262-0626. FAX: 203-262-6734. Web Site: www.southburylibrary.org. *Head Librn,* Shirley Thorson; Tel: 203-262-0626, Ext 140, E-mail: sthorson@biblio.org; *Circ & ILL,* Christine Healy; E-mail: cghealy@biblio.org; *Ref,* Rebecca Randall; E-mail: rrandall@biblio.org; *Teen Serv,* Elizabeth Kelly; E-mail: eakelly@biblio.org; *Youth Serv,* Heather Aronson; E-mail: haronson@biblio.org; Staff 5 (MLS 5)
Founded 1969. Pop 19,877; Circ 315,749
Library Holdings: Bk Vols 92,955; Per Subs 78
Automation Activity & Vendor Info: (Acquisitions) Evergreen; (Cataloging) Evergreen; (Circulation) Evergreen; (ILL) Evergreen; (OPAC) Evergreen; (Serials) Evergreen
Wireless access
Function: Activity rm, Adult bk club, After school storytime, Art exhibits, Audiobks via web, AV serv, Bk club(s), Bks on cassette, Bks on CD, Children's prog, Computer training, Computers for patron use, E-Readers, Electronic databases & coll, Free DVD rentals, Holiday prog, Homebound delivery serv, ILL available, Instruction & testing, Internet access, Jazz prog, Life-long learning prog for all ages, Magazines, Magnifiers for reading, Mango lang, Microfiche/film & reading machines, Movies, Museum passes, Music CDs, Online cat, Outreach serv, OverDrive digital audio bks, Photocopying/Printing, Preschool outreach, Preschool reading prog, Printer for laptops & handheld devices, Prog for adults, Prog for children & young adult, Ref serv available, Scanner, Senior outreach, Spanish lang bks, Spoken cassettes & CDs, Spoken cassettes & DVDs, Story hour, Summer reading prog, Tax forms, Teen prog, Telephone ref, Wheelchair accessible, Workshops
Publications: Monthly calendar
Partic in Bibliomation Inc; Connecticut Library Consortium
Special Services for the Deaf - Assisted listening device; Closed caption videos
Special Services for the Blind - Bks on CD; Large print bks; Low vision equip
Open Mon, Wed & Fri 9:30-4:30, Tues & Thurs 9:30-8:30
Friends of the Library Group

SOUTHINGTON

P SOUTHINGTON PUBLIC LIBRARY & MUSEUM*, Southington Library, 255 Main St, 06489. SAN 302-363X. Tel: 860-628-0947. FAX: 860-628-0488. Web Site: www.southingtonlibrary.org. *Exec Dir,* Kristi Sadowski; *Head, Children's Servx,* Cindy Wall; E-mail: wallc@southington.org; *Cataloger, Head, Coll Mgt,* Billie Gaber; E-mail: witkovicb@southington.org; *Head, Lending Serv,* Shelley Holley; E-mail: holleys@southington.org; *Ch,* Lynn Pawloski; E-mail: pawloskil@southington.org; *Ch,* Molly Verillo; E-mail: verillom@southington.org; *Ref Librn,* Louisa Champagne; E-mail: champagnel@southington.org; *Ref Librn,* Lynn Gardner; E-mail: gardnerl@southington.org; *Ref Librn, Teen Serv Librn,* Nicole Kent; E-mail: kentn@southington.org; *Acq, Pub Relations,* Elizabeth Chubet; E-mail: chubete@southington.org; Staff 19 (MLS 10, Non-MLS 9)
Founded 1902. Pop 43,817; Circ 313,100
Jul 2015-Jun 2016 Income $1,406,029
Library Holdings: Audiobooks 2,246; CDs 3,576; DVDs 16,207; e-books 111,246; Bk Vols 145,745; Per Subs 147
Automation Activity & Vendor Info: (Acquisitions) Innovative Interfaces, Inc - Sierra; (Cataloging) Innovative Interfaces, Inc; (Circulation) Innovative Interfaces, Inc; (ILL) Innovative Interfaces, Inc; (OPAC) Innovative Interfaces, Inc; (Serials) EBSCO Online
Wireless access
Function: 24/7 Electronic res, 24/7 Online cat, Adult bk club, Adult literacy prog, Art exhibits, Audiobks via web, AV serv, Bk club(s), Bks on CD, Children's prog, Computer training, Digital talking bks, Distance learning, Electronic databases & coll, Free DVD rentals, Health sci info serv, ILL available, Instruction & testing, Internet access, Jazz prog, Large print keyboards, Magazines, Magnifiers for reading, Mail & tel request accepted, Movies, Music CDs, Notary serv, Online cat, Online info literacy tutorials on the web & in blackboard, Online ref, Photocopying/Printing, Preschool reading prog, Printer for laptops & handheld devices, Prog for adults, Prog for children & young adult, Ref & res, Ref serv available, Res libr, Res performed for a fee, Spoken cassettes & CDs, Spoken cassettes & DVDs, Summer & winter reading prog, Summer reading prog, Tax forms, Teen prog, Telephone ref, Workshops, Writing prog
Partic in Library Connection, Inc
Special Services for the Deaf - Closed caption videos
Open Mon-Thurs (Winter) 9-9, Fri & Sat 9-5; Mon-Thurs (Summer) 9-9, Fri 9-5
Friends of the Library Group

SOUTHPORT

P PEQUOT LIBRARY*, 720 Pequot Ave, 06890-1496. SAN 302-3648. Tel: 203-259-0346. FAX: 203-259-5602. Web Site: www.pequotlibrary.com. *Exec Dir,* Stephanie J Coakley; E-mail: director@pequotlibrary.org; *Chief Librn,* Christine Catallo; E-mail: catallo@pequotlibrary.org; *Ch Serv,* Jane Manners; E-mail: manners@pequotlibrary.org
Founded 1887. Circ 59,352
Library Holdings: Bk Titles 110,000; Per Subs 140
Special Collections: 19th Century Periodicals; Americana; Genealogy & Local History Coll
Automation Activity & Vendor Info: (Circulation) SirsiDynix; (ILL) OCLC Online; (OPAC) SirsiDynix
Publications: Catalogue of the Monroe, Wakeman & Holman Collection of the Pequot Library Southport, Connecticut Deposited in the Yale University Library; Clare Leighton; The Kelmscott Press
Open Mon-Fri 10-6, Sat 10-4

STAFFORD SPRINGS

P STAFFORD LIBRARY*, Ten Levinthal Run, 06075. SAN 302-3672. Tel: 860-684-2852. FAX: 860-684-2128. E-mail: stafforddesk@biblio.org. Web Site: www.staffordlibrary.org. *Dir,* Christopher Frank; E-mail: cfrank@biblio.org; *Ch Serv,* Deborah Muska; E-mail: dmuska@biblio.org; *Prog Serv,* Debra Galotta; Staff 3 (MLS 2, Non-MLS 1)
Founded 1876. Pop 12,000; Circ 83,000
Library Holdings: CDs 305; DVDs 800; Large Print Bks 546; Bk Vols 55,000; Per Subs 100; Videos 2,172
Special Collections: Local History
Automation Activity & Vendor Info: (Acquisitions) Evergreen; (Cataloging) Evergreen; (Circulation) Evergreen; (ILL) Evergreen; (OPAC) Evergreen; (Serials) Evergreen
Wireless access
Function: Computer training, E-Reserves, Electronic databases & coll, Home delivery & serv to seniorr ctr & nursing homes, Homebound delivery serv, Homework prog, ILL available, Online ref, Photocopying/Printing, Prog for adults, Prog for children & young adult, Ref serv available, Senior computer classes, Spoken cassettes & CDs, Summer reading prog, Tax forms, Telephone ref, VHS videos, Wheelchair accessible
Partic in Bibliomation Inc; Connecticut Library Consortium
Open Mon-Thurs 10-8, Fri & Sat 10-5
Friends of the Library Group

STAMFORD

L CUMMINGS & LOCKWOOD*, Law Library, Six Landmark Sq, 06901. SAN 372-3399. Tel: 203-351-4375. FAX: 203-708-3847. Web Site: www.cl-law.com. *Mgr,* Barbara J Bentley; E-mail: bbentley@cl-law.com; *Libr Asst,* Shawn M McKeon; Staff 2 (MLS 1, Non-MLS 1)

Library Holdings: Bk Vols 20,000
Automation Activity & Vendor Info: (Acquisitions) Inmagic, Inc.; (Cataloging) Inmagic, Inc.; (OPAC) Inmagic, Inc.; (Serials) Inmagic, Inc.
Wireless access
Partic in Connecticut Library Consortium

P THE FERGUSON LIBRARY*, One Public Library Plaza, 06904. SAN 336-4925. Tel: 203-964-1000. Circulation Tel: 203-351-8261. Interlibrary Loan Service Tel: 203-351-8237. Reference Tel: 203-351-8222. Information Services Tel: 203-351-8231. FAX: 203-357-9098. E-mail: comments@fergusonlibrary.org. Web Site: www.fergusonlibrary.org. *Pres,* Alice Knapp; Tel: 203-351-8201, E-mail: aknapp@fergusonlibrary.org; *Admin Serv Dir,* Nicholas A Bochicchio, Jr; Tel: 203-351-8202, E-mail: nboch@fergusonlibrary.org; *Dir, Develop & Communications,* Avellar Linda; Tel: 203-351-8208, E-mail: linda@fergusonlibrary.org; *Dir, Human Res,* Constance Hubbard; Tel: 203-351-8203, E-mail: chubbard@fergusonlibrary.org; *Dir, Pub Serv,* Susan LaPerla; E-mail: slaperla@fergusonlibrary.org; *Bus Off Mgr,* Cheryl Harper; Tel: 203-351-8210, E-mail: charper@fergusonlibrary.org; *Acq, Cat/Circ, IT Supvr,* Alex Lee; Tel: 203-351-8260, E-mail: alee@fergusonlibrary.org; *Adult/Info Serv Coordr,* Elizabeth Joseph; Tel: 203-351-8224, E-mail: ejoseph@fergusonlibrary.org; *Youth Serv Coordr,* Elizabeth McKay; Staff 75.9 (MLS 25.3, Non-MLS 50.6)
Founded 1880. Pop 130,824; Circ 728,914
Jul 2017-Jun 2018 Income (Main & Associated Libraries) $9,455,356, State $1,763, City $8,100,000, Federal $19,000, Other $1,334,593. Mats Exp $9,863,303. Sal $4,942,808
Library Holdings: AV Mats 58,246; Bk Titles 274,193
Wireless access
Function: 24/7 Electronic res, 24/7 Online cat, 3D Printer, Activity rm, Adult bk club, Adult literacy prog, After school storytime, Archival coll, Art exhibits, Art programs, Audio & video playback equip for onsite use, Audiobks on Playaways & MP3, Audiobks via web, AV serv, BA reader (adult literacy), Bilingual assistance for Spanish patrons, Bk club(s), Bk reviews (Group), Bks on cassette, Bks on CD, Bus archives, CD-ROM, Chess club, Children's prog, Citizenship assistance, Computer training, Computers for patron use, Digital talking bks, E-Readers, E-Reserves, Electronic databases & coll, Family literacy, For res purposes, Games & aids for people with disabilities, Govt ref serv, Health sci info serv, Holiday prog, Home delivery & serv to seniorr ctr & nursing homes, Homebound delivery serv, Homework prog, ILL available, Instruction & testing, Internet access, Large print keyboards, Learning ctr, Life-long learning prog for all ages, Literacy & newcomer serv, Magazines, Mail & tel request accepted, Mail loans to mem, Makerspace, Mango lang, Meeting rooms, Microfiche/film & reading machines, Movies, Museum passes, Music CDs, Online cat, Online info literacy tutorials on the web & in blackboard, Online ref, Outreach serv, Outside serv via phone, mail, e-mail & web, OverDrive digital audio bks, Passport agency, Photocopying/Printing, Preschool outreach, Preschool reading prog, Prog for adults, Prog for children & young adult, Ref & res, Ref serv available, Res assist avail, Res libr, Scanner, Senior computer classes, Senior outreach, Serves people with intellectual disabilities, Spanish lang bks, Spoken cassettes & CDs, Spoken cassettes & DVDs, STEM programs, Story hour, Study rm, Summer & winter reading prog, Summer reading prog, Tax forms, Teen prog, Visual arts prog, Wheelchair accessible, Winter reading prog, Words travel prog, Workshops, Writing prog
Publications: Focus (Monthly newsletter)
Open Mon-Thurs 10-9, Fri 10-6, Sat 10-5, Sun 1-5
Friends of the Library Group
Branches: 3
HARRY BENNETT BRANCH, 115 Vine Rd, 06905, SAN 336-495X. Tel: 203-351-8290. Circulation Tel: 203-351-8291. FAX: 203-968-2728. *Supvr,* Erin Shea; E-mail: eshea@fergusonlibrary.org
Friends of the Library Group
SOUTH END, 34 Woodland Ave, 06902, SAN 336-4941. Tel: 203-351-8280. FAX: 203-969-0797. *Supvr,* Josephine Fulcher-Anderson; Tel: 203-351-8281, E-mail: janderson@fergusonlibrary.org
Friends of the Library Group
WEED MEMORIAL & HOLLANDER, 1143 Hope St, 06907, SAN 336-4984. Tel: 203-351-8284. Circulation Tel: 203-351-8285. FAX: 203-321-7024. *Supvr,* Erin Shea
Friends of the Library Group
Bookmobiles: 1. Bkmobile Supvr, Josephine Fulcher-Anderson. Bk vols 6,000

E PURDUE PHARMA LP*, Digital Resources & Information Center, One Stamford Forum, 201 Tresser Blvd, 06901. SAN 302-296X. Tel: 203-588-7267. *Dir,* Cynthia Geremia; Tel: 203-588-7267, E-mail: cynthia.geremia@pharma.com; Staff 3 (MLS 3)
Founded 1970
Library Holdings: e-books 500; e-journals 5,100; Bk Vols 2,500; Per Subs 15
Subject Interests: Bus, Med, Pharmaceuticals
Automation Activity & Vendor Info: (Cataloging) Sydney; (Circulation) Sydney; (OPAC) Sydney; (Serials) Sydney
Wireless access
Function: AV serv
Restriction: 24-hr pass syst for students only

S STAMFORD HISTORY CENTER (HISTORICAL SOCIETY), Marcus Research Library, 1508 High Ridge Rd, 06903-4107. SAN 302-3842. Tel: 203-329-1183. E-mail: history@stamfordhistory.org. Web Site: stamfordhistory.org/marcus-research-library. *Librn,* Ronald Marcus
Founded 1901
Library Holdings: Bk Vols 11,000
Special Collections: 17th-21st Century Americana, Maps & Atlases of Stamford & Fairfield County, Photographic Coll, Stamford Business & Industry, Stamford Government, Stamford Postcard
Subject Interests: Local hist
Wireless access
Open Thurs & Fri 11-4, Sat 10-4

M STAMFORD HOSPITAL*, Health Sciences Library, One Hospital Plaza, 06904. (Mail add: PO Box 9317, 06904-9317), SAN 324-4202. Tel: 203-325-7523. E-mail: library@stamhealth.org. Web Site: stamfordhealth.org. *Dir,* Guillaume Van Moorsel
Founded 1963
Library Holdings: e-journals 1,200; Bk Vols 2,100; Per Subs 200
Special Collections: Medicine, Allied Health & Nursing Coll
Automation Activity & Vendor Info: (Cataloging) CyberTools for Libraries
Wireless access
Partic in Conn Asn of Health Scis Librs; North Atlantic Health Sciences Libraries, Inc
Open Mon-Fri 8-4

S UKRAINIAN MUSEUM & LIBRARY OF STAMFORD, 39 Clovelly Rd, 06902-3004. (Mail add: 161 Glenbrook Rd, 06902-3099). Tel: 203-323-8866, 203-324-0488. FAX: 203-967-9948. E-mail: ukrmulrec@optonline.net. Web Site: www.ukrainianmuseumlibrary.org. *Librn,* John Terlecky; E-mail: jmterlecky@aol.com; *Curator,* Lubow Wolynetz. Subject Specialists: *Ethnography,* Lubow Wolynetz; Staff 5 (MLS 2, Non-MLS 3)
Founded 1938. Highest Degree: Bachelor
Library Holdings: Music Scores 200; Bk Titles 31,875; Bk Vols 50,230; Spec Interest Per Sub 40
Special Collections: Church history & Liturgy of the Ukrainian people; Rare books
Subject Interests: Ukrainian culture
Automation Activity & Vendor Info: (Cataloging) OCLC; (ILL) OCLC
Wireless access
Partic in OCLC Online Computer Library Center, Inc
Open Wed-Fri 1-5
Restriction: Private libr

STONINGTON

P STONINGTON FREE LIBRARY*, 20 High St, 06378. (Mail add: PO Box 232, 06378-0232), SAN 302-3907. Tel: 860-535-0658. Administration Tel: 860-535-0268. FAX: 860-535-3945. E-mail: stonlib@stoningtonfreelibrary.org. Web Site: stoningtonfreelibrary.org. *Exec Dir,* Belinda De Kay; E-mail: director@stoningtonfreelibrary.org; *Asst Dir,* Micayla Hall; E-mail: micaylahall@stoningtonfreelibrary.org; *Libr Develop Coordr,* Suzanne G Kerr; E-mail: development@stoningtonfreelibrary.org; *Youth Serv,* Maris Frey; E-mail: marisfrey@stoningtonfreelibrary.org; Staff 9 (MLS 1, Non-MLS 8)
Founded 1887. Pop 17,903
Jul 2013-Jun 2014 Income $503,413, State $1,503, City $147,000, Locally Generated Income $354,910. Mats Exp $56,644, Books $47,500, Per/Ser (Incl. Access Fees) $4,944, AV Mat $4,200. Sal $264,000 (Prof $63,654)
Library Holdings: Audiobooks 1,450; DVDs 550; e-books 450; e-journals 10; High Interest/Low Vocabulary Bk Vols 95; Large Print Bks 1,075; Bk Titles 38,925; Bk Vols 41,478; Per Subs 64; Videos 100
Subject Interests: Genealogy, Local hist
Automation Activity & Vendor Info: (Cataloging) TLC (The Library Corporation); (Circulation) TLC (The Library Corporation); (OPAC) TLC (The Library Corporation)
Wireless access
Function: Audiobks via web, Bks on CD, Children's prog, Computers for patron use, E-Readers, Free DVD rentals, ILL available, Magazines, Magnifiers for reading, Museum passes, Online cat, OverDrive digital audio bks, Photocopying/Printing, Preschool outreach, Preschool reading prog, Prog for adults, Prog for children & young adult, Scanner, Summer & winter reading prog, Summer reading prog, Tax forms, Wheelchair accessible
Publications: e-Librarian (Monthly); The Librarian (Newsletter)
Partic in Connecticut Library Consortium
Special Services for the Deaf - Bks on deafness & sign lang

Special Services for the Blind - Aids for in-house use; Assistive/Adapted tech devices, equip & products; Audio mat; Bks on cassette; Bks on CD; Cassettes; Closed circuit TV; Computer with voice synthesizer for visually impaired persons; Large print & cassettes; Large print bks; Magnifiers; Talking bks
Open Mon, Tues & Thurs 10-6, Wed 10-7, Fri 10-5, Sat 10-1

S STONINGTON HISTORICAL SOCIETY*, Richard W Woolworth Library & Research Center, 40 Palmer St, 06378. (Mail add: PO Box 103, 06378-0103), SAN 326-7989. Tel: 860-535-1131. E-mail: library@stoningtonhistory.org. Web Site: www.stoningtonhistory.org. *Exec Dir,* Elizabeth Wood; E-mail: director@stoningtonhistory.org; *Libr Dir,* Chelsea Ordner; *Asst Librn,* Joan Rowler; Staff 4 (MLS 1, Non-MLS 3)
Founded 1895
Library Holdings: Bk Vols 3,500
Special Collections: Photographs & Postcards, primarily Stonington Area & People; Stonington Banks
Subject Interests: Genealogy, Local hist
Wireless access
Function: Ref & res, Wheelchair accessible
Open Mon & Wed 1-5, Fri (May-Oct) 1-5, Sat 9-1
Restriction: Non-circulating, Not a lending libr

STONY CREEK

P WILLOUGHBY WALLACE MEMORIAL LIBRARY*, 146 Thimble Islands Rd, 06405-5739. SAN 302-3915. Tel: 203-488-8702. FAX: 203-315-3347. Web Site: www.wwml.org. *Dir,* Alice Pentz; E-mail: apentz@branford-ct.gov; *Circ Supvr,* Lissie Smith
Founded 1958. Pop 3,000; Circ 45,000
Library Holdings: Bk Vols 23,000; Per Subs 30
Subject Interests: Art
Automation Activity & Vendor Info: (Cataloging) Innovative Interfaces, Inc; (Circulation) Innovative Interfaces, Inc; (OPAC) Innovative Interfaces, Inc
Wireless access
Open Mon-Thurs 10-8, Fri & Sat 10-5, Sun (Winter) 1-4
Friends of the Library Group

STORRS

S MANSFIELD HISTORICAL SOCIETY*, Edith Mason Library, 954 Storrs Rd, 06268. (Mail add: PO Box 145, 06268), SAN 328-1663. Tel: 860-429-6575. E-mail: mansfield.historical@snet.net. Web Site: www.mansfieldct-history.org. *Mus Dir,* Ann Galonska; *Librn,* Position Currently Open; Staff 1 (MLS 1)
Library Holdings: Bk Titles 815; Bk Vols 2,804
Special Collections: Photograph Coll. Oral History
Subject Interests: Genealogy, Local hist
Wireless access
Publications: Local History Pamphlets (Annual)
Open Sat (June-Sept) 1:30-4:30
Restriction: Non-circulating to the pub

C UNIVERSITY OF CONNECTICUT, Homer D Babbidge Library, 369 Fairfield Rd, 06269-1005. SAN 336-5042. Circulation Tel: 860-486-2518. Interlibrary Loan Service Tel: 860-486-4959. FAX: 860-486-0584. Web Site: www.lib.uconn.edu. *Dean, Univ Libr Serv,* Anne Langley; E-mail: anne.langley@uconn.edu; *Univ Archivist,* Betsy Pittman; E-mail: betsy.pittman@uconn.edu; Staff 80 (MLS 46, Non-MLS 34)
Founded 1881. Enrl 31,624; Fac 1,489; Highest Degree: Doctorate
Library Holdings: Bk Titles 3,900,000; Per Subs 110,000
Special Collections: Alternative Press; American Socialism & Communism; Belgium History (Revolution, 1830-1839); Black Mountain Poets; Bookplates; Charles Olson Coll; Chilean History & Literature; Conneticut History (primarily 1850-, emphasis on business, labor, ethnicity, public affairs); French History (including Paris Commune 1871); French Language & Linguistics; French Renaissance Literature; French Restoration Pamphlets; French Satirical Magazines, 19th Century; Italian History (including Italian Risorgimento, 1815-1870); Italian Risorgionento, 1815-1870; Labor History; Latin America; Little Magazines; Luis Camoens Coll; Madrid History; Medina Coll; Modern German Drama; Napoleonic Period; Paris Commune, 1871; Powys Brothers Coll; Sermons (Connecticut); Spanish Periodicals & Newspapers; University & Historical Archives; William Berkson. Oral History; State Document Depository; US Document Depository
Subject Interests: Children's lit, Latin Am, Maps
Automation Activity & Vendor Info: (Acquisitions) Ex Libris Group; (Cataloging) Ex Libris Group; (Circulation) Ex Libris Group; (Media Booking) Ex Libris Group; (OPAC) Ex Libris Group; (Serials) Ex Libris Group
Wireless access
Function: 24/7 Electronic res, 24/7 Online cat, Archival coll, Art exhibits, ILL available, Res libr
Partic in Association of Research Libraries; Boston Library Consortium, Inc; Center for Research Libraries; OCLC Online Computer Library Center, Inc
Special Services for the Deaf - Assistive tech
Special Services for the Blind - Assistive/Adapted tech devices, equip & products

Departmental Libraries:

ARCHIVES & SPECIAL COLLECTIONS, 405 Babbidge Rd, Unit 1205, 06269-1205. Tel: 860-486-2524. E-mail: archives@uconn.edu. Web Site: lib.uconn.edu/location/asc. *Head, Archives & Spec Coll,* Rebecca Parmer; Tel: 860-486-3646, E-mail: rebecca.parmer@uconn.edu; *Univ Archivist,* Betsy Pittman; Tel: 860-486-4507, E-mail: betsy.pittman@uconn.edu

AVERY POINT CAMPUS LIBRARY, 1084 Shennecossett Rd, Groton, 06340, SAN 302-1599. Tel: 860-405-9146. FAX: 860-405-9150. E-mail: averypoint.circulation@uconn.edu. Web Site: lib.uconn.edu/location/avery-point-campus-library. *Interim Libr Dir,* David Avery; Tel: 860-486-1582, E-mail: david.avery@uconn.edu; *Res & Instruction Librn,* Elizabeth Rumery; Tel: 860-405-9148, E-mail: elizabeth.rumery@uconn.edu; *Access Serv Coordr,* Chay Reed; Tel: 860-486-9147, E-mail: chay.reed@uconn.edu; Staff 1 (MLS 1)
Founded 1967. Enrl 800; Fac 50; Highest Degree: Doctorate
Library Holdings: Bk Vols 40,100; Per Subs 120
Special Collections: Dredging Data; Hydrographic Charts (East Coast) 1832-1876; Literature of the Sea. US Document Depository
Automation Activity & Vendor Info: (Acquisitions) Ex Libris Group; (Cataloging) Ex Libris Group; (Circulation) Ex Libris Group; (Course Reserve) Ex Libris Group; (OPAC) Ex Libris Group
Partic in LYRASIS
Open Mon-Thurs 8:30-6, Fri 8:30-4; Mon-Fri 10-4 (Summer)

HARTFORD CAMPUS, Uconn Library at Hartford Public Library, 500 Main St, Hartford, 06103, SAN 336-5506. Tel: 959-200-3466. FAX: 860-246-0436. Web Site: lib.uconn.edu/location/hartford-campus-library. *Res & Instruction Librn,* Steve Batt; Tel: 959-200-3465, E-mail: steve.batt@uconn.edu; *Res & Instruction Librn,* Marsha Lee; Tel: 959-200-3467, E-mail: marsha.m.lee@uconn.edu; *Res & Instruction Librn,* Janice Mathews; Tel: 959-200-3461, E-mail: janice.mathews@uconn.edu; *Coordr, Access Serv,* Claudia Lopes; Tel: 959-200-3462, E-mail: claudia.lopes@uconn.edu. Subject Specialists: *Humanities, Soc work, Undergrad educ,* Marsha Lee; *Soc sci, Urban studies,* Janice Mathews; Staff 4.3 (MLS 3, Non-MLS 1.3)
Founded 1939. Enrl 2,100; Fac 120; Highest Degree: Doctorate
Special Collections: Social Work History Coll, vintage bks & journals
Subject Interests: Soc sci
Automation Activity & Vendor Info: (Acquisitions) Ex Libris Group; (Cataloging) Ex Libris Group; (Circulation) Ex Libris Group; (ILL) OCLC ILLiad; (OPAC) Ex Libris Group; (Serials) SerialsSolutions
Function: Art exhibits, Computers for patron use, Electronic databases & coll, Microfiche/film & reading machines, Online cat, Photocopying/Printing, Printer for laptops & handheld devices, Scanner, Study rm
Special Services for the Deaf - Assistive tech
Open Mon-Thurs 9-9, Fri 10-5, Sat 12-5
Restriction: Circ limited, In-house use for visitors, Open to pub for ref & circ; with some limitations

CL THOMAS J MESKILL LAW LIBRARY, 39 Elizabeth St, Hartford, 06105, SAN 336-5492. Tel: 860-570-5200. Reference Tel: 860-570-5068. Administration Tel: 860-570-5109. Information Services Tel: 860-570-5158. Administration FAX: 860-570-5109. TDD: 860-570-5063. E-mail: lawlibrary@uconn.edu, refdesk.lawlib@uconn.edu. Web Site: library.law.uconn.edu. *Dir, Law Libr,* Jessica de Perio Wittman; Tel: 860-570-5109, E-mail: jessica.deperio@law.uconn.edu; *Head, Access & Admin Services,* Jessica Panella; Tel: 860-570-5106, E-mail: jessica.panella@uconn.edu; *Head, Ref Serv,* Anne Rajotte; Tel: 860-510-5081, E-mail: anne.rajotte@uconn.edu; *Head, Tech Serv,* Elisabeth Umpleby; Tel: 860-570-5007, E-mail: elisabeth.umpleby@uconn.edu; *Digital Services Reference Librn,* Maryanne Daly-Doran; Tel: 860-570-5167, E-mail: maryanne.daly-doran@uconn.edu; *Metadata & E-Resource Management Librn,* Susanna French; Tel: 860-570-5009, E-mail: susanna.french@uconn.edu; *Ref Librn,* Tanya Johnson; Tel: 860-570-5072, E-mail: tanya.johnson@uconn.edu; *Ref Librn,* Adam Mackie; Tel: 860-570-5071, E-mail: adam.mackie@uconn.edu; *Syst & Emerging Tech Librn,* Timothy Dannay; Tel: 860-570-5028, E-mail: timothy.dannay@uconn.edu; *Tech Serv Librn,* Ryan Barber; Tel: 860-570-5011, E-mail: ryan.barber@uconn.edu. Subject Specialists: *Educ tech,* Jessica de Perio Wittman; Staff 12 (MLS 8, Non-MLS 4)
Founded 1921. Enrl 704; Fac 54; Highest Degree: Doctorate
Library Holdings: Bk Titles 70,000; Bk Vols 103,471
Subject Interests: Law
Automation Activity & Vendor Info: (Acquisitions) Ex Libris Group; (Cataloging) Ex Libris Group; (Circulation) Ex Libris Group; (Course Reserve) Ex Libris Group; (Media Booking) OCLC ILLiad; (OPAC) Ex Libris Group; (Serials) Ex Libris Group
Function: Electronic databases & coll, ILL available, Internet access, Microfiche/film & reading machines, Online cat, Online ref, Outside serv

via phone, mail, e-mail & web, Photocopying/Printing, Ref serv available, Scanner, Telephone ref, Wheelchair accessible
Partic in OCLC Online Computer Library Center, Inc
Special Services for the Deaf - TDD equip
Special Services for the Blind - Scanner for conversion & translation of mats
Open Mon-Thurs 9-7, Fri & Sat 9-5, Sun 11-7
Restriction: Borrowing privileges limited to fac & registered students, Circ limited, Non-circulating to the pub, Pub ref by request, Pub use on premises

MUSIC & DRAMATIC ARTS LIBRARY, 1295 Storrs Rd, Unit 1153, 06269-1153. Tel: 860-486-2502. FAX: 860-486-5551. Web Site: lib.uconn.edu/location/music-dramatic-arts-library. *Access Serv Coordr,* Nanette Addesso; Tel: 860-486-2033, E-mail: nanette.addesso@uconn.edu; Staff 3 (MLS 2, Non-MLS 1)
Highest Degree: Doctorate
Automation Activity & Vendor Info: (Cataloging) Follett Software; (Circulation) Follett Software; (OPAC) Follett Software
Open Mon-Thurs 8am-10pm, Fri 8-5, Sat Noon-5, Sun 1-10

CM PHARMACY LIBRARY, Pharmacy/Biology Bldg, 2nd Flr, 69 North Eagleville Rd, Rm 228, 06269-3092. Tel: 860-486-2218. FAX: 860-486-4998. Web Site: lib.uconn.edu/location/pharmacy-library. *Pharm Librn,* Roslyn Grandy; E-mail: roslyn.grandy@uconn.edu; Staff 1 (MLS 1)
Highest Degree: Doctorate
Subject Interests: Medicinal chem, Pharmaceutical sci, Pharmacology
Friends of the Library Group

JEREMY RICHARD LIBRARY, STAMFORD CAMPUS, One University Pl, Stamford, 06901-2315, SAN 302-3877. Tel: 203-251-8500. FAX: 203-251-8501. Web Site: lib.uconn.edu/location/stamford-campus-library. *Dir,* Phara Bayonne; Tel: 203-251-8523, E-mail: phara.bayonne@uconn.edu; *Res & Instruction Librn,* Nancy Dryden; Tel: 203-251-8439, E-mail: nancy.dryden@uconn.edu; *Access Serv Coordr,* Jenny Gregory; Tel: 203-251-8518, E-mail: jenny.gregory@uconn.edu. Subject Specialists: *Soc sci,* Phara Bayonne; Staff 4.5 (MLS 3, Non-MLS 1.5)
Founded 1962. Enrl 1,700; Fac 33; Highest Degree: Master
Library Holdings: Bk Vols 90,000; Per Subs 88
Subject Interests: Bus & mgt, Econ, Lit, Soc sci & issues
Automation Activity & Vendor Info: (Acquisitions) Ex Libris Group; (Cataloging) Ex Libris Group; (Circulation) Ex Libris Group; (Course Reserve) Ex Libris Group; (OPAC) Ex Libris Group
Partic in Boston Library Consortium, Inc; LYRASIS; Northeast Research Libraries Consortium
Open Mon-Fri (Spring) 8:30am-9pm, Sat 10-7, Sun 12-4; Mon-Fri (Winter) 8:30-4

WATERBURY REGIONAL CAMPUS LIBRARY, 99 E Main St, Waterbury, 06702, SAN 302-4202. Tel: 203-236-9900. Administration Tel: 203-236-9908. FAX: 203-236-9905. Web Site: www.lib.uconn.edu/location/waterbury-campus-library. *Libr Dir, Res & Instruction Librn,* Shelley Goldstein; Tel: 203-236-9908, E-mail: shelley.goldstein@uconn.edu; *Access Serv, ILL,* Stephen Bustamante; Tel: 203-236-9901, E-mail: steve.bustamante@uconn.edu. Subject Specialists: *Bus,* Stephen Bustamante; Staff 3 (MLS 3)
Founded 1946
Library Holdings: Bk Vols 35,000; Per Subs 100
Subject Interests: Art
Automation Activity & Vendor Info: (Acquisitions) Ex Libris Group; (Circulation) Ex Libris Group; (Course Reserve) Ex Libris Group; (ILL) OCLC; (OPAC) Ex Libris Group; (Serials) Ex Libris Group
Partic in Boston Library Consortium, Inc; Connecticut Library Consortium; LYRASIS; NELLCO Law Library Consortium, Inc.; OCLC Online Computer Library Center, Inc
Open Mon-Thurs 9-3

SR EDWINA WHITNEY LIBRARY OF THE STORRS CONGREGATIONAL CHURCH, Two N Eagleville Rd, 06268-1710. Tel: 860-429-9382. FAX: 860-429-9693. E-mail: scoffice@storrscongchurch.org. Web Site: www.storrscongchurch.org/forming-faith/library. *Librn,* Janet Atkins; Tel: 860-423-5930, E-mail: janetatkins275@gmail.com
Library Holdings: Bk Titles 4,000
Open Tues 9:30-11

STRATFORD

S STRATFORD HISTORICAL SOCIETY LIBRARY*, 967 Academy Hill, 06615. (Mail add: PO Box 382, 06615-0382), SAN 325-657X. Tel: 203-378-0630. FAX: 203-378-2562. Web Site: stratfordhistoricalsociety.info, www.stratfordhistoricalsociety.org. *Dir & Curator,* Sandra Rutkowski
Founded 1925
Library Holdings: Bk Titles 650
Subject Interests: Local hist
Open Tues & Thurs 9-2:30

P STRATFORD LIBRARY ASSOCIATION*, 2203 Main St, 06615. SAN 302-3931. Tel: 203-385-4161. Circulation Tel: 203-385-4160. Reference Tel: 203-385-4164. Administration Tel: 203-381-4166. E-mail: ask@stratfordlibrary.org. Web Site: stratfordlibrary.org. *Libr Dir,* Sheri Szymanski; *Asst Libr Dir,* Geri Diorio; E-mail: gdiorio@stratfordlibrary.org; *Head, Info Tech Serv,* Diane Kurtz; Tel: 203-385-4163, E-mail: dkurtz@stratfordlibrary.org; *Head, Adult Serv,* Katie McFadden; *Head, Children's Servx,* Martha Simpson; Tel: 203-385-4165, E-mail: msimpson@stratfordlibrary.org; *Head, Teen Serv,* Beth Grimes; Tel: 203-385-4167, E-mail: bgrimes@stratfordlibrary.org; *Pub Relations,* Tom Holehan; Tel: 203-385-4162, E-mail: tholehan@stratfordlibrary.org; Staff 28.2 (MLS 12.1, Non-MLS 16.1)
Founded 1886. Pop 51,901; Circ 459,055
Library Holdings: AV Mats 18,292; Electronic Media & Resources 3,891; Bk Vols 140,000; Per Subs 100
Special Collections: ESOL Coll; Leading to Reading Kits; Local History Coll; Raymark EPA Documents
Automation Activity & Vendor Info: (Acquisitions) SirsiDynix; (Cataloging) SirsiDynix; (Circulation) SirsiDynix; (ILL) OCLC; (OPAC) SirsiDynix; (Serials) SirsiDynix
Wireless access
Function: Adult bk club, After school storytime, Art exhibits, Audiobks via web, AV serv, Bk club(s), Bks on CD, Children's prog, Computer training, Computers for patron use, Digital talking bks, Electronic databases & coll, Family literacy, Free DVD rentals, Holiday prog, Homework prog, ILL available, Internet access, Magnifiers for reading, Mail & tel request accepted, Microfiche/film & reading machines, Museum passes, Music CDs, Online cat, Online ref, Outreach serv, Outside serv via phone, mail, e-mail & web, OverDrive digital audio bks, Photocopying/Printing, Preschool outreach, Preschool reading prog, Printer for laptops & handheld devices, Prof lending libr, Prog for adults, Prog for children & young adult, Ref serv available, Scanner, Senior outreach, Spanish lang bks, Story hour, Summer & winter reading prog, Tax forms, Teen prog, Telephone ref, Wheelchair accessible, Workshops
Publications: Annual Report; Monthly Calendar
Partic in Connecticut Library Consortium
Special Services for the Deaf - Assistive tech; Bks on deafness & sign lang; Closed caption videos; High interest/low vocabulary bks
Special Services for the Blind - Assistive/Adapted tech devices, equip & products; Audio mat; Bks on cassette; Bks on CD; Digital talking bk; Large print bks; Low vision equip; Magnifiers; Playaways (bks on MP3); Recorded bks
Open Mon-Thurs 10-8, Fri & Sat 10-5, Sun (Oct-May) 1-5

SUFFIELD

P KENT MEMORIAL LIBRARY*, 50 N Main St, 06078-2117. SAN 302-3958. Tel: 860-668-3896. FAX: 860-668-3895. E-mail: circ@suffield-library.org, ref@suffield-library.org. Web Site: www.suffield-library.org. *Libr Dir,* Garrett Pinder; E-mail: gpinder@suffieldct.gov; *Asst Dir,* Kim Lord; *Cat,* Sabine Schneider; *Ch Serv,* Wendy Taylor; *Circ,* Lois Gracey; Staff 7 (MLS 4, Non-MLS 3)
Founded 1884. Pop 13,800; Circ 79,000
Jul 2016-Jun 2017 Income $542,400. Mats Exp $540,700, Books $64,300, Per/Ser (Incl. Access Fees) $70, Manu Arch $3,700, AV Mat $16,170, Electronic Ref Mat (Incl. Access Fees) $25,500. Sal $350,000 (Prof $269,620)
Library Holdings: Audiobooks 7,810; CDs 7,810; DVDs 8,359; e-books 6,833; e-journals 50; Electronic Media & Resources 48; Large Print Bks 1,114; Microforms 176; Bk Vols 64,300; Per Subs 68
Special Collections: Local Suffield History, bks, doc
Automation Activity & Vendor Info: (Acquisitions) Bibliomation Inc; (Cataloging) Bibliomation Inc; (Circulation) Bibliomation Inc; (ILL) Bibliomation Inc; (OPAC) Bibliomation Inc; (Serials) Bibliomation Inc
Wireless access
Function: 24/7 Electronic res, 24/7 Online cat, Activity rm, Adult bk club, Archival coll, Art exhibits, Audiobks via web, Bk club(s), Bks on CD, Children's prog, Computer training, Computers for patron use, Electronic databases & coll, Equip loans & repairs, Free DVD rentals, Holiday prog, Home delivery & serv to seniorr ctr & nursing homes, Homebound delivery serv, ILL available, Internet access, Laminating, Life-long learning prog for all ages, Magazines, Magnifiers for reading, Mail & tel request accepted, Meeting rooms, Movies, Museum passes, Music CDs, Notary serv, Online cat, Online ref, Orientations, Outreach serv, Outside serv via phone, mail, e-mail & web, OverDrive digital audio bks, Photocopying/Printing, Preschool outreach, Preschool reading prog, Prog for adults, Prog for children & young adult, Ref serv available, Scanner, Spoken cassettes & CDs, Spoken cassettes & DVDs, STEM programs, Story hour, Study rm, Summer & winter reading prog, Summer reading prog, Tax forms, Teen prog, Telephone ref, VHS videos, Wheelchair accessible, Winter reading prog, Workshops, Writing prog
Publications: Weekly & Monthly Events Newsletter
Partic in Bibliomation Inc; CLA; Connecticut Library Consortium
Open Mon-Thurs 10-8:30, Fri & Sat 10-5, Sat (Summer) 10-1
Friends of the Library Group

TERRYVILLE

S LOCK MUSEUM OF AMERICA, INC LIBRARY*, 230 Main St, 06786-5900. (Mail add: PO Box 104, 06786-0104), SAN 326-2537. Tel: 860-589-6359. FAX: 860-589-6359. E-mail: tlockmuseum@gmail.com. Web Site: www.lockmuseumofamerica.org. *Curator,* Thomas Hennessy, Jr
Founded 1972
Library Holdings: Bk Titles 1,000; Per Subs 500
Special Collections: Lockmaking Research Materials; Patent Indexes, 1790-1977
Open Tues-Fri (May-Oct) 1:30-4

P TERRYVILLE PUBLIC LIBRARY*, 238 Main St, 06786. SAN 302-3974. Tel: 860-582-3121. Reference Tel: 860-583-4467. FAX: 860-585-4068. E-mail: tplstaff@biblio.org. Web Site: www.terryvillepl.info. *Libr Dir,* Gretchen DelCegno; E-mail: gdelcegno@biblio.org; Staff 13 (MLS 2, Non-MLS 11)
Founded 1895. Pop 11,800; Circ 60,000
Library Holdings: Bks on Deafness & Sign Lang 15; High Interest/Low Vocabulary Bk Vols 250; Large Print Bks 1,000; Bk Titles 56,000; Per Subs 101; Talking Bks 800
Special Collections: Career Corner; Terryville-Plymouth Room
Subject Interests: Literacy
Automation Activity & Vendor Info: (Cataloging) Bibliomation Inc; (Circulation) Bibliomation Inc; (OPAC) Bibliomation Inc
Wireless access
Function: 24/7 Electronic res, 24/7 Online cat
Publications: The Footnote (Newsletter)
Partic in Bibliomation Inc; Region I Coop Libr Servs Unit
Open Mon-Wed 10-8, Thurs 10-6, Fri & Sat (Sept-June) 10-5
Friends of the Library Group

THOMASTON

P THOMASTON PUBLIC LIBRARY, 248 Main St, 06787. SAN 302-3990. Tel: 860-283-4339. FAX: 860-283-4330. Web Site: www.thomastonlibrary.org. *Libr Dir,* Debra Radosevich; E-mail: dradosevich@biblio.org; *Adult Serv,* Ruth Fields; E-mail: rfields@biblio.org
Founded 1898. Pop 6,276; Circ 70,000
Library Holdings: Bk Vols 50,000; Per Subs 115
Special Collections: Art Techniques (Bradshaw Coll); Career Information; Conklin Coll of the Arts, bks, fs; Connecticut History (Allan C Innes Coll); Innes Coll (J P Seth) Thomaston Centennial (Seth Thomas Clock Company & Family Coll). Oral History
Automation Activity & Vendor Info: (Acquisitions) Horizon; (Cataloging) Horizon; (Circulation) Horizon; (Course Reserve) Horizon; (ILL) Horizon; (OPAC) Horizon; (Serials) Horizon
Publications: Thomaston Public Library Gazette
Partic in Bibliomation Inc
Open Mon-Thurs 10-8, Fri 10-5, Sat (Sept-June) 10-3
Friends of the Library Group

TOLLAND

S FRENCH-CANADIAN GENEALOGICAL SOCIETY OF CONNECTICUT, INC LIBRARY*, 53 Tolland Green, 06084. (Mail add: PO Box 928, 06084-0928), SAN 326-9698. Tel: 860-872-2597. E-mail: fcgsc@fcgsc.comcastbiz.net. Web Site: www.fcgsc.org. *Pres,* Maryanne LeGrow; *Dir,* Germaine Hoffman; Tel: 860-623-8721
Founded 1981
Library Holdings: Bk Titles 3,000
Special Collections: Brown New England Coll; Hebert Acadian Coll; Tolland Library Association Genealogical Coll
Subject Interests: Acadian genealogy, Fr Can
Wireless access
Publications: Connecticut Maple Leaf (semi annual)
Partic in Area Libr Serv Authority
Open Mon & Wed 1-5, Sat 9-4, Sun 1-4
Restriction: Authorized patrons, Circ to mem only, Free to mem, Limited access for the pub, Non-circulating, Not a lending libr, Private libr

P TOLLAND PUBLIC LIBRARY*, 21 Tolland Green, 06084. SAN 302-4008. Tel: 860-871-3620. FAX: 860-871-3626. Web Site: www.tolland.org/library. *Dir,* Barbara Pettijohn; E-mail: bpettijohn@tolland.org; Staff 9 (MLS 2, Non-MLS 7)
Founded 1899. Pop 12,036; Circ 134,969
Library Holdings: Bk Titles 71,568; Per Subs 80
Automation Activity & Vendor Info: (Acquisitions) Bibliomation Inc; (Cataloging) Bibliomation Inc; (Circulation) Bibliomation Inc; (OPAC) Bibliomation Inc
Wireless access
Function: ILL available, Photocopying/Printing
Partic in Bibliomation Inc; Connecticut Library Consortium
Open Mon-Thurs 10-7 Fri & Sat 10-4:45
Friends of the Library Group

TORRINGTON

S TORRINGTON HISTORICAL SOCIETY, John Thompson Memorial Library, 192 Main St, 06790. SAN 302-4016. Tel: 860-482-8260. E-mail: torringtonhistorical@snet.net. Web Site: www.torringtonhistoricalsociety.org/research-library. *Dir,* Mark McEachern; *Archivist, Assoc Dir,* Gail Kruppa
Founded 1944
Library Holdings: Bk Titles 2,000
Special Collections: CT Journal (1782-1813), newsp; General Archives; Litchfield Enquirer (1842-1941), newsp; Litchfield Monitor (1791-1795), newsp; Torrington Building Co, blueprints; Torrington History; Torrington Register (1874-present)
Subject Interests: Genealogy, Local hist
Open Wed-Fri 1-4

P TORRINGTON LIBRARY, 12 Daycoeton Pl, 06790. SAN 302-4024. Tel: 860-489-6684. FAX: 860-482-4664. E-mail: info@torringtonlibrary.org. Web Site: www.torringtonlibrary.org. *Libr Dir,* Jessica Gueniat; E-mail: jessh@torringtonlibrary.org
Founded 1864. Pop 35,202; Circ 111,121
Library Holdings: AV Mats 1,400; Large Print Bks 2,826; Bk Vols 54,596; Per Subs 74; Talking Bks 800
Special Collections: Large Print Coll
Automation Activity & Vendor Info: (Cataloging) Follett Software; (Circulation) Follett Software; (ILL) Auto-Graphics, Inc; (OPAC) Follett Software
Wireless access
Publications: The Bookworm (Newsletter)
Partic in Region I Coop Libr Servs Unit
Open Mon, Tues & Fri 10-6, Wed & Thurs 10-8, Sat 10-3

TRUMBULL

P TRUMBULL LIBRARY SYSTEM*, 33 Quality St, 06611. SAN 336-5190. Tel: 203-452-5197. FAX: 203-452-5125. Web Site: www.trumbull-ct.gov/662/Library. *Dir,* Stefan Lyhne-Nielsen; E-mail: slyhne@trumbull-ct.gov; *Assoc Dir, Info Syst,* Mary Rogers; E-mail: mrogers@trumbull-ct.gov; *Asst Dir,* Louis Sheehy; E-mail: lsheehy@trumbull-ct.gov; *Circ Supvr,* Megan Norrell; E-mail: mnorrell@trumbull-ct.gov; Staff 48 (MLS 7, Non-MLS 41)
Founded 1975. Pop 34,857; Circ 367,180
Library Holdings: Bk Vols 172,000; Per Subs 200; Talking Bks 1,700; Videos 11,000
Automation Activity & Vendor Info: (Acquisitions) Horizon; (Cataloging) Horizon; (Circulation) Horizon; (OPAC) Horizon
Wireless access
Open Mon-Thurs 9-8, Fri & Sat 9-5, Sun 1-5
Friends of the Library Group
Branches: 1
FAIRCHILD NICHOLS MEMORIAL, 1718 Huntington Tpk, 06611, SAN 336-5220. Tel: 203-452-5196. E-mail: fairchildlibrary@trumball-ct.gov. *Circ,* Paula Carlson; E-mail: pcarlson@trumbull-ct.gov; Staff 6 (MLS 1, Non-MLS 5)
Library Holdings: Bk Vols 34,000
Open Mon & Wed 10-8, Tues & Thurs 10-5, Sat 10-2, Sun (Oct-May) 1-5
Friends of the Library Group

UNCASVILLE

S RADGOWSKI CORRECTIONAL INSTITUTION LIBRARY*, 982 Norwich-New London Tpk, 06382. Tel: 860-848-5070. Web Site: portal.ct.gov/DOC/Facility/Corrigan-Radgowski-CC. *Librn,* Position Currently Open
Library Holdings: Bk Vols 2,800
Restriction: Not open to pub

UNION

P UNION FREE PUBLIC LIBRARY*, 979 Buckley Hwy, 06076. SAN 302-3680. Tel: 860-684-4913. FAX: 860-684-4913. E-mail: littlelibrary979@gmail.com, littlelibrary979@unionctfreepubliclibrary.org. Web Site: unionctfreepubliclibrary.org. *Librn,* Cailin Rae
Founded 1894. Pop 755; Circ 6,233
Library Holdings: Bk Titles 11,000; Bk Vols 12,300
Automation Activity & Vendor Info: (Cataloging) Bibliomation Inc; (Circulation) Bibliomation Inc; (ILL) Bibliomation Inc; (OPAC) Bibliomation Inc
Wireless access
Function: Computers for patron use, Family literacy, Free DVD rentals, Holiday prog, Internet access, Museum passes, Music CDs, Online cat, Photocopying/Printing, Prog for adults, Prog for children & young adult, Ref serv available, Scanner, Story hour, Summer reading prog, Teen prog, VHS videos

Partic in Bibliomation Inc; Connecticut Library Consortium
Open Mon 1-4, Wed 5-8, Sat 9-1

VERNON

P ROCKVILLE PUBLIC LIBRARY, George Maxwell Memorial Library, 52 Union St, 06066-3155. SAN 302-4067. Tel: 860-875-5892. Administration Tel: 860-872-4431. FAX: 860-875-9795. E-mail: rockvillelibrary@vernon-ct.gov. Web Site: rockvillepubliclibrary.org. *Dir,* Jennifer Johnston-Marius; E-mail: jjohnston@vernon-ct.gov; *Asst Dir,* Caitlin Kelley; E-mail: ckelley@vernon-ct.gov; *Head, Children's Servx, Head, Teen Serv,* Kara Morse; E-mail: kmorse@vernon-ct.gov; *ILL,* Jean Luddy; Staff 1 (MLS 1)
Founded 1893. Pop 29,672; Circ 162,000
Library Holdings: Bk Titles 60,000; Per Subs 90
Subject Interests: Local hist
Automation Activity & Vendor Info: (Cataloging) Bibliomation Inc; (Circulation) Bibliomation Inc
Wireless access
Function: Adult bk club, Bks on cassette, Bks on CD, Children's prog, Computers for patron use, Homebound delivery serv, ILL available, Museum passes, Online cat, Online ref, Photocopying/Printing, Prog for adults, Prog for children & young adult, Ref serv available, Senior outreach, Spoken cassettes & CDs, Story hour, Summer reading prog, Tax forms, VHS videos
Partic in Bibliomation Inc
Open Mon-Thurs 10-8, Fri & Sat 10-5
Friends of the Library Group

VOLUNTOWN

P VOLUNTOWN PUBLIC LIBRARY*, 107 Main St, 06384-1820. (Mail add: PO Box 26, 06384-0026), SAN 302-4075. Tel: 860-376-0485. FAX: 860-376-4324. E-mail: vpl@voluntown.gov. Web Site: www.voluntownlibrary.com. *Dir,* Emily Allard; E-mail: allard@voluntown.gov; Staff 4 (MLS 1, Non-MLS 3)
Founded 1940. Pop 2,558
Library Holdings: Bk Vols 18,000
Special Collections: Finnish Culture & Language Coll; Parenting/Home Education Coll
Subject Interests: Local hist
Automation Activity & Vendor Info: (Cataloging) Follett Software; (Circulation) Follett Software; (ILL) Auto-Graphics, Inc; (OPAC) Auto-Graphics, Inc
Wireless access
Function: Bi-weekly Writer's Group, Home delivery & serv to seniorr ctr & nursing homes, Homebound delivery serv, ILL available, Photocopying/Printing, Prog for children & young adult, Summer reading prog, Telephone ref, Wheelchair accessible
Partic in CLA
Special Services for the Deaf - Bks on deafness & sign lang; Closed caption videos
Special Services for the Blind - Cassettes; Home delivery serv; Large print bks
Open Mon 12-4 (2-6 April-Oct), Wed & Fri 12-4, Tues 10:30-7:30, Thurs 1:30-6:30, Sat 10-1
Friends of the Library Group

WALLINGFORD

M GAYLORD HOSPITAL*, Tremaine Library & Resource Center, Jackson Pavilion Ground Flr, 50 Gaylord Farm Rd, 06492. SAN 328-4697. Tel: 203-741-3481. FAX: 203-284-2892. Web Site: www.gaylord.org/patient-info/library-resources. *Med Librn,* Muriel Garvey; E-mail: mgarvey@gaylord.org; Staff 1 (MLS 1)
Library Holdings: Bk Vols 1,500; Per Subs 18
Wireless access
Publications: Newsletter
Partic in Basic Health Sciences Library Network; Conn Asn of Health Scis Librs
Open Mon-Fri 8-7:30

S WALLINGFORD HISTORICAL SOCIETY INC, LIBRARY*, Samuel Parsons House, 180 S Main St, 06492. (Mail add: PO Box 73, 06492-0073), SAN 326-9981. Tel: 203-294-1996. *Pres,* Raymond Chappell; *Library Contact, VPres,* Bob Beaumont
Founded 1916
Library Holdings: Bk Vols 500
Subject Interests: Local genealogy, Local hist
Function: Res libr
Publications: Wallingford - Images of America Series
Restriction: Open by appt only

P WALLINGFORD PUBLIC LIBRARY*, 200 N Main St, 06492-3791. SAN 336-5255. Tel: 203-265-6754. FAX: 203-269-5698. Web Site: www.wallingford.lioninc.org. *Dir,* Jane Fisher; *Asst Dir,* Amy Humphries; Tel: 203-284-6422, E-mail: amyh@lioninc.org; *Head, Children's Servx,* Sunnie Scarpa; *Head, Circ,* Barbara Cangiano; *Head, Innovation & Emerging Tech,* Janet Flewelling; *Head, Tech Serv,* Elizabeth Gatter; *Head, Teen Serv,* Jennifer Nash; *Ch,* Kari Hamad; *Ch,* Alyssa Johnson; *Ch,* Allison Murphy; *Commun Serv Librn,* Julie Rio; *Ref Librn,* Christopher Ciemniewski; Staff 16 (MLS 16)
Founded 1881. Pop 44,680; Circ 646,244
Special Collections: Oneida Community, Holocaust
Subject Interests: Local hist
Automation Activity & Vendor Info: (Acquisitions) Innovative Interfaces, Inc; (Cataloging) Innovative Interfaces, Inc; (Circulation) Innovative Interfaces, Inc; (ILL) Innovative Interfaces, Inc; (OPAC) Innovative Interfaces, Inc; (Serials) Innovative Interfaces, Inc
Wireless access
Function: 24/7 Online cat, 3D Printer, Adult bk club, Archival coll, Audio & video playback equip for onsite use, Bk club(s), Bks on CD, Chess club, Children's prog, Computer training, Computers for patron use, Digital talking bks, Electronic databases & coll, Equip loans & repairs, Free DVD rentals, Homebound delivery serv, Homework prog, ILL available, Magazines, Makerspace, Meeting rooms, Microfiche/film & reading machines, Museum passes, Music CDs, Online cat, OverDrive digital audio bks, Photocopying/Printing, Prog for children & young adult, Ref & res, STEM programs, Wheelchair accessible
Publications: WORDS (Newsletter)
Partic in Libraries Online, Inc
Open Mon-Fri 9:30-9, Sat 9:30-5, Sun (Winter) 1-5
Friends of the Library Group
Branches: 1
YALESVILLE BRANCH, 400 Church St, Yalesville, 06492, SAN 336-528X. Tel: 203-269-3688. *Dir,* Jane Fisher
Automation Activity & Vendor Info: (Circulation) Innovative Interfaces, Inc - Millennium
Open Tues & Thurs 12-7, Sat 10-2
Friends of the Library Group

WARREN

P WARREN PUBLIC LIBRARY*, 15 Sackett Hill Rd, 06754. SAN 302-4105. Tel: 860-868-2195. E-mail: warrenpl@optonline.net. Web Site: www.warrenctlibrary.org. *Dir,* Louise J Manteuffel; *Asst Librn,* Susan Bates; *Ch,* Melissa Fillie; E-mail: Filliewpl@optonline.net; Staff 3 (Non-MLS 3)
Pop 1,400; Circ 7,000
Library Holdings: Bk Vols 14,000
Automation Activity & Vendor Info: (Acquisitions) Bibliomation Inc; (Cataloging) Bibliomation Inc; (Circulation) Bibliomation Inc
Wireless access
Function: Audio & video playback equip for onsite use, Bks on cassette, Bks on CD, Children's prog, Computers for patron use, Free DVD rentals, Homebound delivery serv, ILL available, Literacy & newcomer serv, Mail & tel request accepted, Music CDs, Photocopying/Printing, Preschool outreach, Prog for adults, Prog for children & young adult, Ref serv available
Partic in Bibliomation Inc; Connecticut Library Consortium; Evergreen Indiana Consortium; Suburban Library Cooperative
Open Tues 10-7, Thurs & Fri 10-5, Sat 10-2

WASHINGTON

S THE FREDERICK GUNN SCHOOL, Tisch Family Library, (Formerly Gunnery), 99 Green Hill Rd, 06793. SAN 326-0054. Tel: 860-868-7334, Ext 224. FAX: 860-868-1614. Web Site: libguides.gunnery.org/home. *Libr Dir,* Ed Surjan; E-mail: surjane@frederickgunn.org; *Asst Librn,* Moira Conlan; E-mail: conlanm@frederickgunn.org; Staff 2 (MLS 2)
Library Holdings: Bk Vols 15,000; Per Subs 90
Special Collections: Alumni bks & publications

P GUNN MEMORIAL LIBRARY, INC*, Five Wykeham Rd, 06793-1308. (Mail add: PO Box 1273, 06793-0273), SAN 302-4113. Tel: 860-868-7586. FAX: 860-868-7247. E-mail: gunnlib@biblio.org. Web Site: www.gunnlibrary.org. *Dir,* Jean Chapin; E-mail: jchapin@biblio.org; *Adult Serv,* Martie Smolka; E-mail: GunnCirc@biblio.org
Founded 1908. Pop 4,000; Circ 66,747
Library Holdings: Audiobooks 3,764; DVDs 2,197; e-books 204; Bk Vols 50,296; Per Subs 82; Videos 1,811
Subject Interests: Connecticut
Automation Activity & Vendor Info: (Cataloging) Bibliomation Inc; (Circulation) Bibliomation Inc; (OPAC) Bibliomation Inc
Wireless access
Partic in Bibliomation Inc
Open Mon & Fri 9:30-5, Tues & Thurs 9:30-8, Sat 9:30-3

S INSTITUTE FOR AMERICAN INDIAN STUDIES*, Research & Education Libraries, 38 Curtis Rd, 06793. SAN 321-0359. Tel: 860-868-0518. FAX: 860-868-1649. Web Site: iaismuseum.org/. *Exec Dir,*

Chris Combs; E-mail: ccombs@iaismuseum.org; *Asst Dir,* Paul Wegner; E-mail: pwegner@iaismuseum.org; *Coll, Res Serv,* Dr Lucianne Lavin; E-mail: llavin@iaismuseum.org
Founded 1975
Library Holdings: Bk Titles 2,400
Subject Interests: Archaeology, Ethnobotany
Wireless access
Restriction: Open by appt only

WATERBURY

P SILAS BRONSON LIBRARY*, 267 Grand St, 06702-1981. SAN 336-531X. Tel: 203-574-8205. Circulation Tel: 203-574-8206. Reference Tel: 203-574-8225. Administration Tel: 203-574-8226. FAX: 203-574-8055. E-mail: sbl-refdesk@waterburyct.org. Web Site: www.bronsonlibrary.org. *Dir,* Raechel Guest; E-mail: rguest@waterburyct.org; Staff 34 (MLS 15, Non-MLS 19)
Founded 1869. Pop 109,676; Circ 154,588
Library Holdings: AV Mats 16,021; Electronic Media & Resources 20; Bk Vols 256,314; Per Subs 195
Subject Interests: Genealogy, Local hist
Automation Activity & Vendor Info: (Cataloging) Horizon; (Circulation) Horizon; (ILL) Horizon; (OPAC) Horizon; (Serials) Horizon
Wireless access
Function: 24/7 Electronic res, 24/7 Online cat, Activity rm, Adult bk club, Archival coll, Art exhibits, Audiobks via web, AV serv, BA reader (adult literacy), Bk club(s), Bks on CD, Chess club, Children's prog, Computer training, Computers for patron use, Digital talking bks, Distance learning, Doc delivery serv, E-Reserves, Electronic databases & coll, For res purposes, Free DVD rentals, Govt ref serv, Holiday prog, Homebound delivery serv, Homework prog, ILL available, Internet access, Jazz prog, Life-long learning prog for all ages, Magazines, Magnifiers for reading, Mail & tel request accepted, Meeting rooms, Microfiche/film & reading machines, Movies, Museum passes, Music CDs, Online cat, Online ref, Outside serv via phone, mail, e-mail & web, OverDrive digital audio bks, Photocopying/Printing, Preschool outreach, Preschool reading prog, Prog for adults, Prog for children & young adult, Ref & res, Ref serv available, Scanner, Senior computer classes, Senior outreach, Spanish lang bks, Spoken cassettes & CDs, Spoken cassettes & DVDs, Story hour, Summer & winter reading prog, Summer reading prog, Tax forms, Teen prog, Telephone ref, VHS videos, Wheelchair accessible, Winter reading prog, Workshops
Publications: Books & Happenings (Newsletter)
Partic in Bibliomation Inc
Special Services for the Deaf - Bks on deafness & sign lang; Closed caption videos; High interest/low vocabulary bks; TTY equip
Special Services for the Blind - Audio mat; Bks on cassette; Bks on CD; Computer with voice synthesizer for visually impaired persons; Extensive large print coll; Internet workstation with adaptive software; Large print bks; Large screen computer & software; Low vision equip; Magnifiers; Newsletter (in large print, Braille or on cassette); PC for people with disabilities; Photo duplicator for making large print; Ref serv; Screen enlargement software for people with visual disabilities; Talking bks; Videos on blindness & physical disabilties
Open Mon-Thurs 9-8, Fri 9-5, Sat 9-4:45
Friends of the Library Group
Branches: 1
BUNKER HILL, 192 Bunker Hill Ave, 06708, SAN 336-5344. Tel: 203-574-8240. *Br Mgr,* Margaret Keating; E-mail: mkeating@waterburyct.org
Library Holdings: Bk Vols 7,000
Open Tues 1-8, Thurs & Fri 12-5
Friends of the Library Group

L CARMODY, TORRANCE, SANDAK, HENNESSEY LLP*, Law Library, 50 Leavenworth St, 06721-1110. SAN 372-3402. Tel: 203-573-1200. FAX: 203-575-2600. E-mail: librarystaff@carmodylaw.com. *Dir, Info Res,* Position Currently Open
Library Holdings: Bk Vols 12,000; Per Subs 100
Automation Activity & Vendor Info: (Cataloging) EOS International; (Circulation) EOS International
Open Mon-Fri 9-5

S MATTATUCK MUSEUM OF THE MATTATUCK HISTORICAL SOCIETY, Max R Traurig Library, 144 W Main St, 06702. SAN 302-4172. Tel: 203-753-0381. Web Site: mattmuseum.org/collections/traurig-library. *Dir,* Robert Burns; Tel: 203-753-0381, Ext 122; *Archivist,* Stephanie Crawford; E-mail: scrawford@mattmuseum.org; *Colls Mgr,* Wayne Eldred; Tel: 203-753-0381, Ext 112; *Curator,* Cynthia Roznoy; Tel: 203-753-0381, Ext 115
Founded 1877
Library Holdings: Bk Vols 1,500; Per Subs 10
Special Collections: Brass Workers History Project Archives; Connecticut Artists Coll; Decorative Arts; Pictorial History of Waterbury, 1674-1974; Platt Brothers Archives; Waterbury Industrial History Archives
Subject Interests: Local hist
Wireless access
Restriction: Open by appt only

J NAUGATUCK VALLEY COMMUNITY COLLEGE*, Max R Traurig Library, 750 Chase Pkwy, Rm K512, 06708. SAN 302-4229. Tel: 203-575-8024. Reference Tel: 203-575-8244. FAX: 203-575-8062. TDD: 203-596-8762. E-mail: library@nv.edu. Web Site: www.nv.edu/Student-Resources/Academic-Support-Resources/Library. *Dir, Libr Serv,* Jaime Hammond; Tel: 203-575-8199, E-mail: jhammond@nv.edu; *Instrul Serv Librn, Ref (Info Servs),* Liz Frechette; Tel: 203-575-8106, E-mail: efrechette@nv.edu; *Instruction Librn, Ref Librn,* Jenna Stebbins; Tel: 203-596-8712, E-mail: jstebbins@nv.edu; *Ref/Instruction/Tech Serv Librn,* John Leonetti; Tel: 203-575-8021, E-mail: jleonetti@nv.edu; *Circ Supvr,* Elaine Milnor; Tel: 203-575-8147, E-mail: emilnor@nv.edu; Staff 5 (MLS 4, Non-MLS 1)
Founded 1964. Enrl 7,000; Fac 120; Highest Degree: Associate
Library Holdings: e-books 26,000; Bk Vols 35,000
Automation Activity & Vendor Info: (Acquisitions) Ex Libris Group; (Cataloging) Ex Libris Group; (Circulation) Ex Libris Group; (Course Reserve) Ex Libris Group; (ILL) Ex Libris Group; (OPAC) Ex Libris Group; (Serials) Ex Libris Group
Wireless access
Special Services for the Deaf - TDD equip
Special Services for the Blind - Braille bks; Closed circuit TV magnifier; Computer with voice synthesizer for visually impaired persons; Magnifiers; Reader equip
Open Mon-Thurs 8-8, Fri 8-4:30, Sat & Sun 10-2
Restriction: Open to pub for ref & circ; with some limitations

C POST UNIVERSITY, Traurig Library & Learning Resources Center, 800 Country Club Rd, 06723-2540. SAN 302-4180. Tel: 203-596-4560. E-mail: library@post.edu. Web Site: post.edu/student-services/library/. *Dir,* Tracy Ralston; Tel: 203-596-4564, E-mail: Tralston@post.edu; *Info Serv Librn,* Susan Garry; Tel: 203-596-4565; *Ref Librn,* Kelly Marchand; Tel: 203-596-4609; Staff 3 (MLS 3)
Founded 1890. Enrl 5,812; Fac 130; Highest Degree: Master
Jul 2015-Jun 2016. Mats Exp $423,887
Special Collections: Equine Coll; Law Library. State Document Depository; US Document Depository
Automation Activity & Vendor Info: (OPAC) Auto-Graphics, Inc
Wireless access
Function: Computers for patron use, Electronic databases & coll, ILL available, Internet access, Online cat, Online info literacy tutorials on the web & in blackboard, Online ref, Photocopying/Printing, Printer for laptops & handheld devices, Ref serv available, Telephone ref
Partic in Connecticut Library Consortium; Council of Connecticut Academic Library Directors; LYRASIS; OCLC Online Computer Library Center, Inc
Open Mon-Wed (Fall-Spring) 8am-10pm, Thurs 8-8, Fri 8-5, Sat 10-4, Sun 2-8; Mon-Thurs (Summer) 8-5, Fri 8-4, Sat 10-4

M SAINT MARY'S HOSPITAL*, Health Science Library, 56 Franklin St, 06706. Tel: 203-709-6408. FAX: 203-709-7738. *Med Librn,* Lori Bradshaw; E-mail: lori.bradshaw@stmh.org; Staff 1.8 (MLS 1, Non-MLS 0.8)
Library Holdings: e-books 10; e-journals 140; Bk Titles 4,000; Per Subs 360
Automation Activity & Vendor Info: (Circulation) CyberTools for Libraries; (OPAC) CyberTools for Libraries
Wireless access
Partic in Conn Asn of Health Scis Librs
Open Mon-Fri 8-4:30

S WATERBURY REPUBLICAN & AMERICAN LIBRARY, 389 Meadow St, 06702. SAN 324-3583. Tel: 203-574-3636, Ext 1497. FAX: 203-596-9277. Web Site: rep-am.com. *Librn,* Michael DeGirolamo, Jr; E-mail: mdegirolamo@rep-am.com
Library Holdings: Bk Titles 700; Bk Vols 2,300; Per Subs 15
Special Collections: Local History Books; Local Newspaper Clippings; Local Photo Coll
Subject Interests: NW Conn
Wireless access
Restriction: Open by appt only

WATERFORD

S EUGENE O'NEILL THEATER CENTER*, Liebling-Wood Library, 305 Great Neck Rd, 06385. SAN 302-4237. Tel: 860-443-5378, Ext 227. Administration Tel: 860-443-5378. FAX: 860-443-9653. E-mail:

litoffice@theoneill.org. Web Site: www.theoneill.org. *Lit Prog Mgr,* Lexy Leuszler; E-mail: literarymanager@theoneill.org; Staff 2 (Non-MLS 2)
Founded 1966
Library Holdings: Bk Titles 4,000
Special Collections: Eugene O'Neill Coll; National Critics Institute; National Music Theater Conference Archive; National Playwrights Conference Archive; National Puppetry Conference; National Theatre Institute Library. Oral History
Subject Interests: Develop of performance art, Standard drama & variations
Wireless access
Function: Prog for children & young adult, Workshops, Writing prog
Restriction: Access at librarian's discretion, Authorized scholars by appt, Circ privileges for students & alumni only, External users must contact libr, In-house use for visitors, Open to fac, students & qualified researchers, Open to pub by appt only
Friends of the Library Group

P WATERFORD PUBLIC LIBRARY, 49 Rope Ferry Rd, 06385. SAN 302-4245. Tel: 860-444-5805. FAX: 860-437-1685. E-mail: waterfordlibrary@waterfordct.org. Web Site: waterfordct.org/library. *Dir,* Christine Johnson; E-mail: cjohnson@waterfordct.org
Founded 1923. Pop 19,100
Library Holdings: CDs 1,000; DVDs 750; Large Print Bks 2,500; Bk Vols 85,000; Per Subs 125; Talking Bks 1,250; Videos 2,000
Special Collections: Travel Coll
Subject Interests: Local hist
Automation Activity & Vendor Info: (Cataloging) SirsiDynix; (Circulation) SirsiDynix; (OPAC) SirsiDynix
Wireless access
Open Mon-Wed 9-8, Thurs-Sat 9-5

WATERTOWN

S WATERTOWN HISTORY MUSEUM LIBRARY, (Formerly Watertown History Society Library), 401 Main St, 06795. (Mail add: PO Box 853, 06795-0853), SAN 302-4253. Tel: 860-274-1050. Web Site: www.watertownhistorymuseum.org. *Curator,* Diane Ciba; E-mail: curator@watertownhistorymuseum.org
Founded 1947
Library Holdings: Bk Vols 600
Subject Interests: Genealogy, Local hist
Open Wed & Sat 10-2

P WATERTOWN LIBRARY ASSOCIATION*, 470 Main St, 06795. SAN 336-5409. Tel: 860-945-5360. FAX: 860-945-5367. E-mail: wtnlib@watertownlibrary.org. Web Site: www.watertownlibrary.org. *Dir,* Joan K Rintelman; E-mail: joankr@watertownlibrary.org; *Asst Dir,* Dona L Rintelman
Founded 1865. Pop 20,000; Circ 113,657
Library Holdings: Bk Vols 107,000; Per Subs 180
Wireless access
Partic in Region I Coop Libr Servs Unit
Open Mon & Fri 10-5, Tues-Thurs 10-8, Sat 10-4
Friends of the Library Group
Branches: 1
OAKVILLE BRANCH, 55 Davis St, Oakville, 06779, SAN 336-5433. Tel: 860-945-5368. FAX: 860-945-7199. *Br Mgr,* Donald Stepanek; *Asst Librn,* Lisa Dalton
Founded 1914
Open Tues & Wed 9-5, Thurs 9-1
Friends of the Library Group

WEST CORNWALL

P THE HUGHES MEMORIAL PUBLIC LIBRARY*, 35 Lower River Rd, 06796. (Mail add: PO Box 4, 06796), SAN 324-3753. E-mail: cornwalllibrary@biblio.org. Web Site: www.cornwallct.org/index.php?id=library.
Circ 5,000
Library Holdings: Bk Titles 16,000
Open Sat 10-1:30

WEST HARTFORD

R CONGREGATION BETH ISRAEL*, Deborah Library, Ellen Jeanne Goldfarb Community Learning Ctr, 701 Farmington Ave, 06119. SAN 372-5820. Tel: 860-233-8215. FAX: 860-523-0223. Web Site: www.cbict.org/learn/learning-center/deborah-library. *Librn,* Karen Beyard; Tel: 860-233-8215, Ext 2230, E-mail: kbeyard@cbict.org; Staff 1 (MLS 1)
Founded 1934
Library Holdings: Bk Titles 15,000
Subject Interests: Judaica
Automation Activity & Vendor Info: (Cataloging) Follett Software; (Circulation) Follett Software
Wireless access
Open Tues 10-3, Wed 2-6, Thurs 10-1, Sun 9-noon
Friends of the Library Group

R EMANUEL SYNAGOGUE LIBRARY*, 160 Mohegan Dr, 06117. SAN 302-4288. Tel: 860-233-2774, 860-236-1275. FAX: 860-231-8890. E-mail: library@emanuelsynagogue.org. Web Site: emanuelsynagogue.org. *Librn,* Beth Katten; Tel: 860-236-1275, Ext 124, E-mail: bethkatten@yahoo.com
Library Holdings: Bk Vols 5,200
Restriction: Mem only

R FIRST CHURCH WEST HARTFORD, John P Webster Library, 12 S Main St, 06107. SAN 370-0305. Tel: 860-232-3893. FAX: 860-232-8183. E-mail: jpwebster@whfirstchurch.org. Web Site: whfirstchurch.org/jpw-library. *Libr Dir,* Jennifer deSimas; E-mail: jpwebsterdir@whfirstchurch.org; *Asst Librn,* Karla Fackler Grafton; E-mail: jpwebsterlib@whfirstchurch.org; Staff 2 (MLS 2)
Founded 1978
Library Holdings: Audiobooks 150; Bk Vols 13,000; Spec Interest Per Sub 1; Videos 300
Special Collections: Ruth Dudley Resource Center for Spiritual Formation
Subject Interests: Relig, Soc issues, Spirituality
Automation Activity & Vendor Info: (Cataloging) Bibliomation Inc; (Circulation) Bibliomation Inc; (OPAC) Bibliomation Inc
Wireless access
Function: 24/7 Online cat, Adult bk club, Archival coll, Art exhibits, Audiobks on Playaways & MP3, Bk club(s), Bks on CD, CD-ROM, Free DVD rentals, Holiday prog, Mail & tel request accepted, Mail loans to mem, Meeting rooms, Online cat, Prog for adults, Prog for children & young adult, Ref & res, Res assist avail, Res libr, Senior outreach, Wheelchair accessible, Workshops
Partic in Bibliomation Inc; Connecticut Library Consortium
Open Mon-Thurs 9-5, Sun 9-12

C SAINT JOSEPH UNIVERSITY*, Pope Pius XII Library, 1678 Asylum Ave, 06117-2791. SAN 302-430X. Tel: 860-232-4571. Circulation Tel: 860-231-5209. Interlibrary Loan Service Tel: 860-231-5750. Reference Tel: 860-231-5435. E-mail: reference@usj.edu. Web Site: www.usj.edu/academics/library. *Dir,* Tim Salm; E-mail: tsalm@usj.edu; *Instruction Librn, Ref Serv,* Lynne Piacentini; Tel: 860-231-5751, E-mail: lpiacentini@usj.edu; *Pharm Librn,* Antoinette Collins; Tel: 860-231-5484, E-mail: acollins@usj.edu; *Cat, Syst Librn,* Ann Williams; Tel: 860-231-5207, E-mail: awilliams@usj.edu; *Access Serv Coordr,* Elizabeth Lesso; E-mail: elesso@usj.edu; *ILL Coordr,* Kathleen Kelley; E-mail: kkelley@usj.edu; Staff 8 (MLS 6, Non-MLS 2)
Founded 1932. Highest Degree: Master
Automation Activity & Vendor Info: (Cataloging) OCLC; (Circulation) SirsiDynix; (Course Reserve) Docutek; (ILL) OCLC; (OPAC) SirsiDynix; (Serials) SerialsSolutions
Wireless access
Function: Archival coll
Partic in Connecticut Library Consortium; Library Connection, Inc; LYRASIS; OCLC Online Computer Library Center, Inc

C UNIVERSITY OF HARTFORD LIBRARIES*, W H Mortensen Library, 200 Bloomfield Ave, 06117. SAN 302-4318. Tel: 860-768-4264. Administration Tel: 860-768-4268. Circulation FAX: 860-768-5298. Administration FAX: 860-768-4274. Web Site: library.hartford.edu. *Dir,* Randi Lynn Ashton-Pritting; E-mail: pritting@hartford.edu; *Head, Pub Serv, Head, Ref,* Nick Wharton; Staff 9 (MLS 2, Non-MLS 7)
Founded 1957. Enrl 6,882; Fac 306; Highest Degree: Doctorate
Library Holdings: Bk Vols 450,000; Per Subs 2,089; Videos 2,000
Special Collections: Black Literature; Judaica (Millie & Irving Bercowetz Family Coll)
Subject Interests: Art, Music
Automation Activity & Vendor Info: (Cataloging) Ex Libris Group; (Circulation) Ex Libris Group; (Course Reserve) Ex Libris Group; (OPAC) Ex Libris Group
Wireless access
Publications: Resources (Newsletter)
Partic in Connecticut Library Consortium; Coun of Conn Acad Libr Dirs; Greater Hartford Consortium for Higher Education; LYRASIS; OCLC Online Computer Library Center, Inc
Special Services for the Blind - Closed circuit TV magnifier
Friends of the Library Group
Departmental Libraries:
MILDRED P ALLEN MEMORIAL, 200 Bloomfield Ave, 06117-0395, SAN 324-3060. Tel: 860-768-4404. FAX: 860-768-5295. *Head Librn,* Tracey Rudnick; E-mail: rudnick@hartford.edu; *Tech Serv Librn,* Jennifer Olson; E-mail: jolson@hartford.edu; Staff 6 (MLS 2, Non-MLS 4)
Founded 1938. Enrl 700; Fac 125; Highest Degree: Doctorate
Library Holdings: AV Mats 23,000; Music Scores 38,000; Bk Vols 12,000; Per Subs 211
Special Collections: Kalmen Opperman Clarinet Coll; Stuart Smith Coll, ms, writings & published works

Subject Interests: Music, Performing arts
Automation Activity & Vendor Info: (Acquisitions) Ex Libris Group; (Cataloging) Ex Libris Group; (Circulation) Ex Libris Group; (Course Reserve) Ex Libris Group; (ILL) Ex Libris Group; (OPAC) Ex Libris Group
Partic in OCLC Online Computer Library Center, Inc
Restriction: Non-circulating to the pub

S NOAH WEBSTER HOUSE & WEST HARTFORD HISTORICAL SOCIETY*, 227 S Main St, 06107-3430. SAN 329-160X. Tel: 860-521-5362. Circulation Tel: 860-521-5362, Ext 17. FAX: 860-521-4036. Web Site: www.noahwebsterhouse.org. *Curator, Spec Project Dir,* Sheila Daley; E-mail: daleys@noahwebsterhouse.org
Founded 1974
Library Holdings: Bk Vols 300; Per Subs 10
Special Collections: 18th Century History, lifestyle, gardening; Lexicography. Oral History
Subject Interests: Decorative art, Hist
Function: Res libr
Partic in W Hartford Libr Syst
Restriction: Non-circulating, Open by appt only

P WEST HARTFORD PUBLIC LIBRARY*, Noah Webster Memorial Library, 20 S Main St, 06107-2432. SAN 336-5522. Tel: 860-561-6950. Circulation Tel: 860-561-6960. Interlibrary Loan Service Tel: 860-561-6968. Reference Tel: 860-561-6990. Administration Tel: 860-561-6970. FAX: 860-561-6976. E-mail: whpl@westhartford.org. Web Site: www.westhartfordlibrary.org. *Dir,* Martha Church; E-mail: mchurch@westhartfordct.gov; *Ch,* Sara Bartelmo; E-mail: sbartelmo@wethartfordct.gov; *Pub Relations & Prog Serv Mgr,* Joe Cadieux; E-mail: cadieux@westhartfordct.gov; *Adult Serv,* Agatha Monahan; E-mail: amonahan@westhartfordct.gov; *Cat,* Jacqueline Douglas; E-mail: jdouglas@westhartfordct.gov; *Ch Serv,* Carol Waxman; E-mail: cwaxman@westhartfordct.gov; *Coll Develop,* Rebecca Nugent; E-mail: rnugent@westhartfordct.gov; *Circ,* Ann Marie Salerno; E-mail: asalerno@westhartfordct.gov; *Commun Outreach Liaison,* Pramod Pradhan; E-mail: ppradhan@westhartfordct.gov; *Info Tech,* Genevienve Francis; E-mail: gfrancis@westhartfordct.gov; *Teen Serv,* Kari Karp; E-mail: kkarp@westhartfordct.gov. Subject Specialists: *Grants,* Joe Cadieux; Staff 24 (MLS 14, Non-MLS 10)
Founded 1897. Pop 63,133; Circ 653,152
Library Holdings: Bk Vols 204,371; Per Subs 400
Special Collections: Local History Coll; Noah Webster Coll; West Hartford News, micro
Automation Activity & Vendor Info: (Cataloging) OCLC; (Circulation) Innovative Interfaces, Inc - Sierra; (Discovery) EBSCO Discovery Service; (ILL) OCLC; (OPAC) Innovative Interfaces, Inc - Sierra; (Serials) SerialsSolutions
Wireless access
Function: 24/7 Electronic res, 24/7 Online cat, Art exhibits, Citizenship assistance, Computers for patron use, ILL available, Internet access, Large print keyboards, Magnifiers for reading, Microfiche/film & reading machines, Online cat, Prog for adults, Prog for children & young adult, Res assist avail, Scanner, Spanish lang bks, Teen prog, Writing prog
Partic in Connecticut Library Consortium; Library Connection, Inc; OCLC Online Computer Library Center, Inc
Special Services for the Deaf - ADA equip; Am sign lang & deaf culture; Assisted listening device; Closed caption videos; Sign lang interpreter upon request for prog; Staff with knowledge of sign lang
Special Services for the Blind - Accessible computers; Assistive/Adapted tech devices, equip & products; Closed circuit TV magnifier; Computer access aids; Computer with voice synthesizer for visually impaired persons; Copier with enlargement capabilities; Dragon Naturally Speaking software; Internet workstation with adaptive software; Large print bks; Large print bks & talking machines; Large screen computer & software; Low vision equip; Magnifiers
Open Mon-Thurs 10-9, Fri & Sat 10-5, Sun (Oct-May) 1-5
Branches: 2
BISHOP'S CORNER, 15 Starkel Rd, 06117, SAN 336-5581. Tel: 860-561-8210. Circulation Tel: 860-561-8211. Reference Tel: 860-561-8212. *Br Operations Mgr,* Karen Polmatier; E-mail: kpolmatier@westhartfordct.gov; *Ch Serv,* Bailey Berardino; E-mail: bberardino@westhartfordct.gov; *Circ,* Desiree Meyer
Library Holdings: Bk Vols 45,135
Open Mon & Wed 10-6, Tues 1-8, Thurs 11-5, Fri & Sat 10-2
FAXON BRANCH, 1073 New Britain Ave, 06110, SAN 336-5557. Tel: 860-561-8200. Circulation Tel: 860-561-8201. Reference Tel: 860-561-8202. *Br Operations Mgr,* Karen Polmatier; E-mail: kpolmatier@westhartfordct.gov; *Ch,* Ellen Phillips; E-mail: ephillips@westhartfordct.gov; *Circ,* Karen Thomson
Library Holdings: Bk Vols 39,448
Special Services for the Deaf - TDD equip
Open Mon & Wed 1-8, Tues & Thurs 10-6, Fri & Sat 10-2

WEST HARTLAND

P HARTLAND PUBLIC LIBRARY*, 61 Center St, Rte 20, 06091. SAN 302-4326. Tel: 860-238-4400. E-mail: hartlandlib@hotmail.com. Web Site: library.hartlandct.org. *Chairperson,* Connie Irwin
Founded 1965. Pop 2,058; Circ 3,483
Library Holdings: AV Mats 155; Large Print Bks 21; Bk Titles 7,732; Bk Vols 8,082; Per Subs 20; Talking Bks 58; Videos 20
Wireless access
Partic in Region I Coop Libr Servs Unit
Open Tues 5-8, Fri 3-6, Sat 9-12
Friends of the Library Group

WEST HAVEN

C UNIVERSITY OF NEW HAVEN*, Marvin K Peterson Library, 300 Boston Post Rd, 06516. SAN 302-4342. Tel: 203-932-7189. Circulation Tel: 203-932-7197. Interlibrary Loan Service Tel: 203-932-7194. Administration Tel: 203-932-7190. FAX: 203-932-1469. E-mail: LibraryHelp@newhaven.edu. Web Site: www.newhaven.edu/library. *Dir,* Hanko H Dobi; Tel: 203-932-7191, E-mail: hdobi@newhaven.edu; *Outreach Librn, Tech Serv,* Anna Malicka; E-mail: amalicka@newhaven.edu; *Access Serv Mgr,* Amber Montano; E-mail: amontano@newhaven.edu; Staff 6 (MLS 6)
Founded 1920. Enrl 3,140; Fac 232; Highest Degree: Master
Library Holdings: Bk Vols 300,000; Per Subs 1,000
Special Collections: US Document Depository
Subject Interests: Criminal law & justice, Engr, Forensic sci
Automation Activity & Vendor Info: (Acquisitions) Ex Libris Group; (Cataloging) Ex Libris Group; (Circulation) Ex Libris Group; (Course Reserve) Ex Libris Group; (ILL) OCLC; (OPAC) Ex Libris Group; (Serials) Ex Libris Group
Wireless access
Publications: Friends (Newsletter); Library Guides; Library Newsletter
Partic in Connecticut Library Consortium; Coun of Conn Acad Libr Dirs; LYRASIS
Open Mon-Thurs 9am-10pm, Fri 8:30-4:30, Sat 9-5, Sun 2-10
Friends of the Library Group

GM VA CONNECTICUT HEALTH CARE SYSTEM*, Library Service, 950 Campbell Ave, 06516-2770. SAN 302-4350. Tel: 203-932-5711, Ext 2898. FAX: 203-937-3822. *Librn,* Jessica Patterson
Founded 1953
Library Holdings: Bk Titles 5,000
Partic in Conn Asn of Health Scis Librs
Open Mon-Fri 7:30-4

P WEST HAVEN PUBLIC LIBRARY*, 300 Elm St, 06516-4692. SAN 336-5611. Tel: 203-937-4233. Reference Tel: 203-937-4233, Ext 4512. FAX: 203-937-4224. TDD: 203-937-4235. E-mail: dir@westhavenlibrary.org. Web Site: whpl.lioninc.org. *Exec Dir,* Colleen Bailie; E-mail: dir@westhavenlibrary.org; *Asst Dir,* Catherine Bushman; E-mail: asstdir@westhavenlibrary.org; *Circ Librn,* Tanarha Smith; E-mail: wmcirc@westhavenlibrary.org; *Digital Serv Librn,* Travis Feder; E-mail: techservices@westhavenlibrary.org; Staff 9 (MLS 7, Non-MLS 2)
Founded 1906. Pop 55,000; Circ 267,580
Library Holdings: Bk Vols 160,000; Per Subs 303
Subject Interests: Connecticut, Hist
Automation Activity & Vendor Info: (Circulation) Innovative Interfaces, Inc
Wireless access
Function: 3D Printer, Activity rm, Adult bk club, Adult literacy prog, Audiobks on Playaways & MP3, Audiobks via web, AV serv, BA reader (adult literacy), Bk club(s), Bks on CD, Children's prog, Computer training, Computers for patron use, E-Reserves, Electronic databases & coll, Family literacy, For res purposes, Free DVD rentals, Holiday prog, Home delivery & serv to seniorr ctr & nursing homes, Homebound delivery serv, ILL available, Internet access, Literacy & newcomer serv, Magazines, Magnifiers for reading, Meeting rooms, Microfiche/film & reading machines, Movies, Museum passes, Online cat, Outreach serv, Outside serv via phone, mail, e-mail & web, OverDrive digital audio bks, Photocopying/Printing, Preschool outreach, Preschool reading prog, Prog for adults, Prog for children & young adult, Ref & res, Ref serv available, Res assist avail, Scanner, Senior computer classes, Senior outreach, Spanish lang bks, Spoken cassettes & CDs, Spoken cassettes & DVDs, Story hour, Summer & winter reading prog, Summer reading prog, Tax forms, Teen prog, Telephone ref, Workshops, Writing prog
Partic in Connecticut Library Consortium; Libraries Online, Inc
Open Mon-Thurs 10-8, Tues & Wed 10-6, Fri & Sat 10-5
Friends of the Library Group
Branches: 2
ORA MASON BRANCH, 260 Benham Hill Rd, 06516-6541, SAN 336-5646. Tel: 203-933-9381. FAX: 203-931-7149. *Br Mgr,* Andrea Zimmermann
Library Holdings: Bk Vols 24,829

Open Mon & Wed 9-5, Tues & Thurs 11-7
Friends of the Library Group
LOUIS PIANTINO BRANCH, One Forest Rd, 06516-1698, SAN 336-5670. Tel: 203-933-9335. Circulation E-mail: lpcirc@westhavenlibrary.org. *Br Mgr,* Aisha Banks
Library Holdings: Bk Vols 30,655
Friends of the Library Group

WESTBROOK

P WESTBROOK PUBLIC LIBRARY*, 61 Goodspeed Dr, 06498. SAN 302-4369. Tel: 860-399-6422. FAX: 860-399-6344. E-mail: westbrook.public.lib@gmail.com. Web Site: westbrooklibrary.lioninc.org. *Dir,* Lewis B Daniels, III; *Asst Librn,* Brittany Pearson; *Ch,* Mary Nyman. Subject Specialists: *Tech, Teen serv,* Brittany Pearson; Staff 4 (MLS 3, Non-MLS 1)
Founded 1895. Pop 6,902; Circ 41,140
Jul 2017-Jun 2018. Mats Exp $38,500, Books $25,000, Per/Ser (Incl. Access Fees) $6,500, AV Mat $7,000
Library Holdings: CDs 1,704; DVDs 2,101; Large Print Bks 788; Bk Titles 50,029; Per Subs 124; Videos 715
Special Collections: Literacy Volunteers Coll
Automation Activity & Vendor Info: (Circulation) Innovative Interfaces, Inc
Wireless access
Function: 24/7 Electronic res, 24/7 Online cat, Activity rm, Adult bk club, Adult literacy prog, Archival coll
Publications: Friends of the Library (Annual)
Partic in Libraries Online, Inc
Open Tues & Thurs 9-8, Wed, Fri & Sat 9-5
Friends of the Library Group

WESTON

P WESTON PUBLIC LIBRARY*, 56 Norfield Rd, 06883. SAN 302-4385. Tel: 203-222-2665. Interlibrary Loan Service Tel: 203-222-2550. FAX: 203-222-2560. E-mail: westonlibrary@westonct.gov. Web Site: www.westonpubliclibrary.org. *Dir,* Karen Tatarka; *Ch Serv, YA Serv,* Alessandra Petrino; Tel: 203-222-2651, E-mail: apetrino@westonct.gov; *Circ,* Nancy Lincoln; Tel: 203-222-2664, E-mail: nlincoln@westonct.gov; *ILL,* Karen Bennett; E-mail: kbennett@westonct.gov
Founded 1963. Pop 10,263; Circ 65,000
Library Holdings: Audiobooks 5,014; AV Mats 5,810; DVDs 3,129; e-books 4,814; Large Print Bks 504; Bk Vols 48,212; Per Subs 45
Automation Activity & Vendor Info: (Circulation) Bibliomation Inc; (OPAC) Bibliomation Inc; (Serials) EBSCO Online
Wireless access
Partic in Bibliomation Inc
Open Mon & Tues 9-6, Wed 9-8, Thurs & Fri 9-5, Sat 10-4, Sun 12-4
Friends of the Library Group

WESTPORT

S WESTPORT HISTORICAL SOCIETY LIBRARY*, 25 Avery Pl, 06880-3215. SAN 302-4458. Tel: 203-222-1424. FAX: 203-221-0981. E-mail: archives@westporthistory.org. Web Site: westporthistory.org. *Exec Dir,* Ramin Ganeshram; Tel: 203-222-1424, Ext 105, E-mail: executivedirector@westporthistory.org; *Asst Dir,* Barbara Peck; Tel: 203-222-1424, Ext 106, E-mail: bpeck@westporthistory.org; *Archivist,* Sven Selinder; E-mail: svenericsr@gmail.com
Library Holdings: Bk Vols 200
Special Collections: Historical Items from 1783 to present
Restriction: Open by appt only, Open to pub for ref only

P THE WESTPORT LIBRARY*, 20 Jesup Rd, 06880. SAN 302-4466. Tel: 203-291-4820. Circulation Tel: 203-291-4800. Interlibrary Loan Service Tel: 203-291-4816. FAX: 203-227-3829. Reference E-mail: ref@westportlibrary.org. Web Site: www.westportlibrary.org. *Exec Dir,* William H Harmer; Tel: 203-291-4801, E-mail: bharmer@westportlibrary.org; *Dir, Mkt & Communications,* Rachel Pegnataro; E-mail: rpegnataro@westportlibrary.org; *Dir, Organization & Mgmt,* Melanie Myers; E-mail: mmyers@westportlibrary.org
Founded 1908. Pop 25,749; Circ 924,058
Library Holdings: Audiobooks 6,546; CDs 6,659; DVDs 18,152; Bk Vols 193,483; Per Subs 323
Special Collections: Picture File, clippings & photos
Subject Interests: Performing arts, Visual arts
Automation Activity & Vendor Info: (Acquisitions) Horizon; (Cataloging) Horizon; (Circulation) Horizon; (ILL) OCLC; (OPAC) Horizon; (Serials) Horizon
Wireless access
Function: Adult bk club, Art exhibits, Audiobks via web, Bk club(s), Bks on CD, Children's prog, Computers for patron use, E-Reserves, Electronic databases & coll, Free DVD rentals, Games & aids for people with disabilities, Home delivery & serv to seniorr ctr & nursing homes, Homebound delivery serv, ILL available, Internet access, Magnifiers for reading, Mail & tel request accepted, Music CDs, Online cat, Online ref, Outside serv via phone, mail, e-mail & web, Photocopying/Printing, Prog for adults, Prog for children & young adult, Ref & res, Ref serv available, Spoken cassettes & CDs, Spoken cassettes & DVDs, Story hour, Summer reading prog, Teen prog, Telephone ref, Wheelchair accessible
Publications: Westport Public Library Annual Report; Westport Public Library Newsletter/Calendar
Special Services for the Deaf - Bks on deafness & sign lang; Closed caption videos
Special Services for the Blind - Bks on cassette; Bks on CD; Closed circuit TV magnifier; Home delivery serv; Large print bks; Magnifiers; Talking bks
Open Mon-Thurs 9-9, Fri 9-6, Sat 9-5, Sun 1-5
Friends of the Library Group

WETHERSFIELD

S WETHERSFIELD HISTORICAL SOCIETY, Old Academy Library, 150 Main St, 06109. SAN 302-4482. Tel: 860-529-7656. FAX: 860-563-2609. E-mail: society@wethersfieldhistory.org. Web Site: www.wethersfieldhistory.org. *Exec Dir,* Amy Northrop Wittorff; *Prog Coordr,* Kevin Andersen; E-mail: kevin.andersen@wethersfieldhistory.org
Founded 1932
Library Holdings: Bk Titles 1,500; Bk Vols 2,000
Special Collections: Old manuscripts, deeds, letters, log books, maps, bibles, textbooks & account books; Pamphlet Coll; Photograph Coll
Subject Interests: Archit, Genealogy, Local hist
Wireless access
Open Tues-Fri 10-4

P WETHERSFIELD PUBLIC LIBRARY*, 515 Silas Deane Hwy, 06109. SAN 302-4490. Tel: 860-529-2665. Information Services Tel: 860-257-2811. FAX: 860-257-2822. E-mail: library@wethersfieldlibrary.org. Web Site: www.wethersfieldlibrary.org. *Dir,* Brook Berry; *Mgr, Ch Serv,* Regina Aleksandravicius; *Mgr, Coll Serv,* Celia Allison
Founded 1893. Pop 26,700; Circ 350,000
Automation Activity & Vendor Info: (Cataloging) Innovative Interfaces, Inc; (Circulation) Innovative Interfaces, Inc; (ILL) OCLC WorldShare Interlibrary Loan; (OPAC) Innovative Interfaces, Inc
Wireless access
Partic in Library Connection, Inc
Open Mon-Sat 10-5
Friends of the Library Group

WILLIMANTIC

C EASTERN CONNECTICUT STATE UNIVERSITY*, J Eugene Smith Library, 83 Windham St, 06226-2295. SAN 302-4512. Tel: 860-465-4506. Interlibrary Loan Service Tel: 860-465-4462. Reference Tel: 860-465-4699. Administration Tel: 860-465-4397. Toll Free Tel: 877-587-8693. FAX: 860-465-5521. Interlibrary Loan Service FAX: 860-465-4355. Administration FAX: 860-465-5522. Web Site: www.easternct.edu/smithlibrary. *Dir, Libr Serv,* Janice A Wilson; Tel: 860-465-4466, E-mail: wilsonj@easternct.edu; *Head, Cat,* Kristin M Jacobi; Tel: 860-465-4508, E-mail: jacobikr@easternct.edu; *Head, Tech Serv,* Sandy Rosado; Tel: 860-465-4464, E-mail: rosados@easternct.edu; *Access Serv Librn,* Kellie O'Donnell-Bobadilla; Tel: 860-465-5719, E-mail: odonnellbobadillak@easternct.edu; *Acq Librn,* Carolyn Coates; Tel: 860-465-5557, E-mail: coatesc@easternct.edu; *Curric Center Librn,* Hope Marie Cook; Tel: 860-465-4456, Fax: 860-465-5517, E-mail: cookh@easternct.edu; *Info Literacy Librn,* David Vrooman; Tel: 860-465-4470, E-mail: vroomand@easternct.edu; *Ref & Instruction Librn,* Angela Walker; Tel: 860-465-5566, E-mail: walkerang@easternct.edu; *Archivist, Spec Coll Librn,* Tara Hurt; Tel: 860-465-5563, E-mail: hurtt@easternct.edu; *Syst Librn,* Bruce Johnston; Tel: 860-465-5552, E-mail: johnstonb@easternct.edu; Staff 28 (MLS 14, Non-MLS 14)
Founded 1889. Enrl 5,261; Fac 499; Highest Degree: Master
Library Holdings: AV Mats 9,108; e-books 125,000; Electronic Media & Resources 125; Microforms 975,423; Bk Vols 406,087
Special Collections: Carribbean Coll, AV, bks; Connecticut History Coll, bks, pamphlets, per, prints, slides; Vocation (Career Information Center), bks, microfiche, per. Canadian and Provincial; State Document Depository; US Document Depository
Automation Activity & Vendor Info: (Acquisitions) Ex Libris Group; (Cataloging) Ex Libris Group; (Circulation) Ex Libris Group; (Course Reserve) Ex Libris Group; (ILL) OCLC ILLiad; (OPAC) Ex Libris Group; (Serials) Ex Libris Group
Wireless access
Function: Electronic databases & coll, ILL available, Music CDs, Online cat, Photocopying/Printing, Ref serv available
Publications: ECSU Library Newsletter
Partic in Connecticut Library Consortium; Connecticut State University Library System; LYRASIS; OCLC Online Computer Library Center, Inc

Special Services for the Deaf - Bks on deafness & sign lang
Special Services for the Blind - Cassettes; PC for people with disabilities; Recorded bks; Scanner for conversion & translation of mats; Videos on blindness & physical disabilties
Open Mon-Thurs 8am-Midnight, Fri 8-6, Sat 10-6, Sun Noon-Midnight

P WILLIMANTIC PUBLIC LIBRARY*, 905 Main St, 06226. SAN 302-4520. Tel: 860-465-3079. FAX: 860-465-3083. Web Site: www.willimanticlibrary.org. *Actg Dir,* Julia Gavin; E-mail: jgavin@biblio.org; *Adult Serv,* Julia Graham; Tel: 860-465-2176, E-mail: wplref@biblio.org; *Ch Serv,* Gail Zeiba; Tel: 860-465-3081; Staff 9 (MLS 2, Non-MLS 7)
Founded 1854. Pop 25,000; Circ 70,000
Library Holdings: Bk Vols 60,000; Per Subs 137
Automation Activity & Vendor Info: (Acquisitions) Bibliomation Inc; (Cataloging) OCLC WorldShare Interlibrary Loan; (Circulation) Evergreen; (ILL) Bibliomation Inc; (OPAC) Evergreen
Wireless access
Function: 24/7 Electronic res, 24/7 Online cat, Audiobks via web, Bks on cassette, Bks on CD, Children's prog, Computers for patron use, Electronic databases & coll, Free DVD rentals, ILL available, Internet access, Magazines, Museum passes, Music CDs, Online cat, OverDrive digital audio bks, Photocopying/Printing, Preschool outreach, Prog for children & young adult, Story hour, Summer reading prog, Tax forms, Wheelchair accessible
Partic in Bibliomation Inc; Connecticut Library Consortium
Open Mon & Wed (Oct-June) 9-6, Tues & Thurs 12-8, Fri 9-5, Sat 10-2; Mon & Wed (Summer) 9-5, Tues & Thurs 12-8, Fri 9-5
Restriction: Fee for pub use
Friends of the Library Group

S WINDHAM TEXTILE & HISTORY MUSEUM, Dunham Hall Library, 411 Main St, 06226. SAN 375-1856. Tel: 860-456-2178. E-mail: themillmuseum@gmail.com. Web Site: www.millmuseum.org. *Exec Dir,* Kira Holmes; *Colls Mgr,* Chelsey Knyff; *Historian,* Jamie Eves; Staff 2 (Non-MLS 2)
Founded 1989
Jan 2013-Dec 2013. Mats Exp $1,000
Library Holdings: AV Mats 25; CDs 50; Music Scores 40; Bk Titles 2,000; Videos 50
Special Collections: Mill Blue Prints. Oral History
Subject Interests: Immigration, Textile
Wireless access
Publications: Willimantic, Industry & Community
Open Fri, Sat & Sun 10-4
Restriction: Open to pub for ref only

WILLINGTON

P WILLINGTON PUBLIC LIBRARY*, Seven Ruby Rd, 06279. SAN 302-4547. Tel: 860-429-3854. FAX: 860-429-2136. Web Site: www.willingtonpubliclibrary.org. *Dir,* Kristine Donnelly
Founded 1923. Pop 5,100; Circ 17,379
Library Holdings: Bk Vols 18,000
Wireless access
Open Mon & Wed 11-5, Tues & Thurs 11-8, Fri & Sat 9-3
Friends of the Library Group

WILTON

P WILTON LIBRARY ASSOCIATION*, 137 Old Ridgefield Rd, 06897-3000. SAN 302-4563. Tel: 203-762-3950. Circulation Tel: 203-762-6334. Reference Tel: 203-762-6350. FAX: 203-834-1166. Web Site: www.wiltonlibrary.org. *Exec Dir,* Elaine Tai-Lauria; E-mail: etailauria@wiltonlibrary.org; *Develop Dir,* Courtney Lilly; E-mail: clilly@wiltonlibrary.org; *Asst Dir, Tech,* Mary Anne Mendola Franco; E-mail: mamfranco@wiltonlibrary.org; *Asst Dir, Coll Mgt, Ref,* Lauren McLaughlin; E-mail: lmclaughlin@wiltonlibrary.org; *Circ Serv Mgr,* Karen Zeibak; E-mail: kzeibak@wiltonlibrary.org; *Children's Mgr,* Andrea Szabo; E-mail: aszabo@wiltonlibrary.org; *ILL Mgr,* Catherine Steele; E-mail: csteele@wiltonlibrary.org; *Makerspace Mrg, Teen Serv,* Susan Lauricella; E-mail: slauricella@wiltonlibrary.org. Subject Specialists: *Events planning,* Mary Anne Mendola Franco; Staff 21 (MLS 12, Non-MLS 9)
Founded 1895. Pop 18,700
Library Holdings: Audiobooks 6,604; CDs 5,257; DVDs 11,107; Large Print Bks 3,403; Bk Vols 118,018; Per Subs 164
Special Collections: Wilton History Coll
Automation Activity & Vendor Info: (Acquisitions) Innovative Interfaces, Inc; (Cataloging) Innovative Interfaces, Inc; (Circulation) Innovative Interfaces, Inc; (ILL) OCLC; (OPAC) Innovative Interfaces, Inc
Wireless access
Function: 24/7 Electronic res, 24/7 Online cat, 3D Printer, Adult bk club, After school storytime, Art exhibits, Art programs, Audiobks via web, Bks on CD, Children's prog, Computers for patron use, E-Readers, Electronic databases & coll, Holiday prog, Homebound delivery serv, ILL available, Internet access, Life-long learning prog for all ages, Magazines, Magnifiers for reading, Makerspace, Meeting rooms, Museum passes, Music CDs, Online cat, OverDrive digital audio bks, Photocopying/Printing, Printer for laptops & handheld devices, Prog for adults, Prog for children & young adult, Ref serv available, Scanner, Spanish lang bks, STEM programs, Story hour, Study rm, Summer reading prog, Teen prog, Telephone ref, Wheelchair accessible
Publications: Annual Report; The Week Ahead (Newsletter); Wilton Obituary Index (Local historical information)
Special Services for the Blind - Bks on cassette; Bks on CD; Computer with voice synthesizer for visually impaired persons; Home delivery serv; Large print bks; Magnifiers
Open Mon-Thurs 10-8, Fri 10-6, Sat 10-5, Sun (Sept-June) 1-5

WINDHAM

P WINDHAM FREE LIBRARY ASSOCIATION*, Seven Windham Green Rd, 06280. (Mail add: PO Box 168, 06280-0168), SAN 302-4571. Tel: 860-423-0636. FAX: 860-423-0636. Web Site: windhamfreelibrary.org. *Dir, Libr Serv,* Carol Santa Lucia; Staff 3 (Non-MLS 3)
Founded 1896. Pop 23,000
Library Holdings: Bk Titles 9,800; Bk Vols 9,900; Per Subs 51
Subject Interests: Connecticut, Local hist
Wireless access
Partic in Bibliomation Inc
Open Tues & Thurs 10-12 & 1-7, Wed 1-5, Sat 9-1

WINDSOR

S LIMRA INFOCENTER, William J Mortimer Library, 300 Day Hill Rd, 06095. SAN 374-468X. Tel: 860-285-7767. FAX: 860-298-9555. E-mail: infocenter@limra.com. Web Site: www.limra.com. *Archivist, Sr Info Spec,* Jennifer Keefe; E-mail: jkeefe@limra.com; Staff 6 (MLS 4, Non-MLS 2)
Founded 1926
Library Holdings: Bk Vols 5,000; Per Subs 200
Subject Interests: Life ins, Market res
Automation Activity & Vendor Info: (Acquisitions) Inmagic, Inc.; (Cataloging) Inmagic, Inc.; (Circulation) Inmagic, Inc.; (ILL) OCLC; (OPAC) Inmagic, Inc.; (Serials) Inmagic, Inc.
Wireless access
Partic in Connecticut Library Consortium; OCLC Online Computer Library Center, Inc
Restriction: Authorized personnel only, Borrowing requests are handled by ILL, Employee & client use only, Mem organizations only, Not open to pub

S WINDSOR HISTORICAL SOCIETY LIBRARY*, 96 Palisado Ave, 06095. SAN 302-4628. Tel: 860-688-3813. FAX: 860-687-1633. E-mail: info@windsorhistoricalsociety.org. Web Site: www.windsorhistoricalsociety.org. *Dir,* Christine Ermenc; E-mail: cermenc@windsorhistoricalsociety.org; *Archivist, Librn,* Michelle Tom; E-mail: mtom@windsorhistoricalsociety.org; Staff 1 (MLS 1)
Founded 1925
Library Holdings: Bk Titles 5,000
Special Collections: Church & School Records & Newspapers; Local History, family papers, genealogies, photogs, slides, town histories; Manuscripts & Deeds. Oral History
Wireless access
Open Wed-Sat 11-4
Restriction: Non-circulating

P WINDSOR PUBLIC LIBRARY*, 323 Broad St, 06095. SAN 336-5700. Tel: 860-285-1910. Reference Tel: 860-285-1918. FAX: 860-285-1889. E-mail: library@townofwindsorct.com. Web Site: www.windsorlibrary.com. *Dir,* Gaye Rizzo; Tel: 860-285-1912, E-mail: rizzo@townofwindsorct.com; *Head, Children's Servx,* Shana Shea; Tel: 860-285-1917, E-mail: shea@townofwindsorct.com; *Head, Lending Serv,* Gail Mannion; Tel: 860-285-1923, E-mail: mannion@townofwindsorct.com; *Head, Ref & Tech Serv,* Andrea O'Shea; Tel: 860-285-1920, E-mail: oshea@townofwindsorct.com; *Ref Librn,* Danielle Tapper; Tel: 860-285-1925, E-mail: tapper@townofwindsorct.com; *Ref & Tech Librn,* Denise Ricotta; Tel: 860-285-1922, E-mail: ricotta@townofwindsorct.com; *Ref & Teen Librn,* Andy Geary; Tel: 860-285-1919, E-mail: Geary@townofwindsorct.com; *Br Mgr,* Gabbie Barnes; Tel: 860-519-5809, E-mail: Barnes@townofwindsorct.com; *Libr Asst,* Laura Pastula; Tel: 860-285-1913, E-mail: Pastula@townofwindsorct.com; Staff 9 (MLS 5, Non-MLS 4)
Founded 1888. Pop 29,069; Circ 245,562
Special Collections: Career Center; Health Info Ctr; Parenting Ctr; Travel Ctr
Automation Activity & Vendor Info: (Cataloging) OCLC; (Circulation) Innovative Interfaces, Inc - Sierra; (ILL) OCLC; (OPAC) Innovative Interfaces, Inc - Sierra
Wireless access

Function: 24/7 Electronic res, 24/7 Online cat, 3D Printer, Activity rm, Adult bk club, Adult literacy prog, After school storytime, Online cat
Partic in Library Connection, Inc
Open Mon-Thurs 10-9, Fri & Sat 10-5, Sun 2-5
Friends of the Library Group
Branches: 1
WILSON, 365 Windsor Ave, 06095-4550, SAN 336-576X. Tel: 860-247-8960. *Br Mgr,* Kevin Sullivan; Tel: 860-285-1931, E-mail: sullivan@townofwindsorct.com; Staff 1 (Non-MLS 1)
Open Mon 10-7:30, Tues-Fri 10-5:30, Sat 10-3

WINDSOR LOCKS

S NEW ENGLAND AIR MUSEUM*, John W Ramsay Research Center, 36 Perimeter Rd, 06096. SAN 302-4636. Tel: 860-623-3305. FAX: 860-406-7910. E-mail: nhurley@neam.org. Web Site: www.neam.org/shell.php?page=library. *Libr Dir,* Dave McChesney; *Research Librn,* Carl Stidsen; Staff 17 (MLS 2, Non-MLS 15)
Founded 1960
Library Holdings: DVDs 1,000; Bk Titles 20,000; Per Subs 97,000; Videos 350
Special Collections: Burnelli Aircraft Coll
Subject Interests: Aviation
Wireless access
Function: Res libr
Publications: Newsletter (Quarterly)
Restriction: Non-circulating

P WINDSOR LOCKS PUBLIC LIBRARY*, 28 Main St, 06096. SAN 302-4660. Tel: 860-627-1495. FAX: 860-627-1496. Web Site: www.windsorlockslibrary.org. *Dir,* Gloria Malec; E-mail: gmalec@libraryconnection.info; *Ad,* Eileen Pearce; E-mail: epearce@libraryconnection.info; Staff 3 (MLS 1, Non-MLS 2)
Founded 1907. Pop 12,400; Circ 87,000
Library Holdings: Bk Vols 65,000; Per Subs 70
Special Collections: ESL (English as a Second Language) Coll; Local Interest Coll
Wireless access
Function: Computer training
Partic in Connecticut Library Consortium; Library Connection, Inc
Open Mon-Thurs 10-8:30, Fri & Sat 10-5 (Sat 10-2 July-Aug)

WINSTED

P BEARDSLEY & MEMORIAL LIBRARY, 40 Munro Pl, 06098. SAN 302-4679. Tel: 860-379-6043. FAX: 860-379-3621. Web Site: www.beardsleylibrary.org. *Dir,* Karin Taylor; E-mail: director@beardsleylibrary.org; Staff 1 (MLS 1)
Founded 1898. Pop 15,616; Circ 1,060,151
Library Holdings: Bk Vols 58,115; Per Subs 105
Special Collections: Oral History
Subject Interests: Genealogy, Hist
Automation Activity & Vendor Info: (Cataloging) TLC (The Library Corporation); (Circulation) TLC (The Library Corporation); (ILL) TLC (The Library Corporation); (OPAC) TLC (The Library Corporation); (Serials) TLC (The Library Corporation)
Wireless access
Open Tues, Wed & Fri 10-6, Thurs 10-8, Sat 10-2
Friends of the Library Group

J NORTHWESTERN CONNECTICUT COMMUNITY COLLEGE LIBRARY*, Park Pl E, 06098. SAN 302-4687. Tel: 860-738-6480. FAX: 860-379-4995. E-mail: NW-LibRequests@nwcc.commnet.edu. Web Site: nwcc.edu/library. *Dir,* James Patterson; E-mail: jpatterson@nwcc.edu; *Librn,* Seth Kershner; Tel: 860-738-6481, E-mail: skershner@nwcc.edu; *Tech Serv,* Ann Marie Hyres; Tel: 860-738-6479, E-mail: ahyres@nwcc.edu; Staff 5 (MLS 2, Non-MLS 3)
Founded 1965. Enrl 1,632; Fac 30; Highest Degree: Associate
Library Holdings: AV Mats 2,511; Bk Vols 42,569; Per Subs 175
Special Collections: Deaf Education; Historical Jazz, compact discs; World War I & II. State Document Depository
Subject Interests: Art, Deaf, Recreation
Automation Activity & Vendor Info: (Acquisitions) Ex Libris Group; (Cataloging) Ex Libris Group; (Circulation) Ex Libris Group; (Course Reserve) Ex Libris Group; (ILL) OCLC Online; (OPAC) Ex Libris Group; (Serials) Ex Libris Group
Wireless access
Function: Audio & video playback equip for onsite use, Bks on cassette, Bks on CD, Computers for patron use, Electronic databases & coll, Instruction & testing, Music CDs, Online cat, Online info literacy tutorials on the web & in blackboard, Online ref, Orientations, Photocopying/Printing, Spoken cassettes & CDs, Spoken cassettes & DVDs, VHS videos
Publications: Periodical List
Partic in OCLC Online Computer Library Center, Inc
Special Services for the Deaf - Bks on deafness & sign lang; Closed caption videos; Coll on deaf educ; Deaf publ; TDD equip; TTY equip
Special Services for the Blind - Assistive/Adapted tech devices, equip & products; Bks on cassette; Bks on CD; Internet workstation with adaptive software; Magnifiers; Screen enlargement software for people with visual disabilities; ZoomText magnification & reading software
Open Mon-Wed 8:30-8, Thurs & Fri 8:30-4:30

S WINCHESTER HISTORICAL SOCIETY LIBRARY*, 265 Prospect St, 06098-1942. (Mail add: PO Box 206, 06098-0206), SAN 370-3029. Tel: 860-379-8433. Reference Tel: 860-379-1677. *Curator, Library Contact,* Milly Hudak; E-mail: milly345@sbcglobal.net
Special Collections: 11 Rooms of Victorian Furnishings; Civil War Coll; Fire Department Museum Coll. Oral History
Subject Interests: Local genealogy, Local hist
Restriction: Open by appt only

WOLCOTT

P WOLCOTT PUBLIC LIBRARY*, 469 Boundline Rd, 06716. SAN 302-4695. Tel: 203-879-8110. FAX: 203-879-8109. Web Site: wolcottlibrary.org. *Dir,* Jessica Jahnke; E-mail: jjahnke@biblio.org; Staff 9 (MLS 2, Non-MLS 7)
Founded 1828. Pop 17,840; Circ 96,000
Library Holdings: CDs 1,898; DVDs 1,160; Bk Vols 54,417; Per Subs 72; Talking Bks 819; Videos 4,352
Special Collections: Foreign Language Cassettes; Job Resource Center
Automation Activity & Vendor Info: (Acquisitions) Bibliomation Inc; (Cataloging) Bibliomation Inc; (Circulation) Bibliomation Inc; (ILL) Bibliomation Inc; (OPAC) Bibliomation Inc; (Serials) Bibliomation Inc
Wireless access
Partic in Bibliomation Inc; Connecticut Library Consortium
Open Mon & Wed 10-8, Tues & Fri 10-6, Thurs 12-8, Sat 10-3
Friends of the Library Group

WOODBRIDGE

P WOODBRIDGE TOWN LIBRARY*, Ten Newton Rd, 06525. SAN 302-4709. Tel: 203-389-3433. Administration Tel: 203-389-3437. Information Services Tel: 203-389-3434. FAX: 203-389-3457. Web Site: www.woodbridge.lioninc.org. *Dir,* Eric Werthmann; Tel: 203-389-3435, E-mail: ewerthmann@woodbridgect.org; *Asst Dir, Head, Tech Serv,* Lynn Serra; Tel: 203-389-3438, E-mail: lserra@lioninc.org; *Head, Adult Serv,* Katherine Ward; E-mail: kward@woodbridgect.org; *Head, Children's Servx,* Judy Rabin; Tel: 203-389-3439; *Head, Circ,* Margaret Routzahn; E-mail: mroutzahn@woodbridgect.org; Staff 23 (MLS 7, Non-MLS 16)
Founded 1940. Pop 9,775; Circ 162,267
Jul 2016-Jun 2017. Mats Exp $84,525, Books $58,093, Per/Ser (Incl. Access Fees) $8,395, AV Mat $17,497, Electronic Ref Mat (Incl. Access Fees) $540
Library Holdings: AV Mats 12,234; Bk Titles 73,171; Per Subs 85
Special Collections: Chinese Language Coll
Subject Interests: Russian (Lang), Travel
Automation Activity & Vendor Info: (Acquisitions) Innovative Interfaces, Inc; (Cataloging) Innovative Interfaces, Inc; (Circulation) Innovative Interfaces, Inc; (OPAC) Innovative Interfaces, Inc; (Serials) Innovative Interfaces, Inc
Wireless access
Function: Art exhibits, Bks on CD, CD-ROM, Children's prog, Computers for patron use, Electronic databases & coll, Homebound delivery serv, ILL available, Museum passes, Music CDs, Preschool outreach, Prog for adults, Prog for children & young adult, Senior outreach, Story hour, Summer reading prog, Tax forms, Teen prog, Wheelchair accessible
Partic in Libraries Online, Inc
Open Mon-Thurs 10-8, Fri & Sat 10-5
Friends of the Library Group

WOODBURY

S SEABURY SOCIETY FOR THE PRESERVATION OF THE GLEBE HOUSE, INC, Glebe House Museum Library, 49 Hollow Rd, 06798. (Mail add: PO Box 245, 06798-0245), SAN 374-8618. E-mail: office@glebehousemuseum.org. *Dir,* LoriAnn Witte; Tel: 203-263-2855
Founded 1926
Library Holdings: Bk Vols 200
Special Collections: 18th Century Social & Religious History Coll; Museum Archives
Subject Interests: Episcopal Church, Gardening
Function: Ref serv available
Restriction: Non-circulating

P WOODBURY PUBLIC LIBRARY, 269 Main St S, 06798. SAN 302-4717. Tel: 203-263-3502. FAX: 203-263-0571. Web Site: www.woodburylibraryct.org. *Libr Dir,* Sue Piel; E-mail: spiel@biblio.org; *Head, Ch,* Bonnie Knapik; E-mail: bknapik@biblio.org; *ILL Librn,* David Makusevich; E-mail: woodburyill@biblio.org; *Programming Librn, Teen &*

Adult Librn, Marla Martin; E-mail: mmartin@biblio.org; *Ref, Tech Librn*, Ron Fairchild; E-mail: rfairchild@biblio.org; *Asst Ch*, Heidi Duchaine; E-mail: hduchaine@biblio.org; *Tech Serv*, Maura Yerger; E-mail: myerger@biblio.org; Staff 15 (MLS 5, Non-MLS 10)
Founded 1772. Pop 9,865; Circ 136,529
Library Holdings: Bk Vols 100,000; Per Subs 145
Subject Interests: Local hist
Automation Activity & Vendor Info: (Cataloging) Evergreen; (Circulation) Evergreen; (ILL) Evergreen; (OPAC) Evergreen; (Serials) Evergreen
Wireless access
Function: 24/7 Electronic res, 24/7 Online cat, Activity rm, Adult bk club, Adult literacy prog
Open Mon, Wed, Fri & Sat 9:30-4:30, Tues & Thurs 9:30-8, Sun (Oct-May) 12:30-4:30
Friends of the Library Group

WOODSTOCK

P BRACKEN MEMORIAL LIBRARY, 57 Academy Rd, 06281. SAN 302-4725. Tel: 860-928-0046. Web Site: www.woodstockacademy.org/library. *Asst Librn*, Michelle Laprade; E-mail: mlaprade@woodstockacademy.org; Staff 1 (MLS 1)
Founded 1926. Pop 5,000; Circ 18,000
Library Holdings: Bk Titles 17,000; Per Subs 30
Automation Activity & Vendor Info: (Cataloging) Follett Software; (Circulation) Follett Software
Wireless access
Partic in Connecticut Library Consortium
Open Mon-Wed & Fri 9-2:30, Thurs 2:30-6:30, Sat 9-12

P NORTH WOODSTOCK LIBRARY*, 1286 Rte 169, 06281. Tel: 860-928-2629. *Dir*, Dawn Hellwig
Founded 1834. Pop 7,854; Circ 6,117
Jul 2012-Jun 2013. Mats Exp $11,492
Library Holdings: CDs 53; DVDs 168; Bk Vols 11,692; Per Subs 3; Videos 273
Wireless access
Partic in Connecticut Library Consortium
Open Mon 9-1, Tues & Thurs 9-12

P WEST WOODSTOCK LIBRARY*, Five Bungay Hill Rd, 06281. SAN 320-6211. Tel: 860-974-0376. Circulation E-mail: circulation@westwoodstocklibrary.org. Web Site: westwoodstocklibrary.org. *Librn*, Su Connor; E-mail: librarian@westwoodstocklibrary.org
Founded 1806. Pop 7,000
Library Holdings: Bk Vols 20,000
Subject Interests: Local hist, State hist
Partic in Connecticut Library Consortium
Open Tues -Thurs 3-6, Sat 9-12
Friends of the Library Group

DELAWARE

Date of Statistics: FY 2020
Population, 2020 U.S. Census: 986,809
Population Served by Public Libraries: 973,764
Total Materials in Public Libraries: 1,954,441
Materials Per Capita: 2.01
Total Public Library Circulation: 4,188,537
Circulation Per Capita: 5.60
Income and Expenditures:
Total Public Library Income: $31,328,896
Number of County Systems: 3
Number of Library Outlets: 35
Number of Bookmobiles in State: 2
Grants-in-Aid to Public Libraries:
Federal: $1,207,081
State Aid: $4,365,600
Information provided courtesy of: Elizabeth Emerson, Management Analyst II; Delaware Division of Libraries

BEAR

P BEAR LIBRARY, 101 Governor's Pl, 19701. Tel: 302-838-3300. FAX: 302-838-3307. E-mail: bear@delawarelibraries.libanswers.com. Web Site: nccde.org/291/bear-library. *Mgr,* Eric Kuhn; E-mail: eric.kuhn@newcastlede.gov; Staff 9 (MLS 5, Non-MLS 4)
Founded 1998. Pop 103,000; Circ 600,000
Library Holdings: Audiobooks 4,682; AV Mats 24,985; CDs 6,778; DVDs 13,525; e-books 31,175; Large Print Bks 3,221; Bk Titles 73,709; Bk Vols 89,496; Per Subs 210; Talking Bks 4,682
Special Collections: Delawareana
Automation Activity & Vendor Info: (Cataloging) SirsiDynix-WorkFlows; (Circulation) SirsiDynix-WorkFlows; (OPAC) SirsiDynix-Enterprise
Wireless access
Function: 24/7 Electronic res, 24/7 Online cat, Adult bk club, Adult literacy prog, Art exhibits, Art programs, Audiobks on Playaways & MP3, Audiobks via web, BA reader (adult literacy), Bilingual assistance for Spanish patrons, Bk club(s), Bks on CD, Chess club, Children's prog, Computer training, Computers for patron use, Digital talking bks, Distance learning, Doc delivery serv, Electronic databases & coll, Family literacy, Genealogy discussion group, Holiday prog, Homebound delivery serv, ILL available, Instruction & testing, Internet access, Life-long learning prog for all ages, Literacy & newcomer serv, Magazines, Mail & tel request accepted, Meeting rooms, Movies, Music CDs, Online cat, Online info literacy tutorials on the web & in blackboard, Online ref, Outreach serv, Outside serv via phone, mail, e-mail & web, OverDrive digital audio bks, Photocopying/Printing, Preschool outreach, Printer for laptops & handheld devices, Prog for adults, Prog for children & young adult, Ref & res, Ref serv available, Scanner, Senior computer classes, Serves people with intellectual disabilities, Spanish lang bks, Spoken cassettes & CDs, Spoken cassettes & DVDs, STEM programs, Story hour, Study rm, Summer & winter reading prog, Summer reading prog, Tax forms, Teen prog, Telephone ref, Visual arts prog, Wheelchair accessible, Winter reading prog, Workshops, Writing prog
Mem of New Castle County Libraries
Open Mon-Wed 10-8, Thurs & Sat 10-5
Friends of the Library Group

BRIDGEVILLE

P BRIDGEVILLE PUBLIC LIBRARY*, 600 S Cannon St, 19933. SAN 302-4733. Tel: 302-337-7401. FAX: 302-337-3270. Web Site: www.bridgevillelibrary.com. *Dir,* Karen Johnson; E-mail: karen.johnson@lib.de.us; Staff 4 (Non-MLS 4)
Founded 1919. Pop 6,922; Circ 95,680
Library Holdings: Bk Vols 25,000; Per Subs 90
Special Collections: Delaware & Eastern Shore; Genealogy Coll
Automation Activity & Vendor Info: (Cataloging) SirsiDynix; (Circulation) SirsiDynix; (OPAC) SirsiDynix
Wireless access
Function: Genealogy discussion group, ILL available, Photocopying/Printing, Prog for children & young adult, Summer reading prog, Telephone ref
Mem of Sussex County Department of Libraries
Open Mon & Fri 10-5, Tues-Thurs 10-7, Sat 10-2
Friends of the Library Group

CLAYMONT

P CLAYMONT PUBLIC LIBRARY*, 400 Lenape Way, 19703. SAN 302-4741. Tel: 302-798-4164. FAX: 302-798-6329. Web Site: www.nccde.org/298/Claymont-Library. *Mgr,* Beth Kloetzer; E-mail: elizabeth.kloetzer@newcastlede.gov; Staff 12 (MLS 2, Non-MLS 10)
Founded 1929. Pop 30,428
Library Holdings: Audiobooks 1,107; CDs 1,324; DVDs 7,052; Electronic Media & Resources 8; Large Print Bks 1,798; Bk Vols 34,783; Per Subs 77
Automation Activity & Vendor Info: (Acquisitions) Baker & Taylor; (Cataloging) SirsiDynix-WorkFlows; (Circulation) SirsiDynix-WorkFlows; (ILL) OCLC; (OPAC) SirsiDynix-WorkFlows; (Serials) EBSCO Online
Wireless access
Function: 24/7 Electronic res, 24/7 Online cat, 3D Printer, Audiobks via web, Bks on CD, Digital talking bks, Electronic databases & coll, Free DVD rentals, ILL available, Magazines, Mail & tel request accepted, Music CDs, Online cat, Online info literacy tutorials on the web & in blackboard, Online ref, OverDrive digital audio bks, Printer for laptops & handheld devices, Spanish lang bks, Summer reading prog, Tax forms, Telephone ref
Mem of New Castle County Libraries
Special Services for the Deaf - Bks on deafness & sign lang; High interest/low vocabulary bks
Special Services for the Blind - Audio mat; Bks on CD; Large print bks
Restriction: Circ to mem only, ID required to use computers (Ltd hrs), Non-resident fee, Not open to pub, Pub access by telephone only
Friends of the Library Group

DELAWARE CITY

P DELAWARE CITY PUBLIC LIBRARY*, 250 Fifth St, 19706. (Mail add: PO Box 541, 19706-0541), SAN 302-475X. Tel: 302-834-4148. Web Site: delawarecity.lib.de.us. *Dir,* Alexandra Monroe; E-mail: alexandra.monroe@lib.de.us; Staff 1 (MLS 1)
Founded 1973. Pop 7,132; Circ 40,183
Library Holdings: Bk Vols 24,293; Per Subs 75
Automation Activity & Vendor Info: (Cataloging) SirsiDynix; (Circulation) SirsiDynix; (OPAC) SirsiDynix; (Serials) SirsiDynix
Wireless access
Mem of New Castle County Libraries
Open Mon-Thurs 12-8, Sat 11-4, Sun 12-3
Friends of the Library Group

DELMAR

P DELMAR PUBLIC LIBRARY, 101 N Bi-State Blvd, 19940. SAN 302-4784. Tel: 302-846-9894. E-mail: delmar.library@lib.de.us. Web Site: delmar.lib.de.us. *Dir,* Susan Upole; E-mail: susan.upole@lib.de.us; Staff 1 (MLS 1)
Founded 1940. Pop 6,049; Circ 64,297
Library Holdings: CDs 1,240; DVDs 2,325; Bk Vols 20,265; Per Subs 42
Automation Activity & Vendor Info: (Cataloging) SirsiDynix; (Circulation) SirsiDynix; (OPAC) SirsiDynix
Wireless access
Function: Bk club(s), Bks on CD, Children's prog, Computer training, Computers for patron use, Electronic databases & coll, Free DVD rentals, ILL available, Internet access, Music CDs, Online cat, Online ref, Photocopying/Printing, Preschool reading prog, Prog for adults, Prog for children & young adult, Story hour, Summer reading prog, Teen prog, Telephone ref
Mem of New Castle County Libraries; Sussex County Department of Libraries
Open Mon-Thurs 10-7, Fri 10-5, Sat 10-2
Friends of the Library Group

DOVER

C DELAWARE STATE UNIVERSITY, William C Jason Library, 1200 N Dupont Hwy, 19901-2277. SAN 302-4814. Tel: 302-857-6191. Reference Tel: 302-857-6180. Administration Tel: 302-857-6136. FAX: 302-857-6177. Reference E-mail: libref@desu.edu. Web Site: desu.edu/academics/library. *Dean, Univ Libr,* Dr Rebecca E Batson; Tel: 302-857-7887, E-mail: rbatson@desu.edu; *Exec Dir, Libr Serv,* Ondrea Murphy; Tel: 302-857-6192, E-mail: omurphy@desu.edu; *Govt Doc Librn, Ref & Ser Librn,* Monifa Carter; Tel: 302-857-7588, E-mail: mtcarter@desu.edu; *Pub Serv Librn, Ref Serv Librn,* Ronald W Davis; Tel: 302-857-6187, E-mail: rdavis@desu.edu; *Pub Serv Librn, Ref Serv Librn,* Rosamond Panda; Tel: 302-857-6197, E-mail: rpanda@desu.edu; *Ref & Access Serv Librn,* Tameca Beckett; Tel: 302-857-7886, E-mail: tbeckett@desu.edu; *Spec Coll Librn, Univ Archivist,* Rejoice Scherry; Tel: 302-857-6130, E-mail: rscherry@desu.edu; *Coordr, Tech Serv,* Position Currently Open; *Circ Tech,* Maurio J Watson; Tel: 302-857-6133, E-mail: mjwatson@desu.edu. Subject Specialists: *Agr, Related sci,* Ronald W Davis; *Educ,* Rosamond Panda; Staff 14 (MLS 7, Non-MLS 7)
Founded 1891. Enrl 4,600; Fac 198; Highest Degree: Doctorate
Jul 2014-Jun 2015 Income $138,011,644. Mats Exp $480,620. Sal $59,382,577 (Prof $47,267,710)
Library Holdings: AV Mats 2,130; Braille Volumes 126; CDs 744; DVDs 1,035; e-books 162,031; e-journals 39,747; Electronic Media & Resources 114; Large Print Bks 99; Microforms 86,000; Music Scores 124; Bk Titles 193,224; Bk Vols 261,136; Per Subs 108; Talking Bks 39; Videos 3,251
Special Collections: Archival Coll; Delaware Coll; Select Government Depository; Special Rare Books Coll
Subject Interests: African-Am studies, Bus, Curric, Del, Educ, Nursing
Automation Activity & Vendor Info: (Acquisitions) SirsiDynix; (Cataloging) SirsiDynix; (Circulation) SirsiDynix; (Course Reserve) SirsiDynix; (OPAC) SirsiDynix; (Serials) SirsiDynix
Wireless access
Partic in OCLC Online Computer Library Center, Inc
Open Mon-Thurs 8am-Midnight, Fri 8-5, Sat 12-5, Sun 2-10 (Winter); Mon-Thurs 8am-10pm, Fri 8-5, Sun 2-10 (Summer)

J DELAWARE TECHNICAL & COMMUNITY COLLEGE*, Terry Campus Library, 100 Campus Dr, 19904. SAN 302-4822. Tel: 302-857-1060. E-mail: terry-library@dtcc.edu. Web Site: dtcc.edu/student-resources/libraries. *Librn,* Debbie Lloyd; E-mail: dlloyd@dtcc.edu; Staff 2.8 (MLS 1.8, Non-MLS 1)
Founded 1974. Enrl 1,964; Fac 76; Highest Degree: Associate
Library Holdings: AV Mats 461; Bk Vols 15,327; Per Subs 98
Automation Activity & Vendor Info: (Acquisitions) SirsiDynix; (Cataloging) SirsiDynix; (Circulation) SirsiDynix; (Course Reserve) SirsiDynix; (ILL) SirsiDynix; (OPAC) SirsiDynix; (Serials) SirsiDynix
Wireless access
Partic in OCLC Online Computer Library Center, Inc
Open Mon-Thurs 8am-9pm, Fri 8-4, Sat 9-1
Restriction: Open to students, fac & staff, Restricted pub use

P DOVER PUBLIC LIBRARY, 35 Loockerman Plaza, 19901. SAN 302-4830. Tel: 302-736-7030. Administration Tel: 302-736-7032. FAX: 302-736-5087. Web Site: dover.lib.de.us. *Libr Dir,* Brian Sylvester; E-mail: brian.sylvester@lib.de.us; *Asst Dir,* Meegs Johnson; E-mail: meegs.johnson@lib.de.us; *Head, Adult Serv,* Audrey Avery; E-mail: audrey.avery@lib.de.us; *ILL, Tech Serv,* David Giglio; E-mail: david.giglio@lib.de.us; Staff 24 (MLS 7, Non-MLS 17)
Founded 1885. Pop 65,000; Circ 398,666
Library Holdings: Bk Vols 115,000; Per Subs 320
Special Collections: Countywide Reference Center; Delaware & Delmarva Peninsula (Delawareana); Kent County Consumer Health Coll
Wireless access
Partic in LYRASIS; OCLC Online Computer Library Center, Inc; Ohio Public Library Information Network
Open Tues, Thurs & Sat 10-2, Wed & Fri 2-6
Friends of the Library Group

GL KENT COUNTY LAW LIBRARY*, Kent County Courthouse, 38 The Green, Ste 100, 19901. SAN 302-4857. Tel: 302-674-7470. FAX: 302-674-7471. Web Site: courts.delaware.gov/lawlibraries/kent.aspx. *Law Librn,* Bethany Geleskie; E-mail: bethany.geleskie@delaware.gov
Library Holdings: Bk Vols 35,000; Per Subs 30
Special Collections: Early & Unusual Law Books
Wireless access
Function: Res libr
Open Mon-Fri 8:30-4:30

P KENT COUNTY PUBLIC LIBRARY*, 497 S Red Haven Ln, 19901. Tel: 302-744-1919. FAX: 302-744-9680. E-mail: KCPL@co.kent.de.us. Web Site: www.co.kent.de.us/kc-library.aspx. *Dir,* Dr Hilary Welliver; E-mail: hilary.welliver@co.kent.de.us; Staff 10 (MLS 2, Non-MLS 8)
Founded 1989. Pop 42,000
Library Holdings: Audiobooks 1,000; DVDs 2,500; e-books 10,000; e-journals 300; Electronic Media & Resources 13; Large Print Bks 1,000; Bk Titles 39,000; Per Subs 50
Automation Activity & Vendor Info: (Cataloging) SirsiDynix; (Circulation) SirsiDynix; (OPAC) SirsiDynix
Wireless access
Function: 24/7 Electronic res, 24/7 Online cat, Activity rm, Adult bk club, Art programs, Audiobks on Playaways & MP3, Audiobks via web, Bi-weekly Writer's Group, Bk club(s), Bk reviews (Group), Bks on CD, CD-ROM, Children's prog, Computer training, Computers for patron use, Digital talking bks, E-Reserves, Electronic databases & coll, Free DVD rentals, Holiday prog, ILL available, Instruction & testing, Internet access, Life-long learning prog for all ages, Magazines, Mango lang, Meeting rooms, Movies, Online cat, Online info literacy tutorials on the web & in blackboard, Online ref, Orientations, Outreach serv, OverDrive digital audio bks, Photocopying/Printing, Preschool outreach, Preschool reading prog, Printer for laptops & handheld devices, Prof lending libr, Prog for adults, Prog for children & young adult, Scanner, Senior computer classes, Senior outreach, Serves people with intellectual disabilities, Spoken cassettes & CDs, Spoken cassettes & DVDs, STEM programs, Story hour, Summer & winter reading prog, Summer reading prog, Tax forms, Teen prog, Visual arts prog, Wheelchair accessible, Winter reading prog, Workshops, Writing prog
Open Mon-Fri 9-8, Sat & Sun 1-5
Friends of the Library Group
Bookmobiles: Librns, Heidi Seldomridge & Olive Keegan-Kelly. Bk vols, 2,500

P STATE OF DELAWARE*, Delaware Division of Libraries, 121 Martin Luther King Jr Blvd N, 19901. SAN 336-5859. Tel: 302-739-4748. Toll Free Tel: 800-282-8696. FAX: 302-739-6787. Web Site: lib.de.us, www.libraries.delaware.gov. *Dir,* Dr Annie Norman; Tel: 302-257-3001, E-mail: annie.norman@state.de.us; *Dep Dir,* Beth-Ann Ryan; Tel: 302-257-3002, E-mail: beth-Ann.ryan@state.de.us; *Sr Librn,* Marie Cunningham; Tel: 302-257-3006, E-mail: marie.cunningham@state.de.us; Staff 11 (MLS 11)
Founded 1901
Special Collections: Delaware Heritage Coll
Automation Activity & Vendor Info: (Cataloging) SirsiDynix; (Circulation) SirsiDynix; (ILL) OCLC; (OPAC) SirsiDynix; (Serials) SirsiDynix
Wireless access
Friends of the Library Group
Branches: 1
P DELAWARE LIBRARY ACCESS SERVICES, 121 Martin Luther King Blvd N, 19901. Tel: 302-257-3015. Toll Free Tel: 800-282-8676. FAX: 302-739-6787. E-mail: debph@lib.de.us. Web Site: libraries.delaware.gov/dlas. *Admin Librn,* John Philos; E-mail: john.phillos@state.de.us; Staff 1 (MLS 1)
Founded 1971. Pop 1,500; Circ 54,000
Library Holdings: Bk Titles 36,000; Bk Vols 50,000; Per Subs 10
Automation Activity & Vendor Info: (Circulation) Keystone Systems, Inc (KLAS); (OPAC) Keystone Systems, Inc (KLAS)
Special Services for the Blind - Audio mat; Bks & mags in Braille, on rec, tape & cassette; Bks on cassette; Cassette playback machines
Open Mon-Fri 8-4:30
Friends of the Library Group

FRANKFORD

P FRANKFORD PUBLIC LIBRARY*, Eight Main St, 19945. (Mail add: PO Box 610, 19945-0610), SAN 302-4873. Tel: 302-732-9351. Web Site: frankford.lib.de.us. *Dir,* Bonnie Elliott; E-mail: bonnie.elliott@lib.de.us
Founded 1930. Pop 7,487; Circ 30,087. Sal $100,583 (Prof $28,132)

Library Holdings: AV Mats 750; CDs 855; DVDs 1,942; Bk Vols 12,212; Per Subs 60
Special Collections: Delaware Coll
Automation Activity & Vendor Info: (Cataloging) SirsiDynix; (Circulation) SirsiDynix; (OPAC) SirsiDynix
Wireless access
Function: ILL available
Mem of Sussex County Department of Libraries
Open Mon-Thurs 10-8, Fri 12-5, Sat 10-2

GEORGETOWN

J DELAWARE TECHNICAL & COMMUNITY COLLEGE*, Stephen J Betze Library, 21179 College Dr, 19947. SAN 302-4881. Tel: 302-259-6199. E-mail: owens-library@dtcc.edu. Web Site: www.dtcc.edu/student-resources/libraries. *Head Librn,* Angelynn King; Staff 8 (MLS 4, Non-MLS 4)
Founded 1967. Enrl 2,928; Fac 250; Highest Degree: Associate
Special Collections: US Document Depository
Wireless access
Open Mon-Thurs 8am-9pm, Fri 8-4:30

P GEORGETOWN PUBLIC LIBRARY*, 123 W Pine St, 19947. SAN 302-489X. Tel: 302-856-7958. E-mail: Georgetown.library@lib.de.us. Web Site: www.georgetownpubliclibrary.org. *Dir,* Elaine D Fike; E-mail: elaine.fike@lib.de.us; Staff 2 (Non-MLS 2)
Circ 41,791
Library Holdings: Audiobooks 1,744; DVDs 1,500; Bk Vols 26,044; Per Subs 65
Special Collections: Delawareana
Subject Interests: Del, Genealogy, Mysteries
Automation Activity & Vendor Info: (Acquisitions) SirsiDynix; (Cataloging) OCLC CatExpress; (Circulation) SirsiDynix-WorkFlows; (Serials) SirsiDynix-WorkFlows
Wireless access
Function: ILL available
Mem of Sussex County Department of Libraries
Special Services for the Deaf - Assistive tech
Open Mon-Thurs 10-8, Fri 10-5, Sat 10-2
Friends of the Library Group

P SUSSEX COUNTY DEPARTMENT OF LIBRARIES*, 22215 DuPont Blvd, 19947-2809. (Mail add: PO Box 589, 19947-0589), SAN 302-4903. Tel: 302-855-7890. FAX: 302-855-7895. Web Site: sussexlibraries.org. *County Librn,* Kathy Graybeal; E-mail: kathy.graybeal@lib.de.us
Founded 1975
Library Holdings: Bk Vols 4,910; Per Subs 42
Special Collections: Eastern Shore Coll
Subject Interests: Libr & info sci
Automation Activity & Vendor Info: (Acquisitions) SirsiDynix; (Cataloging) SirsiDynix; (Circulation) SirsiDynix; (OPAC) SirsiDynix; (Serials) SirsiDynix
Wireless access
Member Libraries: Bridgeville Public Library; Delmar Public Library; Frankford Public Library; Georgetown Public Library; Laurel Public Library; Lewes Public Library; Milford Public Library; Millsboro Public Library; Rehoboth Beach Public Library; Seaford District Library; Selbyville Public Library
Open Mon-Fri 8:30-4:30
Branches: 3
GREENWOOD PUBLIC, 100 Mill St, Greenwood, 19950. (Mail add: PO Box 839, Greenwood, 19950). Tel: 302-349-5309. E-mail: greenwood.library@lib.de.us. Web Site: greenwood.lib.de.us. *Dir,* Christina Woitas; E-mail: christina.woitas@lib.de.us
Library Holdings: Bk Titles 15,000; Per Subs 200
Open Mon, Tues, Thurs & Fri 10-8, Wed 10-5, Sat 10-2
Friends of the Library Group
MILTON PUBLIC, 121 Union St, Milton, 19968, SAN 321-1312. Tel: 302-684-8856. E-mail: milton.library@lib.de.us. Web Site: milton.lib.de.us. *Dir,* Mary Catherine Hopkins; E-mail: milton-director@lib.de.us
Library Holdings: Bk Vols 38,507; Per Subs 294
Open Mon-Fri 10-8, Sat 10-4
Friends of the Library Group
SOUTH COASTAL PUBLIC LIBRARY, 43 Kent Ave, Bethany Beach, 19930. Tel: 302-539-5231. E-mail: southcoastal.library@lib.de.us. Web Site: southcoastal.lib.de.us. *Dir,* Sue Keefe; E-mail: sue.keefe@lib.de.us; Staff 3.5 (MLS 2.6, Non-MLS 0.9)
Founded 1978. Pop 13,441; Circ 117,270
Library Holdings: AV Mats 1,016; CDs 648; DVDs 2,200; Large Print Bks 1,385; Music Scores 769; Bk Titles 25,080; Bk Vols 26,361; Per Subs 190; Videos 1,179
Function: Adult bk club, Adult literacy prog, Audiobks via web, Bk club(s), Bk reviews (Group), Bks on cassette, Bks on CD, Children's prog, Computer training, Computers for patron use, Digital talking bks, Electronic databases & coll, Genealogy discussion group, Homebound delivery serv, ILL available, Internet access, Music CDs, Notary serv, Online cat, Photocopying/Printing, Prog for adults, Prog for children & young adult, Ref serv available, Summer reading prog, Tax forms, Telephone ref, VHS videos, Wheelchair accessible
Open Mon-Thurs 10-8, Fri 1-5, Sat 9-3
Friends of the Library Group
Bookmobiles: 1. Mgr, Kathy McFadden. Bk vols 10,898

HARRINGTON

P HARRINGTON PUBLIC LIBRARY*, 110 Center St, 19952. Tel: 302-398-4647. FAX: 302-398-3847. E-mail: harrington.library@lib.de.us. Web Site: harrington.delaware.gov/public-library. *Dir,* Christine Hayward; *Asst Dir, Youth Serv Librn,* Marleena Scott; Staff 3 (Non-MLS 3)
Founded 1979. Pop 11,000
Library Holdings: AV Mats 1,000; Bk Vols 22,000; Per Subs 26; Talking Bks 300
Automation Activity & Vendor Info: (Acquisitions) SirsiDynix; (Cataloging) SirsiDynix; (Circulation) SirsiDynix; (Course Reserve) SirsiDynix; (ILL) SirsiDynix; (Media Booking) SirsiDynix; (OPAC) SirsiDynix; (Serials) SirsiDynix
Wireless access
Function: Adult literacy prog, ILL available, Large print keyboards, Photocopying/Printing, Prog for children & young adult, Ref serv available, Summer reading prog, Telephone ref, Wheelchair accessible
Open Mon, Wed & Fri 10-6, Tues & Thurs 11:30-8, Sat 10-2
Friends of the Library Group

HOCKESSIN

P HOCKESSIN PUBLIC LIBRARY*, 1023 Valley Rd, 19707. SAN 302-4946. Tel: 302-239-5160. FAX: 302-239-1519. Web Site: nccde.org/329/Hockessin-Library. *Mgr,* Sue Rekart; E-mail: srekart@nccde.org; Staff 12 (MLS 3, Non-MLS 9)
Founded 1977. Pop 26,795; Circ 490,689
Library Holdings: AV Mats 8,000; Bk Vols 70,700; Per Subs 150
Special Collections: Delaware Coll
Automation Activity & Vendor Info: (Cataloging) SirsiDynix; (Circulation) SirsiDynix; (OPAC) SirsiDynix
Function: ILL available, Photocopying/Printing
Mem of New Castle County Libraries
Partic in OCLC Online Computer Library Center, Inc
Open Mon-Wed 10-9, Fri & Sat 10-5, Sun 1-5
Friends of the Library Group

LAUREL

P LAUREL PUBLIC LIBRARY, 101 E Fourth St, 19956-1567. SAN 302-4954. Tel: 302-875-3184. Web Site: laurel.lib.de.us. *Dir,* Gail Bruce; E-mail: gail.bruce@lib.de.us; Staff 3 (MLS 3)
Founded 1909. Pop 12,500; Circ 107,000
Library Holdings: Bk Vols 51,000; Per Subs 132
Special Collections: Local History (Delaware Coll)
Wireless access
Function: Adult bk club, After school storytime, Archival coll, Art exhibits, Bk club(s), Bks on cassette, Bks on CD, Children's prog, Computers for patron use, Doc delivery serv, Electronic databases & coll, Free DVD rentals, Genealogy discussion group, Holiday prog, ILL available, Music CDs, Online cat, Photocopying/Printing, Prog for adults, Prog for children & young adult, Story hour, Summer reading prog, Tax forms, Teen prog, Wheelchair accessible
Mem of Sussex County Department of Libraries
Open Mon 10-6:30, Tues-Fri 10-5, Sat 10-2
Friends of the Library Group

LEWES

M BEEBE HEALTHCARE*, Health Sciences Library, 424 Savannah Rd, 19958. SAN 336-5948. Tel: 302-645-3100, Ext 5472. FAX: 302-644-2319. *Librn,* Jean Winstead; E-mail: jwinstead@bbmc.org; Staff 1 (MLS 1)
Founded 1921
Library Holdings: Bk Vols 150; Per Subs 40
Subject Interests: Med, Nursing
Wireless access
Partic in Basic Health Sciences Library Network; National Network of Libraries of Medicine Region 1
Branches:
MARGARET H ROLLINS NURSING SCHOOL LIBRARY, 424 Savannah Rd, 19958, SAN 336-5972. Tel: 302-645-3100, Ext 5667. FAX: 302-645-3488. Web Site: www.beebehealthcare.org. *Librn,* Mary Beth Orbin; E-mail: morbin@beebehealthcare.org; Staff 1 (MLS 1)
Founded 1921
Library Holdings: DVDs 10; Bk Vols 2,273; Per Subs 3; Videos 70
Subject Interests: Nursing
Restriction: Borrowing privileges limited to fac & registered students

P LEWES PUBLIC LIBRARY*, 111 Adams Ave, 19958. SAN 302-4962. Tel: 302-645-2733. FAX: 302-645-6235. E-mail: lewes.library@gmail.com. Web Site: lewes.lib.de.us. *Libr Dir,* Lea Rosell; *Adult Prog Coordr, Develop Dir,* Rebecca Lowe; *Asst Dir,* Kristen Gramer; *Ch, Prog Coordr,* Jennifer Noona; *Teen Serv Librn,* Emily Ellinger; *Operations Mgr,* Heather Lachmann; Staff 9 (MLS 3.5, Non-MLS 5.5)
Founded 1935. Pop 17,073; Circ 184,174
Jul 2015-Jun 2016 Income $526,983, State $73,574, City $10,000, Federal $1,570, County $263,198, Locally Generated Income $178,641. Mats Exp $45,000, Books $40,000, Per/Ser (Incl. Access Fees) $5,000. Sal $348,960
Library Holdings: Audiobooks 1,206; CDs 1,147; DVDs 1,994; Electronic Media & Resources 9; Large Print Bks 2,210; Bk Titles 44,806; Bk Vols 47,653; Per Subs 111; Videos 575
Special Collections: Delaware Coll; Writer's Library
Wireless access
Function: Accelerated reader prog, Adult bk club, Archival coll, Art exhibits, Audiobks via web, Bk club(s), Bks on cassette, Bks on CD, Children's prog, Computer training, Computers for patron use, Digital talking bks, Electronic databases & coll, Free DVD rentals, Genealogy discussion group, ILL available, Music CDs, Online cat, Online ref, OverDrive digital audio bks, Photocopying/Printing, Preschool outreach, Preschool reading prog, Prog for adults, Prog for children & young adult, Senior computer classes, Spanish lang bks, Spoken cassettes & CDs, Story hour, Summer reading prog, Tax forms, Teen prog, Telephone ref, VHS videos, Wheelchair accessible, Workshops, Writing prog
Mem of Sussex County Department of Libraries
Open Mon-Thurs 10-8, Fri 10-5, Sat 10-2
Friends of the Library Group

MIDDLETOWN

P APPOQUINIMINK COMMUNITY LIBRARY*, 651 N Broad St, 19709. SAN 302-4989. Tel: 302-378-5588. FAX: 302-378-5594. E-mail: appoquinimink@delawarelibraries.libanswers.com. Web Site: nccde.org/288/Appoquinimink-Community-Library. *Mgr,* Kevin Swed; Staff 17 (MLS 3, Non-MLS 14)
Pop 32,000; Circ 195,000
Library Holdings: AV Mats 3,501; Bk Vols 46,644; Per Subs 128
Automation Activity & Vendor Info: (Cataloging) SirsiDynix; (Circulation) SirsiDynix; (OPAC) SirsiDynix; (Serials) SirsiDynix
Function: 24/7 Electronic res, 24/7 Online cat, Activity rm, Adult bk club, Audio & video playback equip for onsite use, Audiobks via web, Bks on CD, Children's prog, Computer training, Computers for patron use, Digital talking bks, Electronic databases & coll, Free DVD rentals, Holiday prog, Homebound delivery serv, Magazines, Meeting rooms, Movies, Music CDs, Online cat, Photocopying/Printing, Preschool outreach, Preschool reading prog, Printer for laptops & handheld devices, Prog for adults, Prog for children & young adult, Ref & res, Ref serv available, Scanner, Senior computer classes, Senior outreach, STEM programs, Story hour, Summer reading prog, Tax forms, Teen prog, Telephone ref
Mem of New Castle County Libraries
Open Mon 10-8, Tues & Wed 1-8, Thurs-Sat 10-5
Restriction: Non-resident fee
Friends of the Library Group

MILFORD

P MILFORD PUBLIC LIBRARY*, 11 SE Front St, 19963. SAN 302-4997. Tel: 302-422-8996. E-mail: milford.library@lib.de.us. Web Site: milford.lib.de.us. *Actg Dir,* Vivian Erickson; E-mail: Vivian.erickson@lib.de.us; *Circ Mgr,* Norma Chalmers; E-mail: norma.chalmers@lib.de.us; Staff 16 (Non-MLS 16)
Founded 1882. Pop 18,112; Circ 140,604
Library Holdings: AV Mats 3,000; Bks on Deafness & Sign Lang 10; CDs 1,200; DVDs 2,480; High Interest/Low Vocabulary Bk Vols 50; Large Print Bks 1,500; Bk Vols 45,000; Per Subs 116; Talking Bks 1,000; Videos 600
Special Collections: Milford Chronicles & Peninsula News from 1886; Quilting Coll
Subject Interests: Del
Automation Activity & Vendor Info: (Acquisitions) SirsiDynix; (Cataloging) SirsiDynix; (Circulation) SirsiDynix; (OPAC) SirsiDynix; (Serials) SirsiDynix
Wireless access
Mem of Sussex County Department of Libraries
Special Services for the Deaf - High interest/low vocabulary bks
Special Services for the Blind - Low vision equip
Open Mon-Fri 9-8, Sat 9-2
Friends of the Library Group

MILLSBORO

P MILLSBORO PUBLIC LIBRARY*, 217 W State St, 19966. (Mail add: PO Box 458, 19966-0458), SAN 302-5012. Tel: 302-934-8743. FAX: 302-934-8623. Web Site: millsboro.lib.de.us. *Dir,* Mary Brittingham; E-mail: mary.brittingham@lib.de.us
Pop 7,518; Circ 38,013
Library Holdings: Bk Vols 35,000; Per Subs 96
Special Collections: Delaware Coll
Automation Activity & Vendor Info: (Cataloging) SirsiDynix; (Circulation) SirsiDynix; (ILL) SirsiDynix; (OPAC) SirsiDynix
Mem of Sussex County Department of Libraries
Open Mon, Wed & Fri 9-5, Tues & Thurs 11-8, Sat 9-1
Friends of the Library Group

NEW CASTLE

M DELAWARE DIVISION OF SUBSTANCE ABUSE & MENTAL HEALTH*, Medical Library, Springer Bldg, 1901 N Dupont Hwy, 19720. SAN 302-5039. Tel: 302-255-2789. FAX: 302-255-4458. E-mail: dhsslibrary@delaware.gov. Web Site: dhss.delaware.gov. *Admin Librn,* Position Currently Open
Library Holdings: Bk Vols 300; Per Subs 40
Subject Interests: Nursing, Psychiat, Psychol, Soc serv (soc work)
Partic in Wilmington Area Biomedical Library Consortium
Open Mon-Fri 8-4:30

P NEW CASTLE COUNTY LIBRARIES*, Department of Community Services, James H Gilliam Bldg, 77 Read's Way, 19720. Tel: 302-395-5617. Web Site: www.nccde.org/286/Libraries.
Member Libraries: Appoquinimink Community Library; Bear Library; Brandywine Hundred Library; Claymont Public Library; Corbit-Calloway Memorial Library; Delaware City Public Library; Delmar Public Library; Elsmere Public Library; Hockessin Public Library; Kirkwood Library; New Castle Public Library; Newark Free Library; Wilmington Public Library; Woodlawn Library

P NEW CASTLE PUBLIC LIBRARY*, 424 Delaware St, 19720. SAN 302-5047. Tel: 302-328-1995. FAX: 302-328-4412. Web Site: nccde.org/337/New-Castle-Public-Library. *Dir,* Julie Kirk; E-mail: julie.kirk@lib.de.us; Staff 5 (MLS 3, Non-MLS 2)
Founded 1811. Pop 35,726; Circ 109,629
Library Holdings: CDs 362; DVDs 398; Large Print Bks 249; Bk Titles 38,972; Per Subs 79; Talking Bks 1,590; Videos 713
Special Collections: Delawareana, Original New Castle Library Company Coll
Automation Activity & Vendor Info: (Cataloging) SirsiDynix; (Circulation) SirsiDynix; (OPAC) SirsiDynix
Wireless access
Function: 24/7 Electronic res, 24/7 Online cat, Adult bk club, Art exhibits, Bks on CD, Children's prog, Computer training, Computers for patron use, Doc delivery serv, Electronic databases & coll, Magazines, Meeting rooms, Movies, Music CDs, Online cat, Online ref, Outreach serv, OverDrive digital audio bks, Photocopying/Printing, Preschool reading prog, Printer for laptops & handheld devices, Prog for adults, Prog for children & young adult, Ref serv available, Scanner, Summer reading prog, Tax forms, Teen prog
Mem of New Castle County Libraries
Open Mon & Tues 10-9, Wed & Thurs 2-9, Fri & Sat 10-5
Friends of the Library Group

C WILMINGTON UNIVERSITY LIBRARY*, Robert C & Dorothy M Peoples Library, 320 N DuPont Hwy, 19720. SAN 302-5055. Tel: 302-356-6879. Toll Free Tel: 800-451-5724. FAX: 302-328-0914. E-mail: librarycontact@wilmu.edu. Web Site: www.wilmu.edu/library. *Libr Dir,* James M McCloskey; Tel: 302-356-6880, E-mail: james.m.mccloskey@wilmu.edu; *Asst Dir,* Adrienne M Johnson; Tel: 302-669-6607, E-mail: adrienne.m.johnson@wilmu.edu; *Librn,* Pamela A Shukitt; Tel: 302-356-6877, E-mail: pamela.a.shukitt@wilmu.edu; *Librn,* Michelle C Reyes; Tel: 302-356-6857, E-mail: michelle.c.reyes@wilmu.edu; *Instruction Librn,* James Bradley; Tel: 302-356-6872, E-mail: james.a.bradley@wilmu.edu; *Librn,* William L Smith; Tel: 302-356-6878, E-mail: william.l.smith@wilmu.edu; *Learning Commons Librn,* Melissa Jones; Tel: 302-356-8610, E-mail: melissa.j.jones@wilmu.edu; *Communications Spec, Pub Serv,* Kailah Neal; Tel: 302-669-6602, E-mail: kailah.r.neal@wilmu.edu; *Libr Tech II,* Craig S Conrad; Tel: 302-356-6876; *Libr Asst,* Erica Jones; Tel: 302-356-6873; Staff 11.5 (MLS 7.5, Non-MLS 4)
Founded 1968. Enrl 14,000; Fac 7; Highest Degree: Doctorate
Library Holdings: AV Mats 3,849; e-books 169,370; Microforms 95,816; Bk Vols 105,252; Per Subs 500
Special Collections: Automobile Advertising Coll
Subject Interests: Bus mgt, Educ, Leadership, Nursing, Soc sci
Automation Activity & Vendor Info: (Acquisitions) SirsiDynix; (Cataloging) SirsiDynix; (Circulation) SirsiDynix; (Course Reserve) SirsiDynix; (Discovery) OCLC Worldshare Management Services; (ILL) OCLC ILLiad; (OPAC) SirsiDynix; (Serials) OCLC
Wireless access
Partic in LYRASIS; OCLC Online Computer Library Center, Inc; OCLC-LVIS

Open Mon-Thurs 8:30am-10pm, Fri 8:30-8, Sat 9:30-4:30, Sun 1-8
Restriction: Non-circulating to the pub

NEWARK

M CHRISTIANA HOSPITAL LIBRARY*, Lewis B Flinn Medical Library, John H Ammon Medical Educ Ctr, 4755 Ogletown-Stanton Rd, 19718-0002. SAN 302-539X. Tel: 302-733-1115. FAX: 302-733-1365.
Founded 1965
Library Holdings: e-books 600; e-journals 1,100; Bk Titles 5,400; Per Subs 30
Subject Interests: Cancer, Clinical med, Consumer health, Preventive med
Automation Activity & Vendor Info: (Cataloging) Marcive, Inc; (Circulation) Softlink America; (OPAC) Softlink America
Wireless access
Function: Doc delivery serv, ILL available, Internet access, Ref serv available
Partic in LYRASIS

Branches:

GAIL P GILL COMMUNITY HEALTH LIBRARY, 4755 Ogletown-Stanton Rd, 19718. Tel: 302-733-1116.
Founded 1997
Library Holdings: Bk Titles 900
Subject Interests: Chronic disease, Consumer health, Wellness
Function: Computers for patron use, Outside serv via phone, mail, e-mail & web, Ref serv available
Restriction: Open to pub for ref & circ; with some limitations

JUNIOR BOARD CANCER RESOURCE LIBRARY, Helen F Graham Cancer Ctr, 4701 Ogletown-Stanton Rd, Rm 1106, 19713. Tel: 302-623-4580.
Founded 2002
Library Holdings: Bk Vols 3,000; Per Subs 40
Automation Activity & Vendor Info: (Serials) Softlink America

J DELAWARE TECHNICAL & COMMUNITY COLLEGE*, Stanton Campus Library, 400 Stanton-Christiana Rd, Rm D 201, 19713-2197. SAN 302-5063. Tel: 302-453-3716. FAX: 302-453-3079. E-mail: stanton-library@dtcc.edu. Web Site: www.library.dtcc.edu. *Head Librn,* Mary Anne Farrell; E-mail: farrell@dtcc.edu; *Tech Serv,* Karen Dower; Staff 4 (MLS 4)
Founded 1968. Enrl 1,800; Fac 106
Library Holdings: Bk Vols 31,448; Per Subs 364
Subject Interests: Careers, Criminal justice, Fire sci, Nursing, Soc sci & issues
Automation Activity & Vendor Info: (Cataloging) SirsiDynix; (Circulation) SirsiDynix; (Course Reserve) SirsiDynix; (ILL) SirsiDynix; (OPAC) SirsiDynix; (Serials) SirsiDynix
Wireless access
Partic in Tri State Col Libr Coop; Wilmington Area Biomedical Library Consortium
Open Mon-Thurs 8am-9pm, Fri 8-4, Sat 9-1

P NEWARK FREE LIBRARY, 750 Library Ave, 19711. SAN 302-508X. Tel: 302-731-7550. FAX: 302-731-4019. Web Site: www.nccde.org/333/Newark-Free-Library. *Mgr,* Martha Birchenall; E-mail: mpbirchenall@nccde.org; Staff 16 (MLS 4, Non-MLS 12)
Founded 1897. Pop 70,160; Circ 617,042
Library Holdings: Bk Vols 106,956; Per Subs 326
Automation Activity & Vendor Info: (Cataloging) SirsiDynix; (Circulation) SirsiDynix; (OPAC) SirsiDynix; (Serials) SirsiDynix
Wireless access
Function: Telephone ref
Mem of New Castle County Libraries
Special Services for the Deaf - High interest/low vocabulary bks; Spec interest per
Open Mon-Wed & Fri 10-9, Sat 10-5, Sun 1-5
Friends of the Library Group

R NEWARK UNITED METHODIST CHURCH*, Bunting Library, 69 E Main St, 19711-4645. SAN 326-2235. Tel: 302-368-8774. Web Site: newark-umc.org/wp/education/library. *Library Contact,* Brenda Cassel
Founded 1955
Library Holdings: High Interest/Low Vocabulary Bk Vols 100; Large Print Bks 25; Bk Vols 2,000
Subject Interests: Children's lit, Family, Relig
Open Mon-Fri 8-4, Sun 8-12

S MARGARET S STERCK SCHOOL FOR THE DEAF LIBRARY*, 630 E Chestnut Hill Rd, 19713. SAN 302-5098. Tel: 302-454-2301. FAX: 302-454-3493. Web Site: www.dsdeaf.org. *Library Contact,* Karen Martin
Library Holdings: Bk Vols 10,000
Special Collections: Captioned Filmstrip Coll; Large Print Books for the Visually Impaired; Professional Library of materials on deafness, deaf culture & visual impairment
Subject Interests: Deaf
Special Services for the Deaf - Staff with knowledge of sign lang
Restriction: Staff use only, Students only

S UNIVERSITY OF DELAWARE*, Education Resource Center, Willard Hall Education Bldg, 16 W Main St, Rm 012, 19716. Tel: 302-831-2335. FAX: 302-831-8404. E-mail: ERC-contact@udel.edu. Web Site: www.erc.udel.edu. *Assoc Dir,* Christine McBride; E-mail: mcbride@udel.edu; Staff 2 (MLS 1, Non-MLS 1)
Founded 1971
Library Holdings: AV Mats 2,000; Bk Vols 41,530; Per Subs 39
Special Collections: Book Examination Site
Subject Interests: Curric related mat for K-12, Young adult bks
Automation Activity & Vendor Info: (Acquisitions) Follett Software; (Cataloging) Follett Software; (Circulation) Follett Software; (Course Reserve) Follett Software; (OPAC) Follett Software; (Serials) Follett Software
Wireless access
Function: Audio & video playback equip for onsite use, Audiobks on Playaways & MP3, Bks on cassette, Bks on CD, CD-ROM, Computers for patron use, Digital talking bks, Games & aids for people with disabilities, ILL available, Internet access, Laminating, Large print keyboards, Magazines, Makerspace, Movies, Music CDs, Online cat, Photocopying/Printing, Scanner, Spanish lang bks, Spoken cassettes & CDs, Spoken cassettes & DVDs, Study rm, Wheelchair accessible
Open Mon-Thurs 8:30-8, Fri 8:30-5
Restriction: Borrowing privileges limited to fac & registered students, Fee for pub use, Open to pub for ref & circ; with some limitations, Open to students, fac & staff

C UNIVERSITY OF DELAWARE LIBRARY*, 181 S College Ave, 19717-5267. SAN 336-609X. Tel: 302-831-2965. Circulation Tel: 302-831-2455. Interlibrary Loan Service Tel: 302-831-2236. Web Site: library.udel.edu. *Vice Provost & May Morris Univ Librn,* Trevor A Dawes; E-mail: lib-vplm@udel.edu; *Assoc Univ Librn, Pub Serv, Dep Univ Librn, Outreach Serv,* Dr Sandra K Millard; E-mail: skm@udel.edu; *Assoc Univ Librn, Budget & Collections,* M Dina Giambi; E-mail: dinag@udel.edu; *Assoc Univ Librn, Human Res, Assoc Univ Librn, Organizational Develop,* Julie Brewer; E-mail: jbrewer@udel.edu; *Assoc Univ Librn, Publishing Preservation, Research & Digital Access,* Monica McCormick; E-mail: mmcc@udel.edu; *Assoc Univ Librn, Planning & Fac, Communications Librn,* Shelly L McCoy; E-mail: smccoy@udel.edu; *Dir of Assessment,* Erin C Daix; E-mail: daix@udel.edu; *Dir of Mus, Dir, Spec Coll,* Dr Janis A Tomlinson; E-mail: jat@udel.edu; *Budget Dir, Dir, Strategic Initiatives,* Justin C Wing; E-mail: wingman@udel.edu; *Dir, External Relations,* Tywanda L Cuffy; E-mail: tywanda@udel.edu; Staff 73 (MLS 47, Non-MLS 26)
Founded 1743. Enrl 24,120; Circ 2,719,392; Fac 1,356; Highest Degree: Doctorate
Jul 2017-Jun 2018. Mats Exp $12,358,392. Sal $8,358,844 (Prof $5,852,921)
Library Holdings: e-books 670,435; e-journals 100,413; Per Subs 100,000
Special Collections: American art of the 20th century to the present, esp. photography, works on papers, African American art, sculpture, and regional paintings; Inuit art; mineralogical coll; Delaware History & Politics; History of Papermaking & Contemporary Fine Printing (Bird & Bull Press Archives, Plough Press Archives); Irish Literature; John De Pol Papers); Senatorial Papers of Vice President Joseph R Biden, Jr; Twentieth-Century American Literature (Alice Dunbar-Nelson Papers, Emily Coleman Papers, Louis Untermeyer Papers, John Malcolm Brinnin Papers, Ishmael Reed Papers, Paul Bowles Papers, Donald Justice Papers, Tennessee Williams Coll, Marguerite & Captain Louis Henry Cohn Ernest Hemingway Coll, Ezra Pound Coll, Archives of Pagany); Unidel History of Chemistry Coll; Unidel History of Horticulture & Landscape Architecture Coll; US Patent Coll. US Document Depository
Subject Interests: Mus, Spec coll
Wireless access
Publications: Collections; Exhibition Catalogs; Friends of the University of Delaware Library Newsletter
Partic in Association of Research Libraries; Center for Research Libraries; Chesapeake Information & Research Library Alliance; Greater Western Library Alliance; LYRASIS; Northeast Research Libraries Consortium; OCLC Online Computer Library Center, Inc; OCLC Research Library Partnership; Philadelphia Area Consortium of Special Collections Libraries
Special Services for the Deaf - Assistive tech
Special Services for the Blind - Assistive/Adapted tech devices, equip & products
Open Mon-Thurs 8am-2am, Fri 8am-10pm, Sat 9am-10pm, Sun 11am-2am
Friends of the Library Group

Departmental Libraries:

CHEMISTRY, Brown Laboratory, Rm 202, 181 S College Ave, 19717, SAN 336-6154. Tel: 302-831-2993. E-mail: circulation@winsor.lib.udel.edu. Web Site: library.udel.edu/branchlibraries/chemistry. *Liaison Librn, Sr Asst Librn,* Sabine Lanteri; Tel: 302-831-6945, E-mail: slanteri@udel.edu; *Libr Asst*

III, Cindy Bailey; Tel: 302-831-2455, E-mail: clbailey@udel.edu. Subject Specialists: *Sci,* Sabine Lanteri
Library Holdings: Bk Vols 28,000; Per Subs 198
Subject Interests: Analytical chem, Biochem, Inorganic chem, Organic chem, Phys chem
Open Mon-Fri 8-5
Friends of the Library Group

ODESSA

P CORBIT-CALLOWAY MEMORIAL LIBRARY*, 115 High St, 19730. SAN 302-511X. Tel: 302-378-8838. FAX: 302-378-7803. E-mail: corbitlibrary@gmail.com. Web Site: corbitlibrary.org. *Dir,* Karen Quinn; E-mail: karen.quinn@lib.de.us; Staff 4 (MLS 1, Non-MLS 3)
Founded 1847. Pop 6,100; Circ 34,660
Library Holdings: AV Mats 300; High Interest/Low Vocabulary Bk Vols 500; Large Print Bks 700; Bk Titles 28,000; Bk Vols 35,000; Per Subs 95; Spec Interest Per Sub 65; Talking Bks 150
Special Collections: DelMarva Coll of History & Culture
Automation Activity & Vendor Info: (Circulation) SirsiDynix; (OPAC) SirsiDynix; (Serials) SirsiDynix
Wireless access
Publications: The Face of a Town: The Corbit-Calloway Memorial Library; Yesterday & Today (Histories of eight towns)
Mem of New Castle County Libraries
Open Mon & Thurs 1-8, Tues & Fri 10-4, Wed 10-8, Sat 9-1
Friends of the Library Group

REHOBOTH BEACH

P REHOBOTH BEACH PUBLIC LIBRARY, 226 Rehoboth Ave, 19971-2134. Tel: 302-227-8044. FAX: 302-227-0597. Web Site: www.rehobothlibrary.org. *Libr Dir,* Alison Miller; Tel: 302-227-8044, Ext 108, E-mail: alison.miller@lib.de.us; *Program Libm,* Lauren McCauley; Tel: 302-227-8044, Ext 109, E-mail: lauren.mccauley@lib.de.us; *Youth Serv Librn,* Sarah Beham; Tel: 302-227-8044, Ext 106, E-mail: sarah.beham@lib.de.us; *Events Coord,* Genevieve Pedley; Tel: 302-227-8044, Ext 107; Staff 5 (MLS 3, Non-MLS 2)
Founded 1912. Circ 58,239
Jul 2020-Jun 2021 Income $480,313, State $52,962, City $30,000, County $250,569, Locally Generated Income $146,782. Mats Exp $382,382, Books $15,000, Per/Ser (Incl. Access Fees) $3,000, AV Mat $5,200, Electronic Ref Mat (Incl. Access Fees) $1,400. Sal $221,693
Library Holdings: Bk Vols 50,000; Per Subs 85
Special Collections: Delaware Coll
Automation Activity & Vendor Info: (Acquisitions) SirsiDynix; (Cataloging) SirsiDynix; (Circulation) SirsiDynix; (OPAC) SirsiDynix
Wireless access
Function: 24/7 Electronic res, 24/7 Online cat, Activity rm, Adult bk club, Audio & video playback equip for onsite use, Audiobks on Playaways & MP3, Audiobks via web, Bk club(s), Bks on CD, Children's prog, Computer training, Computers for patron use, E-Readers, Electronic databases & coll, Homebound delivery serv, ILL available, Internet access, Life-long learning prog for all ages, Literacy & newcomer serv, Magazines, Meeting rooms, Microfiche/film & reading machines, Movies, Music CDs, Notary serv, Online cat, Online ref, OverDrive digital audio bks, Photocopying/Printing, Printer for laptops & handheld devices, Prog for adults, Prog for children & young adult, Ref serv available, Scanner, Story hour, Study rm, Summer reading prog, Teen prog
Mem of Sussex County Department of Libraries
Open Mon-Wed 10-8, Thurs & Fri 10-5, Sat 10-3, Sun (May-Sept) 10-2
Friends of the Library Group

SEAFORD

P SEAFORD DISTRICT LIBRARY, 600 N Market St Extended, 19973. SAN 302-5136. Tel: 302-629-2524. E-mail: seaford.reference@lib.de.us. Web Site: seaforddistrictlibrary.org. *Dir,* Jerry Keiser; E-mail: jerry.keiser@lib.de.us; Staff 9 (MLS 1, Non-MLS 8)
Founded 1902. Pop 25,000; Circ 107,435
Library Holdings: Bk Vols 44,265; Per Subs 40
Special Collections: Classic Cars Coll; Delaware History (Delawareana Coll); Large Print Coll; Parents & Children (Parenting Coll)
Automation Activity & Vendor Info: (Cataloging) SirsiDynix; (Circulation) SirsiDynix; (OPAC) SirsiDynix
Wireless access
Function: ILL available
Mem of Sussex County Department of Libraries
Open Mon-Fri 9-5
Friends of the Library Group

SELBYVILLE

P SELBYVILLE PUBLIC LIBRARY*, 11 Main & McCabe Sts, 19975. (Mail add: PO Box 739, 19975-0739), SAN 302-5144. Tel: 302-436-8195. FAX: 302-436-1508. Web Site: www.selbyvillelibrary.org. *Dir,* Kelly Kline; E-mail: Kelly.Kline@lib.de.us
Pop 3,000
Library Holdings: Bk Vols 21,833; Per Subs 21
Wireless access
Mem of Sussex County Department of Libraries
Open Mon & Fri 10-2, Wed 3-7
Friends of the Library Group

SMYRNA

P SMYRNA PUBLIC LIBRARY*, 107 S Main St, 19977. SAN 302-5160. Tel: 302-653-4579. FAX: 302-653-2650. Web Site: www.smyrna.delaware.gov/84/Library. *Dir,* Beverly Hirt; E-mail: Beverly.Hirt@lib.de.us
Founded 1858. Circ 37,895
Library Holdings: CDs 102; DVDs 39; Large Print Bks 515; Bk Titles 23,000; Per Subs 67; Talking Bks 659; Videos 770
Special Collections: Delaware Authors
Subject Interests: Del
Partic in OCLC Online Computer Library Center, Inc
Open Mon, Wed & Fri 8:30-6, Tues & Thurs 10-8, Sat 9-2
Friends of the Library Group

S JAMES T VAUGHN CORRECTIONAL CENTER LAW LIBRARY*, 1181 Paddock Rd, 19977. SAN 302-5152. Tel: 302-653-9261. FAX: 302-659-6687. Web Site: doc.delaware.gov/views/jtvcc.blade.shtml. *Legal Serv Adminr,* Andrew Peruchi; E-mail: andrew.peruchi@delaware.gov
Founded 1971
Library Holdings: Bk Titles 4,000
Restriction: Not open to pub

WILMINGTON

P BRANDYWINE HUNDRED LIBRARY*, 1300 Foulk Rd, 19803. SAN 302-5217. Tel: 302-477-3150. FAX: 302-477-4545. Web Site: www.nccde.org/294/Brandywine-Hundred-Library. *Mgr,* Jean Kaufman; E-mail: jkaufman@nccde.org; Staff 31 (MLS 6, Non-MLS 25)
Founded 1959
Library Holdings: Bk Vols 151,725; Per Subs 330
Special Collections: Coin Coll; Delawareana Coll; Holocaust
Automation Activity & Vendor Info: (Acquisitions) SirsiDynix; (Cataloging) SirsiDynix; (Circulation) SirsiDynix; (OPAC) SirsiDynix
Wireless access
Function: ILL available, Outside serv via phone, mail, e-mail & web, Photocopying/Printing, Prog for children & young adult, Ref serv available, Summer reading prog, Telephone ref, Wheelchair accessible
Publications: Friends of the Brandywine Hundred Library (Newsletter)
Mem of New Castle County Libraries
Open Mon-Wed & Fri 10-9, Sat 10-5, Sun 1-5
Friends of the Library Group

R CONGREGATION BETH EMETH*, William, Vitellia & Topkis Library, 300 W Lea Blvd, 19802. SAN 302-5365. Tel: 302-764-2393. FAX: 302-764-2395. Web Site: www.bethemethde.org. *Exec Dir,* Jonathan Yulish; E-mail: jyulish@bethemethde.org
Library Holdings: Bk Vols 3,000
Subject Interests: Judaica (lit or hist of Jews)
Wireless access
Open Mon-Thurs 9-5, Fri 8:30-4

S DELAWARE ART MUSEUM*, Helen Farr Sloan Library & Archives, 2301 Kentmere Pkwy, 19806. SAN 302-5233. Tel: 302-351-8540. Web Site: www.delart.org. *Archivist/Librn,* Rachael DiEleuterio; E-mail: rdieleuterio@delart.org; Staff 1 (MLS 1)
Founded 1912
Library Holdings: Bk Vols 40,000; Per Subs 50
Special Collections: Bancroft Pre-Raphaelite Library, archival rec, bks, cat, mss; Everett Shinn Archives; Frank Schoonover Coll, archives, bks, illus, photog; Gayle Hoskins Coll, memorabilia, photog, complete published works; Howard Pyle Library & Archives, illus, photog, complete published works; Jerome Myers Coll, archival rec, memorabilia; John Sloan Coll, bks, cat, personal papers, photog; N C Wyeth Coll, bks, illus, per; Stanley Arthurs Coll, bks, illus, clippings
Automation Activity & Vendor Info: (Cataloging) Follett Software; (OPAC) Follett Software
Function: Res libr
Restriction: Open by appt only

S DELAWARE HISTORICAL SOCIETY RESEARCH LIBRARY*, 505 N Market St, 19801. SAN 302-5276. Tel: 302-655-7161. FAX: 302-655-7844. E-mail: deinfo@dehistory.org. Web Site: dehistory.org. *Exec Dir,* Dr David W Young; E-mail: dyoung@dehistory.org; *Chief Curator,* Leigh Rifenburg; Tel: 302-295-2386, E-mail: lrifenburg@dehistory.org; *Curator, Printed Mat,* Edward Richi; Tel: 302-295-2387, E-mail: erichi@dehistory.org; *Curator of Objects & Textiles,* Jennifer Potts; E-mail: jpotts@dehistory.org; *Curator, Spec Coll,* Brenton Grom; E-mail: bgrom@dehistory.org; *Presv Librn,* Bill Robinson; E-mail: brobinson@dehistory.org; Staff 4 (Non-MLS 4)
Founded 1864
Library Holdings: Bk Vols 32,000; Per Subs 73
Special Collections: Ephemera; Manuscripts; Maps; Newspapers; Photographs. Oral History
Subject Interests: Del hist, Genealogy, US hist
Automation Activity & Vendor Info: (Cataloging) Cuadra Associates, Inc; (OPAC) Cuadra Associates, Inc
Wireless access
Publications: Delaware History (Biannually)
Open Mon 11-7, Tues & Thurs 9-1, Fri 9-5
Friends of the Library Group

S DELAWARE MUSEUM OF NATURAL HISTORY LIBRARY*, 4840 Kennett Pike, 19807. (Mail add: PO Box 3937, 19807-0937), SAN 302-492X. Tel: 302-658-9111. FAX: 302-658-2610. Web Site: www.delmnh.org/collections-research/research-lirbary-archives. *Dir,* Dr Jean Woods; Tel: 302-658-9111, Ext 314, E-mail: jwoods@delmnh.org
Founded 1972
Library Holdings: Bk Vols 10,000; Per Subs 130
Subject Interests: Birds, Mollusks
Wireless access
Function: Res libr
Publications: Nemouria: Occasional Papers of the Delaware Museum of Natural History (Journal)
Restriction: Non-circulating, Open by appt only

J DELAWARE TECHNICAL & COMMUNITY COLLEGE*, John Eugene Derrickson Memorial Library, Wilmington Campus, West Bldg, First Flr, 300 N Orange St, 19801. SAN 302-525X. Tel: 302-573-5422. FAX: 302-577-2038. E-mail: wilm-library@dtcc.edu. Web Site: www.library.dtcc.edu. *Actg Head Librn,* Joan Harden; E-mail: jharden3@dtcc.edu; *Libr Tech,* Monica Smallwood; E-mail: msmallw@dtcc.edu; Staff 4 (MLS 4)
Founded 1973. Enrl 3,000; Fac 125; Highest Degree: Associate
Library Holdings: Bk Vols 36,400; Per Subs 410
Subject Interests: Allied health, Bus & mgt, Computer tech
Automation Activity & Vendor Info: (Acquisitions) SirsiDynix; (Cataloging) SirsiDynix; (Circulation) SirsiDynix; (Course Reserve) SirsiDynix; (ILL) SirsiDynix; (OPAC) SirsiDynix; (Serials) SirsiDynix
Wireless access
Partic in LYRASIS; OCLC Online Computer Library Center, Inc; Tri State Col Libr Coop
Open Mon-Thurs 7:30am-9pm, Fri 8-4:30

P ELSMERE PUBLIC LIBRARY*, 30 Spruce Ave, 19805. SAN 377-0974. Tel: 302-892-2210. FAX: 302-892-2213. E-mail: elsmere@delawarelibraries.libanswers.com. Web Site: www.nccde.org/327/Elsmere-Library. *Mgr,* Tanya Moye; E-mail: tmoye@nccde.org; Staff 3.5 (MLS 1.5, Non-MLS 2)
Founded 1995. Pop 44,294; Circ 271,992
Library Holdings: Audiobooks 4,824; DVDs 4,693; Electronic Media & Resources 64; Bk Vols 34,521; Per Subs 102
Automation Activity & Vendor Info: (Acquisitions) SirsiDynix; (Cataloging) SirsiDynix; (Circulation) SirsiDynix; (OPAC) SirsiDynix; (Serials) EBSCO Online
Wireless access
Mem of New Castle County Libraries
Partic in OCLC Online Computer Library Center, Inc; Tipcat
Open Mon 10-8, Tues & Thurs 12-8, Fri & Sat 10-5
Friends of the Library Group

C GOLDEY-BEACOM COLLEGE*, J Wilbur Hirons Library, Jones Ctr, 4701 Limestone Rd, 19808. SAN 302-5268. Tel: 302-225-6247. FAX: 302-998-6189. E-mail: hirons@gbc.edu. Web Site: www.gbc.edu/academics/academic-resources/library-technology-services. *Dir,* Rusty Michalak; Tel: 303-225-6227, E-mail: michalr@gbc.edu; *Librn,* Bethany Geleskie; E-mail: geleskb@gbc.edu; *Libr Asst,* Sandy McNeal; Staff 4 (MLS 3, Non-MLS 1)
Founded 1969. Enrl 1,800; Fac 85; Highest Degree: Master
Library Holdings: AV Mats 1,320; Bk Titles 40,346; Bk Vols 44,602; Per Subs 1,051
Special Collections: College Archives; Delaware Business
Subject Interests: Bus & mgt
Automation Activity & Vendor Info: (Cataloging) SirsiDynix; (Circulation) SirsiDynix; (OPAC) SirsiDynix
Wireless access
Partic in LYRASIS
Open Mon-Thurs 8:30am-10pm, Fri 8-5, Sat 8-6, Sun 11-5

S HAGLEY MUSEUM & LIBRARY*, 298 Buck Rd E, 19807. (Mail add: PO Box 3630, 19807-0630), SAN 302-4938. Tel: 302-658-2400. FAX: 302-658-0568. E-mail: AskHagley@hagley.org. Web Site: www.hagley.org. *Dir, Libr Serv,* Erik Rau; E-mail: erau@hagley.org; *Ref Librn,* Linda Gross; E-mail: lgross@hagley.org; *Curator,* Max Moeller; E-mail: mmoeller@hagley.org; Staff 13 (MLS 4, Non-MLS 9)
Founded 1955
Library Holdings: Bk Vols 250,000; Per Subs 259
Special Collections: Chemical history, bks, flm, ms; Dupont Company & Family Papers; Iron & Steel, bks & ms; Pennsylvania Power & Light Coll; Petroleum Bks & ms; Railroad Firms; Reading Railroad Coll, ms; Textile Bks & ms; Trade Catalogs & Journals; World's Fairs & International Expositions
Subject Interests: Bus & mgt, Consumerism, Econ hist, Hist of tech, Indust design, Indust hist
Automation Activity & Vendor Info: (Cataloging) EOS International; (OPAC) EOS International
Wireless access
Function: Res libr
Publications: A Guide to the Manuscripts in the Eleutherian Mills Historical Library (1970) & Supplement (1978); Pennsylvania Power & Light: A Guide to the Records (1985)
Partic in Independent Res Libr Asn; OCLC Research Library Partnership
Open Mon-Fri 8:30-4:30
Restriction: Non-circulating to the pub

R IMMANUEL CHURCH LIBRARY*, 2414 Pennsylvania Ave, 19806. Tel: 302-652-3121. FAX: 302-652-1078. E-mail: immanuellibrary@comcast.net. Web Site: www.immanuelchurch.us. *Librn,* Betty Jean Helms
Founded 1865
Library Holdings: AV Mats 400; DVDs 60; Bk Vols 3,500; Videos 200
Special Collections: Immanuel History, newsclippings
Restriction: Mem only

P KIRKWOOD LIBRARY, 6000 Kirkwood Hwy, 19808. SAN 302-5284. Tel: 302-995-7663. FAX: 302-995-7687. Web Site: nccde.org/332/kirkwood-library. *Mgr,* Steven Davis; E-mail: steven.davis@newcastlede.gov; Staff 10 (MLS 3, Non-MLS 7)
Founded 1967. Pop 52,702; Circ 418,634
Library Holdings: Bk Vols 85,934; Per Subs 206
Automation Activity & Vendor Info: (Cataloging) SirsiDynix; (Circulation) SirsiDynix; (OPAC) SirsiDynix; (Serials) SirsiDynix
Wireless access
Mem of New Castle County Libraries
Open Mon-Wed 10-9, Thurs & Sat 10-5, Sun 1-5
Friends of the Library Group

L MORRIS JAMES LLP*, Law Library, 500 Delaware Ave, Ste 1500, 19801-1494. SAN 370-6672. Tel: 302-888-6863. FAX: 302-571-1750. Web Site: www.morrisjames.com. *Librn,* Sandra J Proctor; E-mail: sproctor@morrisjames.com; Staff 2 (MLS 1, Non-MLS 1)
Subject Interests: Bankruptcy, Corporate law, Family law, Real estate law, Tax law
Automation Activity & Vendor Info: (Cataloging) Inmagic, Inc.; (Serials) Inmagic, Inc.
Function: ILL available
Restriction: By permission only

L MORRIS, NICHOLS, ARSHT & TUNNELL, LLP*, Law Library, 1201 N Market St, 19801. (Mail add: PO Box 1347, 19899). Tel: 302-658-9200. FAX: 302-658-3989. Web Site: www.mnat.com. *Librn,* Pamela Reed; E-mail: preed@mnat.com; Staff 2 (MLS 1, Non-MLS 1)
Library Holdings: Bk Vols 2,500; Per Subs 25
Subject Interests: Bankruptcy, Corporate law, Intellectual property law, Securities law
Function: ILL available, Photocopying/Printing
Restriction: Staff use only

S MT CUBA ASTRONOMICAL OBSERVATORY MEMORIAL LIBRARY, 1610 Hillside Mill Rd, 19807. (Mail add: PO Box 3915, Greenville, 19807), SAN 326-9787. Tel: 302-654-6407. Web Site: mountcuba.org.
Founded 1958
Library Holdings: Bk Titles 608
Subject Interests: Astronomy

GL NEW CASTLE COUNTY LAW LIBRARY*, New Castle Courthouse, 500 N King St, Ste 2500, 19801. SAN 302-5322. Tel: 302-255-0847. FAX: 302-255-2223. Web Site: courts.delaware.gov/lawlibraries/newcastle.aspx. *Sr Law Librn,* Galen Wilson; E-mail: galen.wilson@delaware.gov
Founded 1911

Library Holdings: Bk Vols 25,000
Wireless access
Open Mon-Fri 8:30-4:30
Restriction: Non-circulating to the pub

L POTTER ANDERSON & CORROON LLP*, Law Library, Hercules Plaza, 1313 N Market St, 19801. (Mail add: PO Box 951, 19899-0951). Tel: 302-984-6000. FAX: 302-658-1192. Web Site: www.potteranderson.com. *Dir, Libr Serv,* Kathleen H Veith; Tel: 302-984-6195, Fax: 302-778-6195, E-mail: kveith@potteranderson.com; Staff 1 (MLS 1)
Subject Interests: Bankruptcy, Corporate law, Estates, Tax law, Trusts
Wireless access
Function: ILL available, Photocopying/Printing
Restriction: Staff use only

L RICHARDS, LAYTON & FINGER LIBRARY*, One Rodney Sq, 920 N King St, 19801. SAN 326-9744. Tel: 302-651-7700. FAX: 302-651-7701. Web Site: www.rlf.com. *Libr Mgr,* Robert L Guerrero; Tel: 302-651-7775, E-mail: guerrero@rlf.com; Staff 2 (MLS 1, Non-MLS 1)
Founded 1929
Library Holdings: Bk Vols 14,000; Per Subs 27
Subject Interests: Law
Restriction: Staff use only

L SKADDEN, ARPS, SLATE, MEAGHER & FLOM LLP RESEARCH & KNOWLEDGE*, One Rodney Sq, 7th Flr, 920 N King St, 19801. SAN 329-1073. Tel: 302-651-3224. FAX: 302-651-3001. *Mgr,* Leslie Corey Leach; Staff 2 (MLS 1, Non-MLS 1)
Founded 1979
Library Holdings: e-books 45; e-journals 30; Bk Titles 850; Bk Vols 9,000; Per Subs 25
Subject Interests: Bankruptcy, Del law, Securities
Automation Activity & Vendor Info: (Acquisitions) EOS International; (Cataloging) OCLC; (Circulation) EOS International; (ILL) EOS International; (OPAC) EOS International; (Serials) EOS International
Wireless access
Restriction: Staff use only

GL UNITED STATES COURT OF APPEALS, Branch Library, US Courts Library, 5122 Federal Bldg, 844 King St, Unit 43, 19801. SAN 302-5373. Tel: 302-573-5880, 302-573-5881. FAX: 302-573-6430. *Librn,* Elizabeth Crowder; E-mail: elizabeth_crowder@ca3.uscourts.gov; Staff 2 (MLS 1, Non-MLS 1)
Founded 1974
Library Holdings: Bk Vols 14,000; Per Subs 25
Partic in Federal Library & Information Network
Open Mon-Fri 8:30-4:30
Restriction: Non-circulating to the pub

WIDENER UNIVERSITY

CL HARRISBURG CAMPUS LAW LIBRARY*, 3800 Vartan Way, Harrisburg, 17110. (Mail add: PO Box 69380, Harrisburg, 17106-9380), SAN 370-3517. Tel: 717-541-3933. FAX: 717-541-3998. Web Site: www.law.widener.edu/LawLibrary. *Dir,* Michael J Slinger; Tel: 302-477-2111, Fax: 302-477-2228, E-mail: mjslinger@widener.edu; *Assoc Dir,* Patricia Fox; Tel: 717-541-3935, E-mail: pfox@widener.edu; *Ref/Emerging Technologies Librn,* Stephanie Engerer; Tel: 717-541-3953, E-mail: sjengerer@widener.edu; *Ref/Tech Serv Librn,* Susan Giusti; Tel: 717-541-3929, E-mail: smgiusti@widener.edu; *Govt Doc, Ref Serv,* Edmund Sonnenberg; Tel: 717-541-3932, E-mail: ejsonnenberg@widener.edu; *Ref Serv,* Brent Johnson; Tel: 717-541-3984, E-mail: bljohnson@widener.edu. Subject Specialists: *State doc,* Brent Johnson; Staff 11 (MLS 6, Non-MLS 5)
Founded 1989
Library Holdings: Bk Titles 28,504; Bk Vols 199,864
Special Collections: US Document Depository
Subject Interests: Penn law, Pub law
Open Mon-Thurs 8am-Midnight, Fri 8am-11pm, Sat 8-8, Sun 10am-Midnight

CL SCHOOL OF LAW LIBRARY*, 4601 Concord Pike, 19803. (Mail add: PO Box 7474, 19083), SAN 302-5241. Tel: 302-477-2244. FAX: 302-477-2240. Reference E-mail: law.libref@law.widener.edu. Web Site: law.widener.edu/lawlibrary. *Assoc Dean, Info Serv & Tech, Dir, Legal Info Ctr,* Michael J Slinger; Tel: 302-477-2111, Fax: 302-477-2228, E-mail: mjslinger@widener.edu; *Assoc Dir,* Mary K Marzolla; Tel: 302-477-2157, E-mail: mkmarzolla@widener.edu; *Head, Outreach Serv,* Mary Alice Peeling; *Ref & ILL Librn,* Enza Klotzbucher; Tel: 302-477-2292; *Ref/Electronic Serv Librn,* Janet Lindenmuth; Tel: 302-477-2245; *Ref/Outreach Librn,* Margaret S Adams; Tel: 302-477-2039; *Tech Serv Librn,* Laurie Palumbo; Staff 8 (MLS 8)
Founded 1973. Enrl 1,100; Fac 100; Highest Degree: Doctorate
Library Holdings: Bk Vols 610,000; Per Subs 8,400
Special Collections: US Document Depository
Subject Interests: Corp, Del, Environ law, Health law
Partic in OCLC Online Computer Library Center, Inc

P WILMINGTON PUBLIC LIBRARY*, Ten E Tenth St, 19801. SAN 336-6480. Tel: 302-571-7400. FAX: 302-654-9132. Reference E-mail: wilmref@lib.de.us. Web Site: wilmington.lib.de.us. *Dir,* Jamar Rahming; E-mail: Jamar.Rahming@lib.de.us; Staff 18 (MLS 9, Non-MLS 9)
Founded 1788. Pop 131,000; Circ 185,463
Library Holdings: AV Mats 26,638; CDs 7,770; DVDs 5,000; Bk Vols 335,329; Per Subs 700; Talking Bks 3,700; Videos 10,168
Special Collections: Delawareana; Periodicals
Automation Activity & Vendor Info: (Acquisitions) SirsiDynix; (Circulation) SirsiDynix; (Media Booking) SirsiDynix
Wireless access
Publications: Institute of the Colonies; So Laudable An Undertaking: Grapevine; Wilmington Library
Mem of New Castle County Libraries
Open Mon-Wed 9:30-8, Thurs 9:30-5, Fri & Sat 9-5
Friends of the Library Group
Branches: 1
NORTH WILMINGTON, 3400 N Market St, 19802, SAN 377-7383. Tel: 302-761-4290. FAX: 302-761-4291. *Br Mgr,* Cathy Hall; E-mail: cathy.hall@lib.de.us
Open Mon-Wed 11:30-8, Thurs 11:30-5, Fri & Sat 11:30-4
Friends of the Library Group

P WOODLAWN LIBRARY, 2020 W Ninth St, 19805. SAN 336-6545. Tel: 302-571-7425. FAX: 302-571-7320. Web Site: nccde.org/344/Woodlawn-Library. *Mgr,* Tanya Moye; E-mail: tanya.moye@newcastlede.gov
Wireless access
Mem of New Castle County Libraries
Open Mon-Wed 10-9, Thurs & Sat 10-5, Sun 1-5
Friends of the Library Group

WINTERTHUR

S THE WINTERTHUR LIBRARY, 5105 Kennett Pike, 19735. SAN 302-5411. Tel: 302-888-4681. FAX: 302-888-4870. E-mail: reference@winterthur.org. Web Site: www.winterthur.org/exhibitions-and-collections/library.
Founded 1951
Library Holdings: Bk Vols 120,000; Per Subs 300
Special Collections: Decorative Arts Photographic Coll; Edward Deming Andrews Memorial Shaker Coll; John & Carolyn Grossman Coll; Joseph Downs Coll of Manuscripts & Printed Ephemera; Winterthur Archives
Automation Activity & Vendor Info: (Cataloging) Innovative Interfaces, Inc; (Circulation) Innovative Interfaces, Inc; (OPAC) Innovative Interfaces, Inc; (Serials) Innovative Interfaces, Inc
Wireless access
Function: Res libr
Publications: An American Cornucopia; Guide to the Winterthur Library: The Joseph Downs Collection & the Winterthur Archives; Personal Accounts of Events, Travels & Everyday Life in America: An Annotated Bibliography; The Edward Deming Andrews Memorial Shaker Collection; The Winterthur Library Revealed; The Winterthur Museum Library Collection of Printed Books & Periodicals (9 Vol); Trade Catalogues at Winterthur
Partic in Independent Res Libr Asn; OCLC Online Computer Library Center, Inc; OCLC Research Library Partnership
Restriction: Open by appt only, Open to pub for ref only

DISTRICT OF COLUMBIA

WASHINGTON

L ADMINISTRATIVE OFFICE OF THE UNITED STATES COURTS LIBRARY*, One Columbus Circle NE, Ste 4-400, 20544. SAN 372-1108. Tel: 202-502-1203. FAX: 202-502-1588. *Law Librn*, Alyson Foster; E-mail: alyson_foster@ao.uscourts.gov; Staff 1 (Non-MLS 1)
Library Holdings: e-journals 3,500; Electronic Media & Resources 25; Bk Vols 2,500; Per Subs 30
Subject Interests: Admin law, Bankruptcy law & Federal rules, Civil law, Criminal law, US & intl judiciary, US courts
Automation Activity & Vendor Info: (Acquisitions) SirsiDynix-WorkFlows; (Cataloging) OCLC Connexion; (Circulation) SirsiDynix-WorkFlows; (ILL) SirsiDynix-WorkFlows
Wireless access
Partic in Law Library Microform Consortium
Restriction: External users must contact libr, Not open to pub, Open by appt only

S ADVOCATES FOR YOUTH, The Mary Lee Tatum Library, 1325 G St NW, Ste 980, 20005. SAN 375-0566. Tel: 202-419-3420. FAX: 202-419-1448. Web Site: www.advocatesforyouth.org. *Pub Serv Librn*, Emily Bridges; Tel: 202-419-3420, Ext 43, E-mail: emily@advocatesforyouth.org; Staff 2 (MLS 2)
Library Holdings: Bk Vols 3,000; Per Subs 150
Subject Interests: Behav, Health, Youth
Automation Activity & Vendor Info: (ILL) OCLC
Restriction: Open by appt only

SR AHMADIYYA MOVEMENT IN ISLAM INC*, Muslim Library, American Fazel Mosque, 2141 LeRoy Pl NW, 20008. SAN 326-9272. Tel: 202-232-3737. E-mail: help@ahmadiyya.us. Information Services E-mail: info@alislam.org. Web Site: www.alislam.org/library. *Librn*, Zaheer Ahmed Bajwa
Library Holdings: Bk Titles 500

L AKIN GUMP STRAUSS HAUER & FELD LLP, Law Library, Robert S Strauss Tower, 2001 K St NW, 20006-1037. SAN 377-3787. Tel: 202-887-4000. FAX: 202-887-4288. E-mail: washdcinfo@akingump.com. Web Site: www.akingump.com. *Ref Librn*, Brian Bevins; E-mail: bbevins@akingump.com
Library Holdings: Bk Vols 15,000
Partic in DC Soc of Law Librs

S ALEXANDER GRAHAM BELL ASSOCIATION FOR THE DEAF & HARD OF HEARING*, Volta Bureau Library, 3417 Volta Pl NW, 20007. SAN 302-5969. Tel: 202-204-4683. FAX: 202-337-8314. Web Site: www.agbell.org. *Mgr*, Gary Yates; E-mail: gyates@agbell.org
Founded 1887
Library Holdings: Bk Vols 12,000; Per Subs 20
Special Collections: Hearing (Alexander Graham Bell Coll), ms, correspondence
Subject Interests: Deaf, Speech & hearing
Restriction: Off-site coll in storage - retrieval as requested, Open by appt only

S AMERICAN ASSOCIATION OF STATE HIGHWAY & TRANSPORTATION OFFICIALS LIBRARY, 444 N Capitol St NW, Ste 249, 20001. SAN 377-1326. Tel: 202-624-8918. FAX: 202-624-5806. E-mail: info@aashto.org. Web Site: www.transportation.org. *Info Res Mgr*, Robert Cullen; E-mail: bcullen@aashto.org
Library Holdings: Bk Vols 5,000; Per Subs 60
Open Mon-Fri 9-4:30

S AMERICAN BAR ASSOCIATION LIBRARY, 1050 Connecticut Ave NW, Ste 400, 20036. SAN 326-9116. Tel: 202-662-1015. FAX: 202-662-1032. *Librn*, Jill Sandor; Tel: 202-662-1015, E-mail: jill.sandor@americanbar.org
Library Holdings: Bk Titles 7,500; Per Subs 140
Function: ILL available
Open Mon-Fri 10-6
Restriction: Borrowing requests are handled by ILL

S AMERICAN CHEMICAL SOCIETY INFORMATION RESOURCE CENTER*, 1155 16th St NW, 20036. SAN 302-5578. Tel: 202-872-4513. Toll Free Tel: 800-227-5556, Ext 4513. FAX: 202-872-6257. E-mail: library@acs.org. *Librn*, Moria Smith; E-mail: m_smith@acs.org; *Asst Librn*, Courtney O'Donnell; E-mail: c_odonnell@acs.org. Subject Specialists: *Chem, Phys & life sci*, Moria Smith; *Phys & life sci*, Courtney O'Donnell; Staff 2 (MLS 2)
Founded 1876
Library Holdings: Bk Titles 7,500; Per Subs 250; Spec Interest Per Sub 150
Special Collections: ACS Materials, print & digital photos
Subject Interests: Chem
Automation Activity & Vendor Info: (Acquisitions) Sydney; (Cataloging) Sydney; (Circulation) Sydney; (ILL) OCLC; (OPAC) Sydney; (Serials) EBSCO Online
Wireless access
Function: Doc delivery serv, For res purposes, ILL available, Photocopying/Printing, Prof lending libr, Ref serv available, Res libr, Wheelchair accessible
Partic in OCLC-LVIS
Open Mon-Fri 8:30-5
Restriction: Circulates for staff only, Open to pub for ref only, Open to pub with supv only

M AMERICAN COLLEGE OF OBSTETRICIANS & GYNECOLOGISTS*, Resource Center, 409 12th St SW, 20024-2188. (Mail add: PO Box 96920, 20090-6920), SAN 303-8068. Tel: 202-863-2518. FAX: 202-484-1595. E-mail: resources@acog.org. Web Site: www.acog.org. *Sr Dir*, Mary A Hyde; *Spec Coll Librn*, Beth DeFrancis Sun; *Ref Serv*, Yvonnada McNeil; *Ref Serv*, Jean E Riedlinger; Staff 5 (MLS 4, Non-MLS 1)
Founded 1969
Library Holdings: Bk Vols 15,000; Per Subs 450

Special Collections: J Bay Jacobs Library for the History of Medicine in Obstetrics & Gynecology in America; Ralph W Hale MD History Museum. Oral History
Subject Interests: Obstetrics & gynecology
Automation Activity & Vendor Info: (Acquisitions) EOS International; (Cataloging) EOS International; (Circulation) EOS International; (OPAC) EOS International; (Serials) EOS International
Wireless access
Publications: Bibliographies
Partic in District of Columbia Area Health Science Libraries

S AMERICAN COUNCIL OF LIFE INSURERS LIBRARY*, Research & Information Center, 101 Constitution Ave NW, 20001-2133. SAN 302-5586. Tel: 202-624-2000. FAX: 202-624-2319. E-mail: library@acli.com. Web Site: www.acli.com. *Library Contact,* Aaron Hoppenstedt; Staff 8 (MLS 7, Non-MLS 1)
Library Holdings: Bk Titles 3,000; Per Subs 1,000
Subject Interests: Benefits, Econ, Statistics
Publications: Acquisitions List; Daily Electronic Newsletter
Open Mon-Fri 9-5
Restriction: Access at librarian's discretion, Non-circulating, Not a lending libr

S AMERICAN FEDERATION OF STATE, COUNTY & MUNICIPAL EMPLOYEES*, Information Center, 1625 L St NW, 20036-5687. SAN 328-6460. Tel: 202-429-1000, 202-429-1215. FAX: 202-223-3255. E-mail: infocenter@afscme.org. Web Site: www.afscmeinfocenter.org. *Dir,* Mark Murphy; *Research Librn,* Lindsay Shapray; E-mail: lshapray@afscme.org; *Research Librn,* Beth Vernaci; E-mail: bvernaci@afscme.org; Staff 4 (MLS 3, Non-MLS 1)
Library Holdings: Bk Vols 5,000; Per Subs 300
Automation Activity & Vendor Info: (Acquisitions) Inmagic, Inc.; (Cataloging) Inmagic, Inc.; (Circulation) Inmagic, Inc.; (OPAC) Inmagic, Inc.; (Serials) Inmagic, Inc.
Wireless access
Restriction: Staff use only

S AMERICAN PHARMACISTS ASSOCIATION LIBRARY*, 2215 Constitution Ave, 20037. SAN 302-5721. Tel: 202-429-7524. FAX: 202-783-2351. Web Site: www.pharmacist.com. *Sr Knowledge Mgmt Specialist,* Gwen Norheim; E-mail: gnorheim@aphanet.org
Founded 1934
Library Holdings: Bk Titles 1,300; Bk Vols 6,000; Per Subs 119
Restriction: Open by appt only

S AMERICAN PSYCHIATRIC ASSOCIATION FOUNDATION, Melvin Sabshin, MD Library & Archives, 800 Maine Ave SW, Ste 900, 20024. SAN 302-5748. Tel: 202-559-3759. E-mail: library@psych.org. Web Site: legacy.psychiatry.org. *Dep Dir,* Amy Porfiri; Tel: 202-683-8312, E-mail: aporfiri@psych.org; *Librn & Archivist,* Deena Gorland; E-mail: dgorland@psych.org; Staff 1 (MLS 1)
Founded 1961
Library Holdings: Bk Titles 2,500
Special Collections: Oral History
Subject Interests: Anthrop, Forensic psychiat & ethics, Hist of psychiat, Neurology, Psychiat
Wireless access
Function: Archival coll, Doc delivery serv, Electronic databases & coll, Health sci info serv, ILL available, Internet access, Mail & tel request accepted, Mail loans to mem, Ref & res
Partic in Association of Mental Health Libraries
Open Mon-Fri 9-4
Restriction: Authorized scholars by appt, External users must contact libr, Fee for pub use, In-house use for visitors, Not a lending libr, Open to researchers by request, Open to staff, students & ancillary prof, Open to students, Researchers by appt only

S AMERICAN PSYCHOLOGICAL ASSOCIATION*, Arthur W Melton Library, 750 First St NE, Rm 3012, 20002-4242. SAN 302-5756. Tel: 202-336-5640. E-mail: lib-staff@apa.org. Web Site: www.apa.org/archives. *Actg Dir,* Elizabeth Deegan; Tel: 202-336-5645, E-mail: edeegan@apa.org; Staff 4 (MLS 2, Non-MLS 2)
Founded 1970
Library Holdings: AV Mats 116; e-journals 62; Bk Titles 7,120; Per Subs 121
Special Collections: American Psychological Association Archives; American Psychological Association Central Office, Division & State Association Publications; Classic Books in Psychology
Subject Interests: Allied disciplines, Mental health, Psychol
Automation Activity & Vendor Info: (Cataloging) Inmagic, Inc.; (Circulation) Inmagic, Inc.; (ILL) Inmagic, Inc.
Wireless access
Function: Archival coll
Publications: APA Convention Directory; Biography Index
Open Mon-Fri 8-5

S AMERICAN PUBLIC TRANSPORTATION ASSOCIATION*, 1300 I St NW, Ste 1200 E, 20005. SAN 371-8654. Tel: 202-496-4800. FAX: 202-496-4324. E-mail: info@apta.com. Web Site: www.apta.com/RESOURCES.
Founded 1915
Library Holdings: Bk Vols 10,000; Per Subs 85
Special Collections: APTA Publications; Fed Transit Agency
Subject Interests: Pub transportation
Automation Activity & Vendor Info: (Cataloging) Inmagic, Inc.
Function: Ref serv available
Publications: Catalog of Member Products & Services (COMPS); Index to Weekly Newspaper; Information Center Brochure; Passenger Transport; Publication Catalog
Restriction: Open by appt only

L AMERICAN SOCIETY OF INTERNATIONAL LAW LIBRARY*, deFord Library & Information Center, 2223 Massachusetts Ave NW, 20008. SAN 302-5802. Tel: 202-939-6017. FAX: 202-319-1670. Web Site: www.asil.org/resources/deford-library-and-information-center. *Dir of Publ(s), Dir, Res,* Justine Stefanelli; E-mail: jstefanelli@asil.org
Founded 1960
Library Holdings: Bk Vols 20,000; Per Subs 125
Subject Interests: Intl law, Intl trade
Publications: Guide to Electronic Resources for International Law
Open Mon-Fri 9-4
Friends of the Library Group

S AMERICAN SOCIETY OF LANDSCAPE ARCHITECTS*, Professional Practice Library, 636 I St NW, 20001-3736. SAN 372-6142. Tel: 202-216-2354. FAX: 202-898-1185. E-mail: aslalibrary@asla.org. Web Site: www.asla.org/LibraryAndResearchServices.aspx. *Dir,* Susan Cahill-Aylward; Tel: 202-216-2320, E-mail: scahill@asla.org; *Archivist, Tech Librn,* Ian Bucacink; E-mail: ibucacink@asla.org; Staff 2 (MLS 2)
Founded 1899
Library Holdings: Bk Titles 2,100; Per Subs 150
Subject Interests: Environ, Hist presv, Infrastructure, Landscape archit, Landscape design, Landscape hist, Planning, Sustainable agr, Transportation, Urban planning, Water
Automation Activity & Vendor Info: (Cataloging) Readerware
Wireless access
Open Mon-Fri 9-5

CL AMERICAN UNIVERSITY*, Pence Law Library, Washington College of Law, 4300 Nebraska Ave NW, 20016-8182. SAN 336-660X. Tel: 202-274-4300. Circulation Tel: 202-274-4351. Interlibrary Loan Service Tel: 202-274-4327. Reference Tel: 202-274-4352. Administration Tel: 202-274-4375. FAX: 202-274-4365. E-mail: reflib@wcl.american.edu. Web Site: library.wcl.american.edu. *Dean,* Camille A Nelson; *Assoc Dean, Info,* Billie Jo Kaufman; Tel: 202-274-4374, E-mail: bkaufman@wcl.american.edu; *Dir, Coll & Circ Operations,* Khelani Clay; Tel: 202-274-4354; *Bibliog Serv, Head, Coll,* Linda Wen; Tel: 202-274-4345; *Acq/Ser Librn,* John A Smith; Tel: 202-274-4354, E-mail: jasmith@wcl.american.edu; *Ref Librn,* John Heywood; Tel: 202-274-4329, E-mail: heywood@american.edu; *Student Serv Librn,* Shannon Roddy; Tel: 202-274-4332, E-mail: roddy@wcl.american.edu; *Assoc Librn, Foreign & Intl Law,* William Ryan; Tel: 202-274-4331, E-mail: wryan@wcl.american.edu; *Cat,* Sima Mirkin; Tel: 202-274-4344, E-mail: smirkin@wcl.american.edu; *Electronic & Ref Serv,* Ripple Weistling; Tel: 202-274-4382, E-mail: rweistling@wcl.american.edu. Subject Specialists: *Intl law,* John Heywood; *Foreign law, Intl law,* William Ryan; *Environ law,* Ripple Weistling; Staff 9 (MLS 9)
Founded 1896. Enrl 1,440; Fac 60; Highest Degree: Doctorate
Library Holdings: Bk Titles 243,746; Bk Vols 585,600; Per Subs 6,761
Special Collections: Goodman Coll of Rare Law Books; National Bankruptcy Review Commission. US Document Depository
Automation Activity & Vendor Info: (Acquisitions) Innovative Interfaces, Inc; (Cataloging) Innovative Interfaces, Inc; (Circulation) Innovative Interfaces, Inc; (Course Reserve) Innovative Interfaces, Inc; (Discovery) EBSCO Discovery Service; (ILL) OCLC; (OPAC) Innovative Interfaces, Inc; (Serials) Innovative Interfaces, Inc
Wireless access
Function: 24/7 Electronic res, 24/7 Online cat, Archival coll, Art exhibits, Computers for patron use, Govt ref serv, Microfiche/film & reading machines, Notary serv, Photocopying/Printing, Printer for laptops & handheld devices, Ref & res, Ref serv available, Scanner, Tax forms, Telephone ref
Partic in NELLCO Law Library Consortium, Inc.; Washington Research Library Consortium
Restriction: Access at librarian's discretion, Authorized patrons, Borrowing privileges limited to fac & registered students, Circ privileges for students & alumni only, In-house use for visitors, Open to students, fac, staff & alumni, Pub access for legal res only, Vols & interns use only

C AMERICAN UNIVERSITY LIBRARY, Jack I & Dorothy G Bender Library & Learning Resources Center, 4400 Massachusetts Ave NW, 20016-8046. SAN 336-657X. Tel: 202-885-3232. Circulation Tel: 202-885-3221. Interlibrary Loan Service Tel: 202-885-3282. Reference Tel: 202-885-3260. Web Site: www.american.edu/library. *Univ Librn,* Jeehyun Davis; E-mail: jeehyundavis@american.edu; *Dir, Acad Tech,* Michael Piller; Tel: 202-885-3228, E-mail: piller@american.edu; *Dir, Admin Serv,* Michele Mikkelsen; Tel: 202-885-3234, E-mail: mmikkel@american.edu; *Dir, Multimedia Coll & Serv,* Christopher Lewis; Tel: 202-885-3257, E-mail: clewis@american.edu; *Dir, Res, Teaching & Learning,* Gwendolyn Reece; Tel: 202-885-3281, E-mail: greece@american.edu; *Dir, Access Serv,* Robert Kelshian; E-mail: calvin@american.edu; *Dir, AV,* Robert Brownlee; Tel: 202-885-2297, E-mail: bbrownlee@american.edu; *Coll Develop,* Martin Shapiro; Tel: 202-885-3854, E-mail: mshapir@american.edu. Subject Specialists: *Media,* Christopher Lewis; Staff 56.6 (MLS 23.6, Non-MLS 33)
Founded 1893. Enrl 11,720; Fac 825; Highest Degree: Doctorate
Library Holdings: DVDs 1,400; e-books 193,000; e-journals 14,374; Music Scores 13,000; Bk Vols 1,000,000; Per Subs 4,200; Videos 9,300
Special Collections: Asia & the East, Japanese Culture (Spinks Coll); Drew Pearson Coll; Friends of Colombia Archives; John Hickman Coll; Mathematics (Artemas Martin Coll); Papers of the National Commission on the Public Service; Peace Corps Community Archive; Records of the National Peace Corps Association Archives; Theatre Play Bill Coll
Subject Interests: Art, Bus & mgt, Econ, Hist, Humanities, Intl studies, Polit sci
Automation Activity & Vendor Info: (Acquisitions) Ex Libris Group; (Cataloging) Ex Libris Group; (Circulation) Ex Libris Group; (Course Reserve) Atlas Systems; (ILL) OCLC ILLiad; (Media Booking) Ex Libris Group; (OPAC) Ex Libris Group; (Serials) SerialsSolutions
Wireless access
Partic in OCLC Online Computer Library Center, Inc
Friends of the Library Group

Departmental Libraries:

MUSIC LIBRARY, Katzen Arts Ctr, Rm 150, 4400 Massachusetts Ave NW, 20016-8046, SAN 336-6634. Tel: 202-885-3524. FAX: 202-885-3226. Web Site: american.edu/library/music. *Music & Performing Arts Librn,* Nobue Matsuoka; Tel: 202-885-3465, E-mail: nobue@american.edu; Staff 2 (MLS 1, Non-MLS 1)
Founded 1966
Library Holdings: CDs 10,000; Music Scores 15,000
Partic in OCLC Online Computer Library Center, Inc
Open Mon-Thurs 9-8, Fri 9-5, Sat 11-4

L ARENT FOX PLLC LIBRARY*, 1717 K St NW, 20006. SAN 326-9191. Tel: 202-857-6000. FAX: 202-857-6395. Web Site: www.arentfox.com. *Librn,* Pamela Lipscomb; E-mail: lipscomb.pamela@arentfox.com
Library Holdings: Bk Vols 60,000; Per Subs 400
Open Mon-Fri 9-5

S ARMY & NAVY CLUB LIBRARY*, 901 17th St NW, 20006. SAN 302-587X. Tel: 202-628-8400, Ext 386, 202-721-2096. FAX: 202-296-8787. E-mail: library@armynavyclub.org. Web Site: www.armynavyclub.org. *Librn,* Aleksandra M Zajackowski
Founded 1885
Library Holdings: Bk Titles 18,000; Bk Vols 20,000; Per Subs 40
Special Collections: Reginald W Oakie Coll of Civil War Stereographs; Writings of Club Members
Wireless access
Open Mon-Sun 7am-11pm

L ARNOLD & PORTER LIBRARY*, 601 Massachusetts Ave NW, 20001-3743. SAN 302-5888. Tel: 202-942-5000. Interlibrary Loan Service Tel: 202-942-5370. Reference Tel: 202-942-5427. FAX: 202-942-5999. Web Site: www.arnoldporter.com. *Dir,* Ellen Callinan; Staff 13 (MLS 6, Non-MLS 7)
Library Holdings: Bk Vols 70,000; Per Subs 350
Subject Interests: Law, Legislation
Automation Activity & Vendor Info: (Acquisitions) EOS International; (Cataloging) EOS International; (Circulation) EOS International; (ILL) EOS International; (OPAC) EOS International; (Serials) EOS International
Publications: Miscellaneous Research Guides; Monthly Accessions List
Restriction: Not open to pub

S ASPIRA ASSOCIATION LIBRARY*, 1220 L St NW, Ste 701, 20005. SAN 373-0379. Tel: 202-759-5181. E-mail: info@aspiradc.org. Web Site: www.aspira.org. *VPres,* Hilda Crespo; E-mail: hcrespo@aspiradc.org
Library Holdings: Electronic Media & Resources 1,000
Special Collections: Puerto Rican Art & Culture Coll
Wireless access
Open Mon-Fri 9-5

S ASSOCIATION OF GOVERNING BOARDS OF UNIVERSITIES & COLLEGES*, Zwingle Library & Resource Center, 1133 20th St NW, Ste 300, 20036. SAN 326-3193. Administration Toll Free Tel: 800-356-6317. FAX: 202-223-7053. Web Site: www.agb.org/zwingle-library-and-resource-center-academic-trusteeship-and-governance. Staff 1.2 (MLS 1.2)
Founded 1975
Library Holdings: Bk Titles 10,000; Per Subs 43
Subject Interests: Govt, Higher educ
Automation Activity & Vendor Info: (OPAC) Inmagic, Inc.
Function: Res libr
Restriction: Circulates for staff only, Mem only

L BAKER & MCKENZIE LLP LIBRARY*, 815 Connecticut Ave NW, Ste 900, 20006. SAN 326-2162. Tel: 202-452-7070. FAX: 202-452-7074. Web Site: www.bakermckenzie.com. Staff 3 (MLS 1, Non-MLS 2)
Library Holdings: Bk Titles 3,500; Bk Vols 20,000; Per Subs 70
Subject Interests: Corporate law, Intl law, Intl trade, Taxation
Automation Activity & Vendor Info: (Acquisitions) SydneyPlus; (Cataloging) SydneyPlus; (Circulation) SydneyPlus; (Course Reserve) SydneyPlus; (ILL) SydneyPlus; (Media Booking) SydneyPlus; (OPAC) SydneyPlus; (Serials) SydneyPlus
Open Mon-Fri 9-5:30

L BAKER BOTTS LLP*, Law Library, 1299 Pennsylvania Ave NW, 20004-2400. SAN 377-3604. Tel: 202-639-7967. FAX: 202-639-7890. Web Site: www.bakerbotts.com. *Libr Mgr,* Edward O'Rourke; E-mail: edward.orourke@bakerbotts.com; Staff 3 (MLS 2, Non-MLS 1)
Library Holdings: Bk Vols 25,000; Per Subs 250
Automation Activity & Vendor Info: (Cataloging) Inmagic, Inc.; (Circulation) Inmagic, Inc.; (OPAC) Inmagic, Inc.
Wireless access
Partic in DC Soc of Law Librs
Open Mon-Fri 9-5

L BAKERHOSTETLER*, Law Library, Washington Sq, Ste 1100, 1050 Connecticut Ave NW, 20036. SAN 377-3019. Tel: 202-861-1500. FAX: 202-861-1783. E-mail: legalcontentservices@bakerlaw.com. Web Site: www.bakerlaw.com/WashingtonDC. *Librn,* Steve LaFalce; Tel: 202-861-1578
Library Holdings: Bk Vols 25,000; Per Subs 50
Open Mon-Fri 8-6

L BALLARD SPAHR LLP*, Law Library, 1909 K St NW, 20006-1157. SAN 372-3887. Tel: 202-661-2200. FAX: 202-661-2299. Web Site: www.ballardspahr.com. *Dir,* John Harbison
Library Holdings: Bk Vols 10,000
Subject Interests: Commercial law
Restriction: Staff use only

L BEVERIDGE & DIAMOND, PC LIBRARY*, 1900 N St NW, Ste 100, 20036. SAN 377-2993. Tel: 202-789-6000. FAX: 202-789-6190. Web Site: www.bdlaw.com. *Librn,* Laura Grimm; *Librn,* Scott Larson; E-mail: slarson@bdlaw.com
Library Holdings: Bk Vols 10,000; Per Subs 300
Subject Interests: Environ law
Restriction: Staff use only

BOARD OF GOVERNORS OF THE FEDERAL RESERVE SYSTEM

GL LAW LIBRARY*, 20th & C St NW, MS 7, 20551, SAN 336-6723. Tel: 202-452-3040. Interlibrary Loan Service Tel: 202-452-2454. Reference Tel: 202-452-3283. FAX: 202-452-3101. Web Site: www.federalreserve.gov. ; Staff 4 (MLS 3, Non-MLS 1)
Founded 1975
Library Holdings: Bk Vols 30,000; Per Subs 500
Special Collections: Congressional (Legislative History Coll of Banking-Related Statutes of the US), micro. US Document Depository
Subject Interests: Admin law, Banking law
Publications: Current Legislative & Regulatory Activity; Recent Law Journal Articles of Interest; Textual Changes in the Federal Reserve Act
Restriction: Open by appt only

G RESEARCH LIBRARY*, 20th & C St NW, MS 102, 20551, SAN 336-6758. Tel: 202-452-3333. FAX: 202-530-6222. *Chief Librn,* Kristin Vajs; *Lead Librn, Data Contracts,* Christine Black; *Lead Librn, Tech Serv,* Jane Olvera; *Sr Librn, Acq & Per,* Anna Harkins; *Sr Librn, Data Contracts,* Jasmine Griffiths; *Sr Librn, Data Contracts,* Alison Labonte; *Sr Librn, Tech Serv,* Marlene Vikor; *Sr Res Librn,* Krista Box; *Sr Res Librn,* Sian Seldin; *Tech & Acq Librn,* Yin Zhu; Staff 14 (MLS 12, Non-MLS 2)
Founded 1914
Library Holdings: Bk Vols 62,000; Per Subs 1,200
Special Collections: Federal Reserve System; Foreign Central Bank Publications
Subject Interests: Banks & banking, Econ, Finance, Monetary policy
Automation Activity & Vendor Info: (Acquisitions) Innovative Interfaces, Inc; (Cataloging) Innovative Interfaces, Inc; (Circulation)

Innovative Interfaces, Inc; (ILL) Innovative Interfaces, Inc; (OPAC) Innovative Interfaces, Inc; (Serials) Innovative Interfaces, Inc
Partic in OCLC Online Computer Library Center, Inc
Publications: Recent Acquisitions
Restriction: Open by appt only
Friends of the Library Group

L BRACEWELL LLP*, Law Library, 2001 M St NW, Ste 900, 20036. SAN 372-1728. Tel: 202-828-5800. FAX: 202-223-1225. Web Site: bracewelllaw.com. *Librn,* Ruth Mendelson
Library Holdings: Bk Vols 10,000; Per Subs 25
Subject Interests: Admin law, Environ law
Automation Activity & Vendor Info: (Acquisitions) Sydney
Partic in OCLC Online Computer Library Center, Inc
Restriction: Staff use only

S BREAD FOR THE WORLD LIBRARY, 425 Third St SW, Ste 1200, 20024. SAN 329-0514. Tel: 202-639-9400. Administration Tel: 202-688-1082. Web Site: www.bread.org. *Librn,* Christine Matthews; E-mail: cmatthews@bread.org; Staff 1 (MLS 1)
Library Holdings: Bk Titles 2,000; Per Subs 20
Subject Interests: Agr, Christian perspective, Climate change, Foreign aid, Gender, Hunger, Immigration, Intl develop, Nutrition, Poverty, Trade, US budget
Automation Activity & Vendor Info: (OPAC) Inmagic, Inc.
Wireless access
Function: For res purposes
Restriction: Open by appt only

S BROOKINGS INSTITUTION LIBRARY*, 1775 Massachusetts Ave NW, 20036. SAN 302-6019. Tel: 202-797-6240. Circulation E-mail: circdesk@brookings.edu. Web Site: brookings.edu/about-us/research-library-and-archives. *Libr Dir,* Cy Behroozi; E-mail: cbehroozi@brookings.edu; *Archives, Sr Res Librn,* Sarah Chilton; E-mail: schilton@brookings.edu; *Coll Develop Librn,* Elif Ecer; E-mail: eecer@brookings.edu; *ILL, Research Librn,* Laura Mooney; E-mail: lmooney@brookings.edu; *Cat, Tech Serv Librn,* David Bair; E-mail: dbair@brookings.edu; Staff 6 (MLS 5, Non-MLS 1)
Founded 1927
Library Holdings: Bk Vols 68,000; Per Subs 250
Subject Interests: Econ, Intl relations, Soc sci, Urban policy, US govt
Automation Activity & Vendor Info: (Cataloging) SirsiDynix; (Circulation) SirsiDynix; (OPAC) SirsiDynix
Wireless access
Restriction: Not open to pub

L BRYAN CAVE LEIGHTON PAISNER LAW LIBRARY*, 1155 F St, 20004-1357. SAN 377-2977. Tel: 202-508-6000. Reference Tel: 202-508-6115. FAX: 202-508-6200. *Chief Libr Officer, Res Officer,* Judith L Harris; Tel: 314-259-2298, E-mail: jlharris@bclplaw.com; Staff 3 (MLS 2, Non-MLS 1)
Library Holdings: Bk Vols 10,000; Per Subs 200
Automation Activity & Vendor Info: (Acquisitions) Inmagic, Inc.; (Cataloging) Inmagic, Inc.; (ILL) Inmagic, Inc.; (Serials) Inmagic, Inc.
Open Mon-Fri 9-6:30

L CADWALADER, WICKERSHAM & TAFT*, Law Library, 700 Sixth St NW, Ste 300, 20001. SAN 372-1442. Tel: 202-862-2289. FAX: 202-862-2400. Web Site: www.cadwalader.com. *Librn,* Jacqueline Henderson; E-mail: jacqueline.henderson@cwt.com; Staff 2 (MLS 1, Non-MLS 1)
Library Holdings: Bk Vols 9,000; Per Subs 45
Automation Activity & Vendor Info: (Cataloging) SIMA, Inc; (Serials) SIMA, Inc
Wireless access
Restriction: Staff use only

L CAHILL, GORDON & REINDEL LIBRARY*, 1990 K St NW, Ste 950, 20006. SAN 302-6043. FAX: 202-862-8958. Web Site: www.cahill.com. *Dir, Libr Res Serv,* Gina Cartusciello; Tel: 212-701-3541, E-mail: gcartusciello@cahill.com
Library Holdings: Bk Vols 3,000; Per Subs 25
Open Mon-Fri 9:30-5:30

L CAPLIN & DRYSDALE LIBRARY*, One Thomas Circle, NW, Ste 1100, 20005-5802. SAN 302-606X. Tel: 202-862-5073. FAX: 202-429-3301. E-mail: library@capdale.com. Web Site: www.caplindrysdale.com. *Mgr, Libr Serv,* Nalini Rajguru; *Ref Librn,* Abby Dos Santos; Tel: 202-862-7835, E-mail: adossantos@capdale.com; Staff 4 (MLS 3, Non-MLS 1)
Founded 1969
Library Holdings: Bk Titles 4,911; Bk Vols 15,010; Per Subs 50
Automation Activity & Vendor Info: (Acquisitions) Inmagic, Inc.; (Cataloging) Inmagic, Inc.; (OPAC) Inmagic, Inc.; (Serials) Inmagic, Inc.
Wireless access
Function: ILL available
Open Mon-Fri 9-5:30

C CAPUCHIN COLLEGE LIBRARY*, 4121 Harewood Rd NE, 20017. SAN 302-6078. Tel: 202-529-2188. FAX: 202-526-6664. *Librn,* Sonia Bernardo; Staff 1 (MLS 1)
Library Holdings: CDs 26; Bk Titles 2,500; Bk Vols 75,000; Per Subs 25
Subject Interests: Catholicism, Theol

S CARNEGIE ENDOWMENT FOR INTERNATIONAL PEACE LIBRARY*, 1779 Massachusetts Ave NW, 20036. SAN 328-5189. Tel: 202-939-2256. FAX: 202-483-4462. E-mail: Library@ceip.org. Web Site: www.carnegieendowment.org/about/library. *Libr Dir,* Martha Higgins; E-mail: martha.higgins@ceip.org
Library Holdings: Bk Vols 8,500; Per Subs 150
Subject Interests: Foreign policy
Automation Activity & Vendor Info: (Acquisitions) EOS International; (Cataloging) EOS International; (Circulation) EOS International; (ILL) OCLC; (OPAC) EOS International
Open Mon-Fri 9-5

C CATHOLIC UNIVERSITY OF AMERICA*, John K Mullen of Denver Memorial Library, 315 Mullen Library, 620 Michigan Ave NE, 20064. SAN 336-6871. Tel: 202-319-5055. Circulation Tel: 202-319-5060. Interlibrary Loan Service Tel: 202-319-5063. Reference Tel: 202-319-5070. Web Site: libraries.cua.edu. *Univ Librn,* Stephen Connaghan; E-mail: connaghan@cua.edu; *Dir, Res Mgt & Digital Serv,* Elzbieta Rymsza-Pawlowska; Tel: 202-319-5554, E-mail: pawlowska@cua.edu; *Dir, Res & Instruction Serv,* Joan Stahl; Tel: 202-319-6473, E-mail: stahlj@cua.edu; *Bus Mgr,* Mary Mathews; Tel: 202-319-5464, E-mail: mathews@cua.edu; Staff 132 (MLS 30, Non-MLS 102)
Founded 1889. Enrl 6,201; Fac 400; Highest Degree: Doctorate
Apr 2012-Mar 2013. Mats Exp $3,847,207, Books $439,600, Per/Ser (Incl. Access Fees) $1,803,000, Other Print Mats $110,000, Micro $34,380, AV Mat $3,267, Electronic Ref Mat (Incl. Access Fees) $1,409,960, Presv $47,000. Sal $3,245,160 (Prof $1,675,208)
Library Holdings: Audiobooks 42,687; AV Mats 52,786; DVDs 507; e-books 51,114; e-journals 42,560; Electronic Media & Resources 9,619; Bk Vols 1,444,018; Per Subs 9,720; Spec Interest Per Sub 46; Videos 8,682
Special Collections: Catholic Americana; Celtic Coll; Knights of Malta Coll; Library of Pope Clement XI (Clementine Library); Luso-Brazilian Studies (Oliveira Lima Library); Semitic & Egyptian Languages & Literatures
Subject Interests: Canon law, Church hist, Greek, Immigration, Labor, Latin, Medieval studies, Patristics
Automation Activity & Vendor Info: (Acquisitions) Ex Libris Group; (Cataloging) Ex Libris Group; (Circulation) Ex Libris Group; (Course Reserve) Ex Libris Group; (ILL) Ex Libris Group; (Media Booking) Ex Libris Group; (OPAC) Ex Libris Group; (Serials) Ex Libris Group
Wireless access
Function: Archival coll, Distance learning, Doc delivery serv, ILL available, Magnifiers for reading, Photocopying/Printing, Ref serv available, Res libr, Telephone ref, Wheelchair accessible
Partic in Washington Research Library Consortium; Washington Theological Consortium
Special Services for the Deaf - Bks on deafness & sign lang; TDD equip; TTY equip
Special Services for the Blind - Reader equip
Open Mon-Thurs 8am-11pm, Fri 8am-10pm, Sat 9-8, Sun 11am-11pm
Restriction: Open to pub for ref & circ; with some limitations, Open to students, fac & staff

Departmental Libraries:

CL JUDGE KATHRYN J DUFOUR LAW LIBRARY, 3600 John McCormack Rd NE, 20064, SAN 336-6995. Tel: 202-319-5156. Reference Tel: 202-319-6284. Web Site: www.law.edu/about-us/law-library. *Dir,* Elizabeth Edinger; Tel: 202-319-5228, E-mail: edinger@law.edu; Staff 22 (MLS 10, Non-MLS 12)
Founded 1898
Library Holdings: Bk Vols 400,000; Per Subs 4,853
Open Mon-Thurs 7:30am-11pm, Fri 7:30am-9pm, Sat 9-9, Sun 10am-10:30pm

OLIVEIRA LIMA LIBRARY, 22 Mullen Library, 620 Michigan Ave NE, 20064, SAN 336-7118. Tel: 202-319-5059. E-mail: cua-limalibrary@cua.edu. Web Site: libraries.catholic.edu/special-collections/oliveira-lima-library. *Dir,* Dr Nathalia Henrich; Tel: 202-319-6442, E-mail: henrich@cua.edu
Library Holdings: Bk Vols 59,000
Open Mon-Fri 10-Noon & 1-4

RARE BOOKS SPECIAL COLLECTIONS, 214 Mullen Library, 620 Michigan Ave NE, 20064, SAN 336-6936. Tel: 202-319-5091. E-mail: lib-rarebooks@cua.edu. Web Site: libraries.catholic.edu/special-collections/rare-books. *Univ Archivist &*

Head, Spec Coll, W John Shepherd; Tel: 202-319-5065, E-mail: shepherw@cua.edu
Function: ILL available
Restriction: Open by appt only, Open to researchers by request
REFERENCE & INSTRUCTIONAL SERVICES DIVISION, 124 Mullen Library, 620 Michigan Ave NE, 20064, SAN 336-7142. Tel: 202-319-5070. *Res & Instruction Librn,* Julie Loy; Tel: 202-319-5548, E-mail: loy@cua.edu

CR RELIGIOUS STUDIES-PHILOSOPHY & CANON LAW, 316A Mullen Library, 620 Michigan Ave NE, 20064, SAN 336-7150. Tel: 202-319-5071. *Relig Studies Librn,* Taras Zvir; E-mail: zvir@cua.edu
Open Mon-Thurs 8am-11pm, Fri 8am-10pm, Sat 9-8, Sun 11am-11pm

CR SEMITICS/ICOR LIBRARY, 035 Mullen Library, 620 Michigan Ave NE, 20064, SAN 336-7207. Tel: 202-319-4532. Web Site: libraries.catholic.edu/special-collections/semitics-icor-library. *Curator,* Dr Monica Blanchard; E-mail: Blanchard@cua.edu
Library Holdings: CDs 35; DVDs 15; Bk Vols 46,950; Per Subs 763
Special Collections: Ostraca & Papyri Colls; Syriac Digital Library Projects, bks, maps, ms, photog & other doc; Syriac Studies Reference Library
Open Mon-Fri 9-5 by appointment

M CENTER FOR MOLECULAR NUTRITION & SENSORY DISORDERS*, Taste & Smell Clinic Library, 5125 MacArthur Blvd NW, Ste 20, 20016. SAN 371-8255. Tel: 202-364-4180. Toll Free Tel: 877-697-6355. FAX: 202-364-9727. E-mail: Doc@TasteandSmell.com. Web Site: www.tasteandsmell.com. *Chief Librn,* Dr Robert I Henkin
Founded 1975
Library Holdings: Bk Titles 1,000; Per Subs 90; Spec Interest Per Sub 60
Special Collections: Dan Bradley Coll; R I Henkin Coll
Subject Interests: Taste & smell pathology & physiology

S CENTER ON CONSCIENCE & WAR LIBRARY, 1830 Connecticut Ave NW, 20009-5706. SAN 370-7547. Tel: 202-483-2220. FAX: 202-483-1246. E-mail: ccw@centeronconscience.org. Web Site: www.centeronconscience.org.
Founded 1940
Library Holdings: Bk Titles 350; Bk Vols 400; Per Subs 15
Special Collections: Conscientious Objection; Military Conscription & Military Service; Selective Service System & the Draft
Wireless access
Restriction: By permission only, Non-circulating of rare bks, Open by appt only, Pub use on premises, Visitors must make appt to use bks in the libr

S COSMOS CLUB LIBRARY*, 2121 Massachusetts Ave NW, 20008. SAN 377-2381. Tel: 202-387-7783, Ext 1525, 202-939-1525. FAX: 202-234-6817. Web Site: www.cosmosclub.org. *Head, Coll Mgt, Librn,* Thad Garrett; E-mail: tgarrett@cosmosclub.org; Staff 1 (MLS 1)
Library Holdings: Audiobooks 50; CDs 100; DVDs 50; e-journals 30; Per Subs 130; Videos 200
Special Collections: Cosmos Club Members Oral History Coll; John Wesley Powell Coll (Powelliana). Oral History
Automation Activity & Vendor Info: (Acquisitions) Inmagic, Inc.; (Cataloging) Inmagic, Inc.; (Circulation) Inmagic, Inc.; (Course Reserve) Inmagic, Inc.; (ILL) Inmagic, Inc.; (Media Booking) Inmagic, Inc.; (OPAC) Inmagic, Inc.; (Serials) Inmagic, Inc.
Wireless access
Function: Archival coll, Bk club(s), Bks on CD, Computers for patron use, Online cat, Ref & res, Spoken cassettes & CDs
Partic in DC Libr Asn
Restriction: Circ to mem only, Not a lending libr, Not open to pub, Private libr

S COUNCIL FOR ADVANCEMENT & SUPPORT OF EDUCATION*, CASE Information Center, 1307 New York Ave, Ste 1000, 20005-4701. SAN 302-6256. Tel: 202-328-2273. E-mail: library@case.org. Web Site: www.case.org.
Founded 1974
Subject Interests: Commun, Fundraising, Mkt
Restriction: Mem only, Open by appt only

S COUNCIL ON FOUNDATIONS, Knowledge Center, 1255 23rd St NW, Ste 200, 20037. SAN 375-1031. Tel: 202-991-2225. E-mail: knowledge@cof.org. Web Site: www.cof.org/person/knowledge-center.
Founded 1985
Library Holdings: Bk Titles 3,000; Bk Vols 4,500; Per Subs 15
Subject Interests: Philanthropy
Automation Activity & Vendor Info: (Acquisitions) Inmagic, Inc.; (Cataloging) Inmagic, Inc.; (Circulation) Inmagic, Inc.; (OPAC) Inmagic, Inc.; (Serials) Inmagic, Inc.
Function: For res purposes
Restriction: Mem only, Open by appt only

L COVINGTON & BURLING LLP*, Law Library, One City Ctr, 850 Tenth St, NW, 20001. SAN 302-6264. Tel: 202-662-6158. FAX: 202-778-6658. Web Site: www.cov.com. *Dir, Libr Serv,* Jennifer Korpacz Pelaia; E-mail: jpelaia@cov.com; *ILL Librn,* Lawrence Simpson Guthrie, II; E-mail: lguthrie@cov.com; Staff 9 (MLS 8, Non-MLS 1)
Founded 1919
Library Holdings: Bk Vols 75,000; Per Subs 200
Special Collections: Food & Drug Library; Legislative History Coll
Subject Interests: Antitrust, Bankruptcy, Drug, Food, Intellectual property, Intl law, Legis, Sports law
Automation Activity & Vendor Info: (Cataloging) EOS International; (Circulation) EOS International; (ILL) OCLC; (Serials) EOS International
Wireless access
Function: ILL available
Partic in OCLC Online Computer Library Center, Inc
Restriction: Borrowing requests are handled by ILL

G DC COURT OF APPEALS LIBRARY*, 430 E St NW, Rm 203, 20001. SAN 374-6143. Tel: 202-879-2767. FAX: 202-879-9912. *Librn,* Laura Moorer; E-mail: lmoorer@dcappeal.gov; Staff 1 (MLS 1)
Founded 1977
Library Holdings: Bk Vols 20,000
Wireless access
Restriction: Staff use only

L DEBEVOISE & PLIMPTON*, Law Library, 801 Pennsylvania Ave NW, 20004. SAN 377-3523. Tel: 202-383-8055, 202-383-8075. FAX: 202-383-8118. Web Site: www.debevoise.com. *Libr Mgr,* Helen Fiori; E-mail: hefiori@debevoise.com
Library Holdings: Bk Titles 10,000; Bk Vols 15,000; Per Subs 65
Open Mon-Fri 9:30-5:30

L DECHERT LLP*, Law Library, 1900 K St NW, 20006-1110. SAN 372-3445. Tel: 202-261-7909. FAX: 202-261-3333. Web Site: www.dechert.com. *Librn,* David W Lang; E-mail: david.lang@dechert.com. Subject Specialists: *Securities law,* David W Lang; Staff 1 (MLS 1)
Library Holdings: Bk Vols 5,000; Per Subs 50
Subject Interests: Securities law
Function: ILL available
Restriction: Not open to pub

M DEPARTMENT OF BEHAVIORAL HEALTH, ST ELIZABETHS HOSPITAL*, Frances N Waldrop Health Sciences Library, 1100 Alabama Ave SE, 20032. SAN 373-0395. Tel: 202-299-5997. Reference Tel: 202-299-5203. E-mail: seh.library@dc.gov. *Health Sci Librn,* Toni Yancey; E-mail: toni.yancey@dc.gov; Staff 2 (MLS 1, Non-MLS 1)
Library Holdings: Bk Vols 12,000
Special Collections: William Alanson White (Coll of over 900 Titles on the social sciences collected by the superintendent of Saint Elizabeths Hospital 1903-1937 dating back to the 1900s.)
Subject Interests: Behav health, Mental health, Psychiat, Psychoanalysis, Psychol
Automation Activity & Vendor Info: (Acquisitions) CyberTools for Libraries; (Cataloging) CyberTools for Libraries; (OPAC) CyberTools for Libraries; (Serials) CyberTools for Libraries
Wireless access
Partic in National Network of Libraries of Medicine Region 1
Restriction: Lending to staff only, Researchers by appt only, Staff use only

DEPARTMENT OF VETERANS AFFAIRS

GM CENTRAL OFFICE LIBRARY*, 810 Vermont Ave NW, 20420, SAN 337-2510. Tel: 202-273-8523. FAX: 202-273-9125. *Chief Librn,* Caryl Kazen; E-mail: caryl.kazen@va.gov; *ILL,* Robyn Washington; Tel: 202-273-8520; Staff 2 (MLS 2)
Founded 1923
Library Holdings: Bk Vols 7,000; Per Subs 208
Special Collections: US Document Depository
Subject Interests: Med, Mil hist, Veterans
Open Mon-Fri 8-5

GM MEDICAL CENTER LIBRARY*, 50 Irving St NW, 20422, SAN 337-260X. Tel: 202-745-8262. FAX: 202-745-8632.
Library Holdings: Bk Vols 2,171; Per Subs 319
Subject Interests: Clinical med
Partic in National Network of Libraries of Medicine Region 1
Open Mon-Fri 8-4:30

GL OFFICE OF THE GENERAL COUNSEL LAW LIBRARY*, 810 Vermont Ave NW, 20420, SAN 337-257X. Tel: 202-273-6558. FAX: 202-273-6645. Web Site: www.va.gov/ogc. *Librn,* Susan Sokoll; E-mail: susan.sokoll@va.gov; Staff 3 (MLS 1, Non-MLS 2)
Library Holdings: Bk Vols 25,120; Per Subs 21
Restriction: Not open to pub

S DISTANCE EDUCATION ACCREDITING COMMISSION*, 1101 17th St NW, Ste 808, 20036. SAN 327-1293. Tel: 202-234-5100. FAX: 202-332-1386. E-mail: info@deac.org. Web Site: www.deac.org. *Exec Dir,* Leah K Matthews; Tel: 202-234-5100, Ext 101, E-mail: leah.matthews@deac.org
Founded 1926
Library Holdings: Bk Titles 1,500
Subject Interests: Distance educ
Restriction: Non-circulating to the pub, Open by appt only

S DISTRICT OF COLUMBIA DEPARTMENT OF CORRECTIONS*, Correctional Treatment Facility Law Library, 1901 D St SE, 20003. SAN 377-1229. Tel: 202-523-7259. FAX: 202-698-3301. *Law Librn,* Gwendolyn Holden; Staff 2 (MLS 2)
Library Holdings: Bk Titles 15,000
Restriction: Not open to pub

P DISTRICT OF COLUMBIA PUBLIC LIBRARY*, Administration, 1990 K St NW, 20006. SAN 336-9366. Tel: 202-727-1101. Information Services Tel: 202-727-0321, 202-727-0324. FAX: 202-727-1129. Web Site: www.dclibrary.org. *Exec Dir,* Richard Reyes-Gavilan; E-mail: richard.reyes-gavilan@dc.gov; *Exec Officer,* Gary Romero; E-mail: gary.romero@dc.gov; *Dir, Communications,* Position Currently Open; *Human Res, Interim Dir,* Jaki Buckley; E-mail: jaki.buckley@dc.gov; *Chief Info Officer, Dir, Info Tech,* Lami Aromire; E-mail: lami.aromire@dc.gov; *Assoc Dir, Coll,* Sheryl Katzin; E-mail: sheryl.katzin@dc.gov
Founded 1896. Pop 591,833; Circ 1,781,862
Library Holdings: Audiobooks 37,346; AV Mats 15,853; Bks on Deafness & Sign Lang 285; Braille Volumes 1,189; CDs 37,117; DVDs 137,999; e-books 29,900; Electronic Media & Resources 77; Large Print Bks 14,860; Microforms 4; Music Scores 25,012; Bk Titles 459,023; Bk Vols 1,802,305; Per Subs 2,309; Talking Bks 88,005; Videos 1,454
Special Collections: African-American Studies; Washingtoniana. Oral History; State Document Depository; US Document Depository
Automation Activity & Vendor Info: (Acquisitions) SirsiDynix; (Cataloging) SirsiDynix; (Circulation) SirsiDynix; (OPAC) SirsiDynix
Wireless access
Publications: Beyond Words (Newsletter)
Special Services for the Deaf - Am sign lang & deaf culture; Assistive tech; Bks on deafness & sign lang; Deaf publ; Lecture on deaf culture; TTY equip; Video relay services
Special Services for the Blind - Accessible computers; Assistive/Adapted tech devices, equip & products; Bks on CD; Large print bks; Playaways (bks on MP3); Spec prog; Talking bks
Open Mon-Fri 9-5
Friends of the Library Group
Branches: 27
ANACOSTIA, 1800 Good Hope Rd SE, 20020. Tel: 202-715-7707, 202-715-7708. E-mail: anacostialibrary@dc.gov. Web Site: www.dclibrary.org/anacostia. *Mgr,* Yvette Davis
Open Mon-Thurs 9:30-9, Fri & Sat 9:30-5:30, Sun 1-5
Friends of the Library Group
CAPITOL VIEW BRANCH, 5001 Central Ave SE, 20019. Tel: 202-645-0755. E-mail: capitolviewlibrary@dc.gov. Web Site: www.dclibrary.org/capitolview. *Br Mgr,* Marcus Wade
Library Holdings: Bk Vols 20,000
Open Mon-Thurs 9:30-9, Fri & Sat 9:30-5:30, Sun 1-5
Friends of the Library Group
CHEVY CHASE, 5625 Connecticut Ave NW, 20015, SAN 336-948X. Tel: 202-282-0021. E-mail: chevychaselibrary@dc.gov. Web Site: www.dclibrary.org/chevychase. *Mgr,* Tracy Myers; E-mail: tracy.myers@dc.gov
Library Holdings: Bk Vols 106,710
Open Mon-Thurs 9:30-9, Fri & Sat 9:30-5:30, Sun 1-5
Friends of the Library Group
CLEVELAND PARK, 3310 Connecticut Ave NW, 20008, SAN 336-9544. Tel: 202-282-3080. E-mail: clevelandparklibrary@dc.gov. Web Site: www.dclibrary.org/clevelandpark. *Mgr,* Heather Scott; E-mail: heather.scott@dc.gov
Library Holdings: Bk Vols 98,976
Open Mon-Thurs 9:30-9, Fri & Sat 9:30-5:30, Sun 1-5
Friends of the Library Group
WATHA T DANIEL/SHAW NEIGHBORHOOD LIBRARY, 1630 Seventh St NW, 20001. Tel: 202-727-1288. E-mail: wathashawlibrary@dc.gov. Web Site: www.dclibrary.org/watha. *Mgr,* Position Currently Open
Special Collections: Graphic Novel Coll
Subject Interests: Adult & young adult prog
Open Mon-Thurs 9:30-9, Fri & Sat 9:30-5:30, Sun 1-5
Friends of the Library Group
DEANWOOD, 1350 49th St NE, 20019. Tel: 202-698-1175. E-mail: deanwoodlibrary@dc.gov. Web Site: www.dclibrary.org/deanwood. *Mgr,* Position Currently Open
Open Mon, Wed & Fri 9:30-5:30, Tues 1-9, Thurs 9:30-9, Sat 9-5, Sun 1-5
GEORGETOWN, 3260 R St NW, 20007, SAN 336-9633. Tel: 202-727-0232. E-mail: georgetownlibrary@dc.gov. Web Site: www.dclibrary.org/georgetown. *Mgr,* Linda Jones; E-mail: linda.jones4@dc.gov
Library Holdings: Bk Vols 90,408
Subject Interests: Local hist
Open Mon-Thurs 9:30-9, Fri & Sat 9:30-5:30, Sun 1-5
Friends of the Library Group
FRANCIS A GREGORY NEIGHBORHOOD, 3660 Alabama Ave SE, 20020, SAN 336-9609. Tel: 202-698-6373. E-mail: francisgregorylibrary@dc.gov. Web Site: www.dclibrary.org/francis. *Mgr,* Maria Escher; E-mail: maria.escher@dc.gov
Library Holdings: Bk Vols 50,000
Open Mon-Thurs 9:30-9, Fri & Sat 9:30-5:30, Sun 1-5
Friends of the Library Group
DOROTHY I HEIGHT/BENNING NEIGHBORHOOD LIBRARY, 3935 Benning Rd NE, 20019, SAN 336-9455. Tel: 202-281-2583. E-mail: benninglibrary@dc.gov. Web Site: www.dclibrary.org/benning. *Mgr,* Winnell Morris Montague; E-mail: winnell.montague@dc.gov. Subject Specialists: *Mgt,* Winnell Morris Montague
Library Holdings: Bk Vols 40,000
Open Mon-Thurs 9:30-9, Fri & Sat 9:30-5:30, Sun 1-5
Friends of the Library Group
MARTIN LUTHER KING JR MEMORIAL, 901 G St NW, 20001-4531. Tel: 202-727-0321. FAX: 202-727-0321. E-mail: mlkjrlibrary@dc.gov.
Library Holdings: Bk Vols 875,580
Special Collections: The Black Studies Center; The Children's Illustrator Coll; The District of Columbia Community Archives; Washingtoniana
Special Services for the Deaf - Accessible learning ctr; ADA equip; Assisted listening device; Assistive tech; Bks on deafness & sign lang; Closed caption videos; Coll on deaf educ; Deaf publ; Described encaptioned media prog; Staff with knowledge of sign lang
Special Services for the Blind - Accessible computers; Assistive/Adapted tech devices, equip & products; Bks on cassette; Braille & cassettes; Braille alphabet card; Braille bks; Braille equip; Cassettes; Large print bks; Magnifiers; Newsp on cassette; Reader equip; Recorded bks; Ref in Braille; Talking bks; Volunteer serv
Friends of the Library Group
LAMOND RIGGS, 5401 S Dakota Ave NE, 20011, SAN 336-965X. Tel: 202-541-6255. E-mail: lamondriggslibrary@dc.gov. Web Site: www.dclibrary.org/lamond. *Mgr,* Robin Imperial; E-mail: robin.imperial@dc.gov
Library Holdings: Bk Vols 50,000
Open Mon-Thurs 9:30-9, Fri & Sat 9:30-5:30, Sun 1-5
Friends of the Library Group
LIBRARY FOR THE BLIND & PHYSICALLY HANDICAPPED
See Separate Entry Under District of Columbia Talking Book & Braille Library
WILLIAM O LOCKRIDGE/BELLEVUE, 115 Atlantic St SW, 20032, SAN 336-9994. Tel: 202-243-1185. E-mail: bellevuelibrary@dc.gov. Web Site: www.dclibrary.org/bellevue. *Mgr,* Maria Perry; E-mail: maria.perry@dc.gov
Library Holdings: Bk Vols 67,435
Open Mon-Thurs 9:30-9, Fri & Sat 9:30-5:30, Sun 1-5
Friends of the Library Group
MOUNT PLEASANT, 3160 16th St NW, 20010, SAN 336-9692. Tel: 202-671-3121. E-mail: mtpleasantlibrary@dc.gov. Web Site: www.dclibrary.org/mtpleasant. *Mgr,* Position Currently Open
Founded 1925
Library Holdings: Bk Vols 60,000
Open Mon-Thurs 9:30-9, Fri & Sat 9:30-5:30, Sun 1-5
Friends of the Library Group
NORTHEAST NEIGHBORHOOD LIBRARY, 330 Seventh St NE, 20002, SAN 336-9722. Tel: 202-698-0058. E-mail: northeastlibrary@dc.gov. Web Site: www.dclibrary.org/northeast. *Mgr,* Position Currently Open
Library Holdings: Bk Vols 57,694
Open Mon-Thurs 9:30-9, Fri & Sat 9:30-5:30, Sun 1-5
Friends of the Library Group
NORTHWEST ONE, 155 L St NW, 20001. Tel: 202-939-5946. E-mail: northwestonelibrary@dc.gov. Web Site: www.dclibrary.org/northwest. *Mgr,* Bobbie Dougherty; E-mail: barbara.dougherty@dc.gov
Open Mon, Wed, Fri & Sat 9:30-5:30, Tues 1-9, Thurs 9:30-9, Sun 1-5
PALISADES, 4901 V St NW, 20007, SAN 336-9757. Tel: 202-282-3139. E-mail: palisadeslibrary@dc.gov. Web Site: www.dclibrary.org/palisades. *Mgr,* Karen Quash; E-mail: karen.quash@dc.gov
Library Holdings: Bk Vols 81,644
Open Mon-Thurs 9:30-9, Fri & Sat 9:30-5:30, Sun 1-5
Friends of the Library Group
PARKLANDS-TURNER COMMUNITY, 1547 Alabama Ave SE, 20032, SAN 337-0178. Tel: 202-645-4532. E-mail: parklandsturnerlibrary@dc.gov. Web Site: www.dclibrary.org/parklands. *Mgr,* Kellye Carter; E-mail: kellye.carter@dc.gov
Library Holdings: Bk Vols 40,701
Open Mon-Thurs 9:30-9, Fri & Sat 9:30-5:30, Sun 1-5
Friends of the Library Group

PETWORTH, 4200 Kansas Ave NW, 20011, SAN 336-9781. Tel: 202-243-1188. E-mail: petworthlibrary@dc.gov. Web Site: www.dclibrary.org/petworth. *Mgr,* Jeff Neher; E-mail: jeff.neher@dc.gov
Library Holdings: Bk Vols 73,239
Open Mon-Thurs 9:30-9, Fri & Sat 9:30-5:30, Sun 1-5
Friends of the Library Group

ROSEDALE, 1701 Gales St NE, 20002. Tel: 202-727-5012. E-mail: rosedalelibrary@dc.gov. Web Site: www.dclibrary.org/rosedale. *Mgr,* Anina Ertel; E-mail: anita.ertel@dc.gov
Open Mon, Wed, Fri & Sat 9:30-5:30, Tues 1-9, Thurs 9:30-9, Sun 1-5
Friends of the Library Group

SOUTHEAST, 403 Seventh St SE, 20003, SAN 336-9811. Tel: 202-698-3377. E-mail: southeastlibrary@dc.gov. Web Site: www.dclibrary.org/southeast. *Mgr,* Julia Strusienski; E-mail: julia.strusienski@dc.gov
Library Holdings: Bk Vols 77,598
Special Collections: Hist of Eastern Mkt & Capital Hill Communities
Open Mon-Thurs 9:30-9, Fri & Sat 9:30-5:30, Sun 1-5
Friends of the Library Group

SOUTHWEST, 425 M St SW, 20024, SAN 336-9846. Tel: 202-724-4752. E-mail: southwestlibrary@dc.gov. Web Site: www.dclibrary.org/southwest. *Mgr,* Melinda MacCall; E-mail: melinda.maccall@dc.gov
Library Holdings: Bk Vols 70,028
Open Mon-Thurs 9:30-9, Fri & Sat 9:30-5:30, Sun 1-5
Friends of the Library Group

TAKOMA PARK, 416 Cedar St NW, 20012, SAN 336-9900. Tel: 202-576-7252. E-mail: takomaparklibrary@dc.gov. Web Site: www.dclibrary.org/takomapark. *Mgr,* Paula Landsam; E-mail: paula.landsam@dc.gov
Library Holdings: Bk Vols 38,637
Open Mon-Thurs 9:30-9, Fri & Sat 9:30-5:30, Sun 1-5
Friends of the Library Group

TENLEY-FRIENDSHIP, 4450 Wisconsin Ave NW, 20016, SAN 336-9935. Tel: 202-727-1488. E-mail: tenleylibrary@dc.gov. Web Site: www.dclibrary.org/tenley. *Mgr,* Regina Harris; E-mail: reginal.harris@dc.gov
Library Holdings: Bk Vols 79,533
Open Mon-Thurs 9:30-9, Fri & Sat 9:30-5:30, Sun 1-5
Friends of the Library Group

JUANITA E THORNTON/SHEPHERD PARK NEIGHBORHOOD LIBRARY, 7420 Georgia Ave NW, 20012, SAN 373-5745. Tel: 202-541-6100. E-mail: shepherdparklibrary@dc.gov. Web Site: www.dclibrary.org/thornton. *Mgr,* Brian Hasbrouck; E-mail: brian.hasbrouck@dc.gov
Library Holdings: Bk Vols 66,942
Open Mon-Thurs 9:30-9, Fri & Sat 9:30-5:30, Sun 1-5
Friends of the Library Group

WEST END, 2301 L St NW, 20037, SAN 337-0054. Tel: 202-724-8707. E-mail: westendlibrary@dc.gov. Web Site: www.dclibrary.org/westend. *Mgr,* Rob Schneider; E-mail: robert.schneider@dc.gov
Library Holdings: Bk Vols 71,664
Open Mon-Thurs 9:30-9, Fri & Sat 9:30-5:30, Sun 1-5
Friends of the Library Group

WOODRIDGE, 1801 Hamlin St NE, 20018, SAN 337-0089. Tel: 202-541-6226. E-mail: woodridgelibrary@dc.gov. Web Site: www.dclibrary.org/woodridge. *Mgr,* Jeanette Graham; E-mail: jeanette.graham@dc.gov
Library Holdings: Bk Vols 87,709
Open Mon-Thurs 9:30-9, Fri & Sat 9:30-5:30, Sun 1-5
Friends of the Library Group

GL DISTRICT OF COLUMBIA SUPERIOR COURT JUDGES LIBRARY*, 500 Indiana Ave NW, Rm 5400, 20001. SAN 302-6353. Tel: 202-879-1435. Web Site: www.dccourts.gov. *Librn,* Yousuf Galeel
Library Holdings: Bk Vols 30,000; Per Subs 30
Restriction: Not open to pub

P DISTRICT OF COLUMBIA TALKING BOOK & BRAILLE LIBRARY*, Center for Accessibility, Rm 215, 901 G St NW, 20001. SAN 302-6345. Tel: 202-727-2142. FAX: 202-727-0322. E-mail: lbph.dcpl@dc.gov. Web Site: www.dclibrary.org/talkingbooks. *Libr Mgr,* Julie Wolhandler; E-mail: julie.wolhandler@dc.gov; *Adaptive Tech Librn,* Patrick Timony; E-mail: james.timony@dc.gov; *Librn for Deaf,* Janice Rosen; E-mail: janice.rosen@dc.gov; Staff 9 (MLS 4, Non-MLS 5)
Founded 1973
Library Holdings: Bks on Deafness & Sign Lang 100; Braille Volumes 200; DVDs 160; Bk Vols 300; Per Subs 50; Talking Bks 200,000; Videos 200
Special Collections: Americans with Disabilities Act Coll; Blindness & Other Disabilities Reference Coll; Deaf Culture & ASL Learning; Friends Group; Services & Agencies for the Handicapped File Coll; Volunteer Tapists; Washington Volunteer Readers for the Blind
Subject Interests: Disabilities, Employment, Rehabilitation
Wireless access
Function: Adult bk club, Audio & video playback equip for onsite use, Audiobks via web, Bk club(s), Children's prog, Computer training, Computers for patron use, Free DVD rentals, Large print keyboards, Magnifiers for reading, OverDrive digital audio bks, Prog for children & young adult, Teen prog, Wheelchair accessible
Publications: Inside the Beltway (Newsletter); Library Services to the Deaf Community (Newsletter)
Special Services for the Deaf - Am sign lang & deaf culture; Assisted listening device; Assistive tech; Bks on deafness & sign lang; Closed caption videos; Coll on deaf educ; Deaf publ; Lecture on deaf culture; Pocket talkers; Sign lang interpreter upon request for prog; Sorenson video relay syst; Spec interest per; Staff with knowledge of sign lang; TTY equip; Video & TTY relay via computer; Video relay services
Special Services for the Blind - Accessible computers; Assistive/Adapted tech devices, equip & products; Bks & mags in Braille, on rec, tape & cassette; Bks on flash-memory cartridges; Braille alphabet card; Braille bks; Cassette playback machines; Cassettes; Children's Braille; Closed circuit TV magnifier; Computer with voice synthesizer for visually impaired persons; Daisy reader; Descriptive video serv (DVS); Digital talking bk machines; Disability awareness prog; Dragon Naturally Speaking software; Home delivery serv; Info on spec aids & appliances; Inspiration software; Internet workstation with adaptive software; Large screen computer & software; Local mags & bks recorded; Low vision equip; Magnifiers; Mags & bk reproduction/duplication; Micro-computer access & training; Networked computers with assistive software; Newsletter (in large print, Braille or on cassette); Newsline for the Blind; Open bk software on pub access PC; Scanner for conversion & translation of mats; Screen enlargement software for people with visual disabilities; Screen reader software; Soundproof reading booth; Talking bks & player equip; Talking calculator; Web-Braille; ZoomText magnification & reading software
Open Mon & Tues 12-9, Wed-Fri 9:30-5:30
Friends of the Library Group

L DLA PIPER US LLP*, Law Library, 500 Eighth St NW, 20004. SAN 372-154X. Tel: 202-799-4000. FAX: 202-799-5000. Web Site: www.dlapiper.com. *Research Librn,* Laura Spence; Staff 4 (MLS 2, Non-MLS 2)
Library Holdings: Bk Vols 6,000; Per Subs 50
Special Collections: Government Contracts
Subject Interests: Environ law, Franchises
Wireless access
Restriction: Not open to pub

CR DOMINICAN THEOLOGICAL LIBRARY, Dominican House of Studies Library, 487 Michigan Ave NE, 20017-1585. SAN 302-752X. Tel: 202-655-4654. FAX: 202-495-3873. Web Site: www.dhs.edu. *Librn,* Fr John Martin Ruiz; Tel: 202-655-4651, E-mail: librarian@dhs.edu; *Circ Librn, Patron Serv Librn,* Hannah Jones; Tel: 202-655-4653; *Tech Serv Librn,* Benjamin Turnbull; Tel: 202-655-4652; Staff 5 (MLS 3, Non-MLS 2)
Founded 1905. Enrl 94; Fac 14; Highest Degree: Doctorate
Library Holdings: AV Mats 800; Bk Vols 64,000; Per Subs 222
Special Collections: Dissertations by Dominican Authors; Dominican History, Liturgy & Authors; St Thomas Aquinas Writings
Subject Interests: Philos, Theol, Thomist
Automation Activity & Vendor Info: (Cataloging) OCLC Worldshare Management Services; (Circulation) OCLC Worldshare Management Services; (Course Reserve) OCLC Worldshare Management Services; (ILL) OCLC WorldShare Interlibrary Loan; (Media Booking) OCLC Worldshare Management Services; (OPAC) OCLC Worldshare Management Services; (Serials) OCLC Worldshare Management Services
Wireless access
Open Mon, Thurs & Fri 8:30-6, Tues & Wed 8:30am-9pm, Sat 9-1; Mon-Fri 8:30-4 (Summer)

S EMBASSY OF OMAN*, Sultan Qaboos Cultural Center Library, 1100 16th St NW, 20036. Tel: 202-677-3967. E-mail: library@sqcc.org. Web Site: www.sqcc.org/library. *Librn,* Walid Sellal; Tel: 202-677-3967, Ext 104, E-mail: wsellal@sqcc.org. Subject Specialists: *Indexing,* Walid Sellal; Staff 1 (MLS 1)
Founded 2014
Library Holdings: DVDs 50; e-books 10; Large Print Bks 200; Bk Titles 3,000; Bk Vols 150; Videos 10
Special Collections: Oman Coll (A coll focusing on the Sultanate of Oman)
Subject Interests: Art, Geog, Handicraft, Hist, Law, Music, Relig, Seafaring
Automation Activity & Vendor Info: (Acquisitions) Koha; (Cataloging) Koha; (Circulation) Koha; (Course Reserve) Koha; (ILL) OCLC WorldShare Interlibrary Loan; (Media Booking) OCLC WorldShare Interlibrary Loan; (OPAC) Koha; (Serials) Koha
Wireless access

Function: After school storytime, Computer training, Free DVD rentals, Govt ref serv, ILL available, Internet access, Magazines, Meeting rooms, Online cat
Open Mon-Fri 10-4

G ENVIRONMENTAL PROTECTION AGENCY*, Headquarters & Chemical Libraries, West Bldg, Rm 3340, 1301 Constitution Ave NW, 20004. (Mail add: 1200 Pennsylvania Ave NW, MC 3404T, 20460), SAN 302-6450. Tel: 202-566-0556. E-mail: hqchemlibraries@epa.gov. Web Site: www.epa.gov/libraries/headquarters-and-chemical-libraries. *Supvry Librn,* Ann-Marie Stewart; Tel: 202-566-0578
Founded 1971
Special Collections: Emergency Planning Community Right-To-Know Act Coll; Toxic Substances Control Act Coll
Automation Activity & Vendor Info: (Cataloging) OCLC Worldshare Management Services; (ILL) OCLC WorldShare Interlibrary Loan
Partic in OCLC Online Computer Library Center, Inc
Open Mon-Fri 8:30-4:30

L EVERSHEDS SUTHERLAND (US) LLP LIBRARY*, 700 Sixth St NW, Ste 700, 20001-3980. SAN 302-7856. Tel: 202-383-0100. Web Site: us.eversheds-sutherland.com. *Library Contact,* Jennifer Eckel; Staff 5 (MLS 2, Non-MLS 3)
Library Holdings: Bk Vols 1,500
Special Collections: Energy, Insurance, Patents, Tax & Trademarks Coll
Subject Interests: Corporate securities, Energy, Intellectual property, Tax
Function: ILL available

G EXECUTIVE OFFICE OF THE PRESIDENT LIBRARY, Library & Research Services, Eisenhower Executive Office Bldg, 20503. SAN 336-7266. Tel: 202-395-4690. E-mail: library@oa.eop.gov. *Dir,* Sarena Burgess; Staff 12 (MLS 11, Non-MLS 1)
Library Holdings: Audiobooks 750; DVDs 40; e-books 400; e-journals 75; Bk Titles 33,000; Bk Vols 53,000; Per Subs 60
Special Collections: Congressional Appropriations Legislation Coll; Federal Budget Documents Coll; Legal Coll; The Presidency
Subject Interests: Econ, Intl trade, Presidents (US)
Automation Activity & Vendor Info: (Acquisitions) OCLC Worldshare Management Services; (Cataloging) OCLC Worldshare Management Services; (Circulation) OCLC Worldshare Management Services; (Discovery) OCLC Worldshare Management Services; (ILL) OCLC Worldshare Management Services; (Serials) OCLC Worldshare Management Services
Wireless access
Partic in Federal Library & Information Network; OCLC Online Computer Library Center, Inc

G FEDERAL BUREAU OF PRISONS LIBRARY*, Bldg 400, 3rd Flr, 320 First St NW, 20534. SAN 302-6507. Tel: 202-307-3029. FAX: 202-307-5756. E-mail: BOP-IPP/Library@bop.gov. Web Site: bop.library.net. *Head of Libr,* Denise W Lomax; E-mail: dlomax@bop.gov; Staff 2 (MLS 1, Non-MLS 1)
Founded 1960
Library Holdings: AV Mats 500; Bk Titles 6,000; Bk Vols 7,000; Per Subs 70
Subject Interests: Corrections, Criminal justice, Psychol, Sociol
Automation Activity & Vendor Info: (Cataloging) OCLC; (Circulation) TLC (The Library Corporation); (OPAC) TLC (The Library Corporation); (Serials) TLC (The Library Corporation)
Function: Prof lending libr, Res libr
Publications: Periodical List; Video List
Partic in Federal Library & Information Network; OCLC Online Computer Library Center, Inc; World Criminal Justice Libr Network

G FEDERAL COMMUNICATIONS COMMISSION LIBRARY*, 445 12th St SW, 20554. SAN 302-6515. Tel: 202-418-0450. E-mail: fcclibrary@fcc.gov. *Dir,* Amanda Costigan
Library Holdings: Bk Titles 9,000; Bk Vols 40,000
Special Collections: Legislative Histories: Communications Act of 1934 & subsequent Amendments
Subject Interests: Computer sci, Econ, Engr, Law
Wireless access
Friends of the Library Group

G FEDERAL DEPOSIT INSURANCE CORP LIBRARY*, 550 17th St NW, 20429-0002. SAN 302-6523. Tel: 202-898-3631. FAX: 202-898-3984. E-mail: library@fdic.gov. Web Site: www.fdic.gov. *Chief, Libr Serv,* Richard Huffine; E-mail: rhuffine@fdic.gov; Staff 11 (MLS 8, Non-MLS 3)
Founded 1934
Library Holdings: Bk Titles 13,000; Bk Vols 15,000; Per Subs 200
Special Collections: FDIC Archival Material
Subject Interests: Banks & banking, Econ, Law, Real estate
Function: ILL available
Partic in OCLC Online Computer Library Center, Inc
Restriction: Open by appt only

GL FEDERAL ELECTION COMMISSION*, Law Library, 999 E St NW, Rm 801, 20463. SAN 325-7975. Tel: 202-694-1516. FAX: 202-208-3579. Web Site: www.fec.gov. *Dir,* Leta Holley; E-mail: holleyleta@gmail.com; Staff 2 (MLS 1, Non-MLS 1)
Library Holdings: Bk Vols 10,000; Per Subs 30
Subject Interests: Law, Polit sci
Automation Activity & Vendor Info: (Acquisitions) Inmagic, Inc.; (Cataloging) OCLC; (Circulation) Inmagic, Inc.; (Serials) Inmagic, Inc.
Partic in DC Soc of Law Librs; Federal Library & Information Network
Open Mon-Fri 9-4:30

G FEDERAL JUDICIAL CENTER*, Information Services Office, One Columbus Circle NE, 20002-8003. SAN 325-7991. Tel: 202-502-4153. FAX: 202-502-4077. Web Site: www.fjc.gov. *Librn,* Deena Smith; E-mail: dsmith@fjc.gov; Staff 2 (MLS 1, Non-MLS 1)
Library Holdings: AV Mats 4,500; Bk Titles 5,800; Bk Vols 12,000; Per Subs 300
Automation Activity & Vendor Info: (Circulation) NOTEbookS Library Automation; (OPAC) NOTEbookS Library Automation
Function: ILL available, Res libr
Partic in Federal Library & Information Network; OCLC Online Computer Library Center, Inc
Restriction: Open by appt only

G FEDERAL MARITIME COMMISSION LIBRARY*, 800 N Capitol St NW, Rm 1085, 20573. SAN 302-6531. Tel: 202-523-5762. FAX: 202-523-5738. E-mail: LibraryInquiries@fmc.gov. Web Site: www.fmc.gov. *Librn,* Ian Lane; Staff 1 (MLS 1)
Founded 1961
Library Holdings: Bk Vols 8,700; Per Subs 50
Open Mon-Fri 8-4:30
Restriction: External users must contact libr

G FEDERAL TRADE COMMISSION LIBRARY*, 600 Pennsylvania Ave NW, Rm 630, 20580. SAN 302-654X. Tel: 202-326-2395. FAX: 202-326-2732. Web Site: www.ftc.gov. *Dir,* John Shimmons; *Librn,* Jack Cunningham; Staff 3 (MLS 3)
Founded 1914
Library Holdings: AV Mats 175; Bk Vols 117,000; Per Subs 350
Special Collections: Archives; Legislative Histories
Subject Interests: Bus, Consumer protection, Econ, Law
Wireless access
Publications: Periodical Holdings List
Partic in OCLC Online Computer Library Center, Inc
Open Mon-Fri 8:30-5

S FEDERATION OF AMERICAN SCIENTISTS LIBRARY*, 1725 DaSales St NW, Ste 600, 20036. SAN 371-1412. Tel: 202-546-3300. FAX: 202-675-1010. E-mail: fas@fas.org. Web Site: fas.org.
Library Holdings: e-books 4,000; Bk Vols 200
Restriction: Open by appt only

S FHI 360, Information Services Center, 1825 Connecticut Ave NW, 20009. SAN 328-5480. Tel: 202-884-8000. FAX: 202-884-8400. Web Site: www.fhi360.org. *Libr Mgr,* Allison Burns; E-mail: aburns@fhi360.org; Staff 3 (MLS 1, Non-MLS 2)
Founded 1980
Library Holdings: Bk Titles 6,000
Automation Activity & Vendor Info: (OPAC) Inmagic, Inc.
Wireless access
Open Mon-Fri 9-5
Restriction: Co libr

L FINNEGAN, HENDERSON, FARABOW, GARRETT & DUNNER*, Law Library, 901 New York Ave, NW, 20001-4413. SAN 370-1166. Tel: 202-408-4000, 202-408-4290. FAX: 202-408-4400. Web Site: www.finnegan.com/en/firm/offices/washington.html. *Mgr, Libr Serv,* Kelley Hayes Greenhill; Staff 7 (MLS 2, Non-MLS 5)
Library Holdings: Bk Titles 3,483; Bk Vols 12,000; Per Subs 40
Subject Interests: Intellectual property law, Patents, Trademarks
Wireless access
Function: Doc delivery serv, Internet access, Online cat, Online ref
Restriction: Private libr

L FOLEY & LARDNER LLP*, Private Law Library, 3000 K St NW, 4th Flr, 20007. SAN 321-7639. Tel: 202-672-5300. FAX: 202-672-5399. Web Site: www.foley.com. *Research Librn,* Robin Evans; E-mail: revans@foley.com; Staff 5 (MLS 2, Non-MLS 3)
Library Holdings: Bk Titles 15,000
Partic in Proquest Dialog
Restriction: Not open to pub, Staff use only

S FOLGER SHAKESPEARE LIBRARY*, 201 E Capitol St SE, 20003-1094. SAN 302-6558. Tel: 202-544-4600. Reference Tel: 202-675-0310. Reference E-mail: reference@folger.edu. Web Site: www.folger.edu. *Dir,* Dr Michael Witmore; E-mail: mwitmore@folger.edu; *Dir of Coll, Librn,* Greg Prickman; Tel: 202-675-4600, E-mail: gprickman@folger.edu; *Head, Circ,* Rosalind Larry; Tel: 202-675-0310, E-mail: rlarry@folger.edu; *Head, Conserv,* Renate Mesmer; Tel: 202-675-0332, E-mail: rmesmer@folger.edu; *Res & Ref Librn,* Abbie Weinberg; Tel: 202-675-0353, E-mail: aweinberg@folger.edu; *Exhibitions Mgr,* Emily Snedden Yates; Tel: 202-675-8776, E-mail: esneddenyates@folger.edu; *Coordr, Acq,* Rachel Hammer; Tel: 202-675-0384, E-mail: rhammer@folger.edu; *Curator of Ms,* Dr Heather Wolfe; Tel: 202-675-0325, E-mail: hwolfe@folger.edu; *Curator, Early Modern Bks & Prints,* Caroline Duroselle-Melish; Tel: 202-675-0356, E-mail: cdmelish@folger.edu; *Sr Cataloger,* Dr Erin Blake; Tel: 202-675-0323, E-mail: eblake@folger.edu. Subject Specialists: *English paleography,* Dr Heather Wolfe
Founded 1932
Library Holdings: Bk Titles 265,000; Per Subs 200
Special Collections: French political pamphlets, Mazarinades; Manuscripts (16th-17th c English; 18th and 19th c theatrical-Shakespeare); Reformation pamphlets; Shakespeare Coll, playbills, promptbooks, theatrical materials; STC/Wing Coll, printed bks
Subject Interests: English lit, Hist, Renaissance, Shakespeare, Theatre
Automation Activity & Vendor Info: (Acquisitions) Ex Libris Group; (Cataloging) Ex Libris Group; (Circulation) Ex Libris Group; (OPAC) Ex Libris Group; (Serials) Ex Libris Group
Wireless access
Publications: Exhibition Catalogues; Folger Digital Editions; Folger Library Edition of the Complete Plays of William Shakespeare; Folger Magazine; Shakespeare Quarterly
Partic in OCLC Online Computer Library Center, Inc; OCLC Research Library Partnership
Open Mon-Fri. 8:45-4:45; Sat. 9-noon, 1-4:30 PM
Friends of the Library Group

SR FRANCISCAN MONASTERY LIBRARY, Commissariat of the Holy Land USA, 1400 Quincy St NE, 20017. SAN 302-6604. Tel: 202-734-3866. FAX: 202-734-3866. Web Site: myfranciscan.org/. *Archivist/Librn,* Karen L Levenback; E-mail: karen@myfranciscan.com. Subject Specialists: *Relig & fraternal groups,* Karen L Levenback; Staff 2 (MLS 1, Non-MLS 1)
Founded 1900
Library Holdings: Bk Vols 20,000; Per Subs 10
Special Collections: Franciscan Coll; Holy Land Coll; Rare Books. Oral History
Subject Interests: Catholic hist, Franciscan hist, Holy Land & Palestine
Wireless access
Restriction: Access at librarian's discretion, Open by appt only

L FRIED, FRANK, HARRIS, SHRIVER & JACOBSON LLP*, Law Library, 801 17th St NW, Ste 600, 20006. Tel: 202-639-7000. FAX: 202-639-7003. Web Site: www.friedfrank.com. *Libr Mgr,* Janet James; E-mail: janet.james@friedfrank.com; *ILL,* Thomas King; *Res,* Sue Ann Orsini; *Tech Serv,* Leigh Beatson; Staff 4 (MLS 3, Non-MLS 1)
Library Holdings: Bk Titles 5,500; Bk Vols 25,000; Per Subs 300
Automation Activity & Vendor Info: (Cataloging) SirsiDynix; (Circulation) SirsiDynix; (OPAC) SirsiDynix; (Serials) SirsiDynix
Wireless access
Restriction: Open by appt only

C GALLAUDET UNIVERSITY LIBRARY*, 800 Florida Ave NE, 20002-3095. SAN 302-6620. Tel: 202-651-5217. E-mail: library.help@gallaudet.edu. Web Site: www.gallaudet.edu/library. *Dir, Pub Libr Serv,* Sarah Hamrick; Tel: 202-651-5214, E-mail: sarah.hamrick@gallaudet.edu; *Instruction & Ref/Electronic Res Librn,* Elizabeth Henry; Tel: 202-651-2855, E-mail: elizabeth.henry@gallaudet.edu; *Instruction & Ref Librn,* Noah Beckman; Tel: 202-651-1724, E-mail: noah.beckman@gallaudet.edu; *Instruction & Ref Librn,* Patrick Oberholtzer; Tel: 202-651-5233, E-mail: patrick.oberholtzer@gallaudet.edu; *Supvr, Instruction & Ref,* Laura Jacobi; Tel: 202-651-5239, E-mail: laura.jacobi@gallaudet.edu; *Circ Spec,* Dianne Shaw; Tel: 202-651-2349, E-mail: dianne.shaw@gallaudet.edu. Subject Specialists: *Sci,* Patrick Oberholtzer; *Human relations,* Laura Jacobi; Staff 12 (MLS 5, Non-MLS 7)
Founded 1876. Enrl 1,500; Fac 250; Highest Degree: Doctorate
Special Collections: Archival Materials, artifacts, bks, doc, microfilm, V-tapes; Deaf Coll, bks, V-tapes. Oral History
Subject Interests: Audiology & hearing, Deafness, Institutional memory & hist
Wireless access
Partic in OCLC Online Computer Library Center, Inc; Washington Research Library Consortium
Special Services for the Deaf - ADA equip; Assisted listening device; Bks on deafness & sign lang; Captioned film dep; Closed caption videos; Coll on deaf educ; Deaf publ; Interpreter on staff; Lecture on deaf culture; Pocket talkers; Sorenson video relay syst; Spec interest per; Staff with knowledge of sign lang; TDD equip; TTY equip; Video & TTY relay via computer
Open Mon-Thurs 8am-Midnight, Fri 8-6, Sat 12-5, Sun 1pm-Midnight

S GENERAL FEDERATION OF WOMEN'S CLUBS, Women's History & Resource Center, 1734 N St NW, 20036-2990. SAN 371-8417. Tel: 202-683-2028. FAX: 202-835-0246. E-mail: WHRC@GFWC.org. Web Site: www.gfwc.org/what-we-do/whrc. *Pres,* Marian St Clair; E-mail: mstclair@gfwc.org; *Mgr,* Alyssa Constad; E-mail: aconstad@gfwc.org; Staff 2 (MLS 1, Non-MLS 1)
Founded 1984
Library Holdings: AV Mats 250; Bk Titles 1,500
Special Collections: Art & Artifacts Coll; GH Coll on UN Decade for Women, bks, ms; Women's History & Volunteerism (General Federation of Women's Clubs Archives), doc. Oral History
Subject Interests: Women's hist
Wireless access
Open Mon-Fri 9:30-4:30
Friends of the Library Group

C THE GEORGE WASHINGTON UNIVERSITY*, Melvin & Estelle Gelman Library, 2130 H St NW, 20052. SAN 336-741X. Tel: 202-994-6558. Circulation Tel: 202-994-6840. Interlibrary Loan Service Tel: 202-994-7128. Reference Tel: 202-994-6048. FAX: 202-994-6464. Interlibrary Loan Service FAX: 202-994-1340. E-mail: gelman@gwu.edu. Web Site: library.gwu.edu. *Dean of Libraries & Acad Innovation,* Geneva Henry; E-mail: genevahenry@gwu.edu; *Dep Univ Librn, Sr Assoc Dean,* Hannah Sommers; E-mail: hsommers@gwu.edu; *Assoc Dean,* Barbra Giorgini; E-mail: btschida@gwu.edu; Staff 109 (MLS 38, Non-MLS 71)
Founded 1821. Enrl 25,116; Fac 1,300; Highest Degree: Doctorate
Special Collections: Africana Research Center (Walter Fauntroy Papers, John A Wilson Papers); American Labor History (International Brotherhood of Teamsters, National Education Association, American Association of University Professors); Art & Design Coll from the Corcoran; I Edward Kiev Judaica Coll; Media & Journalism (Jack Anderson Papers, Mutual Broadcasting System Records); Middle East Institute Rare Book Coll; University Archives (University Historical Material, Freeman-Watts Coll, Janet Travell Papers, Mount Vernon Seminary & College Coll); Washington Area & Holy Land (Map Coll); Washingtoniana (Washington Writers' Archive, PNC-Riggs Coll, C&O Canal Association, DC City Councilmember Papers, Metro History Coll). US Document Depository
Subject Interests: Art hist, Asian studies, Bus & mgt, Educ, Engr, European studies, Intl affairs, Polit sci, Slavic studies
Automation Activity & Vendor Info: (Acquisitions) Ex Libris Group; (Cataloging) Ex Libris Group; (Circulation) Ex Libris Group; (Course Reserve) Ex Libris Group; (ILL) OCLC; (Media Booking) Ex Libris Group; (OPAC) Ex Libris Group; (Serials) Ex Libris Group
Wireless access
Publications: GW Libraries: Vision (Annual)
Partic in Northeast Research Libraries Consortium; OCLC Research Library Partnership; Washington Research Library Consortium
Special Services for the Blind - Accessible computers; Assistive/Adapted tech devices, equip & products; Braille equip; Disability awareness prog

Departmental Libraries:

CL JACOB BURNS LAW LIBRARY, 716 20th St NW, 20052, SAN 336-7444. Tel: 202-994-6648. Interlibrary Loan Service Tel: 202-994-4156. Reference Tel: 202-994-6647. FAX: 202-994-2874. Interlibrary Loan Service FAX: 202-994-0433. Web Site: www.law.gwu.edu/library. *Dir,* Scott B Pagel; Tel: 202-994-7337, Fax: 202-994-1430, E-mail: spagel@law.gwu.edu; *Dir, Spec Coll,* Jennie C Meade; Tel: 202-994-6857, E-mail: jmeade@law.gwu.edu; *Asst Dir, Admin,* Leslie A Lee; Tel: 202-994-2385, E-mail: llee@law.gwu.edu; *Asst Dir, Info Syst,* Nicole Harris; Tel: 202-994-4225, E-mail: nharris@law.gwu.edu; *Asst Dir, Pub Serv,* Deborah Norwood; Tel: 202-994-7338, E-mail: dnorwood@law.gwu.edu; *Asst Dir, Tech Serv, Head, Cat,* Virginia Bryant; Tel: 202-994-1378, E-mail: vbryant@law.gwu.edu; *Head, Acq,* Trina Robinson; Tel: 202-994-8550, E-mail: trrobinson@law.gwu.edu; *Head, Coll Serv,* Iris M Lee; Tel: 202-994-2733, E-mail: ilee@law.gwu.edu; *Head, Doc Serv,* Lesliediana Jones; Tel: 202-994-9017, E-mail: ljones@law.gwu.edu; *Head, Info Serv,* Larry Ross; Tel: 202-994-0037, E-mail: lross@law.gwu.edu; *Head, Ref,* Germaine Leahy; Tel: 202-994-8551, E-mail: gleahy@law.gwu.edu. Subject Specialists: *Info serv,* Nicole Harris; *Media,* Larry Ross; *Environ law,* Germaine Leahy; Staff 42 (MLS 22, Non-MLS 20)
Founded 1865. Enrl 1,749; Fac 97; Highest Degree: Doctorate
Library Holdings: Bk Titles 379,988; Bk Vols 677,379; Per Subs 5,006
Special Collections: Early French Law (French Coll)
Subject Interests: Environ law, Fr law, Intellectual property law, Intl law, Law, Legal hist
Automation Activity & Vendor Info: (Acquisitions) Innovative Interfaces, Inc; (Cataloging) Innovative Interfaces, Inc; (Circulation) Innovative Interfaces, Inc; (OPAC) Innovative Interfaces, Inc; (Serials) Innovative Interfaces, Inc

Publications: A Legal Miscellanea (Newsletter); Basic Legal Research Guide Series; Guide to the Law Library (Library handbook); Specialized Legal Research Guide Series; The French Collection (Collection catalog)
Friends of the Library Group

ECKLES LIBRARY, 2100 Foxhall Rd NW, 20007, SAN 302-6973. Tel: 202-242-6620. FAX: 202-242-6632. E-mail: eckles@gwu.edu. Web Site: library.gwu.edu/eckles. *Dean of Libr,* Geneva Henry; E-mail: genevahenry@gwu.edu; *Libr Mgr,* David Lemmons; Tel: 202-242-6621, E-mail: davlem@email.gwu.edu; Staff 2 (MLS 1, Non-MLS 1)
Founded 1875. Enrl 700; Fac 35; Highest Degree: Doctorate
Special Collections: Les Dames d'Escoffier Culinary Book Coll; Walter Beach Archives of the American Political Science Association
Subject Interests: Art, Art hist, Interior design, Women's studies

CM PAUL HIMMELFARB HEALTH SCIENCES LIBRARY, 2300 I St NW, 20037, SAN 336-7479. Tel: 202-994-2850. Circulation Tel: 202-994-2962. Interlibrary Loan Service Tel: 202-994-2860. FAX: 202-994-4343. E-mail: himmelfarb@gwu.edu. Web Site: himmelfarb.gwu.edu, www.gwumc.edu/library. *Dir,* Anne Linton; Tel: 202-994-1826, E-mail: alinton@gwu.edu; *Dep Dir,* Alexandra Gomes; Tel: 202-994-1825, E-mail: gomesa@gwu.edu; Staff 14 (MLS 14)
Founded 1857. Enrl 1,000; Fac 400; Highest Degree: Doctorate
Library Holdings: e-journals 1,500; Bk Titles 27,000; Per Subs 500
Special Collections: Interviews with George Washington University VIPs from 1930-50's. Oral History
Automation Activity & Vendor Info: (Circulation) SirsiDynix; (Serials) SirsiDynix
Partic in OCLC Online Computer Library Center, Inc
Publications: Information Interface

VIRGINIA SCIENCE & TECHNOLOGY CAMPUS LIBRARY, 44983 Knoll Sq, Ste 179, Ashburn, 20147-2604, SAN 371-9642. Tel: 571-553-8230. E-mail: virginia@gwu.edu. Web Site: library.gwu.edu/virginia. *Libr Mgr,* Tara Patterson; E-mail: tarap@email.gwu.edu; Staff 1 (Non-MLS 1)
Founded 1991. Enrl 555; Highest Degree: Doctorate
Special Collections: Foundation Center Funding Information Network (Foundation Center database assistance available by appointment)
Subject Interests: Computer sci, Engr sci, Environ sci, Higher educ, Nursing, Pharmacogenomics, Physics, Transportation engr, Transportation safety
Function: Computers for patron use, Distance learning, Doc delivery serv, E-Reserves, Electronic databases & coll, Homebound delivery serv, ILL available, Ref serv available, Res libr, Scanner, Telephone ref, Workshops
Restriction: Limited access for the pub, Open to qualified scholars, Open to researchers by request, Photo ID required for access, Pub use on premises, Restricted pub use

S THE GEORGE WASHINGTON UNIVERSITY MUSEUM & THE TEXTILE MUSEUM, Arthur D Jenkins Library, 701 21st St NW, 20052. SAN 302-7880. Tel: 202-994-5918. E-mail: museumlibrary@gwu.edu. Web Site: museum.gwu.edu/library. *Librn,* Tracy Meserve; Staff 1 (MLS 1)
Founded 1926
Library Holdings: Bk Titles 20,000; Per Subs 144
Special Collections: Cultural History of the Americas, Asia, Africa, the Middle East & the Pacific Rim; History of Rugs, Textiles, Costume
Subject Interests: Costume design, Textile hist, Textile tech
Wireless access

C GEORGETOWN UNIVERSITY*, Joseph Mark Lauinger Library, 37th & O St NW, 20057-1174. SAN 336-7533. Tel: 202-687-7607. Reference Tel: 202-687-7452. Administration Tel: 202-687-7425. FAX: 202-687-7501. Web Site: www.library.georgetown.edu/libraries/lauinger. *Dean of Libr,* Harriette Hemmasi; E-mail: hh749@georgetown.edu; *Dep Univ Librn,* Peggy Fry; E-mail: Fry@georgetown.edu; *Assoc Univ Librn, Digital Serv & Tech Planning,* Shu-Chen Tsung; Tel: 202-687-7429, E-mail: tsungs@georgetown.edu; *Dir, Finance & Operations,* Phyllis Barrow; Tel: 202-687-7454, E-mail: barrowp@georgetown.edu; Staff 112 (MLS 43, Non-MLS 69)
Founded 1789. Enrl 17,044; Fac 1,635; Highest Degree: Doctorate
Library Holdings: Bk Vols 3,858,079
Special Collections: Archives of Dag Hammarskjold College; Archives of Maryland Province, Society of Jesus; Archives of the American Political Science Association; Archives of Woodstock College; Catholic History; Diplomacy & Foreign Affairs; Political Science; United States-American & English Literature; University Archives; Woodstock Theological Library Coll. US Document Depository
Automation Activity & Vendor Info: (ILL) OCLC
Wireless access
Publications: Library Associates (Newsletter); Special Collections at Georgetown, A Descriptive Catalog
Partic in OCLC Online Computer Library Center, Inc; Washington Research Library Consortium
Restriction: Photo ID required for access
Friends of the Library Group

Departmental Libraries:

S BIOETHICS RESEARCH LIBRARY, Kennedy Institute of Ethics, 37th & O St NW, 20057. (Mail add: Box 571212, 20057-1212), SAN 336-8289. Tel: 202-687-3885. E-mail: bioethics@georgetown.edu. Web Site: bioethics.georgetown.edu. *Archivist/Ref Librn,* John Zarrillo; E-mail: john.zarrillo@georgetown.edu; *Tech Serv Mgr,* Patricia Martin; E-mail: martinp@georgetown.edu; *Reference & Prog Specialist,* Roxie France-Nuriddin; E-mail: roxie.francenuriddin@georgetown.edu; Staff 3 (MLS 1, Non-MLS 2)
Founded 1973
Library Holdings: Bk Vols 32,000; Per Subs 25
Special Collections: Archives Colls of Federal Bioethics & Human Experimentation Commissions; Archives National Bioethics Advisory Commission (NBAC); Curriculum Development Clearinghouse for Bioethics (Syllubus Exchange Coll); Kampelman Coll of Jewish Ethics; Shriver Coll of Christian Ethics
Function: ILL available, Photocopying/Printing, Scanner
Partic in National Network of Libraries of Medicine Region 1; OCLC Online Computer Library Center, Inc
Restriction: Open to students, fac, staff & alumni

BLOMMER SCIENCE LIBRARY, 302 Reiss Science Bldg, 20057. (Mail add: PO Box 571230, 20057-1230). Tel: 202-687-5687. Web Site: www.library.georgetown.edu/blommer. *Ref Librn,* Jill Hollingsworth; Tel: 202-662-2573, E-mail: hollingj@georgetown.edu; *Ref Librn,* Holly Surbaugh; Tel: 202-662-5685, E-mail: hs880@georgetown.edu; Staff 4.5 (MLS 2, Non-MLS 2.5)
Open Mon-Wed 8:30am-Midnight, Thurs 8:30am-9pm, Fri 8:30-6, Sat Noon-6, Sun Noon-Midnight

CM DAHLGREN MEMORIAL LIBRARY, Preclinical Science Bldg GM-7, 3900 Reservoir Rd NW, 20007. (Mail add: PO Box 571420, 20057-1420), SAN 336-7568. Tel: 202-687-1448. Interlibrary Loan Service Tel: 202-687-1029. Administration Tel: 202-687-1187. FAX: 202-687-1862. Reference E-mail: dmlreference@georgetown.edu. Web Site: dml.georgetown.edu. *Dir, Sr Assoc Dean,* Jett McCann; E-mail: jm594@georgetown.edu; *Asst Dean,* Douglas Varner; Tel: 202-431-9503, E-mail: dlv2@georgetown.edu; *Access Serv, Asst Dean, Resource Management,* Linda Van Keuren; Tel: 202-687-1168, E-mail: lav30@georgetown.edu; *Dir, Discovery & Integrated Syst Librn,* Jonathan Hartmann; Tel: 202-687-1308, E-mail: jth52@georgetown.edu; *Dir, Info & Delivery Services,* Meghan Hupe; Tel: 202-687-1173, E-mail: Meghan.Hupe@georgetown.edu; *Dir, Instrul Tech,* Dr Taeyeol Park; Tel: 202-687-5089, E-mail: tp3@georgetown.edu; *Assoc Dir, Edu Servs,* Grant Connors; Tel: 202-687-2914, E-mail: gc275@georgetown.edu; *Assoc Dir, Research Servs,* C Scott Dorris; Tel: 202-687-2942, E-mail: csd24@georgetown.edu; *Asst Dir for Res,* Katherine Greene; Tel: 202-687-8670, E-mail: kg615@georgetown.edu; *Clinical Serv Librn, Data Mgt,* Emily Alagha; Tel: 202-687-2486, E-mail: ec1094@georgetown.edu; *Evening Librn,* Latoya Singleton; Tel: 202-687-3791, E-mail: lds34@georgetown.edu; *Ref & Digital Librn,* Angela Barr; Tel: 202-687-1535; *Fac Mgr,* Benjamin Sussman; Tel: 202-687-1665, E-mail: bls50@georgetown.edu; *Access Serv,* Amanda Hall; Tel: 202-687-1013, E-mail: halla@georgetown.edu; *ILL Serv,* Eugennie Buckley; E-mail: buckleye@georgetown.edu; Staff 13 (MLS 11, Non-MLS 2)
Founded 1912. Highest Degree: Doctorate
Library Holdings: e-books 4,500; e-journals 6,500; Bk Vols 6,000
Function: Computers for patron use, For res purposes, Health sci info serv, Internet access, Online cat, Online ref, Ref & res, Ref serv available, Res assist avail, Res libr
Restriction: Authorized patrons, Authorized personnel only, Badge access after hrs, Borrowing privileges limited to fac & registered students, Circ limited, Hospital employees & physicians only, ID required to use computers (Ltd hrs), Med & health res only, Med & nursing staff, patients & families, Med staff & students, Med staff only, Non-circulating to the pub, Open to authorized patrons, Open to fac, students & qualified researchers, Open to hospital affiliates only, Open to students, fac & staff, Photo ID required for access, Restricted pub use

CL GEORGETOWN LAW LIBRARY (EDWARD BENNETT WILLIAMS LIBRARY), 111 G St NW, 20001, SAN 336-7592. Tel: 202-662-9131. Interlibrary Loan Service Tel: 202-662-9152. Reference Tel: 202-662-9140. Administration Tel: 202-662-9160. FAX: 202-662-9168. Reference E-mail: lawlibref@georgetown.edu. Web Site: www.law.georgetown.edu/library. *Dir, Law Libr,* Michelle M Wu; Tel: 202-662-9161, E-mail: mmw84@law.georgetown.edu; *Assoc Dir, Coll Develop, Res,* Marylin J Raisch; Tel: 202-662-9159, E-mail: mjr47@georgetown.edu; *Head, Access Serv,* Craig Lelansky; Tel: 202-662-9155, E-mail: cdl3@law.georgetown.edu; *Head, Ref,* Cattleya M Concepcion; Tel: 202-662-9144, E-mail: cmc462@georgetown.edu; *Head, Res Serv,* Thanh Nguyen; Tel: 202-662-9073, E-mail: nguyent2@georgetown.edu; *Head, Tech,* Kimberli Kelmor; Tel: 202-662-9158, E-mail: kk1210@georgetown.edu; *Electronic Res Librn, Integrated Syst Librn,* Smita Parkhe; Tel: 202-662-9191, E-mail: svp6@georgetown.edu; *Foreign & Intl Ref Librn,* Charles Bjork; Tel: 202-662-4264, E-mail: chb39@georgetown.edu; *Foreign & Intl Ref Librn,* Heather Casey; Tel: 202-662-6573, E-mail:

hec29@georgetown.edu; *Instrul Tech Librn,* Jill Smith; Tel: 202-662-9165, E-mail: jas515@georgetown.edu; *Ref Librn,* Anne M Guha; Tel: 202-662-9180, E-mail: amg300@georgetown.edu; *Ref Librn,* Rachel O Jorgensen; Tel: 202-662-9139, E-mail: rojz@georgetown.edu; *Ref Librn,* Savanna Nolan; Tel: 202-662-9143, E-mail: sn647@georgetown.edu; *Research Servs Librn,* Jeremy J McCabe; Tel: 202-662-9145, E-mail: jjm323@georgetown.edu; *Research Servs Librn,* Andrea Muto; Tel: 202-662-6598, E-mail: amm574@georgetown.edu; *Assoc Law Librn, Digital Initiatives, Spec Coll,* Leah Prescott; Tel: 202-662-4065, E-mail: lp627@georgetown.edu; Staff 54 (MLS 28, Non-MLS 26)
Founded 1870
Library Holdings: Bk Titles 800,000; Bk Vols 1,000,000
Special Collections: US Document Depository
Subject Interests: Intl law
Automation Activity & Vendor Info: (Acquisitions) Innovative Interfaces, Inc; (Cataloging) Innovative Interfaces, Inc; (Circulation) Innovative Interfaces, Inc; (Course Reserve) Innovative Interfaces, Inc; (ILL) Innovative Interfaces, Inc; (Media Booking) Innovative Interfaces, Inc; (OPAC) Innovative Interfaces, Inc; (Serials) Innovative Interfaces, Inc
Partic in OCLC Online Computer Library Center, Inc
Publications: Friends of the Library (Newsletter); Guides
Restriction: Restricted access
Friends of the Library Group

S GERMAN HISTORICAL INSTITUTE LIBRARY, 1607 New Hampshire Ave NW, 20009-2562. SAN 323-8350. Tel: 202-387-3355. FAX: 202-387-6437. E-mail: library@ghi-dc.org. Web Site: www.ghi-dc.org/library. *Head Librn,* Anna Maria Boss; E-mail: boss@ghi-dc.org; Staff 3 (MLS 1, Non-MLS 2)
Founded 1987
Library Holdings: DVDs 100; e-journals 220; Bk Vols 50,000; Per Subs 220; Videos 30
Subject Interests: German hist, German-Am relations
Wireless access
Open Mon-Thurs 9-5, Fri 9-4 & by appointment
Restriction: In-house use for visitors
Friends of the Library Group

S HILLWOOD ESTATE, MUSEUM & GARDENS LIBRARY, 4155 Linnean Ave NW, 20008. SAN 374-6011. Tel: 202-243-3953. FAX: 202-966-7846. Web Site: www.hillwoodmuseum.org/archives-and-special-collections. *Head, Archives & Spec Coll,* Jason Speck; E-mail: jspeck@hillwoodmuseum.org; Staff 3 (MLS 2, Non-MLS 1)
Founded 1958
Library Holdings: Bk Titles 35,000; Per Subs 30
Special Collections: 18th Century French Decorative Arts; Art and Art History; Country Houses and Decorative Gardens; Imperial Russian Decorative Arts; Imperial Russian History; Washington, DC History
Automation Activity & Vendor Info: (Acquisitions) Koha; (OPAC) Koha
Wireless access
Function: 24/7 Online cat, Archival coll, For res purposes, ILL available, Internet access, Microfiche/film & reading machines, Ref & res, Ref serv available, Res libr, Scanner, Wheelchair accessible
Open Mon-Thurs 10-4
Restriction: Closed stack, Limited access based on advanced application, Limited access for the pub, Not a lending libr, Open to pub by appt only

L HOLLAND & KNIGHT LAW LIBRARY*, 800 17th St NW, 20006. SAN 370-7636. Tel: 202-955-3000. FAX: 202-955-5564. Web Site: hklaw.com/Offices/Washington-DC. *Info & Res Mgr,* Katherine Baer; E-mail: katherine.baer@hklaw.com; Staff 3 (MLS 2, Non-MLS 1)
Library Holdings: Bk Vols 3,000; Per Subs 40
Subject Interests: Aviation, Construction, Housing, Real estate, Securities
Restriction: Open by appt only

C HOWARD UNIVERSITY LIBRARIES*, Founders Library, 500 Howard Pl NW, Ste 203, 20059. Circulation Tel: 202-806-7250. Interlibrary Loan Service Tel: 202-806-5716, 202-806-7132. Reference Tel: 202-806-7252. Administration Tel: 202-806-7275. Information Services Tel: 202-806-7443. Administration FAX: 202-806-5903. E-mail: refdept@howard.edu. Web Site: library.howard.edu. *Exec Dir,* Rhea Ballard-Thrower; Tel: 202-806-7236, E-mail: rballard@howard.edu; *Interim Dir, Univ Archivist,* Dr Clifford L Muse, Jr; Tel: 202-806-7498, E-mail: cmuse@howard.edu; *Assoc Dir,* Carrie M Hackney; Tel: 202-806-0768, E-mail: chackney@howard.edu; *Curator, Interim Chief Librn,* Joellen ElBashir; Tel: 202-806-7480, E-mail: jelbashir@howard.edu; *Fac Adminr & Head, Multimedia Serv,* Errol Watkis; Tel: 202-806-7238, E-mail: ewatkis@howard.edu; *Head, Acq & Ser,* Alliah V Humber; Tel: 202-884-7502, E-mail: ahumber@howard.edu; *Head, Metadata & Res Description Serv,* Dr Andrew Sulavik; Tel: 202-806-4224, E-mail: andrew.sulavik@howard.edu; *Head, Access Serv,* Ruth M Rasby; Tel: 202-806-7213, E-mail: ruth.rasby@howard.edu; *Head, Ref & Instruction,* Celia C Daniel; Tel: 202-806-7446, E-mail: ccdaniel@howard.edu; *Bus Librn,* Tommy Waters; Tel: 202-806-1599, E-mail: tommy.waters@howard.edu; *First Year Experience Librn,* Niketha McKenzie; Tel: 202-806-7301, E-mail: niketha.mckenzie@howard.edu.
Subject Specialists: *Relig,* Carrie M Hackney; *Art,* Alliah V Humber; *Classics, Philos, Theol,* Dr Andrew Sulavik; *African-Am studies, Engr,* Celia C Daniel; *Bus, Polit sci,* Tommy Waters; Staff 27 (MLS 17, Non-MLS 10)
Founded 1939. Enrl 8,941; Fac 1,024; Highest Degree: Doctorate
Jul 2012-Jun 2013 Income (Main & Associated Libraries) $5,875,762. Mats Exp $2,955,862. Sal $2,889,900
Library Holdings: Bk Vols 2,402,648
Special Collections: African Diaspora (Moorland Spingarn Research Center); Channing Pollock Theatre Coll
Subject Interests: Humanities, Soc sci, STEM
Automation Activity & Vendor Info: (Acquisitions) SerialsSolutions; (Cataloging) OCLC; (Serials) SerialsSolutions
Wireless access
Function: Archival coll, AV serv, Computers for patron use, Doc delivery serv, E-Reserves, Electronic databases & coll, ILL available, Internet access, Mail & tel request accepted, Microfiche/film & reading machines, Notary serv, Online cat, Online info literacy tutorials on the web & in blackboard, Online ref, Orientations, Outreach serv, Outside serv via phone, mail, e-mail & web, Photocopying/Printing, Ref & res, Ref serv available, Res libr, Wheelchair accessible, Workshops
Open Mon-Thurs 8am-Midnight, Fri 8-5, Sat 9-6, Sun 1-9:30
Restriction: 24-hr pass syst for students only
Friends of the Library Group

Departmental Libraries:

AFRO-AMERICAN STUDIES RESOURCE CENTER, 500 Howard Pl NW, Rm 300, 20059, SAN 336-8076. Tel: 202-806-7242. FAX: 202-986-0538. *Dir,* E Ethelbert Miller; Tel: 202-806-7686, E-mail: emiller@howard.edu; *Librn,* Celia Daniel; E-mail: ccdaniel@howard.edu
Founded 1969
Library Holdings: Bk Vols 32,000
Subject Interests: African-Am studies, Lit

ARCHITECTURE, 500 Howard Pl NW, 20059, SAN 336-7835. *Curator,* Alliah Humber; Tel: 202-806-7502, E-mail: ahumber@howard.edu; Staff 2 (Non-MLS 2)
Founded 1971. Enrl 180; Fac 19; Highest Degree: Bachelor
Library Holdings: Bk Vols 33,876; Per Subs 62
Subject Interests: Archit, Bldg construction, Design, Environ planning, Interior design, Landscape archit, Urban planning
Function: Res libr
Open Mon-Thurs 8:30-6, Fri 8:30-5

BUSINESS, 2600 Sixth St NW, 20059, SAN 336-786X. Tel: 202-806-1561. FAX: 202-797-6393. *Bus Librn,* Tommy Waters; Tel: 202-806-1599, E-mail: tommy.waters@howard.edu; Staff 5 (MLS 1, Non-MLS 4)
Founded 1970. Enrl 1,366; Fac 80; Highest Degree: Doctorate
Library Holdings: Bk Vols 94,331; Per Subs 1,100
Subject Interests: Acctg, Electronic commerce, Finance, Housing, Info syst, Mgt, Mkt, Real estate
Open Mon-Thurs 8am-10pm, Fri 8-5, Sat 9:30-6
Restriction: Open to students, fac & staff, Restricted pub use

CR DIVINITY, 2929 Van Ness St NW, 4th Flr, 20017, SAN 336-7924. Tel: 202-806-8206. Interlibrary Loan Service Tel: 202-806-5716. FAX: 202-806-0711. *Head Librn,* Carrie Hackney; Tel: 202-806-0768, E-mail: chackney@howard.edu; Staff 3 (MLS 1, Non-MLS 2)
Founded 1935. Enrl 286; Fac 14; Highest Degree: Doctorate
Library Holdings: Bk Vols 121,000; Per Subs 240
Special Collections: African Heritage Coll
Subject Interests: Biblical studies, Church hist, Ethics, Pastoral counseling, World relig
Automation Activity & Vendor Info: (Acquisitions) Innovative Interfaces, Inc; (Cataloging) Innovative Interfaces, Inc; (Circulation) Innovative Interfaces, Inc; (Course Reserve) Innovative Interfaces, Inc; (ILL) Innovative Interfaces, Inc; (Media Booking) Innovative Interfaces, Inc; (OPAC) Innovative Interfaces, Inc; (Serials) Innovative Interfaces, Inc
Open Mon-Fri 7am-11pm, Sat 9am-10pm, Sun 11-11
Friends of the Library Group

CL LAW LIBRARY, 2929 Van Ness St NW, 20008, SAN 336-8106. Tel: 202-806-8045. Reference Tel: 202-806-8208. Web Site: library.law.howard.edu. *Assoc Dir, Interim Dir,* Eileen Santos; Tel: 202-806-8301, Fax: 202-806-8590, E-mail: esantos@law.howard.edu; *Access Serv Librn,* Jason Happ; Tel: 202-806-8104, E-mail: jason.happ@law.howard.edu; *Acq Librn,* Kwei Hung; Tel: 202-806-8051, E-mail: khung@law.howard.edu; *Ref Librn,* Victoria Capatosto; Tel: 202-806-8175, E-mail: victoria.capatosto@law.howard.edu; *Fac Mgr,* Jerome Roberson, PhD; Tel: 202-806-8224, E-mail: jroberson@law.howard.edu; *Archivist,* Seth Kronemer; Tel: 202-806-8304, E-mail: smkronemer@law.howard.edu; *ILL,* Zachary

Knatt; Tel: 202-806-8203, E-mail: zknatt@law.howard.edu; Staff 9 (MLS 8, Non-MLS 1)
Founded 1868. Enrl 450; Fac 36; Highest Degree: Doctorate
Library Holdings: Bk Titles 28,500; Bk Vols 253,000; Per Subs 621
Special Collections: Indritz Papers
Subject Interests: Civil rights
Special Services for the Blind - Braille equip
Open Mon-Fri 7am-11pm, Sat 9am-10pm, Sun 11-11
Restriction: Non-circulating to the pub

MOORLAND-SPINGARN RESEARCH CENTER, 500 Howard Pl NW, 20059, SAN 336-8130. Tel: 202-806-7480. Reference Tel: 202-806-4237. Web Site: library.howard.edu/MSRC. *Curator, Interim Chief Librn,* Joellen El Bashir; E-mail: jelbashir@howard.edu; *Manuscript Librn,* Alhaji Conteh, PhD; E-mail: alhaji.conteh@howard.edu; *Sr Archivist,* Tewodros Abebe; Tel: 202-806-7498, E-mail: tabebe@howard.edu; *Archivist,* Sonja N Woods; E-mail: sonja.n.woods@howard.edu
Founded 1914
Library Holdings: Bk Vols 200,000; Per Subs 632
Special Collections: Africa; Afro-American & Afro-Latin Authors (Spingarn Coll); Arthur B Spingarn Music Coll, sheet music; Civil Rights (Ralph J Bunche Oral History Coll), tapes; Journalism (Documentary Series on the Black Press), tapes; Mary O'H Williamson Photograph Coll; Rose McClendon-Carl Van Vechten Photograph Coll. Oral History
Subject Interests: Africa, African-Am, Caribbean, S Am
Open Mon-Fri 9-4:30
Restriction: Non-circulating
Friends of the Library Group

SOCIAL WORK, 601 Howard Pl NW, Rm 200, 20059, SAN 336-7959. Tel: 202-806-7316. *Interim Librn,* Tommy Waters; Tel: 202-806-7316; *Libr Tech 1,* Chelton Johnson; Tel: 202-806-4735, E-mail: cjohnson1@howard.edu; *Libr Tech 1,* Cherette J Sanders; Tel: 202-806-4737, E-mail: jsanders@howard.edu; Staff 3 (MLS 1, Non-MLS 2)
Library Holdings: Bk Vols 40,000; Per Subs 344
Subject Interests: Hist, Philos, Soc work mat
Open Mon-Thurs (Fall-Spring) 8:30am-10pm, Fri 8:30-5, Sat & Sun 1-5; Mon-Fri (Summer) 8:30-5

CM LOUIS STOKES HEALTH SCIENCES LIBRARY, 501 W St NW, 20059, SAN 336-7711. Tel: 202-884-1500. Circulation Tel: 202-884-1520. Reference Tel: 202-884-1522. Administration Tel: 202-884-1732. Circulation FAX: 202-884-1506. E-mail: HealthSciencesLibrary@howard.edu. Web Site: hsl-howard.libguides.com/library. *Exec Dir,* Fatima Barnes; Tel: 202-884-1722, E-mail: fatima.barnes@howard.edu; *Digital Res Librn,* Yelena Suprunova; Tel: 202-884-1730, E-mail: yelena.suprunova@howard.edu; *Access Services Tech,* Vermille Davis; Tel: 202-884-1521, E-mail: vermille.davis@howard.edu; *Access Services Tech,* Lawrence Tucker; E-mail: lawrence.tucker@howard.edu; *Archivist,* Joni Floyd; Tel: 202-884-1729, E-mail: joni.floyd@howard.edu; Staff 15 (MLS 8, Non-MLS 7)
Founded 1927. Highest Degree: Doctorate
Library Holdings: Bk Vols 100,000; Per Subs 350
Special Collections: Allied Health & Pharmacy; Biographical Files on Blacks in Medicine, Dentistry & Nursing; Local History (Howard University, Colleges of Medicine, Dentistry & Nursing)
Partic in National Network of Libraries of Medicine Region 1
Open Mon-Thurs 8am-2am, Fri 8am-10pm, Sat 10-10, Sun Noon-Midnight

L HUGHES, HUBBARD & REED LLP LIBRARY*, 1775 I St NW, Ste 600, 20006-2401. SAN 375-0213. Tel: 202-721-4600. FAX: 202-721-4646. Web Site: www.hugheshubbard.com. *Dir, Libr Serv,* Patricia Barbone; E-mail: patricia.barbone@hugheshubbard.com
Library Holdings: Bk Vols 5,000; Per Subs 10
Wireless access
Restriction: Staff & mem only

G JOHN T HUGHES LIBRARY*, Defense Intelligence Agency, Attn: NIU-3A, 7400 Pentagon, 20301-7400. SAN 374-597X. Information Services Tel: 202-231-3839. E-mail: JTH_Library@dodiis.mil. Web Site: ni-u.edu/wp/jth-library. *Libr Dir,* Elizabeth Ventura; Staff 10 (MLS 8, Non-MLS 2)
Founded 1992
Library Holdings: Audiobooks 375; CDs 450; DVDs 1,000; e-journals 456; Bk Titles 83,789; Bk Vols 97,989; Per Subs 854; Talking Bks 975; Videos 1,500
Special Collections: Diaries & Personal Papers of Ambassador Vernon A Walters
Automation Activity & Vendor Info: (Cataloging) Ex Libris Group; (Circulation) Ex Libris Group; (Course Reserve) Ex Libris Group; (ILL) Ex Libris Group; (OPAC) Ex Libris Group; (Serials) Ex Libris Group
Function: ILL available
Publications: Guide to Library Services
Partic in Federal Library & Information Network
Restriction: Restricted access

S INSTITUTE OF INTERNATIONAL FINANCE LIBRARY*, 1333 H St NW, Ste 800E, 20005-4770. SAN 329-1634. Tel: 202-857-3600. FAX: 202-775-1430. E-mail: info@iif.com. Web Site: www.iif.com. *Database Mgr,* Charlotte Hannagan
Library Holdings: Bk Titles 2,000; Per Subs 450
Restriction: Staff use only

S INSTITUTE OF TRANSPORTATION ENGINEERS*, ITE Technical Library, 1627 Eye St NW, Ste 600, 20006. SAN 377-4112. Tel: 202-785-0060, Ext 120. Web Site: www.ite.org/resources/library/search. *Sr Dir, Info Serv,* Zach Pleasant; E-mail: zpleasant@ite.org

S INTER-AMERICAN DEVELOPMENT BANK, Felipe Herrera Library, 1300 New York Ave NW, Stop W-0102, 20577. SAN 336-8165. Tel: 202-623-3210. FAX: 202-623-3183. E-mail: BID-Library@IABD.ORG. Web Site: www.iadb.org/en/library/library-app/felipe-herrera-library. *Team Leader,* Carolina Osorio; E-mail: cosorio@iadb.org; Staff 5 (MLS 2, Non-MLS 3)
Founded 1960
Library Holdings: Bk Titles 100,000; Per Subs 1,500
Special Collections: International Documents Coll (UN, OECD, World Bank, FAO, etc); Latin American & Caribbean History
Subject Interests: Latin Am & Caribbean soc & econ develop
Automation Activity & Vendor Info: (Acquisitions) OCLC Worldshare Management Services; (Cataloging) OCLC Worldshare Management Services; (Circulation) OCLC Worldshare Management Services; (ILL) OCLC WorldShare Interlibrary Loan; (OPAC) OCLC; (Serials) OCLC
Wireless access
Function: Online cat, Ref & res
Partic in OCLC Online Computer Library Center, Inc
Open Mon-Fri 10-5
Restriction: Borrowing requests are handled by ILL, Internal circ only, Non-circulating to the pub, Res pass required for non-affiliated visitors

S INTERNATIONAL FOOD POLICY RESEARCH INSTITUTE LIBRARY*, 1201 I St NW, 20005. SAN 302-6817. Tel: 202-862-5600. Reference Tel: 202-862-5616. E-mail: ifpri-library@cgiar.org. Web Site: library.ifpri.info. *Libr Mgr,* Indira Yerramareddy; Staff 2 (MLS 2)
Founded 1975
Library Holdings: Bk Vols 8,200; Per Subs 129
Subject Interests: Develop countries, Environ, Food admin, Intl trade, Nutrition
Wireless access
Publications: New Acquisitions List
Restriction: Open by appt only

L IVINS, PHILIPS & BARKER LIBRARY*, 1717 K St NW, Ste 600, 20006. SAN 377-4635. Tel: 202-393-7600. FAX: 202-393-7601. Web Site: www.ipbtax.com. *Librn,* Jeffrey Freilich; E-mail: jfreilich@ipbtax.com
Library Holdings: Bk Vols 3,000; Per Subs 25
Subject Interests: Employee benefits, Tax
Open Mon-Fri 8:30-5

S JAPAN-AMERICAN SOCIETY OF WASHINGTON DC LIBRARY, 1819 L St NW, Level 410, 20036. SAN 375-7773. Tel: 202-833-2210. FAX: 202-833-2456. E-mail: info@jaswdc.org. Web Site: jaswdc.org. *Pres,* Ryan Shaffer
Library Holdings: Bk Titles 1,000; Per Subs 10
Subject Interests: Japanese studies

C JOHNS HOPKINS UNIVERSITY SCHOOL OF ADVANCED INTERNATIONAL*, Sydney R & Elsa W Mason Library, 1740 Massachusetts Ave NW, 6th Flr, 20036. SAN 302-6868. Tel: 202-663-5900. Interlibrary Loan Service Tel: 202-663-5908. Reference Tel: 202-663-5901. FAX: 202-663-5916. E-mail: saislibrary@jhu.edu. Web Site: www.sais-jhu.edu/library. *Libr Dir,* Sheila Thalhimer; Tel: 202-663-5905, E-mail: sthalhimer@jhu.edu; *Assoc Dir,* Stephen A Sears; Tel: 202-663-5907, E-mail: sasears@jhu.edu; *Circ Supvr,* Susan High; Tel: 202-663-5900, E-mail: shigh1@jhu.edu; Staff 15 (MLS 5, Non-MLS 10)
Founded 1943. Enrl 550; Fac 100; Highest Degree: Doctorate
Library Holdings: Bk Titles 70,000; Bk Vols 110,000; Per Subs 950
Automation Activity & Vendor Info: (Acquisitions) SirsiDynix; (Cataloging) SirsiDynix; (Circulation) SirsiDynix; (Course Reserve) Docutek; (ILL) OCLC ILLiad; (OPAC) SirsiDynix
Wireless access
Partic in OCLC Online Computer Library Center, Inc
Restriction: Not open to pub

C JOHNS HOPKINS UNIVERSITY-SHERIDAN LIBRARIES*, Washington Library Resource Center, 1717 Massachusetts Ave, Ste 100, 20036. Tel: 202-452-0714. E-mail: washrocklibraries@jhu.edu. Web Site:

www.library.jhu.edu/library-hours/sheridan-libraries-columbia-dc-montgomery/sheridan-libraries-at-dc. *Dir, Regional Libraries,* Sharon Morris; Tel: 410-440-8963, E-mail: smorris@jhu.edu; *Regional Campus Librn,* Feraz Ashraf; E-mail: fashraf@jhu.edu
Open Mon-Thurs 11-8, Fri 11-5, Sat 9:30-1:30

S JOINT WORLD BANK-INTERNATIONAL MONETARY FUND LIBRARY, 700 19th St NW, Rm HQ1-CN-650J, 20431. SAN 321-9062. Tel: 202-623-7054. FAX: 202-623-6417. E-mail: jointlib@imf.org. Web Site: external.worldbankimflib.org. *Dep Div Chief,* Mr Sai Chinnaswamy; Tel: 202-623-5995, E-mail: schinnaswamy@imf.org; Staff 32 (MLS 21, Non-MLS 11)
Founded 1946
Library Holdings: e-books 3,000; e-journals 3,000; Bk Titles 149,332; Per Subs 593
Special Collections: Bretton Woods Coll
Subject Interests: Banking, Econ develop, Intl econ, Intl finance, Money
Publications: A Basic Collection for Central Bank Libraries (1984); Blueprint: Bibliolist Updates in Print (Monthly); Economics & Finance Indexes: Index to Periodical Articles, 1947-1971 (1972, 4 vol); First Supplement, 1972-1974; IntlEc: Index to International Economics, Development & Finance, 1981-1991; Second Supplement, 1975-1977; The Developing Areas, a Classified Bibliography of the Joint Bank-Fund Library (1975, 3 vols)
Restriction: Staff use only

L JONES DAY*, Law Library, 51 Louisiana Ave NW, 20001-2113. SAN 372-3232. Tel: 202-879-3939, 202-879-3953. FAX: 202-626-1700. Web Site: www.jonesday.com. *Librn,* Todd Weaver; E-mail: tweaver@jonesday.com
Library Holdings: Bk Vols 10,000

L K&L GATES LLP*, Law Library, 1601 K St NW, 20006-1600. SAN 371-0319. Tel: 202-778-9000 (main), 202-778-9160. FAX: 202-778-9100. Web Site: www.klgates.com. *Assoc Dir, Library & Info Services,* Walker Chaffin; Tel: 202-778-9162, E-mail: walker.chaffin@klgates.com
Library Holdings: Bk Vols 11,000; Per Subs 350
Subject Interests: Securities
Open Mon-Fri 9-5:30
Restriction: Staff use only

L KATTEN MUCHIN ROSENMAN LLP*, Law Library, 2900 K St NW, Ste 200, 20007. SAN 372-3879. Tel: 202-625-3500. FAX: 202-298-7570. Web Site: www.kattenlaw.com.
Founded 1974
Library Holdings: Bk Vols 10,000; Per Subs 100
Subject Interests: Corporate, Real estate
Automation Activity & Vendor Info: (Cataloging) EOS International; (Circulation) EOS International; (Serials) EOS International
Partic in OCLC Online Computer Library Center, Inc
Restriction: Private libr

L KING & SPALDING*, Law Library, 1700 Pennsylvania Ave NW, Ste 200, 20006-4706. SAN 320-4340. Tel: 202-737-0500. FAX: 202-626-3737. E-mail: kingspalding@kslaw.com. Web Site: www.kslaw.com. *Librn,* Sara Uehlein
Library Holdings: Bk Vols 10,000
Restriction: Staff use only

L KIRKLAND & ELLIS LLP LIBRARY*, 655 15th St NW, Ste 1200, 20005-5793. SAN 302-6892. Tel: 202-879-5000. FAX: 202-879-5200. Web Site: www.kirkland.com. *Assoc Dir, Res Serv,* Ansley Calhoun; Tel: 202-879-5113, E-mail: acalhoun@kirkland.com; Staff 8 (MLS 3, Non-MLS 5)
Founded 1951
Library Holdings: Bk Titles 6,500; Bk Vols 10,000; Per Subs 100
Subject Interests: Law, Legislation
Wireless access
Restriction: Not open to pub

S KUTAK & ROCK LIBRARY, 1625 Eye St NW, Ste 800, 20006-4061. SAN 370-1476. Tel: 202-828-2400. FAX: 202-828-2488. Web Site: www.kutakrock.com.
Library Holdings: Bk Vols 2,500; Per Subs 200
Special Collections: Security Exchange Commission (microfiche)
Partic in Proquest Dialog
Restriction: Open by appt only

S LEAGUE OF ARAB STATES*, Arab Information Center, 1100 17th St NW, Ste 602, 20036-3602. SAN 325-741X. Tel: 202-265-3210. E-mail: arableague@aol.com. Web Site: arableague-us.org. *Library Contact,* Salah A Sarhan
Library Holdings: Bk Vols 1,000; Per Subs 12
Restriction: Staff use only

L LEWIS BAACH KAUFMANN MIDDLEMISS PLLC LIBRARY*, 1899 Pennsylvania Ave NW, Ste 600, 20006. SAN 377-4546. Tel: 202-833-8900. FAX: 202-466-5738. Web Site: www.baachrobinson.com. *Fac Mgr,* Thomas D McBride; E-mail: thomas.mcbride@baachrobinson.com
Library Holdings: Bk Vols 5,000; Per Subs 30
Restriction: Open by appt only

G LIBRARY OF CONGRESS*, James Madison Memorial Bldg, 101 Independence Ave SE, 20540. SAN 336-8343. Tel: 202-707-5000. Interlibrary Loan Service Tel: 202-707-5444. FAX: 202-707-1925. Web Site: www.loc.gov. *Librn of Congress,* Dr Carla Hayden; E-mail: librarian@loc.gov; *Deputy Librarian of Congress, Principal,* J Mark Sweeney; *Chief Coms Officer,* Roswell Encina; *Chief Info Officer,* Judith Conklin; *Chief of Research & Ref Servs Div,* Dennis Clark; *Chief of Staff,* Ryan Ramsey; *Chief Operating Officer,* Edward R Jablonski; *Deputy Chief Info Officer,* John Rutledge; *Dir, Res Serv,* Mary B Mazanec; *Dir, U.S. Copyright Office, Register of Copyrights,* Shira Perlmupper; *Assoc Librn, Libr Serv,* Robin L Dale. Subject Specialists: *Congressional,* Mary B Mazanec; *Copyright,* Shira Perlmupper
Founded 1800
Special Collections: Gutenberg Bible; Manuscripts of Eminent Americans; Papers of the first 23 Presidents
Automation Activity & Vendor Info: (Acquisitions) Ex Libris Group; (Cataloging) Ex Libris Group; (Circulation) Ex Libris Group; (OPAC) Ex Libris Group; (Serials) Ex Libris Group
Wireless access
Publications: Library of Congress Magazine (bimonthly); The Gazette (weekly staff newsp)
Partic in Association of Research Libraries; OCLC Online Computer Library Center, Inc; OCLC Research Library Partnership
Special Services for the Deaf - Spec interest per; Staff with knowledge of sign lang; TTY equip
Special Services for the Blind - Reader equip
Open Mon-Sat 8:30-5
Friends of the Library Group
Branches:
JOHN W KLUGE CENTER, LIBRARY COLLECTIONS & SERVICES GROUP, Thomas Jefferson Bldg, LJ-120, First St SE, 20540-4860. Tel: 202-707-3302. FAX: 202-707-3595. *Dir,* John Haskell; *Dep Librn,* Robin Dale
LIBRARY SERVICES - ACQUISITIONS & BIBLIOGRAPHIC ACCESS DIRECTORATE, James Madison Memorial Bldg, LM Rm 642, 101 Independence Ave SE, 20540. Tel: 202-707-5325. Web Site: www.loc.gov/aba. *Dir,* Mr Beacher Wiggins; E-mail: bwig@loc.gov
Open Mon-Fri 8-5
LIBRARY SERVICES - GENERAL & INTERNATIONAL COLLECTIONS DIRECTORATE, James Madison Memorial Bldg, LM 642, 101 Independence Ave SE, 20540. Web Site: loc.gov/rr/coll-overview.html. *Dir,* Eugene Flanagan
NATIONAL LIBRARY SERVICE FOR THE BLIND & PRINT DISABLED, Library Collections & Services Group, 1291 Taylor St NW, 20542, SAN 336-8610. Tel: 202-707-5100. Toll Free Tel: 800-424-8567. FAX: 202-707-0712. E-mail: nls@loc.gov. Web Site: www.loc.gov/nls. *Dir,* Jason Broughton; *Dep Dir,* Jason Yasner
Founded 1931
Function: Digital talking bks, Wheelchair accessible
Publications: Braille Book Review (Bimonthly); Musical Mainstream (Periodical); News (Newsletter); Talking Book Topics (Bimonthly); Update (Newsletter)
Special Services for the Blind - Audio mat; Bks & mags in Braille, on rec, tape & cassette; Bks on flash-memory cartridges; Digital talking bk machines; Music instrul cassettes; Musical scores in Braille & large print; Production of talking bks; Ref serv; Web-Braille
Open Mon-Fri 8-4:30
PRESERVATION DIRECTORATE, 101 Independence Ave SE, 20540-4530. Web Site: www.loc.gov/preservation. *Dir,* Jacob Nadal

L MANATT, PHELPS & PHILLIPS LLP*, Law Library, 1050 Connecticut Ave NW, Ste 600, 20036. SAN 377-287X. Tel: 202-585-6500. Interlibrary Loan Service Tel: 202-585-6681. FAX: 202-585-6600. Web Site: www.manatt.com. *ILL,* Patrick Eugene; E-mail: peugene@manatt.com; Staff 3 (MLS 1, Non-MLS 2)
Founded 1965
Library Holdings: Per Subs 300
Subject Interests: Gen law, Litigation
Automation Activity & Vendor Info: (Acquisitions) SirsiDynix; (Cataloging) SirsiDynix; (Circulation) SirsiDynix; (OPAC) SirsiDynix
Open Mon-Fri 9:30-6

CR MARIST COLLEGE LIBRARY, 815 Varnum St NE, 20017-2199. SAN 302-6922. Tel: 202-529-2821, Ext 21. *Librn,* Paul Osmanski
Founded 1898

Library Holdings: Bk Titles 4,355; Bk Vols 5,444; Per Subs 47
Subject Interests: Philos, Theol
Restriction: Not open to pub, Open to students, fac & staff

S MAYER, BROWN LLP*, Law Library, 1999 K St NW, Ste 1200, 20006-1101. SAN 329-8868. Tel: 202-263-3000. FAX: 202-263-3300. Web Site: www.mayerbrownrowe.com. *Librn,* Gloria Miccioli; Staff 5 (MLS 3, Non-MLS 2)
Library Holdings: Bk Vols 5,000
Subject Interests: Law, Litigation
Wireless access
Restriction: Staff use only

L MCMANUS & FELSEN LLP*, 1990 M St, Ste 600, 20005. Tel: 202-296-9260. FAX: 202-659-3732. Web Site: www.mcmanus-felsen.com. *Adminr,* Emily Whittington; E-mail: ewhittington@mcmanus-felsen.com
Library Holdings: Bk Titles 175
Wireless access
Restriction: Not a lending libr

S METROPOLITAN CLUB OF THE CITY OF WASHINGTON LIBRARY*, 1700 H St, NW, 20006. Tel: 202-835-2556. Administration FAX: 202-835-2582. E-mail: library@metroclub.org. Web Site: www.metroclub.org. *Dir, Libr & Archives,* Michael J Higgins; *Libr Tech,* Robin W Higgins; E-mail: RHiggins@metroclub.org; Staff 1 (MLS 1)
Founded 1863
Sept 2016-Aug 2017. Mats Exp $24,000, Books $18,000, Per/Ser (Incl. Access Fees) $5,000, Presv $1,000
Library Holdings: Audiobooks 200; Bk Vols 18,000; Per Subs 80
Special Collections: Club Member Publications; Metropolitan Club Archives
Automation Activity & Vendor Info: (Cataloging) EOS International; (Circulation) EOS International; (OPAC) EOS International; (Serials) EBSCO Online
Publications: An Annotated Guide to New Books in the Library (Monthly bulletin)
Restriction: Authorized patrons

S MIDDLE EAST INSTITUTE*, The Oman Library, 1761 N St NW, 20036. SAN 302-6949. Tel: 202-785-1141, Ext 222. FAX: 202-331-8861. E-mail: library@mei.edu. Web Site: www.mideasti.org/library. *Cat, Coll Develop Librn,* Walid Sellal; E-mail: wsellal@sqcc.org; Staff 1 (MLS 1)
Founded 1946
Library Holdings: AV Mats 100; e-books 500; Bk Vols 21,000; Per Subs 300
Special Collections: 18th & 19th Century travel accounts of the Middle East
Subject Interests: Africa, Archit, Caucasus, Cent Asia, Islam, Middle East, North Africa, Political
Automation Activity & Vendor Info: (Cataloging) Inmagic, Inc.; (Circulation) Inmagic, Inc.; (OPAC) Inmagic, Inc.; (Serials) Inmagic, Inc.
Open Mon-Fri 10-5

L MIGRANT LEGAL ACTION PROGRAM LIBRARY*, 1001 Connecticut Ave NW, Ste 915, 20036. SAN 373-0980. Tel: 202-775-7780. E-mail: mlap@mlap.org. Web Site: www.mlap.org. *Exec Dir,* Roger C Rosenthal
Library Holdings: Bk Vols 500
Subject Interests: Farming, Rural
Restriction: Staff use only

L MILLER & CHEVALIER*, Law Library, 900 Sixteenth St, NW, 20006. SAN 372-1361. Tel: 202-626-6094. FAX: 202-626-5801. Web Site: www.millerchevalier.com. *Dir, Libr Serv,* Christine Ciambella; E-mail: cciambella@milchev.com; *Asst Librn,* Karen Polk
Automation Activity & Vendor Info: (Cataloging) SIMA, Inc; (Circulation) SIMA, Inc; (OPAC) SIMA, Inc
Open Mon-Fri 8:30-5:30

L MORGAN LEWIS & BOCKIUS LLP*, Law Library, 1111 Pennsylvania Ave NW, 20004-2541. Tel: 202-739-4636. FAX: 202-739-3001. Web Site: www.morganlewis.com. *Libr Serv Mgr,* Andy Zimmerman; Staff 9 (MLS 4, Non-MLS 5)
Library Holdings: Bk Titles 11,000; Bk Vols 45,000; Per Subs 750
Subject Interests: Employment, Environ law, Finance, Intellectual property, Labor, Law, US Congress
Automation Activity & Vendor Info: (Cataloging) Innovative Interfaces, Inc
Wireless access
Publications: ML&B Library Bulletin
Partic in OCLC Online Computer Library Center, Inc; Proquest Dialog
Restriction: Not open to pub

G NASA HEADQUARTERS LIBRARY*, Dr T Keith Glennan Memorial Library, 300 E St SW, Rm 1W53, 20546. SAN 302-699X. Tel: 202-358-0168. FAX: 202-358-3251. E-mail: library@hq.nasa.gov. Web Site: www.hq.nasa.gov/office/hqlibrary. *Librn,* Claudia Jones; Tel: 202-358-0171, E-mail: claudia.m.jones@nasa.gov; *Ref Librn,* Donna Pallotta; Tel: 202-358-2000, E-mail: donna.m.pallotta@nasa.gov; *Ref Librn,* Richard Spencer; Tel: 202-358-0172, E-mail: richard.d.spencer@nasa.gov; Staff 3 (MLS 2, Non-MLS 1)
Founded 1958
Library Holdings: DVDs 60; Bk Titles 16,000; Per Subs 100; Videos 100
Subject Interests: Aerospace sci
Automation Activity & Vendor Info: (Cataloging) OCLC; (ILL) OCLC
Function: 24/7 Electronic res, 24/7 Online cat, Computers for patron use, ILL available, Internet access, Mail & tel request accepted, Ref & res, Ref serv available, Res libr
Publications: Alerts
Partic in OCLC Online Computer Library Center, Inc
Open Mon-Fri 7:30-5
Restriction: Circ to mem only, Open to pub for ref only

S THE NATIONAL ACADEMIES, Transportation Research Board Library, Keck 439, 500 Fifth St NW, 20001. SAN 302-7015. Tel: 202-334-2989. E-mail: trblibrary@nas.edu. Web Site: www.trb.org/InformationServices/TRBLibrary1.aspx. *Indexer, Mgr,* Janet Daly; E-mail: jdaly@nas.edu; *Sr Librn,* Alexandra Briseno; E-mail: abriseno@nas.edu; *Database Librn,* Sam Saffer; E-mail: ssaffer@nas.edu; *Mgr, Info Serv,* William McLeod; E-mail: wmcleod@nas.edu; *Libr Asst,* Shaakira Jackson; E-mail: sjackson@nas.edu; Staff 5 (MLS 4, Non-MLS 1)
Founded 1946
Library Holdings: Bk Titles 11,850; Per Subs 500
Special Collections: Highway Research Board & Transportation Research Board Publications; Marine Board; Strategic Highway Research Program (SHRP & SHRP2) Publications
Subject Interests: Civil engr, Transportation
Automation Activity & Vendor Info: (Acquisitions) EOS International; (Cataloging) EOS International; (Circulation) EOS International; (ILL) OCLC; (OPAC) EOS International; (Serials) EOS International
Partic in OCLC Online Computer Library Center, Inc
Open Mon-Fri 8:30-5

S THE NATIONAL ACADEMIES OF SCIENCES, ENGINEERING & MEDICINE*, George E Brown Jr Library/Research Center, 500 Fifth St NW, Keck 304, 20001-2721. SAN 302-7023. Tel: 202-334-2125. Interlibrary Loan Service Tel: 202-334-1309. FAX: 202-334-1651. E-mail: research@nas.edu. Web Site: www.nationalacademies.org/researchcenter. *Mgr,* Colleen Willis; *Sr Librn,* Anne Marie Houppert; *Sr Librn,* Christopher Lao-Scott; *Sr Librn,* Jorge Mendoza; *Sr Librn,* Rebecca Morgan; Staff 5 (MLS 5)
Founded 1945
Library Holdings: e-books 220,000; e-journals 17,000; Bk Titles 15,000
Special Collections: National Academy of Sciences Reports Archives
Subject Interests: Educ, Engr, Global affairs, Med, Policy, Sci, Soc sci
Automation Activity & Vendor Info: (Cataloging) OCLC Worldshare Management Services; (Circulation) OCLC Worldshare Management Services; (Discovery) OCLC Worldshare Management Services; (ILL) OCLC ILLiad; (OPAC) OCLC Worldshare Management Services; (Serials) OCLC Worldshare Management Services
Wireless access
Function: Res libr
Partic in Docline; OCLC Online Computer Library Center, Inc
Restriction: Authorized scholars by appt, Borrowing requests are handled by ILL, Circ limited, Closed stack, External users must contact libr, In-house use for visitors, Open by appt only, Visitors must make appt to use bks in the libr

S NATIONAL ACADEMY OF SOCIAL INSURANCE LIBRARY*, 1200 New Hampshire Ave NW, Ste 830, 20036. SAN 374-9959. Tel: 202-452-8097. FAX: 202-452-8111. E-mail: nasi@nasi.org. Web Site: www.nasi.org. *Library Contact,* Gloria Kim
Library Holdings: Bk Titles 3,000; Per Subs 12
Subject Interests: Soc ins progs
Function: For res purposes
Restriction: Mem only

S NATIONAL ENDOWMENT FOR DEMOCRACY LIBRARY*, Democracy Resource Center, 1025 F St NW, Ste 800, 20004. SAN 377-4554. Tel: 202-378-9700. FAX: 202-378-9407. E-mail: drc@ned.org, info@ned.org. Web Site: www.ned.org, www.ned.org/research/democracy-resource-center. *Libr Mgr,* Tim Myers; E-mail: tim@ned.org; *Archivist/Librn,* Anna Yevropina; *Sr Librn,* Emily Vaughan; E-mail: emilyv@ned.org; Staff 5 (MLS 4, Non-MLS 1)
Founded 1994
Library Holdings: DVDs 300; Electronic Media & Resources 4,000; Bk Vols 20,000; Per Subs 300
Subject Interests: Govt, Intl affairs, Politics

Automation Activity & Vendor Info: (Acquisitions) OCLC WorldShare Interlibrary Loan; (Cataloging) OCLC WorldShare Interlibrary Loan; (Circulation) OCLC WorldShare Interlibrary Loan; (ILL) OCLC WorldShare Interlibrary Loan; (OPAC) OCLC WorldShare Interlibrary Loan; (Serials) OCLC WorldShare Interlibrary Loan
Wireless access
Partic in OCLC Online Computer Library Center, Inc
Open Mon-Fri 9-5:30

G NATIONAL ENDOWMENT FOR THE HUMANITIES LIBRARY*, NEH Library, 4th Flr, 400 Seventh St SW, 20506. SAN 325-9854. Tel: 202-606-8244. FAX: 202-208-0781. Web Site: www.neh.gov. *Sr Librn,* Janice Bell; E-mail: jbell@neh.gov; *Tech Info Spec,* Donna McClish; E-mail: dmcclish@neh.gov; Staff 1 (Non-MLS 1)
Founded 1965
Library Holdings: Bk Vols 11,000
Partic in OCLC Online Computer Library Center, Inc
Open Mon-Fri 8:30-4:45

S NATIONAL GALLERY OF ART LIBRARY*, Fourth St & Constitution Ave NW, 20565. (Mail add: 2000B S Club Dr, Door 7, Landover, 20785-3230), SAN 302-7228. Tel: 202-842-6511. Circulation Tel: 202-842-6516. Interlibrary Loan Service Tel: 202-842-6512. Administration Tel: 202-842-6505. FAX: 202-789-3068. E-mail: library@nga.gov. Web Site: library.nga.gov. *Exec Librn,* Roger Lawson; *Spec Coll Librn,* Yuri Long; *Automation Coordr,* Karen Cassedy; *Libr Syst Spec,* Yuning Zhou; *Image Coll,* Andrea Gibbs; *Image Coll,* Gregory Most; *Ref (Info Servs),* John Hagood; Staff 40 (MLS 21, Non-MLS 19)
Founded 1941
Library Holdings: Bk Titles 450,000; Bk Vols 480,000; Per Subs 958
Special Collections: Art Exhibition Catalogs; Art Sales Records; Artists Book Coll; Leonardo da Vinci Coll; Museum & Private Art Coll; Photographic Archives of European & American Art
Subject Interests: Archit, Graphic arts, Paintings, Sculpture
Automation Activity & Vendor Info: (Acquisitions) Ex Libris Group; (Cataloging) Ex Libris Group; (Circulation) Ex Libris Group; (ILL) OCLC; (OPAC) Ex Libris Group; (Serials) Ex Libris Group
Publications: Annotated Bibliography of Microforms (1991); Documenting the Salon: Paris Salon Catalogs 1673-1945 (2016) (Research guide); Guide to the National Gallery of Art Library (1994); Guide to the National Gallery of Art Photo Archives (2002); The Patricia G England Collection of Fine Press & Artists' Books (2000)
Partic in Federal Library & Information Network; OCLC Online Computer Library Center, Inc; OCLC Research Library Partnership
Open Mon 12-4:30, Tues-Fri 10-4:30

Branches:

DEPARTMENT OF EDUCATION RESOURCES, Fourth St & Constitution Ave NW, 20565. (Mail add: 2000B S Club Dr, Landover, 20785), SAN 329-9686. Tel: 202-842-6280. FAX: 202-842-6935. E-mail: edresources@nga.gov. Web Site: www.nga.gov/education/classroom/loanfinder. *Head, Dept of Educ Res,* Leo J Kasun
Library Holdings: AV Mats 140; CDs 10; DVDs 22; Electronic Media & Resources 2; Bk Titles 43; Videos 63
Subject Interests: Educ
Open Mon-Fri 9-5

S NATIONAL GEOGRAPHIC LIBRARY & ARCHIVES*, 1146 16th St NW, 20036. (Mail add: 1145 17th St NW, 20036), SAN 336-9129. Tel: 202-857-7783. FAX: 202-429-5731. E-mail: library@ngs.org. Web Site: ngslis.org. *Libr Dir,* Maggie Turqman; *Archives Dir,* Renee Braden; E-mail: ngarchives@ngs.org; *Archives Dir,* Karen Cerka; *Photo Archivist,* Sara Manco. Subject Specialists: *Manuscripts,* Renee Braden; *Video,* Karen Cerka; Staff 9 (MLS 4, Non-MLS 5)
Founded 1920
Library Holdings: Bk Vols 30,000; Per Subs 60
Special Collections: Hakluyt Society Publications; National Geographic publications
Subject Interests: Exploration, Geog, Natural hist, Travel
Automation Activity & Vendor Info: (Acquisitions) Innovative Interfaces, Inc; (Cataloging) Innovative Interfaces, Inc; (Circulation) Innovative Interfaces, Inc; (ILL) OCLC; (OPAC) Innovative Interfaces, Inc; (Serials) Innovative Interfaces, Inc
Function: Online cat, Online ref
Publications: Staff Brochure
Partic in OCLC Online Computer Library Center, Inc
Restriction: Access for corporate affiliates, Authorized scholars by appt, Circulates for staff only, Open to pub by appt only, Photo ID required for access, Use of others with permission of librn

A NATIONAL GUARD MEMORIAL LIBRARY*, One Massachusetts Ave NW, 20001. SAN 326-1786. Tel: 202-408-5890, 202-789-0031. Web Site: www.ngef.org/national-guard-memorial-library. *Dir, Archives,* Anne Armstrong; E-mail: anne.armstrong@ngaus.org; Staff 2 (MLS 1, Non-MLS 1)
Founded 1975
Library Holdings: Bk Vols 6,000; Per Subs 1
Special Collections: Air National Guard and Army National Guard Photos; National Guard Association Archives; State Guard Histories, bks, correspondence, clippings. Oral History
Wireless access
Open Mon-Fri 9-4

GL NATIONAL INSTITUTE OF JUSTICE*, Online Research & Information Center, 810 Seventh St NW, Rm 6304, 20531. SAN 377-4228. Tel: 202-307-6742. FAX: 202-307-6742. Web Site: www.nij.gov. *Dir,* William Ford; E-mail: william.ford@usdoj.gov
Library Holdings: Bk Vols 500; Per Subs 30
Open Mon-Fri 8:30-5

S NATIONAL LABOR RELATIONS BOARD LIBRARY*, 1015 Half St SE, Ste 6038, 20570-0001. SAN 302-7260. Tel: 202-273-3720. FAX: 202-273-2906. Web Site: www.nlrb.gov. *Chief Librn,* Andrew Martin; E-mail: andrew.martin@nlrb.gov; Staff 9 (MLS 3, Non-MLS 6)
Library Holdings: Bk Vols 37,000; Per Subs 30
Special Collections: Publications By or About National Labor Relations Board, National Labor Relations Act, Labor; Relations Act of 1947 & Landrum-Griffin Act, Title VII
Subject Interests: Bus, Employment law, Labor, Law
Automation Activity & Vendor Info: (Cataloging) EOS International; (Circulation) EOS International; (Serials) EOS International
Publications: New Books & Current Labor Articles
Partic in OCLC Online Computer Library Center, Inc
Open Mon-Fri 9-4

G NATIONAL LIBRARY OF EDUCATION*, 400 Maryland Ave SW, BE-101, 20202-5523. SAN 336-9242. Tel: 202-205-5015. E-mail: askalibrarian@ed.gov. Web Site: ies.ed.gov/ncee/projects/nle. *Dep Dir,* Barbara Holton; E-mail: barbara.holton@ed.gov
Founded 1994
Oct 2016-Sept 2017 Income $2,000,000
Library Holdings: Bk Vols 100,000; Per Subs 500
Special Collections: ERIC (Educational Resources Information Center), 1966-2003, micro; Rare Books Coll; US Department of Education Historical Coll. US Document Depository
Subject Interests: Educ policy, Educ psychol, Educ res, Educ statistics, Soc sci res methodology
Automation Activity & Vendor Info: (Acquisitions) SirsiDynix-iBistro; (Cataloging) SirsiDynix-iBistro; (Circulation) SirsiDynix-iBistro; (ILL) OCLC; (OPAC) SirsiDynix-iBistro; (Serials) SirsiDynix-iBistro
Wireless access
Function: 24/7 Online cat, Archival coll, Govt ref serv, ILL available, Photocopying/Printing, Ref & res, Telephone ref
Partic in Coalition for Networked Information; Federal Library & Information Network; OCLC Online Computer Library Center, Inc
Special Services for the Deaf - TTY equip
Open Mon-Fri 9-5
Restriction: Authorized scholars by appt, Circulates for staff only, External users must contact libr, Lending to staff only, Non-circulating of rare bks, Non-circulating to the pub, Open to pub by appt only, Open to researchers by request, Photo ID required for access

S NATIONAL MUSEUM OF AMERICAN JEWISH MILITARY HISTORY COLLECTIONS*, 1811 R St NW, 20009. SAN 377-1172. Tel: 202-265-6280. FAX: 202-462-3192. E-mail: nmajmh@nmajmh.org. Web Site: www.nmajmh.org. *Archives Coll Mgr,* Pamela Elbe; E-mail: pelbe@nmajmh.org
Library Holdings: Bk Vols 22,000
Open Mon-Fri 9-5

S NATIONAL MUSEUM OF WOMEN IN THE ARTS*, Betty Boyd Dettre Library & Research Center, 1250 New York Ave NW, 20005. Tel: 202-266-2835, 202-783-5000. E-mail: lrc@nmwa.org. Web Site: nmwa.org/learn/library-research/. Staff 3 (MLS 2, Non-MLS 1)
Founded 1982
Library Holdings: Bk Titles 18,000; Bk Vols 18,500; Per Subs 50
Special Collections: Archives on Women Artists; Artists' Books Coll; Irene Rice Pereira Library
Automation Activity & Vendor Info: (Acquisitions) Ex Libris Group; (Cataloging) Ex Libris Group; (Circulation) Ex Libris Group; (OPAC) Ex Libris Group; (Serials) Ex Libris Group
Open Mon-Fri 10-12 & 1-5
Friends of the Library Group

R THE NATIONAL PRESBYTERIAN CHURCH*, William Smith Culbertson Memorial Library, Administration Bldg, 2nd Flr, 4101 Nebraska Ave NW, 20016. SAN 302-7317. Tel: 202-537-7529. Administration Tel: 202-537-0800. FAX: 202-686-0031. E-mail:

Library@NationalPres.org. Web Site: www.nationalpres.org/library. *Dir, Libr & Archives,* J Theodore Anderson
Founded 1969
Jan 2019-Dec 2019 Income $78,000, Locally Generated Income $70,000, Parent Institution $8,000. Mats Exp $14,150, Books $5,000, Per/Ser (Incl. Access Fees) $650, Manu Arch $1,000, Other Print Mats $2,000, AV Mat $500, Electronic Ref Mat (Incl. Access Fees) $1,000, Presv $4,000. Sal $55,000
Library Holdings: AV Mats 4,200; Bks on Deafness & Sign Lang 100; Braille Volumes 125; DVDs 350; Bk Titles 16,000; Per Subs 38; Spec Interest Per Sub 8; Talking Bks 200; Videos 900
Special Collections: Chambers Theology Coll; Chapman Memorial Archives. Oral History
Subject Interests: Children's lit, Hist, Music, Relig, Theol
Automation Activity & Vendor Info: (Acquisitions) Surpass; (Cataloging) Surpass; (Circulation) Surpass; (Course Reserve) Surpass; (Media Booking) Surpass; (OPAC) Surpass; (Serials) Surpass
Wireless access
Publications: Current Awareness Bulletin; New Book Lists; Reading for Special Days
Special Services for the Blind - Aids for in-house use
Open Mon-Fri 9-5, Sun 8-1
Friends of the Library Group

S NATIONAL PRESS CLUB*, Eric Friedheim Library, 529 14th St NW, 13th Flr, 20045. SAN 326-128X. Tel: 202-662-7523. FAX: 202-879-6725. E-mail: info@press.org. Web Site: www.press.org/library. *Dir,* Julie Schoo; Tel: 202-662-7507; *Archivist,* Jeffrey Schlosberg; Tel: 202-662-7598, E-mail: archives@press.org; Staff 5 (MLS 2, Non-MLS 3)
Founded 1908
Library Holdings: Bk Vols 3,000
Special Collections: Hammond Photographs (John Hay Hammond Coll); NPC Cartoon Coll, original art & political cartoons; Sigma Delta Chi DC Chapter, docs; Washington Press Club Archives
Subject Interests: Current news
Open Mon-Fri 9-6
Friends of the Library Group

S NATIONAL RIGHT TO LIFE LIBRARY*, 512 Tenth St NW, 20004. SAN 371-8689. Tel: 202-626-8800. E-mail: NRLC@nrlc.org. Web Site: www.nrlc.org. *Dir of Educ, Dir, Res Serv,* Dr Randall O'Bannon
Library Holdings: Bk Titles 1,000
Special Collections: Abortion; Euthanasia; Infanticide
Function: Res libr

NATIONAL SOCIETY OF THE DAUGHTERS OF THE AMERICAN REVOLUTION

S DAR LIBRARY*, 1776 D St NW, 20006-5303, SAN 302-7368. Tel: 202-879-3229. Reference Tel: 202-777-2366. FAX: 202-879-3227. E-mail: library@dar.org. Web Site: www.dar.org. *Coll Develop, Dir,* Eric G Grundset; *Tech Serv,* Bertha Mutz; Staff 16 (MLS 3, Non-MLS 13)
Founded 1896
Mar 2014-Feb 2015 Income $1,120,000, Locally Generated Income $120,000, Parent Institution $1,000,000. Mats Exp $47,000, Books $30,000, Per/Ser (Incl. Access Fees) $15,000, Micro $2,000. Sal $800,000 (Prof $200,000)
Library Holdings: CDs 700; Bk Titles 175,000; Bk Vols 230,000; Per Subs 1,100
Special Collections: American Indians Coll; Minority Participants in the American Revolution (African American & American Indian Patriots); Women's History Coll
Subject Interests: Genealogy, State hist, US hist
Automation Activity & Vendor Info: (Acquisitions) TLC (The Library Corporation); (Cataloging) TLC (The Library Corporation); (Circulation) TLC (The Library Corporation); (OPAC) TLC (The Library Corporation); (Serials) TLC (The Library Corporation)
Function: CD-ROM, Computers for patron use, Microfiche/film & reading machines, Online ref, Orientations, Photocopying/Printing, Ref serv available, Telephone ref, Workshops
Publications: America's Women in the Revolutionary Era (Bibliographies); Forgotten Patriots: African American & American Indian Patriots in the Revolutionary War: Service (Reference guide); Georgia in the American Revolution (Research guide); New York in the American Revolution (Research guide); Rhode Island in the American Revolution (Research guide); South Carolina in the American Revolution (Research guide); Virginia in the American Revolution (Research guide)
Special Services for the Deaf - Sorenson video relay syst; Staff with knowledge of sign lang
Special Services for the Blind - Closed circuit TV magnifier
Open Mon-Fri 8:30-4, Sat 9-5
Restriction: Non-circulating, Open to pub for ref only, Open to students
Friends of the Library Group

S MUSEUM REFERENCE LIBRARY*, 1776 D St NW, 20006, SAN 321-2262. Tel: 202-879-3241. FAX: 202-628-0820. E-mail: museum@dar.org. Web Site: www.dar.org/museum. *Dir,* Heidi Campbell-Shoaf; Staff 10 (Non-MLS 10)
Founded 1970
Library Holdings: Bk Vols 3,000; Per Subs 30
Subject Interests: Decorative art
Function: For res purposes
Open Mon-Fri 9:30-4, Sat 9-5

A NAVAL HISTORY & HERITAGE COMMAND*, Navy Department Library, Bldg 44, 1st Flr, 805 Kidder-Breese St SE, 20374-5060. SAN 337-1670. Tel: 202-433-2060. Web Site: www.history.navy.mil/research/library.html. *Libr Dir,* Dr Rondelle M Price, Sr; E-mail: rondelle.price@navy.mil; *Cat Librn,* Dr Young Park; *Tech Info Spec/Fed Dep Libr,* Position Currently Open; Staff 11 (MLS 6, Non-MLS 5)
Founded 1800
Library Holdings: Bk Titles 102,000; Per Subs 375
Special Collections: Administrative Histories of World War II Coll; Cruise Books; Cryptologic Documents; Dissertations on Naval & Military History; Navy Officer Registers; Rare Books & Manuscripts; US Navy Shipbuilding Contracts. US Document Depository
Subject Interests: Maritime hist, Naval hist
Automation Activity & Vendor Info: (Cataloging) EOS International; (Circulation) EOS International; (ILL) OCLC Online; (OPAC) EOS International; (Serials) EOS International
Function: Ref serv available
Publications: Accessions List; Subject Bibliographies
Partic in OCLC Online Computer Library Center, Inc
Open Mon-Fri 9-4
Restriction: Open to pub for ref & circ; with some limitations

G NAVAL RESEARCH LABORATORY*, Ruth H Hooker Research Library, 4555 Overlook Ave SW, Code 5500, 20375-5337. SAN 302-7392. Tel: 202-767-2357. FAX: 202-767-3352. Reference E-mail: ref@library.nrl.navy.mil. Web Site: infoweb.nrl.navy.mil. *Chief Librn,* Suzanne Ryder; E-mail: suzanne.ryder@library.nrl.navy.mil; Staff 19 (MLS 9, Non-MLS 10)
Library Holdings: Bk Vols 46,000; Per Subs 2,506
Subject Interests: Atmospheric sci, Biomolecular sci, Chem, Computer sci, Electronics sci & tech, Info tech, Mat sci, Nanotechnologies, Ocean sci, Optical sci, Physics, Radar
Automation Activity & Vendor Info: (Cataloging) SirsiDynix; (Circulation) SirsiDynix; (ILL) OCLC; (Serials) SirsiDynix
Partic in Consortium of Naval Libraries; National Research Library Alliance

S NEW YORK TIMES*, Washington Bureau Library, 1627 I St NW, 20006. SAN 302-7422. Tel: 202-862-0300. FAX: 202-862-0428. Web Site: nytimes.com.
Founded 1932
Library Holdings: Bk Titles 4,500; Per Subs 30
Subject Interests: Fed govt, Politics
Partic in NY Times Info Bank
Restriction: Not open to pub, Staff use only

L NIXON PEABODY LLP*, Law Library, 799 Ninth St NW, Ste 500, 20001. SAN 371-5582. Tel: 202-585-8000, Ext 8320. FAX: 202-585-8080. Web Site: www.nixonpeabody.com. *Dir, Libr & Res Serv,* Sara G Eakes; E-mail: seakes@nixonpeabody.com; *Librn,* Beverly Miller; *Librn,* Tamie Tobe; Staff 3 (MLS 3)
Library Holdings: Bk Titles 1,500; Bk Vols 5,000; Per Subs 150
Automation Activity & Vendor Info: (Cataloging) SydneyPlus; (Circulation) SydneyPlus; (OPAC) SydneyPlus; (Serials) SydneyPlus
Wireless access
Restriction: Not open to pub

S NPR RAD-RESEARCH ARCHIVE & DATA STRATEGY*, 1111 N Capitol St NE, 20002. SAN 326-2189. Administration Tel: 202-513-2355. E-mail: RAD@npr.org. Web Site: www.npr.org. *Chief,* Laura Soto-Barra; E-mail: lsotobarra@npr.org; *Deputy Chief,* Mary Glendinning. Subject Specialists: *Bus, Strategy,* Laura Soto-Barra; *Operations, Strategy,* Mary Glendinning; Staff 17 (MLS 12, Non-MLS 5)
Founded 1971
Special Collections: NPR Archives, audio, metadata, transcripts 1971 to present, different formats
Wireless access

S NUCLEAR ENERGY INSTITUTE LIBRARY*, 1201 F St NW, Ste 1100, 20004-1218. SAN 302-5926. Tel: 202-739-8002. FAX: 202-785-4019. Web Site: www.nei.org. *Library Contact,* Position Currently Open; Staff 1 (MLS 1)
Founded 1954

Library Holdings: Bk Titles 10,000; Per Subs 250
Subject Interests: Energy, Environ studies, Nuclear energy, Radiation
Automation Activity & Vendor Info: (Cataloging) EOS International; (Circulation) EOS International; (OPAC) EOS International
Wireless access
Restriction: Researchers by appt only, Staff & mem only

L O'MELVENY & MYERS LLP*, Law Library, 1625 Eye St NW, 20006. SAN 372-3208. Tel: 202-383-5300. FAX: 202-383-5414. Web Site: www.omm.com. *Mgr,* Martha Cocker; E-mail: mcocker@omm.com; Staff 5 (MLS 3, Non-MLS 2)
Special Collections: In-house Legislative History Coll
Subject Interests: Antitrust, Employee benefits, Employment law, Estate planning, Financial institutions, Intellectual property, Intl trade, Labor law, Litigation, Mergers, Telecommunication
Automation Activity & Vendor Info: (Acquisitions) OCLC; (Cataloging) OCLC; (Circulation) OCLC; (Course Reserve) OCLC Online; (OPAC) OCLC
Restriction: Open by appt only

S ORGANIZATION OF AMERICAN STATES, Columbus Memorial Library, 19th & Constitution Ave NW, 20006-4499. SAN 302-7465. Tel: 202-370-0628. FAX: 202-458-3914. E-mail: cmlibrary@oas.org. Web Site: www.oas.org/en/columbus. *Libr Spec,* Rocio Suarez; E-mail: rsuarez@oas.org; *Doc Librn,* Rene L Gutierrez; Tel: 202-370-6233, E-mail: rgutierrez@oas.org; Staff 3 (MLS 2, Non-MLS 1)
Founded 1890
Library Holdings: Bk Vols 500,000; Per Subs 2,679
Special Collections: Democracy; Drugs; Historical Photographs; Human Rights Coll; Inter-American System; International Orgns; Latin America, Caribbean, Canada & the US; Sustainable Development; Trade; Women in the Americas. UN Document Depository
Wireless access
Function: Archival coll, Bilingual assistance for Spanish patrons, For res purposes, ILL available, Online cat, Ref & res, Ref serv available, Res libr, Spanish lang bks
Publications: Guide to the Columbus Memorial Library; Hipolito Unanue Bibliographic Servs; Indice Analitico de Documentos Oficiales; Information & Documentation Series; List of Recently Catalogued Books; Lista General de Documentos Oficiales; OAS Records Management Handbook; OAS Records Management Manual; Periodical Articles of Interest
Restriction: Access at librarian's discretion, Authorized patrons, Authorized scholars by appt, Borrowing requests are handled by ILL, Closed stack, External users must contact libr, Non-circulating to the pub, Open to pub by appt only, Open to pub for ref & circ; with some limitations

G OSHA*, Technical Data Center, 200 Constitution Ave NW, Rm N-2625, 20210-2001. SAN 323-9233. Tel: 202-693-2350. FAX: 202-693-1648. E-mail: technicaldatacenter@dol.gov. Web Site: www.osha.gov/dts/tdc. *Dir,* Michelle Walker; E-mail: walker.michelle@dol.gov; Staff 1 (MLS 1)
Library Holdings: Bk Titles 6,000; Bk Vols 12,500; Per Subs 206
Special Collections: OSHA Rulemaking Records
Subject Interests: Engr, Med, Occupational safety
Function: ILL available
Partic in Federal Library & Information Network; OCLC Online Computer Library Center, Inc
Open Mon-Fri 8:15-4:45
Restriction: Non-circulating to the pub

S PAI LIBRARY, (Formerly Population Action International Library), 1300 19th St NW, Ste 200, 20036. SAN 320-1368. Tel: 202-557-3400. FAX: 202-728-4177. E-mail: library@pai.org. Web Site: pai.org. *Digital Design & Editorial Content Mgr,* Katie Unthank
Library Holdings: Bk Titles 2,000; Per Subs 30
Subject Interests: Ecology, Reproductive health
Automation Activity & Vendor Info: (Cataloging) Sydney Enterprise; (Circulation) Sydney Enterprise; (OPAC) Sydney Enterprise
Wireless access
Restriction: External users must contact libr, Staff use only

S PAN AMERICAN HEALTH ORGANIZATION HEADQUARTERS LIBRARY*, 525 23rd St NW, 20037. SAN 302-749X. Tel: 202-974-3160, 202-974-3734. E-mail: libraryhq@paho.org. Web Site: www.paho.org/english/DD/IKM/LI/library.htm. *Advisor, Knowledge Mgmt & Networks,* Eliane Santos. Subject Specialists: *Pub health,* Eliane Santos; Staff 5 (MLS 3, Non-MLS 2)
Founded 1926
Library Holdings: Bk Titles 50,000; Per Subs 30
Special Collections: PAHO Institutional Repository of Information Sharing (IRIS); Pan American Health Organization/World Health Organization Documents
Subject Interests: Pub health
Wireless access
Partic in US National Library of Medicine
Restriction: Open by appt only

S PENSION BENEFIT GUARANTY CORPORATION*, Corporate Library, 1200 K St NW, Ste 360, 20005-4026. SAN 320-135X. Tel: 202-326-4000, Ext 3091. E-mail: librarystaff2@pbgc.gov. Web Site: www.pbgc.gov. *Libr Mgr,* Judith M Weiss; E-mail: weiss.judith@pbgc.gov; *Ref Librn,* Ann Wakefield; Tel: 202-326-4000, Ext 3550, E-mail: wakefield.ann@pbgc.gov; *Tech Info Spec,* Lynn Artabane; Tel: 202-326-4000, Ext 6061, E-mail: artabane.lynn@pbgc.gov; Staff 4 (MLS 2, Non-MLS 2)
Founded 1976
Library Holdings: Bk Vols 12,000; Per Subs 65
Subject Interests: Bankruptcy, Pensions
Restriction: Open to pub by appt only

S PEW CHARITABLE TRUSTS LIBRARY, 901 E St, 20004. SAN 374-5430. Tel: 215-575-9050. Administration Tel: 215-575-4920. FAX: 215-575-4939. E-mail: library@pewtrusts.org. Web Site: www.pewresearch.org/. *Digital Archivist, Librn,* Caitlin Curran; Tel: 202-540-6560, E-mail: ccurran@pewtrusts.org; *Research Librn,* Melissa Jordan; Tel: 202-540-6611, E-mail: mjordan@pewtrusts.org; *Syst Librn,* Shari Clayman; Tel: 202-552-2209, E-mail: sclayman@pewtrusts.org; *Res Officer,* Melanie Sciochetti; E-mail: msciochetti@pewtrusts.org; Staff 5 (MLS 5)
Founded 1989
Special Collections: Internal Digital Documents Coll. Oral History
Subject Interests: Philanthropy
Automation Activity & Vendor Info: (Acquisitions) EOS International; (Cataloging) EOS International; (Circulation) EOS International; (Discovery) EBSCO Discovery Service; (ILL) OCLC; (OPAC) EOS International; (Serials) EOS International
Wireless access
Restriction: Not open to pub

S THE PHILLIPS COLLECTION LIBRARY*, 1600 21st St NW, 20009. SAN 321-2297. Tel: 202-387-2151, Ext 212. FAX: 202-387-2436. Web Site: www.phillipscollection.org. *Head Librn,* Karen Schneider; E-mail: kschneider@phillipscollection.org; Staff 3 (MLS 2, Non-MLS 1)
Founded 1976
Library Holdings: Bk Vols 10,000; Per Subs 6
Special Collections: 19th & 20th Century European & American Artists, monographs; Duncan Phillips Coll, Correspondence, ms & journals; Exhibition Catalogues; History of American Art Museums & Collecting; Phillips Coll Artists & Correspondence & monographs
Restriction: Authorized scholars by appt, Open by appt only

L PORTER, WRIGHT, MORRIS & ARTHUR LLP*, Law Library, 2020 K St, NW, Ste 600, 20006. SAN 377-4279. Tel: 202-778-3000, 202-778-3044. Toll Free Tel: 800-456-7962. FAX: 202-778-3063. Web Site: www.porterwright.com. *Librn,* Robert Oszakiewski; E-mail: roszakiewski@porterwright.com
Library Holdings: Bk Vols 2,000; Per Subs 8
Open Mon-Fri 9-6

L PROSKAUER LLP LIBRARY*, 1001 Pennsylvania Ave NW, Ste 600 S, 20004-2533. SAN 377-4473. Tel: 202-416-6823. FAX: 202-416-6899. *Librn,* Carla Evans; E-mail: cevans@proskauer.com; Staff 2 (MLS 1, Non-MLS 1)
Library Holdings: Bk Vols 5,000; Per Subs 40
Restriction: Open to pub by appt only

S PUBLIC CITIZEN LIBRARY*, 215 Pennsylvania Ave SE, 3rd Flr, 20003. SAN 325-8580. Tel: 202-546-4996. FAX: 202-547-7392. Web Site: www.citizen.org. *Mgr,* Kevin Rice; E-mail: krice@citizen.org
Library Holdings: Bk Titles 1,000; Per Subs 20
Subject Interests: Consumer
Open Mon-Fri 9-6

L REED SMITH LLP*, Law Library, 1301 K St NW, Ste 1100, E Tower, 20005-3317. SAN 325-8564. Tel: 202-414-9200. Interlibrary Loan Service Tel: 202-414-9415. FAX: 202-414-9299. Web Site: www.reedsmith.com. *Sr Mgr,* Lorraine DeSouza; E-mail: ldesouza@reedsmith.com; *Sr Res Librn,* Amy Denniston; E-mail: adenniston@reedsmith.com
Library Holdings: Bk Vols 21,041; Per Subs 250
Automation Activity & Vendor Info: (Acquisitions) SirsiDynix
Open Mon-Fri 8:30-6

S RESOURCES FOR THE FUTURE INC LIBRARY, 1616 P St NW, Ste 600, 20036. SAN 374-471X. Tel: 202-328-5089. FAX: 202-939-3460. Web Site: www.rff.org. *Librn,* Christopher B Clotworthy; E-mail: clotwort@rff.org; Staff 1 (MLS 1)
Founded 1985

Library Holdings: Bk Titles 5,500; Per Subs 180
Subject Interests: Environ policy
Restriction: Open by appt only

S SCOTTISH RITE LIBRARY*, 1733 16th St NW, 20009-3103. SAN 302-7686. Tel: 202-232-3579. FAX: 202-464-0487. E-mail: library@scottishrite.org. Web Site: www.scottishrite.org. *Dir,* Sean Graystone; Tel: 202-777-3131, E-mail: temple@scottishrite.org; *Librn,* Joan O Kleinknecht; Tel: 202-777-3139; *Archivist,* Arturo deHoyos; Tel: 202-777-3107, E-mail: archives@scottishrite.org
Founded 1881
Library Holdings: Bk Vols 193,000
Special Collections: Abraham Lincoln Coll; Goethe Coll; J Edgar Hoover Coll; Masonic Coll; Panama Canal (Thatcher Coll); Robert Burns Coll
Subject Interests: Freemasonry, Hist
Automation Activity & Vendor Info: (Cataloging) SirsiDynix
Wireless access
Open Mon-Thurs 8-5
Friends of the Library Group

S SEYFARTH SHAW*, Washington Branch Office Library, 975 F St NW, 20004. SAN 302-7694. Tel: 202-828-5345. Web Site: www.seyfarth.com. *Librn,* Susan Ryan; E-mail: sryan@seyfarth.com; Staff 2 (MLS 1, Non-MLS 1)
Founded 1978
Library Holdings: Bk Vols 11,000; Per Subs 150
Subject Interests: Construction, Employment law, Labor law, Law
Automation Activity & Vendor Info: (Cataloging) OCLC
Function: ILL available
Partic in Illinois Library & Information Network; OCLC Online Computer Library Center, Inc
Restriction: Not open to pub

L SHEARMAN & STERLING LLP*, Law Library, 401 Ninth St NW, Ste 800, 20004-2128. SAN 373-0972. Tel: 202-508-8055. FAX: 202-508-8100. Web Site: www.shearman.com. *Coordr, Info Serv, Research Coordr,* Eleanor Gonzalez; E-mail: eleanor.gonzalez@shearman.com; Staff 6 (MLS 3, Non-MLS 3)
Library Holdings: Bk Vols 1,800; Per Subs 35
Subject Interests: Antitrust, Corporate, Intl trade, Litigation, Securities
Wireless access
Restriction: Open by appt only

L SIDLEY AUSTIN LLP*, Law Library, 1501 K St NW, 20005. SAN 371-6317. Tel: 202-736-8525. Interlibrary Loan Service Tel: 202-736-8505. FAX: 202-736-8711. Web Site: www.sidley.com. *Dir,* Jeffrey V Bosh; E-mail: jbosh@sidley.com; *Res Analyst,* Ronnie Schulman; E-mail: rschulman@sidley.com; Staff 2 (MLS 2)
Library Holdings: Per Subs 300
Special Collections: Legislative Histories
Wireless access
Partic in OCLC Online Computer Library Center, Inc
Open Mon-Fri 9-5

L SKADDEN, ARPS, SLATE, MEAGHER & FLOM LLP*, Law Library, 1440 New York Ave NW, 20005. SAN 372-1434. Tel: 202-371-7000. FAX: 202-393-5760. Web Site: www.skadden.com. *Knowledge Serv Analyst,* Kelly McGlynn
Library Holdings: Bk Vols 30,000; Per Subs 400
Subject Interests: Energy, Intl trade, Litigation, Mergers, Securities, Tax
Restriction: Private libr

S SMITHSONIAN LIBRARIES*, Natural History Bldg, Tenth St & Constitution Ave NW, 20560. (Mail add: PO Box 37012, MRC154, 20013-7012), SAN 337-0321. Tel: 202-633-2240. Interlibrary Loan Service Tel: 202-633-1245. Administration Tel: 202-633-1940. FAX: 202-633-4315. E-mail: libmail@si.edu. Web Site: www.library.si.edu. *Dir of Libr,* Position Currently Open; *Interim Dir,* Scott Miller; Tel: 647-264-7328, E-mail: millers@si.edu; *Assoc Dir, Digital Serv,* Martin Kalfatovic; Tel: 202-633-1705, E-mail: kalfatovicm@si.edu; *Admin Officer,* Kathy Hill; Tel: 202-633-1945, E-mail: hillka@si.edu; *Public Affairs Mgr,* Elizabeth O'Brien; Tel: 203-633-1522, E-mail: obriene@si.edu; Staff 112 (MLS 60, Non-MLS 52)
Founded 1846
Library Holdings: Bk Vols 1,587,735
Special Collections: History of Science & Technology; Natural History, Trade Literature
Subject Interests: African art, Am art, Am cultural hist, Asian art, Aviation hist, Ethnology, Mus studies, Natural hist, Sci tech, Trade
Automation Activity & Vendor Info: (Acquisitions) SirsiDynix; (Cataloging) SirsiDynix; (Circulation) SirsiDynix; (ILL) OCLC ILLiad; (OPAC) SirsiDynix; (Serials) SirsiDynix
Wireless access
Publications: Information (Newsletter)
Partic in Association of Research Libraries; Chesapeake Information & Research Library Alliance; Metropolitan New York Library Council; OCLC Online Computer Library Center, Inc; OCLC Research Library Partnership
Open Mon-Fri 9-5
Restriction: Open to others by appt
Branches:
ANACOSTIA COMMUNITY MUSEUM LIBRARY, 1901 Fort Pl SE, Rm 215, 20020. (Mail add: 1901 Fort Pl SE, MRC 777, 20020-3230), SAN 302-5845. Tel: 202-633-4862. FAX: 202-633-0211. Web Site: library.si.edu/libraries/anacostia. *Librn,* Baasil Wilder; E-mail: wilderb@si.edu
Library Holdings: Bk Vols 8,000; Per Subs 100
Subject Interests: Abolitionism, African, African-Am, Local hist, Slavery
Publications: Newsletter
Restriction: Open by appt only
BOTANY & HORTICULTURE LIBRARY, Natural History Bldg, Rm W422, Tenth St & Constitution Ave NW, 20560. (Mail add: PO Box 37012, MRC 154, 20013-7012), SAN 374-8073. Tel: 202-633-1685. FAX: 202-357-1896. Web Site: library.si.edu/libraries/botany. *Librn,* Robin Everly; E-mail: everlyr@si.edu
Library Holdings: Bk Vols 51,313
Special Collections: Agrostology (Hitchcock-Chase Coll); Algology (Dawson Coll); General Botany (John Donnell Smith Coll)
Subject Interests: Botany, Hort
Restriction: Open to pub by appt only
COOPER-HEWITT, NATIONAL DESIGN LIBRARY, Two E 91st St, New York, 10128, SAN 312-0651. Tel: 212-849-8330. FAX: 212-849-8339. E-mail: CooperHewittLibrary@si.edu. Web Site: library.si.edu/libraries/cooper-hewitt. *Actg Head Librn,* Jennifer Cohlman Bracchi; Tel: 212-848-8333, E-mail: bracchij@si.edu; *Colls Librn,* Stephen H Van Dyk; Tel: 212-849-8335, E-mail: vandyks@si.edu; *Ref Librn,* Elizabeth Broman; Tel: 212-633-8336, E-mail: bromane@si.edu; Staff 2 (MLS 2)
Library Holdings: Bk Vols 71,166
Special Collections: American & Foreign Auction Catalogs; Donald Deskey Archive; Henry Dreyfuss Archive; Ladislav Sutnar Archive; Pop-Up Book Coll; Therese Bonney Photographs; World's Fair Coll, 1844-1964
Subject Interests: Archit, Decorative art, Decorative design, Interior design, Rare bks, Textiles
Restriction: Open by appt only
JOSEPH F CULLMAN III, LIBRARY OF NATURAL HISTORY, Nat Museum of Natural History, Tenth St & Constitution Ave NW, 20560. (Mail add: PO Box 37012, MRC 154, 20013-7012). Tel: 202-633-1184. FAX: 202-633-0219. Web Site: library.si.edu/libraries/cullman. *Curator, Natural Hist Rare Bks,* Leslie K Overstreet; Tel: 202-633-1176, E-mail: overstreetl@si.edu; *Ref Librn,* Alexandra Alvis; Tel: 202-633-1177, E-mail: alvisa@si.edu; Staff 2 (MLS 1, Non-MLS 1)
Library Holdings: Bk Vols 20,000
Special Collections: James Smithson Library; Natural History & Natural Sciences Coll
Subject Interests: Anthrop, Botany, Hist of mus & sci coll, Hort, Mineral sci, Paleontology, Voyages, Zoology
Restriction: Open by appt only
VINE DELORIA, JR LIBRARY, NATIONAL MUSEUM OF THE AMERICAN INDIAN, Cultural Resource Ctr, MRC 538, 4220 Silver Hill Rd, Suitland, 20746-0537. Tel: 301-238-1376. FAX: 301-238-3038. Web Site: library.si.edu/libraries/american-indian. *Librn,* Elayne Silversmith; E-mail: silversmithe@si.edu; Staff 2 (MLS 1, Non-MLS 1)
Library Holdings: Bk Vols 37,000
Function: Res libr
Restriction: Open to pub by appt only
THE DIBNER LIBRARY OF THE HISTORY OF SCIENCE & TECHNOLOGY, Nat Museum of American Hist, Rm 1041, 14th St & Constitution Ave NW, 20560-0672. (Mail add: PO Box 37012, MRC 672, 20013-7012), SAN 375-5266. Tel: 202-633-3872. E-mail: dibnerlibrary@si.edu. Web Site: library.si.edu/libraries/dibner. *Head, Spec Coll,* Lilla Vekerdy; E-mail: vekerdyl@si.edu; Staff 2 (MLS 1, Non-MLS 1)
Library Holdings: Bk Vols 35,000
Special Collections: A G Bell & Joseph Henry Coll; Burndy Library Donation; Comegys Library; Wetmore Bequest; World's Fair Coll
Subject Interests: Applied arts, Astronomy, Engr, Natural hist, Phys sci, Tech
Publications: Dibner Library Lecture (Annual); Heralds of Science; Manuscripts of the Dibner Collection
Open Mon-Fri 10-5:30 or by appointment
FREER GALLERY OF ART & ARTHUR M SACKLER GALLERY LIBRARY, Arthur M Sackler Gallery, Rm 2058, 1050 Independence Ave NW, 20560. (Mail add: PO Box 37012, MRC 707, 20013-7012), SAN 337-047X. Tel: 202-633-0477. FAX: 202-786-2936. Web Site: library.si.edu/libraries/freer-sackler. *Head Librn,* Reiko Yoshimura; Tel: 202-633-0481, E-mail: yoshire@si.edu; *Librn,* Kathryn Phillips; Tel: 202-633-0478, E-mail: phillka@si.edu; *Librn,* Yue Shu; Tel:

202-633-0479, E-mail: shuyuex@si.edu; *Librn,* Mike Smith; Tel: 202-633-0480, E-mail: smithmi@si.edu; Staff 3 (MLS 3)
Founded 1923
Library Holdings: Bk Vols 86,804
Special Collections: Charles Lang Freer Coll, archives; Herzfeld Coll, archives; James M Whistler & His Contemporaries
Subject Interests: Arts, Asia, E Asian, Far East, Near East, S Asia, SE Asia
Automation Activity & Vendor Info: (OPAC) Innovative Interfaces, Inc
Open Mon-Fri 10-5
Restriction: Non-circulating to the pub

HIRSHHORN MUSEUM & SCULPTURE GARDEN LIBRARY, Hirshhorn Museum, 4th Flr, 700 Independence Ave SW, 20560. (Mail add: PO Box 37012, MRC 361, 20013-7012), SAN 337-050X. Tel: 202-633-2776. FAX: 202-633-8796. E-mail: HMSGLibrary@si.edu. Web Site: library.si.edu/libraries/hirshhorn. *Br Librn,* Jacqueline Protka; Tel: 202-633-2774, E-mail: protkaj@si.edu; *Libr Tech,* Rebecca Bruner; Tel: 202-633-2775, E-mail: brunerr@si.edu; Staff 2 (MLS 1, Non-MLS 1)
Founded 1969
Library Holdings: Bk Vols 67,353
Special Collections: Press Books, photogs, slides
Subject Interests: 19th Century, 20th Century, Memorabilia, Painting, Sculpture
Restriction: Open by appt only

MUSEUM SUPPORT CENTER LIBRARY, Smithsonian Museum Support Center, Rm C-2000, 4210 Silver Hill Rd, Suitland, 20746-2863. (Mail add: PO Box 37012, MRC 534, 20013-7012), SAN 376-9348. Tel: 301-238-1030. Web Site: library.si.edu/libraries/museum-support-center-library. *Coll Mgt Librn,* Sharad J Shah; E-mail: shahs@si.edu; *Coll Mgt, Libr Tech,* Amanda E Landis; Tel: 301-238-1027, E-mail: landisae@si.edu; Staff 2 (MLS 2)
Library Holdings: Bk Vols 25,647
Subject Interests: Art conserv, Mat & conserv sci, Object conserv, Restoration
Function: Audio & video playback equip for onsite use
Restriction: Open by appt only

NATIONAL AIR & SPACE MUSEUM LIBRARY, Steven F Udar-Hazy Center Room, 203.10 14390 Air & Space Museum Pkwy, Chantilly, 20151. Tel: 703-572-4175. FAX: 703-572-4161. Web Site: library.si.edu/libraries/air-and-space. *Head Librn,* Chris Cottrill; Tel: 703-572-4048, E-mail: cottrillc@si.edu; Staff 4 (MLS 1, Non-MLS 3)
Library Holdings: Bk Titles 44,000
Special Collections: Aerospace (Bella Landauer Sheet Music & Children's Book Coll); Aerospace (Institute of Aeronautical Sciences Historical Coll), bk, per, photog; Ballooning (William A M Burden Coll), bks, per; Rare & Scarce Aeronautica & Astronautica (Ramsey Room)
Subject Interests: Aeronaut, Astronautics, Astronomy, Astrophysics, Earth sci, Planetary sci
Open Tues-Fri 10-4 or by appointment

NATIONAL MUSEUM OF AMERICAN HISTORY LIBRARY, NMAH Rm 5016, 14th & Constitution Ave NW, 20560. (Mail add: PO Box 37012, MRC 630, 20013-7012), SAN 337-0593. Tel: 202-633-3865. FAX: 202-633-3427. Web Site: library.si.edu/libraries/american-history. *Head Librn,* Tina Brown; Tel: 202-633-3867, E-mail: brownkm@si.edu; *Ref Librn,* Jim Roan; Tel: 202-633-3860, E-mail: roanj@si.edu
Founded 1958
Library Holdings: Microforms 500; Bk Vols 468,857
Special Collections: Exhibitions & Expositions; History of Science & Technology; Radioana; Trade Literature
Subject Interests: Am hist, Culture, Decorative art, Graphic arts, Mil hist, Numismatics, Photog, Textiles
Restriction: Open to pub by appt only

NATIONAL MUSEUM OF NATURAL HISTORY LIBRARY, Tenth St & Constitution Ave NW, 1st Flr, 20013-0712. (Mail add: PO Box 37012, MRC 154, 20013-7012), SAN 337-0623. Tel: 202-633-1680. FAX: 202-357-1896. Web Site: library.si.edu/libraries/natural-history. *Dept Head,* Barbara P Ferry; Tel: 202-633-1785, E-mail: ferryb@si.edu; *Librn,* Robin Everly; Tel: 202-633-1685, E-mail: everlyr@si.edu; *Ref Librn,* Polly Lasker; Tel: 202-633-1702, E-mail: laskerp@si.edu; *Libr Tech,* Richard Greene; Tel: 202-633-1672, E-mail: greener@si.edu; *Libr Tech,* Ronald Lindsey; Tel: 202-633-1673, E-mail: lindseyr@si.edu. Subject Specialists: *Natural sci, Phys sci,* Barbara P Ferry; Staff 9 (MLS 5, Non-MLS 4)
Library Holdings: Bk Vols 129,544
Special Collections: Entomology (Casey Coleoptera Coll); Foraminifera (Cushman Coll); Invertebrate Zoology (Wilson Copepoda Coll); Meteorites (Paneth Coll)
Subject Interests: Botany, Ecology, Entomology, Evolution, Geol, Oceanography, Zoology
Open Mon-Fri 9-5 or by appointment

NATIONAL POSTAL MUSEUM LIBRARY, Two Massachusetts Ave NE, MRC 570, Rm 106, 20013, SAN 375-5258. Tel: 202-633-5543. FAX: 202-633-8876. Web Site: library.si.edu/libraries/postal-museum. *Librn,* Baasil Wilder; E-mail: wilderb@si.edu; Staff 1 (MLS 1)
Library Holdings: Bk Vols 22,190
Special Collections: Postal History (Thaddeus Hyatt Postcard & Clipping Files); Sydnor Zip-Code File; US Post Office Department Files
Subject Interests: Philately
Open Mon-Fri 10-3:30 or by appointment

NATIONAL ZOOLOGICAL PARK LIBRARY, Nat Zoological Park, Education Bldg-Visitor Ctr, 3000 Block of Connecticut Ave NW, 20008-0551. (Mail add: PO Box 37012, MRC 5501, 20013-7012), SAN 337-0712. Tel: 202-673-1030. FAX: 202-673-4900. E-mail: nzplibrary@si.edu. Web Site: library.si.edu/libraries/national-zoo. *Br Librn,* Stephen H Cox, Jr; Tel: 202-633-1798, E-mail: coxsh@si.edu; Staff 1 (MLS 1)
Library Holdings: Bk Vols 14,500
Subject Interests: Animal husbandry, Animals, behavior of, Clinical med, Pathology, Veterinary med, Wildlife
Restriction: Open by appt only

JOHN WESLEY POWELL LIBRARY OF ANTHROPOLOGY, Natural History Bldg, Rm 331, Tenth St & Constitution Ave NW, 20560-0112. (Mail add: PO Box 37012, MRC 154, 20013-7012), SAN 374-8081. Tel: 202-633-1640. FAX: 202-357-1896. Web Site: library.si.edu/libraries/anthropology. *Libr Tech,* Ronald Lindsey; E-mail: lindseyr@si.edu; *Librn Emeritus,* Margaret Dittemore; E-mail: dittemorem@si.edu; Staff 3 (MLS 2, Non-MLS 1)
Library Holdings: Bk Vols 84,223
Special Collections: Asian Cultural History (Echols Coll); Bureau of American Ethnology Library Coll; Mesoamerican Codices; Native American Languages/Linguistics; Physical Anthropology (Hrdlicka Coll)
Subject Interests: Anthrop, Archaeology
Restriction: Open to pub by appt only

WARREN M ROBBINS LIBRARY, NATIONAL MUSEUM OF AFRICAN ART, National Museum of African Art, 950 Independence Ave SW, Rm 2138, 20560. (Mail add: PO Box 37012, MRC 708, 20013-7012), SAN 302-637X. Tel: 202-633-4680. FAX: 202-357-4879. Web Site: library.si.edu/libraries/african-art. *Librn,* Janet L Stanley; Tel: 202-633-4681, E-mail: janet@si.edu; *Libr Tech,* Karen Brown; Tel: 202-633-4682, E-mail: brownkf@si.edu; Staff 1 (MLS 1)
Library Holdings: Bk Vols 40,500
Subject Interests: Africa, Archaeology, Art, Folklore, Hist, Mat culture, Music, Relig
Restriction: Open to pub by appt only

SMITHSONIAN AMERICAN ART MUSEUM/NATIONAL PORTRAIT GALLERY LIBRARY, Victor Bldg, Rm 2100, 750 Ninth St NW, 20560. (Mail add: PO Box 37012, MRC 975, 20013-7012), SAN 337-0569. Tel: 202-633-8230. FAX: 202-633-8232. E-mail: AAPGLibrary@si.edu. Web Site: library.si.edu/libraries/american-art-and-portrait-gallery-library. *Head Librn,* Anne Evenhaugen; Tel: 202-633-8227, E-mail: evenhaugena@si.edu; *Ref Librn,* Alexandra Reigle; Tel: 202-633-8235, E-mail: reiglea@si.edu; Staff 5 (MLS 2, Non-MLS 3)
Founded 1964
Library Holdings: Bk Vols 180,000
Special Collections: California Art & Artists (Ferdinand Perret Art Reference Library), scrapbks; Mallet Library of Art Reproductions
Subject Interests: 20th Century art, Am art, Biog, Hist, Portraiture
Partic in Proquest Dialog; Wilsonline
Publications: Brochure
Open Mon-Fri 10-5

SMITHSONIAN ENVIRONMENTAL RESEARCH CENTER LIBRARY, 647 Contees Wharf Rd, Edgewater, 21037, SAN 307-0174. Tel: 443-482-2273. FAX: 443-482-2286. Web Site: library.si.edu/libraries/environmental-research-center. *Librn,* Susan Zwicker; Tel: 202-633-1675, E-mail: zwickers@si.edu; Staff 1 (Non-MLS 1)
Founded 1977
Library Holdings: Bk Vols 13,850
Subject Interests: Ecology, Environ mgt, Land use
Restriction: Open to pub by appt only

R SOCIETY OF MOUNT CARMEL, Carmelitana Collection, Whitefriars Hall, 1600 Webster St NE, 20017. Tel: 202-526-1221, Ext 204, 202-892-4077. E-mail: carmelitanacoll@gmail.com. Web Site: carmeliteinstitute.net/the-carmelitana-collection. *Librn,* Patricia O'Callaghan; Staff 3 (MLS 2, Non-MLS 1)
Founded 1948
Library Holdings: Bk Titles 15,500; Per Subs 32
Special Collections: Carmelite Tradition in Roman Catholic Spirituality (Carmelitana Coll), AV mat, microfilm, rare & modern bks
Automation Activity & Vendor Info: (Cataloging) OCLC Connexion; (ILL) OCLC WorldShare Interlibrary Loan; (OPAC) Inmagic, Inc.
Wireless access
Restriction: Open by appt only

S SOCIETY OF THE CINCINNATI LIBRARY, 2118 Massachusetts Ave NW, 20008. SAN 302-7767. Tel: 202-785-2040, Ext 411. FAX: 202-785-0729. E-mail: library@societyofthecincinnati.org. Web Site: www.societyofthecincinnati.org. *Libr Dir,* Ellen Clark; Tel: 202-785-2040, Ext 426, E-mail: emclark@societyofthecincinnati.org; *Research Servs*

Librn, Rachel Nellis; Tel: 202 785-2040, Ext 424, E-mail: rnellis@societyofthecincinnati.org; *Cataloger,* E K Hong; Tel: 202-785-2040, Ext 425, E-mail: ekhong@societyofthecincinnati.org; Staff 3 (MLS 3)
Founded 1968
Library Holdings: Per Subs 100
Special Collections: 18th Century, American Revolution, Art of War & Military History, engravings, maps, ms, prints, rare bks; Archives of the Society of the Cincinnati
Wireless access
Function: Archival coll, Art exhibits, Online cat
Publications: Cincinnati Fourteen (Biennial); Exhibition Catalogs
Partic in OCLC Online Computer Library Center, Inc
Restriction: Open by appt only

L SPIEGEL & MCDIARMID LLP, Law Library, 1875 Eye St NW, Ste 700, 20006. SAN 372-1744. Tel: 202-879-4055. FAX: 202-393-2866. E-mail: library@spiegelmcd.com. Web Site: www.spiegelmcd.com. *Librn,* Jeffrey J Berns; E-mail: jeff.berns@spiegelmcd.com; Staff 1 (MLS 1)
Founded 1967
Library Holdings: e-books 580; Microforms 10; Bk Titles 4,465; Bk Vols 11,925; Per Subs 45; Videos 170
Subject Interests: Admin law, Energy law, Environ law, Telecommunications law
Automation Activity & Vendor Info: (Acquisitions) Inmagic, Inc.; (Cataloging) LibraryWorld, Inc; (Circulation) LibraryWorld, Inc; (ILL) Inmagic, Inc.; (OPAC) LibraryWorld, Inc; (Serials) LibraryWorld, Inc
Wireless access
Publications: Library Blog (Online only)
Open Mon-Fri 9-5:30

L SQUIRE PATTON & BOGGS LLP*, Law Library, 2550 M St NW, 20037. SAN 376-0669. Tel: 202-457-6000. FAX: 202-457-6315. Web Site: www.squirepattonboggs.com/en/locations/washington-dc. *Librn,* Kevin McCall; E-mail: kevin.mccall@squirepb.com
Library Holdings: Bk Titles 3,500; Bk Vols 20,000; Per Subs 200
Open Mon-Fri 9-5:30

L STEPTOE & JOHNSON LIBRARY*, 1330 Connecticut Ave NW, 20036. SAN 302-7805. Tel: 202-828-3620. FAX: 202-429-3902. Web Site: www.steptoe.com. *Dir,* Ellen Brondfield; Tel: 202-429-6429, E-mail: ebrondfield@steptoe.com; Staff 9 (MLS 8, Non-MLS 1)
Founded 1972
Library Holdings: Bk Vols 60,000
Subject Interests: Law, Legislation
Partic in OCLC Online Computer Library Center, Inc
Restriction: Not open to pub

L STERNE, KESSLER, GOLDSTEIN & FOX LIBRARY*, 1100 New York Ave NW, Ste 600, 20005. SAN 371-7666. Tel: 202-371-2600. Interlibrary Loan Service Tel: 202-772-8808. FAX: 202-371-2540. E-mail: info@skgf.com. Web Site: www.skgf.com. *Dir,* LiMin Fields; E-mail: lfields@skgf.com; *Libr Asst,* Jackie Canty-Tisdale; E-mail: jtisdale@skgf.com; Staff 2 (MLS 1, Non-MLS 1)
Library Holdings: Bk Titles 700
Wireless access

L STONE MATTHEIS XENOPOULOS & BREW, PC LIBRARY*, 1025 Thomas Jefferson St NW, Ste 800 W, 20007-5201. Tel: 202-342-0800. FAX: 202-342-0807. Web Site: www.smxblaw.com. *Library Contact,* Pam Ingram; E-mail: pdi@smxblaw.com
Library Holdings: Bk Titles 400
Function: Res libr
Restriction: Authorized personnel only, Borrowing requests are handled by ILL, Co libr

C STRAYER UNIVERSITY*, Wilkes Library, 1133 15th St NW, 20005. SAN 302-7813. Tel: 202-419-0483. FAX: 202-419-1463. *Univ Librn,* Mary Snyder; *Learning Resource Ctr Mgr,* Chris Kosko
Founded 1965. Highest Degree: Master
Library Holdings: AV Mats 1,000; e-books 80,000; Bk Vols 105,000; Per Subs 500
Subject Interests: Acctg, Bus admin, Criminal justice, Educ, Health serv admin, Info syst, Mkt, Pub admin
Automation Activity & Vendor Info: (Cataloging) SirsiDynix; (Circulation) SirsiDynix; (OPAC) SirsiDynix
Partic in LYRASIS; OCLC Online Computer Library Center, Inc

L SULLIVAN & CROMWELL LLP*, Law Library, 1700 New York Ave NW, Ste 700, 20006-5215. SAN 372-1477. Tel: 202-956-7500. FAX: 202-293-6330. E-mail: library.dc@sullcrom.com. Web Site: www.sullcrom.com. *Librn,* Denise Noller; E-mail: nollerd@sullcrom.com
Library Holdings: Bk Vols 8,000; Per Subs 25
Wireless access
Open Mon-Fri 9-5 by appointment

GL SUPREME COURT OF THE UNITED STATES LIBRARY, One First St NE, 20543. (Mail add: 3035 V St NE, 20018), SAN 302-7848. Tel: 202-479-3037. FAX: 202-479-3477. *Librn,* Linda Maslow; E-mail: lmaslow@supremecourt.gov; *Asst Librn, Coll Mgt, Tech,* Melissa Williams; E-mail: mhuyck@supremecourt.gov; *Asst Librn, Res Serv,* Karin Johnsrud; E-mail: kjohnsrud@supremecourt.gov; *Asst Librn, Spec Coll, Tech Serv,* William Sleeman; E-mail: wsleeman@supremecourt.gov; Staff 28 (MLS 15, Non-MLS 13)
Founded 1887
Library Holdings: Bk Vols 600,000; Per Subs 6,370
Special Collections: Supreme Court of the United States Coll, recs & briefs
Subject Interests: Law
Automation Activity & Vendor Info: (OPAC) Innovative Interfaces, Inc
Function: For res purposes
Partic in Law Library Microform Consortium
Open Mon-Fri 9-4:30
Restriction: Private libr

G SURFACE TRANSPORTATION BOARD LIBRARY*, 395 E St SW, 20024. SAN 302-6841. Tel: 202-245-0238. E-mail: rcpa@stb.gov. Web Site: www.stb.gov/stb/public/inquiries_library.html. *Dep Dir,* Michael Higgins; Staff 1 (MLS 1)
Founded 1894
Library Holdings: Bk Vols 10,000; Per Subs 10
Special Collections: Congressional Materials; Transportation in the US, doc, rare bks; US & Canada Regulatory Commissions, rpts
Subject Interests: Admin law, Statistics, Transportation
Automation Activity & Vendor Info: (Cataloging) Inmagic, Inc.
Restriction: Open by appt only

R TEMPLE SINAI LIBRARY*, 3100 Military Rd NW, 20015. SAN 302-7872. Tel: 202-363-6394. FAX: 202-363-6396. Web Site: www.templesinaidc.org/learn/library. *Librn,* Ruth Polk; Tel: 202-363-6394, Ext 218, E-mail: rpolk@templesinaidc.org
Founded 1955
Library Holdings: Audiobooks 3; DVDs 88; Bk Vols 9,000; Per Subs 15
Special Collections: Bill Rabin Art Coll; Children's Literature (Lisa Sanders Ressell Coll); Comparative Religion (Celia Freedman Coll); Hebrew Texts
Subject Interests: Biblical studies, Holocaust, Jewish hist & lit, Judaica, Philos, Relig
Wireless access
Function: 24/7 Online cat, Adult bk club
Publications: Selected Bibliographies on Judaica
Restriction: Authorized patrons, Congregants only

L THOMPSON COBURN LIBRARY*, DC Branch, 1909 K St NW, Ste 600, 20006. SAN 377-4449. Tel: 202-585-6900. FAX: 202-585-6969. Web Site: www.thompsoncoburn.com. *Legislative Librn,* Charlotte Osborn-Bensaada; E-mail: cbensaada@thompsoncoburn.com

L THREE CROWNS LLP*, Law Library, 3000 K St NW, Ste 101, 20007. Tel: 202-540-9500. FAX: 202-350-9439. *Res Mgr,* Kelly Renehan; Tel: 202-540-9460, E-mail: kelly.renehan@threecrownship.com; *Research Coordr,* Mailise Johnson; Tel: 202-540-9491, E-mail: mailise.johnson@threecrownsllp.com; Staff 2 (Non-MLS 2)
Library Holdings: Bk Titles 500
Restriction: Not open to pub

C TRINITY UNIVERSITY, Sister Helen Sheehan Library, 125 Michigan Ave NE, 20017. SAN 302-7929. Tel: 202-884-9350. Interlibrary Loan Service Tel: 202-884-9357. FAX: 202-884-9241. E-mail: trinitylibrary@trinitydc.edu. Web Site: www.trinitydc.edu/library. *Univ Librn,* Trisha Smith; Tel: 202-884-9351, E-mail: smithtri@trinitydc.edu; *Coll Develop Librn,* Alexander Salopek; Tel: 202-884-9359, E-mail: salopeka@trinitydc.edu; *Instruction Librn,* Bridgette Comanda; Tel: 202-884-9352, E-mail: comandab@trinitydc.edu; Staff 3 (MLS 2, Non-MLS 1)
Founded 1897. Enrl 1,600; Fac 100; Highest Degree: Master
Subject Interests: Hist, Lit, Women's studies
Automation Activity & Vendor Info: (Acquisitions) Ex Libris Group; (Cataloging) Ex Libris Group; (Circulation) Ex Libris Group; (ILL) OCLC; (OPAC) Ex Libris Group; (Serials) Ex Libris Group
Wireless access
Function: Distance learning, Doc delivery serv, Electronic databases & coll, Homework prog, ILL available, Internet access, Online ref, Outside serv via phone, mail, e-mail & web, Photocopying/Printing, Ref & res, Ref serv available, Telephone ref, VHS videos, Wheelchair accessible, Workshops
Partic in OCLC Online Computer Library Center, Inc; Washington Research Library Consortium

S UNITED NATIONS INFORMATION CENTER*, 1775 K St NW, Ste 400, 20006. SAN 302-7937. Tel: 202-331-8670. FAX: 202-331-9191. E-mail: unicdc@unic.org. Web Site: www.unicwash.org. *Librn, Pub Info,* Liam Murphy
Founded 1946
Library Holdings: Bk Titles 2,000; Bk Vols 3,000; Per Subs 10
Special Collections: Film Library; United Nations Chronicles & Publications; United Nations Official Reports. UN Document Depository
Subject Interests: Econ, Energy, Finance, Human rights, Intl law, Soc sci & issues, United Nations
Restriction: Open by appt only

G US AGENCY FOR INTERNATIONAL DEVELOPMENT*, USAID Library, 1300 Pennsylvania Ave NW, Rm M01-010, 20523-1000. SAN 302-5497. Tel: 202-712-0579. E-mail: ksc@usaid.gov. Web Site: www.usaid.gov/results-and-data/information-resources/about-library. *Libr Team Lead,* Susan G. Press; E-mail: spress@usaid.gov; *Electronic Res Librn,* Mary B. Fry; E-mail: mfry@usaid.gov; *Syst & Cat Librn,* Sean E. Crumley; E-mail: scrumley@usaid.gov; *Librn,* Fatmata McCormack; E-mail: fmccormack@usaid.gov; *ILL Librn,* Susan Press; E-mail: ksc@usaid.gov; Staff 4 (MLS 4)
Founded 1967
Library Holdings: DVDs 500; e-books 7,000; e-journals 200; Bk Vols 16,000; Per Subs 200
Automation Activity & Vendor Info: (Acquisitions) SirsiDynix; (Cataloging) SirsiDynix; (Circulation) SirsiDynix; (ILL) OCLC; (Serials) SirsiDynix
Wireless access
Function: 24/7 Electronic res, 24/7 Online cat, Doc delivery serv, Electronic databases & coll, ILL available
Publications: DEC Express (Acquisition list); New Books In The USAID Library (Acquisition list)
Partic in OCLC Online Computer Library Center, Inc
Open Mon-Fri 9-5
Restriction: Secured area only open to authorized personnel

UNITED STATES AIR FORCE

A ANDREWS AIR FORCE BASE LIBRARY FL4425*, 89 SVS/SVMG, Brookley & D St, Bldg 1642, Andrews AFB, 20762, SAN 337-0836. Tel: 301-981-6454. FAX: 301-981-4231. *Dir,* Anette Powell; Tel: 301-981-1637, E-mail: anette.powell@andrews.af.mil; Staff 5 (MLS 1, Non-MLS 4)
Library Holdings: Bk Vols 30,714; Per Subs 140
Special Collections: Air War College; Children's Coll
Subject Interests: Bus & mgt, Intl relations, Polit sci
Automation Activity & Vendor Info: (Cataloging) SirsiDynix; (Circulation) SirsiDynix; (ILL) OCLC; (OPAC) SirsiDynix
Open Mon 9-8, Tues, Wed & Fri 9-6, Thurs 11-8

A BOLLING AIR FORCE BASE LIBRARY*, FL 7054 HQ 11 MSG/SVMG, 410 Tinker St Bolling AFB, 20032-0703, SAN 337-0895. Tel: 202-767-5578. FAX: 202-404-8526. *Dir,* Shirley Foster; E-mail: shirley.foster@afncr.af.mil
Founded 1931
Library Holdings: Bk Vols 28,090; Per Subs 33
Subject Interests: Mil hist
Automation Activity & Vendor Info: (Cataloging) Softlink America; (Circulation) Softlink America; (OPAC) Softlink America
Restriction: Not open to pub

S UNITED STATES BOTANIC GARDEN LIBRARY*, 245 First St SW, 20024. SAN 374-7689. Tel: 202-225-8333. FAX: 202-225-1561. E-mail: usbg@aoc.gov. Web Site: www.usbg.gov. *Exec Dir,* Dr Saharah Moon Chapotin, PhD; E-mail: schapotin@aoc.gov
Library Holdings: Bk Vols 1,200; Per Subs 10
Subject Interests: Botany, Hort, Landscape design
Restriction: Open by appt only

G UNITED STATES COMMISSION ON CIVIL RIGHTS*, Robert S Rankin Memorial Library, Publications Office, 1331 Pennsylvania Ave NW, Ste 1150, 20425. SAN 302-7953. Tel: 202-376-8110. FAX: 202-376-7597. E-mail: publications@usccr.gov. Web Site: www.usccr.gov. *Libr Tech,* Position Currently Open
Founded 1957
Library Holdings: Per Subs 95
Special Collections: Civil Rights (US Commission on Civil Rights Coll); Federal Register, micro
Subject Interests: Aging, Civil rights, Educ, Handicaps
Automation Activity & Vendor Info: (Cataloging) OCLC; (ILL) OCLC
Partic in OCLC Online Computer Library Center, Inc
Special Services for the Deaf - TDD equip
Open Mon-Fri 10-4
Restriction: Restricted pub use

SR UNITED STATES CONFERENCE OF CATHOLIC BISHOPS -CATHOLIC NEWS SERVICE*, Department of Communications Library & Archives, 3211 Fourth St NE, 20017-1194. SAN 371-6341. Tel: 202-541-3286. Web Site: www.catholicnews.com, www.usccb.org. *Mgr, Info & Archive Serv,* Katherine Nuss; E-mail: knuss@usccb.org; Staff 1 (MLS 1)
Founded 1917
Library Holdings: Bk Vols 3,500; Per Subs 20
Special Collections: Catholic News Service; NCWC American Bishops, books & pamphlets; United States Conference of Catholic Bishops Publications, books & pamphlets
Subject Interests: Church hist, Human rights, Theol
Wireless access
Function: 24/7 Electronic res, Archival coll, Electronic databases & coll, For res purposes, Ref & res
Restriction: Access at librarian's discretion, Non-circulating coll, Not a lending libr, Open by appt only

GL UNITED STATES COURT OF APPEALS FOR THE ARMED FORCES LIBRARY*, 450 E St NW, 20442-0001. SAN 302-7988. Tel: 202-761-1466. Web Site: www.armfor.uscourts.gov/newcaaf/library.htm. *Law Librn,* Agnes Kiang; Staff 2 (MLS 1, Non-MLS 1)
Founded 1951
Library Holdings: Bk Vols 20,000; Per Subs 40
Subject Interests: Criminal law, Mil justice
Wireless access
Function: For res purposes, ILL available
Restriction: By permission only

GL UNITED STATES COURT OF APPEALS FOR THE DISTRICT OF COLUMBIA*, Circuit Library, US Court House, 333 Constitution Ave NW, Rm 3205, 20001. SAN 302-7961. Tel: 202-216-7400. Web Site: www.cadc.uscourts.gov. *Circuit Librn,* Patricia Michalowskij; *Dep Circuit Librn,* Theresa Santella
Library Holdings: Bk Vols 90,000; Per Subs 160
Automation Activity & Vendor Info: (Acquisitions) SirsiDynix; (Cataloging) SirsiDynix; (Circulation) SirsiDynix; (ILL) SirsiDynix; (Serials) SirsiDynix
Wireless access
Partic in OCLC Online Computer Library Center, Inc

G UNITED STATES DEPARTMENT OF COMMERCE*, Commerce Research Library, 1401 Constitution Ave NW, Rm 1894, 20230. SAN 337-1042. Tel: 202-482-1154. FAX: 202-482-0221. E-mail: research@doc.gov. Web Site: library.doc.gov.
Founded 1913
Wireless access
Partic in OCLC Online Computer Library Center, Inc
Restriction: Open to dept staff only, Open to pub by appt only

G US DEPARTMENT OF DEFENSE*, National Defense University Library, Fort McNair, Marshall Hall, 20319-5066. (Mail add: Fort Leslie J McNair, Bldg 62, 300 Fifth Ave SW, 20319-5066), SAN 302-7163. Tel: 202-685-3511. Interlibrary Loan Service Tel: 202-685-3968. Reference Tel: 202-685-3511, 202-685-3513. FAX: 202-685-3733. *Dir,* David Gansz; *Chief, Info Archit Div,* Michael McNulty; *Spec Coll & Archives Librn,* Susan K Lemke; Tel: 202-685-3957, E-mail: lemkes@ndu.edu. Subject Specialists: *Mil hist,* Susan K Lemke; Staff 30 (MLS 18, Non-MLS 12)
Founded 1976. Enrl 4,500; Fac 261; Highest Degree: Master
Library Holdings: e-journals 18,000; Electronic Media & Resources 75; Bk Titles 320,000; Bk Vols 675,000; Per Subs 1,200
Special Collections: Archives of the Hudson Institute; Conduct of the Persian Gulf War; Correspondence of Bernard Baruch & Julius A Krug; Ft McNair History, including photographs & materials of the Lincoln assassination; Library & Papers of Dr Ralph L Powell (China); Library of Hoffman Nickerson (military history); Mallahan World War I Coll; Military Classics, including the early editions of Marshal de Saxe; NDU Academic & Institutional Archives; Personal Papers (Restricted) of Generals Frank S Besson Jr, John Galvin, Andreu J Goodpaster, George Joulwan, Lyman L Lemnitzer, Colin Powell, John Shalikashvili, Maxwell D Taylor; Speeches on Industrial Mobilization & Papers of J Carlton Ward Jr; Working Papers for the Presidential Commission on Women in the Combat. US Document Depository
Subject Interests: Intl relations, Logistics, Mil hist, Nat security, Polit sci
Automation Activity & Vendor Info: (Acquisitions) SirsiDynix; (Cataloging) SirsiDynix; (Circulation) SirsiDynix; (Course Reserve) SirsiDynix; (ILL) OCLC; (OPAC) SirsiDynix; (Serials) SirsiDynix
Function: Archival coll, Art exhibits, Computer training, Distance learning, E-Reserves, Electronic databases & coll, Govt ref serv, ILL available, Internet access, Online info literacy tutorials on the web & in blackboard, Online ref, Orientations, Outside serv via phone, mail, e-mail & web, Ref & res, Ref serv available, Telephone ref
Publications: Military Policy Awareness Links (Current awareness service); Subject Bibliographies

Partic in Federal Library & Information Network
Restriction: Not open to pub, Open to students, fac & staff

G UNITED STATES DEPARTMENT OF DEFENSE, WASHINGTON HEADQUARTERS SERVICES*, The Pentagon Library, 1155 Defense Pentagon, 20301-1155. SAN 337-1611. Circulation Tel: 703-695-1992. Reference Tel: 703-695-1997. Web Site: www.whs.mil/library. *Libr Tech,* Peggy Poirier; Staff 21 (MLS 9, Non-MLS 12)
Founded 1944
Special Collections: DoD/DA Regulatory Publications & Manuals; Law Coll; Legislative Histories Relating to DoD Issues; Military Arts & Sciences Coll; Military History Coll; Regulatory Publications
Subject Interests: Foreign affairs, Intl relations, Mil hist (US), Mil sci
Automation Activity & Vendor Info: (Cataloging) EOS International; (Circulation) EOS International
Wireless access
Partic in Federal Library & Information Network
Restriction: Not open to pub

G UNITED STATES DEPARTMENT OF HEALTH & HUMAN SERVICES*, Office of the General Counsel, Law Library, Cohen Bldg, Rm 4541, 330 Independence Ave SW, 20201. SAN 377-399X. Tel: 202-619-0190. FAX: 202-619-3719. E-mail: law.library@hhs.gov. *Legal Info Mgr,* Susan Panasik; *Libr Tech,* Luan Tang; Staff 2 (MLS 1, Non-MLS 1)
Founded 1987
Library Holdings: Bk Vols 10,000; Per Subs 10
Subject Interests: Admin law, Health law
Open Mon-Fri 9-5
Restriction: Authorized personnel only, Circ limited

G UNITED STATES DEPARTMENT OF HOUSING & URBAN DEVELOPMENT*, HUD Library, 451 Seventh St SW, Rm 8141, 20410. SAN 302-802X. Tel: 202-708-2370. FAX: 202-708-1485. E-mail: library@hud.gov. Web Site: www.hud.gov. *Librn,* Eric Erickson; Tel: 202-402-4269, E-mail: eric.c.erickson@hud.gov. Subject Specialists: *Econ, Soc sci,* Eric Erickson
Founded 1934
Library Holdings: Bk Vols 680,000; Per Subs 2,200
Special Collections: Comprehensive Housing Affordability Strategy Reports; Housing in the 70's Background Papers; Management Evaluation Reports
Subject Interests: Am housing, Archit, Bldg construction, Bldg tech, Commun develop, Econ, Environ, Fed govt, Homelessness, Law, Local govt, Metrop area problems, Regional data, Regional planning, Sociologic data, State govt, Urban land use
Wireless access
Publications: Library Periodicals List: internal distribution; Recent Library Acquisitions
Partic in Federal Library & Information Network
Open Mon-Fri 9-4:30

GL UNITED STATES DEPARTMENT OF JUSTICE*, Justice Libraries, 950 Pennsylvania Ave, Ste 5313, 20530. SAN 337-1190. Tel: 202-514-2133. Reference Tel: 202-514-3775. Web Site: www.justice.gov/jmd/ls. *Dir,* Dennis Feldt; Staff 78 (MLS 35, Non-MLS 43)
Founded 1831
Library Holdings: Bk Titles 85,000; Bk Vols 300,000; Per Subs 1,700
Special Collections: American, Canadian & British Law; Department of Justice Publications; United States Supreme Court Records & Briefs
Subject Interests: Antitrust, Civil, Civil rights, Criminal, Environ, Natural res, Tax
Automation Activity & Vendor Info: (Acquisitions) Ex Libris Group; (Cataloging) OCLC; (Circulation) SirsiDynix; (OPAC) SirsiDynix; (Serials) SirsiDynix
Wireless access
Partic in OCLC Online Computer Library Center, Inc
Special Services for the Deaf - TDD equip
Restriction: Open by appt only

G UNITED STATES DEPARTMENT OF LABOR*, Wirtz Labor Library, 200 Constitution Ave NW, Rm N-2445, 20210. SAN 337-1344. Tel: 202-693-6600. FAX: 202-693-6644. E-mail: library@dol.gov. Web Site: www.dol.gov/oasam/wirtzlaborlibrary. *Libr Dir,* Macaire Carroll-Gavula; Staff 11 (MLS 5, Non-MLS 6)
Founded 1917
Library Holdings: e-journals 4,500; Bk Titles 140,000; Per Subs 4,500
Special Collections: Labor Unions, doc, mat
Subject Interests: Econ, Labor
Special Services for the Deaf - ADA equip; Am sign lang & deaf culture; Assisted listening device
Special Services for the Blind - Aids for in-house use
Open Mon-Fri 8:15-4:45
Restriction: Fee for pub use

G UNITED STATES DEPARTMENT OF STATE*, Ralph J Bunche Library, A/GIS/IPS/LIBR, Rm 3239, 2201 C St NW, 20520-2442. SAN 302-8038. Tel: 202-647-1099. E-mail: library@state.gov. Web Site: www.state.gov/about-us-library-services. *Chief Librn,* Julie Arrighetti; Tel: 202-647-3002; Staff 29 (MLS 17, Non-MLS 12)
Founded 1789
Library Holdings: e-books 7,000; e-journals 8,136; Electronic Media & Resources 51; Bk Vols 400,000; Per Subs 800
Special Collections: Department of State Publications; Diplomatic Lists
Subject Interests: Diplomatic hist, Foreign affairs, Intl law
Automation Activity & Vendor Info: (Cataloging) Ex Libris Group; (Circulation) Ex Libris Group; (OPAC) Ex Libris Group
Publications: Acquisitions List (Monthly)
Restriction: Open by appt only

G UNITED STATES DEPARTMENT OF THE INTERIOR LIBRARY*, 1849 C St NW, MS 1151, 20240. SAN 302-8046. Tel: 202-208-5815. FAX: 202-208-6773. E-mail: library@ios.doi.gov. Web Site: www.doi.gov/library. *Libr Dir,* George Franchois; Tel: 202-208-3796, E-mail: george_franchois@ios.doi.gov; *Head, Ref Serv,* Jennifer Klang; Tel: 202-208-3396, E-mail: jennifer_klang@ios.doi.gov; *ILL, Ref Librn,* Shyamalika Ghoshal; Tel: 202-208-3309, E-mail: shyamalika_ghoshal@ios.doi.gov; *Law Librn,* Shannon Lynch; Tel: 202-208-3686, E-mail: Mary_Lynch@ios.doi.gov; *Tech Serv Mgr,* Judy Din; Tel: 202-208-3402, E-mail: judy_din@ios.doi.gov. Subject Specialists: *Hist,* George Franchois; Staff 8 (MLS 7, Non-MLS 1)
Founded 1949
Library Holdings: Bk Vols 950,000; Per Subs 1,000
Special Collections: Conservation & Natural Resources; Dept of the Interior; Rare Book Coll. US Document Depository
Subject Interests: Am hist, Energy, Land mgt, Mining, Natural res, Nature, Parks, Recreation, Wildlife
Automation Activity & Vendor Info: (Acquisitions) SirsiDynix; (Cataloging) SirsiDynix; (Circulation) SirsiDynix; (Serials) SirsiDynix
Partic in OCLC Online Computer Library Center, Inc
Open Mon-Fri 7:45-5

UNITED STATES DEPARTMENT OF THE NAVY

AL NAVY GENERAL COUNSEL LAW LIBRARY*, Bldg 36, Rm 213, 720 Kennon St SE, 20374, SAN 337-1948. Tel: 202-685-6944. FAX: 202-685-6959.
Founded 1949
Library Holdings: Bk Vols 30,000
Special Collections: Law & Legislation (Legislative Histories)
Function: ILL available

A OFFICE OF NAVAL INTELLIGENCE RESEARCH LIBRARY*, 4251 Suitland Rd, 20395-5720, SAN 337-1859. Tel: 301-669-4386. FAX: 301-669-4282. *Chief Librn,* Magen Dane; Tel: 301-669-3116, E-mail: mdane@nmic.navy.mil; Staff 9 (MLS 2, Non-MLS 7)
Library Holdings: Bk Vols 10,000; Per Subs 1,000
Subject Interests: Maritime
Partic in OCLC Online Computer Library Center, Inc

UNITED STATES DEPARTMENT OF TRANSPORTATION

GL FEDERAL HIGHWAY ADMINISTRATION-CHIEF COUNSEL'S LAW LIBRARY*, 1200 New Jersy Ave SE, Rm E84-464, 20590, SAN 323-8725. Tel: 202-366-1387. FAX: 202-366-1380. Web Site: www.fhwa.dot.gov. *Librn,* Shelia Taylor; Staff 4 (MLS 1, Non-MLS 3)
Library Holdings: Bk Vols 500
Special Collections: Highway Legislative Histories (1893-present)
Partic in CQ Washington Alert
Publications: Federal Laws & Materials Relating to the Federal Highway Administration

G NATIONAL HIGHWAY TRAFFIC SAFETY ADMINISTRATION-TECHNICAL INFORMATION SERVICES*, NPO-411, 1200 New Jersey Ave SE, 20590, SAN 302-7252. Tel: 202-366-2588. FAX: 202-493-2833. E-mail: tis@nhtsa.dot.gov. Web Site: www.nhtsa.dot.gov. *Lead, Info Spec/Analyst,* Shirlene D Ball; E-mail: shirlene.ball@dot.gov; *Info Spec,* Derrick Lewis; E-mail: derrick.lewis@dot.gov; Staff 5 (MLS 1, Non-MLS 4)
Founded 1967
Library Holdings: CDs 450; Electronic Media & Resources 15,000; Bk Vols 100; Per Subs 30
Special Collections: Automotive Safety (Research & Test Reports of National Highway Traffic Safety Administration); Defect Investigation Files Coll; Record of Rulemaking Activity of National Highway Traffic Safety Administration
Function: For res purposes, ILL available, Internet access, Photocopying/Printing, Telephone ref
Partic in Federal Library & Information Network; TRIS File
Open Mon-Fri 9:30-4

S UNITED STATES EQUAL EMPLOYMENT OPPORTUNITY COMMISSION LIBRARY*, 131 M St NE, Rm 4SW16N, 20507. SAN 302-8070. Tel: 202-663-4630. FAX: 202-663-4629. E-mail: eeoclibrary@eeoc.gov. *Research Librn,* Linda Hutchinson; *Tech Serv Librn,* Fran O'Neill; *Res Analyst,* Douglas Huemmer; Staff 5 (MLS 4, Non-MLS 1)
Founded 1966
Special Collections: EEOC (Agency) Archives
Subject Interests: Civil rights, Employment, Labor
Publications: What's New in the Library? (Newsletter)
Partic in OCLC Online Computer Library Center, Inc

G UNITED STATES GOVERNMENT ACCOUNTABILITY OFFICE*, Library Services, 441 G St NW, Rm 6H19, 20548. SAN 337-2154. E-mail: gaolibrary@gao.gov. *Dir, Libr Serv,* Meg Tulloch; E-mail: mtulloch@loc.gov; Staff 7 (MLS 7)
Founded 1972
Special Collections: US Document Depository
Subject Interests: Acctg, Auditing, Econ, Law, Soc serv (soc work)
Automation Activity & Vendor Info: (OPAC) Innovative Interfaces, Inc
Partic in OCLC Online Computer Library Center, Inc
Restriction: Access at librarian's discretion, Authorized patrons, Borrowing requests are handled by ILL, Circulates for staff only, Open by appt only, Photo ID required for access, Use of others with permission of librn

G UNITED STATES HOLOCAUST MEMORIAL MUSEUM LIBRARY*, 100 Raoul Wallenberg Pl SW, 20024. SAN 376-2009. Tel: 202-479-9717. FAX: 202-479-9726. E-mail: library@ushmm.org. Reference E-mail: reference@ushmm.org. Web Site: www.ushmm.org/research/library. *Dir,* Lenore Bell; Tel: 202-488-0417, E-mail: lbell@ushmm.org; *Ref Asst,* Ron Coleman; *Ref Asst,* Megan Lewis; *Cat,* Amy Alderfer; *Cat,* Steven Kanaley; *Cat,* Holly Vorhies; *Libr Tech,* Shiela Hoburtes; *Ref Serv,* Vincent Slatt; Staff 6 (MLS 5, Non-MLS 1)
Founded 1993
Library Holdings: CDs 500; DVDs 400; Bk Titles 110,000; Per Subs 100; Videos 800
Special Collections: Memorial Books
Subject Interests: Holocaust
Automation Activity & Vendor Info: (OPAC) Ex Libris Group
Wireless access
Function: Res libr
Open Mon-Fri 8-5

G UNITED STATES HOUSE OF REPRESENTATIVES LIBRARY, 292 Cannon House Office Bldg, 20515-6612. SAN 302-8100. Tel: 202-225-9000. E-mail: library@mail.house.gov. Web Site: clerk.house.gov. *Librn,* Rae Ellen Best; E-mail: rae.best@mail.house.gov; Staff 9 (MLS 6, Non-MLS 3)
Founded 1792
Library Holdings: Bk Vols 200,000
Wireless access
Open Mon-Fri 9-6
Restriction: Mem only, Non-circulating

GL UNITED STATES INTERNATIONAL TRADE COMMISSION LAW LIBRARY*, 500 E St SW, Rm 614, 20436, SAN 337-2219. Tel: 202-205-3287. FAX: 202-205-3111. *Librn,* Maureen Bryant; E-mail: maureen.bryant@usitc.gov; Staff 1 (MLS 1)
Founded 1972
Library Holdings: Bk Vols 10,000
Special Collections: Legislative Histories dealing with Trade & Tariff Acts
Subject Interests: Anti-dumping, Countervailing duties, Imports, Intellectual property, Tariffs, US trade law
Automation Activity & Vendor Info: (Cataloging) OCLC
Publications: Bibliography of Law Journal Articles on Statutes Administered by the United States International Trade Commission & Related Subjects
Restriction: Borrowing requests are handled by ILL, External users must contact libr

G NATIONAL LIBRARY OF INTERNATIONAL TRADE*, 500 E St SW, Rm 300, 20436, SAN 337-2189. Tel: 202-205-2630. FAX: 202-205-2316. Web Site: www.usitc.gov. ; Staff 8 (MLS 5, Non-MLS 3)
Founded 1916
Library Holdings: Bk Vols 40,000; Per Subs 2,500
Subject Interests: Agr products, Econ, Electronics, Energy, Forest products, Intl trade, Machinery manufacturers, Misc manufacturers, Textiles, Transportation
Partic in OCLC Online Computer Library Center, Inc
Open Mon-Fri 9-5
Restriction: Open to pub for ref only
Friends of the Library Group

A UNITED STATES MARINE BAND*, Music Library, Marine Barracks Annex & Band Support Facility, Seventh & L Sts SE, 20003. SAN 302-8135. Tel: 202-433-4298. FAX: 202-433-2221. E-mail: marineband.publicaffairs@usmc.mil. Web Site: www.marineband.marines.mil/About/Library-and-Archives. *Chief Librn,* Kira Wharton
Founded 1798
Library Holdings: Music Scores 50,000; Bk Vols 1,000; Per Subs 25
Special Collections: Band Music; Dance Band; Historical & Program Files; Instrumental Ensembles; John Philip Sousa Coll; Marine Band Archives & Historical Coll, ms, photogs; Military & Wind Music; Orchestra Music; Piano Sheet Music; Reference Books & Scores
Restriction: Open by appt only

G UNITED STATES MERIT SYSTEMS PROTECTION BOARD LIBRARY, 1615 M St NW, 20419. SAN 328-3488. Tel: 202-653-7200. FAX: 202-653-7130. E-mail: mspb@mspb.gov. Web Site: www.mspb.gov. *Librn,* Felicia Moss; Staff 1 (MLS 1)
Library Holdings: Per Subs 20
Wireless access
Function: Archival coll, Govt ref serv, ILL available, Ref & res
Restriction: Open by appt only

S US NATIONAL PARK SERVICE, Frederick Douglass NHS Library, 1411 W St SE, 20020. SAN 370-291X. Tel: 202-426-5961. FAX: 202-426-0880. Web Site: www.nps.gov/frdo. *Curator,* Mike Antonioni; E-mail: mike_antonioni@nps.gov
Founded 1962
Library Holdings: Bk Vols 2,000
Special Collections: Cartes-de-visite; Lantern Slides; Photographic Prints Coll
Special Services for the Deaf - TTY equip

G UNITED STATES NAVAL OBSERVATORY*, James Melville Gilliss Library, 3450 Massachusetts Ave NW, 20392. SAN 302-8143. Tel: 202-762-1463. FAX: 202-762-1516. E-mail: NOBS_LIBRARY@navy.mil. Web Site: www.usno.navy.mil/usno/library. *Librn,* Morgan Aronson; E-mail: morgan.aronson@navy.mil; Staff 2 (MLS 2)
Founded 1830
Library Holdings: Bk Vols 90,000; Per Subs 60
Special Collections: Astronomy, Mathematics, Physics & Navigation (Pre-19th Century Books)
Automation Activity & Vendor Info: (OPAC) Inmagic, Inc.
Partic in Federal Library & Information Network; OCLC Online Computer Library Center, Inc; OCLC-LVIS
Open Mon-Fri 8-5

G UNITED STATES POSTAL SERVICE LIBRARY*, 475 L'Enfant Plaza SW, Rm 11800, 20260-1540. SAN 302-816X. Tel: 202-268-2074. E-mail: phistory@usps.gov. *Historian, Info Serv Mgr,* Jenny Lynch
Founded 1955
Library Holdings: Bk Titles 50,000; Bk Vols 115,000
Special Collections: Congressional Reports (US Congressional Serial Document Set)
Subject Interests: Data proc, Econ, Human resources, Law, Mkt
Open Mon-Fri 8:30-12:30 & 1:30-5

G UNITED STATES SECURITIES & EXCHANGE COMMISSION LIBRARY*, 100 F St NE, Rm 1500, 20549-0002. SAN 302-8178. Tel: 202-551-5450. E-mail: library@sec.gov. *Dir,* Jennifer Davitt; *Ref Librn,* Lillian Hatch; Staff 9 (MLS 6, Non-MLS 3)
Founded 1934
Library Holdings: Bk Vols 62,000; Per Subs 425
Special Collections: Legislative Histories of Statutes Administered by Agency
Subject Interests: Acctg, Bus, Econ, Finance, Securities laws & regulations
Publications: Library Information Bulletin; Periodical Holdings
Partic in OCLC Online Computer Library Center, Inc
Open Mon-Fri 8:30-5
Friends of the Library Group

G UNITED STATES SENATE LIBRARY*, SRB-15 Senate Russell Bldg, 20510. SAN 302-8186. Tel: 202-224-7106. FAX: 202-224-0879. *Head, Ref,* Meghan Dunn; *Librn,* Leona Faust; Staff 20 (MLS 17, Non-MLS 3)
Founded 1871
Library Holdings: Bk Vols 200,000; Per Subs 115
Special Collections: Bills & Resolutions, bk, micro; Congressional Hearings, bk, micro; Congressional Record, bk, micro; Serial Set, bk, micro. US Document Depository
Automation Activity & Vendor Info: (Acquisitions) TLC (The Library Corporation); (Cataloging) TLC (The Library Corporation); (Circulation) TLC (The Library Corporation); (OPAC) TLC (The Library Corporation); (Serials) TLC (The Library Corporation)

Publications: Presidential Vetoes
Partic in OCLC Online Computer Library Center, Inc; Proquest Dialog
Special Services for the Deaf - TDD equip

L UNITED STATES SENTENCING COMMISSION LIBRARY*, One Columbus Circle NE, Ste 2-500 S Lobby, 20002-8002. SAN 372-3097. Tel: 202-502-4500. FAX: 202-502-4699. Web Site: www.ussc.gov. *Librn,* Brittany Davis; E-mail: bdavis@ussc.gov
Library Holdings: Bk Vols 10,000
Partic in OCLC Online Computer Library Center, Inc

GL UNITED STATES TAX COURT LIBRARY*, 400 Second St NW, 20217. SAN 302-8194. Tel: 202-521-4585. FAX: 202-521-4574. E-mail: tclib@ustaxcourt.gov. Web Site: www.ustaxcourt.gov.
Founded 1924
Library Holdings: Bk Titles 36,000; Per Subs 1,500
Special Collections: Tax Laws
Automation Activity & Vendor Info: (Acquisitions) SIMA, Inc; (Cataloging) OCLC Connexion
Function: ILL available
Publications: Monthly Bulletin
Partic in OCLC Online Computer Library Center, Inc
Restriction: Not open to pub

UNIVERSITY OF THE DISTRICT OF COLUMBIA

CL DAVID A CLARKE SCHOOL OF LAW, CHARLES N & HILDA H M MASON LAW LIBRARY*, Bldg 39, Rm B-16, 4200 Connecticut Ave NW, 20008, SAN 371-9952. Tel: 202-274-7310. FAX: 202-274-7311. E-mail: lawlibrary@udc.edu. Web Site: catalog.law.udc.edu, www.law.udc.edu. *Dir,* Vinenc Feliu; Tel: 202-274-7354, E-mail: vfeliu@udc.edu; *Assoc Dir, Pub Serv,* Helen Frazer; Tel: 202-274-7356, E-mail: hfrazer@udc.edu; *Asst Dir, Tech Serv,* Han Ouyang; Tel: 202-274-7358, E-mail: houyang@udc.edu; *Acq Librn,* John Jensen; Tel: 202-274-5214, E-mail: jjensen@udc.edu; *Cat Librn,* Yasmin Morais; *Circ Librn,* Gail Mathapo; Tel: 202-274-7357, E-mail: gmathapo@udc.edu; *Emerging Tech Librn,* Brittany Kolonay; *Network Adminr,* Lewis Perry; *Ser Tech,* Kim Walker; *Ser Tech,* Marvin Williams; *Tech Support,* Lachelle Cooper; Staff 7 (MLS 7)
Founded 1987. Enrl 280; Fac 20
Library Holdings: Bk Vols 255,000
Automation Activity & Vendor Info: (Acquisitions) Innovative Interfaces, Inc
Publications: Guide
Open Mon-Fri 8am-11:30pm, Sat 10-10, Sun Noon-11:30

C LEARNING RESOURCES DIVISION*, 4200 Connecticut Ave NW, 20008, SAN 337-2391. Tel: 202-274-6370. Circulation Tel: 202-274-6009. Interlibrary Loan Service Tel: 202-274-6011. Reference Tel: 202-274-6122. FAX: 202-274-6012. Web Site: www.lrdudc.wrlc.org. *Dean of Libr,* Albert J Casciero; *Electronic Serv Librn,* Michael Fitzgerald; *Info Literacy Librn,* Rachel Jorgensen; *Ref Librn,* John Page; *Ref/Archives Librn,* Christopher Anglim; *Acq,* Gemma Park; *Electronic Ref Librn,* Lindsay Sarin; Staff 28 (MLS 10, Non-MLS 18)
Founded 1976. Enrl 5,200; Fac 211; Highest Degree: Master
Library Holdings: Bk Vols 549,678; Per Subs 594
Subject Interests: Educ, Health sci, Humanities
Partic in Washington Research Library Consortium
Publications: Access; Learning Link; Learning Resources Division Annual Report
Special Services for the Blind - Scanner for conversion & translation of mats

S URBAN LAND INSTITUTE*, Information Center & Library, 2001 L St NW, Ste 200, 20036. SAN 302-8216. Tel: 202-624-7000, 202-624-7137. FAX: 202-624-7140. Web Site: www.uli.org. *Librn/Mgr,* Joan Campbell; E-mail: joan.campbell@uli.org
Founded 1936
Library Holdings: Bk Vols 10,000; Per Subs 275
Subject Interests: Real estate
Restriction: Open by appt only

G US ACCESS BOARD, US ARCHITECTURAL & TRANSPORTATION BARRIERS COMPLIANCE BOARD*, Technical Resources Library, 1331 F St NW, Ste 1000, 20004-1111. SAN 325-9811. Tel: 202-272-0080. Toll Free Tel: 800-872-2253. FAX: 202-272-0081. TDD: 202-272-0082, 800-993-2822. E-mail: info@access-board.gov. Web Site: www.access-board.gov. *Info Mgt Spec,* Anita Kinney
Library Holdings: Bk Vols 5,300; Per Subs 50
Special Collections: State, Local & Model Code on Accessibility
Special Services for the Deaf - TTY equip
Restriction: Open by appt only

G US CUSTOMS & BORDER PROTECTION INFORMATION RESOURCES CENTER*, CBP IRC Library, 90 K St NE, 20229. Tel: 202-325-0130. Interlibrary Loan Service Tel: 202-325-0171. FAX: 202-325-0170. E-mail: cbp.library@cbp.dhs.gov. Web Site: www.cbp.gov. *Dir,* Carolina Menendez; *Access & Discovery Librn,* Maura Martinez; *Cat/Syst Librn,* Tamara L B Wilson; *Law Librn,* MaryAnn Keeling; *Outreach Librn, Ref Librn,* Carisa Pastuch; *IT Spec,* Salvin Dave; *ILL, Libr Tech-Mats,* Mark Hempstead. Subject Specialists: *Law, Legal res,* MaryAnn Keeling; *Web design,* Salvin Dave; Staff 7 (MLS 5, Non-MLS 2)
Founded 1975
Special Collections: Anti-Terrorism Coll
Subject Interests: Bus, Human resources, Intl trade, Law enforcement, Mgt
Automation Activity & Vendor Info: (Acquisitions) EOS International; (Cataloging) EOS International; (Circulation) EOS International; (Course Reserve) EOS International; (ILL) EOS International; (OPAC) EOS International; (Serials) EOS International
Wireless access
Function: ILL available
Partic in Federal Library & Information Network; OCLC Online Computer Library Center, Inc
Restriction: Access at librarian's discretion

G US INTERNATIONAL DEVELOPMENT FINANCE CORP, 1100 New York Ave NW, 20527. SAN 302-7473. Tel: 202-336-8400. Interlibrary Loan Service Tel: 202-336-8568. FAX: 202-408-9860. Web Site: www.dfc.gov. *Ref Librn,* Angel Dang; E-mail: angel.dang@dfc.gov; *Ref, Tech Serv Librn,* Fawn Rooke; E-mail: fawn.rooke@dfc.gov; Staff 4 (MLS 3, Non-MLS 1)
Founded 1974
Subject Interests: Econ, Finance
Automation Activity & Vendor Info: (Acquisitions) SirsiDynix; (Cataloging) SirsiDynix; (Circulation) SirsiDynix; (OPAC) SirsiDynix; (Serials) SirsiDynix
Partic in Federal Library & Information Network; OCLC Online Computer Library Center, Inc

L VAN NESS FELDMAN LIBRARY*, 1050 Thomas Jefferson St NW, 20007. SAN 371-8948. Tel: 202-298-1800. FAX: 202-338-2416. Web Site: www.vnf.com. *Librn,* Susan Pries; Staff 3 (MLS 2, Non-MLS 1)
Founded 1976
Library Holdings: Bk Titles 12,000; Bk Vols 35,000; Per Subs 250
Subject Interests: Energy
Automation Activity & Vendor Info: (Cataloging) Inmagic, Inc.
Wireless access
Restriction: Private libr

L VENABLE LLP LIBRARY*, Washington, DC Office, 600 Massachusetts Ave NW, 20001. SAN 325-3902. Tel: 202-344-4000. Reference Tel: 202-344-8325. FAX: 202-344-8300. *Mgr, Libr Syst, Mgr, Tech Serv,* David Konieczko; Tel: 202-344-8377, E-mail: dkonieczko@venable.com; Staff 6 (MLS 5, Non-MLS 1)
Founded 1981
Library Holdings: Bk Vols 27,500; Per Subs 50
Subject Interests: Banks & banking, Corporate law, Drug laws, Energy, Environ law, Estates, Govt, Intl trade, Labor, Litigation, Patents, Real estate law, Securities, Taxation, Trademarks, Trusts
Automation Activity & Vendor Info: (Cataloging) Sydney; (Circulation) Sydney; (OPAC) Sydney; (Serials) Sydney
Partic in CourtLink; Dun & Bradstreet Info Servs; LexisNexis; LivEdgar; Proquest Dialog

L VORYS, SATER, SEYMOUR & PEASE LIBRARY*, 1909 K St NW, Ste 900, 20006-1152. SAN 377-3930. Tel: 202-467-8800. FAX: 202-467-8900. Web Site: www.vorys.com. *Librn,* Mick Baugh
Library Holdings: Bk Titles 1,000; Per Subs 40

R WASHINGTON HEBREW CONGREGATION LIBRARIES*, 3935 Macomb St NW, 20016-3741. SAN 302-8259. Tel: 301-354-3212. FAX: 301-354-3200. Web Site: whctemple.org. *Librn,* Ellen Share; E-mail: eshare@whctemple.org; Staff 2 (MLS 1, Non-MLS 1)
Library Holdings: Bk Vols 15,000
Subject Interests: Biblical studies, Holocaust, Jewish hist & lit
Automation Activity & Vendor Info: (Cataloging) Follett Software; (Circulation) Follett Software
Wireless access
Friends of the Library Group

M WASHINGTON HOSPITAL CENTER*, William B Glew MD Health Sciences Library, 110 Irving St NW, Rm 2A-21, 20010-2975. SAN 302-8267. Tel: 202-877-6221. E-mail: libraryreferenceservices@medstar.net. Web Site: www.medstarwashington.org. *Library Contact,* Layla Heimlich; Staff 9 (MLS 5, Non-MLS 4)
Founded 1958
Library Holdings: Bk Titles 10,000; Bk Vols 29,800; Per Subs 700
Subject Interests: Med, Nursing

Automation Activity & Vendor Info: (Cataloging) SirsiDynix; (Circulation) SirsiDynix; (OPAC) SirsiDynix; (Serials) SirsiDynix
Publications: Annual Report; Newsletter
Partic in National Network of Libraries of Medicine Region 1; OCLC Online Computer Library Center, Inc
Friends of the Library Group

G WASHINGTON METROPOLITAN AREA TRANSIT AUTHORITY, General Counsel's Office Law Library, 600 Fifth St NW, 20001. SAN 377-3914. Tel: 202-962-1012. FAX: 202-962-2550. Web Site: www.wmata.com. *Librn,* Jeanette Richmond; E-mail: jrichmond@wmata.com
Library Holdings: Bk Vols 7,000; Per Subs 50

S WASHINGTON NATIONAL CATHEDRAL, Cathedral Rare Book Library, 3101 Wisconsin Ave NW, 20016. SAN 371-1129. Tel: 202-537-6200. E-mail: info@cathedral.org. Web Site: cathedral.org. *Head Archivist,* Diane Ney; E-mail: dney@cathedral.org
Library Holdings: Bk Vols 8,000
Restriction: Not open to pub

L WEIL, GOTSHAL & MANGES LLP*, Law Library, 2001 M St NW, Ste 600, 20036. SAN 372-1132. Tel: 202-682-7000, 202-682-7117. Interlibrary Loan Service Tel: 202-682-7270. Web Site: www.weil.com. *Libr Mgr,* Laura Gaudio-Hint; E-mail: laura.gaudio@weil.com; *Libr Asst,* Kelly Booker; E-mail: kelly.booker@weil.com
Library Holdings: Bk Titles 30,000
Subject Interests: Banking, Corporate, Environ law, Intl trade, Litigation, Securities, Tax
Wireless access

L WEINER BRODSKY & KIDER PC*, Law Library, 1300 19th St NW, 5th Flr, 20036-1609. SAN 372-1736. Tel: 202-628-2000. FAX: 202-628-2011. Web Site: www.thewbkfirm.com.
Founded 1992
Library Holdings: Bk Vols 6,500; Per Subs 40
Function: ILL available
Restriction: Not open to pub

R WESLEY THEOLOGICAL SEMINARY LIBRARY*, 4500 Massachusetts Ave NW, 20016-5690. SAN 302-8313. Tel: 202-885-8695. FAX: 202-885-8691. E-mail: library@wesleyseminary.edu. Web Site: wesleyseminary.edu/library. *Dir,* James D Estes; Tel: 202-885-8696, E-mail: jestes@wesleyseminary.edu; *Coll Develop Librn,* Andrew Klenklen; Tel: 202-885-8692, E-mail: aklenklen@wesleyseminary.edu; *Metadata Librn, Syst Librn,* Hope Cooper; Tel: 202-885-8658, E-mail: hcooper@wesleyseminary.edu; *Pub Serv Librn,* Position Currently Open; Staff 5 (MLS 4, Non-MLS 1)
Founded 1882. Enrl 630; Fac 38; Highest Degree: Doctorate
Library Holdings: Bk Vols 171,500; Per Subs 600
Special Collections: Early American Methodism Coll; Methodist Protestant Church Coll
Subject Interests: Relig, Theol
Automation Activity & Vendor Info: (Acquisitions) Ex Libris Group; (Cataloging) Ex Libris Group; (Circulation) Ex Libris Group; (Course Reserve) Ex Libris Group; (ILL) OCLC WorldShare Interlibrary Loan; (OPAC) Ex Libris Group; (Serials) Ex Libris Group
Wireless access
Partic in Washington Theological Consortium
Open Mon-Thurs 8:30-8:30, Fri 8:30-4:30, Sat 12-4

L WHITE & CASE LLP*, Law Library, 701 13th St NW, 20005-3807. SAN 372-1469. Tel: 202-626-3600, 202-626-6475. FAX: 202-639-9355. Web Site: www.whitecase.com. *Sr Researcher,* Tim McAllister; *Res Asst,* Roshni Santiago
Library Holdings: Bk Titles 1,000; Per Subs 10
Subject Interests: Intl law
Wireless access
Partic in OCLC Online Computer Library Center, Inc
Restriction: Private libr

SR WHITEFRIARS HALL, Order of Carmelites Library, 1600 Webster St NE, 20017. SAN 371-8662. Tel: 202-526-1221, Ext 203. FAX: 202-526-9217. E-mail: carmelitana@gmail.com. *Librn,* Patricia O'Callaghan; Staff 1 (Non-MLS 1)
Founded 1948
Library Holdings: Microforms 109; Bk Titles 12,000; Per Subs 87; Videos 100
Special Collections: Whitefriars Hall (Theology)
Wireless access
Restriction: Open by appt only

L WILEY REIN LLC LIBRARY*, 1776 K St NW, 20006. SAN 377-3833. Tel: 202-719-7000. FAX: 202-719-7049. Web Site: www.wileyrein.com. *Mgr, Libr Serv,* Kent Boese; E-mail: kboese@wileyrein.com
Library Holdings: Bk Vols 25,000; Per Subs 200
Wireless access
Restriction: Not open to pub

L WILKINSON BARKER KNAUER LLP LIBRARY*, 1800 M St NW, Ste 800N, 20036. Tel: 202-383-3420. FAX: 202-783-5851. Web Site: www.wbklaw.com. *Librn/Mgr,* Tera Brostoff; E-mail: tbrostoff@wbklaw.com; Staff 1 (MLS 1)
Library Holdings: Bk Vols 1,000; Per Subs 11
Wireless access
Function: ILL available
Restriction: Access at librarian's discretion, Circ limited, Not open to pub

L WILLIAMS & CONNOLLY LIBRARY, 725 12th St NW, 20005. SAN 302-833X. Tel: 202-434-5303. FAX: 202-434-5029. Web Site: www.wc.com. *Dir, Libr Serv,* Caitlin Lietzan; Tel: 202-434-5306, E-mail: clietzan@wc.com; *Head, Res Serv,* Alicia Julian; E-mail: ajulian@wc.com; *Research Librn,* Shannon Coffey; E-mail: scoffey@wc.com; *Research Librn,* Matt Foley; Tel: 202-434-5308, E-mail: mfoley@wc.com; *Research Librn,* Michele Penn; E-mail: mpenn@wc.com; *Research Librn,* Chelsea Seddon; E-mail: cseddon@wc.com; *Tech Serv Librn,* Jackie Vick; E-mail: jvick@wc.com; *ILL,* Patti Hennessy; E-mail: phennessy@wc.com; Staff 13 (MLS 7, Non-MLS 6)
Founded 1970
Library Holdings: Bk Vols 75,000; Per Subs 300
Subject Interests: Law
Automation Activity & Vendor Info: (Acquisitions) Softlink America; (Cataloging) Softlink America; (Circulation) Softlink America; (ILL) Softlink America; (OPAC) Softlink America; (Serials) Softlink America
Wireless access
Partic in OCLC Online Computer Library Center, Inc
Restriction: Not open to pub

L WILMER, CUTLER, HALE & DORR LIBRARY*, 1875 Pennsylvnia Ave NW, 20006. SAN 302-8348. Tel: 202-663-6000. FAX: 202-663-6363. Web Site: www.wilmerhale.com. *Librn,* Donna Lombardo; Staff 18 (MLS 13, Non-MLS 5)
Founded 1963
Library Holdings: Bk Vols 55,750
Subject Interests: Antitrust law, Banks & banking, Legislation, Securities
Partic in Dow Jones News Retrieval; Proquest Dialog

S WOODROW WILSON INTERNATIONAL CENTER FOR SCHOLARS LIBRARY*, 1300 Pennsylvania Ave NW, 20004-3027. SAN 302-7732. Tel: 202-691-4150. FAX: 202-691-4001. E-mail: library.email@wilsoncenter.org. Web Site: www.wilsoncenter.org. *Librn,* Janet Spikes; E-mail: janet.spikes@wilsoncenter.org; *Libr Tech,* Michelle Kamalich; E-mail: michelle.kamalich@wilsoncenter.org; Staff 3 (MLS 1, Non-MLS 2)
Founded 1970
Library Holdings: Bk Titles 8,000; Bk Vols 12,000; Per Subs 250
Subject Interests: Russia
Restriction: Open by appt only
Branches:
KENNAN INSTITUTE FOR ADVANCED RUSSIAN STUDIES LIBRARY, 1300 Pennsylvania Ave NW, 20004-3027. *Librn,* Janet Spikes; E-mail: janet.spikes@wilsoncenter.org; Staff 3 (MLS 1, Non-MLS 2)
Founded 1975
Library Holdings: Bk Titles 8,000; Bk Vols 10,000; Per Subs 50
Subject Interests: Hist, Literary criticism, Soviet studies
Restriction: Open by appt only

SR WOODSTOCK THEOLOGICAL CENTER LIBRARY*, Georgetown University, Lauinger Library, PO Box 571170, 20057-1170. SAN 322-8568. Tel: 202-687-7513. FAX: 202-687-7473. E-mail: woodstocktheology@georgetown.edu. Web Site: www.library.georgetown.edu/woodstock. *Dept Head,* J Leon Hooper; Tel: 202-687-4250, E-mail: jlh3@georgetown.edu; *Libr Asst,* Susan Karp; E-mail: karps@georgetown.edu; *Spec Coll Cataloger,* Amy Phillips; Tel: 202-687-2902, E-mail: aep49@georgetown.edu; Staff 4 (MLS 3, Non-MLS 1)
Founded 1869
Library Holdings: Microforms 325; Bk Vols 210,000; Per Subs 747
Special Collections: 16th-19th Century Counter-Reformational Coll; Palestinian Antiquities (Halpern Coll), engravings; Theology & Jesuitica (Joques, Shrub Oak & Parsons Coll)
Subject Interests: Relig, Scriptures, Theol
Automation Activity & Vendor Info: (Cataloging) Innovative Interfaces, Inc; (OPAC) Innovative Interfaces, Inc - Millennium
Wireless access

Partic in Washington Research Library Consortium; Washington Theological Consortium
Open Mon-Thurs 9-7:45, Fri 9-4:45

S THE WORLD BANK GROUP LIBRARY, 1818 H St NW, MSN MC-C3-220, 20433. SAN 377-4619. Tel: 202-473-2000, 202-473-8670. FAX: 202-522-1160. E-mail: LADevelopment@worldbank.org. Web Site: external.worldbankimflib.org/external.htm, openknowledge.worldbank.org. *Sr Info Officer,* Eliza McLeod
Library Holdings: Bk Vols 60,000; Per Subs 200
Function: ILL available
Restriction: Staff use only

S WORLD RESOURCES INSTITUTE, Library & Information Center, Ten G St NE, Ste 800, 20002. Tel: 202-729-7602. FAX: 202-729-7610. E-mail: library@wri.org. Web Site: www.wri.org/about/library-information-center. *Dir, Libr Serv,* Mary Maguire; *Librn,* Julia Hussey; E-mail: jhussey@wri.org; Staff 4 (MLS 2, Non-MLS 2)
Founded 1982
Library Holdings: Bk Titles 10,000; Per Subs 200
Automation Activity & Vendor Info: (Circulation) Inmagic, Inc.
Function: ILL available
Restriction: Open by appt only

L WRIGHT & TALISMAN PC*, Law Library, 1200 G St NW, Ste 600, 20005-3898. SAN 370-1174. Tel: 202-393-1200. FAX: 202-393-1240. Web Site: www.wrightlaw.com. *Library Contact,* Sarah Gordon
Library Holdings: Per Subs 37
Wireless access
Restriction: Staff use only

FLORIDA

Date of Statistics: FY 2020
Population, 2020 U.S. Census: 21,596,068
Population Served by Public Libraries: 21,944,846
Total Public Library Circulation: 78,559,457
Income and Expenditures:
Total Public Library Income (incl. Grants-in-Aid): $690,239,542
Source of Income: Local 93.74%; State 3.18%; Federal 0.25%; Other 2.83%
Expenditures Per Capita: $28.07
Number of County Systems: 40
Regional Systems: 8 Multi-County Systems covering 27 counties
Counties Served: 67
Number of Bookmobiles in State: 20
Grants-in-Aid to Public Libraries: $21,977,189
Formula for Apportionment of State Aid: Legally established county, municipality or multi-county libraries receive grants based on local support; additional funds are provided to 32 poorest counties and to multi-county systems.
Information provided courtesy of: Nancy Guidry-Hall, State Data Coordinator; Bureau of Library Development

ALTAMONTE SPRINGS

P ALTAMONTE SPRINGS CITY LIBRARY*, 281 N Maitland Ave, 32701. SAN 302-8380. Tel: 407-571-8830. FAX: 407-571-8834. E-mail: library@altamonte.org. Web Site: altamonte.mysurpass.net, www.altamonte.org/356/Library. *Dir,* Diana Long; E-mail: dllong@altamonte.org; *Ch,* Fazana Baksh; *Ref Librn, YA Serv,* Heather Eger; Staff 5 (MLS 1, Non-MLS 4)
Founded 1959. Pop 42,000; Circ 47,730
Library Holdings: Bk Vols 36,000; Per Subs 24
Special Collections: Local Historical Coll
Subject Interests: Fla
Automation Activity & Vendor Info: (Acquisitions) Mandarin Library Automation; (Cataloging) Mandarin Library Automation; (Circulation) Mandarin Library Automation
Wireless access
Open Mon-Thurs 10-7, Fri & Sat 10-4

J CITY COLLEGE*, Altamonte Springs Library, 177 Montgomery Rd, 32714. Tel: 407-831-9816. FAX: 407-831-1147. Web Site: www.citycollege.edu. *Librn,* Patricia Bivin; E-mail: pbivin@citycollege.edu; Staff 1 (MLS 1)
Founded 1996. Enrl 300; Highest Degree: Associate
Library Holdings: e-books 14,000; e-journals 1,000; Bk Vols 2,000; Per Subs 50; Spec Interest Per Sub 25
Wireless access
Partic in Florida Library Information Network; LYRASIS
Open Mon-Thurs 8am-10pm, Fri 8-5

APALACHICOLA

P APALACHICOLA MARGARET KEY LIBRARY, (Formerly Apalachicola Municipal Library), 80 12th St, 32320. SAN 370-4610. Tel: 850-653-8436. FAX: 850-653-1350. E-mail: amklibrary2017@gmail.com. Web Site: www.apalachicolalibrary.com. *Dir,* Caroline Kienzle
Library Holdings: Bk Titles 14,000
Wireless access
Open Mon-Fri 10-5, Sun 12-5
Friends of the Library Group

APOPKA

C UNIVERSITY OF FLORIDA, Mid Florida Research & Education Center Library, 2725 S Binion Rd, 32703-8504. SAN 322-9009. Tel: 407-410-6929, 407-884-2034, Ext 140. Web Site: mrec.ifas.ufl.edu. *Librn,* Carmen Nazario; E-mail: cnazario@ufl.edu
Library Holdings: Bk Vols 5,000
Subject Interests: Agr
Wireless access
Open Mon-Fri 9-5

C UNIVERSITY OF FLORIDA*, Mid-Florida Research & Education Center, 2725 S Binion Rd, 32703-8504. SAN 323-715X. Tel: 407-884-2034. FAX: 407-814-6186. Web Site: mrec.ifas.ufl.edu. *Dir,* Dr Roger Kjelgren; Tel: 407-884-2035, E-mail: rkjelgren@ufl.edu
Library Holdings: Bk Vols 12,000; Per Subs 132
Open Mon-Fri 8:30-5

ARCADIA

P DESOTO COUNTY LIBRARY*, 125 N Hillsborough Ave, 34266. SAN 302-8402. Tel: 863-993-4851. Web Site: myhlc.org/libraries/desoto. *Dir,* Linda Waters; E-mail: lindaw@myhlc.org
Founded 1963. Pop 23,865; Circ 167,811
Library Holdings: Bk Vols 59,000; Per Subs 63
Automation Activity & Vendor Info: (Cataloging) Innovative Interfaces, Inc; (Circulation) Innovative Interfaces, Inc
Wireless access
Mem of Heartland Library Cooperative
Partic in Tampa Bay Library Consortium, Inc
Open Tues-Fri 9-6, Sat 9-2:30
Friends of the Library Group

AUBURNDALE

P AUBURNDALE PUBLIC LIBRARY*, 100 W Bridgers Ave, 33823. SAN 302-8437. Tel: 863-965-5548. FAX: 863-965-5554. Web Site: www.auburndalefl.com/library. *Librn,* Kristal Holmes; E-mail: kholmes@auburndalefl.com; *Ch,* Rhonda Hayes; E-mail: rhayes@auburndalefl.com
Founded 1951. Pop 10,000; Circ 62,000
Library Holdings: DVDs 4,225; Bk Titles 56,433; Per Subs 51
Wireless access
Partic in Polk County Libr Coop; Tampa Bay Library Consortium, Inc
Open Mon-Fri 10-7, Sat 9-5

AVE MARIA

CR CANIZARO LIBRARY AT AVE MARIA UNIVERSITY*, 5251 Donahue St, 34142. Tel: 239-280-2557. E-mail: library@avemaria.edu. Web Site: www.avemaria.edu/majorsprograms/library. *Dir, Libr Serv,* Jennifer Nodes; Tel: 239-348-4710, E-mail: jennifer.nodes@avemaria.edu; *Head, Pub Serv,* Sarah DeVille; Tel: 239-280-2422, E-mail: sarah.deville@avemaria.edu; *Librn, Tech Serv,* Mary Coniglio; Tel: 239-280-2426, E-mail: mary.coniglio@avemaria.edu; Staff 6 (MLS 3, Non-MLS 3)
Founded 2003. Enrl 1,080; Fac 60; Highest Degree: Doctorate
Library Holdings: CDs 700; DVDs 1,400; e-books 2,000; Electronic Media & Resources 80; Music Scores 1,000; Bk Titles 160,000; Bk Vols 190,000; Per Subs 280; Videos 200
Special Collections: Catholic Americana; Natural Family Planning Archives
Automation Activity & Vendor Info: (Acquisitions) Baker & Taylor; (Cataloging) OCLC Connexion; (Circulation) OCLC; (Course Reserve) OCLC; (ILL) OCLC; (OPAC) OCLC; (Serials) OCLC

Wireless access
Function: Art exhibits, Audio & video playback equip for onsite use, ILL available, Instruction & testing, Music CDs, Online cat, Online ref, Photocopying/Printing, Ref serv available, Scanner
Publications: Lanthorn (Newsletter)
Partic in Southwest Florida Library Network
Open Mon-Thurs 8am-1am, Fri 8-8, Sat 9-8, Sun 1pm-1am
Restriction: 24-hr pass syst for students only, Authorized scholars by appt, In-house use for visitors, Open to students, fac & staff

AVON PARK

J SOUTH FLORIDA STATE COLLEGE LIBRARY*, 600 W College Dr, 33825-9356. SAN 302-847X. Tel: 863-784-7306. Reference Tel: 863-784-7304. FAX: 863-452-6042. E-mail: sfsc-library@southflorida.edu. Web Site: www.southflorida.edu/current-students/library/highlands-campus-library. *Interim Dean,* Lynn MacNeill; E-mail: macneill@southflorida.edu; *Chair, Libr Serv, Lead Librn,* Lena Phelps; Tel: 863-784-7303, E-mail: phelpsl@southflorida.edu; *Librn,* Claire Miller; Tel: 863-784-7305, E-mail: millerc@southflorida.edu; Staff 2 (MLS 2)
Founded 1966. Enrl 2,500; Fac 68; Highest Degree: Bachelor
Automation Activity & Vendor Info: (Acquisitions) Ex Libris Group; (Cataloging) Ex Libris Group; (Circulation) Ex Libris Group; (Course Reserve) Ex Libris Group; (ILL) Ex Libris Group; (Media Booking) Ex Libris Group; (OPAC) Ex Libris Group; (Serials) Ex Libris Group
Wireless access
Partic in Tampa Bay Library Consortium, Inc
Open Mon-Thurs 7:30am-9pm, Fri 7:30-5

BABSON PARK

C WEBBER INTERNATIONAL UNIVERSITY, Grace & Roger Babson Learning Center, 1201 N Scenic Hwy, 33827. (Mail add: PO Box 97, 33827-0097), SAN 302-8496. Tel: 863-638-1431, Ext 3001. E-mail: library@webber.edu. Web Site: www.webber.edu. *Dir, Head Librn,* Sue Dunning; E-mail: dunningcs@webber.edu; *Libr Asst,* Billie Kayworth; Staff 2 (MLS 1, Non-MLS 1)
Founded 1927. Enrl 630; Highest Degree: Master
Library Holdings: DVDs 120; e-books 200,000; Electronic Media & Resources 15; Bk Titles 3,220; Bk Vols 3,850; Per Subs 10
Special Collections: Civil War Coll
Subject Interests: Bus & mgt, Econ
Automation Activity & Vendor Info: (Cataloging) Book Systems; (Circulation) Book Systems; (Discovery) EBSCO Discovery Service; (OPAC) Book Systems
Wireless access
Function: Computers for patron use, Electronic databases & coll
Partic in Independent Cols & Univs of Fla; Library & Information Resources Network
Open Mon-Thurs 8am-10pm, Fri 8-5, Sun 6pm-11; Mon-Thurs 8-5 (Summer)
Restriction: Borrowing privileges limited to fac & registered students

BARTOW

P BARTOW PUBLIC LIBRARY*, 2150 S Broadway Ave, 33830. SAN 302-850X. Tel: 863-534-0131. FAX: 863-534-0913. E-mail: bartowpubliclibrary@gmail.com. *Actg Dir, Ref Serv,* Paul Wartenberg; *Cat,* Wendy Hiers; *Youth Serv,* Melissa Causey; Staff 5 (MLS 4, Non-MLS 1)
Founded 1897. Pop 17,000; Circ 161,000
Library Holdings: DVDs 1,700; Bk Titles 57,000; Per Subs 122
Automation Activity & Vendor Info: (Acquisitions) SirsiDynix; (Cataloging) SirsiDynix; (Circulation) SirsiDynix
Wireless access
Function: Adult bk club, After school storytime, Art exhibits, Audiobks via web, AV serv, Bk club(s), Bks on cassette, Bks on CD, Children's prog, Computer training, Computers for patron use, Distance learning, Electronic databases & coll, Free DVD rentals, Holiday prog, Homebound delivery serv, ILL available, Internet access, Mail & tel request accepted, Mail loans to mem, Music CDs, Notary serv, Online cat, Photocopying/Printing, Preschool outreach, Prog for adults, Prog for children & young adult, Ref serv available, Spoken cassettes & CDs, Spoken cassettes & DVDs, Story hour, Summer reading prog, Tax forms, Teen prog, Telephone ref, VHS videos, Wheelchair accessible
Partic in Polk County Libr Coop; Tampa Bay Library Consortium, Inc
Open Mon-Thurs 9-8, Fri & Sat 9-5
Restriction: 24-hr pass syst for students only
Friends of the Library Group

S FLORIDA INSTITUTE OF PHOSPHATE RESEARCH*, FIPR Library & Info Clearinghouse, 1855 W Main St, 33830-4338. SAN 324-5594. Tel: 863-534-7160. FAX: 863-534-7165. Web Site: www.fipr.state.fl.us/library-publications. *Dir,* Gary R Albarelli; E-mail: galbarel@mail.usf.edu; Staff 3 (MLS 2, Non-MLS 1)
Founded 1980
Library Holdings: Bk Titles 7,800; Per Subs 110
Subject Interests: Beneficiation, Environ incl radon, Phosphate mining, Reclamation
Automation Activity & Vendor Info: (Circulation) Follett Software; (OPAC) Follett Software
Wireless access
Publications: Annual Report
Partic in LYRASIS; OCLC Online Computer Library Center, Inc; Proquest Dialog; Tampa Bay Library Consortium, Inc
Open Mon-Fri 8:30-5

S POLK COUNTY HISTORICAL & GENEALOGICAL LIBRARY*, Historic Courthouse, 100 E Main St, 33830. SAN 302-8526. Tel: 863-534-4380. Web Site: www.polk-county.net/history-center/historical-and-genealogical-library. *Genealogy Librn, Research Historian,* Preston Petermeier; E-mail: prestonpetermeier@polk-county.net
Founded 1940
Library Holdings: Bk Titles 12,800; Per Subs 40
Special Collections: Genealogy & History of the Southeastern US
Automation Activity & Vendor Info: (Cataloging) SirsiDynix
Wireless access
Partic in Tampa Bay Library Consortium, Inc
Open Tues-Sat 9-5
Restriction: Open to pub for ref only

GL POLK COUNTY LAW LIBRARY*, Justice Steven H Grimes Law Library, Courthouse, Rm 3076, 255 N Broadway, 33830. SAN 302-8534. Tel: 863-534-4013. Administration Tel: 863-534-4016. FAX: 863-534-7443. *Dir,* Amanda Horton; E-mail: ahorton@jud10.flcourts.org
Founded 1956
Library Holdings: Bk Vols 25,000; Per Subs 60
Automation Activity & Vendor Info: (Cataloging) Follett Software; (Circulation) Follett Software
Partic in Polk County Libr Coop; Tampa Bay Library Consortium, Inc
Open Mon-Fri 8:30-5
Restriction: Non-circulating to the pub

BAY PINES

GM BAY PINES VETERANS AFFAIRS HEALTHCARE SYSTEM*, 10000 Bay Pines Blvd, 33744. (Mail add: PO Box 5005, 33744-5005), SAN 302-8542. Tel: 727-398-9366. FAX: 727-398-9367. Web Site: www.baypines.va.gov. *Librn,* Diana Akins; Staff 6 (MLS 2, Non-MLS 4)
Founded 1930
Library Holdings: AV Mats 200; e-books 60,000; e-journals 700; Bk Titles 100
Subject Interests: Allied health, Consumer health, Geriatrics & gerontology, Med, Nursing
Automation Activity & Vendor Info: (Cataloging) OCLC; (Circulation) Follett Software; (Serials) SerialsSolutions
Function: Audio & video playback equip for onsite use, Computers for patron use, Digital talking bks, Doc delivery serv, Electronic databases & coll, Health sci info serv, ILL available, Internet access, Photocopying/Printing, Scanner, VHS videos, Wheelchair accessible
Publications: Library Service (Newsletter)
Partic in Medical Library Association; Tampa Bay Library Consortium, Inc; Tampa Bay Medical Library Network
Special Services for the Deaf - ADA equip; Closed caption videos
Special Services for the Blind - Audio mat; BiFolkal kits; Bks & mags in Braille, on rec, tape & cassette
Open Mon-Thurs 7-4:30, Fri 7-1:30
Restriction: Circulates for staff only, In-house use for visitors

BELLE GLADE

J PALM BEACH STATE COLLEGE*, Belle Glade-Campus Library/Learning Resource Center, 1977 College Dr, Mail Sta 43, 33430. SAN 302-8577. Tel: 561-993-1150. FAX: 561-993-1157. E-mail: WestLibraryLRC@palmbeachstate.edu. Web Site: www.palmbeachstate.edu/library/belle-glade-library. *Dir,* Patricia Caldwell; E-mail: caldwelp@palmbeachstate.edu; *Fac Librn,* Iris Fiallos; E-mail: fiallosi@palmbeachstate.edu; *Libr Tech II,* Halimeh Shatara; Tel: 561-993-1155, E-mail: shatarah@palmbeachstate.edu; Staff 2 (MLS 2)
Highest Degree: Associate
Library Holdings: Bk Vols 11,000; Per Subs 82
Automation Activity & Vendor Info: (Cataloging) Ex Libris Group; (Circulation) Ex Libris Group; (Course Reserve) Ex Libris Group; (OPAC) Ex Libris Group; (Serials) Ex Libris Group
Open Mon-Thurs 8-8, Fri 8-12

C UNIVERSITY OF FLORIDA, Everglades Research & Education Center, 3200 E Palm Beach Rd, 33430. SAN 302-8585. Tel: 561-993-1517. FAX: 561-993-1582. *AV/Multimedia Spec,* David Stevens; E-mail: dstevens55@ufl.edu
Founded 1926
Library Holdings: Per Subs 50
Subject Interests: Agr, Turfgrass, Water quality
Wireless access
Publications: Journal Series; Research Reports
Open Mon-Fri 8-5

BEVERLY HILLS

P CITRUS COUNTY LIBRARY SYSTEM*, Administrative Offices, 425 W Roosevelt Blvd, 34465-4281. SAN 328-8633. Tel: 352-746-9077. FAX: 352-746-9493. E-mail: suggestions@citruslibraries.org. Web Site: www.citruslibraries.org. *Dir, Libr Serv,* Eric C Head; *Communications Facilitator,* Taylor Keeran; Staff 14 (MLS 4, Non-MLS 10)
Founded 1987. Pop 143,621; Circ 588,789
Library Holdings: Audiobooks 8,643; AV Mats 23,256; Bks on Deafness & Sign Lang 111; Braille Volumes 41; CDs 4,551; DVDs 9,431; e-books 11,097; High Interest/Low Vocabulary Bk Vols 2,931; Large Print Bks 11,291; Bk Titles 145,826; Bk Vols 200,944; Per Subs 221
Automation Activity & Vendor Info: (Acquisitions) Koha; (Cataloging) Koha; (Circulation) Koha; (Discovery) Koha; (ILL) OCLC WorldShare Interlibrary Loan; (Media Booking) Koha; (OPAC) Koha
Wireless access
Function: 24/7 Electronic res, 24/7 Online cat, Adult bk club, Adult literacy prog, Art exhibits, Art programs, Audio & video playback equip for onsite use, Bk club(s), Bks on CD, CD-ROM, Chess club, Children's prog, Citizenship assistance, Computer training, Computers for patron use, Electronic databases & coll, Family literacy, Free DVD rentals, Genealogy discussion group, Govt ref serv, Holiday prog, Home delivery & serv to seniorr ctr & nursing homes, Homebound delivery serv, ILL available, Instruction & testing, Internet access, Life-long learning prog for all ages, Literacy & newcomer serv, Magazines, Magnifiers for reading, Mail & tel request accepted, Meeting rooms, Microfiche/film & reading machines, Movies, Music CDs, Online cat, Online ref, Outreach serv, OverDrive digital audio bks, Photocopying/Printing, Preschool outreach, Preschool reading prog, Prog for adults, Prog for children & young adult, Ref & res, Ref serv available, Scanner, Senior computer classes, Senior outreach, Serves people with intellectual disabilities, Spanish lang bks, Spoken cassettes & CDs, Spoken cassettes & DVDs, STEM programs, Story hour, Study rm, Summer & winter reading prog, Summer reading prog, Tax forms, Teen prog, Telephone ref, Wheelchair accessible, Writing prog
Partic in Tampa Bay Library Consortium, Inc
Open Mon-Fri 8-5
Friends of the Library Group
Branches: 5
CENTRAL RIDGE, 425 W Roosevelt Blvd, 34465-4281, SAN 337-8780. Tel: 352-746-6622. FAX: 352-746-4170. *Br Mgr,* Debbie Reilly; *Circ Supvr,* Cheryl Green
Open Mon-Wed 9-7, Thurs & Fri 9-5, Sat 10-4
Friends of the Library Group
COASTAL REGION, 8619 W Crystal St, Crystal River, 34428-4468, SAN 337-8608. Tel: 352-795-3716. FAX: 352-795-3103. *Br Mgr,* Susan Mutschler; *Circ Supvr,* Jacky Moore
Open Mon-Wed 9-7, Thurs & Fri 9-5
Friends of the Library Group
FLORAL CITY PUBLIC, 8360 E Orange Ave, Floral City, 34436-3200, SAN 337-8667. Tel: 352-726-3671. FAX: 352-726-1159. *Br Mgr,* Debbie Reilly; *Circ Supvr,* TerriAnne Caraluzzo
Open Mon-Wed 9-7, Thurs & Fri 9-5
Friends of the Library Group
HOMOSASSA PUBLIC, 4100 S Grandmarch Ave, Homosassa, 34446-1120, SAN 337-8721. Tel: 352-628-5626. FAX: 352-628-3011. *Br Mgr,* Susan Mutschler; *Circ Supvr,* Renee' Thompson
Open Mon-Wed 9-7, Thurs & Fri 9-5, Sat 10-4
Friends of the Library Group
LAKES REGION, 1511 Druid Rd, Inverness, 34452-4507, SAN 337-8756. Tel: 352-726-2357. FAX: 352-726-2814. *Br Mgr,* Debbie Reilly; *Circ Supvr,* Adam Chang
Open Mon-Wed 9-7, Thurs & Fri 9-5, Sat 10-4
Friends of the Library Group

BLOUNTSTOWN

P CALHOUN COUNTY PUBLIC LIBRARY*, 17731 NE Pear St, 32424. SAN 370-4688. Tel: 850-674-8773. FAX: 850-674-2843. Web Site: www.ccpl-fl.net. *Dir,* Rita Maupin; E-mail: maupinr@yahoo.com; *Asst Dir, Tech Serv,* Karen Bryant
Library Holdings: Bk Titles 30,705; Per Subs 10
Automation Activity & Vendor Info: (Acquisitions) SirsiDynix; (Cataloging) SirsiDynix; (Circulation) SirsiDynix; (OPAC) SirsiDynix
Wireless access
Mem of Panhandle Public Library Cooperative System
Open Mon-Thurs 9-5:30, Sat 9-3
Branches: 5
ALTHA BRANCH, 15525 NW County Rd 274, Altha, 32421, SAN 370-4696. Tel: 850-762-8280. FAX: 850-762-4547.
Library Holdings: AV Mats 83; Large Print Bks 292; Bk Titles 2,447; Bk Vols 4,952; Videos 221
Open Mon-Thurs 2-5, Sat 9-12
HUGH CREEK PARK, 11442 SE County Rd 69, 32424. Tel: 850-674-3334. FAX: 850-674-3334.
Library Holdings: Bk Vols 900
Open Mon-Thurs 2-5, Sat 9-12
KINARD BRANCH, 5416 SW State Rd 73, Kinard, 32449, SAN 370-470X. Tel: 850-639-5125. FAX: 850-639-5125.
Library Holdings: AV Mats 18; Large Print Bks 175; Bk Titles 1,814; Bk Vols 4,501; Videos 47
Open Mon-Thurs 2-5, Sat 9-12
MOSSY POND PARK, 22216 NW Lake McKenzie Blvd, Altha, 32421-4163. Tel: 850-762-2400.
SHELTON'S PARK, 25008 NW State Rd 73, Altha, 32421, SAN 377-8355. Tel: 850-762-3992. FAX: 850-762-3992 (call first).
Library Holdings: Bk Titles 908
Open Mon-Thurs 2-5, Sat 9-12

BOCA RATON

P BOCA RATON PUBLIC LIBRARY*, Downtown Library, 400 NW Boca Raton Blvd, 33432-3798. SAN 302-8593. Tel: 561-393-7852. Circulation Tel: 561-367-7019. Reference Tel: 561-393-7906. FAX: 561-393-7823. Web Site: www.myboca.us/957/Library. *Dir,* Ellen Randolph; E-mail: erandolph@myboca.us; Staff 76.5 (MLS 8, Non-MLS 68.5)
Founded 1938. Pop 96,114; Circ 910,830
Library Holdings: Audiobooks 9,056; AV Mats 57,994; Bks on Deafness & Sign Lang 94; Braille Volumes 2; CDs 11,581; DVDs 36,664; High Interest/Low Vocabulary Bk Vols 139; Large Print Bks 11,017; Music Scores 86; Bk Titles 112,474; Bk Vols 168,745; Per Subs 286
Special Collections: American Girl Dolls Coll; Cake Pans Coll; Early Literacy Backpacks Coll; Spanish Language Coll
Automation Activity & Vendor Info: (Acquisitions) Innovative Interfaces, Inc; (Cataloging) Innovative Interfaces, Inc; (Circulation) Innovative Interfaces, Inc; (ILL) OCLC WorldShare Interlibrary Loan; (OPAC) Innovative Interfaces, Inc; (Serials) Innovative Interfaces, Inc
Wireless access
Function: 24/7 Electronic res, 24/7 Online cat, 3D Printer, Activity rm, Adult bk club, Adult literacy prog, After school storytime, Art exhibits, Audiobks on Playaways & MP3, Audiobks via web, Bilingual assistance for Spanish patrons, Bk club(s), Bk reviews (Group), Bks on cassette, Bks on CD, Children's prog, Citizenship assistance, Computer training, Computers for patron use, Digital talking bks, Distance learning, Electronic databases & coll, Govt ref serv, Health sci info serv, Holiday prog, ILL available, Internet access, Large print keyboards, Learning ctr, Life-long learning prog for all ages, Magazines, Magnifiers for reading, Makerspace, STEM programs, Wheelchair accessible
Partic in Southeast Florida Library Information Network, Inc
Special Services for the Deaf - Assistive tech; Bks on deafness & sign lang; Closed caption videos; Staff with knowledge of sign lang
Special Services for the Blind - Accessible computers; Aids for in-house use; Assistive/Adapted tech devices, equip & products; Bks available with recordings; Bks on CD; Computer access aids; Copier with enlargement capabilities; Internet workstation with adaptive software; Large print bks; Low vision equip; Magnifiers; Networked computers with assistive software; Playaways (bks on MP3); Screen enlargement software for people with visual disabilities; Screen reader software; Talking bk serv referral
Open Mon-Thurs 9-9, Fri & Sat 9-6, Sun 12-6
Restriction: Circ to mem only, Non-resident fee
Friends of the Library Group
Branches: 1
SPANISH RIVER LIBRARY, 1501 NW Spanish River Blvd, 33431. Tel: 561-393-7852. *Mgr, Libr Serv,* Ann Nappa; E-mail: anappa@myboca.us; Staff 76.5 (MLS 8, Non-MLS 68.5)
Founded 2008. Pop 96,114; Circ 910,830
Library Holdings: Audiobooks 20,834; AV Mats 37,396; Bks on Deafness & Sign Lang 94; Braille Volumes 2; CDs 11,581; DVDs 36,664; Large Print Bks 11,017; Music Scores 86; Bk Titles 112,474; Bk Vols 168,745; Per Subs 410
Automation Activity & Vendor Info: (Acquisitions) Innovative Interfaces, Inc - Millennium; (Cataloging) Innovative Interfaces, Inc - Millennium; (Circulation) Innovative Interfaces, Inc - Millennium; (ILL) OCLC WorldShare Interlibrary Loan; (OPAC) Innovative Interfaces, Inc - Millennium; (Serials) Innovative Interfaces, Inc - Millennium
Function: 24/7 Electronic res, 24/7 Online cat, Activity rm, Archival coll, Art exhibits, Audiobks on Playaways & MP3, Audiobks via web, Bilingual assistance for Spanish patrons, Bks on CD, Children's prog, Citizenship assistance, Computer training, Computers for patron use,

Distance learning, Electronic databases & coll, Games & aids for people with disabilities, Govt ref serv, Health sci info serv, ILL available, Internet access, Large print keyboards, Learning ctr, Magazines, Magnifiers for reading, Makerspace, Meeting rooms, Music CDs, Online cat, Online info literacy tutorials on the web & in blackboard, Online ref, Outreach serv, OverDrive digital audio bks, Photocopying/Printing, Preschool reading prog, Prog for adults, Prog for children & young adult, Ref & res, Ref serv available, Res assist avail, Senior computer classes, STEM programs, Wheelchair accessible
Special Services for the Deaf - Assistive tech; Bks on deafness & sign lang; Closed caption videos; Staff with knowledge of sign lang
Special Services for the Blind - Accessible computers; Aids for in-house use; Assistive/Adapted tech devices, equip & products; Bks available with recordings; Bks on CD; Computer access aids; Copier with enlargement capabilities; Internet workstation with adaptive software; Large print bks; Low vision equip; Magnifiers; Networked computers with assistive software; Playaways (bks on MP3); Screen enlargement software for people with visual disabilities; Screen reader software; Talking bk serv referral
Open Mon-Thurs 9-9, Fri & Sat 9-6, Sun 12-6
Restriction: Circ to mem only, Non-resident fee
Friends of the Library Group

M BOCA RATON REGIONAL HOSPITAL*, Medical Staff Library, 800 Meadows Rd, 33486. SAN 324-5632. Tel: 561-955-4088. FAX: 561-955-4825. Web Site: www.brrh.com/Healthcare-Professionals/Medical-Library.aspx. *Med Librn*, Rana Dole; E-mail: rdole@brrh.com; Staff 1 (MLS 1)
Founded 1969
Library Holdings: Bk Titles 4,800; Per Subs 125
Partic in Fla Health Sci Libr Asn; National Network of Libraries of Medicine Region 2
Open Mon-Fri 8-5

C EVERGLADES UNIVERSITY LIBRARIES*, Boca Raton Campus, 5002 T-REX Ave, Ste 100, 33431. Tel: 561-912-1211. Toll Free Tel: 888-772-6077. FAX: 561-912-1191. Web Site: www.evergladesuniversity.edu/library. *Dir, Libr Serv*, Adam Brody; E-mail: abrody@evergladesuniversity.edu; Staff 3 (MLS 3)
Highest Degree: Master
Wireless access
Partic in Library & Information Resources Network; Southeast Florida Library Information Network, Inc
Open Mon, Tues & Thurs 8:30am-9pm, Wed & Fri 10-7, Sat 8:30-5
Departmental Libraries:
ORLANDO CAMPUS, 850 Trafalgar Ct, Ste 100, Maitland, 32751. Tel: 407-277-0311. Toll Free Tel: 866-289-1078. FAX: 407-482-9801. Web Site: www.evergladesuniversity.edu/locations/contact-orlando. *Dir, Libr Serv*, Adam Brody; E-mail: abrody@evergladesuniversity.edu
Open Mon-Thurs 9am-9:30pm, Fri 8:30-5, Sat 9-5
SARASOTA CAMPUS, 6001 Lake Osprey Dr, Ste 110, Sarasota, 34240. Tel: 941-907-2262. Toll Free Tel: 888-854-5645. FAX: 941-907-6634. Web Site: www.evergladesuniversity.edu/locations/contact-sarasota. *Dir, Libr Serv*, Danielle O'Donnell
Open Mon, Tues & Thurs 7:30am-9pm, Wed 7:30am-10pm, Fri 7:30-5, Sat 9-5
TAMPA CAMPUS, 5010 W Kennedy Blvd, Tampa, 33609. Tel: 813-961-2837. Toll Free Tel: 844-297-1715. FAX: 813-885-6031. Web Site: www.evergladesuniversity.edu/locations/contact-tampa. *Librn*, James Evans
Partic in Tampa Bay Library Consortium, Inc
Open Mon-Thurs 9am-10pm, Fri & Sat 9-5

C FLORIDA ATLANTIC UNIVERSITY*, S E Wimberly Library, 777 Glades Rd, 33431. (Mail add: PO Box 3092, 33431-0992), SAN 337-2693. Tel: 561-297-3165. Circulation Tel: 561-297-0350. Interlibrary Loan Service Tel: 561-297-0563. Reference Tel: 561-297-3785. Information Services Tel: 561-297-3770. FAX: 561-297-2189. Interlibrary Loan Service FAX: 561-297-2232. E-mail: library@fau.edu. Web Site: library.fau.edu. *Interim Dean*, Amy Kornblau; Tel: 561-297-3789, E-mail: kornblau@fau.edu; *Asst Dean, Pub Serv*, Dawn Smith; Tel: 561-297-1029, E-mail: dsmith@fau.edu; *Asst Dir, Support Serv*, Steven Matthew; Tel: 561-297-4027, E-mail: matthew@fau.edu; *Head, Coll Mgt*, Maris Hayashi; Tel: 561-297-4317, E-mail: mhayashi@fau.edu; *Head, Engagement & Instructional Servs*, Kenneth Frankel; Tel: 561-297-0079, E-mail: frankel@fau.edu; *Head, Spec Coll*, Victoria Thur; Tel: 561-297-3787, E-mail: vthur@fau.edu; Staff 35 (MLS 35)
Founded 1961. Enrl 30,364; Fac 1,045; Highest Degree: Doctorate
Jul 2014-Jun 2015. Mats Exp $3,233,551, Books $223,798, Per/Ser (Incl. Access Fees) $25,354, AV Mat $18,129, Electronic Ref Mat (Incl. Access Fees) $2,810,091, Presv $9,164
Library Holdings: CDs 7,705; DVDs 9,501; e-books 1,212,331; e-journals 30,671; Bk Vols 1,146,661; Per Subs 668; Videos 8,482
Special Collections: Arlyn Austin Katims Civil War Coll; Clarke Family Papers; Harold L Glasser Coll; Jaffe Books as Aesthetic Objects; K Frank Korf Papers; Marvin & Sybil Weiner Spirit of America Coll; Marvin Kemery Letters; Print Music Coll; Recorded Sound Archives; Theodore Pratt Papers; University Archives; Virginia Snyder Coll; Walter Wadepuhl Papers. State Document Depository; US Document Depository
Subject Interests: Am hist, Art, Engr, Ethnic studies, Film studies, Music, Nursing, Women's studies
Automation Activity & Vendor Info: (Acquisitions) Ex Libris Group; (Cataloging) Ex Libris Group; (Circulation) Ex Libris Group; (Course Reserve) Ex Libris Group; (ILL) OCLC; (OPAC) Ex Libris Group; (Serials) Ex Libris Group
Wireless access
Partic in LYRASIS; Southeast Florida Library Information Network, Inc
Open Mon-Fri 8:30-5:30
Friends of the Library Group

C LYNN UNIVERSITY LIBRARY, 3601 N Military Trail, 33431-5598. SAN 302-8607. Tel: 561-237-7254. E-mail: library@lynn.edu. Web Site: lynn-library.libguides.com. *Dir*, Amy Filiatreau; Tel: 561-237-7067, E-mail: afiliatreau@lynn.edu; *Digital Res Librn*, Jared Wellman; Tel: 561-237-7073, E-mail: jwellman@lynn.edu; *Music Librn*, Tuskasa Cherkaoui; Tel: 561-237-7214, E-mail: tcherkaoui@lynn.edu; *Outreach Librn*, Sabine Dantus; Tel: 561-237-7708, E-mail: sdantus@lynn.edu; *Ref & Instruction Librn*, Amy An; Tel: 561-237-7072, E-mail: aan@lynn.edu; Staff 8 (MLS 7, Non-MLS 1)
Founded 1963. Enrl 2,500; Fac 85; Highest Degree: Doctorate
Library Holdings: AV Mats 4,000; Bk Vols 100,000; Per Subs 300
Subject Interests: Bus & mgt, Humanities, Intl commun, Leadership
Automation Activity & Vendor Info: (Acquisitions) Mandarin Library Automation; (Cataloging) Mandarin Library Automation; (Circulation) Mandarin Library Automation; (Course Reserve) Mandarin Library Automation; (OPAC) Mandarin Library Automation; (Serials) Mandarin Library Automation
Wireless access
Partic in Southeast Florida Library Information Network, Inc
Open Mon-Thurs 7:30am-Midnight, Fri 7:30-6, Sat 11-6, Sun Noon-Midnight

BONIFAY

P HOLMES COUNTY PUBLIC LIBRARY*, 303 N J Harvey Etheridge, 32425. SAN 376-2718. Tel: 850-547-3573. FAX: 850-547-2801. E-mail: hcpl32425@yahoo.com. Web Site: myhcpl.org. *Dir*, Susan Harris; E-mail: director@myhcpl.org; *Asst Dir*, Becky Marsh; *Cat, Tech Serv*, Rachel Darling; *Ch Serv*, Joan Biddle; *Circ*, Iris Smith; *ILL*, Michelle Cross; Staff 4 (Non-MLS 4)
Founded 1973. Pop 19,564; Circ 29,689
Library Holdings: DVDs 1,500; Large Print Bks 2,000; Bk Titles 19,053; Per Subs 10; Talking Bks 1,509; Videos 100
Automation Activity & Vendor Info: (Cataloging) SirsiDynix; (Circulation) SirsiDynix-WorkFlows; (ILL) SirsiDynix-WorkFlows
Wireless access
Function: Computers for patron use, ILL available, Prog for children & young adult
Mem of Panhandle Public Library Cooperative System
Open Tues-Fri 8-5, Sat 8-12
Friends of the Library Group

BOYNTON BEACH

M BETHESDA HEALTH - BETHESDA HOSPITAL EAST*, Robert E Raborn Medical Library, 2815 S Seacrest Blvd, 33435-7934. SAN 302-864X. Tel: 561-737-7733, Ext 84439. FAX: 561-735-7080. Web Site: www.bethesdaweb.com. *Libr Asst*, Cynthia DeMarco; E-mail: cdemarco@bhinc.org
Founded 1967
Library Holdings: Bk Vols 3,500; Per Subs 35
Special Collections: NCME Tapes
Wireless access
Restriction: Not open to pub

P BOYNTON BEACH CITY LIBRARY*, 115 N Federal Hwy, 33435. SAN 302-8658. Tel: 561-742-6390. Administration Tel: 561-742-6380. FAX: 561-742-6381. E-mail: boyntonref@gmail.com. Web Site: www.boyntonlibrary.org. *Libr Dir*, Craig B Clark; E-mail: clarkc@bbfl.us; *Asst Dir*, Jeannie Taylor; E-mail: taylorjd@bbfl.us; *Head, Ref Serv*, Ellen Mancuso; E-mail: mancusoe@boyntonlibrary.org; *Head, Tech*, Michael Naughton; E-mail: naughtonm@bbfl.us; *Cat Librn*, Meghan Hoffman; E-mail: hoffmanm@boyntonlibrary.org; *Ref Librn*, Patricia Gabaldon; E-mail: gabaldonp@boyntonlibrary.org; *Teen Librn*, Kristine Kreidler; E-mail: kreidlerk@boyntonlibrary.org; *Youth Serv Librn*, Rebecca Feinsilber; E-mail: feinsilber@boyntonlibrary.org; *Head, Customer Serv*, Position Currently Open; Staff 33 (MLS 9, Non-MLS 24)
Founded 1961. Pop 76,000
Library Holdings: Bk Titles 120,000; Bk Vols 129,200; Per Subs 110

Special Collections: Florida Coll; History & Archives (local history). Oral History
Subject Interests: Gardening, Investing, Songbooks
Automation Activity & Vendor Info: (Acquisitions) SirsiDynix; (Cataloging) SirsiDynix; (Circulation) SirsiDynix; (OPAC) SirsiDynix-Enterprise
Wireless access
Function: 24/7 Electronic res, 24/7 Online cat, Adult literacy prog
Partic in Coop Authority for Libr Automation; Library Cooperative of the Palm Beaches; Southeast Florida Library Information Network, Inc
Special Services for the Deaf - TDD equip
Open Mon-Thurs 9-8:30, Sat 9-5
Friends of the Library Group

R ST VINCENT DE PAUL REGIONAL SEMINARY LIBRARY, 10701 S Military Trail, 33436-4811. SAN 302-8666. Tel: 561-732-4424, Ext 174. FAX: 561-737-2205. Web Site: www.svdp.edu. *Libr Dir,* Arthur G Quinn; E-mail: aquinn@svdp.edu. Subject Specialists: *Theol,* Arthur G Quinn; Staff 1 (MLS 1)
Founded 1963. Enrl 139; Fac 20; Highest Degree: Master
Jul 2019-Jun 2020. Mats Exp $60,929, Books $20,000, Per/Ser (Incl. Access Fees) $26,081, Manu Arch $2,314, AV Mat $565, Electronic Ref Mat (Incl. Access Fees) $10,560, Presv $1,409. Sal $78,593
Library Holdings: AV Mats 2,143; e-books 579; Electronic Media & Resources 8; Bk Titles 51,157; Bk Vols 57,355; Per Subs 204
Special Collections: Loeb Series; Sources Chretiennes Series
Subject Interests: Latin Am, Philos, Theol
Automation Activity & Vendor Info: (Cataloging) EOS International; (Circulation) EOS International; (Course Reserve) EOS International; (ILL) OCLC WorldShare Interlibrary Loan; (OPAC) EOS International; (Serials) EOS International
Wireless access
Function: 24/7 Electronic res, 24/7 Online cat, Bilingual assistance for Spanish patrons, Computers for patron use, Electronic databases & coll, ILL available, Internet access, Magazines, Music CDs, Online cat, Orientations, Photocopying/Printing, Res libr, Spanish lang bks, Wheelchair accessible
Open Mon-Fri 8am-11pm, Sat & Sun 10am-11pm
Restriction: Authorized patrons, Borrowing privileges limited to fac & registered students, Non-circulating of rare bks, Open to authorized patrons, Open to students, fac & staff, Photo ID required for access

BRADENTON

S ART CENTER MANATEE*, McKelvey Memorial Library, 209 Ninth St W, 34205. SAN 302-8674. Tel: 941-746-2862. FAX: 941-746-2319. E-mail: acm@artcentermanatee.org. Web Site: www.artcentermanatee.org. *Exec Dir,* Carla Nierman; E-mail: carla@artcentermanatee.org
Founded 1955
Library Holdings: Bk Titles 1,400; Bk Vols 1,500; Videos 50
Restriction: Mem only

L MANATEE COUNTY LAW LIBRARY*, Manatee County Judicial Ctr, Rm 1101, 1051 Manatee Ave W, 34205. (Mail add: PO Box 25400, 34205), SAN 302-8682. Tel: 941-741-4090. FAX: 941-741-4085. Web Site: www.manateeclerk.com/Departments/Law-Library. *Law Librn,* James Murga; E-mail: james.murga@manateeclerk.com; Staff 1 (Non-MLS 1)
Library Holdings: CDs 68; Bk Vols 16,000
Wireless access
Open Mon-Fri 8:30-4:30

P MANATEE COUNTY PUBLIC LIBRARY SYSTEM*, Downtown Library, 1301 Barcarrota Blvd W, 34205-7522. SAN 337-2723. Tel: 941-748-5555. Circulation Tel: 941-748-5555, Ext 6321. Interlibrary Loan Service Tel: 941-748-5555, Ext 6333. Reference Tel: 941-234-0394 (ref by text), 941-748-5555, Ext 6309. Administration Tel: 941-748-5555, Ext 6303. Information Services Tel: 941-748-5555, Ext 6311. FAX: 941-749-7191. Reference E-mail: reference@mymanatee.org. Web Site: www.mymanatee.org/library. *Mgr, Libr Serv,* Ava Ehde; Tel: 941-748-5555, Ext 6301, E-mail: ava.ehde@mymanatee.org; *Asst Libr Serv Mgr,* Glenda Lammers; Tel: 941-748-5555, Ext 6325, E-mail: glenda.lammers@mymanatee.org; *Head Cataloger,* Cindy Ardelle; Tel: 941-748-5555, Ext 6327, E-mail: cindy.ardelle@mymanatee.org; *Supvr, Ad Serv,* Ericka Dow; Tel: 941-748-5555, Ext 6311, E-mail: ericka.dow@mymanatee.org; *Supvr, Circ,* Zenobia Giles; E-mail: zenobia.giles@mymanatee.org; *Acq, Supvr, Coll Develop,* Courtney DeSear; Tel: 941-748-5555, Ext 6333, E-mail: courtney.desear@mymanatee.org; *Automation Coordr, Info Tech,* Robbie Taylor; Tel: 941-748-5555, Ext 6330, E-mail: robbie.taylor@mymanatee.org; *Coordr, Youth Serv,* Chris O'Hara; Tel: 941-748-5555, Ext 6319, E-mail: chris.ohara@mymanatee.org; *Literacy Coordr,* Jodie Williams; Tel: 941-748-5555, Ext 3820, E-mail: jodie.williams@mymanatee.org; *Mkt Coordr,* Kelly Foster; Tel: 941-748-5555, Ext 6307, E-mail: kelly.foster@mymanatee.org; *Prog Coordr,* Jyna Scheeren; Tel: 941-748-5555, Ext 6308, E-mail: jyna.scheeren@mymanatee.org. Subject Specialists: *Early childhood educ, Literacy,* Jodie Williams; Staff 70 (MLS 33, Non-MLS 37)
Founded 1964. Pop 364,000; Circ 4,100,000
Library Holdings: Bk Vols 499,567; Per Subs 300
Special Collections: Digitized Local History Archival Negatives and Documents. Oral History; US Document Depository
Subject Interests: Fla hist, Genealogy, Local hist, Musical instruments, Spanish (Lang), Tools
Automation Activity & Vendor Info: (Acquisitions) Innovative Interfaces, Inc; (Cataloging) Innovative Interfaces, Inc; (Circulation) Innovative Interfaces, Inc; (OPAC) Innovative Interfaces, Inc; (Serials) Innovative Interfaces, Inc
Wireless access
Function: 24/7 Electronic res, 24/7 Online cat, 3D Printer, Accelerated reader prog, Activity rm, Adult bk club, After school storytime, Archival coll, Art exhibits, Audio & video playback equip for onsite use, Audiobks via web, AV serv, Bilingual assistance for Spanish patrons, Bk club(s), Bks on CD, Children's prog, Computer training, Computers for patron use, Electronic databases & coll, Equip loans & repairs, Family literacy, Free DVD rentals, Govt ref serv, ILL available, Internet access, Magazines, Magnifiers for reading, Mango lang, Microfiche/film & reading machines, Music CDs, Online cat, Online ref, Outreach serv, OverDrive digital audio bks, Photocopying/Printing, Preschool outreach, Prog for adults, Prog for children & young adult, Ref & res, Ref serv available, Res libr, Serves people with intellectual disabilities, Spanish lang bks, Spoken cassettes & CDs, Story hour, Study rm, Summer reading prog, Tax forms, Teen prog, Telephone ref, VHS videos, Wheelchair accessible
Publications: 805 Literary Journal (805lit.org) (Quarterly); Update (Newsletter)
Partic in Tampa Bay Library Consortium, Inc
Special Services for the Deaf - Am sign lang & deaf culture; Bks on deafness & sign lang; Closed caption videos; Staff with knowledge of sign lang
Special Services for the Blind - Accessible computers; Aids for in-house use; Bks available with recordings; Bks on CD; Descriptive video serv (DVS); Extensive large print coll; Home delivery serv; Large print bks; PC for people with disabilities; Playaways (bks on MP3); Sound rec; Talking bks
Open Mon 10-8, Tues 10-6, Wed 12-8, Thurs & Fri 9-5, Sat 11-5
Restriction: Non-resident fee
Friends of the Library Group
Branches: 5
BRADEN RIVER, 4915 53rd Ave E, 34203, SAN 371-3709. Tel: 941-727-6079. FAX: 941-727-6059. *Br Mgr,* Cathryn Laird; Staff 8 (MLS 3, Non-MLS 5)
Library Holdings: Bk Vols 84,787
Open Wed & Fri 10-6, Tues 10-8, Thurs 12-8, Sat 10-5
Friends of the Library Group
ISLAND BRANCH, 5701 Marina Dr, Holmes Beach, 34217-1516, SAN 337-2758. Tel: 941-778-6341. FAX: 941-749-7184. *Supvr,* Inez Tamanaha; Tel: 941-778-6341, Ext 6373, E-mail: inez.tamanaha@mymanatee.org; Staff 6 (MLS 2, Non-MLS 4)
Open Tues & Thurs-Sat 9-5, Wed 12-8
Friends of the Library Group
PALMETTO BRANCH, 923 Sixth St W, Palmetto, 34221, SAN 337-2812. Tel: 941-722-3333. FAX: 941-749-7193. *Br Mgr,* Yoshira Castro; Staff 5 (MLS 3, Non-MLS 2)
Open Mon, Wed, Fri & Sat 9-5, Thurs 9-8
Friends of the Library Group
ROCKY BLUFF, 7016 US Hwy 301 N, Ellenton, 34222, SAN 374-5244. Tel: 941-723-4821. FAX: 941-723-4825. *Br Mgr,* Kate Lippincott; E-mail: kate.lippincott@mymanatee.org; Staff 6 (MLS 3, Non-MLS 3)
Open Tues, Thurs & Fri 10-6, Wed 12-8, Sat 10-5
Friends of the Library Group
SOUTH MANATEE COUNTY, 6081 26th St N, 34207, SAN 337-2847. Tel: 941-755-3892. FAX: 941-751-7098. *Br Mgr,* Linda Noyes; Tel: 941-727-6081, E-mail: linda.noyes@mymanatee.org; Staff 8 (MLS 3, Non-MLS 5)
Open Mon & Tues 9-8, Wed-Sat 9-5
Friends of the Library Group

J STATE COLLEGE OF FLORIDA MANATEE-SARASOTA LIBRARY*, 5840 26th St W, 34207. SAN 302-8690. Tel: 941-752-5305. Interlibrary Loan Service Tel: 941-752-5657. Reference Tel: 941-752-5304. Administration Tel: 941-752-5306. FAX: 941-752-5308. Reference E-mail: reference@scf.edu. Web Site: www.scf.edu. *Dir, Libr Serv,* Meg Hawkins; E-mail: hawkinm@scf.edu; *Digital Presence Librn,* Rhonda Kitchens; Tel: 941-408-1431, E-mail: kitcher@scf.edu; *Evening Librn,* Kirsten Beauchamp; E-mail: beauck@scf.edu; *Info Literacy Librn,* Mark Marino; Tel: 941-752-5317, E-mail: marinom@scf.edu; *Libr Supvr, Digital Initiatives,* Dana Bowker; Tel: 941-408-1434, E-mail: bowkerd@scf.edu; *Acq, Tech Serv Supvr,* Judy Born; Tel: 941-752-5262, E-mail: bornj@scf.edu. Subject Specialists: *Knowledge mgt,* Dana Bowker; Staff 8 (MLS 8)

Founded 1958. Enrl 11,500; Fac 650; Highest Degree: Bachelor
Library Holdings: AV Mats 4,098; e-books 9,502; Bk Vols 66,000; Per Subs 355
Subject Interests: Lit, Nursing
Automation Activity & Vendor Info: (Acquisitions) Ex Libris Group; (Cataloging) Ex Libris Group; (Circulation) Ex Libris Group; (ILL) OCLC; (OPAC) Ex Libris Group; (Serials) Ex Libris Group
Wireless access
Function: 24/7 Electronic res, Archival coll, Art exhibits, Bk reviews (Group), Computer training, Computers for patron use, Digital talking bks, Distance learning, Doc delivery serv, E-Readers, E-Reserves, Electronic databases & coll, Health sci info serv, Internet access, Life-long learning prog for all ages, Movies, Online cat, Online info literacy tutorials on the web & in blackboard, Online ref, Orientations, Outreach serv, Outside serv via phone, mail, e-mail & web, OverDrive digital audio bks, Photocopying/Printing, Ref & res, Ref serv available, Study rm, Wheelchair accessible, Workshops
Partic in Tampa Bay Library Consortium, Inc
Open Mon-Thurs 7:45am-9pm, Sun 5pm-9pm
Restriction: 24-hr pass syst for students only, Access at librarian's discretion, Access for corporate affiliates, Authorized patrons
Departmental Libraries:
VENICE CAMPUS, 8000 S Tamiami Trail, Venice, 34293, SAN 371-3660. Tel: 941-408-1435. FAX: 941-486-2687. *Libr Supvr,* Dana Bowker; Tel: 941-408-1434; *Digital Presence Librn,* Rhonda Kitchens; E-mail: kitcher@scf.edu; Staff 4 (MLS 2, Non-MLS 2)
Library Holdings: AV Mats 2,964; e-books 9,502; Bk Vols 27,916; Per Subs 137
Open Mon-Thurs 8:30-8, Fri 8:30-2

BRADENTON BEACH

P TINGLEY MEMORIAL LIBRARY*, Bradenton Beach Public Library, 111 Second St N, 34217-2465. SAN 375-3360. Tel: 941-779-1208. Web Site: www.cityofbradentonbeach.com/175/Tingley-Library. *Librn,* Eveann Adams; Staff 26 (MLS 1, Non-MLS 25)
Founded 1959
Oct 2013-Sept 2014. Mats Exp $7,000
Library Holdings: Audiobooks 200; CDs 200; DVDs 600; Large Print Bks 400; Bk Vols 8,000; Per Subs 20; Videos 20
Special Collections: Municipal Document Depository
Subject Interests: Fla
Wireless access
Function: Art exhibits, Bk club(s), Bks on cassette, Bks on CD, Computers for patron use, Photocopying/Printing, Spoken cassettes & CDs, Spoken cassettes & DVDs, VHS videos, Wheelchair accessible
Open Tues-Sat 10-3

BRONSON

P LEVY COUNTY PUBLIC LIBRARY SYSTEM*, Administration Office, 7871 NE 90th St, 32621. (Mail add: PO Box 1210, 32621-1210). Tel: 352-486-5552. FAX: 352-486-5553. Web Site: levycounty.org/cd_library.aspx. *Interim Dir,* Jeanine Turner; E-mail: jturner@neflin.org
Library Holdings: Bk Vols 75,950
Automation Activity & Vendor Info: (Acquisitions) SirsiDynix; (Cataloging) SirsiDynix; (Circulation) SirsiDynix
Wireless access
Open Mon-Fri 8-5
Branches: 5
BRONSON PUBLIC, 600 Gilbert St, 32621. Tel: 352-486-2015. *Mgr,* Sandy Moseley; E-mail: smoseley@neflin.org
Automation Activity & Vendor Info: (Acquisitions) Auto-Graphics, Inc; (Cataloging) Auto-Graphics, Inc; (Circulation) Auto-Graphics, Inc
Partic in Northeast Florida Library Information Network
Open Tues & Thurs 1-7, Wed & Fri 11-5, Sat 10-3
Friends of the Library Group
LUTHER CALLAWAY PUBLIC, 104 NE Third St, Chiefland, 32626-0937, SAN 374-4523. Tel: 352-493-2758. *Mgr,* Sue Ann Burkhardt; E-mail: sburkhardt@neflin.org
Open Mon, Wed & Fri 10-5, Tues & Thurs 1-8, Sat 10-3
Friends of the Library Group
CEDAR KEY PUBLIC, 460 Second St, Cedar Key, 32625. (Mail add: PO Box 550, Cedar Key, 32625-0550), SAN 337-8543. Tel: 352-543-5777. *Mgr,* Molly Jubitz; E-mail: mjubitz@neflin.org
Open Mon, Wed & Thurs 10-4, Tues 4-8, Fri 1-4, Sat 10-1
Friends of the Library Group
AF KNOTTS PUBLIC, 11 56th St, Yankeetown, 34498, SAN 374-454X. Tel: 352-447-4212. *Mgr,* L Cohan; E-mail: lcohan@neflin.org
Open Tues 3-8, Wed & Thurs 9-5, Sat 9-1
Friends of the Library Group
WILLISTON PUBLIC, Ten SE First St, Williston, 32696-2671. (Mail add: PO Box 373, Williston, 32696), SAN 337-8845. Tel: 352-528-2313. *Mgr,* Lonna Bear; E-mail: lbear@neflin.org
Open Mon, Wed, Fri & Sat 10-4, Tues & Thurs 12-8

BROOKSVILLE

P HERNANDO COUNTY PUBLIC LIBRARY SYSTEM*, Lykes Memorial Library, 238 Howell Ave, 34601. SAN 337-2871. Tel: 352-754-4043. E-mail: libacct@hernandocounty.us. Web Site: www.hernandocountylibrary.us. *Libr Serv Dir,* Cynthia Loftis-Culp; E-mail: cluftis-culp@co.hernandofl.us; *Youth Serv Librn,* Justin King; E-mail: jking@co.hernandofl.us; *Coll Mgr,* Lauren Rouhana; E-mail: lrouhana@co.hernandofl.us; *Br Supvr,* Susan Cataldo; E-mail: scataldo@co.hernandofl.us; Staff 57 (MLS 12, Non-MLS 45)
Founded 1926. Circ 595,714. Sal $1,583,556
Library Holdings: Audiobooks 6,813; AV Mats 9,317; e-books 8,916; Electronic Media & Resources 61; Bk Titles 184,163; Per Subs 457
Subject Interests: Fla
Automation Activity & Vendor Info: (Cataloging) ByWater Solutions; (Circulation) ByWater Solutions
Wireless access
Function: Adult bk club, Audiobks via web, Bks on cassette, Bks on CD, Children's prog, Computer training, Computers for patron use, Holiday prog, ILL available, Jail serv, Mail & tel request accepted, Music CDs, Online cat, Online ref, OverDrive digital audio bks, Photocopying/Printing, Prog for adults, Prog for children & young adult, Ref & res, Ref serv available, Tax forms, Teen prog, Telephone ref, VHS videos, Wheelchair accessible
Partic in Florida Library Information Network; Tampa Bay Library Consortium, Inc
Special Services for the Deaf - Closed caption videos
Special Services for the Blind - Audio mat; Bks on cassette; Bks on CD
Open Mon-Thurs 10-6, Fri 9-5
Friends of the Library Group
Branches: 4
EAST HERNANDO, 6457 Windemere Rd, 34602, SAN 373-806X. Tel: 352-754-4043. *Br Supvr,* Glorea Charland; E-mail: gcharland@co.hernandofl.us
Open Tues & Wed 10-6, Thurs 12-8, Fri & Sat 9-5
Friends of the Library Group
SPRING HILL BRANCH, 9220 Spring Hill Dr, Spring Hill, 34608, SAN 337-2995. Tel: 352-754-4043. *Br Supvr,* Colleen Ludington; E-mail: cludington@co.hernandofl.us
Open Tues & Wed 10-6, Thurs 12-8, Fri 9-5
Friends of the Library Group
WEST HERNANDO, 6335 Blackbird Ave, 34613, SAN 325-4429. Tel: 352-754-4043. Reference Tel: 352-540-6392. *Br Supvr,* Darla Steward; E-mail: dsteward@co.hernandofl.us
Open Mon-Wed 10-6, Thurs 12-8, Fri 9-5
Friends of the Library Group

C PASCO-HERNANDO STATE COLLEGE-NORTH CAMPUS, Alfred A McKethan Library, 11415 Ponce de Leon Blvd, Rm C125, 34601-8698. SAN 302-8720. Tel: 352-797-5007. FAX: 352-797-5080. Web Site: libguides.phsc.edu/c.php?g=846660&p=6445400, phsc.edu/academics/libraries. *Assoc Dir of Libr,* Nava Cohen; Tel: 352-797-5139, E-mail: cohenn@phsc.edu
Founded 1974
Library Holdings: Bk Vols 20,000; Per Subs 100
Automation Activity & Vendor Info: (Cataloging) Ex Libris Group; (Circulation) Ex Libris Group; (Course Reserve) Ex Libris Group; (ILL) OCLC; (OPAC) Ex Libris Group; (Serials) Ex Libris Group
Wireless access
Open Mon-Thurs 8-7:30; Fri 8-4:30

CAPE CANAVERAL

P CAPE CANAVERAL PUBLIC LIBRARY*, 201 Polk Ave, 32920-3067. SAN 302-8755. Tel: 321-868-1101. FAX: 321-868-1103. Web Site: www.brevardfl.gov/PublicLibraries/Branches/CapeCanaveral. *Dir,* Lisa Olzewski; E-mail: lolzewski@brev.org; *Circ Supvr,* Lauren Cynova; E-mail: lcynova@brev.org; *Youth Serv,* Brittany Wilson; E-mail: bwilson@brev.org; Staff 3 (MLS 2, Non-MLS 1)
Founded 1966
Library Holdings: Bk Vols 44,191; Per Subs 82
Wireless access
Mem of Brevard County Public Libraries
Open Mon 12-8, Tues-Fri 9-5, Sat 10-2
Friends of the Library Group

CASSELBERRY

P SEMINOLE COUNTY PUBLIC LIBRARY SYSTEM*, 215 N Oxford Rd, 32707. SAN 338-0645. Tel: 407-665-1500. FAX: 407-665-1510. Web Site: www.seminolelibrary.org. *Mgr, Libr Serv,* Christine Patten; E-mail: cpatten@seminolecountyfl.gov; Staff 71 (MLS 29, Non-MLS 42)
Founded 1987. Pop 422,718; Circ 1,768,647
Library Holdings: Audiobooks 29,949; DVDs 5,828; Electronic Media & Resources 40,468; Bk Titles 224,740; Bk Vols 585,266; Per Subs 511
Automation Activity & Vendor Info: (Acquisitions) SirsiDynix-WorkFlows; (Cataloging) SirsiDynix-WorkFlows; (Circulation) SirsiDynix-WorkFlows; (OPAC) SirsiDynix; (Serials) SirsiDynix-WorkFlows
Wireless access
Function: 24/7 Electronic res, Adult bk club, Bks on CD, Chess club, Children's prog, Computer training, Computers for patron use, E-Readers, Electronic databases & coll, Free DVD rentals, Genealogy discussion group, Home delivery & serv to seniorr ctr & nursing homes, Homebound delivery serv, Internet access, Life-long learning prog for all ages, Magazines, Meeting rooms, Movies, Online cat, Online ref, Orientations, OverDrive digital audio bks, Photocopying/Printing, Prog for adults, Prog for children & young adult, Ref serv available, Spanish lang bks, Story hour, Summer reading prog, Tax forms, Teen prog, Telephone ref, Wheelchair accessible
Open Mon-Thurs 9-8, Sat 9-5, Sun 1-5
Friends of the Library Group
Branches: 5
EAST BRANCH, 310 Division St, Oviedo, 32765, SAN 328-8978. Tel: 407-665-1560. FAX: 407-665-1585. *Br Mgr,* Norma Medina-Ortiz; E-mail: nmedinaortiz@seminolecountyfl.gov
Open Mon-Thurs 9-8, Sat 9-5, Sun 1-5
NORTH BRANCH, 150 N Palmetto Ave, Sanford, 32771, SAN 338-067X. Tel: 407-665-1620. FAX: 407-665-1615. *Br Mgr,* Norma Medina-Ortiz
Open Mon-Thurs 9-8, Fri & Sat 9-5, Sun 1-5
NORTHWEST BRANCH, 580 Greenway Blvd, Lake Mary, 32746, SAN 328-8994. Tel: 407-665-1640. FAX: 407-665-1645. *Br Mgr,* Barbara McCullough; E-mail: bmccullough@seminolecountyfl.gov
Open Mon-Thurs 9-8, Fri & Sat 9-5, Sun 1-5
JEAN RHEIN CENTRAL LIBRARY, 215 N Oxford Rd, 32707, SAN 338-070X. *Br Mgr,* Caroline Quintanilla; E-mail: cquintanilla@seminolecountyfl.gov
Open Mon-Thurs 9-8, Sat 9-5, Sun 1-5
WEST, 245 Hunt Club Blvd N, Longwood, 32779, SAN 328-901X. Tel: 407-665-1670. FAX: 407-665-1675. *Br Mgr,* Barbara McCullough
Open Mon-Thurs 9-8, Sat 9-5, Sun 1-5

CHATTAHOOCHEE

M FLORIDA STATE HOSPITAL*, Library Services, Main Library Bldg 1260, 32324. (Mail add: PO Box 1000, 32324-1000), SAN 302-881X. Tel: 850-663-7671. *Dir, Libr Serv,* Marcia Duggar; E-mail: marcia.duggar@myflfamilies.com. Subject Specialists: *Mental illness,* Marcia Duggar; Staff 2 (MLS 2)
Library Holdings: Bk Titles 35,000; Per Subs 22
Subject Interests: Law, Music, Psychol, Relig
Open Mon-Fri 8-4:30

CHIPLEY

P WASHINGTON COUNTY LIBRARY*, 1444 Jackson Ave, 32428. SAN 376-5016. Tel: 850-638-1314. FAX: 850-638-9499. Web Site: wcplfl.com. *Dir,* Renae Rountree; E-mail: director@wcplfl.com
Automation Activity & Vendor Info: (Cataloging) Koha; (Circulation) Koha
Wireless access
Open Mon-Thurs 9-6, Fri 9-1
Friends of the Library Group
Branches: 3
SAM MITCHELL PUBLIC LIBRARY, 3731 Roche Ave, Vernon, 32462, SAN 376-8287. Tel: 850-535-1208. FAX: 850-535-1208. *Mgr,* Dorothy Pichardo
Open Mon & Thurs 9-6, Tues & Wed 12-6, Fri 9-3
SUNNY HILLS LIBRARY, 4083 Challenger Blvd, Sunny Hills, 32428. Tel: 850-773-3588.
Open Tues, Wed & Thurs 9-6
WAUSAU PUBLIC LIBRARY, Town Hall, 1607 Second Ave, Wausau, 32463, SAN 376-8295. Tel: 850-638-2532. FAX: 850-638-2532. *Mgr,* Susan Cook
Open Mon 9-3, Tues & Thurs 10-6, Wed 1-6

CITRUS SPRINGS

P CITRUS SPRINGS MEMORIAL LIBRARY, 1826 W Country Club Blvd, 34434. SAN 376-3005. Tel: 352-489-2313. E-mail: cslibrary@hotmail.com. Web Site: www.facebook.com/citrusspringslibrary.
Library Holdings: AV Mats 600; Bk Vols 14,000; Talking Bks 124
Wireless access
Open Mon-Fri 10-4, Sat 10-1

CLEARWATER

M BAY CARE*, Medical Library, Morton Plant Hospital, 300 Pinellas St, 33756. (Mail add: PO Box 210, 33756-0210), SAN 322-7219. Tel: 727-462-7889. FAX: 727-461-8755. E-mail: medical.library@baycare.org. Web Site: baycare.org. *Mgr, Libr Serv,* Lori Brown; E-mail: lori.brown@baycare.org; Staff 2 (MLS 1, Non-MLS 1)
Founded 1955
Library Holdings: Bk Vols 2,500; Per Subs 200
Subject Interests: Allied health, Med, Nursing
Automation Activity & Vendor Info: (Cataloging) EOS International; (Circulation) EOS International; (OPAC) EOS International; (Serials) EOS International
Wireless access
Partic in National Network of Libraries of Medicine Region 2; Tampa Bay Medical Library Network

P CLEARWATER PUBLIC LIBRARY SYSTEM*, 100 N Osceola Ave, 33755. SAN 337-3053. Tel: 727-562-4970. Automation Services Tel: 727-286-6894. FAX: 727-562-4977. E-mail: referencedesk@myclearwater.com. Web Site: www.myclearwaterlibrary.com. *Dir,* Barbara Pickell; *Asst Dir,* Jennifer Obermaier; E-mail: jennifer.obermaier@myclearwater.com; *Asst Dir,* Linda Rothstein; E-mail: linda.rothstein@myclearwater.com; *Financial Serv Adminr,* Paula Chaplinsky; E-mail: paula.chaplinsky@myclearwater.com; *Head, Prog,* Kayla Grant; E-mail: kayla.grant@myclearwater.com; *Head, Youth Serv,* Mercedes Bleattler; E-mail: mercedes.bleattler@myclearwater.com; *Br Mgr, Librn,* Christa Smith; E-mail: christa.smith@myclearwater.com; *Ref Supvr,* Michelle Arnold; E-mail: michelle.arnold@myclearwater.com; *Ref Supvr,* Adriana Topel; E-mail: adriana.topel@myclearwater.com; *Tech Serv Mgr,* Bonnie Potters; E-mail: bonnie.potters@myclearwater.com; Staff 20.5 (MLS 18.5, Non-MLS 2)
Founded 1916. Pop 107,000
Library Holdings: AV Mats 20,415; Bk Vols 229,556; Per Subs 427
Special Collections: US Document Depository
Automation Activity & Vendor Info: (Acquisitions) SirsiDynix; (Cataloging) SirsiDynix; (Circulation) SirsiDynix; (OPAC) SirsiDynix; (Serials) SirsiDynix
Wireless access
Function: Adult bk club, Archival coll, Art exhibits, Audiobks via web, Bk club(s), Bks on CD, Children's prog, Computer training, Computers for patron use, Digital talking bks, E-Reserves, Electronic databases & coll, Free DVD rentals, Govt ref serv, Internet access, Mail & tel request accepted, Microfiche/film & reading machines, Music CDs, Online cat, OverDrive digital audio bks, Photocopying/Printing, Preschool outreach, Preschool reading prog, Prog for adults, Prog for children & young adult, Ref & res, Ref serv available, Spanish lang bks, Story hour, Summer reading prog, Tax forms, Teen prog, Telephone ref, Wheelchair accessible
Mem of Pinellas Public Library Cooperative
Partic in Tampa Bay Library Consortium, Inc
Special Services for the Blind - ABE/GED & braille classes for the visually impaired
Open Mon-Thurs 10-7, Fri-Sun 12-5
Friends of the Library Group
Branches: 4
BEACH, 69 Bay Esplanade, 33767, SAN 337-3088. Tel: 727-562-4970. *Br Librn,* Joyce Kirchoffer; E-mail: joyce.kirchoffer@myclearwater.com; Staff 1 (Non-MLS 1)
Founded 1961
Open Mon & Tues 10-5, Wed 1-7, Thurs & Fri 1-5
Friends of the Library Group
COUNTRYSIDE, 2642 Sabal Springs Dr, 33761, SAN 329-6741. Tel: 727-562-4970. *Br Mgr,* Tracey Reed; E-mail: tracey.reed@myclearwater.com; *Ref Serv,* Stephanie Catlyn; E-mail: stephanie.catlyn@myclearwater.com; Staff 7 (MLS 7)
Founded 1988
Open Mon-Thurs 10-7, Fri-Sun 12-5
EAST, 2465 Drew St, 33765, SAN 326-8586. Tel: 727-562-4970. *Ref Librn,* Kristina Pasley; E-mail: kristina.pasley@myclearwater.com; Staff 6 (MLS 6)
Founded 1985
Open Mon & Thurs 10-7, Tues & Wed 11-8, Fri & Sat 12-5
Friends of the Library Group
NORTH GREENWOOD, 905 N Martin Luther King Jr Ave, 33755, SAN 337-3142. Tel: 727-562-4970. *Br Mgr,* Valerie Mathre; *Youth Serv,* Sarah Jameson; E-mail: sarah.jameson@myclearwater.com
Founded 1950
Special Collections: African-American Coll; Christine Wigfall Morris African American Coll
Open Mon & Thurs 10-6, Tues & Wed 10-8, Fri 1-5
Friends of the Library Group

GL PINELLAS COUNTY LAW LIBRARY*, Clearwater, 324 S Ft Harrison Ave, 33756-5165. SAN 302-8852. Tel: 727-464-3411. FAX: 727-464-4571. E-mail: clwllib@jud6.org. Web Site: www.jud6.org/LegalCommunity/LawLibraries.html. *Law Libr Dir/Law Libn,* Michelle Howard
Founded 1950
Library Holdings: Bk Vols 34,000
Special Collections: Laws of Florida
Wireless access
Function: Computers for patron use, Internet access, Notary serv, Photocopying/Printing
Partic in Southeastern Chapter of the American Association of Law Libraries
Open Mon-Fri 8:30-4:30
Restriction: Mem only, Non-circulating, Not a lending libr, Pub use on premises, Ref only

P PINELLAS PUBLIC LIBRARY COOPERATIVE*, 1330 Cleveland St, 33755-5103. Tel: 727-441-8408. FAX: 727-441-8938. Web Site: www.pplc.us. *Exec Dir,* Cheryl Morales; E-mail: cmorales@pplc.us; *County Coordr,* Gary Earl; E-mail: gearl@pplc.us
Member Libraries: Barbara S Ponce Public Library; Clearwater Public Library System; Dunedin Public Library; East Lake Community Library; Gulf Beaches Public Library; Gulfport Public Library; Oldsmar Public Library; Palm Harbor Library; Pinellas Talking Book Library; Safety Harbor Public Library; Saint Petersburg Public Library; Seminole Community Library at St Petersburg College; St Pete Beach Public Library; Tarpon Springs Public Library

P PINELLAS TALKING BOOK LIBRARY*, 1330 Cleveland St, 33755-5103. Tel: 727-441-9958. FAX: 727-441-9068. TDD: 727-441-3168. E-mail: talkingbooks@pplc.us. Web Site: www.pplc.us/tbl. *Exec Dir,* Cheryl Morales; E-mail: cmorales@pplc.us; *Pub Serv Coordr,* Meagan Magee; E-mail: mmagee@pplc.us
Library Holdings: Talking Bks 69,000
Automation Activity & Vendor Info: (Cataloging) Keystone Systems, Inc (KLAS); (Circulation) Keystone Systems, Inc (KLAS); (OPAC) Keystone Systems, Inc (KLAS)
Wireless access
Mem of Pinellas Public Library Cooperative
Partic in Tampa Bay Library Consortium, Inc
Special Services for the Blind - Bks & mags in Braille, on rec, tape & cassette; Braille bks
Open Mon-Fri 8:30-4:30

S PROVIDENCE HISTORICAL SOCIETY*, 28051 US Hwy 19 N, 33761. SAN 300-1717. Tel: 813-855-4635. FAX: 813-855-2309. *Librn,* Nancy Stewart; Staff 10 (MLS 4, Non-MLS 6)
Founded 1971
Library Holdings: Bk Titles 11,000; Bk Vols 15,000

CLEWISTON

P HENDRY COUNTY LIBRARY SYSTEM*, Clewiston Public Library (Headquarters), 120 W Osceola Ave, 33440. SAN 302-8895. Tel: 863-983-1493. FAX: 863-983-9194. E-mail: library@clewiston-fl.gov. Web Site: www.hendrylibraries.org. *Dir,* Natasha Hayes; E-mail: natasha.hayes@clewiston-fl.gov
Founded 1962. Pop 10,000; Circ 39,366
Library Holdings: Bk Vols 71,385; Per Subs 152
Automation Activity & Vendor Info: (Cataloging) TLC (The Library Corporation); (Circulation) TLC (The Library Corporation); (OPAC) TLC (The Library Corporation)
Wireless access
Open Mon & Thurs 9-8, Tues, Wed & Fri 9-5, Sat 9-1
Friends of the Library Group
Branches: 3
BARRON LIBRARY, 461 N Main St, Labelle, 33935. (Mail add: PO Box 785, Labelle, 33935-0785), SAN 302-9948. Tel: 863-675-0833, 863-675-0839. FAX: 863-675-7544. E-mail: barronlibrary2013@gmail.com. *Libr Dir,* Karen Hildebrand; E-mail: khildebrand.barron@gmail.com
Pop 8,000; Circ 40,000
Library Holdings: Bk Vols 24,126; Per Subs 25
Open Mon & Thurs 10-8, Tues, Wed & Fri 10-5, Sat 10-1
Friends of the Library Group
HARLEM COMMUNITY PUBLIC LIBRARY, 1010 J Harlem Academy Ave, 33440. Tel: 863-902-3322, 863-902-3324. FAX: 863-902-3323. E-mail: harlem.library1@gmail.com. *Libr Dir,* Gretchen Debree; E-mail: gretchen.debree@hendryfla.net
Library Holdings: Bk Vols 11,000
Open Mon-Thurs 10-6, Fri 12-5
Friends of the Library Group
MONTURA LIBRARY, 255 N Hacienda St, 33440. *Librn,* Maria Antunez
Open Tues & Wed 3-6

COCOA

P BREVARD COUNTY PUBLIC LIBRARIES*, 308 Forrest Ave, 2nd Flr, 32922. SAN 303-0393. Tel: 321-633-1801. Automation Services Tel: 855-210-0357. FAX: 321-633-1798. Web Site: www.brevardfl.gov//PublicLibraries. *Dir, Libr Serv,* Jeffrey Thompson; E-mail: jthompson@brev.org; *Asst Libr Serv Dir,* Jeri Prieth; E-mail: jprieth@brev.org
Founded 1972. Pop 460,977; Circ 5,132,773
Oct 2013-Sept 2014 Income $14,801,276. Mats Exp $1,056,072, Books $592,150, Other Print Mats $333,662, Electronic Ref Mat (Incl. Access Fees) $130,260. Sal $9,196,568
Library Holdings: Bk Vols 1,184,819; Per Subs 1,111; Talking Bks 39,897; Videos 114,567
Automation Activity & Vendor Info: (Circulation) TLC (The Library Corporation)
Wireless access
Member Libraries: Cape Canaveral Public Library; Catherine Schweinsberg Rood Central Library; Cocoa Beach Public Library; Dr Martin Luther King Jr Library; Eau Gallie Public Library; Franklin T Degroodt Library; Melbourne Beach Public Library; Melbourne Public Library; Merritt Island Public Library; Mims/Scottsmoor Public Library; Palm Bay Public Library; Port St John Public Library; Satellite Beach Public Library; South Mainland Library; Suntree/Viera Public Library; Titusville Public Library; West Melbourne Public Library
Partic in Cent Fla Libr Consortium; Northeast Florida Library Information Network
Special Services for the Blind - Talking bks
Open Mon-Fri 8-5
Friends of the Library Group
Bookmobiles: 1. Libr Supvr, Tammy Moon

C EASTERN FLORIDA STATE COLLEGE*, Cocoa Campus Joint Use Library, 1519 Clearlake Rd, 32922. SAN 337-3266. Circulation Tel: 321-433-7250. Interlibrary Loan Service Tel: 321-433-7662. FAX: 321-433-7678. E-mail: LibraryB@easternflorida.edu. Web Site: www.easternflorida.edu/library. *Cat Librn,* Karen MacArthur; Tel: 321-433-7266, E-mail: macarthurk@easternflorida.edu; *Acq & Ser Librn,* Michelle Rezeau; Tel: 321-433-7189, E-mail: rezeaum@easternflorida.edu; *Circ Librn, E-Resources Librn,* Holly Tkaczyk; Tel: 321-433-7252, E-mail: tkaczykh@easternflorida.edu; *ILL Spec,* Gina Rippins; Tel: 321-433-7262, E-mail: rippinsg@easternflorida.edu; Staff 30 (MLS 11, Non-MLS 19)
Founded 1960. Highest Degree: Bachelor
Library Holdings: e-books 60,000; Electronic Media & Resources 80; Bk Vols 196,700; Per Subs 1,300
Automation Activity & Vendor Info: (Acquisitions) Ex Libris Group; (Cataloging) Ex Libris Group; (Circulation) Ex Libris Group; (Course Reserve) Ex Libris Group; (OPAC) Ex Libris Group; (Serials) Ex Libris Group
Wireless access
Function: Audio & video playback equip for onsite use, Doc delivery serv, ILL available, Ref serv available, Telephone ref
Partic in LYRASIS; Northeast Florida Library Information Network
Open Mon-Thurs 8-5

S FLORIDA HISTORICAL SOCIETY*, Library of Florida History, 435 Brevard Ave, 32922. SAN 338-196X. Tel: 321-690-1971, Ext 211. FAX: 321-690-4388. E-mail: archivist@myfloridahistory.org. Web Site: www.myfloridahistory.org. *Dir, Educ Res,* Ben DiBiase; E-mail: ben.dibiase@myfloridahistory.org; *Archivist,* Position Currently Open
Founded 1856
Library Holdings: Bk Vols 7,000; Per Subs 75
Subject Interests: State hist
Publications: Florida Historical (Quarterly); The Society Report
Open Tues-Sat 10-4:30
Friends of the Library Group

P PORT ST JOHN PUBLIC LIBRARY, 6500 Carole Ave, 32927. SAN 376-5105. Tel: 321-633-1867. Web Site: brevardcounty.us/PublicLibraries/Branches/PortStJohn. *Dir,* Mary Lena Penna; E-mail: mpenna@brev.org
Library Holdings: Bk Vols 45,000; Per Subs 15
Automation Activity & Vendor Info: (Cataloging) TLC (The Library Corporation); (Circulation) TLC (The Library Corporation); (OPAC) TLC (The Library Corporation)
Wireless access
Mem of Brevard County Public Libraries
Open Mon, Tues, Thurs & Fri 9-5, Wed 12-8, Sat 10-2
Friends of the Library Group

P CATHERINE SCHWEINSBERG ROOD CENTRAL LIBRARY*, 308 Forrest Ave, 32922. SAN 302-8909. Tel: 321-633-1792. Circulation Tel: 321-633-1793. FAX: 321-633-1806. Web Site:

brevardfl.gov/PublicLibraries/Branches/CatherineSchweinsbergRood. *Libr Dir,* Marian H Griffin; E-mail: mgriffin@brev.org; *Head, Circ,* Joyce Higgins; *Youth Serv Supvr,* Theresa O'Brien
Founded 1895. Circ 439,161
Library Holdings: AV Mats 14,191; DVDs 7,232; Bk Vols 186,960; Per Subs 397; Talking Bks 60,718
Special Collections: Municipal Document Depository; US Document Depository
Subject Interests: Fla, Genealogy
Automation Activity & Vendor Info: (OPAC) TLC (The Library Corporation); (Serials) Brodart
Wireless access
Mem of Brevard County Public Libraries
Partic in Cent Fla Libr Consortium
Special Services for the Blind - Closed circuit TV; Reader equip; Talking bks
Open Mon, Wed, Fri & Sat 9-5, Tues & Thurs 9-8, Sun 1-5
Friends of the Library Group

COCOA BEACH

P COCOA BEACH PUBLIC LIBRARY, 550 N Brevard Ave, 32931. SAN 302-8917. Tel: 321-868-1104. FAX: 321-868-1141. Web Site: www.brevardcounty.us/PublicLibraries/Branches/CocoaBeach. *Libr Dir,* Lisa Olzewski; Tel: 321-868-1106, E-mail: lolzewski@brev.org; *Head, Circ,* Laurie Baumann; *Head, Ref,* Michael Perini; E-mail: mperini@brev.org; *Head, Youth Serv,* Position Currently Open; *Programming Librn,* Lauren Biller; Staff 3 (MLS 3)
Founded 1955. Pop 20,000; Circ 286,488
Library Holdings: AV Mats 23,819; Bk Vols 106,714; Per Subs 221
Special Collections: Cocoa Beach Artists, oil, watercolor, batik & bronze
Subject Interests: Fiction, Fla
Automation Activity & Vendor Info: (Cataloging) TLC (The Library Corporation); (Circulation) TLC (The Library Corporation); (OPAC) TLC (The Library Corporation)
Wireless access
Publications: Footnotes (Newsletter)
Mem of Brevard County Public Libraries
Open Mon & Thurs-Sat 9-5, Tues & Wed 9-8, Sun 1-5
Friends of the Library Group

CORAL GABLES

M DOCTOR'S HOSPITAL, BAPTIST HEALTH*, Medical Library, 5000 University Dr, 33146. SAN 324-6388. Tel: 305-669-2360. FAX: 305-669-2456. E-mail: library@baptisthealth.net. Web Site: www.baptisthealth.net. *Dir,* Devica Samsundar; E-mail: devicas@baptisthealth.net
Founded 1954
Library Holdings: Bk Vols 500
Special Collections: Oral History
Partic in LYRASIS

R TEMPLE JUDEA, Mel Harrison Memorial Library, 5500 Granada Blvd, 33146. SAN 302-8941. Tel: 305-667-5657. FAX: 305-665-5834. E-mail: edoffice@judeagables.org. Web Site: judeagables.org/library.html. *Librn,* Anna Forer; Staff 1 (MLS 1)
Founded 1970
Library Holdings: Bk Vols 5,000
Special Collections: Judaica Coll & Holocaust Coll
Automation Activity & Vendor Info: (Cataloging) Follett Software; (Circulation) Follett Software; (OPAC) Follett Software
Wireless access
Restriction: Mem only, Staff use only

CL UNIVERSITY OF MIAMI*, School of Law Library, 1311 Miller Dr, 33146. (Mail add: PO Box 248087, 33124-0247), SAN 337-338X. Tel: 305-284-2251. Circulation Tel: 305-284-3563. Reference Tel: 305-284-3585. FAX: 305-284-3554. Web Site: law.miami.edu/library. *Dir,* Michael Chiorazzi; Tel: 305-284-2755, E-mail: mchiorazzi@law.miami.edu; *Assoc Dir,* Robin Schard; *Head, Acq & Coll Develop,* Helen Wohl; *Head, Ref,* Pam Lucken; *Circ Librn,* William Latham; *Foreign & Intl Law Librn, Ref Librn,* Bianca Anderson; *Syst Librn,* Emerita Cuesta; *Adjunct Cat Librn,* Renee Meyer; *Adjunct Ref Librn,* Carlos Espinosa; *Adjunct Ref Librn,* Patricia Patdo; *Ref Librn,* Nicholas Mignanelli; E-mail: nxm765@law.miami.edu; *Ref Librn,* Sarah Slinger; E-mail: sslinger@law.miami.edu; Staff 12 (MLS 11, Non-MLS 1)
Highest Degree: Doctorate
Automation Activity & Vendor Info: (Acquisitions) Ex Libris Group; (Cataloging) Ex Libris Group; (Circulation) Ex Libris Group; (Course Reserve) Ex Libris Group; (ILL) OCLC; (OPAC) Ex Libris Group; (Serials) Ex Libris Group
Wireless access
Publications: Law Library Research Guides
Partic in Consortium of Southern Biomedical Libraries; LYRASIS
Open Mon-Thurs 7am-Midnight, Fri 7am-10pm, Sat 9am-10pm, Sun 9am-Midnight

C UNIVERSITY OF MIAMI LIBRARIES*, Otto G Richter Library, 1300 Memorial Dr, 33146. (Mail add: PO Box 248214, 33124-0320), SAN 337-3290. Tel: 305-284-3233. Interlibrary Loan Service Tel: 305-284-6102. FAX: 305-284-4027. Web Site: www.library.miami.edu. *Dean of Libr,* Charles D Eckman; E-mail: ceckman@miami.edu; *Dir, Info Mgt & Syst,* Cheryl Gowing; E-mail: cgowing@miami.edu; *Head, Monographic Ordering & Database Maintenance,* Carmen Civieta-Gaskell; Staff 38 (MLS 38)
Founded 1926. Enrl 14,685; Fac 1,865; Highest Degree: Doctorate
Library Holdings: Bk Vols 3,000,000; Per Subs 70,000
Special Collections: Amigos of the University of Miami Library Cuban Heritage Coll; Floridiana; Latin American (especially Cuban, Caribbean & Colombian); Marine & Atomospheric Sciences. State Document Depository; US Document Depository
Automation Activity & Vendor Info: (Acquisitions) Innovative Interfaces, Inc; (Cataloging) Innovative Interfaces, Inc; (Circulation) Innovative Interfaces, Inc
Wireless access
Publications: Context (Friends of the Library Newsletter)
Partic in Association of Southeastern Research Libraries; LYRASIS; OCLC Online Computer Library Center, Inc; OCLC Research Library Partnership; Southeast Florida Library Information Network, Inc
Open Mon-Thurs 7:30am-2am, Fri 7:30am-10pm, Sat 9am-10pm, Sun 9am-2am
Friends of the Library Group

Departmental Libraries:

ARCHITECTURE RESEARCH CENTER (ARC), 1223 Dickinson Dr, Bldg 48, 33146. Tel: 305-284-5282. FAX: 305-284-1894. Web Site: library.miami.edu/architecture. *Head, Archit Libr,* Gilda Santana; E-mail: gsantana@miami.edu
Library Holdings: Bk Vols 5,000
Open Mon-Fri 9-8:30

S JUDI PROKOP NEWMAN INFORMATION RESOURCE CENTER, University of Miami, Miami Herbert Business School, 33124-6520. Tel: 305-284-6516. E-mail: irc.reference@miami.edu. Web Site: www.library.miami.edu/business. *Head, Info Resource Ctr,* Doris Jui; E-mail: djui@bus.miami.edu. Subject Specialists: *Bus, Econ,* Doris Jui
Founded 1999

MARTA & AUSTIN WEEKS MUSIC LIBRARY, 5501 San Amaro Dr, 33124. (Mail add: PO Box 248165, 33124-7610). Tel: 305-284-9885. FAX: 305-284-1041. Web Site: www.library.miami.edu/musiclib. *Head Music Libr,* Joy Doan; E-mail: joymdoan@miami.edu; Staff 8 (MLS 2, Non-MLS 6)
Library Holdings: CDs 22,000; DVDs 1,060; Music Scores 75,000; Bk Titles 24,200; Per Subs 130; Videos 1,133
Special Collections: Larry Taylor-Billy Matthews Musical Theater Archive Coll, CDs, LPs, playbills, scores, scripts
Open Mon-Thurs 8:30am-11pm, Fri 8:30-6, Sat 10-6, Sun 12-11
Restriction: Open to pub for ref only

§CM UNIVERSITY OF ST AUGUSTINE FOR HEALTH SCIENCES, Miami Campus Library, 800 Douglas Rd, 33134. Tel: 786-725-4031. E-mail: library@usa.edu. Web Site: library.usa.edu. *Librn,* Shaina Berlant; E-mail: sberlant@usa.edu; *Circ Mgr,* Sade Gordon; E-mail: sgordon1@usa.edu
Wireless access
Function: ILL available, Photocopying/Printing, Scanner
Open Mon-Sun 7am-10pm

CRAWFORDVILLE

P WAKULLA COUNTY PUBLIC LIBRARY, 4330 Crawfordville Hwy, 32326. (Mail add: PO Box 1300, 32326-1300), SAN 320-4685. Tel: 850-926-7415. Web Site: wcpl.wildernesscoast.org. *Dir,* Robyn Drummond; E-mail: robyn@wakullalibrary.org; Staff 5 (MLS 1, Non-MLS 4)
Founded 1972. Pop 22,500; Circ 57,000
Library Holdings: Bk Titles 30,000; Per Subs 18
Special Collections: Florida & Local History (The Elizabeth Smith Coll), bks, publications; Hi Lo Literary Coll. Oral History
Automation Activity & Vendor Info: (Circulation) SirsiDynix; (OPAC) SirsiDynix
Wireless access
Mem of Wilderness Coast Public Libraries
Partic in Panhandle Library Access Network
Open Tues & Thurs 9-8, Wed & Fri 9-6, Sat 9-1
Friends of the Library Group

CRESTVIEW

P ROBERT L F SIKES PUBLIC LIBRARY*, Crestview Public Library, 1445 Commerce Dr, 32539. SAN 302-8976. Tel: 850-682-4432. FAX: 850-689-4788. Web Site: www.cityofcrestview.org/library.php. *Dir,* Marie

Heath; *Ad,* Augusta Whittle; E-mail: awhittle@readokaloosa.org; *Ref Librn,* Sandra Dreaden; E-mail: sdreaden@okaloosa.lib.fl.us; *Youth Serv Librn,* Heather Nitzel; E-mail: hnitzel@okaloosa.lib.fl.us; Staff 3 (MLS 1, Non-MLS 2)
Founded 1976. Pop 85,000; Circ 205,000
Library Holdings: CDs 2,900; DVDs 4,200; e-books 400; Large Print Bks 2,000; Bk Vols 48,000; Per Subs 60; Videos 600
Automation Activity & Vendor Info: (Cataloging) SirsiDynix; (Circulation) SirsiDynix; (ILL) OCLC FirstSearch; (OPAC) SirsiDynix
Wireless access
Partic in Okaloosa County Public Library Cooperative
Open Mon & Tues 10-8, Wed & Thurs 10-6, Fri 8:30-4:30, Sat 10-4
Friends of the Library Group

CROSS CITY

P DIXIE COUNTY PUBLIC LIBRARY, 16328 SE Hwy 19, 32628. SAN 337-680X. Tel: 352-498-1219. FAX: 352-498-1408. E-mail: dixie@3riverslibrary.com. Web Site: 3riverslibrary.com. *Dir,* Cindy Bellot; E-mail: cbellot@3riverslibrary.com; Staff 4 (Non-MLS 4)
Founded 1961. Pop 16,422
Library Holdings: Audiobooks 1,399; DVDs 3,735; Large Print Bks 2,041; Bk Vols 28,549; Per Subs 42
Automation Activity & Vendor Info: (Cataloging) Koha; (Circulation) Koha
Wireless access
Function: 24/7 Electronic res, 24/7 Online cat, Audiobks via web, Bks on CD, Children's prog, Computer training, Computers for patron use, Electronic databases & coll, Free DVD rentals, ILL available, Internet access, Life-long learning prog for all ages, Magazines, Meeting rooms, Movies, Music CDs, Online cat, OverDrive digital audio bks, Photocopying/Printing, Preschool reading prog, Prog for adults, Prog for children & young adult, Satellite serv, Spanish lang bks, Summer reading prog, Workshops
Mem of Three Rivers Regional Library System
Partic in Three Rivers Regional Library Consortium
Open Mon-Fri 8:30-5:30
Restriction: Circ to mem only, In-house use for visitors

DADE CITY

C PASCO-HERNANDO STATE COLLEGE-EAST CAMPUS, Charles E Conger Library, 36727 Blanton Rd, Rm C124, 33523-7599. SAN 302-900X. Tel: 352-518-1211. FAX: 352-518-1350. Web Site: phsc.edu/academics/libraries. *Assoc Dir of Libr,* Ingrid Purrenhage; E-mail: purreni@phsc.edu
Founded 1972. Enrl 2,800; Highest Degree: Associate
Library Holdings: Bk Titles 19,000; Bk Vols 24,000; Per Subs 110
Subject Interests: Agr, Data proc, Law enforcement, Nursing, Paramedics
Automation Activity & Vendor Info: (Cataloging) Ex Libris Group; (Circulation) Ex Libris Group; (Course Reserve) Ex Libris Group; (ILL) OCLC; (OPAC) Ex Libris Group; (Serials) Ex Libris Group
Wireless access
Partic in Tampa Bay Library Consortium, Inc
Open Mon-Thurs 8-7:30

DANIA BEACH

S INTERNATIONAL GAME FISH ASSOCIATION, E K Harry Library of Fishes, 300 Gulf Stream Way, 33004. SAN 325-8823. Tel: 954-927-2628. FAX: 954-924-4299. Web Site: www.igfa.org. *Librn,* Gail Morchower; E-mail: gmorchower@igfa.org; Staff 1 (MLS 1)
Founded 1973
Library Holdings: AV Mats 2,200; Bk Vols 15,000; Per Subs 150
Special Collections: Art; Historical Photos; Stamps
Wireless access

DAVIE

C BROWARD COLLEGE*, University/College Library, Bldg 17, 3501 SW Davie Rd, 33314. SAN 337-3959. Tel: 954-201-6648. Circulation Tel: 954-201-6649. Administration Tel: 954-201-6480. FAX: 954-201-6490. Web Site: ucl.broward.edu. *Dean,* Monique Blake; E-mail: mblake@broward.edu; *Archives,* Andrew Dutka; Tel: 954-201-6577, E-mail: adutka@broward.edu; *Automation Serv,* Dennis Levine; *Coll Develop, Ref,* Michelle Apps; Tel: 954-201-6330, E-mail: mapps@broward.edu; *ILL,* Grushenska Elusta; Tel: 954-201-6658, E-mail: gelusta@broward.edu; *Tech Serv,* Jan Rothhaar; Tel: 954-201-6655, E-mail: jrothhaa@broward.edu; Staff 11.5 (MLS 11.5)
Founded 1960. Enrl 21,000; Fac 375; Highest Degree: Bachelor
Library Holdings: AV Mats 3,795; CDs 898; e-books 8,632; Microforms 1,471; Bk Titles 239,420; Bk Vols 276,105; Per Subs 195
Automation Activity & Vendor Info: (Acquisitions) Ex Libris Group; (Cataloging) Ex Libris Group; (Circulation) Ex Libris Group; (Course Reserve) Ex Libris Group; (ILL) Ex Libris Group; (OPAC) Ex Libris Group; (Serials) Ex Libris Group
Wireless access
Partic in LYRASIS; Southeast Florida Library Information Network, Inc
Open Mon-Thurs 7:30am-10pm, Fri 7:30-5, Sat 9-5, Sun 2-10
Departmental Libraries:
NORTH CAMPUS LIBRARY LRC, 1100 Coconut Creek Blvd, Coconut Creek, 33066, SAN 321-1878. Tel: 954-201-2600. FAX: 954-201-2650. *Br Mgr,* Ronnie Kowal; Staff 2 (MLS 2)
Founded 1994
Library Holdings: Bk Vols 225,000
Open Mon-Thurs 7:30am-8pm, Fri 7:30-4, Sat & Sun 10-6
Friends of the Library Group
SOUTH CAMPUS LIBRARY LRC, Bldg 81, 7300 Pines Blvd, Pembroke Pines, 33024, SAN 321-1886. Tel: 954-201-8825, 954-201-8896. Web Site: libguides.broward.edu/southcampuslibrary. *Librn,* Lori Albrizio; E-mail: lalbriz@broward.edu; *Librn,* Chris Casper; E-mail: ccasper@broward.edu; *Librn,* Tiffany Walker; E-mail: twalker3@broward.edu
Library Holdings: Bk Titles 155,000; Per Subs 850
Automation Activity & Vendor Info: (Cataloging) TLC (The Library Corporation); (Circulation) TLC (The Library Corporation)
Open Mon-Thurs 7:30am-8pm, Fri 7:30-4, Sat & Sun 10-6
Friends of the Library Group

DAYTONA BEACH

C BETHUNE-COOKMAN UNIVERSITY*, Carl S Swisher Library & Learning Resource Center, 640 Mary McLeod Bethune Blvd, 32114. SAN 302-9018. Tel: 386-481-2186. FAX: 386-481-2182. Web Site: www.cookman.edu/academics/library. *Chief Librn, Dean of Libr,* Dr Tasha Lucas-Youmans; Tel: 368-481-2181, E-mail: youmanst@cookman.edu; *Ref Librn,* Andre Jansons; E-mail: jansonsa@cookman.edu; *Librn, Tech Proc,* Angelo Salvo; E-mail: salvoa@cookman.edu
Founded 1904. Enrl 3,090; Fac 147; Highest Degree: Master
Library Holdings: Bk Vols 175,483; Per Subs 770
Special Collections: Africa & the Negro, bk, micro; Archival (Mary McLeod Bethune & others); Art (Peter Turcheon); Attica Coll; Children's Coll; Rosewood Exhibit. Oral History; State Document Depository; US Document Depository
Automation Activity & Vendor Info: (Cataloging) TLC (The Library Corporation); (Circulation) TLC (The Library Corporation); (OPAC) TLC (The Library Corporation)
Wireless access
Publications: Annual Library Report; Faculty Library Manual; Nonprint Media Newsletter
Partic in LYRASIS; Northeast Florida Library Information Network; OCLC Online Computer Library Center, Inc
Open Mon-Thurs 7:30am-Midnight, Fri 8-5, Sat 9-5, Sun 3pm-Midnight; Mon-Fri (Summer) 8am-10pm, Sat 10-2

P BUREAU OF BRAILLE & TALKING BOOK LIBRARY SERVICES*, 421 Platt St, 32114-2804. SAN 302-9042. Tel: 386-239-6000. Toll Free Tel: 800-226-6075. FAX: 386-239-6069. Web Site: dbs.myflorida.com/library/index.html. *Bur Chief,* James Woolyhand; Tel: 386 239-6060, E-mail: james.woolyhand@dbs.fldoe.org; Staff 23 (MLS 3, Non-MLS 20)
Founded 1950
Library Holdings: Braille Volumes 120,982; DVDs 2,484; Large Print Bks 657; Spec Interest Per Sub 1,020; Talking Bks 1,087,112
Special Collections: Florida related topics and authors. US Document Depository
Automation Activity & Vendor Info: (Cataloging) Keystone Systems, Inc (KLAS); (Circulation) Keystone Systems, Inc (KLAS); (OPAC) Keystone Systems, Inc (KLAS)
Function: 24/7 Electronic res, 24/7 Online cat, Bilingual assistance for Spanish patrons, Homebound delivery serv, Online cat, Outreach serv, Outside serv via phone, mail, e-mail & web, Prof lending libr, Ref serv available, Wheelchair accessible
Publications: Quarterly Patron Newsletter in large print,and on the web site.
Special Services for the Deaf - Assisted listening device
Special Services for the Blind - Audio mat; Bks on flash-memory cartridges; Blind students ctr; Braille alphabet card; Braille bks; Braille music coll; Children's Braille; Descriptive video serv (DVS); Digital talking bk; Digital talking bk machines; Free checkout of audio mat; Home delivery serv; Info on spec aids & appliances; Newsline for the Blind; Newsp reading serv; PC for people with disabilities; Production of talking bks; Rec; Recorded bks; Ref in Braille; Ref serv; Spanish Braille mags & bks; Talking bk & rec for the blind cat; Talking bk serv referral; Talking bks; Talking bks from Braille Inst; Volunteer serv; Web-Braille
Open Mon-Fri 8-5
Restriction: Authorized patrons
Friends of the Library Group

C DAYTONA STATE COLLEGE LIBRARY*, Bldg 115, Rm 314, 1200 W International Speedway Blvd, 32114. (Mail add: PO Box 2811, 32120-2811), SAN 302-9026. Tel: 386-506-3055. Reference Tel: 386-506-3518. FAX: 386-506-3008. *Assoc VP, Academic Services,* Kathy Hoellen; Tel: 386-506-4430, E-mail: Kathy.Hoellen@daytonastate.edu; *Chair, Libr Serv,* Mercedes Clement; Tel: 386-506-3440, E-mail: Mercedes.Clement@daytonastate.edu; *Asst Chair, Library Services,* Dustin Weeks; Tel: 386-506-3593, E-mail: Dustin.Weeks@daytonastate.edu; *Emerging Tech Librn,* Anibal Delgado; Tel: 386-506-3608, E-mail: Anibal.DelgadoGonzalez@daytonastate.edu; *Coll Develop, Fac Serv Librn,* Rachel Owens; Tel: 386-506-3842, E-mail: Rachel.Owens@daytonastate.edu; *Instruction & Outreach Librn,* Maxwell Hackman; Tel: 386-506-3521, E-mail: Maxwell.Hackman@daytonastate.edu; Staff 6 (MLS 6)
Founded 1957. Highest Degree: Bachelor
Automation Activity & Vendor Info: (Cataloging) Ex Libris Group; (Circulation) Ex Libris Group; (Course Reserve) Ex Libris Group; (Discovery) Ex Libris Group; (ILL) Ex Libris Group; (OPAC) Ex Libris Group; (Serials) Ex Libris Group
Wireless access
Partic in Florida Academic Library Services Cooperative

Departmental Libraries:

DELAND CAMPUS LIBRARY, Bldg One, 1155 County Rd 4139, Deland, 32724. Tel: 386-785-2017. *Campus Librn,* Christina Hastie; Tel: 386-785-2018, E-mail: Christina.Hastie@DaytonaState.edu; *Libr Spec,* Eric Jenkins; Tel: 386-785-2099, E-mail: Eric.Jenkins@DaytonaState.edu
Open Mon-Fri 8-5

C EMBRY-RIDDLE AERONAUTICAL UNIVERSITY*, Hunt Library, One Aerospace Blvd, 32114. SAN 302-9034. Tel: 386-226-7656. Circulation Tel: 386-226-6592. Reference Tel: 386-226-6604. Administration Tel: 386-226-6933. Toll Free Tel: 800-678-9428. E-mail: library@erau.edu. Web Site: huntlibrary.erau.edu. *Libr Dir,* Anne Marie Casey; Tel: 386-226-6593, E-mail: Anne.Casey@erau.edu; *Assoc Dir, Access Serv,* Melanie West; Tel: 386-226-6591, E-mail: Melanie.West@erau.edu; *Assoc Dir, Electronic/Tech Libr Serv,* Suzanne Sprague; Tel: 386-226-6932, E-mail: Suzanne.Sprague@erau.edu; *Assoc Dir, Res/Worldwide Libr Serv,* Karen Bronshteyn; Tel: 386-226-6602, E-mail: Karen.Bronshteyn@erau.edu; *ILL Librn,* Elizabeth Sterthaus; Tel: 386-323-8774, E-mail: Elizabeth.Sterthaus@erau.edu; Staff 34 (MLS 20, Non-MLS 14)
Founded 1965. Enrl 5,538; Fac 414; Highest Degree: Doctorate
Jul 2015-Jun 2016. Mats Exp $932,466, Books $191,000, Per/Ser (Incl. Access Fees) $325,000, AV Mat $9,000, Electronic Ref Mat (Incl. Access Fees) $407,466. Sal $1,754,855
Library Holdings: AV Mats 5,148; e-books 6,038; Microforms 318,077; Bk Titles 53,216; Bk Vols 76,464; Per Subs 996
Special Collections: Aviation History & Aeronautical Engineering Coll, bks, doc, per; FAA & NTSB documents
Subject Interests: Aeronaut engr, Aerospace engr, Aviation
Automation Activity & Vendor Info: (Acquisitions) Ex Libris Group; (Cataloging) Ex Libris Group; (Circulation) Ex Libris Group; (Course Reserve) Ex Libris Group; (ILL) Clio; (Media Booking) Ex Libris Group; (OPAC) Ex Libris Group; (Serials) Ex Libris Group
Wireless access
Partic in Florida Library Information Network; Independent Cols & Univs of Fla; LYRASIS; Northeast Florida Library Information Network; OCLC Online Computer Library Center, Inc
Special Services for the Deaf - Assistive tech
Open Mon-Thurs & Sun 8-8, Fri 8-5

S MUSEUM OF ARTS & SCIENCES*, Margaret & John Wilkinson Library, 352 S Nova Rd, 32114. SAN 302-9093. Tel: 386-255-0285. FAX: 386-255-5040. Web Site: www.moas.org. *Dir, Operations,* Stephanie Mason-Teague; E-mail: stephanie@moas.org; Staff 46 (MLS 28, Non-MLS 18)
Founded 1956
Library Holdings: Bk Vols 5,000
Special Collections: American Art; Florida history books, periodicals & manuscripts; Lucy Shepard Bequest; Natural history; Ornithology Coll; Rare Cuban books (General Fulgencio Batista Coll); World Art. Oral History
Subject Interests: Art, Astronomy, Cuba, Fla, Natural hist
Wireless access
Function: Ref serv available
Partic in Lee County
Restriction: Open by appt only

GL VOLUSIA COUNTY LAW LIBRARY*, Courthouse Annex, Rm 208, 125 E Orange Ave, 32114. SAN 302-9107. Tel: 386-257-6041. FAX: 386-257-6052. Web Site: www.vclawlib.org/daytona-beach. *Dir,* Deborah Patterson
Library Holdings: Bk Vols 25,000
Open Mon-Fri 8:30-12 & 1-4:30

P VOLUSIA COUNTY PUBLIC LIBRARY*, 1290 Indian Lake Rd, 32124. SAN 337-3444. Tel: 386-248-1745. Reference Tel: 386-257-6037. FAX: 386-248-1746. Web Site: volusialibrary.org. *Libr Dir,* Lucinda Colee; E-mail: llcolee@volusia.org; *Regional Librn,* Ann Collins; Tel: 386-822-6430, E-mail: acollins@volusia.org; *Regional Librn,* Melissa Reynolds; Tel: 386-257-6036, E-mail: mreynolds@volusia.org; *Regional Librn,* Jane Weimer; Tel: 386-322-5152, E-mail: jweimer@volusia.org; *Coll Develop Mgr,* Mr Brook White; E-mail: bwhite@volusia.org; *Mgr, Info Tech,* Annie Powers; E-mail: apowers@volusia.org; *Support Serv Mgr,* Tammy Heuring; Staff 23 (MLS 6, Non-MLS 17)
Founded 1961. Pop 456,000; Circ 3,274,066
Library Holdings: e-books 31,118; Bk Vols 859,415; Per Subs 1,380; Talking Bks 71,118; Videos 123,813
Special Collections: Genealogy Coll. US Document Depository
Subject Interests: Genealogy
Automation Activity & Vendor Info: (Circulation) Infor Library & Information Solutions; (OPAC) Infor Library & Information Solutions
Wireless access
Publications: Annual Report; Happenings (Monthly newsletter)
Partic in LYRASIS; Northeast Florida Library Information Network
Special Services for the Deaf - Bks on deafness & sign lang; High interest/low vocabulary bks; Staff with knowledge of sign lang
Open Mon-Fri 8-4:30
Friends of the Library Group

Branches: 14

DAYTONA BEACH REGIONAL, 105 E Magnolia Ave, 32114, SAN 337-3533. Tel: 386-257-6036. FAX: 386-257-6026. *Br Mgr,* Dedra Roman; Staff 21 (MLS 8, Non-MLS 13)
Open Mon-Thurs 9-7, Fri & Sat 9-5, Sun 1-5
Friends of the Library Group

DEBARY PUBLIC LIBRARY, 200 N Charles R Beall Blvd, DeBary, 32713, SAN 337-3568. Tel: 386-668-3835. FAX: 386-668-3837. *Br Head,* Cammie Newton; Staff 5 (MLS 2, Non-MLS 3)
Open Mon & Wed 9:30-6, Tues & Thurs 9:30-7:30, Fri & Sat 9:30-5
Friends of the Library Group

DELAND REGIONAL LIBRARY, 130 E Howry Ave, DeLand, 32724, SAN 337-3592. Tel: 386-822-6430. FAX: 386-822-6435. *Br Mgr,* Chabha Shams; Staff 19 (MLS 9, Non-MLS 10)
Special Services for the Deaf - TDD equip
Open Mon-Thurs 9:30-7:30, Fri & Sat 9:30-5, Sun 1-5
Friends of the Library Group

DELTONA REGIONAL, 2150 Eustace Ave, Deltona, 32725, SAN 337-3622. Tel: 386-789-7207, 407-328-4912 (osteen). FAX: 386-789-7211. *Br Mgr,* Char Purdy; Staff 18 (MLS 8, Non-MLS 10)
Founded 1976
Open Mon-Thurs 9:30-7:30, Fri & Sat 9:30-5, Sun 1-5
Friends of the Library Group

JOHN H DICKERSON HERITAGE LIBRARY, 411 S Keech St, 32114, SAN 337-3509. Tel: 386-239-6478. *Br Head,* Charles Dansby; Staff 4 (MLS 1, Non-MLS 3)
Founded 1977
Open Mon-Wed 9-6, Thurs 9-7, Fri & Sat 9-5

EDGEWATER PUBLIC LIBRARY, 103 W Indian River Blvd, Edgewater, 32132, SAN 337-3681. Tel: 386-424-2916. FAX: 386-424-2918. *Br Head,* Jane Wright; Staff 6 (MLS 3, Non-MLS 3)
Open Mon & Wed 9:30-6, Tues & Thurs 9:30-7:30, Fri & Sat 9:30-5
Friends of the Library Group

HOPE PLACE PUBLIC LIBRARY, 1310 Wright St, 32117. Tel: 386-258-4027. *Br Head,* Mary Renee Galloway
Open Mon-Wed 9-6, Thurs 9-7, Fri & Sat 9-5

LAKE HELEN PUBLIC, 221 N Euclid Ave, Lake Helen, 32744, SAN 337-3746. Tel: 386-228-1152. FAX: 386-228-1154. *Br Head,* Tabitha Gregg; Staff 2 (Non-MLS 2)
Open Mon, Wed & Fri 9-12 & 1-5, Tues & Thurs 11:30-1 & 2-7:30
Friends of the Library Group

NEW SMYRNA BEACH PUBLIC, 1001 S Dixie Freeway, New Smyrna Beach, 32168, SAN 337-3479. Tel: 386-424-2910. FAX: 386-424-2913. *Br Mgr,* Kristin Bennett; Staff 14 (MLS 5, Non-MLS 9)
Open Mon-Thurs 9-7, Fri & Sat 9-5, Sun 1-5
Friends of the Library Group

OAK HILL PUBLIC LIBRARY, 125 E Halifax Ave, Oak Hill, 32759, SAN 337-3770. Tel: 386-345-5510. FAX: 386-345-5510. *Br Head,* Jane Wright; Staff 1 (Non-MLS 1)
Open Mon, Tues & Fri 10-1 & 2-5, Wed 1-5, Thurs 12-3 & 4-7
Friends of the Library Group

ORANGE CITY PUBLIC LIBRARY, 148 Albertus Way, Orange City, 32763, SAN 337-3657. Tel: 386-775-5270. *Br Head,* Mary Clogston; Staff 2 (Non-MLS 2)
Open Mon-Thurs 9:30-1 & 2-5:30, Fri 9:30-1 & 2-5
Friends of the Library Group

ORMOND BEACH PUBLIC LIBRARY, 30 S Beach St, Ormond Beach, 32174, SAN 337-3789. Tel: 386-676-4191. FAX: 386-676-4194. *Br Mgr,* Position Currently Open
Open Mon-Thurs 9-7, Fri & Sat 9-5, Sun 1-5
Friends of the Library Group

PIERSON PUBLIC LIBRARY, 115 N Volusia Ave, Pierson, 32180, SAN 378-0090. Tel: 386-749-6930. *Regional Librn,* Ann Collins; E-mail: acollins@volusia.org; Staff 2 (MLS 1, Non-MLS 1)
Open Mon, Wed & Fri 10-12 & 1-5, Tues & Thurs 11-2 & 3-7
PORT ORANGE PUBLIC LIBRARY, 1005 City Center Circle, Port Orange, 32119, SAN 322-6174. Tel: 386-322-5152. FAX: 386-322-5155. *Br Mgr,* Cindy Moore; Staff 17 (MLS 7, Non-MLS 10)
Open Mon-Thurs 9-7, Fri & Sat 9-5, Sun 1-5
Friends of the Library Group

DE FUNIAK SPRINGS

P WALTON COUNTY PUBLIC LIBRARY SYSTEM*, Walton-DeFuniak Library, Three Circle Dr, 32435-2542. SAN 302-9115. Tel: 850-892-3624. FAX: 850-892-4438. E-mail: dfslibrary@co.walton.fl.us. Web Site: www1.youseemore.com/walton. *Libr Dir,* Caitie Cerise; E-mail: cercaitlin@co.walton.fl.us; *Br Mgr,* Laura Moree; E-mail: MorLaura@co.walton.fl.us; Staff 15 (MLS 3, Non-MLS 12)
Founded 1886
Library Holdings: Audiobooks 5,547; AV Mats 314; CDs 3,876; DVDs 639; e-books 1,256; High Interest/Low Vocabulary Bk Vols 6,413; Large Print Bks 4,474; Bk Titles 87,000; Bk Vols 98,856; Per Subs 60; Talking Bks 517; Videos 639
Special Collections: Antique Record Player; Armor Coll; Shell Coll
Automation Activity & Vendor Info: (Acquisitions) TLC (The Library Corporation); (Cataloging) TLC (The Library Corporation); (Circulation) TLC (The Library Corporation); (OPAC) TLC (The Library Corporation)
Wireless access
Function: 24/7 Online cat, Activity rm, Adult bk club, Art exhibits, Audio & video playback equip for onsite use, Audiobks via web, Bk club(s), Bks on cassette, Bks on CD, Butterfly Garden, CD-ROM, Children's prog, Computer training, Computers for patron use, Digital talking bks, Doc delivery serv, Electronic databases & coll, Equip loans & repairs, Family literacy, Free DVD rentals, ILL available, Internet access, Magazines, Magnifiers for reading, Meeting rooms, Microfiche/film & reading machines, Music CDs, Online cat, Photocopying/Printing, Preschool outreach, Preschool reading prog, Printer for laptops & handheld devices, Prog for adults, Prog for children & young adult, Ref serv available, Scanner, Spanish lang bks, Spoken cassettes & DVDs, Story hour, Study rm, Summer & winter reading prog, Summer reading prog, Tax forms, VHS videos, Wheelchair accessible, Writing prog
Open Mon & Wed-Sat 9-5, Tues 9-8
Restriction: Internal use only
Friends of the Library Group
Branches: 3
COASTAL, 437 Greenway Trail, Santa Rosa Beach, 32459-5589, SAN 328-641X. Tel: 850-267-2809. FAX: 850-267-9452. *Br Mgr,* Linda Thompson; E-mail: ThoLinda@co.walton.fl.us; Staff 5 (MLS 1, Non-MLS 4)
Founded 1986
Automation Activity & Vendor Info: (Acquisitions) TLC (The Library Corporation); (Cataloging) TLC (The Library Corporation); (Circulation) TLC (The Library Corporation); (ILL) OCLC WorldShare Interlibrary Loan; (OPAC) TLC (The Library Corporation)
Open Mon 10-6, Tues-Sat 9-5
Friends of the Library Group
FREEPORT PUBLIC, 76 Hwy 20 W, Freeport, 32439, SAN 328-6436. Tel: 850-835-2040. FAX: 850-835-2154. *Br Mgr,* Ms Robbie Daniels; E-mail: DanRoberta@co.walton.fl.us; Staff 3 (MLS 1, Non-MLS 2)
Founded 1986
Open Mon-Sat 9-5
Friends of the Library Group
NORTH WALTON COUNTY - GLADYS N MILTON MEMORIAL, 261 Flowersview Rd, Laurel Hill, 32567. Tel: 850-834-5383. FAX: 850-834-5487. *Library Contact,* Debra Hogans; Staff 2 (Non-MLS 2)
Open Mon-Tues, Thurs-Sat 9-5
Friends of the Library Group
Bookmobiles: 1. Libr Contact, Jesse Rushing

DELAND

C STETSON UNIVERSITY, duPont-Ball Library, 421 N Woodland Blvd, Unit 8418, 32723. SAN 337-3835. Tel: 386-822-7175. Interlibrary Loan Service Tel: 386-822-7183. Reference Tel: 386-747-9028. Web Site: www.stetson.edu/library. *Dean of the Library & Learning Technologies,* Susan M Ryan; Tel: 386-822-7181, E-mail: sryan@stetson.edu; *Assoc Dean,* Debora Dinkins; Tel: 386-822-7179, E-mail: ddinkins@stetson.edu; *Dir, Pub Serv,* Jennifer Corbin; Tel: 386-822-7178, E-mail: jcorbin1@stetson.edu; *Engagement Librn, Learning Librn,* Hunter Murphy; Tel: 386-822-7176, E-mail: thmurphy@stetson.edu; *Govt Doc & Res Librn,* Barbara Costello; Tel: 386-822-7185, E-mail: bcostell@stetson.edu; *Learning & Info Literacy Librn,* Grace Kaletski-Maisel; Tel: 386-822-7190, E-mail: gkaletsk@stetson.edu; *Cat,* Laura Kirkland; Tel: 386-822-4027, E-mail: lkirklan@stetson.edu; *Circ,* Colby Cilento; Tel: 386-822-7187, E-mail: ccilento@stetson.edu; *ILL,* Elizabeth Martino; Tel: 386-822-4034, E-mail: ecmartino@stetson.edu; Staff 9.5 (MLS 8.5, Non-MLS 1)
Founded 1883. Enrl 4,462; Fac 413; Highest Degree: Master
Jul 2021-Jun 2022. Mats Exp $799,081, Books $68,156, Per/Ser (Incl. Access Fees) $359,392, Other Print Mats $5,538, AV Mat $45,388, Electronic Ref Mat (Incl. Access Fees) $315,448, Presv $0. Sal $953,828 (Prof $623,425)
Library Holdings: AV Mats 17,021; CDs 7,141; DVDs 4,834; e-books 234,624; e-journals 188,064; Electronic Media & Resources 404,856; Microforms 14,811; Music Scores 20,738; Bk Titles 176,041; Bk Vols 221,740; Per Subs 337; Videos 4,834
Special Collections: Bert Fish Coll (Ambassador to Egypt); Congressional Papers & Memorabilia (Congressman E Clay Shaw Coll); Faculty & Alumni Authors (Stetson Coll); Government Documents Coll; Juvenile Literature (Greenlaw Coll); Political Memorabilia (Senator J Maxwell Cleland Coll); University Archives. State Document Depository; US Document Depository
Subject Interests: Bus, Educ, Humanities, Lit, Music, Relig, Russia
Automation Activity & Vendor Info: (Acquisitions) OCLC Worldshare Management Services; (Cataloging) OCLC Worldshare Management Services; (Circulation) OCLC Worldshare Management Services; (Course Reserve) OCLC Worldshare Management Services; (Discovery) OCLC Worldshare Management Services; (ILL) OCLC WorldShare Interlibrary Loan; (OPAC) OCLC Worldshare Management Services; (Serials) OCLC Worldshare Management Services
Wireless access
Function: 24/7 Electronic res, 24/7 Online cat, 3D Printer
Publications: Library Brochure (Annual); Newsletter (Biannually)
Partic in Independent Cols & Univs of Fla; LYRASIS; Northeast Florida Library Information Network
Open Mon-Thurs 8am-Midnight, Fri 8-6, Sat 11-6, Sun 11am-Midnight
Restriction: Authorized patrons, Open to authorized patrons, Open to students, fac & staff

DELRAY BEACH

P DELRAY BEACH PUBLIC LIBRARY*, 100 W Atlantic Ave, 33444. SAN 302-9174. Tel: 561-266-0194. Reference Tel: 561-266-0196. FAX: 561-266-9757. E-mail: info.delraylibrary@gmail.com. Web Site: www.delraylibrary.org. *Dir,* Karen Ronald; Tel: 561-266-9488, E-mail: karen.ronald@delraylibrary.org; *Asst Dir,* Mykal Banta; Tel: 561-266-0198, E-mail: mykal.banta@delraylibrary.org; *Ref Librn,* Loanis Menendez-Cuesta; E-mail: loanis.menendez@delraylibrary.org; *ILL, Ref Librn,* Alyson Walzer; E-mail: alyson.walzer@delraylibrary.org; *Cat, Tech Serv,* Esther Robinson Coine; E-mail: dbpl.cat@delraylibrary.org; *Ch Serv,* Ilene Glickman; E-mail: ilene.glickman@delraylibrary.org; Staff 9 (MLS 5, Non-MLS 4)
Founded 1939. Pop 62,040; Circ 257,950
Library Holdings: AV Mats 9,276; Bk Vols 250,000; Per Subs 350
Subject Interests: Fla
Automation Activity & Vendor Info: (Circulation) SirsiDynix; (OPAC) SirsiDynix
Wireless access
Function: Adult bk club, After school storytime, Art exhibits, AV serv, Bilingual assistance for Spanish patrons, Bk club(s), Bk reviews (Group), Bks on cassette, Bks on CD, CD-ROM, Children's prog, Computer training, Computers for patron use, Electronic databases & coll, Holiday prog, Homework prog, ILL available, Instruction & testing, Internet access, Literacy & newcomer serv, Magnifiers for reading, Music CDs, Online cat, Outreach serv, Outside serv via phone, mail, e-mail & web, Photocopying/Printing, Prog for adults, Prog for children & young adult, Ref & res, Ref serv available, Senior computer classes, Story hour, Summer & winter reading prog, Summer reading prog, Tax forms, Teen prog, Telephone ref, VHS videos, Wheelchair accessible, Workshops, Writing prog
Publications: Newsletter (Bimonthly)
Partic in Coop Authority for Libr Automation; Library Cooperative of the Palm Beaches; Southeast Florida Library Information Network, Inc
Open Mon-Wed 9-8, Thurs-Sat 9-5, Sun (Sept-May) 1-5

S MORIKAMI MUSEUM*, Colonel Donald B Gordon Memorial Library, 4000 Morikami Park Rd, 33446. SAN 322-8770. Tel: 561-495-0233, Ext 217. FAX: 561-499-2557. Web Site: morikami.org. *Chief Curator, Dep Dir,* Tamara Joy; E-mail: tjoy@pbcgov.org; Staff 1 (Non-MLS 1)
Founded 1977
Library Holdings: Bk Titles 6,500; Bk Vols 7,000; Spec Interest Per Sub 8
Special Collections: Japanese culture, language, people
Subject Interests: Japanese (Lang), Japanese culture
Function: For res purposes
Open Tues-Sun 10-5
Restriction: Non-circulating to the pub

L PALM BEACH COUNTY LAW LIBRARY*, 200 W Atlantic Ave, Rm 2E-205, 33444. SAN 373-0409. Tel: 561-274-1440. E-mail: cad-lawlibrary@pbcgov.org. Web Site: 15thcircuit.com/services/law-library. *Libr Mgr,* Joseph Crisco
Library Holdings: Bk Vols 4,500
Wireless access
Open Mon-Fri 8-4:45

DESTIN

P DESTIN LIBRARY*, 150 Sibert Ave, 32541-1523. Tel: 850-837-8572. E-mail: library@cityofdestin.com. Web Site: www.cityofdestin.com/105/Library. *Dir,* Wen Livingston; E-mail: wlivingston@cityofdestin.com; *Ch,* Laura Harris; E-mail: lharris@cityofdestin.com; *Programming Spec, Technology Spec,* Skylar Dennis; E-mail: sdennis@cityofdestin.com; *Circ,* Kitti Capps; E-mail: kcapps@cityofdestin.com; *Tech Serv,* Sandra Kelly; E-mail: skelly@okaloosa.lib.fl.us; Staff 9 (MLS 2, Non-MLS 7)
Founded 1940. Circ 69,907
Oct 2015-Sept 2016 Income $421,845, City $349,330, County $53,805, Locally Generated Income $18,710. Mats Exp $45,000, Books $33,320, Per/Ser (Incl. Access Fees) $1,000, AV Mat $3,100, Electronic Ref Mat (Incl. Access Fees) $7,580. Sal $260,504 (Prof $73,500)
Library Holdings: Audiobooks 1,531; AV Mats 2,982; DVDs 2,982; e-books 62,140; Electronic Media & Resources 2; Large Print Bks 2,500; Bk Titles 31,000; Bk Vols 34,649; Per Subs 40; Videos 40
Special Collections: Florida Coll, bks, ms; Library of America Coll; Sea Life Coll, art, artifacts, bks, films, ms
Subject Interests: Rare bks
Automation Activity & Vendor Info: (Acquisitions) SirsiDynix; (Cataloging) SirsiDynix; (Circulation) SirsiDynix; (Course Reserve) SirsiDynix; (Discovery) SirsiDynix-WorkFlows; (OPAC) SirsiDynix
Wireless access
Function: 24/7 Electronic res, 24/7 Online cat, Activity rm, Adult bk club, Art exhibits, Audio & video playback equip for onsite use, Audiobks on Playaways & MP3, Audiobks via web, AV serv, Bk club(s), Bks on CD, Butterfly Garden, Children's prog, Computer training, Computers for patron use, E-Readers, E-Reserves, Electronic databases & coll, Free DVD rentals, Holiday prog, ILL available, Internet access, Life-long learning prog for all ages, Magazines, Mail & tel request accepted, Makerspace, Meeting rooms, Microfiche/film & reading machines, Movies, Notary serv, Online cat, Outside serv via phone, mail, e-mail & web, OverDrive digital audio bks, Photocopying/Printing, Preschool reading prog, Printer for laptops & handheld devices, Prog for adults, Prog for children & young adult, Scanner, Senior computer classes, Spanish lang bks, STEM programs, Story hour, Study rm, Summer reading prog, Tax forms, Teen prog, Wheelchair accessible
Partic in Okaloosa County Public Library Cooperative; Panhandle Library Access Network
Open Mon 9-5, Tues & Thurs 9-8, Wed 1-5, Fri 9-6, Sat 9-1
Restriction: Non-resident fee
Friends of the Library Group

DUNDEE

P DUNDEE PUBLIC LIBRARY*, 202 E Main St, PO Box 1000, 33838. Tel: 863-439-9424. Administration Tel: 863-439-9425. FAX: 863-439-9426. Web Site: townofdundee.com/our-community/libraries. *Libr Dir,* Vivian Godfrey; E-mail: vgodfrey@townofdundee.com; *Circ,* Gayle Hilburn; *Circ,* Kaliyah Monroe; *Circ,* LaShanta Wade; Staff 4 (MLS 1, Non-MLS 3)
Founded 1990. Pop 4,500
Library Holdings: AV Mats 200; High Interest/Low Vocabulary Bk Vols 350; Large Print Bks 400; Bk Titles 12,000; Per Subs 11; Talking Bks 30; Videos 200
Special Collections: Home School Coll
Subject Interests: Fla, Spanish
Automation Activity & Vendor Info: (Acquisitions) SirsiDynix; (Cataloging) SirsiDynix; (Circulation) SirsiDynix; (ILL) OCLC; (OPAC) SirsiDynix
Wireless access
Function: 24/7 Electronic res, 24/7 Online cat, Accelerated reader prog, Children's prog, Computers for patron use, Free DVD rentals, Internet access, Photocopying/Printing, Preschool outreach, Prog for adults, Prog for children & young adult, Ref serv available, Spoken cassettes & CDs, Summer reading prog, Telephone ref, Wheelchair accessible
Partic in Polk County Libr Coop; Tampa Bay Library Consortium, Inc
Special Services for the Deaf - Bks on deafness & sign lang
Special Services for the Blind - Bks on CD
Open Mon-Fri 10-6, Sat 9-1
Friends of the Library Group

DUNEDIN

P DUNEDIN PUBLIC LIBRARY, 223 Douglas Ave, 34698. SAN 302-9182. Tel: 727-298-3080. Circulation Tel: 727-298-3080, Ext 1713. Reference Tel: 727-298-3080, Ext 1707. FAX: 727-298-3088. E-mail: dunedinlibrary@dunedinfl.net. Web Site: www.dunedingov.com/city-departments/library. *Dir,* Phyllis Gorshe; Tel: 727-298-3080, Ext 1701, E-mail: pgorshe@dunedinfl.net; *Circ,* Kari Morrel; Tel: 727-298-3080, Ext 1706, E-mail: kmorrel@dunedinfl.net; *Info Serv,* Kathy Smuz; Tel: 727-298-3080, Ext 1702, E-mail: ksmuz@dunedinfl.net; *Tech Serv,* Doreen Chonko; Tel: 727-298-3080, Ext 1739; *Youth Serv,* Olivia Wilson; Tel: 727-298-3080, Ext 1732, E-mail: owilson@dunedinfl.net; Staff 27 (MLS 11, Non-MLS 16)
Founded 1895. Pop 37,000; Circ 473,683
Oct 2021-Sept 2022. Mats Exp $198,500
Library Holdings: Bk Titles 98,000; Bk Vols 109,000; Per Subs 198
Special Collections: Scottish Coll
Automation Activity & Vendor Info: (Acquisitions) SirsiDynix-WorkFlows; (Cataloging) SirsiDynix-WorkFlows; (Circulation) SirsiDynix-WorkFlows; (ILL) OCLC WorldShare Interlibrary Loan; (OPAC) SirsiDynix; (Serials) SirsiDynix
Wireless access
Function: 24/7 Online cat, Activity rm, Adult bk club, Adult literacy prog, After school storytime, Audiobks on Playaways & MP3, Audiobks via web, Bks on CD, CD-ROM, Chess club, Children's prog, Computer training, Computers for patron use, E-Reserves, Electronic databases & coll, Free DVD rentals, Holiday prog, Home delivery & serv to seniorr ctr & nursing homes, Homebound delivery serv, Homework prog, ILL available, Internet access, Life-long learning prog for all ages, Magazines, Meeting rooms, Movies, Music CDs, Notary serv, Online cat, OverDrive digital audio bks, Photocopying/Printing, Preschool outreach, Printer for laptops & handheld devices, Prog for adults, Prog for children & young adult, Ref serv available, Satellite serv, Scanner, Spanish lang bks, Story hour, Study rm, Summer & winter reading prog, Summer reading prog, Tax forms, Teen prog, Telephone ref, Wheelchair accessible, Workshops, Writing prog
Publications: Friends (Newsletter)
Mem of Pinellas Public Library Cooperative
Partic in Tampa Bay Library Consortium, Inc
Open Mon-Wed 9:30-8, Thurs & Fri 9:30-6, Sat 9:30-5, Sun 1-5
Friends of the Library Group

EAGLE LAKE

P EAGLE LAKE PUBLIC LIBRARY*, 75 N Seventh St, 33839-3430. (Mail add: PO Box 129, 33839-0129), SAN 370-4718. Tel: 863-293-2914. FAX: 863-292-0210. *Dir,* Rita Childress; E-mail: ritac@eaglelake-fla.com
Library Holdings: Audiobooks 25; AV Mats 250; DVDs 2,400; Large Print Bks 162; Bk Vols 3,000; Videos 2,400
Automation Activity & Vendor Info: (Cataloging) SirsiDynix; (Circulation) SirsiDynix
Wireless access
Partic in Polk County Libr Coop; Tampa Bay Library Consortium, Inc
Open Mon-Fri 9-5

EASTPOINT

P FRANKLIN COUNTY PUBLIC LIBRARY*, 160 Hickory Dip, 32328. (Mail add: PO Box 722, 32328-0722), SAN 377-2888. Tel: 850-670-8151. FAX: 850-670-4423. Web Site: fcpl.wildernesscoast.org. *Libr Dir,* Whitney Roundtree; E-mail: whitneyn@franklincountyflorida.com
Library Holdings: Bk Vols 30,000; Per Subs 12
Automation Activity & Vendor Info: (Cataloging) SirsiDynix; (Circulation) SirsiDynix; (OPAC) SirsiDynix
Wireless access
Mem of Wilderness Coast Public Libraries
Open Mon-Fri 9-5
Friends of the Library Group
Branches:
CARRABELLE BRANCH, 311 Saint James Ave, Carrabelle, 32322. (Mail add: PO Box 722, 32328-0722), SAN 376-7604. Tel: 850-697-2366. FAX: 850-697-4562.
Open Mon-Fri 9-6, Sat 10-2
Friends of the Library Group

EGLIN AFB

A AIR FORCE RESEARCH LABORATORY MUNITIONS DIRECTORATE TECHNICAL LIBRARY*, 203 W Eglin Blvd, Ste 300, 32542-6843, SAN 377-3108. Tel: 850-882-5586. FAX: 850-882-4476. *Info Spec,* Cheryl Mack; E-mail: cheryl.mack@eglin.af.mil; Staff 5 (MLS 1, Non-MLS 4)
Library Holdings: Bk Titles 10,000; Bk Vols 12,000; Per Subs 200
Subject Interests: Aerospace, Chem, Math, Physics
Automation Activity & Vendor Info: (Cataloging) EOS International; (Circulation) EOS International; (ILL) OCLC; (OPAC) EOS International; (Serials) EOS International
Function: Computers for patron use, Electronic databases & coll, Govt ref serv, ILL available, Internet access, Online cat, Online ref,

Orientations, Outside serv via phone, mail, e-mail & web, Photocopying/Printing, Scanner, Wheelchair accessible
Restriction: Govt use only, Open to mil & govt employees only, Photo ID required for access

A TECHNICAL LIBRARY*, 203 W Eglin Blvd, Ste 300, 32542-6843, SAN 337-3924. Tel: 850-882-3212, 850-882-5586. FAX: 850-882-3214. *Dir,* Cheryl Mack; Tel: 850-882-6849, E-mail: cheryl.mack@eglin.af.mil; *Ref Librn,* Eleanor Baudouin; E-mail: eleanor.baudouin@eglin.af.mil; *Info Spec,* Christi Rountree; E-mail: christina.rountree.ctr@eglin.af.mil; Staff 5 (MLS 1, Non-MLS 4)
Founded 1955
Library Holdings: e-journals 440; Electronic Media & Resources 64; Large Print Bks 488; Bk Titles 10,000; Per Subs 450
Subject Interests: Aeronaut, Biology, Chem, Electronics, Math, Physics
Automation Activity & Vendor Info: (Acquisitions) EOS International; (Cataloging) EOS International; (Circulation) EOS International; (OPAC) EOS International; (Serials) EOS International
Function: Computers for patron use, Doc delivery serv, Electronic databases & coll, Govt ref serv, Internet access, Online cat, Online ref, Photocopying/Printing, Ref serv available, Scanner, Telephone ref
Partic in Federal Library & Information Network; OCLC-LVIS; Panhandle Library Access Network
Restriction: Not open to pub, Restricted access, Secured area only open to authorized personnel

ENGLEWOOD

P ELSIE QUIRK PUBLIC LIBRARY OF ENGLEWOOD*, 100 W Dearborn St, 34223. SAN 302-9190. Tel: 941-861-1200. Circulation Tel: 941-861-1225. Administration Tel: 941-861-1205. Web Site: www.scgov.net/government/libraries/hours-and-locations. *Libr Mgr,* Zina Jayne; E-mail: zjayne@scgov.net; *Asst Mgr,* Michele Strickland; Tel: 941-861-1216, E-mail: mstrickland@scgov.net; Staff 11 (MLS 4, Non-MLS 7)
Founded 1962. Pop 28,000; Circ 221,464
Special Collections: Englewood History Information
Automation Activity & Vendor Info: (Acquisitions) Baker & Taylor; (Cataloging) Innovative Interfaces, Inc - Millennium; (Circulation) Innovative Interfaces, Inc - Millennium; (OPAC) Innovative Interfaces, Inc - Millennium
Wireless access
Function: Adult bk club, Audiobks via web, Bi-weekly Writer's Group, Bk club(s), Bks on cassette, Bks on CD, Children's prog, Computer training, Computers for patron use, Digital talking bks, E-Reserves, Electronic databases & coll, Family literacy, Free DVD rentals, Genealogy discussion group, Internet access, Literacy & newcomer serv, Music CDs, Online cat, Online ref, Outreach serv, OverDrive digital audio bks, Photocopying/Printing, Prog for adults, Prog for children & young adult, Ref serv available, Spoken cassettes & CDs, Spoken cassettes & DVDs, Story hour, Summer reading prog, Tax forms, Teen prog, VHS videos, Wheelchair accessible
Mem of Sarasota County Library System
Special Services for the Deaf - TTY equip
Special Services for the Blind - Accessible computers; Assistive/Adapted tech devices, equip & products; Bks on cassette; Bks on CD
Open Mon-Thurs 10-6, Fri & Sat 10-5
Friends of the Library Group

EUSTIS

P EUSTIS MEMORIAL LIBRARY*, 120 N Center St, 32726. SAN 302-9212. Tel: 352-357-5686. Circulation Tel: 352-357-5003. Reference Tel: 352-357-6110. FAX: 352-357-5794. E-mail: EMLContact@eustis.org. Web Site: www.eustismemoriallibrary.org. *Dir,* Ann Ivey; E-mail: iveya@ci.eustis.fl.us; *Ref Librn,* Jasmine Wilkins; *Ref & Ad Serv Librn,* Lauren McLaughlin; *Youth Serv Librn,* Bernadette Niedermeier; Tel: 352-357-0896; *Circ Mgr,* Celeste Bringard; Staff 5 (MLS 5)
Founded 1902. Pop 19,129; Circ 118,000
Library Holdings: Audiobooks 1,725; CDs 1,505; DVDs 3,767; e-books 1,051; Bk Vols 100,048; Per Subs 152; Talking Bks 1,929; Videos 603
Special Collections: Florida Coll
Automation Activity & Vendor Info: (Cataloging) SirsiDynix; (Circulation) SirsiDynix; (OPAC) SirsiDynix
Wireless access
Function: Bks on CD, Children's prog, Computers for patron use, Holiday prog, ILL available, Magazines, Magnifiers for reading, Microfiche/film & reading machines, Movies, Online cat, Online ref, Photocopying/Printing, Preschool outreach, Preschool reading prog, Prog for children & young adult, Ref serv available, Summer reading prog, Tax forms, Teen prog, Telephone ref, Wheelchair accessible
Partic in Tampa Bay Library Consortium, Inc
Special Services for the Blind - Bks on cassette; Bks on CD
Open Mon-Fri 10-5
Restriction: Non-resident fee

FERNANDINA BEACH

P NASSAU COUNTY PUBLIC LIBRARY SYSTEM*, Fernandina Beach Branch, 25 N Fourth St, 32034-4123. Tel: 904-530-6500, Ext 1. E-mail: libraryinfo@nassaucountyfl.com. Web Site: nassaureads.com. *Dir, Pub Libr Serv,* Dawn S Bostwick; E-mail: dbostwick@nassaucounty.com; *Asst Dir,* Janet W Loveless; E-mail: jloveless@nassaucountyfl.com; Staff 10 (MLS 4, Non-MLS 6)
Founded 1966. Pop 68,188; Circ 176,912
Library Holdings: Bk Titles 80,000; Bk Vols 166,000; Per Subs 95
Special Collections: AIGS; Genealogy & Local History (Permanent loan from Amelia Island Genealogical Society)
Automation Activity & Vendor Info: (Acquisitions) SirsiDynix; (Cataloging) SirsiDynix; (Circulation) SirsiDynix; (ILL) OCLC; (OPAC) SirsiDynix
Wireless access
Function: Bk club(s), Bks on CD, Computers for patron use, Free DVD rentals, Govt ref serv, Holiday prog, ILL available, Music CDs, Online cat, Online ref, Orientations, OverDrive digital audio bks, Photocopying/Printing, Preschool outreach, Prog for adults, Prog for children & young adult, Summer reading prog, Telephone ref, Wheelchair accessible
Partic in Florida Library Information Network; Northeast Florida Library Information Network; OCLC Online Computer Library Center, Inc
Open Mon & Thurs 10-8, Tues, Wed, Fri & Sat 10-6
Restriction: Non-resident fee
Friends of the Library Group
Branches: 4
BRYCEVILLE BRANCH, 7280 Motes Rd, Bryceville, 32009. *ILL, Libr Asst II,* Susan McKenney; Staff 1 (Non-MLS 1)
Founded 2003
Oct 2018-Sept 2019 Income $66,529
Library Holdings: Bk Vols 7,394; Per Subs 10
Automation Activity & Vendor Info: (Acquisitions) SirsiDynix; (Cataloging) SirsiDynix-WorkFlows; (Circulation) SirsiDynix-WorkFlows; (OPAC) SirsiDynix-iBistro
Function: Bks on CD, Children's prog, Computers for patron use, Electronic databases & coll, Free DVD rentals, Govt ref serv, Holiday prog, ILL available, Online cat, Online ref, Orientations, OverDrive digital audio bks, Photocopying/Printing, Summer reading prog, Tax forms, Telephone ref
Partic in OCLC Online Computer Library Center, Inc
Open Tues, Wed & Sat 10-6, Thurs Noon-8
Restriction: Non-resident fee
Friends of the Library Group
CALLAHAN BRANCH, 450077 State Rd 200, Callahan, 32011-3767. Tel: 904-530-6533. *Br Librn,* Elizabeth McKibben-Nee; E-mail: emckibben-nee@nassaucountyfl.com; Staff 2 (MLS 1, Non-MLS 1)
Founded 1985. Circ 41,503
Library Holdings: Bk Titles 39,907; Bk Vols 42,920; Per Subs 7
Automation Activity & Vendor Info: (Circulation) SirsiDynix-WorkFlows; (ILL) OCLC; (OPAC) SirsiDynix-iBistro
Function: Bk club(s), Bks on CD, Children's prog, Computers for patron use, Free DVD rentals, Govt ref serv, Holiday prog, ILL available, Music CDs, Online cat, Orientations, OverDrive digital audio bks, Photocopying/Printing, Prog for adults, Summer reading prog, Tax forms
Open Mon & Wed-Fri 10-6, Tues 12-8
Restriction: Non-resident fee
Friends of the Library Group
HILLIARD BRANCH, 15821 CR 108, Hilliard, 32046. Tel: 904-530-6544. *Br Librn,* Susan Stanley; E-mail: sstanley@nassaucountyfl.com; Staff 2 (MLS 1, Non-MLS 1)
Founded 1994
Automation Activity & Vendor Info: (Circulation) SirsiDynix-WorkFlows; (ILL) OCLC; (OPAC) SirsiDynix-iBistro
Function: Bks on CD, Children's prog, Computers for patron use, Free DVD rentals, Govt ref serv, Holiday prog, ILL available, Magazines, Meeting rooms, Music CDs, Online cat, Orientations, Photocopying/Printing, Prog for adults, Prog for children & young adult, Summer reading prog, Tax forms
Partic in OCLC Online Computer Library Center, Inc
Open Mon-Wed & Fri 10-6, Thurs 12-8
Restriction: Non-resident fee
Friends of the Library Group
YULEE BRANCH, 76346 William Burgess Blvd, Yulee, 32097. *Libr, Circ,* Position Currently Open; Staff 2 (Non-MLS 2)
Founded 2001
Library Holdings: Bk Vols 7,935; Per Subs 1
Automation Activity & Vendor Info: (Circulation) SirsiDynix-WorkFlows; (OPAC) SirsiDynix-iBistro
Function: Bks on CD, Children's prog, Computers for patron use, Free DVD rentals, Govt ref serv, Holiday prog, ILL available, Online cat, Orientations, OverDrive digital audio bks, Photocopying/Printing, Prog for adults, Summer reading prog, Tax forms
Open Mon-Thurs 8-8, Fri 8am-Noon

Restriction: Non-resident fee
Friends of the Library Group

FLAGLER BEACH

P FLAGLER BEACH LIBRARY*, 315 S Seventh St, 32136-3640. (Mail add: PO Box 449, 32136-0449), SAN 370-4629. Tel: 386-517-2030. FAX: 386-517-2234. Web Site: www.cityofflaglerbeach.com/125/Library. *Librn*, Melissa Parish; E-mail: mparish@cityofflaglerbeach.com; Staff 2 (Non-MLS 2)
Library Holdings: Audiobooks 553; Bks on Deafness & Sign Lang 15; DVDs 308; Large Print Bks 700; Music Scores 226; Bk Titles 23,323; Per Subs 50
Wireless access
Special Services for the Blind - Bks on cassette
Open Tues 1-7, Wed-Fri 10-5, Sat 10-2

FLEMING ISLAND

P CLAY COUNTY PUBLIC LIBRARY SYSTEM*, Fleming Island Branch (Headquarters), 1895 Town Center Blvd, 32003. (Mail add: PO Box 10109, 32006-0109). Tel: 904-278-3720. Administration Tel: 904-278-4745. Web Site: www.claycountygov.com/departments/library. *Dir, Libr Serv*, Pat Coffman; E-mail: Pat.Coffman@claycountygov.com; *Dep Dir, Libr Serv*, Lynn Pinilla; E-mail: Lynn.Pinilla@claycountygov.com; *Asst Dir, Libr Serv*, Jason Black; E-mail: Jason.Black@claycountygov.com; *Br Mgr*, Kelly Bohannan; E-mail: Kelly.Bohannan@claycountygov.com
Library Holdings: Bk Vols 267,881
Automation Activity & Vendor Info: (Cataloging) SirsiDynix; (Circulation) SirsiDynix; (OPAC) SirsiDynix
Wireless access
Partic in Florida Library Information Network; Northeast Florida Library Information Network
Open Mon-Thurs 10-8, Fri & Sat 9-5
Friends of the Library Group
Branches: 4
GREEN COVE SPRINGS BRANCH, 403 Ferris St, Green Cove Springs, 32043, SAN 337-5544. Tel: 904-269-6315, 904-284-6315. FAX: 904-284-4053. *Br Mgr*, Jennifer Parker; E-mail: jennifer.parker@claycountygov.com
Founded 1961
Library Holdings: Bk Titles 58,672; Per Subs 189
Subject Interests: Fla, Genealogy
Partic in LYRASIS
Open Mon-Thurs 10-8, Fri & Sat 9-5
Friends of the Library Group
KEYSTONE HEIGHTS BRANCH, 175 Oriole St, Keystone Heights, 32656, (Mail add: PO Box 710, Keystone Heights, 32656-0710), SAN 337-5579. Tel: 352-473-4286. FAX: 352-473-5123. *Br Mgr*, Margaret Whipple; E-mail: margaret.whipple@claycountygov.com
Library Holdings: Bk Vols 37,194; Per Subs 25
Open Mon-Thurs 10-8, Fri & Sat 9-5
Friends of the Library Group
MIDDLEBURG CLAY-HILL BRANCH, 2245 Aster Ave, Middleburg, 32068, SAN 322-5712. Tel: 904-541-5855. *Br Mgr*, Brandy Black; E-mail: brandy.black@claycountygov.com
Library Holdings: Bk Vols 36,141; Per Subs 25
Open Mon-Thurs 10-8, Fri & Sat 9-5
Friends of the Library Group
ORANGE PARK PUBLIC LIBRARY, 2054 Plainfield Ave, Orange Park, 32073-5498, SAN 337-5609. Tel: 904-278-4750. FAX: 904-278-3618. *Br Mgr*, Karen Walker; E-mail: Karen.Walker@claycountygov.com
Library Holdings: Bk Vols 83,960
Open Mon-Thurs 10-8, Fri & Sat 9-5
Friends of the Library Group

FORT LAUDERDALE

P BROWARD COUNTY LIBRARIES DIVISION*, Broward County Library, 100 S Andrews Ave, 33301. SAN 337-3983. Tel: 954-357-7444. Circulation Tel: 954-357-7407. Interlibrary Loan Service Tel: 954-357-7442. Reference Tel: 954-357-7439. Administration Tel: 954-357-7377. Automation Services Tel: 954-357-8620. FAX: 954-357-5733. TDD: 954-357-7528. E-mail: LIB-CustomerSvc@browardlibrary.org. Web Site: www.broward.org/library. *Dir*, Kelvin Watson; E-mail: kelvinwatson@broward.org; *Asst Dir*, Allison Grubbs; Tel: 954-357-6592, E-mail: jsears@broward.org; *Regional Mgr*, Ellen Lindenfield; Tel: 954-201-8834, E-mail: elindenfield@broward.org; *Regional Mgr*, Lisa Manners; E-mail: lmanners@broward.org; *Regional Mgr*, Valerie Simpson; Tel: 954-765-1596, E-mail: vsimpson@broward.org; Staff 636 (MLS 242, Non-MLS 394)
Founded 1974. Pop 1,759,591; Circ 10,530,000. Sal $46,223,653
Library Holdings: Audiobooks 102,134; AV Mats 2,524; Bks-By-Mail 2,134; Bks on Deafness & Sign Lang 284; Braille Volumes 407; CDs 187,617; DVDs 399,553; e-books 65,871; Electronic Media & Resources 392; High Interest/Low Vocabulary Bk Vols 1,664; Large Print Bks 101,532; Microforms 22,750; Music Scores 7,417; Bk Titles 377,631; Bk Vols 2,632,730; Per Subs 2,850; Talking Bks 52,536; Videos 51,225
Special Collections: African-American Research Library; Bienes Rare Books Coll; Florida Diagnostic & Learning Resource System; Judaica (Isaac Mayer Wise Coll); Music Scores; Small Business Resource Center
Subject Interests: Fla, Genealogy, Intl trade, Patents
Automation Activity & Vendor Info: (Acquisitions) CARL.Solution (TLC); (Cataloging) CARL.Solution (TLC); (Circulation) CARL.Solution (TLC); (ILL) OCLC WorldShare Interlibrary Loan; (Serials) CARL.Solution (TLC)
Wireless access
Function: 24/7 Electronic res, 24/7 Online cat, 3D Printer, Accelerated reader prog, Activity rm, Adult literacy prog, Archival coll, Art exhibits, Audiobks via web, AV serv, Bilingual assistance for Spanish patrons, Bks on CD, Children's prog, Computer training, Computers for patron use, Digital talking bks, Distance learning, E-Readers, E-Reserves, Electronic databases & coll, For res purposes, Free DVD rentals, Genealogy discussion group, Govt ref serv, Health sci info serv, Holiday prog, Homebound delivery serv, ILL available, Internet access, Learning ctr, Life-long learning prog for all ages, Literacy & newcomer serv, Magazines, Magnifiers for reading, Mail & tel request accepted, Mail loans to mem, Meeting rooms, Microfiche/film & reading machines, Movies, Music CDs, Online cat, Online info literacy tutorials on the web & in blackboard, Online ref, Orientations, Outreach serv, Outside serv via phone, mail, e-mail & web, OverDrive digital audio bks, Photocopying/Printing, Preschool outreach, Preschool reading prog, Printer for laptops & handheld devices, Prog for adults, Prog for children & young adult, Ref serv available, Res assist avail, Res libr, Scanner, Wheelchair accessible
Publications: WOW Update (Bimonthly)
Partic in LYRASIS; OCLC Online Computer Library Center, Inc; Southeast Florida Library Information Network, Inc
Special Services for the Deaf - Assisted listening device; Bks on deafness & sign lang; Closed caption videos; Spec interest per; Staff with knowledge of sign lang; TTY equip
Special Services for the Blind - Braille bks; Closed circuit TV; Large print bks; Magnifiers; Talking bks; Videos on blindness & physical disabilties
Open Mon & Wed 9-8, Thurs-Sat 10-6
Friends of the Library Group
Branches: 40
AFRICAN-AMERICAN RESEARCH LIBRARY & CULTURAL CENTER, 2650 Sistrunk Blvd, 33311, SAN 337-4378. Tel: 954-357-6282. FAX: 954-357-6257. Web Site: www.broward.org/library/Pages/BranchDetails.aspx?branches=1.
Founded 2002. Circ 41,382
Special Collections: Black Heritage Coll
Function: 24/7 Electronic res, 24/7 Online cat, Activity rm, Adult literacy prog, Archival coll, Art exhibits, Audiobks via web, AV serv, BA reader (adult literacy), Bks on CD, Bus archives, Children's prog, Citizenship assistance, Computer training, Computers for patron use, Digital talking bks, Distance learning, E-Readers, E-Reserves, Electronic databases & coll, Family literacy, For res purposes, Free DVD rentals, Genealogy discussion group, Holiday prog, Homework prog, ILL available, Internet access, Large print keyboards, Learning ctr, Life-long learning prog for all ages, Literacy & newcomer serv, Magazines, Magnifiers for reading, Mail & tel request accepted, Meeting rooms, Microfiche/film & reading machines, Movies, Music CDs, Online cat, Online info literacy tutorials on the web & in blackboard, Online ref, Orientations, Outreach serv, Outside serv via phone, mail, e-mail & web, OverDrive digital audio bks, Photocopying/Printing, Preschool outreach, Preschool reading prog, Printer for laptops & handheld devices, Prog for adults, Prog for children & young adult, Ref serv available, Res assist avail, Res libr, Scanner, Wheelchair accessible
Open Mon & Wed 12-8, Tues & Thurs-Sun 10-6
Friends of the Library Group
BEACH BRANCH, 3250 NE Second St, Pompano Beach, 33062, SAN 373-5192. Tel: 954-357-7830. FAX: 954-357-4908. Web Site: www.broward.org/library/Pages/BranchDetails.aspx?branches=2.
Founded 1991. Circ 66,632
Function: 24/7 Electronic res, 24/7 Online cat, Activity rm, Adult bk club, Audiobks via web, AV serv, Bilingual assistance for Spanish patrons, Bk club(s), Bks on CD, Computer training, Computers for patron use, Digital talking bks, Doc delivery serv, E-Reserves, Electronic databases & coll, For res purposes, Free DVD rentals, Games & aids for people with disabilities, Govt ref serv, Health sci info serv, ILL available, Internet access, Life-long learning prog for all ages, Magazines, Magnifiers for reading, Music CDs, Online cat, Online info literacy tutorials on the web & in blackboard, Online ref, Orientations, Outreach serv, Outside serv via phone, mail, e-mail & web, OverDrive digital audio bks, Photocopying/Printing, Prog for adults, Ref serv available, Res assist avail, Scanner, Wheelchair accessible
Open Tues-Sat 10-6
Friends of the Library Group

BOOKS BY MAIL, 100 S Andrews Ave, 3rd Flr, 33301, SAN 378-0678. Tel: 954-357-5757. Web Site: www.broward.org/library/Pages/BooksByMail.aspx.
Circ 21,471
Open Mon-Fri 10-6
Friends of the Library Group

TYRONE BRYANT BRANCH, 2230 NW 21st Ave, 33311, SAN 337-4327. Tel: 954-357-8210. FAX: 954-357-8216. Web Site: www.broward.org/library/Pages/BranchDetails.aspx?branches=38.
Founded 1980. Circ 26,387
Function: 24/7 Electronic res, 24/7 Online cat, Audiobks via web, AV serv, Bks on CD, Children's prog, Computer training, Computers for patron use, Digital talking bks, E-Reserves, Electronic databases & coll, For res purposes, Free DVD rentals, ILL available, Internet access, Large print keyboards, Learning ctr, Life-long learning prog for all ages, Magazines, Mail & tel request accepted, Meeting rooms, Movies, Music CDs, Online cat, Online info literacy tutorials on the web & in blackboard, Outreach serv, OverDrive digital audio bks, Photocopying/Printing, Preschool outreach, Prog for adults, Prog for children & young adult, Ref serv available, Scanner, Wheelchair accessible
Open Mon & Thurs 12-8, Tues, Wed, Fri & Sat 10-6
Friends of the Library Group

CARVER RANCHES, 4735 SW 18th St, West Park, 33023, SAN 337-4025. Tel: 954-357-6245. FAX: 954-357-6316. Web Site: www.broward.org/library/Pages/BranchDetails.aspx?branches=6.
Founded 1982. Circ 40,130
Library Holdings: Bk Titles 2,000
Function: 24/7 Electronic res, 24/7 Online cat, Activity rm, Adult literacy prog, After school storytime, Audiobks via web, Bks on CD, CD-ROM, Children's prog, Computers for patron use, Family literacy, Free DVD rentals, ILL available, Internet access, Laminating, Life-long learning prog for all ages, Literacy & newcomer serv, Magazines, Mail & tel request accepted, Meeting rooms, Movies, Music CDs, Online cat, Outreach serv, OverDrive digital audio bks, Photocopying/Printing, Preschool outreach, Prof lending libr, Prog for adults, Prog for children & young adult, Ref serv available, Res assist avail, Scanner
Open Mon & Wed 12-8, Tues, Thurs, Fri & Sat 10-6
Friends of the Library Group

CYBRARY CENTER, 100 S Andrews Ave, 1st & 7th Flr, 33301, SAN 378-0988. Tel: 954-357-7485. FAX: 954-357-7792.
Open Mon, Thurs & Fri 10-6, Tues & Wed 12-8

DAVIE-COOPER CITY BRANCH, 4600 SW 82nd Ave, Davie, 33328, SAN 337-4068. Tel: 954-357-6399. FAX: 954-357-6058. Web Site: www.broward.org/library/Pages/BranchDetails.aspx?branches=9.
Circ 152,432
Function: 24/7 Electronic res, 24/7 Online cat, Accelerated reader prog, Activity rm, Adult bk club, Adult literacy prog, After school storytime, Art exhibits, Audio & video playback equip for onsite use, Audiobks via web, AV serv, Bilingual assistance for Spanish patrons, Bk club(s), Bks on CD, Butterfly Garden, CD-ROM, Children's prog, Citizenship assistance, Computer training, Computers for patron use, Digital talking bks, Distance learning, Doc delivery serv, Electronic databases & coll, Family literacy, For res purposes, Free DVD rentals, Games & aids for people with disabilities, Govt ref serv, Health sci info serv, Holiday prog, Home delivery & serv to seniorr ctr & nursing homes, ILL available, Internet access, Large print keyboards, Life-long learning prog for all ages, Literacy & newcomer serv, Magazines, Magnifiers for reading, Mail & tel request accepted, Masonic res mat, Meeting rooms, Movies, Music CDs, Online cat, Online info literacy tutorials on the web & in blackboard, Online ref, Orientations, Outreach serv, Outside serv via phone, mail, e-mail & web, OverDrive digital audio bks, Photocopying/Printing, Preschool outreach, Preschool reading prog, Prog for adults, Prog for children & young adult, Ref serv available, Res assist avail, Scanner, Wheelchair accessible
Open Mon & Tues 12-8, Wed-Sat 10-6
Friends of the Library Group

DEERFIELD BEACH PERCY WHITE BRANCH, 837 E Hillsboro Blvd, Deerfield Beach, 33441, SAN 337-4084. Tel: 954-357-7680. FAX: 954-357-7735. Web Site: www.broward.org/library/Pages/BranchDetails.aspx?branches=10.
Circ 105,569
Function: 24/7 Electronic res, 24/7 Online cat, Accelerated reader prog, Activity rm, Adult bk club, Adult literacy prog, After school storytime, Art exhibits, Audio & video playback equip for onsite use, Audiobks on Playaways & MP3, Audiobks via web, AV serv, Bilingual assistance for Spanish patrons, Bk club(s), Bks on CD, Children's prog, Citizenship assistance, Computer training, Computers for patron use, Electronic databases & coll, Family literacy, Free DVD rentals, Govt ref serv, Health sci info serv, Holiday prog, Home delivery & serv to seniorr ctr & nursing homes, Homework prog, ILL available, Instruction & testing, Internet access, Large print keyboards, Life-long learning prog for all ages, Literacy & newcomer serv, Magazines, Magnifiers for reading, Mail & tel request accepted, Meeting rooms, Microfiche/film & reading machines, Movies, Music CDs, Online cat, Online info literacy tutorials on the web & in blackboard, Online ref, Orientations, Outreach serv, Outside serv via phone, mail, e-mail & web, OverDrive digital audio bks, Photocopying/Printing, Preschool outreach, Preschool reading prog, Prog for adults, Prog for children & young adult, Ref serv available, Scanner, Wheelchair accessible
Open Mon, Wed, Fri & Sat 10-6, Tues & Thurs 12-8
Friends of the Library Group

DANIA BEACH-PAUL DEMAIO LIBRARY, One Park Ave E, Dania Beach, 33004, SAN 337-4076. Tel: 954-357-7073. FAX: 954-357-7069. Web Site: www.broward.org/library/Pages/BranchDetails.aspx?branches=8.
Founded 1979. Circ 77,265
Function: 24/7 Electronic res, 24/7 Online cat, Adult bk club, Art exhibits, Bk club(s), Bks on CD, CD-ROM, Children's prog, Computers for patron use, Electronic databases & coll, Free DVD rentals, ILL available, Internet access, Large print keyboards, Literacy & newcomer serv, Meeting rooms, Movies, Music CDs, Online cat, Photocopying/Printing, Prog for adults, Prog for children & young adult, Ref serv available, Scanner
Open Mon & Thurs 12-8, Tues, Wed, Fri & Sat 10-6
Friends of the Library Group

FORT LAUDERDALE READING CENTER, 1300 E Sunrise Blvd, 33304, SAN 337-4106. Tel: 954-357-7890. FAX: 954-357-7868. Web Site: www.broward.org/library/Pages/BranchDetails.aspx?branches=11.
Circ 30,469
Function: 24/7 Electronic res, 24/7 Online cat, Adult bk club, Audiobks via web, AV serv, Bilingual assistance for Spanish patrons, Bk club(s), Bk reviews (Group), Bks on CD, CD-ROM, Computers for patron use, Digital talking bks, E-Reserves, Electronic databases & coll, Free DVD rentals, Govt ref serv, Health sci info serv, ILL available, Internet access, Large print keyboards, Magazines, Mail & tel request accepted, Music CDs, Online cat, Online info literacy tutorials on the web & in blackboard, Online ref, Outside serv via phone, mail, e-mail & web, OverDrive digital audio bks, Photocopying/Printing, Prog for adults, Ref serv available, Res assist avail, Scanner, Wheelchair accessible
Open Mon & Wed-Fri 10-6, Tues 12-8
Friends of the Library Group

FOSTER PARK COMMUNITY CENTER MICRO-LIBRARY, 609 NW Sixth Ave, Hallandale Beach, 33009. Tel: 954-455-0310. Web Site: www.broward.org/library/Pages/BranchDetails.aspx?branches=12.
Open Mon-Fri 6pm-9pm, Sat & Sun 12-5
Friends of the Library Group

GALT OCEAN MILE READING CENTER, 3403 Galt Ocean Dr, 33308, SAN 373-5206. Tel: 954-357-7840. FAX: 954-357-7854. Web Site: www.broward.org/library/Pages/BranchDetails.aspx?branches=13.
Circ 47,515
Function: 24/7 Electronic res, 24/7 Online cat, Activity rm, Adult bk club, Audiobks via web, AV serv, Bilingual assistance for Spanish patrons, Bk club(s), Bk reviews (Group), Bks on CD, Chess club, Computer training, Computers for patron use, Digital talking bks, Doc delivery serv, E-Reserves, Electronic databases & coll, For res purposes, Free DVD rentals, Games & aids for people with disabilities, Govt ref serv, Health sci info serv, Holiday prog, ILL available, Instruction & testing, Internet access, Life-long learning prog for all ages, Literacy & newcomer serv, Magazines, Magnifiers for reading, Mail & tel request accepted, Movies, Music CDs, Online cat, Online info literacy tutorials on the web & in blackboard, Online ref, Orientations, Outreach serv, Outside serv via phone, mail, e-mail & web, OverDrive digital audio bks, Photocopying/Printing, Prog for adults, Ref serv available, Res assist avail, Scanner, Wheelchair accessible
Open Mon, Tues, Fri & Sat 10-6, Thurs 12-8
Friends of the Library Group

HALLANDALE BEACH BRANCH, 300 S Federal Hwy, Hallandale, 33009, SAN 337-4130. Tel: 954-357-6380. FAX: 954-357-5324. Web Site: www.broward.org/library/Pages/BranchDetails.aspx?branches=14.
Circ 138,423
Function: 24/7 Electronic res, 24/7 Online cat, Activity rm, Adult bk club, Adult literacy prog, After school storytime, Art exhibits, Audio & video playback equip for onsite use, Audiobks on Playaways & MP3, Audiobks via web, Bi-weekly Writer's Group, Bilingual assistance for Spanish patrons, Bk club(s), Bk reviews (Group), Bks on CD, Bus archives, Chess club, Children's prog, Citizenship assistance, Computers for patron use, Distance learning, Electronic databases & coll, For res purposes, Free DVD rentals, Govt ref serv, Health sci info serv, Homebound delivery serv, ILL available, Internet access, Jazz prog, Large print keyboards, Life-long learning prog for all ages, Literacy & newcomer serv, Magazines, Magnifiers for reading, Mail & tel request accepted, Meeting rooms, Movies, Music CDs, Online cat, Online ref, Orientations, Outreach serv, Outside serv via phone, mail, e-mail & web, OverDrive digital audio bks, Photocopying/Printing, Preschool outreach, Prog for adults, Prog for children & young adult, Ref serv available, Res assist avail, Res libr, Satellite serv, Scanner, Wheelchair accessible
Open Mon & Tues 12-8, Wed-Sat 10-6
Friends of the Library Group

HOLLYWOOD BRANCH, 2600 Hollywood Blvd, Hollywood, 33020, SAN 337-4165. Tel: 954-357-7760. FAX: 954-357-6582. Web Site: www.broward.org/library/Pages/BranchDetails.aspx?branches=16.
Circ 24,280
Function: 24/7 Electronic res, 24/7 Online cat, Adult bk club, Adult literacy prog, Audiobks via web, AV serv, Bi-weekly Writer's Group, Bilingual assistance for Spanish patrons, Bks on CD, CD-ROM, Children's prog, Citizenship assistance, Computer training, Computers for patron use, Digital talking bks, Electronic databases & coll, Free DVD rentals, Health sci info serv, Holiday prog, ILL available, Internet access, Large print keyboards, Life-long learning prog for all ages, Literacy & newcomer serv, Magazines, Magnifiers for reading, Meeting rooms, Movies, Music CDs, Online cat, Online info literacy tutorials on the web & in blackboard, Online ref, Orientations, Outreach serv, OverDrive digital audio bks, Photocopying/Printing, Preschool outreach, Prog for adults, Prog for children & young adult, Ref & res, Scanner, Wheelchair accessible
Open Mon-Wed 10-8, Thurs-Sat 10-6
Friends of the Library Group

IMPERIAL POINT BRANCH, 5985 N Federal Hwy, 33308, SAN 328-9036. Tel: 954-357-6530. FAX: 954-357-6694. Web Site: www.broward.org/library/Pages/BranchDetails.aspx?branches=17.
Circ 119,158
Function: 24/7 Electronic res, 24/7 Online cat, Accelerated reader prog, Activity rm, Adult bk club, Adult literacy prog, Audiobks via web, AV serv, Bilingual assistance for Spanish patrons, Bks on CD, CD-ROM, Chess club, Children's prog, Citizenship assistance, Computer training, Computers for patron use, Digital talking bks, Doc delivery serv, E-Readers, E-Reserves, Electronic databases & coll, Family literacy, For res purposes, Free DVD rentals, Govt ref serv, Health sci info serv, Holiday prog, ILL available, Internet access, Large print keyboards, Life-long learning prog for all ages, Literacy & newcomer serv, Magazines, Mail & tel request accepted, Mail loans to mem, Meeting rooms, Movies, Music CDs, Notary serv, Online cat, Online info literacy tutorials on the web & in blackboard, Online ref, Outreach serv, OverDrive digital audio bks, Photocopying/Printing, Preschool outreach, Preschool reading prog, Prog for adults, Prog for children & young adult, Ref serv available, Res assist avail, Res libr, Scanner, Wheelchair accessible
Open Mon & Thurs-Sat 10-6, Tues & Wed 12-8
Friends of the Library Group

LAUDERDALE LAKES BRANCH/EDUCATIONAL & CULTURAL CENTER, 3580 W Oakland Park Blvd, Lauderdale Lakes, 33311, SAN 337-419X. Tel: 954-357-8650. FAX: 954-357-8653. Web Site: www.broward.org/library/Pages/BranchDetails.aspx?branches=19.
Circ 50,123
Function: 24/7 Electronic res, 24/7 Online cat, Activity rm, Adult literacy prog, Art exhibits, Audiobks via web, AV serv, BA reader (adult literacy), Bks on CD, Children's prog, Citizenship assistance, Computer training, Computers for patron use, Electronic databases & coll, Family literacy, Free DVD rentals, Govt ref serv, Health sci info serv, Holiday prog, Homework prog, ILL available, Internet access, Large print keyboards, Life-long learning prog for all ages, Magazines, Meeting rooms, Microfiche/film & reading machines, Movies, Music CDs, Online cat, Outreach serv, OverDrive digital audio bks, Photocopying/Printing, Preschool outreach, Preschool reading prog, Prog for adults, Prog for children & young adult, Ref serv available, Res assist avail, Scanner, Wheelchair accessible
Open Mon, Wed, Fri & Sat 10-6 Tues & Thurs 12-8
Friends of the Library Group

LAUDERHILL CENTRAL PARK LIBRARY BRANCH, 3810 NW 11 Pl, Lauderhill, 33311, SAN 337-422X. Tel: 954-357-7833. FAX: 954-357-7837. Web Site: www.broward.org/library/Pages/BranchDetails.aspx?branches=20.
Circ 28,516
Function: 24/7 Electronic res, 24/7 Online cat, Activity rm, Adult literacy prog, After school storytime, Art exhibits, Audiobks via web, AV serv, Bilingual assistance for Spanish patrons, Bks on CD, Children's prog, Computers for patron use, Electronic databases & coll, Family literacy, For res purposes, Free DVD rentals, Home delivery & serv to seniorr ctr & nursing homes, ILL available, Internet access, Large print keyboards, Life-long learning prog for all ages, Literacy & newcomer serv, Magazines, Meeting rooms, Movies, Music CDs, Online cat, Online info literacy tutorials on the web & in blackboard, Online ref, Orientations, Outreach serv, Outside serv via phone, mail, e-mail & web, OverDrive digital audio bks, Photocopying/Printing, Preschool outreach, Preschool reading prog, Prog for adults, Prog for children & young adult, Ref serv available, Res assist avail, Scanner, Wheelchair accessible
Open Mon & Wed 12-8, Tues, Thurs, Fri & Sat 10-6
Friends of the Library Group

LAUDERHILL TOWNE CENTRE LIBRARY, 6399 W Oakland Park Blvd, Lauderhill, 33313, SAN 337-4238. Tel: 954-357-6406. FAX: 954-357-6479. Web Site: www.broward.org/library/Pages/BranchDetails.aspx?branches=21.
Circ 74,493
Function: 24/7 Electronic res, 24/7 Online cat, Accelerated reader prog, Adult bk club, Adult literacy prog, Audiobks via web, AV serv, Bilingual assistance for Spanish patrons, Bk club(s), Bks on CD, CD-ROM, Children's prog, Citizenship assistance, Computer training, Computers for patron use, Distance learning, E-Reserves, Electronic databases & coll, Family literacy, Free DVD rentals, Homework prog, ILL available, Internet access, Large print keyboards, Learning ctr, Life-long learning prog for all ages, Literacy & newcomer serv, Magazines, Meeting rooms, Movies, Music CDs, Online cat, Online info literacy tutorials on the web & in blackboard, Online ref, Orientations, Outreach serv, Outside serv via phone, mail, e-mail & web, OverDrive digital audio bks, Photocopying/Printing, Preschool outreach, Preschool reading prog, Prog for adults, Prog for children & young adult, Ref serv available, Scanner, Wheelchair accessible
Open Mon & Tues 12-8, Wed-Sat 10-6
Friends of the Library Group

MARGATE CATHARINE YOUNG BRANCH, 5810 Park Dr, Margate, 33063, SAN 337-4246. Tel: 954-357-7500. FAX: 954-357-7523. Web Site: www.broward.org/library/Pages/BranchDetails.aspx?branches=23.
Circ 85,974
Function: 24/7 Electronic res, 24/7 Online cat, Adult bk club, Audio & video playback equip for onsite use, Audiobks via web, Bilingual assistance for Spanish patrons, Bks on cassette, Bks on CD, CD-ROM, Children's prog, Citizenship assistance, Computer training, Computers for patron use, Electronic databases & coll, Free DVD rentals, Health sci info serv, ILL available, Internet access, Life-long learning prog for all ages, Literacy & newcomer serv, Magazines, Magnifiers for reading, Mail & tel request accepted, Meeting rooms, Music CDs, Online cat, OverDrive digital audio bks, Photocopying/Printing, Prog for adults, Prog for children & young adult, Ref serv available, Scanner, Wheelchair accessible
Special Services for the Blind - Talking bks
Open Mon, Wed, Fri & Sat 10-6, Tues & Thurs 12-8
Friends of the Library Group

MIRAMAR BRANCH LIBRARY & EDUCATION CENTER, 2050 Civic Center Pl, Miramar, 33025. Tel: 954-357-8090. FAX: 954-357-8564. Web Site: www.broward.org/library/Pages/BranchDetails.aspx?branches=24.
Circ 276,108
Function: 24/7 Electronic res, 24/7 Online cat, Activity rm, Adult bk club, Adult literacy prog, Art exhibits, Audiobks via web, Bi-weekly Writer's Group, Bilingual assistance for Spanish patrons, Bk club(s), Bks on CD, CD-ROM, Children's prog, Citizenship assistance, Computer training, Computers for patron use, Digital talking bks, Electronic databases & coll, For res purposes, Free DVD rentals, Games & aids for people with disabilities, Govt ref serv, Health sci info serv, Holiday prog, ILL available, Internet access, Large print keyboards, Magazines, Mail & tel request accepted, Meeting rooms, Music CDs, Online cat, Orientations, Outreach serv, Outside serv via phone, mail, e-mail & web, OverDrive digital audio bks, Photocopying/Printing, Preschool outreach, Prog for adults, Prog for children & young adult, Ref serv available, Scanner, Wheelchair accessible
Open Mon-Wed 10-8, Thurs-Sat 10-6
Friends of the Library Group

JAN MORAN COLLIER CITY LEARNING LIBRARY, 2800 NW Ninth Ct, Pompano Beach, 33069-2149, SAN 337-4033. Tel: 954-357-7670. FAX: 954-357-8630. Web Site: www.broward.org/library/Pages/BranchDetails.aspx?branches=18.
Founded 1985. Circ 14,881
Special Collections: Adult Literacy Coll
Subject Interests: Family literacy
Function: 24/7 Electronic res, 24/7 Online cat, Accelerated reader prog, Activity rm, Adult literacy prog, Audio & video playback equip for onsite use, Audiobks via web, AV serv, Bk club(s), Bks on CD, Children's prog, Citizenship assistance, Computer training, Computers for patron use, Doc delivery serv, Electronic databases & coll, Family literacy, Free DVD rentals, Govt ref serv, Homework prog, ILL available, Internet access, Learning ctr, Literacy & newcomer serv, Magazines, Magnifiers for reading, Meeting rooms, Movies, Music CDs, Online cat, Online info literacy tutorials on the web & in blackboard, Online ref, Orientations, Outreach serv, Outside serv via phone, mail, e-mail & web, OverDrive digital audio bks, Photocopying/Printing, Preschool outreach, Prog for adults, Prog for children & young adult, Ref serv available, Res assist avail, Scanner
Open Mon 12-8, Tues, Thurs & Fri 10-6, Wed 10-9
Friends of the Library Group

NORTH LAUDERDALE SARANIERO BRANCH, 6901 Kimberly Blvd, North Lauderdale, 33068, SAN 337-4262. Tel: 954-357-6660. FAX: 954-357-6663. Web Site: www.broward.org/library/Pages/BranchDetails.aspx?branchinfo=25.
Circ 79,999
Function: 24/7 Electronic res, 24/7 Online cat, Activity rm, Adult bk club, Adult literacy prog, Art exhibits, Audiobks via web, Bk club(s), Bks on CD, Children's prog, Computers for patron use, Electronic databases & coll, Family literacy, For res purposes, Free DVD rentals, ILL available, Internet access, Large print keyboards, Life-long learning

prog for all ages, Literacy & newcomer serv, Magazines, Mail & tel request accepted, Meeting rooms, Movies, Music CDs, Online cat, Online ref, Outreach serv, Outside serv via phone, mail, e-mail & web, OverDrive digital audio bks, Photocopying/Printing, Preschool outreach, Preschool reading prog, Prog for adults, Prog for children & young adult, Ref serv available, Res assist avail, Scanner, Wheelchair accessible
Open Mon & Tues 12-8, Wed-Sat 10-6
Friends of the Library Group

NORTH REGIONAL-BROWARD COLLEGE LIBRARY, 1100 Coconut Creek Blvd, Coconut Creek, 33066, SAN 373-5214. Tel: 954-201-2600. FAX: 954-201-2650. Web Site: www.broward.org/library/Pages/BranchDetails.aspx?branches=26.
Circ 333,046
Function: 24/7 Electronic res, 24/7 Online cat, Accelerated reader prog, Activity rm, Adult literacy prog, After school storytime, Art exhibits, Audio & video playback equip for onsite use, Audiobks via web, AV serv, Bilingual assistance for Spanish patrons, Bk club(s), Bk reviews (Group), Bks on CD, Children's prog, Computer training, Computers for patron use, Digital talking bks, Doc delivery serv, E-Readers, Electronic databases & coll, Family literacy, For res purposes, Free DVD rentals, Govt ref serv, Health sci info serv, Holiday prog, Home delivery & serv to seniorr ctr & nursing homes, ILL available, Internet access, Large print keyboards, Life-long learning prog for all ages, Literacy & newcomer serv, Magazines, Magnifiers for reading, Mail & tel request accepted, Meeting rooms, Microfiche/film & reading machines, Movies, Music CDs, Online cat, Online info literacy tutorials on the web & in blackboard, Online ref, Orientations, Outreach serv, Outside serv via phone, mail, e-mail & web, OverDrive digital audio bks, Photocopying/Printing, Preschool outreach, Preschool reading prog, Printer for laptops & handheld devices, Prog for adults, Prog for children & young adult, Ref serv available, Res assist avail, Scanner, Wheelchair accessible
Open Mon-Wed 7:30am-8pm, Thurs 7:30-6, Fri 7:30-4, Sat & Sun 10-6
Friends of the Library Group

NORTHWEST BRANCH, 1580 NW Third Ave, Pompano Beach, 33060, SAN 373-5222. Tel: 954-357-6599. FAX: 954-357-6625. Web Site: www.broward.org/library/Pages/BranchDetails.aspx?branches=27.
Circ 25,180
Function: 24/7 Electronic res, 24/7 Online cat, Accelerated reader prog, Activity rm, Adult bk club, Adult literacy prog, Audiobks via web, AV serv, Bk club(s), Bks on CD, Children's prog, Citizenship assistance, Computer training, Computers for patron use, Electronic databases & coll, For res purposes, Free DVD rentals, Govt ref serv, Health sci info serv, Homework prog, ILL available, Internet access, Large print keyboards, Literacy & newcomer serv, Magazines, Mail & tel request accepted, Meeting rooms, Movies, Music CDs, Online cat, Online info literacy tutorials on the web & in blackboard, Orientations, Outreach serv, OverDrive digital audio bks, Photocopying/Printing, Preschool outreach, Preschool reading prog, Prof lending libr, Prog for adults, Prog for children & young adult, Ref serv available, Res assist avail, Scanner, Wheelchair accessible
Open Mon & Wed 12-8, Tues & Thurs-Sat 10-6
Friends of the Library Group

NORTHWEST REGIONAL, 3151 University Dr, Coral Springs, 33065. Tel: 954-357-7990. FAX: 954-357-7864. Web Site: www.broward.org/library/Pages/BranchDetails.aspx?branches=28.
Circ 518,366
Function: 24/7 Electronic res, 24/7 Online cat, 3D Printer, Activity rm, Adult bk club, Adult literacy prog, After school storytime, Art exhibits, Audiobks via web, Bilingual assistance for Spanish patrons, Bk club(s), Bks on CD, CD-ROM, Children's prog, Citizenship assistance, Computer training, Computers for patron use, Digital talking bks, Electronic databases & coll, Free DVD rentals, Govt ref serv, Holiday prog, Homebound delivery serv, Homework prog, ILL available, Internet access, Large print keyboards, Life-long learning prog for all ages, Literacy & newcomer serv, Magazines, Magnifiers for reading, Mail & tel request accepted, Mail loans to mem, Meeting rooms, Movies, Music CDs, Online cat, Online ref, Outreach serv, OverDrive digital audio bks, Photocopying/Printing, Preschool outreach, Preschool reading prog, Printer for laptops & handheld devices, Prog for adults, Prog for children & young adult, Ref serv available, Scanner, Wheelchair accessible
Special Services for the Blind - Large print bks; Talking bks
Open Mon-Wed 10-8, Thurs-Sun 10-6
Friends of the Library Group

HOLLYWOOD BEACH-BERNICE P OSTER READING CENTER, 1301 S Ocean Dr, Hollywood, 33019, SAN 374-8049. Tel: 954-357-4798. FAX: 954-357-4791. Web Site: www.broward.org/library/Pages/BranchDetails.aspx?branches=15.
Circ 58,485
Function: 24/7 Electronic res, 24/7 Online cat, Adult bk club, Art exhibits, Audiobks via web, AV serv, Bk club(s), Bk reviews (Group), Bks on CD, CD-ROM, Computers for patron use, Digital talking bks, Electronic databases & coll, Free DVD rentals, Govt ref serv, Health sci info serv, ILL available, Internet access, Large print keyboards, Magazines, Movies, Online cat, Online info literacy tutorials on the web & in blackboard, Online ref, OverDrive digital audio bks, Photocopying/Printing, Prog for adults, Ref serv available, Res assist avail, Scanner, Wheelchair accessible
Open Mon-Fri 10-6
Friends of the Library Group

POMPANO BEACH BRANCH & CULTURAL CENTER, 50 W Atlantic Blvd, Pompano Beach, 33060, SAN 373-5230. Tel: 954-357-7595. FAX: 954-357-7656. Web Site: www.broward.org/library/Pages/BranchDetails.aspx?branches=31.
Circ 83,498
Function: 24/7 Electronic res, 24/7 Online cat, 3D Printer, Activity rm, Adult bk club, Art exhibits, Audiobks via web, Bks on CD, CD-ROM, Chess club, Children's prog, Computer training, Computers for patron use, Digital talking bks, Distance learning, Doc delivery serv, Electronic databases & coll, Free DVD rentals, Games & aids for people with disabilities, Govt ref serv, Health sci info serv, Homework prog, ILL available, Large print keyboards, Life-long learning prog for all ages, Magazines, Meeting rooms, Movies, Music CDs, Online cat, Online info literacy tutorials on the web & in blackboard, Online ref, Outreach serv, OverDrive digital audio bks, Photocopying/Printing, Preschool outreach, Prog for children & young adult, Satellite serv, Scanner, Wheelchair accessible
Open Mon-Wed 10-8, Thurs-Sat 10-6
Friends of the Library Group

RIVERLAND BRANCH, 2710 W Davie Blvd, 33312, SAN 337-4319. Tel: 954-357-7455. FAX: 954-357-7493. Web Site: www.broward.org/library/Pages/BranchDetails.aspx?branches=32.
Circ 59,715
Function: 24/7 Electronic res, 24/7 Online cat, Activity rm, Adult bk club, Adult literacy prog, After school storytime, Audiobks via web, AV serv, Bilingual assistance for Spanish patrons, Bk club(s), Bks on CD, Chess club, Children's prog, Citizenship assistance, Computer training, Computers for patron use, Electronic databases & coll, Family literacy, Free DVD rentals, Holiday prog, Homework prog, ILL available, Internet access, Large print keyboards, Literacy & newcomer serv, Magazines, Meeting rooms, Movies, Music CDs, Online cat, Online info literacy tutorials on the web & in blackboard, Online ref, Orientations, Outreach serv, Outside serv via phone, mail, e-mail & web, OverDrive digital audio bks, Photocopying/Printing, Preschool outreach, Prog for adults, Prog for children & young adult, Ref serv available, Res assist avail, Scanner, Wheelchair accessible
Open Mon & Thurs 12-8, Tues, Wed, Fri & Sat 10-6
Friends of the Library Group

ALVIN SHERMAN LIBRARY, RESEARCH & INFORMATION TECHNOLOGY CENTER AT NOVA SOUTHEASTERN UNIVERSITY, 3100 Ray Ferrero Jr Blvd, 33314, SAN 378-0651. Tel: 954-262-5477. FAX: 954-262-3805. Web Site: sherman.library.nova.edu, www.broward.org/library/Pages/BranchDetails.aspx?branches=29.
Circ 139,707
Open Mon-Thurs 7:30am-11pm, Fri 7:30am-9pm, Sat 8-8, Sun 11am-11:30pm
Friends of the Library Group

CENTURY PLAZA LEON SLATIN BRANCH, 1856A W Hillsboro Blvd, Deerfield Beach, 33442, SAN 337-405X. Tel: 954-357-7740. FAX: 954-357-8597. Web Site: www.broward.org/library/Pages/BranchDetails.aspx?branches=7.
Founded 1982. Circ 155,641
Function: 24/7 Electronic res, 24/7 Online cat, Accelerated reader prog, Activity rm, Adult bk club, Adult literacy prog, Audiobks via web, AV serv, Bk club(s), Bks on CD, CD-ROM, Children's prog, Computer training, Computers for patron use, Digital talking bks, Electronic databases & coll, Free DVD rentals, Holiday prog, Homebound delivery serv, ILL available, Internet access, Literacy & newcomer serv, Magazines, Magnifiers for reading, Mail & tel request accepted, Meeting rooms, Movies, Music CDs, Online cat, Outreach serv, Outside serv via phone, mail, e-mail & web, OverDrive digital audio bks, Photocopying/Printing, Preschool outreach, Preschool reading prog, Prog for adults, Prog for children & young adult, Ref serv available, Res assist avail, Scanner, Wheelchair accessible
Open Mon-Sat 10-6
Friends of the Library Group

SOUTH REGIONAL - BROWARD COLLEGE LIBRARY, 7300 Pines Blvd, Pembroke Pines, 33024, SAN 337-4343. Tel: 954-201-8825. FAX: 954-964-0282. Web Site: www.broward.org/library/Pages/BranchDetails.aspx?branches=33.
Circ 279,958
Function: 24/7 Electronic res, 24/7 Online cat, Accelerated reader prog, Activity rm, Adult bk club, Adult literacy prog, After school storytime, Art exhibits, Audiobks via web, Bi-weekly Writer's Group, Bilingual assistance for Spanish patrons, Bk club(s), Bks on CD, Chess club, Children's prog, Citizenship assistance, Computer training, Computers for patron use, Digital talking bks, E-Reserves, Electronic databases & coll, Family literacy, Free DVD rentals, ILL available, Internet access, Large print keyboards, Literacy & newcomer serv, Magazines, Magnifiers for reading, Mail & tel request accepted, Meeting rooms, Microfiche/film

& reading machines, Movies, Music CDs, Notary serv, Online cat, Online ref, Orientations, Outside serv via phone, mail, e-mail & web, OverDrive digital audio bks, Photocopying/Printing, Preschool outreach, Printer for laptops & handheld devices, Prog for adults, Prog for children & young adult, Ref serv available, Res assist avail, Scanner, Wheelchair accessible
Special Services for the Deaf - TDD equip
Open Mon-Thurs 7:30am-8pm, Fri 7:30-4, Sat & Sun 10-6
Friends of the Library Group

SOUTHWEST REGIONAL, 16835 Sheridan St, Pembroke Pines, 33331. Tel: 954-357-6580. FAX: 954-357-7150. Web Site: www.broward.org/library/Pages/BranchDetails.aspx?branches=34. Founded 2000. Circ 375,759
Function: 24/7 Electronic res, 24/7 Online cat, Accelerated reader prog, Activity rm, Adult bk club, Adult literacy prog, After school storytime, Art exhibits, Audiobks via web, Bi-weekly Writer's Group, Bilingual assistance for Spanish patrons, Bk club(s), Bks on CD, Chess club, Children's prog, Citizenship assistance, Computer training, Computers for patron use, Digital talking bks, E-Reserves, Electronic databases & coll, Family literacy, Free DVD rentals, ILL available, Internet access, Large print keyboards, Literacy & newcomer serv, Magazines, Magnifiers for reading, Mail & tel request accepted, Meeting rooms, Microfiche/film & reading machines, Movies, Music CDs, Notary serv, Online cat, Online ref, Orientations, Outside serv via phone, mail, e-mail & web, OverDrive digital audio bks, Photocopying/Printing, Preschool outreach, Printer for laptops & handheld devices, Prog for adults, Prog for children & young adult, Ref serv available, Res assist avail, Scanner, Wheelchair accessible
Special Services for the Blind - Large print bks; Talking bks
Open Mon-Wed 10-8, Thurs-Sun 10-6
Friends of the Library Group

STIRLING ROAD BRANCH, 3151 Stirling Rd, Hollywood, 33312-6526. Tel: 954-357-7550. FAX: 954-357-7404. Web Site: www.broward.org/library/Pages/BranchDetails.aspx?branches=35. Founded 2003. Circ 199,066
Function: 24/7 Electronic res, 24/7 Online cat, Accelerated reader prog, Activity rm, Adult bk club, Adult literacy prog, Art exhibits, Audiobks via web, BA reader (adult literacy), Bilingual assistance for Spanish patrons, Bk club(s), Bk reviews (Group), Bks on CD, Chess club, Children's prog, Computer training, Computers for patron use, Digital talking bks, Distance learning, Doc delivery serv, Electronic databases & coll, For res purposes, Free DVD rentals, Genealogy discussion group, Govt ref serv, Holiday prog, Homework prog, ILL available, Internet access, Large print keyboards, Life-long learning prog for all ages, Literacy & newcomer serv, Magazines, Magnifiers for reading, Mail & tel request accepted, Meeting rooms, Movies, Music CDs, Online cat, Online info literacy tutorials on the web & in blackboard, Orientations, Outreach serv, Outside serv via phone, mail, e-mail & web, OverDrive digital audio bks, Photocopying/Printing, Preschool outreach, Prof lending libr, Prog for adults, Prog for children & young adult, Ref serv available, Res assist avail, Scanner, Wheelchair accessible
Open Mon, Fri & Sun 10-6, Tues-Thurs 12-8
Friends of the Library Group

SUNRISE/DAN PEARL BRANCH, 10500 W Oakland Park Blvd, Sunrise, 33351, SAN 375-605X. Tel: 954-357-7440. FAX: 954-357-7445. Web Site: www.broward.org/library/Pages/BranchDetails.aspx?branches=36. Circ 119,591
Function: 24/7 Electronic res, 24/7 Online cat, Activity rm, Adult bk club, Adult literacy prog, Audiobks via web, AV serv, Bilingual assistance for Spanish patrons, Bk club(s), Bks on CD, Chess club, Children's prog, Citizenship assistance, Computer training, Computers for patron use, Electronic databases & coll, Family literacy, For res purposes, Free DVD rentals, Govt ref serv, Health sci info serv, Holiday prog, Home delivery & serv to seniorr ctr & nursing homes, ILL available, Internet access, Life-long learning prog for all ages, Literacy & newcomer serv, Magazines, Magnifiers for reading, Mail & tel request accepted, Meeting rooms, Movies, Music CDs, Online cat, Online info literacy tutorials on the web & in blackboard, Online ref, Orientations, Outreach serv, Outside serv via phone, mail, e-mail & web, OverDrive digital audio bks, Photocopying/Printing, Preschool outreach, Preschool reading prog, Prog for adults, Prog for children & young adult, Ref serv available, Res assist avail, Scanner, Wheelchair accessible
Open Mon & Thurs-Sat 10-6, Tues & Wed 12-8
Friends of the Library Group

P TALKING BOOK LIBRARY, 100 S Andrews Ave, 33301, SAN 337-4017. Tel: 954-357-7555. FAX: 954-357-7420. TDD: 954-357-7528. E-mail: talkingbooks@broward.org. Web Site: www.broward.org/library/Pages/TalkingBookLibrary.aspx. Founded 1977. Circ 146,841
Special Services for the Blind - Closed circuit TV; Magnifiers; Talking bks & player equip
Open Mon-Fri 10-6
Friends of the Library Group

TAMARAC BRANCH, 8701 W Commercial Blvd, Tamarac, 33351, SAN 337-4424. Tel: 954-765-1500. FAX: 954-765-1550. Web Site: www.broward.org/library/Pages/BranchDetails.aspx?branches=37. Founded 2003. Circ 279,449
Function: 24/7 Electronic res, 24/7 Online cat, Accelerated reader prog, Activity rm, Adult bk club, Adult literacy prog, After school storytime, Art exhibits, Audiobks on Playaways & MP3, Audiobks via web, BA reader (adult literacy), Bilingual assistance for Spanish patrons, Bk club(s), Bk reviews (Group), Bks on CD, Children's prog, Citizenship assistance, Computer training, Computers for patron use, E-Reserves, Electronic databases & coll, Family literacy, Free DVD rentals, Health sci info serv, Holiday prog, Homework prog, ILL available, Internet access, Large print keyboards, Learning ctr, Life-long learning prog for all ages, Literacy & newcomer serv, Magazines, Mail & tel request accepted, Meeting rooms, Movies, Music CDs, Online cat, Orientations, Outreach serv, OverDrive digital audio bks, Photocopying/Printing, Preschool outreach, Preschool reading prog, Prog for adults, Prog for children & young adult, Ref serv available, Scanner, Wheelchair accessible
Open Mon-Wed 10-8, Thurs-Sat 10-6
Friends of the Library Group

WEST REGIONAL, 8601 W Broward Blvd, Plantation, 33324, SAN 337-4416. Tel: 954-765-1560. FAX: 954-765-1536. Web Site: www.broward.org/library/Pages/BranchDetails.aspx?branches=39. Circ 445,335
Function: 24/7 Electronic res, 24/7 Online cat, Adult bk club, Adult literacy prog, Art exhibits, Audiobks on Playaways & MP3, Audiobks via web, Bi-weekly Writer's Group, Bilingual assistance for Spanish patrons, Bk club(s), Bk reviews (Group), Bks on CD, CD-ROM, Chess club, Children's prog, Citizenship assistance, Computer training, Computers for patron use, Digital talking bks, E-Reserves, Electronic databases & coll, Family literacy, For res purposes, Free DVD rentals, Genealogy discussion group, Govt ref serv, Holiday prog, ILL available, Internet access, Life-long learning prog for all ages, Literacy & newcomer serv, Magazines, Mail & tel request accepted, Meeting rooms, Microfiche/film & reading machines, Movies, Music CDs, Outside serv via phone, mail, e-mail & web, OverDrive digital audio bks, Preschool outreach, Printer for laptops & handheld devices, Prog for adults, Prog for children & young adult, Ref serv available, Scanner, Wheelchair accessible
Special Services for the Deaf - TDD equip
Open Mon-Wed 10-8, Thurs-Sun 10-6
Friends of the Library Group

WESTON BRANCH, 4205 Bonaventure Blvd, Weston, 33332, SAN 374-8065. Tel: 954-357-5420. FAX: 954-357-7891. Web Site: www.broward.org/library/Pages/BranchDetails.aspx?branches=40. Circ 368,563
Function: 24/7 Electronic res, 24/7 Online cat, Accelerated reader prog, Activity rm, Adult bk club, Adult literacy prog, Art exhibits, Audio & video playback equip for onsite use, Audiobks via web, AV serv, Bilingual assistance for Spanish patrons, Bk club(s), Bks on CD, CD-ROM, Children's prog, Citizenship assistance, Computer training, Computers for patron use, Digital talking bks, Distance learning, Electronic databases & coll, Equip loans & repairs, For res purposes, Free DVD rentals, Genealogy discussion group, Govt ref serv, Health sci info serv, Holiday prog, Home delivery & serv to seniorr ctr & nursing homes, Homebound delivery serv, ILL available, Internet access, Life-long learning prog for all ages, Literacy & newcomer serv, Magazines, Mail & tel request accepted, Mail loans to mem, Meeting rooms, Movies, Music CDs, Online cat, Online info literacy tutorials on the web & in blackboard, Online ref, Outreach serv, Outside serv via phone, mail, e-mail & web, OverDrive digital audio bks, Preschool outreach, Preschool reading prog, Prof lending libr, Prog for adults, Prog for children & young adult, Ref serv available, Res assist avail, Res libr, Scanner, Wheelchair accessible
Open Mon-Wed 10-8, Thurs-Sat 10-6
Friends of the Library Group

YOUNG AT ART MUSEUM & BROWARD COUNTY LIBRARY, 751 SW 121st Ave, Davie, 33325. Tel: 954-357-5437. FAX: 954-357-5799. Web Site: www.broward.org/library/Pages/BranchDetails.aspx?branches=41. Circ 123,282
Library Holdings: CDs 307,757; DVDs 475,796; e-books 115,810; Bk Titles 2,764,321; Per Subs 2,850
Function: 24/7 Electronic res, 24/7 Online cat, Activity rm, Adult bk club, After school storytime, Audio & video playback equip for onsite use, Audiobks via web, Bilingual assistance for Spanish patrons, Bk club(s), Bks on CD, Chess club, Children's prog, Computers for patron use, E-Readers, Electronic databases & coll, Family literacy, Free DVD rentals, Govt ref serv, Health sci info serv, ILL available, Internet access, Life-long learning prog for all ages, Literacy & newcomer serv, Magazines, Meeting rooms, Movies, Music CDs, Online cat, Orientations, Outreach serv, Outside serv via phone, mail, e-mail & web, OverDrive digital audio bks, Photocopying/Printing, Preschool outreach,

Preschool reading prog, Prog for adults, Prog for children & young adult, Ref serv available, Scanner, Wheelchair accessible
Open Mon-Sat 10-6, Sun 11-6
Friends of the Library Group
PEMBROKE PINES BRANCH-WALTER C YOUNG RESOURCE CENTER, 955 NW 129th Ave, Pembroke Pines, 33028. Tel: 954-357-6750. FAX: 954-357-6718. Web Site: www.broward.org/library/Pages/BranchDetails.aspx?branches=30.
Circ 148,836
Subject Interests: Middle sch
Function: 24/7 Electronic res, 24/7 Online cat, Activity rm, Adult bk club, Adult literacy prog, Art exhibits, Audio & video playback equip for onsite use, Audiobks via web, AV serv, BA reader (adult literacy), Bilingual assistance for Spanish patrons, Bk club(s), Bk reviews (Group), Bks on CD, CD-ROM, Chess club, Children's prog, Citizenship assistance, Computers for patron use, Digital talking bks, Distance learning, Doc delivery serv, Electronic databases & coll, Family literacy, For res purposes, Free DVD rentals, Games & aids for people with disabilities, Govt ref serv, Health sci info serv, Holiday prog, Homebound delivery serv, ILL available, Internet access, Large print keyboards, Learning ctr, Life-long learning prog for all ages, Literacy & newcomer serv, Magazines, Magnifiers for reading, Mail & tel request accepted, Mail loans to mem, Meeting rooms, Movies, Music CDs, Online cat, Online info literacy tutorials on the web & in blackboard, Online ref, Orientations, Outreach serv, Outside serv via phone, mail, e-mail & web, OverDrive digital audio bks, Photocopying/Printing, Preschool outreach, Preschool reading prog, Prog for adults, Prog for children & young adult, Ref serv available, Res assist avail, Res libr, Scanner, Wheelchair accessible
Open Mon & Wed 8-8, Tues, Thurs & Fri 8-4, Sat 10-6
Friends of the Library Group

J CITY COLLEGE LIBRARY - FORT LAUDERDALE*, 2000 W Commercial Blvd, Ste 200, 33309-3001. Tel: 954-492-5353. FAX: 954-491-1965. Web Site: www.citycollege.edu. *Libr Dir,* Juliette Felde; E-mail: jfelde@citycollege.edu; *Libr Asst,* Gabrielle Gramazio; Staff 2 (MLS 1, Non-MLS 1)
Highest Degree: Bachelor
Library Holdings: AV Mats 102; DVDs 102; Bk Titles 2,055; Per Subs 71
Wireless access
Open Mon-Thurs 8am-10pm, Fri 8-5, Sat 9-1

S FORT LAUDERDALE HISTORICAL SOCIETY*, Hoch Research Library, 219 SW Second Ave, 33301. SAN 325-853X. Tel: 954-463-4431. E-mail: info@flhc.org. Web Site: www.historyfortlauderdale.org. *Exec Dir,* Patricia Zeiler; E-mail: pzeiler@flhc.org; *Dep Dir,* Ellery Andrews; E-mail: eandre3s@historyfortlauderdale.org; *Research Librn,* Margaret Miller; E-mail: mmiller@flhc.org; *Colls Mgr, Historian,* Barbara Poleo; E-mail: bpoleo@historyfortlauderdale.org; *Historian,* Rodney Dillon; E-mail: rdillon@historyfortlauderdale.org. Subject Specialists: *Historic presv,* Patricia Zeiler; *Anthrop, Archaeology,* Ellery Andrews; *Fla hist,* Barbara Poleo; *Fla hist,* Rodney Dillon; Staff 8 (MLS 1, Non-MLS 7)
Founded 1962
Library Holdings: Bk Titles 3,000; Bk Vols 3,500
Special Collections: Architectural Blueprints & Drawings; August Burghard Coll Manuscripts, Photos; Florida History Coll, rare bks; Gene Hyde Photographic Coll; Sanborn Fire Insurance Maps; Stranahan Coll; Vertical History Files, Phone Directories & Historic Maps. Oral History
Subject Interests: Anthrop, Archaeology, Bus hist, Ecology, Fla hist, Genealogy
Wireless access
Function: Archival coll, Art exhibits, Art programs, Bus archives, For res purposes, Life-long learning prog for all ages, Magnifiers for reading, Mail & tel request accepted, Meeting rooms, Museum passes, Notary serv, Photocopying/Printing, Prog for adults, Prog for children & young adult, Ref & res, Ref serv available, Res assist avail, Res libr, Res performed for a fee, Scanner, STEM programs, Visual arts prog, Wheelchair accessible
Publications: Businesses That Built Greater Fort Lauderdale (Local historical information); Checkered Sunshine (Local historical information); New River Innsider (Newsletter)
Open Mon-Fri 9-5
Restriction: Access at librarian's discretion, Authorized scholars by appt, Circ limited, External users must contact libr, Fee for pub use, Free to mem, Non-circulating of rare bks, Not a lending libr, Open evenings by appt, Open to qualified scholars, Open to researchers by request, Open to students, fac & staff, Pub use on premises, Researchers by appt only, Visitors must make appt to use bks in the libr

L GREENSPOON MARDER*, Law Library, 200 E Broward Blvd, Ste 1800, 33301. SAN 327-781X. Tel: 954-491-1120. FAX: 954-771-9264. E-mail: info@gmlaw.com. Web Site: www.gmlaw.com. *Librn,* Joanne Camejo; E-mail: joanne.camejo@gmlaw.com; *Mkt Coordr,* Natalie Villanueva; E-mail: natalie.villanueva@gmlaw.com; *Marketing Specialist,* Michelle Martinez Reyes; E-mail: michelle.martinez.reyes@gmlaw.com; Staff 2 (MLS 1, Non-MLS 1)
Library Holdings: Bk Vols 10,000; Per Subs 25
Wireless access
Partic in S Fla Law Libr Asn

C KEISER UNIVERSITY LIBRARY SYSTEM, 1500 NW 49th St, 33309. SAN 373-1294. Tel: 954-351-4035. Web Site: keiseruniversity.libguides.com. *Assoc Vice Chancellor, Univ Libr Syst,* Benjamin Williams; E-mail: ben@keiseruniversity.edu; *Libr Dir, Clearwater Campus,* Micheal McGuire; E-mail: mimcguire@keiseruniversity.edu; *Libr Dir, New Port Richey Campus,* Jessica Swanson; E-mail: jeswanson@keiseruniversity.edu; *Campus Libr Dir, San Marcos, Nicaragua,* Lissette Ruiz; E-mail: lissette.ruiz@keiseruniversity.edu; *Daytona Beach Campus Libr Dir,* Diane Scot; E-mail: dscot@keiseruniversity.edu; *Ft Lauderdale Campus Libr Dir,* Fay Cottoy; E-mail: fcottoy@keiseruniversity.edu; *Ft Myers Campus Libr Dir,* Rob Martinez; E-mail: rmartinez@keiseruniversity.edu; *Jacksonville Campus Libr Dir,* Patricia Lynn Mayfield; E-mail: lmayfield@keiseruniversity.edu; *Lakeland Campus Libr Dir,* Elizabeth Kolbe; E-mail: elikolbe@keiseruniversity.edu; *Melbourne Campus Libr Dir,* Carol Crawford; E-mail: ccrawford@keiseruniversity.edu; *Miami Campus Libr Dir,* Kelly Ribeiro; E-mail: kribeiro@keiseruniversity.edu; *Orlando Campus Libr Dir,* David Poremba; E-mail: dporemba@keiseruniversity.edu; *Pembroke Pines Campus Libr Dir,* Fadi Dagher; E-mail: fdagher@keiseruniversity.edu; *Port St Lucie Campus Libr Dir,* Justin Rogers; E-mail: jrogers@keiseruniversity.edu; *Sarasota Campus Libr Dir,* Abby Gilman; E-mail: agilman@keiseruniversity.edu; *Tallahassee Campus Libr Dir,* Lifeng Yu; E-mail: lifengy@keiseruniversity.edu; *Tampa Campus Libr Dir,* Debra Bogart; E-mail: dbogart@keiseruniversity.edu; *W Palm Beach Campus Libr Dir,* Timothy Guillen; E-mail: tguillen@keiseruniversity.edu; *Librn, Ft Lauderdale Campus,* Rebecca Rodriguez; E-mail: rguillen@keiseruniversity.edu; *Librn, Tallahassee Campus,* Anna Lybbert; E-mail: anroldan@keiseruniversity.edu. Subject Specialists: *Humanities,* Benjamin Williams; Staff 40 (MLS 34, Non-MLS 6)
Founded 1976. Enrl 17,000; Highest Degree: Doctorate
Library Holdings: e-journals 24; Electronic Media & Resources 240; Bk Vols 155,000; Per Subs 205
Automation Activity & Vendor Info: (Acquisitions) Auto-Graphics, Inc; (Cataloging) Auto-Graphics, Inc; (Circulation) Auto-Graphics, Inc; (OPAC) Auto-Graphics, Inc; (Serials) Auto-Graphics, Inc
Wireless access
Function: 24/7 Electronic res, 24/7 Online cat, Activity rm, Bilingual assistance for Spanish patrons, Bk club(s), Computers for patron use, Doc delivery serv, E-Reserves, Electronic databases & coll, Free DVD rentals, Internet access, Online cat, Online info literacy tutorials on the web & in blackboard, Online ref, Orientations, Outside serv via phone, mail, e-mail & web, Photocopying/Printing, Ref & res, Ref serv available, Spanish lang bks, Telephone ref
Publications: Bibliographies; New Books; Student Manuals; Style Sheets
Partic in Library & Information Resources Network; Northeast Florida Library Information Network; Panhandle Library Access Network; Southeast Florida Library Information Network, Inc; Southwest Florida Library Network; Tampa Bay Library Consortium, Inc
Open Mon-Thurs 7:30am-9pm, Fri 7:30-5, Sat 8-5
Restriction: Open to pub for ref & circ; with some limitations

CM NOVA SOUTHEASTERN UNIVERSITY, Martin & Gail Press Health Professions Division Library, 3200 S University Dr, 33328. SAN 373-420X. Tel: 954-262-3106. E-mail: hpdlibrary@nova.edu. Reference E-mail: hpdref@nova.edu. Web Site: www.nova.edu/hpdlibrary. *Exec Dir,* Todd Puccio; Tel: 954-262-3114, E-mail: puccio@nova.edu; *Circ Mgr,* Steve Roberts; Tel: 954-262-3110; *Supvr, Tech Serv,* Star Andrews; Tel: 954-262-3129, E-mail: sa11@nova.edu; Staff 14 (MLS 9, Non-MLS 5)
Founded 1979. Enrl 4,692; Highest Degree: Doctorate
Library Holdings: e-books 201; e-journals 1,969; Electronic Media & Resources 38; Bk Titles 23,790; Bk Vols 70,381; Per Subs 3,388
Subject Interests: Audiology, Dentistry, Nursing, Occupational therapy, Optometry, Osteopathic med, Pharmacology, Phys therapy
Automation Activity & Vendor Info: (Acquisitions) Innovative Interfaces, Inc; (Cataloging) Innovative Interfaces, Inc; (Circulation) Innovative Interfaces, Inc; (Course Reserve) Innovative Interfaces, Inc
Wireless access
Function: Online cat, Online ref
Partic in Fla Health Sci Libr Asn; LYRASIS; OCLC Online Computer Library Center, Inc; South Florida Health Sciences Library Consortium
Open Mon-Thurs 7am-Midnight, Fri 7am-9pm, Sat & Sun 10am-Midnight
Restriction: Badge access after hrs, Borrowing privileges limited to fac & registered students, Circ privileges for students & alumni only, Open to pub for ref only, Open to students, fac, staff & alumni, Prof mat only, Restricted borrowing privileges

C NOVA SOUTHEASTERN UNIVERSITY LIBRARIES, Alvin Sherman Library, Research & Information Technology Center, 3100 Ray Ferrero Jr Blvd, 33314. SAN 337-4432. Tel: 954-262-4600. Circulation Tel: 954-262-4601. Interlibrary Loan Service Tel: 954-262-4619, 954-262-4660. Reference Tel: 954-262-4613. Administration Tel: 954-262-4545, 954-262-4578. Toll Free Tel: 800-541-6682. FAX: 954-262-3805. Circulation FAX: 954-262-4038. Interlibrary Loan Service FAX: 954-262-3944. Reference FAX: 954-262-6830. E-mail: refdesk@nova.edu. Web Site: sherman.library.nova.edu. *Exec Dir, Library Systems,* Piya Chayanuwat; Tel: 954-262-4696, E-mail: piya@nova.edu; *Dir of Circ,* Constantinos Andreou; Tel: 954-262-4682, E-mail: constant@nsu.nova.edu; *Dir of Library Computing Servs,* John Vempala; Tel: 954-262-4695, E-mail: vempala@nova.edu; *Dir, Mkt & Outreach,* Marcia Silverstein; Tel: 954-262-4562, E-mail: msilvers@nova.edu; *Dir, Ref Serv, Dir, Instrul Serv,* Nora Quinlan; Tel: 954-262-4637, E-mail: nora@nsu.nova.edu; *Dir, Tech Serv,* Natasha Grando; Tel: 954-262-4665, E-mail: ngrando@nsu.nova.edu; *Interim Dir of Reference,* Laura Ramirez; Tel: 954-262-8423, E-mail: lucio@nova.edu; *Interim Dir, Public Library Services,* LeThesha Harris; Tel: 954-262-4639, E-mail: lethesha@nova.edu; *Univ Librn,* James Hutchens; Tel: 954-262-4648, E-mail: jamesh@nova.edu; *Mgr, Bus Serv,* Dina Azpiri; Tel: 954-262-4546, E-mail: dinan@nova.edu; *Univ Archivist,* Gena Meroth; Tel: 954-262-4641, E-mail: gmeroth@nova.edu; Staff 71 (MLS 31, Non-MLS 40)
Founded 1966. Enrl 20,888; Fac 2,154; Highest Degree: Doctorate
Library Holdings: AV Mats 25,983; Bks on Deafness & Sign Lang 187; e-books 181,157; e-journals 111,410; High Interest/Low Vocabulary Bk Vols 150; Large Print Bks 507; Bk Vols 570,906; Per Subs 3,235
Automation Activity & Vendor Info: (Acquisitions) Innovative Interfaces, Inc; (Cataloging) Innovative Interfaces, Inc; (Circulation) Innovative Interfaces, Inc; (Course Reserve) Innovative Interfaces, Inc; (ILL) Innovative Interfaces, Inc; (Media Booking) Innovative Interfaces, Inc; (OPAC) Innovative Interfaces, Inc; (Serials) Innovative Interfaces, Inc
Wireless access
Partic in Florida Library Information Network; Independent Cols & Univs of Fla; Southeast Florida Library Information Network, Inc
Open Mon-Thurs 7:30am-11pm, Fri 7:30am-9pm, Sat 8-8, Sun 11am-11:30pm
Friends of the Library Group
Departmental Libraries:
HEALTH PROFESSIONS DIVISION LIBRARY
See Separate Entry
OCEANOGRAPHIC CAMPUS LIBRARY, 8000 N Ocean Dr, Dania Beach, 33004. SAN 337-4580. Tel: 954-262-3643, 954-262-3681. Toll Free Tel: 800-541-6882, Ext 23643. FAX: 954-262-4021. E-mail: oclibrary@nova.edu. Web Site: nsufl.libguides.com/oclibrary. *Reference Librarian III,* Keri Baker; Tel: 954-262-3643, E-mail: kbaker1@nova.edu; *Reference Librarian III,* Jaime Goldman; E-mail: hjaime@nova.edu. Subject Specialists: *Marine sci,* Jaime Goldman; Staff 3 (MLS 2, Non-MLS 1)
Founded 1970. Enrl 253; Fac 16; Highest Degree: Doctorate
Library Holdings: AV Mats 130; e-journals 64; Bk Vols 15,291; Per Subs 37
Open Mon-Thurs 8-6, Fri 8:30-4:30
Restriction: Borrowing privileges limited to fac & registered students

CL PANZA MAURER LAW LIBRARY, Shepard Broad College of Law, Leo Goodwin Sr Bldg, 3305 College Ave, Davie, 33314. SAN 337-4491. Tel: 954-262-6100. Circulation Tel: 954-262-6202. Reference Tel: 954-262-6201. Administration Tel: 954-262-6211. Administration FAX: 954-262-3838. E-mail: referencedesk@nsu.law.nova.edu. Web Site: law.nova.edu/library. *Assoc Dean, Libr Serv,* Vicenc Feliu; E-mail: vfeliu@nova.edu; *Assoc Dir, Operations & Colls,* Beth Parker; Tel: 954-262-6204, E-mail: mparker@nova.edu; *Assoc Dir, Reference & Research,* Dr Cheryl Booth; Tel: 954-262-6215, E-mail: cbooth1@nova.edu; *Research & Technical Servs Librn,* Marin Dell; Tel: 954-262-6224, E-mail: ddell@nova.edu; *Research & Technical Servs Librn,* Will Geeslin; Tel: 954-262-6226, E-mail: wgeeslin@nova.edu; *Research & Technical Servs Librn,* Emily Mayers-Twist; Tel: 954-262-6223, E-mail: emayerst@nova.edu; *Research & Technical Servs Librn,* Brian Quigley; Tel: 954-262-6213, E-mail: bquigley@nova.edu
Founded 1974. Enrl 830
Library Holdings: Bk Vols 360,067; Per Subs 5,466
Special Collections: UN Document Depository; US Document Depository
Automation Activity & Vendor Info: (Acquisitions) Innovative Interfaces, Inc; (Cataloging) Innovative Interfaces, Inc; (Circulation) Innovative Interfaces, Inc; (Course Reserve) Innovative Interfaces, Inc; (ILL) OCLC FirstSearch; (OPAC) Innovative Interfaces, Inc
Publications: Book Docket (Monthly); Tydbytes (Quarterly)
Open Mon-Sun 8am-Midnight (Winter)

S STONEWALL NATIONAL MUSEUM & ARCHIVES, Stonewall Library, 1300 E Sunrise Blvd, 33304. Tel: 954-763-8565. E-mail: inquiry@stonewall-museum.org. Web Site: stonewall-museum.org. *Exec Dir,* Hunter O'Hanian; E-mail: hunter@stonewall-museum.org; *Chief Librn,* Robert Lee
Library Holdings: CDs 1,000; Bk Titles 28,000; Per Subs 60
Automation Activity & Vendor Info: (Cataloging) Inmagic, Inc.; (Circulation) Inmagic, Inc.
Wireless access
Open Mon-Fri 11-5, Sat 10-3

GL LAMAR WARREN LAW LIBRARY OF BROWARD COUNTY*, Broward County Judicial Complex, North Wing, Rm 1800, 201 SE Sixth St, 33301. SAN 302-9255. Tel: 954-831-6226. Web Site: www.browardbar.org/law-library. *Dir,* Barbara Brush; Staff 3 (MLS 1, Non-MLS 2)
Founded 1956
Library Holdings: Bk Vols 30,000
Special Collections: Retrospective Florida Law Coll
Wireless access
Special Services for the Blind - Reader equip
Open Mon-Fri 8:30-4:45

FORT MEADE

P FORT MEADE PUBLIC LIBRARY*, 75 E Broadway, 33841-2998. SAN 302-9328. Tel: 863-285-8287. FAX: 863-285-8093. Web Site: www.cityoffortmeade.com/departments/library.php. *Dir, Ref/Tech Proc,* Jacqueline Rose; E-mail: jrose@cityoffortmeade.com; *ILL,* Savanna Britt; E-mail: sbritt@cityoffortmeade.com; Staff 4 (MLS 1, Non-MLS 3)
Pop 6,203; Circ 19,574
Oct 2020-Sept 2021 Income $238,668. Mats Exp $15,000. Sal $107,776 (Prof $47,151)
Library Holdings: CDs 900; Bk Vols 17,742; Per Subs 17
Special Collections: Fort Meade History
Automation Activity & Vendor Info: (Cataloging) SirsiDynix; (Circulation) SirsiDynix; (OPAC) SirsiDynix
Wireless access
Function: 24/7 Electronic res, 24/7 Online cat, Adult bk club, Audiobks on Playaways & MP3, Bk club(s), Bks on CD, Children's prog, Computer training, Computers for patron use, For res purposes, Free DVD rentals, Holiday prog, Homebound delivery serv, Homework prog, Internet access, Magazines, Movies, Music CDs, Notary serv, Online cat, Outreach serv, Photocopying/Printing, Preschool outreach, Preschool reading prog, Prog for adults, Prog for children & young adult, Ref & res, Story hour, Summer & winter reading prog
Partic in Polk County Libr Coop; Tampa Bay Library Consortium, Inc
Open Mon-Fri 8:30-5
Friends of the Library Group

FORT MYERS

C FLORIDA GULF COAST UNIVERSITY LIBRARY*, 10501 FGCU Blvd S, 33965. SAN 377-6719. Circulation Tel: 239-590-7610. Reference Tel: 239-590-7630. Administration Tel: 239-590-7600. Administration FAX: 239-590-7609. TDD: 239-590-7618. E-mail: libcirc@fgcu.edu. Web Site: library.fgcu.edu. *Dean of Libr,* Tracy Elliott; Tel: 239-590-7602, E-mail: telliott@fgcu.edu; *Assoc Dean,* Jeremy Brown; Tel: 239-590-7605, E-mail: jerbrown@fgcu.edu; *Assoc Dir, Univ Librn,* Rebecca Donlan; Tel: 239-590-7641, E-mail: rdonlan@fgcu.edu; *Assoc Dir,* Donna Vazquez; Tel: 239-590-7603, E-mail: devazque@fgcu.edu; *Head, Ref, Res & Instruction,* Dr Linda Colding; Tel: 239-590-7604, E-mail: lcolding@fgcu.edu; *Head, Archives & Spec Coll, Head, Digital Initiatives,* Melissa VandeBurgt; Tel: 239-590-7658, E-mail: mvandeburgt@fgcu.edu; *Head, Customer Serv,* Peggy Glatthaar; Tel: 239-590-1429, E-mail: mglatthaar@fgcu.edu; *Asst Librn, Head, Tech Serv,* Christopher Boyd; Tel: 239-590-7640, E-mail: cboyd@fgcu.edu; *Head, Tech, Univ Librn,* Danielle Zino Rosenthal; Tel: 239-590-7633, E-mail: drosenth@fgcu.edu; *Univ Librn,* Anjana Bhatt; Tel: 239-590-7634, E-mail: abhatt@fgcu.edu; *Univ Librn,* Rachel Cooke; Tel: 239-590-7606, E-mail: rcooke@fgcu.edu; *First Year Experience & Outreach Librn,* Heather Snapp; Tel: 239-745-4224, E-mail: hsnapp@fgcu.edu; *Instrul Tech Librn,* Anna Carlin; Tel: 239-590-7663, E-mail: acarlin@fgcu.edu; *Asst Librn,* Kim Reycraft; Tel: 239-590-1339, E-mail: kreycraf@fgcu.edu; *Asst Librn,* Steve Rokusek; Tel: 239-590-7632, E-mail: srokusek@fgcu.edu; *Asst Librn,* Rachel Tait-Ripperdan; Tel: 239-590-7661, E-mail: rtait@fgcu.edu; *Assoc Librn,* Regina Beard; Tel: 239-590-4372, E-mail: rmbeard@fgcu.edu. Subject Specialists: *Educ, The arts,* Rachel Cooke; *STEM,* Kim Reycraft; *Soc sci,* Steve Rokusek; *Hist, Lit, Philos,* Rachel Tait-Ripperdan; *Hospital mgt, Resort mgt,* Regina Beard; Staff 42 (MLS 18, Non-MLS 24)
Founded 1997. Enrl 15,000; Fac 18; Highest Degree: Doctorate. Sal $1,651,536
Library Holdings: AV Mats 16,324; e-books 33,552; Per Subs 6,585; Videos 4,880
Automation Activity & Vendor Info: (Acquisitions) Ex Libris Group; (Cataloging) Ex Libris Group; (Circulation) Ex Libris Group; (ILL) OCLC ILLiad; (OPAC) Ex Libris Group; (Serials) SerialsSolutions
Wireless access
Partic in ISI; LYRASIS; Southwest Florida Library Network

Special Services for the Deaf - TTY equip
Open Sun 11-1, Mon-Thurs 7am-1am, Fri 7-8, Sat 8-6

J FLORIDA SOUTHWESTERN STATE COLLEGE*, Richard H Rush Library - Lee Campus, 8099 College Pkwy SW, Bldg J-212, 33919. (Mail add: PO Box 60210, 33906-6210), SAN 302-9336. Tel: 239-489-9220. FAX: 239-489-9465. Web Site: www.fsw.edu/library. *Head Librn,* William Shuluk; Tel: 239-489-9356, E-mail: wshuluk@fsw.edu; *Fac Librn,* Jane V Charles; Tel: 239-489-8345, E-mail: jane.charles@fsw.edu; *Fac Librn,* Frank Dowd; Tel: 239-489-9449, E-mail: fdowd@fsw.edu; *Circ Serv Coordr,* Peggy Phetterplace; Tel: 239-489-9299, E-mail: pphetterplace@fsw.edu; *Acq,* Cindy Campbell; Tel: 239-489-9367, E-mail: ccampbell@fsw.edu; Staff 18.5 (MLS 6.5, Non-MLS 12)
Founded 1962. Enrl 11,000; Fac 200; Highest Degree: Bachelor
Library Holdings: Electronic Media & Resources 25; Bk Titles 75,000; Per Subs 250
Publications: User's Brochure
Partic in Florida Asn of Commun Col; Southwest Florida Library Network
Open Mon-Thurs (Sept-May) 7:30-9, Fri 7:30-4, Sat & Sun 10-6; Mon-Thurs (Summer) 7:30-9, Fri 7:30-4, Sat 10-6

GL LEE COUNTY LAW LIBRARY*, Judge Lynn Gerald Law Library, Lee County Justice Ctr, 1700 Monroe St, 33901. SAN 302-9352. Tel: 239-533-9195. FAX: 239-485-2598. Web Site: www.ca.cjis20.org/home/main/lawlibrary.asp. *Law Librn,* Guyatri Sharon Heerah; E-mail: gheerah@ca.cjis20.org
Founded 1959
Library Holdings: Bk Vols 1,800
Wireless access
Open Mon-Fri 8:30-5

P LEE COUNTY LIBRARY SYSTEM, 2345 Union St, 33901-3924. SAN 337-4610. Tel: 239-533-4800. Interlibrary Loan Service Tel: 239-533-4199. Reference Tel: 239-479-4636. FAX: 239-485-1100. Interlibrary Loan Service FAX: 239-485-1121. E-mail: lcls@leegov.com. Web Site: www.leegov.com/library. *Dir,* Mindi Simon; E-mail: msimon@leegov.com; *Dep Dir,* Nancy Roark; E-mail: nroark@leegov.com; *Mgr, Prog & Outreach,* Melissa Baker; E-mail: mbaker@leegov.com; *District Libr Mgr,* Anita Pintado; E-mail: apintado@leegov.com; *Digital Serv Mgr,* Anne Simpson; E-mail: asimpson@leegov.com; *Fiscal Mgr,* Lori Arends; E-mail: larends@leegov.com; *Internal Services, Mgr,* Jill Horrom; E-mail: jhorrom@leegov.com; *Libr Mgr, Support Serv,* Amy Krueger; E-mail: akrueger@leegov.com; Staff 253 (MLS 84, Non-MLS 169)
Founded 1964. Pop 698,468; Circ 6,054,016
Oct 2018-Sept 2019. Mats Exp $3,795,755, Books $1,583,000, Per/Ser (Incl. Access Fees) $101,875, Micro $29,000, AV Mat $634,480, Electronic Ref Mat (Incl. Access Fees) $1,447,400. Sal $13,088,175
Library Holdings: Audiobooks 42,318; AV Mats 4,061; Bks-By-Mail 985; CDs 35,682; DVDs 221,457; e-books 527,515; e-journals 49,529; Electronic Media & Resources 98,362; Large Print Bks 46,498; Microforms 7,351; Bk Vols 883,665; Per Subs 1,757
Automation Activity & Vendor Info: (Acquisitions) Innovative Interfaces, Inc; (Cataloging) Innovative Interfaces, Inc; (Circulation) Innovative Interfaces, Inc; (ILL) OCLC; (OPAC) Innovative Interfaces, Inc; (Serials) Innovative Interfaces, Inc
Wireless access
Partic in Southwest Florida Library Network
Friends of the Library Group
Branches: 16
BONITA SPRINGS PUBLIC LIBRARY, 26876 Pine Ave, Bonita Springs, 34135-5009, SAN 302-8631. Tel: 239-533-4860. *Sr Librn,* Karen Gravlin; E-mail: kgravlin@leegov.com; Staff 12 (MLS 3, Non-MLS 9)
Circ 195,184
Open Mon, Wed & Thurs 10-6, Tues 12-8, Fri & Sat 9-5
Friends of the Library Group
CAPE CORAL-LEE COUNTY PUBLIC LIBRARY, 921 SW 39th Terrace, Cape Coral, 33914-5721, SAN 337-467X. Tel: 239-533-4500. *Principal Librn,* Dora Schilling; E-mail: dschilling@leegov.com; Staff 24 (MLS 9, Non-MLS 15)
Circ 663,518
Open Mon-Wed 9-8, Thurs 9-6, Fri & Sat 9-5
Friends of the Library Group
CAPTIVA MEMORIAL LIBRARY, 11560 Chapin Lane, Captiva, 33924, SAN 302-8801. Tel: 239-533-4890. *Sr Librn,* Colleen Barany; E-mail: cbarany@leegov.com; Staff 3 (MLS 1, Non-MLS 2)
Circ 15,036
Open Tues & Thurs 10-6, Wed 12-8, Fri & Sat 9-5
Friends of the Library Group
DUNBAR-JUPITER HAMMON PUBLIC LIBRARY, 3095 Blount St, 33916-2032, SAN 337-4734. Tel: 239-533-4150. *Sr Librn,* Jubilee Brainerd; E-mail: jbrainerd@leegov.com; Staff 5 (MLS 1, Non-MLS 4)
Circ 54,181
Special Collections: African-American Literature Coll
Open Tues 12-8, Wed & Thurs 10-6, Fri & Sat 9-5
Friends of the Library Group
EAST COUNTY REGIONAL LIBRARY, 881 Gunnery Rd N, Lehigh Acres, 33971. Tel: 239-533-4200. *Principal Librn,* Lori Lowery; E-mail: llowery@leegov.com; Staff 26 (MLS 7, Non-MLS 19)
Circ 493,622
Open Mon-Wed 9-8, Thurs 9-6, Fri & Sat 9-5
Friends of the Library Group
FORT MYERS REGIONAL LIBRARY, 2450 First St, 33901, SAN 302-9344. Tel: 239-533-4600. TDD: 239-485-1162. *Principal Librn,* Tori Hersh; E-mail: thersh@leegov.com; Staff 26 (MLS 9, Non-MLS 17)
Circ 474,012
Special Collections: Genealogy. State Document Depository
Special Services for the Deaf - TTY equip
Open Mon-Wed 9-8, Thurs 9-6, Fri & Sat 9-5
Friends of the Library Group
LAKES REGIONAL LIBRARY, 15290 Bass Rd, 33919, SAN 372-0233. Tel: 239-533-4000. *Principal Librn,* Carolyn MacDonald; E-mail: cmacdonald@leegov.com; Staff 28 (MLS 9, Non-MLS 19)
Circ 940,452
Open Mon-Wed 9-8, Thurs 9-6, Fri & Sat 9-5
Friends of the Library Group
LIBRARY PROCESSING, 881 Gunnery Rd N, Ste 2, Lehigh Acres, 33971-1246, SAN 372-0217. Tel: 239-533-4170. *Adult Coll Develop Librn, Principal Librn,* Rollie Welch; E-mail: rwelch@leegov.com; *Principal Librn, Youth Coll Develop Librn,* Diane Lettieri; E-mail: dlettieri@leegov.com; *ILL, Sr Librn,* Eileen Downing; E-mail: edowning@leegov.com; *Sr Librn, Acq,* Nicole Parsons; E-mail: nparsons@leegov.com; *Colls Mgr,* Judy Shannon; E-mail: jshannon@leegov.com; *ILS Syst Mgr, Mgr, Cat Serv,* Cecilia Smiley; E-mail: msmiley@leegov.com; *Sr Libr Supvr, Tech Serv,* Chris Barber; E-mail: cbarber@leegov.com; Staff 22 (MLS 10, Non-MLS 12)
Automation Activity & Vendor Info: (ILL) OCLC FirstSearch
Partic in LYRASIS
Open Mon-Fri 8-5
Friends of the Library Group
NORTH FORT MYERS PUBLIC LIBRARY, 2001 N Tamiami Trail NE, North Fort Myers, 33903-2802, SAN 337-4823. Tel: 239-533-4320. *Sr Librn,* Kathy Chumley; E-mail: kchumley@leegov.com; Staff 13 (MLS 3, Non-MLS 10)
Circ 248,170
Open Mon, Wed & Thurs 10-6, Tues 12-8, Fri & Sat 9-5
Friends of the Library Group
NORTHWEST REGIONAL LIBRARY, 519 N Chiquita Blvd, Cape Coral, 33993. Tel: 239-533-4700. *Principal Librn,* Cynthia Loftis-Culp; E-mail: cloftis-culp@leegov.com; Staff 21 (MLS 7, Non-MLS 14)
Circ 525,189
Open Mon, Wed & Thurs 10-6, Tues 12-8, Fri & Sat 9-5
Friends of the Library Group
PINE ISLAND PUBLIC LIBRARY, 10701 Russell Rd, Bokeelia, 33922, SAN 337-4858. Tel: 239-533-4350. *Sr Librn,* Linda Kroeker; E-mail: lkroeker@leegov.com; Staff 6 (MLS 1, Non-MLS 5)
Circ 91,763
Open Tues & Thurs 10-6, Wed 12-8, Fri & Sat 9-5
Friends of the Library Group
RIVERDALE BRANCH LIBRARY, 2421 Buckingham Rd, 33905, SAN 372-0225. Tel: 239-533-4370. *Sr Librn,* Alyssa Diekman; E-mail: adiekman@leegov.com; Staff 7 (MLS 1, Non-MLS 6)
Circ 121,457
Open Tues 12-8, Wed & Thurs 10-6, Fri & Sat 9-5
Friends of the Library Group
SOUTH COUNTY REGIONAL LIBRARY, 21100 Three Oaks Pkwy, Estero, 33928-3020, SAN 376-9453. Tel: 239-533-4400. *Principal Librn,* Barb Swenson; E-mail: bswenson@leegov.com; Staff 23 (MLS 9, Non-MLS 14)
Circ 605,469
Open Mon-Wed 9-8, Thurs 9-6, Fri & Sat 9-5
Friends of the Library Group
P TALKING BOOKS LIBRARY, 1651 Lee St, 33901, SAN 372-0241. Tel: 239-533-4780. Toll Free Tel: 800-854-8195. *Sr Librn,* Karin McLeish-Delgado; E-mail: kmcleishdelgado@leegov.com; *Libr Assoc,* Lisa Cooke; E-mail: lcooke@leegov.com; Staff 4 (MLS 1, Non-MLS 3)
Circ 97,122
Special Services for the Blind - Assistive/Adapted tech devices, equip & products; Audio mat; Bks & mags in Braille, on rec, tape & cassette; Children's Braille; Recorded bks; Spanish Braille mags & bks; Talking bks
Open Mon-Fri 9-5
TELEPHONE & VIRTUAL REFERENCE SERVICES, 2450 First St, 33901, SAN 374-406X. Information Services Tel: 239-479-4636. *Sr Librn,* Laura Cifelli; E-mail: lcifelli@leegov.com; Staff 7 (MLS 2, Non-MLS 5)
Open Mon-Wed 9-8, Thurs 9-6, Fri & Sat 9-5
Bookmobiles: 1. Sr Librn, Kelly Palma. Bk vols 13,630

M LEE MEMORIAL HEALTH SYSTEM LIBRARY*, 2776 Cleveland Ave, 1st Flr, 33901. Tel: 239-343-2410. FAX: 239-343-3422. Web Site: www.leehealth.org/health-and-Wellness/Medical-library. *Librn,* Narges Ahmadi; E-mail: narges.ahmadi@leememorial.org; *Libr Assoc,* Kathleen More; Staff 1 (MLS 1)
Library Holdings: e-journals 1,800; Bk Titles 6,000; Per Subs 115
Subject Interests: Healthcare, Hist of med, Nursing
Wireless access
Partic in Southwest Florida Library Network; Tampa Bay Medical Library Network
Open Mon 7-6, Tues-Fri 7:30-4

C SOUTHERN TECHNICAL COLLEGE, Learning Resource Center, 1685 Medical Lane, 33907. Tel: 239-939-4766, Ext 1403. FAX: 239-936-4040. Web Site: southerntechlibraries.org. *Librn,* Ashleigh Carner; E-mail: acarner@southerntech.edu; Staff 1 (MLS 1)
Automation Activity & Vendor Info: (Acquisitions) LibraryWorld, Inc; (Cataloging) LibraryWorld, Inc; (Circulation) LibraryWorld, Inc; (ILL) OCLC; (Serials) LibraryWorld, Inc
Wireless access
Function: Online cat
Open Mon-Thurs 8-8, Fri 8-5
Departmental Libraries:
AUBURNDALE CAMPUS, 450 Havendale Blvd, Auburndale, 33823. Tel: 863-551-1112. Web Site: southerntechlibraries.org/lrc-hours/auburndale. *Librn,* Luis Perez; E-mail: luisperez@southerntech.edu
Function: ILL available
Partic in Tampa Bay Library Consortium, Inc
Open Mon-Thurs 8am-7pm
BRANDON CAMPUS, 608 E Bloomingdale Ave, Brandon, 33511. Tel: 813-820-0200. Web Site: southerntechlibraries.org/lrc-hours/brandon-library. *Librn,* Dawn Parker; E-mail: dparker1@southerntech.edu
Partic in Tampa Bay Library Consortium, Inc
Open Mon-Thurs 9-8, Fri 8-5
ORLANDO CAMPUS, 1485 Florida Mall Ave, Orlando, 32809. Tel: 407-438-6000. Web Site: southerntechlibraries.org/lrc-hours/orlando. *Librn,* Renae Hamilton; E-mail: rhamilton@southerntech.edu; *Librn,* Lillian D Soler-Lopez; E-mail: lsolerlopez@southerntech.edu
Function: ILL available
Partic in Tampa Bay Library Consortium, Inc
Open Mon & Wed 8:30-6:30, Fri 9-1
PORT CHARLOTTE CAMPUS, 950 Tamiami Trail, No 109, Port Charlotte, 33953. Tel: 941-391-8888. Web Site: southerntechlibraries.org/lrc-hours/port-charlotte. *Librn,* Janet Sordan; E-mail: jsordan@southerntech.edu
Open Mon-Thurs 8am-10pm, Fri 8-5
SANFORD CAMPUS, 2910 S Orlando Dr, Sanford, 32773. Tel: 407-323-4141. Web Site: southerntechlibraries.org/lrc-hours/sanford-library. *Librn,* Rachel Gault; E-mail: rgault@southerntech.edu; *Librn,* Sharon Langlois; E-mail: slanglois@southerntech.edu
Open Mon & Wed 10-7:30, Tues & Thurs 10:30-7:30, Fri 9-5
TAMPA CAMPUS, 3910 Riga Blvd, Tampa, 33619. Tel: 813-630-4401. FAX: 813-630-4272. *Librn,* Cynthia Dixon; E-mail: cdixon@southerntech.edu; Staff 1 (MLS 1)
Highest Degree: Bachelor

FORT MYERS BEACH

P FORT MYERS BEACH PUBLIC LIBRARY*, 2755 Estero Blvd, 33931. SAN 302-9379. Tel: 239-765-8162. Reference Tel: 239-765-8163. FAX: 239-463-8776. TDD: 239-233-8179. E-mail: library@fmb.lib.fl.us. Web Site: www.fmb.lib.fl.us. *Dir,* Cletus Poser; Tel: 239-463-9691, E-mail: cletusp@fmb.lib.fl.us; *Cataloger,* John Lukow; E-mail: johnl@fmb.lib.fl.us; Staff 12 (MLS 3, Non-MLS 9)
Founded 1955. Pop 16,500; Circ 110,944
Library Holdings: AV Mats 10,100; Bk Titles 81,000; Per Subs 173
Special Collections: Florida Coll
Automation Activity & Vendor Info: (Cataloging) TLC (The Library Corporation)
Wireless access
Partic in Southwest Florida Library Network
Open Mon-Fri 9-5, Sat 9-1
Friends of the Library Group

FORT PIERCE

C FLORIDA ATLANTIC UNIVERSITY, Harbor Branch Oceanographic Institute Library, 5600 US 1 N, 34946. SAN 302-9387. Tel: 772-242-2486. Web Site: www.fau.edu/hboi/library. *Libr Dir,* Pamela Alderman; E-mail: palderm1@fau.edu; Staff 1 (MLS 1)
Founded 1975
Library Holdings: Bk Vols 30,000
Subject Interests: Aquaculture, Marine drug discovery, Ocean engr, Ocean exploration, Ocean health
Automation Activity & Vendor Info: (Acquisitions) Main Library Systems; (Cataloging) Main Library Systems; (Circulation) Main Library Systems; (Course Reserve) Main Library Systems; (OPAC) Main Library Systems
Wireless access
Publications: Acquisitions List; Publications List
Open Mon-Fri 8-6
Restriction: Badge access after hrs

C INDIAN RIVER STATE COLLEGE*, Miley Library, 3209 Virginia Ave, 34981-5599. SAN 302-9395. Tel: 772-462-7600. FAX: 772-462-4780. E-mail: library@irsc.edu. Web Site: www.irsc.edu. *Dean, Learning Res,* Dr Akos Delneky; Tel: 772-462-7590; *Emerging Tech Librn,* Mia Tignor; Tel: 772-462-7124; *Ref/Outreach Librn,* Alexis Carlson; Tel: 772-462-7194; *Ref/Outreach Librn,* Katie Williams; Tel: 772-462-7587; Staff 6 (MLS 4, Non-MLS 2)
Founded 1960. Fac 167; Highest Degree: Bachelor
Library Holdings: e-books 108,000; Bk Vols 81,000; Per Subs 200
Special Collections: Florida; Instructional Effectiveness. US Document Depository
Automation Activity & Vendor Info: (Cataloging) Ex Libris Group; (Circulation) Ex Libris Group; (ILL) OCLC Online; (OPAC) Ex Libris Group
Wireless access
Partic in OCLC Online Computer Library Center, Inc; Tampa Bay Library Consortium, Inc
Open Mon-Thurs (Fall & Spring) 7:45am-9pm, Fri 7:45-5, Sun 1-5; Mon-Thurs (Summer) 7am-8pm
Departmental Libraries:
BRACKETT LIBRARY - MUELLER CAMPUS, Indian River State College, Mueller Campus, 6155 College Lane, Vero Beach, 32966. Tel: 772-226-2544, 772-226-3080. FAX: 772-226-2542. *Ref Librn,* Angie Neely-Sardon; Tel: 772-226-2544
Founded 2009
Open Mon, Thurs & Fri 9-5, Tues & Wed 12-8
DIXON HENDRY CAMPUS LIBRARY, 2229 NW Ninth Ave, Okeechobee, 34972. Tel: 863-763-8017. *Emerging Tech Librn,* Mia Tignor; Tel: 863-462-7124; *Ref/Outreach Librn,* Alexis Carlson; Tel: 863-462-7194; *Ref/Outreach Librn,* Dan Hood; Tel: 863-462-7587
Library Holdings: Bk Vols 500
Open Mon-Thurs 8-8, Fri 8-2
MORGADE LIBRARY - CHASTAIN CAMPUS, 5851 SE Community Dr, Stuart, 34997. Tel: 772-463-3245. *Tech Asst,* Deborah Kent; E-mail: dkent@irsc.edu
Open Mon, Tues & Thurs-Sat 10-5:30, Wed 12-8
KEN PRUITT CAMPUS LIBRARY, 500 NW California Blvd, Port Saint Lucie, 34986. Tel: 772-336-6380. FAX: 772-873-3409. *Ref Librn,* Brett Williams; Tel: 772-336-6383
Library Holdings: Bk Vols 12,000; Per Subs 50
Open Mon-Thurs 9-9, Fri 9-5, Sat & Sun 1-5

P SAINT LUCIE COUNTY LIBRARY SYSTEM*, Susan B Kilmer Branch Library, 101 Melody Lane, 34950-4402. SAN 337-4912. Tel: 772-462-1615. Reference Tel: 772-462-2188. FAX: 772-462-2750. Web Site: library.stlucieco.gov. *Libr Mgr,* Susan Jacob; E-mail: jacobs@stlucieco.org; *Head, Br Libr,* Mark Freed; Tel: 772-462-1618, E-mail: freedm@stlucieco.org; *Head, Info Syst,* Randy Miller; Tel: 772-462-1802, E-mail: millerra@stlucieco.org; *Br Supvr,* Amanda Carranza; Tel: 772-462-1607, E-mail: carranzaa@stlucieco.org; *Tech Serv Supvr,* Jill Siekman; Tel: 772-462-2198, E-mail: Siekmanj@stlucieco.org; Staff 63 (MLS 10, Non-MLS 53)
Founded 1953
Library Holdings: Audiobooks 7,831; DVDs 19,865; e-books 5,309; Bk Vols 232,461; Per Subs 357
Special Collections: Black History; Florida Coll, bks
Subject Interests: Genealogy, Local hist
Automation Activity & Vendor Info: (Acquisitions) SirsiDynix; (Circulation) SirsiDynix; (OPAC) SirsiDynix
Wireless access
Function: 24/7 Electronic res, 24/7 Online cat, 3D Printer, Activity rm, Adult bk club, After school storytime, Archival coll, Art exhibits, Art programs, Audiobks via web, AV serv, Bk club(s), Bks on cassette, Bks on CD, Children's prog, Computer training, Computers for patron use, Digital talking bks, Electronic databases & coll, Free DVD rentals, Genealogy discussion group, Holiday prog, Homebound delivery serv, ILL available, Internet access, Magazines, Magnifiers for reading, Meeting rooms, Microfiche/film & reading machines, Movies, Music CDs, Online cat, Online ref, OverDrive digital audio bks, Photocopying/Printing, Printer for laptops & handheld devices, Prog for adults, Prog for children & young adult, Ref & res, Ref serv available, Res assist avail, Scanner, Spanish lang bks, Spoken cassettes & CDs, Spoken cassettes & DVDs, STEM programs, Story hour, Study rm, Summer reading prog, Teen prog, Telephone ref, VHS videos, Wheelchair accessible

Partic in Tampa Bay Library Consortium, Inc
Open Tues & Thurs 9-8, Wed 9-5:30, Fri 9-5, Sat 8:30-5
Friends of the Library Group
Branches: 5
ZORA NEALE HURSTON BRANCH, 3008 Avenue D, 34947, SAN 328-6398. Tel: 772-462-2154. ; Staff 1 (MLS 1)
Founded 1991
Library Holdings: Bk Vols 25,500
Special Collections: Zora Neale Hurston Coll
Open Tues & Thurs 10-7, Sat 9-5
LAKEWOOD PARK BRANCH, 7605 Santa Barbara Dr, 34951, SAN 322-6239. Tel: 772-462-6870. FAX: 772-462-6874. *Br Head,* Carol Shroyer; Staff 1 (MLS 1)
Founded 1989
Special Services for the Deaf - TDD equip
Open Tues 9-5:30, Wed & Thurs 9-7, Fri & Sat 9-5
Friends of the Library Group
PAULA A LEWIS BRANCH LIBRARY, 2950 SW Rosser Blvd, Port Saint Lucie, 34953. Tel: 772-871-5470. *Br Supvr,* Maureen Gallagher; E-mail: gallagherm@stlucieco.org; Staff 1 (MLS 1)
Open Tues & Thurs 9-8, Wed 9-5:30, Fri 9-5, Sat 8:30-5
Friends of the Library Group
MORNINGSIDE BRANCH, 2410 Morningside Blvd, Port Saint Lucie, 34952. SAN 372-7904. Tel: 772-337-5632. *Br Mgr,* Sandy Henry-Gordon; Staff 1 (MLS 1)
Founded 1993
Library Holdings: Bk Vols 48,000
Open Tues & Thurs 9-8, Wed 9-5:30, Fri & Sat 9-5
Friends of the Library Group
PORT SAINT LUCIE BRANCH, 180 SW Prima Vista Blvd, Port Saint Lucie, 34983. SAN 337-4947. Tel: 772-871-5450. *Br Mgr,* Mark Freed; E-mail: freedm@stlucieco.org; Staff 1 (MLS 1)
Founded 1970
Library Holdings: Bk Vols 27,000
Special Services for the Deaf - TDD equip
Open Tues 9-5:30, Wed & Thurs 9-8, Fri & Sat 9-5
Friends of the Library Group

G SAINT LUCIE COUNTY REGIONAL HISTORY CENTER, Research Library, 414 Seaway Dr, 34949. SAN 327-3113. Tel: 772-462-1795. FAX: 772-462-1877. Web Site: www.stlucieco.gov/history. *Registrar,* Harry Quatraro; E-mail: quatraroh@stlucieco.org
Founded 1968
Library Holdings: CDs 30; Bk Vols 1,500; Videos 75
Subject Interests: Hist of Fla
Wireless access
Restriction: Open to pub by appt only

GL RUPERT J SMITH LAW LIBRARY OF SAINT LUCIE COUNTY*, Saint Lucie County Law Library, 221 S Indian River Dr, 34950. SAN 302-9409. Tel: 772-462-2370. FAX: 772-462-2145. E-mail: lucielaw@bellsouth.net. Web Site: rjslawlibrary.org. *Librn,* Nora J Everlove; E-mail: nora@rjslawlibrary.org; *Librn,* Merrilyn Phillips
Library Holdings: Bk Vols 15,000
Wireless access
Open Mon-Thurs 9-5, Sat 9-4:30
Friends of the Library Group

C UNIVERSITY OF FLORIDA*, Indian River Research & Education Center, 2199 S Rock Rd, 34945-3138. SAN 325-3503. Tel: 772-468-3922. FAX: 772-468-5668. Web Site: www.irrec.ifas.ufl.edu. *Dir,* Charles A Powell; E-mail: capowell@ufl.edu
Founded 1960
Library Holdings: Bk Titles 500; Bk Vols 525; Per Subs 20
Wireless access
Open Mon-Fri 8-5

FORT WALTON BEACH

P FORT WALTON BEACH LIBRARY, 185 Miracle Strip Pkwy SE, 32548. SAN 302-9417. Tel: 850-833-9590. FAX: 850-833-9659. E-mail: library@fwb.org. Web Site: fwb.org/library. *Libr Dir,* Patricia Gould; E-mail: pgould@fwb.org; *Ch Serv Librn,* Nancy Cardinal; E-mail: ncardinal@fwb.org; Staff 7.5 (MLS 1, Non-MLS 6.5)
Founded 1954. Pop 25,000; Circ 118,368
Library Holdings: AV Mats 4,656; Bk Vols 62,000; Per Subs 184
Special Collections: Daily News Archives, microfilm back to 1915
Automation Activity & Vendor Info: (Cataloging) SirsiDynix; (Circulation) SirsiDynix
Wireless access
Partic in LYRASIS; Okaloosa County Public Library Cooperative; Panhandle Library Access Network
Open Mon-Thurs 10-6, Fri 10-5, Sat 10-4

S INDIAN TEMPLE MOUND MUSEUM LIBRARY, 139 Miracle Strip Pkwy SE, 32548. SAN 373-0417. Tel: 850-833-9595. FAX: 850-833-9675. Web Site: www.fwb.org/museums/indian-temple-mound-museum. *Mgr,* Gail Meyer; E-mail: gmeyer@fwb.org
Founded 1970
Library Holdings: Bk Vols 2,500; Per Subs 25
Subject Interests: Archaeology, Local hist, Native American
Function: For res purposes
Open Mon-Sat 10-2
Restriction: Not a lending libr

C UNIVERSITY OF WEST FLORIDA, Emerald Coast Library, 1170 Martin Luther King Jr Blvd, 32547. Tel: 850-863-6578. Web Site: libguides.uwf.edu/emeraldcoast. *Librn,* Paul Williford; Tel: 850-863-6577, E-mail: williford@uwf.edu; Staff 3 (MLS 1, Non-MLS 2)
Highest Degree: Doctorate
Library Holdings: e-books 350,000; e-journals 80; Bk Titles 25,000; Bk Vols 30,000
Wireless access
Open Mon-Thurs 8am-9pm, Fri 8-5, Sat 1-5

FROSTPROOF

P LATT MAXCY MEMORIAL LIBRARY*, 15 N Magnolia Ave, 33843. SAN 329-143X. Tel: 863-635-7857. FAX: 863-635-8502. Web Site: pclc.ent.sirsi.net/client/en_US/mypclc. *Dir,* Missy Hadden; E-mail: Missy.Hadden@mypclc.org; Staff 4 (Non-MLS 4)
Founded 1922. Pop 2,800; Circ 38,217
Library Holdings: Bk Titles 33,000; Bk Vols 35,478; Per Subs 41
Special Collections: Florida Coll, large print bks; Spanish Coll, vertical file
Automation Activity & Vendor Info: (Cataloging) TLC (The Library Corporation); (Circulation) TLC (The Library Corporation); (OPAC) TLC (The Library Corporation)
Function: ILL available
Partic in Polk County Libr Coop; Tampa Bay Library Consortium, Inc
Special Services for the Deaf - Bks on deafness & sign lang
Special Services for the Blind - Bks on cassette
Open Mon & Thurs 8:30-7, Tues, Wed & Fri 8:30-5, Sat 9-12
Friends of the Library Group

FRUITLAND PARK

P FRUITLAND PARK LIBRARY, 604 W Berckman St, 34731. SAN 302-9433. Tel: 352-360-6561. FAX: 352-278-9500. Web Site: www.fruitlandpark.org/library. *Dir,* Jo-Ann Glendinning; E-mail: JGlendinning@lakeline.lib.fl.us; Staff 5 (Non-MLS 5)
Founded 1936
Library Holdings: Bk Vols 37,000; Per Subs 35
Automation Activity & Vendor Info: (Acquisitions) SirsiDynix-WorkFlows; (Cataloging) SirsiDynix; (Circulation) SirsiDynix
Wireless access
Mem of Lake County Library System
Open Mon-Fri 10-4
Friends of the Library Group

GAINESVILLE

P ALACHUA COUNTY LIBRARY DISTRICT*, Headquarters Library, 401 E University Ave, 32601-5453. SAN 337-503X. Tel: 352-334-3900. Circulation Tel: 352-334-3950. Interlibrary Loan Service Tel: 352-334-3938. Reference Tel: 352-334-3939. Administration Tel: 352-334-3910. Automation Services Tel: 352-334-3998. FAX: 352-334-3918. Web Site: www.aclib.us. *Libr Dir,* Shaney T Livingston; E-mail: slivingston@aclib.us; *Asst to the Dir,* Devonia Andrew; E-mail: dandrew@aclib.us; *Div Dir, Admin Serv,* Michael D Durham; Tel: 352-334-3914, E-mail: mdurham@aclib.us; *Div Dir, Pub Serv,* Christine Culp; Tel: 352-334-3922, E-mail: cculp@aclib.us; *Human Res Dir,* Wantanisha Morant; Tel: 352-334-0158, E-mail: wmorant@aclib.us; *Auromated Serv Adminr,* Christopher Cochran; Tel: 352-334-3995, E-mail: ccochran@aclib.us; *Fac/Safety Serv Adminr,* Michael McLaughlin; Tel: 352-334-3915, E-mail: mmclaughlin@aclib.us; *Financial Serv Adminr,* Tamika A Gadson; Tel: 352-334-3913, E-mail: tgadson@aclib.us; *Pub Serv Adminr,* Phillis Filer; Tel: 352-334-3957, E-mail: pfiler@aclib.us; *Tech Serv Adminr,* Renee Patterson; Tel: 352-334-3960, Fax: 352-334-3999, E-mail: rpatterson@aclib.us; *E-Br Mgr,* Otto Pleil; Tel: 352-334-3936, E-mail: opleil@aclib.us; *Outreach Serv Mgr,* Alicia Antone; Tel: 352-334-3991, E-mail: aantone@aclib.us; *Pub Relations Mgr,* Rachel Cook; Tel: 352-334-3909, E-mail: rcook@aclib.us; *Pub Serv Adminr,* Joyce West; Tel: 352-334-3968, E-mail: jwest@aclib.us; *Youth Serv Sr Libr Mgr,* Susan Wright; Tel: 352-334-3947, E-mail: swright@aclib.us; Staff 58.5 (MLS 56.5, Non-MLS 2)
Founded 1906. Pop 257,062; Circ 4,289,325
Oct 2015-Sept 2016 Income (Main & Associated Libraries) $17,158,258, State $478,610, County $16,014,161, Locally Generated Income $37,773, Other $627,714. Mats Exp $1,902,343, Books $573,287, Per/Ser (Incl.

Access Fees) $106,727, Micro $4,620, AV Mat $383,135, Electronic Ref Mat (Incl. Access Fees) $834,574. Sal $10,288,988 (Prof $3,900,152)
Library Holdings: Audiobooks 23,286; AV Mats 173,778; Bks-By-Mail 1,809; Bks on Deafness & Sign Lang 442; Braille Volumes 283; CDs 38,876; DVDs 111,053; e-books 84,779; Electronic Media & Resources 104,946; High Interest/Low Vocabulary Bk Vols 5,386; Large Print Bks 16,555; Microforms 821; Bk Titles 265,246; Bk Vols 538,592; Per Subs 1,228; Spec Interest Per Sub 62; Videos 547
Special Collections: Digital Heritage Coll; Genealogy Coll; Local Government Documents (Gainesville, Alachua County, North Central Florida), bd doc, microfilm & minutes; Local History (Alachua County/Gainesville), a-tapes, index to local newsp, maps, pamphlets, photog & v-tapes; Snuggle Up Coll; Spanish Language Materials. Municipal Document Depository
Subject Interests: Genealogy
Automation Activity & Vendor Info: (Acquisitions) Innovative Interfaces, Inc; (Cataloging) Innovative Interfaces, Inc; (Circulation) Innovative Interfaces, Inc; (ILL) OCLC ILLiad; (OPAC) Innovative Interfaces, Inc; (Serials) Innovative Interfaces, Inc
Wireless access
Function: 24/7 Electronic res, 24/7 Online cat, Accelerated reader prog, Activity rm, Adult bk club, Adult literacy prog, After school storytime, Archival coll, Art exhibits, Audio & video playback equip for onsite use, Audiobks on Playaways & MP3, Audiobks via web, Bk club(s), Bk reviews (Group), Bks on cassette, Bks on CD, Children's prog, Computer training, Computers for patron use, E-Reserves, Electronic databases & coll, Family literacy, For res purposes, Free DVD rentals, Games & aids for people with disabilities, Govt ref serv, Holiday prog, Home delivery & serv to seniorr ctr & nursing homes, Homebound delivery serv, Homework prog, ILL available, Internet access, Jail serv, Life-long learning prog for all ages, Literacy & newcomer serv, Magazines, Magnifiers for reading, Mail & tel request accepted, Meeting rooms, Microfiche/film & reading machines, Movies, Music CDs, Online cat, Online ref, Orientations, Outreach serv, Outside serv via phone, mail, e-mail & web, OverDrive digital audio bks, Photocopying/Printing, Preschool outreach, Preschool reading prog, Prog for adults, Prog for children & young adult, Ref & res, Ref serv available, Senior computer classes, Senior outreach, Serves people with intellectual disabilities, Spanish lang bks, Spoken cassettes & CDs, Spoken cassettes & DVDs, Story hour, Study rm, Summer reading prog, Tax forms, Teen prog, Telephone ref, VHS videos, Wheelchair accessible, Workshops
Partic in Northeast Florida Library Information Network; PAL Library Cooperative
Special Services for the Deaf - ADA equip; Am sign lang & deaf culture; Assistive tech; Bks on deafness & sign lang; Closed caption videos; High interest/low vocabulary bks; Lecture on deaf culture; Sign lang interpreter upon request for prog; Staff with knowledge of sign lang; Video & TTY relay via computer
Special Services for the Blind - Accessible computers; Aids for in-house use; Assistive/Adapted tech devices, equip & products; Audio mat; Bks & mags in Braille, on rec, tape & cassette; Bks available with recordings; Bks on cassette; Bks on CD; Braille bks; Children's Braille; Computer access aids; Copier with enlargement capabilities; Descriptive video serv (DVS); Extensive large print coll; Free checkout of audio mat; Home delivery serv; Info on spec aids & appliances; Internet workstation with adaptive software; Large print & cassettes; Large print bks; Large print bks & talking machines; Large screen computer & software; Low vision equip; Magnifiers; Playaways (bks on MP3); Recorded bks; Ref serv; Screen enlargement software for people with visual disabilities; Sound rec; Talking bk & rec for the blind cat; Talking bk serv referral; Talking bks; Talking bks & player equip; Videos on blindness & physical disabilties; ZoomText magnification & reading software
Open Mon-Thurs 9:30-9, Fri 9:30-6, Sat 9:30-5, Sun 1-5
Restriction: Non-resident fee
Friends of the Library Group
Branches: 12
ALACHUA BRANCH, 14913 NW 140 St, Alachua, 32615, SAN 337-5048. Tel: 386-462-2592. FAX: 386-462-5537. Web Site: www.aclib.us/alachua. *Br Mgr,* Ross Woodbridge; E-mail: rwoodbridge@aclib.us
Open Mon-Thurs 11-7, Fri & Sat 11-5, Sun 1-5
Friends of the Library Group
ARCHER BRANCH, 13266 SW State Rd 45, Archer, 32618-5524, SAN 373-5680. Tel: 352-495-3367. FAX: 352-495-3061. Web Site: www.aclib.us/archer. *Br Mgr,* Taryn Brown; E-mail: tbrown@aclib.us
Open Mon-Thurs 10-7, Sun 1-5
Friends of the Library Group
CONE PARK BRANCH, 2801 E University Ave, 32641. Tel: 352-334-0720. FAX: 352-334-0310. Web Site: www.aclib.us/cone-park. *Br Mgr,* Diane Johnson; E-mail: djohnson@aclib.us
Open Mon-Thurs 10-6, Fri & Sat 10-5
Friends of the Library Group
HAWTHORNE BRANCH, 6640 SE 221 St, Hawthorne, 32640-3815, SAN 337-5064. Tel: 352-481-1920. FAX: 352-481-1921. Web Site: www.aclib.us/hawthorne. *Br Mgr,* Keith Harmon; E-mail: kharmon@aclib.us
Open Mon-Thurs 10-7, Fri-Sun 1-5
Friends of the Library Group
HIGH SPRINGS BRANCH, 23779 W US Hwy 27, High Springs, 32643, SAN 337-5099. Tel: 386-454-2515. FAX: 386-454-3439. Web Site: www.aclib.us/high-springs. *Br Mgr,* David Fuller; E-mail: dfuller@aclib.us
Open Mon, Wed & Fri 10-5, Tues & Thurs 10-8, Sat 10-2, Sun 1-5
Friends of the Library Group
LIBRARY PARTNERSHIP, 912 NE 16th Ave, 32601. Tel: 352-334-0165. FAX: 352-334-0167. Web Site: www.aclib.us/library-partnership. *Br Mgr,* Tina Bushnell; E-mail: tbushnell@aclib.us
Open Mon & Tues 9-6, Wed & Thurs 11-7, Fri 9-5, Sat 10-3
Friends of the Library Group
MICANOPY BRANCH, Micanopy Town Hall, 706 NE Cholokka Blvd, Micanopy, 32667-4113, SAN 337-5129. Tel: 352-466-3122. FAX: 352-466-3124. Web Site: www.aclib.us/micanopy. *Br Mgr,* Carolyn Wallace; E-mail: cwallace@aclib.us
Open Mon 11-7, Tues-Thurs 1-7, Sun 1-5
Friends of the Library Group
MILLHOPPER BRANCH, 3145 NW 43rd St, 32606-6107, SAN 373-5664. Tel: 352-334-1272. FAX: 352-334-1280. Web Site: www.aclib.us/millhopper. *Br Mgr,* Emily Young; E-mail: eyoung@aclib.us
Open Mon-Thurs 9:30-8:30, Fri & Sat 9:30-5, Sun 1-5
Friends of the Library Group
NEWBERRY BRANCH, 110 S Seaboard Dr, Newberry, 32669, SAN 373-5699. Tel: 352-472-1135. FAX: 352-472-1136. Web Site: www.aclib.us/newberry. *Br Mgr,* Marlin Day; E-mail: mday@aclib.us
Open Mon-Thurs 10-8, Fri & Sat 10-5, Sun 1-5
Friends of the Library Group
SHERIFF'S DEPARTMENT OF THE JAIL, 3333 NE 39th Ave, 32609-2699. (Mail add: 401 E University Ave, 32601), SAN 328-9672. Tel: 352-334-3991. FAX: 352-334-3994. *Outreach Serv Mgr,* David Fuller
Restriction: Not open to pub
Friends of the Library Group
TOWER ROAD BRANCH, 3020 SW 75th St, 32608, SAN 373-5672. Tel: 352-333-2840. FAX: 352-333-2846. Web Site: www.aclib.us/tower-road. *Sr Br Mgr,* Jodie Patterson; E-mail: jpatterson@aclib.us
Open Mon-Thurs 9:30-8:30, Fri & Sat 9:30-5, Sun 1-5
Friends of the Library Group
WALDO BRANCH, 14257 Cole St, Waldo, 32694, SAN 376-9178. Tel: 352-468-3298. FAX: 352-468-3299. Web Site: www.aclib.us/waldo. *Br Mgr,* Kerry Dowd; E-mail: kdowd@aclib.us
Open Mon-Thurs 12:30-7, Sun 1-5
Friends of the Library Group
Bookmobiles: 2. Sr Libr Spec, Geraldine Hall-Harris

S CENTER FOR APPLICATIONS OF PSYCHOLOGICAL TYPE*, Isabel Briggs Myers Memorial Library, 2815 NW 13th St, Ste 401, 32609. SAN 325-1683. Tel: 352-375-0160. FAX: 352-378-0503. E-mail: library@capt.org. Web Site: www.capt.org. *Research Librn,* Logan Abbitt; Staff 1 (MLS 1)
Founded 1975
Library Holdings: AV Mats 1,499; Bk Vols 1,680; Per Subs 11
Special Collections: Articles & Papers; Conference Proceedings; Dissertations & Theses
Subject Interests: Jungian psychol
Open Mon-Fri 9-5
Restriction: Not a lending libr

J CITY COLLEGE - GAINESVILLE LIBRARY*, 7001 NW Fourth Blvd, 32607. Tel: 352-335-4000, Ext 1429. FAX: 352-335-4303. Web Site: citycollege.libguides.com/content.php?pid=318874&sid=2609389. *Libr Dir,* Diane Colson; E-mail: dcolson@citycollege.edu
Highest Degree: Bachelor
Library Holdings: Bk Vols 6,600; Per Subs 15
Automation Activity & Vendor Info: (Cataloging) OCLC CatExpress; (Circulation) Follett Software
Wireless access
Function: ILL available, Online cat
Partic in LYRASIS
Open Mon-Thurs 8-8, Fri 8-5, Sat 9-1
Restriction: Borrowing privileges limited to fac & registered students

FIRST UNITED METHODIST CHURCH
R EPWORTH LIBRARY & SUSANNAH WESLEY MEDIA CENTER*, 419 NE First St, 32601, SAN 302-9476. Tel: 352-372-8523. FAX: 352-372-2524. Web Site: www.fumcgnv.org. *Library Contact,* Pat Jennings

Founded 1950
Library Holdings: Large Print Bks 25; Bk Vols 3,500
Subject Interests: Theol
Open Mon-Thurs 1-4:30, Sun 8:30-12

R LAURA KNIGHT CHILDREN'S LIBRARY*, 419 NE First St, 32601, SAN 320-9628. Tel: 352-372-8523. FAX: 352-372-2524. *Library Contact,* Joan Van Winkle
Founded 1978
Library Holdings: Bk Vols 630
Open Mon-Thurs 1-4:30

G FLORIDA DEPARTMENT OF AGRICULTURE & CONSUMER SERVICES*, Division of Plant Industry Library, 1911 SW 34th St, 32608. (Mail add: PO Box 147100, 32614-7100), SAN 302-9484. Tel: 352-395-4722. FAX: 352-395-4614. E-mail: dpi-library@freshfromflorida.com. Web Site: www.neflin.org/dpi. *Libr Spec,* Jeff Eby; E-mail: jeffrey.eby@freshfromflorida.com; Staff 1 (Non-MLS 1)
Founded 1915
Library Holdings: Bk Titles 17,000; Per Subs 300
Subject Interests: Entomology
Automation Activity & Vendor Info: (Cataloging) NOTIS
Function: Archival coll, Electronic databases & coll, For res purposes, Govt ref serv, ILL available, Internet access, Online cat, Outside serv via phone, mail, e-mail & web, Photocopying/Printing, Ref & res, Ref serv available, Res assist avail, Res libr, Scanner
Partic in Northeast Florida Library Information Network
Open Mon-Fri 8-5
Restriction: Access at librarian's discretion, Borrowing privileges limited to anthropology fac & libr staff, Borrowing requests are handled by ILL, Non-circulating of rare bks, Open to pub for ref only, Restricted borrowing privileges

GL JOHN A H MURPHREE LAW LIBRARY*, Alachua County Courthouse, Family/ Civil Justice Ctr, 201 E University Ave, Rm 413, 32601. Tel: 352-548-3781. Web Site: circuit8.org/law-library. *Dir,* Annemarie Schuller; E-mail: schullera@circuit8.org; *Library Contact,* Wendy Jenkins; Staff 1 (Non-MLS 1)
Founded 1957
Library Holdings: Bk Vols 10,000
Wireless access
Partic in Southeastern Chapter of the American Association of Law Libraries
Open Mon-Fri 8-5
Restriction: Non-circulating, Open to pub for ref only

J SANTA FE COLLEGE*, Lawrence W Tyree Library, 3000 NW 83rd St, Bldg Y, 32606. SAN 337-4971. Tel: 352-395-5409. Circulation Tel: 352-395-5412. Administration Tel: 352-381-3638. FAX: 352-395-5102. Administration FAX: 352-395-7326. E-mail: library@sfcollege.edu. Web Site: www.sfcollege.edu/library. *Interim Libr Dir,* Nance Lempinen-Leedy; Tel: 352-395-5256, E-mail: nance.lempinen-leedy@sfcollege.edu; *Ref Librn,* Diana Matthews; Tel: 352-395-5408, E-mail: diana.matthews@sfcollege.edu; *Ref Librn,* Jenna Miller; Tel: 352-395-5329, E-mail: jenna.miller@fscc.edu; *Ref Librn,* Ramona Miller-Ridlon; Tel: 352-381-3637, E-mail: ramona.miller-ridlon@sfcollege.edu; *Ref Librn,* Scott Tarbox; Tel: 352-395-5233, E-mail: scott.tarbox@sfcollege.edu; *Tech Serv Librn,* Trenita White; Tel: 352-395-5771, E-mail: trenita.white@sfcollege.edu; *Circ Supvr,* Sarah Ingley; Tel: 352-395-5411, E-mail: sarah.ingley@sfcollege.edu; *Evening Circ Supvr,* Mike Muhlhauser; Tel: 352-395-5937, E-mail: mike.muhlhauser@sfcollege.edu; Staff 13 (MLS 7, Non-MLS 6)
Founded 1966. Enrl 14,000; Fac 300; Highest Degree: Associate
Library Holdings: Bk Vols 86,470; Per Subs 435
Automation Activity & Vendor Info: (Acquisitions) Ex Libris Group; (Cataloging) Ex Libris Group; (Circulation) Ex Libris Group; (OPAC) Ex Libris Group; (Serials) Ex Libris Group
Wireless access
Partic in Northeast Florida Library Information Network
Open Mon-Thurs 7-7, Fri 7-4:30, Sun 12-8

GM UNITED STATES DEPARTMENT OF VETERANS AFFAIRS, Gainesville VA Medical Center, 1601 SW Archer Rd, 32608-1197. SAN 302-9506. Tel: 352-548-6316. FAX: 352-384-7609. Web Site: www.northflorida.va.gov/locations/gainesville.asp. *Supv Librn,* Lisa Huang; E-mail: lisa.huang@va.gov; Staff 4 (MLS 2, Non-MLS 2)
Founded 1967
Library Holdings: Bk Titles 7,000; Per Subs 350
Automation Activity & Vendor Info: (Acquisitions) LibraryWorld, Inc; (Cataloging) LibraryWorld, Inc; (Circulation) LibraryWorld, Inc; (Discovery) EBSCO Discovery Service; (OPAC) LibraryWorld, Inc; (Serials) SerialsSolutions
Wireless access
Partic in Northeast Florida Library Information Network; Veterans Affairs Library Network
Special Services for the Blind - Bks on CD
Open Mon-Fri 8-4:30

C UNIVERSITY OF FLORIDA LIBRARIES*, George A Smathers Libraries, 1545 W University Ave, 32611-7000. (Mail add: PO Box 117000, 32611-7000), SAN 337-5153. Tel: 352-273-2505. Circulation Tel: 352-273-2525. Interlibrary Loan Service Tel: 352-273-2535. Reference Tel: 352-273-2665. FAX: 352-392-7251. Interlibrary Loan Service FAX: 352-392-7598. Web Site: www.uflib.ufl.edu. *Dean, Univ Libr,* Judith C Russell; E-mail: jcrussell@ufl.edu; *Assoc Dean, Dir, Health Sci Ctr Libr,* Melissa Rethlefsen; Tel: 352-273-8404, E-mail: mlo.rethlefsen@ufl.edu; *Sr Assoc Dean,* Patrick J Reakes; E-mail: pjr@uflib.ufl.edu; *Assoc Dean, Digital Serv & Shared Coll,* Ben F Walker; Tel: 352-273-2545, E-mail: benwalk@uflib.ufl.edu; *Assoc Dean, Admin & Faculty Affairs,* Brian W Keith; Tel: 352-273-2595, Fax: 352-392-4538, E-mail: bwkeith@ufl.edu; *Chair, Humanities & Soc Sci Librn,* Jana Ronan; Tel: 352-273-2623, Fax: 352-392-8118, E-mail: jronan@ufl.edu; *Chair, Info Tech,* Todd Digby; E-mail: digby@ufl.edu; *Chair, Marston Sci Libr,* Val Minson; Tel: 352-273-2880, E-mail: vdavis@ufl.edu; *Chair, Spec & Area Studies Coll,* Haven Hawley; Tel: 352-273-2765, E-mail: ehh@ufl.edu; *Head, Access Serv, Head, Resource Sharing,* Lily Pang; Tel: 352-273-2910, E-mail: xpang@ufl.edu; *Coll Serv, Head, Acq,* Trey Shelton; Tel: 352-273-2700, E-mail: tshelton@ufl.edu; *Head, Archit & Fine Arts Libr,* Ann Lindell; Tel: 352-273-2805, Fax: 352-846-2747, E-mail: annlind@uflib.ufl.edu; *Head, Educ Libr,* Rachael Elrod; Tel: 352-273-2627, Fax: 352-392-4789, E-mail: relrod@ufl.edu; *Head, Fac & Security,* Peter Miller; Tel: 352-273-2578, Fax: 352-392-4507, E-mail: petmill@uflib.ufl.edu; *Head, Map & Imagery Libr,* Carol McAuliffe; Tel: 352-273-2825, Fax: 352-392-4787, E-mail: carolmc@uflib.ufl.edu; *Govt Doc Librn,* Sarah Erekson; Tel: 352-273-2635, E-mail: sarah.erekson@ufl.edu; *Grants Mgr,* Bess de Farber; Tel: 352-273-2519, E-mail: besdefa@uflib.ufl.edu; *ILL Coordr,* Melanie Davis; Tel: 352-273-2522, E-mail: davism@ufl.edu; *Digital Coll Curator,* Chelsea Dinsmore; Tel: 352-273-0369, Fax: 352-846-3702, E-mail: chedins@uflib.ufl.edu; Staff 265 (MLS 80, Non-MLS 185)
Founded 1853. Enrl 50,000; Fac 4,000; Highest Degree: Doctorate
Special Collections: African Studies Coll; Architecture Archives; Archives and Manuscripts; Baldwin-Historical Children's Literature; Harold & Mary Jean Hanson Rare Book Coll; Latin American and Caribbean Coll; Map & Imagery Library; P K Yonge Library of Florida History; Popular Culture; Price Library of Judaica; University Archives. State Document Depository; UN Document Depository; US Document Depository
Subject Interests: Archit, Educ, Fine arts, Humanities, Journalism, Sciences
Automation Activity & Vendor Info: (Acquisitions) Ex Libris Group; (Cataloging) Ex Libris Group; (Circulation) Ex Libris Group; (Course Reserve) Docutek; (ILL) OCLC ILLiad; (OPAC) Ex Libris Group; (Serials) Ex Libris Group
Wireless access
Function: Res libr
Publications: Chapter One; News from the Source (Biannually)
Partic in Association of Research Libraries; Consortium of Southern Biomedical Libraries; Northeast Florida Library Information Network
Special Services for the Deaf - Assisted listening device
Friends of the Library Group

CL UNIVERSITY OF FLORIDA LIBRARIES, Lawton Chiles Legal Information Center, Holland Law Ctr, 309 Village Dr, 32611. SAN 337-5420. Tel: 352-273-0700. Reference Tel: 352-273-0723. FAX: 352-392-5093. Web Site: guides.law.ufl.edu. *Assoc Dir,* Jane O'Connell; Tel: 352-273-0715, E-mail: janeoconnell@law.ufl.edu; *Asst Dir, Pub Serv,* Elizabeth Hilkin; Tel: 352-273-0702, E-mail: hilkin@lw.ufl.edu; Staff 27 (MLS 11, Non-MLS 16)
Founded 1909. Enrl 1,196; Fac 87; Highest Degree: Doctorate
Library Holdings: Bk Vols 600,000; Per Subs 5,437
Special Collections: Brazilian Law Coll; Great Britain Law Coll. State Document Depository; US Document Depository
Wireless access
Publications: Legal Bibliography; Library Handbook
Partic in Northeast Florida Library Information Network

GRACEVILLE

CR THE BAPTIST COLLEGE OF FLORIDA*, Ida J McMillan Library, 5400 College Dr, 32440-1833. SAN 302-9514. Tel: 850-263-3261, Ext 424. Toll Free Tel: 800-328-2660. Circulation Toll Free Tel: 800-328-2660, Ext 424. FAX: 850-263-5704. E-mail: library@baptistcollege.edu. Web Site: www.baptistcollege.edu/Library/page.asp?content=lib-home. *Asst to the Dir,* Elayna Peacock; E-mail: espeacock@baptistcollege.edu; Staff 2 (MLS 2)
Founded 1943. Highest Degree: Master
Library Holdings: Bk Vols 72,222; Per Subs 327
Special Collections: Baptist Coll; College Archives
Subject Interests: Educ, Humanities, Leadership, Music, Psychol, Relig

Automation Activity & Vendor Info: (Cataloging) OCLC; (OPAC) TLC (The Library Corporation)
Wireless access
Partic in OCLC Online Computer Library Center, Inc; Panhandle Library Access Network
Open Mon, Tues & Thurs 7:30am-10:30pm, Wed & Fri 7:30-4:30, Sat 10-4; Mon-Thurs (Summer) 8-4:30, Fri 8-Noon

GULF BREEZE

G UNITED STATES ENVIRONMENTAL PROTECTION*, Gulf Ecology Division Library, One Sabine Island Dr, 32561-5299. SAN 302-9530. Tel: 850-934-9318. E-mail: epalibrarynetwork@epa.gov. Web Site: www.epa.gov/libraries/ordnheerlgulf-ecology-division-library-services. *Libr I, Supvr,* Sonya M Doten; E-mail: doten.sonya@epa.gov; Staff 1 (MLS 1)
Founded 1967
Library Holdings: Bk Titles 6,750; Per Subs 15
Special Collections: Environmental Issues-Northwest Florida
Subject Interests: Environ analysis (water), Estuarine biol, Water pollution
Automation Activity & Vendor Info: (Cataloging) OCLC; (ILL) OCLC WorldShare Interlibrary Loan
Function: ILL available
Publications: Laboratory Publications Bibliography; Periodicals List
Partic in Federal Library & Information Center Committee
Open Mon-Thurs 7:30-4

GULFPORT

P GULFPORT PUBLIC LIBRARY, 5501 28th Ave S, 33707. SAN 302-9549. Tel: 727-893-1074. Reference Tel: 727-893-1073. FAX: 727-344-6386. E-mail: libraryinfo@mygulfport.us. Web Site: mygulfport.us/gpl. *Libr Dir,* Dave Mather; Tel: 727-893-1075, E-mail: dmather@mygulfport.us; *Librn,* Alex Hooks; E-mail: ahooks@mygulfport.us; *Ch,* Cailey Klasson; Tel: 727-893-1134, E-mail: cklasson@mygulfport.us; *Tech Serv,* Carol Parker; Tel: 727-893-1076, E-mail: cparker@mygulfport.us; Staff 14 (MLS 5, Non-MLS 9)
Founded 1935. Pop 12,000; Circ 115,894
Library Holdings: Bk Vols 70,000; Per Subs 100
Special Collections: Russian Books (popular)
Automation Activity & Vendor Info: (Cataloging) Innovative Interfaces, Inc; (Circulation) Innovative Interfaces, Inc; (OPAC) Innovative Interfaces, Inc
Wireless access
Mem of Pinellas Public Library Cooperative
Partic in Florida Library Information Network; Tampa Bay Library Consortium, Inc
Open Mon-Fri 10-7, Sat 10-4
Friends of the Library Group

CL STETSON UNIVERSITY COLLEGE OF LAW LIBRARY*, 1401 61st St S, 33707. SAN 338-0580. Tel: 727-562-7820. Reference Tel: 727-562-7821. FAX: 727-562-7678. E-mail: lawrefgp@law.stetson.edu. Web Site: libguides.law.stetson.edu. *Syst Adminr,* Jason Buckmelter; E-mail: jbuckmel@law.stetson.edu; Staff 16 (MLS 6, Non-MLS 10)
Founded 1901. Enrl 895; Fac 45; Highest Degree: Master
Library Holdings: Bk Titles 120,248; Bk Vols 398,443; Per Subs 4,061
Special Collections: US Document Depository
Automation Activity & Vendor Info: (Acquisitions) Innovative Interfaces, Inc; (Cataloging) Innovative Interfaces, Inc; (Circulation) Innovative Interfaces, Inc; (OPAC) Innovative Interfaces, Inc; (Serials) Innovative Interfaces, Inc
Wireless access
Partic in OCLC Online Computer Library Center, Inc; Tampa Bay Library Consortium, Inc

HAINES CITY

P HAINES CITY PUBLIC LIBRARY*, 111 N Sixth St, 33844. SAN 302-9557. Tel: 863-421-3633. Web Site: hainescity.com/171/Library. *Librn,* Mary Ellin Barrett; E-mail: MBarrett@hainescity.com; Staff 6 (MLS 1, Non-MLS 5)
Founded 1920. Pop 18,780
Library Holdings: Bk Titles 53,000; Per Subs 35
Special Collections: Florida Coll
Automation Activity & Vendor Info: (Cataloging) SirsiDynix; (Circulation) SirsiDynix; (ILL) OCLC FirstSearch
Wireless access
Partic in Polk County Libr Coop; Tampa Bay Library Consortium, Inc
Open Mon 10-7, Tues 10-8, Wed & Thurs 10-6, Fri 10-5, Sat 10-3

HIALEAH

§C FLORIDA NATIONAL UNIVERSITY LIBRARY, Hialeah Campus, 4425 W Jose Regueiro Ave, 33012. Tel: 305-821-3333, Ext 1020. E-mail: hllibrary@fnu.edu. Web Site: www.fnu.edu/library. *Libr Dir,* Ida Tomshinsky; E-mail: itomshinsky@fnu.edu; *Librn,* Maria E de la Cruz; E-mail: mcruz@fnu.edu
Wireless access
Function: Computers for patron use, Photocopying/Printing, Ref serv available
Partic in Southeast Florida Library Information Network, Inc
Open Mon-Fri 8am-9pm
Departmental Libraries:
SOUTH CAMPUS RESOURCE ROOM, 11865 SW 26th St, Unit H-3, Miami, 33175. Tel: 305-226-9999, Ext 1320. E-mail: sclibrary@fnu.edu. *Librn,* Martha Rodriguez; E-mail: mrodriguez@fnu.edu
Open Mon-Fri 8am-10pm

P HIALEAH PUBLIC LIBRARIES*, John F Kennedy Memorial Library, 190 W 49th St, 33012-3712. SAN 337-5633. Tel: 305-821-2700. FAX: 305-818-9144. E-mail: jfklib@hialeahfl.gov. Web Site: www.hialeahfl.gov/library. *Dir,* Grisel Torralbas; E-mail: gtorralbas@hialeahfl.gov; Staff 16 (MLS 6, Non-MLS 10)
Founded 1964
Special Collections: Cuba Coll; Florida Coll; Hialeah History Coll
Automation Activity & Vendor Info: (Cataloging) SirsiDynix; (Circulation) SirsiDynix; (OPAC) SirsiDynix
Wireless access
Function: 24/7 Electronic res, 24/7 Online cat, 3D Printer, Activity rm, Adult bk club, Adult literacy prog, After school storytime, Archival coll, Art exhibits, Art programs, Audio & video playback equip for onsite use, Audiobks via web, Bilingual assistance for Spanish patrons, Bk club(s), Bks on CD, Chess club, Children's prog, Citizenship assistance, Computer training, Computers for patron use, Electronic databases & coll, Family literacy, Free DVD rentals, Govt ref serv, Holiday prog, Internet access, Life-long learning prog for all ages, Literacy & newcomer serv, Magazines, Makerspace, Movies, Notary serv, Online cat, Online ref, Outreach serv, Photocopying/Printing, Preschool outreach, Preschool reading prog, Prog for adults, Prog for children & young adult, Ref serv available, Res assist avail, Scanner, Senior computer classes, Senior outreach, Spanish lang bks, STEM programs, Story hour, Study rm, Summer reading prog, Tax forms, Teen prog, Telephone ref, Wheelchair accessible, Workshops, Writing prog
Partic in Southeast Florida Library Information Network, Inc
Open Mon-Thurs Noon-8, Sat 9-5
Friends of the Library Group
Branches: 5
LUA CURTISS E-LIBRARY, 501 E Fourth Ave, 33010, SAN 337-5668. Tel: 305-883-6950. FAX: 305-863-2205.
Automation Activity & Vendor Info: (Cataloging) SirsiDynix; (Circulation) SirsiDynix; (OPAC) SirsiDynix
Function: 24/7 Electronic res, 24/7 Online cat, Activity rm, Audiobks via web, Bilingual assistance for Spanish patrons, Computer training, Computers for patron use, Electronic databases & coll, Internet access, Magazines, Online cat, Outreach serv, Photocopying/Printing, Ref serv available, Scanner, Senior computer classes, Spanish lang bks, Study rm, Summer reading prog, Tax forms, Telephone ref
Open Mon-Thurs 3pm-8pm
Friends of the Library Group
NORTH HIALEAH E-LIBRARY, 7400 W Tenth Ave, 33014. Tel: 305-816-4470. FAX: 305-816-4473.
Automation Activity & Vendor Info: (Cataloging) SirsiDynix; (Circulation) SirsiDynix; (Discovery) SirsiDynix; (OPAC) SirsiDynix
Function: 24/7 Electronic res, 24/7 Online cat, Audiobks via web, Bilingual assistance for Spanish patrons, Computers for patron use, Electronic databases & coll, Internet access, Magazines, Online cat, Outreach serv, Photocopying/Printing, Ref serv available, Scanner, Spanish lang bks, Summer reading prog, Tax forms, Telephone ref
Open Mon-Thurs 3pm-8pm
Friends of the Library Group
WALKER E-LIBRARY, 800 W 29th St, 33012. Tel: 305-883-6317. FAX: 305-883-6319.
Automation Activity & Vendor Info: (Cataloging) SirsiDynix; (Circulation) SirsiDynix; (Discovery) SirsiDynix; (OPAC) SirsiDynix
Function: 24/7 Electronic res, 24/7 Online cat, Audiobks via web, Bilingual assistance for Spanish patrons, Bks on CD, Computer training, Computers for patron use, Electronic databases & coll, Internet access, Magazines, Movies, Online cat, Outreach serv, Photocopying/Printing, Scanner, Senior computer classes, Spanish lang bks, Summer reading prog, Tax forms, Telephone ref
Open Mon-Thurs 3pm-8pm
Friends of the Library Group
WEST HIALEAH E-LIBRARY, 7400 W 24th Ave, 33016. Tel: 305-698-3615. FAX: 305-698-3604.
Automation Activity & Vendor Info: (Cataloging) SirsiDynix; (Circulation) SirsiDynix; (Discovery) SirsiDynix; (OPAC) SirsiDynix
Function: 24/7 Electronic res, 24/7 Online cat, Audiobks via web, Bilingual assistance for Spanish patrons, Bks on CD, Computers for patron use, Electronic databases & coll, Internet access, Magazines, Movies, Online cat, Outreach serv, Photocopying/Printing, Ref serv

available, Scanner, Spanish lang bks, Summer reading prog, Tax forms, Telephone ref
Open Mon-Thurs 3pm-8pm
Friends of the Library Group
WILDE E-LIBRARY, 1701 W 53rd Terrace, 33012. Tel: 305-818-9766. FAX: 305-818-9932. *Library Contact,* Position Currently Open
Automation Activity & Vendor Info: (Cataloging) SirsiDynix; (Circulation) SirsiDynix; (Discovery) SirsiDynix; (OPAC) SirsiDynix
Function: 24/7 Electronic res, 24/7 Online cat, Audiobks via web, Bilingual assistance for Spanish patrons, Computers for patron use, Electronic databases & coll, Internet access, Magazines, Movies, Online cat, Outreach serv, Photocopying/Printing, Prog for adults, Prog for children & young adult, Ref serv available, Scanner, Senior computer classes, Spanish lang bks, Summer reading prog, Tax forms, Telephone ref
Open Mon-Thurs 3pm-8pm
Friends of the Library Group

HIGHLAND BEACH

P HIGHLAND BEACH LIBRARY*, 3618 S Ocean Blvd, 33487. SAN 376-4990. Tel: 561-278-5455. FAX: 561-278-0156. Web Site: highlandbeach.us/departments/library. *Dir,* Lois Albertson; E-mail: lalbertson@highlandbeach.us; Staff 5 (MLS 2, Non-MLS 3)
Founded 1986
Special Collections: Florida Coll
Wireless access
Open Mon-Thurs 10-8, Fri 10-4:30, Sat 9-1
Friends of the Library Group

HOBE SOUND

CR HOBE SOUND BIBLE COLLEGE LIBRARY*, 11440 SE Gomez Ave, 33455-3378. (Mail add: PO Box 1065, 33475-1065), SAN 302-9603. Tel: 772-545-1400. FAX: 772-545-1422. E-mail: info@hsbc.edu. Web Site: www.hsbc.edu/academics/library. *Librn,* Phil Jones; Staff 2 (MLS 1, Non-MLS 1)
Founded 1960. Enrl 144; Fac 24; Highest Degree: Doctorate
Library Holdings: Bk Vols 36,000; Per Subs 220
Special Collections: Albert Burr Earth Sciences Coll; Child Evangelism Coll
Subject Interests: Humanities, Music
Automation Activity & Vendor Info: (Circulation) Follett Software
Wireless access
Open Mon, Tues & Thurs 8-4:45 & 6:30-10:30, Wed & Fri 8-4:45, Sat 1-4:45 & 7-10

HOLLYWOOD

M MEMORIAL HEALTHCARE SYSTEM*, Memorial Regional Hospital Knowledge Services Library, 3501 Johnson St, 33021. SAN 302-962X. Tel: 954-265-5840. FAX: 954-967-2951. Web Site: www.mhs.net. *Librn,* Sally E Haff; E-mail: shaff@mhs.net; Staff 1 (MLS 1)
Founded 1963
Library Holdings: Bk Titles 300; Per Subs 35
Subject Interests: Allied health, Clinical med
Partic in South Florida Health Sciences Library Consortium
Restriction: Clients only, Med staff only, Non-circulating

R TEMPLE BETH EL*, Billie Davis Rodenberg Memorial Library, 1351 S 14th Ave, 33020-6499. SAN 302-9638. Tel: 954-920-8225. FAX: 954-920-7026. E-mail: temple@tbehollywood.com. Web Site: templebethelhollywood.org. *Dir Learning Ctr,* Barbara Segal; E-mail: barbara@tbehollywood.com
Founded 1962
Library Holdings: Bk Titles 5,500
Subject Interests: Judaica (lit or hist of Jews)
Wireless access
Restriction: Mem only

HOMESTEAD

C MIAMI DADE COLLEGE*, Homestead Campus Library, 500 College Terrace, Bldg D, Rm D-101, 33030-6009. Tel: 305-237-5153. Web Site: www.mdc.edu/learning-resources/libraries. *Campus Libr Dir, Dir, Learning Res,* Lindsey Schriftman; Tel: 305-237-5245, E-mail: lschrift@mdc.edu
Library Holdings: Bk Titles 20,000; Per Subs 150
Automation Activity & Vendor Info: (Acquisitions) Ex Libris Group; (Cataloging) Ex Libris Group; (Circulation) Ex Libris Group; (Course Reserve) Ex Libris Group; (ILL) Ex Libris Group; (Media Booking) Ex Libris Group; (OPAC) Ex Libris Group; (Serials) Ex Libris Group
Open Mon-Thurs 7:30am-9pm, Fri 7:30-5, Sat 8-1

C UNIVERSITY OF FLORIDA, TROPICAL RESEARCH & EDUCATION CENTER, Institute of Food & Agricultural Sciences Library, 18905 SW 280th St, 33031. SAN 302-9662. Tel: 305-246-7000. FAX: 305-246-7003. Web Site: trec.ifas.ufl.edu. *Library Contact,* Dr Edward Evans; Tel: 786-217-9263, E-mail: eaevans@ufl.edu
Library Holdings: Bk Vols 4,000; Per Subs 71
Wireless access
Open Mon-Fri 8-5

HOWEY IN THE HILLS

P MARIANNE BECK MEMORIAL LIBRARY*, Howey-in-the-Hills Library, 112 W Central Ave, 34737. Tel: 352-324-0254. FAX: 352-324-1115. E-mail: howeylibrary@howey.org. Web Site: howeylibrary.org. *Chair,* Robert Latshaw; *Dir,* Tara Hall
Library Holdings: Audiobooks 100; DVDs 1,200; e-books 40; Large Print Bks 200; Bk Titles 12,000
Wireless access
Mem of Lake County Library System
Open Mon, Wed & Fri 10-5, Tues & Thurs 10-7, Sat 10-1
Friends of the Library Group

HUDSON

P PASCO COUNTY LIBRARY SYSTEM*, Administration & Support Services, 8012 Library Rd, 34667. SAN 324-8003. Tel: 727-861-3020. Reference Tel: 727-861-3040. FAX: 727-861-3025. Web Site: pascolibraries.org. *Libr Adminr,* Nancy Fredericks; E-mail: nancyfredericks@pascolibraries.org; *Libr Adminr,* Kevin Griffith; E-mail: keving@pascolibraries.org; *Libr Adminr,* Sean McGarvey; E-mail: seanm@pascolibraries.org; *Coll Develop Serv Mgr,* Dorothy Dibiasi
Founded 1980
Subject Interests: Fla
Automation Activity & Vendor Info: (Acquisitions) Koha; (Cataloging) Koha; (Circulation) Koha; (OPAC) Koha; (Serials) Koha
Wireless access
Function: 24/7 Electronic res, 24/7 Online cat, Activity rm, Adult bk club, Art exhibits, Audiobks on Playaways & MP3, Audiobks via web, Bk club(s), Bks on CD, Chess club, Children's prog, Computer training, Computers for patron use, Digital talking bks, E-Readers, Electronic databases & coll, Family literacy, Free DVD rentals, Govt ref serv, Holiday prog, ILL available, Internet access, Life-long learning prog for all ages, Magazines, Movies, Online cat, Online ref, Outreach serv, Outside serv via phone, mail, e-mail & web, OverDrive digital audio bks, Photocopying/Printing, Preschool outreach, Preschool reading prog, Prog for adults, Prog for children & young adult, Ref serv available, Senior computer classes, Senior outreach, Spanish lang bks, Spoken cassettes & CDs, Story hour, Study rm, Summer reading prog, Tax forms, Teen prog, Telephone ref, VHS videos, Wheelchair accessible, Workshops
Publications: Friends of Pasco County Newsletter; Friends Voices (Newsletter)
Member Libraries: Zephyrhills Public Library
Partic in LYRASIS; Tampa Bay Library Consortium, Inc
Special Services for the Deaf - Closed caption videos; Staff with knowledge of sign lang
Special Services for the Blind - Audio mat; Bks on CD; Large print bks
Open Mon-Fri 8-5
Friends of the Library Group
Branches: 7
CENTENNIAL PARK, 5740 Moog Rd, Holiday, 34690, SAN 370-3622. Tel: 727-834-3204. FAX: 727-834-3225. *Regional Br Mgr,* Mary Beth Isaacson; Staff 2 (MLS 2)
Founded 1986. Pop 117,988
Function: 24/7 Electronic res, Adult bk club, Audiobks on Playaways & MP3, Audiobks via web, Bk club(s), Bks on CD, Children's prog, Computer training, Computers for patron use, Electronic databases & coll, Free DVD rentals, Govt ref serv, Health sci info serv, ILL available, Internet access, Life-long learning prog for all ages, Magazines, Meeting rooms, Movies, Online cat, Online ref, Outreach serv, Outside serv via phone, mail, e-mail & web, OverDrive digital audio bks, Preschool outreach, Preschool reading prog, Prog for adults, Prog for children & young adult, Ref serv available, Scanner, Senior computer classes, Senior outreach, Spanish lang bks, Story hour, Summer reading prog, Tax forms, Teen prog, Telephone ref, Wheelchair accessible
Open Tues 10-8, Wed & Thurs 10-6, Fri & Sat 10-5
Friends of the Library Group
HUGH EMBRY BRANCH, 14215 Fourth St, Dade City, 33523, SAN 302-8992. Tel: 352-567-3576. FAX: 352-521-6670. *Regional Br Mgr,* Angelo Liranzo; Staff 2 (MLS 2)
Founded 1904. Pop 15,100
Function: Adult bk club, Audiobks on Playaways & MP3, Audiobks via web, AV serv, Bk club(s), Bks on CD, Children's prog, Citizenship assistance, Computers for patron use, Electronic databases & coll, Family literacy, Free DVD rentals, ILL available, Internet access, Life-long learning prog for all ages, Magazines, Meeting rooms, Microfiche/film & reading machines, Movies, Online cat, Online ref, Outreach serv, OverDrive digital audio bks, Photocopying/Printing, Preschool outreach, Preschool reading prog, Prog for adults, Prog for children & young adult,

Ref serv available, Senior outreach, Spoken cassettes & CDs, Story hour, Summer reading prog, Teen prog, Telephone ref, Wheelchair accessible
Open Mon & Wed 10-8, Tues & Thurs 10-6, Fri & Sat 10-5
Friends of the Library Group

HUDSON BRANCH LIBRARY, 8012 Library Rd, 34667, SAN 370-6257. Tel: 727-861-3040. FAX: 727-861-3025. *Div Mgr,* Lisa Morgan; *Br Mgr,* Katrina Rash; Staff 4 (MLS 4)
Founded 1990. Pop 69,919
Function: Adult bk club, Art exhibits, Audiobks on Playaways & MP3, Audiobks via web, Bk club(s), Bks on CD, Children's prog, Computers for patron use, Electronic databases & coll, Govt ref serv, Health sci info serv, ILL available, Internet access, Life-long learning prog for all ages, Magazines, Magnifiers for reading, Meeting rooms, Movies, Online cat, Online ref, Outreach serv, Outside serv via phone, mail, e-mail & web, Photocopying/Printing, Preschool outreach, Preschool reading prog, Prog for adults, Prog for children & young adult, Ref serv available, Scanner, Senior computer classes, Senior outreach, Spoken cassettes & CDs, Spoken cassettes & DVDs, Story hour, Study rm, Summer reading prog, Tax forms, Teen prog, Telephone ref, Wheelchair accessible
Special Services for the Blind - Audio mat; Bks on CD; Large print bks
Open Mon & Tues 10-6, Wed & Thurs 10-8, Fri & Sat 10-5
Friends of the Library Group

LAND O' LAKES BRANCH, 2818 Collier Pkwy, Land O'Lakes, 34639, SAN 370-6265. Tel: 813-929-1214. FAX: 813-929-1235. *Regional Br Mgr,* Kathleen Rothstein; *Br Mgr,* Robert Speich; Staff 5 (MLS 5)
Founded 1991. Pop 69,531
Function: 24/7 Electronic res, Adult bk club, Audiobks on Playaways & MP3, Audiobks via web, Bk club(s), Bks on CD, Children's prog, Computer training, Computers for patron use, Electronic databases & coll, Family literacy, Free DVD rentals, Govt ref serv, ILL available, Internet access, Life-long learning prog for all ages, Magazines, Meeting rooms, Movies, Online cat, Online ref, Outreach serv, Outside serv via phone, mail, e-mail & web, OverDrive digital audio bks, Photocopying/Printing, Preschool outreach, Preschool reading prog, Prog for adults, Prog for children & young adult, Ref serv available, Scanner, Senior computer classes, Senior outreach, Spanish lang bks, Story hour, Study rm, Summer reading prog, Tax forms, Telephone ref, Wheelchair accessible
Open Mon & Tues 10-8, Wed & Thurs 10-6, Fri & Sat 10-5
Friends of the Library Group

NEW RIVER, 34043 State Rd 54, Zephyrhills, 33543, SAN 371-3687. Tel: 813-788-6375. FAX: 813-788-6977. *Regional Br Mgr,* Angelo Liranzo; *Br Mgr,* Danielle Lee; Staff 2 (MLS 2)
Founded 1991. Pop 45,802
Function: 24/7 Electronic res, Adult bk club, Audiobks on Playaways & MP3, Audiobks via web, AV serv, Bk club(s), Bks on CD, Children's prog, Computer training, Computers for patron use, Electronic databases & coll, Govt ref serv, Health sci info serv, ILL available, Internet access, Life-long learning prog for all ages, Magazines, Meeting rooms, Movies, Online cat, Outreach serv, Outside serv via phone, mail, e-mail & web, OverDrive digital audio bks, Photocopying/Printing, Preschool outreach, Preschool reading prog, Prog for adults, Prog for children & young adult, Ref serv available, Senior computer classes, Senior outreach, Spanish lang bks, Story hour, Summer reading prog, Tax forms, Teen prog, Telephone ref, Wheelchair accessible
Open Tues 10-6, Wed 11-6, Thurs 10-8, Fri & Sat 10-5
Friends of the Library Group

REGENCY PARK, 9701 Little Rd, New Port Richey, 34654, SAN 370-6273. Tel: 727-861-3049. FAX: 727-861-3011. *Regional Br Mgr,* Tracy Blimes; *Br Mgr,* Mary Kate Downing; Staff 3 (MLS 3)
Founded 1990. Pop 99,243
Function: 24/7 Electronic res, Adult bk club, Audiobks on Playaways & MP3, Audiobks via web, AV serv, Bk club(s), Bks on CD, Children's prog, Computer training, Computers for patron use, Electronic databases & coll, Family literacy, Free DVD rentals, Govt ref serv, Health sci info serv, ILL available, Internet access, Life-long learning prog for all ages, Magazines, Meeting rooms, Movies, Online cat, Outreach serv, Outside serv via phone, mail, e-mail & web, OverDrive digital audio bks, Photocopying/Printing, Preschool outreach, Preschool reading prog, Prog for adults, Prog for children & young adult, Ref serv available, Scanner, Senior computer classes, Senior outreach, Spanish lang bks, Story hour, Study rm, Summer reading prog, Tax forms, Teen prog, Telephone ref, Wheelchair accessible
Open Mon & Tues 10-8, Wed & Thurs 10-6, Fri & Sat 10-5
Friends of the Library Group

SOUTH HOLIDAY BRANCH, 4649 Mile Stretch Rd, Holiday, 34690, SAN 371-3695. Tel: 727-834-3331. FAX: 727-942-6740. *Regional Br Mgr,* Mary Beth Isaacson; *Br Mgr,* Kim Nordon-Parks
Pop 103,113
Function: 24/7 Electronic res, Adult bk club, Audiobks on Playaways & MP3, Audiobks via web, AV serv, Bk club(s), Bks on CD, Children's prog, Computer training, Computers for patron use, Electronic databases & coll, Family literacy, Free DVD rentals, Govt ref serv, Health sci info serv, ILL available, Internet access, Life-long learning prog for all ages, Magazines, Magnifiers for reading, Meeting rooms, Movies, Online cat, Outreach serv, Outside serv via phone, mail, e-mail & web, OverDrive digital audio bks, Photocopying/Printing, Preschool outreach, Preschool reading prog, Prog for adults, Prog for children & young adult, Ref serv available, Scanner, Senior computer classes, Senior outreach, Spanish lang bks, Story hour, Summer reading prog, Tax forms, Teen prog, Telephone ref, VHS videos, Wheelchair accessible
Open Tues & Thurs 10-6, Wed 10-8, Fri & Sat 10-5
Friends of the Library Group

HURLBURT FIELD

A UNITED STATES AIR FORCE, Hurlburt Field Base Library, Base Library, 443 Cody Ave, 32544. SAN 337-3894. Tel: 850-884-6266, 850-884-6947. FAX: 850-884-6050. E-mail: hurlburtlibrary@yahoo.com. Web Site: www.hurlburtlibrary.org. *Libr Dir,* Megan Walters; Staff 5 (MLS 1, Non-MLS 4)
Founded 1955
Library Holdings: Bk Vols 20,000; Per Subs 50
Special Collections: Special Operations (Military)
Automation Activity & Vendor Info: (OPAC) SirsiDynix
Wireless access
Function: Bks on CD, STEM programs, Story hour, Study rm, Summer & winter reading prog
Publications: Selected Resources on Special Operations
Restriction: Authorized personnel only

INDIAN ROCKS BEACH

§P INDIAN ROCKS BEACH LIBRARY, 1507 Bay Palm Blvd, 33785. Tel: 727-596-1822. E-mail: indianrocksbeachlibrary@gmail.com. Web Site: www.indian-rocks-beach.com/irb_library.php. *Librn,* Lee Miller; E-mail: lmiller@irbcity.com
Automation Activity & Vendor Info: (Cataloging) Biblionix; (OPAC) Biblionix
Wireless access
Partic in Tampa Bay Library Consortium, Inc
Open Mon-Fri 10-4
Friends of the Library Group

INDIANTOWN

S MARTIN CORRECTIONAL INSTITUTION LIBRARY*, 1150 SW Allapattah Rd, 34956-4310. SAN 377-290X. Tel: 772-597-3705. FAX: 772-597-4529. *Librn,* Position Currently Open
Library Holdings: Bk Vols 19,152; Per Subs 79
Special Collections: Major Law Coll

JACKSONVILLE

S CUMMER MUSEUM OF ART & GARDENS LIBRARY*, 829 Riverside Ave, 32204. SAN 326-5846. Tel: 904-356-6857. FAX: 904-353-4101. Web Site: www.cummermuseum.org. *Chief Curator,* Holly Keris; E-mail: hkeris@cummermuseum.org
Founded 1961
Library Holdings: Bk Vols 15,000; Per Subs 43
Special Collections: European Porcelains
Subject Interests: Art hist
Restriction: Non-circulating to the pub

GL DUVAL COUNTY LAW LIBRARY*, 501 W Adams St, Rm 2291, 32202. SAN 302-9719. Tel: 904-255-1150. FAX: 904-255-1164. Web Site: www.jud4.org/Court-Services/Duval-County-Law-Library-1. *Dir,* Bud Maurer; E-mail: bmaurer@coj.net; *Asst Dir,* Tracey Murphy; E-mail: traceym@coj.net; Staff 8 (MLS 1, Non-MLS 7)
Founded 1939
Library Holdings: Bk Vols 47,000
Subject Interests: Fla, Law
Automation Activity & Vendor Info: (Cataloging) LibraryWorld, Inc; (Circulation) LibraryWorld, Inc
Wireless access
Open Mon-Fri 8-5

C THE EDWARD WATERS COLLEGE LIBRARY*, 1658 Kings Rd, 32209-6199. SAN 302-9727. Tel: 904-470-8080. Reference Tel: 904-470-8081. FAX: 904-470-8032. *Libr Dir,* Brenda M Harrell; E-mail: b.harrell@ewc.edu; *Circ Librn,* Michael A Wolfe; Tel: 904-470-8086, E-mail: michael.wol0911@ewc.edu; *Ref Librn,* Emma Kent; Tel: 904-470-8082, E-mail: emma.kent@ewc.edu; *Ref Librn,* Alicisa Nelson; Tel: 904-470-8084, E-mail: a.nelson@ewc.edu; *Cataloger, Tech Asst,* Gwen Gatson; Tel: 904-470-8083, E-mail: ggatson@ewc.edu; Staff 5 (MLS 4, Non-MLS 1)
Founded 1945. Enrl 900; Fac 49; Highest Degree: Bachelor
Library Holdings: AV Mats 1,000; Bk Titles 17,000; Per Subs 60
Special Collections: Afro-American
Wireless access

Function: AV serv, ILL available, Photocopying/Printing, Ref serv available, Wheelchair accessible
Open Mon-Fri 8am-9pm, Sat & Sun 2-6

CL FLORIDA COASTAL SCHOOL OF LAW*, Library & Technology Center, 8787 Baypine Rd, 32256. SAN 378-4266. Tel: 904-680-7600. Interlibrary Loan Service Tel: 904-680-7611. Reference Tel: 904-680-7612. Administration Tel: 904-680-7604. FAX: 904-680-7677. E-mail: refdesk@fcsl.edu. Web Site: www.fcsl.edu/library.html. *Assoc Dean of Libr & Tech,* Ms Korin Munsterman; Tel: 904-680-7601, E-mail: kmunsterman@fcsl.edu; *Libr Coord,* Stephanie Hughes; E-mail: shughes@fcsl.edu; Staff 7 (MLS 7)
Founded 1996. Enrl 1,000; Fac 42; Highest Degree: Doctorate
Library Holdings: AV Mats 191; Bk Titles 21,566; Bk Vols 139,432; Per Subs 3,139
Automation Activity & Vendor Info: (Acquisitions) Innovative Interfaces, Inc; (Cataloging) Innovative Interfaces, Inc; (Circulation) Innovative Interfaces, Inc; (Course Reserve) Innovative Interfaces, Inc; (OPAC) Innovative Interfaces, Inc; (Serials) Innovative Interfaces, Inc
Wireless access
Function: ILL available, Ref serv available
Partic in LYRASIS
Restriction: Not open to pub

C FLORIDA STATE COLLEGE AT JACKSONVILLE*, Kent Campus Library & Learning Commons, 3939 Roosevelt Blvd, C-100, 32205. SAN 337-5846. Tel: 904-381-3522. Reference Tel: 904-381-3545. FAX: 904-381-3579. Web Site: guides.fscj.edu/KentCampus, www.fscj.edu/student-services/student-resources/llc. *Dir, Libr Serv, Libr Mgr,* Victoria McGlone, PhD; E-mail: victoria.mcglone@fscj.edu; *Librn,* Sharon Uskokovich; Staff 1 (MLS 1)
Founded 1966
Wireless access
Partic in Florida Library Information Network; Northeast Florida Library Information Network
Open Mon-Thurs 7:30am-9pm, Fri & Sat 8-3
Friends of the Library Group

Departmental Libraries:

DEERWOOD CENTER LIBRARY, 9911 Old Baymeadows Rd, 32256. Tel: 904-997-2562. Web Site: guides.fscj.edu/Open. *Dir, Online Library Servs,* Shannon Dew; *Libr Mgr,* Peggi Patrick; *Fac Librn,* Barbara Markham; *Adjunct Librn,* Lea Cason; Staff 2 (MLS 1, Non-MLS 1)
Founded 2000. Enrl 9,337; Highest Degree: Associate
Library Holdings: Bk Titles 13,709; Per Subs 120
Automation Activity & Vendor Info: (ILL) Ex Libris Group; (Media Booking) Ex Libris Group; (Serials) Ex Libris Group
Function: ILL available
Partic in LINCC
Open Mon-Thurs 8-8, Fri 8-2, Sat 9-1

DOWNTOWN CAMPUS LIBRARY & LEARNING COMMONS, 101 W State St, Bldg A, Rm A-2102 & A-3040, 32202-3056, SAN 337-5811. Tel: 904-633-8368. Reference Tel: 904-633-8169. Web Site: guides.fscj.edu/downtown. *Mgr,* Nick Bodnar; *Librn,* Sheri Brown; Tel: 904-633-8414, E-mail: sheri.a.brown@fscj.edu; *Pub Serv Coordr,* Jennifer Grey
Library Holdings: Bk Vols 50,000; Per Subs 285
Open Mon-Thurs 7:45am-8pm, Fri 7:45-3, Sat 9-3

NASSAU CENTER LIBRARY & LEARNING COMMONS, 76346 William Burgess Blvd, Yulee, 32097. Tel: 904-548-4467. Web Site: guides.fscj.edu/nassau. *Dir,* Youlanda Henry; *Fac Librn,* Melonee Slocum; *Libr Mgr,* Patrick Bertram
Open Mon-Thurs 8-6, Fri 8-12

NORTH CAMPUS & LEARNING COMMONS, 4501 Capper Rd, 32218-4499, SAN 337-5870. Tel: 904-766-6717. Reference Tel: 904-766-6635. Administration Tel: 904-766-6765. Web Site: guides.fscj.edu/North. *Dir,* Youlanda Henry; *Librn,* Mary Dumbleton; *Mgr,* Susan Mythen; Staff 3 (MLS 3)
Enrl 7,700; Highest Degree: Bachelor
Library Holdings: Bk Vols 38,000; Per Subs 325
Open Mon-Thurs 7:30am-9pm, Fri 7:30-4 Sat 7:30-2

SOUTH CAMPUS LIBRARY & LEARNING COMMONS, 11901 Beach Blvd, 32246-6624, SAN 337-5781. Tel: 904-646-2174. Web Site: guides.fscj.edu/SouthCampusLLC. *Exec Dean,* Tom Messner; E-mail: tom.messner@fscj.edu; *Librn,* Emily O'Neil; *Libr Mgr,* Trina McCowan
Library Holdings: AV Mats 7,200; Bk Vols 79,531; Per Subs 523
Open Mon-Thurs 7:30am-9pm, Fri 7:30-3, Sat 8-3, Sun 1-5

J ITT TECHNICAL INSTITUTE*, Learning Resource Center, 7011 A C Skinner Pkwy, Ste 140, 32256. Tel: 904-573-9100, Ext 135. Toll Free Tel: 800-318-1264. FAX: 904-573-0512. Web Site: www.itt-tech.edu. *Librn,* Position Currently Open; Staff 2 (MLS 1, Non-MLS 1)
Founded 1991. Enrl 600; Fac 30; Highest Degree: Bachelor
Library Holdings: AV Mats 2,000; e-books 20,000; Bk Vols 7,000; Per Subs 45
Automation Activity & Vendor Info: (Cataloging) Follett Software; (Circulation) Follett Software
Wireless access
Partic in Fla Libr Asn
Open Mon-Fri 8am-10:30pm, Sat 8-2

P JACKSONVILLE PUBLIC LIBRARY, 303 N Laura St, 32202-3505. SAN 337-5935. Tel: 904-630-2665. Circulation Tel: 904-630-1984. Interlibrary Loan Service Tel: 904-630-2986. Reference Tel: 904-630-1962. Administration Tel: 904-630-1994. Administration FAX: 904-630-1343. E-mail: libdir@coj.net. Web Site: jaxpubliclibrary.org. *Libr Dir,* Tim Rogers; *Dep Dir, Admin & Finance,* Chuck McNeil; Tel: 904-630-1171, E-mail: cmcneil@coj.net; *Asst Dir, Commun Relations & Mkt,* Christian Boivin; Tel: 904-630-7595, E-mail: cboivin@coj.net; *Asst Dir, Learning Res,* Amber Holley; Tel: 904-630-2982, E-mail: amberh@coj.net; *Asst Dir, Pub Serv,* Julie McNeil; Tel: 904-630-1181, E-mail: jmcneil@coj.net; *Asst Dir, Support Serv,* Gretchen Mitchell; Tel: 904-630-1666, E-mail: gmitch@coj.net; *Mgr, Strategic Initiatives,* Richard Mott; Tel: 904-630-2407, E-mail: rmott@coj.net; *Bibliog Syst & Access Mgr,* Lynn Jacobson; Tel: 904-630-1318, E-mail: jacobson@coj.net; Staff 189 (MLS 44, Non-MLS 145)
Founded 1903. Pop 879,602; Circ 508,984
Oct 2015-Sept 2016 Income (Main & Associated Libraries) $33,469,084, State $1,024,351, County $32,194,512, Locally Generated Income $250,221. Mats Exp $3,718,047, Books $2,118,546, Other Print Mats $433,797, AV Equip $26,000, AV Mat $500, Electronic Ref Mat (Incl. Access Fees) $1,139,204. Sal $12,126,212 (Prof $16,969,679)
Library Holdings: AV Mats 307,487; CDs 154,155; DVDs 149,154; e-books 13,400; Electronic Media & Resources 58,918; Microforms 39,941; Bk Vols 1,864,057; Per Subs 2,826; Spec Interest Per Sub 3; Talking Bks 64,986; Videos 2,317
Special Collections: African-American Coll; Delius Coll, mss,music, secondary sources; Digital Library Coll; Florida Coll; Genealogy Coll, Southeast Region; Holocaust Coll; Lewis Ansbacher Map Coll; Nonprofit Resources. State Document Depository; US Document Depository
Automation Activity & Vendor Info: (Acquisitions) SirsiDynix; (Cataloging) SirsiDynix; (Circulation) SirsiDynix; (ILL) OCLC; (OPAC) SirsiDynix; (Serials) SirsiDynix
Wireless access
Function: 24/7 Electronic res, 24/7 Online cat, Activity rm, Adult bk club, Adult literacy prog, After school storytime, Archival coll, Art exhibits, Audiobks via web, Bilingual assistance for Spanish patrons, Bk club(s), Bks on cassette, Bks on CD, Children's prog, Citizenship assistance, Computer training, Computers for patron use, E-Reserves, Electronic databases & coll, Free DVD rentals, Govt ref serv, Holiday prog, Homework prog, ILL available, Internet access, Learning ctr, Literacy & newcomer serv, Microfiche/film & reading machines, Music CDs, Online cat, Online ref, Outreach serv, OverDrive digital audio bks, Photocopying/Printing, Preschool outreach, Prog for adults, Prog for children & young adult, Ref serv available, Spanish lang bks, Spoken cassettes & CDs, Spoken cassettes & DVDs, Summer reading prog, Tax forms, Teen prog, Telephone ref, VHS videos, Wheelchair accessible
Publications: All About E-Services (Brochure); Annual Report; Center for Adult Learning (Brochure); Discovery Awaits Online (Brochure); E-newsletter (Monthly); Find a Job, Start a Business (Brochure); GET CARDED (Brochure); Jean Ribault Mural (Brochure); Quarterly Update; Special Collections (Brochure); The Conference Center (Brochure); Traveling Tales (Brochure); Youth Services for Educators (Brochure); Youth Services for Parents & Caregivers (Brochure)
Partic in Fla Computer Catalogue of Monographic Holdings; Northeast Florida Library Information Network; OCLC Online Computer Library Center, Inc; Urban Libraries Council
Special Services for the Deaf - Closed caption videos
Special Services for the Blind - Talking bks
Restriction: Borrowing requests are handled by ILL
Friends of the Library Group

Branches: 21

ARGYLE BRANCH, 7973 Old Middleburg Rd S, 32222-1817. Tel: 904-573-3164. FAX: 904-573-3162. *Br Mgr,* Kristi Dorney; Staff 12 (MLS 2, Non-MLS 10)
Circ 224,369
Library Holdings: Bk Vols 55,625
Open Tues & Thurs 1-9, Wed, Fri & Sat 10-6

BEACHES BRANCH, 600 Third St, Neptune Beach, 32266-5014, SAN 337-6087. Tel: 904-241-1141. FAX: 904-241-4965. *Br Mgr,* Position Currently Open; Staff 15 (MLS 3, Non-MLS 12)
Circ 343,398
Library Holdings: Bk Vols 92,477
Special Collections: Joe Gill Business Coll
Open Tues & Wed 1-9, Thurs-Sat 10-6
Friends of the Library Group

BRADHAM-BROOKS NORTHWEST BRANCH, 1755 Edgewood Ave W, 32208-7206, SAN 371-4748. Tel: 904-765-5402. FAX: 904-768-7609. *Br Mgr,* Laura Minor; Staff 11 (MLS 2, Non-MLS 9)
Circ 71,300

Library Holdings: Bk Vols 44,216
Open Mon, Tues, Fri & Sat 10-6, Wed & Thurs 1-9
Friends of the Library Group
BRENTWOOD BRANCH, 3725 Pearl St, 32206-6401, SAN 337-6141. Tel: 904-630-0924. FAX: 904-630-0441. *Br Mgr,* Kathleen Krizek; Staff 7 (MLS 2, Non-MLS 5)
Circ 60,821
Library Holdings: Bk Vols 11,745
Open Mon & Thurs Noon-8, Tues, Wed, Fri & Sat 10-6
Friends of the Library Group
RAIFORD A BROWN EASTSIDE BRANCH, 1390 Harrison St, 32206-5324, SAN 337-6028. Tel: 904-630-5466. FAX: 904-630-5463. *Br Mgr,* Gray Phenessa; Staff 6 (MLS 1, Non-MLS 5)
Circ 19,713
Library Holdings: Bk Vols 8,903
Open Mon & Tues Noon-8, Wed-Sat 10-6
DALLAS JAMES GRAHAM BRANCH, 2304 N Myrtle Ave, 32209-5099, SAN 337-5994. Tel: 904-630-0922. FAX: 904-630-0439. *Br Mgr,* Susan Arthur; Staff 7 (MLS 2, Non-MLS 5)
Circ 64,793
Library Holdings: Bk Vols 20,945
Open Mon, Wed, Fri & Sat 10-6, Tues & Thurs Noon-8
Friends of the Library Group
HIGHLANDS BRANCH, 1826 Dunn Ave, 32218-4712, SAN 325-416X. Tel: 904-757-7702. FAX: 904-696-4328. *Br Mgr,* Pat Morrison; Staff 21 (MLS 5, Non-MLS 16)
Circ 270,909
Library Holdings: Bk Vols 97,920
Open Mon, Tues & Thurs 1-9, Wed, Fri & Sat 10-6
MANDARIN BRANCH, 3330 Kori Rd, 32257-5454, SAN 328-7254. Tel: 904-262-5201. FAX: 904-292-1029. *Br Mgr,* Theresa Rooney; Staff 15 (MLS 3, Non-MLS 12)
Circ 370,880
Library Holdings: Bk Vols 93,381
Open Mon, Thurs & Sat 10-6, Tues & Wed 1-9
MAXVILLE BRANCH, 8375 Maxville Rd, 32234-2748. Tel: 904-289-7563. FAX: 904-289-9285. *Br Mgr,* Sharon Kirkes
Circ 22,706
Library Holdings: Bk Vols 20,519
Open Mon, Wed & Sat 10-6, Tues & Thurs Noon-8
Friends of the Library Group
MURRAY HILL BRANCH, 918 Edgewood Ave S, 32205-5341, SAN 337-6117. Tel: 904-384-2665. FAX: 904-381-1104. *Br Mgr,* Guy Adkins; Staff 8 (MLS 2, Non-MLS 6)
Circ 103,358
Library Holdings: Bk Vols 27,539
Open Tues & Wed 1-9, Thurs-Sat 10-6
Friends of the Library Group
PABLO CREEK REGIONAL, 13295 Beach Blvd, 32246-7259. Tel: 904-992-7101. FAX: 904-992-3987. *Br Mgr,* Jackie Spiritas; Staff 24 (MLS 6, Non-MLS 18)
Circ 579,307
Library Holdings: Bk Vols 127,423
Open Mon, Wed & Thurs 1-9, Tues, Fri & Sat 10-6
REGENCY SQUARE BRANCH, 9900 Regency Square Blvd, 32225-6539. Tel: 904-726-5142. FAX: 904-726-5153. TDD: 904-726-5152. *Br Mgr,* Donna Carroll; Staff 18 (MLS 3, Non-MLS 15)
Circ 330,218
Library Holdings: Bk Vols 85,580
Special Services for the Deaf - TDD equip
Open Mon, Tues, Fri & Sat 10-6, Wed & Thurs 1-9
SAN MARCO BRANCH, 1513 LaSalle St, 32207-8653, SAN 337-6206. Tel; 904-858-2907. FAX: 904-306-2182. *Br Mgr,* Lilia Simonton; Staff 10 (MLS 2, Non-MLS 8)
Circ 166,098
Library Holdings: Bk Vols 42,947
Open Tues & Thurs 1-9, Wed, Fri & Sat 10-6
SOUTH MANDARIN BRANCH, 12125 San Jose Blvd, 32223-2636. Tel: 904-288-6385. FAX: 904-288-6399. *Br Mgr,* Ann Fridl; Staff 15 (MLS 2, Non-MLS 13)
Circ 354,897
Library Holdings: Bk Vols 81,420
Open Tues, Fri & Sat 10-6, Wed & Thurs 1-9
Friends of the Library Group
SOUTHEAST REGIONAL, 10599 Deerwood Park Blvd, 32256-0507, SAN 377-6204. Tel: 904-996-0325. FAX: 904-996-0340. *Br Mgr,* Erica Brown; Staff 24 (MLS 5, Non-MLS 19)
Circ 562,804
Library Holdings: Bk Vols 147,868
Open Mon, Tues & Thurs 1-9, Wed, Fri & Sat 10-6

P TALKING BOOKS FOR THE BLIND & PHYSICALLY HANDICAPPED, 303 N Laura St, Conference Level, 32202, SAN 375-5770. Tel: 904-630-1999. *Talking Bks Libr Mgr,* Janet Ducat; Staff 6 (MLS 2, Non-MLS 4)
Founded 1974. Circ 100,078
Library Holdings: DVDs 619; Per Subs 3; Talking Bks 64,896
Function: Writing prog
Special Services for the Blind - Assistive/Adapted tech devices, equip & products; Computer with voice synthesizer for visually impaired persons
Open Mon-Fri 9-6
UNIVERSITY PARK BRANCH, 3435 University Blvd N, 32277-2464. Tel: 904-630-1265. FAX: 904-744-6892. *Br Mgr,* Sandra Ostroski; Staff 14 (MLS 3, Non-MLS 11)
Circ 250,667
Library Holdings: Bk Vols 60,265
Open Mon, Thurs, Fri & Sat 10-6, Tues & Wed 1-9
CHARLES WEBB WESCONNETT REGIONAL, 6887 103rd St, 32210-6897, SAN 337-6230. Tel: 904-778-7305. FAX: 904-777-2262. *Br Mgr,* Kathy Tekin; Staff 23 (MLS 5, Non-MLS 18)
Circ 386,847
Library Holdings: Bk Vols 91,436
Open Mon, Wed & Thurs 1-9, Tues, Fri & Sat 10-6
WEST REGIONAL, 1425 Chaffee Rd S, 32221-1119. Tel: 904-693-1448. FAX: 904-693-1470. *Br Mgr,* Sharon Kirkes; Staff 18 (MLS 3, Non-MLS 15)
Circ 295,619
Library Holdings: Bk Vols 140,540
Open Tues & Wed 1-9, Thurs, Fri & Sat 10-6
WESTBROOK BRANCH, 2809 Commonwealth Ave, 32254-2599, SAN 337-596X. Tel: 904-384-7424. FAX: 904-381-1107. *Br Mgr,* Susan Arthur; Staff 6 (MLS 1, Non-MLS 5)
Founded 1959. Circ 39,844
Library Holdings: Bk Vols 8,818
Open Mon, Wed, Fri & Sat 10-6, Tues & Thurs Noon-8
WILLOWBRANCH BRANCH, 2875 Park St, 32205-8099, SAN 337-6265. Tel: 904-381-8490. FAX: 904-381-8495. *Br Mgr,* Scott Adams; Staff 10 (MLS 2, Non-MLS 8)
Circ 103,647
Library Holdings: Bk Vols 23,351
Open Tues, Fri & Sat 10-6, Wed & Thurs 1-9
Friends of the Library Group

C JACKSONVILLE UNIVERSITY*, Carl S Swisher Library, 2800 University Blvd N, 32211-3394. SAN 302-976X. Tel: 904-256-7277. Interlibrary Loan Service Tel: 904-256-7275. Reference Tel: 904-256-7263. Administration Tel: 904-256-7267. E-mail: library@ju.edu. Web Site: library.ju.edu, www.ju.edu/library. *Libr Dir,* Jessica M Collogan; E-mail: jcollog@ju.edu; *Access Serv Librn,* Allison Crowford; Tel: 904-256-7934, E-mail: acrowfo4@ju.edu; *Circ Serv Mgr,* Julia McKenna; Tel: 904-256-7944, E-mail: jmckenn1@ju.edu; *Coll Develop Librn,* Paula McIntyre; Tel: 904-256-7265, E-mail: pmcinty@ju.edu; *Ref & Instruction Librn,* Nancy Tucker; Tel: 904-256-7266, E-mail: ntucker2@ju.edu; Staff 13 (MLS 5, Non-MLS 8)
Founded 1934. Enrl 3,400; Fac 242; Highest Degree: Master
Library Holdings: Bks on Deafness & Sign Lang 114; CDs 6,051; DVDs 801; e-books 68,972; e-journals 51,959; Electronic Media & Resources 2,571; Music Scores 9,197; Bk Vols 273,986; Per Subs 350; Videos 616
Special Collections: Delius Coll; Jacksonville Historical Society Archives; Jacksonville University Archives; Rare Books. State Document Depository; US Document Depository
Subject Interests: Bus, Educ, Fine arts, Liberal arts, Nursing, Orthodontics
Automation Activity & Vendor Info: (Acquisitions) Ex Libris Group; (Cataloging) Ex Libris Group; (Circulation) Ex Libris Group; (Course Reserve) Ex Libris Group; (ILL) OCLC WorldShare Interlibrary Loan; (OPAC) Ex Libris Group; (Serials) EBSCO Online
Wireless access
Function: Telephone ref
Partic in Florida Library Information Network; LYRASIS; Northeast Florida Library Information Network; OCLC Online Computer Library Center, Inc
Open Mon-Thurs 7:30am-11pm, Fri 7:30-5, Sat 9-5, Sun 2-10
Friends of the Library Group

CR TRINITY BAPTIST COLLEGE LIBRARY*, 800 Hammond Blvd, 32221. Tel: 904-596-2508. Administration Tel: 904-596-2507. Web Site: www.tbc.edu/library. *Dir,* Dr John Lucy; E-mail: jlucy@tbc.edu; *Asst Librn,* Janice Claxton; E-mail: jclaxton@tbc.edu; Staff 2 (MLS 1, Non-MLS 1)
Founded 1974. Enrl 469; Fac 41; Highest Degree: Master
Library Holdings: Bks on Deafness & Sign Lang 50; CDs 185; DVDs 240; e-books 365; Music Scores 50; Bk Vols 35,000; Per Subs 120; Videos 690
Subject Interests: Baptist hist, Educ, Relig
Automation Activity & Vendor Info: (Acquisitions) A-G Canada Ltd; (Cataloging) Book Systems; (Circulation) Follett Software; (OPAC) Follett Software
Wireless access
Partic in Library & Information Resources Network; Northeast Florida Library Information Network
Open Mon, Tues, Thurs & Fri 8am-10pm, Wed 8-5, Sat Noon-6

A UNITED STATES ARMY, Corps of Engineers Technical Library, 701 San Marco Blvd, Rm 430-W, 32207. (Mail add: PO Box 4970, 32232-0019), SAN 337-629X. Tel: 904-232-3643. FAX: 904-232-1838. *Librn,* Oriana B Armstrong; E-mail: oriana.b.armstrong@usace.army.mil; Staff 1 (MLS 1)
Founded 1978
Library Holdings: Bk Vols 27,000; Per Subs 400
Special Collections: Cross Florida Barge Canal Study
Subject Interests: Civil engr, Construction, Engr, Recreation, Sci tech
Automation Activity & Vendor Info: (Cataloging) OCLC; (ILL) OCLC
Wireless access
Partic in Legislate; LePac; OCLC Online Computer Library Center, Inc; Proquest Dialog
Open Mon-Fri 6:30am-3pm

M UNIVERSITY OF FLORIDA HEALTH SCIENCE CENTER-JACKSONVILLE*, Borland Health Sciences Library, 653-1 W Eighth St, 32209-6511. SAN 302-9751. Tel: 904-244-3240. Web Site: borland.ufl.edu. *Dir,* Gretchen Kuntz; Tel: 904-244-2143, E-mail: gkuntz@ufl.edu; *Sr Libr Tech,* Cynthia Ellison; Tel: 904-244-2155, E-mail: cellison@ufl.edu; Staff 5 (MLS 3, Non-MLS 2)
Founded 1961
Library Holdings: Bk Vols 6,000; Per Subs 560
Special Collections: Florida Public Health History
Subject Interests: Allied health, Dentistry, Med, Nursing
Wireless access
Open Mon-Fri 8-5

C UNIVERSITY OF NORTH FLORIDA*, Thomas G Carpenter Library, Bldg 12-Library, One UNF Dr, 32224-2645. SAN 320-9385. Tel: 904-620-2615. Administration Tel: 904-620-2553. FAX: 904-620-2719. Web Site: www.unf.edu/library. *Dean of Libr,* Brent Mai; E-mail: brent.mai@unf.edu; *Dir, Pub Serv,* Thomas Caswell; Tel: 904-620-5455, E-mail: t.caswell@unf.edu; *Dir, Libr Syst & Tech Serv,* Jennifer Murray; Tel: 904-620-5160, E-mail: jennifer.murray@unf.edu; *Head of Instruction,* Laura Newton; *Head, Acq & Coll Develop,* Apryl Price; Tel: 904-620-1516, E-mail: a.price@unf.edu; *Head, Digital Projects, Head, Presv,* Coutenay McLeland; *Head, Discovery Serv,* Susan Massey; *Head, Outreach Serv, Head, Res Serv,* Stephanie Race; *Head, Spec Coll & Archives,* Susan Swiatosz; Staff 46.5 (MLS 21, Non-MLS 25.5)
Founded 1970. Enrl 16,000; Fac 540; Highest Degree: Doctorate
Library Holdings: AV Mats 30,718; CDs 13,544; DVDs 782; Music Scores 486; Bk Titles 511,858; Bk Vols 813,389; Per Subs 2,350; Videos 7,977
Special Collections: Arthur N Sollee Papers; Eartha White Memorial Coll, memorabilia, photog; Senator Jack E Mathews Papers; University Archives
Subject Interests: Bus & mgt, Econ, Educ, Nursing
Automation Activity & Vendor Info: (Acquisitions) Ex Libris Group; (Cataloging) Ex Libris Group; (Circulation) Ex Libris Group; (Course Reserve) Ex Libris Group; (ILL) OCLC ILLiad; (OPAC) Ex Libris Group; (Serials) Ex Libris Group
Wireless access
Publications: Annual Report
Partic in LYRASIS; Northeast Florida Library Information Network; OCLC Online Computer Library Center, Inc
Special Services for the Deaf - TDD equip
Open Mon-Thurs 7am-3:30am, Fri 7am-8pm, Sat 8-6, Sun 1pm-3am
Restriction: Open to fac, students & qualified researchers

JUPITER

C FLORIDA ATLANTIC UNIVERSITY*, John D MacArthur Campus Library, 5353 Parkside Dr, 33458. SAN 371-375X. Tel: 561-799-8530. FAX: 561-799-8587. Web Site: www.library.fau.edu/npb/npb.htm. *Interim Dean,* Amy Kornblau; E-mail: kornblau@fau.edu; *Dir,* Ethan J Allen, Jr; Tel: 561-799-8030, E-mail: eallen@fau.edu; *Asst Dir,* Leah Plocharczyk; Tel: 561-799-8685, E-mail: lplochar@fau.edu; Staff 6 (MLS 2, Non-MLS 4)
Founded 1972. Enrl 1,300; Fac 77; Highest Degree: Doctorate
Library Holdings: DVDs 3,000; Bk Vols 80,000; Per Subs 19; Videos 336
Special Collections: Children's Books; Senior Theses
Automation Activity & Vendor Info: (Acquisitions) Ex Libris Group; (Cataloging) Ex Libris Group; (Circulation) Ex Libris Group; (Course Reserve) Ex Libris Group; (ILL) OCLC ILLiad; (OPAC) Ex Libris Group; (Serials) Ex Libris Group
Wireless access
Function: Art exhibits, Audio & video playback equip for onsite use, Bks on CD, CD-ROM, Computers for patron use, Digital talking bks, Doc delivery serv, Electronic databases & coll, For res purposes, ILL available, Internet access, Music CDs, Online cat, Online info literacy tutorials on the web & in blackboard, Orientations, Photocopying/Printing, Ref & res, Scanner, Telephone ref, Wheelchair accessible
Partic in Fla Ctr for Libr Automation; LYRASIS
Special Services for the Blind - Reader equip
Restriction: Open to fac, students & qualified researchers, Open to pub for ref & circ; with some limitations

KENNEDY SPACE CENTER

G NASA*, John F Kennedy Space Center Library, 32899. SAN 302-9905. Tel: 321-867-3600. FAX: 321-867-4534. E-mail: ksc-dl-library@mail.nasa.gov. Web Site: www.kennedyspacecenter.com. *Chief Librn,* Bennett Wight; *Acq,* Deborah Guelzow; *Archivist,* Elaine Liston; *Doc,* Lori Uffner
Founded 1962
Library Holdings: Bk Titles 18,000; Per Subs 900
Special Collections: Archives Coll; Kennedy Space Center History Coll, photog
Subject Interests: Aerospace sci
Automation Activity & Vendor Info: (Cataloging) SirsiDynix; (Circulation) SirsiDynix; (ILL) OCLC
Wireless access
Publications: Chronology of KSC & Related Events (Annual); Index for the Space Transportation System; Index of KSC Specifications & Standards; Index to Spaceport News (official Space Center newspaper)
Partic in Aerospace Res Info Network; Cent Fla Libr Consortium; Florida Library Information Network; NASA Library Network; OhioNET
Restriction: Open by appt only

KEY WEST

J FLORIDA KEYS COMMUNITY COLLEGE LIBRARY*, Bldg A, 2nd Fl, 5901 College Rd, 33040. SAN 302-9913. Tel: 305-809-3194. Administration Tel: 305-809-3206. E-mail: library@fkcc.edu. Web Site: libguides.fkcc.edu/lrc/library. *Dir, Learning Res Ctr,* Kristina Neihouse; E-mail: kristina.neihouse@fkcc.edu; Staff 4 (MLS 2, Non-MLS 2)
Founded 1965. Enrl 259; Fac 36
Library Holdings: AV Mats 2,865; Bk Titles 29,769; Bk Vols 32,746; Per Subs 163
Automation Activity & Vendor Info: (Acquisitions) Ex Libris Group; (Cataloging) Ex Libris Group; (Circulation) Ex Libris Group; (Course Reserve) Ex Libris Group; (ILL) OCLC; (Media Booking) Ex Libris Group; (OPAC) Ex Libris Group; (Serials) Ex Libris Group
Wireless access
Open Mon-Thurs 8-8, Fri 8-5

P MONROE COUNTY PUBLIC LIBRARY*, 700 Fleming St, 33040. SAN 337-6443. Tel: 305-292-3595. FAX: 305-295-3368. Web Site: www.keyslibraries.org. *Dir of Libr,* Norma Kula; Tel: 305-853-7349, E-mail: kula-norma@monroecounty-fl.gov; *Libr Adminr,* Anne Layton Rice; E-mail: rice-anne@monroecounty-fl.gov; *Sr Librn,* Tom Hambright; E-mail: hambright-tom@monroecounty-fl.gov; *Mgr,* Michael Nelson; E-mail: nelson-michael@monroecounty-fl.gov; Staff 13 (MLS 6, Non-MLS 7)
Founded 1892. Pop 76,000; Circ 392,524
Library Holdings: Bk Vols 183,757; Per Subs 120
Subject Interests: Local hist
Automation Activity & Vendor Info: (Acquisitions) Innovative Interfaces, Inc; (Cataloging) Innovative Interfaces, Inc; (Circulation) Innovative Interfaces, Inc; (ILL) OCLC FirstSearch; (OPAC) Innovative Interfaces, Inc
Wireless access
Function: Adult bk club, Archival coll, Art exhibits, Audiobks via web, Bilingual assistance for Spanish patrons, Bk club(s), Bks on cassette, Bks on CD, Children's prog, Computer training, Computers for patron use, Digital talking bks, Electronic databases & coll, Free DVD rentals, Holiday prog, ILL available, Mail & tel request accepted, Music CDs, Online cat, Online ref, Outside serv via phone, mail, e-mail & web, OverDrive digital audio bks, Photocopying/Printing, Preschool outreach, Prog for adults, Prog for children & young adult, Ref serv available, Senior outreach, Spanish lang bks, Spoken cassettes & CDs, Spoken cassettes & DVDs, Story hour, Summer reading prog, Tax forms, Teen prog, Telephone ref, Wheelchair accessible
Partic in Southeast Florida Library Information Network, Inc
Open Mon, Tues, Thurs & Fri 9:30-6, Wed 9:30-8, Sat 10-6
Friends of the Library Group
Branches: 4
BIG PINE KEY BRANCH, 213 Key Deer Blvd, Big Pine Key, 33043, SAN 376-9143. Tel: 305-872-0992. FAX: 305-872-7106. *Mgr,* Kim Rinaldi; E-mail: rinaldi-kim@monroecounty-fl.gov; Staff 1 (MLS 1)
Open Mon & Wed-Fri 9:30-6, Tues 9:30-8, Sat 10-6
Friends of the Library Group
ISLAMORADA BRANCH, 81830 Overseas Hwy, Islamorada, 33036, SAN 337-6478. Tel: 305-664-4645. FAX: 305-664-4875. *Mgr,* Walt Johnson; E-mail: johnson-walt@monroecounty-fl.gov
Open Mon & Wed-Fri 9:30-6, Tues 9:30-8, Sat 10-6
Friends of the Library Group
KEY LARGO BRANCH, Tradewinds Shopping Ctr, 101485 Overseas Hwy, Key Largo, 33037, SAN 337-6508. Tel: 305-451-2396. FAX: 305-451-4536. *Mgr,* Paulette Sullivan; E-mail: sullivan-paulette@monroecounty-fl.gov

Open Mon, Tues, Thurs & Fri 9:30-6, Wed 9:30-8, Sat 10-6
Friends of the Library Group
MARATHON BRANCH, 3251 Overseas Hwy, Marathon, 33050, SAN 337-6532. Tel: 305-743-5156. FAX: 305-289-6093. *Mgr,* Lorenia Diaz; E-mail: diaz-lorenia@monroecounty-fl.gov
Open Mon, Tues, Thurs & Fri 9:30-6, Wed 9:30-8, Sat 10-6
Friends of the Library Group

KISSIMMEE

CR JOHNSON UNIVERSITY FLORIDA LIBRARY*, 1011 Bill Beck Blvd, 34744. Tel: 407-569-1385. E-mail: LibraryFL@JohnsonU.edu. Web Site: johnsonu.edu/library/florida. *Assoc Librn,* Marla Black; E-mail: mblack@johnsonu.edu; Staff 1 (MLS 1)
Founded 1976. Enrl 300; Fac 11; Highest Degree: Master
Special Collections: Fayetta Storm Davis Restoration Coll; Robert E Reeves Missions Coll
Subject Interests: Missions, Restoration movement
Automation Activity & Vendor Info: (Cataloging) TLC (The Library Corporation); (Circulation) TLC (The Library Corporation); (Discovery) EBSCO Discovery Service; (ILL) OCLC WorldShare Interlibrary Loan; (OPAC) TLC (The Library Corporation); (Serials) OCLC WorldShare Interlibrary Loan
Wireless access
Function: 24/7 Electronic res, 24/7 Online cat, Wheelchair accessible
Partic in Christian Library Consortium

P OSCEOLA LIBRARY SYSTEM*, Hart Memorial Central Library & Ray Shanks Law Library, 211 E Dakin Ave, 34741. SAN 323-5947. Tel: 407-742-8888. FAX: 407-742-8897. E-mail: thelibrary@osceolalibrary.org. Web Site: www.myosceolalibrary.org. *Libr Dir,* Denise Galarraga; E-mail: Denise.Galarraga@osceolalibrary.org
Founded 1989. Pop 275,000; Circ 1,266,573
Automation Activity & Vendor Info: (Acquisitions) SirsiDynix; (Cataloging) OCLC Online; (Circulation) SirsiDynix; (ILL) OCLC Online; (OPAC) SirsiDynix
Wireless access
Partic in Tampa Bay Library Consortium, Inc
Special Services for the Deaf - TDD equip
Open Mon-Thurs 9-9, Fri & Sat 9-6, Sun 12-6
Friends of the Library Group
Branches: 5
BUENAVENTURA LAKES BRANCH, 405 Buenaventura Blvd, 34743, SAN 376-9224. Tel: 407-742-8888. *Libr Dir,* Denise Galarraga; E-mail: Denise.Galarraga@osceolalibrary.org
Open Mon-Thurs 9-9, Fri & Sat 9-6, Sun 12-6
Friends of the Library Group
KENANSVILLE BRANCH, 1154 S Canoe Creek Rd, Kenansville, 34739. Tel: 407-742-8888.
Open Tues, Thurs & Fri 3-7, Wed & Sat 10-2 & 3-7
Friends of the Library Group
POINCIANA BRANCH, 101 N Doverplum Ave, 34758. Tel: 407-742-8888.
Open Mon-Thurs 9-9, Fri & Sat 9-6, Sun 12-6
Friends of the Library Group
VETERANS MEMORIAL LIBRARY, 810 13th St, Saint Cloud, 34769, SAN 376-2688. Tel: 407-742-8888.
Open Mon-Thurs 9-9, Fri & Sat 9-6, Sun 12-6
Friends of the Library Group
WEST OSCEOLA BRANCH, Water Tower Shoppes, 21 Blake Blvd, Celebration, 34747. Tel: 407-742-8888.
Open Mon-Sat 10-7
Friends of the Library Group

C VALENCIA COLLEGE*, Osceola Campus Library, Bldg 4, Rm 202, 1800 Denn John Lane, 6-4, 34744, SAN 376-8309. Tel: 407-582-4155. Reference Tel: 407-582-4154. Web Site: valenciacollege.edu/students/library/. *Librn,* Sarah Dockray; Tel: 407-582-4156, E-mail: sdockray@valenciacollege.edu; *Libr Spec,* Marcie Rhodes; Tel: 407-582-4153, E-mail: mrhodes@valenciacollege.edu; Staff 13 (MLS 6, Non-MLS 7)
Founded 1967. Fac 2; Highest Degree: Bachelor
Library Holdings: Audiobooks 63; AV Mats 564; DVDs 1,359; e-books 172,483; Bk Titles 38,887; Per Subs 40
Automation Activity & Vendor Info: (Acquisitions) Ex Libris Group; (Cataloging) Ex Libris Group; (Circulation) Ex Libris Group; (Course Reserve) Ex Libris Group; (ILL) Ex Libris Group; (Media Booking) Ex Libris Group; (OPAC) Ex Libris Group; (Serials) Ex Libris Group
Wireless access
Function: Electronic databases & coll, Free DVD rentals, ILL available, Instruction & testing, Magnifiers for reading, Online cat, Online info literacy tutorials on the web & in blackboard, Photocopying/Printing, Ref serv available, Scanner, Telephone ref, Wheelchair accessible
Partic in Tampa Bay Library Consortium, Inc
Open Mon-Thurs 7am-10pm, Fri 7-5, Sat 8-1
Restriction: Borrowing privileges limited to fac & registered students, ID required to use computers (Ltd hrs)

LADY LAKE

P LADY LAKE PUBLIC LIBRARY*, 225 W Guava St, 32159. SAN 376-2661. Tel: 352-753-2957. FAX: 352-753-3361. Web Site: www.ladylake.org/departments/library. *Dir,* Lori Sadler; E-mail: lsadler@mylakelibrary.org; *Admin Coordr,* Mary Ellen Petrucelli; E-mail: mpetrucelli@lakeline.lib.fl.us; *Prog & Youth Coordr,* Thom Mazak; *Circ/Acq,* Beth Gobeil; E-mail: bgobeil@lakeline.lib.fl.us. Subject Specialists: *Computer art, Youth,* Thom Mazak; Staff 7 (MLS 1, Non-MLS 6)
Founded 1992. Pop 30,000; Circ 117,000
Library Holdings: Bk Titles 46,000; Per Subs 77
Subject Interests: Civil War, Collectibles, Fla, Gardening
Automation Activity & Vendor Info: (Acquisitions) SirsiDynix; (Cataloging) SirsiDynix; (Circulation) SirsiDynix; (OPAC) SirsiDynix; (Serials) SirsiDynix
Wireless access
Mem of Lake County Library System
Special Services for the Blind - Talking bks
Open Mon 9-7, Tues-Fri 9-6
Friends of the Library Group

LAKE ALFRED

S CITRUS RESEARCH & EDUCATION CENTER LIBRARY*, Ben Hill Griffin Jr. Citrus Hall, 700 Experiment Station Rd, 33850-2243. SAN 302-9964. Tel: 863-956-1151. FAX: 863-956-4631. Web Site: www.crec.ifas.ufl.edu/services/library. *Librn,* Jennifer Dawson; Tel: 863-956-5890, E-mail: jdawson@ufl.edu
Founded 1947
Library Holdings: Bk Titles 6,980; Bk Vols 15,000; Per Subs 50
Wireless access
Function: For res purposes, Ref serv available, Res libr
Open Mon-Fri 8-5
Friends of the Library Group

P LAKE ALFRED PUBLIC LIBRARY*, 245 N Seminole Ave, 33850. SAN 302-9956. Tel: 863-291-5378. FAX: 863-878-0344. Web Site: www.lakealfredlibrary.org, www.mypclc.org/library/lake-alfred-public-library. *Head Librn,* Linda Hitchcock; E-mail: lhitchcock@mylakealfred.com; *Asst Librn,* Linda Snell; E-mail: lsnell@mylakealfred.com; *Asst Librn,* Kimberly Walker; E-mail: kwalker@mylakealfred.com; *Ch Serv,* Keri Jones; E-mail: mcarr@mylakealfred.com; Staff 3 (MLS 1, Non-MLS 2)
Founded 1973. Pop 4,000; Circ 14,000
Library Holdings: Bk Vols 24,000; Per Subs 20
Subject Interests: Fla
Automation Activity & Vendor Info: (Cataloging) Horizon; (Circulation) Horizon
Wireless access
Function: Photocopying/Printing, Prog for children & young adult, Summer reading prog
Partic in Polk County Libr Coop; Tampa Bay Library Consortium, Inc
Open Mon-Fri 9-6, Sat 9-3
Friends of the Library Group

LAKE BUTLER

P NEW RIVER PUBLIC LIBRARY COOPERATIVE*, 110 N Lake Ave, 32054. SAN 377-8800. Tel: 386-496-2526. FAX: 386-496-3394. E-mail: newriver@neflin.org. Web Site: www.newriverlibrary.org. *Dir,* Tricia Wylie; Staff 4 (MLS 1, Non-MLS 3)
Founded 1996. Pop 70,000
Library Holdings: Bk Titles 152,000; Per Subs 200
Automation Activity & Vendor Info: (Cataloging) SirsiDynix; (Circulation) SirsiDynix; (OPAC) SirsiDynix
Wireless access
Member Libraries: Bradford County Public Library; Emily Taber Public Library; Union County Public Library
Partic in Northeast Florida Library Information Network
Open Mon-Fri 8-4
Bookmobiles: 1. Bk vols 5,000

P UNION COUNTY PUBLIC LIBRARY*, 250 SE Fifth Ave, 32054. SAN 323-7516. Tel: 386-496-3432. E-mail: union@neflin.org. Web Site: www.newriverlibrary.org/ucpl. *Dir,* Mary C Brown; E-mail: marycb@neflin.org
Founded 1989. Pop 14,200
Library Holdings: Bk Titles 40,000; Per Subs 35
Subject Interests: Local hist
Automation Activity & Vendor Info: (Circulation) SirsiDynix
Wireless access

Mem of New River Public Library Cooperative
Partic in Northeast Florida Library Information Network
Open Mon & Wed-Fri 9-6, Tues 9-8, Sat 9-3
Friends of the Library Group

LAKE CITY

P COLUMBIA COUNTY PUBLIC LIBRARY*, 308 NW Columbia Ave, 32055. SAN 323-7761. Tel: 386-758-2101. Administration Tel: 386-758-1018. FAX: 386-758-2135. Web Site: ccpl.ent.sirsi.net. *Dir,* Katrina Evans; E-mail: kevans@columbiacountyfla.com; Staff 18.7 (MLS 5, Non-MLS 13.7)
Founded 1959. Pop 70,503; Circ 276,076
Library Holdings: Audiobooks 7,005; DVDs 11,496; e-books 69,086; e-journals 25; Bk Vols 118,153; Per Subs 151
Automation Activity & Vendor Info: (Acquisitions) SirsiDynix; (Cataloging) SirsiDynix; (Circulation) SirsiDynix; (OPAC) SirsiDynix; (Serials) SirsiDynix
Wireless access
Function: 24/7 Electronic res, 24/7 Online cat, Adult bk club, Adult literacy prog, After school storytime, Art exhibits, Audiobks via web, Bilingual assistance for Spanish patrons, Bk club(s), Bks on CD, Children's prog, Citizenship assistance, Computers for patron use, Electronic databases & coll, Family literacy, Free DVD rentals, ILL available, Internet access, Large print keyboards, Magazines, Meeting rooms, Online cat, OverDrive digital audio bks, Preschool outreach, Prog for adults, Prog for children & young adult, Ref serv available, Spanish lang bks, Story hour, Summer reading prog, Tax forms, Teen prog, Telephone ref, VHS videos, Wheelchair accessible
Publications: Friends Newsletter; Various Bibliographies
Partic in Northeast Florida Library Information Network
Open Mon & Tues 9-9, Wed, Thurs & Fri 9-6, Sat & Sun 1-5
Friends of the Library Group
Branches: 2
FORT WHITE BRANCH, 17700 SW State Rd 47, Fort White, 32038, SAN 376-821X. Tel: 386-497-1108. FAX: 386-497-2066. *Br Mgr,* June Green; Staff 3 (Non-MLS 3)
Founded 1988
Function: Adult bk club, Adult literacy prog, Bks on CD, Children's prog, Citizenship assistance, Computers for patron use, Free DVD rentals, ILL available, Internet access, Magazines, Meeting rooms, Online cat, Preschool outreach, Ref serv available, Summer reading prog, Tax forms, Wheelchair accessible
Open Mon-Thurs 10-6, Fri & Sat 10-5
Friends of the Library Group
WEST BRANCH, 435 NW Hall of Fame Dr, 32055. Tel: 386-758-1321. *Br Mgr,* Mary Williams; Staff 3 (Non-MLS 3)
Founded 2004
Function: Adult literacy prog, Bks on CD, Citizenship assistance, Computers for patron use, Free DVD rentals, ILL available, Internet access, Magazines, Meeting rooms, Online cat, Ref serv available, Summer reading prog, Tax forms, Wheelchair accessible
Open Tues 10-8, Wed & Thurs 10-6, Fri & Sat 10-5

J FLORIDA GATEWAY COLLEGE*, Wilson S Rivers Library & Media Center, 149 SE College Pl, 32025-2006. SAN 302-9980. Tel: 386-754-4401. Reference Tel: 386-754-4391. FAX: 386-754-4901. Reference FAX: 386-754-4891. E-mail: library@fgc.edu. Web Site: www.fgc.edu/students/library. *Dir, Libr Serv,* Christine Boatright; Tel: 386-754-4337, E-mail: christine.boatright@fgc.edu; *Coordr, Libr Res,* Patricia Morris; Tel: 386-754-4391, E-mail: patricia.morris@fgc.edu; *Cat, ILL,* Jo Ann Bailey; Tel: 386-754-4338, E-mail: joann.bailey@fgc.edu; *Cat, Ser,* Kristin Corbin; Tel: 386-754-4339, E-mail: kristin.corbin@fgc.edu; *Circ, Reserves,* Lynnda White; Tel: 386-754-4400, E-mail: lynnda.white@fgc.edu; Staff 5 (MLS 2, Non-MLS 3)
Founded 1962. Enrl 3,361; Fac 68; Highest Degree: Bachelor. Sal $197,948
Library Holdings: e-books 56,217; Bk Titles 100,028
Subject Interests: Allied health, Art, Water res
Automation Activity & Vendor Info: (Acquisitions) GRCI; (Cataloging) Ex Libris Group; (Circulation) Ex Libris Group; (Course Reserve) Ex Libris Group; (ILL) Ex Libris Group; (OPAC) Ex Libris Group; (Serials) Ex Libris Group
Wireless access
Publications: Annual Report; Orientation Brochures; Student Handbook
Partic in LINCC; Northeast Florida Library Information Network
Open Mon-Thurs (Fall-Spring) 7:30-7:30, Fri 9-4:30; Mon-Thurs (Summer) 7:30-6:30

GM NORTH FLORIDA/SOUTH GEORGIA VETERANS HEALTH SYSTEM*, VA Medical Center Library, 619 S Marion Ave, 32025. SAN 302-9999. Tel: 386-755-3016, Ext 2232. FAX: 386-758-3218. *Chief Librn,* Position Currently Open
Founded 1955
Library Holdings: Audiobooks 300; CDs 75; DVDs 850; e-books 150; e-journals 220; Electronic Media & Resources 51; Large Print Bks 188; Microforms 400; Bk Vols 8,342; Per Subs 82
Special Collections: Index Medicus, Current List Medical Literature 1941-1959; Index Medicus, Quarterly Cumulative Index Medicus 1927-1956
Subject Interests: Consumer health, Patient health educ
Automation Activity & Vendor Info: (Cataloging) CyberTools for Libraries; (Circulation) CyberTools for Libraries; (ILL) OCLC WorldShare Interlibrary Loan; (OPAC) CyberTools for Libraries; (Serials) SerialsSolutions
Function: Audio & video playback equip for onsite use, Audiobks on Playaways & MP3, Bks on CD, CD-ROM, Computers for patron use, Electronic databases & coll, Health sci info serv, ILL available, Internet access, Magazines, Magnifiers for reading, Mail & tel request accepted, Mail loans to mem, Microfiche/film & reading machines, Movies, Music CDs, Online cat, Online ref, Orientations, Ref serv available, Telephone ref, Wheelchair accessible
Partic in Veterans Affairs Library Network
Open Mon-Fri 8-4:30

LAKE MARY

S INSTITUTE OF INTERNAL AUDITORS LIBRARY*, 1035 Greenwood Blvd, Ste 401, 32746. SAN 302-8399. Tel: 407-937-1246. Information Services Tel: 407-937-1100. FAX: 407-937-1101. Web Site: na.theiia.org/Pages/IIAHome.aspx. *Library Contact,* Lisa Krist; E-mail: lisa.krist@theiia.org
Founded 1941
Library Holdings: Bk Vols 1,000; Per Subs 52
Special Collections: Institute of Internal Auditors publications
Subject Interests: Acctg, Bus & mgt, Data proc
Restriction: Staff use only

LAKE PARK

P LAKE PARK PUBLIC LIBRARY, 529 Park Ave, 33403. SAN 303-0008. Tel: 561-881-3330. Web Site: www.lakeparkflorida.gov/Government/Departments/Lake-Park-Public-Library. *Dir,* Karen H Mahnk; Tel: 561-881-3331, E-mail: kmahnk@lakeparkflorida.gov; Staff 6 (MLS 2, Non-MLS 4)
Pop 11,452; Circ 27,683
Library Holdings: Bks on Deafness & Sign Lang 2; Bk Titles 38,000; Per Subs 10
Subject Interests: Fla
Automation Activity & Vendor Info: (Acquisitions) Koha; (Cataloging) Koha; (Circulation) Koha; (OPAC) Koha
Wireless access
Function: 24/7 Electronic res, 24/7 Online cat, Adult bk club, After school storytime, Art exhibits, Audiobks on Playaways & MP3, Audiobks via web, AV serv, Bi-weekly Writer's Group, Bks on CD, Children's prog, Computer training, Computers for patron use, Electronic databases & coll, Family literacy, Free DVD rentals, Home delivery & serv to seniorr ctr & nursing homes, Homebound delivery serv, Homework prog, ILL available, Internet access, Magazines, Meeting rooms, Movies, Museum passes, Music CDs, Online cat, Online info literacy tutorials on the web & in blackboard, Online ref, Outreach serv, OverDrive digital audio bks, Photocopying/Printing, Preschool outreach, Preschool reading prog, Printer for laptops & handheld devices, Prog for adults, Prog for children & young adult, Ref & res, Scanner, Senior outreach, Serves people with intellectual disabilities, Story hour, Study rm, Summer & winter reading prog, Summer reading prog, Tax forms, Teen prog, Telephone ref, Visual arts prog, Wheelchair accessible, Winter reading prog, Workshops, Writing prog
Publications: E-blast (Periodical); Lake Park Library (Newsletter)
Partic in Coop Authority for Libr Automation; Library Cooperative of the Palm Beaches; Southeast Florida Library Information Network, Inc
Open Mon-Thurs 9-6, Fri 9-4, Sat 10-4
Restriction: ID required to use computers (Ltd hrs), In-house use for visitors
Friends of the Library Group

LAKE WALES

S BOK TOWER GARDENS*, Anton Brees Carillon Library, 1151 Tower Blvd, 33853-3412. SAN 371-7933. Tel: 863-734-1227. E-mail: library@boktowergardens.org. Web Site: boktowergardens.org/library. *Colls Mgr,* Jamie Fogel; E-mail: jfogel@boktower.org; Staff 2 (MLS 2)
Founded 1968
Library Holdings: AV Mats 179; CDs 1,455; Music Scores 2,988; Bk Vols 3,030; Per Subs 20
Special Collections: Personal Archives
Automation Activity & Vendor Info: (Cataloging) Mandarin Library Automation; (OPAC) Mandarin Library Automation
Wireless access
Function: Archival coll, Audio & video playback equip for onsite use, Online cat, Ref serv available

Partic in Tampa Bay Library Consortium, Inc
Restriction: Access at librarian's discretion, Authorized scholars by appt, Limited access based on advanced application, Limited access for the pub, Non-circulating, Not a lending libr, Open by appt only

P LAKE WALES PUBLIC LIBRARY*, 290 Cypress Garden Lane, 33853. SAN 303-0032. Tel: 863-678-4004. FAX: 863-678-4051. E-mail: library@lakewalesfl.gov. Web Site: www.cityoflakewales.com/309/Library. *Dir,* Tina M Peak; E-mail: tpeak@lakewalesfl.gov; *Bks by Mail Supvr,* Lisa Eisemann; Tel: 863-679-4441, E-mail: leisemann@lakewalesfl.gov; *Circ Supvr,* Melissa Mayer; E-mail: mmayer@lakewalesfl.gov; *Youth Serv Supvr,* Kara Wiseman; E-mail: kwiseman@lakewalesfl.gov; *Teen Coordr,* Position Currently Open; *Coll Develop, ILL, Ref (Info Servs),* Marcia Loveman; E-mail: mloveman@lakewalesfl.gov; *Tech Serv,* Marie Zero; E-mail: mzero@lakewalesfl.gov; *Bkmobile/Outreach Serv, Libr Asst,* Sydney MacDonald; Tel: 863-678-4004, Ext 230; Staff 9 (MLS 4, Non-MLS 5)
Founded 1919. Pop 16,000; Circ 235,000
Library Holdings: Audiobooks 4,500; Bks on Deafness & Sign Lang 20; CDs 3,800; DVDs 7,000; e-books 3,500; Electronic Media & Resources 10; High Interest/Low Vocabulary Bk Vols 200; Large Print Bks 18,000; Microforms 50; Bk Titles 86,000; Per Subs 182; Spec Interest Per Sub 10; Talking Bks 3,350
Special Collections: Florida; Local History Archives. Oral History
Subject Interests: Bus, Careers, Fla, Genealogy, Spanish (Lang)
Automation Activity & Vendor Info: (Acquisitions) SirsiDynix; (Cataloging) SirsiDynix; (Circulation) SirsiDynix; (OPAC) SirsiDynix; (Serials) SirsiDynix
Wireless access
Function: 24/7 Electronic res, 24/7 Online cat, Activity rm, Adult bk club, Archival coll, Art exhibits, Audiobks via web, Bks on CD, Chess club, Children's prog, Computer training, Computers for patron use, E-Reserves, Electronic databases & coll, Free DVD rentals, Home delivery & serv to seniorr ctr & nursing homes, Homebound delivery serv, ILL available, Internet access, Magnifiers for reading, Mail & tel request accepted, Mail loans to mem, Microfiche/film & reading machines, Music CDs, Online cat, Online ref, OverDrive digital audio bks, Photocopying/Printing, Preschool outreach, Preschool reading prog, Printer for laptops & handheld devices, Prog for adults, Prog for children & young adult, Ref serv available, Senior computer classes, Senior outreach, Spanish lang bks, Story hour, Summer & winter reading prog, Summer reading prog, Tax forms, Teen prog, Telephone ref, Wheelchair accessible, Workshops, Writing prog
Publications: America Libraries; Booklist; Library Journal
Partic in Fla Libr Asn; Polk County Libr Coop; Tampa Bay Library Consortium, Inc
Open Mon, Tues & Thurs 9-6:30, Wed & Fri 9-5:30, Sat 9-3
Friends of the Library Group

C WARNER UNIVERSITY, Pontious Learning Resource Center, 13895 Hwy 27, 33859. SAN 303-0040. Tel: 863-638-7674. Circulation Tel: 863-638-7235. Reference Tel: 863-638-7666. FAX: 863-638-7675. E-mail: askalibrarian@warner.edu. Web Site: libguides.warner.edu/general/library, warner.edu/royal-resources/library-services. *Libr Dir,* Sherill L Harriger; *Head, Access Serv,* Mary Thorsen; Tel: 863-638-7586, E-mail: mary.thorsen@warner.edu; *Research Librn,* Virginia Schnarre; Tel: 863-638-7620, E-mail: virginia.schnarre@warner.edu. Subject Specialists: *Hist,* Virginia Schnarre; Staff 4 (MLS 3, Non-MLS 1)
Founded 1967. Enrl 1,100; Highest Degree: Master
Library Holdings: AV Mats 2,407; DVDs 943; e-books 216,188; e-journals 30,420; Bk Titles 73,831; Per Subs 200; Videos 300
Subject Interests: Educ, Liberal arts, Music, Recreation, Relig, Soc sci & issues
Automation Activity & Vendor Info: (Acquisitions) OCLC Worldshare Management Services; (Cataloging) OCLC Worldshare Management Services; (Circulation) OCLC Worldshare Management Services; (Discovery) EBSCO Discovery Service; (ILL) OCLC WorldShare Interlibrary Loan; (OPAC) OCLC Worldshare Management Services
Wireless access
Function: 24/7 Electronic res, Archival coll, Art exhibits, Computers for patron use, Distance learning, Free DVD rentals, ILL available, Internet access, Laminating, Learning ctr, Magazines, Online cat, Orientations, Photocopying/Printing, Scanner, Telephone ref, Wheelchair accessible
Partic in Christian Library Consortium; Independent Cols & Univs of Fla; Library & Information Resources Network; LYRASIS; Tampa Bay Library Consortium, Inc
Special Services for the Blind - Accessible computers
Open Mon-Thurs 7:30am-10pm, Fri 7:30-5, Sat 12-4, Sun 6pm-10
Restriction: Authorized patrons, Non-circulating of rare bks, Open to students, fac & staff, Restricted pub use

LAKE WORTH

P LAKE WORTH PUBLIC LIBRARY*, 15 North M St, 33460. SAN 303-0059. Tel: 561-533-7354. FAX: 561-586-1651. E-mail: lwlibrary@lakeworth.org. Web Site: www.lakeworth.org/residents/library. *Libr Serv Mgr,* Vickie Joslin; E-mail: vjoslin@lakeworth.org; Staff 8.5 (MLS 1, Non-MLS 7.5)
Founded 1912. Pop 34,500; Circ 125,000
Library Holdings: Audiobooks 500; CDs 450; DVDs 800; e-books 14,000; Bk Titles 55,400; Bk Vols 60,000; Per Subs 102; Videos 150
Special Collections: Lake Worth History (Florida Coll), clipping, micro; Large Print Books Coll
Automation Activity & Vendor Info: (Cataloging) Innovative Interfaces, Inc; (Circulation) Innovative Interfaces, Inc; (OPAC) Innovative Interfaces, Inc
Wireless access
Function: After school storytime, Bks on CD, Children's prog, Computers for patron use, E-Reserves, ILL available, Magnifiers for reading, Music CDs, Online cat, Photocopying/Printing, Ref serv available, Story hour, Summer reading prog, Tax forms, Teen prog
Partic in Library Cooperative of the Palm Beaches; Southeast Florida Library Information Network, Inc
Open Tues & Wed 10-7, Thurs 10-6, Fri & Sat 10-5
Friends of the Library Group

J PALM BEACH STATE COLLEGE*, Harold C Manor Library, 4200 Congress Ave, Mail Sta 17, 33461. SAN 337-6591. Tel: 561-868-3800. Circulation Tel: 561-868-3710. Reference Tel: 561-868-3713. FAX: 561-868-3708. Web Site: www.palmbeachstate.edu. *Dir, Libr Serv,* Rob C Krull; *Ref Librn, Student Serv/Outreach Librn,* Alyse McKeal; *Digital Serv Librn,* Robbie Allen; *Fac Outreach Librn, Info Literacy/Ref,* Connie Tuisku; *ILL,* Penny Brown; *Per,* Patricia Alvarez; *Ref (Info Servs),* Doug Cornwell; *Tech Serv,* Kenneth Myers; *Media Spec,* Ricardo Reyes; Staff 15 (MLS 15)
Founded 1965. Enrl 25,000; Fac 247; Highest Degree: Bachelor
Library Holdings: Audiobooks 2,341; e-books 120,000; e-journals 19,000; Bk Titles 161,121; Bk Vols 210,567; Per Subs 1,863; Videos 8,500
Special Collections: Roosevelt Jr College Coll. Oral History
Automation Activity & Vendor Info: (Acquisitions) Ex Libris Group; (Cataloging) Ex Libris Group; (Circulation) Ex Libris Group; (Course Reserve) Ex Libris Group; (ILL) Ex Libris Group; (OPAC) Ex Libris Group; (Serials) Ex Libris Group
Wireless access
Partic in LYRASIS; OCLC Online Computer Library Center, Inc; Southeast Florida Library Information Network, Inc
Open Mon-Thurs 7:30am-9pm, Fri 7:30am-8pm, Sat 10-3

LAKELAND

§E FLORIDA POLYTECHNIC UNIVERSITY LIBRARY, 4700 Research Way, 33805. Tel: 863-874-8643. E-mail: library@floridapoly.edu. Web Site: floridapoly.edu/student-affairs/library.php. *Library Contact,* Marcie Hoecker; E-mail: mhoecker@floridapoly.edu
Automation Activity & Vendor Info: (Cataloging) Ex Libris Group; (OPAC) Ex Libris Group
Function: ILL available
Partic in Tampa Bay Library Consortium, Inc

C FLORIDA SOUTHERN COLLEGE*, Roux Library, 111 Lake Hollingsworth Dr, 33801-5698. SAN 303-0067. Tel: 863-680-4164. FAX: 863-680-4126. Web Site: www.flsouthern.edu/library. *Libr Dir,* Randall M MacDonald; Tel: 863-680-4165, E-mail: rmacdonald1@flsouthern.edu; *Instrul Serv Librn,* Julie Hornick; Tel: 863-680-4496, E-mail: jhornick@flsouthern.edu; *Instrul Serv Librn,* Steven Wade; Tel: 863-616-6451, E-mail: swade@flsouthern.edu; *Metadata Librn,* Marina Morgan; Tel: 863-616-6450, E-mail: mmorgan@flsouthern.edu; *Res Sharing Librn,* Nora E Galbraith; Tel: 863-616-6454, E-mail: ngalbraith@flsouthern.edu; *Circ Supvr,* Robert Hernandez; Tel: 863-616-6453, E-mail: rhernandez@flsouthern.edu; *Evening Circ Supvr,* Andy Franzoni; Tel: 863-616-6452, E-mail: afranzoni@flsouthern.edu; *Libr Asst,* Elizabeth Partington; E-mail: epartington@flsouthern.edu; *Evening Libr Asst,* Mallory Moxley; E-mail: mmoxley@flsouthern.edu; *Tech Serv Asst,* Donna Kahelin; Tel: 863-680-4470, E-mail: dkahelin@flsouthern.edu; *Col Archivist,* Gerrianne Schaad; Tel: 863-680-4994, E-mail: gschaad@flsouthern.edu; *Archives, Tech,* Amy Skillen; Tel: 863-616-6487, E-mail: askillen@flsouthern.edu; Staff 12 (MLS 6, Non-MLS 6)
Founded 1885. Enrl 2,339; Fac 125; Highest Degree: Doctorate
Jun 2020-May 2021. Mats Exp $479,591, Books $24,867, Electronic Ref Mat (Incl. Access Fees) $435,800, Presv $18,924. Sal $164,029 (Prof $364,388)
Library Holdings: AV Mats 8,077; e-books 167,631; e-journals 97,722; Electronic Media & Resources 45,285; Bk Vols 160,232; Per Subs 69
Special Collections: Andy Ireland Coll; Florida United Methodist History Coll; Frank Lloyd Wright Coll; James A Haley Coll

Automation Activity & Vendor Info: (Acquisitions) Innovative Interfaces, Inc; (Cataloging) Innovative Interfaces, Inc; (Circulation) Innovative Interfaces, Inc; (Course Reserve) Innovative Interfaces, Inc; (Discovery) EBSCO Discovery Service; (ILL) OCLC; (OPAC) Innovative Interfaces, Inc; (Serials) Innovative Interfaces, Inc
Wireless access
Partic in LYRASIS; Tampa Bay Library Consortium, Inc; Westchester Academic Library Directors Organization
Open Mon-Thurs 7:30am-1am, Fri & Sat 8-5, Sun 10am-1am

P LAKELAND PUBLIC LIBRARY*, 100 Lake Morton Dr, 33801-5375. SAN 337-6621. Tel: 863-834-4280. Interlibrary Loan Service Tel: 863-834-4263. Administration Tel: 863-834-4271. FAX: 863-834-4329. Web Site: www.lakelandgov.net/library. *City Librn,* Lisa Lilyquist; E-mail: lisa.lilyquist@lakelandgov.net; *Librn Supvr,* Monica Fisher; E-mail: monica.fisher@lakelandgov.net; *Librn Supvr,* Jackson Hager; E-mail: jackson.hager@lakelandgov.net; Staff 16 (MLS 13, Non-MLS 3)
Founded 1927
Oct 2014-Sept 2015 Income (Main & Associated Libraries) $3,270,160, City $2,395,640, County $874,520. Mats Exp $477,128. Sal $2,155,409
Library Holdings: Bk Vols 196,267; Per Subs 106
Special Collections: Lakeland Chapter DAR; Lakeland Coll; Lakeland Photographs; Polk County Citrus Labels
Subject Interests: Local hist
Automation Activity & Vendor Info: (Cataloging) SirsiDynix; (Circulation) SirsiDynix; (OPAC) SirsiDynix
Wireless access
Function: Adult bk club, Archival coll, Audiobks via web, AV serv, Bks on CD, Children's prog, Computer training, Computers for patron use, Electronic databases & coll, Free DVD rentals, ILL available, Large print keyboards, Magazines, Meeting rooms, Microfiche/film & reading machines, Movies, Music CDs, Notary serv, Online cat, OverDrive digital audio bks, Photocopying/Printing, Prog for adults, Scanner, Summer reading prog, Tax forms, Telephone ref, Wheelchair accessible
Partic in OCLC Online Computer Library Center, Inc; Polk County Libr Coop; Tampa Bay Library Consortium, Inc
Open Mon-Thurs 9-7, Fri & Sat 9-5, Sun 1:30-5
Friends of the Library Group
Branches: 1
LARRY R JACKSON BRANCH, 1700 N Florida Ave, 33805, SAN 337-6656. Tel: 863-834-4288. FAX: 863-834-4327. *Librn Supvr,* Angel Davis; E-mail: angel.davis@lakelandgov.net; Staff 9 (MLS 1, Non-MLS 8)
Founded 1995
Function: Prog for children & young adult, Summer reading prog
Open Mon-Thurs 9-7, Fri & Sat 9-5, Sun 1:30-5
Friends of the Library Group

M LAKELAND REGIONAL MEDICAL CENTER*, Medical Library, 1324 Lakeland Hills Blvd, 33805. (Mail add: PO Box 95448, 33804-5448), SAN 325-8920. Tel: 863-687-1176. FAX: 863-687-1488. E-mail: medlibdesk@mylrh.org. *Med Librn,* Cindy Emery; Staff 5 (Non-MLS 5)
Library Holdings: Audiobooks 100; CDs 100; DVDs 20; Bk Titles 1,000; Per Subs 175; Videos 100
Special Collections: Leadership Development
Partic in SEND; Tampa Bay Medical Library Network

S POLK MUSEUM OF ART*, Penfield Library, 800 E Palmetto St, 33801-5529. SAN 303-0075. Tel: 863-688-7743. FAX: 863-688-2611. Web Site: polkmuseumofart.org. *Chief Curator, Exec Dir,* Claire Orologas; E-mail: COrologas@PolkMuseumofArt.org; Staff 1 (Non-MLS 1)
Founded 1966
Library Holdings: Bk Vols 2,000; Per Subs 20
Special Collections: Florida Contemporary Artists
Subject Interests: Archit, Art, Craft, Exhibition catalogs
Wireless access
Function: For res purposes
Restriction: Non-circulating, Open by appt only

CR SOUTHEASTERN UNIVERSITY*, Steelman Library, 1000 Longfellow Blvd, 33801. SAN 303-0083. Tel: 863-667-5089. Interlibrary Loan Service Tel: 863-667-5059. Reference Tel: 863-667-5060, 863-667-5949. Automation Services Tel: 863-667-5309. FAX: 863-669-4160. E-mail: library@seu.edu. Web Site: library.seu.edu. *Dean, Libr Serv,* Amy Harris; Tel: 863-667-5572, E-mail: ajharris@seu.edu; *Asst Dir, Ref, Ser Librn,* Glenn Pearl; E-mail: gapearl@seu.edu; *Head, Circ,* Kathy Kempa; E-mail: kfkempa@seu.edu; *Ref & Instruction Librn,* Amy Beatty; Tel: 863-667-5523, E-mail: arbeatty@seu.edu; *Syst Librn,* Nathan R Schwartz; E-mail: nrschwartz@seu.edu; *Tech Serv,* Debbie Rusch; Tel: 863-667-5522, E-mail: dfrusch@seu.edu; *ILL,* Cynthia Childs; E-mail: cchilds@seu.edu. Subject Specialists: *Educ,* Amy Harris; *Relig,* Glenn Pearl; *Bus, Health sci, Natural sci,* Kathy Kempa; *Communication, English, Film, Graphic design,* Amy Beatty; *Hist, Leadership studies, Legal,* Nathan R Schwartz; *Behav & soc sci, Math, Natural sci,* Debbie Rusch; Staff 11 (MLS 6, Non-MLS 5)
Founded 1935. Enrl 3,500; Highest Degree: Doctorate
Automation Activity & Vendor Info: (Acquisitions) OCLC; (Cataloging) OCLC; (Circulation) OCLC; (Course Reserve) OCLC; (ILL) OCLC; (OPAC) OCLC; (Serials) OCLC
Wireless access
Function: Distance learning, ILL available, Photocopying/Printing, Ref serv available
Partic in Independent Cols & Univs of Fla; Tampa Bay Library Consortium, Inc; Westchester Academic Library Directors Organization
Restriction: Open to students, fac & staff

LANTANA

A G HOLLEY STATE HOSPITAL
M BENJAMIN L BROCK MEDICAL LIBRARY*, 1199 W Lantana Rd, 33462. (Mail add: PO Box 3084, 33465-3084), SAN 322-8215. Tel: 561-582-5666. FAX: 561-540-3710. Web Site: www.agholley.com. *Librn,* Markesha Burgess
Library Holdings: Bk Titles 200; Per Subs 10
Special Collections: Oral History
Restriction: Staff use only

M PATIENTS LIBRARY*, 1199 W Lantana Rd, 33465, SAN 303-0105. Tel: 561-582-5666, Ext 3799. FAX: 561-540-3753. *Librn,* Tim Thompson
Library Holdings: Bk Titles 9,800

P LANTANA PUBLIC LIBRARY*, 205 W Ocean Ave, 33462. SAN 303-0113. Tel: 561-540-5740. FAX: 561-540-5742. E-mail: lib.lantana@gmail.com. Web Site: www.lantanalibrary.org. *Dir,* Position Currently Open; *Libr Asst,* Ellen Tuggle; Staff 1 (MLS 1)
Founded 1947. Pop 10,300
Oct 2014-Sept 2015. Mats Exp $108,000, Books $20,000, Per/Ser (Incl. Access Fees) $85,000, Electronic Ref Mat (Incl. Access Fees) $3,000
Library Holdings: e-books 1,300; e-books 1,300; e-journals 28; e-journals 28; Large Print Bks 1,000; Large Print Bks 1,000; Bk Titles 20,000; Bk Titles 20,000; Bk Vols 23,000; Per Subs 58
Special Collections: Florida & Lantana History (Linehan Coll), bks, slides
Automation Activity & Vendor Info: (Cataloging) ByWater Solutions; (Circulation) ByWater Solutions; (OPAC) ByWater Solutions
Wireless access
Function: Adult bk club, Online cat
Partic in Library Cooperative of the Palm Beaches
Open Mon & Thurs 10-8, Tues, Wed & Fri 10-6, Sat (Sept-May)10-2
Friends of the Library Group

LARGO

P LARGO PUBLIC LIBRARY, 120 Central Park Dr, 33771. SAN 303-0156. Tel: 727-587-6715. E-mail: libraryinfo@largo.com. Web Site: www.largopubliclibrary.org. *Libr Dir,* Casey McPhee; E-mail: librarydirector@largo.com; Staff 10 (MLS 9, Non-MLS 1)
Founded 1916. Pop 68,244; Circ 713,488
Library Holdings: Bk Vols 231,000; Per Subs 198
Subject Interests: Arts & crafts, Genealogy, Local hist
Automation Activity & Vendor Info: (Cataloging) SirsiDynix; (Circulation) SirsiDynix; (OPAC) SirsiDynix
Wireless access
Partic in Tampa Bay Library Consortium, Inc
Special Services for the Deaf - Bks on deafness & sign lang; High interest/low vocabulary bks
Open Mon-Wed 9-8, Thurs & Fri 10-6, Sat 10-5
Friends of the Library Group

G PINELLAS COUNTY GOVERNMENT*, Heritage Village Archives & Library, 11909 125th St N, 33774. SAN 372-6053. Tel: 727-582-2128. FAX: 727-582-2211. Web Site: www.pinellascounty.org/heritage/archives_library.htm. *Mus Spec,* Patricia Landon; E-mail: plandon@pinellascounty.org; Staff 1 (MLS 1)
Founded 1961
Library Holdings: Bk Vols 3,500
Special Collections: Pinellas County History, photographs, postcards, yearbooks, city directories
Wireless access
Function: Archival coll
Partic in Tampa Bay Library Consortium, Inc
Restriction: Closed stack, In-house use for visitors, Not a lending libr, Open by appt only
Friends of the Library Group

LECANTO

J COLLEGE OF CENTRAL FLORIDA LEARNING RESOURCES CENTER*, Citrus Campus Library, 3800 S Lecanto Hwy, C2-202, 34461. Tel: 352-249-1205. TDD: 352-249-1201. E-mail: citruslb@cf.edu. Web Site: cf.libguides.com, www.cf.edu/go/learn/library. *Librn/Mgr,* Edith Ramlow; E-mail: ramlowe@cf.edu; *Sr Libr Tech,* Rachel Baril; E-mail: barilr@cf.edu; *Libr Tech,* Kimberly Moore; E-mail: moorek@cf.edu.

Subject Specialists: *Genealogy, Mkt, Photog,* Edith Ramlow; *Psychol,* Rachel Baril; *Bus, Statistics,* Kimberly Moore; Staff 2.5 (MLS 1, Non-MLS 1.5)
Founded 1996. Enrl 9,500; Highest Degree: Bachelor
Library Holdings: Bk Vols 9,000
Special Collections: Florida & Ecological Sciences (David E Walker Environmental Sciences Coll)
Automation Activity & Vendor Info: (Acquisitions) Ex Libris Group; (Cataloging) Ex Libris Group; (Circulation) Ex Libris Group; (Course Reserve) Ex Libris Group; (ILL) OCLC FirstSearch; (OPAC) Ex Libris Group; (Serials) Ex Libris Group
Wireless access
Function: 24/7 Electronic res, 3D Printer, Audio & video playback equip for onsite use, AV serv, Computers for patron use, Distance learning, E-Reserves, Electronic databases & coll, Equip loans & repairs, For res purposes, Free DVD rentals, Games & aids for people with disabilities, Health sci info serv, ILL available, Instruction & testing, Internet access, Learning ctr, Magazines, Magnifiers for reading, Mail & tel request accepted, Makerspace, Online cat, Online ref, Photocopying/Printing, Printer for laptops & handheld devices, Ref & res, Scanner, Telephone ref
Open Mon-Fri 8-4:30 (Aug-April); Mon-Thurs 8-4:30 (May-July)
Restriction: Borrowing privileges limited to fac & registered students, Borrowing requests are handled by ILL, External users must contact libr

LEESBURG

C BEACON COLLEGE LIBRARY*, 105 E Main St, 34748. Tel: 352-638-9707. Web Site: beaconcollege.edu/academics/resources, www.youseemore.com/beacon/default.asp. *Dir, Libr Res,* Tiffany Reitz; E-mail: treitz@beaconcollege.edu; Staff 2 (MLS 1, Non-MLS 1)
Founded 1995. Enrl 190; Fac 27; Highest Degree: Bachelor
Library Holdings: AV Mats 211; e-books 154,000; e-journals 30,876; Bk Titles 19,000; Per Subs 50; Spec Interest Per Sub 18; Videos 1,186
Subject Interests: Learning disabilities
Automation Activity & Vendor Info: (Cataloging) TLC (The Library Corporation); (Circulation) TLC (The Library Corporation); (ILL) TLC (The Library Corporation); (OPAC) TLC (The Library Corporation); (Serials) TLC (The Library Corporation)
Wireless access
Partic in Florida Library Information Network
Open Mon-Thurs 7:30am-8pm, Fri 7:30-5, Sat 9-4, Sun 11-7
Restriction: Borrowing requests are handled by ILL, Open to students, fac & staff

C LAKE-SUMTER STATE COLLEGE LIBRARY*, 9501 US Hwy 441, 34788-8751. SAN 303-0164. Tel: 352-365-3563, 352-365-3590. Web Site: libguides.lssc.edu/new_homepage. *Dean of Libr,* Kathleen Sacco; E-mail: SaccoK@lssc.edu; *Access Serv,* Kevin Arms; E-mail: armsk@lssc.edu; *Acq, Coll Develop,* James Cason; Tel: 352-435-5030, E-mail: casonj@lssc.edu; *Cat, ILL,* David Goff; Tel: 352-365-3527, E-mail: goffd@lssc.edu; *Govt Doc, Ser,* Nora Rackley; Tel: 352-365-3586, E-mail: rackleyn@lssc.edu; Staff 5 (MLS 5)
Founded 1962. Enrl 6,042; Fac 87; Highest Degree: Associate
Library Holdings: AV Mats 1,481; e-books 222,832; Bk Vols 70,870; Per Subs 117
Special Collections: US Document Depository
Automation Activity & Vendor Info: (Acquisitions) Ex Libris Group; (Cataloging) Ex Libris Group; (Circulation) Ex Libris Group; (Course Reserve) Ex Libris Group; (ILL) Ex Libris Group; (OPAC) Ex Libris Group; (Serials) Ex Libris Group
Wireless access
Partic in LYRASIS; OCLC Online Computer Library Center, Inc; Tampa Bay Library Consortium, Inc
Open Mon-Thurs 7:45am-9pm, Fri 7:45-7

P LEESBURG PUBLIC LIBRARY*, 100 E Main St, 34748. SAN 337-6680. Tel: 352-728-9790. E-mail: librarian@leesburgflorida.gov. Web Site: www.leesburgflorida.gov/government/departments/library, www.mylakelibrary.org/libraries/leesburg_public_library.aspx. *Libr Dir,* Lucy B Gangone; E-mail: lucy.gangone@leesburgflorida.gov; *Ad,* Emily Morgan; E-mail: emily.morgan@leesburgflorida.gov; *Ad,* Tom Wilcox; E-mail: tom.wilcox@leesburgflorida.gov; *Support Serv Mgr,* Claudia Procko; E-mail: claudia.procko@leesburgflorida.gov; *Adult Serv Supvr,* Dusty Matthews; E-mail: dusty.matthews@leesburgflorida.gov; *Youth Serv Supvr,* Melissa Curry; E-mail: melissa.curry@leesburgflorida.gov; *Prog Coordr,* Deborah Bussinger; E-mail: deborah.bussinger@leesburgflorida.gov. Subject Specialists: *Genealogy, Local hist,* Tom Wilcox; Staff 8 (MLS 6, Non-MLS 2)
Founded 1883. Pop 70,000; Circ 317,582
Oct 2016-Sept 2017 Income $1,477,248, City $1,143,775, Federal $16,804, County $282,565, Locally Generated Income $34,104. Mats Exp $195,400, Books $89,983, Per/Ser (Incl. Access Fees) $10,000, Other Print Mats $19,025, AV Mat $60,325, Electronic Ref Mat (Incl. Access Fees) $16,067. Sal $634,614
Library Holdings: Audiobooks 10,856; DVDs 8,969; e-books 11,600; Electronic Media & Resources 83; Bk Vols 121,541; Per Subs 220; Videos 163
Special Collections: Genealogy & Local History
Subject Interests: Genealogy, Local hist
Automation Activity & Vendor Info: (Acquisitions) Baker & Taylor; (Cataloging) Koha; (Circulation) Koha; (OPAC) Koha; (Serials) Koha
Wireless access
Function: 24/7 Electronic res, 24/7 Online cat, Accelerated reader prog, Activity rm, Adult bk club, Adult literacy prog, Archival coll, Audiobks on Playaways & MP3, Audiobks via web, Bilingual assistance for Spanish patrons, Bk club(s), Bks on CD, Butterfly Garden, Chess club, Children's prog, Citizenship assistance, Computer training, Computers for patron use, Digital talking bks, Electronic databases & coll, Family literacy, Free DVD rentals, Homework prog, Internet access, Jazz prog, Life-long learning prog for all ages, Literacy & newcomer serv, Magazines, Magnifiers for reading, Mail & tel request accepted, Meeting rooms, Microfiche/film & reading machines, Movies, Music CDs, Online cat, Online info literacy tutorials on the web & in blackboard, Orientations, Outreach serv, OverDrive digital audio bks, Passport agency, Photocopying/Printing, Preschool outreach, Preschool reading prog, Prog for adults, Prog for children & young adult, Ref & res, Ref serv available, Scanner, Senior computer classes, Senior outreach, Spanish lang bks, STEM programs, Story hour, Study rm, Summer reading prog, Tax forms, Teen prog, Telephone ref, Wheelchair accessible, Writing prog
Mem of Lake County Library System
Partic in Tampa Bay Library Consortium, Inc
Open Mon-Thurs 9-8, Sat 9-5
Friends of the Library Group

LIGHTHOUSE POINT

P LIGHTHOUSE POINT LIBRARY*, 2200 NE 38th St, 33064-3913. SAN 303-0180. Tel: 954-946-6398. FAX: 954-781-1950. E-mail: info@lighthousepointlibrary.com. Web Site: lighthousepointlibrary.com. *Dir,* Christy Keyes; E-mail: ckeyes@lighthousepoint.com; *Librn,* Pam Eldana; E-mail: peldana@lighthousepoint.com; Staff 4 (MLS 1, Non-MLS 3)
Founded 1965. Pop 10,767
Library Holdings: AV Mats 2,216; Bks on Deafness & Sign Lang 15; High Interest/Low Vocabulary Bk Vols 60; Large Print Bks 3,707; Bk Titles 33,280; Bk Vols 32,251; Per Subs 143; Talking Bks 715
Subject Interests: Fla
Automation Activity & Vendor Info: (Cataloging) Follett Software; (Circulation) Follett Software; (ILL) OCLC FirstSearch; (OPAC) Follett Software
Wireless access
Partic in Southeast Florida Library Information Network, Inc
Open Mon & Wed-Fri 10-6, Tues 10-8, Sat 9-2
Friends of the Library Group

LIVE OAK

P SUWANNEE RIVER REGIONAL LIBRARY*, 1848 Ohio Ave S, 32064-4517. SAN 337-6745. Tel: 386-362-2317. FAX: 386-364-6071. Reference E-mail: srrlref@neflin.org. Web Site: srrlib.org, suwcounty.org/county/index.php/departments/library. *Dir,* Betty Lawrence; E-mail: blawrence@neflin.org; Staff 1 (Non-MLS 1)
Founded 1958. Pop 68,140; Circ 331,297
Library Holdings: Bk Titles 71,401; Bk Vols 160,787; Per Subs 507
Automation Activity & Vendor Info: (Acquisitions) SirsiDynix; (Cataloging) SirsiDynix; (Circulation) SirsiDynix; (OPAC) SirsiDynix
Wireless access
Partic in LYRASIS; Northeast Florida Library Information Network
Special Services for the Deaf - TDD equip
Open Mon & Thurs 8:30-8, Tues, Wed & Fri 8:30-5:30, Sat 8:30-4
Friends of the Library Group
Branches: 8
BRANFORD PUBLIC LIBRARY, 703 NW Suwannee Ave, Branford, 32008-3279, SAN 337-677X. Tel: 386-935-1556. FAX: 386-935-6351. E-mail: branford@neflin.org. *Mgr,* Donna Koon
Open Mon 9-8, Tues-Fri 9-5:30, Sat 9-4
Friends of the Library Group
GREENVILLE PUBLIC LIBRARY, 1325 SW Main St, Greenville, 32331, SAN 337-6834. Tel: 850-948-2529. FAX: 850-948-5220. E-mail: greenville@neflin.org. *Mgr,* Kerry Cohen; Staff 2 (MLS 1, Non-MLS 1)
Open Mon 9-12:30 & 1:30-5:30, Wed-Fri 10-12:30 & 1:30-5
JASPER PUBLIC LIBRARY, 311 Hatley St NE, Jasper, 32052, SAN 337-6869. Tel: 386-792-2285. FAX: 386-792-1966. E-mail: jasper@neflin.org. *Mgr,* Becky Adams
Open Mon 9-8, Tues-Fri 9-5:30, Sat 9-12:30

JENNINGS PUBLIC LIBRARY, 1322 Plum St, Jennings, 32053-2221. Tel: 386-938-1143. FAX: 386-938-1153. E-mail: jennings@neflin.org. *Mgr,* Barbara McClain
Library Holdings: Bk Vols 11,000; Per Subs 47
Open Mon & Wed-Fri 1-6, Tues 10-6
JO KENNON PUBLIC LIBRARY, 10655 Dowling Park Dr, 32064. Tel: 386-658-2670. E-mail: dpark@neflin.org. *Mgr,* Rhoda Odom
Open Mon & Wed-Fri 9-6, Tues 9-7:30, Sat 9-4
LEE PUBLIC LIBRARY, 7883 E US Hwy 90, Lee, 32059-0040, SAN 377-0508. Tel: 850-971-5665. FAX: 850-971-4333. E-mail: lee@neflin.org. *Mgr,* Linda Swann
Open Mon & Wed 10-12:30 & 1:30-7:30, Tues & Fri 10-12:30 &1:30-5:30
MADISON PUBLIC LIBRARY, 378 NW College Loop, Madison, 32340-1446, SAN 337-6958. Tel: 850-973-6814. FAX: 850-973-8322. E-mail: madison@neflin.org. *Mgr,* Vicki Donaldson
Open Mon-Fri 9-5:30
WHITE SPRINGS PUBLIC LIBRARY, 16403 Jewett St, White Springs, 32096, SAN 377-6689. Tel: 386-397-1389. FAX: 386-397-4460. E-mail: wsprings@neflin.org. *Mgr,* Tracy Woodard
Founded 1997
Library Holdings: Bk Vols 3,300
Open Mon-Wed & Fri 1-5:30, Thurs 10-12 & 1-5:30

LONGBOAT KEY

S LONGBOAT LIBRARY, INC*, 555 Bay Isles Rd, 34228-3102. SAN 324-7104. Tel: 941-383-2011. Web Site: www.longboatlibrary.org. *Co-Pres,* Mary Baker; *Co-Pres,* Hazel Steskal
Founded 1957. Pop 15,000
Library Holdings: Bk Titles 15,100
Wireless access
Open Mon-Fri (Winter) 9-4; Tues-Sat (Summer) 9-Noon

LYNN HAVEN

P LYNN HAVEN PUBLIC LIBRARY*, 901 Ohio Ave, 32444. SAN 376-2734. Tel: 850-265-2781. FAX: 850-265-7311. E-mail: library@cityoflynnhaven.com. Web Site: www.lynnhavenlibrary.com. *Libr Mgr,* Alice Fritze; *Cat,* Julia Cuff; *Ch Serv,* Kris Horst; *ILL,* Jill Snipes; Staff 4 (Non-MLS 4)
Pop 18,000
Library Holdings: Audiobooks 945; Large Print Bks 1,001; Bk Titles 25,810; Bk Vols 27,266; Per Subs 12; Videos 1,018
Automation Activity & Vendor Info: (Cataloging) TLC (The Library Corporation); (Circulation) TLC (The Library Corporation); (ILL) OCLC FirstSearch; (OPAC) TLC (The Library Corporation)
Wireless access
Open Mon & Fri 9-5, Tues & Thurs 12-8, Wed 1-5, Sat 10-3

MACCLENNY

P EMILY TABER PUBLIC LIBRARY, 14 McIver Ave W, 32063. SAN 377-8789. Tel: 904-259-6464. E-mail: etaber@neflin.org. Web Site: newriverlibrary.org/etpl. *Dir,* April Teel
Founded 1961. Pop 22,000
Library Holdings: Bk Titles 35,041; Bk Vols 36,383; Per Subs 85
Automation Activity & Vendor Info: (Cataloging) SirsiDynix; (Circulation) SirsiDynix
Wireless access
Mem of New River Public Library Cooperative
Partic in Northeast Florida Library Information Network
Open Mon-Fri 11-6
Friends of the Library Group

MACDILL AFB

A UNITED STATES AIR FORCE*, MacDill Air Force Base Library, 8102 Condor St, 33621-5408. (Mail add: MacDill AFB Library, 8102 Condor St, Bldg 252, Tampa, 33621), SAN 337-7105. Tel: 813-828-3607. FAX: 813-828-4416. E-mail: 6SVS.library@macdill.af.mil. Web Site: tinyurl.com/macdill-lib. *Libr Dir,* Carrie Brang; E-mail: carrie.brang@us.af.mil; Staff 6 (MLS 1, Non-MLS 5)
Library Holdings: Audiobooks 2,500; AV Mats 150; CDs 200; DVDs 4,000; e-books 10,000; Electronic Media & Resources 20,000; Large Print Bks 500; Bk Titles 24,900; Bk Vols 26,500
Subject Interests: Middle East, Mil hist
Automation Activity & Vendor Info: (Cataloging) SirsiDynix; (Circulation) SirsiDynix; (ILL) OCLC; (OPAC) SirsiDynix
Wireless access
Function: Accelerated reader prog, After school storytime, Art exhibits, Audio & video playback equip for onsite use, Bks on CD, Children's prog, Computers for patron use, Doc delivery serv, Electronic databases & coll, Free DVD rentals, Holiday prog, ILL available, Internet access, Music CDs, Online cat, Orientations, OverDrive digital audio bks, Photocopying/Printing, Preschool outreach, Prog for children & young adult, Ref serv available, Scanner, Senior outreach, Spoken cassettes & CDs, Story hour, Summer reading prog, Tax forms, Teen prog, Wheelchair accessible
Partic in Tampa Bay Library Consortium, Inc
Restriction: Not open to pub, Open to authorized patrons

MADEIRA BEACH

P GULF BEACHES PUBLIC LIBRARY*, 200 Municipal Dr, 33708. SAN 303-0229. Tel: 727-391-2828. FAX: 727-399-2840. E-mail: gulfbeacheslibrary@icloud.com. Web Site: www.gulfbeacheslibrary.org. *Dir,* Vincent Gadrix; E-mail: librarydirector@zoho.com
Founded 1952. Pop 16,900; Circ 165,000
Library Holdings: Bk Vols 70,000; Per Subs 127
Special Collections: Florida Coll
Automation Activity & Vendor Info: (Cataloging) Innovative Interfaces, Inc; (Circulation) Innovative Interfaces, Inc
Wireless access
Mem of Pinellas Public Library Cooperative
Partic in Tampa Bay Library Consortium, Inc
Open Mon & Wed-Fri 10-6, Tues 10-8, Sat 10-5
Friends of the Library Group

MADISON

J NORTH FLORIDA COLLEGE LIBRARY*, Marshall W Hamilton Library, 325 NW Turner Davis Dr, 32340. SAN 303-0237. Tel: 850-973-1624. E-mail: learningresources@nfc.edu, library@nfc.edu. Web Site: www.nfc.edu/learning-resources. *Dir,* Lynn Wyche; E-mail: wychel@nfc.edu; *Libr Coord,* Ellie Morgan; Staff 2 (MLS 2)
Founded 1958. Enrl 1,700; Fac 33; Highest Degree: Associate
Library Holdings: AV Mats 3,688; Bks on Deafness & Sign Lang 85; CDs 117; DVDs 191; e-books 34,920; Bk Titles 32,000; Bk Vols 35,475; Per Subs 222; Videos 2,541
Special Collections: Florida Coll; Madison History Coll
Automation Activity & Vendor Info: (Acquisitions) Ex Libris Group; (Cataloging) Ex Libris Group; (Circulation) Ex Libris Group; (OPAC) Ex Libris Group; (Serials) Ex Libris Group
Wireless access
Partic in Florida Library Information Network; LYRASIS; Northeast Florida Library Information Network
Special Services for the Deaf - TDD equip
Special Services for the Blind - Magnifiers
Open Mon-Thurs 8-7, Fri 8-4:30

MAITLAND

P MAITLAND PUBLIC LIBRARY*, 501 S Maitland Ave, 32751-5672. SAN 303-0261. Tel: 407-647-7700. Web Site: maitlandpubliclibrary.org. *Libr Dir,* Stacie Larson; *Pub Serv Librn,* Colleen Whittall; *Digital Serv Mgr,* Catherine Keating; *Mgr, Pub Serv,* Amber Downs; E-mail: adowns@maitlandpl.org; *Circ,* Veronica Dailey; E-mail: circulation@maitlandpl.org; *Youth Serv,* Mary Daniels; Staff 7 (MLS 5, Non-MLS 2)
Founded 1896. Pop 16,919; Circ 121,471
Library Holdings: Bk Vols 69,185; Per Subs 57
Special Collections: Natural History & Environment (Audubon Coll)
Automation Activity & Vendor Info: (Cataloging) TLC (The Library Corporation); (Circulation) TLC (The Library Corporation); (Discovery) TLC (The Library Corporation); (OPAC) TLC (The Library Corporation)
Wireless access
Function: 24/7 Electronic res, 24/7 Online cat, Adult bk club, Art exhibits, Audiobks via web, Bk club(s), Bks on CD, Children's prog, Computers for patron use, Digital talking bks, Distance learning, Electronic databases & coll, Internet access, Life-long learning prog for all ages, Magazines, Movies, Music CDs, Online cat, Online ref, OverDrive digital audio bks, Photocopying/Printing, Preschool reading prog, Prog for adults, Prog for children & young adult, Ref serv available, Story hour, Summer reading prog, Tax forms, Writing prog
Publications: Directors Newsletter; Living Well at MPL (Adult Newsletter) (Monthly newsletter)
Partic in Tampa Bay Library Consortium, Inc
Open Mon-Thurs 10-9, Fri & Sat 10-6, Sun 1-6
Restriction: Non-resident fee
Friends of the Library Group

MANALAPAN

P J TURNER MOORE MEMORIAL LIBRARY, 1330 Lands End Rd, 33462. (Mail add: 600 S Ocean Blvd, 33462). Tel: 561-383-2541, 561-588-7577. E-mail: librarian@manalapan.org. Web Site: www.manalapan.org/index.aspx?nid=379. *Libr Dir,* Lisa Petersen; E-mail: lpetersen@manalapan.org
Founded 1970

MARIANNA

C CHIPOLA COLLEGE LIBRARY*, 3094 Indian Circle, 32446. SAN 303-0288. Tel: 850-718-2274. FAX: 850-718-2349. Web Site: www.chipola.edu/library. *Dir, Learning Res,* Vikki Milton; Tel: 850-718-2371, E-mail: miltonv@chipola.edu; *Coordr, Circ,* Jane Stephens; Tel: 850-718-2279, E-mail: stephensj@chipola.edu; *Libr Serv Coordr,* Wilson Ivey; Tel: 850-718-2372, E-mail: iveyw@chipola.edu; *Acq, ILL,* Nell Donaldson; Tel: 850-718-2273, E-mail: donaldsonn@chipola.edu; Staff 2 (MLS 1, Non-MLS 1)
Founded 1948. Enrl 1,300; Highest Degree: Bachelor
Library Holdings: DVDs 900; e-books 67,000; e-journals 18,000; Electronic Media & Resources 16,000; Bk Titles 33,500; Bk Vols 35,000; Per Subs 150
Special Collections: Florida Coll; Blue Springs Coll
Automation Activity & Vendor Info: (Cataloging) SirsiDynix; (Circulation) SirsiDynix; (Course Reserve) SirsiDynix; (ILL) SirsiDynix; (OPAC) SirsiDynix; (Serials) SirsiDynix
Wireless access
Function: ILL available
Partic in Florida Library Information Network; OCLC Online Computer Library Center, Inc; Panhandle Library Access Network
Open Mon-Thurs 7am-8pm, Fri 7:30-4

P JACKSON COUNTY PUBLIC LIBRARY SYSTEM*, 2929 Green St, 32446. SAN 303-0296. Tel: 850-482-1257. FAX: 850-482-9511. E-mail: jcpl@jacksoncountyfl.com. Web Site: www.jcplfl.org. *Libr Dir,* Deborah Hynes; E-mail: dhynes@jacksoncountyfl.com; *Asst Dir,* Susanna Gaston; *Ch Mgr,* Lynn Lowenthal
Founded 1977. Pop 43,000
Library Holdings: Bk Vols 78,000; Per Subs 192
Special Collections: Genealogy Coll; Local History Coll
Automation Activity & Vendor Info: (Cataloging) SirsiDynix; (Circulation) SirsiDynix
Wireless access
Mem of Panhandle Public Library Cooperative System
Partic in LYRASIS
Open Mon & Wed-Fri 9-6, Tues 9-8, Sat 9-5
Friends of the Library Group
Branches: 2
GRACEVILLE BRANCH, 5314 Brown St, Graceville, 32440. Tel: 850-263-3659. FAX: 850-263-3652. *Br Mgr,* Jennifer Thomas
Library Holdings: Bk Vols 3,526
Open Mon 10-8, Tues-Fri 10-6, Sat 10-2
GREENWOOD BRANCH, 4207 Bryan St, Greenwood, 32443. Tel: 850-594-4961. *Library Contact,* Ann Bryan
Open Mon-Thurs 12-4:30

P PANHANDLE PUBLIC LIBRARY COOPERATIVE SYSTEM*, 2862 Madison St, 32448. Tel: 850-482-9296. FAX: 850-482-9297. E-mail: admin@pplcs.net. Web Site: pplcs.net. *Adminr,* Mary Balint; Staff 2 (MLS 1, Non-MLS 1)
Founded 1992. Pop 80,136
Automation Activity & Vendor Info: (Cataloging) Koha; (Circulation) Koha; (OPAC) Koha
Function: 24/7 Electronic res, 24/7 Online cat, Audiobks via web, Electronic databases & coll, Online cat, OverDrive digital audio bks
Member Libraries: Calhoun County Public Library; Holmes County Public Library; Jackson County Public Library System
Partic in Panhandle Library Access Network
Restriction: Not a lending libr

MARY ESTHER

P MARY ESTHER PUBLIC LIBRARY*, 100 Hollywood Blvd W, 32569-1957. SAN 303-0318. Tel: 850-243-5731. FAX: 850-243-4931. E-mail: maryestherlibrary@gmail.com. Web Site: www.readokaloosa.org. *Dir,* Sheila Ortyl; E-mail: sortyl@okaloosa.lib.fl.us
Founded 1974. Pop 6,000
Library Holdings: Bk Vols 25,000; Per Subs 30; Talking Bks 600
Automation Activity & Vendor Info: (Acquisitions) SirsiDynix; (Cataloging) SirsiDynix; (Circulation) SirsiDynix
Partic in Okaloosa County Public Library Cooperative
Open Mon 12-6, Tues & Thurs 9-8, Wed & Fri 9-6, Sat 9-5
Friends of the Library Group

MAYO

P LAFAYETTE COUNTY PUBLIC LIBRARY*, 120 NE Crawford St, 32066. (Mail add: PO Box 418, 32066-0418), SAN 337-6982. Tel: 386-294-1021. FAX: 386-294-3396. E-mail: lafayette@neflin.org. Web Site: 3riverslibrary.com. *Mgr,* Deborah Johnson; E-mail: djohnson@3riverslibrary.com
Founded 1995
Library Holdings: Bk Vols 12,500; Per Subs 45
Automation Activity & Vendor Info: (Cataloging) LibLime; (Circulation) LibLime
Wireless access
Partic in Three Rivers Regional Library Consortium
Open Mon-Wed & Fri 8:30-5:30, Thurs 8:30-6

MELBOURNE

J EASTERN FLORIDA STATE COLLEGE*, Melbourne Campus Library, Philip F Nohrr Learning Resource Ctr, 3865 N Wickham Rd, 32935-2399. SAN 303-0326. Tel: 321-433-5575, 321-433-5580. Reference Tel: 321-433-5576. Web Site: www.easternflorida.edu/library. *Librn,* Jessica Cerny; E-mail: cernyj@easternflorida.edu; Staff 2 (MLS 2)
Founded 1968
Library Holdings: Bk Titles 48,000; Per Subs 225
Automation Activity & Vendor Info: (Acquisitions) Ex Libris Group; (Cataloging) Ex Libris Group; (Circulation) Ex Libris Group; (Course Reserve) Ex Libris Group; (Media Booking) Ex Libris Group; (OPAC) Ex Libris Group; (Serials) Ex Libris Group
Wireless access
Open Mon-Thurs 8-8, Fri 9-1

P EAU GALLIE PUBLIC LIBRARY*, 1521 Pineapple Ave, 32935-6594. SAN 303-0342. Tel: 321-255-4304. FAX: 321-255-4323. Web Site: www.brevardfl.gov/PublicLibraries/Branches/EauGallie. *Dir,* Jenny Morrison; E-mail: jmorrison@brev.org; Staff 6.2 (MLS 4, Non-MLS 2.2)
Founded 1939. Pop 47,000; Circ 245,075
Library Holdings: AV Mats 7,585; Bk Vols 72,957; Per Subs 213
Automation Activity & Vendor Info: (Cataloging) TLC (The Library Corporation); (Circulation) TLC (The Library Corporation); (OPAC) TLC (The Library Corporation)
Wireless access
Function: Adult bk club, Bks on cassette, Bks on CD, Children's prog, Computers for patron use, Free DVD rentals, Holiday prog, ILL available, Music CDs, Online cat, Online ref, Photocopying/Printing, Preschool outreach, Prog for adults, Prog for children & young adult, Ref serv available, Spoken cassettes & CDs, Spoken cassettes & DVDs, Story hour, Summer reading prog, Telephone ref, VHS videos, Wheelchair accessible
Mem of Brevard County Public Libraries
Open Mon 12-8, Tues & Thurs-Sat 9-5, Wed 9-8
Friends of the Library Group

C FLORIDA INSTITUTE OF TECHNOLOGY, Evans Library, 150 W University Blvd, 32901-6988. SAN 337-713X. Tel: 321-674-8000. Circulation Tel: 321-674-8086. Interlibrary Loan Service Tel: 321-674-7539. FAX: 321-724-2559. E-mail: libadmin@fit.edu. Web Site: lib.fit.edu. *Dean of Libr,* Dr Holly Miller; Tel: 321-674-8871, E-mail: hmiller@fit.edu; *Asst Dean, Head, User Experience,* Nancy Garmer; Tel: 321-674-7542; Staff 20 (MLS 12, Non-MLS 8)
Founded 1958. Enrl 8,601; Fac 475; Highest Degree: Doctorate
Library Holdings: Bk Vols 419,274; Per Subs 6,318
Special Collections: Congressman Dave Weldon, MD; Dr Jerome Penn Keuper Coll; Edmund Skellings Poet Laureate, FL; Edwin A Link Coll (Ocean Related Personal Papers, electronic archives); General John Bruce Medaris Coll (Personal Papers & Memorabilia); Radiation Inc Archives; Scott Frisch Coll; University Archives. US Document Depository
Subject Interests: Aeronaut, Engr, Marine & environ syst, Psychol
Automation Activity & Vendor Info: (Cataloging) Koha; (Circulation) Koha; (Serials) Koha
Wireless access
Partic in LYRASIS; Northeast Florida Library Information Network; OCLC Online Computer Library Center, Inc
Open Mon-Thurs 7:45-Midnight, Fri 7:45-6, Sat 10-6, Sun 10-Midnight

S FLORIDA TODAY NEWSPAPER LIBRARY*, One Gannett Plaza, 32940. SAN 324-4512. Tel: 321-242-3500. FAX: 321-242-6620. Web Site: www.floridatoday.com. *Library Contact,* Christina LaFortune; E-mail: clafortune@floridatoday.com; Staff 1 (MLS 1)
Founded 1966
Library Holdings: Bk Titles 200
Special Collections: Newspaper 1917-Present
Publications: Library Clips (Quarterly)
Restriction: Staff use only

P DR MARTIN LUTHER KING JR LIBRARY*, 955 E University Blvd, 32920. SAN 376-2750. Tel: 321-952-4511. FAX: 321-952-4512. Web Site: www.brevardfl.gov/PublicLibraries/Branches/MLK. *Libr Dir,* Irma Fordham; E-mail: ifordham@brev.org
Library Holdings: Audiobooks 850; CDs 1,189; DVDs 3,031; Bk Vols 21,275; Per Subs 53
Automation Activity & Vendor Info: (Cataloging) Infor Library & Information Solutions; (Circulation) Infor Library & Information Solutions; (OPAC) Infor Library & Information Solutions
Wireless access
Mem of Brevard County Public Libraries

Open Mon, Wed & Fri 9-5, Tues & Thurs Noon-8
Friends of the Library Group

P MELBOURNE PUBLIC LIBRARY, 540 E Fee Ave, 32901. SAN 303-0377. Tel: 321-952-4514. FAX: 321-952-4518. Web Site: brevardfl.gov/PublicLibraries/Branches/Melbourne. *Libr Dir,* Irma Fordham; E-mail: ifordham@brev.org; *Asst Dir,* Geraldine Prieth; E-mail: gprieth@brev.org; Staff 5 (MLS 5)
Founded 1918. Pop 66,970; Circ 459,601
Library Holdings: Bk Vols 107,513; Per Subs 298
Special Collections: Florida Coll; Genealogy Coll; Investing Coll
Automation Activity & Vendor Info: (Cataloging) Infor Library & Information Solutions; (Circulation) Infor Library & Information Solutions; (OPAC) Infor Library & Information Solutions
Wireless access
Mem of Brevard County Public Libraries
Open Mon & Wed 9-8, Tues & Thurs-Sat 9-5, Sun 1-5
Friends of the Library Group

P SUNTREE/VIERA PUBLIC LIBRARY, 902 Jordan Blass Dr, 32940. Tel: 321-255-4404. FAX: 321-255-4406. Reference FAX: 321-253-6640. Web Site: brevardfl.gov/publiclibraries/branches/suntreeviera. *Dir,* Heather Palmer; E-mail: hpalmer@brev.org; Staff 14.5 (MLS 3, Non-MLS 11.5)
Circ 222,000
Library Holdings: AV Mats 1,700; CDs 950; DVDs 4,800; Large Print Bks 2,650; Bk Titles 51,000; Per Subs 66
Special Collections: LEAF Lib
Automation Activity & Vendor Info: (Cataloging) Infor Library & Information Solutions; (Circulation) Infor Library & Information Solutions
Wireless access
Mem of Brevard County Public Libraries
Open Mon & Tues 9-8, Wed-Sat 9-5
Friends of the Library Group

MELBOURNE BEACH

P MELBOURNE BEACH PUBLIC LIBRARY*, 324 Ocean Ave, 32951. Tel: 321-956-5642. FAX: 321-953-6942. Web Site: www.brevardfl.gov/PublicLibraries/Branches/MelbourneBeach. *Libr Dir,* Ashley Link; E-mail: alink@brev.org; Staff 4 (MLS 2, Non-MLS 2)
Founded 2002
Library Holdings: Bk Vols 53,000; Per Subs 65
Automation Activity & Vendor Info: (Cataloging) Infor Library & Information Solutions; (Circulation) Infor Library & Information Solutions; (OPAC) Infor Library & Information Solutions
Wireless access
Mem of Brevard County Public Libraries
Open Mon & Thurs 10-6, Tues 12-8, Wed & Fri 9-5, Sat 10-2
Friends of the Library Group

MERRITT ISLAND

P MERRITT ISLAND PUBLIC LIBRARY*, 1195 N Courtenay Pkwy, 32953-4596. SAN 303-0407. Tel: 321-455-1369. Web Site: www.brevardcounty.us/PublicLibraries/Branches/MerrittIsland. *Dir,* Janice Murray; E-mail: jmurray@brev.org
Founded 1965. Pop 36,090; Circ 316,681
Library Holdings: Bk Titles 101,000; Per Subs 200
Automation Activity & Vendor Info: (Circulation) Infor Library & Information Solutions; (OPAC) Infor Library & Information Solutions
Wireless access
Function: Archival coll, AV serv, For res purposes, Homebound delivery serv, ILL available, Internet access, Magnifiers for reading, Photocopying/Printing, Prog for children & young adult, Ref serv available, Telephone ref, Wheelchair accessible
Mem of Brevard County Public Libraries
Open Mon 9-8, Tues, Wed, Fri & Sat 9-5, Thurs 12-8

MIAMI

L BAKER & MCKENZIE*, Law Library, 1111 Brickell Ave, Ste 1700, 33131. SAN 372-1337. Tel: 305-789-8900, 305-789-8951. FAX: 305-789-8953. Web Site: www.bakermckenzie.com. *Dir,* Wendy Richards
Library Holdings: Bk Vols 5,000; Per Subs 75
Automation Activity & Vendor Info: (Cataloging) SydneyPlus
Wireless access
Restriction: Staff use only

M BAPTIST HOSPITAL OF MIAMI*, Jaffee Medical Library, 8900 N Kendall Dr, 33176. SAN 303-0423. Tel: 786-596-6506. FAX: 786-596-5910. E-mail: library@baptisthealth.net. Web Site: www.baptisthealth.net. *Dir,* Devica Samsundar; E-mail: devicas@baptisthealth.net; Staff 2 (MLS 2)
Founded 1966
Library Holdings: e-journals 900; Bk Titles 600; Per Subs 50
Special Collections: Antique Surgical Instruments
Subject Interests: Allied health, Consumer health, Hist of med, Hospital admin, Med, Nursing
Automation Activity & Vendor Info: (Cataloging) CyberTools for Libraries; (Circulation) CyberTools for Libraries; (OPAC) CyberTools for Libraries; (Serials) EBSCO Online
Publications: Newsletter
Partic in National Network of Libraries of Medicine Region 2; SE-Atlantic Regional Med Libr Servs; South Florida Health Sciences Library Consortium
Restriction: Non-circulating to the pub

R BETH DAVID CONGREGATION*, Harry Simons Library, 2625 SW Third Ave, 33129. SAN 303-0431. Tel: 305-854-3911. FAX: 305-285-5841. E-mail: info@bethdavid.miami.org. Web Site: bethdavidmiami.org. *Children's Serv Coordr,* Reiz Farah
Founded 1962
Library Holdings: Bk Vols 7,000
Subject Interests: Biology, Children's lit, Educ, Fiction, Hist, Relig
Restriction: Mem only, Students only

C CARLOS ALBIZU UNIVERSITY LIBRARY, 2173 NW 99 Ave, 33172. SAN 375-3565. Tel: 305-593-1223, Ext 3131. Reference Tel: 305-593-1223, Ext 3220. Administration Tel: 305-593-1223, Ext 3221. FAX: 305-593-8318. E-mail: aumiamilibrary@albizu.edu. Web Site: albizu.ent.sirsi.net/client/en_us/miami. *Dir,* Juan Zaragoza; E-mail: jzaragoza@albizu.edu; *Ref & Instruction Librn,* Julian Perez; E-mail: juperez@albizu.edu; Staff 4 (MLS 1, Non-MLS 3)
Enrl 850; Fac 80; Highest Degree: Doctorate
Library Holdings: Bks on Deafness & Sign Lang 21; Bk Titles 25,000; Bk Vols 30,000; Per Subs 350
Subject Interests: Bus, Cross-cultural studies, Psychol
Automation Activity & Vendor Info: (Cataloging) Follett Software; (Circulation) Follett Software; (OPAC) Follett Software
Wireless access
Publications: Library Report
Partic in Florida Library Information Network; LYRASIS; Southeast Florida Library Information Network, Inc
Open Mon-Fri 10-9, Sat 9-3

J CITY COLLEGE - MIAMI LIBRARY*, 9300 S Dadeland Blvd, Ste 200, 33156. Tel: 305-666-9242, Ext 1136. FAX: 305-666-9243. Web Site: www.citycollege.edu. *Exec Dir,* Narion Damour
Highest Degree: Bachelor
Library Holdings: Bk Vols 2,000; Per Subs 50; Spec Interest Per Sub 20; Videos 400
Special Collections: Florida Legal Coll
Automation Activity & Vendor Info: (Cataloging) Winnebago Software Co
Wireless access
Partic in OCLC Online Computer Library Center, Inc
Open Mon-Thurs 8am-9:30pm, Fri 8-5, Sat 9-1

S FAIRCHILD TROPICAL BOTANIC GARDEN*, Montgomery Library, 11935 Old Cutler Rd, 33156. SAN 303-0504. Tel: 305-667-1651, Ext 3424. FAX: 305-669-4074. E-mail: library@fairchildgarden.org. Web Site: www.fairchildgarden.org. *Dir,* Carl E Lewis; E-mail: clewis@fairchildgarden.org; Staff 1 (MLS 1)
Founded 1941
Library Holdings: Bk Vols 16,000; Per Subs 60
Special Collections: David Fairchild Coll, papers & photos; Florida Botanists
Subject Interests: Botany, Hort
Automation Activity & Vendor Info: (OPAC) CyberTools for Libraries
Function: Archival coll, For res purposes
Restriction: Not a lending libr, Open by appt only

C FLORIDA INTERNATIONAL UNIVERSITY*, Steven & Dorothea Green Library, 11200 SW Eighth St, 33199. SAN 337-7199. Tel: 305-348-2461. Circulation Tel: 305-348-2451. Interlibrary Loan Service Tel: 305-348-4054. Reference Tel: 305-348-2470. Automation Services Tel: 305-348-3127. FAX: 305-348-3408. Interlibrary Loan Service FAX: 305-348-6055. Reference FAX: 305-348-6579. TDD: 305-348-1295. Web Site: library.fiu.edu. *Dean, Univ Libr,* Anne M Prestamo; E-mail: anne.prestamo@fiu.edu; *Assoc Dean, Tech & Digital Serv,* Dr Bryan Cooper; Tel: 305-348-2982, Fax: 305-348-0122, E-mail: lbcooper@fiu.edu; *Dir, Admin Serv, Head, Operations & Budget,* Diana Cardenas; Tel: 305-348-1900, E-mail: dicarden@fiu.edu; *Head of GIS Ctr,* Jennifer Fu; Tel: 305-348-3138, Fax: 305-348-6445, E-mail: fujen@fiu.edu; *Head, Cat,* Rita Cauce; Tel: 305-348-0547, E-mail: rita.cauce@fiu.edu; *Bibliog Instr, Head, Ref Serv,* Elana Karshmer; Tel: 305-348-1843, E-mail: ekarshme@fiu.edu; *Head, Spec Coll, Univ Archivist,* Vicki Silvera; Tel: 305-348-3136, Fax: 305-348-4739, E-mail: silverav@fiu.edu; *Head, Syst,* George Fray; Tel: 305-348-2488, Fax: 305-348-6450, E-mail:

frayg@fiu.edu. Subject Specialists: *Admin, Fr opera, Musicology,* Anne M Prestamo; *Admin, Automation, Digitization,* Dr Bryan Cooper; *Budgeting, Human resources,* Diana Cardenas; *Info literacy,* Elana Karshmer; *Archives, Caribbean area, Latin Am,* Vicki Silvera; Staff 40 (MLS 26, Non-MLS 14)
Founded 1972. Enrl 33,540; Fac 891; Highest Degree: Doctorate
Library Holdings: Audiobooks 1,061; AV Mats 48,540; e-books 122,297; e-journals 87,257; Electronic Media & Resources 85,681; Microforms 2,843,669; Bk Vols 1,379,635; Per Subs 1,531; Videos 15,950
Special Collections: Diaz-Ayala Music Coll; European Documentation Center; Geological Survey Maps; Latin American & Caribbean Coll; Urban & Regional Documents. State Document Depository; UN Document Depository; US Document Depository
Automation Activity & Vendor Info: (Acquisitions) Ex Libris Group; (Cataloging) Ex Libris Group; (Circulation) Ex Libris Group; (Course Reserve) Ex Libris Group; (ILL) OCLC ILLiad; (OPAC) Ex Libris Group; (Serials) Ex Libris Group
Wireless access
Function: Archival coll, Art exhibits, Audio & video playback equip for onsite use, AV serv, Bilingual assistance for Spanish patrons, Bks on cassette, Bks on CD, Computers for patron use, Digital talking bks, Distance learning, Doc delivery serv, E-Reserves, Electronic databases & coll, Govt ref serv, Health sci info serv, ILL available, Internet access, Large print keyboards, Music CDs, Online cat, Online info literacy tutorials on the web & in blackboard, Online ref, Orientations, Outside serv via phone, mail, e-mail & web, Photocopying/Printing, Ref serv available, Scanner, Spoken cassettes & CDs, Tax forms, Telephone ref, VHS videos, Wheelchair accessible
Partic in Association of Southeastern Research Libraries; Center for Research Libraries; Consortium of Southern Biomedical Libraries; Florida Library Information Network; LYRASIS
Special Services for the Deaf - TDD equip
Special Services for the Blind - Computer with voice synthesizer for visually impaired persons
Open Mon-Thurs 7:30am-1am, Fri 7:30am-10pm, Sat 8-8, Sun 10am-1am

L GREENBERG TRAURIG LLP*, Research Center Law Library, 333 SE Second Ave, Ste 4400, 33131. (Mail add: Doral Concourse, 8400 NW 36th St, Ste 400, Doral, 33166), SAN 328-0705. Tel: 305-579-0500. FAX: 305-579-0717. Web Site: www.gtlaw.com/en/locations/miami. *Supvr,* Denise Mason; Staff 13 (MLS 3, Non-MLS 10)
Founded 1975
Library Holdings: Bk Titles 8,000; Bk Vols 20,000; Per Subs 450
Function: Doc delivery serv, For res purposes, ILL available, Internet access, Ref serv available, Telephone ref
Restriction: Access at librarian's discretion

L HOLLAND & KNIGHT LLP*, Law Library, 701 Brickell Ave, Ste 3300, 33131. SAN 372-1329. Tel: 305-374-8500. FAX: 305-789-7799. *Librn,* Jackie Norton; E-mail: jackie.norton@hklaw.com; Staff 1 (MLS 1)
Library Holdings: Bk Vols 10,000; Per Subs 75

M MERCY HOSPITAL LIBRARY SERVICES*, 3663 S Miami Ave, 33133. SAN 303-0601. Tel: 305-285-2160. FAX: 305-285-2128. Web Site: mercymiami.com/professionals/physicians/online-medical-library.dot. *Med Librn,* Jean Garrison; E-mail: jgarrison@mercymiami.org; Staff 1 (Non-MLS 1)
Founded 1951
Library Holdings: e-books 118; e-journals 1,500; Bk Titles 500; Per Subs 25
Partic in National Network of Libraries of Medicine Region 2; South Florida Health Sciences Library Consortium
Restriction: Staff use only

M MIAMI CHILDREN'S HEALTH SYSTEM*, Nicklaus Children's Hospital Medical Library, 3100 SW 62nd Ave, 33155-3009. SAN 328-1329. Tel: 305-666-6511, Ext 4470. FAX: 305-284-1145. Web Site: www.nicklauschildrens.org/medical-professionals/for-physicians/medical-library. *Dir,* Roumiana Katzarkov; E-mail: Roumiana.Katzarkov@mch.com; Staff 3 (MLS 1, Non-MLS 2)
Library Holdings: e-books 65; e-journals 400; Bk Vols 3,700; Per Subs 150
Subject Interests: Pediatrics
Automation Activity & Vendor Info: (Cataloging) EOS International; (Circulation) EOS International; (OPAC) EOS International; (Serials) EOS International
Partic in South Florida Health Sciences Library Consortium
Restriction: Employees only

MIAMI DADE COLLEGE

C KENDALL CAMPUS LIBRARY*, 11011 SW 104th St, 33176-3393, SAN 337-7253. Tel: 305-237-0996, 305-237-2015, 305-237-2291. Interlibrary Loan Service Tel: 305-237-2783. Reference Tel: 305-237-2292. FAX: 305-237-2923. Interlibrary Loan Service FAX: 305-237-2864. Administration FAX: 305-237-0302. Web Site: www.mdc.edu/kendall/library. *Dir,* Eric Dominicis; *Asst Dir,* Jennifer Diptee; *Librn,* Barbara Feldman-Joy; *Librn,* Laurie Hime; *Librn,* Steven Kronen; *Librn,* David Picca; *Librn,* Jennifer Saxton; Staff 23.8 (MLS 7.9, Non-MLS 15.9)
Founded 1965. Enrl 63,092; Fac 204; Highest Degree: Bachelor
Library Holdings: Bk Titles 126,194; Bk Vols 139,798; Per Subs 431
Special Collections: Archival Coll
Automation Activity & Vendor Info: (Acquisitions) Ex Libris Group; (Cataloging) LAC Group; (Circulation) Ex Libris Group; (OPAC) Ex Libris Group
Publications: Kendall Campus Library Fact Sheet
Open Mon-Thurs 7am-10pm, Fri 7-6, Sat 10-4

CM MEDICAL CENTER CAMPUS LIBRARY & INFORMATION RESOURCE CENTER*, 950 NW 20th St, 33127, SAN 337-7318. Tel: 305-237-4129. FAX: 305-237-4301. *Dir,* Elisa Abella; Tel: 305-237-4498, E-mail: elisa.abella@mdc.edu; *Asst Dir,* Ivan Toledo; Tel: 305-237-4325; *Librn,* Carla Clark; Tel: 305-237-4342; Staff 3 (MLS 3)
Founded 1975. Enrl 41,000; Fac 100
Library Holdings: Bk Titles 11,000; Bk Vols 12,000; Per Subs 96
Subject Interests: Allied health, Nursing
Partic in SE Fla Educ Consortium
Open Mon-Thurs 7:30am-9pm, Fri 7:30-5, Sat 9-4

C NORTH CAMPUS LEARNING RESOURCES*, 11380 NW 27th Ave, 33167, SAN 337-7229. Tel: 305-237-1142. Reference Tel: 305-237-1183. FAX: 305-237-8276. Web Site: www.mdc.edu/north/library. *Dir,* Estrella Iglesias; Tel: 305-237-1471; *Assoc Dir,* Dr Sara Alegria; Tel: 305-237-1777; *ILL,* Devi Singh; Staff 7 (MLS 7)
Founded 1960. Enrl 25,000; Fac 350; Highest Degree: Bachelor
Library Holdings: Bk Titles 107,760; Bk Vols 130,000; Per Subs 650
Partic in LYRASIS; South Florida Health Sciences Library Consortium

C WOLFSON CAMPUS LIBRARY*, 300 NE Second Ave, 33132, SAN 337-7288. Tel: 305-237-3144. Interlibrary Loan Service Tel: 305-237-3454. Reference Tel: 305-237-3451. Web Site: www.mdc.edu/main/library. *Dir, Learning Res,* Zoila De Yurre Fatemian; Tel: 305-237-7454, E-mail: zdeyurre@mdc.edu; *Assoc Dir, Learning Res,* Katia Nunez; Tel: 305-237-7385, E-mail: knunez1@mdc.edu; *Librn,* Adria Leal; Tel: 305-237-3449, E-mail: aleal2@mdc.edu; Staff 11 (MLS 5, Non-MLS 6)
Founded 1972
Library Holdings: AV Mats 3,821; Bk Vols 45,015; Per Subs 170; Talking Bks 236
Automation Activity & Vendor Info: (Cataloging) Ex Libris Group; (Circulation) Ex Libris Group; (OPAC) Ex Libris Group; (Serials) Ex Libris Group
Open Mon-Thurs 7:30am-9pm, Fri 7:30-5, Sat 8-1

L MIAMI-DADE COUNTY LAW LIBRARY*, County Courthouse, Rm 321A, 73 W Flagler St, 33130. SAN 303-0466. Tel: 305-349-7548. FAX: 305-349-7552. E-mail: refdesk@mdcll.org. Web Site: www.mdcll.org. *Dir,* Johanna Porpiglia; *Ref,* Claudette Calixte; Staff 14 (MLS 7, Non-MLS 7)
Founded 1937
Library Holdings: Bk Vols 127,270; Per Subs 30
Subject Interests: State law
Automation Activity & Vendor Info: (Acquisitions) Inmagic, Inc.; (Cataloging) Inmagic, Inc.; (Serials) Inmagic, Inc.
Wireless access
Partic in Southeastern Chapter of the American Association of Law Libraries
Open Mon-Thurs 8:15-4, Fri 8:15-Noon
Restriction: Pub use on premises

P MIAMI-DADE PUBLIC LIBRARY SYSTEM*, Main Library, 101 W Flagler St, 33130-1523. SAN 337-7342. Tel: 305-375-2665. Circulation Tel: 305-375-2493. Reference Tel: 305-375-5231, 305-375-5575. Administration Tel: 305-375-5026. FAX: 305-375-3048. TDD: 305-679-7977. Web Site: www.mdpls.org. *Dir,* Raymond Baker; E-mail: director@mdpls.org; *Asst Dir,* Mike Iturrey; Tel: 305-375-5044, E-mail: iturreym@mdpls.org; *Asst Dir, Fac Mgt & Develop,* Leo Gomez; Tel: 305-375-5051, E-mail: gomezl@mdpls.org; *Operations Adminr,* Ralph Costa; Tel: 305-375-5183, E-mail: costar@mdpls.org; *Operations Adminr,* Wil Fowler; Tel: 305-375-3873, E-mail: fowlerw@mdpls.org; *Operations Adminr,* Michele Stiles; Tel: 305-375-5008, E-mail: stilesm@mdpls.org; *Mgr,* Shana Hinze; E-mail: hinzes@mdpls.org; Staff 218 (MLS 200, Non-MLS 18)
Founded 1971. Pop 2,121,798; Circ 8,132,818
Library Holdings: Audiobooks 53,133; AV Mats 25,328; Bks on Deafness & Sign Lang 1,152; Braille Volumes 432; CDs 23,575; DVDs 158,360; e-books 4,850; Electronic Media & Resources 3,789; High Interest/Low Vocabulary Bk Vols 899; Large Print Bks 52,795; Microforms 66,751; Music Scores 28,893; Bk Titles 621,509; Bk Vols 2,588,195; Per Subs 1,265; Videos 30,099
Special Collections: Florida Room, bks, rare bks, clippings, photog; Foundations Center Regional Coll; Patent. State Document Depository; US Document Depository
Subject Interests: Fla, Intl, Latin Am, Patents, Spanish lang

Automation Activity & Vendor Info: (Acquisitions) Innovative Interfaces, Inc; (Cataloging) Innovative Interfaces, Inc; (Circulation) Innovative Interfaces, Inc; (OPAC) Innovative Interfaces, Inc; (Serials) Innovative Interfaces, Inc
Wireless access
Function: Homebound delivery serv
Publications: Guide to Services; Library Happenings (Newsletter); Long Range Plan; Schedule of Programs (Monthly)
Partic in Southeast Florida Library Information Network, Inc
Special Services for the Deaf - Staff with knowledge of sign lang; TDD equip
Special Services for the Blind - Assistive/Adapted tech devices, equip & products; Audio mat; Bks & mags in Braille, on rec, tape & cassette; Talking bks
Open Mon-Sat 9:30-6
Friends of the Library Group
Branches: 50
ALLAPATTAH BRANCH, 1799 NW 35th St, 33142-5421, SAN 337-7407. Tel: 305-638-6086. Web Site: www.mdpls.org/branches/allapattah-branch-library.asp. *Mgr,* Harry Varela; E-mail: varelah@mdpls.org
Open Mon-Wed, Fri & Sat 9:30-6, Thurs 11:30-8
ARCOLA LAKES BRANCH, 8240 NW 7 Ave, 33150. Tel: 305-694-2707. Web Site: www.mdpls.org/branches/arcola-lakes-branch-library.asp. *Mgr,* Paul Lefrak; E-mail: lefrakp@mdpls.org
Open Mon, Tues, Fri & Sat 9:30-6, Wed & Thurs 11:30-8
BAY HARBOR ISLANDS BRANCH, 1175 95 St, Bay Harbor Islands, Miami Beach, 33154. Tel: 786-646-9961. Web Site: www.mdpls.org/branches/bay-harbor-islands-branch-library.asp. *Mgr,* Hector Vazquez; E-mail: vazquezh@mdpls.org
Open Tues-Thurs 10:30-7, Fri 9:30-6, Sat 10-6
P BRAILLE & TALKING BOOKS LIBRARY, c/o North Dade Regional Library, 2455 NW 183rd St, 33056, SAN 337-7377. Tel: 305-751-8687. Toll Free Tel: 800-451-9544. FAX: 305-757-8401. E-mail: talkingbooks@mdpls.org. Web Site: www.mdpls.org/services/talking-books.asp. *Mgr,* Patrick Noel
Special Collections: Blindness & Other Handicaps Reference Material; Spanish Language Coll, cassettes
Open Mon-Thurs 9:30-8, Fri-Sun 9:30-6
CALIFORNIA CLUB BRANCH, 700 Ives Dairy Rd, 33179. Tel: 305-770-3161. Web Site: www.mdpls.org/branches/california-club-branch-library.asp. *Mgr,* Pablo Lopez; E-mail: lopezp@mdpls.org
Open Mon, Thurs, Fri & Sat 9:30-6, Tues & Wed 11:30-8
CIVIC CENTER PORTA KIOSK, Metrorail Civic Ctr Sta, 1501 NW 12th Ave, 33136. (Mail add: 227 22nd St, Miami Beach, 33139), SAN 377-7138. Tel: 305-324-0291. Web Site: www.mdpls.org/branches/civic-center-branch-library.asp. *Mgr,* Shana Hinze; E-mail: hinzes@mdpls.org
Open Mon-Fri 7-6
COCONUT GROVE BRANCH, 2875 McFarlane Rd, Coconut Grove, 33133, SAN 337-7431. Tel: 305-442-8695. Web Site: www.mdpls.org/branches/coconut-grove-branch-library.asp. *Mgr,* Krystle Smith; E-mail: smithk@mdpls.org
Open Mon, Wed, Thurs & Sat 9:30-6, Tues 11:30-8
CONCORD BRANCH, 3882 SW 112th Ave, 33165. Tel: 305-207-1344. Web Site: www.mdpls.org/branches/concord-branch-library.asp. *Mgr,* Melinda Meyer; E-mail: meyerm@mdpls.org
Open Mon, Wed & Thurs-Sat 9:30-6, Tues 11:30-8
CORAL GABLES BRANCH, 3443 Segovia St, Coral Gables, 33134, SAN 337-7466. Tel: 305-442-8706. Web Site: www.mdpls.org/branches/coral-gables-branch-library.asp. *Mgr,* Will Runyan; E-mail: runyanw@mdpls.org
Open Mon-Thurs 9:30-8, Fri-Sun 9:30-6
CORAL REEF BRANCH, 9211 SW 152nd St, 33157, SAN 337-7474. Tel: 305-233-8324. Web Site: www.mdpls.org/branches/coral-reef-branch-library.asp. *Mgr,* Miriam Quiros-Laso; E-mail: quiroslasom@mdpls.org
Open Mon & Tues 11:30-8, Wed & Thurs 9:30-8, Fri & Sat 9:30-6
COUNTRY WALK BRANCH, 15433 SW 137th Ave, 33177. Tel: 786-293-4577. FAX: 786-293-4582. Web Site: www.mdpls.org/branches/country-walk-branch-library.asp. *Mgr,* Ellen Book; E-mail: booke@mdpls.org
Open Mon & Thurs-Sat 9:30-6, Tues & Wed 11:30-8
CULMER OVERTOWN BRANCH, 350 NW 13th St, 33136, SAN 337-7490. Tel: 305-579-5322. Web Site: www.mdpls.org/branches/culmer-overtown-branch-library.asp. *Mgr,* Latoya Darbeau; E-mail: darbeaul@mdpls.org
Open Mon-Fri 9:30-6
DORAL BRANCH, 8551 NW 53rd St, Ste A107, Doral, 33166. Tel: 305-716-9598. Web Site: www.mdpls.org/branches/doral-branch-library.asp. *Mgr,* Marie Blanco; E-mail: blancom@mdpls.org
Open Mon-Thurs 9:30-7, Fri & Sat 9:30-6
EDISON CENTER BRANCH, 531 NW 62nd St, 33150, SAN 337-7520. Tel: 305-757-0668. FAX: 305-757-3975. Web Site: www.mdpls.org/branches/edison-center-branch-library.asp. *Mgr,* Candice Pinder; E-mail: pinderc@mdpls.org
Open Mon-Fri 9:30-6
FAIRLAWN BRANCH, 6376 SW Eighth St, 33144, SAN 337-7555. Tel: 305-261-1571. FAX: 305-264-1716. Web Site: www.mdpls.org/branches/fairlawn-branch-library.asp. *Mgr,* Janelle Gonzalez; E-mail: gonzalezja@mdpls.org
Open Mon, Tues & Thurs-Sat 9:30-6, Wed 11:30-8
GOLDEN GLADES BRANCH, 100 NE 166 St, 33162. Tel: 305-787-1544. FAX: 305-787-8297. Web Site: www.mdpls.org/branches/golden-glades-branch-library.asp. *Mgr,* Pamela Jefferson; E-mail: jeffersonp@mdpls.org
Open Mon & Tues 11:30-8, Wed-Sat 9:30-6
HIALEAH GARDENS BRANCH, 11300 NW 87th Ct, Ste 112-114, Hialeah Gardens, 33018. Tel: 305-820-8520. FAX: 305-820-8577. Web Site: www.mdpls.org/branches/hialeah-gardens-branch-library.asp. *Mgr,* Ana Barreto; E-mail: barretoa@mdpls.org
Open Mon-Wed, Fri & Sat 9:30-6, Thurs 11:30-8
HISPANIC BRANCH, 1398 SW First St, 33135, SAN 337-761X. Tel: 305-643-8574. FAX: 305-643-8578. Web Site: www.mdpls.org/branches/hispanic-branch-library.asp. *Mgr,* Camilo Barrero; E-mail: barreroc@mdpls.org
Subject Interests: Latin Am, Spanish (Lang)
Open Mon & Wed 11:30-8, Tues & Thurs-Sat 9:30-6
HOMESTEAD BRANCH, 700 N Homestead Blvd, Homestead, 33030, SAN 337-7644. Tel: 305-246-0168. FAX: 305-248-7817. Web Site: www.mdpls.org/branches/homestead-branch-library.asp. *Mgr,* Fatima Centeno; E-mail: centenof@mdpls.org
Open Mon & Thurs-Sat 9:30-6, Tues & Wed 11:30-8
INTERNATIONAL MALL BRANCH, 10315 NW 12 St, 33172. Tel: 305-594-2514. FAX: 305-418-2746. Web Site: www.mdpls.org/branches/international-mall-branch-library.asp. *Mgr,* Raquel Fernandez; E-mail: fernandezr@mdpls.org
Open Mon, Wed, Fri & Sat 9:30-6, Tues & Thurs 11:30-8
KENDALE LAKES BRANCH, 15205 SW 88 St, 33196. Tel: 305-388-0326. FAX: 305-388-2259. Web Site: www.mdpls.org/branches/kendale-lakes-branch-library.asp. *Mgr,* Athanasia Fitos; E-mail: fitosa@mdpls.org
Open Mon & Thurs 11:30-8, Tues, Wed, Fri & Sat 9:30-6
KENDALL BRANCH, 9101 SW 97th Ave, 33176, SAN 337-7679. Tel: 305-279-0520. FAX: 305-270-2983. Web Site: www.mdpls.org/branches/kendall-branch-library.asp. *Mgr,* Javier Corredor; E-mail: corredorj@mdpls.org
Open Mon & Wed 11:30-8, Tues & Thurs-Sat 9:30-6
KEY BISCAYNE BRANCH, 299 Crandon Blvd, Key Biscayne, 33149, SAN 322-5941. Tel: 305-361-6134. FAX: 305-365-0496. Web Site: www.mdpls.org/branches/key-biscayne-branch-library.asp. *Mgr,* Alexandra Gutierrez; E-mail: gutierreza@mdpls.org
Open Mon & Thurs-Sat 9:30-6, Tues & Wed 11:30-8
LAKES OF THE MEADOW BRANCH, 4284 SW 152nd Ave, 33185. Tel: 305-222-2149. FAX: 305-222-2146. Web Site: www.mdpls.org/branches/lakes-of-the-meadow-branch-library.asp. *Mgr,* Athanasia Fitos; E-mail: fitosa@mdpls.org
Open Mon, Tues, Thurs & Sat 9:30-6, Wed 11:30-8
LEMON CITY BRANCH, 430 NE 61st St, 33137, SAN 337-7709. Tel: 305-757-0662. FAX: 305-757-5747. Web Site: www.mdpls.org/branches/lemon-city-branch-library.asp. *Mgr,* Jameliya Hall; E-mail: hallj@mdpls.org
Founded 1894
Open Mon, Tues & Thurs-Sat 9:30-6, Wed 11:30-8
LITTLE RIVER BRANCH, 160 NE 79th St, 33138, SAN 337-7733. Tel: 305-751-8689. FAX: 305-757-5237. Web Site: www.mdpls.org/branches/little-river-branch-library.asp. *Mgr,* Tristan Miller; E-mail: millert@mdpls.org
Open Mon-Sat 9:30-6
MIAMI BEACH REGIONAL, 227 22nd St, Miami Beach, 33139, SAN 328-6452. Tel: 305-535-4219. FAX: 305-535-4224. Web Site: www.mdpls.org/branches/miami-beach-regional-library.asp. *Mgr,* Bryant Capley; E-mail: capleyb@mdpls.org
Open Mon-Thurs 9:30-8, Fri-Sun 9:30-6
MIAMI LAKES BRANCH, 6699 Windmill Gate Rd, Miami Lakes, 33014, SAN 337-775X. Tel: 305-822-6520. FAX: 305-364-0802. Web Site: www.mdpls.org/branches/miami-lakes-branch-library.asp. *Mgr,* Carmen Docurro; E-mail: docurroc@mdpls.org
Open Mon 11:30-8, Tues & Wed 9:30-8, Thurs-Sat 9:30-6
MIAMI SPRINGS BRANCH, 401 Westward Dr, Miami Springs, 33166, SAN 337-7768. Tel: 305-805-3811. FAX: 305-805-1611. Web Site: www.mdpls.org/branches/miami-springs-branch-library.asp. *Mgr,* Rita Mayer; E-mail: mayerr@mdpls.org
Open Mon, Wed, Thurs & Sat 9:30-6, Tues 11:30-8

MODEL CITY BRANCH, 2211 NW 54th St, 33142, SAN 337-7792. Tel: 305-636-2233. FAX: 305-638-6828. Web Site: www.mdpls.org/branches/model-city-branch-library.asp. *Mgr,* Jemmy Pierre-Louis; E-mail: pierrelouisj@mdpls.org
Open Mon-Fri 9-5

NARANJA BRANCH, 14850 SW 280 St, 33032. Tel: 305-242-2290. FAX: 305-242-2297. Web Site: www.mdpls.org/branches/naranja-branch-library.asp. *Mgr,* Milena Gonzalez; E-mail: gonzalezmi@mdpls.org
Open Mon, Wed, Fri & Sat 9:30-6, Tues & Thurs 11:30-8

NORTH CENTRAL BRANCH, 9590 NW 27th Ave, 33147, SAN 371-3431. Tel: 305-693-4541. FAX: 305-694-0315. Web Site: www.mdpls.org/branches/north-central-branch-library.asp. *Mgr,* Sylvia Brown; E-mail: browns@mdpls.org
Open Mon-Wed, Fri & Sat 9:30-6, Thurs 11:30-6

NORTH DADE REGIONAL, 2455 NW 183rd St, 33056, SAN 337-7822. Tel: 305-625-6424. FAX: 305-628-3854. Web Site: www.mdpls.org/branches/north-dade-regional-library.asp. *Mgr,* Patrick Noel; E-mail: noelp@mdpls.org
Special Collections: Schomburg Clipping & Index File
Open Mon-Thurs 9:30-8, Fri-Sun 9:30-6

NORTH SHORE BRANCH, 7501 Collins Ave, Miami Beach, 33141, SAN 328-6479. Tel: 305-864-5392. FAX: 305-861-2032. Web Site: www.mdpls.org/branches/north-shore-branch-library.asp. *Mgr,* Katherine Ehlers; E-mail: ehlersk@mdpls.org
Open Mon, Tues, Fri & Sat 9:30-6, Wed 11:30-8

NORTHEAST DADE - AVENTURA BRANCH, 2930 Aventura Blvd, 33180, SAN 337-7857. Tel: 305-931-5512. FAX: 305-931-5515. Web Site: www.mdpls.org/branches/northeast-dade-aventura-branch-library.asp. *Mgr,* David Larsen; E-mail: larsend@mdpls.org
Open Mon 9:30-9, Tues-Thurs 9:30-8, Fri-Sun 9:30-6

OPA-LOCKA BRANCH, 780 Fisherman St, Ste 140, Opa-Locka, 33054. Tel: 305-688-1134. FAX: 305-769-4045. Web Site: www.mdpls.org/branches/opa-locka-branch-library.asp. *Mgr,* Sylvia Brown; E-mail: browns@mdpls.org
Open Mon-Fri 9:30-6

PALM SPRINGS NORTH BRANCH, 17601 NW 78th Ave, Ste 111, Hialeah, 33015. Tel: 305-820-8564. FAX: 305-557-2173. Web Site: www.mdpls.org/branches/palm-springs-north-branch-library.asp. *Mgr,* Carmen Docurro; E-mail: docurroc@mdpls.org
Open Mon, Tues, Fri & Sat 9:30-6, Wed 11:30-8

PALMETTO BAY BRANCH, 17641 Old Cutler Rd, 33157. Tel: 305-232-1771. FAX: 305-232-1706. Web Site: www.mdpls.org/branches/palmetto-bay-branch-library.asp. *Mgr,* Jennifer Stockment; E-mail: stockmentj@mdpls.org
Open Mon, Tues, Fri & Sat 9:30-6, Wed & Thurs 11:30-8

PINECREST BRANCH, 5835 SW 111 St, Pinecrest, 33156. Tel: 305-668-4571. FAX: 305-668-4480. Web Site: www.mdpls.org/branches/pinecrest-branch-library.asp. *Mgr,* Ellen Book; E-mail: booke@mdpls.org
Open Mon & Thurs 11:30-8, Tues & Wed 9:30-8, Fri & Sat 9:30-6

SHENANDOAH BRANCH, 2111 SW 19th St, 33145, SAN 337-7881. Tel: 305-250-4688. FAX: 305-250-4687. Web Site: www.mdpls.org/branches/shenandoah-branch-library.asp. *Mgr,* Jessica Iglesias; E-mail: iglesiasj@mdpls.org
Open Mon, Wed, Fri & Sat 9:30-6, Tues & Thurs 11:30-8

SOUTH DADE REGIONAL, 10750 SW 211th St, 33189, SAN 337-7911. Tel: 305-233-8140. FAX: 305-233-4419. Web Site: www.mdpls.org/branches/south-dade-regional-library.asp. *Mgr,* Maria Crespi; E-mail: crespim@mdpls.org
Open Mon-Thurs 9:30-8, Fri-Sun 9:30-6

SOUTH MIAMI BRANCH, 6000 Sunset Dr, South Miami, 33143, SAN 337-7946. Tel: 305-667-6121. FAX: 305-661-6558. Web Site: www.mdpls.org/branches/south-miami-branch-library.asp. *Mgr,* Pamela Hogue; E-mail: hoguep@mdpls.org
Open Mon & Thurs-Sat 9:30-6, Tues & Wed 11:30-8

SOUTH SHORE BRANCH, 131 Alton Rd, Miami Beach, 33139, SAN 328-6495. Tel: 305-535-4223. FAX: 305-535-4225. Web Site: www.mdpls.org/branches/south-shore-branch-library.asp. *Mgr,* Katherine Ehlers; E-mail: ehlersk@mdpls.org
Open Mon, Tues, Thurs & Sat 9:30-6, Wed 11:30-8

SUNNY ISLES BEACH BRANCH, 18070 Collins Ave, Sunny Isles Beach, 33160. Tel: 305-682-0726. FAX: 305-682-0781. Web Site: www.mdpls.org/branches/sunny-isles-beach-branch-library.asp. *Mgr,* Hector Vazquez; E-mail: vazquezh@mdpls.org
Open Mon, Tues, Fri & Sat 9:30-6, Wed & Thurs 11:30-8

SUNSET BRANCH, 10855 SW 72 St, No 13-14, 33173. Tel: 305-270-6368. FAX: 305-273-6074. Web Site: www.mdpls.org/branches/sunset-branch-library.asp. *Mgr,* Javier Corredor; E-mail: corredorj@mdpls.org
Open Mon, Thurs & Sat 9:30-6, Tues & Wed 11:30-8

TAMIAMI BRANCH, 13250-52 SW Eighth St, 33184. Tel: 305-223-4758. FAX: 305-480-8571. Web Site: www.mdpls.org/branches/tamiami-branch-library.asp. *Mgr,* Alice Connors-Suarez; E-mail: connorsa@mdpls.org
Open Mon-Wed, Fri & Sat 9:30-6, Thurs 11:30-8

VIRRICK PARK BRANCH, 3255 Plaza St, Coconut Grove, 33133. Tel: 305-442-7872. FAX: 305-442-7876. Web Site: www.mdpls.org/branches/virrick-park-branch-library.asp. *Mgr,* Pamela Hogue; E-mail: hoguep@mdpls.org
Open Mon & Wed-Sat 9:30-6

WEST DADE REGIONAL, 9445 Coral Way, 33165, SAN 337-7970. Tel: 305-553-1134. FAX: 305-226-5343. Web Site: www.mdpls.org/branches/west-dade-regional-library.asp. *Mgr,* Julio Rodriguez; E-mail: rodriguezj@mdpls.org
Open Mon-Thurs 9:30-8, Fri-Sun 9:30-6

WEST FLAGLER BRANCH, 5050 W Flagler St, 33134, SAN 337-8004. Tel: 305-442-8710. FAX: 305-445-5495. Web Site: www.mdpls.org/branches/west-flagler-branch-library.asp. *Mgr,* Janelle Gonzalez; E-mail: gonzalezj@mdpls.org
Open Mon & Thurs 11:30-8, Tues, Wed, Fri & Sat 9:30-6

WEST KENDALL REGIONAL, 10201 Hammocks Blvd, 33196, SAN 371-3016. Tel: 305-385-7135. FAX: 305-385-5285. Web Site: www.mdpls.org/branches/west-kendall-regional-library.asp. *Mgr,* Elizabeth Pearson; E-mail: pearsone@mdpls.org
Open Mon-Thurs 9:30-8, Fri-Sun 9:30-6

Bookmobiles: 1

C MIAMI INTERNATIONAL UNIVERSITY OF ART & DESIGN LIBRARY*, 1501 Biscayne Blvd, Ste 100, 33132-1418. SAN 375-3220. Tel: 305-428-5674. Toll Free Tel: 800-225-9023. FAX: 305-374-7946. Web Site: www.artinstitutes.edu/miami/. *Dir, Libr Serv,* Position Currently Open; Staff 2 (MLS 2)
Founded 1967. Enrl 1,600; Fac 115; Highest Degree: Master
Library Holdings: Bk Titles 25,000; Per Subs 211
Special Collections: History of Costume Coll; Vogue Magazine, 1947-present
Subject Interests: Animation, Fashion, Film, Graphic design, Interior design, Visual arts
Automation Activity & Vendor Info: (Cataloging) OCLC; (Circulation) Follett Software
Wireless access
Function: Res libr
Publications: TWIS
Partic in Library & Information Resources Network
Open Mon-Thurs 7:30am-9:30pm, Fri 7:30-6, Sat 10-5
Restriction: Open to students, fac & staff

GM MIAMI VA HEALTHCARE SYSTEM*, Medical Library, 1201 NW 16th St, 33125-1693. SAN 337-8128. Tel: 305-575-3187. Toll Free Tel: 888-276-1785, Ext 3187. FAX: 305-575-3118. E-mail: vhamialibrary@va.gov. Web Site: www.miami.va.gov. *Supvr,* Monica Bamio; E-mail: monica.bamio@va.gov; *ILL, Libr Tech,* Christine A Kittler; E-mail: christine.kittler@va.gov; Staff 2 (MLS 1, Non-MLS 1)
Founded 1947
Library Holdings: DVDs 200
Automation Activity & Vendor Info: (Cataloging) CyberTools for Libraries; (Circulation) CyberTools for Libraries; (Discovery) EBSCO Discovery Service; (ILL) OCLC
Wireless access
Partic in Docline; OCLC Online Computer Library Center, Inc; Veterans Affairs Library Network
Open Mon-Fri 7-4:30

P MICCOSUKEE COMMUNITY LIBRARY*, Tamiami Sta, 33144. (Mail add: PO Box 440021, 33144-0021), SAN 377-3140. Tel: 305-223-8380, Ext 2248. FAX: 305-223-1011. *Librn,* Sharon Logan
Library Holdings: Bk Vols 25,000; Per Subs 35
Restriction: Mem only
Friends of the Library Group

L MORGAN LEWIS LLP*, Law Library, 200 S Biscayne Blvd, Ste 5300, 33131. SAN 372-1310. Tel: 305-415-3000. FAX: 305-415-3001. Web Site: www.morganlewis.com.
Library Holdings: Bk Titles 100; Per Subs 10
Wireless access
Restriction: Staff use only

G NATIONAL MARINE FISHERIES SERVICE*, Southeast Fisheries Science Center Library, 75 Virginia Beach Dr, 33149. SAN 303-0660. Tel: 305-361-4229. FAX: 305-365-4104. Web Site: www.sefsc.noaa.gov. *Librn,* Maria Bello; E-mail: Maria.Bello@noaa.gov
Founded 1965
Library Holdings: Bk Titles 5,000; Per Subs 180

Special Collections: Fish, Fish Eggs, Larvae, Systematics & Scallops, reprints & micro
Subject Interests: Ecology, Environ studies, Marine biol
Partic in NOAA Libraries Network; OCLC Online Computer Library Center, Inc; Proquest Dialog

G NATIONAL OCEANIC & ATMOSPHERIC ADMINISTRATION*, Miami Regional Library, Atlantic Oceanographic & Meteorlogical Lab, 4301 Rickenbacker Causeway, 33149. SAN 377-7405. Tel: 305-361-4428. FAX: 305-361-4452. E-mail: aoml.library@noaa.gov. Web Site: www.aoml.noaa.gov/general/lib. *Librn,* Gloria Aversano; E-mail: gloria.aversano@noaa.gov. Subject Specialists: *Atmospheric sci,* Gloria Aversano; Staff 3 (MLS 3)
Library Holdings: Microforms 60,000; Bk Vols 20,776; Per Subs 190
Special Collections: Oceanography
Subject Interests: Atmospheric, Earth, Geoscience
Automation Activity & Vendor Info: (Cataloging) SirsiDynix; (Circulation) SirsiDynix
Function: ILL available, Ref & res
Partic in NOAA Libraries Network
Open Mon-Fri 8-4:30
Restriction: Non-circulating, Open to pub by appt only

R SAINT JOHN VIANNEY COLLEGE SEMINARY*, Maytag Library, 2900 SW 87th Ave, 33165. SAN 303-0687. Tel: 305-223-4561. FAX: 305-223-0650. Web Site: www.sjvcs.edu/maytag-library-department. *Head Librn,* Maria Rodriguez; E-mail: rodriguez@sjvcs.edu; *Asst Librn,* Ximena Lopez; E-mail: lopez@sjvcs.edu; Staff 3 (MLS 2, Non-MLS 1)
Founded 1960. Enrl 55; Fac 20; Highest Degree: Bachelor
Library Holdings: Bk Titles 44,451; Bk Vols 52,802; Per Subs 155
Special Collections: Philosophy & Literature Bi-lingual Coll
Subject Interests: Philos, Relig, Theol
Automation Activity & Vendor Info: (Acquisitions) Follett Software; (Cataloging) Follett Software; (Circulation) Follett Software
Partic in Southeast Florida Library Information Network, Inc
Restriction: Open to pub with supv only

M SOUTH MIAMI HOSPITAL*, Health Sciences Library, 6200 SW 73rd St, 33143. SAN 328-1035. Tel: 786-662-8219. FAX: 786-662-5124. E-mail: library@baptisthealth.net. Web Site: www.baptisthealth.net. *Dir,* Devica Samsundar; E-mail: devicas@baptisthealth.net; Staff 2 (MLS 1, Non-MLS 1)
Founded 1977
Library Holdings: e-books 60; e-journals 900; Bk Titles 800; Per Subs 160
Subject Interests: Allied health, Med, Nursing
Automation Activity & Vendor Info: (Cataloging) CyberTools for Libraries; (Circulation) CyberTools for Libraries; (ILL) CyberTools for Libraries; (OPAC) CyberTools for Libraries; (Serials) CyberTools for Libraries
Wireless access
Publications: Library Letter
Partic in South Florida Health Sciences Library Consortium
Open Mon-Fri 8:30-5

L SQUIRE PATTON BOGGS LIBRARY*, 200 S Biscayne Blvd, Ste 4700, 33131. SAN 327-0939. Tel: 305-577-7000, 800-743-5773. FAX: 305-577-7001. Web Site: www.squirepattonboggs.com. *Res Serv Mgr,* Jeffrey Nelson
Library Holdings: Bk Vols 30,000; Per Subs 700
Restriction: Not open to pub

L STEARNS, WEAVER, MILLER, WEISSLER, ALHADEFF & SITTERSON, Law Library, 2200 Museum Tower, 150 W Flagler St, 33130. SAN 372-1345. Tel: 305-789-3251. FAX: 305-789-3395. Web Site: www.stearnsweaver.com. *Dir, Res Serv,* Jeanne S Korman; E-mail: jkorman@stearnsweaver.com; *Res Asst,* Carmen Freire; Tel: 305-789-3250, E-mail: cfreire@stearnsweaver.com; *Res Asst,* Kathryn G Rodriguez; Tel: 813-222-5020, E-mail: krodriguez@stearnsweaver.com; Staff 2 (MLS 1, Non-MLS 1)
Library Holdings: Bk Vols 15,000; Per Subs 186
Subject Interests: Banking, Bankruptcy, Bus law, Corporate law, Employment, Labor, Real estate, State law
Automation Activity & Vendor Info: (Acquisitions) Inmagic, Inc.; (Cataloging) Inmagic, Inc.; (Circulation) Inmagic, Inc.; (OPAC) Inmagic, Inc.; (Serials) Inmagic, Inc.
Restriction: Not open to pub

GL THIRD DISTRICT COURT OF APPEALS*, Law Library, 2001 SW 117th Ave, 33175. SAN 303-0555. Tel: 305-229-3200. *Librn,* Sarah Lanciault; E-mail: lanciault@flcourts.org
Founded 1957
Library Holdings: Bk Vols 25,000; Per Subs 65
Wireless access
Open Mon-Fri 8-5

G UNITED STATES NATIONAL OCEANIC & ATMOSPHERIC ADMINISTRATION*, National Hurricane Center/Tropical Prediction Center Library, 11691 SW 17 St, 33165-2149. SAN 302-8933. Tel: 305-229-4406. FAX: 305-553-9879. E-mail: Nhclibrary@noaa.gov. Web Site: www.aoml.noaa.gov/general/lib/lib1/nhclib. *Librn,* Gloria Aversano
Founded 1956
Library Holdings: Bk Vols 10,000; Per Subs 30
Special Collections: Technical Reports Coll; Tropical Typhoons & Cyclones
Subject Interests: Meteorology
Automation Activity & Vendor Info: (Acquisitions) SirsiDynix; (Cataloging) SirsiDynix; (Circulation) SirsiDynix
Publications: Acquisitions; Database listing; Newsletter; Serials listing
Partic in NOAA Libraries Network; OCLC Online Computer Library Center, Inc; Proquest Dialog
Open Tues-Thurs 9-5
Restriction: Open to pub for ref only

C UNIVERSITY OF MIAMI*, Rosenstiel School of Marine & Atmospheric Science Library, 4600 Rickenbacker Causeway, SLAB 160 Library, 33149-1098. SAN 337-8039. Tel: 305-421-4060. FAX: 305-361-9306. Circulation E-mail: libcirc@rsmas.miami.edu. Web Site: library.miami.edu/rsmaslib. *Librn,* Angela Clark-Hughes; Tel: 305-421-4020, E-mail: aclark@rsmas.miami.edu; *Access Serv Supvr,* Ann Campbell; Tel: 305-421-4060, E-mail: acampbell@rsmas.miami.edu. Subject Specialists: *Atmospheric sci, Environ sci, Marine sci, Ocean sci,* Angela Clark-Hughes; Staff 3 (MLS 1, Non-MLS 2)
Founded 1943. Highest Degree: Doctorate
Library Holdings: Bk Vols 70,151; Per Subs 765
Special Collections: Expedition reports; Marine & Atmospheric Atlases; Nautical Charts
Subject Interests: Atmospheric sci, Geol, Geophysics, Marine sci
Automation Activity & Vendor Info: (Acquisitions) EBSCO Online; (ILL) OCLC FirstSearch; (OPAC) Innovative Interfaces, Inc; (Serials) EBSCO Online
Wireless access
Publications: Serials list
Partic in OCLC Online Computer Library Center, Inc
Open Mon-Thurs 8:30am-9pm, Fri 8:30-5, Sat 1-5, Sun 1-5
Restriction: Restricted borrowing privileges

Departmental Libraries:

LOUIS CALDER MEMORIAL LIBRARY, Miller School of Medicine, 1601 NW Tenth Ave, 33136. (Mail add: PO Box 016950 R950, 33101), SAN 337-8063. Tel: 305-243-6403. Reference Tel: 305-243-6648. Administration Tel: 305-243-6441. Interlibrary Loan Service FAX: 305-243-9670. Reference FAX: 305-325-9670. Administration FAX: 305-325-8853. E-mail: circulation@med.miami.edu. Web Site: calder.med.miami.edu. *Dir of Libr Operations,* JoAnn Van Schaik; Tel: 305-243-6441, E-mail: jvanschaik@miami.edu; *Dep Dir,* Kimberly Loper; Tel: 305-243-6424, E-mail: kloper@miami.edu; *Dir of Serv, ILL,* David Goolabsingh; Tel: 305-243-6749, E-mail: dgoulabsingh@miami.edu; *Asst Dir, Libr Serv,* Yesenia Navarro; Tel: 305-243-6403, E-mail: y.navarro1@miami.edu; *Head, Ref & Educ Serv,* Carmen Bou-Crick; Tel: 305-243-1967, E-mail: cbou@miami.edu; *Sr Ref Librn,* Yanira Garcia-Barcena; Tel: 305-243-5439, E-mail: ygarcia@med.miami.edu; *Emerging Tech Librn,* Shidan Hemmat; Tel: 305-243-6424, E-mail: sxh275@miami.edu; *Instrul & Ref Librn,* John Reazer; Tel: 305-243-3999, E-mail: jxr1217@miami.edu; *Metadata & Spec Coll Librn,* Erica Powell; Tel: 305-243-6931, E-mail: epowell@miami.edu; *Ref & Educ Librn,* John Reynolds; Tel: 305-243-5439, E-mail: jxr1327@miami.edu; *ILL/Doc Delivery Serv, Libr Mgr,* Manuel Pasos; Tel: 305-243-6749, E-mail: jmp209@miami.edu; *Mgr, Acq & Ser, Tech Serv,* Amalia de la Vega; Tel: 305-243-6901, E-mail: adelavega@miami.edu; *Mgr, Ref & Educ Serv,* Kelsa Bartley; Tel: 305-243-5530, E-mail: k.bartley@miami.edu; Staff 11 (MLS 11)
Founded 1952. Enrl 1,018; Fac 1,193; Highest Degree: Doctorate
Library Holdings: AV Mats 3,000; e-books 450; e-journals 13,000; Bk Titles 61,000; Bk Vols 133,000; Per Subs 1,159
Special Collections: Florida Coll; Floridiana, bks, pamphlets; History of Medicine Archives & Faculty Publications
Partic in OCLC Online Computer Library Center, Inc; South Florida Health Sciences Library Consortium
Publications: Biennial Report; Calder Communications (Newsletter)
Open Mon-Thurs 7:30am-Midnight, Fri 7:30am-10pm, Sat & Sun 10-10
Friends of the Library Group

MARY & EDWARD NORTON LIBRARY OF OPHTHALMOLOGY, Bascom Palmer Eye Inst, 900 NW 17th St, 33136, SAN 337-8098. Tel: 305-326-6078. FAX: 305-326-6066. Web Site: www.bascompalmer.org. *Supvr,* Dennis Bermudez; E-mail: dbermudez@med.miami.edu
Founded 1962
Library Holdings: Bk Vols 18,000; Per Subs 230
Special Collections: AV Coll; Historical Coll

Subject Interests: Ophthalmology
Open Mon-Fri 9-5

MIAMI BEACH

M MOUNT SINAI MEDICAL CENTER*, Medical Library, 4300 Alton Rd, 33140. SAN 303-0768. Tel: 305-674-2840. FAX: 305-674-2843. Web Site: www.msmc.com. *Librn,* Andre Peres; E-mail: aperes@msmc.com; Staff 1 (MLS 1)
Founded 1946
Library Holdings: Bk Vols 15,000; Per Subs 300
Automation Activity & Vendor Info: (Cataloging) Surpass; (Circulation) Surpass
Partic in South Florida Health Sciences Library Consortium
Restriction: Staff use only

MIAMI GARDENS

C FLORIDA MEMORIAL UNIVERSITY*, Nathan W Collier Library, 15800 NW 42nd Ave, 33054. SAN 303-0539. Tel: 305-626-3640. Reference Tel: 305-626-3647. FAX: 305-626-3625. Reference E-mail: libref@fmuniv.edu. Web Site: www.fmuniv.edu/library. *Dir,* O D Alexander; Tel: 305-626-3641. Subject Specialists: *Bus,* O D Alexander; Staff 11 (MLS 5, Non-MLS 6)
Founded 1879. Enrl 1,500; Fac 70; Highest Degree: Master
Library Holdings: Bk Vols 131,000; Per Subs 715
Special Collections: Archives Coll; Florida Coll, bks, mats; Laban C Connor Black Coll; Theological, Pastoral & Sermonic Materials (Reverend I C Mickins Coll)
Subject Interests: Soc sci & issues
Automation Activity & Vendor Info: (Cataloging) Innovative Interfaces, Inc; (Circulation) Innovative Interfaces, Inc; (OPAC) Innovative Interfaces, Inc
Wireless access
Function: Ref serv available
Publications: Handbook; Newsletter
Partic in Independent Cols & Univs of Fla; Southeast Florida Library Information Network, Inc
Open Mon-Thurs 8am-11pm, Fri 8-5, Sat 8-4, Sun 2-10

C ST THOMAS UNIVERSITY LIBRARY*, 16401 NW 37th Ave, 33054. SAN 321-5415. Tel: 305-628-6667. FAX: 305-628-6666. Web Site: www.stu.edu/library. *Assoc Dir, Metadata Librn,* Jessica M Orozco; Tel: 305-474-6863, E-mail: jmorozco@stu.edu; Staff 11 (MLS 5, Non-MLS 6)
Founded 1962. Enrl 2,100; Fac 80; Highest Degree: Doctorate
Library Holdings: Bk Vols 215,000; Per Subs 700
Special Collections: Black Catholic Archives; Dorothy Day Coll; Jackie Gleason Kinescope Archives; Walt Whitman Coll. US Document Depository
Automation Activity & Vendor Info: (Cataloging) OCLC WorldShare Interlibrary Loan; (Circulation) OCLC WorldShare Interlibrary Loan
Wireless access
Publications: Library Handbook; Library Newsletter
Partic in OCLC Online Computer Library Center, Inc; Southeast Florida Library Information Network, Inc

Departmental Libraries:

CL ALEX A HANNA LAW LIBRARY, 16401 NW 37th Ave, 33054. Tel: 305-623-2330. Circulation Tel: 305-623-2332. Reference Tel: 305-623-2331. FAX: 305-623-2337. Web Site: www.stu.edu/law/library. *Dir,* Roy Balleste; E-mail: rballeste@stu.edu; *Assoc Dir, Head, Tech Serv,* Sonia Luna-Lamas; Tel: 305-623-2387, E-mail: slamas@stu.edu; *Ref/Fac Serv Librn,* John O'Donnell; Tel: 305-623-2339, E-mail: jodonnell@stu.edu; *Tech Serv Librn,* Elias Royal; Tel: 305-623-2336, E-mail: eliasroyal@stu.edu
Library Holdings: Bk Vols 120,000
Automation Activity & Vendor Info: (Acquisitions) OCLC WorldShare Interlibrary Loan; (ILL) Clio; (OPAC) OCLC WorldShare Interlibrary Loan; (Serials) OCLC WorldShare Interlibrary Loan
Open Mon-Thurs 7:30am-Midnight, Fri 7:30am-9pm, Sat 8-6, Sun 11am-Midnight

MIAMI SHORES

CR BARRY UNIVERSITY, Monsignor William Barry Memorial Library, 11300 NE Second Ave, 33161-6695. SAN 303-0806. Tel: 305-899-3760. Reference Tel: 305-899-3772. Administration Tel: 305-899-4095. Toll Free Tel: 800-756-6000, Ext 3760. Interlibrary Loan Service FAX: 305-899-3775. E-mail: libraryhelp@barry.edu. Web Site: my.barry.edu/library-services. *Dir, Libr Serv,* Dr Jan Figa; Tel: 305-899-3768, E-mail: jfiga@barry.edu; *Assoc Dir, Tech Serv,* Marietta DeWinter; Tel: 305-899-4813, E-mail: mdewinter@barry.edu; *Sr Ref & Instruction Librn,* Philip M O'Neill; Tel: 305-899-3762, E-mail: poneill@barry.edu; *Ref & Instruction Librn,* Bonnie DiGiallonardo; Tel: 305-899-3773, E-mail: bdigiallonardo@barry.edu; *Ref & Instruction Librn,* Maria Gonzalez; Tel: 305-899-3761, E-mail: magonzalez@barry.edu; *Ref & Instruction Librn,* Eduardo Porben; Tel: 305-981-1195, E-mail: eporben@barry.edu; *Electronic Res Coordr, Ref Librn,* Merlene Nembhard; Tel: 305-899-4051, E-mail: mnembhard@barry.edu; *Tech Serv Librn,* Frances Sciurba; Tel: 305-899-4029, E-mail: fsciurba@barry.edu; *Archives, Libr Tech, Spec Coll,* St Victor Dominique; Tel: 305-899-3852, E-mail: dstvictor@barry.edu; *ILL, Libr Tech,* Marcia Dixon; Tel: 305-899-4050, E-mail: mdixon@barry.edu. Subject Specialists: *Fine arts,* Marietta DeWinter; *Hist of philosophy, Polit sci, Theol,* Philip M O'Neill; *Adult educ, Continuing educ, Fine arts,* Maria Gonzalez; *Computer sci, Math, Psychol,* Merlene Nembhard; Staff 12 (MLS 12)
Founded 1940. Enrl 8,112; Fac 255; Highest Degree: Doctorate
Library Holdings: Bk Titles 800,000; Bk Vols 980,000; Per Subs 1,200
Special Collections: Atonement Coll
Subject Interests: Catholicism
Automation Activity & Vendor Info: (Acquisitions) Innovative Interfaces, Inc - Millennium; (Cataloging) Innovative Interfaces, Inc - Millennium; (Circulation) Innovative Interfaces, Inc - Millennium; (Course Reserve) Innovative Interfaces, Inc - Millennium; (ILL) Innovative Interfaces, Inc - Millennium; (OPAC) Innovative Interfaces, Inc - Millennium; (Serials) Innovative Interfaces, Inc - Millennium
Wireless access
Partic in LYRASIS; Southeast Florida Library Information Network, Inc
Open Mon-Thurs 7:30am-10pm, Fri 7:30am-8pm, Sat 9-8, Sun 10-10

P BROCKWAY MEMORIAL LIBRARY*, 10021 NE Second Ave, 33138. SAN 303-0814. Tel: 305-758-8107. FAX: 805-756-8972. Web Site: brockwaylibrary.org. *Dir,* Michelle Brown; E-mail: brownm@msvfl.gov; *Ad,* Francis Walsh; *Youth Serv Librn,* Brenda Holsing; Staff 6.1 (MLS 3, Non-MLS 3.1)
Founded 1949. Pop 10,250; Circ 76,060
Library Holdings: Audiobooks 1,980; AV Mats 5,281; DVDs 3,301; e-books 16,000; Electronic Media & Resources 2; Large Print Bks 1,867; Bk Vols 65,000; Per Subs 115
Automation Activity & Vendor Info: (Acquisitions) Baker & Taylor; (Cataloging) Follett Software; (Circulation) Follett Software; (OPAC) Follett Software
Wireless access
Function: Adult bk club, Art exhibits, Bk club(s), Bks on cassette, Bks on CD, Children's prog, Computers for patron use, Electronic databases & coll, Free DVD rentals, ILL available, Magnifiers for reading, Online cat, Photocopying/Printing, Prog for adults, Prog for children & young adult, Ref & res, Story hour, Summer reading prog, Teen prog
Partic in Southeast Florida Library Information Network, Inc
Open Mon, Tues & Thurs 9-8, Wed & Fri 9-6, Sat 9-1
Restriction: Circ to mem only

MICCO

P SOUTH MAINLAND LIBRARY*, 7921 Ron Beatty Blvd, 32976. SAN 370-3592. Tel: 772-664-4066. FAX: 772-664-0534. Web Site: www.brevardfl.gov//PublicLibraries/Branches/SouthMainlandMicco. *Libr Dir,* Heather Palmer; E-mail: hpalmer@brev.org; *Head, Ref, Head, Youth Serv,* Emily Derrough; E-mail: ederrough@brev.org; *Supvr, Circ,* Susan Getter; E-mail: sgetter@brev.org; Staff 8 (MLS 1, Non-MLS 7)
Founded 1987. Circ 250,000
Library Holdings: Audiobooks 2,500; CDs 2,000; DVDs 10,000; Bk Titles 45,000; Per Subs 96; Videos 2,000
Wireless access
Function: Adult bk club, Bk club(s), Bks on CD, Computers for patron use, Electronic databases & coll, Free DVD rentals, Holiday prog, Music CDs, Notary serv, Online cat, OverDrive digital audio bks, Photocopying/Printing, Prog for adults, Prog for children & young adult, Ref serv available, Wheelchair accessible
Mem of Brevard County Public Libraries
Open Mon & Fri 9-5, Tues & Thurs 12-8, Wed & Sat 10-2
Friends of the Library Group

MILTON

P SANTA ROSA COUNTY LIBRARY SYSTEM*, 6275 Dogwood Dr, 32570. Tel: 850-981-7323. FAX: 850-626-3085. E-mail: libraries@santarosa.fl.gov. Web Site: www.santarosa.fl.gov/libraries. *Dir,* Gwen Wilson; E-mail: gwenw@santarosa.fl.gov; Staff 6 (MLS 6)
Founded 2006. Pop 117,500; Circ 705,000
Library Holdings: AV Mats 15,000; Bk Vols 125,000; Per Subs 40
Wireless access

MIMS

P MIMS/SCOTTSMOOR PUBLIC LIBRARY*, 3615 Lionel Rd, 32754. Tel: 321-264-5080. FAX: 321-264-5081. Web Site: www.brevardfl.gov/PublicLibraries/Branches/MimsScottsmoor. *Dir,* Mary Toupin; E-mail: mtoupin@brev.org; *Ch Serv,* Sandra Chafin; E-mail: schafin@brev.org; *Ref Serv,* Beth Doud; E-mail: bdoud@brev.org
Library Holdings: Bk Vols 33,500; Per Subs 55

Automation Activity & Vendor Info: (Cataloging) Infor Library & Information Solutions; (Circulation) Infor Library & Information Solutions; (OPAC) Infor Library & Information Solutions
Wireless access
Mem of Brevard County Public Libraries
Open Mon 10-6, Tues, Wed & Fri 9-5, Thurs 12-8
Friends of the Library Group

MIRAMAR

C TRINITY INTERNATIONAL UNIVERSITY, Florida Regional Center Library, 3700 Lakeside Dr, Ste 200, 33027. SAN 303-0628. Tel: 954-382-6400. FAX: 954-382-6420. E-mail: studentservicesfl@tiu.edu. Web Site: www.tiu.edu/florida/student-services. *Dir, Libr Serv,* Rebecca Donald; Tel: 847-317-4013, E-mail: rldonald@tiu.edu; Staff 1 (MLS 1)
Founded 1949. Enrl 672; Fac 65; Highest Degree: Master
Library Holdings: Bk Titles 6,500
Subject Interests: Bus, Educ, Psychol, Relig
Wireless access
Partic in Association of Chicago Theological Schools
Open Mon, Tues, Thurs & Fri 1-10, Sat 8:30-2:30

MONTICELLO

P JEFFERSON COUNTY PUBLIC LIBRARY*, R J Bailar Public Library, 375 S Water St, 32344. SAN 303-0830. Tel: 850-342-0205, 850-342-0206. FAX: 850-342-0207. Web Site: jcpl.wildernesscoast.org. *Dir,* Natalie Binder; E-mail: nbinder@jeffersoncountyfl.gov
Founded 1984. Pop 15,000
Library Holdings: Bk Vols 35,000; Per Subs 52
Special Collections: Florida Coll; Keyston Genealogy Library; Literacy, Prof, Equipment
Automation Activity & Vendor Info: (Cataloging) LibLime; (Circulation) LibLime
Wireless access
Mem of Wilderness Coast Public Libraries
Open Mon, Wed & Fri 9-5:30, Tues & Thurs 9-7:30, Sat 9-3
Friends of the Library Group

P WILDERNESS COAST PUBLIC LIBRARIES, 1180 W Washington St, 32344. (Mail add: PO Box 551, 32345), SAN 375-3190. Tel: 850-997-7400. FAX: 850-997-7403. Web Site: www.wildernesscoast.org. *Adminr,* Courtney Whitaker; E-mail: courtney@wildernesscoast.org; Staff 3 (MLS 1, Non-MLS 2)
Founded 1992. Pop 50,218; Circ 161,526
Library Holdings: AV Mats 10,087; e-books 23,572; Electronic Media & Resources 30; Bk Vols 107,210; Per Subs 158
Special Collections: Florida Coll. Oral History
Automation Activity & Vendor Info: (Cataloging) OCLC; (Circulation) SirsiDynix; (OPAC) SirsiDynix
Wireless access
Publications: Annual Plan of Service & Budget
Member Libraries: Franklin County Public Library; Jefferson County Public Library; Wakulla County Public Library
Partic in Panhandle Library Access Network
Friends of the Library Group
Bookmobiles: 1. Extension Mgr, Linda Norton. Bk vols 2,500

MONTVERDE

P HELEN LEHMANN MEMORIAL LIBRARY*, Montverde Library, 17435 Fifth St, 34756. Tel: 407-469-3838. FAX: 407-469-2083. Web Site: mylakelibrary.org/libraries/helen_lehmann_memorial_library.aspx. *Libr Dir,* Kathleen Gifford; E-mail: kgifford@mymontverde.com
Wireless access
Mem of Lake County Library System
Open Mon-Thurs 8:30-6:30

MOORE HAVEN

P GLADES COUNTY PUBLIC LIBRARY*, 201 Riverside Dr SW, 33471. (Mail add: PO Box 505, 33471), SAN 338-0254. Tel: 863-946-0744. FAX: 863-946-1661. Web Site: myhlc.org/libraries/glades-county. *Librn,* Iris Perkins; E-mail: iris@myhlc.org; Staff 2 (Non-MLS 2)
Circ 8,143
Library Holdings: Bk Titles 17,043; Per Subs 60; Talking Bks 519; Videos 255
Special Collections: County History Coll
Mem of Heartland Library Cooperative
Partic in Tampa Bay Library Consortium, Inc
Open Mon-Fri 9-5

S MOORE HAVEN CORRECTIONAL FACILITY LIBRARY*, 1282 E State Rd 78, 33471. Tel: 863-946-2420. *Libr Supvr,* Thomas Eggers; Staff 3 (MLS 1, Non-MLS 2)
Founded 1995
Library Holdings: Bk Vols 6,000; Per Subs 4
Open Mon, Tues, Thurs & Fri 8:15-11:15 & 1:15-4, Wed 8:15-11:15 & 1:15-4 & 6-8, Sat 9-11 & 2-3

MOUNT DORA

P W T BLAND PUBLIC LIBRARY, 1995 N Donnelly St, 32757. SAN 303-0849. Tel: 352-735-7180. FAX: 352-735-0074. E-mail: library@cityofmountdora.com. Web Site: ci.mount-dora.fl.us/1045/WT-Bland-Public-Library, www.mylakelibrary.org/libraries/wt_bland_public_library.aspx. *Libr Mgr,* Cathy Lunday; E-mail: lundayc@cityofmountdora.com; *Youth Serv Librn,* Lynn Gonzales; E-mail: gonzalesl@cityofmountdora.com; *Circ Supvr,* Jill Santos; Staff 12 (MLS 3, Non-MLS 9)
Founded 1905. Circ 150,132
Library Holdings: Bk Titles 60,000; Per Subs 150; Talking Bks 2,187
Special Collections: Florida Coll; Large Print Coll
Automation Activity & Vendor Info: (Cataloging) Horizon; (Circulation) Horizon; (OPAC) Horizon
Wireless access
Mem of Lake County Library System
Open Mon, Thurs & Fri 10-6, Tues & Wed 10-8, Sat 10-5
Friends of the Library Group

MULBERRY

P MULBERRY PUBLIC LIBRARY*, 905 NE Fifth St, 33860. Tel: 863-425-3246. FAX: 863-425-8818. Web Site: mulberrylibrary.com. *Dir,* Cheri Schisler; E-mail: cschisler@cityofmulberryfl.com; Staff 4.5 (MLS 1, Non-MLS 3.5)
Founded 1949. Pop 3,650; Circ 64,000
Library Holdings: CDs 2,100; e-books 800; Bk Titles 19,500
Automation Activity & Vendor Info: (Cataloging) SirsiDynix; (Circulation) SirsiDynix; (ILL) OCLC
Wireless access
Function: 24/7 Electronic res, 24/7 Online cat, 3D Printer, Accelerated reader prog, Adult bk club, Adult literacy prog, Art programs, Audiobks via web, Bilingual assistance for Spanish patrons, Bk club(s), Bks on CD, CD-ROM, Children's prog, Computer training, Computers for patron use, E-Readers, Electronic databases & coll, Free DVD rentals, Holiday prog, Homebound delivery serv, ILL available, Internet access, Magazines, Makerspace, Meeting rooms, Movies, Music CDs, Online cat, Photocopying/Printing, Preschool outreach, Printer for laptops & handheld devices, Prog for adults, Prog for children & young adult, Ref & res, Ref serv available, Scanner, Senior computer classes, Spoken cassettes & CDs, Spoken cassettes & DVDs, STEM programs, Story hour, Study rm, Summer & winter reading prog, Summer reading prog, Tax forms, Teen prog, Wheelchair accessible
Partic in Polk County Libr Coop; Tampa Bay Library Consortium, Inc
Open Mon, Tues & Wed 9-6, Thurs 9-7, Fri 9-5, Sat 10-3
Friends of the Library Group

NAPLES

CL AVE MARIA SCHOOL OF LAW LIBRARY, 1025 Commons Circle, 34119. Tel: 239-687-5500. Reference Tel: 239-687-5506. FAX: 239-353-3172. E-mail: circulation@avemarialaw.edu, librarian@avemarialaw.edu. Web Site: www.avemarialaw.edu/library. *Dir, Law Libr,* Ulysses Jaen; Tel: 239-687-5501, E-mail: ujaen@avemarialaw.edu; Staff 7 (MLS 4, Non-MLS 3)
Founded 2000. Enrl 380; Fac 21; Highest Degree: Doctorate
Library Holdings: Bk Titles 177,204; Bk Vols 200,000; Per Subs 3,000
Special Collections: Canon Law Coll
Automation Activity & Vendor Info: (Acquisitions) Innovative Interfaces, Inc; (Cataloging) Innovative Interfaces, Inc; (Circulation) Innovative Interfaces, Inc; (OPAC) Innovative Interfaces, Inc; (Serials) Innovative Interfaces, Inc
Wireless access
Open Mon-Fri 8-5
Restriction: Open to students, fac & staff, Pub use on premises

P COLLIER COUNTY PUBLIC LIBRARY*, 2385 Orange Blossom Dr, 34109. Tel: 239-593-0334. Administration Tel: 239-593-3511. FAX: 239-254-8167. Web Site: www.collierlibrary.org. *Dir,* Tanya Williams; E-mail: tanya.williams@colliercountyfl.gov; *Asst Dir,* Catherine Cowser; E-mail: catherine.cowser@colliercountyfl.gov; *Br Mgr,* April Ristau; E-mail: april.ristau@colliercountyfl.gov; Staff 22 (MLS 22)
Pop 260,000; Circ 2,500,000
Library Holdings: Bk Vols 631,830; Per Subs 1,300
Automation Activity & Vendor Info: (Acquisitions) Innovative Interfaces, Inc; (Cataloging) Innovative Interfaces, Inc; (Circulation) Innovative Interfaces, Inc; (OPAC) Innovative Interfaces, Inc; (Serials) Innovative Interfaces, Inc
Wireless access

Publications: Bibliographies; Calendar (Monthly); Friends of Library (Newsletter)
Partic in National Network of Libraries of Medicine Region 2; Southwest Florida Library Network
Open Mon-Thurs 9-8, Fri & Sat 9-5, Sun 1-5
Friends of the Library Group
Branches: 9
EAST NAPLES BRANCH, 8787 E Tamiami Trail, 34113, SAN 337-8322. Tel: 239-775-5592. FAX: 239-774-5148. *Librn,* Marilyn McKay; Staff 1 (MLS 1)
Open Mon-Thurs 9-8, Fri & Sat 9-5
ESTATES, 1266 Golden Gate Blvd W, 34120, SAN 374-7514. Tel: 239-455-8088. FAX: 239-455-8113. *Librn,* Nina Metzel; Staff 1 (MLS 1)
Open Mon-Thurs 9-8, Fri & Sat 9-5
EVERGLADES BRANCH, City Hall, Everglades City, 34139, SAN 375-0175. Tel: 239-695-2511. FAX: 239-695-2511. *Mgr,* Roberta Stone. Subject Specialists: *Customer serv,* Roberta Stone; Staff 1 (Non-MLS 1)
Open Mon-Thurs 9-5, Fri 9-12
GOLDEN GATE, 2432 Lucerne Rd, 34116, SAN 337-8330. Tel: 239-455-1441. FAX: 239-455-8921. *Librn,* David Chalick; *Ch Serv,* Katherine Hemmat; Staff 2 (MLS 2)
Open Mon-Thurs 9-8, Fri & Sat 9-5
IMMOKALEE BRANCH, 417 N First St, Immokalee, 34142, SAN 337-8365. Tel: 239-657-2882. FAX: 239-657-4901. *Librn,* Tanya Saldivar; Staff 1 (MLS 1)
Open Mon & Thurs 11-7, Tues, Wed & Fri 9-5
MARCO ISLAND BRANCH, 210 S Heathwood Dr, Marco Island, 34145, SAN 337-839X. Tel: 239-394-3272. FAX: 239-394-2383. *Librn,* Gwynn Goodman; Staff 1 (MLS 1)
Open Mon-Thurs 9-8, Fri & Sat 9-5
Friends of the Library Group
NAPLES REGIONAL LIBRARY, 650 Central Ave, 34102, SAN 337-8306. Tel: 239-262-4130. Reference Tel: 239-263-7768. FAX: 239-649-1293. *Br Mgr,* Kay Oistad; *Extn Serv, Outreach Serv Librn,* Marilyn Norris; Tel: 239-261-8208; Staff 27 (MLS 8, Non-MLS 19)
Founded 1957
Open Mon-Thurs 9-8, Fri & Sat 9-5, Sun (Jan-March) 1-5
Friends of the Library Group
SOUTH REGIONAL BRANCH, 8065 Lely Cutural Pkwy, 34113. Tel: 239-252-7542. *Br Mgr,* Denise McMahon; E-mail: denise.mchahon@colliercountyfl.gov
Open Mon-Thurs 9-7, Fri & Sat 9-5
VANDERBILT BEACH, 788 Vanderbilt Beach Rd, 34108, SAN 337-8314. Tel: 239-597-8444. FAX: 239-597-3653. *Librn,* Blane Halliday; E-mail: bhalliday@collier-lib.org; Staff 1 (MLS 1)
Open Mon-Thurs 10-7

J FLORIDA SOUTHWESTERN STATE COLLEGE, Collier Library - Collier Campus, 7505 Grand Lely Dr, Bldg G, 34113. Tel: 239-732-3774. Web Site: www.fsw.edu/library. *Fac Librn,* Anthony P Valenti; E-mail: anthony.valenti@fsw.edu; Staff 5 (MLS 1, Non-MLS 4)
Founded 1992. Enrl 5,000; Fac 45; Highest Degree: Associate
Library Holdings: Bk Titles 10,000; Per Subs 60
Automation Activity & Vendor Info: (Acquisitions) Ex Libris Group; (Cataloging) Ex Libris Group; (Circulation) Ex Libris Group; (Course Reserve) Ex Libris Group; (ILL) Ex Libris Group; (OPAC) Ex Libris Group; (Serials) Ex Libris Group
Wireless access
Open Mon-Thurs 7:30am-9pm, Fri 7:30-4, Sat 9-2

C HODGES UNIVERSITY*, Terry P McMahan Library, 2655 Northbrooke Dr, 34119. SAN 374-6240. Tel: 239-598-6109, 239-938-7812. Web Site: library.hodges.edu/home, www.hodges.edu/library. *Libr Dir,* Gayle Haring; Tel: 800-466-8017, Ext 7811, E-mail: gharing@hodges.edu; Staff 7 (MLS 4, Non-MLS 3)
Founded 1990. Enrl 2,439; Fac 5; Highest Degree: Master
Library Holdings: e-books 1,400; Bk Titles 26,000; Bk Vols 37,400; Per Subs 225; Videos 500
Special Collections: Marco Island, Florida Incorporation Files-Archives; Rare Books College Archives; Travel & Far East Rare Books Coll. US Document Depository
Automation Activity & Vendor Info: (Acquisitions) OCLC WorldShare Interlibrary Loan; (Cataloging) OCLC WorldShare Interlibrary Loan; (Circulation) OCLC WorldShare Interlibrary Loan; (ILL) OCLC WorldShare Interlibrary Loan; (OPAC) OCLC WorldShare Interlibrary Loan
Wireless access
Publications: Odyssey (Newsletter); Research Guides
Partic in Florida Library Information Network; Library & Information Resources Network; LYRASIS; Southwest Florida Library Network
Open Mon-Thurs 9am-9:50pm

M NAPLES COMMUNITY HOSPITAL*, William J Bailey Library, 350 Seventh St N, 34102-5730. (Mail add: PO Box 413029, 34101-3029), SAN 375-4863. Tel: 239-436-5384. Web Site: www.nchmd.org. *Librn,* Annette Campbell; E-mail: annette.campbell@nchmd.org; Staff 2 (MLS 1, Non-MLS 1)
Founded 1975
Library Holdings: Bk Titles 2,250; Bk Vols 3,000
Subject Interests: Clinical med
Partic in SEND; Southwest Florida Library Network; Tampa Bay Medical Library Network

NEW PORT RICHEY

P NEW PORT RICHEY PUBLIC LIBRARY*, 5939 Main St, 34652. SAN 303-0865. Tel: 727-853-1279. FAX: 727-853-1280. Web Site: www.nprlibrary.org. *Dir,* Susan D Dillinger; Tel: 727-853-1262, E-mail: LibDir@NPRLibrary.org; *Asst Libr Dir,* Ann Scott; Tel: 727-853-1265, E-mail: AsstDir@NPRLibrary.org; *Instruction Librn,* Stephanie Jones; Tel: 727-853-1273, E-mail: InfoLib@NPRLibrary.org; *Outreach Librn,* Kayla Kuni; Tel: 727-853-1274, E-mail: TechLib@NPRLibrary.org; *Youth Librn,* Jessica Meredith; Tel: 727-853-1264, E-mail: YouthLib@NPRLibrary.org; *Libr Asst,* Vivienne MacDonald; Tel: 727-853-1263, E-mail: AdmAsst@NPRLibrary.org; Staff 17 (MLS 5, Non-MLS 12)
Founded 1919. Pop 15,000; Circ 782,962
Oct 2015-Sept 2016 Income (Main & Associated Libraries) $1,010,593, State $28,163, City $943,411, Locally Generated Income $30,669, Other $8,350. Mats Exp $117,148, Books $48,016, Per/Ser (Incl. Access Fees) $5,000, AV Mat $17,610, Electronic Ref Mat (Incl. Access Fees) $46,522. Sal $447,374 (Prof $254,000)
Library Holdings: CDs 4,835; e-books 20,544; Electronic Media & Resources 6,369; Bk Vols 96,306; Per Subs 137; Videos 9,837
Special Collections: Avery Coll; Florida Coll; Genealogy Coll
Automation Activity & Vendor Info: (Acquisitions) Innovative Interfaces, Inc - Sierra; (Cataloging) Innovative Interfaces, Inc - Sierra; (Circulation) Innovative Interfaces, Inc - Sierra; (ILL) Innovative Interfaces, Inc - Sierra; (OPAC) Innovative Interfaces, Inc - Sierra; (Serials) Innovative Interfaces, Inc - Sierra
Wireless access
Function: 24/7 Electronic res, 24/7 Online cat, Adult bk club, Adult literacy prog, Archival coll, Art exhibits, Audio & video playback equip for onsite use, Audiobks on Playaways & MP3, Audiobks via web, AV serv, BA reader (adult literacy), Bi-weekly Writer's Group, Bilingual assistance for Spanish patrons, Bk club(s), Bk reviews (Group), Bks on cassette, Bks on CD, Bus archives, CD-ROM, Children's prog, Citizenship assistance, Computer training, Computers for patron use, Digital talking bks, E-Readers, E-Reserves, Electronic databases & coll, Family literacy, Free DVD rentals, Govt ref serv, Health sci info serv, Holiday prog, Home delivery & serv to seniorr ctr & nursing homes, Homebound delivery serv, ILL available, Instruction & testing, Internet access, Jail serv, Jazz prog, Laminating, Large print keyboards, Learning ctr, Life-long learning prog for all ages, Literacy & newcomer serv, Magazines, Magnifiers for reading, Mail & tel request accepted, Mail loans to mem, Mango lang, Meeting rooms, Microfiche/film & reading machines, Movies, Museum passes, Music CDs, Online cat, Online ref, Orientations, Outreach serv, Outside serv via phone, mail, e-mail & web, OverDrive digital audio bks, Photocopying/Printing, Preschool outreach, Preschool reading prog, Printer for laptops & handheld devices, Prog for adults, Prog for children & young adult, Ref serv available, Scanner, Senior computer classes, Senior outreach, Serves people with intellectual disabilities, Spanish lang bks, Spoken cassettes & CDs, Spoken cassettes & DVDs, Story hour, Study rm, Summer reading prog, Tax forms, Teen prog, Telephone ref, Wheelchair accessible, Workshops, Writing prog
Publications: Library Happenings (Newsletter)
Partic in Tampa Bay Library Consortium, Inc
Special Services for the Deaf - Sorenson video relay syst
Special Services for the Blind - Talking bk serv referral
Open Mon & Thurs 10-8, Fri & Sat 10-2
Restriction: In-house use for visitors, Non-circulating of rare bks
Friends of the Library Group

C PASCO-HERNANDO STATE COLLEGE-WEST CAMPUS*, Alric CT Pottberg Library, 10230 Ridge Rd, Rm C124, 34654-5122. SAN 337-842X. Tel: 727-816-3229. FAX: 727-816-3346. Web Site: phsc.edu/library. *Dir of Libr,* Ray Calvert; E-mail: calverr@phsc.edu; Staff 4.5 (MLS 1, Non-MLS 3.5)
Founded 1972. Enrl 4,000; Fac 200; Highest Degree: Associate
Library Holdings: e-books 75,000; Bk Titles 30,000; Per Subs 85
Automation Activity & Vendor Info: (Cataloging) Ex Libris Group; (Circulation) Ex Libris Group; (Course Reserve) Ex Libris Group; (OPAC) Ex Libris Group; (Serials) Ex Libris Group
Partic in LYRASIS; OCLC Online Computer Library Center, Inc; Tampa Bay Library Consortium, Inc
Open Mon-Thurs 8am-9pm, Fri 8-4:30

NICEVILLE

P NICEVILLE PUBLIC LIBRARY*, 206 Partin Dr N, 32578. SAN 370-4661. Circulation Tel: 850-279-6436, Ext 1500. Reference Tel: 850-279-6436, Ext 1504. FAX: 850-279-6516. E-mail: ncvlibrary@okaloosa.lib.fl.us. Web Site: cityofniceville.org/169/Library. *Dir,* Sheila K Bishop; Fax: 850-729-4093, E-mail: sbishop@okaloosa.lib.fl.us; *Acq, Tech Serv,* Lee Luton; Tel: 850-279-6436, Ext 1508, E-mail: lluton@okaloosa.lib.fl.us; *ILL, Ref (Info Servs),* Lora Glass; Tel: 850-279-6436, Ext 1507, E-mail: lglass@okaloosa.lib.fl.us; *ILL, Ref,* William Prince; E-mail: wprince@okaloosa.lib.fl.us; *Youth & Teen Serv,* Karen Houston; Tel: 850-279-6436, Ext 1514, E-mail: khouston@okaloosa.lib.fl.us; Staff 18 (Non-MLS 18)
Founded 1974
Library Holdings: AV Mats 2,709; Bk Vols 540,627; Per Subs 149; Talking Bks 2,986
Automation Activity & Vendor Info: (Cataloging) SirsiDynix; (Circulation) SirsiDynix; (OPAC) SirsiDynix
Wireless access
Function: 24/7 Electronic res, 24/7 Online cat, Adult bk club, Art exhibits, Audiobks via web, Bk club(s), Bks on CD, Children's prog, Computers for patron use, Electronic databases & coll, Holiday prog, Homebound delivery serv, ILL available, Internet access, Magazines, Mail & tel request accepted, Movies, Music CDs, Notary serv, Online cat, Online ref, Outreach serv, OverDrive digital audio bks, Photocopying/Printing, Prog for adults, Prog for children & young adult, Spanish lang bks, STEM programs, Story hour, Study rm, Summer reading prog, Tax forms, Teen prog, Telephone ref, Wheelchair accessible, Workshops, Writing prog
Partic in Okaloosa County Public Library Cooperative; Panhandle Library Access Network
Open Tues & Thurs 9-8, Wed & Fri 9-6, Sat 9-2
Friends of the Library Group

J NORTHWEST FLORIDA STATE COLLEGE*, Learning Resources Center, 100 College Blvd E, 32578. SAN 303-0873. Tel: 850-729-5318. Reference Tel: 850-729-5395. FAX: 850-729-5295. E-mail: reference@nwfsc.edu. Web Site: lrc.nwfsc.edu, www.nwfsc.edu/raider-central/learning-commons. *Dir,* Janice W Henderson; E-mail: hendersj@nwfsc.edu; *Assoc Libm,* Marni Chidsey; E-mail: chidseym@nwfsc.edu; Staff 17.6 (MLS 5.3, Non-MLS 12.3)
Founded 1964. Enrl 4,830; Fac 250; Highest Degree: Bachelor
Library Holdings: AV Mats 7,973; e-books 29,767; Electronic Media & Resources 451; Bk Titles 74,354; Bk Vols 106,383; Per Subs 480; Videos 2,246
Special Collections: Florida & Works of Floridians
Automation Activity & Vendor Info: (Acquisitions) Ex Libris Group; (Cataloging) Ex Libris Group; (Circulation) Ex Libris Group; (Course Reserve) Ex Libris Group; (ILL) OCLC; (OPAC) Ex Libris Group; (Serials) Ex Libris Group
Wireless access
Partic in Florida Library Information Network; OCLC Online Computer Library Center, Inc; Panhandle Library Access Network
Open Mon-Thurs 7:30am-9pm, Fri 7:30-5, Sat 9-1

NORTH MIAMI

C FLORIDA INTERNATIONAL UNIVERSITY*, Glenn Hubert Library, 3000 NE 151st St, 33181-3600. SAN 303-089X. Tel: 305-919-5726. Circulation Tel: 305-919-5718. Interlibrary Loan Service Tel: 305-919-5715. Administration Tel: 305-919-5730. FAX: 305-919-5914. Interlibrary Loan Service FAX: 305-949-1591. Information Services FAX: 305-940-6865. Web Site: library.fiu.edu. *Dean of Libr,* Anne M Prestamo; E-mail: anne.prestamo@fiu.edu; *Assoc Dean,* Dr Bryan Cooper; Tel: 305-348-5764, E-mail: lbcooper@fiu.edu; *Head, Res Develop,* Position Currently Open; *Head, Cat,* Rita Cauce; Tel: 305-348-0547, E-mail: caucer@fiu.edu; *Head, Res & Info Serv,* Gricel Dominguez; Tel: 305-348-5719, E-mail: gdoming@fiu.edu; *LTA Supvr, Circ,* Jude Cobham; Tel: 305-919-5797, E-mail: cobhamj@fiu.edu. Subject Specialists: *Admin, Fr opera, Musicology,* Anne M Prestamo; Staff 9 (MLS 8, Non-MLS 1)
Founded 1977. Enrl 7,383; Fac 110; Highest Degree: Doctorate
Library Holdings: AV Mats 7,803; e-books 122,297; e-journals 87,257; Electronic Media & Resources 85,681; Microforms 689,155; Bk Vols 313,103; Per Subs 439; Videos 7,541
Special Collections: Holocaust Oral History Video Coll
Automation Activity & Vendor Info: (Acquisitions) Ex Libris Group; (Cataloging) Ex Libris Group; (Circulation) Ex Libris Group; (Course Reserve) Ex Libris Group; (ILL) OCLC ILLiad; (OPAC) Ex Libris Group; (Serials) Ex Libris Group
Wireless access
Function: Art exhibits, Audio & video playback equip for onsite use, AV serv, Bks on CD, Bus archives, Computer training, Computers for patron use, Digital talking bks, Distance learning, Doc delivery serv, E-Reserves, Electronic databases & coll, Equip loans & repairs, Govt ref serv, Health sci info serv, ILL available, Internet access, Mail & tel request accepted, Music CDs, Notary serv, Online cat, Online info literacy tutorials on the web & in blackboard, Online ref, Orientations, Outside serv via phone, mail, e-mail & web, Photocopying/Printing, Prog for adults, Ref & res, Ref serv available, Scanner, Spoken cassettes & CDs, Spoken cassettes & DVDs, Tax forms, Telephone ref, VHS videos, Wheelchair accessible, Workshops
Partic in LYRASIS; Southeast Florida Library Information Network, Inc
Special Services for the Deaf - Assistive tech; Closed caption videos; TDD equip
Special Services for the Blind - Assistive/Adapted tech devices, equip & products; Audio mat; Bks on cassette; Braille equip; Cassette playback machines; Closed caption display syst; Computer with voice synthesizer for visually impaired persons; Reader equip
Open Mon-Thurs 7:30am-1am, Fri 7:30am-10pm, Sat 8-8, Sun 10am-1am
Friends of the Library Group

P NORTH MIAMI PUBLIC LIBRARY*, E May Avil Library, 835 NE 132nd St, 33161. SAN 303-0903. Tel: 305-891-5535. E-mail: library@northmiamifl.gov. Web Site: www.northmiamifl.gov/departments/library. *Dir,* Lucia M Gonzalez; E-mail: lgonzalez@northmiamifl.gov; *Tech Serv,* Audrey Ryan; E-mail: aryan@northmiamifl.gov; Staff 5.8 (MLS 2.1, Non-MLS 3.7)
Founded 1949. Pop 59,310; Circ 71,232
Library Holdings: AV Mats 2,653; DVDs 4,500; High Interest/Low Vocabulary Bk Vols 800; Large Print Bks 10,000; Bk Vols 65,000; Per Subs 33
Special Collections: Art (Smik Memorial Coll); Bicentennial of the US Constitution Coll; Civil War Coll; Filipiniana Coll; Florida Coll; Literacy Coll; Parenting Coll; Stage & Studio Coll
Automation Activity & Vendor Info: (Cataloging) Innovative Interfaces, Inc; (Circulation) Innovative Interfaces, Inc; (OPAC) Innovative Interfaces, Inc
Wireless access
Function: ILL available
Special Services for the Deaf - TDD equip
Special Services for the Blind - Braille equip
Open Mon-Thurs 9:30-8, Fri & Sat 9:30-5
Friends of the Library Group

NORTH MIAMI BEACH

P NORTH MIAMI BEACH PUBLIC LIBRARY, 1601 NE 164th St, 33162. SAN 303-0911. Tel: 305-948-2970. FAX: 305-787-6007. E-mail: nmblib@citynmb.com. Web Site: nmblib.weebly.com, www.citynmb.com/305/library. *Libr Dir,* Edenia Hernandez; E-mail: Edenia.hernandez@citynmb.com. Subject Specialists: *Develop, Educ, Tech mgt,* Edenia Hernandez; Staff 4 (MLS 2, Non-MLS 2)
Founded 1961. Pop 44,000; Circ 137,683
Library Holdings: AV Mats 8,025; Bk Vols 58,523; Per Subs 200
Subject Interests: Chinese, Creole, Spanish
Automation Activity & Vendor Info: (Acquisitions) SirsiDynix; (Cataloging) SirsiDynix; (Circulation) SirsiDynix; (Course Reserve) SirsiDynix; (OPAC) SirsiDynix
Wireless access
Function: Ref serv available
Partic in Southeast Florida Library Information Network, Inc
Open Mon-Thurs 9:30-7:30, Fri & Sat 9:30-5

NORTH PALM BEACH

P NORTH PALM BEACH PUBLIC LIBRARY*, 303 Anchorage Dr, 33408. SAN 303-0938. Tel: 561-841-3383. FAX: 561-848-2874. E-mail: library@village-npb.org. Web Site: www.npblibrary.org. *Libr Dir,* Zakariya Sherman; E-mail: zsherman@village-npb.org; *Circ Supvr,* Lynn Ruiz; *Libr Asst,* Mark Mork; *Teen Serv,* Meagan Hurd; *Youth Serv,* Julie Morrell; E-mail: Jmorrell@village-NPB.org; Staff 7 (MLS 2, Non-MLS 5)
Founded 1963. Pop 13,000; Circ 86,745
Oct 2017-Sept 2018 Income $873,637, City $873,637. Mats Exp $87,000, Books $38,000, Per/Ser (Incl. Access Fees) $3,000, AV Mat $22,000, Electronic Ref Mat (Incl. Access Fees) $24,000. Sal $442,000 (Prof $75,000)
Library Holdings: Audiobooks 1,732; AV Mats 188; CDs 858; DVDs 4,272; e-books 7,844; Electronic Media & Resources 4; Large Print Bks 2,059; Bk Vols 35,679; Per Subs 97
Special Collections: Local History & Archives
Automation Activity & Vendor Info: (Acquisitions) SirsiDynix; (Cataloging) SirsiDynix; (Circulation) SirsiDynix; (OPAC) SirsiDynix-iBistro; (Serials) SirsiDynix
Wireless access
Function: 24/7 Electronic res, 24/7 Online cat, Activity rm, Adult bk club, Art programs, Audiobks on Playaways & MP3, Bk club(s), Bks on CD, Chess club, Children's prog, Computers for patron use, Digital talking bks, E-Readers, Electronic databases & coll, Genealogy discussion group, ILL available, Internet access, Meeting rooms, Movies, Music CDs, Online cat, OverDrive digital audio bks, Photocopying/Printing, Prog for adults, Prog

for children & young adult, Scanner, Story hour, Study rm, Summer & winter reading prog, Summer reading prog, Winter reading prog
Partic in Library Cooperative of the Palm Beaches; Southeast Florida Library Information Network, Inc
Open Mon-Thurs 9-7, Fri & Sat 9-5, Sun 1-5
Friends of the Library Group

NORTH PORT

P NORTH PORT PUBLIC LIBRARY*, 13800 S Tamiami Trail, 34287. SAN 370-3614. Tel: 941-861-1300. FAX: 941-426-6564. Web Site: www.scgov.net/library. *Mgr,* Holly Anderson; E-mail: handerso@scgov.net; *Asst Mgr,* Janita Wisch; E-mail: jwisch@scgov.net; Staff 12.3 (MLS 6, Non-MLS 6.3)
Founded 1975
Library Holdings: Bk Vols 55,000; Per Subs 122
Automation Activity & Vendor Info: (Cataloging) Innovative Interfaces, Inc; (Circulation) Innovative Interfaces, Inc; (OPAC) Innovative Interfaces, Inc
Wireless access
Mem of Sarasota County Library System
Special Services for the Deaf - TDD equip
Special Services for the Blind - BC CILS
Open Mon, Thurs, Fri & Sat 10-5, Tues & Wed 10-8
Friends of the Library Group

OAKLAND PARK

P OAKLAND PARK CITY LIBRARY, 1298 NE 37th St, 33334. SAN 303-0946. Tel: 954-630-4370. Administration Tel: 954-630-4366. Information Services Tel: 954-630-4378. Web Site: oaklandparkfl.gov/200/Ethel-M-Gordon-Oakland-Park-Library, oaklandparkfl.org/oakland-park-library. *Dir, Cultural Serv, Libr Dir,* Heidi Burnett; E-mail: HeidiB@oaklandparkfl.gov; *Youth Serv Librn,* Brittney Farley; Tel: 954-630-4372, E-mail: brittney.farley@oaklandparkfl.gov; *Libr Mgr,* Danielle Giguere; E-mail: danielleg@oaklandparkfl.gov; Staff 7.4 (MLS 3.8, Non-MLS 3.6)
Founded 1963. Pop 42,000; Circ 100,000
Library Holdings: Bk Vols 40,508; Per Subs 125
Special Collections: Urban fiction. Municipal Document Depository
Subject Interests: Fla, Spanish (Lang)
Automation Activity & Vendor Info: (Cataloging) SirsiDynix; (Circulation) SirsiDynix
Wireless access
Function: Accelerated reader prog, Adult bk club, After school storytime, Art exhibits, Bks on CD, CD-ROM, Children's prog, Citizenship assistance, Computer training, Computers for patron use, Free DVD rentals, Holiday prog, ILL available, Internet access, Music CDs, Online cat, Outside serv via phone, mail, e-mail & web, Photocopying/Printing, Preschool outreach, Prog for children & young adult, Ref & res, Ref serv available, Senior computer classes, Spoken cassettes & CDs, Spoken cassettes & DVDs, Story hour, Summer reading prog, Tax forms, Teen prog, Telephone ref, VHS videos, Wheelchair accessible
Partic in LYRASIS; Southeast Florida Library Information Network, Inc
Open Mon, Wed, Fri & Sat 9-6, Tues & Thurs Noon-8
Friends of the Library Group

OCALA

J COLLEGE OF CENTRAL FLORIDA, Learning Resources Center, 3001 SW College Rd, 34474-4415. SAN 303-0954. Tel: 352-873-5805. FAX: 352-873-5818. E-mail: library@cf.edu. Web Site: cf.libguides.com/libraryhome. *Dean,* Dr Tammi Viviano-Broderick; E-mail: vivianot@cf.edu; *Libr Dir,* Teresa Faust; E-mail: faustt@cf.edu; Staff 14.1 (MLS 6.3, Non-MLS 7.8)
Founded 1958. Fac 130; Highest Degree: Bachelor
Library Holdings: DVDs 2,800; e-books 70,000; e-journals 46,000; Bk Vols 70,000; Per Subs 70
Special Collections: Equine; Wisdom Traditions
Automation Activity & Vendor Info: (Acquisitions) Ex Libris Group; (Cataloging) Ex Libris Group; (Circulation) Ex Libris Group; (Course Reserve) Ex Libris Group; (Discovery) Ex Libris Group; (ILL) OCLC; (OPAC) Ex Libris Group; (Serials) Ex Libris Group
Wireless access
Partic in Ex Libris Aleph; Northeast Florida Library Information Network
Open Mon-Thurs 7:30am-9pm, Fri 7:30-4:30, Sat 10-5

G MARION CORRECTIONAL INSTITUTION LIBRARY*, 3269 NW 105th St, 34482. (Mail add: PO Box 158, Lowell, 32663-0158), SAN 322-6689. Tel: 352-401-6400. *Librn,* Position Currently Open
Founded 1977
Library Holdings: Bks on Deafness & Sign Lang 12; High Interest/Low Vocabulary Bk Vols 300; Bk Titles 20,000; Bk Vols 23,000; Per Subs 40
Special Collections: Major Law Library Coll
Subject Interests: Gen ref
Special Services for the Blind - Bks available with recordings

P MARION COUNTY PUBLIC LIBRARY SYSTEM*, 2720 E Silver Springs Blvd, 34470. SAN 337-8454. Tel: 352-671-8551. Administration Tel: 352-368-4500. FAX: 352-368-4545. TDD: 352-368-4578. Web Site: library.marioncountyfl.org. *Dir,* Julie H Sieg; E-mail: julie.sieg@marioncountyfl.org; *Asst Dir,* Patsy Marsee; *Br Serv Mgr,* Roseanne Russo; *Automation Syst Coordr,* Linda Watson; *Ch Serv,* Jennifer Ransone; *Coll Develop,* Suzanne Brown; *Info Serv,* Domina Daughtrey; *ILL, Tech Serv,* Susan Reynolds
Founded 1961. Pop 330,000
Library Holdings: Bk Vols 561,302; Per Subs 700
Automation Activity & Vendor Info: (Cataloging) SirsiDynix; (Circulation) SirsiDynix
Wireless access
Publications: WORDS (Quarterly)
Partic in Northeast Florida Library Information Network
Open Mon-Thurs 10-8, Fri & Sat 10-6
Friends of the Library Group
Branches: 8
BELLEVIEW PUBLIC LIBRARY, 13145 SE Hwy 484, Belleview, 34420, SAN 337-8489. Tel: 352-438-2500. FAX: 352-438-2502. *Br Supvr,* Lee Schwartz
Open Mon & Tues 10-8, Wed-Sat 10-6
Friends of the Library Group
DUNNELLON PUBLIC LIBRARY, 20351 Robinson Rd, Dunnellon, 34431, SAN 337-8632. Tel: 352-438-2520. FAX: 352-438-2522. *Br Supvr,* Kate O'Brien
Founded 1961
Open Mon, Wed, Fri & Sat 10-6, Tues & Thurs 10-8
Friends of the Library Group
FOREST PUBLIC LIBRARY, 905 S County 314A, Ocklawaha, 32179, SAN 374-4515. Tel: 352-438-2540. FAX: 352-438-2545. *Br Supvr,* Dave Freudenburg
Founded 1987
Open Mon, Wed, Fri & Sat 10-6, Tues & Thurs 10-8
Friends of the Library Group
FORT MCCOY PUBLIC LIBRARY, 14660 NE Hwy 315, Fort McCoy, 32134, SAN 377-7618. Tel: 352-438-2560. FAX: 352-438-2562. *Br Supvr,* Position Currently Open
Founded 1996
Open Mon-Wed 10-6, Sat 10-4
Friends of the Library Group
FREEDOM PUBLIC LIBRARY, 5870 SW 95 St, 34476. Tel: 352-438-2580. FAX: 352-438-2582. *Br Supvr,* Tina Knight
Open Mon, Wed, Fri & Sat 10-6, Tues & Thurs 10-8
MARION OAKS PUBLIC LIBRARY, 294 Marion Oaks Lane, 34473, SAN 377-7634. Tel: 352-438-2570. FAX: 352-438-2572. *Br Supvr,* Robyne Fraize
Founded 1996
Open Mon-Fri 10-6, Sat 10-4
Friends of the Library Group
OCALA PUBLIC LIBRARY (HEADQUARTERS), 2720 E Silver Springs Blvd, 34470. Tel: 352-671-8551. FAX: 352-368-4545. *Dir,* Julie Sieg
Automation Activity & Vendor Info: (Acquisitions) SirsiDynix; (Cataloging) SirsiDynix; (Circulation) SirsiDynix; (OPAC) SirsiDynix; (Serials) SirsiDynix
Open Mon-Thurs 10-8, Fri & Sat 10-6, Sun 1-5
Friends of the Library Group
REDDICK PUBLIC LIBRARY, 15150 NW Gainsville Rd, Reddick, 32686-3221. (Mail add: PO Box 699, Reddick, 32686-0699), SAN 374-4531. Tel: 352-438-2566. FAX: 352-438-2567. *Br Supvr,* Christine Knowles
Open Mon-Wed 10-6, Sat 10-4
Friends of the Library Group

OKEECHOBEE

P OKEECHOBEE COUNTY PUBLIC LIBRARY*, 206 SW 16th St, 34974. SAN 370-3789. Tel: 863-763-3536. FAX: 863-763-5368. Web Site: myhlc.org/libraries/okeechobee-county. *Dir,* Kresta L King; E-mail: kresta@myhlc.org; *Cat & Adult Serv,* Deb Cason; *Children's Spec, Libr Spec I,* Kim Bass; *Libr Spec I,* Kellie Bailey; *Libr Spec I,* Sonya Chapa; Staff 8 (MLS 1, Non-MLS 7)
Founded 1967. Pop 40,140; Circ 153,606
Oct 2012-Sept 2013 Income $414,090, State $93,123, County $316,967, Locally Generated Income $4,000. Mats Exp $30,130, Books $25,000, Per/Ser (Incl. Access Fees) $1,000, Micro $130, AV Mat $4,000. Sal $198,000 (Prof $52,000)
Library Holdings: AV Mats 11,859; DVDs 8,916; Electronic Media & Resources 77; Bk Vols 69,134; Per Subs 20
Subject Interests: Fla, Genealogy
Automation Activity & Vendor Info: (Circulation) Innovative Interfaces, Inc

Wireless access
Function: Accelerated reader prog, Adult bk club, After school storytime, Art exhibits, Audiobks via web, Bi-weekly Writer's Group, Bilingual assistance for Spanish patrons, Bk club(s), Bks on cassette, Bks on CD, Children's prog, Computers for patron use, E-Reserves, Electronic databases & coll, Free DVD rentals, Govt ref serv, Holiday prog, ILL available, Internet access, Magnifiers for reading, Mail & tel request accepted, Microfiche/film & reading machines, Music CDs, Online cat, Online ref, Orientations, Outside serv via phone, mail, e-mail & web, OverDrive digital audio bks, Photocopying/Printing, Preschool reading prog, Prog for adults, Prog for children & young adult, Ref serv available, Serves people with intellectual disabilities, Spanish lang bks, Story hour, Summer reading prog, Tax forms, Telephone ref, VHS videos, Wheelchair accessible
Mem of Heartland Library Cooperative
Partic in Tampa Bay Library Consortium, Inc
Open Mon-Sat 10-6
Friends of the Library Group

P SEMINOLE TRIBE OF FLORIDA*, Billy Osceola Memorial Library, 5658 E Village St, 34974. SAN 323-7842. Tel: 863-763-4236. FAX: 863-763-0679. Web Site: www.semtribe.com/stof/services/tribal-library-program. *Mgr,* Dinorah Marie Johns; E-mail: djohns@semtribe.com; Staff 12 (MLS 7, Non-MLS 5)
Library Holdings: Bk Titles 22,000; Per Subs 25
Special Collections: Seminole Indians of Florida
Partic in Southwest Florida Library Network
Open Mon-Fri 8-12 & 1-5
Friends of the Library Group
Branches: 3
WILLIE FRANK MEMORIAL, 30901 Josie Billie Hwy, Clewiston, 33440, SAN 376-9577. Tel: 863-902-3200. FAX: 863-902-3223. *Mgr,* Claudia Doctor; E-mail: claudiadoctor@semtribe.com
Open Mon-Fri 8-12 & 1-5
DOROTHY SCOTT OSCEOLA MEMORIAL, 3100 NW 63rd Ave, Hollywood, 33024, SAN 378-0139. Tel: 954-989-6840. FAX: 954-233-9536. *Mgr,* Cecelia Vickers; E-mail: CeceliaVickers@semtribe.com
Open Mon-Fri 8-12 & 1-5
DIANE YZAGUIRRE MEMORIAL LIBRARY, 295 Stockade Rd, Immokalee, 34142. Tel: 239-867-8305. FAX: 239-658-1163. *Mgr,* Dolores Lopez; E-mail: DoloresLopez@semtribe.com
Open Mon-Fri 8-12 & 1-5

OLDSMAR

P OLDSMAR PUBLIC LIBRARY*, 400 St Petersburg Dr E, 34677. SAN 323-9454. Tel: 813-749-1178. FAX: 813-854-1881. E-mail: information@oldsmarlibrary.org. Web Site: oldsmarlibrary.org/index.php. *Dir,* Susan Hurley; E-mail: shurley@myoldsmar.com; *Head, Support Serv,* Jane Lingle; E-mail: jlingle@myoldsmar.com; *Ch,* Anthony Casale; E-mail: acasale@myoldsmar.com; *Circ, ILL,* Darlene Cadwallader; E-mail: dcadwallader@myoldsmar.com; *Ref Serv, Ad,* Claire LeBlanc; E-mail: cleblanc@myoldsmar.com; Staff 14 (MLS 4, Non-MLS 10)
Founded 1920. Pop 14,200; Circ 200,000
Automation Activity & Vendor Info: (Circulation) SirsiDynix
Wireless access
Function: 24/7 Electronic res, 24/7 Online cat, Activity rm, Adult bk club, Audiobks via web, Bi-weekly Writer's Group, Bks on CD, Children's prog, Computer training, Computers for patron use, Electronic databases & coll, Free DVD rentals, ILL available, Internet access, Magazines, Magnifiers for reading, Meeting rooms, Movies, Museum passes, Online cat, Online ref, OverDrive digital audio bks, Photocopying/Printing, Prog for adults, Prog for children & young adult, Scanner, Spanish lang bks, Story hour, Summer reading prog, Tax forms, Teen prog
Mem of Pinellas Public Library Cooperative
Partic in Tampa Bay Library Consortium, Inc
Open Mon-Thurs 9-8, Fri & Sat 9-5
Friends of the Library Group

ORLANDO

M ADVENTHEALTH ORLANDO*, Medical Library, 601 E Rollins, 32803. SAN 303-2515. Tel: 407-303-1860. FAX: 407-303-1786. E-mail: medical.library@adventhealth.com. Web Site: www.adventhealth.com/hospital/adventhealth-orlando. *Librn/Mgr,* Nancy Aldrich; Staff 3 (MLS 2, Non-MLS 1)
Founded 1964
Library Holdings: Bk Titles 3,100; Per Subs 249
Wireless access
Open Mon-Thurs 8-4:30, Fri 8-1
Restriction: Badge access after hrs

C ADVENTIST UNIVERSITY OF HEALTH SCIENCES*, R A Williams Library, 671 Winyah Dr, 32803. SAN 303-1063. Tel: 407-303-1851. Interlibrary Loan Service Tel: 407-303-7747. FAX: 407-303-9622. Web Site: library.ahu.edu. *Interim Dir,* Neal Smith, Jr; Tel: 407-303-7747, Ext 110-9894, E-mail: neal.smith@ahu.edu; *Cat Librn, Ref Librn,* Mary Rickelman; Tel: 407-303-7747, Ext 110-6046, E-mail: mary.rickelman@ahu.edu; *ILL & Ser,* Sylvia Dominguez; Tel: 407-303-7747, Ext 110-9890, E-mail: sylvia.dominguez@ahu.edu; *Coll, Instruction Librn,* Becky Fisher; Tel: 407-303-7747, Ext 110-9882, E-mail: rebecca.fisher@ahu.edu; Staff 6.5 (MLS 3.5, Non-MLS 3)
Enrl 2,100; Highest Degree: Bachelor
Library Holdings: AV Mats 1,600; Bk Vols 15,585; Per Subs 174
Subject Interests: Health sci, Nursing
Automation Activity & Vendor Info: (OPAC) Book Systems
Wireless access
Function: ILL available
Publications: Infolink
Partic in Consortium of College & University Media Centers; Independent Cols & Univs of Fla; Tampa Bay Library Consortium, Inc; Tampa Bay Medical Library Network
Open Mon-Thurs 8am-9pm, Fri 8-3, Sun 3-9

C ANA G MENDEZ UNIVERSITY SYSTEM*, Learning Resource Center, 5601 Semoran Blvd, Ste 55, 32822. Tel: 407-207-3363, Ext 1813. FAX: 407-207-3373. Web Site: usa.uagm.edu/en/content/metro-orlando. *Learning Res Ctr Dir,* Juan Lopez; E-mail: julopez@suagm.edu. Subject Specialists: *Info literacy,* Juan Lopez; Staff 5 (MLS 2, Non-MLS 3)
Founded 2003. Enrl 1,213; Fac 256; Highest Degree: Master
Library Holdings: AV Mats 29; Bk Vols 3,500; Per Subs 35
Automation Activity & Vendor Info: (Cataloging) Ex Libris Group; (Circulation) Ex Libris Group; (Course Reserve) Ex Libris Group; (OPAC) Ex Libris Group
Open Mon-Thurs 9am-10pm, Fri 8-6, Sat 8-5

§CL BARRY UNIVERSITY, Dwayne O Andreas School of Law Library, 6441 E Colonial Dr, 32807. Tel: 321-206-5700. E-mail: lawcirc@barry.edu, lawreferencelibrarians@barry.edu. Web Site: eguides.barry.edu/barrylawlibraryhome. *Assoc Dir, Head, Pub Serv,* Diana Botluk; Tel: 321-206-5727, E-mail: dbotluk@barry.edu
Wireless access
Function: Computers for patron use, Res assist avail, Study rm
Partic in Tampa Bay Library Consortium, Inc
Open Mon-Thurs 8am-10pm, Fri & Sat 8-6, Sun 10am-10pm

S CENTRAL FLORIDA RECEPTION CENTER, Main Unit Library, 7000 H C Kelley Rd, 32831. SAN 377-340X. Tel: 407-208-8283. *Educ Supvr,* Leticia Silva; E-mail: leticia.silva@fdc.myflorida.com
Library Holdings: Large Print Bks 80; Bk Titles 5,900; Bk Vols 8,800

CL FLORIDA AGRICULTURAL & MECHANICAL UNIVERSITY, Law Library, 201 Beggs Ave, 32801. Tel: 407-254-3263. Reference Tel: 407-254-3289. FAX: 407-254-3273. E-mail: famulawlibrary@gmail.com. Web Site: library.famu.edu/lawlibrary. *Dir,* Dr Yolanda Jones; Tel: 407-254-3231, E-mail: yolanda.jones@famu.edu
Library Holdings: Bk Vols 350,000
Wireless access
Partic in Tampa Bay Library Consortium, Inc
Open Mon-Fri 7-7

J FLORIDA TECHNICAL COLLEGE LIBRARY*, 12900 Challenger Pkwy, Ste 130, 32826. Tel: 407-447-7300. Toll Free Tel: 844-402-3337. FAX: 407-447-7301. Web Site: www.ftccollege.edu/campuses/college-in-orlando-fl.html. *Librn,* Ricardo Ruiz; *Libr Asst,* Christopher Plaza
Library Holdings: Bk Vols 7,000; Per Subs 100
Automation Activity & Vendor Info: (Acquisitions) LibraryWorld, Inc; (Cataloging) LibraryWorld, Inc; (Circulation) LibraryWorld, Inc; (ILL) LibraryWorld, Inc
Wireless access
Open Mon-Thurs 8am-10pm, Fri 8-5

L HOLLAND & KNIGHT LLP*, Law Library, 200 S Orange Ave, Ste 2600, 32801. (Mail add: PO Box 1526, 32802-1526), SAN 327-2702. Tel: 407-425-8500. FAX: 407-244-5288. Web Site: www.hklaw.com. *Librn,* Margie Hawkins; Tel: 407-244-1153, E-mail: margie.hawkins@hklaw.com; Staff 2 (MLS 1, Non-MLS 1)
Library Holdings: Bk Vols 25,000; Per Subs 72
Subject Interests: Law
Automation Activity & Vendor Info: (Acquisitions) Inmagic, Inc.; (Cataloging) Inmagic, Inc.; (Circulation) Inmagic, Inc.; (ILL) OCLC; (Serials) Inmagic, Inc.
Partic in LYRASIS
Restriction: Staff use only

P ORANGE COUNTY LIBRARY SYSTEM*, Orlando Public Library, 101 E Central Blvd, 32801. SAN 337-8969. Tel: 407-835-7323. Automation Services Tel: 407-835-7323, Ext 2. E-mail: circulation@ocls.info. Web Site: www.ocls.info. *Dir/Chief Exec Officer,* Mary Anne Hodel; E-mail: hodel.maryanne@ocls.info; *Adminr, Pub Relations,* Erin Sullivan; E-mail: sullivan.erin@ocls.info; *Chief of Lifelong Learning,* Debbie Tour; *Chief Finance Officer,* Kris Shoemaker; *Chief Info Officer,* Ricardo Viera; E-mail: viera.ricardo@ocls.info; *Chief Operating Officer,* Steve Powell; *Br Chief,* Danielle King; E-mail: king.danielle@ocls.info; *Br Chief,* Bethany Stone; E-mail: stone.bethany@ocls.info; *Acq Mgr,* Jo Ann Sampson; E-mail: sampson.joann@ocls.info; Staff 123 (MLS 58, Non-MLS 65)
Founded 1923. Pop 1,000,000; Circ 13,262,020
Library Holdings: AV Mats 252,000; e-books 21,430; Bk Vols 2,300,000; Per Subs 2,097
Special Collections: Florida Coll; Genealogy (Florida DAR); Walt Disney World Coll. State Document Depository
Automation Activity & Vendor Info: (Acquisitions) Innovative Interfaces, Inc; (Cataloging) Innovative Interfaces, Inc; (Circulation) Innovative Interfaces, Inc; (OPAC) Innovative Interfaces, Inc; (Serials) Innovative Interfaces, Inc
Wireless access
Function: Art exhibits, AV serv, Bk club(s), Bks on CD, Children's prog, Citizenship assistance, Computer training, Computers for patron use, E-Reserves, Electronic databases & coll, Family literacy, Free DVD rentals, Homework prog, Internet access, Magnifiers for reading, Mail & tel request accepted, Music CDs, Online cat, Online ref, Outreach serv, OverDrive digital audio bks, Photocopying/Printing, Preschool outreach, Prog for adults, Prog for children & young adult, Ref & res, Ref serv available, Spoken cassettes & CDs, Story hour, Summer reading prog, Telephone ref, Wheelchair accessible
Partic in Florida Library Information Network; LYRASIS; OCLC Online Computer Library Center, Inc
Special Services for the Deaf - Assistive tech; High interest/low vocabulary bks; Staff with knowledge of sign lang; TDD equip; TTY equip
Special Services for the Blind - Aids for in-house use; Assistive/Adapted tech devices, equip & products; Audio mat; Bks on cassette; Bks on CD; Braille bks; Closed circuit TV; Computer with voice synthesizer for visually impaired persons; Copier with enlargement capabilities; Descriptive video serv (DVS); Home delivery serv; Large print bks; Low vision equip; Magnifiers; Talking bk & rec for the blind cat; Talking bks
Friends of the Library Group

Branches: 16

ALAFAYA BRANCH, 12000 E Colonial Dr, 32826, SAN 337-8993. Web Site: www.ocls.info/locations-hours/alafaya-branch. *Br Mgr,* Lynette Schimpf; E-mail: schimph.lynette@ocls.info
Library Holdings: Bk Vols 123,962
Open Mon-Thurs 10-9, Fri & Sat 10-5
Friends of the Library Group

CHICKASAW BRANCH, 870 N Chickasaw Trail, 32825. Web Site: www.ocls.info/locations-hours/chickasaw-branch. *Br Mgr,* Lisa Stewart; E-mail: stewart.lisa@ocls.info
Open Mon-Thurs 10-9, Fri & Sat 10-5

EATONVILLE BRANCH, 200 E Kennedy Blvd, Eatonville, 32751. Web Site: www.ocls.info/locations-hours/eatonville-branch. *Br Mgr,* Patrice Florence-Walker; E-mail: florence-walker.patrice@ocls.info
Open Mon-Thurs 10-8, Fri & Sat 10-5

FAIRVIEW SHORE BRANCH, 902 Lee Rd, Ste 26, 32810, SAN 329-6210. Web Site: www.ocls.info/locations-hours/edgewater-branch. *Br Mgr,* Griselda Clarke; E-mail: clarke.griselda@ocls.info
Library Holdings: Bk Vols 110,000; Per Subs 20
Open Mon-Thurs 10-9, Fri & Sat 10-5
Friends of the Library Group

HERNDON BRANCH, 4324 E Colonial Dr, 32803, SAN 378-0392. Web Site: www.ocls.info/locations-hours/herndon-branch. *Br Mgr,* Edward Booker; E-mail: booker.edward@ocls.info
Library Holdings: Bk Vols 72,262
Open Mon-Thurs 10-9, Fri & Sat 10-5
Friends of the Library Group

HIAWASSEE BRANCH, 7391 W Colonial Dr, 32818, SAN 371-9855. Web Site: www.ocls.info/locations-hours/hiawassee-branch. *Br Mgr,* Ken Gibert; E-mail: gilbert.ken@ocls.info
Library Holdings: Bk Vols 113,721
Open Mon-Thurs 10-9, Fri & Sat 10-5
Friends of the Library Group

NORTH ORANGE BRANCH, 1211 E Semoran Blvd, Apopka, 32703, SAN 337-9116. Web Site: www.ocls.info/locations-hours/north-orange-branch. *Br Mgr,* Maritza Alicea; E-mail: alicea.maritza@ocls.info
Library Holdings: Bk Vols 109,381
Open Mon-Thurs 10-9, Fri & Sat 10-5, Sun 1-6
Friends of the Library Group

SOUTH CREEK BRANCH, 1702 Deerfield Blvd, 32837, SAN 371-9847. Web Site: www.ocls.info/locations-hours/south-creek-branch. *Br Mgr,* Julie Ventura; E-mail: ventura.julie@ocls.info
Library Holdings: Bk Vols 104,350
Open Mon-Thurs 10-9, Fri & Sat 10-5, Sun 1-6
Friends of the Library Group

SOUTH TRAIL BRANCH, 4600 S Orange Blossom Trail, 32839, SAN 337-9027. Web Site: www.ocls.info/locations-hours/south-trail-branch. *Br Mgr,* Carolyn McClendon; E-mail: mcclendon.carolyn@ocls.info
Library Holdings: Bk Vols 93,909
Open Mon-Thurs 10-8, Fri & Sat 10-5
Friends of the Library Group

SOUTHEAST BRANCH, 5575 S Semoran Blvd, 32822, SAN 328-6517. Web Site: www.ocls.info/locations-hours/southeast-branch. *Br Mgr,* Paolo Melillo; E-mail: melillo.paolo@ocls.info
Library Holdings: Bk Vols 89,895
Open Mon-Thurs 10-9, Fri & Sat 10-5
Friends of the Library Group

SOUTHWEST BRANCH, 7255 Della Dr, 32819, SAN 329-6253. Web Site: www.ocls.info/locations-hours/southwest-branch. *Br Mgr,* Position Currently Open
Library Holdings: Bk Vols 107,592
Open Mon-Thurs 10-9, Fri & Sat 10-5
Friends of the Library Group

P TALKING BOOKS SECTION, 101 E Central Blvd, 32801, SAN 337-8977. Tel: 407-835-7464.
Special Services for the Deaf - TDD equip
Open Mon-Thurs 9-8, Fri & Sat 9-6, Sun 1-6
Friends of the Library Group

WASHINGTON PARK BRANCH, 5151 Raleigh St, Ste A, 32811, SAN 337-923X. Web Site: www.ocls.info/locations-hours/washington-park-branch. *Br Mgr,* David Matthew; E-mail: matthew.david@ocls.info
Library Holdings: Bk Vols 51,612
Open Mon-Thurs 10-8, Fri & Sat 10-5
Friends of the Library Group

WEST OAKS BRANCH & GENEALOGY CENTER, 1821 E Silver Star Rd, Ocoee, 34761. Web Site: www.ocls.info/locations-hours/west-oaks-branch. *Br Mgr,* Gregg Gronlund; E-mail: gronlund.gregg@ocls.info
Library Holdings: Bk Vols 45,179
Open Mon-Thurs 10-9, Fri & Sat 10-5, Sun 1-6
Friends of the Library Group

WINDERMERE BRANCH, 530 Main St, Windermere, 34786, SAN 371-9871. Web Site: www.ocls.info/locations-hours/windermere-branch. *Br Mgr,* Leila Higgins; E-mail: higgins.leila@ocls.info
Library Holdings: Bk Vols 49,276
Open Tues-Thurs 10-9, Fri & Sat 10-5
Friends of the Library Group

WINTER GARDEN BRANCH, 805 E Plant St, Winter Garden, 34787, SAN 337-9264. Web Site: www.ocls.info/locations-hours/winter-garden-branch. *Br Mgr,* August Calabrese; E-mail: calabrese.august@ocls.info
Library Holdings: Bk Vols 66,026
Open Tues-Thurs 10-9, Fri & Sat 10-5
Friends of the Library Group

S ORANGE COUNTY REGIONAL HISTORY CENTER*, Joseph L Brechner Research Center, 65 E Central Blvd, 32801. SAN 326-1883. Tel: 407-836-8500. Web Site: www.thehistorycenter.org/resources/research-center. *Research Librn,* Noelia Irizarry-Roman; Tel: 407-836-8581, E-mail: Noelia.IrizarryRoman@ocfl.net; *Archives, Coll,* Lesleyanne Drake; Tel: 407-836-8584, E-mail: Lesleyanne.Drake@ocfl.net; Staff 3 (Non-MLS 3)
Library Holdings: Bk Titles 7,000; Bk Vols 8,000; Per Subs 11
Special Collections: Joseph L Brechner Coll. Oral History
Function: Archival coll, For res purposes, Ref serv available, Res libr, Telephone ref
Restriction: Closed stack, Non-circulating to the pub, Open by appt only

M ORLANDO HEALTH*, Health Sciences Library, 1400 S Orange Ave, 32806. SAN 328-3895. Tel: 321-841-5454. FAX: 321-843-6825. E-mail: library@orlandohealth.com. Web Site: www.orlandohealth.com/library. *ILL,* Tracy Lau; E-mail: tracy.lau@orlandohealth.com; Staff 3.5 (MLS 2, Non-MLS 1.5)
Library Holdings: Bk Titles 2,000; Per Subs 375
Subject Interests: Allied health, Med, Nursing
Automation Activity & Vendor Info: (Cataloging) OCLC; (Circulation) LibraryWorld, Inc; (OPAC) LibraryWorld, Inc
Wireless access
Function: Computers for patron use, Doc delivery serv, Electronic databases & coll, ILL available, Online cat, Photocopying/Printing
Partic in National Network of Libraries of Medicine Region 2; Tampa Bay Medical Library Network
Restriction: Badge access after hrs, Circulates for staff only, Open to staff only, Photo ID required for access

Branches:
CLIFFORD E GRAESE COMMUNITY HEALTH LIBRARY, 1400 S Orange Ave, 32806. Tel: 321-841-5454. E-mail: library@orlandohealth.com. *Librn,* Jessica Daly; Tel: 321-841-7234, E-mail: jessica.daly@orlandohealth.com. Subject Specialists: *Med,* Jessica Daly; Staff 1 (MLS 1)
Library Holdings: AV Mats 144; Bk Titles 555; Per Subs 27
Subject Interests: Chronic disease, Elderly concerns, Fitness, Growth, Health, Nutrition, Obgyn, Pain mgt, Palliative care
Function: Health sci info serv
Open Mon-Fri 8-4:30

L RUMBERGER KIRK*, Law Library, 300 S Orange Ave, Ste 1400, 32801. (Mail add: PO Box 1873, 32802-1873), SAN 323-6838. Tel: 407-872-7300. FAX: 407-841-2133. Web Site: www.rumberger.com. *Librn,* Terri Lamb; E-mail: tlamb@rumberger.com; Staff 2 (MLS 1, Non-MLS 1)
Founded 1978
Library Holdings: Bk Titles 2,500; Bk Vols 15,000
Special Collections: Continuing Legal Education Audiovisuals; Engineering & Automotive Technical Publications; Florida Attorney & Judge Vertical Files; Florida Legislative Histories
Subject Interests: Law
Wireless access
Publications: Library News (Newsletter)
Partic in LYRASIS; OCLC Online Computer Library Center, Inc
Open Mon-Fri 9-5
Restriction: Access at librarian's discretion

C UNIVERSITY OF CENTRAL FLORIDA LIBRARIES*, 12701 Pegasus Dr, 32816-8030. (Mail add: PO Box 162666, 32816-2666), SAN 303-1098. Tel: 407-823-2564. Circulation Tel: 407-823-2580. Interlibrary Loan Service Tel: 407-823-2383. Reference Tel: 407-823-3379. Automation Services Tel: 407-823-3685. Information Services Tel: 407-823-2562. FAX: 407-823-2529. Circulation FAX: 407-823-6327. Interlibrary Loan Service FAX: 407-823-3047. Reference FAX: 407-823-5865. E-mail: libadmin@ucf.edu. Web Site: library.ucf.edu. *Dir of Libr,* Barry B Baker; E-mail: barry.baker@ucf.edu; *Asst Dir, Info Tech & Digital Initiatives,* Selma K Jaskowski; Tel: 407-823-5444, Fax: 407-823-4627, E-mail: selmaj@ucf.edu; *Admin Serv, Sr Assoc Dir,* Frank R Allen; Tel: 407-823-2892, E-mail: frank.allen@ucf.edu; *Assoc Dir, Res,* Penny M Beile; Tel: 407-823-5488, E-mail: pbeile@ucf.edu; *Head, ILL & Doc Delivery,* Kristine Shrauger; Tel: 407-823-5422, E-mail: kristine.shrauger@ucf.edu; *Head, Acq & Coll Serv,* Ying Zhang; Tel: 407-883-4253, E-mail: Ying.Zhang@ucf.edu; *Head, Circ Serv,* Lindsey A Ritzert; Tel: 407-823-2527, Fax: 407-823-6347, E-mail: Lindsey.Ritzert@ucf.edu; *Head, Curric Mat Ctr,* Amy Dovydaitis; Tel: 407-823-2327, Fax: 407-823-3984, E-mail: amy.dovydaitis@ucf.edu; *Head, Res & Info Serv,* Barbara Tierney; Tel: 407-823-5464, E-mail: barbara.tierney@ucf.edu; *Head, Spec Coll & Univ Archives,* David R Benjamin; Tel: 407-823-2788, E-mail: David.Benjamin@ucf.edu; Staff 132 (MLS 55, Non-MLS 77)
Founded 1963. Enrl 63,000; Fac 1,965; Highest Degree: Doctorate
Jul 2015-Jun 2016 Income $14,980,268. Mats Exp $6,917,395, Books $809,821, Per/Ser (Incl. Access Fees) $4,104,079, AV Mat $20,584, Electronic Ref Mat (Incl. Access Fees) $1,968,357, Presv $14,554. Sal $5,415,187 (Prof $2,746,075)
Library Holdings: AV Mats 58,294; e-books 156,190; e-journals 52,337; Microforms 3,291,584; Bk Titles 1,671,450; Bk Vols 2,042,990; Per Subs 53,544
Special Collections: African American Legacy: The Carol Mundy Coll, 1794-2010; Albin Polasek Coll, 1897-2004; Book Arts Coll; Bromeliad Society International (BSI) Archive, 1942-2009; Carey Hand Funeral Home Records, 1891-1955; Children's Home Society of Florida Coll, 1862-2012; Democratic Women's Club of Florida, 1957-2006; Educator's Oral History Coll, 1997-2002; Florida Ephemera Coll, 1841-2007; Florida State Music Teachers Association Records, 1934-2013; George & Anne Millay Coll, 1959-2006; Glenn "Marty" Stein Coll of Cartoon Art, 1955-2013; Harris Rosen Scrapbooks Coll, 1939-2012; Harrison "Buzz" Price Papers, 1952-2006; Henry Nehrling Papers, 1886-1970; Howard J. Duerr Coll, 1915-1978; John L Ducker Personal Papers, 1944-2002; Joy Postle Coll, 1912-2006; Judith & Warren Kaplan Coll, Women's & Gender Studies, ca 1800s-2000s; Lou Frey Papers, 1947-2006; Mary Monroe Theatre Coll, 1973-2016; Michael A Spencer Bromeliad Research Coll, 1754-2014; NASA Ephemera Coll, 1969-2006; NASA Photographs Coll, 1974-2001; Otto Frohlich Coll, 1897, 1956-1969; Robert P Foster Coll; Sol & Sadie Malkoff Papers, 1939-1999; Stephen Danks Lodwick Papers, 1964-2002; Susan King Papers & Library; UCF 25th Anniversary Records, 1967-1989; UCF Athletics Coll, 1968-2009; UCF Audio, Visual, and Multi-Media Coll, 1967-2007; UCF Faculty Senate papers, 1968-2008; UCF News and Information Coll, 1968-2003; UCF Office of the President Records, 1968-2008; UCF Office of Vice President of University Relations Records, 1968-1992; UCF Photograph Coll, 1963-2012; UCF Staff Council Papers, 1971-2010; UCF Student Development and Enrollment Services Records, 1968-2002; UCF Student Government Association Records, 1983-2002; UCF Theatre Program Coll, 1969-2009; UCF Women's Club Papers, 1968-2007; University Archives; Van Sickle Leftist Pamphlet Coll, 1900-1993; Walter Gaudnek Coll, 1945-2009; William L Bryant West Indies Coll, 1712-1996. State Document Depository; US Document Depository
Subject Interests: Chem, Civil engr, Criminal justice, Educ res, Electrical engr, Indust engr, Math, Mechanical engr, Nursing, Physics, Polit sci, Psychol, Pub admin, Soc work
Automation Activity & Vendor Info: (Acquisitions) Ex Libris Group; (Cataloging) Ex Libris Group; (Circulation) Ex Libris Group; (Course Reserve) Ex Libris Group; (Discovery) EBSCO Discovery Service; (ILL) OCLC ILLiad; (Media Booking) Ex Libris Group; (OPAC) Ex Libris Group; (Serials) Ex Libris Group
Wireless access
Function: Res libr
Special Services for the Deaf - Sorenson video relay syst
Special Services for the Blind - Dragon Naturally Speaking software; Telesensory screen enlarger

VALENCIA COMMUNITY COLLEGE
C EAST CAMPUS*, 701 N Econlockhatchee Trail, 32825, SAN 329-269X. Tel: 407-582-2467. Circulation Tel: 407-582-2459. Interlibrary Loan Service Tel: 407-582-2461. Reference Tel: 407-582-2456. FAX: 407-582-8914. Web Site: www.valenciacollege.edu/east/. *Dir,* Dr Dennis Weeks; E-mail: dweeks@valenciacollege.edu; *Librn,* Erich Heintzelman; *AV,* Steven Suarez; *Circ,* Maria Moreno; *Computer Serv,* Joshua Chapkin; *ILL, Ref Serv,* Mark Bollenback; *Ref Serv,* Chris Wettstein; Staff 14 (MLS 5, Non-MLS 9)
Founded 1975. Enrl 14,000; Fac 200; Highest Degree: Associate
Library Holdings: Bk Titles 46,360; Bk Vols 57,734; Per Subs 385
Special Collections: College Archives
Automation Activity & Vendor Info: (Acquisitions) Ex Libris Group; (Cataloging) Ex Libris Group; (Circulation) Ex Libris Group; (Course Reserve) Ex Libris Group; (ILL) Ex Libris Group; (OPAC) Ex Libris Group; (Serials) Ex Libris Group
Partic in Cent Fla Libr Consortium; Florida Library Information Network; LYRASIS
Open Mon-Thurs (Winter) 7am-10pm, Fri 7am-9pm, Sat 8-4, Sun 2-8; Mon-Thurs (Summer) 7am-10pm, Fri 7am-12:30pm, Sat 8-2

C RAYMER MAGUIRE JR LEARNING RESOURCES CENTER, WEST CAMPUS*, 1800 S Kirkman Rd, 32811, SAN 303-1012. Tel: 407-582-1210. FAX: 407-582-1686. Web Site: www.valenciacc.edu/library/west. *Dir,* Karen Blondeau; Tel: 407-582-1601; *Coordr, Ref (Info Servs),* Donna J Carver; *Ref (Info Servs),* Suzanne Johnson; *Ref (Info Servs),* Paulette Smith; *Tech Serv,* Kusum Aneja; Staff 5 (MLS 5)
Founded 1967. Enrl 10,500
Library Holdings: Bk Titles 70,284; Bk Vols 80,500; Per Subs 131
Subject Interests: Educ, Hort, Hotel admin, Nursing
Automation Activity & Vendor Info: (Acquisitions) Ex Libris Group; (Cataloging) Ex Libris Group; (Circulation) Ex Libris Group; (ILL) Ex Libris Group; (OPAC) Ex Libris Group; (Serials) Ex Libris Group
Partic in Cent Fla Libr Consortium; LYRASIS; OCLC Online Computer Library Center, Inc
Publications: Handbook; Instructional Materials in Various Formats; LRC Alert (Biannually); Pathfinders
Open Mon-Thurs 7:30am-10pm, Fri 7-5, Sat 9-1, Sun 2-6

OVIEDO

R REFORMED THEOLOGICAL SEMINARY LIBRARY*, Orlando Campus, 1231 Reformation Dr, 32765. SAN 371-8921. Tel: 407-366-9493, Ext 217. FAX: 407-366-9425. E-mail: library.orlando@rts.edu. Web Site: library.rts.edu. *Dean of Libr,* Dr John R Muether; *Dir,* Michael Farrell; Tel: 407-278-4635; Staff 3 (MLS 2, Non-MLS 1)
Founded 1989. Enrl 255; Fac 15; Highest Degree: Master
Library Holdings: Bk Vols 100,000; Per Subs 300
Subject Interests: Biblical studies, Church hist, Theol
Automation Activity & Vendor Info: (Cataloging) TLC (The Library Corporation); (Circulation) TLC (The Library Corporation); (ILL) OCLC FirstSearch; (OPAC) TLC (The Library Corporation)
Wireless access
Partic in LYRASIS
Open Mon-Thurs 8am-10pm, Fri 8-5, Sat 9-4

J SEMINOLE COMMUNITY COLLEGE*, Oviedo Campus Library, 2505 Lockwood Blvd, 32765-9189. Tel: 407-971-5061. Reference Tel: 407-971-5062. FAX: 407-971-5067. E-mail: library@seminolestate.edu. Web Site: www.seminolestate.edu/library. *Campus Librn,* Kellie Diaz; Tel: 407-971-5051, E-mail: diazk@seminolestate.edu
Founded 2001
Library Holdings: AV Mats 159; Bk Titles 12,000; Per Subs 56
Automation Activity & Vendor Info: (Cataloging) Ex Libris Group; (Circulation) Ex Libris Group; (OPAC) Ex Libris Group
Wireless access

Open Mon-Thurs (Winter) 8am-9pm, Fri 8-12; Mon-Thurs (Summer) 8am-9pm
Friends of the Library Group

PALATKA

P PUTNAM COUNTY LIBRARY SYSTEM*, Palatka Public Library, 601 College Rd, 32177-3873. SAN 303-1136. Tel: 386-329-0126. Toll Free Tel: 800-826-1437. FAX: 386-329-1240. Web Site: www.putnam-fl.com/lib. *Dir,* Stella Brown; E-mail: stella.brown@putnam-fl.com; *Cat Librn,* Aida Marino Smith; E-mail: aida.smith@putnam-fl.com; *Children's Serv Coordr, Manager, Family Services,* Position Currently Open; *Coordr, Spec Projects,* Jeremy Yates; Tel: 386-329-0441, E-mail: jeremy.yates@putnam-fl.com; *Archivist, Spec Coll,* Mischa Johns; E-mail: mischa.johns@putnam-fl.com; *Circ,* Position Currently Open; *ILL,* Marian Purifoy; Staff 12 (MLS 2, Non-MLS 10)
Founded 1895. Pop 73,586
Library Holdings: Large Print Bks 2,531; Bk Titles 101,000; Per Subs 275; Talking Bks 1,581
Special Collections: Genealogy (Materials of the Southeast); Putnam County Archives & History Coll. Municipal Document Depository; Oral History
Subject Interests: Genealogy
Automation Activity & Vendor Info: (Acquisitions) TLC (The Library Corporation); (Cataloging) TLC (The Library Corporation); (Circulation) TLC (The Library Corporation); (ILL) OCLC FirstSearch; (OPAC) TLC (The Library Corporation)
Function: Archival coll, AV serv, BA reader (adult literacy), Home delivery & serv to seniorr ctr & nursing homes, Homebound delivery serv, ILL available, Magnifiers for reading, Prog for children & young adult, Ref serv available, Serves people with intellectual disabilities, Summer reading prog
Member Libraries: GFWC Women's Club of Welaka Library
Partic in Northeast Florida Library Information Network
Open Mon & Wed 9-6, Tues & Thurs 9-9, Fri 9-5, Sat 9-1
Branches: 4
BOSTWICK PUBLIC, 125 Tillman St, 32177. Tel: 386-326-2750. FAX: 386-326-2733. E-mail: bostwicklib@putnam-fl.com. *Br Mgr,* Claudia W Wilkinson
Founded 1999
Library Holdings: Large Print Bks 22; Bk Titles 101; Per Subs 15; Talking Bks 36
Function: ILL available, Prog for children & young adult, Summer reading prog
Open Tues 12-6, Wed & Fri 10-3, Thurs 2:30-8, Sat 9-12:30
Friends of the Library Group
CRESCENT CITY PUBLIC LIBRARY, 610 N Summit, Crescent City, 32112-2148, SAN 328-9001. Tel: 386-698-2600. FAX: 386-698-4212. E-mail: crescentcitylib@putnam-fl.com. *Br Mgr,* Adia Smith; Staff 3 (Non-MLS 3)
Founded 1990. Pop 7,022
Library Holdings: Large Print Bks 95; Bk Titles 20,959; Per Subs 43; Talking Bks 178
Function: BA reader (adult literacy), ILL available, Summer reading prog, Telephone ref, Wheelchair accessible
Special Services for the Blind - Large screen computer & software
Open Tues 9-5:30, Wed 10-7, Thurs & Fri 9-5, Sat 9-1
Friends of the Library Group
INTERLACHEN PUBLIC LIBRARY, 133 N County Rd 315, Interlachen, 32148. (Mail add: PO Box 260, Interlachen, 32148-0260), SAN 372-7882. Tel: 386-684-1600. FAX: 386-684-1601. E-mail: interlachenlib@putnam-fl.com. *Br Mgr,* Marilyn Meetz; Staff 3 (Non-MLS 3)
Founded 1984
Library Holdings: Large Print Bks 308; Bk Vols 15,914; Per Subs 49; Talking Bks 144
Function: ILL available, Summer reading prog, Telephone ref
Open Tues-Fri 9:30-6, Sat 9-12:30
Friends of the Library Group
MELROSE PUBLIC LIBRARY, 312 Wynnwood Ave, Melrose, 32666, SAN 324-2617. Tel: 352-475-3382. FAX: 352-475-5779. E-mail: melroselib@putnam-fl.com. *Br Mgr,* Sheree Simms; Staff 3 (Non-MLS 3)
Founded 1984
Library Holdings: Large Print Bks 201; Bk Titles 20,395; Per Subs 35; Talking Bks 92
Function: ILL available, Prog for children & young adult, Summer reading prog, Telephone ref
Open Tues-Fri 9:30-6, Sat 9-12:30
Friends of the Library Group

C SAINT JOHNS RIVER STATE COLLEGE*, B C Pearce Learning Resources Center, 5001 St Johns Ave, 32177-3897. SAN 303-1144. Tel: 386-312-4200. Circulation Tel: 386-312-4150. Reference Tel: 386-312-4154. Administration Tel: 386-312-4152. FAX: 386-325-4292. Web Site: www.sjrstate.edu/libraries.html. *Dean, Libr Serv,* Christina Will; E-mail: christinawill@sjrstate.edu; *Pub Serv,* Robbie Allen; E-mail: robbieallen@sjrstate.edu; *Pub Serv,* Joyce Smith; E-mail: joycesmith@sjrstate.edu; Staff 14 (MLS 7, Non-MLS 7)
Founded 1958. Highest Degree: Bachelor
Library Holdings: e-books 30,000; Bk Vols 65,000; Per Subs 350
Special Collections: Civil War Coll
Automation Activity & Vendor Info: (Cataloging) Ex Libris Group; (Circulation) Ex Libris Group; (Course Reserve) Ex Libris Group; (ILL) OCLC; (OPAC) Ex Libris Group
Wireless access
Publications: Civil War Collection Bibliography; Faculty Handbook (Annual); Library Handbook (Annual)
Partic in Northeast Florida Library Information Network
Special Services for the Deaf - ADA equip; Assistive tech; Closed caption videos
Special Services for the Blind - Newsletter (in large print, Braille or on cassette); Playaways (bks on MP3); Text reader
Open Mon-Thurs (Winter) 8am-9pm, Fri 8-5; Mon-Thurs (Summer) 8-7
Departmental Libraries:
ORANGE PARK CENTER LIBRARY, 283 College Dr, Orange Park, 32065-6751, SAN 374-4558. Tel: 904-276-6830. FAX: 904-276-6796. *Librn,* Dixie Yaeger; Tel: 904-276-6840; *Pub Serv,* Eric Biggs; Tel: 904-276-6831
Open Mon-Thurs (Aug-April) 8am-9pm, Fri 8-5, Sat 12-4; Mon-Thurs (May-July) 8-7, Fri 8-5, Sat 12-4
SAINT AUGUSTINE CENTER LIBRARY, 2990 College Dr, Saint Augustine, 32084, SAN 323-5440. Tel: 904-808-7474. FAX: 904-808-7478. *Librn,* Christina Will; *Pub Serv,* Royce Bass
Library Holdings: Bk Vols 10,000; Per Subs 95
Open Mon-Thurs 8-9, Fri 8-5, Sat 9-1; Mon-Thurs 8-7, Fri 8-5, Sat (Summer) 9-1

G ST JOHN'S RIVER WATER MANAGEMENT DISTRICT*, Scientific Reference Center, 4049 Reid St, 32177. (Mail add: PO Box 1429, 32178-1429), SAN 322-6654. Tel: 386-329-4190. Web Site: www.sjrwmd.com. *Sci Ref Spec,* Susie Hallowell; E-mail: shallowell@sjrwmd.com; Staff 1 (MLS 1)
Founded 1975
Library Holdings: Bk Titles 20,100; Per Subs 217
Subject Interests: Ecology, Engr, Geol, Hydrol, Water res
Automation Activity & Vendor Info: (Cataloging) EOS International; (OPAC) EOS International
Wireless access

PALM BAY

P FRANKLIN T DEGROODT LIBRARY*, 6475 Minton Rd SE, 32909. SAN 325-0768. Tel: 321-952-6317. Web Site: www.brevardfl.gov/PublicLibraries/Branches/FranklinTDegroodt. *Dir,* Christine Sullivan; E-mail: csullivan@brev.org; Staff 26 (MLS 2, Non-MLS 24)
Founded 1992. Pop 90,000
Library Holdings: Bk Vols 68,136; Per Subs 205; Talking Bks 2,144
Automation Activity & Vendor Info: (Cataloging) Infor Library & Information Solutions; (Circulation) Infor Library & Information Solutions; (OPAC) Infor Library & Information Solutions
Wireless access
Mem of Brevard County Public Libraries
Special Services for the Deaf - Bks on deafness & sign lang; High interest/low vocabulary bks; TDD equip
Open Mon, Wed, Fri & Sat 9-5, Tues & Thurs 9-8
Friends of the Library Group

J EASTERN FLORIDA STATE COLLEGE*, Palm Bay Campus Library, 250 Community College Pkwy, 32909. SAN 370-7822. Tel: 321-433-5270. Interlibrary Loan Service Tel: 321-433-5262. Reference Tel: 321-433-5275. Administration Tel: 321-433-5260. FAX: 321-433-5309. Web Site: www.easterflorida.edu/library. *Librn,* Deborah F Anderson; E-mail: andersond@easternflorida.edu; *Asst Librn,* Duke Darkwolf; E-mail: darkwolfd@easternflorida.edu; Staff 5.8 (MLS 2.3, Non-MLS 3.5)
Founded 1989. Enrl 3,000; Fac 30; Highest Degree: Bachelor
Library Holdings: e-books 30,000; Bk Titles 26,000; Per Subs 60
Automation Activity & Vendor Info: (Acquisitions) Ex Libris Group; (Cataloging) Ex Libris Group; (Circulation) Ex Libris Group; (Course Reserve) Ex Libris Group; (ILL) OCLC; (OPAC) Ex Libris Group; (Serials) Ex Libris Group
Wireless access
Partic in OCLC Online Computer Library Center, Inc
Open Mon-Thurs 8-8, Fri 9-1

S HARRIS CORPORATION*, Harris Engineering Library, Harris Corp, 1000 Charles J Herbert Dr, MS HTC-1N, 32905. SAN 303-0350. Tel: 321-727-4220. *Head Librn,* Mary B Briand; Staff 1 (MLS 1)
Founded 1952

Library Holdings: Bk Vols 10,000; Per Subs 5
Subject Interests: Electronics, Engr
Automation Activity & Vendor Info: (Acquisitions) SirsiDynix; (Cataloging) SirsiDynix; (Circulation) SirsiDynix; (ILL) SirsiDynix; (OPAC) SirsiDynix; (Serials) SirsiDynix
Function: Archival coll, Doc delivery serv, ILL available, Outside serv via phone, mail, e-mail & web, Photocopying/Printing, Ref serv available, Telephone ref
Publications: IEEE (Periodical)
Partic in LYRASIS
Restriction: Employees only
Friends of the Library Group

P PALM BAY PUBLIC LIBRARY*, 1520 Port Malabar Blvd NE, 32905. SAN 372-7572. Tel: 321-952-4519. FAX: 321-952-4543. Web Site: www.brevardfl.gov/PublicLibraries/Branches/PalmBay. *Dir,* Christine Sullivan; E-mail: CSullivan@brev.org; Staff 3 (MLS 1, Non-MLS 2)
Founded 1980
Library Holdings: Bk Vols 37,000; Per Subs 60
Automation Activity & Vendor Info: (Cataloging) TLC (The Library Corporation); (Circulation) TLC (The Library Corporation); (OPAC) TLC (The Library Corporation)
Wireless access
Mem of Brevard County Public Libraries
Open Mon, Tues, Thurs & Fri 9-5, Wed 12-8
Friends of the Library Group

PALM BEACH

S THE SOCIETY OF THE FOUR ARTS, King & Children's Libraries, 101 Four Arts Plaza, 33480. SAN 303-1160. Tel: 561-655-2766. E-mail: kinglibrary@fourarts.org. Web Site: www.fourarts.org/kinglibrary. *Libr Dir,* Dr Rachel Schipper; Staff 9 (MLS 5, Non-MLS 4)
Founded 1936
Library Holdings: Audiobooks 3,000; CDs 1,500; DVDs 8,020; e-books 5,000; e-journals 125; Large Print Bks 2,238; Bk Vols 70,000; Per Subs 50
Special Collections: Addison Mizner Coll; Jessup Coll
Subject Interests: Archit, Fine arts, Paintings
Wireless access
Function: 24/7 Electronic res, 24/7 Online cat, 3D Printer, Activity rm, Adult bk club
Partic in Southeast Florida Library Information Network, Inc
Special Services for the Blind - Audio mat
Open Mon-Fri 10-4:45, Sat (Nov-April) 10-12:45

PALM BEACH GARDENS

J PALM BEACH STATE COLLEGE*, Eissey Campus Library Learning Resource Center, 3160 PGA Blvd, 33410-2893. SAN 303-2396. Tel: 561-207-5800. Interlibrary Loan Service Tel: 561-207-5801. Administration Tel: 561-207-5811. FAX: 561-207-5805. Web Site: www.palmbeachstate.edu/library/palm-beach-gardens-library. *Dir,* David Pena; Tel: 561-207-5810, E-mail: penad@palmbeachstate.edu; *Librn,* Susan Setterlund; E-mail: setterls@palmbeachstate.edu; *Tech Serv Librn,* Lisa Hogan; E-mail: hoganl@palmbeachstate.edu; *Circ Mgr,* Amanda Chick; E-mail: chicka@palmbeachstate.edu; *Ref (Info Servs),* Joanne Cameron; E-mail: cameronj@palmbeachstate.edu; Staff 3 (MLS 3)
Founded 1974
Library Holdings: AV Mats 3,050; Bk Titles 34,108; Bk Vols 38,055; Per Subs 198
Wireless access
Partic in Libr Info Network for Commun Cols; LYRASIS; OCLC Online Computer Library Center, Inc
Open Mon-Thurs 7:30am-9:30pm, Fri 7:30-5, Sat 10-3

PALM COAST

P FLAGLER COUNTY PUBLIC LIBRARY, 2500 Palm Coast Pkwy NW, 32137. SAN 323-7044. Tel: 386-446-6763. FAX: 386-446-6773. Reference E-mail: reference@flaglercounty.org. Web Site: www.flaglerlibrary.org. *Dir,* Holly Albanese; E-mail: halbanese@flaglercounty.org; *Asst Dir,* Joe Saloom; E-mail: jsaloom@flaglercounty.org; *Head, Circ,* Jacqueline Brown-Jackson; E-mail: jbrown@flaglerlibrary.org; *Head, Circ,* Monette England; E-mail: mengland@flaglerlibrary.org; *Ch Serv,* Jessica Robayo; E-mail: jrobayo@flaglerlibrary.org; *Tech Serv,* Lisa Catalano; E-mail: lcatalano@flaglerlibrary.org; Staff 18 (MLS 4, Non-MLS 14)
Founded 1987
Library Holdings: Bks on Deafness & Sign Lang 22; High Interest/Low Vocabulary Bk Vols 80; Bk Titles 55,000; Bk Vols 78,000; Per Subs 150
Special Collections: Flagler County Coll; Genealogy Coll; Local History Center; Palm Coast Coll
Automation Activity & Vendor Info: (Acquisitions) Innovative Interfaces, Inc. - Polaris; (Cataloging) Innovative Interfaces, Inc. - Polaris; (Circulation) Innovative Interfaces, Inc. - Polaris; (ILL) OCLC FirstSearch; (OPAC) Innovative Interfaces, Inc. - Polaris
Wireless access
Function: 24/7 Electronic res, 24/7 Online cat, Adult bk club, Audiobks via web, Bk club(s), Bks on CD, Butterfly Garden, CD-ROM, Children's prog, Computer training, Computers for patron use, Digital talking bks, Electronic databases & coll, Free DVD rentals, Genealogy discussion group, Holiday prog, Homework prog, ILL available, Internet access, Large print keyboards, Life-long learning prog for all ages, Magazines, Mail & tel request accepted, Microfiche/film & reading machines, Movies, Online cat, Online ref, Outside serv via phone, mail, e-mail & web, OverDrive digital audio bks, Passport agency, Photocopying/Printing, Printer for laptops & handheld devices, Prog for adults, Prog for children & young adult, Ref & res, Ref serv available, Res assist avail, Scanner, Senior computer classes, Spanish lang bks, STEM programs, Story hour, Summer reading prog, Tax forms, Teen prog, Telephone ref, Visual arts prog, Wheelchair accessible, Workshops
Partic in Northeast Florida Library Information Network
Open Mon & Wed 9-8,Tues,Thurs & Fri 9-6, Sat 9-5
Restriction: Fee for pub use, Non-resident fee
Friends of the Library Group
Branches: 1
BUNNELL BRANCH, 103 E Moody Blvd, Bunnell, 32110. (Mail add: 2500 Palm Coast Pkwy NW, 32137). Tel: 386-437-7390. FAX: 386-437-7390. E-mail: bunnell@flaglercounty.org. *Br Coordr,* Jonathan Nemergut; E-mail: jnemergut@flaglercounty.org; Staff 2 (Non-MLS 2)
Founded 2004
Special Collections: Flagler County Law Library
Function: 24/7 Electronic res, 24/7 Online cat, Bks on CD, Children's prog, Computers for patron use, Free DVD rentals, Holiday prog, ILL available, Internet access, Magazines, Online cat, Online ref, Passport agency, Photocopying/Printing, Printer for laptops & handheld devices, Ref & res, Tax forms, Telephone ref
Open Mon-Fri 9-6
Restriction: Fee for pub use, Non-resident fee
Friends of the Library Group

PALM HARBOR

P EAST LAKE COMMUNITY LIBRARY*, 4125 East Lake Rd, 34685. Tel: 727-773-2665. FAX: 727-773-9583. Web Site: www.eastlakelibrary.org. *Dir,* Lois Eannel; E-mail: lois-e@eastlakelibrary.org; Staff 6 (MLS 2, Non-MLS 4)
Founded 1999. Pop 30,000; Circ 157,027
Library Holdings: Audiobooks 2,837; AV Mats 7,500; Bks on Deafness & Sign Lang 143; DVDs 4,791; Bk Vols 38,469; Per Subs 25
Special Collections: Florida Coll
Subject Interests: Fla
Automation Activity & Vendor Info: (Cataloging) Innovative Interfaces, Inc; (Circulation) Innovative Interfaces, Inc
Wireless access
Function: Adult bk club, Art exhibits, Audio & video playback equip for onsite use, AV serv, Bi-weekly Writer's Group, Bk club(s), Computer training, Digital talking bks, E-Reserves, Electronic databases & coll, Home delivery & serv to seniorr ctr & nursing homes, Homebound delivery serv, Homework prog, ILL available, Internet access, Mail & tel request accepted, Mail loans to mem, Music CDs, Online ref, Photocopying/Printing, Prog for adults, Prog for children & young adult, Ref & res, Ref serv available, Senior computer classes, Serves people with intellectual disabilities, Spoken cassettes & CDs, Spoken cassettes & DVDs, Summer reading prog, Tax forms, Telephone ref, Wheelchair accessible, Workshops
Mem of Pinellas Public Library Cooperative
Partic in Tampa Bay Library Consortium, Inc
Open Mon-Wed & Fri 10-6, Thurs 12-8, Sat 10-4
Friends of the Library Group

P PALM HARBOR LIBRARY*, 2330 Nebraska Ave, 34683. SAN 323-9217. Tel: 727-784-3332. FAX: 727-785-6534. Web Site: www.palmharborlibrary.org. *Dir,* Gene Coppola; Tel: 727-784-3332, Ext 3001, E-mail: gene@phlib.org; *Asst Dir,* Elisabeth Roen; Tel: 727-784-3332, Ext 3007, E-mail: elisabeth@phlib.org; *Head, Circ,* Betzaida Harris; Tel: 727-784-3332, Ext 3011, E-mail: betsy@phlib.org; *Head, Youth Serv,* Marisa Steuer; Tel: 727-784-3332, Ext 3018, E-mail: marisa@phlib.org; Staff 22 (MLS 6, Non-MLS 16)
Founded 1978. Pop 59,000; Circ 371,156
Library Holdings: Bk Vols 215,000; Per Subs 45
Special Collections: Florida Coll; New Readers Literacy Coll; Toys to Go (Adaptive Toys for Special Needs)
Subject Interests: Genealogy, Handcrafts
Wireless access
Function: Adult literacy prog, AV serv, Games & aids for people with disabilities, Home delivery & serv to seniorr ctr & nursing homes, Homebound delivery serv, ILL available, Internet access, Large print keyboards, Prog for adults, Prog for children & young adult, Ref serv available, Summer reading prog, Telephone ref, Wheelchair accessible, Workshops

Publications: Annual Report; Find Your Roots Genealogy Guide; Friends of the Library Newsletter
Mem of Pinellas Public Library Cooperative
Partic in Tampa Bay Library Consortium, Inc
Special Services for the Deaf - Adult & family literacy prog
Special Services for the Blind - Assistive/Adapted tech devices, equip & products
Open Mon-Thurs 10-8, Fri & Sat 10-5
Friends of the Library Group

PALM SPRINGS

P PALM SPRINGS PUBLIC LIBRARY, 217 Cypress Lane, 33461-1698. SAN 324-0274. Tel: 561-584-8350. FAX: 561-964-2803. Web Site: vpsfl.org/269/library. *Dir,* Jossie Maliska; E-mail: jmaliska@vpsfl.org; *Ch,* Karen Garcia; E-mail: kgarcia@vpsfl.org; *Circ Supvr,* Lisa Veres; E-mail: lveres@vpsfl.org; Staff 10 (MLS 2, Non-MLS 8)
Pop 26,890
Library Holdings: Bk Titles 42,119; Per Subs 49
Automation Activity & Vendor Info: (Acquisitions) Koha
Wireless access
Partic in Library Cooperative of the Palm Beaches
Open Mon, Wed, Fri & Sat 9-5, Tues & Thurs 9-7
Friends of the Library Group

PANAMA CITY

C GULF COAST STATE COLLEGE LIBRARY*, 5230 W US Hwy 98, 32401. SAN 303-1195. Tel: 850-872-3893. E-mail: librarian@gulfcoast.edu. Web Site: www.gulfcoast.edu/academics/library. *Dir,* Lori Driscoll; E-mail: ldriscoll@gulfcoast.edu; *Colls Librn, Tech Serv Librn,* David Russell; E-mail: drussel10@gulfcoast.edu; *Distance Learning & Outreach Librn,* Wendy Dover; E-mail: wdover@gulfcoast.edu; *Instruction Librn,* Connie Head; E-mail: chead@gulfcoast.edu; *Coordr, Libr Serv,* Carrie Lewis; E-mail: clewis16@gulfcoast.edu. Subject Specialists: *Visual arts,* David Russell; *Soc sci,* Wendy Dover; *Lang, Lit,* Connie Head; *Math,* Carrie Lewis; Staff 9 (MLS 6, Non-MLS 3)
Founded 1957. Enrl 4,000; Highest Degree: Bachelor
Automation Activity & Vendor Info: (Acquisitions) Ex Libris Group; (Cataloging) Ex Libris Group; (Circulation) Ex Libris Group; (Course Reserve) Ex Libris Group; (ILL) OCLC; (OPAC) Ex Libris Group; (Serials) Ex Libris Group
Wireless access
Partic in Panhandle Library Access Network

G NATIONAL MARINE FISHERIES SERVICE*, Panama City Laboratory Library, 3500 Delwood Beach Rd, 32408. SAN 303-1209. Tel: 850-234-6541, Ext 227. FAX: 850-235-3559. Web Site: www.sefsc.noaa.gov/labs/panama/library/library.htm. *Librn,* Emily Harrell; E-mail: emily.harrell@noaa.gov; Staff 1 (MLS 1)
Founded 1973
Library Holdings: Bk Vols 4,000; Per Subs 400
Special Collections: St Andrew Bay Research
Subject Interests: Marine biol, Oceanography
Function: ILL available
Publications: Reprints list; Serials list
Partic in NOAA Libraries Network; OCLC Online Computer Library Center, Inc
Open Mon-Fri 8-Noon
Restriction: Limited access for the pub

A NAVAL SURFACE WARFARE CENTER, Panama City Division Technical Library, 110 Vernon Ave, 32407. SAN 337-9655. Tel: 850-234-4848. FAX: 850-234-4844. *Lead Librn,* Deborah Caldwell; *Librn,* Anthony Waterman; Tel: 850-234-4848; *Libr Tech,* Elga Huggins; Staff 2 (MLS 1, Non-MLS 1)
Founded 1948
Library Holdings: Bk Titles 16,000; Per Subs 95
Subject Interests: Diving, Hydrodynamics, Underwater acoustics
Automation Activity & Vendor Info: (Cataloging) SirsiDynix; (Circulation) SirsiDynix; (Serials) SirsiDynix
Restriction: Not open to pub

P NORTHWEST REGIONAL LIBRARY SYSTEM*, Bay County Public Library, 898 W 11th St, 32401. (Mail add: PO Box 59625, 32412-0625), SAN 337-9353. Tel: 850-522-2100. Interlibrary Loan Service Tel: 850-522-2107. FAX: 850-522-2138. Web Site: www.nwrls.com. *Libr Dir,* Robin Shader; E-mail: rshader@nwrls.com; *Circ,* Ann Robbins; Staff 39.8 (MLS 8, Non-MLS 31.8)
Founded 1942. Pop 167,631; Circ 440,295
Library Holdings: Audiobooks 4,519; Bk Titles 170,151; Bk Vols 187,278; Per Subs 483
Special Collections: Local History Coll; Local Newspaper Coll; Local Photographic Coll
Automation Activity & Vendor Info: (Acquisitions) TLC (The Library Corporation); (Cataloging) TLC (The Library Corporation); (Circulation) TLC (The Library Corporation); (ILL) OCLC WorldShare Interlibrary Loan; (OPAC) TLC (The Library Corporation); (Serials) TLC (The Library Corporation)
Wireless access
Partic in Panhandle Library Access Network
Open Mon-Wed 9-7, Thurs-Sat 9-5
Branches: 6
CORINNE COSTIN GIBSON MEMORIAL PUBLIC LIBRARY, 110 Library Dr, Port Saint Joe, 32456, SAN 337-9531. Tel: 850-229-8879. FAX: 850-229-8313. *Coordr,* Mimi Minnick
Founded 1965
Open Mon & Tues 10-8, Thurs & Fri 10-6, Sat 10-4
Friends of the Library Group
HARRELL MEMORIAL LIBRARY OF LIBERTY COUNTY, 13016 NW CR 12, Bristol, 32321, SAN 337-9477. Tel: 850-643-2247. FAX: 850-643-2208. *Asst Mgr,* Amy Miller
Open Mon 9-7, Tues 9-6, Wed & Thurs 9-5, Sat 9-3
Friends of the Library Group
PANAMA CITY BEACH PUBLIC LIBRARY, 12500 Hutchison Blvd, Panama City Beach, 32407, SAN 337-9523. Tel: 850-233-5055. FAX: 850-233-5019. *Libr Mgr,* Laura Laspee
Open Mon-Wed 9-6, Thurs & Fri 9-5, Sat 9-4
Friends of the Library Group
PARKER PUBLIC LIBRARY, 4710 Second St, Parker, 32404, SAN 370-9329. Tel: 850-871-3092. FAX: 850-874-8978. *Libr Mgr,* Debbie Daniels
Open Mon, Tues, Thurs & Sat 10-5
Friends of the Library Group
CHARLES WHITEHEAD WEWAHITCHKA PUBLIC LIBRARY, 314 North Second St, Wewahitchka, 32465, SAN 337-9620. Tel: 850-639-2419. FAX: 850-639-3862. *Br Mgr,* Joyelle Linton
Open Mon & Wed-Fri 10-5, Tues 10-8, Sat 10-2
Friends of the Library Group

PARKLAND

P PARKLAND LIBRARY, 6620 University Dr, 33067. Tel: 954-757-4200. FAX: 954-753-5223. E-mail: library@cityofparkland.org. Web Site: cityofparkland.org/103/library-homepage. *Libr Dir,* Jacqueline Wehmeyer; E-mail: jwehmeyer@cityofparkland.org; *Libr Mgr,* Michele Andrews; E-mail: mandrews@cityofparkland.org; Staff 8 (MLS 3, Non-MLS 5)
Founded 2003
Library Holdings: Audiobooks 1,500; DVDs 3,500; Electronic Media & Resources 30; Large Print Bks 1,000; Bk Vols 37,000; Per Subs 10
Automation Activity & Vendor Info: (Cataloging) Mandarin Library Automation; (Circulation) Mandarin Library Automation; (OPAC) Mandarin Library Automation
Wireless access
Open Mon-Thurs 10-7:30, Fri & Sat 10-5
Restriction: Residents only
Friends of the Library Group

PATRICK AFB

A UNITED STATES AIR FORCE*, Patrick Air Force Base Library, Bldg 722, 842 Falcon Ave, 32925-3439. SAN 337-971X. Tel: 321-494-6881. FAX: 321-494-4190. E-mail: base.library@us.af.mil. Web Site: www.gopatrickfl.com/library.html. *Dir,* Marta Demopoulos; Staff 5 (MLS 2, Non-MLS 3)
Founded 1950
Library Holdings: AV Mats 875; CDs 450; DVDs 500; Large Print Bks 300; Bk Vols 40,000; Per Subs 90; Videos 850
Special Collections: CLEP/DANTES Testing Materials; Leadership/Management Coll; Professional Military Education Coll
Subject Interests: Mil hist
Automation Activity & Vendor Info: (Acquisitions) EOS International; (Cataloging) EOS International; (Circulation) EOS International; (ILL) OCLC; (OPAC) EOS International; (Serials) EOS International
Wireless access
Restriction: Authorized patrons, Mil only

PEMBROKE PINES

GM FLORIDA DEPARTMENT OF CHILDREN & FAMILIES*, Correct Care Recovery Solutions Library, 800 E Cypress Dr, 33025. SAN 377-3736. Tel: 954-392-3000. Web Site: www.correctcarers.com/sfsh. *Commun Liaison Librn,* Gwen Henry; E-mail: ghenry@correctcarers.com
Library Holdings: Bk Vols 1,600; Per Subs 200
Special Services for the Blind - Bks on cassette
Restriction: Not open to pub

PENSACOLA

M ASCENSION SACRED HEART HEALTH SYSTEM*, Medical Library, 5151 N Ninth Ave, 32504. SAN 337-9892. Tel: 850-416-7109. FAX: 850-416-6864. *Med Librn,* Joseph King; Staff 1 (MLS 1)
Founded 1959
Library Holdings: e-books 30; Bk Vols 933
Wireless access
Open Mon-Fri 8-4:30

GL FIRST JUDICIAL CIRCUIT OF FLORIDA ESCAMBIA COUNTY*, Ernest E Mason Law Library, M C Blanchard Judicial Bldg, 190 Governmental Ctr, 32502. SAN 303-1241. Tel: 850-595-4468. FAX: 850-595-4470. *Librn,* Susan Dobinson; E-mail: susan.dobinson@flcourts1.gov
Library Holdings: Bk Vols 27,000; Per Subs 5
Open Mon-Fri 8-5

A NAVAL AIR STATION PENSACOLA LIBRARY, Station Library, 250 Chambers Ave, Bldg 634, 32508-5217. Tel: 850-452-4362. FAX: 850-452-3961. *Dir,* Amy Parrot; E-mail: amy.parrot@navy.mil; Staff 6 (MLS 1, Non-MLS 5)
Founded 1914
Library Holdings: Bk Titles 11,000; Bk Vols 14,000; Per Subs 65; Talking Bks 2,000; Videos 100
Subject Interests: Aviation, Mil art, Mil sci, Navy hist, US hist
Automation Activity & Vendor Info: (Acquisitions) EOS International; (Cataloging) EOS International; (Circulation) EOS International; (OPAC) EOS International; (Serials) EOS International
Wireless access
Function: Bks on CD, Computers for patron use, Digital talking bks, Electronic databases & coll, Free DVD rentals, Photocopying/Printing, Prog for children & young adult, Ref serv available, Scanner, Summer reading prog, Wheelchair accessible
Open Mon-Fri 8-8, Sat & Sun 12-6

S PENSACOLA MUSEUM OF ART*, Harry Thornton Library, 407 S Jefferson St, 32502-5901. SAN 303-1276. Tel: 850-432-6247. Web Site: www.pensacolamuseum.org. *Chief Curator,* Anna Wall; E-mail: awall@uwf.edu
Founded 1960
Library Holdings: Bk Titles 300
Subject Interests: Art hist

C PENSACOLA STATE COLLEGE*, Edward M Chadbourne Library, Bldg 20, 1000 College Blvd, 32504-8998. SAN 337-9809. Tel: 850-484-2002. Reference Tel: 850-484-2006. FAX: 850-484-1991. Web Site: www.pensacolastate.edu/library. *District Dept Head of Libr,* LisaMarie Bartusik; Tel: 850-484-2007, E-mail: lbartusik@pensacolastate.edu; *Dir, Tech Serv,* Linda Broyles; Tel: 850-484-1107, E-mail: lbroyles@pensacolastate.edu; *Librn,* Sarah Addison; Tel: 850-484-2084, E-mail: saddison@pensacolastate.edu; *Librn,* Stephanie Johnson; Tel: 850-484-2091, E-mail: sajohnson@pensacolastate.edu; Staff 7 (MLS 7)
Founded 1948. Enrl 35,000; Fac 261; Highest Degree: Associate
Library Holdings: AV Mats 4,392; CDs 261; DVDs 1,820; e-books 3,122; High Interest/Low Vocabulary Bk Vols 82; Bk Titles 125,879; Bk Vols 147,853; Per Subs 202; Videos 1,256
Automation Activity & Vendor Info: (Cataloging) Ex Libris Group; (Circulation) Ex Libris Group; (Course Reserve) Ex Libris Group; (OPAC) Ex Libris Group; (Serials) Ex Libris Group
Wireless access
Publications: PJC LRC News (Newsletter)
Partic in LYRASIS; OCLC Online Computer Library Center, Inc; Panhandle Library Access Network
Special Services for the Blind - Assistive/Adapted tech devices, equip & products; VisualTek equip
Open Mon-Thurs 7:30am-8:30pm, Fri 7:30-4, Sun 1-5

Departmental Libraries:

MILTON CAMPUS, Bldg 4100, 5988 Hwy 90, Milton, 32583-1798, SAN 337-9833. Tel: 850-484-4450. Reference Tel: 850-484-4452. FAX: 850-484-4453. *Campus Librn,* Charlotte Sweeney; Tel: 850-484-4465, E-mail: csweeney@pensacolastate.edu; Staff 4 (MLS 1, Non-MLS 3)
Library Holdings: Bk Titles 12,627; Bk Vols 15,822; Per Subs 24
Open Mon, Tues & Thurs 7:30-7, Wed & Fri 7:30-4

WARRINGTON CAMPUS, Bldg 3500, 5555 West Hwy 98, 32507-1097, SAN 337-9868. Tel: 850-484-2289. Reference Tel: 850-471-4626. FAX: 850-484-2355. *Campus Librn,* Melissa Davis; Tel: 850-484-2263, E-mail: mtdavis@pensacolastate.edu; Staff 3 (MLS 1, Non-MLS 2)
Library Holdings: Bk Titles 27,578; Bk Vols 30,657; Per Subs 82
Open Mon, Tues & Thurs 7:30-7, Wed & Fri 7:30-4

UNITED STATES NAVY

AM MEDICAL LIBRARY, CODE 185*, 6000 W Hwy 98, Code 185, 32512-0003, SAN 338-0025. Tel: 850-505-6635. FAX: 850-505-7063. *Library Contact,* Cortiz Stewart; Staff 1 (MLS 1)
Library Holdings: AV Mats 1,864; Bk Vols 1,260; Per Subs 75
Function: Internet access
Partic in DOD-Drols
Open Mon-Fri 7:30-4
Restriction: Authorized patrons, Circulates for staff only

AM NAVAL OPERATIONAL MEDICINE INSTITUTE LIBRARY*, 340 Hulse Rd, 32508-1089. Tel: 850-452-2256. FAX: 850-452-2304. Web Site: www.nomi.med.navy.mil/NAMI/library.htm. *Librn,* Valerie S McCann; E-mail: valerie.mccann@med.navy.mil; Staff 2 (MLS 1, Non-MLS 1)
Founded 1940
Library Holdings: Bk Titles 8,000; Bk Vols 10,000; Per Subs 51
Special Collections: Naval Aerospace Medical Research Laboratory Reports
Function: Res libr
Partic in Consortium of Naval Libraries
Open Mon-Fri 8-4

C UNIVERSITY OF WEST FLORIDA*, John C Pace Library, 11000 University Pkwy, 32514-5750. SAN 303-1306. Tel: 850-474-2492. Circulation Tel: 850-474-2414. Interlibrary Loan Service Tel: 850-474-2411. Reference Tel: 850-474-2424. FAX: 850-474-3338. TDD: 850-474-2190. Web Site: library.uwf.edu. *Dean of Libr,* Robert Dugan; Tel: 850-474-3135, E-mail: rdugan@uwf.edu; *Spec Coll & Archives Librn,* Dean DeBolt; Tel: 850-474-2213, E-mail: ddebolt@uwf.edu; Staff 43 (MLS 15, Non-MLS 28)
Founded 1966. Enrl 10,380; Fac 368; Highest Degree: Doctorate
Library Holdings: Audiobooks 410; AV Mats 9,042; Bks on Deafness & Sign Lang 543; CDs 1,304; DVDs 2,003; e-books 90,786; e-journals 3,321; Electronic Media & Resources 333; Microforms 1,162,896; Music Scores 3,959; Bk Titles 497,817; Bk Vols 724,067; Per Subs 5,019; Videos 5,021
Special Collections: Langston Hughes Coll; Panton Leslie & Company Papers; West Florida History, bks, mss, maps, photos. Oral History; State Document Depository; US Document Depository
Automation Activity & Vendor Info: (Acquisitions) Ex Libris Group; (Cataloging) OCLC Connexion; (Circulation) Ex Libris Group; (Course Reserve) Ex Libris Group; (ILL) OCLC ILLiad; (Media Booking) Ex Libris Group; (OPAC) Endeca Technologies, Inc; (Serials) Ex Libris Group
Wireless access
Partic in Florida Library Information Network; LYRASIS; OCLC Online Computer Library Center, Inc; Panhandle Library Access Network
Special Services for the Deaf - TDD equip
Special Services for the Blind - Braille equip; Computer with voice synthesizer for visually impaired persons; Reader equip; ZoomText magnification & reading software
Open Mon-Thurs 7:30am-10pm, Fri 7:30-6, Sat 10-6, Sun 1-9

S UNIVERSITY OF WEST FLORIDA HISTORIC TRUST, Hilton-Green Research Room, 117 E Government St, 32502. (Mail add: PO Box 12866, 32591-2866), SAN 303-1284. Tel: 850-595-5985, Ext 125. FAX: 850-595-5989. E-mail: hparchives@uwf.edu. Web Site: www.historicpensacola.org. *Exec Dir,* Robert Overton, Jr; Tel: 850-595-5985, Ext 106, E-mail: roverton@uwf.edu; *Interim Archivist,* Adrianne Walker; Tel: 850-595-5840, Ext 126, E-mail: asams@uwf.edu
Founded 1960
Library Holdings: DVDs 3; Bk Titles 5,000; Bk Vols 5,500; Per Subs 20; Spec Interest Per Sub 5
Special Collections: Architecture & Preservation Coll, blueprints, bks, photog, slides, VF; Artifact ID & Dating Coll, bks, pamphlets, VF; Cartography Coll-Southeastern US, Florida & Local Area, Circa 1500-present; Civil War Coll, archival mat, bks, doc & personal papers, pamphlets, photos, VF; Family Histories Coll, archival items; General Florida History, bks, pamphlets; History Districts & Pensacola Architectural Review Board File; History of Pensacola & Northwest Florida, archival papers & objects, bks, pamphlets, photos, VF; Museum Studies Coll, bks, VF; Pensacola Genealogy Coll, bks, pamphlets, personal papers, VF; Photograph Coll-Pensacola & Escambia County, Florida, daguerreotypes, digital images, photos, slides, tintypes. Oral History
Subject Interests: Hist presv, Mus mgt, Northwest Fla hist
Wireless access
Function: Archival coll, Computers for patron use, Mail & tel request accepted, Microfiche/film & reading machines, Photocopying/Printing, Printer for laptops & handheld devices, Scanner, Telephone ref, Wheelchair accessible
Publications: Pensacola History Illustrated: A Journal of Pensacola & West Florida History (Biannually); Pensacola History Today (Newsletter)
Open Tues & Thurs 10-4
Restriction: Fee for pub use, Free to mem, In-house use for visitors, Not a lending libr, Pub use on premises

P WEST FLORIDA PUBLIC LIBRARY*, 239 N Spring St, 32502. SAN 338-0041. Tel: 850-436-5060. Reference Tel: 850-436-5064. Administration Toll Free Tel: 850-436-5033. E-mail: refstaff@mywfpl.com. Web Site: mywfpl.com. *Dir,* Todd Humbell; E-mail: tjhumble@mywfpl.com; *Asst to the Dir,* John Shelton; E-mail: jshelton@mywfpl.com; *Libr Mgr,* Kimberly Ball; E-mail: kaball@mywfpl.com; *Eng & Math Librn, Sci & Tech Librn,* Alan Davis; E-mail: acdavis@mywfpl.com; *Coord, Ad Serv,* Amy Horosky; E-mail: ajhorosky@mywfpl.com; *Circ Serv Coordr,* Susan White; E-mail: skwhite@mywfpl.com; *Youth Serv Coordr,* Stevie Thomas; E-mail: sethomas@mywfpl.com; Staff 14 (MLS 12, Non-MLS 2)
Founded 1937. Pop 303,343; Circ 778,052
Library Holdings: Audiobooks 8,956; CDs 3,553; DVDs 10,063; e-books 27,411; Electronic Media & Resources 66; Bk Vols 209,318; Per Subs 450; Talking Bks 22,498; Videos 2,240
Subject Interests: Genealogy, Local hist
Automation Activity & Vendor Info: (Acquisitions) SirsiDynix; (Cataloging) SirsiDynix; (Circulation) SirsiDynix; (OPAC) SirsiDynix; (Serials) SirsiDynix
Wireless access
Publications: PPL Friends Newsletter (Bimonthly)
Partic in Panhandle Library Access Network
Special Services for the Blind - Talking bk & rec for the blind cat
Open Mon-Thurs 9-8, Fri & Sat 9-5, Sun 2-7
Friends of the Library Group
Branches: 6
CENTURY BRANCH, 7991 N Century Blvd, Century, 32535. Tel: 850-256-6217. *Br Mgr,* Deanna McCarthy-Perkins; E-mail: DMMcCarthy-Perkins@mywfpl.com
Open Tues-Fri 10-7, Sat 10-4
Friends of the Library Group
MOLINO BRANCH, 6450-A Hwy 95A, Molino, 32577. Tel: 850-435-1760. *Br Mgr,* Rachel Nicholas-Kahalley; E-mail: rnkahalley@myescambia.com
Open Mon-Fri 10-7, Sat 10-4
Friends of the Library Group
SOUTHWEST, 12248 Gulf Beach Hwy, 32507, SAN 378-1410. Tel: 850-453-7780. *Br Mgr,* Chris Hare; E-mail: ckhare@mywfpl.com
Open Tues-Thurs 9-8, Fri & Sat 9-5
Friends of the Library Group
LUCIA M TRYON BRANCH, 1200 Langley Ave, 32504, SAN 338-0076. Tel: 850-471-6980. *Br Mgr,* Rachel Wallace; E-mail: rmwallace@mywfpl.com
Open Tues-Thurs 9-8, Fri & Sat 9-5
Friends of the Library Group
WEST FLORIDA GENEALOGY, 5740 N Ninth Ave, 32504. Tel: 850-494-7373. *Br Mgr,* Michael Taranto; E-mail: mjtaranto@mywfpl.com
WESTSIDE, 1301 W Gregory St, 32502. Tel: 850-595-1047. *Br Mgr,* Position Currently Open
Open Mon-Fri 10-7
Friends of the Library Group

PERRY

P TAYLOR COUNTY PUBLIC LIBRARY, 403 N Washington St, 32347. SAN 303-1314. Tel: 850-838-3512. FAX: 850-838-3514. E-mail: taylor@3riverslibrary.com. *Libr Mgr,* Jo-Ann Morgan
Pop 17,150; Circ 53,923
Library Holdings: Bk Vols 42,000; Per Subs 80
Automation Activity & Vendor Info: (Cataloging) Innovative Interfaces, Inc; (Circulation) Innovative Interfaces, Inc
Wireless access
Partic in Three Rivers Regional Library Consortium
Special Services for the Deaf - Bks on deafness & sign lang; Captioned film dep; High interest/low vocabulary bks
Open Mon-Fri 8:30-5:30
Friends of the Library Group

PINELLAS PARK

P BARBARA S PONCE PUBLIC LIBRARY*, 7770 52nd St, 33781. SAN 303-1322. Tel: 727-369-0669. Reference Tel: 727-369-0667. Automation Services Tel: 727-369-7786. FAX: 727-541-0818. E-mail: library@pinellas-park.com. Web Site: www.pinellas-park.com/336/Library-Leisure-Services. *Dir,* Angela Pietras; Tel: 727-369-0590, E-mail: apietras@pinellas-park.com; *Asst Dir,* David McMurrin; Tel: 727-369-0679, E-mail: dmcmurrin@pinellas-park.com; *Borrower Serv Librn,* Bonnie Vincent; Tel: 727-369-0592, E-mail: bvincent@pinellas-park.com; *Adult Coll, Adult Serv,* Cathy Wos; Tel: 727-369-0676, E-mail: cwos@pinellas-park.com; Staff 6 (MLS 6)
Founded 1948. Pop 48,835; Circ 369,728
Library Holdings: AV Mats 9,184; e-books 36,593; High Interest/Low Vocabulary Bk Vols 225; Large Print Bks 7,005; Bk Vols 111,159; Per Subs 315
Automation Activity & Vendor Info: (Cataloging) SirsiDynix; (Circulation) SirsiDynix; (OPAC) SirsiDynix
Wireless access
Function: ILL available, Ref serv available
Publications: Newsletter
Mem of Pinellas Public Library Cooperative
Partic in Tampa Bay Library Consortium, Inc
Special Services for the Deaf - Bks on deafness & sign lang; TDD equip; Video relay services
Open Mon-Thurs 9-8:30, Fri & Sat 9-5, Sun 1-5
Friends of the Library Group

C SAINT PETERSBURG COLLEGE*, M M Bennett Libraries, 7200 66th St N, 33781. (Mail add: PO Box 13489, Saint Petersburg, 33733-3489), SAN 337-3185. Tel: 727-341-3604. Reference Tel: 727-341-3775. Web Site: go.spcollege.edu/Libraries. *Dir,* Lynn McCormick McDonald; Tel: 727-341-7183, E-mail: mccormickmcdonald.lynn@spcollege.edu; Staff 36 (MLS 12, Non-MLS 24)
Founded 1927. Enrl 16,933; Highest Degree: Bachelor
Library Holdings: Bk Vols 88,000
Special Collections: US Document Depository
Automation Activity & Vendor Info: (Circulation) SirsiDynix
Wireless access
Partic in Tampa Bay Library Consortium, Inc
Open Mon-Thurs 7:30am-9pm, Fri 7:30-4, Sat 10-5
Departmental Libraries:
CLEARWATER CAMPUS LIBRARY, 2465 Drew St, Clearwater, 33765, SAN 337-3177. Tel: 727-791-2614. FAX: 727-791-2601. Web Site: www.spcollege.edu/central/libonline. *Head Librn/Prog Dir II,* Kim Wolff; Tel: 727-791-2417, E-mail: wolff.kim@spcollege.edu; *Librn,* Paula Bagwell; Tel: 727-791-2415, E-mail: bagwell.paula@spcollege.edu; *Librn,* Pat Barbier; Tel: 727-791-2603, E-mail: barbierp@spcollege.edu; *Librn,* Antoinette Caraway; Tel: 727-791-2416, E-mail: caraway.antoinette@spcollege.edu; *Librn,* Donna Kelly; Tel: 727-341-3771, E-mail: kelly.donna@spcollege.edu; Staff 4 (MLS 4)
CM HEALTH EDUCATION CENTER, 7200 66th St N, 33781, SAN 370-2014. Tel: 727-341-3657. FAX: 727-341-3658. *Head Librn/Prog Dir,* Hector Perez-Gilbe; Staff 4 (MLS 1, Non-MLS 3)
Partic in Tampa Bay Medical Library Network
PROCESSING CENTER, 6021 142nd Ave N, Clearwater, 33760, SAN 370-2022. Tel: 727-341-3693. FAX: 727-341-3399. *Head Librn/Prod Dir I,* Rebecca Frank; Tel: 727-341-3759, E-mail: frank.rebecca@spcollege.edu; Staff 3 (MLS 1, Non-MLS 2)
SAINT PETERSBURG-GIBBS CAMPUS LIBRARY, 6605 Fifth Ave N, Saint Petersburg, 33710, SAN 338-0432. Tel: 727-341-7198. FAX: 727-341-7188. *Head Librn/Prog Dir II,* Tracy Elliott; Tel: 727-341-7197, E-mail: elliott.tracy@spcollege.edu; *Librn,* Betty Jo Gaston; Tel: 727-341-7179, E-mail: gaston.betty@spcollege.edu; *Librn,* Gail Lancaster; Tel: 727-341-4793, E-mail: lancasterg@spcollege.edu; *Librn,* Chad Mairn; Tel: 727-341-7188, E-mail: mairn.chad@spcollege.edu; Staff 9 (MLS 4, Non-MLS 5)
TARPON SPRINGS CAMPUS LIBRARY, 600 Klosterman Rd, Tarpon Springs, 34689, SAN 370-226X. Tel: 727-712-5728. FAX: 727-712-5706. *Head Librn,* Jorge Perez; E-mail: perez.jorge@spcollege.edu; *Librn,* Mathew Bodie; Tel: 727-712-5240, E-mail: bodie.mathew@spcollege.edu; Staff 4 (MLS 2, Non-MLS 2)
Open Mon-Thurs 7:30am-9pm, Fri 7:30-4, Sat 10-5, Sun 1-5

S TAMPA BAY REGIONAL PLANNING COUNCIL*, Research & Information Center, 4000 Gateway Center Blvd, Ste 100, 33782. SAN 303-1632. Tel: 727-570-5151. FAX: 727-570-5118. E-mail: info@tbrpc.org. Web Site: www.tbrpc.org. *Dir, Res,* Randy Deshazo; E-mail: randy@tbrpc.org
Library Holdings: Bk Vols 3,000; Per Subs 90
Special Collections: Developments of Regional Impact for Pinellas, Hillsborough, Pasco & Manatee Counties Coll
Subject Interests: Housing, Planning, Transportation
Open Mon-Fri 8:30-12 & 1-5

PLANTATION

P HELEN B HOFFMAN PLANTATION LIBRARY, 501 N Fig Tree Lane, 33317. SAN 303-1357. Tel: 954-797-2140. Reference Tel: 954-797-2144. Administration Tel: 954-797-2141. FAX: 954-797-2767. E-mail: library@plantation.org. Web Site: www.plantation.org/library. *Dir,* Monika L Knapp; E-mail: mknapp@plantation.org; *Sr Librn,* Jenny Kajatt; Staff 5 (MLS 2, Non-MLS 3)
Founded 1963. Pop 89,000
Library Holdings: Bk Vols 70,000
Special Collections: Florida Coll; Large Print Coll; Spanish Coll
Automation Activity & Vendor Info: (Cataloging) Mandarin Library Automation; (Circulation) Mandarin Library Automation; (OPAC) Mandarin Library Automation; (Serials) Mandarin Library Automation
Open Mon 12-9, Tues-Thurs 10-9, Fri 12-7, Sat 10-5

Restriction: Non-resident fee
Friends of the Library Group

POLK CITY

P SUZETTE PENTON POLK CITY COMMUNITY LIBRARY, 215 S Bougainvillea Ave, 33868. (Mail add: 123 Broadway Blvd, 33868), SAN 377-2705. Tel: 863-984-4340. FAX: 863-984-6385. Web Site: mypolkcity.org/departments/administration/library. *Librn,* Mikayla Osso; E-mail: mikayla.osso@mypolkcity.org; Staff 1 (Non-MLS 1)
Library Holdings: Bk Vols 10,000; Per Subs 20
Automation Activity & Vendor Info: (Cataloging) SirsiDynix; (Circulation) SirsiDynix; (OPAC) SirsiDynix
Wireless access
Function: ILL available
Partic in Polk County Libr Coop; Tampa Bay Library Consortium, Inc
Open Mon-Fri 9-12:30 & 1:30-5

PORT CHARLOTTE

P CHARLOTTE COUNTY LIBRARY SYSTEM*, Library Administration, 2050 Forrest Nelson Blvd, 33952. SAN 338-019X. Tel: 941-613-3200. Interlibrary Loan Service Tel: 941-613-3198. FAX: 941-613-3196. E-mail: CharlotteCountyLibraries@charlottecountyfl.gov. Web Site: www.charlottecountyfl.com/library. *Div Mgr,* Lanette Hart; E-mail: Lanette.Hart@charlottecountyfl.gov; *Regional Librn,* Evelyn Kennedy; E-mail: Terri.Crawford@charlottecountyfl.gov; Staff 31.5 (MLS 10, Non-MLS 21.5)
Founded 1963. Pop 160,000; Circ 792,548
Library Holdings: Audiobooks 18,149; DVDs 25,146; e-books 12,082; Bk Vols 208,692; Per Subs 329
Special Collections: Florida Coll; Genealogy Coll; Large Print Book Coll; Local Author Coll
Automation Activity & Vendor Info: (Acquisitions) TLC (The Library Corporation); (Cataloging) TLC (The Library Corporation); (Circulation) TLC (The Library Corporation); (OPAC) TLC (The Library Corporation); (Serials) TLC (The Library Corporation)
Wireless access
Function: Adult bk club, Art exhibits, AV serv, Bk club(s), Bks on CD, Children's prog, Computer training, Computers for patron use, Electronic databases & coll, Free DVD rentals, Genealogy discussion group, ILL available, Large print keyboards, Magnifiers for reading, Mail & tel request accepted, Music CDs, Notary serv, Online cat, Outside serv via phone, mail, e-mail & web, Photocopying/Printing, Preschool outreach, Prog for adults, Prog for children & young adult, Ref & res, Ref serv available, Scanner, Senior computer classes, Story hour, Tax forms, Teen prog, Telephone ref, Wheelchair accessible
Publications: Friend's Newsletters; Information pamphlets
Partic in Southwest Florida Library Network
Special Services for the Deaf - ADA equip; Assisted listening device; Closed caption videos; Pocket talkers
Special Services for the Blind - Accessible computers; Assistive/Adapted tech devices, equip & products; Audio mat; Copier with enlargement capabilities; Internet workstation with adaptive software; Large print bks; Screen reader software
Open Mon-Thurs 10-7, Fri & Sat 10-5
Restriction: Non-resident fee
Friends of the Library Group
Branches: 4
ENGLEWOOD CHARLOTTE PUBLIC, 3450 N Access Rd, Englewood, 34224, SAN 338-022X. Tel: 941-681-3736. Circulation Tel: 941-681-3735. FAX: 941-681-3740. *Librn,* Lynda L Citro; Tel: 941-681-3739, E-mail: lynda.citro@charlottefl.com; Staff 5 (MLS 1, Non-MLS 4)
Circ 68,557
Function: Adult bk club, Bks on CD, Children's prog, Computers for patron use, E-Reserves, Electronic databases & coll, Free DVD rentals, Music CDs, Online cat, Online ref, Photocopying/Printing, Summer reading prog, Teen prog
Publications: Friend's Newsletters
Special Services for the Blind - Talking bks
Open Tues-Thurs 10-6, Fri 10-5, Sat 10-2
Restriction: Non-resident fee
Friends of the Library Group
MID-COUNTY REGIONAL LIBRARY, 2050 Forrest Nelson Blvd, 33952, SAN 326-7377. Reference Tel: 941-613-3166. FAX: 941-613-3177. ; Staff 18.5 (MLS 6, Non-MLS 12.5)
Founded 2005. Circ 397,052
Special Collections: Genealogy Coll
Function: Art exhibits, Bk club(s), Bks on CD, Children's prog, Computer training, Computers for patron use, Electronic databases & coll, Free DVD rentals, Genealogy discussion group, ILL available, Internet access, Large print keyboards, Music CDs, Notary serv, Online cat, Photocopying/Printing, Prog for adults, Prog for children & young adult, Ref serv available, Scanner, Senior computer classes, Story hour, Summer reading prog, Tax forms, Teen prog, Telephone ref, Wheelchair accessible
Publications: Newsletters
Open Mon-Thurs 10-7, Fri & Sat 10-5
Restriction: Non-resident fee
Friends of the Library Group
PORT CHARLOTTE PUBLIC, 2280 Aaron St, 33952, SAN 338-0289. Reference Tel: 941-764-5562. FAX: 941-764-5571. *Librn,* Tarcy Herman; Tel: 941-764-5570, E-mail: Tracy.Herman@Charlottecountyfl.gov; Staff 4.5 (MLS 1, Non-MLS 3.5)
Circ 100,672
Function: Adult bk club, Art exhibits, Bks on CD, Children's prog, Computers for patron use, Electronic databases & coll, Free DVD rentals, ILL available, Magnifiers for reading, Music CDs, Online cat, Photocopying/Printing, Prog for adults, Prog for children & young adult, Summer reading prog, Tax forms, Telephone ref, Wheelchair accessible
Publications: Newsletters
Special Services for the Blind - Talking bks
Open Tues-Thurs 10-6, Fri 10-5
Restriction: Non-resident fee
Friends of the Library Group
PUNTA GORDA PUBLIC, 424 W Henry St, Punta Gorda, 33950, SAN 338-0319. Reference Tel: 941-833-5460. FAX: 941-833-5463. *Librn Supvr,* LeeAnn Beckwith; Tel: 941-833-5459, E-mail: LeeAnn.Beckwith@Charlottecountyfl.gov; Staff 5 (MLS 1, Non-MLS 4)
Circ 175,971
Special Collections: Florida Coll
Publications: Newsletters
Special Services for the Blind - Talking bks
Open Tues & Wed 10-6, Thurs 10-7, Fri 10-5
Restriction: Non-resident fee
Friends of the Library Group

PORT ORANGE

§CM PALMER COLLEGE OF CHIROPRACTIC, Florida Campus Library, 4777 City Center Pkwy, 32129. Tel: 386-763-2670. Web Site: www.palmer.edu/academics/library. *Librn/Br Mgr,* Edward Murphy; E-mail: edward.murphy@palmer.edu
Special Collections: Chiropractic Archives
Wireless access
Function: Computers for patron use, ILL available, Study rm
Partic in Northeast Florida Library Information Network
Open Mon-Thurs 7am-11pm, Fri 7-5, Sat 8:30-5, Sun 2:30pm-11pm

PUNTA GORDA

J FLORIDA SOUTHWESTERN STATE COLLEGE*, Vernon Peeples Library-Charlotte Campus, 26300 Airport Rd, 33950. Tel: 941-637-5620. FAX: 941-637-3501. Web Site: www.fsw.edu/charlotte/library. *Fac Librn,* Mary Ann Walton; Tel: 941-637-5644, E-mail: mwalton@fsw.edu; Staff 6 (MLS 3, Non-MLS 3)
Founded 1996. Enrl 1,400; Fac 15; Highest Degree: Associate
Library Holdings: Bk Titles 10,000; Per Subs 90
Automation Activity & Vendor Info: (Acquisitions) Ex Libris Group; (Cataloging) Ex Libris Group; (Circulation) Ex Libris Group; (Course Reserve) Ex Libris Group; (ILL) OCLC; (OPAC) Ex Libris Group; (Serials) Ex Libris Group
Wireless access
Open Mon-Thurs 7:30am-9pm, Fri 7:30-4, Sat 9-1

QUINCY

P GADSDEN COUNTY PUBLIC LIBRARY*, William A "Bill" McGill Pubic Library & Administrative Office, 732 S Pat Thomas Pkwy, 32351. SAN 320-4715. Tel: 850-627-7106. FAX: 850-627-7775. Web Site: www2.youseemore.com/gadsden. *Dir,* Tabitha Washington; E-mail: twashington@gadsdencountyfl.gov; *Outreach Serv Librn,* Shannon Powell Allen; *Ch Serv,* Kris Odahowski; Staff 2 (MLS 2)
Founded 1979. Pop 45,000
Library Holdings: Bk Titles 83,559; Bk Vols 85,000; Per Subs 76
Automation Activity & Vendor Info: (Cataloging) TLC (The Library Corporation); (Circulation) TLC (The Library Corporation)
Wireless access
Open Mon-Thurs 10-8, Fri & Sat 10-6
Friends of the Library Group
Branches: 2
COWEN PUBLIC LIBRARY, 300 Maple St, Chattahoochee, 32324, SAN 320-5088. Tel: 850-663-2707. FAX: 850-663-4598. *Br Mgr,* Brittany Green; *Libr Tech,* Marie Parker
Open Mon & Tues 11-8, Wed-Fri 11-6, Sat 10-3
Friends of the Library Group

HAVANA PUBLIC LIBRARY, 203 E Fifth Ave, Havana, 32333, SAN 320-9954. Tel: 850-539-2844. E-mail: hsrc@macneal.com. *Librn,* Virginia Green
Library Holdings: Bk Vols 4,000
Open Mon & Tues 11-8, Wed-Fri 11-6, Sat 10-3
Friends of the Library Group
Bookmobiles: 1

S GADSEN CORRECTIONAL INSTITUTION LIBRARY*, 6044 Greensboro Hwy, 32351-9100. SAN 377-0885. Tel: 850-875-9701, Ext 2261. *Librn,* William Miller
Library Holdings: Bk Vols 12,000; Per Subs 71
Open Mon-Fri 8-11 & 1-5, Sat 8-12

RIVERVIEW

CL WESTERN MICHIGAN UNIVERSITY-COOLEY LAW SCHOOL LIBRARIES, Tampa Campus, 9445 Camden Field Pkwy, 33578. Tel: 813-419-5100. Circulation Tel: 813-419-5100, Ext 5120. Reference Tel: 813-419-5100, Ext 5121. FAX: 813-405-3402. Web Site: cooley.edu/locations/tampa-bay. *Head, Pub Serv,* Chad Brown; Tel: 813-419-5100, Ext 5113, E-mail: browncha@cooley.edu
Wireless access
Open Mon-Thurs 8am-Midnight, Fri 8am-10pm, Sat & Sun Noon-10pm

RIVIERA BEACH

P RIVIERA BEACH PUBLIC LIBRARY*, 600 W Blue Heron Blvd, 33404-4398. (Mail add: PO Box 11329, 33419-1329), SAN 303-1403. Tel: 561-845-4195. FAX: 561-881-7308. E-mail: library@rivierabeach.org. Web Site: www.rivierabch.com/library. *Dir,* Cynthia Cobb; Tel: 561-845-4195, E-mail: ccobb@rivierabeach.org; *Asst Dir,* Amy Dickinson; Tel: 561-840-0155, E-mail: ADickinson@rivierabeach.org; *Ch Serv,* Sharmain Arnold; Tel: 561-845-3428, E-mail: SArnold@rivierabeach.org; Staff 7 (MLS 2, Non-MLS 5)
Founded 1950. Pop 34,674; Circ 79,230
Special Collections: African-American Studies Coll; Florida Coll
Automation Activity & Vendor Info: (Cataloging) Auto-Graphics, Inc; (Circulation) Auto-Graphics, Inc; (OPAC) Auto-Graphics, Inc
Wireless access
Function: 24/7 Electronic res, 24/7 Online cat, Adult bk club, Art exhibits, Bks on CD, Children's prog, Computer training, Computers for patron use, Digital talking bks, Electronic databases & coll, Free DVD rentals, Holiday prog, ILL available, Instruction & testing, Internet access, Magazines, Meeting rooms, Movies, Music CDs, Notary serv, Online cat, Orientations, OverDrive digital audio bks, Prog for adults, Prog for children & young adult, Ref & res, Ref serv available, Scanner, Senior computer classes, Story hour, Study rm, Wheelchair accessible
Partic in Library Cooperative of the Palm Beaches; Southeast Florida Library Information Network, Inc
Open Mon 9-6, Tues, Wed & Thurs 9-8, Fri & Sat 9-5

ROYAL PALM BEACH

C SOUTH UNIVERSITY, West Palm Beach Campus Library, 9801 Belvedere Rd, 33411-3640. SAN 375-3786. Tel: 561-273-6402. Administration Tel: 561-273-6403. FAX: 561-273-6420. Web Site: www.southuniversity.edu/west-palm-beach.aspx. *Libr Dir,* Sal Greco; E-mail: sgreco@southuniversity.edu; Staff 1 (MLS 1)
Enrl 1,000; Fac 75; Highest Degree: Doctorate
Library Holdings: AV Mats 1,824; e-books 412,998; Electronic Media & Resources 103; Bk Titles 20,000; Bk Vols 22,226; Per Subs 25
Subject Interests: Advan practice nursing, Bus, Counseling, Criminal justice, Health sci, Healthcare mgt, Info tech, Legal studies, Nursing, Occupational therapy, Paralegal studies, Phys therapy, Psychol
Automation Activity & Vendor Info: (Circulation) Ex Libris Group; (OPAC) Ex Libris Group
Wireless access
Open Mon-Wed 9-4, Thurs 9-6, Fri 9-3
Restriction: Borrowing privileges limited to fac & registered students

SAFETY HARBOR

P SAFETY HARBOR PUBLIC LIBRARY, 101 Second St N, 34695. SAN 323-7575. Tel: 727-724-1525. FAX: 727-724-1533. TDD: 727-724-1529. Reference E-mail: shplref@cityofsafetyharbor.com. Web Site: cityofsafetyharbor.com/60/library. *Libr Dir,* Lisa Kothe; E-mail: lkothe@cityofsafetyharbor.com; *Circ Supvr,* Gail Geraci; E-mail: ggeraci@cityofsafetyharbor.com; *Outreach Serv Librn,* Desiree Spano; E-mail: dspano@cityofsafetyharbor.com; Staff 5 (MLS 4, Non-MLS 1)
Founded 1938. Pop 17,300; Circ 276,528
Library Holdings: AV Mats 7,881; Bks on Deafness & Sign Lang 1,842; e-books 3,598; High Interest/Low Vocabulary Bk Vols 100; Large Print Bks 1,797; Bk Titles 53,218; Bk Vols 65,000; Per Subs 113; Talking Bks 3,456; Videos 10,163
Special Collections: Books & Videos on Deafness & Sign Language
Subject Interests: Deafness, Sign lang
Automation Activity & Vendor Info: (Acquisitions) SirsiDynix; (Cataloging) SirsiDynix; (Circulation) SirsiDynix; (OPAC) SirsiDynix; (Serials) SirsiDynix
Mem of Pinellas Public Library Cooperative
Partic in Tampa Bay Library Consortium, Inc
Special Services for the Deaf - Adult & family literacy prog; Bks on deafness & sign lang; Captioned film dep; Deaf publ; TDD equip
Open Mon-Thurs 9:30-8, Fri 9:30-6, Sat 9:30-5
Friends of the Library Group

SAINT AUGUSTINE

C FLAGLER COLLEGE, Proctor Library, 44 Sevilla St, 32084-4302. (Mail add: 74 King St, 32084), SAN 303-1411. Tel: 904-819-6206. Reference Tel: 904-819-6331. E-mail: library@flagler.edu. Web Site: library.flagler.edu. *Dir, Libr Serv,* Brian Nesselrode; E-mail: bness@flagler.edu; *Access Serv Librn,* Caitlin Trachim; E-mail: ctrachim@flagler.edu; *Coll Develop Librn,* Jessie Rutland; E-mail: jrutland@flagler.edu; *Evening/Weekend Librn,* Stephen Derrig; E-mail: sderrig@flagler.edu; *Spec Coll Librn,* Katherine Owens; E-mail: kowens@flagler.edu; *Teaching & Learning Librn,* Jack Daniels; E-mail: danielsj@flagler.edu; *Web Serv Librn,* Blake Pridgen; E-mail: bpridgen@flagler.edu; *Archive Spec,* Jolene DuBray; E-mail: JDubray679@flagler.edu; *Circ Spec,* Maria Dintino; E-mail: mdintino@flagler.edu; *Circ Spec,* Virginia Luteran; E-mail: vluteran@flagler.edu; Staff 7 (MLS 7)
Founded 1968. Enrl 2,958; Fac 400; Highest Degree: Bachelor
Library Holdings: AV Mats 5,134; e-books 317,346; e-journals 41,860; Bk Vols 102,242; Per Subs 76
Special Collections: Deaf Studies Coll
Automation Activity & Vendor Info: (Discovery) EBSCO Discovery Service; (ILL) OCLC Connexion
Wireless access
Partic in Florida Library Information Network; Independent Cols & Univs of Fla; LYRASIS; Northeast Florida Library Information Network
Open Mon-Thurs 7:30am-Midnight, Fri 7:30-5, Sat 10-5, Sun 11am-Midnight

S SAINT AUGUSTINE HISTORICAL SOCIETY*, Research Library, Six Artillery Lane, 2nd Flr, 32084. (Mail add: 271 Charlotte St, 32084-5099), SAN 303-1438. Tel: 904-825-2333. E-mail: sahslibrary@bellsouth.net. Web Site: saintaugustinehistoricalsociety.org/reserach-library. *Chief Librn,* Bob Nawrocki; E-mail: bobnawrocki@sahs1883.com; *Asst Librn,* Chad Germany; E-mail: chadgermany@sahs1883.com; *Sr Res Librn,* Charles Tingley; E-mail: charlestingley@sahs1883.com; Staff 3 (MLS 1, Non-MLS 2)
Founded 1883
Library Holdings: Microforms 1,200; Bk Titles 8,000; Per Subs 10
Special Collections: Card Calendar of Spanish Documents, 1512-1764; Card Index of St Augustine Residents; Cathedral Parish Records, 1594-1763 & 1784-1882, including Baptisms, Marriages & Burials; Ceiba Mocha Parish, Cuban Archives, 1797-1920, microfilm; Census Records for Northeast Florida, 1784-1920; Colonial Office Records, 1763-1784, British period, microfilm; Court Records for St Johns County, 1812-1960; East Florida Papers on microfilm, 1783-1821; Florida Times Union Newspaper, 1881-1895, microfilm; Maps of Florida & St Augustine (copies), 16th Century to present; Photographs of the St Augustine Area, 19th Century to present; St Augustine Newspapers, 1821 to Present, with gaps; Stetson Coll, 1500's-1817; Various Manuscript Coll. Oral History
Subject Interests: Fla colonial hist, St Augustine, Fla, St Johns County
Automation Activity & Vendor Info: (Cataloging) TLC (The Library Corporation)
Publications: East Florida Gazette (Biannually); El Escribano, St Augustine Journal of History (Annual)
Open Tues-Fri 9-4:30
Friends of the Library Group

P SAINT JOHNS COUNTY PUBLIC LIBRARY SYSTEM*, Southeast Branch Library & Administrative Headquarters, 6670 US 1 South, 32086. SAN 338-0408. Tel: 904-827-6900. Circulation Tel: 904-827-6904. Interlibrary Loan Service Tel: 904-827-6934. Reference Tel: 904-827-6902. Administration Tel: 904-827-6925. Automation Services Tel: 904-827-6924. Circulation FAX: 904-827-6905. Administration FAX: 904-827-6930. Web Site: www.sjcpls.org. *Dir,* Debra Rhodes Gibson; Tel: 904-827-6926, E-mail: dgibson@sjcfl.us; *Tech Serv Adminr,* Jae Bass; E-mail: jbass@sjcfl.us; *Circ Mgr,* Kris Mangus; Tel: 904-827-6916, E-mail: kmangus@sjcfl.us; *Extn Serv Mgr,* Harold George; Tel: 904-827-6928, E-mail: hgeorge@sjcfl.us; *Ch Serv,* Alex Phillips; Tel: 904-827-6912, E-mail: aphillips@sjcfl.us; *ILL,* Karlene Adams; E-mail: kadams@sjcfl.us; *Br Mgr,* Todd Booth; Tel: 904-827-6913, E-mail: tbooth@sjcfl.us; *Ref Serv,* Juli Wald; Tel: 904-827-6918, E-mail: jwald@sjcfl.us; Staff 24.5 (MLS 9, Non-MLS 15.5)
Founded 1975

Oct 2016-Sept 2017. Mats Exp Electronic Ref Mat (Incl. Access Fees) $60,000
Library Holdings: Audiobooks 36,987; AV Mats 76,220; CDs 283,534; e-books 184,084; Electronic Media & Resources 88; Bk Vols 277,399; Per Subs 300
Special Collections: Genealogy
Subject Interests: Fla
Automation Activity & Vendor Info: (Acquisitions) SirsiDynix; (Cataloging) SirsiDynix; (Circulation) SirsiDynix; (ILL) OCLC WorldShare Interlibrary Loan; (OPAC) SirsiDynix
Wireless access
Function: 24/7 Online cat, Adult bk club, Art exhibits, Audiobks via web, Bks on CD, Children's prog, Computer training, Computers for patron use, Electronic databases & coll, Holiday prog, Home delivery & serv to seniorr ctr & nursing homes, Homebound delivery serv, ILL available, Instruction & testing, Internet access, Laminating, Magazines, Mail & tel request accepted, Meeting rooms, Movies, Music CDs, Notary serv, Online cat, Online ref, Outreach serv, Outside serv via phone, mail, e-mail & web, OverDrive digital audio bks, Photocopying/Printing, Preschool outreach, Prog for adults, Prog for children & young adult, Ref serv available, Scanner, Senior outreach, Spanish lang bks, Story hour, Summer reading prog, Tax forms, Teen prog, Telephone ref, Wheelchair accessible
Partic in LYRASIS; Northeast Florida Library Information Network
Special Services for the Deaf - Assistive tech; Bks on deafness & sign lang; Sign lang interpreter upon request for prog; Staff with knowledge of sign lang; Video relay services
Special Services for the Blind - Assistive/Adapted tech devices, equip & products; BiFolkal kits; Bks on CD; Braille bks; Dragon Naturally Speaking software; Extensive large print coll; Large screen computer & software; Magnifiers; Talking bk serv referral
Open Mon, Tues & Thurs 10-8, Wed & Fri 10-6, Sat 10-5
Restriction: Non-resident fee
Friends of the Library Group
Branches: 5
ANASTASIA ISLAND BRANCH, 124 Seagrove Main St, Saint Augustine Beach, 32080. Tel: 904-209-3730. FAX: 904-209-3735. E-mail: libai@sjcfl.us. *Br Mgr,* Mikki Sampo; Tel: 904-209-3731, E-mail: msampo@sjcfl.us; *Circ Supvr,* Deborah Braden; Tel: 904-209-3734, E-mail: dbraden@sjcfl.us; *Ch Serv,* Nicole Jebbia; Tel: 904-209-3732, E-mail: njebbia@sjcfl.us; Staff 8.8 (MLS 2, Non-MLS 6.8)
Founded 2007
Function: 24/7 Online cat, Adult bk club, Bks on CD, Children's prog, Computers for patron use, Electronic databases & coll, Holiday prog, ILL available, Internet access, Meeting rooms, Movies, OverDrive digital audio bks, Photocopying/Printing, Preschool outreach, Prog for adults, Prog for children & young adult, Ref serv available, Scanner, Story hour, Summer reading prog, Tax forms, Wheelchair accessible
Open Tues & Thurs 10-8, Wed & Fri 10-6, Sat 10-5
Friends of the Library Group
BARTRAM TRAIL BRANCH, 60 Davis Pond Blvd, Fruit Cove, 32259-4390, SAN 325-4100. Tel: 904-827-6960. Reference Tel: 904-827-4748. FAX: 904-827-6965. *Br Mgr,* Dan Markus; Tel: 904-827-6961, E-mail: libbt@sjcfl.us; *Circ Supvr,* Melissa Burke; Tel: 904-827-6964, E-mail: mburke@sjcfl.us; *Ch Serv,* Lisa Darenberg; Tel: 904-827-6962, E-mail: ldarenberg@sjcfl.us; *Ref Serv,* Maribeth Wood; Tel: 904-827-6963, E-mail: mwood@sjcfl.us; Staff 11 (MLS 4, Non-MLS 7)
Founded 1997
Function: 24/7 Online cat, Adult bk club, Bks on CD, Children's prog, Computer training, Computers for patron use, Electronic databases & coll, Holiday prog, ILL available, Internet access, Life-long learning prog for all ages, Magazines, Meeting rooms, Music CDs, Notary serv, OverDrive digital audio bks, Photocopying/Printing, Prog for adults, Prog for children & young adult, Ref serv available, Scanner, Summer reading prog, Tax forms, Teen prog, Wheelchair accessible
Open Mon, Wed, Thurs & Fri 10-6, Tues 12-8 Sat 10-5
Friends of the Library Group
HASTINGS BRANCH, 6195 S Main St, Hastings, 32145, SAN 338-0416. Tel: 904-827-6970. FAX: 904-827-6975. E-mail: libh@sjcfl.us. *Br Mgr,* Brad Powell; Tel: 904-827-6971, E-mail: bpowell@sjcfl.us; *Ch Serv Librn,* Michelle Kiley; Tel: 904-827-6976, E-mail: mkiley@sjcfl.us; *Circ Supvr,* Terri Beverly; Tel: 904-827-6974, E-mail: tbeverly@sjcfl.us; Staff 4.7 (MLS 2, Non-MLS 2.7)
Founded 1997. Pop 7,569
Automation Activity & Vendor Info: (Circulation) Horizon
Function: 24/7 Online cat, Adult bk club, Art exhibits, Bks on CD, Children's prog, Computer training, Computers for patron use, Electronic databases & coll, ILL available, Internet access, Meeting rooms, Movies, Music CDs, Notary serv, Outreach serv, OverDrive digital audio bks, Photocopying/Printing, Prog for adults, Prog for children & young adult, Ref serv available, Scanner, Summer reading prog, Tax forms
Open Tues & Thurs 10-7, Wed & Fri 10-6, Sat 10-3
Friends of the Library Group
MAIN BRANCH, 1960 N Ponce de Leon Blvd, 32084. Tel: 904-827-6940. Circulation Tel: 904-827-4707. Reference Tel: 904-827-4702. FAX: 904-827-6945. E-mail: libm@sjcfl.us. *Br Mgr,* Valerie Peischel Mull; Tel: 904-827-6941, E-mail: vpeischel@sjcfl.us; *Ch Serv Librn,* Andy Calvert; Tel: 904-827-6943, E-mail: acalvert@sjcfl.us; *Ref Librn,* Amy Ackerman; Tel: 904-827-6942, E-mail: aackerman@sjcfl.us; *Circ Supvr,* Richard Steinmeyer; Tel: 904-827-6946, E-mail: rsteinmeyer@sjcfl.us; Staff 13.3 (MLS 3.5, Non-MLS 9.8)
Founded 1977
Function: 24/7 Online cat, Adult bk club, Art exhibits, Children's prog, Computers for patron use, Electronic databases & coll, Genealogy discussion group, Holiday prog, ILL available, Internet access, Magazines, Meeting rooms, Movies, Notary serv, OverDrive digital audio bks, Photocopying/Printing, Preschool outreach, Prog for adults, Prog for children & young adult, Ref serv available, Scanner, Spanish lang bks, Tax forms, Visual arts prog, Wheelchair accessible
Open Mon & Tues 11-7, Wed, Thurs & Fri 10-6, Sat 10-5
Friends of the Library Group
PONTE VEDRA BEACH BRANCH, 101 Library Blvd, Ponte Vedra Beach, 32082, SAN 325-4127. Tel: 904-827-6950. Circulation Tel: 904-827-4762. Reference Tel: 904-827-4766. FAX: 904-827-6955. E-mail: libpv@sjcfl.us. *Br Mgr,* Amy Ring; Tel: 904-827-6951, E-mail: aring@sjcfl.us; *Circ Supvr,* Lidia Wolfcale; Tel: 904-827-6956, E-mail: lwolfcale@sjcfl.us; *Ch Serv,* Anne Crawford; Tel: 904-827-6952, E-mail: acrawford@sjcfl.us; *Ref Serv,* Joan Hakala; Tel: 904-827-6953, E-mail: jhakala@sjcfl.us; Staff 10.9 (MLS 3, Non-MLS 7.9)
Founded 1993
Function: 24/7 Online cat, Adult bk club, Art exhibits, Bks on CD, Children's prog, Electronic databases & coll, ILL available, Internet access, Magazines, Meeting rooms, Movies, Music CDs, Notary serv, OverDrive digital audio bks, Photocopying/Printing, Prog for adults, Prog for children & young adult, Ref serv available, Scanner, Tax forms, Wheelchair accessible
Open Mon-Wed 10-8, Thurs & Fri 10-6, Sat 10-5
Friends of the Library Group

§CM UNIVERSITY OF ST AUGUSTINE FOR HEALTH SCIENCES, St Augustine Campus Library, One University Blvd, 32086. Tel: 904-770-3593. E-mail: library@usa.edu. Web Site: library.usa.edu. *Dir, Libr Serv,* Julie Evener; E-mail: jevener@usa.edu; *Librn,* Alexia Sheck; E-mail: asheck@usa.edu; *Circ Mgr,* Adam Mills; E-mail: amills@usa.edu
Wireless access
Function: ILL available, Photocopying/Printing, Scanner
Partic in Northeast Florida Library Information Network
Open Mon-Sun 7am-10pm

SAINT LEO

C SAINT LEO UNIVERSITY*, Cannon Memorial Library, 33701 State Rd 52, 33574. (Mail add: PO Box 6665, MC2128, 33574-6665), SAN 303-1446. Tel: 352-588-8258. FAX: 352-588-8484. Web Site: slulibrary.saintleo.edu. *Interim Dir, Libr Serv,* Doris Van Kampen; Tel: 352-588-8485, E-mail: doris.vankampen@saintleo.edu; *Coll Develop Librn,* Renee Gould; Tel: 352-588-8265, E-mail: renee.gould@saintleo.edu; *Ref Librn,* Janet Franks; Tel: 352-588-8478, E-mail: janet.franks@saintleo.edu; *Ref & Instrul Outreach Librn,* Carolann Moon; Tel: 352-588-8261, E-mail: carol.moon@saintleo.edu; *Ref & Instrul Serv Librn,* Jackie Bryan; Tel: 352-588-7437, E-mail: jacalyn.bryan@saintleo.edu; *Circ Evening Coordr,* Franisco Narvaez-Rodriguez; Tel: 352-588-8273, E-mail: francisco.narvaez@saintleo.edu; *Libr Tech Spec,* Christopher Wiginton; Tel: 352-588-7206, E-mail: christopher.wiginton@saintleo.edu; *ILL Asst,* Emilee Leathers; Tel: 352-588-8328, E-mail: emilee.leathers@saintleo.edu; Staff 16 (MLS 12, Non-MLS 4)
Founded 1959. Enrl 8,376; Fac 70; Highest Degree: Master
Library Holdings: e-books 235,000; Bk Titles 101,311; Bk Vols 111,138; Per Subs 474
Subject Interests: Catholic Church, Humanities, Monasticism, Theol
Automation Activity & Vendor Info: (Acquisitions) Ex Libris Group; (Cataloging) Ex Libris Group; (Circulation) Ex Libris Group; (Course Reserve) Ex Libris Group; (ILL) OCLC; (OPAC) Ex Libris Group; (Serials) Ex Libris Group
Wireless access
Publications: Acquisitions List; Bibliographies; Handbook; Library Guides; Newsletter; Periodicals Lists
Partic in LYRASIS; OCLC Online Computer Library Center, Inc; Tampa Bay Library Consortium, Inc
Open Sun-Thurs 8am-2am, Fri & Sat 8-7

SAINT PETE BEACH

P ST PETE BEACH PUBLIC LIBRARY*, 365 73rd Ave, 33706-1996. SAN 303-1683. Tel: 727-363-9238. FAX: 727-552-1760. Web Site: www.spblibrary.com. *Dir,* Betcinda Kettells; E-mail: bkettells@stpetebeach.org; *Librn,* Maureen Marton; E-mail: mmarton@stpetebeach.org; Staff 10 (MLS 2, Non-MLS 8)

Founded 1951. Pop 9,200; Circ 153,406
Oct 2012-Sept 2013 Income $517,978, City $355,841, County $162,137. Mats Exp $57,440. Sal $312,434 (Prof $135,000)
Library Holdings: AV Mats 3,009; DVDs 4,345; e-books 6,647; Bk Titles 50,544; Per Subs 61
Special Collections: Florida Coll; Sister City Coll
Automation Activity & Vendor Info: (Acquisitions) Innovative Interfaces, Inc; (Cataloging) Innovative Interfaces, Inc; (Circulation) Innovative Interfaces, Inc
Wireless access
Mem of Pinellas Public Library Cooperative
Partic in Tampa Bay Library Consortium, Inc
Open Mon & Wed 10-8, Tues, Thurs & Fri 10-6, Sat 10-2
Friends of the Library Group

SAINT PETERSBURG

M BAYFRONT HEALTH ST PETERSBURG*, Aucremann Medical Library, 701 Sixth St S, 33701. SAN 303-1462. Tel: 727-893-6751. FAX: 727-893-6819. Web Site: www.bayfront.org. *Libr Mgr,* Julie Hunt
Founded 1937
Library Holdings: Bk Vols 1,500; Per Subs 50
Subject Interests: Clinical med, Neurosurgery, Obstetrics & gynecology
Partic in SE-Atlantic Regional Med Libr Servs; Tampa Bay Medical Library Network
Open Mon-Fri 8-5

S SALVADOR DALI FOUNDATION INC*, Dali Museum Library, One Dali Blvd, 33701. SAN 322-7421. Tel: 727-623-4734. Web Site: thedali.org/library-2. *Librn,* Shaina Buckles Harkness; E-mail: sharkness@thedali.org; Staff 2 (MLS 1, Non-MLS 1)
Founded 1982
Library Holdings: CDs 30; DVDs 128; e-journals 18; Bk Titles 4,402; Bk Vols 6,122
Special Collections: Salvador Dali Coll
Subject Interests: Surrealism
Automation Activity & Vendor Info: (Acquisitions) LibraryWorld, Inc; (Cataloging) OCLC Connexion; (OPAC) LibraryWorld, Inc
Wireless access
Function: 24/7 Online cat, Archival coll, Art exhibits, For res purposes, Internet access, Online cat, Res libr
Publications: Books on Dali: Dali in the Nude; Dali the Passions; Dali, A Panorama; Exhibit Catalogs; Newsletter
Partic in Tampa Bay Library Consortium, Inc
Restriction: Authorized scholars by appt, Circulates for staff only, External users must contact libr, Non-circulating

C ECKERD COLLEGE*, Peter H Armacost Library, 4200 54th Ave S, 33711. SAN 303-1489. Tel: 727-864-8337. Interlibrary Loan Service Tel: 727-864-8475. Administration Tel: 727-864-8336. FAX: 727-864-8997. E-mail: libref@eckerd.edu. Web Site: www.eckerd.edu/library. *Dir, Libr Serv,* Lisa Johnston; E-mail: johnstln@eckerd.edu; *E-Resources, Coll Dev & Instructional Servs Librarian,* Nancy Schuler; E-mail: schulenl@eckerd.edu; *Instrul & Access Serv Librn,* Kim Copenhaver; E-mail: copenhka@eckerd.edu; *Technical Servs, Serials & Instruction Librn,* Alyssa Koclanes; E-mail: koclanan@eckerd.edu; *Visiting Access Services & Instruction Librn,* Heather Bush; E-mail: bushhk@eckerd.edu; *Circ Supvr,* Liz Pritchard; E-mail: pritcher@eckerd.edu; Staff 12 (MLS 5, Non-MLS 7)
Founded 1959. Enrl 1,608; Fac 124; Highest Degree: Bachelor
Library Holdings: Bk Titles 131,976; Bk Vols 165,085; Per Subs 821
Automation Activity & Vendor Info: (Acquisitions) Ex Libris Group; (Cataloging) Ex Libris Group; (Circulation) Ex Libris Group; (Course Reserve) Ex Libris Group
Wireless access
Partic in Florida Library Information Network; Independent Cols & Univs of Fla; Library & Information Resources Network; OCLC Online Computer Library Center, Inc; Tampa Bay Library Consortium, Inc
Friends of the Library Group

G FISH & WILDLIFE RESEARCH INSTITUTE*, Research Information Center, 100 Eighth Ave SE, 33701-5095. SAN 303-1497. Tel: 727-896-8626. FAX: 727-823-0166. Web Site: www.myfwc.com/research/publications/ric. *Librn,* Robin Grunwald; E-mail: robin.grunwald@myfwc.com; Staff 4 (MLS 1, Non-MLS 3)
Founded 1955
Library Holdings: Bk Titles 6,500; Per Subs 170
Subject Interests: Biological, Environ studies, Ichthyology, Marine biol, Wildlife res
Publications: Florida Marine Research Publications; Memoirs of the Hourglass Cruises; Reprints of Articles in Outside Journals; Technical Reports
Partic in Tampa Bay Library Consortium, Inc
Open Mon-Fri 8-5

M JOHNS HOPKINS ALL CHILDREN'S HOSPITAL*, Medical Library, 501 Sixth Ave S, 33701. SAN 303-1454. Tel: 727-767-4278. FAX: 727-767-8557. E-mail: achmedicallibrary@jhmi.edu. *Dir,* Pamela Williams; E-mail: pwilli78@jhmi.edu; Staff 2 (MLS 2)
Library Holdings: CDs 300; Bk Titles 900; Per Subs 50
Subject Interests: Cardiology, Med, Neurology, Nursing, Pediatrics
Automation Activity & Vendor Info: (Cataloging) LibraryWorld, Inc; (OPAC) LibraryWorld, Inc; (Serials) LibraryWorld, Inc
Wireless access
Function: Doc delivery serv, For res purposes, Health sci info serv, ILL available, Internet access, Ref serv available
Partic in Florida Health Sciences Library Association; SEND; Tampa Bay Medical Library Network
Open Mon-Fri 9-5:30
Restriction: Badge access after hrs, Staff & prof res

S MUSEUM OF FINE ARTS*, Reference Library, 255 Beach Dr NE, 33701. SAN 303-156X. Tel: 727-896-2667. FAX: 727-894-4638. Web Site: mfastpete.org. *Librn,* Position Currently Open
Founded 1962
Library Holdings: Bk Titles 27,000; Per Subs 21
Subject Interests: Art & archit, Decorative art
Temporarily Closed 2020-
Open Tues, Wed & Sat 10-5, Thurs & Fri 12-8, Sun 12-5
Restriction: Non-circulating

R PASADENA PRESBYTERIAN CHURCH LIBRARY*, Maxine Perry Library, 100 Pasadena Ave N, 33710-8315. SAN 303-1578. Tel: 727-345-0148. FAX: 727-347-6836. Web Site: www.pasadenapc.com. *Librn,* Laurie Smith; Staff 1 (Non-MLS 1)
Founded 1960
Library Holdings: Audiobooks 20; CDs 40; DVDs 154; Large Print Bks 20; Bk Titles 4,800; Bk Vols 4,850; Spec Interest Per Sub 2; Videos 159
Special Collections: Christian Children's & Youth Books (Including an Easy Section & Reading-Level Books)
Subject Interests: Bible study, Christian bks, Christian fiction, Christian life
Function: Bks on cassette, Bks on CD, VHS videos
Open Sun 8:30-Noon

P SAINT PETERSBURG PUBLIC LIBRARY*, 3745 Ninth Ave N, 33713. SAN 338-0467. Tel: 727-893-7724. FAX: 727-892-5432. Web Site: splibraries.org. *Dir,* Mika Slaughter Nelson; Tel: 727-893-7736; *Libr Operations Mgr,* Beth Lindsay; Tel: 727-892-5003, E-mail: mary.lindsay@stpete.org; *Coordr, Support Serv,* Linda Branson; Tel: 727-893-7318
Founded 1910. Pop 240,318; Circ 1,051,108
Library Holdings: Bk Vols 435,634; Per Subs 886
Special Collections: Florida History. State Document Depository; US Document Depository
Automation Activity & Vendor Info: (Acquisitions) Innovative Interfaces, Inc; (Cataloging) Innovative Interfaces, Inc; (Circulation) Innovative Interfaces, Inc
Wireless access
Mem of Pinellas Public Library Cooperative
Partic in Tampa Bay Library Consortium, Inc
Open Mon, Wed, Fri & Sat 10-6, Tues & Thurs 10-8, Sun 12-6
Friends of the Library Group
Branches: 5
JAMES WELDON JOHNSON BRANCH, 1059 18th Ave S, 33705, SAN 338-0491. Tel: 727-893-7113. FAX: 727-821-4845. *Coordr, Librn II,* Susan Dickson; E-mail: susan.dickson@stpete.org
Open Mon & Wed 10-8, Tues, Thurs & Fri 10-6, Sat Noon-6
Friends of the Library Group
MIRROR LAKE, 280 Fifth St N, 33701, SAN 338-0521. Tel: 727-893-7268. FAX: 727-821-4975. *Coordr, Librn II,* Elizabeth Felix-Discussion; E-mail: elizabeth.discussion@stpete.org
Open Mon & Wed 10-7, Tues, Thurs & Fri 10-6, Sat 9-5
Friends of the Library Group
NORTH, 861 70th Ave N, 33702, SAN 338-0556. Tel: 727-893-7214. FAX: 727-522-6902. *Coordr, Librn II,* Sharon Coppola; E-mail: sharon.coppola@stpete.org
Open Mon, Wed, Fri & Sat 9-6, Tues & Thurs 10-8
Friends of the Library Group
SOUTH, 2300 Roy Hanna Dr S, 33712, SAN 338-0564. Tel: 727-893-7244. FAX: 727-864-2470. *Coordr, Librn II,* Sandy Allen; E-mail: sandy.allen@stpete.org
Open Mon, Wed & Fri 10-6, Tues & Thurs 10-8, Sat Noon-6
Friends of the Library Group
WEST SAINT PETERSBURG COMMUNITY LIBRARY, 6700 Eighth Ave N, 33710, SAN 323-9195. Tel: 727-341-7199. *Coordr, Librn II,* Sandra Gordon; E-mail: sandra.gordon@stpete.org
Open Mon-Thurs 7:30am-9pm, Fri 7:30-4, Sat 10-5

Friends of the Library Group
Bookmobiles: 1

S ST PETERSBURG MUSEUM OF HISTORY, Archival Library, 335 Second Ave NE, 33701. SAN 303-1608. Tel: 727-894-1052, Ext 202. E-mail: archives@spmoh.org. Web Site: www.spmoh.org. *Archivist,* Jessica Breckenridge; E-mail: jessica@spmoh.org
Founded 1922
Library Holdings: Bk Vols 1,020
Special Collections: Baseball Coll 1930-60's; Florida Tourism Materials; Railroad & Early Florida Settlement (Peter Demens Coll); Regional Photgraph Coll; Regional Postcard Coll; St Petersburg Area History (Blocker Coll)
Subject Interests: Aviation, Baseball, Hist of Fla
Wireless access
Open Tues, Thurs & Sat 11-4

C UNIVERSITY OF SOUTH FLORIDA SAINT PETERSBURG*, Nelson Poynter Memorial Library, 140 Seventh Ave S, POY118, 33701. SAN 303-1667. Tel: 727-873-4405. Interlibrary Loan Service Tel: 727-873-4549. FAX: 727-873-4196. Web Site: www.lib.usfsp.edu/home. *Dean of Libr,* Catherine Cardwell; Tel: 727-873-4400, E-mail: ccardwell@mail.usf.edu; *Dir, Instrul Tech, Online Learning Librn,* David Brodosi; Tel: 727-873-4126, E-mail: brodusi@mail.usf.edu; *Head, Coll & Tech Serv,* Patricia Pettijohn; Tel: 727-873-4407, E-mail: patricia@mail.usf.edu; *Head, Syst & Digital Tech,* Berrie Watson; Tel: 727-873-4402, E-mail: bwatson@mail.usf.edu; *Head, Access Serv,* Virginia Champion; Tel: 727-873-4843, E-mail: vchampio@mail.usf.edu; *Head, Res & Instruction,* Kaya van Beynen; Tel: 727-873-4626, E-mail: kayatown@mail.usf.edu; *Distance Learning/Bus Librn, Res & Instruction Librn,* Gary Austin; Tel: 727-873-4404, E-mail: glaustin@mail.usf.edu; *Ref & Instruction Librn,* Tina Neville; Tel: 727-873-4081, E-mail: neville@mail.usf.edu; *Student Serv Librn,* Anthony Stamatoplos; Tel: 727-873-4124, E-mail: stamatoplos@mail.usf.edu; *Mgr, Libr Operations,* Christine Dunleavy; Tel: 727-873-4718, E-mail: cdunleavy@mail.usf.edu; Staff 12 (MLS 9, Non-MLS 3)
Founded 1968. Enrl 5,500; Fac 166; Highest Degree: Master
Jul 2013-Jun 2014. Mats Exp $87,606, Books $32,334, Per/Ser (Incl. Access Fees) $54,635, AV Mat $498, Presv $139
Library Holdings: Audiobooks 437; AV Mats 15,948; CDs 1,076; DVDs 3,776; Bk Titles 208,370; Bk Vols 214,701; Per Subs 290; Videos 7,069
Special Collections: Florida & Local History Coll; Ichthyology, Natural History & Zoology (Dr John C Briggs Coll); Mark Twain (Dr David Hubbell Coll); Papers of Nelson Poynter, Publisher of the St Petersburg Times; University of South Florida St Petersburg Archives. Oral History
Subject Interests: Bus & mgt, Educ, Humanities, Marine sci, Soc sci
Automation Activity & Vendor Info: (Acquisitions) Ex Libris Group; (Cataloging) Ex Libris Group; (Circulation) Ex Libris Group; (Course Reserve) Ex Libris Group; (ILL) OCLC; (OPAC) Ex Libris Group; (Serials) Ex Libris Group
Wireless access
Function: Archival coll, AV serv, Distance learning, E-Reserves, Electronic databases & coll, Ref & res
Publications: The Library Connection (Newsletter)
Partic in LYRASIS; Tampa Bay Library Consortium, Inc
Open Mon-Thurs 8am-2am, Fri 8-6, Sat 9-5, Sun 1-9
Restriction: Pub use on premises
Friends of the Library Group

SANFORD

J SEMINOLE STATE COLLEGE OF FLORIDA LIBRARY, 100 Weldon Blvd, 32773-6199. SAN 303-1691. Tel: 407-328-2295. Circulation Tel: 407-328-2618. Reference Tel: 407-328-2305. FAX: 407-328-2233. E-mail: library@seminolestate.edu. Web Site: www.seminolestate.edu/library. *Dir, College Libraries,* Morgan Tracy; Tel: 407-708-2136, E-mail: tracyma@seminolestate.edu; Staff 25 (MLS 11, Non-MLS 14)
Founded 1966. Enrl 29,000; Highest Degree: Bachelor
Library Holdings: Bk Titles 75,000; Per Subs 50
Automation Activity & Vendor Info: (Acquisitions) Ex Libris Group; (Cataloging) Ex Libris Group; (Circulation) Ex Libris Group; (Course Reserve) Ex Libris Group; (ILL) Ex Libris Group; (Media Booking) Ex Libris Group; (OPAC) Ex Libris Group; (Serials) Ex Libris Group
Wireless access
Partic in Northeast Florida Library Information Network; OCLC Online Computer Library Center, Inc
Special Services for the Blind - Assistive/Adapted tech devices, equip & products
Open Mon-Thurs 7:45am-8pm, Fri 7:45-4:30, Sat 9-1, Sun 1-6

SANIBEL

P SANIBEL PUBLIC LIBRARY DISTRICT, 770 Dunlop Rd, 33957. SAN 303-1705. Tel: 239-472-2483. FAX: 239-472-9524. E-mail: notices@sanlib.org. Web Site: www.sanlib.org. *Dir,* Margaret Mohundro; E-mail: mmohundro@sanlib.org; *Youth Serv Librn,* Deanna Evans; *Adult Serv Coordr,* Candy Heise; *Coll Develop,* Duane Shaffer; Staff 9 (MLS 4, Non-MLS 5)
Founded 1962. Pop 6,500
Library Holdings: AV Mats 6,000; e-books 3,500; e-journals 50; Bk Titles 58,000; Bk Vols 62,000; Per Subs 226
Special Collections: Oral History
Subject Interests: Fla, Local hist, Paintings
Automation Activity & Vendor Info: (Cataloging) TLC (The Library Corporation); (Circulation) TLC (The Library Corporation); (ILL) OCLC FirstSearch; (OPAC) TLC (The Library Corporation)
Wireless access
Function: 24/7 Electronic res, 24/7 Online cat, Accelerated reader prog, Activity rm, Adult bk club, After school storytime
Publications: Palm Reader (Newsletter)
Partic in National Network of Libraries of Medicine Region 2; OCLC Online Computer Library Center, Inc; Southwest Florida Library Network
Open Mon & Thurs 9-8, Tues, Wed, Fri & Sat 9-5
Friends of the Library Group

SARASOTA

§S ELLING EIDE CENTER, Research Library, 8000 S Tamiami Trail, 34231. Tel: 941-921-4304. E-mail: info@ellingoeide.org. Web Site: ellingoeide.org/homepage/libraryhome. *Librn,* Hannah Liu; E-mail: hliu@ellingoeide.org
Library Holdings: Bk Vols 60,000
Special Collections: Elling Eide Archives, correspondence, doc, papers, photogs; Rare Books Coll
Subject Interests: Asian studies, Chinese hist, Medieval China, Poetry
Wireless access
Partic in Tampa Bay Library Consortium, Inc
Open Mon-Thurs 9-5, Fri 9-Noon

P FRUITVILLE PUBLIC LIBRARY*, 100 Apex Rd, 34240. Tel: 941-861-2500. Circulation Tel: 941-861-2512. Reference Tel: 941-861-2517. FAX: 941-861-2528. *Libr Mgr,* Peggy Border; E-mail: pborder@scgov.net; *Asst Libr Mgr,* Faith Lipton; E-mail: flipton@scgov.net; *Ref Librn,* Lisa Backer; E-mail: lbacker@scgov.net; *Ref Librn,* Kristen Bott; E-mail: kbott@scgov.net; *Youth Ref Librn,* Barbara Davis; *Youth Ref Librn,* Jennifer Hitchcock
Founded 2001
Library Holdings: AV Mats 17,000; Bk Vols 75,000; Per Subs 52; Talking Bks 3,000
Special Collections: Spanish Language
Automation Activity & Vendor Info: (Acquisitions) Innovative Interfaces, Inc; (Cataloging) Innovative Interfaces, Inc; (Circulation) Innovative Interfaces, Inc; (OPAC) Innovative Interfaces, Inc
Wireless access
Mem of Sarasota County Library System
Special Services for the Deaf - Bks on deafness & sign lang
Special Services for the Blind - Bks on CD; Descriptive video serv (DVS); Large print bks; Low vision equip; Talking bk serv referral
Open Mon-Wed 10-8, Thurs-Sat 10-5
Friends of the Library Group

P GULF GATE PUBLIC LIBRARY*, 7112 Curtiss Ave, 34231. Tel: 941-861-1230. FAX: 941-316-1221. Web Site: www.sclibs.net. *Mgr,* Christine Aston; E-mail: caston@scgov.net; Staff 15 (MLS 5, Non-MLS 10)
Library Holdings: DVDs 10,000; Bk Vols 80,000; Per Subs 70
Automation Activity & Vendor Info: (Acquisitions) Innovative Interfaces, Inc; (Cataloging) Innovative Interfaces, Inc; (Circulation) Innovative Interfaces, Inc
Wireless access
Mem of Sarasota County Library System
Open Mon-Wed 10-8, Fri & Sat 10-5
Friends of the Library Group

S MOTE MARINE LABORATORY LIBRARY & ARCHIVES*, Arthur Vining Davis Library & Archives, 1600 Ken Thompson Pkwy, 34236-1096. SAN 303-173X. Tel: 941-388-4441, Ext 333. E-mail: libarc@mote.org. Web Site: mote.org/research/research-library. *Archivist, Sci Librn,* Kay L Garsnett; Staff 1 (MLS 1)
Founded 1978
Library Holdings: DVDs 25; e-books 5,000; e-journals 3,500; Bk Titles 15,000; Bk Vols 17,000; Per Subs 425; Videos 50
Special Collections: Bass Biological Laboratory Papers, 1931-1942 (Biological Research Florida); Charles M Breder, Jr Manuscripts, 1921-1974; Mina Walther Newspaper Columns, 1971-2003 (Nature Articles); Perry W Gilbert, PhD Papers
Subject Interests: Aquaculture, Biomed res, Coral reefs, Ecotoxicology, Fisheries, Marine biol

Automation Activity & Vendor Info: (Cataloging) OCLC CatExpress; (Circulation) EOS International; (ILL) OCLC WorldShare Interlibrary Loan; (OPAC) EOS International
Wireless access
Function: Ref serv available
Publications: Collected Papers of MML; Mote Magazine (Periodical); Mote Technical Reports; Protect Our Reefs Reports
Partic in Florida Library Information Network; Tampa Bay Library Consortium, Inc
Restriction: Open by appt only

C NEW COLLEGE OF FLORIDA UNIVERSITY OF SOUTH FLORIDA SARASOTA MANATEE*, Jane Bancroft Cook Library, 5800 Bay Shore Rd, 34243-2109. SAN 303-1748. Tel: 941-487-4305. Interlibrary Loan Service Tel: 941-487-4410. FAX: 941-487-4307. E-mail: library@ncf.edu. Web Site: www.ncf.edu/library. *Dean of Libr,* Brian Doherty; Tel: 941-487-4401, E-mail: bdoherty@ncf.edu; *Assessment Librn, Syst Librn,* Tammera Race; Tel: 941-487-4405, E-mail: trace@ncf.edu; *Res & Instruction Librn,* Helen Gold; Tel: 941-487-4416, E-mail: hgold@ncf.edu; *Res & Instruction Librn,* Cal Murgu; Tel: 941-487-4412, E-mail: cmurgu@ncf.edu. Subject Specialists: *Sci,* Tammera Race; Staff 19 (MLS 7, Non-MLS 12)
Founded 1962. Enrl 800; Fac 70; Highest Degree: Bachelor
Library Holdings: AV Mats 8,400; CDs 4,951; DVDs 3,449; e-books 69,780; e-journals 23,000; Bk Vols 275,000; Per Subs 855
Special Collections: Helen N Fagin Holocaust Coll. US Document Depository
Automation Activity & Vendor Info: (Acquisitions) Ex Libris Group; (Cataloging) Ex Libris Group; (Circulation) Ex Libris Group; (Course Reserve) Ex Libris Group; (ILL) Ex Libris Group; (OPAC) Ex Libris Group; (Serials) Ex Libris Group
Wireless access
Partic in Tampa Bay Library Consortium, Inc
Open Mon-Thurs 8am-1am, Fri 8-6, Sat 12-6, Sun 1pm-1am

S THE RINGLING ART LIBRARY*, The John and Mable Ringling Museum of Art, 5401 Bay Shore Rd, 34243. SAN 303-1756. Tel: 941-359-5700, Ext 2701. FAX: 941-360-7370. E-mail: library@ringling.org. Web Site: www.ringling.org. *Head, Libr Serv,* Elisa Marie Hansen; E-mail: elisa.hansen@ringling.org; *Asst Librn,* Christopher Bonadio; Tel: 941-359-5700, Ext 2704, E-mail: christopher.bonadio@ringling.org. Subject Specialists: *Art,* Elisa Marie Hansen; Staff 3 (MLS 3)
Founded 1946
Special Collections: A Everett Austin Jr Coll; John Ringling Book Coll; Mrs Potter Palmer Library Coll
Subject Interests: Art, Art hist, Rare bks
Automation Activity & Vendor Info: (Acquisitions) Follett Software; (Cataloging) OCLC Connexion; (Circulation) Follett Software; (ILL) OCLC; (OPAC) Follett Software
Wireless access
Function: 24/7 Online cat, Electronic databases & coll, Instruction & testing, Online cat, Online ref, Prog for adults, Ref & res, Ref serv available, Res libr
Publications: Rare Books from the Library of the Ringling Museum of Art Sarasota, Florida
Partic in Florida Library Information Network; OCLC Online Computer Library Center, Inc; Tampa Bay Library Consortium, Inc
Open Mon-Fri 1-5
Restriction: Access at librarian's discretion, Non-circulating, Pub use on premises
Friends of the Library Group

C RINGLING COLLEGE OF ART & DESIGN*, Alfred R Goldstein Library, 2700 N Tamiami Trail, 34234-5895. SAN 303-1764. Tel: 941-359-7587. Interlibrary Loan Service Tel: 941-359-7630. FAX: 941-359-7632. E-mail: library@ringling.edu. Web Site: www.ringling.edu/library. *Dir, Libr Serv,* Kristina Keogh; E-mail: kkeogh@ringling.edu; *Tech Serv Librn,* Janet K Thomas; Tel: 941-359-7586, E-mail: jthomas@ringling.edu; *Circ Mgr,* Tim DeForest; E-mail: tdeforest@ringling.edu; Staff 14 (MLS 6, Non-MLS 8)
Founded 1931. Enrl 1,600; Fac 160; Highest Degree: Bachelor
Library Holdings: CDs 863; DVDs 5,000; e-books 40,200; Electronic Media & Resources 334; Bk Titles 50,427; Bk Vols 55,470; Per Subs 370; Videos 2,500
Special Collections: Brizdle-Schoenberg Coll, artist publ projects, prints, illustrations, rare bks; Brizdle-Schoenberg Special Colls Center; Ringling College Archives
Automation Activity & Vendor Info: (Acquisitions) Ex Libris Group; (Cataloging) Ex Libris Group; (Circulation) Ex Libris Group; (Course Reserve) Ex Libris Group; (ILL) OCLC; (OPAC) Ex Libris Group; (Serials) Ex Libris Group
Wireless access
Function: Art exhibits, Audio & video playback equip for onsite use, CD-ROM, Computers for patron use, Electronic databases & coll, ILL available, Instruction & testing, Online cat, Photocopying/Printing, Ref & res, VHS videos
Partic in Independent Cols & Univs of Fla; LYRASIS; Tampa Bay Library Consortium, Inc
Special Services for the Deaf - Closed caption videos
Open Mon-Thurs 8am-11pm, Fri 8-7, Sat 12-6, Sun 10am-11pm
Restriction: Open to pub for ref & circ; with some limitations
Friends of the Library Group

P SARASOTA COUNTY LIBRARY SYSTEM*, 1600 Ringling Blvd, 5th Flr, 34236. Tel: 941-861-5481. Web Site: www.scgov.net/Library. *Dir,* Renee DiPilato; E-mail: rdipilato@scgov.net
Wireless access
Member Libraries: Elsie Quirk Public Library of Englewood; Frances T Bourne Jacaranda Public Library; Fruitville Public Library; Gulf Gate Public Library; North Port Public Library; Selby Public Library; Venice Public Library
Partic in Tampa Bay Library Consortium, Inc

S MARIE SELBY BOTANICAL GARDENS, Research Library, 1534 Mound St, 34236. SAN 371-6457. Tel: 941-366-5731, Ext 248. FAX: 941-366-9807. Web Site: selby.org/botany/collections/research-library. *Dir,* Bruce Holst; Tel: 941-955-7553, Ext 312, E-mail: bholst@selby.org
Founded 1975
Library Holdings: Bk Titles 4,900; Bk Vols 7,200; Per Subs 310; Videos 100
Special Collections: Early Botanical Reference Microfiche Coll; Rare Botanical Book Coll
Subject Interests: Botany, Conserv, Ecology, Hort, Orchids
Automation Activity & Vendor Info: (Cataloging) ComPanion Corp
Publications: Field Guide to the Mangroves of Florida; Icones; Selbyana; The Nature Trail at Pine View School - Plants of Sarasota County, Florida, Part 1 (Research guide); The Tropical Dispatch (Newsletter)
Restriction: Non-circulating, Open by appt only, Researchers only

P SELBY PUBLIC LIBRARY, 1331 First St, 34236. SAN 338-0734. Tel: 941-861-1100. Web Site: www.scgov.net/library. *Libr Mgr,* Steven Thomas; E-mail: smthomas@scgov.net; *YA Serv,* Nadia Ingram; Staff 48 (MLS 17, Non-MLS 31)
Founded 1907. Pop 371,155; Circ 1,922,992
Library Holdings: Bk Titles 100,000; Bk Vols 192,747; Per Subs 350
Special Collections: US Document Depository
Subject Interests: Genealogy
Automation Activity & Vendor Info: (Cataloging) Innovative Interfaces, Inc - Sierra; (Circulation) Innovative Interfaces, Inc - Sierra
Wireless access
Mem of Sarasota County Library System
Partic in OCLC Online Computer Library Center, Inc
Special Services for the Deaf - TDD equip
Open Mon-Thurs 10-6, Fri & Sat 10-5
Friends of the Library Group

SATELLITE BEACH

P SATELLITE BEACH PUBLIC LIBRARY*, 751 Jamaica Blvd, 32937. SAN 303-1772. Tel: 321-779-4004. FAX: 321-779-4036. Web Site: www.brevardfl.gov/PublicLibraries/Branches/SatelliteBeach. *Dir,* Lucinda Dann; E-mail: ldann@brev.org; *Youth Serv,* Marlena Harold; E-mail: marharold@brev.org; Staff 12.3 (MLS 3.5, Non-MLS 8.8)
Founded 1966. Circ 293,000
Library Holdings: Bk Titles 83,000; Per Subs 218
Special Collections: Florida Coll
Automation Activity & Vendor Info: (Circulation) Infor Library & Information Solutions
Wireless access
Mem of Brevard County Public Libraries
Special Services for the Deaf - High interest/low vocabulary bks; TDD equip
Open Mon 9-8, Tue 12-8, Wed-Sat 9-5
Friends of the Library Group

SEBRING

P HEARTLAND LIBRARY COOPERATIVE*, 319 W Center Ave, 33870. Tel: 863-402-6716. Web Site: myhlc.org. *Chair,* June Fisher; *Vice Chair,* Don Elwell; *Coordr,* Kresta King; E-mail: kresta@myhlc.org
Member Libraries: Desoto County Library; Glades County Public Library; Hardee County Public Library; Highlands County Library; Okeechobee County Public Library
Partic in Tampa Bay Library Consortium, Inc

P HIGHLANDS COUNTY LIBRARY*, Sebring Public Library, 319 W Center Ave, 33870-3109. SAN 303-1780. Tel: 863-402-6716. FAX: 863-385-2883. Web Site: myhlc.org/libraries/sebring. *Librn,* Vikki Brown; Staff 5 (MLS 5)

Founded 1926. Pop 95,000; Circ 345,362
Library Holdings: Bk Titles 75,916; Bk Vols 102,477; Per Subs 145
Special Collections: Florida Coll
Automation Activity & Vendor Info: (Circulation) Innovative Interfaces, Inc; (OPAC) Innovative Interfaces, Inc
Wireless access
Mem of Heartland Library Cooperative
Partic in Tampa Bay Library Consortium, Inc
Open Tues-Thurs 10:30-6:30, Fri & Sat 9:30-5:30
Friends of the Library Group
Branches: 2
AVON PARK PUBLIC LIBRARY, 100 N Museum Ave, Avon Park, 33825, SAN 302-8453. Tel: 863-452-3803. FAX: 863-452-3809. Web Site: www.myhlc.org/libraries/avon-park. *Libr Syst Mgr,* Vikki Brown; E-mail: vikki@myhlc.org
Pop 8,200
Library Holdings: Bk Vols 70,000
Special Collections: Large Print Coll
Automation Activity & Vendor Info: (Cataloging) Innovative Interfaces, Inc; (Circulation) Innovative Interfaces, Inc; (OPAC) Innovative Interfaces, Inc
Open Tues 10:30-6:30, Wed-Sat 9:30-5:30
Friends of the Library Group
LAKE PLACID MEMORIAL LIBRARY, 205 W Interlake Blvd, Lake Placid, 33852, SAN 376-5008. Tel: 863-699-3705. FAX: 863-699-3713. Web Site: www.myhlc.org/libraries/lake-placid. *Librn,* Samantha Roll; E-mail: samantha@myhlc.org; Staff 1 (MLS 1)
Founded 1929. Pop 19,500; Circ 98,000
Library Holdings: AV Mats 5,000; Bk Vols 49,000; Per Subs 30
Subject Interests: Genealogy
Automation Activity & Vendor Info: (Circulation) Innovative Interfaces, Inc; (ILL) OCLC FirstSearch; (OPAC) Innovative Interfaces, Inc; (Serials) EBSCO Online
Function: AV serv, CD-ROM, Digital talking bks, ILL available, Magnifiers for reading, Music CDs, Photocopying/Printing, Prog for adults, Prog for children & young adult, Ref serv available, Spoken cassettes & CDs, Summer reading prog, Telephone ref, VHS videos, Wheelchair accessible
Open Tues 10:30-6, Wed-Sat 9:30-5:30
Friends of the Library Group

SEMINOLE

P SEMINOLE COMMUNITY LIBRARY AT ST PETERSBURG COLLEGE*, 9200 113th St N, 33772. SAN 323-7966. Tel: 727-394-6905. E-mail: scl@myseminole.com. Web Site: go.spcollege.edu/scl. *Libr Dir,* Michael Bryan; Tel: 727-394-6923, E-mail: mbryan@myseminole.com; *Adult Serv Supvr, Info Serv Supvr,* Stephanie Young; Tel: 727-394-6921, E-mail: syoung@myseminole.com; *Circ Supvr,* Marion Chamberlain; Tel: 727-394-6909, E-mail: mchamberlain@myseminole.com; *Youth Serv Supvr,* Jill Storm; Tel: 727-394-6915, E-mail: jstorm@myseminole.com; Staff 25 (MLS 6, Non-MLS 19)
Founded 1960. Pop 18,000
Oct 2017-Sept 2018. Mats Exp $74,191, Books $54,564, AV Mat $12,101, Electronic Ref Mat (Incl. Access Fees) $7,436. Sal $702,357
Library Holdings: CDs 4,060; DVDs 5,660; Bk Vols 81,971; Per Subs 127
Special Collections: Parent-Teacher
Automation Activity & Vendor Info: (Acquisitions) SirsiDynix; (Cataloging) SirsiDynix; (Circulation) SirsiDynix; (OPAC) SirsiDynix
Wireless access
Function: 24/7 Electronic res, 24/7 Online cat, 3D Printer, Adult bk club, Audiobks via web, Bk club(s), Bks on CD, Chess club, Children's prog, Computer training, Computers for patron use, Digital talking bks, Electronic databases & coll, Free DVD rentals, Holiday prog, Homework prog, ILL available, Internet access, Magazines, Magnifiers for reading, Mail & tel request accepted, Makerspace, Meeting rooms, Movies, Museum passes, Music CDs, Online cat, Outreach serv, OverDrive digital audio bks, Photocopying/Printing, Preschool outreach, Preschool reading prog, Prog for adults, Prog for children & young adult, Ref & res, Ref serv available, Scanner, Senior computer classes, Spoken cassettes & CDs, Spoken cassettes & DVDs, Story hour, Study rm, Summer reading prog, Tax forms, Teen prog, Telephone ref, Wheelchair accessible
Mem of Pinellas Public Library Cooperative
Partic in Tampa Bay Library Consortium, Inc
Special Services for the Blind - Accessible computers; Bks on CD; Large print bks; Low vision equip; PC for people with disabilities
Open Mon-Thurs 7:30am-9pm, Fri 7:30-4, Sat 10-5, Sun 1-5
Friends of the Library Group

SHALIMAR

P SHALIMAR PUBLIC LIBRARY*, 115 Richbourg Ave, 32579. Tel: 850-609-1515. E-mail: shalimarlibrary@embarqmail.com. Web Site: www.atplus.com/library. *Mgr, Libr Serv,* Alice Brown; *Youth Serv,* Gloria Crews
Library Holdings: Bk Vols 14,000
Open Mon 11-5, Tues, Thurs & Sat 10-2, Wed 12-6, Fri 12-4
Friends of the Library Group

SOUTH BAY

S THE GEO GROUP INC*, South Bay Correctional Facility Library, 600 US Hwy 27 S, 33493. Tel: 561-992-9505. FAX: 561-992-9551. Web Site: www.dc.state.fl.us/facilities/region3/405.html. *Librn,* Gabriel Hedgyes
Library Holdings: Bk Vols 4,300; Per Subs 45

SPRING HILL

C PASCO-HERNANDO STATE COLLEGE-SPRING HILL*, Campus Library, 450 Beverly Ct, Rm C109, 34606-5307. Tel: 352-340-4881. FAX: 352-340-4966. *Assoc Dir of Libr,* Andrew Beman-Cavallaro; E-mail: bemanca@phsc.edu
Open Mon-Thurs 8am-9pm, Fri 8-4:30

STARKE

P BRADFORD COUNTY PUBLIC LIBRARY, 456 W Pratt St, 32091. SAN 303-1802. Tel: 904-368-3911. FAX: 904-964-2164. E-mail: bradford@neflin.org. Web Site: newriverlibrary.org/bradford. *Dir,* Robert Perone; *Asst Dir,* Cindy Weeks; E-mail: cweeks@neflin.org; *Circ Supvr,* Lori Butcher; E-mail: lbutcher@neflin.org; Staff 14 (MLS 1, Non-MLS 13)
Founded 1935. Pop 26,080; Circ 120,000
Library Holdings: Bk Vols 42,000; Per Subs 100
Special Collections: Florida Coll; Genealogy Coll
Automation Activity & Vendor Info: (Cataloging) SirsiDynix; (Circulation) SirsiDynix; (OPAC) SirsiDynix
Wireless access
Function: 24/7 Electronic res, 24/7 Online cat, Adult bk club
Mem of New River Public Library Cooperative
Partic in Northeast Florida Library Information Network
Open Mon & Thurs 8-6, Tues & Wed 8-5, Fri 9-5
Friends of the Library Group

STUART

P MARTIN COUNTY LIBRARY SYSTEM*, Blake Library, 2351 SE Monterey Rd, 34996. SAN 303-1837. Tel: 772-288-5702. Administration Tel: 772-221-1408. FAX: 772-219-4959. Circulation FAX: 772-221-1358. Web Site: www.library.martin.fl.us. *Libr Dir,* Jennifer Salas; Tel: 772-221-1410, E-mail: jsalas@martin.fl.us; *Dep Dir,* Richard Reilly; Tel: 772-219-4964, E-mail: rreilly@martin.fl.us; *Br Mgr,* Nancy Keough; Tel: 772-221-1402, E-mail: nkeough@martin.fl.us; *Coll Mgr,* Katherine Noe; Tel: 772-219-4968, E-mail: knoe@martin.fl.us; *Fac Mgr,* Nicole Lebeau; Tel: 772-221-1404, E-mail: nlebeau@martin.fl.us; *Literacy, Educ & Outreach Mgr,* Darlene Encomio; Tel: 772-219-4908, E-mail: dencomio@martin.fl.us; *Electronic Res Coordr,* Riki Donnelly; Tel: 772-463-3296, E-mail: rdonnelly@martin.fl.us; Staff 46 (MLS 11, Non-MLS 35)
Founded 1957. Circ 926,376
Oct 2014-Sept 2015 Income (Main & Associated Libraries) $4,568,382, State $123,748, County $3,925,453, Locally Generated Income $519,181. Mats Exp $585,205, Books $261,023, Per/Ser (Incl. Access Fees) $36,272, Micro $1,730, AV Equip $26,514, AV Mat $79,187, Electronic Ref Mat (Incl. Access Fees) $180,479. Sal $2,511,572 (Prof $1,227,441)
Library Holdings: Audiobooks 11,282; AV Mats 60,865; Bks on Deafness & Sign Lang 69; Braille Volumes 8; CDs 15,810; DVDs 33,673; e-books 4,928; e-journals 20; Electronic Media & Resources 82; Large Print Bks 13,073; Microforms 3,306; Bk Titles 251,056; Bk Vols 326,392; Per Subs 273
Special Collections: Anne M & Joel L Pearl Cancer Resource Center; Florida Coll; Genealogy Coll
Subject Interests: Alaskana
Automation Activity & Vendor Info: (Acquisitions) SirsiDynix; (Cataloging) SirsiDynix; (Circulation) SirsiDynix; (OPAC) SirsiDynix; (Serials) SirsiDynix
Wireless access
Function: 24/7 Electronic res, Activity rm, Adult bk club, Adult literacy prog, After school storytime, Art exhibits, Audiobks via web, BA reader (adult literacy), Bilingual assistance for Spanish patrons, Bk club(s), Bk reviews (Group), Bks on CD, CD-ROM, Children's prog, Citizenship assistance, Computer training, Computers for patron use, Digital talking bks, E-Reserves, Electronic databases & coll, Equip loans & repairs, Family literacy, Free DVD rentals, Games & aids for people with disabilities, Genealogy discussion group, Health sci info serv, Holiday prog, Homework prog, ILL available, Internet access, Jail serv, Large print

keyboards, Learning ctr, Life-long learning prog for all ages, Literacy & newcomer serv, Magazines, Magnifiers for reading, Mail & tel request accepted, Microfiche/film & reading machines, Movies, Museum passes, Music CDs, Online cat, Online info literacy tutorials on the web & in blackboard, Online ref, Orientations, Outreach serv, Outside serv via phone, mail, e-mail & web, OverDrive digital audio bks, Photocopying/Printing, Preschool outreach, Preschool reading prog, Prof lending libr, Prog for adults, Prog for children & young adult, Ref & res, Ref serv available, Scanner, Senior computer classes, Senior outreach, Serves people with intellectual disabilities, Spanish lang bks, Spoken cassettes & CDs, Spoken cassettes & DVDs, Story hour, Study rm, Summer reading prog, Tax forms, Teen prog, Telephone ref, Visual arts prog, Wheelchair accessible, Words travel prog, Workshops, Writing prog
Partic in LYRASIS; OCLC Online Computer Library Center, Inc; Southeast Florida Library Information Network, Inc
Special Services for the Deaf - TTY equip
Special Services for the Blind - Closed circuit TV; Magnifiers; Screen reader software; ZoomText magnification & reading software
Open Mon, Wed & Fri-Sun 10-5:30, Tues & Thurs 10-8
Restriction: Lending limited to county residents
Friends of the Library Group
Branches: 6
BLAKE LIBRARY (MAIN), 2351 SE Monterey Rd, 34996. Tel: 772-288-5702. E-mail: library@martin.fl.us.
Open Mon, Wed & Fri-Sun 10-5:30, Tues & Thurs 10-8
Friends of the Library Group
PETER & JULIE CUMMINGS LIBRARY, 2551 SW Matheson Ave, Palm City, 34990, SAN 375-5924. Tel: 772-288-2551, FAX: 772-288-5563. *Br Mgr,* Carolyn Smith; E-mail: csmith@martin.fl.us
Founded 1995
Open Tues-Thurs & Sat 10-5:30, Fri 12-8
Friends of the Library Group
HOBE SOUND BRANCH, 10595 SE Federal Hwy, Hobe Sound, 33455, SAN 328-6533. Tel: 772-546-2257. FAX: 772-546-3816. *Br Mgr,* Pat Riker; E-mail: priker@martin.fl.us
Founded 1985
Open Mon, Tues & Thurs-Sat 10-5:30, Wed 12-8
Friends of the Library Group
HOKE LIBRARY, 1150 NW Jack Williams Way, Jensen Beach, 34957, SAN 329-5915. Tel: 772-463-2870. FAX: 772-463-2874. *Br Mgr,* Emma Castle; E-mail: ecastle@martin.fl.us
Founded 1986
Open Tues-Thurs & Sat 10-5:30, Fri 12-8
Friends of the Library Group
ELISABETH LAHTI LIBRARY, 15200 SW Adams Ave, Indiantown, 34956, SAN 328-655X. Tel: 772-597-4200. *Br Mgr,* Katie Kerns; E-mail: kkerns@martin.fl.us
Founded 1991
Open Tues & Thurs-Sat 10-5:30, Wed 12-8
Friends of the Library Group
MARTIN COUNTY LAW LIBRARY, 2351 SE Monterey Rd, 34996, SAN 371-9146. Tel: 772-221-1427. *Librn,* Katherine Kremers; E-mail: kkremers@martin.fl.us
Open Mon-Fri 9-5

SUMTERVILLE

P CLARK MAXWELL JR LIBRARY, 1405 CR 526A, 33585. Tel: 352-568-3074. FAX: 352-568-3376. *Librn,* Dr Richard Morrill; *Libr Tech II,* Scott Perry; E-mail: perrys@lssc.edu
Library Holdings: Bk Vols 8,000; Per Subs 50
Automation Activity & Vendor Info: (Cataloging) SirsiDynix; (Circulation) SirsiDynix
Wireless access
Open Mon-Thurs 8-7, Fri 8-4, Sat 10-2

TALLAHASSEE

P LEROY COLLINS LEON COUNTY PUBLIC LIBRARY SYSTEM*, 200 W Park Ave, 32301-7720. SAN 303-2035. Tel: 850-606-2665. FAX: 850-606-2601. Interlibrary Loan Service FAX: 850-606-2606. TDD: 850-606-2603. E-mail: answersquad@leoncountyfl.gov. Web Site: www.leoncountylibrary.org. *Dir,* Cay Hohmeister; E-mail: hohmeisterc@leoncountyfl.gov; *Budget & Coll Develop Mgr,* Mercedes Carey; E-mail: carym@leoncountyfl.gov; *Coll Mgt Mgr,* Christopher Gorsuch; Fax: 850-606-2607, E-mail: gorsuchc@leoncountyfl.gov; *Extn Serv Mgr,* Debra Sears; E-mail: searsd@leoncountyfl.gov; *Operations Mgr,* Scott Joyner; E-mail: joyners@leoncountyfl.gov; *Adult, Tech & Media Serv Coordr,* Michelle Ray; E-mail: raym@leoncountyfl.gov; *Circ Serv Coordr,* Jennifer Taylor; E-mail: taylorje@leoncountyfl.gov; *Libr Serv Coordr, Bkmobile/Outreach Serv,* Danielle Daguerre; E-mail: daguerred@leoncountyfl.gov; *Youth Serv Coordr,* Mary Douglas; E-mail: douglasm@leoncountyfl.gov; Staff 102 (MLS 34, Non-MLS 68)
Founded 1955. Pop 272,896; Circ 1,423,260
Oct 2016-Sept 2017 Income (Main & Associated Libraries) $6,798,554, State $172,272, County $6,866,639. Mats Exp $622,300, Books $371,521, AV Mat $188,211, Electronic Ref Mat (Incl. Access Fees) $132,575. Sal $3,805,740
Library Holdings: Audiobooks 31,243; DVDs 35,810; e-books 3,767; Electronic Media & Resources 70; Bk Vols 667,408; Per Subs 218
Automation Activity & Vendor Info: (Acquisitions) SirsiDynix; (Cataloging) SirsiDynix; (Circulation) SirsiDynix
Wireless access
Function: 24/7 Online cat, Accelerated reader prog, Activity rm, Adult bk club, Adult literacy prog, Art exhibits, Audio & video playback equip for onsite use, Audiobks on Playaways & MP3, Audiobks via web, AV serv, Bilingual assistance for Spanish patrons, Bk club(s), Bks on cassette, Bks on CD, Children's prog, Citizenship assistance, Computer training, Computers for patron use, Digital talking bks, Distance learning, Electronic databases & coll, Family literacy, Free DVD rentals, Games & aids for people with disabilities, Govt ref serv, Health sci info serv, Home delivery & serv to seniorr ctr & nursing homes, ILL available, Internet access, Literacy & newcomer serv, Magazines, Magnifiers for reading, Mail & tel request accepted, Meeting rooms, Microfiche/film & reading machines, Music CDs, Online cat, Online ref, Outreach serv, Outside serv via phone, mail, e-mail & web, OverDrive digital audio bks, Photocopying/Printing, Prog for adults, Prog for children & young adult, Ref & res, Ref serv available, Res assist avail, Scanner, Senior outreach, Serves people with intellectual disabilities, Spanish lang bks, Spoken cassettes & CDs, Spoken cassettes & DVDs, Story hour, Study rm, Summer & winter reading prog, Summer reading prog, Tax forms, Teen prog, Telephone ref, VHS videos, Wheelchair accessible
Partic in LYRASIS; OCLC Online Computer Library Center, Inc; Panhandle Library Access Network
Special Services for the Deaf - Deaf publ; TDD equip; Videos & decoder
Special Services for the Blind - Reader equip
Open Mon-Thurs 10-9, Fri 10-6, Sat 10-5, Sun 1-6
Friends of the Library Group
Branches: 6
EASTSIDE BRANCH, 1583 Pedrick Rd, 32317. Tel: 850-606-2750.
FORT BRADEN, 16327 Blountstown Hwy, 32310. Tel: 850-606-2900. FAX: 850-606-2901. *Br Mgr,* Teretha Scott; E-mail: scottte@leoncountyfl.gov
Open Tues & Thurs 11-8, Wed & Fri 10-6, Sat 10-4
NORTHEAST BRANCH, THE BRUCE J HOST CENTER, 5513 Thomasville Rd, 32309, SAN 374-6844. Tel: 850-606-2800. FAX: 850-606-2801. *Br Mgr,* Muriel Llewellyn
Open Wed & Fri 10-6, Tues & Thurs 11-8, Sat 10-4
LAKE JACKSON, Huntington Oaks Plaza, 3840-302 N Monroe, 32303, SAN 371-3768. Tel: 850-606-2850. FAX: 850-606-2851. *Br Mgr,* Bart Pisapia; E-mail: pisapiab@leoncountyfl.gov
Special Services for the Deaf - TDD equip
Open Wed & Fri 10-6, Tues & Thurs 11-8, Sat 10-4
DR B L PERRY JR BRANCH, 2817 S Adams St, 32301, SAN 321-9119. Tel: 850-606-2950. FAX: 850-606-2951. TDD: 850-922-2518. *Br Mgr,* Beverly Bass; E-mail: bassb@leoncountyfl.gov
Open Wed & Fri 10-6, Tues & Thurs 11-8, Sat 10-4
Friends of the Library Group
WOODVILLE BRANCH, 8000 Old Woodvile Rd, 32305. Tel: 850-606-2925. *Br Mgr,* Verna Brock

S FEDERAL CORRECTIONAL INSTITUTION LIBRARY, 501 Capital Circle NE, 32301. SAN 303-1861. Tel: 850-878-2173. FAX: 850-671-6105. E-mail: tal-execassistant@bop.gov. *Library Contact,* Sisi Smith
Founded 1947
Library Holdings: Bk Vols 11,000; Per Subs 90

GL FIRST DISTRICT COURT OF APPEAL LIBRARY*, 2000 Drayton Dr, 32399. SAN 377-3221. Tel: 850-487-1000. E-mail: marshal@1dca.org. *Librn,* Kevin Taylor
Library Holdings: Bk Vols 15,000
Open Mon-Fri 8-5

C FLORIDA AGRICULTURAL & MECHANICAL UNIVERSITY LIBRARIES*, Samuel H Coleman Memorial Library, 525 Orr Dr, 32307-4700. (Mail add: 1500 S Martin Luther King Blvd, 32307-4700), SAN 338-0793. Tel: 850-599-3370. Circulation Tel: 850-599-3376. Reference Tel: 850-599-3330. FAX: 850-561-2293. Interlibrary Loan Service FAX: 850 561-2651. Web Site: library.famu.edu. *Dean,* Faye Watkins; E-mail: faye.watkins@famu.edu; *Assoc Dean,* Brenda Wright; E-mail: brenda.wright@famu.edu; *Asst Dir, Pub Serv,* Position Currently Open; *Head, Acq,* Ernestine Holmes; Tel: 850-599-3314, E-mail: ernestine.holmes@famu.edu; *Head, Ref,* Pamela Monroe; Tel: 850-599-8576, E-mail: pamela.monroe@famu.edu; *Archit Librn,* Jacqueline Menzel; Tel: 850-599-8770, E-mail: jacqueline.menzel@famu.edu; *Electronic Res Librn,* Brian Crowell; Tel: 850-599-8675, E-mail: brian.crowell@famu.edu; *Sci Res Ctr Librn,* Shuchun Liang; Tel: 850-599-3423, E-mail: shuchun.liang@famu.edu; *Syst Librn,* Keith Fagg;

Tel: 850-561-2131, E-mail: keith.fagg@famu.edu; *Access Serv, Govt Doc,* Priscilla B Henry; E-mail: priscilla.henry@famu.edu; *Journalism & Graphic Communication Res,* Karen Southwood; Tel: 850-599-3704, Fax: 850-599-2769, E-mail: karen.southwood@famu.edu; *Spec Coll,* Gloria T Woody; E-mail: gloria.woody@famu.edu. Subject Specialists: *Psychol,* Ernestine Holmes; *Criminal justice, Soc work, Sociol,* Pamela Monroe; *Archit, Art,* Jacqueline Menzel; *Agr, Food sci, Music,* Brian Crowell; *Environ sci, Health sci,* Shuchun Liang; *Computer sci,* Keith Fagg; *Educ,* Priscilla B Henry; *Graphic arts, Journalism,* Karen Southwood; *African-Am culture, African-Am hist,* Gloria T Woody; Staff 43 (MLS 15, Non-MLS 28)
Founded 1887. Fac 543; Highest Degree: Doctorate
Jul 2017-Jun 2018 Income Parent Institution $6,090,264. Mats Exp $6,090,264, Books $198,992, Per/Ser (Incl. Access Fees) $2,372,391. Sal $2,348,392
Library Holdings: e-books 468,561; e-journals 405,711; Electronic Media & Resources 314; Bk Vols 1,014,339; Per Subs 17,167; Videos 1,228
Special Collections: 1890 Land Grant Publications; African American Culture & History; Materials About Florida A&M University (FAMUANA), publications, memorabilia. US Document Depository
Automation Activity & Vendor Info: (Acquisitions) Ex Libris Group; (Cataloging) Ex Libris Group; (Circulation) Ex Libris Group; (Course Reserve) Ex Libris Group; (ILL) OCLC ILLiad; (OPAC) Ex Libris Group; (Serials) Ex Libris Group
Wireless access
Publications: A classified Catalogue of the Negro Collection in the Samuel H Coleman Memorial Library; A National Network for the Acquisition, Organization, Processing & Dissemination of Materials By & About Blacks; Instructional Media Film & Video Catalog; Library Handbook
Partic in Florida Library Information Network; LYRASIS; Panhandle Library Access Network
Special Services for the Deaf - Assistive tech; TTY equip
Special Services for the Blind - Accessible computers
Friends of the Library Group

Departmental Libraries:

FLORIDA STATE UNIVERSITY COLLEGE OF ENGINEERING LIBRARY, 2525 Potsdamer St, 32306. Tel: 850-410-6328. Web Site: www.eng.famu.fsu.edu/library. *Libr Mgr,* Cynthia Harley; E-mail: charley@fsu.edu

GL FLORIDA ATTORNEY GENERAL'S LAW LIBRARY*, Collins Bldg, 107 W Gaines St, Rm 437, 32399-1050. (Mail add: PL-01 The Capitol, 32301), SAN 303-1950. Tel: 850-414-3300. FAX: 850-921-5784. E-mail: library@myfloridalegal.com. Web Site: myfloridalegal.com/direct.nsf/offices. *Dir, Libr Serv,* Betsy L Stupski; *Libr Asst,* Travis Dudley; *Libr Asst,* Aditi Jamwal; Staff 3 (MLS 1, Non-MLS 2)
Subject Interests: Law
Function: Ref serv available
Open Mon-Fri 8-5

G FLORIDA AUDITOR GENERAL LIBRARY*, Claude Pepper Bldg, Rm G-74, 111 W Madison St, 32399-1450. Tel: 850-412-2722. FAX: 850-488-6975. E-mail: flaudgen@aud.state.fl.us. Web Site: www.FLAuditor.gov. *Library Contact,* Bernice Keaton
Library Holdings: Bk Titles 4,000; Per Subs 15
Restriction: Staff use only

G FLORIDA DEP-GEOLOGICAL SURVEY RESEARCH LIBRARY, Herman Gunter Library, 3000 Commonwealth Blvd, Ste 1, 32303. SAN 303-1969. Tel: 850-617-0316. FAX: 850-617-0341. Web Site: www.dep.state.fl.us/geology/publications/library.htm. *Librn Spec,* Katie Etheridge; E-mail: kathryn.etheridge@floridadep.gov; Staff 1 (MLS 1)
Founded 1908
Library Holdings: Bk Vols 33,000; Per Subs 40
Special Collections: Florida Aerial Photographs; Florida Sinkhole Research Institute Archives; Florida Topographic Maps; Photo Archives Coll
Subject Interests: Environ protection, Fla, Geol
Automation Activity & Vendor Info: (Cataloging) OCLC CatExpress; (Circulation) Follett Software; (ILL) OCLC; (OPAC) Follett Software; (Serials) EBSCO Online
Wireless access
Function: Archival coll, For res purposes, Internet access, Mail & tel request accepted, Ref serv available, Scanner, Telephone ref, Wheelchair accessible
Partic in Florida Library Information Network; OCLC-LVIS; Panhandle Library Access Network; Soline
Open Mon-Fri 8:30-11:45 & 12:45-5:30
Restriction: Circulates for staff only, In-house use for visitors, Non-circulating of rare bks, Open to pub for ref only

G FLORIDA DEPARTMENT OF ELDER AFFAIRS*, Reference, 4040 Esplanade Way, Ste 360, 32399-7000. Tel: 850-414-2000, 850-414-2344. Toll Free Tel: 800-963-5337. FAX: 850-414-2008. TDD: 800-955-8771. *Librn,* Fae Wilkes; Staff 1 (Non-MLS 1)
Library Holdings: Bk Titles 3,500; Per Subs 17
Special Collections: Emergency Management (Elder Update Editions)
Subject Interests: Disabled, Spec needs
Wireless access
Restriction: Authorized personnel only, Circulates for staff only, Closed stack, Not a lending libr, Not open to pub, Open to employees & special libr, Open to govt employees only, Prof mat only

P FLORIDA DEPARTMENT OF STATE, DIVISION OF LIBRARY & INFORMATION SERVICES*, State Library & Archives of Florida, R A Gray Bldg, 500 S Bronough St, 32399-0250. SAN 303-2051. Tel: 850-245-6600. Interlibrary Loan Service Tel: 850-245-6680. Reference Tel: 850-245-6682. FAX: 850-245-6735. Interlibrary Loan Service FAX: 850-245-6744. Reference FAX: 850-487-6651. TDD: 850-922-4085. E-mail: library@dos.myflorida.com. Web Site: dos.myflorida.com/library-archives. *State Librn,* Amy L Johnson; Tel: 850-245-6603, E-mail: amy.johnson@dos.myflorida.com; *Libr Mgr,* Cathy Moloney; Tel: 850-245-6687, E-mail: cathy.moloney@dos.myflorida.com; *Archives Mgr,* Elisabeth Golding; Tel: 850-245-6639, E-mail: beth.golding@dos.myflorida.com; *Libr Develop Coordr,* Claudia Holland; Tel: 850-245-6622, E-mail: Claudia.Holland@dos.myflorida.com; Staff 14 (MLS 8, Non-MLS 6)
Founded 1845
Special Collections: Florida Coll, bks, mss, maps, memorabilia, per; State Planning Coll, 1970 to present. State Document Depository; US Document Depository
Subject Interests: Educ, Govt, Libr & info sci
Automation Activity & Vendor Info: (Cataloging) SirsiDynix; (Circulation) SirsiDynix; (Discovery) EBSCO Discovery Service; (ILL) OCLC; (OPAC) SirsiDynix; (Serials) SirsiDynix
Wireless access
Publications: Florida Public Documents (State publication)
Partic in Florida Library Information Network; LYRASIS
Special Services for the Deaf - ADA equip; TDD equip
Special Services for the Blind - Accessible computers; Braille equip; Computer access aids; Copier with enlargement capabilities; Internet workstation with adaptive software; Magnifiers
Open Mon-Fri 9-4:30
Friends of the Library Group

G FLORIDA DEPARTMENT OF TRANSPORTATION, Research Management Library, Burns Bldg, 605 Suwannee St, Mail Sta 30, 32399. SAN 303-1985. Tel: 850-414-4615. FAX: 850-414-4696. Web Site: myflorida.com. *Div Mgr,* Darryll Dockstader; E-mail: darryll.dockstader@dot.state.fl.us
Founded 1967
Library Holdings: Bk Vols 15,000; Per Subs 20
Special Collections: Historical DOT Coll; HRD Materials; Transportation Research-Related Reports
Subject Interests: Transportation
Restriction: Non-circulating, Not open to pub

G FLORIDA OFFICE OF FINANCIAL REGULATION*, Legal Library, Fletcher Bldg, 200 E Gaines St, Ste 526, 32399-0379. SAN 325-8548. Tel: 850-487-9687. FAX: 850-410-9645. Web Site: www.flofr.com. *Librn,* Mary Howell; E-mail: mary.howell@fldfs.com
Library Holdings: Bk Vols 2,000
Open Mon-Fri 9-5

C FLORIDA STATE UNIVERSITY LIBRARIES*, Robert Manning Strozier Library, Strozier Library Bldg, 116 Honors Way, 32306. Tel: 850-644-2706. Circulation Tel: 850-644-1486. Interlibrary Loan Service Tel: 850-644-4466. Administration Tel: 850-644-5211. Interlibrary Loan Service FAX: 850-644-4702. Reference FAX: 850-644-1231. Administration FAX: 850-644-5016. Web Site: www.lib.fsu.edu/robert-manning-strozier-library. *Dean, Univ Libr,* Gale A Etschmaier; E-mail: getschmaier@fsu.edu; *Assoc Dean, Spec Coll,* Kathleen McCormick; E-mail: kmccormick@fsu.edu; *Assoc Dean, Admin Serv,* Susanna Miller; E-mail: scmiller@fsu.edu; *Univ Librn for External Relations,* Roy Ziegler; E-mail: rziegler@fsu.edu; Staff 160 (MLS 88, Non-MLS 72)
Founded 1888. Enrl 41,861; Fac 2,351; Highest Degree: Doctorate
Library Holdings: AV Mats 250,484; e-journals 29,485; Bk Vols 2,889,810; Per Subs 42,076
Special Collections: Carothers Memorial Coll of Bibles & Rare Books; Florida Coll; FSU Archives; Herbal Coll; Lois Lenski Coll; Mildred & Claude Pepper Coll; Napoleon & French Revolution; Press Works (including Kelmscott Press); Rare Books & Manuscripts Coll; Scottish Coll; Shaw Poetry Coll. State Document Depository; UN Document Depository; US Document Depository

Automation Activity & Vendor Info: (Acquisitions) Ex Libris Group; (Cataloging) Ex Libris Group; (Circulation) Ex Libris Group; (ILL) OCLC ILLiad; (Serials) Ex Libris Group
Wireless access
Function: Res libr
Partic in LYRASIS; OCLC Online Computer Library Center, Inc
Special Services for the Deaf - Assistive tech
Special Services for the Blind - Assistive/Adapted tech devices, equip & products
Friends of the Library Group

Departmental Libraries:

WARREN D ALLEN MUSIC LIBRARY, Housewright Music Bldg, 122 N Copeland St, 32306. Tel: 850-644-5028. Administration Tel: 850-644-3999. FAX: 850-644-3982. E-mail: AMLRef@fsu.edu. Web Site: music.fsu.edu/library. *Head of Libr, Univ Librn,* Laura Gayle Green; E-mail: lgreen3@fsu.edu; *Head, Tech Serv, Univ Librn,* Sarah Hess Cohen; Tel: 850-644-4137, E-mail: shess@fsu.edu; *Circ, Reserves Mgr,* Miles Bozeman; Tel: 850-644-7068, E-mail: mbozeman@fsu.edu; *Cat Spec,* Elizabeth Uchimura; Tel: 850-644-7064, E-mail: euchimura@fsu.edu; Staff 7 (MLS 3, Non-MLS 4)
Highest Degree: Doctorate
Library Holdings: Bk Titles 150,000
Open Mon-Thurs 7:50am-11pm, Fri 7:50-7, Sat 10-7, Sun 1-11

THE CAREER CENTER LIBRARY, Dunlap Success Ctr 1200, 100 S Woodward Ave, 32304. Tel: 850-644-9779. FAX: 850-644-3273. Web Site: career.fsu.edu/resources/career-center-library. *Librn,* Sarah Pearson; E-mail: sarah.pearson@fsu.edu
Library Holdings: Bk Titles 1,500; Spec Interest Per Sub 25
Open Mon-Fri 8-5

CENTER FOR DEMOGRAPHY & POPULATION HEALTH, 601 Bellamy Bldg, 113 Collegiate Loop, 32306-2240, SAN 338-1218. Tel: 850-644-1762. FAX: 850-644-8818. E-mail: popctr@fsu.edu. Web Site: popcenter.fsu.edu. *Library Contact,* Kathryn Harker Tillman; E-mail: ktillman@fsu.edu
Library Holdings: Bk Vols 7,500; Per Subs 15
Special Collections: Charles M Grigg Memorial Coll; Soviet Population Materials (Galina Selegan Coll)
Open Mon-Fri 8-3
Restriction: Open to students, fac & staff

CL COLLEGE OF LAW LIBRARY, 425 W Jefferson St, 32306, SAN 338-1242. Tel: 850-644-4578. Circulation Tel: 850-644-3405. Reference Tel: 850-644-4095. Web Site: www.law.fsu.edu/research-center. *Dir,* Elizabeth Farrell Clifford; E-mail: efarrell@law.fsu.edu; *Assoc Dir,* Katie Crandall; E-mail: kcrandall@fsu.edu; *Asst Dir, Intl Legal Res,* Margaret Clark; Tel: 850-644-9244, E-mail: maclark@law.fsu.edu; *Asst Dir for Res,* Amy Lipford; E-mail: alipford@law.fsu.edu; Staff 10 (MLS 10)
Founded 1966. Enrl 766; Fac 45; Highest Degree: Doctorate
Library Holdings: AV Mats 1,349; Bk Titles 199,619; Bk Vols 510,662; Per Subs 3,580
Special Collections: Works by or about US Supreme Court Justices. US Document Depository
Automation Activity & Vendor Info: (Cataloging) Ex Libris Group; (Circulation) Ex Libris Group; (Course Reserve) Ex Libris Group; (OPAC) Ex Libris Group; (Serials) Ex Libris Group
Partic in LYRASIS; OCLC Online Computer Library Center, Inc
Open Mon-Thurs 8-7, Fri 8-5, Sat & Sun 1-5

JOHN A DEGEN RESOURCE ROOM, 239 Fine Arts Bldg, 540 W Call St, Rm 204, 32306-1160. Tel: 850-645-7247. FAX: 850-644-7408. Web Site: theatre.fsu.edu/about/facilities-performance-spaces/the-john-a-degen-resource-room. *Finance & Operations Mgr, Library Contact,* Lauren Snyder; Tel: 850-644-7259, E-mail: lasnyder@fsu.edu
Library Holdings: CDs 430; DVDs 100; Bk Titles 8,500
Special Collections: Historic Playbills Coll
Subject Interests: Theatre
Automation Activity & Vendor Info: (Cataloging) SirsiDynix-WorkFlows; (Circulation) SirsiDynix-WorkFlows; (OPAC) SirsiDynix
Open Mon & Fri 9-2:20, Tues 8:30-10:30, 11-2:20 & 3-5, Thurs 830am-10:30am
Restriction: Open to students, fac & staff

CR DEPARTMENT OF RELIGION LIBRARY, 301-B Dodd Hall, 641 University Way, 32306-1520. Tel: 850-644-1020. FAX: 850-644-7225. *Library Contact,* David Levenson; E-mail: dlevenson@fsu.edu
Restriction: Not open to pub, Open to students

PAUL A M DIRAC SCIENCE LIBRARY, 110 N Woodward Ave, 32301. Tel: 850-644-5534. FAX: 850-644-0025. Web Site: lib.fsu.edu/dirac. *Dir,* Renaine Julian; E-mail: rjulian@fsu.edu; Staff 12 (MLS 4, Non-MLS 8)
Founded 1988
Subject Interests: Applied sci, Pure sci
Open Mon-Wed 8am-3am, Thurs 8am-1am, Fri 8-5, Sun 1-9

HERBARIUM LIBRARY, Biology Unit 1, Rm 100, 116 Honors Way, 32306-4370. Tel: 850-644-6278. FAX: 850-644-0481. E-mail: herbarium@bio.fsu.edu. Web Site: herbarium.bio.fsu.edu. *Dir,* Dr Austin Mast; E-mail: amast@bio.fsu.edu
Function: Res libr
Restriction: By permission only, Open by appt only, Open to students, fac & staff

LEARNING RESOURCE CENTER, COLLEGE OF EDUCATION, 1301 Stone Bldg, 32306-4450, SAN 338-1161. Tel: 850-644-4553. Web Site: education.fsu.edu/student-resources/learning-resource-center. *Dir,* Dina Vyortkina; E-mail: dvyortkina@admin.fsu.edu
Library Holdings: Bk Titles 1,000
Open Mon-Thurs 8am-10pm, Fri 8-6
Restriction: Open to students, fac & staff

CM CHARLOTTE EDWARDS MAGUIRE MEDICAL LIBRARY, 1115 W Call St, 32306-4300. Tel: 850-644-3883. Interlibrary Loan Service Tel: 850-644-6683. FAX: 850-644-9942. E-mail: MedLibrary@med.fsu.edu. Web Site: med.fsu.edu/library. *Dir,* Martin Wood; Tel: 850-645-7304, E-mail: martin.wood@med.fsu.edu; *Head, Res Serv,* Robyn Rosasco; Tel: 850-645-0348, E-mail: robyn.rosasco@med.fsu.edu; *Head, Scholarly Communications,* Roxann Mouratidis; Tel: 850-645-9398, E-mail: roxann.mouratidis@med.fsu.edu; *Syst Librn,* Susan Epstein; E-mail: susan.epstein@med.fsu.edu; Staff 5 (MLS 5)
Founded 2000. Enrl 488; Fac 2,100; Highest Degree: Doctorate
Automation Activity & Vendor Info: (Course Reserve) Ex Libris Group; (ILL) Ex Libris Group; (Serials) SerialsSolutions
Partic in Consortium of Southern Biomedical Libraries; Fla Ctr for Libr Automation
Open Mon-Fri 8-5

CLAUDE PEPPER LIBRARY & ARCHIVES, 636 W Call St, 32304. Tel: 850-644-3271, 850-644-9217. E-mail: lib-specialcollections@fsu.edu. Web Site: www.lib.fsu.edu/pepper-library. *Archivist,* Robert Rubero; E-mail: rlr02e@fsu.edu; Staff 3 (MLS 1, Non-MLS 2)
Open Mon-Fri 11-4

GL FLORIDA SUPREME COURT LIBRARY, 500 S Duval St, 32399-1926. SAN 303-2027. Tel: 850-488-8919. FAX: 850-922-5219. E-mail: library@flcourts.org. Web Site: www.floridasupremecourt.org/library/index.shtml. *Ref Serv,* Teresa Farley; *Cat Librn,* Jeff Spalding; *Archivist,* Erik Robinson; Staff 3 (MLS 3)
Founded 1845
Library Holdings: Bk Titles 12,157; Bk Vols 114,587; Per Subs 1,476
Special Collections: Florida Supreme Court Historical Society. Oral History; US Document Depository
Automation Activity & Vendor Info: (Cataloging) Innovative Interfaces, Inc; (OPAC) Innovative Interfaces, Inc
Partic in LYRASIS; Proquest Dialog
Open Mon-Fri 8-5

L HOPPING, GREEN & SAMS*, Law Library, 119 S Monroe St, Ste 300, 32301. (Mail add: PO Box 6526, 32314-6526). Tel: 850-222-7500. FAX: 850-224-8551. Web Site: www.hgslaw.com. *Librn,* Marisol Roberts; Staff 1 (MLS 1)
Library Holdings: e-journals 5; Bk Vols 6,000; Per Subs 10; Spec Interest Per Sub 35
Subject Interests: Admin law, Environ law
Wireless access
Restriction: Not open to pub, Private libr

G STATE LIBRARY OF FLORIDA, Capitol Branch Library, The Capitol, Rm 701, 32399. SAN 303-1993. Tel: 850-245-6612. Web Site: dos.myflorida.com/library-archives. *State Librn,* Amy Johnson; E-mail: amy.johnson@dos.myflorida.com; Staff 2 (MLS 1, Non-MLS 1)
Founded 1949
Library Holdings: Bk Titles 10,000; Bk Vols 22,000; Per Subs 410
Special Collections: Public Administration & Legislative Mats
Automation Activity & Vendor Info: (Cataloging) SirsiDynix; (Circulation) SirsiDynix
Publications: Checklist of Recent Acquisitions (Monthly); Checklist of Recent Legislative Publications (Quarterly); The Florida Legislative Library: Functions, Scope, Procedures (revised as needed)
Open Mon-Fri 9-4:30

J TALLAHASSEE COMMUNITY COLLEGE LIBRARY*, 444 Appleyard Dr, 32304-2895. SAN 303-2078. Tel: 850-201-8376. Reference Tel: 850-201-8383. FAX: 850-201-8380. E-mail: library@tcc.fl.edu. Web Site: www.tcc.fl.edu/academics/academic-divisions/library. *Dir,* Position Currently Open; *Fac Librn,* Tricia Elton; Tel: 850-201-6181, E-mail: eltont@tcc.fl.edu; *Library Contact,* Tanja Waller; Tel: 850-201-6108, E-mail: wallerta@tcc.fl.edu; Staff 7 (Non-MLS 7)
Founded 1966. Enrl 11,200; Fac 490; Highest Degree: Associate
Library Holdings: Bk Titles 95,157; Bk Vols 121,462; Per Subs 782
Special Collections: Florida (Beatrice Shaw Coll)
Subject Interests: Paramedics
Wireless access
Publications: Acquisitions (newsletter); Library Handbook; Library Staff Newsletter

Partic in Panhandle Library Access Network
Open Mon-Thurs (Fall-Spring) 7:30am-9pm, Fri 7:30-5, Sat 10-2; Mon-Thurs (Summer) 7:30-7:30, Fri 7:30-5

TAMPA

M ADVENTHEALTH TAMPA*, Medical Library, 3100 E Fletcher Ave, 33613-4688. SAN 324-5616. Tel: 813-615-7236. FAX: 813-615-7854. *Mgr,* Sharon Henrich; E-mail: sharon.henrich@adventhealth.com; Staff 1 (MLS 1)
Founded 1974
Library Holdings: Bk Titles 1,000; Per Subs 50
Automation Activity & Vendor Info: (Cataloging) TLC (The Library Corporation); (Circulation) TLC (The Library Corporation)
Wireless access
Partic in National Network of Libraries of Medicine Region 2; Regional Med Libr - Region 2; Tampa Bay Medical Library Network
Open Mon-Fri 8-4:30

C ALTIERUS CAREER COLLEGE*, Tampa Campus Library, 3319 W Hillsborough Ave, 33614. SAN 376-9615. Tel: 813-879-6000. *Dir,* Betty Martinez; E-mail: bettym@altierus.edu; Staff 1 (MLS 1)
Enrl 200; Highest Degree: Bachelor
Automation Activity & Vendor Info: (Circulation) LibraryWorld, Inc; (OPAC) LibraryWorld, Inc
Wireless access
Function: 24/7 Electronic res, 24/7 Online cat, Audio & video playback equip for onsite use, Computers for patron use, Distance learning, Electronic databases & coll, Internet access, Learning ctr, Magazines, Movies, Online cat, Orientations, Outside serv via phone, mail, e-mail & web, Photocopying/Printing, Ref serv available, Scanner, Spoken cassettes & DVDs, Telephone ref
Partic in LYRASIS; Tampa Bay Library Consortium, Inc
Open Mon-Thurs 9-9, Fri 9-5
Restriction: ID required to use computers (Ltd hrs), Limited access for the pub, Open to students, fac, staff & alumni

S CAE USA, INC LIBRARY*, 4908 Tampa West Blvd, 33634. SAN 326-7865. Tel: 813-885-7481, 813-887-1540. FAX: 813-901-6417. Web Site: www.cae.com/cae-usa. *Librn,* Bridget Diffenderfer; E-mail: bridget.diffenderfer@caemilusa.com; Staff 4 (MLS 3, Non-MLS 1)
Subject Interests: Aeronaut, Engr
Restriction: Not open to pub

L CARLTON FIELDS*, Law Library, 4221 W Boy Scout Blvd, Ste 1000, 33607. (Mail add: PO Box 3239, 33601-3239), SAN 303-2086. Tel: 813-223-7000. Toll Free Tel: 888-223-9191. FAX: 813-229-4133. Web Site: www.carltonfields.com/about-us/offices/tampa. *Mgr, Libr Serv,* Terry Psarras; E-mail: tpsarras@carltonfields.com
Founded 1915
Library Holdings: Bk Titles 30,000; Per Subs 200
Automation Activity & Vendor Info: (Cataloging) Inmagic, Inc.
Restriction: Not open to pub

L GRAY-ROBINSON, PA*, Law Library, 401 E Jackson St, Ste 2700, 33602. (Mail add: PO Box 3324, 33601-3324), SAN 373-6598. Tel: 813-273-5000. FAX: 813-273-5145. Web Site: www.gray-robinson.com.
Library Holdings: Bk Titles 3,500; Bk Vols 25,000; Per Subs 75
Restriction: Staff use only

J HILLSBOROUGH COMMUNITY COLLEGE*, District Library Technical Services, Collaboration Studio, Rm 139, 1602 N 15th St, 33605. SAN 338-1390. Tel: 813-259-6059. Automation Services Tel: 813-259-6058. FAX: 813-253-7510. Web Site: libguides.hccfl.edu/dlts. *Info Analyst,* Andrea Dufault; E-mail: adufault@hccfl.edu. Subject Specialists: *Bus,* Andrea Dufault
Founded 1968. Highest Degree: Associate
Special Collections: Opthalmology (Stimson Coll)
Automation Activity & Vendor Info: (Acquisitions) Ex Libris Group; (Cataloging) Ex Libris Group; (Circulation) Ex Libris Group; (Course Reserve) Ex Libris Group; (ILL) Ex Libris Group; (OPAC) Ex Libris Group; (Serials) Ex Libris Group
Wireless access
Partic in Florida Library Information Network; LYRASIS; Tampa Bay Library Consortium, Inc
Open Mon-Fri 7:30-4:30
Restriction: ID required to use computers (Ltd hrs), Restricted borrowing privileges, Restricted loan policy, Restricted pub use
Departmental Libraries:
BRANDON CAMPUS LIBRARY, 10451 Nancy Watkins Dr, 33619-7850, SAN 322-8983. Tel: 813-253-7803. Interlibrary Loan Service Tel: 813-253-7847. Reference Tel: 813-253-7886.
Open Mon-Thurs 8-8, Fri 8-4:30, Sat 8-2
DALE MABRY CAMPUS LIBRARY, 4001 Tampa Bay Blvd, 33614-7820, SAN 338-1420. Tel: 813-253-7381. FAX: 813-253-7400. Web Site: www.hccfl.edu/library. ; Staff 1 (MLS 1)
Founded 1968. Enrl 22,000
Special Collections: Literary Criticism File; Slide Library
Partic in OCLC Online Computer Library Center, Inc
Open Mon-Thurs 8-8, Fri 8-2, Sat 8-3
PLANT CITY CAMPUS LIBRARY, 1206 N Park Rd, Plant City, 33563, SAN 303-1330. Tel: 813-757-2163. FAX: 813-757-2167. ; Staff 3 (MLS 1, Non-MLS 2)
Open Mon-Thurs 8-8, Fri 8-4:30
SOUTH SHORE CAMPUS LIBRARY, 551 24th St NE, Ruskin, 33570. Tel: 813-253-7000, Ext 5726.
YBOR CITY CAMPUS LIBRARY, 1512 E Ninth Ave, 33605, SAN 329-5729. Tel: 813-253-7645. Reference Tel: 813-253-7729.
Partic in OCLC Online Computer Library Center, Inc
Open Mon-Thurs 8-8, Fri 8-4:30

L HOLLAND & KNIGHT LLP*, Library & Research Services, 100 N Tampa St, Ste 4100, 33602. SAN 372-1396. Tel: 813-227-8500. Web Site: www.hklaw.com.
Library Holdings: Bk Vols 30,000
Restriction: Not open to pub

GL JAMES J LUNSFORD (HILLSBOROUGH COUNTY) LAW LIBRARY, 701 E Twiggs St, 33602. SAN 303-2132. Tel: 813-272-5818. FAX: 813-272-5226. *Br Mgr,* Norma Wise; E-mail: WiseN@HillsboroughCounty.org; *Libr Supvr,* Donna L Barnes; Staff 4 (MLS 1, Non-MLS 3)
Founded 1937
Library Holdings: Bk Vols 40,000; Per Subs 75
Mem of Tampa-Hillsborough County Public Library System
Partic in Hillsborough County Public Library Cooperative
Open Mon-Thurs 8-8, Fri 8-5, Sat & Sun 12-5
Restriction: Non-circulating
Friends of the Library Group

M H LEE MOFFITT CANCER CENTER & RESEARCH INSTITUTE*, Biomedical Library, 12902 USF Magnolia Dr, 33612. Tel: 813-745-4673. FAX: 813-745-3084. Web Site: library.moffitt.org. *Mgr, Libr Serv,* Susan Sharpe; E-mail: susan.sharpe@moffitt.org; *Med Librn,* Mary-Kate Haver; E-mail: marykatherine.haver@moffitt.org; Staff 1.5 (MLS 1, Non-MLS 0.5)
Library Holdings: e-books 8,000; Bk Vols 800
Subject Interests: Molecular biol, Oncology
Wireless access
Function: Health sci info serv, ILL available, Res libr
Partic in Tampa Bay Library Consortium, Inc; Tampa Bay Medical Library Network
Open Mon-Fri 10-4
Restriction: Circ limited, Non-circulating coll

P TAMPA-HILLSBOROUGH COUNTY PUBLIC LIBRARY SYSTEM*, Administration, 102 E Seventh Ave, 33602-3704. SAN 338-1455. Administration Tel: 813-273-3660. TDD: 813-273-3610. Web Site: www.hcplc.org. *Dir of Libr,* Andrew Breidenbaugh
Founded 1915
Special Collections: State Document Depository; US Document Depository
Subject Interests: Fla, Genealogy, Local hist
Wireless access
Member Libraries: James J Lunsford (Hillsborough County) Law Library
Partic in Florida Library Information Network; Hillsborough County Public Library Cooperative
Open Mon-Thurs 10-9, Fri & Sat 10-6, Sun 12:30-5
Friends of the Library Group
Branches: 28
C BLYTHE ANDREWS JR PUBLIC LIBRARY, 2607 E Dr Martin Luther King Jr Blvd, 33610-7770, SAN 370-0917. Web Site: www.hcplc.org/locations/c-blythe-andrews-jr.
Open Mon & Tues 10-8, Wed-Sat 10-6
Friends of the Library Group
BLOOMINGDALE REGIONAL PUBLIC LIBRARY, 1906 Bloomingdale Ave, Valrico, 33596. Web Site: www.hcplc.org/locations/bloomingdale.
Open Mon-Thurs 10-9, Fri & Sat 10-6, Sun 12:30-5
Friends of the Library Group
BRANDON REGIONAL LIBRARY, 619 Vonderburg Dr, Brandon, 33511-5972, SAN 338-151X. Web Site: www.hcplc.org/locations/brandon.
Open Mon-Thurs 10-9, Fri & Sat 10-6, Sun 12:30-5
Friends of the Library Group
BRUTON MEMORIAL LIBRARY, 302 W McLendon St, Plant City, 33563, SAN 303-1349. Tel: 813-757-9215. Web Site: www.plantcitygov.com/Library. *Dir,* Tonda Morris; E-mail: tmorris@plantcitygov.com; *Tech Serv Librn,* Susan Ambrose Miles;

E-mail: smiles@plantcitygov.com; *Tech Librn,* Lori Thibert; E-mail: lthibert@plantcitygov.com; Staff 6 (MLS 3, Non-MLS 3)
Founded 1929. Pop 73,000; Circ 254,898
Library Holdings: Bk Vols 118,000; Per Subs 175
Special Collections: Florida Coll
Function: 24/7 Electronic res, 24/7 Online cat, Activity rm, Adult bk club, Adult literacy prog, After school storytime
Partic in Hillsborough County Public Library Cooperative; Tampa Bay Library Consortium, Inc
Publications: Digital newsletter via email
Open Mon-Thurs 10-9, Fri 10-6, Sat 10-5, Sun 1-5
Friends of the Library Group

AUSTIN DAVIS PUBLIC LIBRARY, 17808 Wayne Rd, Odessa, 33556-4720, SAN 338-1544. Web Site: www.hcplc.org/locations/austin-davis.
Open Mon 12-8, Tues 10-8, Wed-Sat 10-6
Friends of the Library Group

EGYPT LAKE PARTNERSHIP LIBRARY, 3403 W Lambright St, 33614-4618. Web Site: www.hcplc.org/locations/egypt-lake.
Open Mon-Wed 2:30-8, Thurs & Fri 2:30-6, Sat 10-6
Friends of the Library Group

CHARLES J FENDIG PUBLIC LIBRARY, 3909 W Neptune St, 33629, SAN 338-1668. Web Site: www.hcplc.org/locations/charles-j-fendig.
Open Mon & Tues 10-8, Wed-Sat 10-6
Friends of the Library Group

MAUREEN B GAUZZA PUBLIC LIBRARY, 11211 Countryway Blvd, 33626-2624. Web Site: www.hcplc.org/locations/maureen-b-gauzza.
Open Mon-Thurs 10-9, Fri & Sat 10-6, Sun 12:30-5
Friends of the Library Group

JOHN F GERMANY PUBLIC LIBRARY, 900 N Ashley Dr, 33602-3704. Tel: 813-273-3652.
Open Mon-Thurs 10-9, Fri & Sat 10-6, Sun 12:30-5

ARTHENIA L JOYNER UNIVERSITY AREA COMMUNITY LIBRARY, 13619 N 22nd St, 33613-5872. Web Site: www.hcplc.org/locations/arthenia-l-joyner.
Function: Meeting rooms
Open Mon 11-7, Tues-Sat 10-6
Friends of the Library Group

JIMMIE B KEEL REGIONAL LIBRARY, 2902 W Bearss Ave, 33618-1828, SAN 328-8927. Web Site: www.hcplc.org/locations/jimmie-b-keel.
Open Mon-Thurs 10-9, Fri & Sat 10-6, Sun 12:30-5
Friends of the Library Group

LUTZ BRANCH LIBRARY, 101 Lutz-Lake Fern Rd W, Lutz, 33548-7220, SAN 338-1609. Web Site: www.hcplc.org/locations/lutz.
Open Mon 12-8, Tues 10-8, Wed-Sat 10-6
Friends of the Library Group

NEW TAMPA REGIONAL LIBRARY, 10001 Cross Creek Blvd, 33647-2581, SAN 377-5798. Web Site: www.hcplc.org/locations/new-tampa.
Open Mon-Thurs 10-9, Fri & Sat 10-6, Sun 12:30-5
Friends of the Library Group

NORTH TAMPA BRANCH LIBRARY, 8916 North Blvd, 33604-1209, SAN 338-1633. Web Site: www.hcplc.org/locations/north-tampa.
Open Mon-Wed 10-8, Thurs-Sat 10-6, Sun 12:30-5
Friends of the Library Group

JAN KAMINIS PLATT REGIONAL LIBRARY, 3910 S Manhattan Ave, 33611-1214. Web Site: www.hcplc.org/locations/jan-kaminis-platt.
Open Mon-Thurs 10-9, Fri & Sat 10-6, Sun 12:30-5
Friends of the Library Group

PORT TAMPA CITY LIBRARY, 4902 W Commerce St, 33616-2704, SAN 338-1692. Web Site: www.hcplc.org/locations/port-tampa.
Open Mon-Sat 10-6
Friends of the Library Group

RIVERVIEW BRANCH LIBRARY, 10509 Riverview Dr, Riverview, 33578-4367, SAN 338-1714. Web Site: www.hcplc.org/locations/riverview.
Open Mon & Tues 10-8, Wed-Sat 10-6
Friends of the Library Group

NORMA & JOSEPH ROBINSON PARTNERSHIP LIBRARY @ SULPHUR SPRINGS, 8412 N 13th St, 33604-1842. Web Site: www.hcplc.org/locations/norma-and-joseph-robinson.
Open Mon-Fri 3-6, Sat 10-6
Friends of the Library Group

RUSKIN BRANCH LIBRARY, 26 Dickman Dr SE, Ruskin, 33570-4313, SAN 338-1722. Web Site: www.hcplc.org/locations/ruskin.
Open Mon, Tues & Thurs-Sat 10-6, Wed 10-8
Friends of the Library Group

ROBERT W SAUNDERS SR PUBLIC LIBRARY, 1505 Nebraska Ave, 33602-2849, SAN 338-1870. Web Site: www.hcplc.org/locations/robert-w-saunders-sr.
Open Mon-Tues 10-8, Wed-Sat 10-6
Friends of the Library Group

SEFFNER-MANGO BRANCH LIBRARY, 410 N Kingsway Rd, Seffner, 33584-3602. Web Site: www.hcplc.org/locations/seffner-mango.
Open Mon 10-8, Tues 12-8, Wed-Sat 10-6
Friends of the Library Group

SEMINOLE HEIGHTS BRANCH LIBRARY, 4711 Central Ave, 33603-3905, SAN 338-1757. Web Site: www.hcplc.org/locations/seminole-heights.
Open Mon & Wed-Sat 10-6, Tues 10-8
Friends of the Library Group

SEVENTY-EIGHTH STREET COMMUNITY LIBRARY, 7625 Palm River Rd, 33619-4135, SAN 377-5771. Web Site: www.hcplc.org/locations/seventy-eighth-st.
Open Mon & Wed-Sat 10-6, Tues 10-8
Friends of the Library Group

SOUTHSHORE REGIONAL LIBRARY, 15816 Beth Shields Way, Ruskin, 33573-4903. Web Site: www.hcplc.org/locations/southshore.
Open Mon-Thurs 10-9, Fri & Sat 10-6, Sun 12:30-5
Friends of the Library Group

TEMPLE TERRACE PUBLIC LIBRARY, 202 Bullard Pkwy, Temple Terrace, 33617-5512, SAN 303-2248. Tel: 813-506-6770. Web Site: www.templeterrace.com/library. *Libr Dir,* Teressa Fraser; E-mail: tfraser@templeterrace.com; Staff 5 (MLS 5)
Founded 1960. Pop 81,570; Circ 482,510
Library Holdings: Bk Titles 82,758; Bk Vols 94,181; Per Subs 90
Function: 24/7 Electronic res, 24/7 Online cat, 3D Printer, Activity rm, Adult bk club, Adult literacy prog, Art exhibits, Audiobks via web, Bi-weekly Writer's Group, Bk club(s), Bks on CD, Chess club, Children's prog, Computer training, Computers for patron use, Electronic databases & coll, Free DVD rentals, Holiday prog, ILL available, Internet access, Magazines, Mango lang, Meeting rooms, Music CDs, Online cat, OverDrive digital audio bks, Photocopying/Printing, Printer for laptops & handheld devices, Prog for adults, Prog for children & young adult, Spanish lang bks, Story hour, Study rm, Summer reading prog, Tax forms, Teen prog
Partic in Hillsborough County Public Library Cooperative; Tampa Bay Library Consortium, Inc
Open Mon & Wed 10-8, Tues & Thurs 12-8, Fri & Sat 10-6
Friends of the Library Group

THONOTOSASSA BRANCH LIBRARY, 10715 Main St, Thonotosassa, 33592-2831, SAN 370-0925. Web Site: www.hcplc.org/locations/thonotosassa.
Open Mon-Sat 10-6
Friends of the Library Group

TOWN 'N COUNTRY REGIONAL PUBLIC LIBRARY, 7606 Paula Dr, Ste 120, 33615-4116, SAN 338-1811. Web Site: www.hcplc.org/locations/town-n-country.
Open Mon-Thurs 10-9, Fri & Sat 10-6, Sun 12:30-5
Friends of the Library Group

WEST TAMPA BRANCH LIBRARY, 2312 W Union St, 33607-3423, SAN 338-1846. Web Site: www.hcplc.org/locations/west-tampa.
Open Mon-Sat 10-6
Friends of the Library Group

Bookmobiles: 1

S TAMPA MUSEUM OF ART*, Judith Rozier Blanchard Library, 120 W Gasparilla Plaza, 33602. SAN 303-2140. Tel: 813-274-8130. FAX: 813-274-8732. Web Site: www.tampamuseum.org. *Educ Curator,* Brittny Bevel; E-mail: brittny.bevel@tampamuseum.org
Library Holdings: Bk Vols 7,845; Per Subs 19
Special Collections: Greek & Roman Antiquities, bks, corpus vasoreum, elephant folios, journals, offprints, rare bks
Publications: Exhibition Catalogs; Newsletter (Monthly)
Restriction: Not open to pub, Private libr

GM UNITED STATES DEPARTMENT OF VETERANS AFFAIRS*, Willard S Harris Medical Library, Library Service (142D), 13000 Bruce B Downs Blvd, 33612. SAN 303-2183. Tel: 813-972-2000, Ext 6570. Interlibrary Loan Service Tel: 813-972-2000, Ext 6569. FAX: 813-978-5917. E-mail: tamlibrary@med.va.gov. Web Site: www.tampa.va.gov/features/health_information_your_va_library.asp. *Clinical Med Librn,* Marilyn Teolis; E-mail: marilyn.teolis@va.gov; Staff 4 (MLS 4)
Founded 1972
Library Holdings: AV Mats 817; Bk Titles 2,506; Per Subs 378
Subject Interests: Med, Nursing
Automation Activity & Vendor Info: (Cataloging) Follett Software; (Circulation) Follett Software; (OPAC) Follett Software
Wireless access
Publications: Medical Library Newsletter
Partic in Tampa Bay Medical Library Network
Restriction: Not open to pub

UNIVERSITY OF SOUTH FLORIDA

GM LOUIS DE LA PARTE FLORIDA MENTAL HEALTH INSTITUTE RESEARCH LIBRARY*, 13301 Bruce B Downs Blvd, 33612-3899, SAN 303-2108. Tel: 813-974-4471. FAX: 813-974-7242. *Access Serv, ILL,* Walter Cone; *Coll Develop,* Patricia C Pettijohn; Staff 5 (MLS 3, Non-MLS 2)
Founded 1974
Library Holdings: Bk Titles 30,000; Per Subs 430
Special Collections: AAD/ADHD Coll; De la Parte Institute Archives; Florida State Behavioral Healthcare Policy Coll; Multicultural Coll; Streaming Video Online Training Coll
Subject Interests: AIDS, Autism, Behav studies, Domestic violence, Epidemiology, Fla, Gerontology, Homelessness, Mental health, Mental health of children, Psychol, Soc serv (soc work), Spec educ
Automation Activity & Vendor Info: (Acquisitions) NOTIS; (Cataloging) NOTIS; (Circulation) NOTIS
Function: Res libr
Partic in Association of Southeastern Research Libraries; Center for Research Libraries; Consortium of Southern Biomedical Libraries; LYRASIS; OCLC Online Computer Library Center, Inc; Tampa Bay Medical Library Network
Open Mon-Thurs 8-8, Fri 8-4

CM HINKS & ELAINE SHIMBERG HEALTH SCIENCES LIBRARY*, 12901 Bruce B Downs Blvd, MDC 31, 33612, SAN 338-1900. Tel: 813-974-2243. Interlibrary Loan Service Tel: 813-974-2123. Reference Tel: 813-974-2288. Web Site: library.hsc.usf.edu. *Dir,* Rose Bland; Tel: 813-974-2390; *Cat/Ref Librn,* Allison Howard; Tel: 813-974-4752; *Libr Operations Supvr/Access Serv, ILL & Doc Delivery,* Jeff Honker; *Acq,* Clint Cherry; Tel: 813-974-9078; Staff 8 (MLS 6, Non-MLS 2)
Founded 1971. Enrl 1,117; Fac 551; Highest Degree: Doctorate
Library Holdings: Bk Titles 29,863; Per Subs 1,373
Subject Interests: Med, Nursing, Pharm, Pub health
Automation Activity & Vendor Info: (Acquisitions) Ex Libris Group; (Cataloging) Ex Libris Group
Partic in National Network of Libraries of Medicine Region 2
Open Mon-Fri 7:30am-11pm, Sat 10-6, Sun Noon-11

C TAMPA CAMPUS LIBRARY*, 4101 USF Apple Dr, LIB122, 33620. (Mail add: 4202 E Fowler Ave, LIB122, 33620-5400). Tel: 813-974-2729. Circulation Tel: 813-974-1611. Interlibrary Loan Service Tel: 813-974-1627. FAX: 813-974-5153. TDD: 813-974-9874. Web Site: www.lib.usf.edu. *Dean,* William A Garrison; Tel: 813-974-1642, E-mail: wgarrison@usf.edu; *Dir, Acad Res,* Todd A Chavez; Tel: 813-974-7905, E-mail: tchavez@usf.edu; *Dir, Acad Serv,* Nancy A Cunningham; Tel: 813-974-0450, E-mail: nancy@usf.edu; *Dir, Admin Serv,* Tom Cetwinski; Tel: 813-974-4592, E-mail: tcetwinski@usf.edu; *Dir, Spec & Digital Coll, Fla Studies Ctr & Holocaust & Genocide Prog,* Dr Mark I Greenberg; Tel: 813-974-4141; Staff 73.5 (MLS 37, Non-MLS 36.5)
Founded 1960. Enrl 47,321; Fac 2,349; Highest Degree: Doctorate
Library Holdings: Audiobooks 16,472; CDs 16,339; DVDs 4,763; e-books 543,452; e-journals 80,112; Electronic Media & Resources 3,125; Microforms 2,894,423; Music Scores 16,717; Bk Vols 2,051,766; Per Subs 82,536; Videos 17,729
Special Collections: 19th Century American Literature (Dobkin Coll); 19th Century American Playscript Coll; 19th Century American Printed Ephemera Coll; 19th Century American Songbook Coll; American Almanac Coll; American Currency (Wollowick Coll); American Juvenile Series Book Coll; American Toybook Coll; Archives & Manuscripts Coll; Bartok Coll; Black Musical Heritage Coll; Cigar Art Coll; Cigar Label Progressive Proof Books (Kane-Greenberg Lithography Coll); Congressman Sam M Gibbons Papers; Dime Novel Coll; Dion Boucicault Theatre Coll; Early American Textbook Coll; Florida (Regional History Coll), bks, journals, maps, ms, photog, postcards; Florida Federal Writers Project Papers; Florida Sheet Music Coll; Floridiana (Hampton Dunn & Tony Pizzo Colls); George Alfred Henty Press Coll; Governor LeRoy Collins Papers; Haldeman-Julius Coll; Miles Hanley Papers; Mosher Press Coll; National Amateur Press Coll; Nations Bank Coll; Piers Anthyony Papers; Rare Books Coll; Rare Map Coll, primarily North America, 1524-1900; Records of Tampa Ethnic Mutual Aid Societies; Robert W & Helen Saunders Papers; US Tobacco Museum Coll. Oral History; State Document Depository; US Document Depository
Automation Activity & Vendor Info: (Acquisitions) Ex Libris Group; (Cataloging) Ex Libris Group; (Circulation) Ex Libris Group; (Course Reserve) Blackboard Inc
Partic in LYRASIS; OCLC Research Library Partnership; Tampa Bay Library Consortium, Inc
Publications: Library Leads (Newsletter); Library Link (Newsletter)

C UNIVERSITY OF TAMPA*, Macdonald-Kelce Library, 401 W Kennedy Blvd, 33606-1490. SAN 303-2175. Tel: 813-253-6231. Reference Tel: 813-257-3057. FAX: 813-258-7426. E-mail: library@ut.edu. Web Site: utopia.ut.edu. *Dir,* Marlyn Pethe; Tel: 813-251-3402, E-mail: mpethe@ut.edu; *Acq Librn, Cat Librn,* Laura Rounds; Tel: 813-257-3649, E-mail: lrounds@ut.edu; *Info Literacy Librn,* David Davisson; Tel: 813-257-3719, E-mail: ddavisson@ut.edu; *Ref Librn,* Elizabeth Barron; Tel: 813-257-3741, E-mail: ebarron@ut.edu; *Per, Ref Librn,* Shannon Spencer; Tel: 813-257-3847, E-mail: sspencer@ut.edu; *Coll Develop, Ref Librn,* Jeanne Vince; Tel: 813-257-3744, E-mail: jvince@ut.edu; *Circ Mgr,* Teresa Brown; Tel: 813-257-3053, E-mail: tbrown@ut.edu; Staff 21 (MLS 9, Non-MLS 12)
Founded 1931. Enrl 6,600; Fac 460; Highest Degree: Master
Library Holdings: AV Mats 1,600; Bk Titles 175,000; Bk Vols 275,000; Per Subs 50,500
Special Collections: Drama (Blanche Yurka Coll), letters, res mat, scrapbks; Florida Military Coll; John Wilkes Booth (Stanley Kimmel Coll), bks, photog, res mat; Local History Coll; University Archives. US Document Depository
Subject Interests: Bus & mgt, Computer sci, Nursing
Automation Activity & Vendor Info: (Acquisitions) Ex Libris Group; (Cataloging) Ex Libris Group; (Circulation) Ex Libris Group; (Course Reserve) Ex Libris Group; (OPAC) Ex Libris Group; (Serials) Ex Libris Group
Wireless access
Publications: Bibliographies; faculty library handbook, library guide, fact sheet
Partic in Florida Library Information Network; LYRASIS; OCLC Online Computer Library Center, Inc; Tampa Bay Library Consortium, Inc
Open Mon-Thurs (Winter) 8am-1am, Fri 8-6, Sat 11-7, Sun Noon-1am night; Mon-Thurs (Summer) 8am-11pm, Sat 10-6, Sun 1-9
Friends of the Library Group

TARPON SPRINGS

P TARPON SPRINGS PUBLIC LIBRARY, 138 E Lemon St, 34689. SAN 303-2221. Tel: 727-943-4922. E-mail: tslibrary@ctsfl.us. Web Site: tarponspringslibrary.org. *Dir,* Cari Rupkalvis; E-mail: crupkalvis@ctsfl.us; *Head, Adult Serv,* Salvatore Miranda; E-mail: smiranda@ctsfl.us; *Head, Tech Serv,* Barbara Aglieri; E-mail: baglieri@ctsfl.us; *Ref & ILL Librn,* Irene Marcus; E-mail: imarcus@ctsfl.us; *Circ,* Terrie Olson; E-mail: tolson@ctsfl.us; Staff 21 (MLS 5, Non-MLS 16)
Founded 1916
Library Holdings: AV Mats 6,066; Bks on Deafness & Sign Lang 60; Large Print Bks 5,000; Bk Vols 77,787; Per Subs 157; Talking Bks 8,488
Subject Interests: Bus, Fla, Greek
Automation Activity & Vendor Info: (Cataloging) OCLC; (Circulation) Innovative Interfaces, Inc; (ILL) OCLC; (OPAC) Innovative Interfaces, Inc; (Serials) Innovative Interfaces, Inc
Wireless access
Publications: Newsletter
Mem of Pinellas Public Library Cooperative
Partic in Tampa Bay Library Consortium, Inc
Open Mon-Wed 10-9, Thurs & Fri 10-6, Sat 10-5
Friends of the Library Group

TAVARES

P CITY OF TAVARES PUBLIC LIBRARY*, 314 N New Hampshire Ave, 32778. SAN 323-651X. Tel: 352-742-6204. Reference Tel: 352-742-6203. FAX: 352-742-6472. Web Site: www.tavares.org. *Dir,* Gary Earl; E-mail: gearl@tavares.org; Staff 11 (MLS 2, Non-MLS 9)
Founded 1959. Pop 10,301; Circ 87,428
Library Holdings: Audiobooks 2,921; AV Mats 3,756; Bks on Deafness & Sign Lang 28; DVDs 3,516; High Interest/Low Vocabulary Bk Vols 168; Large Print Bks 2,365; Bk Vols 33,368; Per Subs 153; Talking Bks 997
Special Collections: Dorothy Young Johnson Dance & Theater Coll; Florida Materials; Large Print Coll
Subject Interests: Dance
Wireless access
Function: Ref serv available
Publications: @ the Library (Newsletter)
Mem of Lake County Library System
Open Mon & Thurs 9:30-8, Tues, Wed & Fri 10-6, Sat 9:30-5
Friends of the Library Group

S LAKE COUNTY HISTORICAL SOCIETY LIBRARY*, 317 W Main St, 32778. (Mail add: PO Box 7800, 32778-7800), SAN 325-1845. Tel: 352-343-9890. FAX: 352-343-9814. E-mail: info@lakecountyhistoricalmuseum.org. Web Site: lakecountyhistoricalmuseum.org, www.lakecountyfl.gov. *Curator,* Bob Grenier
Founded 1954
Library Holdings: Bk Titles 600
Special Collections: Poll Tax Books, 1887-1937
Subject Interests: Maps, Rare bks
Function: Res libr
Publications: Lake County Florida: A Pictorial History
Open Thurs-Sat 10-2

P LAKE COUNTY LIBRARY SYSTEM*, 418 W Alfred St, Ste C, 32778. (Mail add: PO Box 7800, 32778-7800), SAN 370-4653. Tel: 352-253-6180. FAX: 352-253-6184. Web Site: www.mylakelibrary.org. *Dir, Libr Serv,* George Taylor; E-mail: gtaylor@mylakelibrary.org; *Support Serv Mgr,* Sean Okeefe; E-mail: sokeefe@mylakelibrary.org; *Youth Serv Coordr,* Linda Goff; Tel: 352-253-6169, E-mail: lgoff@mylakelibrary.org; *Tech Serv Mgr,* Donna Gray-Williams; Tel: 352-253-6161, E-mail: dgwilliams@mylakelibrary.org; Staff 47.5 (MLS 29.5, Non-MLS 18)
Founded 1982. Pop 293,478; Circ 2,113,840
Library Holdings: Audiobooks 33,399; DVDs 64,117; Bk Vols 547,991; Per Subs 1,549
Special Collections: Florida Environment Coll
Subject Interests: Genealogy
Automation Activity & Vendor Info: (Acquisitions) SirsiDynix; (Cataloging) SirsiDynix; (Circulation) SirsiDynix; (OPAC) SirsiDynix
Wireless access
Member Libraries: City of Tavares Public Library; Fruitland Park Library; Helen Lehmann Memorial Library; Lady Lake Public Library; Leesburg Public Library; Marianne Beck Memorial Library; Umatilla Public Library; W T Bland Public Library
Partic in OCLC Online Computer Library Center, Inc; Tampa Bay Library Consortium, Inc
Friends of the Library Group
Branches: 7
ASTOR COUNTY LIBRARY, 54905 Alco Rd, Astor, 32102. Tel: 352-759-9913. FAX: 352-759-9923. *Br Supvr,* Jonathan Dolce
Founded 2002
Open Mon & Wed 9-5, Tues & Thurs 9-8, Sat 9-1
Friends of the Library Group
MARION BAYSINGER MEMORIAL COUNTY LIBRARY, 756 W Broad St, Groveland, 34736, SAN 370-4645. Tel: 352-429-5840. FAX: 352-429-9924. *Br Supvr,* Daniel Velez-Rubio
Open Mon & Wed 10-6, Tues & Thurs 10-8, Fri & Sat 10-3
Friends of the Library Group
CAGAN CROSSINGS COMMUNITY LIBRARY, 16729 Cagan Oaks, Clermont, 34714. Tel: 352-243-1840. FAX: 352-243-3230. *Br Supvr,* Rachael Smoyak; *Youth Serv Librn,* Kim Roccanti
Founded 2000
Open Mon-Thurs 10-7:30, Fri & Sat 10-2
Friends of the Library Group
COOPER MEMORIAL LIBRARY, 2525 Oakley Seaver Dr, Clermont, 34711, SAN 302-8887. Tel: 352-536-2275. FAX: 352-536-2259. *Br Supvr,* Boyd Bruce; *Head, Ref,* Beth Reichardt; *Head, Youth Serv,* Amy Stultz; *Ref Librn,* Dennis Smolarek; Staff 4 (MLS 3, Non-MLS 1)
Founded 1914
Special Collections: Oral History; US Document Depository
Subject Interests: Fla, Genealogy, Local hist
Open Mon-Thurs 8-8, Fri & Sat 9-5
Friends of the Library Group
EAST LAKE COUNTY LIBRARY, 31340 County Rd 437, Sorrento, 32776. Tel: 352-383-9980. FAX: 352-383-9982. *Br Supvr,* Pamela Edwards-Goodson
Founded 2000
Open Mon & Tues 10-8, Wed & Thurs 10-6, Fri & Sat 10-3
Friends of the Library Group
MINNEOLA SCHOOLHOUSE LIBRARY, 100 S Main St, Minneola, 34715. Tel: 352-432-3921, Ext 380. Web Site: www.minneola.us/library. *Libr Mgr,* Josephine Dix; Tel: 352-432-3921, Ext 381, E-mail: jdix@minneola.us
Open Mon-Thurs 9:30-6:30, Fri 9:30-5
Friends of the Library Group
PAISLEY COUNTY LIBRARY, 24954 County Rd 42, Paisley, 32767. Tel: 352-669-1001. FAX: 352-669-2180. *Br Supvr,* Jonathan Dolce
Founded 2001
Open Mon & Wed 9:30-6, Tues & Thurs 9:30-8, Sat 10-2
Friends of the Library Group

TEMPLE TERRACE

C FLORIDA COLLEGE*, Chatlos Library, 119 N Glen Arven Ave, 33617-5578. SAN 303-223X. Tel: 813-988-5131, Ext 210. Interlibrary Loan Service Tel: 813-988-5131, Ext 215. Web Site: www.floridacollege.edu/library. *Libr Dir,* Wanda D Dickey; Tel: 813-988-5131, Ext 211, E-mail: dickeyw@floridacollege.edu; *Archives, Ser Librn,* Brooke Ward; Tel: 813-988-5131, Ext 212, E-mail: wardb@floridacollege.edu; *Cataloger, ILL,* Jennifer Kearney; E-mail: kearneyj@floridacollege.edu; Staff 3 (MLS 3)
Founded 1946. Enrl 500; Fac 40; Highest Degree: Bachelor
Library Holdings: CDs 696; e-books 40,000; Bk Titles 122,482; Per Subs 290; Videos 979
Subject Interests: Hist, Music, Relig
Automation Activity & Vendor Info: (Cataloging) OCLC CatExpress; (Circulation) EOS International; (Course Reserve) EOS International; (ILL) OCLC FirstSearch; (OPAC) EOS International; (Serials) EOS International
Wireless access
Partic in Christian Col Libr; Independent Cols & Univs of Fla; Tampa Bay Library Consortium, Inc

TITUSVILLE

J EASTERN FLORIDA STATE COLLEGE*, Titusville Campus Library, Dr Frank Elbert Williams Learning Resource Ctr, 1311 N US 1, 32796-2192. SAN 303-2256. Tel: 321-433-5036. Circulation Tel: 321-433-5066. FAX: 321-433-5114. Web Site: www.easternflorida.edu/library. *Librn,* Joanne Connell; Staff 2 (MLS 2)
Founded 1973. Enrl 2,000; Fac 18
Library Holdings: Bk Vols 22,000; Per Subs 200
Automation Activity & Vendor Info: (Acquisitions) Ex Libris Group; (Cataloging) Ex Libris Group; (Circulation) Ex Libris Group; (Course Reserve) Ex Libris Group; (ILL) Ex Libris Group; (OPAC) Ex Libris Group; (Serials) Ex Libris Group
Wireless access
Partic in LINCC
Open Mon-Thurs 8-8, Fri 9-1

P TITUSVILLE PUBLIC LIBRARY*, 2121 S Hopkins Ave, 32780. SAN 303-2272. Tel: 321-264-5026. FAX: 321-264-5030. Web Site: www.brev.org, www.brevardfl.gov/PublicLibraries/Branches/Titusville/Home. *Libr Dir,* Mary Toupin; E-mail: mtoupin@brev.org; *Youth Serv,* Denise Ambrosait; E-mail: dambrosait@brev.org; Staff 15.9 (MLS 3, Non-MLS 12.9)
Founded 1906. Pop 45,000; Circ 433,630
Library Holdings: Audiobooks 5,284; Bk Vols 94,990; Per Subs 69
Subject Interests: Genealogy
Automation Activity & Vendor Info: (Cataloging) TLC (The Library Corporation); (Circulation) TLC (The Library Corporation); (OPAC) TLC (The Library Corporation)
Wireless access
Function: 24/7 Online cat, Activity rm, Bk club(s), Bks on CD, Children's prog, Computers for patron use, Electronic databases & coll, Free DVD rentals, Genealogy discussion group, Internet access, Magazines, Magnifiers for reading, Meeting rooms, Microfiche/film & reading machines, Music CDs, Notary serv, OverDrive digital audio bks, Photocopying/Printing, Prog for adults, Prog for children & young adult, Ref serv available, Scanner, Study rm, Summer reading prog, Tax forms, Teen prog, Telephone ref, Wheelchair accessible
Mem of Brevard County Public Libraries
Special Services for the Deaf - TTY equip
Open Mon & Tues 9-8, Wed-Sat 9-5, Sun 1-5
Friends of the Library Group

TRENTON

P GILCHRIST COUNTY PUBLIC LIBRARY*, 105 NE 11th Ave, 32693-3803. Tel: 352-463-3176. FAX: 352-463-3164. E-mail: gilchrist@3riverslibrary.com. Web Site: gilchrist.fl.us/gilchrist-county-public-library. *Mgr,* Sylvia Hiers; E-mail: shiers@3riverslibrary.com
Pop 17,000
Library Holdings: Bk Vols 20,000; Per Subs 43
Automation Activity & Vendor Info: (Circulation) SirsiDynix
Wireless access
Partic in Three Rivers Regional Library Consortium
Open Mon-Fri 9-6
Friends of the Library Group

TRINITY

C TRINITY COLLEGE, Raymond H Center Library, 2430 Welbilt Blvd, 34655. Tel: 727-376-6911, Ext 341. FAX: 727-376-0781. Web Site: library.trinitycollege.edu. *Librn,* Cindy Hyer; Tel: 727-376-6911, Ext 343, E-mail: cindy.hyer@trinitycollege.edu; Staff 2 (MLS 2)
Founded 1932. Enrl 230; Fac 6; Highest Degree: Bachelor
Library Holdings: e-books 160,000; Bk Vols 35,000; Per Subs 24
Special Collections: Theology Books of the 1890s (E C Bragg Coll)
Wireless access
Function: ILL available, Internet access, Orientations, Photocopying/Printing, VHS videos, Wheelchair accessible
Partic in Christian Library Consortium; Independent Cols & Univs of Fla; OCLC Online Computer Library Center, Inc; Tampa Bay Library Consortium, Inc
Open Mon-Thurs 9-9, Fri 9-4, Sat Noon-5
Restriction: Open to students, fac & staff, Use of others with permission of librn
Friends of the Library Group

TYNDALL AFB

UNITED STATES AIR FORCE

A AIR FORCE RESEARCH LAB, TYNDALL RESEARCH SITE TECHNICAL INFORMATION CENTER*, 139 Barnes Dr, Ste 2, 32403-5323, SAN 324-5845. Tel: 850-283-6285. FAX: 850-283-6500. E-mail: tic@tyndall.af.mil. *Chief Librn,* Amber Collins; E-mail: amber.collins@tyndall.af.mil; *Ref Librn,* Mariana Grey; E-mail: mariana.grey.ctr@tyndall.af.mil; Staff 2 (MLS 2)
Founded 1968
Special Collections: Air Base Survivability; Air-Bird Strikes; Aircraft Fire Research Studies; Chemical/Biological Decontamination, especially Military Equipment; Corrosion Control of Military Facilities; Hazardous Materials; Rapid Runway Repair
Subject Interests: Chem engr, Civil engr, Energy, Mat sci, Structural engr
Automation Activity & Vendor Info: (Acquisitions) Mandarin Library Automation; (Cataloging) Mandarin Library Automation; (Circulation) Mandarin Library Automation
Partic in Air Force Res Lab Virtual Libr Team; OCLC Online Computer Library Center, Inc
Publications: Early Alert Services; Periodicals Listing; Tic Talk
Open Mon-Thurs 8-4, Fri 8-3

A TYNDALL AIR FORCE BASE LIBRARY FL4819*, 325 SVS/SVMG/45, 640 Suwanee Rd, Bldg 916, 32403-5531, SAN 338-1994. Tel: 850-283-4287. FAX: 850-283-4994.
Founded 1982
Library Holdings: Bk Vols 27,000; Per Subs 300
Subject Interests: Aeronaut, Mil hist
Automation Activity & Vendor Info: (Cataloging) SirsiDynix; (Circulation) SirsiDynix; (OPAC) SirsiDynix
Partic in OCLC Online Computer Library Center, Inc
Publications: Substance (Monthly newsletter)
Restriction: Authorized patrons, Authorized personnel only

UMATILLA

P UMATILLA PUBLIC LIBRARY*, 412 Hatfield Dr, 32784-8913. SAN 303-2280. Tel: 352-669-3284. FAX: 352-669-2927. TDD: 352-669-2927. E-mail: umatillalibrary@gmail.com. Web Site: umatillalibrary.org. *Dir,* Janet Lewis; E-mail: jlewis@mylakelibrary.org; *Circ Supvr,* Brandy Padgett
Founded 1917. Pop 3,600; Circ 103,353
Library Holdings: Bk Vols 33,974; Per Subs 12
Automation Activity & Vendor Info: (Cataloging) Koha; (Circulation) Koha; (OPAC) Koha
Wireless access
Function: 24/7 Electronic res, 24/7 Online cat, Adult literacy prog, After school storytime, Audiobks on Playaways & MP3, Audiobks via web, AV serv, Bks on CD, CD-ROM, Children's prog, Citizenship assistance, Computer training, Computers for patron use, Distance learning, Electronic databases & coll, Free DVD rentals, Holiday prog, Internet access, Life-long learning prog for all ages, Literacy & newcomer serv, Magazines, Magnifiers for reading, Mail & tel request accepted, Movies, Music CDs, Online cat, Online info literacy tutorials on the web & in blackboard, Online ref, Outreach serv, Outside serv via phone, mail, e-mail & web, OverDrive digital audio bks, Photocopying/Printing, Preschool outreach, Preschool reading prog, Prog for adults, Prog for children & young adult, Scanner, Senior computer classes, Story hour, Summer & winter reading prog, Summer reading prog, Teen prog, Wheelchair accessible, Winter reading prog
Mem of Lake County Library System
Open Mon & Tues 12-6, Wed & Thurs 9-5, Fri 9-6, Sat 9-Noon
Friends of the Library Group

VALPARAISO

P VALPARAISO COMMUNITY LIBRARY, 459 Valparaiso Pkwy, 32580. SAN 303-2299. Tel: 850-729-5406. FAX: 850-729-1120. Web Site: vcl.valp.org. *Dir,* Hope Willis; E-mail: hwillis@valp.org; Staff 6 (MLS 2, Non-MLS 4)
Founded 1973. Pop 178,000
Library Holdings: Bk Titles 40,000; Per Subs 50
Subject Interests: Genealogy
Automation Activity & Vendor Info: (Circulation) SirsiDynix
Wireless access
Partic in Okaloosa County Public Library Cooperative
Open Mon-Wed 9-8, Thurs 9-6, Fri 9-5
Friends of the Library Group

VENICE

P FRANCES T BOURNE JACARANDA PUBLIC LIBRARY*, 4143 Woodmere Park Blvd, 34293. SAN 376-267X. Tel: 941-861-1260. FAX: 941-486-2725. Web Site: www.scgov.net/government/libraries/hours-and-locations. *Libr Mgr,* Stacey Ogea; Tel: 941-861-1277, E-mail: sogea@scgov.net; *Asst Mgr,* Mary Louise Fischer; Tel: 941-861-1272, E-mail: mfischer@scgov.net; Staff 12 (MLS 6, Non-MLS 6)
Founded 1994. Pop 35,000; Circ 360,000
Library Holdings: Bk Titles 55,100; Per Subs 188
Special Collections: College & Career Coll; Florida Coll; Reader Development Coll
Automation Activity & Vendor Info: (Acquisitions) Innovative Interfaces, Inc; (Cataloging) Innovative Interfaces, Inc; (Circulation) Innovative Interfaces, Inc; (Course Reserve) Innovative Interfaces, Inc; (ILL) Innovative Interfaces, Inc; (Media Booking) Innovative Interfaces, Inc; (OPAC) Innovative Interfaces, Inc; (Serials) Innovative Interfaces, Inc
Wireless access
Mem of Sarasota County Library System
Partic in National Network of Libraries of Medicine Region 2
Special Services for the Deaf - Assistive tech; Bks on deafness & sign lang; Closed caption videos
Special Services for the Blind - Assistive/Adapted tech devices, equip & products; Children's Braille; Closed circuit TV; Descriptive video serv (DVS); Large print bks; Lending of low vision aids; Magnifiers; Talking bks
Open Mon-Thurs 10-6, Fri & Sat 10-5
Friends of the Library Group

P VENICE PUBLIC LIBRARY, 260 Nokomis Ave S, 34285, SAN 303-2302. Tel: 941-861-1336. Circulation Tel: 941-861-1331. Reference Tel: 941-861-1347. Web Site: sclibs.net. *Libr Mgr,* Katie Dow; Tel: 941-861-1350, E-mail: kdow@scgov.net; *Asst Libr Mgr,* Roland Marcotte; E-mail: rmarcotte@scgov.net; *Ref Serv,* Melanie Odom; *Youth Serv,* Anisa Hitt; *Libr Asst,* Marion Mikruta. Subject Specialists: *Genealogy,* Melanie Odom; Staff 13 (MLS 5, Non-MLS 8)
Founded 1965. Pop 46,441; Circ 465,486
Library Holdings: Bk Vols 90,000; Per Subs 135
Automation Activity & Vendor Info: (Acquisitions) Innovative Interfaces, Inc; (Cataloging) Innovative Interfaces, Inc; (Circulation) Innovative Interfaces, Inc
Wireless access
Publications: Bookbits; FOL Newsletter (Quarterly)
Mem of Sarasota County Library System
Open Mon-Thurs 10-6, Fri & Sat 10-5
Friends of the Library Group

VENUS

S ARCHBOLD BIOLOGICAL STATION LIBRARY, 123 Main Dr, 33960. SAN 303-0024. Tel: 863-465-2571. FAX: 863-699-1927. E-mail: library@archbold-station.org. Web Site: archbold-station.org/html/datapub/library/library.html. *Librn,* Joseph Gentili; E-mail: jgentili@archbold-station.org; Staff 1 (Non-MLS 1)
Founded 1941
Library Holdings: Bk Vols 7,200; Per Subs 200
Special Collections: Biology of North American Land Tortoise-Gopherus, cataloged reprints; Florida Department of Geology Publications; Florida Natural History
Subject Interests: Agro-ecology, Animal behavior, Conserv biol, Ecology, Entomology, Evolution, Herpetology, Ichthyology, Mammalogy, Ornithology
Automation Activity & Vendor Info: (Cataloging) Innovative Interfaces, Inc
Wireless access
Restriction: Non-circulating, Open by appt only

VERO BEACH

P INDIAN RIVER COUNTY LIBRARY SYSTEM*, Main Branch, 1600 21st St, 32960. SAN 303-2329. Tel: 772-770-5060. FAX: 772-770-5066. E-mail: refdesk@irclibrary.org. Web Site: www.irclibrary.org. *Dir, Libr Serv,* Anne M Shepherd; E-mail: ashepherd@irclibrary.org; *Asst Libr Dir,* Tanya M Huff; E-mail: thuff@irclibrary.org; *Head Ref Librn,* Elizabeth Stenger; E-mail: estenger@irclibrary.org; *Ch,* Patti Fuchs; E-mail: pfuchs@irclibrary.org; *Circ Supvr,* Pansey Jhagroo; *Syst Coordr,* Joshua Perez; E-mail: jperez@irclibrary.org; *Cat,* Darlene Hadsell; E-mail: dhadsell@irclibrary.org; *Local Hist/Genealogy,* Michelle Wagner; E-mail: mwagner@irclibrary.org. Subject Specialists: *Fla hist,* Michelle Wagner; Staff 1 (MLS 1)
Founded 1915. Pop 140,000; Circ 1,392,560
Oct 2015-Sept 2016 Income (Main & Associated Libraries) $3,745,481, State $98,318, County $3,647,163. Mats Exp $721,318. Sal $1,681,948
Library Holdings: Audiobooks 15,911; DVDs 23,378; e-books 9,718; Bk Vols 445,807; Per Subs 22,422
Special Collections: Oral History
Subject Interests: Bus, Civil War, Genealogy, Health, Law, Lit, State hist, Wars
Automation Activity & Vendor Info: (Acquisitions) Innovative Interfaces, Inc; (Cataloging) Innovative Interfaces, Inc; (Circulation) Innovative

Interfaces, Inc; (ILL) OCLC Online; (OPAC) Innovative Interfaces, Inc; (Serials) Innovative Interfaces, Inc
Wireless access
Function: Adult literacy prog, Archival coll, Audiobks via web, Bks on CD, Children's prog, Computers for patron use, Electronic databases & coll, Free DVD rentals, ILL available, Internet access, Magazines, Magnifiers for reading, Mango lang, Meeting rooms, Microfiche/film & reading machines, Music CDs, Online cat, Online ref, OverDrive digital audio bks, Photocopying/Printing, Prog for adults, Prog for children & young adult, Ref & res, Scanner, Spanish lang bks, Study rm, Tax forms, Teen prog, Telephone ref
Partic in Tampa Bay Library Consortium, Inc
Special Services for the Deaf - TDD equip
Special Services for the Blind - Bks on cassette
Open Mon-Thurs 10-8, Tues, Wed & Fri 10-5, Sat 10-4, Sun 1-5
Restriction: Non-resident fee
Friends of the Library Group
Branches: 3
GIFFORD BRANCH, 4875 43rd Ave, 32967. Tel: 772-794-1005. FAX: 772-569-5563.
Open Tues-Thurs 1-5
Friends of the Library Group
NORTH INDIAN RIVER COUNTY LIBRARY, 1001 Sebastian Blvd, CR 512, Sebastian, 32958, SAN 370-3584. Tel: 772-589-1355. FAX: 772-388-3697. TDD: 772-581-7654. *Br Mgr,* Kathleen Bowman; E-mail: kmbowman@irclibrary.org; *Ch,* Patti Fuchs; E-mail: pfuchs@irclibrary.org; *YA Librn,* Amanda Atwater; E-mail: aatwater@irclibrary.org; *Circ Supvr,* Sandy Bachmann; E-mail: sbachmann@irclibrary.org; *Ch Serv,* Joann Jedlinski; *Computer Spec,* Tracy Galentine; E-mail: tgalentine@irclibrary.org; Staff 6 (MLS 1, Non-MLS 5)
Founded 1983. Pop 47,222; Circ 369,650
Function: Adult bk club, Art exhibits, Audio & video playback equip for onsite use, Bi-weekly Writer's Group, Bks on cassette, Bks on CD, Chess club, Children's prog, Computer training, Computers for patron use, Electronic databases & coll, Free DVD rentals, Homebound delivery serv, ILL available, Music CDs, Notary serv, Online cat, Photocopying/Printing, Preschool outreach, Prog for adults, Prog for children & young adult, Ref serv available, Scanner, Story hour, Summer reading prog, Tax forms, VHS videos, Wheelchair accessible
Special Services for the Deaf - TDD equip
Open Mon-Wed 10-8, Thurs & Fri 10-5, Sat 10-4
Friends of the Library Group

G UNIVERSITY OF FLORIDA*, Florida Medical Entomology Laboratory Library, 200 Ninth St SE, 32962. SAN 303-2310. Tel: 772-778-7200, Ext 120. FAX: 772-778-7205. Web Site: www.fmel.ifas.ufl.edu. *Dir,* Jorge R Rey; E-mail: jrey@ufl.edu
Library Holdings: Bk Titles 5,600; Per Subs 105
Subject Interests: Biochem, Biology, Ecology, Entomology, Ornithology, Virology
Restriction: Not open to pub

VIERA

L A MAX BREWER MEMORIAL LAW LIBRARY*, Brevard County Law Library, Harry T & Harriette V Moore Justice Ctr, 2825 Judge Fran Jamieson Way, 32940. SAN 324-7627. Tel: 321-617-7295. FAX: 321-617-7303. Web Site: www.brevardfl.gov/SpecialDistricts/BrewerLawLibrary. *Dir, Law Libr,* Teresa Cassella; E-mail: Teresa.Cassella@flcourts18.org; *Law Librn,* Mari Andrews; E-mail: Mari.Andrews@flcourts18.org; *Law Librn,* Teri Elgin-Smith; E-mail: Teri.Elgin-Smith@flcourts18.org; Staff 3 (MLS 3)
Founded 1955
Library Holdings: Bk Vols 32,640; Per Subs 20
Special Collections: Harry T Moore Coll
Automation Activity & Vendor Info: (Cataloging) OCLC
Wireless access
Open Mon-Fri 8-5
Restriction: Non-circulating to the pub

WAUCHULA

P HARDEE COUNTY PUBLIC LIBRARY, 315 N Sixth Ave, 33873. SAN 303-2337. Tel: 863-773-6438. Web Site: myhlc.org/hardee-county-library. *Librn,* Dee Shackelford; E-mail: dee@myhlc.org
Circ 15,000
Library Holdings: Bk Titles 45,000; Per Subs 30
Wireless access
Mem of Heartland Library Cooperative
Partic in Tampa Bay Library Consortium, Inc
Open Mon 10-6:30, Tues 9-5:30, Wed & Thurs 9-5, Fri 9-4
Friends of the Library Group

WELAKA

P GFWC WOMEN'S CLUB OF WELAKA LIBRARY*, 644 County Rd 309, 32193. (Mail add: PO Box 154, 32193-0154), SAN 320-4723. Tel: 386-467-9706. *Librn,* Peggy Williams
Founded 1960. Pop 1,000; Circ 2,100
Library Holdings: Bk Vols 3,000
Subject Interests: Fla
Wireless access
Mem of Putnam County Library System
Open Tues, Thurs & Fri 10-Noon

WESLEY CHAPEL

C PASCO-HERNANDO STATE COLLEGE-PORTER CAMPUS*, Wiregrass Ranch Library, 2727 Mansfield Blvd, Rm C428, 33543-7168. Tel: 813-527-6651. FAX: 813-527-6992. *Assoc Dir of Libr,* Ingrid Purrenhage; E-mail: purreni@phsc.edu
Open Mon-Thurs 8am-9pm, Fri 8-4:30

WEST MELBOURNE

P WEST MELBOURNE PUBLIC LIBRARY*, 2755 Wingate Blvd, 32904. Tel: 321-952-4508. Web Site: www.brevardfl.gov//PublicLibraries/Branches/westMelbourne. *Libr Dir,* Mauri Baumann; E-mail: mbaumann@brev.org; *Youth Serv,* Michelle Hutto; E-mail: mhutto@brev.org; Staff 16 (MLS 2, Non-MLS 14)
Founded 1970. Pop 10,000; Circ 140,000
Library Holdings: Bk Vols 68,000; Per Subs 98
Automation Activity & Vendor Info: (Circulation) CARL.Solution (TLC); (OPAC) CARL.Solution (TLC); (Serials) EBSCO Online
Wireless access
Mem of Brevard County Public Libraries
Open Mon & Wed 12-8, Tues, Thurs, Fri & Sat 9-5
Friends of the Library Group

WEST PALM BEACH

M GOOD SAMARITAN MEDICAL CENTER*, Richard S Beinecke Medical Library, 1309 N Flagler Dr, 33401. SAN 303-2361. Tel: 561-650-6315. Administration Tel: 561-655-5511. FAX: 561-671-7428. Administration FAX: 561-650-6127. *Mgr,* Anjana Roy; E-mail: anjana.roy@tenethealth.com; Staff 1 (MLS 1)
Founded 1967
Jan 2019-Dec 2019 Income $65,000. Mats Exp $65,000, Books $15,000, Electronic Ref Mat (Incl. Access Fees) $50,000
Library Holdings: Bk Titles 3,000; Bk Vols 4,000; Per Subs 225
Special Collections: Medicine (Rare Book Coll)
Subject Interests: Hospital admin, Med, Nursing, Surgery
Wireless access
Partic in Basic Health Sciences Library Network; North Atlantic Health Sciences Libraries, Inc; SE-Atlantic Regional Med Libr Servs; South Florida Health Sciences Library Consortium
Restriction: Hospital employees & physicians only, Non-circulating, Not open to pub

S HISTORICAL SOCIETY OF PALM BEACH COUNTY*, 300 N Dixie Hwy, 33401. (Mail add: PO Box 4364, 33402-4364), SAN 303-1152. Tel: 561-832-4164. Reference Tel: 561-832-4164, Ext 112. FAX: 561-832-7965. E-mail: archive@hspbc.org. Web Site: www.hspbc.org. *Dir, Res,* Rose Guerrero; E-mail: rguerrero@hspbc.org; *Chief Curator,* Debi Murray; Tel: 561-832-4164, Ext 105, E-mail: dmurray@historicalsocietypbc.org. Subject Specialists: *Fla hist,* Rose Guerrero; *Fla hist,* Debi Murray; Staff 3 (Non-MLS 3)
Founded 1937
Library Holdings: Bk Vols 4,000
Special Collections: Addison Mizner Coll, architectural drawings, house photog; Boca News Photo Coll; Gustav Maass Coll, architectural drawings; Maurice Fatio, Trainor & Fatio Coll, architectural drawings, house photos; Miami Herald Palm Beach Bureau Photo Coll, 1970-1980; Palm Beach Daily News Photograph Coll; Palm Beach Post Photograph Coll; Pioneer Manuscripts; Sam R Quincey Coll, 1945-mid 1970, photos. Oral History
Subject Interests: Hist of Fla
Publications: Guide to the Archives; Palm Beach Life Index (Index to periodicals); The Newsletter; Tustenegee (Online only)
Restriction: Open to pub for ref only

P MANDEL PUBLIC LIBRARY OF WEST PALM BEACH*, 411 Clematis St, 33401. SAN 303-2469. Tel: 561-868-7700. Circulation Tel: 561-868-7702. Information Services Tel: 561-868-7701. FAX: 561-868-7706. E-mail: mpl@wpbcitylibrary.org. Web Site: www.wpb.org/government/mandel-public-library-of-west-palm-beach. *Dir,* Lisa Hathaway; E-mail: hathawayl@mycitylibrary.org; *Head, Circ, Head, Tech Serv,* Theresa Salantrie; E-mail: salantriet@mycitylibrary.org; *Head, Ref, Head, Tech,* Janice Collins; Tel: 561-868-7765, E-mail:

collinsj@mycitylibrary.org; *Youth Serv Mgr*, Jennifer McQuown; Tel: 561-868-7722, E-mail: mcquownj@mycitylibrary.org; *Supvr, Coll Develop*, Tina Maura; Tel: 561-868-7765, E-mail: maurat@mycitylibrary.org; Staff 20.5 (MLS 20.5)
Founded 1894. Pop 99,919; Circ 862,956
Oct 2012-Sept 2013 Income $4,576,764, State $113,172, City $3,812,056, Locally Generated Income $651,536. Mats Exp $398,520, Books $202,887, Per/Ser (Incl. Access Fees) $14,406, AV Mat $127,020, Electronic Ref Mat (Incl. Access Fees) $54,207. Sal $2,570,394
Library Holdings: Audiobooks 6,239; AV Mats 60,441; CDs 17,951; DVDs 42,490; e-books 2,110; Electronic Media & Resources 51; Large Print Bks 3,374; Bk Vols 162,513; Per Subs 318
Special Collections: Florida Coll
Automation Activity & Vendor Info: (Acquisitions) Innovative Interfaces, Inc - Millennium; (Cataloging) Innovative Interfaces, Inc - Millennium; (Circulation) Innovative Interfaces, Inc - Millennium; (ILL) Innovative Interfaces, Inc - Millennium; (OPAC) Innovative Interfaces, Inc - Millennium; (Serials) Innovative Interfaces, Inc - Millennium
Wireless access
Function: Art exhibits, Bks on CD, Computers for patron use, Electronic databases & coll, Free DVD rentals, Homework prog, ILL available, Internet access, Life-long learning prog for all ages, Magazines, Magnifiers for reading, Microfiche/film & reading machines, Movies, Music CDs, Online cat, Online ref, Outside serv via phone, mail, e-mail & web, Photocopying/Printing, Preschool outreach, Preschool reading prog, Prog for adults, Prog for children & young adult, Ref & res, Ref serv available, Scanner, Spanish lang bks, Story hour, Study rm, Summer reading prog, Tax forms, Teen prog, Telephone ref, Visual arts prog, Wheelchair accessible, Writing prog
Partic in Southeast Florida Library Information Network, Inc
Open Mon-Thurs 9:30-8:30, Fri & Sat 9:30-5, Sun 1-5
Friends of the Library Group

CR PALM BEACH ATLANTIC UNIVERSITY*, Warren Library, 300 Pembroke Pl, 33401-6503. (Mail add: PO Box 24708, 33416-4708), SAN 303-237X. Tel: 561-803-2226. Interlibrary Loan Service Tel: 561-803-2228. Reference Tel: 561-803-2227. Information Services Tel: 561-803-2240. FAX: 561-803-2235. E-mail: library@pba.edu. Reference E-mail: reference@pba.edu. Web Site: library.pba.edu. *Dir*, John Doncevic; E-mail: John_Doncevic@pba.edu; *Ref Librn*, Michelle Keba; Tel: 561-803-2230, E-mail: michelle_keba@pba.edu; *Ref Librn*, Robert K Triplett; Tel: 561-803-2234, E-mail: bob_triplett@pba.edu; *Ref Librn*, Anthony Verdesca; Tel: 561-803-2238, E-mail: anthony_verdesca@pba.edu; *Access Serv Librn*, Kellie Barbato; Tel: 561-803-2210, E-mail: kellie_barbato@pba.edu; *Digital Serv Librn*, Elizabeth Fairall; Tel: 561-803-2224, E-mail: Elizabeth_Fairall@pba.edu; *Access Serv Coordr, Archives Asst*, Megan Nance; Tel: 561-803-2231, E-mail: megan_nance@pba.edu; *Coordr, Acq*, Deirdre Kilduff; Tel: 561-803-2229, E-mail: deirdre_kilduff@pba.edu; *ILL, Ser*, Nerolie Ceus; E-mail: nerolie_ceus@pba.edu; *Metadata Serv*, Julia Pichette; Tel: 561-803-2225, E-mail: julia_pichette@pba.edu; *Syst*, Chris Lovell; Tel: 561-803-2221, E-mail: christopher_lovell@pba.edu; Staff 13 (MLS 6, Non-MLS 7)
Founded 1968. Enrl 3,444; Fac 163; Highest Degree: Doctorate
Special Collections: Dr. Jess Moody Papers; Dr. Ray Robinson Coll; James Mallory Willson Coll; Sen. George S. LeMieux Papers
Automation Activity & Vendor Info: (Acquisitions) Ex Libris Group; (Cataloging) Ex Libris Group; (Circulation) Ex Libris Group; (Course Reserve) Ex Libris Group; (Discovery) Ex Libris Group; (ILL) Ex Libris Group; (OPAC) Ex Libris Group; (Serials) Ex Libris Group
Wireless access
Function: Art exhibits, Computers for patron use, Electronic databases & coll, Free DVD rentals, ILL available, Magnifiers for reading, Mail & tel request accepted, Music CDs, Online cat, Online ref, Orientations, Outside serv via phone, mail, e-mail & web, Photocopying/Printing, Printer for laptops & handheld devices, Ref serv available, Scanner, Telephone ref, VHS videos, Wheelchair accessible
Partic in LYRASIS; National Network of Libraries of Medicine Region 2; Southeast Florida Library Information Network, Inc
Open Mon-Thurs 7am-Midnight, Fri 7-6, Sat 9-6, Sun Noon-Midnight

GL PALM BEACH COUNTY LAW LIBRARY*, County Courthouse, Rm 12200, 205 N Dixie Hwy, 33401. SAN 303-2388. Tel: 561-355-2928. FAX: 561-355-1654. *Mgr*, Position Currently Open
Founded 1947
Library Holdings: Bk Vols 30,000; Per Subs 30
Wireless access
Open Mon-Fri 8-5
Restriction: Non-circulating to the pub

P PALM BEACH COUNTY LIBRARY SYSTEM*, 3650 Summit Blvd, 33406-4198. SAN 338-2028. Tel: 561-233-2600. Toll Free Tel: 888-780-4962. E-mail: pbclref@pbclibrary.org. Web Site: www.pbclibrary.org. *Dir*, Douglas Crane; E-mail: craned@pbclibrary.org; *Asst Dir*, Aurora Arthay; E-mail: arthaya@pbclibrary.org; *Syst Serv Dir*, Adam Davis; E-mail: davisa@pbclibrary.org; *Branch Services*, Elizabeth Prior; E-mail: priore@pbclibrary.org; *Tech Serv*, Sue Bermann; E-mail: bermanns@pbclibrary.org; Staff 474.4 (MLS 123.5, Non-MLS 350.9)
Founded 1967. Pop 909,448; Circ 9,117,499
Special Collections: Audubon Coll; Florida Coll; Large Print Coll
Automation Activity & Vendor Info: (Cataloging) SirsiDynix; (Circulation) SirsiDynix; (OPAC) SirsiDynix
Wireless access
Function: Adult literacy prog, Health sci info serv, Homebound delivery serv, ILL available, Internet access, Magnifiers for reading, Photocopying/Printing, Prof lending libr, Prog for adults, Prog for children & young adult, Ref serv available, Summer reading prog, Telephone ref, VHS videos, Wheelchair accessible
Publications: Brochures; Happenings (Newsletter); Staff Newsletter
Partic in Library Cooperative of the Palm Beaches; National Network of Libraries of Medicine Region 2; OCLC Online Computer Library Center, Inc; Southeast Florida Library Information Network, Inc
Special Services for the Deaf - TDD equip; TTY equip
Special Services for the Blind - Talking bks
Open Mon-Thurs 9-9, Fri 9-6, Sat 9-5, Sun 12-5
Friends of the Library Group
Branches: 17
ACREAGE BRANCH, 15801 Orange Blvd, Loxahatchee, 33470. Tel: 561-681-4100. Web Site: www.pbclibrary.org/branches/acreage. *Br Mgr*, Doris Mendez-DeMaio
Founded 2012
Open Mon-Thurs 10-9, Fri 10-6, Sat 10-5, Sun Noon-5
Friends of the Library Group
CLARENCE E ANTHONY BRANCH, 375 SW Second Ave, South Bay, 33493, SAN 375-5894. Tel: 561-992-8393. Web Site: www.pbclibrary.org/branches/clarence-e-anthony. *Br Mgr*, Position Currently Open
Founded 1992
Open Mon & Wed 11-7, Tues & Thurs-Sat 9-5
Friends of the Library Group
BELLE GLADE BRANCH, 725 NW Fourth St, Belle Glade, 33430, SAN 302-8550. Tel: 561-996-3453. Web Site: www.pbclibrary.org/branches/belle-glade. *Br Mgr*, Position Currently Open
Open Mon-Wed 10-8, Thurs-Sat 10-5
Friends of the Library Group
GARDENS BRANCH, 11303 Campus Dr, Palm Beach Gardens, 33410, SAN 377-0486. Tel: 561-626-6133. Web Site: www.pbclibrary.org/branches/gardens. *Br Mgr*, Carol Roggenstein
Open Mon-Thurs 10-9, Fri 10-6, Sat 10-5, Sun 12-5
Friends of the Library Group
GLADES ROAD BRANCH, 20701 95th Ave S, Boca Raton, 33434, SAN 338-2230. Tel: 561-482-4554. Web Site: www.pbclibrary.org/branches/glades-road. *Br Mgr*, Lynlee Lebensart
Open Mon-Wed 10-8, Thurs & Fri 10-6, Sat 10-5
Friends of the Library Group
GREENACRES BRANCH, 3750 Jog Rd, Greenacres, 33467, SAN 338-2117. Tel: 561-641-9100. Web Site: www.pbclibrary.org/branches/greenacres. *Br Mgr*, David Scott
Open Mon & Tues 10-8, Wed-Fri 10-6, Sat 10-5
Friends of the Library Group
HAGEN RANCH ROAD BRANCH, 14350 Hagen Ranch Rd, Delray Beach, 33446, SAN 338-2087. Tel: 561-894-7500. Web Site: www.pbclibrary.org/branches/hagen-ranch-road. *Br Mgr*, Elizabeth Locke
Open Mon-Wed 9-8, Thurs & Fri 9-6, Sat 9-5, Sun 12-5
Friends of the Library Group
JUPITER BRANCH, 705 N Military Trail, Jupiter, 33458, SAN 326-7598. Tel: 561-744-2301. Web Site: www.pbclibrary.org/branches/jupiter. *Br Mgr*, Henrik Laursen
Open Mon-Thurs 9-8, Fri 9-6, Sat 9-5, Sun 12-5
Friends of the Library Group
LANTANA ROAD BRANCH, 4020 Lantana Rd, Lake Worth, 33462. Tel: 561-304-4500. Web Site: www.pbclibrary.org/branches/lantana. *Br Mgr*, Susan Kelly
Founded 2009
Open Mon-Thurs 10-9, Fri 10-6, Sat 10-5, Sun 12-5
Friends of the Library Group
OKEECHOBEE BOULEVARD BRANCH, 5689 Okeechobee Blvd, 33417, SAN 338-2176. Tel: 561-233-1880. Web Site: www.pbclibrary.org/branches/okeechobee-blvd. *Br Mgr*, James Larson
Open Mon-Wed 10-8, Thurs & Fri 10-6, Sat 10-5
Friends of the Library Group
PALM BEACH COUNTY LIBRARY ANNEX, 4249 Cherry Rd, 33409, SAN 338-2052. Tel: 561-649-5500. Toll Free Tel: 888-780-5151. *Head, Outreach Serv*, Adam Davis; *Head, Tech Serv*, Sue Bermann
Restriction: Open by appt only

ROYAL PALM BEACH BRANCH, 500 Civic Center Way, Royal Palm Beach, 33411, SAN 338-2249. Tel: 561-790-6030. Web Site: www.pbclibrary.org/branches/royal-palm-beach. *Br Mgr,* Karen Crisco
Open Mon-Wed 9-8, Thurs & Fri 9-6, Sat 9-5
Friends of the Library Group
TEQUESTA BRANCH, 461 Old Dixie Hwy N, Tequesta, 33469, SAN 338-2141. Tel: 561-746-5970. Web Site: www.pbclibrary.org/branches/tequesta. *Br Mgr,* Henrik Laursen
Open Mon-Wed 10-8, Thurs-Sat 10-5
Friends of the Library Group
WELLINGTON BRANCH, 1951 Royal Fern Dr, Wellington, 33414, SAN 377-6530. Tel: 561-790-6070. Web Site: www.pbclibrary.org/branches/wellington. *Br Mgr,* Margaret Barry
Open Mon-Thurs 10-9, Fri 10-6, Sat 10-5, Sun 12-5
Friends of the Library Group
WEST BOCA BRANCH, 18685 State Rd 7, Boca Raton, 33498. Tel: 561-470-1600. Web Site: www.pbclibrary.org/branches/west-boca. *Br Mgr,* Laura Connors
Open Mon-Thurs 10-9, Fri 10-6, Sat 10-5, Sun 12-5
Friends of the Library Group
WEST BOYNTON BRANCH, 9451 Jog Rd, Boynton Beach, 33437, SAN 375-5908. Tel: 561-734-5556. Web Site: www.pbclibrary.org/branches/west-boynton. *Br Mgr,* Cindi Permenter
Open Mon-Thurs 10-9, Fri 10-6, Sat 10-5, Sun 12-5
Friends of the Library Group
LOULA V YORK BRANCH, 525 Bacom Point Rd, Pahokee, 33476, SAN 370-0186. Tel: 561-924-5928. Web Site: www.pbclibrary.org/branches/loula-v-york. *Br Mgr,* Position Currently Open
Open Mon & Wed 11-7, Tues & Thurs-Sat 9-5
Friends of the Library Group
Bookmobiles: 1. In Charge, Ronald Glass. Bk titles 3,000

S SOUTH FLORIDA WATER MANAGEMENT DISTRICT, Reference Center Library, 3301 Gun Club Rd, 33406. (Mail add: PO Box 24680, 33416-4680), SAN 303-2418. Tel: 561-686-8800. Web Site: www.sfwmd.gov. *Bus Support Unit Supvr,* Doris Lopez; E-mail: dlopez@sfwmd.gov
Founded 1949
Special Collections: Florida Environmental History Coll; Technical Reports & Documents
Subject Interests: Agr, Conserv, Environ engr, Water pollution, Water res
Restriction: Open to pub for ref only

WEWAHITCHKA

S GULF CORRECTIONAL INSTITUTION LIBRARY*, 500 Ike Steel Rd, 32465. SAN 377-2675. Tel: 850-639-1000. FAX: 850-639-1182. *Librn,* Candice Mills; E-mail: candice.mills@fdc.myflorida.com
Library Holdings: Bk Vols 13,229; Per Subs 72
Branches:
ANNEX BRANCH, 699 Ike Steel Rd, 32465. Tel: 850-639-1780. *Libr Tech,* William Weeks
Library Holdings: Bk Vols 6,558; Per Subs 45

WILDWOOD

P SUMTER COUNTY LIBRARY SYSTEM*, Administrative Office, 7375 Powell Rd, Ste 150, 34785. Tel: 352-689-4567. FAX: 352-689-4561. Web Site: sumter.librarycatalog.info/polaris, www.sumtercountyfl.gov/853/About-the-Library. *Libr Dir,* Lisa Taylor; Tel: 352-689-4560, E-mail: lisa.taylor@lsslibraries.com; *Admin Serv Mgr,* Leslie Smith; Tel: 352-689-4400, E-mail: leslie.smith@sumtercountyfl.gov
Pop 114,350; Circ 749,821
Library Holdings: Bk Titles 94,761; Bk Vols 164,733
Automation Activity & Vendor Info: (Acquisitions) Innovative Interfaces, Inc; (Cataloging) Innovative Interfaces, Inc; (Circulation) Innovative Interfaces, Inc
Wireless access
Function: 24/7 Electronic res, Adult bk club, After school storytime, Audiobks via web, Bks on CD, Children's prog, Computer training, Computers for patron use, E-Readers, E-Reserves, Electronic databases & coll, Free DVD rentals, ILL available, Magazines, Mango lang, Music CDs, Online cat, Outreach serv, OverDrive digital audio bks, Photocopying/Printing, Preschool reading prog, Summer reading prog, Tax forms
Partic in Tampa Bay Library Consortium, Inc
Open Mon-Fri 8:30-5
Friends of the Library Group
Branches: 5
BUSHNELL PUBLIC LIBRARY, 402 N Florida St, Bushnell, 33513, SAN 376-2998. FAX: 352-569-1791.
Library Holdings: Bk Vols 6,565; Per Subs 15
Automation Activity & Vendor Info: (Cataloging) SirsiDynix; (Circulation) SirsiDynix; (OPAC) SirsiDynix
Open Mon-Thurs 9-7, Fri 9-5, Sat 9-6
Friends of the Library Group
PANASOFFKEE COMMUNITY LIBRARY, 1500 County Rd 459, Lake Panasoffkee, 33538, SAN 376-2742. FAX: 352-569-1941.
Library Holdings: Bk Titles 15,200; Per Subs 40
Automation Activity & Vendor Info: (Cataloging) Innovative Interfaces, Inc; (Circulation) Innovative Interfaces, Inc
Open Mon & Tues 10-7, Wed, Thurs & Sat 10-6, Fri 10-5
Friends of the Library Group
E C ROWELL PUBLIC LIBRARY, 2810 CR 478A, Webster, 33597. FAX: 352-569-1534.
Library Holdings: Bk Titles 15,000; Bk Vols 17,000; Per Subs 40
Automation Activity & Vendor Info: (Cataloging) SirsiDynix; (Circulation) SirsiDynix
Open Mon & Tues 10am-7pm, Wed, Thurs & Sat 10-6, Fri 10-5
VILLAGES PUBLIC LIBRARY AT BELVEDERE, 325 Belvedere Blvd, The Villages, 32162. FAX: 352-689-4691.
Library Holdings: Bk Vols 45,000
Automation Activity & Vendor Info: (Cataloging) SirsiDynix; (Circulation) SirsiDynix; (OPAC) SirsiDynix
Open Mon-Thurs & Sat 9-6, Fri 9-5
Friends of the Library Group
VILLAGES PUBLIC LIBRARY AT PINELLAS PLAZA, 7375 Powell Rd, Ste 100, 34785. FAX: 352-689-4581.
Open Mon-Thurs 9-7, Fri 9-5, Sat 9-6

WILTON MANORS

P RICHARD C SULLIVAN PUBLIC LIBRARY OF WILTON MANORS*, 500 NE 26th St, 33305. SAN 303-2477. Tel: 954-390-2195. FAX: 954-390-2183. Web Site: www.wiltonmanors.com/library. *Dir,* Rick Sterling; E-mail: rsterling@wiltonmanors.com; *Pub Serv,* Cynthia Exterkamp; E-mail: cexterkamp@wiltonmanors.com; *Tech Serv,* Mike Hesson; E-mail: mhesson@wiltonmanors.com; *Youth Serv,* Jill Epsilantis; E-mail: jepsilantis@wiltonmanors.com; Staff 7 (MLS 6, Non-MLS 1)
Founded 1957. Pop 12,108; Circ 54,109
Oct 2014-Sept 2015 Income $766,375, State $19,243, City $725,232, Locally Generated Income $21,900. Mats Exp $47,136, Books $27,465, Per/Ser (Incl. Access Fees) $5,612, AV Mat $5,500, Electronic Ref Mat (Incl. Access Fees) $8,559. Sal $401,140
Library Holdings: Audiobooks 1,106; CDs 912; DVDs 2,144; e-books 2,591; Large Print Bks 1,213; Bk Vols 31,791; Per Subs 84
Special Collections: Florida Coll
Automation Activity & Vendor Info: (Cataloging) Auto-Graphics, Inc; (Circulation) Auto-Graphics, Inc; (OPAC) Auto-Graphics, Inc
Wireless access
Function: 24/7 Electronic res, 24/7 Online cat, Adult bk club, Bilingual assistance for Spanish patrons, Bks on CD, Children's prog, Computers for patron use, Free DVD rentals, Homebound delivery serv, ILL available, Internet access, Magazines, Magnifiers for reading, Mango lang, Music CDs, Online cat, Photocopying/Printing, Story hour, Summer reading prog, Tax forms
Partic in Southeast Florida Library Information Network, Inc
Open Mon, Tues, Thurs & Fri 9:30-5:30, Wed Noon-8, Sat 9:30-1
Friends of the Library Group

WINTER HAVEN

C POLK STATE COLLEGE*, James W Dowdy Library, 999 Ave H NE, 33881. SAN 303-2485. Tel: 863-297-1040. Web Site: www.polk.edu/library. *Dir, Learning Res,* Christina Fullerton; Tel: 863-292-1040, Ext 5302, E-mail: cfullerton@polk.edu; *Librn,* Beverly Chapa; Tel: 863-298-6813, E-mail: bchapa@polk.edu; *Librn,* Jarrod Jones; E-mail: jajones@polk.edu; Staff 12 (MLS 5, Non-MLS 7)
Founded 1965. Enrl 6,600; Fac 125; Highest Degree: Associate
Library Holdings: e-books 49,000; Bk Titles 93,000; Per Subs 350; Videos 4,500
Subject Interests: Fla, State hist
Automation Activity & Vendor Info: (Cataloging) Ex Libris Group; (Circulation) Ex Libris Group; (Course Reserve) Ex Libris Group; (ILL) OCLC; (OPAC) Ex Libris Group; (Serials) Ex Libris Group
Wireless access
Partic in LYRASIS; OCLC Online Computer Library Center, Inc; Tampa Bay Library Consortium, Inc
Special Services for the Deaf - Assistive tech; Bks on deafness & sign lang; Closed caption videos; TDD equip
Special Services for the Blind - Assistive/Adapted tech devices, equip & products; Cassette playback machines; Closed circuit TV; Computer with voice synthesizer for visually impaired persons; Low vision equip; ZoomText magnification & reading software
Open Mon-Thurs 7:30am-9pm, Fri 7:30-4, Sat 9-1
Departmental Libraries:
LAKELAND CAMPUS LIBRARY, 3425 Winter Lake Rd, Sta 62, Lakeland, 33803, SAN 374-6771. Tel: 863-297-1042. FAX: 863-297-1064. *Dir, Learning Res, Lakeland,* William C Foege, Jr;

E-mail: bfoege@polk.edu; *Librn,* Helen Schmidt; E-mail: hschmidt@polk.edu; *Ref (Info Servs),* Helen Schmidt; E-mail: hschmidt@polk.edu; *Learning Res Asst, Cir/Reserve,* Lynn Heil; *Learning Res Asst, Ser & ILL,* Kristen Jernigan; Staff 6.2 (MLS 3.3, Non-MLS 2.9)
Founded 1988. Enrl 3,120; Highest Degree: Bachelor
Open Mon-Thurs 8am-9pm, Fri 8-4, Sat 9-1

S RIDGE TECHNICAL COLLEGE LIBRARY, 7700 State Rd 544, 33881. SAN 377-3264. Tel: 863-419-3060, Ext 52738. FAX: 863-419-3062. Web Site: www.polkedpathways.com/ridge-technical-college. *Media Spec,* Darlene Lyon; E-mail: darlene.lyon@polk-fl.net
Founded 1979
Library Holdings: Bks on Deafness & Sign Lang 15; High Interest/Low Vocabulary Bk Vols 2,000; Bk Titles 8,500; Per Subs 40
Subject Interests: Career, Vocational
Automation Activity & Vendor Info: (Acquisitions) Brodart; (Circulation) Follett Software; (Serials) EBSCO Online
Wireless access
Restriction: Students only
Friends of the Library Group

P WINTER HAVEN PUBLIC LIBRARY*, Kathryn L Smith Memorial, 325 Ave A NW, 33881. SAN 303-2493. Tel: 863-291-5880. FAX: 863-291-5889. Web Site: www.mywinterhaven.com/library. *Libr Dir,* Jane Martin; E-mail: jmartin@mywinterhaven.com; *Info & Tech Librn,* Linda Babli; E-mail: lbabli@mywinterhaven.com; *Pub Serv Librn,* Cori Greear; E-mail: cgreear@mywinterhaven.com; *Youth Serv Librn,* Kristen Barnes; E-mail: kbarnes@mywinterhaven.com
Founded 1910. Pop 25,000; Circ 237,414
Library Holdings: Bk Titles 80,000
Automation Activity & Vendor Info: (Acquisitions) SirsiDynix; (Cataloging) SirsiDynix; (Circulation) SirsiDynix
Wireless access
Partic in Tampa Bay Library Consortium, Inc
Open Mon & Wed 9-6, Tues & Thurs 10-7, Fri & Sat 9-5
Friends of the Library Group

WINTER PARK

C HERZING UNIVERSITY LIBRARY, Orlando Campus, 1865 SR 436, 32792. Tel: 407-749-1126. Web Site: www.herzing.edu/orlando.
Highest Degree: Bachelor
Library Holdings: AV Mats 320; Bk Vols 4,000; Per Subs 30
Automation Activity & Vendor Info: (Cataloging) Follett Software; (Circulation) Follett Software; (OPAC) Follett Software
Open Mon-Thurs 8:30am-9pm, Fri 8:30-5

C ROLLINS COLLEGE*, Olin Library, 1000 Holt Ave, Campus Box 2744, 32789-2744. SAN 338-232X. Tel: 407-646-2521. Interlibrary Loan Service Tel: 407-646-1554. E-mail: askolinlibrary@rollins.edu. Web Site: www.rollins.edu/library. *Interim Dir,* Wenxian Zhang; E-mail: wzhang@rollins.edu; *Head, Coll, Syst,* Jonathan Harwell; Tel: 407-646-2148, E-mail: jharwell@rollins.edu; *Head, Pub Serv,* Dorothy Mays; Tel: 407-646-1533, E-mail: dmays@rollins.edu; *Emerging Serv Librn,* William Svitavsky; Tel: 407-646-2679, E-mail: wsvitavsky@rollins.edu; *Pub Serv Librn,* Susan Montgomery; Tel: 407-646-2295, E-mail: smontgomery@rollins.edu; *Electronic Res, Ser Librn,* Maridath Wilson; Tel: 407-691-6431, E-mail: mwilson@rollins.edu; *Sci Librn,* Patti McCall; Tel: 407-646-2683, E-mail: pmccall@rollins.edu; *Discovery Serv, Syst Adminr,* Paul Gindlesperger; Tel: 407-646-1372, E-mail: pgindlesperger@rollins.edu; *Digital Archivist,* Rachel Walton; Tel: 407-691-1127, E-mail: rwalton@rollins.edu; *Digital Serv Spec,* Juan Gonzalez; Tel: 407-691-1157, E-mail: jagonzalez@rollins.edu; Staff 11 (MLS 9, Non-MLS 2)
Founded 1885. Enrl 3,240; Fac 235; Highest Degree: Doctorate
Library Holdings: CDs 1,697; DVDs 3,305; e-books 293,165; e-journals 153,333; Electronic Media & Resources 110; Music Scores 1,226; Bk Titles 512,152; Bk Vols 225,713
Special Collections: Constance F Woolson Coll; Floridiana; Hamilton Holt Papers; M P Shiel Coll; Poetry & Letters (Jessie B Rittenhouse Coll); Rollins College Archives; Walt Whitman Coll
Automation Activity & Vendor Info: (Acquisitions) Ex Libris Group; (OPAC) Ex Libris Group
Publications: Olin Info (Newsletter)
Partic in Associated Colleges of the South; LYRASIS; Oberlin Group; Tampa Bay Library Consortium, Inc
Open Mon-Thurs 7:45am-Midnight, Fri 7:45-5, Sat 9-5, Sun 11am-Midnight

J VALENCIA COLLEGE*, Winter Park Campus Library, 850 W Morse Blvd, 32789. Tel: 407-582-6814. FAX: 407-582-6014. Web Site: valenciacollege.edu/library. *Interim Dir,* Benjamin Mittag; E-mail: bmittag@valenciacollege.edu; Staff 7 (MLS 3, Non-MLS 4)
Library Holdings: Bk Vols 18,000
Wireless access
Open Mon-Thurs 8-7, Fri 8-5

P WINTER PARK PUBLIC LIBRARY*, 460 E New England Ave, 32789. SAN 303-2523. Tel: 407-623-3300. FAX: 407-623-3489. Web Site: www.wppl.org. *Exec Dir,* Sabrina Bernat; Tel: 407-623-3458, E-mail: sbernat@wppl.org; *Head, Adult Serv,* Nicole Heintzelman; Tel: 407-623-3300, Ext 104, E-mail: nheintzelman@wppl.org; *Head, Circ,* Melissa Schneider; Tel: 407-623-3300, Ext 107, E-mail: mschneider@wppl.org; *Head, Youth Serv,* Evelyn Malles; Tel: 407-623-3300, Ext 115, E-mail: emalles@wppl.org; *Teen Librn,* Grace Moore; Tel: 407-623-3300, Ext 114, E-mail: gmoore@wppl.org; *YA Librn,* Lisa Blue; E-mail: lblue@wppl.org; *Archivist,* Rachel Simmons; Tel: 407-623-3300, Ext 106, E-mail: rsimmons@wppl.org; Staff 17 (MLS 13, Non-MLS 4)
Founded 1885. Pop 27,200; Circ 530,865
Library Holdings: Bk Titles 153,000; Bk Vols 175,000; Per Subs 326
Special Collections: Winter Park History Archive
Automation Activity & Vendor Info: (Circulation) SirsiDynix; (OPAC) SirsiDynix
Wireless access
Publications: Read All About It (Newsletter)
Open Mon-Thurs 9-9, Fri & Sat 9-5, Sun 1-5
Friends of the Library Group

ZEPHYRHILLS

P ZEPHYRHILLS PUBLIC LIBRARY*, 5347 Eighth St, 33542. SAN 303-2531. Tel: 813-780-0064. FAX: 813-780-0664. E-mail: library@ci.zephyrhills.fl.us. Web Site: www.ci.zephyrhills.fl.us. *Dir,* Lori Brightwell; *Asst Dir,* Peggy L Panak; *Circ,* Debbie Lopez; *Circ,* Victoria DeGeorge; Staff 2 (MLS 1, Non-MLS 1)
Founded 1912. Pop 30,000; Circ 120,745
Library Holdings: Audiobooks 761; AV Mats 1,968; Bk Vols 29,000; Per Subs 60
Special Collections: Civil War Coll; World War II Coll
Subject Interests: Civil War, Fla, Gardening
Automation Activity & Vendor Info: (Acquisitions) TLC (The Library Corporation); (Cataloging) TLC (The Library Corporation); (Circulation) TLC (The Library Corporation)
Wireless access
Mem of Pasco County Library System
Partic in Tampa Bay Library Consortium, Inc
Open Tues 9-7, Wed-Fri 9-6, Sat 9-12

GEORGIA

Date of Statistics: FY 2020
Population, 2020 U.S. Census: 10,710,017
Total Volumes in Public Libraries: 14,744,448
Volumes Per Capita: 1.36
Total Public Library Circulation: 28,930,791
Circulation Per Capita: 2.67
Digital Resources:
Total e-books: 2,955,286
Total e-books Per Capita: 0.27
Total computers for use by the public: 10,149
Total annual wireless sessions: 4,221,869
Income and Expenditures:
Total Public Library Income: $225,807,139
Source of Income: Public Funds; Local; State & Federal; Library Fines; Fees, & Donations.
Income Per Capita: $20.84
Federal Library Services and Technology Act: $4,586,119
State Service Grants to Libraries & Statewide Services Funding: $39,476,895
Information provided courtesy of: Whitney Payne, Director of Research and Statistics; Georgia Public Library Service

ALBANY

C ALBANY STATE UNIVERSITY*, Harold B Wetherbee Library, Bldg G, 2400 Gillionville Rd, 31707. SAN 303-254X. Tel: 229-500-3613. Circulation Tel: 229-317-6766. Interlibrary Loan Service Tel: 229-500-3464. Web Site: www.asurams.edu/academic-affairs/library/about-wetherbee-library.php. *Dir, Univ Libr,* Dr Laverne McLaughlin; Tel: 229-500-3468, E-mail: laverne.mclaughlin@asurams.edu; Staff 7 (MLS 3, Non-MLS 4)
Founded 1966. Enrl 5,800; Fac 125; Highest Degree: Associate
Library Holdings: AV Mats 5,182; e-books 27,417; Bk Vols 98,000; Per Subs 247
Subject Interests: Allied health, Nursing
Automation Activity & Vendor Info: (Acquisitions) Ex Libris Group; (Cataloging) Ex Libris Group; (Circulation) Ex Libris Group; (ILL) OCLC; (OPAC) Ex Libris Group
Wireless access
Function: Distance learning, ILL available, Magnifiers for reading, Ref serv available, Wheelchair accessible
Partic in GOLD Resource Sharing Network for Georgia's Libraries; OCLC Online Computer Library Center, Inc
Special Services for the Deaf - Assistive tech
Special Services for the Blind - Assistive/Adapted tech devices, equip & products; Computer with voice synthesizer for visually impaired persons
Open Mon-Thurs 7:30am-8pm, Fri 7:30-5, Sat Noon-4, Sun 2-8

C ALBANY STATE UNIVERSITY*, James Pendergrast Memorial Library, 504 College Dr, 31705-2796. SAN 303-2558. Tel: 229-430-4799. Circulation Tel: 229-430-4805. E-mail: circulation@asurams.edu. Web Site: www.asurams.edu/academic-affairs/library-home. *Dir, Libr Serv,* LaVerne McLaughlin; E-mail: laverne.mclaughlin@asurams.edu
Founded 1903. Enrl 4,024; Fac 300; Highest Degree: Master
Library Holdings: CDs 139; DVDs 10; e-books 27,442; Bk Vols 200,000; Per Subs 323
Special Collections: History & Literature (Black Studies); Library of American Civilization; US Govt Census Data
Automation Activity & Vendor Info: (Acquisitions) Ex Libris Group; (Cataloging) Ex Libris Group; (Circulation) Ex Libris Group; (Course Reserve) Ex Libris Group; (ILL) Ex Libris Group; (Media Booking) Ex Libris Group; (OPAC) Ex Libris Group; (Serials) Ex Libris Group
Wireless access
Publications: New Acquisitions List
Partic in LYRASIS; OCLC Online Computer Library Center, Inc
Open Mon-Thurs 7:30am-10pm, Fri 7:30-5, Sat 12-4, Sun 2-10

P DOUGHERTY COUNTY PUBLIC LIBRARY*, 300 Pine Ave, 31701-2533. SAN 338-2419. Tel: 229-420-3200. Reference Tel: 229-420-3210. Administration Tel: 229-420-3214. FAX: 229-420-3215. E-mail: dcpl@docolib.org. Web Site: www.docolib.org. *Dir,* Pauline Abidde; E-mail: pabidde@docolib.org; *Head, Ref,* Christina Shepherd; *Finance Mgr,* Sabrina Little; *Ch Serv,* Melinda Vest; Staff 35 (MLS 7, Non-MLS 28)
Founded 1905. Pop 99,880
Subject Interests: Genealogy, Local hist
Automation Activity & Vendor Info: (Cataloging) Evergreen; (Circulation) Evergreen; (ILL) OCLC; (OPAC) Evergreen
Wireless access
Partic in GOLD Resource Sharing Network for Georgia's Libraries; Public Information Network for Electronic Services
Open Mon-Fri 10-5:30, Sat 11-3
Friends of the Library Group
Branches: 4
TALLULAH MASSEY BRANCH, 2004 Stratford Dr, 31705, SAN 338-2532. Tel: 229-420-3250. *Br Mgr,* Micah Kloberdanz
Open Mon-Fri 10-5:30, Sat 11-3
NORTHWEST, 2507 Dawson Rd, 31707, SAN 322-7189. Tel: 229-420-3270. *Br Mgr,* Patricia Perles
Open Mon-Fri 10-5:30, Sat 11-3
SOUTHSIDE, 2114 Habersham Rd, 31705, SAN 370-1085. Tel: 229-420-3260. *Br Mgr,* Wanda Brown
Open Mon-Thurs 10-5:30
WESTTOWN, 2124 Waddell Ave, 31707, SAN 371-2982. Tel: 229-420-3280. *Mgr,* Katrina Holloman
Open Mon-Thurs 10-5:30

A MARINE CORPS LOGISTICS BASES*, MCCS Library, Base Library, Bldg 7122, 814 Radford Blvd, Ste 20311, 31704-0311. SAN 338-2591. Tel: 229-639-5242. FAX: 229-639-5197. Web Site: library.usmc-mccs.org/cgi-bin/get_data.pl?library=Albany. *Librn,* Amos Tookes; E-mail: amos.tookes@usmc-mccs.org
Library Holdings: Bk Titles 6,000; Per Subs 10
Wireless access
Open Mon-Fri 9:30-6

ALTO

S GEORGIA DEPARTMENT OF CORRECTIONS, OFFICE OF LIBRARY SERVICES*, Arrendale State Prison, 2023 Gainesville Hwy S, 30510. (Mail add: PO Box 709, 30510-0709). Tel: 706-776-4700, Ext 4858. Web Site: www.dcor.state.ga.us/Facilities/arrendale-state-prison. *Librn,* Regina Bell
Library Holdings: Bk Vols 10,000
Restriction: Not open to pub

AMERICUS

C GEORGIA SOUTHWESTERN STATE UNIVERSITY, James Earl Carter Library, 800 Georgia Southwestern State University Dr, 31709. SAN 303-2582. Tel: 229-931-2259. FAX: 229-931-2265. E-mail: libcirc@gsw.edu, library@gsw.edu. Web Site: gsw.edu/library. *Dean, Libr Serv,* Ru Story-Huffman; E-mail: ru.story-huffman@gsw.edu; *Bibliog Database Mgr, Cat Librn,* Bokshim Fox; Tel: 229-931-2258, E-mail: bokshim.fox@gsw.edu; *Govt Info Coordr, Ref Librn,* John Wilson; Tel: 229-931-2850, E-mail: john.wilson@gsw.edu; *Access Serv Supvr,* Jennifer

Griffin; Tel: 229-931-2266, E-mail: jennifer.griffin@gsw.edu; Staff 5 (MLS 4, Non-MLS 1)
Founded 1928. Enrl 2,900; Fac 125; Highest Degree: Master
Library Holdings: e-books 30,000; Bk Titles 131,658; Bk Vols 143,557; Per Subs 400
Special Collections: POW Coll; Third World Studies Coll. US Document Depository
Subject Interests: Educ
Automation Activity & Vendor Info: (Acquisitions) Ex Libris Group; (Cataloging) Ex Libris Group; (Circulation) Ex Libris Group; (Course Reserve) Ex Libris Group; (ILL) Ex Libris Group; (OPAC) Ex Libris Group
Wireless access
Partic in Georgia Library Learning Online
Special Services for the Blind - ZoomText magnification & reading software
Open Mon-Thurs 9am-10pm, Fri 10-5, Sat 1-5, Sun 5pm-10pm

P LAKE BLACKSHEAR REGIONAL LIBRARY SYSTEM*, 307 E Lamar St, 31709-3633. SAN 338-2621. Tel: 229-924-8091. FAX: 229-928-4445. E-mail: info@lbrls.org. Web Site: www.lbrls.org. *Dir,* Anne M Isbell; E-mail: amisbell@lbrls.org; *Asst Dir, Cat,* Cheryl Brown; Staff 3 (MLS 3)
Founded 1878. Pop 68,000; Circ 90,852
Special Collections: Andersonville Prison, bks, photog; Genealogy Coll, bks, microfiche, microfilm; Jimmy Carter Coll, multi-media; Local History Coll, bks, photog
Automation Activity & Vendor Info: (Acquisitions) Evergreen; (Cataloging) Evergreen; (Circulation) Evergreen; (ILL) OCLC; (OPAC) Evergreen
Wireless access
Publications: Index to the Roster of Confederate Soldiers
Partic in LYRASIS; Public Information Network for Electronic Services
Open Mon 10-6, Tues-Thurs 10-8, Fri & Sat 10-4
Friends of the Library Group
Branches: 5
BYROMVILLE PUBLIC, 452 Main St, Byromville, 31007-2500. (Mail add: PO Box 6, Byromville, 31007-0006), SAN 338-2656. Tel: 478-433-5100. *Br Mgr,* Rose Grimmett
Open Tues & Thurs 2:30-5:30
Friends of the Library Group
CORDELE-CRISP CARNEGIE, 115 E 11th Ave, Cordele, 31010. (Mail add: PO Box 310, Cordele, 31010-0310), SAN 338-2680. Tel: 229-276-1300. FAX: 229-276-1151. *Br Mgr,* Mari Mills
Open Mon & Wed 10-6, Tues & Thurs 10-8, Fri & Sat 10-4
Friends of the Library Group
DOOLY COUNTY, 1200 E Union St, Vienna, 31092-7545, SAN 338-2710. Tel: 229-268-4687. FAX: 229-268-4687. *Br Mgr,* Hope E Henderson
Open Mon-Wed 9-5, Thurs 9-6, Fri 9:30-4
Friends of the Library Group
ELIZABETH HARRIS LIBRARY, 312 Harman St, Unadilla, 31091. (Mail add: PO Box 930, Unadilla, 31091-0930), SAN 326-8411. Tel: 478-627-9303. FAX: 478-627-9303. *Br Mgr,* Rhonda Bartlett
Open Tues-Thurs 8:30-6, Fri 9-4, Sat 9-Noon
Friends of the Library Group
SCHLEY COUNTY, 54 S Broad St, Ellaville, 31806-3457. (Mail add: PO Box 365, Ellaville, 31806-0365), SAN 338-2745. Tel: 229-937-2004. FAX: 229-937-2004. *Br Mgr,* Mary Ann Roper
Open Mon & Fri 10-4:30, Tues & Thurs 10-6:30, Sat 10-2
Friends of the Library Group
Bookmobiles: 1. Outreach Servs, Jill Kloberdanz

J SOUTH GEORGIA TECHNICAL COLLEGE*, Americus Campus Library, Hicks Hall, Rm 115, 900 S Georgia Tech Pkwy, 31709. Tel: 229-931-2562. FAX: 229-931-2732. Web Site: www.southgatech.edu. *Dir,* Jerry Stovall; E-mail: jstovall@southgatech.edu; Staff 2 (MLS 1, Non-MLS 1)
Founded 1948. Enrl 1,400; Highest Degree: Associate
Library Holdings: e-journals 27,000; Bk Vols 13,000; Per Subs 105
Automation Activity & Vendor Info: (Cataloging) TLC (The Library Corporation); (Circulation) TLC (The Library Corporation); (OPAC) TLC (The Library Corporation)
Wireless access
Partic in Georgia Library Learning Online
Open Mon-Thurs 7:30am-8pm, Fri 8-Noon

ATHENS

SR ATHENS FIRST UNITED METHODIST CHURCH LIBRARY*, 327 N Lumpkin St, 30601. SAN 303-2604. Tel: 706-543-1442. Web Site: athensfirstumc.org. *Library Contact,* Cindy Kuhlman; E-mail: kuhlman.gc@gmail.com
Library Holdings: AV Mats 80; Bk Vols 2,100; Spec Interest Per Sub 3
Special Collections: UMW Holdings
Subject Interests: Local authors

P ATHENS REGIONAL LIBRARY SYSTEM*, Athens-Clarke County Library, 2025 Baxter St, 30606-6331. SAN 338-277X. Tel: 706-613-3650. E-mail: contact_us@arlsmail.org. Web Site: www.athenslibrary.org/athens. *Dir,* Valerie Bell; E-mail: vbell@athenslibrary.org; *Asst to the Dir,* Lisa Moncrief; Tel: 706-613-3650, Ext 351, E-mail: lmoncrief@athenslibrary.org; *Pub Info Officer,* Rhiannon Eades; E-mail: reades@athenslibrary.org
Founded 1936. Pop 228,644; Circ 1,215,173
Special Collections: County Library; Genealogy & Georgia; Genealogy, Daughters of American Revolution
Subject Interests: Local hist, State hist
Wireless access
Partic in GOLD Resource Sharing Network for Georgia's Libraries; OCLC Online Computer Library Center, Inc; Public Information Network for Electronic Services
Special Services for the Deaf - Bks on deafness & sign lang; Closed caption videos; High interest/low vocabulary bks
Special Services for the Blind - Aids for in-house use; Computer with voice synthesizer for visually impaired persons
Friends of the Library Group
Branches: 10
BIBLIOTECA CENTRO EDUCATIVO DE LA COMMUNIDAD DE PINEWOODS (PINEWOODS LIBRARY & LEARNING CENTER), North Lot F-12, 1465 US Hwy 29 N, 30601-1103. (Mail add: 2025 Baxter St, 30606). Tel: 706-613-3708. FAX: 706-613-3708. Web Site: www.athenslibrary.org/pinewoods. *Br Mgr,* Aida Quinones
Founded 2005
Open Mon-Thurs 1-8, Fri 11-1
BOGART BRANCH, 200 S Burson Ave, Bogart, 30622. (Mail add: PO Box 218, Bogart, 30622), SAN 338-280X. Tel: 770-725-9443. Web Site: www.athenslibrary.org/bogart. *Br Mgr,* Donna Butler
Founded 1940
Open Mon, Wed, Fri & Sat 10-6, Tues & Thurs 12-8
Friends of the Library Group
EAST ATHENS RESOURCE CENTER, East Athens Community Ctr, 3rd Flr, 400 McKinley Dr, 30601. Tel: 706-613-3657. Reference Tel: 706-613-3650, Ext 356. Web Site: www.athenslibrary.org/eastathens. *Br Mgr,* Tonya Sands
Founded 1998
Open Mon-Thurs 2-6
LAVONIA-CARNEGIE BRANCH, 28 Hartwell Rd, Lavonia, 30553. (Mail add: PO Box 237, Lavonia, 30553-0237), SAN 338-2869. Tel: 706-356-4307. Information Services Tel: 706-769-3950. FAX: 706-356-4307. Web Site: www.athenslibrary.org/lavonia. *Br Mgr,* Maggie West
Founded 1904
Open Mon & Wed 10-8, Tues & Fri 10-6, Sat 10-2
Friends of the Library Group
LAY PARK RESOURCE CENTER, Lay Park Community Ctr, 3rd Flr, 297 Hoyt St, 30601. (Mail add: 2025 Baxter St, 30606). Tel: 706-613-3667. FAX: 706-613-3667. Web Site: www.athenslibrary.org/laypark. *Br Mgr,* Dorothy Harrison
Founded 1998
Open Mon-Fri 2-6
MADISON COUNTY BRANCH, 1315 Hwy 98 W, Danielsville, 30633. (Mail add: PO Box 38, Danielsville, 30633-0038), SAN 338-2893. Tel: 706-795-5597. FAX: 706-795-0830. Web Site: www.athenslibrary.org/madison. *Br Mgr,* Jennifer Ivey
Founded 1935
Automation Activity & Vendor Info: (Acquisitions) Baker & Taylor; (Cataloging) Baker & Taylor; (Circulation) Evergreen; (OPAC) Evergreen
Function: Art exhibits, Audiobks via web, Bks on cassette, Bks on CD, Children's prog, Computer training, Computers for patron use, Digital talking bks, Electronic databases & coll, Free DVD rentals, Holiday prog, Home delivery & serv to seniorr ctr & nursing homes, ILL available, Large print keyboards, Music CDs, Online cat, OverDrive digital audio bks, Photocopying/Printing, Prog for children & young adult, Scanner, Senior computer classes, Story hour, Summer reading prog, Tax forms, Teen prog, Telephone ref, VHS videos, Wheelchair accessible
Open Mon, Wed, Fri & Sat 10-6, Tues & Thurs 10-8, Sun 2-6
Friends of the Library Group
OCONEE COUNTY-WATKINSVILLE BRANCH, 1080 Experiment Station Rd, Watkinsville, 30677. (Mail add: PO Box 837, Watkinsville, 30677-0019), SAN 338-2923. Tel: 706-769-3950. FAX: 706-769-3952. Web Site: www.athenslibrary.org/oconee. *Br Mgr,* Cara Karnes; Tel: 706-769-3951
Founded 1940
Open Mon & Wed 10-9, Tues, Thurs, Fri & Sat 10-6, Sun 2-6
Friends of the Library Group
OGLETHORPE COUNTY BRANCH, 858 Athens Rd, Hwy 78, Lexington, 30648. (Mail add: PO Box 100, Lexington, 30648-0100), SAN 338-2958. Tel: 706-743-8817. FAX: 706-743-8817. Web Site: www.athenslibrary.org/oglethorpe. *Br Mgr,* Austin Jenkins

Founded 1940
Open Mon, Wed & Thurs 10-6, Tues 10-8, Fri & Sat 10-2
Friends of the Library Group
ROYSTON BRANCH, 634 Franklin Springs St, Royston, 30662, SAN 338-2982. Tel: 706-245-6748. Web Site: www.athenslibrary.org/royston. *Br Mgr,* Maggie West
Founded 1920
Open Mon & Fri 10-6, Tues & Thurs 10-8, Sat 10-2
Friends of the Library Group
WINTERVILLE BRANCH, 115 Marigold Lane, Winterville, 30683. (Mail add: PO Box 89, Winterville, 30683-0089), SAN 338-3016. Tel: 706-742-7735. FAX: 706-742-7735. Web Site: www.athenslibrary.org/winterville. *Br Mgr,* Deirdre Murray
Founded 1974
Open Mon, Tues & Thurs 3-7, Wed 9-12, Sat 10-2
Friends of the Library Group

J ATHENS TECHNICAL COLLEGE LIBRARY*, 800 US Hwy 29 N, 30601-1500. SAN 323-5513. Tel: 706-355-5020. Interlibrary Loan Service Tel: 706-355-5164. Administration Tel: 706-355-5019. FAX: 706-355-5162. E-mail: alibrary@athenstech.edu, elibrary@athenstech.edu. Web Site: library.athenstech.edu. *Dir, Libr Serv,* Carol Stanley; *Librn,* Qian Fang; E-mail: qfang@athenstech.edu; Staff 5 (MLS 3, Non-MLS 2)
Founded 1984. Enrl 9,000; Fac 150; Highest Degree: Associate
Library Holdings: AV Mats 4,250; e-books 120,000; Electronic Media & Resources 310; Bk Titles 37,841; Per Subs 512; Videos 10,000
Special Collections: Allied Health Coll; Technical Education
Automation Activity & Vendor Info: (Acquisitions) SirsiDynix; (Cataloging) SirsiDynix; (Circulation) SirsiDynix; (Discovery) EBSCO Discovery Service; (OPAC) SirsiDynix; (Serials) SirsiDynix
Wireless access
Function: Audio & video playback equip for onsite use, CD-ROM, Distance learning, Electronic databases & coll, Health sci info serv, ILL available, Mail & tel request accepted, Orientations, Photocopying/Printing, Ref serv available, Spoken cassettes & CDs, VHS videos, Wheelchair accessible
Partic in GOLD Resource Sharing Network for Georgia's Libraries
Open Mon-Thurs 7:30am-10pm, Fri & Sat 7:30-4
Restriction: Authorized personnel only
Departmental Libraries:
ELBERT COUNTY CAMPUS, 1317 Athens Hwy, Elberton, 30635, SAN 377-7863. Tel: 706-213-2116. FAX: 706-213-2149. *Br Librn, Cat, ILL,* Carol Stanley; Staff 1 (MLS 1)
Founded 1997
Automation Activity & Vendor Info: (Cataloging) OCLC; (ILL) OCLC; (Serials) EBSCO Online
Function: Audio & video playback equip for onsite use, CD-ROM, Distance learning, Electronic databases & coll, Homebound delivery serv, ILL available, Orientations, Photocopying/Printing, Ref serv available, Telephone ref, VHS videos, Wheelchair accessible
Open Mon-Thurs 7:30am-10pm, Fri 7:30-4
GREENE COUNTY CAMPUS, 1051 Athens Tech Dr, Greensboro, 30642. Tel: 706-453-0536. *Support Serv Coordr,* Marjorie Heimer
Automation Activity & Vendor Info: (Cataloging) OCLC; (ILL) OCLC; (Serials) EBSCO Online
Function: Audio & video playback equip for onsite use, CD-ROM, Distance learning, Electronic databases & coll, Homebound delivery serv, ILL available, Orientations, Photocopying/Printing, Ref serv available, Telephone ref, VHS videos, Wheelchair accessible
Open Mon-Thurs 7:30am-10pm, Fri 7:30-4
WALTON COUNTY CAMPUS, 212 Bryant Rd, Monroe, 30648. Tel: 770-207-3126. *Support Serv Coordr,* Marjorie Heimer
Automation Activity & Vendor Info: (Cataloging) OCLC; (ILL) OCLC; (Serials) EBSCO Online
Function: Audio & video playback equip for onsite use, CD-ROM, Distance learning, Electronic databases & coll, Homebound delivery serv, ILL available, Orientations, Photocopying/Printing, Ref serv available, Telephone ref, VHS videos, Wheelchair accessible
Open Mon-Thurs 7:30am-10pm, Fri 7:30-4

UNIVERSITY OF GEORGIA
CL ALEXANDER CAMPBELL KING LAW LIBRARY*, 225 Herty Dr, 30602-6018, SAN 338-3105. Tel: 706-542-1922. Interlibrary Loan Service Tel: 706-542-6670. Reference Tel: 706-542-6591. Administration Tel: 706-542-8480. FAX: 706-542-5001. Web Site: www.law.uga.edu/library. *Dir,* Carol A Watson; E-mail: cwatson@uga.edu; *Adminr,* Deborah Baker; E-mail: debbb@uga.edu; *Acq Librn,* Wendy Moore; Tel: 706-542-5081, E-mail: wemoore@uga.edu; *Cat Serv Librn,* Suzanne R Graham; Tel: 706-542-5082, Fax: 706-542-5130, E-mail: srgraham@uga.edu; *Copyright Librn, Research Librn,* Stephen Wolfson; E-mail: stephen.wolfson@uga.edu; *Fac Serv Librn,* Thomas J Striepe; Tel: 706-542-5077, E-mail: tstriepe@uga.edu; *Foreign & Intl Law Librn,* Anne E Burnett; Tel: 702-542-5298; *IT Librn,* Jason Tubinis; Tel: 706-542-7365; *Metadata Librn,* Rachel Evans; E-mail: rsevans@uga.edu; *Spec Coll Librn,* Sharon A Bradley; Tel: 706-542-5083, E-mail: bradleys@uga.edu; *Student Serv Librn,* Maureen Cahill; Tel: 706-542-3825, E-mail: mcahill@uga.edu; *Access Serv Mgr,* Marie Mize; E-mail: mmize@uga.edu; *Coll Serv Mgr,* David Rutland; E-mail: drutlan@uga.edu; *Access Serv, Libr Assoc,* Szilvia Somodi; E-mail: somodi@uga.edu; Staff 25 (MLS 8, Non-MLS 17)
Founded 1859. Enrl 675; Fac 40
Special Collections: The Louis B Sohn Library on International Studies
Subject Interests: Intl law
Automation Activity & Vendor Info: (Acquisitions) Innovative Interfaces, Inc; (Cataloging) Innovative Interfaces, Inc; (Circulation) Innovative Interfaces, Inc; (Course Reserve) Innovative Interfaces, Inc; (ILL) Innovative Interfaces, Inc; (Media Booking) Innovative Interfaces, Inc; (Serials) Innovative Interfaces, Inc
Function: Res libr
Partic in LYRASIS

C OWENS LIBRARY*, School of Environmental Design, G14 Caldwell Hall, 30602. (Mail add: College of Environment & Design, 609 Caldwell Hall, 30602-1845), SAN 377-6220. Tel: 706-542-8292. FAX: 706-542-4485. Web Site: www.sed.uga.edu/facilities/owenslibrary.htm. *Dir,* Rene D Shoemaker, IV; E-mail: rds@uga.edu; Staff 1 (MLS 1)
Library Holdings: Bk Vols 6,000
Subject Interests: Landscape archit, Planning
Automation Activity & Vendor Info: (Cataloging) Inmagic, Inc.; (Circulation) Inmagic, Inc.; (Serials) Inmagic, Inc.
Open Mon-Fri 8:30-6

C UNIVERSITY OF GEORGIA LIBRARIES*, 320 S Jackson St, 30602-1641. SAN 338-3075. Tel: 706-542-3251. Circulation Tel: 706-542-3256. Interlibrary Loan Service Tel: 706-542-0643. Administration Tel: 706-542-0621. Web Site: www.libs.uga.edu. *Assoc Provost, Univ Librn,* Toby Graham; E-mail: tgraham@uga.edu; *Head, Coll Develop,* Nan McMurry; Tel: 706-542-8474, E-mail: nmcmurry@uga.edu; Staff 261 (MLS 75, Non-MLS 186)
Founded 1785. Enrl 33,418; Fac 1,832; Highest Degree: Doctorate
Library Holdings: Bk Vols 4,028,611; Per Subs 67,268
Special Collections: Hargrett Rare Book & Manuscript Library; Richard B Russell Library for Political Research & Studies; Walter J Brown Media Archives & Peabody Awards Coll. State Document Depository; UN Document Depository; US Document Depository
Subject Interests: Ecology, Intl relations, Law, Math, Med, Photog
Automation Activity & Vendor Info: (Acquisitions) Ex Libris Group; (Cataloging) Ex Libris Group; (Circulation) Ex Libris Group; (Course Reserve) Ex Libris Group; (ILL) Ex Libris Group; (Media Booking) Ex Libris Group; (OPAC) Ex Libris Group; (Serials) Ex Libris Group
Wireless access
Function: Res libr
Partic in Association of Southeastern Research Libraries; Center for Research Libraries; National Network of Libraries of Medicine Region 2
Open Mon-Thurs 7:30am-2am, Fri 7:30am-9pm, Sat 10-7, Sun 1pm-2am
Departmental Libraries:
ART, Main Art Bldg, Rm N201, Lamar Dodd School of Art, 30602. Tel: 706-542-2712. E-mail: artlibrary@uga.edu. Web Site: art.uga.edu/school/facilities/art-library. *Art Librn,* Lindsey Reynolds; E-mail: lwreyn@uga.edu
Special Collections: Dodd Gallery Publications
Function: Computers for patron use, Scanner, Study rm
CARNEGIE LIBRARY, 101 Fox Rd, 30602. Tel: 706-713-2724. E-mail: carnegielibrary@uga.edu. Web Site: www.libs.uga.edu/carnegie. *Libr Coord,* Scott Blackwell; E-mail: sblackwe@uga.edu
Founded 1910
Function: Computers for patron use, Photocopying/Printing, Scanner
Open Mon-Thurs 9am-10pm, Sun 2-10; Mon-Fri 9-6 (Summer)
CURRICULUM MATERIALS, 207 Aderhold Hall, 110 Carlton St, 30602. Tel: 706-542-2957. FAX: 706-583-0764. E-mail: cml@uga.edu. Web Site: www.libs.uga.edu/cml. *Librn,* Carla Wilson Buss; E-mail: cbuss@uga.edu; *Coordr,* Jason Matherly; E-mail: matherly@uga.edu
Special Collections: Juvenile Literature Coll; K-12 Curriculum Materials; Science Education Kits; The Aaron Coll
Open Mon-Fri 8-5
MAP & GOVERNMENT INFORMATION, 320 S Jackson St, 30602. Tel: 706-542-0690. E-mail: mapsinfo@uga.edu. Web Site: www.libs.uga.edu/magil. *Head of Libr,* Valerie Glenn; Tel: 706-542-0664, E-mail: valerie.glenn@uga.edu; *Libr Assoc II, Pub Serv, Student Asst Supvr,* Rebecca Hartle; Tel: 706-542-0662, E-mail: rebecca.hartle@uga.edu; *Govt Doc, Libr Assoc,* Taylor Ross; Tel: 706-542-0489, E-mail: taylor.ross@uga.edu
Founded 2012
Special Collections: State Document Depository; US Document Depository
Function: Ref & res, Scanner
Open Mon-Fri 10-3 or by appointment
MUSIC, School of Music, Rm 250, 250 River Rd, 30602. Tel: 706-542-2712. E-mail: muslib@uga.edu. Web Site: www.libs.uga.edu/music. *Librn III,* Guy Leach; E-mail: gleach@uga.edu;

Circ Assoc, Library Reserve, Elizabeth Durusau; E-mail: edurusau@uga.edu
Library Holdings: AV Mats 45,000; Music Scores 75,000; Bk Titles 40,000; Per Subs 525
Open Mon-Thurs 8am-10pm, Fri 8-5, Sun 2pm-10pm

SCIENCE, Boyd Graduate Studies Bldg, 210 D W Brooks Dr, 30602. Tel: 706-542-0698. Circulation Tel: 706-542-4535. E-mail: science@uga.edu. Web Site: www.libs.uga.edu/science. *Head, Scholarly Communications,* Mariann Samuel; E-mail: mariann@uga.edu; *Science Reference Librn,* Cynthia Prosser; E-mail: cprosser@uga.edu; *Sci Res & Instruction Librn,* Kelsey Forester; E-mail: kelsey.forester@uga.edu; *Sci Res & Instruction Librn,* Colleen Gardina; E-mail: colleen.gardina@uga.edu; *Instruction Coordr, Sci Res & Instruction Librn,* Ian Thomas; E-mail: ithomas@uga.edu
Subject Interests: Life sci, Med sci, Natural sci, Tech
Function: Computers for patron use
Open Mon-Thurs 7:30am-2am, Fri 7:30am-9pm, Sat 10-7, Sun 1pm-1am; Mon-Thurs 7:30am-10pm, Fri 7:30-6, Sat 10-6, Sun 1-10 (Summer)

SKIDAWAY INSTITUTE OF OCEANOGRAPHY LIBRARY
See Separate Entry in Savannah

SPECIAL COLLECTIONS, Richard B Russell Bldg, 300 S Hull St, 30602. Tel: 706-542-7123. FAX: 706-542-0672. E-mail: sclib@uga.edu. Web Site: www.libs.uga.edu/scl. *Cat,* Jamie Jedlicka; E-mail: jmej@uga.edu; *Cat,* Erin Leach; E-mail: eleach@uga.edu
Special Collections: Hargrett Rare Book & Manuscript Library; Richard B Russell Library for Political Research & Studies; Walter J Brown Media Archives & Peabody Awards Coll
Open Mon, Wed & Fri 8-5, Tues & Thurs 8-7

ATLANTA

C ACA LIBRARY OF SAVANNAH COLLEGE OF ART & DESIGN*, 1600 Peachtree St NW, 30309. SAN 303-2647. Tel: 404-253-3196. E-mail: ref_atl@scad.edu. Web Site: library.scad.edu. *Dir,* Teresa Burk; Staff 7 (MLS 5, Non-MLS 2)
Founded 1905. Enrl 2,000; Highest Degree: Master
Library Holdings: Bk Vols 67,000; Per Subs 175
Special Collections: Artists' Books Coll; Rare Book Coll
Subject Interests: Animation, Art, Art hist, Design, Drawing, Film, Liberal arts, Painting, Photog, Printmaking, Sculpture, Video
Automation Activity & Vendor Info: (Cataloging) Innovative Interfaces, Inc; (Circulation) Innovative Interfaces, Inc; (Course Reserve) Innovative Interfaces, Inc; (OPAC) Innovative Interfaces, Inc; (Serials) Innovative Interfaces, Inc
Wireless access
Function: Art exhibits, ILL available, Workshops
Partic in Atlanta Regional Council for Higher Education
Restriction: External users must contact libr

AMERICAN INTERCONTINENTAL UNIVERSITY

C ATLANTA CAMPUS LIBRARY*, 500 Embassy Row, 6600 Peachtree-Dunwoody Rd, 30328. Tel: 404-965-6533. E-mail: atllib@aiuniv.edu. *Campus Librn,* Jessica Epstein; Tel: 404-965-6527, E-mail: jepstein@aiuniv.edu; Staff 2 (MLS 2)
Founded 1977. Enrl 1,200; Fac 21; Highest Degree: Master
Library Holdings: DVDs 2,500; Bk Vols 6,500; Per Subs 85
Automation Activity & Vendor Info: (Cataloging) TLC (The Library Corporation); (Circulation) TLC (The Library Corporation); (OPAC) TLC (The Library Corporation)
Partic in Georgia Library Learning Online
Open Mon-Thurs 7am-10pm, Fri 7-5, Sat 9-4

C DUNWOODY CAMPUS-MEDIA CENTER*, 6600 Peachtree-Dunwoody Rd, 500 Embassy Row, 30328. Tel: 404-965-6533. Web Site: www.aiuniv.edu. *Dir, IT,* Rahem Gaines; Staff 2 (MLS 2)
Founded 1998. Highest Degree: Master
Library Holdings: e-books 22,000; Bk Vols 3,700; Per Subs 56; Videos 160
Special Collections: Global Culture Coll
Subject Interests: Bus, Criminal justice, Game design, Info tech, Visual communications
Automation Activity & Vendor Info: (Cataloging) TLC (The Library Corporation); (Circulation) TLC (The Library Corporation); (OPAC) TLC (The Library Corporation)
Partic in Georgia Library Learning Online
Open Mon-Thurs 7:30am-10pm, Fri & Sat 9-3

C ART INSTITUTE OF ATLANTA LIBRARY*, 6600 Peachtree-Dunwoody Rd, 100 Embassy Row, 30328-1635. Tel: 770-689-4885. FAX: 770-730-8767. E-mail: ailibrary@aii.edu. Web Site: www.artinstitutes.edu. *Campus Librn,* Dr Michael W Wilson; E-mail: miwilson@aii.edu; Staff 1 (MLS 1)
Founded 1949. Highest Degree: Bachelor
Library Holdings: CDs 1,534; DVDs 3,332; Electronic Media & Resources 54; Bk Vols 52,127; Per Subs 185; Videos 325
Subject Interests: Culinary arts, Design, Digital film, Fashion, Media arts
Automation Activity & Vendor Info: (Cataloging) Ex Libris Group; (Circulation) Ex Libris Group; (ILL) OCLC WorldShare Interlibrary Loan; (OPAC) Ex Libris Group
Wireless access
Open Mon-Thurs 8am-9pm, Fri 8-5, Sat 9-4
Restriction: Borrowing privileges limited to fac & registered students

S ATLANTA BOTANICAL GARDEN, Sheffield Botanical Library & Orchid Reference Library, 1345 Piedmont Ave NE, 30309-3366. SAN 374-5597. Tel: 404-591-1546, 404-591-1725. FAX: 404-876-7472. E-mail: info@atlantabg.org. Web Site: www.atlantabg.org. *Librn,* Dr Clara R Williams; E-mail: cwilliams@atlantabg.org; Staff 1 (MLS 1)
Founded 1985
Library Holdings: Bk Vols 11,900; Per Subs 125
Subject Interests: Botany, Hort
Automation Activity & Vendor Info: (Cataloging) TLC (The Library Corporation); (OPAC) TLC (The Library Corporation)
Function: 24/7 Online cat, Archival coll, Children's prog, Computers for patron use, For res purposes, Magazines, Mail & tel request accepted, Online cat, Outreach serv, Prog for children & young adult, Ref & res, Ref serv available, Res assist avail, Res libr, Story hour, Wheelchair accessible
Partic in Council on Botanical & Horticultural Libraries, Inc
Restriction: Authorized patrons, Authorized personnel only, Authorized scholars by appt, Badge access after hrs, By permission only, Circ limited, Circulates for staff only, Employees only, External users must contact libr, Non-circulating of rare bks, Non-circulating to the pub, Open by appt only, Open to authorized patrons, Open to dept staff only, Open to employees & special libr, Open to others by appt, Open to researchers by request

P ATLANTA-FULTON PUBLIC LIBRARY SYSTEM*, Central Library & Library System Headquarters, One Margaret Mitchell Sq, 30303-1089. SAN 338-313X. Tel: 404-612-3189. Reference Tel: 404-730-4636. FAX: 404-612-0644. Web Site: www.afpls.org. *Dir,* Dr Gabriel Morley; *Admin Coordr,* Zenobia Claxton; E-mail: zenobia.claxton@fultoncountyga.gov; Staff 454 (MLS 144, Non-MLS 310)
Founded 1902. Pop 969,033; Circ 2,534,636
Library Holdings: Bk Titles 600,000; Bk Vols 2,219,609; Per Subs 6,000
Special Collections: Coll on the History of Atlanta, Georgia & the Southeast; Genealogy Coll; Margaret Mitchell Exhibit. Oral History; US Document Depository
Automation Activity & Vendor Info: (Acquisitions) SirsiDynix; (Cataloging) SirsiDynix; (Circulation) SirsiDynix; (Course Reserve) SirsiDynix; (ILL) OCLC WorldShare Interlibrary Loan; (OPAC) SirsiDynix; (Serials) SirsiDynix
Wireless access
Publications: Access (Newsletter)
Partic in National Network of Libraries of Medicine Region 2
Special Services for the Deaf - Bks on deafness & sign lang; Captioned film dep; High interest/low vocabulary bks; Spec interest per; TTY equip
Special Services for the Blind - Reader equip
Closed for Renovations until 2020
Friends of the Library Group
Branches: 33

ADAMS PARK BRANCH, 2231 Campbellton Rd SW, 30311, SAN 338-3164. Tel: 404-752-8763. FAX: 404-752-8765. Web Site: www.afplweb.com/adams-park-branch.
Library Holdings: Bk Vols 39,704
Closed for renovations 2019-
Friends of the Library Group

ADAMSVILLE-COLLIER HEIGHTS BRANCH, 3424 Martin Luther King Jr Dr, 30331, SAN 338-3288. Tel: 404-699-4206. FAX: 404-699-6380. Web Site: www.afplweb.com/adamsville-collier-branch. *Br Mgr,* Gabrielle Taylor; *Ch,* Emma Laster; E-mail: emma.laster@fultoncountyga.gov
Library Holdings: Bk Vols 49,327
Closed for renovations August 2019-
Friends of the Library Group

ALPHARETTA BRANCH, Ten Park Plaza, Alpharetta, 30009, SAN 338-3199. Tel: 404-613-6735. FAX: 770-740-2427. Web Site: www.afpls.org/alpharetta-branch. *Br Mgr,* Jeffrey Stinson; *Asst Br Mgr,* Michael Salpeter
Library Holdings: Bk Vols 78,562
Open Mon & Thurs 10-8, Tues, Wed, Fri & Sat 10-6, Sun 2-6
Friends of the Library Group

AUBURN AVENUE RESEARCH LIBRARY ON AFRICAN-AMERICAN CULTURE & HISTORY, 101 Auburn Ave NE, 30303-2503, SAN 375-1465. Tel: 404-613-4001. Reference Tel: 404-613-4101. FAX: 404-730-5879. Web Site: afpls.org/aarl. *Sr Librn,* Okezie Amalaha; Tel: 404-730-4001, Ext 207, E-mail: okezie.amalaha@fultoncountyga.gov; *Mgr, Sr Librn,* Morris Gardner; E-mail: morris.gardner@fultoncountyga.gov; *Sr Librn,* Charmaine Johnson; Tel: 407-730-4001, Ext 104, E-mail: charmaine.johnson@fultoncountyga.gov; *Sr Librn,* Gloria Mims; Tel: 404-730-4001, Ext 108, E-mail: gloria.mims@fultoncountyga.gov; *Librn,* Eleanor Hunter; Tel: 404-730-4001, Ext 107, E-mail: eleanor.hunter@fultoncountyga.gov; *Libr Assoc,* Angela Ahmad; Tel: 404-730-4001, Ext 308, E-mail:

angela.ahmad@fultoncountyg; *Libr Assoc,* Anita Martin; E-mail: anita.martin@fultoncountyga.gov; *Libr Assoc,* Alvin R Robinson; *Libr Assoc,* Marquita Gooch; E-mail: marquita.gooch@fultoncountyga.gov; *Rec Doc Spec,* Jerome Huff; E-mail: jerome.huff@fultoncountyga.gov
Founded 1994
Library Holdings: Bk Vols 54,457
Special Collections: Ambassador Andrew Young Papers; Hosea Williams Coll; Weems Photographic Coll
Function: For res purposes
Open Mon & Fri 12-6, Tues & Sat 10-6, Wed & Thurs 12-8, Sun 2-6
Restriction: Non-circulating coll
Friends of the Library Group

BUCKHEAD BRANCH, 269 Buckhead Ave NE, 30305, SAN 338-361X. Tel: 404-814-3500. FAX: 404-814-3503. Web Site: www.afplweb.com/buckhead-branch. *Br Mgr,* Jane Taylor; *Asst Br Mgr, Sr Ref Librn,* Angela Simpson; E-mail: simpson.angela1@fultoncountyga.gov
Library Holdings: Bk Vols 113,608
Closed for renovations 2019-
Friends of the Library Group

CLEVELAND AVENUE BRANCH, 47 Cleveland Ave SW, 30315, SAN 373-9333. Tel: 404-762-4116. FAX: 404-762-4118. Web Site: www.afplweb.com/cleveland-ave-branch. *Br Mgr,* Gloria Dennis; E-mail: gloria.dennis@fultoncountyga.gov; *Ch,* Vanessa Slaton; E-mail: vanessa.slaton@fultoncountyga.gov
Library Holdings: Bk Vols 56,238
Closed for renovations 2019-
Friends of the Library Group

COLLEGE PARK BRANCH, 3647 Main St, College Park, 30337, SAN 338-3253. Tel: 404-762-4060. FAX: 404-762-4062. Web Site: www.afplweb.com/college-park-branch. *Br Mgr,* Bonita McZorn; E-mail: bonita.mczorn@fultoncountyga.gov; *Ch,* Kimara Mason
Closed for renovations 2019-
Friends of the Library Group

GLADYS S DENNARD LIBRARY AT SOUTH FULTON, 4055 Flat Shoals Rd, Union City, 30291-1590, SAN 373-9341. Tel: 770-306-3092. FAX: 770-306-3127. Web Site: afplweb.com/south-fulton-branch6. *Actg Br Mgr,* David Thrash; E-mail: david.thrash@fultoncountyga.gov; *Ch,* Cassie Gwyn; E-mail: cassie.gwyn@fultoncountyga.gov; *Ref Librn,* Dinah Baldwin; E-mail: dinah.baldwin@fultoncountyga.gov; *Ref Librn,* Elizabeth Costello; E-mail: elizabeth.costello@fultoncountyga.gov
Library Holdings: Bk Vols 100,751
Open Mon, Wed, Fri & Sat 10-6, Tues & Thurs 10-8, Sun 2-6
Friends of the Library Group

DOGWOOD BRANCH, 1838 Donald L Hollowell Pkwy NW, 30318, SAN 338-3342. Tel: 404-612-3900. FAX: 404-792-4963. Web Site: www.afplweb.com/dogwood-branch. *Librn,* Debra Perry; E-mail: debra.perry@fultoncountyga.gov; *Ch,* Vincent Chukumah; E-mail: vincent.chukumah@fultoncountyga.gov
Library Holdings: Bk Vols 39,350
Open Mon, Fri & Sat 12-6, Tues 10-8, Wed & Thurs 10-6
Friends of the Library Group

EAST ATLANTA BRANCH, 400 Flat Shoals Ave SE, 30316, SAN 338-3407. Tel: 404-730-5438. FAX: 404-730-5436. Web Site: www.afplweb.com/east-atlanta-branch. *Br Mgr,* Shannon Duffy; *Asst Br Mgr, Ch,* Oscar Gittemeier
Library Holdings: Bk Vols 38,621
Open Mon 10-8, Tues-Thurs & Sat 10-6, Fri 12-6
Friends of the Library Group

EAST POINT BRANCH, 2757 Main St, East Point, 30344, SAN 376-8546. Tel: 404-613-1050. FAX: 404-762-4844. Web Site: www.afplweb.com/east-point-branch. *Br Mgr,* Michael Hickman; E-mail: michael.hickman@fultoncountyga.gov; *Asst Br Mgr,* Derek Wilson; *Ch,* Kaleema Abdurrahman
Library Holdings: Bk Vols 68,331
Open Mon & Thurs 10-8, Tues, Wed & Sat 10-6, Fri 12-6, Sun 2-6
Friends of the Library Group

EAST ROSWELL BRANCH, 2301 Holcomb Bridge Rd, Roswell, 30076. Tel: 404-613-4050. *Br Mgr,* Swalena Griffin
Library Holdings: Bk Vols 39,848
Open Mon & Wed 10-8, Tues, Thurs & Sat 10-6, Fri 12-6, Sun 2-6
Friends of the Library Group

FAIRBURN BRANCH, 60 Valley View Dr, Fairburn, 30213, SAN 338-358X. Tel: 404-613-5750. FAX: 770-306-3140. Web Site: afpls.org/fairburn-branch. *Br Mgr,* Eugene Haston; E-mail: eugene.haston@fultoncountyga.gov; *Asst Br Mgr, Ch,* Evette Bridges; E-mail: evette.bridges@fultoncountyga.gov
Library Holdings: Bk Vols 38,371
Open Mon, Wed & Thurs 10-6, Tues 10-8, Fri & Sat 12-6

JOAN P GARDNER LIBRARY, 980 Ponce de Leon Ave NE, 30306, SAN 338-3555. Tel: 404-885-7820. FAX: 404-885-7822. Web Site: www.afplweb.com/ponce-branch6. *Youth/Young Adult Librn,* Madigan McGillicuddy
Library Holdings: Bk Vols 86,171
Open Mon, Thurs & Sat 10-6, Tues & Wed 10-8, Fri 12-6, Sun 2-6

HAPEVILLE BRANCH, 525 King Arnold St, Hapeville, 30354, SAN 338-3520. Tel: 404-762-4065. FAX: 404-762-4067. Web Site: www.afplweb.com/hapeville-branch. *Br Mgr,* Marquita Washington; E-mail: marquita.washington@fultoncountyga.gov; *Ch,* Andrea Robinson
Library Holdings: Bk Vols 32,246
Open Mon 10-7, Tues-Thurs 10-6, Fri & Sat 12-6
Friends of the Library Group

MARTIN LUTHER KING JR BRANCH, 409 John Wesley Dobbs Ave, 30312-1342, SAN 338-3709. Tel: 404-730-1185. FAX: 404-893-6858. Web Site: www.afplweb.com/mlk-branch. *Br Mgr,* Denise Barbour; E-mail: denise.barbour@fultoncountyga.gov
Library Holdings: Bk Vols 24,764
Function: Children's prog, Computer training, Computers for patron use, Homework prog, Music CDs, Prog for adults, VHS videos
Open Mon-Thurs 10-6, Fri & Sat 12-6

KIRKWOOD BRANCH, 11 Kirkwood Rd SE, 30317, SAN 338-3679. Tel: 404-613-7200. FAX: 404-373-5024. Web Site: www.afplweb.com/kirkwood-branch. *Ch,* Leilani McWilliams; E-mail: leilani.mcwilliams@fultoncountyga.gov
Library Holdings: Bk Vols 31,024
Open Mon 10-8, Tues-Thurs 10-6, Fri & Sat 12-6
Friends of the Library Group

EVELYN G LOWERY LIBRARY AT SOUTHWEST, 3665 Cascade Rd SW, 30331, SAN 370-4777. Tel: 404-699-6363. FAX: 404-699-6381. Web Site: www.afpls.org/southwest-branch6. *Br Mgr,* Eugene Haston; E-mail: eugene.haston@fultoncountyga.gov; *Asst Mgr,* Darlene McDade; E-mail: darlene.mcdade@fultoncountyga.gov; *Ch,* Teffany Edmondson; E-mail: teffany.edmondson@fultoncountyga.gov; *Ch,* Eileen Slough; E-mail: eileen.slough@fultoncountyga.gov; *Ref Librn,* Malik Grohse; E-mail: malik.grohse@fultoncountyga.gov; *Ref Librn,* Valerie Lewis; E-mail: valeire.lewis@fultoncountyga.gov; *Ref Librn,* Martaire Walker; E-mail: martaire.walker@fultoncountyga.gov; *YA Serv,* William Hutchinson, III; E-mail: william.hutchinson@fultoncountyga.gov
Library Holdings: Bk Vols 133,198
Open Mon & Tues 10-8, Wed-Sat 10-6, Sun 2-6
Friends of the Library Group

MECHANICSVILLE BRANCH, 400 Formwalt St SW, 30312, SAN 338-3377. Tel: 404-730-4779. FAX: 404-730-4778. Web Site: www.afplweb.com/mechanicsville-branch. *Br Mgr,* David Thrash; *Ch,* Denise Barbour
Library Holdings: Bk Vols 36,352
Closed for renovations 2019-
Friends of the Library Group

METROPOLITAN BRANCH, 1332 Metropolitan Pkwy, 30310. Tel: 404-613-5722. Web Site: www.afpls.org/metropolitan-branch6.
Open Mon & Wed 10-8, Tues & Thurs-Sat 10-6, Sun 2-6

MILTON BRANCH, 855 Mayfield Rd, Milton, 30009. Tel: 404-613-4402. Web Site: www.afpls.org/locations/locations2/1610-milton-branch.
Open Mon & Thurs-Sat 10-6, Tues & Wed 10-8, Sun 2-6

NORTHEAST/SPRUILL OAKS BRANCH, 9560 Spruill Rd, Johns Creek, 30022. Tel: 770-360-8820. Web Site: www.afpls.org/northeast-spruill-oaks-branch.
Closed for renovations 2019-

NORTHSIDE BRANCH, 3295 Northside Pkwy NW, 30327, SAN 338-3768. Tel: 404-814-3508. FAX: 404-814-3511. Web Site: www.afplweb.com/northside-branch. *Br Mgr,* Howell Williams; E-mail: howell.williams@fultoncountyga.gov; *Asst Br Mgr, Ch,* Swalena Griffin; E-mail: swalena.griffin@fultoncountyga.gov; *Ref Librn,* Sandra Anderson; E-mail: sandra.alexander@fultoncountyga.gov
Library Holdings: Bk Vols 64,861
Closed for renovations 2019-
Friends of the Library Group

NORTHWEST BRANCH AT SCOTTS CROSSING, 2489 Perry Blvd, 30318. Tel: 404-613-4364. FAX: 404-893-6795. Web Site: www.afpls.org/northwest-branch6. *Br Mgr,* Kysh Clemons
Library Holdings: Bk Vols 14,740

OCEE BRANCH, 5090 Abbotts Bridge Rd, Johns Creek, 30005-4601. Tel: 770-360-8897. FAX: 770-360-8892. Web Site: www.afpls.org/ocee-branch6. *Br Mgr,* Carla Burton; E-mail: carla.burton@fultoncountyga.gov; *Asst Br Mgr, Head, Children's Servx,* Marcia Divack; E-mail: marcia.divack@fultoncountyga.gov; *Ch,* Karen Kennedy; E-mail: karen.kennedy@fultoncountyga.gov; *Ref Librn,* John Offerdahl; E-mail: john.offerdahl@fultoncountyga.gov; *YA Serv,* Virginia Cline; E-mail: virginia.cline@fultoncountyga.gov
Library Holdings: Bk Vols 141,000
Closed for renovations 2019-
Friends of the Library Group

PALMETTO BRANCH, 9111 Cascade Palmetto Hwy, Palmetto, 30268. Tel: 404-613-4075. Web Site: www.afpls.org/palmetto-branch.

PEACHTREE BRANCH, 1315 Peachtree St NE, 30309, SAN 329-7438. Tel: 404-885-7830. FAX: 404-885-7833. Web Site: afplweb.com/peachtree-branch6. *Br Mgr,* Hensley Roberts; E-mail: hensley.roberts@fultoncountyga.gov
Library Holdings: Bk Vols 55,133

Open Mon, Tues & Thurs 10-6, Wed 10-8, Fri & Sat 12-6
Friends of the Library Group
ROSWELL BRANCH, 115 Norcross St, Roswell, 30075, SAN 338-3857. Tel: 770-640-3075. FAX: 770-640-3077. Web Site: www.afplweb.com/roswell-branch6. *Br Mgr,* Juliet Padgett; *Asst Br Mgr,* Todd Williamson; E-mail: todd.williamson@fultoncountyga.gov; *Ch,* Virginia Collier; *Ch,* Angela Whelchel; E-mail: angela.whelchel@fultoncountyga.gov
Founded 1946
Library Holdings: Bk Vols 125,000
Closed for renovations 2019-
Friends of the Library Group
SANDY SPRINGS BRANCH, 395 Mount Vernon Hwy NE, Sandy Springs, 30328, SAN 338-3822. Tel: 404-612-7000. FAX: 404-303-6133. Web Site: www.afplweb.com/sandy-springs-branch6. *Br Mgr,* Dorothy Parker; E-mail: dorothy.parker@fultoncountyga.gov; *Adult Ref Librn,* Karen Reynolds; E-mail: karen.reynolds@fultoncountyga.gov; *Ch,* Leah Germon; *Ref Librn,* Ruby Allen; E-mail: ruby.allen@fultoncountyga.gov
Library Holdings: Bk Vols 123,185
Open Mon & Wed 10-8, Tues & Thurs-Sat 10-6, Sun 2-6
Friends of the Library Group
SOUTHEAST ATLANTA BRANCH - LOUISE WATLEY LIBRARY, 1463 Pryor Rd, 30315. Tel: 404-613-5771. FAX: 404-730-5429. *Br Mgr,* Joia Ellis-Dinkins
Library Holdings: Bk Vols 31,185
Open Mon, Wed & Thurs 10-6, Tues 10-8, Fri & Sat 12-6
WASHINGTON PARK BRANCH, 1116 Martin Luther King Jr Dr, 30314, SAN 338-3946. Tel: 404-612-0110. FAX: 404-752-8762. Web Site: www.afpls.org/washington-park-branch6. *Br Mgr,* Sharon D Washington; E-mail: sharon.washington@fultoncountyga.gov
Library Holdings: Bk Vols 30,923
Open Mon, Wed & Thurs 10-6, Tues 10-8, Fri & Sat 12-6
WEST END BRANCH, 525 Peeples St SW, 30310, SAN 338-3911. Tel: 404-613-8000. FAX: 404-752-8742. *Br Mgr,* Rosie Meadows; E-mail: rosie.meadows@fultoncountyga.gov; *Ch,* Cathy Gwyn; E-mail: cathy.gwyn@fultoncountyga.gov
Library Holdings: Bk Vols 31,277
Open Mon 10-8, Tues-Thurs 10-6, Fri & Sat 12-6
WOLF CREEK BRANCH, 3100 Enon Rd SW, 30331. Tel: 404-613-4255. *Br Mgr,* Valdoshia Hunt; E-mail: valdoshia.hunt@fultoncountyga.gov
Library Holdings: Bk Vols 17,570
Open Mon & Wed 10-8, Tues & Thurs-Sat 10-6, Sun 2-6

S ATLANTA HISTORY CENTER*, Kenan Research Center, 3101 Andrews Dr NW, 30305. (Mail add: 130 W Paces Ferry Rd, 30305), SAN 303-2655. Tel: 404-814-4000, 404-814-4040. FAX: 404-814-4175. Reference E-mail: reference@atlantahistorycenter.com. Web Site: www.atlantahistorycenter.com. *Dir,* Paul Crater; *Librn,* Helen Matthews; Tel: 404-814-4048, E-mail: hmatthews@atlantahistorycenter.com
Founded 1926
Library Holdings: Bk Vols 25,000; Per Subs 90
Special Collections: Decorative Art Books; DuBose Civil War Coll; Joel Chandler Harris Coll; Revolutionary War in Georgia; Shillinglaw Cookbook Coll; Shutze Architecture Coll
Subject Interests: Ga, Genealogy
Automation Activity & Vendor Info: (OPAC) OCLC Worldshare Management Services
Wireless access
Function: Archival coll
Publications: History Matters (Newsletter)
Partic in GOLD Resource Sharing Network for Georgia's Libraries; LYRASIS
Open Tues-Sat 10-5
Restriction: Non-circulating
Branches:
CHEROKEE GARDEN LIBRARY, 130 W Paces Ferry Rd, 30305. Tel: 404-814-4046. Web Site: www.atlantahistorycenter.com/research/cherokee-garden-library. *Libr Dir,* Staci Catron; E-mail: scatron@atlantahistorycenter.com; *Librn,* Jennie Oldfield; Tel: 404-814-4124, E-mail: joldfield@atlantahistorycenter.com
Library Holdings: Bk Vols 32,000
Open Wed-Sat 10-5

C ATLANTA METROPOLITAN STATE COLLEGE LIBRARY, 1630 Metropolitan Pkwy SW, 30310. SAN 303-2663. Tel: 404-756-4010. *Libr Dir,* Robert Quarles; E-mail: rquarles@atlm.edu; *Ref Librn,* Tarita Chambers; E-mail: tchambers@atlm.edu; *Libr Asst III,* Carolyn Harmon; E-mail: charmon@atlm.edu; Staff 3 (MLS 2, Non-MLS 1)
Founded 1974. Highest Degree: Bachelor
Library Holdings: e-books 500,000; e-journals 11,000; Bk Vols 45,000; Per Subs 3
Automation Activity & Vendor Info: (Cataloging) Ex Libris Group; (Circulation) Ex Libris Group; (ILL) Ex Libris Group; (OPAC) Ex Libris Group; (Serials) EBSCO Online
Wireless access
Function: ILL available, Internet access, Ref serv available, Wheelchair accessible
Partic in Georgia Library Learning Online; GOLD Resource Sharing Network for Georgia's Libraries; LYRASIS; OCLC Online Computer Library Center, Inc
Open Mon-Thurs 8-7
Restriction: Open to students, fac & staff

G ATLANTA REGIONAL COMMISSION INFORMATION CENTER*, 229 Peachtree St NE, Ste 100, 30303. SAN 303-2698. Tel: 404-463-3100. FAX: 404-463-3205. E-mail: infocenter@atlantaregional.com. Web Site: atlantaregional.com. *Dir,* Douglas Hooker
Founded 1947
Library Holdings: Bk Titles 850
Special Collections: Atlanta Regional Commission Planning Reports
Subject Interests: Planning, Transportation
Open Mon-Fri 8:30-5

J ATLANTA TECHNICAL COLLEGE*, Library & Media Services, 1560 Metropolitan Pkwy SW, 30310. Tel: 404-225-4595. E-mail: atclibrary@atlantatech.edu. Web Site: www.atlantatech.edu/library. *Dir, Libr Serv,* Tosha Bussey; Tel: 404-225-4596, E-mail: tbussey@atlantatech.edu; *Cat Librn,* Priscilla Dickerson; E-mail: pdickerson@atlantatech.edu; *Circ Librn,* Cordelia Riley; E-mail: criley@atlantatech.edu; Staff 4 (MLS 3, Non-MLS 1)
Founded 1967. Enrl 5,066; Highest Degree: Associate
Library Holdings: Audiobooks 20; CDs 75; DVDs 210; e-books 26,000; Bk Titles 12,860; Bk Vols 20,284; Per Subs 170; Videos 414
Special Collections: Paralegal Law Library
Automation Activity & Vendor Info: (Acquisitions) Ex Libris Group; (Cataloging) Ex Libris Group; (Circulation) Ex Libris Group; (Course Reserve) FileMaker; (ILL) OCLC WorldShare Interlibrary Loan; (OPAC) Ex Libris Group; (Serials) EBSCO Discovery Service
Wireless access
Partic in Georgia Library Learning Online; GOLD Resource Sharing Network for Georgia's Libraries
Open Mon-Thurs 8-7, Fri & Sat 8-2

C ATLANTA UNIVERSITY CENTER*, Robert W Woodruff Library, 111 James P Brawley Dr SW, 30314. SAN 303-2701. Tel: 404-978-2000. Circulation Tel: 404-978-2097. Interlibrary Loan Service Tel: 404-978-2025. Reference Tel: 404-978-2067. Administration Tel: 404-978-2018. FAX: 404-577-5158. E-mail: adminres@auctr.edu. Web Site: www.auctr.edu. *Dir,* Loretta Parham; E-mail: lparham@auctr.edu; *Tech Librn,* Robert Fallen; Tel: 404-978-2058, E-mail: rfallen@auctr.edu; *Archivist,* Karen Jefferson; Tel: 404-978-2045, E-mail: kjefferson@auctr.edu; *Circ,* William Holt; Tel: 404-978-2048, E-mail: wholt@auctr.edu; Staff 51 (MLS 24, Non-MLS 27)
Founded 1964. Enrl 9,965; Fac 776; Highest Degree: Doctorate
Library Holdings: Bk Vols 400,000; Per Subs 1,419
Special Collections: Abraham Lincoln Coll, memorabilia; Black History & Literature (Cullen-Jackman, Henry P Slaughter & Hoytt Fuller Coll); C Eric Lincoln (African American Coll); Freedman's Aid Society Records; John Henrik Clarke Coll; Music (Cuney-Hare Coll); Southern Regional Council Archival Coll on Race Relations. US Document Depository
Subject Interests: Acctg, African-Am, Art, Chem, Computer sci, Criminal law & justice, Econ, English (Lang), English lit, Hist, Mass communications, Nursing, Physics, Polit sci, Relig, Soc serv (soc work), Sociol, Theol, Zoology
Wireless access
Publications: Index to Theses
Partic in Atlanta Regional Council for Higher Education; Proquest Dialog
Open Mon-Thurs 7:30am-Midnight, Fri 7:30-6, Sat Noon-6, Sun Noon -Midnight
Friends of the Library Group

CR BEULAH HEIGHTS UNIVERSITY*, Barth Memorial Library, 892 Berne St SE, 30316. (Mail add: PO Box 18145, 30316-0145), SAN 303-2728. Tel: 404-627-2681, Ext 116. Toll Free Tel: 888-777-2422. FAX: 404-627-0702. Web Site: www.beulah.edu/Library. *Dir, Libr Serv,* Pradeep Das; E-mail: pradeep.das@beulah.org; Staff 2 (MLS 2)
Founded 1918. Enrl 815; Fac 45; Highest Degree: Master
Library Holdings: AV Mats 1,850; Bk Titles 44,320; Bk Vols 48,000; Per Subs 290
Subject Interests: Biblical studies, Bus, Christian educ, Econ, Finance Bus ethics, Intl trade, Leadership, Missions, Relig, Urban studies
Automation Activity & Vendor Info: (Cataloging) Follett Software; (Circulation) Follett Software; (OPAC) Follett Software
Wireless access
Partic in Georgia Private Acad Librs Consortium; GOLD Resource Sharing Network for Georgia's Libraries; LYRASIS
Restriction: Not open to pub, Open to students

L BRYAN CAVE*, Law Library & Information Center, One Atlantic Ctr 14th Flr, 1201 W Peachtree St NW, 30309. SAN 327-8980. Tel: 404-572-6696. FAX: 404-572-6999. Web Site: www.bryancave.com. *Chief Librn,* Judith Harris; Tel: 314-259-2298, E-mail: jlharris@bryancave.com; *Regional Mgr,* Herb Barnes
Restriction: Staff use only

CR CARVER BIBLE COLLEGE LIBRARY*, 3870 Cascade Rd, 30331. SAN 303-2736. Tel: 404-527-4520. FAX: 404-527-4524. Web Site: www.carver.edu. *Dir, Libr Serv,* Debra Milligan; E-mail: dmilligan@carver.edu; Staff 3 (MLS 1, Non-MLS 2)
Founded 1943. Enrl 153; Fac 14; Highest Degree: Bachelor
Library Holdings: Bk Titles 14,434; Bk Vols 15,600; Per Subs 60
Wireless access
Open Mon-Fri 9am-10pm

G CENTERS FOR DISEASE CONTROL & PREVENTION*, Stephen B Thacker CDC Library, Tom Harkin Global Communications Ctr, Bldg 19, 1st Flr, MS C04, 1600 Clifton Rd NE, 30333. SAN 303-2744. Tel: 404-639-1717. Toll Free Tel: 800-232-4636. FAX: 404-639-1160. E-mail: cdclibrary@cdc.gov. Web Site: www.cdc.gov/library/index.html. *Head Librn,* Julie Fishman; E-mail: jbf4@cdc.gov
Founded 1947
Library Holdings: Bk Vols 25,000; Per Subs 1,531
Special Collections: CDC Publications; CDC Thesis Coll; PHS (HHS) Pamphlet Coll
Subject Interests: Biochem, Environ health, Microbiology, Pub health, Toxicology, Virology
Automation Activity & Vendor Info: (Acquisitions) Ex Libris Group; (Cataloging) Ex Libris Group; (Circulation) Ex Libris Group; (ILL) OCLC ILLiad; (OPAC) Ex Libris Group; (Serials) Ex Libris Group
Wireless access
Partic in Federal Library & Information Network; GOLD Resource Sharing Network for Georgia's Libraries
Open Mon-Fri 8-4:30
Restriction: Badge access after hrs

S COURT OF APPEALS ELEVENTH CIRCUIT LIBRARY*, Elbert P Tuttle US Court of Appeals Bldg, 56 Forsyth St NW, 30303. SAN 327-8107. Tel: 404-335-6500. FAX: 404-335-6510. Web Site: www.ca11.uscourts.gov/eleventh-circuit-library. *Librn,* Nancy Adams; E-mail: nancy_adams@ca11.uscourts.gov; Staff 9 (MLS 5, Non-MLS 4)
Founded 1981
Library Holdings: Bk Vols 50,000; Per Subs 300
Special Collections: US Document Depository
Subject Interests: Law
Automation Activity & Vendor Info: (Acquisitions) SirsiDynix; (Cataloging) SirsiDynix; (Circulation) SirsiDynix; (Course Reserve) SirsiDynix; (ILL) SirsiDynix; (Media Booking) SirsiDynix; (OPAC) SirsiDynix; (Serials) SirsiDynix
Wireless access
Partic in OCLC Online Computer Library Center, Inc
Open Mon-Fri 8:30-4
Restriction: Circ limited

L DENTONS US LLP*, Law Library, 303 Peachtree St, Ste 5300, 30308. SAN 325-6456. Tel: 404-527-4057. FAX: 404-527-8474. *Librn,* Mica Maddry
Library Holdings: Bk Titles 4,000
Wireless access
Restriction: Not open to pub

M EMORY UNIVERSITY HOSPITAL MIDTOWN*, Clinical Branch Library, Davis-Fisher Bldg, 1st Flr, Rm 1312, 550 Peachtree St NE, 30308. SAN 303-3082. Tel: 404-686-1978. Web Site: health.library.emory.edu, www.emoryhealthcare.org. *Informationist,* John Nemeth; E-mail: jnemeth@emory.edu
Founded 1942
Special Collections: Performance Improvement Management
Subject Interests: Allied health, Consumer health, Hospital admin, Med, Nursing, Surgery
Automation Activity & Vendor Info: (Acquisitions) SirsiDynix; (Cataloging) SirsiDynix; (Circulation) SirsiDynix; (Course Reserve) SirsiDynix; (OPAC) SirsiDynix; (Serials) SirsiDynix
Function: ILL available
Publications: Annual Report
Partic in Atlantic Health Sci Librs Consortium
Restriction: Not open to pub, Staff use only

EMORY UNIVERSITY LIBRARIES
GOIZUETA BUSINESS LIBRARY*, 540 Asbury Circle, 30322. Tel: 404-727-1641. FAX: 404-727-1012. Web Site: www.business.library.emory.edu. *Exec Dir,* Susan Klopper; E-mail: susan.kloper@emory.edu; *Bus Librn,* Malisa Anderson-Strait; E-mail: malisa.anderson@emory.edu; *Bus Librn,* Ann Cullen; E-mail: ann.cullen@emory.edu; *Bus Librn,* Marilyn Pahr; E-mail: marilyn.pahr@emory.edu; *Bus Librn,* Lee Pasackow; E-mail: lee.pasackow@emory.edu

CR PITTS THEOLOGY LIBRARY*, Candler School of Theology, 1531 Dickey Dr, Ste 560, 30322-2810, SAN 338-4063. Tel: 404-727-4166. FAX: 404-727-1219. E-mail: libmpg@emory.edu. Web Site: www.pitts.emory.edu. *Dir,* Dr Matt Patrick Graham; *Ref/Outreach Librn,* Rebekah Bedard; Tel: 404-727-5094, E-mail: rebekah.bedard@emory.edu; *Archivist,* Robert Presutti; *Cat,* Dr Denise Hanusek; *Cat,* Armin Siedlecki; *Per,* Tracy Powell; *Pub Serv, Reader Serv,* Dr Richard Adams. Subject Specialists: *Ancient Near East,* Rebekah Bedard; Staff 7 (MLS 7)
Founded 1914. Highest Degree: Doctorate
Library Holdings: Microforms 121,000; Bk Vols 610,000; Per Subs 1,041
Special Collections: A Christian Sermon; A Selective Bibliography of Recent Acquisitions Spring 1984; An Annotated Bibliograph; Archives & Manuscript Coll; Early Book Coll incl pre-1750 books published outside the US, pre-1820 US Imprints & Incunabula; Early Reformation Imprints; Elisabeth Creutziger, the Magdeburg Enchiridion, 1536 & Reformation Theology; European Theological Dissertations Printed in the 16th-19th Centuries; Kessler Coll comes to Emory; Luther, Bach & the Early Reformation Chorale; Preserving the Traditions of Faith: A History of the Pitts Theology Library; Richard C Kessler Reformation Coll, incl 16th Century vols by Martin Luther; The Politics of Manning's Conversion; Thomas Menton Coll; Warrington-Paine-Pratt Hymnology Coll; Wesleyana Coll, bks & pamphlets, incl First Edition of the Works of John & Charles Wesley
Subject Interests: Relig, Theol
Partic in LYRASIS; Research Libraries Information Network
Friends of the Library Group

CM WOODRUFF HEALTH SCIENCES CENTER LIBRARY*, 1462 Clifton Rd NE, 30322, SAN 338-4187. Tel: 404-727-8727. Reference Tel: 404-727-3760. Administration Tel: 404-727-5820. FAX: 404-727-9821. Web Site: health.library.emory.edu. *Dir,* Sandra G Franklin; E-mail: librsf@emory.edu; *Coordr, Coll Serv,* Bonita Bryan; E-mail: libbrb@emory.edu; *Info Serv Coordr,* Barbara Abu-Zeid; E-mail: babuzei@emory.edu; Staff 12.8 (MLS 12.8)
Founded 1923
Special Collections: History of Medicine in Georgia
Partic in LYRASIS; National Network of Libraries of Medicine Region 2
Open Mon-Thurs 8am-Midnight, Fri 8-7, Sat 10-7, Sun Noon-Midnight

C ROBERT W WOODRUFF LIBRARY*, 540 Asbury Circle, 30322-2870, SAN 338-4039. Tel: 404-727-6861. Circulation Tel: 404-727-6873. Reference Tel: 404-727-6875. FAX: 404-727-0805. Web Site: web.library.emory.edu. *Univ Librn,* Yolanda Cooper; E-mail: yolanda.cooper@emory.edu; *Bus Librn,* Susan Klopper; Tel: 404-727-0177, Fax: 404-727-1641, E-mail: skloppe@emory.edu; *Sr Leader, Content Div,* Lars Meyer; Tel: 404-727-2437, Fax: 404-727-1132, E-mail: lmeyer2@emory.edu; *Media Spec, Music,* Joyce Clinkscales; Tel: 404-727-1066, Fax: 404-727-2257, E-mail: libjm01@emory.edu; Staff 212 (MLS 88, Non-MLS 124)
Founded 1915. Enrl 12,059; Fac 718; Highest Degree: Doctorate
Library Holdings: Bk Vols 3,619,813; Per Subs 66,992
Special Collections: 19th Century English Prose Fiction; African-American History & Culture (James Weldon Johnson Coll, Raymond Andrews Family Papers); American & Asian Communism (Theodore Draper & Philip Jaffe Coll), ms, printed mat; Antebellum, Civil War & Post Civil War (Alexander Stephens & Others), ms; British & Irish Literature (W B Yeats, Lady Gregory, Ted Hughes Colls); Confederate Imprints; Early American History (McGregor Coll); Southern Economic History (Charles Herty Papers & Harrold Coll of Business & Family Letters & Records, Georgia 1836-1953), ms; Southern Literary & Journalistic History (Joel Chandler Harris, Henry Grady, Ralph McGill Coll), ms; Wesleyana & Methodist History, ms & printed mat; Yeats & 20th Century Irish Literature. US Document Depository
Automation Activity & Vendor Info: (Acquisitions) Ex Libris Group; (Cataloging) Ex Libris Group; (Circulation) Ex Libris Group; (Course Reserve) Ex Libris Group; (OPAC) Ex Libris Group; (Serials) Ex Libris Group
Partic in Association of Research Libraries; Association of Southeastern Research Libraries; Atlanta Regional Council for Higher Education; Center for Research Libraries; Coalition for Networked Information; Consortium of Southern Biomedical Libraries; Digital Libr Fedn; Georgia Libr Info Network; LYRASIS; OCLC Research Library Partnership
Publications: Imprint (Newsletter); Library Directions
Special Services for the Deaf - TDD equip
Friends of the Library Group

CL EMORY UNIVERSITY SCHOOL OF LAW*, Hugh F MacMillan Law Library, 1301 Clifton Rd, 30322. SAN 338-4128. Tel: 404-727-6823. Circulation Tel: 404-727-6824. Reference Tel: 404-727-0059. FAX:

404-727-2202. Circulation E-mail: lawcirch@mail.library.emory.edu. Web Site: library.law.emory.edu. *Dir, Libr Serv,* Mark Engsberg; E-mail: mark.engsberg@emory.edu; Staff 11 (MLS 10, Non-MLS 1)
Founded 1916
Library Holdings: e-books 146,017; e-journals 19,390; Bk Titles 185,904; Bk Vols 215,897; Per Subs 1,442
Special Collections: US Document Depository
Automation Activity & Vendor Info: (Acquisitions) Ex Libris Group; (Cataloging) Ex Libris Group; (Circulation) Ex Libris Group; (OPAC) Ex Libris Group; (Serials) Ex Libris Group
Wireless access
Function: ILL available
Partic in OCLC Online Computer Library Center, Inc

S FEDERAL RESERVE BANK OF ATLANTA, Research Library, 1000 Peachtree St NE, 30309-4470. SAN 303-2841. Tel: 404-498-8927. Web Site: www.atlantafed.org. *Knowledge & Info Mgmt,* Ernie Evangelista; E-mail: ernie.m.evangelista@atl.frb.org; Staff 5 (MLS 3, Non-MLS 2)
Founded 1938
Library Holdings: Bk Titles 11,000; Per Subs 1,800
Special Collections: Federal Reserve Bank & Federal Reserve Board Publications; Southeastern Regional Economics
Subject Interests: Banks & banking, Econ, Finance, Trade
Publications: Monthly Accessions List
Partic in Dow Jones News Retrieval; GOLD Resource Sharing Network for Georgia's Libraries; Proquest Dialog
Special Services for the Deaf - TDD equip
Restriction: Open to pub by appt only

S FERNBANK SCIENCE CENTER LIBRARY*, 156 Heaton Park Dr NE, 30307-1398. SAN 303-2795. Tel: 678-874-7116. FAX: 678-874-7110. Web Site: fsc.fernbank.edu/faculty/mediacenter.htm. *Librn,* Sue Levine; E-mail: sue_m_levine@dekalbschoolsga.org; Staff 1 (MLS 1)
Founded 1967
Library Holdings: Bk Titles 14,658; Bk Vols 22,000; Per Subs 35
Subject Interests: Astronomy, Botany, Environ studies, Hort, Sci tech
Automation Activity & Vendor Info: (Cataloging) OCLC; (ILL) OCLC
Wireless access
Partic in LYRASIS
Open Mon-Sat 10-5

GL FULTON COUNTY COURTS, Justice Resource Center, (Formerly Fulton County Law Library), Justice Center Tower, J1-7001, 185 Central Ave SW, 30303. SAN 303-2868. Tel: 404-612-4544. Web Site: www.fultoncourt.org/library. *Info Serv, Libr Mgr,* Jeannie Ashley; E-mail: jeannie.ashley@fultoncountyga.gov
Wireless access
Open Mon-Fri 8:30-4:30

C GEORGIA INSTITUTE OF TECHNOLOGY LIBRARY*, Georgia Tech Library, 266 Fourth St NW, 30332-0900. SAN 303-2922. Tel: 404-894-4500. Toll Free Tel: 888-225-7804. FAX: 404-894-6084. Web Site: www.library.gatech.edu. *Dean of Libr,* Catherine Murray-Rust; E-mail: catherine.murray-rust@library.gatech.edu; *Assoc Dean, Learning Services, Res Serv,* Bruce Henson; *Assoc Dean, Scholarly Communications & Access,* Jeff Carrico; *Asst Dean, Copyright & Info Adv,* Ms Bing Wang; *Finance Mgr, Sr Dir,* Vanessa Payne; *Dir, Service Experience & Program Design,* Ameet Doshi; *Head, Archives & Spec Coll,* Jody Thompson; *Head Campus Engagement & Scholarly Outreach, Subj Librn,* Cathy Carpenter; *Pub Serv Mgr,* Emy Decker; Staff 101 (MLS 30, Non-MLS 71)
Founded 1885. Enrl 25,034; Fac 1,076; Highest Degree: Doctorate
Jul 2015-Jun 2016 Income (Main & Associated Libraries) $17,141,026. Mats Exp $9,044,584. Sal $5,325,294 (Prof $3,478,323)
Library Holdings: e-books 632,230; Bk Titles 1,410,804; Bk Vols 1,542,955
Special Collections: ASERL Center of Excellence (NASA, USPTO, EPA); Patent & Trademark Resource Center; Technical Reports (National Technical Information Services, NASA, DOE), micro. US Document Depository
Subject Interests: Archit, Bus & mgt, Econ, Engr, Environ studies, Natural sci, Phys sci, Sci tech
Automation Activity & Vendor Info: (Acquisitions) Ex Libris Group; (Cataloging) Ex Libris Group; (Circulation) Ex Libris Group; (Course Reserve) Atlas Systems; (Discovery) Ex Libris Group; (ILL) OCLC ILLiad; (OPAC) Ex Libris Group; (Serials) Ex Libris Group
Wireless access
Partic in Association of Southeastern Research Libraries; GALILEO; LYRASIS
Special Services for the Blind - Assistive/Adapted tech devices, equip & products

Departmental Libraries:

ARCHITECTURE CORE COLLECTION, Hinman Bldg, Ground Flr, 723 Cherry St NW, 30332, SAN 321-222X. Tel: 404-894-4500.
Subject Interests: Archit, Construction, Design
Open Mon, Wed & Fri 8am-12:30pm

P GEORGIA LIBRARY FOR ACCESSIBLE STATEWIDE SERVICES*, One Margaret Mitchell Sq, 4th Flr, 30303-1089. SAN 303-2949. Tel: 404-657-1452. Administration Tel: 404-756-4476. Toll Free Tel: 800-248-6701. FAX: 404-657-1459. E-mail: glass@georgialibraries.org. Web Site: georgialibraries.org/glass/atlanta. *Dir,* Pat Herndon; E-mail: pherndon@georgialibraries.org; *Librn,* Beverly Williams; E-mail: bwilliams@georgialibraries.org; Staff 18.5 (MLS 7, Non-MLS 11.5)
Founded 1931. Pop 149,000; Circ 349,000
Library Holdings: Bk Titles 57,000; Bk Vols 300,000; Talking Bks 57,000
Automation Activity & Vendor Info: (Acquisitions) Keystone Systems, Inc (KLAS); (Cataloging) Keystone Systems, Inc (KLAS); (Circulation) Keystone Systems, Inc (KLAS); (Course Reserve) Keystone Systems, Inc (KLAS); (ILL) Keystone Systems, Inc (KLAS); (Media Booking) Keystone Systems, Inc (KLAS); (OPAC) Keystone Systems, Inc (KLAS); (Serials) Keystone Systems, Inc (KLAS)
Wireless access
Function: 24/7 Electronic res, Adult bk club, Art exhibits, Audio & video playback equip for onsite use, Chess club, Children's prog, Computer training, Computers for patron use, Digital talking bks, Equip loans & repairs, Holiday prog, Internet access, Large print keyboards, Magnifiers for reading, Mail & tel request accepted, Mail loans to mem, Online cat, Outreach serv, Photocopying/Printing, Prog for adults, Senior outreach, Summer reading prog, VHS videos, Wheelchair accessible
Partic in Atlanta Health Science Libraries Consortium
Special Services for the Blind - Bks on cassette; Braille bks; Closed circuit TV; Computer with voice synthesizer for visually impaired persons; Local mags & bks recorded; Photo duplicator for making large print
Open Mon, Fri & Sat 8-5, Tues-Thurs 8-6
Restriction: Authorized patrons, Closed stack
Friends of the Library Group

C GEORGIA STATE UNIVERSITY*, Atlanta Campus Library, 100 Decatur St SE, 30303-3202. (Mail add: PO Box 3967, 30302-3967), SAN 303-2957. Tel: 404-413-2700. Circulation Tel: 404-413-2820. Interlibrary Loan Service Tel: 404-413-2790. Reference Tel: 404-413-2800. FAX: 404-413-2701. Circulation FAX: 404-413-2821. Interlibrary Loan Service FAX: 404-413-2791. E-mail: libcirc@gsu.edu. Web Site: library.gsu.edu. *Dean of Libr,* Jeff Steely; E-mail: jsteely@gsu.edu; *Assoc Dean, Digital Serv & Scholarly Communications, Tech Serv,* Laura Burtle; Tel: 404-413-2706, E-mail: lburtle@gsu.edu; *Assoc Dean, Pub Serv,* Bryan Sinclair; Tel: 404-413-2721, E-mail: bsinclair@gsu.edu; *Admin Officer,* Ernest Duncan; Tel: 404-413-2713, E-mail: eduncan19@gsu.edu; *Head, Coll Develop,* Skye Hardesty; Tel: 404-413-2786, E-mail: skye@gsu.edu; *Head, Digital Libr Serv,* Krista Graham; Tel: 404-413-2752, E-mail: kgraham13@gsu.edu; *Head, Libr Serv,* Tamika Barnes; Tel: 770-274-5084, E-mail: tbarnes24@gsu.edu; *Head, Research & Engagment,* Laura Carscaddon; Tel: 404-413-2804, E-mail: lcarscaddon1@gsu.edu; *Head, Spec Coll & Univ Archives,* Christina Zamon; Tel: 404-413-2889, E-mail: czamon1@gsu.edu; *Head, User Services & Tech Support,* Kara Mullen; Tel: 404-413-2822, E-mail: kmullen@gsu.edu; Staff 70 (MLS 58, Non-MLS 12)
Founded 1931. Enrl 52,000; Fac 1,658; Highest Degree: Doctorate
Special Collections: Georgia Government Documentation Project; Georgia Women's Coll; Labor History (Southern Labor Archives); Lane Brothers & Tracy O'Neal (Photographic Coll); Popular Music (Johnny Mercer Coll); Rare Book Coll; University Archives. Oral History; US Document Depository
Automation Activity & Vendor Info: (Acquisitions) Ex Libris Group; (Cataloging) Ex Libris Group; (Circulation) Ex Libris Group; (Course Reserve) Ex Libris Group; (ILL) OCLC ILLiad; (Media Booking) Ex Libris Group; (OPAC) Ex Libris Group; (Serials) Ex Libris Group
Wireless access
Function: Computers for patron use, Photocopying/Printing
Partic in Atlanta Regional Council for Higher Education; Center for Research Libraries; GALILEO; OCLC Online Computer Library Center, Inc
Open Mon-Thurs 7am-2am, Fri 7-6, Sat 12-6, Sun 12pm-2am
Restriction: Badge access after hrs, ID required to use computers (Ltd hrs), In-house use for visitors, Open to students, fac, staff & alumni, Photo ID required for access, Restricted pub use

Departmental Libraries:

ALPHARETTA CAMPUS, 3705 Brookside Pkwy, Alpharetta, 30022. Tel: 678-240-6135. *Dept Head,* Tamika Barnes; Tel: 770-274-5084, E-mail: tbarnes24@gsu.edu; *Asst Dept Head,* Mary Ann Cullen; Tel: 678-240-6139, E-mail: mcullen@gsu.edu

CLARKSTON CAMPUS, 555 N Indian Creek Dr, Clarkston, 30021. Tel: 678-891-3645. Circulation FAX: 678-891-3652. *Dept Head,* Tamika Barnes; Tel: 770-274-5084, E-mail: tbarnes24@gsu.edu; *Asst Dept Head,* Christopher Moffat; Tel: 678-891-3697, E-mail: cmoffat1@gsu.edu
Function: Computers for patron use, Photocopying/Printing
Restriction: ID required to use computers (Ltd hrs)

CL COLLEGE OF LAW LIBRARY, 140 Decatur St, 30302. (Mail add: PO Box 4008, 30302-4008), SAN 324-2684. Circulation Tel: 404-413-9100. Reference Tel: 404-651-4143. Web Site: lawlibrary.gsu.edu. *Assoc Dean, Libr & Info Serv,* Kris Niedringhaus; Tel: 404-413-9140, E-mail: krisn@gsu.edu; Staff 19 (MLS 7, Non-MLS 12)
Founded 1982. Enrl 600; Fac 40; Highest Degree: Doctorate
Special Collections: US Document Depository
Automation Activity & Vendor Info: (Acquisitions) Ex Libris Group; (Cataloging) Ex Libris Group; (Circulation) Ex Libris Group; (Course Reserve) Ex Libris Group; (OPAC) Ex Libris Group; (Serials) Ex Libris Group
Partic in Association of Southeastern Research Libraries; LYRASIS
DECATUR CAMPUS, 3251 Panthersville Rd, Decatur, 30034. Tel: 678-891-2585. Circulation Tel: 678-891-2591. Reference Tel: 678-891-2592. FAX: 678-891-2860. *Dept Head,* Tamika Barnes; Tel: 770-274-5084, E-mail: tbarnes24@gsu.edu; *Asst Dept Head,* Scott Pieper; Tel: 678-891-2587, E-mail: spieper1@gsu.edu
Highest Degree: Associate
Function: Computers for patron use
Restriction: ID required to use computers (Ltd hrs), In-house use for visitors, Open to students, fac, staff & alumni, Photo ID required for access
DUNWOODY CAMPUS, 2101 Womack Rd, Dunwoody, 30338. Tel: 770-274-5085. Reference Tel: 770-274-5100. FAX: 770-274-5090. *Dept Head,* Tamika Barnes; Tel: 770-274-5084, E-mail: tbarnes24@gsu.edu; *Asst Dept Head,* Amy Stalker; Tel: 770-274-5088, E-mail: astalker@gsu.edu
NEWTON CAMPUS, 239 Cedar Lane, Newton, 30014. Tel: 770-278-1260. FAX: 770-278-1439. *Dept Head,* Tamika Barnes; Tel: 770-274-5084, E-mail: tbarnes24@gsu.edu; *Asst Dept Head,* Laura Tartak; Tel: 770-278-1342, E-mail: ttartak@gsu.edu

S GERMAN CULTURAL CENTER, Goethe-Zentrum Atlanta Library, (Formerly Friends of Goethe, Inc), Colony Sq, Plaza Level, 1197 Peachtree St NE, 30361-2401. SAN 324-136X. Tel: 404-892-2388. FAX: 404-875-0475. E-mail: info@german-institute.org, info@goetheatlanta.org. Web Site: www.german-institute.org. *Exec Dir,* Oliver Gorf; E-mail: oliver.gorf@goetheatlanta.org
Founded 1977
Library Holdings: Bk Titles 8,500; Per Subs 35
Special Collections: German Language Materials
Subject Interests: Geog, German affairs, German art, Hist, Lit
Function: For res purposes, Wheelchair accessible
Open Mon-Thurs 10-6, Fri 10-4
Restriction: Mem only
Friends of the Library Group

R GLENN MEMORIAL UNITED METHODIST CHURCH, Edward G Mackay Library, 1660 N Decatur Rd NE, Rm 309, 30307. SAN 303-2973. Tel: 404-634-3936. FAX: 404-634-1994. E-mail: library@glennumc.org. Web Site: www.glennumc.org. *Librn,* Position Currently Open
Library Holdings: Bk Vols 3,000
Wireless access

C HERZING UNIVERSITY LIBRARY, Atlanta Campus, 50 Hurt Plaza SE, Ste 400, 30303. Tel: 404-586-4265. Web Site: www.herzing.edu/atlanta.
Founded 1965. Enrl 350; Highest Degree: Bachelor
Library Holdings: Bk Vols 7,000; Per Subs 60; Videos 45
Automation Activity & Vendor Info: (Cataloging) Follett Software; (Circulation) Follett Software; (OPAC) Follett Software
Partic in Georgia Library Learning Online; Georgia Private Acad Librs Consortium
Open Mon-Fri 8-8, Sat 8-2, Sun 1-9

CL JOHN MARSHALL LAW SCHOOL, Michael J Lynch Law Library, 245 Peachtree Center Ave NE, 18th Flr, 30303. SAN 303-3031. Tel: 678-916-2664. FAX: 404-873-3802. Web Site: www.johnmarshall.edu/libguides.com/library. *Dir, Law Libr,* Michael J Lynch; Tel: 678-916-2661, E-mail: mlynch@johnmarshall.edu; *Head, Pub Serv,* Mary Wilson; Tel: 678-916-2663, E-mail: mewilson@johnmarshall.edu; *Head, Tech Serv,* Mark Durbin; Tel: 678-916-2662, E-mail: mdurbin@johnmarshall.edu; Staff 9 (MLS 5, Non-MLS 4)
Founded 1935. Enrl 270; Fac 30; Highest Degree: Doctorate
Library Holdings: e-books 10,000; Bk Titles 147,500; Bk Vols 250,000; Per Subs 2,500
Automation Activity & Vendor Info: (ILL) OCLC
Wireless access
Partic in Georgia Private Acad Librs Consortium
Open Mon 8am-11pm, Tues-Fri 8am-10pm, Sat 11-7, Sun 1-9
Restriction: Open to fac, students & qualified researchers

L KILPATRICK TOWNSEND & STOCKTON LLP*, Law Library, 1100 Peachtree St, Ste 2800, 30309-4528. SAN 303-304X. Tel: 404-815-6500. FAX: 404-815-6555. *Info & Res Mgr,* Louise Adams; E-mail: ladams@kilpatricktownsend.com
Founded 1904
Library Holdings: Bk Vols 30,000
Publications: Recent Acquisitions; Seminar list (Monthly)
Partic in Proquest Dialog

L KING & SPALDING*, Law Library, 1180 Peachtree St NE, Ste 1600, 30309. SAN 303-3058. Tel: 404-572-4600, Ext 3300. FAX: 404-572-5123.
Library Holdings: Bk Vols 50,000

S KING LIBRARY & ARCHIVES, 449 Auburn Ave NE, 30312. SAN 303-3066. Tel: 404-526-8983. E-mail: archives@thekingcenter.org. Web Site: www.thekingcenter.org. *Dir,* Cynthia Patterson Lewis; Tel: 404-526-8986, E-mail: clewis@thekingcenter.org; Staff 3 (MLS 1, Non-MLS 2)
Founded 1969
Library Holdings: Bk Vols 5,000; Per Subs 25
Special Collections: Black American History; Civil Rights Movement, 1954-1968, Post 1968; Nonviolence. Oral History
Subject Interests: Civil rights

C MERCER UNIVERSITY ATLANTA*, Monroe F Swilley Jr Library, 3001 Mercer University Dr, 30341. SAN 303-3104. Tel: 678-547-6284. Reference Tel: 678-547-6282. FAX: 678-547-6270. Web Site: libraries.mercer.edu. *Dean of Libr,* Jeffrey Waldrop; Tel: 678-547-6274, E-mail: waldrop_ja@mercer.edu; *Asst Dean, Res Serv,* Kim Eccles; Tel: 678-547-6271, E-mail: eccles_kl@mercer.edu; *Assoc Dean,* Scott Gilliies; Tel: 678-547-6274, E-mail: gillies_sf@mercer.edu; *Research Servs Librn,* Arlene Desselles; Tel: 678-547-6283, E-mail: desselles_af@mercer.edu; *Research Servs Librn,* Beth Perry; Tel: 678-547-6435, E-mail: perry_sb@mercer.edu; *Research Servs Librn,* Florence Tang; Tel: 678-547-6261, E-mail: tang_fy@mercer.edu. Subject Specialists: *Bus,* Kim Eccles; *Theol,* Beth Perry; Staff 9 (MLS 9)
Founded 1968. Enrl 2,878; Highest Degree: Doctorate
Library Holdings: e-journals 4,000; Bk Titles 128,615; Bk Vols 146,872; Per Subs 586
Special Collections: British & American Literature Coll, 18th-19th Century, 1st ed
Subject Interests: Counseling, Educ, Nursing, Pharm, Theol
Automation Activity & Vendor Info: (Acquisitions) Innovative Interfaces, Inc; (Cataloging) Innovative Interfaces, Inc; (Circulation) Innovative Interfaces, Inc; (ILL) Innovative Interfaces, Inc; (OPAC) Innovative Interfaces, Inc; (Serials) Innovative Interfaces, Inc
Wireless access
Function: Archival coll, Art exhibits, AV serv, Bks on CD, CD-ROM, Computers for patron use, E-Reserves, Electronic databases & coll, Health sci info serv, ILL available, Internet access, Magnifiers for reading, Online cat, Online ref, Orientations, Outside serv via phone, mail, e-mail & web, Photocopying/Printing, Ref serv available, Scanner, Spoken cassettes & CDs, Spoken cassettes & DVDs, Telephone ref, VHS videos, Wheelchair accessible, Workshops
Partic in Atlanta Health Science Libraries Consortium; Atlanta Regional Council for Higher Education; Georgia Interactive Network for Medical Information; Georgia Library Learning Online; LYRASIS; National Network of Libraries of Medicine Region 2; OCLC Online Computer Library Center, Inc
Open Mon-Thurs 7:30am-Midnight, Fri 7:30-6, Sat 10-6
Restriction: Open to students, fac & staff, Photo ID required for access, Staff use only, Students only

CM MOREHOUSE SCHOOL OF MEDICINE*, M Delmar Edwards MD Library, Medical Education Bldg, 1st Flr, Ste 100, 720 Westview Dr SW, 30310-1495. SAN 320-1457. Tel: 404-752-1530, 404-752-1536. Interlibrary Loan Service Tel: 404-752-1528. Reference Tel: 404-752-1533. FAX: 404-752-1049. Web Site: www.msm.edu/Library/index.php. *Dir,* Joe Swanson, Jr; Tel: 404-752-1542, E-mail: jswanson@msm.edu; *Mgr, Info Serv,* Tara Douglas-Williams; E-mail: tdouglas-williams@msm.edu; *Mgr, Tech Serv,* Roland Welmaker; Tel: 404-752-1534, E-mail: rwelmaker@msm.edu; Staff 9 (MLS 3, Non-MLS 6)
Founded 1978. Enrl 500; Highest Degree: Doctorate
Library Holdings: CDs 435; e-books 601; e-journals 9,893; Electronic Media & Resources 22; Bk Vols 14,039; Per Subs 182
Subject Interests: Health sci
Automation Activity & Vendor Info: (Cataloging) CyberTools for Libraries; (Circulation) CyberTools for Libraries; (Course Reserve) CyberTools for Libraries; (OPAC) CyberTools for Libraries
Wireless access
Function: 24/7 Electronic res, Art exhibits, Computers for patron use, E-Reserves, ILL available, Internet access, Mail & tel request accepted, Online cat, Online ref, Outreach serv, Photocopying/Printing, Printer for

laptops & handheld devices, Ref serv available, Scanner, Study rm, Telephone ref, Wheelchair accessible, Workshops
Publications: Library Guide
Partic in Atlanta Health Science Libraries Consortium; Atlanta Regional Council for Higher Education; Consortium of Southern Biomedical Libraries; Georgia Health Sciences Library Association; LYRASIS; National Network of Libraries of Medicine Region 2
Restriction: 24-hr pass syst for students only

S NATIONAL ARCHIVES & RECORDS ADMINISTRATION*, Jimmy Carter Presidential Library & Museum, 441 Freedom Pkwy, 30307-1498. SAN 328-5650. Tel: 404-865-7100. FAX: 404-865-7102. E-mail: carter.library@nara.gov. Web Site: www.jimmycarterlibrary.gov. *Dir,* Dr Meredith Evans; *Pub Affairs,* Tony Clark; Tel: 404-865-7109, E-mail: tony.clark@nara.gov
Founded 1986
Library Holdings: Bk Titles 6,500; Per Subs 50; Videos 1,550
Special Collections: Presidental Papers of Jimmy Carter
Wireless access
Function: Res libr
Publications: Historical Materials in the Jimmy Carter Library (Online only)
Open Mon-Fri 8:30-4:30
Friends of the Library Group

S NATIONAL FOOTBALL FOUNDATION'S COLLEGE*, College Football Hall of Fame Library, 250 Marietta St, 30313-1591. SAN 313-5527. Tel: 404-880-4800. E-mail: info@cfbhall.com. Web Site: www.cfbhall.com. *Curator, Historian,* Jeremy Swick; E-mail: jswick@cfbhall.com; Staff 4 (MLS 1, Non-MLS 3)
Library Holdings: AV Mats 1,580; CDs 109; Bk Titles 10,100; Bk Vols 12,300; Per Subs 68; Videos 410
Special Collections: Oral History
Subject Interests: Col football hist
Wireless access
Restriction: Open by appt only

M NORTHSIDE HOSPITAL*, Health Resource Center, 1000 Johnson Ferry Rd NE, 30342-1611. SAN 303-3155. Tel: 404-851-6431. FAX: 404-851-6167. *Dir, Libr Serv,* Todd Prusin; E-mail: todd.prusin@northside.com
Founded 1970
Library Holdings: e-journals 400; Bk Titles 1,400; Per Subs 150
Subject Interests: Med, Nursing, Obstetrics & gynecology
Wireless access
Partic in Atlanta Health Science Libraries Consortium
Open Mon-Fri 7-4
Friends of the Library Group

C OGLETHORPE UNIVERSITY*, Philip Weltner Library, 4484 Peachtree Rd NE, 30319. SAN 303-3163. Tel: 404-364-8511. FAX: 404-364-8517. Web Site: library.oglethorpe.edu. *Dir & Univ Librn,* Anne Salter; *Cat,* Jean Hudgins; E-mail: jhudgins@oglethorpe.edu; *Ref (Info Servs),* Eli Arnold; E-mail: earnold@oglethorpe.edu; Staff 3 (MLS 3)
Founded 1916. Enrl 920; Fac 48; Highest Degree: Master
Library Holdings: Bk Titles 157,000; Per Subs 745
Special Collections: James E Oglethorpe Coll; Sidney Lanier Coll
Automation Activity & Vendor Info: (Cataloging) Ex Libris Group; (Circulation) Ex Libris Group
Wireless access
Partic in Atlanta Regional Council for Higher Education
Open Mon-Thurs 8:30am-10pm, Fri 8:30-5, Sat 12-5, Sun 2pm-10pm

R PEACHTREE PRESBYTERIAN CHURCH*, Pattillo Library, 3434 Roswell Rd NW, 30305. SAN 303-3171. Tel: 404-842-5810. Web Site: www.peachtreechurch.org. *Library Contact,* Liz Tash; E-mail: ltash@peachtreepres.org
Founded 1960
Library Holdings: Bk Vols 10,000
Restriction: Mem only

CR RICHMONT GRADUATE UNIVERSITY*, Atlanta Campus Library, 1900 The Exchange SE, Bldg 100, 30339. SAN 329-8361. Tel: 404-835-6120. FAX: 404-239-9460. Web Site: www.richmont.edu/library. *Dir of Libr,* John Hughes; E-mail: jhughes@richmont.edu; *Librn,* Alison Mead; Tel: 405-835-6133, E-mail: amead@richmont.edu; Staff 1 (MLS 1)
Enrl 100; Highest Degree: Master
Library Holdings: Bk Vols 14,000; Per Subs 39
Automation Activity & Vendor Info: (Cataloging) Follett Software
Wireless access
Partic in GOLD Resource Sharing Network for Georgia's Libraries; Tenn-Share
Open Mon & Wed 8:30-7, Tues & Thurs 8:30am-9pm, Fri 9-5

L SCHREEDER, WHEELER & FLINT LLP*, Law Library, 1100 Peachtree St NE, Ste 800, 30309. SAN 372-1426. Tel: 404-681-3450. FAX: 404-681-1046. Web Site: www.swfllp.com. *Library Contact,* Debbie Wilson; E-mail: dwilson@swfllp.com
Library Holdings: Bk Vols 5,000; Per Subs 10
Subject Interests: Real estate

L SMITH, GAMBRELL & RUSSELL*, Law Library, Prominade II, 1230 Peachtree St NE, Ste 3100, 30309. SAN 303-3228. Tel: 404-815-3538. Information Services Tel: 404-815-3618. FAX: 404-685-6838, 404-815-3509. E-mail: library@sgrlaw.com. Web Site: www.sgrlaw.com/locations/atlanta. *Dir,* Sarah Mauldan; Staff 4 (MLS 1, Non-MLS 3)
Founded 1893
Library Holdings: Bk Vols 50,000; Per Subs 100
Wireless access
Partic in CT Advantage; Dun & Bradstreet Info Servs; Pacer; Proquest Dialog; Thompson Saegis

UNITED STATES ENVIRONMENTAL PROTECTION

G REGION 4 LIBRARY*, Atlanta Federal Ctr, 61 Forsyth St SW, 30303-3104, SAN 303-2809. Tel: 404-562-8190. FAX: 404-562-8114. E-mail: r4-library@epa.gov. *Sr Librn,* Ora Mims Howell; Tel: 404-562-8125; Staff 1 (MLS 1)
Founded 1973
Library Holdings: Bk Titles 24,000; Per Subs 50
Special Collections: EPA Reports; Public Display; Superfund Docket; USGS Reports
Subject Interests: Air pollution, Environ law, Noise pollution, Water pollution
Partic in OCLC Online Computer Library Center, Inc; OLS
Open Mon-Fri 8-4
Friends of the Library Group

G REGION 4 OEA INFORMATION-RESEARCH CENTER*, 61 Forsyth St SW, 30303-3104, SAN 374-7034. Tel: 404-562-9654. FAX: 404-562-9663. *Dir,* Pat Strougal; Staff 1 (MLS 1)
Founded 1992
Library Holdings: Bk Titles 600; Bk Vols 6,200; Videos 75
Special Collections: EPA Guidances
Subject Interests: Environ law
Function: For res purposes, Ref serv available, Telephone ref
Restriction: Circulates for staff only, Not open to pub

M WELLSTAR ATLANTA MEDICAL CENTER*, Fay E Evatt Medical Library, 303 Parkway Dr NE, Box 415, 30312-1212. SAN 338-4217. Tel: 404-265-4000. FAX: 404-265-3559. E-mail: medicallibrary@wellstar.org. *Med Librn,* Lisa Mastin; Tel: 404-265-4605, E-mail: lisa.mastin@wellstar.org; Staff 1 (MLS 1)
Founded 1930
Library Holdings: Bk Titles 3,500; Per Subs 398
Special Collections: Archives
Automation Activity & Vendor Info: (Cataloging) CyberTools for Libraries; (Circulation) CyberTools for Libraries; (OPAC) CyberTools for Libraries; (Serials) CyberTools for Libraries
Wireless access
Function: Health sci info serv
Partic in Atlanta Health Science Libraries Consortium; Georgia Health Sciences Library Association
Open Mon-Fri 8-4
Restriction: Access at librarian's discretion, Authorized patrons, Badge access after hrs, Circulates for staff only, Hospital staff & commun, Lending to staff only, Med & health res only

AUGUSTA

S AUGUSTA RICHMOND COUNTY HISTORICAL SOCIETY LIBRARY*, c/o Reese Library @ GRU, 2500 Walton Way, 30904-2200. SAN 303-3368. Tel: 706-737-1532. FAX: 706-667-4415. E-mail: archs1946@gmail.com. Web Site: www.thearchs.org. *Dir,* Elaine Benton
Founded 1946
Library Holdings: Bk Titles 2,091; Bk Vols 3,072
Subject Interests: Ga, Genealogy
Publications: An Augusta Scrapbook - Twentieth Century Memories; Augusta: A Pictorial History; Confederate City, Augusta, Georgia; Historical Markers and monuments of Augusta, Richmond County; Journal of Archibald Campbell in His Majesty's Service, 1778; Reminiscences of Augusta Marines; Richmond County History, The Journal of the Society (annual); Summerville: A Pictorial History; The Story of Augusta; Touring Historic Augusta
Open Wed & Thurs 10-4

P AUGUSTA-RICHMOND COUNTY PUBLIC LIBRARY*, 823 Telfair St, 30901. SAN 338-4519. Tel: 706-821-2600. FAX: 706-724-6762. Web Site: arcpls.org. *Dir,* Mashell Fashion; E-mail: fashionm@arcpls.org; *Asst Dir,*

Tracey Busbee; E-mail: busbeet@arcpls.org; *Syst Adminr,* Benjamin Dudley; *Head, Pub Serv,* Russell Liner; E-mail: linerr@arcpls.org; *Head, Tech Serv,* Jennie Feinberg; E-mail: feinbergj@arcpls.org; *Ch,* Carrie Koerber; *Outreach Librn,* Erin Prentiss; *Circ Mgr,* Jennifer Stallings; Staff 58 (MLS 14, Non-MLS 44)
Founded 1848. Pop 338,000; Circ 113,743
Library Holdings: Audiobooks 3,952; AV Mats 30,250; CDs 1,728; DVDs 12,162; e-books 2,200; Bk Vols 618,439; Per Subs 188; Talking Bks 33,836; Videos 18,092
Subject Interests: Ga
Automation Activity & Vendor Info: (Cataloging) Evergreen; (Circulation) Evergreen; (OPAC) Evergreen
Wireless access
Function: ILL available, Magnifiers for reading, Photocopying/Printing, Prog for children & young adult, Ref serv available, Summer reading prog, Wheelchair accessible
Publications: Library Links (Newsletter); Personal Name Index to the Augusta Chronicle Newspaper
Partic in Public Information Network for Electronic Services
Special Services for the Deaf - TDD equip; TTY equip
Special Services for the Blind - Bks on cassette; Bks on CD; Computer with voice synthesizer for visually impaired persons; Large print bks; Reader equip
Open Mon-Thurs 9-8, Fri & Sat 9-5:30, Sun 2-5:30
Friends of the Library Group
Branches: 6
APPLEBY BRANCH, 2260 Walton Way, 30904, SAN 338-4578. Tel: 706-736-6244. FAX: 706-481-0616. *Br Mgr,* Nicole Ashworth; E-mail: ashworthn@arcpls.org; Staff 2 (Non-MLS 2)
Founded 1955
Library Holdings: DVDs 216; Bk Vols 36,621; Per Subs 44; Talking Bks 381
Function: Photocopying/Printing, Prog for children & young adult, Summer reading prog
Special Services for the Blind - Bks on CD; Computer with voice synthesizer for visually impaired persons; Large print bks; Talking bks
Open Mon-Sat 9-5:30
Friends of the Library Group
DIAMOND LAKES, 101 Diamond Lakes Way, Hephzibah, 30815. Tel: 706-772-2432. FAX: 706-772-2433. *Br Mgr,* Cathy Joseph; E-mail: josephc@arcpls.org
Founded 2005
Library Holdings: DVDs 455; Bk Vols 14,723; Per Subs 70; Talking Bks 110; Videos 355
Function: Adult bk club, Bks on cassette, Bks on CD, Children's prog, Computer training, Computers for patron use, Electronic databases & coll, Free DVD rentals, ILL available, Magazines, Music CDs, Online cat, Photocopying/Printing, Prog for adults, Prog for children & young adult, Story hour, Summer reading prog, Tax forms
Special Services for the Blind - Bks on cassette; Bks on CD; Computer with voice synthesizer for visually impaired persons
Open Mon & Wed 9-7, Tues & Thurs-Sat 9-5:30
Friends of the Library Group
FRIEDMAN BRANCH, 1447 Jackson Rd, 30909, SAN 328-7882. Tel: 706-736-6758. FAX: 706-737-2034. *Br Mgr,* Paulette Scurry; E-mail: scurryp@arcpls.org; Staff 3 (MLS 1, Non-MLS 2)
Founded 1986. Circ 117,463
Library Holdings: DVDs 362; Bk Vols 43,290; Per Subs 36; Talking Bks 111; Videos 1,000
Function: Photocopying/Printing, Prog for children & young adult, Ref serv available, Summer reading prog, Telephone ref, Wheelchair accessible
Special Services for the Blind - Bks on cassette; Bks on CD; Computer with voice synthesizer for visually impaired persons; Large print bks
Open Mon & Wed 9-7, Tues & Thurs-Sat 9-5:30
Friends of the Library Group
JEFF MAXWELL BRANCH, 1927 Lumpkin Rd, 30906, SAN 338-4608. Tel: 706-793-2020. FAX: 706-790-1023. *Br Mgr,* Joshua Sheffield; E-mail: sheffieldj@arcpls.org; Staff 3 (MLS 1, Non-MLS 2)
Founded 1973. Circ 130,555
Library Holdings: DVDs 1,200; Bk Vols 59,809; Per Subs 37; Videos 500
Function: Photocopying/Printing, Prog for children & young adult, Ref serv available, Summer reading prog, Telephone ref, Wheelchair accessible
Special Services for the Blind - Bks on cassette; Bks on CD; Large print bks
Open Mon, Wed, Fri & Sat 9-5:30, Tues & Thurs 9-7
Friends of the Library Group
TALKING BOOK CENTER, 823 Telfair St, 30901, SAN 338-4543. Tel: 706-821-2625. FAX: 706-724-5403. *Br Mgr,* Jayne Andrews; E-mail: andrewsj@arcpls.org; Staff 4 (Non-MLS 4)
Founded 1981. Circ 82,524
Library Holdings: DVDs 896; Large Print Bks 1,158; Talking Bks 34,641; Videos 7,739
Subject Interests: Blind, Physically handicapped
Function: AV serv
Publications: Augusta Talking Book Center News (Newsletter)
Special Services for the Blind - Talking bks
Open Mon-Thurs 9-8, Fri & Sat 9-5:30, Sun 2-5:30
Friends of the Library Group
WALLACE BRANCH, 1237 Laney-Walker Blvd, 30901, SAN 338-4632. Tel: 706-722-6275. FAX: 706-724-0715. *Br Mgr,* Sandra May; E-mail: mays@arcpls.org; Staff 2 (Non-MLS 2)
Founded 1959. Circ 18,855
Library Holdings: Bk Vols 28,000; Per Subs 39; Talking Bks 22
Function: Photocopying/Printing, Prog for children & young adult, Summer reading prog, Wheelchair accessible
Special Services for the Blind - Bks on CD; Computer with voice synthesizer for visually impaired persons
Open Mon-Sat 9-5:30
Friends of the Library Group
Bookmobiles: 1. In Charge, Diane Evans

J AUGUSTA TECHNICAL COLLEGE*, Jack B Patrick Information Tech Center, 3200 Augusta Tech Dr, 30906. SAN 326-6605. Tel: 706-771-4164, 706-771-4165. FAX: 706-771-4169. Web Site: www.augustatech.edu/library.html. *Dir, Libr Serv,* Bonnie Owen; E-mail: bowen@augustatech.edu; Staff 9 (MLS 5, Non-MLS 4)
Library Holdings: Bk Titles 100,000; Per Subs 500
Special Collections: US Document Depository
Subject Interests: Electronics
Wireless access
Partic in LYRASIS
Open Mon-Thurs 7:30am-8:30pm, Fri 7:30-3, Sun 2-6
Departmental Libraries:
BURKE CAMPUS LIBRARY, 216 Hwy 24 S, Waynesboro, 30830. Tel: 706-437-6805, 706-437-6806. *Librn,* Teresa Evans; E-mail: tevans@augustatech.edu
Open Mon-Thurs 8-8, Fri 8-3
MCDUFFIE CAMPUS LIBRARY, 338 Tech Dr NW, Thomson, 30824. Tel: 706-595-0166. *Librn,* Brenda Norman; E-mail: bnorman@augustatech.edu
Open Mon-Thurs 8-8, Fri 8-3

C AUGUSTA UNIVERSITY, Reese Library, 2500 Walton Way, 30904-2200. SAN 303-3333. Tel: 706-737-1744. E-mail: reference@augusta.edu. Web Site: www.augusta.edu/library/reese. *Assoc Prof, Interim Libr Dir,* Kathy Davies; E-mail: kadavies@augusta.edu; Staff 29 (MLS 10, Non-MLS 19)
Founded 1957. Enrl 6,900; Fac 310; Highest Degree: Master
Library Holdings: Bk Vols 497,172; Per Subs 36,124
Special Collections: Cumming Family Papers; Edison Marshall Papers; Local History Coll (Augusta-Richmond County Historical Society). US Document Depository
Automation Activity & Vendor Info: (Cataloging) Ex Libris Group; (Circulation) Ex Libris Group; (Course Reserve) Ex Libris Group; (ILL) OCLC ILLiad; (Media Booking) Ex Libris Group; (OPAC) Ex Libris Group; (Serials) Ex Libris Group
Wireless access
Partic in Georgia Library Learning Online; LYRASIS; OCLC Online Computer Library Center, Inc
Special Services for the Deaf - TTY equip

CM AUGUSTA UNIVERSITY*, Robert B Greenblatt MD Library, 1459 Laney-Walker Blvd, 30912-0004. (Mail add: 1120 15th St, 30912), SAN 303-3341. Tel: 706-721-3441. Interlibrary Loan Service Tel: 706-721-6374. FAX: 706-721-2018. Interlibrary Loan Service FAX: 706-721-6006. Reference E-mail: libref@augusta.edu. Web Site: www.augusta.edu/library/greenblatt/. *Interim Dir, Libr Serv,* Kathy Davies, PhD; Tel: 706-721-9911, E-mail: kadavies@augusta.edu; *Chair, Content Mgt,* Sandra Bandy; Tel: 706-721-0299, E-mail: sbandy@gru.edu; *Chair, Res & Educ Serv,* Gail Kouame; Tel: 706-721-9904, E-mail: gkouame@augusta.edu; *Access Serv Librn,* Natalie Logue; Tel: 706-721-6473, E-mail: nlogue@augusta.edu; *Bus Mgr,* Marianne Brown; E-mail: marbrown@augusta.edu; Staff 23 (MLS 9, Non-MLS 14)
Founded 1834. Enrl 8,995; Fac 1,575; Highest Degree: Doctorate
Jul 2012-Jun 2013. Mats Exp $1,485,093. Sal $1,058,903
Library Holdings: AV Mats 1,772; e-books 548; Bk Titles 27,167; Bk Vols 32,285; Per Subs 6,134
Special Collections: 19th Century Library; Greenblatt Archive; Landmarks in Modern Medicine Coll; Medical Artifacts
Subject Interests: Allied health, Dentistry, Med, Nursing
Automation Activity & Vendor Info: (Cataloging) Ex Libris Group; (Circulation) Ex Libris Group; (Course Reserve) Ex Libris Group; (ILL) OCLC ILLiad; (Media Booking) Ex Libris Group; (OPAC) Ex Libris Group; (Serials) Ex Libris Group
Wireless access

Function: Res libr
Partic in Consortium of Southern Biomedical Libraries; National Network of Libraries of Medicine Region 2; OCLC Online Computer Library Center, Inc; Regents Acad Comt on Librs

GM CHARLIE NORWOOD VA MEDICAL CENTER LIBRARY*, One Freedom Way, 30904-6285. SAN 303-3384. Tel: 706-733-0188, Ext 7518. FAX: 706-823-3920. *Chief Librn,* Brian Rothwell; Staff 2 (MLS 1, Non-MLS 1)
Founded 1937
Library Holdings: Bk Vols 5,226; Per Subs 321
Subject Interests: Geriatrics, Med, Nursing, Psychiat, Psychol, Soc serv (soc work), Surgery
Partic in National Network of Libraries of Medicine Region 2
Restriction: Staff & patient use

C PAINE COLLEGE, Collins Callaway Library & Learning Resources Center, 1235 15th St, 30901-3105. SAN 303-335X. Tel: 706-821-8308. Administration Tel: 706-821-8253. FAX: 706-821-8698. Web Site: www.paine.edu/web/academics/library. *Libr Dir,* Alana Lewis; Tel: 708-821-8361, E-mail: alewis@paine.edu; *Mgr,* Rosa L Martin; Tel: 706-821-8365, E-mail: rmartin@paine.edu
Founded 1882. Enrl 900; Highest Degree: Bachelor
Special Collections: African-American Special Coll
Wireless access
Partic in Georgia Private Acad Librs Consortium; LYRASIS
Open Mon-Thurs 8am-10pm, Fri 8-5, Sun 4-8
Restriction: In-house use for visitors

BAINBRIDGE

P SOUTHWEST GEORGIA REGIONAL LIBRARY*, Decatur County - Gilbert H Gragg Library, 301 S Monroe St, 39819. SAN 338-4667. Tel: 229-248-2665. FAX: 229-248-2670. E-mail: librarian@swgrl.org. Web Site: www.swgrl.org. *Dir,* Susan S Whittle; E-mail: swhittle@swgrl.org; *Asst Dir, Tech, Training & Develop,* Catherine Vanstone; E-mail: cvanstone@swgrl.org; Staff 19.5 (MLS 3, Non-MLS 16.5)
Founded 1902. Pop 44,008; Circ 221,715
Jul 2013-Jun 2014 Income (Main & Associated Libraries) $1,217,940, State $426,752, City $1,621, County $719,701, Other $69,866. Mats Exp $74,775, Books $56,516, Per/Ser (Incl. Access Fees) $5,006, AV Mat $12,803, Electronic Ref Mat (Incl. Access Fees) $450. Sal $582,765 (Prof $209,530)
Library Holdings: AV Mats 15,442; Electronic Media & Resources 3; Bk Vols 171,075; Per Subs 79; Talking Bks 38,609
Special Collections: Andrew Avery Film Coll; E Ashby Woods World War II Coll; Georgia Author Coll; Jack Wingate Hunters & Anglers Coll. Oral History
Subject Interests: Genealogy, Local hist, World War II
Automation Activity & Vendor Info: (Cataloging) Evergreen; (Circulation) Evergreen; (ILL) OCLC; (OPAC) Evergreen
Wireless access
Function: After school storytime, Art exhibits, Bk club(s), Bks on CD, Children's prog, Computer training, Computers for patron use, Digital talking bks, Electronic databases & coll, Free DVD rentals, Holiday prog, ILL available, Music CDs, Online cat, Online ref, Outreach serv, Photocopying/Printing, Preschool outreach, Prog for adults, Prog for children & young adult, Ref serv available, Senior computer classes, Senior outreach, Spoken cassettes & CDs, Story hour, Summer reading prog, Tax forms, Teen prog, VHS videos, Wheelchair accessible
Publications: Bainbridge Subregional Library & Physically Handicapped of Southwest Georgia (Monthly newsletter); SWGRL Spotlight (Monthly newsletter)
Partic in Public Information Network for Electronic Services
Special Services for the Deaf - Assistive tech; TTY equip
Special Services for the Blind - Accessible computers; Assistive/Adapted tech devices, equip & products; Audio mat; Bks & mags in Braille, on rec, tape & cassette; Bks on cassette; Bks on CD; Braille alphabet card; Braille equip; Cassette playback machines; Cassettes; Children's Braille; Digital talking bk; Home delivery serv; Info on spec aids & appliances; Internet workstation with adaptive software; Large print bks; Low vision equip; Magnifiers; Newsletter (in large print, Braille or on cassette); Newsline for the Blind; Recorded bks; Screen reader software; Talking bks; Talking bks & player equip
Open Mon 9-8, Tues, Wed & Fri 9-6, Thurs 9-7, Sat 9-4
Friends of the Library Group
Branches: 3

P BAINBRIDGE SUBREGIONAL LIBRARY FOR THE BLIND & PHYSICALLY HANDICAPPED-TALKING BOOK CENTER, 301 S Monroe St, 39819. Tel: 229-248-2680. Toll Free Tel: 800-795-2680. FAX: 229-248-2670. E-mail: Lbph@swgrl.org. *Librn,* Susan Whittle; Staff 3 (MLS 1, Non-MLS 2)
Founded 1971
Library Holdings: Talking Bks 38,609
Automation Activity & Vendor Info: (Circulation) Keystone Systems, Inc (KLAS)
Publications: Talking Book Newsletter (Monthly)
Special Services for the Blind - Aids for in-house use; Assistive/Adapted tech devices, equip & products; Bks & mags in Braille, on rec, tape & cassette; Braille equip; Cassette playback machines; Cassettes; Digital talking bk; Digital talking bk machines; Info on spec aids & appliances; Internet workstation with adaptive software; Newsletter (in large print, Braille or on cassette); Newsline for the Blind; Ref serv; Talking bk & rec for the blind cat; Talking bks; Talking bks & player equip
Open Mon 9-8, Tues, Wed & Fri 9-6, Thurs 9-7, Sat 9-4

MILLER COUNTY-JAMES W MERRITT JR MEMORIAL LIBRARY, 259 E Main St, Colquitt, 39837, SAN 338-4721. Tel: 229-758-3131. FAX: 229-758-9267. *Br Mgr,* Donna Weeks
Open Mon-Fri 10-5:30
Friends of the Library Group

SEMINOLE COUNTY PUBLIC LIBRARY, 103 W Fourth St, Donalsonville, 39845, SAN 338-4756. Tel: 229-524-2665. FAX: 229-524-8913. *Br Mgr,* Judy Smith
Subject Interests: Genealogy, Local hist
Open Mon-Sat 9:30-5:30
Bookmobiles: 1. Outreach Coordr, Arlene Freeman. Bk vols 3,751

BARNESVILLE

J GORDON STATE COLLEGE*, Dorothy W Hightower Collaborative Learning Center & Library, 419 College Dr, 30204. SAN 303-3406. Tel: 678-359-5076. FAX: 678-359-5240. E-mail: library@gordonstate.edu. Web Site: www.gordonstate.edu/library/home.html. *Interim Dir, Res Sharing Librn, Ser Librn,* Brenda Rutherford; E-mail: brendar@gordonstate.edu; *Circ Librn, Media Librn,* Beverly Eskridge; E-mail: beverly@gordonstate.edu; *Ref & Instrul Serv Librn,* Beth Pye; E-mail: bethp@gordonstate.edu; *Tech Serv Asst,* Lisa Millican; E-mail: lisam@gordonstate.edu; Staff 7 (MLS 4, Non-MLS 3)
Founded 1939. Enrl 3,800; Fac 96; Highest Degree: Bachelor
Library Holdings: AV Mats 4,785; e-books 27,417; Microforms 9,637; Bk Vols 103,000; Per Subs 45
Subject Interests: Ga
Automation Activity & Vendor Info: (Acquisitions) Ex Libris Group; (Cataloging) OCLC; (Circulation) Ex Libris Group; (Course Reserve) Ex Libris Group; (ILL) OCLC; (OPAC) Ex Libris Group; (Serials) Ex Libris Group
Wireless access
Partic in LYRASIS
Open Mon-Wed 8am-10pm, Thurs 8-8, Fri 8-5, Sun 2-10

BLAIRSVILLE

J NORTH GEORGIA TECHNICAL COLLEGE LIBRARY*, Blairsville Campus, 121 Meeks Ave, 30512. Tel: 706-439-6326. FAX: 706-439-6301. E-mail: library@northgatech.edu. Web Site: www.northgatech.edu/library. *Supvr,* Samantha Marchant; E-mail: smarchan@northgatech.edu; *Libr Asst,* Tina Dellaposta; E-mail: tdellaposta@northgatech.edu; Staff 1 (MLS 1)
Founded 1998. Enrl 500; Fac 20; Highest Degree: Associate
Library Holdings: AV Mats 925; CDs 100; DVDs 500; e-books 39,000; Bk Titles 5,000; Bk Vols 5,100; Per Subs 50
Automation Activity & Vendor Info: (Cataloging) OCLC CatExpress; (Circulation) SirsiDynix; (OPAC) SirsiDynix
Wireless access
Partic in LYRASIS

BRUNSWICK

J COLLEGE OF COASTAL GEORGIA*, Clara Wood Gould Memorial Library, One College Dr, 31520-3644. SAN 303-3414. Tel: 912-279-5700. Circulation Tel: 912-279-5874. Toll Free Tel: 800-675-7235. Web Site: www.ccga.edu/page.cfm?p=688. *Dean, Libr Serv,* Debbie Holmes; Tel: 912-279-5787, E-mail: dholmes@ccga.edu; *Pub Serv Librn,* Karen Haven; Tel: 954-279-5784, E-mail: khaven@ccga.edu; *Pub Serv Librn,* Lynda Kennedy; Tel: 912-279-5782, E-mail: lkennedy@ccga.edu; *Pub Serv Librn,* Cary Knapp; Tel: 912-279-5781, E-mail: cknapp@ccga.edu; Staff 9 (MLS 5, Non-MLS 4)
Founded 1961. Enrl 3,200; Fac 54; Highest Degree: Associate
Library Holdings: e-books 53,000; Electronic Media & Resources 150; Bk Titles 48,894; Bk Vols 51,211; Per Subs 250
Special Collections: Coastal Georgia History
Automation Activity & Vendor Info: (Acquisitions) Ex Libris Group; (Cataloging) Ex Libris Group; (Circulation) Ex Libris Group; (ILL) OCLC ILLiad; (Media Booking) Ex Libris Group; (OPAC) Ex Libris Group; (Serials) Ex Libris Group
Wireless access
Function: ILL available
Partic in LYRASIS
Special Services for the Blind - Reader equip

Open Mon-Thurs 8am-10pm, Fri 8-5, Sat 1-5, Sun 1-9
Restriction: Employees & their associates, In-house use for visitors, Non-circulating to the pub, Open to pub for ref only, Open to students, fac & staff
Departmental Libraries:
CAMDEN CENTER LEARNING RESOURCES CENTER, 8001 Lakes Blvd, Kingsland, 31548. Tel: 912-510-3331. Web Site: www.ccga.edu/page.cfm?p=1093. *Pub Serv Librn,* John Kissinger; E-mail: jkissinger@ccga.edu; *Info Spec,* Angela Hughes
Open Mon-Thurs 8am-9pm, Fri 8-5

P MARSHES OF GLYNN LIBRARIES*, Brunswick-Glynn County Library, 208 Gloucester St, 31520. SAN 338-4780. Tel: 912-279-3740. Web Site: moglibraries.org/brunswick-glynn-county-library. *Dir,* Gerri Mullis; *Asst Dir,* Ben Bryson; Tel: 912-229-3735, E-mail: bbryson@glynncounty-ga.gov; *Libr Mgr,* Lori Hull; E-mail: lhull@glenncounty-ga.gov; Staff 2 (MLS 1, Non-MLS 1)
Founded 1883. Pop 80,000
Library Holdings: Bk Vols 67,000
Special Collections: Brunswick & Glynn County History Coll, maps & photo; Genealogy, Georgia & Southeast United States Coll; Georgia History Coll
Automation Activity & Vendor Info: (Acquisitions) Evergreen; (Cataloging) Evergreen; (Circulation) Evergreen; (ILL) OCLC; (OPAC) Evergreen
Wireless access
Member Libraries: Saint Simons Island Public Library
Partic in Public Information Network for Electronic Services
Open Mon, Wed, Fri & Sat 9:30-5, Tues & Thurs 9:30-8
Friends of the Library Group

BUFORD

S PHILLIPS STATE PRISON*, Law & General Library, 2989 W Rock Quarry Rd, 30519-4198. SAN 371-0971. Tel: 770-932-4500, 770-932-4732. *Librn,* Princess Shellman
Library Holdings: Bk Vols 8,000; Per Subs 45
Special Services for the Deaf - High interest/low vocabulary bks
Restriction: Staff & inmates only

CAIRO

P RODDENBERY MEMORIAL LIBRARY, 320 N Broad St, 39828-2109. SAN 338-4993. Tel: 229-377-3632. FAX: 229-377-7204. E-mail: rml@rmlibrary.org. Web Site: www.rmlibrary.org. *Dir,* Janet R Boudet; E-mail: jboudet@rmlibrary.org; *Assoc Dir,* Jessica Wilson; Staff 9 (MLS 2, Non-MLS 7)
Founded 1939. Pop 24,845; Circ 92,085
Jul 2021-Jun 2022 Income $607,915, State $134,688, City $237,500, County $100,000, Locally Generated Income $25,000, Other $110,727. Sal $416,124 (Prof $178,501)
Library Holdings: Audiobooks 869; AV Mats 2,495; Bks on Deafness & Sign Lang 59; CDs 538; DVDs 485; Electronic Media & Resources 157; High Interest/Low Vocabulary Bk Vols 64; Large Print Bks 4,278; Microforms 309; Bk Titles 59,085; Bk Vols 64,419; Per Subs 127; Talking Bks 47; Videos 544
Special Collections: Genealogy Coll. Oral History
Subject Interests: Gardening, Local authors
Automation Activity & Vendor Info: (Cataloging) Evergreen; (Circulation) Evergreen; (ILL) OCLC; (OPAC) Evergreen
Wireless access
Function: 24/7 Electronic res, 24/7 Online cat, 3D Printer, Activity rm, Adult literacy prog, Art programs, Audiobks via web, AV serv, Bks on cassette, Bks on CD, CD-ROM, Children's prog, Computers for patron use, E-Reserves, Electronic databases & coll, Free DVD rentals, Genealogy discussion group, Homework prog, ILL available, Instruction & testing, Internet access, Laminating, Large print keyboards, Magazines, Magnifiers for reading, Mail & tel request accepted, Mango lang, Meeting rooms, Museum passes, Music CDs, Notary serv, Online cat, OverDrive digital audio bks, Photocopying/Printing, Preschool outreach, Printer for laptops & handheld devices, Prog for adults, Prog for children & young adult, Ref serv available, Scanner, Spoken cassettes & CDs, Story hour, Study rm, Summer reading prog, Tax forms, Teen prog, Telephone ref, VHS videos, Wheelchair accessible
Publications: Gleanings from Grady County (Local historical information); Grady County Information & Referral Guide; I Remember Wessie
Partic in GOLD Resource Sharing Network for Georgia's Libraries; National Network of Libraries of Medicine Region 2; Public Information Network for Electronic Services
Special Services for the Blind - Large print bks; Magnifiers; Screen enlargement software for people with visual disabilities; Talking bks & player equip; VisualTek equip
Open Mon-Thurs 10-6, Fri 10-3, Sat 10-2
Friends of the Library Group

CAMILLA

P DE SOTO TRAIL REGIONAL LIBRARY SYSTEM*, 145 E Broad St, 31730. SAN 338-5051. Tel: 229-336-8372. FAX: 229-336-9353. Web Site: www.desototrail.org. *Dir,* Lisa Rigsby; E-mail: rigsby@desototrail.org; *Asst Dir,* Lauren Culpepper Brookins; Staff 3 (MLS 3)
Library Holdings: Bk Vols 50,000; Per Subs 76
Automation Activity & Vendor Info: (Cataloging) SirsiDynix; (Circulation) SirsiDynix
Wireless access
Function: 24/7 Electronic res, 24/7 Online cat, 3D Printer, Activity rm, Butterfly Garden, Computer training, Computers for patron use, Genealogy discussion group, ILL available, Internet access, Laminating, Life-long learning prog for all ages, Magazines, Mango lang, Meeting rooms, Notary serv, Online cat, Photocopying/Printing, Printer for laptops & handheld devices, Prog for children & young adult, Scanner, STEM programs, Story hour, Summer reading prog, Tax forms
Partic in Public Information Network for Electronic Services
Open Mon, Tues & Thurs 9-6, Wed & Fri 9-5:30, Sat 9-12:30
Branches: 3
BAKER COUNTY, 398 Ga Hwy 37 SW, Newton, 39870. Tel: 229-734-3025. *Librn,* Tammy Hawkins
Open Mon-Fri 2-5, Sat 10-12
LUCY MADDOX MEMORIAL, 11880 Columbia St, Blakely, 39823, SAN 338-5116. Tel: 229-723-3079. FAX: 229-723-6429. *Br Mgr,* Brenda Wall
Open Mon-Fri 9-5:30, Sat 9-12
PELHAM CARNEGIE BRANCH, 133 Hand Ave, Pelham, 31779, SAN 338-5140. Tel: 229-294-6030. FAX: 229-294-6030. *Br Mgr,* Kelly Hancock
Open Mon-Fri 9:30-12:30 & 1:30-5:30

CANTON

P SEQUOYAH REGIONAL LIBRARY SYSTEM*, R T Jones Memorial Library, Headquarters, 116 Brown Industrial Pkwy, 30114. SAN 338-5264. Tel: 770-479-3090. Circulation Tel: 770-479-3090, Ext 234. Reference Tel: 770-479-3090, Ext 228. FAX: 770-479-3069. E-mail: sequoyahregional@gmail.com. Web Site: www.sequoyahregionallibrary.org/r-t-jones. *Exec Dir,* Anita Summers; Tel: 770-479-3090, Ext 221, E-mail: summersa@seqlib.org; *Dep Dir,* Angela Glowcheski; Tel: 770-479-3090, Ext 230, E-mail: glowcheskia@seqlib.org; *Asst Dir,* Vicki Gazaway; E-mail: gazawayv@seqlib.org; *Libr Syst Adminr,* Donna Ferguson; E-mail: fergusod@seqlib.org; *Br Mgr,* Lisa Huskey; E-mail: huskeyl@seqlib.org; *Circ Mgr,* Rebecca Camp; E-mail: campr@seqlib.org; *Mgr, Coll Develop,* Jeff Fisher; *Tech Serv Mgr,* Christy Southard; E-mail: southac0@seqlib.org; *Youth Serv Supvr,* Melanie Pullen; E-mail: mpullen@seqlib.org; Staff 26 (MLS 3, Non-MLS 23)
Founded 1956. Pop 148,800; Circ 974,618
Library Holdings: Bk Vols 333,345
Special Collections: Career Center; Georgia History; Homeschooling Center; Spanish Center
Automation Activity & Vendor Info: (Acquisitions) TLC (The Library Corporation); (Cataloging) TLC (The Library Corporation); (Circulation) TLC (The Library Corporation); (Course Reserve) TLC (The Library Corporation); (ILL) TLC (The Library Corporation); (Media Booking) TLC (The Library Corporation); (OPAC) TLC (The Library Corporation); (Serials) TLC (The Library Corporation)
Wireless access
Partic in Georgia Libr Info Network; GOLD Resource Sharing Network for Georgia's Libraries; LYRASIS
Open Mon & Wed 10-8, Tues & Thurs-Sat 10-6, Sun 2-6
Friends of the Library Group
Branches: 7
BALL GROUND PUBLIC, 435 Old Canton Rd, Ball Ground, 30107. Tel: 770-735-2025. FAX: 770-735-6050. *Mgr,* Laura Sheehan; E-mail: sheehanl@seqlib.org
Founded 1997
Library Holdings: Bk Vols 32,378
Open Mon, Wed, Fri & Sat 10-6, Tues & Thurs 10-8
Friends of the Library Group
GILMER COUNTY PUBLIC, 268 Calvin Jackson Dr, Ellijay, 30540, SAN 338-5299. Tel: 706-635-4528. FAX: 706-635-3528. *Mgr,* Alex Thomerson; E-mail: thomersona@seqlib.org; Staff 1 (MLS 1)
Founded 1940
Special Collections: Genealogy Coll; Local History Coll
Open Mon-Thurs 9-8, Fri & Sat 9-6
Friends of the Library Group
HICKORY FLAT PUBLIC, 2740 E Cherokee Dr, 30115, SAN 374-4108. Tel: 770-345-7565. FAX: 770-345-7660. *Mgr,* Laurie Darrow; E-mail: darrowl@seqlib.org; Staff 7 (Non-MLS 7)
Founded 1993
Open Mon & Wed 10-8, Tues & Thurs-Sat 10-6
Friends of the Library Group

LAW LIBRARY, Frank C Mills III Justice Ctr, 90 North St, Ste 250, 30114. Tel: 678-493-6175. *Mgr,* Melissa Kelley; E-mail: robertsm@seqlib.org; Staff 1 (Non-MLS 1)
Founded 1996
Open Mon-Fri 8-5
Restriction: Non-circulating

PICKENS COUNTY PUBLIC, 100 Library Lane, Jasper, 30143, SAN 338-5329. Tel: 706-692-5411. FAX: 706-692-9518. *Mgr,* Stacy Hill; E-mail: hills@seqlib.org; Staff 8 (MLS 1, Non-MLS 7)
Founded 1958
Open Mon-Thurs 9-9, Fri & Sat 9-5, Sun 2-6
Friends of the Library Group

ROSE CREEK PUBLIC, 4476 Towne Lake Pkwy, Woodstock, 30189, SAN 371-3636. Tel: 770-591-1491. FAX: 770-591-1693. *Mgr,* Jill Green; E-mail: greenj@seqlib.org; Staff 7 (Non-MLS 7)
Founded 1991
Open Mon, Wed, Fri & Sat 10-6, Tues & Thurs 10-8
Friends of the Library Group

WOODSTOCK PUBLIC, 7735 Main St, Woodstock, 30188, SAN 338-5353. Tel: 770-926-5859. FAX: 770-591-8476. *Mgr,* Joey Dye; E-mail: dyej@seqlib.org; Staff 10 (Non-MLS 10)
Founded 1964
Open Mon, Wed, Fri & Sat 10-6, Tues & Thurs 10-8, Sun 2-6
Friends of the Library Group

CARROLLTON

R OAK GROVE BAPTIST CHURCH LIBRARY, 2829 Oak Grove Church Rd, 30117. SAN 303-3430. Tel: 770-834-7019. FAX: 770-834-8218. E-mail: info@ogbc.church. Web Site: www.ogbc.church. *Asst Librn,* Zelda Loftin; *Vols Librn,* Charlotte Culwell
Founded 1967
Library Holdings: Bk Vols 3,500
Subject Interests: Biblical studies, Relig

R TABERNACLE BAPTIST CHURCH LIBRARY*, 150 Tabernacle Dr, 30117. SAN 303-3457. Tel: 770-832-7063. FAX: 770-834-2777. Web Site: www.tabernacle.org. *Librn,* Linda Hale
Library Holdings: Bk Vols 9,335
Wireless access
Open Sun 9-10:30

C UNIVERSITY OF WEST GEORGIA*, Irvine Sullivan Ingram Library, 1601 Maple St, 30118. SAN 303-3473. Tel: 678-839-6495. Circulation Tel: 678-839-6502. Interlibrary Loan Service Tel: 678-839-6354. Administration Tel: 678-839-6498. Information Services Tel: 678-839-6350. FAX: 678-839-6511. Web Site: www.westga.edu/library. *Interim Dean of Libr,* Andrea Stanfield; E-mail: astanfie@westga.edu; *Head, Acq, Head, Electronic Res,* Charlie Sicignano; E-mail: charlie@westga.edu; *Head, Assessment & Outreach,* Anne Barnhart; E-mail: barnhart@westga.edu; *Head, Learning Serv, Head, Res Support Serv,* Angela Pashia; E-mail: apashia@westga.edu; *Head, Spec Coll,* Blynne Olivieri; Tel: 678-839-5455, E-mail: bolivier@westga.edu; *Instruction Librn,* CJ Ivory; E-mail: civory@westga.edu; *Ref Coordr, Sci Librn,* Jean Cook; E-mail: jcook@westga.edu; *Circ Mgr,* Sarah Cooper; E-mail: scooper@westga.edu; *Res Sharing Mgr,* Angela Mehaffey; E-mail: amehaffe@westga.edu; *Sr Cataloger,* Shelley Rogers; E-mail: srogers@westga.edu; *Proc Archivist,* Catherine Hendricks; E-mail: chendric@westga.edu; Staff 32 (MLS 14, Non-MLS 18)
Founded 1933. Enrl 11,252; Fac 551; Highest Degree: Doctorate
Library Holdings: AV Mats 11,634; Bk Vols 534,446; Per Subs 50,000
Special Collections: Georgia's Political Heritage Program Coll (Twentieth Century Georgia Politicians); Humanistic Psychology. US Document Depository
Automation Activity & Vendor Info: (Acquisitions) Ex Libris Group; (Cataloging) Ex Libris Group; (Course Reserve) Docutek; (ILL) OCLC ILLiad
Wireless access
Function: Archival coll, Art exhibits, Audio & video playback equip for onsite use, Computers for patron use, E-Reserves, Electronic databases & coll, Govt ref serv, ILL available, Music CDs, Online cat, Online info literacy tutorials on the web & in blackboard, Orientations, Photocopying/Printing
Partic in Cent Ga Associated Librs; LYRASIS; N Ga Associated Librs
Open Mon-Thurs 7:30am-2am, Fri 7:30am-11pm, Sat 10am-6pm, Sun 2pm-2am

P WEST GEORGIA REGIONAL LIBRARY*, Neva Lomason Memorial Library, 710 Rome St, 30117. SAN 338-5388. Tel: 770-836-6711. FAX: 770-836-4787. Web Site: www.wgrls.org. *Dir,* Jessica Everingham; Tel: 770-830-2233, Ext 1010, E-mail: jeveringham@wgrls.org; *Libr Mgr,* Rachel Linn; E-mail: rlinn@wgrls.org; Staff 5 (Non-MLS 5)
Founded 1944. Pop 425,000; Circ 1,756,518
Library Holdings: Audiobooks 32,469; DVDs 47,307; Bk Vols 640,274; Per Subs 300
Subject Interests: Genealogy, Local hist
Wireless access
Function: 24/7 Online cat, Adult bk club, After school storytime, Archival coll, Audiobks via web, Bk club(s), Bks on CD, Children's prog, Computer training, Computers for patron use, Electronic databases & coll, Free DVD rentals, Holiday prog, ILL available, Internet access, Magazines, Mail & tel request accepted, Mango lang, Meeting rooms, Microfiche/film & reading machines, Museum passes, Music CDs, Online cat, Online ref, Photocopying/Printing, Preschool outreach, Prog for adults, Prog for children & young adult, Res assist avail, Spanish lang bks, Story hour, Summer reading prog, Teen prog, Telephone ref, VHS videos, Wheelchair accessible
Partic in LYRASIS; N Ga Associated Librs; Public Information Network for Electronic Services
Special Services for the Blind - Audio mat; Bks on CD; Home delivery serv; Large print bks; Ref serv
Open Mon, Wed & Fri 9-5, Tues & Thurs 9-7
Friends of the Library Group
Branches: 18

BUCHANAN-HARALSON PUBLIC LIBRARY, 145 Van Wert St, Buchanan, 30113. Tel: 770-646-3369. FAX: 770-646-1103. *Mgr,* Jana Gentry; E-mail: jgentry@wgrls.org
Founded 2003. Pop 5,000; Circ 15,899
Library Holdings: CDs 302; DVDs 52; Bk Vols 9,000; Per Subs 15; Talking Bks 370; Videos 410
Open Mon-Thurs 11-6, Sat 10-2
Friends of the Library Group

CENTRALHATCHEE PUBLIC LIBRARY, 171 Motnomis Rd, Franklin, 30217. Tel: 678-853-9047. Web Site: www.wgrls.org/visit/centralhatchee. *Mgr,* Christa Phillips; E-mail: cphillips@wgrls.org
Open Tues 11-7, Wed 11-5, Thurs & Fri 9-5

CROSSROADS PUBLIC LIBRARY, 909 Harmony Grove Church Rd, Acworth, 30101. Tel: 770-975-0197. *Mgr,* Kristen Milton; E-mail: kmilton@wgrls.org
Open Mon-Thurs 10-7, Fri 9-5, Sat 1-5
Friends of the Library Group

DALLAS PUBLIC LIBRARY, 1010 E Memorial Dr, Dallas, 30132, SAN 338-5531. Tel: 770-445-5680. FAX: 770-443-7626. *Mgr,* Amy Mollenkamp; E-mail: amollenkamp@wgrls.org
Open Mon-Thurs 10-9, Fri & Sat 9-5
Friends of the Library Group

DOG RIVER PUBLIC LIBRARY, 6100 Georgia Hwy 5, Douglasville, 30135. Tel: 770-577-5186. *Mgr,* Trisha Salisbury; E-mail: tsalisbury@wgrls.org; Staff 1 (MLS 1)
Open Mon-Thurs 9-7, Fri 10-5, Sat 10-4
Friends of the Library Group

DOUGLAS COUNTY PUBLIC LIBRARY, 6810 Selman Dr, Douglasville, 30134, SAN 338-5418. Tel: 770-920-7125. FAX: 770-920-3121. *Mgr,* Jill Hernandez; E-mail: jhernandez@wgrls.org
Open Mon-Thurs 9-7, Fri 10-5, Sat 10-4
Friends of the Library Group

EPHESUS PUBLIC LIBRARY, 200 Rogers St, Roopville, 30170. Tel: 770-854-7323. FAX: 770-854-7326. *Mgr,* Donna Alvis; E-mail: dalvis@wgrls.org
Library Holdings: DVDs 100; Bk Vols 10,000; Per Subs 20; Talking Bks 50
Open Mon-Wed 9-5, Thurs 11-7, Sat 9-1
Friends of the Library Group

HEARD COUNTY PUBLIC LIBRARY, 564 Main St, Franklin, 30217, SAN 338-5477. Tel: 706-675-6501. FAX: 706-675-1065. *Mgr,* Leslie Stokes; E-mail: lstokes@wgrls.org
Open Mon & Thurs 10-1 & 1:30-7:30, Tues & Fri 9-1 & 1:30-6, Wed 1-6, Sat 9-2
Friends of the Library Group

RUTH HOLDER PUBLIC LIBRARY, 337 Sage St, Temple, 30179. Tel: 770-562-5145. Web Site: www.wgrls.org/visit/ruth-holder-public-library. *Mgr,* Laura Burton; E-mail: lburton@wgrls.org
Open Mon-Wed & Fri 10-5, Thurs 10-7, Sat 10-3

LITHIA SPRINGS PUBLIC LIBRARY, 7100 Turner Dr, Lithia Springs, 30122, SAN 338-5507. Tel: 770-944-5931. FAX: 770-944-5932. *Mgr,* Katie Gordon; E-mail: kgordon@wgrls.org
Open Mon-Thurs 9-7, Fri 10-5, Sat 10-4
Friends of the Library Group

MOUNT ZION PUBLIC LIBRARY, 4455 Mount Zion Rd, Mount Zion, 30150. (Mail add: PO Box 597, Mount Zion, 30150-0597). Tel: 770-832-0056, Ext 104. FAX: 770-834-7228. *Mgr,* Vicki Sizemore; E-mail: vsizemore@wgrls.org
Library Holdings: Bk Titles 1,000
Open Mon-Thurs 9-4:30
Friends of the Library Group

NEW GEORGIA PUBLIC LIBRARY, 94 Ridge Rd, Dallas, 30157, SAN 377-7278. Tel: 770-459-8163. FAX: 770-459-9343. *Mgr,* Hannah LeGrande; E-mail: hlegrand@wgrls.org
Open Mon-Thurs 10-7, Fri 9-5, Sat 1-5
Friends of the Library Group

MAUDE P RAGSDALE PUBLIC LIBRARY, 1815 Hiram-Douglasville Hwy, Hiram, 30141, SAN 375-5134. Tel: 770-439-3964. FAX: 770-943-8720. *Mgr,* Kendra Winters; E-mail: kwinters@wgrls.org
Open Mon-Thurs 10-7, Fri & Sat 9-5
Friends of the Library Group

WARREN P SEWELL MEMORIAL LIBRARY OF BOWDON, 450 West Ave, Bowdon, 30108, SAN 338-5590. Tel: 770-258-8991. FAX: 770-258-8990. *Mgr,* Cindy Inman; E-mail: cinman@wgrls.org
Open Mon & Tues 9-6, Wed & Sat 9-1, Thurs & Fri 9-5
Friends of the Library Group

WARREN P SEWELL MEMORIAL LIBRARY OF BREMEN, 315 Hamilton Ave, Bremen, 30110, SAN 338-5620. Tel: 770-537-3937. FAX: 770-537-1660. *Mgr,* Lisa Walton-Cagle; E-mail: lwalton-cagle@wgrls.org
Open Mon & Wed 10-5:30, Tues & Thurs 12-7, Fri 12-5:30, Sat 10-3
Friends of the Library Group

TALLAPOOSA PUBLIC LIBRARY, 388 Bowden St, Tallapoosa, 30176, SAN 338-5442. Tel: 770-574-3124. FAX: 770-574-3124. *Mgr,* Karen Boling; E-mail: kboling@wgrls.org
Open Mon, Tues & Fri 10-5, Thurs 10-8, Sat 10-4
Friends of the Library Group

VILLA RICA PUBLIC LIBRARY, 869 Dallas Hwy, Villa Rica, 30180, SAN 338-5566. Tel: 770-459-7012. FAX: 770-459-7960. *Mgr,* Evette Bridges; E-mail: ebridges@wgrls.org
Founded 1969
Automation Activity & Vendor Info: (Circulation) Evergreen
Open Mon-Wed 9-7, Thurs 9-8, Fri 9-5:30, Sat 9-2

WHITESBURG PUBLIC LIBRARY, 800 Main St, Whitesburg, 30185. Tel: 770-834-0713. *Mgr,* Ruth Fuller; E-mail: rfuller@wgrls.org
Library Holdings: Bk Titles 5,000
Automation Activity & Vendor Info: (Cataloging) Evergreen; (Circulation) Evergreen
Open Mon & Thurs 12-8, Tues 12-6, Fri & Sat 12-4, Sun 2-6
Friends of the Library Group

CARTERSVILLE

P BARTOW COUNTY PUBLIC LIBRARY SYSTEM*, 429 W Main St, 30120. SAN 324-0800. Tel: 770-382-4203. FAX: 770-386-3056. E-mail: info@bartowlibrary.org. Web Site: www.bartowlibraryonline.org. *Dir,* Carmen Melinda Sims; E-mail: carmen@bartowlibrary.org; Staff 20 (MLS 5, Non-MLS 15)
Founded 1981. Pop 79,244; Circ 188,721
Library Holdings: Bk Titles 55,935; Bk Vols 80,763; Per Subs 121
Subject Interests: Local hist
Automation Activity & Vendor Info: (Cataloging) SirsiDynix; (Circulation) SirsiDynix; (OPAC) SirsiDynix
Function: Photocopying/Printing
Partic in GOLD Resource Sharing Network for Georgia's Libraries; OCLC Online Computer Library Center, Inc
Open Mon, Wed & Fri 9-6, Tues & Thurs 9-8, Sat 9-5
Friends of the Library Group
Branches: 3

ADAIRSVILLE BRANCH, 202 N Main St, Adairsville, 30123, SAN 324-0827. Tel: 770-769-9200. FAX: 770-769-9201. *Br Mgr,* Position Currently Open
Library Holdings: Bk Vols 17,000
Open Mon-Wed & Fri 10-6, Thurs 12-8, Sat 9-1
Friends of the Library Group

CARTERSVILLE MAIN STREET, 429 W Main St, 30120, SAN 324-0843. Tel: 770-382-4203. FAX: 770-386-3056. *Br Mgr,* Becky Stiles
Library Holdings: Bk Vols 55,769
Open Mon-Wed & Fri 9-6, Tues & Thurs 9-8, Sat 9-5
Friends of the Library Group

EMMIE NELSON BRANCH, 108 Covered Bridge Rd, 30120, SAN 328-7467. Tel: 770-382-2057. FAX: 770-382-6316. *Br Mgr,* Christina Jedziniak
Library Holdings: Bk Vols 9,784
Open Mon & Wed-Fri 10-6, Tues 12-8
Friends of the Library Group

CHESTER

S GEORGIA DEPARTMENT OF CORRECTIONS, OFFICE OF LIBRARY SERVICES*, Dodge State Prison, 2971 Old Bethel Rd, 31012. (Mail add: PO Box 276, 31012-0276). Tel: 478-358-7201. FAX: 478-358-7303. Web Site: www.dcor.state.ga.us/Facilities/dodge-state-prison. *Librn,* Carolyn McCune
Library Holdings: Bk Vols 10,000
Special Collections: Law Coll

CLARKESVILLE

P CLARKESVILLE-HABERSHAM COUNTY LIBRARY, 178 E Green St, 30523. Tel: 706-754-4413. FAX: 762-230-0003. E-mail: clarksvillelib@gmail.com. Web Site: clarkesvillelibrary.org. *Br Mgr,* Shawna Meers-Ernst; Staff 3 (MLS 1, Non-MLS 2)
Founded 1928
Special Collections: Genealogy-Heritage Room
Wireless access
Mem of Northeast Georgia Regional Library System
Open Mon-Thurs 10-6, Fri 10-5, Sat 10-2

J NORTH GEORGIA TECHNICAL COLLEGE LIBRARY, Clarkesville Campus, 1500 Hwy 197 N, 30523. (Mail add: PO Box 65, 30523-0065), SAN 303-349X. Tel: 706-754-7720. FAX: 706-754-7777. E-mail: library@northgatech.edu. Web Site: libguides.northgatech.edu/home. *Dir, Libr Serv,* Jamey Wilkes; E-mail: jwilkes@northgatech.edu; *Currahee Campus Librn,* Melissa Hozey; Tel: 706-779-8104, E-mail: mhozey@northgatech.edu; Staff 2 (MLS 2)
Enrl 2,500; Fac 85
Automation Activity & Vendor Info: (Cataloging) Ex Libris Group; (Circulation) Ex Libris Group; (ILL) OCLC; (OPAC) Ex Libris Group
Wireless access

P NORTHEAST GEORGIA REGIONAL LIBRARY SYSTEM, 204 Ellison St, Ste F, 30523. (Mail add: PO Box 2020, 30523-0034), SAN 338-5655. Tel: 706-754-0416. FAX: 762-230-0010. E-mail: webadmin@negeorgialibraries.org. Web Site: www.negeorgialibraries.org. *Librn, Syst Serv Dir,* Delana Knight; E-mail: dknight@negeorgialibraries.org; *ILL/Tech Serv Librn,* John McConnell; E-mail: jmcconnell@negeorgialibraries.org; *Tech & Syst Librn,* Michael Metzger; E-mail: mmetzger@negeorgialibraries.org; *Bus Mgr,* Stacey Naddor; E-mail: snaddor@negeorgialibraries.org; Staff 4 (MLS 3, Non-MLS 1)
Founded 1951
Library Holdings: Audiobooks 7,892; DVDs 4,529; e-books 333; Electronic Media & Resources 1,374; Bk Vols 184,242; Per Subs 166; Videos 14,622
Automation Activity & Vendor Info: (Cataloging) Evergreen; (Circulation) Evergreen; (OPAC) Evergreen
Wireless access
Member Libraries: Clarkesville-Habersham County Library; Cornelia-Habersham County Library; Rabun County Public Library; Toccoa-Stephens County Public Library; White County Public Library
Partic in Public Information Network for Electronic Services
Friends of the Library Group

CLAXTON

P EVANS COUNTY PUBLIC LIBRARY*, 701 W Main St, 30417. SAN 339-2252. Tel: 912-739-1801. FAX: 912-739-0522. E-mail: reservesclay@strl.info. Web Site: strl.info/claxton-library. *Dir,* Jennifer Durham; E-mail: jennd@strl.info; *Mgr,* Charlotte DeLoach; Staff 2 (Non-MLS 2)
Pop 10,074; Circ 18,778
Automation Activity & Vendor Info: (Acquisitions) SirsiDynix; (Cataloging) SirsiDynix; (Circulation) SirsiDynix; (ILL) OCLC
Wireless access
Mem of Statesboro Regional Public Libraries
Partic in Public Information Network for Electronic Services
Open Mon-Thurs 10:30-5:30

CLAYTON

P RABUN COUNTY PUBLIC LIBRARY, 73 Jo Dotson Circle, 30525. SAN 338-568X. Tel: 706-782-3731. Web Site: www.rabuncountylibrary.org. *Libr Mgr,* Caroline Frick; E-mail: cfrick@negeorgialibraries.org
Wireless access
Mem of Northeast Georgia Regional Library System
Open Mon & Wed-Fri 10-5, Tue 10-6
Friends of the Library Group

CLEVELAND

C TRUETT-MCCONNELL UNIVERSITY*, Cofer Library, 100 Alumni Dr, 30528-9799. SAN 303-3511. Tel: 706-865-2134, Ext 2200. FAX: 706-243-4837. E-mail: library@truett.edu. Web Site: tmc.tlcdelivers.com/truett. *Dir, Libr Serv,* Teresa P Haymore; Tel: 706-865-2134, Ext 2201, E-mail: thaymore@truett.edu; *Cat, Instrul Serv Librn,* Vonda Henderson; Tel: 706-865-2134, Ext 2202, E-mail: vhenderson@truett.edu; Staff 3 (MLS 2, Non-MLS 1)
Founded 1946. Enrl 1,776; Fac 55; Highest Degree: Master
Library Holdings: AV Mats 500; CDs 1,900; DVDs 400; e-books 1,400,000; e-journals 300; Electronic Media & Resources 3,400; Microforms 40,000; Music Scores 500; Bk Titles 40,000; Bk Vols 42,000; Per Subs 140; Videos 1,900
Special Collections: Baptist History Coll; Religion (George W Truett Coll)
Automation Activity & Vendor Info: (Acquisitions) TLC (The Library Corporation); (Cataloging) TLC (The Library Corporation); (Circulation) TLC (The Library Corporation); (Course Reserve) TLC (The Library

Corporation); (ILL) OCLC WorldShare Interlibrary Loan; (OPAC) TLC (The Library Corporation)
Wireless access
Function: 24/7 Electronic res, 24/7 Online cat, Archival coll, AV serv, Bks on cassette, Bks on CD, CD-ROM, Computers for patron use, Digital talking bks, Distance learning, E-Reserves, Electronic databases & coll, Free DVD rentals, ILL available, Instruction & testing, Internet access, Laminating, Magazines, Mail & tel request accepted, Microfiche/film & reading machines, Music CDs, Online cat, Online ref, Orientations, Photocopying/Printing, Ref & res, Ref serv available, Res assist avail, Res libr, Scanner, Study rm, Telephone ref, VHS videos, Wheelchair accessible
Partic in Association of Christian Librarians; Georgia Private Acad Libs Consortium
Open Mon-Thurs 8am-10pm, Fri 8-4:30, Sun 7pm-10pm; Mon-Fri (Summer) 8-4:30

P WHITE COUNTY PUBLIC LIBRARY*, Cleveland Branch, Ten Colonial Dr, 30528. (Mail add: PO Box 657, 30528-0657), SAN 338-571X. Tel: 706-865-5572. FAX: 706-219-3621. Web Site: gapines.org/eg/opac/library/NEG-CLVLND, www.whitecounty.net/departments/libraries. *Mgr,* Michael Humphrey; E-mail: mhumphrey@negeorgialibraries.org
Library Holdings: CDs 276; DVDs 393; Bk Vols 47,481
Wireless access
Mem of Northeast Georgia Regional Library System
Open Mon 9-7, Tues-Fri 9-5, Sat 9-12
Friends of the Library Group
Branches: 1
HELEN BRANCH, 90 Petes Park Rd, Helen, 30545. (Mail add: PO Box 1088, Helen, 30545-1088), SAN 338-5779. Tel: 706-878-2438. FAX: 706-878-1479. *Mgr,* Deborah Kelley
Open Mon, Wed & Fri 9-5, Tues & Thurs 9-6, Sat 10-1

COCHRAN

C MIDDLE GEORGIA STATE UNIVERSITY*, Cochran Campus Library - Roberts Memorial, 1100 Second St SE, 31014. SAN 303-352X. Tel: 478-934-3179. FAX: 478-934-3378. *Asst Dir, Libr Serv,* Ann Williams; E-mail: ann.williams@mga.edu; *Cat Librn,* April Warren; Tel: 478-934-3071, E-mail: april.renfroewarren@mga.edu; Staff 7 (MLS 4, Non-MLS 3)
Founded 1928. Enrl 8,450; Highest Degree: Master
Library Holdings: Bk Titles 28,976; Bk Vols 32,084; Per Subs 13; Videos 454
Special Collections: Archives; County Histories; Georgianna Genealogy
Automation Activity & Vendor Info: (Acquisitions) Ex Libris Group; (Cataloging) Ex Libris Group; (Circulation) Ex Libris Group; (Course Reserve) Ex Libris Group; (ILL) Ex Libris Group; (Media Booking) Ex Libris Group; (OPAC) Ex Libris Group; (Serials) Ex Libris Group
Wireless access
Partic in LYRASIS; OCLC Online Computer Library Center, Inc
Open Mon-Thurs 7:30am-10pm, Fri 7:30-Noon, Sun 1-7

COLUMBUS

P CHATTAHOOCHEE VALLEY LIBRARIES*, Columbus Public Library, Headquarters, 3000 Macon Rd, 31906-2201. SAN 338-5868. Tel: 706-243-2669. Circulation Tel: 706-243-2689. Interlibrary Loan Service Tel: 706-243-2683. Reference Tel: 706-243-2790. Administration Tel: 706-243-2670. FAX: 706-565-8667. Interlibrary Loan Service FAX: 706-565-8665. Administration FAX: 706-565-8668. Reference E-mail: pachelp@cvlga.org. Web Site: www.cvlga.org. *Dir,* Alan Harkness; E-mail: aharkness@cvlga.org; *Dep Dir,* Gabriel Lundeen; Tel: 706-243-2671, E-mail: glundeen@cvlga.org; *Finance Mgr,* Tracie Price; Tel: 706-243-2672, E-mail: tprice@cvlga.org; *Commun Coordr,* Tiffany Wilson; Tel: 706-243-2673, E-mail: twilson@cvlga.org; *IT Coordr,* Van Montesclaros; Tel: 706-243-2686, E-mail: vmontesclaros@cvlga.org; *Libr Operations Coordr,* Tammy Battley; Tel: 706-243-2702, E-mail: tbattley@cvlga.org; *Media Coordr,* Henry McCoy; E-mail: hmccoy@cvlga.org; *Tech Serv,* Amber Brookins; Tel: 706-243-2820, E-mail: abrookins@cvlga.org; Staff 15 (MLS 15)
Founded 1908. Pop 215,952; Circ 702,739
Library Holdings: Bk Vols 327,639; Per Subs 1,100
Special Collections: Genealogy & Local History; Local Newspapers
Automation Activity & Vendor Info: (Acquisitions) Brodart; (Cataloging) Innovative Interfaces, Inc; (Circulation) Innovative Interfaces, Inc; (ILL) OCLC; (OPAC) Innovative Interfaces, Inc; (Serials) Innovative Interfaces, Inc
Wireless access
Function: 24/7 Electronic res, 24/7 Online cat, 3D Printer, Activity rm, Adult bk club, Adult literacy prog, After school storytime, Art exhibits, Audiobks via web, Bk club(s), Bks on CD, CD-ROM, Chess club, Children's prog, Computer training, Computers for patron use, Electronic databases & coll, Free DVD rentals, Holiday prog, Home delivery & serv to seniorr ctr & nursing homes, ILL available, Internet access, Jail serv, Life-long learning prog for all ages, Magazines, Magnifiers for reading, Meeting rooms, Microfiche/film & reading machines, Movies, Museum passes, Music CDs, Online cat, Online ref, Outreach serv, OverDrive digital audio bks, Photocopying/Printing, Preschool outreach, Printer for laptops & handheld devices, Prog for adults, Prog for children & young adult, Ref serv available, Scanner, Senior computer classes, Senior outreach, Spanish lang bks, Story hour, Summer reading prog, Tax forms, Teen prog, Telephone ref, Wheelchair accessible, Writing prog
Partic in LYRASIS
Special Services for the Blind - Aids for in-house use; Assistive/Adapted tech devices, equip & products; Audio mat; Bks on cassette; Bks on CD; Braille bks; Cassette playback machines; Cassettes; Children's Braille; Closed circuit TV; Computer with voice synthesizer for visually impaired persons; Disability awareness prog; Home delivery serv; Large print bks; Large screen computer & software; Talking bks & player equip; Tel Pioneers equip repair group
Open Mon-Thurs 10-8, Fri & Sat 10-6, Sun 1:30-6
Friends of the Library Group
Branches: 6
CUSSETA-CHATTAHOOCHEE PUBLIC LIBRARY, 262 Broad St, Cusseta, 31805. (Mail add: PO Box 539, Cusseta, 31805-0539), SAN 338-5957. Tel: 706-989-3700. FAX: 706-989-1850. *Br Mgr,* Pamela Burgamy; E-mail: pburgamy@cvlga.org; Staff 3 (Non-MLS 3)
Open Mon, Tues & Thurs 9:30-1 & 1:30-6, Fri & Sat 9:30-1:30
Friends of the Library Group
MARION COUNTY PUBLIC LIBRARY, 123 E Fifth Ave, Buena Vista, 31803-2113. (Mail add: PO Box 12, Buena Vista, 31803-0012), SAN 338-6015. Tel: 229-649-6385. FAX: 229-649-6385. *Br Mgr,* Kim Scott; E-mail: kscott@cvlga.org; Staff 4 (Non-MLS 4)
Open Mon, Wed & Fri 10-5
Friends of the Library Group
NORTH COLUMBUS BRANCH, 5689 Armour Rd, 31909-4513, SAN 373-9325. Tel: 706-748-2795. FAX: 706-748-2859. *Br Mgr,* Jeannine Scott; E-mail: jscott@cvlga.org; Staff 13 (MLS 1, Non-MLS 12)
Open Mon-Wed, Fri & Sat 10-6, Thurs 10-8
Friends of the Library Group
PARKS MEMORIAL PUBLIC LIBRARY, 890 Wall St, Richland, 31825-0112, SAN 338-6104. Tel: 229-887-2103. FAX: 229-887-2103. Web Site: www.cvlga.org/branches/parks. *Br Mgr,* Pepper Grimmett; E-mail: pgrimmett@cvlga.org; Staff 2 (Non-MLS 2)
Open Tues & Thurs 10-5, Wed 1:30-5
Friends of the Library Group
SOUTH COLUMBUS BRANCH, 2034 S Lumpkin Rd, 31903-2728, SAN 338-5922. Tel: 706-683-8805. FAX: 706-683-8809. *Br Mgr,* Natalie Couch; E-mail: ncouch@cvlga.org; Staff 7 (MLS 1, Non-MLS 6)
Open Mon, Tues & Thurs-Sat 10-6, Wed 10-8
Friends of the Library Group
MILDRED L TERRY BRANCH, 640 Veterans Pkwy, 31901, SAN 338-5981. Tel: 706-748-2851. FAX: 706-748-2853. *Br Mgr,* Silvia Bunn; E-mail: sbunn@cvlga.org; Staff 8 (MLS 2, Non-MLS 6)
Open Mon & Wed-Sat 10-6, Tues 10-8
Friends of the Library Group

M COLUMBUS REGIONAL HEALTHCARE SYSTEM*, Simon Schwob Medical Library, 710 Center St, 31902. (Mail add: PO Box 951, 31902-0951), SAN 303-3562. Tel: 706-571-1178, 706-571-1179. FAX: 706-660-2674. *Librn,* Dionne Lyme; Staff 1 (MLS 1)
Founded 1949
Library Holdings: Bk Titles 2,810; Per Subs 222
Subject Interests: Cancer, Geriatrics & gerontology, Med, Neonatology, Nursing, Pediatrics, Trauma
Wireless access
Partic in Atlantic Health Sci Librs Consortium; Georgia Health Sciences Library Association; Medical Library Association
Open Mon-Fri 8-4:30

C COLUMBUS STATE UNIVERSITY LIBRARIES, Simon Schwob Memorial Library, 4225 University Ave, 31907. SAN 303-3538. Tel: 706-507-8670. FAX: 706-507-8697. Web Site: library.columbusstate.edu. *Dean, Libr Serv,* Alan C Karass; E-mail: karass_alan@columbusstate.edu; *Head, Archives & Spec Coll,* David Owings; Tel: 706-507-8674, E-mail: owings_david@columbusstate.edu; *Head, Ref Serv,* Michelle Jones; Tel: 706-507-8688, E-mail: jones_michelle@columbusstate.edu; *Instruction Librn,* Thomas Ganzevoort; Tel: 706-507-8686, E-mail: ganzevoort_thomas@columbusstate.edu; *Archival Assoc,* Jessie T Merrell; Tel: 706-507-8673, E-mail: merrell_jessie@columbusstate.edu. Subject Specialists: *Music,* Alan C Karass; *Educ,* Michelle Jones; *Art, Communication, Hist,* Thomas Ganzevoort; Staff 10 (MLS 8, Non-MLS 2)
Founded 1961. Enrl 8,179; Fac 296; Highest Degree: Doctorate
Library Holdings: AV Mats 11,500; e-books 600,000; e-journals 14,000; Microforms 1,132,896; Bk Vols 398,432; Per Subs 395
Special Collections: Architectural Drawings; Chattahoochee Valley Historical Coll; Columbus State University Archives. Oral History; US Document Depository

Automation Activity & Vendor Info: (Acquisitions) Ex Libris Group; (Cataloging) Ex Libris Group; (Circulation) Ex Libris Group; (ILL) OCLC; (OPAC) Ex Libris Group; (Serials) Ex Libris Group
Wireless access
Function: Computers for patron use, Distance learning, Govt ref serv, ILL available, Online cat, Online ref, Photocopying/Printing, Ref & res, Scanner, Tax forms, VHS videos, Wheelchair accessible, Workshops
Publications: Muscogiana (Local historical information); Simon Says (Newsletter)
Partic in LYRASIS
Special Services for the Blind - Closed circuit TV; Computer with voice synthesizer for visually impaired persons; ZoomText magnification & reading software
Open Mon-Fri 8-5
Restriction: Borrowing privileges limited to fac & registered students, In-house use for visitors, Open to pub for ref & circ; with some limitations, Open to students, fac & staff
Friends of the Library Group

Departmental Libraries:

MUSIC LIBRARY, 900 Broadway, 31901-2735. (Mail add: 4225 University Ave, 31907). Tel: 706-641-5045. FAX: 706-649-7261. Web Site: library.columbusstate.edu/music. *Assoc Dean, Music Librn,* Roberta C Ford; Tel: 706-641-5047, E-mail: ford_roberta@columbusstate.edu; *Access Serv Mgr,* Judy Moore; Tel: 706-641-5044, E-mail: moore_judith@columbusstate.edu; Staff 3 (MLS 1, Non-MLS 2)
Founded 2001
Open Mon-Fri 9-5
Restriction: Open to pub for ref only

J COLUMBUS TECHNICAL COLLEGE LIBRARY*, 928 Manchester Expressway, 31904-6577. Tel: 706-649-1852. FAX: 706-649-1885. E-mail: library@columbustech.edu. Web Site: www.columbustech.edu/academics/library.cms. *Dir, Libr & Media Serv,* Stephanie Middleton; E-mail: smiddleton@columbustech.edu; *Assoc Librn,* Alice McCown; *ILL,* Evelyn Willis
Founded 1961. Enrl 3,456; Highest Degree: Associate
Library Holdings: AV Mats 50; CDs 22,293; DVDs 22; e-books 52,000; Bk Vols 28,000; Per Subs 255; Videos 654
Automation Activity & Vendor Info: (Cataloging) TLC (The Library Corporation); (Circulation) TLC (The Library Corporation); (OPAC) TLC (The Library Corporation)
Partic in Georgia Library Learning Online
Open Mon-Thurs 7:30am-9:30pm, Fri 9-1

S GEORGIA DEPARTMENT OF CORRECTIONS, OFFICE OF LIBRARY SERVICES*, Rutledge State Prison, 7175 Manor Rd, 31907. Tel: 706-568-2439. FAX: 706-568-2126. Web Site: www.dcor.state.ga.us/Facilities/rutledge-state-prison. *Dir, Libr Serv,* Emanuel Mitchell; E-mail: emanuel.mitchell@gdc.ga.gov
Library Holdings: Bk Vols 7,000; Per Subs 15
Special Collections: Law Coll
Restriction: Not open to pub

S HISTORIC WESTVILLE LIBRARY*, 3557 S Lumpkin Rd, 31903. (Mail add: PO Box 1850, Lumpkin, 31815-1850), SAN 303-3880. Tel: 706-940-0057. Toll Free Tel: 888-733-1850. FAX: 229-838-4000. E-mail: info@westville.org. Web Site: www.westville.org. *Exec Dir,* Allen Sistrunk
Founded 1966
Library Holdings: Bk Titles 1,475
Special Collections: African-American Architecture & History Survey of West Georgia; John West Coll; Pre-Columbian Seminars Transcripts
Subject Interests: Decorative art, Ga, Hort
Open Tues-Sat 9-4
Restriction: Not a lending libr

M HUGHSTON FOUNDATION LIBRARY, 6262 Veterans Pkwy, 31909-3540. SAN 370-6400. Tel: 706-494-3390. FAX: 706-494-3348. Web Site: hughston.com/hughston-foundation/facilities-and-services. *Med Librn,* Dennise Brogdon; E-mail: dbrogdon@hughston.com; Staff 1 (Non-MLS 1)
Library Holdings: Bk Titles 1,200; Per Subs 42
Wireless access
Partic in National Network of Libraries of Medicine Region 2
Restriction: Staff use only

CONYERS

P CONYERS-ROCKDALE LIBRARY SYSTEM*, Nancy Guinn Memorial Library, 864 Green St, 30012. SAN 372-5995. Tel: 770-388-5040. FAX: 770-388-5043. E-mail: publiccomment@conyersrockdalelibrary.org. Web Site: conyersrockdalelibrary.org. *Dir,* Brenda Poku; E-mail: bpoku@conyersrockdalelibrary.org; *Head, Info Tech,* Alex Boardman; E-mail: jboardman@conyersrockdalelibrary.org; *Tech Serv,* Christina Hodgens; E-mail: chodgens@conyersrockdalelibrary.org; Staff 5 (MLS 1, Non-MLS 4)
Library Holdings: Bk Vols 100,000; Per Subs 34
Special Collections: Law
Subject Interests: Genealogy
Automation Activity & Vendor Info: (Acquisitions) Evergreen; (Cataloging) Evergreen; (Circulation) Evergreen; (ILL) OCLC; (OPAC) Evergreen; (Serials) Evergreen
Wireless access
Partic in GOLD Resource Sharing Network for Georgia's Libraries; LYRASIS; OCLC Online Computer Library Center, Inc; Public Information Network for Electronic Services
Open Mon-Thurs 10-8, Fri & Sat 10-5
Friends of the Library Group

CORDELE

J SOUTH GEORGIA TECHNICAL COLLEGE*, Crisp County Campus Library, Crisp County Ctr, Rm A37, 402 N Midway Rd, 31015. Tel: 229-271-4071. FAX: 229-271-4050. Web Site: www.southgatech.edu. *Dir,* Jerry Stovall; E-mail: jstovall@southgatech.edu; *Media Spec,* Dianne Trueblood; E-mail: dtrueblood@southgatech.edu
Founded 2000. Highest Degree: Associate
Library Holdings: e-books 27,000; e-journals 27,000; Bk Vols 3,078; Per Subs 20
Automation Activity & Vendor Info: (Cataloging) TLC (The Library Corporation); (Circulation) TLC (The Library Corporation); (OPAC) TLC (The Library Corporation)
Wireless access
Partic in Georgia Library Learning Online
Open Mon-Thurs 7:30am-8pm, Fri 8-Noon

CORNELIA

P CORNELIA-HABERSHAM COUNTY LIBRARY, 301 Main St N, 30531. SAN 338-5744. Tel: 706-778-2635. FAX: 706-903-1000. Web Site: www.cornelialibrary.org. *Libr Mgr,* Josh Smith; E-mail: jsmith@negeorgialibraries.org; Staff 4.5 (Non-MLS 4.5)
Founded 1988. Pop 42,000; Circ 78,000
Automation Activity & Vendor Info: (Acquisitions) Evergreen; (Course Reserve) Evergreen; (ILL) Evergreen; (Media Booking) Evergreen; (Serials) Evergreen
Wireless access
Mem of Northeast Georgia Regional Library System
Open Mon & Tues 9-6, Wed & Fri 9-5, Thurs 9-7
Friends of the Library Group

COVINGTON

J GEORGIA PIEDMONT TECHNICAL COLLEGE*, Newton Campus Learning Resource Center, Bldg B, Rm 109, 16200 Alcovy Rd, 30014. Tel: 770-786-9522, Ext 3212, 770-786-9522, Ext 3233. Web Site: libguides.gptc.edu. *Librn,* Caroline Dial; E-mail: dialc@gptc.edu; Staff 2 (MLS 1, Non-MLS 1)
Founded 1997. Highest Degree: Associate
Wireless access
Function: Computers for patron use, Electronic databases & coll, Learning ctr, Online ref, Photocopying/Printing, Ref & res, Scanner
Partic in Georgia Library Learning Online
Open Mon-Thurs 9-8

P NEWTON COUNTY LIBRARY SYSTEM*, 7116 Floyd St NE, 30014. SAN 338-6880. Tel: 770-787-3231. Information Services Tel: 770-385-6449. FAX: 770-784-2092. TDD: 770-784-2091. Web Site: www.newtonlibrary.org. *Dir,* Lace Keaton; E-mail: lace@newtonlibrary.org; Staff 27 (MLS 4, Non-MLS 23)
Founded 1969. Pop 103,528; Circ 660,102
Library Holdings: Audiobooks 11,987; AV Mats 2,217; CDs 2,205; DVDs 6,800; High Interest/Low Vocabulary Bk Vols 1,600; Large Print Bks 7,000; Bk Titles 123,055; Bk Vols 148,000; Per Subs 192; Videos 6,216
Special Collections: Porter Foundation Garden Coll
Subject Interests: Local hist
Automation Activity & Vendor Info: (Cataloging) Evergreen; (Circulation) Evergreen; (ILL) OCLC
Wireless access
Function: ILL available
Publications: Bookworm Notes: Friends of the Library Newsletter
Partic in GOLD Resource Sharing Network for Georgia's Libraries; LYRASIS; Public Information Network for Electronic Services
Special Services for the Blind - Computer with voice synthesizer for visually impaired persons
Open Tues & Thurs 10-8, Wed & Fri 10-6, Sat 10-2
Friends of the Library Group

Branches: 1

PORTER MEMORIAL BRANCH LIBRARY, 6191 Hwy 212, 30016. *Br Mgr,* Ginny VanOrsdale

CUMMING

P FORSYTH COUNTY PUBLIC LIBRARY*, Cumming Library & FCPL Headquarters, 585 Dahlonega St, 30040-2109. SAN 375-4162. Tel: 770-781-9840. Web Site: www.forsythpl.org. *Dir,* Anna Lyle; E-mail: lylea@forsythpl.org; *Asst Dir, Mat,* Linda Kelly; E-mail: kellyl@forsythpl.org; *Asst Dir, Info Tech,* Holly Barfield; E-mail: barfieldh@forsythpl.org; *Asst Dir, Pub Serv,* Stephen Kight; E-mail: kights@forsythpl.org; *Br Mgr,* Denise Leeson; Staff 84 (MLS 10, Non-MLS 74)
Founded 1996. Pop 220,000; Circ 2,475,542
Library Holdings: Audiobooks 17,330; CDs 11,394; DVDs 19,615; e-books 10,283; e-journals 122; Electronic Media & Resources 28; Large Print Bks 4,497; Bk Titles 135,996; Bk Vols 311,758
Automation Activity & Vendor Info: (Acquisitions) Innovative Interfaces, Inc; (Cataloging) Innovative Interfaces, Inc; (Circulation) Innovative Interfaces, Inc; (ILL) Innovative Interfaces, Inc; (OPAC) Innovative Interfaces, Inc; (Serials) Innovative Interfaces, Inc
Wireless access
Function: 24/7 Electronic res, 24/7 Online cat, 3D Printer, Adult bk club, Audiobks via web, AV serv, Bi-weekly Writer's Group, Bilingual assistance for Spanish patrons, Bk club(s), Bk reviews (Group), Bks on CD, Butterfly Garden, Chess club, Children's prog, Computer training, Computers for patron use, Electronic databases & coll, Holiday prog, Homebound delivery serv, Homework prog, ILL available, Internet access, Large print keyboards, Life-long learning prog for all ages, Magazines, Magnifiers for reading, Mail & tel request accepted, Mango lang, Meeting rooms, Microfiche/film & reading machines, Movies, Museum passes, Music CDs, Online cat, Outreach serv, Outside serv via phone, mail, e-mail & web, OverDrive digital audio bks, Photocopying/Printing, Preschool outreach, Preschool reading prog, Prog for adults, Prog for children & young adult, Ref & res, Ref serv available, Res assist avail, Scanner, Senior computer classes, Senior outreach, Serves people with intellectual disabilities, Spanish lang bks, Story hour, Study rm, Summer reading prog, Tax forms, Teen prog, Telephone ref, Wheelchair accessible, Writing prog
Open Mon-Thurs 10-8:30, Fri & Sat 10-5:30, Sun 1:30-5:30
Friends of the Library Group
Branches: 3
SHARON FORKS, 2820 Old Atlanta Rd, 30041. Tel: 770-781-9840. *Br Mgr,* Mendy Gunter
Library Holdings: AV Mats 14,231; Large Print Bks 721; Bk Vols 97,907; Per Subs 158; Talking Bks 4,553
Open Mon-Thurs 10-8:30, Fri & Sat 10-5:30, Sun 1:30-5:30

J LANIER TECHNICAL COLLEGE*, Forsyth Campus Library, 7745 Majors Rd, 30041. Tel: 770-533-6969. FAX: 770-533-6328. Web Site: www.laniertech.edu/library. *Dir, Libr Serv,* Kathryn Thompson; Tel: 770-533-6968, E-mail: kthompson@laniertech.edu; *Librn,* Min Su; Tel: 678-341-6636, E-mail: msu@laniertech.edu
Library Holdings: e-books 23,000; Bk Vols 5,000; Per Subs 90
Automation Activity & Vendor Info: (Cataloging) TLC (The Library Corporation); (Circulation) TLC (The Library Corporation); (OPAC) TLC (The Library Corporation)
Partic in Georgia Library Learning Online
Open Mon-Thurs 7:30am-8pm

CUTHBERT

J ANDREW COLLEGE*, Pitts Library, 501 College St, 39840. SAN 303-3589. Tel: 229-732-5956. FAX: 229-732-5957. Web Site: www.andrewcollege.edu/pitts/library. *Dir, Libr Serv,* McKenzie Ragan; E-mail: mckenzieragan@andrewcollege.edu; Staff 2.4 (MLS 1, Non-MLS 1.4)
Founded 1854. Enrl 278; Fac 25; Highest Degree: Associate
Library Holdings: AV Mats 6,550; DVDs 84; Microforms 6,500; Bk Vols 34,600; Per Subs 170; Videos 618
Special Collections: Andrew College Archives, bks, doc, ms, pamphlets, pictures
Automation Activity & Vendor Info: (Acquisitions) Ex Libris Group; (Cataloging) Ex Libris Group; (Circulation) Ex Libris Group; (Course Reserve) Ex Libris Group; (ILL) Ex Libris Group; (OPAC) Ex Libris Group; (Serials) EBSCO Online
Wireless access
Function: Archival coll, Computers for patron use, Electronic databases & coll, ILL available, Online cat, Orientations, Photocopying/Printing, Ref & res, Ref serv available
Partic in Georgia Private Acad Librs Consortium; GOLD Resource Sharing Network for Georgia's Libraries; LYRASIS; OCLC Online Computer Library Center, Inc
Open Mon-Thurs (Fall-Spring) 8:30am-10pm, Fri 8:30-4:30; Mon-Fri (Summer) 8:30-4:30

DAHLONEGA

P CHESTATEE REGIONAL LIBRARY SYSTEM*, Headquarters, 56 Mechanicsville Rd, 30533. SAN 377-6859. Tel: 706-864-3668. FAX: 706-344-3692. E-mail: crls@chestateelibrary.org. Web Site: www.chestateelibrary.org. *Dir,* Leslie Clark; E-mail: lclark@chestateelibrary.org; *Coll Mgt Librn,* Elizabeth Stipek; E-mail: estipek@chestateelibrary.org; Staff 15 (MLS 3, Non-MLS 12)
Founded 1953. Pop 56,985; Circ 312,251
Jul 2012-Jun 2013 Income $962,761, State $211,272, County $674,354, Locally Generated Income $77,135. Mats Exp $109,650, Books $75,297, Electronic Ref Mat (Incl. Access Fees) $4,680. Sal $502,137 (Prof $153,763)
Library Holdings: Audiobooks 15,805; e-books 10,127; Bk Titles 106,115; Per Subs 131; Videos 10,661
Automation Activity & Vendor Info: (Cataloging) Evergreen; (Circulation) Evergreen; (OPAC) Evergreen
Wireless access
Function: Adult bk club, After school storytime, Archival coll, Audio & video playback equip for onsite use, AV serv, Bk club(s), Bks on CD, Children's prog, Computer training, Computers for patron use, Digital talking bks, Doc delivery serv, Electronic databases & coll, Family literacy, Free DVD rentals, Homebound delivery serv, ILL available, Instruction & testing, Microfiche/film & reading machines, Music CDs, Notary serv, Online cat, Outside serv via phone, mail, e-mail & web, OverDrive digital audio bks, Photocopying/Printing, Printer for laptops & handheld devices, Prog for adults, Prog for children & young adult, Ref & res, Ref serv available, Satellite serv, Scanner, Spoken cassettes & CDs, Story hour, Summer & winter reading prog, Summer reading prog, Tax forms, Teen prog, Telephone ref, Wheelchair accessible, Workshops
Publications: Chestatee Highlighter (Newsletter)
Partic in GOLD Resource Sharing Network for Georgia's Libraries
Open Mon-Fri 8-4:30
Friends of the Library Group
Branches: 2
DAWSON COUNTY LIBRARY, 342 Allen St, Dawsonville, 30534, SAN 374-7336. Tel: 706-344-3690. FAX: 706-344-3691. E-mail: dawson@chestateelibrary.org. *Br Mgr,* Stacey Leonhardt; Tel: 706-344-3690, Ext 21, E-mail: sleonhardt@chestateelibrary.org; Staff 7 (Non-MLS 7)
Founded 1958. Pop 26,368; Circ 145,845
Jul 2012-Jun 2013 Income $390,549, County $357,545, Locally Generated Income $33,347. Mats Exp $51,363. Sal $144,026
Subject Interests: Local hist
Open Mon-Thurs 9-5:30, Fri & Sat 9-2:30
Friends of the Library Group
LUMPKIN COUNTY LIBRARY, 56 Mechanicsville Rd, 30533. FAX: 706-864-3937. E-mail: lumpkin@chestateelibrary.org. *Br Mgr,* Tracey Thomaswick; E-mail: tthomaswick@chestateelibrary.org; Staff 8 (Non-MLS 8)
Founded 1917. Pop 30,617; Circ 166,406
Jul 2012-Jun 2013 Income $360,195, County $316,809, Locally Generated Income $43,386. Mats Exp $51,457. Sal $113,698
Subject Interests: Genealogy, Local hist
Open Mon-Thurs 9-5:30, Fri & Sat 9-2:30
Friends of the Library Group

DALTON

C DALTON STATE COLLEGE*, Derrell C Roberts Library, 650 College Dr, 30720-3778. SAN 303-3600. Tel: 706-272-4585. Reference Tel: 706-272-4575. FAX: 706-272-4511. Web Site: www.daltonstate.edu/library/about-roberts-library.cms. *Libr Dir,* Melissa Whitesell; E-mail: mwhitesell@daltonstate.edu; *Archives, Cat & Tech Serv Librn,* Lee Ann Cline; E-mail: lcline@daltonstate.edu; *Govt Doc Librn, ILL,* Barbara Jones; E-mail: bjones@daltonstate.edu; *Ref & Instruction Librn,* Amy Burger; E-mail: aburger1@daltonstate.edu; *Ref & Instruction Librn,* Betsy Whitley; Tel: 706-272-4527, E-mail: bwhitley@daltonstate.edu; Staff 9 (MLS 5, Non-MLS 4)
Founded 1967. Enrl 4,239; Fac 5; Highest Degree: Bachelor
Library Holdings: AV Mats 10,461; e-books 99,973; Microforms 214,464; Bk Vols 143,415; Per Subs 248
Special Collections: College Archives; Dalton Room. US Document Depository
Automation Activity & Vendor Info: (Cataloging) Ex Libris Group; (Circulation) Ex Libris Group; (Course Reserve) Ex Libris Group; (Discovery) EBSCO Discovery Service; (ILL) OCLC; (OPAC) Ex Libris Group; (Serials) Ex Libris Group
Wireless access
Function: Art exhibits, Computers for patron use, Electronic databases & coll, Govt ref serv, ILL available, Internet access, Magazines, Microfiche/film & reading machines, Online cat, Online ref, Outside serv via phone, mail, e-mail & web, Photocopying/Printing, Ref & res, Ref serv available, Scanner, Spanish lang bks, Study rm, Wheelchair accessible
Partic in Georgia Library Learning Online; LYRASIS

Special Services for the Deaf - Assistive tech; Closed caption videos
Special Services for the Blind - Accessible computers; Assistive/Adapted tech devices, equip & products; Closed circuit TV magnifier; Computer with voice synthesizer for visually impaired persons; Dragon Naturally Speaking software; Internet workstation with adaptive software; Large print bks; Magnifiers; PC for people with disabilities; Reader equip; Screen reader software; Text reader
Open Mon-Thurs 7:30am-8pm, Fri 7:30-Noon, Sun 1-7
Restriction: Open to students, fac, staff & alumni

M HAMILTON MEDICAL CENTER*, Medical Library, 1200 Memorial Dr, 30720-2529. (Mail add: PO Box 1168, 30722-1168), SAN 374-8650. Tel: 706-272-6056. FAX: 706-272-6094. *Med Librn,* Sarah Russell; E-mail: srussell@hhcs.org; Staff 1 (Non-MLS 1)
Library Holdings: Bk Vols 1,000; Per Subs 90
Wireless access

P NORTHWEST GEORGIA REGIONAL LIBRARY SYSTEM*, Dalton-Whitfield Regional Library (Headquarters), 310 Cappes St, 30720. SAN 338-6139. Tel: 706-876-1360. FAX: 706-272-2977. Web Site: www.ngrl.org. *Syst Dir,* Darla Chambliss; E-mail: dchambliss@ngrl.org; *Br Adminr,* Brandy Wyatt; Staff 5 (MLS 5)
Founded 1924. Pop 197,000; Circ 320,000
Library Holdings: Bk Vols 210,000; Per Subs 65
Special Collections: Georgia Coll; Newspapers, micro
Subject Interests: Genealogy
Automation Activity & Vendor Info: (Acquisitions) SirsiDynix; (Cataloging) SirsiDynix; (Circulation) SirsiDynix; (ILL) OCLC
Wireless access
Partic in Georgia Libr Info Network; Public Information Network for Electronic Services
Open Mon-Thurs 10-7, Fri 10-6, Sat 10-1:30
Friends of the Library Group
Branches: 2
CALHOUN-GORDON COUNTY, 100 N Park Ave, Calhoun, 30701, SAN 338-6163. Tel: 706-624-1456. *Mgr,* Nyala Edwards
Special Collections: Dr Henry T Malone Coll
Open Mon, Wed & Fri 10-6, Tues & Thurs 10-7, Sat 10-3
Friends of the Library Group
CHATSWORTH-MURRAY COUNTY, 100 N Third Ave, Chatsworth, 30705, SAN 338-6287. Tel: 706-695-4200. *Mgr,* Diane Davis
Open Mon-Fri 9-5
Friends of the Library Group

S WHITFIELD-MURRAY HISTORICAL SOCIETY*, Crown Gardens & Archives, 715 Chattanooga Ave, 30720. (Mail add: PO Box 6180, 30722), SAN 373-4250. Tel: 706-278-0217. E-mail: wmhs@optilink.us. Web Site: www.whitfield-murrayhistoricalsociety.org. *Exec Dir,* Vallarie Pratt; Staff 1 (MLS 1)
Founded 1976
Library Holdings: Bk Vols 750
Subject Interests: Genealogy, Local hist
Wireless access
Open Mon-Fri 10-4

DARIEN

P IDA HILTON PUBLIC LIBRARY*, 1105 North Way, 31305. (Mail add: PO Box 1227, 31305-1227), SAN 329-0077. Tel: 912-437-2124. FAX: 912-437-5113. Web Site: threeriverslibraries.org/woodpress-dev/library-locations/ida-hilton-public-library. *Libr Mgr,* Barbara Sawyer; E-mail: bsawyer@trrl.org
Special Collections: Fanny Kemble Coll; Gullah Coll; Sapelo Island Coll
Subject Interests: Genealogy
Mem of Three Rivers Regional Library System
Open Tues & Thurs 10-7, Wed & Fri 10-4
Friends of the Library Group

DAWSON

P KINCHAFOONEE REGIONAL LIBRARY SYSTEM*, 913 Forrester Dr SE, 39842-2106. Tel: 229-995-6331. FAX: 229-995-3383. Web Site: www.krlibrary.org. *Dir,* Gary McNeely; E-mail: mcneelyg@krlibrary.org; *Asst Dir,* Leslie Partridge; E-mail: partridgel@krlibrary.org; *Bus Mgr,* Denise Schmidt; Staff 3 (MLS 2, Non-MLS 1)
Founded 1954. Pop 28,253
Subject Interests: Ga
Automation Activity & Vendor Info: (Cataloging) Evergreen
Partic in LYRASIS; Public Information Network for Electronic Services
Open Mon-Fri 8-5
Branches: 6
CALHOUN COUNTY LIBRARY, 19379 E Hartford St, Edison, 39846-5626. (Mail add: PO Box 365, Edison, 39846-0365), SAN 338-6341. Tel: 229 835-2012. FAX: 229 835-2355. *Libr Mgr,* Dianna Carter; E-mail: dcarter@krlibrary.org; Staff 2 (Non-MLS 2)
Founded 1989. Pop 4,970; Circ 13,704
Library Holdings: CDs 40; DVDs 116; Bk Titles 11,436; Per Subs 29; Talking Bks 170; Videos 886
Special Collections: Georgia
Subject Interests: Local hist
Open Mon-Wed & Fri 9-5
Friends of the Library Group
CLAY COUNTY LIBRARY, 208 S Hancock St, Fort Gaines, 39851-9506. (Mail add: PO Box 275, Fort Gaines, 39851-0275), SAN 338-6406. Tel: 229-768-2248. FAX: 229-768-2275. *Libr Mgr,* Tara Williams; E-mail: twilliams@krlibrary.org; Staff 2 (MLS 1, Non-MLS 1)
Founded 1988. Pop 3,489; Circ 19,738
Library Holdings: CDs 17; DVDs 172; Bk Titles 15,209; Per Subs 42; Talking Bks 324; Videos 1,113
Special Collections: Georgia
Subject Interests: Local hist
Publications: Clay County History
Open Mon-Fri 8-5, Sat 9-1
QUITMAN COUNTY LIBRARY, 39 Old School Rd, Georgetown, 39854. (Mail add: PO Box 278, Georgetown, 39854-0278), SAN 338-6074. Tel: 229-334-8972. FAX: 229-234-3241. *Libr Mgr,* Betty Fair; E-mail: bfair@krlibrary.org; Staff 2 (Non-MLS 2)
Open Mon-Wed 9-5, Fri 9-4
Friends of the Library Group
RANDOLPH COUNTY LIBRARY, 106 Pearl St, Cuthbert, 39840-1474, SAN 338-649X. Tel: 229-732-2566. FAX: 229-732-6824. *Libr Mgr,* Dianna Carter; Staff 3 (MLS 1, Non-MLS 2)
Founded 1997. Pop 6,851; Circ 34,720
Library Holdings: CDs 128; DVDs 272; Bk Titles 14,895; Per Subs 31; Talking Bks 59; Videos 796
Special Collections: Georgia; Local history
Subject Interests: Photog
Publications: Monthly Newsletter
Open Mon, Tues & Fri 10-5, Thurs 10-6, Sat 10-2
TERRELL COUNTY LIBRARY, 913 Forrester Dr SE, 39842-2106, SAN 370-7865. Tel: 229-995-2902. FAX: 229-995-5989. *Librn,* Gary McNeely; *Libr Mgr,* Pearlie Bishop; E-mail: bishopp@krlibrary.org; Staff 3 (MLS 1, Non-MLS 2)
Founded 1997. Pop 10,720; Circ 29,009
Library Holdings: CDs 35; DVDs 175; e-books 12; Bk Titles 37,984; Per Subs 28; Talking Bks 520; Videos 2,778
Special Collections: Georgia; Local History
Publications: Friends (Newsletter); Terrell County History
Open Mon-Fri 10-5
Friends of the Library Group
WEBSTER COUNTY LIBRARY, 40 Cemetey Rd, Preston, 31824, SAN 338-652X. Tel: 229-828-5740. FAX: 229-828-5740. *Libr Mgr,* Nicholas Storey; E-mail: nstorey@krlibrary.org; *Librn,* Leslie Partridge; Staff 2 (Non-MLS 2)
Founded 1989. Pop 1,947; Circ 4,993
Library Holdings: DVDs 125; Bk Titles 8,009; Per Subs 17; Videos 507
Open Mon, Wed & Fri 1:30-4:30, Tues & Thurs 11-2

DECATUR

C AGNES SCOTT COLLEGE, McCain Library, 141 E College Ave, 30030-3770. SAN 303-3619. Circulation Tel: 404-471-6094. Interlibrary Loan Service Tel: 404-471-5342. Reference Tel: 404-471-6096. E-mail: library@agnesscott.edu. Web Site: www.agnesscott.edu/library. *Dir,* Elizabeth Leslie Bagley; E-mail: ebagley@agnesscott.edu; *Head, Access Serv, Liaison Librn,* Christopher Bishop; Tel: 404-471-6337; *Head, Res & Instrul Serv, Ref,* Casey Long; Tel: 404-471-6343, E-mail: clong@agnesscott.edu; *Acq, Automation Syst Coordr, E-Res Licensing,* Kathryn (Kat) Greer; Tel: 404-471-6141, E-mail: kgreer@agnesscott.edu; *Archivist, Spec Coll,* Casey Westerman; Tel: 404-471-6344, E-mail: cwesterman@agnesscott.edu; *ILL,* Stephany Kurth; Tel: 404-471-5342, E-mail: skurth@agnesscott.edu; Staff 8.5 (MLS 5, Non-MLS 3.5)
Founded 1889. Enrl 1,040; Fac 81; Highest Degree: Master
Library Holdings: e-books 372,772; e-journals 158,462; Electronic Media & Resources 395; Bk Titles 173,734; Bk Vols 193,366; Per Subs 862
Special Collections: Catherine Marshall Papers; Faculty, Student & Alumnae Publications; Frontier Religion; Robert Frost Coll
Subject Interests: Liberal arts, Sciences
Automation Activity & Vendor Info: (Acquisitions) OCLC Worldshare Management Services; (Cataloging) OCLC Worldshare Management Services; (Circulation) OCLC Worldshare Management Services; (Course Reserve) OCLC Worldshare Management Services; (Discovery) EBSCO Discovery Service; (ILL) OCLC WorldShare Interlibrary Loan; (Media Booking) OCLC Worldshare Management Services; (OPAC) OCLC Worldshare Management Services; (Serials) OCLC Worldshare Management Services
Wireless access
Function: 24/7 Electronic res, 24/7 Online cat, Art exhibits, Electronic databases & coll, Photocopying/Printing

Partic in Georgia Library Learning Online; LYRASIS; Oberlin Group; OCLC Online Computer Library Center, Inc
Open Mon-Thurs 8am-10:30pm, Fri 8-6, Sat 10-4, Sun 1-10:30; Mon-Thurs (Summer) 8-5:15
Restriction: Badge access after hrs, Borrowing requests are handled by ILL, Open to students, fac & staff

GM ATLANTA VA MEDICAL CENTER LIBRARY*, 1670 Clairmont Rd, 30033. SAN 303-3678. Tel: 404-321-6111, Ext 1027672. Web Site: www.atlanta.va.gov. *Chief Librn,* Shirley Avin; Staff 1 (Non-MLS 1)
Founded 1945
Library Holdings: Bk Titles 2,000; Per Subs 482
Subject Interests: Health sci, Med
Partic in Atlanta Health Science Libraries Consortium
Open Mon-Fri 8-4:30

R CLAIRMONT PRESBYTERIAN CHURCH LIBRARY*, 1994 Clairmont Rd, 30033. SAN 303-3635. Tel: 404-634-3355. FAX: 404-321-5057. E-mail: office@clairmontpres.org. Web Site: www.clairmontpres.org. *Librn,* Position Currently Open
Library Holdings: Bk Vols 2,750
Subject Interests: Fiction, Relig
Open Wed 8am-9pm, Sun 8-12:30

R COLUMBIA THEOLOGICAL SEMINARY*, John Bulow Campbell Library, 701 S Columbia Dr, 30030. SAN 303-3643. Tel: 404-687-4610. FAX: 404-687-4687. E-mail: ref-desk@ctsnet.edu. Web Site: www.ctsnet.edu. *Dir & Assoc Dean for Info Serv,* Dr Kelly D Campbell; Tel: 404-687-4547, E-mail: CampbellK@CTSnet.edu; *Pub Serv Librn,* Erica Durham; Tel: 404-687-4661, E-mail: durhame@ctsnet.edu; *Circ,* Mary Martha Riviere; Tel: 404-687-4617, E-mail: rivierem@ctsnet.edu; *Ser,* Griselda Lartey; Tel: 404-687-4548, E-mail: larteyg@ctsnet.edu; Staff 7 (MLS 5, Non-MLS 2)
Founded 1828. Enrl 625
Library Holdings: Bk Vols 200,000; Per Subs 862
Subject Interests: Philos, Relig
Automation Activity & Vendor Info: (Acquisitions) SirsiDynix; (Cataloging) SirsiDynix; (Circulation) SirsiDynix; (Course Reserve) SirsiDynix; (ILL) SirsiDynix; (OPAC) SirsiDynix; (Serials) SirsiDynix
Wireless access
Partic in OCLC Online Computer Library Center, Inc
Restriction: Open to students, fac & staff, Restricted pub use, Use of others with permission of librn

P DEKALB COUNTY PUBLIC LIBRARY*, Darro C Willey Administrative Offices, 3560 Kensington Rd, 30032. SAN 338-6589. Tel: 404-508-7190. FAX: 404-370-8469. TDD: 404-508-7179. Web Site: www.dekalblibrary.org. *Dir,* Alison Weissinger; E-mail: weissingera@dekalblibrary.org; *Asst Libr Dir,* Nancy Wright; E-mail: wrightn@dekalblibrary.org; *Br Operations Coordr,* George Ford; E-mail: fordg@dekalblibrary.org; *Br Operations Coordr,* Kitty Wilson; E-mail: wilsonk@dekalblibrary.org; *Coordr, Coll Mgt,* Lesley Barber; Staff 230.3 (MLS 58.5, Non-MLS 171.8)
Founded 1925. Pop 721,520; Circ 2,916,460
Jul 2013-Jun 2014 Income (Main & Associated Libraries) $15,567,689, State $1,046,695, City $279,247, Federal $4,675, County $13,230,068, Locally Generated Income $1,000,190, Other $6,814. Mats Exp $930,804, Books $461,783, Per/Ser (Incl. Access Fees) $46,887, Other Print Mats $42,253, Micro $1,750, AV Mat $176,797, Electronic Ref Mat (Incl. Access Fees) $201,334. Sal $11,513,215
Library Holdings: AV Mats 74,063; CDs 42,861; DVDs 31,202; Large Print Bks 6,044; Bk Vols 812,792; Per Subs 1,417
Special Collections: Georgia & DeKalb County History Coll
Automation Activity & Vendor Info: (Acquisitions) SirsiDynix; (Cataloging) SirsiDynix; (Circulation) SirsiDynix; (ILL) OCLC; (OPAC) SirsiDynix
Wireless access
Friends of the Library Group
Branches: 22

BROOKHAVEN BRANCH, 1242 N Druid Hills Rd NE, Atlanta, 30319, SAN 338-6619. Tel: 404-848-7140. Web Site: www.dekalblibrary.org/branches/broo.
Open Mon & Tues 10-8, Wed-Sat 10-5
Friends of the Library Group

WESLEY CHAPEL-WILLIAM C BROWN BRANCH, 2861 Wesley Chapel Rd, 30034, SAN 370-8012. Tel: 404-286-6980. Web Site: www.dekalblibrary.org/branches/wesl.
Open Mon-Wed 10-8, Thurs-Sat 10-5
Friends of the Library Group

SCOTT CANDLER BRANCH, 1917 Candler Rd, 30032, SAN 338-6643. Tel: 404-286-6986. Web Site: www.dekalblibrary.org/branches/cand.
Open Mon-Wed 10-8, Thurs-Sat 10-5
Friends of the Library Group

CHAMBLEE BRANCH, 4115 Clairmont Rd, Chamblee, 30341, SAN 338-6678. Tel: 770-936-1380. Web Site: www.dekalblibrary.org/branches/cham.
Open Mon-Wed 10-8, Thurs-Sat 10-5
Friends of the Library Group

CLARKSTON BRANCH, 951 N Indian Creek Dr, Clarkston, 30021, SAN 372-0101. Tel: 404-508-7175. Web Site: www.dekalblibrary.org/branches/clar.
Open Mon-Wed 10-8, Thurs-Sat 10-5
Friends of the Library Group

COVINGTON, 3500 Covington Hwy, 30032, SAN 372-0152. Tel: 404-508-7180. Web Site: www.dekalblibrary.org/branches/covi.
Open Mon-Wed 10-8, Thurs-Sat 10-5
Friends of the Library Group

DECATUR LIBRARY, 215 Sycamore St, 30030, SAN 338-6597. Tel: 404-370-3070. Web Site: www.dekalblibrary.org/branches/deca.
Open Mon-Wed 9-9, Thurs-Sat 9-6, Sun 1-6
Friends of the Library Group

DORAVILLE BRANCH, 3748 Central Ave, Doraville, 30340, SAN 338-6732. Tel: 770-936-3852. Web Site: www.dekalblibrary.org/branches/dora.
Open Mon, Wed, Thurs & Sat 10-6, Tues 12-8
Friends of the Library Group

DUNWOODY BRANCH, 5339 Chamblee-Dunwoody Rd, Dunwoody, 30338, SAN 321-4605. Tel: 770-512-4640. Web Site: www.dekalblibrary.org/branches/dunw.
Open Mon-Wed 10-8, Thurs-Sat 10-5
Friends of the Library Group

EMBRY HILLS BRANCH, 3733 Chamblee-Tucker Rd, Chamblee, 30341, SAN 370-7970. Tel: 770-270-8230. Web Site: www.dekalblibrary.org/branches/emhi.
Open Mon & Tues 10-8, Wed-Sat 10-5
Friends of the Library Group

FLAT SHOALS BRANCH, 4022 Flat Shoals Pkwy, 30034, SAN 372-011X. Tel: 404-244-4370. Web Site: www.dekalblibrary.org/branches/flat.
Open Mon-Wed 10-8, Thurs-Sat 10-5
Friends of the Library Group

GRESHAM BRANCH, 2418 Gresham Rd SE, Atlanta, 30316, SAN 372-0128. Tel: 404-244-4374. Web Site: www.dekalblibrary.org/branches/gres.
Open Mon & Tues 10-8, Wed-Sat 10-5
Friends of the Library Group

HAIRSTON CROSSING BRANCH, 4911 Redan Rd, Stone Mountain, 30088, SAN 370-7989. Tel: 404-508-7170. Web Site: www.dekalblibrary.org/branches/hair.
Open Mon-Wed 10-8, Thurs-Sat 10-5
Friends of the Library Group

STONE MOUNTAIN-SUE KELLOGG BRANCH, 952 Leon St, Stone Mountain, 30083, SAN 338-6821. Tel: 770-413-2020. Web Site: www.dekalblibrary.org/branches/ston.
Open Mon-Wed 10-8, Thurs-Sat 10-5
Friends of the Library Group

LITHONIA-DAVIDSON BRANCH, 6821 Church St, Lithonia, 30058, SAN 338-6856. Tel: 770-482-3820. Web Site: www.dekalblibrary.org/branches/lith.
Open Mon & Tues 10-8, Wed-Sat 10-5
Friends of the Library Group

NORTHLAKE-BARBARA LOAR BRANCH, 3772 La Vista Rd, Tucker, 30084, SAN 372-0136. Tel: 404-679-4408. Web Site: www.dekalblibrary.org/branches/nolk.
Open Mon-Wed 10-8, Thurs-Sat 10-5
Friends of the Library Group

REDAN-TROTTI BRANCH, 1569 Wellborn Rd, Redan, 30074, SAN 372-0144. Tel: 770-482-3821. Web Site: www.dekalblibrary.org/branches/reda.
Open Mon-Wed 10-8, Thurs-Sat 10-5
Friends of the Library Group

SALEM-PANOLA BRANCH, 5137 Salem Rd, Lithonia, 30038, SAN 370-7997. Tel: 770-987-6900. Web Site: www.dekalblibrary.org/branches/sapa.
Open Mon-Wed 10-8, Thurs-Sat 10-5
Friends of the Library Group

SCOTTDALE-TOBIE GRANT HOMEWORK CENTER, 644 Parkdale Dr, Scottdale, 30079, SAN 338-6767. Tel: 404-508-7174. Web Site: www.dekalblibrary.org/branches/gran.
Open Mon-Thurs 12-5

STONECREST BRANCH, 3123 Klondike Rd, Lithonia, 30038. Tel: 770-482-3828. Web Site: dekalblibrary.org/branches/stcr.
Open Mon-Wed 10-8, Thurs-Sat 10-5
Friends of the Library Group

TUCKER-REID H COFER BRANCH, 5234 LaVista Rd, Tucker, 30084, SAN 338-6708. Tel: 770-270-8234. Web Site: www.dekalblibrary.org/branches/tuck.
Open Mon-Wed 10-8, Thurs-Sat 10-5
Friends of the Library Group

TOCO HILL-AVIS G WILLIAMS BRANCH, 1282 McConnell Dr, 30033, SAN 338-6910. Tel: 404-679-4404. Web Site: www.dekalblibrary.org/branches/toco.
Open Mon-Wed 10-8, Thurs-Sat 10-5
Friends of the Library Group

DEMOREST

C PIEDMONT UNIVERSITY, Arrendale Library, 1021 Central Ave, 30535. (Mail add: PO Box 40, 30535-0040), SAN 303-3686. Tel: 706-776-0111. E-mail: libraries@piedmont.edu. Web Site: library.piedmont.edu. *Col Librn, Dean of Libr,* Bob Glass; E-mail: bglass@piedmont.edu; *Sr Librn for Assessment & Instruction,* Joseph Brenes-Dawsey; E-mail: jdawsey@piedmont.edu; *Assoc Librn for Coll Dev & Info Servs,* Davy Gibbs; E-mail: dgibbs@piedmont.edu; Staff 4.5 (MLS 3.5, Non-MLS 1)
Founded 1897. Enrl 2,076; Fac 140; Highest Degree: Doctorate
Library Holdings: CDs 1,200; DVDs 1,600; e-books 425,000; e-journals 22,000; Music Scores 1,260; Bk Titles 83,000; Bk Vols 95,000; Per Subs 50
Automation Activity & Vendor Info: (Acquisitions) SirsiDynix; (Cataloging) SirsiDynix; (Circulation) SirsiDynix; (Course Reserve) SirsiDynix; (Discovery) EBSCO Discovery Service; (ILL) OCLC Tipasa; (OPAC) SirsiDynix; (Serials) SirsiDynix
Wireless access
Function: 24/7 Electronic res, 24/7 Online cat, Computers for patron use, Doc delivery serv, Electronic databases & coll, ILL available, Online cat, Online info literacy tutorials on the web & in blackboard, Online ref, Photocopying/Printing, Ref serv available, Res assist avail, Telephone ref
Partic in Georgia Libr Info Network; Georgia Library Learning Online; Georgia Private Acad Librs Consortium; LYRASIS; OCLC Online Computer Library Center, Inc
Open Mon-Thurs 7:45am-11pm, Fri 7:45-5, Sat 11-5, Sun 2-10 (Fall-Spring); Mon-Thurs 8am-7pm, Fri 8-2, Sat 11-5 (Summer)
Friends of the Library Group

DOUGLAS

P SATILLA REGIONAL LIBRARY*, Douglas/Coffee County Public Library, 200 S Madison Ave, Ste D, 31533. SAN 338-6945. Tel: 912-384-4667. FAX: 912-389-4365. E-mail: douglib@srlsys.org. Web Site: www.srlsys.org. *Dir,* Rodney McElveen; E-mail: rmcelveen@srlsys.org; *Circ,* Regina Bennett
Founded 1914. Circ 218,275
Library Holdings: Bk Titles 77,329; Per Subs 317; Talking Bks 701
Subject Interests: Genealogy
Wireless access
Partic in Georgia Libr Info Network; GOLD Resource Sharing Network for Georgia's Libraries; LYRASIS; Public Information Network for Electronic Services
Open Mon-Thurs 10-6, Fri 10-4, Sat 10-2
Branches: 5

AMBROSE PUBLIC LIBRARY, 1070 Cypress St, Ambrose, 31512, SAN 376-9550. Tel: 912-359-2536. FAX: 912-359-2536. E-mail: ambrlib@srlsys.org. *Mgr,* Hannah Harper
Circ 3,738
Library Holdings: Bk Titles 4,017
Open Mon-Thurs 1:30-6

BROXTON PUBLIC LIBRARY, 105 Church St, Broxton, 31519, SAN 338-6953. Tel: 912-359-3887. FAX: 912-359-3887. E-mail: broxlib@srlsys.org. *Mgr,* Ketziah Harper
Circ 3,477
Library Holdings: Bk Vols 8,413
Open Mon-Thurs 1:30-6

NICHOLLS PUBLIC LIBRARY, 108 N Liberty St, Nicholls, 31554, SAN 338-7011. Tel: 912-345-2534. FAX: 912-345-2534. E-mail: nichlib@srlsys.org. *Mgr,* Bobbie McGray
Circ 14,532
Library Holdings: Bk Titles 4,885
Open Mon-Thurs 1:30-6

PEARSON PUBLIC LIBRARY, 56 E Bullard Ave, Pearson, 31642, SAN 338-7038. Tel: 912-422-3500. FAX: 912-422-3500. E-mail: pearlib@srlsys.org. *Mgr,* Cathy Koch; *Mgr,* Cristina Ornelas
Pop 3,500; Circ 7,398
Library Holdings: Bk Titles 11,924; Talking Bks 11
Open Mon-Fri 12-6, Sat 10-2

WILLACOOCHEE PUBLIC LIBRARY, 165 E Fleetwood Ave, Willacoochee, 31650, SAN 338-7062. Tel: 912-534-5252. FAX: 912-534-5252. E-mail: willalib@srlsys.org. *Mgr,* Lisa Cater
Pop 3,500; Circ 13,515
Library Holdings: Bk Titles 10,993
Open Mon-Thurs 2:30-6, Sat 10-2
Bookmobiles: 1. Librn, Lorrinda Johnson. Bk titles 2,645

C SOUTH GEORGIA STATE COLLEGE*, William S Smith Library, 100 W College Park Dr, 31533-5098. SAN 303-3694. Tel: 912-260-4323. Interlibrary Loan Service Tel: 912-260-4335. Administration Tel: 912-260-4234. Information Services Tel: 912-260-4331. FAX: 912-260-4452. Web Site: www.sgsc.edu. *Dir of Libr,* Sharon Lynn Kelly; E-mail: lynn.kelly@sgsc.edu; *Info Serv Librn,* Ashley Wilson; E-mail: ashley.wilson@sgsc.edu; *Cat, Tech Serv,* Yolanda Crosby; E-mail: yolanda.crosby@sgsc.edu; *Cat, Tech Serv Asst,* Position Currently Open; Staff 5 (MLS 2, Non-MLS 3)
Founded 1906. Enrl 2,213; Fac 50; Highest Degree: Bachelor
Library Holdings: AV Mats 3,511; Bks on Deafness & Sign Lang 37; DVDs 189; e-books 180,000; Microforms 48,293; Bk Titles 82,545; Bk Vols 94,296; Per Subs 30
Special Collections: US Geological Survey Maps
Automation Activity & Vendor Info: (Cataloging) Ex Libris Group; (Circulation) Ex Libris Group; (Course Reserve) Ex Libris Group; (Discovery) Ex Libris Group; (ILL) OCLC WorldShare Interlibrary Loan; (OPAC) Ex Libris Group
Wireless access
Partic in Galileo/GIL
Open Mon-Thurs 8am-9pm, Fri 8-Noon, Sun 4-8

J WIREGRASS GEORGIA TECHNICAL COLLEGE, Coffee Campus Library, 706 W Baker Hwy, Rm 2125, 31533. Tel: 229-468-2226. FAX: 912-389-4308. Web Site: wiregrass.edu/library. *Libr Serv Dir,* Patrice Toomer; E-mail: patrice.toomer@wiregrass.edu; Staff 2 (MLS 1, Non-MLS 1)
Founded 2010. Enrl 750; Fac 20; Highest Degree: Associate
Jul 2020-Jun 2021. Mats Exp $7,203, Books $3,600, Per/Ser (Incl. Access Fees) $33, AV Mat $1,800, Electronic Ref Mat (Incl. Access Fees) $1,770
Library Holdings: AV Mats 4; CDs 23; DVDs 257; Bk Titles 3,825; Per Subs 22; Videos 59
Automation Activity & Vendor Info: (Cataloging) Ex Libris Group; (Circulation) Ex Libris Group; (ILL) OCLC ILLiad; (OPAC) Ex Libris Group
Wireless access
Open Mon-Thurs 7:30-5:30

DUBLIN

P OCONEE REGIONAL LIBRARY*, Laurens County, 801 Bellevue Ave, 31021. SAN 338-7097. Tel: 478-272-5710. FAX: 478-275-5381. Web Site: www.ocrl.org/lc-home. *Interim Dir,* Beverly Brown; E-mail: bbrown@ocrl.org; Staff 27 (MLS 6, Non-MLS 21)
Founded 1904. Pop 79,516; Circ 334,627
Library Holdings: Bk Vols 92,950; Per Subs 135
Special Collections: Georgia Coll
Subject Interests: Local hist
Wireless access
Function: ILL available
Partic in GOLD Resource Sharing Network for Georgia's Libraries; LYRASIS; Public Information Network for Electronic Services
Open Mon-Thurs 9-7, Fri 9-5, Sat 10-2
Friends of the Library Group
Branches: 5

HARLIE FULFORD MEMORIAL, 301 Elm St, Wrightsville, 31096. (Mail add: PO Box 69, Wrightsville, 31096-0069), SAN 338-7127. Tel: 478-864-3940. FAX: 478-864-0626. *Mgr,* Marolyn Fortner
Library Holdings: Bk Vols 12,298; Per Subs 22
Open Mon-Fri 9:30-6

GLASCOCK COUNTY LIBRARY, 738 Railroad Ave, Gibson, 30810. (Mail add: PO Box 128, Gibson, 30810-0128). Tel: 706-598-9837. FAX: 706-598-2670. *Br Mgr,* Betty Cook; Staff 1 (Non-MLS 1)
Founded 2000. Pop 2,547; Circ 11,139
Library Holdings: DVDs 121; Bk Vols 3,596; Per Subs 16; Talking Bks 33; Videos 239
Function: Photocopying/Printing, Prog for children & young adult, Summer reading prog
Special Services for the Blind - Bks on cassette; Bks on CD; Computer with voice synthesizer for visually impaired persons
Open Tues 9-7, Wed & Sat 9-1, Thurs & Fri 12-6

P TALKING BOOK CENTER, 801 Bellevue Ave, 31021. (Mail add: PO Box 100, 31040-0100). Tel: 478-275-5382. Toll Free Tel: 800-453-5541. FAX: 478-275-3821. *Mgr,* Wanda Daniel
Publications: Talking Book News (Newsletter)
Special Services for the Blind - Cassette playback machines; Closed circuit TV; Duplicating spec requests; Home delivery serv; Large screen computer & software; Newsletter (in large print, Braille or on cassette); Reader equip; Screen enlargement software for people with visual disabilities; Spanish Braille mags & bks; Talking bks & player equip; Textbks on audio-cassettes; ZoomText magnification & reading software
Open Mon-Fri 9:30-6

TREUTLEN COUNTY, 585 Second St, Soperton, 30457. (Mail add: PO Box 49, Soperton, 30457), SAN 338-7186. Tel: 912-529-6683. FAX: 912-529-6050. *Br Mgr,* Mary Jane Gabriel-Smith; E-mail: mjsmith@ocrl.org
Library Holdings: Bk Vols 14,921; Per Subs 29
Open Mon-Fri 12-6

WASHINGTON COUNTY, 314 S Harris St, Sandersville, 31082-2669. (Mail add: PO Box 268, Sandersville, 31082-0268), SAN 338-7240. Tel: 478-552-7466. FAX: 478-552-6064. *Mgr,* Diane Meeks
Library Holdings: Bk Vols 41,979; Per Subs 91
Open Mon-Fri 9:30-6, Sat 9-3
Friends of the Library Group

DULUTH

S NATIONAL RAILWAY HISTORICAL SOCIETY, ATLANTA CHAPTER*, Southeastern Railway Museum Library, 3595 Buford Hwy, 30096. (Mail add: PO Box 1267, 30096-1267), SAN 375-0590. Tel: 770-476-2013. Web Site: www.nrhs.com, www.train-museum.org. *Libr Dir,* Ed Berntsen
Founded 1959
Library Holdings: Bk Vols 2,000; Per Subs 2; Videos 100
Subject Interests: Rail transportation
Open Thurs-Sat 10-5
Friends of the Library Group

CR NEW ORLEANS BAPTIST THEOLOGICAL SEMINARY*, North Georgia Campus Library, 1800 Satellite Blvd NW, 30097. Tel: 470-655-6717. Web Site: www.nobts.edu. *Dean of Libr,* Dr Jeff Griffin; E-mail: jgriffin@nobts.edu; *Librn,* Helen Shin; Tel: 770-321-1606, E-mail: hshin@nobts.edu; Staff 1 (MLS 1)
Founded 1975. Enrl 350; Highest Degree: Doctorate
Library Holdings: Bk Vols 21,000; Per Subs 25
Automation Activity & Vendor Info: (Cataloging) Horizon; (Circulation) Horizon; (OPAC) Horizon
Wireless access
Open Mon-Thurs 8-8 (Winter); Mon-Thurs 8-5 (Summer)

EASTMAN

P OCMULGEE REGIONAL LIBRARY SYSTEM*, Dodge County Library (System Headquarters), 531 Second Ave, 31023. Tel: 478-374-4711. FAX: 478-374-5646. E-mail: circulation@orls.org. Web Site: www.orls.org. *Dir,* Anne H Bowen; E-mail: ahb@orls.org; *Dep Dir,* Chris Woodburn; E-mail: ccw@orls.org; *Librn,* Josh Sheffield; Staff 7 (MLS 5, Non-MLS 2)
Founded 1954. Pop 6,600; Circ 496,344
Library Holdings: Bk Vols 209,584; Per Subs 262
Special Collections: American Indian (Ethlyn P Rolfe Coll); Genealogy (Burch-Harrell-Smallwood Coll)
Subject Interests: Ethnic studies, Local hist, Natural sci, Relig
Automation Activity & Vendor Info: (Acquisitions) Baker & Taylor
Wireless access
Partic in Public Information Network for Electronic Services
Open Mon, Tues & Thurs-Sat 9-5
Branches: 5

TESSIE W NORRIS PUBLIC LIBRARY, 103 N Third St, Cochran, 31014, SAN 338-7305. Tel: 478-934-2904. FAX: 478-934-0705.
Open Mon-Fri 9-5:30, Sat 9-2
Friends of the Library Group

M E RODEN MEMORIAL LIBRARY, 151 Commerce St, Hawkinsville, 31036, SAN 338-7364. Tel: 478-892-3155. FAX: 478-892-3155.
Open Mon-Fri 10-5:30
Friends of the Library Group

TELFAIR COUNTY LIBRARY, 101 W College St, McRae, 31055, SAN 338-7399. Tel: 229-868-2978.
Open Mon 10-7, Tues-Fri 10-5
Friends of the Library Group

WHEELER COUNTY LIBRARY, 61 W Main St, Alamo, 30411, SAN 338-7216. Tel: 912-568-7321. FAX: 912-568-7116.
Open Mon 1-7, Tues-Thurs 10-5, Fri 9-4

WILCOX COUNTY LIBRARY, Historic Courthouse Sq, 104 N Broad St, Abbeville, 31001, SAN 338-7429. Tel: 229-467-2075. FAX: 229-467-2075.
Founded 1936
Open Mon-Fri 11:30-5

ELBERTON

P ELBERT COUNTY PUBLIC LIBRARY*, 345 Heard St, 30635. SAN 338-7453. Tel: 706-283-5375. Administration Tel: 706-283-9299. FAX: 706-283-5456. Web Site: elbertlibrary.org. *Dir,* Jan L Burroughs; E-mail: jburroughs@elbertcountypl.org; Staff 5 (MLS 2, Non-MLS 3)
Founded 1925. Pop 19,478; Circ 83,987
Library Holdings: AV Mats 1,314; CDs 293; DVDs 241; Bk Vols 72,201; Per Subs 118; Videos 2,623
Automation Activity & Vendor Info: (Acquisitions) SirsiDynix; (Cataloging) SirsiDynix; (Circulation) SirsiDynix
Wireless access
Function: Home delivery & serv to seniorr ctr & nursing homes, ILL available, Internet access, Mail loans to mem, Photocopying/Printing, Prog for children & young adult, Ref serv available, Summer reading prog, Telephone ref
Partic in Public Information Network for Electronic Services
Special Services for the Deaf - Bks on deafness & sign lang; Closed caption videos; High interest/low vocabulary bks
Special Services for the Blind - Audio mat; Bks on cassette; Bks on CD; Extensive large print coll; Home delivery serv; Large print bks; Talking bks; Videos on blindness & physical disabilties
Open Mon, Tues & Thurs 10-8, Wed & Fri 10-5, Sat 9-1
Friends of the Library Group
Branches: 1

BOWMAN BRANCH, 21 Prince Ave, Bowman, 30624. Tel: 706-245-0705. *Librn,* Vivian Barnes; E-mail: vbarnes@elbertcountypl.org
Open Mon-Fri 12-6
Friends of the Library Group
Bookmobiles: 1

EVANS

P GREATER CLARKS HILL REGIONAL LIBRARY SYSTEM*, Columbia County Public Library, 7022 Evans Town Center Blvd, 30809. SAN 373-9406. Tel: 706-863-1946. Circulation Tel: 706-868-3353. Reference Tel: 706-447-7660. Administration Tel: 706-447-7663. FAX: 706-868-3351. Web Site: www.gchrl.org. *Syst Dir,* Mary Lin Maner; E-mail: mlmaner@columbiacountyga.gov; *Ch,* Natalie Pulley; Tel: 706-447-7664, E-mail: npulley@columbiacountyga.gov; *YA Librn,* Mallory Harris; E-mail: mharris@columbiacountyga.gov; *Regional Mgr,* Jeanne Peloquin; E-mail: jpeloquin@columbiacountyga.gov; *Circ Mgr,* Kathy Hebert; Tel: 706-447-7662, E-mail: khebert@columbiacountyga.gov; *Ref Mgr,* Natalie Gibson; Tel: 706-447-7671, E-mail: ngibson@columbiacountyga.gov; Staff 11 (MLS 4, Non-MLS 7)
Founded 1982. Pop 122,000; Circ 418,132
Jul 2012-Jun 2013 Income $1,349,900. Mats Exp $560,500. Sal Prof $594,770
Library Holdings: Bk Vols 153,000; Per Subs 120; Talking Bks 250
Wireless access
Function: Adult bk club, After school storytime, AV serv, Children's prog, Computer training, Computers for patron use, Digital talking bks, Electronic databases & coll, Free DVD rentals, Holiday prog, Microfiche/film & reading machines, Music CDs, Notary serv, Online cat, OverDrive digital audio bks, Photocopying/Printing, Preschool outreach, Prog for children & young adult, Senior computer classes, Spanish lang bks, Story hour, Summer reading prog, Tax forms, Teen prog, Wheelchair accessible
Partic in Public Information Network for Electronic Services
Special Services for the Blind - Bks on cassette; Bks on CD; Computer with voice synthesizer for visually impaired persons; Large print bks
Open Mon, Tues & Thurs 12-8, Wed & Fri 12-5, Sat 1-5, Sun 2-5
Friends of the Library Group
Branches: 7

BURKE COUNTY LIBRARY, 130 Hwy 24 S, Waynesboro, 30830, SAN 373-9422. Tel: 706-554-3277. FAX: 706-554-0313. E-mail: burke@gchrl.org. *Br Mgr,* Gwendolyn Jackson; E-mail: gjackson@gchrl.org; Staff 3 (Non-MLS 3)
Founded 1959. Pop 23,424; Circ 59,505
Library Holdings: DVDs 2,000; Bk Vols 28,892; Per Subs 49; Talking Bks 59; Videos 2,553
Subject Interests: Local hist
Function: Photocopying/Printing, Prog for children & young adult, Ref serv available, Summer reading prog, Telephone ref
Special Services for the Blind - Bks on cassette; Bks on CD; Computer with voice synthesizer for visually impaired persons; Large print bks
Open Mon 9-8, Tues & Thurs 9-7, Wed 9-6, Fri 8-5, Sat 9-2
Friends of the Library Group

GROVETOWN LIBRARY, 105 Old Wrightsboro Rd, Grovetown, 30813, SAN 374-8162. Tel: 706-868-3401. FAX: 706-868-3402. *Br Mgr,* Keisha Evans; E-mail: krevans@columbiacountyga.gov; Staff 4 (MLS 1, Non-MLS 3)
Founded 1994. Pop 97,389; Circ 104,915
Library Holdings: Bk Vols 53,000; Per Subs 61; Talking Bks 150; Videos 3,500
Function: Photocopying/Printing, Prog for children & young adult, Wheelchair accessible
Special Services for the Blind - Bks on cassette; Bks on CD; Computer with voice synthesizer for visually impaired persons; Large print bks; Text reader
Open Mon & Tues 10-8, Wed-Fri 10-5, Sat 1-5
Friends of the Library Group

HARLEM BRANCH, 145 N Louisville St, Harlem, 30814, SAN 373-9414. Tel: 706-650-5009. FAX: 706-556-2576. E-mail: harlem@columbiacountyga.gov. *Br Mgr,* Amanda Ham; E-mail: adove@columbiacountyga.gov; Staff 1 (Non-MLS 1)
Founded 1981. Pop 97,389
Library Holdings: Bk Vols 10,680; Per Subs 25; Talking Bks 25; Videos 2,000
Function: Photocopying/Printing, Prog for children & young adult, Summer reading prog
Special Services for the Blind - Bks on cassette; Bks on CD; Large print bks
Open Mon, Wed & Fri 10-5, Tues & Thurs 10-8, Sat 10-2
Friends of the Library Group

LINCOLN COUNTY LIBRARY, 181 N Peachtree St, Lincolnton, 30817. (Mail add: PO Box 310, Lincolnton, 30817-0310), SAN 373-9392. Tel: 706-359-4014. FAX: 706-359-1105. E-mail: lcpl@lincolncountyga.gov. *Br Mgr,* Shirley Dawkins; E-mail: sdawkins@gchrl.org; Staff 2 (Non-MLS 2)
Founded 1986. Pop 8,484; Circ 41,804
Library Holdings: DVDs 1,000; Bk Vols 11,712; Per Subs 10; Talking Bks 51; Videos 907
Function: Photocopying/Printing, Summer reading prog
Special Services for the Blind - Bks on cassette; Bks on CD; Computer with voice synthesizer for visually impaired persons
Open Mon & Thurs 9-6, Tues 9-7, Wed 9-4, Fri & Sat 9-2
Friends of the Library Group

MIDVILLE BRANCH, 149 Trout St, Midville, 30441. (Mail add: PO Box 428, Midville, 30441-0428), SAN 373-9449. Tel: 478-589-7825. FAX: 478-589-7825. E-mail: midville@gchrl.org. *Br Mgr,* Robert Daughtry; E-mail: rdaughtry@gchrl.org; Staff 1 (Non-MLS 1)
Founded 1994. Pop 23,424; Circ 3,830
Library Holdings: Bk Vols 5,341; Per Subs 14
Function: Internet access, Summer reading prog
Special Services for the Blind - Computer with voice synthesizer for visually impaired persons
Open Mon 12-6, Wed 12-4, Fri 9:30-5:30
Friends of the Library Group

SARDIS COUNTY LIBRARY, 750 Charles Perry Ave, Sardis, 30456. (Mail add: PO Box 57, Sardis, 30456), SAN 373-9430. Tel: 478-569-4866. FAX: 478-569-9510. E-mail: sardis@gchrl.org. *Br Mgr,* Jacqueline Jordan; E-mail: jjordan@gchrl.org; Staff 1 (Non-MLS 1)
Founded 1980. Pop 23,424
Library Holdings: Bk Vols 6,131; Per Subs 10
Function: Internet access
Open Mon & Wed 12-6, Fri 9:30-5:30
Friends of the Library Group

WARREN COUNTY LIBRARY, Ten Warren St, Warrenton, 30828, SAN 303-4348. Tel: 706-465-2656. FAX: 706-465-2656. *Br Mgr,* Beth Bean; E-mail: bbean@classicsouth.net; Staff 2 (Non-MLS 2)
Founded 1988. Pop 6,380; Circ 19,419
Library Holdings: DVDs 1,000; Bk Vols 12,108; Per Subs 17; Talking Bks 125; Videos 425
Function: Photocopying/Printing, Summer reading prog, Wheelchair accessible
Special Services for the Blind - Bks on cassette; Bks on CD; Computer with voice synthesizer for visually impaired persons
Open Tues 10-8, Wed-Fri 10-6, Sat 10-3
Friends of the Library Group

FAYETTEVILLE

S FAYETTE COUNTY HISTORICAL SOCIETY, INC LIBRARY*, 195 Lee St, 30214. (Mail add: PO Box 421, 30214-0421), SAN 371-6368. Tel: 770-461-9270. E-mail: fayettehistoricalsocietyga@gmail.com. Web Site: www.fayettehistoricalsociety.com. *Pres,* Alice Reeves
Library Holdings: Bk Titles 1,000
Special Collections: Civil War (War of the Rebellion Records Coll & Confederate Veteran Coll); Genealogy (Family History Coll), bks, ms
Open Tues 6pm-9pm, Thurs 10-1, Sat 9-1

FITZGERALD

P FITZGERALD-BEN HILL COUNTY LIBRARY*, 123 N Main St, 31750-2591. SAN 303-3775. Tel: 229-426-5080. FAX: 229-426-5084. Web Site: fitzgeraldbenhillcountylibrary.org. *Br Mgr,* Andrew Vickers; E-mail: avickers@cprl.org; Staff 3 (MLS 1, Non-MLS 2)
Founded 1915. Pop 18,298; Circ 47,251
Library Holdings: Bk Titles 60,000; Per Subs 200
Special Collections: Georgia Room
Subject Interests: Ga, Local hist
Automation Activity & Vendor Info: (Acquisitions) Evergreen; (Cataloging) Evergreen; (Circulation) Evergreen; (OPAC) Evergreen; (Serials) Evergreen
Wireless access
Function: 24/7 Electronic res, 24/7 Online cat, Activity rm, Adult literacy prog, Audiobks via web, AV serv, Bks on cassette, Bks on CD, CD-ROM, Children's prog, Computer training, Computers for patron use, Digital talking bks, Electronic databases & coll, Family literacy, Free DVD rentals, Holiday prog, Home delivery & serv to seniorr ctr & nursing homes, Homebound delivery serv, ILL available, Internet access, Laminating, Large print keyboards, Life-long learning prog for all ages, Literacy & newcomer serv, Magazines, Magnifiers for reading, Mango lang, Meeting rooms, Microfiche/film & reading machines, Movies, Museum passes, Music CDs, Notary serv, Online cat, Outreach serv, OverDrive digital audio bks, Photocopying/Printing, Preschool outreach, Preschool reading prog, Printer for laptops & handheld devices, Prog for adults, Prog for children & young adult, Ref & res, Scanner, Senior computer classes, Senior outreach, Serves people with intellectual disabilities, Spanish lang bks, Story hour, Study rm, Summer reading prog, Tax forms, Teen prog, VHS videos, Wheelchair accessible
Partic in GOLD Resource Sharing Network for Georgia's Libraries
Open Mon-Fri 9-7
Restriction: Borrowing requests are handled by ILL, ID required to use computers (Ltd hrs)
Friends of the Library Group

J WIREGRASS GEORGIA TECHNICAL COLLEGE, Lewis I Brinson Sr Library - Ben Hill-Irwin Campus Library, 667 Perry House Rd, 31750. Tel: 229-468-2012. FAX: 229-468-2110. Web Site: wiregrass.edu/library. *Dir, Libr Serv,* Patrice Bennett; E-mail: patrice.bennett@wiregrass.edu; Staff 2 (MLS 1, Non-MLS 1)
Founded 2006. Enrl 765; Highest Degree: Associate
Jul 2020-Jun 2021. Mats Exp $5,801, Books $4,101, Per/Ser (Incl. Access Fees) $1,200, AV Mat $500
Library Holdings: DVDs 392; e-books 34,497; Bk Vols 7,029; Per Subs 29; Videos 92
Automation Activity & Vendor Info: (Acquisitions) Ex Libris Group; (Cataloging) Ex Libris Group; (Circulation) Ex Libris Group; (ILL) OCLC ILLiad; (OPAC) Ex Libris Group
Wireless access

FOLKSTON

P CHARLTON PUBLIC LIBRARY, INC*, 1291 Indian Trail, 31537. SAN 338-4845. Tel: 912-496-2041. FAX: 912-496-1144. Web Site: threeriverslibraries.org/woodpress-dev/library-locations/charlton-county-public-library. *Libr Mgr,* Barbara Parker; E-mail: bparker@trrl.org
Subject Interests: Local hist
Mem of Three Rivers Regional Library System
Open Mon-Thurs 10-6, Fri 10-2

FORSYTH

S GEORGIA DEPARTMENT OF CORRECTIONS, OFFICE OF LIBRARY SERVICES*, Burruss Correctional Training Center, 1000 Indian Springs Dr, 31029. (Mail add: PO Box 5849, 31029-5849). Tel: 478-994-7512. FAX: 478-994-7561. Web Site: www.dcor.state.ga.us/Facilities/burruss-correctional-training-ctr. *Librn,* James Jackson
Library Holdings: Bk Vols 3,000; Per Subs 10; Talking Bks 80
Special Collections: Law Coll

FORT BENNING

UNITED STATES ARMY

AM MARTIN ARMY COMMUNITY HOSPITAL MEDICAL LIBRARY*, Bldg 9200, Rm 010 MCXB-IL, 7950 Martin Loop, 31905-5637, SAN 338-7682. Tel: 706-544-3533. FAX: 706-544-3215. Web Site: www.martin.amedd.army.mil/medlib.html. *Librn,* Beverly A McMaster; *Libr Tech,* Susan O Waldrop; Staff 2 (MLS 1, Non-MLS 1)
Library Holdings: Per Subs 90
Automation Activity & Vendor Info: (Acquisitions) Ex Libris Group; (Cataloging) Ex Libris Group; (Circulation) Ex Libris Group; (Course Reserve) Ex Libris Group; (ILL) OCLC; (Media Booking) Ex Libris Group; (OPAC) Ex Libris Group; (Serials) Ex Libris Group
Function: Health sci info serv, ILL available, Internet access, Photocopying/Printing, Ref serv available
Partic in Army Medical Department - Medical Library & Information Network; OCLC Online Computer Library Center, Inc
Open Mon-Fri 8-4:30

A MWR LIBRARY*, Bldg 93, Wold Ave, 31905, SAN 338-7518. Tel: 706-545-7141. FAX: 706-545-6363. Web Site: www.benningmwr.com. *Dir,* Renolds Trent; Tel: 706-545-8932; *Tech Serv,* Nancy Wahlstrom; Staff 6 (MLS 3, Non-MLS 3)
Founded 1942
Library Holdings: Bk Titles 51,700; Bk Vols 54,900; Per Subs 227
Subject Interests: Bus & mgt, Hist, Music, Polit sci
Partic in Georgia Libr Info Network; Telecommunications Libr Info Network

A US ARMY MANEUVER CENTER OF EXCELLENCE*, Donovan Research Library, 7533 Holtz St, Bldg 70, Ste 1025, 31905. SAN 338-7666. Tel: 706-545-5661. FAX: 706-545-8590. E-mail: usarmy.benning.mcoe.mbx.donovan-ref-desk@mail.mil. Web Site: www.benning.army.mil/library. *Chief,* Ericka Loze-Hudson; Tel: 706-545-8591, E-mail: ericka.l.loze-hudson.civ@us.army.mil; Staff 4 (MLS 2, Non-MLS 2)
Founded 1919
Library Holdings: Bk Vols 58,435; Per Subs 84
Special Collections: After Action Reports; Army Unit Histories; Classified Documents; Rare Books; Staff Studies; The Digitized Monograph Coll of Student Papers, WWI forward
Subject Interests: Mil hist
Automation Activity & Vendor Info: (Acquisitions) SirsiDynix; (Cataloging) SirsiDynix; (Circulation) SirsiDynix; (ILL) OCLC; (OPAC) SirsiDynix
Wireless access
Publications: Bibliographies; Library Handbook; Periodical Holdings List
Open Mon-Thurs 8-4
Friends of the Library Group

FORT GORDON

UNITED STATES ARMY
A CONSUMER HEALTH LIBRARY*, Eisenhower Army Medical Ctr, Rm 3-D-15, 30905, SAN 338-778X. Tel: 706-787-6765. FAX: 706-787-2327. *Librn,* Janet Millar
Founded 1942
Library Holdings: Bk Vols 1,100; Per Subs 400
Restriction: Not open to pub
AM EISENHOWER ARMY MEDICAL CENTER*, Health Sciences Libr, DDEAMC, 30905-5650, SAN 338-7755. Tel: 706-787-6765. FAX: 706-787-2327. *Librn,* Janet Millar
Library Holdings: Bk Vols 16,000; Per Subs 500
Partic in OCLC Online Computer Library Center, Inc
Restriction: Not open to pub
A WOODWORTH CONSOLIDATED LIBRARY/FORT GORDON POST LIBRARY*, 549 Rice Rd, Bldg 33500, 30905-5081, SAN 338-7720. Tel: 706-791-7323. Interlibrary Loan Service Tel: 706-791-3086. Reference Tel: 706-791-2449. Administration Tel: 706-791-6993. FAX: 706-791-3282. Web Site: gordon.army.mil/library. *Libr Dir,* Susanna Joyner; E-mail: susie.joyner@us.army.mil; Staff 13 (MLS 5, Non-MLS 8)
Founded 1950
Special Collections: US Army Signal Corps
Subject Interests: Computer sci
Automation Activity & Vendor Info: (Acquisitions) Innovative Interfaces, Inc - Millennium; (Cataloging) Innovative Interfaces, Inc - Millennium; (Circulation) Innovative Interfaces, Inc - Millennium; (ILL) OCLC WorldShare Interlibrary Loan; (OPAC) Innovative Interfaces, Inc - Millennium; (Serials) Innovative Interfaces, Inc - Millennium
Function: Adult bk club, Art exhibits, Audio & video playback equip for onsite use, Audiobks via web, Bk club(s), Bks on CD, CD-ROM, Chess club, Children's prog, Computer training, Computers for patron use, Digital talking bks, Electronic databases & coll, Free DVD rentals, Govt ref serv, Holiday prog, ILL available, Instruction & testing, Internet access, Jazz prog, Mail & tel request accepted, Music CDs, Online cat, Online ref, Orientations, Outreach serv, OverDrive digital audio bks, Photocopying/Printing, Preschool outreach, Prog for adults, Prog for children & young adult, Ref & res, Ref serv available, Scanner, Spoken cassettes & CDs, Spoken cassettes & DVDs, Story hour, Summer reading prog, Tax forms, Teen prog, Telephone ref, Visual arts prog, Wheelchair accessible, Workshops, Writing prog
Partic in Georgia Libr Info Network; OCLC Online Computer Library Center, Inc
Open Mon-Thurs 9-8, Sat & Sun 10-6
Restriction: Authorized patrons, Limited access for the pub, Open to mil & govt employees only, Photo ID required for access, Restricted loan policy

FORT OGLETHORPE

S NATIONAL PARK SERVICE*, Chickamauga Chattanooga National Military Park, Thomas Longstreet Library, 3370 LaFayette Rd, 30742. SAN 373-0425. Tel: 706-866-9241. Web Site: nps.gov/chch. *Historian,* James Ogden, III; E-mail: james_ogden@nps.gov
Founded 1890
Library Holdings: Bk Vols 5,000
Special Collections: Chattanooga Campaign, ms
Subject Interests: Civil War
Restriction: Open by appt only

FORT STEWART

UNITED STATES ARMY
A FORT STEWART MAIN POST LIBRARY*, 316 Lindquist Rd, 31314-5126, SAN 338-7879. Tel: 912-767-2260, 912-767-2828. FAX: 912-767-3794. Web Site: www.stewlib3.stewart.army.mil. *Dir,* Faye Couture; *Ref Librn,* Patricia Alcorn; *Tech Serv,* Meriam D Simmons
Founded 1942
Library Holdings: Bk Titles 55,000; Bk Vols 68,000; Per Subs 250
Subject Interests: Mil hist
Automation Activity & Vendor Info: (Acquisitions) Ex Libris Group; (Cataloging) Ex Libris Group; (Circulation) Ex Libris Group; (OPAC) Ex Libris Group
Partic in Georgia Libr Info Network; News Bank; OCLC Online Computer Library Center, Inc
AM WINN ARMY COMMUNITY HOSPITAL MEDICAL LIBRARY*, 1061 Harman Ave, Ste 2J11B, 31314-5611, SAN 338-7895. Tel: 912-435-6542. FAX: 912-435-5480. *Librn,* Laura Harvell
Library Holdings: Bk Titles 300; Bk Vols 600; Per Subs 36
Subject Interests: Allied health
Restriction: Open by appt only

FORT VALLEY

S AMERICAN CAMELLIA SOCIETY LIBRARY, 100 Massee Lane, 31030-6974. SAN 326-8578. Tel: 478-967-2358. Toll Free Tel: 877-422-6355. FAX: 478-967-2083. E-mail: ask@americancamellias.org. Web Site: www.americancamellias.com/publications-and-library. *Exec Dir,* Matthew Israel; E-mail: misrael@americancamellias.org
Founded 1945
Library Holdings: Bk Vols 500; Per Subs 10
Restriction: Open by appt only

C FORT VALLEY STATE UNIVERSITY*, Henry Alexander Hunt Memorial Library, 1005 State University Dr, 31030-4313. SAN 303-3791. Tel: 478-825-6753. FAX: 478-825-6663. Web Site: www.fvsu.edu/huntlibrary. *Dir, Libr Serv,* Frank Mahitab; E-mail: mahitabf@fvsu.edu; *Asst Dir,* Agnes Muriuki; E-mail: muriukia@fvsu.edu; Staff 12 (MLS 5, Non-MLS 7)
Founded 1925. Enrl 2,466; Fac 161; Highest Degree: Master
Library Holdings: Bk Vols 189,417; Per Subs 805
Special Collections: Materials and books by and about Blacks
Subject Interests: Agr, Art, Econ, Educ, Ethnic studies, Home econ, Sci tech
Automation Activity & Vendor Info: (Acquisitions) Ex Libris Group; (Cataloging) Ex Libris Group; (Circulation) Ex Libris Group; (ILL) Ex Libris Group; (OPAC) Ex Libris Group; (Serials) Ex Libris Group
Wireless access
Publications: LRC Student Handbook; Newsletter; The Info
Partic in Galileo/GIL

P PEACH PUBLIC LIBRARIES*, Thomas Public Library (Syst Hq), 315 Martin Luther King Jr Dr, 31030-4196. SAN 338-7933. Tel: 478-825-1640. FAX: 478-825-2061. Web Site: www.peach.public.lib.ga.us. *Dir,* Billy Tripp; E-mail: trippb@mail.peach.public.lib.ga.us; *Pub Serv Librn,* Andrew Vickers; E-mail: vickersa@mail.peach.public.lib.ga.us; *Circ Mgr,* Maria Zepeda Aguilar; E-mail: aguilarm@mail.peach.public.lib.ga.us; *Children's Spec, Outreach Serv Spec, Youth Spec,* Maira Hernandez; E-mail: hernandezm@mail.peach.public.lib.ga.us; Staff 6 (MLS 2, Non-MLS 4)
Founded 1915. Pop 22,881; Circ 85,849
Library Holdings: CDs 580; DVDs 1,068; Bk Vols 48,080; Per Subs 25
Subject Interests: Local hist
Partic in Public Information Network for Electronic Services
Open Mon 9:30-7, Tues-Thurs 9:30-5:30, Fri & Sat 9:30-1:30
Friends of the Library Group
Branches: 1
BYRON PUBLIC, 105 W Church St, Byron, 31008. (Mail add: PO Box 1120, Byron, 31008-1120), SAN 338-7968. Tel: 478-956-2200. FAX: 478-956-5688. *Br Mgr,* Susan Halbedel
Library Holdings: Bk Vols 19,639
Open Tues (Winter) 10-8, Wed & Thurs 10-6, Fri & Sat 10-4; Mon-Thurs (Summer) 9-6, Fri 9-1

FRANKLIN SPRINGS

CR EMMANUEL COLLEGE, Shaw-Leslie Library, 2261 W Main St, 30639. (Mail add: PO Box 69, 30639-0069), SAN 303-3805. Tel: 706-245-7226, Ext 2850. FAX: 706-245-4424. E-mail: eclibrary@ec.edu. Web Site: ec.edu/library, libguides.ec.edu/home. *Dir, Libr Serv,* Deborah Millier; Tel: 706-245-2852, E-mail: dmillier@ec.edu; *Sr Libr Assoc,* Beth Cochran; E-mail: bcochran@ec.edu; *Libr Asst,* Ann Ashworth; E-mail: aashworth@ec.edu; Staff 3 (MLS 1, Non-MLS 2)
Founded 1935. Enrl 845; Fac 52; Highest Degree: Bachelor
Jul 2020-Jun 2021. Mats Exp $5,000, Books $500, Per/Ser (Incl. Access Fees) $4,500

Library Holdings: CDs 332; DVDs 158; Music Scores 184; Per Subs 80
Special Collections: Archive of Emmanuel College
Automation Activity & Vendor Info: (Cataloging) Follett Software; (Circulation) Follett Software; (ILL) OCLC; (OPAC) Follett Software; (Serials) EBSCO Online
Wireless access
Partic in Christian Libr Network; Georgia Private Acad Libs Consortium; OCLC-LVIS
Open Mon-Thurs 7:45am-11pm, Fri 7:45-4, Sat 1-5, Sun 7pm-11pm
Restriction: Open to fac, students & qualified researchers, Restricted pub use

GAINESVILLE

C BRENAU UNIVERSITY, Trustee Library, 625 Academy St, 30501-3343. SAN 303-3813. Tel: 770-534-6113. Toll Free Tel: 800-252-5119, Ext 6113. FAX: 770-534-6254. E-mail: library@brenau.edu. Web Site: library.brenau.edu. *Dean, Libr Serv,* Linda Kern; E-mail: lkern@brenau.edu; *Head, Res & Instruction,* Kimberly Boyd; Tel: 770-534-6213, E-mail: kboyd2@brenau.edu; *Coll Develop Librn,* Benjamin Barton; Tel: 770-538-4723, E-mail: bbarton@brenau.edu; *Tech Serv Librn,* Thomas Waters; Tel: 770-718-5303, E-mail: twaters1@brenau.edu; Staff 9 (MLS 6, Non-MLS 3)
Founded 1878. Enrl 2,100; Fac 110; Highest Degree: Master
Library Holdings: e-books 50,000; Music Scores 1,200; Bk Vols 80,000; Per Subs 150; Videos 2,900
Special Collections: Elson Judaica Coll; Rare Book Gallery (18th & 19th century fiction); Senator Tom Watson Library
Subject Interests: Educ, Music, Nursing
Automation Activity & Vendor Info: (Acquisitions) Ex Libris Group; (Cataloging) Ex Libris Group; (Circulation) Ex Libris Group; (OPAC) Ex Libris Group
Wireless access
Function: For res purposes
Publications: Library Handbook
Partic in Atlanta Regional Council for Higher Education; LYRASIS
Open Mon-Thurs 7:45am-10pm, Fri 7:45-6, Sun 1-10
Restriction: Circ limited

P HALL COUNTY LIBRARY SYSTEM*, Gainesville Branch, 127 Main St NW, 30501-3699. SAN 338-8026. Tel: 770-532-3311. Circulation Tel: 770-532-3311, Ext 110. Reference Tel: 770-532-3311, Ext 114. FAX: 770-532-4305. Circulation E-mail: circdesk@hallcountylibrary.org. Web Site: www.hallcountylibrary.org. *Dir,* Lisa MacKinney; E-mail: lmackinney@hallcountylibrary.org; *Br Mgr,* Jeanne Jimerson; Tel: 770-532-3311, Ext 107, E-mail: jjimerson@hallcountylibrary.org; *Youth Serv Mgr,* Adrianne Junius; Tel: 770-532-3311, Ext 126, E-mail: ajunius@hallcountylibrary.org; Staff 59 (MLS 7, Non-MLS 52)
Founded 1997. Pop 203,894; Circ 1,005,688
Library Holdings: Bk Vols 300,449; Per Subs 200
Special Collections: James Longstreet Coll, papers
Subject Interests: Genealogy, Local hist, Spanish
Automation Activity & Vendor Info: (Cataloging) Evergreen; (Circulation) Evergreen; (ILL) OCLC; (OPAC) Evergreen
Wireless access
Publications: e-link (Monthly newsletter); Friends Footnotes (Quarterly); Staff Newsletter (Monthly)
Partic in Georgia Library Learning Online; LYRASIS; OCLC Online Computer Library Center, Inc; Public Information Network for Electronic Services
Special Services for the Deaf - ADA equip; Am sign lang & deaf culture; Assisted listening device; Assistive tech; Closed caption videos; Described encaptioned media prog; TDD equip
Special Services for the Blind - Accessible computers; Assistive/Adapted tech devices, equip & products; Audio mat; BiFolkal kits; Bks & mags in Braille, on rec, tape & cassette; Bks available with recordings; Bks on cassette; Bks on CD; Cassette playback machines; Cassettes; Compressed speech equip; Computer access aids; Computer with voice synthesizer for visually impaired persons; Copier with enlargement capabilities; Digital talking bk; Duplicating spec requests; Extensive large print coll; Info on spec aids & appliances; Large print bks; Large screen computer & software; Lending of low vision aids; Low vision equip; Machine repair; Magnifiers; Micro-computer access & training; Networked computers with assistive software; Newsletter (in large print, Braille or on cassette); PC for people with disabilities; Ref serv; Screen enlargement software for people with visual disabilities; Talking bks; Talking bks & player equip; Text reader; Volunteer serv
Open Mon & Thurs 10-8, Tues & Wed 10-6, Fri & Sat 10-5
Friends of the Library Group
Branches: 3
BLACKSHEAR PLACE, 2927 Atlanta Hwy, 30507, SAN 370-9264. Tel: 770-532-3311, Ext 151. FAX: 770-287-3653. *Br Mgr,* Veronica Gomez; E-mail: vgomez@hallcountylibrary.org; Staff 8.5 (Non-MLS 8.5)
Circ 115,135
Library Holdings: Bk Vols 70,000; Per Subs 64
Open Mon & Thurs 12-8, Tues & Wed 9-6, Fri 9-5
Friends of the Library Group
MURRAYVILLE BRANCH, 4796 Thompson Bridge Rd, Murrayville, 30507, SAN 374-7352. Tel: 770-532-3311, Ext 171. FAX: 770-503-9298. *Mgr,* Kathy Evans; E-mail: kevans@hallcountylibrary.org; Staff 3 (Non-MLS 3)
Circ 49,613
Library Holdings: Bk Vols 16,796; Per Subs 12
Open Mon & Thurs 12-8, Tues & Wed 9-6, Fri 9-5
Friends of the Library Group
SPOUT SPRINGS BRANCH, 6488 Spout Springs Rd, Flowery Branch, 30542. Tel: 770-532-3311, Ext 191. FAX: 770-965-9501. *Br Mgr,* Angela Glowcheski; Staff 11.5 (MLS 1, Non-MLS 10.5)
Library Holdings: Bk Vols 82,322; Per Subs 38
Open Mon & Thurs 12-8, Tues & Wed 9-6, Fri 9-5

M NORTHEAST GEORGIA HEALTH SYSTEM, Fraser Resource Center & Health Sciences Library, 743 Spring St NE, 30501-3715. SAN 320-9393. Tel: 770-219-5216. FAX: 770-219-7330. E-mail: library@nghs.com. Web Site: www.nghs.com/library. *Libr Coord,* Shannon Glover; E-mail: shannon.glover@nghs.com; Staff 3 (MLS 2, Non-MLS 1)
Founded 1963
Subject Interests: Allied health, Consumer health, Med, Nursing
Automation Activity & Vendor Info: (Cataloging) EOS International; (Circulation) EOS International; (OPAC) EOS International; (Serials) EBSCO Online
Wireless access
Partic in Southeastern Regional Med Libr Program
Open Mon-Fri 8-4:30
Restriction: Hospital staff & commun

GARDEN CITY

S GEORGIA DEPARTMENT OF CORRECTIONS, OFFICE OF LIBRARY SERVICES*, Coastal State Prison, 200 Gulfstream Rd, 31418. (Mail add: PO Box 7150, 31418-7150). Tel: 912-965-6306. FAX: 912-966-6799. Web Site: www.dcor.state.ga.us. *Librn,* Doris Liggins
Library Holdings: Bk Vols 15,000
Special Collections: Law Coll
Restriction: Not open to pub

GLENNVILLE

S GEORGIA DEPARTMENT OF CORRECTIONS, OFFICE OF LIBRARY SERVICES*, Smith State Prison, 9676 Hwy 301 N, 30427. (Mail add: PO Box 726, 30427-0726). Tel: 912-654-5090. Web Site: www.dcor.state.ga.us/GDC/FacilityMap/html/S_50000207.html. *Librn,* Mr Tracy Hilton
Library Holdings: AV Mats 150; Bk Vols 11,000; Per Subs 40; Talking Bks 10; Videos 300
Special Collections: Law Coll
Restriction: Not open to pub

GLYNCO

G FEDERAL LAW ENFORCEMENT TRAINING CENTER LIBRARY*, Bldg 262, 1131 Chapel Crossing Rd, 31524. SAN 303-3848. Tel: 912-267-2320. E-mail: fletc-libraryservices@fletc.dhs.gov. Web Site: fltc.ent.sirsi.net. *Librn,* Position Currently Open; Staff 3 (MLS 1, Non-MLS 2)
Founded 1975
Library Holdings: Bk Titles 4,000; Bk Vols 40,000
Automation Activity & Vendor Info: (Cataloging) Follett Software
Wireless access
Restriction: Open to students, fac & staff

GRIFFIN

P FLINT RIVER REGIONAL LIBRARY SYSTEM*, Griffin-Spalding County Library & Library System Headquarters, 800 Memorial Dr, 30223. SAN 338-8174. Tel: 770-412-4770. Web Site: frrls.net. *Acq Librn, Exec Dir,* Natalie Marshall; E-mail: natalie@frrls.net; *Asst Dir, Pub Serv,* Lois Griffin; E-mail: lgriffin@frrls.net; *ILL Librn,* Karin Fulton; *Local Hist Librn,* Evans Millican; E-mail: evans@frrls.net; *Tech Librn,* Scott T Martin; E-mail: stmartin@frrls.net; *Youth Serv Librn,* Bea Mengel; E-mail: bmengel@frrls.net; *Circ Mgr,* Amy Cook; E-mail: amyc@frrls.net; *Tech Serv Mgr,* Stephen Hart; E-mail: stephenhart@frrls.net; Staff 14 (MLS 8, Non-MLS 6)
Founded 1949. Pop 272,943; Circ 1,071,130
Library Holdings: Audiobooks 17,746; DVDs 8,958; Bk Vols 506,046; Videos 5,090
Subject Interests: County hist, State hist
Automation Activity & Vendor Info: (Acquisitions) Evergreen; (Cataloging) Evergreen; (Circulation) Evergreen; (OPAC) Evergreen
Wireless access

Function: Adult bk club, Audiobks via web, Bks on CD, Children's prog, Computers for patron use, Electronic databases & coll, ILL available, Internet access, Magazines, Meeting rooms, Microfiche/film & reading machines, Movies, Notary serv, Online cat, Photocopying/Printing, Ref serv available, Scanner, Story hour, Study rm, Summer reading prog, Tax forms, Teen prog, Telephone ref, Wheelchair accessible
Partic in GOLD Resource Sharing Network for Georgia's Libraries; LYRASIS; Public Information Network for Electronic Services
Open Mon & Thurs 9-8, Tues, Wed, Fri & Sat 9-5
Friends of the Library Group
Branches: 7
BARNESVILLE-LAMAR COUNTY LIBRARY, 401 Thomaston St, Barnesville, 30204, SAN 338-8239. Tel: 770-358-3270. *Libr Mgr,* Kelly Hughes; Staff 5 (MLS 1, Non-MLS 4)
Library Holdings: Audiobooks 768; DVDs 636; Bk Vols 39,119; Videos 1,597
Subject Interests: County hist, State hist
Open Mon & Wed 10-7:30, Tues, Thurs & Fri 10-4:30, Sat 10-12:30
Friends of the Library Group
J JOEL EDWARDS PUBLIC LIBRARY, 7077 Hwy 19 S, Zebulon, 30295. (Mail add: PO Box 574, Zebulon, 30295), SAN 338-8573. Tel: 770-567-2014. *Libr Mgr,* Rosemary Bunn; Staff 4 (Non-MLS 4)
Library Holdings: Bk Vols 22,851
Subject Interests: State hist
Open Mon, Wed & Fri 11-5, Tues & Thurs 11-7, Sat 11-3
FAYETTE COUNTY PUBLIC LIBRARY, 1821 Heritage Pkwy, Fayetteville, 30214, SAN 338-8441. Tel: 770-305-5426. Web Site: www.fayettecountyga.gov. *Libr Mgr,* Michelle Bennett-Copeland; Staff 10 (MLS 4, Non-MLS 6)
Library Holdings: Audiobooks 7,850; DVDs 2,172; Bk Vols 127,517; Videos 1,941
Special Collections: Margaret Mitchell Coll
Subject Interests: State hist
Open Mon-Thurs 9-9, Fri & Sat 9-6
Friends of the Library Group
JACKSON-BUTTS COUNTY PUBLIC LIBRARY, 436 E College St, Jackson, 30233, SAN 338-8387. Tel: 770-775-7524. *Libr Mgr,* Cathy Kelly; Staff 4 (MLS 1, Non-MLS 3)
Library Holdings: Audiobooks 748; DVDs 340; Bk Vols 44,746
Subject Interests: County hist, State hist
Partic in National Network of Libraries of Medicine Region 2
Open Mon-Fri 9:30-3
Friends of the Library Group
MONROE COUNTY LIBRARY, 62 W Main St, Forsyth, 31029, SAN 338-8476. Tel: 478-994-7025. *Libr Mgr,* Kimberly Clayton; Staff 4 (Non-MLS 4)
Library Holdings: Audiobooks 594; DVDs 138; Bk Vols 44,703; Videos 65
Subject Interests: County hist, State hist
Open Mon & Tues 9-8, Wed 9-6
Friends of the Library Group
PEACHTREE CITY LIBRARY, 201 Willowbend Rd, Peachtree City, 30269, SAN 338-8565. Tel: 770-631-2520. *Libr Adminr,* Jill Prouty; Staff 11 (MLS 4, Non-MLS 7)
Founded 1973
Library Holdings: Audiobooks 5,324; DVDs 6,247; Bk Vols 98,457; Videos 1,141
Subject Interests: Ga
Open Mon, Wed & Fri 10-5, Tues & Thurs 12-7, Sat 10-3
Friends of the Library Group
TYRONE PUBLIC LIBRARY, 143 Commerce Dr, Tyrone, 30290, SAN 338-859X. Tel: 770-487-1565. *Libr Mgr,* Patty Newland; Staff 4 (Non-MLS 4)
Library Holdings: Audiobooks 342; DVDs 393; Bk Vols 26,144; Videos 203
Open Mon-Fri 9-5

J SOUTHERN CRESCENT TECHNICAL COLLEGE*, Griffin Campus Library, 501 Varsity Rd, 30223. Tel: 770-228-7348, 770-412-4755. Toll Free Tel: 877-897-0006. E-mail: library@sctech.edu. Web Site: www.sctech.edu/libraries. *Dir, Libr Serv,* Denise Barbour; E-mail: Denise.Barbour@sctech.edu; Staff 3 (MLS 1, Non-MLS 2)
Founded 1963. Enrl 2,450
Library Holdings: e-books 25,000; Bk Titles 17,518; Bk Vols 18,010; Per Subs 135
Automation Activity & Vendor Info: (Cataloging) Surpass; (Circulation) Surpass; (OPAC) Surpass
Wireless access
Partic in Georgia Library Learning Online
Open Mon-Thurs 8am-9pm

C UNIVERSITY OF GEORGIA LIBRARIES, Griffin Campus, 1109 Experiment St, 30223-1797. SAN 303-3759. Tel: 770-228-7238. FAX: 770-229-3213. Web Site: site.caes.uga.edu/library-griffin. *Librn,* John W Cruickshank; E-mail: johnlc@uga.edu; Staff 1 (MLS 1)
Founded 1888
Library Holdings: Bk Vols 10,000; Per Subs 300
Special Collections: Oral History
Subject Interests: Agr
Wireless access
Function: ILL available
Partic in Atlanta Regional Council for Higher Education; OCLC Online Computer Library Center, Inc
Open Mon-Fri 8-5
Restriction: Non-circulating to the pub

GROVETOWN

S GEORGIA DEPARTMENT OF CORRECTIONS, OFFICE OF LIBRARY SERVICES*, Augusta State Medical Prison, 3001 Gordon Hwy, 30813. Tel: 706-855-4882. FAX: 706-855-4924. Web Site: www.dcor.state.ga.us/Facilities/augusta-state-med-prison. *Dir, Libr Serv,* Position Currently Open
Library Holdings: Audiobooks 127; Bks on Deafness & Sign Lang 2; Bk Vols 21,000; Per Subs 27; Talking Bks 96
Special Collections: Law Coll
Restriction: Not open to pub

HARDWICK

S GEORGIA DEPARTMENT OF CORRECTIONS, OFFICE OF LIBRARY SERVICES*, Baldwin State Prison, 140 Laying Farm Rd, 31034. (Mail add: PO Box 218, 31034-0218). Tel: 478-445-4175. Web Site: www.dcor.state.ga.us/Facilities/baldwin-state-prison. *Librn,* Position Currently Open
Library Holdings: Bk Vols 7,000; Per Subs 15
Special Collections: Law Coll
Restriction: Not open to pub

HARTWELL

P HART COUNTY LIBRARY*, 150 Benson St, 30643. SAN 303-3864. Tel: 706-376-4655. FAX: 706-376-1157. E-mail: info@hartcountylibrary.com. Web Site: www.hartcountylibrary.com. *Dir,* Richard Sanders; Staff 5 (MLS 2, Non-MLS 3)
Founded 1936. Pop 21,500; Circ 162,000
Library Holdings: Bk Vols 52,000; Per Subs 32
Special Collections: History of Hart County, A-tapes. Oral History
Open Mon, Tues & Fri 10-6, Wed & Sat 10-2, Thurs 10-8
Friends of the Library Group

HAWKINSVILLE

S GEORGIA DEPARTMENT OF CORRECTIONS, OFFICE OF LIBRARY SERVICES*, Pulaski State Prison, 373 Upper River Rd, 31036. (Mail add: PO Box 839, 31036-0839). Tel: 478-783-6000, Ext 6102. FAX: 478-783-6008. Web Site: www.dcor.state.ga.us/Facilities/pulaski-state-prison. *Librn,* Janice Postell
Library Holdings: Bk Vols 3,500; Per Subs 25; Talking Bks 150; Videos 200
Special Collections: Law Coll
Restriction: Not open to pub

HELENA

S GEORGIA DEPARTMENT OF CORRECTIONS, OFFICE OF LIBRARY SERVICES*, Telfair State Prison, 210 Longbridge Rd, 31037. (Mail add: PO Box 549, 31037-0549). Tel: 229-868-7721. FAX: 229-868-6509. Web Site: www.dcor.state.ga.us/GDC/FacilityMap/html/S_50000199.html. *Librn,* Mildred Hamilton; E-mail: mildred.hamilton@gdc.ga.gov
Library Holdings: Bk Vols 3,000
Special Collections: Law Coll
Restriction: Not open to pub

HINESVILLE

J SAVANNAH TECHNICAL COLLEGE*, Liberty County Campus Library, 100 Technology Dr, 31313. Tel: 912-408-3024, Ext 6017. FAX: 912-408-3038. E-mail: reference@savannahtech.edu. Web Site: www.savannahtech.edu/academics/library. *Dir, Libr & Info Serv,* James Burch; Tel: 912-443-5874, E-mail: jburch@savannahtech.edu; *Librn,* Troy Cook; E-mail: tcook@savannahtech.edu
Founded 1989. Highest Degree: Associate
Library Holdings: e-books 50,000; e-journals 15,000; Bk Vols 3,000; Per Subs 30
Automation Activity & Vendor Info: (Cataloging) TLC (The Library Corporation); (Circulation) TLC (The Library Corporation); (OPAC) TLC (The Library Corporation)
Wireless access
Partic in Georgia Library Learning Online
Open Mon-Thurs 7-7, Fri 8-Noon

HOMERVILLE

S HUXFORD GENEALOGICAL SOCIETY INC*, Huxford-Spear Genealogical Library, 20 S College St, 31634. (Mail add: PO Box 595, 31634-0595), SAN 375-7730. Tel: 912-487-2310. FAX: 912-487-3881. E-mail: huxford.spearlibrary@windstream.net, huxford@windstream.net. Web Site: huxford.com. *Libr Dir,* Cathy Wells; Staff 2 (Non-MLS 2)
Founded 1972
Library Holdings: Bk Titles 4,000; Per Subs 1,500
Wireless access
Publications: Pioneers of Wiregrass Georgia (Quarterly)
Open Tues-Fri 9-4

JACKSON

S GEORGIA DEPARTMENT OF CORRECTIONS, OFFICE OF LIBRARY SERVICES*, Georgia Diagnostic & Classification State Prison, 2978 Hwy 36 W, 30233. (Mail add: PO Box 3877, 30233-0078). Tel: 770-504-2000. FAX: 770-504-2006. Web Site: www.dcor.state.ga.us/Facilities/ga-diag-class-prison. *Law Librn,* John Young
Library Holdings: Bk Vols 3,000
Special Collections: Law Coll

JEFFERSON

P PIEDMONT REGIONAL LIBRARY SYSTEM*, Regional Office, 990 Washington St, 30549-1011. SAN 339-3399. Tel: 706-367-9399. FAX: 706-367-8032. Web Site: prlib.org. *Dir,* Beth McIntyre; E-mail: bmcintyre@prlib.org; *Asst Dir,* Kelli McDaniel; *Head, Tech Serv,* Nancy Holmes; *Info Technician, Librn,* George Tuttle; Staff 4 (MLS 4)
Founded 1954. Pop 148,247; Circ 582,027
Library Holdings: Bk Vols 582,027; Per Subs 262
Automation Activity & Vendor Info: (ILL) OCLC
Wireless access
Partic in Public Information Network for Electronic Services
Open Mon-Fri 8:30-5
Friends of the Library Group
Branches: 10
AUBURN PUBLIC LIBRARY, 24 Fifth St, Auburn, 30011-3280. Tel: 770-513-2925. Web Site: auburn.prlib.org. *Libr Mgr,* Belinda Outwater; E-mail: boutwater@prlib.org
Open Mon-Thurs 10-7, Fri & Sat 10-5
BANKS COUNTY PUBLIC LIBRARY, 226 Hwy 51 S, Homer, 30547, SAN 339-3429. Tel: 706-677-3164. Web Site: banks.prlib.org. *Libr Mgr,* Stacy G Krumnow; E-mail: skrumnow@prlib.org; Staff 6 (Non-MLS 6)
Function: 24/7 Online cat, Accelerated reader prog, Bks on CD, Children's prog, Computers for patron use, Free DVD rentals, Internet access, Laminating, Large print keyboards, Magazines, Mango lang, Notary serv, Online cat, OverDrive digital audio bks, Photocopying/Printing, Preschool reading prog, Prog for adults, Prog for children & young adult, Senior computer classes, Story hour, Summer & winter reading prog, Summer reading prog, Tax forms, Teen prog, Wheelchair accessible
Open Mon, Tues & Thurs 10-7, Wed 10-6, Fri 10-4, Sat 10-2
BRASELTON LIBRARY, 15 Brassie Lane, Braselton, 30517. Tel: 706-654-1992. Web Site: braselton.prlib.org. *Libr Mgr,* Lori Hayes; E-mail: lhayes@prlib.org
Open Mon, Wed & Fri 10-5, Tues & Thurs 10-7, Sat 10-2
Friends of the Library Group
COMMERCE PUBLIC LIBRARY, 1344 S Broad St, Commerce, 30529-2053, SAN 339-3453. Tel: 706-335-5946. Web Site: commerce.prlib.org. *Libr Mgr,* Angel Abounader; E-mail: aabounader@prlib.org
Open Mon-Wed 10-6, Thurs 10-8, Fri 10-5, Sat 10-4
Friends of the Library Group
JEFFERSON PUBLIC LIBRARY, 100 Washington St, 30549, SAN 339-3488. Tel: 706-367-8012. Web Site: jefferson.prlib.org. *Libr Mgr,* Laura Gentle; E-mail: lgentle@prlib.org
Open Mon-Thurs 9-7, Fri 9-5, Sat 10-4
Friends of the Library Group
MAYSVILLE PUBLIC LIBRARY, 9247 Gillsville Rd, Maysville, 30558, SAN 374-6534. Tel: 706-652-2323. Web Site: maysville.prlib.org. *Libr Mgr,* Melanie Weatherby; E-mail: mweatherby@prlib.org; Staff 3 (Non-MLS 3)
Founded 1933. Pop 1,831
Library Holdings: Audiobooks 200; DVDs 1,500; Large Print Bks 100; Bk Titles 8,000; Per Subs 15
Function: 24/7 Online cat, Accelerated reader prog, Adult bk club, Art exhibits, Bilingual assistance for Spanish patrons, Bks on CD, Children's prog, Computers for patron use, Family literacy, Free DVD rentals, Govt ref serv, Holiday prog, Internet access, Jail serv, Life-long learning prog for all ages, Magazines, Mango lang, Movies, Museum passes, Online cat, Online info literacy tutorials on the web & in blackboard, Online ref, OverDrive digital audio bks, Photocopying/Printing, Preschool outreach, Preschool reading prog, Prog for children & young adult, Serves people with intellectual disabilities, Spanish lang bks, Story hour, Summer & winter reading prog, Summer reading prog, Tax forms, Wheelchair accessible
Special Services for the Blind - Assistive/Adapted tech devices, equip & products
Open Mon & Fri 10-5, Tues & Thurs 10-7, Sat 10-2
Friends of the Library Group
STATHAM PUBLIC LIBRARY, 1928 Railroad St, Statham, 30666. Tel: 770-725-4785. Web Site: statham.prlib.org. *Libr Mgr,* Suzy Dukes; E-mail: sdukes@prlib.org; Staff 5 (MLS 1, Non-MLS 4)
Function: 24/7 Electronic res, 24/7 Online cat, Online cat, Wheelchair accessible
Open Mon-Thurs 10-7, Fri 10-5, Sat 10-3
Friends of the Library Group
HAROLD S SWINDLE PUBLIC LIBRARY, 5466 US Hwy 441 S, Nicholson, 30565, SAN 339-3607. Tel: 706-757-3577. Web Site: nicholson.prlib.org. *Libr Mgr,* Rhonda O'Keeffe; E-mail: rokeeffe@prlib.org; Staff 1 (Non-MLS 1)
Pop 2,000
Function: Bk club(s), Bks on CD, Children's prog, Computer training, Computers for patron use, Free DVD rentals, Holiday prog, Internet access, Large print keyboards, Magazines, Mango lang, Museum passes, Music CDs, Online cat, Photocopying/Printing, Prog for adults, Prog for children & young adult, Scanner, Senior computer classes, Story hour, Summer reading prog, Tax forms, Wheelchair accessible
Open Mon-Fri 10-6, Sat 10-2
Friends of the Library Group
TALMO PUBLIC LIBRARY, 45 A J Irvin Rd, Talmo, 30575. Tel: 706-693-1905. Web Site: talmo.prlib.org. *Libr Mgr,* Jenna McBurney; E-mail: jmcburney@prlib.org
Open Mon & Wed-Fri 9-6, Tues 10-7
WINDER PUBLIC LIBRARY, 189 Bellview St, Winder, 30680-1706. Tel: 770-867-2762. Web Site: winder.prlib.org. *Libr Mgr,* Julia Simpson; E-mail: jsimpson@prlib.org
Library Holdings: Bk Vols 60,550
Open Mon 9-8, Tues-Thurs 9-7, Fri & Sat 9-5
Friends of the Library Group
Bookmobiles: 1

JESUP

P THREE RIVERS REGIONAL LIBRARY SYSTEM*, 280 S Mahogany St, 31546. Tel: 912-559-2391. Web Site: www.threeriverslibraries.org. *Dir,* Dr Diana J Very; E-mail: dvery@trrl.org; *Digital Serv Librn,* Jessica Anderson; E-mail: janderson@trrl.org
Member Libraries: Brantley County Library; Camden County Public Library; Charlton Public Library, Inc; Hog Hammock Public Library; Ida Hilton Public Library; Long County Library; St Mary's Library; Wayne County Library; Woodbine Public Library
Partic in Public Information Network for Electronic Services

P WAYNE COUNTY LIBRARY*, 759 Sunset Blvd, 31545-4409. SAN 338-4969. Tel: 912-427-2500. FAX: 912-427-0071. Web Site: threeriverslibraries.org/woodpress-dev/library-locations/wayne-county-public-library. *Libr Mgr,* Debbie Turner; E-mail: dturner@trrl.org
Subject Interests: Ga, Gardening, Local hist
Mem of Three Rivers Regional Library System
Open Mon, Tues & Thurs 10-8, Wed & Fri 10-6, Sat 10-2
Friends of the Library Group

JONESBORO

P CLAYTON COUNTY LIBRARY SYSTEM*, 865 Battlecreek Rd, 30236. SAN 338-8417. Tel: 770-473-3850. FAX: 770-473-3858. E-mail: cclsit@gmail.com. Web Site: www.claytonpl.org. *Dir, Libr Serv,* Rosalind Lett; E-mail: rosalind.lett@claytoncountyga.gov; *Asst Dir, Access Serv,* David Thrash; E-mail: David.Thrash@claytoncountyga.gov; *Asst Dir, Br Serv,* Robyn Saint-Paen; E-mail: robyn.saint-paen@claytoncountyga.gov; *Asst Dir, Develop, Project Mgr,* Scott Parham; E-mail: Scott.Parham@claytoncountyga.gov; *Asst Dir, Youth Serv,* Rebecca James; E-mail: rebecca.james@claytoncountyga.gov; *Virtual Serv Librn,* Marquita Gooch; E-mail: marquita.gooch@claytoncountyga.gov; Staff 62 (MLS 13, Non-MLS 49)
Founded 1941. Pop 287,677; Circ 680,049
Library Holdings: AV Mats 13,128; CDs 1,957; Bk Vols 439,338; Per Subs 184
Special Collections: Clayton County History
Subject Interests: Ga
Automation Activity & Vendor Info: (Acquisitions) Evergreen; (Cataloging) Evergreen; (Circulation) Evergreen; (OPAC) Evergreen
Wireless access
Function: Chess club, Children's prog, Citizenship assistance, Computers for patron use, E-Reserves, Electronic databases & coll, Family literacy, Homework prog, ILL available, Magnifiers for reading,

Photocopying/Printing, Preschool outreach, Prog for adults, Prog for children & young adult, Spoken cassettes & CDs, Summer reading prog, Tax forms, Teen prog, VHS videos
Publications: Monthly Calendar of Events
Partic in Public Information Network for Electronic Services
Special Services for the Blind - Large print bks
Open Mon-Thurs 9-9, Fri 9-6, Sat 9-5, Sun 1:30-5:30
Branches: 5
FOREST PARK BRANCH, 696 Main St, Forest Park, 30297, SAN 338-8298. Tel: 404-366-0850. FAX: 404-366-0884. *Br Mgr,* Erica Ware
Library Holdings: AV Mats 1,470; Bk Vols 57,865; Per Subs 55
Open Mon & Tues 9-9, Wed-Fri 9-6, Sat 9-5
Friends of the Library Group
JONESBORO BRANCH, 124 Smith St, 30236, SAN 328-8897. Tel: 770-478-7120. FAX: 770-473-3846. *Br Mgr,* Kimberly Oliver
Library Holdings: AV Mats 1,582; Bk Vols 61,475; Per Subs 64
Open Mon & Tues 9-9, Wed-Fri 9-6, Sat 9-5
LOVEJOY, 1721 McDonough Rd, Hampton, 30228. Tel: 770-472-8129. FAX: 770-472-8136. *Br Mgr,* Lisa Bowens
Library Holdings: AV Mats 1,441; Bk Vols 32,006; Per Subs 68
Open Mon & Tues 9-9, Wed-Fri 9-6, Sat 9-5
Friends of the Library Group
MORROW BRANCH, 6225 Maddox Rd, Morrow, 30260, SAN 338-8506. Tel: 404-366-7749. FAX: 404-363-4569. *Br Mgr,* Rachel Briggs
Library Holdings: AV Mats 2,223; Bk Vols 67,540; Per Subs 58
Open Mon & Tues 9-9, Wed-Fri 9-6, Sat 9-5
RIVERDALE BRANCH, 420 Valley Hill Rd, Riverdale, 30274, SAN 324-086X. Tel: 770-472-8100. FAX: 770-472-8106. *Br Mgr,* Lawanza Griffin
Library Holdings: AV Mats 2,513; Bk Vols 77,679; Per Subs 72
Open Mon & Tues 9-9, Wed-Fri 9-6, Sat 9-5
Friends of the Library Group

KENNESAW

C KENNESAW STATE UNIVERSITY LIBRARY SYSTEM*, Horace W Sturgis Library, 385 Cobb Ave NW, MD 1701, 30144. SAN 303-3937. Tel: 470-578-7276. FAX: 470-578-9122. Web Site: www.kennesaw.edu/library. *Dean, Libr Serv,* Dr David Evans; Tel: 470-578-6194, E-mail: devans@kennesaw.edu; *Assoc Dean,* Dr Linda Golian-Lui; Tel: 470-578-6199, E-mail: lgolian@kennesaw.edu; *Interim Dept Chair, Pub Serv,* Ana Guimaraes; Tel: 470-578-7920, E-mail: aguimar1@kennesaw.edu; *Interim Dept Chair, Resource Management,* Ariel Turner; Tel: 470-578-6273, E-mail: aturne93@kennesaw.edu; *Dir of Libr Grad & Res Serv,* Cheryl Stiles; Tel: 470-578-6003, E-mail: cstiles@kennesaw.edu; *Dir, Facilities,* Alan Lebish; Tel: 470-578-6192, E-mail: alebish@kennesaw.edu; *Dir, Virtual Serv,* Jon Hansen; Tel: 470-578-6248, E-mail: jhansen@kennesaw.edu; *Access Serv, Interim Dir,* Chris Sharp; Tel: 470-578-6190, E-mail: csharp@kennesaw.edu; *Coll Develop, Interim Dir,* Laurie Aycock; Tel: 470-578-4825, E-mail: laycock8@kennesaw.edu; *Interim Dir, Instrul Serv, Res,* Amy Barker; Tel: 470-578-2861, E-mail: abarke24@kennesaw.edu; *Interim Dir, Instrul Serv, Res,* Ashley Hoffman; Tel: 470-578-2735, E-mail: ahoffm18@kennesaw.edu; *Head, Syst,* Li Chen; E-mail: lchen12@kennesaw.edu; *Assessment Librn,* Manda Sexton; Tel: 470-578-6511, E-mail: asexto16@kennesaw.edu; *Coll Develop Librn, Electronic Res,* Jackie Watkins; Tel: 470-578-2983, E-mail: jwatki35@kennesaw.edu; *Acq, Continuing Resources Librn,* Hyun (Leah) Kim; Tel: 470-578-6660, E-mail: hkim53@kennesaw.edu; *Discovery Librn, Res Mgt Librn,* Christin Collins; Tel: 470-578-4445, E-mail: crc6945@kennesaw.edu; *First Year Experience Librn,* Leslie Drost; Tel: 470-578-3884, E-mail: ldrost@kennesaw.edu; *Graduate Bus Librn, Humanities & Soc Sci Librn,* Nashieli Marcano; Tel: 470-578-2791, E-mail: nmarcano@kennesaw.edu; *Graduate Education Librn,* Dr Olga Koz; Tel: 470-578-6004, E-mail: okoz@kennesaw.edu; *Graduate Engineering Librn,* Crystal Renfro; Tel: 470-578-4530, E-mail: crenfro1@kennesaw.edu; *Graduate Health & Human Services Librn,* Barbara Wood; Tel: 470-578-2560, E-mail: bwood53@kennesaw.edu; *Learning Commons Librn,* LaTiffany Davis; Tel: 470-578-3228, E-mail: ldavi211@kennesaw.edu; *Math Librn, Scholarly Communications Librn, Sci Librn,* April Schweikhard; Tel: 470-578-7639, E-mail: aschwei2@kennesaw.edu; *Res & Instruction Librn,* Carey Huddlestun; Tel: 470-578-6534, E-mail: ahuddle3@kennesaw.edu; *Res Sharing Librn,* Rosemary Humphrey; Tel: 470-578-7277, E-mail: rhumph13@kennesaw.edu; *Monographs Coord, STEM Coll Dev Librn,* Xueying Chen; Tel: 470-578-7465, E-mail: xchen8@kennesaw.edu; *Strategic Marketing Librn,* Jennifer Jacobs; Tel: 470-578-3167, E-mail: jjacob73@kennesaw.edu; *Syst Librn,* Jason Penwell; Tel: 470-578-6189, E-mail: jpenwell@kennesaw.edu; *Syst Librn,* Li Chen; Tel: 470-578-7467, E-mail: lchen12@kennesaw.edu; *Undergrad Support Librn,* Mary Margaret Cornwell; Tel: 470-578-6188, E-mail: mcornwe2@kennesaw.edu; *Web Librn,* Chris Morris; Tel: 470-578-3909, E-mail: cmorri54@kennesaw.edu; *Instruction Coordr,* Christina Holm; Tel: 470-578-6197, E-mail: cholm1@kennesaw.edu; *Ref Coordr,* Position Currently Open; *Undergraduate Liaison Coord,* Position Currently Open; Staff 38 (MLS 37, Non-MLS 1)
Founded 1963. Enrl 35,420; Fac 1,151; Highest Degree: Doctorate
Jul 2018-Jun 2019. Mats Exp $1,903,271, Books $331,573, Electronic Ref Mat (Incl. Access Fees) $1,571,698. Sal $3,006,009
Library Holdings: AV Mats 88,482; e-books 833,275; e-journals 155,672; Electronic Media & Resources 276,803; Music Scores 3,863; Bk Titles 375,407; Bk Vols 398,015; Per Subs 1,439
Special Collections: US Document Depository
Automation Activity & Vendor Info: (Acquisitions) Ex Libris Group; (Cataloging) Ex Libris Group; (Circulation) Ex Libris Group; (Course Reserve) Ex Libris Group; (ILL) OCLC ILLiad; (OPAC) Ex Libris Group; (Serials) Ex Libris Group
Wireless access
Partic in Atlanta Regional Council for Higher Education; Galileo/GIL
Open Mon-Thurs 7am-Midnight, Fri 7am-8pm, Sat 8-6, Sun 1-10
Friends of the Library Group
Departmental Libraries:
LAWRENCE V JOHNSON LIBRARY, 1100 S Marietta Pkwy, Marietta, 30060-2896, SAN 303-3961. Tel: 678-470-578-7276. Web Site: library.kennesaw.edu. *Dean, Libr Serv,* Dr David Evans; E-mail: devans@kennesaw.edu; *Libr Dir,* Alan Lebish; E-mail: alebish@kennesaw.edu; *Head, Syst, Librn,* Li Chen; Tel: 678-915-7467, E-mail: lchen12@kennesaw.edu; Staff 9 (MLS 6, Non-MLS 3)
Founded 1948. Enrl 4,000; Fac 120; Highest Degree: Master
Library Holdings: Bk Titles 117,887; Bk Vols 119,780; Per Subs 1,216
Special Collections: American Architectural History; Architectural drawings; Geological Survey; Surveying maps; University archives
Subject Interests: Art & archit, Bus & mgt, Sci tech
Automation Activity & Vendor Info: (Cataloging) Ex Libris Group; (Circulation) Ex Libris Group; (Course Reserve) Ex Libris Group; (ILL) Ex Libris Group; (OPAC) Ex Libris Group; (Serials) Ex Libris Group
Partic in Georgia Libr Info Network; GOLD Resource Sharing Network for Georgia's Libraries; LYRASIS; SOQUIJ
Open Mon-Thurs 8am-10pm, Fri 8-6, Sat 11-6, Sun 1-8
Friends of the Library Group

S NATIONAL PARK SERVICE*, Kennesaw Mountain National Battlefield Park Archives, 900 Kennesaw Mountain Dr, 30152. SAN 303-3953. Tel: 770-427-4686. FAX: 770-528-8398. E-mail: kemo_archives@nps.gov. Web Site: www.nps.gov/kemo. *Superintendent,* Nancy Walther; E-mail: nancy_walther@nps.gov
Founded 1935
Library Holdings: Bk Titles 1,000
Special Collections: Atlanta Campaign-1864
Function: Res libr
Restriction: Non-circulating, Open by appt only

KINGSLAND

P CAMDEN COUNTY PUBLIC LIBRARY*, 1410 Hwy 40 E, 31548-9380. SAN 338-487X. Tel: 912-729-3741. Web Site: threeriverslibraries.org/woodpress-dev/library-locations/camden-county-public-library. *Libr Mgr,* Mellissa Clark; E-mail: mclark@trrl.org
Mem of Three Rivers Regional Library System
Open Mon & Wed 10-6, Tues & Thurs 10-8, Fri & Sat 10-5
Friends of the Library Group

LAFAYETTE

P CHEROKEE REGIONAL LIBRARY SYSTEM*, La Fayette-Walker County Public Library, 305 S Duke St, 30728. SAN 338-8980. Tel: 706-638-2992. Administration Tel: 706-638-8312. Automation Services Tel: 706-638-1958. FAX: 706-638-3979. Administration FAX: 706-638-4028. Web Site: www.chrl.org. *Dir,* Lecia Eubanks; E-mail: leubanks@chrl.org; *Mgr,* Tim York; Tel: 706-638-0288, E-mail: tyork@chrl.org; *Bus & Human Res Mgr,* Misty Reyes; E-mail: mreyes@chrl.org; *Br Serv Librn,* Chelsea Kovalevskiy; Tel: 706-638-8311, E-mail: chelseak@chrl.org; *Genealogy Serv,* Carol Smith; Tel: 706-638-4912; Staff 14 (MLS 2, Non-MLS 12)
Founded 1938. Pop 86,000; Circ 65,041
Library Holdings: CDs 339; Bk Vols 67,328; Per Subs 18; Talking Bks 1,244; Videos 1,662
Special Collections: Local History of Dade & Walker Counties (Georgia History), bk, micro, CD
Subject Interests: Ga, Genealogy, Local hist
Automation Activity & Vendor Info: (Acquisitions) SirsiDynix; (Cataloging) SirsiDynix; (Circulation) SirsiDynix; (ILL) SirsiDynix; (OPAC) SirsiDynix; (Serials) SirsiDynix
Function: 24/7 Online cat, Activity rm, After school storytime, Art programs, Audio & video playback equip for onsite use, Audiobks on Playaways & MP3, AV serv, Bks on CD, Children's prog, Computers for patron use, Doc delivery serv, Electronic databases & coll, Free DVD rentals, Holiday prog, ILL available, Internet access, Large print keyboards, Life-long learning prog for all ages, Magazines, Mail & tel request accepted, Mango lang, Meeting rooms, Microfiche/film & reading

machines, Notary serv, Online info literacy tutorials on the web & in blackboard, Outreach serv, Outside serv via phone, mail, e-mail & web, OverDrive digital audio bks, Photocopying/Printing, Preschool outreach, Preschool reading prog, Printer for laptops & handheld devices, Prog for adults, Prog for children & young adult, Ref serv available, Scanner, STEM programs, Story hour, Study rm, Summer & winter reading prog, Summer reading prog, Tax forms, Teen prog, Telephone ref, Wheelchair accessible
Partic in Public Information Network for Electronic Services
Special Services for the Blind - Closed circuit TV; Computer with voice synthesizer for visually impaired persons; Descriptive video serv (DVS); Magnifiers; Soundproof reading booth; Talking bks
Open Mon 10-6, Tues 10-7, Thurs 1-7, Fri 11-2, Sat 10-2
Friends of the Library Group
Branches: 3
CHICKAMAUGA PUBLIC, 306 Cove Rd, Chickamauga, 30707, SAN 338-9073. Tel: 706-375-3004. FAX: 706-375-7034. *Br Mgr,* Renee Roeder; Staff 4 (Non-MLS 4)
Founded 1966. Circ 46,981
Library Holdings: CDs 306; Bk Vols 29,870; Per Subs 14; Talking Bks 595; Videos 769
Subject Interests: Civil War, Local hist
Function: ILL available, Photocopying/Printing, Ref serv available, Telephone ref
Open Tues & Thurs 9-7, Fri 9-5, Sat 9-Noon
Friends of the Library Group
DADE COUNTY PUBLIC LIBRARY, 102 Court St, Trenton, 30752, SAN 338-9103. Tel: 706-657-7857. FAX: 706-657-7860. *Br Mgr,* Marshana Sharp; Staff 6 (MLS 1, Non-MLS 5)
Founded 1938. Pop 15,541; Circ 52,370
Library Holdings: Bk Vols 32,772; Per Subs 30; Videos 895
Subject Interests: Local hist
Open Tues 10-7, Wed 10-5, Thurs 10-6, Fri 10-4, Sat 10-2
Friends of the Library Group
ROSSVILLE PUBLIC, 504 McFarland Ave, Rossville, 30741, SAN 338-9162. Tel: 706-866-1368. FAX: 706-858-9251. *Br Mgr,* Carmella Clark; Staff 4 (Non-MLS 4)
Founded 1944. Circ 81,488
Library Holdings: CDs 211; Bk Vols 36,078; Per Subs 60; Talking Bks 500; Videos 1,211
Subject Interests: Local hist
Function: ILL available, Photocopying/Printing, Ref serv available, Telephone ref
Open Tues 9-7, Wed 9-5, Thurs 10-7, Sat 10-2
Friends of the Library Group

LAGRANGE

C LA GRANGE COLLEGE*, Frank & Laura Lewis Library, 601 Broad St, 30240-2999. SAN 338-8743. Tel: 706-880-8312. FAX: 706-880-8040. Web Site: www.lagrange.edu/library. *Libr Dir,* Kelly Ansley; Tel: 706-880-8311, E-mail: kansley@lagrange.edu; *Access Serv Librn,* Position Currently Open; *Electronic Res Librn,* Position Currently Open; *Ref & Info Serv Librn,* Dr Arthur Robinson; Tel: 706-880-8289, E-mail: arobinson@lagrange.edu; *Circ Mgr,* April Butler; Tel: 706-880-8012; *Acq, Ser,* David Wiggins; Tel: 706-880-8233; *Archives Asst,* Felecia Moore; Tel: 706-880-8995; *Circ Assoc,* Lisa Farrow; *Tech Serv Asst,* Stacey Davis; Staff 9 (MLS 4, Non-MLS 5)
Founded 1836. Enrl 1,000; Fac 80; Highest Degree: Doctorate
Library Holdings: AV Mats 7,299; e-books 110,410; Electronic Media & Resources 237; Bk Vols 119,791; Per Subs 704
Automation Activity & Vendor Info: (Cataloging) SirsiDynix; (Circulation) SirsiDynix; (ILL) OCLC; (OPAC) SirsiDynix
Wireless access
Partic in OCLC Online Computer Library Center, Inc
Open Mon-Thurs 8am-11pm, Fri 8-5, Sat 1-5, Sun 2-10
Friends of the Library Group

P TROUP-HARRIS REGIONAL LIBRARY SYSTEM*, La Grange Memorial Library, 115 Alford St, 30240. SAN 338-8808. Tel: 706-882-7784. E-mail: info@thrl.org. Web Site: www.thrl.org/lagrange-memorial-library. *Libr Mgr, Regional Libr Dir,* Keith Schuermann; E-mail: kschuermann@thrl.org; Staff 5 (MLS 4, Non-MLS 1)
Founded 1926. Pop 95,000
Library Holdings: AV Mats 2,943; High Interest/Low Vocabulary Bk Vols 375; Bk Titles 183,191; Per Subs 158; Talking Bks 1,389
Special Collections: Historic Photograph Coll Online; Troup County Marriage & Deed Records Online. Oral History
Subject Interests: Ga, Spanish (Lang)
Automation Activity & Vendor Info: (Cataloging) OCLC; (Circulation) Evergreen; (ILL) OCLC; (OPAC) Evergreen
Wireless access
Function: Accelerated reader prog, Adult bk club, Audio & video playback equip for onsite use, Audiobks via web, BA reader (adult literacy), Bilingual assistance for Spanish patrons, Bk club(s), Bks on cassette, Bks on CD, Children's prog, Computers for patron use, Digital talking bks, Distance learning, E-Reserves, Electronic databases & coll, Free DVD rentals, ILL available, Internet access, Music CDs, Notary serv, Online cat, OverDrive digital audio bks, Photocopying/Printing, Prog for adults, Prog for children & young adult, Ref serv available, Spoken cassettes & CDs, Spoken cassettes & DVDs, Story hour, Summer reading prog, Tax forms, Teen prog, Telephone ref, VHS videos, Wheelchair accessible
Publications: Friends of the LaGrange Memorial Library (Newsletter)
Partic in GOLD Resource Sharing Network for Georgia's Libraries; Public Information Network for Electronic Services
Open Mon-Thurs 10-6, Fri 10-5, Sat 10-4
Friends of the Library Group
Branches: 2
HARRIS COUNTY PUBLIC LIBRARY, 7511 George Hwy 116, Hamilton, 31811, SAN 338-8867. Tel: 706-628-4685. FAX: 706-628-4198. *Br Mgr,* Stephanie Green; E-mail: sgreen@thrl.org; *Asst Br Mgr,* Alyson Nesnick; E-mail: anesnick@thrl.org; Staff 4 (Non-MLS 4)
Founded 1992. Pop 36,000; Circ 63,000
Jul 2012-Jun 2013 Income $212,000. Mats Exp $13,438, Books $10,387, Per/Ser (Incl. Access Fees) $2,200, AV Mat $851. Sal $130,000
Library Holdings: AV Mats 3,200; Bk Titles 27,000; Per Subs 45; Talking Bks 415
Function: Distance learning, ILL available, Internet access, Photocopying/Printing, Satellite serv, Summer reading prog
Open Mon-Wed 10-6, Thurs 10-7, Fri 10-5, Sat 10-4
HOGANSVILLE PUBLIC LIBRARY, 310 Johnson St, Hogansville, 30230, SAN 338-8891. Tel: 706-637-6230. *Br Mgr,* Rebecca Keller; E-mail: rkeller@thrl.org; Staff 2 (Non-MLS 2)
Founded 1991. Pop 5,000; Circ 12,955
Library Holdings: AV Mats 1,127; Bk Titles 16,139; Per Subs 40; Talking Bks 240
Function: ILL available, Internet access, Photocopying/Printing, Summer reading prog, Wheelchair accessible
Open Mon-Thurs 10-6, Fri 10-5
Bookmobiles: 1

LAWRENCEVILLE

L GWINNETT COUNTY JUDICIAL CIRCUIT*, Homer M Stark Law Library, Justice & Adminisration Ctr, Lower Level, 75 Langley Dr, 30046. SAN 372-1752. Tel: 770-822-8575. FAX: 770-822-8570. E-mail: StarkLawLibrary@gwinnettcounty.com. Web Site: www.gcll.org. *Dir,* Grace Holloway; Tel: 770-822-8571, E-mail: grace.holloway@gwinnettcounty.com
Founded 1988
Library Holdings: Bk Vols 13,000; Per Subs 25
Wireless access
Open Mon-Fri 8-5

P GWINNETT COUNTY PUBLIC LIBRARY*, 1001 Lawrenceville Hwy NW, 30046-4707. SAN 338-9197. Tel: 770-978-5154. Administration Tel: 770-822-4522. Administration FAX: 770-822-5379. E-mail: askgcpl@gwinnettpl.org. Web Site: ask.gwinnettpl.org, www.gwinnettpl.org. *Exec Dir,* Charles Pace; E-mail: cpace@gwinnettpl.org; *Chief Financial Officer, Dir, Admin Serv,* Dana Russell; E-mail: drussell@gwinnettpl.org; *Dir, Br Serv,* Margaret Penn; E-mail: mpenn@gwinnettpl.org; *Customer Experience Dir,* Michael Casey; Tel: 770-822-5334, E-mail: mcasey@gwinnettpl.org; *Develop Mgr,* Shelly Schwerzler; E-mail: sschwerzler@gwinnettpl.org; *Mkt & Communications Mgr,* Dee Driver; E-mail: ddriver@gwinnettpl.org
Founded 1935. Pop 877,922; Circ 5,500,000
Special Collections: Gwinnett Authors (Central Coll)
Automation Activity & Vendor Info: (Acquisitions) Innovative Interfaces, Inc; (Cataloging) Innovative Interfaces, Inc; (Circulation) Innovative Interfaces, Inc; (ILL) OCLC FirstSearch; (OPAC) Innovative Interfaces, Inc; (Serials) Innovative Interfaces, Inc
Wireless access
Function: 24/7 Electronic res, Art exhibits, Audiobks via web, Bk club(s), Bks on CD, Children's prog, Citizenship assistance, Computer training, Computers for patron use, Distance learning, Electronic databases & coll, Family literacy, Free DVD rentals, Homebound delivery serv, Internet access, Large print keyboards, Life-long learning prog for all ages, Literacy & newcomer serv, Magazines, Magnifiers for reading, Mango lang, Meeting rooms, Museum passes, Online cat, Online ref, Outreach serv, OverDrive digital audio bks, Photocopying/Printing, Preschool outreach, Senior computer classes, Senior outreach, Summer reading prog, Teen prog, Wheelchair accessible, Workshops
Special Services for the Deaf - Assistive tech; Bks on deafness & sign lang; Closed caption videos; High interest/low vocabulary bks; TTY equip
Special Services for the Blind - Assistive/Adapted tech devices, equip & products; Computer with voice synthesizer for visually impaired persons

Open Mon-Thurs 10-8, Fri & Sat 10-5, Sun 12-5
Friends of the Library Group
Branches: 15
BUFORD-SUGAR HILL BRANCH, 2100 Buford Hwy, Buford, 30518-6035, SAN 338-9251.
Friends of the Library Group
CENTERVILLE BRANCH, 3025 Bethany Church Rd, Snellville, 30039-6109.
Friends of the Library Group
COLLINS HILL, 455 Camp Perrin Rd, 30043-2408.
Friends of the Library Group
DACULA BRANCH, 265 Dacula Rd, Dacula, 30019-2131.
Friends of the Library Group
DULUTH BRANCH, 3480 Duluth Park Lane, Duluth, 30096-3257, SAN 338-9316.
Friends of the Library Group
FIVE FORKS BRANCH, 2780 Five Forks Trickum Rd, 30044-5865, SAN 373-8736.
Friends of the Library Group
GRAYSON BRANCH, 700 Grayson Pkwy, Grayson, 30017-1208.
Friends of the Library Group
HAMILTON MILL BRANCH, 3690 Braselton Hwy, Dacula, 30019-1067.
Friends of the Library Group
LAWRENCEVILLE BRANCH, 1001 Lawrenceville Hwy, 30046-4707, SAN 338-9227.
Friends of the Library Group
LILBURN BRANCH, 4817 Church St, Lilburn, 30047-6827, SAN 338-9375.
Friends of the Library Group
MOUNTAIN PARK BRANCH, 1210 Pounds Rd SW, Lilburn, 30047-6744, SAN 338-9405.
Friends of the Library Group
NORCROSS BRANCH, 6025 Buford Hwy, Norcross, 30071-2408, SAN 338-943X.
Friends of the Library Group
PEACHTREE CORNERS BRANCH, 5570 Spalding Dr, Norcross, 30092-2501, SAN 329-7039.
Friends of the Library Group
SNELLVILLE BRANCH (ELIZABETH H WILLIAMS LIBRARY), 2740 Lenora Church Rd, Snellville, 30078-3226, SAN 338-9464.
Friends of the Library Group
SUWANEE BRANCH, 361 Main St, Suwanee, 30024-2233.
Friends of the Library Group

J GWINNETT TECHNICAL COLLEGE LIBRARY*, 5150 Sugarloaf Pkwy, 30043. Tel: 770-962-7580, Ext 6270, 770-962-7580, Ext 6388. FAX: 770-962-7985. E-mail: gtclibrary@gwinnetttech.edu. Web Site: www.gwinnetttech.edu. *Mgr, Libr Serv,* Elissa Checov
Founded 1984. Enrl 4,500; Highest Degree: Associate
Library Holdings: AV Mats 1,300; e-books 26,000; e-journals 30; Bk Vols 14,000; Per Subs 182
Automation Activity & Vendor Info: (Cataloging) TLC (The Library Corporation); (Circulation) TLC (The Library Corporation); (OPAC) TLC (The Library Corporation)
Partic in Georgia Library Learning Online
Open Mon-Thurs 8am-8:30pm, Fri 8-4

LEESBURG

S GEORGIA DEPARTMENT OF CORRECTIONS, OFFICE OF LIBRARY SERVICES*, Lee State Prison, 153 Pinewood Rd, 31763. Tel: 229-759-3110. FAX: 229-759-3065. Web Site: www.dcor.state.ga.us/Facilities/lee-state-prison. *Librn,* W C McDaniel
Library Holdings: Bk Vols 3,000; Per Subs 15
Special Collections: Law Coll

P LEE COUNTY PUBLIC LIBRARY*, Headquarters, 245 Walnut Ave S, 31763-4367. Tel: 229-759-2369. FAX: 229-759-2326. Reference E-mail: reference@leecountylibrary.org. Web Site: leecountylibrary.org. *Dir,* Claire Leavy
Library Holdings: Bk Vols 45,000
Automation Activity & Vendor Info: (Cataloging) Evergreen; (Circulation) Evergreen; (OPAC) Evergreen
Wireless access
Function: AV serv, Photocopying/Printing
Friends of the Library Group
Branches: 3
OAKLAND BRANCH, 445 Oakland Pkwy W, 31763. Tel: 229-889-0300. FAX: 229-889-0408.
Open Mon, Wed & Fri 9-6, Tues & Thurs 9-8, Sat 10-2
REDBONE, 104 Thundering Springs Rd, 31763. Tel: 229-903-8871. FAX: 229-903-8872. *Br Mgr,* Leslie Partridge
Open Mon-Thurs 2-8, Fri 2-6, Sat 10-2
Friends of the Library Group
SMITHVILLE BRANCH, 116 Main St, Smithville, 31787. Tel: 229-846-6625. FAX: 229-846-6625. *Br Mgr,* Eva Majors
Library Holdings: Bk Vols 2,500
Open Mon & Wed 3-8, Tues & Thurs 3-6
Friends of the Library Group

LITHONIA

R LUTHER RICE UNIVERSITY & SEMINARY*, Bertha Smith Library, 3038 Evans Mill Rd, 30038. SAN 302-9786. Tel: 770-484-1204, Ext 5756. Toll Free Tel: 800-442-1577, Ext 5756. E-mail: library@lutherrice.edu. Web Site: library.lutherrice.edu. *Dir,* Prasada Sajja; E-mail: prasada.sajja@lutherrice.edu; *Asst Dir,* Alisha Blevins; E-mail: alisha.blevins@lutherrice.edu; Staff 1 (MLS 1)
Founded 1962
Library Holdings: DVDs 200; e-books 126; e-journals 38; Electronic Media & Resources 28,170; Bk Titles 58,835; Bk Vols 60,000; Per Subs 100
Special Collections: Religion (Christian Ministry), dissertations
Subject Interests: Biblical studies, Theol
Wireless access
Open Mon, Tues, Thurs & Fri 8:30-5, Wed 8:30-4:30

LOOKOUT MOUNTAIN

CR COVENANT COLLEGE*, Anna Emma Kresge Memorial Library, 14049 Scenic Hwy, 30750. SAN 315-8411. Tel: 706-419-1430. Reference Tel: 706-419-1565. Administration Tel: 706-419-1434. E-mail: library@covenant.edu. Web Site: library.covenant.edu. *Dir, Libr Serv,* John Holberg; E-mail: john.holberg@covenant.edu; *Assoc Dir, Libr Serv,* Kimberly Crocker; Staff 6.7 (MLS 3, Non-MLS 3.7)
Founded 1955. Enrl 1,150; Fac 75; Highest Degree: Master
Jul 2013-Jun 2014 Income $744,400. Mats Exp $439,400, Books $95,000, Per/Ser (Incl. Access Fees) $53,000, AV Mat $10,000, Electronic Ref Mat (Incl. Access Fees) $162,000. Sal $305,000 (Prof $175,000)
Library Holdings: AV Mats 6,735; e-books 98,000; Microforms 122,000; Bk Vols 84,687; Per Subs 300
Special Collections: 19th Century Central & Southern Africa (Carroll R Stegall, Jr Coll); East Asian Studies - English Language Resources (Alvin D Coox Coll); John Bunyan Coll; John Hamm Coll, audio recs, bks, scores, video recs; Puritan & 16th Century Protestant Works (Ian Tait Coll)
Automation Activity & Vendor Info: (Acquisitions) OCLC; (Cataloging) OCLC; (Circulation) OCLC; (Course Reserve) Atlas Systems; (ILL) Atlas Systems; (OPAC) OCLC; (Serials) OCLC
Wireless access
Function: Archival coll, Doc delivery serv, ILL available, Ref serv available
Partic in Georgia Private Acad Librs Consortium; LYRASIS
Open Mon-Thurs 7:45am-Midnight, Fri 7:45-5:30

LOUISVILLE

P JEFFERSON COUNTY LIBRARY SYSTEM*, 306 E Broad St, 30434. SAN 338-9499. Tel: 478-625-7079. FAX: 478-625-9256. Web Site: www.jefferson.public.lib.ga.us. *Dir,* Carol Taylor; E-mail: ctaylor@mail.jefferson.public.lib.ga.us; Staff 7.8 (MLS 2, Non-MLS 5.8)
Founded 1953. Pop 16,430; Circ 49,868. Sal $245,693 (Prof $114,996)
Library Holdings: Audiobooks 996; Bk Vols 47,726; Per Subs 102; Videos 2,900
Subject Interests: Genealogy, Local hist
Automation Activity & Vendor Info: (Cataloging) Evergreen; (Circulation) Evergreen; (OPAC) Evergreen
Wireless access
Function: Bks on cassette, Bks on CD, Computers for patron use, Electronic databases & coll, ILL available, Magnifiers for reading, Microfiche/film & reading machines, Notary serv, Photocopying/Printing, Ref serv available, Scanner, Tax forms, VHS videos, Wheelchair accessible
Partic in Georgia Library Learning Online; GOLD Resource Sharing Network for Georgia's Libraries; Public Information Network for Electronic Services
Open Mon-Fri 8:30-1 & 2-5:30
Friends of the Library Group
Branches: 2
MCCOLLUM PUBLIC, 405 N Main St, Wrens, 30833-1142, SAN 338-9529. Tel: 706-547-7567. FAX: 706-547-7544. *Mgr,* Wanda McGahee; Staff 1.4 (Non-MLS 1.4)
Special Collections: Local History & Genealogy (Heritage Coll)
Open Mon-Fri 8:30-1 & 2-5:30
Friends of the Library Group
WADLEY PUBLIC, 11 W College Ave, Wadley, 30477. Tel: 478-252-5392. FAX: 478-252-8972. *Mgr,* Position Currently Open
Open Mon-Fri 8:30-1 & 2-5:30

LUDOWICI

P LONG COUNTY LIBRARY*, 270 S Main St, 31316. SAN 338-490X. Tel: 912-545-2521. FAX: 912-545-8887. Web Site: threeriverslibraries.org/woodpress-dev/library-locations/long-county-public-library. *Libr Mgr,* Tammy Goober; E-mail: tgoober@trrl.org
Subject Interests: Local hist
Wireless access
Mem of Three Rivers Regional Library System
Open Mon, Thurs & Fri 10-8, Tues & Sat 10-6, Wed 10-5

MACON

J CENTRAL GEORGIA TECHNICAL COLLEGE LIBRARY*, Macon Campus, I Bldg, 2nd Flr, 3300 Macon Tech Dr, 31206-3628. SAN 375-4898. Tel: 478-757-3549. FAX: 478-757-3545. E-mail: library@centralgatech.edu. Web Site: www.centralgatech.edu/library. *Exec Dir, Libr Serv,* W Neil McArthur; Tel: 478-757-3548, E-mail: nmcarthur@centralgatech.edu; *Librn,* Sara Boyd; E-mail: sboyd@centralgatech.edu; *Librn,* Allison Repzynski; Tel: 478-757-3547, E-mail: arepzynski@centralgatech.edu; *Librn,* Lyn Young; E-mail: lyoung@centralgatech.edu; Staff 4.8 (MLS 3, Non-MLS 1.8)
Founded 1993. Enrl 6,000; Fac 200; Highest Degree: Associate
Jul 2013-Jun 2014 Income $230,000
Library Holdings: AV Mats 2,500; e-books 60,000; Bk Vols 20,000; Per Subs 300
Subject Interests: Bus, Educ, Health, Indust, Info tech, Pub serv, Tech, Trade
Automation Activity & Vendor Info: (Cataloging) TLC (The Library Corporation); (Circulation) TLC (The Library Corporation); (ILL) OCLC; (OPAC) TLC (The Library Corporation)
Wireless access
Function: Audio & video playback equip for onsite use, ILL available, Photocopying/Printing, Ref serv available, Telephone ref, Wheelchair accessible
Partic in Soline
Open Mon-Thurs 7:45am-8pm, Fri 7:45-3

MERCER UNIVERSITY

CL WALTER F GEORGE SCHOOL OF LAW, FURMAN SMITH LAW LIBRARY*, 1021 Georgia Ave, 31201-1001. (Mail add: 1400 Coleman Ave, 31207-0003), SAN 338-9618. Tel: 478-301-2612. Reference Tel: 478-301-2334. FAX: 478-301-2284. Web Site: www.law.mercer.edu/library. *Dir,* Suzanne L Cassidy; E-mail: cassidy_sl@law.mercer.edu; *IT Supvr,* Chris Bombardo; Tel: 478-301-2182; *Digital Ser & Scholarly Res Librn,* Sharon Bradley; E-mail: bradley_s@law.mercer.edu; *Asst Librn,* Denise M Gibson; Tel: 478-301-5905; *Assoc Librn,* Ismael Gullon; Tel: 478-301-5904; *Ref (Info Servs),* John M Perkins; Tel: 478-301-2667; *Ref (Info Servs),* James P Walsh; Tel: 478-301-2625; Staff 6 (MLS 6)
Founded 1850. Enrl 432; Fac 25; Highest Degree: Doctorate
Library Holdings: Bk Titles 57,064; Bk Vols 333,000; Per Subs 1,100
Special Collections: Griffin B Bell Papers. US Document Depository
Subject Interests: Law
Automation Activity & Vendor Info: (Acquisitions) Innovative Interfaces, Inc; (Cataloging) Innovative Interfaces, Inc; (Circulation) Innovative Interfaces, Inc; (OPAC) Innovative Interfaces, Inc; (Serials) Innovative Interfaces, Inc
Partic in Georgia Interactive Network for Medical Information; OCLC Online Computer Library Center, Inc
Open Mon-Thurs 8-8, Fri 8-5, Sat 1-5, Sun 1-8

CM SCHOOL OF MEDICINE, MEDICAL LIBRARY & LRC*, 1550 College St, 31207, SAN 338-9626. Tel: 478-301-2515. Circulation Tel: 478-301-4056. Interlibrary Loan Service Tel: 478-301-2549. Toll Free Tel: 800-425-4246. FAX: 478-301-2051. E-mail: reference.ill@gain.mercer.edu. Web Site: med.mercer.edu/library. *Interim Dir,* Kim K Meeks; Tel: 478-301-2519, E-mail: meeks_k@mercer.edu; Staff 21 (MLS 9, Non-MLS 12)
Founded 1974. Enrl 313; Fac 837; Highest Degree: Doctorate
Special Collections: Southern History of Medicine. Oral History
Subject Interests: Med
Automation Activity & Vendor Info: (Acquisitions) Innovative Interfaces, Inc; (Cataloging) Innovative Interfaces, Inc; (Circulation) Innovative Interfaces, Inc; (Course Reserve) Innovative Interfaces, Inc; (ILL) OCLC ILLiad; (OPAC) Innovative Interfaces, Inc; (Serials) Innovative Interfaces, Inc
Partic in Atlanta Regional Council for Higher Education; Consortium of Southern Biomedical Libraries; National Network of Libraries of Medicine Region 2; OCLC Online Computer Library Center, Inc
Open Mon-Thurs 8am-11pm, Fri 8-6, Sat 10-6, Sun 1-11
Restriction: Non-circulating to the pub, Restricted pub use

C JACK TARVER LIBRARY*, 1300 Edgewood Ave, 31207, SAN 338-9588. Tel: 478-301-2960. Circulation Tel: 478-301-2961. Reference Tel: 478-301-2055. FAX: 478-301-2111. Web Site: libraries.mercer.edu/. *Dean of Libr,* Elizabeth D Hammond; E-mail: hammond_bd@mercer.edu; *Assoc Dir, Coll Mgt, Assoc Dir, Pub Serv,* Theresa Preuit; *Assoc Dir, Tech Serv, Spec Coll & Archives Librn,* Susan G Broome; Tel: 478-301-2193; *ILL/Circ Supvr, Ref Librn,* Andrew Shuping; Tel: 478-301-2251; *Syst Librn,* Robert Frasier; Tel: 478-301-2027; *Media Librn, Outreach Librn, Ref Librn,* Lee Twombly; Tel: 478-301-2852; *ILL,* Cecilia Williams; Tel: 478-301-2102; *Coordr, Libr Instruction, Coordr, Ref (Info Serv),* Consuela Cline; Tel: 478 301-5334; *Head, Spec Coll,* Laura Botts; Tel: 478-301-2968; *Acq,* Brenda Medlin; Tel: 478-301-2505; *Ser,* Brenda Mays; Tel: 478-301-2966; Staff 31 (MLS 12, Non-MLS 19)
Founded 1833. Enrl 6,800; Fac 210; Highest Degree: Doctorate
Library Holdings: Electronic Media & Resources 200; Bk Titles 210,000; Bk Vols 250,000; Per Subs 4,500; Videos 1,500
Special Collections: Cooperative Baptist Fellowship Archives; Georgia Baptist History & Archives; Mercer University Archives. US Document Depository
Subject Interests: Baptist hist, Baptists, Civil War, Southern culture, Southern hist
Automation Activity & Vendor Info: (Acquisitions) Innovative Interfaces, Inc; (Cataloging) Innovative Interfaces, Inc; (OPAC) Innovative Interfaces, Inc; (Serials) Innovative Interfaces, Inc
Function: Photocopying/Printing
Partic in LYRASIS; NELLCO Law Library Consortium, Inc.

P MIDDLE GEORGIA REGIONAL LIBRARY SYSTEM*, Washington Memorial Library (Main Library), 1180 Washington Ave, 31201-1790. SAN 338-9642. Tel: 478-744-0800, 478-744-0841. Reference Tel: 478-744-0825. FAX: 478-742-3161. Web Site: bibblib.org. *Dir,* Jennifer Lautzenheiser; Tel: 478-744-0850, E-mail: lautzenheiserj@bibblib.org; *Head Librn,* Lauren Mullins; Tel: 478-744-0828, E-mail: mullinsl@bibblib.org; *Head, Circ,* Ashley O'Neal; *Head, Pub Serv,* James O'Neal; Tel: 478-744-0836; *Head, Tech Serv,* Hetal Vyas; Tel: 478-744-0813; Staff 20 (MLS 20)
Founded 1889. Pop 257,687
Library Holdings: Bk Vols 483,291
Automation Activity & Vendor Info: (ILL) OCLC
Wireless access
Partic in GOLD Resource Sharing Network for Georgia's Libraries; Public Information Network for Electronic Services
Open Mon-Thurs 9-9, Fri & Sat 9-6
Friends of the Library Group
Branches: 13
CRAWFORD COUNTY PUBLIC LIBRARY, 340 McCrary Ave, Roberta, 31078-0580, SAN 338-9677. Tel: 478-836-4478. FAX: 478-836-4478. E-mail: mgrlro@bibblib.org. *Br Mgr,* Leda Starnes
Library Holdings: Bk Vols 17,143
Open Mon 1-7, Tues-Thurs 10-12 & 1-7
Friends of the Library Group
EAST WILKINSON COUNTY PUBLIC LIBRARY, 154 E Main St, Irwinton, 31042-2602, SAN 325-4437. Tel: 478-946-2778. FAX: 478-946-2778. E-mail: mgrlew@bibblib.org. *Br Mgr,* Arlene Bache
Library Holdings: Bk Vols 10,011
Open Mon-Wed 10-6, Thurs Noon-8, Fri 10-5
Friends of the Library Group
GENEALOGICAL & HISTORICAL ROOM & GEORGIA ARCHIVES, 1180 Washington Ave, 31201-1790. Tel: 478-744-0821. E-mail: mgrlgh@bibblib.org. *Head of Libr,* Muriel Jackson; E-mail: jacksonm@bibblib.org
Library Holdings: Bk Vols 131,706
Special Collections: African-American; Archives; Business Reference; Genealogy; Georgiana; Local Hist; Telephone indexes
Subject Interests: Bus & mgt, Genealogy, Local hist
Open Mon 9-9, Tues-Sat 9-6
Friends of the Library Group
GORDON PUBLIC LIBRARY, 284 Milledgeville Hwy W, Gordon, 31031, SAN 338-9707. Tel: 478-628-5352. FAX: 478-628-5352. E-mail: mgrlgo@bibblib.org. *Br Mgr,* Judy Brown
Library Holdings: Bk Vols 9,304
Open Mon-Fri 9-7
Friends of the Library Group
IDEAL PUBLIC LIBRARY, 605 Tom Watson Ave, Ideal, 31041, SAN 325-4399. Tel: 478-949-2720. FAX: 478-949-2720. E-mail: mgrlid@bibblib.org. *Br Mgr,* Betty Rainey
Library Holdings: Bk Vols 1,250
Open Mon & Wed 8-12 & 1-5, Fri 8-12 & 1-4
Friends of the Library Group
JONES COUNTY PUBLIC LIBRARY, 146 Railroad Ave, Gray, 31032, SAN 338-9766. Tel: 478-986-6626. FAX: 478-986-6626. E-mail: mgrljo@bibblib.org. *Br Mgr,* Leisl Hammond
Founded 1936
Library Holdings: Bk Vols 24,425
Open Mon-Thurs 9-6, Fri 8-5
Friends of the Library Group

CHARLES A LANFORD MD LIBRARY, 6504 Houston Rd, 31216-6702, SAN 338-9944. Tel: 478-621-6970. FAX: 478-621-6985. *Br Librn,* Dean Maddox; E-mail: maddoxd@bibblib.org
Library Holdings: Bk Vols 44,202
Open Mon-Wed & Fri 9:30-6, Thurs 10:30-7, Sun 1-5
Friends of the Library Group

MARSHALLVILLE PUBLIC LIBRARY, 106 Camellia Blvd, Marshallville, 31057, SAN 338-9790. Tel: 478-967-2413. FAX: 478-967-2413. E-mail: mgrlma@bibblib.org. *Br Mgr,* Robbie Robinson
Library Holdings: Bk Vols 4,550
Open Mon-Fri 9-12 & 3-6
Friends of the Library Group

MONTEZUMA PUBLIC LIBRARY, 506 N Dooly St, Montezuma, 31063-1308, SAN 338-9820. Tel: 478-472-6095. FAX: 478-472-6095. E-mail: mgrlmo@bibblib.org. *Br Mgr,* Darneisha Ivey
Library Holdings: Bk Vols 17,441
Open Mon-Wed 10-5, Thurs 9:30-5:30, Fri 10-2
Friends of the Library Group

OGLETHORPE PUBLIC LIBRARY, 115 Chatham St, Oglethorpe, 31068, SAN 338-9855. Tel: 478-472-7116. FAX: 478-472-7116. E-mail: mgrlog@bibblib.org. *Br Mgr,* Cindy Law
Library Holdings: Bk Vols 4,978
Open Mon-Thurs 8-6
Friends of the Library Group

RIVERSIDE BRANCH, Rivergate Shopping Ctr, 110 Holiday Dr N, 31210, SAN 338-991X. Tel: 478-757-8900. FAX: 478-757-1094. *Br Librn,* Suzy McCullough; E-mail: suzymc@bibblib.org
Library Holdings: Bk Vols 53,124
Open Mon-Wed & Fri 9:30-6, Thurs 10:30-7, Sun 1-5
Friends of the Library Group

SHURLING BRANCH, Shurlington Plaza, 1769 Shurling Dr, 31211-2152, SAN 338-9979. Tel: 478-744-0875. *Br Librn,* Samantha Wilcox; E-mail: wilcoxs@bibblib.org
Library Holdings: Bk Vols 43,889
Open Mon-Wed & Fri 9:30-6, Thurs 10:30-7, Sun 1-5
Friends of the Library Group

TWIGGS COUNTY PUBLIC LIBRARY, 109 Main St, Jeffersonville, 31044, SAN 338-9731. Tel: 478-945-3814. FAX: 478-945-3814. E-mail: mgrltw@bibblib.org. *Br Mgr,* Eudoxie Finch
Library Holdings: Bk Vols 13,653
Open Mon & Wed 9-5, Tues & Thurs 10-6
Friends of the Library Group

C MIDDLE GEORGIA STATE UNIVERSITY*, Macon Campus Library, 100 University Pkwy, 31206. SAN 303-3902. Tel: 478-471-2709. FAX: 478-471-2869. Web Site: www.mga.edu/library. *Dir,* Tamatha Lambert; Tel: 478-471-2865, E-mail: tamatha.lambert@mga.edu; *Asst Dir, Libr Serv,* Felicia Haywood; Tel: 478-471-2867, E-mail: felicia.haywood@mga.edu; *Electronic Res Librn,* Ashley Bennett; Tel: 478-471-2866, E-mail: ashley.bennett@mga.edu; *Grad Serv Librn,* Dana Casper; Tel: 478-471-2042, E-mail: dana.casper@mga.edu; *Ref & Instruction Librn,* Abbie Holmes; Tel: 478-471-2093, E-mail: abbie.holmes@mga.edu; Staff 8 (MLS 5, Non-MLS 3)
Founded 1968. Enrl 6,615; Fac 194; Highest Degree: Master
Library Holdings: Bk Titles 88,000; Bk Vols 90,000
Special Collections: College Archives; Horticulture Coll
Automation Activity & Vendor Info: (Acquisitions) Ex Libris Group; (Cataloging) Ex Libris Group; (Circulation) Ex Libris Group; (Course Reserve) Ex Libris Group; (ILL) Ex Libris Group; (Media Booking) Ex Libris Group; (OPAC) Ex Libris Group; (Serials) Ex Libris Group
Wireless access
Partic in LYRASIS; OCLC Online Computer Library Center, Inc
Special Services for the Blind - Computer with voice synthesizer for visually impaired persons; ZoomText magnification & reading software
Open Mon-Thurs 7:30am-10pm, Fri 7:30-Noon, Sun 2-6

S NATIONAL PARK SERVICE*, Ocmulgee National Monument Library, 1207 Emery Hwy, 31217. SAN 303-3910. Tel: 478-752-8257, Ext 224. FAX: 478-752-8259. Web Site: www.nps.gov/ocmu. *Library Contact,* Lonnie Davis; E-mail: lonnie_davis@nps.gov
Founded 1936
Library Holdings: Bk Titles 700; Per Subs 15
Subject Interests: Anthrop, Archaeology, Environ studies, Native Americans
Restriction: Staff use only

C WESLEYAN COLLEGE*, Willet Memorial Library, 4760 Forsyth Rd, 31210-4462. SAN 303-3929. Tel: 478-757-5200. FAX: 478-757-3898. E-mail: wlibrary@wesleyancollege.edu. Web Site: www.wesleyancollege.edu/library/willetlibrary-Home.cfm. *Libr Dir,* Kristina C Peavy; Tel: 478-757-5201, E-mail: kpeavy@wesleyancollege.edu; *Archivist, Pub Serv Librn,* Virginia Blake; Tel: 478-757-5274, E-mail: vblake@wesleyancollege.edu; *Electronic Res Mgr,* Rhiannon Bruner; Tel: 478-757-5204, E-mail: rbruner@wesleyancollege.edu; *Supvr, Pub Serv,* Malise Fathi; Tel: 478-757-5202, E-mail: mfathi@wesleyancollege.edu; Staff 4 (MLS 3, Non-MLS 1)
Founded 1836. Fac 50; Highest Degree: Master
Library Holdings: AV Mats 1,991; CDs 299; DVDs 86; e-books 16,463; Microforms 33,912; Bk Vols 142,337; Per Subs 456; Videos 240
Special Collections: Americana (McGregor Coll); Georgiana (Park Coll)
Automation Activity & Vendor Info: (Acquisitions) OCLC; (Cataloging) OCLC; (Circulation) OCLC; (Course Reserve) OCLC; (ILL) OCLC WorldShare Interlibrary Loan; (OPAC) OCLC
Wireless access
Function: Archival coll, Audio & video playback equip for onsite use, Electronic databases & coll, ILL available, Photocopying/Printing, Ref serv available
Partic in Georgia Library Learning Online; GOLD Resource Sharing Network for Georgia's Libraries; LYRASIS
Open Mon-Thurs 8am-10pm, Fri 8-5, Sat 12-7, Sun 2:30-10
Restriction: Open to pub for ref only, Open to students, fac & staff

MADISON

P AZALEA REGIONAL LIBRARY SYSTEM*, 1121 East Ave, 30650. SAN 339-0063. Tel: 706-342-4974. FAX: 706-342-4510. Web Site: www.azalealibraries.org. *Regional Dir,* Stacy L Brown; Tel: 706-342-4974, Ext 1010, E-mail: sbrown@azalealibraries.org; *Admin Serv, Librn,* Mary Young; Tel: 706-342-4974, Ext 1026, E-mail: myoung@azalealibraries,org; *Librn, Tech Serv,* Holly Jarrell; Tel: 706-342-4974, Ext 1018, E-mail: hjarrell@azalealibraries.org; Staff 34 (MLS 7, Non-MLS 27)
Founded 1952. Pop 162,000; Circ 484,098
Library Holdings: AV Mats 15,737; CDs 1,015; DVDs 1,040; Electronic Media & Resources 41; Bk Titles 75,262; Bk Vols 215,034; Per Subs 126; Talking Bks 8,321; Videos 7,416
Special Collections: Joel Chandler Harris Coll
Subject Interests: Ga, Genealogy
Automation Activity & Vendor Info: (Cataloging) SirsiDynix; (Circulation) SirsiDynix; (OPAC) SirsiDynix
Wireless access
Member Libraries: Azalea Regional Library System
Partic in Georgia Library Learning Online; LYRASIS; Public Information Network for Electronic Services
Open Mon-Fri 8-5
Friends of the Library Group
Branches: 8

EATONTON-PUTNAM COUNTY LIBRARY, 309 N Madison Ave, Eatonton, 31024, SAN 339-0098. Tel: 706-485-6768. FAX: 706-485-5896. Web Site: www.azalealibraries.org/member-libraries/eatonton-putnam-county-library. *Br Mgr,* Lachelle Jordan; E-mail: ljordan@azalealibraries.org
Subject Interests: Ga, Genealogy
Mem of Azalea Regional Library System
Open Mon-Wed & Fri 10-6, Thurs 10-8, Sat 10-4, Sun 2-6

GREENE COUNTY LIBRARY, 610 S Main St, Greensboro, 30642, SAN 339-3038. Tel: 706-453-7276. FAX: 706-453-0500. Web Site: www.azalealibraries.org/member-libraries/greene-county-library. *Br Mgr,* Lonya Jackson-Sarden; E-mail: ljsarden@azalealibraries.org
Subject Interests: Ga, Genealogy
Mem of Azalea Regional Library System
Open Mon & Wed-Fri 9-6, Tues 9-8, Sat 10-4, Sun 2-6
Friends of the Library Group

HANCOCK COUNTY LIBRARY, 8984 E Broad St, Sparta, 31087, SAN 339-0128. Tel: 706-444-5389. FAX: 706-444-6056. Web Site: www.azalealibraries.org/member-libraries/hancock-county-library. *Br Mgr,* Kathy Ransom; E-mail: kransom@azalealibraries.org
Subject Interests: Ga, Genealogy
Mem of Azalea Regional Library System
Open Mon, Wed & Fri 10-6, Thurs 10-8, Sat 10-2, Sun 2-6

JASPER COUNTY LIBRARY, 319 E Green St, Monticello, 31064, SAN 339-0152. Tel: 706-468-6292. FAX: 706-468-2060. Web Site: www.azalealibraries.org/member-libraries/jasper-county-library. *Br Mgr,* Tamala Alexander; E-mail: talexander@azalealibraries.org
Subject Interests: Ga, Genealogy
Mem of Azalea Regional Library System
Open Mon-Wed & Fri 10-6, Thurs 10-8, Sat 10-2

MONROE - WALTON COUNTY LIBRARY, 217 W Spring St, Monroe, 30655, SAN 339-3577. Tel: 770-267-4630. FAX: 770-267-6682. Web Site: www.azalealibraries.org/member-libraries/monroe-walton-county-library. *Br Mgr,* Dana Seger; E-mail: dseger@azalealibraries,org; Staff 1 (MLS 1)
Subject Interests: Ga, Genealogy
Mem of Azalea Regional Library System
Open Mon-Thurs 9-7, Fri 9-6, Sat 10-4, Sun 2-6
Friends of the Library Group

MORGAN COUNTY LIBRARY, 1131 East Ave, 30650, SAN 370-0178. Tel: 706-342-1206. FAX: 706-342-0883. Web Site: www.azalealibraries.org/member-libraries/morgan-county-library. *Br Mgr,* Covy Hunter; E-mail: chunter@azalealibraries.org
Special Collections: Joel Chandler Harris Coll
Subject Interests: Ga, Genealogy
Mem of Azalea Regional Library System
Open Mon-Wed & Fri 10-6, Thurs 10-8, Sat 10-4, Sun 2-6
Friends of the Library Group

O'KELLY MEMORIAL LIBRARY, 363 Conyers Rd, Loganville, 30052, SAN 339-3518. Tel: 770-466-2895. FAX: 770-466-3700. Web Site: www.azalealibraries.org/member-libraries/okelly-memorial-library. *Br Mgr,* Rick Vetsch; E-mail: rvetsch@azalealibraries.org
Mem of Azalea Regional Library System
Open Mon-Thurs 9-7, Fri 9-6, Sat 10-4, Sun 2-6
Friends of the Library Group

W H STANTON MEMORIAL LIBRARY, 407 W Hightower Trail, Social Circle, 30025, SAN 339-3631. Tel: 770-464-2444. FAX: 770-464-1596. Web Site: www.azalealibraries.org/member-libraries/w-h-stanton-memorial-library. *Br Mgr,* Amy Hicks; E-mail: ahicks@azalealibraries.org
Subject Interests: Ga, Genealogy
Mem of Azalea Regional Library System
Open Mon, Wed & Fri 10-6, Tues & Thurs 9-7, Sat 10-4, Sun 2-6

MANCHESTER

P PINE MOUNTAIN REGIONAL LIBRARY*, 218 Perry St NW, 31816. (Mail add: PO Box 709, 31816-0709), SAN 339-0187. Tel: 706-846-2186. FAX: 706-846-8455. Web Site: www.pinemtnlibrary.org. *Dir,* Cynthia Kilby; E-mail: ckilby@pinemtnlibrary.org; *Tech Coordr,* Lorraine Smalley; Staff 21 (MLS 5, Non-MLS 16)
Founded 1938. Pop 65,712; Circ 157,728
Library Holdings: Bk Vols 118,936
Subject Interests: Genealogy, Local hist
Automation Activity & Vendor Info: (Acquisitions) Evergreen; (Cataloging) Evergreen; (Circulation) Evergreen; (ILL) OCLC; (OPAC) Evergreen; (Serials) Evergreen
Partic in Public Information Network for Electronic Services
Open Mon-Fri 8:30-5:30
Branches: 7

BUTLER PUBLIC, 56 W Main St, Butler, 31006-0508. (Mail add: PO Box 508, Butler, 31006-0508), SAN 339-0217. Tel: 478-862-5428. FAX: 478-862-2924. *Mgr,* Johnnie Harris
Open Tues, 10-1 & 2-6, Wed & Fri 2-6, Thurs 2-8, Sat 9-1

GREENVILLE AREA PUBLIC, 2323 Gilbert St, Greenville, 30222-0710. (Mail add: PO Box 710, Greenville, 30222-0710), SAN 339-0241. Tel: 706-672-4004. FAX: 706-672-9223. E-mail: libraryg@pinemtnlibrary.org.
Open Tues-Fri 2-6, Sat 9-12

HIGHTOWER MEMORIAL, 800 W Gordon St, Thomaston, 30286-3417. (Mail add: PO Box 631, Thomaston, 30286-0008), SAN 339-0330. Tel: 706-647-8649. FAX: 706-647-3977. *Br Mgr,* Shirley Fogarty; *Librn,* Cynthia Kilby
Open Mon-Wed & Fri 10-6, Thurs 10-9, Sat 9-1

MANCHESTER PUBLIC, 218 Perry St, 31816-0709, SAN 373-6229. Tel: 706-846-3851. FAX: 706-846-9632. E-mail: librarym@pinemtnlibrary.org. *Mgr,* Diane Rakhshani
Open Mon-Wed & Fri 8:30-5:30, Thurs 8:30-8:30, Sat 9-1

REYNOLDS COMMUNITY, 208 N Winston St, Reynolds, 31076. (Mail add: PO Box 467, Reynolds, 31076-0467), SAN 339-0276. Tel: 478-847-3468. FAX: 478-847-4553. *Mgr,* Melinda Hortman
Open Mon, Tues & Thurs 1-6, Sat 10-2

TALBOT COUNTY, 75 N Jefferson St, Talbotton, 31827-9732. (Mail add: PO Box 477, Talbotton, 31827-0477), SAN 339-0306. Tel: 706-665-3134. FAX: 706-665-8777. *Br Mgr,* Shamona L Willis
Open Tues & Thurs 12-8, Wed 10-6, Fri 12-6, Sat 1-5

YATESVILLE PUBLIC, 77 Childs Ave, Yatesville, 31097-3661. (Mail add: PO Box 87, Yatesville, 31097-0087). Tel: 706-472-3048. FAX: 706-472-3049. *Br Mgr,* Connie Moncrief
Founded 2002
Open Tues & Wed 2-7, Thurs 2-8, Fri 2-6

MARIETTA

J CHATTAHOOCHEE TECHNICAL COLLEGE LIBRARY*, 980 S Cobb Dr, 30060. (Mail add: 1046 S Cobb Dr, MD202, 30060), SAN 375-4154. Tel: 770-528-4536. E-mail: library@chattahoocheetech.edu. Web Site: www.chattahoocheetech.edu/library. *Dir of Libr,* Leigh Hall; Tel: 770-528-6461, E-mail: lhall@chattahoocheetech.edu; *Cataloger, Librn,* Don Auensen; Tel: 770-528-6466, E-mail: dauensen@chattahoocheetech.edu; *Appalachian Campus Librn,* Samantha Carder; Tel: 706-253-4571, E-mail: scarder@chattahoocheetech.edu; *Canton Campus Librn,* Colin Eade; Tel: 770-345-1392, E-mail: colin.eade@chattahoocheetech.edu; *Mountain View Campus Librn,* Mary Platt; E-mail: mary.platt@chattahoocheetech.edu; *N Metro Campus Librn,* Shannon Gibson; Tel: 770-975-4054, E-mail: shannon.gibson@chattahoocheetech.edu; *Paulding Campus Librn,* Janice Levine; Tel: 770-443-3632, Fax: 770-443-3631, E-mail: jlevine@chattahoocheetech.edu; Staff 14 (MLS 8, Non-MLS 6)
Founded 1986. Highest Degree: Associate
Library Holdings: e-books 442,000; Bk Vols 50,000; Per Subs 116
Special Collections: Georgia Topics & Authors
Automation Activity & Vendor Info: (Acquisitions) SirsiDynix; (Cataloging) SirsiDynix; (Circulation) SirsiDynix; (Course Reserve) SirsiDynix; (Discovery) EBSCO Discovery Service; (ILL) OCLC; (OPAC) SirsiDynix
Wireless access
Partic in Georgia Library Learning Online
Open Mon-Thurs 8:30am-3:30pm, Fri 9:30am-12:30pm
Restriction: Borrowing privileges limited to fac & registered students
Departmental Libraries:

APPALACHIAN CAMPUS LIBRARY, 100 Campus Dr, Jasper, 30143. Tel: 706-253-4572. *Librn, Library Services,* Samantha Carder; Tel: 770-975-4134, E-mail: scarder@chattahoocheetech.edu

CANTON CAMPUS LIBRARY, 1645 Bluffs Pkwy, Canton, 30114. Tel: 770-345-1390. *Librn, Library Services,* Colin M Eade; Tel: 770-345-1052, E-mail: colin.eade@chattahoocheetech.edu

MOUTAIN VIEW CAMPUS LIBRARY, 2680 Gordy Pkwy, 30066. Tel: 770-509-6320. *Librn, Library Services,* Dylan Priddy; Tel: 770-509-6320, E-mail: dylan.priddy@chattahoocheetech.edu

NORTH METRO CAMPUS LIBRARY, 5198 Ross Rd, Acworth, 30102. Tel: 770-975-4054. FAX: 770-975-4284. *Librn,* Shannon Gibson; Staff 3 (MLS 3)
Founded 1989. Enrl 2,000; Highest Degree: Associate
Library Holdings: CDs 40; DVDs 15; e-books 34,000; e-journals 3,000; Bk Vols 6,000; Per Subs 35; Talking Bks 50; Videos 500
Automation Activity & Vendor Info: (Cataloging) Surpass; (Circulation) Surpass; (OPAC) Surpass
Open Mon-Thurs 8:30am-3:30pm, Fri 9:30am-2:30pm

PAULDING CAMPUS LIBRARY, 400 Nathan Dean Blvd, Dallas, 30132. Tel: 770-443-3630. *Librn, Library Services,* Janice Levine; Tel: 770-443-3632, E-mail: jlevine@chattahoocheetech.edu

WOODSTOCK CAMPUS LIBRARY, 8371 Main St, Woodstock, 30188. Tel: 770-720-6687. *Librn, Library Services,* Mary Platt; E-mail: mary.platt@chattahoocheetech.edu

P COBB COUNTY PUBLIC LIBRARY SYSTEM*, 266 Roswell St, 30060-2004. SAN 339-0365. Tel: 770-528-2320. Interlibrary Loan Service Tel: 770-528-2339. Reference Tel: 770-528-2377. FAX: 770-528-2349. Interlibrary Loan Service FAX: 770-528-2367. E-mail: contactus@cobbcat.org. Web Site: www.cobbcat.org. *Dir,* Helen Poyer; *Assoc Dir, Br Serv,* Teresa Tresp; *Assoc Dir, Tech Serv,* Zhang Shelley; Staff 44 (MLS 43, Non-MLS 1)
Founded 1958. Pop 679,325; Circ 4,014,576
Library Holdings: Bk Vols 301,464
Special Collections: Georgia Room
Automation Activity & Vendor Info: (Acquisitions) SirsiDynix; (Circulation) SirsiDynix; (ILL) SirsiDynix; (OPAC) SirsiDynix; (Serials) Sydney
Wireless access
Open Mon-Thurs 9-9:30, Fri & Sat 9-6, Sun 1-5
Friends of the Library Group
Branches: 15

ACWORTH LIBRARY, 4569 Dallas St, Acworth, 30101, SAN 339-039X. Tel: 770-917-5165. FAX: 770-917-5177. Web Site: www.cobbcat.org/venue/acworth-library. *Mgr,* Nicole Knox
Founded 1958. Circ 116,181
Library Holdings: Bk Vols 31,347
Open Mon-Wed 10-7, Thurs & Fri 1-6, Sat 10-5
Friends of the Library Group

EAST COBB LIBRARY, 4880 Lower Roswell Rd, 30068, SAN 339-0551. Tel: 770-509-2730. FAX: 770-509-2733. Web Site: www.cobbcat.org/venue/east-cobb-library. *Mgr,* Ansie Krige
Founded 1958. Circ 485,869
Library Holdings: Bk Vols 71,078
Open Mon-Wed 10-9, Thurs & Fri 10-6, Sat 10-5
Friends of the Library Group

GRITTERS LIBRARY, 880 Shaw Park Rd, 30066, SAN 339-0489. Tel: 770-528-2524. FAX: 770-528-2533. Web Site: www.cobbcat.org/venue/gritters-library. *Mgr,* Pam Finley
Founded 1958. Circ 162,418
Library Holdings: Bk Vols 44,944
Open Mon-Wed 10-8, Thurs & Fri 10-6, Sat 10-5
Friends of the Library Group

KEMP MEMORIAL LIBRARY, 4029 Due West Rd, 30064, SAN 370-8039. Tel: 770-528-2527. FAX: 770-528-2592. Web Site: www.cobbcat.org/venue/kemp-memorial-library. *Mgr,* Maria Dominguez
Founded 1958. Circ 182,864
Library Holdings: Bk Vols 52,460
Open Mon-Wed 10-8, Thurs & Fri 10-6, Sat 10-5
Friends of the Library Group

KENNESAW LIBRARY, 2250 Lewis St, Kennesaw, 30144, SAN 339-0519. Tel: 770-528-2529. FAX: 770-528-2593. Web Site: www.cobbcat.org/venue/kennesaw-library. *Mgr,* Jenny Everett
Founded 1958. Circ 252,560
Library Holdings: Bk Vols 53,836
Open Mon-Wed 10-8, Thurs & Fri 10-6, Sat 10-5
Friends of the Library Group

MOUNTAIN VIEW REGIONAL LIBRARY, 3320 Sandy Plains Rd, 30066, SAN 370-8047. Tel: 770-509-2725. FAX: 770-509-2726. Web Site: www.cobbcat.org/venue/mountain-view-regional-library. *Regional Mgr,* Deborah Jackson; *Mgr,* Deborah Feanny
Founded 1958. Circ 554,749
Library Holdings: Bk Vols 124,236
Open Mon-Wed 10-9, Thurs & Fri 10-6, Sat 10-5, Sun 1-5
Friends of the Library Group

POWDER SPRINGS LIBRARY, 4181 Atlanta St, Bldg 1, Powder Springs, 30127, SAN 339-0578. Tel: 770-439-3600. FAX: 770-439-3620. Web Site: www.cobbcat.org/venue/powder-springs-library. *Mgr,* Jennifer Rapier
Founded 1958. Circ 159,643
Library Holdings: Bk Vols 51,009
Open Mon-Wed 10-8, Thurs & Fri 10-6, Sat 10-5
Friends of the Library Group

LEWIS A RAY LIBRARY, 4500 Oakdale Rd, Smyrna, 30080, SAN 339-0608. Tel: 770-801-5335. FAX: 770-801-5316. Web Site: www.cobbcat.org/venue/lewis-a-ray-library. *Mgr,* Margaret Eves
Founded 1958. Circ 61,749
Library Holdings: Bk Vols 22,466
Open Mon-Wed 10-7, Thurs & Fri 1-6, Sat 10-5
Friends of the Library Group

SEWELL MILL LIBRARY & CULTURAL CENTER, 2051 Lower Roswell Rd, 30068, SAN 339-042X. Tel: 770-509-2711. FAX: 770-509-2714. Web Site: www.cobbcat.org/venue/sewell-mill-library-cultural-center. *Br Mgr,* Bruce Thompson
Founded 1967. Circ 183,401
Library Holdings: Bk Vols 58,302
Open Mon-Wed 10-9, Thurs & Fri 10-6, Sat 10-5
Friends of the Library Group

SIBLEY LIBRARY, 1539 S Cobb Dr, 30060, SAN 339-0632. Tel: 770-528-2520. FAX: 770-528-2594. Web Site: www.cobbcat.org/venue/sibley-library. *Mgr,* Beth Baldwin
Founded 1958. Circ 41,781
Library Holdings: Bk Vols 28,403
Open Mon-Wed 10-7, Thurs & Fri 1-6, Sat 10-5
Friends of the Library Group

SOUTH COBB REGIONAL LIBRARY, 805 Clay Rd, Mableton, 30126, SAN 339-0667. Tel: 678-398-5828. FAX: 678-398-5833. Web Site: www.cobbcat.org/venue/south-cobb-regional-library. *Regional Mgr,* Jo Lahmon; *Mgr,* Roxanne Magaw
Founded 1958. Circ 321,829
Library Holdings: Bk Vols 88,255
Open Mon-Wed 10-9, Thurs & Fri 10-6, Sat 10-5, Sun 1-5
Friends of the Library Group

STRATTON LIBRARY, 1100 Powder Springs Rd SW, 30064, SAN 339-0691. Tel: 770-528-2522. FAX: 770-528-2595. Web Site: www.cobbcat.org/venue/stratton-library. *Mgr,* Patricia Ball
Founded 1958. Circ 129,070
Library Holdings: Bk Vols 41,085
Open Mon-Wed 10-8, Thurs & Fri 10-6, Sat 10-5
Friends of the Library Group

SWEETWATER VALLEY LIBRARY, 5000 Austell-Powder Springs Rd, Ste 123, Austell, 30106, SAN 339-0721. Tel: 770-819-3290. FAX: 770-819-3293. Web Site: www.cobbcat.org/venue/sweetwater-valley-library. *Mgr,* Position Currently Open
Founded 1958. Circ 57,197
Library Holdings: Bk Vols 27,891
Open Mon-Wed 10-7, Thurs & Fri 1-6, Sat 10-5
Friends of the Library Group

VININGS LIBRARY, 4290 Paces Ferry Rd, Atlanta, 30339, SAN 370-8055. Tel: 770-801-5330. FAX: 770-801-5319. Web Site: www.cobbcat.org/venue/vinings-library. *Mgr,* Susan Irvin
Founded 1958. Circ 152,043
Library Holdings: Bk Vols 43,651
Open Mon-Wed 10-8, Thurs & Fri 10-6, Sat 10-5
Friends of the Library Group

WEST COBB REGIONAL LIBRARY, 1750 Dennis Kemp Lane, Kennesaw, 30152. Tel: 770-528-4699. FAX: 770-528-4619. Web Site: www.cobbcat.org/venue/west-cobb-regional-library. *Regional Mgr,* Steve Powell; *Mgr,* Jennifer Wells
Founded 1958. Circ 456,721
Library Holdings: Bk Vols 95,773
Open Mon-Wed 10-9, Thurs & Fri 10-6, Sat 10-5, Sun 1-5
Friends of the Library Group

CM LIFE UNIVERSITY*, Drs Sid E & Nell K Williams Library, 1269 Barclay Circle, 30060. SAN 370-5730. Tel: 770-426-2688. FAX: 770-426-2745. E-mail: Library@LIFE.edu. Web Site: www.life.edu/campus-life-pages/sid-and-nell-williams-library/library-resources. *Dir,* Karen Preston; Tel: 770-426-2692, E-mail: kpreston@life.edu; *Asst Dir,* Geetha Sridaran; Tel: 770-426-2691, E-mail: gsridaran@life.edu; *Ref & Instruction,* Pam Shadrix; E-mail: pshadrix@life.edu. Subject Specialists: *Sci ref,* Geetha Sridaran; Staff 3 (MLS 3)
Founded 1975. Enrl 2,300; Fac 167; Highest Degree: Doctorate
Library Holdings: Audiobooks 94; AV Mats 10,442; CDs 196; DVDs 239; e-books 23,090; e-journals 33,470; Bk Titles 32,603; Bk Vols 40,000; Per Subs 60; Videos 6,240
Special Collections: Chiropractic Coll
Subject Interests: Biology, Bus, Chiropractic, Computer info, Dietetics, Health sci, Nutrition, Psychol, Sports health sci
Automation Activity & Vendor Info: (Acquisitions) OCLC Worldshare Management Services; (Cataloging) OCLC Worldshare Management Services; (Circulation) OCLC Worldshare Management Services; (Discovery) OCLC Worldshare Management Services; (ILL) OCLC Worldshare Management Services; (OPAC) OCLC Worldshare Management Services; (Serials) OCLC Worldshare Management Services
Wireless access
Function: Archival coll, AV serv, CD-ROM, Computers for patron use, Digital talking bks, Doc delivery serv, Electronic databases & coll, For res purposes, Health sci info serv, ILL available, Online cat, Orientations, Outside serv via phone, mail, e-mail & web, Photocopying/Printing, Ref serv available, Telephone ref, VHS videos, Workshops
Publications: Today's Chiropractic Lifestyle
Partic in Chiropractic Libr Consortium; Georgia Private Acad Librs Consortium; OCLC Online Computer Library Center, Inc
Open Mon-Thurs 6:45am-11:45pm, Fri 6:45-6:45, Sat 10:30-6:45, Sun Noon-11:45
Restriction: In-house use for visitors, Open to students, fac & staff

M WELLSTAR LIBRARY SERVICES*, Health Sciences Library, 677 Church St, 30060. SAN 329-1715. Tel: 770-793-7178. FAX: 770-793-7956. E-mail: medical.library@wellstar.org. Web Site: www.wellstar.org. *Supvr, Libr Serv,* Benedette Wright; Staff 1 (MLS 1)
Library Holdings: e-books 134; e-journals 3,400; Bk Vols 1,100; Per Subs 148
Subject Interests: Allied health, Med, Nursing
Automation Activity & Vendor Info: (Cataloging) LibraryWorld, Inc; (OPAC) LibraryWorld, Inc; (Serials) Prenax, Inc
Wireless access
Function: Health sci info serv
Partic in Atlanta Health Science Libraries Consortium; Georgia Health Sciences Library Association; Medical Library Association; Southern Chapter of Med Libr Asn
Restriction: Authorized personnel only, Badge access after hrs

MCDONOUGH

P HENRY COUNTY PUBLIC LIBRARY SYSTEM*, 1001 Florence McGarity Blvd, 30252. SAN 378-5726. Tel: 678-432-5353. Web Site: henrylibraries.org. *Dir,* Kathy Pillatzki; E-mail: director@henrylibraries.org; *Asst Dir, Coll Develop,* Gail Evans; E-mail: gail.evans@henrylibraries.org; *Asst Dir, Pub Serv,* Dr Adam Townes; E-mail: adam.townes@henrylibraries.org; *Asst Dir, Tech Serv,* Pamela Bagby; E-mail: pamela.bagby@henrylibraries.org; *Network Adminr,* Amanda Cox; E-mail: amanda.cox@henrylibraries.org; *Br Mgr,* Ruthina Ozoh; E-mail: ruthina.ozoh@henrylibraries.org; Staff 4 (MLS 4)
Library Holdings: Audiobooks 9,643; Braille Volumes 85; DVDs 1,759; Electronic Media & Resources 35; Large Print Bks 17,745; Bk Vols 207,901; Per Subs 14; Videos 3,719
Automation Activity & Vendor Info: (Cataloging) Evergreen; (Circulation) Evergreen; (OPAC) Evergreen
Wireless access
Partic in Public Information Network for Electronic Services
Open Mon & Thurs 12-8, Tues & Wed 10-6, Sun 1-5
Friends of the Library Group
Branches: 4

COCHRAN PUBLIC LIBRARY, 174 Burke St, Stockbridge, 30281. Tel: 678-432-5353, Ext 7. *Mgr,* Jacqueline Johnson; E-mail: jacqueline.johnson@henrylibraries.org
Founded 1991. Pop 12,541; Circ 249,855
Library Holdings: Audiobooks 2,148; CDs 1,123; DVDs 344; Electronic Media & Resources 4; Large Print Bks 1,473; Bk Vols 53,292; Per Subs 14; Videos 894
Special Services for the Blind - Audio mat; Bks available with recordings; Bks on cassette; Bks on CD; Large print bks; Reader equip
Open Mon & Thurs 12-8, Tues & Wed 1-6, Fri 10-2
Friends of the Library Group

FAIRVIEW PUBLIC LIBRARY, 28 Austin Rd, Stockbridge, 30281. Tel: 770-389-6277. FAX: 678-432-5353, Ext 3. *Mgr,* Phoenix Light; E-mail: phoenix.light@henrylibraries.org
Founded 2006. Pop 13,622; Circ 245,868
Library Holdings: CDs 884; DVDs 137; Large Print Bks 1,705; Bk Titles 53,662; Bk Vols 56,000; Per Subs 82; Talking Bks 1,027; Videos 881
Special Services for the Deaf - Adult & family literacy prog; Assistive tech; Bks on deafness & sign lang; Closed caption videos; High interest/low vocabulary bks
Special Services for the Blind - Audio mat; Bks on cassette; Bks on CD; Large print bks; Reader equip; Ref serv
Open Mon-Thurs 9:30-8, Fri 9:30-6, Sat 9:30-5
Friends of the Library Group

FORTSON PUBLIC LIBRARY, 61 McDonough St, Hampton, 30228. Tel: 770-288-7233. *Mgr,* Tangela McKibbens; E-mail: tangela.mckibbens@henrylibraries.org
Circ 89,296
Library Holdings: Audiobooks 1,800; CDs 293; DVDs 340; Large Print Bks 1,313; Bk Vols 40,984; Per Subs 14; Videos 587
Function: Bks on cassette, Bks on CD, Computers for patron use, Free DVD rentals, ILL available, Internet access, Music CDs, OverDrive digital audio bks, Photocopying/Printing, Prog for children & young adult, Ref serv available, Spoken cassettes & CDs, Story hour, Summer reading prog, Tax forms, Teen prog, VHS videos
Special Services for the Deaf - Closed caption videos; High interest/low vocabulary bks
Special Services for the Blind - Audio mat; Bks on cassette; Bks on CD; Cassettes; Large print bks; Reader equip
Open Mon & Thurs 12-8, Tues & Wed 10-6, Fri 10-2
Friends of the Library Group

LOCUST GROVE PUBLIC LIBRARY, 115 Martin Luther King Jr Blvd, Locust Grove, 30248. Tel: 678-432-5353, Ext 4. *Mgr,* Jarian Jones; E-mail: jarian.jones@henrylibraries.org
Library Holdings: Audiobooks 1,482; CDs 244; DVDs 372; Large Print Bks 487; Bk Vols 27,904; Per Subs 56; Talking Bks 456; Videos 470
Function: Bks on cassette, Bks on CD, Children's prog, Computers for patron use, Free DVD rentals, ILL available, Internet access, Music CDs, Online cat, Photocopying/Printing, Preschool outreach, Prog for children & young adult, Ref serv available, Spoken cassettes & CDs, Story hour, Summer reading prog, Tax forms, Teen prog, VHS videos
Special Services for the Deaf - Bks on deafness & sign lang; High interest/low vocabulary bks
Special Services for the Blind - Audio mat; Bks on cassette; Bks on CD; Large print bks; Recorded bks; Talking bk serv referral
Open Mon-Thurs 9:30-8, Fri 9:30-6, Sat 9:30-5
Friends of the Library Group

METTER

P L C ANDERSON MEMORIAL LIBRARY*, 50 S Kennedy St, 30439-4442. SAN 339-2228. Tel: 912-685-2455. FAX: 912-685-4462. E-mail: lca@strl.info. Web Site: www.facebook.com/metterlibrary. *Mgr,* Edith Rolison; Staff 4 (Non-MLS 4)
Pop 9,454; Circ 23,931
Library Holdings: Bk Vols 19,300; Per Subs 30
Automation Activity & Vendor Info: (Acquisitions) SirsiDynix; (Cataloging) SirsiDynix; (Circulation) SirsiDynix; (ILL) OCLC
Wireless access
Mem of Statesboro Regional Public Libraries
Partic in Public Information Network for Electronic Services
Open Mon-Thurs 10-5, Sat 10-12 & 1-5
Friends of the Library Group

MILLEDGEVILLE

J CENTRAL GEORGIA TECHNICAL COLLEGE LIBRARY*, Milledgeville Campus, 54 Hwy 22 W, 31061. Tel: 478-445-2333. FAX: 478-445-2346. E-mail: library@centralgatech.edu. Web Site: www.centralgatech.edu/library. *Librn,* Joelle Etheridge; E-mail: jetheridge@centralgatech.edu; *Librn,* Carter Nipper; Tel: 478-445-2319, E-mail: cnipper@centralgatech.edu; *Libr Asst,* Teri Garnto; E-mail: tgarnto@centralgatech.edu; Staff 2.8 (MLS 1.8, Non-MLS 1)
Founded 1997. Enrl 800; Highest Degree: Associate
Library Holdings: AV Mats 750; e-books 46,000; Bk Vols 6,000; Per Subs 60
Wireless access
Open Mon-Thurs 7:45am-8pm, Fri 7:45-3

C GEORGIA COLLEGE*, Ina Dillard Russell Library, 320 N Wayne St, 31061. (Mail add: Campus Box 043, 31061), SAN 339-0780. Tel: 478-445-4047. Reference Tel: 478-445-0979. FAX: 478-445-6847. E-mail: reference@gcsu.edu. Circulation E-mail: circ@gcsu.edu. Web Site: www.gcsu.edu/library. *Interim Dir,* Shaundra Walker; Tel: 478-445-0982, E-mail: shaundra.walker@gcsu.edu; *Instruction & Ref Librn,* Edward Whatley; E-mail: edward.whatley@gcsu.edu; Staff 39 (MLS 14, Non-MLS 25)
Founded 1889. Enrl 6,000; Fac 230; Highest Degree: Master
Library Holdings: e-books 27,441; Bk Titles 196,919; Bk Vols 199,729; Per Subs 415
Special Collections: Branham Cookbook Coll; Flannery O'Conner Coll, bks, ms, per; Georgia College Archives Coll; Georgia College Horology Coll, clocks, watches; Georgia History Coll, bks, ms; Middle Georgia Towns & Cities Coll; US Senator Paul Coverdell Paners Coll. US Document Depository
Subject Interests: Educ, Nursing, Psychol
Automation Activity & Vendor Info: (Acquisitions) Ex Libris Group; (Cataloging) Ex Libris Group; (Circulation) Ex Libris Group; (ILL) OCLC; (Media Booking) Ex Libris Group; (Serials) Ex Libris Group
Wireless access
Partic in GOLD Resource Sharing Network for Georgia's Libraries; LYRASIS; OCLC Online Computer Library Center, Inc; Proquest Dialog; Ser Holdings Network
Open Mon-Fri 8-5, Sat 10-6

J GEORGIA MILITARY COLLEGE*, Sibley-Cone Memorial Library, 201 E Greene St, 31061. SAN 303-3988. Tel: 478-387-4849. Web Site: gmcga.libguides.com/milledgeville, www.gmc.edu/academic-programs/26.cms. *Dir, Libr Serv,* Erin Newton; Tel: 478-387-4729, E-mail: enewton@gmc.edu; *Ref & Instruction Librn,* Beth Jones; Tel: 478-387-4733, E-mail: criggs@gmc.edu; *Cat/Syst Librn,* Dylan Stephens; E-mail: dstephens@gmc.edu; Staff 3 (MLS 2, Non-MLS 1)
Founded 1879. Enrl 2,773; Fac 75; Highest Degree: Associate
Library Holdings: Bk Titles 31,000; Bk Vols 36,000; Per Subs 150
Subject Interests: Ga, Hist, Local hist
Automation Activity & Vendor Info: (Acquisitions) Mandarin Library Automation; (Cataloging) Mandarin Library Automation; (Circulation) Mandarin Library Automation
Wireless access
Function: Archival coll, ILL available, Photocopying/Printing
Partic in Cent Ga Associated Librs; GOLD Resource Sharing Network for Georgia's Libraries
Open Mon-Thurs 7:45am-9:30pm, Fri 7:45-4, Sun 5pm-9:30pm

P TWIN LAKES LIBRARY SYSTEM*, Mary Vinson Memorial Library - Headquarters, 151 S Jefferson St SE, 31061-3419. SAN 339-0004. Tel: 478-452-0677. FAX: 478-452-0680. Web Site: www.tllsga.org. *Dir,* Stephen Houser; E-mail: shouser@tllsga.org; Staff 16 (MLS 2, Non-MLS 14)
Founded 1938. Pop 144,000
Library Holdings: Bk Vols 75,000
Subject Interests: Local hist
Wireless access
Open Mon & Tues 9-9, Wed-Fri 9-6, Sat 10-4
Friends of the Library Group
Branches: 1
LAKE SINCLAIR, 130 Log Cabin Rd, Unit D, 31061. Tel: 478-452-6522. FAX: 478-452-6524. *Br Mgr, Mgr Digital Initiatives,* Virginia Greene; E-mail: vgreene@tllsga.org
Open Mon-Fri 12-6

MOODY AFB

A UNITED STATES AIR FORCE, Moody Air Force Base Library FL4830, 23 FSS/FSDL, 3010 Robinson Rd, Bldg 328, 31699-1594. SAN 339-0845. Tel: 229-257-3539. FAX: 229-257-4119. Web Site: www.moodyafblibrary.com. *Libr Dir,* Jess G Echord; E-mail: jess.echord.1@us.af.mil; Staff 6 (MLS 1, Non-MLS 5)
Founded 1952
Library Holdings: Bk Vols 40,000; Per Subs 250
Subject Interests: Mil hist
Wireless access
Partic in OCLC Online Computer Library Center, Inc
Open Mon-Wed & Fri 8-4, Thurs 8-8, Sat 10-2

MORGAN

S GEORGIA DEPARTMENT OF CORRECTIONS, OFFICE OF LIBRARY SERVICES*, Calhoun State Prison, 27823 Main St, 39866. (Mail add: PO Box 249, 39866-0249). Tel: 229-849-5000, Ext 5058. Web Site: www.dcor.state.ga.us/Facilities/calhoun-state-prison. *Librn,* Dr Patricia Pierce; E-mail: patricia.pierce@gdc.ga.gov
Library Holdings: Bk Vols 4,000; Per Subs 15
Special Collections: Law Coll
Restriction: Not open to pub

MORROW

C CLAYTON STATE UNIVERSITY*, 2000 Clayton State Blvd, 30260. SAN 303-3996. Tel: 678-466-4325. Circulation Tel: 678-466-4331. Interlibrary Loan Service Tel: 678-466-4326. Reference Tel: 678-466-4329. Administration Tel: 678-466-4332. Automation Services Tel: 678-466-4336. Information Services Tel: 678-466-4345. FAX: 678-466-4349. TDD: 678-466-4346. Reference E-mail: reference@clayton.edu. Web Site: www.clayton.edu/library. *Dean of Libr,* Dr Sonya S Gaither; Tel: 678-466-4334, E-mail: sonyagaither@clayton.edu; *Assoc Dean,* Position Currently Open; *Dept Head, Instrul Serv, Res,* Bonnie Parker; Tel: 678-466-4340, E-mail: bonnieparker@clayton.edu; *Head, Electronic Res & Serv,* Christopher Stotelmyer; Tel: 678-466-4347, E-mail: christopherstotelmyer@clayton.edu; *Head, Res Mgt,* Adam Kubik; Tel: 678-466-4337, E-mail: adamkubik@clayton.edu; *Assessment & Mkt Librn,* Erin Nagel; Tel: 678-466-4330; *Electronic Serv Librn,* Jim Rickerson; Tel: 678-466-4339, E-mail: jimrickerson@clayton.edu; *Pub Serv Librn/Weekend Coordr,* Thomas Jackson, Jr; Tel: 678-466-4338, E-mail: thomasjacksonjr@clayton.edu; *Ref & Instruction Librn,* David Greenbaum; E-mail: DavidGreenebaum@clayton.edu; *Ref & Instruction Librn,* Ashley Woodruff; Tel: 678-466-4348, E-mail: ashleywoodruff@clayton.edu; *Ser Librn,* Laura Herndon; Tel: 678-466-4335, E-mail: lauraherndon@clayton.edu; *Circ Supvr,* Stephanie Schweighardt; Tel: 678-466-4332, E-mail: stephanieschweighardt@clayton.edu; *Acq/CatAsst,* Heather Walls; Tel: 678-466-4341, E-mail: heatherwalls@clayton.edu; *Evening Circ,* Elizabeth Smedley; Tel: 678-466-4331, E-mail: elizabethsmedley@Clayton.edu; *ILL & Reserves Asst,* Rhonda Boozer; E-mail: rhondaboozer@clayton.edu; *Univ Archivist,* Feechi Hall; Tel: 678-466-4333, E-mail: feechihall@clayton.edu. Subject Specialists: *English, Legal studies, Soc sci,* Bonnie Parker; *Health, Nursing, Physics,* Christopher Stotelmyer; *Music,* Adam Kubik; *Psychol,* Erin Nagel; *Performing arts,* Jim Rickerson; *Interdisciplinary studies, Teacher educ,* Thomas Jackson, Jr; *Bus,* David Greenbaum; *Humanities,* Ashley Woodruff; *Life sci,* Laura Herndon; *Archives,* Feechi Hall; Staff 17 (MLS 11, Non-MLS 6)
Founded 1969. Enrl 6,996; Fac 247; Highest Degree: Master
Library Holdings: CDs 6,493; DVDs 1,236; e-books 392,567; e-journals 46,609; Electronic Media & Resources 38,641; Microforms 280,618; Bk Vols 111,404; Per Subs 248
Special Collections: Civil War (War of the Rebellion); Georgia (Southern History); The Foundation Center's Funding Information Network
Subject Interests: Bus, Educ, Music, Nursing
Automation Activity & Vendor Info: (Acquisitions) Ex Libris Group; (Cataloging) Ex Libris Group; (Circulation) Ex Libris Group; (Course Reserve) Ex Libris Group; (ILL) OCLC; (OPAC) Ex Libris Group; (Serials) Ex Libris Group
Wireless access
Publications: Library Source
Partic in Atlanta Regional Council for Higher Education; LYRASIS; OCLC Online Computer Library Center, Inc
Open Mon-Thurs 8am-10pm, Fri 8-6, Sat 9-6, Sun 1-10

G GEORGIA ARCHIVES, Reference Library, 5800 Jonesboro Rd, 30260. SAN 303-2884. Tel: 678-364-3710. FAX: 678-364-3856. Web Site: www.georgiaarchives.org. *Asst Vice Chancellor, State Archivist,* Christopher Davidson; E-mail: christopher.davidson@usg.edu; *Dir, Archives,* Kayla Barrett; Tel: 678-364-3781
Founded 1918
Special Collections: County & Family Histories; DAR Coll; Family Charts; Georgia & Eastern United States Genealogy; Georgia History; Georgia Map Coll; Georgia Newspapers; Georgia Photographs; Local Government Records; Official State Records; Private Papers; Surname Card File
Subject Interests: Local genealogy, Local hist
Automation Activity & Vendor Info: (Cataloging) Ex Libris Group; (OPAC) Ex Libris Group
Wireless access
Function: 24/7 Online cat, Res libr
Partic in LYRASIS
Open Tues-Sat 8:30-5
Restriction: In-house use for visitors, Internal use only, Non-circulating, Not a lending libr
Friends of the Library Group

P GEORGIA PUBLIC LIBRARY SERVICE*, Unit of the Board of Regents of the University System of Georgia, 5800 Jonesboro Rd, 30260. SAN 338-4306. Tel: 678-364-3722. FAX: 404-235-7201. Web Site: www.georgialibraries.org. *State Librn,* Julie Walker; Tel: 404-235-7140, E-mail: jwalker@georgialibraries.org; *Asst State Librn,* Ben Carter; Tel: 404-235-7123, E-mail: bcarter@georgialibraries.org; *Asst State Librn,* Wendy Cornelisen; Tel: 404-235-7122, E-mail: wcornelisen@georgialibraries.org; Staff 40 (MLS 20, Non-MLS 20)
Founded 1897
Library Holdings: Audiobooks 38; DVDs 193; Per Subs 26; Videos 300
Subject Interests: Libr & info sci
Automation Activity & Vendor Info: (Cataloging) Evergreen; (Circulation) Evergreen; (ILL) OCLC WorldShare Interlibrary Loan; (OPAC) Evergreen
Wireless access
Function: ILL available
Publications: Collection Development Statement; Georgia Public Library Service News (Bimonthly); Georgia Public Library Statistics (Annual); Georgia Public Library Trustees Handbook; GOLD ILL Procedures Manual; GOLD Serials Manual; Periodicals List
Partic in Association for Rural & Small Libraries; Association of Southeastern Research Libraries; GOLD Resource Sharing Network for Georgia's Libraries; LYRASIS; OCLC Online Computer Library Center, Inc; Soline
Restriction: Not open to pub
Branches: 1
GEORGIA LIBRARY FOR ACCESSIBLE STATEWIDE SERVICES
See Separate Entry

G NATIONAL ARCHIVES & RECORDS ADMINISTRATION*, National Archives at Atlanta, 5780 Jonesboro Rd, 30260. SAN 329-8280. Tel: 770-968-2100. FAX: 770-968-2457. E-mail: atlanta.archives@nara.gov. Web Site: archives.gov/atlanta. *Archives Dir,* Rob Richards; Tel: 770-968-2485, E-mail: rob.richards@nara.gov; *Archivist,* Shane Bell; E-mail: shane.bell@nara.gov; *Archivist,* Guy Hall; E-mail: guy.hall@nara.gov; *Archivist,* Maureen E Hill; E-mail: maureen.hill@nara.gov
Special Collections: Archival records of Federal agencies & courts in Alabama, Florida, Georgia, Kentucky, Mississippi, North Carolina, South Carolina & Tennessee
Subject Interests: Arts, Bus, Census, Civil War, Constitutional, Crime, Econ develop, Space, World War I, World War II
Wireless access
Open Mon-Fri 8:30-5
Restriction: Ref only to non-staff

MOULTRIE

P MOULTRIE-COLQUITT COUNTY LIBRARY*, 204 Fifth St SE, 31768. SAN 339-087X. Tel: 229-985-6540. FAX: 229-985-0936. E-mail: mccls@mccls.org. Web Site: www.mccls.org. *Dir,* Holly Phillips; E-mail: hbp@mccls.org; *Ch,* Erin Honeycutt; E-mail: ehoneycutt@mccls.org; *Cat, Circ Mgr,* Monique Green; E-mail: mlg@mccls.org; *Adult Serv,* Melody Jenkins; E-mail: msj@mccls.org; *Circ/Tech,* Amanda Burroughs; E-mail: acb@mccls.org; Staff 12.8 (MLS 2, Non-MLS 10.8)
Founded 1907. Pop 47,620; Circ 117,460
Library Holdings: Audiobooks 1,596; DVDs 228; Large Print Bks 2,094; Microforms 1,295; Bk Vols 124,170; Per Subs 59; Videos 739
Special Collections: Ellen Payne Odom Genealogy Library
Automation Activity & Vendor Info: (Acquisitions) Evergreen; (Cataloging) OCLC Connexion; (Circulation) Evergreen; (ILL) OCLC; (OPAC) Evergreen
Wireless access
Function: Adult bk club, Bks on cassette, Bks on CD, Children's prog, Computer training, Computers for patron use, Electronic databases & coll, Free DVD rentals, ILL available, Magnifiers for reading, Mail & tel request accepted, Online cat, Photocopying/Printing, Prog for children & young adult, Ref serv available, Summer reading prog, Tax forms, VHS videos, Wheelchair accessible
Member Libraries: Moultrie-Colquitt County Library
Partic in Georgia Libr Info Network; Public Information Network for Electronic Services
Special Services for the Blind - Closed circuit TV magnifier; Large print bks; Magnifiers; Talking bks
Open Mon-Fri 11-3
Friends of the Library Group
Branches: 1
DOERUN MUNICIPAL LIBRARY, 185 N Freeman St, Doerun, 31744, SAN 339-0993. Tel: 229-782-5507. *Library Contact,* Stephanie Enfinger; E-mail: senfinger@mccls.org
Function: Computers for patron use, Electronic databases & coll, ILL available, Online cat, Ref serv available, Summer reading prog, Tax forms, Wheelchair accessible
Mem of Moultrie-Colquitt County Library
Open Mon, Tues & Thurs 2-6, Wed 9-1
Bookmobiles: 2. Librns, Sheila Houston & Kimberly Millan

J MOULTRIE TECHNICAL COLLEGE LIBRARY*, Veterans Parkway Campus, 800 Veterans Pkwy N, 31788. Tel: 229-217-4159. FAX: 229-891-7010. E-mail: library@southernregional.edu. Web Site: www.moultrietech.edu/library. *Dir, Libr Serv,* Udella Spicer; Tel: 229-891-7020, E-mail: uspicer@southernregional.edu
Founded 1964. Enrl 2,000; Fac 140; Highest Degree: Associate
Library Holdings: Bk Titles 3,842; Bk Vols 95
Automation Activity & Vendor Info: (Cataloging) TLC (The Library Corporation); (Circulation) TLC (The Library Corporation)

Wireless access
Open Mon-Thurs 8-7, Fri 8-4
Departmental Libraries:
TIFTON CAMPUS, 52 Tech Dr, Tifton, 31794. Tel: 229-391-2623. FAX: 229-391-3717. *Librn,* Priscilla Hunter; E-mail: phunter@moultrietech.edu
Highest Degree: Associate
Library Holdings: Bk Vols 1,760
Open Mon & Wed 8-7:15, Tues 8-6:15, Thurs 2-5

MOUNT BERRY

C BERRY COLLEGE, Memorial Library, 2277 Martha Berry Hwy, 30149. SAN 339-1086. Tel: 706-236-1739. E-mail: library@berry.edu. Web Site: www.berry.edu/academics/library. *Dir,* Sherre L Harrington; Tel: 706-236-2285, E-mail: sharrington@berry.edu; *Assoc Dir,* Jeremy Worsham; Tel: 706-368-6707, E-mail: jworsham@berry.edu; *Digital Initiatives Librn,* Jessica Hornbuckle; Tel: 706-236-1705, E-mail: jhornbuckle@berry.edu; *Engagement Librn, Student Serv Librn,* Position Currently Open; *Evening Supvr,* Carolina Ritcher-Sanchez; Tel: 706-238-5887, E-mail: CRitcherSanchez@berry.edu; *Access Serv Coordr,* Morgan Stansell; Tel: 706-233-2938, E-mail: mstansell@berry.edu; *Acq, E-Res Coordr,* Position Currently Open; *Coll Spec, ILL Spec,* Cetoria Tomberlin; Tel: 706-368-6706, E-mail: ctomberlin@berry.edu; *Archivist,* Michael O'Malley; Tel: 706-238-5886, E-mail: momalley@berry.edu. Subject Specialists: *English, Math, Natural sci,* Sherre L Harrington; *Educ, Nursing, World lang,* Jeremy Worsham; *Fine arts, Hist, Philos,* Jessica Hornbuckle; Staff 10 (MLS 5, Non-MLS 5)
Founded 1926. Enrl 1,995; Fac 167; Highest Degree: Master
Special Collections: Institutional Historical Documents (Berry College Archives). Oral History; US Document Depository
Automation Activity & Vendor Info: (Acquisitions) OCLC Worldshare Management Services; (Cataloging) OCLC Worldshare Management Services; (Circulation) OCLC Worldshare Management Services; (Course Reserve) OCLC Worldshare Management Services; (Discovery) OCLC Worldshare Management Services; (ILL) OCLC Tipasa; (OPAC) OCLC; (Serials) OCLC Worldshare Management Services
Wireless access
Partic in Georgia Library Learning Online; Georgia Private Acad Librs Consortium; LYRASIS

MOUNT VERNON

C BREWTON-PARKER COLLEGE*, Fountain-New Library, 201 David-Eliza Fountain Circle, 30445. (Mail add: PO Box 197, 30445), SAN 303-4003. Tel: 912-583-3235. Interlibrary Loan Service Tel: 912-583-3232. Reference Tel: 912-583-3234. Administration Tel: 912-583-3230. Toll Free Tel: 800-342-1087. FAX: 912-583-3454. Web Site: www.bpc.edu/academics/library. *Dir, Libr Serv,* Ms Tanvi Chauhan; E-mail: tchauhan@bpc.edu; Staff 2 (MLS 2)
Founded 1988. Enrl 1,036; Fac 61; Highest Degree: Bachelor
Library Holdings: AV Mats 8,400; Bk Titles 71,000; Bk Vols 81,000; Per Subs 410
Special Collections: Brewton-Parker College Historical Coll
Subject Interests: Christianity, Educ, Music
Automation Activity & Vendor Info: (Acquisitions) SirsiDynix; (Cataloging) SirsiDynix; (Circulation) SirsiDynix; (OPAC) SirsiDynix
Wireless access
Publications: Handbook
Open Mon-Thurs 8am-11pm, Fri 8-5, Sun 2-11

S GEORGIA DEPARTMENT OF CORRECTIONS, OFFICE OF LIBRARY SERVICES*, Montgomery State Prison, 650 Alston Rd, 30445. (Mail add: PO Box 256, 30445-0256). Tel: 912-583-3600. FAX: 912-583-3667, 912-583-4240. Web Site: www.dcor.state.ga.us. *Librn,* Autumn Turner; E-mail: autumn.turner@gdc.ga.gov
Library Holdings: Bk Vols 3,400; Per Subs 21; Videos 30

NAHUNTA

P BRANTLEY COUNTY LIBRARY*, 14046 Cleveland St E, 31553-9470. (Mail add: PO Box 1090, 31553-1090), SAN 338-4837. Tel: 912-462-5454. FAX: 912-462-5329. Web Site: threeriverslibraries.org/woodpress-dev/library-locations/brantley-county-public-library. *Libr Mgr,* Kathy Moody; E-mail: kmoody@trrl.org
Founded 1980
Subject Interests: Local hist
Mem of Three Rivers Regional Library System
Open Mon-Fri 8:30-5
Friends of the Library Group

NEWBORN

NEWTON COUNTY LIBRARY SYSTEM*, Jeanette Adams Ziegler Library, 4224 Hwy 142, 30056. Tel: 770-787-1126.

NEWNAN

P COWETA PUBLIC LIBRARY SYSTEM*, Central Library, 85 Literary Lane, 30265. Tel: 770-683-2052. FAX: 770-683-0065. Web Site: www.cowetapubliclibrary.org. *Dir of Libr,* Jimmy Bass; E-mail: jebass@coweta.ga.us; *Libr Assoc/Ch,* Kristin Rubenstein; E-mail: krubenstein@coweta.ga.us; *Libr Assoc/Tech Serv,* Miriam Veale; E-mail: mveale@coweta.ga.us; *Libr Assoc/Teen Serv,* Shamika Pearson; E-mail: spearson@coweta.ga.us
Library Holdings: Audiobooks 1,281; CDs 589; DVDs 1,871; Bk Vols 65,325; Per Subs 133
Automation Activity & Vendor Info: (Cataloging) SirsiDynix; (Circulation) SirsiDynix; (OPAC) SirsiDynix
Wireless access
Open Mon, Wed & Fri 9-6, Tues & Thurs 9-8, Sat 10-5
Friends of the Library Group
Branches: 3
GRANTVILLE PUBLIC LIBRARY, 100 Park Dr, Grantville, 30220, SAN 373-8752. Tel: 770-683-0535. *Br Mgr,* Marie Vielot; E-mail: mvielot@coweta.ga.us
Founded 1992. Pop 5,000; Circ 1,316
Library Holdings: AV Mats 158; Bk Titles 6,915
Function: ILL available, Internet access, Summer reading prog
Open Mon-Wed 10-6, Thurs 11-7, Fri 2-6, Sat 10-2
A MITCHELL POWELL JR PUBLIC LIBRARY, 25 Hospital Rd, 30263, SAN 338-8921. Tel: 770-253-3625. FAX: 770-254-7262. *Br Mgr,* Aime Oswald; E-mail: aoswald@newnan-coweta.org; Staff 16 (MLS 4, Non-MLS 12)
Founded 1988. Pop 95,000; Circ 306,000
Library Holdings: AV Mats 2,700; Bk Titles 91,000; Per Subs 141; Talking Bks 1,300
Subject Interests: Law
Function: ILL available, Internet access, Photocopying/Printing, Prog for adults, Prog for children & young adult, Summer reading prog, Telephone ref, Wheelchair accessible
Special Services for the Deaf - TDD equip
Open Mon, Wed & Fri 10-4, Tues & Thurs 1-6, Sat 10-2
SENOIA AREA PUBLIC LIBRARY, 148 Plyant St, Senoia, 30276, SAN 338-8832. Tel: 770-599-3537. FAX: 770-599-3537. *Br Mgr,* Marie Vielot; E-mail: mvielot@coweta.ga.us; Staff 2 (Non-MLS 2)
Founded 1974. Pop 10,000; Circ 15,744
Library Holdings: AV Mats 218; Bk Titles 13,000; Talking Bks 329
Automation Activity & Vendor Info: (OPAC) TLC (The Library Corporation)
Function: ILL available, Internet access, Photocopying/Printing, Prog for children & young adult, Summer reading prog
Open Mon-Fri 10-6, Sat 10-5

NICHOLLS

S GEORGIA DEPARTMENT OF CORRECTIONS, OFFICE OF LIBRARY SERVICES*, Coffee Correctional Facility (Privatization Unit), 1153 N Liberty St, 31554. Tel: 912-345-5058, Ext 25473. FAX: 912-345-5086. Web Site: www.dcor.state.ga.us/GDC/FacilityMap/html/S_50000067.html. *Librn,* Paul Cason; E-mail: travis.cason@corecivic.com
Founded 1998
Library Holdings: Bk Vols 6,100; Per Subs 40
Special Collections: Law Coll
Automation Activity & Vendor Info: (Cataloging) LRMS, Inc (Library Resource Management Systems); (Circulation) LRMS, Inc (Library Resource Management Systems)
Restriction: Not open to pub

NORCROSS

C ALTIERUS CAREER COLLEGE*, Norcross Campus Library, 1750 Beaver Ruin Rd, Ste 500, 30093. Tel: 770-921-1085. FAX: 770-923-4533. *Coordr,* Kelly Gooden; E-mail: kgooden@altierus.edu
Wireless access

OAKWOOD

J LANIER TECHNICAL COLLEGE*, Oakwood Campus Library, 2990 Landrum Education Dr, 30566. Tel: 770-531-6969. FAX: 770-531-6328. Web Site: www.laniertech.edu/library. *Dir, Libr Serv,* Kathryn Thompson; Tel: 770-533-6968, E-mail: kthompson@laniertech.edu
Library Holdings: e-books 100,000; Bk Vols 8,000; Per Subs 50
Automation Activity & Vendor Info: (Cataloging) TLC (The Library Corporation); (Circulation) TLC (The Library Corporation); (OPAC) TLC (The Library Corporation)
Wireless access
Partic in Georgia Library Learning Online
Open Mon-Thurs 7:30am-9pm, Fri 8-Noon

C UNIVERSITY OF NORTH GEORGIA*, Gainesville Campus Library, 3820 Mundy Mill Rd, 30566. (Mail add: PO Box 1358, Gainesville, 30503), SAN 303-3597. Tel: 678-717-3653. Interlibrary Loan Service Tel: 678-717-3662. Administration Tel: 678-717-3466. FAX: 678-717-3657. E-mail: askus@ung.edu. Web Site: ung.edu/libraries. *Dean of Libr,* Deborah Prosser, PhD; E-mail: deborah.prosser@ung.edu; *Head Librn - Gainesville Campus,* Amanda Nash; Tel: 678-717-3825, E-mail: amanda.nash@ung.edu; Staff 28 (MLS 13, Non-MLS 15)
Founded 1873. Enrl 15,000; Fac 825; Highest Degree: Master
Library Holdings: Bk Vols 229,250; Per Subs 580
Special Collections: Curriculum Development; Leadership. US Document Depository
Subject Interests: Mil hist
Automation Activity & Vendor Info: (Acquisitions) Ex Libris Group; (Cataloging) Ex Libris Group; (Circulation) Ex Libris Group; (Course Reserve) Ex Libris Group; (ILL) OCLC ILLiad; (OPAC) Ex Libris Group; (Serials) Ex Libris Group
Wireless access
Partic in LYRASIS
Restriction: Open to pub for ref & circ; with some limitations
Departmental Libraries:
CUMMING CAMPUS LIBRARY, 300 Aquatic Circle, Cumming, 30040. Tel: 470-239-3120. *Head Librn,* Rose Rebecca; Tel: 470-239-3119, E-mail: rebecca.rose@ung.edu
DAHLONEGA CAMPUS LIBRARY, 117 Georgia Circle, Dahlonega, 30597. Tel: 706-864-1889. FAX: 706-864-1867. *Head Librn,* Jay Bolt; Tel: 706-864-1514, E-mail: jay.bolt@ung.edu
OCONEE CAMPUS LIBRARY, 1201 Bishop Farms Pkwy, Watkinsville, 30677. (Mail add: PO Box 1748, Watkinsville, 30677). Tel: 706-310-6238. FAX: 706-310-6237. *Head Librn,* Virginia Faher; Tel: 706-310-6305, E-mail: virginia.faher@ung.edu

OGLETHORPE

S GEORGIA DEPARTMENT OF CORRECTIONS, OFFICE OF LIBRARY SERVICES*, Macon State Prison, 2728 Hwy 49 S, 31068. (Mail add: PO Box 426, 31068-0426). Tel: 478-472-3486. Web Site: www.dcor.state.ga.us/Facilities/macon-state-prison. *Librn,* Barbara Brown; E-mail: barbara.brown@gdc.ga.gov
Library Holdings: Bk Vols 3,000; Per Subs 35; Talking Bks 15
Special Collections: Law Coll
Restriction: Not open to pub

PELHAM

S GEORGIA DEPARTMENT OF CORRECTIONS, OFFICE OF LIBRARY SERVICES*, Autry State Prison, 3178 Mt Zion Church Rd, 31779. Tel: 229-294-2940. Web Site: www.dcor.state.ga.us/Facilities/autry-state-prison. *Librn,* James Blocker; E-mail: james.blocker@gdc.ga.gov
Library Holdings: Bk Vols 1,700; Per Subs 30
Special Collections: Law Coll
Restriction: Not open to pub

PEMBROKE

P PEMBROKE PUBLIC LIBRARY*, 1018 Camelia Dr, 31321. (Mail add: PO Box 7, 31321-0007), SAN 339-2317. Tel: 912-653-2822. FAX: 912-653-2802. Web Site: pembrokelibrary.info. *Libr Mgr,* Nancy Nubern; E-mail: nancyn@strl.info; Staff 4 (Non-MLS 4)
Pop 12,999; Circ 27,457
Library Holdings: Bk Vols 20,000; Per Subs 32
Wireless access
Mem of Statesboro Regional Public Libraries
Partic in SAILS Library Network
Open Mon-Fri 10-5:30, Sat 10-2
Friends of the Library Group

PERRY

P HOUSTON COUNTY PUBLIC LIBRARY SYSTEM*, 1201 Washington Ave, 31069. SAN 339-1140. Tel: 478-987-3050. FAX: 478-987-4572. Web Site: houpl.org. *Dir,* J Sara Paulk; E-mail: jspaulk@houpl.org; *Head, Info Tech,* Dixie Henning; *Br Mgr,* Judith Malone; *Bus Mgr,* Cynthia Spratling; *Cat, Tech Serv,* Janet Sayre; Staff 4 (MLS 4)
Founded 1974. Pop 165,000; Circ 425,000
Library Holdings: Bk Vols 200,000; Per Subs 125
Automation Activity & Vendor Info: (Cataloging) Evergreen; (Circulation) Evergreen; (ILL) OCLC
Function: 24/7 Electronic res, 24/7 Online cat, Adult bk club, Audiobks via web, AV serv, Bks on CD, Children's prog, Computers for patron use, Electronic databases & coll, Free DVD rentals, Holiday prog, ILL available, Internet access, Large print keyboards, Magazines, Magnifiers for reading, Mail & tel request accepted, Mango lang, Meeting rooms, Microfiche/film & reading machines, Museum passes, Online cat, Outreach serv, OverDrive digital audio bks, Photocopying/Printing, Preschool outreach, Prog for adults, Prog for children & young adult, Ref serv available, Scanner, Spanish lang bks, Spoken cassettes & CDs, Story hour, Study rm, Summer reading prog, Teen prog, Wheelchair accessible, Winter reading prog
Partic in Public Information Network for Electronic Services
Friends of the Library Group
Branches: 3
NOLA BRANTLEY MEMORIAL LIBRARY, 721 Watson Blvd, Warner Robins, 31093, SAN 339-123X. Tel: 478-923-0128. FAX: 478-929-8611. E-mail: wrlibrary@houpl.org. *Br Mgr,* Mark Bohnstedt; Staff 1 (MLS 1)
Founded 1948
Library Holdings: Bk Titles 90,000; Per Subs 400
Automation Activity & Vendor Info: (Cataloging) Evergreen; (Circulation) Evergreen; (OPAC) Evergreen
Friends of the Library Group
CENTERVILLE BRANCH, 206 Gunn Rd, Centerville, 31028, SAN 339-1175. Tel: 478-953-4500. FAX: 478-953-7850. *Br Mgr,* Nancy Granger; E-mail: ngranger@houpl.org
Friends of the Library Group
PERRY BRANCH, 1201 Washington Ave, 31069, SAN 339-1205. Tel: 478-987-3050. FAX: 478-987-4572. *Head Librn,* Nancy Granger
Friends of the Library Group

R PERRY UNITED METHODIST CHURCH LIBRARY*, 1002 Carroll St, 31069. (Mail add: PO Box 73, 31069-0073), SAN 303. Tel: 478-987-1852. FAX: 478-988-1428. Web Site: www.perryumc.org/welcome.
Founded 1967
Library Holdings: Bk Vols 4,500
Subject Interests: Hist
Restriction: Mem only

QUITMAN

P BROOKS COUNTY PUBLIC LIBRARY, 404 Barwick Rd, 31643. SAN 303-4062. Tel: 229-263-4412. FAX: 229-263-8002. Web Site: www.brooks.public.lib.ga.us. *Dir,* Scott Routsong; E-mail: sroutsong@mail.brooks.public.lib.ga.us
Pop 16,450; Circ 50,000
Library Holdings: Bk Vols 60,000; Per Subs 45
Subject Interests: African-Am, Genealogy
Automation Activity & Vendor Info: (Cataloging) Evergreen; (Circulation) Evergreen
Wireless access
Publications: Library Edition (Friends)
Partic in Public Information Network for Electronic Services
Open Mon-Thurs 9-6, Fri & Sat 9-3
Friends of the Library Group

REIDSVILLE

GEORGIA DEPARTMENT OF CORRECTIONS, OFFICE OF LIBRARY SERVICES
S GEORGIA STATE PRISON*, 300 First Ave S, 30453. Tel: 912-557-7301. FAX: 912-557-7241. Web Site: www.dcor.state.ga.us. *Librn,* Hortense Moody
Library Holdings: Bk Vols 1,500; Per Subs 15
Special Collections: Law Coll
Open Mon-Fri 8:30-10:30 & 1-3
S ROGERS STATE PRISON*, 1978 Georgia Hwy 147, 30453. Tel: 912-557-7771. FAX: 912-557-7051. Web Site: www.dcor.state.ga.us. *Librn,* Andre L Bateman; Tel: 912-557-7019, E-mail: dreb8man@yahoo.com
Library Holdings: Bk Vols 14,000; Per Subs 30
Special Collections: Law Coll
Open Mon-Thurs 8:30-10, 1-3 & 5-7

RICHMOND HILL

P RICHMOND HILL-BRYAN COUNTY LIBRARY, 9607 Ford Ave, 31324. (Mail add: PO Box 939, 31324-0939), SAN 339-2341. Tel: 912-756-3580. FAX: 912-756-2976. Web Site: strl.info/richmond-hill-public-library. *Libr Mgr,* Samantha Moose; E-mail: samantham@strl.info; Staff 6 (Non-MLS 6)
Pop 15,000; Circ 97,000
Library Holdings: Bk Vols 21,838; Per Subs 25
Automation Activity & Vendor Info: (ILL) OCLC
Wireless access
Function: Computers for patron use
Mem of Statesboro Regional Public Libraries
Partic in Public Information Network for Electronic Services
Open Mon-Fri 10-5:30, Sat 10-3
Friends of the Library Group

RINGGOLD

P CATOOSA COUNTY LIBRARY*, 108 Catoosa Circle, 30736. SAN 338-6198. Tel: 706-965-3600. FAX: 706-965-3608. E-mail: info@catoosacountylibrary.org. Web Site: www.catoosacountylibrary.org. *Dir,* Richard Groves; E-mail: rpg@catoosacountylibrary.org
Wireless access
Function: Children's prog, Teen prog
Partic in Public Information Network for Electronic Services
Open Mon & Wed 10-6, Tues & Thurs 10-7, Fri 10-5, Sat 10-3
Friends of the Library Group

ROME

J GEORGIA HIGHLANDS COLLEGE LIBRARIES*, 3175 Cedartown Hwy SE, 30161. SAN 303-4089. Tel: 706-295-6318. FAX: 706-295-6365. Web Site: www.highlands.edu/library. *Dean of Libr,* Julius Fleschner; E-mail: jfleschn@highlands.edu; *Asst Dir,* Susan Vines; *Libr Assoc,* Jennifer Jacobs; *Libr Assoc,* Sumer Lang; *Libr Asst,* Melissa Jones; *Acq,* Susanna Smith; *Pub Serv,* Karin Bennedsen; *Pub Serv,* Carmel Brunson; *Pub Serv,* Betsy Clark; *Pub Serv,* Christin Collins; *Pub Serv,* Laura Gargis; *Pub Serv,* Marla Means; *Pub Serv,* Maggie Murphy; *Tech Serv,* Jeannie Blakely; Staff 16 (MLS 11, Non-MLS 5)
Founded 1970. Fac 11; Highest Degree: Bachelor
Library Holdings: e-books 110,000; Bk Vols 70,000; Per Subs 100
Automation Activity & Vendor Info: (Acquisitions) Ex Libris Group; (Cataloging) Ex Libris Group; (Circulation) Ex Libris Group; (Course Reserve) Ex Libris Group; (ILL) OCLC; (OPAC) Ex Libris Group; (Serials) Ex Libris Group
Partic in Galileo/GIL; Georgia Library Learning Online
Open Mon-Thurs 8-9, Fri 8-2

J GEORGIA NORTHWESTERN TECHNICAL COLLEGE*, Floyd County Campus Library, Bldg H, Rm 156 & 148, One Maurice Culberson Dr, 30161. Tel: 706-295-6845. Interlibrary Loan Service Tel: 678-757-2043. Administration Tel: 706-295-6511. FAX: 706-295-6843. Interlibrary Loan Service FAX: 678-757-1673. Web Site: gntc.libguides.com/library. *Dir, Libr Serv,* John Lassiter; E-mail: jlassiter@gntc.edu; *Evening Librn,* John Rivest; *Coordr, Cat,* Stephen Meeks; Tel: 706-295-6263, E-mail: smeeks@gntc.edu; Staff 3.5 (MLS 2.5, Non-MLS 1)
Founded 1962. Enrl 6,000; Highest Degree: Associate
Library Holdings: Audiobooks 150; CDs 20; DVDs 2,000; e-books 22,300; Bk Titles 10,000; Bk Vols 12,000; Per Subs 75; Videos 100
Automation Activity & Vendor Info: (Cataloging) Surpass; (Circulation) Surpass; (Course Reserve) Surpass; (ILL) OCLC; (OPAC) Surpass; (Serials) Surpass
Wireless access
Function: Audio & video playback equip for onsite use, AV serv, Bks on CD, CD-ROM, Computers for patron use, Electronic databases & coll, Free DVD rentals, ILL available, Large print keyboards, Music CDs, Online cat, Orientations, Photocopying/Printing, Ref serv available, Scanner, Wheelchair accessible
Partic in Georgia Interactive Network for Medical Information; Georgia Library Learning Online; LYRASIS
Special Services for the Deaf - Bks on deafness & sign lang; Closed caption videos; Sorenson video relay syst
Special Services for the Blind - Accessible computers; Bks on CD; Copier with enlargement capabilities; Internet workstation with adaptive software; Networked computers with assistive software; Reader equip; Screen enlargement software for people with visual disabilities; Screen reader software
Open Mon-Thurs 8:30am-9pm, Fri 7:30-Noon

Departmental Libraries:

GORDON COUNTY CAMPUS LIBRARY, Bldg 400, 1151 Hwy 53 Spur, Calhoun, 30701. Tel: 706-378-1718. FAX: 706-624-1107. *Coordr,* Bonnie Moore; E-mail: bmoore@gntc.edu; Staff 1.2 (MLS 0.2, Non-MLS 1)
Founded 2003. Enrl 800; Fac 1; Highest Degree: Associate
Library Holdings: AV Mats 1,200; e-books 22,300; Bk Vols 3,300; Per Subs 54
Automation Activity & Vendor Info: (Cataloging) Surpass; (Circulation) Surpass; (Course Reserve) Surpass; (ILL) OCLC; (OPAC) Surpass; (Serials) Surpass
Function: Adult bk club, Audio & video playback equip for onsite use, AV serv, Bks on cassette, Bks on CD, CD-ROM, Computers for patron use, Distance learning, Electronic databases & coll, Free DVD rentals, ILL available, Internet access, Music CDs, Online cat, Orientations, Outside serv via phone, mail, e-mail & web, Photocopying/Printing, Ref & res, Ref serv available, Scanner, VHS videos, Wheelchair accessible
Partic in Georgia Library Learning Online
Special Services for the Deaf - Sorenson video relay syst
Open Mon-Thurs 8-4
Restriction: Borrowing privileges limited to fac & registered students, Limited access for the pub

POLK COUNTY CAMPUS LIBRARY, Rm D103, 466 Brock Rd, Rockmart, 30153. Tel: 706-378-1781. FAX: 678-757-1673. *Coordr,* Bonnie Moore; *Libr Asst,* Nancy Coley
Founded 2004. Enrl 200; Highest Degree: Associate
Library Holdings: AV Mats 1,000; e-books 22,300; Bk Vols 3,500; Per Subs 45
Automation Activity & Vendor Info: (Cataloging) Surpass; (Circulation) Surpass; (ILL) OCLC; (OPAC) Surpass; (Serials) Surpass
Function: CD-ROM, Computers for patron use, Distance learning, E-Reserves, Electronic databases & coll, ILL available, Music CDs, Orientations, Photocopying/Printing, Ref & res, Wheelchair accessible
Partic in Georgia Library Learning Online
Special Services for the Deaf - Assistive tech; Closed caption videos; Sorenson video relay syst
Special Services for the Blind - Accessible computers
Open Mon, Tues & Thurs 8-4, Wed 8:30-4
Restriction: Open to students, fac, staff & alumni, Use of others with permission of librn

WALKER COUNTY CAMPUS LIBRARY, Bldg 500, 265 Bicentennial Trail, Rock Spring, 30739. Tel: 706-764-3533. FAX: 706-764-3567. *Coordr,* Pete Bursi; Tel: 706-764-3568, E-mail: pbursi@gntc.edu; Staff 3 (MLS 2, Non-MLS 1)
Founded 1966. Enrl 2,300; Highest Degree: Associate
Library Holdings: CDs 37; e-books 15,000; Bk Vols 13,000; Per Subs 140; Videos 250
Automation Activity & Vendor Info: (Cataloging) Surpass; (Circulation) Surpass; (OPAC) Surpass
Partic in Georgia Library Learning Online
Open Mon-Thurs 7:30am-9pm, Fri 9-3

P SARA HIGHTOWER REGIONAL LIBRARY*, Rome-Floyd County Library, 205 Riverside Pkwy NE, 30161-2922. SAN 339-1264. Tel: 706-236-4600, 706-236-4601. Interlibrary Loan Service Tel: 706-236-4603. Reference Tel: 706-236-4604. FAX: 706-236-4605. Web Site: rome.shrls.org. *Dir,* Delana Sissel; Tel: 706-236-4609, E-mail: dsissel@shrls.org; Staff 68 (MLS 4, Non-MLS 64)
Founded 1911. Pop 121,327; Circ 760,000
Library Holdings: Per Subs 184
Special Collections: Audio-Visual Materials; Cherokee Indians; Genealogy & Local History; Marshall Forest Coll; Video Studio Coll
Wireless access
Partic in GOLD Resource Sharing Network for Georgia's Libraries; Public Information Network for Electronic Services
Special Services for the Deaf - Adult & family literacy prog; Assistive tech; Bks on deafness & sign lang; Closed caption videos; TDD equip
Special Services for the Blind - Duplicating spec requests; Home delivery serv; Large print bks; Magnifiers; Newsp on cassette; Reader equip
Open Mon-Thurs 8:30-8:30, Sat 10-5
Friends of the Library Group

Branches: 3

CAVE SPRING BRANCH, 17 Cedartown St SW, Cave Spring, 30124-2702. (Mail add: PO Box 329, Cave Spring, 30124-0329), SAN 339-1418. Tel: 706-777-3346. FAX: 706-777-0947. Web Site: cavespring.shrls.org. *Br Mgr,* Diana Mills; E-mail: dmills@shrls.org; Staff 5 (MLS 1, Non-MLS 4)
Pop 2,153
Special Collections: Municipal Document Depository
Automation Activity & Vendor Info: (Acquisitions) Evergreen; (Cataloging) Evergreen; (Circulation) Evergreen; (OPAC) Evergreen
Function: 24/7 Electronic res, Children's prog, Computer training, Computers for patron use, Digital talking bks, Doc delivery serv, Electronic databases & coll, Home delivery & serv to seniorr ctr & nursing homes, Online cat, Photocopying/Printing
Special Services for the Deaf - Bks on deafness & sign lang; Closed caption videos; Sign lang interpreter upon request for prog; Staff with knowledge of sign lang
Open Mon-Fri 12-6
Restriction: Non-resident fee

CEDARTOWN BRANCH, 245 East Ave, City Complex, Cedartown, 30125-3001, SAN 339-1442. Tel: 770-748-5644. FAX: 770-748-4399. Web Site: cedartown.shrls.org. *Br Mgr,* Allison Robinson; E-mail: arobinson@shrls.org; Staff 2 (MLS 1, Non-MLS 1)
Founded 1921
Function: Bks on CD, Children's prog, Computers for patron use, E-Reserves, Free DVD rentals, ILL available, Magnifiers for reading, Mail & tel request accepted, Microfiche/film & reading machines, Music CDs, Online cat, OverDrive digital audio bks, Photocopying/Printing, Prog for children & young adult, Scanner, Spanish lang bks, Story hour, Summer reading prog, Tax forms
Open Mon-Thurs 9-6, Fri 9-5, Sat 9-4

ROCKMART BRANCH, Bldg 201, 316 N Piedmont Ave, Rockmart, 30153-2402, SAN 339-1477. Tel: 770-684-3022. FAX: 770-684-7876. Web Site: rockmart.shrls.org. *Br Mgr,* Sharon Cleveland; E-mail: scleveland@shrls.org; Staff 3 (Non-MLS 3)
Library Holdings: Bk Vols 46,430; Per Subs 32

Open Mon-Thurs 9-6, Fri 9-5, Sat 9-4
Friends of the Library Group

C SHORTER UNIVERSITY, Livingston Library, 315 Shorter Ave NW, 30165. SAN 303-4127. Tel: 706-233-7296, 770-748-0231, Ext 7296. Interlibrary Loan Service Tel: 706-233-7299. Toll Free Tel: 800-868-6980. FAX: 706-233-7999. Web Site: shorter.edu/libraries. *Libr Dir,* John Shaffett; Tel: 706-233-7357, E-mail: jshaffett@shorter.edu; *Pub Serv Librn,* Dorothy Smith; E-mail: djsmith@shorter.edu; *Online Serv, Ref, Resources Librn,* Mary Wilson; Tel: 706-233-7822, E-mail: mwilson@shorter.edu; Staff 4 (MLS 3, Non-MLS 1)
Founded 1873. Enrl 1,700; Fac 62; Highest Degree: Master
Library Holdings: Bk Vols 139,488; Per Subs 832
Special Collections: Baptist Convention & Association Minutes; Georgia Baptist History
Subject Interests: Music, Relig
Automation Activity & Vendor Info: (Cataloging) TLC (The Library Corporation); (Circulation) TLC (The Library Corporation); (OPAC) TLC (The Library Corporation)
Wireless access
Publications: Livingston Library Handbook
Partic in Georgia Library Learning Online; Georgia Private Acad Librs Consortium; LYRASIS; OCLC Online Computer Library Center, Inc
Open Mon-Thurs 8am-11pm, Fri 8:30-3, Sun 6pm-11pm

SAINT MARYS

P ST MARY'S LIBRARY*, 100 Herb Bauer Dr, 31558-3300. SAN 338-4934. Tel: 912-882-4800. FAX: 912-882-2453. Web Site: threeriverslibraries.org/woodpress-dev/library-locations/st-marys-public-library. *Libr Mgr,* Judy Britt; E-mail: jbritt@trrl.org
Mem of Three Rivers Regional Library System
Open Mon-Thurs 10-8, Fri 10-5, Sat 10-1

SAINT SIMONS ISLAND

G FORT FREDERICA NATIONAL MONUMENT LIBRARY, 6515 Frederica Rd, 31522. SAN 373-4285. Tel: 912-638-3639, Ext 114. FAX: 912-638-3639. Web Site: www.nps.gov/fofr. *Cultural Res Spec,* Denise Spear; E-mail: denise_spear@nps.gov
Library Holdings: Bk Vols 300
Restriction: Open by appt only

P SAINT SIMONS ISLAND PUBLIC LIBRARY, 530A Beachview Dr, 31522. SAN 303-4143. Tel: 912-279-3750. FAX: 912-638-8254. Web Site: moglibraries.org/st-simons-public-library. *Dir,* Geri Lynn Mullis; E-mail: gmullis@glynncounty-ga.gov
Founded 1937. Pop 14,000; Circ 26,000
Library Holdings: Bk Vols 47,000; Per Subs 30
Wireless access
Mem of Marshes of Glynn Libraries
Partic in Public Information Network for Electronic Services
Open Mon, Tues, Thurs & Fri 9:30-5, Wed 9:30-7, Sat 9:30-1
Friends of the Library Group

SR UNITED METHODIST CHURCH - SOUTH GEORGIA CONFERENCE, Arthur J Moore Methodist Museum & Library, Epworth-by-the-Sea, 100 Arthur Moore Dr, 31522. (Mail add: PO Box 24081, 31522-7081), SAN 373-0433. Tel: 912-638-4050. FAX: 912-638-9050. Web Site: www.sgaumc.org/mooremuseum. *Dir,* Anne Packard; E-mail: director@mooremuseum.org; *Asst Dir,* Cindy Angelich; E-mail: assistantdirector@mooremuseum.org
Library Holdings: Bk Vols 6,000
Wireless access
Open Mon-Sat 10-4
Friends of the Library Group

SANDERSVILLE

S THIELE KAOLIN CO*, Research & Development Library, 520 Kaolin Rd, 31082. (Mail add: PO Box 1056, 31082), SAN 303-4151. Tel: 478-552-3951. FAX: 478-552-4138. *Library Contact,* Elizabeth Archer; E-mail: elizabeth.archer@thielekaolin.com
Founded 1965
Library Holdings: Bk Vols 1,500; Per Subs 44
Open Mon-Fri 8-5

SAPELO ISLAND

P HOG HAMMOCK PUBLIC LIBRARY*, 1023 Hillery Ln, 31327. (Mail add: PO Box 69, 31327-0006). Tel: 912-485-2291. Web Site: threeriverslibraries.org/woodpress-dev/library-locations/hog-hammock-public-library. *Libr Mgr,* Shun Gaskins; E-mail: sgaskins@trrl.org
Library Holdings: Bk Vols 1,000
Mem of Three Rivers Regional Library System
Open Tues & Thurs 9-4, Sat 9:30-Noon

C UNIVERSITY OF GEORGIA*, Marine Institute Library, One Turkey Fountain Way, 31327. (Mail add: PO Box 32, 31327), SAN 325-0210. Tel: 912-485-2106. FAX: 912-485-2133. E-mail: ugami@uga.edu. *Dir,* Merryl Alber; *Libr Asst,* Maryam Payne; E-mail: ugami@uga.edu
Founded 1953
Library Holdings: Bk Vols 5,000; Per Subs 65
Subject Interests: Local hist
Wireless access
Publications: Collected Reprint Series

SAVANNAH

S GEORGIA HISTORICAL SOCIETY*, Research Center, 501 Whitaker St, 31401. (Mail add: 104 W Gaston St, 31401), SAN 303-4186. Tel: 912-651-2128. Administration Tel: 912-651-2125. FAX: 912-651-2831. E-mail: library@georgiahistory.com. Web Site: www.georgiahistory.com.
Founded 1839
Library Holdings: Bk Vols 20,000; Per Subs 50
Subject Interests: Ga hist, Genealogy, Southern hist
Automation Activity & Vendor Info: (Cataloging) EOS International; (OPAC) EOS International
Wireless access
Publications: Georgia Historical Quarterly (Journal); Georgia History Today (Newsletter); Headlines (Online only)
Partic in OCLC Online Computer Library Center, Inc
Open Wed, Thurs & Fri 12-5
Restriction: Non-circulating to the pub

C GEORGIA SOUTHERN UNIVERSITY*, Lane Library, 11935 Abercorn St, 31419. SAN 303-416X. Tel: 912-344-3027. Reference Tel: 912-344-3026. FAX: 912-344-3457. Web Site: library.georgiasouthern.edu. *Dean,* Dr Lisandra Carmichael; Tel: 912-478-5116, E-mail: lcarmichael@georgiasouthern.edu; *Assoc Dean,* Doug Frazier; Tel: 912-344-2818, E-mail: drfrazier@georgiasouthern.edu; *Head, Circ/ILL,* Ann Fuller; Tel: 912-344-3006, E-mail: aofuller@georgiasouthern.edu; *Head, Learning Commons,* Position Currently Open; *Head, Ref & Instruction,* Ms Vivian Bynoe; Tel: 912-344-3028, E-mail: vbynoe@georgiasouthern.edu; Staff 20 (MLS 11, Non-MLS 9)
Founded 1935. Enrl 5,200; Fac 228; Highest Degree: Doctorate
Special Collections: Educational Resources Information Center Coll, fiche; First Editions of Conrad Aiken & other Savannah authors; Library of American Civilization, fiche; Library of English Literature, fiche; Savannah Authors; Savannah History
Subject Interests: Ga
Automation Activity & Vendor Info: (Acquisitions) Ex Libris Group; (Cataloging) Ex Libris Group; (Circulation) Ex Libris Group; (Discovery) EBSCO Discovery Service; (ILL) OCLC ILLiad; (OPAC) Ex Libris Group; (Serials) Ex Libris Group
Wireless access
Publications: Library Guides
Partic in Galileo/GIL; LYRASIS

S GIRL SCOUTS OF THE USA*, Juliette Gordon Low Birthplace Library, Ten E Oglethorpe Ave, 31401. SAN 377-3965. Tel: 912-233-4501. E-mail: birthplace@girlscouts.org. Web Site: www.juliettegordonlowbirthplace.org. *Exec Dir,* Shannon Browning-Mullis; E-mail: sbrowning-mullis@girlscouts.org
Library Holdings: Bk Vols 550
Special Collections: Gordon Family Archives, letters, papers, photog & scrapbks
Restriction: Open by appt only

P LIVE OAK PUBLIC LIBRARIES*, 2002 Bull St, 31401. SAN 339-1655. Tel: 912-652-3600. Circulation Tel: 912-652-3629. Reference Tel: 912-652-3627. FAX: 912-652-3638. Web Site: liveoakpl.org. *Exec Dir,* Tom Sloan; E-mail: sloant@liveoakpl.org; *Dir, Cent Libr Serv,* Beatrice Saba; E-mail: sabab@liveoakpl.org; Staff 176 (MLS 35, Non-MLS 141)
Founded 1903. Pop 339,150; Circ 1,088,837
Library Holdings: AV Mats 26,589; Large Print Bks 14,124; Bk Titles 161,726; Bk Vols 302,100; Per Subs 1,148; Talking Bks 18,404
Special Collections: Local History (Gamble Coll)
Subject Interests: Genealogy
Automation Activity & Vendor Info: (Acquisitions) SirsiDynix; (Cataloging) SirsiDynix; (Circulation) SirsiDynix; (OPAC) SirsiDynix
Wireless access
Partic in OCLC Online Computer Library Center, Inc; Public Information Network for Electronic Services
Special Services for the Deaf - TDD equip; Videos & decoder
Open Mon & Tues 10-7, Wed-Fri 10-6, Sat 10-4
Friends of the Library Group

Branches: 15
CARNEGIE BRANCH, 537 E Henry St, 31401, SAN 339-168X. Tel: 912-651-1973. FAX: 912-651-2001. Web Site: liveoakpl.org/locations/carnegie. *Libr Mgr,* Cassie Jones; E-mail: jonesc@liveoakpl.org; Staff 3 (MLS 1, Non-MLS 2)
Library Holdings: Bk Vols 2,098
Subject Interests: African-Am
Open Mon 10-7, Tues-Fri 10-6
FOREST CITY BRANCH, 1501 Stiles Ave, 31415, SAN 339-1701. Tel: 912-651-0942. FAX: 912-651-1958. Web Site: liveoakpl.org/locations/forestcity. *Branch Lead,* Tonya Johnson; E-mail: johnsonto@liveoakpl.org; Staff 3 (Non-MLS 3)
Library Holdings: Bk Vols 23,439
Open Mon & Tues 10-6, Wed 2-6, Thurs 2-7, Fri 10-2
GARDEN CITY BRANCH, 104 Sunshine Ave, Garden City, 31405. Tel: 912-644-5932. FAX: 912-644-5967. Web Site: liveoakpl.org/friendly.php?s=locations/gardencity. *Libr Mgr,* Kathryn Wade; E-mail: wadek@liveoakpl.org
Open Mon & Tues 10-7, Wed-Fri 10-6, Sat 10-4
HINESVILLE BRANCH, 236 W Memorial Dr, Hinesville, 31313, SAN 339-1833. Tel: 912-368-4003. FAX: 912-368-4422. Web Site: liveoakpl.org/locations/hinesville. *Sr Libr Mgr,* Jo Fortner; E-mail: fortnere@liveoakpl.org; Staff 15 (MLS 3, Non-MLS 12)
Library Holdings: Bk Vols 53,922
Open Mon-Thurs 9-8, Fri & Sat 9-6
ISLANDS BRANCH, 50 Johnny Mercer Blvd, 31410, SAN 339-1752. Tel: 912-897-4061. FAX: 912-897-2029. Web Site: liveoakpl.org/locations/islands. *Libr Mgr,* Mary Rogers; E-mail: rogersm@liveoakpl.org; Staff 7 (MLS 1, Non-MLS 6)
Library Holdings: Bk Vols 33,586
Open Mon & Tues 10-7, Wed-Fri 10-6, Sat 10-4
W W LAW BRANCH, 909 E Bolton St, 31401, SAN 339-1809. Tel: 912-644-5903. FAX: 912-644-5920. Web Site: liveoakpl.org/locations/wwlaw. *Branch Lead,* Sandra McKiver; E-mail: mckivers@liveoakpl.org; Staff 2 (Non-MLS 2)
Library Holdings: Bk Vols 4,632
Open Mon & Fri 2-6, Tues-Thurs 10-6
MIDWAY-RICEBORO BRANCH, 9397 E Oglethorpe Hwy, Midway, 31320, SAN 375-5479. Tel: 912-884-5742. FAX: 912-884-5741. Web Site: liveoakpl.org/locations/midway. *Libr Mgr,* Bonnie Boccio; E-mail: bocciob@liveoakpl.org; Staff 2 (Non-MLS 2)
Library Holdings: Bk Vols 10,000
Open Mon, Tues & Thurs-Sat 10-6, Wed 12-8
OGLETHORPE MALL BRANCH, Seven Mall Annex, 31406, SAN 339-1892. Tel: 912-921-2082. FAX: 912-921-2088. Web Site: liveoakpl.org/locations/oglethorpe. *Sr Libr Mgr,* Alissa Boyd; E-mail: boyda@liveoakpl.org; Staff 16 (MLS 4, Non-MLS 12)
Library Holdings: Bk Vols 81,298
Open Mon & Wed 10-7, Tues, Thurs & Fri 10-6, Sat 10-4
POOLER BRANCH, 216 S Rogers St, Pooler, 31322, SAN 339-1922. Tel: 912-748-6979. FAX: 912-330-8112. Web Site: liveoakpl.org/locations/pooler. *Libr Mgr,* Jennifer Taylor-Pack; E-mail: taylorpackj@liveoakpl.org; Staff 6 (MLS 1, Non-MLS 5)
Library Holdings: Bk Vols 32,167
Open Mon & Tues 10-7, Wed & Thurs 10-6, Fri & Sat 10-2
PORT CITY BRANCH, 3501 Houlihan Ave, 31408, SAN 339-1949. Tel: 912-965-0102. FAX: 912-965-0104. Web Site: liveoakpl.org/locations/portcity. *Libr Mgr,* Sheila Henderson-Moore; E-mail: hendersons@liveoakpl.org; Staff 4 (Non-MLS 4)
Library Holdings: Bk Vols 24,771
Open Mon, Wed & Fri 12-6, Tues & Thurs 10-6, Fri 12-6
RINCON BRANCH, 17th St & Hwy 21, Rincon, 31326. (Mail add: PO Box 1939, Rincon, 31326-1939), SAN 329-6059. Tel: 912-826-2222. FAX: 912-826-6304. Web Site: liveoakpl.org/locations/rincon. *Libr Mgr,* Catherine Driggers; E-mail: driggersc@liveoakpl.org; Staff 10 (MLS 2, Non-MLS 8)
Library Holdings: Bk Vols 42,448
Open Mon, Wed & Thurs 10-7, Tues, Fri & Sat 10-6
SOUTHWEST CHATHAM BRANCH, 14097 Abercorn St, 31419. Tel: 912-927-4079. Circulation Tel: 912-927-4079, Ext 303. Reference Tel: 912-927-4079, Ext 310. FAX: 912-927-4083. Web Site: liveoakpl.org/locations/southwest. *Sr Libr Mgr,* Maryann Brickey; E-mail: brickeym@liveoakpl.org
Open Mon & Tues 10-7, Wed-Fri 10-6, Sat 10-4
SPRINGFIELD BRANCH, 810 Hwy 119 S, Springfield, 31329. (Mail add: PO Box 189, Springfield, 31329), SAN 339-171X. Tel: 912-754-3003. FAX: 912-754-9494. Web Site: liveoakpl.org/locations/springfield. *Libr Mgr,* Melissa Nicolaus; E-mail: nicolausm@liveoakpl.org
Library Holdings: Bk Vols 35,315
Open Mon, Wed, Thurs & Sat 10-6, Tues 10-7
TYBEE ISLAND BRANCH, 403 Butler Ave, Tybee Island, 31328. (Mail add: PO Box 1619, Tybee Island, 31328), SAN 339-2015. Tel: 912-786-7733. FAX: 912-786-7734. Web Site: liveoakpl.org/locations/tybee. *Branch Lead,* Laurel Powers; E-mail: powersl@liveoakpl.org; Staff 2 (Non-MLS 2)
Library Holdings: Bk Vols 12,094
Open Mon & Fri 1-6, Tues & Wed 10-6, Thurs 2-6, Sat 10-2
WEST BROAD BRANCH, YMCA Bldg, 1110 May St, 31415. Tel: 912-201-9246. FAX: 912-201-9247. Web Site: liveoakpl.org/locations/westbroad. *Branch Lead,* Denitra Reynolds; E-mail: reynoldsde@liveoakpl.org
Open Mon & Fri 2-6, Tues-Thurs 10-6
Bookmobiles: 1

M MEMORIAL HEALTH UNIVERSITY MEDICAL CENTER*, Health Sciences Library, 1250 E 66 St, 31404. SAN 323-7370. Tel: 912-721-8230. E-mail: savmedlibrary@mercer.edu. *Assoc Dir, Library & Info Services,* Carolyn Klatt; E-mail: klatt_ca@mercer.edu; *Access Serv Mgr,* Vanessa Wallace Lonon; E-mail: lonon_vw@mercer.edu; Staff 2 (MLS 1, Non-MLS 1)
Library Holdings: Bk Titles 4,200; Per Subs 325
Wireless access
Open Mon-Fri 7:30-5
Restriction: Non-circulating

C SAVANNAH STATE UNIVERSITY, Asa H Gordon Library, 2200 Tompkins Rd, 31404. (Mail add: PO Box 20394, 31404-9705), SAN 303-4216. Tel: 912-358-4324. FAX: 912-358-3184. Web Site: www.savannahstate.edu/library. *Interim Univ Librn,* Louise Wyche; E-mail: wychel@savannahstate.edu; *Student Success Librn,* Patrick Morgan; E-mail: morganp@savannahstate.edu; Staff 3 (MLS 3)
Founded 1891. Enrl 2,900; Highest Degree: Master
Library Holdings: Bk Vols 189,000; Per Subs 566
Special Collections: Educational Resources Information Center
Subject Interests: African-Am (ethnic)
Automation Activity & Vendor Info: (Acquisitions) Ex Libris Group; (Cataloging) Ex Libris Group; (Circulation) Ex Libris Group; (Serials) EBSCO Online
Wireless access
Function: ILL available
Publications: Bibliographies; Library Handbook
Partic in LYRASIS
Open Mon-Fri 9-5; Mon-Fri 8-5 (Summer)

J SAVANNAH TECHNICAL COLLEGE*, Savannah Campus Library, 5717 White Bluff Rd, 31405-5521. Tel: 912-443-5700, 912-443-5870. E-mail: reference@savannahtech.edu. Web Site: www.savannahtech.edu/academics/library. *Dir, Libr & Info Serv,* James Burch; Tel: 912-443-5874, E-mail: jburch@savannahtech.edu; *Libr Asst,* Franck Kuraogo; Tel: 912-443-4780, E-mail: fkuraogo@savannahtech.edu; Staff 3 (MLS 2, Non-MLS 1)
Founded 1929. Enrl 3,708; Highest Degree: Associate
Library Holdings: e-books 58,000; e-journals 15,000; Bk Vols 33,000; Per Subs 150; Talking Bks 100; Videos 2,800
Automation Activity & Vendor Info: (Cataloging) TLC (The Library Corporation); (Circulation) TLC (The Library Corporation); (OPAC) TLC (The Library Corporation)
Wireless access
Partic in Georgia Library Learning Online
Open Mon-Thurs 8-7, Fri 8-Noon

S SKIDAWAY INSTITUTE OF OCEANOGRAPHY LIBRARY*, John F McGowan Library, Ten Ocean Science Circle, 31411-1011. SAN 303-4224. Tel: 912-598-2474. FAX: 912-598-2391. Web Site: www.skio.uga.edu/resources/john-mcgowan-library. *Librn,* Dee King; E-mail: dee.king@skio.uga.edu; Staff 1 (MLS 1)
Founded 1970
Library Holdings: Bk Vols 4,000; Per Subs 110
Subject Interests: Ecology, Geochemistry, Geol, Marine biol, Oceanography
Automation Activity & Vendor Info: (Acquisitions) Ex Libris Group; (Cataloging) Ex Libris Group; (Circulation) Ex Libris Group; (Course Reserve) Ex Libris Group; (ILL) Ex Libris Group; (Media Booking) Ex Libris Group; (OPAC) Ex Libris Group; (Serials) Ex Libris Group
Function: Photocopying/Printing
Publications: Serials Holdings List
Partic in NOAA Libraries Network
Open Mon-Fri 8-4:30

C SOUTH UNIVERSITY LIBRARY, 709 Mall Blvd, 31406. SAN 322-8800. Tel: 912-201-8047. Interlibrary Loan Service Tel: 912-201-8046. Web Site: inside.southuniversity.edu. *Libr Dir,* Valerie E Yaughn; Staff 1 (MLS 1)
Founded 1975. Enrl 1,200; Fac 95; Highest Degree: Doctorate
Library Holdings: AV Mats 300; DVDs 50; e-books 275,000; e-journals 100; Electronic Media & Resources 75; Bk Vols 50,000; Per Subs 30; Videos 250
Subject Interests: Allied health, Behav sci, Bus, Legal studies, Theol
Automation Activity & Vendor Info: (Acquisitions) Ex Libris Group; (Cataloging) Ex Libris Group; (Circulation) Ex Libris Group; (OPAC) Ex Libris Group; (Serials) Ex Libris Group

Wireless access
Function: AV serv, Computers for patron use, Distance learning, Electronic databases & coll, ILL available, Instruction & testing, Learning ctr, Online cat, Online ref, Orientations, Outside serv via phone, mail, e-mail & web, Photocopying/Printing, Ref & res, Ref serv available, Telephone ref, VHS videos, Wheelchair accessible
Partic in LYRASIS; National Network of Libraries of Medicine Region 2
Open Mon-Thurs 8am-10pm, Fri 8-5, Sat 9-5
Restriction: Authorized patrons, Borrowing privileges limited to fac & registered students, Open to pub by appt only, Open to students, fac & staff

S TELFAIR MUSEUM OF ART*, Anderson Library/Jepson Center for the Arts, 207 W York St, 31401. (Mail add: PO Box 10081, 31412), SAN 371-1196. Tel: 912-790-8802. FAX: 912-790-8803. Web Site: www.telfair.org. *Chief Curator,* Courtney McNeil; *Asst Curator,* Beth Moore; E-mail: mooreb@telfair.org; Staff 10 (Non-MLS 10)
Founded 1886
Library Holdings: Bk Titles 6,000; Per Subs 10
Subject Interests: 18th Century decorative arts, 19th Century Am lit, 20th Century art, 21st Century fine art, Decorative art
Wireless access
Restriction: Not a lending libr, Staff use only

SR ABE & ESTHER TENENBAUM LIBRARY*, c/o Congregation Augudath Achim, Nine Lee Blvd, 31405. SAN 329-7365. Tel: 912-352-4737. FAX: 912-352-3477. *Exec Dir,* Motti Locker; E-mail: mottilocker@aol.com; Staff 1 (Non-MLS 1)
Library Holdings: Bk Vols 2,000
Special Collections: Judaica, bks
Open Mon-Thurs 8:30-5, Fri 8:30-3

S US NATIONAL PARK SERVICE*, Fort Pulaski Monument Library, PO Box 30757, 31410-0757. SAN 370-2901. Tel: 912-786-8182. FAX: 912-786-6023. *Cultural Res Spec,* Laura Waller; E-mail: laura_waller@nps.gov
Library Holdings: Bk Vols 800; Per Subs 10
Subject Interests: Natural hist
Restriction: Open by appt only

SMYRNA

P SMYRNA PUBLIC LIBRARY*, 100 Village Green Circle, 30080-3478. SAN 303-4232. Tel: 770-431-2860. Reference E-mail: sreference@smyrnaga.gov. Web Site: www.smyrna-library.com. *Dir,* Mary Wallace Moore; E-mail: mwmoore@smyrnaga.gov; *ILL,* Kate Reinecke; E-mail: rkreinecke@smyrnaga.gov; *Tech Serv,* Ruth Hayden; E-mail: rhayden@smyrnaga.gov; *Youth Serv,* Rebecca Power; E-mail: rpower@smyrnaga.gov; Staff 11 (MLS 4, Non-MLS 7)
Founded 1936. Pop 51,271; Circ 310,300
Jul 2018-Jun 2019 Income $780,842
Special Collections: Archives Coll, docs, ephemera, photos; Genealogy Coll (Southern focus with particular emphasis on Virginia resources.); Smyrna Coll (Circulating and reference books on local, state and regional history.)
Automation Activity & Vendor Info: (Acquisitions) Baker & Taylor; (Cataloging) TLC (The Library Corporation); (Circulation) TLC (The Library Corporation); (OPAC) TLC (The Library Corporation); (Serials) TLC (The Library Corporation)
Wireless access
Function: 24/7 Electronic res, 24/7 Online cat, Adult bk club, Archival coll, Art exhibits, Audiobks via web, AV serv, Bk club(s), Bks on CD, Children's prog, Computers for patron use, Digital talking bks, Distance learning, Electronic databases & coll, Free DVD rentals, Holiday prog, ILL available, Internet access, Large print keyboards, Life-long learning prog for all ages, Magazines, Mango lang, Meeting rooms, Microfiche/film & reading machines, Movies, Museum passes, Music CDs, Online cat, Orientations, Photocopying/Printing, Preschool outreach, Preschool reading prog, Printer for laptops & handheld devices, Prog for adults, Prog for children & young adult, Ref & res, Ref serv available, Senior computer classes, Spanish lang bks, Spoken cassettes & CDs, Spoken cassettes & DVDs, STEM programs, Story hour, Study rm, Summer & winter reading prog, Summer reading prog, Tax forms, Teen prog, Telephone ref, Visual arts prog, Wheelchair accessible, Workshops, Writing prog
Partic in GALILEO
Special Services for the Deaf - Closed caption videos
Special Services for the Blind - Bks on CD; Digital talking bk; Large print bks
Open Mon-Thurs 10-8, Fri 10-6, Sat 10-5, Sun 1-6
Restriction: Non-resident fee
Friends of the Library Group

SPARKS

J WIREGRASS GEORGIA TECHNICAL COLLEGE LIBRARY*, Cook County Workforce Development Resource Center, 1676 Elm St, Rm 204, 31647. (Mail add: 4089 Val Tech Rd, Valdosta, 31602). Tel: 229-549-7368, Ext 7941. Circulation Tel: 229-259-5177. Administration Tel: 229-259-5178. FAX: 229-549-6286. Circulation FAX: 229-259-5179. E-mail: library@wiregrass.edu. Web Site: wiregrass.edu/library. *Dir, Libr Serv,* Kathryn Tomlinson; Staff 1 (MLS 1)
Founded 2005. Enrl 102; Fac 10; Highest Degree: Associate
Library Holdings: CDs 35; DVDs 76; Electronic Media & Resources 100; Bk Vols 731; Per Subs 3; Videos 28
Automation Activity & Vendor Info: (Acquisitions) TLC (The Library Corporation); (Cataloging) TLC (The Library Corporation); (Circulation) TLC (The Library Corporation); (ILL) OCLC ILLiad; (OPAC) TLC (The Library Corporation); (Serials) EBSCO Online
Wireless access

SPARTA

S GEORGIA DEPARTMENT OF CORRECTIONS, OFFICE OF LIBRARY SERVICES*, Hancock State Prison, 701 Prison Blvd, 31087. (Mail add: PO Box 339, 31087-0339). Tel: 706-444-1026. Web Site: www.dcor.state.ga.us/Facilities/hancock-state-prison. *Librn,* Ashkea Lewis
Library Holdings: Bk Vols 1,700; Per Subs 10; Talking Bks 20
Special Collections: Law Coll
Restriction: Not open to pub

STATESBORO

C GEORGIA SOUTHERN UNIVERSITY*, Zach S Henderson Library, 1400 Southern Dr, 30458. (Mail add: PO Box 8074, 30460), SAN 303-4240. Tel: 912-478-5115. Circulation Tel: 912-478-5647. Interlibrary Loan Service Tel: 912-478-5405. Reference Tel: 912-478-5645. FAX: 912-478-0093. Web Site: library.georgiasouthern.edu. *Dean of Libr,* Dr Lisandra R Carmichael; E-mail: lcarmichael@georgiasouthern.edu; *Head, Access Serv,* Jessica Garner; E-mail: jgarner@georgiasouthern.edu; *Head, Coll Serv,* Debra Skinner; Tel: 912-478-5114, E-mail: dskinner@georgiasouthern.edu; *Actg Head, Res Serv,* Lori Gwinett; E-mail: lgwinett@georgiasouthern.edu; *Head, Syst,* David Lowder; Tel: 912-478-0161, E-mail: dlowder@georgiasouthern.edu; Staff 55 (MLS 19, Non-MLS 36)
Founded 1906. Enrl 21,749; Fac 905; Highest Degree: Doctorate
Jul 2018-Jun 2019. Mats Exp $3,807,159
Library Holdings: AV Mats 97,892; e-books 652,207; e-journals 138,495; Electronic Media & Resources 185,561; Bk Titles 716,539; Bk Vols 930,997
Special Collections: Commander William M Rigdon Coll, 1940-1950; Congressman Ronald "Bo" Ginn Coll; Geer Coll; Gulver Kidd Coll; McTell Papers (Michael Gray Coll); Zachert Coll of Private Press Books. State Document Depository; US Document Depository
Automation Activity & Vendor Info: (Acquisitions) Ex Libris Group; (Cataloging) Ex Libris Group; (Circulation) Ex Libris Group; (Course Reserve) Ex Libris Group; (Discovery) EBSCO Discovery Service; (ILL) OCLC; (Media Booking) Ex Libris Group; (OPAC) Ex Libris Group; (Serials) Ex Libris Group
Wireless access
Partic in Galileo/GIL; Georgia Library Learning Online; LYRASIS; National Network of Libraries of Medicine Region 2
Friends of the Library Group

J OGEECHEE TECHNICAL COLLEGE LIBRARY*, One Joe Kennedy Blvd, 30458. Tel: 912-871-1886. Administration Tel: 912-871-3524. FAX: 912-486-7003. E-mail: library@ogeecheetech.edu. Web Site: www.ogeecheetech.edu/index.php/current-students/library. *Dir, Libr Serv,* Lisa Lanier; E-mail: llanier@ogeecheetech.edu; *Librn,* Charles Davis; E-mail: codavis@ogeecheetech.edu; Staff 4 (MLS 2, Non-MLS 2)
Founded 1989. Enrl 1,853; Highest Degree: Associate
Library Holdings: AV Mats 421; e-books 20,851; Bk Vols 9,834; Per Subs 40
Automation Activity & Vendor Info: (Cataloging) OCLC WorldShare Interlibrary Loan; (OPAC) OCLC WorldShare Interlibrary Loan
Wireless access
Partic in Georgia Library Learning Online
Open Mon-Thurs 8-8

P STATESBORO REGIONAL PUBLIC LIBRARIES, 124 S Main St, 30458. SAN 339-2198. Tel: 912-764-1341. FAX: 912-764-1350. E-mail: sboro@strl.info. Web Site: strl.info. *Regional Libr Dir,* Jennifer Durham; E-mail: director@strl.info; *Asst Dir,* Bridgid McCalister; Staff 5 (MLS 4, Non-MLS 1)
Founded 1937. Pop 163,000; Circ 182,011
Library Holdings: Bk Vols 196,095; Per Subs 303
Special Collections: Genealogy Coll, bks, micro
Automation Activity & Vendor Info: (Cataloging) Evergreen; (Circulation) Evergreen; (ILL) OCLC Connexion; (OPAC) Evergreen

Wireless access
Function: 24/7 Electronic res, 24/7 Online cat, 3D Printer, Audiobks via web, Bk club(s), Bks on CD, Children's prog, Computer training, Computers for patron use, E-Readers, E-Reserves, Electronic databases & coll, Equip loans & repairs, Family literacy, Free DVD rentals, Genealogy discussion group, Home delivery & serv to seniorr ctr & nursing homes, Homebound delivery serv, Homework prog, ILL available, Internet access, Laminating, Large print keyboards, Life-long learning prog for all ages, Magazines, Magnifiers for reading, Mango lang, Meeting rooms, Microfiche/film & reading machines, Museum passes, Online cat, Outreach serv, OverDrive digital audio bks, Photocopying/Printing, Prog for adults, Prog for children & young adult, Scanner, Spanish lang bks, STEM programs, Story hour, Summer reading prog, Teen prog, Telephone ref, Wheelchair accessible
Publications: 1909 Map (Bulloch County Georgia); Genealogy (incl cemetery rec, census, newspaper abstracts)
Member Libraries: Evans County Public Library; Franklin Memorial Library; L C Anderson Memorial Library; Pembroke Public Library; Richmond Hill-Bryan County Library
Partic in Georgia Libr Info Network; Public Information Network for Electronic Services
Open Mon-Thurs 8-7, Fri & Sat 9-6
Restriction: ID required to use computers (Ltd hrs), Non-resident fee
Friends of the Library Group

SUMMERVILLE

P CHATTOOGA COUNTY LIBRARY*, 360 Farrar Dr, 30747. SAN 338-9049. Tel: 706-857-2553. FAX: 706-857-7841. Web Site: www.chattoogacountylibrary.org. *Dir,* Susan Stephens; E-mail: sstephens@chattoogacountylibrary.org; Staff 9 (MLS 2, Non-MLS 7)
Founded 1941. Pop 25,000; Circ 85,005
Library Holdings: CDs 300; DVDs 200; Bk Vols 40,000; Per Subs 68; Videos 1,200
Automation Activity & Vendor Info: (Cataloging) Evergreen; (Circulation) Evergreen; (OPAC) Evergreen
Member Libraries: Trion Public Library
Partic in Public Information Network for Electronic Services
Open Mon & Fri 10-6, Tues & Thurs 10-8, Sat 10-5
Friends of the Library Group

SWAINSBORO

C EAST GEORGIA STATE COLLEGE LIBRARY*, 131 College Circle, 30401-2699. SAN 303-4259. Tel: 478-289-2083. Interlibrary Loan Service Tel: 478-289-2085. FAX: 478-289-2089. TDD: 478-289-2159. E-mail: library@ega.edu. Web Site: ega.libguides.com/home. *Interim Dir,* Meghan Crews; Tel: 478-289-2087, E-mail: mmcrews@ega.edu; *Libr Assoc,* Bonnie Nash; Tel: 478-289-2085, E-mail: bnnash@ega.edu; *Libr Asst,* Amber Amerson; Tel: 478-289-2086, E-mail: aamerso2@ega.edu; Staff 4 (MLS 2, Non-MLS 2)
Founded 1973. Enrl 2,944; Fac 103; Highest Degree: Bachelor
Special Collections: Ehrlich Military History Coll, bks, media items; The Heritage Center (includes Emanual County, GA hist, Swainsboro, GA hist), mats, artifacts
Automation Activity & Vendor Info: (Acquisitions) Ex Libris Group; (Cataloging) Ex Libris Group; (Circulation) Ex Libris Group; (Course Reserve) Ex Libris Group; (Discovery) EBSCO Discovery Service; (ILL) OCLC Connexion; (OPAC) Ex Libris Group; (Serials) Ex Libris Group
Wireless access
Function: 24/7 Online cat, Archival coll, Art exhibits, Audio & video playback equip for onsite use, Bks on CD, Chess club, Computers for patron use, Distance learning, Doc delivery serv, Electronic databases & coll, For res purposes, Free DVD rentals, ILL available, Instruction & testing, Internet access, Learning ctr, Magazines, Meeting rooms, Microfiche/film & reading machines, Music CDs, Online cat, Online info literacy tutorials on the web & in blackboard, Online ref, Orientations, Photocopying/Printing, Prog for adults, Ref & res, Ref serv available, Scanner, Spanish lang bks, Study rm, Telephone ref, VHS videos, Wheelchair accessible, Workshops
Partic in GALILEO; Georgia Library Learning Online; GOLD Resource Sharing Network for Georgia's Libraries; LYRASIS; OCLC-LVIS
Open Mon-Thurs 7:30am-8pm, Fri 7:30-5
Restriction: Non-circulating of rare bks, Open to pub for ref & circ; with some limitations, Open to students, fac & staff

P FRANKLIN MEMORIAL LIBRARY*, 331 W Main St, 30401. SAN 339-2287. Tel: 478-237-7791. FAX: 478-237-3553. E-mail: swainsborolibrary@gmail.com. Web Site: strl.info/swainsboro-library. *Libr Mgr,* Gladys Collins; E-mail: gladysc@strl.info; Staff 7 (Non-MLS 7)
Pop 21,536; Circ 44,628
Library Holdings: Bk Vols 32,000; Per Subs 45
Automation Activity & Vendor Info: (Acquisitions) SirsiDynix; (Cataloging) SirsiDynix; (Circulation) SirsiDynix; (ILL) OCLC
Wireless access
Mem of Statesboro Regional Public Libraries
Partic in Public Information Network for Electronic Services
Open Mon-Fri 9-6, Sat 9-1
Friends of the Library Group

J SOUTHEASTERN TECHNICAL COLLEGE LIBRARY*, 346 Kite Rd, 30401. Tel: 478-289-2322. Web Site: library.southeasterntech.edu. *Dir, Libr Serv,* Leah Dasher; E-mail: ldasher@southeasterntech.edu; *Asst Librn,* Bera Booker; E-mail: bbooker@southeasterntech.edu; Staff 1.5 (MLS 1.5)
Founded 1998. Enrl 714; Highest Degree: Associate
Library Holdings: AV Mats 147; CDs 620; e-books 49,646; Bk Titles 9,985; Bk Vols 12,531; Per Subs 80; Videos 865
Automation Activity & Vendor Info: (Cataloging) Surpass; (Circulation) Surpass; (OPAC) Surpass
Wireless access
Function: Audio & video playback equip for onsite use, CD-ROM, Electronic databases & coll, Internet access, Online ref, Orientations, Photocopying/Printing, VHS videos, Wheelchair accessible
Partic in Georgia Library Learning Online
Open Mon-Thurs 8-6, Fri 8-2:30
Restriction: Open to students, fac & staff

SYLVANIA

P SCREVEN-JENKINS REGIONAL LIBRARY*, 106 S Community Dr, 30467. SAN 339-2376. Tel: 912-564-7526. FAX: 912-564-7580. Web Site: sjrls.org. *Regional Libr Dir,* Kathyrn Youles; E-mail: kathryny@sjrls.org; *Asst Dir,* Sharon L Blank; E-mail: sblank@sjrls.org; Staff 7 (MLS 2, Non-MLS 5)
Founded 1951. Pop 24,713; Circ 153,163
Library Holdings: Bk Vols 144,000; Per Subs 86
Subject Interests: Ga, Genealogy, Local hist
Wireless access
Partic in LYRASIS; Public Information Network for Electronic Services
Open Mon 10-6, Tues-Fri 9-6, Sat 10-5
Friends of the Library Group
Branches: 1
JENKINS COUNTY MEMORIAL LIBRARY, 223 Daniel St, Millen, 30442, SAN 339-2406. Tel: 478-982-4244. FAX: 478-982-2192.
Library Holdings: Bk Vols 25,000; Per Subs 35
Open Mon-Wed & Fri 10:30-6, Sat 10:30-2:30
Friends of the Library Group
Bookmobiles: 1

SYLVESTER

P WORTH COUNTY LIBRARY, Margaret Jones Public, 205 E Pope St, 31791. SAN 338-523X. Tel: 229-776-2096. FAX: 229-776-0079. Web Site: www.worthlib.org. *Dir,* Leigh Wiley; E-mail: leigh@worthlib.org
Library Holdings: Bk Vols 38,675
Wireless access
Partic in Public Information Network for Electronic Services
Open Mon 9-5, Tues & Thurs 9-7, Wed & Fri 9-5:30, Sat 9-1

THOMASTON

J SOUTHERN CRESCENT TECHNICAL COLLEGE*, Flint River Campus Library, Bldg B, 1533 Hwy 19 S, 30286. Tel: 706-646-6173. FAX: 706-646-6240. E-mail: flintlibrary@sctech.edu. Web Site: www.sctech.edu/libraries. *Dir, Libr Serv,* Denise Barbour; E-mail: Denise.Barbour@sctech.edu; Staff 2 (MLS 2)
Founded 1963. Enrl 700; Highest Degree: Associate
Library Holdings: AV Mats 350; e-books 16,000; Bk Vols 11,000; Per Subs 93
Automation Activity & Vendor Info: (Cataloging) Surpass; (Circulation) Surpass; (OPAC) Surpass
Wireless access
Publications: Library Newsletter
Partic in Georgia Library Learning Online; GOLD Resource Sharing Network for Georgia's Libraries
Open Mon-Thurs 8-6, Fri 8-Noon
Restriction: Open to students, fac & staff

THOMASVILLE

J SOUTHERN REGIONAL TECHNICAL COLLEGE LIBRARY*, 15689 US Hwy 19 N, 31792. Tel: 229-225-4096. FAX: 229-225-3959. E-mail: library@southernregional.edu. Web Site: southernregional.edu/library. *Dir, Libr Serv,* Polly Swilley; E-mail: pswilley@southernregional.edu; Staff 2 (MLS 2)
Founded 1947. Enrl 1,700; Highest Degree: Associate
Library Holdings: CDs 2,000; DVDs 200; e-books 23,000; e-journals 8,000; Bk Vols 23,000; Per Subs 90; Videos 200
Automation Activity & Vendor Info: (Cataloging) TLC (The Library Corporation); (Circulation) TLC (The Library Corporation); (OPAC) TLC (The Library Corporation)

Partic in Georgia Library Learning Online
Open Mon-Thurs 8-7

P THOMAS COUNTY PUBLIC LIBRARY SYSTEM*, 201 N Madison St, 31792-5414. SAN 373-2967. Tel: 229-225-5252. FAX: 229-225-5258. Web Site: www.tcpls.org. *Dir,* Trent Reynolds; E-mail: trent@tcpls.org; *Bus Mgr,* Donna Jones; E-mail: business@tcpls.org; *Children's Mgr,* Amanda Redker; E-mail: amanda@tcpls.org; *Circ Mgr,* Joanita Cook; *Ref (Info Servs),* Perida Mitchell; E-mail: perida@tcpls.org; Staff 20 (MLS 2, Non-MLS 18)
Founded 1988. Pop 17,421; Circ 159,079
Jul 2014-Jun 2015 Income (Main & Associated Libraries) $1,192,341, State $159,272, County $904,161, Locally Generated Income $128,908. Mats Exp $94,218, Books $74,707, Per/Ser (Incl. Access Fees) $4,000, AV Mat $10,137, Electronic Ref Mat (Incl. Access Fees) $5,374. Sal $431,016 (Prof $105,597)
Library Holdings: Audiobooks 2,364; CDs 3,941; DVDs 27,238; e-books 2,855; Electronic Media & Resources 61; Bk Vols 74,735; Per Subs 87
Special Collections: Black Culture/History (Flipper Coll); Black obituaries; Plantation Project for South Georgia; Thomas County, Georgia, a History (Heritage Room Coll), bks, microfilm & oral hist. Oral History
Automation Activity & Vendor Info: (Acquisitions) Evergreen; (Cataloging) Evergreen; (Circulation) Evergreen
Wireless access
Function: Accelerated reader prog, Adult bk club, Adult literacy prog, Art exhibits, Audiobks via web, AV serv, Bk club(s), Bks on CD, CD-ROM, Children's prog, Citizenship assistance, Computer training, Computers for patron use, Digital talking bks, E-Readers, Electronic databases & coll, Equip loans & repairs, Family literacy, Free DVD rentals, Holiday prog, Home delivery & serv to seniorr ctr & nursing homes, Homebound delivery serv, Homework prog, ILL available, Internet access, Jail serv, Large print keyboards, Magazines, Magnifiers for reading, Mango lang, Meeting rooms, Microfiche/film & reading machines, Movies, Music CDs, Online cat, Online ref, Outreach serv, OverDrive digital audio bks, Photocopying/Printing, Preschool outreach, Preschool reading prog, Printer for laptops & handheld devices, Prog for adults, Prog for children & young adult, Ref serv available, Scanner, Senior computer classes, Senior outreach, Serves people with intellectual disabilities, Spanish lang bks, Spoken cassettes & CDs, Spoken cassettes & DVDs, Story hour, Study rm, Summer & winter reading prog, Summer reading prog, Tax forms, Teen prog, Telephone ref, Wheelchair accessible, Workshops
Publications: Friends (Newsletter)
Partic in GOLD Resource Sharing Network for Georgia's Libraries; Public Information Network for Electronic Services
Special Services for the Deaf - Assisted listening device; Bks on deafness & sign lang; High interest/low vocabulary bks; Spec interest per; TDD equip
Special Services for the Blind - Accessible computers; Assistive/Adapted tech devices, equip & products
Open Mon & Tues 9:30-8, Wed-Fri 9:30-6, Sat 9:30-3:30, Sun 2-5
Restriction: Non-resident fee, Open to students
Friends of the Library Group
Branches: 5

BOSTON CARNEGIE PUBLIC LIBRARY, 250 S Main St, Boston, 31626-3674. (Mail add: PO Box 310, Boston, 31626-0310), SAN 373-2975. Tel: 229-498-5101. FAX: 229-498-5101. E-mail: boston@tcpls.org. *Mgr,* Suzanne Moore; E-mail: suzanne@tcpls.org; Staff 2 (Non-MLS 2)
Founded 1914. Pop 430; Circ 5,137
Library Holdings: Audiobooks 21; DVDs 689; e-books 8,462; Bk Vols 10,073; Per Subs 7; Videos 976
Function: Bks on CD, Children's prog, Computers for patron use, Digital talking bks, Electronic databases & coll, Free DVD rentals, Homebound delivery serv, Homework prog, ILL available, Internet access, Large print keyboards, Magazines, Mango lang, Meeting rooms, Movies, Online cat, OverDrive digital audio bks, Photocopying/Printing, Printer for laptops & handheld devices, Prog for adults, Prog for children & young adult, Summer reading prog, Tax forms, Wheelchair accessible
Friends of the Library Group

GLADYS H CLARK MEMORIAL LIBRARY, 1060 NE Railroad St, Ochlocknee, 31773. (Mail add: PO Box 89, Ochlocknee, 31773-0089), SAN 373-5966. Tel: 229-574-5884. FAX: 229-574-5884. *Libr Mgr,* Susan King; E-mail: susank@tcpls.org; Staff 2 (Non-MLS 2)
Founded 1946. Pop 520; Circ 3,038
Library Holdings: Audiobooks 44; DVDs 492; e-books 3,073; Electronic Media & Resources 61; Bk Vols 8,462; Per Subs 5
Function: Bks on CD, Children's prog, Computers for patron use, Electronic databases & coll, Free DVD rentals, Homework prog, ILL available, Internet access, Large print keyboards, Magazines, Mango lang, Movies, Online cat, OverDrive digital audio bks, Photocopying/Printing, Prog for adults, Prog for children & young adult, Summer reading prog
Friends of the Library Group

COOLIDGE PUBLIC LIBRARY, 1029 E Verbena Ave, Coolidge, 31738. (Mail add: PO Box 429, Coolidge, 31738-0429), SAN 373-2983. Tel: 229-346-3463. FAX: 229-346-3463. *Libr Mgr,* Susan Leik; E-mail: susanl@tcpls.org; Staff 2 (Non-MLS 2)
Founded 1993. Pop 626; Circ 3,769
Library Holdings: Audiobooks 43; DVDs 377; e-books 8,462; Electronic Media & Resources 61; Bk Vols 8,903; Per Subs 6; Videos 13
Function: Audiobks via web, Children's prog, Computer training, Electronic databases & coll, Free DVD rentals, ILL available, Internet access, Large print keyboards, Magazines, Mango lang, Movies, OverDrive digital audio bks, Photocopying/Printing, Prog for adults, Prog for children & young adult, Ref serv available, Summer reading prog, Tax forms, VHS videos, Wheelchair accessible
Friends of the Library Group

MEIGS PUBLIC LIBRARY, 3058 NE Railroad St, Meigs, 31765. (Mail add: PO Box 176, Meigs, 31765-0176), SAN 373-2991. Tel: 229-683-3853. FAX: 229-683-3853. *Libr Mgr,* Brieana Hayes; E-mail: brieana@tcpls.org; Staff 2 (Non-MLS 2)
Founded 1976. Pop 684; Circ 3,274
Library Holdings: Audiobooks 14; DVDs 300; e-books 8,462; Electronic Media & Resources 165; Bk Vols 7,426; Per Subs 4
Function: Audiobks via web, Children's prog, Computer training, Computers for patron use, Electronic databases & coll, Free DVD rentals, ILL available, Internet access, Large print keyboards, Magazines, Mango lang, Meeting rooms, Movies, Online cat, OverDrive digital audio bks, Photocopying/Printing, Printer for laptops & handheld devices, Prog for children & young adult, Ref serv available, Summer reading prog, Tax forms, Wheelchair accessible
Friends of the Library Group

PAVO PUBLIC LIBRARY, 3031 E Harris St, Pavo, 31778, SAN 373-5974. Tel: 229-859-2697. FAX: 229-859-2697. *Libr Mgr,* Melissa Denham; E-mail: melissa@tcpls.org; Staff 2 (Non-MLS 2)
Founded 1987. Pop 731; Circ 5,911
Library Holdings: Audiobooks 17; DVDs 453; e-books 3,073; Electronic Media & Resources 61; Bk Vols 9,739; Per Subs 6
Function: Children's prog, Computer training, Computers for patron use, Digital talking bks, Electronic databases & coll, Family literacy, Free DVD rentals, ILL available, Internet access, Large print keyboards, Magazines, Mango lang, Movies, OverDrive digital audio bks, Photocopying/Printing, Printer for laptops & handheld devices, Prog for adults, Prog for children & young adult, Ref serv available, Summer reading prog, Tax forms, Wheelchair accessible
Friends of the Library Group

C THOMAS UNIVERSITY, Library & Learning Commons, 1501 Millpond Rd, 31792. SAN 303-4275. Tel: 229-227-6959. E-mail: tulibrary@thomasu.edu. Web Site: www.thomasu.edu/student-life/library. *Dir,* Tara Hagan; Tel: 229-226-1621, Ext 1107, E-mail: thagan@thomasu.edu; *Access Serv, Tech Serv Asst,* Tiffany McCardel; Staff 3 (MLS 2, Non-MLS 1)
Founded 1950. Enrl 800; Highest Degree: Master
Library Holdings: Bk Vols 85,000; Per Subs 412
Wireless access
Partic in GOLD Resource Sharing Network for Georgia's Libraries; LYRASIS
Open Mon & Wed 10-6, Tues & Thurs 12-6

TIFTON

C ABRAHAM BALDWIN AGRICULTURAL COLLEGE*, Baldwin Library, 2802 Moore Hwy, 31793. SAN 303-4283. Tel: 229-391-4990. E-mail: baldwinlibrary@abac.edu. Web Site: www.abac.edu/academics/abac-libraries. *Dir of Libr,* Laura K Clark; E-mail: laura.clark@abac.edu; *Instrul Serv Librn,* David Edens; Tel: 229-391-4986, E-mail: dedens@abac.edu; Staff 3 (MLS 3)
Founded 1908. Enrl 3,300; Fac 82; Highest Degree: Bachelor
Jul 2013-Jun 2014 Income $252,160. Sal $170,665
Library Holdings: AV Mats 2,126; CDs 76; DVDs 50; e-books 17,862; Bk Vols 79,321; Per Subs 132; Videos 1,124
Special Collections: Dorothy King & Betty King Carr Children's Classic Coll; Georgiana Coll
Automation Activity & Vendor Info: (Cataloging) OCLC; (Circulation) Ex Libris Group; (ILL) OCLC; (OPAC) Ex Libris Group
Wireless access
Function: ILL available
Publications: Library+ (Newsletter)
Partic in Georgia Library Learning Online; OCLC Online Computer Library Center, Inc
Open Mon-Thurs 8am-9pm, Fri 8-3, Sun 2-9
Restriction: Circ limited
Departmental Libraries:

C BAINBRIDGE CAMPUS LIBRARY, 2500 E Shotwell St, Bainbridge, 39819, SAN 303-3392. Tel: 229-248-3797. FAX: 229-248-2589. E-mail: bainbridgelibrary@abac.edu. *Libr Asst,* Chandra Casteel; Tel: 229-248-3795, E-mail: chandra.casteel@abac.edu; Staff 3 (MLS 3)

Founded 1973. Enrl 1,900; Fac 68; Highest Degree: Bachelor
Library Holdings: Audiobooks 497; CDs 365; DVDs 727; Music Scores 20; Bk Titles 38,198; Bk Vols 45,366; Per Subs 90
Special Collections: Apollo Lunar Surface EVA Video Coll; Walter E Cox Political Archives
Automation Activity & Vendor Info: (Acquisitions) Ex Libris Group; (Cataloging) Ex Libris Group; (Circulation) Ex Libris Group; (Course Reserve) Ex Libris Group; (ILL) OCLC FirstSearch; (OPAC) Ex Libris Group; (Serials) Ex Libris Group
Partic in Georgia Libr Info Network; GOLD Resource Sharing Network for Georgia's Libraries; LYRASIS
Open Mon-Thurs 7:30-6

P COASTAL PLAIN REGIONAL LIBRARY*, Headquarters, 2014 Chestnut Ave, 31794. SAN 339-2430. Tel: 229-386-3400. FAX: 229-386-7007. E-mail: cprl@cprl.org. Web Site: www.cprl.org. *Dir,* Sandy Hester; E-mail: shester@cprl.org; *Asst Dir,* Jennifer Golden; E-mail: jgolden@cprl.org; *Tech Serv,* Todd Roberson; Staff 3 (MLS 3)
Founded 1956. Pop 88,911; Circ 334,936
Library Holdings: AV Mats 7,948; Bk Vols 220,666; Per Subs 186
Automation Activity & Vendor Info: (Acquisitions) Infor Library & Information Solutions; (Cataloging) SirsiDynix; (Circulation) SirsiDynix; (ILL) OCLC Connexion; (OPAC) SirsiDynix
Wireless access
Partic in GOLD Resource Sharing Network for Georgia's Libraries; National Network of Libraries of Medicine Region 2; Public Information Network for Electronic Services
Special Services for the Deaf - Assisted listening device; Closed caption videos; TDD equip
Special Services for the Blind - Large print bks; Low vision equip; Magnifiers; Talking bks
Open Mon-Fri 9-6
Friends of the Library Group
Branches: 5
COOK COUNTY, 213 E Second St, Adel, 31620, SAN 339-249X. Tel: 229-896-3652. FAX: 229-896-5746. E-mail: ccl@cprl.org. *Br Mgr,* Nyisha Key; E-mail: nkey@cprl.org
Open Mon 9-7, Tues-Fri 9-6
Friends of the Library Group
IRWIN COUNTY, 310 S Beech St, Ocilla, 31774, SAN 339-2554. Tel: 229-468-2148. FAX: 229-468-2160. E-mail: id@cprl.org. *Br Mgr,* Deborah Moorman; E-mail: dmoorman@cprl.org
Open Mon-Fri 10-4
Friends of the Library Group
CARRIE DORSEY PERRY MEMORIAL, 315 W Marion Ave, Nashville, 31639, SAN 339-2465. Tel: 229-686-2782. FAX: 229-686-9185. E-mail: cdpml@cprl.org. *Br Mgr,* Angi Hughes; E-mail: ahughes@cprl.org
Open Mon, Wed & Fri 12-5, Tues & Thurs 10-2
Friends of the Library Group
TIFTON-TIFT COUNTY PUBLIC, 245 Love Ave, 31794, SAN 339-2619. Tel: 229-386-7148. FAX: 229-386-7205. E-mail: ttcpl@cprl.org. *Br Mgr,* Victoria Horst; E-mail: vhorst@cprl.org
Open Mon-Fri 9-6, Sat 10-3
Friends of the Library Group
TURNER COUNTY-VICTORIA EVANS MEMORIAL, 605 North St, Ashburn, 31714, SAN 339-252X. Tel: 229-567-4027. FAX: 229-567-4033. E-mail: veml@cprl.org. *Br Mgr,* JoAnne M High; E-mail: jhigh@cprl.org
Open Mon 10-3, Tues-Fri 9-3

C UNIVERSITY OF GEORGIA COLLEGE OF AGRICULTURAL & ENVIRONMENTAL SCIENCES*, Tifton Campus Library, 2360 Rainwater Rd, 31793. SAN 303-4291. Tel: 912-386-3447. FAX: 912-391-2501. E-mail: librtif@uga.edu. Web Sites: www.libs.uga.edu/tifton. *Librn,* Duncan McClusky; E-mail: mcclusky@uga.edu; Staff 1 (MLS 1)
Founded 1924. Fac 100; Highest Degree: Bachelor
Library Holdings: Bk Titles 7,000; Bk Vols 8,000; Per Subs 70
Subject Interests: Agr, Biology
Wireless access
Open Mon-Fri 8-12 & 1-5

TOCCOA

P TOCCOA-STEPHENS COUNTY PUBLIC LIBRARY*, 53 W Savannah St, 30577. SAN 338-5809. Tel: 706-886-6082. FAX: 706-886-7561. Web Site: www.toccoastephenslibrary.org. *Libr Mgr,* Leslie Allen; E-mail: lallen@negeorgialibraries.org
Wireless access
Mem of Northeast Georgia Regional Library System
Open Mon-Fri 10-5:30, Sat 10-1

TOCCOA FALLS

C TOCCOA FALLS COLLEGE*, Seby Jones Library, 107 Kincaid Dr, MSC 749, 30598. SAN 303-4305. Tel: 706-886-7299, Ext 5337. Web Site: www.tfc.edu/library. *Libr Dir,* Armand Ternak; E-mail: aternak@tfc.edu; *Asst Dir,* Selina Slate; Tel: 706-886-729, Ext 5302, E-mail: sslate@tfc.edu; *Cat, Online Serv,* Torri Beck; Tel: 706-886-7299, Ext 5300, E-mail: tbeck@tfc.edu; Staff 15 (MLS 3, Non-MLS 12)
Founded 1911. Enrl 1,330; Fac 50; Highest Degree: Master
Special Collections: Religion (R A Forrest Coll-Founder & First President of College)
Subject Interests: Educ, Music, Relig
Automation Activity & Vendor Info: (Cataloging) OCLC Worldshare Management Services; (Circulation) OCLC Worldshare Management Services; (ILL) OCLC Worldshare Management Services; (OPAC) OCLC Worldshare Management Services; (Serials) EBSCO Discovery Service
Wireless access
Partic in Association of Christian Librarians; Christian Library Consortium; GALILEO; Georgia Private Acad Librs Consortium; GOLD Resource Sharing Network for Georgia's Libraries; OCLC Online Computer Library Center, Inc
Open Mon-Thurs 7:45am-10pm, Fri 7:45-5, Sun 6pm-10pm

TRION

S GEORGIA DEPARTMENT OF CORRECTIONS, OFFICE OF LIBRARY SERVICES*, Hays State Prison, 777 Underwood Rd, 30753. (Mail add: PO Box 668, 30753-0668). Tel: 706-857-0400. FAX: 706-857-0624. Web Site: www.dcor.state.ga.us/Facilities/hays-state-prison. *Librn,* Position Currently Open
Library Holdings: Bk Vols 10,000; Per Subs 15
Special Collections: Law Coll

P TRION PUBLIC LIBRARY*, 15 Bulldog Blvd, 30753. Tel: 706-734-7594. FAX: 706-734-7504. Web Site: chattoogacountylibrary.org. *Br Mgr,* Gail Renfroe; E-mail: grenfroe@chattoogacountylibrary.org
Library Holdings: CDs 245; DVDs 170; Bk Vols 10,343; Talking Bks 23; Videos 1,096
Automation Activity & Vendor Info: (ILL) OCLC
Mem of Chattooga County Library
Open Mon-Fri 11-6
Friends of the Library Group

UNADILLA

S GEORGIA DEPARTMENT OF CORRECTIONS, OFFICE OF LIBRARY SERVICES*, Dooly State Prison, 1412 Plunkett Rd, 31091. (Mail add: PO Box 750, 31091-0750). Tel: 478-627-2000. Web Site: www.dcor.state.ga.us/Facilities/dooly-state-prison. *Librn,* Ms M Chaney
Library Holdings: CDs 61; Bk Vols 5,000; Per Subs 24; Talking Bks 100
Special Collections: Law Coll
Restriction: Not open to pub

VALDOSTA

S GEORGIA DEPARTMENT OF CORRECTIONS, OFFICE OF LIBRARY SERVICES*, Valdosta State Prison, 3259 Valtech Rd, 31601. (Mail add: PO Box 310, 31603). Tel: 229-333-7900, 229-333-7991. FAX: 229-333-5387. Web Site: www.dcor.state.ga.us/Facilities/valdosta-state-prison.
Library Holdings: Bk Vols 10,697; Per Subs 24

P LOWNDES COUNTY HISTORICAL SOCIETY & MUSEUM*, 305 W Central Ave, 31601. (Mail add: PO Box 56, 31603-0056), SAN 370-520X. Tel: 229-247-4780. E-mail: Research.LCHS@gmail.com. Web Site: valdostamuseum.com. *Dir,* Donald Davis
Founded 1967. Pop 55,000
Library Holdings: Bk Titles 1,200
Special Collections: Civil War (Colonel T A Faries Coll)
Subject Interests: Local hist
Function: Ref serv available
Open Mon-Fri 10-5, Sat 10-2

P SOUTH GEORGIA REGIONAL LIBRARY SYSTEM*, Valdosta-Lowndes County Public, 300 Woodrow Wilson Dr, 31602. SAN 339-2643. Tel: 229-333-0086. Reference Tel: 229-333-0086, Ext 220. FAX: 229-333-7669. E-mail: sgrl@sgrl.org. Web Site: www.sgrl.org/index.php/find-a-branch/valdosta-lowndes-county-library. *Dir,* Miguel Vicente; E-mail: mvicente@sgrl.org; *Managing Librn,* David Peeples; *Librn for Blind & Physically Handicapped,* Diane Jernigan; *Adult Serv,* Eric Mathis; *Youth Serv,* Christie Paulk; Staff 35 (MLS 4, Non-MLS 31)
Founded 1876. Pop 100,000; Circ 500,000
Library Holdings: AV Mats 18,000; Bk Vols 229,669; Per Subs 280
Special Collections: Birds

Automation Activity & Vendor Info: (Cataloging) Evergreen; (Circulation) Evergreen; (ILL) OCLC; (OPAC) Evergreen
Wireless access
Partic in National Network of Libraries of Medicine Region 2; Public Information Network for Electronic Services
Special Services for the Blind - Talking bks
Open Mon-Thurs 9:30-8, Fri 9:30-5:30, Sat 11-5:30, Sun 2-6
Friends of the Library Group
Branches: 5
ALLEN STATENVILLE BRANCH, 123 US Hwy 129, Statenville, 31648, SAN 339-2791. Tel: 229-559-8182. *Mgr,* Jackie Culpepper; Staff 1.2 (MLS 0.2, Non-MLS 1)
Library Holdings: Bk Vols 11,576
Special Collections: Echols County History
Function: Senior computer classes, Story hour, Summer reading prog, Teen prog, VHS videos
Partic in OCLC Online Computer Library Center, Inc
Open Mon, Tues, Thurs & Fri 11-5
Friends of the Library Group
EDITH G JOHNSTON LAKES BRANCH, 720 Lakes Blvd, Lake Park, 31636, SAN 372-0063. Tel: 229-559-8016. *Mgr,* Megan Brown
Library Holdings: Bk Vols 27,681
Open Mon-Thurs 11-7, Fri 11-5:30
Friends of the Library Group
MAE WISENBAKER MCMULLEN MEMORIAL SOUTHSIDE LIBRARY, 527 Griffin Ave, 31601-6343, SAN 373-7128. Tel: 229-253-8313. *Librn,* Cathy Jans
Library Holdings: Bk Vols 23,000
Open Mon-Thurs 11-7, Fri 11-5:30
Friends of the Library Group
MILLER LAKELAND BRANCH, 18 S Valdosta Rd, Lakeland, 31635, SAN 339-2767. Tel: 229-482-2904. *Librn,* Kim Brouse; Staff 1.6 (MLS 1, Non-MLS 0.6)
Founded 1988. Pop 15,000; Circ 11,203
Library Holdings: Bk Vols 22,000
Function: Computer training, Computers for patron use, Electronic databases & coll, Family literacy, Free DVD rentals, Music CDs, Online cat, Photocopying/Printing, Prog for adults, Prog for children & young adult, Spoken cassettes & CDs, VHS videos, Wheelchair accessible
Partic in OCLC Online Computer Library Center, Inc
Open Tues-Thurs 11-6, Fri 10-5:30
Friends of the Library Group
SALTER HAHIRA BRANCH, 220 E Main St, Hahira, 31632, SAN 339-2732. Tel: 229-794-3063. *Librn,* Janet Register
Library Holdings: Bk Vols 27,631
Open Mon-Thurs 11-7, Fri 11-5:30
Friends of the Library Group

C VALDOSTA STATE UNIVERSITY, Odum Library, 1500 N Patterson St, 31698-0150. SAN 303-4313. Tel: 229-333-5860. Interlibrary Loan Service Tel: 229-333-5867. Reference Tel: 229-333-7149. FAX: 229-259-5055. Interlibrary Loan Service FAX: 229-333-5862. Web Site: www.valdosta.edu/academics/library. *Dean of Libr,* Dr Alan Bernstein; E-mail: abernste@valdosta.edu; *Dir, Ref, Lending Servs,* Dr Laura Wright; Tel: 229-245-3746, E-mail: lbwright@valdosta.edu; *Dir, Archives & Spec Coll,* Deborah Davis; Tel: 229-259-7756, E-mail: dsdavis@valdosta.edu; *Dir, Coll Serv, Dir, Res Serv,* Ken Smith; Tel: 229-259-3734, E-mail: kensmith@valdosta.edu; *ILL Librn,* Amy Chew; Tel: 229-245-3717, E-mail: achew@valdosta.edu; *Circ, Lending Serv Coordr,* Steven Scheuler; Tel: 229-259-5363, E-mail: sascheul@valdosta.edu; Staff 36 (MLS 13, Non-MLS 23)
Founded 1913. Enrl 10,200; Fac 488; Highest Degree: Doctorate
Library Holdings: Bk Titles 367,417; Bk Vols 548,229; Per Subs 987
Special Collections: Archives of Contemporary South Georgia History; Georgia History & Culture (Emily Hendree Park Memorial Coll). US Doc Dep, US Maps
Automation Activity & Vendor Info: (Acquisitions) Ex Libris Group; (Cataloging) Ex Libris Group; (Circulation) Ex Libris Group; (Course Reserve) Ex Libris Group; (Media Booking) Ex Libris Group; (OPAC) Ex Libris Group; (Serials) Ex Libris Group
Wireless access
Partic in LYRASIS; OCLC Online Computer Library Center, Inc; Peachnet
Open Mon-Thurs 7am-Midnight, Fri 7am-9pm, Sat 12-8, Sun Noon-Midnight

J WIREGRASS GEORGIA TECHNICAL COLLEGE*, Valdosta Campus Library, Lowndes Hall, 4089 Val Tech Rd, Rm 7147A, 31602. Tel: 229-259-5177. FAX: 229-259-5179. E-mail: library@wiregrass.edu. Web Site: wiregrass.edu/library. *Dir, Circ & Archives,* Kathryn S Tomlinson; Tel: 229-259-5178, E-mail: kathryn.tomlinson@wiregrass.edu; *Libr Asst,* Dorisanne Cardwell; E-mail: dorisanne.cardwell@wiregrass.edu; *Libr Asst,* Jennifer Whinnery; E-mail: jennifer.mcwilliams@wiregrass.edu; Staff 2 (MLS 1, Non-MLS 1)
Founded 1997. Enrl 2,500; Fac 180; Highest Degree: Associate
Jul 2013-Jun 2014. Mats Exp $27,700, Books $20,000, Per/Ser (Incl. Access Fees) $4,500, Electronic Ref Mat (Incl. Access Fees) $3,200
Library Holdings: AV Mats 75; Bks on Deafness & Sign Lang 16; Braille Volumes 1; CDs 723; DVDs 815; e-books 35,000; Electronic Media & Resources 650; High Interest/Low Vocabulary Bk Vols 9; Bk Vols 10,000; Per Subs 80; Videos 499
Automation Activity & Vendor Info: (Acquisitions) TLC (The Library Corporation); (Cataloging) TLC (The Library Corporation); (Circulation) TLC (The Library Corporation); (ILL) OCLC ILLiad; (OPAC) TLC (The Library Corporation); (Serials) EBSCO Online
Wireless access
Function: CD-ROM, Computers for patron use, Electronic databases & coll, Free DVD rentals, ILL available, Notary serv, Online cat, Orientations, Photocopying/Printing, Ref serv available, Scanner, VHS videos, Wheelchair accessible
Special Services for the Deaf - Bks on deafness & sign lang; Closed caption videos
Special Services for the Blind - Large screen computer & software; Low vision equip; Screen enlargement software for people with visual disabilities; ZoomText magnification & reading software
Open Mon-Thurs 7:30-7, Fri 7:30-3

VIDALIA

P OHOOPEE REGIONAL LIBRARY SYSTEM*, Vidalia-Toombs County Library Headquarters, 610 Jackson St, 30474-2835. SAN 339-2821. Tel: 912-537-9283, Ext 104. FAX: 912-537-3735. Web Site: ohoopeelibrary.org. *Regional Libr Dir,* Cameron Asbell; E-mail: asbellc@ohoopeelibrary.org; *Br Mgr,* Jan Outler; E-mail: outlerj@ohoopeelibrary.org; Staff 9 (MLS 4, Non-MLS 5)
Founded 1938. Pop 52,000; Circ 150,000
Library Holdings: Bk Vols 130,000; Per Subs 110
Special Collections: Genealogy Coll; Local Newspaper (Vidalia Advance Coll, 1920 to date), micro
Automation Activity & Vendor Info: (Cataloging) Evergreen; (Circulation) Evergreen
Wireless access
Partic in Public Information Network for Electronic Services
Open Mon-Thurs 10-6, Sat 10-2
Branches: 6
NELLE BROWN MEMORIAL LIBRARY, 166 W Liberty St, Lyons, 30436-1432, SAN 339-2910. Tel: 912-526-6511. FAX: 912-526-6511. *Br Mgr,* Hannah Parker; E-mail: parkerh@ohoopeelibrary.org; Staff 1 (Non-MLS 1)
Open Mon-Thurs 2-5, Fri 10-1
JEFF DAVIS COUNTY PUBLIC LIBRARY, 189 E Jarman St, Hazlehurst, 31539, SAN 338-697X. Tel: 912-375-2386. *Librn,* Lynn Hall; E-mail: halll@ohoopeelibrary.org; *Br Mgr,* Ashley Walls; E-mail: walls@ohoopeelibrary.org
Library Holdings: Bk Titles 12,500
Open Mon-Thurs 10-6, Sat 10-2
Friends of the Library Group
GLENNVILLE PUBLIC, 408 E Barnard St, Glennville, 30427, SAN 339-2856. Tel: 912-654-3812. FAX: 912-654-3812. *Br Mgr,* Patty Wilson; E-mail: wilsonp@ohoopeelibrary.org; Staff 2 (Non-MLS 2)
Open Mon 10-5:30, Tues & Thurs 10-7, Wed, Fri & Sat 10-1:30
LADSON GENEALOGICAL LIBRARY, 125 Church St, 30474, SAN 339-2880. Tel: 912-537-8186. FAX: 912-537-8186. *Librn,* Stacey Wright; E-mail: wrights@ohoopeelibrary.org
Open Wed 9-3, Thurs & Fri 9-1 & 2-6
Restriction: Non-circulating
MONTGOMERY COUNTY PUBLIC LIBRARY, 215 S Railroad Ave, Mount Vernon, 30445, SAN 339-2945. Tel: 912-583-2780. FAX: 912-583-2780. *Br Mgr,* Nadine Kelly; E-mail: kellyn@ohoopeelibrary.org
Founded 1976
Open Mon, Tues & Thurs 11-6, Wed & Fri 10-3
TATTNALL COUNTY LIBRARY, 129 Tattnall St, Reidsville, 30453-0338, SAN 339-297X. Tel: 912-557-6247. FAX: 912-557-6247. *Br Mgr,* Anecia Peterson; E-mail: petersona@ohoopeelibrary.org; Staff 1 (Non-MLS 1)
Open Mon 10-5:30, Tues & Thurs 10-7, Wed, Fri & Sat 10-1:30
Bookmobiles: 1

J SOUTHEASTERN TECHNICAL COLLEGE*, Vidalia Campus Library, 3001 E First St, Rm 143, 30474. Tel: 912-538-3132. FAX: 912-538-3156. Web Site: library.southeasterntech.edu, www.southeasterntech.edu/other-pages/library.php. *Dir, Libr Serv,* Leah Dasher; Tel: 912-538-3186, E-mail: ldasher@southeasterntech.edu; Staff 2 (MLS 2)
Founded 1990. Enrl 1,200; Highest Degree: Associate
Library Holdings: DVDs 40; e-books 29,000; Bk Vols 7,000; Per Subs 50; Talking Bks 10; Videos 350
Automation Activity & Vendor Info: (Cataloging) TLC (The Library Corporation); (Circulation) TLC (The Library Corporation); (OPAC) TLC (The Library Corporation)

Wireless access
Partic in Georgia Library Learning Online
Open Mon-Thurs 8am-9pm

WACO

J WEST GEORGIA TECHNICAL COLLEGE*, Mary McClung Library-Murphy Campus, 176 Murphy Campus Blvd, 30182. Tel: 770-537-6066. FAX: 770-537-7997. Web Site: www.westgatech.edu/library. *Exec Dir, Libr Serv,* Chris Carroll; E-mail: chris.carroll@westgatech.edu; *Librn,* Farley Jenkins; E-mail: farley.jenkins@westgatech.edu; *Librn,* Matt Sunrich; E-mail: matthew.sunrich@westgatech.edu; Staff 3 (MLS 2, Non-MLS 1)
Founded 2002. Highest Degree: Associate
Library Holdings: AV Mats 2,438; Bk Vols 24,000; Per Subs 215
Automation Activity & Vendor Info: (Cataloging) SirsiDynix; (Circulation) SirsiDynix; (OPAC) SirsiDynix
Wireless access
Partic in Georgia Library Learning Online
Open Mon-Thurs 7:30am-9pm, Fri 7:30-Noon
Departmental Libraries:
DOUGLAS CAMPUS LIBRARY, 4600 Timber Ridge Dr, Douglasville, 30135. Tel: 770-947-7238. FAX: 770-947-4361. *Librn,* Gary Frizzell; E-mail: gary.frizzell@westgatech.edu; *Librn,* Mike Stephens; Tel: 770-947-7240, E-mail: michael.stephens@westgatech.edu; *Libr Asst,* Bob Abdich; E-mail: robert.abdich@westgatech.edu
Founded 1995. Highest Degree: Associate
Open Mon-Thurs 7:30am-9pm, Fri 7:30-Noon
LAGRANGE CAMPUS LIBRARY, One College Circle, LaGrange, 30240. Tel: 770-756-4557. FAX: 706-756-4631. *Librn,* Carla Fredd; E-mail: carla.fredd@westgatech.edu; *Librn,* Linda Gavin; E-mail: linda.gavin@westgatech.edu; Staff 2 (MLS 2)
Founded 1966. Enrl 1,950; Highest Degree: Associate
Library Holdings: AV Mats 70; e-books 15,000; Bk Vols 14,511; Per Subs 218; Videos 700
Automation Activity & Vendor Info: (Cataloging) TLC (The Library Corporation); (Circulation) TLC (The Library Corporation); (OPAC) TLC (The Library Corporation)
Partic in Georgia Library Learning Online
Open Mon-Thurs 7:30am-9pm, Fri 7:30am-Noon
ROGER SCHOERNER TECHNICAL LIBRARY-CARROLL CAMPUS, 997 S Hwy 16, Carrollton, 30116. Tel: 770-836-4711. FAX: 770-836-6807. *Librn,* Chris Carroll; E-mail: chris.carroll@westgatech.edu; *Libr Asst,* Cathy Bost; E-mail: cathy.bost@westgatech.edu; Staff 1 (MLS 1)
Founded 1970. Highest Degree: Associate
Open Mon-Thurs 7:30am-9pm, Fri 7:30am-Noon

WALESKA

C REINHARDT UNIVERSITY*, Hill Freeman Library & Spruill Learning Center, 7300 Reinhardt Circle, 30183. SAN 303-4321. Tel: 770-720-9120. Interlibrary Loan Service Tel: 770-720-5584. FAX: 770-720-5944. E-mail: library@reinhardt.edu. Web Site: www.reinhardt.edu/library. *Libr Dir,* Joel C Langford; Tel: 770-720-5585, E-mail: jcl@reinhardt.edu; Staff 6 (MLS 2, Non-MLS 4)
Founded 1883. Enrl 1,600; Fac 65; Highest Degree: Master
Library Holdings: e-books 100,000; e-journals 37,000; Bk Titles 68,375; Bk Vols 71,000; Per Subs 300
Automation Activity & Vendor Info: (Acquisitions) Ex Libris Group; (Cataloging) Ex Libris Group; (Circulation) Ex Libris Group; (OPAC) Ex Libris Group; (Serials) Ex Libris Group
Wireless access
Partic in Georgia Private Acad Librs Consortium; LYRASIS
Open Mon-Thurs 8am-11pm, Fri 8-5, Sat 1-5, Sun 2-11

WARNER ROBINS

J CENTRAL GEORGIA TECHNICAL COLLEGE LIBRARY*, Warner Robins Campus, 80 Cohen Walker Dr, 31088. Tel: 478-988-6863. E-mail: library@centralgatech.edu. Web Site: www.centralgatech.edu/library. *Librn,* Belle Bush; Tel: 478-218-3290, E-mail: ibush@centralgatech.edu; *Librn,* Stephanie Crane; Tel: 378-218-3291, E-mail: scrane@centralgatech.edu; Staff 4.5 (MLS 2, Non-MLS 2.5)
Founded 1998. Enrl 4,768; Highest Degree: Associate
Jul 2013-Jun 2014 Income $100,000. Mats Exp $72,807, Books $37,019, Per/Ser (Incl. Access Fees) $14,500, AV Equip $98, AV Mat $14,000, Electronic Ref Mat (Incl. Access Fees) $6,890, Presv $300
Library Holdings: AV Mats 2,079; CDs 686; DVDs 478; e-books 61,000; Bk Titles 24,993; Bk Vols 27,367; Per Subs 150; Videos 838
Automation Activity & Vendor Info: (Cataloging) TLC (The Library Corporation); (Circulation) TLC (The Library Corporation); (ILL) OCLC CatExpress; (OPAC) TLC (The Library Corporation)
Wireless access
Partic in GALILEO
Open Mon-Thurs 7:30am-9pm, Fri 7:30-3:30

WASHINGTON

P BARTRAM TRAIL REGIONAL LIBRARY*, Mary Willis Library Headquarters, 204 E Liberty St, 30673. SAN 339-3003. Tel: 706-678-7736. FAX: 706-678-1615. E-mail: willism@btrl.net. Web Site: www.btrl.net. *Dir,* Katherine Gregory; E-mail: katherine@btrl.net; Staff 4 (MLS 3, Non-MLS 1)
Founded 1888. Pop 33,615; Circ 10,410
Library Holdings: Bk Vols 101,000; Per Subs 75
Subject Interests: Ga, Local hist
Automation Activity & Vendor Info: (Cataloging) Evergreen; (Circulation) Evergreen; (ILL) OCLC; (OPAC) Evergreen
Wireless access
Partic in Public Information Network for Electronic Services
Special Services for the Deaf - High interest/low vocabulary bks
Open Mon-Fri 9-5
Friends of the Library Group
Branches: 2
TALIAFERRO COUNTY, 117 Askin St, Crawfordville, 30631. (Mail add: PO Box 129, Crawfordville, 30631-0129), SAN 339-3097. Tel: 706-456-2531. FAX: 706-456-2531. E-mail: tcl@btrl.net. *Mgr,* Sharon DuBois; *Mgr,* Barbara Wolter
Open Mon, Tues, Thurs & Fri 10-5
Friends of the Library Group
THOMSON-MCDUFFIE COUNTY, 338 Main St, Thomson, 30824, SAN 339-3062. Tel: 706-595-1341. FAX: 706-597-9458. E-mail: thomsonmcduffielibrary@gmail.com. *Librn,* Suzan Harris
Open Mon-Fri 9-3
Friends of the Library Group
Bookmobiles: 1

WAYCROSS

J COASTAL PINES TECHNICAL COLLEGE*, Waycross Campus Library, 1701 Carswell Ave, 31503. Tel: 912-287-6655. FAX: 912-287-4865. Web Site: libguides.coastalpines.edu/libraryservices/waycross. *Dir, Libr Serv,* Cassie Clemons; Tel: 912-287-5834, E-mail: cclemons@coastalpines.edu; Staff 1.5 (MLS 1.5)
Enrl 1,100; Highest Degree: Associate
Library Holdings: DVDs 453; e-books 50,000; Bk Vols 7,000; Per Subs 120
Automation Activity & Vendor Info: (Cataloging) TLC (The Library Corporation); (Circulation) TLC (The Library Corporation); (ILL) OCLC FirstSearch; (OPAC) TLC (The Library Corporation)
Wireless access
Partic in Georgia Library Learning Online
Open Mon-Thurs 7:45am-9pm
Departmental Libraries:
ALMA LEARNING RESOURCE CENTER, 101 W 17th St, Rm 1106, Alma, 31510. Tel: 912-632-0951. *Libr Asst,* Kira Johnson; E-mail: kjohnson@coastalpines.edu
Open Mon-Thurs 8-6
BAXLEY LEARNING RESOURCE CENTER, 1334 Golden Isles Pkwy W, Rm 1110, Baxley, 31513. Tel: 912-367-1700. *Libr Asst,* Joanne White; E-mail: jwhite@coastalpines.edu
Open Mon, Tues & Thurs 8am-9pm, Wed 8-5
GOLDEN ISLES LIBRARY, 3700 Glynco Pkwy, Brunswick, 31525. Tel: 912-262-4314. *Librn,* Michele Nicole Johnson; Tel: 912-262-4315, E-mail: mnjohnson@coastalpines.edu
Open Mon-Thurs 7:30-6:30, Fri 8-Noon
HAZLEHURST LEARNING RESOURCE CENTER, 677 Douglas Hwy, Rm 102, Hazlehurst, 31513. Tel: 912-379-0041. *Libr Asst,* Rhonda Miles; E-mail: rmiles@coastalpines.edu
Open Mon & Wed 8-8, Tues & Thurs 8-6
JESUP LIBRARY, 1777 W Cherry St, Jesup, 31545. Tel: 912-427-5800. *Librn,* Caroline Culver; Tel: 912-427-1929, E-mail: cculver@coastalpines.edu; Staff 2 (MLS 1, Non-MLS 1)
Highest Degree: Associate
Library Holdings: CDs 25; Bk Vols 9,000; Per Subs 115
Automation Activity & Vendor Info: (Cataloging) TLC (The Library Corporation); (Circulation) TLC (The Library Corporation); (OPAC) TLC (The Library Corporation)
Partic in Georgia Library Learning Online
Open Mon & Tues 7:30-6:30, Wed & Thurs 7:30-6, Fri 8-Noon

S GEORGIA DEPARTMENT OF CORRECTIONS, OFFICE OF LIBRARY SERVICES, Ware State Prison, 3620 N Harris Rd, 31503. Tel: 912-285-6400. FAX: 912-287-6520. Web Site: www.dcor.state.ga.us/facilities/ware-state-prison. *Librn,* Position Currently Open
Library Holdings: Bk Vols 15,000; Per Subs 6
Special Collections: Law Coll
Restriction: Staff & inmates only

P OKEFENOKEE REGIONAL LIBRARY*, Waycross-Ware County Public Library, 401 Lee Ave, 31501. SAN 339-3127. Tel: 912-287-4978. FAX: 912-284-2533. Web Site: okrls.org. *Mgr,* John Miller; E-mail: jmiller@okrls.org; *Circ,* Rosanne Moore; *Ref (Info Servs),* James Britton, III; *Tech Serv,* Linda K Lightfoot; Staff 5 (MLS 5)
Founded 1955. Pop 85,519; Circ 185,407
Library Holdings: Bk Titles 10,000; Bk Vols 230,000; Per Subs 123
Special Collections: Oral History
Subject Interests: Ga, Genealogy
Automation Activity & Vendor Info: (Cataloging) SirsiDynix; (Circulation) SirsiDynix; (ILL) OCLC WorldShare Interlibrary Loan; (OPAC) SirsiDynix
Wireless access
Partic in Public Information Network for Electronic Services
Open Mon & Thurs 10-8, Tues, Wed & Fri 10-6, Sat 10-2
Friends of the Library Group
Branches: 4
ALMA-BACON COUNTY PUBLIC, 201 N Pierce St, Alma, 31510, SAN 339-3216. Tel: 912-632-4710. FAX: 912-632-4512. *Mgr,* Theressa Anderson
Open Mon 9-12:30 & 1:30-8, Tues-Fri 9-12:30 & 1:30-5:30, Sat 9-12:30
APPLING COUNTY PUBLIC, 301 City Hall Dr, Baxley, 31513, SAN 339-3186. Tel: 912-367-8103. FAX: 912-367-8104. *Mgr,* Annette Osborne
Open Mon 10-8, Tues-Thurs 10-6, Fri 10-4, Sat 9-1
BLACKSHEAR MEMORIAL LIBRARY, 600 S Main St, Blackshear, 31516, SAN 339-3240. Tel: 912-449-7040. FAX: 912-449-2265. *Mgr,* Anita Bunkley
Open Mon, Tues, Thurs & Fri 9:30-1 & 2-6, Wed & Sat 9-1
Friends of the Library Group
CLINCH COUNTY PUBLIC, 478 W Dame St, Homerville, 31634, SAN 339-3275. Tel: 912-487-3200. FAX: 912-487-3304. *Mgr,* Jane Welch
Open Mon-Wed 10-1 & 2-6, Thurs 2-8, Fri 10-1, Sat 2-5
Friends of the Library Group
Bookmobiles: 1. In Charge, Katherine Smith

J SOUTH GEORGIA STATE COLLEGE*, Waycross Campus Library, 2001 S Georgia Pkwy, 31503. SAN 303-4356. Tel: 912-449-7515, 912-449-7518. FAX: 912-449-7611. Web Site: www.sgsc.edu/academics/homepage.cms. *Dir of Libr,* Sharon Lynn Kelly; Tel: 912-260-4324, E-mail: lynn.kelly@sgsc.edu; *Coordr,* Janice Williams; Tel: 912-449-7519, E-mail: janice.williams@sgsc.edu; Staff 4 (MLS 2, Non-MLS 2)
Founded 1976. Enrl 1,027; Fac 25; Highest Degree: Associate
Library Holdings: e-books 27,501; Bk Titles 27,500; Bk Vols 28,536; Per Subs 178
Special Collections: Okefenokee Swamp
Automation Activity & Vendor Info: (Cataloging) Ex Libris Group; (Circulation) Ex Libris Group; (OPAC) Ex Libris Group; (Serials) Ex Libris Group
Wireless access
Publications: Bay Leaf (Newsletter)
Partic in Georgia Libr Info Network
Open Mon-Thurs 8-8, Fri 8-Noon

WEST POINT

P HAWKES LIBRARY, 100 W Eighth St, 31833. SAN 303-4364. Tel: 706-645-1549. FAX: 706-645-1549. E-mail: friendsofhawkes@gmail.com. *Librn,* Rebecca Cotney
Founded 1922. Pop 40,000
Library Holdings: Bk Vols 21,500; Per Subs 15
Special Collections: Confederate Memorabilia; Georgia Culture Coll
Subject Interests: Local hist
Wireless access
Open Mon, Tues, Thurs & Fri 10-5:30
Friends of the Library Group

C POINT UNIVERSITY*, Library of Point University, 507 W Tenth St, 31833-1200. SAN 303-3716. Tel: 706-385-1000. Web Site: intranet.point.edu/library. *Dir, Libr Res,* Michael Bain; E-mail: michael.bain@point.edu; Staff 1 (MLS 1)
Founded 1937. Enrl 1,985; Fac 125; Highest Degree: Master
Library Holdings: e-books 175,000; e-journals 50,000; Bk Titles 15,000; Bk Vols 15,000; Per Subs 12
Wireless access
Partic in Association of Christian Librarians; Christian Libr Network; Georgia Private Acad Libs Consortium

WOODBINE

S BRYAN-LANG HISTORICAL LIBRARY, 311 Camden Ave, 31569. (Mail add: PO Box 715, 31569-0715), SAN 371-5337. Tel: 912-576-5841. FAX: 912-576-5841. Web Site: www.co.camden.ga.us/66/bryan-lang-library. *Archivist,* Harland Harris; E-mail: aharris@co.camden.ga.us
Founded 1984
Library Holdings: Bk Titles 4,500
Special Collections: Berrie Coll; Lang Coll
Function: Res libr
Open Mon-Fri 9-4:30
Restriction: Not a lending libr

P WOODBINE PUBLIC LIBRARY*, 103 E Eight St, 31569. Tel: 912-559-2391. Web Site: threeriverslibraries.org/woodpress-dev/woodbine-public-library-inc. *Libr Mgr,* Tiffany Levin; E-mail: tlevin@trrl.org
Mem of Three Rivers Regional Library System

WRIGHTSVILLE

S GEORGIA DEPARTMENT OF CORRECTIONS, OFFICE OF LIBRARY SERVICES, Johnson State Prison, 290 Donovan-Harrison Rd, 31096. (Mail add: PO Box 344, 31096-0344). Tel: 478-864-4100, Ext 4141. FAX: 478-864-4104. Web Site: www.dcor.state.ga.us/facilities/johnson-state-prison. *Librn,* William D Wicker
Library Holdings: Bk Vols 6,944; Per Subs 10; Talking Bks 10
Special Collections: Law Coll
Restriction: Not open to pub

YOUNG HARRIS

P MOUNTAIN REGIONAL LIBRARY SYSTEM*, Mountain Regional Library, 698 Miller St, 30582. (Mail add: PO Box 159, 30582-0159), SAN 339-3720. Tel: 706-379-3732. FAX: 706-379-2047. Web Site: www.mountainregionallibrary.org. *Regional Libr Dir,* Heath Lee; E-mail: director@mountainregionallibrary.org; *Bus Mgr,* Vicki Adkinson; E-mail: vadkinson@mountainregionallibrary.org; *Cat Supvr, ILL,* Vanessa Pittman; E-mail: pittmanv@mountainregionallibrary.org; *Pub Serv Coordr,* Marlene Cannon; E-mail: mcannon@mountainregionallibrary.org; Staff 6.2 (MLS 2, Non-MLS 4.2)
Founded 1946. Pop 59,444; Circ 303,409
Special Collections: Appalachian Coll; Rare & Special Local Coll
Automation Activity & Vendor Info: (Acquisitions) Evergreen; (Cataloging) Evergreen; (Circulation) Evergreen; (ILL) OCLC; (OPAC) Evergreen
Wireless access
Function: Adult bk club, Art exhibits, Audio & video playback equip for onsite use, Audiobks via web, AV serv, Bks on cassette, Bks on CD, Children's prog, Computer training, Computers for patron use, Digital talking bks, Electronic databases & coll, Free DVD rentals, ILL available, Instruction & testing, Magnifiers for reading, Mail & tel request accepted, Museum passes, Music CDs, Notary serv, Online cat, Outreach serv, Outside serv via phone, mail, e-mail & web, OverDrive digital audio bks, Photocopying/Printing, Preschool outreach, Preschool reading prog, Prog for adults, Prog for children & young adult, Ref serv available, Senior computer classes, Senior outreach, Spoken cassettes & CDs, Story hour, Summer reading prog, Tax forms, Teen prog, Telephone ref, Wheelchair accessible
Partic in Georgia Library Learning Online; LYRASIS; OCLC Online Computer Library Center, Inc; Public Information Network for Electronic Services
Special Services for the Deaf - Assistive tech; Bks on deafness & sign lang
Special Services for the Blind - Accessible computers; Aids for in-house use; Assistive/Adapted tech devices, equip & products; Audio mat; Bks & mags in Braille, on rec, tape & cassette; Computer with voice synthesizer for visually impaired persons; Copier with enlargement capabilities; Digital talking bk; Digital talking bk machines; Extensive large print coll; Free checkout of audio mat; Home delivery serv; Internet workstation with adaptive software; Large print bks; Large screen computer & software; Lending of low vision aids; Magnifiers; Playaways (bks on MP3); Reader equip; Talking bk serv referral; Talking bks & player equip
Open Mon, Wed & Fri 9-5, Tues & Thurs 9-7, Sat 10-2
Friends of the Library Group
Branches: 3
FANNIN COUNTY PUBLIC LIBRARY, 400 W Main St, Ste 104, Blue Ridge, 30513, SAN 339-378X. Tel: 706-632-5263. FAX: 706-632-7719. E-mail: fcpl@mountainregionallibrary.org. *Br Mgr,* Monica Clark; Staff 1 (MLS 1)
Pop 24,949; Circ 101,133
Automation Activity & Vendor Info: (Acquisitions) Evergreen; (Cataloging) Evergreen; (Circulation) Evergreen; (ILL) OCLC; (OPAC) Evergreen
Function: Art exhibits, Audio & video playback equip for onsite use, Audiobks via web, AV serv, Bks on cassette, Bks on CD, Children's prog, Computers for patron use, Digital talking bks, Free DVD rentals, ILL available, Magnifiers for reading, Music CDs, Online cat, Outside serv via phone, mail, e-mail & web, OverDrive digital audio bks, Photocopying/Printing, Prog for adults, Prog for children & young adult, Story hour, Summer reading prog, Tax forms, Teen prog, Telephone ref, Wheelchair accessible

Special Services for the Deaf - Bks on deafness & sign lang
Special Services for the Blind - Accessible computers; Assistive/Adapted tech devices, equip & products; Audio mat; Bks & mags in Braille, on rec, tape & cassette; Bks on cassette; Bks on CD; Internet workstation with adaptive software; Large print & cassettes; Large print bks; Reader equip; Recorded bks; Talking bks & player equip
Open Mon & Fri 9-5, Tues 9-7, Thurs 11-7, Sat 9-1
Friends of the Library Group

TOWNS COUNTY PUBLIC LIBRARY, 99 S Berrong St, Hiawassee, 30546, SAN 328-8951. Tel: 706-896-6169. FAX: 706-896-2309. E-mail: tcpl@mountainregionallibrary.org. *Br Mgr,* Deborah Phillips; Staff 3 (Non-MLS 3)
Pop 11,469; Circ 41,747
Function: Audio & video playback equip for onsite use, Audiobks via web, AV serv, Bks on cassette, Bks on CD, Computers for patron use, Digital talking bks, Electronic databases & coll, Free DVD rentals, ILL available, Magnifiers for reading, Mail & tel request accepted, Notary serv, Online cat, OverDrive digital audio bks, Photocopying/Printing, Preschool outreach, Prog for adults, Prog for children & young adult, Story hour, Summer reading prog, Tax forms, VHS videos, Wheelchair accessible
Special Services for the Deaf - Bks on deafness & sign lang
Special Services for the Blind - Bks on CD; Digital talking bk; Digital talking bk machines; Free checkout of audio mat; Large print bks; Local mags & bks recorded; Magnifiers; Playaways (bks on MP3); Screen enlargement software for people with visual disabilities; Talking bks & player equip
Open Mon-Wed & Fri 9-5, Thurs 10-6
Friends of the Library Group

UNION COUNTY PUBLIC LIBRARY, 303 Hunt Martin St, Blairsville, 30512, SAN 339-3755. Tel: 706-745-7491. FAX: 706-745-5652. E-mail: ucpl@mountainregionallibrary.org. *Br Mgr,* Susie Brendle; Staff 4.5 (MLS 1, Non-MLS 3.5)
Pop 22,269; Circ 175,657
Function: Adult bk club, Art exhibits, Audiobks via web, Bks on CD, Children's prog, Computer training, Computers for patron use, Digital talking bks, Electronic databases & coll, Free DVD rentals, ILL available, Instruction & testing, Magnifiers for reading, Museum passes, Music CDs, Notary serv, Online cat, Online ref, Outreach serv, OverDrive digital audio bks, Photocopying/Printing, Preschool outreach, Preschool reading prog, Prog for adults, Prog for children & young adult, Ref serv available, Scanner, Senior computer classes, Story hour, Summer reading prog, Tax forms, Wheelchair accessible
Open Mon, Wed & Fri 9-5, Tues & Thurs 9-7, Sat 10-2
Friends of the Library Group

C YOUNG HARRIS COLLEGE*, Zell & Shirley Miller Library Library, One College St, 30582. (Mail add: PO Box 39, 30582-0039), SAN 303-4372. Tel: 706-379-4313. E-mail: library@yhc.edu. Web Site: www.yhc.edu. *Dean, Libr Serv,* Debra March; E-mail: dbmarch@yhc.edu; *Access Serv Librn, Instruction Librn,* Kyle DeBell; E-mail: kdebell@yhc.edu; *User Serv,* Ginia Wood Magers; E-mail: gwmagers@yhc.edu; Staff 5 (MLS 3, Non-MLS 2)
Founded 1886. Enrl 1,150; Fac 145; Highest Degree: Bachelor
Library Holdings: e-books 152,000; Bk Vols 48,000; Per Subs 12
Special Collections: Byron Herbert Reece & J A Sharp Coll; Merle Mann Indian Artifacts; Ogletree Lincolniana Coll; Vietnam Veterans Oral History Project. Oral History
Subject Interests: Hist, Humanities, Music, Relig
Automation Activity & Vendor Info: (Cataloging) SirsiDynix; (Circulation) SirsiDynix; (ILL) OCLC; (OPAC) SirsiDynix
Wireless access
Partic in Georgia Private Acad Librs Consortium; GOLD Resource Sharing Network for Georgia's Libraries; LYRASIS
Open Mon-Thurs 7:45am-Midnight, Fri 7:45-6, Sat 1-6, Sun 1-Midnight
Friends of the Library Group

ZEBULON

S GEORGIA DEPARTMENT OF CORRECTIONS, OFFICE OF LIBRARY SERVICES*, West Central Probation Detention Center Library, 1070 County Farm Rd, 30295. Tel: 770-567-0531. FAX: 770-567-0257. Web Site: www.dcor.state.ga.us/GDC/FacilityMap/html/S_50000533.html. *Library Contact,* Lindolyn Green
Library Holdings: Bk Vols 530; Per Subs 20
Restriction: Not open to pub

HAWAII

Date of Statistics: FY 2020
Population, 2020 U.S. Census: 1,407,006
Population Served by Public Libraries Statewide: 1,415,872
Total Volumes in Public Libraries (including State Library): 3,250,313
Volumes Per Capita: 2.3
Digital Resources:
- **Total e-books:** 116,195
- **Total audio items (physical and downloadable units):** 198,118
- **Total video items (physical and downloadable units):** 176,098
- **Total computers for use by the public:** 735
- **Total annual wireless sessions:** 341,736

Total Public Library Circulation (Includes Library for the Blind and Physically Handicapped): 4,752,618
Income and Expenditures:
Total Public Library Income: $36,968,892
- **Source of Income:** State Legislative Appropriation (FY 2020), Federal LSTA Funds, and Special Funds
- **Expenditures Per Capita:** $28.90

Number of County Libraries: The Hawaii State Public Library System is made up of 51 branches across six islands.
Number of Bookmobiles in State: 2
Grants-in-Aid to Public Libraries: zero
- **Library Services and Technology Act, FY 2020:** $844,463
- **State Aid:** State funded

Information provided courtesy of: Jessica Hogan, Librarian; Hawaii State Public Library System

FORT SHAFTER

A UNITED STATES ARMY*, Fort Shafter Library, 181 Chapplear Rd, Bldg 650, 96858. SAN 339-5677. Tel: 808-438-9521. E-mail: ftslib@yahoo.com. Web Site: hawaii.armymwr.com/programs/fort-shafter-library. *Librn,* Chris Kobayashi; Staff 3 (MLS 1, Non-MLS 2)
Founded 1943
Library Holdings: Bk Vols 18,000; Per Subs 86
Subject Interests: Hawaii
Wireless access
Open Mon-Thurs 10-6, Fri-Sun 10-4
Restriction: Mil only

HICKAM AFB

A JOINT BASE PEARL HARBOR-HICKAM LIBRARY*, Bldg 595, 990 Mills Blvd, 96853. SAN 339-3844. Tel: 808-449-8299. FAX: 808-449-8298. E-mail: hickamlibrary@gmail.com. Web Site: jbphh.greatlifehawaii.com/recreation/library. *Dir,* Phyllis Frenzel; E-mail: phyllis.frenzel@navy.mil; *Ref Serv,* Jeff Boling; Staff 7 (MLS 2, Non-MLS 5)
Founded 1957
Library Holdings: Bk Vols 36,000; Per Subs 75
Subject Interests: Hawaii
Automation Activity & Vendor Info: (Acquisitions) EOS International; (Cataloging) EOS International; (Circulation) EOS International
Wireless access
Open Mon-Sat 11-8
Friends of the Library Group

HILO

S HAWAII COMMUNITY CORRECTIONAL CENTER LIBRARY*, 60 Punahele St, 96720. Tel: 808-933-0428. FAX: 808-933-0425. Web Site: dps.hawaii.gov/about/divisions/corrections/about-corrections/hccc.
Library Holdings: Bk Vols 6,000
Subject Interests: Law, Recreation
Restriction: Staff & inmates only

GL STATE SUPREME COURT*, Third Circuit Court-Law Library, Hale Kaulike Bldg, 777 Kilauea Ave, 96720-4212. SAN 303-4429. Tel: 808-961-7438. Web Site: histatelawlibrary.com. *Librn,* Jasmine Thompson
Library Holdings: Bk Vols 30,000
Open Mon-Fri 7:45-4:30

C UNIVERSITY OF HAWAII AT HILO LIBRARY*, Edwin H Mookini Library, 200 W Kawili St, 96720. SAN 339-3933. Tel: 808-932-7286. Interlibrary Loan Service Tel: 808-932-7288. Administration Tel: 808-932-7280. FAX: 808-932-7306. E-mail: mookini@hawaii.edu. Web Site: hilo.hawaii.edu/library. *Dir,* Joseph Sanchez; Tel: 808-932-7315, E-mail: josephs7@hawaii.edu; *Coll Serv Librn,* Kathleen Stacey; Tel: 808-932-7285, E-mail: kstacey@hawaii.edu; *Distance Learning Librn,* Amy Saxton; Tel: 808-932-7331, E-mail: saxton@hawaii.edu; *Pub Serv Librn,* Brian Bays; Tel: 808-932-7310, E-mail: bbays@hawaii.edu; Staff 22 (MLS 8, Non-MLS 14)
Founded 1947. Enrl 3,800; Fac 216; Highest Degree: Doctorate
Library Holdings: AV Mats 10,000; e-books 132,000; e-journals 35,000; Microforms 440,000; Bk Vols 230,000
Special Collections: Hawaiiana, bks & per. State Document Depository; US Document Depository
Subject Interests: Pacific Islands
Automation Activity & Vendor Info: (Acquisitions) Ex Libris Group; (Cataloging) Ex Libris Group; (Circulation) Ex Libris Group; (Course Reserve) Ex Libris Group; (ILL) Ex Libris Group; (Media Booking) Ex Libris Group; (OPAC) Ex Libris Group; (Serials) Ex Libris Group
Wireless access
Function: ILL available, Ref serv available
Open Mon-Thurs 8am-10:30pm, Fri 8-6, Sun 2-10:30

HONOLULU

S BERNICE P BISHOP MUSEUM, Library & Archives, 1525 Bernice St, 96817. SAN 303-447X. Tel: 808-848-4148. FAX: 808-847-8241. E-mail: archives@bishopmuseum.org, library@bishopmuseum.org. Web Site: www.bishopmuseum.org/library-and-archives. *Dir,* Leah Caldeira
Founded 1891
Library Holdings: Bk Vols 115,000; Per Subs 1,100; Videos 90
Special Collections: Hawaii Maritime Center Coll; Hawaiian Language Newspapers; Hawaiiana (Carter Coll); Japanese Hawaii Imprints; Jerome Baker Coll; Pacific Island Languages; Pacificana (Fuller Coll); United States Geological Survey & South Pacific Commission
Subject Interests: Anthrop, Archaeology, Botany, Ethnology, Geog, Hawaii, Museology, Pacific, Photog, Zoology
Automation Activity & Vendor Info: (Cataloging) Ex Libris Group; (OPAC) Ex Libris Group
Publications: Journal (Quarterly)
Partic in OCLC Online Computer Library Center, Inc
Restriction: Open by appt only

L CADES SCHUTTE*, Law Library, 1000 Bishop St, Ste 1200, 96813-4212. SAN 303-4488. Tel: 808-521-9200. FAX: 808-521-9210. E-mail: cades@cades.com. Web Site: www.cades.com. *Librn,* Elizabeth Hamilton; E-mail: bhamilton@cades.com; Staff 3 (Non-MLS 3)
Founded 1922
Library Holdings: Bk Titles 5,000; Bk Vols 15,000; Per Subs 215
Special Collections: Ecology (Hawaiian Water Rights); Hawaii Legislative Reports
Subject Interests: Corporate law, Med, Real estate, Securities
Function: Res libr
Restriction: Private libr

L CARLSMITH BALL LLP LIBRARY*, ASB Tower, Ste 2200, 1001 Bishop St, 96813. SAN 303-4496. Tel: 808-523-2500. FAX: 808-523-0842. Web Site: www.carlsmith.com. *Librn, Supvr,* Grace Yamada; E-mail: gyamada@carlsmith.com
Library Holdings: Bk Vols 20,000; Per Subs 150
Restriction: Not open to pub

C CHAMINADE UNIVERSITY OF HONOLULU*, Sullivan Family Library, 3140 Waialae Ave, 96816-1578. SAN 303-4518. Tel: 808-735-4725. Circulation Tel: 808-739-4665. Reference Tel: 808-739-4660. FAX: 808-735-4891. E-mail: library@chaminade.edu. Web Site: lib.chaminade.edu. *Librn,* Valerie Coleman; Tel: 808-739-4661, E-mail: vcoleman@chaminade.edu; *Librn,* Sharon LePage; Tel: 808-739-4263; *Librn,* Lynette Teruya; Tel: 808-739-4860; Staff 3.8 (MLS 3.8)
Founded 1955. Enrl 2,400; Fac 80; Highest Degree: Master
Library Holdings: DVDs 1,200; e-books 36,000; e-journals 17,000; Bk Vols 75,000; Per Subs 230
Special Collections: Catholic Authors; Hawaiiana; Judaica
Automation Activity & Vendor Info: (Cataloging) SirsiDynix; (Circulation) SirsiDynix; (ILL) OCLC; (OPAC) SirsiDynix; (Serials) SirsiDynix
Wireless access
Partic in Hawaii Library Consortium; OCLC Online Computer Library Center, Inc
Open Mon-Thurs 8:15am-11pm, Fri 8:15-6, Sat 11-4, Sun 4-11

G CITY & COUNTY OF HONOLULU MUNICIPAL REFERENCE CENTER*, 558 S King St, 96813-3006. SAN 303-4895. Tel: 808-768-3765. E-mail: mrc@honolulu.gov. Web Site: www.honolulu.gov/csd/mrc. *Libr Tech,* Robin Ballentyne; Staff 1 (Non-MLS 1)
Founded 1929
Special Collections: Ordinances & Repository for Publications of the City & County of Honolulu. Municipal Document Depository
Subject Interests: Municipal govt
Wireless access
Restriction: Open by appt only

S EAST-WEST CENTER*, Research Information Services, John A Burns Hall, Rm 4063 & 4066, 1601 East-West Rd, 96848-1601. SAN 326-7520. Tel: 808-944-7345. FAX: 808-944-7600. E-mail: EWCcontact@eastwestcenter.org, ris@eastwestcenter.org. Web Site: www.eastwestcenter.org/research/research-information-services. *Info Spec,* Phyllis Tabusa; Tel: 808-944-7450, E-mail: tabusap@eastwestcenter.org; *Libr Spec,* Jerilyn Sumida; Tel: 808-944-7379, E-mail: sumidaj@eastwestcenter.org; Staff 4 (MLS 4)
Founded 1971
Library Holdings: Bk Titles 50,000; Bk Vols 66,000; Per Subs 40
Special Collections: Asian & Pacific Census; World Fertility Survey
Subject Interests: Econ, Energy, Environ, Intl relations
Automation Activity & Vendor Info: (Cataloging) EOS International; (Circulation) EOS International; (ILL) OCLC; (OPAC) EOS International; (Serials) EOS International
Function: Doc delivery serv, ILL available, Ref serv available
Publications: Acquisitions Lists
Partic in OCLC Online Computer Library Center, Inc
Open Mon-Fri 8-Noon
Restriction: Restricted pub use

S HAWAII CHINESE HISTORY CENTER ARCHIVES*, 111 N King St, Rm 307, 96817. SAN 303-4593. Tel: 808-521-5948. E-mail: hchc71989@gmail.com. Web Site: sites.google.com/site/hawaiichinesehistorycenter. *Pres,* Douglas Chong
Founded 1970
Library Holdings: AV Mats 20; Bk Vols 850
Subject Interests: Chinese lang, Chinese-Am, Genealogy, Hawaii
Restriction: Open by appt only

M HAWAII PACIFIC HEALTH STRAUB MEDICAL CENTER*, Arnold Library, 888 S King St, 96813. SAN 303-495X. Tel: 808-522-4471. E-mail: libraryservices@hawaiipacifichealth.org. Web Site: www.straubhealth.com. *Med Librn,* David Coleman
Founded 1922
Library Holdings: Bk Vols 300; Per Subs 15
Special Collections: Physicians' Articles Coll
Subject Interests: Med
Wireless access
Function: Doc delivery serv, ILL available, Photocopying/Printing, Ref serv available, Res libr
Partic in National Network of Libraries of Medicine Region 5; Proquest Dialog
Restriction: Staff use only

C HAWAII PACIFIC UNIVERSITY LIBRARIES*, Meader Library, 1060 Bishop St, 96813-3192. SAN 303-4674. Tel: 808-544-0210. Reference Tel: 808-544-1133. Administration Tel: 808-544-0292. FAX: 808-521-7998. Reference E-mail: reference@hpu.edu. Web Site: www.hpu.edu/libraries. *Actg Dir,* Valentina Abordonado, PhD; E-mail: vabordonado@hpu.edu; Staff 26 (MLS 14, Non-MLS 12)
Founded 1965. Highest Degree: Master
Library Holdings: DVDs 3,000; e-books 50,000; e-journals 25,000; High Interest/Low Vocabulary Bk Vols 1,000; Bk Titles 90,000; Bk Vols 110,000; Per Subs 1,000
Special Collections: Atlas Coll; Closed Coll; Foreign Language Coll; Graduate Professional Paper Coll; Hawaiian-Pacific Coll; Index Center Coll; Topic Assistance Center Coll
Automation Activity & Vendor Info: (Circulation) TLC (The Library Corporation); (ILL) OCLC Online
Wireless access
Function: AV serv, Photocopying/Printing, Ref serv available, VHS videos
Open Mon-Fri 8-5
Restriction: Open to students, fac & staff

Departmental Libraries:

ATHERTON LIBRARY, Cook Academic Ctr, 45-045 Kamehameha Hwy, Kaneohe, 96744, SAN 303-5050. Tel: 808-236-3505. Reference Tel: 808-236-5803. FAX: 808-236-5806. E-mail: atherton@hpu.edu. *Head, Pub Serv,* Elizabeth Torres; E-mail: etorres@hpu.edu; Staff 6 (MLS 4, Non-MLS 2)
Founded 1967. Highest Degree: Master
Subject Interests: Hawaii, Nursing, Pacific, Sci
Function: Electronic databases & coll, Photocopying/Printing
Open Mon-Fri 8-5

S HAWAII SCHOOL FOR THE DEAF & BLIND LIBRARY*, Bldg E, 3440 Leahi Ave, 96815. SAN 303-4690. Tel: 808-733-4999, Ext 264. FAX: 808-733-4824. Web Site: www.hsdb.k12.hi.us/library.html. *Librn,* Jan Khil; Staff 2 (MLS 1, Non-MLS 1)
Founded 1976
Library Holdings: Bks on Deafness & Sign Lang 100; Braille Volumes 100; Large Print Bks 100; Bk Titles 6,000; Videos 5,000
Special Collections: Braille Textbooks; Captioned Media Program, VHS; Large Print Textbooks
Automation Activity & Vendor Info: (Acquisitions) Follett Software
Function: Accelerated reader prog, Online cat
Restriction: Open to students, fac & staff

G HAWAII STATE ARCHIVES*, Iolani Palace Grounds, 364 S King St, 96813. SAN 303-4704. Tel: 808-586-0329. FAX: 808-586-0330. E-mail: archives@hawaii.gov. Web Site: ags.hawaii.gov/archives. *Head, Coll Mgt,* Gina S Vergara-Bautista; E-mail: gina.s.vergara-bautista@hawaii.gov; *State Archivist,* Adam Jansen; *Dep State Archivist,* Ju Sun Yi; E-mail: ju.sun.yi@hawaii.gov; *Archivist,* Alice Y Tran; E-mail: alice.y.tran@hawaii.gov; *Archivist,* Dr Ronald C Williams; E-mail: ron.c.williams@hawaii.gov; *Supvr,* Gina S Vergara-Bautista; E-mail: gina.s.vergara-bautista@hawaii.gov; *Libr Tech,* Fredericka P Aikau; E-mail: fredericka.p.aikau@hawaii.gov; *Libr Asst,* Melissa Shimonishi; E-mail: melissa.shimonishi@hawaii.gov; Staff 12 (MLS 6, Non-MLS 6)
Founded 1905
Library Holdings: Bk Vols 25,000
Special Collections: 19th Century Hawaiian Newspapers; Captain James Cook Memorial Coll; Hawaiian Government Publications Coll; Immigration Records to 1900; National Territorial & State Archives, 1790 to date; Paul M Kahn Coll
Open Mon-Fri 9-4

P HAWAII STATE PUBLIC LIBRARY SYSTEM*, Office of the State Librarian, 44 Merchant St, 96813. SAN 339-3992. Tel: 808-586-3704. Circulation Tel: 808-586-3500. Interlibrary Loan Service Tel: 808-586-3624. Reference Tel: 808-586-3621. FAX: 808-586-3715. Web Site: www.librarieshawaii.org. *State Librn,* Stacey Aldrich; E-mail: stlib@librarieshawaii.org; Staff 179 (MLS 176, Non-MLS 3)
Founded 1961. Pop 1,427,538; Circ 5,887,611
Jul 2017-Jun 2018 Income $39,229,791, State $35,961,873, Federal $794,628, Other $2,473,290. Mats Exp $4,242,675, Books $2,491,491, Per/Ser (Incl. Access Fees) $120,461, Other Print Mats $43,698, Micro $43,895, Electronic Ref Mat (Incl. Access Fees) $1,120,394. Sal $24,976,710
Library Holdings: Audiobooks 152,768; AV Mats 60; Braille Volumes 23,689; CDs 108,095; DVDs 174,127; e-books 135,098; Large Print Bks 30,665; Microforms 589; Bk Vols 3,173,711; Per Subs 2,609; Videos 1,644
Special Collections: Pacific Coll. State Document Depository; US Document Depository
Subject Interests: Chinese lang, Hawaii, Japanese (Lang), Korean (Lang)
Automation Activity & Vendor Info: (Acquisitions) SirsiDynix; (Cataloging) SirsiDynix; (Circulation) SirsiDynix; (OPAC) SirsiDynix
Wireless access
Function: 24/7 Electronic res, 24/7 Online cat, Activity rm, Adult bk club, Archival coll, Art exhibits, Art programs, Audiobks on Playaways & MP3,

Bk club(s), Bks on cassette, Bks on CD, CD-ROM, Chess club, Children's prog, Computer training, Computers for patron use, E-Readers, Electronic databases & coll, Life-long learning prog for all ages, Magazines, Mail & tel request accepted, Makerspace, Mango lang, Meeting rooms, Microfiche/film & reading machines, Movies, Music CDs, Online cat, Orientations, Outreach serv, OverDrive digital audio bks, Passport agency, Photocopying/Printing, Preschool outreach, Preschool reading prog, Prog for adults, Prog for children & young adult, Ref serv available, Res assist avail, Res performed for a fee, STEM programs, Story hour, Summer reading prog, Tax forms, Teen prog, Telephone ref, VHS videos, Workshops, Writing prog
Partic in Hawaii Library Consortium
Special Services for the Deaf - TTY equip
Special Services for the Blind - Braille bks; Braille servs; Descriptive video serv (DVS); Large print bks; Radio reading serv; Talking bks
Friends of the Library Group

Branches: 51

AIEA PUBLIC LIBRARY, 99-374 Pohai Pl, Aiea, 96701, SAN 339-4654. Tel: 808-483-7333. FAX: 808-483-7336. Web Site: www.librarieshawaii.org/branch/aiea-public-library. *Br Mgr,* Tina Takamoto; E-mail: tina.takamoto@librarieshawaii.org; Staff 3 (MLS 3)
Founded 1964. Circ 108,339
Library Holdings: Bk Vols 80,840
Function: 24/7 Electronic res, 24/7 Online cat, Art exhibits, Art programs, Children's prog, Computers for patron use, Holiday prog, ILL available, Internet access, Life-long learning prog for all ages, Magazines, Mango lang, Meeting rooms, Movies, Music CDs, Online cat, OverDrive digital audio bks, Photocopying/Printing, Prog for adults, Prog for children & young adult, Ref serv available, Summer reading prog, Teen prog, VHS videos
Special Services for the Deaf - TTY equip
Open Mon-Wed & Sat 10-5, Thurs 1-8
Friends of the Library Group

AINA HAINA PUBLIC LIBRARY, 5246 Kalanianaole Hwy, 96821, SAN 339-4263. Tel: 808-377-2456. FAX: 808-377-2455. Web Site: www.librarieshawaii.org/branch/aina-haina-public-library. *Br Mgr,* Holly Kwok; E-mail: holly.kwok@librarieshawaii.org; Staff 3 (MLS 3)
Founded 1962. Circ 86,233
Library Holdings: Bk Vols 60,350
Function: 24/7 Electronic res, 24/7 Online cat, Art programs, CD-ROM, Children's prog, Computers for patron use, Holiday prog, ILL available, Internet access, Life-long learning prog for all ages, Magazines, Mango lang, Movies, Music CDs, Online cat, OverDrive digital audio bks, Photocopying/Printing, Preschool reading prog, Prog for adults, Prog for children & young adult, Ref serv available, Summer reading prog, Teen prog
Open Tues 1-8, Wed-Sat 10-5
Friends of the Library Group

EWA BEACH PUBLIC & SCHOOL LIBRARY, 91-950 North Rd, Ewa Beach, 96706, SAN 339-4689. Tel: 808-689-1204. FAX: 808-689-1349. Web Site: www.librarieshawaii.org/branch/ewa-beach-public-and-school-library. *Br Mgr,* Shari-Lynn Murphy; E-mail: shari-lynn.murphy@@librarieshawaii.org; Staff 2 (MLS 2)
Founded 1971. Circ 61,463
Library Holdings: Bk Vols 62,003
Special Collections: Oral History
Function: 24/7 Electronic res, 24/7 Online cat, Art exhibits, Art programs, CD-ROM, Children's prog, Computers for patron use, Electronic databases & coll, Holiday prog, ILL available, Internet access, Life-long learning prog for all ages, Magazines, Mango lang, Movies, Music CDs, Online cat, OverDrive digital audio bks, Photocopying/Printing, Preschool reading prog, Prog for adults, Prog for children & young adult, Ref serv available, Story hour, Summer reading prog, Teen prog, VHS videos
Open Mon & Tues 1-8, Wed-Fri 10-5
Friends of the Library Group

HANA PUBLIC & SCHOOL LIBRARY, 4111 Hana Hwy, Hana, 96713. (Mail add: PO Box 490, Hana, 96713-0490), SAN 339-5480. Tel: 808-248-4848. FAX: 808-248-4849. Web Site: www.librarieshawaii.org/branch/hana-public-and-school-library. *Br Mgr,* Irene Pavao; E-mail: irene.pavao@librarieshawaii.org; Staff 1 (MLS 1)
Founded 1984. Circ 9,025
Library Holdings: Bk Vols 25,597
Function: 24/7 Electronic res, 24/7 Online cat, Art programs, CD-ROM, Children's prog, Computers for patron use, Electronic databases & coll, ILL available, Internet access, Life-long learning prog for all ages, Mango lang, Movies, Music CDs, Online cat, Outreach serv, OverDrive digital audio bks, Photocopying/Printing, Preschool outreach, Prog for adults, Prog for children & young adult, Story hour, Summer reading prog, VHS videos
Open Mon & Fri 8-4, Tues 9-4, Wed & Thurs 11-7
Friends of the Library Group

HANAPEPE PUBLIC LIBRARY, 4490 Kona Rd, Hanapepe, 96716. (Mail add: PO Box 557, Hanapepe, 96716), SAN 339-5316. Tel: 808-335-8418. FAX: 808-335-2120. Web Site: www.librarieshawaii.org/branch/hanapepe-public-library. *Br Mgr,* Mindy Gipson; Staff 1 (MLS 1)
Founded 1950. Circ 17,932
Library Holdings: Bk Vols 25,230
Function: 24/7 Electronic res, 24/7 Online cat, Art programs, Children's prog, Computers for patron use, Electronic databases & coll, ILL available, Internet access, Life-long learning prog for all ages, Magazines, Mango lang, Meeting rooms, Music CDs, Online cat, OverDrive digital audio bks, Photocopying/Printing, Prog for adults, Prog for children & young adult, Ref serv available, Summer reading prog, VHS videos
Open Tues, Wed & Fri 9-5, Thurs 12-8, Sat 8:30-4
Friends of the Library Group

HAWAII KAI PUBLIC LIBRARY, 249 Lunalilo Home Rd, 96825, SAN 339-4298. Tel: 808-397-5833. FAX: 808-397-5832. Web Site: www.librarieshawaii.org/branch/hawaii-kai-public-library. *Br Mgr,* Colleen Lashway; E-mail: colleen.lashway@librarieshawaii.org; Staff 4 (MLS 4)
Founded 1973. Circ 89,324
Library Holdings: Bk Vols 65,539
Function: 24/7 Electronic res, 24/7 Online cat, Activity rm, Art programs, CD-ROM, Children's prog, Computers for patron use, Holiday prog, ILL available, Internet access, Life-long learning prog for all ages, Magazines, Mango lang, Meeting rooms, Movies, Music CDs, Online cat, OverDrive digital audio bks, Photocopying/Printing, Prog for adults, Prog for children & young adult, Ref serv available, Story hour, Summer reading prog, VHS videos
Special Services for the Deaf - TTY equip
Open Mon 12-7, Tues-Thurs & Sat 9-5
Friends of the Library Group

HAWAII STATE LIBRARY, 478 S King St, 96813, SAN 339-4050. Tel: 808-586-3500. FAX: 808-586-3943. TDD: 808-586-3471. Web Site: www.librarieshawaii.org/branch/hawaii-state-library. *Actg Dir,* Marya Zoller; E-mail: marya.zoller@librarieshawaii.org; Staff 39 (MLS 38, Non-MLS 1)
Founded 1913. Circ 183,954
Library Holdings: Bk Vols 542,891
Special Collections: Asian Language Materials; Federal Documents; Hawaii & Pacific Coll; Patent & Trademark Depository; Telephone References
Subject Interests: Art, Hist, Lit, Music, Philos, Recreation, Sci tech, Soc sci & issues, Tech
Function: 24/7 Electronic res, 24/7 Online cat, Adult bk club, Archival coll, Art exhibits, Art programs, Bk club(s), Bks on cassette, Bks on CD, CD-ROM, Children's prog, Computer training, Computers for patron use, Electronic databases & coll, Govt ref serv, Holiday prog, ILL available, Internet access, Life-long learning prog for all ages, Magazines, Mango lang, Microfiche/film & reading machines, Movies, Music CDs, Online cat, Online ref, Outreach serv, OverDrive digital audio bks, Passport agency, Photocopying/Printing, Preschool reading prog, Prog for adults, Prog for children & young adult, Ref serv available, Res performed for a fee, Story hour, Summer reading prog, Tax forms, Teen prog, Telephone ref, VHS videos, Visual arts prog, Wheelchair accessible
Special Services for the Deaf - TTY equip
Open Mon & Wed 10-5, Tues, Fri & Sat 9-5, Thurs 9-8
Friends of the Library Group

HILO PUBLIC LIBRARY, 300 Waianuenue Ave, Hilo, 96720, SAN 339-4891. Tel: 808-933-8890. FAX: 808-933-8895. Web Site: www.librarieshawaii.org/branch/hilo-public-library. *Br Mgr,* Position Currently Open; Staff 6 (MLS 6)
Founded 1880. Circ 219,315
Library Holdings: Bk Vols 203,531
Function: 24/7 Electronic res, 24/7 Online cat, Art programs, CD-ROM, Chess club, Children's prog, Computer training, Computers for patron use, Electronic databases & coll, ILL available, Internet access, Life-long learning prog for all ages, Magazines, Mango lang, Movies, Music CDs, Online cat, OverDrive digital audio bks, Prog for adults, Prog for children & young adult, Ref serv available, Story hour, Summer reading prog, Teen prog, VHS videos
Special Services for the Deaf - TTY equip
Open Tues & Wed 11-7, Thurs & Sat 9-5, Fri 10-5
Friends of the Library Group

HONOKAA PUBLIC LIBRARY, Bldg 3, 45-3380 Mamane St, Honokaa, 96727, SAN 339-4980. Tel: 808-775-8881. FAX: 808-775-8882. Web Site: www.librarieshawaii.org/branch/honokaa-public-library. *Br Mgr,* Position Currently Open; Staff 1 (MLS 1)
Founded 1937. Circ 18,109
Library Holdings: Bk Vols 17,069
Function: 24/7 Electronic res, 24/7 Online cat, Art programs, Children's prog, Computers for patron use, Electronic databases & coll, Internet access, Life-long learning prog for all ages, Magazines, Mango lang,

Music CDs, Online cat, Photocopying/Printing, Prog for adults, Prog for children & young adult, Summer reading prog
Open Mon & Thurs 11-7, Tues & Wed 9-5, Fri 9-3
Friends of the Library Group
KAHUKU PUBLIC & SCHOOL LIBRARY, 56-490 Kamehameha, Kahuku, 96731. Tel: 808-293-8935. FAX: 808-293-8937. Web Site: www.librarieshawaii.org/branch/kahuku-public-and-school-library. *Br Mgr,* Tamara King; E-mail: tamara.king@libarieshawaii.org; Staff 2 (MLS 2)
Founded 1968. Circ 35,871
Library Holdings: Bk Vols 45,478
Function: 24/7 Electronic res, 24/7 Online cat, Art programs, Children's prog, Computers for patron use, ILL available, Internet access, Life-long learning prog for all ages, Magazines, Mango lang, Movies, Music CDs, Online cat, OverDrive digital audio bks, Photocopying/Printing, Prog for adults, Prog for children & young adult, Ref serv available, Story hour, Summer reading prog, VHS videos
Open Mon, Wed & Thurs 9-5, Tues 12-8, Fri 9-3
Friends of the Library Group
KAHULUI PUBLIC LIBRARY, 90 School St, Kahului, 96732, SAN 339-5499. Tel: 808-873-3097. FAX: 808-873-3094. Web Site: www.librarieshawaii.org/branch/kahului-public-library. *Br Mgr,* Position Currently Open; Staff 3 (MLS 3)
Founded 1963. Circ 85,700
Library Holdings: Bk Vols 100,182
Function: 24/7 Electronic res, 24/7 Online cat, Art programs, CD-ROM, Computers for patron use, ILL available, Internet access, Life-long learning prog for all ages, Magazines, Mango lang, Music CDs, Online cat, OverDrive digital audio bks, Photocopying/Printing, Prog for adults, Prog for children & young adult, Ref serv available, Summer reading prog, VHS videos
Open Tues 12-8, Wed-Sat 9-5
Friends of the Library Group
KAILUA-KONA PUBLIC LIBRARY, 75-138 Hualalai Rd, Kailua-Kona, 96740, SAN 339-5014. Tel: 808-327-4327. FAX: 808-327-4326. Web Site: www.librarieshawaii.org/branch/kailua-kona-public-library. *Br Mgr,* Position Currently Open; Staff 3 (MLS 3)
Founded 1972. Circ 96,788
Library Holdings: Bk Vols 54,595
Function: 24/7 Electronic res, 24/7 Online cat, Art programs, Children's prog, Computers for patron use, Holiday prog, ILL available, Internet access, Life-long learning prog for all ages, Magazines, Mango lang, Movies, Music CDs, Online cat, OverDrive digital audio bks, Photocopying/Printing, Prog for adults, Prog for children & young adult, Story hour, Summer reading prog, VHS videos
Open Tues 12-7, Wed, Thurs & Sat 9-5, Fri 11-5
Friends of the Library Group
KAILUA PUBLIC LIBRARY, 239 Kuulei Rd, Kailua, 96734, SAN 339-4352. Tel: 808-266-9911. FAX: 808-266-9915. Web Site: www.librarieshawaii.org/branch/kailua-public-library. *Br Mgr,* Patti Meerians; E-mail: patti.meerians@librarieshawaii.org; Staff 3.5 (MLS 3.5)
Founded 1960. Circ 156,704
Library Holdings: Bk Vols 69,169
Function: 24/7 Electronic res, 24/7 Online cat, Adult bk club, Art programs, Bk club(s), CD-ROM, Children's prog, Computers for patron use, Electronic databases & coll, ILL available, Internet access, Life-long learning prog for all ages, Magazines, Mango lang, Music CDs, Online cat, OverDrive digital audio bks, Photocopying/Printing, Prog for adults, Prog for children & young adult, Ref serv available, Story hour, Summer reading prog, Teen prog, VHS videos
Open Mon, Wed, Fri & Sat 10-5, Tues & Thurs 1-8
Friends of the Library Group
KAIMUKI PUBLIC LIBRARY, 1041 Koko Head Ave, 96816, SAN 339-4387. Tel: 808-733-8422. FAX: 808-733-8426. Web Site: www.librarieshawaii.org/branch/kaimuki-public-library. *Br Mgr,* Lea Domingo; E-mail: lea.domingo@librarieshawaii.org; Staff 5 (MLS 5)
Founded 1940. Circ 162,030
Library Holdings: Bk Vols 80,832
Function: 24/7 Electronic res, 24/7 Online cat, Adult bk club, Art programs, Bk club(s), CD-ROM, Children's prog, Computers for patron use, Electronic databases & coll, Holiday prog, ILL available, Internet access, Life-long learning prog for all ages, Magazines, Mango lang, Online cat, OverDrive digital audio bks, Photocopying/Printing, Prog for adults, Prog for children & young adult, Ref serv available, Story hour, Summer reading prog, Teen prog, VHS videos, Wheelchair accessible
Open Mon & Tues 10-8, Wed & Thurs 10-6, Fri 1-5, Sun 10-5
Friends of the Library Group
KALIHI-PALAMA PUBLIC LIBRARY, 1325 Kalihi St, 96819, SAN 339-4417. Tel: 808-832-3466. FAX: 808-832-3469. Web Site: www.librarieshawaii.org/branch/kalihi-palama-public-library. *Br Mgr,* Trisha Murakami; E-mail: trisha.murakami@librarieshawaii.org; Staff 3 (MLS 3)
Founded 1935. Circ 75,094
Library Holdings: Bk Vols 54,923
Function: 24/7 Electronic res, 24/7 Online cat, Art programs, CD-ROM, Computers for patron use, Electronic databases & coll, ILL available, Internet access, Life-long learning prog for all ages, Magazines, Mango lang, Movies, Online cat, OverDrive digital audio bks, Photocopying/Printing, Preschool reading prog, Prog for adults, Prog for children & young adult, Ref serv available, Story hour, Summer reading prog, Teen prog, VHS videos
Open Mon & Wed 1-8, Tues & Thurs-Sat 10-5
Friends of the Library Group
KANEOHE PUBLIC LIBRARY, 45-829 Kamehameha Hwy, Kaneohe, 96744, SAN 339-4441. Tel: 808-233-5676. FAX: 808-233-5672. Web Site: www.librarieshawaii.org/branch/kaneohe-public-library. *Br Mgr,* Cynthia Chow; E-mail: cyndi.chow@librarieshawaii.org; Staff 5 (MLS 5)
Founded 1961. Circ 139,429
Library Holdings: Bk Vols 92,690
Function: 24/7 Electronic res, 24/7 Online cat, Art programs, CD-ROM, Chess club, Children's prog, Computers for patron use, Electronic databases & coll, Holiday prog, ILL available, Internet access, Life-long learning prog for all ages, Magazines, Mango lang, Microfiche/film & reading machines, Movies, Music CDs, Online cat, OverDrive digital audio bks, Photocopying/Printing, Prog for adults, Prog for children & young adult, Ref serv available, STEM programs, Story hour, Summer reading prog, Teen prog, VHS videos
Open Mon & Wed 10-8, Tues, Thurs & Sun 10-5, Fri 1-5
Friends of the Library Group
KAPAA PUBLIC LIBRARY, 4-1464 Kuhio Hwy, Kapaa, 96746, SAN 339-5340. Tel: 808-821-4422. FAX: 808-821-4423. TDD: 808-821-4438. Web Site: www.librarieshawaii.org/branch/kapaa-public-library. *Br Mgr,* Lani Kawahara; E-mail: lani.kawahara@librarieshawaii.org; Staff 1 (MLS 1)
Founded 1955. Circ 52,770
Library Holdings: Bk Vols 36,331
Function: 24/7 Electronic res, 24/7 Online cat, Art programs, Computers for patron use, Electronic databases & coll, ILL available, Internet access, Magazines, Makerspace, Mango lang, Music CDs, Online cat, OverDrive digital audio bks, Photocopying/Printing, Prog for adults, Prog for children & young adult, Ref serv available, Summer reading prog, VHS videos
Special Services for the Deaf - TTY equip
Open Mon & Wed-Fri 9-5, Tues 12-8
Friends of the Library Group
KAPOLEI PUBLIC LIBRARY, 1020 Manawai St, Kapolei, 96707, SAN 991-0018. Tel: 808-693-7050. FAX: 808-693-7062. Web Site: www.librarieshawaii.org/branch/kapolei-public-library. *Br Mgr,* Position Currently Open; Staff 7 (MLS 7)
Founded 2004. Circ 205,832
Library Holdings: Bk Vols 143,436
Function: 24/7 Electronic res, 24/7 Online cat, Adult bk club, Art programs, Bk club(s), CD-ROM, Children's prog, Computers for patron use, Electronic databases & coll, Holiday prog, ILL available, Internet access, Life-long learning prog for all ages, Magazines, Mango lang, Music CDs, Online cat, OverDrive digital audio bks, Prog for adults, Prog for children & young adult, Ref serv available, Story hour, Summer reading prog, Teen prog, VHS videos, Wheelchair accessible
Open Mon & Thurs-Sat 10-5, Tues & Wed 10-8
Friends of the Library Group
KEAAU PUBLIC & SCHOOL LIBRARY, 16-571 Keaau-Pahoa Rd, Keaau, 96749, SAN 339-5049. Tel: 808-982-4281. FAX: 808-982-4242. Web Site: www.librarieshawaii.org/branch/keaau-public-and-school-library. *Br Mgr,* Maxine Aki; E-mail: maxine.aki@librarieshawaii.org; Staff 1 (MLS 1)
Founded 1974. Circ 33,439
Library Holdings: Bk Vols 34,970
Function: 24/7 Electronic res, 24/7 Online cat, Art programs, Computers for patron use, Electronic databases & coll, Internet access, Life-long learning prog for all ages, Magazines, Mango lang, Music CDs, Online cat, OverDrive digital audio bks, Summer reading prog, VHS videos
Open Mon 9-4:30, Tues & Thurs 1-8, Wed 10-4:30, Fri 8:30-4:30
KEALAKEKUA PUBLIC LIBRARY, 81-6619 Mamalahoa Hwy, Kealakekua, 96750. (Mail add: PO Box 768, Kealakekua, 96750). Tel: 808-323-7585. FAX: 808-323-7586. Web Site: www.librarieshawaii.org/branch/kealakekua-public-library. *Br Mgr,* Judith Andrews; E-mail: judith.andrews@librarieshawaii.org; Staff 1 (MLS 1)
Founded 1950. Circ 41,935
Library Holdings: Bk Vols 21,990
Function: 24/7 Electronic res, 24/7 Online cat, Art programs, Children's prog, Electronic databases & coll, Internet access, Life-long learning prog for all ages, Magazines, Mango lang, Online cat, OverDrive digital audio bks, Photocopying/Printing, Prog for adults, Prog for children & young adult, Summer reading prog, VHS videos
Open Mon 10-5, Tues, Thurs & Fri 11-5, Wed 12-7
Friends of the Library Group

KIHEI PUBLIC LIBRARY, 35 Waimahaihai St, Kihei, 96753, SAN 326-8667. Tel: 808-875-6833. FAX: 808-875-6834. Web Site: www.librarieshawaii.org/branch/kihei-public-library. *Br Mgr,* Tracy Latimer; E-mail: tracy.latimer@librarieshawaii.org; Staff 2 (MLS 2)
Founded 1988. Circ 82,342
Library Holdings: Bk Vols 65,279
Function: 24/7 Electronic res, 24/7 Online cat, Art programs, CD-ROM, Children's prog, Computers for patron use, Holiday prog, ILL available, Internet access, Life-long learning prog for all ages, Magazines, Mango lang, Music CDs, OverDrive digital audio bks, Prog for adults, Prog for children & young adult, Ref serv available, Story hour, Summer reading prog, VHS videos
Open Tues 12-8, Wed-Sat 10-5
Friends of the Library Group

KOLOA PUBLIC & SCHOOL LIBRARY, 3451 Poipu Rd, Koloa, 96756. (Mail add: PO Box 9, Koloa, 96756-0009), SAN 339-5375. Tel: 808-742-8455. FAX: 808-742-8454. Web Site: www.librarieshawaii.org/branch/koloa-public-and-school-library. *Br Mgr,* David Thorp; E-mail: david.thorp@librarieshawaii.org; Staff 1 (MLS 1)
Founded 1976. Circ 40,959
Library Holdings: Bk Vols 32,833
Special Collections: Koloa, Kauai History Materials
Function: 24/7 Electronic res, 24/7 Online cat, Computers for patron use, Electronic databases & coll, ILL available, Internet access, Magazines, Mango lang, Music CDs, Online cat, OverDrive digital audio bks, Photocopying/Printing, Ref serv available, Summer reading prog
Open Mon, Tues & Fri 8:30-5, Wed 12-8, Thurs 9-5
Friends of the Library Group

LAHAINA PUBLIC LIBRARY, 680 Wharf St, Lahaina, 96761, SAN 339-5529. Tel: 808-662-3950. FAX: 808-662-3951. Web Site: www.librarieshawaii.org/branch/lahaina-public-library. *Br Mgr,* Alayna Davies-Smith; Staff 1 (Non-MLS 1)
Founded 1956. Circ 34,333
Library Holdings: Bk Vols 25,085
Function: 24/7 Electronic res, 24/7 Online cat, Art programs, CD-ROM, Children's prog, Computers for patron use, Electronic databases & coll, ILL available, Internet access, Life-long learning prog for all ages, Magazines, Mango lang, Online cat, OverDrive digital audio bks, Photocopying/Printing, Prog for adults, Prog for children & young adult, Ref serv available, Story hour, Summer reading prog, VHS videos
Open Tues 12-8, Wed & Thurs 9-5, Fri & Sat 10:30-4:30
Friends of the Library Group

LANAI PUBLIC & SCHOOL LIBRARY, 555 Fraser Ave, Lanai City, 96763. (Mail add: PO Box 630550, Lanai City, 96763-0550), SAN 339-5553. Tel: 808-565-7920. FAX: 808-565-7922. TDD: 808-565-6996. Web Site: www.librarieshawaii.org/branch/lanai-public-and-school-library. *Br Mgr,* Peggy Fink; E-mail: peggy.fink@librarieshawaii.org; Staff 1 (MLS 1)
Founded 1975. Circ 22,793
Library Holdings: Bk Vols 34,529
Function: 24/7 Electronic res, 24/7 Online cat, Art programs, CD-ROM, Children's prog, Computers for patron use, Electronic databases & coll, ILL available, Internet access, Life-long learning prog for all ages, Magazines, Mango lang, Movies, Music CDs, Online cat, OverDrive digital audio bks, Photocopying/Printing, Prog for adults, Prog for children & young adult, Ref serv available, Story hour, Summer reading prog
Special Services for the Deaf - TTY equip
Open Mon-Wed & Fri 9-5, Thurs 1-8
Friends of the Library Group

LAUPAHOEHOE PUBLIC & SCHOOL LIBRARY, 35-2065 Old Mamalahoa Hwy, Laupahoehoe, 96764. (Mail add: PO Box 249, Laupahoehoe, 96764-0249), SAN 339-5103. Tel: 808-962-2229. FAX: 808-962-2230. Web Site: www.librarieshawaii.org/branch/laupahoehoe-public-and-school-library. *Br Mgr,* Position Currently Open; Staff 1 (MLS 1)
Founded 1973. Circ 19,364
Library Holdings: Bk Vols 25,123
Function: 24/7 Electronic res, 24/7 Online cat, Bk club(s), Children's prog, Computers for patron use, Electronic databases & coll, Internet access, Magazines, Mango lang, Music CDs, Online cat, Online ref, OverDrive digital audio bks, Prog for adults, Prog for children & young adult, Ref serv available, Summer reading prog, Telephone ref
Open Mon 12-8, Tues-Thurs 9-5, Fri 9-4
Friends of the Library Group

LIBRARY FOR THE BLIND & PHYSICALLY HANDICAPPED
See Separate Entry

LIHUE PUBLIC LIBRARY, 4344 Hardy St, Lihue, 96766, SAN 339-5286. Tel: 808-241-3222. FAX: 808-241-3225. Web Site: www.librarieshawaii.org/branch/lihue-public-library. *Br Mgr,* Position Currently Open; Staff 3 (MLS 3)
Founded 1969. Circ 61,595
Library Holdings: Bk Vols 61,595
Function: 24/7 Electronic res, 24/7 Online cat, Children's prog, Computers for patron use, ILL available, Internet access, Magazines, Mango lang, Music CDs, OverDrive digital audio bks, Photocopying/Printing, Prog for adults, Prog for children & young adult, Ref serv available, Story hour, Summer reading prog, VHS videos
Special Services for the Deaf - TTY equip
Open Mon & Wed 11-7, Tues, Thurs & Fri 9-4:30
Friends of the Library Group

LILIHA PUBLIC LIBRARY, 1515 Liliha St, 96817, SAN 339-4476. Tel: 808-587-7577. FAX: 808-587-7579. Web Site: www.librarieshawaii.org/branch/liliha-public-library. *Br Mgr,* Linda Mediati; E-mail: linda.mediati@librarieshawaii.org; Staff 3 (MLS 3)
Founded 1966. Circ 146
Library Holdings: Bk Vols 72,671
Special Collections: Chinese Language Coll
Function: 24/7 Electronic res, 24/7 Online cat, Activity rm, Art programs, CD-ROM, Children's prog, Computers for patron use, Electronic databases & coll, Holiday prog, ILL available, Internet access, Life-long learning prog for all ages, Magazines, Mango lang, Meeting rooms, Movies, Music CDs, Online cat, OverDrive digital audio bks, Prog for adults, Prog for children & young adult, Ref serv available, Story hour, Summer reading prog, VHS videos
Special Services for the Deaf - TTY equip
Library is temporarily closed for repairs 2021
Restriction: Not open to pub
Friends of the Library Group

MAKAWAO PUBLIC LIBRARY, 1159 Makawao Ave, Makawao, 96768, SAN 339-5588. Tel: 808-573-8785. FAX: 808-573-8787. Web Site: www.librarieshawaii.org/branch/makawao-public-library. *Br Mgr,* Laurie Barker-Perez; E-mail: laurie.barkerperez@librarieshawaii.org; Staff 2 (MLS 2)
Founded 1969. Circ 91,757
Library Holdings: Bk Vols 33,687
Function: 24/7 Electronic res, 24/7 Online cat, Adult bk club, Art programs, Chess club, Children's prog, Computers for patron use, Holiday prog, ILL available, Internet access, Life-long learning prog for all ages, Magazines, Mango lang, Movies, Online cat, OverDrive digital audio bks, Photocopying/Printing, Prog for adults, Prog for children & young adult, Ref serv available, Story hour, Summer reading prog, VHS videos
Open Mon & Wed 12-8, Tues, Thurs & Sat 9:30-5
Friends of the Library Group

MANOA PUBLIC LIBRARY, 2716 Woodlawn Dr, 96822, SAN 339-4506. Tel: 808-988-0459. FAX: 808-988-0458. Web Site: www.librarieshawaii.org/branch/manoa-public-library. *Br Mgr,* Christel Collins; E-mail: christel.collins@librarieshawaii.org; Staff 3 (MLS 3)
Founded 1966. Circ 171,425
Library Holdings: Bk Vols 65,176
Function: 24/7 Electronic res, 24/7 Online cat, Activity rm, Art exhibits, Art programs, Children's prog, Computers for patron use, Electronic databases & coll, ILL available, Internet access, Life-long learning prog for all ages, Magazines, Mango lang, Movies, Music CDs, Online cat, OverDrive digital audio bks, Photocopying/Printing, Prog for adults, Prog for children & young adult, Ref serv available, Story hour, Summer reading prog, Teen prog, VHS videos, Wheelchair accessible
Open Mon, Tues & Sat 10-5, Wed & Thurs 12-8, Fri 1-5
Friends of the Library Group

MCCULLY-MOILIILI PUBLIC LIBRARY, 2211 S King St, 96826, SAN 339-4530. Tel: 808-973-1099. FAX: 808-973-1095. Web Site: www.librarieshawaii.org/branch/mccully-moiliili-public-library. *Br Mgr,* Hillary Chang; E-mail: hillary.chang@librarieshawaii.org; Staff 4 (MLS 4)
Founded 1969. Circ 138,167
Library Holdings: Bk Vols 63,084
Special Collections: Korean Language Coll
Function: 24/7 Electronic res, 24/7 Online cat, Activity rm, Art programs, Children's prog, Computers for patron use, Electronic databases & coll, Holiday prog, ILL available, Internet access, Life-long learning prog for all ages, Magazines, Mango lang, Meeting rooms, Movies, Music CDs, Online cat, OverDrive digital audio bks, Photocopying/Printing, Prog for adults, Prog for children & young adult, Ref serv available, STEM programs, Story hour, Summer reading prog, Teen prog, VHS videos
Special Services for the Deaf - TTY equip
Library closed for renovation.
Friends of the Library Group

MILILANI PUBLIC LIBRARY, 95-450 Makaimoimo St, Mililani, 96789, SAN 339-4700. Tel: 808-627-7470. FAX: 808-627-7309. Web Site: www.librarieshawaii.org/branch/mililani-public-library. *Br Mgr,* Wendi Woodstrup; E-mail: wendi.woodstrup@librarieshawaii.org; Staff 4 (MLS 4)
Founded 1984. Circ 173,904
Library Holdings: Bk Vols 77,615
Function: 24/7 Electronic res, 24/7 Online cat, Art programs, Children's prog, Computers for patron use, Electronic databases & coll, Holiday prog, ILL available, Internet access, Life-long learning prog for all ages, Magazines, Mango lang, Movies, Music CDs, OverDrive digital audio

bks, Photocopying/Printing, Prog for adults, Prog for children & young adult, Ref serv available, Story hour, Teen prog, VHS videos
Special Services for the Deaf - TTY equip
Open Mon & Wed 1-8, Tues & Thurs-Sat 10-5
Friends of the Library Group

MOLOKAI PUBLIC LIBRARY, 15 Ala Malama Ave, Kaunakakai, 96748. (Mail add: PO Box 395, Kaunakakai, 96748-0395), SAN 339-5618. Tel: 808-553-1765. FAX: 808-553-1766. Web Site: www.librarieshawaii.org/branch/molokai-public-library. *Br Mgr,* Cynthia Delanty; E-mail: cynthia.delanty@librarieshawaii.org; Staff 1 (MLS 1)
Founded 1937. Circ 22,338
Library Holdings: Bk Vols 26,939
Function: 24/7 Electronic res, 24/7 Online cat, Art exhibits, Art programs, CD-ROM, Children's prog, Computers for patron use, Electronic databases & coll, ILL available, Internet access, Life-long learning prog for all ages, Magazines, Mango lang, Music CDs, Online cat, Preschool outreach, Prog for adults, Prog for children & young adult, Ref serv available, Story hour, Summer reading prog, VHS videos
Special Services for the Deaf - TTY equip
Open Mon, Tues, Thurs & Fri 9:30-5, Wed 12:30-8
Friends of the Library Group

MOUNTAIN VIEW PUBLIC & SCHOOL LIBRARY, 18-1235 Volcano Hwy, Mountain View, 96771. (Mail add: PO Box 380, Mountain View, 96771-0380), SAN 339-5138. Tel: 808-968-2322. FAX: 808-968-2323. Web Site: www.librarieshawaii.org/branch/mountain-view-public-and-school-library. *Br Mgr,* Bonnie Perry; E-mail: bonnie.perry@librarieshawaii.org; Staff 1 (MLS 1)
Founded 1977. Circ 21,448
Library Holdings: Bk Vols 21,950
Function: 24/7 Electronic res, 24/7 Online cat, Art programs, Magazines, Mango lang, Movies, Online cat, Online ref, OverDrive digital audio bks, Photocopying/Printing, Prog for adults, Prog for children & young adult, Ref serv available, Summer reading prog, Telephone ref
Open Mon & Tues 12-7:30, Wed & Thurs 10-6, Fri 10-4
Friends of the Library Group

NAALEHU PUBLIC LIBRARY, 95-5669 Mamalahoa Hwy, Naalehu, 96772. (Mail add: PO Box 653, Naalehu, 96772-0653), SAN 339-5146. Tel: 808-939-2442. FAX: 808-939-2443. Web Site: www.librarieshawaii.org/branch/naalehu-public-library. *Br Mgr,* Sara Kamibayashi; E-mail: sara.kamibayashi@librarieshawaii.org; Staff 1 (MLS 1)
Founded 1994. Circ 16,934
Library Holdings: Bk Vols 10,485
Function: 24/7 Electronic res, 24/7 Online cat, Art programs, Audiobks via web, Electronic databases & coll, Internet access, Magazines, Mango lang, Movies, Music CDs, Online cat, Photocopying/Printing, Prog for adults, Prog for children & young adult, Story hour, Summer reading prog, VHS videos
Closed for library renovations starting 9/16/19 - current date.
Restriction: Not open to pub
Friends of the Library Group

NANAKULI PUBLIC LIBRARY, 89-070 Farrington Hwy, Waianae, 96792, SAN 991-0026. Tel: 808-668-5844. FAX: 808-668-5847. Web Site: www.librarieshawaii.org/branch/nanakuli-public-library. *Br Mgr,* Kelsey Domingo; E-mail: kelsey.domingo@librarieshawaii.org; Staff 3 (MLS 3)
Founded 2018. Circ 40,015
Library Holdings: Bk Vols 37,089
Function: 24/7 Electronic res, 24/7 Online cat, Activity rm, Art programs, Audiobks via web, Bks on CD, Children's prog, Computers for patron use, Free DVD rentals, Holiday prog, Internet access, Life-long learning prog for all ages, Magazines, Mango lang, Meeting rooms, Music CDs, Online cat, OverDrive digital audio bks, Photocopying/Printing, Prog for adults, Prog for children & young adult, Ref serv available, Story hour, Summer & winter reading prog, Summer reading prog, Telephone ref, Wheelchair accessible, Winter reading prog
Open Mon & Thurs 1-8, Tues, Wed, Fri & Sat 10-5
Friends of the Library Group

NORTH KOHALA PUBLIC LIBRARY, 54-3645 Akoni Pule Hwy, Kapaau, 96755. (Mail add: PO Box 248, Kapaau, 96755-0248). Tel: 808-889-6655. FAX: 808-889-6656. Web Site: www.librarieshawaii.org/branch/north-kohala-public-library. *Br Mgr,* Angela Weisner; Staff 2 (MLS 2)
Founded 2010. Circ 36,748
Library Holdings: Bk Vols 21,805
Function: 24/7 Electronic res, 24/7 Online cat, Art programs, Bk club(s), Electronic databases & coll, Internet access, Magazines, Mango lang, Movies, Music CDs, Online cat, Online ref, OverDrive digital audio bks, Photocopying/Printing, Prog for adults, Prog for children & young adult, Summer reading prog, Writing prog
Open Mon 12-8, Tues-Thurs 9-5, Fri 9-4
Friends of the Library Group

PAHALA PUBLIC & SCHOOL LIBRARY, 96-3150 Pikake St, Pahala, 96777. (Mail add: PO Box 400, Pahala, 96777-0400), SAN 339-5162. Tel: 808-928-2015. FAX: 808-928-2016. Web Site: www.librarieshawaii.org/branch/pahala-public-and-school-library. *Br Mgr,* Position Currently Open
Founded 1963. Circ 7,221
Library Holdings: Bk Vols 12,378
Function: 24/7 Electronic res, 24/7 Online cat, Art programs, Computers for patron use, Internet access, Magazines, Mango lang, Movies, Music CDs, Online cat, Online ref, Photocopying/Printing, Prog for adults, Prog for children & young adult, Ref serv available, Summer reading prog
Open Mon, Wed & Thurs 10-1 & 2-5, Tues 12-3 & 4-7, Fri 12-5
Friends of the Library Group

PAHOA PUBLIC & SCHOOL LIBRARY, 15-3070 Pahoa-Kalapana Rd, Pahoa, 96778, SAN 339-5197. Tel: 808-965-2171. FAX: 808-965-2199. Web Site: www.librarieshawaii.org/branch/pahoa-public-and-school-library. *Br Mgr,* Jennifer Gordon; E-mail: jennifer.gordon@librarieshawaii.org; Staff 1 (MLS 1)
Founded 1967. Circ 56,524
Library Holdings: Bk Vols 64,439
Function: 24/7 Electronic res, 24/7 Online cat, Computers for patron use, Electronic databases & coll, Internet access, Magazines, Mango lang, Online cat, Prog for children & young adult, Ref serv available, Summer reading prog, VHS videos
Open Mon 1-8, Tues-Fri 10-5
Friends of the Library Group

THELMA PARKER MEMORIAL PUBLIC & SCHOOL LIBRARY, 67-1209 Mamalahoa Hwy, Kamuela, 96743. (Mail add: PO Box 698, Kamuela, 96743-0698), SAN 339-5227. Tel: 808-887-6067. FAX: 808-887-6066. Web Site: www.librarieshawaii.org/branch/thelma-parker-memorial-public-and-school-library. *Br Mgr,* Pamela Akao; E-mail: pamela.akao@librarieshawaii.org; Staff 2 (MLS 2)
Founded 1978. Circ 55,870
Library Holdings: Bk Vols 44,553
Function: 24/7 Electronic res, 24/7 Online cat, Art programs, Audiobks via web, Children's prog, Computers for patron use, Electronic databases & coll, Internet access, Magazines, Mango lang, Movies, Music CDs, Online cat, Online ref, OverDrive digital audio bks, Photocopying/Printing, Prog for adults, Prog for children & young adult, Ref serv available, Story hour, Summer reading prog, Teen prog, VHS videos, Writing prog
Open Tues & Thurs-Sat 9:30-4:30, Wed 12:30-7:30
Friends of the Library Group

PEARL CITY PUBLIC LIBRARY, 1138 Waimano Home Rd, Pearl City, 96782, SAN 339-4719. Tel: 808-453-6566. FAX: 808-453-6570. Web Site: www.librarieshawaii.org/branch/pearl-city-public-library. *Br Mgr,* Vicky Bowie; E-mail: vicky.bowie@librarieshawaii.org; Staff 5 (MLS 5)
Founded 1969. Circ 98,319
Library Holdings: Bk Vols 79,786
Function: 24/7 Electronic res, 24/7 Online cat, Activity rm, Art programs, CD-ROM, Children's prog, Computers for patron use, Electronic databases & coll, Holiday prog, ILL available, Internet access, Life-long learning prog for all ages, Magazines, Mango lang, Meeting rooms, Movies, Music CDs, Online cat, OverDrive digital audio bks, Photocopying/Printing, Prog for adults, Prog for children & young adult, Ref serv available, STEM programs, Story hour, Summer reading prog, Teen prog, VHS videos, Workshops
Special Services for the Deaf - TTY equip
Open Mon & Tues 12-8, Wed & Thurs 9-5, Fri 1-5, Sun 10-5
Friends of the Library Group

PRINCEVILLE PUBLIC LIBRARY, 4343 Emmalani Dr, Princeville, 96722, SAN 991-0034. Tel: 808-826-4310. FAX: 808-826-4311. Web Site: www.librarieshawaii.org/branch/princeville-public-library. *Br Mgr,* Katherine Bengston; E-mail: katherine.bengston@librarieshawaii.org; Staff 1 (MLS 1)
Founded 1999. Circ 51,656
Library Holdings: Bk Vols 43,550
Function: 24/7 Electronic res, 24/7 Online cat, Adult bk club, Bk club(s), Children's prog, Computers for patron use, Electronic databases & coll, ILL available, Internet access, Magazines, Mango lang, Music CDs, Online cat, Photocopying/Printing, Prog for adults, Prog for children & young adult, Ref serv available, Summer reading prog, VHS videos
Open Tues & Thurs-Sat 9-5, Wed 12-7
Friends of the Library Group

SALT LAKE-MOANALUA PUBLIC LIBRARY, 3225 Salt Lake Blvd, 96818, SAN 326-7393. Tel: 808-831-6831. FAX: 808-831-6834. Web Site: www.librarieshawaii.org/branch/salt-lake-moanalua-public-library. *Br Mgr,* Duane Wenzel; E-mail: duane.wenzel@librarieshawaii.org; Staff 3 (MLS 3)
Founded 1984. Circ 129,983
Library Holdings: Bk Vols 68,947
Special Collections: Martial Art Coll

Function: 24/7 Electronic res, 24/7 Online cat, Art programs, CD-ROM, Children's prog, Computers for patron use, Holiday prog, ILL available, Internet access, Life-long learning prog for all ages, Magazines, Mango lang, Movies, Music CDs, Online cat, OverDrive digital audio bks, Photocopying/Printing, Prog for adults, Prog for children & young adult, Ref serv available, Story hour, Summer reading prog, Teen prog, VHS videos
Open Mon & Tues 12-7, Wed-Fri 10-5, Sat 10-3
Friends of the Library Group

WAHIAWA PUBLIC LIBRARY, 820 California Ave, Wahiawa, 96786, SAN 339-4743. Tel: 808-622-6345. FAX: 808-622-6348. Web Site: www.librarieshawaii.org/branch/wahiawa-public-library. *Br Mgr,* Sharrese Castillo; E-mail: sharrese.castillo@librarieshawaii.org; Staff 2 (MLS 2)
Founded 1940. Circ 32,207
Library Holdings: Bk Vols 49,793
Function: 24/7 Electronic res, 24/7 Online cat, Art exhibits, Art programs, CD-ROM, Children's prog, Computers for patron use, Electronic databases & coll, Holiday prog, ILL available, Internet access, Life-long learning prog for all ages, Magazines, Mango lang, Movies, Online cat, OverDrive digital audio bks, Photocopying/Printing, Prog for adults, Prog for children & young adult, Ref serv available, Story hour, Summer reading prog, VHS videos
Open Tues-Thurs 12-8, Fri & Sat 9-5
Friends of the Library Group

WAIALUA PUBLIC LIBRARY, 67-068 Kealohanui St, Waialua, 96791, SAN 339-4778. Tel: 808-637-8286. FAX: 808-637-8288. Web Site: www.librarieshawaii.org/branch/waialua-public-library. *Br Mgr,* Timothy Littlejohn; E-mail: timothy.littlejohn@librarieshawaii.org; Staff 2 (MLS 2)
Founded 1952. Circ 35,461
Library Holdings: Bk Vols 40,385
Function: 24/7 Electronic res, 24/7 Online cat, Adult bk club, Art programs, Children's prog, Computer training, Computers for patron use, Electronic databases & coll, ILL available, Internet access, Life-long learning prog for all ages, Magazines, Mango lang, Movies, Music CDs, Online cat, Photocopying/Printing, Prog for adults, Prog for children & young adult, Ref serv available, Summer reading prog, VHS videos, Writing prog
Open Tues-Thurs 9-6, Fri 9-5, Sat 9-2
Friends of the Library Group

WAIANAE PUBLIC LIBRARY, 85-625 Farrington Hwy, Waianae, 96792, SAN 339-4808. Tel: 808-697-7868. FAX: 808-697-7870. Web Site: www.librarieshawaii.org/branch/waianae-public-library. *Br Mgr,* Sheryl Lynch; E-mail: sheryl.lynch@librarieshawaii.org; Staff 2 (MLS 2)
Founded 1966. Circ 29,724
Library Holdings: Bk Vols 46,456
Function: 24/7 Electronic res, 24/7 Online cat, Adult bk club, Art programs, Children's prog, Computer training, Computers for patron use, Electronic databases & coll, Holiday prog, ILL available, Internet access, Life-long learning prog for all ages, Magazines, Mango lang, Movies, Music CDs, Online cat, OverDrive digital audio bks, Photocopying/Printing, Prog for adults, Prog for children & young adult, Ref serv available, Summer reading prog, VHS videos
Open Mon, Tues, Thurs & Sat 9-5, Wed 1-8, Fri 1-5
Friends of the Library Group

WAIKIKI-KAPAHULU PUBLIC LIBRARY, 400 Kapahulu Ave, 96815, SAN 339-4565. Tel: 808-733-8488. FAX: 808-733-8490. Web Site: www.librarieshawaii.org/branch/waikiki-kapahulu-public-library. *Br Mgr,* Melissa LePage; E-mail: mellisa.lepage@librarieshawaii.org; Staff 3 (MLS 3)
Founded 1952. Circ 73,831
Library Holdings: Bk Vols 35,635
Function: 24/7 Electronic res, 24/7 Online cat, Art programs, CD-ROM, Children's prog, Computers for patron use, Holiday prog, ILL available, Internet access, Life-long learning prog for all ages, Magazines, Mango lang, Movies, Music CDs, Online cat, OverDrive digital audio bks, Photocopying/Printing, Prog for adults, Prog for children & young adult, Ref serv available, Story hour, Summer reading prog, VHS videos
Open Tues, Wed, Fri & Sat 10-5, Thurs 12-7
Friends of the Library Group

WAILUKU PUBLIC LIBRARY, 251 S High St, Wailuku, 96793, SAN 339-5464. Tel: 808-243-5766. FAX: 808-243-5768. Web Site: www.librarieshawaii.org/branch/wailuku-public-library. *Br Mgr,* Alison Costanzo; E-mail: alison.costanzo@librarieshawaii.org; Staff 3 (MLS 3)
Founded 1929. Circ 44,265
Library Holdings: Bk Vols 47,719
Function: 24/7 Electronic res, 24/7 Online cat, Art programs, CD-ROM, Children's prog, Computers for patron use, Electronic databases & coll, Holiday prog, ILL available, Internet access, Life-long learning prog for all ages, Magazines, Mango lang, Movies, Music CDs, Online cat, Outreach serv, OverDrive digital audio bks, Photocopying/Printing, Preschool outreach, Preschool reading prog, Prog for adults, Prog for children & young adult, Ref serv available, Story hour, Summer reading prog, Teen prog, VHS videos
Open Mon-Wed & Fri 9-5, Thurs 1-8
Friends of the Library Group

WAIMANALO PUBLIC & SCHOOL LIBRARY, 41-1320 Kalanianaole Hwy, Waimanalo, 96795, SAN 339-459X. Tel: 808-259-2610. FAX: 808-259-2612. Web Site: www.librarieshawaii.org/branch/waimanalo-public-and-school-library. *Br Mgr,* Cora Eggerman; E-mail: cora.eggerman@librarieshawaii.org; Staff 1.5 (MLS 1.5)
Founded 1978. Circ 25,899
Library Holdings: Bk Vols 42,132
Function: 24/7 Electronic res, 24/7 Online cat, Art programs, Children's prog, Computers for patron use, Electronic databases & coll, ILL available, Internet access, Life-long learning prog for all ages, Magazines, Mango lang, Movies, Music CDs, Online cat, OverDrive digital audio bks, Photocopying/Printing, Prog for adults, Prog for children & young adult, Ref serv available, Story hour, Summer reading prog, VHS videos
Open Mon, Tues, Thurs & Fri 9-5, Wed 1-8, Sat 10-2
Friends of the Library Group

WAIMEA PUBLIC LIBRARY, 9750 Kaumualii Hwy, Waimea, 96796. (Mail add: PO Box 397, Waimea, 96796-0397), SAN 339-5405. Tel: 808-338-6848. FAX: 808-338-6847. Web Site: www.librarieshawaii.org/branch/waimea-public-library. *Br Mgr,* Michelle Young; E-mail: michelle.young@librarieshawaii.org; Staff 1 (MLS 1)
Founded 1950. Circ 26,384
Library Holdings: CDs 512; DVDs 1,390; Bk Vols 20,978; Per Subs 10; Videos 13
Function: 24/7 Electronic res, 24/7 Online cat, Art programs, Children's prog, Computers for patron use, Electronic databases & coll, ILL available, Internet access, Magazines, Mango lang, Music CDs, Online cat, Photocopying/Printing, Prog for adults, Prog for children & young adult, Ref serv available, Summer reading prog, VHS videos
Open Mon & Wed 12-8, Tues & Thurs 9-5, Fri 10-5
Friends of the Library Group

WAIPAHU PUBLIC LIBRARY, 94-275 Mokuola St, Waipahu, 96797. Tel: 808-675-0358. FAX: 808-675-0360. Web Site: www.librarieshawaii.org/branch/waipahu-public-library. *Br Mgr,* Christine Madayag; E-mail: christine.madayag@librarieshawaii.org; Staff 3 (MLS 3)
Founded 1952. Circ 45,241
Library Holdings: Bk Vols 63,720
Function: 24/7 Electronic res, 24/7 Online cat, Art programs, CD-ROM, Children's prog, Computers for patron use, Life-long learning prog for all ages, Magazines, Mango lang, Movies, Music CDs, Online cat, OverDrive digital audio bks, Photocopying/Printing, Prog for adults, Prog for children & young adult, Ref serv available, STEM programs, Story hour, Summer reading prog, VHS videos
Open Tues, Thurs & Fri 10-5, Wed 1-8, Sat 9-4
Friends of the Library Group

Bookmobiles: 2

P HAWAII STATE PUBLIC LIBRARY SYSTEM*, Library for the Blind & Physically Handicapped, 402 Kapahulu Ave, 96815. SAN 303-4712. Tel: 808-733-8444. FAX: 808-733-8449. E-mail: olbcirc@librarieshawaii.org. Web Site: www.librarieshawaii.org/branch/library-for-the-blind-and-physically-handicapped. *Br Mgr,* Baron Baroza; E-mail: baron.baroza@librarieshawaii.org; Staff 2 (MLS 2)
Founded 1931. Pop 20,000; Circ 20,546
Library Holdings: Audiobooks 57,398; AV Mats 41; Braille Volumes 23,689; CDs 2; DVDs 24; Large Print Bks 15,257; Bk Vols 15,895; Per Subs 13; Videos 102
Special Collections: Braille, Large Print, Audiobooks; Hawaiiana Titles, Described Videos & DVDs; Reference Material on Various Handicaps
Wireless access
Function: 24/7 Electronic res, 24/7 Online cat, Audio & video playback equip for onsite use, Audiobks via web, AV serv, Bks on cassette, Bks on CD, Computers for patron use, Electronic databases & coll, Homebound delivery serv, ILL available, Internet access, Life-long learning prog for all ages, Magazines, Mango lang, Music CDs, Online cat, Orientations, Outreach serv, OverDrive digital audio bks, Photocopying/Printing, Prog for adults, Ref serv available, Spoken cassettes & CDs, Spoken cassettes & DVDs, Summer reading prog, Telephone ref, VHS videos
Publications: New Large Type Books (Newsletter); News is Getting Around the Pacific (Newsletter)
Special Services for the Deaf - Bks on deafness & sign lang; Deaf publ; Spec interest per; Staff with knowledge of sign lang; TTY equip
Special Services for the Blind - Accessible computers; Audio mat; Bks & mags in Braille, on rec, tape & cassette; Bks on cassette; Bks on CD; Braille bks; Braille equip; Braille music coll; Braille servs; Children's Braille; Closed circuit radio for broadcast serv; Closed circuit TV; Club for the blind; Computer with voice synthesizer for visually impaired persons; Copier with enlargement capabilities; Digital talking bk; Digital talking bk machines; Duplicating spec requests; Extensive large print coll; Internet workstation with adaptive software; Large print bks; Large screen computer & software; Mags & bk reproduction/duplication; Merlin electronic

magnifier reader; Musical scores in Braille & large print; Newsletter (in large print, Braille or on cassette); Newsline for the Blind; Newsp reading serv; PC for people with disabilities; Production of talking bks; Radio reading serv; Recorded bks; Ref in Braille; Ref serv; Screen enlargement software for people with visual disabilities; Soundproof reading booth; Talking bk serv referral; Talking bks; Talking bks & player equip; Transcribing serv; Videos on blindness & physical disabilties; Volunteer serv; ZoomText magnification & reading software
Open Mon & Wed-Fri 8:30-4:30, Tues 10-6
Friends of the Library Group

S HAWAIIAN HISTORICAL SOCIETY LIBRARY, 560 Kawaiahao St, 96813. SAN 303-4763. Tel: 808-537-6271. FAX: 808-537-6271. E-mail: hhsoffice@hawaiianhistory.org. Web Site: www.hawaiianhistory.org/research. *Exec Dir,* Cynthia Engle; E-mail: executivedirector@hawaiianhistory.org; Staff 1 (MLS 1)
Founded 1892
Library Holdings: Bk Titles 16,000; Per Subs 20
Special Collections: History of Hawaii & Pacific Coll (Late 18th & 19th Centuries)
Automation Activity & Vendor Info: (OPAC) LibraryWorld, Inc
Wireless access
Publications: The Hawaiian Historical Society: A Guide to the Library Collections, 1991; The Hawaiian Journal of History (Annual)
Open Tues-Sat 10-4
Restriction: Open to pub for ref only

S HAWAIIAN MISSION CHILDREN'S SOCIETY LIBRARY*, Hawaiian Mission Houses Archives, 553 S King St, 96813. SAN 303-4771. Tel: 808-531-0481. FAX: 808-545-2280. E-mail: info@missionhouses.org. Web Site: www.missionhouses.org. *Dir of Coll, Dir, Operations,* Elizabeth Pooloa; E-mail: epooloa@missionhouses.org; *Archivist,* John Barker; E-mail: archives@missionhouses.org; Staff 1 (MLS 1)
Founded 1908
Library Holdings: AV Mats 50; Electronic Media & Resources 41; Bk Vols 13,000; Per Subs 10
Special Collections: American Board of Commissioners for Foreign Missions, including letters, ledgers, reports written by missionaries to the ABCFM in Boston; Hawaiian Evangelical Association Archives,including reports of native Hawaiian ministers; Hawaiian Language Imprints, 19th century; Lahainaluna Copperplate Engravings, 1830-1840; Marquesas Coll, including letters written by native Hawaiian missionaries to the Hawaiian Board of Missions in Hawaii; Micronesian Mission-HEA Papers, including letters from native Hawaiian ministers in Micronesia to the Hawaiian Board of Missions in Hawaii; Missionary Manuscripts, letters, reports, journals
Subject Interests: Hawaii
Wireless access
Function: Archival coll, Doc delivery serv, For res purposes, Magnifiers for reading, Photocopying/Printing, Prog for children & young adult, Ref serv available, Res libr, Telephone ref, Wheelchair accessible
Publications: A Guide to the Holdings of the Hawaiian Mission Children's Society Library; Engraved at Lahainaluna by David Forbes, 2012; Grapes of Canaan by Albertine Loomis; Hawaiian Language Imprints, 1822-1899; Ka Pai Palapala: Early Printing in Hawaii; Mission Houses Museum Guidebook, Na Hale Hoikeike o Na Mikanele, Honolulu, 2001; Missionary Album: Biographical Sketches & Portraits of the American Protestant Missionaries to Hawaii, HMCS, 1969; The Hawaii Journals of the New England Missionaries, 1813-1894; The Journals of Cochran Forbes; Voyages to Hawaii before 1860 by Bernice Judd, UH Press, 1974
Restriction: Closed stack, Non-circulating, Not a lending libr, Open to fac, students & qualified researchers, Open to pub for ref only, Private libr

J HONOLULU COMMUNITY COLLEGE LIBRARY, 874 Dillingham Blvd, 96817-4598. SAN 303-4801. Tel: 808-845-9199. Circulation Tel: 808-845-9221. E-mail: honcclib@hawaii.edu. Web Site: library.honolulu.hawaii.edu/home. *Head Librn,* Stefanie Sasaki; Tel: 808-845-9463; *Assoc Prof, Librn,* Sarah Myhre; Tel: 808-845-9194; Staff 7 (MLS 3, Non-MLS 4)
Founded 1965. Highest Degree: Associate
Special Collections: Hawaii/Pacific Coll
Subject Interests: Liberal arts, Occupational
Automation Activity & Vendor Info: (Cataloging) Ex Libris Group; (Circulation) Ex Libris Group
Wireless access

S HONOLULU MUSEUM OF ART*, Robert Allerton Art Library, 900 S Beretania St, 96814-1495. SAN 303-4798. Tel: 808-532-8754. FAX: 808-532-3683. E-mail: library@honolulumuseum.org. Web Site: honolulumuseum.org/4977-robert_allerton_research_library. *Dir of Coll,* Cynthia Low; E-mail: clow@honolulumuseum.org; Staff 1 (MLS 1)
Founded 1927
Library Holdings: Bk Titles 40,000; Bk Vols 55,000; Per Subs 40
Automation Activity & Vendor Info: (Cataloging) OCLC Connexion; (OPAC) Ex Libris Group
Wireless access
Open Wed 10-4

CM JOHN A BURNS SCHOOL OF MEDICINE*, Health Sciences Library, 651 Ilalo St, MEB 101, 96813. SAN 303-500X. Tel: 808-692-0810. FAX: 808-692-1244. E-mail: hslinfo@hawaii.edu. Web Site: hslib.jabsom.hawaii.edu. *Libr Dir,* Kristen Anderson; Tel: 808-692-0823, E-mail: krisa@hawaii.edu; *Info Serv & Instrul Librn,* Melissa Kahili-Heede; Tel: 808-692-0825, E-mail: mkahili@hawaii.edu; *Circ Mgr,* Hilda Baroza; Tel: 808-692-0816, E-mail: baroza@hawaii.edu; Staff 8.5 (MLS 4.5, Non-MLS 4)
Founded 2005. Highest Degree: Doctorate
Library Holdings: Bk Titles 8,000; Bk Vols 11,000; Per Subs 150
Subject Interests: Med, Pub health
Automation Activity & Vendor Info: (Cataloging) OCLC; (Circulation) Ex Libris Group; (OPAC) Ex Libris Group; (Serials) SerialsSolutions
Wireless access
Partic in OCLC Online Computer Library Center, Inc; Pacific Southwest Regional Medical Library
Open Mon-Fri 8-5

J KAPI'OLANI COMMUNITY COLLEGE LIBRARY*, Lama Library, 4303 Diamond Head Rd, 96816. SAN 303-4852. Tel: 808-734-9268. Reference Tel: 808-734-9359. Administration Tel: 808-734-9259. FAX: 808-734-9453. Reference E-mail: kapccref@hawaii.edu. Web Site: library.kcc.hawaii.edu. *Interim Vice Chancellor, Academic Affairs,* Susan Kuzama; Tel: 808-734-9155, E-mail: smurata@hawaii.edu; *Digital Initiatives Librn,* Sunny Pai; Tel: 808-734-9755, E-mail: sunyeen@hawaii.edu; *Electronic Res Librn,* Stephanie Nelson; Tel: 808-734-9254, E-mail: stephnel@hawaii.edu; *Info Literacy Librn,* Joy Oehlers; Tel: 808-734-9352, E-mail: aichin@hawaii.edu; *Learning Res Librn,* Joyce Tokuda; Tel: 808-734-9357, E-mail: jtokuda@hawaii.edu; *Tech Serv Librn,* Michelle Sturges; Tel: 808-734-9163, E-mail: sturges@hawaii.edu; *Educ Spec,* Guy Inaba; Tel: 808-734-9206, E-mail: inaba@hawaii.edu; *Hawaiian Res Spec,* Annie Thomas; Tel: 808-734-9599, E-mail: athomas@hawaii.edu; *Res Support Spec,* Alva Kodama; Tel: 808-734-9217, E-mail: kodama@hawaii.edu. Subject Specialists: *Hawaii, Pacific,* Annie Thomas; Staff 22 (MLS 9, Non-MLS 13)
Founded 1992. Enrl 7,757; Fac 360; Highest Degree: Associate
Library Holdings: e-books 1,311; e-journals 17,000; Bk Titles 58,810; Bk Vols 73,114; Per Subs 300
Special Collections: Chinese History & Culture (Char Coll); Read (Developmental)
Subject Interests: Hawaii, Japan
Automation Activity & Vendor Info: (Cataloging) Ex Libris Group; (Circulation) Ex Libris Group; (OPAC) Ex Libris Group
Wireless access
Function: AV serv, Distance learning, Doc delivery serv, ILL available, Magnifiers for reading, Photocopying/Printing, Ref serv available, Telephone ref, Wheelchair accessible
Open Mon-Thurs 7:30-7, Fri 7:30-4, Sat 8:30-4

P MASONIC PUBLIC LIBRARY*, 1611 Kewalo St, 96822. Tel: 808-521-2070. FAX: 808-533-6493. *Mgr,* Jami Kaneshiro
Library Holdings: Bk Vols 6,000
Special Collections: Masonic Archival Coll
Subject Interests: Hawaii, Masonic heritage
Function: Photocopying/Printing
Open Mon-Fri 9-1

G PACIFIC ISLANDS FISHERIES SCIENCE CENTER LIBRARY, NOAA IRC-NMFS/PIFSC/SOD/Library, 1845 Wasp Blvd, Bldg 176, 96818. Tel: 808-725-5579. *Librn,* Jacquelyn Crossman; E-mail: pifsc.librarian@noaa.gov
Partic in NOAA Libraries Network
Open Mon-Fri 6-6

M SHRINERS HOSPITALS FOR CHILDREN*, Honolulu Library, 1310 Punahou St, 96826-1099. SAN 303-4941. Tel: 808-941-4466, Ext 638. FAX: 808-942-8573. Web Site: www.shrinershospitalsforchildren.org/honolulu. *Library Contact,* Rob Miyamoto, PhD; Tel: 808-951-3693, E-mail: rmiyamoto@shrinenet.org
Founded 1923
Library Holdings: Bk Vols 650; Per Subs 13
Wireless access
Restriction: Not open to pub

GL SUPREME COURT LAW LIBRARY, 417 S King St, Rm 119, 96813. Tel: 808-539-4964. FAX: 808-539-4974. E-mail: lawlibrary@courts.hawaii.gov. Web Site: histatelawlibrary.com. *State Law Librn,* Jenny Silbiger; *Pub Serv Librn,* Marlene Cuenco; *Tech Serv,* Mark Skrimstad; Staff 7 (MLS 3, Non-MLS 4)
Founded 1851
Library Holdings: Bk Vols 85,000; Per Subs 206

Open Mon-Fri 7:45-4:15
Restriction: Open to pub for ref only

AM TRIPLER ARMY MEDICAL CENTER*, Medical Library, One Jarrett White Rd, 96859-5000. SAN 339-5790. Tel: 808-433-6391. FAX: 808-433-4892. *Librn,* Mabel Trafford; Tel: 808-433-4534, E-mail: mabel.a.trafford.civ@mail.mil; Staff 4 (MLS 2, Non-MLS 2)
Founded 1946
Library Holdings: Bk Vols 8,000; Per Subs 400
Partic in OCLC Online Computer Library Center, Inc

G UNESCO-INTERGOVERNMENTAL OCEANOGRAPHIC COMMISSION & NATIONAL WEATHER SERVICE*, International Tsunami Information Center Library, NOAA IRC-NWS/ITIC, 1845 Wasp Blvd, Bldg 176, 96818. SAN 326-3436. Tel: 808-725-6050. FAX: 808-725-6055. Web Site: itic.ioc-unesco.org. *Tech Info Spec,* Position Currently Open
Founded 1965
Library Holdings: Bk Titles 2,000
Special Collections: Catalog of Tsunamis in Pacific, bks; Marigrams 2/65-1978, microfiche. UN Document Depository
Subject Interests: Earthquakes, Geophysics, Oceanography
Wireless access
Function: Ref serv available
Publications: Tsunami Newsletter; Tsunami Reports
Open Mon-Fri 8-4
Restriction: In-house use for visitors

GL UNITED STATES COURTS LIBRARY*, 300 Ala Moana Blvd C-341, 96850. SAN 303-4992. Tel: 808-541-1797. Web Site: www.hid.uscourts.gov. *Librn,* Shannon Lashbrook
Library Holdings: Bk Vols 30,000; Per Subs 25
Automation Activity & Vendor Info: (Acquisitions) SirsiDynix
Wireless access
Restriction: Not open to pub

CL UNIVERSITY OF HAWAII*, William S Richardson School of Law Library, 2525 Dole St, 96822-2328. SAN 326-5188. Tel: 808-956-5581, 808-956-7583. FAX: 808-956-4615. TDD: 808-956-9577. Web Site: library.law.hawaii.edu. *Dir, Law Libr & Assoc Prof of Law,* Victoria Szymczak; E-mail: vjs777@hawaii.edu; *Ref & Instrul Serv Librn,* Roberta Lian Woods; Tel: 808-956-0478, E-mail: rfwoods@hawaii.edu; *Syst Librn,* Keiko Okuhara; Tel: 808-956-9953, E-mail: keikooku@hawaii.edu; *Pub Serv Mgr,* Lynette Rudolfo; E-mail: rudolfo@hawaii.edu; *Tech Serv,* Storm Stoker; Tel: 808-956-5582, E-mail: sstoker@hawaii.edu; Staff 9 (MLS 5, Non-MLS 4)
Enrl 253; Fac 18; Highest Degree: Doctorate
Library Holdings: Bk Titles 304,000; Bk Vols 304,934; Per Subs 3,748
Special Collections: Pacific-Asian law. US Document Depository
Subject Interests: Environ law
Automation Activity & Vendor Info: (Acquisitions) Ex Libris Group; (Cataloging) Ex Libris Group; (Circulation) Ex Libris Group; (ILL) Ex Libris Group; (Media Booking) Ex Libris Group; (OPAC) Ex Libris Group; (Serials) Ex Libris Group
Wireless access
Partic in Hawaii Library Consortium; OCLC Online Computer Library Center, Inc
Open Mon-Thurs (Winter) 8am-11pm, Fri 8-7, Sat 9-7, Sun 10am-11pm; Mon-Fri (Summer) 8-5

C UNIVERSITY OF HAWAII AT MANOA LIBRARY*, Thomas Hale Hamilton Library, 2550 McCarthy Mall, 96822. SAN 339-6096. Tel: 808-956-7203. Interlibrary Loan Service Tel: 808-956-8568. Reference Tel: 808-956-7214. Administration Tel: 808-956-7207. Automation Services Tel: 808-956-7853. FAX: 808-956-5968. E-mail: library@hawaii.edu. Web Site: manoa.hawaii.edu/library/. Staff 130 (MLS 51, Non-MLS 79)
Founded 1907. Enrl 18,000; Highest Degree: Doctorate
Library Holdings: AV Mats 62,616; e-books 132,374; Music Scores 23,641; Bk Vols 3,206,032; Per Subs 44,000
Special Collections: Asia Coll; Book Arts; Congressional Papers Coll; Hawaiian Coll; Japanese American Veterans Coll; Jean Charlot Coll; Pacific Coll; Tsuzaki Reinecke Creole Coll; University Archives. State Document Depository; UN Document Depository; US Document Depository
Automation Activity & Vendor Info: (Acquisitions) Ex Libris Group; (Cataloging) Ex Libris Group; (Circulation) Ex Libris Group; (Course Reserve) Ex Libris Group; (ILL) OCLC ILLiad; (Media Booking) Ex Libris Group; (OPAC) Ex Libris Group; (Serials) Ex Libris Group
Wireless access
Publications: Acquisitions List of the Pacific Collection; Annual Report of the Univerity of Hawaii at Manoa Library; Current Hawaiiana; Ke Kukini (Newsletter); Selected Acquisitions of the Asia Collection
Partic in Association of Research Libraries; Greater Western Library Alliance; Hawaii Library Consortium; OCLC Online Computer Library Center, Inc
Open Mon-Thurs 8am-10pm, Fri 8-6, Sat 9-5, Sun 12-10

Departmental Libraries:
GREGG M SINCLAIR LIBRARY, 2425 Campus Rd, 96822. (Mail add: 2550 McCarthy Mall, 96822), SAN 339-6126. Tel: 808-956-8308. FAX: 808-956-5952. E-mail: sinc@hawaii.edu. Web Site: guides.library.manoa.hawaii.edu/sinclairlibrary. *Dept Chair, Librarian V,* James Adamson; E-mail: adamson@hawaii.edu
Founded 1956
Restriction: Badge access after hrs

S USS BOWFIN SUBMARINE MUSEUM & PARK LIBRARY*, 11 Arizona Memorial Dr, 96818-3145. SAN 371-8395. Tel: 808-423-1341. FAX: 808-422-5201. E-mail: info@bowfin.org. Web Site: www.bowfin.org. *Dir of Educ,* Charles R Hinman; *Curator,* Nancy Richards; E-mail: curator@bowfin.org. Subject Specialists: *Submarines, World War II,* Charles R Hinman; Staff 3 (Non-MLS 3)
Founded 1981
Library Holdings: Bk Titles 2,500; Bk Vols 5,000
Special Collections: Oral Histories of World War II Submariners; Submarine Photo Archives; US Navy Training Manuals for Submariners; USS Bowfin; War Patrol Reports of US Submarines in World War II; World War II Crew '35. Oral History
Subject Interests: Naval hist, Submarines, World War II
Function: Res libr
Publications: On Eternal Patrol
Open Mon-Sun 7-5
Restriction: Not a lending libr

KAHULUI

C UNIVERSITY OF HAWAII, Maui Community College Library, 310 Kaahumanu Ave, 96732. SAN 303-5026. Tel: 808-984-3233, 808-984-3715. Administration Tel: 808-984-3582. FAX: 808-244-9644. E-mail: uhmclib@hawaii.edu. Web Site: www.maui.hawaii.edu/library. *Head Librn,* Ellen Peterson; E-mail: epeterso@hawaii.edu; *Librn,* Jeffrey Marzluft; E-mail: marzluft@hawaii.edu; *Librn,* Shavonn Matsuda; E-mail: shavonn@hawaii.edu; Staff 8 (MLS 4, Non-MLS 4)
Founded 1970. Enrl 2,794; Fac 92; Highest Degree: Bachelor
Library Holdings: AV Mats 3,703; DVDs 1,000; Bk Titles 49,258; Bk Vols 61,572; Per Subs 250; Videos 2,700
Subject Interests: Hawaii
Automation Activity & Vendor Info: (Cataloging) Ex Libris Group; (Circulation) Ex Libris Group; (Course Reserve) Ex Libris Group; (ILL) Ex Libris Group; (Media Booking) Ex Libris Group; (OPAC) Ex Libris Group
Wireless access
Partic in OCLC Online Computer Library Center, Inc
Open Mon-Thurs 8-8, Fri & Sat (Fall & Spring) 8-4:30

KALAHEO

S NATIONAL TROPICAL BOTANICAL GARDEN LIBRARY*, 3530 Papalina Rd, 96741. SAN 371-7852. Tel: 808-332-7324, Ext 214. FAX: 808-332-9765. Web Site: www.ntbg.org/resources/library.php. *Dir,* David H Lorence; E-mail: lorence@ntbg.org; Staff 1 (MLS 1)
Founded 1971
Library Holdings: Bk Titles 15,500; Bk Vols 16,800; Per Subs 400
Special Collections: Tropical Botany, bks, journals. Oral History
Subject Interests: Botany, Hort
Open Mon-Fri 8-5
Friends of the Library Group

KANEOHE

M HAWAII STATE HOSPITAL*, Medical Library, 45-710 Keaahala Rd, 96744-3528. SAN 303-5069. Tel: 808-236-8201. FAX: 808-247-7335. *Librn,* Lisa Anne Matsumoto; E-mail: lisa.matsumoto@doh.hawaii.gov; Staff 1 (MLS 1)
Founded 1950
Library Holdings: Bk Titles 4,500; Per Subs 251
Subject Interests: Mental health, Neuropsychology, Psychiat, Psychol
Partic in Pacific Southwest Regional Medical Library
Restriction: Open to pub by appt only

J UNIVERSITY OF HAWAII*, Windward Community College Library, 45-720 Kea'ahala Rd, 96744. SAN 303-5077. Tel: 808-235-7436. Circulation Tel: 808-235-7441. Reference Tel: 808-235-7338. FAX: 808-235-7344. E-mail: wccref@hawaii.edu. Web Site: library.wcc.hawaii.edu. *Head Librn,* Sarah Gilman Sur; Tel: 808-235-7435, E-mail: sgilman@hawaii.edu; *Tech Serv Librn,* Mariko Kershaw; Tel: 808-235-7439, E-mail: kershaw@hawaii.edu; Staff 3 (MLS 3)
Founded 1972. Enrl 1,800; Fac 77; Highest Degree: Associate
Library Holdings: AV Mats 4,648; Bk Titles 40,800; Bk Vols 48,552; Per Subs 147
Special Collections: Hawaiian Coll

Automation Activity & Vendor Info: (Cataloging) Ex Libris Group; (Circulation) Ex Libris Group; (Course Reserve) Ex Libris Group; (OPAC) Ex Libris Group
Wireless access
Publications: Audiovisual Materials in the WCC Library; Periodicals in the WCC Library
Open Mon-Thurs 8am-9pm, Fri 8-5
Friends of the Library Group

KANEOHE BAY

A MARINE CORPS BASE HAWAII LIBRARIES*, Marine Corps Base Hawaii, Bldg 219, 96863. (Mail add: PO Box 63073, 96863-3073), SAN 339-6037. Tel: 808-254-7624. E-mail: mcbhawaii.baselibrary@usmc-mccs.org. Web Site: www.mccshawaii.com/library. *Supvry Librn,* Meredith Healey; E-mail: meredith.healey@usmc-mccs.org; Staff 6 (MLS 1, Non-MLS 5)
Founded 1964
Library Holdings: Audiobooks 500; CDs 1,379; DVDs 385; Electronic Media & Resources 4; Microforms 1,199; Bk Titles 50,475; Bk Vols 58,368; Per Subs 239; Videos 8
Special Collections: Board Games; Children's Coll; Hawaiiana; Professional Military Education; Rosetta Stone Language Modules, 16 languages; US Marine (Professional) Reading List; US Marine Corps Coll
Subject Interests: Mil art & sci, Voluntary educ
Automation Activity & Vendor Info: (Acquisitions) SirsiDynix-WorkFlows; (Cataloging) SirsiDynix-WorkFlows; (Circulation) SirsiDynix-WorkFlows; (ILL) SirsiDynix-WorkFlows; (OPAC) SirsiDynix-WorkFlows; (Serials) SirsiDynix-WorkFlows
Wireless access
Partic in OCLC Online Computer Library Center, Inc
Open Mon-Sat 9-4
Restriction: Mil, family mem, retirees, Civil Serv personnel NAF only

KAPOLEI

C UNIVERSITY OF HAWAII - WEST OAHU LIBRARY*, 91-1001 Farrington Hwy, 96707. SAN 303-4399. Tel: 808-689-2700. Reference Tel: 808-689-2703. E-mail: uhwolib@hawaii.edu. Web Site: www2.hawaii.edu/~uhwolib. *Interim Libr Dir, Pub Serv,* Michiko Joseph; E-mail: msjoseph@hawaii.edu
Founded 1976. Enrl 823; Fac 51; Highest Degree: Bachelor
Library Holdings: AV Mats 1,500; e-books 40,000; e-journals 25,000; Microforms 1,150; Bk Titles 28,000; Per Subs 40
Automation Activity & Vendor Info: (Cataloging) Ex Libris Group; (Circulation) Ex Libris Group; (Course Reserve) Ex Libris Group; (ILL) Ex Libris Group; (Media Booking) Ex Libris Group; (OPAC) Ex Libris Group; (Serials) Ex Libris Group
Wireless access
Partic in Hawaii Library Consortium
Open Mon-Thurs 7:30am-9pm, Fri 7:30-5, Sat 10-5

KEALAKEKUA

C UNIVERSITY OF HAWAII WEST HAWAII CENTER*, Library & Learning Center, 81-964 Halekii St, 96750. SAN 370-3800. Tel: 808-322-4858, 808-934-2530. Web Site: hawaii.hawaii.edu/node/1208. *Dir,* Laurel Gregory; E-mail: lgregory@hawaii.edu; *Educ Spec,* Karen Au; E-mail: karenau@hawaii.edu; Staff 2 (MLS 1, Non-MLS 1)
Founded 1989. Enrl 500; Highest Degree: Master
Library Holdings: Bk Vols 5,500
Subject Interests: Hawaii
Automation Activity & Vendor Info: (Acquisitions) TLC (The Library Corporation); (Cataloging) TLC (The Library Corporation); (Circulation) TLC (The Library Corporation); (Course Reserve) TLC (The Library Corporation); (ILL) TLC (The Library Corporation); (Media Booking) TLC (The Library Corporation); (OPAC) TLC (The Library Corporation); (Serials) TLC (The Library Corporation)
Wireless access
Open Mon-Fri 8-4:15

LAIE

C BRIGHAM YOUNG UNIVERSITY-HAWAII*, Joseph F Smith Library, BYU-Hawaii, No 1966, 55-220 Kulanui St, 96762-1294. SAN 303-5123. Tel: 808-675-3878. Circulation Tel: 808-675-3876. E-mail: library@byuh.edu. Web Site: library.byuh.edu. *Univ Librn,* Michael Aldrich; Tel: 808-675-3851, E-mail: michael.aldrich@byuh.edu; *Coll & Access Serv Librn,* Marynelle Chew; Tel: 808-675-3863, E-mail: chewm@byuh.edu; *Info & Instruction Librn,* Becky DeMartini; Tel: 808-675-3946, E-mail: becky.demartini@byuh.edu; *ILL,* Moana Kalua'u; E-mail: kaluaum@byuh.edu; Staff 10.5 (MLS 6, Non-MLS 4.5)
Founded 1955. Enrl 2,600; Fac 110; Highest Degree: Bachelor
Library Holdings: e-books 80,000; e-journals 50,000; Bk Vols 207,474; Per Subs 400
Special Collections: Mormonism Coll; Pacific Islands Coll. US Document Depository
Subject Interests: Pacific Islands
Automation Activity & Vendor Info: (Acquisitions) SirsiDynix; (Cataloging) SirsiDynix; (Circulation) SirsiDynix; (Course Reserve) SirsiDynix; (ILL) OCLC ILLiad; (Media Booking) SirsiDynix; (OPAC) SirsiDynix; (Serials) SirsiDynix
Wireless access
Partic in OCLC Online Computer Library Center, Inc
Open Mon-Thurs 7am-Midnight, Fri 7am-8pm, Sat 9-9

LIHUE

C KAUAI COMMUNITY COLLEGE*, S W Wilcox II Learning Resource Center, 3-1901 Kaumualii Hwy, 96766. SAN 303-5131. Tel: 808-245-8233. Circulation Tel: 808-245-8322. Reference Tel: 808-245-8253. Administration Tel: 808-245-8236. FAX: 808-245-8294. E-mail: kccisl@hawaii.edu. Web Site: libguides.kauai.hawaii.edu/main. *Head Librn,* Robert M Kajiwara; E-mail: kajiwara@hawaii.edu; *Distance Educ,* Anne McKenna; Tel: 808-245-8374, E-mail: mckenna@hawaii.edu; *Tech Serv,* Diane M Johnson; Tel: 808-245-8240, E-mail: dianej@hawaii.edu. Subject Specialists: *Hist,* Robert M Kajiwara; *Bus, Health, Med,* Anne McKenna; *Fiction, Sports,* Diane M Johnson; Staff 7 (MLS 4, Non-MLS 3)
Founded 1967. Enrl 1,115; Fac 77; Highest Degree: Master
Library Holdings: CDs 169; Electronic Media & Resources 6,000; Bk Titles 42,023; Bk Vols 60,269; Per Subs 169; Videos 1,544
Special Collections: Hawaii & the Pacific, v-tapes
Subject Interests: Allied health, Nursing
Automation Activity & Vendor Info: (Cataloging) Ex Libris Group; (Circulation) Ex Libris Group; (Course Reserve) Ex Libris Group; (OPAC) Ex Libris Group
Wireless access
Function: Ref serv available
Publications: Circulation Policies; How to Locate Library Resources; Quick Reference
Open Mon-Thurs (Winter) 7:30-7, Fri 7:30-4; Mon-Fri (Summer) 8-4

S KAUAI COMMUNITY CORRECTIONAL CENTER LIBRARY*, 3-5351 Kuhio Hwy, 96766. Tel: 808-241-3050. FAX: 808-241-3059. Web Site: dps.hawaii.gov/kccc. *Librn,* Jeannie Renaud
Library Holdings: Bk Titles 2,100; Per Subs 50
Restriction: Not open to pub
Friends of the Library Group

PEARL CITY

J LEEWARD COMMUNITY COLLEGE LIBRARY*, 96-045 Ala Ike St, 96782. SAN 303-5182. Tel: 808-455-0210. Reference Tel: 808-455-0379. FAX: 808-453-6729. E-mail: lcccirc@hawaii.edu. Reference E-mail: lccref@hawaii.edu. Web Site: www2.leeward.hawaii.edu/library. *Head Librn,* Wayde Oshiro; Tel: 808-455-0378, E-mail: waydeo@hawaii.edu; *Pub Serv Librn,* Junie Hayashi; Tel: 808-455-0680, E-mail: junie@hawaii.edu; *Syst Librn,* Ralph Toyama; Tel: 808-455-0682, E-mail: rtoyama@hawaii.edu; *Tech Serv Librn,* Jue Wang; Tel: 808-455-0672, E-mail: juewang@hawaii.edu; *Circ Serv Mgr,* Kalekona Kingsbury; Tel: 808-455-0209, E-mail: kalekona@hawaii.edu; Staff 5 (MLS 5)
Founded 1968. Highest Degree: Associate
Library Holdings: Bk Titles 61,051; Bk Vols 76,169; Per Subs 249
Special Collections: Hawaiian/Pacific Coll, bks, pers. US Document Depository
Automation Activity & Vendor Info: (Cataloging) Ex Libris Group; (Circulation) Ex Libris Group; (Course Reserve) Ex Libris Group; (OPAC) Ex Libris Group
Wireless access
Publications: LCC Periodicals List
Open Mon-Thurs 7:30am-8pm, Fri 7:30-4:30

SCHOFIELD BARRACKS

A UNITED STATES ARMY*, SGT Yano Library, Bldg 560, 1565 Kolekole Ave, 96857. SAN 339-5707. Tel: 808-655-8002. Reference Tel: 808-655-8001. FAX: 808-655-6375. E-mail: yanolibrary@gmail.com. Web Site: hawaii.armymwr.com/programs/sgt-yano-library.
Founded 1915
Library Holdings: AV Mats 1,000; Bk Vols 80,000; Per Subs 200
Special Collections: Hawaiian Islands (Hawaiiana)
Subject Interests: Mil hist
Wireless access
Partic in OCLC Online Computer Library Center, Inc
Open Mon & Tues 11-8, Wed-Sat 11-6

WAILUKU

GL HAWAII STATE CIRCUIT COURT-SECOND CIRCUIT*, Law Library, 2145 Main St, Rm 207, 96793. SAN 303-5212. Tel: 808-244-2959.
Library Holdings: Bk Vols 17,963

Automation Activity & Vendor Info: (Acquisitions) SirsiDynix
Restriction: By permission only

S MAUI COMMUNITY CORRECTIONAL CENTER MCCC LIBRARY*, 600 Waiale Rd, 96793. Tel: 808-243-5855. FAX: 808-244-9101. *Librn III, Mgr, Coll Mgt,* Jeanne Linn; E-mail: jeanne.l.linn@hawaii.gov; Staff 2 (MLS 1, Non-MLS 1)
Library Holdings: Large Print Bks 10; Bk Titles 5,500; Bk Vols 5,800; Per Subs 10
Wireless access
Restriction: Not open to pub
Friends of the Library Group
Bookmobiles: 1. Librn, Jessica Gleason

S MAUI HISTORICAL SOCIETY*, Archival Resource Center, 2375 A Main St, 96793. SAN 326-3118. Tel: 808-244-3326. E-mail: info@mauimuseum.org. Web Site: www.mauimuseum.org. *Exec Dir,* Naomi Lake-Farm
Founded 1957
Library Holdings: Bk Titles 7,650
Special Collections: Photographs
Publications: Index to the Maui News 1900-1973; Island of Maui Cemetery Directories
Restriction: Open by appt only

S PACIFIC WHALE FOUNDATION LIBRARY*, 300 Ma'alaea Rd, Ste 211, 96793. SAN 373-4315. Tel: 808-249-8811. Toll Free Tel: 800-942-5311. FAX: 808-243-9021. E-mail: education@pacificwhale.org, info@pacificwhale.org. Web Site: www.pacificwhale.org.
Library Holdings: Bk Vols 500; Per Subs 150
Wireless access
Restriction: Not open to pub, Staff use only

IDAHO

Date of Statistics: FY 2020
Population, 2020 U.S. Census: 1,841,377
Population Served by Public Libraries: 1,613,547
Unserved: 227,830
Total Volumes in Public Libraries: 6,646,256
Volumes Per Capita: 3.6
Circulation Per Capita: 6.2
Digital Resources:
Total e-books: 1,300,365
Total audio items (physical and downloadable units): 675,822
Total video items (physical and downloadable units): 396,897
Total computers for use by the public: 1,837
Total annual wireless sessions: 1,623,752 (uses of library wireless networks).

Income and Expenditures:
Total Public Library Income: $73,340,333
Local Taxes: $65,326,524
Local Taxes (ad valorem): 89.1%
Percent State Sales Tax: 2,069,956 (2.8%)
Federal (LSTA): 391,558
Percent Other: 3,159,068 (4.3%)
Total Expenditures: $61,361,777
Expenditures Per Capita: $33.32
Number of County or District Libraries: 56 (Includes 3 school/community libraries)
Number of Public Libraries: 104 (includes city/county/district/school/community libraries)
Number of Bookmobiles in State: 13
Information provided courtesy of: Idaho Commission for Libraries

ABERDEEN

P ABERDEEN DISTRICT LIBRARY, 76 E Central, 83210. (Mail add: PO Box 207, 83210-0207), SAN 303-5247. Tel: 208-397-4427. E-mail: aberdeenlib@gmail.com. Web Site: aberdeen.lili.org. *Dir,* Stephanie Adamson
Circ 14,844
Library Holdings: Bk Vols 18,000; Per Subs 30
Automation Activity & Vendor Info: (Cataloging) OCLC; (Circulation) SirsiDynix; (ILL) OCLC; (OPAC) SirsiDynix
Wireless access
Open Tue-Fri 10:30-6, Sat Noon-3

AMERICAN FALLS

P AMERICAN FALLS DISTRICT LIBRARY*, 308 Roosevelt St, 83211. SAN 303-5255. Tel: 208-226-2335. FAX: 208-226-2303. Web Site: www.aflibrary.org. *Dir,* Kindra Munk; E-mail: kindra@aflibrary.org; Staff 5 (Non-MLS 5)
Pop 6,700; Circ 78,286
Library Holdings: Audiobooks 1,500; Bks on Deafness & Sign Lang 18; CDs 725; DVDs 1,600; Large Print Bks 3,612; Bk Titles 36,476; Bk Vols 36,700; Per Subs 100; Talking Bks 1,250; Videos 812
Special Collections: Idaho Coll; Large Print Coll; Music Coll; Spanish Lang Coll, bks on tape; Young Adult Coll
Automation Activity & Vendor Info: (Acquisitions) Winnebago Software Co; (Cataloging) OCLC; (Circulation) Follett Software; (ILL) OCLC
Wireless access
Open Mon-Thurs (Winter) 10-8, Fri 10-6, Sat 10-5; Mon-Fri (Summer) 10-6, Sat 10-5
Restriction: Badge access after hrs
Friends of the Library Group

ARCO

P LOST RIVERS DISTRICT LIBRARY*, 126 S Front St, 83213. (Mail add: PO Box 170, 83213-0170), SAN 303-5263. Tel: 208-527-8511. E-mail: lrdl8511@outlook.com. Web Site: lostriverscommunitylibrary.wordpress.com/about. *Dir,* Bettina Blattner; E-mail: bettina_6@hotmail.com
Pop 2,907; Circ 15,716
Library Holdings: Bk Vols 13,000; Per Subs 50
Special Collections: American Classics; Antique Book Coll
Automation Activity & Vendor Info: (Acquisitions) Winnebago Software Co; (Cataloging) Winnebago Software Co; (Circulation) Winnebago Software Co; (Course Reserve) Winnebago Software Co; (ILL) Winnebago Software Co; (Media Booking) Winnebago Software Co; (OPAC) Winnebago Software Co; (Serials) Winnebago Software Co
Publications: Library Journal
Open Mon-Thurs 10-5:30, Fri 10-5

Branches: 1
HOWE BRANCH, 1523 Hwy 22, Howe, 83244. Tel: 208-767-3018. *Librn,* Janene Williams
Library Holdings: Bk Vols 2,500
Open Mon, Wed & Fri 1:30-6

BELLEVUE

P BELLEVUE PUBLIC LIBRARY*, 117 E Pine St, 83313. (Mail add: PO Box 825, 83313). Tel: 208-788-4503. FAX: 208-788-2128. E-mail: bellevuelibrary@bellevueidaho.us. Web Site: bellevue.lili.org, www.bellevueidaho.us. *Libr Dir,* Kristin Gearhart; E-mail: kgearhart@bellevueidaho.us
Library Holdings: Bk Vols 8,000; Per Subs 10
Automation Activity & Vendor Info: (Cataloging) Follett Software; (Circulation) Follett Software; (OPAC) Follett Software
Wireless access
Open Mon & Wed 10-5, Tues & Thurs 11-6:30, Fri 10-Noon
Friends of the Library Group

BLACKFOOT

M BINGHAM MEMORIAL HOSPITAL*, Medical Library, 98 Poplar St, 83221. SAN 371-2052. Tel: 208-785-4100. FAX: 208-785-7606. Web Site: www.binghammemorial.org. *Librn,* Margaret Davis
Library Holdings: Bk Vols 500; Per Subs 50

P BLACKFOOT PUBLIC LIBRARY, 129 N Broadway, 83221-2204. (Mail add: PO Box 610, 83221-0610), SAN 303-5298. Tel: 208-785-8628. E-mail: library@cityofblackfoot.org. Web Site: blackfootlibrary.org. *Dir,* Lisa Harral; Staff 2 (Non-MLS 2)
Founded 1916. Pop 20,000; Circ 223,000
Library Holdings: CDs 2,027; DVDs 6,595; Large Print Bks 1,138; Bk Titles 46,454; Bk Vols 51,781; Per Subs 65
Special Collections: Local Newspaper Coll, 1880-, micro
Automation Activity & Vendor Info: (Cataloging) Follett Software; (Circulation) Follett Software; (OPAC) Follett Software
Wireless access
Partic in Idaho Libr Asn
Open Mon-Thurs 9:30-8:30, Fri 9:30-5:30
Friends of the Library Group

P SNAKE RIVER SCHOOL COMMUNITY LIBRARY*, 924 W Hwy 39, 83221. SAN 303-5301. Tel: 208-684-3063. FAX: 208-684-3141. E-mail: snakeriverlibrary@gmail.com. Web Site: snakeriverlibrary.com. *Dir,* Lorrie Surerus
Founded 1951. Pop 7,900; Circ 90,473
Library Holdings: Bk Vols 34,000; Per Subs 16
Automation Activity & Vendor Info: (Cataloging) Follett Software; (Circulation) Follett Software; (ILL) OCLC; (OPAC) Follett Software
Wireless access
Open Mon-Thurs 7am-8pm, Fri 10-4

BOISE

P ADA COMMUNITY LIBRARY*, Victory Branch, 10664 W Victory Rd, 83709. SAN 323-9756. Tel: 208-362-0181. FAX: 208-362-0303. Web Site: www.adalib.org. *Assoc Dir, Br Mgr,* Kristi Haman; Tel: 208-362-0181, Ext 24, E-mail: khaman@adalib.org; *Div Coordr, Financial Serv,* Martha Beller; *IT Coordr,* Dylan Baker; Tel: 208-362-0181, Ext 132, E-mail: dbaker@adalib.org; Staff 15 (MLS 4, Non-MLS 11)
Founded 1984. Pop 50,000; Circ 700,000
Library Holdings: CDs 3,164; DVDs 2,491; e-books 6,616; Bk Vols 138,000; Per Subs 200; Talking Bks 9,000; Videos 8,000
Automation Activity & Vendor Info: (Cataloging) Horizon; (Circulation) Horizon; (ILL) OCLC; (OPAC) Horizon; (Serials) Horizon
Function: 24/7 Electronic res, 24/7 Online cat, Activity rm, Adult bk club, After school storytime, Art exhibits, Audio & video playback equip for onsite use, Audiobks on Playaways & MP3, Audiobks via web, AV serv, Bk club(s), Bks on cassette, Bks on CD, Children's prog, Computer training, Computers for patron use, E-Readers, E-Reserves, Electronic databases & coll, Free DVD rentals, Holiday prog, Homework prog, ILL available, Internet access, Jail serv, Life-long learning prog for all ages, Magazines, Mail & tel request accepted, Movies, Music CDs, Online cat, Online ref, Outreach serv, Outside serv via phone, mail, e-mail & web, OverDrive digital audio bks, Photocopying/Printing, Preschool outreach, Prog for adults, Prog for children & young adult, Ref & res, Scanner, Senior outreach, Serves people with intellectual disabilities, Spanish lang bks, Spoken cassettes & CDs, Story hour, Study rm, Summer & winter reading prog, Summer reading prog, Tax forms, Teen prog, Telephone ref, Visual arts prog, Wheelchair accessible, Winter reading prog, Workshops
Partic in LYNX! Consortium; OCLC Online Computer Library Center, Inc
Open Mon-Thurs 9-8, Fri & Sat 11-6
Friends of the Library Group
Branches: 3
HIDDEN SPRINGS BRANCH, 5868 W Hidden Springs Dr, 83714. Tel: 208-229-2665. *Div Coordr,* Mary Allington; E-mail: mallington@adalib.org; Staff 4 (MLS 2, Non-MLS 2)
Founded 2001. Pop 2,400
Function: 24/7 Electronic res, 24/7 Online cat, Activity rm, Adult bk club, Audiobks on Playaways & MP3, Audiobks via web, Bk reviews (Group), Bks on cassette, Bks on CD, Children's prog, Computer training, Computers for patron use, Digital talking bks, E-Readers, E-Reserves, Electronic databases & coll, Free DVD rentals, Holiday prog, Homework prog, ILL available, Internet access, Life-long learning prog for all ages, Magazines, Mail & tel request accepted, Meeting rooms, Movies, Music CDs, Online cat, Online ref, Outreach serv, Outside serv via phone, mail, e-mail & web, OverDrive digital audio bks, Photocopying/Printing, Preschool outreach, Preschool reading prog, Prog for adults, Prog for children & young adult, Ref serv available, Spoken cassettes & CDs, Spoken cassettes & DVDs, Story hour, Summer & winter reading prog, Summer reading prog, Tax forms, Teen prog, Telephone ref, VHS videos, Wheelchair accessible, Winter reading prog, Workshops
Open Mon-Fri 12-6
Friends of the Library Group
LAKE HAZEL BRANCH, 10489 W Lake Hazel Rd, 83709. *Assoc Dir, Br Mgr,* Alex Hartman; E-mail: ahartman@adalib.org; Staff 14 (MLS 2, Non-MLS 12)
Founded 2011. Pop 20,000
Function: 24/7 Electronic res, 24/7 Online cat, Activity rm, After school storytime, Audio & video playback equip for onsite use, Audiobks on Playaways & MP3, Audiobks via web, AV serv, Bk club(s), Bks on cassette, Bks on CD, Children's prog, Computer training, Computers for patron use, Digital talking bks, E-Reserves, Electronic databases & coll, Family literacy, For res purposes, Free DVD rentals, Holiday prog, Homework prog, ILL available, Internet access, Jail serv, Life-long learning prog for all ages, Literacy & newcomer serv, Magazines, Meeting rooms, Movies, Music CDs, Online cat, Online ref, Outreach serv, Outside serv via phone, mail, e-mail & web, OverDrive digital audio bks, Photocopying/Printing, Preschool outreach, Preschool reading prog, Printer for laptops & handheld devices, Prog for adults, Prog for children & young adult, Ref & res, Scanner, Story hour, Study rm, Summer & winter reading prog, Summer reading prog, Tax forms, Teen prog, Telephone ref, Visual arts prog, Wheelchair accessible, Workshops
STAR BRANCH, 10706 W State St, Star, 83669. Tel: 208-286-9755. FAX: 208-286-9755. *Br Mgr,* Joy Lear
Library Holdings: Audiobooks 2,998; Bk Titles 30,254; Bk Vols 38,634; Per Subs 60; Videos 3,899
Open Mon-Thurs 10-7, Fri & Sat 10-5
Friends of the Library Group

S BOISE ART MUSEUM LIBRARY*, 670 Julia Davis Dr, 83702. SAN 320-149X. Tel: 208-345-8330, Ext 110. FAX: 208-345-2247. Web Site: www.boiseartmuseum.org. *Library Contact,* MacKenzie Buie; E-mail: mackenzie@boiseartmuseum.org
Library Holdings: Bk Titles 2,500; Per Subs 10
Subject Interests: Art hist
Function: Res libr
Open Tues-Sat 10-5, Sun 12-5
Restriction: Non-circulating

CR BOISE BIBLE COLLEGE LIBRARY*, 8695 W Marigold St, 83714-1220. SAN 303-5328. Tel: 208-376-7731. FAX: 208-376-7743. Web Site: boisebible.edu/academics/library-information. *Librn,* Amber Grove; E-mail: agrove@boisebible.edu; Staff 1 (Non-MLS 1)
Founded 1945. Enrl 201; Fac 10; Highest Degree: Bachelor
Library Holdings: Bk Titles 29,731; Bk Vols 35,268; Per Subs 77; Videos 200
Special Collections: Oregon Trail Society Coll; Rare Book Coll; Restoration Movement materials
Subject Interests: Biblical studies, Church hist, Missions & missionaries
Automation Activity & Vendor Info: (Circulation) Follett Software; (OPAC) Follett Software
Wireless access
Open Mon-Thurs 8am-10pm, Fri 8-5, Sat 10-1 & 6-9, Sun 6-9
Restriction: Borrowing privileges limited to fac & registered students, In-house use for visitors

P BOISE PUBLIC LIBRARY*, Main Library, 715 S Capitol Blvd, 83702. SAN 303-5344. Tel: 208-972-8200. Administration Tel: 208-972-8258. TDD: 800-377-3529. E-mail: librarycomments@cityofboise.org. Web Site: www.boisepubliclibrary.org. *Libr Dir,* Jessica Dorr; E-mail: LibraryDirector@cityofboise.org; *Mgr,* Heidi Lewis; *Acq/Tech Serv Mgr,* Shanna Decker; Tel: 208-972-8219, E-mail: sdecker@cityofboise.org; *Operations & Outreach Mgr,* Denise McNeley; Tel: 208-972-8210, E-mail: dmcneley@cityofboise.org; *Mgr, Pub Serv,* Sarah Keller-Chase; Tel: 208-972-8202, E-mail: schase@cityofboise.org; Staff 106.3 (MLS 19, Non-MLS 87.3)
Founded 1895. Pop 208,219; Circ 1,510,530
Library Holdings: AV Mats 28,588; Large Print Bks 5,043; Bk Titles 261,797; Bk Vols 356,772; Per Subs 299
Special Collections: Newspaper (Idaho Stateman), micro; Northwest & Idaho History. US Document Depository
Automation Activity & Vendor Info: (Acquisitions) SirsiDynix; (Cataloging) SirsiDynix; (Circulation) SirsiDynix; (ILL) OCLC Online; (OPAC) SirsiDynix; (Serials) SirsiDynix
Wireless access
Function: Home delivery & serv to seniorr ctr & nursing homes, Homebound delivery serv, ILL available, Magnifiers for reading, Outside serv via phone, mail, e-mail & web, Photocopying/Printing, Prog for children & young adult, Ref serv available, Summer reading prog, Wheelchair accessible
Partic in LYNX! Consortium
Special Services for the Deaf - TTY equip
Special Services for the Blind - Assistive/Adapted tech devices, equip & products
Open Mon-Thurs 10-9, Fri 10-6, Sat 10-5, Sun 12-5
Friends of the Library Group
Branches: 4
LIBRARY! AT BOWN CROSSING, 2153 E Riverwalk Dr, 83706. Tel: 208-972-8630. *Br Supvr,* Joni Hansen
Friends of the Library Group
LIBRARY! AT COLE & USTICK, 7557 W Ustick Rd, 83704, SAN 370-3649. Tel: 208-972-8300. *Br Supvr,* Trisha Mick
Founded 2009
Open Tues-Thurs 10-9, Fri 10-6, Sat Noon-5, Sun 1-5
Friends of the Library Group
LIBRARY! AT COLLISTER, 4724 W State St, 83703. Tel: 208-972-8320. *Br Supvr,* Jennifer Villalobos
Founded 2008
Open Tues-Thurs 10-9, Fri 10-6, Sat Noon-5, Sun 1-5
Friends of the Library Group
LIBRARY! AT HILLCREST, 5246 W Overland Rd, 83705. Tel: 208-972-8340. *Br Supvr,* Huda Shaltry
Founded 2008
Open Tues-Thurs 10-9, Fri 10-6, Sat Noon-5, Sun 1-5
Friends of the Library Group
Bookmobiles: 1

C BOISE STATE UNIVERSITY*, Albertsons Library, 1865 Cesar Chavez Lane, 83725. (Mail add: 1910 University Dr, 83725), SAN 339-624X. Tel: 208-426-1204. Reference Tel: 208-426-3301. Administration Tel: 208-426-1234. FAX: 208-334-2111. Web Site: library.boisestate.edu. *Dean,* Dr Tracy Bicknell-Holmes; E-mail: tracybicknell-holmes@boisestate.edu; *Assoc Dean,* Michelle Armstrong; E-mail: michellearmstrong1@boisestate.edu; *Head, Acq,* Nancy Rosenheim; Tel: 208-426-1660, E-mail: nrosenhe@boisestate.edu; *Head, Spec Coll & Archives,* Cheryl Oestriecher; Tel: 208-426-3958, E-mail: cheryloestreicher@boisestate.edu; Staff 61.9 (MLS 22.9, Non-MLS 39)
Founded 1932. Enrl 18,936; Fac 611; Highest Degree: Doctorate
Special Collections: Cenarrusa Papers; Idaho Historical Manuscripts & Photos; Idaho Writers Archive, literary ms; Papers of Governor Cecil

Andrus; Rare Books Coll; Senatorial Papers of Frank Church & Len B Jordan. US Document Depository
Automation Activity & Vendor Info: (Acquisitions) Ex Libris Group; (Cataloging) Ex Libris Group; (Circulation) Ex Libris Group; (Course Reserve) Docutek; (OPAC) Ex Libris Group; (Serials) Ex Libris Group
Wireless access
Open Mon-Fri 7am-Midnight, Sat & Sun 9am-Midnight; Mon-Fri (Summer) 7-7, Sat & Sun 9-6

GM DEPARTMENT OF VETERANS AFFAIRS*, Medical Center Library, 500 W Fort St, 531/142D, 83702. SAN 303-545X. Tel: 208-422-1306. FAX: 208-422-1390. E-mail: vhaboilibrab@va.gov. Web Site: www.boise.va.gov. *Library Contact,* Rob Lyons; Staff 1 (Non-MLS 1)
Founded 1930
Library Holdings: AV Mats 464; CDs 175; DVDs 183; e-books 3,000; e-journals 5,000; Microforms 1,440; Bk Titles 5,060; Per Subs 98; Videos 423
Special Collections: Clinical Medicine, bks, AV; Patient Education, bks, AV
Automation Activity & Vendor Info: (Acquisitions) Follett Software; (Cataloging) Follett Software; (Circulation) Follett Software; (Course Reserve) Follett Software; (Media Booking) Follett Software; (OPAC) Follett Software; (Serials) Follett Software
Wireless access
Function: For res purposes, Govt ref serv, ILL available, Magnifiers for reading, Wheelchair accessible
Partic in National Network of Libraries of Medicine Region 4; Pacific NW Regional Health Sci Libr
Open Mon-Fri 8-4:30

L HAWLEY TROXELL ENNIS & HAWLEY*, Law Library, 877 Main St, Ste 1000, 83702-1617. Tel: 208-344-6000. FAX: 208-342-3829. Web Site: www.hawleytroxell.com. *Librn,* Allison Perry; E-mail: aperry@hawleytroxell.com
Library Holdings: Bk Vols 12,000; Per Subs 50
Restriction: Not open to pub

S HEALTHWISE INC*, Research Library, 2601 N Bogus Basin Rd, 83702. SAN 377-2276. Tel: 208-331-6958. FAX: 208-345-1897. E-mail: hwlibrary@healthwise.org. *Med Librn,* Karri Alderson; E-mail: kalderson@healthwise.org; Staff 2 (MLS 2)
Library Holdings: Bk Titles 200
Function: ILL available, Res libr
Restriction: Co libr, Open to staff only

G IDAHO COMMISSION FOR LIBRARIES*, 325 W State St, 83702-6072. SAN 339-6363. Tel: 208-334-2150. FAX: 208-334-4016. E-mail: lili@libraries.idaho.gov. Web Site: libraries.idaho.gov. *State Librn,* Stephanie Bailey-White; E-mail: stephanie.bailey-white@libraries.idaho.gov; *Dep State Librn,* Stephanie Bailey-White; E-mail: stephanie.bailey-white@libraries.idaho.gov; *Admin Serv Mgr,* Roger Dubois; E-mail: roger.dubois@libraries.idaho.gov; *Prog Supvr,* Randy Kemp; E-mail: randall.kemp@libraries.idaho.gov
Founded 1901
Special Collections: NLS (Talking Book Service Coll); Shelf Project (Talking Book Service Coll); Stacks (Digital Repository of State Publications). State Document Depository
Automation Activity & Vendor Info: (Circulation) Keystone Systems, Inc (KLAS); (ILL) OCLC WorldShare Interlibrary Loan; (OPAC) Keystone Systems, Inc (KLAS)
Wireless access
Publications: Connections: TBS News (Quarterly newsletter); Envoy - Trustee News (Quarterly); Idaho Library Laws (Annual); Nexus - ICFL News (Bimonthly); Public Library Statistics; The Bookworm (Monthly newsletter); The Scoop (Monthly newsletter)
Partic in Association for Rural & Small Libraries
Special Services for the Blind - Digital talking bk; Digital talking bk machines; Newsletter (in large print, Braille or on cassette); Production of talking bks; Tel Pioneers equip repair group
Open Mon-Fri 8-5

P IDAHO COMMISSION FOR LIBRARIES*, Talking Book Service, 325 W State St, 83702-6072. SAN 303-5379. Tel: 208-334-2150. Toll Free Tel: 800-458-3271. E-mail: talkingbooks@libraries.idaho.gov. Web Site: libraries.idaho.org. *State Librn,* Stephanie Bailey-White; E-mail: stephanie.bailey-white@libraries.idaho.gov; Staff 7 (MLS 1, Non-MLS 6)
Founded 1973. Pop 3,679; Circ 186,960
Special Collections: Braille & Audio Reading Download; Idaho & Pacific Northwest Recorded Books; Idaho Shelf Project
Automation Activity & Vendor Info: (OPAC) Keystone Systems, Inc (KLAS)
Wireless access
Publications: Connections: TBS News (Quarterly); Large Print Calendar
Special Services for the Blind - Audio mat; Bks & mags in Braille, on rec, tape & cassette; Children's Braille; Newsletter (in large print, Braille or on cassette); Newsline for the Blind; Newsp reading serv
Open Mon-Fri 8-5

G IDAHO LEGISLATIVE RESEARCH LIBRARY*, State Capitol, 700 W Jefferson St, 83702. (Mail add: PO Box 83720, 83720), SAN 320-1759. Tel: 208-334-4822. E-mail: library@lso.idaho.gov. Web Site: legislature.idaho.gov/lso/research/#hcode-tab-style2legislative-research-library. *Legislative Librn,* Eric Glover; E-mail: eglover@lso.idaho.gov; Staff 3 (MLS 1, Non-MLS 2)
Founded 1978
Library Holdings: CDs 50; Bk Titles 2,500; Bk Vols 3,100; Per Subs 40
Subject Interests: Legislation
Automation Activity & Vendor Info: (Cataloging) Follett Software; (Circulation) Follett Software
Wireless access
Function: Govt ref serv, Photocopying/Printing, Ref & res, Ref serv available, Res assist avail, Res libr, Telephone ref
Open Mon-Fri 8-5
Restriction: Circulates for staff only

S IDAHO POWER CO*, Corporate Library, 1221 W Idaho St, 83702. (Mail add: PO Box 70, 83707-0070), SAN 328-7890. Tel: 208-388-2696. Web Site: www.idahopower.com. *Librn,* Daralie Kane; E-mail: dkane@idahopower.com
Library Holdings: Bks on Deafness & Sign Lang 2; Bk Titles 3,000; Per Subs 30
Wireless access
Open Mon-Fri 8-5

S IDAHO STATE CORRECTIONAL INSTITUTION LIBRARY, 13500 S Pleasant Valley Rd, 83707. (Mail add: PO Box 14, 83707-0014). Tel: 208-336-0740. FAX: 208-424-3731. *Librn,* Karen Bassford; E-mail: kbassfo@corr.state.id.us; Staff 1 (MLS 1)
Founded 1974
Library Holdings: Bk Titles 34,349; Per Subs 32
Restriction: Not open to pub
Branches:
IDAHO CORRECTIONAL INSTITUTION-OROFINO LIBRARY, 23 Hospital Dr N, Orofino, 83544. Tel: 208-476-3655. *Dir,* Jim Rehder
Library Holdings: Bk Vols 2,000; Per Subs 30
Automation Activity & Vendor Info: (Cataloging) Follett Software; (Circulation) Follett Software
Restriction: Not open to pub
POCATELLO WOMEN'S CORRECTIONAL CENTER LIBRARY, 1451 Fore Rd, Pocatello, 83204. Tel: 208-236-6360. FAX: 208-236-6362.
Library Holdings: Bk Vols 13,075; Per Subs 19
Automation Activity & Vendor Info: (Cataloging) Follett Software; (Circulation) Follett Software
SOUTH BOISE WOMEN'S CORRECTIONAL CENTER LIBRARY, 13200 S Pleasant Valley Rd, Kuna, 83634. (Mail add: PO Box 8509, 83707-8509). Tel: 208-336-1260.
Library Holdings: Bk Vols 5,000
SOUTH IDAHO CORRECTIONAL INSTITUTION LIBRARY, 13900 S Pleasant Valley Rd, Kuna, 83634. (Mail add: PO Box 8509, 83707-8509). Tel: 208-336-1260. *Librn,* Robyn Patterson
Library Holdings: Bk Vols 7,000

S IDAHO STATE HISTORICAL SOCIETY, Idaho State Archives Research Center, Idaho History Ctr, 2205 Old Penitentiary Rd, 83712-8250. SAN 339-6304. Tel: 208-334-2620, 208-334-3356. FAX: 208-334-2626. E-mail: public.archives@ishs.idaho.gov. Web Site: history.idaho.gov/archives. *Adminr, State Archivist,* David Matte; Tel: 208-514-2328, E-mail: david.matte@ishs.idaho.gov; *Govt Reference Mger,* Mackenzie Stone; Tel: 208-514-2316, E-mail: mackenzie.stone@ishs.idaho.gov; *Outreach Mgr,* Danielle Worthy; Tel: 208-514-2323, E-mail: danielle.worthy@ishs.idaho.gov; *Ref Mgr,* Elizabeth Westenburg; Tel: 208-514-2324, E-mail: elizabeth.westenburg@ishs.idaho.gov. Subject Specialists: *State govt,* David Matte; Staff 11 (MLS 4, Non-MLS 7)
Founded 1907
Library Holdings: Microforms 40,000; Bk Titles 37,000; Per Subs 170
Special Collections: Idaho & Pacific Northwest history; Idaho Newspapers, microfilm, photographs; Manuscripts including State & Local governmental records; Maps Coll. Municipal Document Depository; Oral History; State Document Depository
Subject Interests: Genealogy, State hist
Wireless access
Function: Archival coll, For res purposes, ILL available, Mail & tel request accepted, Microfiche/film & reading machines, Photocopying/Printing, Ref serv available, Res libr, Res performed for a fee, Scanner
Publications: Idaho Landscapes (Periodical); Idaho Yesterdays (Periodical)

Open Tues-Sat 11-4
Restriction: In-house use for visitors, Non-circulating, Pub use on premises

L IDAHO STATE LAW LIBRARY*, 514 W Jefferson St, 2nd Flr, 83702. (Mail add: PO Box 83720, 83720-0051), SAN 303-5395. Tel: 208-364-4555. E-mail: lawlibrary@idcourts.net. Web Site: www.isll.idaho.gov. *Libr Dir, Ref & Instruction Librn,* Stacy Etheredge; Tel: 208-364-4558, E-mail: stacye@uidaho.edu; *Ref & Instruction Librn,* Sam Williams; Tel: 208-364-4554, E-mail: sawilliams@uidaho.edu; Staff 3 (MLS 2, Non-MLS 1)
Founded 1869
Library Holdings: Bk Vols 31,000
Special Collections: US Document Depository
Subject Interests: Law, Legislation
Automation Activity & Vendor Info: (Acquisitions) Ex Libris Group; (Cataloging) Ex Libris Group; (Circulation) Ex Libris Group; (ILL) OCLC FirstSearch; (OPAC) Ex Libris Group; (Serials) Ex Libris Group
Wireless access
Function: Computers for patron use, ILL available, Photocopying/Printing, Ref & res, Ref serv available, Scanner
Open Mon-Fri 8-5
Restriction: Borrowing requests are handled by ILL, Circ limited, Non-circulating coll, Non-circulating to the pub

M SAINT ALPHONSUS HEALTH SYSTEM*, Kissler Library, Central Tower, 1055 N Curtis Rd, 2nd Flr, 83706. SAN 303-5417. Tel: 208-367-2271. FAX: 208-367-2702. Web Site: www.saintalphonsus.org/kissler-family-library. *Librn,* Tina Slanc; E-mail: tina.slanc@saintalphonsus.org
Founded 1970
Library Holdings: e-journals 10,000; Bk Titles 600; Per Subs 210
Wireless access
Open Mon-Fri 7:30-3:30

M SAINT LUKE'S HEALTH SYSTEM LIBRARIES*, Dr Maurice M Burkholder Health Sciences Library, 190 E Bannock St, 83712-6297. SAN 303-5425. Tel: 208-381-2276. Automation Services Tel: 208-381-2277. E-mail: library@slhs.org. Web Site: www.stlukesonline.org/health-services/health-information/health-library. *Libr Mgr,* Sara Loree; *ILL, Libr Asst,* Madi Vershum
Founded 1971
Library Holdings: Bk Titles 1,300; Bk Vols 1,500; Per Subs 1,100
Subject Interests: Cardiology, Internal med, Obstetrics & gynecology, Oncology, Pediatrics
Automation Activity & Vendor Info: (Cataloging) Softlink America; (Circulation) Softlink America; (OPAC) Softlink America
Wireless access
Open Mon-Fri 8-4:30

BONNERS FERRY

P BOUNDARY COUNTY LIBRARY*, 6370 Kootenai St, 83805. (Mail add: PO Box Y, 83805-1276), SAN 303-5468. Tel: 208-267-3750. FAX: 208-267-5231. E-mail: boundarycountylibrary1@frontier.com. Web Site: www.boundarycountylibrary.com. *Libr Dir,* Sandra Ashworth
Founded 1914. Pop 11,000; Circ 100,000
Library Holdings: Bk Vols 41,000; Per Subs 184
Subject Interests: Environ studies, Forestry
Automation Activity & Vendor Info: (Cataloging) OCLC WorldShare Interlibrary Loan; (Circulation) OCLC WorldShare Interlibrary Loan
Wireless access
Open Mon & Fri 9-8, Tues-Thurs 9-6, Sat 10-4

BRUNEAU

P BRUNEAU DISTRICT LIBRARY*, 32073 Ruth St, 83604. (Mail add: PO Box 253, 83604). Tel: 208-845-2131. FAX: 208-845-2131. E-mail: bruneau_library@yahoo.com. *Dir,* Pamela Landis
Library Holdings: DVDs 50; Bk Titles 10,500; Videos 420
Wireless access
Open Tues 10-6, Wed 8:30-4, Thurs 8:30-5

BUHL

P BUHL PUBLIC LIBRARY, 215 Broadway Ave N, 83316. SAN 303-5476. Tel: 208-543-6500. FAX: 208-543-2318. E-mail: library@cityofbuhl.us. Web Site: buhlpubliclibrary.org. *Libr Dir,* Reba Puente; E-mail: reba.p@cityofbuhl.us; *Ch Serv,* Linda Henderson
Pop 3,516; Circ 38,744
Library Holdings: Bk Vols 25,664; Per Subs 56; Talking Bks 1,688; Videos 1,191
Special Collections: Children's Art Coll; Idaho Coll; Quilting Coll
Automation Activity & Vendor Info: (Cataloging) Follett Software; (Circulation) Follett Software; (OPAC) Follett Software
Wireless access
Open Mon & Wed 9-5, Tues & Thurs 1-7, Sat 1-5

BURLEY

P BURLEY PUBLIC LIBRARY*, 1300 Miller Ave, 83318-1729. SAN 303-5492. Tel: 208-878-7708. FAX: 208-878-7018. E-mail: library@bplibrary.org. Web Site: www.bplibrary.org. *Dir,* Julie Woodford
Founded 1922. Pop 9,316; Circ 55,909
Library Holdings: Bk Vols 46,194; Per Subs 40
Special Collections: Idaho Coll
Automation Activity & Vendor Info: (Cataloging) Follett Software; (Circulation) Follett Software; (ILL) OCLC FirstSearch; (OPAC) Follett Software
Wireless access
Open Mon 9:30-7, Tues-Thurs 10-7, Fri 9:30-6, Sat 10-5
Friends of the Library Group

CALDWELL

P CALDWELL PUBLIC LIBRARY*, 1010 Dearborn St, 83605. SAN 303-5506. Tel: 208-459-3242. FAX: 208-459-7344. E-mail: infolibrary@cityofcaldwell.org. Web Site: www.caldwellpubliclibrary.org. *Dir,* Lacey Welt; E-mail: lwelt@cityofcaldwell.org; *Ad,* Marina Rose; E-mail: mrose@cityofcaldwell.org; *Tech Serv Librn,* Abraham Valadez; E-mail: avaladez@cityofcaldwell.org; *Circ Supvr,* Lori Shirley; E-mail: lshirley@cityofcaldwell.org; *Tech Serv Supvr,* Annalea Martinez; E-mail: amartinez@cityofcaldwell.org; *Youth Serv Supvr,* Fiona May; E-mail: fmay@cityofcaldwell.org; Staff 6 (MLS 2, Non-MLS 4)
Founded 1887. Pop 48,957; Circ 183,944
Oct 2016-Sept 2017 Income $611,575, City $534,476, Locally Generated Income $77,099. Mats Exp $81,571, Books $64,851, AV Mat $5,411, Electronic Ref Mat (Incl. Access Fees) $11,309. Sal $351,024
Library Holdings: AV Mats 1,844; Bk Vols 95,092; Per Subs 153; Videos 1,821
Special Collections: Historical Photograph Coll. Oral History
Subject Interests: Local hist
Automation Activity & Vendor Info: (Acquisitions) Innovative Interfaces, Inc; (Cataloging) Innovative Interfaces, Inc; (Circulation) Innovative Interfaces, Inc; (ILL) OCLC WorldShare Interlibrary Loan; (OPAC) Innovative Interfaces, Inc; (Serials) Innovative Interfaces, Inc
Wireless access
Function: 24/7 Electronic res, 24/7 Online cat, Adult bk club, Archival coll, Audiobks via web, AV serv, Bilingual assistance for Spanish patrons, Bk club(s), Bks on CD, Children's prog, Citizenship assistance, Computer training, Computers for patron use, Electronic databases & coll, For res purposes, Free DVD rentals, Holiday prog, Home delivery & serv to seniorr ctr & nursing homes, Homebound delivery serv, ILL available, Instruction & testing, Internet access, Magazines, Meeting rooms, Microfiche/film & reading machines, Movies, Music CDs, Online cat, Online info literacy tutorials on the web & in blackboard, OverDrive digital audio bks, Photocopying/Printing, Preschool reading prog, Prog for adults, Prog for children & young adult, Ref & res, Ref serv available, Scanner, Serves people with intellectual disabilities, Spanish lang bks, Story hour, Summer reading prog, Tax forms, Teen prog, Wheelchair accessible
Partic in Canyon Owyhee Library Group, Ltd; LYNX! Consortium; OCLC Online Computer Library Center, Inc
Special Services for the Deaf - ADA equip; Bks on deafness & sign lang
Special Services for the Blind - Bks & mags in Braille, on rec, tape & cassette; Bks on CD; Braille bks; Children's Braille; Digital talking bk; Home delivery serv; Large print bks
Open Mon-Thurs 10-9, Fri 10-6, Sat 10-5, Sun (Sept-May) 2-5
Restriction: Circ to mem only, Non-resident fee
Friends of the Library Group

C THE COLLEGE OF IDAHO*, Cruzen-Murray Library, 2112 Cleveland Blvd, 83605. SAN 303-5514. E-mail: library@collegeofidaho.edu. Web Site: www.collegeofidaho.edu/library. *Libr Dir,* Christine Schutz; E-mail: cschutz@collegeofidaho.edu; *Libr Serv Coordr,* Dayle Winbigler; E-mail: dwinbigler@collegeofidaho.edu; Staff 5 (MLS 2, Non-MLS 3)
Founded 1891. Enrl 1,010; Highest Degree: Master
Automation Activity & Vendor Info: (Acquisitions) OCLC Worldshare Management Services; (Cataloging) OCLC Worldshare Management Services; (Circulation) OCLC Worldshare Management Services; (Course Reserve) OCLC Worldshare Management Services; (Discovery) OCLC Worldshare Management Services; (ILL) OCLC WorldShare Interlibrary Loan; (OPAC) OCLC Worldshare Management Services
Wireless access
Partic in LYRASIS
Restriction: Not open to pub, Open to students, fac & staff
Friends of the Library Group

CAMBRIDGE

P CAMBRIDGE COMMUNITY LIBRARY, 120 S Superior St, 83610. (Mail add: PO Box 436, 83610-0436), SAN 303-5522. Tel: 208-257-3434. E-mail: cambplib@ctcweb.net. Web Site: www.cambridge.lili.org. *Dir,* Lorrie Robertson
Founded 1973. Pop 249; Circ 9,000
Library Holdings: Bk Titles 16,000
Wireless access
Special Services for the Blind - Bks on cassette
Open Mon-Sat 1-6

CAREY

P LITTLE WOOD RIVER DISTRICT LIBRARY*, 16 Panther Ave, 83320-5063. (Mail add: PO Box 10, 83320-0218), SAN 303-5530. Tel: 208-823-4510. E-mail: lwrlibrary@yahoo.com. *Dir,* Mary Bowman
Founded 1976. Pop 1,000; Circ 15,000
Library Holdings: AV Mats 100; CDs 50; DVDs 360; Bk Titles 6,000; Videos 700
Wireless access
Open Mon 10-7:30, Wed 3:30-7:30

CASCADE

P CASCADE PUBLIC LIBRARY, 105 Front St, 83611. (Mail add: PO Box 10, 83611-0010), SAN 303-5549. Tel: 208-382-4757. FAX: 208-382-4757. E-mail: librarydesk@cascadeid.us. Web Site: cascade.lili.org. *Libr Dir,* Casey Taylor; E-mail: librarydirector@cascadeid.us; Staff 1 (Non-MLS 1)
Founded 1914. Pop 1,001; Circ 12,250
Library Holdings: Audiobooks 305; CDs 96; DVDs 308; Large Print Bks 310; Bk Titles 15,200; Bk Vols 15,232; Per Subs 2; Videos 1,002
Special Collections: Genealogy Coll; Idaho Coll; National Geographic 1914-2010
Automation Activity & Vendor Info: (Cataloging) Biblionix; (Circulation) Biblionix; (ILL) OCLC FirstSearch
Wireless access
Function: 24/7 Electronic res, 24/7 Online cat, Adult bk club, Audio & video playback equip for onsite use, Audiobks on Playaways & MP3, Audiobks via web, Bk club(s), Bks on cassette, Bks on CD, CD-ROM, Children's prog, Citizenship assistance, Computer training, Computers for patron use, Digital talking bks, Distance learning, E-Readers, E-Reserves, Electronic databases & coll, Free DVD rentals, Govt ref serv, Homebound delivery serv, ILL available, Instruction & testing, Internet access, Laminating, Literacy & newcomer serv, Magazines, Magnifiers for reading, Mail & tel request accepted, Mail loans to mem, Masonic res mat, Meeting rooms, Movies, Music CDs, Online cat, Online info literacy tutorials on the web & in blackboard, Online ref, Orientations, Outreach serv, Outside serv via phone, mail, e-mail & web, OverDrive digital audio bks, Photocopying/Printing, Preschool outreach, Preschool reading prog, Printer for laptops & handheld devices, Prog for adults, Prog for children & young adult, Ref & res, Ref serv available, Scanner, Senior outreach, Serves people with intellectual disabilities, Spoken cassettes & CDs, Spoken cassettes & DVDs, Story hour, Study rm, Summer reading prog, Tax forms, Teen prog, Telephone ref, VHS videos, Wheelchair accessible
Partic in Valley Mountain Library Consortium
Special Services for the Blind - Bks on cassette; Cassette playback machines; Cassettes; Home delivery serv; Large print & cassettes; Talking bk serv referral; Talking bks; Talking bks & player equip
Open Mon-Fri 11-6, Sat 10-2
Friends of the Library Group

CHALLIS

P CHALLIS PUBLIC LIBRARY*, 531 W Main St, 83226. (Mail add: PO Box 186, 83226-0186), SAN 303-5557. Tel: 208-879-4267. FAX: 208-879-2027. E-mail: cpl@custertel.net. Web Site: challis.lili.org. *Dir,* Becky Mitchell; Staff 1 (MLS 1)
Founded 1935. Pop 1,990; Circ 9,291
Library Holdings: Audiobooks 250; Bk Titles 16,000; Per Subs 20
Automation Activity & Vendor Info: (Cataloging) New Generation Technologies Inc. (LiBRARYSOFT); (Circulation) New Generation Technologies Inc. (LiBRARYSOFT); (OPAC) New Generation Technologies Inc. (LiBRARYSOFT)
Wireless access
Open Tues-Thurs 12-6, Fri & Sat 12-3

CHUBBUCK

P PORTNEUF DISTRICT LIBRARY*, 5210 Stuart Ave, 83202. SAN 303-6308. Tel: 208-237-2192. E-mail: notices@portneuflibrary.org. Web Site: www.portneuflibrary.org. *Dir,* Holly Jackson; E-mail: holly.jackson@portneuflibrary.org; *Asst Dir,* Josh Barnes; E-mail: josh.barnes@portneuflibrary.org; *Ch,* Amanda Bowden; E-mail: amanda.bowden@portneuflibrary.org; Staff 3 (MLS 1, Non-MLS 2)
Founded 1958. Pop 22,000; Circ 117,717
Library Holdings: Audiobooks 4,633; Bks on Deafness & Sign Lang 10; CDs 500; DVDs 2,689; Large Print Bks 500; Bk Titles 43,190; Per Subs 29
Special Collections: Idaho Authors
Subject Interests: Idaho hist
Automation Activity & Vendor Info: (ILL) OCLC; (Serials) EBSCO Online
Wireless access
Function: 24/7 Electronic res, Activity rm, After school storytime, Audiobks via web, Bilingual assistance for Spanish patrons, Bks on CD, Chess club, Children's prog, Citizenship assistance, Computer training, Computers for patron use, Digital talking bks, Electronic databases & coll, Free DVD rentals, Holiday prog, Homework prog, ILL available, Instruction & testing, Internet access, Life-long learning prog for all ages, Literacy & newcomer serv, Magazines, Mango lang, Movies, Music CDs, Notary serv, Online cat, Online ref, Photocopying/Printing, Preschool outreach, Preschool reading prog, Prog for adults, Prog for children & young adult, Ref serv available, Senior computer classes, Senior outreach, Serves people with intellectual disabilities, Spanish lang bks, Spoken cassettes & CDs, Spoken cassettes & DVDs, Story hour, Study rm, Summer & winter reading prog, Summer reading prog, Teen prog, Wheelchair accessible, Winter reading prog, Workshops
Partic in Library Consortium of Eastern Idaho
Open Mon-Fri 9-7, Sat 10-6

CLARKIA

P CLARKIA DISTRICT LIBRARY, 377 Poplar St, 83812. (Mail add: PO Box 1126, 83812-1126). Tel: 208-245-2908. FAX: 208-245-2908. E-mail: clarkialibrary@yahoo.com. Web Site: clarkia.lili.org. *Dir,* Dawn Kruger
Library Holdings: Bk Vols 7,000
Open Mon & Wed 3-8, Tues, Thurs & Sat 9-Noon

COEUR D'ALENE

P COEUR D'ALENE PUBLIC LIBRARY*, 702 E Front Ave, 83814-2373. SAN 303-5573. Tel: 208-769-2315. FAX: 208-769-2381. E-mail: info@cdalibrary.org. Web Site: www.cdalibrary.org. *Dir,* Bette Ammon; E-mail: bammon@cdalibrary.org; *Youth Serv Librn,* Mandi Harris; E-mail: mharris@cdalibrary.org; *Circ Mgr,* Tyler McClane; E-mail: tmclane@cdalibrary.org; *Communications Coordr,* David Townsend; E-mail: dtownsend@cdalibrary.org; *Young Adult Serv Coordr,* Angela Flock; E-mail: aflock@cdalibrary.org; *Info Serv,* Christopher Brannon; E-mail: christopher@cdalibrary.org; *ILL,* Lindsay Moore; E-mail: lmoore@cdalibrary.org; *Ref/Tech Serv,* Melissa Searle; E-mail: msearle@cdalibrary.org; Staff 7 (MLS 2, Non-MLS 5)
Founded 1904
Special Collections: Idaho Coll
Subject Interests: Local hist
Automation Activity & Vendor Info: (Acquisitions) Koha; (Cataloging) OCLC FirstSearch; (Circulation) Koha; (ILL) OCLC FirstSearch; (OPAC) Koha
Wireless access
Function: 24/7 Electronic res, 24/7 Online cat, Activity rm, Adult bk club
Publications: Page Turner (Monthly newsletter)
Partic in Cooperative Information Network
Open Mon-Thurs 10-8, Fri & Sat 10-6, Sun 12-5
Friends of the Library Group

S MUSEUM OF NORTH IDAHO*, Research Library, 115 Northwest Blvd, 83814. (Mail add: PO Box 812, 83816-0812), SAN 371-2966. Tel: 208-664-3448. Web Site: www.museumni.org. *Dir,* Dorothy Dahlgren; E-mail: dd@museumni.org
Library Holdings: Bk Vols 7,000
Subject Interests: County hist, Forest, Logging, Transportation
Publications: Newsletter (Quarterly)
Open Tues-Sat 11-5 by appointment only
Restriction: Researchers only

J NORTH IDAHO COLLEGE LIBRARY*, Molstead Library, 1000 W Garden Ave, 83814-2199. SAN 303-5581. Tel: 208-769-3355. Interlibrary Loan Service Tel: 208-769-3269. Administration Tel: 208-769-3215. Information Services Tel: 208-769-3265. FAX: 208-769-3428. E-mail: librarian@nic.edu. Web Site: www.nic.edu/websites/default.aspx?dpt=38&pageId=6167. *Libr Dir,* George McAlister; Tel: 208-769-3393, E-mail: george.mcalister@nic.edu; *Coll Develop Librn, Pub Serv,* Brian Seguin; Tel: 208-769-3255, E-mail: brian.seguin@nic.edu; *Ref & Instruction Librn,* Lisa Kellerman; Tel: 208-769-3253, E-mail: lisa.kellerman@nic.edu; *Tech Serv Librn,* Ann Johnston; Tel: 208-769-3240, E-mail: ann.johnston@nic.edu; *ILL/Circ Supvr,* Brooke Urbaniak; Tel: 208-769-3269, E-mail: brooke.urbaniak@nic.edu; *Learning Res Coordr,* Andy Finney; Tel: 208-769-3266, E-mail: andy_finney@nic.edu; Staff 6.5 (MLS 4.5, Non-MLS 2)
Founded 1933. Enrl 3,405; Fac 175; Highest Degree: Associate

Library Holdings: CDs 2,000; DVDs 4,000; Electronic Media & Resources 20,858; Bk Vols 78,000
Special Collections: Pacific Northwest History & Indian Affairs (Special Coll & Veeder Coll). Oral History; State Document Depository
Automation Activity & Vendor Info: (Acquisitions) Ex Libris Group; (Cataloging) Ex Libris Group; (Circulation) Ex Libris Group; (OPAC) Ex Libris Group
Wireless access
Open Mon-Thurs 7:30-5, Fri 7:30-2:30

COTTONWOOD

S NORTH IDAHO CORRECTIONAL INSTITUTION LIBRARY*, 236 Radar Rd, 83522. Tel: 208-962-3276, Ext 174. Web Site: www.idoc.idaho.gov/content/locations/prisons/north_idaho_correctional_institution. *Librn,* Emmett Wilson
Library Holdings: Bk Titles 7,800; Bk Vols 8,300; Per Subs 23

P PRAIRIE COMMUNITY LIBRARY, 506 King St, 83522. (Mail add: PO Box 65, 83522-0065). Tel: 208-962-3714. E-mail: cottonwoodlib@gmail.com.
Pop 350; Circ 2,000
Library Holdings: DVDs 50; Large Print Bks 100; Bk Vols 13,000; Per Subs 1; Talking Bks 100; Videos 50
Wireless access
Open Tues & Thurs 10-5, Wed 1-5

COUNCIL

P COUNCIL DISTRICT LIBRARY*, Council Valley Free Library, 104 California Ave, 83612. (Mail add: PO Box E, 83612-0804), SAN 303-5611. Tel: 208-253-6004. FAX: 208-253-6004. E-mail: cvfl@ctcweb.net. Web Site: council.lili.org. *Dir,* Patty Gross; *Youth Serv,* Krissi Hansen
Circ 36,000. Sal $30,141
Library Holdings: AV Mats 670; Bk Vols 22,500; Per Subs 10
Wireless access
Special Services for the Blind - Bks on cassette
Open Tues & Thurs 9:30-6, Sat 9:30-5:30
Friends of the Library Group

DOWNEY

P SOUTH BANNOCK LIBRARY DISTRICT*, 18 N Main St, 83234. (Mail add: PO Box D, 83234-0160), SAN 303-562X. Tel: 208-897-5270. FAX: 208-897-5270. E-mail: downylib@dcdi.net. Web Site: www.southbannocklibrary.org. *Dir,* Marcy Price; *Asst Dir,* Debbie Anderson
Pop 7,807; Circ 44,165
Library Holdings: AV Mats 800; Bk Titles 32,000; Per Subs 137
Automation Activity & Vendor Info: (Cataloging) Follett Software; (Circulation) Follett Software
Wireless access
Open Mon, Tues & Thurs 1-5, Wed & Fri 11-5
Friends of the Library Group
Branches: 2
LAVA HOT SPRINGS BRANCH, 33 E Main St, Lava Hot Springs, 83246-9999. (Mail add: PO Box 369, Lava Hot Springs, 83246-0369). Tel: 208-776-5301. FAX: 208-776-5301. E-mail: lavalib@dcdi.net.
Library Holdings: Bk Titles 17,000; Per Subs 69
Open Mon, Tues & Thurs 1-5, Wed & Fri 11-5
Friends of the Library Group
MCCAMMON LIBRARY, 808 Center St, McCammon, 83250. (Mail add: PO Box 360, McCammon, 83250). Tel: 208-254-9003. E-mail: mccammonlib@yahoo.com.
Open Mon Noon-3, Tues-Fri 11-5
Friends of the Library Group
Bookmobiles: 1

DUBOIS

P CLARK COUNTY LIBRARY*, 21 E Main St, 83423. (Mail add: PO Box 67, 83423-0067), SAN 303-5638. Tel: 208-374-5267. E-mail: clarkcolib10@gmail.com. Web Site: clarkcounty.lili.org. *Dir,* Brenda Laird
Pop 1,022
Library Holdings: Bk Titles 7,500
Wireless access
Special Services for the Deaf - Bks on deafness & sign lang
Open Mon-Fri 3:30-6

EAGLE

P EAGLE PUBLIC LIBRARY*, 100 N Stierman Way, 83616. SAN 303-5646. Tel: 208-939-6814. E-mail: eaglelibrary@cityofeagle.org. Web Site: eaglepubliclibrary.org. *Libr Dir,* Steve Bumgarner; E-mail: sbumgarner@cityofeagle.org; *Educ Librn,* Irene Benvenuti; *Patron Serv Supvr,* Carol Berry; E-mail: cberry@cityofeagle.org; Staff 13.5 (MLS 2, Non-MLS 11.5)
Founded 1963. Pop 24,600; Circ 345,000
Oct 2015-Sept 2016 Income $1,140,000
Library Holdings: AV Mats 11,419; Bk Vols 86,964; Per Subs 151
Automation Activity & Vendor Info: (Acquisitions) SirsiDynix; (Cataloging) SirsiDynix; (Circulation) SirsiDynix; (ILL) OCLC FirstSearch; (OPAC) SirsiDynix; (Serials) SirsiDynix
Wireless access
Partic in LYNX! Consortium
Special Services for the Blind - Large print bks
Open Mon-Thurs 9-6:30, Fri & Sat 9-4
Friends of the Library Group

ELK CITY

P ELK CITY COMMUNITY LIBRARY*, 100 School Rd, 83525. (Mail add: PO Box 419, 83525-0419), *Librn,* Penny Parker
Library Holdings: Bk Vols 5,500
Open Tues 3:15-5

ELK RIVER

P ELK RIVER FREE LIBRARY DISTRICT*, 203 Main St, 83827. (Mail add: PO Box 187, 83827-0187), SAN 321-0294. Tel: 208-826-3539. E-mail: elkriverfreelibrarydistrict@gmail.com. *Dir,* Tonya Delphous
Pop 265; Circ 2,872
Library Holdings: Bk Vols 10,000; Per Subs 30
Wireless access
Open Mon-Fri 1-5

EMMETT

P EMMETT PUBLIC LIBRARY*, 275 S Hayes Ave, 83617. SAN 303-5654. Tel: 208-365-6057. FAX: 208-365-6060. E-mail: library@cityofemmett.org. Web Site: www.cityofemmett.org/library. *Dir,* Alyce Kelley; E-mail: akelley@cityofemmett.org
Founded 1924. Pop 6,000; Circ 53,178
Library Holdings: Bk Vols 61,000
Wireless access
Partic in LYNX! Consortium
Open Mon-Fri 11-6, Sat 12-4
Friends of the Library Group

FAIRFIELD

P CAMAS COUNTY PUBLIC LIBRARY*, 607 Soldier Rd, 83327. (Mail add: PO Box 292, 83327-0292), SAN 303-5662. Tel: 208-764-2553. FAX: 208-764-2553. E-mail: camaslibrary@rtci.net. Web Site: camas.lili.org. *Libr Dir,* Marilyn Ballard
Pop 1,000
Library Holdings: Bk Vols 12,000
Wireless access
Open Mon 12:30-7, Tues, Wed & Fri 12:30-5:30, Thurs 10-5:30

FERNWOOD

P BENEWAH COUNTY DISTRICT LIBRARY*, Tri Community Branch, 46 Isaacson St, 83830. SAN 377-4104. Tel: 208-245-4883. FAX: 208-245-0129. E-mail: tricomm@idaho.net. Web Site: tricommunity.lili.org. *Head Librn,* Teri Wood
Library Holdings: Bk Vols 18,500
Wireless access
Open Mon 12-6, Tues, Thurs & Sat 10-3, Wed & Fri 10-5
Friends of the Library Group

FILER

P FILER PUBLIC LIBRARY, 219 Main St, 83328-5349. (Mail add: PO Box 52, 83328-0052), SAN 303-5670. Tel: 208-326-4143. E-mail: filerpubliclibrary@gmail.com. *Librn,* Margaret Holley
Founded 1923. Pop 1,850; Circ 13,567
Library Holdings: Bk Vols 15,000
Special Collections: Local History Archives
Subject Interests: Idaho
Automation Activity & Vendor Info: (Cataloging) Follett Software
Open Mon-Wed & Fri 2-6:30, Thurs 10:30-12 & 2-6:30, Sat 1:30-4:30

FORT HALL

P SHOSHONE-BANNOCK LIBRARY*, Fort Hall Library, Pima & Bannock Dr, 83203. (Mail add: PO Box 306, 83203-0306), SAN 303-5689. Tel: 208-478-3882. *Dir,* Ardith Peyope; E-mail: apeyope@shoshonebannocktribes.com
Circ 18,169
Library Holdings: Bk Titles 5,500
Special Collections: Oral History

Subject Interests: Indians
Open Mon-Fri 8-5

GARDEN CITY

P GARDEN CITY PUBLIC LIBRARY*, 6015 Glenwood St, 83714. SAN 303-5360. Tel: 208-472-2941. E-mail: gcpl@gardencitylibrary.org. Reference E-mail: reference@gardencitylibrary.org. Web Site: www.notaquietlibrary.org. *Libr Dir,* Lindsey Pettyjohn
Founded 1962. Pop 12,000
Wireless access
Partic in LYNX! Consortium
Open Mon & Fri 9:30-5:30, Tues, Wed & Thurs 9:30-8, Sat 10-4
Friends of the Library Group
Bookmobiles: 1

GARDEN VALLEY

P GARDEN VALLEY DISTRICT LIBRARY*, 342 Village Circle, 83622-8040. SAN 303-5697. Tel: 208-462-3317. FAX: 208-462-4418. *Dir,* Kerri Hart; E-mail: director@gvlibrary.org; Staff 5 (Non-MLS 5)
Pop 2,000; Circ 4,200
Library Holdings: AV Mats 3,000; Bks on Deafness & Sign Lang 20; Bk Titles 16,000; Per Subs 30
Special Collections: Idaho History
Automation Activity & Vendor Info: (Cataloging) Follett Software; (Circulation) Follett Software
Partic in Valley Mountain Library Consortium
Open Mon-Fri 10-6, Sat 10-4
Friends of the Library Group

GLENNS FERRY

P GLENNS FERRY PUBLIC LIBRARY*, 298 S Lincoln, 83623. (Mail add: PO Box 910, 83623-0910), SAN 303-5719. Tel: 208-366-2045. FAX: 208-366-2238. *Dir,* Jennifer Trail; E-mail: jtrail@gflibrary.org; Staff 1 (Non-MLS 1)
Founded 1930. Pop 1,500; Circ 16,000
Library Holdings: Audiobooks 450; CDs 30; Large Print Bks 2,500; Bk Vols 14,500; Talking Bks 400; Videos 53
Special Collections: Christian Fiction
Wireless access
Function: ILL available
Open Mon, Tues & Thurs 12-5, Wed 12-4
Restriction: Non-circulating

GOODING

P GOODING PUBLIC LIBRARY, 306 Fifth Ave W, 83330-1205. SAN 303-5727. Tel: 208-934-4089. E-mail: goodingpubliclibrary@gmail.com. Web Site: gooding.lili.org. *Dir,* Cindy Bigler
Founded 1910. Pop 3,230; Circ 24,100
Library Holdings: Bk Vols 22,000; Per Subs 52
Special Collections: Idaho Coll
Automation Activity & Vendor Info: (Cataloging) Follett Software; (Circulation) Follett Software
Wireless access
Open Mon & Fri 10-5, Tues-Thurs 10-6, Sat 9-12
Friends of the Library Group

P IDAHO SCHOOL FOR THE DEAF & BLIND LIBRARY*, 1450 Main St, 83330. Tel: 208-934-1050. FAX: 208-934-8352. Web Site: www.isdb.idaho.gov. *Librn,* Sharlyn Jackson; Tel: 208-934-1052, E-mail: sharlyn.jackson@iesdb.org; Staff 2 (MLS 1, Non-MLS 1)
Founded 1910
Jul 2016-Jun 2017 Income $2,043. Mats Exp $4,160, Books $2,924, Other Print Mats $1,236. Sal $62,491 (Prof $19,231)
Library Holdings: Audiobooks 200; AV Mats 250; Bks on Deafness & Sign Lang 200; Braille Volumes 500; CDs 150; DVDs 250; High Interest/Low Vocabulary Bk Vols 500; Large Print Bks 650; Bk Titles 20,000; Bk Vols 22,000; Per Subs 10; Spec Interest Per Sub 5; Talking Bks 75; Videos 750
Subject Interests: Am sign lang, Blindness, Deaf culture, Deaf hist, Hearing impaired, Visually impaired
Automation Activity & Vendor Info: (Acquisitions) Follett Software; (Cataloging) Follett Software; (Circulation) Follett Software
Wireless access
Special Services for the Blind - Assistive/Adapted tech devices, equip & products; Audio mat; Bks & mags in Braille, on rec, tape & cassette; Digital talking bk; Large print bks; Newsline for the Blind
Open Mon-Thurs 7-4:30

GRACE

P GRACE DISTRICT LIBRARY*, 204 S Main, 83241. (Mail add: PO Box B, 83241-0200), SAN 303-5735. Tel: 208-425-3695. FAX: 208-425-3695. E-mail: gracedistlibra@dcdi.net. Web Site: grace.lili.org. *Libr Dir,* April Smith
Founded 1941. Pop 2,200; Circ 45,685
Library Holdings: Bk Titles 18,000; Per Subs 26
Partic in Library Consortium of Eastern Idaho
Open Mon 10-7, Tues-Fri 10-5
Friends of the Library Group

GRAND VIEW

P EASTERN OWYHEE COUNTY LIBRARY*, 520 Boise Ave, 83624. (Mail add: PO Box 100, 83624-0100), SAN 303-5743. Tel: 208-834-2785. E-mail: eoclibrary@gmail.com. *Dir,* Tammy L Gray
Founded 1974. Pop 5,000
Library Holdings: Audiobooks 602; DVDs 522; Music Scores 18; Bk Vols 20,799; Per Subs 26; Videos 18
Wireless access
Open Mon-Thurs 10-6, Fri & Sat 10-2
Friends of the Library Group

GRANGEVILLE

P GRANGEVILLE CENTENNIAL LIBRARY*, 215 W North St, 83530. SAN 303-5751. Tel: 208-983-0951. FAX: 208-983-2336. E-mail: library@grangeville.us. Web Site: grangeville.us/centennial-library. *Libr Dir,* Angela Norman; *Asst Librn,* Danielle Reynolds; Staff 2 (Non-MLS 2)
Founded 1899. Pop 3,228; Circ 26,275
Library Holdings: AV Mats 475; CDs 121; DVDs 82; Large Print Bks 133; Bk Vols 12,235; Per Subs 28; Talking Bks 241
Subject Interests: Genealogy
Automation Activity & Vendor Info: (Cataloging) Ex Libris Group; (Circulation) Ex Libris Group
Open Mon-Fri 10-6, Sat 10-2
Friends of the Library Group

HAILEY

P HAILEY PUBLIC LIBRARY*, Seven W Croy St, 83333. SAN 303-5778. Tel: 208-788-2036. FAX: 208-788-7646. Web Site: www.haileypubliclibrary.org. *Dir,* Lyn Drewien; E-mail: lyn.drewien@haileypubliclibrary.org; Staff 6 (Non-MLS 6)
Founded 1919. Pop 5,500; Circ 50,500
Library Holdings: Bk Titles 33,000; Bk Vols 34,000; Per Subs 85
Special Collections: Idaho Coll; Mallory Photo Coll - Historical Photographs of Wood River Valley
Automation Activity & Vendor Info: (Cataloging) Horizon; (Circulation) Horizon; (OPAC) Horizon
Wireless access
Partic in LYNX! Consortium
Open Mon, Fri & Sat 10-6, Tues-Thurs 10-7
Friends of the Library Group

HAMER

P HAMER PUBLIC LIBRARY*, 2450 E 2100 N, 83425. (Mail add: PO Box 240, 83425-0240), SAN 303-5786. Tel: 208-662-5275. FAX: 208-662-5213. Web Site: hamer.lili.org. *Dir,* Rosemary Dixon; *Head Asst Librn,* Laurel Dalling; E-mail: dalllaur@mudlake.net
Founded 1972. Pop 800
Library Holdings: AV Mats 800; Bk Titles 15,000; Bk Vols 15,500; Per Subs 20; Talking Bks 500
Special Collections: Oral History
Automation Activity & Vendor Info: (Cataloging) SirsiDynix; (Circulation) SirsiDynix; (OPAC) SirsiDynix
Function: ILL available
Publications: Sands of Time - Desert in Bloom
Mem of Jefferson County District Library
Open Tues & Wed 9-4, Thurs 11-5
Friends of the Library Group

HANSEN

P HANSEN COMMUNITY LIBRARY*, 120 W Maple Ave, 83334-4975. Tel: 208-423-4122. E-mail: hanlib@cableone.net. Web Site: hansen.lili.org. *Dir,* Linda Oatman; Staff 1 (Non-MLS 1)
Founded 1975. Pop 2,811
Library Holdings: AV Mats 381; CDs 24; DVDs 1,181; Large Print Bks 83; Bk Vols 12,610; Per Subs 27; Talking Bks 75
Wireless access
Function: Accelerated reader prog, Adult literacy prog, Bks on cassette, Bks on CD, Children's prog, Computers for patron use, Free DVD rentals,

ILL available, Music CDs, Photocopying/Printing, Prog for adults, Ref serv available, Summer reading prog, VHS videos, Wheelchair accessible
Open Mon & Fri 1-6, Wed 1-7

HAYDEN

P COMMUNITY LIBRARY NETWORK*, Hayden Branch, 8385 N Government Way, 83835-9280. SAN 303-5816. Tel: 208-772-5612. FAX: 208-215-2259. E-mail: hayden@communitylibrary.net. Web Site: www.communitylibrary.net. *Dir,* John W Hartung; E-mail: johnh@communitylibrary.net; *Mgr,* Darla Gunning; Staff 50 (MLS 4, Non-MLS 46)
Founded 1976. Pop 66,750; Circ 467,000
Library Holdings: Bk Titles 103,500; Per Subs 103
Special Collections: North Idaho Genealogy Coll; North Idaho Land Surveyors Materials
Automation Activity & Vendor Info: (Cataloging) Ex Libris Group; (Circulation) Ex Libris Group; (ILL) Ex Libris Group; (OPAC) Ex Libris Group
Wireless access
Function: Adult bk club, ILL available, Mail & tel request accepted, Music CDs, Photocopying/Printing, Preschool outreach, Prog for adults, Prog for children & young adult, Ref serv available, Spoken cassettes & CDs, Summer reading prog, Tax forms, Telephone ref, VHS videos, Wheelchair accessible
Partic in Cooperative Information Network
Open Mon-Thurs 10-8, Fri & Sat 10-5, Sun 12-5
Friends of the Library Group
Branches: 6
ATHOL BRANCH, 30399 Third St, Athol, 83801. (Mail add: PO Box 70, Athol, 83801-0070), SAN 328-2228. Tel: 208-683-2979. FAX: 208-683-2979. *Mgr,* Jill Roche; Staff 3 (Non-MLS 3)
Function: After school storytime, ILL available, Photocopying/Printing, Prog for adults, Prog for children & young adult, Wheelchair accessible
Open Mon-Wed 1-6, Thurs 10-6, Fri 1-5, Sat 12-4
Friends of the Library Group
HARRISON PUBLIC, 111 Coeur d'Alene Ave, Harrison, 83833, SAN 303-5808. Tel: 208-689-3976. FAX: 208-689-3976. *Mgr,* Dorothy Blackmore; Staff 2 (Non-MLS 2)
Pop 1,200; Circ 10,168
Function: Adult bk club, ILL available, Music CDs, Photocopying/Printing, Prog for children & young adult, Wheelchair accessible
Open Mon, Wed & Sat 10-5, Fri 1-5
Friends of the Library Group
PINEHURST-KINGSTON BRANCH, 107 Main St, Pinehurst, 83850, SAN 303-6251. Tel: 208-682-3483. FAX: 208-682-3483. *Mgr,* Position Currently Open
Pop 4,100; Circ 35,882
Function: ILL available, Music CDs, Photocopying/Printing, Prog for children & young adult, Summer reading prog, Tax forms, VHS videos, Wheelchair accessible
Open Mon 11-8, Tues-Fri 11-5, Sat 11-2
Friends of the Library Group
POST FALLS BRANCH, 821 N Spokane St, Post Falls, 83854, SAN 303-6316. Tel: 208-773-1506. FAX: 208-773-1507. *Mgr,* Jennifer Craft; Staff 10 (MLS 2, Non-MLS 8)
Founded 1915
Library Holdings: AV Mats 4,500; Large Print Bks 3,000; Bk Titles 50,000; Per Subs 110; Talking Bks 2,000
Open Mon-Thurs 10-8, Fri 10-6, Sat 10-5, Sun 12-5
Friends of the Library Group
RATHDRUM BRANCH, 16320 Hwy 41, Rathdrum, 83858, SAN 303-6359. Tel: 208-687-1029. FAX: 208-687-1029. *Mgr,* Linda Mahon; Staff 4 (Non-MLS 4)
Pop 11,800; Circ 62,828
Function: Adult bk club, Electronic databases & coll, ILL available, Mail & tel request accepted, Music CDs, Photocopying/Printing, Preschool outreach, Prog for adults, Prog for children & young adult, Spoken cassettes & CDs, Spoken cassettes & DVDs, Summer reading prog, Tax forms, Telephone ref, VHS videos, Wheelchair accessible
Open Mon, Wed & Thurs 10-6, Tues 10-7, Fri 10-5, Sat 10-4
Friends of the Library Group
SPIRIT LAKE BRANCH, 32575 N Fifth Ave, Spirit Lake, 83869. (Mail add: PO Box 186, Spirit Lake, 83869-0186), SAN 328-2260. Tel: 208-623-5353. FAX: 208-623-5353. *Mgr,* Carol Furguson; Staff 2 (Non-MLS 2)
Pop 5,100; Circ 23,849
Function: Adult bk club, ILL available, Music CDs, Photocopying/Printing, Preschool outreach, Prog for adults, Prog for children & young adult, Spoken cassettes & CDs, Spoken cassettes & DVDs, Summer reading prog, Tax forms, VHS videos, Wheelchair accessible
Open Mon 10-5, Tues-Thurs 1-6, Fri 12-5, Sat 12-4
Friends of the Library Group
Bookmobiles: 1. Mgr, Twylla Rehder

HOMEDALE

P HOMEDALE PUBLIC LIBRARY, Gypsy Jackson Memorial Library, 125 W Owyhee, 83628. (Mail add: PO Box 1087, 83628-1087), SAN 303-5824. Tel: 208-337-4228. E-mail: citylibrary@cityofhomedale.org. Web Site: homedale.lili.org. *Dir,* Sharla Jensen
Founded 1921. Pop 2,619; Circ 8,759
Library Holdings: AV Mats 382; Bk Vols 8,790
Wireless access
Partic in Valley Mountain Library Consortium
Open Mon-Wed 12-6, Thurs 12-7, Fri 10-5, Sat 10-1
Friends of the Library Group

HORSESHOE BEND

P HORSESHOE BEND DISTRICT LIBRARY, 392 Hwy 55, 83629-9701. SAN 303-5832. Tel: 208-793-2460. FAX: 208-793-1311. E-mail: hsblibrary@gmail.com. Web Site: horseshoebend.lili.org. *Exec Dir/Librn,* Teresa Cooper
Founded 1917
Library Holdings: Bk Vols 14,000; Per Subs 37
Special Collections: Idaho History Coll
Automation Activity & Vendor Info: (Cataloging) Follett Software; (Circulation) Follett Software
Wireless access
Open Mon-Fri 10-5, Sat 10-12

IDAHO CITY

P BOISE BASIN LIBRARY DISTRICT*, 123 Montgomery St, 83631. SAN 303-5840. Tel: 208-392-4558. FAX: 208-392-4920. Web Site: boisebasin.lili.org. *Dir,* Marcy Moore; E-mail: director.bbld@gmail.com; Staff 5 (Non-MLS 5)
Founded 1962. Pop 3,700; Circ 21,009
Library Holdings: CDs 139; Large Print Bks 500; Bk Titles 11,000; Per Subs 24; Talking Bks 337; Videos 409
Special Collections: Boise Basin History Room; History of Idaho City Coll; The Idaho World Coll, photo
Automation Activity & Vendor Info: (Cataloging) Follett Software; (Circulation) Follett Software; (ILL) OCLC; (OPAC) Follett Software; (Serials) EBSCO Online
Wireless access
Function: Homebound delivery serv, ILL available, Internet access, Photocopying/Printing, Prog for adults, Prog for children & young adult, Ref serv available, Summer reading prog, Telephone ref
Open Tues-Sat 11-6
Friends of the Library Group
Bookmobiles: 1

IDAHO FALLS

J COLLEGE OF EASTERN IDAHO*, Richard & Lila J Jordon Library, Alexander Creek Bldg, Rm 551, 1600 S 25th E, 83404. SAN 371-8247. Tel: 208-535-5349. Circulation Tel: 208-535-5312. Web Site: www.cei.edu/library. *Librn,* Nathan Brown; E-mail: nathan.brown@cei.edu; Staff 4 (MLS 1, Non-MLS 3)
Founded 1989. Enrl 2,500; Fac 43; Highest Degree: Associate
Library Holdings: AV Mats 590; e-books 2,061; Bk Titles 18,500; Bk Vols 20,000; Per Subs 125; Spec Interest Per Sub 25; Videos 315
Automation Activity & Vendor Info: (Cataloging) SirsiDynix; (Circulation) SirsiDynix; (ILL) OCLC WorldShare Interlibrary Loan; (OPAC) SirsiDynix
Wireless access
Function: Mail loans to mem, Ref serv available, Wheelchair accessible
Partic in Library Consortium of Eastern Idaho
Open Mon-Thurs 7:30am-8pm, Fri 7:30-4:30; Mon-Fri (Summer) 8-4
Restriction: Open to students, fac & staff

P IDAHO FALLS PUBLIC LIBRARY*, 457 W Broadway, 83402. SAN 303-5891. Tel: 208-612-8460. Reference Tel: 208-612-8462. Administration Tel: 208-612-8155. Automation Services Tel: 208-612-8198. FAX: 208-612-8467. Web Site: www.ifpl.org. *Dir,* Robert Wright; E-mail: rwright@ifpl.org; *Adult Serv,* Jenniffer Hentzen; E-mail: jhentzen@ifpl.org; *Ch Serv,* Kim Bryant; E-mail: kimb@ifpl.org; Staff 5 (MLS 4, Non-MLS 1)
Founded 1909. Pop 105,772; Circ 1,200,006
Library Holdings: Audiobooks 9,576; Braille Volumes 20; CDs 12; DVDs 20,762; e-books 300; Large Print Bks 24,809; Bk Vols 254,863; Per Subs 225; Talking Bks 3,669
Special Collections: Vardis Fisher Coll. State Document Depository
Automation Activity & Vendor Info: (Acquisitions) SirsiDynix; (Cataloging) SirsiDynix; (Circulation) SirsiDynix; (ILL) OCLC; (OPAC) SirsiDynix; (Serials) SirsiDynix

Wireless access
Function: Adult bk club, After school storytime, Audiobks via web, Bk club(s), Bks on cassette, Bks on CD, Children's prog, Computers for patron use, Digital talking bks, Electronic databases & coll, Free DVD rentals, Homebound delivery serv, ILL available, Microfiche/film & reading machines, Music CDs, Online cat, Orientations, Outreach serv, OverDrive digital audio bks, Photocopying/Printing, Preschool outreach, Printer for laptops & handheld devices, Prog for adults, Prog for children & young adult, Ref serv available, Scanner, Story hour, Summer & winter reading prog, Summer reading prog, Teen prog, VHS videos, Wheelchair accessible, Winter reading prog
Open Mon-Thurs 10-9, Fri & Sat 10-6
Friends of the Library Group
Branches: 2
IONA BRANCH, 3548 N Main St, Iona, 83427. Tel: 208-523-2358.
Open Mon-Sat 1-6
Friends of the Library Group
SWAN VALLEY BRANCH, Swan Valley School, 3389 Hwy 26, Irwin, 83428. Tel: 208-483-2405.
Open Mon-Thurs 3:30-6:30, Sat 9-Noon

S IDAHO NATIONAL LABORATORY, Research Library, 1955 N Fremont Ave, 83415. (Mail add: PO Box 1625, 83415), SAN 303-5859. Tel: 208-526-2926. FAX: 208-526-0211. E-mail: lib@inl.gov. Web Site: inl.gov/about-inl/general-information/research-library. *Library Contact,* Leslie Wright; E-mail: leslie.wright@inl.gov; Staff 2 (MLS 1, Non-MLS 1)
Founded 1960
Library Holdings: AV Mats 128; e-books 1,604; e-journals 2,479; Bk Titles 33,900; Bk Vols 46,527; Per Subs 400
Subject Interests: Chem, Computer sci, Metallurgy, Nuclear engr, Nuclear sci, Physics
Wireless access
Publications: New Materials List
Partic in OCLC Online Computer Library Center, Inc; Proquest Dialog
Restriction: Staff use only

S IDAHO NATIONAL LABORATORY RESEARCH LIBRARY*, 2251 North Blvd, MS 2300, 83415. (Mail add: MS 2300, PO Box 1625, 83415), SAN 303-5875. Tel: 208-526-1185. Interlibrary Loan Service Tel: 208-526-1195. Automation Services Tel: 208-526-1196. FAX: 208-526-0211. E-mail: lib@inl.gov. Web Site: www.inl.gov/about-inl/general-information/research-library. *Mgr,* Leslie Wright; Tel: 208-526-2926, E-mail: leslie.wright@inl.gov; *ILL,* Tamera Waldron; E-mail: Tamera.Waldron@inl.gov; *Ref,* Jackie Loop; E-mail: Jackie.Loop@inl.gov; Staff 3 (MLS 1, Non-MLS 2)
Founded 1951
Library Holdings: e-books 3,000; e-journals 4,000; Bk Titles 20,000; Per Subs 250
Special Collections: AEC, ERDA & DOE Reports; DOE Public Reading Room: TMI-2 Research & Develop Program Files; Standards & Compliance Information
Subject Interests: Biochem, Chem, Chem engr, Computer sci, Earth sci, Energy, Engr, Environ sci, Geoscience, Mat sci, Math, Mgt, Nuclear engr, Nuclear physics, Nuclear safety, Nuclear sci, Occupational health, Occupational safety, Optics, Physics, Radioactive waste
Automation Activity & Vendor Info: (Cataloging) Ex Libris Group; (Circulation) Ex Libris Group; (OPAC) Ex Libris Group; (Serials) Ex Libris Group
Wireless access
Restriction: Secured area only open to authorized personnel

JEROME

P JEROME PUBLIC LIBRARY*, 100 First Ave E, 83338-2302. SAN 303-5921. Tel: 208-324-5427. FAX: 208-324-6426. Web Site: jerome.lili.org. *Dir,* Linda Mecham; E-mail: lmecham@ci.jerome.id.us; Staff 1 (MLS 1)
Founded 1921. Circ 72,300
Library Holdings: Bk Vols 38,000; Per Subs 14
Special Collections: Idaho History Coll; Large Print Coll
Automation Activity & Vendor Info: (Cataloging) SirsiDynix; (Circulation) SirsiDynix
Wireless access
Open Mon-Thurs 9-7, Fri 9-5, Sat 10-5
Friends of the Library Group

KELLOGG

P KELLOGG PUBLIC LIBRARY*, 16 W Market Ave, 83837. SAN 303-593X. Tel: 208-786-7231. FAX: 208-784-1100. E-mail: kellogglibrary@yahoo.com. Web Site: kellogg.lili.org. *Dir,* Danni Boylan
Pop 2,491; Circ 14,533
Library Holdings: Bk Vols 11,500; Per Subs 30
Automation Activity & Vendor Info: (Cataloging) Ex Libris Group; (Circulation) Ex Libris Group; (OPAC) Ex Libris Group
Wireless access
Open Mon 12:30-7, Tues-Fri 12:30-5:30

KETCHUM

P THE COMMUNITY LIBRARY*, 415 Spruce Ave N, 83340. (Mail add: PO Box 2168, 83340-2168), SAN 303-5948. Tel: 208-726-3493. E-mail: info@comlib.org. Web Site: www.comlib.org. *Exec Dir,* Jenny Emery Davidson; *Ch,* DeAnn Campbell; *Circ Coordr,* Pam Parker
Founded 1955. Pop 25,000; Circ 125,000
Library Holdings: AV Mats 12,853; Bk Titles 89,000; Per Subs 164; Talking Bks 5,380
Special Collections: John Lister Coll of Astrology & Occult Sciences; Sun Valley Ski Coll; Wood River Valley Coll, diaries, doc & letters. Oral History
Automation Activity & Vendor Info: (Cataloging) TLC (The Library Corporation); (Circulation) TLC (The Library Corporation); (ILL) TLC (The Library Corporation); (Media Booking) TLC (The Library Corporation)
Wireless access
Open Mon, Fri & Sat 10-6, Tues-Thurs 10-8
Friends of the Library Group

KIMBERLY

P KIMBERLY PUBLIC LIBRARY*, 120 Madison St W, 83341. (Mail add: PO Box 369, 83341-0369), SAN 303-5956. Tel: 208-423-4556. FAX: 208-423-4556. E-mail: kimblib@safelink.net. Web Site: kimberly.lili.org. *Dir,* Helen McCord; Tel: 208-423-4262; *Children's & Youth Serv,* Kerri-Lynn Harris; Tel: 208-212-1565; Staff 1.3 (Non-MLS 1.3)
Founded 1978. Pop 3,216; Circ 31,317
Oct 2012-Sept 2013 Income $61,957, City $57,957, Locally Generated Income $3,000, Other $1,000. Mats Exp $7,715, Books $7,405, Other Print Mats $135, AV Mat $175. Sal $38,461
Library Holdings: Audiobooks 191; CDs 40; DVDs 275; Large Print Bks 66; Bk Titles 16,335; Bk Vols 16,350; Per Subs 25; Videos 200
Special Collections: Idaho Coll; Kipling's Works; Mark Twain Coll; O'Henry Coll; Writings of Abraham Lincoln
Wireless access
Function: Accelerated reader prog, After school storytime, AV serv, Bks on cassette, Bks on CD, Children's prog, Computers for patron use, Free DVD rentals, ILL available, Music CDs, Photocopying/Printing, Preschool reading prog, Prog for adults, Prog for children & young adult, Story hour, Summer & winter reading prog, VHS videos, Wheelchair accessible
Open Mon & Thurs 11-6, Tues 3-8, Wed & Fri 3-6, Sat 10-2

G UNITED STATES DEPARTMENT OF AGRICULTURE, Agricultural Research Service, Northwest Irrigation & Soils Research Laboratory, 3793 N 3600 E, 83341-5776. SAN 321-771X. Tel: 208-423-5582. FAX: 208-423-6555. Web Site: sand.nwisrl.ars.usda.gov. *Prog Serv,* Michelle Wayment; E-mail: michelle.wayment@usda.gov
Library Holdings: Bk Titles 1,800
Subject Interests: Agr engr, Gen agr, Irrigation, Plants, Pollution, Soils, Water
Open Mon-Fri 8-4:30

KUNA

P KUNA LIBRARY DISTRICT*, 457 N Locust, 83634-1926. (Mail add: PO Box 129, 83634-0129), SAN 303-5964. Tel: 208-922-1025. FAX: 208-922-1026. E-mail: admin1@kunalibrary.org. Web Site: kunalibrary.org. *Co-Dir,* Jana Cutforth; *Co-Dir,* Tam Svedin
Founded 1964. Pop 30,000; Circ 67,000
Library Holdings: AV Mats 2,600; Bk Vols 68,000; Per Subs 65; Talking Bks 1,350
Subject Interests: Idaho
Automation Activity & Vendor Info: (Cataloging) Follett Software; (Circulation) Follett Software
Function: 24/7 Electronic res, 24/7 Online cat, Activity rm, Adult literacy prog, Art programs, Audiobks via web, Bilingual assistance for Spanish patrons, Bk club(s), Bks on CD, Children's prog, Computers for patron use, E-Reserves, Family literacy, Free DVD rentals, Holiday prog, ILL available, Internet access, Laminating, Magazines, Mail & tel request accepted, Meeting rooms, Movies, Music CDs, Online cat, Outreach serv, OverDrive digital audio bks, Passport agency, Photocopying/Printing, Preschool outreach, Preschool reading prog, Prof lending libr, Prog for adults, Prog for children & young adult, Ref & res, Ref serv available, Scanner, Senior outreach, Spanish lang bks, STEM programs, Story hour, Study rm, Summer & winter reading prog, Summer reading prog, Tax forms, Teen prog, Telephone ref, Wheelchair accessible, Winter reading prog
Partic in LYNX! Consortium
Open Mon, Fri & Sat 10-5, Tues, Wed & Thurs 10-8
Friends of the Library Group

LAPWAI

P PRAIRIE-RIVER LIBRARY DISTRICT*, 103 N Main St, 83540. (Mail add: PO Box 1200, 83540-1200), SAN 339-6517. Tel: 208-843-7254. E-mail: lapwai.library@prld.org. Web Site: www.prld.org. *Dir,* Michael Priest; *Br Mgr,* Julie Seely
Founded 1959. Pop 14,904; Circ 79,641
Library Holdings: Bk Vols 92,051; Per Subs 50; Talking Bks 1,287; Videos 2,029
Automation Activity & Vendor Info: (Cataloging) Ex Libris Group; (Circulation) Ex Libris Group; (OPAC) Ex Libris Group
Wireless access
Partic in Association for Rural & Small Libraries
Open Mon-Fri 10-6
Branches: 7
CRAIGMONT COMMUNITY, 113 W Main St, Craigmont, 83523-9700. (Mail add: PO Box 191, Craigmont, 83523), SAN 339-6533. Tel: 208-924-5510. E-mail: craigmont.library@prld.org. Web Site: www.prld.org/craigmont. *Br Mgr,* Doreen Schmidt
Open Mon, Wed & Fri 10-4
Friends of the Library Group
CULDESAC COMMUNITY, 714 Main St, Culdesac, 83524-7806, SAN 339-6525. Tel: 208-843-5215. E-mail: culdesac.library@prld.org. Web Site: www.prld.org/culdesac. *Br Mgr,* Lynda Crow
Open Tues & Wed 11-4:30, Thurs 10:30-5:30
Friends of the Library Group
KAMIAH COMMUNITY, 505 Main St, Kamiah, 83536-9702. (Mail add: PO Box 846, Kamiah, 83536-0846), SAN 339-6541. Tel: 208-935-0428. E-mail: kamiah.library@prld.org. Web Site: www.prld.org/kamiah. *Br Mgr,* April Blankenship
Open Mon-Fri 10-4
Friends of the Library Group
KOOSKIA COMMUNITY, 26 S Main St, Kooskia, 83539. (Mail add: PO Box 146, Kooskia, 83539-0146), SAN 377-8495. Tel: 208-926-4539. E-mail: kooskia.library@prld.org. Web Site: www.prld.org/kooskia. *Br Mgr,* Dena Puderbaugh
Open Mon-Fri 12-6
Friends of the Library Group
NEZPERCE COMMUNITY, 602 Fourth Ave, Nezperce, 83543. (Mail add: PO Box 124, Nezperce, 83543-0124), SAN 321-8902. Tel: 208-937-2458. E-mail: nezperce.library@prld.org. Web Site: www.prld.org/nezperce. *Br Mgr,* Terra Baldus
Open Mon & Fri 10:30-5:30, Wed 10:30-6:30
Friends of the Library Group
PECK COMMUNITY, 217 N Main St, Peck, 83545. (Mail add: PO Box 112, Peck, 83545-0112), SAN 339-655X. Tel: 208-486-6161. E-mail: peck.library@prld.org. Web Site: www.prld.org/peck. *Br Mgr,* Doreen Schmidt
Open Tues & Thurs 10-5:30
Friends of the Library Group
WINCHESTER COMMUNITY, 314 Nezperce St, Winchester, 83555. (Mail add: PO Box 275, Winchester, 83555-0275). Tel: 208-924-5164. E-mail: winchester.library@prld.org. Web Site: www.prld.org/winchester. *Br Mgr,* Ms Chris Case
Open Mon-Thurs 12-5:30
Friends of the Library Group

LEADORE

P LEADORE COMMUNITY LIBRARY*, 202 S Railroad St, 83464. (Mail add: PO Box 106, 83464-0106), SAN 303-5972. Tel: 208-768-2640. E-mail: leadorelibrary@centurytel.net. Web Site: leadore.lili.org. *Actg Dir,* Jeri Ann Beyeler
Founded 1961. Pop 114; Circ 200
Library Holdings: AV Mats 143; Bk Vols 5,175; Talking Bks 11
Wireless access
Partic in Library Consortium of Eastern Idaho
Open Tues 10-5, Wed 2-6, Thurs 11-6, Sat 10-2
Friends of the Library Group

LEWISTON

C LEWIS-CLARK STATE COLLEGE LIBRARY*, 500 Eighth Ave, 83501. SAN 303-5980. Tel: 208-792-2236. Circulation Tel: 208-792-2396. Interlibrary Loan Service Tel: 208-792-2394. FAX: 208-792-2831. Web Site: www.lcsc.edu/library. *Dir,* Johanna Bjork; Tel: 208-792-2395, E-mail: jcbjork@lcsc.edu; *Coll Mgt, Librn,* Samantha Thompson-Franklin; Tel: 208-792-2557, E-mail: sfranklin@lcsc.edu; *Electronic Res, Librn,* Lynne Bidwell; Tel: 208-792-2438, E-mail: lbidwell@lcsc.edu; *Instruction Librn,* Guarina Grullon; Tel: 208-792-2235, E-mail: ggrullon@lcsc.edu; *Circ, Pub Serv Librn,* Jennifer Cromer; Tel: 208-792-2829, E-mail: jjcromer@lcsc.edu; *Cat,* Shannon Casteel; Tel: 208-792-2229, E-mail: scasteel@lcsc.edu; *Circ,* Sarah Rogers; Tel: 208-792-2833, E-mail: sarogers@lcsc.edu; *ILL, Ser,* Amanda Klone; E-mail: alklone@lcsc.edu; *Asst to the Dir,* Claudia O'Connor; Tel: 208-792-2230, E-mail: coconnor@lcsc.edu; Staff 9 (MLS 5, Non-MLS 4)
Founded 1893. Fac 5; Highest Degree: Bachelor
Special Collections: Audio-Visual Coll; Children's Literature; Curriculum Library; Pacific Northwest Coll. US Document Depository
Automation Activity & Vendor Info: (Acquisitions) Ex Libris Group; (Cataloging) Ex Libris Group; (Circulation) Ex Libris Group; (Course Reserve) Ex Libris Group; (ILL) OCLC; (OPAC) Ex Libris Group; (Serials) Ex Libris Group
Wireless access
Partic in OCLC Online Computer Library Center, Inc
Open Mon-Thurs 7:30am-9:55pm, Fri 8-5:55, Sat Noon-5:55, Sun Noon-9:55

P LEWISTON CITY LIBRARY*, 411 D St, 83501. SAN 339-6428. Tel: 208-798-2525. E-mail: library@cityoflewiston.org. Web Site: lewistonlibrary.org. *Dir,* Lynn Johnson; Tel: 208-798-2501, E-mail: ljohnson@cityoflewiston.org; *Ad,* Barrie Olmstead; E-mail: bolmstead@cityoflewiston.org; *Tech Librn,* Bonnie Gardner; E-mail: bgardner@cityoflewiston.org; *Pub Serv Mgr,* William Younger; E-mail: wyounger@cityoflewiston.org; Staff 8 (MLS 3, Non-MLS 5)
Founded 1901. Pop 30,906; Circ 211,904
Library Holdings: Bk Vols 75,000; Per Subs 128
Special Collections: Genealogy Coll; Idaho Coll
Automation Activity & Vendor Info: (Cataloging) Ex Libris Group; (Circulation) Ex Libris Group; (ILL) OCLC; (OPAC) Ex Libris Group; (Serials) Ex Libris Group
Wireless access
Function: After school storytime, Audiobks via web, Bk club(s), Bks on CD, Children's prog, Computers for patron use, Family literacy, Homebound delivery serv, Magnifiers for reading, Online cat, Photocopying/Printing, Preschool outreach, Prog for adults, Prog for children & young adult, Ref serv available, Story hour, Summer reading prog, Tax forms, Teen prog, Telephone ref
Special Services for the Blind - Audio mat; Bks available with recordings; Bks on cassette; Bks on CD; Cassettes; Digital talking bk; Extensive large print coll; Home delivery serv; Large print bks; Large type calculator; Lending of low vision aids; Magnifiers; Volunteer serv
Open Mon-Thurs 10-7, Fri & Sat 10-5
Friends of the Library Group

LEWISVILLE

P LEWISVILLE LEGACY LIBRARY*, 3453 E 480 N, 83431. (Mail add: PO Box 158, 83431-0158). Tel: 208-754-8608. E-mail: lewisvillelibrary@live.com. Web Site: lewisville.lili.org. *Libr Dir,* Merideth McElprang
Pop 467; Circ 3,634
Oct 2016-Sept 2017 Income City $11,300. Mats Exp $3,000. Sal $6,000
Library Holdings: Audiobooks 424; AV Mats 3; DVDs 193; e-books 284; Electronic Media & Resources 51; Bk Vols 6,811; Per Subs 8
Automation Activity & Vendor Info: (Cataloging) ResourceMATE; (Circulation) ResourceMATE
Wireless access
Function: Bks on CD, Computers for patron use, E-Readers, Free DVD rentals, Internet access, Magazines, Photocopying/Printing, Summer reading prog
Open Mon, Tues & Thurs (Winter) 4-6, Wed 4-7, Sat 10-12; Mon & Sat (Summer) 10-12, Tues & Thurs 4-6, Wed 10-1
Friends of the Library Group

MACKAY

P MACKAY DISTRICT LIBRARY*, 320 Capitol Ave, 83251. (Mail add: PO Box 355, 83251-0355). Tel: 208-588-3333. FAX: 208-588-3333. E-mail: library@atcnet.net. Web Site: mackay.lili.org. *Dir,* Tina Bethoulle
Pop 1,500; Circ 9,000
Library Holdings: Large Print Bks 50; Bk Vols 9,000; Per Subs 12; Talking Bks 300
Automation Activity & Vendor Info: (Cataloging) Follett Software; (Circulation) Follett Software
Open Tues-Thurs 10-12 & 1-5, Fri & Sat 10-1:30

MALAD CITY

P ONEIDA COUNTY LIBRARY*, 31 N 100 W, 83252-1234. (Mail add: PO Box 185, 83252-0185), SAN 303-6049. Tel: 208-766-2229. FAX: 208-647-4006. E-mail: oclib3@hotmail.com. Web Site: oneidacountylibrary.org. *Dir,* Kathy Kent; Staff 10 (Non-MLS 10)
Founded 1912. Pop 2,945; Circ 42,407
Library Holdings: Bk Vols 26,000; Per Subs 50
Special Collections: Local History Coll
Automation Activity & Vendor Info: (Cataloging) Follett Software; (Circulation) Follett Software; (OPAC) Follett Software
Wireless access
Function: 24/7 Electronic res, 24/7 Online cat, 3D Printer, Accelerated reader prog, Activity rm, Adult bk club, After school storytime

Open Mon 11:30-6, Tues-Fri 11:30-5:30, Sat 10-1
Friends of the Library Group

MARSING

P LIZARD BUTTE PUBLIC LIBRARY, 111 Third Ave W, 83639. SAN 325-3058. Tel: 208-896-4690. FAX: 208-226-2692. E-mail: lizardbuttelibrary@yahoo.com. Web Site: lizardbutte.lili.org. *Dir,* Catriona Hardy; Staff 2 (Non-MLS 2)
Founded 1982. Pop 10,000
Library Holdings: Bk Titles 36,000
Wireless access
Function: ILL available
Open Mon, Wed & Fri 12-6, Tues & Thurs 12-7, Sat 10-2

MCCALL

P MCCALL PUBLIC LIBRARY*, 218 E Park St, 83638. SAN 303-6030. Tel: 208-634-5522. E-mail: library@mccall.id.us. Web Site: www.mccall.id.us/departments/library. *Libr Dir,* Meg Lojek; Staff 5 (MLS 1, Non-MLS 4)
Founded 1930. Pop 2,950
Library Holdings: Bk Titles 35,000; Per Subs 54
Special Collections: Building Trades; Idaho History Coll; Nature Studies Coll; Valley County Historical Coll
Subject Interests: Health promotion
Automation Activity & Vendor Info: (Cataloging) OCLC
Wireless access
Function: 24/7 Electronic res, Activity rm, Adult bk club, Adult literacy prog, Audiobks via web, Bilingual assistance for Spanish patrons, Bk club(s), Bks on CD, Chess club, Children's prog, Citizenship assistance, Computer training, Computers for patron use, Digital talking bks, Distance learning, E-Reserves, Electronic databases & coll, Family literacy, Free DVD rentals, Holiday prog, Home delivery & serv to seniorr ctr & nursing homes, ILL available, Instruction & testing, Internet access, Literacy & newcomer serv, Magazines, Movies, Music CDs, Online cat, Outreach serv, OverDrive digital audio bks, Photocopying/Printing, Preschool outreach, Preschool reading prog, Printer for laptops & handheld devices, Prog for adults, Prog for children & young adult, Ref & res, Ref serv available, Scanner, Spanish lang bks, Spoken cassettes & CDs, Spoken cassettes & DVDs, Story hour, Study rm, Summer reading prog, Tax forms, Teen prog
Partic in Idaho Libr Asn; Valley Mountain Library Consortium
Special Services for the Blind - Large print bks & talking machines
Open Mon-Fri 10-6, Sat 10-2
Friends of the Library Group

MENAN

P JEFFERSON COUNTY DISTRICT LIBRARY*, 623A N 3500 E, 83434. SAN 377-4988. Tel: 208-754-0021. FAX: 208-754-4155. *Dir,* Laurie Willmore
Founded 1972
Wireless access
Member Libraries: Hamer Public Library; Heart of the Valley Public Library; Menan-Annis, Grant Public Library

P MENAN-ANNIS, GRANT PUBLIC LIBRARY*, 623A N 3500 E, 83434. Tel: 208-754-0021. FAX: 208-754-4155. E-mail: menanlibrary@gmail.com. *Dir,* Laurie Willmore; Staff 3 (Non-MLS 3)
Founded 1972
Library Holdings: Bk Titles 11,921; Per Subs 25
Automation Activity & Vendor Info: (Cataloging) Follett Software; (Circulation) Follett Software
Wireless access
Mem of Jefferson County District Library
Open Mon 1-7, Tues, Thurs & Fri 1-5, Wed 10-5
Friends of the Library Group

MERIDIAN

P MERIDIAN LIBRARY DISTRICT*, 1326 W Cherry Lane, 83642. SAN 303-6057. Tel: 208-888-4451. FAX: 208-968-1297. Web Site: www.mld.org. *Libr Dir,* Gretchen Caserotti; E-mail: director@mld.org; *Asst Dir,* John Thill; *Mgr, Main Libr,* Kristi Haman; *Mgr, Mat Serv,* Cheri Rendler; *District Prog Mgr,* Megan Egbert; *Outreach Mgr,* Audra Green; Staff 61 (MLS 14, Non-MLS 47)
Founded 1924
Automation Activity & Vendor Info: (Acquisitions) Innovative Interfaces, Inc; (Cataloging) Innovative Interfaces, Inc; (Circulation) Innovative Interfaces, Inc; (OPAC) Innovative Interfaces, Inc
Wireless access
Function: 24/7 Electronic res, 24/7 Online cat, Accelerated reader prog, Activity rm, Adult bk club, After school storytime, Art exhibits, Audio & video playback equip for onsite use, Audiobks on Playaways & MP3, Audiobks via web, AV serv, Bi-weekly Writer's Group, Bk club(s), Bks on CD, CD-ROM, Children's prog, Computer training, Computers for patron use, Digital talking bks, Distance learning, Doc delivery serv, E-Readers, Electronic databases & coll, Equip loans & repairs, Family literacy, Free DVD rentals, Home delivery & serv to seniorr ctr & nursing homes, Homebound delivery serv, ILL available, Instruction & testing, Internet access, Learning ctr, Magazines, Movies, Music CDs, Notary serv, Online cat, Online ref, Outreach serv, Outside serv via phone, mail, e-mail & web, OverDrive digital audio bks, Photocopying/Printing, Preschool outreach, Preschool reading prog, Prof lending libr, Prog for adults, Prog for children & young adult, Ref & res, Ref serv available, Scanner, Senior computer classes, Senior outreach, Serves people with intellectual disabilities, Spanish lang bks, Spoken cassettes & CDs, Spoken cassettes & DVDs, Story hour, Study rm, Summer & winter reading prog, Summer reading prog, Tax forms, Teen prog, Telephone ref, Wheelchair accessible, Winter reading prog, Workshops, Writing prog
Partic in LYNX! Consortium
Open Mon-Thurs 9-8, Fri 9-6, Sat 10-5, Sun 1-5
Restriction: Borrowing requests are handled by ILL, Free to mem, Non-circulating, Non-resident fee
Friends of the Library Group
Branches: 3
SILVERSTONE BRANCH, 3531 E Overland Rd, 83642. Tel: 208-884-2616. *Br Mgr,* Dusty Waltner; E-mail: dwaltner@mld.org
Open Mon-Thurs 9-8, Fri 9-6, Sat 10-5, Sun 1-5
TINY LIBRARY, 5159 S Hillsdale Ave, 83642. (Mail add: 1326 W Cherry Lane, 83646). Tel: 208-576-3511.
UNBOUND TECHNOLOGY LIBRARY, 722 NE Second St, 83642. *Br Mgr,* Nick Grove; Tel: 208-258-2000, E-mail: nick@mld.org
Founded 2015
Friends of the Library Group
Bookmobiles: 2

MIDDLETON

P MIDDLETON PUBLIC LIBRARY*, 307 Cornell St, 83644. SAN 303-6065. Tel: 208-585-3931. Web Site: middleton.lili.org. *Dir,* Kate Lovan; E-mail: klovan@mymiddletonlibrary.org; *Libr Mgr,* Robyn Millar; *Coll Develop, Libr Assoc,* Jennifer Kuhn; Staff 3 (Non-MLS 3)
Founded 1960. Pop 5,500
Library Holdings: Bk Vols 20,000; Per Subs 10
Automation Activity & Vendor Info: (ILL) Surpass
Wireless access
Partic in WiLS
Open Mon-Fri 10:30-6:30, Sat 10:30-4
Friends of the Library Group

MIDVALE

P MIDVALE COMMUNITY LIBRARY, 70 E Bridge St, 83645-2012. (Mail add: PO Box 127, 83645-0127), SAN 303-6073. Tel: 208-355-2213. E-mail: mcl@mtecom.net. Web Site: midvale.lili.org. *Librn,* Suzanne Ash
Founded 1976. Pop 800; Circ 10,606
Library Holdings: Bk Titles 12,038
Special Collections: Idaho Authors & History, bks & pamphlets. Oral History
Automation Activity & Vendor Info: (Cataloging) Follett Software
Wireless access
Open Mon-Sat 1-5
Friends of the Library Group

MONTPELIER

P BEAR LAKE COUNTY FREE LIBRARY*, 138 N Sixth St, 83254-1556. SAN 303-609X. Tel: 208-847-1664. FAX: 208-847-1664. E-mail: blcirc@dcdi.net. Web Site: bearlake.lili.org.
Founded 1959. Pop 7,250
Library Holdings: Bk Vols 60,000; Per Subs 120
Automation Activity & Vendor Info: (Cataloging) SirsiDynix; (Circulation) SirsiDynix; (OPAC) SirsiDynix
Wireless access
Open Mon-Fri 10-6, Sat 10-2
Branches: 1
PARIS BRANCH, 62 S Main, Paris, 83261. Tel: 208-945-2253.
Pop 7,250
Library Holdings: Bk Vols 5,000
Open Mon, Wed & Fri 1-5

MOSCOW

S APPALOOSA MUSEUM & HERITAGE CENTER*, Appaloosa Museum Library, 2720 W Pullman Rd, 83843. SAN 376-0820. Tel: 208-882-5578, Ext 279. FAX: 208-882-8150. E-mail: museum@appaloosa.com. Web Site: appaloosamuseum.com. *Dir,* Crystal White; Tel: 208-882-5578
Library Holdings: AV Mats 40; Bk Titles 400
Open Mon-Fri (Fall & Winter) 10-3, Sat 11-3; Mon-Sat (Spring & Summer) 11-4

S LATAH COUNTY HISTORICAL SOCIETY LIBRARY*, 327 E Second St, 83843. SAN 303-6103. Tel: 208-882-1004. E-mail: lchslibrary@latah.id.us. Web Site: www.latahcountyhistoricalsociety.org. *Exec Dir,* Dulce Kersting; E-mail: dkersting@latah.id.us; *Curator,* Zavhary X Wnek; E-mail: zwnek@latah.id.us
Founded 1968
Library Holdings: Bk Titles 450; Per Subs 500
Special Collections: Carol Ryrie Brink Coll (letters, interviews, photos, ms); Historic Preservation Coll; Psychiana Papers; Washington, Idaho & Montana Railroad Paper. Oral History
Publications: Guide to Historical & Genealogical Records in Latah County; Guide to the Latah County Oral History Collection; Guide to the Local History Library at the Latah County Historical Society; Latah Legacy (Quarterly); Newsletter (Quarterly)
Open Tues-Fri 8-4
Restriction: Not a lending libr

P LATAH COUNTY LIBRARY DISTRICT*, 110 S Jefferson St, 83843-2833. SAN 339-6576. Tel: 208-882-3925. FAX: 208-882-5098. E-mail: moscow@latahlibrary.org. Web Site: www.latahlibrary.org. *Dir,* Chris Sokol; E-mail: director@latahlibrary.org; Staff 7 (MLS 1, Non-MLS 6)
Founded 1901. Pop 35,000; Circ 235,000
Library Holdings: Bk Vols 98,518; Per Subs 237
Subject Interests: Local hist, Sci fict
Wireless access
Open Mon-Thurs 10-7, Fri 10-6, Sat 10-5
Friends of the Library Group
Branches: 6
BOVILL BRANCH, 310 First Ave, Bovill, 83806. (Mail add: PO Box 210, Bovill, 83806-0210), SAN 371-3644. Tel: 208-826-3451. FAX: 208-826-3451. E-mail: bovill@latahlibrary.org. *Br Mgr,* Brittany Griffin
Library Holdings: Bk Vols 2,500
Open Mon & Thurs 10-2, Tues & Wed 3-6
Friends of the Library Group
DEARY BRANCH, 304 Second Ave, Deary, 83823. (Mail add: PO Box 213, Deary, 83823-0213), SAN 339-6592. Tel: 208-877-1664. FAX: 208-877-1664. E-mail: deary@latahlibrary.org. *Br Mgr,* Brittany Griffin
Library Holdings: Bk Vols 5,000
Open Mon & Thurs 3-6, Tues & Wed 10-4
Friends of the Library Group
GENESEE BRANCH, 140 E Walnut St, Genesee, 83832. (Mail add: PO Box 278, Genesee, 83832-0278), SAN 339-6606. Tel: 208-285-1398. FAX: 208-285-1398. E-mail: genesee@latahlibrary.org. *Br Mgr,* Connie Sobczyk
Library Holdings: Bk Vols 5,000
Open Mon & Wed 1-7, Thurs 10-4
Friends of the Library Group
JULIAETTA BRANCH, 205 Main St, Juliaetta, 83535. (Mail add: PO Box 471, Juliaetta, 83535-0470), SAN 339-6630. Tel: 208-276-7071. FAX: 208-276-7071. E-mail: juliaetta@latahlibrary.org. *Br Mgr,* Erin Davis
Library Holdings: Bk Vols 5,000
Open Mon & Thurs 10-3, Tues & Wed 2-6
Friends of the Library Group
POTLATCH BRANCH, 1010 Onaway Rd, Potlatch, 83855. (Mail add: PO Box 335, Potlatch, 83855-0335), SAN 339-6665. Tel: 208-875-1036. FAX: 208-875-1036. E-mail: potlatch@latahlibrary.org. *Br Mgr,* Beth Tunnell
Library Holdings: Bk Vols 5,000
Open Mon & Wed 2-7, Tues & Thurs 3-7, Fri 10-2
Friends of the Library Group
TROY BRANCH, 402 S Main St, Troy, 83871. (Mail add: PO Box 477, Troy, 83871-0477), SAN 339-669X. Tel: 208-835-4311. FAX: 208-835-4311. E-mail: troy@latahlibrary.org. *Br Supvr,* Michelle Sturdy
Library Holdings: Bk Vols 5,000
Open Mon & Wed 12-6, Thurs 10-4
Friends of the Library Group

C UNIVERSITY OF IDAHO LIBRARY*, Rayburn St, 83844. (Mail add: 875 Perimeter Dr, MS 2350, 83844-2350), SAN 339-672X. Tel: 208-885-6534. Circulation Tel: 208-885-6559. Interlibrary Loan Service Tel: 208-885-6843. Reference Tel: 208-885-6235, 208-885-6584. FAX: 208-885-6817. Web Site: www.lib.uidaho.edu. *Dean, Univ Libr,* Dr Lynn Baird; Fax: 208-885-7070, E-mail: lbaird@uidaho.edu; *Assoc Dean,* Benjamin Hunter; Tel: 208-885-5858, E-mail: bhunter@uidaho.edu; *Head, Data Serv, Head, Digital Serv,* Devin Becker; Tel: 208-885-7040, E-mail: dbecker@uidaho.edu; *Head, Govt Doc, Head, Tech Serv,* Dr Ramirose Attebury; Tel: 208-885-2503, E-mail: rattebur@uidaho.edu; *Head, Spec Coll & Archives,* Erin Passehl Stoddart; Tel: 208-885-5813, E-mail: estoddart@uidaho.edu; *Head, User & Res Serv,* Kristin Henrich; Tel: 208-885-6514, E-mail: khenrich@uidaho.edu; *Ref Coordr,* Rochelle Smith; Tel: 208 885-7850, E-mail: rsmith@uidaho.edu; *Ref & Instrul Serv, Instr Coordr,* Diane Prorak; Tel: 208-885-2508, E-mail: prorak@uidaho.edu; Staff 47 (MLS 22, Non-MLS 25)
Founded 1889. Enrl 11,780; Fac 871; Highest Degree: Doctorate
Jul 2016-Jun 2017 Income (Main Library Only) $7,490,019, State $7,100,607, Locally Generated Income $265,216, Other $124,196. Mats Exp $4,318,101. Sal $2,133,807
Library Holdings: AV Mats 10,728; Bks on Deafness & Sign Lang 2,194; Braille Volumes 253; CDs 3,150; DVDs 6,652; e-books 706,595; e-journals 100,582; Electronic Media & Resources 132,800; Microforms 2,556,150; Music Scores 17,696; Bk Titles 1,576,680; Per Subs 13,500; Videos 7,687
Special Collections: Ezra Pound Coll; Idaho History (Day-Northwest Coll); Idaho State Publications; Imprints (Caxton Printers, Idaho); International Jazz Coll; Sir Walter Scott Coll. Oral History; State Document Depository; US Document Depository
Subject Interests: Mining, Natural res
Automation Activity & Vendor Info: (Acquisitions) Ex Libris Group; (Cataloging) OCLC; (Circulation) Ex Libris Group; (ILL) OCLC Online; (OPAC) OCLC WorldShare Interlibrary Loan; (Serials) Ex Libris Group
Wireless access
Function: Archival coll, Art exhibits, Audio & video playback equip for onsite use, Bus archives, CD-ROM, Computers for patron use, Distance learning, Doc delivery serv, E-Reserves, Electronic databases & coll, For res purposes, Free DVD rentals, Govt ref serv, Homework prog, ILL available, Internet access, Jazz prog, Music CDs, Online cat, Online info literacy tutorials on the web & in blackboard, Online ref, Orientations, Outreach serv, Outside serv via phone, mail, e-mail & web, Photocopying/Printing, Prog for adults, Ref & res, Ref serv available, Res libr, Tax forms, Telephone ref, VHS videos, Wheelchair accessible
Publications: Towers
Partic in Orbis Cascade Alliance
Special Services for the Blind - Reader equip
Restriction: In-house use for visitors, Non-circulating of rare bks
Friends of the Library Group
Departmental Libraries:
CL COLLEGE OF LAW, 711 Rayburn St, 83844. (Mail add: 875 Perimeter Dr, PO Box 442324, 83844-2324). Tel: 208-885-6521. Interlibrary Loan Service Tel: 208-885-2159. Reference Tel: 208-885-5899. FAX: 208-885-2743. E-mail: lawlib@uidaho.edu. Web Site: www.uidaho.edu/law/library. *Dir,* John Hasko; E-mail: jhasko@uidaho.edu; *Head, Pub Serv,* Diana Gleason; Tel: 208-885-2161; *Head, Tech Serv,* Ruth Funabiki; E-mail: funabiki@uidaho.edu; *Ref & Coll Develop Librn,* Jean Mattimoe; Tel: 208-885-2162, E-mail: mattimoe@uidaho.edu; Staff 9 (MLS 4, Non-MLS 5)
Founded 1914. Enrl 360; Fac 33; Highest Degree: Doctorate
Library Holdings: Bk Titles 41,274; Bk Vols 250,747
Special Collections: Idaho Supreme Court Briefs. US Document Depository
Subject Interests: Native Am law, Natural res, Trial practice
Function: Ref serv available
Open Mon-Thurs 7:30am-10pm, Fri 7:30am-9pm, Sat 12-5, Sun 12-10
Restriction: Badge access after hrs

MOUNTAIN HOME

P MOUNTAIN HOME PUBLIC LIBRARY*, 790 N Tenth E, 83647. SAN 303-6111. Tel: 208-587-4716. FAX: 208-587-6645. Web Site: www.mhlibrary.org. *Libr Dir,* William Lamb; E-mail: wlamb@mountain-home.us
Founded 1908. Pop 14,562; Circ 82,071
Library Holdings: Audiobooks 1,517; DVDs 2,144; e-books 19,157; Bk Vols 31,698; Per Subs 75
Wireless access
Function: 24/7 Electronic res, 24/7 Online cat, 3D Printer, Adult bk club, Adult literacy prog, Audiobks via web, Bilingual assistance for Spanish patrons, Bks on CD, Children's prog, Computer training, Computers for patron use, Digital talking bks, Distance learning, Doc delivery serv, Electronic databases & coll, Free DVD rentals, Holiday prog, ILL available, Internet access, Laminating, Life-long learning prog for all ages, Magazines, Meeting rooms, Movies, Notary serv, Online cat, Outreach serv, OverDrive digital audio bks, Photocopying/Printing, Prog for adults, Prog for children & young adult, Scanner, Senior computer classes, Spanish lang bks, STEM programs, Summer reading prog, Tax forms, Teen prog, Telephone ref, Wheelchair accessible, Winter reading prog
Partic in LYNX! Consortium
Open Mon & Fri 10-7, Sat 9-5
Friends of the Library Group

MOUNTAIN HOME AFB

A UNITED STATES AIR FORCE*, Mountain Home Air Force Base Library FL4897, Bldg 2610, Ste 100, 480 Fifth Ave, 83648. SAN 339-6789. Tel: 208-828-2326, 208-828-2743. FAX: 208-832-9840. E-mail: mhafblibrary15@gmail.com. Web Site: accc.ent.sirsi.net/client/en_US/mountainhome, www.mhafbfun.com/directory_listing/library. *Libr Dir,* Debbie Worthington; E-mail: deborah.worthington.1@us.af.mil; Staff 3.7 (MLS 1.3, Non-MLS 2.4)
Founded 1952

Library Holdings: CDs 2,100; DVDs 6,000; Bk Vols 39,540
Subject Interests: Aeronaut, Idaho, Mil hist
Automation Activity & Vendor Info: (Cataloging) SirsiDynix; (Circulation) SirsiDynix; (ILL) OCLC WorldShare Interlibrary Loan; (OPAC) SirsiDynix; (Serials) SirsiDynix
Wireless access
Partic in OCLC Online Computer Library Center, Inc
Open Tues-Thurs 10-7, Fri 10-6, Sat 12-5

MULLAN

P MULLAN PUBLIC LIBRARY, 117 Hunter Ave, 83846. (Mail add: PO Box 479, 83846-0479), SAN 303-612X. Tel: 208-744-1220. FAX: 208-744-1220. E-mail: mplibrary@frontier.com. Web Site: mullan.lili.org. *Libr Dir,* Tamara Lindroos; *Asst Librn,* Danielle King; Staff 2 (Non-MLS 2)
Founded 1950. Pop 840; Circ 1,850
Library Holdings: AV Mats 600; Bk Vols 7,000
Wireless access
Open Mon, Tues, Thurs & Fri 3-7, Wed 11-7
Friends of the Library Group

MURPHY

S OWYHEE COUNTY HISTORICAL SOCIETY*, Museum & Library Complex, 17085 Basey St, 83650. SAN 303-6138. Tel: 208-495-2319. FAX: 208-495-9824. Administration E-mail: administration@owyheemuseum.org. Web Site: www.owyheemuseum.org. *Dir,* Eriks Garsvo; E-mail: owyheemuseumdirector@gmail.com
Founded 1960
Library Holdings: Bk Titles 1,000; Per Subs 13; Talking Bks 30
Special Collections: Newspaper (Owyhee Avalanche, Silver City), micro. Oral History; State Document Depository
Subject Interests: Archaeology, Genealogy, Geol, Hist, Mining
Wireless access
Publications: Owyhee Outpost (Annual historical book)
Restriction: Open by appt only, Open to pub for ref only

NAMPA

J COLLEGE OF WESTERN IDAHO*, Nampa Library, Nampa Campus Multipurpose Bldg, 1st Flr, Rm 105/103, 6042 Birch Lane, 83687. (Mail add: MS1300, PO Box 3010, 85653-3010). Tel: 208-562-3115. E-mail: library@cwidaho.cc. Web Site: cwi.edu/current-students/library. *Dir, Libr Serv,* Ms Kim Reed; Tel: 208-562-3114, E-mail: kimreed@cwidaho.cc; *Asst Dir, Libr Serv,* Jean-Louise Zancanella; Tel: 205-562-3118, E-mail: jeanlouisezancanella@cwidaho.cc
Wireless access
Open Mon-Thurs 8:30-8, Fri 8:30-5, Sat 10-2

Departmental Libraries:

ADA LIBRARY, Ada County Campus Pintail Ctr, Rm 1301, 1360 S Eagle Flight Way, Boise, 83709. (Mail add: MS 5000, PO Box 3010, Boise, 83653-3010). Tel: 208-562-2502.
Open Mon-Thurs 8:30-8, Fri 8:30-5, Sat 10-2

P NAMPA PUBLIC LIBRARY*, 215 12th Ave S, 83651. SAN 303-6146. Tel: 208-468-5800. FAX: 208-318-0530. E-mail: info@nampalibrary.org. Web Site: nampalibrary.org. *Dir,* Claire Connley; E-mail: connleyc@nampalibrary.org; *Adult Serv Supvr,* Beth Neunaber; Tel: 208-468-5807, E-mail: neunaberb@nampalibrary.org; *Circ Supvr,* Ezequiel Luna; Tel: 208-468-5801, E-mail: lunae@nampalibrary.org; Staff 23 (MLS 5, Non-MLS 18)
Founded 1904. Pop 83,000; Circ 749,000
Library Holdings: Audiobooks 10,161; AV Mats 8,142; e-books 500; Bk Vols 93,561; Per Subs 173
Special Collections: Local History Coll
Automation Activity & Vendor Info: (Acquisitions) SirsiDynix; (Cataloging) SirsiDynix; (Circulation) SirsiDynix; (ILL) OCLC Online; (OPAC) SirsiDynix; (Serials) SirsiDynix
Wireless access
Function: Children's prog, Computer training
Partic in LYNX! Consortium
Open Mon-Thurs 10-7, Fri 10-6, Sat 10-5
Friends of the Library Group

C NORTHWEST NAZARENE UNIVERSITY*, John E Riley Library, 804 E Dewey St, 83686. (Mail add: 623 S University Blvd, 83686). Circulation Tel: 208-467-8607. Interlibrary Loan Service Tel: 208-467-8605. Reference Tel: 208-467-8611. E-mail: library@nnu.edu. Web Site: library.nnu.edu. *Dir, Libr & Archives,* Amy C Rice; Tel: 208-467-8609, E-mail: arice@nnu.edu; *Coll Mgt Librn,* Sheryll Hampton; E-mail: sheryllhampton@nnu.edu; *Instruction & Res Serv Librn,* Dr Rodney Birch; Tel: 208-467-8606, E-mail: rbirch@nnu.edu; *Circ Supvr, Learning Commons Supvr,* Deanna Wilde; Tel: 208-467-8614, E-mail: dwilde@nnu.edu; *Tech Serv Supvr,* Coral Mattei; E-mail: clmattei@nnu.edu; *Libr Tech,* Carol Poe; Tel: 208-467-8616, E-mail: cjpoe@nnu.edu; Staff 4 (MLS 4)
Founded 1913. Enrl 2,020; Highest Degree: Master
Library Holdings: Bk Titles 112,250; Bk Vols 174,533; Per Subs 855
Automation Activity & Vendor Info: (Acquisitions) OCLC WorldShare Interlibrary Loan; (Cataloging) OCLC Worldshare Management Services; (Circulation) OCLC Worldshare Management Services; (Course Reserve) OCLC Worldshare Management Services; (ILL) Clio; (OPAC) OCLC Worldshare Management Services; (Serials) OCLC Worldshare Management Services
Wireless access
Open Mon-Thurs 8am-midnight, Fri 8-5, Sat 11-5, Sun 4-midnight
Restriction: Open to pub for ref & circ; with some limitations

NEW MEADOWS

P MEADOWS VALLEY PUBLIC LIBRARY DISTRICT*, 400 Virginia St, 83654. (Mail add: PO Box 436, 83654-0436), SAN 303-6162. Tel: 208-347-3147. FAX: 208-347-3147. *Dir,* Audrey Crogh; E-mail: audrey@mvpubliclibrary.com
Founded 1997. Pop 1,800
Library Holdings: Bk Vols 13,500
Subject Interests: Idaho
Automation Activity & Vendor Info: (Cataloging) Surpass; (Circulation) Surpass; (ILL) OCLC WorldShare Interlibrary Loan
Function: 24/7 Electronic res, 24/7 Online cat, Adult bk club, Bk club(s), Bks on CD, Children's prog, Computer training, Computers for patron use, Electronic databases & coll, Free DVD rentals, ILL available, Instruction & testing, Internet access, Magazines, Meeting rooms, Movies, Online cat, Photocopying/Printing, Prog for adults, Prog for children & young adult, Spanish lang bks, Story hour, Summer reading prog, Tax forms, Teen prog
Special Services for the Blind - Braille bks; Descriptive video serv (DVS); Large print bks; Talking bks
Open Mon-Fri 11-6, Sat (Summer) 11-2
Friends of the Library Group

NEW PLYMOUTH

P ARMORAL TUTTLE PUBLIC LIBRARY*, 301 N Plymouth Ave, 83655. (Mail add: PO Box 158, 83655-0158), SAN 303-6170. Tel: 208-278-5338. E-mail: atplibrary@fmtc.com. Web Site: newplymouth.lili.org. *Dir,* Melanie Cope
Founded 1916. Pop 1,186; Circ 11,810
Library Holdings: Large Print Bks 319; Bk Vols 9,361; Talking Bks 206
Automation Activity & Vendor Info: (Cataloging) Follett Software; (Circulation) Follett Software
Open Mon 10-2, Tues 10-4, Wed & Thurs 1-7
Friends of the Library Group

NOTUS

P NOTUS PUBLIC LIBRARY*, 387 First St, PO Box 169, 83656-0169. Tel: 208-459-8247. E-mail: notuspubliclibrary@gmail.com. *Dir,* Ann Misner
Library Holdings: Bk Vols 12,000
Wireless access
Partic in Canyon Owyhee Library Group, Ltd
Open Tues, Wed & Thurs (Summer) 1-6:30; Wed, Thurs & Fri (Fall-Spring) 1:6:30

OAKLEY

P OAKLEY FREE LIBRARY DISTRICT*, 185 E Main St, 83346. SAN 303-6197. Tel: 208-862-3434. E-mail: oaklib@pmt.org. Web Site: oakley.lili.org. *Libr Dir,* AriAnn Hale; *Asst Librn,* Brittane Higley
Founded 1973. Pop 1,500
Library Holdings: Bk Vols 9,884
Special Collections: Idaho History Coll
Automation Activity & Vendor Info: (Acquisitions) DEMCO; (Cataloging) OCLC Connexion; (Circulation) JayWil Software Development, Inc; (ILL) OCLC FirstSearch
Wireless access
Publications: Dusty Memories; History of the Latter Day Saints Community of Oakley; My Book & Me; The Twin Falls-Oakley Irrigation Project
Open Tues, Thurs & Sat 2-6
Friends of the Library Group

OROFINO

P CLEARWATER MEMORIAL PUBLIC LIBRARY*, 402 Michigan Ave, 83544. (Mail add: PO Box 471, 83544-0471), SAN 303-6200. Tel: 208-476-3411. FAX: 208-476-4527. E-mail: cmpvalnet@orofino-id.com. Web Site: www.orofinolibrary.com. *Dir,* Marcia Player; Staff 5 (MLS 1, Non-MLS 4)
Founded 1949. Pop 8,446; Circ 47,371

Library Holdings: AV Mats 646; Bks on Deafness & Sign Lang 12; Electronic Media & Resources 16; Bk Titles 33,630; Per Subs 75; Talking Bks 692
Special Collections: Lewis & Clark Coll; Pacific Northwest
Automation Activity & Vendor Info: (Cataloging) OCLC; (Circulation) LibLime
Wireless access
Special Services for the Blind - Talking bks
Open Mon-Fri 9-6, Sat 9-2
Friends of the Library Group
Bookmobiles: 1

OSBURN

P OSBURN PUBLIC LIBRARY*, 921 E Mullan, 83849. (Mail add: PO Box 809, 83849-0809), SAN 303-6219. Tel: 208-752-9711. FAX: 208-753-8585. E-mail: osburnlibrary@cityofosburn.org. Web Site: osburn.lili.org. *Libr Dir,* Jamee Sperry
Founded 1960. Pop 1,545; Circ 9,700
Library Holdings: AV Mats 340; Bk Vols 9,400; Per Subs 20; Talking Bks 96
Automation Activity & Vendor Info: (Cataloging) Ex Libris Group; (Circulation) Ex Libris Group; (OPAC) Ex Libris Group
Open Mon & Wed (Winter) 12-8, Tues, Thurs & Fri 12-5; Mon & Wed (Summer) 11-8, Tues & Thurs 11-5
Friends of the Library Group

PARMA

P PATRICIA ROMANKO PUBLIC LIBRARY*, 121 N Third St, 83660. (Mail add: PO Box 309, 83660-0309), SAN 303-6227. Tel: 208-722-6605. E-mail: parmalibrarymatters@gmail.com. Web Site: parma.lili.org. *Dir,* Gina Day
Pop 3,138; Circ 9,614
Library Holdings: Bk Titles 18,900
Subject Interests: Idaho
Automation Activity & Vendor Info: (Cataloging) Follett Software; (Circulation) Follett Software
Wireless access
Partic in Idaho Libr Asn
Open Tues & Wed 11-6, Thurs 12-6, Fri 12-5, Sat 11-5
Friends of the Library Group

PAYETTE

P PAYETTE PUBLIC LIBRARY, 24 S Tenth St, 83661-2861. SAN 303-6235. Tel: 208-642-6029. E-mail: library@cityofpayette.com. Web Site: payette.lili.org. *Dir,* Clay Ritter; Staff 3 (Non-MLS 3)
Founded 1920. Pop 6,170; Circ 36,755
Library Holdings: Bk Vols 40,800; Per Subs 88
Special Collections: Northwest Coll
Wireless access
Open Mon-Fri 10-6, Sat 10-4
Friends of the Library Group

PIERCE

P PIERCE DISTRICT LIBRARY*, 208 S Main St, 83546. (Mail add: PO Box 386, 83546-0386), SAN 303-6243. Tel: 208-464-2823. FAX: 208-464-2823. Web Site: piercelibrary.lili.org. *Dir,* Kim Ward; E-mail: kward@piercepubliclibrary.com
Founded 1919. Pop 1,000; Circ 13,899
Library Holdings: Bk Titles 14,945; Per Subs 51
Special Collections: Local History Artifacts
Automation Activity & Vendor Info: (Cataloging) Ex Libris Group; (Circulation) Ex Libris Group; (OPAC) Ex Libris Group
Wireless access
Open Mon-Thurs 9-5, Fri 10-4

PLUMMER

P PLUMMER PUBLIC LIBRARY*, 849 D St, 83851. (Mail add: PO Box 309, 83851-0309). Tel: 208-686-1812. E-mail: plummerlibrary@gmail.com. Web Site: plummer.lili.org. *Dir,* Paulina Freeburg
Library Holdings: Bk Vols 17,000; Per Subs 12
Automation Activity & Vendor Info: (Cataloging) Baker & Taylor; (Circulation) Baker & Taylor; (OPAC) Baker & Taylor
Wireless access
Open Mon-Wed 10-6, Thurs 2-6, Sat 10-2
Friends of the Library Group

POCATELLO

C IDAHO STATE UNIVERSITY*, Eli M Oboler Library, 850 S Ninth Ave, 83209. (Mail add: 921 S Eighth Ave, Stop 8089, 83209-8089), SAN 303-6294. Tel: 208-282-2958. Interlibrary Loan Service Tel: 208-282-3127. Administration Tel: 208-282-2997. Web Site: www.isu.edu/library. *Interim Dean,* Sandra Shropshire; E-mail: shrosand@isu.edu; *Adminr, Info Syst,* Michael Gower; Tel: 208-282-2882, E-mail: gowemich@isu.edu; *Head, Spec Coll,* Ellen M Ryan; Tel: 208-282-3608, E-mail: ryanelle@isu.edu; *Assoc Univ Librn, Res Serv,* Jenny Semenza; Tel: 208-282-2581, E-mail: semejen@isu.edu; *Coordr, Instruction,* Spencer Jardine; Tel: 208-282-5609, E-mail: jardspen@isu.edu; Staff 39 (MLS 15, Non-MLS 24)
Founded 1902. Enrl 14,664; Fac 621; Highest Degree: Doctorate
Library Holdings: Audiobooks 1,282; AV Mats 4,370; CDs 3,202; DVDs 653; e-books 741; e-journals 5,855; Microforms 2,004,535; Bk Titles 516,208; Bk Vols 541,668; Per Subs 8,185; Videos 2,435
Special Collections: Book Arts; Childrens' Readers; Early English Dictionaries; Elocution Coll; Samuel Johnson Coll. State Document Depository; US Document Depository
Subject Interests: Health sci, Law
Automation Activity & Vendor Info: (Acquisitions) Ex Libris Group; (Cataloging) Ex Libris Group; (Circulation) Ex Libris Group; (Course Reserve) Ex Libris Group; (ILL) Ex Libris Group; (Media Booking) Ex Libris Group; (OPAC) Ex Libris Group; (Serials) Ex Libris Group
Wireless access
Function: Archival coll, Distance learning, Doc delivery serv, For res purposes, Govt ref serv, Health sci info serv, ILL available, Internet access, Photocopying/Printing, Ref serv available, Telephone ref, Wheelchair accessible, Workshops
Publications: Between-the-Lines (Newsletter)
Partic in OCLC Online Computer Library Center, Inc
Special Services for the Deaf - Assistive tech
Special Services for the Blind - Assistive/Adapted tech devices, equip & products
Open Mon-Thurs 7:30am-Midnight, Fri 7:30-7, Sat 10-7, Sun Noon-Midnight
Friends of the Library Group

Departmental Libraries:

CM IDAHO HEALTH SCIENCES LIBRARY, 850 S Ninth Ave, 83201-5314. (Mail add: 921 S Eighth Ave, Stop 8089, 83209-8089). Tel: 208-282-4685. FAX: 202-282-4295. Web Site: www.isu.edu/library/libandcoll/ihsl/. *Interim Dean,* Sandra Shropshire; E-mail: shrosand@isu.edu
Publications: Liaison (Newsletter)
Open Mon-Fri 8am-9pm, Sat 12-5

UNIVERSITY LIBRARY CENTER, 1784 Science Center Dr, Rm 225, Idaho Falls, 83402. Tel: 208-282-7906. Web Site: isu.edu/library/libandcoll/isu-library—idaho-falls. *Coordr, Libr Serv,* Catherine Gray; E-mail: graycath@isu.edu; Staff 2 (MLS 1, Non-MLS 1)
Founded 1993. Enrl 2,180; Highest Degree: Doctorate
Library Holdings: Bk Vols 1,196
Function: Distance learning, Doc delivery serv, Ref serv available, Wheelchair accessible
Open Mon-Thurs 9-8, Fri & Sat 9-3
Restriction: Pub use on premises

P MARSHALL PUBLIC LIBRARY, 113 S Garfield Ave, 83204. SAN 339-6819. Tel: 208-232-1263. FAX: 208-232-9266. Reference E-mail: ref@marshallpl.org. Web Site: www.marshallpl.org. *Dir,* Eric Suess; E-mail: esuess@marshallpl.org; *Assoc Dir,* Trina Bonman; E-mail: tbonman@marshallpl.org; *Readers' Advisor Librn,* Becky Hadley; E-mail: bhadley@marshallpl.org; *Ref Librn,* Amy Campbell; E-mail: acampbell@marshallpl.org; *YA Librn,* Kath Ann Hendricks; E-mail: khendricks@marshallpl.org; Staff 10 (Non-MLS 10)
Founded 1905. Pop 50,600; Circ 463,159
Library Holdings: Bk Vols 151,903; Per Subs 198
Special Collections: Idaho Coll. State Document Depository
Automation Activity & Vendor Info: (Cataloging) SirsiDynix; (Circulation) SirsiDynix; (OPAC) SirsiDynix
Wireless access
Partic in Library Consortium of Eastern Idaho
Open Mon-Thurs 10-9, Fri & Sat 10-6
Friends of the Library Group

PRAIRIE

P PRAIRIE DISTRICT LIBRARY, 71 Smith Creek Rd, 83647. Tel: 208-868-3269. E-mail: prairielibrarydistrict@gmail.com. *Librn,* Position Currently Open
Library Holdings: Bk Vols 6,000
Open Mon, Wed & Fri (Summer) 9-5; Mon-Fri (Winter) 9-4

PRESTON

P FRANKLIN COUNTY LIBRARY DISTRICT, Larsen-Sant Public Library, 109 S First E, 83263. SAN 303-6324. Tel: 208-852-0175. FAX: 208-852-7148. E-mail: larsensantlib@gmail.com. Web Site: larsen-sant.lili.org. *Dir,* Laura Wheatley; *Asst Dir,* Teresa Rasmussen
Pop 11,000; Circ 90,000
Library Holdings: Bk Vols 36,000; Per Subs 52
Wireless access

Partic in Library Consortium of Eastern Idaho
Open Mon-Thurs 10-7, Fri 10-6, Sat 11-4
Friends of the Library Group

PRIEST LAKE

P PRIEST LAKE PUBLIC LIBRARY*, 28769 Hwy 57, 83856. SAN 303-6332. Tel: 208-443-2454. FAX: 208-443-3121. E-mail: plplibrary@hotmail.com. Web Site: www.priestlake.lili.org. *Dir,* Jaime Yob; *Asst to the Dir,* Cassandra Wood; *Asst Librn,* Kristine Ostler; *Asst Librn,* Marnie Mason
Founded 1974. Pop 1,786
Library Holdings: Audiobooks 500; DVDs 1,500; Large Print Bks 100; Bk Titles 11,000; Per Subs 50; Videos 120
Special Collections: History of Priest Lake
Wireless access
Function: 24/7 Electronic res, 24/7 Online cat, 3D Printer, Adult bk club, Art programs, Audio & video playback equip for onsite use, Audiobks via web, Bks on cassette, Bks on CD, CD-ROM, Children's prog, Computers for patron use, Free DVD rentals, ILL available, Internet access, Laminating, Magazines, Mail & tel request accepted, Meeting rooms, Movies, Music CDs, Notary serv, Online cat, Photocopying/Printing, Preschool reading prog, Printer for laptops & handheld devices, Prog for adults, Prog for children & young adult, Satellite serv, Scanner, Spanish lang bks, Spoken cassettes & CDs, Spoken cassettes & DVDs, STEM programs, Summer & winter reading prog, Teen prog, Telephone ref, VHS videos, Wheelchair accessible
Open Mon-Wed & Fri 10-4, Thurs 10-6, Sat 10-3 (Fall/Winter); Mon-Fri 10-5, Sat 10-3 (Summer)
Restriction: Pub use on premises

PRIEST RIVER

P WEST BONNER LIBRARY DISTRICT*, 118 Main St, 83856-5059. SAN 303-6340. Tel: 208-448-2207. E-mail: library@westbonnerlibrary.org. Web Site: westbonner.lili.org. *Dir,* Katie Crill; Staff 4 (Non-MLS 4)
Founded 1926. Pop 8,800; Circ 42,690
Library Holdings: Bk Vols 21,958
Wireless access
Function: Adult literacy prog, For res purposes, ILL available, Photocopying/Printing, Prog for children & young adult, Summer reading prog, Telephone ref, Wheelchair accessible
Special Services for the Deaf - Bks on deafness & sign lang
Special Services for the Blind - Audio mat; Bks on CD; Large print bks; Talking bks
Open Mon, Wed & Fri 10-5, Tues & Thurs 10-7, Sat 10-2
Friends of the Library Group
Branches: 1
BLANCHARD BRANCH, 412 Railroad Ave, Blanchard, 83804. (Mail add: PO Box 27, Blanchard, 83804). Tel: 208-437-0801.
Founded 1926. Pop 8,000; Circ 32,000
Automation Activity & Vendor Info: (Cataloging) Koha; (Circulation) Koha; (Discovery) Koha; (ILL) OCLC WorldShare Interlibrary Loan; (OPAC) Koha
Function: 24/7 Electronic res, 24/7 Online cat, Activity rm, Adult bk club, Art programs, Audiobks via web, Bk club(s), Bks on CD, Children's prog, Computers for patron use, Digital talking bks, Electronic databases & coll, Free DVD rentals, ILL available, Internet access, Life-long learning prog for all ages, Magazines, Meeting rooms, Music CDs, Online cat, OverDrive digital audio bks, Photocopying/Printing, Preschool reading prog, Prog for adults, Prog for children & young adult, Serves people with intellectual disabilities, Spoken cassettes & CDs, STEM programs, Story hour, Summer & winter reading prog, Summer reading prog, Tax forms, Teen prog, Wheelchair accessible, Winter reading prog, Workshops
Open Mon & Thurs 11-5, Tues Noon-6, Wed 10-5, Sat 10-2
Friends of the Library Group

REXBURG

C BRIGHAM YOUNG UNIVERSITY-IDAHO*, David O McKay Library, 525 S Center St, 83460. SAN 303-6375. Tel: 208-496-9522. Interlibrary Loan Service Tel: 208-496-9524. Web Site: library.byui.edu. *Univ Librn,* Laurie Francis; Tel: 208-496-9510, E-mail: francisl@byui.edu; *Assoc Univ Librn, Pub Serv,* Holly Green; E-mail: greenh@byui.edu; *Acq & Ser Librn,* Debora Scholes; E-mail: scholesde@byui.edu; Staff 17 (MLS 10, Non-MLS 7)
Founded 1906. Enrl 13,368; Fac 603; Highest Degree: Bachelor
Library Holdings: Audiobooks 220; CDs 6,300; DVDs 1,600; e-books 432,000; e-journals 82,000; Electronic Media & Resources 336; Microforms 95,000; Music Scores 136,000; Bk Titles 157,000; Bk Vols 193,000; Per Subs 704; Videos 9,000
Special Collections: History of Writing (Scriptorium Coll); LDS Church Coll; Southeast Idaho Coll
Subject Interests: Genealogy
Automation Activity & Vendor Info: (Acquisitions) Horizon; (Cataloging) Horizon; (Circulation) Horizon; (Course Reserve) Horizon; (ILL) OCLC ILLiad; (OPAC) Horizon; (Serials) Horizon
Wireless access
Partic in LYRASIS; OCLC Online Computer Library Center, Inc
Open Mon-Thurs 7am-11:30pm, Fri 7am-9pm, Sat 9-9

P MADISON LIBRARY DISTRICT, 73 N Center St, 83440. SAN 303-6367. Tel: 208-356-3461. E-mail: askmadisonlibrary@madisonlib.org. Web Site: www.madisonlib.org. *Dir,* Valerie Lloyd; Tel: 208-356-341, Ext 10, E-mail: director@madisonlib.org; *Asst Dir, YA Librn,* Miranda Galbraith; Tel: 208-356-3461, Ext 26, E-mail: miranda.g@madisonlib.org; Staff 7 (MLS 2, Non-MLS 5)
Founded 1920. Pop 32,000; Circ 393,379
Library Holdings: Bk Titles 65,000; Per Subs 105
Subject Interests: Idaho
Automation Activity & Vendor Info: (Cataloging) Horizon; (Circulation) Horizon; (ILL) OCLC FirstSearch; (OPAC) Horizon
Wireless access
Partic in Library Consortium of Eastern Idaho
Open Mon-Thurs 9-8, Fri 10-6, Sat 10-4
Friends of the Library Group

RICHFIELD

P RICHFIELD DISTRICT LIBRARY*, 105 S Main St, 83349. (Mail add: PO Box 146, 83349-0146), SAN 303-6383. Tel: 208-487-1242. E-mail: richdislib@gmail.com. Web Site: richfield.lili.org. *Dir,* Cheryl Patterson
Pop 1,050; Circ 3,373
Library Holdings: AV Mats 250; Bk Vols 10,000
Wireless access
Function: Bks on cassette, Bks on CD, CD-ROM, Children's prog, Computers for patron use, Digital talking bks, Free DVD rentals, ILL available, Photocopying/Printing, Summer reading prog, VHS videos
Open Mon 2-6, Tues 10-6, Wed & Thurs 12-6

RIGBY

P RIGBY PUBLIC LIBRARY*, 110 N State St, 83442. (Mail add: PO Box 328, 83442), SAN 303-6391. Tel: 208-745-8231. FAX: 208-745-8231. E-mail: rcity1@ida.net. Web Site: www.rigby.lili.org. *Dir,* Marilynn Kamoe; *Asst Dir,* Bari Trost
Founded 1948. Pop 3,000; Circ 93,306
Library Holdings: Bk Vols 26,000; Per Subs 31
Automation Activity & Vendor Info: (Cataloging) SirsiDynix; (Circulation) SirsiDynix; (OPAC) SirsiDynix
Partic in Library Consortium of Eastern Idaho
Open Tues & Thurs 11-7, Wed & Fri 11-5, Sat 11-3
Friends of the Library Group

RIGGINS

P SALMON RIVER PUBLIC LIBRARY*, 126 N Main St, 83549. (Mail add: PO Box 249, 83549-0249). Tel: 208-628-3394. FAX: 208-628-3792. E-mail: srplinfo@frontiernet.net. Web Site: rigginsidaho.org/library.html. *Dir,* Susan Hollenbeak
Library Holdings: Bk Titles 10,000; Bk Vols 13,000
Automation Activity & Vendor Info: (Cataloging) Follett Software; (Circulation) Follett Software; (OPAC) Follett Software
Wireless access
Open Mon-Fri 10-5
Friends of the Library Group

RIRIE

P RIRIE CITY LIBRARY*, 464 Main St, 83443. (Mail add: PO Box 97, 83443-0097). Tel: 208-538-7974. FAX: 208-538-7974. E-mail: ririelibrary@yahoo.com. Web Site: ririelibrary.lili.org. *Dir,* Wendy Mullins
Pop 545; Circ 6,315
Library Holdings: AV Mats 101; Bk Vols 11,000
Automation Activity & Vendor Info: (Cataloging) Follett Software; (Circulation) Follett Software; (OPAC) Follett Software
Wireless access
Open Mon, Tues, Thurs & Fri 1-5, Wed 11-5
Friends of the Library Group

ROBERTS

P ROBERTS CITY LIBRARY, (Formerly Roberts Public Library), 2870 E 650 N, 83444. Tel: 208-228-2210. E-mail: robertslibrary@gmail.com. Web Site: www.roberts.lili.org. *Libr Dir,* April Galbraith
Library Holdings: DVDs 150; Bk Vols 10,000
Automation Activity & Vendor Info: (Cataloging) Koha; (Circulation) Koha; (OPAC) Koha
Wireless access
Open Mon & Wed 2-6, Fri & Sat 11-3

ROCKLAND

P ROCKLAND SCHOOL COMMUNITY LIBRARY*, 321 E Center St, 83271. (Mail add: PO Box 119, 83271-0119), SAN 303-6405. Tel: 208-548-2221, Ext 2. FAX: 208-548-2224. E-mail: library@rbulldogs.org. *Libr Dir,* Hanalorraine Miller
Founded 1974. Pop 450; Circ 17,500
Library Holdings: Bk Vols 12,354; Per Subs 33
Automation Activity & Vendor Info: (Cataloging) ComPanion Corp; (Circulation) ComPanion Corp
Wireless access
Function: Accelerated reader prog, Children's prog, Computers for patron use, Electronic databases & coll, Equip loans & repairs, Family literacy, For res purposes, Free DVD rentals, Instruction & testing, Internet access, Laminating, Learning ctr, Magnifiers for reading, Online ref, Photocopying/Printing, Preschool reading prog, Prog for children & young adult, Ref & res, Scanner, Spoken cassettes & CDs, STEM programs, Story hour, Summer & winter reading prog, Summer reading prog, Tax forms, Wheelchair accessible
Special Services for the Deaf - Bks on deafness & sign lang
Special Services for the Blind - Bks on CD; Blind Club (monthly newsletter); Copier with enlargement capabilities; Digital talking bk; Digital talking bk machines; Large print bks
Open Mon, Wed & Thurs 7:45-3:30, Tues 7:45-3:30 & 5-7
Restriction: Authorized patrons, Authorized personnel only, In-house use for visitors

RUPERT

P DEMARY MEMORIAL LIBRARY*, 417 Seventh St, 83350. SAN 303-6413. Tel: 208-436-3874. FAX: 208-436-9719. E-mail: demary@pmt.org. Web Site: demary.lili.org. *Dir,* Ms Shambry Emero; Staff 3.4 (Non-MLS 3.4)
Founded 1958. Pop 5,645; Circ 43,024
Library Holdings: Bk Vols 43,500; Per Subs 48
Special Collections: Idaho Coll; Local Archives
Wireless access
Open Mon-Fri 11-7, Sat 11-3
Friends of the Library Group

SAINT ANTHONY

P FREMONT COUNTY DISTRICT LIBRARY*, Saint Anthony Branch, 420 N Bridge, Ste E, 83445. Tel: 208-624-3192. FAX: 208-624-3192. E-mail: fcstalib@gmail.com. Web Site: www.fremont.lili.org. *District Dir,* Rashell Cardell
Founded 1920. Pop 3,182; Circ 47,924
Library Holdings: Bk Vols 16,000; Per Subs 30
Automation Activity & Vendor Info: (Cataloging) SirsiDynix; (Circulation) SirsiDynix; (OPAC) SirsiDynix
Open Mon-Thurs 10-6, Fri 10-5, Sat 10-1
Friends of the Library Group
Branches: 2
ASHTON BRANCH, 925 Main, Ashton, 83420. (Mail add: PO Box 854, Ashton, 83420-0854), SAN 303-5271. Tel: 208-652-7280. E-mail: ashlib@ida.net. Web Site: fremont.lili.org. *Dir,* Cardell Rashell; *Ch Serv,* Barbara Moon
Pop 11,719; Circ 16,658
Library Holdings: Bk Vols 17,000; Per Subs 26
Subject Interests: Rare bks
Automation Activity & Vendor Info: (Cataloging) SirsiDynix; (Circulation) SirsiDynix; (OPAC) SirsiDynix
Open Mon-Thurs 10-6, Fri 10-5, Sat 10-1
ISLAND PARK BRANCH, 3350 Hwy 20, Island Park, 83429. (Mail add: PO Box 134, Macks Inn, 83433). Tel: 208-558-0991. E-mail: Iplibrary1@gmail.com. *District Dir,* Rashell Cardell
Library Holdings: Bk Vols 7,450
Automation Activity & Vendor Info: (Cataloging) SirsiDynix; (Circulation) SirsiDynix; (OPAC) SirsiDynix
Open Tues-Thurs (May-Oct) 10-6, Fri 10-5, Sat 10-1; Thurs-Sat (Nov-April) 10-4
Friends of the Library Group

S JUVENILE CORRECTION CENTER LIBRARY*, 2220 E 600 North, 83445. Tel: 208-624-3462. FAX: 208-624-0973. Web Site: www.idjc.idaho.gov. *Librn,* Lorene Hall; E-mail: lorene.hall@idjc.idaho.gov
Library Holdings: Bk Vols 5,000
Open Mon-Fri 8-2

SAINT MARIES

P SAINT MARIES PUBLIC LIBRARY*, 822 College Ave, 83861. SAN 303-643X. Tel: 208-245-3732. FAX: 208-245-7102. E-mail: smlibrary@smgazette.com. Web Site: stmarieslibrary.lili.org. *Librn,* Ms Pinky Humphrey
Founded 1912. Pop 2,872; Circ 23,811
Library Holdings: Bk Vols 15,500; Per Subs 36
Automation Activity & Vendor Info: (Cataloging) Ex Libris Group; (Circulation) Ex Libris Group; (OPAC) Ex Libris Group
Wireless access
Open Mon 10-5, Tues & Fri 12-5, Thurs 12-7, Sat 9-2
Friends of the Library Group

SALMON

P SALMON PUBLIC LIBRARY*, 300 Main St, 83467-4111. SAN 303-6456. Tel: 208-756-2311. FAX: 208-756-2444. E-mail: salmonlibrary1@gmail.com. Web Site: www.salmonlibrary.org. *Libr Dir,* Ramona Stauffer; Staff 1 (Non-MLS 1)
Founded 1916. Pop 7,806; Circ 51,922
Library Holdings: AV Mats 689; Large Print Bks 489; Bk Vols 22,722; Per Subs 60
Special Collections: Idaho Territorial & State Census Coll (1870-1930), microfilm; Lemhi Indian Agency Records, microfilm; Lewis & Clark Coll; Local Newspaper Coll (1882-2004), microfilm. Oral History
Automation Activity & Vendor Info: (Cataloging) SirsiDynix; (Circulation) SirsiDynix; (OPAC) SirsiDynix
Wireless access
Publications: History of Lemhi County
Partic in Library Consortium of Eastern Idaho
Open Mon-Wed 10-6, Thurs 10-7, Fri & Sat 10-5
Friends of the Library Group

SANDPOINT

S BONNER COUNTY HISTORICAL SOCIETY*, Research Library, 611 S Ella Ave, 83864. SAN 323-5378. Tel: 208-263-2344. E-mail: bcmuseum@frontier.com. Web Site: www.bonnercountyhistory.org. *Dir,* Olivia Luther; *Curator,* Heather Upton; E-mail: bchscuratorial@frontier.com
Founded 1972
Library Holdings: Bk Titles 1,000
Special Collections: Bonner County newspapers, 1891-present; Bonner County School Records, historic photos. Oral History
Subject Interests: Family hist, Idaho
Wireless access
Publications: Beautiful Bonner History & Memories, Vol 2; Beautiful Bonner History of Bonner County, Idaho; Morton Memories, History of Morton Community, Bonner County, Idaho
Open Tues-Fri 10-4

P EAST BONNER COUNTY LIBRARY DISTRICT*, 1407 Cedar St, 83864-2052. SAN 303-6464. Tel: 208-263-6930. Circulation Tel: 208-263-6930, Ext 1257. Reference Tel: 208-263-6930, Ext 1209. Administration Tel: 208-263-6930, Ext 1208. Automation Services Tel: 208-263-6930, Ext 1202. FAX: 208-263-8320. E-mail: infodesk@ebonnerlibrary.org. Web Site: ebonnerlibrary.org, www.ebcl.lib.id.us. *Dir,* Ann Nichols; E-mail: ann@ebonnerlibrary.org; *Adult Programming, Coordr,* Mike Bauer; *Teen Prog, Teen Serv,* Kimber Glidden; *Youth & Teen Serv,* Kimber Glidden
Founded 1912. Pop 34,500; Circ 490,944
Library Holdings: AV Mats 25,464; Large Print Bks 4,719; Bk Vols 77,468; Per Subs 215
Special Collections: Pacific Northwest (Northwest Coll). State Document Depository
Automation Activity & Vendor Info: (Acquisitions) TLC (The Library Corporation); (Cataloging) TLC (The Library Corporation); (Circulation) TLC (The Library Corporation); (Course Reserve) TLC (The Library Corporation); (ILL) TLC (The Library Corporation); (OPAC) TLC (The Library Corporation)
Wireless access
Function: Homebound delivery serv, ILL available, Prog for children & young adult, Summer reading prog, Wheelchair accessible
Special Services for the Blind - Videos on blindness & physical disabilties
Open Mon-Thurs (Winter) 9-8, Fri & Sat 10-5; Mon-Thurs (Summer) 9-7, Fri & Sat 10-5
Friends of the Library Group
Branches: 1
CLARK FORK BRANCH, 601 Main St, Clark Fork, 83811. (Mail add: PO Box 219, Clark Fork, 83811-0219), SAN 328-6991. Tel: 208-266-1321. FAX: 208-266-1663.
Function: Adult bk club, Art exhibits, Bks on CD, Children's prog, Citizenship assistance, Computer training, Computers for patron use, Digital talking bks, Electronic databases & coll, Free DVD rentals, Home delivery & serv to seniorr ctr & nursing homes, Homebound delivery serv, Homework prog, ILL available, Instruction & testing, Learning ctr, Magnifiers for reading, Mail & tel request accepted, Music CDs, Notary serv, Online cat, Online info literacy tutorials on the web & in blackboard, Outreach serv, Outside serv via phone, mail, e-mail & web, OverDrive digital audio bks, Photocopying/Printing, Preschool outreach,

Printer for laptops & handheld devices, Prog for adults, Prog for children & young adult, Ref & res, Ref serv available, Res libr, Scanner, Senior computer classes, Senior outreach, Spoken cassettes & CDs, Spoken cassettes & DVDs, Story hour, Summer & winter reading prog, Summer reading prog, Tax forms, Teen prog, Telephone ref, Wheelchair accessible, Winter reading prog
Special Services for the Blind - Audio mat
Open Mon-Thurs 10-6, Fri & Sat 10-5
Friends of the Library Group

SHELLEY

P NORTH BINGHAM COUNTY DISTRICT LIBRARY*, 197 W Locust St, 83274-1139. SAN 303-6472. Tel: 208-357-7801. FAX: 208-357-2272. Web Site: northbingham.lili.org/. *Librn,* Heidi Riddoch; E-mail: hriddoch@cableone.net; Staff 1 (Non-MLS 1)
Pop 11,000; Circ 150,000
Library Holdings: AV Mats 1,000; Bk Vols 50,000; Talking Bks 600
Subject Interests: Local hist
Automation Activity & Vendor Info: (Cataloging) SirsiDynix
Open Mon, Tues, Thurs & Fri 10-6, Wed 10-8, Sat 10-2
Friends of the Library Group

SHOSHONE

P SHOSHONE PUBLIC LIBRARY*, 211 S Rail St W, 83352-0236. SAN 303-6499. Tel: 208-886-2843. FAX: 208-886-2426. E-mail: library@shoshonecity.com. Web Site: shoshone.lili.org. *Dir,* Catherine Tanner; E-mail: ctanner@shoshonecity.com; Staff 3 (MLS 1, Non-MLS 2)
Pop 2,312; Circ 22,678
Library Holdings: Bks on Deafness & Sign Lang 10; Bk Titles 16,000; Per Subs 20
Special Collections: Idaho History
Subject Interests: Popular mat
Wireless access
Open Mon & Fri 12-5, Tues 2-7, Wed 12-7, Thurs 10-4
Friends of the Library Group

SODA SPRINGS

P SODA SPRINGS PUBLIC LIBRARY*, 149 S Main, 83276. SAN 303-6502. Tel: 208-547-2606. FAX: 208-547-2606. E-mail: sspl@sodaspringsid.com. Web Site: soda.lili.org. *Dir,* Cindy Erickson; *Ch,* Dorajo Messerly; Staff 2 (Non-MLS 2)
Founded 1951. Pop 3,600; Circ 51,000
Library Holdings: Bks on Deafness & Sign Lang 12; High Interest/Low Vocabulary Bk Vols 100; Bk Vols 38,000; Per Subs 70
Special Collections: Idaho History (Southeast Idaho-especially Caribou County); Literature (Vardis Fisher Coll); Oregon Trail Newspapers (Caribou County Sun)
Subject Interests: Idaho
Automation Activity & Vendor Info: (Cataloging) SirsiDynix; (Circulation) SirsiDynix; (OPAC) SirsiDynix
Wireless access
Partic in Library Consortium of Eastern Idaho
Open Mon-Thurs 9-7, Fri 10-5
Friends of the Library Group

STANLEY

P STANLEY COMMUNITY PUBLIC LIBRARY, 240 Niece Ave, 83278. (Mail add: PO Box 230, 83278-0230). Tel: 208-774-2470. FAX: 208-774-2471. E-mail: stanley.id.library@gmail.com. Web Site: stanley.lili.org. *Libr Dir,* Jane Somerville
Automation Activity & Vendor Info: (Cataloging) Innovative Interfaces, Inc; (Circulation) Innovative Interfaces, Inc; (ILL) OCLC Online; (OPAC) Innovative Interfaces, Inc
Wireless access
Partic in Library Consortium of Eastern Idaho
Open Mon & Thurs 12-6, Tues & Wed 12-4, Fri & Sat 10-6
Friends of the Library Group

SUGAR CITY

P SUGAR-SALEM SCHOOL COMMUNITY LIBRARY*, One Digger Dr, 83448. SAN 303-6529. Tel: 208-356-0271. Web Site: www.sugarlib.org. *Libr Dir,* Cami Dodson; E-mail: cdodson@sugarsalem.com; Staff 1 (Non-MLS 1)
Pop 4,012
Library Holdings: Bk Vols 24,800; Per Subs 65; Videos 420
Automation Activity & Vendor Info: (Cataloging) Innovative Interfaces, Inc; (Circulation) Innovative Interfaces, Inc; (OPAC) Innovative Interfaces, Inc
Wireless access
Partic in Library Consortium of Eastern Idaho
Open Mon-Thurs 7:30-7, Fri 7:30-5, Sat 10-2 (Fall-Spring); Mon, Tues & Fri 10-2, Wed & Thurs 2-6 (Summer)

TERRETON

P HEART OF THE VALLEY PUBLIC LIBRARY*, 1252 E 1500 N, 83450. (Mail add: PO Box 45, 83450-0045), SAN 377-5429. Tel: 208-663-4834. FAX: 208-663-4834. E-mail: hvpl@mudlake.net. Web Site: heart.lili.org. *Dir,* Elaine Davies
Library Holdings: Bk Vols 21,000
Automation Activity & Vendor Info: (Cataloging) SirsiDynix; (Circulation) SirsiDynix; (OPAC) SirsiDynix
Mem of Jefferson County District Library
Open Mon, Tues, Thurs & Fri (Winter) 9-4, Wed 9-6; Tues & Thurs (Summer) 10-5, Wed 1-7
Friends of the Library Group

TWIN FALLS

J COLLEGE OF SOUTHERN IDAHO LIBRARY*, 315 Falls Ave, 83301-3367. (Mail add: PO Box 1238, 83303-1238), SAN 303-6545. Tel: 208-732-6500. Interlibrary Loan Service Tel: 208-732-6503. Reference Tel: 208-732-6504. Administration Tel: 208-732-6501. FAX: 208-736-3087. Web Site: www.csi.edu/library. *Dept Chair, Libr Dir,* Dr Teri Fattig; E-mail: tfattig@csi.edu; *Ref (Info Servs),* Stephen Poppino; E-mail: spoppino@csi.edu; Staff 7 (MLS 3, Non-MLS 4)
Founded 1965. Enrl 6,896; Fac 496; Highest Degree: Bachelor
Library Holdings: AV Mats 5,311; Bk Titles 62,901; Bk Vols 69,000; Per Subs 312
Automation Activity & Vendor Info: (Cataloging) SirsiDynix; (Circulation) SirsiDynix; (Course Reserve) SirsiDynix; (OPAC) SirsiDynix; (Serials) SirsiDynix
Wireless access
Function: 24/7 Electronic res, 24/7 Online cat, Audio & video playback equip for onsite use, Audiobks on Playaways & MP3, Audiobks via web, Bks on CD, CD-ROM, Computers for patron use, Electronic databases & coll, Free DVD rentals, ILL available, Instruction & testing, Internet access, Magazines, Magnifiers for reading, Music CDs, Online cat, Online info literacy tutorials on the web & in blackboard, Orientations, Photocopying/Printing, Ref & res, Ref serv available, Res assist avail, Scanner, Study rm, Telephone ref, Wheelchair accessible
Open Mon-Thurs (Fall & Spring) 7:30am-10pm, Fri 7:30-6, Sat & Sun 10-5; Mon, Wed & Fri (Summer & Winter) 7:30-5, Tues & Thurs 7:30am-8pm, Sat 10-5

P TWIN FALLS PUBLIC LIBRARY, 201 Fourth Ave E, 83301-6397. SAN 303-6561. Tel: 208-733-2964. FAX: 208-733-2965. E-mail: tfpl@twinfallspubliclibrary.org. Web Site: www.twinfallspubliclibrary.org. *Dir,* Tara Bartley; E-mail: tbartley@twinfallspubliclibrary.org; *Admin/Personnel Mgr,* Karolee Sorenson; E-mail: ksorenson@twinfallspubliclibrary.org; *Head, Adult Serv, Head, Ref, ILL Supvr,* Jennifer Hill; E-mail: jhill@twinfallspubliclibrary.org; *Head, Circ Serv,* Jill Fleming; E-mail: jfleming@twinfallspubliclibrary.org; *Head, Outreach Serv,* Katie Johnson; E-mail: kjohnson@twinfallspubliclibrary.org; *Head, Youth Serv,* Erica Littlefield; E-mail: elittlefield@twinfallspubliclibrary.org; *Cat, Tech Serv Supvr,* Kathleen Lambert; E-mail: klambert@twinfallspubliclibrary.org; *Computer Support Spec,* Adam Day; E-mail: aday@twinfallspubliclibrary.org; Staff 10 (MLS 8, Non-MLS 2)
Founded 1909. Pop 44,564; Circ 464,343
Library Holdings: Bk Vols 170,629; Per Subs 411
Special Collections: Early Local Photography (Bisbee Coll); Idaho & Pacific Northwest History Coll; Large Print Coll; Pacific Northwest Americana Coll. State Document Depository
Subject Interests: Agr, Bus & mgt, Hist
Automation Activity & Vendor Info: (Acquisitions) Innovative Interfaces, Inc; (Cataloging) Innovative Interfaces, Inc; (Circulation) Innovative Interfaces, Inc; (OPAC) Innovative Interfaces, Inc; (Serials) Innovative Interfaces, Inc
Wireless access
Function: Activity rm, Adult bk club, After school storytime, Audio & video playback equip for onsite use, Audiobks on Playaways & MP3, Audiobks via web, Bks on CD, Children's prog, Computer training, Computers for patron use, E-Readers, Electronic databases & coll, Free DVD rentals, Home delivery & serv to seniorr ctr & nursing homes, ILL available, Internet access, Magazines, Mango lang, Meeting rooms, Microfiche/film & reading machines, Music CDs, Notary serv, Online cat, Outreach serv, Outside serv via phone, mail, e-mail & web, OverDrive digital audio bks, Photocopying/Printing, Preschool outreach, Printer for laptops & handheld devices, Prog for children & young adult, Senior computer classes, Senior outreach, Serves people with intellectual disabilities, Spanish lang bks, Story hour, Summer reading prog, Teen prog, Wheelchair accessible, Workshops
Partic in LYNX! Consortium

Open Mon-Thurs 9-9, Fri & Sat 10-6
Bookmobiles: 1. Outreach Librn, Katie Volle. Bk vols 473

VICTOR

P VALLEY OF THE TETONS DISTRICT LIBRARY*, 56 N Main, 83455. (Mail add: PO Box 37, 83455-0037), SAN 303-657X. Tel: 208-787-2201. FAX: 208-787-2204. E-mail: library@silverstar.com. Web Site: www.tetons.lili.org. *Dir,* Chris Johnson; Staff 9 (MLS 1, Non-MLS 8)
Founded 1966. Pop 10,275; Circ 73,324
Oct 2015-Sept 2016 Income $509,862, State $26,624, Locally Generated Income $467,844, Other $15,394. Mats Exp $431,854, Books $33,893, Per/Ser (Incl. Access Fees) $82, Electronic Ref Mat (Incl. Access Fees) $51. Sal $251,610 (Prof $298,589)
Library Holdings: Audiobooks 33,893; DVDs 3,717; Large Print Bks 618; Bk Titles 33,893; Per Subs 82
Automation Activity & Vendor Info: (Cataloging) Follett Software; (Circulation) Follett Software; (OPAC) Follett Software
Wireless access
Function: 24/7 Electronic res, 24/7 Online cat, Activity rm, Archival coll, Audio & video playback equip for onsite use, Audiobks on Playaways & MP3, Audiobks via web, Bk club(s), Bks on cassette, Bks on CD, Children's prog, Computers for patron use, Digital talking bks, Doc delivery serv, E-Readers, Electronic databases & coll, Free DVD rentals, ILL available, Instruction & testing, Internet access, Laminating, Magazines, Mail & tel request accepted, Meeting rooms, Microfiche/film & reading machines, Music CDs, Online cat, Online info literacy tutorials on the web & in blackboard, OverDrive digital audio bks, Photocopying/Printing, Preschool reading prog, Prog for children & young adult, Ref serv available, Scanner, Spanish lang bks, Spoken cassettes & CDs, Story hour, Study rm, Summer reading prog, Tax forms, Teen prog, Wheelchair accessible, Writing prog
Partic in Association for Rural & Small Libraries
Special Services for the Blind - Talking bk serv referral
Open Mon-Fri 10-6, Sat 10-2
Friends of the Library Group

WALLACE

P WALLACE PUBLIC LIBRARY*, 415 River St, 83873. SAN 303-6596. Tel: 208-752-4571. FAX: 208-752-4571. E-mail: wallacelibrary@yahoo.com. Web Site: wallace.lili.org. *Dir,* Annette Kologi
Founded 1902. Pop 1,010; Circ 14,154
Library Holdings: Bk Titles 16,367; Per Subs 30
Special Collections: Idaho & Pacific Northwestern History, bks, microfiche, microfilm, slides; Large Print Coll; Scandinavian History & Literature
Automation Activity & Vendor Info: (Cataloging) Ex Libris Group; (Circulation) Ex Libris Group; (OPAC) Ex Libris Group
Publications: Booklist
Open Mon & Thurs 12-8, Tues, Wed & Fri 12-5:30

WEIPPE

P CLEARWATER COUNTY FREE LIBRARY DISTRICT*, Weippe Public Library, 204 Wood St, 83553. (Mail add: PO Box 435, 83553-0435). Tel: 208-435-4058. FAX: 208-435-4374. E-mail: weippelibrary@weippe.com. Web Site: ccfldatweippe.lili.org. *Dir,* Terri Summerfield; *Youth Serv,* Jenni Tissel
Founded 1956
Library Holdings: Bk Vols 8,000; Per Subs 45
Automation Activity & Vendor Info: (Cataloging) Ex Libris Group; (Circulation) Ex Libris Group; (OPAC) Ex Libris Group
Wireless access
Function: ILL available, Photocopying/Printing
Open Mon, Thurs & Fri 10-5, Tues & Wed 10-7, Sat 10-1
Friends of the Library Group

WEISER

P WEISER PUBLIC LIBRARY, 628 E First St, 83672-2241. SAN 303-660X. Tel: 208-549-1243. Web Site: weiserlibrary.net. *Dir,* Kimbra Long; E-mail: librarydirector@cityofweiser.com
Founded 1890. Pop 4,900; Circ 40,000
Library Holdings: DVDs 300; Large Print Bks 200; Bk Titles 26,000; Per Subs 40
Automation Activity & Vendor Info: (Acquisitions) Follett Software; (Cataloging) Follett Software; (Circulation) Follett Software; (Course Reserve) Follett Software
Wireless access
Open Mon-Fri 9-6
Friends of the Library Group

WENDELL

P WENDELL PUBLIC LIBRARY, 375 First Ave E, 83355. SAN 303-6618. Tel: 208-536-6195. E-mail: wendellcitylibrary@wendell.id.gov. *Dir,* Annie Burke
Pop 2,338; Circ 18,000
Library Holdings: Bk Vols 20,000
Wireless access
Open Mon-Fri 10-5

WHITEBIRD

P WHITEBIRD COMMUNITY LIBRARY*, 245 River St, 83554. Tel: 208-839-2805. E-mail: whitebirdlib@gmail.com. Web Site: visitwhitebird.com/library. *Mgr,* Leah Harvey
Library Holdings: Bk Vols 5,500
Wireless access
Open Tues & Sat 10-1, Thurs 1-4

WILDER

P WILDER PUBLIC LIBRARY DISTRICT*, 111 Second St, 83676-6099. (Mail add: PO Box 128, 83676-0128), SAN 303-6626. Tel: 208-482-7880. FAX: 208-482-7880. E-mail: wpl@cableone.net. *Librn,* Susan Waldemer
Founded 1978. Pop 3,958; Circ 9,467
Library Holdings: Bk Vols 27,070
Wireless access
Partic in Canyon Owyhee Library Group, Ltd
Open Mon, Tues & Thurs 11-5:30, Fri 12-5, Sat 10-1
Friends of the Library Group

ILLINOIS

Date of Statistics: FY 2021
Population, 2020 U.S. Census: 12,812,508
Population Served by Tax-Supported Public Libraries: 11,831,674
Total Volumes in Public Libraries: 36,889,960 (books plus serials)
Volumes Per Capita: 2.9
Volumes Per Capita Served: 3.0
Total Public Library Circulation Transactions: 96,903,701
Circulation Transactions Per Capita: 7.6
Circulation Transactions Per Capita Served: 8.0
Digital Resources:
6,712 total electronic collections (includes 16 statewide database collections)
Total e-books: 51,032,620
Total audio items (physical and downloadable units): 28,175,450
Total video items (physical and downloadable units): 6,433,528
Total computers for use by the public: 14,773
Total annual wireless sessions: 12,772,855
Total Non-book Resources Held: 34,608,978 (audio plus video)
Income and Expenditures:
Total Public Library Income (including some State & Federal Grants & Capital Income): $931,045,176
Source of Income: Primarily property tax
Total Operating Expenditures: $797,799,457
Expenditures Per Capita: $62.0
Expenditures Per Capita Served: $67.0
Number of System (Regional Libraries): 2 multi-type; 1 public
Number of Central Public Libraries: 642
Counties Served: 102 whole or partial
Grants, awarded & monitored: 1,976 grants for $67,740,980.23 (Grants to all types of libraries including state funds, CARES Act funds, LSTA and other federal funds)
Information provided courtesy of: Patricia Burg, State Data Coordinator; Library Development Group, Illinois State Library

ABINGDON

P JOHN MOSSER PUBLIC LIBRARY DISTRICT*, 106 W Meek St, 61410-1451. SAN 303-6634. Tel: 309-462-3129. FAX: 309-462-3129. E-mail: j_mosser_pld@hotmail.com. Web Site: johnmosserpubliclibrary.com. *Dir,* Jamie Lynn Beil; *Youth Librn,* Michelle L Dunbar; *Asst Librn,* Jenna Dean; *Asst Librn,* Carol Holliday; *Asst Librn,* Marcy Koller; Staff 4 (Non-MLS 4)
Founded 1895. Pop 3,300; Circ 20,500
Library Holdings: Bk Titles 22,618; Bk Vols 23,966; Per Subs 43
Special Collections: Abingdon Pottery Coll; County Histories; Cramer Coll, miniature vases; DAR Lineages from 1900; Hedding College Coll, memorabilia; Mosser Coll
Subject Interests: Genealogy
Wireless access
Open Tues & Fri 10-5, Wed 10-7, Sat 10-1
Friends of the Library Group

ADDISON

P ADDISON PUBLIC LIBRARY*, Four Friendship Plaza, 60101. SAN 303-6642. Tel: 630-543-3617. Reference Tel: 630-458-3318. FAX: 630-543-6645. E-mail: director@addisonlibrary.org. Web Site: www.addisonlibrary.org. *Libr Dir,* Mary A Medjo-Me-Zengue; Tel: 630-458-3300, E-mail: medjo@addisonlibrary.org; *Asst Dir, Head, Mat Mgt,* Brooke Sievers; Tel: 630-458-3329, E-mail: sievers@addisonlibrary.org; *Dept Head, Adult Serv,* Michael Monahan; Tel: 630-458-3314, E-mail: monahan@addisonlibrary.org; *Head, Children's Servx,* Louise Dimick; E-mail: dimick@addisonlibrary.org; *Head, Community Engagement,* Kathy Welko; E-mail: welko@addisonlibrary.org; *Head, Guest Serv,* Jenny Cuevas; E-mail: cuevas@addsionlibrary.org; *Head, Info Tech,* Yabin Liu; Tel: 630-458-3350, E-mail: liu@addisonlibrary.org; *Head, Teen Serv,* Elizabeth Lynch; E-mail: lynch@addisonlibrary.org; *Soc Serv Librn,* Marcella Hernandez; E-mail: mhernandez@addisonlibrary.org; *Coord, Coll Develop,* Karen Dini; E-mail: dini@addisonlibrary.org; *Communications Coordr, Mkt,* Emily Glimco; Tel: 630-458-3303, E-mail: glimco@addisonlibrary.org; *Digital Serv Coordr,* Ben Eggler; Tel: 630-458-3354, E-mail: eggler@addisonlibrary.org; Staff 70 (MLS 18, Non-MLS 52)
Founded 1962. Pop 36,946
Automation Activity & Vendor Info: (Acquisitions) Innovative Interfaces, Inc - Sierra; (Cataloging) Innovative Interfaces, Inc - Sierra; (Circulation) Innovative Interfaces, Inc - Sierra; (Serials) Innovative Interfaces, Inc - Sierra
Wireless access
Function: 24/7 Electronic res, 24/7 Online cat, 3D Printer, Activity rm, Adult bk club, Adult literacy prog, Art exhibits, Audiobks on Playaways & MP3, Audiobks via web, AV serv, Bilingual assistance for Spanish patrons, Bk club(s), Bks on CD, Children's prog, Citizenship assistance, Computer training, Computers for patron use, Digital talking bks, Distance learning, E-Reserves, Electronic databases & coll, Family literacy, Free DVD rentals, Holiday prog, Home delivery & serv to seniorr ctr & nursing homes, Homebound delivery serv, Homework prog, ILL available, Instruction & testing, Internet access, Laminating, Life-long learning prog for all ages, Literacy & newcomer serv, Magazines, Makerspace, Mango lang, Meeting rooms, Movies, Music CDs, Notary serv, Online cat, Online ref, Outreach serv, OverDrive digital audio bks, Photocopying/Printing, Preschool outreach, Preschool reading prog, Printer for laptops & handheld devices, Prof lending libr, Prog for adults, Prog for children & young adult, Ref serv available, Scanner, Senior computer classes, Senior outreach, Serves people with intellectual disabilities, Spanish lang bks, Story hour, Study rm, Summer & winter reading prog, Summer reading prog, Tax forms, Teen prog, Telephone ref, Wheelchair accessible, Winter reading prog, Workshops, Writing prog
Mem of Reaching Across Illinois Library System (RAILS)
Partic in Marmot Library Network
Open Mon-Thurs 9-9, Fri & Sat 9-5, Sun 1-5
Friends of the Library Group

ALBANY

P ALBANY PUBLIC LIBRARY*, 302 S Main St, 61230. (Mail add: PO Box 516, 61230-0516), SAN 376-0952. Tel: 309-887-4193. *Librn,* Susie Boston
Library Holdings: Bk Titles 6,000; Per Subs 15
Open Mon, Tues & Thurs 6pm-7pm, Sat 9:30-10:30
Friends of the Library Group

ALBION

P ALBION PUBLIC LIBRARY*, Six N Fourth St, 62806. SAN 303-6669. Tel: 618-445-3314. E-mail: albion.public@gmail.com. Web Site: www.albion.lib.il.us. *Dir,* Roxanna Behnke; E-mail: rbehnke59@gmail.com
Founded 1819. Pop 7,000; Circ 19,044
Library Holdings: Bk Vols 14,798; Per Subs 50
Wireless access
Mem of Illinois Heartland Library System
Open Tues 1-7, Wed-Fri 10-5, Sat 10-1
Friends of the Library Group

ALEDO

P EDWARDS RIVER PUBLIC LIBRARY DISTRICT*, 412 E Main St, 61231. SAN 303-6677. Tel: 309-582-2032. FAX: 309-582-5155. E-mail: edwardsriverlibrary@gmail.com. Web Site: edwardsriverpubliclibrary.blogspot.com. *Dir,* Courtney Wright; Staff 1 (MLS 1)
Founded 1915. Pop 4,826
Library Holdings: Bk Titles 16,000; Per Subs 45
Subject Interests: Local hist
Wireless access
Mem of Reaching Across Illinois Library System (RAILS)
Open Mon, Wed & Fri 9-6, Tues & Thurs 9-7, Sat 9-2
Friends of the Library Group

ALGONQUIN

P ALGONQUIN AREA PUBLIC LIBRARY DISTRICT*, 2600 Harnish Dr, 60102-5900. SAN 303-6685. Tel: 847-458-6060, 847-658-4343. FAX: 847-458-9370. Interlibrary Loan Service FAX: 847-458-9359. TDD: 847-458-9573. Web Site: www.aapld.org. *Dir,* Sara Murray; E-mail: smurray@aapld.org; *Br Mgr,* Steven Slavick; *Head, Adult Serv,* Patrice Pearsall; *Head, Youth Serv,* Alicia Parmele; *Teen/YA Librn,* Lindsey Tomsu; *Access Serv,* Gary Christopherson; Staff 62 (MLS 19, Non-MLS 43)
Founded 1921. Pop 40,809; Circ 749,430
Jul 2016-Jun 2017 Income (Main & Associated Libraries) $6,014,244, State $31,000, Locally Generated Income $5,933,244, Other $50,000
Library Holdings: DVDs 23,066; e-books 11,893; Bk Vols 171,704; Per Subs 400
Subject Interests: Local hist
Automation Activity & Vendor Info: (Acquisitions) SirsiDynix; (Cataloging) SirsiDynix; (Circulation) SirsiDynix; (Discovery) SirsiDynix; (OPAC) SirsiDynix
Wireless access
Function: 24/7 Electronic res, 24/7 Online cat, 3D Printer, Adult bk club, Art exhibits, Audiobks on Playaways & MP3, Audiobks via web, AV serv, Bi-weekly Writer's Group, Bilingual assistance for Spanish patrons, Bk club(s), Bks on CD, Children's prog, Computer training, Computers for patron use, E-Reserves, Electronic databases & coll, Free DVD rentals, Genealogy discussion group, Home delivery & serv to seniorr ctr & nursing homes, Homebound delivery serv, ILL available, Internet access, Life-long learning prog for all ages, Magazines, Mango lang, Meeting rooms, Microfiche/film & reading machines, Movies, Museum passes, Music CDs, Notary serv, Online cat, Online ref, Outreach serv, Outside serv via phone, mail, e-mail & web, OverDrive digital audio bks, Photocopying/Printing, Preschool outreach, Printer for laptops & handheld devices, Prog for adults, Prog for children & young adult, Ref & res, Ref serv available, Scanner, Senior outreach, Spanish lang bks, Story hour, Study rm, Summer & winter reading prog, Teen prog, Telephone ref, Wheelchair accessible, Writing prog
Publications: Library Leaves (Newsletter)
Mem of Reaching Across Illinois Library System (RAILS)
Partic in Cooperative Computer Services - CCS
Special Services for the Deaf - TDD equip
Open Mon-Thurs 9-9, Fri & Sat 9-5, Sun 12-5
Friends of the Library Group

ALSIP

P ALSIP-MERRIONETTE PARK PUBLIC LIBRARY DISTRICT*, 11960 S Pulaski Rd, 60803. SAN 303-6693. Tel: 708-371-5666. Interlibrary Loan Service Tel: 708-371-5666, Ext 139. E-mail: ampl@alsiplibrary.info. Web Site: www.alsiplibrary.info. *Dir,* Sarah Cottonaro; *Adult Serv Mgr,* Sue Pajor; E-mail: spajor@alsiplibrary.info; *Mgr, Youth Serv,* Amy Malysa; Tel: 708-371-5666, Ext 140, E-mail: amalysa@alsiplibrary.info; *Patron Serv,* Sandra Leyva; E-mail: sleyva@alsiplibrary.info; Staff 29.6 (MLS 8.5, Non-MLS 21.1)
Founded 1973. Pop 22,280; Circ 165,948
Library Holdings: CDs 6,947; DVDs 9,332; Bk Vols 96,633; Per Subs 279
Automation Activity & Vendor Info: (Acquisitions) Innovative Interfaces, Inc; (Cataloging) Innovative Interfaces, Inc; (Circulation) Innovative Interfaces, Inc; (OPAC) Innovative Interfaces, Inc
Wireless access
Publications: NewsAmpler (Newsletter)
Mem of Reaching Across Illinois Library System (RAILS)
Partic in System Wide Automated Network
Open Mon-Thurs 9-9, Fri & Sat 9-5, Sun 1-5

ALTAMONT

P ALTAMONT PUBLIC LIBRARY*, 121 W Washington Ave, 62411. SAN 303-6707. Tel: 618-483-5457. FAX: 618-483-5457. Web Site: www.altamontpubliclibrary.com. *Libr Dir,* Beth Speers; E-mail: apldirector@yahoo.com
Founded 1908. Pop 2,296; Circ 25,689
Library Holdings: Bk Vols 20,000; Per Subs 28
Wireless access
Mem of Illinois Heartland Library System
Open Mon-Wed 2-7, Thurs 5-8, Fri 2-6, Sat 9-1

ALTON

P HAYNER PUBLIC LIBRARY DISTRICT*, 326 Belle St, 62002. SAN 303-6723. Tel: 618-462-0677. FAX: 618-462-0665. Administration FAX: 618-462-4919. Web Site: www.haynerlibrary.org. *Exec Dir,* Bernadette Duvernoy; *Asst Dir, Circ,* Mary Cordes; *Ref Librn,* Sharon Schaefer; *Delivery Serv Mgr,* Esther Gillespie; *ILL Mgr,* Susan McConnell; *Vols Mgr,* Stephanie Munson; Staff 3 (MLS 3)
Founded 1891. Pop 58,155
Library Holdings: Bk Vols 208,267; Per Subs 374
Special Collections: Illinois History (Illinois Room), bks, microfilm, vf. Municipal Document Depository
Subject Interests: Hist
Automation Activity & Vendor Info: (Acquisitions) Innovative Interfaces, Inc; (Cataloging) Innovative Interfaces, Inc; (Circulation) Innovative Interfaces, Inc; (Course Reserve) Innovative Interfaces, Inc; (ILL) Innovative Interfaces, Inc; (Media Booking) Innovative Interfaces, Inc; (OPAC) Innovative Interfaces, Inc; (Serials) Innovative Interfaces, Inc
Wireless access
Publications: The Hayner Public Library District (Newsletter)
Mem of Illinois Heartland Library System
Open Mon-Thurs 8:30-8, Fri & Sat 8:30-5, Sun 1-6
Friends of the Library Group
Branches: 2
ALTON SQUARE, 132 Alton Sq, 62002-6115. E-mail: branch.library@haynerlibrary.org. *Libr Mgr,* Janet Schweppe
Open Mon-Sat 8:30am-9pm, Sun 12-5
GENEALOGY & LOCAL HISTORY, 401 State St, 62002-6113. *Libr Mgr,* Lacy McDonald
Open Mon, Tues, Thurs & Fri 8:30-5, Wed 12-7, Sat 8:30-1

ALTONA

P RANSOM MEMORIAL PUBLIC LIBRARY*, 110 E Main St, 61414. SAN 303-6758. Tel: 309-484-6193. E-mail: ransompl@mymctc.net. *Dir,* Donna Naslund; Staff 1 (Non-MLS 1)
Founded 1889. Pop 864; Circ 14,227
Library Holdings: Bk Vols 21,000; Per Subs 30
Wireless access
Function: ILL available
Mem of Reaching Across Illinois Library System (RAILS)
Open Mon, Wed & Thurs 1-6:30, Sat 9-12:30

AMBOY

P PANKHURST MEMORIAL LIBRARY, Three S Jefferson Ave, 61310-1400. SAN 303-6766. Tel: 815-857-3925. FAX: 815-857-3065. E-mail: pmlamboy@gmail.com. Web Site: www.amboy.lib.il.us. *Dir,* Emily Goff; Staff 3 (Non-MLS 3)
Founded 1928. Pop 2,561
Library Holdings: High Interest/Low Vocabulary Bk Vols 60; Bk Titles 19,280; Bk Vols 20,000; Per Subs 25
Wireless access
Mem of Reaching Across Illinois Library System (RAILS)
Partic in OWLSnet
Open Mon & Wed 11:30-6:30, Tues & Thurs 9-3, Fri & Sat 9-1
Friends of the Library Group

ANDALUSIA

P ANDALUSIA TOWNSHIP LIBRARY, 503 W Second St, 61232. (Mail add: PO Box 268, 61232-0268), SAN 303-6774. Tel: 309-798-2542. FAX: 309-798-2310. E-mail: and@andalusialibrary.org. Web Site: andalusialibrary.org. *Dir,* Leann Bredberg; Staff 2 (MLS 1, Non-MLS 1)
Pop 2,261; Circ 12,041
Library Holdings: Bk Vols 7,500; Per Subs 20
Wireless access
Mem of Reaching Across Illinois Library System (RAILS)
Open Mon-Thurs 1-7, Fri 2-6, Sat 9-1

ANNA

P STINSON MEMORIAL PUBLIC LIBRARY DISTRICT*, 409 S Main St, 62906. SAN 303-6790. Tel: 618-833-2521. FAX: 618-833-3560. Web Site: www.stinsonlibrary.org. *Interim Dir,* Beth Sisler; E-mail: bsisler@stinsonlibrary.org; *Asst Dir,* Thomas Sisler; Staff 11 (MLS 1, Non-MLS 10)
Founded 1914. Pop 15,408
Library Holdings: Bk Vols 32,658; Per Subs 44
Wireless access
Mem of Illinois Heartland Library System
Partic in Association for Rural & Small Libraries
Open Mon-Fri 10-6, Sat 10-3
Friends of the Library Group
Branches: 1
COBDEN BRANCH, 100 S Front St, Cobden, 62920. (Mail add: 409 S Main St, 62906). Tel: 618-893-4637. FAX: 618-893-4637.
Open Tues 2-6, Thurs 9-Noon

ANNAWAN

P ANNAWAN-ALBA TOWNSHIP LIBRARY*, 200 N Meadow Lane, Ste 2, 61234-7607. SAN 303-6804. Tel: 309-935-6483. FAX: 309-935-6483. Web Site: www.annawanil.org/library.html. *Head Librn,* Michele Thurston; E-mail: thurstonm2003@gmail.com; *Asst Librn,* Renee Jackson
Founded 1930. Pop 1,332; Circ 25,989

Library Holdings: Bk Vols 13,320; Per Subs 27
Wireless access
Mem of Reaching Across Illinois Library System (RAILS)
Open Mon 1-5, Tues & Fri 9-12 & 1-5, Wed 1-7, Sat 9-3
Friends of the Library Group

ANTIOCH

P ANTIOCH PUBLIC LIBRARY DISTRICT*, 757 Main St, 60002. SAN 303-6812. Tel: 847-395-0874. FAX: 847-395-5399. TDD: 847-395-0916. *Dir,* Jennifer Drinka; Tel: 847-395-0874, Ext 9051, E-mail: jdrinka@apld.info; *Ch Serv,* Kim Zupkoff; Tel: 847-395-0874, Ext 9064, E-mail: kzupkoff@apld.info; *Circ,* Lynn Floyd; Tel: 847-395-0874, Ext 9058, E-mail: lfloyd@apld.info; *Ref (Info Servs),* Amy Blue; Tel: 847-395-0874, Ext 9059, E-mail: ablue@apld.info; *Tech Serv,* Jennifer Norris; Tel: 847-395-0874, Ext 9057, E-mail: jnorris@apld.info; Staff 5 (MLS 3, Non-MLS 2)
Founded 1921. Pop 26,111
Library Holdings: Audiobooks 9,557; CDs 12,951; DVDs 15,315; e-books 6,163; e-journals 65; Microforms 168; Bk Titles 122,716; Bk Vols 123,009; Per Subs 168; Videos 5,129
Subject Interests: City hist, Cooking, Craft, Games, Parenting
Automation Activity & Vendor Info: (Cataloging) TLC (The Library Corporation); (Circulation) TLC (The Library Corporation); (ILL) OCLC; (OPAC) TLC (The Library Corporation); (Serials) OCLC
Wireless access
Mem of Reaching Across Illinois Library System (RAILS)
Open Mon-Thurs 9-9, Fri & Sat 9-5, Sun 1-5
Friends of the Library Group

ARCOLA

P ARCOLA PUBLIC LIBRARY DISTRICT*, 407 E Main St, 61910. SAN 303-6820. Tel: 217-268-4477. FAX: 217-268-4478. E-mail: arcolapl@consolidated.net. Web Site: www.arcola.lib.il.us. *Dir,* Cheryl Switzer; Staff 4 (Non-MLS 4)
Founded 1904. Pop 4,072; Circ 26,947
Library Holdings: DVDs 100; Bk Titles 25,000; Per Subs 50
Wireless access
Mem of Illinois Heartland Library System
Open Mon 9:30-8, Tues-Fri 9:30-6, Sat 9-3

ARGENTA

P ARGENTA-OREANA PUBLIC LIBRARY DISTRICT, Argenta Public Library, 100 E Water St, 62501. (Mail add: PO Box 278, Oreana, 62554), SAN 303-6839. Tel: 217-468-2340, 217-795-2144. Web Site: www.aopld.org. *Dir,* Donna Schaal; E-mail: director@aopld.lib.il.us; Staff 3 (MLS 2, Non-MLS 1)
Pop 4,138
Library Holdings: AV Mats 1,000; CDs 350; DVDs 1,000; High Interest/Low Vocabulary Bk Vols 1,000; Large Print Bks 3,000; Bk Titles 32,837; Per Subs 250; Talking Bks 1,000; Videos 1,755
Wireless access
Mem of Illinois Heartland Library System
Open Mon & Wed 9-5, Tues & Thurs 9-7, Sat 9-1

ARLINGTON HEIGHTS

P ARLINGTON HEIGHTS MEMORIAL LIBRARY*, 500 N Dunton Ave, 60004-5966. SAN 303-6863. Tel: 847-392-0100. FAX: 847-506-2650. Web Site: www.ahml.info. *Exec Dir,* Mike Driskell; E-mail: mdriskell@ahml.info; *Dir, Customer Serv,* Shannon Distel; E-mail: sdistel@ahml.info; Staff 17.5 (MLS 17.5)
Founded 1926. Pop 76,031; Circ 2,300,000
Library Holdings: Audiobooks 34,710; DVDs 46,401; e-books 10,143; Bk Titles 246,705; Per Subs 814
Subject Interests: Am lit, Educ, Fiction, Foreign lang, Genealogy, Illinois, Law, Local hist
Automation Activity & Vendor Info: (Acquisitions) Innovative Interfaces, Inc - Millennium; (Cataloging) Innovative Interfaces, Inc - Millennium; (Circulation) Innovative Interfaces, Inc - Millennium; (ILL) Innovative Interfaces, Inc - Millennium; (OPAC) Innovative Interfaces, Inc - Millennium; (Serials) Innovative Interfaces, Inc - Millennium
Wireless access
Mem of Reaching Across Illinois Library System (RAILS)
Open Mon-Fri 9am-10pm, Sat 9-8, Sun 11-8
Friends of the Library Group
Bookmobiles: 1. Bkmobile Servs Supvr, Teri Scallon

S THE CENTER - RESOURCES FOR TEACHING & LEARNING LIBRARY, 2626 S Clearbrook Dr, 60005-4626. SAN 324-3370. Tel: 224-366-8500. FAX: 224-366-8514. Web Site: library.thecenterweb.org. *Librn,* Kim Scannell; Tel: 224-366-8590, E-mail: kscannell@cntrmail.org; Staff 3 (MLS 1, Non-MLS 2)
Founded 1974
Library Holdings: Bk Titles 20,000; Per Subs 60
Subject Interests: Adult basic educ, Bilingual educ, Early childhood educ, English as a second lang, GED programs, Literacy
Automation Activity & Vendor Info: (Cataloging) Evergreen; (ILL) OCLC; (OPAC) Evergreen
Function: ILL available
Mem of Reaching Across Illinois Library System (RAILS)
Open Mon, Tues, Thurs & Fri 9-4:45, Wed 9-7

M NORTHWEST COMMUNITY HOSPITAL*, Health Resource Library, 800 W Central Rd, 60005-2392. SAN 303-6871. Tel: 847-618-5180. Interlibrary Loan Service Tel: 847-618-5181. FAX: 847-618-5189. E-mail: library@nch.org. Web Site: www.nch.org. *Libr Dir,* Mary O'Connell
Founded 1963
Library Holdings: Bk Titles 6,189; Per Subs 281
Subject Interests: Consumer health, Med, Mgt, Nursing, Oncology
Automation Activity & Vendor Info: (Cataloging) Professional Software; (Circulation) Professional Software; (ILL) OCLC Connexion; (OPAC) Professional Software; (Serials) Professional Software
Wireless access
Partic in Metrop Consortium of Healthcare Librs
Open Mon-Fri 9-4

ARTHUR

P ARTHUR PUBLIC LIBRARY*, 225 S Walnut, 61911. SAN 303-6898. Tel: 217-543-2037. FAX: 217-543-2037. E-mail: apld@arthurlibrary.org. Web Site: www.arthurlibrary.org. *Libr Dir,* Kelsey Pruitt; E-mail: kelsey.pruitt@gmail.com; Staff 3 (MLS 1, Non-MLS 2)
Founded 1901. Pop 5,097; Circ 71,000
Library Holdings: Bk Vols 20,000; Per Subs 53
Subject Interests: Amish
Automation Activity & Vendor Info: (Cataloging) SirsiDynix; (Circulation) SirsiDynix; (OPAC) SirsiDynix
Wireless access
Open Mon-Thurs 9-8, Fri & Sat 9-5

ASHLAND

P PRAIRIE SKIES PUBLIC LIBRARY DISTRICT*, 125 W Editor St, 62612. (Mail add: PO Box 498, 62612-0498), SAN 303-6901. Tel: 217-476-3417. FAX: 217-476-8076. E-mail: pskiesld@gmail.com. Web Site: www.pspld.com. *Dir,* Kathy Roegge; *Cat,* Beth Harris; Staff 7 (MLS 1, Non-MLS 6)
Founded 1999. Pop 7,500; Circ 31,281
Library Holdings: Bk Vols 22,000; Per Subs 80
Wireless access
Function: 24/7 Online cat, Activity rm, Adult bk club, Audiobks via web, Bks on CD, Children's prog, Computer training, Computers for patron use, Free DVD rentals, ILL available, Internet access, Magazines, Movies, Notary serv, Online cat, OverDrive digital audio bks, Photocopying/Printing, Scanner, Senior computer classes, Story hour, Summer reading prog
Mem of Reaching Across Illinois Library System (RAILS)
Partic in Association for Rural & Small Libraries; Resource Sharing Alliance
Open Mon-Wed & Fri 9-5, Thurs 9-7, Sat 9-Noon
Branches: 1
PLEASANT PLAINS BRANCH, 555 Buckeye Rd, Pleasant Plains, 62677. (Mail add: PO Box 498, 62612-0498). Tel: 217-626-1553. FAX: 217-626-2433. *Dir,* Kathy Roegge; Tel: 217-476-3417, E-mail: pskiesld@gmail.com; *Librn,* Beth Harris
Founded 2002
Library Holdings: Bk Titles 2,000; Per Subs 10
Automation Activity & Vendor Info: (Acquisitions) SirsiDynix
Open Mon, Wed & Fri 9-5, Tues & Thurs 9-7, Sat 9-2
Friends of the Library Group

ASHLEY

P ASHLEY PUBLIC LIBRARY DISTRICT, 70 N Second St, 62808. (Mail add: PO Box 246, 62808-0246), SAN 303-691X. Tel: 618-485-2295. FAX: 618-485-2295. E-mail: maindesk@ashleypubliclibrary.org. *Dir,* Carol Tomaszewski
Pop 922; Circ 5,441
Library Holdings: Bk Vols 9,000; Per Subs 20
Mem of Illinois Heartland Library System
Open Mon 6pm-8pm, Tues & Fri 1-4:30, Sat 9-12
Friends of the Library Group

ASHTON

P MILLS & PETRIE MEMORIAL LIBRARY*, 704 N First St, 61006. (Mail add: PO Box 308, 61006), SAN 303-6928. Tel: 815-453-2213. FAX: 815-453-2723. E-mail: library@ashtonusa.com. Web Site: millspetrielibrary.weebly.com. *Librn,* Linda Dallam

Pop 1,142; Circ 9,090
Library Holdings: Bk Vols 12,200; Per Subs 60
Wireless access
Mem of Reaching Across Illinois Library System (RAILS)
Open Mon-Thurs 1-6:30, Sat 10-1

ASSUMPTION

P ASSUMPTION PUBLIC LIBRARY DISTRICT*, 205 N Oak St, 62510. SAN 303-6936. Tel: 217-226-3915. FAX: 217-226-3915. E-mail: assumptionpub@consolidated.net. Web Site: assumptionpubliclibrary.com. *Dir,* Anna Adermann
Founded 1903. Pop 2,101; Circ 12,637
Library Holdings: Bk Titles 14,000; Per Subs 20
Automation Activity & Vendor Info: (Cataloging) SirsiDynix; (Circulation) SirsiDynix; (OPAC) SirsiDynix
Mem of Illinois Heartland Library System
Open Mon, Thurs & Fri 9-5, Wed 9-6, Sat 9-3

ASTORIA

P ASTORIA PUBLIC LIBRARY DISTRICT*, 220 W Broadway, 61501-9630. SAN 376-091X. Tel: 309-329-2423. FAX: 309-329-2842. E-mail: astorlib@astoriail.net. *Libr Dir,* Jennifer Willard; Staff 1 (Non-MLS 1)
Founded 1940. Pop 2,506
Function: For res purposes, Home delivery & serv to seniorr ctr & nursing homes, Internet access, Large print keyboards, Magnifiers for reading, Mail loans to mem, Photocopying/Printing, Prog for adults, Prog for children & young adult, Ref serv available, Summer reading prog, Wheelchair accessible, Workshops
Special Services for the Blind - Audio mat; Cassette playback machines; Cassettes; Copier with enlargement capabilities; Home delivery serv; Large print & cassettes; Large print bks & talking machines; Large screen computer & software; Magnifiers; Screen enlargement software for people with visual disabilities; Talking bk & rec for the blind cat; Talking bks
Open Mon-Thurs 9:30-12 & 12:30-5:30, Fri 1:30-5:30
Restriction: Access at librarian's discretion
Friends of the Library Group

ATHENS

P ATHENS MUNICIPAL LIBRARY*, 410 E Hargrave St, 62613-9702. Tel: 217-636-8047. FAX: 217-636-8763. E-mail: athenslibrary@casscomm.com. Web Site: www.athenslibrary.weebly.com. *Libr Dir,* Donna Cunningham
Pop 2,000
Library Holdings: Bk Titles 12,000
Automation Activity & Vendor Info: (Acquisitions) Horizon
Wireless access
Function: 24/7 Online cat, Activity rm, Adult bk club, Archival coll, Audiobks via web, Bks on CD, Children's prog, Computers for patron use, Electronic databases & coll, Homebound delivery serv, ILL available, Internet access, Meeting rooms, Microfiche/film & reading machines, Movies, Online cat, OverDrive digital audio bks, Photocopying/Printing, Prog for adults, Prog for children & young adult, Story hour, Summer reading prog, Wheelchair accessible
Mem of Illinois Heartland Library System
Open Mon-Thurs 10-7, Sun 12-4
Friends of the Library Group

ATKINSON

P ATKINSON PUBLIC LIBRARY DISTRICT*, 109 S State, 61235. SAN 303-6944. Tel: 309-936-7606. FAX: 309-936-7606. E-mail: apld1.il.lib@gmail.com. Web Site: www.atkinson-library.com. *Libr Dir,* Ninette Carton; *Asst Dir,* Ruthann Carton
Founded 1920. Pop 1,498; Circ 15,516
Library Holdings: AV Mats 620; DVDs 100; Large Print Bks 75; Bk Vols 16,974; Per Subs 69; Talking Bks 900
Special Collections: Bound local newspapers - 70 volumes (yearly)
Automation Activity & Vendor Info: (Cataloging) SirsiDynix; (Circulation) SirsiDynix; (ILL) OCLC; (OPAC) SirsiDynix
Wireless access
Function: Accelerated reader prog
Mem of Reaching Across Illinois Library System (RAILS)
Special Services for the Deaf - Closed caption videos
Special Services for the Blind - Talking bks
Open Mon & Thurs 2-6, Tues 9-12 & 2-6, Wed 2-8, Fri 2-5, Sat 9-12

ATLANTA

P ATLANTA PUBLIC LIBRARY DISTRICT*, 100 Race St, 61723. (Mail add: PO Box 568, 61723-0568), SAN 303-6952. Tel: 217-648-2112. FAX: 217-648-5269. E-mail: apldinformation@gmail.com. Web Site: www.atlantapld.org. *Libr Dir,* Catherine Maciariello; *Mus Dir,* Rachel Neisler; Staff 4 (Non-MLS 4)
Founded 1908. Pop 2,325; Circ 6,116
Library Holdings: Bk Vols 13,468
Special Collections: Local Newspaper Coll, micro. Oral History
Subject Interests: Abraham Lincoln
Wireless access
Mem of Reaching Across Illinois Library System (RAILS)
Open Mon 10-12:30, Tues & Thurs 10-7, Wed & Fri 10-4:30, Sat 9-3

ATWOOD

P ATWOOD-HAMMOND PUBLIC LIBRARY*, 123 N Main St, 61913. (Mail add: PO Box 440, 61913-0440), SAN 303-6960. Tel: 217-578-2727. FAX: 217-578-2727. E-mail: ahlibrary@hotmail.com. Web Site: www.ahlibrary.com. *Dir,* Marsha Burgener
Pop 2,996; Circ 23,000
Library Holdings: Bk Titles 18,000; Per Subs 42
Subject Interests: Local hist
Automation Activity & Vendor Info: (Cataloging) SirsiDynix; (Circulation) SirsiDynix; (OPAC) SirsiDynix
Wireless access
Mem of Illinois Heartland Library System
Open Mon & Fri 9-5, Tues-Thurs 12-8, Sat 9-1
Friends of the Library Group

AUBURN

P AUBURN PUBLIC LIBRARY, 338 W Jefferson, 62615. SAN 303-6979. Tel: 217-438-6211. FAX: 217-438-9317. Web Site: auburnpubliclibraryil.org. *Librn,* Amanda Kendall; E-mail: apldlibrarian@gmail.com
Founded 1932. Pop 4,317; Circ 27,084
Library Holdings: AV Mats 1,500; Large Print Bks 1,700; Bk Vols 35,000; Per Subs 36; Talking Bks 870
Wireless access
Mem of Illinois Heartland Library System
Open Mon, Tues & Thurs 2-6:30, Wed 10-6:30, Fri 10-4:30, Sat 9-1
Friends of the Library Group

AUGUSTA

P GREATER WEST CENTRAL PUBLIC LIBRARY DISTRICT*, Augusta Branch, 202 Center St, 62311. (Mail add: PO Box 235, 62311-0235), SAN 303-6987. Tel: 217-392-2211. FAX: 217-392-2211. E-mail: gwcaugustalibrary@yahoo.com. Web Site: greaterwestcentral.org. *Dir,* Jennifer Gorsuch
Founded 1915. Pop 5,015; Circ 55,130
Library Holdings: Bk Titles 72,025; Per Subs 135
Subject Interests: Educ, Hist
Wireless access
Open Tues & Thurs 1-8, Wed 9-Noon, Sat 9-2
Branches: 3
BOWEN BRANCH, 116 W Fifth St, Bowen, 62316. (Mail add: PO Box 235, 62311), SAN 303-7436. Tel: 217-842-5573. FAX: 217-842-5573. E-mail: gwcbowenlibrary@yahoo.com. *Librn,* Dixie Campbell
Founded 1972. Pop 1,348; Circ 11,220
Library Holdings: Bk Vols 20,000; Per Subs 25
Open Tues 9-Noon, Thurs 2-5, Sat 9-11
GOLDEN BRANCH, 309 Quincy St, Golden, 62339. (Mail add: PO Box 87, Golden, 62339-0087), SAN 372-5235. Tel: 217-696-2428. FAX: 217-696-2428. E-mail: gwcgoldenlibrary@yahoo.com. *Librn,* Shelly Jones
Library Holdings: Bk Titles 10,000; Per Subs 30
Open Tues 9-12 & 2-5, Wed 2-5, Thurs 9-12 & 5-8, Sat 9-Noon
PLYMOUTH BRANCH, 129 W Side Sq, Plymouth, 62367. (Mail add: PO Box 251, Plymouth, 62367-0251), SAN 325-3929. Tel: 309-458-6616. FAX: 309-458-6616. E-mail: gwcplymouthlibrary@yahoo.com. *Librn,* Linda Switzer
Library Holdings: Bk Vols 10,000; Per Subs 10
Open Tues 10-1 & 3-6, Wed 3-6, Thurs 9-12 & 3-7, Sat 9-12

AURORA

P AURORA PUBLIC LIBRARY DISTRICT*, 101 S River St, 60506. SAN 303-7002. Tel: 630-264-4100. Administration Tel: 630-264-4106. FAX: 630-896-3209. Administration FAX: 630-859-1909. E-mail: businessoffice@aurorapubliclibrary.org. Web Site: www.aurorapubliclibrary.org. *Exec Dir,* Michaela Haberkern; E-mail: michaela@aurorapubliclibrary.org; *Dep Dir,* Tom Spicer; *Dir of Finance,* Kathy Fennell; Tel: 630-264-4118; *Dir, Neighborhood Servs,* Heather Sturm; Tel: 630-264-3410, E-mail: heather.sturm@aurorapubliclibrary.org; Staff 158 (MLS 33, Non-MLS 125)
Founded 1881. Pop 199,963; Circ 14,000,000
Library Holdings: Bk Vols 524,008; Per Subs 8,891
Subject Interests: Local hist
Automation Activity & Vendor Info: (Circulation) Innovative Interfaces, Inc; (ILL) OCLC

Wireless access
Function: 24/7 Electronic res, 24/7 Online cat, 3D Printer, Adult bk club, After school storytime, Art exhibits, Audiobks via web, Bilingual assistance for Spanish patrons, Bk club(s), Bks on CD, Children's prog, Citizenship assistance, Computer training, Computers for patron use, Digital talking bks, E-Readers, Electronic databases & coll, Family literacy, For res purposes, Free DVD rentals, Holiday prog, Home delivery & serv to seniorr ctr & nursing homes, Homebound delivery serv, Homework prog, ILL available, Internet access, Learning ctr, Life-long learning prog for all ages, Literacy & newcomer serv, Magazines, Mail & tel request accepted, Makerspace, Meeting rooms, Microfiche/film & reading machines, Movies, Museum passes, Music CDs, Online cat, Online ref, Orientations, Outreach serv, OverDrive digital audio bks, Photocopying/Printing, Preschool outreach, Preschool reading prog, Printer for laptops & handheld devices, Prog for adults, Prog for children & young adult, Ref & res, Ref serv available, Res assist avail, Scanner, Senior computer classes, Senior outreach, Spanish lang bks, STEM programs, Story hour, Study rm, Summer & winter reading prog, Summer reading prog, Teen prog, Telephone ref, Wheelchair accessible, Winter reading prog, Workshops
Mem of Reaching Across Illinois Library System (RAILS)
Partic in OCLC-LVIS
Special Services for the Blind - Accessible computers; Bks on CD; Large print bks; Large screen computer & software
Open Mon-Thurs 9-8, Fri & Sat 9-5, Sun (Sept-May) 1-5
Branches: 2
EOLA ROAD BRANCH, 555 S Eola Rd, 60504-8992. Tel: 630-264-3400. FAX: 630-898-5220. Reference FAX: 630-264-3409. *Dir, Neighborhood Servs,* Heather Sturm; *Br Mgr,* Rebecca Clark; E-mail: rclark@aurorapubliclibrary.org; Staff 35 (MLS 8, Non-MLS 27)
Founded 1993
Automation Activity & Vendor Info: (Circulation) Innovative Interfaces, Inc
Open Mon-Thurs 9-8, Fri & Sat 9-6, Sun (Sept-May) 12-6
WEST BRANCH, 233 S Constitution Dr, 60506-0506. Tel: 630-264-3600. FAX: 630-844-8695. *Br Mgr,* Scott Grotto; E-mail: sgrotto@aurorapubliclibrary.org; Staff 14 (MLS 5, Non-MLS 9)
Library Holdings: Bk Titles 75,000; Per Subs 150
Automation Activity & Vendor Info: (Circulation) Innovative Interfaces, Inc
Open Mon, Wed & Sat 9-6, Tues & Thurs 11-8, Fri 2-6, Sun (Sept-May) 1-5
Bookmobiles: 1. Outreach Serv Mgr, Jessica Cantarero

C AURORA UNIVERSITY*, Charles B Phillips Library, 315 S Gladstone, 60506-4892. (Mail add: 347 S Gladstone Ave, 60506-4877), SAN 303-6995. Tel: 630-844-5437. Circulation Tel: 630-844-7583. Interlibrary Loan Service Tel: 630-844-5439. Reference Tel: 630-844-7534. Toll Free Tel: 800-742-5281. FAX: 630-844-3848. Web Site: libguides.aurora.edu/libraryinfo, www.aurora.edu/academics/library. *Dir, Univ Libr,* Kathy Clark; Tel: 630-844-5443, E-mail: kclark@aurora.edu; *Electronic Res Librn,* Jayna Leipart Guttilla; Tel: 630-844-5525, E-mail: jleipartguttilla@aurora.edu; *Info Serv Librn,* Sarah Kooistra; Tel: 630-844-5440, E-mail: skooistra@aurora.edu; *Info Serv Librn,* Allyson Palagi; Tel: 630-844-5653, E-mail: apalagi@aurora.edu; *Curator,* Dr Susan Palmer; Tel: 630-844-5445, E-mail: spalmer@aurora.edu; Staff 10 (MLS 7, Non-MLS 3)
Founded 1893. Enrl 4,700; Highest Degree: Doctorate
Library Holdings: Bk Titles 78,893; Bk Vols 99,000; Per Subs 210
Special Collections: Adventism (Jenks Coll), bks, per
Subject Interests: Educ, English lit, Native Americans, Nursing, Soc serv (soc work)
Automation Activity & Vendor Info: (Cataloging) Ex Libris Group; (Circulation) Ex Libris Group; (OPAC) Ex Libris Group
Wireless access
Function: Ref serv available
Mem of Reaching Across Illinois Library System (RAILS)
Partic in Consortium of Academic & Research Libraries in Illinois; LIBRAS, Inc; OCLC-LVIS

S ENGINEERING SYSTEMS INC LIBRARY*, 4215 Campus Dr, 60504-7900. SAN 375-3298. Tel: 630-851-4566, Ext 1238. FAX: 630-851-4870. *Librn,* Cheryl A Hansen; E-mail: cahansen@engsys.com; Staff 1 (MLS 1)
Founded 1990
Library Holdings: Bk Titles 2,000
Automation Activity & Vendor Info: (Cataloging) SydneyPlus; (OPAC) SydneyPlus
Wireless access
Mem of Reaching Across Illinois Library System (RAILS)
Partic in Illinois Library & Information Network

S ILLINOIS MATHEMATICS & SCIENCE ACADEMY, Leto M Furnas Information Resource Center, 1500 Sullivan Rd, 60506-1000. SAN 375-9539. Tel: 630-907-5920. Interlibrary Loan Service Tel: 630-907-5075. Reference Tel: 630-907-5973. FAX: 630-907-5004. E-mail: irc@imsa.edu. Web Site: staff.imsa.edu/irc. *Coll Develop Librn, Electronic Res, Ref,* Connie James-Jenkin; E-mail: cjames-jenkin@imsa.edu; *Institutional Repository Librn, Tech Serv,* Jean Bigger; *Circ & ILL,* Angela Richardson; Staff 4 (MLS 1, Non-MLS 3)
Founded 1986
Library Holdings: Bk Titles 42,000; Per Subs 120
Special Collections: DigitalCommons@IMSA (Institutional repository); IMSA Archives. Oral History
Automation Activity & Vendor Info: (Cataloging) Ex Libris Group; (Circulation) Ex Libris Group; (OPAC) Ex Libris Group
Wireless access
Mem of Reaching Across Illinois Library System (RAILS)
Partic in Consortium of Academic & Research Libraries in Illinois
Special Services for the Blind - Aids for in-house use
Restriction: Not open to pub

S MARMION ACADEMY LIBRARY*, 1000 Butterfield Rd, 60502. SAN 375-9806. Tel: 630-897-6936. FAX: 630-897-7086. Web Site: www.marmion.org. *Librn,* Fr Abbott Vincent
Library Holdings: Bk Titles 10,316
Wireless access
Open Mon-Fri 7:30-4

M RUSH COPLEY MEDICAL CENTER*, Health Science Library, 2000 Ogden Ave, 60504. SAN 376-0065. Tel: 630-499-2324. Web Site: www.rushcopley.com. *Dir,* Amanda Bolander; E-mail: abolander@rushcopley.com
Library Holdings: Bk Vols 829
Special Collections: Management Coll; Nursing Coll
Automation Activity & Vendor Info: (Cataloging) OCLC; (ILL) OCLC; (OPAC) OCLC FirstSearch
Mem of Reaching Across Illinois Library System (RAILS)
Restriction: Not open to pub

AVON

P VILLAGE OF AVON PUBLIC LIBRARY*, 105 S Main St, 61415. (Mail add: PO Box 598, 61415-0598), SAN 303-7037. Tel: 309-465-3933. FAX: 309-465-3933. E-mail: avonillibrary@hotmail.com. *Dir,* Courtney Young; Staff 1 (Non-MLS 1)
Founded 1913. Pop 799; Circ 1,468
Library Holdings: DVDs 124; Large Print Bks 172; Bk Vols 8,774; Per Subs 19
Automation Activity & Vendor Info: (Cataloging) SirsiDynix-WorkFlows; (Circulation) SirsiDynix-WorkFlows
Wireless access
Function: 24/7 Online cat, Audiobks via web, Digital talking bks, Free DVD rentals, Homebound delivery serv, ILL available, Internet access, Laminating, Magazines, Meeting rooms, Online cat, Photocopying/Printing, Printer for laptops & handheld devices, Ref & res, Scanner, Summer reading prog
Mem of Reaching Across Illinois Library System (RAILS)
Partic in Resource Sharing Alliance
Open Mon, Wed, Thurs, & Fri 2-6, Sat 9-Noon

BARRINGTON

P BARRINGTON AREA LIBRARY*, 505 N Northwest Hwy, 60010. SAN 303-7053. Tel: 847-382-1300. FAX: 847-382-1261. Web Site: www.balibrary.org, www.barringtonarealibrary.org. *Exec Dir,* Vicki Rakowski; E-mail: vrakowski@barringtonarealibrary.org; *Head, Adult Serv,* Jason Pinshower; E-mail: jpinshower@barringtonarealibrary.org; *Head, Tech Serv,* Maripat Olson; E-mail: molson@barringtonarealibrary.org; *Head, Youth Serv,* Alyson Prchal; E-mail: aprchal@barringtonarealibrary.org; Staff 39 (MLS 23, Non-MLS 16)
Founded 1913. Pop 42,127; Circ 978,703
Library Holdings: CDs 18,681; DVDs 18,802; e-books 9,697; Bk Vols 243,847; Per Subs 439
Automation Activity & Vendor Info: (Acquisitions) SirsiDynix; (Cataloging) SirsiDynix; (Circulation) SirsiDynix; (ILL) OCLC; (OPAC) SirsiDynix; (Serials) SirsiDynix
Wireless access
Function: Computer training, E-Reserves, Electronic databases & coll, Homebound delivery serv, Homework prog, ILL available, Internet access, Magnifiers for reading, Mail & tel request accepted, Music CDs, Online ref, Photocopying/Printing, Preschool outreach, Prog for adults, Prog for children & young adult, Ref serv available, Spoken cassettes & CDs, Spoken cassettes & DVDs, Summer reading prog, Tax forms, Telephone ref, VHS videos, Wheelchair accessible
Publications: Check It Out (Newsletter)
Open Mon-Fri 9-9, Sat 9-5, Sun 1-5

BARRY

P BARRY PUBLIC LIBRARY, 880 Bainbridge St, 62312. SAN 303-7096. Tel: 217-335-2149. FAX: 217-335-2149. E-mail; barrypublic@adams.net. Web Site: www.barrypubliclibrary.org. *Librn,* Ginny Lister
Founded 1856. Pop 1,391; Circ 17,492
Library Holdings: Bk Vols 12,000; Per Subs 100
Wireless access
Open Mon-Wed 12-6, Thurs 12-7, Sat 10-12

BARTLETT

P BARTLETT PUBLIC LIBRARY DISTRICT*, 800 S Bartlett Rd, 60103. SAN 303-710X. Tel: 630-837-2855. Interlibrary Loan Service Tel: 630-837-3560. FAX: 630-837-2669. TDD: 630-837-2922. Reference E-mail: bpldref@bartlett.lib.il.us. Web Site: www.bartlett.lib.il.us. *Dir,* Karolyn Nance; E-mail: knance@bartlettlibrary.org; *Adult & Tech Serv Mgr,* Mary Jane O'Brien; *IT Mgr,* Al Ramirez; *Teen Serv Mgr, Youth Serv,* Ruth Anne Mielke; Staff 11 (MLS 11)
Founded 1972. Pop 35,942; Circ 510,000
Library Holdings: AV Mats 18,000; Bk Vols 107,000
Automation Activity & Vendor Info: (Cataloging) OCLC; (ILL) OCLC
Wireless access
Mem of Reaching Across Illinois Library System (RAILS)
Special Services for the Deaf - TDD equip
Open Mon-Thurs 9-9, Fri 9-6, Sat 9-5, Sun Noon-5
Friends of the Library Group

BARTONVILLE

P ALPHA PARK PUBLIC LIBRARY DISTRICT*, 3527 S Airport Rd, 61607-1799. SAN 303-7118. Tel: 309-697-3822. Circulation Tel: 309-697-3822, Ext 10. Reference Tel: 309-697-3822, Ext 13. Administration Tel: 309-697-3822, Ext 12. FAX: 309-697-9681. TDD: 309-697-9470. E-mail: alpha@alphapark.org. Web Site: www.alphapark.org. *Dir,* Melissa Sierra; E-mail: melissa@alphapark.org; Staff 25 (MLS 1, Non-MLS 24)
Founded 1972. Pop 28,545; Circ 195,089
Library Holdings: Bk Vols 72,667; Per Subs 378
Special Collections: Peoria State Hospital Coll
Automation Activity & Vendor Info: (Circulation) TLC (The Library Corporation)
Wireless access
Function: ILL available
Publications: Library Times (Bimonthly)
Partic in Association for Rural & Small Libraries; LYRASIS; Resource Sharing Alliance
Special Services for the Deaf - TDD equip
Special Services for the Blind - Reader equip
Open Mon-Thurs 9-9, Fri 9-6, Sat 9-5
Friends of the Library Group

BATAVIA

P BATAVIA PUBLIC LIBRARY DISTRICT*, Ten S Batavia Ave, 60510-2793. SAN 303-7126. Tel: 630-879-1393. Circulation Tel: 630-879-1393, Ext 100. Reference Tel: 630-879-1393, Ext 200. FAX: 630-879-9118. Web Site: www.bataviapubliclibrary.org. *Dir,* George H Scheetz; E-mail: gscheetz@bataviapubliclibrary.org; *Dep Dir, Youth Serv Mgr,* Joanne C Zillman; E-mail: jzillman@bataviapubliclibrary.org; *Adult Serv Mgr, Outreach Serv Mgr,* Stacey Peterson; E-mail: speterson@bataviapubliclibrary.org; *Circ Serv Mgr,* Stephanie W DeYoung; E-mail: sdeyoung@bataviapubliclibrary.org; Staff 12.6 (MLS 9.8, Non-MLS 2.8)
Founded 1881. Pop 25,723; Circ 663,001
Library Holdings: AV Mats 24,831; Electronic Media & Resources 32; Bk Vols 185,139; Per Subs 249
Special Collections: American-Style Windmills Coll
Subject Interests: Batavia & Kane County hist
Automation Activity & Vendor Info: (Cataloging) SirsiDynix; (Circulation) SirsiDynix; (OPAC) SirsiDynix
Wireless access
Publications: Neighbors of Batavia (Periodical); Wired (Monthly newsletter)
Mem of Reaching Across Illinois Library System (RAILS)
Partic in System Wide Automated Network
Special Services for the Deaf - Closed caption videos; TDD equip
Special Services for the Blind - BiFolkal kits; Descriptive video serv (DVS)
Open Mon-Thurs 9-9, Fri & Sat 9-5, Sun 12-5 (1-4 Summer)
Friends of the Library Group

S FERMI NATIONAL ACCELERATOR LABORATORY*, Fermilab Library, Kirk & Wilson Sts, 60510. (Mail add: PO Box 500, MS109, 60510), SAN 303-7134. Tel: 630-840-3401. FAX: 630-840-4636. E-mail: library@fnal.gov. Web Site: library.fnal.gov. *Mgr,* Heath O'Connell; E-mail: hoc@fnal.gov; *Librn II,* Sandra Lee; E-mail: sllee@fnal.gov; Staff 3 (MLS 2, Non-MLS 1)
Founded 1967
Library Holdings: Bk Vols 20,000; Per Subs 160
Special Collections: High Energy Physics Preprints
Subject Interests: Computer sci, Energy, Engr
Wireless access
Function: Res libr
Open Mon-Fri 8:30-5

BEARDSTOWN

P BEARDSTOWN HOUSTON MEMORIAL LIBRARY*, 13 Boulevard Rd, 62618-8119. SAN 303-7142. Tel: 217-323-4204. FAX: 217-323-4217. E-mail: beard.h.ml.rsa@gmail.com. Web Site: cityofbeardstown.org/library. *Dir,* Ethan McIntyre; Staff 1 (Non-MLS 1)
Founded 1904. Pop 6,000; Circ 21,000
Library Holdings: High Interest/Low Vocabulary Bk Vols 25; Bk Vols 25,000; Per Subs 60
Special Collections: Oral History
Automation Activity & Vendor Info: (Circulation) Follett Software
Wireless access
Partic in Resource Sharing Alliance
Open Mon-Fri 10-6, Sat 10-2

BEDFORD PARK

P BEDFORD PARK PUBLIC LIBRARY DISTRICT*, 7816 W 65th Pl, 60501. SAN 303-6847. Tel: 708-458-6826. FAX: 708-458-9827. E-mail: bplib@bplib.net. Web Site: bedfordparklibrary.com. *Dir,* Anne M Murphy; E-mail: amurphy@bedfordparklibrary.com; *Ad,* Barbara Weber; E-mail: bweber@bedforparklibrary.com
Founded 1963. Pop 988; Circ 89,000
Library Holdings: Bk Vols 88,000; Per Subs 223
Automation Activity & Vendor Info: (Acquisitions) Innovative Interfaces, Inc; (Cataloging) Innovative Interfaces, Inc; (Circulation) Innovative Interfaces, Inc; (OPAC) Innovative Interfaces, Inc
Publications: Calendar & Booklist (Monthly); Newsletter (Quarterly)
Mem of Reaching Across Illinois Library System (RAILS)
Partic in System Wide Automated Network
Open Mon-Thurs 9-8, Fri & Sat 9-4

S ILLINOIS INSTITUTE OF TECHNOLOGY*, Institute for Food Safety & Health Library, Moffett Campus, 6502 S Archer Rd, 60501-1957. SAN 375-5363. Tel: 708-563-8160. FAX: 708-563-1873. Web Site: library.iit.edu/about/libraries/ifsh. *Librn, Webmaster,* David Griesemer; E-mail: dgriesem@iit.edu; Staff 2 (MLS 1, Non-MLS 1)
Founded 1993
Library Holdings: Bk Titles 5,000; Bk Vols 6,800; Per Subs 200
Automation Activity & Vendor Info: (Cataloging) EOS International; (Serials) EOS International
Wireless access
Partic in OCLC Online Computer Library Center, Inc

BEECHER

P BEECHER COMMUNITY LIBRARY*, 660 Penfield St, 60401. (Mail add: PO Box 818, 60401-0818). Tel: 708-946-9090. FAX: 708-946-2896. Web Site: beecherlibrary.org. *Dir,* Jill Grosso; E-mail: director@beecherlibrary.com
Founded 1994. Pop 4,302
Library Holdings: Bk Titles 20,000; Per Subs 35
Special Collections: Local history
Automation Activity & Vendor Info: (Cataloging) Innovative Interfaces, Inc; (Circulation) Innovative Interfaces, Inc; (OPAC) Innovative Interfaces, Inc
Mem of Reaching Across Illinois Library System (RAILS)
Partic in System Wide Automated Network
Open Mon-Fri 10-7, Sat 9-Noon

BELLEVILLE

P BELLEVILLE PUBLIC LIBRARY*, 121 E Washington St, 62220. SAN 339-7203. Tel: 618-234-0441. FAX: 618-234-9474. E-mail: mainlibrary@bellevillepubliclibrary.org. Web Site: www.belleville.net/350/Library. *Dir,* Leander Spearman; E-mail: leander.spearman@bellevillepubliclibrary.org; *Circ Supvr,* Andy Rowe; E-mail: andy.rowe@bellevillepubliclibrary.org; *Archives Supvr, Ref Supvr,* Anna Kimball; E-mail: anna.kimball@bellevillepubliclibrary.org; *Youth Serv Supvr,* Becky Cline; E-mail: becky.cline@bellevillepubliclibrary.org; Staff 26 (MLS 1, Non-MLS 25)
Founded 1836. Pop 44,165; Circ 221,203
Library Holdings: Bk Vols 135,000; Per Subs 443
Special Collections: Geneology. State Document Depository
Subject Interests: Area hist, Local hist

Automation Activity & Vendor Info: (Acquisitions) SirsiDynix; (Cataloging) SirsiDynix; (Circulation) SirsiDynix; (OPAC) SirsiDynix
Wireless access
Function: ILL available
Publications: Anniversary booklet, Walking Tour Guide & Archives Bibliography
Mem of Illinois Heartland Library System
Open Mon-Thurs 9-8, Fri & Sat 9-5
Friends of the Library Group
Branches: 1
WEST BRANCH, 3414 W Main St, 62226, SAN 339-7238. Tel: 618-233-4366. FAX: 618-233-1482. E-mail: westbranch@bellevillepubliclibrary.org. *Br Supvr,* Maggie Bacon; E-mail: maggie.bacon@bellevillepubliclibrary.org
Open Mon, Wed & Sat 9-5, Tues & Thurs 12-8
Friends of the Library Group

M MEMORIAL HOSPITAL LIBRARY*, 4500 Memorial Dr, 62226-5360. SAN 321-6594. Tel: 618-233-7750. FAX: 618-257-6946. Web Site: www.memhosp.com. *Librn,* Amanda Pankey; Staff 2 (MLS 1, Non-MLS 1)
Founded 1974
Library Holdings: Bk Titles 5,000; Per Subs 430
Wireless access
Publications: library infobooklet; Newsletter
Partic in Areawide Hospital Library Consortium of Southwestern Illinois; National Network of Libraries of Medicine Region 6; Regional Med Libr - Region 3
Open Mon-Fri 8-4:30
Friends of the Library Group

J SOUTHWESTERN ILLINOIS COLLEGE*, Belleville Campus Library, 2500 Carlyle Ave, 62221. SAN 303-7150. Tel: 618-235-2700, Ext 5204. Interlibrary Loan Service Tel: 618-222-5353. Reference Tel: 618-222-5236, 618-222-5597. Toll Free Tel: 866-942-7942. Web Site: swic.edu/students/services/library. *Ref Librn,* Jennifer Bone; E-mail: jennifer.bone@swic.edu; Staff 2 (MLS 2)
Founded 1946. Enrl 5,009; Highest Degree: Associate
Library Holdings: AV Mats 251; Bk Titles 61,072; Bk Vols 62,917; Per Subs 200
Automation Activity & Vendor Info: (Cataloging) Ex Libris Group; (Circulation) Ex Libris Group; (OPAC) Ex Libris Group
Mem of Illinois Heartland Library System
Partic in Consortium of Academic & Research Libraries in Illinois
Open Mon-Thurs 8-8, Fri 8-4

BELLWOOD

P BELLWOOD PUBLIC LIBRARY, 600 Bohland Ave, 60104-1896. SAN 303-7177. Tel: 708-547-7393. FAX: 708-547-9352. TDD: 708-547-7475. E-mail: info@bellwoodlibrary.org. Web Site: www.bellwoodlibrary.org. *Dir,* Amy Crump; E-mail: crumpa@bellwoodlibrary.org; *Bus Mgr,* Ashley Matthews; E-mail: matthewsa@bellwoodlibrary.org; *Head, Adult Serv, Head, Ref,* Kara Spizziri; E-mail: spizzirik@bellwoodlibrary.org; *Head, Youth Serv,* Sophia Brown; *Info Tech,* Tony Brown; E-mail: brownt@bellwoodlibrary.org; Staff 4 (MLS 2, Non-MLS 2)
Founded 1932. Pop 19,071; Circ 54,140
Library Holdings: Audiobooks 832; CDs 1,372; DVDs 3,073; e-books 18,722; Large Print Bks 1,214; Bk Vols 77,699; Per Subs 96
Subject Interests: Illinois
Wireless access
Publications: Bellwood, 1900-1975 (history)
Mem of Reaching Across Illinois Library System (RAILS)
Partic in System Wide Automated Network
Special Services for the Deaf - TDD equip
Open Mon-Thurs 9:30-8, Fri 9:30-6
Friends of the Library Group

BELVIDERE

P IDA PUBLIC LIBRARY*, 320 N State St, 61008-3299. SAN 303-7193. Tel: 815-544-3838. E-mail: localhistory@idapubliclibrary.org. Web Site: idapubliclibrary.org. *Dir,* Louis Carlile; E-mail: louisc@idapubliclibrary.org; *Circ Mgr,* Kaitlin Woodward; E-mail: kaitlinw@idapubliclibrary.org; Staff 3 (MLS 3)
Founded 1885. Pop 23,532; Circ 165,000
Library Holdings: Bk Vols 77,000; Per Subs 250
Subject Interests: Local hist
Automation Activity & Vendor Info: (Cataloging) Innovative Interfaces, Inc; (Circulation) Innovative Interfaces, Inc; (ILL) Innovative Interfaces, Inc; (OPAC) Innovative Interfaces, Inc; (Serials) Innovative Interfaces, Inc
Wireless access
Publications: Ida-Lites (Newsletter)
Mem of Reaching Across Illinois Library System (RAILS)
Open Mon-Fri 10-8, Sat 9-5
Friends of the Library Group

BEMENT

P BEMENT PUBLIC LIBRARY DISTRICT*, 349 S Macon St, 61813. SAN 303-7207. Tel: 217-678-7101. FAX: 217-678-7034. E-mail: bementlibrary@gmail.com. Web Site: bementpubliclibrary.net. *Dir,* Melinda Glover
Founded 1877. Pop 2,445; Circ 22,679
Library Holdings: Bk Vols 16,435; Per Subs 75
Subject Interests: Genealogy, Local hist, Ref bks
Wireless access
Function: ILL available, Photocopying/Printing
Mem of Illinois Heartland Library System
Open Mon & Wed 12-8, Tues, Thurs & Fri 12-5, Sat 9-2
Friends of the Library Group

BENLD

P FRANK BERTETTI BENLD PUBLIC LIBRARY*, 308 E Central Ave, 62009. Tel: 217-835-4045. FAX: 217-835-4045. E-mail: benldlibrary@gmail.com. Web Site: www.benldlibrary.org. *Librn,* Mary Newman
Founded 1997
Library Holdings: Bk Titles 9,000
Mem of Illinois Heartland Library System
Open Mon & Thurs 2-6, Tues 2-7, Wed & Fri 9-5, Sat 9-Noon

BENSENVILLE

P BENSENVILLE COMMUNITY PUBLIC LIBRARY*, 200 S Church Rd, 60106. SAN 303-7215. Tel: 630-766-4642. FAX: 630-766-0788. Reference E-mail: reference@benlib.org. Web Site: benlib.org. *Libr Dir,* David Sieffert; Tel: 630-766-4642, Ext 426, E-mail: dsieffert@benlib.org; *Youth Serv Librn,* Diane McReynolds; *Admin Serv Coordr,* Tekolya Brown; *Adult Serv Coordr,* Chris Sloan; Staff 37 (MLS 7, Non-MLS 30)
Founded 1960. Pop 21,640; Circ 130,000
Library Holdings: Bk Titles 80,000; Bk Vols 87,000; Per Subs 370
Special Collections: Large Print Books; Local History. Oral History
Automation Activity & Vendor Info: (Acquisitions) SirsiDynix; (Cataloging) SirsiDynix; (Circulation) SirsiDynix; (Course Reserve) SirsiDynix; (OPAC) SirsiDynix
Publications: Community News (Bimonthly); Serendipity E News (Newsletter)
Mem of Reaching Across Illinois Library System (RAILS)
Partic in System Wide Automated Network
Open Mon-Thurs 9-9, Fri & Sat 9-5, Sun 1-5

BENTON

P BENTON PUBLIC LIBRARY DISTRICT*, 502 S Main St, 62812. SAN 303-7223. Tel: 618-438-7511. FAX: 618-439-6139. Web Site: www.bentonlibrary.com. *Dir,* Susan Stickel; E-mail: susanstickel.bpl@gmail.com; Staff 1 (Non-MLS 1)
Founded 1916. Pop 10,170; Circ 60,000
Library Holdings: Bk Vols 42,000; Per Subs 60
Special Collections: Southern Illinois History
Subject Interests: Fiction, Genealogy, Local hist
Automation Activity & Vendor Info: (Cataloging) Innovative Interfaces, Inc; (Circulation) Innovative Interfaces, Inc; (OPAC) Innovative Interfaces, Inc
Wireless access
Mem of Illinois Heartland Library System
Partic in Illinois Library & Information Network
Open Mon-Thurs 9-8, Fri & Sat 9-5, Sun 1-5

BERKELEY

P BERKELEY PUBLIC LIBRARY*, 1637 N Taft Ave, 60163-1499. SAN 303-7231. Tel: 708-544-6017. FAX: 708-544-7551. E-mail: mail@berkeleypl.org. Web Site: www.berkeleypl.org. *Dir,* Ryan Cox; E-mail: rcox@berkeleypl.org; *Bus Mgr,* Isabel LaBarbera; E-mail: ilabarbera@berkeleypl.org; *Adult Serv Coordr,* Cathy Johnson; *Circ Serv Coordr,* Loretta Bohn; *Tech Serv Coordr,* Sonia Stetkus; *Youth Serv Coordr,* Rachel Schukat; Staff 2 (MLS 2)
Pop 5,409
Automation Activity & Vendor Info: (Acquisitions) Baker & Taylor; (Cataloging) Innovative Interfaces, Inc; (Circulation) Innovative Interfaces, Inc; (ILL) OCLC WorldShare Interlibrary Loan; (OPAC) Innovative Interfaces, Inc
Wireless access
Function: 24/7 Electronic res, Adult bk club, Audiobks via web, Bilingual assistance for Spanish patrons, Bk club(s), Bks on CD, Children's prog, Computer training, Computers for patron use, Electronic databases & coll, Family literacy, Free DVD rentals, Govt ref serv, Holiday prog, Homebound delivery serv, ILL available, Magazines, Mail & tel request accepted, Movies, Museum passes, Music CDs, Online cat, Online info literacy tutorials on the web & in blackboard, Outreach serv, Outside serv

via phone, mail, e-mail & web, OverDrive digital audio bks, Photocopying/Printing, Preschool outreach, Printer for laptops & handheld devices, Ref & res, Ref serv available, Scanner, Senior outreach, Spanish lang bks, Story hour, Study rm, Summer & winter reading prog, Teen prog, Telephone ref, Wheelchair accessible, Workshops
Mem of Reaching Across Illinois Library System (RAILS)
Partic in System Wide Automated Network
Open Mon-Thurs 10-9, Fri 10-6, Sat 10-5
Restriction: ID required to use computers (Ltd hrs)
Friends of the Library Group

BERWYN

P BERWYN PUBLIC LIBRARY, 2701 S Harlem Ave, 60402. SAN 339-7262. Tel: 708-795-8000. Administration Tel: 708-795-8000, Ext 3029. FAX: 708-795-8101. TDD: 708-795-5998. E-mail: askus@berwynlibrary.org. Web Site: www.berwynlibrary.org. *Dir,* Tammy Sheedy; E-mail: tsheedy@berwynlibrary.org; Staff 54 (MLS 7, Non-MLS 47)
Pop 54,016; Circ 367,210
Library Holdings: Bk Vols 200,000; Per Subs 388
Special Collections: Czechoslovakian Language Coll
Wireless access
Publications: Newsletter (Quarterly)
Mem of Reaching Across Illinois Library System (RAILS)
Partic in System Wide Automated Network
Open Mon-Thurs 9-7, Fri & Sat 9-5
Friends of the Library Group

M MACNEAL HOSPITAL*, Health Sciences Resource Center, 3249 S Oak Park Ave, 60402. SAN 303-724X. Tel: 708-783-3089. FAX: 708-783-3369. E-mail: hsrc@macneal.com. *Library Contact,* Lili Wang; E-mail: lili.wang@luhs.org; Staff 1 (MLS 1)
Founded 1950
Subject Interests: Med, Nursing
Automation Activity & Vendor Info: (OPAC) CyberTools for Libraries; (Serials) SERHOLD
Wireless access
Mem of Reaching Across Illinois Library System (RAILS)
Partic in National Network of Libraries of Medicine Region 6; OCLC Online Computer Library Center, Inc
Restriction: Hospital employees & physicians only

BETHALTO

P BETHALTO PUBLIC LIBRARY DISTRICT*, 321 S Prairie St, 62010-1525. SAN 303-7266. Tel: 618-377-8141. FAX: 618-377-3520. E-mail: info@bethaltolibrary.org. Web Site: www.bethaltolibrary.org. *Dir,* Mary Brewster; Staff 8 (MLS 1, Non-MLS 7)
Founded 1947. Pop 15,828; Circ 128,560
Library Holdings: Audiobooks 825; DVDs 5,454; e-books 23,172; Bk Vols 38,934; Per Subs 143
Automation Activity & Vendor Info: (Circulation) Innovative Interfaces, Inc
Wireless access
Function: 24/7 Electronic res, 24/7 Online cat, Adult bk club, Audiobks on Playaways & MP3, Audiobks via web, Bks on CD, Children's prog, Computers for patron use, Free DVD rentals, ILL available, Internet access, Large print keyboards, Magazines, Photocopying/Printing, Scanner, Story hour, Summer reading prog, Tax forms, Wheelchair accessible
Mem of Illinois Heartland Library System
Open Mon-Thurs 9-8, Fri 9-7, Sat 10-5, Sun 1-5

BETHANY

P MARROWBONE PUBLIC LIBRARY DISTRICT*, 216 W Main St, 61914. SAN 303-7274. Tel: 217-665-3014. FAX: 217-665-3246. Web Site: marrowbonepld.com. *Co-Dir,* Sally Ellen Ascenzo; *Co-Dir,* Lisa Marie Spracklen; *Ch,* Lesa Oathout; Staff 4 (Non-MLS 4)
Founded 1939. Pop 2,261; Circ 37,297
Library Holdings: Bks on Deafness & Sign Lang 10; High Interest/Low Vocabulary Bk Vols 100; Bk Titles 27,000; Per Subs 193
Automation Activity & Vendor Info: (Circulation) Innovative Interfaces, Inc
Wireless access
Mem of Illinois Heartland Library System
Open Mon 9-8, Tues-Fri 9-6, Sat 10-4

BIGGSVILLE

P HENDERSON COUNTY PUBLIC LIBRARY DISTRICT*, 110 Hillcrest Dr, 61418-9736. SAN 303-7282. Tel: 309-627-2450. FAX: 309-627-2830. E-mail: hcpl61418@hotmail.com. Web Site: www.hendersoncolibrary.com. *Libr Dir,* Anita Smith
Founded 1959. Pop 7,331; Circ 54,265
Library Holdings: Bk Vols 40,000; Per Subs 10
Subject Interests: Genealogy
Automation Activity & Vendor Info: (Cataloging) SirsiDynix; (Circulation) SirsiDynix; (OPAC) SirsiDynix
Wireless access
Function: Adult bk club, Bks on CD, Children's prog, Computers for patron use, Digital talking bks, Free DVD rentals, Genealogy discussion group, Microfiche/film & reading machines, Music CDs, Online cat, OverDrive digital audio bks, Photocopying/Printing, Preschool outreach, Preschool reading prog, Prog for children & young adult, Scanner, Senior outreach, Story hour, Summer & winter reading prog, Tax forms, Wheelchair accessible
Mem of Reaching Across Illinois Library System (RAILS)
Partic in RSA
Open Mon-Fri 9-5, Sat 9-12 & 1-5
Bookmobiles: 1. In Charge, Crystal Parsons

BLANDINSVILLE

P BLANDINSVILLE-HIRE DISTRICT LIBRARY*, 130 S Main St, 61420. (Mail add: PO Box 50, 61420-0050), SAN 303-7290. Tel: 309-652-3166. FAX: 309-652-3166. E-mail: blanhire@mtcnow.net. Web Site: blanhirelib.weebly.com. *Dir,* Sherry Talbott; *Asst Dir,* Lura Krueger
Founded 1953. Pop 2,345; Circ 30,120
Library Holdings: AV Mats 1,550; Large Print Bks 580; Bk Titles 23,000; Bk Vols 23,200; Per Subs 91; Talking Bks 450
Subject Interests: Antiques, Genealogy, Hist, Local hist
Partic in RSA
Open Mon 12:30-8, Tues & Sat 8:30-5, Wed 8:30-8, Fri 12:30-5

BLOOMINGDALE

P BLOOMINGDALE PUBLIC LIBRARY*, 101 Fairfield Way, 60108. SAN 303-7304. Tel: 630-529-3120. FAX: 630-529-3243. Reference E-mail: bdref@mybpl.org. Web Site: www.mybpl.org. *Dir,* Timothy Jarzemsky; E-mail: tjarzemsky@mybpl.org; *Adult Serv,* Abby Budzynski; E-mail: abudzynski@mybpl.org; *Circ,* Christine Sporleder; E-mail: csporleder@mybpl.org; *Computer Serv,* Sean Luster; E-mail: sluster@mybpl.org; *Youth Serv,* Katie Richert; E-mail: krichert@mybpl.org; Staff 56 (MLS 12, Non-MLS 44)
Founded 1974. Pop 22,018; Circ 301,731
Library Holdings: Audiobooks 31,317; DVDs 12,607; e-books 15,839; Electronic Media & Resources 68; Bk Titles 107,289; Per Subs 229
Automation Activity & Vendor Info: (Acquisitions) SirsiDynix; (Circulation) SirsiDynix; (OPAC) SirsiDynix-iBistro
Wireless access
Publications: Off the Shelf (Newsletter)
Mem of Reaching Across Illinois Library System (RAILS)
Partic in System Wide Automated Network
Open Mon-Thurs 9-9, Fri & Sat 9-5, Sun 1-5
Friends of the Library Group

BLOOMINGTON

P BLOOMINGTON PUBLIC LIBRARY*, 205 E Olive St, 61701. SAN 303-7312. Tel: 309-828-6091. FAX: 309-828-7312. Interlibrary Loan Service FAX: 309-821-9314. Web Site: www.bloomingtonlibrary.org. *Dir,* Jeanne Hamilton; *Bus Mgr,* Kathy Jeakins; E-mail: kathyj@bloomingtonlibrary.org; *Circ Mgr,* Position Currently Open; *Human Res Mgr,* Gayle Tucker; E-mail: gaylet@bloomingtonlibrary.org; *Mgr, Info Tech,* Jon Whited; *Tech Serv Mgr,* Allison Schmid; *Adult Serv,* Carol Torrens; *Ch Serv,* Melissa Robinson; E-mail: melissar@bloomingtonlibrary.org; *Mkt,* Rhonda Massie; E-mail: rhondam@bloomingtonlibrary.org; Staff 47 (MLS 15, Non-MLS 32)
Founded 1867. Pop 81,000
Library Holdings: AV Mats 25,281; Bks on Deafness & Sign Lang 162; Bk Titles 178,864; Per Subs 500; Talking Bks 3,063
Special Collections: Illinois Coll
Subject Interests: Genealogy, Illinois
Automation Activity & Vendor Info: (Cataloging) SirsiDynix; (Circulation) SirsiDynix; (OPAC) SirsiDynix
Wireless access
Publications: Business Connection, News & Reviews (Newsletter)
Mem of Reaching Across Illinois Library System (RAILS)
Partic in Illinois Library & Information Network; OCLC Online Computer Library Center, Inc
Special Services for the Blind - Talking bks
Open Mon-Thurs 9-9, Fri & Sat 9-5, Sun 1-5
Bookmobiles: 1. Bk titles 25,378

C ILLINOIS WESLEYAN UNIVERSITY, The Ames Library, One Ames Plaza, 61701-7188. (Mail add: PO Box 2899, 61702-2899), SAN 339-7351. Tel: 309-556-3350. Interlibrary Loan Service Tel: 309-556-1040. FAX: 309-556-3706. Administration FAX: 309-556-3261. Web Site: www.iwu.edu/library. *Univ Librn,* Dr Stephanie Davis-Kahl; Tel: 309-556-3010, E-mail: sdaviska@iwu.edu; *Libr Tech & Res Dir,* Suzanne Wilson; Tel: 309-556-3144, E-mail: swilson@iwu.edu; *Info Literacy Librn,*

Scholarly Communications Librn, Christopher Sweet; Tel: 309-556-3984, E-mail: csweet@iwu.edu; *Spec Coll Librn, Univ Archivist,* Meg Miner; Tel: 309-556-1538, E-mail: mminer@iwu.edu; *Circ Mgr,* Katy Ritter; Tel: 309-556-3172, E-mail: kritter@iwu.edu; *Operations Mgr, Tech Serv Mgr,* Gloria Redinger; Tel: 309-556-3526, E-mail: gredinge@iwu.edu; *Doc Delivery Spec, ILL,* Tony Heaton; Tel: 309-556-1040, E-mail: theaton@iwu.edu; *Media Spec,* Michael Limacher; Tel: 309-556-3323, E-mail: limacher@iwu.edu; *Archives, Metadata Specialist,* Julie Wood; Tel: 309-56-3620, E-mail: jwood@iwu.edu; *Digital Initiatives,* Amy Sutter; Tel: 309-556-3728, E-mail: asutter@iwu.edu. Subject Specialists: *Copyrights,* Dr Stephanie Davis-Kahl; Staff 24 (MLS 9, Non-MLS 15)
Founded 1850. Enrl 1,900; Fac 175; Highest Degree: Bachelor
Library Holdings: Per Subs 3,000
Special Collections: Beat literature; Dave Kindred papers; Political Science & Government (Leslie Arends Coll), flm, memorabilia
Automation Activity & Vendor Info: (Cataloging) Ex Libris Group; (Circulation) Ex Libris Group; (OPAC) Ex Libris Group; (Serials) Ex Libris Group
Wireless access
Mem of Reaching Across Illinois Library System (RAILS)
Partic in Consortium of Academic & Research Libraries in Illinois; Illinois Library & Information Network; OCLC Online Computer Library Center, Inc
Special Services for the Deaf - ADA equip
Special Services for the Blind - Accessible computers; Aids for in-house use; Bks available with recordings; Disability awareness prog; Large print bks & talking machines; Large screen computer & software; Mags & bk reproduction/duplication; Reader equip
Open Mon-Thurs 7:45am-1:30am, Fri 7:45am-10pm, Sat 10-10, Sun Noon-1:30am
Restriction: Authorized patrons, Authorized scholars by appt

S MCLEAN COUNTY MUSEUM OF HISTORY, Stevenson-Ives Library, 200 N Main, 61701. SAN 303-7347. Tel: 309-827-0428. FAX: 309-827-0100. E-mail: library@mchistory.org. Web Site: www.mchistory.org. *Exec Dir,* Julie Emig; *Librn,* Bill Kemp; E-mail: bkemp@mchistory.org; *Archivist,* George Perkins; E-mail: gperkins@mchistory.org; Staff 2 (Non-MLS 2)
Founded 1892
Library Holdings: CDs 25; Music Scores 50; Bk Vols 16,000; Per Subs 10
Special Collections: Arthur L. Pillsbury Coll; Chicago and Alton Railroad; Childrens Home Papers; Edward J Lewis Diaries & Civil War Correspondence; Ensenberger Furniture; Ezra M Prince Manuscripts & Correspondence; Hutton Family Coll; Illinois Soldiers & Sailors Coll; Illinois Traction System/ Illinois Terminal Railroad; International Affairs (Adlai Stevenson Lectures), papers; McLean County Home Bureau Papers; McLean County Photographs, 1850-; McLean County, Civil War & Illinois History Coll; Milo Cluster Manuscripts; Minnie Salzman Stevens Papers; Moon Family Coll; Phoenix Nursery; Political & Social History of McLean County Archives; Sons of Union Veterans' Coll; William Brigham Papers; William Wantling Coll, correspondence, papers, poetry ms
Subject Interests: Genealogy, Local hist, Mat culture
Wireless access
Publications: Archive Index with Unpublished Calendar; Indexes
Mem of Reaching Across Illinois Library System (RAILS)
Partic in RSA
Open Mon & Wed-Sat 9-5, Tues 9-9
Restriction: Non-circulating to the pub

SR ST JOHN'S LUTHERAN CHURCH LIBRARY, 1617 E Emerson St, 61701. SAN 371-9987. Tel: 309-827-6121. FAX: 309-829-3866. E-mail: info@stjohnsbloomington.org. Web Site: www.stjohnsbloomington.org.
Founded 1970
Library Holdings: AV Mats 50; Bk Titles 800
Subject Interests: Bible hist, Biblical, Christian educ, Family life

SR SECOND PRESBYTERIAN CHURCH*, Capen Memorial Library, 404 N Prairie St, 61701. SAN 303-7355. Tel: 309-828-6297. FAX: 309-828-7038. Web Site: secondpres.com. *Library Contact,* Dorothy Kennett; E-mail: dkenne2@ilstu.edu; Staff 3 (Non-MLS 3)
Library Holdings: Audiobooks 4; CDs 200; DVDs 100; Large Print Bks 17; Bk Vols 3,000; Spec Interest Per Sub 1; Talking Bks 30; Videos 400
Open Mon-Fri 8:30-4:30, Sun 8:30-11

BLUE ISLAND

P BLUE ISLAND PUBLIC LIBRARY*, 2433 York St, 60406-2011. SAN 303-738X. Tel: 708-388-1078. FAX: 708-388-1143. E-mail: info@blueislandlibrary.org. Web Site: blueislandlibrary.org. *Dir,* Anna Wassenaar; Tel: 708-388-1078, Ext 14, E-mail: awassenaar@blueislandlibrary.org; *Circ Serv,* David Boras; Tel: 708-388-1078, Ext 15, E-mail: dboras@blueislandlibrary.org; *Events & Outreach,* Meghan White; Tel: 708-388-1078, Ext 30, E-mail: mwhite@blueislandlibrary.org; *Ref Serv, Tech Serv,* Oscar Arellano; Tel: 708-388-1078, Ext 16, E-mail: oarellano@blueislandlibrary.org; *Youth Serv,* Deborah Beasley; Tel: 708-388-1078, Ext 22, E-mail: dbeasley@blueislandlibrary.org; Staff 3 (MLS 3)
Founded 1897. Pop 23,463; Circ 112,000
Library Holdings: Bk Vols 79,000; Per Subs 315
Subject Interests: City hist
Wireless access
Publications: The Bookworm (Newsletter)
Mem of Reaching Across Illinois Library System (RAILS)
Partic in System Wide Automated Network
Open Mon-Thurs 9-9, Fri & Sat 9-5, Sun (Sept-May) 1-5
Friends of the Library Group

BLUE MOUND

P BLUE MOUND MEMORIAL LIBRARY DISTRICT*, 213 N St Marie, 62513. (Mail add: PO Box 317, 62513-0317), SAN 303-7401. Tel: 217-692-2774. FAX: 217-692-2191. E-mail: bluemoundlibrary@hotmail.com. Web Site: www.bluemoundlibrary.lib.il.us. *Dir,* Julie Jones
Founded 1948. Pop 2,554; Circ 24,872
Library Holdings: Bk Titles 21,500; Per Subs 42
Mem of Illinois Heartland Library System
Partic in Heartland Consortia; Illinois Library & Information Network
Open Mon-Wed & Fri 10-6, Thurs 10-8, Sat 10-2

BLUFFS

P BLUFFS PUBLIC LIBRARY*, 110 N Bluffs St, 62621. (Mail add: PO Box 177, 62621-0177), SAN 303-741X. Tel: 217-754-3804. FAX: 217-754-3804. *Librn,* Ellen Graves
Pop 715; Circ 1,187
Library Holdings: Bk Vols 8,000; Per Subs 7
Mem of Reaching Across Illinois Library System (RAILS)
Open Tues, Thurs & Fri 1-5, Wed 9-12 & 1-7, Sat 9-12

BOLINGBROOK

P FOUNTAINDALE PUBLIC LIBRARY DISTRICT*, 300 W Briarcliff Rd, 60440. SAN 339-7475. Tel: 630-759-2102. FAX: 630-759-6180. TDD: 630-754-4949, 815-886-4638. E-mail: info@fountaindale.org. Web Site: www.fountaindale.org. *Exec Dir,* Paul Mills; Tel: 630-685-4157, E-mail: pmills@fountaindale.org; *Dep Dir,* Nancy Castellanos; E-mail: ncastellanos@fountaindale.org; *Adult & Teen Serv Mgr,* Debra Dudek; Tel: 630-685-4201, E-mail: ddudek@fountaindale.org; *Ch Mgr,* Wendy Birkemeier; Tel: 630-685-4198, E-mail: wbirkemeier@fountaindale.org; *Mgr, Outreach Serv,* Marianne M Thompson; Tel: 630-685-4231, E-mail: mmthompson@fountaindale.org; Staff 75 (MLS 18, Non-MLS 57)
Founded 1970. Pop 71,474; Circ 826,075
Library Holdings: Bk Vols 285,727
Automation Activity & Vendor Info: (Circulation) SirsiDynix; (OPAC) SirsiDynix
Wireless access
Mem of Reaching Across Illinois Library System (RAILS)
Partic in Pinnacle Library Cooperative
Special Services for the Deaf - TDD equip
Open Mon-Thurs 9-9, Fri & Sat 9-6, Sun 12-6
Friends of the Library Group
Bookmobiles: 1

BOURBONNAIS

P BOURBONNAIS PUBLIC LIBRARY DISTRICT*, 250 W John Casey Rd, 60914. SAN 324-5713. Tel: 815-933-1727. FAX: 815-933-1961. E-mail: library@bourbonnaislibrary.org. Web Site: www.bourbonnaislibrary.org. *Dir,* Kelly McCully; *Adult Serv Supvr,* Cassidy Steinke; E-mail: csteinke@bourbonnaislibrary.org; *Children's & Teen Serv, Youth Serv Supvr,* Rory Parilac; Tel: 815-295-1366, E-mail: rparilac@bourbonnaislibrary.org; *Mkt, Outreach Coordr,* Katelyn Moore; E-mail: kmoore@bourbonnaislibrary.org
Founded 1982. Pop 25,242; Circ 138,162
Library Holdings: Bk Titles 44,796; Per Subs 103
Automation Activity & Vendor Info: (Circulation) SirsiDynix
Wireless access
Function: 24/7 Electronic res, 24/7 Online cat, Activity rm, Adult bk club, After school storytime, Art programs, Audiobks on Playaways & MP3, Audiobks via web, Bk club(s), Bks on CD, Children's prog, Computer training, Computers for patron use, E-Readers, Free DVD rentals, Holiday prog, ILL available, Internet access, Life-long learning prog for all ages, Magazines, Meeting rooms, Movies, Music CDs, Outreach serv, OverDrive digital audio bks, Preschool outreach, Preschool reading prog, Printer for laptops & handheld devices, Prog for adults, Prog for children & young adult, Scanner, Spanish lang bks, STEM programs, Story hour, Study rm, Summer reading prog, Tax forms, Teen prog, Wheelchair accessible
Mem of Reaching Across Illinois Library System (RAILS)

Open Mon-Thurs 9-9, Fri & Sat 9-4
Friends of the Library Group

CR OLIVET NAZARENE UNIVERSITY*, Benner Library & Resource Center, One University Ave, 60914-2271. SAN 303-7428. Tel: 815-939-5354. Interlibrary Loan Service Tel: 815-928-5439. Reference Tel: 815-939-5355. Administration Tel: 815-939-5211. FAX: 815-939-5170. Web Site: library.olivet.edu. *Dir, Libr Serv,* Pam Greenlee; E-mail: pgreenle@olivet.edu; *Access Serv Librn,* Kyle Olney; Tel: 815-928-5490, E-mail: kolney1@olivet.edu; *Curric Librn, Informatics Librn,* Ann Johnston; Tel: 815-939-5061, E-mail: ajohnsto@olivet.edu; *Digital Initiatives Librn,* Bethany Nummela-Hanel; Tel: 815-939-5145; *Instrul Serv Librn,* Jasmine Cieszynski; Tel: 815-928-5449, E-mail: jcieszyn@olivet.edu; *Ref Librn,* Judson Strain; Tel: 815-928-5438, E-mail: jlstrain@olivet.edu. Subject Specialists: *Church hist,* Kyle Olney; *Educ,* Ann Johnston; *Digitization,* Bethany Nummela-Hanel; *Psychol,* Jasmine Cieszynski; *Law,* Judson Strain; Staff 7 (MLS 7)
Founded 1909. Enrl 4,162; Fac 271; Highest Degree: Doctorate
Jul 2014-Jun 2015. Mats Exp $1,839,268, Books $28,071, Per/Ser (Incl. Access Fees) $32,600, AV Mat $1,987, Electronic Ref Mat (Incl. Access Fees) $385,149, Presv $1,614. Sal $723,860 (Prof $289,423)
Library Holdings: CDs 888; DVDs 373; e-books 178,808; e-journals 38,767; Electronic Media & Resources 140; Music Scores 14,330; Bk Titles 141,120; Bk Vols 155,648; Per Subs 682; Videos 2,088
Special Collections: Jacob Arminus Coll, bks, microflm; John Wesley Coll; Olivet Nazarene Univ Archives. US Document Depository
Subject Interests: Educ, Nursing, Theol
Automation Activity & Vendor Info: (Acquisitions) Ex Libris Group; (Cataloging) Ex Libris Group; (Circulation) Ex Libris Group; (ILL) Ex Libris Group; (OPAC) Ex Libris Group; (Serials) Ex Libris Group
Wireless access
Function: 24/7 Electronic res, Archival coll, Audio & video playback equip for onsite use, Computers for patron use, Distance learning, Doc delivery serv, E-Reserves, Electronic databases & coll, Govt ref serv, ILL available, Internet access, Laminating, Magazines, Microfiche/film & reading machines, Music CDs, Online cat, Online ref, Orientations, Photocopying/Printing, Ref & res, Ref serv available, Res libr, Scanner, Study rm
Mem of Reaching Across Illinois Library System (RAILS)
Partic in Consortium of Academic & Research Libraries in Illinois; Illinois Library & Information Network
Special Services for the Blind - Reader equip
Open Mon-Thurs 8am-Midnight, Fri 8-5, Sat 11-4, Sun 6pm-Midnight
Restriction: In-house use for visitors

BRADFORD

P BRADFORD PUBLIC LIBRARY DISTRICT*, 111 S Peoria St, 61421. (Mail add: PO Box 249, 61421-0249), SAN 303-7444. Tel: 309-897-8400. FAX: 309-897-8314. E-mail: bdford.pld.rsa@gmail.com. Web Site: www.bpld.org. *Dir,* Sarah Boehm; *Youth Serv Librn,* Nicholas Poignant
Founded 1924. Pop 1,699; Circ 14,123
Library Holdings: Bk Vols 7,079; Per Subs 20
Automation Activity & Vendor Info: (Cataloging) CARL.Solution (TLC); (Circulation) CARL.Solution (TLC)
Wireless access
Function: 24/7 Online cat, Adult bk club, Art programs, Audiobks on Playaways & MP3, Audiobks via web, Bks on CD, Children's prog, Computers for patron use, Digital talking bks, Electronic databases & coll, Free DVD rentals, Holiday prog, Homebound delivery serv, ILL available, Internet access, Laminating, Magazines, Mail & tel request accepted, Movies, Music CDs, Online cat, OverDrive digital audio bks, Photocopying/Printing, Preschool reading prog, Prog for adults, Prog for children & young adult, Ref & res, Scanner, Story hour, Summer & winter reading prog, Summer reading prog, Tax forms, Teen prog, Winter reading prog
Mem of Reaching Across Illinois Library System (RAILS)
Open Mon & Thurs 10-7, Tues, Wed & Fri 10-5, Sat 9-Noon
Friends of the Library Group

BRADLEY

P BRADLEY PUBLIC LIBRARY DISTRICT*, 296 N Fulton Ave, 60915. SAN 303-7452. Tel: 815-932-6245. FAX: 815-932-6278. E-mail: info@bradleylibrary.org. Web Site: www.bradleylibrary.org. *Dir,* Jodie DePatis; Staff 5 (MLS 1, Non-MLS 4)
Founded 1944. Pop 13,295; Circ 100,250
Jul 2015-Jun 2016 Income (Main Library Only) $751,300
Library Holdings: Audiobooks 1,450; DVDs 2,600; e-books 39,100; e-journals 22; Bk Vols 38,700; Per Subs 98
Automation Activity & Vendor Info: (Cataloging) Innovative Interfaces, Inc; (Circulation) Innovative Interfaces, Inc; (OPAC) Innovative Interfaces, Inc
Wireless access
Function: 24/7 Electronic res, 24/7 Online cat, Adult bk club, Audiobks via web, Bk club(s), Bks on CD, Chess club, Children's prog, Computer training, Computers for patron use, Electronic databases & coll, Free DVD rentals, Homebound delivery serv, ILL available, Internet access, Life-long learning prog for all ages, Magazines, Meeting rooms, Notary serv, Online cat, Outreach serv, OverDrive digital audio bks, Photocopying/Printing, Preschool reading prog, Printer for laptops & handheld devices, Prog for adults, Prog for children & young adult, Scanner, Story hour, Study rm, Summer reading prog, Tax forms, Wheelchair accessible
Mem of Reaching Across Illinois Library System (RAILS)
Partic in Prairienet
Open Mon-Thurs 9-8, Fri 9-6, Sat 9-5, Sun (Sept-May) 1-4
Friends of the Library Group

BRAIDWOOD

P FOSSIL RIDGE PUBLIC LIBRARY*, 386 W Kennedy Rd, 60408. SAN 303-7460. Tel: 815-458-2187. FAX: 815-458-2042. Web Site: www.fossilridge.org. *Libr Dir,* Richard Ashley; E-mail: rashley@fossilridge.org
Founded 1970. Pop 14,803; Circ 71,493
Library Holdings: Bk Vols 46,754; Per Subs 151
Wireless access
Function: 24/7 Electronic res, 24/7 Online cat, Activity rm, Adult bk club, Bk club(s), Bks on CD, Children's prog, Computer training, Computers for patron use, E-Readers, Electronic databases & coll, Free DVD rentals, Holiday prog, ILL available, Internet access, Laminating, Life-long learning prog for all ages, Magazines, Meeting rooms, Microfiche/film & reading machines, Movies, Museum passes, Music CDs, Notary serv, Online cat, Outreach serv, OverDrive digital audio bks, Photocopying/Printing, Preschool outreach, Prog for adults, Prog for children & young adult, Ref serv available, Scanner, Serves people with intellectual disabilities, Story hour, Study rm, Summer & winter reading prog, Summer reading prog, Tax forms, Teen prog, Wheelchair accessible, Winter reading prog
Mem of Reaching Across Illinois Library System (RAILS)
Open Mon-Thurs 9-8, Fri 9-5, Sat 9-3
Friends of the Library Group
Bookmobiles: 1

BREESE

P BREESE PUBLIC LIBRARY, 530 N Third St, 62230. SAN 303-7479. Tel: 618-526-7361. FAX: 618-526-0143. Web Site: www.breeselibrary.org. *Dir,* Kelly Zurliene; E-mail: librarydirector@breeselibrary.org; *Asst Librn,* Diane Holtgrave; Staff 3 (MLS 1, Non-MLS 2)
Founded 1962. Pop 4,048; Circ 124,124
Library Holdings: Large Print Bks 200; Bk Titles 30,000; Bk Vols 32,000; Per Subs 75; Talking Bks 350
Automation Activity & Vendor Info: (Acquisitions) SirsiDynix; (Cataloging) SirsiDynix; (Circulation) SirsiDynix
Wireless access
Function: 24/7 Electronic res, 24/7 Online cat, Adult bk club, After school storytime
Mem of Illinois Heartland Library System
Open Mon & Wed 10-8, Tues, Thurs & Fri 10-4:30, Sat 8-1

BRIDGEVIEW

P BRIDGEVIEW PUBLIC LIBRARY*, 7840 W 79th St, 60455. SAN 303-7487. Tel: 708-458-2880. FAX: 708-458-3553. E-mail: bridgeviewlibrary@bridgeviewlibrary.org. Web Site: www.bridgeviewlibrary.org. *Dir,* Chris Sebuck; Tel: 708-458-2880, Ext 100, E-mail: csebuck@bridgeviewlibrary.org
Founded 1966. Pop 14,402; Circ 112,355
Library Holdings: AV Mats 2,859; Bk Vols 72,000; Per Subs 172
Automation Activity & Vendor Info: (Cataloging) TLC (The Library Corporation); (Circulation) TLC (The Library Corporation)
Mem of Reaching Across Illinois Library System (RAILS)
Partic in System Wide Automated Network
Open Mon-Thurs 10-8, Fri & Sat 10-6

J NORTHWESTERN COLLEGE, Bridgeview Campus, 7725 S Harlem Ave, 60455. Tel: 708-237-5050. FAX: 708-237-5005. Web Site: nc.edu/library. *Dir, Libr Serv,* Sarah Dulay; E-mail: sdulay@nc.edu; Staff 1 (MLS 1)
Library Holdings: CDs 13; DVDs 15; e-books 30; Bk Titles 6,406; Bk Vols 7,215; Per Subs 8; Videos 49
Automation Activity & Vendor Info: (Cataloging) OCLC Connexion; (Circulation) Mandarin Library Automation; (ILL) OCLC WorldShare Interlibrary Loan; (OPAC) Mandarin Library Automation
Wireless access
Mem of Reaching Across Illinois Library System (RAILS)
Partic in Network of Illinois Learning Resources in Community Colleges
Open Mon-Thurs 8-6, Fri 8-4

BRIGHTON

P BRIGHTON MEMORIAL LIBRARY*, 110 N Main St, 62012. (Mail add: PO Box 183, 62012-0183), SAN 375-9911. Tel: 618-372-8450. FAX: 618-372-7450. E-mail: books@brightonpubliclibrary.org. Web Site: www.brightonpubliclibrary.org. *Dir,* Holly Hasquin; *Librn,* Joni Blackenship; *Librn,* Abigail Harper; *Librn,* Becky Woods
Pop 2,500; Circ 26,000
Library Holdings: Audiobooks 517; Bks on Deafness & Sign Lang 5; CDs 120; DVDs 166; Electronic Media & Resources 5; Large Print Bks 505; Bk Titles 13,633; Per Subs 14; Videos 1,079
Automation Activity & Vendor Info: (Acquisitions) Innovative Interfaces, Inc - Millennium; (Cataloging) Innovative Interfaces, Inc - Millennium; (Circulation) Innovative Interfaces, Inc - Millennium; (ILL) Innovative Interfaces, Inc - Millennium; (Media Booking) Innovative Interfaces, Inc - Millennium; (OPAC) Innovative Interfaces, Inc - Millennium; (Serials) Innovative Interfaces, Inc - Millennium
Wireless access
Function: Art exhibits, Audiobks via web, Bk club(s), Bks on cassette, Bks on CD, Children's prog, Computers for patron use, Electronic databases & coll, Free DVD rentals, Home delivery & serv to seniorr ctr & nursing homes, Homebound delivery serv, ILL available, Internet access, Music CDs, Online cat, Online ref, OverDrive digital audio bks, Photocopying/Printing, Preschool outreach, Prog for adults, Prog for children & young adult, Ref serv available, Scanner, Spoken cassettes & CDs, Spoken cassettes & DVDs, Story hour, Summer & winter reading prog, Summer reading prog, VHS videos, Wheelchair accessible
Mem of Illinois Heartland Library System
Special Services for the Deaf - Bks on deafness & sign lang; Closed caption videos
Special Services for the Blind - Audio mat; Bks on cassette; Bks on CD; Cassette playback machines; Cassettes; Large print & cassettes; Large print bks; Large type calculator; Photo duplicator for making large print; Recorded bks; Sound rec; Talking bk & rec for the blind cat
Open Mon, Wed & Thurs 10-6, Tues 10-7:30, Fri 10-5, Sat 10-3
Friends of the Library Group

BRIMFIELD

P BRIMFIELD PUBLIC LIBRARY DISTRICT*, 111 S Galena Ave, 61517. (Mail add: PO Box 207, 61517-0207), SAN 303-7495. Tel: 309-446-9575. FAX: 309-446-9357. Web Site: www.brimfieldlibrary.org. *Libr Dir,* Cheryl Harlow; E-mail: charlow@brimfieldlibrary.org; *Asst Dir,* Tina Kellstadt; E-mail: tkellstadt@brimfieldlibrary.org
Founded 1924. Circ 17,373
Library Holdings: Bk Vols 34,000; Per Subs 38
Automation Activity & Vendor Info: (Cataloging) SirsiDynix; (Circulation) SirsiDynix; (OPAC) SirsiDynix
Wireless access
Open Mon-Thurs 10-7, Fri 10-6, Sat 10-2

BROADVIEW

P BROADVIEW PUBLIC LIBRARY DISTRICT*, 2226 S 16th Ave, 60155. SAN 303-7509. Tel: 708-345-1325. FAX: 708-345-0302. E-mail: brs@broadviewlibrary.org. Web Site: www.broadviewlibrary.org. *Exec Dir,* Keisha Hester; Tel: 708-345-1325, Ext 6, E-mail: hester@broadviewlibrary.org; *Asst Dir, Data Mgr, Mat Mgr,* Robert Lafferty; Tel: 708-345-1325, Ext 14, E-mail: lafferty@broadviewlibrary.org; *Instruction & Research Mgr,* Joseph Bondi; Tel: 708-345-1325, Ext 18, E-mail: bondi@broadviewlibrary.org
Founded 1955. Pop 8,713; Circ 68,922
Library Holdings: Bk Vols 51,000; Per Subs 125
Automation Activity & Vendor Info: (Acquisitions) Innovative Interfaces, Inc - Millennium; (Cataloging) Innovative Interfaces, Inc - Millennium; (Circulation) Innovative Interfaces, Inc - Millennium
Wireless access
Mem of Reaching Across Illinois Library System (RAILS)
Partic in System Wide Automated Network
Open Mon-Thurs 10-9, Fri & Sat 10-5
Friends of the Library Group

BROOKFIELD

S AMERICAN SOKOL EDUCATIONAL & PHYSICAL CULTURE ORGANIZATION*, Library & Archives, 9126 Ogden Ave, 60513. SAN 326-7873. Tel: 708-255-5397. FAX: 708-255-5398. E-mail: aso@american-sokol.org. Web Site: www.american-sokol.org. *Curator,* Position Currently Open
Founded 1976
Library Holdings: Bk Titles 3,166; Per Subs 3,836
Restriction: Open by appt only

P BROOKFIELD PUBLIC LIBRARY*, 3609 Grand Blvd, 60513. SAN 303-7525. Tel: 708-485-6917. FAX: 708-485-5172. Web Site: www.brookfieldlibrary.info. *Libr Dir,* Kimberly Coughran; E-mail: kcoughran@brookfieldlibrary.info
Founded 1913. Pop 18,978; Circ 296,000
Library Holdings: Bk Vols 73,366; Per Subs 164
Automation Activity & Vendor Info: (Acquisitions) Innovative Interfaces, Inc; (Cataloging) Innovative Interfaces, Inc; (Circulation) Innovative Interfaces, Inc; (OPAC) Innovative Interfaces, Inc; (Serials) Innovative Interfaces, Inc
Wireless access
Mem of Reaching Across Illinois Library System (RAILS)
Partic in OCLC Online Computer Library Center, Inc; System Wide Automated Network
Open Mon-Fri 11-6, Sat 11-5
Friends of the Library Group

S CHICAGO ZOOLOGICAL SOCIETY*, Brookfield Zoo Library, 3300 Golf Rd, 60513. SAN 303-7533. Tel: 708-688-8583. FAX: 708-688-7583. Web Site: www.czs.org/Brookfield-ZOO/About/History/80th-Anniversary.aspx. *Mgr, Libr Serv,* Carla Owens; Staff 1 (MLS 1)
Founded 1964
Library Holdings: AV Mats 100; Bk Vols 8,000; Per Subs 100
Special Collections: Zoo Archives 1919 to present
Subject Interests: Animal behavior, Natural hist, Veterinary med, Zoology
Automation Activity & Vendor Info: (Cataloging) SirsiDynix-Enterprise
Wireless access
Function: 24/7 Online cat
Publications: Gateways
Mem of Reaching Across Illinois Library System (RAILS)
Partic in Chicago Collections Consortium
Restriction: Authorized scholars by appt, In-house use for visitors, Open by appt only, Open to pub upon request, Open to researchers by request, Open to staff, students & ancillary prof, Pub by appt only, Visitors must make appt to use bks in the libr

BRUSSELS

P SOUTH COUNTY PUBLIC LIBRARY DISTRICT, 106 Main St, 62013. (Mail add: PO Box 93, 62013-0093), SAN 303-7541. Tel: 618-883-2522. E-mail: scpld@frontiernet.net. *Librn,* Nancy Moennig
Founded 1974. Pop 1,298; Circ 3,046
Library Holdings: Bk Vols 9,025
Wireless access
Mem of Illinois Heartland Library System
Open Tues 10-7, Wed 10-4

BUDA

P MASON MEMORIAL PUBLIC LIBRARY, 104 W Main St, 61314. (Mail add: PO Box 55, 61314-0055), SAN 303-755X. Tel: 309-895-7701. FAX: 309-895-7701. E-mail: budalib61314@gmail.com. *Head Librn,* Peg Foster; E-mail: pegfost@yahoo.com
Pop 597; Circ 5,357
Library Holdings: Bk Vols 13,770; Per Subs 44
Subject Interests: Genealogy, Local hist
Wireless access
Function: Homebound delivery serv, ILL available, Photocopying/Printing, Summer reading prog, Wheelchair accessible
Mem of Reaching Across Illinois Library System (RAILS)
Open Mon 9-4, Tues 11-5, Wed 1-6, Fri & Sat 1-5

BUNKER HILL

P BUNKER HILL PUBLIC LIBRARY DISTRICT*, 220 E Warren St, 62014. (Mail add: PO Box P, 62014-0664), SAN 303-7568. Tel: 618-585-4736. FAX: 618-585-6073. E-mail: library@bunkerhilllibrary.org. Web Site: www.bunkerhilllibrary.org. *Libr Dir,* Kelsey Lasswell; *Librn,* Kimberly Albers; *Librn,* Pat Sims; Staff 2 (Non-MLS 2)
Founded 1867. Pop 4,270
Wireless access
Mem of Illinois Heartland Library System
Open Mon-Fri 10-6, Sat 10-2

BURBANK

P PRAIRIE TRAILS PUBLIC LIBRARY DISTRICT, 8449 S Moody, 60459-2525. SAN 303-7576. Tel: 708-430-3688. FAX: 708-430-5596. E-mail: pts@prairietrailslibrary.org. Web Site: www.prairietrailslibrary.org. *Dir,* Mary Ann Lema; E-mail: mlema@prairietrailslibrary.org; *Asst Librn,* Kendall Harvey; E-mail: kharvey@prairietrailslibrary.org; *Adult Serv,* Sean O'Malley; E-mail: somalley@prairietrailslibrary.org; Staff 30 (MLS 7, Non-MLS 23)
Founded 1969. Pop 30,031; Circ 194,104

Library Holdings: Audiobooks 5,480; CDs 19,959; DVDs 40,529; Bk Titles 124,262; Per Subs 181
Special Collections: Arabic Language Coll; Polish Language Coll; Spanish Language Coll. Oral History
Subject Interests: Adult fiction
Automation Activity & Vendor Info: (Circulation) SirsiDynix-Enterprise; (OPAC) SirsiDynix-WorkFlows; (Serials) EBSCO Online
Wireless access
Function: 24/7 Electronic res, 24/7 Online cat, Adult bk club, After school storytime, Audio & video playback equip for onsite use, Audiobks via web, AV serv, Bilingual assistance for Spanish patrons, Bk club(s), Bks on CD, Children's prog, Computer training, Computers for patron use, Digital talking bks, E-Readers, E-Reserves, Electronic databases & coll, Free DVD rentals, Holiday prog, Homebound delivery serv, ILL available, Internet access, Life-long learning prog for all ages, Magazines, Magnifiers for reading, Mail & tel request accepted, Movies, Museum passes, Music CDs, Notary serv, Online cat, Outreach serv, Photocopying/Printing, Preschool outreach, Printer for laptops & handheld devices, Prog for adults, Prog for children & young adult, Ref serv available, Scanner, Senior computer classes, Senior outreach, Serves people with intellectual disabilities, Spanish lang bks, Story hour, Study rm, Summer & winter reading prog, Summer reading prog, Tax forms, Teen prog, Telephone ref, Wheelchair accessible, Workshops
Publications: Newsletter (Monthly)
Mem of Reaching Across Illinois Library System (RAILS)
Partic in System Wide Automated Network
Open Mon-Thurs 9-9, Fri & Sat 9-5

BUREAU

P LEEPERTOWN TOWNSHIP PUBLIC LIBRARY*, 201 E Nebraska, 61315. (Mail add: PO Box 80, 61315), SAN 303-7584. Tel: 815-659-3283. FAX: 815-659-3263. Web Site: leepertown.lib.il.us. *Libr Dir,* Rose M Thompson; E-mail: rosemt@leepertown.lib.il.us
Founded 1976. Pop 518
Library Holdings: Bk Titles 4,500
Special Collections: Spanish language
Wireless access
Mem of Reaching Across Illinois Library System (RAILS)
Open Mon, Wed & Fri 2-6, Thurs 5-7, Sat 12-3

BURR RIDGE

P REACHING ACROSS ILLINOIS LIBRARY SYSTEM (RAILS)*, 125 Tower Dr, 60527. Tel: 630-734-5000. Toll Free Tel: 866-940-4081. Web Site: www.railslibraries.info. *Exec Dir,* Deirdre Brennan; E-mail: dee.brennan@railslibraries.info
Member Libraries: Acorn Public Library District; Addison Public Library; Adler Planetarium & Astronomy Museum; Advocate Trinity Hospital; Algonquin Area Public Library District; Alsip-Merrionette Park Public Library District; Alzheimer's Association; American College of Surgeons Library; American Dental Association Library & Archives; American Health Information Management Association; American Library Association Library; Amita Health; AMITA Health Adventist Hinsdale Hospital; AMITA Health Saint Joseph Medical Center; AMITA Resurrection Medical Center Chicago; Andalusia Township Library; Ann & Robert H Lurie Children's Hospital of Chicago; Annawan-Alba Township Library; Antioch Public Library District; Appraisal Institute; Argosy University; Arlington Heights Memorial Library; Arnstein & Lehr LLP Library; Atkinson Public Library District; Atlanta Public Library District; Aurora Public Library District; Aurora University; Bartlett Public Library District; Batavia Public Library District; Bedford Park Public Library District; Beecher Community Library; Bellwood Public Library; Benedictine University Library; Bensenville Community Public Library; Berkeley Public Library; Bertolet Memorial Library District; Berwyn Public Library; Black Hawk College; Bloomingdale Public Library; Bloomington Public Library; Blue Island Public Library; Bluffs Public Library; Bond Public Library; Boston Consulting Group; Bourbonnais Public Library District; Bradford Public Library District; Bradley Public Library District; Bridgeview Public Library; Brinks, Gilson & Lione; Broadview Public Library District; Brookfield Public Library; Byron Public Library District; Calumet City Public Library; Calumet Park Public Library; Camp Point Public Library; Carol Stream Public Library; Carthage Public Library District; Carus Chemical Co; Caterpillar Inc; Catholic Theological Union; Centegra Health System; CGH Medical Center; Chadwick Public Library District; Cherry Valley Public Library District; Chicago Community Trust Library; Chicago Heights Public Library; Chicago History Museum; Chicago Mercantile Exchange Library; Chicago Psychoanalytic Institute; Chicago Ridge Public Library; Chicago School of Professional Psychology Library; Chicago Sinai Congregation; Chicago State University; Chicago Theological Seminary; Chicago Transit Authority-Law Library; Chicago Urban League; Chicago Zoological Society; Cicero Public Library; City Colleges of Chicago; City of Chicago; Clarendon Hills Public Library; Clausen Miller Research Services; Clinton Township Public Library; Clover Public Library District; Coal City Public Library District; Colchester District Library; College of DuPage Library; College of Lake County; Colona District Public Library; Columbia College Chicago Library; Cook Memorial Public Library District; Cordova District Library; Cortland Community Library; Creston-Dement Public Library District; Crestwood Public Library District; Crete Public Library District; Creve Coeur Public Library; Danvers Township Library; Deere & Co Library; DeKalb Public Library; Dentons US LLP; DePaul University Libraries; Dixon Public Library; DLA Piper US LLP; Dolton Public Library District; Dominy Memorial Library; Downers Grove Public Library; Duff & Phelps; Earlville Library District; East Dubuque District Library; East Moline Public Library; Edward Chipman Public Library; Edward Hospital; Edwards River Public Library District; Eisenhower Public Library District; El Paso Public Library; Elgin Mental Health Center Library; Elizabeth Township Library; Ella Johnson Memorial Public Library District; Elmhurst Memorial Healthcare; Elmhurst Public Library; Elmwood Park Public Library; Encyclopaedia Britannica Inc; Energy BBDO; Engineering Systems Inc Library; Erie Public Library District; Erikson Institute; Evergreen Park Public Library; Exelon Corporate Library; Fabricators & Manufacturers Association International; Federal Reserve Bank of Chicago; FHN Memorial Hospital; Field Museum of Natural History; First Division Museum at Cantigny; Flagg-Rochelle Public Library District; Flewellin Memorial Library; Flossmoor Public Library; Fondulac Public Library District; Forefront Library; Forest Park Public Library; Forreston Public Library; Fossil Ridge Public Library; Fountaindale Public Library District; Fox College Library; Fox Lake Public District Library; Fox River Grove Public Library District; Fox River Valley Public Library District; Frankfort Public Library District; Franklin Park Public Library District; Freeport Public Library; Gail Borden Public Library District; Galena Public Library District; Galesburg Public Library; Galva Public Library District; Geneseo Public Library District; Genesis Medical Center, Illini Campus; Geneva Public Library District; Genoa Public Library District; Glen Ellyn Public Library; Glenside Public Library District; Glenview Public Library; Glenwood-Lynwood Public Library District; Graham Hospital Association; Grande Prairie Public Library District; Grant Park Public Library; Graves-Hume Public Library District; Greeley & Hansen Engineering Library; Green Hills Public Library District; Greig Memorial Library; Group Technology Library & Information Services; H Douglas Singer Mental Health Center; Hamilton Public Library; Hamilton Sundstrand; Hanover Township Library; Harrington College of Design Library; Harvard Diggins Public Library; Harvey Public Library District; Havana Public Library District; Heartland Institute; Helen M Plum Memorial Public Library District; Henderson County Public Library District; Henry C Adams Memorial Library; Heyworth Public Library District; Highland Community College Library; Highwood Public Library; Hinckley Public Library District; Historical Society of Quincy & Adams County Library; Hodgkins Public Library District; Homer Township Public Library District; Hometown Public Library; Honeywell Sensing & Control; Hudson Area Public Library District; Huntley Area Public Library District; Ida Public Library; Illinois Agricultural Association; Illinois College; Illinois College of Optometry Library; Illinois Department of Corrections; Illinois Historic Preservation Agency; Illinois Institute of Art - Chicago Library; Illinois Institute of Technology; Illinois Mathematics & Science Academy; Illinois School for the Visually Impaired Library; Illinois Valley Community College; Illinois Wesleyan University; Illinois Youth Center; Indian Prairie Public Library District; Institute for Clinical Social Work Library; Itasca Community Library; John G Shedd Aquarium Library; John H Stroger Jr Hospital of Cook County; John Wood Community College Library; Johnsburg Public Library District; Joliet Junior College Library; Joliet Public Library; Judson University; Julia Hull District Library; Justice Public Library District; Kane County Law Library & Self Help Legal Center; Kaneville Public Library District; Kankakee Community College; Kankakee Public Library; Katten, Muchin, Rosenman LLP Library; Kendall College; Kewanee Public Library District; Kirkland Public Library; Kishwaukee College Library; Knowledge Systems Institute Library; La Grange Park Public Library District; La Grange Public Library; La Harpe Carnegie Public Library District; Lacon Public Library District; Ladd Public Library District; LAF Library; LaMoille-Clarion Public Library District; Lanark Public Library; Lansing Public Library; LaSalle Public Library; Learning Point Associates; Leepertown Township Public Library; Lemont Public Library District; Lena Community District Library; Lenhardt Library of the Chicago Botanic Garden; Lewis University Library; Lillie M Evans Library District; Limestone Township Library District; Lisle Library District; Lostant Community Library; MacCormac College Library; MacMurray College; MacNeal Hospital; Malta Township Public Library; Manhattan-Elwood Public Library District; Maple Park Public Library District; Marengo-Union Library District; Markham Public Library; Marquette Heights Public Library; Marseilles Public Library; Martin Township Public Library; Mason Memorial Public Library; Matteson Area Public Library District; Mayer Brown LLP; Maywood Public Library District; McCook Public Library District; McLean County Museum of History; Melrose Park Public Library; Mercy Hospital & Medical Center; Messenger Public Library of North Aurora; MetroSouth Medical Center; Midlothian Public Library; Milledgeville Public Library; Mills & Petrie Memorial Library; Mineral-Gold Public Library District; Mokena Community Public Library

District; Moline Public Library; Monmouth College; Moody Bible Institute; Moore Memorial Library District; Moraine Valley Community College Library; Morris Area Public Library District; Morrison & Mary Wiley Library District; Morton College Library; Morton Grove Public Library; Morton Public Library District; Mount Carroll Township Public Library; Mount Hope-Funks Grove Townships Library District; Mount Morris Public Library; Mount Prospect Public Library; NAES College; Nancy L McConathy Public Library; Naperville Public Library; National Association of Realtors; National Safety Council Library; National University of Health Sciences Learning Resource Center; Nauvoo Public Library; New Gracanica Monastery; New Lenox Public Library District; Newberry Library; Nicor Gas; Niles-Maine District Library; Nippersink Public Library District; Normal Public Library; North East Multi-Regional Training; North Park University; North Pike District Library; North Riverside Public Library District; North Suburban Library District; Northbrook Public Library; Northeastern Illinois University; Northern Illinois University Libraries; Northlake Public Library District; Northwestern College; Northwestern Medicine Central DuPage Hospital; Northwestern Medicine-Delnor Hospital; Northwestern University Libraries; Oak Brook Public Library; Oak Lawn Public Library; Oak Park Public Library; Oakton Community College Library; Odell Public Library; Odell Public Library District; Oglesby Public Library; Ohio Public Library District; Olivet Nazarene University; Oregon Public Library District; Orland Hills Public Library District; Orland Park Public Library; OSF Saint Anthony Medical Center; Oswego Public Library District; Our Lady of the Resurrection Medical Center Library; Packer Engineering Inc; Palatine Public Library District; Palos Heights Public Library; Palos Park Public Library; Pankhurst Memorial Library; Park Forest Public Library; Parlin Ingersoll Public Library; Paw Paw Public Library District; Pearl City Public Library District; Pecatonica Public Library District; Pedersen & Houpt Library; Peotone Public Library District; Peru Public Library; Plainfield Public Library District; Plano Community Library District; Polish Museum of America Library; Polo Public Library District; Poplar Creek Public Library District; Posen Public Library District; Prairie Skies Public Library District; Prairie State College Library; Prairie Trails Public Library District; Presence Mercy Medical Center; Presence Saint Francis Medical Library; Presence Saint Joseph Medical Library; Prevention First Inc; Prospect Heights Public Library District; Provena Saint Joseph Hospital; Putnam County Public Library District; Quincy Public Library; Quincy University; Ransom Memorial Public Library; Raymond A Sapp Memorial Township Library; Reddick Public Library District; Richard A Mautino Memorial Library; Richton Park Public Library District; River Forest Public Library; River Grove Public Library District; River Valley District Library; Riverdale Public Library District; Riverside Public Library; Robert Morris University; Robert R Jones Public Library; Robert W Rowe Public Library District; Rock Falls Public Library District; Rock Island County Law Library; Rock Island Public Library; Rock River Library District; Rock Valley College; Rockford Memorial Hospital; Rockford Public Library; Rockford University; Roseland Community Hospital; Roselle Public Library District; Round Lake Area Public Library District; Rush Copley Medical Center; Saint Xavier University; Sandwich Public Library District; Sanford-Brown College; Sargent & Lundy, LLC; Sauk Valley Community College; Savanna Public Library District; Schaumburg Township District Library; Schiller Park Public Library; Schmaling Memorial Public Library District; School of the Art Institute of Chicago; Selby Township Library District; Seneca Public Library District; Seyfarth Shaw LLP; Sheffield Public Library; Shorewood-Troy Public Library District; Shriners' Hospital for Children; Silver Cross Hospital Medical Library; Skidmore, Owings & Merrill Library; Skokie Public Library; Society of Actuaries Library; Somonauk Public Library District; South Beloit Public Library; South Holland Public Library; South Suburban College Library; Spencer Stuart Library; Spertus Institute of Jewish Studies; St Charles Public Library District; Stateville Correctional Center Libraries; Steger-South Chicago Heights Public Library District; Sterling Public Library; Stickney-Forest View Public Library District; Stockton Township Public Library; Streator Public Library; Sugar Grove Public Library District; Summit Public Library District; Swedish Covenant Hospital; Sycamore Public Library; Talcott Free Public Library; Tetra-Tech Em Inc; The Center - Resources for Teaching & Learning Library; The Morton Arboretum; Theosophical Society in America; Thomas Ford Memorial Library; Thornton Public Library; Three Rivers Public Library District; Tinley Park Public Library; Tiskilwa Public Library; Toluca Public Library; Town & Country Public Library District; Tremont District Public Library; Trinity Christian College; Trinity Iowa Health System; Triton College Library; United States Army; United States Environmental Protection Agency; United States Railroad Retirement Board Library; University of St Francis; University Park Public Library District; Utica Public Library District; Vandercook College of Music; Villa Park Public Library; Village of Avon Public Library; Viola Public Library District; Walnut Public Library District; Warren Township Public Library; Warren-Newport Public Library District; Warrenville Public Library District; Wauconda Area Public Library District; West Chicago Public Library District; Westchester Public Library; Western District Library; Western Illinois Area Agency on Aging; Westmont Public Library; Wheaton College; Wheaton Public Library; White Oak Library District; William Blair & Co LLC; William Leonard Public Library District; Wilmette Public Library District; Wilmington Public Library District; Winfield Public Library; Winifred Knox Memorial Library; Winnebago County Law Library; Winnebago Public Library District; Wiss, Janney, Elstner Associates, Inc; Wood Dale Public Library District; Woodridge Public Library; Woodstock Public Library; Worth Public Library District; York Township Public Library; Yorkville Public Library

BUSHNELL

P BUSHNELL PUBLIC LIBRARY*, 455 N Dean, 61422-1299. SAN 303-7592. Tel: 309-772-2060. FAX: 309-772-9038. E-mail: plibrary@frontier.com. *Dir,* Laurie Hockenberry
Pop 4,706; Circ 25,639
Library Holdings: Bk Titles 25,000; Bk Vols 26,000; Per Subs 65
Special Collections: Peter Newell Coll
Automation Activity & Vendor Info: (Cataloging) Follett Software; (Circulation) Follett Software
Wireless access
Open Mon-Fri 9-6, Sat 9-Noon

BYRON

P BYRON PUBLIC LIBRARY DISTRICT*, 100 S Washington St, 61010. (Mail add: PO Box 434, 61010-0434), SAN 303-7606. Tel: 815-234-5107. FAX: 815-234-5582. E-mail: library@byron.lib.il.us. Web Site: byron.lib.il.us. *Dir,* Emily Porter; E-mail: emilyp@byron.lib.il.us; *Head, Teen Serv,* Nancy McKay; E-mail: nancym@byron.lib.il.us; *Head, Youth Serv,* Julie Reckamp; E-mail: julier@byron.lib.il.us; Staff 2 (MLS 2)
Founded 1916. Pop 7,989; Circ 138,289
Library Holdings: Audiobooks 2,411; CDs 2,059; DVDs 4,067; e-books 170; Large Print Bks 3,284; Bk Vols 53,466; Per Subs 108
Special Collections: Commonwealth Edison
Automation Activity & Vendor Info: (Cataloging) Innovative Interfaces, Inc - Sierra; (Circulation) Innovative Interfaces, Inc - Sierra; (OPAC) Innovative Interfaces, Inc - Sierra; (Serials) Innovative Interfaces, Inc - Sierra
Wireless access
Mem of Reaching Across Illinois Library System (RAILS)
Open Mon-Thurs 9-8, Fri & Sat 9-5, Sun 1-5

CAHOKIA

P CAHOKIA PUBLIC LIBRARY DISTRICT*, 140 Cahokia Park Dr, 62206-2129. SAN 303-7614. Tel: 618-332-1491. FAX: 618-332-1104. E-mail: info@cahokialibrary.org. Web Site: www.cahokialibrary.org. *Dir,* Kathleen Armstrong
Founded 1963. Pop 17,550; Circ 70,453
Library Holdings: Bk Vols 37,659; Per Subs 79
Automation Activity & Vendor Info: (Circulation) Innovative Interfaces, Inc
Wireless access
Mem of Illinois Heartland Library System
Open Mon-Thurs 9-7:30, Fri & Sat 9-5
Friends of the Library Group

CAIRO

P CAIRO PUBLIC LIBRARY, 1609 Washington Ave, 62914. (Mail add: PO Box 151, 62914-0151), SAN 303-7630. Tel: 618-734-1840. FAX: 618-734-4799. E-mail: cairopl1884@gmail.com. *Librn,* Monica L Smith
Founded 1884. Pop 2,846; Circ 32,800
Library Holdings: Bk Vols 52,000; Per Subs 60
Special Collections: Army & Navy Records; Census Microfilm for 16 Southern Illinois Counties; Civil War Coll; Jesuit Relations; Local Newspapers on Microfilm from 1848; WPA Art
Mem of Illinois Heartland Library System
Open Mon-Fri 9:30-4:30

CALUMET CITY

P CALUMET CITY PUBLIC LIBRARY*, 660 Manistee Ave, 60409. SAN 303-7649. Tel: 708-862-6220. Administration Tel: 708-862-6220, Ext 241. FAX: 708-862-0872. E-mail: info@calumetcitypl.org. Web Site: www.calumetcitypl.org. *Dir,* Jane Rowland; Tel: 708-862-6220, Ext 244, E-mail: jrowland@calumetcitypl.org; *Head, Adult Serv,* Denise Benson; Tel: 708-862-6220, Ext 249, E-mail: dbenson@calumetcitypl.org; *Head, Circ,* Lisa Trevino; Tel: 708-862-6220, Ext 240, E-mail: ltrevino@calumetcitypl.org; *Head, Tech Serv,* Warren Zachary; Tel: 708-862-6220, Ext 224, E-mail: zwarren@calumetcitypl.org; *Head, Youth Serv,* Gale Krekovich; Tel: 708-862-6220, Ext 233, E-mail: gkrekovich@calumetcitypl.org; Staff 6 (MLS 5, Non-MLS 1)
Pop 39,071; Circ 174,726
Library Holdings: AV Mats 13,537; Large Print Bks 2,017; Bk Vols 126,932; Per Subs 33; Talking Bks 1,371

Automation Activity & Vendor Info: (Circulation) Innovative Interfaces, Inc; (OPAC) Innovative Interfaces, Inc; (Serials) Innovative Interfaces, Inc
Wireless access
Publications: Library Links (Quarterly newsletter)
Mem of Reaching Across Illinois Library System (RAILS)
Partic in System Wide Automated Network
Open Mon-Thurs 10-9, Fri & Sat 10-4

CALUMET PARK

P CALUMET PARK PUBLIC LIBRARY*, 1500 W 127th St, 60827. SAN 303-7657. Tel: 708-385-5768. FAX: 708-385-8816. E-mail: CAS@calumetparklibrary.org. Web Site: librarylearning.org/calumet-park-public-library. *Dir,* Debra Woods; E-mail: wooddebrann1@gmail.com
Pop 8,788; Circ 15,770
Library Holdings: Bk Vols 25,000; Per Subs 80
Special Collections: Lupus
Automation Activity & Vendor Info: (Cataloging) Innovative Interfaces, Inc; (Circulation) Innovative Interfaces, Inc; (OPAC) Innovative Interfaces, Inc
Mem of Reaching Across Illinois Library System (RAILS)
Partic in System Wide Automated Network
Open Tues-Fri 10-1

CAMBRIDGE

P CAMBRIDGE PUBLIC LIBRARY DISTRICT*, 212 W Center St, 61238-1239. SAN 303-7665. Tel: 309-937-2233. FAX: 309-937-2873. E-mail: cambpld@gmail.com. *Dir,* John Sayers
Pop 3,394
Library Holdings: Bk Vols 28,000; Per Subs 65
Subject Interests: Local hist
Automation Activity & Vendor Info: (Cataloging) Follett Software; (Circulation) Follett Software
Open Mon-Thurs (Winter) 11-8, Fri 11-5, Sat 11-4; Mon-Thurs (Summer) 11-8, Fri & Sat 11-4

CAMP POINT

P CAMP POINT PUBLIC LIBRARY*, 206 E State St, 62320. (Mail add: PO Box 377, 62320-0377), SAN 303-7673. Tel: 217-593-7021. FAX: 217-593-6121. E-mail: caseytownshiplibrary@gmail.com. Web Site: www.camppointpubliclibrary.com. *Dir,* Debra Rossiter
Founded 1906. Pop 3,058; Circ 12,736
Jul 2013-Jun 2014 Income $60,897, State $3,835, County $56,462, Locally Generated Income $600. Mats Exp $8,879, Books $6,670, Per/Ser (Incl. Access Fees) $569, Electronic Ref Mat (Incl. Access Fees) $1,640. Sal $26,213
Library Holdings: Large Print Bks 750; Bk Titles 15,874; Per Subs 36
Automation Activity & Vendor Info: (Circulation) Follett Software
Wireless access
Function: Archival coll, Home delivery & serv to seniorr ctr & nursing homes, Homebound delivery serv, Homework prog, ILL available, Internet access, Photocopying/Printing, Prog for adults, Prog for children & young adult, Ref serv available, Summer reading prog, Telephone ref, VHS videos, Wheelchair accessible
Mem of Reaching Across Illinois Library System (RAILS)
Open Mon & Fri 2-6, Tues 10-7, Wed & Thurs 2-7, Sat 10-2
Restriction: Authorized patrons, In-house use for visitors, Non-circulating coll, Non-resident fee, Open to pub with supv only

CANTON

M GRAHAM HOSPITAL ASSOCIATION, Medical Staff Library & School of Nursing Library, 210 W Walnut St, 61520. SAN 303-7681. Tel: 309-647-5240, Ext 2343. FAX: 309-649-5105. E-mail: library@grahamhospital.org. Web Site: www.grahamschoolofnursing.org/library. *Dir, Libr Serv,* Michelle Quinones; Tel: 309-647-5240, Ext 3388, E-mail: mquinones@grahamhospital.org; *Tech Coordr,* Lynette Murphy; Staff 1 (MLS 1)
Founded 1909
Library Holdings: AV Mats 600; Bk Vols 2,093; Per Subs 109
Special Collections: Oral History
Subject Interests: Med, Nursing
Automation Activity & Vendor Info: (Cataloging) OCLC Connexion; (Circulation) SirsiDynix-WorkFlows; (ILL) OCLC; (OPAC) SirsiDynix-WorkFlows; (Serials) EBSCO Online
Wireless access
Mem of Reaching Across Illinois Library System (RAILS)
Partic in Health Science Library of Illinois; Heart of Illinois Library Consortium
Open Mon-Fri 7-5
Restriction: Authorized patrons

S ILLINOIS DEPARTMENT OF CORRECTIONS*, Illinois River Correctional Center Library, 1300 W Locust St, 61520-8791. (Mail add: PO Box 999, 61520), SAN 371-6600. Tel: 309-647-7030, Ext 549, 309-647-7030, Ext 550. FAX: 309-647-0353. Web Site: www2.illinois.gov/idoc/facilities/Pages/illinoisrivercorrectionalcenter.aspx. *Librn,* Jake Nebergal; Staff 1 (MLS 1)
Founded 1989
Library Holdings: High Interest/Low Vocabulary Bk Vols 50; Bk Titles 9,000; Bk Vols 19,000
Subject Interests: Law
Function: Ref serv available
Partic in Resource Sharing Alliance
Special Services for the Blind - Talking bks
Open Tues-Fri 7-5
Restriction: Circ limited

P PARLIN INGERSOLL PUBLIC LIBRARY, 205 W Chestnut St, 61520. SAN 303-769X. Tel: 309-647-0328. FAX: 309-647-8117. E-mail: parlin@parliningersoll.org. Web Site: www.parliningersoll.org. *Dir,* Kimberly Bunner; *Pub Serv,* Ben Smith; *Youth Serv,* Tiffany Kaufmann; Staff 2 (MLS 1, Non-MLS 1)
Pop 14,704
Library Holdings: Audiobooks 5,419; CDs 5,297; DVDs 8,641; Bk Titles 82,702; Per Subs 67
Special Collections: Fulton County History Coll
Automation Activity & Vendor Info: (Cataloging) OCLC; (Circulation) Innovative Interfaces, Inc; (ILL) OCLC; (OPAC) Innovative Interfaces, Inc
Wireless access
Function: 24/7 Online cat, Bk club(s), Bks on CD, Children's prog, Homebound delivery serv, ILL available, Internet access, Magazines, Notary serv, Online cat, OverDrive digital audio bks, Photocopying/Printing, Prog for children & young adult, Scanner, Story hour, Wheelchair accessible
Mem of Reaching Across Illinois Library System (RAILS)
Partic in OCLC Online Computer Library Center, Inc
Open Mon, Wed & Fri 9-6, Tues & Thurs 9-8, Sat 9-1

J SPOON RIVER COLLEGE LIBRARY*, Russell Learning Resource Center, 23235 N County Hwy 22, 61520. SAN 303-7703. Tel: 309-649-6603. Interlibrary Loan Service Tel: 309-649-6278. Information Services Tel: 309-649-6603. FAX: 309-649-6235. Reference E-mail: reference@src.edu. Web Site: www.src.edu/services/lrc/library/Pages/default.aspx. *Librn,* Marla Turgeon; E-mail: marla.turgeon@src.edu; *ILL,* Natalie Orwig; Staff 2 (MLS 1, Non-MLS 1)
Founded 1951. Enrl 1,560; Fac 60; Highest Degree: Associate
Jul 2015-Jun 2016. Mats Exp $52,000, Books $7,000, AV Mat $3,000, Electronic Ref Mat (Incl. Access Fees) $42,000. Sal Prof $42,000
Library Holdings: AV Mats 29; DVDs 769; e-books 150,000; Electronic Media & Resources 27; Bk Titles 11,384
Special Collections: College History; Local History
Subject Interests: Humanities, Sciences
Automation Activity & Vendor Info: (Acquisitions) SirsiDynix-WorkFlows; (Cataloging) SirsiDynix-WorkFlows; (Circulation) SirsiDynix-WorkFlows; (Course Reserve) SirsiDynix-WorkFlows; (Discovery) EBSCO Discovery Service; (ILL) OCLC Online; (OPAC) SirsiDynix-Enterprise
Wireless access
Function: 24/7 Online cat, Computers for patron use, Free DVD rentals
Partic in Consortium of Academic & Research Libraries in Illinois; Network of Illinois Learning Resources in Community Colleges; Northern Ill Learning Resources Coop; OCLC Online Computer Library Center, Inc; Resource Sharing Alliance
Special Services for the Deaf - Assistive tech
Special Services for the Blind - Assistive/Adapted tech devices, equip & products; Reader equip; Scanner for conversion & translation of mats; ZoomText magnification & reading software
Open Mon-Fri 8-4:30
Restriction: 24-hr pass syst for students only

CARBONDALE

P CARBONDALE PUBLIC LIBRARY*, 405 W Main St, 62901-2995. SAN 303-7711. Tel: 618-457-0354. FAX: 618-457-0353. E-mail: cpllib@carbondale.lib.il.us. Web Site: www.carbondale.lib.il.us. *Dir,* Diana Brawley Sussman; Staff 6 (MLS 3, Non-MLS 3)
Founded 1923. Pop 25,902; Circ 151,671
Library Holdings: Electronic Media & Resources 30; Per Subs 186
Wireless access
Function: 24/7 Electronic res, 24/7 Online cat, Adult bk club, After school storytime, Art exhibits, Bks on cassette, Bks on CD, Children's prog, Computer training, Computers for patron use, E-Readers, Electronic databases & coll, Family literacy, Free DVD rentals, Holiday prog, Homework prog, ILL available, Instruction & testing, Internet access, Jail serv, Life-long learning prog for all ages, Magazines, Magnifiers for

reading, Mail & tel request accepted, Meeting rooms, Movies, Museum passes, Music CDs, Notary serv, Online cat, Online ref, Orientations, OverDrive digital audio bks, Photocopying/Printing, Preschool outreach, Printer for laptops & handheld devices, Prog for adults, Prog for children & young adult, Ref serv available, Senior computer classes, Serves people with intellectual disabilities, Spoken cassettes & CDs, Spoken cassettes & DVDs, Story hour, Summer & winter reading prog, Summer reading prog, Tax forms, Teen prog, Telephone ref, VHS videos, Wheelchair accessible, Winter reading prog, Workshops, Writing prog
Mem of Illinois Heartland Library System
Partic in Share NW Consortium
Open Mon-Thurs 9-8, Fri & Sat 9-6, Sun 1-6
Friends of the Library Group

C SOUTHERN ILLINOIS UNIVERSITY CARBONDALE*, Delyte W Morris Library, 605 Agriculture Dr, Mailcode 6632, 62901. SAN 339-7599. Tel: 618-453-2522. Circulation Tel: 618-453-1455. Information Services Tel: 618-453-2818. Administration FAX: 618-453-3440. Web Site: www.lib.siu.edu. *Assoc Dean,* Susan Tulis; E-mail: stulis@lib.siu.edu; Staff 40 (MLS 30, Non-MLS 10)
Founded 1869. Highest Degree: Doctorate
Library Holdings: Bk Vols 2,800,000; Per Subs 36,000
Special Collections: American Philosophy Coll; Expatriates Coll; Irish Literary Renaissance Coll; John Dewey Coll; Lawrence Durrell Coll; Private Presses; Robert Graves, James Joyce, D H Lawrence & Henry Miller Colls, bks & mss; Ulysses S Grant Coll. Oral History; State Document Depository; UN Document Depository; US Document Depository
Automation Activity & Vendor Info: (Acquisitions) Ex Libris Group; (Cataloging) Ex Libris Group; (Circulation) Ex Libris Group; (Course Reserve) Ex Libris Group; (ILL) Ex Libris Group; (Media Booking) Ex Libris Group; (OPAC) Ex Libris Group; (Serials) Ex Libris Group
Wireless access
Publications: Bibliographic Contributions (irregular)
Partic in Association of Research Libraries; Center for Research Libraries; Consortium of Academic & Research Libraries in Illinois; Greater Western Library Alliance; Illinois Library & Information Network; OCLC Online Computer Library Center, Inc
Open Mon-Thurs 7:30am-Midnight, Fri 7:30am-9pm, Sat 10-6, Sun 1-9
Friends of the Library Group

Departmental Libraries:

CL LAW LIBRARY, Lesar Law Bldg Mailcode 6803, 1150 Douglas Dr, 62901, SAN 325-3295. Tel: 618-453-8796. FAX: 618-453-8728. E-mail: lawlib@siu.edu. Web Site: www.law.siu.edu/lawlib. *Dir, Law Libr,* Doug Lind; Tel: 618-453-8713, E-mail: dlind@siu.edu; *Head, Pub Serv,* Nolan Wright; Tel: 618-453-8791, E-mail: nwright@siu.edu; *Ref Librn,* Alicia Granby Jones; Tel: 618-453-8780, E-mail: agjones@siu.edu; Staff 5 (MLS 5)
Founded 1973. Enrl 341; Fac 35; Highest Degree: Doctorate
Jul 2013-Jun 2014. Mats Exp $598,056, Books $424,556, Electronic Ref Mat (Incl. Access Fees) $169,000, Presv $2,000
Library Holdings: DVDs 1,093; Bk Vols 230,646; Per Subs 2,116
Special Collections: Dillard Coll; Lincoln as a Lawyer; Self-Help Legal Coll. State Document Depository; US Document Depository
Subject Interests: Law
Automation Activity & Vendor Info: (Acquisitions) Innovative Interfaces, Inc; (Cataloging) Innovative Interfaces, Inc; (Circulation) Innovative Interfaces, Inc; (Course Reserve) Innovative Interfaces, Inc; (ILL) OCLC WorldShare Interlibrary Loan; (OPAC) Innovative Interfaces, Inc; (Serials) Innovative Interfaces, Inc
Function: ILL available, Ref serv available
Partic in Mid-America Law Library Consortium
Open Mon-Thurs 8-9, Fri 8-4, Sun 1-9
Restriction: 24-hr pass syst for students only

CARLINVILLE

C BLACKBURN COLLEGE*, Lumpkin Learning Commons, 700 College Ave, 62626. SAN 303-772X. Tel: 217-854-5665. FAX: 217-854-5712. Web Site: blackburn.edu/why-blackburn/academics/lumpkin-learning-commons/lumpkin/. *Dir,* Rachel Stull; E-mail: rachel.stull@blackburn.edu; Staff 3 (MLS 2, Non-MLS 1)
Founded 1867. Enrl 560; Fac 35; Highest Degree: Bachelor
Library Holdings: Bk Titles 55,000; Bk Vols 80,000; Per Subs 45
Special Collections: US Document Depository
Wireless access
Function: 24/7 Electronic res, 24/7 Online cat, Activity rm, Archival coll, Art exhibits, Audio & video playback equip for onsite use, AV serv, Bilingual assistance for Spanish patrons, Children's prog, Citizenship assistance, Computer training, Computers for patron use, Electronic databases & coll, Equip loans & repairs, For res purposes, Free DVD rentals, Govt ref serv, Health sci info serv, Holiday prog, ILL available, Instruction & testing, Internet access, Laminating, Learning ctr, Literacy & newcomer serv, Magazines, Magnifiers for reading, Mail & tel request accepted, Mail loans to mem, Meeting rooms, Movies, Online cat, Online info literacy tutorials on the web & in blackboard, Online ref, Orientations, Outreach serv, Outside serv via phone, mail, e-mail & web, Photocopying/Printing, Printer for laptops & handheld devices, Prog for adults, Ref & res, Ref serv available, Res assist avail, Res libr, Scanner, Spanish lang bks, Study rm, Tax forms, Telephone ref, Visual arts prog, Workshops, Writing prog
Mem of Illinois Heartland Library System
Partic in Consortium of Academic & Research Libraries in Illinois; OCLC-LVIS
Open Mon-Thurs (Fall & Spring) 8am-11pm, Fri 8-5, Sun 5-11; Mon-Fri (Summer) 8-4

P CARLINVILLE PUBLIC LIBRARY*, 510 N Broad St, 62626-1019. (Mail add: PO Box 17, 62626-0017), SAN 303-7738. Tel: 217-854-3505. FAX: 217-854-5349. E-mail: mail@carlinvillelibrary.org. Web Site: www.carlinvillelibrary.org. *Dir,* Janet Howard; Staff 1 (Non-MLS 1)
Founded 1927. Pop 5,416
Library Holdings: Bk Titles 24,000; Per Subs 120
Subject Interests: Genealogy
Automation Activity & Vendor Info: (Cataloging) SirsiDynix; (Circulation) SirsiDynix
Wireless access
Mem of Illinois Heartland Library System
Open Mon-Thurs 9-8, Fri 9-5, Sat 9-1, Sun 1-4

CARLOCK

P CARLOCK PUBLIC LIBRARY DISTRICT*, 202 E Washington, 61725. (Mail add: PO Box 39, 61725-0039), SAN 321-2718. Tel: 309-376-5651. FAX: 309-376-4027. E-mail: carlockpatron@hotmail.com. Web Site: carlocklibrary.com. *Dir,* Linda Spencer; Staff 3 (MLS 3)
Founded 1979. Pop 2,600; Circ 10,501
Library Holdings: Bk Vols 13,000; Per Subs 37
Automation Activity & Vendor Info: (Circulation) Follett Software
Open Mon, Tues & Thurs 9-Noon & 1-8:30, Wed & Fri 9-Noon & 1-6, Sat 9-1
Friends of the Library Group

CARLYLE

P CASE-HALSTEAD PUBLIC LIBRARY*, 550 Sixth St, 62231. SAN 303-7746. Tel: 618-594-5210. FAX: 618-594-8415. E-mail: librarian@carlylelake.com. Web Site: casehalstead.com. *Dir,* Keith Housewright
Founded 1938. Pop 3,474; Circ 38,500
Library Holdings: Bk Titles 26,200; Per Subs 60
Subject Interests: Genealogy, Local hist
Automation Activity & Vendor Info: (Cataloging) Innovative Interfaces, Inc; (Circulation) Innovative Interfaces, Inc; (OPAC) Innovative Interfaces, Inc
Mem of Illinois Heartland Library System
Open Mon-Thurs 9-8, Fri 9-5, Sat 9-2
Friends of the Library Group

CARMI

P CARMI PUBLIC LIBRARY*, 103 Slocumb St, 62821. SAN 303-7754. Tel: 618-382-5277. FAX: 618-384-3118. E-mail: carmilib@yahoo.com. Web Site: www.cityofcarmi.org/carmi-public-library. *Dir,* Stephanie Dennis
Founded 1914. Pop 5,422; Circ 37,220
Library Holdings: Bk Vols 31,060; Per Subs 66; Talking Bks 602
Mem of Illinois Heartland Library System
Open Mon-Thurs 10-7, Fri 10-6, Sat 11-5
Friends of the Library Group

CAROL STREAM

P CAROL STREAM PUBLIC LIBRARY*, 616 Hiawatha Dr, 60188. SAN 303-7762. Tel: 630-653-0755. FAX: 630-653-6809. E-mail: cstream@cslibrary.org. Web Site: www.cslibrary.org. *Dir,* Susan Westgate; Tel: 630-344-6101, E-mail: director@cslibrary.org; *Asst Dir, Head, Tech Serv,* Mary Clemens; E-mail: mclemens@cslibrary.org; *Mgr, Ad Serv,* Laura Hays; E-mail: lhays@cslibrary.org; *Mgr, Circ Serv,* Jeri Cain; E-mail: jcain@cslibrary.org; *Mgr, Youth Serv,* Amy Teske; E-mail: ateske@cslibrary.org; Staff 39 (MLS 17, Non-MLS 22)
Founded 1962. Pop 39,711; Circ 351,686
May 2017-Apr 2018 Income $3,258,100, State $31,000, Locally Generated Income $3,151,750, Other $75,350. Mats Exp $398,600, Books $125,100, Per/Ser (Incl. Access Fees) $12,500, AV Mat $82,000, Electronic Ref Mat (Incl. Access Fees) $179,000. Sal $1,443,000 (Prof $535,000)
Library Holdings: Audiobooks 4,845; CDs 5,337; DVDs 14,187; e-books 44,605; e-journals 107; Electronic Media & Resources 58; Large Print Bks 2,906; Bk Vols 95,946; Per Subs 230
Automation Activity & Vendor Info: (Acquisitions) SirsiDynix-WorkFlows; (Cataloging) SirsiDynix-WorkFlows; (Circulation) SirsiDynix-WorkFlows; (Serials) SirsiDynix-WorkFlows

Wireless access
Function: 24/7 Electronic res, 24/7 Online cat, Audiobks on Playaways & MP3, Bk club(s), Bks on CD, Children's prog, Computer training, Electronic databases & coll, Free DVD rentals, Homebound delivery serv, ILL available, Internet access, Magazines, Mango lang, Meeting rooms, Museum passes, Music CDs, Online cat, Online ref, OverDrive digital audio bks, Photocopying/Printing, Preschool outreach, Preschool reading prog, Prog for adults, Prog for children & young adult, Ref serv available, Scanner, Senior outreach, Spanish lang bks, STEM programs, Study rm, Summer reading prog, Tax forms, Teen prog
Publications: Carol Stream Public Library (Monthly newsletter)
Mem of Reaching Across Illinois Library System (RAILS)
Partic in System Wide Automated Network
Open Mon-Thurs 9-9, Fri 9-6, Sat 9-5, Sun 1-5
Friends of the Library Group

CARRIER MILLS

P CARRIER MILLS-STONEFORT PUBLIC LIBRARY DISTRICT*, 109 W Oak St, 62917. (Mail add: PO Box 338, 62917-0338), SAN 303-7770. Tel: 618-994-2011. FAX: 618-994-2303. *Librn,* Beth Thomason; *Bus Mgr,* Louis Shaw; Staff 2 (Non-MLS 2)
Founded 1962. Pop 2,952; Circ 3,931
Library Holdings: AV Mats 47; DVDs 100; Large Print Bks 400; Bk Vols 21,722; Per Subs 45; Videos 100
Special Collections: Genealogy Coll; Local History Coll
Mem of Illinois Heartland Library System
Open Mon, Tues & Thurs 9-12 & 1-7, Wed & Fri 9-12 & 1-5

CARROLLTON

P CARROLLTON PUBLIC LIBRARY*, 509 S Main St, 62016. SAN 303-7789. Tel: 217-942-6715. FAX: 217-942-6005. E-mail: carrolltonpl@gmail.com. *Dir,* Angie Custer
Founded 1901. Pop 2,605
Library Holdings: Bk Titles 22,000; Per Subs 50
Subject Interests: Genealogy, Illinois
Wireless access
Mem of Illinois Heartland Library System
Open Mon & Thurs 12-5, Tues & Wed 2-7, Fri 10-5, Sat 10-2
Friends of the Library Group

CARTERVILLE

P ANNE WEST LINDSEY DISTRICT LIBRARY*, 600 N Division St, 62918. SAN 303-7797. Tel: 618-985-3298. FAX: 618-985-9474. Web Site: awlindsey.com. *Dir,* Mary Stoner; E-mail: mstoner@awlindsey.com; Staff 3 (MLS 1, Non-MLS 2)
Founded 2010. Pop 11,309; Circ 31,983
Library Holdings: Bk Vols 40,000
Special Collections: Genealogy Coll; Local History Coll
Wireless access
Function: 24/7 Electronic res, 24/7 Online cat, Adult bk club, Audiobks on Playaways & MP3, Audiobks via web, Bk club(s), Bks on CD, Butterfly Garden, Children's prog, Computer training, Computers for patron use, ILL available, Internet access, Magazines, Meeting rooms, Music CDs, Online cat, Photocopying/Printing, Prog for adults, Prog for children & young adult, STEM programs, Story hour, Summer reading prog, Tax forms, Teen prog
Mem of Illinois Heartland Library System
Open Mon & Wed 10-7, Tues, Thurs & Fri 10-5, Sat 10-4
Friends of the Library Group

J JOHN A LOGAN COLLEGE LIBRARY*, 700 Logan College Dr, 62918. SAN 303-7800. Tel: 618-985-3741, Ext 8338. FAX: 618-985-3899. E-mail: library@jalc.edu. Web Site: www.jalc.edu/library. *Dir, Libr Serv,* J Adam Rubin; E-mail: adamrubin@jalc.edu; *Ref Librn,* Elizabeth Hartman; E-mail: elizabethhartmen@jalc.edu; Staff 13 (MLS 4, Non-MLS 9)
Founded 1968. Enrl 6,000; Fac 92
Library Holdings: AV Mats 500; Bk Titles 57,338; Bk Vols 69,866; Per Subs 450
Special Collections: John A Logan Memorial Coll
Subject Interests: Genealogy, Illinois, Nursing
Wireless access
Partic in Consortium of Academic & Research Libraries in Illinois; Illinois Library & Information Network; Network of Illinois Learning Resources in Community Colleges
Open Mon-Thurs (Winter) 7:30-7:30, Fri 7:30-4:30, Sat 10-Noon; Mon-Thurs (Summer) 7:30-7:30, Fri 8-4:30

CARTHAGE

P CARTHAGE PUBLIC LIBRARY DISTRICT*, 500 Wabash Ave, 62321. SAN 303-7827. Tel: 217-357-3232. FAX: 217-357-2392. E-mail: cartlib@mtcnow.net. Web Site: www.carthagepubliclibrary.com. *Libr Dir,* Amy Gee; E-mail: CarthageLibraryDirector@gmail.com
Founded 1894. Pop 4,250; Circ 37,500
Library Holdings: Audiobooks 1,056; CDs 750; DVDs 2,816; Large Print Bks 3,400; Microforms 190; Bk Vols 39,648; Per Subs 94; Videos 813
Special Collections: Local History & Genealogy
Automation Activity & Vendor Info: (Cataloging) SirsiDynix-WorkFlows; (Circulation) SirsiDynix-WorkFlows; (OPAC) SirsiDynix
Wireless access
Function: 24/7 Online cat, Activity rm, Bilingual assistance for Spanish patrons, Bks on cassette, Bks on CD, CD-ROM, Children's prog, Computers for patron use, Digital talking bks, E-Readers, Free DVD rentals, Home delivery & serv to seniorr ctr & nursing homes, ILL available, Internet access, Laminating, Magazines, Meeting rooms, Music CDs, Online cat, OverDrive digital audio bks, Photocopying/Printing, Preschool reading prog, Prog for adults, Prog for children & young adult, Scanner, Spanish lang bks, Story hour, Summer reading prog, Tax forms, Telephone ref, VHS videos, Wheelchair accessible
Mem of Reaching Across Illinois Library System (RAILS)
Partic in Resource Sharing Alliance
Open Mon-Thurs 11-8, Fri 11-5, Sat 9-5
Friends of the Library Group

CARY

P CARY AREA PUBLIC LIBRARY DISTRICT, 1606 Three Oaks Rd, 60013-1637. SAN 303-7843. Tel: 847-639-4210. Circulation Tel: 847-639-4210, Ext 221. Reference Tel: 847-693-4210, Ext 229. FAX: 847-639-8890. E-mail: libraryboard@caryarealibrary.info. Web Site: www.caryarealibrary.info. *Exec Dir,* Diane R McNulty; Tel: 847-639-4210, Ext 224, E-mail: dmcnulty@cary.lib.il.us; Staff 40 (MLS 3, Non-MLS 37)
Founded 1951. Pop 28,245; Circ 282,085
Jul 2020-Jun 2021 Income $2,150,888, State $56,118, Federal $5,700, Locally Generated Income $2,130,760, Other $27,345. Mats Exp $201,852, Other Print Mats $117,376, AV Mat $29,855, Electronic Ref Mat (Incl. Access Fees) $55,851. Sal $1,199,979
Library Holdings: CDs 6,927; DVDs 5,409; e-books 51,143; Electronic Media & Resources 27,586; Bk Vols 79,769; Per Subs 140
Automation Activity & Vendor Info: (Acquisitions) Innovative Interfaces, Inc. - Polaris; (Cataloging) Innovative Interfaces, Inc. - Polaris; (Circulation) Innovative Interfaces, Inc. - Polaris; (Discovery) Innovative Interfaces, Inc. - Polaris; (ILL) OCLC; (OPAC) Innovative Interfaces, Inc. - Polaris; (Serials) Innovative Interfaces, Inc. - Polaris
Wireless access
Function: 24/7 Electronic res, 24/7 Online cat, Adult bk club, Art exhibits, Art programs, Audiobks via web, Bk club(s), Bk reviews (Group), Bks on CD, Butterfly Garden, Children's prog, Computers for patron use, Electronic databases & coll, For res purposes, Free DVD rentals, Genealogy discussion group, Holiday prog, Home delivery & serv to seniorr ctr & nursing homes, Homebound delivery serv, ILL available, Internet access, Life-long learning prog for all ages, Magazines, Mail & tel request accepted, Mango lang, Meeting rooms, Museum passes, Music CDs, Online cat, Online ref, Outreach serv, Outside serv via phone, mail, e-mail & web, OverDrive digital audio bks, Passport agency, Photocopying/Printing, Preschool outreach, Preschool reading prog, Printer for laptops & handheld devices, Prog for adults, Prog for children & young adult, Ref serv available, Scanner, Senior outreach, Spanish lang bks, Spoken cassettes & CDs, Spoken cassettes & DVDs, STEM programs, Story hour, Study rm, Summer & winter reading prog, Summer reading prog, Teen prog, Telephone ref, Visual arts prog, Wheelchair accessible, Winter reading prog, Workshops, Writing prog
Publications: Books & Bytes (Newsletter)
Partic in Cooperative Computer Services - CCS
Open Mon-Thurs 9-9, Fri & Sat 9-5, Sun 1-5
Restriction: Non-resident fee
Friends of the Library Group

CASEY

P CASEY TOWNSHIP LIBRARY*, 307 E Main St, 62420. SAN 303-7851. Tel: 217-932-2105. FAX: 217-932-2105. E-mail: caseytownshiplibrary@gmail.com. Web Site: sites.google.com/site/caseytownshiplib. *Dir, Head Librn,* Gretchen Murphy; Staff 3 (Non-MLS 3)
Founded 1938. Pop 4,021; Circ 41,000
Library Holdings: Audiobooks 700; Bk Titles 22,000; Per Subs 51; Videos 1,000
Wireless access
Mem of Illinois Heartland Library System
Open Mon-Fri 11-5, Sat 10-5
Friends of the Library Group

CASEYVILLE

P CASEYVILLE PUBLIC LIBRARY DISTRICT*, 419 S Second St, 62232. SAN 303-786X. Tel: 618-345-5848. FAX: 618-345-0081. E-mail: admin@caseylibrary.org. Web Site: www.caseyvillelibrary.org. *Dir,* Ashley Stewart; E-mail: acstewart@caseyvillelibrary.org; Staff 1 (Non-MLS 1)

Founded 1962. Pop 4,772
Library Holdings: Bk Titles 38,000; Per Subs 3
Automation Activity & Vendor Info: (Acquisitions) Innovative Interfaces, Inc - Millennium
Wireless access
Mem of Illinois Heartland Library System
Open Mon, Tues & Wed 9-5, Thurs 12-8, Fri & Sat 10-4

CATLIN

P CATLIN PUBLIC LIBRARY DISTRICT*, 101 Mapleleaf Dr, 61817. (Mail add: PO Box 350, 61817-0350), SAN 303-7878. Tel: 217-427-2550. FAX: 217-427-9830. E-mail: catlinlibrary03@yahoo.com. Web Site: catlinlibrary03.wixsite.com/website. *Librn,* Kathleen Bennett
Founded 1972. Pop 3,402; Circ 20,422
Library Holdings: Bk Vols 15,115; Per Subs 43
Mem of Illinois Heartland Library System
Open Mon & Thurs 9-5, Tues, Wed & Fri 9-7, Sat 9-12

CENTRALIA

S CENTRALIA CORRECTIONAL CENTER LIBRARY*, 9330 Shattuc Rd, 62801. (Mail add: PO Box 1266, 62801-1266), SAN 371-5280. Tel: 618-533-4111. *Libr Assoc,* Christopher Boehler
Founded 1980
Library Holdings: Bk Vols 18,000; Per Subs 66
Open Tues-Fri 7-5

P CENTRALIA REGIONAL LIBRARY DISTRICT*, 515 E Broadway, 62801. SAN 303-7886. Tel: 618-532-5222. FAX: 618-532-8578. Web Site: www.centralialibrary.org. *Dir,* Diana Donahoo; E-mail: director@centralia.lib.il.us; *Asst Dir,* Tammy Wendling; *Circ Supvr,* Cindy Payne; *Asst Circ Supvr,* Mary Hanks; *Ch Serv,* Rita Lewis
Founded 1874. Pop 30,100; Circ 130,300
Library Holdings: Audiobooks 4,300; DVDs 7,582; Bk Vols 84,921
Special Collections: Oral History
Automation Activity & Vendor Info: (Acquisitions) Innovative Interfaces, Inc; (Cataloging) Innovative Interfaces, Inc; (Circulation) Innovative Interfaces, Inc
Wireless access
Mem of Illinois Heartland Library System
Open Mon, Tues, Thurs & Fri 10-6, Wed 10-4:30
Friends of the Library Group

J KASKASKIA COLLEGE LIBRARY*, 27210 College Rd, 62801. SAN 303-7894. Tel: 618-545-3130. Toll Free Tel: 800-642-0859. FAX: 618-532-9241. E-mail: library@kaskaskia.edu. Web Site: www.kaskaskia.edu/campus-life/academic-center-for-excellence/library. *Lead Librn, Learning Res Spec,* Shannon Zelasko; E-mail: szelasko@kaskaskia.edu; *Circ, Libr Asst,* Michele Hill; E-mail: mhill@kaskaskia.edu; *Circ, Libr Asst,* Beth Moore; Tel: 618-545-3133, E-mail: bmoore@kaskaskia.edu; Staff 3 (Non-MLS 3)
Founded 1940. Highest Degree: Associate
Library Holdings: CDs 10; DVDs 57; Per Subs 27; Talking Bks 90; Videos 17
Special Collections: Accounting; African-American Studies; Agriculture/Horticulture; Anatomy; Animal Rights; Animation; Art; Athletes/Sports; Automotive; Biography; Biology; Body, Mind, Spirit; Botany; Business; Career; Chemistry; Child Care; Cinema; Construction; Cosmetology; Criminal Justice; Culinary Arts; Dance; Dentistry; Drafting; Economics; EMT; Environmental; Exercise/Nutrition; Fairy Tales/Folklore; Family & Relationships; Fiction; Finance; Gardening; Illinois Coll; Juvenile Literature; Literature; Mathematics; Music; Mythology; Nature; Nursing; Philosophy; Photography; Physical Therapy; Physics; Psychology; Radiology; Religion; Respiratory; Sociology; Space Exploration; Special Needs; Theatre; Travel; U.S. History; U.S. Presidents; U.S. Wars & Conflicts; Welding; World History; World Politics
Automation Activity & Vendor Info: (ILL) OCLC WorldShare Interlibrary Loan
Wireless access
Function: ILL available
Mem of Illinois Heartland Library System
Partic in Consortium of Academic & Research Libraries in Illinois; Northern Ill Learning Resources Coop
Open Mon, Tues & Thurs 7:30-7, Wed 7:30am-8pm
Friends of the Library Group

CERRO GORDO

P HOPE WELTY PUBLIC LIBRARY DISTRICT*, 100 S Madison St, 61818. (Mail add: PO Box 260, 61818-0260), SAN 303-7908. Tel: 217-763-5001. FAX: 217-763-5391. E-mail: hopeweltylibrary@gmail.com. Web Site: site-rpls-cerphwp.ploud.net. *Dir,* Shari Rawlings; *Head, Circ,* Tina Henderson
Pop 3,624; Circ 41,279
Library Holdings: Bk Vols 15,628; Per Subs 116
Automation Activity & Vendor Info: (Acquisitions) Horizon; (Cataloging) Horizon; (Circulation) Horizon; (ILL) Horizon
Wireless access
Mem of Illinois Heartland Library System
Partic in Illinois Library & Information Network
Open Mon 3-7, Tues, Wed & Fri 10-5, Thurs 10-7, Sat 10-Noon

CHADWICK

P CHADWICK PUBLIC LIBRARY DISTRICT*, 110 Main St, 61014. (Mail add: PO Box 416, 61014-0416), SAN 375-9946. Tel: 815-684-5215. FAX: 815-684-5215. Web Site: www.chadwicklibrary.org. *Dir,* Jo Nell Castellani; E-mail: jonell_castellani@yahoo.com
Founded 1988. Pop 1,221
Library Holdings: Bk Titles 10,000; Per Subs 20
Wireless access
Mem of Reaching Across Illinois Library System (RAILS)
Open Mon-Wed & Fri 1:30-6:30, Thurs 10:30-6:30, Sat 9-1

CHAMPAIGN

S CHAMPAIGN COUNTY HISTORY MUSEUM, Research Library, Cattle Bank Bldg, 102 E University Ave, 61820-4111. SAN 373-4374. Tel: 217-356-1010. Web Site: www.champaigncountyhistory.org. *Pres,* T J Blakeman; E-mail: president@champaigncountyhistory.org
Founded 1974
Library Holdings: Bk Vols 1,000
Special Collections: History of the Champaign County Area, incl Historic Preservation Issues, Memorabilia, Volumes Owned by Historic Figures, Local Histories & Studies of Local Buildings of Historic Value. Oral History
Subject Interests: Local hist
Wireless access
Function: Archival coll, For res purposes, Photocopying/Printing, Res libr
Publications: Champaign County History Museum Electronic Newsletter (Quarterly)
Restriction: In-house use for visitors, Non-circulating

P CHAMPAIGN PUBLIC LIBRARY*, 200 W Green St, 61820-5193. SAN 339-7831. Tel: 217-403-2000. Administration Tel: 217-403-2050. FAX: 217-403-2053. E-mail: librarian@champaign.org. Web Site: www.champaign.org. *Dir,* Donna Pittman; E-mail: dpittman@champaign.org; *Dep Dir,* Brittany Millington; E-mail: bmillington@champaign.org; *Access Serv Mgr,* Kristina L Hoerner; E-mail: khoerner@champaign.org; *Ch Mgr,* Mike Rogalla; E-mail: mrogalla@champaign.org; *Tech Mgr,* Amy Al-Shabibi; E-mail: aal-shabibi@champaign.org
Founded 1876. Pop 81,055; Circ 2,500,000
Library Holdings: Audiobooks 8,000; CDs 29,000; DVDs 40,000; e-books 12,000; Bk Vols 270,000; Per Subs 506
Automation Activity & Vendor Info: (Acquisitions) Innovative Interfaces, Inc; (Cataloging) Innovative Interfaces, Inc; (Circulation) Innovative Interfaces, Inc; (ILL) Innovative Interfaces, Inc; (OPAC) Innovative Interfaces, Inc; (Serials) Innovative Interfaces, Inc
Wireless access
Function: Online info literacy tutorials on the web & in blackboard
Publications: The Last Word (Monthly newsletter)
Mem of Illinois Heartland Library System
Partic in Illinois Library & Information Network
Special Services for the Deaf - TDD equip
Open Mon-Sat 9-6, Sun 12-6
Friends of the Library Group
Branches: 1
DOUGLASS BRANCH, 504 E Grove St, 61820-3239, SAN 339-7866. Tel: 217-403-2090. FAX: 217-356-9561. *Br Mgr,* Essie Harris; E-mail: eharris@champaign.org
Open Mon-Fri 10-6, Sat 10-4
Friends of the Library Group

S ILLINOIS EARLY INTERVENTION CLEARINGHOUSE*, Univ of Illinois-Urbana-Champaign, Children's Research Ctr, 51 Gerty Dr, 61820-7469. SAN 371-523X. Tel: 217-333-1386. Toll Free Tel: 877-275-3227. FAX: 217-244-7732. E-mail: Illinois-eic@illinois.edu. Web Site: www.eiclearinghouse.org. *Librn,* Sarah Isaacs; E-mail: isaacs@illinois.edu; Staff 2 (MLS 1, Non-MLS 1)
Founded 1986
Library Holdings: AV Mats 1,582; Bks on Deafness & Sign Lang 240; Bk Titles 8,864; Per Subs 25
Special Collections: Austism
Subject Interests: Disabilities, Early childhood, Parenting
Automation Activity & Vendor Info: (Cataloging) SirsiDynix; (Circulation) SirsiDynix; (ILL) OCLC; (OPAC) SirsiDynix; (Serials) EBSCO Online
Publications: Bibliography Series; Early Intervention (Newsletter)

Mem of Illinois Heartland Library System
Partic in Health Sci Libr Info Consortium; Illinois Library & Information Network
Special Services for the Deaf - Bks on deafness & sign lang; TDD equip; Videos & decoder
Open Mon-Fri 8-5

J PARKLAND COLLEGE LIBRARY*, 2400 W Bradley Ave, 61821-1899, SAN 303-7940. Tel: 217-351-2223. Reference Tel: 217-373-3839. Administration Tel: 217-351-2365. FAX: 217-351-2581. E-mail: library@parkland.edu. Web Site: www.parkland.edu/library. *Dir,* Morgann Quilty; E-mail: mquilty@parkland.edu; *Cat, Electronic Res, Tech Serv,* Cliff Bishop; E-mail: clbishop@parkland.edu; *Info Serv,* Raeann Dossett; E-mail: rdossett@parkland.edu; *Ref (Info Servs),* Frances Drone-Silvers; E-mail: fdrone-silvers@parkland.edu; Staff 12 (MLS 5, Non-MLS 7)
Founded 1967. Enrl 9,536; Highest Degree: Associate
Library Holdings: AV Mats 9,047; e-books 1,400; Bk Vols 122,330; Per Subs 331
Subject Interests: Career, Tech subjects
Automation Activity & Vendor Info: (Cataloging) Ex Libris Group; (Circulation) Ex Libris Group; (Course Reserve) Ex Libris Group; (ILL) OCLC; (OPAC) Ex Libris Group
Function: Ref serv available
Partic in Consortium of Academic & Research Libraries in Illinois; Network of Illinois Learning Resources in Community Colleges
Open Mon-Thurs 7:30am-9pm, Fri 7:30-5, Sat 10-2; Mon-Thurs 7:30am-8pm (Summer)

A UNITED STATES ARMY CORPS OF ENGINEERS*, Engineer Research & Development Center, 2902 Newmark Dr, 61822. (Mail add: PO Box 9005, 61826-9005), SAN 303-7959. Tel: 217-373-7217. FAX: 217-373-7258. E-mail: library-il@usace.army.mil. Web Site: www.erdc.usace.army.mil/library. *Br Chief,* Molly McMullon; Staff 2 (Non-MLS 2)
Founded 1969
Library Holdings: Bk Titles 19,000
Subject Interests: Civil engr, Construction, Environ engr
Automation Activity & Vendor Info: (Acquisitions) SirsiDynix; (Cataloging) SirsiDynix; (Circulation) SirsiDynix; (OPAC) SirsiDynix
Function: Res libr
Mem of Illinois Heartland Library System
Partic in Illinois Library & Information Network; OCLC Online Computer Library Center, Inc
Restriction: Staff use only

CHANNAHON

P THREE RIVERS PUBLIC LIBRARY DISTRICT*, 25207 W Channon Dr, 60410-5028. (Mail add: PO Box 300, 60410-0300), SAN 321-0308. Tel: 815-467-6200. FAX: 815-467-4012. Web Site: www.trpld.org. *Exec Dir,* Lauren Offerman; Tel: 815-467-6200, Ext 303, E-mail: laureno@trpld.org; *Asst Dir,* Debbie Griggs; Tel: 815-467-6200, Ext 204, E-mail: debbieg@trpld.org; *Ad,* Sarah Robertson; Tel: 815-467-6200, Ext 306, E-mail: sarahr@trpld.org; *Librn, Tech Serv Mgr,* Michele Houchens; Tel: 815-467-6200, Ext 208, E-mail: micheleh@trpld.org; *Youth Serv Librn,* Amber Maxwell; Tel: 815-467-6200, Ext 308, E-mail: amberm@trpld.org; *Circ Serv Mgr,* Wendy Hoffman; Tel: 815-467-6200, Ext 305, E-mail: wendyh@trpld.org; Staff 6 (MLS 4, Non-MLS 2)
Founded 1976. Pop 26,600; Circ 191,764
Library Holdings: Audiobooks 2,969; CDs 2,500; DVDs 2,118; High Interest/Low Vocabulary Bk Vols 50; Large Print Bks 1,200; Bk Vols 80,280; Per Subs 203; Talking Bks 744; Videos 60
Special Collections: Local History, Channahon & Minooka, IL
Automation Activity & Vendor Info: (Circulation) SirsiDynix; (ILL) OCLC; (OPAC) SirsiDynix
Wireless access
Function: 24/7 Electronic res, 24/7 Online cat, Adult bk club, Audiobks on Playaways & MP3, Audiobks via web, Bks on CD, Children's prog, Computer training, Computers for patron use, E-Readers, Electronic databases & coll, Free DVD rentals, Homebound delivery serv, Homework prog, ILL available, Internet access, Laminating, Large print keyboards, Life-long learning prog for all ages, Magazines, Magnifiers for reading, Mango lang, Meeting rooms, Microfiche/film & reading machines, Movies, Museum passes, Music CDs, Notary serv, Online cat, Online ref, Outreach serv, Outside serv via phone, mail, e-mail & web, OverDrive digital audio bks, Photocopying/Printing, Preschool outreach, Printer for laptops & handheld devices, Prog for adults, Prog for children & young adult, Ref serv available, Scanner, Serves people with intellectual disabilities, Spoken cassettes & CDs, STEM programs, Story hour, Summer reading prog, Tax forms, Teen prog, Telephone ref, Wheelchair accessible
Publications: Newsletter (Quarterly)
Mem of Reaching Across Illinois Library System (RAILS)
Open Mon-Thurs 9-9, Fri 9-6, Sat 9-5, Sun 1-5; Mon-Thurs (Summer) 9-9, Fri 9-6, Sat 9-3

CHARLESTON

P CHARLESTON CARNEGIE PUBLIC LIBRARY*, 712 Sixth St, 61920. SAN 303-7967. Tel: 217-345-4913. FAX: 217-348-5616. E-mail: information@charlestonlibrary.org. *Libr Dir,* Chris Houchens; E-mail: director@charlestonlibrary.org; *Adult Serv Mgr,* Kattie Livingston; *Coll Serv Mgr,* Leeanne Reed; *Operations Mgr,* Rita Harper; *Youth Serv Mgr,* Beth Lugar
Founded 1896. Pop 20,398; Circ 163,143
Library Holdings: Bk Titles 48,000; Per Subs 175
Subject Interests: Educ, Med, Relig
Mem of Illinois Heartland Library System
Open Mon-Thurs 10-8, Fri & Sat 10-6, Sun 1-5

S COLES COUNTY HISTORICAL SOCIETY*, Research Library & Museum, Dudley House, 895 Seventh St, 61920. (Mail add: PO Box 1398, Mattoon, 61938), SAN 370-8969. Tel: 217-235-6744. E-mail: coleshistory@consolidated.net. Web Site: www.coleshistory.net. *Spec Coll,* Norma Winkleblack; E-mail: nwink26@consolidated.net
Library Holdings: Bk Vols 2,000
Special Collections: Coles County Coll; Illinois History Coll
Restriction: Open by appt only

C EASTERN ILLINOIS UNIVERSITY*, Booth Library, 600 Lincoln Ave, 61920. SAN 303-7975. Circulation Tel: 217-581-6071. Interlibrary Loan Service Tel: 217-581-6074. Reference Tel: 217-581-6072. Administration Tel: 217-581-6061. Interlibrary Loan Service FAX: 217-581-6066. Reference FAX: 217-581-6911. Administration FAX: 217-581-7534. Web Site: www.library.eiu.edu. *Dean, Libr Serv,* Dr Allen Lanham; E-mail: aklanham@eiu.edu; *Head, Acq,* Marlene Slough; Tel: 217-581-6021, E-mail: mmslough@eiu.edu; *Head Archivist,* Position Currently Open; *Head, Cat,* John Whisler; Tel: 217-581-7561, E-mail: jawhisler@eiu.edu; *Head, Circ,* Bradley Tolppanen; Tel: 217-581-6006, E-mail: bptolppanen@eiu.edu; *Head, Coll Develop,* Karen Whisler; Tel: 217-581-7551, E-mail: klwhisler@eiu.edu; *Head, Ref,* Steve Brantley; Tel: 217-581-7542, E-mail: jsbrantley@eiu.edu; *Head, Tech Serv,* Stacey Knight-Davis; Tel: 217-581-6091, E-mail: slknight@eiu.edu; *Archives, Cat Librn,* Bill Schultz; Tel: 217-581-8457, E-mail: wnschultz@eiu.edu; *Cat/Digitization Libr,* Ellen Corrigan; Tel: 217-581-8456, E-mail: ekcorrigan@eiu.edu; *Institutional Repository Librn,* Todd Bruns; Tel: 217-581-8381, E-mail: tabruns@eiu.edu; *Circ, Night Supvr Librn,* Position Currently Open; *Ref Librn,* David Bell; Tel: 217-581-7547, E-mail: dsbell@eiu.edu; *Ref Librn,* Ann Brownson; Tel: 217-581-6099, E-mail: aebrownson@eiu.edu; *Ref Librn,* Janice Derr; Tel: 217-581-5090, E-mail: jmderr@eiu.edu; *Ref Librn,* Kirstin Duffin; Tel: 217-581-7550, E-mail: kduffin@eiu.edu; *Ref Librn,* Pamela Ferrell; Tel: 217-581-7548, E-mail: pferrell@eiu.edu; *Ref Librn,* Sarah Johnson; Tel: 217-581-7538, E-mail: sljohnson2@eiu.edu. Subject Specialists: *Music,* Dr Allen Lanham; *Art, Family & consumer sci,* Marlene Slough; *Africana studies, Hist, Mil sci,* Bradley Tolppanen; *English, Libr sci, Philos,* Karen Whisler; *Communication studies, Film, Media,* Steve Brantley; *Health studies, Nursing,* Stacey Knight-Davis; *Anthrop, Psychol, Sociol,* Bill Schultz; *Tech,* Todd Bruns; *Counseling, Journalism, Juv, Physics, Spec educ, Theatre arts,* David Bell; *Curric, Elem educ, Juv, Spec educ,* Ann Brownson; *Bus,* Janice Derr; *Biol sci, Chemistry, Geog, Geol,* Kirstin Duffin; *Communication sci & disorders, Foreign lang, Latin Am studies, Polit sci, Sciences, Women studies,* Pamela Ferrell; *Computer sci, Econ, Math,* Sarah Johnson; Staff 35 (MLS 16, Non-MLS 19)
Founded 1896. Enrl 8,250; Fac 597; Highest Degree: Master
Jul 2015-Jun 2016 Income $4,198,716, State $4,112,089, Federal $26,287, Locally Generated Income $45,396, Other $14,944. Mats Exp $1,346,146, Books $206,181, Per/Ser (Incl. Access Fees) $588,445, Micro $17,741, AV Mat $15,397, Electronic Ref Mat (Incl. Access Fees) $477,418, Presv $40,964. Sal $1,228,862 (Prof $1,532,104)
Library Holdings: Audiobooks 10,171; AV Mats 29,325; CDs 5,658; DVDs 13,192; e-books 75,362; e-journals 45,437; Microforms 96,296; Bk Vols 1,004,224; Videos 17,805
Special Collections: Art & Architecture in Illinois Libraries; Ballenger Teacher Center; Garner Sheet Music; Illinois Landscape Artists; Ned Brasel Coll of the Southwest; Remo Belli International Percussion Library. State Document Depository; US Document Depository
Subject Interests: Bus, Educ, Liberal arts
Wireless access
Function: 24/7 Electronic res, 24/7 Online cat, Archival coll, Art exhibits, Audio & video playback equip for onsite use, Audiobks via web, Bks on CD, Children's prog, Computers for patron use, Digital talking bks, Doc delivery serv, E-Reserves, Electronic databases & coll, Games & aids for people with disabilities, Govt ref serv, Health sci info serv, ILL available, Instruction & testing, Internet access, Laminating, Magazines, Magnifiers for reading, Mail & tel request accepted, Meeting rooms, Microfiche/film & reading machines, Movies, Music CDs, Online cat, Online ref, Orientations, Outside serv via phone, mail, e-mail & web, OverDrive digital audio bks, Photocopying/Printing, Printer for laptops & handheld devices, Prog for adults, Prog for children & young adult, Ref & res, Ref serv available, Res libr, Scanner, Serves people with intellectual disabilities,

Spanish lang bks, Tax forms, Telephone ref, VHS videos, Wheelchair accessible, Workshops
Mem of Illinois Heartland Library System
Partic in Consortium of Academic & Research Libraries in Illinois; East Central Illinois Consortium; OCLC Online Computer Library Center, Inc
Special Services for the Deaf - TTY equip
Special Services for the Blind - Accessible computers; Audio mat; Bks available with recordings; Cassette playback machines; Cassettes; HP Scan Jet with photo-finish software
Open Mon-Thurs (Winter) 8am-1am, Fri 8-5, Sat 9-5, Sun Noon-1am; Mon-Thurs (Summer) 8am-10pm, Fri 8-5, Sat 9-5, Sun 2-10
Restriction: Open to students, fac, staff & alumni, Pub use on premises

CHATHAM

P CHATHAM AREA PUBLIC LIBRARY DISTRICT*, 600 E Spruce St, 62629. SAN 376-0022. Tel: 217-483-2713. FAX: 217-483-2361. E-mail: info@chathamlib.org. Web Site: www.chatham.lib.il.us. *Dir,* Amy Ihnen; E-mail: Director@chathamlib.org; Staff 4 (MLS 1, Non-MLS 3)
Pop 13,139; Circ 134,914
Library Holdings: Bk Vols 62,000; Per Subs 124
Automation Activity & Vendor Info: (Cataloging) SirsiDynix; (Circulation) SirsiDynix; (OPAC) SirsiDynix
Mem of Illinois Heartland Library System
Open Mon-Thurs 10-7, Fri 10-5, Sat 10-2
Friends of the Library Group

CHATSWORTH

P CHATSWORTH TOWNSHIP LIBRARY*, 501 E School St, 60921. (Mail add: PO Box 638, 60921-0638), SAN 303-7983. Tel: 815-635-3004. FAX: 815-635-3004. E-mail: chatslib@hotmail.com. *Dir,* Mary Fisher-Miller; *Asst Dir,* Cory Zimmerman
Pop 1,366; Circ 10,592
Library Holdings: Bk Vols 12,000; Per Subs 24
Wireless access
Function: 24/7 Online cat, 3D Printer, After school storytime
Open Mon-Wed & Fri 10-5, Thurs 2-7

CHENOA

P CHENOA PUBLIC LIBRARY*, 211 S Division St, 61726. SAN 303-7991. Tel: 815-945-4253. FAX: 815-945-4203. E-mail: chenoapl@frontier.com. Web Site: chenoalibrary.org. *Dir,* Sheryl Siebert
Pop 2,305; Circ 12,850
Library Holdings: AV Mats 150; Bks on Deafness & Sign Lang 10; DVDs 59; Large Print Bks 50; Bk Titles 14,083; Per Subs 70; Talking Bks 432; Videos 320
Wireless access
Open Mon & Wed 2-7, Tues & Thurs 10-12 & 2-7, Fri 2-5, Sat 9-Noon

CHERRY VALLEY

P CHERRY VALLEY PUBLIC LIBRARY DISTRICT*, 755 E State St, 61016-9699. SAN 320-4731. Tel: 815-332-5161. FAX: 815-332-2441. Web Site: www.cherryvalleylib.org. *Exec Dir,* Jane Lenser; E-mail: janel@cherryvalleylib.org; *Asst Dir,* Michele Arms; Tel: 815-332-5161, Ext 35, E-mail: michelea@cherryvalleylib.org; *Bus Mgr,* Benthe Sloniker; *Circ Mgr,* Jenny Hansen-Peterson; Tel: 815-332-5161, Ext 25, E-mail: jennyh@cherryvalleylib.org; *Tech Serv Mgr,* Fran Schaible; Tel: 815-332-5161, Ext 32, E-mail: frans@cherryvalleylib.org; *Youth Serv Mgr,* Stacey Chester; Tel: 815-332-5161, Ext 33, E-mail: staceyc@cherryvalleylib.org; *Tech Serv,* Becky Yerk; Tel: 815-332-5161, Ext 34, E-mail: beckyy@cherryvalleylib.org; *Youth Serv,* Blaine Cornelius; Tel: 815-332-5161, Ext 26, E-mail: blainec@cherryvalleylib.org; Staff 22 (MLS 1, Non-MLS 21)
Founded 1977. Pop 17,000; Circ 172,510
Library Holdings: AV Mats 4,928; CDs 567; e-books 6,796; Electronic Media & Resources 11; Large Print Bks 1,248; Bk Titles 44,748; Bk Vols 46,855; Per Subs 160; Talking Bks 2,078; Videos 2,283
Subject Interests: Local hist
Automation Activity & Vendor Info: (Acquisitions) Innovative Interfaces, Inc; (Cataloging) Innovative Interfaces, Inc; (Circulation) Innovative Interfaces, Inc; (OPAC) Innovative Interfaces, Inc; (Serials) Innovative Interfaces, Inc
Wireless access
Function: Audio & video playback equip for onsite use, AV serv, ILL available, Magnifiers for reading, Photocopying/Printing, Prog for adults, Prog for children & young adult, Summer reading prog, Wheelchair accessible
Mem of Reaching Across Illinois Library System (RAILS)
Special Services for the Deaf - TDD equip
Special Services for the Blind - Assistive/Adapted tech devices, equip & products; Audio mat; Bks on cassette; Bks on CD; Large print bks; Reader equip; Talking bks
Open Mon-Thurs 9-8, Fri & Sat 9-5, Sun (Sept-May) 1-5
Friends of the Library Group

CHESTER

S CHESTER MENTAL HEALTH CENTER*, Patient Library, 1315 Lehmen Rd, 62233-2542. (Mail add: PO Box 31, 62233-0031), SAN 339-7955. Tel: 618-826-4571, Ext 539. FAX: 618-826-3581.
Founded 1968
Library Holdings: CDs 120; DVDs 50; Large Print Bks 200; Bk Titles 8,500; Per Subs 30; Videos 200
Special Collections: Large Print
Restriction: Staff & patient use

P CHESTER PUBLIC LIBRARY*, 733 State St, 62233. SAN 303-8009. Tel: 618-826-3711. FAX: 618-826-2733. E-mail: chesterpubliclib@gmail.com. Web Site: www.chesterpubliclibrary.com. *Admin Librn,* Tammy Grah; E-mail: tammygrah@gmail.com; *Librn II,* Lisa Wittenborne
Founded 1928. Pop 8,194; Circ 71,424
Library Holdings: Bk Vols 39,000; Per Subs 50
Special Collections: Rare Books (First Books Room)
Subject Interests: Environ studies, Ethnic studies, Genealogy, Local hist, Med, Relig, Sci tech
Automation Activity & Vendor Info: (Cataloging) Innovative Interfaces, Inc; (Circulation) Innovative Interfaces, Inc; (OPAC) Innovative Interfaces, Inc
Mem of Illinois Heartland Library System
Open Mon-Thurs 10-7, Fri 10-5, Sat 10-1
Friends of the Library Group

CHICAGO

C ADLER UNIVERSITY, Harold & Birdie Mosak Library, 17 N Dearborn St, 15th Flr, 60602. SAN 303-8025. Tel: 312-662-4230. FAX: 312-662-4298. E-mail: library@adler.edu. Web Site: library.adler.edu. *Mgr, Libr Serv,* Ms Ariel Orlov; E-mail: aorlov@adler.edu; *Access Serv Librn,* Sreedevi Satyavolu; E-mail: ssatyavolu@adler.edu; *Pub Serv Librn,* Frances Brady; E-mail: fbrady@adler.edu; *Resources Librn, Syst Librn,* Heather Cannon; E-mail: hcannon@adler.edu
Founded 1952. Enrl 1,125; Fac 160; Highest Degree: Doctorate
Library Holdings: e-books 370,000; Bk Titles 14,300
Special Collections: Adlerian Athenaeum Coll; Adlerian Psychology Coll; Individual Psychology Coll
Subject Interests: Art therapy, Cultural diversity, Family, Forensic psychol, Gender, Gerontology, Marriage, Psychiat, Psychol, Psychotherapy, Substance abuse
Automation Activity & Vendor Info: (Cataloging) Ex Libris Group; (Circulation) Ex Libris Group; (Course Reserve) Ex Libris Group; (Discovery) SerialsSolutions; (ILL) Atlas Systems; (OPAC) Ex Libris Group; (Serials) Ex Libris Group
Wireless access
Partic in Asn Col & Res Librs; Consortium of Academic & Research Libraries in Illinois; Illinois Library & Information Network; OCLC Online Computer Library Center, Inc; OCLC-LVIS; US National Library of Medicine
Restriction: Not open to pub

M ADVOCATE ILLINOIS MASONIC MEDICAL CENTER*, Medical Library, 836 W Wellington Ave, Rm 7501, 60657. SAN 320-4499. Tel: 773-296-5084. FAX: 773-296-7421. *Mgr,* Victoria Koren; E-mail: victoria.koren@aah.org; *Ref Serv Librn,* Olivia Baldwin; E-mail: olivia.baldwin@aah.org; Staff 2 (MLS 2)
Founded 1963
Library Holdings: Bk Vols 5,000; Per Subs 340
Subject Interests: Health sci
Automation Activity & Vendor Info: (Cataloging) SirsiDynix; (Circulation) SirsiDynix; (ILL) OCLC; (OPAC) SirsiDynix; (Serials) SirsiDynix
Wireless access
Publications: @ The Library (Intranet Newsletter)
Partic in National Network of Libraries of Medicine Region 6

M ALZHEIMER'S ASSOCIATION*, Benjamin B Green-Field National Alzheimer's Library & Resource Center, 225 N Michigan Ave, 17th Flr, 60601. SAN 371-9901. Toll Free Tel: 800-272-3900. E-mail: greenfield@alz.org. Web Site: www.alz.org/library. *Sr Assoc Dir,* Mary Ann Urbashich; Tel: 312-335-5199, E-mail: maryann.urbashich@alz.org. Subject Specialists: *Alzheimer's disease,* Mary Ann Urbashich; Staff 1 (MLS 1)
Founded 1991
Subject Interests: Aging, Care, Geriatrics, Gerontology, Nonprofit mgt
Automation Activity & Vendor Info: (Acquisitions) EOS International; (Cataloging) EOS International; (Circulation) EOS International; (ILL) OCLC; (OPAC) EOS International; (Serials) EOS International
Wireless access

Publications: Brochure; Resource Bibliographies
Mem of Reaching Across Illinois Library System (RAILS)
Partic in National Network of Libraries of Medicine Region 6
Open Mon-Fri 8-5

S AMERICAN DENTAL ASSOCIATION LIBRARY & ARCHIVES*, 211 E Chicago Ave, American Dental Association, 60611-2637. SAN 303-8106. Tel: 312-440-2653. FAX: 312-440-2774. E-mail: library@ada.org. Web Site: ADA.org/library.
Founded 1927
Special Collections: Archives of American Dental Association; History of Dentistry
Subject Interests: Dentistry
Wireless access
Function: Archival coll, Doc delivery serv, ILL available, Internet access, Online cat, Photocopying/Printing, Ref serv available, Res performed for a fee, Scanner, Telephone ref
Mem of Reaching Across Illinois Library System (RAILS)
Restriction: Employee & client use only, Free to mem, Non-circulating, Not open to pub, Open by appt only, Private libr, Researchers by appt only, Staff & mem only

S AMERICAN HOSPITAL ASSOCIATION, Resource Center, 155 N Wacker Dr, Ste 400, 60606. SAN 303-9455. Tel: 312-422-2050. FAX: 312-422-4700. E-mail: rc@aha.org. Web Site: www.aha.org/data-insights/resource-center.
Founded 1929
Library Holdings: Bk Vols 64,000; Per Subs 250
Special Collections: Center for Hospital & Healthcare Administration History; Ray E Brown Management Coll
Automation Activity & Vendor Info: (Cataloging) CyberTools for Libraries; (ILL) CyberTools for Libraries; (OPAC) CyberTools for Libraries
Wireless access
Partic in National Network of Libraries of Medicine Region 6; OCLC Online Computer Library Center, Inc
Open Mon-Fri 8:30-4:30

S AMERICAN LIBRARY ASSOCIATION LIBRARY*, 50 E Huron St, 60611-2729. SAN 303-8122. Tel: 312-280-2153. Toll Free Tel: 800-545-2433, Ext 2153. FAX: 312-280-3255. E-mail: library@ala.org. Web Site: www.ala.org/library. *Dir,* Kathy Rosa; E-mail: krosa@ala.org; Staff 2.5 (MLS 1.5, Non-MLS 1)
Founded 1924
Sept 2017-Aug 2018 Income $275,000. Mats Exp $42,300, Books $12,000, Per/Ser (Incl. Access Fees) $15,300, Electronic Ref Mat (Incl. Access Fees) $15,000. Sal $150,000
Library Holdings: DVDs 25; Microforms 1,500; Bk Vols 16,000; Per Subs 200
Special Collections: Library Annual Reports
Subject Interests: Hist of the Asn, Issues & hist of librarianship, Libr & info sci
Automation Activity & Vendor Info: (Cataloging) OCLC; (Circulation) OCLC; (ILL) OCLC; (OPAC) OCLC; (Serials) EBSCO Online
Wireless access
Mem of Reaching Across Illinois Library System (RAILS)
Partic in Illinois Library & Information Network; OCLC Online Computer Library Center, Inc
Open Mon-Fri 8:30-4:30
Restriction: Circulates for staff only, External users must contact libr, Prof mat only

S AMERICAN PLANNING ASSOCIATION LIBRARY*, 205 N Michigan Ave, Ste 1200, 60601. SAN 303-9714. Tel: 312-431-9100, Ext 6353. E-mail: library@planning.org. Web Site: www.planning.org/library. *Librn,* Nick Ammerman; *Head, Communication Serv,* Harriet Bogdanowicz; E-mail: hbogdanowicz@planning.org
Founded 1932
Library Holdings: e-books 300; Bk Vols 6,000; Per Subs 100
Special Collections: Ira Bach Coll
Subject Interests: Urban planning
Wireless access
Function: Electronic databases & coll, Internet access, Online cat, Online ref, Ref serv available
Restriction: Co libr, In-house use for visitors, Non-circulating coll, Open by appt only

M AMITA RESURRECTION MEDICAL CENTER CHICAGO, Dr Martin R Sullivan Library & Medical Information Center, 7435 W Talcott Ave, 60631-3746. SAN 304-0062. Tel: 773-990-7638. *Regional Mgr, Libr Serv,* Laura Wimmer; E-mail: Laura.Wimmer@amitahealth.org; Staff 1 (MLS 1)
Founded 1953
Library Holdings: e-books 2,000; e-journals 2,000; Bk Titles 900
Automation Activity & Vendor Info: (Cataloging) LibraryWorld, Inc; (Circulation) LibraryWorld, Inc; (Discovery) OVID Technologies; (OPAC) LibraryWorld, Inc; (Serials) LibraryWorld, Inc
Wireless access
Mem of Reaching Across Illinois Library System (RAILS)
Partic in Illinois Library & Information Network; Metro Consortium of Chicago; National Network of Libraries of Medicine Region 6
Open Mon-Fri 8-4

S APPRAISAL INSTITUTE, Y T & Louise Lee Lum Library, 200 W Madison, Ste 1500, 60606. SAN 370-999X. Tel: 312-335-4467. FAX: 312-335-4486. E-mail: ailibrary@appraisalinstitute.org. Web Site: www.appraisalinstitute.org. *Libr Dir,* Eric B Goodman; E-mail: egoodman@appraisalinstitute.org; Staff 1 (MLS 1)
Founded 1992
Library Holdings: e-books 71; Bk Titles 1,200; Per Subs 25
Subject Interests: Real estate
Automation Activity & Vendor Info: (Acquisitions) Softlink America; (Cataloging) Softlink America; (Circulation) Softlink America; (OPAC) Softlink America; (Serials) Softlink America
Wireless access
Mem of Reaching Across Illinois Library System (RAILS)
Open Mon-Fri 8:30-4

S ART INSTITUTE OF CHICAGO*, Ryerson & Burnham Libraries, 111 S Michigan Ave, 60603. SAN 339-8013. Tel: 312-443-3671. Circulation Tel: 312-443-7279. Reference Tel: 312-443-3666. E-mail: rbarchives@artic.edu, reference@artic.edu, ryerson@artic.edu. Web Site: www.artic.edu/library. *Dir,* Douglas Litts; *Head, Reader Serv,* Autumn Mather; *Head, Tech Serv,* Karen Stafford; E-mail: kstafford2@artic.edu; *Digital Initiatives Librn, Tech Librn,* Alvin Dantes; E-mail: adantes@artic.edu; *Archivist,* Nathaniel Parks; E-mail: nparks@artic.edu; *Archivist,* Bart Ryckbosch; E-mail: bryckbosch@artic.edu; *Conservator,* Christine Fabian; E-mail: cfabian@artic.edu. Subject Specialists: *Archit, Art,* Nathaniel Parks; Staff 23 (MLS 12, Non-MLS 11)
Founded 1879
Library Holdings: Bk Titles 508,000; Per Subs 1,500
Special Collections: Architecture, 18th & 19th Century (Percier & Fontaine Coll), bk, drawings; Catalan Art & Architectural (George R Collins Coll); Chicago & Midwestern Architecture, Archives, photog; Chicago Art & Artists Scrapbook, newsp 1890-to-date, micro: Russian Art (Ernest Hamill Coll); Surrealism (Mary Reynolds Coll); Whistler (Walter Brewster Coll). Oral History
Automation Activity & Vendor Info: (Acquisitions) Innovative Interfaces, Inc; (Cataloging) Innovative Interfaces, Inc; (Circulation) Innovative Interfaces, Inc; (Course Reserve) Innovative Interfaces, Inc; (OPAC) Innovative Interfaces, Inc; (Serials) Innovative Interfaces, Inc
Wireless access
Publications: Annual Exhibition Record of the Art Institute of Chicago 1888-1950 (1991); Architectural Records in Chicago (1981); Burnham Index to Architectural Literature (1990); Final Official Report of the Director of Works of the World's Columbian Exposition (1990); P B Wright (1980); Plan of Chicago (1909-1979); Ryerson Index to Art Periodicals; Surrealism & Its Affinities: The Mary Reynolds Coll; The Burnham Library of Architecture (1912-1987)
Partic in OCLC Online Computer Library Center, Inc; OCLC Research Library Partnership
Restriction: Mem only, Open to students, fac & staff
Friends of the Library Group

S BALZEKAS MUSEUM OF LITHUANIAN CULTURE*, Reference & Research Library, 6500 S Pulaski Rd, 60629. SAN 303-822X. Tel: 773-582-6500. FAX: 773-582-5133. E-mail: info@balzekasmuseum.org. Web Site: balzekasmuseum.org. *Pres,* Stanley Balzekas
Founded 1966
Library Holdings: Bk Titles 65,000; Per Subs 1,700
Special Collections: Art Archives; History (Rare Books Coll); Lithuanian Genealogy, Personality & Photography Archives; Manuscripts, Pamphlets, Periodicals, Records
Subject Interests: Heraldry
Publications: Museum Review
Friends of the Library Group

L BANNER & WITCOFF, LTD LIBRARY*, Ten S Wacker Dr, Ste 3000, 60606. SAN 376-0944. Tel: 312-463-5455. FAX: 312-463-5001. Web Site: www.bannerwitcoff.com. *Librn,* Megan Gluchman; E-mail: mgluchman@bannerwitcoff.com
Library Holdings: Bk Titles 6,290; Per Subs 10
Subject Interests: Law
Automation Activity & Vendor Info: (Cataloging) Inmagic, Inc.
Wireless access
Restriction: Staff use only

L BARACK, FERRAZZANO, KIRSHBAUM & NAGELBERG LIBRARY*, 200 W Madison St, Ste 3900, 60606. SAN 376-1339. Tel: 312-984-3100. FAX: 312-984-3150. Web Site: www.bfkn.com. *Librn,* Carol Brosk
Library Holdings: Bk Titles 300
Automation Activity & Vendor Info: (Cataloging) EOS International; (OPAC) EOS International
Wireless access
Restriction: Staff use only

L BRINKS, GILSON & LIONE*, Law Library, NBC Tower, 455 N Cityfront Plaza Dr, Ste 3600, 60611-5599. SAN 371-8506. Tel: 312-321-4200. FAX: 312-321-4299. Web Site: www.brinksgilson.com. *Librn,* Jenny Koertge; E-mail: jkoertge@brinksgilson.com; Staff 2 (MLS 1, Non-MLS 1)
Founded 1986
Library Holdings: Bk Titles 1,200; Per Subs 100
Special Collections: Patent Law
Automation Activity & Vendor Info: (Cataloging) Inmagic, Inc.
Wireless access
Mem of Reaching Across Illinois Library System (RAILS)
Restriction: Open to pub by appt only

L BUTLER, RUBIN, SALTARELLI & BOYD LLP*, Law Library, 321 N Clark St, Ste 400, 60654. Tel: 312-223-1690, 312-444-9660. FAX: 312-444-9287. Web Site: www.butlerrubin.com. *Dir, Operations,* David Cruz; E-mail: dcruz@butlerrubin.com
Library Holdings: Bk Titles 250; Bk Vols 375; Per Subs 25
Open Mon-Fri 9-5

SR CATHOLIC THEOLOGICAL UNION, Paul Bechtold Library, 5416 S Cornell Ave, 60615-5698. SAN 303-8335. Tel: 773-371-5464. FAX: 773-753-5340. Web Site: ctu.edu/library. *Libr Dir,* Kris Veldheer; E-mail: kveldheer@ctu.edu; Staff 4 (MLS 4)
Founded 1968. Enrl 250; Fac 25; Highest Degree: Doctorate
Jul 2020-Jun 2021 Income $515,000. Mats Exp $160,000, Books $40,000, Per/Ser (Incl. Access Fees) $40,000, Manu Arch $4,000, Electronic Ref Mat (Incl. Access Fees) $34,000, Presv $5,000. Sal $390,000
Library Holdings: AV Mats 1,001; Microforms 227; Music Scores 437; Bk Vols 133,000; Per Subs 384
Special Collections: Franciscan; Religious Orders and Life
Subject Interests: Roman Catholic theol
Automation Activity & Vendor Info: (Acquisitions) Ex Libris Group; (Cataloging) Ex Libris Group; (Circulation) Ex Libris Group; (Course Reserve) Ex Libris Group; (Discovery) EBSCO Discovery Service; (ILL) OCLC WorldShare Interlibrary Loan; (Media Booking) Ex Libris Group; (OPAC) Ex Libris Group; (Serials) Ex Libris Group
Wireless access
Publications: various monographs (Online only)
Mem of Reaching Across Illinois Library System (RAILS)
Partic in Association of Chicago Theological Schools; Consortium of Academic & Research Libraries in Illinois
Restriction: Circ privileges for students & alumni only, Open to pub by appt only

L CHAPMAN & CUTLER*, Law Library, 111 W Monroe, 60603-4096. SAN 303-8416. Tel: 312-845-3000, 312-845-3749. Interlibrary Loan Service Tel: 312-701-2372. FAX: 312-701-6620. Web Site: www.chapman.com/offices-Chicago.html. *Dir, Knowledge Mgt, Dir, Res,* Sarah Andeen; E-mail: sandeen@chapman.com; *Asst Librn,* David P Fanta; Tel: 312-845-3450, E-mail: fanta@chapman.com; *Asst Librn,* Robert Luberda; Tel: 312-845-3437, E-mail: luberda@chapman.com; *Asst Librn,* Jamie Stewart; Tel: 312-845-3435, E-mail: stewart@chapman.com; *Libr Asst,* Emily Byrne; E-mail: byrne@chapman.com; Staff 5 (MLS 4, Non-MLS 1)
Library Holdings: Bk Titles 3,000; Per Subs 50
Automation Activity & Vendor Info: (Acquisitions) EOS International; (Cataloging) EOS International; (Circulation) EOS International; (OPAC) EOS International; (Serials) EOS International
Partic in Illinois Library & Information Network
Restriction: Private libr

S CHICAGO ACADEMY OF SCIENCES/PEGGY NOTEBAERT NATURE MUSEUM*, Reference Library, CAS/PNNM Collections Facility, 4001 N Ravenswood Ave, Ste 201, 60613. SAN 303-8424. Tel: 773-755-5100. E-mail: collectionsinfo@naturemuseum.org. Web Site: www.naturemuseum.org. *Dir of Coll,* Dawn Roberts; E-mail: droberts@naturemuseum.org. Subject Specialists: *Natural hist,* Dawn Roberts
Founded 1857
Library Holdings: Bk Titles 5,000
Subject Interests: Botany, Ecology, Geol, Herpetology, Mammalogy, Natural hist, Ornithology, Paleontology
Publications: Annual Reports (1878-1945); Bulletin (1883-1995); Bulletin of the Natural History Survey (1896-1927); Leaflets (1938-1943); Museum Activities (1950-1979) (Annual report); Natural History Miscellanea (1946-1982); Proceedings (1866); Program of Activities (1930-1937); Science Notes (1959); Special Publications (1902-1959); The Chicago Naturalist (1938-1948); Transactions (1867-1870)
Restriction: Non-circulating, Not open to pub, Open by appt only

S CHICAGO HISTORY MUSEUM*, Research Center, 1601 N Clark St, 60614-6099. SAN 303-8483. Tel: 312-642-4600. FAX: 312-266-2076. E-mail: research@chicagohistory.org. Web Site: libguides.chicagohistory.org/research, www.chicagohistory.org/. *Chief Librn, Dir of Res & Access,* Ellen Keith; Tel: 312-799-2030, E-mail: keith@chicagohistory.org; Staff 6 (MLS 4, Non-MLS 2)
Founded 1856
Library Holdings: Bk Vols 150,000; Per Subs 175
Subject Interests: Civil War, Illinois, Metrop Chicago
Automation Activity & Vendor Info: (OPAC) Horizon
Wireless access
Function: Bus archives, Computers for patron use, For res purposes, Online cat, Photocopying/Printing, Ref serv available
Mem of Reaching Across Illinois Library System (RAILS)
Partic in Consortium of Academic & Research Libraries in Illinois; Illinois Library & Information Network; OCLC Online Computer Library Center, Inc
Open Tues-Fri 1-4:30, Sat 10-4:30
Restriction: Internal circ only, Non-circulating, Not a lending libr, Off-site coll in storage - retrieval as requested, Open to pub for ref only, Photo ID required for access

S CHICAGO PSYCHOANALYTIC INSTITUTE*, McLean Library, 122 S Michigan Ave, Ste 1300, 60603. SAN 320-3719. Tel: 312-897-1419, 312-922-7474. FAX: 312-922-5656. Web Site: mcleanlibrary.chicagoanalysis.org. *Librn,* John Leonard; E-mail: jleonard@chicagoanalysis.org; Staff 1 (MLS 1)
Founded 1932
Library Holdings: Bk Titles 14,000; Per Subs 45
Special Collections: Franz Alexander Archives; Gitelson Film Library Coll; Institute Archives; Kohut Archives; Therese Benedek Archives
Subject Interests: Psychoanalysis, Psychol
Wireless access
Mem of Reaching Across Illinois Library System (RAILS)
Restriction: Open to fac, students & qualified researchers

P CHICAGO PUBLIC LIBRARY*, 400 S State St, 60605. SAN 339-8102. Tel: 312-747-4300. Interlibrary Loan Service Tel: 312-747-4344. E-mail: info@chipublib.org. Web Site: www.chipublib.org. *Commissioner,* Andrea Telli; Tel: 312-747-4212, E-mail: atelli@chipublib.org; *Deputy Commissioner for Admin & Finance,* Baronica Roberson; Tel: 312-747-4030; *First Dep Commissioner,* Mary Ellen Messner; *Dir, Adult Serv,* Craig Davis; Tel: 312-747-4252, E-mail: cdavis@chipublib.org; *Div Chief, Subject Area Services,* Michael Peters; Tel: 312-747-4485, E-mail: mpeters@chipublib.org
Founded 1872. Pop 2,695,598; Circ 9,556,918
Jan 2016-Dec 2016 Income (Main & Associated Libraries) $126,525,066, State $17,017,000, City $99,619,000, Federal $1,104,264. Mats Exp $57,388,281. Sal $69,136,785
Library Holdings: AV Mats 365,282; Bk Vols 5,790,289
Special Collections: US Document Depository
Automation Activity & Vendor Info: (Acquisitions) TLC (The Library Corporation); (Cataloging) TLC (The Library Corporation); (Circulation) TLC (The Library Corporation); (OPAC) TLC (The Library Corporation); (Serials) TLC (The Library Corporation)
Wireless access
Partic in Illinois Library & Information Network; OCLC Online Computer Library Center, Inc
Special Services for the Deaf - Bks on deafness & sign lang; High interest/low vocabulary bks; Spec interest per; TDD equip; TTY equip; Videos & decoder
Special Services for the Blind - Assistive/Adapted tech devices, equip & products; Bks on cassette; Braille bks; Large print bks
Open Mon-Thurs 9-9, Fri & Sat 9-5, Sun 1-5
Friends of the Library Group
Branches: 86
ALBANY PARK, 3401 W Foster Ave, 60625, SAN 339-8374. Tel: 773-539-5450. E-mail: albanypark@chipublib.org. *Br Mgr,* John Glynn
Open Mon & Wed 10-6, Tues & Thurs 12-8, Fri & Sat 9-5
ALTGELD, 13281 S Corliss Ave, 60827. Tel: 312-747-3270. E-mail: altgeld@chipublib.org. *Br Mgr,* Nicholas Saunders
Open Mon & Wed 12-8, Tues & Thurs 10-6, Fri & Sat 9-5
ARCHER HEIGHTS, 5055 S Archer Ave, 60632, SAN 339-8439. Tel: 312-747-9241. E-mail: archerheights@chipublib.org. *Br Mgr,* Elzbieta Ptasik
Open Mon & Wed 12-8, Tues & Thurs 10-6, Fri & Sat 9-5
AUSTIN, 5615 W Race Ave, 60644, SAN 339-8498. Tel: 312-746-5038. E-mail: austin@chipublib.org. *Br Mgr,* JoAnne Willis
Open Mon & Wed 12-8, Tues & Thurs 10-6, Fri & Sat 9-5

AUSTIN-IRVING, 6100 W Irving Park Rd, 60634, SAN 339-8528. Tel: 312-744-6222. E-mail: austin-irving@chipublib.org. *Br Mgr,* Anthony Powers
Open Mon & Wed 12-8, Tues & Thurs 10-6, Fri & Sat 9-5
AVALON, 8148 S Stony Island Ave, 60617, SAN 339-8552. Tel: 312-747-5234. E-mail: avalon@chipublib.org. *Br Mgr,* John-Luke Hamilton
Open Mon & Wed 12-8, Tues & Thurs 10-6, Fri & Sat 9-5
Friends of the Library Group
BACK OF THE YARDS, 2111 W 47th St, 60609. Tel: 312-747-9595. E-mail: backoftheyards@chipublib.org. *Br Mgr,* Pedro Leon
Open Mon & Wed 10-6, Tues & Thurs 12-8, Fri & Sat 9-5
BEVERLY, 1962 W 95th St, 60643, SAN 339-8617. Tel: 312-747-9673. E-mail: beverly@chipublib.org. *Br Mgr,* Joyce Colander
Open Mon & Wed 12-8, Tues & Thurs 10-6, Fri & Sat 9-5
BEZAZIAN, 1226 W Ainslie St, 60640, SAN 339-8641. Tel: 312-744-0019. E-mail: bezazian@chipublib.org. *Br Mgr,* Mark Kaplan
Open Mon & Wed 12-8, Tues & Thurs 10-6, Fri & Sat 9-5
BLACKSTONE, 4904 S Lake Park Ave, 60615, SAN 339-8676. Tel: 312-747-0511. E-mail: blackstone@chipublib.org. *Br Mgr,* Anne Keough
Special Services for the Deaf - TDD equip
Open Mon & Wed 12-8, Tues & Thurs 10-6, Fri & Sat 9-5
BRAINERD, 1350 W 89th St, 60620, SAN 339-8706. Tel: 312-747-6291. E-mail: brainerd@chipublib.org. *Br Mgr,* Mary Jones
Open Mon & Wed 10-6, Tues & Thurs 12-8, Fri & Sat 9-5
Friends of the Library Group
BRIGHTON PARK, 4314 S Archer Ave, 60632, SAN 339-8765. Tel: 312-747-0666. E-mail: brightonpark@chipublib.org. *Br Mgr,* Michael Conlon
Open Mon & Wed 10-6, Tues & Thurs 12-8, Fri & Sat 9-5
BUCKTOWN-WICKER PARK, 1701 N Milwaukee Ave, 60647. Tel: 312-744-6022. E-mail: bucktownwickerpark@chipublib.org. *Br Mgr,* Lisa Roe
Open Mon & Wed 12-8, Tues & Thurs 10-6, Fri & Sat 9-5
BUDLONG WOODS, 5630 N Lincoln Ave, 60659. Tel: 312-742-9590. E-mail: budlongwoods@chipublib.org. *Br Mgr,* Thomas Stark
Open Mon & Wed 12-8, Tues & Thurs 10-6, Fri & Sat 9-5
CANARYVILLE, 642 W 43rd St, 60609, SAN 374-6542. Tel: 312-747-0644. E-mail: canaryville@chipublib.org. *Br Mgr,* Shelley Zawadzki
Open Mon & Wed 12-8, Tues & Thurs 10-6, Fri & Sat 9-5
CHICAGO BEE, 3647 S State St, 60609, SAN 376-8902. Tel: 312-747-6872. E-mail: chicagobee@chipublib.org. *Br Mgr,* Marvin Bowen
Open Mon & Wed 12-8, Tues & Thurs 10-6, Fri & Sat 9-5
CHICAGO LAWN, 6120 S Kedzie Ave, 60629, SAN 339-882X. Tel: 312-747-0639. E-mail: chicagolawn@chipublib.org. *Br Mgr,* Esmeralda Cossyleon
Open Mon & Wed 10-6, Tues & Thurs 12-8, Fri & Sat 9-5
CHINATOWN, 2100 S Wentworth Ave, 60616, SAN 339-8854. Tel: 312-747-8013. E-mail: chinatown@chipublib.org. *Br Mgr,* Si Chen
Open Mon & Wed 12-8, Tues & Thurs 10-6, Fri & Sat 9-5
CLEARING, 6423 W 63rd Pl, 60638, SAN 339-8889. Tel: 312-747-5657. E-mail: clearing@chipublib.org. *Br Mgr,* Robert Bitunjac
Open Mon & Wed 12-8, Tues & Thurs 10-6, Fri & Sat 9-5
BESSIE COLEMAN BRANCH, 731 E 63rd St, 60637, SAN 340-0689. Tel: 312-747-7760. E-mail: coleman@chipublib.org. *Br Mgr,* Shenita Mack
Open Mon & Wed 12-8, Tues & Thurs 10-6, Fri & Sat 9-5
RICHARD J DALEY-BRIDGEPORT BRANCH, 3400 S Halsted St, 60608, SAN 339-8730. Tel: 312-747-8990. E-mail: daley@chipublib.org. *Br Mgr,* Jeremy Kitchen
Open Mon & Wed 10-6, Tues & Thurs 12-8, Fri & Sat 9-5
RICHARD M DALEY-W HUMBOLDT BRANCH, 733 N Kedzie Ave, 60612. Tel: 312-743-0555. E-mail: richardmdaley@chipublib.org. *Br Mgr,* Jacob Cleary
Open Mon & Wed 10-6, Tues & Thurs 12-8, Fri & Sat 9-5
DOUGLASS, 3353 W 13th St, 60623, SAN 339-8943. Tel: 312-747-3725. *Br Mgr,* Eaton LaBrunesha
Open Mon-Thurs 9-9, Fri & Sat 9-5, Sun 1-5
DUNNING, 7455 W Cornelia Ave, 60634. Tel: 312-743-0480. E-mail: dunning@chipublib.org. *Br Mgr,* Melissa Kaszyski
Open Mon & Wed 12-8, Tues & Thurs 10-6, Fri & Sat 9-5
EDGEBROOK, 5331 W Devon Ave, 60646, SAN 339-9036. Tel: 312-744-8313. E-mail: edgebrook@chipublib.org. *Br Mgr,* Jennifer Reynolds
Open Mon & Wed 12-8, Tues & Thurs 10-6, Fri & Sat 9-5
EDGEWATER, 6000 N Broadway, 60660. Tel: 312-742-1945. E-mail: edgewater@chipublib.org. *Br Mgr,* Joanna Hazelden
Open Mon & Wed 10-6, Tues & Thurs 12-8, Fri & Sat 9-5
GAGE PARK, 2807 W 55th St, 60632, SAN 339-915X. Tel: 312-747-0032. E-mail: gagepark@chipublib.org. *Br Mgr,* Junkoo Yun
Open Mon & Wed 10-6, Tues & Thurs 12-8, Fri & Sat 9-5
GALEWOOD-MONT CLARE, 6871 W Belden Ave, 60707, SAN 339-9184. Tel: 312-746-0165. E-mail: galewoodmontclare@chipublib.org. *Br Mgr,* Melissa Kaszyski
Open Mon & Wed 12-8, Tues & Thurs 10-6, Fri 9-5
GARFIELD RIDGE, 6348 S Archer Ave, 60638, SAN 339-9214. Tel: 312-747-6094. E-mail: garfieldridge@chipublib.org. *Br Mgr,* Guillermina Duarte
Open Mon & Wed 10-6, Tues & Thurs 12-8, Fri & Sat 9-5
GENERAL INFORMATION SERVICES DIVISION, 400 S State St, 60605. Tel: 312-747-4472. Information Services FAX: 312-747-4329. *Div Chief,* Shenita Mack; E-mail: smack@chipublib.org
Special Collections: Chicago Biography Index File; Chicago Curio Information; Early American Newspapers; National & International Telephone Directories & Newspapers; National, US, Foreign & Trade Bibliographies
Publications: CPL Serials List
GOVERNMENT PUBLICATIONS DIVISION, 400 S State St, 60605. Tel: 312-747-4512. FAX: 312-747-4516. *Mgr,* Shah Tiwana; E-mail: stiwana@chipublib.org
Special Collections: American Statistics Index Microfiche Library (1974 retrospective-current); Chicago Municipal Reference Coll; CIS-Microfiche Library (1970-present); Congressional Committee Hearings (prior to 1953), microfiche; Congressional Committee Prints (prior to 1970), microfiche; Declassified Documents Reference System; Serial Set (1st-91st Congresses), microfiche. State Document Depository; US Document Depository
GREATER GRAND CROSSING, 1000 E 73rd St, 60619. Tel: 312-745-1608. E-mail: greatergrandcrossing@chipublib.org. *Br Mgr,* Ashley Rayner
Open Mon & Wed 12-8, Tues & Thurs 10-6, Fri & Sat 9-5
HALL, 4801 S Michigan Ave, 60615, SAN 339-9249. Tel: 312-747-2541. E-mail: hall@chipublib.org. *Br Mgr,* Kimberly Hagen
Open Mon & Wed 10-6, Tues & Thurs 12-8, Fri & Sat 9-5
Friends of the Library Group
HEGEWISCH, 3048 E 130th St, 60633, SAN 339-9362. Tel: 312-747-0046. E-mail: hegewisch@chipublib.org. *Br Mgr,* Kyleen Kenney
Special Services for the Deaf - TDD equip
Open Mon & Wed 10-6, Tues & Thurs 12-8, Fri & Sat 9-5
THOMAS HUGHES CHILDREN'S LIBRARY, 400 S State St, 2nd Flr, 60605. Tel: 312-747-4200. *Dir, Ch Serv,* Elizabeth McChesney; Tel: 312-747-4784, E-mail: emcchesn@chipublib.org
Special Collections: Dissertations on Children's Literature, microfiche; Mother Goose Coll; Opie Coll, microfiche; Retrospective Children's Literature (mostly 1900-1950); Walt Disney Coll
Subject Interests: Children's lit
Open Mon-Thurs 9-9, Fri & Sat 9-5, Sun 1-5
HUMBOLDT PARK, 1605 N Troy St, 60647, SAN 339-9427. Tel: 312-744-2244. E-mail: humboldtpark@chipublib.org. *Br Mgr,* Amber Proksa
Open Mon & Wed 12-8, Tues & Thurs 10-6, Fri & Sat 9-5
Friends of the Library Group
INDEPENDENCE, 4024 N Elston Ave, 60618, SAN 339-9540. Tel: 312-744-0900. E-mail: independence@chipublib.org. *Br Mgr,* Rory Brown
Open Mon & Wed 10-6, Tues & Thurs 12-8, Fri & Sat 9-5
JEFFERSON PARK, 5363 W Lawrence Ave, 60630, SAN 339-9575. Tel: 312-744-1998. *Br Mgr,* Eileen Dohnalek
Open Mon & Wed 10-6, Tues & Thurs 12-8, Fri & Sat 9-5
JEFFERY MANOR, 2401 E 100th St, 60617, SAN 339-9605. Tel: 312-747-6479. E-mail: jefferymanor@chipublib.org. *Br Mgr,* Lindsay Holbrook
Open Mon & Wed 10-6, Tues & Thurs 12-8, Fri & Sat 9-5
KELLY, 6151 S Normal Blvd, 60621, SAN 339-963X. Tel: 312-747-8418. E-mail: kellylibrary@chipublib.org. *Br Mgr,* Greg McClain
Open Mon & Wed 10-6, Tues & Thurs 12-8, Fri & Sat 9-5
MARTIN LUTHER KING JR BRANCH, 3436 S King Dr, 60616, SAN 339-9664. Tel: 312-747-7543. E-mail: king@chipublib.org. *Br Mgr,* Rosetta Coleman
Open Mon & Wed 10-6, Tues & Thurs 12-8, Fri & Sat 9-5
LEGLER, 115 S Pulaski Rd, 60624, SAN 339-9729. Tel: 312-746-7730. E-mail: legler@chipublib.org. *Br Mgr,* Jason Driver
Closed for renovations 2019-
LINCOLN BELMONT, 1659 W Melrose St, 60657, SAN 339-9303. Tel: 312-744-0166. E-mail: lincolnbelmont@chipublib.org. *Br Mgr,* Richard Dohnalek
Open Mon & Wed 10-6, Tues & Thurs 12-8, Fri & Sat 9-5
LINCOLN PARK, 1150 W Fullerton Ave, 60614, SAN 339-9753. Tel: 312-744-1926. E-mail: lincolnpark@chipublib.org. *Br Mgr,* Mary Jo O'Toole
Open Mon & Wed 10-6, Tues & Thurs 12-8, Fri & Sat 9-5
LITTLE ITALY, 1336 W Taylor St, 60607. Tel: 312-746-5656. E-mail: littleitaly@chipublib.org. *Br Mgr,* Shelley Hughes
Open Mon & Wed 12-8, Tues & Thurs 10-6, Fri & Sat 9-5

LITTLE VILLAGE, 2311 S Kedzie Ave, 60623. Tel: 312-745-1862. E-mail: littlevillage@chipublib.org. *Br Mgr,* Teresa Madrigal
Open Mon & Wed 10-6, Tues & Thurs 12-8, Fri & Sat 9-5
LOGAN SQUARE, 3030 W Fullerton Ave, 60647, SAN 339-9788. Tel: 312-744-5295. E-mail: logansquare@chipublib.org. *Br Mgr,* Shirley Yee
Open Mon & Wed 10-6, Tues & Thurs 12-8, Fri & Sat 9-5
RUDY LOZANO LIBRARY, 1805 S Loomis St, 60608, SAN 340-014X. Tel: 312-746-4329. E-mail: lozano@chipublib.org. *Br Mgr,* Hector Hernandez
Open Mon & Wed 10-6, Tues & Thurs 12-8, Fri & Sat 9-5
MABEL MANNING BRANCH, Six S Hoyne Ave, 60612, SAN 374-6550. Tel: 312-746-6800. E-mail: manning@chipublib.org. *Br Mgr,* Louis Kujawa
Open Mon & Wed 12-8, Tues & Thurs 10-6, Fri & Sat 9-5
THURGOOD MARSHALL BRANCH, 7506 S Racine Ave, 60620, SAN 374-6569. Tel: 312-747-5927. E-mail: thurgoodmarshall@chipublib.org. *Br Mgr,* Jan Brooks
Open Mon & Wed 12-8, Tues & Thurs 10-6, Fri & Sat 9-5
MAYFAIR, 4400 W Lawrence Ave, 60630, SAN 339-9877. Tel: 312-744-1254. E-mail: mayfair@chipublib.org. *Br Mgr,* Rebecca Berg
Open Mon & Wed 12-8, Tues & Thurs 10-6, Fri & Sat 9-5
MCKINLEY PARK, 1915 W 35th St, 60609, SAN 339-9818. Tel: 312-747-6082. E-mail: mckinleypark@chipublib.org. *Br Mgr,* Sheryll Adams
Open Mon & Wed 12-8, Tues & Thurs 10-6, Fri & Sat 9-5
JOHN MERLO BRANCH, 644 W Belmont Ave, 60657, SAN 339-9699. Tel: 312-744-1139. E-mail: merlo@chipublib.org. *Br Mgr,* Position Currently Open
Closed for renovation until 2020
MOUNT GREENWOOD, 11010 S Kedzie Ave, 60655, SAN 339-9931. Tel: 312-747-2805, 312-747-5693. E-mail: mountgreenwood@chipublib.org. *Br Mgr,* Shannon Arends
Open Mon & Wed 10-6, Tues & Thurs 12-8, Fri & Sat 9-5
NEAR NORTH, 310 W Division St, 60610, SAN 339-879X. Tel: 312-744-0991. E-mail: nearnorth@chipublib.org. *Br Mgr,* Scott Drawe
Open Mon & Wed 12-8, Tues & Thurs 10-6, Fri & Sat 9-5
NORTH AUSTIN, 5724 W North Ave, 60639, SAN 339-9990. Tel: 312-746-4233. E-mail: northaustin@chipublib.org. *Br Mgr,* Arystine Danner
Open Mon & Wed 12-8, Tues & Thurs 10-6, Fri & Sat 9-5
NORTH PULASKI, 4300 W North Ave, 60639, SAN 340-0085. Tel: 312-744-9573. E-mail: northpulaski@chipublib.org. *Br Mgr,* Denise Sebanc
Open Mon & Wed 10-6, Tues & Thurs 12-8, Fri & Sat 9-5
NORTHTOWN, 6800 N Western Ave, 60645, SAN 340-0050. Tel: 312-744-2292. E-mail: northtown@chipublib.org. *Br Mgr,* Catherine Wilson
Open Mon & Wed 10-6, Tues & Thurs 12-8, Fri & Sat 9-5
ORIOLE PARK, 7454 W Balmoral Ave, 60656, SAN 340-0115. Tel: 312-744-1965. E-mail: oriolepark@chipublib.org. *Br Mgr,* Peter Iwanec
Open Mon & Wed 12-8, Tues & Thurs 10-6, Fri & Sat 9-5
Friends of the Library Group
POPULAR LIBRARY, 400 S State St, 1st Flr, 60605. Tel: 312-747-4100. *Unit Mgr,* Position Currently Open
Special Collections: Current Fiction & Non-Fiction, bks, music CDs; Educational & Entertainment Coll, audio bks, DVDs
PORTAGE-CRAGIN, 5108 W Belmont Ave, 60641, SAN 340-0174. Tel: 312-744-0152. E-mail: portage-cragin@chipublib.org. *Br Mgr,* Susan Jorgensen
Open Mon & Wed 12-8, Tues & Thurs 10-6, Fri & Sat 9-5
PULLMAN, 11001 S Indiana Ave, 60628, SAN 340-0204. Tel: 312-747-2033. E-mail: pullman@chipublib.org. *Br Mgr,* Lolita Griffin
Open Mon & Wed 10-6, Tues & Thurs 12-8, Fri & Sat 9-5
RODEN, 6083 N Northwest Hwy, 60631, SAN 340-0263. Tel: 312-744-1478. E-mail: roden@chipublib.org. *Br Mgr,* Sarah Tansley
Open Mon & Wed 10-6, Tues & Thurs 12-8, Fri & Sat 9-5
Friends of the Library Group
ROGERS PARK, 6907 N Clark St, 60626, SAN 340-0298. Tel: 312-744-0156. E-mail: rogerspark@chipublib.org. *Br Mgr,* Jacqueline Hui
Open Mon & Wed 12-8, Tues & Thurs 10-6, Fri & Sat 9-5
SCOTTSDALE, 4101 W 79th St, 60652, SAN 340-0352. Tel: 312-747-0193. E-mail: scottsdale@chipublib.org. *Br Mgr,* Bogdan Ptasik
Open Mon & Wed 10-6, Tues & Thurs 12-8, Fri & Sat 9-5
SHERMAN PARK, 5440 S Racine Ave, 60609, SAN 340-0387. Tel: 312-747-0477. E-mail: shermanpark@chipublib.org. *Br Mgr,* Lala Rogers
Open Mon & Wed 12-8, Tues & Thurs 10-6, Fri & Sat 9-5
SOUTH CHICAGO, 9055 S Houston Ave, 60617, SAN 340-0441. Tel: 312-747-8065. E-mail: southchicago@chipublib.org. *Br Mgr,* Gregory Diaz
Open Mon & Wed 12-8, Tues & Thurs 10-6, Fri & Sat 9-5
SOUTH SHORE, 2505 E 73rd St, 60649, SAN 340-0476. Tel: 312-747-5281. E-mail: southshore@chipublib.org. *Br Mgr,* Sandra Mohammad
Open Mon & Wed 10-6, Tues & Thurs 12-8, Fri & Sat 9-5
SPECIAL COLLECTIONS & PRESERVATION DIVISION, 400 S State St, 60605. Tel: 312-747-4875. E-mail: specoll@chipublib.org. *Head, Spec Coll,* Glenn Humphreys; Tel: 312-747-1941, E-mail: ghumphre@chipublib.org; *Exhibits Curator, Spec Coll,* Elizabeth M Holland; Tel: 312-747-4883, E-mail: eholland@chipublib.org
Special Collections: Chicago History Coll; Chicago Public Library Achives; Chicago Public Library Art Coll; Chicago Theater Coll; Grand Army of the Republic & Civil War Coll; Harold Washinton Achives & Coll; Millennium Park Archives; World's Columbian Exposition Coll
Open Mon & Tues 12-6, Fri & Sat 12-4
CONRAD SULZER REGIONAL, 4455 N Lincoln Ave, 60625, SAN 339-9397. Tel: 312-744-7616. E-mail: sulzerregional@chipublib.org. *Dir,* Dana Revilla
Special Collections: Northside Neighborhood History Coll, 1880s-present, artifacts, city directories, maps, memorabilia, newsclippings, sch year bks, transcribed interviews
Special Services for the Deaf - TDD equip
Open Mon-Thurs 9-9, Fri & Sat 9-5, Sun 1-5
TOMAN, 2708 S Pulaski Rd, 60623, SAN 340-059X. Tel: 312-745-1660. E-mail: toman@chipublib.org. *Br Mgr,* Portia Latalladi
Open Mon & Wed 12-8, Tues & Thurs 10-6, Fri & Sat 9-5
UPTOWN, 929 W Buena Ave, 60613, SAN 374-6577. Tel: 312-744-8400. E-mail: uptown@chipublib.org. *Br Mgr,* Mary Clark
Open Mon & Wed 10-6, Tues & Thurs 12-8, Fri & Sat 9-5
VODAK-EAST SIDE, 3710 E 106th St, 60617, SAN 339-8978. Tel: 312-747-5500. E-mail: vodak-eastside@chipublib.org. *Br Mgr,* David Guilliams
Open Mon & Wed 12-8, Tues & Thurs 10-6, Fri & Sat 9-5
WALKER, 11071 S Hoyne Ave, 60643, SAN 340-0654. Tel: 312-747-1920. E-mail: walker@chipublib.org. *Br Mgr,* Christina Matera
Open Mon & Wed 10-6, Tues & Thurs 12-8, Fri & Sat 9-5
HAROLD WASHINGTON LIBRARY CENTER, 400 S State St, 60605. Tel: 312-747-4300. *Deputy Commissioner, Public Services,* Andrea M Telli; Tel: 312-747-4212, E-mail: atelli@chipublib.org
Special Collections: US Document Depository
Partic in OCLC Online Computer Library Center, Inc
Special Services for the Deaf - Bks on deafness & sign lang; High interest/low vocabulary bks; Spec interest per; Videos & decoder
Open Mon-Thurs 9-9, Fri & Sat 9-5, Sun 1-5
WATER WORKS, 163 E Pearson St, 60611. Tel: 312-742-8811. E-mail: waterworks@chipublib.org. *Br Mgr,* Yolanda Barker
Open Mon-Thurs 9-7, Fri & Sat 9-5, Sun 1-5
WEST BELMONT, 3104 N Narragansett Ave, 60634, SAN 340-0743. Tel: 312-746-5142. E-mail: westbelmont@chipublib.org. *Br Mgr,* Layne Arens
Open Mon & Wed 10-6, Tues & Thurs 12-8, Fri & Sat 9-5
WEST CHICAGO AVENUE, 4856 W Chicago Ave, 60651. Tel: 312-743-0260. E-mail: westchicago@chipublib.org. *Br Mgr,* Shirley Wallace
Open Mon & Wed 10-6, Tues & Thurs 12-8, Fri & Sat 9-5
WEST ENGLEWOOD, 1745 W 63rd St, 60636. Tel: 312-747-3481. E-mail: westenglewood@chipublib.org. *Br Mgr,* Maurice Thomas, Jr
Open Mon & Wed 12-8, Tues & Thurs 10-6, Fri & Sat 9-5
WEST LAWN, 4020 W 63rd St, 60629, SAN 340-0778. Tel: 312-747-7381. E-mail: westlawn@chipublib.org. *Br Mgr,* Marvin Blackwell
Open Mon & Wed 12-8, Tues & Thurs 10-6, Fri & Sat 9-5
WEST LOOP, 122 N Aberdeen St, 60607. Tel: 312-744-2995. E-mail: westloop@chipublib.org. *Br Mgr,* Melissa Wagner
Open Mon & Wed 10-6, Tues & Thurs 12-8, Fri & Sat 9-5
WEST PULLMAN, 830 W 119th St, 60628. Tel: 312-747-1425. E-mail: westpullman@chipublib.org. *Br Mgr,* Dewana Dorsey
Open Mon & Wed 12-8, Tues & Thurs 10-6, Fri & Sat 9-5
WEST TOWN, 1625 W Chicago Ave, 60622. Tel: 312-743-0450. E-mail: westtown@chipublib.org. *Br Mgr,* Stephanie Flinchbaugh
Open Mon & Wed 10-6, Tues & Thurs 12-8, Fri & Sat 9-5
CARTER G WOODSON REGIONAL, 9525 S Halsted St, 60628, SAN 340-0891. Tel: 312-747-6900. E-mail: woodsonregional@chipublib.org. *Dir,* Lynda Schoop
Special Collections: Afro-American History & Literature (Vivian G Harsh Coll), monographs; Afro-American Newspapers, 1927 to date, microfilm; Annual Reports of the National Association for the Advancement of Colored People, 1910-1970; Literary Manuscripts, such as Richard Wright & Langston Hughes; Papers of the American Missionary Association
Special Services for the Deaf - TDD equip
Open Mon-Thurs 9-9, Fri & Sat 9-5, Sun 1-5
WRIGHTWOOD-ASHBURN, 8530 S Kedzie Ave, 60652, SAN 340-0921. Tel: 312-747-2696. E-mail: wrightwood-ashburn@chipublib.org. *Br Mgr,* Veyshon Edmond
Open Mon & Wed 12-8, Tues & Thurs 10-6, Fri & Sat 9-5
WHITNEY M YOUNG JR BRANCH, 415 E 79th St, 60619, SAN 340-0956. Tel: 312-747-0039. E-mail: whitneyyoung@chipublib.org. *Br Mgr,* Mitchell Smith
Open Mon & Wed 10-6, Tues & Thurs 12-8, Fri & Sat 9-5

S CHICAGO SCHOOL OF PROFESSIONAL PSYCHOLOGY LIBRARY*, 325 N Wells St, 6th Flr, 60654. SAN 329-7381. Tel: 312-329-6630. FAX: 312-644-6075. E-mail: library@thechicagoschool.edu. Web Site: www.thechicagoschool.edu/content.cfm/library. *Univ Librn,* David Sibley; *Instructional & Student Engagement Librn,* Fay Kallista; Tel: 312-467-2374, E-mail: fkallista@thechicagoschool.edu; Staff 3.5 (MLS 3.5)
Founded 1979. Enrl 1,600; Fac 100; Highest Degree: Doctorate
Library Holdings: e-books 90,000; e-journals 3,000; Bk Titles 8,500; Bk Vols 14,000; Per Subs 220
Special Collections: Israel Goldiamond Special Coll
Subject Interests: Adolescent psychol, Assessment, Child psychology, Clinical psychol, Forensic psychol, Interpretation, Multicultural studies, Psychotherapy
Automation Activity & Vendor Info: (Cataloging) OCLC; (ILL) OCLC; (OPAC) OCLC; (Serials) OCLC
Wireless access
Function: 24/7 Electronic res, Computers for patron use, Distance learning, Doc delivery serv, E-Reserves, Electronic databases & coll, ILL available, Online cat, Online ref, Outside serv via phone, mail, e-mail & web, Photocopying/Printing
Mem of Reaching Across Illinois Library System (RAILS)
Partic in Health Science Libraries of Illinois; Illinois Library & Information Network; OCLC Online Computer Library Center, Inc; OCLC-LVIS
Open Mon-Thurs 8am-9pm, Fri & Sat 8-5, Sun 11-5

R CHICAGO SINAI CONGREGATION*, James & Leah Davis Memorial Library, 15 W Delaware Pl, 60610. SAN 303-8513. Tel: 312-867-7000. FAX: 312-867-7006. E-mail: library@chicagosinai.org. Web Site: www.chicagosinai.org. *Library Contact,* Judy Genesen; E-mail: ljgenesen@aol.com; Staff 1 (MLS 1)
Founded 1950
Library Holdings: DVDs 100; Bk Titles 5,000; Per Subs 5
Subject Interests: Judaica
Wireless access
Function: Archival coll, Computers for patron use, ILL available, Online cat, Ref serv available
Mem of Reaching Across Illinois Library System (RAILS)
Restriction: Circ to mem only
Friends of the Library Group

C CHICAGO STATE UNIVERSITY*, University Library, 9501 S Martin Luther King Jr Dr, LIB 440, 60628-1598. SAN 303-8521. Tel: 773-995-2235. Circulation Tel: 773-995-2341. Interlibrary Loan Service Tel: 773-995-2222. Administration Tel: 773-995-2253. FAX: 773-995-3772. Interlibrary Loan Service FAX: 773-821-2581. E-mail: reference@csu.edu. Web Site: www.library.csu.edu. *Dean of Libr,* Dr Richard Darga; E-mail: rdarga@csu.edu; *Chair, Libr & Instruction Serv,* Gabrielle Toth; Tel: 773-995-2562, E-mail: gtoth@csu.edu; *Access Serv Librn,* Position Currently Open; *Electronic Res Librn,* Joanna Kolendo; Tel: 773-995-2542, E-mail: jkolendo@csu.edu; *Ref & Instruction Librn, Educ,* Position Currently Open; *Ref & Instruction Librn, Sci,* Position Currently Open; *Ref Librn,* Rosalind Fielder; Tel: 773-821-2431, E-mail: rfielder@csu.edu; *Ref & Instruction Coordr,* Charlene Snelling; Tel: 773-995-2557; *Syst Coordr,* Martin Kong; Tel: 773-995-3908, E-mail: mkong@csu.edu; *Tech Serv & Acq Librn/Coordr,* Azungwe Kwembe; Tel: 995-821-2848, E-mail: akwembe@csu.edu; *Spec Formats Cataloger,* Gayle Porter; Tel: 773-995-2551; *Univ Archivist,* Raquel Flores-Clemons. Subject Specialists: *Foreign lang, Geog, Govt info,* Gabrielle Toth; *Humanities, Lit, Philos,* Joanna Kolendo; *Polit sci, Soc sci,* Rosalind Fielder; *Health sci, Pharm,* Charlene Snelling; *Econ,* Martin Kong; *Mkt,* Azungwe Kwembe; *Sociol,* Gayle Porter; Staff 25 (MLS 8, Non-MLS 17)
Founded 1867. Enrl 3,600; Fac 250; Highest Degree: Doctorate
Jul 2012-Jun 2013. Mats Exp $938,747, Books $92,004. Sal $1,886,684 (Prof $1,285,166)
Library Holdings: AV Mats 8,688; e-books 33,371; e-journals 17,000; Bk Titles 467,544; Per Subs 1,005
Special Collections: Education (Learning Materials, Children's Books). State Document Depository; US Document Depository
Automation Activity & Vendor Info: (Acquisitions) Ex Libris Group; (Cataloging) Ex Libris Group; (Circulation) Ex Libris Group; (Course Reserve) Ex Libris Group; (ILL) Ex Libris Group; (OPAC) Ex Libris Group; (Serials) Ex Libris Group
Wireless access
Mem of Reaching Across Illinois Library System (RAILS)
Partic in Center for Research Libraries; Consortium of Academic & Research Libraries in Illinois; Illinois Library & Information Network
Open Mon-Thurs 8am-10pm, Fri 8-5, Sat 9-5, Sun 2-10

R CHICAGO THEOLOGICAL SEMINARY*, Learning Commons, 1407 E 60th St, 60637-2902. SAN 303-8556. Tel: 773-896-2450. FAX: 773-643-1284. E-mail: library@ctschicago.edu. Web Site: commons.ctschicago.edu/www.ctschicago.edu/library. *Dir,* Yasmine Abou-El-Kheir; E-mail: yasmine.abou-el-kheir@ctschicago.edu; Staff 2 (MLS 1, Non-MLS 1)
Founded 1855. Enrl 224; Fac 15; Highest Degree: Doctorate
Library Holdings: e-books 382,800; e-journals 364; Bk Titles 116,000; Bk Vols 117,000; Per Subs 144
Subject Interests: Biblical studies, Counseling, Relig, Sexuality, Theol
Automation Activity & Vendor Info: (Cataloging) LibLime Koha; (Circulation) LibLime Koha; (Course Reserve) LibLime Koha; (Discovery) EBSCO Discovery Service; (ILL) OCLC WorldShare Interlibrary Loan; (OPAC) LibLime Koha; (Serials) LibLime Koha
Wireless access
Mem of Reaching Across Illinois Library System (RAILS)
Partic in Association of Chicago Theological Schools; Consortium of Academic & Research Libraries in Illinois; Illinois Library & Information Network; OCLC Online Computer Library Center, Inc
Open Mon-Wed 8:30am-10pm, Thurs 8:30-8, Fri 8:30-5, Sat Noon-4

CITY COLLEGES OF CHICAGO

J RICHARD J DALEY COLLEGE LIBRARY*, 7500 S Pulaski Rd, 60652-1200, SAN 376-2564. Tel: 773-838-7667. Circulation Tel: 773-838-7668. Interlibrary Loan Service Tel: 773-838-7676. Reference Tel: 773-838-7669. FAX: 773-838-7524. Web Site: daley.ccc.edu. *Chairperson,* Siew-Ben Chin; Tel: 773-838-7674, E-mail: schin@ccc.edu; Staff 11 (MLS 7, Non-MLS 4)
Founded 1965. Enrl 4,900; Fac 112; Highest Degree: Associate
Library Holdings: Bk Titles 65,000; Per Subs 200
Subject Interests: Local hist
Automation Activity & Vendor Info: (Acquisitions) Innovative Interfaces, Inc; (Cataloging) Innovative Interfaces, Inc; (Circulation) Innovative Interfaces, Inc; (Course Reserve) Innovative Interfaces, Inc; (ILL) OCLC FirstSearch; (OPAC) Innovative Interfaces, Inc; (Serials) Innovative Interfaces, Inc
Function: ILL available
Partic in Network of Illinois Learning Resources in Community Colleges; Northern Illinois Learning Resources Cooperative
Mem of Reaching Across Illinois Library System (RAILS)
Open Mon-Thurs 7:45am-10pm, Fri 7:45-5, Sat 8-2
Restriction: Circ limited

J KENNEDY-KING COLLEGE LIBRARY*, 6403 S Halsted, 60621. (Mail add: 747 W 63rd St, 60621), SAN 303-9390. Tel: 773-602-5449. Information Services Tel: 773-602-5491. FAX: 773-602-5450. E-mail: kkclibrarian@ccc.edu. Web Site: www.ccc.edu/colleges/kennedy/departments/Pages/Library-System.aspx. *Chairperson, Res Mgt Librn,* Ruth A Inman; *Ref & Instruction Librn,* Alecia Kerr. Subject Specialists: *Fine arts, Music,* Ruth A Inman; *Humanities,* Alecia Kerr; Staff 4 (MLS 4)
Founded 1934. Enrl 5,000; Fac 4; Highest Degree: Associate
Library Holdings: Bk Vols 51,000; Per Subs 40
Special Collections: Washburne Cookbook Coll
Automation Activity & Vendor Info: (Acquisitions) Ex Libris Group; (Cataloging) Ex Libris Group; (Circulation) Ex Libris Group; (Course Reserve) Ex Libris Group; (ILL) Ex Libris Group; (OPAC) Ex Libris Group; (Serials) Ex Libris Group
Function: 24/7 Electronic res, Archival coll, Art exhibits, CD-ROM, Computers for patron use, Distance learning, Electronic databases & coll, ILL available, Large print keyboards, Magnifiers for reading, Online cat, Online info literacy tutorials on the web & in blackboard, Orientations, Photocopying/Printing, Ref serv available, Study rm, Telephone ref, Wheelchair accessible, Workshops
Partic in Consortium of Academic & Research Libraries in Illinois; Illinois Library & Information Network; Network of Illinois Learning Resources in Community Colleges; Northern Illinois Learning Resources Cooperative
Mem of Reaching Across Illinois Library System (RAILS)
Open Mon-Thurs 8:30-8, Fri 8:30-4, Sat 9-1
Restriction: Open to pub for ref only

J MALCOLM X COLLEGE - CARTER G WOODSON LIBRARY*, 1900 W Jackson St, 2nd Flr, 60612, SAN 303-9609. Tel: 312-850-7244. E-mail: mxc-library@ccc.edu. Web Site: library.ccc.edu, www.ccc.edu/colleges/malcolm-x/departments/Pages/Library-System.aspx. *Dept Chair,* CM! Winters Palacio; E-mail: cwinterspalacio@ccc.edu; *Archives, Cat, Tech Serv,* Fumilayo Rufai; E-mail: frufai@ccc.edu; *Evening Coordr, ILL,* Dennis Whiteside; E-mail: dwhiteside@ccc.edu. Subject Specialists: *Info literacy,* CM! Winters Palacio; Staff 3 (MLS 2, Non-MLS 1)
Founded 1934. Enrl 12,016; Fac 2; Highest Degree: Associate
Jul 2015-Jun 2016. Mats Exp $56,000, Books $32,000, Per/Ser (Incl. Access Fees) $14,000, Other Print Mats $7,000, AV Mat $3,000
Library Holdings: Bk Titles 35,000; Per Subs 30
Automation Activity & Vendor Info: (Acquisitions) Ex Libris Group
Function: 24/7 Electronic res, Computers for patron use, Digital talking bks, E-Reserves, Electronic databases & coll, Health sci info serv, ILL available, Instruction & testing, Internet access, Magazines, Magnifiers for reading, Movies, Music CDs, Online cat, Online info literacy tutorials on the web & in blackboard, Online ref, Orientations, Outreach serv, Photocopying/Printing, Ref serv available, Scanner, Spanish lang bks,

Spoken cassettes & CDs, Spoken cassettes & DVDs, Study rm, Tax forms, Telephone ref, VHS videos, Wheelchair accessible, Workshops
Partic in Network of Illinois Learning Resources in Community Colleges
Open Mon-Thurs 8-8, Fri 9-1
Restriction: Borrowing privileges limited to fac & registered students, Borrowing requests are handled by ILL, Circ limited, Circ privileges for students & alumni only, In-house use for visitors, Non-circulating coll, Non-circulating of rare bks, Photo ID required for access, Restricted borrowing privileges, Restricted loan policy, Restricted pub use

J OLIVE-HARVEY COLLEGE LIBRARY*, 10001 S Woodlawn Ave, Rm 2423, 60628, SAN 303-9978. Tel: 773-291-6354, 773-291-6477. FAX: 773-291-6463. Web Site: www.ccc.edu. *Librn,* Willa Lyn Fox; Tel: 773-291-6360, E-mail: wfox@ccc.edu; Staff 3 (MLS 1, Non-MLS 2)
Founded 1957. Enrl 7,000; Fac 123; Highest Degree: Doctorate
Library Holdings: Bk Titles 47,601; Bk Vols 57,095; Per Subs 260
Subject Interests: Spanish (Lang)
Automation Activity & Vendor Info: (OPAC) SirsiDynix
Partic in Network of Illinois Learning Resources in Community Colleges
Special Services for the Blind - Braille Webster's dictionary
Open Mon-Thurs (Winter) 8am-9pm, Fri 8-3, Sat 8-1; Mon-Thurs (Summer) 8-8

J HARRY S TRUMAN COLLEGE - COSGROVE LIBRARY*, 1145 W Wilson Ave, 60640-5691, SAN 304-0380. Tel: 773-907-4865. FAX: 773-907-6803. *Chairperson,* Leone McDermot; Tel: 773-907-4877, E-mail: lmcdermott@ccc.edu; *Pub Serv,* Kwan-Yau Lam; Tel: 773-907-4869, E-mail: klam@ccc.edu; Staff 4 (MLS 4)
Founded 1956. Enrl 4,900; Fac 180; Highest Degree: Associate
Library Holdings: Bk Titles 63,000; Bk Vols 66,800; Per Subs 251
Partic in Network of Illinois Learning Resources in Community Colleges; OCLC Online Computer Library Center, Inc
Open Mon-Thurs 8:30-8:30

J HAROLD WASHINGTON COLLEGE LIBRARY*, 30 E Lake St, 60601-9996, SAN 303-9501. Tel: 312-553-5760. FAX: 312-553-5783. E-mail: hwc-library@ccc.edu. Web Site: hwclibrary.ccc.edu. *Instr,* Celia Perez; Tel: 312-553-5635, E-mail: cperez2@ccc.edu; Staff 10 (MLS 4, Non-MLS 6)
Founded 1962. Enrl 8,400; Fac 8; Highest Degree: Associate
Library Holdings: CDs 1,300; Bk Titles 69,802; Bk Vols 70,704; Per Subs 175; Videos 3,000
Subject Interests: Ethnic studies
Automation Activity & Vendor Info: (Acquisitions) Ex Libris Group; (Cataloging) Ex Libris Group; (Circulation) Ex Libris Group; (Course Reserve) Ex Libris Group; (ILL) Ex Libris Group; (Media Booking) Ex Libris Group; (OPAC) Ex Libris Group; (Serials) Ex Libris Group
Partic in Ill Regional Libr Coun; Network of Illinois Learning Resources in Community Colleges; Northern Illinois Learning Resources Cooperative
Open Mon-Fri 8am-9pm, Sat 8:30-1:30

J WILBUR WRIGHT COLLEGE LIBRARY*, 4300 N Narragansett Ave, L-200, 60634-1500, SAN 304-0542. Tel: 773-481-8400. FAX: 773-481-8407. Web Site: www.ccc.edu/colleges/wright/departments/Pages/Library-System.aspx. *Libr Asst II,* Myrna Favors; E-mail: mfavors1@ccc.edu; Staff 3 (MLS 3)
Founded 1934. Enrl 6,250
Library Holdings: Bk Titles 48,000; Bk Vols 52,000; Per Subs 100
Automation Activity & Vendor Info: (Cataloging) Innovative Interfaces, Inc; (Circulation) Innovative Interfaces, Inc; (OPAC) Innovative Interfaces, Inc
Partic in Network of Illinois Learning Resources in Community Colleges
Mem of Reaching Across Illinois Library System (RAILS)
Open Mon-Thurs 8am-9:30pm, Fri 8-4, Sat 8-2

GL CITY OF CHICAGO*, Department of Law Library, 30 N LaSalle, Ste 800, 60602. SAN 373-6172. Tel: 312-744-5124. FAX: 312-744-1974. Web Site: cityofchicago.org. *Librn,* Michael McMurray; Staff 3 (MLS 2, Non-MLS 1)
Library Holdings: Bk Titles 700; Bk Vols 16,000
Wireless access
Mem of Reaching Across Illinois Library System (RAILS)
Restriction: Staff use only

L CLAUSEN MILLER RESEARCH SERVICES*, Ten S LaSalle St, 16th Flr, 60603-1098. SAN 371-635X. Tel: 312-606-7887. FAX: 312-606-7777. Web Site: www.clausen.com. *Sr Res Spec,* Anton Kresich; E-mail: akresich@clausen.com; Staff 20 (MLS 2, Non-MLS 18)
Founded 1936
Library Holdings: Bk Vols 15,000; Per Subs 300
Mem of Reaching Across Illinois Library System (RAILS)
Partic in Illinois Library & Information Network; OCLC Online Computer Library Center, Inc
Open Mon-Fri 8:30-6

S COLLECTORS CLUB OF CHICAGO LIBRARY, 1029 N Dearborn St, 60610. SAN 372-574X. Tel: 312-642-7981. Web Site: www.collectorsclubchicago.org/the-ccc-library. *Chairperson, Librn,* Edward W Waterous; E-mail: ewwaterous@hotmail.com
Founded 1928
Library Holdings: Bk Titles 10,000; Per Subs 50
Special Collections: US Document Depository
Publications: Philatelic Hard Bound, bks

C COLUMBIA COLLEGE CHICAGO LIBRARY*, 624 S Michigan Ave, 60605-1996. SAN 340-0980. Tel: 312-344-7900. Circulation Tel: 312-344-7152. Interlibrary Loan Service Tel: 312-344-7370. Reference Tel: 312-344-7153. FAX: 312-344-8062. Web Site: library.colum.edu. *Libr Dir,* Jo Cates; Tel: 312-369-8781, E-mail: jcates@colum.edu; *Asst Dir,* Dennis McGuire; Tel: 773-220-0223, E-mail: dmcguire@colum.edu; *Head, Access Serv,* Jennifer Sauzer; Tel: 312-369-8540, E-mail: jsauzer@colum.edu; *Head, Archives & Spec Coll,* Heidi Marshall; Tel: 312-369-8689, E-mail: hmarshall@colum.edu; *Head, Ref,* Arlie Sims; Tel: 312-369-7059, E-mail: asims@colum.edu; *Academic Engagement Librn,* Kim Hale; Tel: 312-369-7355, E-mail: khale@colum.edu; Staff 19 (MLS 19)
Founded 1890. Enrl 11,500; Fac 1,100; Highest Degree: Master
Library Holdings: AV Mats 40,000; e-books 131,083; e-journals 1,393,290; Bk Vols 207,365; Per Subs 274
Special Collections: Center for Black Music Research; Center for Book & Paper Arts; Fashion Columbia Study Coll
Subject Interests: Art, Dance, Films & filmmaking, Journalism, Photog, Radio, Television
Wireless access
Mem of Reaching Across Illinois Library System (RAILS)
Partic in Consortium of Academic & Research Libraries in Illinois; Illinois Library & Information Network; LIBRAS, Inc
Friends of the Library Group

S COMPASS LEXECON*, 332 S Michigan Ave, Ste 1300, 60604. SAN 376-0111. Tel: 312-322-0200. FAX: 312-322-0218. Web Site: www.compasslexecon.com. *Librn,* Ray Thomas
Library Holdings: Bk Titles 2,000; Per Subs 82
Wireless access

SR CONGREGATION RODFEI ZEDEK*, The Joseph J & Dora Abbell Library, 5200 S Hyde Park Blvd, 60615-4213. SAN 303-8653. Tel: 773-752-2770, Ext 106. FAX: 773-752-0330. Web Site: rodfei.org/Abbell_Library. *Exec Dir,* Juliet Ratowitz; E-mail: execdir@rodfei.org
Founded 1950
Library Holdings: Bk Vols 8,000; Per Subs 30
Subject Interests: Americana, Judaica (lit or hist of Jews)
Wireless access
Open Mon-Thurs 8:30-4:30, Fri & Sat 8:30-3, Sun 10-1

GL COOK COUNTY LAW LIBRARY, 50 W Washington St, Rm 2900, 60602. SAN 303-8718. Tel: 312-603-5423. FAX: 312-603-4716. E-mail: law.lawlibrary@cookcountyil.gov. Web Site: cookcountyil.gov/agency/law-library. *Exec Law Librn,* Montell Davenport; E-mail: montell.davenport@cookcountyil.gov; *Dep Law Librn,* Jean Wenger; Tel: 312-603-5131, E-mail: jean.wenger@cookcountyil.gov; *Head, Tech Serv,* Carolyn Hayes; Tel: 312-603-2433, E-mail: carolyn.hayes@cookcountyil.gov
Founded 1966
Library Holdings: e-journals 2,100; Bk Vols 375,000
Special Collections: Contemporary & Historical Federal & State Law Coll; Foreign & International Law Coll; Government Documents Coll
Automation Activity & Vendor Info: (Cataloging) Innovative Interfaces, Inc - Sierra; (OPAC) Innovative Interfaces, Inc - Sierra
Wireless access
Function: Computers for patron use, Electronic databases & coll, Internet access, Microfiche/film & reading machines, Online cat, Orientations, Photocopying/Printing, Printer for laptops & handheld devices, Ref & res, Ref serv available, Scanner, Wheelchair accessible
Special Services for the Blind - Accessible computers; Computer with voice synthesizer for visually impaired persons; Copier with enlargement capabilities; Internet workstation with adaptive software; Low vision equip; Screen enlargement software for people with visual disabilities; Screen reader software
Open Mon-Fri 8:30-7, Sat 12:30-4:30
Restriction: Circ limited
Branches:
BRIDGEVIEW BRANCH, 10220 S 76th Ave, Bridgeview, 60455, SAN 370-0313. Tel: 708-974-6201. FAX: 708-974-6053. *Law Librn,* Tracy Harmon; E-mail: tracy.harmon@coolcountyil.gov
Automation Activity & Vendor Info: (Cataloging) Innovative Interfaces, Inc - Sierra; (OPAC) Innovative Interfaces, Inc - Sierra
Function: Computers for patron use, Electronic databases & coll, Internet access, Online cat, Photocopying/Printing

Open Mon-Fri 8:30-4:30
Restriction: Circ limited
CRIMINAL COURT, 2650 S California, 4th Flr, 60608, SAN 320-9903. Tel: 773-674-5039. FAX: 773-674-3413.
Automation Activity & Vendor Info: (Cataloging) Innovative Interfaces, Inc - Sierra; (OPAC) Innovative Interfaces, Inc - Sierra
Function: Computers for patron use, Electronic databases & coll, Internet access, Online cat, Photocopying/Printing
Open Mon-Fri 9-5
MARKHAM BRANCH, 16501 S Kedzie Pkwy, Markham, 60426, SAN 321-3900. Tel: 708-232-4125. FAX: 708-232-4374. *Law Librn,* Eugene Granberry; E-mail: eugene.granberry@cookcountyil.gov
Automation Activity & Vendor Info: (Cataloging) Innovative Interfaces, Inc - Sierra; (OPAC) Innovative Interfaces, Inc - Sierra
Function: Computers for patron use, Electronic databases & coll, Internet access, Online cat, Photocopying/Printing
Open Mon-Fri 8:30-4:30
Restriction: Circ limited
MAYWOOD BRANCH, 1500 Maybrook Dr, Maywood, 60153, SAN 321-3919. Tel: 708-865-6020. FAX: 708-865-5152.
Automation Activity & Vendor Info: (Cataloging) Innovative Interfaces, Inc - Sierra; (OPAC) Innovative Interfaces, Inc - Sierra
Function: Computers for patron use, Electronic databases & coll, Internet access, Online cat, Photocopying/Printing
Open Mon-Fri 8:30-4:30
Restriction: Circ limited
SKOKIE BRANCH, 5600 W Old Orchard Rd, Skokie, 60077, SAN 321-8570. Tel: 847-470-7298. FAX: 847-470-7526. *Law Librn,* Colleen McCarroll; E-mail: colleen.mccarroll@cookcountyil.gov
Library Holdings: Bk Vols 2,500
Automation Activity & Vendor Info: (Cataloging) Innovative Interfaces, Inc - Sierra; (OPAC) Innovative Interfaces, Inc - Sierra
Function: Computers for patron use, Electronic databases & coll, Internet access, Online cat, Photocopying/Printing
Open Mon-Fri 8:30-4:30
Restriction: Circ limited

S DAWSON TECHNICAL INSTITUTE, Learning Resource Center, 3901 S State St, 60609. SAN 325-6758. Tel: 773-602-5555. Web Site: www.ccc.edu/colleges/kennedy/departments/pages/dawson-technical-institute.aspx. *Library Contact,* Jacqueline Crosby; E-mail: jcrosby@ccc.edu
Library Holdings: Bk Titles 15,200; Bk Vols 16,250; Per Subs 45
Wireless access
Function: Photocopying/Printing
Open Mon-Fri 8:30-4

L DENTONS US LLP*, Law Library, 233 S Wacker Dr, Ste 5900, 60606-6361. SAN 304-0275. Tel: 312-876-8000. FAX: 312-876-7934. Web Site: www.dentons.com. *Head, Res Serv,* Nancy Henry; E-mail: nancy.henry@dentons.com; *Res Analyst,* Janice Collins
Library Holdings: Bk Titles 1,200; Bk Vols 15,000; Per Subs 200
Subject Interests: US Law
Automation Activity & Vendor Info: (Acquisitions) EOS International; (Cataloging) EOS International; (Circulation) EOS International; (Course Reserve) EOS International; (ILL) EOS International; (Media Booking) EOS International; (OPAC) EOS International; (Serials) EOS International
Mem of Reaching Across Illinois Library System (RAILS)
Partic in CLS; OCLC Online Computer Library Center, Inc

C DEPAUL UNIVERSITY LIBRARIES*, John T Richardson Library, 2350 N Kenmore, 60614. SAN 340-1103. Tel: 773-325-7862, 773-325-7863. Interlibrary Loan Service Tel: 773-325-7818. Administration Tel: 773-325-7849. FAX: 773-325-7870. Web Site: www.lib.depaul.edu. *VPres, Teaching & Learning Res,* Edward Udovic; E-mail: eudovic@depaul.edu; *Univ Librn,* Scott Walter; *Assoc Univ Librn, Admin Serv,* Christopher Hoeppner; E-mail: choeppne@depaul.edu; *Assoc Univ Librn, Discovery Librn,* Megan Bernal; *Assoc Univ Librn, Res & Info Serv Librn,* Terry Taylor; E-mail: ttaylor@depaul.edu; Staff 67 (MLS 31, Non-MLS 36)
Founded 1898. Enrl 21,363; Fac 1,500; Highest Degree: Doctorate
Library Holdings: Bk Vols 848,846; Per Subs 5,778
Special Collections: Art Books; Charles Dickens; Horace; Napoleon; Sports
Automation Activity & Vendor Info: (Acquisitions) Ex Libris Group; (Cataloging) Ex Libris Group; (Circulation) Ex Libris Group; (Course Reserve) Ex Libris Group; (ILL) Ex Libris Group; (Media Booking) Ex Libris Group; (OPAC) Ex Libris Group; (Serials) Ex Libris Group
Wireless access
Mem of Reaching Across Illinois Library System (RAILS)
Partic in Consortium of Academic & Research Libraries in Illinois; Illinois Library & Information Network
Open Mon-Thurs 7:30am-2am, Fri 7:30am-9pm, Sat 10am-9pm, Sun 10am-2am

Departmental Libraries:
LOOP LIBRARY, One E Jackson Blvd, 10th Flr, 60604, SAN 340-1138. Tel: 312-362-8433. Reference Tel: 312-362-8432. FAX: 312-362-6186.
Open Mon-Fri 8am-10pm, Sat 10am-6pm, Sun 12pm-6pm
CL VINCENT G RINN LAW LIBRARY, 25 E Jackson Blvd, 5th Flr, 60604-2287, SAN 340-1197. Tel: 312-362-8121, 312-362-8701. FAX: 312-362-6908. Web Site: law.depaul.edu/library. *Assoc Dean for IT & Library Servs,* Allen Moye; Tel: 312-362-6893; *Assoc Dir, Computing Serv,* Michael Schiffer; Tel: 312-362-6311, E-mail: mschiffe@depaul.edu; *Assoc Dir, Pub Serv,* Milta Hall; Tel: 312-362-5093; *Assoc Dir, Tech Serv,* Mary Lu Linnane; Tel: 312-362-6895; *Head, Cat,* Denise Glynn; *Acq Mgr,* Lenore Boehm; Tel: 312-362-5224; *Circ Mgr,* Heather Hummons; Tel: 312-362-8958, E-mail: hhummons@depaul.edu; *Mgr, Ser,* Candis Collins; Tel: 312-362-6155; *Cat, Doc,* Walter Baumann; Tel: 312-362-5225, E-mail: wbaumann@depaul.edu; *ILL,* Kimyatta Gainey; Tel: 312-362-5123, E-mail: kgainey@depaul.edu; Staff 18 (MLS 7, Non-MLS 11)
Founded 1920. Enrl 1,100; Fac 50; Highest Degree: Master
Library Holdings: Bk Titles 70,980; Bk Vols 402,000; Per Subs 5,348
Special Collections: Graduate Taxation Law; Health Law Coll; International Human Rights Law; Supreme Court Justices' Signatures (Nathan Schwartz Coll). US Document Depository
Subject Interests: Constitutional law, Environ law
Automation Activity & Vendor Info: (OPAC) Ex Libris Group
Partic in Chicago Legal Acad Syst; Mid-America Law Library Consortium; OCLC Online Computer Library Center, Inc
Open Mon-Fri (Winter) 8am-11pm, Sat 9-6, Sun 12-10; Mon-Fri (Summer) 8am-10pm, Sat 9-6
Restriction: Photo ID required for access

L DLA PIPER US LLP*, Law Library, 444 W Lake St, Ste 900, 60606-0089. SAN 372-1116. Tel: 312-849-3841. Interlibrary Loan Service Tel: 312-984-5855. FAX: 312-251-5845. *Sr Mgr, Knowledge Resource Mgmt,* John Klasey; Tel: 312-984-5222, E-mail: john.klasey@us.dlapiper.com; *Business & Legal Research Analyst,* Valerie Kropf; Tel: 312-984-5703, E-mail: valerie.kropf@us.dlapiper.com; *Knowledge Resource Coord,* Lee Howell; Tel: 312-849-8690, E-mail: lee.howell@us.dlapiper.com; Staff 3 (MLS 2, Non-MLS 1)
Wireless access
Mem of Reaching Across Illinois Library System (RAILS)
Partic in OCLC Online Computer Library Center, Inc

L DRINKER, BIDDLE & REATH*, Library & Research Services, 191 N Wacker Dr, Ste 3700, 60606. SAN 376-1428. Tel: 312-569-1869. FAX: 312-569-3000. Web Site: www.drinkerbiddle.com. *Sr Res Librn,* Susane Yesnick
Library Holdings: Bk Titles 2,700
Automation Activity & Vendor Info: (Acquisitions) SydneyPlus; (Cataloging) SydneyPlus; (Circulation) SydneyPlus; (OPAC) SydneyPlus
Wireless access
Open Mon-Fri 9-5

S DUFF & PHELPS*, Research Library, 311 S Wacker Dr, Ste 4200, 60606. SAN 325-6367. Tel: 312-697-4600. Web Site: www.duffandphelps.com. *Dir, Info & Res,* Michael Tebbe; Tel: 312-697-4535, E-mail: michael.tebbe@duffandphelps.com; Staff 3 (MLS 2, Non-MLS 1)
Library Holdings: Bk Titles 3,700; Bk Vols 4,500; Per Subs 200
Subject Interests: Finance
Automation Activity & Vendor Info: (Acquisitions) Inmagic, Inc.; (Cataloging) Inmagic, Inc.; (Circulation) Inmagic, Inc.; (Serials) Inmagic, Inc.
Wireless access
Mem of Reaching Across Illinois Library System (RAILS)
Restriction: Not open to pub

§C EAST-WEST UNIVERSITY LIBRARY, 816 S Michigan Ave, 60605. Tel: 312-939-0111, Ext 3500. Web Site: www.eastwest.edu/library-resources. *Librn,* Michelle Kopteros; Tel: 312-939-0111, Ext 3503, E-mail: michellek@eastwest.edu; *Librn,* Huston Lawrence; Tel: 312-939-0111, Ext 3502, E-mail: huston@eastwest.edu
Wireless access
Function: ILL available, Res assist avail
Partic in Consortium of Academic & Research Libraries in Illinois
Open Mon-Thurs 8am-8pm, Fri 8:30-4:30

SR EMANUEL CONGREGATION*, Joseph Taussig Memorial Library, 5959 N Sheridan Rd, 60660. SAN 371-6597. Tel: 773-561-5173. FAX: 773-561-5420. E-mail: info@emanuelcong.org. Web Site: www.emanuelcong.org.
Library Holdings: Bk Titles 5,012; Bk Vols 6,000; Per Subs 10
Subject Interests: Judaica
Restriction: Open by appt only, Open to pub for ref only

C ERIKSON INSTITUTE*, Edward Neisser Library, 451 N LaSalle St, Ste 210, 60654. SAN 320-6459. Tel: 312-893-7210. FAX: 312-893-7213. E-mail: library@erikson.edu. Web Site: library.erikson.edu. *Libr Dir,* Karen Janke; E-mail: kjanke@erikson.edu; *Access Serv Librn,* Brittany Poku; E-mail: bpoku@erikson.edu; *Pub Serv Librn,* Lindsey Sturch; Staff 3 (MLS 3)
Founded 1966. Enrl 250; Fac 15; Highest Degree: Doctorate
Jul 2020-Jun 2021. Mats Exp $54,137, Books $13,374, Per/Ser (Incl. Access Fees) $40,763. Sal $189,455
Library Holdings: e-books 15,907; e-journals 15,255; Electronic Media & Resources 6,933; Bk Titles 18,473; Bk Vols 22,918; Per Subs 116; Videos 1,293
Subject Interests: Child develop, Early childhood educ, Soc work
Automation Activity & Vendor Info: (Cataloging) OCLC; (Circulation) ByWater Solutions; (Course Reserve) Atlas Systems; (ILL) OCLC ILLiad; (OPAC) ByWater Solutions; (Serials) EBSCO Online
Wireless access
Function: Archival coll, Audio & video playback equip for onsite use, Computer training, Computers for patron use, Distance learning, Doc delivery serv, Electronic databases & coll, ILL available, Online info literacy tutorials on the web & in blackboard, Online ref, Photocopying/Printing, Ref serv available, Telephone ref
Mem of Reaching Across Illinois Library System (RAILS)
Partic in Consortium of Academic & Research Libraries in Illinois
Restriction: Borrowing privileges limited to fac & registered students, Borrowing requests are handled by ILL, Circ privileges for students & alumni only, External users must contact libr, In-house use for visitors

S FEDERAL RESERVE BANK OF CHICAGO*, Knowledge Center, 230 S LaSalle St, 60604-1413. (Mail add: PO Box 834, 60690-0834), SAN 303-8912. Tel: 312-322-5824. FAX: 312-322-5091. E-mail: chi.knowledgecenter@chi.frb.org. Web Site: www.chicagofed.org. *Mgr,* Susan Chenoweth. Subject Specialists: *Bus finance,* Susan Chenoweth; Staff 8 (MLS 6, Non-MLS 2)
Founded 1920
Library Holdings: Bk Titles 13,600; Per Subs 350
Subject Interests: Banks & banking, Econ, Finance, Monetary policy, Statistics
Automation Activity & Vendor Info: (Cataloging) SirsiDynix; (Circulation) SirsiDynix; (ILL) OCLC; (OPAC) SirsiDynix; (Serials) SirsiDynix
Mem of Reaching Across Illinois Library System (RAILS)
Partic in Illinois Library & Information Network

S FIELD MUSEUM OF NATURAL HISTORY, Marie Louise Rosenthal Library, 1400 S DuSable Lake Shore Dr, 60605-2496. SAN 303-8955. Tel: 312-665-7892. FAX: 312-665-7893. E-mail: library@fieldmuseum.org, reflib@fieldmuseum.org. Web Site: fieldmuseum.org/science/research/area/library. *Head, Coll, Mus Librn,* Gretchen Rings; E-mail: grings@fieldmuseum.org; *Tech Serv Librn,* Diana Duncan; E-mail: dduncan@fieldmuseum.org; *Coord, Libr Coll,* Melissa Anderson; E-mail: manderson@fieldmuseum.org; *Museum Archivist,* Armand Esai; E-mail: aesai@fieldmuseum.org; *Photo Archivist,* Nina Cummings; E-mail: ncummings@fieldmuseum.org; *Archives Asst,* Rebecca Wilke; E-mail: rwilke@fieldmuseum.org; *Tech Asst,* Michael Trombley; E-mail: mtrombley@fieldmuseum.org; Staff 7 (MLS 2, Non-MLS 5)
Founded 1893
Library Holdings: Bk Vols 275,000; Per Subs 1,400
Special Collections: Berthold Laufer Coll of Far Eastern Studies; Edward E Ayer Ornithology Library Coll; Karl P Schmidt Herpetology Library Coll, bks & reprints
Subject Interests: Anthrop, Archaeology, Botany, Geol, Museology, Paleontology, Zoology
Wireless access
Mem of Reaching Across Illinois Library System (RAILS)
Partic in Consortium of Academic & Research Libraries in Illinois; OCLC Online Computer Library Center, Inc
Restriction: Open by appt only

L FOLEY & LARDNER*, Law Library, 321 N Clark St, Ste 2800, 60654-5313. SAN 373-8019. Tel: 312-832-4500. FAX: 312-832-4700. Web Site: www.foley.com. *Librn,* Christina Wagner; E-mail: cwagner@foley.com
Founded 1988
Library Holdings: Bk Vols 10,000
Subject Interests: Commodities, Real estate, Securities

S FOREFRONT LIBRARY, 200 W Madison St, 2nd Flr, 60606. SAN 303-884X. Tel: 312-578-0175. E-mail: library@myforefront.org. Web Site: library.myforefront.org/library, myforefront.org/programs-services/. *Librn,* Sarah Rice; E-mail: srice@myforefront.org; *Knowledge Servs, Mgr,* Zoe Magierek; E-mail: zmagierek@myforefront.org; Staff 2 (MLS 2)
Founded 1974
Library Holdings: Bk Titles 2,500; Bk Vols 2,700; Per Subs 60
Special Collections: Foundation Center Regional Coll
Subject Interests: Philanthropy
Automation Activity & Vendor Info: (Cataloging) Inmagic, Inc.
Wireless access
Function: 24/7 Electronic res, 24/7 Online cat, Electronic databases & coll, Orientations, Outside serv via phone, mail, e-mail & web, Photocopying/Printing, Ref & res, Wheelchair accessible, Workshops
Publications: A Guide to Funding Youth Development Programs; Chicago Area Grant Application; Chicago Area Grant Report; Duties & Responsibilities of Directors & Trustees of Illinois Private Foundations; Giving in Illinois; Principles for Community Health Care; The Directory of Illinois Foundations
Mem of Reaching Across Illinois Library System (RAILS)
Restriction: Circulates for staff only, Non-circulating coll, Open by appt only, Photo ID required for access

S FREEBORN & PETERS LIBRARY*, 311 S Wacker Dr, Ste 3000, 60606. SAN 376-1711. Tel: 312-360-6000, Ext 6258. FAX: 312-360-6520. E-mail: info@freeborn.com. Web Site: www.freeborn.com. *Librn,* Deborah Rusin
Library Holdings: Bk Titles 1,500; Per Subs 200
Subject Interests: Law
Automation Activity & Vendor Info: (Cataloging) Inmagic, Inc.; (Circulation) Inmagic, Inc.; (Serials) Inmagic, Inc.
Open Mon-Fri 9-5

S GREELEY & HANSEN ENGINEERING LIBRARY*, 100 S Wacker Dr, Ste 1400, 60606-4004. SAN 303-9005. Tel: 312-578-2328. Web Site: www.greeley-hansen.com. *Libr Dir,* Rachel Neithercut; E-mail: rneithercut@greeley-hansen.com; Staff 2 (MLS 1, Non-MLS 1)
Founded 1914
Library Holdings: Bk Titles 1,500; Per Subs 3
Subject Interests: Sewage, Water treatment
Automation Activity & Vendor Info: (Cataloging) Inmagic, Inc.; (Circulation) Inmagic, Inc.; (OPAC) Inmagic, Inc.
Function: Doc delivery serv, Electronic databases & coll, Internet access, Mail & tel request accepted, Online cat, Ref serv available
Mem of Reaching Across Illinois Library System (RAILS)
Restriction: Employees & their associates

S HEARTLAND INSTITUTE, Michael Parry Mazur Library, 3939 N Wilke Rd, 60004. SAN 377-5232. Tel: 312-377-4000. FAX: 312-275-7942. E-mail: librarian@heartland.org. Web Site: www.heartland.org/about-us/what-we-do/library. *Head Librn,* Joseph Davis; Staff 1 (MLS 1)
Founded 2016. Pop 500
Library Holdings: DVDs 109; Microforms 822; Bk Vols 21,844; Spec Interest Per Sub 10
Subject Interests: Biog, Church-state, Conservatism, Econ, Educ, Environ, Fiction, Health, Hist, Investing, Law, Math, Mgt, Philos, Polit sci, Psychosocial aspects, Pub policy, Relig, Sci, Socialism, Soviet studies
Automation Activity & Vendor Info: (Cataloging) OCLC Connexion
Wireless access
Function: 24/7 Electronic res, 24/7 Online cat, Online cat, Ref & res, Ref serv available, Res assist avail, Res libr
Mem of Reaching Across Illinois Library System (RAILS)
Open Mon-Fri 9-5
Restriction: In-house use for visitors, Open to pub upon request, Open to researchers by request, Private libr

L HOLLAND & KNIGHT LLP*, Law Library, 150 N Riverside Plaza, 60606. SAN 325-6200. Tel: 312-263-3600. FAX: 312-578-6666. Web Site: www.hklaw.com. *Res Analyst,* Keely Ward; E-mail: keely.ward@hklaw.com; Staff 3 (MLS 1, Non-MLS 2)
Library Holdings: Bk Vols 10,000; Per Subs 200
Automation Activity & Vendor Info: (Cataloging) Inmagic, Inc.; (Circulation) Inmagic, Inc.
Wireless access
Restriction: Staff use only

S J ALLEN HYNEK CENTER FOR UFO STUDIES, Information Center, PO Box 31335, 60631. SAN 370-615X. Tel: 773-271-3611. E-mail: infocenter@cufos.org. Web Site: www.cufos.org. *Librn,* George M Eberhart
Founded 1973
Library Holdings: Bk Titles 5,000
Special Collections: UFO Case Files, early 1900s-present
Wireless access
Restriction: Non-circulating to the pub, Open by appt only

CM ILLINOIS COLLEGE OF OPTOMETRY LIBRARY*, 3241 S Michigan Ave, 60616-3878. Tel: 312-949-7150. Circulation Tel: 312-949-7160. Interlibrary Loan Service Tel: 312-949-7152. Administration Tel: 312-949-7153. Automation Services Tel: 312-949-7158. FAX: 312-949-7337. E-mail: cshepard@ico.edu, icolibrary@ico.edu. Web Site: library.ico.edu. *Sr Dir,* Christine A Weber; E-mail: cweber@ico.edu; *Asst Libr Dir,* Darlene Ward; Tel: 312-949-7151, E-mail: dward@ico.edu;

Librn, Brandon Driver; Tel: 312-949-7149, E-mail: bdriver@ico.edu; *Electronic Serv Librn,* Graham Stephenson; E-mail: gstephenson@ico.edu; *Pub Serv Librn,* Sandra Engram; E-mail: sengram@ico.edu; *Libr Asst,* Natalie Bubrowska; E-mail: bubrowska@ico.edu. Subject Specialists: *Vision sci,* Christine A Weber; *Electronic databases, Spanish,* Graham Stephenson; Staff 6 (MLS 5, Non-MLS 1)
Founded 1955. Enrl 680; Fac 75; Highest Degree: Doctorate
Library Holdings: AV Mats 929; Bks on Deafness & Sign Lang 46; DVDs 100; e-journals 100,000; Microforms 1,522; Bk Titles 14,305; Bk Vols 23,305; Per Subs 250; Videos 700
Subject Interests: Aging, Allied health, Bus, Health sci, Med, Natural sci, Ophthalmology, Optics, Optometry
Automation Activity & Vendor Info: (Acquisitions) Ex Libris Group; (Cataloging) Ex Libris Group; (Circulation) Ex Libris Group; (Course Reserve) Ex Libris Group; (Discovery) Ex Libris Group; (ILL) OCLC; (Media Booking) Ex Libris Group; (OPAC) Ex Libris Group; (Serials) Ex Libris Group
Wireless access
Function: 24/7 Electronic res, 24/7 Online cat, Audiobks on Playaways & MP3, Computers for patron use, Digital talking bks, Doc delivery serv, E-Reserves, Electronic databases & coll, Health sci info serv, ILL available, Internet access, Magazines, Magnifiers for reading, Mango lang, Microfiche/film & reading machines, Notary serv, Online cat, Online info literacy tutorials on the web & in blackboard, Online ref, Photocopying/Printing, Ref & res, Scanner, Tax forms, Telephone ref, Wheelchair accessible
Publications: VisionCite (Index to science materials)
Mem of Reaching Across Illinois Library System (RAILS)
Partic in Association of Vision Science Librarians; Center for Research Libraries; Consortium of Academic & Research Libraries in Illinois; Medical Library Association; National Network of Libraries of Medicine Region 6; OCLC Online Computer Library Center, Inc
Special Services for the Blind - Aids for in-house use; Assistive/Adapted tech devices, equip & products; Bks & mags in Braille, on rec, tape & cassette; Bks available with recordings; Closed circuit TV magnifier; Computer with voice synthesizer for visually impaired persons; Digital talking bk; Digital talking bk machines; Internet workstation with adaptive software; Large print bks; Large print bks & talking machines; Large screen computer & software; Magnifiers; Screen enlargement software for people with visual disabilities; Talking bks; Talking bks & player equip; Text reader; ZoomText magnification & reading software
Restriction: 24-hr pass syst for students only, Access at librarian's discretion, Authorized patrons, Borrowing privileges limited to fac & registered students, Borrowing requests are handled by ILL, By permission only, Circ limited, Circ to mem only, External users must contact libr, Internal circ only, Non-circulating of rare bks, Non-circulating to the pub, Not open to pub, Open to authorized patrons, Open to others by appt, Open to students, fac & staff, Photo ID required for access, Private libr, Pub by appt only, Researchers by appt only, Restricted access, Restricted borrowing privileges, Restricted loan policy, Secured area only open to authorized personnel, Visitors must make appt to use bks in the libr

C ILLINOIS INSTITUTE OF TECHNOLOGY, Paul V Galvin Library, 35 W 33rd St, 60616. SAN 340-1340. Tel: 312-567-3616. Circulation Tel: 312-567-6847. Interlibrary Loan Service Tel: 312-567-6846. FAX: 312-567-5318. E-mail: library@iit.edu. Web Site: library.iit.edu. *Dean of Libr,* Devin Savage; Tel: 312-567-3615, E-mail: dsavage@iit.edu; *Asst to the Dean of Libraries,* Jennifer Worrell; Tel: 312-567-5136, E-mail: jworrell@iit.edu; Staff 29 (MLS 17, Non-MLS 12)
Founded 1891. Enrl 8,200; Highest Degree: Doctorate
Library Holdings: Bk Titles 294,066; Bk Vols 597,594; Per Subs 9,678
Special Collections: IIT Archives; Marvin Camras Coll, papers, inventions. Oral History; US Document Depository
Subject Interests: Art & archit, Computer sci, Econ, Engr, Environ studies, Math, Sci tech
Automation Activity & Vendor Info: (Acquisitions) Ex Libris Group; (OPAC) VuFind
Wireless access
Mem of Reaching Across Illinois Library System (RAILS)
Partic in Chicago Academic Libr Coun; Consortium of Academic & Research Libraries in Illinois; Illinois Library & Information Network; LCS; LIBRAS, Inc; OCLC Online Computer Library Center, Inc
Special Services for the Deaf - TDD equip

Departmental Libraries:

CENTER FOR THE STUDY OF ETHICS IN THE PROFESSIONS LIBRARY, 10 W 35th St, 60616, SAN 326-6842. Tel: 312-567-6913. FAX: 312-567-3016. E-mail: cseplibrary@iit.edu. *Librn,* Kelly Laas; E-mail: laas@iit.edu; Staff 1 (MLS 1)
Founded 1976. Enrl 7,000; Fac 200; Highest Degree: Doctorate
Library Holdings: AV Mats 90; e-journals 50; Bk Titles 2,500; Per Subs 34; Videos 60
Special Collections: Codes of Ethics Coll; Codes of Ethics Online Archive; Software Engineering Code of Ethics Archive
Function: Computers for patron use, Internet access, Online cat, Online ref, Orientations, Photocopying/Printing, Res libr, Res performed for a fee
Publications: Perspectives on the Professions (Newsletter)
Open Mon-Fri 9-5
Restriction: Non-circulating to the pub

CL CHICAGO-KENT COLLEGE OF LAW LIBRARY, 565 W Adams St, 9th Flr, 60661, SAN 340-1375. Tel: 312-906-5600. Interlibrary Loan Service Tel: 312-906-5662. Reference Tel: 312-906-5670. FAX: 312-906-5280. E-mail: library@kentlaw.iit.edu. Web Site: kentlaw.iit.edu/library. *Libr Dir,* Jean Wenger; Tel: 312-906-5610, E-mail: jwenger@kentlaw.iit.edu; *Assoc Dir for Operations,* Eric Neagle; E-mail: eneagle@kentlaw.iit.edu; *Digital Education & Internal Resource Librn,* Emily Barney; Tel: 312-906-5630, E-mail: ebarney@kentlaw.iit.edu; *Educ Tech Librn,* Julie Tedjeske Crane; E-mail: jtedjeske@kentlaw.iit.edu; *Res & Instrul Serv Librn,* Mandy Lee; E-mail: mlee19@kentlaw.iit.edu; Staff 9 (MLS 9)
Enrl 1,100; Fac 70; Highest Degree: Doctorate
Library Holdings: Bk Titles 193,194; Bk Vols 560,940
Special Collections: UN Document Depository; US Document Depository
Subject Interests: Finance, Intl relations, Law
Automation Activity & Vendor Info: (Acquisitions) Ex Libris Group; (Cataloging) Ex Libris Group; (Circulation) Ex Libris Group; (Course Reserve) Ex Libris Group; (OPAC) Ex Libris Group; (Serials) Ex Libris Group
Open Mon-Thurs 8:30-8, Fri 8:30-5, Sat 9-3:30, Sun 12:30-5:30

M INTERNATIONAL MUSEUM OF SURGICAL SCIENCE LIBRARY, 1524 N Lake Shore Dr, 60610. SAN 303-9269. Tel: 312-642-6502. FAX: 312-642-9516. E-mail: info@imss.org. Web Site: imss.org/thorek-library-rare-manuscripts-collection. *Educ Curator, Operations Mgr,* Shannon Marie Fox; Tel: 312-642-6502, Ext 3113, E-mail: shannon@imss.org; *Asst Mgr,* Parker Kohl; E-mail: parker@imss.org; *Spec Projects,* Michelle Rinard; Tel: 312-642-6502, Ext 3118, E-mail: michelle@imss.org. Subject Specialists: *Events planning, Health educ,* Parker Kohl
Founded 1956
Library Holdings: Bk Vols 7,000
Subject Interests: Dentistry, Hist, Med, Surgery
Wireless access
Function: Archival coll, For res purposes
Restriction: Non-circulating to the pub, Open by appt only

L JENNER & BLOCK LIBRARY*, 353 N Clark St, Ste 4300, 60654. SAN 303-9323. Tel: 312-222-9350. FAX: 312-527-0484. E-mail: reference@jenner.com. *Dir,* Mitchell Klaich; *Ref (Info Servs),* Mary Ruddy; Staff 8 (MLS 6, Non-MLS 2)
Founded 1914
Library Holdings: Bk Vols 35,000
Subject Interests: Law
Partic in Illinois Library & Information Network
Open Mon-Fri 8:45-5

L JONES DAY*, Law Library, 77 W Wacker Dr, Ste 3500, 60601-1692. SAN 371-8611. Tel: 312-782-3939. FAX: 312-782-8585. Web Site: www.jonesday.com. *Research Librn,* Edison Ellenberger; Tel: 312-269-4128, E-mail: elellenberger@jonesday.com; Staff 3 (MLS 2, Non-MLS 1)
Restriction: Private libr

L K&L GATES LLP*, 70 W Madison, Ste 2800, 60602-4207. SAN 376-1320. Tel: 312-372-1121. FAX: 312-827-8000. Web Site: www.klgates.com. *Assoc Dir, Library & Info Services,* Walker Chaffin; E-mail: walker.chaffin@klgates.com
Library Holdings: Bk Titles 3,500; Bk Vols 30,000
Automation Activity & Vendor Info: (Cataloging) SirsiDynix
Restriction: Staff use only

L KATTEN, MUCHIN, ROSENMAN LLP LIBRARY*, 525 W Monroe St, Ste 1900, 60661-3693. SAN 321-3994. Tel: 312-902-5200. *Dir, Libr & Res Serv,* Cathy Huff; Staff 8 (MLS 5, Non-MLS 3)
Founded 1974
Library Holdings: Bk Vols 26,000; Per Subs 350
Automation Activity & Vendor Info: (Acquisitions) EOS International; (Cataloging) EOS International; (Circulation) EOS International; (OPAC) EOS International; (Serials) EOS International
Wireless access
Mem of Reaching Across Illinois Library System (RAILS)
Partic in OCLC Online Computer Library Center, Inc
Restriction: Staff use only

L KIRKLAND & ELLIS LLP LIBRARY*, 300 N LaSalle St, 11th Flr, 60654. SAN 303-9412. Tel: 312-862-2358. FAX: 312-862-2200. *Libr Dir,* Joan Batchen; E-mail: joan.batchen@kirkland.com; Staff 14 (MLS 9, Non-MLS 5)

Founded 1918
Wireless access
Restriction: Staff use only

S KORN FERRY RESEARCH LIBRARY*, Willis Tower, Ste 700, 233 S Wacker Dr, 60606. SAN 375-8117. Tel: 312-466-1834. FAX: 312-466-0451. Web Site: www.kornferry.com/office/chicago. *Library Contact,* Sandy George; E-mail: Sandy.George@KornFerry.com
Library Holdings: Bk Titles 300; Per Subs 64

L LAF LIBRARY*, 120 S La Salle St, Ste 900, 60603. SAN 320-1775. Tel: 312-341-1070. FAX: 312-341-1041. E-mail: librarian@LAFChicago.org. Web Site: www.lafchicago.org. *Library Contact,* Meghan Buckman
Founded 1974
Library Holdings: Bk Titles 13,000; Bk Vols 18,000; Per Subs 160
Mem of Reaching Across Illinois Library System (RAILS)
Partic in Illinois Library & Information Network
Open Wed & Fri 9am-11am

L LATHAM & WATKINS*, Law Library, 330 N Wabash Ave, Ste 2800, 60611. SAN 371-4071. Tel: 312-876-7700. FAX: 312-993-9767. Web Site: www.lw.com/offices/chicago. *Libr Mgr, Mgr, Res,* Julie Pabarja; E-mail: julie.pabarja@lw.com; Staff 4 (MLS 3, Non-MLS 1)
Library Holdings: Bk Vols 12,000; Per Subs 142
Wireless access
Open Mon-Fri 9-5

CM LIBRARY OF RUSH UNIVERSITY MEDICAL CENTER*, Armour Academic Ctr, 600 S Paulina St, Ste 571, 60612. SAN 340-2304. Tel: 312-942-5950. Interlibrary Loan Service Tel: 312-942-5220. FAX: 312-942-3143. Reference E-mail: lib_ref@rush.edu. Web Site: rushu.libguides.com. *Dir,* Scott Thomson; Tel: 312-942-8735, E-mail: scott_thomson@rush.edu; *Asst Dir, Content Mgt,* Sandra Wenner; Tel: 312-942-2282, E-mail: sandra_wenner@rush.edu; *Circ Serv Mgr,* Toby Gibson; Tel: 312-942-2279, E-mail: toby_gibson@rush.edu; *Acq & Ser Coordr,* Christopher Gilliam; Tel: 312-942-2107, E-mail: christopher_gilliam@rush.edu; *Res Info Spec,* Patricia Chavez; Tel: 312-942-2731, E-mail: patricia_chavez@rush.edu; *Res Info Spec,* Jennifer Westrick; Tel: 312-563-2679, E-mail: jennifer_westrick@rush.edu; *Technology Spec,* Peter Tubbs; Tel: 312-942-8558, E-mail: peter_tubbs@rush.edu; *Archivist,* Nathalie Wheaton; Tel: 312-942-6358, E-mail: nathalie_wheaton@rush.edu; Staff 13.6 (MLS 6.6, Non-MLS 7)
Founded 1899. Enrl 2,200; Highest Degree: Doctorate
Special Collections: Imprints
Subject Interests: Health sci
Automation Activity & Vendor Info: (Acquisitions) Ex Libris Group; (Cataloging) Ex Libris Group; (Circulation) Ex Libris Group; (Course Reserve) Docutek; (ILL) OCLC ILLiad; (OPAC) Ex Libris Group; (Serials) Ex Libris Group
Wireless access
Function: 24/7 Electronic res, Computers for patron use, Doc delivery serv, E-Reserves, Electronic databases & coll, Health sci info serv, Internet access, Learning ctr, Online cat, Orientations, Photocopying/Printing, Ref & res, Ref serv available, Workshops
Partic in Consortium of Academic & Research Libraries in Illinois; Greater Midwest Regional Medical Libr Network; OCLC Online Computer Library Center, Inc; Serials of Illinois Libraries Online
Open Mon-Fri 7am-Midnight, Sat & Sun 9am-Midnight

GL LIBRARY OF THE US COURTS OF THE SEVENTH CIRCUIT, William J Campbell Library, 219 S Dearborn St, Rm 1637, 60604-1769. SAN 304-0410. Tel: 312-435-5660. FAX: 312-408-5031. Web Site: www.lb7.uscourts.gov, www.lb7.uscourts.gov/ChicagoHome.html. *Circuit Librn,* Heidi Kuehl; E-mail: heidi_kuehl@ca7.uscourts.gov; *Cat Librn,* Kathleen Powers Goodridge; *HQ Librn,* Stephanie Crawford; *HQ Librn,* John Klaus; *HQ Librn,* Jerry Lewis; *HQ Librn,* Erin Schlicht
Library Holdings: Bk Vols 30,000
Subject Interests: Govt publ
Partic in OCLC Online Computer Library Center, Inc
Open Mon-Fri 8:30-5
Restriction: Non-circulating to the pub

S LITHUANIAN RESEARCH & STUDIES CENTER, INC*, 5620 S Claremont Ave, 60636-1039. SAN 325-2728. Tel: 773-434-4545. FAX: 773-434-9363. E-mail: info@lithuanianresearch.org. Web Site: www.lithuanianresearch.org. *Dir of Libr,* Enata Skrupskelis; *Dir, Archives,* Skirmante Miglinas; Staff 10 (MLS 3, Non-MLS 7)
Founded 1982
Library Holdings: Bk Titles 146,000; Bk Vols 182,000; Per Subs 1,600
Special Collections: Cartography Dept; Dainauskas History Library; Krupavicius Coll; Lithuanian Historical Society; Lithuanian Institute of Education; Marian Fathers Coll; Pakstas Coll; Rare Book Coll; World Lithuanian Archives; World Lithuanian Community Coll; Zilevicius-Kreivenas Lithuanian Musicology Archive
Subject Interests: Costume, Culture, Customs, Dance, Economy, Educ, Folklore, Geog, Hist, Immigration, Lit, Lithuanian, Lithuanian-Am Art, Mil, Music, Politics, Sports, Traditions
Restriction: Open by appt only

L LOCKE LORD BISSELL & LIDDELL LLP*, Law Library, 111 S Wacker Dr, 60606. SAN 303-951X. Tel: 312-443-0646. FAX: 312-443-0336. Web Site: www.lockelord.com/offices/chicago. *Dir,* Susan Berg; *Ref Librn,* Julie Swanson; E-mail: julie.swanson@lockelord.com; Staff 8 (MLS 4, Non-MLS 4)
Library Holdings: Bk Vols 10,000
Partic in Illinois Library & Information Network
Restriction: Private libr

CR LOYOLA UNIVERSITY CHICAGO LIBRARIES, 1032 W Sheridan Rd, 60660. SAN 340-143X. Tel: 773-508-2641. Circulation Tel: 773-508-2632. E-mail: librarycirculation@luc.edu. Web Site: libraries.luc.edu. *Dean of Libr,* Marianne Ryan; Tel: 773-508-2657, E-mail: mryan21@luc.edu; *Associate Dean, Collection Services,* Emma Heet; Tel: 773-508-7727, E-mail: eheet@luc.edu; *Head, Libr Syst,* Hong Ma; Tel: 773-508-2590, E-mail: hma2@luc.edu; Staff 63 (MLS 28, Non-MLS 35)
Founded 1870. Enrl 14,649; Fac 885; Highest Degree: Doctorate
Library Holdings: AV Mats 12,862; e-books 565,308; e-journals 52,963; Microforms 1,403,552; Bk Vols 1,854,100
Special Collections: Jesuitica; Paul Claudel Coll; Women & Leadership Archives. Oral History; State Document Depository; US Document Depository
Automation Activity & Vendor Info: (Acquisitions) Ex Libris Group; (Cataloging) Ex Libris Group; (Circulation) Ex Libris Group; (Course Reserve) Ex Libris Group; (Media Booking) Ex Libris Group; (OPAC) Ex Libris Group; (Serials) Ex Libris Group
Wireless access
Partic in Association of Jesuit Colleges & Universities; Chicago Area Theological Libr Asn; Chicago Collections Consortium; Consortium of Academic & Research Libraries in Illinois; Illinois Library & Information Network
Restriction: Limited access for the pub
Friends of the Library Group

Departmental Libraries:

ELIZABETH M CUDAHY MEMORIAL LIBRARY, 1032 W Sheridan Rd, 60660, SAN 340-1464. Tel: 773-508-2632. Interlibrary Loan Service Tel: 773-508-6022. Reference Tel: 773-508-2654. Circulation FAX: 773-508-2993. E-mail: cud-circ@luc.edu, cud-ref@luc.edu. Web Site: libraries.luc.edu/cudahy. *Head, Access Serv,* Chris Martin; Tel: 773-508-2636, E-mail: cmartin15@luc.edu; *Head, Ref Serv,* Niamh McGuigan; Tel: 773-508-2637, E-mail: mmcguigan@luc.edu
Library Holdings: Bk Vols 900,000; Per Subs 3,200
Subject Interests: Arts, Humanities, Sciences, Soc sci
Special Services for the Deaf - Assistive tech
Special Services for the Blind - Assistive/Adapted tech devices, equip & products
Open Mon-Thurs 7:30am-Midnight, Fri 7:30am-9pm, Sat 10-6, Sun 10am-Midnight
Friends of the Library Group

CM HEALTH SCIENCES LIBRARY, Bldg 125, Rm 1526, 2160 S First Ave, Maywood, 60153, SAN 340-1529. Tel: 708-216-9192. E-mail: hsl@luc.edu. Web Site: library.luhs.org/hslibrary. *Assoc Provost, Libr Dir,* Gail Y Hendler; Tel: 708-216-5303, E-mail: ghendler@luc.edu; *Assoc Dir,* Jonna Peterson; Tel: 708-216-6328, E-mail: jpeterson2@luc.edu; *Access Services & Emerging Technologies Librn,* Tiffany Tawzer; Tel: 708-216-5308, E-mail: ttawzer@luc.edu; *Research & Education Librn,* Elizabeth Huggins; Tel: 708-216-5305, E-mail: ehuggins@luc.edu; Staff 25 (MLS 8, Non-MLS 17)
Enrl 627; Fac 1,642; Highest Degree: Doctorate
Library Holdings: AV Mats 6,789; e-books 172; e-journals 1,487; Electronic Media & Resources 7,432; Bk Titles 40,382; Bk Vols 198,189; Per Subs 4,943
Special Collections: History of Medicine
Subject Interests: Health sci, Med, Nursing
Automation Activity & Vendor Info: (Cataloging) Ex Libris Group; (Circulation) Ex Libris Group; (Course Reserve) Ex Libris Group; (ILL) Ex Libris Group; (OPAC) Ex Libris Group; (Serials) Ex Libris Group
Partic in National Network of Libraries of Medicine Region 6
Publications: Circulation Manual; Collection Development Manual; Interlibrary Loan Manual
Open Mon-Fri 9-5

LEWIS LIBRARY, 25 E Pearson St, 60611, SAN 340-1499. Tel: 312-915-6622. Circulation Tel: 312-915-6625. Reference Tel: 312-915-6631. E-mail: lewislib@luc.edu. Web Site: libraries.luc.edu/lewis. *Head of Libr,* Yolande Wersching; Tel: 312-915-6623, E-mail: ywersch@luc.edu
Library Holdings: e-journals 35,000; Bk Vols 250,000; Per Subs 1,500
Subject Interests: Bus admin, Communication, Computer sci, Criminal justice, Econ, Educ, Pastoral studies, Soc work
Open Mon-Thurs 7:30am-8pm, Fri 7:30-6

CL SCHOOL OF LAW LIBRARY, Philip H Corboy Law Ctr, 25 E Pearson St, 60611, SAN 340-1553. Tel: 312-915-7200. Circulation Tel: 312-915-6986. Interlibrary Loan Service Tel: 312-915-7202. Reference Tel: 312-915-7205. FAX: 312-915-6797. E-mail: loyolalawreference@luc.edu. Web Site: www.luc.edu/law/academics/library/index.cfm. *Dir,* Patricia Scott; Tel: 312-915-8515, E-mail: pscott2@luc.edu; *Asst Dir, Access & Technical Servs,* Lucy Robbins; Tel: 312-915-7198, E-mail: lrobbi2@luc.edu; *Reference & Electronic Services Librn,* Joe Mitzenmacher; Tel: 312-915-6844, E-mail: jmitze1@luc.edu; *Foreign & Intl Research Specialist, Ref Librn,* Julienne Grant; Tel: 312-915-8520, E-mail: jgrant6@luc.edu; *Ref Librn,* Tom Keefe; Tel: 312-915-8516, E-mail: tkeefe@luc.edu; *Ref Librn,* Nan Norton; Tel: 312-915-8517, E-mail: nnorton@luc.edu; Staff 16 (MLS 9, Non-MLS 7)
Founded 1909. Enrl 773; Fac 41; Highest Degree: Master
Library Holdings: Bk Titles 61,640; Bk Vols 180,732; Per Subs 1,313
Special Collections: GPO Depository; Medical Jurisprudence; Child Law. US Document Depository
Subject Interests: Antitrust law
Automation Activity & Vendor Info: (ILL) OCLC
Function: ILL available
Partic in Chicago Legal Acad Syst; Jesuit Law Libr Consortium; Mid-America Law Library Consortium
Open Mon-Thurs 8am-11pm, Fri 8-7, Sat 9-5, Sun Noon-10
Restriction: Circ limited
Friends of the Library Group

M ANN & ROBERT H LURIE CHILDREN'S HOSPITAL OF CHICAGO*, Health Sciences Library, 225 E Chicago Ave, Box 12, 60611-2605. SAN 303-8599. Tel: 312-227-4707. FAX: 312-227-9707. Web Site: www.luriechildrens.org. *Ref Librn,* Andrea Fawcett; E-mail: AFawcett@luriechildrens.org. Subject Specialists: *Pediatrics,* Andrea Fawcett; Staff 2 (MLS 1, Non-MLS 1)
Founded 1935
Library Holdings: e-journals 3,000; Bk Vols 600; Per Subs 50
Subject Interests: Adolescent psychol, Child psychology, Pediatrics
Automation Activity & Vendor Info: (Acquisitions) Ex Libris Group; (Cataloging) Ex Libris Group; (Circulation) Ex Libris Group; (OPAC) Ex Libris Group; (Serials) Ex Libris Group
Wireless access
Function: Computer training, Computers for patron use, Health sci info serv, ILL available, Internet access, Online cat, Photocopying/Printing, Ref & res, Ref serv available, VHS videos
Mem of Reaching Across Illinois Library System (RAILS)
Partic in Illinois Library & Information Network; Medical Library Association; National Network of Libraries of Medicine Region 6; OCLC Online Computer Library Center, Inc
Restriction: Authorized personnel only

R LUTHERAN SCHOOL OF THEOLOGY AT CHICAGO & MCCORMICK THEOLOGICAL SEMINARY*, JKM Library, 1100 E 55th St, 60615-5199. SAN 303-9331. Tel: 773-256-0739. Reference Tel: 773-256-0703. FAX: 773-256-0737. E-mail: refdesk@jkmlibrary.org. Web Site: www.jkmlibrary.org. *Libr Dir,* Dr Christine Wenderoth; Tel: 773-256-0735, E-mail: cwenderoth@jkmlibrary.org; *Metadata Librn,* Emilie Pulver; Tel: 773-256-0730, E-mail: epulver@jkmlibrary.org; *Assoc Librn, Pub Serv,* Barry C Hopkins; Tel: 773-256-0738, E-mail: bhopkins@jkmlibrary.org; *Mgr, Access Serv,* Elaine D Bonner; Tel: 773-256-0732, E-mail: ebonner@jkmlibrary.org; Staff 5 (MLS 3, Non-MLS 2)
Founded 1975. Enrl 409; Fac 32; Highest Degree: Doctorate
Jul 2016-Jun 2017 Income $985,356. Mats Exp $964,855, Books $30,754, Per/Ser (Incl. Access Fees) $37,859, AV Mat $414, Electronic Ref Mat (Incl. Access Fees) $35,511, Presv $1,739. Sal Prof $315,804
Library Holdings: CDs 643; DVDs 880; e-books 47,797; e-journals 90; Electronic Media & Resources 11; Microforms 117,468; Music Scores 16; Bk Vols 288,977; Per Subs 383
Special Collections: Reformation Imprints (L Franklin Gruber Coll)
Subject Interests: Biblical studies, Lutheranism, Ministry, Reformation hist, Reformed theol, Theol
Automation Activity & Vendor Info: (ILL) OCLC WorldShare Interlibrary Loan
Wireless access
Function: 24/7 Electronic res, 24/7 Online cat, Doc delivery serv, Outside serv via phone, mail, e-mail & web, Photocopying/Printing, Printer for laptops & handheld devices, Ref & res, Ref serv available, Res libr, Scanner, Study rm, Telephone ref
Partic in Association of Chicago Theological Schools; Consortium of Academic & Research Libraries in Illinois; Illinois Library & Information Network; OCLC Online Computer Library Center, Inc
Open Mon-Fri 8:30am-10:30pm, Sat 10-4:30, Sun 5-10
Restriction: Photo ID required for access

S JOHN D & CATHERINE T MACARTHUR FOUNDATION LIBRARY, 140 S Dearborn St, Ste 1200, 60603-5285. SAN 375-8281. Tel: 312-726-8000. FAX: 312-579-3457. TDD: 312-920-6285. E-mail: 4answers@macfound.org. Web Site: www.macfound.org. *Found Librn,* Elizabeth Quinlan; E-mail: equinlan@macfound.org
Library Holdings: Bk Titles 5,000; Per Subs 200
Restriction: Private libr

L THE JOHN MARSHALL LAW SCHOOL*, Louis L Biro Law Library, 300 S State St, 6th Flr, 60604. SAN 303-9358. Tel: 312-427-2737. Circulation Tel: 312-427-2737, Ext 710. Reference Tel: 312-427-2737, Ext 729. FAX: 312-427-8307. E-mail: library@jmls.edu. Web Site: jmls.uic.edu. *Dir, Libr & Tech,* Ramsey Donnell; E-mail: rdonnell@jmls.edu; *Asst Dir, Acad Tech,* Jessica Wittman; *Assoc Dir, Access & Organization,* Gregory Cunningham; *Assoc Dir, Res & Instruction,* Claire Toomey Durkin; *Head, Cat,* Liping Qin; *Evening Ref Librn,* Victor Salas; *Foreign & Intl Law Librn,* Anne Abramson; *Instrul Serv Librn, Student Serv Librn,* Philip Johnson; Staff 16 (MLS 8, Non-MLS 8)
Founded 1899. Enrl 1,600; Fac 60; Highest Degree: Doctorate
Library Holdings: Bk Titles 92,935; Bk Vols 392,150; Per Subs 6,047
Special Collections: CCH Tax Library Coll, ultrafiche; Chicago Bar Association Core Coll; IHS Legislative Histories; Illinois Appellate Court Unpublished Opinions; Illinois Supreme Court Briefs; National Reporter System Coll, First Series, ultrafiche; United States Circuit Court of Appeals 7th Circuit Briefs; United States Congressional Publications, 1970-date, micro; United States Supreme Court Records & Briefs, 1930-date. US Document Depository
Subject Interests: Anglo-Am law
Wireless access
Publications: The John Marshall Law School Publication Series
Partic in Chicago Legal Acad Syst; Illinois Library & Information Network; Mid-America Law Library Consortium; OCLC Online Computer Library Center, Inc
Open Mon-Thurs 8am-11pm, Fri 8-8, Sat 9-8, Sun 9am-10pm

L MAYER BROWN LLP*, Law Library, 71 S Wacker Dr, 60606. SAN 303-9668. Tel: 312-782-0600. FAX: 312-701-7711. Web Site: www.mayerbrown.com. *Libr Serv Mgr,* Bobby Towns; E-mail: btowns@mayerbrown.com
Mem of Reaching Across Illinois Library System (RAILS)
Partic in Proquest Dialog
Open Mon-Fri 9-5

L MCDERMOTT, WILL & EMERY LAW LIBRARY*, 444 West Lake St, 60606. SAN 303-9587. Tel: 312-984-7650. FAX: 312-984-2094. Web Site: www.mwe.com. *Dir, Res,* Jerry Trenholm; Tel: 312-984-3289, E-mail: jtrenholm@mwe.com
Library Holdings: Bk Titles 60,000; Per Subs 500
Partic in Illinois Library & Information Network
Restriction: Not open to pub

CR MEADVILLE LOMBARD THEOLOGICAL SCHOOL*, Wiggin Library, 610 S Michigan Ave, 60605. SAN 303-9684. Tel: 312-546-6483. Web Site: www.meadville.edu/library-and-archives. *Dir, Libr & Archives,* John Leeker; E-mail: jleeker@meadville.edu; *Librn, Project Archivist,* Sarah Levine; Tel: 773-256-3000, Ext 630, E-mail: slevine@meadville.edu; Staff 2 (MLS 2)
Founded 1844. Enrl 100; Fac 5; Highest Degree: Master
Special Collections: English Philosophy; Ethics & Society; Unitarian-Universalist History & Liberal Religion; World Religion
Wireless access
Partic in Association of Chicago Theological Schools; Consortium of Academic & Research Libraries in Illinois

CR MOODY BIBLE INSTITUTE*, Crowell Library, 820 N LaSalle Blvd, 60610-3284. SAN 340-1618. Tel: 312-329-4136. Interlibrary Loan Service Tel: 312-329-2068. Administration Tel: 312-329-4140. Information Services Tel: 312-329-4122. E-mail: library@moody.edu. Web Site: library.moody.edu. *Dir,* James Preston; E-mail: james.preston@moody.edu; *Head Librn, Pub Serv,* Christopher Ullman. Subject Specialists: *Theol,* James Preston; Staff 7 (MLS 4, Non-MLS 3)
Founded 1889. Enrl 2,022; Fac 90; Highest Degree: Master
Library Holdings: Bks on Deafness & Sign Lang 27; Braille Volumes 128; CDs 11,428; DVDs 635; e-books 1,977; e-journals 16,025; Electronic Media & Resources 63; Large Print Bks 47; Music Scores 5,733; Bk Titles 121,450; Bk Vols 170,890; Per Subs 349; Videos 4,063
Special Collections: Curriculum Lab; Juvenile; D L Moody (Moodyana Coll), artifacts & bks; Moody Bible Institute Archives, docs, letters, newsp & photos
Subject Interests: Relig
Automation Activity & Vendor Info: (Acquisitions) OCLC; (Cataloging) SirsiDynix; (Circulation) SirsiDynix; (Course Reserve) SirsiDynix; (ILL) OCLC; (OPAC) SirsiDynix; (Serials) SirsiDynix
Wireless access

Function: Archival coll, ILL available, Online ref, Photocopying/Printing, Ref serv available
Mem of Reaching Across Illinois Library System (RAILS)
Partic in Asn of Christian Librs; Consortium of Academic & Research Libraries in Illinois; Illinois Library & Information Network; LIBRAS, Inc; OCLC Online Computer Library Center, Inc
Special Services for the Blind - Braille bks
Open Mon-Sat 7:30am-Midnight
Restriction: Photo ID required for access, Restricted pub use

M MOUNT SINAI HOSPITAL MEDICAL CENTER*, Lewison Memorial Library, California Ave at 15th St, 60608. SAN 340-1677. Tel: 773-257-6558. FAX: 773-257-6135. *Interim Mgr,* Trina Coleman; E-mail: trina.coleman@sinai.org; *ILL,* Merly M Arceo
Founded 1942
Library Holdings: Bk Vols 3,000; Per Subs 268
Subject Interests: Med, Nursing

S MUSEUM OF CONTEMPORARY ART LIBRARY*, 220 E Chicago Ave, 60611. SAN 303-9773. Tel: 312-280-2660. FAX: 312-397-4099. E-mail: library@mcachicago.org. Web Site: www.mcachicago.org/learn/library. *Curator,* Lynne Warren; Tel: 312-397-3894; Staff 1 (Non-MLS 1)
Founded 1981
Library Holdings: Bk Vols 13,500; Per Subs 40
Special Collections: Artist & Gallery Files; Artists' books; MCA Exhibition Catalogs
Subject Interests: Art
Automation Activity & Vendor Info: (ILL) OCLC FirstSearch
Function: Res libr
Partic in Illinois Library & Information Network; OCLC Online Computer Library Center, Inc; Research Libraries Information Network
Restriction: Not open to pub, Open by appt only

G NATIONAL ARCHIVES & RECORDS ADMINISTRATION*, Great Lakes Region, 7358 S Pulaski Rd, 60629-5898. Tel: 773-948-9001. FAX: 773-948-9050. E-mail: chicago.archives@nara.gov. Web Site: www.archives.gov/chicago. *Archivist,* Douglas Bicknese; E-mail: douglas.bicknese@nara.gov; *Archivist,* Glenn Longacre; Staff 4 (MLS 2, Non-MLS 2)
Library Holdings: Bk Vols 1,000
Special Collections: Archival Records of Federal Military, Civilian Agencies & Courts in Illinois, Indiana, Michigan, Minnesota, Ohio & Wisconsin from 1800 to 1990's; Indian Affairs Records, microfilm; Passenger Arrival & Naturalization Records, microfilm; Population Censuses for All States, 1790-1930, microfilm; Pre-Federal & Early Federal History Records, microfilm; Pre-World War I Military Service Records, microfilm; US Diplomatic Records, microfilm
Subject Interests: Fed govt rec
Function: Archival coll, Computers for patron use, Photocopying/Printing, Workshops
Open Mon-Fri 8-4:15
Restriction: Closed stack, Internal use only, Non-circulating, Photo ID required for access

S NATIONAL ASSOCIATION OF REALTORS, Information Services, 430 N Michigan Ave, 60611-4087. SAN 303-982X. Tel: 312-329-8577. Toll Free Tel: 800-874-6500. FAX: 312-329-8835. Information Services E-mail: infoservices@realtors.org. Web Site: www.nar.realtor/library. *Managing Dir,* Frederik Heller; *Libr & Archives Mgr,* Sarah Hogan; *Archivist,* Hathaway Hester; E-mail: hhester@realtors.org; Staff 15 (MLS 5, Non-MLS 10)
Founded 1923
Library Holdings: CDs 50; DVDs 50; e-books 4,000; e-journals 7,300; Bk Vols 15,000; Per Subs 150; Spec Interest Per Sub 600
Special Collections: NAR historical archives
Subject Interests: Real estate
Wireless access
Function: 24/7 Electronic res, 24/7 Online cat, Archival coll, Audiobks via web, Bks on CD, Bus archives, CD-ROM, Doc delivery serv, Electronic databases & coll, Literacy & newcomer serv, Magazines, Mail & tel request accepted, Online cat, Online ref, OverDrive digital audio bks, Prof lending libr, Ref & res, Ref serv available, Res libr, Res performed for a fee, Spanish lang bks, Wheelchair accessible
Mem of Reaching Across Illinois Library System (RAILS)
Restriction: Authorized patrons, Authorized scholars by appt, Circ to mem only, Not open to pub, Open to researchers by request

C NATIONAL LOUIS UNIVERSITY LIBRARY, 18 S Michigan Ave, 3rd Flr, 60603. SAN 340-1820. Tel: 312-261-3376. Interlibrary Loan Service Tel: 847-947-5503. Toll Free Tel: 800-443-5522, Ext 3376. FAX: 312-261-3376. Interlibrary Loan Service FAX: 847-947-5110. E-mail: library@nl.edu. Web Site: nl.edu/library. *Exec Dir,* Alexis Carscadden; Tel: 312-261-3645, E-mail: acarscadden@nl.edu; *Librn,* Amy Hall; Tel: 312-261-3565, E-mail: amy.hall@nl.edu; *Librn,* Sarah Leeman; Tel: 312-261-3439, E-mail: sleeman@nl.edu; *Spec Coll Cat Librn,* Meghan Ryan; Tel: 312-261-3122, E-mail: mryan26@nl.edu; *Assoc Librn,* Rob Morrison; Tel: 312-261-3372, E-mail: rob.morrison@nl.edu; *ILL Coordr,* Joanna Siudut; Tel: 312-261-5502, E-mail: joanna.siudut@nl.edu; Staff 17 (MLS 8, Non-MLS 9)
Founded 1920. Enrl 4,384; Fac 896; Highest Degree: Doctorate
Library Holdings: Audiobooks 134; AV Mats 40,547; e-books 295,810; e-journals 17,978; Electronic Media & Resources 76; Bk Titles 76,929; Bk Vols 84,804; Videos 3,028
Special Collections: Children's Literature & Illustration (Weinstein Coll); Digital Commons; Elizabeth Harrison Early Childhood Education Archives
Automation Activity & Vendor Info: (Acquisitions) Ex Libris Group; (Cataloging) Ex Libris Group; (Circulation) Ex Libris Group; (Course Reserve) Ex Libris Group; (ILL) Ex Libris Group; (Media Booking) Ex Libris Group; (OPAC) Ex Libris Group; (Serials) Ex Libris Group
Wireless access
Partic in Consortium of Academic & Research Libraries in Illinois; LIBRAS, Inc
Open Mon-Thurs 9-7, Fri 9-5, Sat 9-2

Departmental Libraries:

LISLE, 850 Warrenville Rd, Lisle, 60532, SAN 321-5695. Tel: 630-874-4530.
Special Collections: Bilingual, Spanish or Latino Themed Children's & Young Adult Books (Americas Coll)
Open Tues & Thurs 2-6 & by appt

NORTH SHORE, 5202 Old Orchard Rd, Skokie, 60077, SAN 340-3866. Toll Free Tel: 888-658-8632, Ext 2222. E-mail: nluskokie@nl.edu. *Library Contact,* Tellier Marion; Tel: 224-233-2000, E-mail: tmarion1@nl.edu
Restriction: Open by appt only

WHEELING, 1000 Capitol Dr, Wheeling, 60090-7201, SAN 378-0732. Tel: 847-947-5503. FAX: 847-947-5110. *Electronic Res & Instruction Librn,* Amy LeFager; Tel: 847-947-5335, E-mail: amy.lefager@nl.edu
Open Mon-Thurs 9-6, Fri 9-5

S NATIONAL OPINION RESEARCH CENTER LIBRARY*, Paul B Sheatsley Library, 1155 E 60th St, Rm 369, 60637-2667. SAN 303-9854. Tel: 773-256-6206. FAX: 773-256-6001. Web Site: www.norc.org. *Librn,* Ernest Tani; E-mail: tani-ernest@norc.org; Staff 3 (Non-MLS 3)
Founded 1941
Library Holdings: Bk Titles 9,000
Subject Interests: Demography, Survey res
Publications: NORC Bibliography of Publications, 1941-1991 (online)
Open Mon-Fri 9-5

L NEAL, GERBER & EISENBERG LLP*, Law Library, Two N La Salle St, Ste 1700, 60602-3801. SAN 323-8458. Tel: 312-269-8000. FAX: 312-578-1747. Web Site: www.nge.com. *Dir, Research & Competitive Intel,* Diana Koppang; E-mail: dkoppang@nge.com; Staff 7 (MLS 5, Non-MLS 2)
Founded 1986
Library Holdings: Bk Titles 3,000; Bk Vols 40,000; Per Subs 300
Subject Interests: Labor, Securities, Tax
Automation Activity & Vendor Info: (Acquisitions) Inmagic, Inc.; (Cataloging) Inmagic, Inc.; (Circulation) Inmagic, Inc.; (ILL) Inmagic, Inc.; (OPAC) Inmagic, Inc.; (Serials) Inmagic, Inc.
Wireless access
Function: 24/7 Electronic res, Online cat
Partic in Illinois Library & Information Network
Restriction: Restricted access

S NEWBERRY LIBRARY, 60 W Walton St, 60610-3305. SAN 303-9900. Tel: 312-943-9090. Web Site: www.newberry.org. *Librn, Pres,* Daniel Greene; Tel: 312-255-3600, E-mail: greened@newberry.org; *VPres, Coll, VPres, Libr Serv,* Alice Schreyer; Tel: 312-255-3590, E-mail: schreyera@newberry.org; *Curator, Americana, Dir, Reader Serv,* Will Hansen; Tel: 312-255-3527, E-mail: hansenw@newberry.org; *Dir, Coll Serv,* Alan Leopold; Tel: 312-255-3629, E-mail: leopolda@newberry.org; *Dir, Conserv Serv,* Lesa Dowd; Tel: 312-255-3549, E-mail: dowdl@newberry.org; *Dir, Digital Initiatives & Serv,* Jennifer Dalzin; Tel: 312-255-3536, E-mail: dalzinj@newberry.org; *Curator of Rare Bks & Ms,* Suzanne Karr Schmidt; Tel: 312-255-3645, E-mail: karrschmidts@newberry.org; *Curator, Genealogy,* Matthew Rutherford; Tel: 312-255-3671, E-mail: rutherfordm@newberry.org; *Curator, Maps,* James Akerman; Tel: 312-255-3523, E-mail: akermanj@newberry.org; *Curator, Modern MS,* Alison Hinderliter; Tel: 312-255-3694, E-mail: hinderlitera@newberry.org; Staff 93 (MLS 29, Non-MLS 64)
Founded 1887
Library Holdings: Bk Titles 980,000; Bk Vols 1,500,000; Per Subs 716
Special Collections: 16th Century Italian Maps (Franco Novacco Map Coll); American & British History (Ruggles Coll); American Indian History & Indigenous Culture (Ayer Coll); Curt Teich Postcard Archives Coll; French Revolution Coll; Historical Geographic Education (Martin M Cassidy Coll); Historical Linguistics (Louis-Lucien Bonaparte Coll); James

Francis Driscoll Coll, American sheet music; John M. Wing Foundation on the History of Printing; Modern Manuscripts & Archives: Chicago & Midwest Arts, Business, Civil War, Clubs & Organizations, Dance, Newberry Library, Politics, Railroads, Social Action, Theater, Family papers, Journalism, Lit, Music; Polar Exploration (Gerald F Fitzgerald Coll); Portuguese & Brazilian History (Greenlee Coll); Rand McNally Co Publications Coll; Roger Baskes Coll, atlases & bks with maps; Theodore Thomas Coll, musical scores; Western Americana (Graff Coll)
Subject Interests: Am hist, Chicago & the Midwest, Genealogy, Hist of the bk, Indian studies, Indigenous studies, Local hist, Maps, travel & exploration, Medieval, Renaissance & early modern studies, Music, Performing arts, Relig
Automation Activity & Vendor Info: (Acquisitions) Ex Libris Group; (Cataloging) Ex Libris Group; (OPAC) Ex Libris Group; (Serials) Ex Libris Group
Wireless access
Function: Res libr
Mem of Reaching Across Illinois Library System (RAILS)
Partic in Black Metropolis Research Consortium; Center for Research Libraries; Chicago Collections Consortium; Consortium of Academic & Research Libraries in Illinois; OCLC Online Computer Library Center, Inc; OCLC Research Library Partnership
Open Tues-Sat 10-4

S NIXON PEABODY*, 70 W Madison St, Ste 3500, 60602. SAN 325-5131. Tel: 312-977-4378. FAX: 312-977-4405. Web Site: www.nixonpeabody.com. *Libr Mgr,* Maria Chavez; E-mail: mchavez@nixonpeabody.com
Subject Interests: Corporate law, Gen bus, Healthcare, Securities, Taxation
Automation Activity & Vendor Info: (Acquisitions) SydneyPlus
Partic in GSI Online; Illinois Library & Information Network; LivEdgar
Restriction: Private libr

NORTH PARK UNIVERSITY
C BRANDEL LIBRARY*, 5114 N Christiana Ave, 60625. (Mail add: 3225 W Foster Ave, 60625), SAN 340-1855. Tel: 773-244-5580, 773-244-6200. Interlibrary Loan Service Tel: 773-244-5588. Reference Tel: 773-244-5247. Administration Tel: 773-244-5583. FAX: 773-244-4891. Web Site: www.northpark.edu/library. *Dir,* Sarah Anderson; Tel: 773-244-5584, E-mail: saanderson@northpark.edu; *Archives Dir,* Anne Jenner; Tel: 773-244-6224, E-mail: ajenner@northpark.edu; *Dir, Media Serv,* Bill Hartley; Tel: 773-244-5579, E-mail: whartley@northpark.edu; *Head, Access Serv,* Richard Schwegel; *Bibliog Instr, Coll Mgt, Head, Ref,* Katie Maier-O'Shea; Tel: 773-244-5582, E-mail: kmaier@northpark.edu; *Bibliog Instr, Database Mgt, Ref Serv,* Laura Burt; Tel: 773-244-5587, E-mail: lburt@northpark.edu; *Ref Serv,* Norma Sutton; Tel: 773-244-6239, E-mail: nsutton@northpark.edu. Subject Specialists: *Music,* Richard Schwegel; *Seminary,* Norma Sutton; Staff 15 (MLS 8, Non-MLS 7)
Founded 1891. Enrl 2,972; Fac 127; Highest Degree: Master
Library Holdings: Bk Titles 203,563; Bk Vols 228,874; Per Subs 961
Special Collections: Bound Scores; China (Harold W Jacobson Coll); Evangelical Covenant Church Archives; G Anderson Coll; Jenny Lind, bks, coins, glass objects, letters, medals, music; Karl A Olsson Coll; Paul L Homer Coll; Scandinavian Coll; Scandinavian Literature (Nils William Olsson Coll); Swedish-American Historical Society Archives; Walter Johnson Coll
Subject Interests: Music, Nursing, Relig, Scandinavia, Theol
Automation Activity & Vendor Info: (Acquisitions) Ex Libris Group; (Cataloging) Ex Libris Group; (Circulation) Ex Libris Group; (ILL) OCLC; (OPAC) Ex Libris Group; (Serials) Ex Libris Group
Partic in Association of Chicago Theological Schools; Consortium of Academic & Research Libraries in Illinois; Illinois Library & Information Network; LIBRAS, Inc
Publications: North Park Faculty Publications & Creative Works (1992 & 1997)
Special Services for the Blind - Magnifiers
Open Mon-Thurs 7:45am-Midnight, Fri 7:45am-10pm, Sat 10-6, Sun 1-Midnight
Restriction: Restricted access

C COVENANT ARCHIVES & HISTORICAL LIBRARY*, Brandel Library, F M Johnson Archives, 3225 W Foster Ave, Box 38, 60625-4823, SAN 325-6731. Tel: 773-244-6224. Toll Free Tel: 800-888-6728. FAX: 773-244-4891. E-mail: archives@northpark.edu. Web Site: www.northpark.edu/Brandel-Library/Archives. *Dir, Archives & Spec Coll,* Anna-Kajsa Anderson; E-mail: aanderson@northpark.edu; *Digitization Coordr, Tech Serv Coordr,* Joanna Wilkinson; Tel: 773-244-5244, E-mail: jwilkinson@northpark.edu; Staff 1 (Non-MLS 1)
Library Holdings: Bk Vols 3,000; Per Subs 15
Subject Interests: Evangelicalism
Restriction: Open by appt only

C SWEDISH-AMERICAN ARCHIVES OF GREATER CHICAGO*, 3225 W Foster Ave, 60625, SAN 304-0348. Tel: 773-244-6223. Toll Free FAX: 800-888-6728. E-mail: archives@northpark.edu. Web Site: www.campus.northpark.edu/library/archives. *Archivist,* Anne Jenner; Tel: 773-244-6224; Staff 1 (Non-MLS 1)
Founded 1968
Library Holdings: Bk Titles 3,000; Per Subs 20
Special Collections: Bengtsor Coll, doc; Chicago Swedes, doc; Chicago Swedes, newsp, orgn rec
Publications: Swedish American Historical Quarterly
Mem of Reaching Across Illinois Library System (RAILS)
Restriction: Open by appt only, Open to pub upon request
Friends of the Library Group

C NORTHEASTERN ILLINOIS UNIVERSITY*, Ronald Williams Library, 5500 N Saint Louis Ave, 60625-4699. SAN 340-191X. Tel: 773-442-4400. Circulation Tel: 773-442-4401. Interlibrary Loan Service Tel: 773-442-4509. Reference Tel: 773-442-4410. Administration Tel: 773-442-4470. E-mail: NEIU-Library@neiu.edu. Web Site: library.neiu.edu. *Dean of Libr,* Steven Harris; *Access Serv Librn,* Zach McMahon; E-mail: z-mcmahon@neiu.edu; *Bus Librn,* Henry Owen, III; E-mail: h-owen3@neiu.edu; *Continuing Resources Librn, Metadata Librn,* Dr Chris Straughn; Tel: 773-442-4477, E-mail: c-straughn@neiu.edu; *Digital Scholarship Librn, First-Year Experience Coord,* Alyssa Vincent; E-mail: a-vincent@neiu.edu; *Educ Librn,* Michelle Oh; E-mail: m-oh@neiu.edu; *E-Resources Librn, Syst Librn,* Lisa Wallis; E-mail: l-wallis@neiu.edu; *Humanities Librn, Ref Coordr,* Mary Thill; E-mail: m-thill@neiu.edu; *Sci Librn,* Geoff Brown; E-mail: g-brown9@neiu.edu; *Soc Sci Librn,* Ed Remus; E-mail: e-remus@neiu.edu; *Tech Serv Coordr,* Position Currently Open; *Univ Archivist,* Hanna Ahn; E-mail: h-ahn2@neiu.edu. Subject Specialists: *Acctg, Bus law, Finance,* Henry Owen, III; *Linguistics,* Dr Chris Straughn; *Art, Media, Theatre,* Alyssa Vincent; *Educ, Phys educ,* Michelle Oh; *Pub health,* Lisa Wallis; *English, Latin Am studies, Teaching English as a second lang,* Mary Thill; *Environ sci, Geol, Physics,* Geoff Brown; *Hist, Polit sci, Psychol,* Ed Remus; Staff 29 (MLS 11, Non-MLS 18)
Founded 1961. Enrl 8,103; Fac 550; Highest Degree: Master
Jul 2017-Jun 2018 Income (Main & Associated Libraries) $3,154,079, State $2,586,423, Locally Generated Income $495,000, Other $72,656. Mats Exp $1,425,028. Sal $1,531,985
Library Holdings: AV Mats 16,520; e-books 308,429; e-journals 66,121; Electronic Media & Resources 217,716; Bk Vols 687,014; Per Subs 18,270
Special Collections: Chicago & Cook County Archives (1831-1955). State Document Depository; US Document Depository
Automation Activity & Vendor Info: (Acquisitions) Ex Libris Group; (Cataloging) Ex Libris Group; (Circulation) Ex Libris Group; (Course Reserve) Ex Libris Group; (Discovery) OCLC Worldshare Management Services; (ILL) OCLC Tipasa; (OPAC) Ex Libris Group; (Serials) Ex Libris Group
Wireless access
Function: 24/7 Electronic res, 24/7 Online cat, Archival coll, Art exhibits, Computer training, Computers for patron use, Electronic databases & coll, Govt ref serv, Internet access, Magazines, Microfiche/film & reading machines, Online cat, Online info literacy tutorials on the web & in blackboard, Online ref, Outside serv via phone, mail, e-mail & web, Photocopying/Printing, Printer for laptops & handheld devices, Ref serv available, Scanner, Telephone ref, Wheelchair accessible
Mem of Reaching Across Illinois Library System (RAILS)
Partic in Consortium of Academic & Research Libraries in Illinois
Open Mon-Thurs 8am-10:45pm, Fri 8-6, Sat 9-6, Sun Noon-8
Restriction: Circ privileges for students & alumni only, ID required to use computers (Ltd hrs), In-house use for visitors, Pub use on premises

Departmental Libraries:

CARRUTHERS CENTER FOR INNER CITY STUDIES LIBRARY, 700 E Oakwood Blvd, 60653, SAN 340-1944. Tel: 773-256-2134. Web Site: www.neiu.edu/library/ccics-library. *Info Serv Librn, Libr Coord,* Robin Harris; E-mail: r-harris14@neiu.edu; Staff 2 (MLS 1, Non-MLS 1)
Subject Interests: Educ, Inner city studies
Open Mon-Thurs 12-8, Fri 10-5

EL CENTRO LIBRARY & LEARNING RESOURCE CENTER, 3390 N Avondale Ave, 60618. Tel: 773-442-4090. Web Site: www.neiu.edu/library/el-centro-library-and-learning-resource-center. *Library & Learning Resource Ctr Librn,* Chrissy Cogswell; E-mail: c-cogswell@neiu.edu. Subject Specialists: *Soc work,* Chrissy Cogswell; Staff 2 (MLS 1, Non-MLS 1)
Open Mon-Thurs 10-8, Fri 10-5, Sat 10-4

M NORTHWESTERN MEMORIAL HOSPITAL*, Alberto Culver Health Learning Center, Galter Pavilion, Ste 3-304, 251 E Huron St, 60611. SAN 373-3556. Tel: 312-926-5465. FAX: 312-926-2125. E-mail: hlc@nmh.org. Web Site: www.nm.org/locations/alberto-culver-health-learning-center. *Mgr,* Nora St. Peter; E-mail: nstpeter@nm.org; *Health Educator,* Moira Workman; Staff 4 (MLS 2, Non-MLS 2)
Founded 1999
Library Holdings: Bk Vols 6,000
Special Collections: Women's Consumer Health
Subject Interests: Health

Wireless access
Function: Computer training, Computers for patron use, Internet access, Learning ctr, Mail & tel request accepted, Online cat, Online ref, Outside serv via phone, mail, e-mail & web, Photocopying/Printing, Ref serv available, Wheelchair accessible
Open Mon-Fri 8:30-3
Restriction: Hospital staff & commun, Med & nursing staff, patients & families, Med staff & students, Non-circulating

§CM OAK POINT UNIVERSITY LIBRARY, 1431 N Claremont Ave, 60622. Tel: 773-235-5537, 773-252-5114. E-mail: library@oakpoint.edu. Web Site: oakpoint.edu/student-resources/library. *Mgr, Libr Serv,* Erin Bell; Tel: 630-537-9790, E-mail: erin.bell@oakpoint.edu
Wireless access
Function: Res assist avail
Partic in Consortium of Academic & Research Libraries in Illinois
Open Mon-Thurs 7am-8pm, Fri 7-4, Sat 8-5

SR ORDER OF SERVANTS OF MARY (SERVITES), USA PROVINCE, Servite Provincial Library, 3121 W Jackson Blvd, 60612. SAN 328-3461. Tel: 773-533-0360. FAX: 773-533-5201. Web Site: www.servite.org. *Archivist,* Fr Paul Gins; Tel: 773-638-5800, Ext 31, E-mail: pbenizi@aol.com
Library Holdings: Bk Vols 3,600; Per Subs 20; Videos 40
Restriction: Open by appt only

SR OUR LADY OF SORROWS BASILICA, Archives Library, 3121 W Jackson Blvd, 60612. SAN 323-4703. Tel: 773-638-5800, Ext 31. Web Site: ols-chicago.org. *Archivist,* Conrad Borntrager; E-mail: conradbosm@yahoo.com
Library Holdings: Bk Vols 300
Restriction: Open by appt only

S POLISH MUSEUM OF AMERICA LIBRARY*, 984 N Milwaukee Ave, 60642-4101. SAN 303-9994. Tel: 773-384-3352, Ext 2111. FAX: 773-384-3799. E-mail: pma@polishmuseumofamerica.org. Web Site: www.polishmuseumofamerica.org/library. *Curator, Head Librn, Head, Spec Coll,* Iwona Bozek; *Archivist/Librn,* Teresa Sromek; Staff 2 (MLS 1, Non-MLS 1)
Founded 1915
Library Holdings: Audiobooks 100; AV Mats 400; CDs 400; DVDs 100; Microforms 300; Music Scores 5,000; Bk Titles 100,000; Bk Vols 120,000; Per Subs 35; Videos 280
Special Collections: 19th Century Polish Emigre Coll; Old Manuscripts; Paderewski Coll; Polish Publishers in the US Coll; Polonica Americana Coll; Polonica in English Coll. Oral History
Subject Interests: Art, Genealogy, Heraldry, Hist, Poland, Polish lit
Wireless access
Function: Archival coll, Art exhibits, Genealogy discussion group, Holiday prog, Photocopying/Printing, Ref serv available, Wheelchair accessible, Workshops
Publications: Polish Past in America
Mem of Reaching Across Illinois Library System (RAILS)
Restriction: Access at librarian's discretion, Authorized patrons, Circ limited, Circ to mem only, Closed stack
Friends of the Library Group

M PRESENCE SAINT JOSEPH MEDICAL LIBRARY*, 2900 N Lake Shore Dr, 12th Flr, 60657. SAN 304-016X. Tel: 773-665-3038. *Med Librn,* Eleanor Truex; Staff 1 (MLS 1)
Library Holdings: AV Mats 2; CDs 20; DVDs 20; e-books 50; Bk Titles 1,900; Per Subs 90
Subject Interests: Med, Nursing
Wireless access
Mem of Reaching Across Illinois Library System (RAILS)
Partic in Greater Midwest Regional Medical Libr Network
Restriction: Authorized personnel only, Badge access after hrs, Hospital employees & physicians only

M PRESENCE SAINTS MARY & ELIZABETH MEDICAL CENTER*, Sister Stella Louise Health Science Library, 2233 W Division St, 60622. SAN 340-2363. Tel: 312-770-2219. FAX: 312-770-2221. E-mail: smemclibrary@presencehealth.org. *Libr Dir,* Eleanor Truex; E-mail: eleanor.truex@amitahealth.org; Staff 2 (MLS 1, Non-MLS 1)
Founded 1949
Library Holdings: Bk Vols 2,250
Subject Interests: Internal med, Surgery
Publications: Acquisition List; Annual Report; Journal List
Partic in Illinois Library & Information Network

§S PRITZKER MILITARY MUSEUM & LIBRARY, 104 S Michigan Ave, 2nd Flr, 60603. Tel: 312-374-9333. FAX: 312-374-9314. E-mail: info@pritzkermilitary.org. Web Site: www.pritzkermilitary.org/explore/library/overview. *Sr Dir,* Roberto Bravo; *Dir, Libr Serv,* Theresa A R Embrey; E-mail: tembrey@pritzkermilitary.org
Library Holdings: Bk Vols 65,000
Special Collections: Military Reading Lists; Rare Book Room
Wireless access
Partic in Consortium of Academic & Research Libraries in Illinois
Open Tues-Sat 10-4

S PRO-LIFE ACTION LEAGUE LIBRARY*, 6160 N Cicero Ave, Ste 600, 60646. SAN 373-3688. Tel: 773-777-2900. FAX: 773-777-3061. E-mail: info@prolifeaction.org. Web Site: prolifeaction.org. *VPres,* Ann Scheidler; *Dir,* Joe Scheidler
Founded 1980
Library Holdings: Bk Vols 1,500; Per Subs 10
Special Collections: Articles on Pro Life
Subject Interests: Abortion, Euthanasia, Life
Wireless access
Publications: Action News (Quarterly)
Open Mon-Fri 9-5

C ROOSEVELT UNIVERSITY*, Murray-Green Library, 430 S Michigan Ave, 60605. SAN 340-224X. Circulation Tel: 312-341-3639, 312-341-3649. Interlibrary Loan Service Tel: 312-341-3638. Reference Tel: 312-341-3643, 312-341-3644. FAX: 312-341-2425. Web Site: www.roosevelt.edu/library. *Interim Dir,* Estevan Montano; E-mail: emontano02@roosevelt.edu; *Dir, Performing Arts Libr,* Richard Schwegel; Tel: 312-341-3648, E-mail: rschwegel@roosevelt.edu; *Head, Access Serv,* Jacob Jeremiah; Tel: 312-341-6965, E-mail: jjeremiah@roosevelt.edu; *Head, Info Literacy & Instruction Serv,* Martinique Hallerduff; Tel: 312-341-2125, E-mail: mhaller@roosevelt.edu; *Head, Tech Serv,* David Pribyl; Tel: 312-341-3647, E-mail: dpribyl@roosevelt.edu; *Coll Develop Librn, Ref,* Geoff Greenburg; Tel: 312-341-2318, E-mail: ggreenberg@roosevelt.edu; *Electronic Res Mgt Librn, Ref & Instruction Librn, Webmaster,* Jefferson Micah; Tel: 312-341-2406, E-mail: mjefferson@roosevelt.edu; *Asst Archivist, Ref & Instruction Librn,* Michael Gabriel; Tel: 312-341-3645, E-mail: mgabriel@roosevelt.edu; *Scholarly Communications Librn,* Freeda Brook; Tel: 312-341-3652, E-mail: fbrook@roosevelt.edu; *Tech Serv Librn,* Erin Carlson; Tel: 312-341-3642, E-mail: ecarlson@roosevelt.edu; *Asst Music Librn,* Deborah Morris; Tel: 312-341-2328, E-mail: dmorris@roosevelt.edu; *Univ Archivist,* Laura Mills; Tel: 312-341-2280, E-mail: lmills@roosevelt.edu; Staff 14 (MLS 14)
Founded 1945. Enrl 5,070; Fac 350; Highest Degree: Doctorate
Library Holdings: Bk Titles 174,907; Bk Vols 187,338; Per Subs 1,165
Special Collections: American Civilization & English Literature Coll; Music Coll, bks, recs, sheet music
Automation Activity & Vendor Info: (Acquisitions) Ex Libris Group; (Cataloging) Ex Libris Group; (Circulation) Ex Libris Group; (Course Reserve) SerialsSolutions; (ILL) OCLC ILLiad; (OPAC) Ex Libris Group; (Serials) EBSCO Online
Wireless access
Publications: Subject Research Guides
Partic in Black Metropolis Research Consortium; Chicago Collections Consortium; Consortium of Academic & Research Libraries in Illinois; LIBRAS, Inc

Departmental Libraries:

ROBERT R MCCORMICK TRIBUNE FOUNDATION LIBRARY, 1400 N Roosevelt Blvd, Schaumburg, 60173, SAN 376-9771. Tel: 847-619-7980. FAX: 847-619-7983. *Univ Librn,* Richard M Uttich; Tel: 312-341-3540, E-mail: ruttich@roosevelt.edu; *Dir, Head, Pub Serv,* Linda Wilkinson; Tel: 312-341-3659, E-mail: lpwilkinson@roosevelt.edu; *Ref & Instruction Librn,* Joseph Davis; *Ref & Instruction Librn,* Laura McLoughlin; *Ref & Instruction Librn,* Renee Roth; Staff 9 (MLS 4, Non-MLS 5)
Library Holdings: Bk Titles 12,400; Per Subs 250
Open Mon-Thurs 9-8, Fri & Sat 9-4

PERFORMING ARTS LIBRARY, 430 S Michigan Ave, Rm 1111, 60605. Tel: 312-341-3651. FAX: 312-341-6394. Web Site: www.roosevelt.edu/library/locations/performingartslibrary.aspx. *Dir,* Richard C Schwegel; Tel: 312-341-3648, E-mail: rschwegel@roosevelt.edu; *Asst Dir,* Morris Deb; Tel: 312-341-2328, E-mail: dmorris@roosevelt.edu; *Tech Asst,* Anita Hwang; Tel: 312-341-2136, E-mail: ahwang@roosevelt.edu; Staff 3.5 (MLS 2, Non-MLS 1.5)
Enrl 500; Highest Degree: Master
Library Holdings: CDs 7,000; Music Scores 40,000; Bk Titles 39,678; Per Subs 90
Automation Activity & Vendor Info: (Course Reserve) Ex Libris Group
Restriction: Pub use on premises

C SAINT AUGUSTINE COLLEGE LIBRARY*, 1345 W Argyle St, 60640. SAN 375-9423. Tel: 773-878-3752. FAX: 773-878-0937. E-mail: library@staugustine.edu. Web Site: library.staugustine.edu. *Head Librn,* Claudia Nickson; E-mail: CNickson@staugustine.edu; Staff 4 (MLS 2, Non-MLS 2)
Founded 1980. Enrl 1,400; Highest Degree: Bachelor

Library Holdings: e-books 150,000; e-journals 1,000,000; Bk Titles 15,000; Bk Vols 17,000; Per Subs 50
Automation Activity & Vendor Info: (Acquisitions) Brodart; (Cataloging) OCLC Online; (Circulation) Follett Software; (ILL) OCLC Online; (OPAC) Follett Software
Wireless access
Partic in Consortium of Academic & Research Libraries in Illinois; Illinois Library & Information Network
Open Mon-Fri 8:30am-9:45pm, Sat 8:30-4
Restriction: By permission only

C SAINT XAVIER UNIVERSITY*, Robert & Mary Rita Murphy Stump, 3700 W 103rd St, 60655-3105. SAN 304-0178. Tel: 773-298-3352, Interlibrary Loan Service Tel: 773-298-3353. Reference Tel: 773-298-3364. FAX: 773-779-5231. Web Site: www.sxu.edu/library. *Libr Dir,* David Stern; Tel: 773-298-3350, E-mail: stern@sxu.edu; Staff 9 (MLS 2, Non-MLS 7)
Founded 1916. Enrl 4,000; Fac 168; Highest Degree: Master
Library Holdings: Bk Vols 73,816; Per Subs 1,607
Automation Activity & Vendor Info: (Acquisitions) Baker & Taylor; (Cataloging) OCLC WorldShare Interlibrary Loan; (Circulation) Ex Libris Group; (Course Reserve) Ex Libris Group; (ILL) OCLC WorldShare Interlibrary Loan; (OPAC) Ex Libris Group
Wireless access
Mem of Reaching Across Illinois Library System (RAILS)
Partic in Consortium of Academic & Research Libraries in Illinois; LIBRAS, Inc; OCLC Online Computer Library Center, Inc
Open Mon-Thurs 7:30am-Midnight, Fri 7:30-5, Sat 12-5, Sun 4-Midnight
Restriction: Authorized patrons

S SARGENT & LUNDY, LLC*, Resource Center, 55 E Monroe St, 24F60, 60603. SAN 340-2428. Tel: 312-269-3525. FAX: 312-269-5932. Web Site: www.sargentlundy.com. *Librn,* Gary Kenny; E-mail: gerard.p.kemy@sargentlundy.com; Staff 3 (MLS 2, Non-MLS 1)
Founded 1969
Library Holdings: Bk Titles 2,000; Per Subs 20
Subject Interests: Archit, Civil engr, Electrical engr, Energy, Mechanical engr
Wireless access
Mem of Reaching Across Illinois Library System (RAILS)
Partic in Illinois Library & Information Network
Restriction: Staff use only

L SCHIFF, HARDIN LLP LIBRARY, 233 S Wacker Dr, Ste 7100, 60606. SAN 304-0186. Tel: 312-258-5500. FAX: 312-258-5600. Web Site: www.schiffhardin.com. *Admin Librn, Sr Res Librn,* Kayla Kotila; E-mail: kkotila@schiffhardin.com; Staff 3 (MLS 2, Non-MLS 1)
Library Holdings: Bk Vols 40,000

C SCHOOL OF THE ART INSTITUTE OF CHICAGO*, John M Flaxman Library, 37 S Wabash Ave, 60603-3103. SAN 339-8048. Tel: 312-899-5097. Reference Tel: 312-899-5096. FAX: 312-899-1851. E-mail: flaxman@saic.edu. Web Site: digital-libraries.saic.edu, www.saic.edu/library. *Exec Dir,* Claire Eike; *Access & Res Serv Librn,* Holly Stec Dankert; *Cat & Acq,* Nathaniel Feis; *Coll Mgt Librn,* Sylvia Choi; *Digital Serv Librn,* Christopher Day; *Digitization Librn, Media Preservation,* Carolyn Faber; *Ref & Instruction Librn,* Nick Ferreira; *Ref & Instruction Librn,* Mackenzie Salisbury; *Spec Coll Librn,* Doro Boehme; *Access Serv Mgr,* Elizabeth Aubrey; *Mgr, Spec Coll,* Kayla Anderson; *Access Serv Asst,* Cristina Garcia; *Acq Asst,* Keith Kostecki; *Cat & Metadata Asst,* Grace Gaynor; *Cat & Metadata Asst,* Michael Donovan; *Coll Mgt Asst,* Anna Di Cesare; *Digital Imaging Tech,* Michelle Brooks; Staff 11 (MLS 9, Non-MLS 2)
Founded 1968. Enrl 3,400; Highest Degree: Master
Library Holdings: AV Mats 30,000; Bk Titles 160,000; Per Subs 700
Special Collections: 16mm Film Study Coll; Correspondence Art; Joan Flasch Artists' Bks Coll; P-form Archives; Randolph Street Gallery Archives; SAIC Digital Libraries; SAIC Publications; Tony Zwicker Archives
Subject Interests: Animation, Archit, Art & tech, Art educ, Art therapy, Arts admin & policy, Contemporary art, Design, Film, Historic presv, New media, Video, Writing
Automation Activity & Vendor Info: (Cataloging) Ex Libris Group; (Circulation) Ex Libris Group; (Discovery) Ex Libris Group; (ILL) OCLC; (OPAC) Ex Libris Group; (Serials) SerialsSolutions
Wireless access
Function: 24/7 Electronic res, Archival coll, Art exhibits, Audio & video playback equip for onsite use, Computers for patron use, Electronic databases & coll, ILL available, Internet access, Magazines, Mango lang, Movies, Music CDs, Online cat, Online ref, Orientations, Outreach serv, Photocopying/Printing, Ref & res, Scanner, VHS videos
Mem of Reaching Across Illinois Library System (RAILS)
Partic in Center for Research Libraries; Chicago Collections Consortium; Consortium of Academic & Research Libraries in Illinois; OCLC Online Computer Library Center, Inc
Special Services for the Deaf - Closed caption videos
Restriction: Open to students, fac & staff, Photo ID required for access

S SEYFARTH SHAW LLP*, Library, 233 Wacker Dr, Ste 8000, 60606-6448. SAN 304-0224. Tel: 312-460-5000. FAX: 312-460-7000. Web Site: www.seyfarth.com. *Dir,* Gabrielle Lewis; E-mail: glewis@seyfarth.com; *Research Librn,* Nancy Faust; Staff 9 (MLS 3, Non-MLS 6)
Founded 1945
Library Holdings: Bk Vols 38,500; Per Subs 484
Special Collections: Arbitration Awards & Legal Memoranda (Seyfarth Shaw Coll), bd vols
Subject Interests: Employment law, Environ law, Labor law, Securities law
Function: ILL available
Mem of Reaching Across Illinois Library System (RAILS)
Partic in OCLC Online Computer Library Center, Inc
Restriction: Co libr

S JOHN G SHEDD AQUARIUM LIBRARY*, 1200 S Lake Shore Dr, 60605. SAN 320-1791. Tel: 312-692-3217. Web Site: www.sheddaquarium.org. *Dir, Integrated Libr Tech Serv, Media Serv,* Amanda Enser; E-mail: aenser@sheddaquarium.org; Staff 1 (MLS 1)
Founded 1975
Library Holdings: AV Mats 100; e-journals 20; Bk Titles 8,000; Per Subs 125
Special Collections: Aquatic Animals Coll, slide images
Subject Interests: Animals, behavior of, Aquarium mgt, Aquatic sci, Great Lakes
Automation Activity & Vendor Info: (Cataloging) SirsiDynix; (Circulation) SirsiDynix; (Discovery) EBSCO Discovery Service; (ILL) OCLC; (OPAC) SirsiDynix; (Serials) SirsiDynix
Wireless access
Function: ILL available
Mem of Reaching Across Illinois Library System (RAILS)
Partic in International Environment Library Consortium; OCLC-LVIS; Serials of Illinois Libraries Online
Restriction: Not open to pub, Staff use only

M SHIRLEY RYAN ABILITYLAB*, LIFE Center, 355 E Erie St, 10th Flr, 60611. SAN 324-7317. Tel: 312-238-5433. FAX: 312-238-2860. E-mail: lifecenter@sralab.org. Web Site: www.sralab.org/lifecenter. *Mgr,* Lisa Rosen; *Med Librn,* Carol Stukey; Staff 1 (MLS 1)
Founded 2003
Library Holdings: DVDs 200; Bk Titles 400; Per Subs 12
Subject Interests: Phys rehabilitation
Wireless access
Function: Health sci info serv
Restriction: Circulates for staff only, In-house use for visitors, Non-circulating to the pub

L SHRIVER CENTER ON POVERTY LAW LIBRARY, 67 E Madison St, Ste 2000, 60603. SAN 326-9574. Tel: 312-263-3830. FAX: 312-263-3846. Web Site: www.povertylaw.org.
Founded 1967
Library Holdings: Per Subs 150
Special Collections: Training Manuals & Poverty Law Analysis Coll
Open Mon-Fri 9-5

L SIDLEY AUSTIN LLP LIBRARY*, One S Dearborn St, 60603. SAN 304-0259. Tel: 312-853-7475. FAX: 312-853-7036. Web Site: www.sidley.com. *Dir, Libr Serv,* Sara Baseggio; E-mail: sbaseggio@sidley.com
Library Holdings: Bk Vols 25,000
Subject Interests: Law
Partic in Illinois Library & Information Network; OCLC Online Computer Library Center, Inc
Restriction: Private libr

L SKADDEN, ARPS, SLATE, MEAGHER & FLOM LLP LIBRARY*, 155 N Wacker Dr, 60606. SAN 375-9652. Tel: 312-407-0700. FAX: 312-407-0411. Web Site: www.skadden.com. *Head Law Librn,* Jessie Lemar; *Sr Librn, Ref,* Sandy Qiu; Staff 5 (MLS 4, Non-MLS 1)
Automation Activity & Vendor Info: (Acquisitions) EOS International; (Cataloging) EOS International; (Circulation) EOS International; (OPAC) EOS International; (Serials) EOS International
Wireless access

S SKIDMORE, OWINGS & MERRILL LIBRARY*, 224 S Michigan Ave, Ste 1000, 60604. SAN 304-0267. Tel: 312-554-9090. FAX: 312-360-4545. Web Site: www.som.com. *Mgr,* Karen Widi
Founded 1972
Library Holdings: Bk Titles 7,000; Per Subs 50
Subject Interests: Art & archit, Engr

Mem of Reaching Across Illinois Library System (RAILS)
Partic in Illinois Library & Information Network
Restriction: Staff use only

S SPENCER STUART LIBRARY*, 353 N Clark, Ste 2400, 60654. SAN 304-0283. Tel: 312-822-0088. FAX: 312-822-0117. *Dir,* Laura Dear; E-mail: ldear@spencerstuart.com; Staff 5 (MLS 5)
Library Holdings: Per Subs 50
Subject Interests: Exec search
Mem of Reaching Across Illinois Library System (RAILS)

CR SPERTUS INSTITUTE OF JEWISH STUDIES*, Norman & Helen Asher Library, 610 S Michigan Ave, 60605. SAN 304-0291. Tel: 312-322-1712. FAX: 312-922-0455. E-mail: resources@spertus.edu. Web Site: www.spertus.edu/library. *Assoc Dir,* Kathleen Bloch; E-mail: kbloch@spertus.edu; *Librn,* Gail Goldberg; E-mail: ggoldberg@spertus.edu; Staff 2 (MLS 1, Non-MLS 1)
Founded 1925. Enrl 900; Highest Degree: Doctorate
Library Holdings: Bk Titles 75,000; Bk Vols 100,000; Per Subs 550
Special Collections: Chicago Jewish Archives; Chicago Jewish History; Jewish Art (Badona Spertus Library of Art in Judaica); Jewish Music (Targ Center for Jewish Music); Non-Profit Management (Lewis Sulkin Human Services Coll)
Subject Interests: Jewish hist, Jewish holocaust, Judaica, Judaism (religion)
Automation Activity & Vendor Info: (Acquisitions) Ex Libris Group; (Cataloging) Ex Libris Group; (Circulation) Ex Libris Group; (OPAC) Ex Libris Group; (Serials) Ex Libris Group
Wireless access
Function: Bks on cassette, Bks on CD, Computers for patron use, Distance learning, Electronic databases & coll, ILL available, Internet access, Mail & tel request accepted, Mail loans to mem, Online cat, Photocopying/Printing, Ref serv available, Spoken cassettes & CDs, Telephone ref, VHS videos, Wheelchair accessible
Mem of Reaching Across Illinois Library System (RAILS)
Partic in Consortium of Academic & Research Libraries in Illinois; Ill Regional Libr Coun
Special Services for the Deaf - TTY equip
Open Mon-Wed 9-5, Thurs 9-6, Fri 9-3, Sun 10-5
Restriction: Open to students, fac, staff & alumni, Restricted borrowing privileges

M JOHN H STROGER JR HOSPITAL OF COOK COUNTY, Academic Center Library, 1950 W Polk St, Rm 5218, 60612. SAN 340-1073. Tel: 312-864-0506. Reference Tel: 312-864-0311. E-mail: library@cookcountyhealth.org. Web Site: cookcountyhealth.org/education-research/research/academic-center-library. *Dir,* Estelle Hu; E-mail: manhwa.hu@cookcountyhealth.org; Staff 2 (MLS 1, Non-MLS 1)
Library Holdings: CDs 10; e-books 264; e-journals 2,560; Electronic Media & Resources 16; Bk Titles 438
Special Collections: Rare Medical Books by Notable Physicians
Subject Interests: Allied health, Med, Nursing
Automation Activity & Vendor Info: (Acquisitions) OCLC Worldshare Management Services; (Cataloging) OCLC Worldshare Management Services; (Course Reserve) OCLC Worldshare Management Services; (Discovery) OCLC Worldshare Management Services; (ILL) OCLC FirstSearch; (OPAC) OCLC; (Serials) OCLC Worldshare Management Services
Wireless access
Function: 24/7 Electronic res, 24/7 Online cat, Health sci info serv
Mem of Reaching Across Illinois Library System (RAILS)
Open Mon-Fri 8-4
Restriction: Authorized patrons, Authorized personnel only, Circulates for staff only, Hospital employees & physicians only
Friends of the Library Group

M SWEDISH COVENANT HOSPITAL*, Joseph G Stromberg Library of the Health Sciences, 5145 N California Ave, 60625. SAN 304-033X. Tel: 773-878-8200, Ext 5312. FAX: 773-878-1624. Web Site: swedishcovenant.org. *Librn,* Liz Giese; E-mail: lgiese@schosp.org; Staff 1 (MLS 1)
Founded 1930
Library Holdings: Bk Titles 1,600; Per Subs 65
Subject Interests: Med
Mem of Reaching Across Illinois Library System (RAILS)
Restriction: Open to others by appt

M UKRAINIAN MEDICAL ASSOCIATION OF NORTH AMERICA*, Medical Archives & Library, 2247 W Chicago Ave, Ste 206, 60622. SAN 325-7185. Tel: 773-278-6262. FAX: 773-278-6962. E-mail: umana@umana.org. Web Site: www.umana.org/library.php. *Archivist, Dir,* Dr M Hrycelak
Founded 1950
Library Holdings: Bk Vols 5,000
Subject Interests: Archives, Med, Ukraine
Function: Archival coll, Res libr
Restriction: Non-circulating, Staff use only

S UNION LEAGUE CLUB OF CHICAGO LIBRARY, George N Leighton Library, 65 W Jackson Blvd, 60604. SAN 304-0399. Tel: 312-435-4818. Web Site: www.ulcc.org/web/pages/library-archives. *Dir, Libr & Archives,* Cheryl Ziegler; E-mail: cziegler@ulcc.org; Staff 1 (MLS 1)
Library Holdings: DVDs 100; Bk Vols 30,000; Per Subs 30
Special Collections: Chicago Metropolitan/Local Interest Fiction & Nonfiction Coll
Subject Interests: Am hist, Art & archit, Fiction, Hist
Wireless access
Function: Archival coll, Bk reviews (Group), Bus archives, Computers for patron use, Electronic databases & coll, Free DVD rentals, Online cat, Photocopying/Printing, Ref serv available, Scanner, Telephone ref, Wheelchair accessible, Writing prog
Publications: Club Life (Monthly newsletter)
Open Mon-Fri 9-5
Restriction: Private libr

G UNITED STATES ENVIRONMENTAL PROTECTION AGENCY, Region 5 Library, 77 W Jackson Blvd (ML-16J), 60604. SAN 303-8882. Tel: 312-886-6822. FAX: 312-886-1492. E-mail: library.r05@epa.gov. Web Site: www.epa.gov/libraries/region-5-library-services. *Fed Libr Mgr,* Jessica Wheatley; *Supvry Librn,* Karen Swanson; Staff 1.3 (MLS 1, Non-MLS 0.3)
Founded 1972
Library Holdings: Bk Titles 3,860
Special Collections: EPA Reports
Subject Interests: Air, Great Lakes, Waste, Water
Automation Activity & Vendor Info: (Cataloging) OCLC; (ILL) OCLC WorldShare Interlibrary Loan
Mem of Reaching Across Illinois Library System (RAILS)
Partic in EPA National Libr Network; Federal Library & Information Network; OCLC Online Computer Library Center, Inc; OCLC-LVIS
Open Mon-Fri 8:30-12 & 12:30-3
Restriction: External users must contact libr, Visitors must make appt to use bks in the libr

S UNITED STATES RAILROAD RETIREMENT BOARD LIBRARY*, 844 N Rush St, 60611-2031. SAN 304-0461. Tel: 312-751-4926. FAX: 312-751-4924. E-mail: library@rrb.gov. Web Site: www.rrb.gov. *Head Librn,* Annie Mentkowski; E-mail: annie.mentkowski@rrb.gov; Staff 1 (MLS 1)
Founded 1940
Library Holdings: Bk Vols 45,000; Per Subs 162
Subject Interests: Law
Function: ILL available
Mem of Reaching Across Illinois Library System (RAILS)
Restriction: By permission only

C THE UNIVERSITY OF CHICAGO LIBRARY*, Joseph Regenstein Library, 1100 E 57th St, 60637-1502. SAN 340-2630. Tel: 773-702-8740. Circulation Tel: 773-702-8701. Interlibrary Loan Service Tel: 773-702-7886, 773-702-8706. Reference Tel: 773-702-4685. FAX: 773-702-6623. Interlibrary Loan Service FAX: 773-834-2598. Web Site: www.lib.uchicago.edu. *Dir & Univ Librn,* Brenda L Johnson; E-mail: brendajohnson@uchicago.edu; *Assoc Univ Librn, Coll & Access,* James Mouw; Tel: 773-702-8732, E-mail: mouw@uchicago.edu; *Assoc Univ Librn, Res & Learning,* Position Currently Open; *Assoc Univ Librn, Info Tech,* Elisabeth Long; Tel: 773-702-3732, E-mail: elong@uchicago.edu; *Dir of Budget & Facilities,* David Borycz; Tel: 773-702-2494, E-mail: dnborycz@uchicago.edu; *Dir, Communications,* Rachel A Rosenberg; Tel: 773-834-1519; *Dir of Develop,* Yasmin Omer; Tel: 773-834-3744, E-mail: yasminomer@uchicago.edu; *Dir, Digital Libr Develop Ctr,* Charles Blair; Tel: 773-702-8459, E-mail: chas@uchicago.edu; *Dir, Human Res,* Shauna Babcock; Tel: 773-702-8755, E-mail: sbabcock@uchicago.edu; *Dir, Res, Teaching & Learning,* Andrea Twiss-Brooks; Tel: 773-702-8777, E-mail: atbrooks@uchicago.edu; *Dir, Head, Sci Libr,* Barbara Kern; Tel: 773-702-8717, E-mail: bkern@uchicago.edu; *Electronic Res Mgt Librn,* Kristin E Martin; E-mail: kmarti@uchicago.edu. Subject Specialists: *Chem, Physics, Sci,* Andrea Twiss-Brooks; *Astronomy, Tech,* Barbara Kern; Staff 290 (MLS 73, Non-MLS 217)
Founded 1891. Enrl 15,300; Fac 2,004; Highest Degree: Doctorate
Jul 2013-Jun 2014. Mats Exp $17,911,128, $19,176,653. Sal $13,689,660 (Prof $5,980,269)
Library Holdings: e-books 1,385,286; Bk Titles 7,102,514; Bk Vols 11,012,065
Special Collections: American Drama (Atkinson & Morton Colls); Anatomical Illustration (Frank Coll); Balzac's Works (Croue Coll); Children's Books, Primarily 19th Century (Encyclopaedia Britannica Coll); Continental Literature (Hirsch-Bernays Coll); Cromwelliana (George Morris Eckels Coll); Dramatic Criticism (Briggs Coll); Early American

School Books (Littlefield Coll); Early Theology & Biblical Criticism (American Bible Union & Hengstenberg Colls); English Bibles (Grant Coll); English Drama to 1800 (Celia & Delia Austrian Coll); Files of Poetry, a Magazine of Verse including The Personal Papers of Harriet Monroe; Fine Printing (Donnelley Coll); German Fiction, 1790-1850 (Lincke Coll); Goethe's Works (Heinemann Coll); History of Kentucky & Ohio River Valley (Durrett Coll); History of Science & Medicine (Crerar Coll); Judaica (Rosenberger Coll); Life Records of Geoffrey Chaucer & Canterbury Tales, in transcripts & photostat; Lincolniana (Barton Coll); Manuscripts of Manorial Records regarding Estates in Norfolk & Suffolk (Bacon Coll); Modern Poetry (Harriet Monroe Coll); New Testament Manuscripts (Edgar J Goodspeed Coll); Notarial Documents of Northern Italy (Rosenthal Coll); Personal Papers of William Beaumont, Stephen A Douglas, William H English (History of Indiana), Frank O Lowden, Ida B Wells; Photostats of German Folksongs (Wieboldt-Rosenwald Coll); Source Material Regarding First Contact of Whites & Indians in Mississippi Valley (Ethno-History Coll); Taschenbuecher; The John Crerar Library Rare Book Coll; University Archives (incl Papers of Edith & Grace Abbott, Thomas C Chamberlin, Enrico Fermi, James Franck, Samuel N Harper, William Rainey Harper, Robert Herrick, George Herbert Mead, William Vaughn Moody, Howard Taylor Ricketts, Marion Talbot, Herman Eduard von Holst). US Document Depository

Automation Activity & Vendor Info: (ILL) OCLC ILLiad; (OPAC) Horizon

Wireless access

Function: Archival coll, Art exhibits, Audio & video playback equip for onsite use, AV serv, CD-ROM, Computers for patron use, Doc delivery serv, E-Reserves, Electronic databases & coll, For res purposes, Health sci info serv, ILL available, Internet access, Magnifiers for reading, Mail & tel request accepted, Music CDs, Online cat, Online ref, Orientations, Outreach serv, Outside serv via phone, mail, e-mail & web, Photocopying/Printing, Ref serv available, Res libr, Scanner, Telephone ref, VHS videos, Wheelchair accessible

Publications: Libra (Newsletter)

Partic in Association of Research Libraries; Big Ten Academic Alliance; Center for Research Libraries; Consortium of Academic & Research Libraries in Illinois; Illinois Library & Information Network; OCLC Online Computer Library Center, Inc; OCLC Research Library Partnership

Special Services for the Deaf - ADA equip; Assisted listening device; Assistive tech

Special Services for the Blind - Accessible computers; Cassette playback machines; Cassettes; Computer access aids; Low vision equip; Magnifiers; Screen enlargement software for people with visual disabilities; Screen reader software; Sound rec

Restriction: Borrowing requests are handled by ILL, In-house use for visitors, Limited access for the pub, Non-circulating of rare bks, Open to pub upon request, Open to students, fac, staff & alumni, Res pass required for non-affiliated visitors, Restricted pub use

Friends of the Library Group

Departmental Libraries:

JOHN CRERAR LIBRARY, 5730 S Ellis Ave, 60637, SAN 303-8750. Tel: 773-702-7715. Circulation Tel: 773-702-7409. Interlibrary Loan Service Tel: 773-702-7031. Administration Tel: 773-702-7469. FAX: 773-702-3317 (Admin). Administration FAX: 773-702-3317. Circulation E-mail: crerar-circulation@lib.uchicago.edu. Reference E-mail: crerar-reference@lib.uchicago.edu. Web Site: www.lib.uchicago.edu/e/crerar. *Co-Dir, Pub Serv, Head of Libr,* Barbara Kern; Tel: 773-702-8717, E-mail: bkern@uchicago.edu; *Co-Dir, Coll Develop, Head of Libr,* Andrea Twiss-Brooks; Tel: 773-702-8777, E-mail: atbrooks@uchicago.edu; *Ref & Instruction Librn,* Debra Werner; Tel: 773-702-8552, E-mail: dwerner@uchicago.edu; *Bibliographer,* Christa Modschiedler; Tel: 773-702-8759, E-mail: mods@uchicago.edu; *Bibliographer,* Brenda Rice; Tel: 773-702-8774, E-mail: bsr2@uchicago.edu. Subject Specialists: *Astronomy, Astrophysics, Tech,* Barbara Kern; *Chem, Geophysical sci, Physics,* Andrea Twiss-Brooks; *Biomed, Nursing,* Debra Werner; *Biomed sci,* Christa Modschiedler; *Computer sci, Math, Statistics,* Brenda Rice; Staff 18 (MLS 6, Non-MLS 12)

Founded 1891

Special Collections: Incunabula; Joseph Regenstein Library

Subject Interests: Astrophysics, Botany, Clinical med, Hist of med, Hist of sci, Oceanography, Physics, Zoology

Partic in Comt for Institutional Coop; National Network of Libraries of Medicine Region 6; OCLC Online Computer Library Center, Inc

Publications: At Your Service (Newsletter)

Open Mon-Thurs 8:30am-10pm, Fri 8:30-6, Sat 9-5, Sun 12-10

Friends of the Library Group

CL D'ANGELO LAW LIBRARY, 1121 E 60th St, 60637-2786, SAN 340-2789. Tel: 773-702-9615. FAX: 773-702-2889. Web Site: www.lib.uchicago.edu/e/law. *Dir,* Sheri Lewis; Tel: 773-702-9614, E-mail: shl@uchicago.edu; *Head, Acq & Electronic Res,* Julie Stauffer; Tel: 773-702-0692; *Head, Cat & Ser,* Patricia Sayre McCoy; Tel: 773-702-9620; *Fac Serv Librn,* Margaret Schilt; Tel: 773-702-6716; *Foreign & Intl Law Librn,* Lyonette Louis-Jacques; Tel: 773-702-9612, E-mail: llou@uchicago.edu; *Ref Librn,* Todd Ito; Tel: 773-702-9617; *Assoc Librn, Tech Serv,* Lorna Tang; Tel: 773-702-9619; *Bibliographer,* William Schwesig; Tel: 773-702-3731, E-mail: w-schwesig@uchicago.edu; *Cataloger,* Michael D Brown; *Ref Serv,* Constance Fleischer; Tel: 773-702-0211, E-mail: mcf0@uchicago.edu. Subject Specialists: *US Law,* Margaret Schilt; *Civil law, Intl law,* Lyonette Louis-Jacques; *US Law,* Todd Ito; *Anglo-Am law,* William Schwesig; *Govt doc,* Constance Fleischer; Staff 26 (MLS 10, Non-MLS 16)

Founded 1902. Enrl 650; Fac 51; Highest Degree: Doctorate

Library Holdings: Bk Vols 672,917; Per Subs 8,450

Special Collections: Henry Simons Papers Coll; US Supreme Court Briefs & Records Depository. US Document Depository

Subject Interests: Anglo-Am law, Intl law

Automation Activity & Vendor Info: (Acquisitions) Innovative Interfaces, Inc; (Cataloging) Horizon; (Circulation) Horizon; (Discovery) EBSCO Discovery Service; (ILL) Relais International; (OPAC) Horizon; (Serials) Horizon

Partic in OCLC Online Computer Library Center, Inc

Restriction: Vols & interns use only

ECKHART LIBRARY, 1118 E 58th St, 60637, SAN 340-272X. Tel: 773-702-8778. FAX: 773-702-7535. E-mail: eckhart-library@lib.uchicago.edu. Web Site: www.lib.uchicago.edu/e/eck. *Librn,* Jennifer Hart; Tel: 773-702-8774; *Libr Asst,* Kiya Moody; Staff 1 (MLS 1)

Library Holdings: Bk Vols 55,000; Per Subs 520

Subject Interests: Computer sci, Math, Statistics

Open Mon, Wed & Thurs 8:30am-10pm, Tues 12-5, Fri 8:30-5, Sat 9-5

SOCIAL SERVICE ADMINISTRATION, 969 E 60th St, 60637-2627, SAN 340-2819. Tel: 773-702-1199. FAX: 773-702-0874. *Librn,* Eileen Libby; E-mail: lib3@midway.uchicago.edu; Staff 1 (MLS 1)

Library Holdings: Bk Vols 35,196; Per Subs 141

Subject Interests: Soc serv (soc work)

Open Mon-Thurs 8:30-8, Fri 8:30-5, Sat 10-5, Sun 12-5

C UNIVERSITY OF ILLINOIS AT CHICAGO*, Richard J Daley Library, MC 234, 801 S Morgan St, 60607. SAN 340-2932. Tel: 312-996-2716. Circulation Tel: 312-996-2724. Interlibrary Loan Service Tel: 312-996-4886. Reference Tel: 312-996-2726. FAX: 312-413-0424. Web Site: www.library.uic.edu. *Interim Univ Librn,* Karen Colley; E-mail: karenc@uic.edu; *Assoc Univ Librn, Health Sci Librn,* Kathryn Carpenter; Tel: 312-996-8974, E-mail: khc@uic.edu; *Asst Univ Librn, Admin Serv,* Linda Naru; Tel: 312-413-0394, E-mail: lnaru@uic.edu; *Assoc Univ Librn, Info Tech,* Robert Sandusky; E-mail: sandusky@uic.edu. Subject Specialists: *Health sci,* Kathryn Carpenter; *Info tech,* Robert Sandusky; Staff 138 (MLS 60, Non-MLS 78)

Founded 1946. Enrl 30,539; Fac 1,941; Highest Degree: Doctorate

Jul 2016-Jun 2017 Income Parent Institution $18,204,718. Mats Exp $7,726,849. Sal $11,784,998

Library Holdings: e-books 671,614; Bk Vols 2,258,519

Special Collections: 17th Century French Political & Intellectual History; Architecture (Mies van der Rohe, Charles Genther, Burnham & Hammond Colls); Archives of the Chicago Rock Island & Pacific Railroad Company; Chicago Design Archive (contains business & organizational records & personal papers, including Institute of Design, Chicago Book Clinic, IDCA, 27 Chicago Designers, R Hunter Middleton, Robert Vogele, Bruce Beck, Gordon Monsen, Phillip Reed & William Stone Colls); Chicago Fairs & Expositions (A Century of Progress World's Fair archives); Chicago Literature & Literary Societies (Chicago literature to the present & Society of Midland Authors, Indiana Society, Boswell Club of Chicago Colls); Chicago Photographic Archive (Phillips, Italian-American Colls); Chicago Railroad Fair, archives; Chicagoana (Lawrence J Gutter Coll), contains pre-fire imprints, maps, lit, literary mss, hist, politics, transportation, archit, crime, prints; Franklin Roosevelt (Joseph M Jacob Coll); Jane Adams Memorial Coll (contains Hull-House Association records, papers of individuals & organizations associated with Hull-House such as: Immigrants Protective League, Travelers Aid Society, Juvenile Protective Association & Wallace Kirkland photographs); Midwest Women's Historical Coll (contains personal & organizational records, including Mary Hastings Bradley, Neva Leona Boyd, Haldeman-Julius Family, Adena-Miller Rich & Esther Saperstein); Papers of Lenox Riley Lohr & Helen Tieken Garaghty; Papers of politicians and records of influential political groups in the Chicago area; Records of the Chicago Urban League; Richard J. Daley papers; Sheet Music (American popular music, 1900-1945); Slavery & Anti-Slavery (Sierra Leone Coll); University Archives (contains the University's official records & papers of prominent members of the university's faculties). State Document Depository; US Document Depository

Automation Activity & Vendor Info: (Acquisitions) Ex Libris Group; (Cataloging) Ex Libris Group; (Circulation) Ex Libris Group; (OPAC) Ex Libris Group; (Serials) Ex Libris Group

Wireless access

Publications: UIC Library newsletter

Partic in Consortium of Academic & Research Libraries in Illinois; Greater Western Library Alliance; National Network of Libraries of Medicine Region 6; OCLC Online Computer Library Center, Inc
Open Mon-Thurs 6:30am-1am, Fri 6:30am-7pm, Sat 8-5, Sun 10am-1am

Departmental Libraries:

CM LIBRARY OF THE HEALTH SCIENCES, CHICAGO, 1750 W Polk St, 60612, SAN 340-3025. Tel: 312-996-8966. Circulation Tel: 312-996-8974. Interlibrary Loan Service Tel: 312-996-8991. Reference Tel: 312-996-9163. FAX: 312-996-9584. *Asst Univ Librn,* Kathryn Carpenter; E-mail: khc@uic.edu
Special Collections: Neurology & Psychiatry (Percival Bailey Coll); Pharmacopoeias, Herbals, Formularies, Dispensatories & History of the Health Sciences (Rare & Early Volumes); Urology & Anomalies (Joseph Kiefer Coll)
Subject Interests: Allied health, Dentistry, Environ studies, Med, Nursing
Open Mon-Thurs 8am- Midnight, Fri 8-7, Sat 9 -7, Sun 11am-Midnight

CM LIBRARY OF THE HEALTH SCIENCES, PEORIA, One Illinois Dr, Peoria, 61605. (Mail add: PO Box 1649, Peoria, 61656-1649), SAN 304-5536. Tel: 309-671-8490. *Regional Head Librn,* Deborah Lauseng; E-mail: dlauseng@uic.edu
Open Mon-Thurs 7:30am-11pm, Fri 7:30-7, Sat Noon-5, Sun Noon- 9

CM LIBRARY OF THE HEALTH SCIENCES, ROCKFORD, Crawford Library of the Health Sciences, 1601 Parkview Ave, Rockford, 61107, SAN 327-9987. Tel: 815-395-5650. E-mail: lib-lhsr@uic.edu. Web Site: library.uic.edu/libraries/lhs-rockford. *Regional Head Librn,* Felicia A Barrett; Tel: 815-395-5660, E-mail: fbarrett@uic.edu
Founded 1972. Highest Degree: Doctorate
Open Mon-Thurs 7:30am-9pm, Fri 7:30-5, Sat 1-5, Sun 1-9

CM LIBRARY OF THE HEALTH SCIENCES, URBANA, 102 Medical Sciences Bldg, MC-714, 506 S Mathews Ave, Urbana, 61801, SAN 340-8604. Tel: 217-333-4893. Reference Tel: 217-244-0607. FAX: 217-333-9559. E-mail: lib-lhsu@uic.edu. *Regional Head Librn,* Ryan Rafferty; Tel: 217-244-2261, E-mail: rraffe2@uic.edu
Open Mon-Thurs 7:30am-10pm, Fri 8:30-8, Sat & Sun Noon-4

C VANDERCOOK COLLEGE OF MUSIC*, Harry Ruppel Memorial Library, 3140 S Federal St, 60616-3731. SAN 304-050X. Tel: 312-225-6288, Ext 260. FAX: 312-225-5211. Web Site: www.vandercook.edu/library. *Archivist, Head Librn,* Rob DeLand; E-mail: rdeland@vandercook.edu. Subject Specialists: *Music,* Rob DeLand; Staff 1 (MLS 1)
Founded 1967. Enrl 150; Fac 25; Highest Degree: Master
Library Holdings: AV Mats 46; CDs 255; Music Scores 225; Bk Vols 332; Per Subs 186
Special Collections: H E Nutt Archives; Rare Book Coll; Ruth Artman Coll
Subject Interests: Educ, Music, Music educ, Psychol
Automation Activity & Vendor Info: (Acquisitions) SirsiDynix; (Cataloging) SirsiDynix; (Circulation) SirsiDynix; (Course Reserve) SirsiDynix; (ILL) OCLC FirstSearch; (OPAC) SirsiDynix; (Serials) SirsiDynix
Wireless access
Function: Res libr
Mem of Reaching Across Illinois Library System (RAILS)
Partic in Consortium of Academic & Research Libraries in Illinois
Open Mon-Thurs 10-10, Fri 9-5
Restriction: Borrowing privileges limited to fac & registered students, Open to pub upon request, Photo ID required for access

L VEDDER, PRICE*, Law Library, 222 N LaSalle, 60601. SAN 304-0518. Tel: 312-609-7500. FAX: 312-609-5005. Web Site: www.vedderprice.com. *Librn,* Deborah Abram
Founded 1952
Library Holdings: Bk Vols 20,000
Subject Interests: Corporate law

L WINSTON & STRAWN LLP LIBRARY*, 35 W Wacker Dr, 60601. SAN 372-3089. Tel: 312-558-5600. FAX: 312-558-5700. E-mail: library@winston.com. Web Site: www.winston.com. *Dir, Libr Serv,* Gwen Watson; Tel: 312-282-5404, E-mail: gwatson@winston.com
Wireless access
Restriction: Lending libr only via mail, Not open to pub

S WORLD BOOK PUBLISHING*, Research Library, 180 N LaSalle St, Ste 900, 60601. SAN 304-0577. Tel: 312-819-8977. FAX: 312-729-5612. Web Site: www.worldbook.com. *Dir,* Scott Richardson; E-mail: srichardson@worldbook.com; Staff 2 (MLS 1, Non-MLS 1)
Founded 1920
Library Holdings: Bk Vols 16,000; Per Subs 100
Special Collections: Archives of Company Products
Automation Activity & Vendor Info: (Acquisitions) EOS International; (Cataloging) EOS International; (Circulation) EOS International; (OPAC) EOS International; (Serials) EOS International
Publications: Quartley Accessions List
Partic in Illinois Library & Information Network; OCLC Online Computer Library Center, Inc

CHICAGO HEIGHTS

P CHICAGO HEIGHTS PUBLIC LIBRARY*, 25 W 15th St, 60411-3488. SAN 304-0585. Tel: 708-754-0323. FAX: 708-754-0325. E-mail: chs@chicagoheightslibrary.org. Web Site: www.chicagoheightslibrary.org. *Prog Dir,* Kelley Nichols; E-mail: nicholsk@chicagoheightslibrary.org; *Head, Adult Serv,* Jennifer Martin; E-mail: martinj@chicagoheightslibrary.org; Staff 21 (MLS 5, Non-MLS 16)
Founded 1901. Pop 32,776; Circ 120,534
Library Holdings: Bk Vols 132,681; Per Subs 294
Subject Interests: Local hist, Spanish (Lang)
Wireless access
Publications: Newsletter
Mem of Reaching Across Illinois Library System (RAILS)
Partic in System Wide Automated Network
Open Mon-Thurs 10-8, Fri 10-5, Sat 10-4, Sun (Sept-June) 1-5
Friends of the Library Group

J PRAIRIE STATE COLLEGE LIBRARY*, 202 S Halsted St, 60411-8200. SAN 304-0593. Tel: 708-709-3552. Interlibrary Loan Service Tel: 708-709-3553. Reference Tel: 708-709-7948. FAX: 708-709-3940. E-mail: librarians@prairiestate.edu. Web Site: library.prairiestate.edu. *Dean, Learning Resources & Assessment,* Carolyn Ciesla; E-mail: cciesla@prairiestate.edu; *Coll Mgt Librn,* Thane Montaner; E-mail: tmontaner@prairiestate.edu; *Col Archivist, ILL Librn,* Alex Altan; E-mail: aallan@prairiestate.edu; *Ref & Instruction Librn,* William Condon; E-mail: wcondon@prairiestate.edu; *Tech Asst,* April Madden; E-mail: amadden@prairiestate.edu; Staff 13 (MLS 6, Non-MLS 7)
Founded 1958. Enrl 9,000; Highest Degree: Associate
Jul 2013-Jun 2014 Income $579,000. Mats Exp $106,400, Books $32,000, Per/Ser (Incl. Access Fees) $30,000, AV Mat $4,000, Electronic Ref Mat (Incl. Access Fees) $40,000, Presv $400. Sal $475,000 (Prof $255,000)
Library Holdings: AV Mats 75; CDs 10; DVDs 25; Bk Titles 34,100; Bk Vols 40,000; Videos 2,010
Subject Interests: Communications, Dental, Nursing, Photog
Automation Activity & Vendor Info: (Acquisitions) Innovative Interfaces, Inc; (Cataloging) Innovative Interfaces, Inc; (Circulation) Innovative Interfaces, Inc; (ILL) OCLC Online; (OPAC) Innovative Interfaces, Inc; (Serials) Innovative Interfaces, Inc
Wireless access
Function: ILL available, Ref serv available
Mem of Reaching Across Illinois Library System (RAILS)
Partic in Consortium of Academic & Research Libraries in Illinois; Network of Illinois Learning Resources in Community Colleges; Northern Illinois Learning Resources Cooperative; System Wide Automated Network
Special Services for the Deaf - Assistive tech; Staff with knowledge of sign lang
Special Services for the Blind - Assistive/Adapted tech devices, equip & products
Open Mon-Thurs 8-8, Fri 8-4:30
Restriction: Open to pub for ref & circ; with some limitations, Open to students, fac & staff

CHICAGO RIDGE

P CHICAGO RIDGE PUBLIC LIBRARY*, 10400 S Oxford Ave, 60415. SAN 304-0615. Tel: 708-423-7753. FAX: 708-423-2758. E-mail: refdesk@chicagoridgelibrary.org. Web Site: chicagoridgelibrary.org. *Libr Dir,* Dana Wishnick; E-mail: dwishnick@chicagoridgelibrary.org; *Admin Mgr,* Brittany Luna; E-mail: bluna@chicagoridgelibrary.org; *Adult Serv Mgr,* Alicia Jackson; E-mail: ajackson@chicagoridgelibrary.org; *Youth Serv Mgr,* Irene Ciciora; E-mail: iciciora@chicagoridgelibrary.org; Staff 19 (MLS 5, Non-MLS 14)
Founded 1966. Pop 14,127; Circ 128,465
Library Holdings: Bk Titles 73,084; Per Subs 456
Automation Activity & Vendor Info: (Acquisitions) Innovative Interfaces, Inc; (Cataloging) Innovative Interfaces, Inc; (Circulation) Innovative Interfaces, Inc
Wireless access
Publications: CR Library Lines (Newsletter)
Mem of Reaching Across Illinois Library System (RAILS)
Partic in System Wide Automated Network
Open Mon-Thurs 11-8, Fri & Sat 11-4
Friends of the Library Group

CHILLICOTHE

P CHILLICOTHE PUBLIC LIBRARY DISTRICT*, 430 N Bradley Ave, 61523-1920. SAN 304-0623. Tel: 309-274-2719. FAX: 309-274-3000. E-mail: ask@chillipld.org. Web Site: www.chillicothepubliclibrary.org. *Libr Dir,* Mary Aylmer; E-mail: maylmer@chillipld.org; *Acq Librn, Tech Serv Librn,* Genevieve Crotz; E-mail: gcrotz@chillipld.org; *ILL/Tech Serv Librn,*

Megan Greenhalgh; E-mail: mgreenhalgh@chillipld.org; *Youth Librn,* Gail Hintz; E-mail: ghintze@chillipld.org; *Adult Serv, YA Serv,* Catherine Barnett; E-mail: cbarnett@chillipld.org; *Circ,* Lisa Jeffries; E-mail: ljeffries@chillipld.org; *Pub Serv, Ref,* Alexander Jeffries; E-mail: ajeffries@chillipld.org; Staff 6 (MLS 1, Non-MLS 5)
Founded 1916. Pop 13,250; Circ 86,000
Library Holdings: AV Mats 4,600; Bks on Deafness & Sign Lang 120; CDs 1,100; DVDs 250; Electronic Media & Resources 100; High Interest/Low Vocabulary Bk Vols 350; Large Print Bks 1,500; Music Scores 25; Bk Titles 33,500; Bk Vols 37,900; Per Subs 120; Spec Interest Per Sub 25; Talking Bks 10; Videos 600
Special Collections: Chillicothe Times-Bulletins, 1883-present; High School Yearbooks, 1918-present
Subject Interests: Local hist
Automation Activity & Vendor Info: (Cataloging) TLC (The Library Corporation); (Circulation) TLC (The Library Corporation); (OPAC) TLC (The Library Corporation)
Function: Adult bk club, Archival coll, Art exhibits, Audiobks via web, Bi-weekly Writer's Group, Bk club(s), Bks on CD, Children's prog, Citizenship assistance, Computer training, Computers for patron use, Digital talking bks, Free DVD rentals, Holiday prog, Home delivery & serv to seniorr ctr & nursing homes, Homebound delivery serv, ILL available, Internet access, Magnifiers for reading, Mail & tel request accepted, Music CDs, Notary serv, Outside serv via phone, mail, e-mail & web, OverDrive digital audio bks, Photocopying/Printing, Prog for adults, Prog for children & young adult, Ref serv available, Scanner, Senior computer classes, Story hour, Summer reading prog, Teen prog, Wheelchair accessible, Writing prog
Partic in Resource Sharing Alliance
Special Services for the Deaf - Staff with knowledge of sign lang
Special Services for the Blind - Accessible computers; Audio mat; Bks available with recordings; Bks on CD; Braille alphabet card; Cassette playback machines; Copier with enlargement capabilities; Extensive large print coll; Home delivery serv; Large print bks; Large screen computer & software; Lending of low vision aids; Magnifiers; Playaways (bks on MP3); Sound rec; Talking bks; Talking bks & player equip
Open Mon-Thurs 7:30am-8pm, Fri 7:30-6, Sat 9-5, Sun Noon-5

CHRISMAN

P CHRISMAN PUBLIC LIBRARY*, 108 N Illinois St, 61924. SAN 304-0631. Tel: 217-269-3011. FAX: 217-269-3011. E-mail: chrismanlib@midwestfirst.com. *Dir,* Paula Daily; *Librn,* Mary E Galway
Founded 1932. Pop 1,318
Library Holdings: Audiobooks 60; CDs 145; DVDs 51; Bk Vols 10,123; Per Subs 37; Videos 982
Automation Activity & Vendor Info: (Cataloging) SirsiDynix; (Circulation) SirsiDynix
Mem of Illinois Heartland Library System
Open Mon, Tues & Fri 1-5:30, Wed & Thurs 1-7

CHRISTOPHER

P CHRISTOPHER PUBLIC LIBRARY*, 202 E Market St, 62822-1759. (Mail add: PO Box 131, 62822-0131), SAN 304-064X. Tel: 618-724-7534. E-mail: christopherlibrary@gmail.com. Web Site: www.cityofchristopher.org/library.html. *Dir, Librn,* Janice Briley
Pop 2,836; Circ 18,117
Library Holdings: Bk Vols 19,200; Per Subs 10
Mem of Illinois Heartland Library System
Open Mon-Fri 12-6, Sat 9-3

CICERO

P CICERO PUBLIC LIBRARY*, 5225 W Cermak Rd, 60804. SAN 304-0658. Tel: 708-652-8084. FAX: 708-652-8095. Web Site: www.cicerolibrary.org. *Dir,* Sandra Tomschin; E-mail: stomschin@cicerolibrary.org; *Head, Acq,* Cheryl Ida; E-mail: cida@cicerolibrary.org; *Head, Circ,* Francisco Cruz; E-mail: fcruz@cicerolibrary.org; *Head, Ref,* Patricia Conroy; E-mail: pconroy@cicerolibrary.org; *Head, Youth Serv,* Colleen Gnat; E-mail: cgnat@cicerolibrary.org; Staff 33 (MLS 5, Non-MLS 28)
Founded 1921. Pop 85,616; Circ 219,688
Library Holdings: Bk Vols 111,770; Per Subs 465; Spec Interest Per Sub 12
Subject Interests: Polish (Lang), Spanish (Lang)
Wireless access
Publications: Cicero Public Library News (Newsletter)
Mem of Reaching Across Illinois Library System (RAILS)
Partic in System Wide Automated Network
Special Services for the Blind - Recorded bks
Open Mon-Thurs 9-9, Fri 9-7, Sat 10-5, Sun 12-5

J MORTON COLLEGE LIBRARY*, 3801 S Central Ave, 60804. SAN 304-0666. Tel: 708-656-8000, Ext 2321. Reference Tel: 708-656-8000, Ext 429. Administration Tel: 708-656-8000, Ext 320. FAX: 708-656-3297. Reference E-mail: reference@morton.edu. Web Site: www.morton.edu/mclibrary. *Libr Dir, Mus Dir,* Jennifer Butler; Tel: 708-656-8000, Ext 2322, E-mail: jennifer.butler@morton.edu; *Circ Librn,* Thomas Mantzakides; E-mail: thomas.mantzakides@morton.edu; *Ref Librn,* Michael Andersen; E-mail: michael.andersen@morton.edu; *Tech Librn,* Heidi Lundquist; E-mail: heidi.lundquist@morton.edu; Staff 9 (MLS 3, Non-MLS 6)
Founded 1924. Enrl 5,244; Fac 263; Highest Degree: Associate
Library Holdings: AV Mats 3,130; Bks on Deafness & Sign Lang 12; High Interest/Low Vocabulary Bk Vols 850; Per Subs 120
Special Collections: Adult New Readers
Subject Interests: Compact discs, Spanish (Lang)
Automation Activity & Vendor Info: (Circulation) Innovative Interfaces, Inc; (ILL) OCLC; (OPAC) Innovative Interfaces, Inc
Mem of Reaching Across Illinois Library System (RAILS)
Partic in Consortium of Academic & Research Libraries in Illinois; Innopac; Network of Illinois Learning Resources in Community Colleges; Proquest Dialog
Open Mon-Thurs 8-7

CISCO

P WILLOW BRANCH TOWNSHIP LIBRARY, 330 N Eldon St, 61830. (Mail add: PO Box 39, 61830), SAN 304-0674. Tel: 217-669-2312. FAX: 217-669-2312. E-mail: willow.branch@hotmail.com. *Dir,* Kelly Frydenger
Pop 829; Circ 4,900
Library Holdings: Bk Vols 5,877; Per Subs 8
Special Collections: Biographies; Classics; Juvenile Fiction & Nonfiction; Westerns
Automation Activity & Vendor Info: (Acquisitions) Innovative Interfaces, Inc; (Cataloging) Innovative Interfaces, Inc; (Circulation) Innovative Interfaces, Inc; (Course Reserve) Innovative Interfaces, Inc; (ILL) Innovative Interfaces, Inc; (Media Booking) Innovative Interfaces, Inc; (OPAC) Innovative Interfaces, Inc; (Serials) Innovative Interfaces, Inc
Wireless access
Mem of Illinois Heartland Library System
Open Mon & Wed 1-8, Tues 10:30-3:30, Fri 1-5, Sat 9-12

CISSNA PARK

P CISSNA PARK COMMUNITY LIBRARY DISTRICT*, 511 N Second St, 60924. SAN 376-1304. Tel: 815-457-2452. FAX: 815-457-3033. Web Site: www.cissnaparklibrary.com. *Librn,* Donna Jean; E-mail: donna.jean@cpschool.org
Founded 1991. Pop 1,806; Circ 32,100
Library Holdings: Bk Titles 36,000; Per Subs 30
Subject Interests: Christian fiction
Mem of Illinois Heartland Library System
Open Mon, Wed & Fri 8-3:45, Tues & Thurs 8-8, Sat 8-2 (Winter); Tues & Thurs 8-6, Wed, Fri & Sat 8-2 (Summer)

CLARENDON HILLS

P CLARENDON HILLS PUBLIC LIBRARY*, Seven N Prospect Ave, 60514. SAN 304-0682. Tel: 630-323-8188. FAX: 630-323-8189. E-mail: info@clarendonhillslibrary.org. Web Site: www.clarendonhillslibrary.org. *Dir,* Lori Craft; E-mail: craftl@clarendonhillslibrary.org; *Adult Serv,* Crissy Barnat; E-mail: barnatc@clarendonhillslibrary.org; *Ch Serv,* Krista Devlin; E-mail: devlink@clarendonhillslibrary.org; *ILL, Ref (Info Servs),* Kathleen Strange; E-mail: strange@clarendonhillslibrary.org; Staff 6 (MLS 3, Non-MLS 3)
Founded 1963. Pop 8,427; Circ 88,123
Library Holdings: AV Mats 1,439; DVDs 3,500; Large Print Bks 253; Bk Titles 48,153; Bk Vols 51,176; Per Subs 146
Subject Interests: Local hist, Travel
Automation Activity & Vendor Info: (Circulation) Innovative Interfaces, Inc
Wireless access
Mem of Reaching Across Illinois Library System (RAILS)
Partic in System Wide Automated Network
Open Mon, Tues & Thurs 9:30-9, Wed & Fri 9:30-5, Sat 9:30-4
Friends of the Library Group

CLAYTON

P CLAYTON PUBLIC LIBRARY DISTRICT*, 211 E Main St, 62324. SAN 304-0690. Tel: 217-894-6519. FAX: 217-894-6519. E-mail: claypld@adams.net. Web Site: www.claytonlibrary.net. *Librn,* Julie Parker
Founded 1943. Pop 1,553
Library Holdings: Bk Vols 10,000; Per Subs 6; Talking Bks 25,000
Wireless access
Open Tues, Wed & Thurs 12:30-6, Fri 9:30-3, Sat 9-12

CLIFTON

P CENTRAL CITIZENS' LIBRARY DISTRICT*, 1134 E 3100 North Rd, Ste C, 60927-7088. Tel: 815-694-2400, 815-694-2800. FAX: 815-694-3200. Web Site: www.ccld.org. *Libr Dir,* Connie Hitchens; E-mail: chitchens@cusd4.org; Staff 2 (MLS 2)
Founded 1995. Pop 5,057; Circ 43,659
Library Holdings: Bk Vols 25,720; Per Subs 85
Automation Activity & Vendor Info: (Cataloging) SirsiDynix; (Circulation) SirsiDynix; (OPAC) SirsiDynix
Mem of Illinois Heartland Library System
Open Mon-Thurs 8-8, Fri 8-4, Sat 9-1; Tues & Wed (Summer) 9-5:30, Thurs 9-8, Fri & Sat 9-2
Friends of the Library Group

P CLIFTON PUBLIC LIBRARY*, 150 E Fourth Ave, 60927. (Mail add: PO Box 452, 60927-0452). Tel: 815-694-2069. FAX: 815-694-2069. E-mail: cliftonpubliclibil@gmail.com. Web Site: www.cliftonpubliclibil.org. *Dir,* Lori Lamping; Staff 1.3 (Non-MLS 1.3)
Founded 1903. Pop 1,317
Library Holdings: DVDs 400; Large Print Bks 60; Bk Titles 7,000; Per Subs 52
Wireless access
Function: Computers for patron use, Digital talking bks, Electronic databases & coll, Internet access, Online ref, Photocopying/Printing, Prog for adults, Prog for children & young adult, Ref & res, Scanner, VHS videos
Open Mon & Wed-Fri 2-7, Tues 10-12 & 2-5, Sat 9-Noon

CLINTON

P VESPASIAN WARNER PUBLIC LIBRARY DISTRICT, 310 N Quincy, 61727. SAN 304-0704. Tel: 217-935-5174. FAX: 217-935-4425. E-mail: library@vwarner.org. Web Site: www.vwarner.org. *Exec Dir,* Ms Bobbi Perryman; E-mail: perryman@vwarner.org; *Bus Mgr,* Samantha Rusk; E-mail: rusk@vwarner.org; *Youth Serv Mgr,* Corey Campbell; E-mail: campbell@vwarner.org
Founded 1901. Pop 10,250; Circ 107,000
Library Holdings: Bk Vols 80,000; Per Subs 200
Special Collections: Early Illinois History & Geography (C H Moore Coll). US Document Depository
Automation Activity & Vendor Info: (Circulation) SirsiDynix
Wireless access
Mem of Illinois Heartland Library System
Open Mon-Thurs 9-7, Fri & Sat 9-4
Friends of the Library Group

COAL CITY

P COAL CITY PUBLIC LIBRARY DISTRICT*, 85 N Garfield St, 60416. SAN 304-0712. Tel: 815-634-4552. FAX: 815-634-2950. E-mail: ccpld@ccpld.org. Web Site: www.ccpld.org. *Libr Dir,* Jolene Franciskovich; E-mail: jolene@ccpld.org; *Asst Dir,* Leah Bill; E-mail: leah@ccpld.org; *Head, Adult Serv,* Dana Abraham; Tel: 815-634-4552, E-mail: dana@ccpld.org; *Head, Circ,* Heather Banks; E-mail: heather@ccpld.org; *Head, Ref,* Bryan Gilligan; E-mail: Bryan@ccpld.org; *Head, Youth Serv,* Rene Norris; E-mail: rene@ccpld.org; *Communications Coordr,* Cindy Starks; E-mail: cindy@ccpld.org; Staff 9 (MLS 1, Non-MLS 8)
Founded 1886. Pop 11,257; Circ 103,536
Jul 2019-Jun 2020 Income $1,354,278, Locally Generated Income $1,332,012, Other $22,266. Mats Exp $75,625, Per/Ser (Incl. Access Fees) $4,479, AV Mat $11,550, Electronic Ref Mat (Incl. Access Fees) $59,596. Sal $668,967 (Prof $469,418)
Library Holdings: Audiobooks 3,417; DVDs 6,417; e-books 488,210; Electronic Media & Resources 13,889
Automation Activity & Vendor Info: (Cataloging) Innovative Interfaces, Inc; (Circulation) Innovative Interfaces, Inc; (OPAC) Innovative Interfaces, Inc
Wireless access
Function: 24/7 Electronic res, 24/7 Online cat, Adult bk club, After school storytime, Art exhibits, Art programs, Audiobks on Playaways & MP3, Audiobks via web, Bk club(s), Bks on CD, Children's prog, Computer training, Computers for patron use, Electronic databases & coll, Free DVD rentals, Holiday prog, Homebound delivery serv, Homework prog, ILL available, Internet access, Laminating, Life-long learning prog for all ages, Magazines, Mail & tel request accepted, Meeting rooms, Microfiche/film & reading machines, Museum passes, Music CDs, Notary serv, Online cat, Online ref, Outreach serv, OverDrive digital audio bks, Passport agency, Photocopying/Printing, Preschool outreach, Preschool reading prog, Printer for laptops & handheld devices, Prog for adults, Prog for children & young adult, Ref serv available, Scanner, Senior computer classes, Senior outreach, STEM programs, Story hour, Summer & winter reading prog, Summer reading prog, Tax forms, Teen prog, Telephone ref, VHS videos, Wheelchair accessible, Winter reading prog
Mem of Reaching Across Illinois Library System (RAILS)
Open Mon-Thurs 9-8, Fri 9-6, Sat 9-4

COAL VALLEY

P ROBERT R JONES PUBLIC LIBRARY*, 900 First St, 61240. (Mail add: PO Box 190, 61240-0190), SAN 304-0720. Tel: 309-799-3047. FAX: 309-799-5528. Web Site: robertrjoneslibrary.org. *Dir,* Jeffrey Stafford; E-mail: jstaf@coalval.lib.il.us
Founded 1967. Pop 4,955; Circ 34,699
Library Holdings: AV Mats 2,211; Bks on Deafness & Sign Lang 10; Large Print Bks 127; Bk Titles 34,194; Per Subs 150
Subject Interests: Coal mining, Coal Valley hist
Automation Activity & Vendor Info: (Circulation) Innovative Interfaces, Inc; (ILL) Innovative Interfaces, Inc; (OPAC) Innovative Interfaces, Inc
Wireless access
Mem of Reaching Across Illinois Library System (RAILS)
Partic in Illinois Library & Information Network; Quad-Link Libr Consortium; RiverShare Libraries
Open Mon-Thurs 10-8, Fri 10-6, Sat 10-3
Friends of the Library Group

COLCHESTER

P COLCHESTER DISTRICT LIBRARY*, 203 Macomb St, 62326. (Mail add: PO Box 237, 62326-0237), SAN 304-0739. Tel: 309-776-4861. FAX: 309-776-4099. E-mail: colchesterlibrary@yahoo.com. Web Site: colchesterlibrary.com. *Dir,* Debbie Sullivan; *Circ Librn,* Waynette Caldwell
Pop 1,645; Circ 12,191
Library Holdings: AV Mats 150; Large Print Bks 200; Bk Vols 11,000; Per Subs 68; Talking Bks 20
Wireless access
Function: ILL available
Mem of Reaching Across Illinois Library System (RAILS)
Open Mon 1-6:45, Wed 9-6:45, Fri 1-5, Sat 9-1

COLFAX

P MARTIN TOWNSHIP PUBLIC LIBRARY*, 132 W Main St, 61728. (Mail add: PO Box 376, 61728-0376), SAN 304-0747. Tel: 309-723-2541. FAX: 309-723-5037. E-mail: martintpl.43@gmail.com. Web Site: www.martintpl.com. *Libr Dir,* Joyce Carmack
Founded 1943. Pop 1,289; Circ 5,000
Library Holdings: Bk Vols 14,000; Per Subs 30
Special Collections: Colfax Press Coll (1896-1992), micro; Cooksville Interprise Coll (1879-1921), micro; Octavia Yearbooks 1940 to 1982; Ridgeview Review (1992-2013), micro
Automation Activity & Vendor Info: (Cataloging) SirsiDynix-WorkFlows; (Circulation) SirsiDynix-WorkFlows; (ILL) OCLC WorldShare Interlibrary Loan
Wireless access
Function: Computers for patron use, Free DVD rentals, ILL available, Photocopying/Printing, Summer reading prog, Tax forms, Wheelchair accessible
Mem of Reaching Across Illinois Library System (RAILS)
Partic in Resource Sharing Alliance
Special Services for the Blind - Large print bks
Open Mon & Fri 1-5, Tues 9-5, Wed 1-8, Sat 9-12

COLLINSVILLE

S ILLINOIS DEPARTMENT OF NATURAL RESOURCES*, Cahokia Mounds State Historic Site Library, 30 Ramey St, 62234. SAN 374-759X. Tel: 618-346-5160. FAX: 618-346-5162. E-mail: cahokia.mounds@sbcglobal.net. Web Site: cahokiamounds.org. *Mgr,* Lori Belknap
Library Holdings: Bk Vols 2,000
Subject Interests: Anthrop, Archaeology, Natural hist
Mem of Illinois Heartland Library System
Open Wed-Sun 9-5
Restriction: Internal circ only

P MISSISSIPPI VALLEY LIBRARY DISTRICT*, Collinsville Memorial Library Center, 408 W Main St, 62234. SAN 304-0755. Tel: 618-344-1112. FAX: 618-345-6401. Web Site: www.collinsvillelibrary.org. *Interim Dir,* Kyla Waltermire; E-mail: kylaw@mvlibdist.org; *ILL Supvr, Supvr, Genealogy Serv,* Leslee Hamilton; *Circ Supvr,* Theresa Beck
Founded 1915. Pop 24,707; Circ 250,756
Library Holdings: AV Mats 4,500; e-books 7,100; Large Print Bks 500; Bk Vols 65,000; Per Subs 250
Subject Interests: Programs
Automation Activity & Vendor Info: (Acquisitions) Innovative Interfaces, Inc; (Cataloging) Innovative Interfaces, Inc; (Circulation) Innovative Interfaces, Inc
Wireless access
Mem of Illinois Heartland Library System

Open Mon-Thurs 9-8, Fri & Sat 9-5, Sun 1-5
Friends of the Library Group
Branches: 1
FAIRMONT CITY LIBRARY CENTER, 4444 Collinsville Rd, Fairmont City, 62201. Tel: 618-482-3966. FAX: 618-482-4058. *Mgr,* Katie Heaton; E-mail: katieh@mvlibdist.org
Open Mon & Wed 10-6, Tues & Thurs 2-6, Fri & Sat 9-5

S SOUTHWESTERN ILLINOIS METROPOLITAN & REGIONAL PLANNING, Technical Library, 2511 Vandalia St, 62234. SAN 326-9558. Tel: 618-344-4250. FAX: 618-344-4253. *Library Contact,* Kevin Terveer; Tel: 618-344-4250, Ext 119, E-mail: kterveer@simapc.com
Publications: Grants & Miscellaneous Municality
Open Mon-Fri 9-5

COLONA

P COLONA DISTRICT PUBLIC LIBRARY*, 911 First St, 61241. SAN 304-2405. Tel: 309-792-0548. FAX: 309-792-2143. E-mail: contact@colonalibrary.com. Web Site: colonalibrary.com. *Dir,* Sarah Alexander, PhD; Staff 8 (Non-MLS 8)
Founded 1972. Pop 6,699; Circ 39,956
Library Holdings: Audiobooks 636; DVDs 2,168; e-books 38,472; Large Print Bks 911; Bk Vols 22,560; Per Subs 23
Subject Interests: Local hist
Wireless access
Function: 24/7 Electronic res, 24/7 Online cat, After school storytime, Audiobks on Playaways & MP3, Audiobks via web, Bks on CD, Children's prog, Computers for patron use, Digital talking bks, Free DVD rentals, ILL available, Internet access, Large print keyboards, Magazines, Meeting rooms, Museum passes, Online cat, OverDrive digital audio bks, Photocopying/Printing, Preschool outreach, Prog for adults, Prog for children & young adult, Scanner, Story hour, Summer reading prog, Tax forms, Wheelchair accessible
Publications: Colona Library Link (Newsletter)
Mem of Reaching Across Illinois Library System (RAILS)
Special Services for the Blind - Talking bks
Open Mon-Fri 10-8, Sat 10-3
Friends of the Library Group

COLUMBIA

P COLUMBIA PUBLIC LIBRARY, 106 N Metter Ave, 62236-2299. SAN 304-0771. Tel: 618-281-4237. FAX: 618-281-6977. E-mail: reference@columbialibrary.org. Web Site: www.columbialibrary.org. *Libr Dir,* Annette Bland; E-mail: annettebland@columbialibrary.org; *Asst Dir, Commun Engagement Librn,* Crystal Snyder; *Cataloger,* Anna Ripplinger; E-mail: annahesterberg@columbialibrary.org; Staff 10 (MLS 2, Non-MLS 8)
Founded 1958. Pop 9,070; Circ 53,354
Subject Interests: Genealogy, Local hist
Automation Activity & Vendor Info: (Circulation) Innovative Interfaces, Inc; (ILL) OCLC WorldShare Interlibrary Loan; (OPAC) Innovative Interfaces, Inc
Wireless access
Function: 24/7 Electronic res, 24/7 Online cat, Activity rm, Archival coll, Audiobks via web, Bks on CD, Children's prog, Computers for patron use, Electronic databases & coll, Family literacy, Free DVD rentals, Holiday prog, ILL available, Instruction & testing, Internet access, Laminating, Magazines, Mail & tel request accepted, Movies, Music CDs, Online cat, Online ref, Outreach serv, Outside serv via phone, mail, e-mail & web, OverDrive digital audio bks, Photocopying/Printing, Preschool reading prog, Prog for adults, Prog for children & young adult, Ref & res, Ref serv available, Scanner, Story hour, Summer reading prog, Tax forms, Teen prog, Telephone ref, Wheelchair accessible, Workshops
Mem of Illinois Heartland Library System
Special Services for the Blind - Extensive large print coll; Large print bks; Talking bk serv referral
Open Mon-Thurs 9-8, Fri 9-4, Sat 9-3
Friends of the Library Group

CORDOVA

P CORDOVA DISTRICT LIBRARY*, 402 Main Ave, 61242. SAN 304-078X. Tel: 309-654-2330. FAX: 309-654-2290. E-mail: cordovalibrary@gmail.com. Web Site: www.cordovalibrary.com. *Dir,* Karen Lonergan; *Librn, Mkt,* Chalyn Fornero-Green; *Tech Serv,* Colette Saathoff; Staff 2 (Non-MLS 2)
Founded 1876. Pop 1,031; Circ 31,625
Library Holdings: Bk Vols 15,000; Per Subs 35
Subject Interests: Miss river
Automation Activity & Vendor Info: (Cataloging) Infor Library & Information Solutions; (Circulation) Infor Library & Information Solutions; (OPAC) Infor Library & Information Solutions
Wireless access
Mem of Reaching Across Illinois Library System (RAILS)
Open Mon & Wed 9-8, Tues & Thurs 1-8, Fri 9-5, Sat 9-1

CORNELL

P AMITY TOWNSHIP PUBLIC LIBRARY*, 604 E Main St, 61319. (Mail add: PO Box 273, 61319-0273), SAN 376-1355. Tel: 815-358-2231, 815-510-0406. *Library Contact,* Sandra Knight
Founded 1981
Library Holdings: Bk Titles 6,000; Per Subs 2
Open Mon & Wed 3-5, Tues 5-7, Thurs 2-4, Sat 10-12

CORTLAND

P CORTLAND COMMUNITY LIBRARY*, 63 S Somonauk Rd, 60112. (Mail add: PO Box 486, 60112-0486). Tel: 815-756-7274. FAX: 815-748-4491. Circulation E-mail: circ@cortlandlibrary.com. Web Site: www.cortlandlibrary.com. *Dir,* Barb Coward; *Asst Libr Dir,* Heather Black
Library Holdings: Bk Titles 23,500; Per Subs 65
Automation Activity & Vendor Info: (Acquisitions) SirsiDynix-iBistro; (Cataloging) SirsiDynix-WorkFlows; (Circulation) SirsiDynix-WorkFlows; (Course Reserve) SirsiDynix-iBistro; (ILL) SirsiDynix-iBistro; (Media Booking) SirsiDynix-iBistro; (OPAC) SirsiDynix-iBistro; (Serials) SirsiDynix-WorkFlows
Wireless access
Mem of Reaching Across Illinois Library System (RAILS)
Special Services for the Blind - Scanner for conversion & translation of mats
Open Mon & Thurs 9-9, Fri & Sat 9-5
Friends of the Library Group

COULTERVILLE

P COULTERVILLE PUBLIC LIBRARY*, 103 S Fourth St, 62237. (Mail add: PO Box 373, 62237-0373), SAN 304-0798. Tel: 618-758-3013. FAX: 618-758-3013. E-mail: coultervillepubliclibrary@gmail.com. Web Site: coultervillelibrary.weebly.com, coultervillepl.org. *Librn,* Jennifer Grafton; *Librn,* Tammy Rieckenberg
Founded 1936. Pop 1,118; Circ 15,951
Library Holdings: Bk Vols 9,173
Special Collections: Education; Genealogy; History; Religion
Wireless access
Mem of Illinois Heartland Library System
Open Mon & Fri 10-3, Tues & Thurs 1-6, Sat 10-2

COWDEN

P DRY POINT TOWNSHIP LIBRARY, S Rte 128, 62422. (Mail add: PO Box 44, 62422-0044), SAN 376-1479. Tel: 217-783-2616. E-mail: drypointtownshiplibrary@yahoo.com. Web Site: cowden-herrick.k12.il.us/elem/Cowdenpl. *Librn,* Charlene Taylor
Founded 1972
Library Holdings: Bk Titles 15,250; Per Subs 15
Automation Activity & Vendor Info: (Cataloging) Innovative Interfaces, Inc. - Polaris; (Circulation) Innovative Interfaces, Inc. - Polaris
Mem of Illinois Heartland Library System
Open Mon & Thurs 2-8, Sat 8-12
Friends of the Library Group

CRESTON

P CRESTON-DEMENT PUBLIC LIBRARY DISTRICT, 107 S Main St, 60113-0056. (Mail add: PO Box 193, 60113-0193). Tel: 815-384-3111. E-mail: crestondementlibrary@gmail.com. Web Site: crestonlib.org. *Dir,* Kristi Scherer; E-mail: kscherer.crestonlib@gmail.com
Founded 1986. Pop 794
Library Holdings: Audiobooks 474; CDs 3; DVDs 800; Large Print Bks 106; Bk Titles 15,000; Per Subs 10
Wireless access
Function: 24/7 Electronic res, 24/7 Online cat, Accelerated reader prog, Adult bk club, ILL available
Mem of Reaching Across Illinois Library System (RAILS)
Open Mon 12-5, Tues-Thurs 10-6, Fri 9-5, Sat 9-2
Friends of the Library Group

CRESTWOOD

P CRESTWOOD PUBLIC LIBRARY DISTRICT*, 4955 W 135th St, 60418. SAN 304-0801. Tel: 708-371-4090. FAX: 708-371-4127. E-mail: cws@crestwoodlibrary.org. Web Site: www.crestwoodlibrary.org. *Dir,* Dan Powers
Founded 1973. Circ 36,640
Library Holdings: Bk Vols 50,000; Per Subs 100
Automation Activity & Vendor Info: (Cataloging) Innovative Interfaces, Inc; (Circulation) Innovative Interfaces, Inc; (OPAC) Innovative Interfaces, Inc

Wireless access
Mem of Reaching Across Illinois Library System (RAILS)
Partic in System Wide Automated Network
Open Mon-Thurs 10-8, Fri & Sat 10-4

CRETE

P CRETE PUBLIC LIBRARY DISTRICT*, 1177 N Main St, 60417. SAN 304-081X. Tel: 708-672-8017. FAX: 708-672-3529. E-mail: info@cretelibrary.org. Web Site: www.cretelibrary.org. *Exec Dir,* Susan Dienes; E-mail: sdienes@cretelibrary.org; *Adult & Teen Serv Mgr, Asst Dir,* Tiffany Amschl; E-mail: tamschl@cretelibrary.org; Staff 21 (MLS 3, Non-MLS 18)
Founded 1985. Pop 19,500; Circ 124,000
Library Holdings: AV Mats 2,400; Bk Titles 61,000; Per Subs 197; Talking Bks 300
Special Collections: Caregiver Resource Center
Subject Interests: Antiques, Collectibles
Automation Activity & Vendor Info: (Acquisitions) Innovative Interfaces, Inc; (Cataloging) Innovative Interfaces, Inc; (Course Reserve) Innovative Interfaces, Inc
Wireless access
Mem of Reaching Across Illinois Library System (RAILS)
Partic in System Wide Automated Network
Open Mon-Thurs 9:30-9, Fri & Sat 9:30-5

CREVE COEUR

P CREVE COEUR PUBLIC LIBRARY*, 311 N Highland St, 61610. SAN 304-0828. Tel: 309-699-7921. FAX: 309-699-0949. E-mail: crcopld@hotmail.com. Web Site: www.crevecoeurlibrary.com. *Dir,* Greg Wydert; Staff 4 (Non-MLS 4)
Founded 1945. Pop 5,448
Library Holdings: Bk Vols 23,279; Per Subs 48
Automation Activity & Vendor Info: (Cataloging) Follett Software; (Circulation) Follett Software
Wireless access
Mem of Reaching Across Illinois Library System (RAILS)
Open Mon 10-8, Tues-Fri 10-6, Sat (Sept-May) 10-2

CRYSTAL LAKE

P CRYSTAL LAKE PUBLIC LIBRARY, 126 Paddock St, 60014. SAN 304-0836. Tel: 815-459-1687. FAX: 815-459-9581. E-mail: ihaveaquestion@crystallakelibrary.org. Web Site: www.crystallakelibrary.org. *Dir,* Kathryn I Martens; E-mail: kmartens@clpl.org; *Asst Dir,* Karen K Migaldi; E-mail: kmigaldi@clpl.org; *Head, Adult Serv,* Nancy Weber; E-mail: nweber@clpl.org; *Head, Automation & Tech Serv,* Penny Ramirez; E-mail: pramirez@clpl.org; *Head, Circ,* Julie Gibson; E-mail: jgibson@clpl.org; *Head, Youth Serv,* Becky Fyolek; E-mail: bfyolek@clpl.org; Staff 86 (MLS 16, Non-MLS 70)
Founded 1913. Pop 39,788; Circ 1,001,075
Library Holdings: AV Mats 32,717; Bk Vols 176,627; Per Subs 360
Automation Activity & Vendor Info: (Acquisitions) SirsiDynix-WorkFlows; (Cataloging) OCLC; (Circulation) SirsiDynix-WorkFlows; (OPAC) SirsiDynix
Wireless access
Function: Adult bk club, Audiobks via web, AV serv, Bks on cassette, Bks on CD, CD-ROM, Chess club, Children's prog, Computer training, Computers for patron use, E-Reserves, Electronic databases & coll, Free DVD rentals, Holiday prog, Home delivery & serv to seniorr ctr & nursing homes, Homebound delivery serv, ILL available, Internet access, Museum passes, Music CDs, Notary serv, Online cat, Online ref, Orientations, Outreach serv, Outside serv via phone, mail, e-mail & web, OverDrive digital audio bks, Photocopying/Printing, Preschool outreach, Prog for adults, Prog for children & young adult, Ref serv available, Senior computer classes, Senior outreach, Story hour, Summer reading prog, Tax forms, Teen prog, Telephone ref, VHS videos, Wheelchair accessible
Publications: Beacon (Newsletter)
Partic in Cooperative Computer Services - CCS
Open Mon-Thurs 9-9, Fri & Sat 9-5, Sun 1-5
Restriction: Access at librarian's discretion

J MCHENRY COUNTY COLLEGE LIBRARY*, 8900 US Hwy 14, 60012-2738. SAN 304-0852. Tel: 815-455-8533. Reference Tel: 815-455-8762. FAX: 815-455-3999. Web Site: www.mchenry.edu/library/. *Exec Dir, Libr Serv,* Kyle McCarrell; Tel: 815-455-8695, E-mail: kmccarrell@mchenry.edu; Staff 15 (MLS 7, Non-MLS 8)
Founded 1968. Enrl 6,602; Highest Degree: Associate
Library Holdings: AV Mats 6,000; Bk Titles 35,000; Bk Vols 41,000; Per Subs 50
Automation Activity & Vendor Info: (Cataloging) OCLC Connexion; (Circulation) Ex Libris Group; (ILL) OCLC WorldShare Interlibrary Loan; (OPAC) Ex Libris Group
Wireless access
Function: ILL available
Partic in Consortium of Academic & Research Libraries in Illinois; Network of Illinois Learning Resources in Community Colleges; Northern Illinois Learning Resources Cooperative
Open Mon-Thurs (Winter) 8am-8:30pm, Fri 8-4:30; Mon-Thurs (Summer) 8-7:30, Fri 8-4:30

CUBA

P SPOON RIVER PUBLIC LIBRARY DISTRICT*, 201 S Third St, 61427. (Mail add: PO Box 140, 61427-0140), SAN 304-0860. Tel: 309-785-5496. FAX: 309-785-5439. E-mail: spoonriverlibrary@gmail.com. Web Site: www.cubaspoonriverlibrary.org. *Dir, Libr Serv,* Gayle Blodgett; Staff 6 (Non-MLS 6)
Founded 1912. Pop 3,402; Circ 27,164
Library Holdings: Bks on Deafness & Sign Lang 12; High Interest/Low Vocabulary Bk Vols 50; Bk Vols 20,000; Per Subs 47
Special Collections: Census on microfilm, Fulton County bks; Cuba High School Yearbook, microfilm; Cuba Journal, microfilm; Genealogy (family history files, obituaries, cemetery plot bks, etc)
Wireless access
Open Mon & Wed 9:30-4, Tues & Thurs 9:30-7, Fri & Sat 9:30-2

CUTLER

P CUTLER PUBLIC LIBRARY*, Civic Ctr, 409 S Main, 62238. SAN 376-1290. Tel: 618-497-2961. FAX: 618-497-8818. E-mail: cutlerpublicl@gmail.com. *Dir,* Jackie Carrothers; *Asst Librn,* Judy Farris
Library Holdings: Bk Titles 2,700
Wireless access
Open Mon & Tues 4-7, Wed & Sat 9-12, Thurs & Fri 2-5

DAHLGREN

P DAHLGREN PUBLIC LIBRARY*, Third & Dale St, 62828. (Mail add: PO Box 237, 62828-0237). Tel: 618-736-2652. FAX: 618-736-2652. *Librn,* Judi Cockrum
Library Holdings: Bk Vols 5,000
Wireless access
Open Thurs-Sun 2-4

DANVERS

P DANVERS TOWNSHIP LIBRARY, 117 E Exchange St, 61732-9347. (Mail add: PO Box 376, 61732-0376), SAN 304-0879. Tel: 309-963-4269. FAX: 309-963-4269. E-mail: danvers.tl.rsa@gmail.com. Web Site: www.danverstownshiplibrary.com. *Dir,* Lori Priebe; *Asst Librn,* Carol Bogue; *Asst Librn,* Jody Cassel; *Asst Librn,* Cathy Frey; *Asst Librn,* Cindy Melick; *Asst Librn,* Chantel Sisco
Pop 1,925; Circ 25,000
Library Holdings: Audiobooks 156; DVDs 3,937; e-books 48,401; Large Print Bks 350; Bk Vols 18,824; Per Subs 74
Wireless access
Function: 24/7 Electronic res, 24/7 Online cat, Audiobks on Playaways & MP3, Bks on CD, Children's prog, Computers for patron use, Electronic databases & coll, Free DVD rentals, Holiday prog, ILL available, Magazines, Meeting rooms, Online cat, OverDrive digital audio bks, Photocopying/Printing, Prog for adults, Prog for children & young adult, Ref serv available, Scanner, Senior outreach, Spoken cassettes & CDs, Story hour, Summer reading prog, Tax forms, Wheelchair accessible, Workshops
Mem of Reaching Across Illinois Library System (RAILS)
Open Mon & Thurs 1-8, Tues 9-8, Wed & Fri 9-5, Sat 9-3

DANVILLE

J DANVILLE AREA COMMUNITY COLLEGE LIBRARY*, 2000 E Main St, 61832-5199. SAN 304-0887. Tel: 217-443-8739. Circulation Tel: 217-443-8883. Interlibrary Loan Service Tel: 217-443-8733. FAX: 217-554-1623. E-mail: library@dacc.edu. Web Site: www.dacc.edu/library. *Dir,* Penny McConnell; *Head, Tech Serv & Cat,* Holly Nordheden; Tel: 217-443-8852; *Ref & Instrul Serv Librn,* Dr Ruth B Lindemann; Tel: 217-443-8735, E-mail: rlinde@dacc.edu; *Circ & ILL,* Kathleen Hantz; E-mail: khantz@dacc.edu; Staff 3 (MLS 2, Non-MLS 1)
Founded 1962. Enrl 1,599; Fac 2; Highest Degree: Associate
Library Holdings: CDs 200; DVDs 3,000; Bk Titles 30,000; Bk Vols 35,000; Per Subs 15
Automation Activity & Vendor Info: (Cataloging) Ex Libris Group; (Circulation) Ex Libris Group; (Discovery) Ex Libris Group; (ILL) Ex Libris Group; (OPAC) Ex Libris Group; (Serials) EBSCO Online
Wireless access
Function: Audio & video playback equip for onsite use, Computers for patron use, Distance learning, Electronic databases & coll, ILL available, Magnifiers for reading, Ref serv available
Mem of Illinois Heartland Library System

Partic in Consortium of Academic & Research Libraries in Illinois; Illinois Library & Information Network; Network of Illinois Learning Resources in Community Colleges
Special Services for the Deaf - Closed caption videos; Described encaptioned media prog
Special Services for the Blind - Playaways (bks on MP3); Screen enlargement software for people with visual disabilities
Open Mon-Fri 8-5
Restriction: Open to pub for ref & circ; with some limitations, Open to students, fac & staff

P DANVILLE PUBLIC LIBRARY*, 319 N Vermilion St, 61832. SAN 304-0895. Tel: 217-477-5220. Reference Tel: 217-477-5228. FAX: 217-477-5230. Web Site: www.danvillepubliclibrary.org. *Exec Dir,* Jennifer Hess; Tel: 217-477-5223, Ext 118, E-mail: jhess@danvillepubliclibrary.org; *Dir, Adult Serv,* Robert Hinton; Tel: 217-477-5228, E-mail: rhinton@danvillepubliclibrary.org; *Dir, Youth Serv,* Lisa Abdelghani; Tel: 217-477-5225, E-mail: labdelghani@danvillepubliclibrary.org; *Outreach Serv Dir,* Jessica Augustson; Tel: 217-477-5227, E-mail: jaugustson@danvillepubliclibrary.org; *Circ Mgr,* Mary Jane Easterday; Tel: 217-477-5220, E-mail: mjeaster@danvillepubliclibrary.org; *Tech Serv Mgr,* Cindy Boroff; Tel: 217-477-5223, Ext 119, E-mail: cboroff@danvillepubliclibrary.org; Staff 9 (MLS 4, Non-MLS 5)
Founded 1883. Pop 33,027
Special Collections: Gardening; Genealogy
Automation Activity & Vendor Info: (Cataloging) Innovative Interfaces, Inc; (Circulation) Innovative Interfaces, Inc; (OPAC) Innovative Interfaces, Inc
Wireless access
Function: 24/7 Electronic res, 24/7 Online cat, 3D Printer, Activity rm, Adult bk club, Archival coll, Art exhibits, Art programs, Audiobks via web, AV serv, Bi-weekly Writer's Group, Bks on CD, Butterfly Garden, Children's prog, Computer training, Computers for patron use, Distance learning, Electronic databases & coll, Free DVD rentals, Genealogy discussion group, Holiday prog, Home delivery & serv to seniorr ctr & nursing homes, Homebound delivery serv, ILL available, Internet access, Jail serv, Life-long learning prog for all ages, Magazines, Magnifiers for reading, Mail & tel request accepted, Makerspace, Mango lang, Meeting rooms, Microfiche/film & reading machines, Movies, Music CDs, Online cat, Outreach serv, Outside serv via phone, mail, e-mail & web, OverDrive digital audio bks, Photocopying/Printing, Preschool outreach, Preschool reading prog, Prog for adults, Prog for children & young adult, Ref & res, Ref serv available, Scanner, Senior outreach, Serves people with intellectual disabilities, STEM programs, Story hour, Study rm, Summer reading prog, Tax forms, Teen prog, Telephone ref, Visual arts prog, Wheelchair accessible
Publications: Danville Public Library News (Newsletter)
Mem of Illinois Heartland Library System
Open Mon-Thurs 9-8, Fri & Sat 9-5:30
Restriction: Non-resident fee
Friends of the Library Group

§CM LAKEVIEW COLLEGE OF NURSING, Danville Campus Library, 903 N Logan Ave, 61832. Tel: 217-709-0920. FAX: 217-709-0955. Web Site: lakeviewcol.edu/library. *Libr Dir,* Miranda Shake; Tel: 217-709-0927, E-mail: mshake@lakeviewcol.edu
Library Holdings: Per Subs 30
Wireless access
Mem of Illinois Heartland Library System
Partic in Consortium of Academic & Research Libraries in Illinois; National Network of Libraries of Medicine Region 6
Open Mon-Fri 8-4:30

DARIEN

P INDIAN PRAIRIE PUBLIC LIBRARY DISTRICT*, 401 Plainfield Rd, 60561-4207. SAN 324-1262. Tel: 630-887-8760. FAX: 630-887-8801. Administration FAX: 630-887-1018. E-mail: ippl@ippl.info. Web Site: www.ippl.info. *Dir,* Jamie Bukovac; E-mail: jamieb@ippl.info; *Asst Dir,* Laura Birmingham; E-mail: laurab@ippl.info; *Adult Serv,* Tony Lucarelli; E-mail: tonyl@ippl.info; *Circ,* Deborah Sheehan; E-mail: debs@ippl.info; *Tech Serv, Tech Serv,* Ann Stovall; E-mail: anns@ippl.info; *Youth Serv,* Natalie Williams; E-mail: nataliew@ippl.info; Staff 94 (MLS 14, Non-MLS 80)
Founded 1988. Pop 42,529; Circ 758,241
Jul 2015-Jun 2016 Income $3,626,759. Mats Exp $440,727, Books $231,228, Per/Ser (Incl. Access Fees) $27,140, AV Mat $115,869, Electronic Ref Mat (Incl. Access Fees) $66,490. Sal $2,098,765
Library Holdings: Audiobooks 19,049; AV Mats 24,825; e-books 45,994; Bk Vols 144,521; Per Subs 419
Automation Activity & Vendor Info: (Acquisitions) SirsiDynix-WorkFlows; (Cataloging) SirsiDynix-WorkFlows; (Circulation) SirsiDynix-WorkFlows; (ILL) SirsiDynix-WorkFlows; (OPAC) SirsiDynix-Enterprise; (Serials) SirsiDynix-WorkFlows
Wireless access
Function: 24/7 Electronic res, 24/7 Online cat, Activity rm, Adult bk club, Adult literacy prog, Audio & video playback equip for onsite use, Audiobks on Playaways & MP3, Audiobks via web, AV serv, BA reader (adult literacy), Bk club(s), Bks on CD, Butterfly Garden, Chess club, Children's prog, Citizenship assistance, Computer training, Computers for patron use, Digital talking bks, E-Readers, E-Reserves, Electronic databases & coll, Equip loans & repairs, Free DVD rentals, Games & aids for people with disabilities, Genealogy discussion group, Govt ref serv, Health sci info serv, Home delivery & serv to seniorr ctr & nursing homes, Homebound delivery serv, ILL available, Internet access, Large print keyboards, Life-long learning prog for all ages, Literacy & newcomer serv, Magazines, Magnifiers for reading, Mail & tel request accepted, Mango lang, Meeting rooms, Microfiche/film & reading machines, Movies, Museum passes, Music CDs, Notary serv, Online cat, Online info literacy tutorials on the web & in blackboard, Online ref, Outside serv via phone, mail, e-mail & web, OverDrive digital audio bks, Passport agency, Photocopying/Printing, Preschool outreach, Preschool reading prog, Printer for laptops & handheld devices, Prog for adults, Prog for children & young adult, Ref serv available, Scanner, Senior computer classes, Senior outreach, Spoken cassettes & CDs, Story hour, Study rm, Summer reading prog, Tax forms, Teen prog, Telephone ref, Wheelchair accessible, Workshops
Publications: Enewsletter; IPPL (Newsletter)
Mem of Reaching Across Illinois Library System (RAILS)
Partic in System Wide Automated Network
Special Services for the Deaf - Assisted listening device; Sign lang interpreter upon request for prog; Video relay services
Special Services for the Blind - Ref serv; Screen enlargement software for people with visual disabilities
Open Mon-Fri 9-9, Sat 9-5, Sun 1-5
Friends of the Library Group

DE LAND

P GOOSE CREEK DISTRICT LIBRARY*, 220 N Highway Ave, 61839. (Mail add: PO Box 237, 61839-0237), SAN 304-095X. Tel: 217-664-3572. FAX: 217-664-3624. E-mail: goosecreeklibrary@yahoo.com. *Dir,* Melinda DelMastro
Pop 852; Circ 6,383
Library Holdings: DVDs 300; Bk Titles 6,000; Per Subs 35
Wireless access
Mem of Illinois Heartland Library System
Open Mon, Tues, Thurs & Fri 1-5:30, Wed 3-7, Sat 9-12

DE PUE

P SELBY TOWNSHIP LIBRARY DISTRICT, 101 Depot St, 61322. (Mail add: PO Box 49, 61322-0049), SAN 304-0968. Tel: 815-447-2660. FAX: 815-447-2598. E-mail: selbytld@gmail.com. *Dir,* Marcia Broady
Founded 1937. Pop 2,536
Library Holdings: Bk Vols 12,500; Per Subs 21
Special Collections: History of De Pue Coll, A-tapes. Oral History
Wireless access
Mem of Reaching Across Illinois Library System (RAILS)
Open Mon, Tues & Fri 12-5, Wed 12-8, Sat 8-12

DECATUR

S DECATUR GENEALOGICAL SOCIETY LIBRARY, 1255 W South Side Dr, 62521-4024. (Mail add: PO Box 1548, 62525-1548), SAN 323-827X. Tel: 217-429-0135. E-mail: decaturgensoc@att.net. Web Site: sites.rootsweb.com/~ildecgs. *Librn,* Cheri Hunter
Founded 1964
Library Holdings: Bk Titles 20,000; Bk Vols 30,000; Per Subs 16
Special Collections: County; Original Macon County IL Probates; Abstracts for Deed,Macon County Vital Records
Subject Interests: Bibles, Genealogy
Wireless access
Publications: Central Illinois Genealogical Quarterly; Central Illinois Newsletter
Open Mon, Wed & Sat 10-4

P DECATUR PUBLIC LIBRARY*, 130 N Franklin St, 62523. SAN 340-3440. Tel: 217-424-2900. Circulation Tel: 217-421-9728. Administration Tel: 217-421-9713. Automation Services Tel: 217-421-9753. Information Services Tel: 217-421-9731. FAX: 217-233-4071. Web Site: www.decaturlibrary.org. *City Librn,* Rick Meyer; E-mail: rmeyer@decaturlibrary.org; *Asst City Librn, Circ Mgr,* Robert Edwards; Tel: 217-421-9702, E-mail: redwards@decaturlibrary.org; *Head, Adult Serv, Head, Children's Servx,* Alissa Henkel; Tel: 217-421-9771, E-mail: ahenkel@decaturlibrary.org; *Head, Archives & Spec Coll,* Rebecca Damptz; Tel: 217-421-9711, E-mail: rdamptz@decaturlibrary.org; *Head, Tech Serv,* Carol Ziese; Tel: 217-421-9739, E-mail: cziese@decaturlibrary.org; *Syst Adminr,* Matthew Wilkerson; E-mail: mwilkerson@decaturlibrary.org; *Asst Tech Serv Librn, ILL,* Julie Martin; E-mail: jmartin@decaturlibrary.org; Staff 61 (MLS 9, Non-MLS 52)

Founded 1876. Pop 76,122; Circ 593,111
May 2012-Apr 2013 Income $3,732,000, State $145,000, City $3,000,000, Other $587,000. Mats Exp $580,000, Books $373,000, Per/Ser (Incl. Access Fees) $24,000, AV Mat $43,000, Electronic Ref Mat (Incl. Access Fees) $140,000. Sal $2,635,201
Library Holdings: Audiobooks 8,540; CDs 9,223; DVDs 8,431; Microforms 3,910; Bk Vols 247,996; Per Subs 362; Videos 6,823
Special Collections: Abraham Lincoln Coll; Local History Coll, Decatur & Macon County. US Document Depository
Automation Activity & Vendor Info: (Acquisitions) SirsiDynix; (Cataloging) SirsiDynix; (Circulation) SirsiDynix; (OPAC) SirsiDynix
Wireless access
Function: Accelerated reader prog, Adult bk club, Adult literacy prog, Archival coll, Art exhibits, Bks on cassette, Bks on CD, Children's prog, Computer training, Computers for patron use, E-Reserves, Electronic databases & coll, Free DVD rentals, Homebound delivery serv, ILL available, Microfiche/film & reading machines, Music CDs, Notary serv, Online cat, OverDrive digital audio bks, Photocopying/Printing, Prog for adults, Prog for children & young adult, Ref & res, Ref serv available, Senior computer classes, Story hour, Summer reading prog, Tax forms, Teen prog, Telephone ref, VHS videos, Wheelchair accessible
Publications: Connections (Bimonthly)
Mem of Illinois Heartland Library System
Open Mon-Thurs 9-8, Fri & Sat 9-5:30
Friends of the Library Group

L MACON COUNTY LEGAL LAW LIBRARY*, Macon County Courthouse, 253 E Wood St, Rm 303, 62523. SAN 326-9531. Tel: 217-424-1372. Web Site: www.illinoislegalaid.org/counties/macon. *Librn,* Sundi Barrett; E-mail: dbarrett@court.co.macon.il.us
Wireless access
Open Mon-Fri 8:30-12 & 1-4:30

C MILLIKIN UNIVERSITY*, Staley Library, 1184 W Main St, 62522. SAN 304-1018. Tel: 217-424-6214. E-mail: refdesk@millikin.edu. Web Site: millikin.edu/staley. *Libr Dir,* Cindy Fuller; E-mail: cfuller@millikin.edu; *Coordr, Educ Tech, Librn,* Rachel Bicicchi; E-mail: rbicicchi@millikin.edu; *Coordr, Access Serv,* Amanda Pippitt; E-mail: apipitt@millikin.edu; *Coordr, Instrul Serv,* Matthew Olsen; E-mail: molsen@millikin.edu; Staff 11 (MLS 5, Non-MLS 6)
Founded 1902. Enrl 2,200; Fac 140; Highest Degree: Master
Library Holdings: Bk Vols 211,539; Per Subs 460; Videos 2,388
Subject Interests: Music
Automation Activity & Vendor Info: (Acquisitions) Ex Libris Group; (Cataloging) Ex Libris Group; (Circulation) Ex Libris Group; (Course Reserve) Ex Libris Group; (ILL) Ex Libris Group; (OPAC) Ex Libris Group; (Serials) Ex Libris Group
Wireless access
Mem of Illinois Heartland Library System
Partic in Consortium of Academic & Research Libraries in Illinois
Open Mon-Fri 7am-Midnight, Sat & Sun 10am-Midnight

J RICHLAND COMMUNITY COLLEGE*, Kitty Lindsay Learning Resources Center, One College Park, 62521. SAN 304-1026. Tel: 217-875-7211, Ext 6303. Interlibrary Loan Service Tel: 217-875-7211, Ext 6301. FAX: 217-875-6961. Web Site: www.richland.edu/current-students/library. *Dir,* Louise W Greene; E-mail: lgreene@richland.edu; *Coordr, Access Serv,* Gavena Dahlman; E-mail: gdahlman@richland.edu; Staff 5 (MLS 3, Non-MLS 2)
Founded 1972. Enrl 3,500; Fac 60; Highest Degree: Associate
Library Holdings: Bk Titles 23,000; Bk Vols 27,000; Per Subs 117
Automation Activity & Vendor Info: (Cataloging) Ex Libris Group; (Circulation) Ex Libris Group; (Course Reserve) Ex Libris Group; (OPAC) Ex Libris Group
Wireless access
Function: Archival coll, Art exhibits, AV serv, Bilingual assistance for Spanish patrons, Computers for patron use, Distance learning, Doc delivery serv, E-Reserves, Electronic databases & coll, ILL available, Instruction & testing, Large print keyboards, Learning ctr, Magnifiers for reading, Outside serv via phone, mail, e-mail & web, Photocopying/Printing, Printer for laptops & handheld devices, Prof lending libr, Ref & res, Ref serv available, Scanner, Spanish lang bks, VHS videos, Wheelchair accessible
Publications: Media Index; Periodical Holdings List
Mem of Illinois Heartland Library System
Partic in Consortium of Academic & Research Libraries in Illinois; Network of Illinois Learning Resources in Community Colleges
Open Mon-Thurs 7:30-7, Fri 7:30-5 (Winter); Mon-Thurs 7:30-7 (Summer)
Restriction: By permission only, Open to pub for ref & circ; with some limitations, Open to students, fac, staff & alumni

M SAINT MARY'S HOSPITAL*, Health Science Library, 1800 E Lake Shore Dr, 62521. SAN 304-1034. Tel: 217-464-2182. FAX: 217-464-1674. Web Site: www.stmarysdecatur.com. *Librn,* Laura Brosamer; Staff 2 (MLS 1, Non-MLS 1)
Founded 1976
Library Holdings: Bk Titles 500
Subject Interests: Hospital admin, Med, Nursing
Automation Activity & Vendor Info: (Cataloging) CyberTools for Libraries; (Circulation) CyberTools for Libraries
Wireless access
Mem of Illinois Heartland Library System
Partic in Basic Health Sciences Library Network; Regional Med Libr - Region 3
Open Mon-Thurs 8-4:30, Fri 8-12

DEER CREEK

P DEER CREEK DISTRICT LIBRARY*, 205 First St, 61733. (Mail add: PO Box 347, 61733-0347), SAN 304-1050. Tel: 309-447-6724. FAX: 309-447-6724. E-mail: dclib1@yahoo.com. Web Site: www.deercreekillinois.org/deer-creek-library.html. *Dir,* Carlene Mathis-Kull
Founded 1965. Pop 1,247; Circ 9,221
Library Holdings: Bk Vols 19,000; Per Subs 36
Wireless access
Partic in Resource Sharing Alliance
Open Mon 9-12 & 1-7, Tues, Thurs & Fri 9-12 & 1-6, Wed 1-8

DEERFIELD

P DEERFIELD PUBLIC LIBRARY*, 920 Waukegan Rd, 60015. SAN 304-1069. Tel: 847-945-3311. Circulation Tel: 847-945-3311, Ext 8822. FAX: 847-945-3402. Reference E-mail: reference@deerfieldlibrary.org. Web Site: deerfieldlibrary.org. *Dir,* Amy Falasz-Peterson; E-mail: afalaszpeterson@deerfieldlibrary.org; Staff 13 (MLS 13)
Founded 1927. Pop 18,400; Circ 384,099
Library Holdings: CDs 10,884; DVDs 8,080; Electronic Media & Resources 31; Bk Vols 152,351; Per Subs 338
Special Collections: Deerfield Local History
Automation Activity & Vendor Info: (Acquisitions) SirsiDynix; (Cataloging) SirsiDynix; (Circulation) SirsiDynix; (OPAC) SirsiDynix; (Serials) SirsiDynix
Wireless access
Function: Adult bk club, After school storytime, Audiobks via web, AV serv, Bk club(s), Bks on cassette, Bks on CD, Children's prog, Computer training, Computers for patron use, Electronic databases & coll, Free DVD rentals, Holiday prog, Home delivery & serv to seniorr ctr & nursing homes, Homebound delivery serv, ILL available, Internet access, Jazz prog, Museum passes, Music CDs, Notary serv, Online cat, Outreach serv, Outside serv via phone, mail, e-mail & web, Photocopying/Printing, Preschool outreach, Prog for adults, Prog for children & young adult, Ref serv available, Senior outreach, Story hour, Summer reading prog, Tax forms, Teen prog, Telephone ref, VHS videos, Wheelchair accessible, Writing prog
Publications: Browsing
Open Mon-Thurs 9-9, Fri 9-6, Sat 9-5, Sun 1-5
Friends of the Library Group

CR TRINITY INTERNATIONAL UNIVERSITY*, James E Rolfing Memorial Library, 2065 Half Day Rd, 60015-1241. SAN 320-1805. Tel: 847-317-4000, 847-317-4001. Circulation Tel: 847-317-4015. Interlibrary Loan Service Tel: 847-317-4008. FAX: 847-317-4012. Reference E-mail: libref@tiu.edu. Web Site: library.tiu.edu/home. *Dir, Libr Serv,* Rebecca Donald; Tel: 847-317-4013, E-mail: rldonald@tiu.edu; *Asst Libr Dir,* Becky Frank; Tel: 847-317-4020, E-mail: rfrank@tiu.edu; *Access Serv Supvr,* Nathan Thebarge; E-mail: nmthebarge@tiu.edu; *Circ Supvr,* Hope Mozo; Tel: 847-317-4002, E-mail: hmozo@tiu.edu; Staff 16 (MLS 7, Non-MLS 9)
Founded 1970. Enrl 4,132; Fac 168; Highest Degree: Doctorate
Library Holdings: AV Mats 5,195; Electronic Media & Resources 51; Bk Titles 172,314; Bk Vols 202,254; Per Subs 1,382
Special Collections: Evangelical Free Church of America Archives (partial); Papers of Wilbur Smith & Carl F H Henry; Trinity International University Archives
Subject Interests: Biblical studies, Bioethics, Church hist, Missions & missionaries, Theol
Automation Activity & Vendor Info: (Acquisitions) Ex Libris Group; (Cataloging) Ex Libris Group; (Circulation) Ex Libris Group; (Course Reserve) Ex Libris Group; (OPAC) Ex Libris Group; (Serials) Ex Libris Group
Function: ILL available
Partic in OCLC Online Computer Library Center, Inc
Open Mon-Thurs 7:30am-Midnight, Fri 7:30am-10pm, Sat 9am-10pm, Sun 2-Midnight

DEKALB

P DEKALB PUBLIC LIBRARY*, Haish Memorial Library Bldg, 309 Oak St, 60115-3369. SAN 304-0941. Tel: 815-756-9568. FAX: 815-756-7837. Reference E-mail: dkplref@dkpl.org. Web Site: www.dkpl.org. *Dir,* Emily Faulkner; E-mail: emilyf@dkpl.org; *Head, Access Serv,* Robert Aspatore;

E-mail: roberta@dkpl.org; *Head, Adult Serv,* Britta Krabill; E-mail: brittak@dkpl.org; *Head, Youth Serv,* Theresa Winterbauer; E-mail: theresaw@dkpl.org; *Tech Serv,* Pat Adamkiewicz; E-mail: pata@dkpl.org; Staff 45 (MLS 8, Non-MLS 37)
Founded 1893. Pop 42,579; Circ 350,000
Library Holdings: AV Mats 9,840; Bk Vols 141,238; Per Subs 238
Subject Interests: Local hist
Automation Activity & Vendor Info: (Cataloging) SirsiDynix; (Circulation) SirsiDynix; (ILL) SirsiDynix; (OPAC) SirsiDynix; (Serials) SirsiDynix
Wireless access
Mem of Reaching Across Illinois Library System (RAILS)
Open Mon-Thurs 9-9, Fri 9-6, Sat 9-5, Sun 1-5
Friends of the Library Group

C NORTHERN ILLINOIS UNIVERSITY LIBRARIES, Founders Memorial Library, 217 Normal Rd, 60115-2828. SAN 340-3297. Tel: 815-753-1094. Circulation Tel: 815-753-9844. Interlibrary Loan Service Tel: 815-753-9842. Reference Tel: 815-753-0152. Interlibrary Loan Service FAX: 815-753-2003. Administration FAX: 815-753-9803. TDD: 815-753-2000. E-mail: lib-admin@niu.edu. Web Site: library.niu.edu/university-libraries. *Dean,* Fred Barnhart; Tel: 815-753-9801, E-mail: fbarnhart@niu.edu; *Interim Assoc Dean, Coll & Serv,* Jana Brubaker; Tel: 815-753-9805, E-mail: jbrubake@niu.edu; *Assoc Dean Coll Mgt,* Gwen Gregory; Tel: 815-753-1746, E-mail: ggregory@niu.edu; *Assoc Dean, Pub Serv,* Leanne VandeCreek; Tel: 815-753-9804, E-mail: lvandecreek@niu.edu; *Asst Dean, Tech Initiatives & Support Serv,* T J Lusher; Tel: 815-753-0521, E-mail: tlusher@niu.edu; *Head, Govt Doc, Head Govt Publ,* Rachel Hradecky; Tel: 815-753-9841, E-mail: rhradecky@niu.edu; *Head, Spec Coll & Archives,* Bradley Wiles; Tel: 815-753-9392, E-mail: bwiles@niu.edu; *Head, User Serv,* Sarah McHone-Chase; Tel: 815-753-9860, E-mail: mchonechase@niu.edu; *Acq Librn,* Michele Hunt; Tel: 815-753-6985, E-mail: mhunt5@niu.edu; *Digital Colls & Metadata Librn,* Matt Short; Tel: 815-753-7663, E-mail: mshort@niu.edu; *Education & Social Sciences Librn,* Alissa Droog; Tel: 815-753-4025, E-mail: adroog@niu.edu; *Humanities & Soc Sci Librn,* Wendell Johnson; Tel: 815-753-1634, E-mail: wjohnso1@niu.edu; *Info Literacy Librn,* Larissa Garcia; Tel: 815-753-4822, E-mail: larissagarcia@niu.edu; *Music Librn,* Sarah Holmes; Tel: 815-753-1426, E-mail: sholmes@niu.edu; *Rare Bks & Spec Coll Librn,* Beth McGowan; Tel: 815-753-1947, E-mail: bmcgowan@niu.edu; *Res & Ref Librn,* Wayne Finley; Tel: 815-753-0991, E-mail: wfinley@niu.edu; *Res & Ref Librn,* Junlin Pan; Tel: 815-753-0530, E-mail: jpan@niu.edu; *Res & Ref Librn,* Robert Ridinger; Tel: 815-753-1367, E-mail: rridinger@niu.edu; *Sci Librn,* Meredith Ayers; Tel: 815-753-1872, E-mail: mayers@niu.edu; *Spec Coll Cat Librn,* Mary Burns; Tel: 815-753-1192, E-mail: mburns6@niu.edu; *Student Success Librn,* Kimberly Shotick; Tel: 815-753-5290, E-mail: kshotick@niu.edu; *Univ Archivist,* Cindy Ditzler; E-mail: cditzler@niu.edu; *Curator,* Hao Phan; Tel: 815-753-1809, E-mail: hphan@niu.edu. Subject Specialists: *Philos, Polit sci, Relig,* Wendell Johnson; *SE Asia,* Hao Phan; Staff 94 (MLS 25, Non-MLS 69)
Founded 1899. Highest Degree: Doctorate
Special Collections: African-American Coll; American Popular Literature Coll; Angus Wilson Coll; Archives; Book Arts Coll; Burns Coll; Byron Coll; Chess Magazines; Chicago Lyric Opera Coll; Colorado-Henkle Coll; Comic Book Coll; Denson Coll; Dos Passos Coll; Drama Coll (includes University & Nisbett-Snydere Coll); Edward Ardizzone Coll; Fine Arts Coll; Gender Studies Coll; Graham Greene Coll; Hanley Manuscript Coll; Horatio Alger Coll; Imprint Society; James D Tobin Coll; Jeremy Taylor Coll; Johannsen Coll; Lovecraft Coll; Motley Coll; Music (Skinner Coll), ms; Private Press; Science Fiction Coll (includes Science Fiction Writers of America & the Science Fiction Magazine Coll); Southeast Asia Coll; Vincent Starrett Coll; Western Fiction Writers of America (WFMWA) Magazine Coll; Whitman Coll; Wordsworth Coll. State Document Depository; US Document Depository
Subject Interests: Bus & mgt, Econ, Educ, Hist, Natural sci, Sci tech
Automation Activity & Vendor Info: (Acquisitions) Ex Libris Group; (Cataloging) Ex Libris Group; (Circulation) Ex Libris Group; (OPAC) Ex Libris Group; (Serials) Ex Libris Group
Wireless access
Mem of Reaching Across Illinois Library System (RAILS)
Partic in Consortium of Academic & Research Libraries in Illinois; Mid-America Law Library Consortium
Open Mon-Thurs 8am-Midnight, Fri 8-6, Sat 9-6, Sun 1pm-Midnight
Friends of the Library Group

Departmental Libraries:

MUSIC, School of Music, Rm 175, 60115. Tel: 815-753-1426. FAX: 815-753-9836. E-mail: musiclibrary@niu.edu. *Music Librn,* Sarah Holmes; E-mail: sholmes@niu.edu; Staff 1 (Non-MLS 1)
Highest Degree: Master
Library Holdings: AV Mats 17,000; CDs 3,000; Music Scores 25,000; Bk Vols 21,000; Per Subs 80
Special Collections: Jazz Recordings & Musical Scores Coll
Function: Audio & video playback equip for onsite use, CD-ROM, Doc delivery serv, ILL available, Music CDs, Orientations, Ref serv available
Open Mon-Thurs 8am-9pm, Fri 8-5, Sat Noon-4, Sun 5-9

REGIONAL HISTORY CENTER, Founders Library, 217 Normal Rd, 60115. Tel: 815-753-1779. *Head, Spec Coll & Archives,* Bradley Wiles; Tel: 815-753-9392, E-mail: bwiles@niu.edu
Special Collections: University Archives Coll
Open Mon-Thurs 9-Noon & 1-4 & by appt

CL DAVID C SHAPIRO MEMORIAL LAW LIBRARY, Swen Parson Hall, 2nd Flr, Normal Rd, 60115-2890. (Mail add: 180 W Stadium Dr, 60115), SAN 304-2227. Tel: 815-753-0507. Reference Tel: 815-753-0519. FAX: 815-753-9499. E-mail: lawreference@niu.edu. Web Site: law.niu.edu/law/library. *Actg Dir, Dep Dir, Research Librn,* Therese Clarke Arado; Tel: 815-753-9497, E-mail: tclarke@niu.edu; *Academic Technologies & Outreach Servs Librn,* Matthew Timko; Tel: 815-753-9492, E-mail: mtimko@niu.edu; *Res Mgt Librn,* Rachel Ford; Tel: 815-753-2021, E-mail: rford2@niu.edu; *Library Operations Assoc,* Kate Hartman; Tel: 815-753-9184, E-mail: khartman@niu.edu; Staff 4 (MLS 4)
Founded 1974. Enrl 307; Fac 21; Highest Degree: Doctorate
Jul 2020-Jun 2021. Mats Exp $429,882
Library Holdings: Bk Titles 272,251
Special Collections: US Document Depository
Subject Interests: Law
Automation Activity & Vendor Info: (ILL) Ex Libris Group
Partic in Chicago Legal Acad Syst; Mid-America Law Library Consortium; NELLCO Law Library Consortium, Inc.; OCLC Online Computer Library Center, Inc
Open Mon-Thurs 8:30-6:30, Fri 8:30-2:30, Sun 4-8 (Fall & Spring); Mon-Thurs 9-5, Fri 9-3 (Summer)
Restriction: Badge access after hrs, Circ privileges for students & alumni only

DELAVAN

P AYER PUBLIC LIBRARY DISTRICT*, 208 Locust St, 61734. (Mail add: PO Box 500, 61734-0500), SAN 304-1107. Tel: 309-244-8236. FAX: 309-244-8237. E-mail: ayerpubliclibrary@yahoo.com. Web Site: www.ayerpubliclibrary.org. *Libr Dir,* Julie Houston; Staff 5 (Non-MLS 5)
Founded 1907. Pop 2,807; Circ 27,668
Library Holdings: AV Mats 550; Bks on Deafness & Sign Lang 30; DVDs 1,100; Large Print Bks 1,000; Bk Vols 21,000; Per Subs 127; Videos 1,120
Special Collections: Delavan Times 1874-present, microfilm
Wireless access
Function: 24/7 Online cat, Adult bk club, Audiobks on Playaways & MP3, Bk club(s), Bks on CD, Children's prog, Computers for patron use, Free DVD rentals, Homebound delivery serv, ILL available, Internet access, Magazines, Microfiche/film & reading machines, Online cat, OverDrive digital audio bks, Photocopying/Printing, Prog for adults, Prog for children & young adult, Ref serv available, Spoken cassettes & CDs, Spoken cassettes & DVDs, Summer reading prog, Tax forms, Telephone ref, Workshops
Open Mon & Thurs 1-8, Tues, Wed & Fri 10-5, Sat 9-Noon

DES PLAINES

S DES PLAINES HISTORICAL SOCIETY LIBRARY*, 781 Pearson St, 60016. SAN 304-1158. Tel: 847-391-5399. FAX: 847-297-4741. E-mail: contact@desplaineshistory.org. Web Site: www.desplaineshistory.org. *Exec Dir,* Philip Mohr; Staff 6 (MLS 4, Non-MLS 2)
Founded 1969
Library Holdings: Bk Vols 500; Per Subs 10
Special Collections: Dr C A Earle Coll
Open Tues-Fri 10-5, Sun 1-4

P DES PLAINES PUBLIC LIBRARY*, 1501 Ellinwood St, 60016. SAN 304-1166. Tel: 847-827-5551. Reference Tel: 847-376-2841. FAX: 847-827-7974. TDD: 847-827-0515. E-mail: help@dppl.org. Web Site: dppl.org. *Dir,* Holly Sorensen; E-mail: hsorensen@dppl.org; *Asst Dir,* Roberta Johnson; E-mail: RJohnson@dppl.org; *Head, Adult Serv,* Jo Bonell; E-mail: jbonell@dppl.org; *Head, Circ Serv,* Susan Farid; Tel: 847-376-2790, E-mail: sfarid@dppl.org; *Head, Youth Serv,* Stephanie Spetter; Tel: 847-376-2839, E-mail: sspetter@dppl.org; Staff 104 (MLS 22, Non-MLS 82)
Founded 1906. Pop 58,617; Circ 1,164,209
Library Holdings: Audiobooks 7,676; CDs 17,672; DVDs 32,688; e-books 11,945; e-journals 75; Large Print Bks 8,920; Bk Vols 254,339; Per Subs 706
Automation Activity & Vendor Info: (Cataloging) SirsiDynix; (Circulation) SirsiDynix; (ILL) SirsiDynix; (OPAC) SirsiDynix; (Serials) SirsiDynix
Wireless access
Publications: eForeword (Newsletter)
Special Services for the Deaf - TDD equip; TTY equip

Special Services for the Blind - Accessible computers; Assistive/Adapted tech devices, equip & products; Copier with enlargement capabilities; Home delivery serv; Low vision equip; Magnifiers; Playaways (bks on MP3)
Open Mon-Fri 9-9, Sat 9-5, Sun 1-5
Friends of the Library Group

S GAS TECHNOLOGY INSTITUTE*, Technical Information Center, 1700 S Mount Prospect Rd, 60018-1804. SAN 303-9226. Tel: 847-768-0664. FAX: 847-768-0669. E-mail: library@gastechnology.org. Web Site: www.gastechnology.org. *Supvr,* Carol Worster; Staff 1 (MLS 1)
Founded 1941
Library Holdings: Bk Vols 36,000; Per Subs 100
Special Collections: American Chemical Society Division of Fuel Chemistry, Preprints 1957 to present; Energy Reports (DOE, EPRI, GRI); Pipeline Simulation Interest Group, Proc
Subject Interests: Natural gas
Partic in Illinois Library & Information Network; OCLC Online Computer Library Center, Inc
Restriction: Access at librarian's discretion, Access for corporate affiliates, Circulates for staff only, External users must contact libr, Non-circulating coll, Open to pub by appt only

J OAKTON COMMUNITY COLLEGE LIBRARY*, 1600 E Golf Rd, Rm 1406, 60016. SAN 304-436X. Tel: 847-635-1642, 847-635-1644. Interlibrary Loan Service Tel: 847-635-1608. Administration Tel: 847-635-1640. Web Site: www.oakton.edu/library. *Asst Dean of Libr,* Jacob Jeremiah; E-mail: jjeremia@oakton.edu; *Co-Chair, Ref & Instruction Librn,* Jane Malik; Tel: 847-635-1715, E-mail: jmalik@oakton.edu; Staff 5 (MLS 5)
Founded 1970. Enrl 5,400; Fac 154; Highest Degree: Associate
Library Holdings: AV Mats 690; DVDs 614; e-books 3,198; High Interest/Low Vocabulary Bk Vols 300; Microforms 4,237; Bk Titles 91,000; Bk Vols 107,578; Per Subs 27,700
Special Collections: US Document Depository
Automation Activity & Vendor Info: (Acquisitions) Ex Libris Group; (Cataloging) Ex Libris Group; (Circulation) Ex Libris Group; (Course Reserve) Ex Libris Group; (ILL) Ex Libris Group; (OPAC) Ex Libris Group; (Serials) Ex Libris Group
Wireless access
Function: Electronic databases & coll
Mem of Reaching Across Illinois Library System (RAILS)
Partic in Consortium of Academic & Research Libraries in Illinois; Network of Illinois Learning Resources in Community Colleges; OCLC Online Computer Library Center, Inc
Open Mon-Thurs (Winter) 7:30am-9pm, Fri 7:30-7:30, Sat 9-3; Mon-Thurs (Summer) 7:30am-9pm
Restriction: Open to pub for ref & circ; with some limitations

DIVERNON

P DIVERNON TOWNSHIP LIBRARY*, 221 S Second St, 62530. SAN 304-1204. Tel: 217-628-3813. FAX: 217-628-3813. Web Site: www.divernontownshiplibrary.org. *Dir,* Trish Austin; *Asst Librn,* Pam Watson
Founded 1967. Pop 1,548
Library Holdings: Audiobooks 30; Bks on Deafness & Sign Lang 1; Large Print Bks 62; Bk Vols 2,500; Per Subs 14
Wireless access
Mem of Illinois Heartland Library System
Open Mon, Tues & Thurs 1-7, Wed & Fri 1-5, Sat 8:30am-12:30pm

DIXON

M KATHERINE SHAW BETHEA HOSPITAL*, Medical Library, 403 E First St, 61021. SAN 377-225X. Tel: 815-285-5622. FAX: 815-285-5870. Web Site: ksbhospital.com. *Library Contact,* Heather Diehl; E-mail: hdiehl@ksbhospital.com; Staff 1 (Non-MLS 1)
Founded 1970
Library Holdings: Bk Vols 158; Per Subs 14
Wireless access
Partic in Health Science Library of Illinois
Open Mon-Fri 8-4:30

S DIXON CORRECTIONAL CENTER LIBRARY, 2600 N Brinton Ave, 61021. (Mail add: PO Box 1200, 61021), SAN 371-7208. Tel: 815-288-5561. Web Site: www2.illinois.gov/idoc/facilities/pages/dixoncorrectionalcenter.aspx.
Library Holdings: Bk Titles 9,000; Bk Vols 10,000
Special Collections: Federal & Illinois Law
Restriction: Staff & inmates only

P DIXON PUBLIC LIBRARY*, 221 S Hennepin Ave, 61021-3093. SAN 304-1212. Tel: 815-284-7261. FAX: 815-288-7323. E-mail: maillibrary@dixonpubliclibrary.org. Web Site: www.dixonpubliclibrary.org. *Dir,* Antony Deter; E-mail: antony.deter@dixonpubliclibrary.org; Staff 8 (MLS 1, Non-MLS 7)
Founded 1872. Pop 15,733; Circ 118,554
Library Holdings: Bks on Deafness & Sign Lang 15; Bk Vols 74,000; Per Subs 125
Special Collections: Dixon Evening Telegraph, 1851-present, micro; Lincoln Coll; Local History-Genealogy Coll; Reagan Coll
Automation Activity & Vendor Info: (Cataloging) TLC (The Library Corporation); (Circulation) TLC (The Library Corporation); (OPAC) TLC (The Library Corporation)
Function: 24/7 Electronic res, 24/7 Online cat, Activity rm, Adult bk club, Adult literacy prog, Audiobks via web, Bk club(s), Bks on CD, Children's prog, Computer training, Computers for patron use, Electronic databases & coll, Free DVD rentals, Govt ref serv, ILL available, Internet access, Magazines, Magnifiers for reading, Mail & tel request accepted, Mango lang, Microfiche/film & reading machines, Movies, Music CDs, Online cat, Photocopying/Printing, Prog for adults, Prog for children & young adult, Ref & res, Ref serv available, Scanner, Spanish lang bks, Summer & winter reading prog, Summer reading prog, Wheelchair accessible
Publications: 1942-1945 (history book); Library Lines (Newsletter); Lincoln in Dixon (history book); Memories of the Green River Ordinance Plant
Mem of Reaching Across Illinois Library System (RAILS)
Special Services for the Deaf - TTY equip
Special Services for the Blind - Closed circuit TV magnifier
Open Mon-Thurs 9-8, Fri 9-5, Sat 10-3
Friends of the Library Group

J SAUK VALLEY COMMUNITY COLLEGE*, Learning Resource Center, 173 IL Rte 2, 61021-9112. SAN 304-1239. Tel: 815-835-6247. FAX: 815-288-5651. Web Site: www.svcc.edu/departments/learning-commons/library. *Coordr,* Melanie Armstrong; Tel: 815-288-5511, Ext 210, E-mail: melanie.s.armstrong@svcc.edu; Staff 2 (MLS 2)
Founded 1966. Highest Degree: Associate
Library Holdings: Audiobooks 430; CDs 2,200; DVDs 1,480; e-books 60,000; e-journals 16,000; Bk Vols 50,000; Per Subs 100; Videos 9,500
Special Collections: Illinois & Local History; Popular Culture (film, music & television)
Automation Activity & Vendor Info: (Acquisitions) Ex Libris Group; (Cataloging) Ex Libris Group; (Circulation) Ex Libris Group; (Course Reserve) Ex Libris Group; (ILL) Ex Libris Group; (OPAC) Ex Libris Group; (Serials) Ex Libris Group
Wireless access
Mem of Reaching Across Illinois Library System (RAILS)
Partic in Consortium of Academic & Research Libraries in Illinois; Northern Ill Learning Resources Coop
Open Mon-Thurs 8-7, Fri 8-2 (Fall & Spring); Mon & Wed 7-7, Tues & Thurs 7-5 (Summer)

DOLTON

P DOLTON PUBLIC LIBRARY DISTRICT, 14037 Lincoln Ave, 60419-1091. SAN 304-1247. Tel: 708-849-2385. FAX: 708-841-6640. Web Site: site-mls-dos.ploud.net. *Dir,* Allyson D Withers; E-mail: allysonw@doltonpubliclibrary.org; Staff 13 (MLS 1, Non-MLS 12)
Founded 1954. Pop 25,614; Circ 114,450
Library Holdings: AV Mats 8,300; Large Print Bks 2,256; Bk Vols 99,746; Per Subs 210; Talking Bks 1,282
Special Collections: Adult New Readers Coll
Subject Interests: African-Am hist, Local hist
Automation Activity & Vendor Info: (Cataloging) Innovative Interfaces, Inc; (Circulation) Innovative Interfaces, Inc; (ILL) Innovative Interfaces, Inc; (OPAC) Innovative Interfaces, Inc
Wireless access
Function: ILL available, Photocopying/Printing, Ref serv available
Mem of Reaching Across Illinois Library System (RAILS)
Partic in System Wide Automated Network
Open Mon-Sat 9-6

DONGOLA

P DONGOLA PUBLIC LIBRARY DISTRICT, 114 NE Front St, 62926. (Mail add: PO Box 113, 62926-0113), SAN 376-1487. Tel: 618-827-3622. FAX: 618-827-3622. E-mail: dongolapld@gmail.com. Web Site: donp.illshareit.com. *Dir,* Heather Miller; Staff 1 (Non-MLS 1)
Founded 1983. Pop 1,907
Library Holdings: Bk Titles 11,000; Per Subs 4
Wireless access
Function: Children's prog, Computers for patron use, Free DVD rentals, Story hour, Summer reading prog, Wheelchair accessible
Mem of Illinois Heartland Library System
Open Tues & Wed 2-6, Thurs 10-12 & 1-7, Sat 9-1

DOWNERS GROVE

P DOWNERS GROVE PUBLIC LIBRARY, 1050 Curtiss St, 60515. SAN 304-1255. Tel: 630-960-1200. FAX: 630-960-9374. E-mail: circdesk@dglibrary.org, info@dglibrary.org. Web Site: www.dglibrary.org. *Libr Dir,* Julie Milavec; Tel: 630-960-1200, Ext 4300, E-mail: jmilavec@dglibrary.org; *Operations Dir,* Ian Knorr; Tel: 630-960-1200, Ext 4244, E-mail: iknorr@dglibrary.org; *Asst Dir,* Jen Ryjewski; Tel: 630-960-1200, Ext 4299, E-mail: jryjewski@dglibrary.org; *Asst Dir, Support Serv,* Sue O'Brien; E-mail: sobrien@dglibrary.org; *Adult & Teen Serv Mgr,* Lizzie Matowski; Tel: 630-960-1200, Ext 4247, E-mail: lmatowski@dglibrary.org; *Mgr, Ch Serv,* Allyson Renell; Tel: 630-960-1200, Ext 4260, E-mail: arenell@dglibrary.org; *Circ Mgr,* Christine Lees; Tel: 630-960-1200, Ext 4264, E-mail: clees@dglibrary.org; *IT Mgr,* Paul Regis; Tel: 630-960-1200, Ext 4291, E-mail: pregis@dglibrary.org; *Pub Relations Mgr,* Cindy Khatri; Tel: 630-960-1200, Ext 4296, E-mail: ckhatri@dglibrary.org; Staff 20 (MLS 20)
Founded 1891. Pop 49,213; Circ 990,982
Jan 2015-Dec 2015 Income $5,104,036, State $128,802, Locally Generated Income $4,708,186, Other $267,048. Mats Exp $644,526, Books $284,534, AV Mat $134,353, Electronic Ref Mat (Incl. Access Fees) $206,319. Sal $2,715,994
Library Holdings: CDs 25,344; DVDs 25,044; e-books 27,790; Bk Vols 227,982; Per Subs 414
Subject Interests: Local hist
Automation Activity & Vendor Info: (Cataloging) SirsiDynix; (Circulation) SirsiDynix; (ILL) SirsiDynix; (OPAC) SirsiDynix
Wireless access
Function: 24/7 Electronic res, 24/7 Online cat, Adult bk club, Art exhibits, Audiobks on Playaways & MP3, Audiobks via web, Bk club(s), Bks on CD, Children's prog, Computer training, Computers for patron use, E-Readers, Electronic databases & coll, Free DVD rentals, Genealogy discussion group, Homebound delivery serv, ILL available, Internet access, Life-long learning prog for all ages, Magazines, Mail & tel request accepted, Mango lang, Meeting rooms, Microfiche/film & reading machines, Movies, Museum passes, Music CDs, Notary serv, Online cat, OverDrive digital audio bks, Photocopying/Printing, Printer for laptops & handheld devices, Prog for adults, Prog for children & young adult, Ref serv available, Scanner, Spanish lang bks, Story hour, Study rm, Summer reading prog, Tax forms, Teen prog, Telephone ref
Publications: Discoveries (Newsletter); E-ssentials (Newsletter)
Mem of Reaching Across Illinois Library System (RAILS)
Partic in System Wide Automated Network
Open Mon-Fri 9-8, Sat 9-5, Sun 1-5
Friends of the Library Group

CM MIDWESTERN UNIVERSITY*, Downers Grove Campus Library, 555 31st St, 60515. SAN 339-8072. Tel: 630-515-6200. FAX: 630-515-6195. Reference E-mail: reference@midwestern.edu. Web Site: library.midwestern.edu. *Dir, Libr Serv,* Rebecca Caton; E-mail: rcaton@midwestern.edu
Founded 1913. Highest Degree: Doctorate
Subject Interests: Biomed sci, Dental, Dentistry, Occupational therapy, Optometry, Osteopathic med, Pharm, Phys therapy, Speech-lang pathology
Wireless access
Publications: Newsletter (Quarterly)
Partic in Consortium of Academic & Research Libraries in Illinois; National Network of Libraries of Medicine Region 6; Regional Med Libr - Region 3
Open Mon-Fri 8am-10pm, Sat & Sun 12-10

DU QUOIN

P DU QUOIN PUBLIC LIBRARY*, 28 S Washington St, 62832. SAN 304-128X. Tel: 618-542-5045. FAX: 618-542-4735. Web Site: duquoinlibrary.org. *Libr Dir,* Kristina Benson; E-mail: kbenson@duquoinlibrary.org
Founded 1934. Pop 6,400
Library Holdings: Bk Vols 22,000; Per Subs 65
Subject Interests: Genealogy
Automation Activity & Vendor Info: (Cataloging) SirsiDynix; (Circulation) SirsiDynix
Wireless access
Mem of Illinois Heartland Library System
Open Mon-Thurs 11-7, Fri 11-5, Sat 9-3
Friends of the Library Group

DUNLAP

P DUNLAP PUBLIC LIBRARY DISTRICT*, 302 S First St, 61525. SAN 304-1301. Tel: 309-243-5716. FAX: 309-243-5874. E-mail: ask@dunlaplibrary.org. Web Site: www.dunlaplibrary.org. *Dir, Ref Serv,* Laura Keyes-Kaplafka; E-mail: director@dunlaplibrary.org; *Head, Circ,* Tina Murphy; E-mail: tmurphy@dunlaplibrary.org; *Ad,* Melissa Weyeneth; E-mail: mweyeneth@dunlaplibrary.org; *Coll Develop, Mkt Coordr,* Kelly Kerckhove; E-mail: kkerckhove@dunlaplibrary.org; Staff 8 (MLS 2, Non-MLS 6)
Founded 1954. Pop 5,184; Circ 59,115
Library Holdings: Bk Titles 30,698; Per Subs 88
Wireless access
Publications: The Library Connection (District newsletter)
Open Mon-Thurs 9-8, Fri 9-6, Sat 9-2

DUPO

P DAUGHERTY PUBLIC LIBRARY DISTRICT*, 220 S Fifth St, 62239. SAN 304-131X. Tel: 618-286-4444. FAX: 618-286-3636. E-mail: dupolibrary@dupolibrary.org. Web Site: www.dupolibrary.org. *Dir,* Carol Brockmeyer; E-mail: carolb@dupolibrary.org
Founded 1971. Pop 7,700; Circ 40,529
Library Holdings: Bk Vols 28,000; Per Subs 53
Wireless access
Mem of Illinois Heartland Library System
Open Mon-Thurs 9-8, Fri & Sat 9-4
Friends of the Library Group

DWIGHT

P PRAIRIE CREEK PUBLIC LIBRARY*, 501 Carriage House Lane, 60420. SAN 304-1328. Tel: 815-584-3061. FAX: 815-584-3120. Web Site: www.prairiecreeklibrary.org. *Dir,* Sherrie Rhodes; E-mail: prairiecreekdirector@gmail.com; Staff 7 (MLS 1, Non-MLS 6)
Founded 1926. Pop 6,234; Circ 39,053
Library Holdings: Bks on Deafness & Sign Lang 20; High Interest/Low Vocabulary Bk Vols 100; Bk Titles 20,000; Bk Vols 31,500; Per Subs 70; Spec Interest Per Sub 10
Subject Interests: Am Civil War, Local hist
Automation Activity & Vendor Info: (Cataloging) Follett Software; (Circulation) Follett Software; (ILL) TLC (The Library Corporation); (OPAC) Follett Software
Wireless access
Publications: American Libraries (Annual report); Public Libraries (Annual report)
Open Mon-Thurs 10-8, Fri 10-5, Sat 10-3
Friends of the Library Group

EARLVILLE

P EARLVILLE LIBRARY DISTRICT*, 205 Winthrop St, 60518. (Mail add: PO Box 420, 60518-0420), SAN 304-1336. Tel: 815-246-9543. FAX: 815-246-6391. E-mail: inquiry@earlvillelibrary.org. Web Site: www.earlvillelibrary.org. *Librn,* Paige Frechman
Pop 2,653; Circ 21,350
Library Holdings: DVDs 234; Large Print Bks 148; Bk Vols 20,000; Per Subs 57; Talking Bks 364; Videos 642
Special Collections: Local Weekly Newspaper, 1914-present, micro. Oral History
Automation Activity & Vendor Info: (Acquisitions) SirsiDynix-WorkFlows; (Cataloging) SirsiDynix-WorkFlows; (Circulation) SirsiDynix-WorkFlows
Wireless access
Mem of Reaching Across Illinois Library System (RAILS)
Open Mon & Wed 10-8, Tues & Fri 10-5, Sat 10-2
Friends of the Library Group

EAST ALTON

P EAST ALTON PUBLIC LIBRARY DISTRICT*, 250 Washington Ave, 62024-1547. SAN 304-1344. Tel: 618-259-0787. FAX: 618-259-0788. E-mail: eastaltonlibrary@gmail.com. Web Site: www.eastaltonlibrary.org. *Dir,* Richard Chartrand; *Asst Dir,* Darlene Pingolt; Staff 10 (MLS 1, Non-MLS 9)
Founded 1936. Pop 14,796; Circ 86,000
Library Holdings: Bk Vols 62,000; Per Subs 186
Automation Activity & Vendor Info: (Acquisitions) Innovative Interfaces, Inc
Wireless access
Mem of Illinois Heartland Library System
Open Mon-Thurs 9:30-6:30, Fri & Sat 9:30-5

EAST DUBUQUE

P EAST DUBUQUE DISTRICT LIBRARY*, 122 Wisconsin Ave, 61025-1325. SAN 304-1352. Tel: 815-747-3052. FAX: 815-747-6062. Web Site: www.eastdubuquelibrary.com. *Dir,* Jessica Arnold; E-mail: director@eastdubuquelibrary.com; *Ch Serv,* Kathy Williams; Staff 3 (Non-MLS 3)
Founded 1937. Pop 4,459; Circ 18,011
Library Holdings: Bks on Deafness & Sign Lang 10; Bk Titles 14,997; Per Subs 33
Wireless access

Publications: Booklist; Illinois Libraries; Newsletter
Mem of Reaching Across Illinois Library System (RAILS)
Special Services for the Deaf - TTY equip
Special Services for the Blind - Bks on cassette; Talking bks
Open Mon-Thurs 10-7, Fri 10-5, Sat 10-2

EAST DUNDEE

P FOX RIVER VALLEY PUBLIC LIBRARY DISTRICT, Dundee Library, 555 Barrington Ave, 60118-1496. SAN 304-1298. Tel: 847-428-3661. FAX: 847-428-4021. Web Site: www.frvpld.info. *Interim Dir,* Roxane Bennett; E-mail: rbennett@frvpld.info; *Asst Dir,* Heather Zabski; E-mail: hzabski@frvpld.info; *Accounts Mgr,* Keri Carroll; E-mail: kcarroll@frvpld.info; *Adult & Teen Serv Mgr,* Jason Katsion; E-mail: jkatsion@frvpld.info; *Acq/Tech Serv Mgr, Purchasing Mgr,* Karin Nelson; E-mail: knelson@frvpld.info; *Br Mgr,* Brittany Berger; E-mail: bberger@frvpld.info; *Fac Mgr,* Michael Lorenzetti; E-mail: mlorenzetti@frvpld.info; *IT Mgr,* John Sabala; E-mail: jsabala@frvpld.info; *Youth Serv Mgr,* Monica Boyer; E-mail: mboyer@frvpld.info; Staff 31 (MLS 11, Non-MLS 20)
Founded 1876. Pop 69,338; Circ 519,734
Jul 2020-Jun 2021. Mats Exp $396,172. Sal $1,633,657
Automation Activity & Vendor Info: (Acquisitions) Innovative Interfaces, Inc. - Polaris; (Cataloging) Innovative Interfaces, Inc. - Polaris; (Circulation) Innovative Interfaces, Inc. - Polaris; (OPAC) Innovative Interfaces, Inc. - Polaris; (Serials) Innovative Interfaces, Inc. - Polaris
Wireless access
Function: 24/7 Electronic res, 24/7 Online cat, 3D Printer, Activity rm, Adult bk club, Adult literacy prog, After school storytime, Archival coll, Art exhibits, Art programs, Audiobks on Playaways & MP3, Audiobks via web, AV serv, Bilingual assistance for Spanish patrons, Bk club(s), Bks on CD, Children's prog, Citizenship assistance, Computer training, Computers for patron use, Electronic databases & coll, Equip loans & repairs, For res purposes, Free DVD rentals, Holiday prog, Home delivery & serv to seniorr ctr & nursing homes, Homebound delivery serv, Homework prog, ILL available, Internet access, Life-long learning prog for all ages, Literacy & newcomer serv, Magazines, Magnifiers for reading, Makerspace, Meeting rooms, Movies, Museum passes, Music CDs, Notary serv, Online cat, Orientations, Outreach serv, OverDrive digital audio bks, Photocopying/Printing, Preschool outreach, Preschool reading prog, Printer for laptops & handheld devices, Prog for adults, Prog for children & young adult, Ref serv available, Senior computer classes, Senior outreach, Serves people with intellectual disabilities, Spanish lang bks, STEM programs, Story hour, Summer & winter reading prog, Summer reading prog, Teen prog, Telephone ref, Wheelchair accessible, Winter reading prog, Workshops
Publications: Newsletter
Mem of Reaching Across Illinois Library System (RAILS)
Partic in Cooperative Computer Services - CCS
Open Mon-Thurs 9-9, Fri & Sat 9-5, Sun 1-5
Friends of the Library Group

EAST MOLINE

S EAST MOLINE CORRECTIONAL CENTER LIBRARY*, 100 Hillcrest Rd, 61244. SAN 376-088X. Tel: 309-755-4511. FAX: 309-755-0498. Web Site: www2.illinois.gov/idoc/facilities/pages/eastmolinecorrectionalcenter.aspx. *Library Contact,* Jenny Wheat
Library Holdings: Bk Titles 7,141
Open Tues-Fri 10-8

P EAST MOLINE PUBLIC LIBRARY*, 740 16th Ave, 61244-2122. SAN 304-1379. Tel: 309-755-9614. FAX: 309-755-3901. E-mail: eastmolinepl@gmail.com. Web Site: www.eastmolinelibrary.org. *Dir,* Laura Long; E-mail: longl@eastmolinelibrary.org; *Asst Dir,* Tami Cox; E-mail: coxt@eastmolinelibrary.org; Staff 14 (MLS 1, Non-MLS 13)
Founded 1915. Pop 21,431; Circ 135,680
Library Holdings: DVDs 3,956; e-books 6,048; Electronic Media & Resources 15; Bk Vols 65,407; Per Subs 130; Talking Bks 6,236
Automation Activity & Vendor Info: (Circulation) SirsiDynix
Wireless access
Publications: EMPL Memo (Newsletter)
Mem of Reaching Across Illinois Library System (RAILS)
Partic in RiverShare Libraries
Friends of the Library Group

EAST PEORIA

P FONDULAC PUBLIC LIBRARY DISTRICT*, 400 Richland St, 61611. SAN 304-1395. Tel: 309-699-3917. FAX: 309-699-7851. E-mail: reference@fondulaclibrary.org. Web Site: fondulaclibrary.org. *Libr Dir,* Genna Buhr; *Bus Mgr,* Tammy Geier
Founded 1935. Pop 20,836; Circ 151,318
Library Holdings: AV Mats 4,613; e-books 325; Bk Vols 72,459; Per Subs 108
Special Collections: East Peoria & Tazewell County History
Subject Interests: Local hist
Automation Activity & Vendor Info: (Acquisitions) TLC (The Library Corporation); (Circulation) TLC (The Library Corporation); (OPAC) CARL.Solution (TLC)
Wireless access
Function: ILL available, Photocopying/Printing, Prog for children & young adult, Ref serv available, Summer reading prog, Telephone ref, Wheelchair accessible
Mem of Reaching Across Illinois Library System (RAILS)
Open Mon-Thurs 9-9, Fri 9-6, Sat 9-5, Sun (Sept-May) 1-5
Friends of the Library Group

J ILLINOIS CENTRAL COLLEGE*, East Peoria Campus Library, Kenneth L Edward Library Administration Bldgs, L312, One College Dr, 61635-0001. SAN 304-1409. Tel: 309-694-5422. Reference Tel: 309-694-5355. FAX: 309-694-5473. Reference E-mail: epref@icc.edu. Web Site: icc.edu/library. *Libr Serv Dir,* Cate Kaufman; Tel: 309-694-8504, E-mail: cathryne.kaufman@icc.edu; *Electronic Res Librn,* Jessica Bastian; Tel: 309-690-6961, E-mail: jessica.bastian@icc.edu; *Ref Librn,* Amy Glass; Tel: 309-694-5748, E-mail: amy.glass@icc.edu; *Tech Serv Librn,* Bryan Clark; Tel: 309-694-5508, E-mail: bryan.clark@icc.edu; Staff 6 (MLS 6)
Founded 1967. Enrl 7,126; Fac 232; Highest Degree: Associate
Library Holdings: AV Mats 5,708; e-books 55,000; Bk Titles 95,000; Bk Vols 100,000; Per Subs 11,000
Automation Activity & Vendor Info: (Cataloging) Ex Libris Group; (Circulation) Ex Libris Group; (Course Reserve) Ex Libris Group; (OPAC) Ex Libris Group
Wireless access
Partic in Consortium of Academic & Research Libraries in Illinois; Network of Illinois Learning Resources in Community Colleges; Northern Illinois Learning Resources Cooperative; OCLC Online Computer Library Center, Inc; OCLC-LVIS
Open Mon-Thurs 7am-10pm, Fri 7-4, Sat 11-4, Sun 12-4

EAST SAINT LOUIS

P EAST SAINT LOUIS PUBLIC LIBRARY*, 5300 State St, 62203. SAN 304-1417. Tel: 618-397-0991. FAX: 618-397-1260. *Head Librn,* Millicent Cason
Founded 1872. Pop 46,000; Circ 175,000
Library Holdings: Bk Vols 53,000; Per Subs 40
Special Collections: Metro-East Journal since 1889, micro
Automation Activity & Vendor Info: (Acquisitions) SirsiDynix; (Cataloging) SirsiDynix; (Circulation) SirsiDynix
Mem of Illinois Heartland Library System
Open Mon-Thurs 9-7:45, Fri & Sat 9-4:45
Friends of the Library Group

S ILLINOIS DEPARTMENT OF CORRECTIONS*, Southwestern Illinois Correctional Center Library, 950 Kingshighway St, 62203. Tel: 618-394-2200, Ext 407. Web Site: www2.illinois.gov/idoc/facilities/Pages/southwesternillinoiscorrectionalcenter.aspx. *Librn,* Steve Bennett; E-mail: steven.bennett@illinois.gov
Library Holdings: Bk Vols 5,000; Per Subs 24
Restriction: Not open to pub

J SOUTHERN ILLINOIS UNIVERSITY EDWARDSVILLE*, East Saint Louis Learning Resource Center, 601 James R Thompson Blvd, Bldg B, 62201. SAN 304-1441. Tel: 618-874-8719. FAX: 618-874-6383. E-mail: siue.esl.library@gmail.com. Administration E-mail: blong@siue.edu. Web Site: eslccc.com/resource-center. *Operations Assoc,* Brittany Long; Tel: 618-874-6357, E-mail: blong@siue.edu; Staff 3 (MLS 1, Non-MLS 2)
Founded 1969. Enrl 1,000; Fac 100; Highest Degree: Associate
Library Holdings: CDs 3,000; DVDs 300; e-books 8,892; Bk Titles 15,000; Per Subs 200; Videos 700
Special Collections: African-American Coll (Authors, Personalities & Local History)
Subject Interests: African-Am
Automation Activity & Vendor Info: (Cataloging) Innovative Interfaces, Inc; (Circulation) Innovative Interfaces, Inc; (Course Reserve) Innovative Interfaces, Inc; (ILL) OCLC; (OPAC) Innovative Interfaces, Inc
Function: Audio & video playback equip for onsite use, Bks on CD, CD-ROM, Computers for patron use, Distance learning, Electronic databases & coll, For res purposes, Free DVD rentals, ILL available, Music CDs, Online cat, Photocopying/Printing, Ref serv available, VHS videos, Wheelchair accessible
Mem of Illinois Heartland Library System
Partic in Association for Rural & Small Libraries
Restriction: Borrowing privileges limited to fac & registered students, Closed stack

GL UNITED STATES COURTS LIBRARY*, Southern District of Illinois, 750 Missouri Ave, 62202. Tel: 618-482-9477. FAX: 618-482-9234. Web Site: www.lb7.uscourts.gov. *Librn,* Chris Tighe
Library Holdings: Bk Vols 5,000
Wireless access
Restriction: Open to pub by appt only

EDWARDSVILLE

P EDWARDSVILLE PUBLIC LIBRARY*, 112 S Kansas St, 62025. SAN 304-145X. Tel: 618-692-7556. FAX: 618-692-9566. Reference E-mail: info@edwardsvillelibrary.org. Web Site: edwardsvillelibrary.org. *Dir,* Jill Schardt; E-mail: jills@edwpl.org; *Asst Dir,* Cary Harvangt; E-mail: caryh@edwpl.org; *Head, Adult Serv,* Jacob Del Rio; E-mail: jacobd@edwpl.org; *Head, Tech Serv,* Gwen Bumpers; E-mail: gwenb@edwpl.org; *Head, Youth Serv, Librn,* Megan Prueter; E-mail: meganp@edwpl.org; Staff 33 (MLS 6, Non-MLS 27)
Founded 1818. Pop 25,073; Circ 281,357
Library Holdings: Bk Vols 112,171
Special Collections: Madison County Genealogical Society Coll
Wireless access
Function: Archival coll, Homebound delivery serv, ILL available, Internet access, Magnifiers for reading, Photocopying/Printing, Prog for adults, Prog for children & young adult, Ref serv available, Summer reading prog, Telephone ref, Wheelchair accessible
Mem of Illinois Heartland Library System
Partic in Coop Libr Agency for Syst & Servs
Open Mon-Thurs 9-9, Fri 9-6, Sat 9-5, Sun 12-5
Friends of the Library Group

P ILLINOIS HEARTLAND LIBRARY SYSTEM*, 6725 Goshen Rd, 62025. Tel: 618-656-3216. FAX: 618-656-9401. Web Site: illinoisheartland.org. *Exec Dir,* Ms Leslie Bednar; Tel: 618-656-3216, Ext 420, E-mail: lbednar@illinoisheartland.org
Member Libraries: A Herr Smith & E E Smith Loda Township Library; Albion Public Library; Allerton Public Library District; Altamont Public Library; Anne West Lindsey District Library; Arcola Public Library District; Argenta-Oreana Public Library District; Ashley Public Library District; Assumption Public Library District; Athens Municipal Library; Atwood-Hammond Public Library; Auburn Public Library; Barclay Public Library District; Belleville Public Library; Bement Public Library District; Benton Public Library District; Bethalto Public Library District; Blackburn College; Blue Mound Memorial Library District; Blue Ridge Township Public Library; Breese Public Library; Brighton Memorial Library; Bryan-Bennett Library; Bunker Hill Public Library District; C E Brehm Memorial Public Library District; Cahokia Public Library District; Cairo Public Library; Camargo Township District Library; Carbondale Public Library; Carlinville Public Library; Carmi Public Library; Carnegie-Schuyler Library; Carrier Mills-Stonefort Public Library District; Carrollton Public Library; Case-Halstead Public Library; Casey Township Library; Caseyville Public Library District; Catlin Public Library District; Central Citizens' Library District; Centralia Regional Library District; Champaign Public Library; Charleston Carnegie Public Library; Chatham Area Public Library District; Chester Public Library; Chrisman Public Library; Christopher Public Library; Cissna Park Community Library District; Columbia Public Library; Coulterville Public Library; Crab Orchard Public Library District; Danville Area Community College Library; Danville Public Library; Daugherty Public Library District; Decatur Public Library; Divernon Township Library; Dodge Memorial Public Library; Dongola Public Library District; Doyle Public Library District; Dry Point Township Library; Du Quoin Public Library; East Alton Public Library District; East Saint Louis Public Library; Eastern Illinois University; Edwardsville Public Library; Effingham Public Library; Eldorado Memorial Public Library District; Elizabeth Titus Memorial Library; Elkhart Public Library District; Elwood Township Carnegie Library; Evans Public Library District; Evansville Public Library; Fairfield Public Library; Fairview Heights Public Library; Flora Public Library; Forsyth Public Library; Frank Bertetti Benld Public Library; Freeburg Area Library; Georgetown Public Library; Germantown Public Library District; Gillespie Public Library; Gilman-Danforth District Library; Girard Township Library; Glen Carbon Centennial Library District; Golconda Public Library; Goose Creek District Library; Grand Prairie of the West Public Library District; Greenfield Public Library; Greenup Township Public Library; Greenville College; Greenville Public Library; Groffe Memorial Library; Hanson Professional Services Inc; Harrisburg Public Library District; Hartford Public Library District; Hayner Public Library District; Herrick Township Public Library; Herrin City Library; Hillsboro Public Library; Homer Community Library; Hoopeston Public Library; Hope Welty Public Library District; Illinois Department of Natural Resources; Illinois Department of Transportation; Illinois Early Intervention Clearinghouse; Illinois Eastern Community College; Illinois Environmental Protection Agency Library; Illinois State Museum Library; Illiopolis-Niantic Public Library District; Jerseyville Public Library; Johnston City Public Library; Jonesboro Public Library; Kansas Community Memorial Library; Kaskaskia College Library; Kinmundy Public Library; Kitchell Memorial Library; Lake Land College Library; Lakeview College of Nursing; Lawrence Public Library District; Lebanon Public Library; Lincoln Christian University; Lincoln College; Lincoln Land Community College Library; Lincoln Library; Lincoln Public Library District; Litchfield Carnegie Public Library; Logan Correctional Center Library; Louis Latzer Memorial Public Library; Lovington Public Library District; Madison Public Library; Mahomet Public Library District; Marion Carnegie Library; Marissa Area Public Library District; Maroa Public Library District; Marrowbone Public Library District; Martinsville Public Library District; Mason City Public Library District; Mattoon Public Library; McCoy Memorial Library; McKendree University; Melvin Public Library; Memorial Medical Center; Metropolis Public Library; Milford District Library; Millikin University; Millstadt Library; Mississippi Valley Library District; Morrison-Talbott Library; Mounds Public Library; Mount Carmel Public Library; Mount Olive Public Library; Mount Pulaski Public Library District; Mount Zion District Library; Moweaqua Public Library; Moyer District Library; Nashville Public Library; National Council of Teachers of English Library; Neoga Public Library District; New Athens District Library; New Baden Public Library; Newman Regional Library District; Newton Public Library & Museum; Nokomis Public Library; Norris City Memorial Public Library District; O'Fallon Public Library; Oakwood Public Library District; Ogden Rose Public Library; Olmsted Public Library; Olney Central College; Olney Public Library; Onarga Community Public Library District; Palestine Public Library District; Paris Carnegie Public Library; Patoka Public Library; Pawnee Public Library; Paxton Carnegie Library; Petersburg Public Library; Philo Public Library District; Pinckneyville Public Library; Piper City Public Library District; Potomac Public Library; Ramsey Public Library; Rantoul Public Library; Red Bud Public Library; Rend Lake College; Richland Community College; Rick Warren Memorial Public Library District; Riverton Village Library; Robinson Public Library District; Rochester Public Library District; Roodhouse Public Library; Rosiclare Memorial Public Library; Roxana Public Library District; Royalton Public Library District; Saint Elmo Public Library District; Saint Mary's Hospital; Sallie Logan Public Library; Sarah Bush Lincoln Health Center; Sesser Public Library; Shawnee Community College Library; Shawneetown Public Library; Shelbyville Public Library; Sheldon Public Library District; Sherman Public Library District; Sidell District Library; Sidney Community Library; Six Mile Regional Library District; Smithton Public Library District; South County Public Library District; South Macon Public Library District; Southern Illinois University Edwardsville; Southern Illinois University School of Medicine; Southwestern Illinois College; Sparta Public Library; Springfield Art Association; St John's Hospital; St Joseph Township-Swearingen Memorial Library; Staunton Public Library; Steeleville Area Public Library District; Stinson Memorial Public Library District; Stonington Township Public Library; Sumpter Township Library; Taylorville Public Library; The Urbana Free Library; Tolono Public Library District; Trenton Public Library; Tri-Township Public Library District; Tuscola Public Library; United States Army Corps of Engineers; University of Illinois at Springfield; University of Illinois Library at Urbana-Champaign; Valmeyer Public Library District; Vance Township Library; Venice Public Library; Vespasian Warner Public Library District; Vienna Carnegie Public Library; Watseka Public Library; Wayne City Public Library; Weldon Public Library District; West Frankfort Public Library; West Salem Public Library; West Sangamon Public Library; West Union District Library; Westville Public Library District; White Hall Township Library; Williamsville Public Library; Willow Branch Township Library; Windsor Storm Memorial Public Library District; Witt Township Memorial Library; Wood River Public Library; Worden Public Library District; Zeigler Public Library
Open Mon-Fri 8-4:30

S MADISON COUNTY HISTORICAL MUSEUM & ARCHIVAL LIBRARY*, 715 N Main St, 62025-1111. SAN 326-601X. Tel: 618-656-7562, 618-656-7569. FAX: 618-659-3457. Web Site: www.madisoncountymuseum.org. *Dir,* John Parkin; *Archives Mgr,* Mary Westerhold; E-mail: mtwesterhold@co.madison.il.us; *Archivist,* LaVerne Bloemker; *Archivist,* Carol Frisse; *Curator of Objects & Textiles,* Mary Louise Brown
Library Holdings: Bk Vols 3,000; Per Subs 12; Spec Interest Per Sub 10
Special Collections: Edwardsville Street Index & Housing Inventory (beginning 1894); Historic Photos; Index to First Sales of Land in Illinois; Madison County Poor Farm Records; N O Nelson-Village of Leclaire Papers; WPA Index to Alton Telegraph 1836-1940; WPA Index to Edwardsville Intelligencer 1862-1937
Subject Interests: Genealogy, Local hist
Wireless access
Publications: General Index for Brink's History of Madison County, Ill 1882; Madison County Poor Farm Index; Military Index for Brink's History of Madison County, Ill; Republication of Brink's History of Madison County Ill 1882
Open Wed-Fri 9-4, Sun 1-4
Restriction: Non-circulating to the pub
Friends of the Library Group

L MADISON COUNTY LAW LIBRARY*, 155 N Main St, 62025. Tel: 618-296-4900, 618-296-5921. FAX: 618-692-7475. E-mail: lawlibrary@co.madison.il.us. Web Site: www.co.madison.il.us/departments/circuit_court/law_library. *Law Librn,* Angela Wille; E-mail: anwille@co.madison.il.us; Staff 1 (Non-MLS 1)
Library Holdings: Bk Vols 5,000
Special Services for the Blind - Computer with voice synthesizer for visually impaired persons
Open Mon-Fri 8:30-4:30

C SOUTHERN ILLINOIS UNIVERSITY EDWARDSVILLE*, Elijah P Lovejoy Library, Campus Box 1063, 30 Hairpin Dr, 62026-1063. SAN 340-3777. Tel: 618-650-4636. Interlibrary Loan Service Tel: 618-650-2174. Web Site: www.siue.edu/lovejoy-library. *Interim Dean of Libr,* Lydia Jackson; Tel: 618-650-2712, E-mail: ljackso@siue.edu; *Interim Asst Dean,* Juliet Gray; Tel: 618-650-3429, E-mail: jkerico@siue.edu
Founded 1957. Enrl 13,295; Fac 518; Highest Degree: Master
Library Holdings: AV Mats 29,495; e-books 1,629; Bk Titles 538,880; Bk Vols 788,003; Per Subs 14,371
Special Collections: Illinois Coll; Illinois, Missouri, & Regional Maps; Mormons in Illinois; Music Coll, sheet music, piano rolls, records, mss, cinema music, hymnals, song bks, instruments, photogs; Slavic-American Imprints Coll. State Document Depository; US Document Depository
Subject Interests: Bus, Educ, Engr, Illinois, Nursing
Automation Activity & Vendor Info: (Acquisitions) Ex Libris Group; (Cataloging) Ex Libris Group; (Circulation) Ex Libris Group; (Course Reserve) Ex Libris Group; (ILL) Ex Libris Group; (OPAC) Ex Libris Group; (Serials) Ex Libris Group
Wireless access
Publications: Lovejoy Imprints (Newsletter)
Partic in Conference of Dirs of State Univ Librns of Ill; Ill Coordinated Coll Mgt Prog; OCLC Online Computer Library Center, Inc
Open Mon-Thurs 7:30am-1am, Fri 7:30-6, Sat 10-6, Sun 10am-1am
Friends of the Library Group
Departmental Libraries:
CM BIOMEDICAL LIBRARY, School of Dental Medicine, 2800 College Ave, Bldg 277, Alton, 62002, SAN 303-674X. Tel: 618-474-7277. FAX: 618-474-7270. *Librn,* Candace Hope; Tel: 618-474-7274, E-mail: cawalte@siue.edu; Staff 2 (MLS 2)
Founded 1970
Library Holdings: Bk Vols 35,000; Per Subs 151
Automation Activity & Vendor Info: (Acquisitions) Ex Libris Group; (Cataloging) Ex Libris Group; (Circulation) Ex Libris Group; (Course Reserve) Ex Libris Group; (ILL) Ex Libris Group; (OPAC) Ex Libris Group; (Serials) Ex Libris Group
Partic in Consortium of Academic & Research Libraries in Illinois; Illinois Library & Information Network
Open Mon-Thurs 7:45am-11pm, Fri 7:45-5, Sat 1-7, Sun 1-10
Friends of the Library Group

EFFINGHAM

P EFFINGHAM PUBLIC LIBRARY*, 200 Third St, 62401. SAN 304-1476. Tel: 217-342-2464. FAX: 217-342-2413. E-mail: info@effinghamlibrary.org. Web Site: www.effinghamlibrary.org. *Dir,* Amanda D McKay; Tel: 217-342-2464, Ext 5, E-mail: amanda@effinghamlibrary.org; *Adult Serv Mgr,* Johnna Schultz; Tel: 217-342-2464, Ext 23, E-mail: johnna@effinghamlibrary.org; *Circ Mgr,* Margo Probst; Tel: 217-342-2464, Ext 2, E-mail: margo@effinghamlibrary.org; *Youth Serv Mgr,* Sara Smith; Tel: 217-342-2464, Ext 6, E-mail: sara@effinghamlibrary.org; Staff 21 (MLS 1, Non-MLS 20)
Founded 1883. Pop 12,300; Circ 165,000
Library Holdings: Bk Vols 56,000; Per Subs 50
Subject Interests: Genealogy, World War II
Automation Activity & Vendor Info: (Cataloging) Innovative Interfaces, Inc; (Circulation) Innovative Interfaces, Inc; (OPAC) Innovative Interfaces, Inc
Wireless access
Function: Ref serv available
Mem of Illinois Heartland Library System
Open Mon-Thurs 9-8, Fri 9-6, Sat 9-5

EL PASO

P EL PASO PUBLIC LIBRARY*, 149 W First St, 61738. SAN 304-1484. Tel: 309-527-4360. FAX: 309-527-7100. E-mail: epplstaff@gmail.com. Web Site: www.elpasopubliclibrary.net. *Dir,* Carla Skare; *Asst Dir, Ch,* Courtney Reid
Founded 1873. Pop 2,695; Circ 24,000
Library Holdings: Large Print Bks 1,000; Bk Vols 25,000; Per Subs 30
Special Collections: Local Newspaper, 1888-present
Automation Activity & Vendor Info: (Circulation) SirsiDynix
Wireless access
Mem of Reaching Across Illinois Library System (RAILS)
Open Mon & Tues 9-7, Wed & Fri 12-6, Thurs 9-6, Sat 10-1

ELBURN

P TOWN & COUNTRY PUBLIC LIBRARY DISTRICT*, 320 E North St, 60119. SAN 304-1492. Tel: 630-365-2244. FAX: 630-365-2358. E-mail: library@elburn.lib.il.us. Web Site: www.elburn.lib.il.us. *Interim Libr Dir,* Dwayne Nelson; E-mail: dnelson@elburn.lib.il.us; Staff 23 (MLS 3, Non-MLS 20)
Founded 1929. Pop 12,392; Circ 144,041
Special Collections: Local History Coll
Automation Activity & Vendor Info: (Acquisitions) SirsiDynix; (Cataloging) SirsiDynix; (Circulation) SirsiDynix; (OPAC) SirsiDynix
Wireless access
Function: Adult bk club, Archival coll, Audiobks via web, Bks on CD, Chess club, Children's prog, Computer training, Computers for patron use, E-Readers, E-Reserves, Electronic databases & coll, Family literacy, Free DVD rentals, Genealogy discussion group, Holiday prog, Homebound delivery serv, Homework prog, ILL available, Internet access, Literacy & newcomer serv, Magnifiers for reading, Museum passes, Music CDs, Notary serv, Online cat, Online ref, Outreach serv, OverDrive digital audio bks, Photocopying/Printing, Preschool outreach, Preschool reading prog, Prog for adults, Prog for children & young adult, Ref serv available, Senior computer classes, Senior outreach, Story hour, Study rm, Summer & winter reading prog, Summer reading prog, Tax forms, Wheelchair accessible
Mem of Reaching Across Illinois Library System (RAILS)
Partic in System Wide Automated Network
Open Mon-Thurs 9-9, Fri & Sat 9-5, Sun 1-5
Friends of the Library Group

ELDORADO

P ELDORADO MEMORIAL PUBLIC LIBRARY DISTRICT*, 1001 Grant St, 62930-1714. (Mail add: PO Box 426, 62930-0426), SAN 304-1506. Tel: 618-273-7922. FAX: 618-273-4402. E-mail: eldoradolibrary@yahoo.com. Web Site: www.eldoradomemoriallibrary.com. *Dir,* Felicia Murray; *Asst Dir,* Miriam Richardson; Staff 4 (MLS 1, Non-MLS 3)
Founded 1987. Pop 7,672; Circ 41,306
Library Holdings: Bk Vols 32,000; Per Subs 30
Automation Activity & Vendor Info: (Cataloging) OCLC Connexion
Wireless access
Mem of Illinois Heartland Library System
Open Mon-Thurs 9-7, Fri & Sat 9-5, Sun 1-5
Friends of the Library Group

ELGIN

P GAIL BORDEN PUBLIC LIBRARY DISTRICT*, 270 N Grove Ave, 60120-5596. SAN 304-1514. Tel: 847-742-2411. Circulation Tel: 847-429-4692. Interlibrary Loan Service Tel: 847-429-4682. Reference Tel: 847-429-4680. FAX: 847-742-0485. Circulation FAX: 847-608-5098. Interlibrary Loan Service FAX: 847-608-5221. Web Site: www.gailborden.info, www.gailborden.info/m/content/view/455/553. *Exec Dir,* Carole Medal; Tel: 847-429-4699, E-mail: cmedal@gailborden.info; *Dep Dir,* Sara Sabo; Tel: 847-429-5984, E-mail: ssabo@gailborden.info; *Div Chief of Access Serv,* Robert Moffett; Tel: 847-429-5989, E-mail: rmoffett@gailborden.info; *Div Chief of Commun Serv & Prog Develop,* Miriam Lytle; Tel: 847-608-5027, E-mail: mlytle@gailborden.info; *Div Chief of Fac & Info Tech,* David Considine; Tel: 847-429-5978, E-mail: dconsidine@gailborden.info; *Div Chief of Public Relations & Develop,* Denise Raleigh; Tel: 847-429-5981, E-mail: draleigh@gailborden.info; *Div Chief of Public Serv,* Margaret Peebles; Tel: 847-429-5983, E-mail: mpeebles@gailborden.info; Staff 26 (MLS 26)
Founded 1873. Pop 144,597; Circ 1,932,057
Jul 2018-Jun 2019 Income $13,420,196, State $180,000, Locally Generated Income $13,240,196. Mats Exp $3,724,200, Books $3,284,000, Per/Ser (Incl. Access Fees) $23,300, Micro $6,000, AV Equip $3,900, AV Mat $197,000, Electronic Ref Mat (Incl. Access Fees) $210,000. Sal $6,600,000 (Prof $2,750,000)
Library Holdings: Audiobooks 7,080; AV Mats 132,662; Bks on Deafness & Sign Lang 190; CDs 15,089; DVDs 31,726; e-books 20,000; High Interest/Low Vocabulary Bk Vols 1,170; Large Print Bks 7,603; Bk Titles 300,418; Bk Vols 437,273; Per Subs 417
Special Collections: Genealogy Coll; Local History Coll (Elgin & Kane County); Spanish Language Materials for Adults & Children
Automation Activity & Vendor Info: (Acquisitions) Innovative Interfaces, Inc; (Cataloging) Innovative Interfaces, Inc; (Circulation) Innovative Interfaces, Inc; (Discovery) BiblioCommons; (ILL) Innovative Interfaces, Inc; (OPAC) Innovative Interfaces, Inc; (Serials) Innovative Interfaces, Inc
Wireless access
Function: 24/7 Electronic res, 24/7 Online cat, 3D Printer, Activity rm, Adult bk club, Adult literacy prog, After school storytime, Archival coll, Art exhibits, Audiobks on Playaways & MP3, Audiobks via web, AV serv, Bilingual assistance for Spanish patrons, Bk club(s), Bk reviews (Group),

Bks on CD, Chess club, Children's prog, Citizenship assistance, Computer training, Computers for patron use, Digital talking bks, Distance learning, Doc delivery serv, E-Readers, E-Reserves, Electronic databases & coll, Equip loans & repairs, Family literacy, Free DVD rentals, Games & aids for people with disabilities, Genealogy discussion group, Holiday prog, Home delivery & serv to seniorr ctr & nursing homes, Homebound delivery serv, Homework prog, ILL available, Internet access, Laminating, Large print keyboards, Life-long learning prog for all ages, Literacy & newcomer serv, Magazines, Magnifiers for reading, Mail & tel request accepted, Meeting rooms, Microfiche/film & reading machines, Movies, Museum passes, Music CDs, Online cat, Outreach serv, Outside serv via phone, mail, e-mail & web, Passport agency, Photocopying/Printing, Preschool outreach, Preschool reading prog, Printer for laptops & handheld devices, Prog for adults, Prog for children & young adult, Ref & res, Ref serv available, Scanner, Senior computer classes, Senior outreach, Serves people with intellectual disabilities, Spanish lang bks, Spoken cassettes & CDs, Spoken cassettes & DVDs, Story hour, Study rm, Summer & winter reading prog, Summer reading prog, Tax forms, Teen prog, Telephone ref, Wheelchair accessible, Winter reading prog, Workshops, Writing prog
Publications: Newsletter (Bimonthly)
Mem of Reaching Across Illinois Library System (RAILS)
Special Services for the Deaf - ADA equip; Assisted listening device; Assistive tech; Bks on deafness & sign lang; Closed caption videos; Sign lang interpreter upon request for prog; Video & TTY relay via computer
Special Services for the Blind - Accessible computers; Aids for in-house use; Assistive/Adapted tech devices, equip & products; BiFolkal kits; Bks available with recordings; Bks on CD; Daisy reader; Disability awareness prog; Ednalite Hi-Vision scope; Extensive large print coll; Free checkout of audio mat; Home delivery serv; Internet workstation with adaptive software; Large print bks; Large screen computer & software; Lending of low vision aids; Low vision equip; Magnifiers; Merlin electronic magnifier reader; Networked computers with assistive software; PC for people with disabilities; Playaways (bks on MP3); Recorded bks; Ref serv; VisualTek equip
Open Mon-Thurs 9-9, Fri & Sat 9-6, Sun 12-5
Friends of the Library Group
Bookmobiles: 1. Librn, Daniel Rick. Bk vols 3,000

SR CHURCH OF THE BRETHREN*, Brethren Historical Library & Archives, 1451 Dundee Ave, 60120-1694. SAN 304-1522. Tel: 847-429-4368. FAX: 847-429-4378. Web Site: www.brethren.org/bhla. *Dir,* William Kostlevy; E-mail: bkostlevy@brethren.org; Staff 1 (Non-MLS 1)
Founded 1936
Library Holdings: Bk Vols 10,407
Special Collections: Archives & Manuscripts Coll; Church of the Brethren History & Doctrines
Automation Activity & Vendor Info: (Cataloging) OCLC; (ILL) OCLC
Function: Archival coll, ILL available, Res libr
Publications: Guide for Local Church Historians; Guide to Research in Brethren Family History; Guide to Research in Brethren History; Guide to the Brethren in Europe
Partic in OCLC Online Computer Library Center, Inc
Restriction: Non-circulating to the pub, Open by appt only

J ELGIN COMMUNITY COLLEGE*, Renner Learning Resources Center, 1700 Spartan Dr, 60123. SAN 304-1530. Tel: 847-214-7337. Interlibrary Loan Service Tel: 847-214-7141. Reference Tel: 847-214-7354. Circulation FAX: 847-214-7995. Interlibrary Loan Service FAX: 847-622-3042. Reference E-mail: libref@elgin.edu. Web Site: library.elgin.edu. *Dean, Learning Res,* Dr Mi Hu; E-mail: mhu@elgin.edu; *Assoc Dean of Libr,* Shannon Pohrte; E-mail: spohrtewenzel@elgin.edu; *Cat/Ref Librn,* Mary Klemundt; E-mail: mklemundt@elgin.edu; *Distance Learning Librn,* Stacey Shah; *Archivist, ILL Librn,* Armando Trejo; *Ref Librn,* Tina Birkholz; *Ref Librn,* Himanshu Trivedi; *Tech Serv Librn,* Ellie Swanson; Staff 21 (MLS 11, Non-MLS 10)
Founded 1949. Enrl 7,010; Fac 470
Library Holdings: Audiobooks 323; CDs 1,782; DVDs 1,598; e-books 33,382; e-journals 43,656; Bk Vols 77,945; Per Subs 365; Videos 90
Automation Activity & Vendor Info: (Acquisitions) Innovative Interfaces, Inc; (Cataloging) Innovative Interfaces, Inc; (Circulation) Innovative Interfaces, Inc; (OPAC) Innovative Interfaces, Inc; (Serials) Innovative Interfaces, Inc
Wireless access
Partic in Consortium of Academic & Research Libraries in Illinois; Illinois Library & Information Network; Network of Illinois Learning Resources in Community Colleges; Northern Ill Learning Resources Coop; OCLC Online Computer Library Center, Inc
Open Mon-Thurs 7:45am-10pm, Fri 7:45-5, Sat 9-2

S ELGIN MENTAL HEALTH CENTER LIBRARY*, Forensic Treatment Program (FTP) Library, 750 S State St, 60123-7692. SAN 340-3807. Tel: 847-742-1040, Ext 3437. FAX: 847-429-4923. *Librn,* David Hagerman; E-mail: david.hagerman@illinois.gov; Staff 1 (MLS 1)
Founded 1995
Library Holdings: CDs 75; Bk Vols 10,000
Mem of Reaching Across Illinois Library System (RAILS)
Restriction: Authorized patrons

CR JUDSON UNIVERSITY, Benjamin P Browne Library, 1151 N State St, 60123. SAN 304-1549. Tel: 847-628-2030. Interlibrary Loan Service Tel: 847-628-2032. Reference Tel: 847-628-2038. Administration Tel: 847-628-2036. FAX: 847-628-2045. Web Site: www.judsonu.edu/library. *Libr Dir,* Larry C Wild; E-mail: lwild@judsonu.edu; *Access Serv Supvr, ILL Supvr,* Emily Tilsy; Tel: 847-628-2034, E-mail: etilsy@judsonu.edu; *Evening/Weekend Supvr,* Jenny Becker; *Evening/Weekend Supvr,* Victor Rivera; E-mail: victor.rivera@judsonu.edu; *Evening/Weekend Supvr,* Fred Versluys; E-mail: fred.versluys@judsonu.edu; *Ref & Instrul Serv, Instr Coordr,* Charlene Thompson; Tel: 847-628-2033, E-mail: cthompson@judsonu.edu; Staff 3 (MLS 2, Non-MLS 1)
Founded 1963. Enrl 920; Highest Degree: Doctorate
Library Holdings: Bk Titles 100,000; Bk Vols 104,693; Per Subs 350
Special Collections: Baptist History & Missions Coll; Edmundson Contemporary Christian Music Coll; Library of American Civilization Coll, micro, ultrafiche
Subject Interests: Archit, Music, Relig
Automation Activity & Vendor Info: (Acquisitions) ProQuest; (Cataloging) ProQuest; (Circulation) ProQuest; (Course Reserve) ProQuest; (Discovery) ProQuest; (ILL) OCLC Online; (OPAC) ProQuest; (Serials) EBSCO Online
Wireless access
Function: 24/7 Electronic res, 24/7 Online cat
Mem of Reaching Across Illinois Library System (RAILS)
Partic in Consortium of Academic & Research Libraries in Illinois; LIBRAS, Inc; OCLC Online Computer Library Center, Inc

ELIZABETH

P ELIZABETH TOWNSHIP LIBRARY*, 210 E Myrtle St, 61028-9785. (Mail add: PO Box 243, 61028-0243), SAN 304-1565. Tel: 815-858-2212. FAX: 815-858-3475. E-mail: elizabethtownshiplibrary@gmail.com. Web Site: www.elizabethlibrary.org. *Adminr,* Deb Wunsch
Founded 1943. Pop 1,063; Circ 6,000
Library Holdings: Bk Vols 11,882; Per Subs 5
Automation Activity & Vendor Info: (Acquisitions) Follett Software; (Cataloging) Follett Software; (Circulation) Follett Software; (ILL) SirsiDynix-WorkFlows; (OPAC) Follett Software
Wireless access
Function: Adult bk club, After school storytime, Art exhibits, Audio & video playback equip for onsite use, Bk club(s), Bks on cassette, Bks on CD, Children's prog, Citizenship assistance, Computer training, Computers for patron use, Digital talking bks, Distance learning, Electronic databases & coll, Family literacy, Free DVD rentals, Games & aids for people with disabilities, Holiday prog, ILL available, Internet access, Mail & tel request accepted, Music CDs, Outreach serv, Photocopying/Printing, Prog for adults, Prog for children & young adult, Ref serv available, Senior outreach, Spoken cassettes & CDs, Spoken cassettes & DVDs, Story hour, Summer reading prog, Tax forms, Teen prog, VHS videos, Wheelchair accessible, Workshops
Mem of Reaching Across Illinois Library System (RAILS)
Open Mon-Wed 1-5:30, Thurs 1-7, Fri 9-5, Sat 9-1
Restriction: Non-resident fee

ELK GROVE VILLAGE

M AMITA HEALTH*, Alexian Brothers Medical Center Library, 800 Biesterfield Rd, 60007-3397. SAN 320-3751. Tel: 847-437-5500. FAX: 847-981-5336. E-mail: alexianlibrary@alexian.net.
Founded 1967
Library Holdings: CDs 250; DVDs 15; e-books 66; e-journals 4,000; Bk Titles 2,000; Per Subs 50
Subject Interests: Med, Nursing
Automation Activity & Vendor Info: (Cataloging) OCLC; (Circulation) CyberTools for Libraries; (OPAC) CyberTools for Libraries; (Serials) CyberTools for Libraries
Partic in Fox Valley Consortium; Greater Midwest Regional Medical Libr Network; Illinois Library & Information Network; OCLC-LVIS
Open Mon-Fri 8-4:30

P ELK GROVE VILLAGE PUBLIC LIBRARY*, 1001 Wellington Ave, 60007-3391. SAN 304-1573. Tel: 847-439-0447. Circulation Tel: 847-725-2176. Administration Tel: 847-725-2150. FAX: 847-439-0475. TDD: 847-439-0885. E-mail: library@egvpl.org. Web Site: www.egvpl.org. *Dir,* Debra Nelson; E-mail: dnelson@egvpl.org; Staff 16.8 (MLS 6.8, Non-MLS 10)
Founded 1959. Pop 33,127; Circ 901,724
Library Holdings: Bks on Deafness & Sign Lang 50; Braille Volumes 21; CDs 35,108; DVDs 29,343; e-books 8,719; Electronic Media & Resources 64; Bk Vols 275,894; Per Subs 523
Subject Interests: Civil War, World War II

Automation Activity & Vendor Info: (Acquisitions) SirsiDynix; (Cataloging) OCLC; (Circulation) SirsiDynix; (OPAC) SirsiDynix; (Serials) SirsiDynix
Wireless access
Publications: Elk Grove-The Peony Village (Local historical information); Highlights (Newsletter)
Special Services for the Deaf - Adult & family literacy prog; Closed caption videos; High interest/low vocabulary bks; Sign lang interpreter upon request for prog; TTY equip
Special Services for the Blind - Accessible computers; BiFolkal kits; Bks on cassette; Bks on CD; Braille bks; Children's Braille; Large print bks; Large screen computer & software; Talking bks from Braille Inst
Open Mon-Thurs 9am-10pm, Fri 9-7, Sat 9-5, Sun 1-5
Friends of the Library Group

ELKHART

P ELKHART PUBLIC LIBRARY DISTRICT*, 121 E Bohan St, 62634. (Mail add: PO Box 170, 62634-0170), SAN 376-1460. Tel: 217-947-2313. FAX: 217-947-2313. E-mail: elkhartlibrary@mchsi.com. Web Site: www.elkhartlibrary.lib.il.us. *Libr Dir,* Vanda Liesman
Founded 1893. Pop 777
Library Holdings: Bk Titles 10,000
Automation Activity & Vendor Info: (Cataloging) Horizon; (Circulation) Horizon
Wireless access
Mem of Illinois Heartland Library System
Special Services for the Blind - Audio mat
Open Mon 4-8, Tues & Fri 9-4, Wed & Thurs 9-8, Sat 9-1

ELKVILLE

P RICK WARREN MEMORIAL PUBLIC LIBRARY DISTRICT*, 114 S Fourth St, 62932-1097. SAN 376-1681. Tel: 618-568-1843. FAX: 618-568-1843. E-mail: rwlibrary@rickwarren.lib.il.us. Web Site: www.rickwarren.lib.il.us. *Librn,* Johnnie Halstead; E-mail: johnnie.halstead@rickwarren.lib.il.us; *Asst Librn,* Tim Fritts; E-mail: assistant@rickwarren.lib.il.us
Founded 1970. Pop 3,301
Library Holdings: High Interest/Low Vocabulary Bk Vols 100; Bk Titles 15,000
Wireless access
Mem of Illinois Heartland Library System
Open Mon, Wed, Thurs & Fri 9-5, Tues 9-8, Sat 9-Noon

ELMHURST

S ELMHURST HISTORICAL MUSEUM LIBRARY*, 120 E Park Ave, 60126. SAN 326-0364. Tel: 630-833-1457. FAX: 630-833-1326. E-mail: ehm@elmhurst.org. Web Site: elmhursthistory.org. *Dir,* Brian F Bergheger; *Curator of Coll,* Daniel Lund; Tel: 630-530-3322
Founded 1975
Library Holdings: Bk Titles 577
Subject Interests: Local hist, Museology, Newsp on microfilm
Open Mon-Fri 1-5
Restriction: Non-circulating

P ELMHURST PUBLIC LIBRARY*, 125 S Prospect Ave, 60126-3298. SAN 304-1603. Tel: 630-279-8696. Interlibrary Loan Service FAX: 630-279-0636. Administration FAX: 630-516-1364. TDD: 630-782-4310. Reference E-mail: reference@elmhurst.org. Web Site: elmhurstpubliclibrary.org. *Dir,* Mary Beth Harper; Tel: 630-530-6300, E-mail: Marybeth.Harper@elmlib.org; *Head, Adult Serv,* Bryan Blank; E-mail: Bryan.Blank@elmhurst.org; *Head, Circ,* Samantha Cresswell; *Head, Kids' Libr,* Sharon Karpiel; *Head, Tech Serv,* Kathleen Murphy; Staff 17.5 (MLS 17.5)
Founded 1916. Pop 44,121; Circ 1,296,436
May 2015-Apr 2016 Income $7,752,931. Mats Exp $4,665,354, Per/Ser (Incl. Access Fees) $40,000. Sal $3,993,204
Library Holdings: Audiobooks 9,224; CDs 17,293; DVDs 24,312; e-books 39,394; Bk Vols 251,183; Per Subs 416
Automation Activity & Vendor Info: (Acquisitions) Innovative Interfaces, Inc; (Circulation) Innovative Interfaces, Inc; (ILL) Innovative Interfaces, Inc; (OPAC) Innovative Interfaces, Inc; (Serials) Innovative Interfaces, Inc
Wireless access
Publications: Newsletter-Fine Print
Mem of Reaching Across Illinois Library System (RAILS)
Partic in OCLC Online Computer Library Center, Inc
Special Services for the Blind - Assistive/Adapted tech devices, equip & products; Screen reader software
Open Mon-Fri 9-9, Sat 9-5, Sun 1-5
Friends of the Library Group

C ELMHURST UNIVERSITY*, A C Buehler Library, 190 Prospect St, 60126. SAN 304-159X. Tel: 630-617-3160. Interlibrary Loan Service Tel: 630-617-3169. Reference Tel: 630-617-3173. FAX: 630-617-3332. Reference E-mail: library@elmhurst.edu. Web Site: library.elmhurst.edu. *Interim Dir,* Peg Cook; Tel: 630-617-3267, E-mail: cookm@elmhurst.edu; *Head, Ref,* Donna Goodwyn; Tel: 630-617-3171, E-mail: donnamg@elmhurst.edu; *Head, Tech Serv,* Elaine Fetyko Page; Tel: 630-617-3166, E-mail: elainep@elmhurst.edu; *Ref & Instruction Librn,* Jacob Hill; Tel: 630-617-3168, E-mail: jacobh@elmhurst.edu; *Asst Librn, Ref & Instruction,* Jennifer Paliatka; Tel: 630-617-3158, E-mail: jenniferp@elmhurst.edu; Staff 6 (MLS 5, Non-MLS 1)
Founded 1871. Enrl 3,068; Fac 156; Highest Degree: Master
Library Holdings: AV Mats 4,085; Bk Titles 219,915; Bk Vols 221,463; Per Subs 1,100
Subject Interests: Nursing
Automation Activity & Vendor Info: (Acquisitions) Ex Libris Group; (Cataloging) Ex Libris Group; (Circulation) Ex Libris Group; (Course Reserve) Ex Libris Group; (Discovery) Ex Libris Group; (ILL) OCLC WorldShare Interlibrary Loan; (OPAC) Ex Libris Group; (Serials) Ex Libris Group
Wireless access
Function: 24/7 Online cat, Computers for patron use, Electronic databases & coll, Free DVD rentals, ILL available, Internet access, Online cat, Online info literacy tutorials on the web & in blackboard, Online ref, Photocopying/Printing, Ref & res, Ref serv available, Res assist avail, Scanner, Study rm
Partic in Consortium of Academic & Research Libraries in Illinois; LIBRAS, Inc; OCLC Online Computer Library Center, Inc
Open Mon-Thurs 7:30am-10pm, Fri 7:30-5, Sun 2-10

ELMWOOD

P MORRISON & MARY WILEY LIBRARY DISTRICT*, 206 W Main St, 61529. (Mail add: PO Box 467, 61529-0467), SAN 304-162X. Tel: 309-742-2431. FAX: 309-742-8298. E-mail: elmwoodlib@gmail.com. Web Site: www.elmwoodpubliclibrary.org. *Libr Dir,* Michelle Armbruster; *Asst Libr Dir,* Pat Keefer; *Librn,* Tracy Burnett; *Librn,* Eulail Huffcutt; Staff 4 (Non-MLS 4)
Founded 1950. Pop 2,598; Circ 17,895
Library Holdings: Audiobooks 814; DVDs 3,305; e-books 2,568; Bk Titles 12,705; Bk Vols 19,000; Per Subs 35
Special Collections: Lorado Taft (Bust of Lorado, bust he made of his father, many books about the famous sculptor from Elmwood.)
Wireless access
Mem of Reaching Across Illinois Library System (RAILS)
Open Mon, Tues & Fri 1-5, Wed 9-6, Thurs 1-8, Sat 9-1

ELMWOOD PARK

P ELMWOOD PARK PUBLIC LIBRARY*, One Conti Pkwy, 60707. SAN 304-1638. Tel: 708-453-7645. Reference Tel: 708-395-1219. FAX: 708-453-4671. E-mail: eps@elmwoodparklibrary.org. Web Site: www.elmwoodparklibrary.org. *Dir,* Tiffany Verzani; Tel: 708-395-1230, E-mail: tverzani@elmwoodparklibrary.org; *Asst Dir,* Jason Stuhlmann; Tel: 708-395-1241, E-mail: jstuhlmann@elmwoodparklibrary.org; *Head, Adult Serv,* Mandy N McGee; Tel: 708-395-1240, E-mail: mmcgee@elmwoodparklibrary.org; *Head, Children's Servx,* Kim Viita; Tel: 708-395-1242, E-mail: kviita@elmwoodparklibrary.org; *Head, Coll Serv,* Mary Moss; Tel: 708-395-1204, E-mail: mmoss@elmwoodparklibrary.org; *Head, Tech Serv,* Marcy Campagna; Tel: 708-395-1205, E-mail: mcampagna@elmwoodparklibrary.org; Staff 26 (MLS 11, Non-MLS 15)
Founded 1936. Pop 24,954; Circ 199,019
Library Holdings: AV Mats 12,730; Bk Vols 84,415; Per Subs 159
Subject Interests: Lit, Local hist, Polish (Lang), Spanish (Lang)
Automation Activity & Vendor Info: (Acquisitions) SirsiDynix-WorkFlows; (Circulation) SirsiDynix-WorkFlows; (OPAC) SirsiDynix-Enterprise
Wireless access
Function: 24/7 Electronic res, 24/7 Online cat, Adult bk club, After school storytime, Audiobks via web, Bilingual assistance for Spanish patrons, Bks on CD, Butterfly Garden, Chess club, Children's prog, Citizenship assistance, Computer training, Computers for patron use, E-Readers, Electronic databases & coll, Free DVD rentals, Homebound delivery serv, ILL available, Internet access, Life-long learning prog for all ages, Magazines, Mango lang, Meeting rooms, Movies, Museum passes, Music CDs, Online cat, Photocopying/Printing, Preschool outreach, Preschool reading prog, Printer for laptops & handheld devices, Prog for adults, Prog for children & young adult, Scanner, Spanish lang bks, Story hour, Study rm, Summer reading prog, Tax forms, Teen prog, Wheelchair accessible
Publications: What's Happening (Newsletter)
Mem of Reaching Across Illinois Library System (RAILS)
Partic in System Wide Automated Network
Open Mon-Thurs 9-9, Fri 9-6, Sat 9-5, Sun (Sept-May) 1-5
Friends of the Library Group

ELSAH

C PRINCIPIA COLLEGE*, Marshall Brooks Library, One Maybeck Pl, 62028-9703. SAN 304-1646. Tel: 618-374-5235. Reference Tel: 618-374-5070. FAX: 618-374-5107. Web Site: library.principiacollege.edu/welcome. *Dir,* Lisa Roberts; E-mail: lisa.roberts@principia.edu; *Assoc Dir,* Edith List; Tel: 618-374-5076, E-mail: edith.list@principia.edu; *Libm,* Chelsea Sutton; *Archives & Spec Coll Librn,* Melody Hauf-Belden; *Acq Mgr,* Cathy Barlow; *Pub Serv Mgr,* Deb Wold; Staff 6 (MLS 4, Non-MLS 2)
Founded 1935. Enrl 500; Fac 62; Highest Degree: Bachelor
Library Holdings: Bk Titles 174,000; Bk Vols 205,000; Per Subs 800
Special Collections: Curriculum; US Govt Documents (Selective Depository)
Subject Interests: Art hist, Biblical studies, Christian scientists, Rare bks
Automation Activity & Vendor Info: (Acquisitions) SirsiDynix; (Cataloging) SirsiDynix; (Circulation) SirsiDynix; (Course Reserve) SirsiDynix; (OPAC) SirsiDynix; (Serials) SirsiDynix
Function: 24/7 Electronic res, 24/7 Online cat, Archival coll
Partic in Consortium of Academic & Research Libraries in Illinois; IAC Expanded Acad, Inc; Illinois Library & Information Network; OCLC Online Computer Library Center, Inc
Open Mon-Thurs 8am-Midnight, Fri 8-6, Sat 9:30-8, Sun 1-Midnight

ERIE

P ERIE PUBLIC LIBRARY DISTRICT*, 802 Eighth Ave, 61250. (Mail add: PO Box 436, 61250-0436), SAN 304-1654. Tel: 309-659-2707. FAX: 309-659-2707. Web Site: eriepubliclibrary.com. *Dir,* Laurel M Reiss; E-mail: lreissepld@gmail.com; *Asst Librn, Ch,* Pamela Ashdown
Founded 1964. Pop 3,345; Circ 18,690
Library Holdings: Audiobooks 954; CDs 702; Bk Titles 27,675; Per Subs 33
Mem of Reaching Across Illinois Library System (RAILS)
Partic in OMNI
Open Mon & Wed 9-11 & 2-8, Tues & Thurs. 2-8, Fri 2-5, Sat 9-2
Friends of the Library Group

EUREKA

C EUREKA COLLEGE, Melick Library, 301 E College Ave, 61530-1563. SAN 304-1662. Tel: 309-467-6380. Reference Tel: 309-467-6892. Administration Tel: 309-467-6382. FAX: 309-467-6386. E-mail: library@eureka.edu. Web Site: www.eureka.edu/academics/melick-library. *Head Librn, Pub Access Librn,* Kelly Fisher; E-mail: kfisher@eureka.edu; *Tech Serv Coordr,* Jennifer Rockey; E-mail: jrockey@eureka.edu; Staff 2 (MLS 1, Non-MLS 1)
Founded 1855. Enrl 500; Fac 40; Highest Degree: Bachelor
Library Holdings: CDs 670; DVDs 735; Microforms 4,900; Bk Titles 80,798; Bk Vols 82,949; Per Subs 15
Special Collections: Christian Church (Disciples of Christ Coll), archives; Eureka College Archives; History of Eureka Archives; Ronald Reagan Research Center
Automation Activity & Vendor Info: (Cataloging) Ex Libris Group; (Circulation) Ex Libris Group; (ILL) Ex Libris Group; (OPAC) Ex Libris Group; (Serials) Ex Libris Group
Wireless access
Partic in Consortium of Academic & Research Libraries in Illinois
Open Mon-Thurs 7:30am-7pm, Fri 7:30-5

P EUREKA PUBLIC LIBRARY DISTRICT*, 202 S Main St, 61530. SAN 304-1670. Tel: 309-467-2922. FAX: 309-467-3527. Web Site: www.eurekapl.org. *Dir,* Ann Reeves; E-mail: directorepld@gmail.com; Staff 7 (MLS 2, Non-MLS 5)
Founded 1930. Pop 6,618; Circ 106,608
Library Holdings: Bk Vols 40,725; Per Subs 251
Special Collections: Local History Coll
Subject Interests: Alaskana
Automation Activity & Vendor Info: (Acquisitions) SirsiDynix; (Cataloging) OCLC Connexion; (Circulation) SirsiDynix-WorkFlows; (OPAC) SirsiDynix
Wireless access
Function: Archival coll, Art exhibits, BA reader (adult literacy), Bi-weekly Writer's Group, Bilingual assistance for Spanish patrons, Bk reviews (Group), Chess club, Citizenship assistance, Genealogy discussion group, Govt ref serv, Health sci info serv, Jail serv, Jazz prog, Large print keyboards, Learning ctr, Legal assistance to inmates, Mail loans to mem, Masonic res mat, Museum passes, Notary serv, Online info literacy tutorials on the web & in blackboard, Online ref, Passport agency, Prof lending libr, Res libr, Res performed for a fee, Satellite serv, Serves people with intellectual disabilities, Specialized serv in classical studies, Words travel prog
Publications: Around the District (Newsletter)
Special Services for the Blind - Web-Braille
Open Mon, Tues & Thurs 9-8, Wed & Fri 8:30-6, Sat (Sept-May) 9-1
Friends of the Library Group

EVANSTON

S EVANSTON HISTORY CENTER LIBRARY & ARCHIVES*, Frank B Foster Research Room, 225 Greenwood St, 60201. SAN 304-1719. Tel: 847-475-3410. FAX: 847-475-3599. Web Site: www.evanstonhistorycenter.org. *Exec Dir,* Eden Juron Pearlman; E-mail: ejpearlman@evanstonhistorycenter.org; *Dir, Archives, Mus Spec,* Grace Lehner; E-mail: glehner@evanstonhistorycenter.org; Staff 1 (Non-MLS 1)
Founded 1898
Library Holdings: Bk Titles 3,000
Special Collections: Charles Gates Dawes Coll
Function: Archival coll, Photocopying/Printing, Ref serv available
Publications: TimeLines (Newsletter)
Open Tues-Thurs & Sat 1-4
Restriction: Fee for pub use, Non-circulating

P EVANSTON PUBLIC LIBRARY*, 1703 Orrington, 60201. SAN 304-1735. Tel: 847-448-8600. Circulation Tel: 847-448-8605. Reference Tel: 847-448-8630. FAX: 847-866-0313. TDD: 847-866-0340. Web Site: www.epl.org. *Dir,* Karen Danczak Lyons; E-mail: kdanczaklyons@cityofevanston.org; *Asst Dir,* Teri Campbell; *Outreach Librn,* Jill Skwerski; *Youth Serv,* Jan Bojda
Founded 1873. Pop 74,239; Circ 868,837
Library Holdings: AV Mats 26,234; Bk Vols 464,830; Per Subs 918
Special Collections: Antique Silver (Berg Coll); Music (Sadie Coe Coll)
Subject Interests: Art
Wireless access
Partic in OCLC Online Computer Library Center, Inc; Proquest Dialog
Open Mon-Thurs 9-9, Fri & Sat 9-6, Sun 12-6
Friends of the Library Group
Branches: 2
CHICAGO AVENUE/MAIN STREET (CAMS), 900 Chicago Ave, Ste 201, 60202. Tel: 847-905-0764. FAX: 847-866-0332. *Br Mgr,* Constance Heneghan
Library Holdings: Bk Vols 25,000; Per Subs 25
Open Mon 10-8, Tues, Wed, Fri & Sat 10-6
NORTH BRANCH, 2026 Central St, 60201. Tel: 847-866-0330, 847-866-5007. FAX: 847-866-0331. *Br Mgr,* Constance Heneghan
Library Holdings: Bk Vols 30,000; Per Subs 39
Open Mon 10-8, Tues, Wed, Fri & Sat 10-6

SR FIRST PRESBYTERIAN CHURCH*, Thomas E Boswell Memorial Library, 1427 Chicago Ave, 60201. SAN 304-1743. Tel: 847-864-1472. FAX: 847-864-1494. E-mail: info@firstpresevanston.org. Web Site: www.firstpresevanston.org. *Librn,* Laurie Oh; Staff 6 (MLS 2, Non-MLS 4)
Founded 1962
Library Holdings: Bk Titles 4,000; Per Subs 13
Subject Interests: Church hist, Fiction, Theol
Open Sun 8-2

R GARRETT-EVANGELICAL THEOLOGICAL SEMINARY*, The Styberg Library, 2121 Sheridan Rd, 60201. SAN 304-1751. Tel: 847-866-3909. Reference Tel: 847-866-3868. Administration Tel: 847-866-3877. Toll Free Tel: 877-600-8753. FAX: 847-866-3894. E-mail: styberg.library@garrett.edu. Web Site: library.garrett.edu. *Dir,* Dr Jaeyeon Lucy Chung; E-mail: jaeyeon.chung@garrett.edu; *Asst Dir,* Lynn Berg; E-mail: lynn.berg@garrett.edu; Staff 5 (MLS 4, Non-MLS 1)
Founded 1981. Fac 30; Highest Degree: Doctorate
Library Holdings: Bk Vols 400,000; Per Subs 400
Special Collections: Egyptology (Hibbard Egyptian Coll); Keen Bible Coll
Subject Interests: Biblical studies, Church hist, Relig, Theol
Wireless access
Partic in Association of Chicago Theological Schools; Consortium of Academic & Research Libraries in Illinois; OCLC Online Computer Library Center, Inc
Open Mon & Wed 8:30am-10pm, Tues & Thurs 7:45am-10pm, Fri 8:30-6, Sat 11-5, Sun 2-8

S NATIONAL WOMAN'S CHRISTIAN TEMPERANCE UNION*, Frances E Willard Memorial Library, 1730 Chicago Ave, 60201. SAN 304-1786. Tel: 847-864-1397. FAX: 847-864-9497. E-mail: archives@franceswillardhouse.org. Web Site: franceswillardhouse.org/research/library-and-archives, www.wctu.org. *Archivist/Librn,* Janet Olsen; Staff 2 (MLS 2)
Founded 1940
Library Holdings: Bk Titles 5,000
Special Collections: Frances E Willard Papers; WCTU Presidential Papers (eg, Anna Gordon, Lillian Stevens); WCTU Records
Subject Interests: Alcohol & drugs, Hist of Woman's Christian Temperance Union, Tobacco, Women's studies
Restriction: Open by appt only
Friends of the Library Group

C NORTHWESTERN UNIVERSITY LIBRARIES*, 1970 Campus Dr, 60208-2300. SAN 340-3920. Tel: 847-491-7658. Circulation Tel: 847-491-7633. Interlibrary Loan Service Tel: 847-491-7630. Reference Tel: 847-491-7656. Administration Tel: 847-491-7640. Interlibrary Loan Service FAX: 847-491-5685. Administration FAX: 847-491-8306. E-mail: library@northwestern.edu. Web Site: www.library.northwestern.edu. *Dean of Libr,* Sarah M Pritchard; E-mail: spritchard@northwestern.edu; *Assoc Univ Librn,* D J Hoek; Staff 104 (MLS 69, Non-MLS 35)
Founded 1851. Enrl 21,000; Fac 3,300; Highest Degree: Doctorate
Sept 2019-Aug 2020. Mats Exp $14,657,972. Sal $13,351,608
Library Holdings: Bk Vols 7,661,190; Per Subs 359,537
Special Collections: African History Coll, lit & culture; Music Coll, 1945-; Transportation Coll. State Document Depository; UN Document Depository; US Document Depository
Automation Activity & Vendor Info: (Acquisitions) Ex Libris Group; (Cataloging) Ex Libris Group; (Circulation) Ex Libris Group; (Course Reserve) Atlas Systems; (Discovery) Ex Libris Group; (ILL) OCLC ILLiad; (Serials) Ex Libris Group
Wireless access
Publications: Footnotes (Newsletter)
Partic in Association of Research Libraries; Big Ten Academic Alliance; Center for Research Libraries; Chicago Collections Consortium; Consortium of Academic & Research Libraries in Illinois; Coun on East Asian Librs; Northeast Research Libraries Consortium; OCLC Online Computer Library Center, Inc
Restriction: Restricted access

Departmental Libraries:

CM GALTER HEALTH SCIENCES LIBRARY, Montgomery Ward Bldg, 303 E Chicago Ave, Chicago, 60611, SAN 340-2061. Tel: 312-503-8133. Circulation Tel: 312-503-8127. Interlibrary Loan Service Tel: 312-503-1908. Reference Tel: 312-503-8109. Information Services Tel: 312-503-8126. FAX: 312-503-1204. Reference E-mail: ghsl-ref@northwestern.edu. Web Site: www.galter.northwestern.edu. *Dir,* James Shedlock; E-mail: j-shedlock@northwestern.edu; *Assoc Dir, Health Sci Libr,* Heidi Nickisch Duggan; Staff 30 (MLS 17, Non-MLS 13)
Founded 1927. Fac 15; Highest Degree: Doctorate
Library Holdings: e-books 849; e-journals 7,966; Electronic Media & Resources 2,887; Bk Titles 125,940; Bk Vols 286,364
Special Collections: Dental History; Medical Classics; Medical History; Rare Books
Subject Interests: Basic med sci, Clinical med, Phys therapy
Automation Activity & Vendor Info: (Acquisitions) Ex Libris Group; (Cataloging) Ex Libris Group; (Circulation) Ex Libris Group; (OPAC) Ex Libris Group; (Serials) Ex Libris Group
Partic in Illinois Library & Information Network; NELLCO Law Library Consortium, Inc.
Publications: Guide Series; Library Guide; Library Notes
Restriction: Not open to pub
Friends of the Library Group

SEELEY G MUDD LIBRARY, 2233 Tech Dr, 60208, SAN 340-4072. Tel: 847-491-3361. FAX: 847-491-4655. E-mail: mudd@northwestern.edu. Web Site: library.northwestern.edu/libraries-collections/mudd-library/index.html. ; Staff 7 (MLS 6, Non-MLS 1)
Subject Interests: Applied math, Astronomy, Chem, Computer sci, Engr, Life sci, Physics

CL PRITZKER LEGAL RESEARCH CENTER, 375 E Chicago Ave, Chicago, 60611, SAN 340-2037. Tel: 312-503-8451. Reference Tel: 312-503-8450. Administration Tel: 312-503-4941. FAX: 312-503-9230. Web Site: www.law.northwestern.edu/lawlibrary/. *Dir,* George H Pike; Tel: 312-503-0295, E-mail: ghpike@law.northwestern.edu; *Acq Librn,* Eric C Parker; Tel: 312-503-7920, E-mail: ecp278@law.northwestern.edu; *Cat Librn,* Terence O'Connell; Tel: 312-503-7364, E-mail: t-oconnell@law.northwestern.edu; *Digital Serv & Emerging Tech Librn,* Kara Young; Tel: 312-503-0252; *Doc Librn,* Pegeen Bassett; Tel: 312-503-7344, E-mail: p-bassett@law.northwestern.edu; *Fac Serv Librn,* Marcia Gold Lehr; Tel: 312-503-4356, E-mail: mglehr@law.northwestern.edu; *Foreign, Comparative & Intl Law Librn,* Heidi Frostestad Kuehl; Tel: 312-503-4725; *Instrul & Access Serv Librn,* Maribel Nash; Tel: 312-503-0300; *Res & Instrul Serv Librn,* Jamie Sommer; Tel: 312-503-0314. Subject Specialists: *Foreign law, Intl law,* Heidi Frostestad Kuehl; Staff 23.5 (MLS 11, Non-MLS 12.5)
Founded 1859. Enrl 988; Fac 160; Highest Degree: Doctorate
Library Holdings: Bk Titles 244,052; Bk Vols 562,601; Per Subs 5,452
Special Collections: Foreign & International Law; Supreme Court Papers of Arthur J Goldberg
Automation Activity & Vendor Info: (Acquisitions) Ex Libris Group; (Cataloging) Ex Libris Group; (Circulation) Ex Libris Group; (Course Reserve) Ex Libris Group; (OPAC) Ex Libris Group; (Serials) Ex Libris Group
Partic in Chicago Legal Acad Syst; OCLC Online Computer Library Center, Inc
Publications: Faculty Publications; Library Guide; New Books List
Mem of Reaching Across Illinois Library System (RAILS)
Open Mon-Thurs 7:30am-11pm, Fri 7:30am-8pm, Sat 9-6, Sun 9am-11pm

JOSEPH SCHAFFNER LIBRARY, Wieboldt Hall, 2nd Flr, 339 E Chicago Ave, Chicago, 60611, SAN 340-2002. Tel: 312-503-8422. FAX: 312-503-8930. Circulation E-mail: schaffner-circulation@northwestern.edu. Reference E-mail: schaffner-reference@northwestern.edu. Web Site: www.library.northwestern.edu/schaffner. *Librn,* Tracy Coyne; Tel: 312-503-6617, E-mail: tracy-coyne@northwestern.edu
Library Holdings: Bk Vols 20,000
Subject Interests: Bus, Humanities

M PRESENCE SAINT FRANCIS MEDICAL LIBRARY*, Ramon E Casas Medical Library, 355 Ridge Ave, 60202. SAN 340-4137. Tel: 847-316-2460. Web Site: www.amitahealth.org/location/amita-health-saint-francis-hospital-evanston. *Med Librn,* Eleanor Truex; Staff 1 (MLS 1)
Founded 1919
Library Holdings: e-books 500; Bk Vols 1,500
Wireless access
Mem of Reaching Across Illinois Library System (RAILS)
Partic in Health Science Libraries of Illinois
Restriction: Badge access after hrs, Hospital employees & physicians only

S SIGMA ALPHA EPSILON FRATERNITY & FOUNDATION, Joseph W Walt Library, 1856 Sheridan Rd, 60201-3837. (Mail add: PO Box 1856, 60204-1856), SAN 304-1808. Tel: 847-475-1856. Toll Free Tel: 800-233-1856. FAX: 847-475-2250. Web Site: www.sae.net. *Chief Info Officer,* Daniel Stanczak; E-mail: dstanczak@sae.net; Staff 1 (Non-MLS 1)
Founded 1930
Library Holdings: Bk Titles 2,000
Special Collections: Books By & About Members of Sigma Alpha Epsilon; Frances Willard Coll; History of SAE, 1856 to present, correspondence, ms, photogs; William C Levere Coll
Subject Interests: Stained glass
Open Mon-Fri 9-4
Restriction: Non-circulating

EVANSVILLE

P EVANSVILLE PUBLIC LIBRARY, 602 Public St, 62242. (Mail add: PO Box 299, 62242-0299), SAN 304-1824. Tel: 618-853-4649. E-mail: evansvillepubliclibrary@yahoo.com. Web Site: evansvillepubliclibrary.weebly.com. *Librn,* Tia Martel; *Asst Librn,* Jean Dobbs
Founded 1965. Pop 724
Library Holdings: Audiobooks 25; CDs 56; DVDs 250; Large Print Bks 40; Bk Vols 9,500; Per Subs 12
Subject Interests: Adult fiction, Hist
Wireless access
Function: 24/7 Online cat, Bk club(s), Bks on CD, Children's prog, Computers for patron use, Free DVD rentals, Internet access, Movies, Music CDs, OverDrive digital audio bks, Photocopying/Printing, Printer for laptops & handheld devices, Prog for children & young adult, Ref & res, Scanner, Story hour, Summer reading prog, Wheelchair accessible
Mem of Illinois Heartland Library System
Open Tues, Thurs & Sat 12-5 (Summer); Tues & Thurs 12-5, Sat 11-4 (Fall)
Friends of the Library Group

EVERGREEN PARK

P EVERGREEN PARK PUBLIC LIBRARY, 9400 S Troy Ave, 60805-2383. SAN 304-1832. Tel: 708-422-8522. FAX: 708-422-8665. Web Site: www.evergreenparklibrary.org. *Dir,* Nicolette Seidl; E-mail: seidln@evergreenparklibrary.org; *Bus Mgr,* Linda McKeown; E-mail: mckeownl@evergreenparklibrary.org; *Adult Serv,* Jenna Harte; E-mail: hartej@evergreenparklibrary.org; *Ch Serv,* Laura Meyer; E-mail: meyerl@evergreenparklibrary.org; Staff 13 (MLS 5, Non-MLS 8)
Founded 1944. Pop 20,860; Circ 125,000
Library Holdings: Bk Vols 70,000
Automation Activity & Vendor Info: (Acquisitions) Innovative Interfaces, Inc; (Cataloging) Innovative Interfaces, Inc; (Circulation) Innovative Interfaces, Inc
Wireless access
Mem of Reaching Across Illinois Library System (RAILS)
Partic in System Wide Automated Network
Open Mon-Thurs 9-9, Fri & Sat 9-5

M LITTLE COMPANY OF MARY HOSPITAL*, Medical Library, 2800 W 95th St, 60805. SAN 304-1840. Tel: 708-229-5299. FAX: 708-229-5885. Web Site: www.osfhealthcare.org/libraries, www.osfhealthcare.org/little-company-of-mary. *Med Librn,* Teresa Luna
Library Holdings: e-journals 16; Bk Vols 50; Per Subs 10

Wireless access
Open Mon-Thurs 7:30-Noon

FAIRBURY

P DOMINY MEMORIAL LIBRARY*, 201 S Third St, 61739. SAN 304-1859. Tel: 815-692-3231. FAX: 815-692-3503. E-mail: dominylibrary@yahoo.com. Web Site: www.dominymemoriallibrary.org. *Head Librn,* Amanda Todd; *Asst Librn,* Marlene Walter; Staff 7 (MLS 1, Non-MLS 6)
Founded 1905. Pop 3,757; Circ 34,266
Library Holdings: High Interest/Low Vocabulary Bk Vols 20; Large Print Bks 382; Bk Vols 20,965; Per Subs 14
Automation Activity & Vendor Info: (Circulation) SirsiDynix-WorkFlows
Wireless access
Function: Home delivery & serv to seniorr ctr & nursing homes, Homebound delivery serv, ILL available, Prog for children & young adult, Summer reading prog
Mem of Reaching Across Illinois Library System (RAILS)
Open Mon, Tues & Thurs 10-7, Wed & Fri 10-5, Sat 9-1
Friends of the Library Group

FAIRFIELD

P FAIRFIELD PUBLIC LIBRARY, 300 SE Second St, 62837. SAN 304-1867. Tel: 618-842-4516. FAX: 618-842-6708. E-mail: fairfieldpubliclibrary@gmail.com. Web Site: www.fairfieldlibrary.org. *Dir, Head Librn,* Michelle Conard; Staff 2 (Non-MLS 2)
Founded 1923. Pop 5,428; Circ 60,119
Library Holdings: Bk Vols 40,000; Per Subs 84
Automation Activity & Vendor Info: (Cataloging) SirsiDynix; (Circulation) SirsiDynix; (OPAC) SirsiDynix
Mem of Illinois Heartland Library System
Open Mon-Thurs 10-6, Fri & Sat 10-2
Friends of the Library Group

J ILLINOIS EASTERN COMMUNITY COLLEGE*, Frontier Community College Learning Resource Center, Two Frontier Dr, 62837-9705. SAN 325-1810. Tel: 618-842-3711. Toll Free Tel: 877-464-3687. FAX: 618-842-4425. Web Site: www.iecc.edu/page.php?page=LIBF. *Dir,* Merna Youngblood; Staff 2 (MLS 1, Non-MLS 1)
Founded 1976. Enrl 650; Fac 500; Highest Degree: Associate
Jul 2019-Jun 2020 Income $106,468. Mats Exp $19,300, Books $6,000, Per/Ser (Incl. Access Fees) $3,500, AV Mat $4,000, Electronic Ref Mat (Incl. Access Fees) $5,800. Sal $72,002
Library Holdings: Audiobooks 396; AV Mats 1,106; CDs 10; DVDs 904; e-journals 63; Bk Titles 11,739; Per Subs 25
Wireless access
Function: Computers for patron use, Electronic databases & coll, ILL available, Internet access, Large print keyboards, Learning ctr, Magnifiers for reading, Online ref, Orientations, Photocopying/Printing, Scanner, Wheelchair accessible
Mem of Illinois Heartland Library System
Partic in Consortium of Academic & Research Libraries in Illinois
Open Mon-Thurs 7:30-6:30, Fri 7:30-4:30

FAIRMOUNT

P VANCE TOWNSHIP LIBRARY*, 107 S Main St, 61841. (Mail add: PO Box 230, 61841-0230), SAN 304-1875. Tel: 217-733-2164. FAX: 217-733-8025. E-mail: vantwplib@yahoo.com. Web Site: vancetownshiplibrary.com. *Dir,* Bonnie B Gilbert; *Libr Asst,* Gabriel Gilbert; Staff 2 (Non-MLS 2)
Founded 1940. Pop 1,027; Circ 4,674
Library Holdings: Bk Vols 10,263; Per Subs 32
Special Collections: History of Fairmount Coll; Jamaica Area; Senior Citizen Info; State of Illinois
Wireless access
Mem of Illinois Heartland Library System
Special Services for the Blind - Talking bk & rec for the blind cat
Open Tues-Fri 12-6, Sat 9-2

FAIRVIEW

P VALLEY DISTRICT PUBLIC LIBRARY*, Fairview Township Library, 515 Carter St, 61432. (Mail add: PO Box 200, 61432-0200), SAN 376-1215. Tel: 309-778-2240. FAX: 309-778-2240. E-mail: vdl61432@hotmail.com. Web Site: www.valleydistrictlibrary.weebly.com. *Dir,* Debbie Canevit
Library Holdings: Large Print Bks 75; Bk Titles 4,700
Open Mon, Wed & Fri 9-5

FAIRVIEW HEIGHTS

P FAIRVIEW HEIGHTS PUBLIC LIBRARY*, 10017 Bunkum Rd, 62208-1703. SAN 321-8961. Tel: 618-489-2070. Circulation Tel: 618-489-2073. Administration Tel: 618-489-2071. FAX: 618-489-2079. E-mail: fhpl@fhplibrary.org. Web Site: www.fairviewheightslibrary.org. *Dir,* Jill Pifer; Staff 11 (MLS 1, Non-MLS 10)
Founded 1972. Pop 15,034; Circ 135,000
Library Holdings: AV Mats 9,094; CDs 3,165; DVDs 2,300; Electronic Media & Resources 100; Large Print Bks 1,500; Bk Vols 40,000; Per Subs 135; Videos 200
Subject Interests: Music
Automation Activity & Vendor Info: (Cataloging) Innovative Interfaces, Inc; (Circulation) Innovative Interfaces, Inc; (ILL) Innovative Interfaces, Inc; (OPAC) Innovative Interfaces, Inc; (Serials) Innovative Interfaces, Inc
Wireless access
Mem of Illinois Heartland Library System
Partic in Illinois Library & Information Network
Open Mon-Thurs 10-8, Fri & Sat 10-5
Friends of the Library Group

FARMER CITY

P FARMER CITY PUBLIC LIBRARY, 109 E Green St, 61842-1508. (Mail add: PO Box 201, 61842-0201), SAN 304-1883. Tel: 309-928-9532. FAX: 309-928-2540. E-mail: farmercitypubliclibrary@gmail.com. Web Site: www.cityoffarmercity.org/library-3. *Dir,* Stephanie Rausch
Pop 2,055; Circ 14,504
Library Holdings: Bk Vols 14,000; Per Subs 29
Subject Interests: Genealogy, Local hist
Wireless access
Open Mon-Wed 10-1 & 4-7, Fri & Sat 9-1

FARMINGTON

P FARMINGTON AREA PUBLIC LIBRARY DISTRICT, 411 N Lightfoot Rd, 61531-1276. SAN 304-1891. Tel: 309-245-2175. FAX: 309-245-2294. E-mail: farmingtonpublic@yahoo.com. Web Site: www.farmingtonpublic.org. *Dir,* Rebecca Seaborn; E-mail: fapldirector@gmail.com; Staff 5 (MLS 1, Non-MLS 4)
Founded 1901. Pop 7,267; Circ 29,258
Library Holdings: Bk Titles 27,000; Per Subs 50
Automation Activity & Vendor Info: (Cataloging) TLC (The Library Corporation)
Wireless access
Function: 24/7 Online cat, Activity rm, Adult bk club, After school storytime, Audiobks on Playaways & MP3, Audiobks via web, Bk club(s), Bks on CD, CD-ROM, Children's prog, Digital talking bks, Free DVD rentals, Games & aids for people with disabilities, Holiday prog, Home delivery & serv to seniorr ctr & nursing homes, Homebound delivery serv, Homework prog, ILL available, Internet access, Magazines, Meeting rooms, Microfiche/film & reading machines, Movies, Museum passes, Music CDs, Notary serv, Online cat, Online ref, Outreach serv, OverDrive digital audio bks, Photocopying/Printing, Preschool reading prog, Prog for children & young adult, Ref serv available, Scanner, Senior computer classes, Senior outreach, Story hour, Study rm, Summer & winter reading prog, Summer reading prog, Tax forms, Teen prog, Wheelchair accessible
Partic in RSA
Open Mon-Thurs 9-8, Fri 9-5, Sat 10-4 (Sept-May); Mon, Wed & Fri 9-5, Tues & Thurs 9-8, Sat 10-4 (June-Aug)

FLORA

P FLORA PUBLIC LIBRARY*, 216 N Main St, 62839-1510. SAN 304-1905. Tel: 618-662-6553. FAX: 618-662-5007. E-mail: florapl@florapubliclibrary.org. Web Site: www.florapubliclibrary.org. *Libr Dir,* Donna L Corry; E-mail: dcorry@florapubliclibrary.org
Founded 1903. Pop 5,070; Circ 47,107
May 2014-Apr 2015 Income $210,514, State $6,338, Locally Generated Income $172,673, Other $31,503. Mats Exp $31,332. Sal $94,096
Library Holdings: Audiobooks 1,037; DVDs 1,617; e-books 30,526; Bk Vols 45,773; Per Subs 89
Wireless access
Mem of Illinois Heartland Library System
Open Mon-Thurs 1:30-8:30, Fri 10-6, Sat 10-3
Friends of the Library Group

FLOSSMOOR

P FLOSSMOOR PUBLIC LIBRARY*, 1000 Sterling Ave, 60422-1295. SAN 304-1913. Tel: 708-798-3600. FAX: 708-798-3603. Reference E-mail: flossref@flossmoorlibrary.org. Web Site: www.flossmoorlibrary.org. *Libr Dir,* Mrs Jamie L Paicely; E-mail: paicelyj@flossmoorlibrary.org
Founded 1953. Pop 9,464; Circ 165,555
May 2015-Apr 2016 Income $1,351,005, State $12,986, Locally Generated Income $1,289,999, Other $48,020

Library Holdings: Bk Vols 56,243; Per Subs 270
Subject Interests: Local hist
Automation Activity & Vendor Info: (Acquisitions) Baker & Taylor; (Cataloging) SirsiDynix; (Circulation) SirsiDynix; (ILL) OCLC FirstSearch; (OPAC) SirsiDynix
Wireless access
Function: 24/7 Electronic res, 24/7 Online cat, Activity rm, Adult bk club, After school storytime, Audiobks via web, AV serv, Bks on CD, Children's prog, Computer training, Computers for patron use, Electronic databases & coll, Free DVD rentals, Home delivery & serv to seniorr ctr & nursing homes, Homework prog, Instruction & testing, Internet access, Magazines, Meeting rooms, Movies, Museum passes, Music CDs, Online cat, OverDrive digital audio bks, Photocopying/Printing, Printer for laptops & handheld devices, Prog for adults, Prog for children & young adult, Ref & res, Scanner, Spoken cassettes & CDs, Spoken cassettes & DVDs, Story hour, Study rm, Summer & winter reading prog, Summer reading prog, Teen prog, Winter reading prog, Workshops
Mem of Reaching Across Illinois Library System (RAILS)
Partic in Illinois Library & Information Network; System Wide Automated Network
Open Mon-Thurs 9:30-9, Fri & Sat 9:30-5, Sun 1-5
Friends of the Library Group

FOREST PARK

P FOREST PARK PUBLIC LIBRARY, 7555 Jackson Blvd, 60130. SAN 304-1921. Tel: 708-366-7171. Reference Tel: 708-689-6125. FAX: 708-366-7185. Web Site: www.fppl.org. *Libr Dir,* Pilar Shaker; E-mail: pshaker@fppl.org; *Adult Serv Mgr,* Skye Lavin; E-mail: slavin@fppl.org; *Bus Mgr, Tech Serv Mgr,* Deb Harris; E-mail: dharris@fppl.org; *Commun Engagement Mgr,* Alicia Hammond; E-mail: ahammond@fppl.org; *Youth Serv Mgr,* Susan Farnum; E-mail: sfarnum@fppl.org; Staff 20 (MLS 5, Non-MLS 15)
Founded 1916. Pop 15,688; Circ 95,000
Library Holdings: Bk Vols 80,000; Per Subs 180
Automation Activity & Vendor Info: (Circulation) Innovative Interfaces, Inc; (OPAC) Innovative Interfaces, Inc
Wireless access
Mem of Reaching Across Illinois Library System (RAILS)
Partic in System Wide Automated Network
Special Services for the Blind - Bks on cassette; Bks on CD; Home delivery serv; Large print bks; Lending of low vision aids; Reader equip
Open Mon-Thurs 9-9, Fri 9-6, Sat 9-5, Sun 1-5
Friends of the Library Group

FORREST

P FORREST PUBLIC LIBRARY DISTRICT*, 301 S James, 61741. (Mail add: PO Box 555, 61741-0555), SAN 304-193X. Tel: 815-657-8805. FAX: 815-657-8837. E-mail: forrestlibrary@sbcglobal.net. *Dir,* Joyce Gulliford
Founded 1939. Pop 2,163; Circ 20,158
Library Holdings: Bk Vols 20,000; Per Subs 49
Special Collections: Louis L'Amour Westerns, large print bks
Subject Interests: Agr, Trains
Wireless access
Publications: Monthly Calendar
Open Mon-Fri 10-5, Sat 9-Noon

FORRESTON

P FORRESTON PUBLIC LIBRARY*, 204 First Ave, 61030. (Mail add: PO Box 606, 61030-0606), SAN 304-1948. Tel: 815-938-2624. FAX: 815-938-2152. E-mail: forlib@frontier.com. Web Site: www.forrestonlibrary.org. *Dir,* Cindy Bahr; Staff 2 (Non-MLS 2)
Pop 1,469; Circ 17,000
Library Holdings: Bks on Deafness & Sign Lang 5; CDs 541; DVDs 440; Large Print Bks 500; Bk Vols 14,313; Per Subs 44; Videos 650
Special Collections: James Grisgby Arts Coll, art books, encyclopedias
Wireless access
Function: Adult bk club, Bks on CD, Children's prog, Computers for patron use, Free DVD rentals, ILL available, Music CDs, Photocopying/Printing, Prog for adults, Prog for children & young adult, Story hour, Tax forms, Wheelchair accessible
Mem of Reaching Across Illinois Library System (RAILS)
Open Mon 9-11:30 & 2:30-8, Tues-Thurs 9-11:30 & 2:30-6, Sat 9-1

FORSYTH

P FORSYTH PUBLIC LIBRARY*, 268 S Elwood, 62535. (Mail add: PO Box 20, 62535-0020), SAN 324-6124. Tel: 217-877-8174. FAX: 217-877-3533. Web Site: www.forsythlibrary.com. *Libr Dir,* Rachel Miller; E-mail: rachelmiller.fpl@gmail.com; Staff 8 (MLS 1, Non-MLS 7)
Founded 1981
Library Holdings: Bk Titles 40,000; Per Subs 153
Wireless access
Function: 24/7 Electronic res, 24/7 Online cat, Adult bk club, Audiobks on Playaways & MP3, Bks on CD, Children's prog, Electronic databases & coll, Internet access, Magazines, OverDrive digital audio bks, Photocopying/Printing, Preschool reading prog, Prog for adults, Prog for children & young adult, Scanner, Story hour, Summer reading prog
Mem of Illinois Heartland Library System
Open Mon, Tues & Thurs 9-8, Wed & Fri 9-5, Sat 9-3

FOX LAKE

P FOX LAKE PUBLIC DISTRICT LIBRARY, 255 E Grand Ave, 60020. SAN 304-1956. Tel: 847-587-0198. FAX: 847-587-9493. Web Site: www.youseemore.com/foxlake. *Dir,* Melissa Villarreal; E-mail: Director@fllib.org; Staff 4 (MLS 4)
Founded 1939. Pop 25,284; Circ 187,024
Library Holdings: Audiobooks 3,500; CDs 3,500; DVDs 42,330; e-books 33,234; Bk Titles 83,284; Per Subs 179
Wireless access
Function: 24/7 Electronic res, 24/7 Online cat, Accelerated reader prog, Activity rm, Adult bk club, After school storytime, Art programs, Audiobks on Playaways & MP3, Audiobks via web, AV serv, Bk club(s), Bk reviews (Group), Bks on CD, Butterfly Garden, Children's prog, Computer training, Computers for patron use, Digital talking bks, Electronic databases & coll, Free DVD rentals, Games & aids for people with disabilities, Govt ref serv, Health sci info serv, Holiday prog, Home delivery & serv to seniorr ctr & nursing homes, Homebound delivery serv, ILL available, Instruction & testing, Internet access, Magazines, Magnifiers for reading, Mail & tel request accepted, Mango lang, Meeting rooms, Movies, Museum passes, Music CDs, Online cat, Online info literacy tutorials on the web & in blackboard, Online ref, Outreach serv, OverDrive digital audio bks, Photocopying/Printing, Preschool outreach, Preschool reading prog, Printer for laptops & handheld devices, Prof lending libr, Prog for adults, Prog for children & young adult, Ref & res, Ref serv available, Res assist avail, Scanner, Senior computer classes, Senior outreach, Serves people with intellectual disabilities, Spanish lang bks, STEM programs, Story hour, Study rm, Summer & winter reading prog, Summer reading prog, Tax forms, Teen prog, Telephone ref, Visual arts prog, Wheelchair accessible, Winter reading prog, Workshops
Publications: Footnotes; Newsletter (Bimonthly)
Mem of Reaching Across Illinois Library System (RAILS)
Open Mon-Fri 9-9, Sat 9-5, Sun (Sept-May) 1-5
Friends of the Library Group

FOX RIVER GROVE

P FOX RIVER GROVE PUBLIC LIBRARY DISTRICT*, 407 Lincoln Ave, 60021-1406. SAN 304-1964. Tel: 847-639-2274. E-mail: frgmlboard@frgml.org. Web Site: www.frgml.org. *Dir,* Nicole Steeves; E-mail: Nsteeves@frgml.org; Staff 9 (MLS 1, Non-MLS 8)
Founded 1936. Pop 4,235; Circ 50,402
Library Holdings: Bk Vols 32,000
Subject Interests: City hist
Automation Activity & Vendor Info: (Circulation) Koha; (OPAC) Koha
Wireless access
Function: 24/7 Electronic res, 24/7 Online cat, Accelerated reader prog, Activity rm, Adult bk club, Archival coll
Publications: Newsletter (Quarterly)
Mem of Reaching Across Illinois Library System (RAILS)
Friends of the Library Group

FRANKFORT

P FRANKFORT PUBLIC LIBRARY DISTRICT*, 21119 S Pfeiffer Rd, 60423-8699. SAN 304-1972. Tel: 815-469-2423. Circulation Tel: 815-534-6170. FAX: 815-469-9307. E-mail: fpl@frankfortlibrary.org. Web Site: www.frankfortlibrary.org. *Dir,* Pierre Gregoire; E-mail: pgregoire@frankfortlibrary.org; Staff 39 (MLS 12, Non-MLS 27)
Founded 1966. Pop 30,484; Circ 315,895
Jul 2014-Jun 2015 Income (Main & Associated Libraries) $2,399,157, State $67,574, County $2,114,842, Other $186,741. Mats Exp $263,365, Books $160,374, AV Mat $43,776, Electronic Ref Mat (Incl. Access Fees) $59,215. Sal $1,065,261 (Prof $306,263)
Library Holdings: Audiobooks 3,686; AV Mats 7,167; CDs 6,909; DVDs 7,167; e-books 7,426; Electronic Media & Resources 2,350; Bk Titles 109,250; Per Subs 159
Automation Activity & Vendor Info: (Acquisitions) SirsiDynix-WorkFlows; (Cataloging) SirsiDynix-WorkFlows; (Circulation) SirsiDynix-WorkFlows; (Discovery) SirsiDynix-Enterprise; (ILL) OCLC FirstSearch; (OPAC) SirsiDynix-Enterprise; (Serials) SirsiDynix-WorkFlows
Wireless access
Function: 24/7 Electronic res, 24/7 Online cat, 3D Printer, Activity rm, Adult bk club, Archival coll, Audio & video playback equip for onsite use, Audiobks on Playaways & MP3, Audiobks via web, Bk club(s), Bks on CD, Children's prog, Computer training, Computers for patron use, Electronic databases & coll, Free DVD rentals, Holiday prog, Home delivery & serv to seniorr ctr & nursing homes, ILL available, Internet

access, Life-long learning prog for all ages, Magazines, Magnifiers for reading, Meeting rooms, Microfiche/film & reading machines, Movies, Museum passes, Music CDs, Notary serv, Online cat, Outreach serv, OverDrive digital audio bks, Photocopying/Printing, Prog for adults, Prog for children & young adult, Ref serv available, Scanner, Senior computer classes, Serves people with intellectual disabilities, Study rm, Summer & winter reading prog, Visual arts prog, Wheelchair accessible, Writing prog
Publications: eNews (Online only)
Mem of Reaching Across Illinois Library System (RAILS)
Partic in System Wide Automated Network
Open Mon-Thurs 10-9, Fri & Sat 9-5, Sun (Sept-May) 1-5
Friends of the Library Group

FRANKLIN GROVE

P WINIFRED KNOX MEMORIAL LIBRARY, Franklin Grove Public Library, 112 S Elm St, 61031. (Mail add: PO Box 326, 61031-0326), SAN 304-1980. Tel: 815-456-2823. FAX: 815-456-2619. E-mail: library@franklingrovelibrary.org. Web Site: www.franklingrovelibrary.org. *Dir,* Jeffrey Munson; E-mail: jmunson@franklingrovelibrary.org
Founded 1916. Pop 1,052
Wireless access
Mem of Reaching Across Illinois Library System (RAILS)
Open Mon-Thurs 10-7, Fri 10-5, Sat 10-2
Friends of the Library Group

FRANKLIN PARK

P FRANKLIN PARK PUBLIC LIBRARY DISTRICT*, 10311 Grand Ave, 60131. SAN 304-1999. Tel: 847-455-6016. FAX: 847-455-6416. E-mail: info@fppld.org. Web Site: www.fppld.org. *Exec Dir,* Marie Saeli; Tel: 847-455-6016, Ext 226, E-mail: msaeli@fppld.org; *Adult Serv,* Vanessa Morrison; Tel: 847-455-6016, Ext 247, E-mail: vmorrison@fppld.org; Staff 7 (MLS 6, Non-MLS 1)
Founded 1962
Library Holdings: CDs 5,000; DVDs 5,000; Bk Vols 170,000; Per Subs 246; Videos 5,000
Special Collections: Local History, artifacts, maps, print; Polish Language, av, print; Spanish Language, av, print
Automation Activity & Vendor Info: (Serials) SirsiDynix
Wireless access
Publications: Franklin Park Public Library Newsletter (Bimonthly); The Franklin Park Library Electronic Newsletter (Monthly bulletin)
Mem of Reaching Across Illinois Library System (RAILS)
Partic in Libr Integrated Network Consortium; System Wide Automated Network
Open Mon-Thurs 9-9, Fri 9-7, Sat 9-5
Friends of the Library Group

FREEBURG

P FREEBURG AREA LIBRARY*, 407 S Belleville, 62243. Tel: 618-539-5454. FAX: 618-539-5854. E-mail: frelib407@gmail.com. Web Site: www.freeburglibrary.com. *Dir,* Kristin Green
Founded 1996
Library Holdings: Bk Titles 37,000; Per Subs 60
Automation Activity & Vendor Info: (Acquisitions) Innovative Interfaces, Inc; (Cataloging) Innovative Interfaces, Inc; (Circulation) Innovative Interfaces, Inc
Wireless access
Mem of Illinois Heartland Library System
Open Mon, Tues & Thurs 11-7, Fri 11-6, Sat 11-2

FREEPORT

M FHN MEMORIAL HOSPITAL*, Health Science Library, 1045 W Stephenson St, 61032. SAN 371-6333. Tel: 815-599-6132. FAX: 815-599-6858. Web Site: www.fhn.org. *Librn,* Mary Pat Gordon; Tel: 815-599-6728, Fax: 815-599-6729, E-mail: mgordon@fhn.org; Staff 1 (MLS 1)
Library Holdings: Bk Titles 750; Per Subs 70
Function: Health sci info serv, ILL available
Mem of Reaching Across Illinois Library System (RAILS)
Partic in Illinois Library & Information Network; OCLC-LVIS
Restriction: Authorized patrons, In-house use for visitors, Lending to staff only, Open by appt only

P FREEPORT PUBLIC LIBRARY*, 100 E Douglas St, 61032. SAN 304-2022. Tel: 815-233-3000. FAX: 815-233-1099. E-mail: information@freeportpubliclibrary.org. Web Site: www.freeportpubliclibrary.org. *Dir,* Ashley Huffines; E-mail: ahuffines@freeportpubliclibrary.org; *Head, Adult Serv,* Laura F Keyes; Tel: 815-233-3000, Ext 221, E-mail: lfkeyes@freeportpubliclibrary.org; *Youth Serv Supvr,* Anna Doyle; Tel: 815-233-3000, Ext 238; *Circ & Outreach,* Geoff Graham; Tel: 815-233-3000, Ext 229; Staff 32 (MLS 3, Non-MLS 29)
Founded 1874. Pop 25,840; Circ 310,324
Library Holdings: Bk Vols 119,688; Per Subs 396
Special Collections: Freeport & Stephenson County History, bks & pamphlet files; Local Newspapers, microfilm; Louis Sullivan Coll, pamphlet file. US Document Depository
Mem of Reaching Across Illinois Library System (RAILS)
Open Mon-Thurs (Winter) 9-9, Fri 9-6, Sat 9-5, Sun 1-4, Mon-Thurs (Summer) 9-8, Fri 9-6, Sat 9-5

J HIGHLAND COMMUNITY COLLEGE LIBRARY, Clarence Mitchell Library, 2998 W Pearl City Rd, 61032-9341. SAN 304-2030. Tel: 815-599-3539. Administration Tel: 815-599-3456. E-mail: library@highland.edu. Web Site: www.highland.edu/library. *Dir, Libr Serv, Ref Librn,* Laura Watson; *User Serv Librn,* Michael Skwara; Tel: 815-599-3657; Staff 3 (MLS 2, Non-MLS 1)
Founded 1962. Enrl 1,100; Highest Degree: Associate
Library Holdings: AV Mats 3,000; Bk Vols 52,000; Per Subs 25
Special Collections: Local Authors Coll
Automation Activity & Vendor Info: (Acquisitions) Innovative Interfaces, Inc; (Cataloging) Innovative Interfaces, Inc; (Circulation) Innovative Interfaces, Inc; (Course Reserve) Innovative Interfaces, Inc; (Discovery) EBSCO Discovery Service; (ILL) Innovative Interfaces, Inc; (Media Booking) Innovative Interfaces, Inc; (OPAC) Innovative Interfaces, Inc; (Serials) Innovative Interfaces, Inc
Wireless access
Mem of Reaching Across Illinois Library System (RAILS)
Partic in Consortium of Academic & Research Libraries in Illinois; Dubuque Area Library Information Consortium; Network of Illinois Learning Resources in Community Colleges
Special Services for the Blind - Assistive/Adapted tech devices, equip & products
Open Mon-Fri 8-5

FULTON

P SCHMALING MEMORIAL PUBLIC LIBRARY DISTRICT, 501 Tenth Ave, 61252. (Mail add: PO Box 125, 61252-0125), SAN 304-2057. Tel: 815-589-2045. FAX: 815-589-4483. E-mail: fulpublib@mchsi.com. Web Site: schmaling.lib.il.us. *Dir,* Britni Hartman; Staff 7 (MLS 3, Non-MLS 4)
Founded 1909. Pop 3,481; Circ 32,445
Library Holdings: Audiobooks 374; CDs 359; DVDs 865; Large Print Bks 742; Microforms 100; Bk Vols 18,367; Per Subs 35
Special Collections: Dutch Costume Patterns & Books in Dutch Language; Local History Coll
Automation Activity & Vendor Info: (Acquisitions) JayWil Software Development, Inc; (Cataloging) JayWil Software Development, Inc; (Circulation) Innovative Interfaces, Inc - Sierra; (ILL) Innovative Interfaces, Inc; (OPAC) Innovative Interfaces, Inc; (Serials) Innovative Interfaces, Inc - Sierra
Wireless access
Function: Adult bk club, Bks on CD, Children's prog, Computer training, Computers for patron use, E-Reserves, Electronic databases & coll, Free DVD rentals, Homebound delivery serv, ILL available, Magazines, Mail & tel request accepted, Microfiche/film & reading machines, Movies, Music CDs, Online cat, Photocopying/Printing, Preschool outreach, Preschool reading prog, Prog for adults, Prog for children & young adult, Ref serv available, Scanner, Story hour, Summer reading prog, Tax forms, Teen prog, Telephone ref, Wheelchair accessible
Mem of Reaching Across Illinois Library System (RAILS)
Open Mon-Wed 10-7, Thurs 10-2, Fri 10-4, Sat 10-1
Restriction: Non-circulating of rare bks, Non-resident fee
Friends of the Library Group

GALENA

P GALENA PUBLIC LIBRARY DISTRICT*, 601 S Bench St, 61036. SAN 304-2065. Tel: 815-777-0200. FAX: 815-777-1542. E-mail: info@galenalibrary.org. Web Site: www.galenalibrary.org. *Libr Dir,* Susi Ludwig; E-mail: ludwigs@galenalibrary.org; *Ad,* Larissa Distler; E-mail: distlerl@galenalibrary.org; *Children & Teen Librn,* Rachel Lenstra; E-mail: lenstrar@galenalibrary.org; *Circ Serv Librn,* Linda Klug; E-mail: klugl@galenalibrary.org; *Tech Serv Librn,* Colleen Keleher; E-mail: keleherc@galenalibrary.org
Founded 1894
Special Collections: Local History Coll, bks, micro, recs
Automation Activity & Vendor Info: (Acquisitions) SirsiDynix; (Cataloging) SirsiDynix; (Circulation) SirsiDynix; (ILL) OCLC WorldShare Interlibrary Loan; (OPAC) SirsiDynix-iBistro; (Serials) SirsiDynix
Wireless access
Mem of Reaching Across Illinois Library System (RAILS)
Partic in Dubuque Area Library Information Consortium
Special Services for the Blind - Braille bks
Open Mon-Thurs 11-8, Fri & Sat 11-5
Friends of the Library Group

S ILLINOIS HISTORIC PRESERVATION AGENCY, Division of Historic Sites-US Grant's Home State Historic Site Library, 307 Decatur St, 61036. (Mail add: PO Box 333, 61036-0333), SAN 325-6839. Tel: 815-777-3310. FAX: 815-777-3310. E-mail: granthome@granthome.com. Web Site: www.granthome.org. *Mgr,* Terry J Miller
Library Holdings: Bk Titles 1,500
Special Collections: E B Washburne Coll; Regional History, decorative arts, architecture, historic sites, local newspapers 1828-1930, historic photographs, 19th century artifacts; U S Grant Coll
Wireless access
Restriction: Open by appt only

GALESBURG

J CARL SANDBURG COLLEGE*, 2400 Tom L Wilson Blvd, 61401. SAN 340-4285. Tel: 309-341-5257. Interlibrary Loan Service Tel: 309-341-5206. FAX: 309-344-3526. E-mail: library@sandburg.edu. Web Site: sandburg.edu/Academics/Library. *Librn,* Claire Ehrlich; E-mail: cehrlich@sandburg.edu; *Info Serv,* Abby Frye; E-mail: afrye@sandburg.edu; Staff 3 (MLS 1, Non-MLS 2)
Founded 1967. Enrl 3,614; Fac 69; Highest Degree: Associate
Library Holdings: Bk Titles 31,644; Bk Vols 38,740; Per Subs 400
Special Collections: Bill Campbell Cartoon Art Coll, original graphic art; Carl Sandburg & Institutional Archives
Subject Interests: Vocational educ
Automation Activity & Vendor Info: (Circulation) TLC (The Library Corporation)
Wireless access
Function: Res libr
Partic in ALS Interlibr Servs; Consortium of Academic & Research Libraries in Illinois; Illinois Library & Information Network; Network of Illinois Learning Resources in Community Colleges; OCLC Online Computer Library Center, Inc
Open Mon-Wed 7:45-6:30, Thur 7:45-6, Fri 7:45-4:45

Departmental Libraries:

CARTHAGE BRANCH CAMPUS, 305 Sandburg Dr, Carthage, 62321, SAN 340-4293. Tel: 217-357-3129. FAX: 217-357-3512. *Dean, Extn Serv,* Debra Miller; E-mail: dmiller@sandburg.edu; Staff 5 (MLS 2, Non-MLS 3)
Highest Degree: Associate
Library Holdings: AV Mats 250; Bk Vols 20,000; Per Subs 125
Function: Res libr
Open Mon-Thurs 7:45am-9pm, Fri 8-4, Sat 9-Noon

P GALESBURG PUBLIC LIBRARY*, 40 E Simmons St, 61401-4591. SAN 340-4315. Tel: 309-343-6118. FAX: 309-343-4877. Reference E-mail: reference@galesburglibrary.org. Web Site: www.galesburglibrary.org. *Dir,* Noelle Thompson; E-mail: noelle.thompson@galesburglibrary.org; *Asst Dir, Head, Adult Serv,* Jane Easterly; E-mail: jane.easterly@galesburglibrary.org; *Head, Children's Servx,* Melinda Jones-Rhoades; E-mail: melindaj@galesburglibrary.org; *Head, Circ,* Kayla Kuffel; E-mail: kayla.kuffel@galesburglibrary.org; *Head, Tech Serv,* Nancy Terpening; E-mail: nancy.terpening@galesburglibrary.org; *Ref Librn,* Faith Burdick; E-mail: faithb@galesburglibrary.org; *Grants Coordr, Ref Librn,* Eileen Castro; E-mail: eileen.castro@galesburglibrary.org; *Ref Librn, YA Librn,* John Driscoll; E-mail: john.driscoll@galesburglibrary.org; *IT Coordr, Ref Librn,* Luke Gorham; E-mail: luke.gorham@galesburglibrary.org; *Archivist,* Emily DuGranrut; E-mail: emily.dugranrut@galesburglibrary.org; Staff 21 (MLS 7, Non-MLS 14)
Founded 1874. Pop 32,195; Circ 279,690
Jan 2013-Dec 2013 Income $1,372,455. Mats Exp $250,000. Sal $776,525 (Prof $150,000)
Library Holdings: CDs 5,778; DVDs 5,931; Bk Titles 184,153; Per Subs 259
Special Collections: Local Newspapers, microfilm. Oral History
Subject Interests: Local hist
Automation Activity & Vendor Info: (Acquisitions) SirsiDynix-WorkFlows; (Cataloging) SirsiDynix-WorkFlows; (Circulation) SirsiDynix-WorkFlows; (ILL) SirsiDynix-WorkFlows; (OPAC) SirsiDynix-WorkFlows; (Serials) SirsiDynix-WorkFlows
Wireless access
Function: Accelerated reader prog, Adult bk club, Archival coll, Art exhibits, Audio & video playback equip for onsite use, Audiobks via web, AV serv, Bk club(s), Bks on cassette, Bks on CD, CD-ROM, Chess club, Children's prog, Computer training, Computers for patron use, E-Reserves, Electronic databases & coll, Free DVD rentals, Holiday prog, Home delivery & serv to seniorr ctr & nursing homes, Homebound delivery serv, ILL available, Instruction & testing, Internet access, Magnifiers for reading, Mail & tel request accepted, Music CDs, Notary serv, Online cat, Online ref, Orientations, Photocopying/Printing, Prof lending libr, Prog for adults, Prog for children & young adult, Ref serv available, Scanner, Senior computer classes, Spoken cassettes & CDs, Story hour, Summer reading prog, Tax forms, Teen prog, Telephone ref, VHS videos, Wheelchair accessible, Workshops
Mem of Reaching Across Illinois Library System (RAILS)
Partic in Resource Sharing Alliance
Special Services for the Deaf - TTY equip
Open Mon-Thurs 9-8, Fri & Sat 9-5
Restriction: Non-circulating of rare bks
Friends of the Library Group

S HILL CORRECTIONAL CENTER LIBRARY*, 600 S Linwood Rd, 61401. (Mail add: PO Box 1700, 61402), SAN 371-6449. Tel: 309-343-4212, Ext 360. *Libr Assoc,* Kellie Dennis
Founded 1986
Library Holdings: Bk Titles 12,000; Per Subs 22
Special Collections: Law Library Coll
Restriction: Staff & inmates only

C KNOX COLLEGE*, Henry W Seymour Library, 371 S West St, 61401. SAN 340-4404. Tel: 309-341-7246. Interlibrary Loan Service Tel: 309-341-7244. Reference Tel: 309-341-7228. Administration Tel: 309-341-7248. FAX: 309-341-7799. Web Site: library.knox.edu. *Dir,* Jeffrey A Douglas; Tel: 309-341-7491, E-mail: jdouglas@knox.edu; *Assoc Librn,* Sharon Clayton; Tel: 309-341-7249, E-mail: sclayton@knox.edu; *IT Librn,* Laurie Sauer; Tel: 309-341-7788, E-mail: lsauer@knox.edu; Staff 7 (MLS 5, Non-MLS 2)
Founded 1837. Enrl 1,339; Fac 116; Highest Degree: Bachelor
Jul 2016-Jun 2017 Income (Main & Associated Libraries) $1,273,000. Mats Exp $405,767, Books $97,055, Per/Ser (Incl. Access Fees) $306,336, Electronic Ref Mat (Incl. Access Fees) $8,046, Presv $6,751. Sal $712,438 (Prof $301,365)
Library Holdings: AV Mats 14,160; Electronic Media & Resources 10,263; Bk Titles 243,659; Bk Vols 338,946; Per Subs 21,166
Special Collections: American Civil War (Smith Coll), bks, mss, maps & photos; Ernest Hemingway & The Lost Generation (Hughes Coll), bks, mss; Lincoln Coll; Old Northwest Territory (Finley Coll), bks & maps; Upper Mississippi River Valley (Player Coll), bks, maps & prints
Automation Activity & Vendor Info: (Acquisitions) Ex Libris Group; (Cataloging) Ex Libris Group; (Circulation) Ex Libris Group; (Course Reserve) Ex Libris Group; (ILL) OCLC ILLiad; (OPAC) Ex Libris Group; (Serials) Ex Libris Group
Wireless access
Partic in Consortium of Academic & Research Libraries in Illinois; OCLC Online Computer Library Center, Inc; OCLC-LVIS
Open Mon-Thurs 8am-1am, Fri 8am-9pm, Sat 10-9, Sun 11am-1am

GALVA

J BLACK HAWK COLLEGE*, Gust E Lundberg Library, 26230 Black Hawk Rd, 61434. SAN 304-3118. Tel: 309-854-1730. E-mail: library@bhc.edu. Web Site: www.bhc.edu/academics/academic-resources/library. *Dir, Libr Serv,* Ashtin Trimble; Tel: 309-796-5143, E-mail: trimblea@bhc.edu; *Lead Libr Asst,* Christine Ernat; E-mail: ernatc@bhc.edu; *Ref & Instruction Librn,* Barbara Bolser; E-mail: bolserb@bhc.edu; Staff 3 (MLS 1, Non-MLS 2)
Founded 1967. Enrl 829; Fac 70; Highest Degree: Associate
Library Holdings: Bk Vols 18,000; Per Subs 128
Special Collections: Local Authors Coll
Subject Interests: Agr, Horses
Wireless access
Partic in Consortium of Academic & Research Libraries in Illinois; Network of Illinois Learning Resources in Community Colleges; Resource Sharing Alliance
Special Services for the Blind - Magnifiers
Open Mon-Thurs (Fall & Spring) 7:30-7:30, Fri 7:30-2; Mon-Thurs (Summer) 8-4, Fri 8-1

P GALVA PUBLIC LIBRARY DISTRICT*, 120 NW Third Ave, 61434. SAN 304-2103. Tel: 309-932-2180. FAX: 309-932-2280. E-mail: galvalibrarystaff@yahoo.com. Web Site: www.galvalibrary.org. *Dir,* Melody Heck; E-mail: galvalib@mchsi.com; *Asst Dir,* Hess Sage; Staff 1 (Non-MLS 1)
Founded 1909. Pop 3,570; Circ 19,819
Jul 2019-Jun 2020 Income $399,476. Mats Exp $31,260, Books $18,328, AV Mat $2,607, Electronic Ref Mat (Incl. Access Fees) $10,325. Sal $174,710
Library Holdings: Audiobooks 504; DVDs 2,533; Large Print Bks 1,368; Bk Vols 21,765; Per Subs 57
Special Collections: Galva News, 1879-present on microfilm; Swedish & Local History
Automation Activity & Vendor Info: (Cataloging) SirsiDynix; (Circulation) SirsiDynix-WorkFlows; (OPAC) SirsiDynix
Wireless access
Function: 24/7 Online cat, Adult bk club
Mem of Reaching Across Illinois Library System (RAILS)
Partic in Resource Sharing Alliance
Open Mon-Wed 8:30-7, Thurs 9:30-5, Fri 1-5, Sat 9-1 (Sept-May); Mon-Thurs 8:30-5, Fri 1-5, Sat 9-12 (June-Aug)

GENESEO

P GENESEO PUBLIC LIBRARY DISTRICT, 805 N Chicago St, 61254. SAN 304-2111. Tel: 309-944-6452. FAX: 309-944-6721. Web Site: geneseo.lib.il.us. *Dir,* Claire Kennefick Crawford; E-mail: ccrawford@geneseo.lib.il.us; Staff 14 (Non-MLS 14)
Founded 1855. Pop 14,633; Circ 149,000
Library Holdings: Audiobooks 2,727; CDs 1,665; DVDs 6,643; e-books 26,158; Electronic Media & Resources 12; Large Print Bks 3,339; Music Scores 62; Bk Vols 62,809; Per Subs 62
Special Collections: Early Geneseo Historical Material 1836-1920, including oral hist tapes, microfilm. Oral History
Subject Interests: Compact discs
Wireless access
Function: 24/7 Electronic res, 24/7 Online cat, Activity rm, Adult bk club, Adult literacy prog, Archival coll, Audiobks on Playaways & MP3, Audiobks via web, Bk club(s), Bks on CD, CD-ROM, Children's prog, Computers for patron use, Digital talking bks, E-Readers, Electronic databases & coll, Free DVD rentals, Genealogy discussion group, ILL available, Internet access, Laminating, Large print keyboards, Life-long learning prog for all ages, Magazines, Mail & tel request accepted, Meeting rooms, Microfiche/film & reading machines, Movies, Museum passes, Music CDs, Notary serv, Online cat, Online ref, Outside serv via phone, mail, e-mail & web, OverDrive digital audio bks, Photocopying/Printing, Preschool outreach, Preschool reading prog, Prog for adults, Prog for children & young adult, Scanner, Serves people with intellectual disabilities, Story hour, Study rm, Summer reading prog, Tax forms, Wheelchair accessible
Publications: Library Events (Newsletter); Online Newletter & Calendar
Mem of Reaching Across Illinois Library System (RAILS)
Special Services for the Blind - Talking bks
Open Mon-Thurs 9-8, Fri 9-6, Sat 9-5
Friends of the Library Group

GENEVA

P GENEVA PUBLIC LIBRARY DISTRICT*, 127 James St, 60134. SAN 304-212X. Tel: 630-232-0780. FAX: 630-232-2040. TDD: 630-845-3176. E-mail: geneva.library@gpld.org. Web Site: www.gpld.org. *Libr Dir,* Christine Lazaris; Tel: 630-232-0780, Ext 302, E-mail: clazaris@gpld.org; *Asst Libr Dir,* Nancy Kendzior; Tel: 630-232-0780, Ext 303, E-mail: nkendzior@gpld.org; *IT Mgr,* Lynnette Singh; Tel: 630-232-0780, Ext 310, E-mail: lsingh@gpld.org; Staff 66 (MLS 13, Non-MLS 53)
Founded 1894. Pop 28,500; Circ 479,000
Library Holdings: AV Mats 17,600; Bks on Deafness & Sign Lang 15; High Interest/Low Vocabulary Bk Vols 300; Large Print Bks 2,800; Bk Titles 127,800; Bk Vols 142,000; Per Subs 270; Talking Bks 9,616
Subject Interests: Art & archit, Folklore, Local hist
Automation Activity & Vendor Info: (Cataloging) SirsiDynix; (Circulation) SirsiDynix; (ILL) OCLC; (OPAC) SirsiDynix; (Serials) SirsiDynix
Wireless access
Publications: Library Link (Newsletter)
Mem of Reaching Across Illinois Library System (RAILS)
Partic in Libraries In Cooperation; System Wide Automated Network
Special Services for the Deaf - TDD equip
Special Services for the Blind - Ednalite Hi-Vision scope; ZoomText magnification & reading software
Open Mon-Thurs 9-9, Fri 9-6, Sat 9-5, Sun 12-5
Friends of the Library Group

M NORTHWESTERN MEDICINE-DELNOR HOSPITAL*, Health Science Library, 300 Randall Rd, 60134. SAN 325-0776. Tel: 630-208-4299. Web Site: www.nm.org. *Librn,* Paula Olson; E-mail: paula.olson@nm.org
Library Holdings: Bk Titles 900; Per Subs 110
Subject Interests: Med
Wireless access
Mem of Reaching Across Illinois Library System (RAILS)
Partic in Illinois Library & Information Network
Open Mon-Fri 7:30-4

GENOA

P GENOA PUBLIC LIBRARY DISTRICT*, 240 W Main St, 60135. SAN 304-2138. Tel: 815-784-2627. FAX: 815-784-4829. E-mail: support@genoalibrary.org. Web Site: www.genoalibrary.org. *Libr Dir,* Jennifer Barton
Founded 1922. Circ 27,153
Library Holdings: Bk Vols 55,000; Per Subs 63
Automation Activity & Vendor Info: (Cataloging) Innovative Interfaces, Inc - Sierra; (Circulation) Innovative Interfaces, Inc - Sierra; (Discovery) Innovative Interfaces, Inc - Sierra; (ILL) Innovative Interfaces, Inc - Sierra; (OPAC) Innovative Interfaces, Inc - Sierra; (Serials) Innovative Interfaces, Inc - Sierra
Wireless access
Function: 24/7 Electronic res, 24/7 Online cat, Activity rm, Adult bk club, Audiobks via web, Bk club(s), Bks on CD, Children's prog, Computer training, Computers for patron use, Digital talking bks, Electronic databases & coll, Free DVD rentals, Holiday prog, ILL available, Internet access, Magazines, Mail & tel request accepted, Meeting rooms, Movies, Music CDs, Online cat, Outside serv via phone, mail, e-mail & web, OverDrive digital audio bks, Photocopying/Printing, Preschool reading prog, Prog for adults, Prog for children & young adult, Ref serv available, Scanner, STEM programs, Story hour, Study rm, Summer reading prog, Tax forms, Teen prog, Telephone ref, Wheelchair accessible, Workshops
Mem of Reaching Across Illinois Library System (RAILS)
Open Mon-Thurs 10-8, Sat 10-2, Sun (Sept-May) 12-4
Restriction: Non-resident fee

GEORGETOWN

P GEORGETOWN PUBLIC LIBRARY*, 102 W West St, 61846. SAN 304-2146. Tel: 217-662-2164. FAX: 217-662-6790. *Librn,* Shannon Whitaker; E-mail: gtwp2019sw@gmail.com
Founded 1936. Pop 3,628; Circ 19,000
Library Holdings: Bk Vols 16,000; Per Subs 30
Automation Activity & Vendor Info: (Acquisitions) SirsiDynix; (Cataloging) SirsiDynix; (Circulation) SirsiDynix; (ILL) SirsiDynix
Wireless access
Mem of Illinois Heartland Library System
Open Mon, Wed & Thurs 12:30-5:30, Tues & Fri 9-5:30, Sat 9-2

GERMANTOWN

P GERMANTOWN PUBLIC LIBRARY DISTRICT, 403 Munster St, 62245. (Mail add: PO Box 244, 62245-0244). Tel: 618-523-4820. FAX: 618-523-4599. E-mail: gma@gtownlibrary.org. Web Site: www.gtownlibrary.org. *Dir,* Kami Komm; E-mail: kamik@gtownlibrary.org; Staff 2 (MLS 1, Non-MLS 1)
Founded 1995. Pop 1,923; Circ 13,732
Library Holdings: AV Mats 379; Large Print Bks 300; Bk Titles 14,359; Per Subs 31
Wireless access
Function: 24/7 Electronic res, 24/7 Online cat, Accelerated reader prog
Mem of Illinois Heartland Library System
Open Mon & Wed 10-4, Tues & Thurs 1-8, Fri 1-6, Sat 9-Noon

GIBSON CITY

P MOYER DISTRICT LIBRARY*, 618 S Sangamon, 60936. SAN 304-2154. Tel: 217-784-5343. FAX: 217-784-5373. E-mail: moyerlibrary@yahoo.com. Web Site: www.moyer.lib.il.us. *Dir,* Sharon Heavilin; Staff 1 (Non-MLS 1)
Founded 1911. Pop 5,402
Library Holdings: Audiobooks 1,517; DVDs 2,655; Bk Titles 42,000; Per Subs 69
Automation Activity & Vendor Info: (Acquisitions) SirsiDynix; (Cataloging) SirsiDynix; (Circulation) SirsiDynix; (Course Reserve) SirsiDynix
Wireless access
Function: After school storytime
Publications: Booklist; Illinois Libraries; Wilson Library Bulletin
Mem of Illinois Heartland Library System
Special Services for the Deaf - TTY equip
Open Mon-Thurs 10-8, Fri 10-5, Sat 10-3
Friends of the Library Group

GILLESPIE

P GILLESPIE PUBLIC LIBRARY*, 201 W Chestnut, 62033. SAN 304-2162. Tel: 217-839-3614. FAX: 217-839-4854. E-mail: gillespiepubliclibrary@gmail.com. *Dir,* Steve Joyce; Staff 3 (MLS 1, Non-MLS 2)
Founded 1944. Pop 3,319; Circ 15,000
Library Holdings: Bk Vols 16,000
Mem of Illinois Heartland Library System
Open Mon 2-8, Tues & Thurs 2-6, Wed & Fri 9-5, Sat 9-1
Friends of the Library Group

GILMAN

P GILMAN-DANFORTH DISTRICT LIBRARY*, 715 N Maple St, 60938. SAN 304-2170. Tel: 815-265-7522. FAX: 815-265-7522. E-mail: gilmandanforthlib@live.com. Web Site: gilmandanforthlib.org. *Libr Dir,* Renee Wellborn
Pop 3,049; Circ 19,000
Library Holdings: Bk Vols 20,000; Per Subs 25
Automation Activity & Vendor Info: (Cataloging) Horizon; (Circulation) Horizon
Wireless access
Mem of Illinois Heartland Library System

Open Mon-Thurs 10-6, Fri 10-5, Sat 10-2
Friends of the Library Group

GIRARD

P GIRARD TOWNSHIP LIBRARY*, 201 W Madison St, 62640-1551. SAN 304-2189. Tel: 217-627-2414. FAX: 217-627-2093. E-mail: library62640@yahoo.com. *Dir,* Diane Seelbach; E-mail: library62640@yahoo.com; Staff 2 (MLS 1, Non-MLS 1)
Founded 1947. Pop 2,642; Circ 16,933
Library Holdings: Audiobooks 100; Bks on Deafness & Sign Lang 6; CDs 90; DVDs 135; Large Print Bks 400; Bk Titles 36,000; Per Subs 18; Talking Bks 100; Videos 250
Special Collections: City Ord/genealogy
Wireless access
Function: 24/7 Electronic res, 24/7 Online cat, Accelerated reader prog, Activity rm, Adult bk club, Adult literacy prog, Archival coll, Art exhibits, Audiobks via web, Bks on cassette, Bks on CD, Children's prog, Computer training, Computers for patron use, Digital talking bks, Electronic databases & coll, Free DVD rentals, Govt ref serv, Home delivery & serv to seniorr ctr & nursing homes, Homebound delivery serv, ILL available, Instruction & testing, Internet access, Magazines, Mail & tel request accepted, Meeting rooms, Microfiche/film & reading machines, Movies, Music CDs, Notary serv, Online cat, Online ref, Outside serv via phone, mail, e-mail & web, Photocopying/Printing, Preschool outreach, Preschool reading prog, Printer for laptops & handheld devices, Prof lending libr, Prog for adults, Prog for children & young adult, Ref & res, Ref serv available, Res assist avail, Res libr, Scanner, Senior computer classes, Senior outreach, Serves people with intellectual disabilities, Study rm, Summer & winter reading prog, Summer reading prog, Tax forms, Teen prog, VHS videos, Wheelchair accessible
Mem of Illinois Heartland Library System
Open Mon 11-5, Tues & Thurs 1-7, Wed & Fri 1-5, Sat 8-Noon
Restriction: Access at librarian's discretion
Friends of the Library Group

GLEN CARBON

P GLEN CARBON CENTENNIAL LIBRARY DISTRICT, 198 S Main St, 62034. Tel: 618-288-1212. FAX: 618-288-1205. E-mail: gle@glencarbonlibrary.org. Web Site: www.glencarbonlibrary.org. *Dir,* Christine Gerrish; E-mail: director@glencarbonlibrary.org; *Youth Serv Dir,* Aimee Villet; E-mail: aimeev@glencarbonlibrary.org; *Circ Mgr,* Cheryl Hager; E-mail: cherylh@glencarbonlibrary.org; Staff 12 (MLS 4, Non-MLS 8)
Founded 1992. Pop 12,900
Library Holdings: Bk Titles 35,000; Per Subs 45
Automation Activity & Vendor Info: (Circulation) Innovative Interfaces, Inc; (OPAC) Innovative Interfaces, Inc
Wireless access
Function: 24/7 Electronic res, 24/7 Online cat, 3D Printer, Activity rm, Adult bk club, Audiobks on Playaways & MP3, Audiobks via web, Bks on CD, Children's prog, Computer training, Computers for patron use, Digital talking bks, E-Readers, Electronic databases & coll, Equip loans & repairs, Free DVD rentals, Homebound delivery serv, ILL available, Internet access, Magazines, Mango lang, Meeting rooms, Movies, Music CDs, Notary serv, Online cat, Online info literacy tutorials on the web & in blackboard, Outside serv via phone, mail, e-mail & web, Photocopying/Printing, Prog for adults, Prog for children & young adult, Ref serv available, Scanner, Senior computer classes, Spanish lang bks, Story hour, Study rm, Summer reading prog, Tax forms, Teen prog, Wheelchair accessible, Writing prog
Mem of Illinois Heartland Library System
Special Services for the Deaf - TDD equip
Open Mon-Thurs 9-8, Fri & Sat 9-5, Sun 1-5
Friends of the Library Group

GLEN ELLYN

J COLLEGE OF DUPAGE LIBRARY*, 425 Fawell Blvd, 60137-6599. SAN 304-2197. Tel: 630-942-2350. Circulation Tel: 630-942-2106. Interlibrary Loan Service Tel: 630-942-2166. Reference Tel: 630-942-3364. FAX: 630-858-8757. Interlibrary Loan Service FAX: 630-942-4646. Web Site: www.cod.edu/library. *Interim Dean of Libr,* Mark Rudisill; Tel: 630-942-3334, E-mail: rudisill@cod.edu; *Assoc Dean of Libr,* Jennifer McIntosh; E-mail: mcintoshj144@cod.edu; *Ref Librn,* Christine Kickles; Tel: 630-942-2021, E-mail: kicklesc@cod.edu; *Ref Librn,* Debra Smith; *Tech Serv Mgr,* Mary S Konkel; Tel: 630-942-2662, E-mail: konkel@cod.edu; *Web Coordr,* Colin Koteles; Tel: 630-942-2923, E-mail: koteles@cod.edu; *Electronic Res, Ref (Info Servs),* Denise Cote; Tel: 630-942-2092, E-mail: cotede@cod.edu; *Ref (Info Servs),* Marianne Berger; Tel: 630-942-2338, E-mail: berger@cod.edu; *Ref (Info Servs),* Daniel Blewett; Tel: 630-942-2279, E-mail: blewett@cod.edu; *Ref (Info Servs),* Jason Ertz; Tel: 630-942-3317, E-mail: ertzja@cod.edu; *Ref (Info Servs),* Jennifer Kelley; Tel: 630-942-2383, E-mail: kelleyj@cod.edu; Staff 46 (MLS 14, Non-MLS 32)
Founded 1967. Enrl 34,000; Fac 308; Highest Degree: Associate
Library Holdings: AV Mats 24,000; Bk Vols 203,500; Per Subs 885
Special Collections: College & Career Information; College of DuPage Archives; Occupational & Technical Colls
Automation Activity & Vendor Info: (Acquisitions) Innovative Interfaces, Inc; (Cataloging) Innovative Interfaces, Inc; (Circulation) Innovative Interfaces, Inc; (Course Reserve) Innovative Interfaces, Inc; (OPAC) Innovative Interfaces, Inc; (Serials) Innovative Interfaces, Inc
Mem of Reaching Across Illinois Library System (RAILS)
Partic in Consortium of Academic & Research Libraries in Illinois; Illinois Library & Information Network; Network of Illinois Learning Resources in Community Colleges; Northern Illinois Learning Resources Cooperative; OCLC Online Computer Library Center, Inc
Special Services for the Deaf - Assistive tech
Special Services for the Blind - Assistive/Adapted tech devices, equip & products
Open Mon-Thurs 7:45am-10pm, Fri 7:45-4:30, Sat 9-4:30, Sun Noon-6

R FIRST UNITED METHODIST CHURCH LIBRARY*, 424 Forest Ave, 60137. SAN 304-2200. Tel: 630-469-3510. FAX: 630-469-2041.
Founded 1954
Library Holdings: AV Mats 300; CDs 50; DVDs 75; Bk Vols 5,500; Videos 200
Special Collections: John Wesley & Church Coll
Special Services for the Blind - Cassettes
Restriction: Mem only

P GLEN ELLYN PUBLIC LIBRARY*, 400 Duane St, 60137-4508. SAN 304-2219. Tel: 630-469-0879. FAX: 630-469-1086. Web Site: www.gepl.org. *Dir,* Dawn A Bussey; E-mail: dawnbussey@gepl.org; *Dir, Adult Serv,* Susan DeRonne; *Dir of Circ,* Carrie Jeffries; *Dir, Youth Serv,* Heather McCammond-Watts; *Head, Mat Proc,* Ann Marie Lindsey; *ILL,* Laurie Gornik; *IT Coordr,* Joe Halter; Staff 13 (MLS 13)
Founded 1907. Pop 27,450; Circ 634,672
Library Holdings: Bk Vols 201,138; Per Subs 800
Automation Activity & Vendor Info: (Circulation) SirsiDynix
Wireless access
Publications: Newsletter
Mem of Reaching Across Illinois Library System (RAILS)
Partic in Libr Integrated Network Consortium; OCLC Online Computer Library Center, Inc; System Wide Automated Network
Open Mon, Wed & Thurs 9-9, Fri & Sat 9-5, Sun 1-5
Friends of the Library Group

GLENCOE

P GLENCOE PUBLIC LIBRARY*, 320 Park Ave, 60022. SAN 304-2243. Tel: 847-835-5056. FAX: 847-835-5648. Web Site: www.glencoe.lib.il.us. *Exec Dir,* Andrew Kim; E-mail: akim@glencoelibrary.org; *Head, Adult Serv,* Liz McClain; E-mail: gckref@glencoelibrary.org; *Head, Circ,* Danny Burdett; E-mail: dburdet@glencoelibrary.org; *Head, Children's Servx,* Ann Finstad; E-mail: childrens@glencoelibrary.org; Staff 31 (MLS 9, Non-MLS 22)
Founded 1909. Pop 8,762; Circ 228,519
Library Holdings: AV Mats 14,170; Bk Vols 82,223
Automation Activity & Vendor Info: (Cataloging) OCLC Connexion; (Circulation) SirsiDynix; (ILL) SirsiDynix; (OPAC) SirsiDynix
Wireless access
Function: AV serv, Homebound delivery serv, ILL available, Internet access, Magnifiers for reading, Outside serv via phone, mail, e-mail & web, Photocopying/Printing, Prog for children & young adult, Ref serv available, Summer reading prog, Telephone ref, Wheelchair accessible
Publications: Excerpts (Newsletter)
Partic in Cooperative Computer Services - CCS
Special Services for the Deaf - TTY equip
Special Services for the Blind - Talking bks
Open Mon-Thurs 9-9, Fri 9-6, Sat 9-5
Friends of the Library Group

S LENHARDT LIBRARY OF THE CHICAGO BOTANIC GARDEN*, 1000 Lake Cook Rd, 60022. SAN 304-2235. Tel: 847-835-8201. Reference Tel: 847-835-8200. E-mail: library@chicagobotanic.org. Web Site: www.chicagobotanic.org/library. *Dir, Libr Serv,* Leora Siegel; Tel: 847-835-8202, E-mail: lsiegel@chicagobotanic.org; *Mgr, Pub Serv, Rare Bks,* Stacy Stoldt; E-mail: sstoldt@chicagobotanic.org; *Mgr, Tech Serv,* Ann Anderson; Tel: 847-835-8381, E-mail: aanderson@chicagobotanic.org; *Digital Spec,* Amanda Lettner; Tel: 847-835-8267, E-mail: alettner@chicagobotanic.org. Subject Specialists: *Digitization,* Amanda Lettner; Staff 5 (MLS 3.5, Non-MLS 1.5)
Founded 1951
Library Holdings: e-journals 50; Bk Titles 40,000; Bk Vols 150,000; Per Subs 400
Special Collections: Rare Book Coll
Subject Interests: Botany, Ecology, Garden design, Gardening, Hort, Hort therapy, Landscape archit

Automation Activity & Vendor Info: (Cataloging) EOS International; (Circulation) EOS International; (OPAC) EOS International; (Serials) EOS International
Wireless access
Function: 24/7 Online cat, Adult bk club, Archival coll, Art exhibits, Children's prog, Computers for patron use, Doc delivery serv, Electronic databases & coll, For res purposes, Free DVD rentals, Internet access, Magazines, Mail & tel request accepted, Online cat, Photocopying/Printing, Ref & res, Ref serv available, Res libr, Spanish lang bks, Story hour, Summer reading prog, Telephone ref, Wheelchair accessible
Mem of Reaching Across Illinois Library System (RAILS)
Partic in Chicago Collections Consortium
Open Wed-Sun Noon-4

GLENDALE HEIGHTS

P GLENSIDE PUBLIC LIBRARY DISTRICT*, 25 E Fullerton Ave, 60139-2697. SAN 304-2251. Tel: 630-260-1550. FAX: 630-260-1433. E-mail: info@glensidepld.org. Web Site: glensidepld.org. *Dir,* Tom Bartenfelder; E-mail: tbartenfelder@glensidepld.org; *Asst Libr Dir,* Ian Peery; E-mail: ipeery@glensidepld.org; *Circ Mgr,* Jane Hebert; E-mail: jhebert@glensidepld.org; *Pub Serv Mgr,* Jill Martorano; E-mail: jmartorano@glensidepld.org; Staff 18.5 (MLS 18.5)
Founded 1974. Pop 36,259; Circ 389,206
Library Holdings: CDs 13,020; DVDs 5,631; e-books 11,093; Electronic Media & Resources 45; Bk Vols 116,773; Per Subs 271
Special Collections: ESL/Literacy; Learning Games; Signed English Children's Books
Automation Activity & Vendor Info: (Acquisitions) Baker & Taylor; (Cataloging) Innovative Interfaces, Inc; (Circulation) Innovative Interfaces, Inc; (OPAC) Innovative Interfaces, Inc
Wireless access
Function: Bk club(s), Bks on CD, Chess club, Children's prog, Computer training, Computers for patron use, Electronic databases & coll, Free DVD rentals, Homebound delivery serv, ILL available, Magnifiers for reading, Music CDs, Notary serv, Online cat, Online ref, Outreach serv, Outside serv via phone, mail, e-mail & web, OverDrive digital audio bks, Photocopying/Printing, Preschool outreach, Prog for adults, Prog for children & young adult, Ref serv available, Scanner, Senior outreach, Spoken cassettes & CDs, Spoken cassettes & DVDs, Story hour, Summer & winter reading prog, Summer reading prog, Tax forms, Teen prog, Telephone ref, Wheelchair accessible
Mem of Reaching Across Illinois Library System (RAILS)
Partic in System Wide Automated Network
Special Services for the Deaf - TDD equip
Special Services for the Blind - VisualTek equip
Open Mon-Thurs 9-9, Fri & Sat 9-5, Sun 1-5
Friends of the Library Group

GLENVIEW

P GLENVIEW PUBLIC LIBRARY*, 1930 Glenview Rd, 60025. SAN 304-226X. Tel: 847-729-7500. FAX: 847-729-7558. TDD: 847-729-7529. E-mail: info@glenviewpl.org. Web Site: www.glenviewpl.org. *Libr Dir,* Lindsey Dorfman; E-mail: ldorfman@glenviewpl.org; *Asst Dir,* Jane D Berry; E-mail: jberry@glenviewpl.org; *Communications Dir,* Hilary Gabel; E-mail: hgabel@glenviewpl.org; *Head, Circ,* Karen Kee; E-mail: kkee@glenviewpl.org; *Head, Reader Serv,* Linda S Burns; E-mail: lburns@glenviewpl.org; *Head, Ref,* Jean Sanders; E-mail: jsanders@glenviewpl.org; *Head, Tech Serv,* Teri Room; E-mail: troom@glenviewpl.org; *Head, Youth Serv,* Barbara Littlefield; E-mail: blittlefield@glenviewpl.org; *Bus Mgr,* Christine Klimusko; E-mail: cklimusko@glenviewpl.org; *Colls Mgr,* Kim Comerford; E-mail: kcomerford@glenviewpl.org; *Fac Mgr,* Mark Depa; E-mail: mdepa@glenviewpl.org; *Technology Spec,* Allen Bettig; E-mail: abettig@glenviewpl.org; *ILL,* Yelena Dereka; Staff 68 (MLS 33, Non-MLS 35)
Founded 1930. Pop 44,692; Circ 689,870
Library Holdings: Audiobooks 21,922; DVDs 15,197; e-books 42,172; Electronic Media & Resources 98; Bk Vols 262,532; Per Subs 548
Special Collections: Genealogy (Lundberg Coll)
Subject Interests: Med
Automation Activity & Vendor Info: (Acquisitions) Innovative Interfaces, Inc; (Cataloging) Innovative Interfaces, Inc; (Circulation) Innovative Interfaces, Inc; (OPAC) Innovative Interfaces, Inc
Wireless access
Function: 24/7 Electronic res, 24/7 Online cat, Activity rm, Adult bk club, Adult literacy prog, After school storytime, Art exhibits, Audio & video playback equip for onsite use, Audiobks on Playaways & MP3, Audiobks via web, Bilingual assistance for Spanish patrons, Bk club(s), Bks on CD, Butterfly Garden, CD-ROM, Chess club, Children's prog, Computer training, Computers for patron use, Digital talking bks, Doc delivery serv, Electronic databases & coll, For res purposes, Free DVD rentals, Games & aids for people with disabilities, Genealogy discussion group, Govt ref serv, Health sci info serv, Holiday prog, Home delivery & serv to seniorr ctr & nursing homes, Homebound delivery serv, Homework prog, ILL available, Internet access, Large print keyboards, Learning ctr, Life-long learning prog for all ages, Literacy & newcomer serv, Magazines, Magnifiers for reading, Mail & tel request accepted, Makerspace, Mango lang, Meeting rooms, Microfiche/film & reading machines, Movies, Museum passes, Music CDs, Online cat, Online ref, Orientations, Outreach serv, OverDrive digital audio bks, Photocopying/Printing, Preschool outreach, Preschool reading prog, Prog for adults, Prog for children & young adult, Ref & res, Ref serv available, Scanner, Senior computer classes, Senior outreach, Serves people with intellectual disabilities, Spanish lang bks, Spoken cassettes & CDs, Spoken cassettes & DVDs, STEM programs, Story hour, Study rm, Summer & winter reading prog, Summer reading prog, Tax forms, Teen prog, Telephone ref, VHS videos, Visual arts prog, Wheelchair accessible, Winter reading prog, Workshops
Publications: Events by Email (Online only); LINES (Quarterly)
Mem of Reaching Across Illinois Library System (RAILS)
Partic in Cooperative Computer Services - CCS
Special Services for the Deaf - ADA equip; Assisted listening device; Closed caption videos; Sign lang interpreter upon request for prog; TTY equip
Special Services for the Blind - Accessible computers; Assistive/Adapted tech devices, equip & products; BiFolkal kits; Bks available with recordings; Bks on cassette; Bks on CD; Cassette playback machines; Cassettes; Children's Braille; Computer access aids; Computer with voice synthesizer for visually impaired persons; Copier with enlargement capabilities; Dragon Naturally Speaking software; Extensive large print coll; Home delivery serv; Internet workstation with adaptive software; Large print bks; Large print bks & talking machines; Lending of low vision aids; Low vision equip; Magnifiers; Mags & bk reproduction/duplication; Open bk software on pub access PC; PC for people with disabilities; Recorded bks; Screen reader software; Sound rec; Talking bks; Talking bks & player equip; ZoomText magnification & reading software
Open Mon-Fri 9-9, Sat 9-5, Sun 1-5
Friends of the Library Group

M NORTH SHORE UNIVERSITY HEALTH SYSTEM-GLENBROOK HOSPITAL*, Medical Library, 2100 Pfingsten Rd, 60026-1301. SAN 374-8308. Tel: 847-657-5618. FAX: 847-657-5995. E-mail: GBH-Library@northshore.org. *Librn,* Hailan Wang; E-mail: hwang@northshore.org; Staff 1 (MLS 1)
Founded 1970
Library Holdings: Bk Titles 1,000; Bk Vols 1,100; Per Subs 115
Function: ILL available
Partic in Illinois Library & Information Network; Northeastern Ill Libr Consortia
Restriction: Staff use only

S TRIODYNE INC*, Beth Hamilton Safety Library, 3054 N Lake Terrace, 60026. SAN 320-5819. Tel: 847-677-4730. FAX: 847-647-2047. E-mail: infoserv@triodyne.com. Web Site: www.triodyne.com/library.htm. *Mgr,* Jenny Warner; E-mail: jennyw@triodyne.com
Founded 1979
Library Holdings: Bk Vols 10,500; Per Subs 200
Special Collections: Expert Transcript Center, Bibcat 2500 (Bibliographies)
Subject Interests: Accident prevention, Automotive engr, Ergonomics, Forensic engr, Human factors, Safety
Function: Doc delivery serv, ILL available, Res libr
Publications: BIBCAT 2500 (Bibliographies)
Restriction: Access at librarian's discretion

GODFREY

J LEWIS & CLARK COMMUNITY COLLEGE, Reid Memorial Library, 5800 Godfrey Rd, 62035. SAN 304-2316. Tel: 618-468-4301. Reference Tel: 618-468-4304. Web Site: www.lc.edu/library. *Dir,* Dennis Krieb; Tel: 618-468-4300, E-mail: dkrieb@lc.edu; *Asst Dir,* Liz Burns; Tel: 618-468-4320, E-mail: lburns@lc.edu; *Asst Dir, Ref,* Greg Cash; Tel: 618-468-4330, E-mail: gcash@lc.edu; *Cat,* Debi Cipriano; *Circ,* Elizabeth Clark; Tel: 618-468-4313, E-mail: eogle@lc.edu; Staff 6 (MLS 3, Non-MLS 3)
Founded 1970. Enrl 4,500; Fac 100
Library Holdings: Bk Titles 45,000; Bk Vols 48,000; Per Subs 3,500
Special Collections: Lewis & Clark Coll; Monticello College History
Subject Interests: Local hist
Automation Activity & Vendor Info: (Cataloging) Ex Libris Group; (Circulation) Ex Libris Group; (Course Reserve) Ex Libris Group; (ILL) Ex Libris Group; (OPAC) Ex Libris Group
Wireless access
Partic in Consortium of Academic & Research Libraries in Illinois; Illinois Library & Information Network; SILRC
Open Mon-Thurs 8-7, Fri 8-4:30

GOLCONDA

P GOLCONDA PUBLIC LIBRARY*, 126 W Main St, 62938. (Mail add: PO Box 523, 62938-0523), SAN 304-2324. Tel: 618-683-6531. FAX: 618-683-6531. E-mail: golillib@shawneelink.net. Web Site: golcondapubliclibrary.webs.com. *Head Librn,* Maxine Houser; *Asst Librn,* Peggy Conley
Founded 1915. Pop 668; Circ 12,450
Library Holdings: Bk Vols 18,267; Per Subs 20
Subject Interests: Genealogy, Local hist
Wireless access
Mem of Illinois Heartland Library System
Open Mon & Tues 9-5, Wed-Fri 1-5, Sat 9-12

GRAFTON

S IYC PERE MARQUETTE CORRECTIONAL INSTITUTION LIBRARY*, 17808 State Hwy 100 W, 62037. Tel: 618-786-2371. Web Site: www.illinois.gov/idjj/Pages/Pere_Marquette_IYC.aspx. *Library Contact,* Alaner Carter
Library Holdings: Bk Vols 1,500
Restriction: Not open to pub

GRANITE CITY

P SIX MILE REGIONAL LIBRARY DISTRICT*, Niedringhaus Bldg, 2001 Delmar Ave, 62040-4590. SAN 304-2332. Tel: 618-452-6238. FAX: 618-876-6317. Web Site: smrld.org. *Exec Dir,* Tina Hubert; E-mail: director@smrld.org; *Asst Dir,* Betsy Mahoney; E-mail: betsymahoney@smrld.org; *Asst Dir, Br Mgr,* Kate Kite; E-mail: katekite@smrld.org; *IT & Fac Mgr,* Tallin Curran; E-mail: ops@smrld.org; *Youth Serv Mgr,* Erica Hanke-Young; E-mail: ericayoung@smrld.org; *Mgr, Mat Serv,* Lynda Seegert; E-mail: lyndaseegert@smrld.org; Staff 11 (MLS 8, Non-MLS 3)
Founded 1912. Pop 43,757; Circ 331,637
Jul 2017-Jun 2018 Income (Main & Associated Libraries) $1,920,863
Wireless access
Function: 24/7 Electronic res, 24/7 Online cat, 3D Printer, Adult bk club, Audiobks via web, Bilingual assistance for Spanish patrons, Bk club(s), Bks on CD, Children's prog, Computer training, Computers for patron use, Electronic databases & coll, Free DVD rentals, Genealogy discussion group, Home delivery & serv to seniorr ctr & nursing homes, Homebound delivery serv, ILL available, Internet access, Life-long learning prog for all ages, Magazines, Mail & tel request accepted, Meeting rooms, Microfiche/film & reading machines, Music CDs, Notary serv, Online cat, Online ref, Orientations, Outreach serv, OverDrive digital audio bks, Passport agency, Photocopying/Printing, Preschool outreach, Printer for laptops & handheld devices, Prog for adults, Prog for children & young adult, Ref & res, Scanner, Spanish lang bks, Story hour, Summer & winter reading prog, Tax forms, Teen prog, Telephone ref, Wheelchair accessible
Mem of Illinois Heartland Library System
Partic in Association for Rural & Small Libraries
Additional Services Include:Illinois Department of Natural Resources Fishing & Hunting Licenses (fee);Illinois License Sticker Renewals (fee);IRS Tax Return Preparation for low- to middle-income customers (free);Register Voters (free)
Open Mon 9-6, Tues-Thurs 11-8, Fri & Sat 9-6
Friends of the Library Group
Branches: 1

P JOHNSON ROAD BRANCH, 2145 Johnson Rd, 62040, SAN 376-2491. Tel: 618-452-6238. FAX: 618-876-6317. *Mgr,* Betsy Mahoney; Tel: 618-452-6238, Ext 785, E-mail: betsymahoney@smrld.org; Staff 2 (MLS 2)
Open Mon & Thurs-Sat 9-5, Tues & Wed 12-8
Friends of the Library Group

J SOUTHWESTERN ILLINOIS COLLEGE*, Sam Wolf Granite City Campus Library, 4950 Maryville Rd, Rm 455, 62040. SAN 371-9111. Tel: 618-797-7353. Circulation Tel: 618-797-7354. Toll Free Tel: 800-222-5131, Ext 7354. E-mail: gcclibrary@swic.edu. Web Site: www.swic.edu/students/services/library. *Librn,* Mark Light; Tel: 618-797-7353, E-mail: mark.light@swic.edu; Staff 3 (MLS 3)
Founded 1983. Enrl 2,770; Fac 200; Highest Degree: Associate
Library Holdings: CDs 94; DVDs 691; Bk Vols 10,409
Automation Activity & Vendor Info: (Course Reserve) Ex Libris Group
Wireless access
Function: Computers for patron use
Mem of Illinois Heartland Library System
Open Mon-Thurs (Winter) 8-8, Fri 8-4, Sat 11-3; Mon-Thurs (Summer) 8-5, Fri 8-2
Restriction: Open to pub for ref & circ; with some limitations, Open to students, fac & staff, Pub use on premises

GRANT PARK

P GRANT PARK PUBLIC LIBRARY*, 107 W Taylor St, 60940. (Mail add: PO Box 392, 60940-0302), SAN 304-2359. Tel: 815-465-6047. E-mail: villageofgrantpark@att.net. Web Site: www.grantpark-il.org/library. *Librn,* Mary Wilkening
Founded 1919. Pop 1,331; Circ 3,151
Library Holdings: Bk Vols 5,070
Special Collections: James Whitcomb Riley; Mark Twain; Zane Grey
Wireless access
Function: Wheelchair accessible
Mem of Reaching Across Illinois Library System (RAILS)
Open Mon 1-6, Wed & Fri 12-6, Thurs 9-2, Sat 9-Noon

GRAYSLAKE

J COLLEGE OF LAKE COUNTY*, John C Murphy Memorial Library, 19351 W Washington St, 60030. SAN 304-2367. Tel: 847-543-2071. Administration Tel: 847-543-2072. E-mail: library@clcillinois.edu. Web Site: library.clcillinois.edu. *Dean of Libr,* Tanya Woltmann; E-mail: twoltmann@clcillinois.edu; *Ref & Instruction Librn,* Erika Behling; Tel: 847-543-2892, E-mail: ebehling@clcillinois.edu; *Ref & Instruction Librn,* Anne Chernaik; Tel: 847-543-2460, E-mail: achernaik@clcillinois.edu; *Ref & Instruction Librn,* Uri Toch; Tel: 847-543-2466, E-mail: utoch@clcillinois.edu; *Syst Librn,* Holly Ledvina; Tel: 847-543-2461, E-mail: hledvina@clcillinois.edu; *Libr Mgr,* Glenn Kahmann; Tel: 847-543-2438, E-mail: gkahmann@clcillinois.edu; *Libr Serv Coordr,* Lori Hansen; Tel: 847-543-2893, E-mail: lhansen2@clcillinois.edu; *ILL,* Scott Emilie; Tel: 847-543-2465, E-mail: ill@clcillinois.edu; Staff 17 (MLS 7, Non-MLS 10)
Founded 1970. Enrl 14,947; Fac 218; Highest Degree: Associate
Library Holdings: Audiobooks 786; CDs 786; DVDs 3,986; e-books 152,227; e-journals 37; Electronic Media & Resources 900; Music Scores 7,430; Bk Vols 44,066; Per Subs 192
Automation Activity & Vendor Info: (Acquisitions) Innovative Interfaces, Inc; (Cataloging) Innovative Interfaces, Inc; (Circulation) Innovative Interfaces, Inc; (Course Reserve) Innovative Interfaces, Inc; (ILL) OCLC Tipasa; (Media Booking) Innovative Interfaces, Inc; (Serials) Innovative Interfaces, Inc
Wireless access
Mem of Reaching Across Illinois Library System (RAILS)
Partic in Consortium of Academic & Research Libraries in Illinois; Network of Illinois Learning Resources in Community Colleges; OCLC Online Computer Library Center, Inc
Open Mon-Thurs 7:30am-9pm, Fri 8-4:30, Sat 9-3

P GRAYSLAKE AREA PUBLIC LIBRARY DISTRICT*, 100 Library Lane, 60030. SAN 304-2375. Tel: 847-223-5313. Circulation Tel: 847-665-1022. FAX: 847-223-6482. TDD: 847-223-5362. Web Site: www.grayslake.info. *Dir,* Sara Brown; E-mail: sbrown@grayslake.info; *Head, Circ,* Ginnie Vehlow; E-mail: gvehlow@grayslake.info; *Head, Youth Serv,* Cassie Carbaugh; E-mail: ccarbaugh@grayslake.info; *Head, Tech Serv,* Jan Davis; E-mail: jdavis@grayslake.info; *Adult Serv,* Carlen DeThorne; E-mail: cdethorne@grayslake.info; Staff 10 (MLS 10)
Founded 1931. Pop 28,172; Circ 551,603
Jul 2014-Jun 2015 Income $2,991,510, State $43,899, Locally Generated Income $178,161, Other $2,769,450. Mats Exp $471,740, Books $230,799, AV Mat $94,432, Electronic Ref Mat (Incl. Access Fees) $146,509
Library Holdings: AV Mats 17,153; Bk Vols 128,447; Per Subs 374
Automation Activity & Vendor Info: (Acquisitions) TLC (The Library Corporation); (Cataloging) TLC (The Library Corporation); (Circulation) TLC (The Library Corporation); (ILL) TLC (The Library Corporation); (OPAC) TLC (The Library Corporation); (Serials) TLC (The Library Corporation)
Wireless access
Function: 24/7 Electronic res, After school storytime, Audiobks via web, AV serv, Bk club(s), Bks on CD, Chess club, Children's prog, Computer training, Computers for patron use, Digital talking bks, E-Readers, E-Reserves, Electronic databases & coll, Free DVD rentals, Homebound delivery serv, ILL available, Internet access, Large print keyboards, Life-long learning prog for all ages, Magazines, Magnifiers for reading, Mail & tel request accepted, Mango lang, Movies, Museum passes, Music CDs, Notary serv, Online cat, Outreach serv, OverDrive digital audio bks, Photocopying/Printing, Preschool outreach, Preschool reading prog, Printer for laptops & handheld devices, Prog for adults, Prog for children & young adult, Ref & res, Scanner, Senior outreach, Spanish lang bks, Story hour, Study rm, Summer & winter reading prog, Teen prog, Telephone ref, Wheelchair accessible
Publications: Front Page (Newsletter)
Open Mon-Thurs 10-8, Fri 10-5, Sat 10-2
Friends of the Library Group

GRAYVILLE

P GROFFE MEMORIAL LIBRARY*, 118 South Middle St, 62844. SAN 304-2383. Tel: 618-375-7121. FAX: 618-375-7173. E-mail: grofflibrary@gmail.com. Web Site: cityofgrayville.com/new/directory/schools/library. *Dir,* Kathleen Rister; Staff 2 (Non-MLS 2)
Founded 1909. Pop 1,725; Circ 8,630
Library Holdings: Bk Titles 12,967; Per Subs 30
Special Collections: Rear Admiral James M Helm Coll, memorabilia
Wireless access
Mem of Illinois Heartland Library System
Open Mon-Thurs 10-7, Fri 10-6, Sat 10-2

GREAT LAKES

A UNITED STATES NAVY*, MWR Library, Bldg 160, 2601E Paul Jones St, 60088-2845. SAN 304-2391. Tel: 847-688-4617. FAX: 847-688-3602. Web Site: mwrgl.cnic.navy.mil/recreation/library/library.htm. *Dir,* Michelle Manfredi; E-mail: michelle.manfredi@navy.mil; *Circ & Staff Develop Coordr,* Anny Swanson; Staff 4 (MLS 1, Non-MLS 3)
Founded 1912. Pop 32,000; Circ 35,000
Library Holdings: AV Mats 600; Bk Vols 22,000; Per Subs 95; Talking Bks 450
Subject Interests: Naval hist, Naval sci
Wireless access
Open Mon-Thurs 9-8, Fri 9-4, Sat 10-2

GREENFIELD

P GREENFIELD PUBLIC LIBRARY*, 515 Chestnut, 62044-1304. SAN 304-2413. Tel: 217-368-2613. FAX: 217-368-2613. E-mail: gfe@greenfieldpl.org. Web Site: www.greenfieldpl.org. *Dir,* Brenda Shipley
Founded 1914. Pop 1,192; Circ 6,000
Library Holdings: AV Mats 1,298; Bk Titles 10,498; Per Subs 18; Talking Bks 455
Wireless access
Mem of Illinois Heartland Library System
Open Mon 1-7, Tues 11-6, Thurs 12-6, Fri & Sat 9-Noon

GREENUP

P GREENUP TOWNSHIP PUBLIC LIBRARY*, 101 N Franklin St, 62428. (Mail add: PO Box 275, 62428-0275), SAN 304-2421. Tel: 217-923-3616. FAX: 217-923-3616. E-mail: greenuptownshiplibrary@gmail.com. Web Site: www.greenup.lib.il.us. *Dir,* Deb Sherrick
Pop 2,500; Circ 14,714
Library Holdings: Bk Vols 15,500; Per Subs 60
Special Collections: Genealogy Coll
Wireless access
Mem of Illinois Heartland Library System
Open Mon 12-8, Tues 12-5, Wed & Sat 9-1, Thurs 12-6, Fri 9-5

GREENVILLE

C GREENVILLE COLLEGE, Ruby E Dare Library, 301 N Elm, 62246. (Mail add: 315 E College Ave, 62246), SAN 304-243X. Tel: 618-664-6603. Reference Tel: 618-664-6599. FAX: 618-664-9578. E-mail: libgen@greenville.edu. Web Site: greenville.libguides.com/library. *Dean, Libr Serv,* Gail Heideman; Tel: 618-664-6609, E-mail: gail.heideman@greenville.edu; Staff 2 (MLS 2)
Founded 1892. Enrl 1,200; Fac 52; Highest Degree: Master
Library Holdings: Audiobooks 18; AV Mats 200; e-books 7,000; e-journals 12,000; Electronic Media & Resources 200; Microforms 17,000; Bk Titles 112,283; Bk Vols 121,350; Per Subs 200; Videos 3,541
Special Collections: Free Methodist Church History Coll; Greenville College History Coll
Automation Activity & Vendor Info: (Acquisitions) Ex Libris Group; (Cataloging) Ex Libris Group; (Circulation) Ex Libris Group; (ILL) OCLC; (OPAC) Ex Libris Group
Wireless access
Publications: Annual report; Library Orientation Packet
Mem of Illinois Heartland Library System
Partic in Consortium of Academic & Research Libraries in Illinois; Illinois Library & Information Network; OCLC Online Computer Library Center, Inc
Special Services for the Deaf - Closed caption videos
Special Services for the Blind - Closed circuit TV; Computer with voice synthesizer for visually impaired persons; Copier with enlargement capabilities
Open Mon-Thurs 8am-11pm, Fri 8-5, Sun 6pm-11pm

P GREENVILLE PUBLIC LIBRARY*, 414 W Main St, 62246-1615. SAN 304-2448. Tel: 618-664-3115. FAX: 618-664-9442. Web Site: www.greenvillepubliclibrary.org. *Dir,* Jo Keillor; E-mail: jo.s.keillor@gmail.com; *Head Librn,* Christal Valentin; E-mail: christalv@greenvillepubliclibrary.org
Founded 1856. Pop 6,955; Circ 40,000
Library Holdings: Bk Vols 29,348; Per Subs 61
Subject Interests: Genealogy
Wireless access
Mem of Illinois Heartland Library System
Partic in Ocean State Libraries
Open Mon & Tues 9-5, Wed & Thurs 10-8, Fri 8-5, Sat 8-Noon

GRIDLEY

P GRIDLEY PUBLIC LIBRARY DISTRICT*, 320 Center St, 61744. (Mail add: PO Box 370, 61744-0370), SAN 304-2456. Tel: 309-747-2284. FAX: 309-747-3195. E-mail: gpld@gridcom.net. *Dir,* Linda Zimmerman
Founded 1916. Pop 2,113
Library Holdings: Audiobooks 375; DVDs 1,300; e-books 25,311; Bk Titles 20,400; Per Subs 72
Special Collections: Library of America Coll
Automation Activity & Vendor Info: (Circulation) SirsiDynix-WorkFlows
Wireless access
Open Mon & Wed 1-7, Tues & Thurs 10-7, Fri 1-5, Sat 10-2

GRIGGSVILLE

P NORTH PIKE DISTRICT LIBRARY*, 119 S Corey St, 62340. (Mail add: PO Box 419, 62340-0419), SAN 304-2464. Tel: 217-833-2633. FAX: 217-833-2283. E-mail: northpike@casscomm.com. Web Site: www.northpikedistrictlibrary.com. *Dir, Libr Serv,* Kimber Martin
Founded 1887. Pop 3,500; Circ 27,960
Library Holdings: Audiobooks 540; AV Mats 700; Bks on Deafness & Sign Lang 5; Braille Volumes 1; DVDs 500; High Interest/Low Vocabulary Bk Vols 1,200; Large Print Bks 1,200; Microforms 24; Bk Titles 25,000; Bk Vols 19,788; Per Subs 32; Spec Interest Per Sub 12; Talking Bks 24; Videos 50
Special Collections: Municipal Document Depository; Oral History
Wireless access
Function: Home delivery & serv to seniorr ctr & nursing homes, Homebound delivery serv, ILL available, Internet access, Large print keyboards, Photocopying/Printing, Preschool reading prog, Prog for children & young adult, Summer reading prog, Telephone ref
Mem of Reaching Across Illinois Library System (RAILS)
Partic in Illinois Library & Information Network; Resource Sharing Alliance
Open Mon & Thurs 11-6, Tues 9-6, Wed 12-6, Fri 10-4

GURNEE

P WARREN-NEWPORT PUBLIC LIBRARY DISTRICT*, 224 N O'Plaine Rd, 60031. SAN 304-2472. Tel: 847-244-5150. FAX: 847-244-3499. E-mail: webcontact@wnpl.info. Web Site: www.wnpl.info. *Exec Dir,* Ryan Livergood; Tel: 847-244-5150, Ext 3008, E-mail: rlivergood@wnpl.info; *Dep Dir,* Noreen Reese; Tel: 847-244-5150, Ext 3026, E-mail: nreese@wnpl.info; *Head, Adult Serv,* Kathie Fifer; Tel: 847-244-5150, Ext 3002, E-mail: kfifer@wnpl.info; *Head, Communications,* Sandy Beda; Tel: 847-244-5150, Ext 3018, E-mail: sbeda@wnpl.info; *Head, Circ,* Meg Schmaus; Tel: 847-244-5150, Ext 3024, E-mail: mschmaus@wnpl.info; *Head, Info Serv,* Kevin Getty; Tel: 847-244-5150, Ext 3015, E-mail: kgetty@wnpl.info; *Head, Outreach Serv,* Angela Clarke; Tel: 847-244-5150, Ext 3025, E-mail: aclarke@wnpl.info; *Head, Tech Serv, ILL,* Amy Meyer; Tel: 847-244-5150, Ext 3048, E-mail: ameyer@wnpl.info; *Head, Youth Serv,* Rebekah Raleigh; Tel: 847-244-5150, Ext 3040, E-mail: rraleigh@wnpl.info; Staff 82 (MLS 16, Non-MLS 66)
Founded 1973
Jul 2017-Jun 2018 Income (Main & Associated Libraries) $7,271,518, State $99,702, Federal $125,927, Locally Generated Income $6,731,460, Other $314,429. Mats Exp $477,743, Books $207,882, AV Mat $133,886, Electronic Ref Mat (Incl. Access Fees) $155,975. Sal $2,885,113
Library Holdings: AV Mats 11,341; Bks on Deafness & Sign Lang 140; CDs 24,019; High Interest/Low Vocabulary Bk Vols 87; Large Print Bks 2,458; Bk Titles 213,749; Per Subs 321; Talking Bks 13,553; Videos 26,930
Subject Interests: Illinois
Automation Activity & Vendor Info: (Acquisitions) Innovative Interfaces, Inc - Millennium; (Cataloging) Innovative Interfaces, Inc - Millennium; (Circulation) Innovative Interfaces, Inc - Millennium; (OPAC) Innovative Interfaces, Inc - Millennium
Wireless access
Function: 24/7 Electronic res, 24/7 Online cat, Adult bk club, Adult literacy prog, Art exhibits, Art programs, Audiobks on Playaways & MP3, Audiobks via web, Bk club(s), Bk reviews (Group), Bks on CD, Children's prog, Computer training, Computers for patron use, Electronic databases & coll, Free DVD rentals, Home delivery & serv to seniorr ctr & nursing homes, Homebound delivery serv, ILL available, Internet access, Magazines, Magnifiers for reading, Mango lang, Meeting rooms, Movies, Museum passes, Music CDs, Online cat, Outreach serv, OverDrive digital

audio bks, Photocopying/Printing, Preschool outreach, Preschool reading prog, Printer for laptops & handheld devices, Prog for adults, Prog for children & young adult, Ref serv available, Res assist avail, Scanner, Senior outreach, Serves people with intellectual disabilities, Spanish lang bks, STEM programs, Story hour, Study rm, Summer reading prog, Tax forms, Teen prog, Wheelchair accessible, Workshops, Writing prog
Publications: Inside Angle (Newsletter)
Mem of Reaching Across Illinois Library System (RAILS)
Partic in OCLC Online Computer Library Center, Inc
Special Services for the Deaf - TDD equip; TTY equip
Special Services for the Blind - Bks on CD; Children's Braille; Large print bks; Playaways (bks on MP3); Screen enlargement software for people with visual disabilities; ZoomText magnification & reading software
Open Mon-Thurs 9-9, Fri 9-6, Sat 9-5, Sun (Sept-May)1-5
Friends of the Library Group
Bookmobiles: 1. Head of Outreach Servs, Angela Clarke

HAMILTON

P HAMILTON PUBLIC LIBRARY*, 861 Broadway St, 62341. SAN 304-2480. Tel: 217-847-2219. FAX: 217-847-3014. E-mail: hamlib@adams.net. Web Site: www.hamiltonpubliclibrary.org. *Dir,* Nancy K Denton; Staff 3 (MLS 1, Non-MLS 2)
Founded 1902. Pop 2,951; Circ 17,610
Library Holdings: Bk Titles 21,595; Per Subs 50
Wireless access
Function: Adult bk club, AV serv, Bks on CD, Children's prog, Computers for patron use, Free DVD rentals, Holiday prog, Home delivery & serv to seniorr ctr & nursing homes, ILL available, Magazines, Online cat, Photocopying/Printing, Preschool outreach, Printer for laptops & handheld devices, Prog for children & young adult, Summer reading prog, Tax forms
Mem of Reaching Across Illinois Library System (RAILS)
Open Mon-Thurs 9-7, Fri 9-5, Sat 11-1
Friends of the Library Group

HAMPSHIRE

P ELLA JOHNSON MEMORIAL PUBLIC LIBRARY DISTRICT, 109 S State St, 60140. (Mail add: PO Box 429, 60140-0429), SAN 304-2499. Tel: 847-683-4490. FAX: 847-683-4493. E-mail: library@ellajohnsonlibrary.org. Web Site: www.ellajohnsonlibrary.org. *Libr Dir,* Nancy A Ashbrook; E-mail: nashbrook@ellajohnsonlibrary.org; *Adult & Teen Serv Mgr,* Angel Flores; E-mail: aflores@ellajohnsonlibrary.org; *Circ Mgr,* Kimberly Alberth; E-mail: kalberth@ellajohnsonlibrary.org; *Youth Serv Mgr,* Heather Swanson; E-mail: hswanson@ellajohnsonlibrary.org; Staff 5 (MLS 3, Non-MLS 2)
Founded 1943. Pop 14,181; Circ 53,000
Library Holdings: Bk Titles 55,000; Per Subs 108
Subject Interests: Local hist
Wireless access
Publications: Library Newsletter (Monthly); Program Flyers (Monthly)
Mem of Reaching Across Illinois Library System (RAILS)
Partic in Association for Rural & Small Libraries
Special Services for the Blind - Newsp on cassette
Open Mon-Thurs 9:30-8, Fri & Sat 12-6
Friends of the Library Group

HANOVER

P HANOVER TOWNSHIP LIBRARY*, 204 Jefferson St, 61041. (Mail add: PO Box 475, 61041-0475), SAN 304-2510. Tel: 815-591-3517. FAX: 815-591-3517. E-mail: hanovertownshiplibrary@gmail.com. Web Site: www.hanover-lib.org. *Dir,* Denise Tollensdorf; Staff 2 (Non-MLS 2)
Founded 1941. Pop 1,229; Circ 11,949
Library Holdings: Audiobooks 347; Large Print Bks 262; Bk Titles 11,041; Per Subs 10; Videos 309
Subject Interests: Local hist
Wireless access
Function: Computers for patron use, Free DVD rentals, ILL available, Internet access, Magazines, Music CDs, Online cat, Outside serv via phone, mail, e-mail & web, OverDrive digital audio bks, Photocopying/Printing, Spoken cassettes & CDs, Summer reading prog, Wheelchair accessible
Mem of Reaching Across Illinois Library System (RAILS)
Open Mon & Thurs 2-7, Tues & Wed 12-5, Sat 9-2

HARRISBURG

P HARRISBURG PUBLIC LIBRARY DISTRICT, Harrisburg District Library, Two W Walnut St, 62946-1261. SAN 304-2529. Tel: 618-253-7455. FAX: 618-252-1239. E-mail: hpld@harrisburglibrary.org. Web Site: www.harrisburglibrary.org. *Dir,* Krystal Gulley; E-mail: kgulley@harrisburglibrary.org; Staff 1 (MLS 1)
Founded 1909. Pop 13,070; Circ 45,000
Library Holdings: Bk Vols 48,000; Per Subs 89
Subject Interests: Genealogy
Automation Activity & Vendor Info: (Cataloging) Innovative Interfaces, Inc; (Circulation) Innovative Interfaces, Inc
Wireless access
Function: ILL available, Prog for children & young adult, Spoken cassettes & CDs, Summer reading prog, Wheelchair accessible
Mem of Illinois Heartland Library System
Open Mon-Fri 9-8, Sat 10-6, Sun 1-5
Friends of the Library Group

J SOUTHEASTERN ILLINOIS COLLEGE*, Melba Patton Library, 3575 College Rd, 62946. SAN 304-2537. Tel: 618-252-5400, Ext 2260. Toll Free Tel: 866-338-2742. Web Site: www.sic.edu/library-resources. *Assoc Dean,* Karla Lewis; E-mail: karla.lewis@sic.edu; Staff 4 (MLS 1, Non-MLS 3)
Founded 1960. Enrl 2,300; Fac 85; Highest Degree: Associate
Library Holdings: Bk Vols 40,000; Per Subs 250
Automation Activity & Vendor Info: (Acquisitions) SirsiDynix; (Cataloging) SirsiDynix; (Circulation) SirsiDynix; (ILL) SirsiDynix; (Media Booking) SirsiDynix; (OPAC) SirsiDynix; (Serials) SirsiDynix
Partic in Consortium of Academic & Research Libraries in Illinois; Northern Illinois Learning Resources Cooperative; Southern Ill Learning Resources Coop
Open Mon-Thurs (Winter) 7:30-6, Fri 7:30-4:30; Mon-Thurs (Summer) 7:30-4:30

HARTFORD

P HARTFORD PUBLIC LIBRARY DISTRICT, 143 W Hawthorne, 62048. SAN 304-2545. Tel: 618-254-9394. FAX: 618-254-6522. E-mail: info@hartfordpubliclibrarydistrict.org. *Dir,* Michelle Prickett; E-mail: michelle@hartfordpubliclibrarydistrict.org; *Children's Activities Dir,* Justin Harrop; E-mail: justin@hartfordpubliclibrarydistrict.org; *Cat,* Christina Hayes; E-mail: christina@hartfordpubliclibrarydistrict.org; Staff 4 (MLS 3, Non-MLS 1)
Founded 1965. Pop 1,185; Circ 13,743
Library Holdings: Audiobooks 146; CDs 90; DVDs 916; Large Print Bks 450; Music Scores 159; Bk Titles 29,812; Bk Vols 29,812; Per Subs 66; Videos 268
Special Collections: Lewis & Clark Reference Center
Wireless access
Function: 24/7 Electronic res, 24/7 Online cat, Bks on cassette, Bks on CD, Bus archives, Children's prog, Computers for patron use, Free DVD rentals, Holiday prog, Homebound delivery serv, ILL available, Internet access, Magazines, Movies, Music CDs, Notary serv, Online cat, Photocopying/Printing, Prog for adults, Scanner, Summer & winter reading prog, Summer reading prog, Tax forms, Teen prog, VHS videos, Wheelchair accessible, Winter reading prog
Publications: Newsletter
Mem of Illinois Heartland Library System
Open Mon & Wed 9-5, Tues & Thurs 9-6, Fri & Sat 10-4

HARVARD

P HARVARD DIGGINS PUBLIC LIBRARY*, 900 E McKinley St, 60033. SAN 304-2553. Tel: 815-943-4671. FAX: 815-943-2312. E-mail: harpgeneral@harvard-diggins.org. Web Site: www.harvard-diggins.org. *Dir,* Karen Sutera; E-mail: karens@harvard-diggins.org
Founded 1908. Pop 9,000; Circ 54,000
Library Holdings: Bks on Deafness & Sign Lang 10; High Interest/Low Vocabulary Bk Vols 100; Bk Titles 24,000; Bk Vols 26,000; Per Subs 80
Special Collections: Butterfly Coll
Automation Activity & Vendor Info: (Cataloging) Innovative Interfaces, Inc; (Circulation) Innovative Interfaces, Inc; (ILL) Innovative Interfaces, Inc; (OPAC) Innovative Interfaces, Inc; (Serials) Innovative Interfaces, Inc
Wireless access
Mem of Reaching Across Illinois Library System (RAILS)
Special Services for the Deaf - Am sign lang & deaf culture
Open Mon-Thurs 9-8, Fri & Sat 9-5

HARVEY

P HARVEY PUBLIC LIBRARY DISTRICT*, 15441 Turlington Ave, 60426. SAN 304-257X. Tel: 708-331-0757. Circulation Tel: 708-331-0757, Ext 3200. Administration Tel: 708-331-0757, Ext 3201. FAX: 708-331-5060. TDD: 708-331-0767. E-mail: has@harvey.lib.il.us. Web Site: www.harvey.lib.il.us. *Libr Dir,* Xavier Menzies; E-mail: xmenzies@harvey.lib.il.us; Staff 10 (MLS 2, Non-MLS 8)
Founded 1903. Pop 25,300; Circ 65,098
Library Holdings: AV Mats 2,584; DVDs 5,674; e-books 680; Bk Vols 85,983; Per Subs 571
Subject Interests: Ethnic studies, Local hist
Automation Activity & Vendor Info: (Acquisitions) Innovative Interfaces, Inc; (Circulation) Innovative Interfaces, Inc
Wireless access
Publications: Internal & Patron Newsletters
Mem of Reaching Across Illinois Library System (RAILS)
Partic in System Wide Automated Network

Special Services for the Deaf - TDD equip
Open Mon-Thurs 10-8, Fri & Sat 10-4

M INGALLS MEMORIAL HOSPITAL MEDICAL LIBRARY*, One Ingalls Dr, 60426. SAN 304-2588. Tel: 708-915-6883. FAX: 708-915-3107. Web Site: www.ingalls.org. *Dir,* Elaine De Young; Staff 1 (MLS 1)
Founded 1968
Library Holdings: Bk Titles 500; Bk Vols 700; Per Subs 50
Subject Interests: Clinical med, Nursing
Function: Health sci info serv, ILL available, Internet access, Ref serv available
Partic in Regional Med Libr - Region 3
Restriction: Staff & prof res

HARWOOD HEIGHTS

P EISENHOWER PUBLIC LIBRARY DISTRICT, 4613 N Oketo Ave, 60706. SAN 304-2596. Tel: 708-867-7828. FAX: 708-867-1535. TDD: 708-867-6362. E-mail: reference@eisenhowerpld.org. Web Site: www.eisenhowerlibrary.org. *Dir,* Stacy Wittmann; *Head, Children's Servx,* Tiffany Lewis; Tel: 708-867-2298; *Head, Circ Serv,* Peggy Tomzik; *Head, Fac & Security,* Tony Sciacotta; *Head, Ref Serv,* Dan McPhillips; Tel: 708-867-2299; *Head, Tech Serv,* Victoria Bitters; *Asst Head, Circ Serv,* Hayley Rightnowar; *Teen Serv Coordr,* Penny Blubaugh; *Asst Head, Ref Serv,* Molly Bitters; *Bus Mgr,* Ellen Bacarella; *Mkt Coordr,* Chris Clark; *Commun Outreach Liaison,* Julie Stam; Staff 24 (MLS 21, Non-MLS 3)
Founded 1972. Pop 23,184
Library Holdings: Audiobooks 2,223; AV Mats 36,237; Bks on Deafness & Sign Lang 37; Braille Volumes 19; CDs 11,650; DVDs 17,062; e-books 103,285; Electronic Media & Resources 74; Large Print Bks 3,605; Music Scores 77; Bk Vols 138,536; Per Subs 178; Videos 17,062
Special Collections: Foreign Languages
Automation Activity & Vendor Info: (Circulation) SirsiDynix
Wireless access
Function: 24/7 Electronic res, 24/7 Online cat, 3D Printer, Adult bk club, After school storytime, Archival coll, Audio & video playback equip for onsite use, Audiobks on Playaways & MP3, Audiobks via web, Bi-weekly Writer's Group, Bk club(s), Bks on CD, CD-ROM, Chess club, Children's prog, Computer training, Computers for patron use, Digital talking bks, E-Readers, Electronic databases & coll, Family literacy, Free DVD rentals, Home delivery & serv to seniorr ctr & nursing homes, Homebound delivery serv, ILL available, Internet access, Life-long learning prog for all ages, Magazines, Magnifiers for reading, Makerspace, Mango lang, Meeting rooms, Movies, Museum passes, Music CDs, Notary serv, Online cat, Outreach serv, Outside serv via phone, mail, e-mail & web, OverDrive digital audio bks, Photocopying/Printing, Preschool outreach, Preschool reading prog, Printer for laptops & handheld devices, Prog for adults, Prog for children & young adult, Ref & res, Ref serv available, Scanner, Senior computer classes, Senior outreach, Spanish lang bks, Story hour, Study rm, Summer reading prog, Tax forms, Teen prog, Telephone ref, Visual arts prog, Wheelchair accessible, Winter reading prog, Workshops, Writing prog
Publications: The Eisenhower Explorer (Newsletter)
Mem of Reaching Across Illinois Library System (RAILS)
Partic in System Wide Automated Network
Special Services for the Deaf - TTY equip
Open Mon-Thurs 9-9, Fri & Sat 9-5, Sun 1-5
Friends of the Library Group

HAVANA

P HAVANA PUBLIC LIBRARY DISTRICT*, 201 W Adams St, 62644-1321. SAN 304-260X. Tel: 309-543-4701. FAX: 309-543-2715. E-mail: info@havana.lib.il.us. Web Site: www.havana.lib.il.us. *Dir,* Vanessa Hall-Bennett; E-mail: director@havana.lib.il.us; *Asst Dir, Children's Serv Coordr,* Ellen R Mibbs; *Young Adult Serv Coordr,* Jessica Hughes; Staff 10 (MLS 1, Non-MLS 9)
Founded 1896. Pop 6,627; Circ 20,000
Library Holdings: Bk Vols 34,000; Per Subs 12
Special Collections: Historic Photograph Coll; Mason County Genealogical & Historical Society Coll
Automation Activity & Vendor Info: (OPAC) SirsiDynix-Unicorn
Wireless access
Function: 24/7 Online cat, Archival coll, Bks on CD, Children's prog, Computers for patron use, Electronic databases & coll, Holiday prog, Home delivery & serv to seniorr ctr & nursing homes, Homebound delivery serv, ILL available, Internet access, Life-long learning prog for all ages, Movies, Online cat, Preschool outreach, Prog for adults, Prog for children & young adult, Ref & res, Ref serv available, Res assist avail, Res performed for a fee, Satellite serv, Scanner, Story hour, Summer reading prog, Teen prog, Telephone ref
Mem of Reaching Across Illinois Library System (RAILS)
Partic in RSA
Special Services for the Blind - Bks on CD; Copier with enlargement capabilities; Home delivery serv; Large print bks; Large print bks & talking machines; Micro-computer access & training; Playaways (bks on MP3); Radio reading serv; Recorded bks; Talking bks; Talking bks & player equip
Open Mon, Wed & Fri 9-6, Tues & Thurs 9-8, Sat (Sep-June) 9-2

HAZEL CREST

P GRANDE PRAIRIE PUBLIC LIBRARY DISTRICT, 3479 W 183rd St, 60429. SAN 304-2618. Tel: 708-798-5563. FAX: 708-798-5874. E-mail: information@grandeprairie.org. Web Site: www.grandeprairie.org. *Dir,* Tracy Ducksworth; E-mail: tracy@grandeprairie.org; *Dir of Circ,* Manuel Vasquez; Tel: 708 798-5563, E-mail: manuel@grandeprairie.org; Staff 22 (MLS 7, Non-MLS 15)
Founded 1960. Pop 30,985; Circ 124,071
Library Holdings: AV Mats 12,804; CDs 10,831; e-books 821; Bk Vols 78,426; Per Subs 210; Videos 3,759
Special Collections: Fiction Works by African American Writers
Automation Activity & Vendor Info: (Acquisitions) Baker & Taylor; (Cataloging) SirsiDynix; (Circulation) SirsiDynix-WorkFlows; (ILL) OCLC WorldShare Interlibrary Loan; (OPAC) SirsiDynix; (Serials) EBSCO Online
Wireless access
Function: 24/7 Online cat, Adult bk club, Bk club(s), Bks on CD, Children's prog, Computer training, Computers for patron use, Electronic databases & coll, Free DVD rentals, Home delivery & serv to seniorr ctr & nursing homes, Homebound delivery serv, ILL available, Internet access, Magazines, Mail & tel request accepted, Mango lang, Museum passes, Music CDs, Notary serv, Online cat, Outreach serv, OverDrive digital audio bks, Photocopying/Printing, Preschool reading prog, Printer for laptops & handheld devices, Prog for adults, Prog for children & young adult, Ref serv available, Story hour, Summer reading prog, Teen prog, Telephone ref
Publications: Grande Prairie Public Library (Newsletter)
Mem of Reaching Across Illinois Library System (RAILS)
Partic in Illinois Library & Information Network; Serials of Illinois Libraries Online; System Wide Automated Network
Open Mon-Thurs 9-8, Fri & Sat 9-5
Restriction: Non-resident fee
Friends of the Library Group

S SOUTH SUBURBAN GENEALOGICAL & HISTORICAL SOCIETY LIBRARY, 3000 W 170th Pl, 60429-1174. SAN 304-6583. Tel: 708-335-3340. E-mail: info@ssghs.org. Web Site: www.ssghs.org. *Pres,* Patty Higgins; *Librn,* Laurie Coolidge
Founded 1972
Library Holdings: CDs 500; Microforms 2,000; Bk Titles 12,000; Spec Interest Per Sub 35
Special Collections: Federal Population Census 1790-1930, micro; Illinois - Cook & Will Counties; Naturalization Records for Calumet City; Obituary Files; Pullman Car Works, personnel rec; Roseland (Chicago) Church Hist; Township Records
Subject Interests: Genealogy, Local hist
Wireless access
Function: Online cat
Publications: Cemetery Readings; Monthly Newsletter; Research Series; Where the Trails Cross (Journal)
Open Mon, Wed & Fri 10-4, Tues 1-5
Restriction: Non-circulating

HENNEPIN

P PUTNAM COUNTY PUBLIC LIBRARY DISTRICT*, 214 N Fourth St, 61327. (Mail add: PO Box 199, 61327-0199), SAN 340-4641. Tel: 815-925-7020. FAX: 815-925-7020. Web Site: www.putnamcountylibrary.org. *Dir,* Jay Kalman; E-mail: jkalman@putnamcountylibrary.org; Staff 4 (Non-MLS 4)
Founded 1938. Pop 6,087; Circ 38,000
Library Holdings: Bk Vols 33,000; Per Subs 40
Wireless access
Mem of Reaching Across Illinois Library System (RAILS)
Partic in Illinois Library & Information Network
Open Mon, Tues & Fri 9-5, Thurs 9-7, Sat 9-Noon
Branches: 5
GRANVILLE BRANCH, 214 S McCoy St, Granville, 61326. (Mail add: PO Box 495, Granville, 61326-0495), SAN 340-4676. Tel: 815-339-2038. FAX: 815-339-2038.
Open Mon, Wed, Thurs & Fri 9-5, Tues 9-7, Sat 9-3
MAGNOLIA BRANCH, 112 N Chicago St, Magnolia, 61336. (Mail add: PO Box 167, Magnolia, 61336-0167), SAN 340-4765. Tel: 815-869-6038. FAX: 815-869-6038. *Librn,* Peggy Smith
Open Tues 3-7, Thurs 3-6, Sat 9-Noon
MCNABB BRANCH, 322 W Main St, McNabb, 61335. (Mail add: PO Box 135, McNabb, 61336-0135). Tel: 815-882-2378. FAX: 815-882-2378. *Librn,* Marilyn Calbow
Open Mon 9-Noon, Wed 3-7, Sat 9-1

PUTNAM COUNTY - CONDIT BRANCH, 105 N Center St, Putnam, 60560. (Mail add: PO Box 4, Putnam, 61560-0004), SAN 340-479X. Tel: 815-437-2811. FAX: 815-437-2811.
Open Tues & Thurs 2-6, Sat 9-Noon
STANDARD BRANCH, 128 First St, Standard, 61363. (Mail add: PO Box 114, Standard, 61363-0217). Tel: 815-339-2471. FAX: 815-339-2471.
Open Tues 1-5

HENRY

P HENRY PUBLIC LIBRARY*, 702 Front St, 61537. (Mail add: PO Box 183, 61537-0183), SAN 304-2634. Tel: 309-364-2516. FAX: 309-364-2717. E-mail: henrypubliclibrary@mchsi.com. Web Site: www.henry.lib.il.us. *Dir,* Elizabeth Wild; *Asst Librn,* Janice Hewett
Founded 1936. Pop 2,591; Circ 27,261
Library Holdings: Bk Vols 23,000; Per Subs 61
Subject Interests: Local hist
Open Mon 1-6, Tues 10-5, Wed 1-8, Thurs & Fri 1-5, Sat 10-3

HERRICK

P HERRICK TOWNSHIP PUBLIC LIBRARY*, 303 N Broadway, 62431. SAN 375-9482. Tel: 618-428-5223. FAX: 618-428-5222. *Librn,* Becky Wilson; E-mail: bewilson78@hotmail.com; Staff 1 (Non-MLS 1)
Founded 1979. Pop 629
Library Holdings: Bk Titles 13,000
Subject Interests: Genealogy
Wireless access
Mem of Illinois Heartland Library System
Open Mon & Tues 12-6, Thurs 9-5

HERRIN

P HERRIN CITY LIBRARY*, 120 N 13th St, 62948-3233. SAN 304-2642. Tel: 618-942-6109. FAX: 618-942-4165. E-mail: herrincitylibrary@gmail.com. Web Site: herrincitylibrary.org. *Libr Dir,* Susan Mullen; E-mail: smullenhcl@gmail.com; *Asst Librn, Ch,* Allison Albert; E-mail: aalberthcl@gmail.com; *Circ Librn,* Kimberley Wild; E-mail: kwildhcl@gmail.com; Staff 4 (MLS 1, Non-MLS 3)
Founded 1917. Pop 12,501; Circ 75,000
May 2013-Apr 2014 Income $296,148, State $12,501, City $256,289, Locally Generated Income $27,358. Mats Exp $25,000, Books $16,000, Per/Ser (Incl. Access Fees) $5,000, AV Mat $1,000, Electronic Ref Mat (Incl. Access Fees) $2,000. Sal $128,131 (Prof $42,000)
Library Holdings: Audiobooks 211; CDs 211; DVDs 1,004; e-books 5,000; Large Print Bks 2,000; Bk Vols 50,000; Per Subs 50; Videos 1,672
Special Collections: Local History & Family Records (Herrin History Room)
Subject Interests: Local hist
Automation Activity & Vendor Info: (Acquisitions) Innovative Interfaces, Inc; (Cataloging) Innovative Interfaces, Inc; (ILL) Innovative Interfaces, Inc; (OPAC) Innovative Interfaces, Inc; (Serials) Innovative Interfaces, Inc
Wireless access
Function: Adult literacy prog, Archival coll, Audio & video playback equip for onsite use, Bks on cassette, Bks on CD, CD-ROM, Children's prog, Computers for patron use, Doc delivery serv, Electronic databases & coll, Family literacy, Free DVD rentals, Homebound delivery serv, ILL available, Internet access, Magnifiers for reading, Mail & tel request accepted, Music CDs, Online cat, Online ref, Outside serv via phone, mail, e-mail & web, OverDrive digital audio bks, Photocopying/Printing, Preschool outreach, Prog for adults, Prog for children & young adult, Ref serv available, Scanner, Spoken cassettes & CDs, Spoken cassettes & DVDs, Story hour, Summer reading prog, Tax forms, Telephone ref, VHS videos, Wheelchair accessible
Mem of Illinois Heartland Library System
Open Mon-Thurs 10-7, Fri 10-6, Sat 12-5
Restriction: In-house use for visitors, Non-resident fee
Friends of the Library Group

HEYWORTH

P HEYWORTH PUBLIC LIBRARY DISTRICT, 119 E Main St, 61745. (Mail add: PO Box 469, 61745-0469), SAN 304-2650. Tel: 309-473-2313. FAX: 309-473-9253. E-mail: questions@heyworthlibrary.com. Web Site: heyworthlibrary.com. *Dir,* Lori Urban; *Asst Librn,* Jacque Stengel; Staff 2 (Non-MLS 2)
Founded 1941. Pop 5,506; Circ 33,863
Library Holdings: Bk Titles 20,000; Bk Vols 22,329; Per Subs 102
Special Collections: Local History/Genealogy Coll. Oral History
Automation Activity & Vendor Info: (Cataloging) SirsiDynix; (Circulation) SirsiDynix; (ILL) OCLC FirstSearch
Wireless access
Function: 24/7 Electronic res, 24/7 Online cat, Adult bk club, Art exhibits, Audiobks via web, Bk club(s), Bks on CD, Children's prog, Computers for patron use, Genealogy discussion group, ILL available, Internet access, Laminating, Magazines, Mail & tel request accepted, Meeting rooms, Microfiche/film & reading machines, Movies, Music CDs, Online cat, OverDrive digital audio bks, Photocopying/Printing, Preschool reading prog, Prog for adults, Prog for children & young adult, Scanner, Story hour, Summer & winter reading prog, Tax forms, Wheelchair accessible
Mem of Reaching Across Illinois Library System (RAILS)
Partic in RSA
Open Mon & Thurs 10-8, Tues 1-8 (10-5 Summer), Wed & Fri 10-5, Sat 10-4

HIGHLAND

P LOUIS LATZER MEMORIAL PUBLIC LIBRARY*, 1001 Ninth St, 62249. SAN 304-2669. Tel: 618-654-5066. FAX: 618-654-1324. E-mail: hie@highlandillibrary.org. Web Site: www.highlandillibrary.org. *Dir,* Angela R Kim; E-mail: akim@highlandillibrary.org; *Ch,* Kay Schuette
Founded 1929. Pop 10,500; Circ 110,000
Library Holdings: DVDs 3,200; Bk Vols 40,000; Per Subs 110
Wireless access
Mem of Illinois Heartland Library System
Partic in Health Science Library of Illinois; OCLC-LVIS
Special Services for the Blind - Rec of textbk mat
Open Mon & Wed 9-6, Tues & Thurs 9-8, Fri 9-5, Sat 9-3
Friends of the Library Group

HIGHLAND PARK

P HIGHLAND PARK PUBLIC LIBRARY, 494 Laurel Ave, 60035-2690. SAN 304-2685. Tel: 847-432-0216. Reference Tel: 847-681-7031. FAX: 847-432-9139. E-mail: hppla@hplibrary.org. Web Site: www.hplibrary.org. *Exec Dir,* Heidi Smith; Tel: 847-432-0216, Ext 121, E-mail: hsmith@hplibrary.org; *Media Serv Mgr,* Juan Reyes; E-mail: jreyes@hplibrary.org; *Membership Serv(s) Mgr,* Robin Smith; E-mail: rsmith@hplibrary.org; *Info & Reader Serv Mgr,* Laurie Unger Skinner; E-mail: lskinner@hplibrary.org; *Interim Tech Serv Mgr,* Michelle London; E-mail: mlondon@hplibrary.org; *Youth Serv Mgr,* Marcia Beach; E-mail: mbeach@hplibrary.org; Staff 89 (MLS 20, Non-MLS 69)
Founded 1887. Pop 30,038; Circ 615,070
Library Holdings: AV Mats 27,049; CDs 15,070; Bk Vols 194,153; Per Subs 350
Subject Interests: Local hist
Automation Activity & Vendor Info: (Acquisitions) SirsiDynix; (Cataloging) SirsiDynix; (Circulation) SirsiDynix; (OPAC) SirsiDynix
Wireless access
Publications: What's New at HPPL (Online only)
Special Services for the Deaf - TDD equip
Open Mon-Thurs 9-9, Fri 9-6, Sat 9-5, Sun 1-5
Friends of the Library Group

R NORTH SUBURBAN SYNAGOGUE BETH EL*, Maxwell Abbell Library, 1175 Sheridan Rd, 60035. SAN 304-2693. Tel: 847-432-8900. FAX: 847-432-9242. E-mail: nssbe@nssbethel.org. Web Site: www.nssbethel.org. *Exec Dir,* Jeffrey T Baden; E-mail: jbaden@nssbethel.org; *Librn,* Rachel Kamin; Tel: 847-432-8900, Ext 242, E-mail: rkamin@nssbethel.org; Staff 2 (MLS 2)
Founded 1959
Library Holdings: Bk Titles 20,000; Per Subs 25
Special Collections: Judaica Video Coll
Subject Interests: Judaica (lit or hist of Jews)
Automation Activity & Vendor Info: (Cataloging) OPALS (Open-source Automated Library System); (Circulation) OPALS (Open-source Automated Library System); (OPAC) OPALS (Open-source Automated Library System)
Wireless access
Function: Adult bk club, Archival coll, Art exhibits, Learning ctr, Magazines, Movies, Online cat
Open Mon-Thurs 9-5, Fri 9-2

HIGHWOOD

P HIGHWOOD PUBLIC LIBRARY*, 102 Highwood Ave, 60040-1597. SAN 304-2707. Tel: 847-432-5404. FAX: 847-432-5806. E-mail: info@highwoodlibrary.org. Web Site: www.highwoodlibrary.org. *Dir,* John Mitchell; E-mail: director@highwoodlibrary.org; Staff 8 (MLS 3, Non-MLS 5)
Founded 1977
Automation Activity & Vendor Info: (Acquisitions) Biblionix; (Cataloging) Biblionix; (Circulation) Biblionix; (ILL) OCLC ILLiad; (OPAC) Biblionix
Wireless access
Function: 24/7 Electronic res, 24/7 Online cat, Adult bk club, Adult literacy prog, Archival coll, Audiobks via web, Bk club(s), Bks on CD, Children's prog, Free DVD rentals, ILL available, Internet access, Magazines, Mail & tel request accepted, Movies, Music CDs, Online cat, OverDrive digital audio bks, Photocopying/Printing, Prog for children & young adult, Ref & res, Scanner, Summer reading prog

Mem of Reaching Across Illinois Library System (RAILS)
Open Mon-Thurs 12-8, Fri & Sat 12-5, Sun 1-5

HILLSBORO

S GRAHAM CORRECTIONAL CENTER LIBRARY*, 12078 Illinois Rte 185, 62049. SAN 376-0871. Tel: 217-532-6961. Web Site: www.illinois.gov/idoc/facilities/pages/grahamcorrectionalcenter.aspx. *Educ Adminr,* Maria Miller; *Librn,* Chris Calderini
Library Holdings: High Interest/Low Vocabulary Bk Vols 50; Large Print Bks 50; Bk Titles 15,000; Per Subs 25

P HILLSBORO PUBLIC LIBRARY*, 214 School St, 62049-1547. SAN 304-2715. Tel: 217-532-3055. FAX: 217-532-6813. E-mail: hillsborocitylibrary@gmail.com. Web Site: www.hillsboropubliclibrary.net. *Dir,* Shelley Kolb
Pop 4,300; Circ 45,000
Library Holdings: Bk Titles 18,000; Bk Vols 20,000; Per Subs 55
Subject Interests: Genealogy
Automation Activity & Vendor Info: (Acquisitions) Follett Software; (Cataloging) Follett Software; (Circulation) Follett Software
Wireless access
Mem of Illinois Heartland Library System
Partic in Washington County Cooperative Library Services
Open Mon & Fri 9:30-5, Tues-Thurs 9:30-5:30, Sat 10-12

HILLSDALE

P MOORE MEMORIAL LIBRARY DISTRICT*, Hillsdale Library, 509 Main St, 61257. (Mail add: PO Box 325, 61257-0325), SAN 304-2723. Tel: 309-658-2666. FAX: 309-658-2666. E-mail: library.hillsdale@gmail.com. Web Site: hillsdale.lib.il.us. *Dir,* Theresa Brooks
Founded 1942. Pop 864; Circ 3,900
Library Holdings: Large Print Bks 120; Bk Vols 6,100; Per Subs 20; Talking Bks 70
Wireless access
Mem of Reaching Across Illinois Library System (RAILS)
Open Mon & Thurs 8-4, Wed 8-3

HILLSIDE

P HILLSIDE PUBLIC LIBRARY*, 405 N Hillside Ave, 60162-1295. SAN 304-2731. Tel: 708-449-7510. FAX: 708-449-6119. E-mail: contact@hillsidelibrary.org. Web Site: hillsidelibrary.org. *Dir,* Doug Losey; E-mail: dlosey@hillsidelibrary.org; *Ad,* Maura Terrado; *Info & Tech Librn,* Louis Trizna; E-mail: ltrizna@hillsidelibrary.org; *YA Librn,* Nicola Covello; E-mail: ncovella@hillsidelibrary.org; *Youth Serv Librn,* Amy Gullo; E-mail: agullo@hillsidelibrary.org; *Circ,* Kathy Zaleta; *Tech Serv,* Carmen Parker; Staff 17 (MLS 5, Non-MLS 12)
Founded 1962. Pop 8,155; Circ 83,056
May 2018-Apr 2019 Income $1,148,923, State $28,253, County $1,071,243, Locally Generated Income $49,427. Mats Exp $172,200, Books $50,000, Per/Ser (Incl. Access Fees) $14,000, AV Equip $7,000, AV Mat $52,000, Electronic Ref Mat (Incl. Access Fees) $40,000. Sal $355,000 (Prof $340,000)
Library Holdings: Audiobooks 1,675; AV Mats 9,023; CDs 1,881; DVDs 4,621; Bk Titles 50,220; Per Subs 102
Automation Activity & Vendor Info: (Cataloging) OCLC Connexion; (Circulation) SirsiDynix-WorkFlows; (ILL) SirsiDynix-WorkFlows; (OPAC) SirsiDynix; (Serials) SirsiDynix-WorkFlows
Wireless access
Function: Adult bk club, Audiobks via web, AV serv, Bilingual assistance for Spanish patrons, Bks on CD, Computer training, Computers for patron use, Electronic databases & coll, Free DVD rentals, ILL available, Life-long learning prog for all ages, Magazines, Mango lang, Meeting rooms, Movies, Museum passes, Online cat, OverDrive digital audio bks, Photocopying/Printing, Prog for adults, Prog for children & young adult, Ref serv available, Scanner, Senior computer classes, Serves people with intellectual disabilities, Spoken cassettes & CDs, Story hour, Summer reading prog, Telephone ref, Wheelchair accessible, Workshops
Publications: Newsletter
Partic in Long Island Library Resources Council; System Wide Automated Network
Open Mon-Thurs 10-9, Fri & Sat 10-5, Sun (Winter) 1-5
Restriction: Authorized patrons, ID required to use computers (Ltd hrs), Non-resident fee
Friends of the Library Group

HINCKLEY

P HINCKLEY PUBLIC LIBRARY DISTRICT*, 100 N Maple St, 60520. SAN 304-2758. Tel: 815-286-3220. FAX: 815-286-3664. Web Site: www.hinckleylibrary.org. *Dir,* Rylie Roubal; E-mail: director@hinckley.lib.il.us; *Youth Serv Dir,* Lisa Carter; E-mail: lcarterhpl@gmail.com; Staff 2 (MLS 1, Non-MLS 1)
Founded 1913. Pop 2,802; Circ 23,941
Jul 2014-Jun 2015 Income $193,197, State $3,503, Locally Generated Income $189,694. Mats Exp $15,407, Books $11,211, Per/Ser (Incl. Access Fees) $1,202, AV Mat $1,494, Electronic Ref Mat (Incl. Access Fees) $1,500. Sal $104,853
Library Holdings: Audiobooks 1,000; DVDs 921; e-books 27,348; Bk Vols 14,748; Per Subs 35
Automation Activity & Vendor Info: (Cataloging) Innovative Interfaces, Inc - Sierra; (Circulation) Innovative Interfaces, Inc - Sierra
Wireless access
Function: 24/7 Electronic res, 24/7 Online cat, Adult bk club, Audiobks via web, Bk club(s), Bks on CD, Children's prog, Computer training, Computers for patron use, Free DVD rentals, Holiday prog, Homebound delivery serv, Homework prog, ILL available, Internet access, Laminating, Magazines, Movies, Music CDs, Online cat, OverDrive digital audio bks, Photocopying/Printing, Preschool reading prog, Prog for adults, Prog for children & young adult, Scanner, Story hour, Summer reading prog, Tax forms, Teen prog, Telephone ref, Wheelchair accessible, Workshops
Mem of Reaching Across Illinois Library System (RAILS)
Open Mon & Wed 10-8, Tues, Thurs & Fri 10-6, Sat 10-2
Restriction: Non-resident fee
Friends of the Library Group

HINES

GM DEPARTMENT OF VETERANS AFFAIRS*, Library Service, PO Box 5000-142D, 60141-5142. SAN 304-2774. Tel: 708-202-2000, Ext 28222. *Librn,* Marielle McNeal; E-mail: marielle.mcneal@va.gov; Staff 6 (MLS 2, Non-MLS 4)
Library Holdings: Bk Vols 9,500
Subject Interests: Allied health
Automation Activity & Vendor Info: (Cataloging) Follett Software; (Circulation) Follett Software
Partic in OCLC Online Computer Library Center, Inc
Open Mon-Fri 8-4:30
Restriction: Non-circulating to the pub, Staff use only

HINSDALE

M AMITA HEALTH ADVENTIST HINSDALE HOSPITAL*, Health Sciences Library, 120 N Oak St, 60521. SAN 304-2790. Tel: 630-856-7230. FAX: 630-856-7239. Web Site: www.amitahealth.org. *Regional Librn,* Bonnie Arnold; E-mail: bonnie.arnold@amitahealth.org; Staff 3 (MLS 1, Non-MLS 2)
Library Holdings: Bk Vols 4,000; Per Subs 230; Spec Interest Per Sub 10
Special Collections: E G White Coll
Subject Interests: Med, Nursing, Seventh Day Adventists
Automation Activity & Vendor Info: (Cataloging) EOS International; (Circulation) EOS International; (OPAC) EOS International
Wireless access
Mem of Reaching Across Illinois Library System (RAILS)
Partic in Illinois Library & Information Network; National Network of Libraries of Medicine Region 6; OCLC-LVIS
Open Mon-Thurs 8-5, Fri 8-3

P HINSDALE PUBLIC LIBRARY*, 20 E Maple St, 60521. SAN 304-2782. Tel: 630-986-1976. Reference Tel: 630-986-1982. FAX: 630-986-9654. E-mail: adultservices@hinsdalelibrary.info. Web Site: www.hinsdalelibrary.info. *Exec Dir,* Karen Kleckner Keefe; E-mail: kkeefe@hinsdalelibrary.info; *Adult Serv Mgr,* Cynthia Dieden; E-mail: cdieden@hinsdalelibrary.info; *Bus Off Mgr,* Nancy Marvan; E-mail: nmarvan@hinsdalelibrary.info; *IT Mgr,* Robert Bell; E-mail: rbell@hinsdalelibrary.info; *Mkt Mgr, Outreach Mgr,* Molly Castor; E-mail: mcastor@hinsdalelibrary.info; *Mat Mgt Mgr,* Ellen Smith; E-mail: esmith@hinsdalelibrary.info; *Patron Serv Mgr,* Martha Kennedy; E-mail: mkennedy@hinsdalelibrary.info; *Youth & Young Adult Mgr,* Ridgeway Burns; E-mail: rburns@hinsdalelibrary.info; Staff 46 (MLS 12, Non-MLS 34)
Founded 1893. Pop 16,594; Circ 333,949
May 2015-Apr 2016 Income $2,942,571. Mats Exp $289,000. Sal $1,700,178
Library Holdings: Bk Vols 114,994; Per Subs 295
Automation Activity & Vendor Info: (Circulation) SirsiDynix; (OPAC) SirsiDynix-WorkFlows
Wireless access
Function: 24/7 Electronic res, Activity rm, Art exhibits, Audio & video playback equip for onsite use, Audiobks via web, AV serv, Bks on CD, Children's prog, Computer training, Computers for patron use, E-Readers, Electronic databases & coll, Homebound delivery serv, ILL available, Internet access, Magazines, Microfiche/film & reading machines, Movies, Music CDs, Online cat, Online ref, Orientations, Outreach serv, Outside serv via phone, mail, e-mail & web, OverDrive digital audio bks, Photocopying/Printing, Preschool outreach, Preschool reading prog, Printer for laptops & handheld devices, Prog for adults, Prog for children & young adult, Ref & res, Ref serv available, Scanner, Story hour, Study rm,

Summer reading prog, Tax forms, Teen prog, Telephone ref, Wheelchair accessible
Publications: Beyond Books (Newsletter)
Partic in System Wide Automated Network
Special Services for the Deaf - TTY equip
Open Mon-Fri 10-6, Sat 10-5
Friends of the Library Group

HODGKINS

P HODGKINS PUBLIC LIBRARY DISTRICT*, 6500 Wenz Ave, 60525. SAN 321-4613. Tel: 708-579-1844. FAX: 708-579-1896. E-mail: contactus@hodgkinslibrary.org. Web Site: www.hodgkinslibrary.org. *Dir,* Tim Prendergast; *Youth Serv Librn,* Carrie Cameron; Staff 1 (MLS 1)
Founded 1975. Pop 2,134
Library Holdings: Bk Vols 40,000; Per Subs 40
Wireless access
Mem of Reaching Across Illinois Library System (RAILS)
Partic in System Wide Automated Network
Open Mon-Thus 2-7, Fri 1-5, Sat 10-2, Sun 1-3

HOMER

P HOMER COMMUNITY LIBRARY, 500 E Second St, 61849. SAN 304-2812. Tel: 217-896-2121. E-mail: homerlibrarian@gmail.com. Web Site: homercommunitylibrary.com. *Head Librn,* Christine Cunningham; Staff 1 (Non-MLS 1)
Founded 1971. Pop 1,200; Circ 18,000
Library Holdings: Audiobooks 200; AV Mats 990; CDs 600; DVDs 2,500; Large Print Bks 100; Bk Titles 21,000; Per Subs 27
Wireless access
Mem of Illinois Heartland Library System
Open Mon, Tues, Thurs & Fri 2-7, Wed 9-2, Sat 10-2
Friends of the Library Group

HOMER GLEN

P HOMER TOWNSHIP PUBLIC LIBRARY DISTRICT*, 14320 W 151st St, 60491. SAN 375-9490. Tel: 708-301-7908. FAX: 708-301-4535. Web Site: homerlibrary.org. *Exec Dir,* Sheree Kozel-La Ha; E-mail: sheree@homerlibrary.org; *Asst Dir,* Sara McCambridge; E-mail: sara@homerlibrary.org; *Info Serv Librn, Teen Serv Coordr,* Heather Colby; E-mail: heather@homerlibrary.org; *Adult Serv Mgr,* Alexandra Annen; E-mail: alex@homerlibrary.org; *Bus Mgr, Tech Serv,* Carol McSweeney; E-mail: carolm@homerlibrary.org; *Circ Mgr, Youth Serv Mgr,* Jody Olivieri; E-mail: jolivieri@homerlibrary.org; Staff 30 (MLS 6, Non-MLS 24)
Founded 1982. Pop 40,000; Circ 267,340
Library Holdings: Audiobooks 5,000; DVDs 2,000; e-books 2,517; Electronic Media & Resources 50; Bk Titles 100,339; Per Subs 136; Talking Bks 5,000
Automation Activity & Vendor Info: (Acquisitions) SirsiDynix; (Cataloging) SirsiDynix; (Circulation) SirsiDynix; (Course Reserve) SirsiDynix; (ILL) SirsiDynix; (Media Booking) SirsiDynix; (OPAC) SirsiDynix; (Serials) SirsiDynix
Wireless access
Mem of Reaching Across Illinois Library System (RAILS)
Special Services for the Blind - Bks on cassette; Bks on CD; Large print bks; Magnifiers; Talking bks; ZoomText magnification & reading software
Open Mon-Thurs 8:30am-9pm, Fri 10-4, Sat 10-3, Sun 4-8
Friends of the Library Group
Bookmobiles: 1. Mgr, Maryellen Reed

HOMETOWN

P HOMETOWN PUBLIC LIBRARY*, Jack R Ladwig Memorial Library, 4331 Southwest Hwy, 60456-1161. SAN 304-2820. Tel: 708-636-0997. FAX: 708-636-8127. E-mail: hometownlibrary@comcast.net. *Head Librn,* Annette Selmeister
Founded 1956. Pop 4,349; Circ 25,814
Library Holdings: Bk Vols 25,186; Per Subs 480
Subject Interests: Hist, Local hist, Relig, Soc sci & issues
Wireless access
Mem of Reaching Across Illinois Library System (RAILS)
Open Mon, Wed & Thurs 1-7, Tues 9-9, Fri 1-5, Sat 10-2

HOMEWOOD

P HOMEWOOD PUBLIC LIBRARY*, 17917 Dixie Hwy, 60430-1703. SAN 304-2839. Tel: 708-798-0121. FAX: 708-798-0662. E-mail: libraryhws@hotmail.com. Web Site: www.homewoodlibrary.org. *Libr Dir,* Colleen Waltman; *Adminr,* Amy Crump; Tel: 708-798-0121, Ext 214, E-mail: amyc@homewoodlibrary.net; *Librn,* Jill Postma; *Mgr,* Judi Wolinsky; Staff 37 (MLS 7, Non-MLS 30)
Founded 1927. Pop 19,274; Circ 390,000
Library Holdings: Bk Vols 161,000; Per Subs 260
Automation Activity & Vendor Info: (Acquisitions) Innovative Interfaces, Inc; (Cataloging) Innovative Interfaces, Inc; (Circulation) Innovative Interfaces, Inc; (Course Reserve) Innovative Interfaces, Inc; (ILL) Innovative Interfaces, Inc; (Media Booking) Innovative Interfaces, Inc; (OPAC) Innovative Interfaces, Inc; (Serials) Innovative Interfaces, Inc
Wireless access
Publications: Homewood Hi-Lites; Novel News
Partic in System Wide Automated Network
Open Mon-Thurs 9-9, Fri & Sat 9-5, Sun 1-5
Friends of the Library Group

HOOPESTON

P HOOPESTON PUBLIC LIBRARY*, 110 N Fourth St, 60942-1422. SAN 304-2847. Tel: 217-283-6711. FAX: 217-283-7077. TDD: 217-283-6999. E-mail: info@hooplib.org. Web Site: www.hooplib.org. *Dir,* Tricia Freeland
Founded 1898. Pop 10,838; Circ 55,412
Library Holdings: Bk Vols 38,000; Per Subs 100
Automation Activity & Vendor Info: (Acquisitions) Horizon; (Cataloging) Horizon; (Circulation) Horizon; (Course Reserve) Horizon; (ILL) Horizon; (Media Booking) Horizon; (OPAC) Horizon; (Serials) Horizon
Wireless access
Mem of Illinois Heartland Library System
Open Mon-Thurs 9:30-8, Fri 9:30-6, Sat 9:30-3
Friends of the Library Group

HUDSON

P HUDSON AREA PUBLIC LIBRARY DISTRICT*, 104 Pearl St, 61748. (Mail add: PO Box 461, 61748-0461), SAN 375-9504. Tel: 309-726-1103. FAX: 309-726-1646. E-mail: hudsonarealibrary@yahoo.com. Web Site: hudsonarealibrary.com. *Libr Dir,* Jenny Losey; *Youth Serv Mgr,* Rhonda Johnson; Staff 9 (Non-MLS 9)
Founded 1992. Pop 3,741; Circ 39,006
Library Holdings: Audiobooks 1,063; CDs 243; DVDs 2,005; e-books 837; Large Print Bks 342; Bk Vols 18,686; Per Subs 40
Special Collections: Hudson History Room
Automation Activity & Vendor Info: (Circulation) SirsiDynix-WorkFlows; (OPAC) SirsiDynix-WorkFlows
Wireless access
Function: 24/7 Electronic res, 24/7 Online cat, Adult bk club, Archival coll, Audiobks via web, Bk club(s), Bks on CD, Children's prog, Computers for patron use, Electronic databases & coll, Free DVD rentals, Holiday prog, ILL available, Internet access, Magazines, Mail & tel request accepted, Music CDs, Online cat, Outside serv via phone, mail, e-mail & web, OverDrive digital audio bks, Photocopying/Printing, Prog for adults, Prog for children & young adult, Ref serv available, Scanner, Spoken cassettes & CDs, Story hour, Summer & winter reading prog, Summer reading prog, Teen prog, Telephone ref, Wheelchair accessible, Winter reading prog
Mem of Reaching Across Illinois Library System (RAILS)
Partic in Resource Sharing Alliance
Open Mon-Thurs 10-8, Fri 10-6, Sat 10-2
Restriction: Non-resident fee

HUNTLEY

P HUNTLEY AREA PUBLIC LIBRARY DISTRICT, 11000 Ruth Rd, 60142-7155. SAN 375-9512. Tel: 847-669-5386. Web Site: www.huntleylibrary.org. *Dir,* Frank Novak; *Head, Pub Serv,* Elizabeth Steffensen; E-mail: esteffensen@huntleylibrary.org; *Head, Tech Serv,* Jo Smolzer; E-mail: jsmolzer@huntleylibrary.org; Staff 43 (MLS 9, Non-MLS 34)
Founded 1989. Pop 39,233; Circ 487,631
Library Holdings: CDs 15,855; DVDs 16,002; e-books 41,347; Electronic Media & Resources 21,183; Bk Vols 97,442; Per Subs 221
Subject Interests: Illinois, Local hist
Wireless access
Function: 24/7 Electronic res, 24/7 Online cat, Adult bk club, Art exhibits, Audiobks on Playaways & MP3, Audiobks via web, AV serv, Bilingual assistance for Spanish patrons, Bk club(s), Bks on CD, Children's prog, Computer training, Computers for patron use, Electronic databases & coll, Free DVD rentals, Home delivery & serv to seniorr ctr & nursing homes, Homebound delivery serv, ILL available, Internet access, Life-long learning prog for all ages, Magazines, Magnifiers for reading, Mango lang, Meeting rooms, Movies, Museum passes, Music CDs, Online cat, Online ref, Outreach serv, OverDrive digital audio bks, Photocopying/Printing, Preschool outreach, Prog for adults, Prog for children & young adult, Ref serv available, Scanner, Senior outreach, Spanish lang bks, Story hour, Summer & winter reading prog, Teen prog, Telephone ref, Wheelchair accessible
Publications: The Whole Story (Newsletter)
Mem of Reaching Across Illinois Library System (RAILS)
Partic in Cooperative Computer Services - CCS

Open Mon-Thurs 9-8, Fri & Sat 9-5, Sun 12-5
Friends of the Library Group

ILLIOPOLIS

P ILLIOPOLIS-NIANTIC PUBLIC LIBRARY DISTRICT, Sixth & Mary Sts, 62539. (Mail add: PO Box 327, 62539-0327), SAN 304-2863. Tel: 217-486-5561. FAX: 217-486-7811. E-mail: illiopolisnianticpld@hotmail.com. Web Site: www.illiopolisniantic.lib.il.us. *Libr Dir,* Shelley Hopkins; *Ch Serv,* Mary Langloss
Founded 1935. Pop 2,198; Circ 19,739
Library Holdings: Bk Vols 16,977; Per Subs 50
Special Collections: War Plants Located at Illiopolis During WWII
Automation Activity & Vendor Info: (Acquisitions) Horizon; (Cataloging) Horizon; (Circulation) Horizon; (ILL) Horizon; (OPAC) Horizon; (Serials) Horizon
Wireless access
Mem of Illinois Heartland Library System
Open Mon & Fri 1-5, Tues & Thurs 1-8, Wed 10-5

INA

S ILLINOIS DEPARTMENT OF CORRECTIONS*, Big Muddy River Correctional Center Library, 251 N Illinois Hwy 37, 62846. (Mail add: PO Box 1000, 62846-1000). Tel: 618-437-5300, Ext 467. FAX: 618-437-5627. Web Site: www2.illinois.gov/idoc/facilities/Pages/bigmuddyriver.aspx. *Libr Mgr,* Jennifer Wilson
Library Holdings: Bk Vols 35,000
Restriction: Not open to pub

J REND LAKE COLLEGE*, Learning Resource Center, 468 N Ken Gray Pkwy, 62846. SAN 304-2871. Tel: 618-437-5321. Circulation Tel: 618-437-5321, Ext 1308. Reference Tel: 618-437-5321, Ext 1276. Administration Tel: 618-437-5321, Ext 1775. Automation Services Tel: 618-437-5321, Ext 1249. Information Services Tel: 618-437-5321, Ext 1259. FAX: 618-437-5677. Web Site: www.rlc.edu/learning-resource-center/electronic-library, www.rlc.edu/student-services/learning-resource-center. *Ref Librn,* Beth Mandrell; E-mail: mandrell@rlc.edu; *Coordr, Tech Serv,* Sandy West; E-mail: wests@rlc.edu; *Libr Asst,* Kim Davis; E-mail: davis@rlc.edu. Subject Specialists: *Info literacy,* Beth Mandrell; Staff 3 (MLS 2, Non-MLS 1)
Founded 1956. Enrl 2,400; Fac 64; Highest Degree: Associate
Jul 2017-Jun 2018 Income $324,580. Mats Exp $100,385, Books $19,700, Per/Ser (Incl. Access Fees) $5,200, AV Mat $2,000, Electronic Ref Mat (Incl. Access Fees) $59,219. Sal $179,261 (Prof $150,461)
Library Holdings: Audiobooks 180; CDs 198; DVDs 1,589; e-books 46,844; e-journals 24,174; Electronic Media & Resources 49; Large Print Bks 145; Bk Titles 12,794; Per Subs 43
Automation Activity & Vendor Info: (Cataloging) Innovative Interfaces, Inc; (Circulation) Innovative Interfaces, Inc; (ILL) OCLC WorldShare Interlibrary Loan; (OPAC) Innovative Interfaces, Inc; (Serials) Innovative Interfaces, Inc
Wireless access
Function: 24/7 Electronic res, Art exhibits, Bks on CD, Distance learning, Doc delivery serv, Electronic databases & coll, Free DVD rentals, ILL available, Learning ctr, Magazines, Online cat, Photocopying/Printing, Ref serv available, Scanner, Wheelchair accessible
Mem of Illinois Heartland Library System
Partic in Consortium of Academic & Research Libraries in Illinois; Network of Illinois Learning Resources in Community Colleges
Special Services for the Blind - Large print bks
Open Mon-Thurs 7-6, Fri 7-4; Mon-Thurs (Summer) 8-4

ITASCA

M AMERICAN ACADEMY OF PEDIATRICS*, Bakwin Library, 345 Park Blvd, 60143. SAN 304-1689. Tel: 630-626-6635. Web Site: www.aap.org. *Dir,* Susan Bolda Marshall; Tel: 630-626-6722; *Libr Mgr,* Chris Kwiat; E-mail: ckwiat@aap.org; *Archivist,* Allison Seagram; Tel: 630-626-7093, E-mail: aseagram@aap.org; Staff 3 (MLS 3)
Founded 1965
Library Holdings: Bk Titles 1,000; Per Subs 130
Special Collections: Pediatric History Center. Oral History
Automation Activity & Vendor Info: (Cataloging) EOS International; (Circulation) EOS International; (OPAC) EOS International
Wireless access
Partic in Illinois Library & Information Network; OCLC Online Computer Library Center, Inc
Open Mon-Fri 8-4:30

P ITASCA COMMUNITY LIBRARY, 500 W Irving Park Rd, 60143. SAN 304-288X. Tel: 630-773-1699. FAX: 630-773-1707. E-mail: itascal@itascalibrary.org. Web Site: www.itascalibrary.org. *Libr Dir,* Position Currently Open; *Ad,* Carrie Straka; E-mail: cstraka@itascalibrary.org; *Youth Serv Librn,* Jackie Stork; E-mail: jstork@itascalibrary.org; *Bus Mgr,* Gail Herff; E-mail: gherff@itascalibrary.org; *Prog Mgr,* Colleen Blanchard; E-mail: cblanchard@itascalibrary.org
Founded 1957. Pop 8,302; Circ 123,781
Library Holdings: Bk Vols 68,521; Per Subs 191
Special Collections: Learning Games Library; Parent Teacher Texts
Automation Activity & Vendor Info: (Cataloging) SirsiDynix; (Circulation) SirsiDynix; (OPAC) SirsiDynix
Wireless access
Mem of Reaching Across Illinois Library System (RAILS)
Partic in System Wide Automated Network
Open Mon-Thurs 9-9, Fri & Sat 9-5, Sun (Winter) 1-5
Friends of the Library Group

S NATIONAL SAFETY COUNCIL LIBRARY*, 1121 Spring Lake Dr, 60143. SAN 303-9870. Tel: 630-285-2199. FAX: 630-285-0765. E-mail: library@nsc.org. Web Site: www.nsc.org/membership/member-resources/nsc-library. *Mgr, Libr & Info Serv,* Alaina Kolosh; Staff 3 (MLS 3)
Founded 1915
Library Holdings: Bk Titles 171,000; Per Subs 90
Subject Interests: Accident prevention, Home & commun safety, Occupational health, Occupational safety, Traffic (safety)
Automation Activity & Vendor Info: (Cataloging) Inmagic, Inc.; (OPAC) Inmagic, Inc.
Publications: Historical Index to the Occupational Safety & Health Data Sheets
Mem of Reaching Across Illinois Library System (RAILS)
Partic in Illinois Library & Information Network
Open Mon-Fri 8:30-4:45

JACKSONVILLE

C ILLINOIS COLLEGE*, Schewe Library, 1101 W College Ave, 62650-2299. Tel: 217-245-3020. Circulation Tel: 217-245-3021. E-mail: schewe@ic.edu. Web Site: www.ic.edu/library. *Libr Dir,* Luke Beatty; E-mail: luke.beatty@ic.edu; *Head, Tech Serv, Librn,* Adam Enz; E-mail: adam.enz@ic.edu; *Cat & Ref Librn,* Garrett Traylor; E-mail: garrett.traylor@ic.edu; Staff 6 (MLS 3, Non-MLS 3)
Founded 1829. Enrl 894; Fac 75; Highest Degree: Bachelor
Library Holdings: AV Mats 12,490; Bk Titles 147,000; Bk Vols 171,500; Per Subs 600
Special Collections: Civil War Coll; Lincoln Coll; Local History Coll
Automation Activity & Vendor Info: (Acquisitions) Ex Libris Group; (Cataloging) Ex Libris Group; (Circulation) Ex Libris Group; (Course Reserve) Ex Libris Group; (ILL) Ex Libris Group; (OPAC) Ex Libris Group; (Serials) Ex Libris Group
Wireless access
Mem of Reaching Across Illinois Library System (RAILS)
Partic in Center for Research Libraries; Consortium of Academic & Research Libraries in Illinois; Illinois Library & Information Network; OCLC Online Computer Library Center, Inc
Open Mon-Thurs 8am-Midnight, Fri 8-7, Sat 1-5, Sun 1-Midnight
Friends of the Library Group

S ILLINOIS DEPARTMENT OF CORRECTIONS*, Jacksonville Correctional Center Library, 2268 E Morton Ave, 62650-9347. SAN 375-5347. Tel: 217-245-1481, Ext 334. FAX: 217-245-1481, Ext 324. Web Site: www2.illinois.gov/idoc/facilities/Pages/jacksonvillecorrectionalcenter.aspx. *Librn,* George Strode; Staff 1 (MLS 1)
Founded 1984
Library Holdings: Bks on Deafness & Sign Lang 10; High Interest/Low Vocabulary Bk Vols 45; Large Print Bks 40; Bk Titles 5,621; Bk Vols 5,669; Per Subs 12
Special Collections: Federal/State Statutory & Case Law Coll; Self-Help Legal Books
Mem of Reaching Across Illinois Library System (RAILS)
Special Services for the Deaf - Bks on deafness & sign lang; TDD equip
Special Services for the Blind - Talking bks
Open Mon-Fri 7-3
Restriction: Inmate patrons, facility staff & vols direct access. All others through ILL only, Restricted access

S ILLINOIS SCHOOL FOR THE DEAF, Library for the Deaf, 125 Webster Ave, 62650. SAN 326-9477. Tel: 217-479-4254. FAX: 217-479-4244. Web Site: www.illinoisdeaf.org/Hs/Hs.html. *Principal,* Christine Good-Deal; E-mail: Christine.Good-Deal@illinois.gov; *Principal,* Position Currently Open; *Learning Res Spec,* Position Currently Open; Staff 5 (Non-MLS 5)
Library Holdings: Bks on Deafness & Sign Lang 1,020; High Interest/Low Vocabulary Bk Vols 4,000; Bk Titles 15,050; Bk Vols 15,150; Per Subs 50
Subject Interests: Deaf educ, Deafness, Educ, Sign lang

Automation Activity & Vendor Info: (Cataloging) Follett Software; (Circulation) Follett Software; (OPAC) Follett Software
Function: ILL available
Publications: Sights & Sounds
Special Services for the Deaf - Captioned film dep; Staff with knowledge of sign lang; TDD equip; TTY equip

S ILLINOIS SCHOOL FOR THE VISUALLY IMPAIRED LIBRARY, 658 E State St, 62650-2130. SAN 326-9582. Tel: 217-479-4471. FAX: 217-479-4479. Web Site: www.dhs.state.il.us/page.aspx?item=87427. *Libr Assoc,* Gina Carr; E-mail: gina.carr@illinois.gov; Staff 1 (Non-MLS 1)
Library Holdings: Braille Volumes 10,000; Bk Titles 29,500; Per Subs 10; Talking Bks 1,500; Videos 450
Subject Interests: Blindness, Spec educ
Mem of Reaching Across Illinois Library System (RAILS)
Special Services for the Blind - Accessible computers; Aids for in-house use; Assistive/Adapted tech devices, equip & products; Audio mat; Audiovision-a radio reading serv; Bks available with recordings; Bks on flash-memory cartridges; Braille bks; Braille equip; Children's Braille; Closed circuit TV magnifier; Computer with voice synthesizer for visually impaired persons; Copier with enlargement capabilities; Dep for Braille Inst; Descriptive video serv (DVS); Digital talking bk; Digital talking bk machines; Internet workstation with adaptive software; Large print bks; Networked computers with assistive software; Talking bks; Talking bks & player equip; Talking bks from Braille Inst
Open Mon-Fri 8-3:30

P JACKSONVILLE PUBLIC LIBRARY, 201 W College Ave, 62650-2497. SAN 304-291X. Tel: 217-243-5435. FAX: 217-243-2182. TDD: 217-245-5022. Web Site: www.jaxpl.org. *Libr Dir,* Chris Ashmore; E-mail: cashmore@jaxpl.org; *Ad,* Sarah Snyder; E-mail: ssnyder@jaxpl.org; *Outreach Serv Librn,* Heidi Estabrook; E-mail: hestabrook@jaxpl.org; *Youth Serv Librn,* Cindy Boehlke; E-mail: cboehlke@jaxpl.org; *Circ Supvr,* Bridget Dean; E-mail: bdean@jaxpl.org; Staff 5 (MLS 2, Non-MLS 3)
Founded 1889. Pop 19,939; Circ 120,000
Library Holdings: AV Mats 7,842; Bk Vols 90,838; Per Subs 100; Talking Bks 4,112
Special Collections: Morgan County History
Automation Activity & Vendor Info: (Acquisitions) TLC (The Library Corporation); (Cataloging) TLC (The Library Corporation); (Circulation) TLC (The Library Corporation); (ILL) OCLC FirstSearch; (OPAC) TLC (The Library Corporation); (Serials) OCLC FirstSearch
Wireless access
Function: Adult bk club, Chess club, Computer training, Doc delivery serv, Home delivery & serv to seniorr ctr & nursing homes, Homebound delivery serv, ILL available, Mail & tel request accepted, Photocopying/Printing, Prog for children & young adult, Ref serv available, Senior computer classes, Serves people with intellectual disabilities, Spoken cassettes & CDs, Spoken cassettes & DVDs, Summer reading prog, VHS videos, Wheelchair accessible
Special Services for the Deaf - Bks on deafness & sign lang; Closed caption videos; TTY equip
Special Services for the Blind - Assistive/Adapted tech devices, equip & products; Audio mat; Bks on cassette; Bks on CD; Computer with voice synthesizer for visually impaired persons; Extensive large print coll; Home delivery serv; Large print bks; Talking bks
Open Mon-Thurs 9-9, Fri 9-6, Sat 9-5, Sun 12-4
Friends of the Library Group

JERSEYVILLE

P JERSEYVILLE PUBLIC LIBRARY*, 105 N Liberty St, 62052-1512. SAN 304-2944. Tel: 618-498-9514. FAX: 618-498-3036. E-mail: jpl@jerseyvillelibrary.org. Web Site: www.jerseyvillelibrary.org. *Dir,* Anita Driver; E-mail: anitad@jerseyvillelibrary.org; *Cataloger,* Chris Maness; E-mail: chrism@jerseyvillelibrary.org; *Circ Serv, ILL,* Beth Tittle; E-mail: betht@jerseyvillelibrary.org; *Youth Serv,* Laurie Ingram; E-mail: lauriei@jerseyvillelibrary.org
Founded 1894. Pop 8,500; Circ 93,735
Library Holdings: CDs 5,771; DVDs 3,599; e-books 16,040; Bk Vols 51,017; Per Subs 145; Talking Bks 806
Automation Activity & Vendor Info: (Cataloging) Innovative Interfaces, Inc; (Circulation) Innovative Interfaces, Inc; (ILL) Innovative Interfaces, Inc; (OPAC) Innovative Interfaces, Inc; (Serials) Innovative Interfaces, Inc
Wireless access
Function: Bks on CD, Computers for patron use, Electronic databases & coll, Homebound delivery serv, ILL available, Microfiche/film & reading machines, Music CDs, Online cat, OverDrive digital audio bks, Photocopying/Printing, Scanner, Story hour, Summer reading prog, Tax forms, Wheelchair accessible
Mem of Illinois Heartland Library System
Partic in Illinois Library & Information Network; OCLC Online Computer Library Center, Inc
Open Mon-Thurs 8:30am-9pm, Fri & Sat 8:30-5, Sun 1-4
Friends of the Library Group

JOHNSBURG

P JOHNSBURG PUBLIC LIBRARY DISTRICT*, 3000 N Johnsburg Rd, 60051. SAN 323-5491. Tel: 815-344-0077. FAX: 815-344-3524. Web Site: www.johnsburglibrary.org. *Dir,* Beth Ryan; E-mail: bryan@johnsburglibrary.org; *Circ,* Melanie Ullrich; Staff 13 (MLS 1, Non-MLS 12)
Founded 1982. Pop 12,421; Circ 103,773
Library Holdings: Bk Vols 60,088; Per Subs 46
Special Collections: Homeschool Resource Center
Automation Activity & Vendor Info: (Cataloging) Follett Software; (Circulation) Follett Software; (OPAC) Follett Software
Wireless access
Publications: Newsletter (Quarterly)
Mem of Reaching Across Illinois Library System (RAILS)
Open Mon-Thurs 8:30am-9pm, Fri & Sat 8:30-5, Sun (Oct-May) 1-4
Friends of the Library Group

JOHNSTON CITY

P JOHNSTON CITY PUBLIC LIBRARY*, 506 Washington Ave, 62951. SAN 304-2952. Tel: 618-983-6359. FAX: 618-983-6359. E-mail: jcpublib@yahoo.com. Web Site: www.johnstoncity-il.com/library. *Head Librn,* Cindy Pulsford
Pop 3,557
Library Holdings: DVDs 70; Bk Titles 15,177; Per Subs 40; Talking Bks 506; Videos 226
Wireless access
Mem of Illinois Heartland Library System
Open Mon & Tues 12-7, Wed & Thurs 12-6, Fri 11-5, Sat 9-1

JOLIET

M AMITA HEALTH SAINT JOSEPH MEDICAL CENTER*, Leon P Gardner Health Science Library, 333 N Madison St, 60435. SAN 304-2995. Tel: 815-725-7133, Ext 3530. FAX: 815-773-7755. Web Site: www.amitahealth.org. *Regional Librn,* Bonnie Arnold; Staff 3 (MLS 1, Non-MLS 2)
Founded 1975
Library Holdings: AV Mats 1,000; Bk Titles 1,500; Bk Vols 2,000; Per Subs 225
Subject Interests: Med, Nursing
Automation Activity & Vendor Info: (Cataloging) EOS International; (OPAC) EOS International
Mem of Reaching Across Illinois Library System (RAILS)

J JOLIET JUNIOR COLLEGE LIBRARY*, Campus Center (A-Bldg), 2nd Flr, 1215 Houbolt Rd, 60431. SAN 304-2987. Tel: 815-280-2665. Reference Tel: 815-280-2344. Administration Tel: 815-729-9020, Ext 2344. FAX: 815-744-2465. E-mail: librarian@jjc.edu, library3@jjc.edu. Web Site: www.jjc.edu/lrc. *Chairperson, Librn,* Susan Prokopeak; Tel: 815-729-2215, E-mail: sprokope@jjc.edu; *Librn,* Cynthia Kramer; Tel: 815-729-6604, E-mail: ckramer@jjc.edu; Staff 9 (MLS 3, Non-MLS 6)
Founded 1902. Enrl 5,000; Fac 150
Library Holdings: AV Mats 361; Bk Titles 53,000; Bk Vols 70,000; Per Subs 275
Special Collections: Children's books, soil surveys
Subject Interests: Agr, Criminal justice, Educ, English, Hist, Hort, Math, Nursing, Psychol, Veterinary tech
Automation Activity & Vendor Info: (Acquisitions) Ex Libris Group
Publications: Acquisitions report; film catalogue; video catalogue
Mem of Reaching Across Illinois Library System (RAILS)
Partic in Consortium of Academic & Research Libraries in Illinois; Ill Regional Libr Coun; Network of Illinois Learning Resources in Community Colleges; Northern Ill Learning Resources Coop
Open Mon-Thurs (Fall & Spring) 7:30am-10pm, Fri 7:30-4:30, Sat 8-3:30; Mon-Thurs (Summer) 7:30am-9pm

P JOLIET PUBLIC LIBRARY*, 150 N Ottawa St, 60432. SAN 340-4854. Tel: 815-740-2660. Reference Tel: 815-740-2666. FAX: 815-740-6161. Web Site: jolietlibrary.org. *Exec Dir,* Megan Millen; Tel: 815-740-2670, E-mail: mmillen@jolietlibrary.org; *Dep Dir,* Catherine Adamowski; E-mail: cyanikoski@jolietlibrary.org; *Head Bldg Serv,* Joe Masters; *Communications Mgr,* Mallory Hewlett; *Tech Mgr,* Jack Kelderhouse; *Access Serv,* Keisha Mandara; *Adult Serv,* Dawn Ritter; *Youth Serv,* Laura Yanchick; Staff 17 (MLS 15, Non-MLS 2)
Founded 1875. Pop 148,600
Library Holdings: Bk Titles 500,000; Per Subs 580
Special Collections: Granger Poetry; Herald News Microfilm Coll (1846-Present); Illinois History
Automation Activity & Vendor Info: (Circulation) Innovative Interfaces, Inc
Wireless access

Function: 24/7 Electronic res, 24/7 Online cat, 3D Printer, Activity rm, Adult bk club, Adult literacy prog, After school storytime, Archival coll
Publications: Public & Staff Newsletters
Mem of Reaching Across Illinois Library System (RAILS)
Partic in Pinnacle Library Cooperative
Open Mon-Thurs 9-9, Fri & Sat 9-5, Sun (Oct-June) 1-5
Friends of the Library Group
Branches: 1
BLACK ROAD BRANCH, 3395 Black Rd, 60431. Tel: 815-846-6500. *Dep Dir,* Catherine Yanikoski Adamowski; Tel: 815-846-6519, E-mail: cyanikoski@jolietlibrary.org
Open Mon-Thurs 9-9, Fri & Sat 9-5, Sun (Oct-June) 9-5

CR UNIVERSITY OF ST FRANCIS*, LaVerne & Dorothy Brown Library, 600 Taylor St, 60435. SAN 304-2960. Tel: 815-740-5041. Circulation Tel: 815-740-3690. Toll Free Tel: 800-726-6500. Web Site: library.stfrancis.edu, stfrancis.edu/academics/usf-library. *Dir, Libr Serv,* Brigette Bell; Tel: 815-740-3447, E-mail: bbell@stfrancis.edu; *Mgr, Ref & Instruction,* Kathleen Gomez; Tel: 815-740-5061, E-mail: kgomez@stfrancis.edu; *Circ Supvr,* Ruth Nelson; *Acq Spec,* Kathy Lindgren; E-mail: klindgren@stfrancis.edu
Founded 1930. Enrl 4,209; Highest Degree: Master
Library Holdings: Bk Vols 110,000; Per Subs 700
Special Collections: Contemporary Business Ethics
Subject Interests: Franciscans, Nursing
Automation Activity & Vendor Info: (Cataloging) Ex Libris Group; (Circulation) Ex Libris Group; (OPAC) Ex Libris Group; (Serials) Ex Libris Group
Wireless access
Mem of Reaching Across Illinois Library System (RAILS)
Partic in Consortium of Academic & Research Libraries in Illinois; Library & Information Resources Network; LIBRAS, Inc; OCLC Online Computer Library Center, Inc; SMRHEC
Open Mon-Thurs (Spring-Fall) 7:30am-10pm, Fri 7:30-4, Sun 3-10; Mon-Thurs (Summer) 9-5, Fri 9:30-4:30

L WILL COUNTY LAW LIBRARY*, 14 W Jefferson St, 4th Flr, 60432-4300. SAN 373-0484. Tel: 815-774-7887. FAX: 815-727-8785. E-mail: lawlib@willcountyillinois.com. Web Site: www.willcountycourts.com/law-library-main. *Librn,* Jeane Fillipitch; E-mail: jfillipitch@willcountyillinois.com; *Asst Librn,* Diane Brandolino
Open Mon-Fri 8:30-4:30

JONESBORO

P JONESBORO PUBLIC LIBRARY*, 412 S Main St, 62952. SAN 304-3010. Tel: 618-833-8121. FAX: 618-833-8121. E-mail: jonesborolibrary@frontier.com. *Librn,* Karen Hallam
Pop 1,853; Circ 4,269
Library Holdings: Bk Vols 8,000
Wireless access
Mem of Illinois Heartland Library System
Open Tues-Sat 1-5

JUSTICE

P JUSTICE PUBLIC LIBRARY DISTRICT*, 7641 Oak Grove Ave, 60458. SAN 320-474X. Tel: 708-496-1790. FAX: 708-496-1898. E-mail: jplonline@yahoo.com. Web Site: justicepubliclibrary.com. *Dir,* Juanita Durkin
Founded 1978. Pop 13,707; Circ 24,450
Library Holdings: Audiobooks 1,100; AV Mats 1,420; Bk Titles 47,123; Per Subs 81
Automation Activity & Vendor Info: (Cataloging) SirsiDynix-WorkFlows; (Circulation) SirsiDynix-WorkFlows; (ILL) SirsiDynix-WorkFlows; (OPAC) SirsiDynix
Wireless access
Function: 24/7 Electronic res, After school storytime, Audiobks via web, Bks on CD, Computers for patron use, Digital talking bks, Electronic databases & coll, ILL available, Internet access, Life-long learning prog for all ages, Magazines, Movies, Museum passes, Music CDs, Notary serv, Online cat, Online ref, OverDrive digital audio bks, Photocopying/Printing, Preschool reading prog, Printer for laptops & handheld devices, Prog for adults, Prog for children & young adult, Summer & winter reading prog, Tax forms
Publications: Cover to Cover (Newsletter)
Mem of Reaching Across Illinois Library System (RAILS)
Partic in System Wide Automated Network
Open Mon-Thurs 9:30-8, Fri & Sat 9:30-5

KAMPSVILLE

S CENTER FOR AMERICAN ARCHEOLOGY*, Research Library, 100 Broadway, 62053. SAN 371-165X. Tel: 618-653-4316. FAX: 618-653-4232. E-mail: caa@caa-archeology.org, museum@caa-archeology.org. Web Site: www.caa-archeology.org. *Exec Dir,* Jason L King, PhD; E-mail: jking@caa-archeology.org
Library Holdings: Bk Vols 1,000
Restriction: Not open to pub

KANEVILLE

P KANEVILLE PUBLIC LIBRARY DISTRICT*, 2S101 Harter Rd, 60144. (Mail add: PO Box 29, 60144-0029), SAN 304-3029. Tel: 630-557-2441. FAX: 630-557-2553. E-mail: info@kanevillelibrary.org. Web Site: www.kanevillelibrary.org. Staff 3 (MLS 3)
Founded 1934. Pop 1,367; Circ 9,750
Library Holdings: Audiobooks 739; Bks on Deafness & Sign Lang 14; DVDs 753; e-books 87,000; Large Print Bks 1,056; Bk Titles 18,765; Bk Vols 23,459; Per Subs 41; Videos 876
Subject Interests: Fiction, Local hist
Automation Activity & Vendor Info: (Cataloging) SirsiDynix; (Circulation) SirsiDynix; (OPAC) SirsiDynix
Wireless access
Function: 24/7 Online cat, Audio & video playback equip for onsite use, Audiobks via web, Bks on CD, CD-ROM, Children's prog, Computers for patron use, Doc delivery serv, Family literacy, Free DVD rentals, Holiday prog, ILL available, Internet access, Magazines, Mail & tel request accepted, Movies, Museum passes, Music CDs, Online cat, Online ref, Photocopying/Printing, Preschool outreach, Prof lending libr, Prog for adults, Prog for children & young adult, Ref & res, Ref serv available, Res assist avail, Story hour, Telephone ref, Wheelchair accessible
Mem of Reaching Across Illinois Library System (RAILS)
Partic in System Wide Automated Network
Open Mon 10-6, Tues & Thurs 2-7, Wed 10-7, Fri 10-4, Sat 10-2
Friends of the Library Group

KANKAKEE

M AMITA HEALTH SAINT MARY'S HOSPITAL*, Medical Library, 500 W Court St, 60901. SAN 375-9466. Tel: 815-937-2400, 815-937-2477. FAX: 815-937-2466. *Librn,* Bonnie Arnold; E-mail: bonita.arnold@amitahealth.org
Library Holdings: Bk Titles 200
Wireless access

J KANKAKEE COMMUNITY COLLEGE*, Harold & Jean Miner Memorial Library, 100 College Dr, 60901-6505. SAN 304-3045. Tel: 815-802-8400. Reference Tel: 815-802-8403. Administration Tel: 815-802-8405. FAX: 815-802-8101. E-mail: library@kcc.edu. Web Site: www.kcc.edu/library. *Dir,* Karen Becker; E-mail: kbecker@kcc.edu; *Librn,* Tracy Connor; E-mail: tconnor@kcc.edu; *Circ Serv,* Barbara Loudy; Tel: 815-802-8404, E-mail: bloudy@kcc.edu; Staff 6 (MLS 2, Non-MLS 4)
Founded 1966. Enrl 3,000; Highest Degree: Associate
Jul 2012-Jun 2013. Mats Exp $105,825, Books $37,000, Per/Ser (Incl. Access Fees) $17,000, AV Mat $7,325, Electronic Ref Mat (Incl. Access Fees) $44,500. Sal $134,602 (Prof $98,992)
Library Holdings: Bk Vols 34,000; Per Subs 100
Special Collections: Gordon Graves Environmental Coll; Reece L Ayers Soil & Water Conservation Coll
Automation Activity & Vendor Info: (Acquisitions) Baker & Taylor; (Cataloging) Ex Libris Group; (Circulation) Ex Libris Group; (Course Reserve) Ex Libris Group; (ILL) Ex Libris Group; (OPAC) Ex Libris Group; (Serials) Ex Libris Group
Wireless access
Mem of Reaching Across Illinois Library System (RAILS)
Partic in Consortium of Academic & Research Libraries in Illinois; Network of Illinois Learning Resources in Community Colleges
Open Mon-Thurs 7am-8pm, Fri 7-4

S KANKAKEE COUNTY HISTORICAL SOCIETY MUSEUM LIBRARY*, 801 S Eighth Ave, 60901-4744. SAN 304-3053. Tel: 815-932-5279. E-mail: kankakeecountymuseum@gmail.com. Web Site: www.kankakeecountymuseum.com/research.html. *Exec Dir,* Connie Licon; E-mail: connielicon.k3museum@gmail.com; *Research Coordr,* Jorie Walters; E-mail: joriewalters.k3musuem@gmail.com
Founded 1906
Library Holdings: Bk Vols 3,500
Special Collections: Biographies; County History; Documents Coll; History of County Townships, bks, photog; Letters Coll; Manuscripts Coll
Subject Interests: Hist
Publications: Newsletter (Quarterly)
Restriction: In-house use for visitors, Open by appt only

P KANKAKEE PUBLIC LIBRARY*, 201 E Merchant St, 60901. SAN 304-3061. Tel: 815-939-4564. Circulation Tel: 815-937-6901. FAX: 815-939-9057. Web Site: www.lions-online.org. *Dir,* Stephen Bertrand; E-mail: sbertrand@lions-online.org; *Asst Dir,* Allison Beasley; E-mail: abeasley@lions-online.org; *Adult Serv Supvr,* Vicki Forquer; E-mail:

vforquer@lions-online.org; *Circ Supvr,* Desnee Thompson; E-mail: dthompson@lions-online.org
Founded 1899. Pop 27,491; Circ 96,000
Library Holdings: Bk Vols 90,000; Per Subs 250
Subject Interests: Genealogy
Automation Activity & Vendor Info: (Acquisitions) SirsiDynix; (Cataloging) SirsiDynix; (Circulation) SirsiDynix; (ILL) SirsiDynix; (OPAC) SirsiDynix; (Serials) SirsiDynix
Publications: Between the Lions Newsletter (Bimonthly)
Mem of Reaching Across Illinois Library System (RAILS)
Open Mon-Thurs 9-9, Fri 9-6, Sat 9-5, Sun (Sept-May) 1-5
Friends of the Library Group

P LIMESTONE TOWNSHIP LIBRARY DISTRICT*, 2701 W Tower Rd, 60901. Tel: 815-939-1696. FAX: 815-939-1748. E-mail: info@limestonelibrary.org. Web Site: www.limestonelibrary.org. *Dir,* Lynne Noffke
Automation Activity & Vendor Info: (Acquisitions) Innovative Interfaces, Inc
Wireless access
Function: Bk club(s), Children's prog, Computer training, Computers for patron use, Free DVD rentals, ILL available, Notary serv, OverDrive digital audio bks, Photocopying/Printing, Prog for adults, Prog for children & young adult, Scanner, Story hour, Summer & winter reading prog, Tax forms, Teen prog
Mem of Reaching Across Illinois Library System (RAILS)
Open Mon-Thurs 10-8, Fri 10-5, Sat 10-3
Friends of the Library Group

KANSAS

P KANSAS COMMUNITY MEMORIAL LIBRARY*, 107 N Front St, 61933. (Mail add: PO Box 365, 61933), SAN 304-3096. Tel: 217-948-5484. FAX: 217-948-5484. E-mail: kansaslibrary@mediacombb.net. Web Site: www.kansaslibrary.jigsy.com. *Librn,* Toni Brandenburg; *Librn,* Cassandra Nichols; E-mail: kansaslibrary1@gmail.com
Founded 1932. Pop 1,114; Circ 9,173
Library Holdings: Bk Vols 10,087; Per Subs 16
Wireless access
Mem of Illinois Heartland Library System
Open Mon & Wed-Fri 1-5, Tues 10-5, Sat 10-Noon

KENILWORTH

S KENILWORTH HISTORICAL SOCIETY*, Kilner Library, 415 Kenilworth Ave, 60043-1134. SAN 304-310X. Tel: 847-251-2565. E-mail: kenilworthhistory@sbcglobal.net. Web Site: www.kenilworthhistory.org. *Curator,* Kyle Mathers; E-mail: kenilworthhistory@sbcglobal.net
Founded 1972
Library Holdings: Bk Titles 665; Bk Vols 674
Special Collections: Photograph Coll
Function: Archival coll
Open Mon 9-4:30, Thurs 9-12
Restriction: Access at librarian's discretion

KEWANEE

S ILLINOIS DEPARTMENT OF CORRECTIONS*, Kewanee Life Skills Reentry Center Library, 2021 Kentville Rd, 61443. Tel: 309-852-4601. FAX: 309-852-4617. Web Site: www2.illinois.gov/idoc/facilities/Pages/KewaneeLifeSkillsReentryCenter.aspx. *Librn,* Ms C Coulter
Library Holdings: Bk Vols 5,561
Restriction: Not open to pub

P KEWANEE PUBLIC LIBRARY DISTRICT*, 102 S Tremont St, 61443. SAN 304-3126. Tel: 309-852-4505. FAX: 309-852-4466. Administration FAX: 309-856-8445. Reference E-mail: reference@kewaneelibrary.org. Web Site: www.kewaneelibrary.org. *Libr Dir,* Barbara E Love; E-mail: loveb@kewaneelibrary.org; *Head, Circ,* Sarah Arnold; E-mail: arnolds@kewaneelibrary.org; *Head, Info Serv,* Ann Turnbull; E-mail: turnbulla@kewaneelibrary.org; *Head, Tech Serv,* Amy Gould; E-mail: goulda@kewaneelibrary.org; *Head, Youth Serv,* Sara Billiet; E-mail: billiets@kewaneelibrary.org; Staff 16 (MLS 1, Non-MLS 15)
Founded 1875. Pop 14,501; Circ 104,389
Library Holdings: AV Mats 7,553; High Interest/Low Vocabulary Bk Vols 451; Large Print Bks 1,463; Bk Vols 57,457; Per Subs 175; Talking Bks 2,218
Special Collections: Genealogy (Henry County Genealogical Coll); Local History
Automation Activity & Vendor Info: (Circulation) SirsiDynix-WorkFlows; (ILL) OCLC; (OPAC) SirsiDynix
Wireless access
Function: 24/7 Electronic res, 24/7 Online cat, Adult bk club, Audiobks on Playaways & MP3, Audiobks via web, Bilingual assistance for Spanish patrons, Bk club(s), Bks on CD, Children's prog, Computers for patron use, Digital talking bks, E-Reserves, Electronic databases & coll, Free DVD rentals, Genealogy discussion group, Holiday prog, Homebound delivery serv, ILL available, Internet access, Laminating, Magazines, Magnifiers for reading, Meeting rooms, Microfiche/film & reading machines, Music CDs, Online cat, Online ref, OverDrive digital audio bks, Photocopying/Printing, Prog for adults, Prog for children & young adult, Ref serv available, Spanish lang bks, Story hour, Study rm, Summer reading prog, Tax forms, Teen prog, Wheelchair accessible
Publications: Between the Lines (Newsletter)
Mem of Reaching Across Illinois Library System (RAILS)
Partic in Resource Sharing Alliance
Open Mon-Thurs (Winter) 9-7, Fri 9-6, Sat 9-1; Mon-Fri (Summer) 9-6, Sat 9-1
Friends of the Library Group

KINMUNDY

P KINMUNDY PUBLIC LIBRARY*, 111 S Monroe St, 62854. (Mail add: PO Box 85, 62854-0085). Tel: 618-547-3250. FAX: 618-547-3258. E-mail: kinmundylibrary@yahoo.com. *Librn,* Alecia Cooper
Pop 892
Library Holdings: Audiobooks 132; DVDs 171; Large Print Bks 200; Bk Titles 19,930; Per Subs 5; Spec Interest Per Sub 1; Videos 100
Wireless access
Mem of Illinois Heartland Library System
Open Mon 9-12 & 1-5, Tues-Fri 1-5, Sat 9-Noon

KIRKLAND

P KIRKLAND PUBLIC LIBRARY*, 513 W Main St, 60146. (Mail add: PO Box 89, 60146), SAN 304-3142. Tel: 815-522-6260. FAX: 815-522-6260. E-mail: kirklandlib@hotmail.com. Web Site: kirklandpubliclibrary.org. *Dir,* Linda Fett; *Asst Librn,* Janet Miller; *Asst Librn,* Martha Valasek; Staff 1 (Non-MLS 1)
Founded 1920. Pop 1,166; Circ 11,000
Library Holdings: High Interest/Low Vocabulary Bk Vols 56; Bk Vols 12,629; Per Subs 16
Automation Activity & Vendor Info: (Circulation) Follett Software
Function: ILL available
Mem of Reaching Across Illinois Library System (RAILS)
Special Services for the Deaf - TDD equip
Open Mon & Thurs 10-7, Tues & Wed 1-7, Sat 9-3
Friends of the Library Group

KNOXVILLE

P KNOXVILLE PUBLIC LIBRARY*, 200 E Main St, 61448-1351. SAN 304-3150. Tel: 309-289-2113. FAX: 309-289-8063. E-mail: kpl2@comcast.net. Web Site: www.knoxvillepubliclibrary.org. *Librn,* Michelle Walker
Founded 1878. Pop 2,911; Circ 21,716
Library Holdings: DVDs 200; Bk Vols 19,000; Per Subs 50
Wireless access
Open Mon-Thurs 11-6, Fri 10-5, Sat 11-3

LA GRANGE

M AMITA HEALTH*, Zitek Medical Library, 5101 Willow Springs Rd, 60525. SAN 304-3169. Tel: 708-245-7230. FAX: 708-245-5613. Web Site: www.keepingyouwell.com/care-services/library-services. *Dir,* Bonnie Arnold; E-mail: bonnie.arnold@ahss.org; Staff 2 (MLS 1, Non-MLS 1)
Founded 1956
Library Holdings: Bk Titles 600; Bk Vols 1,700; Per Subs 225
Subject Interests: Med, Nursing
Wireless access
Mem of Reaching Across Illinois Library System (RAILS)
Partic in Greater Midwest Regional Medical Libr Network; Illinois Library & Information Network; Medical Library Association; OCLC-LVIS
Open Mon-Thurs 8-5, Fri 8-4

R GRACE LUTHERAN CHURCH LIBRARY*, 200 N Catherine Ave, 60525-1826. (Mail add: PO Box 207, 60525-0207), SAN 304-3185. Tel: 708-352-0730. FAX: 708-352-0737. E-mail: administrator@gracelutheran-lg.org. *Librn,* Grace Puls; Staff 12 (MLS 1, Non-MLS 11)
Founded 1954
Library Holdings: Bk Vols 3,452
Subject Interests: Relig
Automation Activity & Vendor Info: (Cataloging) Follett Software
Open Thurs 10-1, Sun 8:30-12

P LA GRANGE PUBLIC LIBRARY*, Ten W Cossitt Ave, 60525. SAN 304-3193. Tel: 708-215-3200. Interlibrary Loan Service Tel: 708-215-3224. FAX: 708-352-1620. E-mail: lgref@lagrangelibrary.org. Web Site: www.lagrangelibrary.org. *Exec Dir,* Charity Gallardo; Tel: 708-215-3273,

E-mail: director@lagrangelibrary.org; *Ad,* Jeanne Jesernik; E-mail: jesernikj@lagrangelibrary.org; *Ad,* Kate Lagerstrom; E-mail: lagerstromk@lagrangelibrary.org; *Ad,* Kenny Tymick; E-mail: tymickk@lagrangelibrary.org; *Ch Serv Librn,* Laura Goldsborough; E-mail: goldsboroughl@lagrangelibrary.org; *Adult & Teen Serv Mgr,* Debbie Darwine; Tel: 708-215-3223, E-mail: darwined@lagrangelibrary.org; *Ch Mgr,* Rachael Dabkey; Tel: 708-215-3212, E-mail: dabkeyr@lagrangelibrary.org; *Coll Serv Mgr,* Rebecca Bartlett; Tel: 708-215-3240, E-mail: bartlettr@lagrangelibrary.org; *Mgr, Mem Serv,* Leslie Hartoonian; Tel: 708-215-3206, E-mail: hartoonianl@lagrangelibrary.org; *Asst Mgr, Adult Serv, Teen Serv,* Lisa Sharkey; Tel: 708-215-3228, E-mail: sharkeyl@lagrangelibrary.org; *Asst Mgr, Ch Serv,* Patti Eaton; E-mail: eatonp@lagrangelibrary.org; *Adult Serv,* Jane Ruback; E-mail: rubackj@lagrangelibrary.org; Staff 12 (MLS 9, Non-MLS 3)
Founded 1905. Pop 15,550; Circ 293,567
May 2019-Apr 2020 Income $2,605,826, State $43,334, City $2,481,251, Locally Generated Income $31,241, Other $50,000. Mats Exp $293,560, Books $175,529, AV Mat $49,567, Electronic Ref Mat (Incl. Access Fees) $68,464. Sal $1,517,741
Library Holdings: CDs 7,472; DVDs 7,638; e-books 78,120; Bk Vols 83,802; Per Subs 241
Special Collections: Business
Subject Interests: Anime, Genealogy, Graphic novels, Local hist
Automation Activity & Vendor Info: (Acquisitions) SirsiDynix-WorkFlows; (Cataloging) SirsiDynix-WorkFlows; (Circulation) SirsiDynix-WorkFlows; (ILL) SirsiDynix-WorkFlows; (OPAC) SirsiDynix; (Serials) SirsiDynix-WorkFlows
Wireless access
Function: Art exhibits, Bk club(s), Bks on CD, Children's prog, Computer training, Computers for patron use, E-Readers, Electronic databases & coll, Equip loans & repairs, Free DVD rentals, Holiday prog, ILL available, Internet access, Life-long learning prog for all ages, Magazines, Mango lang, Meeting rooms, Microfiche/film & reading machines, Movies, Museum passes, Music CDs, Online cat, Outside serv via phone, mail, e-mail & web, OverDrive digital audio bks, Photocopying/Printing, Preschool outreach, Preschool reading prog, Printer for laptops & handheld devices, Prog for adults, Prog for children & young adult, Ref serv available, Scanner, Spanish lang bks, Spoken cassettes & CDs, Story hour, Study rm, Summer & winter reading prog, Summer reading prog, Tax forms, Teen prog, Telephone ref, Wheelchair accessible, Winter reading prog, Writing prog
Publications: BookNews (Online only); The Book Report (Newsletter)
Mem of Reaching Across Illinois Library System (RAILS)
Partic in System Wide Automated Network
Special Services for the Blind - Braille bks; Large print bks; Large screen computer & software; Low vision equip; Reader equip
Open Mon-Fri 9-9, Sat 9-5, Sun (Sept-May) 1-5
Friends of the Library Group

LA GRANGE PARK

P LA GRANGE PARK PUBLIC LIBRARY DISTRICT*, 555 N LaGrange Rd, 60526-5644. SAN 304-3215. Tel: 708-352-0100. Web Site: www.lplibrary.org. *Exec Dir,* Kate Buckson; E-mail: kateb@lplibrary.org; *Dir, Adult Serv,* Gabriel Oppenheim; E-mail: gabe@lplibrary.org; *Dir, Ch Serv,* Rose Hopkins-LaRocco; E-mail: rose@lplibrary.org; *Dir of Circ, Dir, Tech Serv,* Maureen Sill; E-mail: maureen@lplibrary.org; Staff 6 (MLS 5, Non-MLS 1)
Founded 1975. Pop 13,295; Circ 141,024
Library Holdings: Bk Vols 70,434; Per Subs 204; Videos 3,228
Automation Activity & Vendor Info: (Cataloging) Innovative Interfaces, Inc; (Circulation) Innovative Interfaces, Inc
Wireless access
Publications: Newsletter (Quarterly)
Mem of Reaching Across Illinois Library System (RAILS)
Partic in System Wide Automated Network
Open Mon-Thurs 10-9, Fri & Sat 10-5, Sun 1-5
Friends of the Library Group

LA HARPE

P LA HARPE CARNEGIE PUBLIC LIBRARY DISTRICT*, 209 E Main St, 61450. (Mail add: PO Box 506, 61450-0506), SAN 304-3223. Tel: 217-659-7729. FAX: 217-659-7735. E-mail: laharpelibrary@gmail.com. Web Site: www.laharpelibrary.com. *Libr Dir,* Mr Terry Brandt; E-mail: laharpelibrary@gmail.com; *Asst Dir,* Sherri Swanson; E-mail: laharpelibrary@gmail.com
Founded 1890. Pop 2,249; Circ 15,280
Library Holdings: Bk Vols 18,000; Per Subs 32
Special Collections: Hancock County Quill 1893-1982 (weekly newsp)
Automation Activity & Vendor Info: (Circulation) CARL.Solution (TLC)
Function: Homebound delivery serv, ILL available, Internet access, Photocopying/Printing, Prog for adults, Prog for children & young adult, Summer reading prog
Mem of Reaching Across Illinois Library System (RAILS)
Open Mon & Tues 9-5, Wed 12-5, Thurs & Sat 9-12

LACON

P LACON PUBLIC LIBRARY DISTRICT*, 205 Sixth St, 61540. SAN 304-3266. Tel: 309-246-2855. FAX: 309-246-4047. E-mail: laconlib@gmail.com. Web Site: laconlibrary.wordpress.com. *Dir,* Elizabeth Reed; Staff 1 (Non-MLS 1)
Founded 1839. Pop 1,979; Circ 25,796
Library Holdings: Audiobooks 670; CDs 115; DVDs 2,822; e-books 4,492; Large Print Bks 852; Bk Titles 10,997; Per Subs 54; Videos 35
Subject Interests: Local hist
Wireless access
Function: ILL available, Photocopying/Printing, Summer reading prog, Tax forms
Mem of Reaching Across Illinois Library System (RAILS)
Partic in RSA
Open Mon & Wed 1-7, Fri 10-5, Sat 9-1

S MARSHALL COUNTY HISTORICAL SOCIETY LIBRARY*, 314 Fifth St, 61540. (Mail add: PO Box 123, 61540-0123), SAN 374-9371. Tel: 309-246-2349. E-mail: marshallcountyhistory@gmail.com.
Founded 1956
Library Holdings: Bk Vols 525
Special Collections: Doll Coll; Lincoln Coll
Subject Interests: Genealogy, Local hist
Publications: Reflections (Newsletter)
Open Mon, Wed & Sat 9-Noon
Restriction: Non-circulating, Ref only

LADD

P LADD PUBLIC LIBRARY DISTRICT*, 125 N Main St, 61329. (Mail add: PO Box 307, 61329-0307), SAN 304-3274. Tel: 815-894-3254. FAX: 815-894-3254. E-mail: ladd_library@frontier.com. *Dir,* Noah Hollinger; *Asst Librn,* Paula Corpus; *Asst Librn,* Ann King; Staff 3 (Non-MLS 3)
Founded 1930. Pop 1,684; Circ 8,088
Library Holdings: Bk Vols 7,000
Special Collections: Library of America Coll
Wireless access
Function: Adult bk club, After school storytime, Bk club(s), Bks on cassette, Bks on CD, Children's prog, Computers for patron use, ILL available, Magnifiers for reading, Music CDs, Online cat, Photocopying/Printing, Prog for adults, Prog for children & young adult, Story hour, Summer reading prog, Tax forms, VHS videos, Wheelchair accessible
Mem of Reaching Across Illinois Library System (RAILS)
Open Mon & Tues 10-7, Wed 3-7, Fri 10-6, Sat 9-1

LAFAYETTE

P IRA C REED PUBLIC LIBRARY*, 302 Commercial St, 61449. (Mail add: PO Box 185, 61449-0185), SAN 304-3282. Tel: 309-995-3042. FAX: 309-995-3042. E-mail: irclibrary@mymctc.net. *Dir,* Judy King; *Librn,* Marcine Rashid; Staff 3 (Non-MLS 3)
Founded 1909. Pop 227
Library Holdings: Large Print Bks 50; Bk Vols 8,355; Per Subs 12; Videos 250
Subject Interests: Local hist
Wireless access
Open Mon-Thurs 12-7, Fri 12-5:30

LAKE BLUFF

P LAKE BLUFF PUBLIC LIBRARY*, 123 E Scranton Ave, 60044. SAN 304-3290. Tel: 847-234-2540. FAX: 847-234-2649. Web Site: www.lakeblufflibrary.org. *Libr Dir,* Eric Bailey; E-mail: ebailey@lakeblufflibrary.org; *Head, Adult Serv,* Martha Cordeniz O'Hara; *Head, Youth Serv,* Eliza Jarvi; Staff 3 (MLS 3)
Founded 1926. Pop 6,056; Circ 71,752
Library Holdings: AV Mats 3,883; e-books 2,426; Bk Vols 47,101; Per Subs 130
Automation Activity & Vendor Info: (Cataloging) TLC (The Library Corporation); (Circulation) TLC (The Library Corporation); (OPAC) TLC (The Library Corporation)
Wireless access
Function: Adult bk club, Bk club(s), Bks on cassette, Bks on CD, Children's prog, Computers for patron use, Electronic databases & coll, Music CDs, Online cat, Online ref, Photocopying/Printing, Preschool outreach, Prog for adults, Prog for children & young adult, Scanner, Summer reading prog, Tax forms, VHS videos, Wheelchair accessible, Workshops
Publications: Quarterly newsletter
Open Mon-Thurs 10-9, Fri 10-6, Sat 10-5, Sun (Sept-May) 1-5
Friends of the Library Group

LAKE FOREST

C LAKE FOREST COLLEGE, Donnelley & Lee Library, 555 N Sheridan Rd, 60045. SAN 340-4978. Tel: 847-735-5056. FAX: 847-735-6297. E-mail: library@lakeforest.edu. Web Site: www.lakeforest.edu/library. *Interim Dir,* Kimberly Hazlett; Tel: 847-735-5063, E-mail: hazlett@lakeforest.edu; *Head, Access Serv, Head, Outreach Serv,* Patrick Hussey; Tel: 847-735-5061, E-mail: phussey@lakeforest.edu; *Cat & Acq,* Eileen Karsten; Tel: 847-735-5066, E-mail: karsten@lakeforest.edu; *Electronic Res Librn, Syst Librn,* Steve Gladwin; Tel: 847-735-5065, E-mail: sgladwin@lakeforest.edu; *Student Success Librn,* Zohra Saulat; E-mail: zsaulat@lakeforest.edu; *ILL Coordr,* Michael Karsten; Tel: 847-735-5062, E-mail: mkarsten@lakeforest.edu; Staff 7 (MLS 5, Non-MLS 2)
Founded 1857. Enrl 1,560; Fac 110; Highest Degree: Master
Library Holdings: Bk Titles 240,000; Per Subs 1,000
Special Collections: Capt Joseph Medill Patterson Papers (NY Daily News Coll); Humanities, Rare Books (Hamill Coll); Printing History, Western Americana (O'Kieffe); Railroad (Elliott Donnelley, Munson Paddock & James Sloss Colls); Scotland (Stuart Coll); Theatre (Garrett Leverton Papers. US Document Depository
Automation Activity & Vendor Info: (Acquisitions) Ex Libris Group; (Cataloging) Ex Libris Group; (Circulation) Ex Libris Group; (OPAC) Ex Libris Group
Wireless access
Partic in Center for Research Libraries; Consortium of Academic & Research Libraries in Illinois; LIBRAS, Inc; Oberlin Group
Open Mon-Thurs 7:30am-11pm, Fri 7:30-4:30, Sun 2-11

P LAKE FOREST LIBRARY, 360 E Deerpath Rd, 60045-2252. SAN 304-3312. Tel: 847-234-0636. Circulation Tel: 847-810-4600. Web Site: www.lakeforestlibrary.org. *Exec Dir,* Catherine A Lemmer; Tel: 847-810-4602, E-mail: clemmer@lakeforestlibrary.org; *Asst Dir, Head, Adult Serv,* Felicia Song; Tel: 847-810-4611, E-mail: fsong@lakeforestlibrary.org; *Operations Dir,* Ed Finn, III; E-mail: efinn@lakeforestlibrary.org; *Head, Children's & Teen Serv,* Lorie Rohrer; Tel: 847-810-4616, E-mail: lrohrer@lakeforestlibrary.org; *Head, Circ,* Tori Sergel; Tel: 847-810-4616, E-mail: tsergel@lakeforestlibrary.org; *Youth & Teen Serv Librn,* Emily Neal; E-mail: eneal@lakeforestlibrary.org; *Adult Serv Mgr,* Kate Buckardt; Tel: 847-810-4613, E-mail: kbuckardt@lakeforestlibrary.org; Staff 14 (MLS 14)
Founded 1898. Pop 19,375; Circ 450,876
May 2021-Apr 2022 Income $4,387,766, State $49,000, City $4,703,816, Locally Generated Income $30,950. Mats Exp $604,500, Books $210,000, Per/Ser (Incl. Access Fees) $21,000, AV Mat $100,000, Electronic Ref Mat (Incl. Access Fees) $195,000. Sal $1,808,504
Library Holdings: Audiobooks 5,231; AV Mats 25,138; CDs 5,543; DVDs 10,758; e-books 26,738; Electronic Media & Resources 58; Bk Vols 94,164; Per Subs 329
Subject Interests: Art & archit, Gardening, Local hist
Automation Activity & Vendor Info: (Acquisitions) Innovative Interfaces, Inc. - Polaris; (Cataloging) Innovative Interfaces, Inc. - Polaris; (Circulation) Innovative Interfaces, Inc. - Polaris; (ILL) OCLC; (OPAC) Innovative Interfaces, Inc. - Polaris
Wireless access
Publications: Beyond Words (Quarterly newsletter)
Partic in Cooperative Computer Services - CCS; OCLC Online Computer Library Center, Inc
Special Services for the Deaf - TDD equip
Special Services for the Blind - Assistive/Adapted tech devices, equip & products
Open Mon-Thurs 9-9, Fri 9-6, Sat 9-5, Sun 1-5
Friends of the Library Group

LAKE ZURICH

P ELA AREA PUBLIC LIBRARY DISTRICT*, 275 Mohawk Trail, 60047. SAN 304-3347. Tel: 847-438-3433. FAX: 847-438-9290. TDD: 847-438-3799. E-mail: administration@eapl.org. Web Site: www.eapl.org. *Exec Dir,* ; *Asst Dir,* Erica Christianson; *Head, Circ,* Lori Sollenberger; *Head, Digital Serv,* Michelle Bourgeois; *Head, Info Tech,* Chris Pedersen; *Head, Ref,* Melissa Keegan; *Head, Tech Serv,* Michelle Walters; *Head, Youth Serv,* Natalie Ziarnik; *ILL,* Laurie White; Staff 21 (MLS 20, Non-MLS 1)
Founded 1972. Pop 32,000; Circ 834,316
Library Holdings: AV Mats 38,336; Large Print Bks 6,824; Bk Vols 184,110; Per Subs 150
Automation Activity & Vendor Info: (Acquisitions) Innovative Interfaces, Inc; (Cataloging) Innovative Interfaces, Inc; (Circulation) Innovative Interfaces, Inc; (OPAC) Innovative Interfaces, Inc
Publications: Footnotes (Newsletter)
Partic in Cooperative Computer Services - CCS
Special Services for the Deaf - TDD equip
Open Mon-Thurs 9-9, Fri 9-6, Sat 9-5, Sun 12-5
Friends of the Library Group

LAMOILLE

P LAMOILLE-CLARION PUBLIC LIBRARY DISTRICT*, 81 Main St, 61330. (Mail add: PO Box 260, 61330-0260), SAN 304-3231. Tel: 815-638-2356. FAX: 815-638-2356. E-mail: llibrary@live.com. *Dir,* Vanessa Zimmerlein; Staff 2 (Non-MLS 2)
Founded 1973. Pop 1,964; Circ 9,038
Library Holdings: DVDs 150; Large Print Bks 175; Bk Titles 16,393; Per Subs 52; Videos 621
Special Collections: Oral History
Wireless access
Mem of Reaching Across Illinois Library System (RAILS)
Open Mon & Wed 12-6, Tues & Fri 10-12 & 1-5, Thurs 1-5, Sat 10-3

LANARK

P LANARK PUBLIC LIBRARY*, 1118 S Broad St, 61046. SAN 304-3355. Tel: 815-493-2166. FAX: 815-493-2166. E-mail: lanarklibrary1@gmail.com. Web Site: lanarkil.gov/lanark-public-library. *Dir,* Janie Dollinger
Founded 1957. Pop 1,583; Circ 16,000
Library Holdings: Large Print Bks 700; Bk Vols 25,000; Per Subs 40; Talking Bks 500
Subject Interests: Genealogy, Local hist
Automation Activity & Vendor Info: (Circulation) Follett Software
Wireless access
Mem of Reaching Across Illinois Library System (RAILS)
Special Services for the Deaf - TDD equip
Open Tues, Wed & Fri 12-5, Thurs 12-7:30, Sat 10-3
Friends of the Library Group

LANSING

P LANSING PUBLIC LIBRARY*, 2750 Indiana Ave, 60438. SAN 304-3363. Tel: 708-474-2447. FAX: 708-474-9466. E-mail: support@lansingpl.org. Web Site: www.lansingpl.org. *Dir,* Debbie Albrecht; E-mail: debbie@lansingpl.org; Staff 12 (MLS 3, Non-MLS 9)
Founded 1936. Pop 28,131; Circ 215,440
Library Holdings: Bk Titles 150,000; Per Subs 195
Automation Activity & Vendor Info: (Acquisitions) SirsiDynix; (Cataloging) SirsiDynix; (Circulation) SirsiDynix; (OPAC) SirsiDynix; (Serials) SirsiDynix
Wireless access
Mem of Reaching Across Illinois Library System (RAILS)
Partic in State of Iowa Libraries Online; System Wide Automated Network
Open Mon-Thurs 9-8, Fri & Sat 9-5, Sun 11-8
Friends of the Library Group

LASALLE

S CARUS CHEMICAL CO*, Research Library, 1500 Eighth St, 61301-3500. SAN 375-9938. Tel: 815-224-6886. FAX: 815-224-6896. Web Site: www.caruscorporation.com. *Tech Info Spec,* Marsha Shepard; E-mail: marsha.shepard@caruschem.com
Library Holdings: Bk Titles 1,400; Per Subs 20
Mem of Reaching Across Illinois Library System (RAILS)
Restriction: Staff use only

P LASALLE PUBLIC LIBRARY*, 305 Marquette St, 61301. SAN 304-324X. Tel: 815-223-2341. FAX: 815-223-2353. Web Site: www.lasalle.lib.il.us. *Dir,* Cristy Stupegia; E-mail: cstupegia@lasalle.lib.il.us; *Youth Serv Librn,* Donna Blomquist; E-mail: dmblomquist@lasalle.lib.il.us; Staff 7 (MLS 2, Non-MLS 5)
Founded 1907. Pop 9,796
Library Holdings: Bk Vols 50,000; Per Subs 20
Special Collections: Local (LaSalle-Peru) History Materials & Original Documents Regarding History of Library; Spanish/Bilingual Coll
Automation Activity & Vendor Info: (Circulation) Innovative Interfaces, Inc - Sierra
Wireless access
Mem of Reaching Across Illinois Library System (RAILS)
Open Mon & Wed 9-6, Tues & Thurs 9-8, Fri & Sat 9-5

LAWRENCEVILLE

P LAWRENCE PUBLIC LIBRARY DISTRICT*, 814 12th St, 62439. SAN 304-3371. Tel: 618-943-3016. FAX: 618-943-3215. E-mail: lawrencepubliclibrary@yahoo.com. Web Site: www.lawpubliclibrary.org. *Libr Dir,* Theresa Marie Tucker; *Asst Dir,* Joyce Abel
Founded 1921. Pop 15,452; Circ 66,702
Library Holdings: Bk Vols 40,000; Per Subs 8; Talking Bks 700; Videos 900
Automation Activity & Vendor Info: (Acquisitions) Baker & Taylor; (Cataloging) OCLC WorldShare Interlibrary Loan; (OPAC) Innovative Interfaces, Inc
Wireless access

Function: 24/7 Electronic res, 24/7 Online cat, Accelerated reader prog, Activity rm, Adult bk club, Archival coll, Art exhibits, AV serv, Bk club(s), Bks on CD, CD-ROM, Children's prog, Computers for patron use, Electronic databases & coll, Free DVD rentals, Holiday prog, ILL available, Internet access, Laminating, Life-long learning prog for all ages, Magazines, Meeting rooms, Microfiche/film & reading machines, Music CDs, Notary serv, Online cat, Photocopying/Printing, Preschool reading prog, Prog for adults, Prog for children & young adult, Ref & res, Ref serv available, Res performed for a fee, Scanner, Story hour, Study rm, Summer reading prog, Tax forms, Wheelchair accessible
Mem of Illinois Heartland Library System
Open Mon, Wed & Fri 10-5, Tues & Thurs 10-7, Sat 10-3
Restriction: Free to mem, ID required to use computers (Ltd hrs), In-house use for visitors, Non-resident fee
Friends of the Library Group

LEAF RIVER

P BERTOLET MEMORIAL LIBRARY DISTRICT*, 705 S Main St, 61047. (Mail add: PO Box 339, 61047-0339), SAN 324-5551. Tel: 815-738-2742. FAX: 815-738-2742. E-mail: bertolib@lrnet1.com. Web Site: www.bertoletmemoriallibrary.org. *Libr Dir,* Linda M Schreiber; Staff 1 (Non-MLS 1)
Founded 1981. Pop 2,145; Circ 9,180
Library Holdings: Bk Titles 8,624; Per Subs 25
Special Collections: Local History Coll, bks, diaries, ledgers
Wireless access
Mem of Reaching Across Illinois Library System (RAILS)
Open Mon-Thurs 10-7, Sat 8-12

LEBANON

P LEBANON PUBLIC LIBRARY*, 314 W Saint Louis St, 62254. SAN 304-3398. Tel: 618-537-4504. FAX: 618-537-4399. Web Site: lebanonpubliclibrary.org. *Dir,* Ramona Witte; E-mail: lpldirector@gmail.com; Staff 6 (MLS 1, Non-MLS 5)
Founded 1946. Pop 3,523; Circ 13,655
Library Holdings: Bk Vols 15,000; Per Subs 35
Special Collections: Charles Dickens Coll
Mem of Illinois Heartland Library System
Partic in Midwest Collaborative for Library Services
Open Mon-Thurs 10-7, Fri 10-5, Sat 10-3

C MCKENDREE UNIVERSITY, Holman Library, 701 College Rd, 62254-1299. SAN 304-3401. Tel: 618-537-6950. Interlibrary Loan Service Tel: 618-537-6515. Reference Tel: 618-537-6952. Administration Tel: 618-537-6951. Toll Free Tel: 800-232-7228. FAX: 618-537-8411. Toll Free FAX: 800-537-6514. E-mail: libraryservices@mckendree.edu. Web Site: www.mckendree.edu/library. *Govt Doc & Tech Serv Librn, Libr Dir, Univ Archivist,* Deborah Houk; E-mail: djhouk@mckendree.edu; *Access Serv Librn,* Jennifer Funk; E-mail: jafunk@mckendree.edu; *Res & Instruction Librn,* Paul Worrell; Tel: 618-537-6514, E-mail: paworrell@mckendree.edu; *Libr Asst,* Kasandra Noble; Tel: 618-537-6558, E-mail: klnoble@mckendree.edu. Subject Specialists: *Computer sci, Soc sci,* Deborah Houk; *Commun, Lang,* Jennifer Funk; Staff 5 (MLS 4, Non-MLS 1)
Founded 1828. Enrl 2,292; Fac 86; Highest Degree: Doctorate
Library Holdings: AV Mats 5,000; DVDs 3,588; Bk Titles 52,977; Bk Vols 57,000; Per Subs 5
Special Collections: Abraham Lincoln (Warren Grauel Coll); Journalism, Illinois History & Literature (Irving Dilliard Coll). US Document Depository
Subject Interests: Computer sci, Educ, Humanities, Nursing, Soc sci & issues
Automation Activity & Vendor Info: (Acquisitions) Ex Libris Group; (Cataloging) Ex Libris Group; (Circulation) Ex Libris Group; (Course Reserve) Ex Libris Group; (ILL) OCLC; (OPAC) Ex Libris Group; (Serials) Ex Libris Group
Wireless access
Mem of Illinois Heartland Library System
Partic in Consortium of Academic & Research Libraries in Illinois; Saint Louis Regional Library Network; SILRC
Open Mon-Thurs 7am-Midnight, Fri 7-5, Sat 12-5, Sun 1pm-Midnight

LEMONT

S ARGONNE NATIONAL LABORATORY, Argonne Research Library, 9700 S Cass Ave, Bldg 240, 60439-4801. SAN 339-6878. Tel: 630-252-0007. Interlibrary Loan Service Tel: 630-252-4208. Administration Tel: 630-252-4275. FAX: 630-252-5024. Web Site: www.anl.gov/argonne-research-library. *Info & Libr Mgr,* Yvette N Woell; E-mail: ywoell@anl.gov; *Acq Librn,* Erika Weir; Tel: 630-252-4509, E-mail: eweir@anl.gov; *Digital Res Librn,* Megan Hertel; E-mail: mhertel@anl.gov; *Scholarly Communications Librn,* Mary Alice Buckley; E-mail: mbuckley@anl.gov; *Scholarly Communications Librn,* Nick Lundvick; E-mail: nlundvick@anl.gov; *Scholarly Communications Librn,* Laniece Miller; E-mail: lmiller@anl.gov; *Sci Librn,* James Thompson; E-mail: jthompson@anl.gov; *Libr Res Serv Mgr,* Mary Straka; Tel: 630-252-7770, E-mail: mstraka@anl.gov. Subject Specialists: *Engr, Mat sci, Physics,* Mary Straka; Staff 8 (MLS 7, Non-MLS 1)
Founded 1946
Oct 2020-Sept 2021. Mats Exp $4,000,000
Library Holdings: e-books 7,600; e-journals 13,000; Bk Titles 85,000
Special Collections: DOE/ERDA/AEC Technical Report
Subject Interests: Chem, Chem engr, Computer sci, Environ sci, Mat sci, Math, Microbiology, Nuclear sci, Physics, Transportation
Automation Activity & Vendor Info: (Acquisitions) Ex Libris Group; (Cataloging) Ex Libris Group; (Circulation) Ex Libris Group; (Discovery) Ex Libris Group; (OPAC) Ex Libris Group; (Serials) Ex Libris Group
Wireless access
Restriction: Badge access after hrs, Employees only

P LEMONT PUBLIC LIBRARY DISTRICT*, 50 E Wend St, 60439-6439. SAN 304-3428. Tel: 630-257-6541. FAX: 630-257-7737. E-mail: info@lemontlibrary.org. Web Site: www.lemontlibrary.org. *Dir,* Sandra Pointon; E-mail: spointon@lemontlibrary.org; Staff 5.5 (MLS 3.5, Non-MLS 2)
Founded 1943. Pop 22,017; Circ 158,876
Library Holdings: CDs 3,713; DVDs 4,707; Bk Vols 91,498; Per Subs 213
Automation Activity & Vendor Info: (Acquisitions) SirsiDynix
Wireless access
Function: Adult bk club; Bks on cassette, Bks on CD, CD-ROM, Children's prog, Computers for patron use, Homework prog, ILL available, Music CDs, Notary serv, Online cat, Online ref, Outreach serv, Photocopying/Printing, Prog for adults, Prog for children & young adult, Ref serv available, Scanner, Senior outreach, Story hour, Summer reading prog, Tax forms, Teen prog, Telephone ref, VHS videos, Wheelchair accessible
Publications: News For Kids (Newsletter); Read All About It (Newsletter)
Mem of Reaching Across Illinois Library System (RAILS)
Partic in Pinnacle Library Cooperative
Open Mon-Thurs 9-9, Fri & Sat 9-5, Sun 1-5
Restriction: Authorized patrons
Friends of the Library Group

LENA

P LENA COMMUNITY DISTRICT LIBRARY*, 300 W Mason St, 61048. SAN 304-3444. Tel: 815-369-3180. FAX: 815-369-3181. E-mail: lenalibrary@le-win.net. Web Site: villageoflena.com/residents/library. *Dir,* Brittany Gaulrapp; *Asst Librn, Ch,* Kathy Andrews; Staff 3 (Non-MLS 3)
Founded 1912. Pop 5,184; Circ 43,000
Library Holdings: Bk Titles 20,000; Per Subs 70
Special Collections: Lena Stars since 1871 (local newspapers for genealogy research, microfilm)
Subject Interests: Child welfare, Health sci, Hist, Relig
Wireless access
Mem of Reaching Across Illinois Library System (RAILS)
Open Mon & Thurs 12-9, Tues 9-5 & 7-9, Wed 9-5, Fri & Sat 9-3

LEROY

P J T & E J CRUMBAUGH MEMORIAL PUBLIC LIBRARY*, 405 E Center St, 61752-1723. (Mail add: PO Box 129, 61752-0129), SAN 304-338X. Tel: 309-962-3911. E-mail: jtejcrumbaughlibrary@hotmail.com. Web Site: www.crumbaugh.org. *Head Librn,* Denise Woltkamp; *Librn,* Kelly Stills
Founded 1927. Circ 39,797
Library Holdings: AV Mats 170; Bks on Deafness & Sign Lang 10; High Interest/Low Vocabulary Bk Vols 150; Large Print Bks 385; Bk Titles 14,000; Per Subs 30; Talking Bks 50
Special Collections: Local Cemetery Records; Spiritualist Section
Subject Interests: Fine arts, Genealogy, Hist, Local hist
Wireless access
Function: Archival coll, Res libr
Publications: J T & E J Crumbaugh Spiritualist Church & Memorial Library (history booklet); Tracing Your Roots (genealogy booklet)
Special Services for the Blind - Talking bks
Open Mon & Wed 9-7, Tues, Thurs & Fri 9-5, Sat 9-2

LEWISTOWN

P LEWISTOWN CARNEGIE PUBLIC LIBRARY DISTRICT, 1126 N Main St, 61542. SAN 304-3452. Tel: 309-547-2860. FAX: 309-547-2865. E-mail: lcpld1906@yahoo.com. Web Site: lewistowncarnegielibrary.com. *Dir,* Jaime Grove
Founded 1985. Pop 5,762; Circ 26,842
Library Holdings: Bk Vols 19,000; Per Subs 60
Subject Interests: Local hist
Open Mon, Tues, Thurs & Fri 9-5, Wed 12-8

LEXINGTON

P LEXINGTON PUBLIC LIBRARY DISTRICT*, 207 S Cedar St, 61753. SAN 304-3460. Tel: 309-365-7801. FAX: 309-365-9028. E-mail: lexingtonl@yahoo.com. Web Site: www.lexington.lib.il.us. *Dir,* Sherrie Patton
Founded 1896. Pop 3,000; Circ 33,500
Library Holdings: Audiobooks 600; CDs 468; DVDs 1,000; Large Print Bks 700; Bk Titles 25,000; Per Subs 80; Videos 500
Special Collections: Art prints, Library of America-Literacy Materials
Automation Activity & Vendor Info: (Acquisitions) SirsiDynix; (Cataloging) SirsiDynix-WorkFlows; (Circulation) SirsiDynix-WorkFlows; (ILL) OCLC FirstSearch; (OPAC) SirsiDynix-WorkFlows
Wireless access
Function: Bks on CD, CD-ROM, Computers for patron use, Electronic databases & coll, Free DVD rentals, Home delivery & serv to seniorr ctr & nursing homes, Homebound delivery serv, Music CDs, Online cat, Online ref, OverDrive digital audio bks, Photocopying/Printing, Prog for adults, Prog for children & young adult, Ref serv available, Scanner, Story hour, Summer reading prog, Tax forms
Partic in Illinois Library & Information Network; OCLC Online Computer Library Center, Inc
Open Mon-Thurs 10-7, Fri 10-6, Sat 10-3

LIBERTYVILLE

M CONDELL MEDICAL CENTER*, Fohrman Library, 900 Garfield Ave, 60048. SAN 375-9385. Tel: 847-990-5265. FAX: 847-990-2806. Web Site: www.advocatehealth.com/condell. *Dir,* Terri L Licari-DeMay; E-mail: tldemay@hotmail.com. Subject Specialists: *Med, Pharmaceuticals, Psychol,* Terri L Licari-DeMay; Staff 1 (MLS 1)
Library Holdings: Bk Titles 500; Per Subs 130; Spec Interest Per Sub 130
Function: Doc delivery serv, Health sci info serv, ILL available, Internet access, Ref serv available
Restriction: Med staff only

P COOK MEMORIAL PUBLIC LIBRARY DISTRICT*, 413 N Milwaukee Ave, 60048-2280. SAN 304-3479. Tel: 847-362-2330. FAX: 847-362-2354. E-mail: info@cooklib.org. Web Site: www.cooklib.org. *Libr Dir,* David Archer; E-mail: darcher@cooklib.org; *Asst Dir,* Lauren Cerniglia; E-mail: lcerniglia@cooklib.org; *Adult Serv, Sr Mgr,* Jennifer Plohr; E-mail: jplohr@cooklib.org; *Ch Serv, Sr Mgr,* Melissa Phillips; E-mail: mphillips@cooklib.org; *Bus Mgr,* Russell Cerqua; E-mail: rcerqua@cooklib.org; Staff 26 (MLS 26)
Founded 1921. Pop 59,842; Circ 1,337,666
Special Collections: Genealogy Coll; Lake County History Coll
Automation Activity & Vendor Info: (Acquisitions) Innovative Interfaces, Inc - Sierra; (Cataloging) Innovative Interfaces, Inc - Sierra; (Circulation) Innovative Interfaces, Inc - Sierra; (ILL) Innovative Interfaces, Inc - Sierra; (OPAC) Innovative Interfaces, Inc
Wireless access
Publications: Ins & Outs (Quarterly newsletter)
Mem of Reaching Across Illinois Library System (RAILS)
Open Mon-Thurs 9-9, Fri 9-6, Sat 9-5, Sun 1-5
Friends of the Library Group
Bookmobiles: 1

S HOLLISTER INCORPORATED*, Minnie Schneider Resource Center, 2000 Hollister Dr, 60048. SAN 326-9604. Tel: 847-680-1000. Web Site: www.hollister.com.
Founded 1983
Library Holdings: Bk Titles 4,500; Per Subs 200
Subject Interests: Med
Wireless access
Function: Archival coll, Audio & video playback equip for onsite use, Computers for patron use, Doc delivery serv, Electronic databases & coll, ILL available, Internet access, Online cat, Online ref, Orientations, Ref & res, Ref serv available, Scanner
Restriction: Co libr

LINCOLN

CR LINCOLN CHRISTIAN UNIVERSITY*, Jessie C Eury Library, 100 Campus View Dr, 62656. SAN 304-3509. Tel: 217-732-7788, Ext 2234. Toll Free Tel: 888-522-5228, Ext 2234. E-mail: library@lincolnchristian.edu. Web Site: libguides.lincolnchristian.edu. *Dir, Libr Serv,* Nancy J Olson; Tel: 217-732-7788, Ext 2281, E-mail: nolson@lincolnchristian.edu; *Info Serv Librn,* Leslie Starasta; Tel: 217-732-7788, Ext 2203, E-mail: lstarasta@lincolnchristian.edu; Staff 2 (MLS 2)
Founded 1944. Enrl 900; Fac 40; Highest Degree: Doctorate
Library Holdings: Audiobooks 20; AV Mats 2,330; CDs 3,640; DVDs 2,082; Microforms 14,566; Bk Vols 92,800; Per Subs 137; Videos 2,137
Special Collections: Restoration Movement, sermons, hymnals
Subject Interests: Biblical studies, Church hist, Theol
Automation Activity & Vendor Info: (Acquisitions) Ex Libris Group; (Cataloging) Ex Libris Group; (Circulation) Ex Libris Group; (Course Reserve) Ex Libris Group; (OPAC) Ex Libris Group; (Serials) Ex Libris Group
Wireless access
Mem of Illinois Heartland Library System
Partic in Christian Library Consortium; Consortium of Academic & Research Libraries in Illinois
Open Mon-Thurs 7:30am-10:30pm, Fri 7:30-4:30, Sat 9:30-3:30, Sun 2:30-10:30

C LINCOLN COLLEGE*, McKinstry Library, 300 Keokuk St, 62656. SAN 304-3517. Tel: 217-735-7292. Toll Free Tel: 800-569-0556. FAX: 217-732-4465. E-mail: mckinstry@lincolncollege.edu. Web Site: library.lincolncollege.edu. *Libr Dir,* Derrick Casey; Tel: 217-735-7290, E-mail: dcasey@lincolncollege.edu; *Tech Serv Librn,* Adrienne Radzvickas; Tel: 217-735-7291, E-mail: aradzvickas@lincolncollege.edu; Staff 3.5 (MLS 2, Non-MLS 1.5)
Founded 1865. Enrl 830; Highest Degree: Bachelor
Library Holdings: Bk Vols 32,000
Special Collections: Lincoln
Wireless access
Mem of Illinois Heartland Library System
Partic in Consortium of Academic & Research Libraries in Illinois
Open Mon-Thurs 8am-10pm, Fri 8-5, Sat 1-5, Sun 3:30-10

S LINCOLN CORRECTIONAL CENTER LIBRARY, 1098 1350th St, 62656. (Mail add: PO Box 549, 62656-0549). Tel: 217-735-5411, Ext 368. FAX: 217-735-1361. Web Site: www2.illinois.gov/idoc/facilities/Pages/lincolncorrectionalcenter.aspx. *Librn,* Stacey Carter; E-mail: stacey.carter@illinois.gov
Library Holdings: Bk Titles 10,000

P LINCOLN PUBLIC LIBRARY DISTRICT*, 725 Pekin, 62656. SAN 304-3525. Tel: 217-732-5732, 217-732-8878. FAX: 217-732-6273. Web Site: www.lincolnpubliclibrary.org. *Libr Dir,* Mike Starasta; E-mail: directorlpld@gmail.com; Staff 5 (MLS 1, Non-MLS 4)
Founded 1902. Pop 14,300
Jul 2015-Jun 2016 Income $676,000. Mats Exp $70,590. Sal $318,600
Library Holdings: CDs 1,877; DVDs 2,199; Bk Titles 55,400; Per Subs 150
Special Collections: Lincoln Coll; Logan County History & Genealogy
Automation Activity & Vendor Info: (OPAC) SirsiDynix
Wireless access
Function: 24/7 Electronic res, Activity rm, Archival coll, Audiobks via web, Bks on CD, Children's prog, Computers for patron use, E-Reserves, Electronic databases & coll, Equip loans & repairs, Free DVD rentals, Homework prog, ILL available, Internet access, Magazines, Microfiche/film & reading machines, Movies, Online cat, Online ref, Outside serv via phone, mail, e-mail & web, OverDrive digital audio bks, Photocopying/Printing, Prog for adults, Prog for children & young adult, Ref & res, Ref serv available, Scanner, Spoken cassettes & CDs, Spoken cassettes & DVDs, Story hour, Summer reading prog, Tax forms, Teen prog, Telephone ref, Wheelchair accessible
Publications: Human Services Directory
Mem of Illinois Heartland Library System
Open Mon, Wed & Fri 9-5, Tues & Thurs 9-7, Sat 9-1

S LOGAN CORRECTIONAL CENTER LIBRARY, 1096 1350th St, 62656. (Mail add: PO Box 1000, 62656-1000), SAN 376-0863. Tel: 217-735-5581, Ext 3396. Web Site: www2.illinois.gov/idoc/facilities/Pages/logancorrectionalcenter.aspx. *Library Contact,* Deanna Bigger
Library Holdings: Bk Titles 6,160; Per Subs 12
Subject Interests: Easy bks, Spanish
Mem of Illinois Heartland Library System
Restriction: Staff & inmates only

LINCOLNSHIRE

P VERNON AREA PUBLIC LIBRARY DISTRICT*, 300 Olde Half Day Rd, 60069-2901. SAN 304-5722. Tel: 847-634-3650. Circulation Tel: 224-543-1459. FAX: 847-634-8449. Web Site: www.vapld.info. *Libr Dir,* Cynthia Fuerst; *Head, Libr Operations,* Stephen D Territo; *Head, Coll Serv,* Judy Nuernberger; *Head, Community Engagement,* Janice Kellman; *Head, Info Serv,* Keith Barlog; *Mgr, Info Tech,* Reed Martin; Staff 130 (MLS 22, Non-MLS 108)
Founded 1974. Pop 43,000; Circ 76,846
Library Holdings: AV Mats 32,735; e-books 20,818; Bk Vols 227,957; Per Subs 924
Subject Interests: Local hist
Automation Activity & Vendor Info: (Acquisitions) Horizon; (Cataloging) Horizon; (Circulation) Horizon; (OPAC) Horizon; (Serials) Horizon
Wireless access

Function: Adult bk club, After school storytime, Bk club(s), CD-ROM, Digital talking bks, Home delivery & serv to seniorr ctr & nursing homes, Homebound delivery serv, Homework prog, ILL available, Internet access, Magnifiers for reading, Music CDs, Photocopying/Printing, Prog for adults, Prog for children & young adult, Ref serv available, Spoken cassettes & CDs, Spoken cassettes & DVDs, Summer reading prog, Telephone ref, VHS videos, Wheelchair accessible
Publications: Columns (Newsletter)
Open Mon-Thurs 9-9, Fri & Sat 9-5, Sun 12-5
Friends of the Library Group

S ZENITH ELECTRONICS LLC*, Technical Library, 2000 Millbrook Dr, 60069. SAN 304-2294. Tel: 847-941-8000. FAX: 847-941-8555. *Dir,* Tim Laud; Staff 1 (Non-MLS 1)
Founded 1956
Library Holdings: Bk Titles 2,099; Per Subs 34
Subject Interests: Bus, Engr, Math
Function: Res libr
Partic in Illinois Library & Information Network
Restriction: Not open to pub

LINCOLNWOOD

SR ASSYRIAN UNIVERSAL ALLIANCE FOUNDATION*, Ashurbanipal Library, 4343 W Touhy Ave, 60712. SAN 375-9903. Tel: 773-274-9262. FAX: 224-251-7620. E-mail: info@auaf.us. Web Site: auaf.us/library. *Librn,* Ninous Yousif; Tel: 773-863-3538, E-mail: nyousif@auaf.us; *Libr Asst,* Montaha Dawood; Tel: 773-863-3575, E-mail: mdawood@auaf.us
Founded 1980
Library Holdings: Bk Titles 7,000; Per Subs 30
Subject Interests: Hist, Linguistics, Lit
Function: Res libr
Open Mon 4pm-8pm, Tues & Wed 8-8, Thurs & Fri 8-4:30, Sat 10-4
Restriction: Circ limited

P LINCOLNWOOD PUBLIC LIBRARY DISTRICT, 4000 W Pratt Ave, 60712. SAN 320-1813. Tel: 847-677-5277. FAX: 847-677-1937. Information Services E-mail: infoservices@lincolnwoodlibrary.org. Web Site: lincolnwoodlibrary.org. *Dir,* Josephine Tucci; E-mail: jtucci@lincolnwoodlibrary.org; *Dep Dir,* Chris Renkosiak; E-mail: crenkosiak@lincolnwoodlibrary.org; *Head, Bus Serv,* Vandana Sehgal; E-mail: vsehgal@lincolnwoodlibrary.org; *Head, Teen Serv, Head, Youth Serv,* Emily Fardoux; E-mail: efardoux@lincolnwoodlibrary.org; Staff 10 (MLS 7, Non-MLS 3)
Founded 1978. Pop 12,500; Circ 148,000
Library Holdings: AV Mats 10,000; Large Print Bks 5,000; Bk Vols 60,000; Per Subs 105; Talking Bks 5,000
Special Collections: David Zemsky Low Vision Center; Lincolnwood Historical Coll; Literacy Coll
Automation Activity & Vendor Info: (Cataloging) SirsiDynix; (Circulation) SirsiDynix; (ILL) SirsiDynix; (OPAC) SirsiDynix
Wireless access
Publications: Lincolnwood Library; The Acorn (quarterly newsletter)
Partic in Illinois Library & Information Network; OCLC Online Computer Library Center, Inc
Open Mon-Thurs 9-9, Fri 9-6, Sat 9-5, Sun 1-5
Friends of the Library Group

LINDENHURST

P LAKE VILLA DISTRICT LIBRARY*, 140 N Munn Rd, 60046. SAN 304-3320. Tel: 847-356-7711. FAX: 847-265-9595. Web Site: www.lvdl.org. *Dir,* Mikael Jacobsen; Tel: 847-245-5100, E-mail: mjacobsen@lvdl.org; *Head, Adult Serv,* Tara Caldara; Tel: 847-245-5106; *Head, Circ Serv,* Lynn Firman; Tel: 847-245-5107; *Head, Tech Serv,* Anita Santoro; Tel: 847-245-5111; *Head, Youth Serv,* Elisa Gueffier; Tel: 847-245-5112; *Admin Serv Coordr,* Julie Binkley; Tel: 847-245-5101, E-mail: jbinkley@lvdl.org; Staff 61 (MLS 7, Non-MLS 54)
Founded 1952. Pop 33,700; Circ 863,453
Library Holdings: AV Mats 27,445; e-books 11; Bk Vols 144,641; Per Subs 463
Automation Activity & Vendor Info: (Circulation) SirsiDynix; (OPAC) SirsiDynix
Wireless access
Publications: Checking Out (Newsletter)
Partic in Cooperative Computer Services - CCS
Special Services for the Deaf - TTY equip
Special Services for the Blind - Closed circuit TV magnifier
Open Mon-Thurs 9-9, Fri 9-6, Sat 9-5, Sun 1-5
Friends of the Library Group

LISLE

C BENEDICTINE UNIVERSITY LIBRARY*, 5700 College Rd, 60532-0900. SAN 304-355X. Tel: 630-829-6050. Circulation Tel: 630-829-6058. Interlibrary Loan Service Tel: 630-829-6056. Reference Tel: 630-829-6057. Administration Tel: 630-829-6060. FAX: 630-960-9451. Web Site: www.ben.edu/library. *Univ Librn,* Jack Fritts; E-mail: jfritts@ben.edu; *Assoc Univ Librn,* Luann DeGreve; Tel: 630-829-6197, E-mail: ldegreve@ben.edu; *Access Serv Librn,* Silvia Larrondo; E-mail: slarrondo@ben.edu; *Bus Outreach Librn,* Kent Carrico; Tel: 630-829-6055, E-mail: kcarrico@ben.edu; *Emerging Tech Librn,* Sarah Kurpiel; E-mail: skurpiel@ben.edu; *Instruction Librn,* Joan Hopkins; E-mail: jhopkins@ben.edu; *Sci Outreach Librn,* Sulbha Wagh; Tel: 630-829-6054, E-mail: swagh@ben.edu; *Archives, Spec Coll Librn,* Jill Walker; *ILL,* Regina Remson; Tel: 630-829-6061, E-mail: rremson@ben.edu; Staff 1 (Non-MLS 1)
Founded 1887. Fac 150; Highest Degree: Doctorate
Special Collections: College Archives; John Erlenborn Papers; Rare Books & Manuscripts
Subject Interests: Humanities, Theol
Automation Activity & Vendor Info: (Acquisitions) Ex Libris Group; (Cataloging) Ex Libris Group; (Circulation) Ex Libris Group; (Course Reserve) Ex Libris Group; (OPAC) Ex Libris Group; (Serials) Ex Libris Group
Wireless access
Function: 24/7 Electronic res, 24/7 Online cat
Mem of Reaching Across Illinois Library System (RAILS)
Partic in Consortium of Academic & Research Libraries in Illinois; LIBRAS, Inc; OCLC Online Computer Library Center, Inc
Restriction: Closed stack

Departmental Libraries:

MESA CAMPUS LIBRARY, 225 E Main St, Mesa, 85201. Toll Free Tel: 877-575-6050. *Br Dir,* Janet Lynch Forde; E-mail: jforde@ben.edu

P LISLE LIBRARY DISTRICT*, 777 Front St, 60532-3599. SAN 304-3568. Tel: 630-971-1675. FAX: 630-971-1701. Web Site: www.lislelibrary.org. *Dir, Libr Serv,* Tatiana Weinstein; E-mail: tatiana@lislelibrary.org; *Asst Dir,* Beth McQuillan; E-mail: mcquil@lislelibrary.org; *Dir, Adult Serv,* Elizabeth Hopkins; E-mail: hopkinse@lislelibrary.org; *Circ Serv Dir,* Paul Hurt; E-mail: paulhurt@lislelibrary.org; *Dir, Tech Serv,* Laura Murff; E-mail: murffl@lislelibrary.org; *Dir, Youth Serv,* Will Savage; E-mail: savagew@lislelibrary.org; Staff 15 (MLS 15)
Founded 1967. Pop 29,568; Circ 480,000
Library Holdings: Bk Vols 115,000; Per Subs 420
Subject Interests: Local hist, Oriental art
Automation Activity & Vendor Info: (Circulation) Innovative Interfaces, Inc; (Serials) EBSCO Online
Wireless access
Function: Adult literacy prog, AV serv, BA reader (adult literacy), Doc delivery serv, Homebound delivery serv, ILL available, Photocopying/Printing, Prog for children & young adult, Summer reading prog, Wheelchair accessible
Publications: Newsletter (Monthly)
Mem of Reaching Across Illinois Library System (RAILS)
Special Services for the Deaf - TTY equip; Videos & decoder
Open Mon-Fri 9:30-9, Sat 9:30-5, Sun 1-5
Friends of the Library Group

S THE MORTON ARBORETUM, Sterling Morton Library, 4100 Illinois Rte 53, 60532-1293. SAN 304-3576. Tel: 630-719-2429. FAX: 630-719-7950. E-mail: library@mortonarb.org. Web Site: www.mortonarb.org, www.sterlingmortonlibrary.org. *Library Colls Mgr,* Rita Hassert; E-mail: rhassert@mortonarb.org; *Digital Assets Librn,* Danielle Nowak; *Archivist,* Kristin Arnold. Subject Specialists: *Botany, Hort, Spec coll,* Rita Hassert; Staff 3 (MLS 3)
Founded 1922
Library Holdings: Bk Titles 28,000; Per Subs 200
Special Collections: Asia (E H Wilson Photo Coll); Botanical Art & Illustration; History & Topography Maps of Arboretum & Vicinity, 1922-present; Landscape Archives (Jens Jensen, Marshall Johnson & O C Simonds Coll) bks, letters, photos/slides, plans; May Theilgaard Watts Coll, ms; Morton Arboretum Archives; Nursery Catalogs, pre-1920
Subject Interests: Birds, Botanical bibliography, Botanical hist, Botany, Environ studies, Forestry, Gardening, Hort, Landscape archit, Mammals, Natural hist, Plant sci
Automation Activity & Vendor Info: (Cataloging) OCLC; (Circulation) SirsiDynix; (ILL) OCLC; (OPAC) SirsiDynix; (Serials) SirsiDynix
Wireless access
Function: Adult bk club, Archival coll, Art exhibits, ILL available, Online cat, Photocopying/Printing, Ref serv available, Telephone ref, Wheelchair accessible
Mem of Reaching Across Illinois Library System (RAILS)
Partic in Illinois Library & Information Network; System Wide Automated Network
Open Tues-Fri 10-2
Restriction: Restricted borrowing privileges

CR NORTHERN BAPTIST THEOLOGICAL SEMINARY*, Northern Seminary Library, 410 Warrenville Rd, Ste 300, 60532. SAN 304-4904. Tel: 630-620-2156. FAX: 630-620-2190. E-mail: library@seminary.edu. Web Site: student.seminary.edu/students/library. *Interim Libr Dir,* Janeane Forrest; Tel: 630-620-2115, E-mail: jlforrest@seminary.edu; Staff 1 (MLS 1)
Founded 1913. Enrl 235; Fac 16; Highest Degree: Doctorate
Library Holdings: e-books 20,000; Bk Titles 30,000; Bk Vols 35,000; Per Subs 32
Subject Interests: Baptist hist, Bible, Christian hist, Christian theol, New Testament, Relig in Am, Theol, Women's studies in relig
Automation Activity & Vendor Info: (Acquisitions) Ex Libris Group; (Cataloging) Ex Libris Group; (Circulation) Ex Libris Group; (Course Reserve) Ex Libris Group; (ILL) OCLC; (OPAC) Ex Libris Group; (Serials) Ex Libris Group
Wireless access
Function: Online cat, Photocopying/Printing, Ref & res, Res libr
Partic in American Theological Library Association; Association of Chicago Theological Schools; Consortium of Academic & Research Libraries in Illinois
Restriction: In-house use for visitors, Non-circulating to the pub, Open to fac, students & qualified researchers

LITCHFIELD

P LITCHFIELD CARNEGIE PUBLIC LIBRARY*, 1205 S State St, 62056. SAN 304-3584. Tel: 217-324-3866. FAX: 217-324-3884. E-mail: library@litchfieldil.com. Web Site: www.litchfieldpubliclibrary.org. *Dir,* Sara Zumwalt; Staff 5 (Non-MLS 5)
Founded 1872. Pop 6,883; Circ 67,348
Library Holdings: Bk Vols 37,000; Per Subs 136
Special Collections: Genealogy & Local History
Subject Interests: Genealogy
Automation Activity & Vendor Info: (Cataloging) Follett Software; (Circulation) Follett Software
Wireless access
Mem of Illinois Heartland Library System
Open Mon-Thurs 10-8, Fri 10-5, Sat 10-2
Friends of the Library Group

LODA

P A HERR SMITH & E E SMITH LODA TOWNSHIP LIBRARY, 105 E Adams St, 60948. (Mail add: PO Box 247, 60948-0247), SAN 304-3592. Tel: 217-386-2783. FAX: 217-386-2223.
Founded 1897. Pop 1,306; Circ 5,010
Library Holdings: Bk Vols 5,100
Wireless access
Mem of Illinois Heartland Library System
Open Mon-Thurs 9-5, Sat 9-1

LOMBARD

S CZECHOSLOVAK HERITAGE MUSEUM, LIBRARY & ARCHIVES*, 2050 Finly Rd, 60148. SAN 326-5250. Tel: 630-472-0500. Toll Free Tel: 800-543-3272. FAX: 630-472-1100. Web Site: www.csafraternallife.org. *Pres,* Cary Mentzer
Founded 1974
Library Holdings: Bk Titles 1,000
Subject Interests: Czechoslovakia genealogy, Czechoslovakia hist, Czechoslovakia/Slovak Am
Temporarily closed, library is in storage pending move to new location. 2019-
Restriction: Open by appt only

S LOMBARD HISTORICAL SOCIETY LIBRARY, 23 W Maple St, 60148. SAN 374-9193. Tel: 630-629-1885. E-mail: info@lombardhistory.org. Web Site: www.lombardhistory.org. *Exec Dir,* Alison Costanzo; E-mail: director@lombardhistory.org; *Archivist,* Jean Cooper; E-mail: archive@lombardhistory.org
Library Holdings: Bk Vols 350; Per Subs 20

CM NATIONAL UNIVERSITY OF HEALTH SCIENCES LEARNING RESOURCE CENTER*, Sordoni-Burich Library, 200 E Roosevelt Rd, Bldg C, 60148-4583. SAN 304-3614. Tel: 630-889-6612. Interlibrary Loan Service Tel: 630-889-6613. Reference Tel: 630-889-6617. Administration Tel: 630-889-6597. FAX: 630-495-6658. E-mail: reference@nuhs.edu. Circulation E-mail: circulation@nuhs.edu. Interlibrary Loan Service E-mail: interlibraryloan@nuhs.edu. Web Site: www.nuhs.edu/lrc. *Dir,* Patricia Genardo; E-mail: pgenardo@nuhs.edu; *Ref Librn,* Russell Iwami; E-mail: riwami@nuhs.edu; *Tech Serv Librn,* Anne Scott Hope; Tel: 630-889-6538, E-mail: ahope@nuhs.edu; *Circ Mgr,* Debbie Walsh; Tel: 630-889-6610, E-mail: dwalsh@nuhs.edu; Staff 8 (MLS 5, Non-MLS 3)
Founded 1920. Enrl 650; Fac 40; Highest Degree: Doctorate
Library Holdings: Bk Vols 16,000; Per Subs 375; Spec Interest Per Sub 300
Special Collections: Chiropractic Coll; History of National University of Health Sciences; Role of STEM in Human Nutrition & Diet; Spiritual Therapies
Subject Interests: Acupuncture, Alternative healing, Alternative med, Biomed sci, Chiropractic, Complementary med, Massage therapy, Naturopathic med, Neurology, Nutrition, Oriental med, Radiology, Sports med
Automation Activity & Vendor Info: (Cataloging) SirsiDynix; (Circulation) SirsiDynix; (OPAC) SirsiDynix; (Serials) SirsiDynix
Wireless access
Function: Archival coll, Computers for patron use, Doc delivery serv, Electronic databases & coll, For res purposes, Health sci info serv, ILL available, Internet access, Learning ctr, Online cat, Orientations, Outside serv via phone, mail, e-mail & web, Photocopying/Printing, Prof lending libr, Ref & res, Ref serv available, Res libr, Res performed for a fee, Study rm, Telephone ref
Mem of Reaching Across Illinois Library System (RAILS)
Partic in Chiropractic Libr Consortium; Consortium of Academic & Research Libraries in Illinois; Illinois Library & Information Network; System Wide Automated Network
Open Mon-Thurs 7:30am-11pm, Fri 7:30-6, Sat & Sun 11-9
Restriction: In-house use for visitors, Non-circulating of rare bks, Off-site coll in storage - retrieval as requested

P HELEN M PLUM MEMORIAL PUBLIC LIBRARY DISTRICT, 110 W Maple St, 60148-2594. SAN 304-3630. Tel: 630-627-0316. FAX: 630-627-0336. Web Site: www.helenplum.org. *Interim Exec Dir,* Claudia Krauspe; E-mail: CKrauspe@helenplum.org; *Dir, Strategic Communications & Marketing,* Sue K Wilsey; E-mail: swilsey@helenplum.org; *Asst Dir,* Anne Luzeniecki; E-mail: aluzeniecki@helenplum.org; Staff 22 (MLS 15, Non-MLS 7)
Founded 1928. Pop 43,894; Circ 568,572
Library Holdings: Audiobooks 439; CDs 11,234; DVDs 3,184; Electronic Media & Resources 1,335; Bk Vols 196,688; Per Subs 432; Videos 759
Subject Interests: Art & archit, Local hist, Music
Automation Activity & Vendor Info: (Acquisitions) Innovative Interfaces, Inc - Millennium; (Cataloging) Innovative Interfaces, Inc - Millennium; (Circulation) Innovative Interfaces, Inc - Millennium; (ILL) Innovative Interfaces, Inc - Millennium; (OPAC) Innovative Interfaces, Inc - Millennium; (Serials) Innovative Interfaces, Inc - Millennium
Wireless access
Function: Adult bk club, Art exhibits, AV serv, Bks on CD, CD-ROM, Children's prog, Computers for patron use, Electronic databases & coll, Free DVD rentals, Homebound delivery serv, ILL available, Magnifiers for reading, Mail & tel request accepted, Music CDs, Online cat, Outreach serv, OverDrive digital audio bks, Photocopying/Printing, Preschool outreach, Prog for adults, Prog for children & young adult, Ref serv available, Spoken cassettes & CDs, Spoken cassettes & DVDs, Story hour, Summer & winter reading prog, Tax forms, Teen prog, Telephone ref, Wheelchair accessible
Publications: PLUM JAM (Monthly); PLUM TREE (Monthly)
Mem of Reaching Across Illinois Library System (RAILS)
Partic in Illinois Library & Information Network
Open Mon-Fri 9-9, Sat 9-5, Sun 1-5
Friends of the Library Group

LOSTANT

P LOSTANT COMMUNITY LIBRARY, 102 W Third St, 61334. (Mail add: PO Box 189, 61334), SAN 304-3657. Tel: 815-368-3530. E-mail: lostantlibrary@yahoo.com. *Dir,* Kimberly Udstrand
Founded 1961. Pop 1,400; Circ 2,059
Library Holdings: Bk Vols 3,775
Subject Interests: Local hist
Wireless access
Mem of Reaching Across Illinois Library System (RAILS)
Open Tues-Thurs 10-5, Sat 8-Noon

LOVES PARK

P NORTH SUBURBAN LIBRARY DISTRICT*, 6340 N Second St, 61111. SAN 304-3665. Tel: 815-633-4247. Administration Tel: 815-636-5042. FAX: 815-633-4249. Web Site: www.northsuburbanlibrary.org. *Dir,* Mary Petro; E-mail: marype@northsld.org; *Adult Serv Supvr,* Nicole Johnson; E-mail: nicolej@northsld.org; *Children's Serv Supvr,* Barb Jacobs; Staff 7 (MLS 7)
Founded 1944. Pop 61,145; Circ 642,228
Library Holdings: Bk Vols 479,235; Per Subs 460
Subject Interests: Local hist
Automation Activity & Vendor Info: (Acquisitions) Innovative Interfaces, Inc; (Cataloging) Innovative Interfaces, Inc; (Circulation) Innovative Interfaces, Inc; (OPAC) Innovative Interfaces, Inc; (Serials) Innovative Interfaces, Inc

Wireless access
Publications: Elementary Education Newsletter; North Suburban District Library Newsletter; Secondary Education Newsletter; Staff Notes; Young Adult Committee Newsletter
Mem of Reaching Across Illinois Library System (RAILS)
Open Mon-Thurs 11-6, Fri & Sat 11-5
Friends of the Library Group
Branches: 1
ROSCOE BRANCH, 5562 Clayton Circle, Roscoe, 61073, SAN 329-2614. Tel: 815-623-6266. FAX: 815-623-8591. *Br Mgr,* Position Currently Open
Open Mon-Thurs 11-6, Fri & Sat 11-5

LOVINGTON

P LOVINGTON PUBLIC LIBRARY DISTRICT*, 110 W State St, 61937. (Mail add: PO Box 199, 61937-0199), SAN 304-3673. Tel: 217-873-4468. FAX: 217-873-4468. E-mail: lovingtonpld@gmail.com. Web Site: www.lovingtonpld.us. *Dir,* Letitia Clough
Founded 1943. Pop 1,954; Circ 11,145
Library Holdings: Bk Vols 20,722; Per Subs 38
Wireless access
Mem of Illinois Heartland Library System
Open Mon 9-7, Tues-Fri 9-12 & 2-5, Sat 9-12

LYNWOOD

P GLENWOOD-LYNWOOD PUBLIC LIBRARY DISTRICT*, 19901 Stony Island Ave, 60411. SAN 304-2308. Tel: 708-758-0090. FAX: 708-758-0106. E-mail: library@glpld.org. Web Site: www.glpld.org. *Libr Dir,* Brian Vagt; E-mail: vagtb@glpld.org; *Bus Off Mgr,* Doreen Berrien; E-mail: berriend@glpld.org; *Circ Mgr,* Sheila Adams; E-mail: adamss@glpld.org; *Info Serv Mgr,* Rhonda Ruffin; E-mail: ruffinr@glpld.org; Staff 24 (MLS 3, Non-MLS 21)
Founded 1974. Pop 17,976; Circ 134,642
Library Holdings: Audiobooks 855; CDs 1,597; DVDs 2,674; Bk Vols 52,184; Per Subs 102
Automation Activity & Vendor Info: (Acquisitions) SirsiDynix; (Cataloging) SirsiDynix; (Circulation) SirsiDynix; (ILL) SirsiDynix; (OPAC) SirsiDynix-Enterprise; (Serials) SirsiDynix
Wireless access
Function: 24/7 Electronic res, Accelerated reader prog, Activity rm, Adult bk club, Audio & video playback equip for onsite use, Audiobks on Playaways & MP3, Bks on CD, Children's prog, Computer training, E-Readers, Free DVD rentals, Holiday prog, Home delivery & serv to seniorr ctr & nursing homes, Homebound delivery serv, Homework prog, ILL available, Instruction & testing, Internet access, Life-long learning prog for all ages, Magazines, Mail & tel request accepted, Mango lang, Meeting rooms, Movies, Museum passes, Music CDs, Notary serv, Online cat, Outreach serv, Outside serv via phone, mail, e-mail & web, OverDrive digital audio bks, Passport agency, Photocopying/Printing, Preschool outreach, Preschool reading prog, Printer for laptops & handheld devices, Prog for adults, Prog for children & young adult, Ref & res, Ref serv available, Res performed for a fee, Scanner, Senior computer classes, Senior outreach, Serves people with intellectual disabilities, Spanish lang bks, Story hour, Study rm, Summer & winter reading prog, Summer reading prog, Tax forms, Teen prog, Telephone ref, Wheelchair accessible, Winter reading prog, Workshops, Writing prog
Publications: Newsletter
Mem of Reaching Across Illinois Library System (RAILS)
Partic in System Wide Automated Network
Open Mon-Thurs 9-9, Fri & Sat 9-5, Sun 1-5
Friends of the Library Group
Bookmobiles: 1

LYONS

P LYONS PUBLIC LIBRARY*, 4209 Joliet Ave, 60534-1597. SAN 304-3681. Tel: 708-447-3577. FAX: 708-447-3589. E-mail: lyons@lyonslibrary.org. Web Site: www.lyonslibrary.org. *Dir,* Dan Hilker; *Adminr,* Audrey Klawiter; Staff 2 (Non-MLS 2)
Founded 1938. Pop 10,735
Library Holdings: Bk Vols 60,197; Per Subs 115
Special Collections: 17th, 18th, 19th Century Passenger Lists; Chicago Metropolitan History & Genealogy
Subject Interests: Genealogy, Illinois
Automation Activity & Vendor Info: (Acquisitions) Innovative Interfaces, Inc; (Cataloging) Innovative Interfaces, Inc; (Circulation) Innovative Interfaces, Inc; (ILL) Innovative Interfaces, Inc; (OPAC) Innovative Interfaces, Inc; (Serials) Innovative Interfaces, Inc
Wireless access
Function: 24/7 Electronic res, 24/7 Online cat, Accelerated reader prog, After school storytime, AV serv, Bks on CD, Children's prog, Computers for patron use, E-Reserves, Electronic databases & coll, Family literacy, Free DVD rentals, Games & aids for people with disabilities, Holiday prog, ILL available, Instruction & testing, Internet access, Magazines, Mail & tel request accepted, Movies, Museum passes, Music CDs, Notary serv, Online cat, Outside serv via phone, mail, e-mail & web, Photocopying/Printing, Preschool outreach, Prog for adults, Prog for children & young adult, Ref serv available, Scanner, Story hour, Summer & winter reading prog, Summer reading prog, Telephone ref, Wheelchair accessible
Publications: Literally Lyons (Newsletter)
Partic in Chemeketa Cooperative Regional Library Service; System Wide Automated Network
Special Services for the Deaf - ADA equip; Bks on deafness & sign lang; Captioned film dep; Closed caption videos; Sign lang interpreter upon request for prog; Staff with knowledge of sign lang; TTY equip; Video & TTY relay via computer
Special Services for the Blind - Bks on CD; Large print bks
Open Mon-Thurs 9-9, Fri 9-6, Sat 10-5

MACKINAW

P MACKINAW DISTRICT PUBLIC LIBRARY*, 117 S Main St, 61755. (Mail add: PO Box 560, 61755-0560), SAN 304-372X. Tel: 309-359-8022. FAX: 309-359-6502. E-mail: maclibrarian84@yahoo.com. Web Site: mackinawlibrary.com. *Dir,* Mrs Kiana Nafziger
Founded 1900. Pop 4,045; Circ 42,831
Library Holdings: CDs 2,090; DVDs 1,358; Bk Titles 28,544; Per Subs 59
Automation Activity & Vendor Info: (Circulation) SirsiDynix
Wireless access
Function: Homebound delivery serv
Partic in Illinois Library & Information Network; RSA
Open Mon & Wed 10-7, Tues & Thurs 10-6, Fri 10-5, Sat 9-12

MACOMB

P MACOMB PUBLIC LIBRARY DISTRICT, 235 S Lafayette St, 61455. SAN 304-3754. Tel: 309-833-2714. FAX: 309-833-2714. E-mail: library@macomb.com. Web Site: www.macomb.lib.il.us. *Libr Dir,* Dennis Danowski; Staff 7 (MLS 2, Non-MLS 5)
Founded 1881. Pop 21,509; Circ 97,000
Jul 2020-Jun 2021 Income $475,000, State $25,000, Locally Generated Income $450,000. Mats Exp $58,500, Books $44,500, Per/Ser (Incl. Access Fees) $5,000, Micro $1,500, AV Mat $5,000, Presv $2,500. Sal $240,000
Library Holdings: Audiobooks 1,500; CDs 2,550; DVDs 329; Large Print Bks 600; Bk Vols 60,000; Per Subs 100; Videos 250
Special Collections: Illinois Local History Coll, bks & photog
Automation Activity & Vendor Info: (Circulation) SirsiDynix
Wireless access
Open Mon-Fri 9-6
Friends of the Library Group

C WESTERN ILLINOIS UNIVERSITY*, Leslie F Malpass Library, One University Circle, 61455. SAN 304-3762. Tel: 309-298-2705. Interlibrary Loan Service Tel: 309-298-2761. FAX: 309-298-2791. Web Site: www.wiu.edu/library. *Dean of Libr,* Jeanne D Stierman; Tel: 309-298-2762, E-mail: JD-Stierman@wiu.edu; Staff 16 (MLS 15, Non-MLS 1)
Founded 1903. Enrl 11,000; Fac 650; Highest Degree: Doctorate
Library Holdings: Bk Titles 868,519; Bk Vols 998,041; Per Subs 3,200
Special Collections: Birds of Prey (Elton Fawks Coll); Center for Icarian Studies; Political Science (US Congressman Tom Railsback Coll); Theatre (Burl Ives Coll); West Central Illinois Local History Coll; Western Illinois University Theses; Wildlife Conservation (Virginia Eifert Coll). Oral History; State Document Depository; US Document Depository
Wireless access
Function: Archival coll
Partic in Consortium of Academic & Research Libraries in Illinois; OCLC Online Computer Library Center, Inc
Open Mon-Thurs 7:30am-Midnight, Fri 7:30-5, Sat 12-6, Sun 1pm-Midnight

MACON

P SOUTH MACON PUBLIC LIBRARY DISTRICT*, 451 W Glenn St, 62544. SAN 304-3770. Tel: 217-764-3356. FAX: 217-764-5490. E-mail: SouthMaconLibrary@gmail.com. Web Site: southmacon.lib.il.us. *Dir,* Kay Burrous; *Asst Librn,* Vicki Carr
Founded 1980. Pop 2,842; Circ 8,426
Library Holdings: AV Mats 1,029; Bk Titles 9,813; Per Subs 46
Wireless access
Mem of Illinois Heartland Library System
Open Mon, Tues & Fri 10-12 & 1:30-5:30, Wed 1:30-8, Thurs 1:30-5:30, Sat 9-12
Friends of the Library Group

MADISON

P MADISON PUBLIC LIBRARY*, 1700 Fifth St, 62060. SAN 304-3789. Tel: 618-876-8448. FAX: 618-876-8316. E-mail: madisonpublibrary@gmail.com. *Dir,* Melissa Broadway; Staff 2 (MLS 2)
Pop 4,545; Circ 123,982
Library Holdings: Bk Vols 27,000
Mem of Illinois Heartland Library System
Open Tues & Fri 8-4:30, Sat 8-2

MAHOMET

P MAHOMET PUBLIC LIBRARY DISTRICT*, 1702 E Oak St, 61853-7427. SAN 304-3797. Tel: 217-586-2611. FAX: 217-586-5710. E-mail: staff@mahometpubliclibrary.org. Web Site: www.mahometpubliclibrary.org. *Dir,* John Howard; E-mail: Director@MahometPublicLibrary.org; *Bus Mgr,* Kate Smith; E-mail: Kate@mahometpubliclibrary.org; Staff 12 (MLS 2, Non-MLS 10)
Founded 1966. Pop 10,113; Circ 84,371
Library Holdings: Bk Vols 24,000; Per Subs 100
Automation Activity & Vendor Info: (Acquisitions) SirsiDynix; (Cataloging) SirsiDynix; (Circulation) SirsiDynix; (Media Booking) SirsiDynix; (OPAC) SirsiDynix; (Serials) SirsiDynix
Wireless access
Mem of Illinois Heartland Library System
Open Mon-Thurs 9-8, Fri 9-6, Sat 9-3, Sun 1-5
Friends of the Library Group

MALTA

J KISHWAUKEE COLLEGE LIBRARY*, 21193 Malta Rd, 60150-9699. SAN 304-3800. Tel: 815-825-9330. Interlibrary Loan Service Tel: 815-825-9330. Reference Tel: 815-825-9547. FAX: 815-825-2072. Web Site: www.kish.edu/services/library. *Dean, Libr & Acad Support,* Anne-Marie Green; Tel: 815-825-9443, E-mail: agreen3@kish.edu; *Ref Librn,* Carol Wubbena; Tel: 815-825-9544, E-mail: cwubbena@kishwaukeecollege.edu; Staff 6 (MLS 2, Non-MLS 4)
Founded 1968. Enrl 2,000; Fac 65; Highest Degree: Associate
Library Holdings: High Interest/Low Vocabulary Bk Vols 815; Bk Titles 38,966; Bk Vols 44,399; Per Subs 248
Special Collections: Oral History
Automation Activity & Vendor Info: (Acquisitions) Ex Libris Group; (Cataloging) Ex Libris Group; (Circulation) Ex Libris Group; (Course Reserve) Ex Libris Group; (Media Booking) Ex Libris Group; (OPAC) Ex Libris Group; (Serials) Ex Libris Group
Mem of Reaching Across Illinois Library System (RAILS)
Partic in Consortium of Academic & Research Libraries in Illinois; Network of Illinois Learning Resources in Community Colleges; Northern Illinois Learning Resources Cooperative
Special Services for the Blind - Computer with voice synthesizer for visually impaired persons
Open Mon-Thurs 8:30-7, Fri 8-4

P MALTA TOWNSHIP PUBLIC LIBRARY*, 203 E Adams St, 60150. (Mail add: PO Box 54, 60150), SAN 304-3819. Tel: 815-825-2525. FAX: 815-825-1525. E-mail: info@MaltaLibrary.org. Web Site: www.maltalibrary.org. *Dir,* Peggy Wogen; E-mail: pjwogen@maltalibrary.org; Staff 2.6 (Non-MLS 2.6)
Founded 1921. Pop 1,608; Circ 13,823
Library Holdings: Audiobooks 717; CDs 446; DVDs 1,110; e-books 19,589; Large Print Bks 534; Bk Vols 12,084; Per Subs 37
Subject Interests: Civil War, Native Americans
Automation Activity & Vendor Info: (Cataloging) Innovative Interfaces, Inc; (Circulation) Innovative Interfaces, Inc; (ILL) Innovative Interfaces, Inc; (OPAC) Innovative Interfaces, Inc
Wireless access
Function: Adult bk club, Art exhibits, Audio & video playback equip for onsite use, Bks on cassette, Bks on CD, CD-ROM, Children's prog, Computers for patron use, Family literacy, ILL available, Internet access, Music CDs, Notary serv, Online cat, Photocopying/Printing, Prog for adults, Prog for children & young adult, Ref serv available, Scanner, Story hour, Summer reading prog, Teen prog, VHS videos, Wheelchair accessible
Mem of Reaching Across Illinois Library System (RAILS)
Open Tues 1-8, Wed-Fri 3:30-8, Sat 10-3

MANHATTAN

P MANHATTAN-ELWOOD PUBLIC LIBRARY DISTRICT*, 240 Whitson St, 60442. (Mail add: PO Box 53, 60442-0053), SAN 304-3827. Tel: 815-478-3987. FAX: 815-478-3988. E-mail: questions@mpld.org. Web Site: www.mpld.org. *Dir,* Ashley Hopper; E-mail: arhopper@mpld.org; Staff 21 (MLS 2, Non-MLS 19)
Founded 1909. Pop 13,166; Circ 162,047
Jul 2012-Jun 2013 Income $687,603, State $13,020, Locally Generated Income $646,833, Other $22,730. Mats Exp $59,637, Books $41,440, Per/Ser (Incl. Access Fees) $4,195, AV Mat $7,001, Electronic Ref Mat (Incl. Access Fees) $7,001. Sal $391,159
Library Holdings: CDs 2,146; DVDs 3,083; e-books 10,767; Electronic Media & Resources 1,625; Large Print Bks 2,227; Bk Vols 56,140; Per Subs 118
Subject Interests: Accelerated readers, Gardening, Local hist, Parenting
Automation Activity & Vendor Info: (Acquisitions) SirsiDynix; (Cataloging) Innovative Interfaces, Inc; (Circulation) SirsiDynix; (ILL) Innovative Interfaces, Inc; (OPAC) Innovative Interfaces, Inc; (Serials) Innovative Interfaces, Inc
Wireless access
Function: Accelerated reader prog, Adult bk club, Audiobks via web, Bks on cassette, Bks on CD, Children's prog, Computers for patron use, Electronic databases & coll, Free DVD rentals, Home delivery & serv to seniorr ctr & nursing homes, Homebound delivery serv, ILL available, Internet access, Magnifiers for reading, Museum passes, Music CDs, Notary serv, Online cat, Online ref, Outreach serv, OverDrive digital audio bks, Photocopying/Printing, Prog for adults, Prog for children & young adult, Ref serv available, Scanner, Senior computer classes, Senior outreach, Story hour, Summer & winter reading prog, Summer reading prog, Tax forms, Teen prog, Telephone ref, VHS videos, Wheelchair accessible
Mem of Reaching Across Illinois Library System (RAILS)
Partic in Prairienet
Special Services for the Blind - Assistive/Adapted tech devices, equip & products
Open Mon-Thurs 10-8, Fri 10-5, Sat 10-3
Friends of the Library Group

MANITO

P FORMAN VALLEY PUBLIC LIBRARY DISTRICT*, 404 1/2 S Harrison, 61546. (Mail add: PO Box 710, 61546-0710), SAN 320-8230. Tel: 309-968-6093. FAX: 309-968-7120. E-mail: Fv.formval.rsa@gmail.com. *Librn,* Debbie Horchem
Pop 6,000
Library Holdings: Bk Vols 19,000; Per Subs 40
Automation Activity & Vendor Info: (Circulation) TLC (The Library Corporation)
Open Mon, Wed & Fri 9-4:30, Tues & Thurs 9-6:30, Sat 9-1

MANSFIELD

P BLUE RIDGE TOWNSHIP PUBLIC LIBRARY*, 116 E Oliver St, 61854. (Mail add: PO Box 457, 61854-0457), SAN 304-3835. Tel: 217-489-9033. E-mail: mansfieldlibrary@yahoo.com. *Libr Dir,* Brenda Edwards
Founded 1923. Pop 1,418; Circ 12,970
Library Holdings: Bk Vols 10,000; Per Subs 55
Special Collections: Oral History
Mem of Illinois Heartland Library System
Open Mon, Wed & Fri 1-7, Tues & Thurs 4-7, Sat 8-12
Friends of the Library Group

MANTENO

S ILLINOIS VETERAN'S HOME LIBRARY*, One Veterans Dr, 60950-9466. Tel: 815-468-6581, Ext 272. FAX: 815-468-0570. *Librn,* Position Currently Open
Founded 1993. Pop 345; Circ 500
Library Holdings: CDs 1,250; DVDs 2,500; Music Scores 1,500; Bk Titles 2,300; Per Subs 140; Videos 1,000
Wireless access
Open Mon-Fri 8-4:30

P MANTENO PUBLIC LIBRARY DISTRICT*, Ten S Walnut St, 60950. SAN 304-3843. Tel: 815-468-3323. FAX: 815-468-3360. Web Site: www.mantenolibrary.org. *Dir,* Jamie Lockwood; E-mail: jlockwood@mantenolibrary.net; *Asst Dir,* Arlene Flint; E-mail: aflint@mantenolibrary.net
Founded 1965. Pop 8,633; Circ 52,763
Library Holdings: Bk Vols 29,842; Per Subs 80
Open Mon-Thurs 9:30-8, Fri 9:30-6, Sat 9:30-3

MAPLE PARK

P MAPLE PARK PUBLIC LIBRARY DISTRICT*, 302 Willow St, 60151. (Mail add: PO Box 159, 60151), SAN 304-386X. Tel: 815-827-3362. FAX: 815-827-4072. E-mail: mppl@maplepark.lib.il.us. Web Site: sites.google.com/site/mapleparklibrary, villageofmaplepark.org/tag/maple-park-public-library. *Dir,* Kimberly A Martin
Founded 1963. Pop 1,706
Library Holdings: Bk Vols 12,000
Automation Activity & Vendor Info: (Acquisitions) Innovative Interfaces, Inc - Sierra; (Cataloging) Innovative Interfaces, Inc - Sierra; (Circulation) Innovative Interfaces, Inc - Sierra; (OPAC) Innovative Interfaces, Inc

Wireless access
Function: 24/7 Electronic res, 24/7 Online cat, 3D Printer, Bks on CD, Children's prog, Computer training, Computers for patron use, Electronic databases & coll, Free DVD rentals, Homebound delivery serv, ILL available, Internet access, Movies, Music CDs, Online cat, OverDrive digital audio bks, Photocopying/Printing, Prog for adults, Prog for children & young adult, Scanner, STEM programs, Story hour, Summer & winter reading prog
Mem of Reaching Across Illinois Library System (RAILS)
Open Mon-Thurs 12:30pm-7pm, Sat 9-1

MAQUON

P MAQUON PUBLIC LIBRARY DISTRICT*, 210 Main St, 61458. (Mail add: PO Box 230, 61458-0230), SAN 304-3878. Tel: 309-875-3573. FAX: 309-875-3573. E-mail: maquon01@mymctc.net. Web Site: www.maquon.org/Services_Library.html. *Dir,* Mardell May
Founded 1943. Circ 10,215
Library Holdings: CDs 53; Large Print Bks 563; Bk Titles 14,920; Videos 395
Wireless access
Open Tues & Thurs 12-7, Wed & Fri 10-5, Sat 9-12

MARENGO

P MARENGO-UNION LIBRARY DISTRICT*, 19714 E Grant Hwy, 60152. SAN 304-3886. Tel: 815-568-8236. FAX: 815-568-5209. Web Site: www.muld.org. *Libr Dir,* Kevin Drinka; E-mail: kdrinka@muld.org; *Info Serv Mgr,* Sondra Terry; E-mail: sondrat@muld.org; *Patron Serv Mgr,* Carol Clark
Founded 1878. Pop 12,110; Circ 70,223
Library Holdings: Bk Vols 52,657
Automation Activity & Vendor Info: (Cataloging) Follett Software; (Circulation) Follett Software; (OPAC) Follett Software
Wireless access
Function: ILL available
Mem of Reaching Across Illinois Library System (RAILS)
Open Mon-Thurs 9-8, Fri & Sat 9-5
Friends of the Library Group

MARION

P CRAB ORCHARD PUBLIC LIBRARY DISTRICT*, 20012 Crab Orchard Rd, 62959. SAN 376-0073. Tel: 618-982-2141. Toll Free Tel: 866-982-2141. Web Site: www.craborchard.lib.il.us. *Dir,* Erin Steinsultz; E-mail: director.craborchardlibrary@gmail.com
Library Holdings: Bk Titles 20,000; Per Subs 55
Subject Interests: Genealogy
Wireless access
Mem of Illinois Heartland Library System
Open Mon-Thurs 11-7, Fri 11-5, Sat 12-5
Branches: 1
PITTSBURG BRANCH, 302 W Avery St, Pittsburg, 62974-1009. Tel: 618-997-8111. FAX: 618-997-8111. *Dir,* Lola Morris
Library Holdings: Bk Titles 2,000
Open Tues, Wed & Fri 2-6, Thurs 11-3

S GREATER EGYPT REGIONAL PLANNING & DEVELOPMENT COMMISSION*, Library Research Center, 3000 W DeYoung St, Ste 800B-3, 62959. SAN 326-9124. Tel: 618-997-9351. FAX: 618-997-9354. Web Site: greateregypt.org. *Dir,* Cary Minnis; E-mail: caryminnis@greateregypt.org; *Prog Dir,* Margie Mitchell; E-mail: margiemitchell@greateregypt.org
Library Holdings: Bk Vols 400
Restriction: Staff & prof res

P MARION CARNEGIE LIBRARY*, 206 S Market St, 62959-2519. SAN 304-3894. Tel: 618-993-5935. FAX: 618-997-6485. Web Site: www.marioncarnegielibrary.org. *Dir,* David Patton; E-mail: dpatton@marioncarnegielibrary.org; Staff 17 (MLS 2, Non-MLS 15)
Founded 1916. Pop 17,193; Circ 105,652
Library Holdings: AV Mats 2,900; Bks on Deafness & Sign Lang 20; Large Print Bks 3,000; Bk Vols 62,217; Per Subs 80; Talking Bks 1,200; Videos 500
Special Collections: Williamson County Local History Coll
Subject Interests: Civil War, Genealogy, Local hist, Small bus
Automation Activity & Vendor Info: (Acquisitions) SirsiDynix; (Cataloging) SirsiDynix; (Circulation) SirsiDynix; (Course Reserve) SirsiDynix; (ILL) SirsiDynix; (Media Booking) SirsiDynix; (OPAC) SirsiDynix; (Serials) SirsiDynix
Wireless access
Function: AV serv, Home delivery & serv to seniorr ctr & nursing homes, Homebound delivery serv, ILL available, Large print keyboards, Magnifiers for reading, Outside serv via phone, mail, e-mail & web, Photocopying/Printing, Prog for adults, Prog for children & young adult, Ref serv available, Summer reading prog, Telephone ref, Wheelchair accessible
Publications: The Container (Monthly newsletter)
Mem of Illinois Heartland Library System
Partic in Illinois Library & Information Network; OCLC Online Computer Library Center, Inc
Special Services for the Deaf - TTY equip
Special Services for the Blind - Computer with voice synthesizer for visually impaired persons
Open Mon-Thurs 9-8, Fri & Sat 9-5
Friends of the Library Group

MARISSA

P MARISSA AREA PUBLIC LIBRARY DISTRICT*, 212 N Main St, 62257. SAN 304-3916. Tel: 618-295-2825. FAX: 618-295-2435. E-mail: marissalibrary@hotmail.com. *Libr Dir,* Robin Geralds; Staff 4 (Non-MLS 4)
Founded 1959. Pop 3,363; Circ 19,230
Jul 2019-Jun 2020 Income $129,160, State $5,811, Federal $7,650, County $103,183, Locally Generated Income $12,516. Mats Exp $27,294, Books $23,528, AV Mat $3,079, Electronic Ref Mat (Incl. Access Fees) $687. Sal $82,012
Library Holdings: Audiobooks 542; CDs 145; DVDs 3,173; Bk Titles 23,672
Wireless access
Function: 24/7 Online cat, Adult bk club, Audiobks on Playaways & MP3, Audiobks via web, Bks on CD, Computers for patron use, Free DVD rentals, Homebound delivery serv, ILL available, Internet access, Laminating, Movies, Music CDs, Notary serv, Online cat, Photocopying/Printing, Prog for adults, Prog for children & young adult, Story hour, Study rm, Summer reading prog, Tax forms, Teen prog, Wheelchair accessible, Workshops
Mem of Illinois Heartland Library System
Open Mon, Wed & Fri 10-5, Tues & Thurs 10-7, Sat 10-1
Restriction: Non-resident fee
Friends of the Library Group

MARKHAM

P MARKHAM PUBLIC LIBRARY*, 16640 Kedzie Ave, 60428. SAN 304-3924. Tel: 708-331-0130. FAX: 708-331-0137. E-mail: markhampl@markhamlibrary.org. Web Site: www.markhamlibrary.org. *Dir,* Xavier Menzies; *Asst Dir,* Bridget Roland; Staff 1 (MLS 1)
Founded 1967. Pop 15,172; Circ 53,321
Library Holdings: Bk Titles 21,000; Bk Vols 27,000; Per Subs 35
Wireless access
Mem of Reaching Across Illinois Library System (RAILS)
Partic in System Wide Automated Network
Open Mon-Thurs 9-8, Fri & Sat 9-5
Friends of the Library Group

MAROA

P MAROA PUBLIC LIBRARY DISTRICT*, 305 E Garfield St, 61756. SAN 304-3932. Tel: 217-794-5111. FAX: 217-794-3005. E-mail: maroalibrary@gmail.com. Web Site: www.maroa.lib.il.us. *Dir,* Sara Gentle; Staff 3 (Non-MLS 3)
Founded 1945. Pop 2,902; Circ 61,661
Library Holdings: Bk Titles 23,160
Automation Activity & Vendor Info: (Cataloging) SirsiDynix; (Circulation) SirsiDynix
Wireless access
Mem of Illinois Heartland Library System
Partic in Association for Rural & Small Libraries
Open Tues-Thurs 9-6, Fri 9-3, Fri 9-1
Friends of the Library Group

MARQUETTE HEIGHTS

P MARQUETTE HEIGHTS PUBLIC LIBRARY*, 715 Lincoln Rd, 61554. SAN 304-3940. Tel: 309-382-3778. E-mail: marquetteheightspl@gmail.com. Web Site: www.mhlibrary.com. *Libr Dir,* Jenny Jackson; E-mail: jjackson.mhlibrary@gmail.com
Founded 1959. Pop 2,824; Circ 5,207
May 2014-Apr 2015 Income $68,743. Mats Exp $67,004
Library Holdings: Audiobooks 251; DVDs 152; Electronic Media & Resources 29; Bk Vols 13,284; Per Subs 44
Wireless access
Mem of Reaching Across Illinois Library System (RAILS)
Partic in RSA
Open Tues & Thurs 12-8, Wed & Fri 10-6, Sat 10-3 (Sept-May); Tues & Thurs 12-8, Wed & Fri 12-6, Sat 10-3 (Summer)

MARSEILLES

P MARSEILLES PUBLIC LIBRARY, 155 E Bluff St, 61341-1499. SAN 304-3959. Tel: 815-795-4437. FAX: 815-795-5137. Web Site: www.marseilleslibrary.com. *Dir,* Jan Ambrose; E-mail: jambrose155@gmail.com; Staff 6 (Non-MLS 6)
Founded 1904. Pop 5,090; Circ 17,691
Library Holdings: Bk Vols 24,979; Per Subs 17
Subject Interests: Local hist
Automation Activity & Vendor Info: (Circulation) Innovative Interfaces, Inc - Sierra
Wireless access
Function: Adult bk club, After school storytime, Bk club(s), Bks on CD, Chess club, Children's prog, Computer training, Computers for patron use, Homebound delivery serv, Magazines, Movies, Notary serv, Online cat, Photocopying/Printing, Preschool reading prog, Spoken cassettes & CDs, Story hour, Summer reading prog, Tax forms
Mem of Reaching Across Illinois Library System (RAILS)
Open Mon-Thurs 10-7, Fri 10-5, Sat 10-2
Friends of the Library Group

MARSHALL

P MARSHALL PUBLIC LIBRARY, 612 Archer Ave, 62441. SAN 304-3967. Tel: 217-826-2535. FAX: 217-826-5529. E-mail: marshallpubliclibrary@gmail.com. Web Site: www.marshalllillibrary.com. *Dir,* Alyson Thompson; *Head Libn,* Jamie Poorman
Pop 3,392; Circ 26,000
Library Holdings: Bk Vols 25,289; Per Subs 70
Automation Activity & Vendor Info: (Acquisitions) SirsiDynix
Wireless access
Special Services for the Deaf - TDD equip
Open Mon-Wed 10-6, Thurs 10-8, Fri & Sat 10-5
Friends of the Library Group

MARTINSVILLE

P MARTINSVILLE PUBLIC LIBRARY DISTRICT*, 120 E Cumberland St, 62442-1000. SAN 304-3975. Tel: 217-382-4113. E-mail: mvillelibrary@hotmail.com. Web Site: martinsvilleil.com/?page_id=106. *Librn,* Jill Goodman
Library Holdings: Bk Vols 14,000; Per Subs 55
Automation Activity & Vendor Info: (Cataloging) SirsiDynix; (Circulation) SirsiDynix
Mem of Illinois Heartland Library System
Open Mon-Wed & Fri 11-5, Thurs 11-7, Sat 10-1
Friends of the Library Group

MARYVILLE

§P MARYVILLE COMMUNITY LIBRARY, Eight Schiber Ct, 62062. Tel: 618-288-3801. FAX: 618-288-4793. E-mail: mve@maryville.lib.il.us. Web Site: www.maryville.lib.il.us. *Libr Dir,* Peggy Pick; E-mail: peggypick@maryville.lib.il.us
Wireless access
Function: Photocopying/Printing
Partic in Association for Rural & Small Libraries
Open Mon-Thurs 9-8, Fri & Sat 9-4
Friends of the Library Group

MASCOUTAH

P MASCOUTAH PUBLIC LIBRARY*, Three W Church St, 62258. SAN 304-3983. Tel: 618-566-2562. FAX: 618-566-2563. Web Site: www.mascoutahlibrary.com. *Dir,* Marian Albers; E-mail: malbers@mascoutah.lib.il.us; Staff 6 (MLS 2, Non-MLS 4)
Founded 1929. Pop 7,483; Circ 72,240
Library Holdings: Bk Titles 46,743; Per Subs 82
Automation Activity & Vendor Info: (Acquisitions) SirsiDynix; (Cataloging) SirsiDynix; (Circulation) SirsiDynix; (Course Reserve) SirsiDynix; (ILL) SirsiDynix; (Media Booking) SirsiDynix; (OPAC) SirsiDynix; (Serials) SirsiDynix
Wireless access
Open Mon-Thurs 10-8:30, Fri & Sat 10-5:30

MASON CITY

P MASON CITY PUBLIC LIBRARY DISTRICT*, 820 W Chestnut St, 62664-9768. SAN 304-3991. Tel: 217-482-3799. FAX: 217-482-3799. Web Site: www.masoncitylibrary.org. *Dir,* Diane Yeoman
Pop 3,431; Circ 14,523
Library Holdings: Bk Vols 20,000; Per Subs 20
Automation Activity & Vendor Info: (Acquisitions) SirsiDynix; (Cataloging) SirsiDynix; (Circulation) SirsiDynix; (Course Reserve) SirsiDynix; (ILL) SirsiDynix; (Media Booking) SirsiDynix; (OPAC) SirsiDynix; (Serials) SirsiDynix
Mem of Illinois Heartland Library System
Open Mon 10-5, Tues-Fri 12-5, Sat 10-12
Friends of the Library Group

MATTESON

P MATTESON AREA PUBLIC LIBRARY DISTRICT, 801 S School St, 60443-1897. SAN 304-4009. Tel: 708-748-4431. FAX: 708-748-0510. Administration FAX: 708-748-0579. E-mail: mtslib@mapld.org. Web Site: www.mapld.org. *Asst Libr Dir, Head, Adult Serv, Pub Serv Coordr,* Lisa Morrison-Korajczyk; E-mail: lkorajczyk2@mapld.org; *Head, Computer Serv,* Andy Murgas; E-mail: amurgas@mapld.org; *Customer Serv Coordr,* Thom Webb; E-mail: twebb@mapld.org; *Ch Serv,* Nikeda Webb; E-mail: nwebb2@mapld.org; *Ref (Info Servs),* Marsha Lotz; E-mail: mlotz2@mapld.org; Staff 20 (MLS 10, Non-MLS 10)
Founded 1964. Pop 19,009; Circ 232,437
Jul 2021-Jun 2022 Income $2,199,381. Mats Exp $253,400, Books $83,000, Per/Ser (Incl. Access Fees) $12,100, AV Mat $45,500, Electronic Ref Mat (Incl. Access Fees) $106,500. Sal $1,582,000
Library Holdings: Audiobooks 4,158; AV Mats 20,443; CDs 4,214; DVDs 12,071; e-books 530,844; Electronic Media & Resources 54; Large Print Bks 3,209; Bk Vols 98,848; Per Subs 119
Special Collections: Library of Things, craft items, culinary tools, games, health-related items, tech devices, tools
Subject Interests: Tools
Automation Activity & Vendor Info: (Acquisitions) Baker & Taylor; (Cataloging) SirsiDynix-WorkFlows; (Circulation) SirsiDynix-WorkFlows; (Discovery) EBSCO Discovery Service; (ILL) SirsiDynix-WorkFlows; (OPAC) SirsiDynix-Enterprise; (Serials) SirsiDynix-WorkFlows
Wireless access
Function: 24/7 Electronic res, 24/7 Online cat, 3D Printer, Accelerated reader prog, Adult bk club, After school storytime, Art exhibits, Audiobks on Playaways & MP3, Audiobks via web, Bk club(s), Bks on CD, Chess club, Children's prog, Computer training, Computers for patron use, Digital talking bks, Electronic databases & coll, Free DVD rentals, Genealogy discussion group, Holiday prog, Home delivery & serv to seniorr ctr & nursing homes, Homebound delivery serv, Homework prog, ILL available, Internet access, Laminating, Life-long learning prog for all ages, Magazines, Magnifiers for reading, Mail & tel request accepted, Meeting rooms, Museum passes, Music CDs, Notary serv, Online cat, Orientations, Outreach serv, Outside serv via phone, mail, e-mail & web, OverDrive digital audio bks, Passport agency, Photocopying/Printing, Preschool outreach, Preschool reading prog, Printer for laptops & handheld devices, Prog for adults, Prog for children & young adult, Ref serv available, Scanner, Senior computer classes, Senior outreach, Spoken cassettes & CDs, Spoken cassettes & DVDs, STEM programs, Story hour, Study rm, Summer reading prog, Tax forms, Teen prog, Telephone ref, Wheelchair accessible, Winter reading prog, Workshops
Publications: Matteson Connection (Newsletter)
Mem of Reaching Across Illinois Library System (RAILS)
Partic in System Wide Automated Network
Special Services for the Blind - Aids for in-house use; Bks on CD; Descriptive video serv (DVS); Home delivery serv; Large print bks; Magnifiers
Open Mon-Thurs 9-9, Fri & Sat 9-5, Sun (Sept-May) 1-5

MATTOON

J LAKE LAND COLLEGE LIBRARY*, 5001 Lake Land Blvd, 61938. SAN 304-4017. Circulation Tel: 217-234-5367. Interlibrary Loan Service Tel: 217-234-5235. Administration Tel: 217-234-5338. Information Services Tel: 217-234-5440. FAX: 217-234-5533. Web Site: www.lakelandcollege.edu/library. *Dir, Libr Serv,* Sarah Hill; Tel: 217-234-5538, E-mail: shilll@lakelandcollege.edu; Staff 7 (MLS 2, Non-MLS 5)
Founded 1968. Enrl 2,605; Fac 120; Highest Degree: Associate
Jul 2019-Jun 2020 Income $571,313. Mats Exp $159,135, Books $31,000, Per/Ser (Incl. Access Fees) $730, AV Mat $1,500, Electronic Ref Mat (Incl. Access Fees) $125,905. Sal $288,825 (Prof $174,214)
Library Holdings: Audiobooks 470; CDs 592; DVDs 1,306; e-books 165,000; e-journals 43,000; Electronic Media & Resources 37; Bk Vols 20,200; Per Subs 12
Automation Activity & Vendor Info: (Acquisitions) Innovative Interfaces, Inc; (Cataloging) Innovative Interfaces, Inc; (Circulation) Innovative Interfaces, Inc; (Course Reserve) Innovative Interfaces, Inc; (Discovery) ProQuest; (ILL) OCLC; (OPAC) Innovative Interfaces, Inc
Wireless access
Function: Bks on CD, Computers for patron use, Electronic databases & coll, ILL available, Online cat, Online info literacy tutorials on the web & in blackboard, Photocopying/Printing, Ref serv available
Mem of Illinois Heartland Library System
Partic in Consortium of Academic & Research Libraries in Illinois; Illinois Library & Information Network; Network of Illinois Learning Resources in Community Colleges
Special Services for the Deaf - Closed caption videos

Open Mon-Thurs 7:30-7:30, Fri 7:30-5, Sun 2-7 (Fall & Spring); Mon-Thurs 7:30-7:30 (Summer)
Restriction: In-house use for visitors, Open to pub for ref & circ; with some limitations, Open to students, fac & staff

M SARAH BUSH LINCOLN HEALTH CENTER*, Medical Library, 1000 Health Center Dr, 61938. (Mail add: PO Box 372, 61938), SAN 375-9474. Tel: 217-258-2262. FAX: 217-258-2288. Web Site: www.sarahbush.org/cord/program/331. *Librn,* Nina Pals; E-mail: npals@sblhs.org; *Librn,* Anieta Trame; E-mail: atrame@sblhs.org
Library Holdings: DVDs 20; e-books 60; e-journals 3,000; Bk Titles 1,000; Per Subs 45
Wireless access
Mem of Illinois Heartland Library System
Open Mon-Fri 8-4:30

P MATTOON PUBLIC LIBRARY*, 1600 Charleston Ave, 61938-3935. (Mail add: PO Box 809, 61938), SAN 304-4025. Tel: 217-234-2621. FAX: 217-234-2660. E-mail: info@mattoonlibrary.org. Web Site: www.mattoonlibrary.org. *Dir,* Carl Walworth; Tel: 217-234-2610, E-mail: Carl@mattoonlibrary.org; Staff 6 (MLS 2, Non-MLS 4)
Founded 1893. Pop 18,291; Circ 82,665
Library Holdings: AV Mats 3,051; Bks on Deafness & Sign Lang 10; Bk Vols 55,000; Per Subs 170
Automation Activity & Vendor Info: (Cataloging) Innovative Interfaces, Inc; (Circulation) Innovative Interfaces, Inc
Wireless access
Function: ILL available
Mem of Illinois Heartland Library System
Open Mon-Fri 9-7, Sat 10-4
Friends of the Library Group

MAYWOOD

P MAYWOOD PUBLIC LIBRARY DISTRICT*, 121 S Fifth Ave, 60153-1307. SAN 340-5095. Tel: 708-343-1847. FAX: 708-343-2115. E-mail: mpld@maywoodlibrary.org. Web Site: maywoodlibrary.org. *Dir,* Stan Huntington; Tel: 703-343-1847, Ext 28, E-mail: shuntington@maywoodlibrary.org; *Asst Dir,* Felipe Altamirano; Tel: 708-343-1847, Ext 11, E-mail: faltamirano@maywoodlibrary.org; *Head, Tech Serv,* Kristin Flanders; Tel: 708-343-1847, Ext 15, E-mail: kflanders@maywoodlibrary.org; *Head, Youth Serv,* Sheila Ferrari; Tel: 708-343-1847, Ext 24, E-mail: sferrari@maywoodlibrary.org; *IT Mgr,* Marcia Burton; Tel: 708-343-1847, Ext 13, E-mail: mburton@maywoodlibrary.org; Staff 25 (MLS 5, Non-MLS 20)
Founded 1874. Pop 26,987
Library Holdings: AV Mats 7,489; Bks on Deafness & Sign Lang 50; CDs 1,351; DVDs 1,761; High Interest/Low Vocabulary Bk Vols 241; Large Print Bks 683; Bk Vols 77,870; Per Subs 97; Talking Bks 993; Videos 3,745
Subject Interests: African-Am, Local hist
Automation Activity & Vendor Info: (Circulation) Innovative Interfaces, Inc; (OPAC) Innovative Interfaces, Inc
Wireless access
Mem of Reaching Across Illinois Library System (RAILS)
Partic in System Wide Automated Network
Open Mon & Wed 12-7, Tues & Thurs 12-5:30, Sat 9-5:30

MCCOOK

P MCCOOK PUBLIC LIBRARY DISTRICT*, 8419 W 50th St, 60525-3187. SAN 376-0146. Tel: 708-442-1242. FAX: 708-442-0148. E-mail: librarymccook@gmail.com. Web Site: www.mccook.lib.il.us. *Librn,* Nancy Casasanto; Staff 3.8 (MLS 1, Non-MLS 2.8)
Founded 1984. Pop 254; Circ 33,997
Library Holdings: CDs 2,559; DVDs 3,827; Large Print Bks 150; Bk Vols 16,269; Per Subs 83
Automation Activity & Vendor Info: (Acquisitions) SirsiDynix; (Cataloging) SirsiDynix; (Circulation) SirsiDynix-WorkFlows; (ILL) OCLC; (OPAC) SirsiDynix; (Serials) SirsiDynix
Wireless access
Function: Adult bk club, Bks on cassette, Bks on CD, Children's prog, Computers for patron use, Electronic databases & coll, ILL available, Internet access, Music CDs, Online cat, Photocopying/Printing, Prog for children & young adult, Ref & res, Ref serv available, Summer reading prog, Tax forms, Teen prog, VHS videos, Wheelchair accessible
Mem of Reaching Across Illinois Library System (RAILS)
Partic in System Wide Automated Network
Open Mon-Thurs 10-8, Fri 10-5, Sat 10-4
Restriction: Non-resident fee

MCHENRY

P MCHENRY PUBLIC LIBRARY DISTRICT*, 809 Front St, 60050. SAN 304-3711. Tel: 815-385-0036. FAX: 815-385-7085. Web Site: www.mchenrylibrary.org. *Exec Dir,* James C Scholtz; E-mail: jscholtz@mchenrylibrary.org; *Asst Dir,* Bill Edminster; *Adult Serv,* Pam Strain; *Circ,* Barb Majka; *ILL,* Bonnie Niepsuj; *Tech Serv,* Kathy Milfajt; *Youth Serv,* Lesley Jakacki; Staff 56 (MLS 11, Non-MLS 45)
Founded 1943. Pop 42,023; Circ 534,264
Jul 2014-Jun 2015 Income $3,382,212, State $52,529, Locally Generated Income $3,212,228, Other $97,455. Mats Exp $375,123, Books $163,270, AV Mat $122,841, Electronic Ref Mat (Incl. Access Fees) $89,012. Sal $1,573,231
Library Holdings: Audiobooks 9,385; AV Mats 2,238; Bks on Deafness & Sign Lang 38; CDs 8,596; DVDs 16,254; e-books 14,742; Electronic Media & Resources 49; Large Print Bks 4,295; Bk Vols 118,658; Per Subs 255
Special Collections: Large-Type Books Coll
Subject Interests: Genealogy
Wireless access
Publications: The Preface (Newsletter)
Partic in Cooperative Computer Services - CCS
Open Mon-Thurs 9-9, Fri & Sat 9-5, Sun 12-4
Friends of the Library Group

P RIVER EAST PUBLIC LIBRARY*, 813 W Rte 120, 60051. SAN 304-3703. Tel: 815-385-6303. FAX: 815-385-6337. Web Site: www.rivereastlibrary.org. *Dir,* Cherie Wright; E-mail: cherie@rivereastlibrary.org; Staff 5 (MLS 1, Non-MLS 4)
Founded 1960. Pop 4,266
Library Holdings: Bk Titles 13,987; Per Subs 41
Automation Activity & Vendor Info: (Circulation) Follett Software
Open Mon-Thurs 10-7, Fri & Sat 10-5
Friends of the Library Group

MCLEAN

P MOUNT HOPE-FUNKS GROVE TOWNSHIPS LIBRARY DISTRICT, 111 S Hamilton St, 61754-7624. (Mail add: PO Box 320, 61754-0320), SAN 304-3738. Tel: 309-874-2291. FAX: 309-874-2291. E-mail: mhfglibrary1@hotmail.com. Web Site: mthopefglibrary.wixsite.com/mysite-1. *Dir,* Stefanie Geitz; *Libr Tech,* Savannah Gobeli; *Libr Tech,* Natalie Peak
Founded 1917. Pop 1,348
Library Holdings: Bk Titles 13,431; Per Subs 35
Special Collections: McLean Lens Digital Coll
Wireless access
Mem of Reaching Across Illinois Library System (RAILS)
Open Tues & Thurs 2-6, Sat 9-1

MCLEANSBORO

P MCCOY MEMORIAL LIBRARY*, 130 S Washington St, 62859. SAN 304-3746. Tel: 618-643-2125. FAX: 618-643-2207. E-mail: mccoylibrary@yahoo.com. *Librn,* Ginger Finley
Founded 1921. Pop 2,945; Circ 12,372
Library Holdings: Bk Titles 13,858; Per Subs 98
Subject Interests: Genealogy
Wireless access
Mem of Illinois Heartland Library System
Open Mon-Wed & Fri 11-5, Thurs 11-7, Sat 8-12

MELROSE PARK

M GOTTLIEB MEMORIAL HOSPITAL*, Medical Library, 701 W North Ave, 60160. SAN 375-9393. Tel: 708-538-4173. FAX: 708-681-3973. Web Site: www.gottliebhospital.org. *Librn,* Gloria Kroc; E-mail: gloria_kroc@luhs.org; Staff 1 (MLS 1)
Founded 1961
Library Holdings: Bk Titles 450; Per Subs 6
Wireless access
Restriction: Not open to pub

P MELROSE PARK PUBLIC LIBRARY*, 801 N Broadway, 60160. SAN 304-405X. Tel: 708-649-7400. FAX: 708-531-5327. E-mail: mps@mpplibrary.org. Web Site: www.mpplibrary.org. *Libr Dir,* Cindy Guecklich; Staff 9 (MLS 3, Non-MLS 6)
Founded 1898. Pop 23,171; Circ 54,234
Library Holdings: Bk Vols 87,000; Per Subs 183
Special Collections: Cinema
Automation Activity & Vendor Info: (Acquisitions) Innovative Interfaces, Inc
Wireless access
Mem of Reaching Across Illinois Library System (RAILS)
Partic in System Wide Automated Network
Open Mon, Wed & Fri 8-5, Tues & Thurs 11-7, Sat 10-2

MELVIN

P MELVIN PUBLIC LIBRARY*, 102 S Center St, 60952. SAN 304-4084. Tel: 217-388-2421. FAX: 217-388-2421. Web Site: melvinpubliclibrary.blogspot.com. *Dir,* Jacqueline Allen
Pop 614; Circ 6,900
Library Holdings: Bk Vols 8,500; Per Subs 40
Wireless access
Mem of Illinois Heartland Library System
Open Mon-Wed 12-6, Fri 12-5, Sat 10-2
Friends of the Library Group

MENDON

P FOUR STAR PUBLIC LIBRARY DISTRICT, 132 W South St, 62351. (Mail add: PO Box 169, 62351-0169), SAN 375-3271. Tel: 217-936-2131. FAX: 217-936-2132. E-mail: fourstar@adams.net. Web Site: www.fourstarlibrary.com. *Libr Dir,* Jill Lucey; *Prog Coordr,* Jenny King
Founded 1990. Pop 4,314
Library Holdings: Bk Titles 14,000; Per Subs 36
Wireless access
Partic in Association for Rural & Small Libraries; Resource Sharing Alliance
Open Mon-Thurs 2-8, Fri & Sat 10-2

MENDOTA

P GRAVES-HUME PUBLIC LIBRARY DISTRICT, 1401 W Main St, 61342. SAN 304-4092. Tel: 815-538-5142. FAX: 815-538-3816. Web Site: graveshume.org. *Dir,* Emily Kofoid; Staff 10 (MLS 1, Non-MLS 9)
Founded 1870. Pop 7,272; Circ 43,677
Library Holdings: Bk Vols 33,557; Per Subs 119
Wireless access
Function: Adult bk club, After school storytime, Audiobks on Playaways & MP3, Audiobks via web, Children's prog, Computers for patron use, Free DVD rentals, Home delivery & serv to seniorr ctr & nursing homes, Homebound delivery serv, ILL available, Internet access, Laminating, Magazines, Meeting rooms, Movies, Notary serv, Online cat, Photocopying/Printing, Preschool outreach, Preschool reading prog, Prog for adults, Prog for children & young adult, Scanner, Story hour, Study rm, Summer & winter reading prog, Summer reading prog, Tax forms
Mem of Reaching Across Illinois Library System (RAILS)
Open Mon-Thurs 10-8, Fri 10-4, Sat 10-2
Friends of the Library Group

MEREDOSIA

P M-C RIVER VALLEY PUBLIC LIBRARY DISTRICT*, 304 Main St, 62665. (Mail add: PO Box 259, 62665-0259), SAN 304-4106. Tel: 217-584-1571. FAX: 217-584-1571. E-mail: vrevircm@adams.net. *Dir,* Janet Wells
Pop 1,904; Circ 16,032
Library Holdings: Bk Vols 17,000; Per Subs 50
Automation Activity & Vendor Info: (Cataloging) Follett Software; (Circulation) Follett Software; (OPAC) Follett Software
Open Mon & Thurs 5-9, Tues 9-5, Wed 9-8, Fri & Sat 1-5

METAMORA

P ILLINOIS PRAIRIE DISTRICT PUBLIC LIBRARY*, 208 E Partridge St, 61548. SAN 340-515X. Tel: 309-921-5074. FAX: 309-921-5075. Web Site: www.ipdpl.org. *Dir,* Joel D Shoemaker; E-mail: joels@mtco.com; *Asst Dir,* Dawn Smith; Staff 1 (MLS 1)
Founded 1950. Pop 21,644; Circ 139,977
Library Holdings: Bk Vols 127,000; Per Subs 381
Special Collections: Local Newspaper (Metamora Herald 1887-present & Washburn Leader 1963-present), micro
Subject Interests: Agr, Antiques, Educ, Hist
Automation Activity & Vendor Info: (Cataloging) TLC (The Library Corporation); (Circulation) TLC (The Library Corporation); (ILL) OCLC; (OPAC) TLC (The Library Corporation)
Partic in OCLC Online Computer Library Center, Inc
Open Mon, Thurs & Fri 10-5, Tues 10-7, Wed 2-7, Sat 10-2
Branches: 6
BENSON BRANCH, 420 E Front St, Benson, 61516. (Mail add: PO Box 17, Benson, 61516-0017), SAN 340-5184. Tel: 309-394-2542. FAX: 309-394-2792. Web Site: www.ipdpl.org/locations-hours/benson. *Librn,* Jane Kolb
Open Mon, Wed & Fri 3-6, Sat 10-12
MARCELLA SCHNEIDER BRANCH, 509 Woodland Knolls Rd, Germantown Hills, 61548, SAN 340-5214. Tel: 309-921-5056. FAX: 309-383-5057. *Librn,* JoEllyn Curry
Open Mon-Thurs 10-7, Fri 10-5, Sat 10-3
METAMORA BRANCH, 208 E Partridge St, 61548, SAN 340-5249. *Librn,* Peggy Bockler
Pop 19,179
Open Mon, Thurs & Fri 10-5, Tues 10-7, Wed 2-7, Sat 10-12
ROANOKE BRANCH, 123 E Broad St, Roanoke, 61561. (Mail add: PO Box 657, Roanoke, 61561-0657), SAN 340-5273. Tel: 309-923-7686. FAX: 309-923-7601. *Librn,* Sandra Steffan
Open Mon 4-7, Tues & Thurs 12-5, Fri 10-1, Sat 10-12
SPRINGBAY BRANCH, 411 Illinois St, Springbay, 61611, SAN 340-5303. Tel: 309-822-0444. FAX: 309-822-0794. *Librn,* Nel Babitske; *Asst Librn,* Linda M Moore
Library Holdings: Bk Titles 5,723
Open Mon & Thurs 1-6, Sat 10-Noon
WASHBURN BRANCH, 102 W Magnolia, Washburn, 61570. (Mail add: PO Box 128, Washburn, 61570-0128), SAN 340-5338. Tel: 309-248-7429. FAX: 309-248-7027. *Librn,* Donna Adami
Open Mon 2-6, Wed 10-2, Thurs 3-7, Sat 10-12

METROPOLIS

P METROPOLIS PUBLIC LIBRARY*, 317 Metropolis St, 62960. SAN 304-4114. Tel: 618-524-4312. FAX: 618-524-3675. E-mail: library@metropolisil.gov. Web Site: www.metropolispubliclibrary.com. *Dir,* Lori L Bruce; *Ad, Outreach Librn,* Amanda Quint; *Ch,* Angela Lockard; E-mail: alockard@cityofmetropolis.com; *Cat, Info Tech,* Colby Kennedy; E-mail: ckennedy@cityofmetropolis.com; *Circ,* Catharine Bass; E-mail: catharine.metlib@gmail.com; *Genealogy Serv, ILL,* Patricia Lockard; E-mail: Plockard@cityofmetropolis.com; Staff 10 (MLS 1, Non-MLS 9)
Founded 1913. Pop 6,537; Circ 51,066
Library Holdings: e-books 3,000; Bk Vols 38,000; Per Subs 150
Special Collections: Genealogy Coll
Automation Activity & Vendor Info: (Cataloging) OCLC FirstSearch; (Course Reserve) OCLC
Wireless access
Function: 24/7 Electronic res, 24/7 Online cat, Accelerated reader prog, Activity rm, Adult bk club, Audio & video playback equip for onsite use, Audiobks on Playaways & MP3, Audiobks via web, AV serv, Bk club(s), Bks on CD, Bus archives, Children's prog, Citizenship assistance, Computer training, Computers for patron use, Digital talking bks, E-Readers, Electronic databases & coll, Equip loans & repairs, Family literacy, Free DVD rentals, Games & aids for people with disabilities, Genealogy discussion group, Govt ref serv, Health sci info serv, Holiday prog, Home delivery & serv to seniorr ctr & nursing homes, Homebound delivery serv, Homework prog, ILL available, Instruction & testing, Internet access, Laminating, Legal assistance to inmates, Literacy & newcomer serv, Magazines, Magnifiers for reading, Mail & tel request accepted, Makerspace, Masonic res mat, Meeting rooms, Microfiche/film & reading machines, Movies, Notary serv, Online cat, Online ref, Outreach serv, Outside serv via phone, mail, e-mail & web, OverDrive digital audio bks, Photocopying/Printing, Preschool outreach, Preschool reading prog, Printer for laptops & handheld devices, Prof lending libr, Prog for adults, Prog for children & young adult, Ref & res, Ref serv available, Res assist avail, Res performed for a fee, Satellite serv, Senior computer classes, Senior outreach, Serves people with intellectual disabilities, Spanish lang bks, Specialized serv in classical studies, Spoken cassettes & CDs, STEM programs, Story hour, Study rm, Summer & winter reading prog, Tax forms, Teen prog, Telephone ref, Wheelchair accessible, Winter reading prog, Workshops, Writing prog
Mem of Illinois Heartland Library System
Special Services for the Deaf - Assisted listening device; Bks on deafness & sign lang
Special Services for the Blind - Aids for in-house use; Assistive/Adapted tech devices, equip & products; Bks on CD; Copier with enlargement capabilities; Digital talking bk; Large print bks; Magnifiers; Playaways (bks on MP3); Recorded bks
Open Mon-Thurs 10-7, Fri & Sat 10-6
Restriction: Access at librarian's discretion, Borrowing requests are handled by ILL

MIDLOTHIAN

P MIDLOTHIAN PUBLIC LIBRARY, 14701 S Kenton Ave, 60445-4122. SAN 304-4122. Tel: 708-535-2027. FAX: 708-535-2053. E-mail: mds@midlothianlibrary.org. Web Site: www.midlothianlibrary.org. *Libr Dir,* Jennifer Cottrill; E-mail: gcottrill@midlothianlibrary.org; *IT Mgr,* Michelle Vanis; E-mail: mvanis@midlothianlibrary.org; *Libr Office Mgr,* Christy Parente; E-mail: cparente@midlothianlibrary.org; *Mgr, Mat Serv,* Sarah Marshall; E-mail: smarshall@midlothianlibrary.org; *Pub Serv Mgr,* Jamie Kallio; E-mail: jkallio@midlothianlibrary.org; Staff 23 (MLS 5, Non-MLS 18)
Founded 1931. Pop 14,315; Circ 106,182
May 2015-Apr 2016 Income $909,043, State $24,973, City $764,390, Federal $9,103, Locally Generated Income $110,577. Mats Exp $98,263, Books $67,740, Per/Ser (Incl. Access Fees) $4,000, AV Mat $11,925,

Electronic Ref Mat (Incl. Access Fees) $14,598. Sal $370,677 (Prof $214,313)
Library Holdings: AV Mats 3,956; CDs 1,588; DVDs 2,368; Electronic Media & Resources 29; Bk Vols 61,560; Per Subs 261
Automation Activity & Vendor Info: (Cataloging) Innovative Interfaces, Inc; (Circulation) Innovative Interfaces, Inc; (ILL) Innovative Interfaces, Inc; (OPAC) Innovative Interfaces, Inc; (Serials) Innovative Interfaces, Inc
Wireless access
Function: Adult bk club, Bks on CD, Children's prog, Computers for patron use, Electronic databases & coll, Museum passes, Music CDs, Online cat, Photocopying/Printing, Prog for adults, Prog for children & young adult, Spoken cassettes & CDs, Story hour, Summer reading prog, Tax forms, Teen prog
Mem of Reaching Across Illinois Library System (RAILS)
Partic in System Wide Automated Network
Open Mon-Thurs 9-8, Fri 9-5, Sat 9-4
Friends of the Library Group

MILFORD

P MILFORD DISTRICT LIBRARY, Two S Grant Ave, 60953-1399. SAN 304-4130. Tel: 815-889-4722. FAX: 815-889-4722. E-mail: info@milfordlib.org. Web Site: www.milfordlib.org. *Dir,* Nina White
Founded 1896. Pop 3,415; Circ 23,284
Library Holdings: Bk Vols 18,000; Per Subs 3
Automation Activity & Vendor Info: (Acquisitions) SirsiDynix; (Cataloging) SirsiDynix; (Circulation) SirsiDynix; (Course Reserve) SirsiDynix; (ILL) SirsiDynix; (Media Booking) SirsiDynix; (OPAC) SirsiDynix; (Serials) SirsiDynix
Wireless access
Mem of Illinois Heartland Library System
Open Mon-Thurs 9-6, Fri 9-5, Sat 9-Noon

MILLEDGEVILLE

P MILLEDGEVILLE PUBLIC LIBRARY*, 18 W Fifth St, 61051-9416. SAN 304-4149. Tel: 815-225-7572. FAX: 815-225-7572. E-mail: milledgevillelibrary@yahoo.com. Web Site: milledgevillelibrary.org. *Libr Dir,* Jennifer Garden
Founded 1923. Pop 1,366; Circ 8,968
Library Holdings: Bk Vols 12,193; Per Subs 24
Wireless access
Function: 24/7 Online cat, Adult bk club, Archival coll, Audiobks via web, Bks on CD, Children's prog, Computers for patron use, Free DVD rentals, Homebound delivery serv, ILL available, Internet access, Magazines, Meeting rooms, Movies, Notary serv, Online cat, Photocopying/Printing, Printer for laptops & handheld devices, Prog for adults, Prog for children & young adult, Ref & res, Ref serv available, Scanner, Summer reading prog, Tax forms, Telephone ref
Mem of Reaching Across Illinois Library System (RAILS)
Open Tues & Thurs 1-7, Wed & Fri 10-6, Sat 10-2

MILLSTADT

P MILLSTADT LIBRARY, 115 W Laurel St, 62260. SAN 376-0901. Tel: 618-476-1887. FAX: 618-476-3600. E-mail: millstadtlib@gmail.com. Web Site: millstadt-library.org. *Dir,* Nichole Lauko; E-mail: n.lauko.millstadtlib@gmail.com; *Librn,* Elizabeth Harter; *Librn,* Penny Jestes; *Librn,* Cinda Leech; Staff 3 (MLS 1, Non-MLS 2)
Founded 1964. Pop 4,011
Library Holdings: Bk Titles 15,000; Per Subs 46
Automation Activity & Vendor Info: (Circulation) SirsiDynix
Wireless access
Function: 24/7 Electronic res, 24/7 Online cat, Adult bk club, Art programs, Audiobks via web, Bk club(s), Bks on CD, Computer training, Computers for patron use, Holiday prog, Homebound delivery serv, ILL available, Internet access, Magazines, Movies, Music CDs, Online cat, Outreach serv, Outside serv via phone, mail, e-mail & web, Photocopying/Printing, Preschool reading prog, Prog for adults, Prog for children & young adult, Ref & res, Scanner, Senior outreach, Story hour, Summer reading prog, Tax forms
Mem of Illinois Heartland Library System
Open Mon-Thurs Noon-8, Fri & Sat 10-2

MINERAL

P MINERAL-GOLD PUBLIC LIBRARY DISTRICT*, 120 E Main St, 61344. (Mail add: PO Box 87, 61344-0087), SAN 304-4157. Tel: 309-288-3971. FAX: 309-288-3971. E-mail: minerallibrary@frontier.com. *Dir,* Connie Baele
Pop 664; Circ 14,764
Library Holdings: Bk Vols 14,638; Per Subs 30
Subject Interests: Gardening, Local hist
Wireless access
Mem of Reaching Across Illinois Library System (RAILS)
Open Mon-Wed 9-12 & 1-6, Fri & Sat 9-12

MINIER

P H A PEINE DISTRICT LIBRARY*, 202 N Main St, 61759. (Mail add: PO Box 19, 61759-0019), SAN 304-4165. Tel: 309-392-3220. FAX: 309-392-2697. E-mail: minierlibrary@gmail.com. *Dir,* Barbara Tarbuck
Founded 1929. Pop 1,262; Circ 9,600
Library Holdings: Bk Vols 15,000; Per Subs 30
Open Mon-Thurs 12-8, Fri 12-6, Sat 9-1

MINONK

P FILGER PUBLIC LIBRARY*, 261 E Fifth St, 61760. SAN 304-4173. Tel: 309-432-2929. FAX: 309-432-2929. E-mail: filgerlibrary@frontier.com, filgerlibraryboard@gmail.com. Web Site: minonklibrary.wordpress.com. *Dir,* Debra Blunier; *Asst Librn,* Susan Ryan
Founded 1915. Pop 1,984; Circ 25,412
Library Holdings: Bk Vols 28,000; Per Subs 65
Wireless access
Open Mon-Wed 9-5, Thurs 9-7, Fri & Sat 9-Noon

MOKENA

P MOKENA COMMUNITY PUBLIC LIBRARY DISTRICT*, 11327 W 195th St, 60448. SAN 304-4181. Tel: 708-479-9663. FAX: 708-479-9684. E-mail: mcpldstaff@mokena.lib.il.us. Web Site: mokenalibrary.org. *Dir,* Cathy Palmer; E-mail: cpalmer@sbcglobal.net; *Coll Develop, Dir,* Michaelene Cervantes-Squires; E-mail: mcervantes@mokena.lib.il.us; *Asst Dir, Ref Serv,* Carol Tracy; E-mail: ctracy@mokena.lib.il.us; *Head, Tech Serv,* Jenifer Sciaky; E-mail: jsciaky@mokena.lib.il.us; Staff 38 (Non-MLS 38)
Founded 1976. Pop 15,821; Circ 160,000
Library Holdings: Bk Vols 130,000; Per Subs 325
Subject Interests: Parenting
Automation Activity & Vendor Info: (Acquisitions) SirsiDynix; (Cataloging) SirsiDynix; (Circulation) SirsiDynix; (Course Reserve) SirsiDynix; (ILL) SirsiDynix; (Media Booking) SirsiDynix; (OPAC) SirsiDynix; (Serials) SirsiDynix
Wireless access
Publications: Newsletter (in-house, monthly)
Mem of Reaching Across Illinois Library System (RAILS)
Open Mon-Thurs 9-9, Fri 9-6, Sat 9-5
Friends of the Library Group

MOLINE

J BLACK HAWK COLLEGE*, Quad-Cities Campus, 6600 34th Ave, 61265. SAN 340-5362. Tel: 309-796-5700. Reference Tel: 309-796-5147. FAX: 309-796-0393. Reference E-mail: libraryref@bhc.edu. Web Site: www.bhc.edu/academics/academic-resources/library. *Dir, Libr Serv,* Ashtin Trimble; E-mail: Trimblea@bhc.edu; *Ref & Instruction Librn,* Barbara Bolster; E-mail: bolserb@bhc.edu; Staff 4.5 (MLS 2, Non-MLS 2.5)
Founded 1946. Enrl 4,887; Fac 312; Highest Degree: Associate
Automation Activity & Vendor Info: (Acquisitions) Innovative Interfaces, Inc; (Cataloging) Innovative Interfaces, Inc; (Circulation) Innovative Interfaces, Inc; (Course Reserve) Innovative Interfaces, Inc; (OPAC) Innovative Interfaces, Inc
Wireless access
Mem of Reaching Across Illinois Library System (RAILS)
Open Mon-Thurs (Fall-Spring) 7:30-7:30, Fri 7:30-3; Mon-Thurs (Summer) 8-5, Fri 8-1

S DEERE & CO LIBRARY, One John Deere Pl, 61265. SAN 340-5397. Interlibrary Loan Service Tel: 309-765-5200. FAX: 309-765-4088. E-mail: library@johndeere.com. Web Site: www.deere.com. *Coop Librn,* Jamie Hosek
Founded 1958
Special Collections: Deere & Company History
Subject Interests: Agr, Bus & mgt, Construction, Econ, Engr, Finance, Forestry, Mkt
Automation Activity & Vendor Info: (Acquisitions) EBSCO Discovery Service; (Cataloging) EBSCO Discovery Service; (Circulation) EBSCO Discovery Service; (Discovery) EBSCO Discovery Service; (OPAC) EBSCO Discovery Service; (Serials) EBSCO Discovery Service
Wireless access
Mem of Reaching Across Illinois Library System (RAILS)

P MOLINE PUBLIC LIBRARY*, 3210 41st St, 61265. SAN 340-5486. Tel: 309-524-2440. Circulation Tel: 309-524-2450. FAX: 309-524-2441. Reference E-mail: reference@molinelibrary.org. Web Site: www.molinelibrary.com. *Libr Dir,* Bryon Lear; Tel: 309-524-2442, E-mail: blear@molinelibrary.org
Library Holdings: Bk Vols 203,417
Wireless access
Partic in RiverShare Libraries

Special Services for the Deaf - TDD equip
Open Mon-Fri 9-5

S ROCK ISLAND COUNTY ILLINOIS GENEALOGICAL SOCIETY LIBRARY*, 822 11th Ave, 61265. (Mail add: PO Box 3912, Rock Island, 61204-3912), SAN 370-8144. E-mail: librarian@ricigs.org. Web Site: www.ricigs.org.
Library Holdings: Bk Vols 2,718; Spec Interest Per Sub 30
Special Collections: Cemetery Records; County Records; Newspaper Abstracts
Subject Interests: Genealogy
Wireless access
Restriction: Non-circulating to the pub

MOMENCE

P EDWARD CHIPMAN PUBLIC LIBRARY*, 126 N Locust St, 60954. SAN 304-4211. Tel: 815-472-2581. FAX: 815-472-2581. E-mail: edwardchipmanpl@gmail.com. Web Site: momencelibrary.org. *Dir,* Robin Adkins
Founded 1907. Pop 6,837; Circ 14,409
Library Holdings: Audiobooks 613; Large Print Bks 530; Microforms 74; Bk Vols 23,143; Per Subs 37; Videos 551
Mem of Reaching Across Illinois Library System (RAILS)
Open Mon-Wed 9:30-6, Thurs 1-8, Fri 9:30-5, Sat 9:30-2

MONMOUTH

C MONMOUTH COLLEGE, Hewes Library, 700 E Broadway, 61462-1963. SAN 304-422X. Tel: 309-457-2190. Reference Tel: 309-457-2303. FAX: 309-457-2226. E-mail: library@monmouthcollege.edu. Web Site: library.monmouthcollege.edu. *Dir,* Sarah Henderson; Tel: 309-457-2192, E-mail: schenderson@monmouthcollege.edu; *Pub Serv Librn,* Anne Giffey; E-mail: agiffey@monmouthcollege.edu; *Tech Serv Librn,* Lynn K Daw; Tel: 309-457-2187, E-mail: ldaw@monmouthcollege.edu; *Acq Mgr,* Marti Carwile; Tel: 309-457-2191, E-mail: mcarwile@monmouthcollege.edu; *Tech Proc Mgr,* Mindy Damewood; Tel: 309-457-2334, E-mail: damewood@monmouthcollege.edu; Staff 3 (MLS 3)
Founded 1853. Enrl 1,144; Fac 98; Highest Degree: Bachelor
Jul 2021-Jun 2022 Income $1,546,656. Mats Exp $343,554, Books $67,764, Per/Ser (Incl. Access Fees) $96,106, AV Mat $11,643, Electronic Ref Mat (Incl. Access Fees) $155,942, Presv $8,007. Sal $333,988 (Prof $199,716)
Library Holdings: AV Mats 12,724; CDs 3,206; DVDs 3,124; e-books 34,058; e-journals 38,529; Microforms 335,870; Bk Titles 157,274; Bk Vols 207,135; Per Subs 315; Videos 861
Special Collections: Government Documents; James Christie Shields Coll of Ancient Art & Antiquities; Monmouth College Archives. US Document Depository
Automation Activity & Vendor Info: (Acquisitions) Ex Libris Group; (Cataloging) Ex Libris Group; (Circulation) Ex Libris Group; (Course Reserve) Ex Libris Group; (Discovery) OCLC; (ILL) OCLC WorldShare Interlibrary Loan; (OPAC) Ex Libris Group; (Serials) Ex Libris Group
Wireless access
Function: Archival coll, Art exhibits, Audio & video playback equip for onsite use, AV serv, CD-ROM, Computers for patron use, Doc delivery serv, Electronic databases & coll, Free DVD rentals, ILL available, Internet access, Mango lang, Microfiche/film & reading machines, Music CDs, Online cat, Online info literacy tutorials on the web & in blackboard, Online ref, Orientations, Photocopying/Printing, Ref & res, Ref serv available, Scanner, Telephone ref, VHS videos, Visual arts prog
Mem of Reaching Across Illinois Library System (RAILS)
Partic in Associated Colleges of the Midwest; Consortium of Academic & Research Libraries in Illinois; Illinois Library & Information Network
Open Mon-Thurs 7:30am-9pm, Fri 7:30-4:30, Sun 1-9

P WARREN COUNTY PUBLIC LIBRARY DISTRICT*, 62 Public Sq, 61462. SAN 340-5516. Tel: 309-734-3166. FAX: 309-734-5955. E-mail: wcpl@wcplibrary.org. Web Site: www.wcplibrary.org. *Head Librn,* Larisa Good; E-mail: lgood@wcplibrary.org; *Ad,* Megan Horack; *Youth Serv Librn,* Rebecca Montroy; Staff 2 (MLS 1, Non-MLS 1)
Founded 1868. Pop 18,735
Library Holdings: Bks on Deafness & Sign Lang 25; CDs 415; DVDs 1,234; Large Print Bks 3,706; Music Scores 3,000; Bk Titles 82,011; Bk Vols 96,029; Per Subs 161; Talking Bks 2,762; Videos 2,879
Special Collections: Lincoln Coll. Oral History
Subject Interests: Agr, Genealogy
Automation Activity & Vendor Info: (Acquisitions) Follett Software; (Cataloging) Follett Software; (Circulation) Follett Software; (Serials) EBSCO Online
Wireless access
Special Services for the Blind - Audio mat
Open Mon-Thurs 8-8 (8-6 Summer), Fri & Sat 8-5
Friends of the Library Group

Branches: 3
ALEXIS BRANCH, 102 W Broadway, Alexis, 61412, SAN 340-5540. Tel: 309-482-6109.
Library Holdings: Bk Titles 3,013; Per Subs 15
Open Mon & Tues 2-5, Wed 9-12 & 3-6, Thurs 3-6
Friends of the Library Group
KIRKWOOD BRANCH, 134 S Kirk, Kirkwood, 61447, SAN 340-5605. Tel: 309-768-2173.
Library Holdings: Bk Titles 2,627; Per Subs 13
Open Mon, Tues, Thurs & Fri 2:30-5:30, Sat 9-Noon
Friends of the Library Group
ROSEVILLE BRANCH, 145 W Penn Ave, Roseville, 61473, SAN 340-5664. Tel: 309-426-2336.
Library Holdings: Bk Vols 4,348; Per Subs 15
Open Mon, Tues, Thurs & Fri 1-4, Sat 9-12
Friends of the Library Group

MONTICELLO

P ALLERTON PUBLIC LIBRARY DISTRICT, 4000 Green Apple Lane, 61856. SAN 304-4238. Tel: 217-762-4676. FAX: 217-762-2021. E-mail: librarian@monticellolibrary.org. Web Site: www.monticellolibrary.org. *Dir,* Sherry Waldrep; *Circ Serv,* Laura Gillespie; E-mail: l.gillespie@monticellolibrary.org; *Tech Serv,* Lorrie Taylor; E-mail: l.taylor@monticellolibrary.org; Staff 4 (MLS 1, Non-MLS 3)
Founded 1897. Pop 5,906
Library Holdings: Bk Vols 36,000; Per Subs 85
Special Collections: Census (Piatt County Coll), micro; Local History; Piatt County Newspaper Coll, micro. Oral History
Subject Interests: Genealogy
Automation Activity & Vendor Info: (Cataloging) SirsiDynix; (Circulation) SirsiDynix; (OPAC) SirsiDynix; (Serials) SirsiDynix
Wireless access
Publications: Monticello 150 Years Later
Mem of Illinois Heartland Library System
Open Mon & Thurs 9-9, Tues, Wed & Fri 9-6, Sat 9-5, Sun 1-5

S PIATT COUNTY HISTORICAL & GENEALOGICAL SOCIETY LIBRARY, 1115 N State St, Ste 119, 61856. SAN 372-5642. Tel: 217-762-9997. E-mail: piatthistory@gmail.com. Web Site: www.piatthistory.org.
Founded 1980
Library Holdings: CDs 25; DVDs 10; Electronic Media & Resources 100; Bk Titles 1,000; Spec Interest Per Sub 10; Videos 10
Special Collections: Piatt County Illinois Local History (PGHGS Coll), bks & microflm
Wireless access
Publications: PCHGS Quarterly (Newsletter)
Open Mon & Wed 1-4

MORRIS

P MORRIS AREA PUBLIC LIBRARY DISTRICT*, 604 Liberty St, 60450. SAN 304-4254. Tel: 815-942-6880. FAX: 815-942-6415. Web Site: www.morrislibrary.com. *Dir,* Roberta Richter; E-mail: rrichter@morrislibrary.com; *Head, Patron Serv,* Nydia Robinson; E-mail: nrobinson@morrislibrary.com; *Head, Adult Serv, Head, Info Tech,* John Fruit; E-mail: jfruit@morrislibrary.com; *Head, Children's Servx,* Matthew Knott; E-mail: mknott@morrislibrary.com; *Bus Mgr,* Vicki Harvey; E-mail: vharvey@morrislibrary.com; *Tech Serv Coordr,* Tammy Baldine; E-mail: tbaldine@morrislibrary.com; *Libr Assoc/Teen Serv,* Rose Nowak; E-mail: rnowak@morrislibrary.com; Staff 7 (MLS 2, Non-MLS 5)
Founded 1913. Pop 18,501; Circ 160,000
Library Holdings: Audiobooks 3,500; CDs 3,200; DVDs 3,366; e-books 200,000; Electronic Media & Resources 5; Bk Vols 56,399; Per Subs 90
Automation Activity & Vendor Info: (Acquisitions) Innovative Interfaces, Inc; (Cataloging) Innovative Interfaces, Inc; (Circulation) Innovative Interfaces, Inc; (ILL) Innovative Interfaces, Inc; (OPAC) Innovative Interfaces, Inc; (Serials) Innovative Interfaces, Inc
Wireless access
Function: 24/7 Online cat, Activity rm, Adult bk club, Art programs, Audio & video playback equip for onsite use, Audiobks on Playaways & MP3, Audiobks via web, AV serv, Bks on CD, Children's prog, Computer training, Computers for patron use, Digital talking bks, E-Readers, Electronic databases & coll, Family literacy, Free DVD rentals, Holiday prog, Homework prog, ILL available, Internet access, Laminating, Life-long learning prog for all ages, Magazines, Mail & tel request accepted, Meeting rooms, Movies, Museum passes, Music CDs, Notary serv, Online cat, OverDrive digital audio bks, Passport agency, Photocopying/Printing, Preschool outreach, Prof lending libr, Prog for adults, Prog for children & young adult, Ref serv available, Res assist avail, Scanner, Senior computer classes, Senior outreach, Serves people with intellectual disabilities, STEM programs, Story hour, Study rm, Summer & winter reading prog, Summer reading prog, Tax forms, Teen

prog, Telephone ref, Visual arts prog, Wheelchair accessible, Winter reading prog, Workshops
Mem of Reaching Across Illinois Library System (RAILS)
Open Mon-Thurs 9-8, Fri & Sat 9-5, Sun 12-4
Friends of the Library Group

MORRISON

P ODELL PUBLIC LIBRARY*, 307 S Madison St, 61270. SAN 304-4270. Tel: 815-772-7323. FAX: 815-772-7323. E-mail: odell.library@gmail.com. Web Site: odellpubliclibrary.com/wp. *Dir,* Lori Matlack
Founded 1879. Pop 4,600; Circ 47,653
Library Holdings: Bk Vols 36,111; Per Subs 100
Subject Interests: Genealogy
Wireless access
Mem of Reaching Across Illinois Library System (RAILS)
Open Mon & Wed 10-8, Tues & Thurs 2-8, Fri 2-5, Sat 10-3
Friends of the Library Group

MORRISONVILLE

P KITCHELL MEMORIAL LIBRARY*, 300 SE Fifth St, 62546. (Mail add: PO Box 49, 62546), SAN 304-4289. Tel: 217-526-4553. FAX: 217-526-3695. E-mail: mvillelibrary@yahoo.com. Web Site: www.morrisonville.lib.il.us. *Librn,* Linda K Sheedy
Founded 1964. Pop 1,272; Circ 5,700
Library Holdings: CDs 70; DVDs 340; Large Print Bks 117; Bk Vols 8,620; Per Subs 25; Talking Bks 65; Videos 800
Special Collections: Historical Books of Christian Counties & Centennial Releases; Maps of Christian County, Morrisonville & Illinois; Morrisonville Public School Mohawk & Tomahawk Yearbooks; Morrisonville Times (1875 to present)
Wireless access
Function: Bks on cassette, Bks on CD, CD-ROM, Children's prog, Computer training, Computers for patron use, Free DVD rentals, Magnifiers for reading, Music CDs, Notary serv, Photocopying/Printing, Prog for children & young adult, Senior computer classes, Spoken cassettes & CDs, Spoken cassettes & DVDs, Summer reading prog, Tax forms, VHS videos, Wheelchair accessible
Mem of Illinois Heartland Library System
Open Mon & Thurs 1-5:30, Tues 1-6:30, Fri 9-12 & 1-5:30, Sat 9-12

MORTON

P MORTON PUBLIC LIBRARY DISTRICT*, 315 W Pershing St, 61550. SAN 304-4300. Tel: 309-263-2200. FAX: 309-266-9604. E-mail: questions@mortonlibrary.org. Web Site: www.mortonlibrary.org. *Dir,* Alissa Williams; E-mail: alissaw@mortonlibrary.org; Staff 11 (MLS 2, Non-MLS 9)
Founded 1924. Pop 16,267; Circ 314,443
Jul 2012-Jun 2013 Income $877,000. Mats Exp $164,000. Sal $445,700
Library Holdings: Audiobooks 1,308; CDs 11,149; DVDs 8,350; e-books 5,329; Electronic Media & Resources 34; Bk Vols 95,854; Per Subs 138
Automation Activity & Vendor Info: (Acquisitions) SirsiDynix; (Cataloging) OCLC Connexion; (Circulation) SirsiDynix-WorkFlows; (OPAC) SirsiDynix
Wireless access
Function: Adult literacy prog, Audiobks via web, Bk club(s), Bks on cassette, Bks on CD, Children's prog, Computer training, Computers for patron use, Digital talking bks, E-Reserves, Electronic databases & coll, Free DVD rentals, Home delivery & serv to seniorr ctr & nursing homes, ILL available, Magnifiers for reading, Music CDs, Notary serv, Online cat, OverDrive digital audio bks, Photocopying/Printing, Prog for adults, Prog for children & young adult, Ref serv available, Tax forms, VHS videos, Wheelchair accessible
Mem of Reaching Across Illinois Library System (RAILS)
Partic in Resource Sharing Alliance
Open Mon-Thurs 9-9, Fri 9-6, Sat 9-5

MORTON GROVE

P MORTON GROVE PUBLIC LIBRARY, 6140 Lincoln Ave, 60053-2989. SAN 304-4351. Tel: 847-965-4220. Interlibrary Loan Service Tel: 847-929-5103. Reference Tel: 847-929-5101. FAX: 847-324-9580. E-mail: info@mgpl.org. Web Site: www.mgpl.org. *Exec Dir,* Pamela Leffler; E-mail: pleffler@mgpl.org; *Head, Adult Serv,* Melissa Mayberry; E-mail: mmayberry@mgpl.org; *Head, Circ,* Jeffrey Ray; E-mail: jray@mgpl.org; *Head, Tech Serv,* Helga Scherer; E-mail: hscherer@mgpl.org; *Head, Youth Serv,* Courtney Schroeder; E-mail: cschroeder@mgpl.org; Staff 14 (MLS 14)
Founded 1938. Pop 22,451; Circ 337,000
Jan 2015-Dec 2015 Income $2,955,944
Library Holdings: Audiobooks 2,400; CDs 7,500; DVDs 5,800; Bk Vols 132,000; Per Subs 350; Videos 600
Automation Activity & Vendor Info: (Acquisitions) SirsiDynix; (Cataloging) SirsiDynix; (Circulation) SirsiDynix; (ILL) SirsiDynix; (OPAC) SirsiDynix; (Serials) SirsiDynix
Wireless access
Publications: Books & Beyond (Newsletter)
Mem of Reaching Across Illinois Library System (RAILS)
Partic in OCLC Online Computer Library Center, Inc
Special Services for the Deaf - TDD equip
Special Services for the Blind - Reader equip
Open Mon-Thurs 9-9, Fri 9-6, Sat 9-5, Sun 1-5

MOSSVILLE

S CATERPILLAR INC*, Technical Information Center, 14009 Old Galena Rd, 61552. (Mail add: PO Box 1875, 61552), SAN 340-6563. Tel: 309-578-6118. FAX: 309-578-6126. Web Site: www.caterpillar.com. *Mgr,* James Blank; E-mail: blank_james_r@cat.com; Staff 7.5 (MLS 5, Non-MLS 2.5)
Founded 1938
Library Holdings: Audiobooks 9; DVDs 26; e-books 2,623; e-journals 395; Electronic Media & Resources 47; Bk Vols 3,640; Videos 4
Subject Interests: Mechanical engr
Wireless access
Mem of Reaching Across Illinois Library System (RAILS)
Partic in OCLC Online Computer Library Center, Inc
Open Mon-Fri 7:30-4

MOUND CITY

P MOUND CITY PUBLIC LIBRARY*, 224 High St, 62963. SAN 304-4386. Tel: 618-748-9427. *Librn,* Vicki Warden
Founded 1935. Pop 692; Circ 2,966
Library Holdings: Bk Vols 5,000
Special Collections: Gun Boats; Naval Hospital
Wireless access
Open Mon-Fri 12-5
Friends of the Library Group

MOUNDS

P MOUNDS PUBLIC LIBRARY, 418 First St, 62964. SAN 304-4394. Tel: 618-745-6610. E-mail: mdspublib@outlook.com. *Dir,* Eunice McClung
Pop 1,700; Circ 4,277
Library Holdings: Bk Vols 7,362; Per Subs 30
Mem of Illinois Heartland Library System
Open Mon-Thurs 4:30-6:30, Sat 9-2

MOUNT CARMEL

P MOUNT CARMEL PUBLIC LIBRARY, 727 N Mulberry St, 62863. SAN 304-4408. Tel: 618-263-3531. FAX: 618-262-4243. E-mail: publiclibrarymountcarmel@gmail.com. Web Site: mtcarmelpubliclibrary.weebly.com. *Dir,* Twilla Coon
Founded 1911. Pop 8,000; Circ 85,025
Library Holdings: Bk Vols 50,000; Per Subs 128
Special Collections: Daily Republican-Register Local Newspaper (1844 to present), microfilm
Automation Activity & Vendor Info: (Acquisitions) SirsiDynix; (Cataloging) SirsiDynix; (Circulation) SirsiDynix
Mem of Illinois Heartland Library System
Open Mon-Fri 10-5, Sat 10-2

J WABASH VALLEY COLLEGE*, Bauer Media Center, 2200 College Dr, 62863. SAN 304-4416. Tel: 618-262-8641, Ext 3400. FAX: 618-262-8962. Web Site: www.iecc.edu. *Dir,* Sandra Craig; Tel: 618-263-5097, Ext 3401, E-mail: craigs@iecc.edu; *Cataloger,* Karissa Anderson; E-mail: andersonk@iecc.edu; *Circ,* Donna Sigler; E-mail: siglerd@iecc.edu; Staff 1 (Non-MLS 1)
Founded 1961. Enrl 1,396
Library Holdings: Bk Titles 30,000; Bk Vols 32,000; Per Subs 85
Special Collections: Children's Book Coll
Subject Interests: Agr, Electronics, Environ studies, Mining, Nursing, Soc sci & issues
Wireless access
Open Mon-Thurs 7:30-7, Fri 7:30-4:30; Mon-Fri (Summer) 7:30-4

MOUNT CARROLL

P MOUNT CARROLL TOWNSHIP PUBLIC LIBRARY*, 208 N Main St, 61053-1022. SAN 304-4424. Tel: 815-244-1751. FAX: 815-244-5203. E-mail: mtcarrolltownshippubliclibrary@gmail.com. Web Site: www.mountcarrollpubliclibrary.org. *Dir,* Pam Naples; Staff 3 (Non-MLS 3)
Founded 1908. Pop 2,473; Circ 10,609
Library Holdings: AV Mats 340; Large Print Bks 70; Bk Titles 17,136; Per Subs 21; Talking Bks 99
Special Collections: County Cemetary Directory Coll

Subject Interests: Genealogy, Local hist
Wireless access
Function: ILL available
Mem of Reaching Across Illinois Library System (RAILS)
Open Mon-Wed & Fri 9-5:30, Thurs 9-7, Sat 9-1
Friends of the Library Group

MOUNT MORRIS

P MOUNT MORRIS PUBLIC LIBRARY, 105 S McKendrie Ave, 61054. SAN 304-4440. Tel: 815-734-4927. FAX: 815-734-6035. E-mail: mmlib@mtmorris-il.org. Web Site: www.mtmorris-il.org. *Dir,* Mary Cheatwood; *Asst Librn,* Mary Head; Staff 2 (Non-MLS 2)
Founded 1931. Pop 2,998; Circ 22,518
Subject Interests: Local hist
Automation Activity & Vendor Info: (Circulation) Innovative Interfaces, Inc - Sierra
Wireless access
Function: 24/7 Electronic res, 24/7 Online cat, Adult bk club, Art exhibits, Audio & video playback equip for onsite use, AV serv, Bks on cassette, Bks on CD, Children's prog, Computers for patron use, Electronic databases & coll, Free DVD rentals, Home delivery & serv to seniorr ctr & nursing homes, Homebound delivery serv, ILL available, Internet access, Laminating, Magazines, Magnifiers for reading, Mail & tel request accepted, Meeting rooms, Microfiche/film & reading machines, Movies, Music CDs, Online cat, OverDrive digital audio bks, Photocopying/Printing, Prog for adults, Prog for children & young adult, Ref serv available, Scanner, Spoken cassettes & CDs, STEM programs, Story hour, Summer reading prog, Tax forms, Teen prog, Telephone ref, Wheelchair accessible
Mem of Reaching Across Illinois Library System (RAILS)
Open Mon-Thurs 11-7, Fri 11-5, Sat 10-3

MOUNT OLIVE

P MOUNT OLIVE PUBLIC LIBRARY, 100 N Plum St, 62069-1755. SAN 304-4459. Tel: 217-999-7311. FAX: 217-999-7360. E-mail: moelibrary@yahoo.com. *Dir,* Tracy Anderson
Founded 1973. Pop 2,099; Circ 21,578
Library Holdings: Bks on Deafness & Sign Lang 10; Bk Vols 10,000; Per Subs 30
Special Collections: Mount Olive Herald Newspaper, 1893-2013
Wireless access
Function: 24/7 Online cat, Bks on CD, Computers for patron use, Free DVD rentals, Internet access, Magazines, Meeting rooms, Microfiche/film & reading machines, Online cat, Photocopying/Printing, Prog for adults, Prog for children & young adult, Story hour, Summer reading prog, Tax forms, Wheelchair accessible
Mem of Illinois Heartland Library System
Special Services for the Deaf - TDD equip
Special Services for the Blind - Bks on CD; Children's Braille
Open Mon-Wed & Fri 10-6, Sat 10-2

MOUNT PROSPECT

P MOUNT PROSPECT PUBLIC LIBRARY*, Ten S Emerson St, 60056. SAN 304-4475. Tel: 847-253-5675. FAX: 847-253-0642. Web Site: www.mppl.org. *Exec Dir,* Su Reynders; E-mail: sreynders@mppl.org; *Dir Bus Ops,* Karen Almeleh; E-mail: kalmeleh@mppl.org; *Dir, Commun Engagement,* Mary Beth Corrigan-Buchen; E-mail: mbuchen@mppl.org; *Dir of Facilities & Security,* Tom Garvin; E-mail: tgarvin@mppl.org; *Dir, IT,* Timothy Loga; E-mail: tloga@mppl.org; *Communications Dir,* Amy Knutson Strack; E-mail: amyks@mppl.org; *Dep Dir, Pub Serv,* Anne Belden; E-mail: abelden@mppl.org; *Head, Bibliog Serv, Head, Coll,* Rosemary Groenwald; E-mail: rosemary@mppl.org; *Head, Circ,* Janine Sarto; E-mail: jsarto@mppl.org; *Head, Commun Serv,* Jennifer Amling; E-mail: jamling@mppl.org; *Head, Fiction/AV/Teen Serv,* John McInnes; E-mail: jmcinnes@mppl.org; *Head, Registration Serv,* Allison Horton; E-mail: ahorton@mppl.org; *Head, Res Serv,* Dale Heath; E-mail: dheath@mppl.org; *Head, Youth Serv,* Mary Smith; E-mail: msmith@mppl.org; *Asst Head, Circ Serv,* Emily Whitmore; E-mail: awhitmore@mppl.org; *Asst Dept Head, Bibliog Serv, Coll,* Shang Liu; E-mail: sliu@mppl.org; *Asst Head, Fiction/AV/Teen,* Cathleen Blair; E-mail: cblair@mppl.org; *Asst Head, Res Serv,* Julie Collins; E-mail: jcollins@mppl.org; *Asst Head, Youth Serv,* Julie Jurgens; E-mail: jjurgens@mppl.org; *Bus Librn,* Joseph Collier; E-mail: jcollier@mppl.org; *Tech Librn,* Dan Criscione; E-mail: dcriscione@mppl.org; *Teen Librn,* Andrea Johnson; E-mail: ajohnson@mppl.org; *Teen Serv Librn,* Abigail Weaver; E-mail: aweaver@mppl.org; *Mgr, Libr Develop,* Pamela Nelson; E-mail: pnelson@mppl.org; *Human Res Mgr,* Suzanne Yazel; E-mail: syazel@mppl.org; *ILL Coordr,* Virginia Schlachter; E-mail: ginnys@mppl.org; *ILS Adminr,* Kevin Medows; E-mail: kmedows@mppl.org. Subject Specialists: *Graphic arts,* Jennifer Amling; Staff 46 (MLS 27, Non-MLS 19)
Founded 1943. Pop 54,167
Jan 2019-Dec 2019 Income (Main & Associated Libraries) $9,669,036, State $67,709, Locally Generated Income $9,601,327. Mats Exp $788,896, Books $326,457, Per/Ser (Incl. Access Fees) $14,805, Other Print Mats $575, Micro $799, AV Mat $94,778, Electronic Ref Mat (Incl. Access Fees) $306,938. Sal $5,573,124
Library Holdings: AV Mats 71,520; e-journals 66; Electronic Media & Resources 42,541; Bk Vols 337,567; Per Subs 439
Special Collections: Oral History; US Document Depository
Subject Interests: Genealogy, Local hist
Automation Activity & Vendor Info: (Acquisitions) Horizon; (Cataloging) Horizon; (Circulation) Horizon; (OPAC) EBSCO Online
Wireless access
Function: 24/7 Electronic res, 24/7 Online cat, 3D Printer, Activity rm, Adult bk club, Adult literacy prog, After school storytime, Audiobks on Playaways & MP3, Audiobks via web, AV serv, Bk club(s), Bks on CD, Children's prog, Computer training, Computers for patron use, Digital talking bks, Electronic databases & coll, Family literacy, Free DVD rentals, Govt ref serv, Holiday prog, Homebound delivery serv, ILL available, Internet access, Magazines, Magnifiers for reading, Mango lang, Meeting rooms, Microfiche/film & reading machines, Movies, Music CDs, Online cat, Online ref, Outreach serv, Photocopying/Printing, Preschool outreach, Preschool reading prog, Prog for adults, Prog for children & young adult, Ref & res, Ref serv available, Scanner, Serves people with intellectual disabilities, Spanish lang bks, Story hour, Study rm, Summer & winter reading prog, Summer reading prog, Tax forms, Teen prog, Telephone ref, Wheelchair accessible, Winter reading prog
Publications: Preview (Bimonthly)
Mem of Reaching Across Illinois Library System (RAILS)
Special Services for the Deaf - Assisted listening device; Assistive tech; Bks on deafness & sign lang; TDD equip
Special Services for the Blind - Accessible computers; Bks on CD; Large print bks; Large screen computer & software; Magnifiers; Recorded bks; Talking bk serv referral; Text reader
Open Mon-Fri 9am-10pm, Sat 9-5, Sun 12-5
Friends of the Library Group
Branches: 1
SOUTH BRANCH, 1711 W Algonquin Rd, 60056. Tel: 847-590-4090. Web Site: www.mppl.org/southbranch. *Br Mgr,* Maria Garstecki; E-mail: mariag@mppl.org
Open Mon-Fri 11am-7:30pm
Friends of the Library Group

MOUNT PULASKI

P MOUNT PULASKI PUBLIC LIBRARY DISTRICT*, 320 N Washington St, 62548. SAN 304-4483. Tel: 217-792-5919. FAX: 217-792-3449. E-mail: mtpulaskipubliclibrary@gmail.com. Web Site: www.mtpulaskiil.com/mtpulaskiilWEBsite/library/libraryp1.htm. *Libr Dir,* Amanda Doherty
Founded 1892. Pop 2,860; Circ 40,059
Library Holdings: Audiobooks 880; DVDs 1,330; Large Print Bks 1,144; Bk Titles 13,652; Per Subs 62
Subject Interests: Genealogy
Wireless access
Mem of Illinois Heartland Library System
Open Mon-Thurs 10-7, Fri 10-5, Sat 9-1

MOUNT STERLING

P BROWN COUNTY PUBLIC LIBRARY DISTRICT*, 143 W Main St, 62353. SAN 304-4491. Tel: 217-773-2013. FAX: 217-773-4723. E-mail: browncty@adams.net. Web Site: bcpubliclibrary.org, www.actionbrowncounty.org/library. *Dir,* Richard Young; E-mail: richard@bcpubliclibrary.org; Staff 7 (Non-MLS 7)
Founded 1915. Pop 5,812; Circ 23,396
Library Holdings: Bk Vols 25,000
Special Collections: Best Seller & Popular Fiction
Automation Activity & Vendor Info: (OPAC) SirsiDynix
Wireless access
Partic in Association for Rural & Small Libraries
Open Mon-Thurs 9-7, Fri 9-4, Sat 9-Noon

S WESTERN ILLINOIS CORRECTIONAL CENTER LIBRARY*, 2500 Rt 99 S, 62353. SAN 376-1207. Tel: 217-773-4441, Ext 640. *Libr Assoc,* Position Currently Open
Library Holdings: Bk Vols 3,466; Per Subs 13
Special Collections: Illinois Legal Coll
Partic in Resource Sharing Alliance
Restriction: Staff & inmates only

MOUNT VERNON

P C E BREHM MEMORIAL PUBLIC LIBRARY DISTRICT, 101 S Seventh St, 62864. SAN 304-4521. Tel: 618-242-6322. FAX: 618-242-0810. Web Site: mtvbrehm.org. *Libr Dir,* Bill Pixley; E-mail:

bpixley@mtvbrehm.lib.il.us; *Asst Dir,* Esther Curry; E-mail: ecurry@mtvbrehm.org; *Ch,* Susan Williams; E-mail: swilliams@mtvbrehm.org; *Circ,* Jan Kreher; *Genealogy Serv,* April Szarek; E-mail: apitman@mtvbrehm.lib.il.us; Staff 22 (MLS 3, Non-MLS 19)
Founded 1899. Pop 37,918; Circ 166,000
Jul 2020-Jun 2021 Income $1,141,000, State $53,000, Federal $5,000, County $1,028,000, Locally Generated Income $55,000. Mats Exp $776,000. Sal $464,000
Special Collections: Genealogy Coll; Southern Illinois History Coll
Automation Activity & Vendor Info: (Acquisitions) Innovative Interfaces, Inc; (Cataloging) Innovative Interfaces, Inc; (Circulation) Innovative Interfaces, Inc; (ILL) Innovative Interfaces, Inc; (OPAC) Innovative Interfaces, Inc; (Serials) Innovative Interfaces, Inc
Wireless access
Function: 24/7 Online cat, Activity rm, Adult bk club, After school storytime, Audio & video playback equip for onsite use, Audiobks via web, Bk club(s), Bks on CD, Computers for patron use, E-Readers, E-Reserves, Free DVD rentals, Genealogy discussion group, Holiday prog, Home delivery & serv to seniorr ctr & nursing homes, ILL available, Internet access, Magazines, Mail & tel request accepted, Meeting rooms, Movies, Music CDs, Online cat, Prog for adults, Prog for children & young adult, Ref serv available, Res assist avail, Res libr, Senior computer classes, Summer reading prog, Tax forms, Wheelchair accessible
Mem of Illinois Heartland Library System
Open Mon-Thurs 9-8, Fri 9-5, Sat 10-4, Sun 1-5

S CEDARHURST CENTER FOR THE ARTS*, Mitchell Museum Library, 2600 Richview Rd, 62864. (Mail add: PO Box 923, 62864-0019), SAN 304-4513. Tel: 618-242-1236, Ext 224. FAX: 618-242-9530. Web Site: www.cedarhurst.org. *Dir of Educ,* Jennifer Sarver; E-mail: jennifer@cedarhurst.org; Staff 1 (Non-MLS 1)
Founded 1973
Library Holdings: AV Mats 117; Bk Vols 3,100; Per Subs 16; Spec Interest Per Sub 15
Subject Interests: Americana, Art, Paintings, Sculpture
Restriction: Circ limited, Open by appt only, Open to pub for ref only

GL ILLINOIS APPELLATE COURT, Fifth District Law Library, 14th & Main Sts, 62864. (Mail add: PO Box 867, 62864-0018), SAN 304-4505. Tel: 618-242-6414. FAX: 618-242-9133. Web Site: www.state.il.us/court/appellatecourt. *Dir, Res,* Michael D Greathouse; *Librn,* Holy Austin
Founded 1857
Library Holdings: Bk Vols 13,000; Per Subs 20
Subject Interests: Law
Restriction: Staff use only

M SSM HEALTH - GOOD SAMARITAN HOSPITAL*, Health Science Library, One Good Samaritan Way, 62864. SAN 329-773X. Tel: 618-242-4600. Web Site: www.ssmhealthillinois.com/locations/good-samaritan-hospital-mt-vernon. *Librn,* Coleen Saxe; Tel: 618-899-3095, E-mail: coleen.saxe@ssmhealth.com
Library Holdings: Bk Vols 1,000
Wireless access
Open Mon-Fri 8-Noon

MOUNT ZION

P MOUNT ZION DISTRICT LIBRARY, 115 W Main St, 62549. SAN 304-453X. Tel: 217-864-3622. FAX: 217-864-5708. E-mail: mtzionlibrary@mtzion.lib.il.us. Web Site: www.mtzion.lib.il.us. *Dir,* Maria Dent; E-mail: director@mtzion.lib.il.us; Staff 5 (MLS 1, Non-MLS 4)
Founded 1975. Pop 11,722; Circ 66,155
Library Holdings: Bk Vols 25,000; Per Subs 119
Automation Activity & Vendor Info: (Circulation) SirsiDynix
Wireless access
Publications: Newsletter (Monthly)
Mem of Illinois Heartland Library System
Special Services for the Deaf - TTY equip
Open Mon-Thurs 9-8, Fri 9-5, Sat 9-3

MOWEAQUA

P MOWEAQUA PUBLIC LIBRARY*, 600 N Putnam St, 62550. SAN 304-4548. Tel: 217-768-4700. FAX: 217-768-9070. E-mail: moweaquapl@gmail.com. Web Site: www.moweaquapl.com. *Libr Dir,* Fran Lower
Founded 1893. Pop 2,850; Circ 25,211
Library Holdings: Audiobooks 364; DVDs 751; Large Print Bks 724; Microforms 100; Bk Vols 13,000; Per Subs 6; Talking Bks 292; Videos 720
Subject Interests: Genealogy
Automation Activity & Vendor Info: (Circulation) SirsiDynix
Wireless access
Mem of Illinois Heartland Library System
Open Mon 9-7, Tues, Wed & Fri 9-5, Sat 9-2
Friends of the Library Group

MUNDELEIN

P FREMONT PUBLIC LIBRARY DISTRICT, 1170 N Midlothian Rd, 60060. SAN 304-4556. Tel: 847-566-8702. FAX: 847-566-0204. Administration FAX: 847-918-3260. Reference E-mail: ref@fremontlibrary.org. Web Site: www.fremontlibrary.org. *Dir,* Scott Davis; *Asst Dir,* Becky Ingram; *Commun Serv Librn,* Rachael Rezek; *School Services Librn,* Katie O'Brian; *Adult Serv Mgr,* Margaret Kulis; *Circ Mgr,* Karen Bolton; *Youth Serv Mgr,* Maggie Kutsunis; Staff 69 (MLS 15, Non-MLS 54)
Founded 1955. Pop 37,500; Circ 770,000
Library Holdings: Bk Vols 170,000; Per Subs 200
Special Collections: Local Newspapers, 1894-present, micro
Automation Activity & Vendor Info: (Cataloging) SirsiDynix; (Circulation) SirsiDynix; (Discovery) SirsiDynix-Enterprise; (ILL) SirsiDynix; (OPAC) SirsiDynix
Wireless access
Function: ILL available
Publications: Fremont (Newsletter)
Partic in Cooperative Computer Services - CCS
Special Services for the Blind - Accessible computers; Bks on CD; Copier with enlargement capabilities; Home delivery serv; Large print bks; Low vision equip; Magnifiers; Playaways (bks on MP3); Talking bk serv referral
Open Mon-Thurs 9-9, Fri 9-6, Sat 9-5, Sun 1-5
Friends of the Library Group

CR UNIVERSITY OF SAINT MARY OF THE LAKE - MUNDELEIN SEMINARY, Feehan Memorial Library & McEssy Theological Resource Center, 1000 E Maple Ave, 60060. SAN 304-4572. Tel: 847-970-4820. Circulation Tel: 847-970-4821. FAX: 847-566-5229. E-mail: requestILL@usml.edu. Web Site: www.usml.edu/library. *Libr Dir,* Christopher Rogers; Tel: 847-970-4833, E-mail: crogers@usml.edu; *Electronic Res Librn,* Matt Isaia; Tel: 847-970-8945, E-mail: misaia@usml.edu; *Circ Mgr,* DeAnne Besetzny; E-mail: dbesetzny@usml.edu; *Acq Asst,* Natalie Jordan; Tel: 847-970-4894, E-mail: njordan@usml.edu; Staff 4.5 (MLS 3, Non-MLS 1.5)
Founded 1929. Enrl 190; Fac 33; Highest Degree: Doctorate
Library Holdings: AV Mats 300; Bk Titles 102,000; Bk Vols 201,000; Per Subs 435
Special Collections: Incunabula Coll; Irish History & Literature (Carry Coll)
Subject Interests: Canon law, Catholicism, Roman Catholic relig, Scripture
Automation Activity & Vendor Info: (Acquisitions) Ex Libris Group; (Cataloging) Ex Libris Group; (Circulation) Ex Libris Group; (Course Reserve) Ex Libris Group; (ILL) OCLC; (OPAC) Ex Libris Group; (Serials) EBSCO Online
Wireless access
Partic in Association of Chicago Theological Schools; Consortium of Academic & Research Libraries in Illinois; Statewide California Electronic Library Consortium
Open Mon-Fri 8:30-4:30
Restriction: Borrowing requests are handled by ILL, In-house use for visitors, Non-circulating of rare bks, Non-circulating to the pub, Open to students, fac, staff & alumni, Use of others with permission of librn

MURPHYSBORO

P SALLIE LOGAN PUBLIC LIBRARY*, 1808 Walnut St, 62966. SAN 304-4580. Tel: 618-684-3271. FAX: 618-684-2392. E-mail: staff.sallielogan@gmail.com. Web Site: sallieloganlibrary.com. *Dir,* Loretta Broomfield; *Asst Librn,* Sherry Carlock; *Cat,* Traci Hunsiker
Founded 1936. Pop 8,950; Circ 89,335
Library Holdings: Large Print Bks 1,200; Bk Titles 56,000; Per Subs 12
Automation Activity & Vendor Info: (Acquisitions) Innovative Interfaces, Inc; (Cataloging) Innovative Interfaces, Inc; (Circulation) Innovative Interfaces, Inc; (ILL) Innovative Interfaces, Inc; (OPAC) Innovative Interfaces, Inc; (Serials) Innovative Interfaces, Inc
Wireless access
Mem of Illinois Heartland Library System
Open Mon-Thurs 10-7, Fri & Sat 10-5
Friends of the Library Group

NAPERVILLE

SR COMMUNITY UMC LIBRARY, 20 N Center St, 60540. SAN 372-641X. Tel: 630-355-1483. FAX: 630-778-2011. E-mail: info@onecumc.net. Web Site: onecumc.net. *Library Contact,* Susan Keaton; *Library Contact,* Kim Petrella Jackson; Staff 2 (MLS 1, Non-MLS 1)
Founded 1958
Library Holdings: Bk Titles 5,000; Per Subs 12

Special Collections: Illinois Evangelical Church 1850-1946, bks, papers, ledgers; Illinois Evangelical United Brethren Church 1946-1968, bks, papers, ledgers
Restriction: Open by appt only

P NAPERVILLE PUBLIC LIBRARY*, Nichols Library, 200 W Jefferson Ave, 60540-5374. SAN 304-4602. Tel: 630-961-4100. FAX: 630-637-6389. Web Site: www.naperville-lib.org/about/nichols-library. *Exec Dir,* Julie Rothenfluh; Tel: 630-961-4100, Ext 6144, E-mail: jrothenfluh@naperville-lib.org; *Dep Dir,* Dave Della Terza; Tel: 630-961-4100, Ext 6100; *Bus Librn,* Kent Palmer; Tel: 630-961-4100, Ext 6328; *Libr Mgr,* Olya Tymciurak; Tel: 630-961-4100, Ext 6307; *Tech Serv Mgr,* Rohini Bokka; Tel: 630-961-4200, Ext 6141; *Adult Serv Supvr,* Anne Bultman; Tel: 630-961-4100, Ext 6106; *Customer Serv Supvr,* Jeanne Harrison; Tel: 630-961-4100, Ext 6321; *Supvr, Ch Serv,* Ellen Fitzgerald; Tel: 630-961-4100,ExT 6123; Staff 60 (MLS 39, Non-MLS 21)
Founded 1897
Automation Activity & Vendor Info: (Acquisitions) Innovative Interfaces, Inc - Sierra; (Cataloging) Innovative Interfaces, Inc - Sierra; (Circulation) Innovative Interfaces, Inc - Sierra
Wireless access
Function: 24/7 Electronic res, 24/7 Online cat, 3D Printer, Adult bk club, Adult literacy prog, After school storytime, Audio & video playback equip for onsite use, Audiobks via web, AV serv, Bk club(s), Bks on CD, Chess club, Children's prog, Computer training, Computers for patron use, Digital talking bks, E-Readers, Electronic databases & coll, Family literacy, Free DVD rentals, Games & aids for people with disabilities, Genealogy discussion group, Health sci info serv, Holiday prog, Home delivery & serv to seniorr ctr & nursing homes, Homebound delivery serv, Homework prog, ILL available, Internet access, Life-long learning prog for all ages, Magazines, Mail & tel request accepted, Mango lang, Meeting rooms, Microfiche/film & reading machines, Movies, Museum passes, Music CDs, Online cat, Online info literacy tutorials on the web & in blackboard, Online ref, Outreach serv, Outside serv via phone, mail, e-mail & web, OverDrive digital audio bks, Photocopying/Printing, Preschool outreach, Preschool reading prog, Printer for laptops & handheld devices, Prof lending libr, Prog for adults, Prog for children & young adult, Ref & res, Ref serv available, Scanner, Senior computer classes, Serves people with intellectual disabilities, Spanish lang bks, Spoken cassettes & CDs, Spoken cassettes & DVDs, Story hour, Study rm, Summer & winter reading prog, Tax forms, Teen prog, Telephone ref, Wheelchair accessible, Writing prog
Mem of Reaching Across Illinois Library System (RAILS)
Partic in Illinois Library & Information Network
Open Mon-Fri 9-9, Sat 9-5, Sun 1-9 (1-5 Summer)

Branches: 2

NAPER BOULEVARD, 2035 S Naper Blvd, 60565-3353, SAN 372-4999. Tel: 630-961-4100. FAX: 630-961-4119. TDD: 630-355-1585. Web Site: www.naperville-lib.org/about/naper-boulevard-library. *Mgr,* Yan Xu; Tel: 630-961-4100, Ext 2210; *Finance Mgr,* Jeff Scheuerman; Tel: 630-961-4100, Ext 2228; *Human Res Mgr,* Sue Ashe; Tel: 630-961-4100, Ext 2229; *Adult Serv Supvr,* Kathleen Longacre; Tel: 630-961-4100, Ext 2232; *Children's Serv Supvr,* Cory Ganbarg; Tel: 630-961-4100, Ext 2235; *Customer Serv Supvr,* Will Degenhard; Tel: 630-961-4100, Ext 2216
Founded 1992
Library Holdings: Bk Vols 153,293
Function: 24/7 Electronic res, 24/7 Online cat, Adult bk club, Adult literacy prog, After school storytime, Audio & video playback equip for onsite use, Audiobks via web, AV serv, Bks on CD, Children's prog, Computer training, Computers for patron use, Digital talking bks, E-Readers, E-Reserves, Electronic databases & coll, Family literacy, Free DVD rentals, Health sci info serv, Holiday prog, Home delivery & serv to seniorr ctr & nursing homes, Homebound delivery serv, Homework prog, ILL available, Instruction & testing, Internet access, Life-long learning prog for all ages, Literacy & newcomer serv, Magazines, Magnifiers for reading, Mail & tel request accepted, Meeting rooms, Microfiche/film & reading machines, Movies, Museum passes, Music CDs, Online cat, Online ref, Orientations, Outreach serv, Outside serv via phone, mail, e-mail & web, OverDrive digital audio bks, Photocopying/Printing, Preschool outreach, Printer for laptops & handheld devices, Prog for adults, Prog for children & young adult, Ref & res, Scanner, Senior computer classes, Senior outreach, Serves people with intellectual disabilities, Spanish lang bks, Spoken cassettes & CDs, Spoken cassettes & DVDs, Story hour, Study rm, Summer & winter reading prog, Tax forms, Teen prog, Telephone ref, Wheelchair accessible, Workshops
Open Mon-Fri 9-9, Sat 9-5, Sun 1-5

95TH STREET, 3015 Cedar Glade Dr, 60564. Tel: 630-961-4100. FAX: 630-637-4870. Web Site: www.naperville-lib.org/about/95th-street-library. *Libr Mgr,* Karen Dunford; Tel: 630-961-4100, Ext 4900; *Emerging Technologies Adminr,* Sue Karas; Tel: 630-961-4100, Ext 4981; *IT Mgr,* John Bender; Tel: 630-961-4100, Ext 4980; *Mkt Mgr,* Kim Neidermyer; Tel: 630-961-4100, Ext 4913; *Adult & Teen Serv Supvr,* Karen Luster; Tel: 630-961-4100, Ext 4940; *Children's Serv Supvr,* Ellen Norton; Tel: 630-961-4100, Ext 4960; *Circ Serv Supvr,* Carla Nolidis; Tel: 630-961-4100, Ext 4920
Founded 2003
Function: 24/7 Electronic res, 24/7 Online cat, Adult bk club, Adult literacy prog, After school storytime, Audio & video playback equip for onsite use, Audiobks via web, AV serv, Bk club(s), Bks on CD, Children's prog, Computer training, Computers for patron use, Digital talking bks, E-Readers, E-Reserves, Electronic databases & coll, Family literacy, Free DVD rentals, Health sci info serv, Holiday prog, Home delivery & serv to seniorr ctr & nursing homes, Homebound delivery serv, Homework prog, ILL available, Instruction & testing, Internet access, Life-long learning prog for all ages, Literacy & newcomer serv, Magazines, Magnifiers for reading, Mail & tel request accepted, Meeting rooms, Microfiche/film & reading machines, Movies, Museum passes, Music CDs, Online cat, Online ref, Orientations, Outreach serv, Outside serv via phone, mail, e-mail & web, OverDrive digital audio bks, Photocopying/Printing, Preschool outreach, Printer for laptops & handheld devices, Prog for adults, Prog for children & young adult, Ref & res, Scanner, Senior computer classes, Senior outreach, Serves people with intellectual disabilities, Spanish lang bks, Spoken cassettes & CDs, Spoken cassettes & DVDs, Story hour, Study rm, Summer & winter reading prog, Tax forms, Teen prog, Telephone ref, Wheelchair accessible, Workshops
Open Mon-Fri 9-9, Sat 9-5, Sun 1-9 (1-5 Summer)

C NORTH CENTRAL COLLEGE, Oesterle Library, 320 E School St, 60540. SAN 304-4610. Tel: 630-637-5700. Interlibrary Loan Service Tel: 630-637-5705. Reference Tel: 630-637-5715. FAX: 630-637-5716. E-mail: library@noctrl.edu. Web Site: library.noctrl.edu. *Coordr, Access Serv,* Belinda Cheek; Tel: 630-637-5703, E-mail: blcheek@noctrl.edu; *Coordr, Archives & Spec Coll,* Rebecca Skirvin; Tel: 630-637-5714, E-mail: rmskirvin@noctrl.edu; *Coord, Digital & Outreach Serv,* Melissa Proulx; Tel: 630-637-5708, E-mail: mlproulx@noctrl.edu; *Tech Serv Coordr,* Cynthia Scott; Tel: 630-637-5712, E-mail: clscott@noctrl.edu; Staff 9 (MLS 7, Non-MLS 2)
Founded 1861. Enrl 3,000; Fac 183; Highest Degree: Master
Jul 2014-Jun 2015. Mats Exp $543,750. Sal $700,000
Library Holdings: AV Mats 3,346; Bk Vols 134,965; Per Subs 38,895
Special Collections: History (Leffler Lincoln Coll); Literature (Sang Limited Edition Coll); Music (Sang Jazz Coll); Tholin Chicagoana Coll
Automation Activity & Vendor Info: (Acquisitions) Ex Libris Group; (Cataloging) Ex Libris Group; (Circulation) Ex Libris Group; (Course Reserve) Ex Libris Group; (ILL) Ex Libris Group; (OPAC) Ex Libris Group; (Serials) Ex Libris Group
Wireless access
Partic in Consortium of Academic & Research Libraries in Illinois; Illinois Library & Information Network; LIBRAS, Inc; OCLC Online Computer Library Center, Inc
Open Mon-Thurs 9-9, Fri 9-4:30, Sat 11-7, Sun 12-9
Restriction: Open to pub for ref & circ; with some limitations, Open to students, fac & staff

NASHVILLE

P NASHVILLE PUBLIC LIBRARY*, 219 E Elm St, 62263. SAN 304-4629. Tel: 618-327-3827. FAX: 618-327-4820. E-mail: nashvillepublib@gmail.com. Web Site: nashvillepl.com. *Libr Dir,* Kelsey Schaepperkoetter; *Asst Librn,* Mary Schnake
Founded 1943. Pop 3,147; Circ 26,585
Library Holdings: Bk Vols 17,000
Subject Interests: Genealogy, Local hist
Wireless access
Mem of Illinois Heartland Library System
Open Mon-Fri 10-7, Sat 10-2
Friends of the Library Group

NAUVOO

P NAUVOO PUBLIC LIBRARY*, 1270 Mulholland St, 62354. (Mail add: PO Box 276, 62354-0276), SAN 304-4637. Tel: 217-453-2707. FAX: 217-453-2707. E-mail: nauvoopl@gmail.com. Web Site: www.nauvoopubliclibrary.com. *Librn,* Amber Bevier
Founded 1913. Pop 1,149; Circ 10,125
Library Holdings: Large Print Bks 450; Bk Titles 10,000; Per Subs 20
Wireless access
Function: Photocopying/Printing, Prog for children & young adult, Summer reading prog
Mem of Reaching Across Illinois Library System (RAILS)
Open Mon 11-6:30, Tues & Thurs 11-6, Wed 9-4, Fri 10-5, Sat 10-2
Friends of the Library Group

NEOGA

P NEOGA PUBLIC LIBRARY DISTRICT*, 550 Chestnut St, 62447. (Mail add: PO Box 888, 62447-0888), SAN 376-0154. Tel: 217-895-3944. FAX: 217-895-3944. E-mail: neogalibrary@hotmail.com. Web Site: www.neoga.lib.il.us. *Dir*, Patricia Andres
Library Holdings: AV Mats 913; Bk Titles 11,000; Bk Vols 15,749; Per Subs 31
Wireless access
Mem of Illinois Heartland Library System
Open Tues & Thurs 10-7, Wed & Fri 10-5:30, Sat 9-12

NEPONSET

P NEPONSET PUBLIC LIBRARY*, 201 W Commercial St, 61345. (Mail add: PO Box 110, 61345-0110), SAN 304-4645. Tel: 309-594-2204. FAX: 309-594-2204. E-mail: neponsetlibrary@yahoo.com. Web Site: neponsetlibrary.org. *Librn*, Carissa Faber
Founded 1875. Pop 819
Special Collections: Clippings File; Local History, bks, cassettes, flm, micro; School & Cemetary Records
Open Mon (Winter) 1-4, Tues 9-12 & 1-6, Wed & Fri 1-6, Sat 10-3; Tues (Summer) 9-12 & 1-6, Wed & Fri 1-4, Sat 10-3

NEW ATHENS

P NEW ATHENS DISTRICT LIBRARY*, 201 N Van Buren St, 62264. SAN 304-4653. Tel: 618-475-3255. FAX: 618-475-9384. E-mail: newathenslibrary@gmail.com, nwalib@gmail.com. Web Site: newathenslibrary.org. *Dir*, Erica Pyle
Founded 1963. Pop 4,032; Circ 14,365
Library Holdings: Bk Vols 40,000; Per Subs 40
Automation Activity & Vendor Info: (Acquisitions) Innovative Interfaces, Inc; (Cataloging) Innovative Interfaces, Inc; (Circulation) Innovative Interfaces, Inc; (Course Reserve) Innovative Interfaces, Inc; (ILL) Innovative Interfaces, Inc; (Media Booking) Innovative Interfaces, Inc; (OPAC) Innovative Interfaces, Inc; (Serials) Innovative Interfaces, Inc
Wireless access
Mem of Illinois Heartland Library System
Open Mon, Tues & Thurs 4-7, Sat 1-5

NEW BADEN

P NEW BADEN PUBLIC LIBRARY*, 210 N First St, 62265. SAN 376-2211. Tel: 618-588-4554. FAX: 618-588-4554. E-mail: NewBadenLibrary@gmail.com. Web Site: newbadenlibrary.org. *Dir*, Brenda Lehr; E-mail: bllehr62789@gmail.com
Library Holdings: Bk Titles 12,000; Bk Vols 15,000; Per Subs 22
Automation Activity & Vendor Info: (Acquisitions) SirsiDynix; (Cataloging) SirsiDynix; (Circulation) SirsiDynix; (Course Reserve) SirsiDynix; (ILL) SirsiDynix; (Media Booking) SirsiDynix; (OPAC) SirsiDynix; (Serials) SirsiDynix
Wireless access
Mem of Illinois Heartland Library System
Open Mon-Thurs 11-7, Fri 1-6, Sat 9-1

NEW BERLIN

P WEST SANGAMON PUBLIC LIBRARY, 112 E Illinois St, 62670. (Mail add: PO Box 439, 62670-0439). Tel: 217-488-7733. FAX: 217-488-7744. E-mail: info@wspld.com. Web Site: wspld.com. *Libr Dir*, Jeanine Benanti
Founded 1999. Pop 4,371
Library Holdings: e-books 40,000; Electronic Media & Resources 16,000; Bk Titles 22,000
Special Collections: Abraham Lincoln Coll
Automation Activity & Vendor Info: (Cataloging) Innovative Interfaces, Inc. - Polaris
Wireless access
Function: Bk club(s), Homebound delivery serv, ILL available, Meeting rooms, Photocopying/Printing, Story hour
Mem of Illinois Heartland Library System
Open Tues & Thurs 10-7, Wed & Fri 10-4, Sat 10-1
Friends of the Library Group

NEW LENOX

P NEW LENOX PUBLIC LIBRARY DISTRICT*, 120 Veterans Pkwy, 60451. SAN 304-4661. Tel: 815-485-2605. FAX: 815-485-2548. TDD: 815-485-3963. E-mail: info@newlenoxlibrary.org. Web Site: www.newlenoxlibrary.org. *Libr Dir*, Michelle Krooswyk; E-mail: mkrooswyk@newlenoxlibrary.org; *Adult Serv Mgr*, Monica Waligorski; E-mail: mwaligorski@newlenoxlibrary.org; *Circ Mgr*, Jolyce Abernathy-Morris; E-mail: jmorris@newlenoxlibrary.org; *Youth Serv Mgr*, Alissa Raschke-Janchenko; E-mail: ajanchenko@newlenoxlibrary.org; Staff 3.2 (MLS 2.6, Non-MLS 0.6)
Founded 1946. Pop 35,000; Circ 283,969
Subject Interests: Quilting
Automation Activity & Vendor Info: (Acquisitions) SirsiDynix-WorkFlows; (Circulation) SirsiDynix; (ILL) OCLC FirstSearch
Wireless access
Function: Adult bk club, Audiobks via web, Bi-weekly Writer's Group, Bks on cassette, Bks on CD, Children's prog, Computers for patron use, E-Reserves, Electronic databases & coll, ILL available, Internet access, Magnifiers for reading, Mail & tel request accepted, Museum passes, Music CDs, Online cat, Online ref, Photocopying/Printing, Prog for adults, Prog for children & young adult, Ref serv available, Spoken cassettes & CDs, Story hour, Summer reading prog, Tax forms, Telephone ref, Wheelchair accessible
Mem of Reaching Across Illinois Library System (RAILS)
Special Services for the Deaf - Bks on deafness & sign lang; Sign lang interpreter upon request for prog; TDD equip
Special Services for the Blind - Aids for in-house use; Bks on cassette; Bks on CD; Cassettes; Large print bks; Magnifiers; Playaways (bks on MP3); Recorded bks; Screen enlargement software for people with visual disabilities; Talking bk serv referral
Open Mon-Thurs 10-8, Fri 10-6, Sat 10-4
Restriction: Non-resident fee
Friends of the Library Group

M SILVER CROSS HOSPITAL MEDICAL LIBRARY*, Virtual Library, 1900 Silver Cross Blvd, 60451-9509. SAN 304-3002. Tel: 815-300-7491. FAX: 815-300-3567. *Coordr*, Nicole Soldat; E-mail: nsoldat@silvercross.org; Staff 1 (MLS 1)
Founded 1956
Library Holdings: e-books 111; e-journals 360
Subject Interests: Health sci, Med
Wireless access
Function: Health sci info serv
Mem of Reaching Across Illinois Library System (RAILS)
Restriction: Med staff only
Friends of the Library Group

NEW WINDSOR

P NEW WINDSOR PUBLIC LIBRARY DISTRICT*, 412 Main St, 61465. SAN 304-467X. Tel: 309-667-2515. FAX: 309-667-2515. *Librn*, David Kruse; E-mail: dkruse@nwctv.net; Staff 3 (MLS 1, Non-MLS 2)
Founded 1959. Pop 1,268; Circ 14,772
Library Holdings: Bk Vols 10,700; Per Subs 22
Special Collections: Oral History
Subject Interests: Cooking, Gardening, Local hist
Open Mon & Thurs 3:30-8, Tues 9-8, Wed 1-8, Fri 9-5, Sat 9-1
Friends of the Library Group

NEWMAN

P NEWMAN REGIONAL LIBRARY DISTRICT*, 207 S Coffin St, North Entrance, 61942. SAN 304-4688. Tel: 217-837-2412. FAX: 217-837-2412. E-mail: librarian@newmanregionallibrary.org. Web Site: www.newmanregionallibrary.org. *Librn*, Darcie Peck; Staff 1 (Non-MLS 1)
Founded 1909. Pop 1,200; Circ 8,873
Library Holdings: AV Mats 1,000; Large Print Bks 200; Bk Titles 10,841; Per Subs 40; Talking Bks 500
Automation Activity & Vendor Info: (Acquisitions) Horizon; (Cataloging) Horizon; (Circulation) Horizon; (ILL) Horizon; (OPAC) Horizon; (Serials) Horizon
Wireless access
Function: ILL available, Internet access, Magnifiers for reading, Prog for adults, Prog for children & young adult, Summer reading prog, Wheelchair accessible
Mem of Illinois Heartland Library System
Partic in OCLC-LVIS
Open Mon 1-7, Wed 11-5, Tues, Thurs & Fri 1-6, Sat 9-Noon

NEWTON

P NEWTON PUBLIC LIBRARY & MUSEUM*, 100 S Van Buren St, 62448. SAN 304-4696. Tel: 618-783-8141. FAX: 618-783-8149. E-mail: newtonp2016@outlook.com. Web Site: www.newtonpl.com. *Dir*, Jacque Holsapple; *Librn*, Roberta Menke
Founded 1927. Pop 3,186; Circ 20,677
Library Holdings: Bk Vols 17,000; Per Subs 45
Automation Activity & Vendor Info: (Acquisitions) SirsiDynix; (Cataloging) SirsiDynix; (Circulation) SirsiDynix; (Course Reserve) SirsiDynix; (ILL) SirsiDynix
Wireless access
Mem of Illinois Heartland Library System
Open Mon, Wed & Fri 10-5, Tues & Thurs 10-7, Sat 10-1
Friends of the Library Group

NILES

P NILES-MAINE DISTRICT LIBRARY*, 6960 Oakton St, 60714. SAN 340-5907. Tel: 847-663-1234. FAX: 847-663-1350. Interlibrary Loan Service FAX: 847-663-6423. Administration FAX: 847-663-1360. TDD: 847-663-6500. E-mail: books@nileslibrary.org. Web Site: www.nileslibrary.org. *Dir,* Susan Lempke; E-mail: slempke@nileslibrary.org; *Asst Dir,* Cyndi Rademacher; E-mail: cyndi.rademacher@nileslibrary.org; *Bus Mgr, Operations Mgr,* Greg Pritz; E-mail: gpritz@nileslibrary.org; Staff 101 (MLS 28, Non-MLS 73)
Founded 1958. Pop 58,218; Circ 935,786
Library Holdings: AV Mats 29,672; Bk Vols 205,802; Per Subs 421
Wireless access
Function: 24/7 Electronic res, 24/7 Online cat, 3D Printer, Adult bk club, Adult literacy prog, Art exhibits, Art programs, Audio & video playback equip for onsite use, Audiobooks on Playaways & MP3, Audiobks via web, AV serv, Bks on CD, Chess club, Children's prog, Citizenship assistance, Computer training, Computers for patron use, Digital talking bks, E-Reserves, Electronic databases & coll, Family literacy, Free DVD rentals, Health sci info serv, Home delivery & serv to seniorr ctr & nursing homes, Homebound delivery serv, Homework prog, ILL available, Instruction & testing, Internet access, Life-long learning prog for all ages, Magazines, Magnifiers for reading, Mail & tel request accepted, Makerspace, Mango lang, Meeting rooms, Movies, Museum passes, Music CDs, Notary serv, Online cat, Online ref, Outreach serv, OverDrive digital audio bks, Passport agency, Photocopying/Printing, Preschool outreach, Preschool reading prog, Printer for laptops & handheld devices, Prog for adults, Prog for children & young adult, Ref & res, Ref serv available, Res assist avail, Scanner, Senior computer classes, Senior outreach, Serves people with intellectual disabilities, Spanish lang bks, STEM programs, Story hour, Study rm, Summer & winter reading prog, Summer reading prog, Tax forms, Teen prog, Telephone ref, Visual arts prog, Wheelchair accessible, Winter reading prog, Workshops, Writing prog
Publications: Chapter One (Newsletter)
Mem of Reaching Across Illinois Library System (RAILS)
Partic in Cooperative Computer Services - CCS; OCLC Online Computer Library Center, Inc
Special Services for the Deaf - TTY equip
Open Mon-Thurs 9-9, Fri & Sat 9-5, Sun (Sept-May) 1-5
Friends of the Library Group

NOKOMIS

P NOKOMIS PUBLIC LIBRARY, 22 S Cedar St, Ste 2, 62075. SAN 304-4742. Tel: 217-563-2734. FAX: 217-803-2454. E-mail: nkmslib@gmail.com. Web Site: www.nokomispl.org. *Dir,* Debra A Lehman; E-mail: dlehman@nokomispl.org; Staff 3 (MLS 1, Non-MLS 2)
Founded 1950. Pop 2,939; Circ 20,738
Apr 2020-Mar 2021 Income $73,427, State $5,922, Federal $840, Locally Generated Income $57,072, Other $9,593
Library Holdings: Audiobooks 1,533; Bks on Deafness & Sign Lang 22; CDs 1,533; DVDs 4,158; e-books 42,916; Large Print Bks 700; Bk Titles 23,754; Per Subs 3
Special Collections: Free Press-Progress, 1880 to present, micro
Subject Interests: Local hist
Wireless access
Function: 24/7 Online cat, Adult bk club, Art exhibits, Audio & video playback equip for onsite use, Audiobks via web, AV serv, Bk club(s), Bks on CD, CD-ROM, Children's prog, Computer training, Computers for patron use, Digital talking bks, E-Readers, Electronic databases & coll, Family literacy, Free DVD rentals, Holiday prog, Homebound delivery serv, ILL available, Internet access, Life-long learning prog for all ages, Magazines, Magnifiers for reading, Mail & tel request accepted, Microfiche/film & reading machines, Music CDs, Online cat, Outside serv via phone, mail, e-mail & web, Photocopying/Printing, Preschool outreach, Preschool reading prog, Printer for laptops & handheld devices, Prog for adults, Prog for children & young adult, Ref serv available, Scanner, Senior computer classes, Senior outreach, Spanish lang bks, Spoken cassettes & CDs, Spoken cassettes & DVDs, STEM programs, Story hour, Summer & winter reading prog, Tax forms, Teen prog, Telephone ref, Wheelchair accessible
Mem of Illinois Heartland Library System
Special Services for the Deaf - Bks on deafness & sign lang; Closed caption videos
Special Services for the Blind - Bks available with recordings; Bks on cassette; Bks on CD; Computer access aids; Copier with enlargement capabilities; Free checkout of audio mat; Large print bks; Large screen computer & software; Lending of low vision aids; Magnifiers; PC for people with disabilities; Screen enlargement software for people with visual disabilities
Open Mon 10-6:30, Tues, Thurs & Fri 9-5, Wed 10-6, Sat 9-2
Restriction: Non-circulating of rare bks, Non-resident fee

NORMAL

M CARLE BROMENN MEDICAL CENTER*, A E Livingston Health Sciences Library, 1304 Franklin Ave, Ste 180, 61761. SAN 339-7416. Tel: 309-268-5281, 309-454-1400. FAX: 309-268-5953. E-mail: library-network@advocatehealth.com. Web Site: carle.org. *Librn,* Brenna Tuite; E-mail: brenna.tuite@carle.com; Staff 2 (MLS 2)
Founded 1973
Library Holdings: Bk Titles 4,500; Per Subs 300
Subject Interests: Med, Nursing
Partic in Heart of Illinois Library Consortium
Open Mon-Fri 8-4:30

SR FIRST UNITED METHODIST CHURCH LIBRARY*, 211 N School St, 61761. SAN 325-6936. Tel: 309-452-2096. FAX: 309-452-1327. Web Site: www.normalfumc.org. *Librn,* Catherine Knight
Library Holdings: Bk Titles 1,000
Wireless access

J HEARTLAND COMMUNITY COLLEGE LIBRARY*, 1500 W Raab Rd, 61761. Tel: 309-268-8292. Reference Tel: 309-268-8293. Administration Tel: 309-268-8000. FAX: 309-268-7989. E-mail: library@heartland.libanswers.com. Web Site: www.heartland.edu/library. *Dir, Libr & Info Serv,* Rachelle Stivers; Tel: 309-268-8274, E-mail: rachelle.stivers@heartland.edu; *Info Serv Librn,* Jill Harter; Tel: 309-268-8277, E-mail: jill.harter@heartland.edu; *Info Serv Librn,* Carol Reid; Tel: 309-268-8279, E-mail: carol.reid@heartland.edu; *Info Serv Librn,* Colleen Shaw; Tel: 309-268-8284, E-mail: Colleen.Shaw@heartland.edu; *Tech Asst, Tech Serv,* Erin Zimmerman; Tel: 309-268-8273, E-mail: erin.zimmerman@heartland.edu
Library Holdings: Bk Titles 13,000; Bk Vols 15,000; Per Subs 209
Automation Activity & Vendor Info: (Cataloging) TLC (The Library Corporation); (Circulation) TLC (The Library Corporation); (OPAC) TLC (The Library Corporation)
Partic in Consortium of Academic & Research Libraries in Illinois; Network of Illinois Learning Resources in Community Colleges
Open Mon-Thurs 7:30am-8pm, Sat 12-5

S ILLINOIS LODGE OF RESEARCH, Louis L Williams Masonic Library, 614 E Lincoln Ave, 61761. Tel: 309-219-1427. E-mail: info@illinoislodgeofresearch.org. Web Site: illinoislodgeofresearch.org/ilor-library. *Library Contact,* Jeffrey Estes; Tel: 309-310-7826, E-mail: muzishn7@yahoo.com
Library Holdings: Bk Vols 10,000
Wireless access
Function: Computers for patron use, Photocopying/Printing, Res libr
Restriction: Open by appt only

C ILLINOIS STATE UNIVERSITY*, Milner Library, Campus Box 8900, 201 N School St, 61790-8900. SAN 304-4777. Tel: 309-438-3451. Circulation Tel: 309-438-7321. Interlibrary Loan Service Tel: 309-438-3461. Administration Tel: 309-438-3481. FAX: 309-438-3676. Web Site: library.illinoisstate.edu. *Assoc Dean,* Dallas Long; E-mail: dlong@ilstu.edu; *Assoc Dean, Pub Serv & Tech,* Chad Kahl; E-mail: cmkahl@ilstu.edu; Staff 94 (MLS 31, Non-MLS 63)
Founded 1890. Enrl 20,104; Fac 940; Highest Degree: Doctorate
Library Holdings: Bk Vols 1,632,215; Per Subs 4,873
Special Collections: 19th Century Elementary & Secondary School Textbooks; Children's Literature (Lenski, 19th Century); Circus & Allied Arts; Lincoln Coll. State Document Depository; US Document Depository
Subject Interests: Am hist, Educ, Math, Psychol
Automation Activity & Vendor Info: (Acquisitions) Ex Libris Group; (Cataloging) Ex Libris Group; (Circulation) Ex Libris Group; (ILL) Ex Libris Group; (OPAC) Ex Libris Group; (Serials) Ex Libris Group
Wireless access
Publications: Milner Memos
Partic in Consortium of Academic & Research Libraries in Illinois
Open Mon-Thurs 7am-3am, Fri 7:30am-10pm, Sat 10-10, Sun 10am-3am
Friends of the Library Group

P NORMAL PUBLIC LIBRARY*, 206 W College Ave, 61761. (Mail add: PO Box 325, 61761-0325), SAN 304-4785. Tel: 309-452-1757. FAX: 309-452-5312. E-mail: ask@normalpl.org. Web Site: normalpl.org. *Dir,* Brian Chase; *Mgr, Ad Serv,* John Fischer; *Ch Serv,* Tori Melican; *ILL,* Brenda Peden; *Tech Serv,* Jeanne Moonan; *Teen Serv,* Kristi Cates
Founded 1939
Library Holdings: Bk Vols 101,335; Per Subs 300
Automation Activity & Vendor Info: (Acquisitions) CARL.Solution (TLC)
Wireless access
Function: 3D Printer, Activity rm, Adult bk club, Art exhibits, Art programs, Bk club(s), Bks on CD, Makerspace, Movies, Museum passes, Music CDs, Notary serv, Online ref, Outreach serv, Prog for adults, Prog for children & young adult, Scanner, Senior outreach, STEM programs,

Story hour, Summer & winter reading prog, Teen prog, Winter reading prog, Writing prog
Publications: Activity Guide (Quarterly)
Mem of Reaching Across Illinois Library System (RAILS)
Partic in RSA
Open Mon-Thurs 9-9, Fri & Sat 9-5, Sun 1-5

NORRIS CITY

P NORRIS CITY MEMORIAL PUBLIC LIBRARY DISTRICT*, 603 S Division St, 62869. SAN 304-4793. Tel: 618-378-3713. FAX: 618-378-3713. E-mail: libraryncil@yahoo.com. *Dir,* Denise Karns
Founded 1945. Pop 4,472; Circ 28,602
Library Holdings: DVDs 500; Large Print Bks 1,200; Bk Titles 28,000; Per Subs 69; Talking Bks 945
Special Collections: Cookbooks
Subject Interests: Gardening, Genealogy, Hist, Illinois, Nutrition
Wireless access
Publications: Periodical Guide
Mem of Illinois Heartland Library System
Open Mon-Thurs 12-7, Fri & Sat 10-5

NORTH AURORA

P MESSENGER PUBLIC LIBRARY OF NORTH AURORA*, 113 Oak St, 60542. SAN 304-4807. Tel: 630-896-0240. Circulation Tel: 630-896-0240, Ext 4330. Administration Tel: 630-801-2345. Information Services Tel: 630-896-0240, Ext 4350. FAX: 630-896-4654. Web Site: www.messengerpl.org. *Dir,* G Kevin Davis; Tel: 630-801-2345, E-mail: gkdavis@messengerpl.org; *Head, Adult Serv,* Jessie Affelder; Tel: 630-896-0240, Ext 4350, E-mail: jaffelder@messengerpl.org. Subject Specialists: *Genealogy, Local hist,* Jessie Affelder; Staff 12 (MLS 8, Non-MLS 4)
Founded 1937. Pop 16,760; Circ 234,413
Jun 2018-May 2019 Income $1,817,489, State $21,801, Locally Generated Income $1,729,425, Other $66,263. Mats Exp $198,185, Books $104,592, Per/Ser (Incl. Access Fees) $15,000, AV Mat $44,560, Electronic Ref Mat (Incl. Access Fees) $49,033. Sal $797,626
Library Holdings: AV Mats 8,658; Braille Volumes 10; DVDs 16,694; e-books 66,669; Electronic Media & Resources 956; Bk Vols 81,723; Per Subs 113
Special Collections: Photos of buildings of the area from late 1800s to early 20th Century; Schneider diaries that date from the 1800s; Schneider diaries that date from the 1800s
Subject Interests: North Aurora hist
Automation Activity & Vendor Info: (Cataloging) SirsiDynix; (Circulation) SirsiDynix
Wireless access
Function: 24/7 Electronic res, 24/7 Online cat, Activity rm, Adult bk club, After school storytime, Archival coll, Art exhibits, Audio & video playback equip for onsite use, Audiobks on Playaways & MP3, Audiobks via web, Bi-weekly Writer's Group, Bilingual assistance for Spanish patrons, Bk club(s), Bk reviews (Group), Bks on CD, Butterfly Garden, Children's prog, Computer training, Computers for patron use, Distance learning, Doc delivery serv, E-Readers, E-Reserves, Electronic databases & coll, Free DVD rentals, Games & aids for people with disabilities, Genealogy discussion group, Holiday prog, Home delivery & serv to seniorr ctr & nursing homes, Homebound delivery serv, Homework prog, ILL available, Internet access, Large print keyboards, Life-long learning prog for all ages, Magazines, Magnifiers for reading, Mail & tel request accepted, Mail loans to mem, Mango lang, Meeting rooms, Microfiche/film & reading machines, Movies, Museum passes, Music CDs, Notary serv, Online cat, Online info literacy tutorials on the web & in blackboard, Online ref, Orientations, Outreach serv, Outside serv via phone, mail, e-mail & web, OverDrive digital audio bks, Photocopying/Printing, Preschool reading prog, Printer for laptops & handheld devices, Prog for adults, Prog for children & young adult, Ref & res, Ref serv available, Scanner, Senior computer classes, Senior outreach, Serves people with intellectual disabilities, Spanish lang bks, Story hour, Study rm, Summer & winter reading prog, Summer reading prog, Tax forms, Teen prog, Telephone ref, Visual arts prog, Wheelchair accessible, Winter reading prog, Workshops, Writing prog
Mem of Reaching Across Illinois Library System (RAILS)
Partic in Multitype Automation Group in Cooperation; System Wide Automated Network
Special Services for the Deaf - ADA equip; Assistive tech; Bks on deafness & sign lang; Closed caption videos; Sign lang interpreter upon request for prog
Open Mon-Thurs 9-9, Fri & Sat 9-5, Sun 1-5
Restriction: Borrowing requests are handled by ILL

NORTH CHICAGO

AM CAPTAIN JAMES A LOVELL FEDERAL HEALTH CARE CENTER, Health Sciences Library, 3001 Green Bay Rd, 60064. SAN 324-0231. Tel: 224-610-3757, Ext 2. FAX: 224-610-3819. *Head, Med Libr,* Anne Baker
Founded 2010
Library Holdings: CDs 250; Bk Titles 3,000; Per Subs 240; Videos 200
Subject Interests: Clinical med, Health admin, Nursing
Open Mon-Fri 8-4

GM DEPARTMENT OF VETERANS AFFAIRS MEDICAL CENTER*, Learning Resource Center, 3001 Green Bay Rd, 60064. SAN 340-5966. Tel: 847-688-1900, Ext 83757. FAX: 847-578-3819. *Librn,* Anne Baker; E-mail: anne.baker1@va.gov; Staff 2 (Non-MLS 2)
Library Holdings: Bk Titles 3,900; Bk Vols 20,000; Per Subs 80
Subject Interests: Med, Psychiat, Psychol, Soc serv (soc work)
Partic in Midwest Health Sci Libr Network; Northeastern Ill Libr Consortia
Restriction: Non-circulating to the pub, Staff use only

CM ROSALIND FRANKLIN UNIVERSITY OF MEDICINE & SCIENCE*, Boxer University Library, 3333 Green Bay Rd, 60064-3095. SAN 340-2878. Tel: 847-578-8808. FAX: 847-578-3401. E-mail: eresources@rosalindfranklin.edu. Web Site: www.rosalindfranklin.edu/library. *Libr Dir,* Charlotte Beyer; E-mail: charlotte.beyer@rosalindfranklin.edu; *Electronic Res Librn,* Katie Rose McEneely; *Instruction & Ref Librn,* Charlotte Beyer; E-mail: charlotte.beyer@rosalindfranklin.edu
Founded 1912. Enrl 1,373; Fac 350; Highest Degree: Doctorate
Library Holdings: e-journals 1,829; Bk Vols 118,853; Per Subs 380
Subject Interests: Health sci, Med
Automation Activity & Vendor Info: (Cataloging) ComPanion Corp; (Circulation) ComPanion Corp; (ILL) OCLC FirstSearch; (OPAC) OCLC FirstSearch
Wireless access
Publications: Audiovisual catalog; Current Monographs & Serials, Resources; LRC Guide
Partic in Consortium of Academic & Research Libraries in Illinois; National Network of Libraries of Medicine Region 6; OCLC Online Computer Library Center, Inc; Proquest Dialog; Regional Med Libr - Region 3
Open Mon-Fri 8am-10pm, Sat & Sun 12-5

P NORTH CHICAGO PUBLIC LIBRARY*, 2100 Argonne Dr, 60064. SAN 304-4831. Tel: 847-689-0125. Reference Tel: 847-689-0125, Ext 113. FAX: 847-689-9117. E-mail: info@ncplibrary.org. Web Site: www.ncplibrary.org. *Dir,* Joan Battley; Tel: 847-689-0125, Ext 110, E-mail: joanb@ncplibrary.org; *Ch,* John Heideman; Tel: 847-689-0125, Ext 103, E-mail: johnh@ncplibrary.org; *Ref Librn,* Walter Theobald; E-mail: jayt@ncplibrary.org; *Circ Mgr,* Rosetta Blakely; Tel: 847-689-0125, Ext 106, E-mail: rosettab@ncplibrary.org; Staff 10 (MLS 2, Non-MLS 8)
Founded 1916. Pop 34,978
Library Holdings: Bk Titles 66,000; Per Subs 140
Special Collections: African American Coll
Automation Activity & Vendor Info: (Cataloging) TLC (The Library Corporation); (Circulation) TLC (The Library Corporation); (ILL) OCLC; (OPAC) TLC (The Library Corporation)
Wireless access
Special Services for the Blind - Bks & mags in Braille, on rec, tape & cassette; Computer with voice synthesizer for visually impaired persons; Newsp on cassette; Talking bks
Open Mon-Thurs 9-7:45, Fri & Sat 9-4:45
Friends of the Library Group

NORTH RIVERSIDE

P NORTH RIVERSIDE PUBLIC LIBRARY DISTRICT, 2400 S Des Plaines Ave, 60546. SAN 376-0197. Tel: 708-447-0869. FAX: 708-447-0526. Web Site: www.northriversidelibrary.org. *Dir,* Natalie Starosta; Tel: 708-447-0869, Ext 225, E-mail: bazann@northriversidelibrary.org; *Adult Serv Mgr,* Marla Curran; E-mail: curranm@northriversidelibrary.org; *Ch Mgr,* Susan Locander; Tel: 708-447-0869, Ext 224, E-mail: locanders@northriversidelibrary.org; *Patron Serv Mgr,* Mike Bradley; E-mail: bradleym@northriversidelibrary.org; *Tech Serv Mgr, Teen Serv Mgr,* Britney Musial; E-mail: musialb@northriversidelibrary.org; Staff 25 (MLS 5, Non-MLS 20)
Founded 1983. Pop 6,672; Circ 95,432
Jul 2020-Jun 2021 Income (Main Library Only) $1,092,971, Locally Generated Income $1,092,971. Mats Exp $60,749, Books $25,943, Per/Ser (Incl. Access Fees) $1,188, Other Print Mats $1,715, AV Mat $5,344, Electronic Ref Mat (Incl. Access Fees) $15,683. Sal $501,254 (Prof $473,539)
Library Holdings: Bk Titles 30,000; Per Subs 110
Special Collections: North Riverside Historical Society Archive
Automation Activity & Vendor Info: (Circulation) Innovative Interfaces, Inc; (ILL) Innovative Interfaces, Inc; (OPAC) Innovative Interfaces, Inc
Wireless access
Function: 24/7 Electronic res, 24/7 Online cat, 3D Printer, Activity rm, Adult bk club, Adult literacy prog, After school storytime, Archival coll, Art exhibits, Art programs, Audio & video playback equip for onsite use, Audiobks on Playaways & MP3, Audiobks via web, AV serv, Bi-weekly Writer's Group, Bilingual assistance for Spanish patrons, Bk club(s), Bks on CD, Children's prog, Citizenship assistance, Computer training,

Computers for patron use, Digital talking bks, Distance learning, E-Readers, Electronic databases & coll, Family literacy, Free DVD rentals, Holiday prog, Homebound delivery serv, ILL available, Instruction & testing, Internet access, Laminating, Life-long learning prog for all ages, Literacy & newcomer serv, Magazines, Magnifiers for reading, Makerspace, Meeting rooms, Movies, Museum passes, Music CDs, Notary serv, Online cat, Online info literacy tutorials on the web & in blackboard, Online ref, Outreach serv, Outside serv via phone, mail, e-mail & web, OverDrive digital audio bks, Photocopying/Printing, Preschool reading prog, Printer for laptops & handheld devices, Prog for adults, Prog for children & young adult, Scanner, Senior computer classes, Senior outreach, Serves people with intellectual disabilities, Spanish lang bks, STEM programs, Story hour, Study rm, Summer & winter reading prog, Summer reading prog, Tax forms, Teen prog, Telephone ref, Visual arts prog, Wheelchair accessible, Winter reading prog, Workshops, Writing prog
Mem of Reaching Across Illinois Library System (RAILS)
Partic in System Wide Automated Network
Open Mon-Thurs 10-8, Fri 10-6, Sat 10-4, Sun (Sept-May) 12-4
Friends of the Library Group

NORTHBROOK

SR CONGREGATION BETH SHALOM, Marian Renee Saltzberg Learning Resource Center, 3433 Walters Ave, 60062-3298. SAN 371-7690. Tel: 847-498-4100. FAX: 847-498-9160. E-mail: library@bethshalomnb.org. Web Site: www.bethshalomnb.org/library-resource-center. *Librn,* Stephanie Gelb; Tel: 847-478-4100, Ext 13
Founded 1969
Library Holdings: Audiobooks 56; CDs 122; DVDs 393; Large Print Bks 100; Bk Titles 9,000; Bk Vols 11,125; Videos 312
Subject Interests: Holocaust
Automation Activity & Vendor Info: (Circulation) Follett Software
Wireless access
Open Tues 2-9, Sun 8-12:30

P NORTHBROOK PUBLIC LIBRARY*, 1201 Cedar Lane, 60062-4581. SAN 304-4866. Tel: 847-272-6224. FAX: 847-272-5362. Web Site: www.northbrook.info. *Dir,* Kate Hall; E-mail: khall@northbrook.info; *Asst Dir,* Brodie Austin; E-mail: baustin@northbrook.info; *Circ Mgr,* Erin Seeger; Tel: 847-272-2011, E-mail: eseeger@northbrook.info; *Digital Serv Mgr,* Cathleen Doyle; E-mail: cdoyle@northbrook.info; *Finance & Operations Mgr,* Anna Amen; E-mail: aamen@northbrook.info; *Human Res Mgr,* Laurie Prioletti; E-mail: lprioletti@northbrook.info; *Mgr,* Maggie Thomann; E-mail: mthomann@northbrook.info; *Ref Mgr,* Susan Wolf; E-mail: swolf@northbrook.info; *Youth Serv Mgr,* Kelly Durov; E-mail: kdurov@northbrook.info; *Tech Serv,* Lori Schlernitzauer; E-mail: lschlernitzauer@northbrook.info. Subject Specialists: *Fiction, Media,* Maggie Thomann; Staff 121 (MLS 40, Non-MLS 81)
Founded 1952. Pop 33,170
May 2017-Apr 2018 Income $7,423,470, State $159,982, County $7,056,605, Other $206,883. Mats Exp $848,148, Books $412,849, AV Mat $126,809, Electronic Ref Mat (Incl. Access Fees) $308,490. Sal $3,532,352
Library Holdings: Audiobooks 9,220; AV Mats 54,651; CDs 18,302; DVDs 20,401; e-books 60,412; e-journals 115; Large Print Bks 8,608; Microforms 5; Music Scores 1,216; Bk Vols 237,449; Per Subs 461; Spec Interest Per Sub 5,091; Videos 24,785
Subject Interests: Archit, Art, Landscape archit, Sci tech
Automation Activity & Vendor Info: (Acquisitions) Innovative Interfaces, Inc; (Cataloging) Innovative Interfaces, Inc; (Circulation) Innovative Interfaces, Inc; (OPAC) Innovative Interfaces, Inc
Wireless access
Function: 24/7 Electronic res, 24/7 Online cat, 3D Printer, Activity rm, Adult bk club, Adult literacy prog, After school storytime, Art exhibits, Art programs, Audio & video playback equip for onsite use, Audiobks on Playaways & MP3, Audiobks via web, AV serv, Bk club(s), Bks on CD, Chess club, Children's prog, Computer training, Computers for patron use, Digital talking bks, E-Readers, Electronic databases & coll, Equip loans & repairs, Free DVD rentals, Govt ref serv, Home delivery & serv to seniorr ctr & nursing homes, Homebound delivery serv, Homework prog, ILL available, Internet access, Large print keyboards, Life-long learning prog for all ages, Magazines, Magnifiers for reading, Makerspace, Mango lang, Meeting rooms, Microfiche/film & reading machines, Movies, Museum passes, Music CDs, Online cat, Outreach serv, Outside serv via phone, mail, e-mail & web, OverDrive digital audio bks, Photocopying/Printing, Preschool outreach, Preschool reading prog, Printer for laptops & handheld devices, Prog for adults, Prog for children & young adult, Ref & res, Ref serv available, Res assist avail, Scanner, Senior computer classes, Senior outreach, Serves people with intellectual disabilities, Spanish lang bks, Spoken cassettes & CDs, Spoken cassettes & DVDs, STEM programs, Story hour, Study rm, Summer & winter reading prog, Summer reading prog, Tax forms, Teen prog, Telephone ref, Visual arts prog, Wheelchair accessible, Winter reading prog, Workshops, Writing prog
Publications: Library (Newsletter)
Mem of Reaching Across Illinois Library System (RAILS)
Partic in Cooperative Computer Services - CCS
Special Services for the Deaf - Staff with knowledge of sign lang; TDD equip
Special Services for the Blind - Assistive/Adapted tech devices, equip & products; Audio mat; Bks on cassette; Bks on CD; Computer with voice synthesizer for visually impaired persons; Home delivery serv; Large print bks; Large screen computer & software; Lending of low vision aids; PC for people with disabilities; Talking bks
Open Mon-Thurs 9-9, Fri 9-6, Sat 9-5, Sun 1-5
Friends of the Library Group

R SAINT GILES' EPISCOPAL CHURCH*, Saint Bede's Library, 3025 Walters Ave, 60062. SAN 304-4874. Tel: 847-272-6622. FAX: 847-272-7664. Web Site: saint-giles.org.
Founded 1952
Library Holdings: Bk Vols 1,100
Subject Interests: Relig
Restriction: Mem only, Open to others by appt

S WISS, JANNEY, ELSTNER ASSOCIATES, INC, 330 Pfingsten Rd, 60062. SAN 373-0492. Tel: 847-272-7400, 847-753-7202. Web Site: www.wje.com. *Librn,* Penny Sympson; E-mail: psympson@wje.com; Staff 2 (MLS 2)
Library Holdings: Bk Vols 15,000
Subject Interests: Archit, Civil engr, Mat sci, Structural engr
Automation Activity & Vendor Info: (Cataloging) EOS International; (Circulation) EOS International
Function: ILL available, Photocopying/Printing
Mem of Reaching Across Illinois Library System (RAILS)
Partic in OCLC Online Computer Library Center, Inc
Restriction: Co libr, In-house use for visitors, Open by appt only

NORTHFIELD

S STEPAN CO*, Information Research Center, 22 W Frontage Rd, 60093. SAN 326-9647. Tel: 847-446-7500. FAX: 847-501-2466. Web Site: www.stepan.com. *Mgr,* Diane Clark; Staff 2 (MLS 1, Non-MLS 1)
Library Holdings: Bk Vols 3,899; Per Subs 155
Subject Interests: Chem
Restriction: Co libr

SR TEMPLE JEREMIAH, Marshall B & Viola R Schwimmer Library, 937 Happ Rd, 60093. (Mail add: PO Box 8209, 60093-8209), SAN 374-5716. Tel: 847-441-5760. FAX: 847-441-5765. E-mail: office@templejeremiah.org. Web Site: www.templejeremiah.org/about-us/our-building/schwimmer-library. *Exec Dir,* Daniel Glassman; Tel: 847-441-5760, Ext 102; *Communications Coordr,* Meredith Beirne; E-mail: meredith@templejeremiah.org
Library Holdings: Bk Titles 4,500; Per Subs 32
Special Collections: Allan Tarshish Rabbinical Coll; Jewish Art
Restriction: Open by appt only

NORTHLAKE

P NORTHLAKE PUBLIC LIBRARY DISTRICT*, 231 N Wolf Rd, 60164. SAN 304-4890. Tel: 708-562-2301. FAX: 708-562-8120. E-mail: askus@northlakelibrary.org. Web Site: www.northlakelibrary.org. *Dir,* Laura Bartnik; E-mail: lbartnik@northlakelibrary.org; *Asst Dir, Head, Guest Serv,* Raleigh Ocampo; E-mail: rocampo@northlakelibrary.org; *Head, Adult Serv,* Marion Olea; E-mail: molea@northlakelibrary.org; *Head, Youth Serv,* Marianne Ryczek; E-mail: ryczek@northlakelibrary.org; Staff 18 (MLS 10, Non-MLS 8)
Founded 1957. Pop 26,653; Circ 192,676
Library Holdings: AV Mats 5,776; CDs 3,198; DVDs 2,578; Electronic Media & Resources 36; High Interest/Low Vocabulary Bk Vols 60; Bk Titles 79,577; Per Subs 230
Subject Interests: Spanish
Automation Activity & Vendor Info: (Circulation) Innovative Interfaces, Inc; (ILL) Innovative Interfaces, Inc; (OPAC) Innovative Interfaces, Inc; (Serials) Innovative Interfaces, Inc
Wireless access
Function: Bilingual assistance for Spanish patrons, Bk club(s), Bks on cassette, Bks on CD, Computer training, Computers for patron use, E-Reserves, Electronic databases & coll, Free DVD rentals, Home delivery & serv to seniorr ctr & nursing homes, ILL available, Music CDs, Online cat, Photocopying/Printing, Prog for adults, Prog for children & young adult, Senior outreach, Spoken cassettes & CDs, Story hour, Summer reading prog, Tax forms, Teen prog, Telephone ref, Wheelchair accessible
Publications: Newsletter
Mem of Reaching Across Illinois Library System (RAILS)
Partic in Ill Regional Libr Coun; System Wide Automated Network
Open Mon-Thurs 9-9, Fri & Sat 9-5

OAK BROOK

S LIZZADRO MUSEUM OF LAPIDARY ART LIBRARY*, 1220 Kensington Rd, 60523. SAN 326-9493. Tel: 630-833-1616. E-mail: info@lizzadromuseum.org. Web Site: www.lizzadromuseum.org. *Dir,* Dorothy Asher
Founded 1962
Library Holdings: Bk Titles 1,000; Spec Interest Per Sub 3
Special Collections: Auction Catalogs; Chinese Jade, Asian Art; Gemstone Jewelry; Hardstone Carvings
Subject Interests: Gemology, Geol, Mineral, Paleontology
Wireless access
Publications: Lizzadro Museum Publication
Restriction: Open by appt only, Private libr

P OAK BROOK PUBLIC LIBRARY*, 600 Oak Brook Rd, 60523. SAN 304-4920. Tel: 630-368-7700. FAX: 630-368-7704. Web Site: www.oak-brook.org/library. *Head Librn,* Jacob Post; Tel: 630-368-7712, E-mail: jpost@oak-brook.org; Staff 20 (MLS 7, Non-MLS 13)
Founded 1960. Pop 8,702; Circ 96,414
Library Holdings: AV Mats 11,574; Bk Titles 87,433; Bk Vols 94,471; Per Subs 10,080
Special Collections: Douglas Coll
Subject Interests: Gardening, Quilting
Automation Activity & Vendor Info: (Acquisitions) SirsiDynix; (Cataloging) SirsiDynix; (Circulation) SirsiDynix; (OPAC) SirsiDynix; (Serials) SirsiDynix
Wireless access
Function: Adult bk club, Art exhibits, Audiobks via web, AV serv, Bk club(s), Bks on cassette, Bks on CD, Computer training, Computers for patron use, Digital talking bks, E-Reserves, Electronic databases & coll, Holiday prog, Homebound delivery serv, ILL available, Internet access, Mail & tel request accepted, Music CDs, Online cat, Photocopying/Printing, Prog for adults, Prog for children & young adult, Ref & res, Senior outreach, Spoken cassettes & CDs, Spoken cassettes & DVDs, Summer reading prog, Tax forms, Teen prog, Telephone ref, VHS videos, Wheelchair accessible
Mem of Reaching Across Illinois Library System (RAILS)
Partic in Dynix Consortium; System Wide Automated Network
Open Mon-Thurs 9:30-9, Fri & Sat 9:30-5, Sun 1-5
Friends of the Library Group

OAK FOREST

P ACORN PUBLIC LIBRARY DISTRICT*, 15624 S Central Ave, 60452-3204. SAN 304-4955. Tel: 708-687-3700. FAX: 708-687-3712. E-mail: acorn@acornlibrary.org. Web Site: www.acornlibrary.org. *Libr Dir,* Dorothy Koll; E-mail: dkoll@acornlibrary.org; *Head, Adult Serv,* Donna Dukes; E-mail: ddukes@acornlibrary.org; *Head, Circ,* Jane Young; E-mail: jyoung@acornlibrary.org; *Head, Tech Serv,* Anna Orzel; E-mail: aorzel@acornlibrary.org; *Head, Youth Serv,* Jennifer Marquardt; E-mail: jmarquardt@acornlibrary.org; *Bus Mgr,* Karen Miner; E-mail: kminer@acornlibrary.org; Staff 28 (MLS 4, Non-MLS 24)
Founded 1966. Pop 37,322; Circ 159,069
Library Holdings: CDs 3,626; DVDs 3,649; e-books 22,456; Bk Titles 67,295; Per Subs 141
Automation Activity & Vendor Info: (Cataloging) SirsiDynix; (Circulation) SirsiDynix; (ILL) SirsiDynix; (OPAC) SirsiDynix; (Serials) SirsiDynix
Wireless access
Function: 24/7 Electronic res, 24/7 Online cat, Activity rm, Adult bk club, Art exhibits, Art programs, Audio & video playback equip for onsite use, Audiobks on Playaways & MP3, Audiobks via web, AV serv, Bilingual assistance for Spanish patrons, Bk club(s), Bks on CD, CD-ROM, Children's prog, Computer training, Computers for patron use, Digital talking bks, E-Readers, E-Reserves, Electronic databases & coll, Equip loans & repairs, Family literacy, Free DVD rentals, Games & aids for people with disabilities, Genealogy discussion group, Govt ref serv, Holiday prog, Homework prog, ILL available, Internet access, Laminating, Magazines, Mail & tel request accepted, Meeting rooms, Movies, Museum passes, Music CDs, Notary serv, Online cat, Online info literacy tutorials on the web & in blackboard, Online ref, Outreach serv, OverDrive digital audio bks, Photocopying/Printing, Preschool outreach, Preschool reading prog, Printer for laptops & handheld devices, Prog for adults, Prog for children & young adult, Ref & res, Ref serv available, Res assist avail, Scanner, Senior computer classes, Serves people with intellectual disabilities, Spanish lang bks, Story hour, Study rm, Summer & winter reading prog, Summer reading prog, Tax forms, Teen prog, Telephone ref, Wheelchair accessible, Winter reading prog, Workshops
Publications: Community Awareness Brochures; Newsletter
Mem of Reaching Across Illinois Library System (RAILS)
Partic in System Wide Automated Network
Special Services for the Blind - Closed circuit TV
Open Mon-Thurs 9-9, Fri & Sat 9-5
Friends of the Library Group

SR MISSIONARY SISTERS OF SAINT BENEDICT LIBRARY*, 5900 W 147th St, 60452-1104. SAN 321-2289. Tel: 708-535-9623. *Library Contact,* Sister Assumpta Wrobel
Library Holdings: Bk Titles 3,500; Per Subs 40
Special Collections: Oral History
Restriction: Not open to pub, Private libr

OAK LAWN

P OAK LAWN PUBLIC LIBRARY*, 9427 S Raymond Ave, 60453. SAN 304-498X. Tel: 708-422-4990. FAX: 708-422-5061. Web Site: www.olpl.org. *Dir,* Jim Deiters; E-mail: jdeiters@olpl.org; *Head, Adult Serv, Head, YA,* Mary Williams; E-mail: mwilliams@olpl.org; *Librn,* Kathy O'Leary; E-mail: koleary@olpl.org; *Librn,* Ang Romano; E-mail: aromano@olpl.org; *Teen Librn,* Izabel Gronski; E-mail: igronski@olpl.org; Staff 90 (MLS 20, Non-MLS 70)
Founded 1943. Pop 56,000; Circ 500,000
Library Holdings: AV Mats 33,153; Bk Vols 281,342; Per Subs 735
Special Collections: Telephone Books on CD ROM & microfiche; US College Catalogs, microfiche. Oral History
Subject Interests: Careers, Law, Local hist
Automation Activity & Vendor Info: (Acquisitions) Brodart; (Circulation) Innovative Interfaces, Inc
Wireless access
Publications: Check It Out! (Newsletter)
Mem of Reaching Across Illinois Library System (RAILS)
Partic in Illinois Library & Information Network; OCLC Online Computer Library Center, Inc; Proquest Dialog; System Wide Automated Network; Wilsonline
Special Services for the Deaf - Bks on deafness & sign lang; Captioned film dep
Special Services for the Blind - Talking bks
Open Mon-Thurs 9-9, Fri & Sat 9-5, Sun 1-5
Friends of the Library Group

OAK PARK

P OAK PARK PUBLIC LIBRARY*, 834 Lake St, 60301. SAN 340-6148. Tel: 708-383-8200. Circulation Tel: 708-452-3409. FAX: 708-697-6900. Administration FAX: 708-697-6917. Web Site: www.oppl.org. *Exec Dir,* David J Seleb; Tel: 708-697-6911, E-mail: d.seleb@oppl.org; *Asst Dir, Admin Serv, Dep Dir,* Jim Madigan; Tel: 708-687-6909, E-mail: jmadigan@oppl.org; *Br Serv Mgr,* Martin Churchouse; E-mail: mchurchouse@oppl.org; Staff 26 (MLS 26)
Founded 1902. Pop 52,524; Circ 961,801
Library Holdings: Bk Vols 315,000; Per Subs 500
Special Collections: Frank Lloyd Wright & Ernest Hemingway (Local Authors), bks, pamphlets, papers; History, bks, photos, papers; Oak Park Local. US Document Depository
Subject Interests: Art & archit, Local hist
Automation Activity & Vendor Info: (Circulation) SirsiDynix
Wireless access
Function: 24/7 Electronic res, 3D Printer, Adult bk club, Adult literacy prog, After school storytime, Archival coll, Art exhibits, Audiobks via web, AV serv, Bk club(s), Children's prog, Citizenship assistance, Computer training, Computers for patron use, Digital talking bks, E-Readers, Electronic databases & coll, Family literacy, For res purposes, Health sci info serv, Holiday prog, Home delivery & serv to seniorr ctr & nursing homes, Homebound delivery serv, Homework prog, ILL available, Instruction & testing, Internet access, Life-long learning prog for all ages, Literacy & newcomer serv, Magazines, Magnifiers for reading, Mango lang, Meeting rooms, Microfiche/film & reading machines, Movies, Museum passes, Notary serv, Online cat, Online info literacy tutorials on the web & in blackboard, Online ref, Outreach serv, Outside serv via phone, mail, e-mail & web, OverDrive digital audio bks, Photocopying/Printing, Preschool outreach, Preschool reading prog, Prog for adults, Prog for children & young adult, Ref & res, Ref serv available, Res assist avail, Scanner, Senior computer classes, Senior outreach, Story hour, Study rm, Summer & winter reading prog, Summer reading prog, Tax forms, Teen prog, Telephone ref, Wheelchair accessible, Winter reading prog, Workshops
Mem of Reaching Across Illinois Library System (RAILS)
Partic in System Wide Automated Network
Open Mon-Thurs 9-9, Fri 9-6, Sat 9-5, Sun 1-6
Friends of the Library Group
Branches: 2
DOLE BRANCH, 255 Augusta St, 60302, SAN 340-6202. Tel: 708-386-9032. FAX: 708-445-2385.
Open Tues-Thurs 10-9, Fri 10-6, Sat 10-5, Sun 1-6
Friends of the Library Group
MAZE BRANCH, 845 S Gunderson Ave, 60304, SAN 340-6172. Tel: 708-386-4751. FAX: 708-386-0023.
Library Holdings: Bk Vols 30,333
Open Mon-Thurs 10-9, Sat 10-5, Sun 1-6
Friends of the Library Group

S FRANK LLOYD WRIGHT TRUST*, Research Center, 951 Chicago Ave, 60302. SAN 325-2949. Tel: 312-994-4035. E-mail: research@flwright.org. Web Site: flwright.org. *Curator, Dir, Coll & Interpretation,* David Bagnall
Founded 1974
Library Holdings: Bk Titles 2,500; Per Subs 20
Special Collections: Artifacts; Frank Lloyd Wright Coll; John L Wright Toy Coll; Large Drawings; Maginal Wright Barney Archive; Prairie School of Architecture, mat; William Drummond Coll. Oral History
Subject Interests: Archit design, Arts & crafts
Publications: Frank Lloyd Wright (Newsletter)
Restriction: Open by appt only

OAKBROOK TERRACE

S THE JOINT COMMISSION*, Resource Center, One Renaissance Blvd, 60181. SAN 375-9784. Tel: 630-792-5474. Web Site: www.jointcommission.org. *Dir,* Jan Aleccia; E-mail: jaleccia@jointcommission.org; Staff 2 (MLS 2)
Founded 1986
Library Holdings: AV Mats 200; Bk Titles 2,500; Per Subs 100
Subject Interests: Health admin
Automation Activity & Vendor Info: (Cataloging) LibraryWorld, Inc
Wireless access
Partic in National Network of Libraries of Medicine Region 6
Restriction: Not open to pub

OAKWOOD

P OAKWOOD PUBLIC LIBRARY DISTRICT*, 110 E Finley, 61858. (Mail add: PO Box 99, 61858-0099), SAN 376-0162. Tel: 217-354-4777. FAX: 217-354-4782. E-mail: OakwoodPublicLibrary@gmail.com. Web Site: www.oakwood.lib.il.us. *Dir,* Tammi Helka
Founded 1987. Pop 7,409
Library Holdings: Bk Titles 15,000; Per Subs 62
Special Collections: Audio Coll; Local History Room
Automation Activity & Vendor Info: (Cataloging) SirsiDynix; (Circulation) SirsiDynix
Mem of Illinois Heartland Library System
Open Mon, Wed & Fri 10-6, Tues & Thurs 12-8, Sat 9-2
Friends of the Library Group

ODELL

P ODELL PUBLIC LIBRARY DISTRICT*, 301 E Richard St, 60460. SAN 304-5021. Tel: 815-998-2012. FAX: 815-998-2339. E-mail: odellpld@yahoo.com. Web Site: www.odelllibrary.com. *Libr Dir,* Cathy Grafton; *Board Pres,* Dale Hoke; Staff 1 (Non-MLS 1)
Founded 1904. Pop 2,341; Circ 10,319
Jul 2020-Jun 2021 Income $124,157, State $1,800, Provincial $2,200, Other $13,150. Mats Exp $22,070. Sal $42,800
Library Holdings: Audiobooks 308; CDs 312; DVDs 1,111; Large Print Bks 594; Bk Vols 14,171; Per Subs 12
Wireless access
Function: 24/7 Online cat, After school storytime, Archival coll, Art exhibits, Audiobks on Playaways & MP3, Audiobks via web, Bks on CD, Children's prog, Computer training, Computers for patron use, Distance learning, Electronic databases & coll, Free DVD rentals, Holiday prog, Homebound delivery serv, ILL available, Internet access, Laminating, Life-long learning prog for all ages, Magazines, Magnifiers for reading, Meeting rooms, Movies, Music CDs, Online cat, Online ref, Photocopying/Printing, Preschool outreach, Printer for laptops & handheld devices, Prog for adults, Prog for children & young adult, Scanner, Senior computer classes, Senior outreach, Story hour, Summer reading prog, Wheelchair accessible
Mem of Reaching Across Illinois Library System (RAILS)
Open Mon & Wed 1-8, Tues, Thurs & Fri 1-5, Sat 9-12

O'FALLON

P O'FALLON PUBLIC LIBRARY*, 120 Civic Plaza, 62269-2692. SAN 304-503X. Tel: 618-632-3783. FAX: 618-632-3759. Reference E-mail: reference@ofpl.info. Web Site: www.ofpl.info. *Dir,* Molly Scanlan; E-mail: molly@ofpl.info; *Asst Dir,* Ryan Johnson; E-mail: ryan@ofpl.info; *Head, Circ & Adult Serv,* Laura Picato; E-mail: laura@ofpl.info; *Head, Youth Serv,* Teri Rankin; E-mail: teri@ofpl.info; Staff 3 (MLS 2, Non-MLS 1)
Founded 1943. Pop 28,396; Circ 348,532
Library Holdings: Audiobooks 4,694; CDs 4,500; DVDs 4,000; e-books 16,831; Electronic Media & Resources 55; Bk Vols 64,668; Per Subs 220
Special Collections: Learning Activities Resource Center (for teachers/homeschoolers)
Subject Interests: Popular mat
Automation Activity & Vendor Info: (Acquisitions) Innovative Interfaces, Inc; (Cataloging) Innovative Interfaces, Inc; (Circulation) Innovative Interfaces, Inc; (Discovery) EBSCO Discovery Service; (ILL) OCLC; (OPAC) Innovative Interfaces, Inc
Wireless access
Mem of Illinois Heartland Library System
Open Mon-Thurs 9-8, Fri 9-5, Sat 9-4, Sun 1-5
Friends of the Library Group

OGDEN

P OGDEN ROSE PUBLIC LIBRARY*, 103 W Main St, 61859. (Mail add: PO Box 297, 61859-0297), SAN 304-5048. Tel: 217-582-2411. FAX: 217-582-8020. E-mail: roselibrary@comcast.net. *Dir,* Lora Holden
Pop 800; Circ 1,500
Library Holdings: Bk Vols 17,000; Per Subs 20
Wireless access
Mem of Illinois Heartland Library System
Open Tues & Thurs 8-1 & 4-8, Wed 1-8, Sat 9-1
Friends of the Library Group

OGLESBY

J ILLINOIS VALLEY COMMUNITY COLLEGE*, Jacobs Memorial Library, 815 N Orlando Smith Rd, 61348-9692. SAN 304-5056. Tel: 815-224-0306. Interlibrary Loan Service Tel: 815-224-0307. FAX: 815-224-9147. E-mail: jacobs_library@ivcc.edu. Web Site: libguides.ivcc.edu/library. *Access Serv Librn, Coll Develop Librn,* Jayna Leipart Guttilla; Tel: 815-224-0387, E-mail: Jayna_LeipartGuttilla@ivcc.edu; *Pub Serv Librn,* Stephanie King; E-mail: Stephanie_King@ivcc.edu; Staff 4 (MLS 2, Non-MLS 2)
Founded 1968. Enrl 4,500; Fac 91; Highest Degree: Associate
Library Holdings: AV Mats 1,214; e-books 10,738; Bk Vols 61,425
Special Collections: State Document Depository; US Document Depository
Automation Activity & Vendor Info: (Cataloging) Ex Libris Group; (Circulation) Ex Libris Group; (OPAC) Ex Libris Group
Wireless access
Mem of Reaching Across Illinois Library System (RAILS)
Partic in Consortium of Academic & Research Libraries in Illinois; Network of Illinois Learning Resources in Community Colleges; Northern Ill Learning Resources Coop; OCLC Online Computer Library Center, Inc; OCLC-LVIS; State of Ill Librs Online
Open Mon-Thurs 7:30am-8pm, Fri 7:30-4:30
Restriction: Open to pub for ref & circ; with some limitations, Open to students, fac & staff

P OGLESBY PUBLIC LIBRARY, 111 S Woodland St, 61348. SAN 304-5064. Tel: 815-883-3619. FAX: 815-883-3615. Web Site: oglesbylibrary.org. *Dir,* Jill Shevokas; E-mail: director@oglesbylibrary.org; Staff 5 (Non-MLS 5)
Founded 1925. Pop 4,019; Circ 21,667
Library Holdings: Bk Vols 23,000; Per Subs 75
Automation Activity & Vendor Info: (Circulation) Innovative Interfaces, Inc - Sierra
Wireless access
Function: 24/7 Online cat, Bks on CD, Children's prog, Computer training, Computers for patron use, Free DVD rentals, ILL available, Internet access, Laminating, Magazines, Movies, Music CDs, Online cat, Photocopying/Printing, Prog for adults, Prog for children & young adult, Ref serv available, Scanner, Senior computer classes, Spoken cassettes & CDs, Summer reading prog, Tax forms
Mem of Reaching Across Illinois Library System (RAILS)
Open Mon, Wed, & Fri 10-6, Tues & Thurs 10-4, Sat 10-2
Friends of the Library Group

OHIO

P OHIO PUBLIC LIBRARY DISTRICT*, 112 N Main St, 61349. (Mail add: PO Box 187, 61349-0187), SAN 304-5072. Tel: 815-376-5422. FAX: 815-376-5422. E-mail: ohiolibrarybc@yahoo.com. Web Site: ohiolibrarybc.com. *Dir,* David Sprung
Founded 1949. Pop 1,043; Circ 6,075
Library Holdings: AV Mats 672; Bks on Deafness & Sign Lang 32; CDs 5; DVDs 120; Large Print Bks 418; Bk Vols 5,799; Per Subs 25; Spec Interest Per Sub 2; Talking Bks 5; Videos 571
Function: Adult bk club, Audio & video playback equip for onsite use, Computer training, Homebound delivery serv, Internet access, Mail & tel request accepted, Music CDs, Online ref, Outside serv via phone, mail, e-mail & web, Photocopying/Printing, Prog for children & young adult, Ref serv available, Serves people with intellectual disabilities, Spoken cassettes & CDs, Summer reading prog, Tax forms, VHS videos, Wheelchair accessible
Mem of Reaching Across Illinois Library System (RAILS)
Special Services for the Blind - Audio mat; Bks on cassette; Bks on CD; Cassette playback machines; Home delivery serv; Large print bks; Talking bk & rec for the blind cat; Talking bks; Talking bks & player equip
Open Mon & Fri 11-6, Wed 10-6, Sat 9-12
Restriction: In-house use for visitors, Non-circulating coll, Non-resident fee, Open to students, Pub ref by request, Pub use on premises, Registered patrons only, Residents only

OLIVE BRANCH

P DODGE MEMORIAL PUBLIC LIBRARY*, 22440 Railroad St, 62969. (Mail add: PO Box 65, 62969-0065), SAN 376-6764. Tel: 618-776-5115. FAX: 618-776-5115. *Librn,* Karen Schultz; E-mail: klschultz57@dodgelibrary1987.com
Library Holdings: Bk Titles 4,500; Bk Vols 10,000
Wireless access
Mem of Illinois Heartland Library System
Open Tues 3-5, Wed-Fri 11-5

OLMSTED

P OLMSTED PUBLIC LIBRARY*, 160 N Front St, 62970. SAN 376-0170. Tel: 618-742-8296. FAX: 618-742-8296. *Librn,* Katherine Robertson; E-mail: krobolmpl@yahoo.com
Pop 299; Circ 1,161
Library Holdings: Bk Vols 5,000; Per Subs 25
Mem of Illinois Heartland Library System
Open Tues-Thurs 12:30-4:30

OLNEY

J OLNEY CENTRAL COLLEGE*, Anderson Learning Resource Center, 305 N West St, 62450. SAN 304-5080. Tel: 618-395-7777, Ext 2260. FAX: 618-392-3293. Web Site: www.iecc.edu/occ/library. *Interim Libr Dir,* Linda Shidler, PhD; Tel: 618-395-7777, Ext 2264, E-mail: shidlerl@iecc.edu; *Libr Asst,* Kaitlyn Weger; Tel: 618-395-777, ext 2262, E-mail: wegerk@iecc.edu
Founded 1963. Enrl 2,000; Fac 42; Highest Degree: Associate
Library Holdings: Audiobooks 70; AV Mats 742; Bks on Deafness & Sign Lang 27; CDs 139; DVDs 78; e-books 600; e-journals 1,600; Electronic Media & Resources 27; High Interest/Low Vocabulary Bk Vols 208; Large Print Bks 23; Music Scores 10; Bk Titles 20,953; Bk Vols 22,504; Per Subs 52; Spec Interest Per Sub 17; Talking Bks 50; Videos 664
Automation Activity & Vendor Info: (Acquisitions) Ex Libris Group; (Cataloging) Ex Libris Group; (Circulation) Ex Libris Group; (Course Reserve) Ex Libris Group; (ILL) Ex Libris Group; (OPAC) Ex Libris Group; (Serials) ADLiB
Wireless access
Function: ILL available
Mem of Illinois Heartland Library System
Special Services for the Deaf - Accessible learning ctr; ADA equip; Assistive tech; Closed caption videos
Special Services for the Blind - Accessible computers; Aids for in-house use; Assistive/Adapted tech devices, equip & products; Audio mat; Bks available with recordings
Open Mon, Tues & Thurs 7:30-6:30, Wed & Fri 7:30-4;30 (Fall-Spring); Mon-Fri 7;30-4 (Summer)
Friends of the Library Group

P OLNEY PUBLIC LIBRARY*, 400 W Main St, 62450. SAN 340-6237. Tel: 618-392-3711. FAX: 618-392-3139. E-mail: info@olneypubliclibrary.org. Web Site: olneypubliclibrary.org. *Dir,* Brittany Bass; Staff 6 (Non-MLS 6)
Founded 1872. Pop 8,631; Circ 80,000
Library Holdings: Bk Titles 38,000; Per Subs 60
Special Collections: Antiques & Collectibles - Toys & Dolls; Civil War; Genealogy
Mem of Illinois Heartland Library System
Open Mon-Thurs 10-7, Fri & Sat 10-5
Friends of the Library Group

ONARGA

P ONARGA COMMUNITY PUBLIC LIBRARY DISTRICT*, 209 W Seminary Ave, 60955-1131. SAN 304-5102. Tel: 815-268-7626. FAX: 815-268-4635. E-mail: libraryonarga@yahoo.com. Web Site: www.onargalibrary.com. *Dir,* Vicky Reetz
Pop 3,943; Circ 14,161
Automation Activity & Vendor Info: (Circulation) SirsiDynix
Wireless access
Mem of Illinois Heartland Library System
Open Mon-Wed 12-6, Thurs 10-6, Fri 10-5, Sat 10-1

ONEIDA

P GREIG MEMORIAL LIBRARY*, 110 S Joy St, 61467. (Mail add: PO Box 446, 61467-0446), SAN 304-5110. Tel: 309-483-3482. FAX: 309-483-3482. E-mail: greigmemlib@gmail.com. Web Site: greigmemlib.webs.com. *Dir,* Dave Sheppard
Founded 1916. Pop 752; Circ 4,638
Library Holdings: Bk Vols 12,000
Wireless access
Mem of Reaching Across Illinois Library System (RAILS)
Open Tues 12-8, Wed 9-12 & 3-8, Fri & Sat 9-1
Friends of the Library Group

OREANA

P ARGENTA-OREANA PUBLIC LIBRARY DISTRICT*, Oreana Public Library, 211 S Rte 48, 62554. (Mail add: PO Box 278, 62554), SAN 304-5129. Tel: 217-468-2340. FAX: 217-468-2467. Web Site: aopld.org. *Dir,* Donna Schaal; E-mail: director@aopld.lib.il.us
Pop 5,507
Library Holdings: CDs 250; DVDs 3,000; Bk Titles 13,000; Per Subs 45; Talking Bks 1,243
Automation Activity & Vendor Info: (Acquisitions) SirsiDynix; (Cataloging) SirsiDynix; (Circulation) SirsiDynix; (ILL) SirsiDynix; (OPAC) SirsiDynix
Wireless access
Function: CD-ROM
Mem of Illinois Heartland Library System
Open Mon & Wed 9-7, Tues, Thurs & Fri 9-5, Sat 9-1

OREGON

P OREGON PUBLIC LIBRARY DISTRICT*, 300 Jefferson St, 61061. SAN 304-5137. Tel: 815-732-2724. FAX: 815-732-6643. E-mail: oregonlibrary@yahoo.com. Web Site: oregonpubliclibrary.com. *Dir,* Andrew Deltman; *Adult Serv,* Laura Hale; *Ch Serv,* Deborah Herman
Pop 6,719; Circ 37,106
Library Holdings: Bk Vols 34,153; Per Subs 62
Special Collections: Laredo Taft Eagles Nest Art Coll
Subject Interests: Genealogy
Wireless access
Mem of Reaching Across Illinois Library System (RAILS)
Open Mon-Thurs 9-8, Fri & Sat 9-4
Friends of the Library Group

ORION

P WESTERN DISTRICT LIBRARY*, 1111 Fourth St, 61273. (Mail add: PO Box 70, 61273-0070), SAN 304-5145, *Dir,* Don Thorsen; E-mail: director@orionlib.org; *Ch,* Mary Ellison; Staff 1 (MLS 1)
Founded 1905. Pop 4,045; Circ 28,131
Wireless access
Function: 24/7 Electronic res, 24/7 Online cat, Adult bk club
Mem of Reaching Across Illinois Library System (RAILS)
Open Mon & Wed 9-8, Tues & Thurs 12-8, Fri 9-6, Sat 9-1

ORLAND PARK

P ORLAND PARK PUBLIC LIBRARY*, 14921 Ravinia Ave, 60462. SAN 304-5153. Tel: 708-428-5100. Circulation Tel: 708-428-5105. Interlibrary Loan Service Tel: 708-428-5104. Automation Services Tel: 708-428-5202. FAX: 708-349-8322. E-mail: askoppl@orlandparklibrary.org. Web Site: www.orlandparklibrary.org. *Libr Dir,* Mary Weimar; Tel: 708-428-5203, E-mail: mweimar@orlandparklibrary.org; *Asst Libr Dir,* Mary Adamowski; Tel: 708-428-5202, E-mail: madamowski@orlandparklibrary.org; *Adult Serv Mgr,* Katie Allan; Tel: 708-428-5155, E-mail: kallan@orlandparklibrary.org; *Communications Mgr,* Jackie Boyd; Tel: 708-428-5205, E-mail: jboyd@orlandparklibrary.org; *Commun Engagement Mgr,* Sarah Kleiva; Tel: 708-428-5114, E-mail: skleiva@orlandparklibrary.org; *Digital Serv Mgr,* Ian Lashbrook; Tel: 708-428-5167, E-mail: ilashbrook@orlandparklibrary.org; *Patron Serv Mgr,* Theresa Hildebrand; Tel: 708-428-5109, E-mail: thildebrand@orlandparklibrary.org; *Tech Serv Mgr,* Wendy Xie; Tel: 708-428-5120, E-mail: wxie@orlandparklibrary.org; *Youth Serv Mgr,* Brandi Smits; Tel: 708-428-5135, E-mail: bsmits@orlandparklibrary.org; Staff 95 (MLS 30, Non-MLS 65)
Founded 1937. Pop 58,590; Circ 929,003
Library Holdings: Bk Vols 124,000; Per Subs 402
Automation Activity & Vendor Info: (Acquisitions) Innovative Interfaces, Inc; (Cataloging) Innovative Interfaces, Inc; (Circulation) Innovative Interfaces, Inc; (ILL) OCLC WorldShare Interlibrary Loan; (OPAC) Innovative Interfaces, Inc; (Serials) Innovative Interfaces, Inc
Wireless access
Function: 24/7 Electronic res, Activity rm, Adult bk club, Art exhibits, Audiobks via web, Bks on CD, Children's prog, Computer training, Computers for patron use, Digital talking bks, E-Readers, E-Reserves, Electronic databases & coll, Free DVD rentals, Holiday prog, Home delivery & serv to seniorr ctr & nursing homes, Homebound delivery serv, ILL available, Internet access, Life-long learning prog for all ages, Magazines, Magnifiers for reading, Mail & tel request accepted, Microfiche/film & reading machines, Movies, Museum passes, Music CDs, Notary serv, Online cat, Online ref, Outreach serv, Outside serv via phone, mail, e-mail & web, OverDrive digital audio bks, Photocopying/Printing, Preschool outreach, Preschool reading prog, Printer for laptops & handheld devices, Prog for adults, Prog for children & young adult, Ref serv available, Scanner, Senior computer classes, Senior outreach, Story hour,

Study rm, Summer & winter reading prog, Tax forms, Teen prog, Telephone ref, VHS videos, Visual arts prog, Wheelchair accessible, Writing prog
Publications: E-Connection (Newsletter); The Connection (Newsletter)
Mem of Reaching Across Illinois Library System (RAILS)
Special Services for the Deaf - Assisted listening device; Sign lang interpreter upon request for prog
Special Services for the Blind - Accessible computers; Assistive/Adapted tech devices, equip & products; BiFolkal kits; Bks on CD; Bks on flash-memory cartridges; Braille bks; Children's Braille; Home delivery serv; Internet workstation with adaptive software; Large print bks; Low vision equip; Magnifiers; Playaways (bks on MP3); Screen enlargement software for people with visual disabilities; Talking bk serv referral
Open Mon-Fri 9-9, Sat 9-5, Sun 1-5
Restriction: Borrowing requests are handled by ILL, Non-resident fee
Friends of the Library Group

OSWEGO

P OSWEGO PUBLIC LIBRARY DISTRICT*, Oswego Campus, 32 W Jefferson St, 60543. SAN 304-5161. Tel: 630-554-3150. Circulation Tel: 630-978-1205. FAX: 630-978-1307. Web Site: www.oswego.lib.il.us. *Dir,* Sarah Skilton; Tel: 630-978-1506, E-mail: sskilton@oswego.lib.il.us; *Asst Dir,* Krista Katzen; Tel: 630-978-1037, E-mail: kkatzen@oswego.lib.il.us; *Br Mgr,* Lu Anne Harkins; E-mail: lharkins@oswego.lib.il.us; *Head, Adult Serv,* Carolyn Leifheit; E-mail: cleifheit@oswego.lib.il.us; *Head, Youth Serv,* Christy Kepler; E-mail: ckepler@oswego.lib.il.us; Staff 72 (MLS 17, Non-MLS 55)
Founded 1964. Pop 61,594; Circ 927,536
Library Holdings: Bk Vols 271,488
Special Collections: Fox Valley Genealogy Society; Illinois Census Coll (1820-1920), micro; Oswego Historical Records, micro
Subject Interests: Antiques, Collectibles
Automation Activity & Vendor Info: (Cataloging) SirsiDynix; (Circulation) SirsiDynix
Wireless access
Function: 24/7 Online cat, Adult bk club
Mem of Reaching Across Illinois Library System (RAILS)
Open Mon-Thurs 9-8, Fri & Sat 9-4, Sun 12-4
Friends of the Library Group
Branches: 1
, Montgomery Campus, 1111 Reading Dr, Montgomery, 60538. Tel: 630-978-1207. *Br Mgr,* Matt Prinos; E-mail: mprinos@oswego.lib.il.us
Open Mon-Thurs 9-8, Fri & Sat 9-4, Sun 12-4

OTTAWA

P REDDICK PUBLIC LIBRARY DISTRICT*, 1010 Canal St, 61350. SAN 304-517X. Tel: 815-434-0509. FAX: 815-434-2634. E-mail: webmaster@reddicklibrary.org. Web Site: www.reddicklibrary.org. *Libr Dir,* Molly DeBernardi; E-mail: mdebernardi@reddicklibrary.org; Staff 3 (MLS 1, Non-MLS 2)
Founded 1888. Pop 18,400; Circ 124,000
Library Holdings: High Interest/Low Vocabulary Bk Vols 200; Bk Vols 72,865; Per Subs 179
Special Collections: State & Local History (Illinois Coll)
Automation Activity & Vendor Info: (Circulation) SirsiDynix
Wireless access
Mem of Reaching Across Illinois Library System (RAILS)
Open Mon-Thurs 9-9, Fri & Sat 9-5, Sun 12-5
Friends of the Library Group

GL THIRD DISTRICT APPELLATE COURT LIBRARY*, 1004 Columbus St, 61350. SAN 304-5188. Tel: 815-434-5050. FAX: 815-434-2442. *Library Contact,* Kim Lukkari
Library Holdings: Bk Vols 15,000
Open Mon-Fri 8:30-4:30
Restriction: Open to pub for ref only

PALATINE

P PALATINE PUBLIC LIBRARY DISTRICT*, 700 N North Ct, 60067-8159. SAN 304-5196. Tel: 847-358-5881. Administration FAX: 847-358-5998. E-mail: palatine@palatinelibrary.org. Web Site: www.palatinelibrary.org. *Exec Dir,* Jeannie Dilger; *Asst Dir, Pub Serv,* Melissa Gardner; *Asst Dir, Support Serv,* Maureen Galvan; *Circ Mgr,* Rosalie Scarpelli; *Fac Mgr,* Gregg Szczesny; *Finance Mgr,* Regina Stapleton; *Info Serv Mgr,* Brian Herner; *Mgr, Communications, Mkt Mgr,* Andrea Lublink; *Mgr, Popular Mats,* Kathy Burns; *Tech Mgr,* Susan Conner; *Tech Serv Mgr,* Kristin Sedivy; Staff 100 (MLS 15, Non-MLS 85)
Founded 1923. Pop 88,983; Circ 1,578,994
Library Holdings: AV Mats 60,962; e-books 16,994; Bk Titles 255,115; Bk Vols 264,222; Per Subs 524
Automation Activity & Vendor Info: (Acquisitions) Innovative Interfaces, Inc; (Cataloging) Innovative Interfaces, Inc; (Circulation) Innovative Interfaces, Inc; (ILL) OCLC; (OPAC) Innovative Interfaces, Inc; (Serials) Innovative Interfaces, Inc
Wireless access
Function: 24/7 Online cat, Adult bk club, Art exhibits, Audio & video playback equip for onsite use, Audiobks on Playaways & MP3, Audiobks via web, Bilingual assistance for Spanish patrons, Bk club(s), Bks on CD, Chess club, Children's prog, Citizenship assistance, Computer training, Computers for patron use, Digital talking bks, E-Readers, Electronic databases & coll, Free DVD rentals, Genealogy discussion group, Homebound delivery serv, ILL available, Internet access, Magazines, Magnifiers for reading, Mail & tel request accepted, Mango lang, Meeting rooms, Microfiche/film & reading machines, Movies, Museum passes, Music CDs, Online cat, Online ref, Outside serv via phone, mail, e-mail & web, OverDrive digital audio bks, Photocopying/Printing, Printer for laptops & handheld devices, Prog for adults, Prog for children & young adult, Ref serv available, Scanner, Senior computer classes, Spanish lang bks, Study rm, Summer & winter reading prog, Tax forms, Teen prog, Telephone ref, Wheelchair accessible
Publications: Newsletter
Mem of Reaching Across Illinois Library System (RAILS)
Special Services for the Deaf - ADA equip; Assistive tech
Special Services for the Blind - Audio mat; Bks on CD; Braille bks; Braille equip; Children's Braille; Copier with enlargement capabilities; Digital talking bk; Dragon Naturally Speaking software; Home delivery serv; Large print bks; Magnifiers; Playaways (bks on MP3); Talking bks
Open Mon-Thurs 9-9, Fri 9-6, Sat 9-5, Sun 12-5
Friends of the Library Group
Branches: 2
NORTH HOFFMAN BRANCH, 3600 Lexington Dr, Hoffman Estates, 60192, SAN 370-3657. Tel: 847-934-0220. *Br Mgr, Circ,* Rosalie Scarpelli; *Supvr,* Karen Bollman; Staff 18 (MLS 15, Non-MLS 3)
Founded 1981. Pop 11,000; Circ 180,396
Library Holdings: Bk Vols 22,000; Per Subs 59
Function: Computers for patron use, ILL available, Magazines, Movies, Music CDs, Photocopying/Printing, Prog for children & young adult, Ref serv available, Summer reading prog, Wheelchair accessible
Publications: Page Turner (Newsletter)
Open Mon-Fri 11-7, Sat 9-3
Friends of the Library Group
RAND ROAD BRANCH, 1585 N Rand Rd, 60074. Tel: 847-202-1194. *Br Mgr, Circ,* Rosalie Scarpelli; *Br Supvr,* Karen Bollman; Staff 4 (Non-MLS 4)
Founded 2000. Pop 10,000; Circ 67,011
Library Holdings: Bk Titles 4,000; Bk Vols 6,800; Per Subs 16
Function: Bilingual assistance for Spanish patrons, Children's prog, Computers for patron use, Magazines, Movies, Music CDs, Online cat, Ref serv available, Spanish lang bks, Story hour
Publications: Page Turner (Newsletter)
Open Mon-Thurs 10-6, Fri 9-4, Sat 9-1
Friends of the Library Group

J WILLIAM RAINEY HARPER COLLEGE LIBRARY*, Resources for Learning, 1200 W Algonguin Rd, 60067. SAN 304-520X. Tel: 847-925-6584. Interlibrary Loan Service Tel: 847-925-6768. Administration Tel: 847-925-6550. Information Services Tel: 847-925-6184. FAX: 847-925-6164. E-mail: library@harpercollege.edu. Web Site: harpercollege.edu/library. *Dean,* Njambi Kamoche; E-mail: nkamoche@harpercollege.edu; *Coordr, Tech,* William Pankey; Tel: 847-925-6498, E-mail: wpankey@harpercollege.edu; *Coordr, Coll Develop,* Kimberly Fournier; Tel: 847-925-6882, E-mail: kfournie@harpercollege.edu; *Ref Serv Coordr,* Tom Goetz; Tel: 847-925-6252, E-mail: tgoetz@harpercollege.edu; *Tech Serv Coordr,* Jim Edstrom; Tel: 847-925-6763, E-mail: jedstrom@harpercollege.edu; *Circ,* Deanna Belt; Tel: 847-925-6584, E-mail: dbelt@harpercollege.edu; *ILL,* Timothy Philbin; E-mail: tphilbin@harpercollege.edu. Subject Specialists: *Adult educ, Sign lang,* William Pankey; *Counseling, Wellness,* Tom Goetz; Staff 26 (MLS 9, Non-MLS 17)
Founded 1967. Enrl 39,124; Highest Degree: Associate
Library Holdings: AV Mats 21,000; e-books 1,900; Bk Titles 120,544; Bk Vols 127,573; Per Subs 279
Special Collections: Harper College Archives
Automation Activity & Vendor Info: (Acquisitions) Ex Libris Group; (Cataloging) Ex Libris Group; (Circulation) Ex Libris Group; (Course Reserve) Ex Libris Group; (OPAC) Ex Libris Group; (Serials) Ex Libris Group
Wireless access
Function: ILL available, Photocopying/Printing, Ref serv available, Wheelchair accessible
Publications: Library E-News (Newsletter)
Partic in Consortium of Academic & Research Libraries in Illinois; Ill State Libr Network; Network of Illinois Learning Resources in Community Colleges; Northern Illinois Learning Resources Cooperative
Special Services for the Deaf - Assistive tech; Bks on deafness & sign lang; Closed caption videos

Special Services for the Blind - Assistive/Adapted tech devices, equip & products
Open Mon-Thurs (Winter) 7:30am-10pm, Fri 7:30-4:30, Sat 9-3:30, Sun 1-5; Mon-Fri (Summer) 7:30-4:30

PALESTINE

P PALESTINE PUBLIC LIBRARY DISTRICT*, 201 S Washington St, 62451. SAN 320-4758. Tel: 618-586-5317. FAX: 618-586-9711. E-mail: palestinelibrary@outlook.com. Web Site: palestinepubliclibrary.org. *Dir,* Kristen McCormack
Founded 1977. Pop 2,446
Library Holdings: Bk Vols 14,000; Per Subs 15
Wireless access
Mem of Illinois Heartland Library System
Open Mon, Wed & Fri 10-4:30, Tues & Thurs 10-6
Friends of the Library Group

PALOS HEIGHTS

M PALOS COMMUNITY HOSPITAL*, Medical Library, 12251 S 80th Ave, 60463. SAN 340-6415. Tel: 708-923-4000. Web Site: www.paloshealth.com. *Libr Dir,* Karen Thier; Tel: 708-923-4662
Founded 1972
Library Holdings: Bk Titles 2,000; Per Subs 68
Wireless access
Restriction: Staff use only

P PALOS HEIGHTS PUBLIC LIBRARY*, 12501 S 71st Ave, 60463. SAN 304-5226. Tel: 708-448-1473. FAX: 708-448-8950. E-mail: palos.library@phlibrary.org. Web Site: www.phlibrary.org. *Dir,* Jesse Blazek; E-mail: jesseb@phlibrary.org
Founded 1944. Pop 12,188; Circ 155,380
Library Holdings: Bk Vols 70,245; Per Subs 223
Special Collections: Oral History
Subject Interests: Local hist
Automation Activity & Vendor Info: (Acquisitions) Innovative Interfaces, Inc; (Cataloging) Innovative Interfaces, Inc; (Circulation) Innovative Interfaces, Inc; (ILL) Innovative Interfaces, Inc; (OPAC) Innovative Interfaces, Inc; (Serials) Innovative Interfaces, Inc
Wireless access
Mem of Reaching Across Illinois Library System (RAILS)
Partic in System Wide Automated Network
Special Services for the Deaf - TTY equip
Open Mon-Thurs 9-9, Fri & Sat 9-5, Sun (Sept-May) 1-5
Friends of the Library Group

C TRINITY CHRISTIAN COLLEGE*, Jennie Huizenga Memorial Library, 6601 W College Dr, 60463. SAN 304-5234. Tel: 708-293-4925. Reference Tel: 708-293-4926. FAX: 708-385-5665. E-mail: library@trnty.edu. Web Site: www.trnty.edu/tcclibrary.html. *Libr Dir,* Cathy Mayer; Tel: 708-239-4797, E-mail: cathy.mayer@trnty.edu; *Ref/Outreach Librn,* Cynthia Bowen; Tel: 708-239-4841, E-mail: cynthia.bowen@trnty.edu; *Access Serv Mgr, Circ,* Sarah Hoeksema; Tel: 708-239-4796, E-mail: sarah.hoeksema@trnty.edu; Staff 4 (MLS 4)
Founded 1959. Enrl 1,147; Fac 80; Highest Degree: Master
Special Collections: DeKruyter Pastor's Library (Selection from the libr of Rev Arthur DeKruyter); Dutch Heritage Center
Subject Interests: Humanities, Music, Natural sci, Relig, Soc sci & issues
Automation Activity & Vendor Info: (Cataloging) Ex Libris Group; (Circulation) Ex Libris Group; (ILL) OCLC; (OPAC) Ex Libris Group
Wireless access
Function: 24/7 Electronic res, 24/7 Online cat, Archival coll, Computers for patron use, E-Reserves, Electronic databases & coll, Free DVD rentals, ILL available, Internet access, Mail & tel request accepted, Movies, Music CDs, Online ref, Orientations, Photocopying/Printing, Ref serv available, Scanner, Spanish lang bks, Study rm, Telephone ref, Wheelchair accessible
Mem of Reaching Across Illinois Library System (RAILS)
Partic in Consortium of Academic & Research Libraries in Illinois; Council for Christian Colleges & Universities; LIBRAS, Inc
Open Mon-Thurs 8am-11pm, Fri 8-5, Sat 10-5, Sun 4:30pm-11pm
Restriction: Open to pub for ref only, Pub use on premises

PALOS HILLS

P GREEN HILLS PUBLIC LIBRARY DISTRICT*, 10331 S Interlochen Dr, 60465. SAN 304-5242. Tel: 708-598-8446. Circulation Tel: 708-598-8446, Ext 110. Reference Tel: 708-598-8446, Ext 120. FAX: 708-598-0856. E-mail: ghpl@greenhillslibrary.org. Web Site: www.greenhills.lib.il.us. *Libr Dir,* Jane Jenkins; Tel: 708-598-8446, Ext 111, E-mail: jjenkins@greenhillslibrary.org; Staff 4 (MLS 3, Non-MLS 1)
Founded 1962. Pop 31,533; Circ 298,590
Jul 2015-Jun 2016 Income $2,661,634, County $2,661,634. Mats Exp $247,153, Books $109,936, AV Mat $48,148, Electronic Ref Mat (Incl. Access Fees) $89,069. Sal $563,538 (Prof $237,311)
Library Holdings: Audiobooks 1,717; AV Mats 13,518; Bks on Deafness & Sign Lang 41; CDs 5,879; DVDs 7,639; e-books 44,983; Large Print Bks 125; Bk Titles 47,992; Per Subs 161
Special Collections: Oral History
Subject Interests: Literary criticism, Local hist, Polish (Lang)
Automation Activity & Vendor Info: (Cataloging) SirsiDynix; (Circulation) SirsiDynix; (OPAC) SirsiDynix
Wireless access
Function: 24/7 Electronic res, 24/7 Online cat, Adult bk club, Audiobks on Playaways & MP3, Bks on CD, Computer training, Computers for patron use, E-Readers, Electronic databases & coll, Free DVD rentals, Homebound delivery serv, ILL available, Internet access, Magazines, Mango lang, Meeting rooms, Movies, Museum passes, Music CDs, Notary serv, Online cat, Online info literacy tutorials on the web & in blackboard, Online ref, OverDrive digital audio bks, Photocopying/Printing, Prog for adults, Prog for children & young adult, Ref & res, Scanner, Spoken cassettes & CDs, Story hour, Study rm, Summer reading prog, Tax forms, Teen prog, Winter reading prog
Publications: Library Link (Newsletter)
Mem of Reaching Across Illinois Library System (RAILS)
Partic in System Wide Automated Network
Special Services for the Blind - Bks on CD
Open Mon-Fri 9-9, Sat 10-5, Sun 12-4
Friends of the Library Group

J MORAINE VALLEY COMMUNITY COLLEGE LIBRARY*, 9000 W College Pkwy, 60465. SAN 304-5250. Tel: 708-974-5709. Circulation Tel: 708-974-5235. Reference Tel: 708-974-5234. Automation Services Tel: 708-974-5262. FAX: 708-974-1184. E-mail: library@morainevalley.edu. Web Site: lib.morainevalley.edu. *Dean,* Terra Jacobson; Tel: 708-974-5467, E-mail: jacobsont6@morainevalley.edu; *Dept Chair, Pub Serv, Teaching & Learning Librn,* Troy Swanson; Tel: 708-974-5439, E-mail: swanson@morainevalley.edu; *Coll Mgt Librn, Pub Serv,* Joseph Mullarkey; Tel: 708-974-5293, E-mail: mullarkeyj@morainevalley.edu; *Syst & Cat Librn,* Marie Martino; E-mail: martinom43@morainevalley.edu; *Distance Educ,* Lee Semmerling; Tel: 708-608-4009, E-mail: semmerling@morainevalley.edu; Staff 23 (MLS 6, Non-MLS 17)
Founded 1967. Enrl 19,249; Fac 991; Highest Degree: Associate
Library Holdings: AV Mats 9,805; Bk Titles 66,095; Bk Vols 77,731; Per Subs 553
Special Collections: Oral History; US Document Depository
Subject Interests: Allied health, Nursing
Automation Activity & Vendor Info: (Acquisitions) Innovative Interfaces, Inc; (Cataloging) Innovative Interfaces, Inc; (Circulation) Innovative Interfaces, Inc; (Course Reserve) Innovative Interfaces, Inc; (ILL) Innovative Interfaces, Inc; (OPAC) Innovative Interfaces, Inc; (Serials) Innovative Interfaces, Inc
Wireless access
Function: ILL available, Photocopying/Printing, Ref serv available, Wheelchair accessible
Mem of Reaching Across Illinois Library System (RAILS)
Partic in Consortium of Academic & Research Libraries in Illinois; Illinois Library & Information Network; Network of Illinois Learning Resources in Community Colleges; Northern Illinois Learning Resources Cooperative
Open Mon-Thurs 7:30am-10pm, Fri 7:30-5

PALOS PARK

P PALOS PARK PUBLIC LIBRARY, 12330 S Forest Glen Blvd, 60464. SAN 304-5269. Tel: 708-448-1530. FAX: 708-448-3492. E-mail: info@palosparklibrary.org. Web Site: www.palosparklibrary.org. *Libr Dir,* Kathryn Sofianos; E-mail: ksofianos@palosparklibrary.org; Staff 10 (MLS 2, Non-MLS 8)
Founded 1936. Pop 4,847; Circ 42,460
Library Holdings: Large Print Bks 100; Bk Vols 37,182; Per Subs 130
Subject Interests: Local hist
Automation Activity & Vendor Info: (Circulation) SirsiDynix-WorkFlows
Wireless access
Function: 24/7 Electronic res, 24/7 Online cat, Activity rm, Adult bk club, After school storytime
Mem of Reaching Across Illinois Library System (RAILS)
Partic in System Wide Automated Network
Open Mon-Thurs 10-7, Fri & Sat 10-4

PANA

P CARNEGIE-SCHUYLER LIBRARY*, Pana Public Library, 303 E Second St, 62557. SAN 304-5277. Tel: 217-562-2326. FAX: 217-562-2343. E-mail: panalibrary@consolidated.net. Web Site: panalibrary.com. *Libr Dir,* Lisa Lynch; *Librn,* Rebecca Hoffman; *Librn,* Lori Kroenlein; *Librn,* Marla Miller; *Librn,* Donna Wagner
Founded 1903. Pop 5,847; Circ 82,728
Library Holdings: Bk Vols 28,000; Per Subs 11
Wireless access
Mem of Illinois Heartland Library System

Open Mon-Fri 11-6, Sat 9-1
Friends of the Library Group

PARIS

P PARIS CARNEGIE PUBLIC LIBRARY*, 207 S Main St, 61944. SAN 304-5285. Tel: 217-463-3950. FAX: 217-463-1155. E-mail: read@parispubliclibrary.org. Web Site: parispubliclibrary.org. *Dir,* Teresa Pennington; Staff 1 (MLS 1)
Founded 1904. Pop 8,837; Circ 48,240
May 2017-Apr 2018 Income $157,801, State $16,095, City $116,812, Locally Generated Income $16,580, Other $8,096. Mats Exp $16,314, Books $11,277, AV Mat $1,685, Electronic Ref Mat (Incl. Access Fees) $3,352. Sal $91,956
Library Holdings: Audiobooks 586; DVDs 1,452; e-books 79,619; Microforms 239; Bk Vols 30,216; Per Subs 30
Automation Activity & Vendor Info: (Cataloging) Innovative Interfaces, Inc; (Circulation) Innovative Interfaces, Inc; (ILL) OCLC WorldShare Interlibrary Loan; (OPAC) Innovative Interfaces, Inc; (Serials) Innovative Interfaces, Inc
Wireless access
Function: Bk club(s), Bks on CD, Children's prog, Computers for patron use, Electronic databases & coll, Free DVD rentals, ILL available, Internet access, Laminating, Meeting rooms, Microfiche/film & reading machines, Online cat, OverDrive digital audio bks, Photocopying/Printing, Prog for adults, Prog for children & young adult, Story hour, Summer reading prog, Tax forms, Telephone ref, Wheelchair accessible
Mem of Illinois Heartland Library System
Open Mon, Wed & Fri 10-6, Tues & Thurs 10-8, Sat 10-4
Friends of the Library Group

PARK FOREST

P PARK FOREST PUBLIC LIBRARY, 400 Lakewood Blvd, 60466. SAN 304-5307. Tel: 708-748-3731. FAX: 708-748-8829. E-mail: parkforestpl@gmail.com. Web Site: www.pfpl.org. *Dir,* Barbara Byrne Osuch; E-mail: barbara.osuch@pfpl.org; *Coordr, Patron Serv,* Vannessa Cameron; *Youth Engagement Coord,* Nikki Coleman; Staff 4.3 (MLS 1.3, Non-MLS 3)
Founded 1955. Pop 26,963
Automation Activity & Vendor Info: (Acquisitions) SirsiDynix; (Cataloging) SirsiDynix; (Circulation) SirsiDynix; (ILL) SirsiDynix; (OPAC) SirsiDynix; (Serials) SirsiDynix
Wireless access
Publications: Oh, Park Forest - Interpretation of Oral History Tapes
Mem of Reaching Across Illinois Library System (RAILS)
Partic in Illinois Library & Information Network; System Wide Automated Network
Open Mon-Thurs 10-7, Fri & Sat 10-5
Friends of the Library Group

PARK RIDGE

M ADVOCATE LUTHERAN GENERAL HOSPITAL*, Advocate Aurora Library, 1775 Dempster St, 60068. SAN 304-5366. Tel: 847-723-5494. *Dir,* Karen Hanus; E-mail: karen.hanus@aah.org
Founded 1966
Subject Interests: Med, Nursing
Automation Activity & Vendor Info: (Circulation) SirsiDynix
Partic in Illinois Library & Information Network; OCLC Online Computer Library Center, Inc
Restriction: Prof mat only

S AMERICAN ASSOCIATION OF NURSE ANESTHETISTS, Archives-Library, 222 S Prospect Ave, 60068. SAN 374-6704. Tel: 847-655-1106. E-mail: archives@aana.com. Web Site: www.aana.com/about-us/aana-archives-library. *Archivist/Librn,* George Kutsunis; E-mail: gkutsunis@aana.com; Staff 1 (MLS 1)
Library Holdings: Bk Titles 750; Bk Vols 1,000; Per Subs 35
Special Collections: AANA Archives; Nurse Anesthesia History. Oral History
Function: Archival coll, ILL available
Restriction: Access at librarian's discretion, Non-circulating, Open by appt only

P PARK RIDGE PUBLIC LIBRARY*, 20 S Prospect, 60068. SAN 304-5374. Tel: 847-825-3123. Circulation Tel: 847-720-3271. Interlibrary Loan Service Tel: 847-720-3235. Reference Tel: 847-720-3230. Administration Tel: 847-720-3202. FAX: 847-825-0001. Web Site: www.parkridgelibrary.org. *Libr Dir,* Joanna Bertucci; Tel: 847-720-3203, E-mail: director@prpl.org; *Fac Mgr,* John Priala; Tel: 847-720-3210, E-mail: jpriala@prpl.org; *Ref Serv Mgr,* Laura Scott; E-mail: lscott@prpl.org; Staff 100 (MLS 23, Non-MLS 77)
Founded 1913. Pop 37,480; Circ 947,943. Sal $2,470,815
Library Holdings: AV Mats 27,736; e-books 6,000; Bk Vols 215,881; Per Subs 400
Special Collections: Park Ridge History, newsp
Automation Activity & Vendor Info: (Acquisitions) Ex Libris Group; (Cataloging) SirsiDynix; (Circulation) SirsiDynix
Wireless access
Function: Adult bk club, After school storytime, Art exhibits, Audiobks via web, Bk club(s), Bks on CD, Children's prog, Computer training, Computers for patron use, Doc delivery serv, E-Reserves, Electronic databases & coll, Free DVD rentals, Holiday prog, Home delivery & serv to seniorr ctr & nursing homes, Homebound delivery serv, ILL available, Internet access, Large print keyboards, Magnifiers for reading, Mail & tel request accepted, Microfiche/film & reading machines, Museum passes, Music CDs, Notary serv, Online cat, Online ref, Outreach serv, Outside serv via phone, mail, e-mail & web, OverDrive digital audio bks, Photocopying/Printing, Preschool outreach, Preschool reading prog, Prog for adults, Prog for children & young adult, Ref & res, Ref serv available, Scanner, Senior computer classes, Senior outreach, Story hour, Summer & winter reading prog, Tax forms, Teen prog, Telephone ref, Wheelchair accessible, Workshops
Publications: Library Newsletter
Partic in Bergen County Cooperative Library System, Inc; Cooperative Computer Services - CCS
Special Services for the Deaf - Assisted listening device; Bks on deafness & sign lang; Closed caption videos; Sign lang interpreter upon request for prog; TDD equip
Special Services for the Blind - Accessible computers; Assistive/Adapted tech devices, equip & products; BiFolkal kits; Bks available with recordings; Bks on CD; Computer with voice synthesizer for visually impaired persons; Copier with enlargement capabilities; Home delivery serv; Info on spec aids & appliances; Internet workstation with adaptive software; Large print bks; Large screen computer & software; Lending of low vision aids; Magnifiers; Playaways (bks on MP3); Talking bk serv referral; ZoomText magnification & reading software
Open Mon-Thurs 9-9, Fri 9-6, Sat 9-5, Sun 12-5
Friends of the Library Group

PATOKA

P PATOKA PUBLIC LIBRARY*, 210 W Bond St, 62875. (Mail add: PO Box 58, 62875-0058), SAN 304-5382. Tel: 618-432-5019. FAX: 618-432-5019. E-mail: patokalibrary@yahoo.com. *Librn,* Nancy Snider
Founded 1934. Pop 633; Circ 1,815
Library Holdings: Bk Vols 5,023; Per Subs 10
Wireless access
Mem of Illinois Heartland Library System
Open Mon, Wed & Thurs 12-5

PAW PAW

P PAW PAW PUBLIC LIBRARY DISTRICT*, 362 Chicago Rd, 61353. (Mail add: PO Box 362, 61353-0362), SAN 304-5390. Tel: 815-627-9396. FAX: 815-627-3707. E-mail: pawpawlibrary@gmail.com. *Dir,* Barbara Zeman
Founded 1936. Pop 870; Circ 6,733
Library Holdings: Bk Vols 18,417
Special Collections: Lee & DeKalb Counties Local History, includes written materials, census, newspaper slides, photos, scrapbooks & memorabilia
Wireless access
Function: 24/7 Electronic res, 24/7 Online cat, Adult bk club, After school storytime, Children's prog, Computers for patron use, Free DVD rentals, Holiday prog, ILL available, Internet access, Laminating, Magazines, Online cat, Prog for children & young adult, Story hour, Wheelchair accessible
Mem of Reaching Across Illinois Library System (RAILS)
Open Tues & Wed 10-6, Thurs 10-7, Sat 9-12

PAWNEE

P PAWNEE PUBLIC LIBRARY*, 613 Douglas St, 62558. SAN 304-5404. Tel: 217-625-7716. FAX: 217-625-7716. E-mail: pawneepubliclibrary@hotmail.com. Web Site: www.pawneepubliclibrary.org. *Dir,* Bennett Bess
Founded 1951. Circ 10,135
Library Holdings: Bk Titles 14,500; Bk Vols 15,000
Subject Interests: Hist, Illinois
Mem of Illinois Heartland Library System
Open Mon & Fri 11-5, Tues 11-8, Wed 10-5 & 7-9, Thurs 10-9, Sat 11-3

PAXTON

P PAXTON CARNEGIE LIBRARY*, 254 S Market St, 60957-1452. SAN 304-5412. Tel: 217-379-3431. E-mail: paxtonlibrary1@gmail.com. Web Site: www.paxtoncarnegielibrary.org. *Librn,* Anne Newman
Founded 1903. Pop 4,289; Circ 36,886

Library Holdings: Audiobooks 500; Bk Vols 24,000; Per Subs 60
Automation Activity & Vendor Info: (Circulation) SirsiDynix
Wireless access
Mem of Illinois Heartland Library System
Special Services for the Deaf - Bks on deafness & sign lang
Open Mon-Thurs 12-5 & 6:30-8:30, Fri 12-5, Sat 10-5

PEARL CITY

P PEARL CITY PUBLIC LIBRARY DISTRICT*, 221 S Main St, 61062. (Mail add: PO Box 158, 61062-0158), SAN 304-5420. Tel: 815-443-2832. FAX: 815-443-2832. E-mail: pearlcitypubliclibrary@yahoo.com. *Chief Librn,* Pennie E Miller; Staff 2 (Non-MLS 2)
Founded 1946. Pop 2,655; Circ 12,912
Library Holdings: Bk Titles 14,450; Per Subs 13
Wireless access
Function: 24/7 Electronic res, 24/7 Online cat, Audiobks via web, Bks on CD, Children's prog, Computers for patron use, Free DVD rentals, ILL available, Laminating, Magazines, Microfiche/film & reading machines, Music CDs, Online cat, Photocopying/Printing, Prog for adults, Story hour, Summer reading prog, Tax forms
Mem of Reaching Across Illinois Library System (RAILS)
Open Mon & Wed 9-5, Tues & Thurs 1-8, Fri & Sat 9-1

PECATONICA

P PECATONICA PUBLIC LIBRARY DISTRICT*, 400 W 11th St, 61063. SAN 304-5439. Tel: 815-239-2616. FAX: 815-239-2250. E-mail: director@pecatonicalibrary.com. Web Site: www.pecatonicalibrary.com/. *Dir,* Penny Lynn Bryant; E-mail: director@pecatonicalibrary.com; Staff 7 (Non-MLS 7)
Founded 1967. Pop 5,261; Circ 22,830
Library Holdings: AV Mats 1,286; Bks on Deafness & Sign Lang 10; Large Print Bks 220; Bk Titles 24,282; Per Subs 46
Special Collections: Local History (Pecatonica, Winnebago Co & Stephenson Co)
Automation Activity & Vendor Info: (Cataloging) PALS; (Circulation) SirsiDynix-WorkFlows; (OPAC) SirsiDynix-Unicorn
Wireless access
Function: 24/7 Electronic res, Accelerated reader prog, Activity rm, Adult bk club, Adult literacy prog, Art exhibits, Audiobks via web, AV serv, Bks on CD, CD-ROM, Children's prog, Computer training, Computers for patron use, Doc delivery serv, E-Reserves, Electronic databases & coll, Govt ref serv, Homebound delivery serv, ILL available, Internet access, Laminating, Magazines, Magnifiers for reading, Mango lang, Microfiche/film & reading machines, Music CDs, Notary serv, Online cat, Outreach serv, OverDrive digital audio bks, Photocopying/Printing, Preschool reading prog, Prog for children & young adult, Ref serv available, Scanner, Senior computer classes, Spanish lang bks, Story hour, Study rm, Summer reading prog, Tax forms, Wheelchair accessible, Workshops
Mem of Reaching Across Illinois Library System (RAILS)
Special Services for the Deaf - TTY equip
Open Mon-Thurs 10-8, Fri & Sat 9-1, Sun 12-4
Friends of the Library Group

PEKIN

P PEKIN PUBLIC LIBRARY*, 301 S Fourth St, 61554-4284. SAN 304-5455. Tel: 309-347-7111. FAX: 309-347-6587. E-mail: library@pekinpubliclibrary.org. Web Site: www.pekinpubliclibrary.org. *Dir,* Jeff Brooks; Tel: 309-347-7111, Ext 228, E-mail: jbrooks@pekinpubliclibrary.org; Staff 4 (MLS 2, Non-MLS 2)
Founded 1896. Pop 33,857; Circ 277,993
Library Holdings: AV Mats 8,190; Bk Vols 129,314; Per Subs 196
Special Collections: History of Pekin; Tazewell Co
Automation Activity & Vendor Info: (Acquisitions) Baker & Taylor; (Cataloging) OCLC; (Circulation) SirsiDynix-WorkFlows; (ILL) OCLC; (OPAC) SirsiDynix-iBistro
Wireless access
Function: Adult bk club, Bks on cassette, Bks on CD, Computers for patron use, Electronic databases & coll, Free DVD rentals, Homebound delivery serv, ILL available, Music CDs, Online cat, Photocopying/Printing, Scanner, Spoken cassettes & CDs, Spoken cassettes & DVDs, Story hour, Summer reading prog, Tax forms, Teen prog, Telephone ref, VHS videos
Publications: Newsletter
Partic in Illinois Library & Information Network; OCLC Online Computer Library Center, Inc
Open Mon-Thurs 9-8, Fri 9-6, Sat 9-5
Friends of the Library Group

PEORIA

C BRADLEY UNIVERSITY*, Cullom-Davis Library, 1501 W Bradley Ave, 61625. SAN 340-6474. Tel: 309-677-2850. Interlibrary Loan Service Tel: 309-677-2837. FAX: 309-677-2558. Web Site: bradley.edu/library. *Exec Dir,* Barbara A Galik; Tel: 309-677-2830, E-mail: barbara@fsmail.bradley.edu; *Coll Develop Librn,* Todd Spires; *Electronic Serv Librn,* Xiaotian Chen; *Info Literacy/Electronic Serv Librn,* Meg Frazier; *Ref Librn,* Dianne Hollister; *Tech Serv Librn,* Deirdre Redington; *ILL Coordr,* Laura Corpuz; *ILL Coordr,* Marina Savoie; *Coordr, Access Serv,* Sarah Crosman; *Coordr, Acq,* Tonica Toyne; Staff 11 (MLS 11)
Founded 1897. Enrl 5,882; Fac 305; Highest Degree: Master
Library Holdings: Bk Titles 281,121; Bk Vols 435,394; Per Subs 1,488
Special Collections: Abraham Lincoln & Civil War (including Martin L Howser Coll); APCO (Public Safety Communications History Coll); Bradleyana; Industrial Arts History (Charles A Bennett Coll); Jubilee College (Philander Chase Coll & Citizens Committee to Preserve Jubilee College Coll); Peoria-Area History (Library of Peoria Historical Society). Oral History; State Document Depository; US Document Depository
Automation Activity & Vendor Info: (Acquisitions) Ex Libris Group; (Cataloging) Ex Libris Group; (Circulation) Ex Libris Group; (Course Reserve) Ex Libris Group; (OPAC) Ex Libris Group; (Serials) Ex Libris Group
Wireless access
Partic in Consortium of Academic & Research Libraries in Illinois; Heart of Ill Consortium; Illinois Library & Information Network
Friends of the Library Group

Departmental Libraries:

VIRGINIUS H CHASE SPECIAL COLLECTIONS CENTER, 1501 W Bradley Ave, 61625. Tel: 309-677-2822. *Spec Coll Librn,* Liz J Bloodworth; E-mail: ebloodworth@fsmail.bradley.edu
Library Holdings: Bk Vols 17,000
Open Mon-Fri 9-12 & 1-4:30

§CM METHODIST COLLEGE LIBRARY, 7600 N Academic Dr, 61615. Tel: 309-672-5513. E-mail: mclibrary@methodistcol.edu. Web Site: library.methodistcol.edu. *Dir, Libr Serv,* Michelle Nielsen Ott; E-mail: mnielsenott@methodistcol.edu; *Assoc Dir, Libr Serv,* Joel Shoemaker
Founded 1900
Library Holdings: e-journals 387,176; Electronic Media & Resources 69; Bk Vols 5,000
Automation Activity & Vendor Info: (Cataloging) CyberTools for Libraries; (OPAC) CyberTools for Libraries
Wireless access
Function: ILL available, Study rm
Partic in Consortium of Academic & Research Libraries in Illinois; National Network of Libraries of Medicine Region 6

J MIDSTATE COLLEGE*, Barbara Fields Memorial Library, 411 W Northmoor Rd, 61614. SAN 321-5032. Tel: 309-692-4092. FAX: 309-692-3893. E-mail: library@midstate.edu. Web Site: www.midstate.edu/academics/library.php. *Dir, Libr Serv,* Jane Bradbury; Tel: 309-692-4092, Ext 4030, E-mail: jbradbury@midstate.edu; Staff 6 (MLS 1, Non-MLS 5)
Founded 1888. Enrl 625; Fac 40; Highest Degree: Bachelor
Library Holdings: Bk Titles 8,150; Per Subs 100
Automation Activity & Vendor Info: (Cataloging) SirsiDynix; (Circulation) SirsiDynix
Wireless access
Partic in RSA
Open Mon-Thurs 8-8, Fri 8-4:30, Sat 9-Noon

L PEORIA COUNTY LAW LIBRARY*, Peoria County Court House, Rm 211, 324 Main St, 61602. SAN 375-9865. Tel: 309-672-6084. FAX: 309-672-6957. Web Site: www.10thcircuitcourtil.org/174/Law-Library. *Library Contact,* Jennifer M Shadid; E-mail: jmshadid@peoriacounty.org
Library Holdings: Bk Vols 1,000
Open Mon-Fri 8:30-5

P PEORIA PUBLIC LIBRARY*, 107 NE Monroe St, 61602-1070. SAN 340-6741. Tel: 309-497-2000. Circulation Tel: 309-497-2164. Interlibrary Loan Service Tel: 309-497-2153. FAX: 309-497-2007. Interlibrary Loan Service FAX: 309-674-0116. TDD: 309-497-2156. Web Site: www.peoriapubliclibrary.org. *Exec Dir,* Randall Yelverton; Tel: 309-497-2140, E-mail: RandallYelverton@ppl.peoria.lib.il.us; *Dep Dir,* Roberta Koscielski; Tel: 309-497-2186, E-mail: robertakoscielski@ppl.peoria.lib.il.us
Founded 1880. Pop 118,135; Circ 778,175
Library Holdings: Audiobooks 8,695; CDs 9,170; DVDs 6,488; Bk Vols 635,048; Videos 9,539
Special Collections: Genealogy, Local History, Government Documents. US Document Depository
Subject Interests: Census, Genealogy, Local hist
Automation Activity & Vendor Info: (Acquisitions) Baker & Taylor; (Cataloging) OCLC Connexion; (Circulation) SirsiDynix-WorkFlows; (Serials) EBSCO Online
Wireless access
Publications: Passages (Newsletter)
Special Services for the Deaf - TDD equip

Open Mon-Sat 9-6
Friends of the Library Group
Branches: 4
LAKEVIEW, 1137 W Lake Ave, 61614-5935, SAN 340-6776. Tel: 309-497-2200. FAX: 309-497-2211. *Br Mgr,* Elise Hearn; Tel: 309-497-2204, E-mail: elisehearn@ppl.peoria.lib.il.us
Library Holdings: CDs 1,081; DVDs 553; Bk Vols 79,931; Talking Bks 1,343; Videos 2,490
Open Mon-Wed 10-8, Fri & Sat 10-6, Sun 12-5
Friends of the Library Group
LINCOLN, 1312 W Lincoln Ave, 61605-1976, SAN 340-6806. Tel: 309-497-2600. FAX: 309-497-2611. *Br Mgr,* Cynthia Smith; Tel: 309-497-2601, E-mail: cynthiasmith@ppl.peoria.lib.il.us
Open Mon, Tues & Thurs 10-8, Fri & Sat 10-6, Sun 12-5
Friends of the Library Group
MCCLURE, 315 W McClure Ave, 61604-3556, SAN 340-6830. Tel: 309-497-2700. FAX: 309-497-2711. *Br Mgr,* Sarah Couri; Tel: 309-497-2701, E-mail: sarahcouri@ppl.peoria.lib.il.us; Staff 2 (MLS 1, Non-MLS 1)
Library Holdings: Audiobooks 500; CDs 191; DVDs 900; Bk Vols 25,838; Videos 300
Open Mon-Sat 9-6
Friends of the Library Group
NORTH BRANCH, 3001 W Grand Pkwy, 61615. Tel: 309-497-2100. *Br Mgr,* Jamie Jones; Tel: 309-497-2110, E-mail: jamiejones@ppl.peoria.lib.il.us
Open Mon, Wed & Thurs 10-8, Fri & Sat 10-6, Sun Noon-5
Friends of the Library Group
Bookmobiles: 1. Outreach Serv, Teri Miller

CM SAINT FRANCIS MEDICAL CENTER COLLEGE OF NURSING*, The Sister Ludgera Library & Learning Resource Center, 511 NE Greenleaf St, 61603. SAN 340-692X. Tel: 309-655-2180. FAX: 309-655-3648. E-mail: CONLibrary@osfhealthcare.org. Web Site: www.sfmccon.edu/library. *Librn,* Bill Komanecki; E-mail: william.g.komanecki@osfhealthcare.org; *Libr Tech,* Becky Rundall; E-mail: rebecca.r.rundall@osfhealthcare.org; Staff 3 (MLS 1, Non-MLS 2)
Founded 1936. Enrl 150; Fac 19; Highest Degree: Master
Library Holdings: Bk Titles 4,900; Bk Vols 5,300; Per Subs 130
Subject Interests: Educ
Partic in Consortium of Academic & Research Libraries in Illinois; Heart of Illinois Library Consortium; Illinois Library & Information Network
Open Mon-Thurs 7:30am-9pm, Fri 7:30-5, Sat 10-2, Sun 1-9

PEORIA HEIGHTS

P PEORIA HEIGHTS PUBLIC LIBRARY*, 816 E Glen Ave, 61616. SAN 304-5560. Tel: 309-682-5578. FAX: 309-682-4457. E-mail: phpl@peoriaheightslibrary.com. Web Site: www.peoriaheightslibrary.com. *Dir,* Shawn Edwards; *Ch,* Kristina Short; Staff 2 (MLS 2)
Founded 1935. Pop 6,930; Circ 42,186
Library Holdings: Bk Vols 32,800; Per Subs 126
Subject Interests: Art, Hist
Automation Activity & Vendor Info: (Circulation) TLC (The Library Corporation)
Wireless access
Publications: Newsletter: Check It Out
Partic in Illinois Library & Information Network
Open Mon & Tues 9-8, Wed & Thurs 9-6, Fri & Sat 9-5

PEOTONE

P PEOTONE PUBLIC LIBRARY DISTRICT*, 515 N First St, 60468. SAN 304-5579. Tel: 708-258-3436. FAX: 708-258-9796. E-mail: information@peotonelibrary.org. Web Site: www.peotonelibrary.org. *Dir,* Noreen Bormet; E-mail: nabormet@peotonelibrary.org; *Asst Dir,* Sharon Garner; *Youth Serv,* Ranea Bruce
Pop 15,513; Circ 75,000
Library Holdings: Bk Vols 65,000; Per Subs 100
Subject Interests: Genealogy
Wireless access
Mem of Reaching Across Illinois Library System (RAILS)
Open Mon-Thurs 9:30-8, Fri 9:30-5, Sat. 9:30-3
Friends of the Library Group

PERU

M ILLINOIS VALLEY COMMUNITY HOSPITAL*, Medical Library, 925 West St, 61354. SAN 304-3258. Tel: 815-780-3485. FAX: 815-224-1747. Web Site: www.ivch.org. *Dir of Educ,* Maureen Rebholz; E-mail: renee.rebholz@ivch.org
Library Holdings: Bk Vols 506
Restriction: Not open to pub

P PERU PUBLIC LIBRARY*, 1409 11th St, 61354. SAN 304-5587. Tel: 815-223-0229. FAX: 815-223-1559. E-mail: perulibrary@perulibrary.org. Web Site: perulibrary.org. *Libr Dir,* Charm N Ruhnke; E-mail: cnruhnke@perulibrary.org; *Asst Dir,* Melissa Keegan; E-mail: mkeegan@perulibrary.org; *Youth Serv Mgr,* Lynn Sheedy; Staff 4 (MLS 1, Non-MLS 3)
Founded 1911. Pop 9,835; Circ 90,000
Library Holdings: Bk Vols 50,000; Per Subs 140
Special Collections: Local newspaper 1906, micro. Oral History
Subject Interests: Local hist
Automation Activity & Vendor Info: (Acquisitions) SirsiDynix; (Cataloging) SirsiDynix; (Circulation) SirsiDynix; (OPAC) SirsiDynix; (Serials) SirsiDynix
Wireless access
Mem of Reaching Across Illinois Library System (RAILS)
Open Mon-Thurs 9-8, Fri & Sat 9-5
Friends of the Library Group

PETERSBURG

S ILLINOIS COLLEGE, Starhill Forest Arboretum Library, 12000 Boy Scout Trail, 62675. SAN 371-5477. Tel: 217-632-3685. Web Site: www.starhillforest.com. *Dir,* Guy Sternberg; E-mail: guy@starhillforest.com; *Curator,* Alana McKean
Founded 1976
Library Holdings: Bk Titles 2,000; Bk Vols 2,200; Per Subs 10
Special Collections: Antiquarian Natural History; Modern Natural History, bks & slides
Subject Interests: Hort, Natural hist
Function: Ref serv available
Restriction: Private libr, Staff use only
Friends of the Library Group

P PETERSBURG PUBLIC LIBRARY*, 220 S Sixth St, 62675. SAN 304-5595. Tel: 217-632-2807. FAX: 217-632-2833. E-mail: petersburglibrary.1906@gmail.com. Web Site: petersburgil.org/library.htm. *Librn,* Mary Kleinschmidt
Founded 1906. Pop 2,419; Circ 29,000
Library Holdings: Bk Vols 12,900; Per Subs 86
Special Collections: Abraham Lincoln & Edgar Lee Masters
Automation Activity & Vendor Info: (Circulation) SirsiDynix
Mem of Illinois Heartland Library System
Open Tues & Thurs 10-8, Wed & Fri 10-5, Sat 9-1
Friends of the Library Group

PHILO

P PHILO PUBLIC LIBRARY DISTRICT*, 115 E Washington St, 61864. (Mail add: PO Box 199, 61864-0199), SAN 304-5609. Tel: 217-684-2896. FAX: 217-684-2719. E-mail: PhiloPubLib@gmail.com. Web Site: www.philolibrary.info. *Dir,* Donald Pippin; *Assoc Dir,* Susan Hale; Staff 5 (MLS 1, Non-MLS 4)
Founded 1961. Pop 1,954; Circ 21,483
Jul 2012-Jun 2013 Income $84,881, State $4,012, Locally Generated Income $75,973, Other $4,896. Mats Exp $9,947, Books $4,702, Per/Ser (Incl. Access Fees) $1,020, AV Mat $1,230, Electronic Ref Mat (Incl. Access Fees) $228. Sal $40,543
Library Holdings: Audiobooks 97; Braille Volumes 4; CDs 178; DVDs 852; Large Print Bks 220; Bk Titles 13,555; Bk Vols 13,575; Per Subs 60
Automation Activity & Vendor Info: (Circulation) Innovative Interfaces, Inc; (OPAC) Innovative Interfaces, Inc
Wireless access
Function: Accelerated reader prog, Adult bk club, Archival coll
Mem of Illinois Heartland Library System
Partic in Illinois Library & Information Network
Open Mon-Fri 9-12 & 3-7, Sat 9-1, Sun 2-5
Friends of the Library Group

PINCKNEYVILLE

P PINCKNEYVILLE PUBLIC LIBRARY, 312 S Walnut St, 62274. SAN 304-5617. Tel: 618-357-2410. FAX: 618-357-2410. E-mail: library@pinckneyville.lib.il.us. Web Site: www.pinckneyvillelibrary.com. *Libr Dir,* Alex Fisher
Founded 1917. Pop 5,648; Circ 16,405
Library Holdings: AV Mats 651; Bk Vols 17,375; Per Subs 50
Wireless access
Function: 24/7 Electronic res, 24/7 Online cat, After school storytime, Audiobks via web, Bks on cassette, Bks on CD, Children's prog, Computers for patron use, Electronic databases & coll, Free DVD rentals, ILL available, Internet access, Magazines, Microfiche/film & reading machines, Movies, Music CDs, Online cat, Photocopying/Printing, Preschool reading prog, Summer reading prog, Tax forms, Winter reading prog, Workshops
Mem of Illinois Heartland Library System
Open Mon & Wed 12-6, Tues & Thurs 12-5, Fri 10-1, Sat 9-1

PIPER CITY

P PIPER CITY PUBLIC LIBRARY DISTRICT*, 39 W Main, 60959. (Mail add: PO Box 248, 60959-0248), SAN 304-5625. Tel: 815-686-9234. FAX: 815-686-9234. E-mail: pipercitylibrary@frontier.com. Web Site: www.pipercitylibrary.com. *Libr Dir,* Julie Kurtenbach
Founded 1927. Pop 1,149; Circ 6,966
Library Holdings: Bk Vols 7,997; Per Subs 37
Subject Interests: Local hist
Wireless access
Mem of Illinois Heartland Library System
Open Mon & Fri 9-12 & 1-5, Wed 9-12 & 1-7, Sat 9-12

PITTSFIELD

P PITTSFIELD PUBLIC LIBRARY*, 205 N Memorial St, 62363-1406. SAN 304-5633. Tel: 217-285-2200. FAX: 217-285-9423. E-mail: pittsfieldlibrary@frontier.com. Web Site: www.pittsfieldpubliclibrary.com. *Dir,* Sara Bernard; *Youth Librn,* Kathy Robinson; *Asst Librn,* Clari Dees
Founded 1906. Pop 4,600
Library Holdings: Bk Vols 35,000; Per Subs 95
Special Collections: Pike County History
Subject Interests: Hist, Miss river
Wireless access
Open Mon, Wed & Fri 10-5:30, Tues & Thurs 1-8, Sat 10-3

PLAINFIELD

P PLAINFIELD PUBLIC LIBRARY DISTRICT*, 15025 S Illinois St, 60544. SAN 304-565X. Tel: 815-436-6639. FAX: 815-439-2878. Web Site: www.plainfieldpubliclibrary.org. *Libr Dir,* Lisa Pappas; Tel; 815-439-2874, E-mail: lpappas@plainfieldpubliclibrary.org; Staff 50 (MLS 13, Non-MLS 37)
Founded 1925. Pop 75,337; Circ 668,332
Library Holdings: e-books 150,000; Bk Vols 160,000; Per Subs 155
Special Collections: Local History (state, county & city); Local Newspaper & Obituary Index (The Enterprise Coll), micro; Tornado (August 28, 1990), newsp clippings & pictures
Automation Activity & Vendor Info: (Acquisitions) Innovative Interfaces, Inc; (Cataloging) Innovative Interfaces, Inc; (Circulation) Innovative Interfaces, Inc; (ILL) OCLC WorldShare Interlibrary Loan; (OPAC) Innovative Interfaces, Inc; (Serials) Innovative Interfaces, Inc
Wireless access
Mem of Reaching Across Illinois Library System (RAILS)
Open Mon-Thurs 9-9, Fri & Sat 9-5
Friends of the Library Group

PLANO

P PLANO COMMUNITY LIBRARY DISTRICT*, 15 W North St, 60545. SAN 304-5668. Tel: 630-552-2009. FAX: 630-552-1008. Web Site: www.planolibrary.info. *Dir,* Deanna Howard; E-mail: dhoward@plano.lib.il.us; *Adult Serv,* Jeanne Valentine; *Circ Serv,* Randy Struthers; Staff 4 (MLS 1, Non-MLS 3)
Founded 1905. Pop 13,107; Circ 136,766
Library Holdings: Bk Vols 47,403; Per Subs 112
Subject Interests: Local hist
Automation Activity & Vendor Info: (Acquisitions) Innovative Interfaces, Inc - Sierra; (Cataloging) Innovative Interfaces, Inc - Sierra; (Circulation) Innovative Interfaces, Inc - Sierra; (ILL) Innovative Interfaces, Inc - Sierra; (OPAC) Innovative Interfaces, Inc - Sierra; (Serials) Innovative Interfaces, Inc - Sierra
Wireless access
Mem of Reaching Across Illinois Library System (RAILS)
Open Mon-Thurs 10-8, Fri 10-6, Sat 10-4
Friends of the Library Group

POLO

P POLO PUBLIC LIBRARY DISTRICT*, Polo Library, 302 W Mason St, 61064. SAN 304-5676. Tel: 815-946-2713. FAX: 815-946-4127. E-mail: library@pololibrary.org. Web Site: pololibrary.org. *Dir,* Ellen E Finfrock; E-mail: ellenf@pololibrary.org; Staff 2 (Non-MLS 2)
Founded 1871. Pop 2,813; Circ 34,124
Library Holdings: Audiobooks 420; DVDs 1,195; Bk Vols 15,558; Per Subs 65
Special Collections: Local hist
Automation Activity & Vendor Info: (Acquisitions) SirsiDynix; (Cataloging) SirsiDynix; (Circulation) SirsiDynix; (OPAC) SirsiDynix
Wireless access
Function: Adult bk club, Audiobks via web, Children's prog, Computer training, Computers for patron use, Electronic databases & coll, Free DVD rentals, Homebound delivery serv, ILL available, Magnifiers for reading, Music CDs, Online cat, Photocopying/Printing, Prog for adults, Scanner, Story hour, Summer & winter reading prog, Tax forms, VHS videos, Wheelchair accessible
Mem of Reaching Across Illinois Library System (RAILS)
Partic in OMNI
Special Services for the Deaf - TTY equip
Special Services for the Blind - Audio mat; Bks on CD; Digital talking bk; Digital talking bk machines; Large print bks; Low vision equip; Magnifiers; Talking bks & player equip
Open Mon-Thurs 10-7, Fri 10-4, Sat 10-3

PONTIAC

S PONTIAC CORRECTIONAL CENTER LIBRARY*, 700 W Lincoln St, 61764-2323. (Mail add: PO Box 99, 61764-0099), SAN 304-5684. Tel: 815-842-2816, Ext 2267. FAX: 815-842-3051. *Libr Mgr,* Beatrice Stanley; *Librn,* Connie Casey; Staff 4 (Non-MLS 4)
Library Holdings: Bk Vols 31,500; Per Subs 14
Subject Interests: Law
Restriction: Not open to pub

P PONTIAC PUBLIC LIBRARY*, 211 E Madison St, 61764. SAN 304-5692. Tel: 815-844-7229. FAX: 815-844-3475. Web Site: www.pontiac.org/index.aspx?nid=505. *Libr Dir,* Kristin Holzhauer; E-mail: director@pontiacpubliclibrary.org; *Cat,* Levada Lee; *Circ,* Susan Strauch; *ILL,* Kimball Butler; *ILL,* Mary Lynn Schopp; Staff 8 (MLS 1, Non-MLS 7)
Founded 1858. Pop 11,500; Circ 70,000
Library Holdings: DVDs 1,000; Bk Vols 60,000; Per Subs 50
Special Collections: Local History (Livingston County & Pontiac, Ill Coll)
Subject Interests: Agr
Automation Activity & Vendor Info: (Cataloging) OCLC Connexion; (Circulation) SirsiDynix-WorkFlows; (OPAC) SirsiDynix-WorkFlows
Wireless access
Open Mon-Thurs 9-7, Fri & Sat 9-5

PORT BYRON

P RIVER VALLEY DISTRICT LIBRARY*, 214 S Main St, 61275. (Mail add: PO Box 10, 61275-0010), SAN 304-5706. Tel: 309-523-3440. FAX: 309-523-3516. E-mail: rivervalley5@mchsi.com. Web Site: rivervalleylibrary.org. *Dir,* Teri Schwenneker; E-mail: director@rivervalleylibrary.org; *Ch Mgr,* Jade Crisp; E-mail: jade@rivervalleylibrary.org; *Circ Mgr,* Tara McKay; E-mail: tara.mckay@rivervalleylibrary.org; *YA Mgr,* Taylor Hurry; E-mail: rivervalley5@mchsi.com; *Circ Supvr,* Heidi Iffland; E-mail: heidi.iffland@rivervalleylibrary.org; Staff 9 (MLS 1, Non-MLS 8)
Founded 1914. Pop 5,173; Circ 82,866
Special Collections: 1800's Local Newspaper Coll, microfilm; Rock Island County History
Automation Activity & Vendor Info: (Acquisitions) Innovative Interfaces, Inc; (Cataloging) Innovative Interfaces, Inc; (Circulation) Innovative Interfaces, Inc; (ILL) Innovative Interfaces, Inc; (OPAC) Innovative Interfaces, Inc; (Serials) Innovative Interfaces, Inc
Wireless access
Function: Audiobks via web, Bks on CD, Children's prog, Computer training, Computers for patron use, Electronic databases & coll, ILL available, Microfiche/film & reading machines, Music CDs, Notary serv, Online cat, OverDrive digital audio bks, Photocopying/Printing, Preschool reading prog, Prog for adults, Prog for children & young adult, Scanner, Senior computer classes, Story hour, Summer reading prog, Tax forms, Teen prog, Wheelchair accessible
Mem of Reaching Across Illinois Library System (RAILS)
Open Mon-Fri 9-8, Sat 9-1
Friends of the Library Group

POTOMAC

P POTOMAC PUBLIC LIBRARY*, 110 E State St, 61865. (Mail add: PO Box 171, 61865-0171), SAN 304-5714. Tel: 217-987-6457. FAX: 217-987-6457. E-mail: potomacpubliclibrary@gmail.com. *Librn,* Elizabeth Osborn
Founded 1939. Pop 681; Circ 987
Library Holdings: Bk Vols 11,902
Special Collections: Large Print Coll
Mem of Illinois Heartland Library System
Open Mon, Wed & Thurs 1-6

PRINCETON

S BUREAU COUNTY HISTORICAL SOCIETY MUSEUM & LIBRARY*, 109 Park Ave W, 61356-1927. SAN 304-5730. Tel: 815-875-2184. E-mail: museum@bureaucountyhistoricalsociety.com. Web Site: bureaucountyhistoricalsociety.com. *Pres,* Linda Gustafson; *Curator,* David Gugerty
Founded 1948
Library Holdings: Bk Titles 1,000
Special Collections: Henry W Immke Photographic Coll

Subject Interests: Genealogy, Local hist
Open Wed-Sat 1-5

P PRINCETON PUBLIC LIBRARY*, 698 E Peru St, 61356. SAN 304-5749. Tel: 815-875-1331. FAX: 815-872-1376. E-mail: help@princetonpl.org. Web Site: www.princetonpl.org. *Dir,* Jane Wayland; E-mail: jwayland@princetonpl.org; *Head, Tech Serv,* Dana Fine; *Head, Youth Serv,* Ron McCutchan; E-mail: rmccutchan@princetonpl.org; *Youth Serv Librn,* Mary Archer; *Youth Serv Librn,* Cheryl Bebej; *Curator, Ref,* Margaret Martinkus; E-mail: mmartinkus@princetonpl.org; *Programming,* Laurie Anderson; E-mail: landerson@princetonpl.org; Staff 1 (MLS 1)
Founded 1886. Pop 7,501; Circ 62,000
Library Holdings: Bk Titles 44,000; Per Subs 110
Special Collections: Bureau County (Illinois) Farm Architecture Exhibit, photog; Local History Coll, art, bks, blueprints, cassettes, Indian artifacts, micro, pamphlets, photog; World War II Coll, posters
Automation Activity & Vendor Info: (Circulation) SirsiDynix; (OPAC) SirsiDynix
Partic in Central & Western Massachusetts Automated Resource Sharing; Evergreen Indiana Consortium; LibraryLinkNJ, The New Jersey Library Cooperative
Open Mon-Thurs 10-9, Fri 10-6, Sat 10-3
Friends of the Library Group

PRINCEVILLE

P LILLIE M EVANS LIBRARY DISTRICT, 207 N Walnut Ave, 61559. (Mail add: PO Box 349, 61559-0349), SAN 304-5757. Tel: 309-385-4540. FAX: 309-385-2661. E-mail: lill@lmelibrary.org. Web Site: www.lmelibrary.org. *Dir,* Beth Duttlinger; Staff 1 (MLS 1)
Founded 1927. Pop 4,007; Circ 45,203
Library Holdings: CDs 1,688; DVDs 3,446; e-books 27,692; Bk Vols 26,037; Per Subs 35
Subject Interests: Local hist, Spanish (Lang)
Automation Activity & Vendor Info: (Circulation) SirsiDynix; (ILL) OCLC Connexion; (OPAC) SirsiDynix
Wireless access
Function: 24/7 Electronic res, 24/7 Online cat, 3D Printer, Adult bk club, Audiobks on Playaways & MP3, Audiobks via web, Bk club(s), Bks on CD, Butterfly Garden, Children's prog, Computer training, Computers for patron use, Electronic databases & coll, Free DVD rentals, Homebound delivery serv, ILL available, Internet access, Magazines, Magnifiers for reading, Meeting rooms, Movies, Museum passes, Music CDs, Online cat, OverDrive digital audio bks, Photocopying/Printing, Prog for adults, Prog for children & young adult, Ref serv available, Scanner, STEM programs, Story hour, Study rm, Summer reading prog, Tax forms, Teen prog, Wheelchair accessible
Mem of Reaching Across Illinois Library System (RAILS)
Partic in Resource Sharing Alliance
Special Services for the Deaf - Closed caption videos
Special Services for the Blind - Assistive/Adapted tech devices, equip & products
Open Mon 9-8, Tues-Fri 9-5, Sat 9-1
Friends of the Library Group

PROPHETSTOWN

P HENRY C ADAMS MEMORIAL LIBRARY*, 209 W Third St, 61277. SAN 304-5765. Tel: 815-537-5462. FAX: 815-537-9181. E-mail: hcadams1@yahoo.com. Web Site: prophetstownlibrary.com. *Dir,* Elizabeth Swatos; Staff 3 (Non-MLS 3)
Founded 1929. Pop 2,023; Circ 15,648
Library Holdings: DVDs 80; e-books 2,644; Large Print Bks 115; Bk Vols 12,484; Talking Bks 274; Videos 129
Special Collections: Civil War Records
Automation Activity & Vendor Info: (Acquisitions) SirsiDynix; (Cataloging) SirsiDynix; (Circulation) SirsiDynix; (Course Reserve) SirsiDynix; (ILL) SirsiDynix; (Media Booking) SirsiDynix; (OPAC) SirsiDynix; (Serials) SirsiDynix
Wireless access
Function: Homebound delivery serv
Mem of Reaching Across Illinois Library System (RAILS)
Partic in RiverShare Libraries
Special Services for the Blind - Aids for in-house use; Computer with voice synthesizer for visually impaired persons; Talking bks
Open Mon, Tues & Thurs 2-8, Wed & Fri 2-5, Sat 9-1

PROSPECT HEIGHTS

P PROSPECT HEIGHTS PUBLIC LIBRARY DISTRICT, 12 N Elm St, 60070-1450. SAN 304-5781. Tel: 847-259-3500. FAX: 847-259-4602. Web Site: www.phpl.info. *Exec Dir,* Alexander C Todd; E-mail: atodd@phpl.info; *Head, Adult Serv,* Kim Murphy; *Head, Youth Serv,* Sue Seggeling; E-mail: sueann@phpl.info; *Circ,* Ann Thomas; E-mail: athomas@phpl.info; Staff 41 (MLS 8, Non-MLS 33)
Founded 1957. Pop 14,073; Circ 214,769
Jul 2017-Jun 2018. Mats Exp $256,000, Books $90,000, Per/Ser (Incl. Access Fees) $9,000, AV Mat $41,500, Electronic Ref Mat (Incl. Access Fees) $115,500. Sal $1,550,000
Library Holdings: Audiobooks 3,467; CDs 3,974; DVDs 4,625; e-books 64,062; Large Print Bks 3,322; Bk Vols 84,609; Per Subs 50
Automation Activity & Vendor Info: (Cataloging) Innovative Interfaces, Inc; (Circulation) Innovative Interfaces, Inc; (Discovery) Innovative Interfaces, Inc; (ILL) OCLC WorldShare Interlibrary Loan; (OPAC) Innovative Interfaces, Inc; (Serials) Innovative Interfaces, Inc
Wireless access
Function: 24/7 Electronic res, 24/7 Online cat, 3D Printer, Art exhibits, Art programs, Audiobks via web, Bks on CD, Children's prog, Computer training, Computers for patron use, E-Readers, Electronic databases & coll, Free DVD rentals, ILL available, Internet access, Life-long learning prog for all ages, Magazines, Makerspace, Meeting rooms, Music CDs, Online cat, Online ref, OverDrive digital audio bks, Passport agency, Photocopying/Printing, Preschool outreach, Printer for laptops & handheld devices, Prog for adults, Prog for children & young adult, Ref serv available, Scanner, Spanish lang bks, STEM programs, Story hour, Study rm, Summer & winter reading prog, Telephone ref
Publications: Elm Leaf (Newsletter)
Mem of Reaching Across Illinois Library System (RAILS)
Partic in Cooperative Computer Services - CCS
Open Mon-Thurs 10-9, Fri 10-6, Sat 10-5, Sun 1-5

QUINCY

M BLESSING-RIEMAN COLLEGE OF NURSING & HEALTH SCIENCES*, Blessing Health Professions Library, 3609 N Marx Dr, 62305. SAN 304-579X. Tel: 217-228-5520, Ext 6970. FAX: 217-223-6400. E-mail: librarian@brcn.edu. Web Site: www.brcn.edu/library. *Coordr, Libr Serv,* Julie D Dietrich; Tel: 217-228-5520, Ext 6971, E-mail: jdietrich@brcn.edu; *Pub Serv Librn,* Lisa Berry; E-mail: lberry@brcn.edu; *Tech Serv Librn,* Shantry Miller; E-mail: smiller@loren.edu; Staff 3 (MLS 1, Non-MLS 2)
Founded 1891
Library Holdings: Bk Titles 5,000; Per Subs 120
Subject Interests: Nursing
Automation Activity & Vendor Info: (Acquisitions) CARL.Solution (TLC); (Cataloging) CARL.Solution (TLC); (Course Reserve) CARL.Solution (TLC); (ILL) OCLC
Wireless access
Partic in Consortium of Academic & Research Libraries in Illinois; Health Science Libraries of Illinois; Illinois Library & Information Network; MCMLA; RSA

S HISTORICAL SOCIETY OF QUINCY & ADAMS COUNTY LIBRARY*, 425 S 12th St, 62301. SAN 326-145X. Tel: 217-222-1835. FAX: 217-222-8212. E-mail: info@hsqac.org. Web Site: www.hsqac.org. *Ref Librn,* Jean Kay
Founded 1896
Library Holdings: Bk Titles 1,060; Bk Vols 1,110
Special Collections: Civil War (Gen James D Morgan Coll), ms
Mem of Reaching Across Illinois Library System (RAILS)
Open Tues-Fri 10-2
Restriction: Non-circulating to the pub

J JOHN WOOD COMMUNITY COLLEGE LIBRARY*, 1301 S 48th St, 62305. SAN 320-1821. Tel: 217-641-4537. Circulation E-mail: circdesk@jwcc.edu. Reference E-mail: reference@jwcc.edu. Web Site: www.jwcc.edu/library. *Dir, Learning Res Ctr,* Barb Lieber; E-mail: blieber@jwcc.edu; *Mgr, Libr Serv,* Erin Ealy; Staff 2 (MLS 2)
Founded 1974. Enrl 2,640; Fac 50; Highest Degree: Associate
Library Holdings: Bk Titles 18,500; Per Subs 190
Subject Interests: Agr, Local hist, Nursing, Vocational educ
Automation Activity & Vendor Info: (Acquisitions) Ex Libris Group; (Cataloging) Ex Libris Group; (Circulation) Ex Libris Group; (Course Reserve) Ex Libris Group; (ILL) OCLC FirstSearch; (OPAC) Ex Libris Group; (Serials) Ex Libris Group
Wireless access
Mem of Reaching Across Illinois Library System (RAILS)
Partic in Consortium of Academic & Research Libraries in Illinois; Network of Illinois Learning Resources in Community Colleges; Northern Illinois Learning Resources Cooperative
Open Mon-Thurs 7:30am-8:30pm, Fri 7:30-5, Sat 12-4

P QUINCY PUBLIC LIBRARY*, 526 Jersey St, 62301-3996. SAN 304-582X. Tel: 217-223-1309. Interlibrary Loan Service Tel: 217-223-1309, Ext 210. Reference Tel: 217-223-1309, Ext 502. Administration Tel: 217-223-1309, Ext 506. FAX: 217-222-5672. Reference FAX: 217-222-3052. Reference E-mail: reference@quincylibrary.org. Web Site: www.quincylibrary.org. *Exec Dir,* Kathleen Helsabeck; Tel: 217-223-1309, Ext 204, E-mail: khelsabeck@quincylibrary.org; *AV Librn,* Melissa DeVerger; Tel:

217-223-1309, Ext 205, E-mail: mdeverger@quincylibrary.org; *Ch Serv Librn,* Bill Waters; Tel: 217-223-1309, Ext 219, E-mail: bwaters@quincylibrary.org; *Coll & Delivery Serv Mgr,* Bobbi Mock; Tel: 217-223-1309, Ext 203, E-mail: rmock@quincylibrary.org; *Info Serv Mgr,* Katie Kraushaar; Tel: 217-223-1309, Ext 213, E-mail: kkraushaar@quincylibrary.org; *Sr Serv,* Patricia Woodworth; Tel: 217-223-1309, Ext 216, E-mail: pwoodworth@quincylibrary.org; Staff 10 (MLS 8, Non-MLS 2)
Founded 1888. Pop 53,000; Circ 701,716
Library Holdings: AV Mats 11,202; DVDs 12,551; e-books 111,266; Bk Titles 138,227; Per Subs 3,291
Special Collections: State Document Depository
Subject Interests: Genealogy, Local hist
Automation Activity & Vendor Info: (Cataloging) SirsiDynix; (Circulation) SirsiDynix; (ILL) SirsiDynix; (Media Booking) EnvisionWare; (OPAC) SirsiDynix
Wireless access
Function: 24/7 Electronic res, 24/7 Online cat, Adult bk club, After school storytime, Archival coll, Audiobks via web, Bk club(s), Bks on CD, Children's prog, Computer training, Computers for patron use, Digital talking bks, E-Readers, Electronic databases & coll, Free DVD rentals, Genealogy discussion group, Holiday prog, Home delivery & serv to seniorr ctr & nursing homes, Homebound delivery serv, ILL available, Internet access, Life-long learning prog for all ages, Magazines, Mail & tel request accepted, Meeting rooms, Microfiche/film & reading machines, Movies, Music CDs, Notary serv, Online cat, Outreach serv, OverDrive digital audio bks, Photocopying/Printing, Preschool reading prog, Prog for adults, Prog for children & young adult, Ref & res, Ref serv available, Senior outreach, Story hour, Study rm, Summer reading prog, Tax forms, Teen prog, Telephone ref, Wheelchair accessible, Workshops
Mem of Reaching Across Illinois Library System (RAILS)
Special Services for the Deaf - TDD equip
Special Services for the Blind - Closed circuit TV; Large print bks; Reader equip; Talking bks
Open Mon-Thurs (Winter) 9-8, Fri & Sat 9-5, Sun 1-5; Mon-Thurs (Summer) 10-7, Fri & Sat 9-5
Restriction: ID required to use computers (Ltd hrs), Non-resident fee
Friends of the Library Group

C QUINCY UNIVERSITY, Brenner Library, 1800 College Ave, 62301-2699. SAN 304-5811. Tel: 217-228-5432, Ext 3801. Circulation Tel: 217-228-5432, Ext 3804. Reference Tel: 217-228-5432, Ext 3805. Administration Tel: 217-228-5432, Ext 3800. Web Site: www.quincy.edu/brenner-library. *Dean of Libr,* Patricia Tomczak; E-mail: tomczpa@quincy.edu; *Asst Librn, Pub Serv,* Byron Holidman; Tel: 217-228-5348, Ext 3802, E-mail: holdiby@quincy.edu; *Evening Librn, Ref,* Brother Terry Santiapillai; *Educ Tech Spec,* Susan Grant; Tel: 217-228-5347, Ext 3806, E-mail: grantsu@quincy.edu. Subject Specialists: *Archives, Rare bks,* Patricia Tomczak; *Educ tech,* Byron Holidman; *Tech,* Susan Grant; Staff 3 (MLS 2, Non-MLS 1)
Founded 1860. Enrl 1,100; Fac 97; Highest Degree: Master
Library Holdings: Audiobooks 50; AV Mats 6,858; Bks on Deafness & Sign Lang 25; CDs 1,628; DVDs 4,302; e-books 283,776; e-journals 100; Electronic Media & Resources 35; Microforms 29,675; Bk Vols 103,230; Per Subs 134
Special Collections: Fr Tolton Coll; Franciscan Rare Book Coll; Genosky Local History Coll; Hyatt Folklore Coll
Automation Activity & Vendor Info: (Acquisitions) Ex Libris Group; (Cataloging) Ex Libris Group; (Circulation) Ex Libris Group; (Course Reserve) Ex Libris Group; (ILL) OCLC Connexion; (Media Booking) Ex Libris Group; (OPAC) Ex Libris Group; (Serials) EBSCO Online
Wireless access
Function: 24/7 Electronic res, 24/7 Online cat, Archival coll, Art exhibits, E-Reserves, Electronic databases & coll, ILL available, Internet access, Magazines, Microfiche/film & reading machines, Movies, Music CDs, Orientations, Photocopying/Printing, Ref & res, Res assist avail, Scanner, Spoken cassettes & CDs
Publications: Bibliographies (Collection catalog); Catalog of the Incunabula in the Franciscan Rare Book Collection, Quincy University Library
Mem of Reaching Across Illinois Library System (RAILS)
Partic in Consortium of Academic & Research Libraries in Illinois; Illinois Library & Information Network; OCLC Online Computer Library Center, Inc
Restriction: Authorized patrons, Borrowing privileges limited to fac & registered students, Borrowing requests are handled by ILL
Friends of the Library Group

RAMSEY

P RAMSEY PUBLIC LIBRARY*, 401 S Superior St, 62080. (Mail add: PO Box 128, 62080-0128), SAN 375-9733. Tel: 618-423-2019. FAX: 618-423-2120. E-mail: ramseylibrary@yahoo.com. *Librn,* Heather Seaton; Staff 1 (Non-MLS 1)
Pop 1,056; Circ 4,420
Library Holdings: Bk Vols 1,225; Per Subs 15
Subject Interests: Christian
Mem of Illinois Heartland Library System
Open Tues 1-4, Wed-Fri 8:30-4

RANTOUL

P RANTOUL PUBLIC LIBRARY*, 106 W Flessner, 61866. SAN 304-5838. Tel: 217-893-3955. FAX: 217-893-3961. E-mail: rantoullib@gmail.com. Web Site: www.rantoul.lib.il.us. *Dir,* Holly Thompson; E-mail: hollysrpl@gmail.com; *Youth Serv Librn,* Joella Travis; E-mail: rantoullibYS@gmail.com
Founded 1934. Pop 17,212; Circ 89,000
Library Holdings: Bk Vols 50,000; Per Subs 175
Special Collections: Aero-Space Coll
Wireless access
Mem of Illinois Heartland Library System
Special Services for the Deaf - TTY equip
Special Services for the Blind - Audio mat; Bks on cassette; Bks on CD; Braille bks; Talking bks
Open Mon-Thurs 9-9, Fri & Sat 9-5, Sun 1-5
Friends of the Library Group

RAYMOND

P DOYLE PUBLIC LIBRARY DISTRICT, 109 S O'Bannon St, 62560-5212. (Mail add: PO Box 544, 62560-0544). Tel: 217-229-4471. E-mail: doylepublic@gmail.com. Web Site: doylepubliclibrary.org. *Libr Dir,* Sharla Riley
Pop 1,888; Circ 10,000
Library Holdings: Audiobooks 189; Bks on Deafness & Sign Lang 22; CDs 370; DVDs 222; e-books 6,744; Electronic Media & Resources 33; Large Print Bks 230; Microforms 108; Per Subs 16; Talking Bks 37
Special Collections: Raymond Independent & Raymond News Coll, newsp
Wireless access
Publications: Raymond Independent; Raymond News
Mem of Illinois Heartland Library System
Open Mon 11-6, Tues & Thurs 11-5, Wed 11-8, Fri 11-4, Sat 9-Noon
Friends of the Library Group

RED BUD

P RED BUD PUBLIC LIBRARY, 925 S Main St, 62278. SAN 304-5846. Tel: 618-282-2255. FAX: 618-282-4055. E-mail: redbudillinoislibrary@gmail.com. Web Site: redbudpubliclibrary.weebly.com. *Dir,* Brenda Gilpatrick; *Librn,* Linda Krebel; *Asst Librn,* Jamie Joost; Staff 2 (Non-MLS 2)
Founded 1945. Pop 3,334; Circ 8,000
Library Holdings: Audiobooks 300; DVDs 400; Bk Titles 16,000; Per Subs 60
Subject Interests: Illinois
Wireless access
Mem of Illinois Heartland Library System
Open Mon-Thurs 12:30-8, Fri 12:30-4:30, Sat 10-2

RICHMOND

P NIPPERSINK PUBLIC LIBRARY DISTRICT*, 5418 Hill Rd, 60071. SAN 304-5854. Tel: 815-678-4014. FAX: 815-678-4484. E-mail: nippersink@nippersinklibrary.org. Web Site: nippersinklibrary.org. *Dir,* Cynthia Cole; E-mail: cynthiac@nippersinklibrary.org; Staff 12 (MLS 1, Non-MLS 11)
Founded 1972. Pop 11,169; Circ 82,500
Library Holdings: AV Mats 5,500; Bk Vols 46,000; Per Subs 68
Automation Activity & Vendor Info: (Circulation) Innovative Interfaces, Inc; (ILL) Innovative Interfaces, Inc; (OPAC) Innovative Interfaces, Inc
Wireless access
Publications: Library News (Quarterly)
Mem of Reaching Across Illinois Library System (RAILS)
Open Mon-Thurs 9-9, Fri & Sat 9-5
Friends of the Library Group

RICHTON PARK

P RICHTON PARK PUBLIC LIBRARY DISTRICT*, 22310 Latonia Lane, 60471. SAN 304-5862. Tel: 708-481-5333. FAX: 708-481-4343. E-mail: library@richtonparklibrary.org. Web Site: www.richtonparklibrary.org. *Libr Dir,* Laura Van Cleve; *Head, Adult Serv, Head, Tech Serv, Librn,* Brian Vagt; *Head, Circ,* Sarah Brown; *Head, Youth Serv,* Laura Van Cleve; Staff 4 (MLS 3, Non-MLS 1)
Founded 1974. Pop 12,533; Circ 87,138
Library Holdings: AV Mats 1,500; Large Print Bks 200; Bk Titles 39,000; Bk Vols 41,000; Per Subs 175; Talking Bks 2,500
Automation Activity & Vendor Info: (Circulation) Innovative Interfaces, Inc; (ILL) Innovative Interfaces, Inc; (OPAC) Innovative Interfaces, Inc
Wireless access

Function: Adult bk club, Bk club(s), Bks on CD, Children's prog, Computers for patron use, Free DVD rentals, ILL available, Internet access, Mail & tel request accepted, Music CDs, Notary serv, Online cat, Photocopying/Printing, Prog for adults, Prog for children & young adult, Ref serv available, Story hour, Summer reading prog, Tax forms, Telephone ref, Wheelchair accessible
Mem of Reaching Across Illinois Library System (RAILS)
Partic in System Wide Automated Network
Open Mon-Fri 10-8, Sat 10-2
Friends of the Library Group

RIDGE FARM

P ELWOOD TOWNSHIP CARNEGIE LIBRARY*, 104 N State St, 61870. (Mail add: PO Box 349, 61870-0349), SAN 304-5889. Tel: 217-247-2820. E-mail: Library@RidgeFarmIllinois.com. Web Site: www.ridgefarmillinois.com/library. *Librn,* Vicki Hayward; *Librn,* Shawn Schendel
Founded 1909. Pop 1,672; Circ 6,213
Library Holdings: Bk Vols 10,751; Per Subs 20
Automation Activity & Vendor Info: (Cataloging) SirsiDynix; (Circulation) SirsiDynix
Mem of Illinois Heartland Library System
Open Tues 2-7, Wed & Thurs 10-6, Fri 9-2, Sat 11-3

RIVER FOREST

C CONCORDIA UNIVERSITY*, Klinck Memorial Library, 7400 Augusta St, 60305-1499. SAN 304-5897. Tel: 708-209-3050. Toll Free Tel: 866-733-8287. FAX: 708-209-3175. E-mail: library@cuchicago.edu. Web Site: www.cuchicago.edu/academics/library. *Dir,* Yana Serdyuk; Tel: 708-209-3053, E-mail: yana.serdyuk@cuchicago.edu; *Access Serv Librn,* Dan Zamudio; Tel: 708-209-3057, E-mail: dan.zamudio@cuchicago.edu; *Ref & Instruction Librn,* Marty J Breen; Tel: 708-209-3181, E-mail: marty.breen@cuchicago.edu; *Tech Serv Librn,* Simon Czerwinskyj; Tel: 708-209-3254, E-mail: simon.czerwinskyj@cuchicago.edu; Staff 5 (MLS 5)
Founded 1864. Enrl 2,781; Fac 88; Highest Degree: Master
Library Holdings: Bk Titles 170,000; Per Subs 534
Special Collections: Curriculum Library; Educational Resources Info Center, micro; Test file. Oral History
Subject Interests: Educ, Music, Relig
Automation Activity & Vendor Info: (Acquisitions) Ex Libris Group; (Cataloging) Ex Libris Group; (Circulation) Ex Libris Group; (Course Reserve) Ex Libris Group; (ILL) Ex Libris Group; (OPAC) Ex Libris Group; (Serials) Ex Libris Group
Wireless access
Partic in Consortium of Academic & Research Libraries in Illinois; Detroit Area Library Network; Illinois Library & Information Network; LIBRAS, Inc; Minitex
Open Mon-Thurs 8-10, Fri 8-4:30, Sat 9:30-5:30

C DOMINICAN UNIVERSITY, Rebecca Crown Library, 7900 W Division St, 60305-1066. SAN 304-5927. Tel: 708-524-6875. Circulation Tel: 708-524-6876. Interlibrary Loan Service Tel: 708-524-6877. FAX: 708-366-5360. E-mail: reference@dom.edu. Web Site: research.dom.edu. *Univ Librn,* Estevan Montaño; Tel: 708-524-6873, E-mail: emontano@dom.edu; *Access Serv Librn,* Jill Bambenek; E-mail: jbambenek@dom.edu; Staff 13.5 (MLS 7, Non-MLS 6.5)
Founded 1918. Enrl 3,100; Fac 150; Highest Degree: Master
Library Holdings: Bk Vols 300,000; Per Subs 16,000
Special Collections: US Document Depository
Subject Interests: Libr & info sci
Automation Activity & Vendor Info: (Acquisitions) Ex Libris Group; (Cataloging) Ex Libris Group; (Circulation) Ex Libris Group; (OPAC) Ex Libris Group
Wireless access
Publications: Bibliographies; Handbooks
Partic in Consortium of Academic & Research Libraries in Illinois; Illinois Library & Information Network; LIBRAS, Inc; OCLC Online Computer Library Center, Inc
Open Mon-Sun 8am-Midnight

P RIVER FOREST PUBLIC LIBRARY*, 735 Lathrop Ave, 60305-1883. SAN 304-5919. Tel: 708-366-5205. Circulation Tel: 708-366-5205, Ext 304. FAX: 708-366-8699. Reference E-mail: reference@rflib.org. Web Site: www.riverforestlibrary.org. *Dir,* Sue Quinn; Tel: 708-366-5205, Ext 319, E-mail: squinn@riverforestlibrary.org; *Mgr, Ad Serv,* Mary Kay Akers Stiff; Tel: 708-366-5205, Ext 318, E-mail: mkakers@riverforestlibrary.org; *Mgr, Ch Serv,* Amy Grossman; Tel: 708-366-5205, Ext 315, E-mail: agrossman@riverforestlibrary.org; Staff 14 (MLS 9, Non-MLS 5)
Founded 1899. Pop 11,635; Circ 143,185
Automation Activity & Vendor Info: (Circulation) Innovative Interfaces, Inc
Wireless access
Publications: Newsletter (Biannually)
Mem of Reaching Across Illinois Library System (RAILS)
Partic in System Wide Automated Network
Open Mon-Thurs 9-9, Fri & Sat 9-5, Sun (Sept-May) 1-5
Friends of the Library Group

RIVER GROVE

P RIVER GROVE PUBLIC LIBRARY DISTRICT*, 8638 W Grand Ave, 60171. SAN 304-5935. Tel: 708-453-4484. FAX: 708-453-4517. Reference E-mail: info@rivergrovelibrary.org. Web Site: rivergrovelibrary.org. *Dir,* Jorge Perez; *Ch Serv,* Dayna Tucker; *Circ,* Yuli Melnyk; Staff 11 (MLS 1, Non-MLS 10)
Founded 1963. Pop 10,600; Circ 27,000
Library Holdings: Bk Vols 30,000; Per Subs 121
Special Collections: Local History
Automation Activity & Vendor Info: (OPAC) Innovative Interfaces, Inc
Wireless access
Publications: Monthly Calender of Events; New Book List
Mem of Reaching Across Illinois Library System (RAILS)
Partic in System Wide Automated Network
Open Mon-Thurs 10-7, Fri & Sat 10-5
Friends of the Library Group

J TRITON COLLEGE LIBRARY*, 2000 N Fifth Ave, 60171. SAN 304-5943. Tel: 708-456-0300, Ext 3698. FAX: 708-583-3120. E-mail: refdesk@triton.edu. Web Site: library.triton.edu. *Chairperson, Fac Librn,* Dr Robert Connor; Tel: 708-456-0300, Ext 3767, E-mail: robertconnor@triton.edu; *Dir, Libr Syst & Tech Serv,* Hilary Meyer; E-mail: hilarymeyer@triton.edu; *Coordr, Circ,* Annette Lee-McCollum; E-mail: annettelee@triton.edu
Founded 1964. Highest Degree: Associate
Library Holdings: Bk Vols 84,000; Per Subs 410
Subject Interests: Nursing, Sci tech
Wireless access
Mem of Reaching Across Illinois Library System (RAILS)
Partic in Consortium of Academic & Research Libraries in Illinois; Network of Illinois Learning Resources in Community Colleges; OCLC Online Computer Library Center, Inc
Open Mon-Thurs 8-8, Fri 9-2, Sat 9-1

RIVERDALE

P RIVERDALE PUBLIC LIBRARY DISTRICT*, 208 W 144th St, 60827-2733. SAN 304-5951. Tel: 708-841-3311. FAX: 708-841-1805. E-mail: rdpl2@earthlink.net. Web Site: www.riverdale.lib.il.us. *Adminr, Head of Libr,* Katrina Harris; *Circ,* Ninon Greene; *Circ,* Precious Knight; *Tech Serv,* Barb Diehl; Staff 1 (MLS 1)
Founded 1973. Pop 13,549; Circ 16,135
Library Holdings: Audiobooks 472; CDs 952; DVDs 2,131; Bk Titles 27,273; Bk Vols 35,881; Per Subs 24
Automation Activity & Vendor Info: (Circulation) SirsiDynix
Wireless access
Mem of Reaching Across Illinois Library System (RAILS)
Partic in System Wide Automated Network
Open Mon-Thurs 10-6

RIVERSIDE

P RIVERSIDE PUBLIC LIBRARY*, One Burling Rd, 60546. SAN 304-596X. Tel: 708-442-6366. FAX: 708-442-9462. Circulation E-mail: circulation@riversidelibrary.org. Reference E-mail: reference@riversidelibrary.org. Web Site: www.riversidelibrary.org. *Dir,* Janice Foley; Tel: 708-442-6366, Ext 100, E-mail: janicefoley@riversidelibrary.org; Staff 35 (MLS 5, Non-MLS 30)
Founded 1930. Pop 8,774; Circ 134,000
Library Holdings: Bk Titles 67,000; Per Subs 125
Special Collections: Frederick Law Olmsted
Subject Interests: Landscape archit, Local hist
Automation Activity & Vendor Info: (Circulation) Innovative Interfaces, Inc
Wireless access
Publications: Bibliography of Frederick Law Olmsted & Calvert Vaux; Local History Index; Local Newspaper Index 1912-39; Newsletter; Origins of Riverside Street Names
Mem of Reaching Across Illinois Library System (RAILS)
Partic in System Wide Automated Network
Open Mon-Thurs 9-9, Fri & Sat 9-5, Sun (Sept-May) 1-5
Friends of the Library Group

RIVERTON

P RIVERTON VILLAGE LIBRARY*, 1200 E Riverton Rd, 62561-8200. Tel: 217-629-6353. FAX: 217-629-6353. E-mail: staff@rivertonvillagelibrary.org. Web Site: www.rivertonvillagelibrary.org. *Dir,* Jennifer Cernich; *Asst Librn,* Lisa Nerone; *Asst Librn,* Robin Rushing
Founded 1996. Pop 3,455

Automation Activity & Vendor Info: (Acquisitions) SirsiDynix; (Cataloging) SirsiDynix; (Circulation) SirsiDynix; (Course Reserve) SirsiDynix; (ILL) SirsiDynix; (Media Booking) SirsiDynix; (OPAC) SirsiDynix; (Serials) SirsiDynix
Wireless access
Mem of Illinois Heartland Library System
Open Mon-Thurs 9-7, Sat 10-2
Friends of the Library Group

RIVERWOODS

G RYERSON NATURE LIBRARY*, 21950 N Riverwoods Rd, 60015. SAN 304-3495. Tel: 847-968-3320. FAX: 847-367-6649. E-mail: ryersonwoods@LCFPD.org. Web Site: lcfpd.org. *Mgr,* Jill Stites
Founded 1974
Library Holdings: Bk Titles 2,500
Special Collections: Botany (Wildflower Coll), pressed plants; Herbarium
Subject Interests: Biology, Botany, Ecology, Entomology, Environ studies, Forestry, Illinois, Landscape archit, Zoology
Restriction: Not a lending libr

ROBBINS

P WILLIAM LEONARD PUBLIC LIBRARY DISTRICT*, 13820 Central Park Ave, 60472-1999. SAN 304-5978. Tel: 708-597-2760. FAX: 708-597-2778. E-mail: ros@thewlpld.org. Web Site: wlpld.wordpress.com. *Dir,* Coatney Priscilla
Founded 1973. Pop 8,853
Library Holdings: Bk Vols 21,000; Per Subs 88
Automation Activity & Vendor Info: (Circulation) Innovative Interfaces, Inc; (Course Reserve) Innovative Interfaces, Inc
Mem of Reaching Across Illinois Library System (RAILS)
Partic in System Wide Automated Network
Open Mon & Wed 12-8, Tues & Thurs 12-6, Fri 3-7, Sat 10-2
Friends of the Library Group

ROBINSON

J LINCOLN TRAIL COLLEGE*, Eagleton Learning Resources Center, 11220 State Hwy 1, 62454-5707. SAN 304-5986. Tel: 618-544-8657, Ext 1425. Web Site: www.iecc.edu/ltc/student-life/library. *Dir, Support Serv,* Rena Gower; Tel: 618-544-8657, Ext 1427, E-mail: gowerr@iecc.edu; *Libr Asst,* Kelly Mullins
Founded 1970. Enrl 1,025
Library Holdings: Bk Vols 18,000; Per Subs 75
Automation Activity & Vendor Info: (Cataloging) Ex Libris Group; (Circulation) Ex Libris Group; (OPAC) Ex Libris Group
Wireless access
Open Mon-Thurs 7:30-4:30, Fri 7:30-4

P ROBINSON PUBLIC LIBRARY DISTRICT*, 606 N Jefferson St, 62454-2665. SAN 304-5994. Tel: 618-544-2917. FAX: 618-544-7172. E-mail: robinsonlibrarydistrict@hotmail.com. Web Site: www.robinson.lib.il.us. *Dir,* Breyanna Weaver; E-mail: breyannaweaver@hotmail.com; Staff 31 (Non-MLS 31)
Founded 1906. Pop 16,188; Circ 84,778
Library Holdings: DVDs 2,216; Electronic Media & Resources 18; Bk Vols 70,374; Per Subs 80; Talking Bks 710; Videos 5,320
Special Collections: Antiques & Collectibles; Crawford County History; Genealogy; Parenting
Subject Interests: Genealogy, Local hist
Automation Activity & Vendor Info: (Acquisitions) SirsiDynix; (Cataloging) SirsiDynix; (Circulation) SirsiDynix; (ILL) SirsiDynix; (OPAC) SirsiDynix; (Serials) SirsiDynix
Wireless access
Function: Homebound delivery serv, Ref serv available
Mem of Illinois Heartland Library System
Special Services for the Deaf - Bks on deafness & sign lang; Closed caption videos; TDD equip
Special Services for the Blind - Closed circuit TV magnifier; Reader equip; Talking bks
Open Mon-Thurs (Fall-Spring) 9-6, Fri & Sat 9-4:30; Mon (Summer) 9-6, Tues-Sat 9-4:30
Restriction: Non-circulating
Branches: 3
HUTSONVILLE BRANCH, 101 S Main St, Hutsonville, 62433. (Mail add: PO Box 08, Hutsonville, 62433-0008). Tel: 618-563-9603. FAX: 618-563-9603. E-mail: hutsonpubliclibrary@gmail.com. *Br Mgr,* Shannon Wells; Staff 2 (Non-MLS 2)
Founded 1994. Pop 1,151
Open Mon 3-5, Tues & Thurs 1-5, Sat 9-Noon
Friends of the Library Group
OBLONG BRANCH, 110 E Main St, Oblong, 62449. Tel: 618-592-3001. FAX: 618-592-3001. E-mail: doblibrary@yahoo.com. *Br Mgr,* Judy Plunkett; Staff 2 (Non-MLS 2)
Founded 1968. Pop 2,490
Open Tues-Fri 11-5, Sat 10-1
Friends of the Library Group
SUSIE WESLEY MEMORIAL, 105 S Main, Flat Rock, 62427. (Mail add: PO Box 185, Flat Rock, 62427-0185). Tel: 618-584-3636. FAX: 618-584-3636. E-mail: swlib@frtci.net. *Br Mgr,* Ellen Roberts; Staff 2 (Non-MLS 2)
Founded 1988. Pop 1,151
Open Tues & Thurs Noon-5, Sat 9-Noon
Friends of the Library Group

ROCHELLE

P FLAGG-ROCHELLE PUBLIC LIBRARY DISTRICT*, 619 Fourth Ave, 61068. SAN 304-6001. Tel: 815-562-3431. FAX: 815-562-3432. E-mail: library@rochelle.net. Web Site: flaggrochellepubliclibrary.org. *Dir,* Sarah K Flanagan; E-mail: director@flaggrochellepubliclibrary.org; *Asst Dir,* Connie Avery; E-mail: conniea@flaggrochellepubliclibrary.org
Founded 1889. Pop 13,370; Circ 91,304
Library Holdings: Bk Vols 53,000; Per Subs 147
Subject Interests: Genealogy, Local hist
Wireless access
Mem of Reaching Across Illinois Library System (RAILS)
Open Mon-Thurs 10-8:30, Fri & Sat 10-5; Mon-Thurs (Summer) 10-7, Fri & Sat 10-5
Friends of the Library Group

ROCHESTER

P ROCHESTER PUBLIC LIBRARY DISTRICT*, One Community Dr, 62563. (Mail add: PO Box 617, 62563), SAN 376-1266. Tel: 217-498-8454. FAX: 217-498-8455. E-mail: library@rochesterpld.org. Web Site: www.rochesterlibrary.org. *Libr Dir,* Janet McAllister; *Circ Mgr,* Lorachelle Purdy; Staff 9 (MLS 2, Non-MLS 7)
Founded 1985. Pop 7,046
Library Holdings: Bk Titles 29,200; Per Subs 73
Automation Activity & Vendor Info: (Cataloging) SirsiDynix; (Circulation) SirsiDynix; (ILL) SirsiDynix; (OPAC) SirsiDynix
Wireless access
Function: Adult bk club, Art exhibits, Audiobks via web, Bks on CD, Children's prog, Computer training, Computers for patron use, Electronic databases & coll, Equip loans & repairs, Free DVD rentals, Holiday prog, Home delivery & serv to seniorr ctr & nursing homes, Homebound delivery serv, ILL available, Magnifiers for reading, Music CDs, Online cat, OverDrive digital audio bks, Photocopying/Printing, Preschool outreach, Prog for adults, Prog for children & young adult, Ref serv available, Senior computer classes, Senior outreach, Story hour, Summer reading prog, Tax forms, Telephone ref, Wheelchair accessible, Workshops, Writing prog
Publications: Bibliobits
Mem of Illinois Heartland Library System
Partic in Association for Rural & Small Libraries
Special Services for the Blind - Bks on cassette; Braille bks; Magnifiers
Open Mon-Thurs 10-8, Fri 10-5, Sat 10-4
Friends of the Library Group

ROCK FALLS

P ROCK FALLS PUBLIC LIBRARY DISTRICT, 1007 Seventh Ave, 61071. SAN 304-601X. Tel: 815-626-3958. E-mail: rfdistrict@yahoo.com. Web Site: www.rockfallslibrary.com. *Dir,* Amy Lego; Staff 7 (Non-MLS 7)
Founded 1939. Pop 11,000; Circ 48,000
Library Holdings: Bk Vols 36,000; Per Subs 131
Automation Activity & Vendor Info: (Cataloging) TLC (The Library Corporation); (Circulation) TLC (The Library Corporation); (OPAC) TLC (The Library Corporation)
Wireless access
Mem of Reaching Across Illinois Library System (RAILS)
Open Mon-Thurs 9-6, Fri 9-4, Sat 9-Noon

ROCK ISLAND

C AUGUSTANA COLLEGE LIBRARY*, Thomas Tredway Library, 3435 9 1/2 Ave, 61201-2296. (Mail add: 639 38th St, 61201), SAN 304-6028. Tel: 309-794-7266. Circulation Tel: 309-794-7310. Interlibrary Loan Service Tel: 309-794-7585. FAX: 309-794-7640. Interlibrary Loan Service FAX: 309-794-7230. E-mail: libraryinfo@augustana.edu. Circulation E-mail: librarycirculation@augustana.edu. Web Site: library.augustana.edu. *Dir,* Chris Schafer; Tel: 309-794-7642, E-mail: chrisschafer@augustana.edu; *Head, Circ,* Christine Aden; Tel: 309-794-7819, E-mail: christineaden@augustana.edu; *Spec Coll Librn,* Emma Saito Lincoln; Tel: 309-794-7317, E-mail: emmalincoln@augustana.edu; *Res & Instruction Librn,* Stefanie Bluemle; Tel: 309-794-7167, E-mail: stefaniebluemle@augustana.edu; *Res & Instruction Librn,* Anne Earel; Tel: 309-794-7315, E-mail: anneearel@augustana.edu; *Res & Instruction Librn,* Lauryn Lehman; Tel: 309-794-7494, E-mail: laurynlehman@augustana.edu; *Res & Instruction Librn,* Maria Emerson; Tel: 309-794-7823, E-mail:

mariaemerson@augustana.edu; *Tech Serv Librn,* Mary Tatro; Tel: 309-794-7824, E-mail: marytatro@augustana.edu; Staff 16 (MLS 10, Non-MLS 6)
Founded 1860. Enrl 2,441; Fac 223; Highest Degree: Bachelor
Library Holdings: Bk Titles 173,734; Bk Vols 199,838; Per Subs 441
Special Collections: French Revolution (Charles XV Coll); John Hauberg Manuscript Coll; Upper Mississippi Valley Coll
Automation Activity & Vendor Info: (Acquisitions) Ex Libris Group; (Cataloging) Ex Libris Group; (Circulation) Ex Libris Group; (Course Reserve) Ex Libris Group; (ILL) OCLC ILLiad; (OPAC) Ex Libris Group
Wireless access
Partic in Consortium of Academic & Research Libraries in Illinois; OCLC Online Computer Library Center, Inc
Open Mon-Thurs 8am-10pm, Fri 8-5, Sat 12-6, Sun 1-10

L ROCK ISLAND COUNTY LAW LIBRARY*, Rock Island County Courthouse, 3rd Flr, Ste 304, 1317 Third Ave, 61201. SAN 375-975X. Tel: 309-558-3259, 309-786-4451, Ext 3259. FAX: 309-558-3263. Web Site: www.rockislandcounty.org/courtAdmin.aspx?id=39780&terms=law7.20library. *Law Librn,* Sherri Lawton
Library Holdings: Bk Titles 10,000
Special Collections: Legal Item Coll
Wireless access
Mem of Reaching Across Illinois Library System (RAILS)
Open Mon-Fri 8-12 & 12:30-4:30

P ROCK ISLAND PUBLIC LIBRARY*, 401 19th St, 61201. SAN 340-7012. Tel: 309-732-7323. Reference Tel: 309-732-7341. FAX: 309-732-7342. Web Site: rockislandlibrary.org. *Dir,* Angela Campbell; E-mail: Campbell.Angela@rigov.org; *Dir, Ch Serv,* Susan Foster; Tel: 309-732-7362; *Dir of Circ,* Victoria Schoess; Tel: 309-732-7350, E-mail: schoess.victoria@rigov.org; *Dir, Ref Serv,* Amy Sisul; Tel: 309-732-7302, E-mail: Sisul.Amy@rigov.org; *Dir, Facilities,* Kellie Kerns; Tel: 309-732-7305, E-mail: Kerns.Kellie@rigov.org; *Dir, Tech Serv,* Kimberly Brozovich; Tel: 309-732-7344, E-mail: Brozovich.Kimberly@rigov.org; *Ch,* Ranell Dennis; Tel: 309-732-7304, E-mail: Dennis.Ranell@rigov.org; Staff 39 (MLS 6, Non-MLS 33)
Founded 1872. Pop 52,543; Circ 277,205
Library Holdings: Bk Titles 124,399; Bk Vols 190,313; Per Subs 382
Special Collections: Local History, Adults & Children's Large Print Bks
Subject Interests: Lit, Literary criticism
Wireless access
Publications: Rock Island Library Lines
Mem of Reaching Across Illinois Library System (RAILS)
Open Mon-Thurs 9-8, Fri 9-5:30, Sat 9-1
Friends of the Library Group
Branches: 2
SOUTHWEST, 9010 Ridgewood Rd, 61201, SAN 340-7071. Tel: 309-732-7338. FAX: 309-732-7337. *Br Mgr,* Tricia Kane; Tel: 309-732-7364
Library Holdings: Bk Titles 22,806; Bk Vols 23,991
Open Mon & Tues 10-8, Wed 9-8, Thurs-Sat 9-5:30
THIRTY-THIRTY-ONE BRANCH, 3059 30th St, 61201, SAN 340-7101. Tel: 309-732-7369. FAX: 309-732-7371. *Br Mgr,* Tricia Kane; Tel: 309-732-7364
Library Holdings: Bk Titles 17,649; Bk Vols 18,322
Open Mon-Thurs 9-8, Fri & Sat 9-5:30
Bookmobiles: 1

S SWENSON SWEDISH IMMIGRATION RESEARCH CENTER*, Augustana College, 3520 Seventh Ave, 61201. (Mail add: Augustana College, 639 38th St, 61201-2296), SAN 326-9833. Tel: 309-794-7204. FAX: 309-794-7443. E-mail: swensoncenter@augustana.edu. Web Site: www.augustana.edu/swenson. *Dir,* Dr Dag Blanck, PhD; E-mail: dagblanck@augustana.edu; *Head, Genealogical Serv,* Jill Seaholm; E-mail: jillseaholm@augustana.edu; *Head, Libr Serv,* Susanne Titus; Tel: 309-794-7807, E-mail: susannetitus@augustana.edu; *Archivist, Librn,* Lisa Huntsha; Tel: 309-794-7496, E-mail: lisahuntsha@augustana.edu. Subject Specialists: *Family hist,* Jill Seaholm
Founded 1981
Library Holdings: Bk Titles 17,000; Per Subs 30
Special Collections: Chicago, Minneapolis & Saint Paul City Directories, microfilm; Name Indexes to Swedish Embarkation Ports, database; Swedish-American Churches, Societies, Organizations, Businesses & Personal Papers; Swedish-American Newspapers Coll, microfilm
Wireless access
Publications: Swedish American Genealogist (Quarterly)
Partic in OCLC Online Computer Library Center, Inc
Restriction: Open by appt only

R TRI-CITY JEWISH CENTER LIBRARY*, 2715 30th St, 61201. SAN 373-0514. Tel: 309-644-2765. *Librn,* Kristine Cawley; E-mail: kristinecawley@gmail.com; Staff 1 (MLS 1)
Founded 1936
Library Holdings: Bk Vols 10,000
Special Collections: Israeli Coin Coll
Wireless access
Open Mon-Fri 9-5

A UNITED STATES ARMY, Corps of Engineers Rock Island District Library, Clock Tower Bldg, 1500 Rock Island Dr, 61204-2004. SAN 340-7160. Tel: 309-794-5576. FAX: 309-794-5807. Web Site: www.mvr.usace.army.mil/library.
Founded 1975
Library Holdings: Bk Vols 11,500; Per Subs 75
Special Collections: Civil Engineering; Corps of Engineers History Coll; Environmental Resources; Hydraulics (Locks & Dams)
Subject Interests: Civil engr, Soil mechanics
Publications: Periodical Holding List
Mem of Reaching Across Illinois Library System (RAILS)
Partic in LYRASIS; OCLC Online Computer Library Center, Inc; Proquest Dialog
Restriction: Open by appt only

S WESTERN ILLINOIS AREA AGENCY ON AGING*, Elderly Living & Learning Facility, 729 34th Ave, 61201. SAN 375-1775. Tel: 309-793-6800. Toll Free Tel: 800-322-1051. FAX: 309-793-6807. Web Site: www.wiaaa.org.
Founded 1988
Library Holdings: Bk Titles 2,100; Per Subs 15
Subject Interests: Aging, Gerontology
Mem of Reaching Across Illinois Library System (RAILS)
Open Mon-Fri 8-5

ROCKFORD

M OSF SAINT ANTHONY MEDICAL CENTER*, Medical Library, 5666 E State St, 61108-2472. SAN 324-5969. Tel: 815-227-2558. FAX: 815-227-2904. E-mail: SAMC.Library@osfhealthcare.org. Web Site: www.osflibrary.org/locations/saint-anthony.html. *Libr Dir,* Heather Klepitsch; E-mail: heather.klepitsch@osfhealthcare.org; *Med Librn,* Roberta Craig; E-mail: Roberta.J.Craig@osfhealthcare.org; *Libr Tech,* Mary Finkbeiner; E-mail: Mary.E.Finkbeiner@osfhealthcare.org; Staff 3 (MLS 2, Non-MLS 1)
Oct 2013-Sept 2014 Income $159,870. Mats Exp $74,330, Books $17,960, Per/Ser (Incl. Access Fees) $55,520, Presv $850. Sal $70,940
Library Holdings: Bks on Deafness & Sign Lang 1; CDs 8; DVDs 10; e-books 225; e-journals 8,550; Electronic Media & Resources 25; Bk Titles 1,250; Bk Vols 1,400; Per Subs 83
Subject Interests: Clinical med, Healthcare admin, Nursing
Automation Activity & Vendor Info: (Acquisitions) Baker & Taylor; (Cataloging) EOS International; (Circulation) EOS International; (Course Reserve) EOS International; (ILL) OCLC; (OPAC) EOS International; (Serials) EOS International
Wireless access
Publications: InTouch (Newsletter)
Mem of Reaching Across Illinois Library System (RAILS)
Partic in Health Science Library of Illinois; Illinois Library & Information Network; National Network of Libraries of Medicine Region 6
Open Mon-Fri 8-4:30

C RASMUSSEN COLLEGE*, Rockford Campus Library, 6000 E State St, 4th Flr, 61108. Tel: 815-316-4800. FAX: 815-316-4801. Web Site: www.rasmussen.edu. *Librn,* Emily Gilbert; E-mail: Emily.Gilbert@rasmussen.edu
Library Holdings: DVDs 100; Bk Vols 1,000; Per Subs 25
Wireless access
Partic in Consortium of Academic & Research Libraries in Illinois
Open Mon-Thurs 9am-9:30pm, Fri 9-5, Sat 9-1

J ROCK VALLEY COLLEGE*, Estelle M Black Library, 3301 N Mulford Rd, 61114. SAN 304-6052. Tel: 815-921-4615, 815-921-7821. Interlibrary Loan Service Tel: 815-921-4607. Reference Tel: 815-921-4619. Administration Tel: 815-921-4626. Toll Free Tel: 800-973-7821. FAX: 815-921-4629. E-mail: rvc-libref@rockvalleycollege.edu. Web Site: www.rockvalleycollege.edu/library. *Archivist, Outreach Librn,* Steven Thompson; Tel: 815-921-4612, E-mail: S.Thompson@rockvalleycollege.edu; *Ref Librn,* Maria Figiel-Krueger; Tel: 815-921-4606, E-mail: M.Figiel-Krueger@rockvalleycollege.edu; *Syst Librn,* Yiluo Song; Tel: 815-921-4602, E-mail: Y.Song@rockvalleycollege.edu; *Tech Serv Librn,* Brent Eckert; Tel: 815-921-4604, E-mail: B.Eckert@rockvalleycollege.edu; *Access Serv Coordr,* Rebecca Whitlow; Tel: 815-921-4603, E-mail: R.Whitlow@rockvalleycollege.edu. Subject Specialists: *Archives,* Steven Thompson; Staff 5 (MLS 4, Non-MLS 1)
Founded 1965. Enrl 3,800; Fac 123; Highest Degree: Associate

Library Holdings: AV Mats 10,903; CDs 5,163; DVDs 2,268; e-books 14,720; e-journals 111; Electronic Media & Resources 52; Bk Vols 92,225; Per Subs 451; Videos 2,208
Automation Activity & Vendor Info: (Acquisitions) Ex Libris Group; (Cataloging) Ex Libris Group; (Circulation) Ex Libris Group; (Course Reserve) Ex Libris Group; (ILL) OCLC; (OPAC) Ex Libris Group; (Serials) Ex Libris Group
Wireless access
Function: Archival coll, Audio & video playback equip for onsite use, Bks on cassette, Bks on CD, CD-ROM, Computers for patron use, Electronic databases & coll, ILL available, Music CDs, Online cat, Photocopying/Printing, Wheelchair accessible
Mem of Reaching Across Illinois Library System (RAILS)
Partic in Consortium of Academic & Research Libraries in Illinois; Illinois Library & Information Network; Network of Illinois Learning Resources in Community Colleges; OCLC Online Computer Library Center, Inc
Open Mon-Thurs 8am-9pm, Fri 8-5
Restriction: Open to pub for ref & circ; with some limitations, Open to students, fac & staff
Friends of the Library Group

S ROCKFORD INSTITUTE LIBRARY*, 928 N Main St, 61103. SAN 377-4309. Tel: 815-964-5053. E-mail: subscriptions@chroniclesmagazine.org. Web Site: www.chroniclesmagazine.org. *Library Contact,* Cindy Link
Library Holdings: Bk Vols 400; Per Subs 30
Wireless access

P ROCKFORD PUBLIC LIBRARY*, Hart Interim Library, 214 N Church St, 61101-1023. SAN 340-7195. Tel: 815-965-7606. FAX: 815-965-0866. Web Site: www.rockfordpubliclibrary.org. *Exec Dir,* Lynn Stainbrook; E-mail: lstainbrook@rockfordpubliclibrary.org; *Asst Dir of Br,* Aaron Carlin; E-mail: acarlin@rockfordpubliclibrary.org; *Asst Dir, Main Libr,* Emily Klonicki; Tel: 815-987-6673, E-mail: EKlonicki@rockfordpubliclibrary.org; *Chief Financial Officer,* Antony Cortez; E-mail: acortez@rockfordpubliclibrary.org; *Develop Officer,* Anne O'Keefe; E-mail: aokeefe@rockfordpubliclibrary.org; *Mgr, Ad Serv,* Leslie Vano; E-mail: lvano@rockfordpubliclibrary.org; *Mgr, Circ Serv,* Donna Hopson; E-mail: dhopson@rockfordpubliclibrary.org; *Mgr, Coll Mgt, Mgr, Info Tech,* Rose Peterson; *Mgr Fac,* Noel Devine; E-mail: ndevine@rockfordpubliclibrary.org; Staff 21 (MLS 13, Non-MLS 8)
Founded 1872. Pop 150,115
Special Collections: Genealogy & Local History, bks, cemetery census, microtext
Automation Activity & Vendor Info: (Circulation) SirsiDynix
Wireless access
Function: 24/7 Electronic res, 24/7 Online cat, 3D Printer, Activity rm, Adult literacy prog, Archival coll, Audiobks via web, AV serv, Bilingual assistance for Spanish patrons, Bk reviews (Group), Bks on CD, Children's prog, Citizenship assistance, Computer training, Computers for patron use, Distance learning, E-Reserves, Electronic databases & coll, Free DVD rentals, Home delivery & serv to seniorr ctr & nursing homes, Homebound delivery serv, ILL available, Internet access, Life-long learning prog for all ages, Magazines, Meeting rooms, Microfiche/film & reading machines, Movies, Music CDs, Online cat, Online info literacy tutorials on the web & in blackboard, Outreach serv, Photocopying/Printing, Preschool outreach, Preschool reading prog, Printer for laptops & handheld devices, Prog for adults, Prog for children & young adult, Ref & res, Ref serv available, Res assist avail, Senior computer classes, Senior outreach, Serves people with intellectual disabilities, Spanish lang bks, Spoken cassettes & CDs, Story hour, Study rm, Summer reading prog, Tax forms, Teen prog, Telephone ref, Wheelchair accessible, Writing prog
Publications: African Americans in Early Rockford; Confluence (Local historical information); That Men Know So Little of Men (Local Black History)
Mem of Reaching Across Illinois Library System (RAILS)
Special Services for the Deaf - Bks on deafness & sign lang; High interest/low vocabulary bks; TDD equip
Open Mon-Thurs 9-8, Fri & Sat 9-5
Friends of the Library Group
Branches: 4
EAST, 6685 E State St, 61108, SAN 340-7268. Tel: 815-965-7606. FAX: 815-226-1538. *Br Mgr,* Michelle Vosberg
Founded 1986
Library Holdings: Bk Vols 27,773
Open Mon-Thurs 10-8, Fri & Sat 10-6
MONTAGUE, 1238 S Winnebago St, 61102-2944, SAN 340-7284. Tel: 815-965-7606, Ext 739. Administration Tel: 815-965-0866. FAX: 815-963-3264. Administration FAX: 815-987-6179. *Br Mgr,* Scharnae Black-Walker; Tel: 815-965-7606, E-mail: swalker@rockfordpubliclibrary.org
Founded 1923
Function: Activity rm, Bks on CD, Children's prog, Internet access, Life-long learning prog for all ages, Literacy & newcomer serv, Magazines, Meeting rooms, Preschool reading prog, Prog for adults, Prog for children & young adult, Spanish lang bks, Story hour, Summer reading prog, Tax forms, Teen prog
Open Mon-Thurs 10-8, Fri & Sat 10-6
ROCKTON CENTRE, 3112 N Rockton Ave, 61103, SAN 340-7349. Tel: 815-965-7606, Ext 778. FAX: 815-963-8855. *Br Mgr,* Donna Hopson; E-mail: dhopson@rockfordpubliclibrary.org
Founded 2000
Open Mon-Thurs 10-8, Fri & Sat 10-6

C ROCKFORD UNIVERSITY*, Howard Colman Library, 5050 E State St, 61108-2393. SAN 304-6079. Tel: 815-226-4000, 815-226-4035. FAX: 815-226-4084. E-mail: HowardColmanLibrary@Rockford.edu. Web Site: www.rockford.edu/academics/library. *Libr Dir, Tech Serv Librn,* Kelly E James; *Archivist, Electronic Res Librn,* Joanna Mladic; *Instrul Librn, Ref Librn,* Andy Newgren; *Circ Mgr,* Lori Erickson; *ILL Mgr,* Audrey Wilson; Staff 5 (MLS 3, Non-MLS 2)
Founded 1847. Enrl 1,200; Fac 78; Highest Degree: Master
Library Holdings: AV Mats 1,000; DVDs 500; e-books 141,000; e-journals 59,500; Bk Titles 135,000; Per Subs 190
Special Collections: Jane Addams Coll
Automation Activity & Vendor Info: (Acquisitions) Innovative Interfaces, Inc; (Cataloging) Innovative Interfaces, Inc; (Circulation) Innovative Interfaces, Inc; (Discovery) EBSCO Discovery Service; (ILL) OCLC; (OPAC) Innovative Interfaces, Inc; (Serials) Innovative Interfaces, Inc
Wireless access
Function: Computers for patron use, Electronic databases & coll, Internet access, Online cat
Mem of Reaching Across Illinois Library System (RAILS)
Partic in Consortium of Academic & Research Libraries in Illinois; Illinois Library & Information Network; Northern Illinois Learning Resources Cooperative; OCLC Online Computer Library Center, Inc
Special Services for the Blind - Aids for in-house use
Open Mon-Fri 7:45am-11pm, Sat 1-5, Sun 1-11
Restriction: Limited access for the pub, Open to students, fac, staff & alumni

S SWEDISH HISTORICAL SOCIETY OF ROCKFORD*, Erlander Home Museum Library, 404 S Third St, 61104-2013. (Mail add: PO Box 5443, 61125-0443), SAN 375-0922. Tel: 815-963-5559. FAX: 815-963-5559. Web Site: www.swedishhistorical.org. *Admin Dir,* Alix Fox
Library Holdings: Bk Vols 2,000
Special Collections: Furniture Making in Rockford Coll; Swedish Immigration Coll. Oral History
Subject Interests: Immigration, Sweden
Publications: Swedish Heritage (Annual)
Restriction: Open by appt only

GL WINNEBAGO COUNTY LAW LIBRARY, 400 W State St, Rm 300, 61101. SAN 304-6117. Tel: 815-319-4965. FAX: 815-319-4801. Web Site: www.illinois17th.com. *Librn,* Brian L Buzard; E-mail: bbuzard@17thcircuit.illinoiscourts.gov
Founded 1975
Library Holdings: Bk Vols 20,000; Per Subs 20
Special Collections: IICLE Handbooks; Illinois Law; Illinois Law School Law Reviews; ISBA Publications
Mem of Reaching Across Illinois Library System (RAILS)
Open Mon-Fri 8-5

ROCKTON

P TALCOTT FREE PUBLIC LIBRARY*, 101 E Main St, 61072. SAN 304-6125. Tel: 815-624-7511. FAX: 815-624-1176. E-mail: contact@talcottfreelibrary.com. Web Site: www.talcottfreelibrary.com. *Dir,* Megan Gove
Founded 1888. Pop 13,534; Circ 115,000
Library Holdings: AV Mats 3,028; Large Print Bks 500; Bk Titles 46,500; Bk Vols 50,000; Per Subs 100; Talking Bks 2,568
Automation Activity & Vendor Info: (Cataloging) Innovative Interfaces, Inc; (Circulation) Innovative Interfaces, Inc; (OPAC) Innovative Interfaces, Inc
Wireless access
Mem of Reaching Across Illinois Library System (RAILS)
Open Mon, Tues & Thurs 9-8, Wed & Fri 9-5:30, Sat 9-3
Friends of the Library Group

ROLLING MEADOWS

P ROLLING MEADOWS LIBRARY*, 3110 Martin Lane, 60008. SAN 304-615X. Tel: 847-259-6050. FAX: 847-259-5319. Web Site: www.rmlib.org. *Libr Dir,* David C Ruff; E-mail: david.ruff@rmlib.org; *Asst Libr Dir, Dir, Youth Serv,* Lucia Khipple; E-mail: lucia.khipple@rmlib.org; *Dir, Adult Serv,* Mary Constance Back; E-mail: mary.back@rmlib.org; *Dir of Circ,* Mary Sebela; E-mail: mary.sebela@rmlib.org; *Spec Serv Dir,* Sharon Montague; E-mail: sharon.montague@rmlib.org; Staff 14.4 (MLS 9.9, Non-MLS 4.5)

Founded 1959. Pop 24,604; Circ 381,518
Library Holdings: Audiobooks 5,242; AV Mats 18,655; CDs 19,001; DVDs 11,864; Electronic Media & Resources 1; Bk Vols 166,812; Per Subs 581
Special Collections: Rolling Meadows History, photog
Automation Activity & Vendor Info: (Acquisitions) Baker & Taylor; (Cataloging) OCLC FirstSearch; (Circulation) Innovative Interfaces, Inc; (ILL) OCLC FirstSearch; (OPAC) Innovative Interfaces, Inc; (Serials) Innovative Interfaces, Inc
Wireless access
Function: Adult bk club, After school storytime, Art exhibits, Audiobks via web, Bi-weekly Writer's Group, Bilingual assistance for Spanish patrons, Bk club(s), Bk reviews (Group), Bks on cassette, Bks on CD, CD-ROM, Children's prog, Computer training, Computers for patron use, E-Reserves, Electronic databases & coll, Free DVD rentals, Games & aids for people with disabilities, Home delivery & serv to seniorr ctr & nursing homes, Homebound delivery serv, ILL available, Internet access, Jazz prog, Music CDs, Online cat, Online ref, Orientations, Outreach serv, Outside serv via phone, mail, e-mail & web, Photocopying/Printing, Preschool outreach, Prog for adults, Prog for children & young adult, Senior computer classes, Spoken cassettes & CDs, Spoken cassettes & DVDs, Story hour, Summer reading prog, Tax forms, Telephone ref, Wheelchair accessible, Writing prog
Publications: They Took the Challenge: The Story of Rolling Meadows
Open Mon-Fri 9-9, Sat 9-5, Sun 1-5
Friends of the Library Group

ROMEOVILLE

CR LEWIS UNIVERSITY LIBRARY*, One University Pkwy, 60446. SAN 340-7403. Tel: 815-836-5300. Reference Tel: 815-836-5306. Toll Free Tel: 800-897-9000. FAX: 815-838-9456. E-mail: reflib@lewisu.edu. Web Site: www.lewisu.edu/academics/library. *Libr Dir,* Andrew Lenaghan; E-mail: lenaghan@lewisu.edu; *Circ Mgr,* Deyanira Reyes; Tel: 815-836-5307, E-mail: dreyeszavala@lewisu.edu; Staff 15 (MLS 10, Non-MLS 5)
Founded 1952. Enrl 5,000; Fac 169; Highest Degree: Doctorate
Library Holdings: Bk Vols 176,000; Per Subs 602
Special Collections: Contemporary Print Archives; Howard & Lois Adelman Regional History Coll, bound vols, ms, maps, mats, reports; I&M Canal Archives; Library of American Civilization, ultrafiche; Library of English Literatures, Part I & II, ultrafiche. US Document Depository
Subject Interests: Aviation, Bus & mgt, Nursing, Relig
Automation Activity & Vendor Info: (Acquisitions) Ex Libris Group; (Cataloging) Ex Libris Group; (Circulation) Ex Libris Group; (Course Reserve) Ex Libris Group; (ILL) Ex Libris Group; (OPAC) Ex Libris Group
Wireless access
Function: ILL available
Mem of Reaching Across Illinois Library System (RAILS)
Partic in Consortium of Academic & Research Libraries in Illinois; Illinois Library & Information Network; LIBRAS, Inc; OCLC Online Computer Library Center, Inc
Open Mon-Thurs 7:30am-10pm, Fri 7:30-5, Sat 9-5, Sun 10-10

P WHITE OAK LIBRARY DISTRICT*, Romeoville Branch, 201 W Normantown Rd, 60446. Tel: 815-886-2030. Web Site: www.whiteoaklibrary.org. *Dir,* Scott Pointon; *Asst Dir, Br Mgr,* Beverly Jean Krakovec; Tel: 815-552-4225, E-mail: bkrakovec@whiteoaklibrary.org; *Bus Mgr,* Debra Chapp; *Fac Mgr,* John Jozwiak; E-mail: jjozwiak@whiteoaklibrary.org; *IT Mgr,* Michael Pezan; *Outreach Serv Mgr,* Tina Williams; Staff 16 (MLS 9, Non-MLS 7)
Founded 1973. Pop 77,893
Automation Activity & Vendor Info: (Cataloging) SirsiDynix; (Circulation) SirsiDynix
Wireless access
Publications: Check It Out (Newsletter)
Mem of Reaching Across Illinois Library System (RAILS)
Partic in Pinnacle Library Cooperative
Open Mon-Thurs 10-8:30, Fri & Sat 10-5, Sun 1-5
Friends of the Library Group
Branches: 2
CREST HILL BRANCH, 20670 Len Kubinski Dr, Crest Hill, 60403, SAN 328-8692. Tel: 815-725-0234. *Br Mgr,* Amy Byrne-Henderson; E-mail: abyrne@whiteoaklibrary.org
Founded 1969
Open Mon-Thurs 10-8:30, Fri & Sat 10-5, Sun 1-5
Friends of the Library Group
LOCKPORT BRANCH, 121 E Eighth St, Lockport, 60441, SAN 340-5036. Tel: 815-838-0755. *Br Mgr,* Patricia Jarog; E-mail: pjarog@whiteoaklibrary.org; Staff 8 (MLS 6, Non-MLS 2)
Founded 1921
Open Mon-Thurs 10-8:30, Fri & Sat 10-5, Sun 1-5
Friends of the Library Group

ROODHOUSE

P ROODHOUSE PUBLIC LIBRARY, 220 W Franklin St, 62082. SAN 304-6176. Tel: 217-589-5123. FAX: 217-589-5123. E-mail: rhe1926@gmail.com. Web Site: roodhouselibrary.org. *Dir & Librn,* Becky Clemons; E-mail: bclemonsrh.library@gmail.com; *Asst Librn,* Carole Wells
Founded 1926. Pop 2,214; Circ 8,195
Library Holdings: Bk Vols 14,782; Per Subs 45
Wireless access
Mem of Illinois Heartland Library System
Open Mon & Tues 1-7, Wed & Thurs 12-5, Fri 9-12

ROSELLE

P ROSELLE PUBLIC LIBRARY DISTRICT, 40 S Park St, 60172-2020. SAN 304-6184. Tel: 630-529-1641. Circulation Tel: 630-529-1641, Ext 222. Reference Tel: 630-529-1641, Ext 211. Administration Tel: 630-529-1641, Ext 311. FAX: 630-529-7579. TDD: 630-529-0394. E-mail: circulation@rosellepld.org. Web Site: www.rosellepld.org. *Actg Dir, Youth Serv Mgr,* Kristen Lawson; Tel: 630-529-1641, Ext 221, E-mail: klawson@rosellepld.org; *Adult & Teen Serv Mgr,* Maureen Garzano; Tel: 630-529-1641, Ext 212, E-mail: mgarzano@rosellepld.org; *Circ Mgr,* Christy Snyders; Tel: 630-529-1641, Ext 241, E-mail: csnyders@rosellepld.org; Staff 34 (MLS 6, Non-MLS 28)
Founded 1940. Pop 22,791
Library Holdings: CDs 498; DVDs 4,089; Electronic Media & Resources 12; Bk Vols 96,811; Per Subs 248; Talking Bks 4,753; Videos 4,089
Automation Activity & Vendor Info: (OPAC) TLC (The Library Corporation); (Serials) EBSCO Online
Wireless access
Publications: Library Lights (Newsletter)
Mem of Reaching Across Illinois Library System (RAILS)
Partic in System Wide Automated Network
Open Mon-Thurs 9:30-9, Fri & Sat 9:30-5, Sun 1-5
Friends of the Library Group

ROSICLARE

P ROSICLARE MEMORIAL PUBLIC LIBRARY, 308 Main St, 62982. (Mail add: PO Box 16, 62982). Tel: 618-285-6213. FAX: 618-285-6213. E-mail: rmpl@shawneelink.net. Web Site: www.rosiclarelibrary.net. *Libr Dir,* Sharon Wiesemann; Staff 2 (Non-MLS 2)
Founded 1936. Pop 1,160; Circ 3,362
Library Holdings: Bk Vols 12,497; Per Subs 27
Wireless access
Mem of Illinois Heartland Library System
Open Mon, Wed & Fri 1-5, Tues 1-6

ROUND LAKE

P ROUND LAKE AREA PUBLIC LIBRARY DISTRICT*, 906 Hart Rd, 60073. SAN 304-6214. Tel: 847-546-7060. FAX: 847-546-7104. TDD: 847-546-7064. Web Site: www.rlalibrary.org. *Exec Dir,* James A DiDonato; Tel: 847-546-7060, Ext 127, E-mail: jdidonato@rlalibrary.org; *Asst Dir,* Marina Stevens; E-mail: mstevens@rlalibrary.org; *Admin Mgr,* Robbyn Allbee; Tel: 847-546-7060, Ext 105, E-mail: rallbee@rlalibrary.org; *Head, Adult Serv,* Rich Erikson; Tel: 847-546-7060, Ext 123, E-mail: rerikson@rlalibrary.org; *Head, Circ,* Margarita Rodriguez; Tel: 847-546-7060, Ext 115, E-mail: mrodriguez@rlalibrary.org; *Head, Outreach Serv,* Sandra Lopez; Tel: 847-546-7060, Ext 122, E-mail: slopez@rlalibrary.org; *Head, Tech Serv,* Penny McMahon; Tel: 847-546-7060, Ext 116, E-mail: pmcmahon@rlalibrary.org; *Head, Tech,* John Haliotis; E-mail: jhaliotis@rlalibrary.org; *Head, Youth Serv,* Sean Gilmartin; Tel: 847-546-7060, Ext 120, E-mail: sgilmartin@rlalibrary.org; Staff 18 (MLS 9, Non-MLS 9)
Founded 1972. Pop 40,400; Circ 270,000
Jul 2014-Jun 2015 Income $2,885,930, State $10,559, Locally Generated Income $2,746,507, Other $128,864. Mats Exp $216,196, Books $162,583, Per/Ser (Incl. Access Fees) $6,758, AV Mat $40,805, Electronic Ref Mat (Incl. Access Fees) $6,050. Sal $1,518,497
Library Holdings: Audiobooks 10,211; AV Mats 12,723; e-books 32,235; Bk Vols 141,463; Per Subs 200
Subject Interests: Spanish lang mat
Automation Activity & Vendor Info: (Acquisitions) SirsiDynix; (Cataloging) SirsiDynix; (Circulation) SirsiDynix; (ILL) OCLC; (OPAC) SirsiDynix; (Serials) SirsiDynix
Wireless access
Publications: Paige Turner (Newsletter)
Mem of Reaching Across Illinois Library System (RAILS)
Partic in Cooperative Computer Services - CCS
Special Services for the Deaf - TDD equip; TTY equip
Special Services for the Blind - Assistive/Adapted tech devices, equip & products; Bks on CD; Copier with enlargement capabilities; Home delivery serv; Large print bks; Magnifiers; PC for people with disabilities; Playaways (bks on MP3); Screen enlargement software for people with visual disabilities; Talking bk serv referral

Open Mon-Thurs 9-9, Fri & Sat 9-5, Sun 12-4
Friends of the Library Group

ROXANA

P ROXANA PUBLIC LIBRARY DISTRICT*, 200 N Central Ave, 62084-1102. SAN 304-6230. Tel: 618-254-6713. FAX: 618-254-6904. E-mail: library@roxanalibrary.org. Web Site: www.roxanalibrary.org. *Dir,* Ms Jamie Wells; E-mail: jamiewells@roxanalibrary.org; Staff 8 (MLS 1, Non-MLS 7)
Founded 1941. Pop 1,562; Circ 31,306
Library Holdings: Bks on Deafness & Sign Lang 25; Bk Vols 26,779; Per Subs 71
Special Collections: Newbery & Caldicott Award Books; Reading Rainbow
Automation Activity & Vendor Info: (Cataloging) SirsiDynix; (Circulation) SirsiDynix; (OPAC) SirsiDynix
Wireless access
Publications: Newsletter (Biannually)
Mem of Illinois Heartland Library System
Open Mon-Thurs 10-8, Fri & Sat 10-5

ROYALTON

P ROYALTON PUBLIC LIBRARY DISTRICT*, 305 S Dean St, 62983. (Mail add: PO Box 460, 62983-0460). Tel: 618-984-4463. FAX: 618-984-4463. E-mail: royaltonlibrary@frontier.com. Web Site: www.royaltonillinois.com/library.html. *Librn,* Bill McPhail; Staff 1 (Non-MLS 1)
Founded 1986. Pop 1,130; Circ 598
Library Holdings: AV Mats 50; CDs 110; Bk Titles 3,893; Per Subs 15; Videos 40
Wireless access
Mem of Illinois Heartland Library System
Open Mon, Wed & Fri 9-12 & 1-5

RUSHVILLE

P RUSHVILLE PUBLIC LIBRARY, 514 Maple Ave, 62681-1044. SAN 304-6249. Tel: 217-322-3030. FAX: 217-322-3030. E-mail: library1@adams.net. Web Site: www.rushvillepubliclibrary.weebly.com. *Libr Dir,* Amy Ambrosius; *Asst Librn,* Sandy Bullard; *Asst Librn,* Darla Kirkham; Staff 3 (MLS 1, Non-MLS 2)
Founded 1878. Pop 3,212; Circ 30,646
Library Holdings: Bk Titles 20,000; Per Subs 74
Wireless access
Special Services for the Deaf - Bks on deafness & sign lang
Open Mon-Thurs 12-6, Fri 10-6, Sat 9-1

SAINT CHARLES

S ILLINOIS YOUTH CENTER, Sam Sublett Library, 3825 Campton Hills Rd, 60175. SAN 376-0448. Tel: 630-584-0506. Web Site: www2.illinois.gov/idjj/pages/st_charles_iyc.aspx. *Librn,* Position Currently Open
Library Holdings: Bk Titles 12,000; Per Subs 14
Wireless access
Restriction: Staff & inmates only

GL KANE COUNTY LAW LIBRARY & SELF HELP LEGAL CENTER, Kane County Judicial Ctr, 2nd Flr, 37W777W IL Rte 38, 60175. Tel: 630-406-7126. Web Site: www.kclawlibrary.org. *Dir,* Halle Cox; E-mail: coxhalle@16thcircuit.illinoiscourts.gov; *Law Librn,* Ellen Schmid; E-mail: schmidellen@16thcircuit.illinoiscourts.gov; *Tech Asst,* Cynthia Lorenzo; E-mail: lorenzocynthia@16thcircuit.illinoiscourts.gov; Staff 2 (MLS 1, Non-MLS 1)
Wireless access
Function: 24/7 Online cat
Mem of Reaching Across Illinois Library System (RAILS)
Open Mon, Tues, Thurs & Fri 8:30-4:30, Wed 8:30-7

P ST CHARLES PUBLIC LIBRARY DISTRICT*, One S Sixth Ave, 60174-2105. SAN 304-6281. Tel: 630-584-0076. FAX: 630-584-3448. Administration FAX: 630-584-9262. Reference E-mail: adultref@stcharleslibrary.org. Web Site: www.scpld.org. *Dir,* Edith Craig; Tel: 630-584-0076, Ext 273, E-mail: ecraig@stcharleslibrary.org; *Asst Dir,* Myung Sung; Tel: 630-584-0076, Ext 228, E-mail: msung@stcharleslibrary.org; *Coll Mgt Librn,* Sue Pfotenhauer; Tel: 630-584-0076, Ext 220, E-mail: spfotenhauer@stcharleslibrary.org; *Reader Serv Librn,* Marlise Schiltz; Tel: 630-584-0076, Ext 270, E-mail: mschiltz@stcharleslibrary.org; *YA Librn,* Marianne Weick; Tel: 630-584-0076, Ext 223; *Youth Serv Librn,* Michele Collette; Tel: 630-584-0076, Ext 235; *Youth Serv Librn,* Valerie Verscaj; Tel: 630-584-0076, Ext 207; *Adult Serv Mgr,* Heidi Krueger; Tel: 630-584-0076, Ext 256; *Circ Serv Mgr,* Bonni Ellis; Tel: 630-584-0076, Ext 257; *Mkt & Communications Mgr,* Pam Salomone; Tel: 630-584-0076, Ext 246; *Outreach Serv Mgr,* David Kelsey; Tel: 630-584-0076, Ext 219; *Tech Serv Mgr,* Amanda Kaiser; Tel: 630-584-0076, Ext 237, E-mail: akaiser@stcharleslibrary.org; *Youth Serv Mgr,* A Denise Farrugia; Tel: 630-584-0076, Ext 236; Staff 25 (MLS 23, Non-MLS 2)
Founded 1906. Pop 55,092; Circ 1,491,873
Library Holdings: AV Mats 64,523; e-books 16,524; Large Print Bks 7,980; Bk Titles 276,362; Bk Vols 277,362; Per Subs 998
Special Collections: Adult New Reader Colls; Municipal
Subject Interests: Genealogy
Automation Activity & Vendor Info: (Acquisitions) SirsiDynix; (Cataloging) SirsiDynix; (Circulation) SirsiDynix; (ILL) SirsiDynix; (OPAC) SirsiDynix; (Serials) SirsiDynix
Wireless access
Publications: A Step Up: From Readers to Chapter Books; Action Rhymes
Mem of Reaching Across Illinois Library System (RAILS)
Partic in Libr Integrated Network Consortium; OCLC Online Computer Library Center, Inc
Special Services for the Deaf - TDD equip
Special Services for the Blind - Closed circuit TV
Open Mon-Thurs 9-9, Fri 9-8, Sat 9-5, Sun 12-5
Friends of the Library Group

SAINT ELMO

P SAINT ELMO PUBLIC LIBRARY DISTRICT*, 311 W Cumberland Rd, 62458. SAN 304-629X. Tel: 618-829-5544. FAX: 618-829-9104. E-mail: stelmolibrarians@gmail.com. Web Site: www.stelmo.lib.il.us. *Dir,* Kimberly Karnes; E-mail: stelmolibrary@gmail.com
Founded 1948. Pop 5,600; Circ 24,750
Library Holdings: Bk Vols 30,000; Per Subs 40
Wireless access
Function: Adult literacy prog
Mem of Illinois Heartland Library System
Open Mon 12-7, Tues, Wed & Fri 12-5, Thurs 4-7, Sat 10-2
Friends of the Library Group
Branches: 2
BEECHER CITY BRANCH, 108 N James St, Beecher City, 62414. Tel: 618-487-9400. *Library Contact,* Allison Buzzard
Library Holdings: Bk Vols 8,000; Per Subs 15
Open Mon 12:30-7, Tues, Wed & Fri 12:30-5, Thurs 3:30-7, Sat 9:30-1
BROWNSTOWN BRANCH, 120 W Main St, Brownstown, 62418. Tel: 618-427-3853. *Library Contact,* Ginny Wilber
Open Mon, Tues, Thurs & Fri 1-5, Wed 10-3

SAINT JOSEPH

P ST JOSEPH TOWNSHIP-SWEARINGEN MEMORIAL LIBRARY, 201 N Third, 61873. (Mail add: PO Box 259, 61873-0259), SAN 304-6303. Tel: 217-469-2159. FAX: 217-469-2159. E-mail: stjosephtownshiplibrary@gmail.com. Web Site: www.stjosephtownshiplibrary.info. *Librn,* Susan Dawn McKinney; E-mail: smckin@gmail.com; Staff 4 (MLS 1, Non-MLS 3)
Founded 1929. Pop 5,876; Circ 36,870
Apr 2020-Mar 2021 Income $167,135. Mats Exp $159,137, Books $13,721, Per/Ser (Incl. Access Fees) $1,000, AV Mat $7,677, Electronic Ref Mat (Incl. Access Fees) $5,122. Sal $92,183 (Prof $45,621)
Library Holdings: Audiobooks 2,124; CDs 875; DVDs 2,304; Electronic Media & Resources 129,002; Large Print Bks 1,297; Bk Vols 24,050; Per Subs 38
Automation Activity & Vendor Info: (Acquisitions) Innovative Interfaces, Inc; (Cataloging) Innovative Interfaces, Inc; (Circulation) Innovative Interfaces, Inc; (ILL) Innovative Interfaces, Inc; (Serials) Innovative Interfaces, Inc
Wireless access
Function: 24/7 Electronic res, 24/7 Online cat, Activity rm, Audiobks via web, AV serv, Bks on CD, Children's prog, Computers for patron use, Electronic databases & coll, Free DVD rentals, Homebound delivery serv, ILL available, Instruction & testing, Internet access, Magazines, Mango lang, Meeting rooms, Movies, Museum passes, Music CDs, Online cat, OverDrive digital audio bks, Photocopying/Printing, Preschool reading prog, Prog for adults, Prog for children & young adult, Ref serv available, Scanner, Spoken cassettes & CDs, Spoken cassettes & DVDs, Story hour, Summer reading prog, Tax forms, Teen prog, Telephone ref, Wheelchair accessible
Mem of Illinois Heartland Library System
Partic in Worldcat
Special Services for the Deaf - Bks on deafness & sign lang; Closed caption videos; Sign lang interpreter upon request for prog
Special Services for the Blind - Bks on CD; Copier with enlargement capabilities; Extensive large print coll; Free checkout of audio mat; Home delivery serv; Large print bks; Talking bk serv referral
Open Mon 1-8, Tues & Thurs 9-6, Wed 1-6, Fri 9-5, Sat 9-1
Restriction: Non-resident fee

SALEM

P BRYAN-BENNETT LIBRARY, 315 S Maple, 62881. (Mail add: PO Box 864, 62881), SAN 304-6311. Tel: 618-548-3006. FAX: 618-548-3096. Web Site: www.salembbl.lib.il.us. *Libr Dir,* Kim Keller
Founded 1909. Pop 7,485; Circ 48,567
Library Holdings: Bk Vols 30,000; Per Subs 28
Automation Activity & Vendor Info: (Acquisitions) SirsiDynix; (Cataloging) SirsiDynix; (Circulation) SirsiDynix; (Serials) SirsiDynix
Wireless access
Mem of Illinois Heartland Library System
Open Mon-Thurs 11-8, Fri & Sat 9-2
Friends of the Library Group

SANDWICH

P SANDWICH PUBLIC LIBRARY DISTRICT*, 925 S Main St, 60548-2304. SAN 304-632X. Tel: 815-786-8308. FAX: 815-786-9231. E-mail: contact@sandwichpld.org. Web Site: www.sandwichpld.org. *Dir,* Amanda Carr; Tel: 815-786-8308, E-mail: bennetta@sandwichpld.org; Staff 9 (MLS 2, Non-MLS 7)
Founded 1925. Pop 7,401; Circ 52,016
Special Collections: Local Newspaper, 1878-present, microfilm
Wireless access
Function: 24/7 Electronic res, 24/7 Online cat, Activity rm, Adult bk club, After school storytime, Home delivery & serv to seniorr ctr & nursing homes, ILL available, Photocopying/Printing, Prog for children & young adult, Summer reading prog, Tax forms
Mem of Reaching Across Illinois Library System (RAILS)
Open Mon & Wed 10-8, Tues & Thurs 10-9, Fri & Sat 10-5
Friends of the Library Group

SAUK VILLAGE

P NANCY L MCCONATHY PUBLIC LIBRARY, 21737 Jeffery Ave, 60411. SAN 304-6338. Tel: 708-757-4771. FAX: 708-757-3580. Web Site: www.at-the-library.org. *Dir,* Rosie Williams-Baig; E-mail: rwilliams-baig@at-the-library.org; *Asst Dir,* Colleen Baughman; E-mail: cbaughman@at-the-library.org
Founded 1973. Pop 10,517; Circ 66,428
Library Holdings: Bk Vols 58,000; Per Subs 42
Special Collections: Cookbooks; Motion Picture Stars Biography
Mem of Reaching Across Illinois Library System (RAILS)
Partic in System Wide Automated Network
Open Mon & Thurs 10-4:30, Tues & Wed 10-6, Fri & Sat 10-3:30

SAVANNA

P SAVANNA PUBLIC LIBRARY DISTRICT*, 326 Third St, 61074. SAN 304-6346. Tel: 815-273-3714. FAX: 815-273-4634, E-mail: savpublib@gmail.com. Web Site: savannalibrary.com. *Dir,* Mary Meyers; Staff 4 (Non-MLS 4)
Founded 1896. Pop 4,353; Circ 11,832
Library Holdings: Bk Vols 15,581; Per Subs 50
Special Collections: Savanna Times Journal, microfilm
Wireless access
Mem of Reaching Across Illinois Library System (RAILS)
Open Mon & Tues 1-7, Wed 10-5, Fri 1-5, Sat 9-1
Friends of the Library Group

SAYBROOK

P CHENEY'S GROVE TOWNSHIP LIBRARY, 204 S State St, 61770. (Mail add: PO Box 58, 61770-0058), SAN 376-7817. Tel: 309-475-6131. FAX: 309-475-6131. E-mail: cheneysgrovelibrary@gmail.com. *Librn,* Ashleigh Enghausen; *Asst Librn,* Angela Enghausen; Staff 2 (Non-MLS 2)
Pop 660
Library Holdings: Audiobooks 32; DVDs 210; Large Print Bks 276; Microforms 40; Bk Vols 15,000; Per Subs 11
Special Collections: Area Family History; Arrowsmith Newspapers 1920-1965, micro; Coins Coll; First Issue Stamps; Saybrook Newspapers 1890s-1985, micro; Township & Town History, photog; WWII Scrapbooks. Municipal Document Depository
Wireless access
Function: Bks on CD, Computers for patron use, Internet access, Magazines, Mail & tel request accepted, Microfiche/film & reading machines, Movies, Photocopying/Printing, Printer for laptops & handheld devices, Ref & res, Scanner, Spanish lang bks, Summer reading prog, Tax forms, Wheelchair accessible
Open Tues, Wed & Fri 10-12 & 1-5, Thurs 2-5, Sat 9-Noon

SCHAUMBURG

M AMERICAN VETERINARY MEDICAL ASSOCIATION LIBRARY, 1931 N Meacham Rd, 60173-4360. Toll Free Tel: 847-285-6770. FAX: 847-925-9329. *Librn/Copyright & Permissions/Archives Electronic Access,* Diane A Fagen; E-mail: dfagen@avma.org
Founded 1863
Library Holdings: AV Mats 634; DVDs 138; Bk Titles 8,524; Bk Vols 8,602; Per Subs 710; Spec Interest Per Sub 703; Videos 125
Special Collections: Veterinary History, 1877-present. Oral History
Subject Interests: Animal welfare, Food safety, Pub health, Veterinary
Wireless access
Function: Archival coll, Health sci info serv, Outside serv via phone, mail, e-mail & web, Ref serv available, Res libr
Open Mon-Fri 8-4
Restriction: Authorized personnel only, Authorized scholars by appt, Borrowing requests are handled by ILL, By permission only, Circ limited, External users must contact libr, In-house use for visitors, Non-circulating of rare bks, Not a lending libr, Private libr, Pub ref by request

P SCHAUMBURG TOWNSHIP DISTRICT LIBRARY*, 130 S Roselle Rd, 60193. SAN 340-7438. Tel: 847-985-4000. Circulation Tel: 847-923-3386. Interlibrary Loan Service Tel: 847-923-3349. Reference Tel: 847-923-3322. FAX: 847-923-3131. Web Site: www.schaumburglibrary.org. *Exec Dir,* Annie Miskewitch; Tel: 847-923-3200, E-mail: amiskewitch@stdl.org; *Dep Dir,* Jennifer Hunt; Tel: 847-923-3209, E-mail: jhunt@stdl.org; Staff 209 (MLS 30, Non-MLS 179)
Founded 1963. Pop 126,849; Circ 2,054,999
Jul 2019-Jun 2020 Income (Main & Associated Libraries) $15,820,110, State $144,561, Federal $49,569, Locally Generated Income $14,891,410, Other $734,570. Mats Exp $1,497,250, Books $793,311, AV Mat $135,572, Electronic Ref Mat (Incl. Access Fees) $568,367. Sal $9,955,915
Library Holdings: Audiobooks 10,038; AV Mats 56,392; CDs 16,271; DVDs 20,637; e-books 128,516; Large Print Bks 12,082; Microforms 32; Music Scores 1,949; Bk Titles 270,203; Bk Vols 319,756
Special Collections: Citizenship; English as a Second Language; Library of Things; Local History; World Languages
Automation Activity & Vendor Info: (Acquisitions) SirsiDynix; (Cataloging) SirsiDynix; (Circulation) SirsiDynix; (ILL) OCLC Tipasa; (Serials) SirsiDynix
Wireless access
Mem of Reaching Across Illinois Library System (RAILS)
Special Services for the Deaf - Closed caption videos; Sign lang interpreter upon request for prog; Spec interest per; Video & TTY relay via computer
Special Services for the Blind - BiFolkal kits; Computer with voice synthesizer for visually impaired persons; Home delivery serv; Large print bks; Large screen computer & software; Lending of low vision aids; Low vision equip; Magnifiers; PC for people with disabilities; Playaways (bks on MP3); Recorded bks; Ref serv; Talking bk serv referral
Open Mon-Thurs 9-8, Fri & Sat 9-5, Sun Noon-5
Branches: 2
HANOVER PARK BRANCH, 1266 Irving Park Rd, Hanover Park, 60133, SAN 373-7136. Tel: 630-372-7800. FAX: 847-923-3488. *Br Coordr,* Gail Tobin; Tel: 847-923-3470; Staff 14 (MLS 1, Non-MLS 13)
Library Holdings: Audiobooks 563; AV Mats 9,957; CDs 1,514; DVDs 5,084; Large Print Bks 349; Bk Titles 21,949; Bk Vols 22,673
Open Mon-Thurs 10-8, Fri & Sat 10-5
HOFFMAN ESTATES BRANCH, 1550 Hassell Rd, Hoffman Estates, 60169, SAN 340-7462. Tel: 847-885-3511. FAX: 847-923-3466. *Br Coordr,* John Ericson; Tel: 847-923-3456; Staff 17 (MLS 1, Non-MLS 16)
Library Holdings: Audiobooks 588; AV Mats 12,274; CDs 1,777; DVDs 7,252; Large Print Bks 971; Bk Titles 22,805; Bk Vols 23,887
Open Mon-Thurs 10-8, Fri & Sat 10-5

S SOCIETY OF ACTUARIES LIBRARY, 475 N Martingale Rd, Ste 600, 60173. SAN 329-2266. Tel: 847-706-3575. Toll Free Tel: 888-697-3900. FAX: 847-706-3599. E-mail: education@soa.org. Web Site: www.soa.org. *Digital Librn,* Dean Ruppert; E-mail: druppert@soa.org; Staff 1 (MLS 1)
Founded 1949
Library Holdings: Bk Titles 1,650; Per Subs 60
Subject Interests: Actuarial sci, Employee benefits, Health ins, Life ins, Math
Wireless access
Mem of Reaching Across Illinois Library System (RAILS)
Partic in Chicago Association of Law Libraries; OCLC Online Computer Library Center, Inc; SLA

M WOOD LIBRARY-MUSEUM OF ANESTHESIOLOGY*, 1061 American Lane, 60173. SAN 304-5331. Tel: 847-825-5586. E-mail: wlm@asahq.org. Web Site: www.woodlibrarymuseum.org. *Dir,* Matthew Toland; Tel: 847-268-9165, E-mail: m.toland@asahq.org; *Libr Spec,* Amanda Helfers; Tel: 847-268-9160, E-mail: a.helfers@asahq.org; *Curator,* Dr George Bause; E-mail: ujyc@aol.com; *Registrar,* Judith Robins; Tel: 847-268-9168, E-mail: j.robins@asahq.org; Staff 3 (MLS 3)

Founded 1933
Library Holdings: Bk Titles 13,000; Per Subs 65
Special Collections: Curare (R Gill Coll), ms; History of Anesthesia Coll; Mesmerism Coll. Oral History
Subject Interests: Anesthesiology
Automation Activity & Vendor Info: (Cataloging) Sydney
Publications: Historical Monographs; History of Anesthesia Reprint Series (Annual)
Friends of the Library Group

SCHILLER PARK

P SCHILLER PARK PUBLIC LIBRARY*, 4200 Old River Rd, 60176-1699. SAN 304-6362. Tel: 847-678-0433. FAX: 847-678-0567. Web Site: schillerparklibrary.org. *Dir,* Tina J Setzer
Founded 1962. Pop 11,189; Circ 59,594
Library Holdings: Bk Vols 80,000; Per Subs 150
Automation Activity & Vendor Info: (Circulation) Innovative Interfaces, Inc
Wireless access
Publications: Schiller Park Library PEN
Mem of Reaching Across Illinois Library System (RAILS)
Partic in System Wide Automated Network
Open Mon-Thurs 9-9, Fri & Sat 9-5

SCOTT AFB

A UNITED STATES AIR FORCE*, Scott Air Force Base Library FL4407, 375 FSS/FSDL, 510 Ward Dr, 62225-5360. SAN 340-7551. Tel: 618-256-5100. Interlibrary Loan Service Tel: 618-256-3028. FAX: 618-256-4558. E-mail: 375FSS.Library@us.af.mil. Web Site: www.375fss.com/BaseLibrary.php. *Libr Dir,* Emily Enderle; E-mail: emily.enderle@us.af.mil; Staff 2 (MLS 2)
Founded 1954
Library Holdings: Audiobooks 1,400; DVDs 3,300; Bk Vols 30,000; Per Subs 50
Special Collections: Professional Military Education Coll; Veteran Literacy Coll
Subject Interests: Mil hist
Wireless access
Function: Adult bk club, After school storytime, Art exhibits, Audio & video playback equip for onsite use, Bks on CD, CD-ROM, Children's prog, Computers for patron use, Doc delivery serv, Free DVD rentals, Govt ref serv, ILL available, Internet access, Music CDs, Online cat, Online ref, Orientations, Outside serv via phone, mail, e-mail & web, OverDrive digital audio bks, Photocopying/Printing, Preschool outreach, Prof lending libr, Prog for adults, Prog for children & young adult, Ref serv available, Scanner, Story hour, Summer reading prog, Tax forms, Teen prog, VHS videos, Wheelchair accessible
Open Mon-Thurs 10-8, Fri & Sat 10-5

SENECA

P SENECA PUBLIC LIBRARY DISTRICT*, 210 N Main St, 61360. SAN 304-6370. Tel: 815-357-6566. FAX: 815-357-6568. Web Site: www.senecalibrary.net. *Dir,* Margie Nolan; E-mail: mnolan@senecalibrary.net; *Adult Serv, Cat,* Jennifer Bilyeu; *Adult Serv, ILL,* Bonnie Anderson; *Cat, YA Serv,* Michelle Lawruk; *Children's Prog, Circ,* Ruthanne Heaton; *Circ Serv,* Karen Einhaus; *Circ,* Ruth Ann Foehringer
Founded 1938. Pop 3,843; Circ 57,250
Library Holdings: CDs 1,473; DVDs 1,845; Large Print Bks 1,247; Bk Vols 51,330; Per Subs 120; Talking Bks 1,081; Videos 942
Special Collections: Seneca LST Shipyard Coll; WW II Coll
Automation Activity & Vendor Info: (Acquisitions) PALS; (Cataloging) SirsiDynix; (Circulation) SirsiDynix
Wireless access
Function: Adult bk club, Audiobks via web, Bk club(s), Bks on cassette, Bks on CD, Children's prog, Computers for patron use, Digital talking bks, Free DVD rentals, ILL available, Internet access, Music CDs, Notary serv, Online cat, Photocopying/Printing, Prog for adults, Prog for children & young adult, Spoken cassettes & CDs, Story hour, Summer reading prog, Tax forms, Teen prog, Telephone ref, VHS videos, Wheelchair accessible
Publications: Seneca Library Newsletter (Bimonthly)
Mem of Reaching Across Illinois Library System (RAILS)
Open Mon-Thurs 9-8, Fri 9-6, Sat 9-5

SESSER

P SESSER PUBLIC LIBRARY*, 303 W Franklin St, 62884. SAN 376-1274. Tel: 618-625-6566. FAX: 618-625-6566. E-mail: sesserlibrary@yahoo.com. Web Site: www.sesser.org/education-schools-and-library. *Librn,* Leandra Wilson
Founded 1983
Library Holdings: AV Mats 45; Bk Titles 8,860; Videos 36
Mem of Illinois Heartland Library System
Open Mon-Fri 1-5, Sat 9-Noon

SHABBONA

P FLEWELLIN MEMORIAL LIBRARY, 108 W Comanche Ave, 60550. (Mail add: PO Box 190, 60550-0190), SAN 304-6389. Tel: 815-824-2079. FAX: 815-824-2708. E-mail: shabbonalibrary@gmail.com. Web Site: www.shabbonalibrary.org. *Dir,* Judy Schrott
Pop 950; Circ 16,000
Library Holdings: Bk Vols 10,000; Per Subs 80
Special Collections: Chief Shabbona Coll
Automation Activity & Vendor Info: (Cataloging) Follett Software; (Circulation) Follett Software
Mem of Reaching Across Illinois Library System (RAILS)
Open Mon-Fri 3-7, Sat 9-Noon

SHAWNEETOWN

P SHAWNEETOWN PUBLIC LIBRARY*, 320 N Lincoln Blvd E, 62984. (Mail add: PO Box 972, 62984-0972), SAN 304-6397. Tel: 618-269-3761. FAX: 618-269-3761. E-mail: shawls.lib.il.us@clearwave.com. Web Site: shawneetownpubliclibrary.org. *Libr Dir,* Trisha M Scates
Founded 1968. Pop 1,239; Circ 7,000
Library Holdings: Large Print Bks 560; Bk Vols 3,500
Subject Interests: Genealogy
Wireless access
Function: Bks on CD, Children's prog, Computers for patron use, Digital talking bks, E-Readers, Genealogy discussion group, Holiday prog, ILL available, Internet access, Magnifiers for reading, Mail & tel request accepted, Microfiche/film & reading machines, Online cat, Photocopying/Printing, Prog for adults, Prog for children & young adult, Scanner, STEM programs, Story hour, Study rm, Summer & winter reading prog, Summer reading prog, Teen prog
Mem of Illinois Heartland Library System
Open Mon & Fri 1-5, Tues-Thurs 11-5

SHEFFIELD

P SHEFFIELD PUBLIC LIBRARY*, 136 E Cook St, 61361. SAN 304-6400. Tel: 815-454-2628. FAX: 815-454-8030. E-mail: sheffieldlib@yahoo.com. Web Site: sheffieldillinoispubliclibrary.com. *Librn,* Sue Lanxon; *Asst Librn,* Lindsey Donaway
Founded 1896. Pop 946; Circ 3,120
Library Holdings: Bk Vols 10,300; Per Subs 29
Special Collections: Lincoln
Subject Interests: Hist
Wireless access
Function: Children's prog, Homebound delivery serv, ILL available, Internet access, Magnifiers for reading, Mail & tel request accepted, Photocopying/Printing, Spoken cassettes & CDs, Summer reading prog, Telephone ref, VHS videos
Mem of Reaching Across Illinois Library System (RAILS)
Open Mon & Tues 9-5, Wed 9-6, Fri 9-1, Sat 9-Noon

SHELBYVILLE

P SHELBYVILLE PUBLIC LIBRARY, 154 N Broadway St, 62565. SAN 304-6419. Tel: 217-774-4432. FAX: 217-774-2634. E-mail: staff@shelbyvillelibrary.org. Web Site: www.shelbyvillelibrary.org. *Dir,* Monica Cameron
Founded 1902. Pop 5,259; Circ 68,219
Library Holdings: Bk Vols 28,000
Special Collections: 144 rolls of local & misc newspapers on microfilm dating 1812 to present
Subject Interests: Annual reports, Genealogy, Hist, Rare bks
Mem of Illinois Heartland Library System
Partic in Association for Rural & Small Libraries; Illinois Library & Information Network
Open Mon-Fri 9-7, Sat 9-1

SHELDON

P SHELDON PUBLIC LIBRARY DISTRICT*, 125 N Fifth, 60966. (Mail add: PO Box 370, 60966-0370), SAN 304-6427. Tel: 815-429-3521. FAX: 815-429-3804. E-mail: sheldonpld@yahoo.com. *Dir,* Tammy Rice; E-mail: tamzr@hotmail.com
Founded 1917. Pop 2,082; Circ 5,339
Library Holdings: Bk Vols 12,151; Per Subs 30
Mem of Illinois Heartland Library System
Open Mon-Fri 1-6:30, Sat 10-3

SHERIDAN

S ILLINOIS DEPARTMENT OF CORRECTIONS*, Sheridan Correctional Center Library, 4017 E 2603 Rd, 60551. SAN 376-1010. Tel: 815-496-2181. Web Site: www2.illinois.gov/idoc/facilities/Pages/sheridancorrectionalcenter.aspx. *Library Contact,* Gail Sessler
Library Holdings: Bk Vols 5,000
Open Mon-Fri 8-4

P ROBERT W ROWE PUBLIC LIBRARY DISTRICT*, 120 E Si Johnson Ave, 60551. (Mail add: PO Box 358, 60551-0358), SAN 375-9741, Tel: 815-496-2031. FAX: 815-496-2067. Web Site: rwrlibrary.org. *Librn,* Debby Smith; E-mail: dsmith@rwrlibrary.org; Staff 1 (Non-MLS 1)
Founded 1991. Pop 4,428; Circ 14,821
Library Holdings: Bk Titles 17,000; Per Subs 40
Automation Activity & Vendor Info: (Cataloging) SirsiDynix; (Circulation) SirsiDynix; (OPAC) SirsiDynix
Wireless access
Mem of Reaching Across Illinois Library System (RAILS)
Open Mon, Thurs & Fri 10-5, Tues & Wed 1-8, Sat 10-2
Friends of the Library Group

SHERMAN

P SHERMAN PUBLIC LIBRARY DISTRICT, 2100 E Andrew Rd, 62684-9676. Tel: 217-496-2496. FAX: 217-496-2357. E-mail: shermanlibrary@casscomm.com. Web Site: www.shermanlibrary.net. *Libr Dir,* Rachel Kocis
Founded 1995. Circ 3,590
Library Holdings: Bk Vols 22,500; Per Subs 20
Automation Activity & Vendor Info: (Cataloging) Innovative Interfaces, Inc. - Polaris; (Circulation) Innovative Interfaces, Inc. - Polaris
Wireless access
Mem of Illinois Heartland Library System
Open Mon-Thurs 8-8, Fri 8-5, Sat 9-2
Friends of the Library Group

SHERRARD

P SHERRARD PUBLIC LIBRARY DISTRICT*, 201 Fifth Ave, 61281. (Mail add: PO Box 345, 61281-0345), SAN 376-1223. Tel: 309-593-2178. FAX: 309-593-2179. E-mail: circstaff@sherrardlibrary.org. Web Site: www.sherrardlibrary.org. *Dir,* Bobbi Jackson; E-mail: director@sherrardlibrary.org; Staff 1 (MLS 1)
Founded 1976. Pop 7,288; Circ 15,000
Library Holdings: AV Mats 1,493; Large Print Bks 94; Bk Vols 18,910; Per Subs 86; Talking Bks 425
Subject Interests: Christian fiction
Partic in RiverShare Libraries
Open Mon-Fri 10-8, Sat 9-Noon
Friends of the Library Group

SHOREWOOD

P SHOREWOOD-TROY PUBLIC LIBRARY DISTRICT, 650 Deerwood Dr, 60404. SAN 321-0278. Tel: 815-725-1715. FAX: 815-725-1722. TDD: 815-725-2173. Reference E-mail: reference@shorewoodtroylibrary.org. Web Site: shorewoodtroylibrary.org. *Dir,* Jennie Cisna Mills; E-mail: jmills@shorewoodtroylibrary.org; *Asst Dir, Ch Mgr,* Shalyn Rodriguez; *Head, Circ,* Samantha Wilhoyt; *Adult & Teen Serv, Outreach Librn,* Becky Goode; *Ch Serv, Outreach Librn,* Mara Barbel; *Adult & Teen Serv, Tech Mgr,* Julie Hornberger; Staff 11 (MLS 4, Non-MLS 7)
Founded 1975. Pop 19,335; Circ 169,190
Library Holdings: Bk Titles 52,529
Automation Activity & Vendor Info: (Cataloging) Innovative Interfaces, Inc. - Polaris
Wireless access
Mem of Reaching Across Illinois Library System (RAILS)
Partic in Pinnacle Library Cooperative
Open Mon-Thurs 9-8, Fri & Sat 9-5
Friends of the Library Group

SIDELL

P SIDELL DISTRICT LIBRARY*, 101 E Market St, 61876. (Mail add: PO Box 19, 61876-0019), SAN 304-6443. Tel: 217-288-9031. FAX: 217-288-9031. E-mail: sidelldist.library@aol.com. *Dir,* Mary Lue Tate; E-mail: mtate14780@aol.com
Founded 1947. Pop 2,445; Circ 16,000
Library Holdings: Bk Vols 9,389; Per Subs 57
Subject Interests: Fiction, Relig
Wireless access
Mem of Illinois Heartland Library System
Open Mon, Wed, Thurs & Sat 9-11:45 & 12:30-5

SIDNEY

P SIDNEY COMMUNITY LIBRARY*, 217 S David, 61877. (Mail add: PO Box 395, 61877), SAN 304-6451. Tel: 217-688-2332. E-mail: sidneylibrary@yahoo.com. *Librn,* Rosemary McCarrey
Founded 1969. Pop 1,233; Circ 10,853
Library Holdings: AV Mats 181; DVDs 1,000; Bk Vols 7,457; Per Subs 16
Automation Activity & Vendor Info: (Acquisitions) OCLC
Wireless access
Mem of Illinois Heartland Library System
Open Mon-Fri 9-12 & 4-7, Sat 9-12

SILVIS

M GENESIS MEDICAL CENTER, ILLINI CAMPUS*, Perlmutter Library of the Health Sciences, 855 Illini Dr, Ste 102, 61282. SAN 329-2231. Tel: 309-281-5110. FAX: 309-281-5119. E-mail: library@genesishealth.com. *Librn,* Karlene Campbell; E-mail: campbellka@genesishealth.com; Staff 1 (Non-MLS 1)
Library Holdings: Bk Titles 1,600; Per Subs 300
Subject Interests: Consumer health, Nursing, Nutrition
Wireless access
Mem of Reaching Across Illinois Library System (RAILS)
Partic in Health Science Libraries of Illinois; Illinois Library & Information Network; National Network of Libraries of Medicine Region 6
Open Mon-Fri 7:30-4

SKOKIE

CR HEBREW THEOLOGICAL COLLEGE*, Saul Silber Memorial Library, 7135 N Carpenter Rd, 60077-3263. SAN 340-7640. Tel: 847-982-2500. FAX: 847-674-6381. Web Site: www.htc.edu/libraries/saul-silber-memorial-library. *Head Librn,* Dr Michael Verderame; E-mail: verderame@htc.edu; Staff 2 (MLS 1, Non-MLS 1)
Founded 1922
Library Holdings: Bk Vols 70,000; Per Subs 182
Special Collections: Bet Midrash Coll; Halakah (Rabbi Simon H Album Coll); Lazar Holocaust Coll; Rev M Newman Coll, per; Woman in Judaism (Moses Wolfe Coll)
Subject Interests: Biblical studies, Jewish hist & lit
Wireless access
Partic in Asn of Jewish Librs
Open Mon-Thurs 9-3
Friends of the Library Group
Departmental Libraries:
BLITSTEIN INSTITUTE, 2606 W Touhy Ave, Chicago, 60645. Tel: 773-973-0241. FAX: 773-973-1627. *Librn,* Sarah Burnstein; E-mail: sburnstein@htc.edu; Staff 2 (MLS 1, Non-MLS 1)
Library Holdings: Bk Vols 7,200
Special Collections: Dr Esther Levy Robinson Coll
Subject Interests: Judaica (lit or hist of Jews)
Friends of the Library Group

C KNOWLEDGE SYSTEMS INSTITUTE LIBRARY, (Formerly Knowledge Systems Institute), 3420 Main St, 60076. SAN 376-0103. Tel: 847-679-3135. FAX: 847-679-3166. E-mail: ksilibrary@ksi.edu. Web Site: www.ksibootcamps.org.
Founded 1975. Enrl 220; Fac 13; Highest Degree: Master
Library Holdings: Bk Vols 2,213; Per Subs 37
Subject Interests: Computer sci, Health informatics
Wireless access
Mem of Reaching Across Illinois Library System (RAILS)
Restriction: Open to students, fac & staff

M NORTHSHORE UNIVERSITY HEALTHSYSTEM*, Carl Davis Jr, MD Medical Library, 9600 Gross Point Rd, 60076. SAN 373-1952. Tel: 847-570-2665. FAX: 847-570-2926. E-mail: webster@northshore.org. Web Site: www.northshore.org.
Founded 1970
Library Holdings: Bk Titles 1,450; Per Subs 77
Wireless access
Function: ILL available
Partic in Metro Consortium of Chicago
Restriction: Staff use only

J OAKTON COMMUNITY COLLEGE LIBRARY*, Ray Hartstein Campus, 7701 N Lincoln Ave, Rm A200, 60076-2895. Circulation Tel: 847-635-1432. Reference Tel: 847-635-1474. FAX: 847-635-1449. Web Site: www.oakton.edu/library. *Asst Dean of Libr,* Jacob Jeremiah; E-mail: jjeremia@oakton.edu; Staff 4 (MLS 1, Non-MLS 3)
Founded 1970. Highest Degree: Associate
Library Holdings: AV Mats 105; Bk Titles 15,000; Bk Vols 21,000; Per Subs 60

Automation Activity & Vendor Info: (Acquisitions) Ex Libris Group; (Cataloging) Ex Libris Group; (Circulation) Ex Libris Group; (Course Reserve) Ex Libris Group; (ILL) Ex Libris Group; (Media Booking) Ex Libris Group; (OPAC) Ex Libris Group; (Serials) Ex Libris Group
Wireless access
Open Mon-Thurs (Fall & Spring) 7:30am-9pm, Fri 7:30-7:30, Sat 9-3

S PORTLAND CEMENT ASSOCIATION*, Library Services, 5420 Old Orchard Rd, 60077-1083. SAN 340-7705. Tel: 847-972-9174. FAX: 847-966-6221. E-mail: library@cement.org. Web Site: www.cement.org/referencelibrary. *Sr Dir,* Rick Bohan; E-mail: rbohen@cement.org; Staff 3 (MLS 2, Non-MLS 1)
Founded 1950
Library Holdings: Bk Vols 105,000; Per Subs 200
Special Collections: ASTM Standards; Foreign Literature Studies; Limited Bibliographies; Occupational Health & Safety Coll; PCA Publications (out-of-print); Translations; TRB Coll
Subject Interests: Cement, Concrete, Construction
Automation Activity & Vendor Info: (Acquisitions) Sydney; (Cataloging) Sydney; (Circulation) Sydney; (OPAC) Sydney; (Serials) Sydney
Publications: Library Update (bimonthly newsletter); Subject Bibliographies
Partic in Illinois Library & Information Network
Open Mon-Fri 8-4

P SKOKIE PUBLIC LIBRARY, 5215 Oakton St, 60077-3680. SAN 304-6516. Tel: 847-673-7774. FAX: 847-673-7797. TDD: 847-673-8926. E-mail: tellus@skokielibrary.info. Web Site: skokielibrary.info. *Dir,* Richard Kong; E-mail: rkong@skokielibrary.info; *Dep Dir,* Laura McGrath; *Access Serv Mgr,* Annabelle Mortensen; *Coms & Multimedia Engagement Mgr,* Jane Hanna; *Commun Engagement Mgr,* Nancy Kim Phillips; *Human Res Mgr,* Beth Dostert; *Learning & Dev Mgr,* Leah White; *Mgr, Info Tech,* Mark Kadzie; *Mgr, Learning Experience,* Amy Koester; *Patron Serv Mgr,* Lynnanne Pearson; *Teen Serv Mgr,* Laurel Dooley; *Youth Serv Mgr,* Shelley Sutherland; Staff 110 (MLS 40, Non-MLS 70)
Founded 1941. Pop 64,784; Circ 1,017,155
May 2020-Apr 2021 Income $13,365,829, State $481,918, City $12,276,686, Federal $30,011, Locally Generated Income $437,836. Mats Exp $1,369,887, Books $262,082, Per/Ser (Incl. Access Fees) $17,940, Other Print Mats $30,934, AV Mat $112,527, Electronic Ref Mat (Incl. Access Fees) $536,291. Sal $6,478,389
Library Holdings: Audiobooks 7,766; AV Mats 73,883; Bks on Deafness & Sign Lang 54; Braille Volumes 60; CDs 14,668; DVDs 48,364; e-books 75,552; e-journals 21,978; Electronic Media & Resources 987,237; Large Print Bks 6,958; Microforms 2,801; Music Scores 602; Bk Titles 200,507; Bk Vols 262,082; Per Subs 325
Special Collections: Local History Digitized Coll
Subject Interests: Am lit, Art & archit, Bus & mgt, English lit, Foreign lang, Holocaust
Automation Activity & Vendor Info: (Acquisitions) Innovative Interfaces, Inc; (Cataloging) Innovative Interfaces, Inc; (Circulation) Innovative Interfaces, Inc; (ILL) Innovative Interfaces, Inc; (OPAC) BiblioCommons; (Serials) Innovative Interfaces, Inc
Wireless access
Function: 24/7 Electronic res, 24/7 Online cat, 3D Printer, Activity rm, Adult bk club, After school storytime, Archival coll, Art exhibits, Art programs, Audio & video playback equip for onsite use, Audiobks on Playaways & MP3, Audiobks via web, AV serv, Bilingual assistance for Spanish patrons, Bk club(s), Bk reviews (Group), Bks on CD, CD-ROM, Children's prog, Citizenship assistance, Computer training, Computers for patron use, Distance learning, E-Readers, E-Reserves, Electronic databases & coll, Equip loans & repairs, Family literacy, For res purposes, Free DVD rentals, Holiday prog, Homebound delivery serv, Homework prog, ILL available, Internet access, Life-long learning prog for all ages, Magazines, Makerspace, Mango lang, Meeting rooms, Microfiche/film & reading machines, Movies, Museum passes, Music CDs, Online cat, Online ref, Outreach serv, Outside serv via phone, mail, e-mail & web, OverDrive digital audio bks, Photocopying/Printing, Preschool outreach, Printer for laptops & handheld devices, Prog for adults, Prog for children & young adult, Ref & res, Ref serv available, Res assist avail, Scanner, Senior computer classes, Senior outreach, Serves people with intellectual disabilities, Spanish lang bks, STEM programs, Story hour, Study rm, Summer & winter reading prog, Tax forms, Teen prog, Telephone ref, Visual arts prog, Wheelchair accessible, Winter reading prog, Workshops, Writing prog
Publications: Skokie Public Library Newsletter (Bimonthly)
Mem of Reaching Across Illinois Library System (RAILS)
Special Services for the Deaf - Assisted listening device; Bks on deafness & sign lang; High interest/low vocabulary bks; Sign lang interpreter upon request for prog; TDD equip
Special Services for the Blind - Assistive/Adapted tech devices, equip & products; Braille bks; Closed circuit TV; Large print bks; VisualTek equip
Open Mon-Fri 9-9, Sat 9-6, Sun 12-6
Bookmobiles: 1

R TEMPLE JUDEA MIZPAH LIBRARY*, 8610 Niles Center Rd, 60077. SAN 304-6532. Tel: 847-676-1566. FAX: 847-676-1579. E-mail: tjm@templejm.org. Web Site: www.templejm.org. *Librn,* Judy Duesenberg
Library Holdings: Bk Vols 4,000
Special Collections: Jewish Authors, bks, publications

SMITHTON

P SMITHTON PUBLIC LIBRARY DISTRICT*, 109 S Main, 62285-1707. SAN 376-4958. Tel: 618-233-8057. FAX: 618-233-3670. E-mail: smithtonpl@smithtonpl.org. Web Site: www.smithtonpl.org. *Dir,* Jenna Dauer; *Asst Librn,* Linda Hill; Staff 7 (MLS 1, Non-MLS 6)
Founded 1988. Pop 4,807
Automation Activity & Vendor Info: (Cataloging) Innovative Interfaces, Inc; (Circulation) Innovative Interfaces, Inc; (OPAC) Innovative Interfaces, Inc
Wireless access
Function: 24/7 Electronic res, 24/7 Online cat, Accelerated reader prog, Adult bk club, Audiobks on Playaways & MP3, Bks on CD, Children's prog, Computers for patron use, Electronic databases & coll, ILL available, Internet access, Laminating, Magazines, Movies, Music CDs, Online cat, Preschool reading prog, Prog for adults, Prog for children & young adult, Scanner, Story hour, Summer & winter reading prog, Tax forms
Mem of Illinois Heartland Library System
Open Mon-Thurs 9-8, Fri 9-6, Sat 9-5
Friends of the Library Group

SOMONAUK

P SOMONAUK PUBLIC LIBRARY DISTRICT*, 700 E LaSalle St, 60552. SAN 304-6540. Tel: 815-498-2440. FAX: 815-498-2135. Web Site: somonauklibrary.org. *Libr Dir,* Julie Harte; E-mail: jharte@somonauklibrary.org; Staff 1 (MLS 1)
Founded 1921. Pop 9,437
Library Holdings: AV Mats 5,000; Bks on Deafness & Sign Lang 50; High Interest/Low Vocabulary Bk Vols 1,500; Large Print Bks 500; Bk Titles 32,000; Bk Vols 40,000; Per Subs 90,000; Spec Interest Per Sub 45; Talking Bks 450
Subject Interests: Native Americans
Automation Activity & Vendor Info: (Circulation) Infor Library & Information Solutions
Wireless access
Function: ILL available
Mem of Reaching Across Illinois Library System (RAILS)
Open Mon-Thurs 10-8, Fri 10-6, Sat 10-5, Sun (Sept-May) 1-5
Friends of the Library Group

SOUTH BELOIT

P SOUTH BELOIT PUBLIC LIBRARY*, 630 Blackhawk Blvd, 61080-1919. SAN 304-6559. Tel: 815-389-2495. FAX: 815-389-0871. E-mail: info@southbeloitlibrary.com. Web Site: www.southbeloitlibrary.com. *Dir,* Doreen Dalman; E-mail: ddalman@southbeloitlibrary.com; Staff 2 (Non-MLS 2)
Founded 1952. Pop 7,892; Circ 16,257
Library Holdings: Bk Titles 21,727; Per Subs 78
Special Collections: Newbery Award & Coretta Scott King Award Books
Wireless access
Mem of Reaching Across Illinois Library System (RAILS)
Open Mon & Thurs 9-8, Tues & Wed 9-6, Fri 9-5, Sat 9-1

SOUTH HOLLAND

P SOUTH HOLLAND PUBLIC LIBRARY*, 16250 Wausau Ave, 60473. SAN 304-6575. Tel: 708-527-3150. FAX: 708-331-6557. E-mail: library@southhollandlibrary.org. Web Site: www.shlibrary.org. *Libr Dir,* Christyn Rayford; Tel: 708-527-3104, E-mail: christyn@southhollandlibrary.org; Staff 36 (MLS 12, Non-MLS 24)
Founded 1961. Pop 22,030; Circ 125,394
May 2017-Apr 2018 Income $2,131,792, State $159,979, City $1,900,354, Federal $1,075, Locally Generated Income $70,384. Mats Exp $1,988,547, Books $77,561, Per/Ser (Incl. Access Fees) $8,457, AV Mat $42,649, Electronic Ref Mat (Incl. Access Fees) $34,376. Sal $1,055,909
Library Holdings: AV Mats 7,252; DVDs 14,585; e-books 107,331; Electronic Media & Resources 30,110; Bk Titles 80,031; Per Subs 133
Automation Activity & Vendor Info: (Cataloging) SirsiDynix-WorkFlows; (Circulation) SirsiDynix-WorkFlows; (Discovery) EBSCO Discovery Service; (ILL) SirsiDynix-WorkFlows; (OPAC) SirsiDynix-Enterprise; (Serials) SirsiDynix-WorkFlows
Wireless access
Function: 24/7 Electronic res, 24/7 Online cat, 3D Printer, Activity rm, Adult bk club, Audiobks on Playaways & MP3, Audiobks via web, Bilingual assistance for Spanish patrons, Bk club(s), Bks on CD, Chess club, Children's prog, Computer training, Computers for patron use, Doc delivery serv, E-Readers, E-Reserves, Electronic databases & coll, Free DVD rentals, Holiday prog, Home delivery & serv to seniorr ctr & nursing

homes, Homework prog, ILL available, Instruction & testing, Internet access, Life-long learning prog for all ages, Magazines, Magnifiers for reading, Mail & tel request accepted, Mango lang, Meeting rooms, Movies, Museum passes, Music CDs, Notary serv, Online cat, Outreach serv, Outside serv via phone, mail, e-mail & web, OverDrive digital audio bks, Photocopying/Printing, Preschool outreach, Preschool reading prog, Printer for laptops & handheld devices, Prog for adults, Prog for children & young adult, Ref & res, Ref serv available, Scanner, Senior computer classes, Senior outreach, Serves people with intellectual disabilities, Spanish lang bks, Spoken cassettes & CDs, Spoken cassettes & DVDs, STEM programs, Story hour, Study rm, Summer & winter reading prog, Summer reading prog, Tax forms, Teen prog, Telephone ref, Wheelchair accessible, Winter reading prog
Mem of Reaching Across Illinois Library System (RAILS)
Partic in System Wide Automated Network
Special Services for the Deaf - Bks on deafness & sign lang; Closed caption videos
Special Services for the Blind - Accessible computers; Aids for in-house use; Assistive/Adapted tech devices, equip & products; Bks on CD; Copier with enlargement capabilities; Extensive large print coll; Large print bks; Lending of low vision aids; Magnifiers; Playaways (bks on MP3); Rental typewriters & computers; Screen enlargement software for people with visual disabilities; Screen reader software; Talking bk & rec for the blind cat
Open Mon-Thurs 10-9, Fri 10-6, Sat 10-5

J SOUTH SUBURBAN COLLEGE LIBRARY*, 15800 S State St, Rm 1249, 60473-1200. SAN 304-6591. Tel: 708-210-5751. Reference Tel: 708-210-5750. FAX: 708-210-5755. Web Site: ssc.edu/services/library. *Dean of Libr,* Devon Powell; E-mail: dpowell@ssc.edu; *Librn,* Sangeeta Kumar; Tel: 708-596-2000, Ext 2574, E-mail: skumar@ssc.edu; *Librn,* Marilyn Wells; Tel: 708-596-2000, Ext 2239, E-mail: mwells@ssc.edu; Staff 7 (MLS 3, Non-MLS 4)
Founded 1927. Enrl 6,211; Fac 364; Highest Degree: Associate
Library Holdings: AV Mats 200; Bks on Deafness & Sign Lang 15; CDs 61; e-journals 1,500; Electronic Media & Resources 10; Music Scores 461; Bk Titles 24,000; Per Subs 55; Videos 800
Special Collections: US Document Depository
Subject Interests: Nursing
Automation Activity & Vendor Info: (Acquisitions) Baker & Taylor; (Serials) EBSCO Online
Wireless access
Function: AV serv, Computers for patron use, Electronic databases & coll, Govt ref serv, ILL available, Instruction & testing, Literacy & newcomer serv, Magnifiers for reading, Music CDs, Online cat, Orientations, Photocopying/Printing, Ref serv available, Telephone ref, VHS videos, Wheelchair accessible
Mem of Reaching Across Illinois Library System (RAILS)
Partic in Consortium of Academic & Research Libraries in Illinois
Special Services for the Blind - Magnifiers
Open Mon-Thurs (Fall & Spring) 8am-9pm, Fri 8-4; Mon-Thurs (Summer) 8-8

SPARTA

P SPARTA PUBLIC LIBRARY*, 211 W Broadway, 62286. SAN 304-6613. Tel: 618-443-5014. FAX: 618-443-2952. E-mail: spartaillinoislibrary@gmail.com. Web Site: www.spartapubliclibrary.com. *Admin Dir,* Susan Colbert; *Circ,* June Cohoon; *Circ,* Kyle Daniels; *Circ,* Jenny Hobeck; E-mail: jennyhobeck@hotmail.com; *Circ,* Lynette Jalivay; *Circ,* Theresa Simpson; *Circ,* Dara Wilson; Staff 7 (Non-MLS 7)
Founded 1944. Pop 4,853; Circ 45,240
Library Holdings: Bks on Deafness & Sign Lang 10; Bk Vols 39,506; Per Subs 292
Subject Interests: Local hist
Automation Activity & Vendor Info: (Cataloging) Horizon; (Circulation) Horizon
Wireless access
Function: Telephone ref
Mem of Illinois Heartland Library System
Special Services for the Deaf - Bks on deafness & sign lang
Open Mon, Tues & Thurs Noon-7, Wed & Fri 10-5, Sat 10-4
Friends of the Library Group

SPRING VALLEY

P RICHARD A MAUTINO MEMORIAL LIBRARY, 215 E Cleveland St, 61362. SAN 304-6621. Tel: 815-663-4741. FAX: 815-663-1040. E-mail: mautinolibrary@yahoo.com. Web Site: spring-valley.il.us/library. *Dir,* Tari Sangston; *Ch Serv,* Jeri Loebach
Founded 1912. Pop 5,558; Circ 29,991
May 2016-Apr 2017. Mats Exp $28,500, Books $24,000, Per/Ser (Incl. Access Fees) $3,000, Electronic Ref Mat (Incl. Access Fees) $1,500. Sal $63,750
Library Holdings: Audiobooks 1,043; CDs 473; DVDs 1,446; Bk Titles 28,731; Per Subs 33; Videos 95
Special Collections: NewsTribune, early 1900's to present; Spring Valley Gazette & Bureau County Republican, early 1900's to present. Oral History
Automation Activity & Vendor Info: (Acquisitions) Innovative Interfaces, Inc - Sierra; (Cataloging) Innovative Interfaces, Inc - Sierra; (Circulation) Innovative Interfaces, Inc - Sierra; (OPAC) Innovative Interfaces, Inc - Sierra
Wireless access
Mem of Reaching Across Illinois Library System (RAILS)
Special Services for the Deaf - TDD equip
Special Services for the Blind - Bks on CD
Open Mon-Wed 10-6, Thurs 2-6, Fri 10-5, Sat 9-2

SPRINGFIELD

S HANSON PROFESSIONAL SERVICES INC*, Technical Library, 1525 S Sixth St, 62703. SAN 304-663X. Tel: 217-747-9241. FAX: 217-747-9416. E-mail: library@hanson-inc.com. Web Site: www.hanson-inc.com. *Librn,* April Becker; Staff 1 (MLS 1)
Founded 1975
Library Holdings: Bk Titles 16,002; Per Subs 278
Special Collections: Geology (Illinois Coll); Illinois Topo, maps; Walter E Hanson Coll
Subject Interests: Archit, Civil engr, Electrical engr, Mechanical engr
Automation Activity & Vendor Info: (Cataloging) Horizon; (Circulation) Horizon; (ILL) OCLC Online; (OPAC) Horizon; (Serials) Horizon
Wireless access
Mem of Illinois Heartland Library System
Partic in Capital Area Health Consortium; OCLC Online Computer Library Center, Inc
Restriction: Staff use only

G ILLINOIS AUDITOR GENERAL LIBRARY*, 740 E Ash St, 62703. SAN 326-9914. Tel: 217-782-3648. E-mail: audgen@auditor.illinois.gov. Web Site: www.auditor.illinois.gov. *Library Contact,* Lisa McQueen
Library Holdings: Bk Titles 2,600
Special Collections: Financial-Compliance & Performance Audits 1974-present
Partic in Illinois Library & Information Network
Open Mon-Fri 8-5

G ILLINOIS DEPARTMENT OF TRANSPORTATION, Policy & Research Center Library, 320 Harry Hanley Bldg, 2300 S Dirksen Pkwy, 62764-0001. SAN 326-9957. Tel: 217-524-3834, 217-782-6680. E-mail: dot.policyresearchcenter@illinois.gov. *Dir,* Karen Waters; Staff 1 (MLS 1)
Founded 1965
Library Holdings: Bk Vols 18,000; Per Subs 271
Subject Interests: Hwy engr, Transportation
Automation Activity & Vendor Info: (Cataloging) OCLC Connexion; (ILL) OCLC FirstSearch; (OPAC) Innovative Interfaces, Inc
Function: ILL available
Publications: Information Connection
Mem of Illinois Heartland Library System
Partic in Midwest Transportation Knowledge Network; OCLC Online Computer Library Center, Inc
Restriction: Use of others with permission of librn

G ILLINOIS ENVIRONMENTAL PROTECTION AGENCY LIBRARY*, 1021 N Grand Ave E, 62702-4072. (Mail add: PO Box 19276, 62794-9276), SAN 321-897X. Tel: 217-782-9691. FAX: 217-524-4916. Web Site: www2.illinois.gov/epa/about-us/Pages/Library-Services.aspx. *Librn I,* Gloria Hendrickson; E-mail: gloria.hendrickson@illinois.gov; Staff 1 (MLS 1)
Founded 1970
Library Holdings: Bk Titles 25,000; Per Subs 50
Subject Interests: Environ law, Environ protection
Mem of Illinois Heartland Library System
Partic in Capital Area Health Consortium; Illinois Library & Information Network; OCLC Online Computer Library Center, Inc
Open Mon-Fri 8:30-5

S ILLINOIS HISTORIC PRESERVATION AGENCY*, Abraham Lincoln Presidential Library, 112 N Sixth St, 62701. SAN 304-6656. Tel: 217-558-8844. FAX: 217-785-6250. Web Site: www.alplm.org. *Dir of Develop,* Phyllis Evans; E-mail: pevans@alplm.org; *Newspaper Librn,* Teri Barnett; Tel: 217-558-0126, E-mail: teri.barnett@illinois.gov; *Ref Librn,* Meghan Harmon; Tel: 217-524-6024, E-mail: meghan.harmon@illinois.gov; Staff 35 (MLS 9, Non-MLS 26)
Founded 1889
Library Holdings: AV Mats 400,000; Microforms 99,000; Bk Titles 199,000; Bk Vols 350,000; Per Subs 1,200
Special Collections: Illinois Newspapers; Lincolniana
Subject Interests: Civil War, Illinois hist, Mormons

Automation Activity & Vendor Info: (Cataloging) Horizon; (ILL) OCLC; (OPAC) Horizon
Wireless access
Function: Res libr
Publications: Journal of Illinois History (Quarterly)
Mem of Reaching Across Illinois Library System (RAILS)
Partic in Consortium of Academic & Research Libraries in Illinois; Illinois Library & Information Network; OCLC Online Computer Library Center, Inc
Open Mon-Fri 9-5
Restriction: Non-circulating to the pub

P ILLINOIS STATE LIBRARY*, Gwendolyn Brooks Bldg, 300 S Second St, 62701-9713. SAN 304-6672. Tel: 217-782-2994, 217-785-6500. Interlibrary Loan Service Tel: 217-782-7573. Reference Tel: 217-785-1497. Toll Free Tel: 800-665-5576 (IL only). FAX: 217-785-4326. TDD: 800-965-0748. E-mail: islinformationline@ilsos.net. Web Site: www.cyberdriveillinois.com/departments/library/home.html. *Dep Dir,* Greg McCormick; Tel: 217-782-3504, E-mail: gmccormick@ilsos.net; *Assoc Dir, Grants & Prog,* Debra Aggertt; Tel: 217-524-5867, E-mail: daggertt@ilsos.net; *Assoc Dir, Libr Automation & Tech,* Suzanne Schriar; Tel: 217-785-1533, E-mail: sschriar@ilsos.net; *Assoc Dir, Libr Operations,* Kathryn Dauksza; Tel: 217-785-0052, E-mail: kdauksza@ilsos.net; *ILL Librn,* Eric Edwards; Tel: 217-558-1928, E-mail: eedwards@ilsos.net; *Communications Mgr,* Kyle Peebles; Tel: 217-558-4029, E-mail: kpeebles@ilsos.net; *Govt Doc Mgr,* Blaine Redemer; Tel: 217-782-5432, E-mail: bredemer@ilsos.net; *Digital Imaging Prog Coordr,* Sandra Fritz; Tel: 217-558-2064, E-mail: sfritz@ilsos.net; *Ill Ctr for the Bk Coordr,* Bonnie Matheis; Tel: 217-558-2065, E-mail: bmatheis@ilsos.net; *Info Syst Coordr,* Jim Shepard; Tel: 217-782-5524, E-mail: jshepard@ilsos.net; *LSTA Coordr,* Karen Egan; Tel: 217-782-7749, E-mail: kegan@ilsos.net; *Outreach Coordr,* Ryan Franklin; Tel: 217-785-5615, E-mail: rfranklin@ilsos.net; *Tech Coordr,* Andrew Bullen; Tel: 312-814-4386, E-mail: abullen@ilsos.net
Founded 1839
Library Holdings: Bk Titles 1,694,500; Bk Vols 1,844,600; Per Subs 1,025
Special Collections: Illinois Authors Coll. State Document Depository; US Document Depository
Subject Interests: Govt, Polit sci
Automation Activity & Vendor Info: (Acquisitions) Ex Libris Group; (Cataloging) Ex Libris Group; (Cataloging) OCLC; (Circulation) Ex Libris Group; (ILL) OCLC; (OPAC) Ex Libris Group; (Serials) Ex Libris Group
Wireless access
Function: Adult literacy prog, Doc delivery serv, For res purposes, Games & aids for people with disabilities, Govt ref serv, Homebound delivery serv, ILL available, Internet access, Photocopying/Printing, Ref serv available, Telephone ref, Wheelchair accessible, Workshops
Publications: E-news from the ISL (Newsletter); Insight (Newsletter)
Partic in OCLC Online Computer Library Center, Inc
Special Services for the Deaf - Assisted listening device; Assistive tech; Captioned film dep; Closed caption videos; Spec interest per
Special Services for the Blind - Assistive/Adapted tech devices, equip & products; Audio mat; Bks & mags in Braille, on rec, tape & cassette; Bks available with recordings; Braille Webster's dictionary; Cassette playback machines; Computer with voice synthesizer for visually impaired persons; GEAC Advance; Home delivery serv; Large print & cassettes; Large print bks & talking machines; Newsline for the Blind; Radio reading serv; Ref serv; Scanner for conversion & translation of mats; Talking bk & rec for the blind cat; Talking bks & player equip; Tel Pioneers equip repair group; Videos on blindness & physical disabilties
Open Mon-Fri 8-4:30

Branches: 1

P TALKING BOOK & BRAILLE SERVICE, Gwendolyn Brooks Bldg, 300 S Second St, 62701-1796. Tel: 217-785-0022. Toll Free Tel: 800-665-5576. FAX: 217-558-4723. TDD: 888-261-2709. E-mail: isltbbs@ilsos.net. Web Site: www.ilbph.org. *Assoc Dir,* Sharon Ruda; Tel: 217-782-9435, E-mail: sruda@ilsos.net; Staff 14.5 (MLS 2, Non-MLS 12.5)
Founded 1931
Library Holdings: DVDs 535; Bk Titles 17,762; Talking Bks 166,754; Videos 2,045
Automation Activity & Vendor Info: (Cataloging) Keystone Systems, Inc (KLAS); (Circulation) Keystone Systems, Inc (KLAS); (OPAC) Keystone Systems, Inc (KLAS)
Function: 24/7 Electronic res, Audiobks via web, Bks on cassette, Computers for patron use, Digital talking bks, E-Readers, E-Reserves, Equip loans & repairs, Free DVD rentals, Home delivery & serv to seniorr ctr & nursing homes, ILL available, Internet access, Magazines, Mail & tel request accepted, Mail loans to mem, Online cat, Ref serv available, Spanish lang bks, Telephone ref, VHS videos, Wheelchair accessible
Special Services for the Blind - Braille alphabet card; Braille bks; Descriptive video serv (DVS); Digital talking bk; Digital talking bk machines; Free checkout of audio mat; Machine repair; Magnifiers; Mags & bk reproduction/duplication; Music instrul cassettes; Musical scores in Braille & large print; Newsletter (in large print, Braille or on cassette); Newsline for the Blind; PC for people with disabilities; Recorded bks; Screen enlargement software for people with visual disabilities; Screen reader software; Spanish Braille mags & bks; Talking bks; Talking bks & player equip; Talking bks plus; Talking machines; Variable speed audiotape players; Web-Braille; ZoomText magnification & reading software
Open Mon-Fri 8-4:30
Restriction: Authorized patrons, Registered patrons only

S ILLINOIS STATE MUSEUM LIBRARY, Research & Collections Ctr, 1011 E Ash St, 62703. SAN 304-6680. Tel: 217-524-0496. FAX: 217-782-1254, 217-785-2857. Web Site: www.illinoisstatemuseum.org. *Librn II,* Tracy Pierceall; E-mail: Tracy.Pierceall@illinois.gov; Staff 1 (Non-MLS 1)
Founded 1877
Library Holdings: Bk Vols 35,000; Per Subs 50
Special Collections: Anthropology (Thorne Deuel Coll); Art (Benjamin F Hunter Coll); Ornithology (R M Barnes Coll); Paleontology (Raymond E Janssen Coll); Zoology (Donald F Hoffmeister Coll)
Subject Interests: Anthrop, Art, Natural sci
Automation Activity & Vendor Info: (Cataloging) Innovative Interfaces, Inc. - Polaris; (Circulation) Innovative Interfaces, Inc. - Polaris; (ILL) OCLC; (OPAC) Innovative Interfaces, Inc. - Polaris
Mem of Illinois Heartland Library System
Partic in Illinois Library & Information Network
Restriction: Open by appt only

S ILLINOIS STATE MUSEUM LIBRARY, Research & Collections Center, 1011 East Ash, 62703. SAN 375-1279. Tel: 217-524-0496. FAX: 217-785-2857. Web Site: www.illinoisstatemuseum.org/content/library-and-archives. *Librn II,* Tracy Pierceall; E-mail: Tracy.Pierceall@illinois.gov
Function: Res libr
Mem of Illinois Heartland Library System
Restriction: Non-circulating, Open by appt only

L LEGISLATIVE REFERENCE BUREAU LAW LIBRARY*, 112 State House, 62706. SAN 304-6702. Tel: 217-782-6625. FAX: 217-785-4583. Web Site: www.ilga.gov. *Librn,* Mike Trudeau; E-mail: michaelt@ilga.gov
Founded 1913
Library Holdings: Bk Vols 20,000; Per Subs 29
Special Collections: Annotated Statutes for all Fifty States, Legislative Synopsis & Digests; Illinois Laws (since 1840)

J LINCOLN LAND COMMUNITY COLLEGE LIBRARY*, 5250 Shepherd Rd, 62794. (Mail add: PO Box 19256, 62794-9256), SAN 304-6710. Tel: 217-786-2354. Circulation Tel: 217-786-2354. Interlibrary Loan Service Tel: 217-786-2354. Reference Tel: 217-786-2352. Administration Tel: 217-786-2353. Automation Services Tel: 217-786-2475. FAX: 217-786-2251. Web Site: www.library.llcc.edu. *Assoc Dean,* Tamara Kuhn-Schnell; Tel: 217-786-2353, E-mail: tammy.kuhn-schnell@llcc.edu; *Fac Librn,* Jill Campbell; Tel: 217-786-2360, E-mail: jill.campbell@llcc.edu; *Fac Librn,* Leslie Rios; Tel: 217-786-4617, E-mail: leslie.rios@llcc.edu; *Fac Librn,* Ryan Roberts; Tel: 217-786-2771, E-mail: ryan.roberts@llcc.edu; *Electronic Res Librn,* Amanda Wiesenhofer; Tel: 217-786-2475; *Access Serv Librn,* Scott Ebbing; Tel: 217-786-2354; Staff 10 (MLS 6.5, Non-MLS 3.5)
Founded 1968. Enrl 3,500; Fac 224; Highest Degree: Associate
Jul 2013-Jun 2014. Mats Exp $211,406, Books $108,280, Per/Ser (Incl. Access Fees) $36,795, AV Mat $3,747, Electronic Ref Mat (Incl. Access Fees) $62,584. Sal $603,881
Library Holdings: AV Mats 5,282; CDs 669; DVDs 1,118; e-books 38,326; e-journals 182; Bk Titles 53,458; Bk Vols 66,461; Per Subs 216; Videos 535
Automation Activity & Vendor Info: (Acquisitions) Ex Libris Group; (Cataloging) Ex Libris Group; (Circulation) Ex Libris Group; (Course Reserve) Ex Libris Group; (ILL) OCLC; (OPAC) Ex Libris Group; (Serials) Ex Libris Group
Wireless access
Mem of Illinois Heartland Library System
Partic in Consortium of Academic & Research Libraries in Illinois; Network of Illinois Learning Resources in Community Colleges
Open Mon-Thurs 7:30am-9pm (Fall-Spring) Fri 7:30-5, Sat 9-4; Mon-Thurs (Summer) 7am-8pm

P LINCOLN LIBRARY, The Public Library of Springfield, Illinois, 326 S Seventh St, 62701. SAN 340-7853. Tel: 217-753-4900. Web Site: www.lincolnlibrary.info. *Dir,* Rochelle Hartman; E-mail: rochelle.hartman@lincolnlibrary.info; *Adult Serv Mgr,* Ms Sam Dunn; E-mail: samantha.dunn@lincolnlibrary.info; *Youth Serv Mgr,* Anna Moser; E-mail: anna.moser@lincolnlibrary.info; Staff 57 (MLS 18, Non-MLS 39)
Founded 1886. Pop 114,000; Circ 950,342

Library Holdings: Bk Vols 302,954; Per Subs 682
Special Collections: Local History; Newspaper Index; Vachel Lindsay (Sangamon Valley Coll)
Subject Interests: Hist, Music, Polit sci
Automation Activity & Vendor Info: (Cataloging) SirsiDynix; (Circulation) SirsiDynix; (OPAC) SirsiDynix
Wireless access
Publications: Lincoln Library Bulletin
Mem of Illinois Heartland Library System
Partic in OCLC Online Computer Library Center, Inc
Special Services for the Deaf - TTY equip
Open Mon-Thurs 10-6, Fri & Sat 10-5
Friends of the Library Group

M ST JOHN'S HOSPITAL*, Hospital Sisters Health System, Health Sciences Libraries, 800 E Carpenter, 62769. SAN 340-8000. Tel: 217-757-6700. Automation Services Tel: 217-544-6464, Ext 44567. Information Services Tel: 217-544-6464, Ext 44566. FAX: 217-525-2895. E-mail: library@hshs.org. Web Site: st-johns.libguides.com/home. *Libr Dir,* Lesley Wolfgang; Tel: 217-544-6464, Ext 44567, E-mail: lesley.wolfgang@hshs.org; *Librn,* Becky Alford; E-mail: Becky.alford@hshs.org; *Librn,* Laura Brosamer; Tel: 217-464-2182, Fax: 217-464-1674; *Librn,* Isabel Silverstein; Tel: 217-544-6464, Ext 44563, E-mail: isabel.silverstein@hshs.org; Staff 4 (MLS 4)
Founded 1931
Subject Interests: Cardiology, Nursing, Pediatrics, Surgery
Automation Activity & Vendor Info: (Acquisitions) CyberTools for Libraries; (Cataloging) CyberTools for Libraries; (Circulation) CyberTools for Libraries; (Discovery) EBSCO Discovery Service; (ILL) OCLC WorldShare Interlibrary Loan; (Media Booking) CyberTools for Libraries; (OPAC) CyberTools for Libraries; (Serials) CyberTools for Libraries
Wireless access
Mem of Illinois Heartland Library System
Partic in Consortium of Academic & Research Libraries in Illinois; Illinois Library & Information Network; OCLC Online Computer Library Center, Inc
Open Mon-Fri 7:30-4:30
Restriction: Authorized patrons, Badge access after hrs, Med & nursing staff, patients & families

CM SOUTHERN ILLINOIS UNIVERSITY SCHOOL OF MEDICINE*, Medical Library, 801 N Rutledge St, 62702. (Mail add: PO Box 19625, 62794-9625), SAN 304-6761. Tel: 217-545-2658. Circulation Tel: 217-545-1684. Reference Tel: 217-545-2122. Interlibrary Loan Service Tel: 217-545-2113. Reference E-mail: reference@siumed.edu. Web Site: www.siumed.edu/lib. *Dir,* Taran Ley; E-mail: tley65@siumed.edu; *Ref & Instrul Serv Librn,* Geoff Pettys; E-mail: gpettys31@siumed.edu; Staff 20.1 (MLS 5.7, Non-MLS 14.4)
Founded 1970. Enrl 475; Highest Degree: Doctorate
Jul 2013-Jun 2014 Income $2,020,201, Locally Generated Income $13,857, Parent Institution $2,006,344. Mats Exp $906,008, Books $78,641, Per/Ser (Incl. Access Fees) $717,707, Electronic Ref Mat (Incl. Access Fees) $101,675, Presv $7,985. Sal $875,102
Library Holdings: AV Mats 3,316; e-books 8,200; e-journals 2,519; Bk Titles 56,635; Bk Vols 66,285; Per Subs 3,381
Special Collections: History of Medicine
Automation Activity & Vendor Info: (Acquisitions) Ex Libris Group; (Cataloging) Ex Libris Group; (Circulation) Ex Libris Group; (OPAC) Ex Libris Group; (Serials) Ex Libris Group
Wireless access
Function: ILL available, Ref serv available
Publications: AV Titles; Serials Subjects; Serials Titles
Mem of Illinois Heartland Library System
Partic in Consortium of Academic & Research Libraries in Illinois; Illinois Library & Information Network; National Network of Libraries of Medicine Region 6
Open Mon-Thurs 8am-10pm, Fri 8-6

S SPRINGFIELD ART ASSOCIATION*, Michael Victor II Art Library, 700 N Fourth St, 62702. SAN 304-677X. Tel: 217-523-2631. FAX: 217-523-3866. E-mail: mvlibrary@springfieldart.org. Web Site: www.springfieldart.org. *Coll Mgr, Librn,* Barbie LaFrance; E-mail: gallerydirector@springfieldart.org; Staff 1 (Non-MLS 1)
Founded 1964
Library Holdings: Bk Titles 3,800
Subject Interests: Art, Art hist, Arts & crafts, Paintings, Photog, Prints
Function: Art exhibits
Mem of Illinois Heartland Library System
Open Mon-Fri 9-5, Sat 10-3
Friends of the Library Group

GL SUPREME COURT OF ILLINOIS LIBRARY*, Supreme Court Bldg, 200 E Capital Ave, 62701-1791. SAN 304-6699. Tel: 217-782-2424. FAX: 217-782-5287. E-mail: sclibrary_questions@court.state.il.us. Web Site: www.illinoiscourts.gov/SupremeCourt/library.asp. *Head Librn,* Geoff Pelzek; E-mail: gpelzek@illinoiscourts.gov; *Librn,* Jennifer Merriman; E-mail: jmerriman@illinoiscourts.gov; Staff 8 (MLS 4, Non-MLS 4)
Founded 1842
Library Holdings: Bk Titles 10,000; Bk Vols 100,000; Per Subs 350
Special Collections: SJI Depository. State Document Depository
Subject Interests: Illinois, Law
Automation Activity & Vendor Info: (Cataloging) SirsiDynix
Wireless access
Partic in OCLC Online Computer Library Center, Inc
Open Mon-Fri 8-4:30

C UNIVERSITY OF ILLINOIS AT SPRINGFIELD*, Norris L Brookens Library, One University Plaza, MS BRK-140, 62703-5407. Tel: 217-206-6597. Circulation Tel: 217-206-6605. Interlibrary Loan Service Tel: 217-206-6601. FAX: 217-206-6354. Web Site: library.uis.edu. *Dean, Libr Instrul Serv, Univ Librn,* Pattie Piotrowski; E-mail: ppiot2@uis.edu; *Cat Librn, Dir, Tech Serv,* Robin Mize; Tel: 217-206-7113, E-mail: rmize3@uis.edu; *Archivist,* Thomas Wood; Tel: 217-206-6520, E-mail: twood1@uis.edu; Staff 26 (MLS 8, Non-MLS 18)
Founded 1970. Enrl 5,174; Fac 362; Highest Degree: Doctorate
Library Holdings: Audiobooks 1,281; AV Mats 11,921; e-books 51,346; e-journals 57,341; Microforms 49,035; Music Scores 442; Bk Titles 476,774; Bk Vols 532,486; Per Subs 1,643; Videos 5,345
Special Collections: Central Illinois Oral Histories; Handy Colony Coll; Illinois Regional Archives Depository. Oral History; State Document Depository; US Document Depository
Subject Interests: Bus & mgt, Econ, Educ, Law
Automation Activity & Vendor Info: (Acquisitions) Ex Libris Group; (Cataloging) Ex Libris Group; (Circulation) Ex Libris Group; (Course Reserve) Ex Libris Group; (ILL) Ex Libris Group; (OPAC) Ex Libris Group; (Serials) Ex Libris Group
Wireless access
Publications: James Jones in Illinois: A Guide to the Handy Colony Collection, 1989
Mem of Illinois Heartland Library System
Partic in Consortium of Academic & Research Libraries in Illinois; OCLC Online Computer Library Center, Inc
Special Services for the Blind - Aids for in-house use
Open Mon-Thurs 8:30am-Midnight, Fri 8:30-6, Sat 10-6, Sun 2-Midnight
Friends of the Library Group

STANFORD

P ALLIN TOWNSHIP LIBRARY*, 116 W Main St, 61774. (Mail add: PO Box 258, 61774-0258), SAN 376-0936. Tel: 309-379-4631. FAX: 309-379-4631. E-mail: allinlib@mchsi.com. Web Site: www.allintownshiplibrary.org. *Librn,* Angie Gaddy
Library Holdings: Bk Vols 5,000
Open Mon & Wed 11:30-8, Fri 9-4:30, Sat 9-2:30
Friends of the Library Group

STAUNTON

P STAUNTON PUBLIC LIBRARY*, 306 W Main St, 62088. SAN 304-6796. Tel: 618-635-3852. FAX: 618-635-2246. E-mail: library@stauntonpl.org. Web Site: stauntonpubliclibrary.weebly.com. *Dir,* Julie Jarman; E-mail: juliej@stauntonpl.org
Founded 1912. Pop 5,139; Circ 23,000
Library Holdings: Bk Vols 22,000; Per Subs 21
Special Collections: House the Macoupin Company Genealogical Coll
Wireless access
Mem of Illinois Heartland Library System
Open Mon-Thurs 10-7, Fri 10-5, Sat 10-3

STEELEVILLE

P STEELEVILLE AREA PUBLIC LIBRARY DISTRICT, 625 S Sparta St, 62288-2147. SAN 376-494X. Tel: 618-965-9732. FAX: 618-965-3504. E-mail: svillelibrary@gmail.com. Web Site: www.steelevillelibrary.org. *Dir,* Rachel Rheinecker; E-mail: director.svplib@gmail.com; *Circ,* Taylor Cathcart; *Circ, Tech Serv,* Drake Foote; Staff 1 (MLS 1)
Founded 1983. Pop 4,698; Circ 7,134
Jul 2020-Jun 2021. Mats Exp $6,600
Library Holdings: Bk Titles 17,100; Bk Vols 17,700; Per Subs 2; Videos 980
Automation Activity & Vendor Info: (Acquisitions) Innovative Interfaces, Inc. - Polaris; (Cataloging) Innovative Interfaces, Inc. - Polaris; (Circulation) Innovative Interfaces, Inc. - Polaris; (ILL) Innovative Interfaces, Inc. - Polaris; (OPAC) Innovative Interfaces, Inc. - Polaris
Wireless access
Mem of Illinois Heartland Library System
Open Mon-Fri 10-6, Sat 10-1

STEGER

P STEGER-SOUTH CHICAGO HEIGHTS PUBLIC LIBRARY DISTRICT*, 54 E 31st St, 60475. SAN 304-6567. Tel: 708-755-5040. FAX: 708-755-2504. E-mail: ref.ssch@gmail.com. Web Site: www.ssch.lib.il.us. *Dir,* Jamie Paicely; *Adult & Teen Serv,* Laura Munoz; *Ch Serv,* Jessica Rodrigues; *Patron Serv,* Bridgette O'Halloran; Staff 9 (MLS 1, Non-MLS 8)
Founded 1975. Pop 13,709
Library Holdings: Bk Vols 37,393; Per Subs 97
Publications: Newsletter (quarterly)
Mem of Reaching Across Illinois Library System (RAILS)
Partic in System Wide Automated Network
Open Mon-Thurs 10-8, Fri & Sat 10-5

STERLING

M CGH MEDICAL CENTER*, Health Sciences Library, 100 E LeFevre Rd, 61081-1278. SAN 375-2739. Tel: 815-625-0400. *Librn,* Tyler Lawson; E-mail: tyler.lawson@cghmc.com; Staff 1 (MLS 1)
Founded 1972
Library Holdings: Per Subs 120
Wireless access
Mem of Reaching Across Illinois Library System (RAILS)
Restriction: Staff use only

P STERLING PUBLIC LIBRARY, 102 W Third St, 61081-3504. SAN 304-680X. Tel: 815-625-1370. E-mail: sterlingpubliclibrary@gmail.com. Web Site: www.sterlingpubliclibrary.org. *Dir,* Jennifer Slaney; E-mail: spl-director@comcast.net; Staff 13 (MLS 2, Non-MLS 11)
Pop 15,350; Circ 118,641
May 2014-Apr 2015 Income $560,335, State $106,282, City $368,514, Federal $5,000, Locally Generated Income $80,539. Mats Exp $85,289, Books $30,000, Electronic Ref Mat (Incl. Access Fees) $8,000. Sal $297,215
Library Holdings: DVDs 2,158; Electronic Media & Resources 9; Bk Vols 54,626; Per Subs 130; Talking Bks 1,162
Subject Interests: Genealogy, Local hist, Polit sci
Automation Activity & Vendor Info: (Cataloging) TLC (The Library Corporation); (Circulation) TLC (The Library Corporation)
Wireless access
Mem of Reaching Across Illinois Library System (RAILS)
Open Mon-Fri 10-5

STICKNEY

P STICKNEY-FOREST VIEW PUBLIC LIBRARY DISTRICT*, 6800 W 43rd St, 60402. SAN 304-6818. Tel: 708-749-1050. FAX: 708-749-1054. Reference E-mail: reference@sfvpld.org. Web Site: www.sfvpld.org. *Libr Dir,* Leighton Shell; E-mail: shelll@sfvpld.org; *Asst Libr Dir,* Sara Henry; *Head, Tech Serv,* Marcos Arellano; *Head, Youth Serv,* Danielle Taylor; *Bus Mgr,* Joanne Chavez Buchanan; Staff 22 (MLS 7, Non-MLS 15)
Founded 1953. Pop 6,657; Circ 64,750
Library Holdings: Bk Vols 56,000; Per Subs 189
Automation Activity & Vendor Info: (Acquisitions) Baker & Taylor; (Cataloging) Innovative Interfaces, Inc; (Circulation) Innovative Interfaces, Inc; (Course Reserve) Innovative Interfaces, Inc
Wireless access
Mem of Reaching Across Illinois Library System (RAILS)
Partic in System Wide Automated Network
Open Mon-Thurs 9-8, Fri 9-5, Sat 9-5
Friends of the Library Group

STILLMAN VALLEY

P JULIA HULL DISTRICT LIBRARY*, 100 Library Lane, 61084. SAN 304-6826. Tel: 815-645-8611. FAX: 815-645-1341. Web Site: www.juliahull.org. *Dir,* Joanna Kluever; E-mail: jkluever@mail.meridian223.org; *Youth Serv,* Kelly Haas; E-mail: khaas@mail.meridian223.org; Staff 8 (MLS 1, Non-MLS 7)
Founded 1924. Pop 6,995; Circ 24,302
Library Holdings: AV Mats 180; CDs 339; DVDs 152; e-books 2,184; Electronic Media & Resources 56; Large Print Bks 341; Bk Vols 25,074; Per Subs 44; Videos 849
Subject Interests: Christian fiction
Wireless access
Mem of Reaching Across Illinois Library System (RAILS)
Open Mon-Thurs 9-8, Fri 9-5, Sat 9-5 (9-2 Summer)
Friends of the Library Group

STOCKTON

P STOCKTON TOWNSHIP PUBLIC LIBRARY*, 140 W Benton Ave, 61085. SAN 304-6834. Tel: 815-947-2030. FAX: 815-947-2030. E-mail: stocktonlibrary@gmail.com. Web Site: www.stocktonlibrary.org. *Dir, Libr Serv,* Kim Scace
Founded 1926. Pop 2,555; Circ 16,915
Library Holdings: AV Mats 400; Large Print Bks 350; Bk Vols 18,000; Per Subs 54
Special Collections: Paintings (J Howard Smith Coll). Oral History
Subject Interests: Local hist
Wireless access
Mem of Reaching Across Illinois Library System (RAILS)
Open Mon & Wed 12:30-7, Tues & Thurs 12:30-6, Fri 12:30-3, Sat 9-1

STONINGTON

P STONINGTON TOWNSHIP PUBLIC LIBRARY*, 500 E North St, 62567. SAN 304-6842. Tel: 217-325-3512. FAX: 217-325-3750. *Dir,* Sandi Klein; *Libr Asst,* Lisa Grover
Founded 1982. Pop 1,180
Library Holdings: CDs 43; Large Print Bks 48; Bk Vols 11,000; Talking Bks 48; Videos 577
Wireless access
Mem of Illinois Heartland Library System
Open Mon & Thurs 1-6, Tues 1-5, Wed 10-12 & 1-5, Fri 9-12 & 1-4
Friends of the Library Group

STREAMWOOD

P POPLAR CREEK PUBLIC LIBRARY DISTRICT*, 1405 S Park Ave, 60107-2997. SAN 304-6850. Tel: 630-837-6800. FAX: 630-837-6823. Web Site: www.pclib.org. *Exec Dir,* Debra Stombres; E-mail: dstombres@pclib.org; *Dep Dir, Pub Serv,* Kristine Kenney; E-mail: kkenney@pclib.org; *Dep Dir, Support Serv,* Ron Pauli; E-mail: rpauli@pclib.org; *Bus Mgr,* Sue Haisan; *Ch Mgr,* Elizabeth Drennan; *Mgr, Mat Serv,* Margaret Maiken; *Mgr, Popular Mats,* Jill Berrill; *Ref Serv Mgr,* Paulette Harding; *YA Serv,* Hannah Sloan; *Tech Serv,* Cassidy Fontana; Staff 23 (MLS 20, Non-MLS 3)
Founded 1966. Pop 66,639
Library Holdings: CDs 11,676; Bk Vols 328,006; Per Subs 11,683; Videos 5,710
Special Collections: State Document Depository; US Document Depository
Automation Activity & Vendor Info: (Circulation) Innovative Interfaces, Inc
Wireless access
Function: 24/7 Electronic res, 24/7 Online cat, Adult bk club, Art exhibits, Audio & video playback equip for onsite use, Audiobks via web, Bks on CD, Children's prog, Citizenship assistance, Computer training, Computers for patron use, Electronic databases & coll, Govt ref serv, Holiday prog, Homebound delivery serv, ILL available, Internet access, Magazines, Magnifiers for reading, Mail & tel request accepted, Meeting rooms, Microfiche/film & reading machines, Movies, Museum passes, Music CDs, Online cat, Outreach serv, Photocopying/Printing, Preschool reading prog, Printer for laptops & handheld devices, Prog for adults, Prog for children & young adult, Ref serv available, Senior outreach, Spanish lang bks, Study rm, Summer & winter reading prog, Tax forms, Teen prog, Telephone ref, Wheelchair accessible
Publications: Library Digest (Newsletter)
Mem of Reaching Across Illinois Library System (RAILS)
Open Mon-Thurs 9-9, Fri & Sat 9-5, Sun 12-5
Branches: 1
SONYA CRAWSHAW BRANCH, 4300 Audrey Lane, Hanover Park, 60133, SAN 374-3578. Tel: 630-372-0052. FAX: 630-372-0024. *Br Coordr,* Steven Zanfardino
Open Mon-Wed 12-9, Thurs 9-9, Fri-Sun 12-5

STREATOR

P STREATOR PUBLIC LIBRARY*, 130 S Park St, 61364. SAN 304-6869. Tel: 815-672-2729. FAX: 815-672-2729. E-mail: streatorplstaff@gmail.com. Web Site: www.streatorpubliclibrary.org. *Libr Dir,* Cynthia Maxwell; E-mail: streatorpl@gmail.com; *Cat,* Thomas Miller; E-mail: streatorpltech@gmail.com; Staff 1 (Non-MLS 1)
Founded 1903. Pop 13,710; Circ 41,731
Jan 2018-Dec 2018 Income $328,632, State $56,713, City $232,369, Federal $342, Locally Generated Income $39,208. Mats Exp $118,390, Books $33,441, Per/Ser (Incl. Access Fees) $5,239, Micro $750, AV Mat $667, Electronic Ref Mat (Incl. Access Fees) $1,875. Sal $128,125
Library Holdings: Audiobooks 947; AV Mats 954; Bks on Deafness & Sign Lang 26; High Interest/Low Vocabulary Bk Vols 130; Large Print Bks 1,000; Bk Titles 42,800; Bk Vols 42,881; Per Subs 112; Talking Bks 947; Videos 954
Special Collections: History of Streator & La Salle County
Automation Activity & Vendor Info: (Acquisitions) Innovative Interfaces, Inc - Sierra; (Cataloging) Innovative Interfaces, Inc - Sierra; (Circulation) Innovative Interfaces, Inc - Sierra; (Course Reserve) Innovative Interfaces, Inc - Sierra; (Discovery) Innovative Interfaces, Inc - Sierra; (ILL) Innovative Interfaces, Inc - Sierra; (Media Booking) Innovative Interfaces, Inc - Sierra; (OPAC) Innovative Interfaces, Inc - Sierra; (Serials) Innovative Interfaces, Inc - Sierra

Wireless access
Function: 24/7 Electronic res, 24/7 Online cat, Activity rm, Adult bk club, Archival coll, Art programs, Audiobks via web, Bk club(s), Bks on CD, Children's prog, Computer training, Computers for patron use, Electronic databases & coll, Free DVD rentals, Holiday prog, Home delivery & serv to seniorr ctr & nursing homes, ILL available, Internet access, Magazines, Magnifiers for reading, Meeting rooms, Microfiche/film & reading machines, Music CDs, Online cat, Outreach serv, OverDrive digital audio bks, Photocopying/Printing, Prog for adults, Prog for children & young adult, Ref & res, Ref serv available, Res assist avail, Res performed for a fee, Scanner, STEM programs, Story hour, Study rm, Summer reading prog, Tax forms, Teen prog, Wheelchair accessible
Mem of Reaching Across Illinois Library System (RAILS)
Partic in OMNI
Open Mon-Thurs (Winter) 9-8, Fri & Sat 9-6; Mon-Fri (Summer) 9-6, Sat 9-1
Friends of the Library Group

SUGAR GROVE

P SUGAR GROVE PUBLIC LIBRARY DISTRICT*, 125 S Municipal Dr, 60554. SAN 304-6877. Tel: 630-466-4686. Circulation Tel: 630-409-1525. Information Services Tel: 630-466-3951. FAX: 630-466-4189. E-mail: circ@sgpl.org. Web Site: www.sgpl.org. *Dir,* Shannon Halikias; E-mail: shannon@sgpl.org; Staff 11 (MLS 1, Non-MLS 10)
Founded 1962. Pop 15,476; Circ 83,582
Library Holdings: Audiobooks 2,211; CDs 1,000; DVDs 300; Bk Vols 43,545; Per Subs 380; Videos 538
Automation Activity & Vendor Info: (Cataloging) SirsiDynix-WorkFlows; (Circulation) SirsiDynix-WorkFlows; (OPAC) SirsiDynix-WorkFlows
Wireless access
Mem of Reaching Across Illinois Library System (RAILS)
Partic in System Wide Automated Network
Open Mon-Thurs 10-8, Sat 10-4
Friends of the Library Group

J WAUBONSEE COMMUNITY COLLEGE*, Todd Library, Collins Hall, 2nd Flr, State Rte 47 at Waubonsee Dr, 60554. SAN 304-6885. Tel: 630-466-2400. Reference Tel: 630-466-2396. FAX: 630-466-7799. E-mail: library@waubonsee.edu. Web Site: www.waubonsee.edu/student-experience/library. *Libr Mgr,* Spencer A Brayton; Tel: 630-466-2405, E-mail: sbrayton@waubonsee.edu; *Librn,* Adam Burke; Tel: 630-466-2421, E-mail: aburke@waubonsee.edu; *Librn,* Stacia Callaway; Tel: 630-466-2396, E-mail: scallaway@waubonsee.edu; *Tech Coordr,* John Wohlers; Tel: 630-466-2587, E-mail: jwohlers@waubonsee.edu; *Circ,* Rhea Hunter-Brodhead; Tel: 630-466-2401, E-mail: rhunter@waubonsee.edu; *ILL,* Kendall Vance; Tel: 630-466-2333, E-mail: kvance@waubonsee.edu; Staff 16 (MLS 6, Non-MLS 10)
Founded 1967. Enrl 9,935; Fac 510; Highest Degree: Associate
Library Holdings: AV Mats 6,502; e-books 9,544; e-journals 14,717; Bk Vols 45,135; Per Subs 568
Automation Activity & Vendor Info: (Cataloging) SirsiDynix; (Circulation) SirsiDynix; (Course Reserve) SirsiDynix; (ILL) OCLC FirstSearch; (OPAC) SirsiDynix; (Serials) EOS International
Wireless access
Partic in Consortium of Academic & Research Libraries in Illinois; Network of Illinois Learning Resources in Community Colleges; Northern Illinois Learning Resources Cooperative
Special Services for the Blind - Closed circuit TV; Screen reader software
Open Mon-Fri 7:30am-9:30pm, Sat 7:30-4:30, Sun 8-4:30

SULLIVAN

S MOULTRIE COUNTY HISTORICAL & GENEALOGICAL SOCIETY LIBRARY*, 117 E Harrison St, 61951. (Mail add: PO Box 588, 61951-0588), SAN 327-7917. Tel: 217-728-4085. E-mail: mocohgs@gmail.com. Web Site: www.moultrieonline.com/moultrie-county-historical-genealogical-society. *Librn,* Ms Pat Cribbet
Special Collections: Family Histories, County Newspapers on Film; Illinois State Death Index (1916-1950)
Wireless access
Open Mon-Sat 11-3

P ELIZABETH TITUS MEMORIAL LIBRARY*, Two W Water St, 61951. SAN 304-6893. Tel: 217-728-7221. FAX: 217-728-2215. E-mail: elizabeth_titus@ymail.com. Web Site: www.sullivanil.us/departments/library. *Dir,* Michelle Nolen; E-mail: mitchy13_69@yahoo.com; *Asst Dir,* Susan Wood; E-mail: susanew10@hotmail.com; *Ch,* Laura Davison; *Circ Librn,* Jessica Beals; *Tech Serv Librn,* Jessica Bathe
Founded 1915. Pop 4,400; Circ 35,880
Library Holdings: AV Mats 4,546; Bk Vols 42,357; Per Subs 90
Automation Activity & Vendor Info: (Acquisitions) Innovative Interfaces, Inc; (Cataloging) Innovative Interfaces, Inc; (Circulation) Innovative Interfaces, Inc; (OPAC) Innovative Interfaces, Inc
Wireless access
Mem of Illinois Heartland Library System
Open Mon-Thurs 8:30-8, Fri 8:30-5, Sat 9-2

SUMMIT

P SUMMIT PUBLIC LIBRARY DISTRICT*, 6233 S Archer Rd, 60501. SAN 304-6915. Tel: 708-458-1545. FAX: 708-458-1842. E-mail: summitlibrary@yahoo.com. Web Site: www.summitlibrary.info. *Dir,* Hadiya Drew; Staff 15 (MLS 1, Non-MLS 14)
Founded 1917. Pop 11,064
Subject Interests: Spanish (Lang)
Automation Activity & Vendor Info: (Circulation) Innovative Interfaces, Inc
Wireless access
Mem of Reaching Across Illinois Library System (RAILS)
Partic in System Wide Automated Network
Open Mon-Thurs 10-8, Fri 12-5, Sat 9-5
Friends of the Library Group

SUMNER

S ILLINOIS DEPARTMENT OF CORRECTIONS, Lawrence Correctional Center Library, 10940 Lawrence Rd, 62466. Tel: 618-936-2064. FAX: 618-936-2577. Web Site: www2.illinois.gov/idoc/facilities/pages/lawrencecorrectionalcenter.aspx. *Libr Assoc,* Brandon Yockey
Library Holdings: Bk Vols 5,000
Restriction: Staff & inmates only

SYCAMORE

P SYCAMORE PUBLIC LIBRARY, 103 E State St, 60178-1440. SAN 304-6923. Tel: 815-895-2500. FAX: 815-895-9816. E-mail: spl@sycamorelibrary.org. Web Site: www.sycamorelibrary.org. Staff 26 (MLS 5, Non-MLS 21)
Founded 1891. Pop 17,519; Circ 224,027
Library Holdings: Audiobooks 5,629; CDs 5,629; DVDs 6,668; e-books 482,671; Bk Vols 72,295; Per Subs 52
Subject Interests: Local hist
Automation Activity & Vendor Info: (Acquisitions) SirsiDynix; (Cataloging) SirsiDynix; (Circulation) SirsiDynix; (Course Reserve) SirsiDynix; (ILL) SirsiDynix; (Media Booking) SirsiDynix; (OPAC) SirsiDynix; (Serials) SirsiDynix
Wireless access
Function: 24/7 Electronic res, 24/7 Online cat, Adult bk club, Audiobks on Playaways & MP3, Bk club(s), Bks on cassette, Bks on CD, Children's prog, Computer training, Computers for patron use, Electronic databases & coll, Free DVD rentals, Holiday prog, Home delivery & serv to seniorr ctr & nursing homes, ILL available, Internet access, Jail serv, Magazines, Magnifiers for reading, Mail & tel request accepted, Mango lang, Meeting rooms, Movies, Museum passes, Music CDs, Notary serv, Online cat, Online ref, Outreach serv, Outside serv via phone, mail, e-mail & web, OverDrive digital audio bks, Photocopying/Printing, Preschool outreach, Printer for laptops & handheld devices, Prog for adults, Prog for children & young adult, Ref & res, Ref serv available, Res assist avail, Scanner, Senior outreach, Spanish lang bks, STEM programs, Story hour, Summer & winter reading prog, Summer reading prog, Tax forms, Teen prog, Telephone ref, Wheelchair accessible, Writing prog
Mem of Reaching Across Illinois Library System (RAILS)
Special Services for the Deaf - TDD equip
Open Mon-Thurs 9-8, Fri 9-6, Sat 9-5, Sun 1-5
Restriction: Non-resident fee
Friends of the Library Group

TAYLORVILLE

S TAYLORVILLE CORRECTIONAL CENTER LIBRARY, 1144 Illinois Rte 29, 62568. (Mail add: PO Box 1000, 62568-1000), SAN 376-1185. Tel: 217-824-4004, Ext 5802. FAX: 217-824-4042. Web Site: www.illinois.gov/idoc/Facilities/Pages/taylorvillecorrectionalcenter.aspx. *Librn,* Amber Roley; E-mail: amber.roley@doc.illinois.gov
Library Holdings: Bk Titles 4,000; Bk Vols 7,000

P TAYLORVILLE PUBLIC LIBRARY*, 121 W Vine St, 62568. SAN 304-6931. Tel: 217-824-4736. FAX: 217-824-8921. E-mail: staff@taylorvillelibrary.org. Web Site: taylorvillelibrary.org. *Dir,* Steven Ward; Staff 7 (MLS 1, Non-MLS 6)
Founded 1899. Pop 11,113; Circ 79,653
Library Holdings: CDs 1,000; High Interest/Low Vocabulary Bk Vols 200; Large Print Bks 2,000; Bk Vols 45,000; Per Subs 120
Subject Interests: Antiques

Automation Activity & Vendor Info: (Acquisitions) Innovative Interfaces, Inc; (Cataloging) Innovative Interfaces, Inc; (Circulation) Innovative Interfaces, Inc; (Course Reserve) Innovative Interfaces, Inc; (ILL) Innovative Interfaces, Inc; (Media Booking) Innovative Interfaces, Inc; (OPAC) Innovative Interfaces, Inc; (Serials) Innovative Interfaces, Inc
Wireless access
Mem of Illinois Heartland Library System
Open Mon-Thurs 10-8, Fri & Sat 10-5
Friends of the Library Group

THIRD LAKE

S NEW GRACANICA MONASTERY, Joe Buley Memorial Library, 35240 W Grant Ave, 60046. (Mail add: PO Box 371, Grayslake, 60030-0371). Tel: 847-223-4300, Ext 6. FAX: 847-223-4312. E-mail: eparhija@newgarcanica.org. Web Site: newgracanica.com/library. *Librn,* Nicholas T Groves, PhD; *Asst Librn,* Marko Kapetanov; Staff 2 (MLS 1, Non-MLS 1)
Founded 2004
Library Holdings: Bk Vols 8,000; Per Subs 50
Subject Interests: Orthodox theol & hist, Scriptural studies, Serbian archival mat, Serbian hist & culture
Automation Activity & Vendor Info: (Cataloging) SirsiDynix
Function: Res libr
Mem of Reaching Across Illinois Library System (RAILS)
Open Mon 2-7, Tues & Wed 9-4, Thurs-Sat 12-7
Restriction: Circ limited

THOMSON

P YORK TOWNSHIP PUBLIC LIBRARY*, 1005 W Main St, 61285. SAN 304-694X. Tel: 815-259-2480. FAX: 815-259-2480. Web Site: www.thomsonlibrary.org. *Dir,* Deeann Kramer; E-mail: director@thomsonlibrary.org
Founded 1919. Pop 2,272; Circ 17,330
Library Holdings: Bk Vols 14,458; Per Subs 22
Subject Interests: Local hist
Wireless access
Mem of Reaching Across Illinois Library System (RAILS)
Open Mon & Wed 3-7, Tues & Thurs 9-4:30, Sat 9-1

THORNTON

P THORNTON PUBLIC LIBRARY, 115 E Margaret St, 60476. SAN 304-6958. Tel: 708-877-2579. FAX: 708-877-2608. E-mail: library@thorntonil.us. Web Site: www.thorntonlibrary.org. *Dir,* John Deyoung; *Ad,* Angie Enright; E-mail: aenright@thorntonlibrary.org; *YA Librn, Youth Librn,* Kathy Dejnowski; E-mail: kdejnowski@thorntonlibrary.org; Staff 1 (Non-MLS 1)
Founded 1940. Pop 2,582; Circ 15,729
Library Holdings: Bk Vols 20,000; Per Subs 60
Special Collections: American Indians
Wireless access
Mem of Reaching Across Illinois Library System (RAILS)
Partic in System Wide Automated Network
Open Mon, Wed & Fri 9-5, Tues & Thurs 9-8, Sat 10-4

TINLEY PARK

§CM FOX COLLEGE LIBRARY, 18020 Oak Park Ave, 60477. Tel: 708-444-4500. E-mail: librarian@foxcollege.edu. Web Site: www.foxcollege.edu/library. *Ref Librn,* Matthew Johnson
Library Holdings: Per Subs 32
Function: ILL available, Photocopying/Printing
Mem of Reaching Across Illinois Library System (RAILS)
Partic in Consortium of Academic & Research Libraries in Illinois; National Network of Libraries of Medicine Region 6
Open Mon-Thurs 7-5:30, Fri 7-4

P TINLEY PARK PUBLIC LIBRARY*, 7851 Timber Dr, 60477-3398. SAN 304-6974. Tel: 708-532-0160. FAX: 708-532-2981. Reference FAX: 708-532-9813. E-mail: tplibrary@tplibrary.org. Web Site: tplibrary.org. *Libr Adminr,* Rich Wolff; E-mail: rwolff@tplibrary.org; *Asst Admin,* Anthony Andros; E-mail: aandros@tplibrary.org; *Mgr, Patron Serv,* Mary Ann Pyrzynski; Tel: 708-532-0160, Ext 3, E-mail: m_pyrzynski@tplibrary.org; *Adult Serv,* Kristina Howard; Tel: 708-532-0160, Ext 1, E-mail: khoward@tplibrary.org; *Ch Serv,* Kerry Reed; Tel: 708-532-0160, Ext 2, E-mail: kreed@tplibrary.org; *Tech Serv,* Joy Anhalt; Tel: 708-532-0160, Ext 7, E-mail: j_anhalt@tplibrary.org
Founded 1959. Pop 63,852
Library Holdings: Per Subs 270
Special Collections: Arabic Language Books; German Language Books; Hindi Language Books; Spanish Language Books
Automation Activity & Vendor Info: (Circulation) Innovative Interfaces, Inc
Wireless access
Mem of Reaching Across Illinois Library System (RAILS)
Partic in System Wide Automated Network
Open Mon-Fri 9-9, Sat 9-5, Sun 12-5
Friends of the Library Group

TISKILWA

P TISKILWA PUBLIC LIBRARY*, 119 E Main, 61368. (Mail add: PO Box 150, 61368), SAN 304-6982. Tel: 815-646-4511. FAX: 815-646-4247. E-mail: tisklib@comcast.net. Web Site: www.tisklib.org. *Head Librn,* Lisa Bettner; *Libr Asst,* S Anderson; *Libr Asst,* J Archer; *Libr Asst,* D Bartolucci; *Libr Asst,* J Cavada; *Libr Asst,* A Kindle
Founded 1875. Pop 1,587; Circ 17,183
Library Holdings: Bk Vols 16,000; Per Subs 44
Special Collections: Oral History
Automation Activity & Vendor Info: (ILL) PALS
Wireless access
Mem of Reaching Across Illinois Library System (RAILS)
Partic in Association for Rural & Small Libraries
Open Mon-Thurs 10-6, Fri 10-5, Sat 9-12

TOLEDO

P SUMPTER TOWNSHIP LIBRARY, 148 Courthouse Sq, 62468. (Mail add: PO Box 67, 62468-0067), SAN 304-6990. Tel: 217-849-2072. FAX: 217-849-2072. E-mail: sumpterlib@gmail.com. *Librn,* Cassandra Stewart
Pop 1,967; Circ 19,371
Library Holdings: Bk Vols 20,000; Per Subs 40
Wireless access
Mem of Illinois Heartland Library System
Open Tues & Thurs 11-6, Wed 9-5, Fri 12-5, Sat 9-Noon

TOLONO

P TOLONO PUBLIC LIBRARY DISTRICT*, 111 E Main St, 61880. (Mail add: PO Box 759, 61880-0759), SAN 304-7008. Tel: 217-485-5558. FAX: 217-485-3088. Web Site: tolonolibrary.org. *Dir,* Janet Cler; E-mail: jcler@tolonolibrary.org; *Librn,* Breana McCracken; E-mail: bmccracken@tolonolibrary.org
Founded 1968. Pop 8,130; Circ 104,000
Library Holdings: Bk Vols 25,000
Special Collections: Local Archives
Wireless access
Mem of Illinois Heartland Library System
Partic in Association for Rural & Small Libraries
Open Mon-Fri 8-8, Sat 10-4, Sun 12-4
Friends of the Library Group

TOLUCA

P TOLUCA PUBLIC LIBRARY*, 102 N Main St, 61369. (Mail add: PO Box 526, 61369), SAN 304-7016. Tel: 815-452-2211. FAX: 815-452-2211. E-mail: tolucalibrary61369@yahoo.com. *Dir,* Dawn Collins; E-mail: tolucalibrary61369@yahoo.com
Founded 1974. Pop 1,339; Circ 5,030
Library Holdings: Bk Vols 8,079
Special Collections: National Geographic 1929-present
Wireless access
Function: Activity rm, After school storytime, Audiobks via web, Bks on CD, Children's prog, Computers for patron use, Doc delivery serv, Free DVD rentals, ILL available, Internet access, Magazines, Meeting rooms, Photocopying/Printing, Preschool reading prog, Printer for laptops & handheld devices, Ref & res, Ref serv available, Res assist avail, Scanner, Story hour, Summer reading prog, Tax forms, Wheelchair accessible
Mem of Reaching Across Illinois Library System (RAILS)
Open Mon & Wed 9-12, Tues & Fri 9-12 & 1-4:30, Thurs 9-12 & 1:30-4:30

TOULON

P TOULON PUBLIC LIBRARY DISTRICT*, 617 E Jefferson St, 61483. SAN 304-7024. Tel: 309-286-5791. FAX: 309-286-4481. E-mail: toulonlibrary@gmail.com. Web Site: www.toulonpld.org. *Dir,* Michael Baumann; E-mail: director.toulonpld@gmail.com; *Lead Librn,* Janet Kamerer; E-mail: leadlibrarian.toulonpld@gmail.com; *Youth Serv,* Crystal McRell
Pop 2,886; Circ 22,254
Library Holdings: CDs 323; DVDs 838; e-books 825; Large Print Bks 865; Bk Vols 20,418; Per Subs 85; Talking Bks 379; Videos 1,542
Automation Activity & Vendor Info: (Circulation) TLC (The Library Corporation)
Wireless access
Publications: The Library Link (Newsletter)
Open Mon, Wed & Fri 9-5, Tues & Thurs 9-8, Sat 9-Noon

TOWANDA

P TOWANDA DISTRICT LIBRARY*, 301 S Taylor St, 61776. SAN 304-7032. Tel: 309-728-2176. FAX: 309-728-2139. E-mail: towandalib@yahoo.com. Web Site: www.towandalibrary.org. *Dir,* Jason Sleet Shirley; E-mail: director@towandalibrary.org; Staff 1.8 (MLS 0.8, Non-MLS 1)
Founded 1939. Pop 2,187; Circ 16,600
Library Holdings: Audiobooks 419; CDs 1,221; DVDs 1,000; Large Print Bks 121; Bk Vols 16,650; Per Subs 53; Videos 362
Special Collections: History Coll; Illinois Coll; National Geographic Coll, 1916-present
Automation Activity & Vendor Info: (Cataloging) SirsiDynix; (Circulation) SirsiDynix; (ILL) SirsiDynix; (OPAC) SirsiDynix
Wireless access
Function: Adult bk club, Bks on cassette, Bks on CD, Children's prog, Computers for patron use, E-Reserves, Free DVD rentals, Homebound delivery serv, ILL available, Music CDs, Online cat, Photocopying/Printing, Prog for adults, Prog for children & young adult, Ref serv available, Spoken cassettes & CDs, Spoken cassettes & DVDs, Story hour, Summer reading prog, Tax forms, VHS videos, Wheelchair accessible
Special Services for the Blind - Duplicating spec requests
Open Mon & Wed 10-6, Tues 1-7, Thurs & Fri 1-6, Sat 9-2
Restriction: Authorized patrons, Borrowing requests are handled by ILL
Friends of the Library Group

TREMONT

P TREMONT DISTRICT PUBLIC LIBRARY*, 215 S Sampson St, 61568. (Mail add: PO Box 123, 61568-0123), SAN 304-7040. Tel: 309-925-5432, 309-925-5597. FAX: 309-925-9953. Circulation E-mail: TremontLibrary.Circulation@gmail.com. Web Site: tremontlibrary.com. *Dir,* Maria Ford; *Youth Serv Dir,* Lizzi Ogle; *Circ & ILL,* Angie Watson
Founded 1928. Pop 5,022; Circ 77,928
Library Holdings: AV Mats 700; Bks on Deafness & Sign Lang 12; CDs 1,130; DVDs 787; High Interest/Low Vocabulary Bk Vols 110; Large Print Bks 400; Bk Titles 22,718; Bk Vols 24,532; Per Subs 83; Talking Bks 641
Subject Interests: Local hist
Automation Activity & Vendor Info: (Circulation) TLC (The Library Corporation); (ILL) OCLC FirstSearch; (OPAC) TLC (The Library Corporation)
Wireless access
Function: Adult bk club, Art exhibits, Computer training, Digital talking bks, Electronic databases & coll, Home delivery & serv to seniorr ctr & nursing homes, Homebound delivery serv, ILL available, Internet access, Mail & tel request accepted, Music CDs, Photocopying/Printing, Prog for adults, Prog for children & young adult, Ref & res, Senior computer classes, Spoken cassettes & CDs, Summer reading prog, Tax forms, Telephone ref, Wheelchair accessible
Mem of Reaching Across Illinois Library System (RAILS)
Partic in Resource Sharing Alliance
Open Mon-Thurs 10-8, Fri 10-5, Sat 9-1

TRENTON

P TRENTON PUBLIC LIBRARY*, 118 E Indiana, 62293. SAN 304-7059. Tel: 618-224-7662. E-mail: trentonpubliclibrary@gmail.com. Web Site: trentonil.org/library. *Libr Dir,* Angie Chute; E-mail: lrich118@gmail.com; *Asst Librn,* Lindy Evans; *Asst Librn,* Tracy Frey; Staff 2 (Non-MLS 2)
Founded 1974. Pop 2,715; Circ 15,236
Library Holdings: DVDs 1,038; Large Print Bks 954; Bk Vols 28,994; Per Subs 78; Talking Bks 290; Videos 303
Wireless access
Mem of Illinois Heartland Library System
Open Tues-Thurs 10-7, Fri 12-5, Sat 9-1

TROY

P TRI-TOWNSHIP PUBLIC LIBRARY DISTRICT*, 209 S Main St, 62294. SAN 375-9709. Tel: 618-667-2133. FAX: 618-667-9866. E-mail: info@troylibrary.org. Web Site: troylibrary.org. *Libr Dir,* David Cassens, II; *Head, Circ,* Debbie Shrewsberry; *Ch,* Coleen Morgan; *Mgr, Digital Assets,* Joel Pikora; *Cataloger,* Denise Putz; Staff 8 (MLS 1, Non-MLS 7)
Pop 13,215; Circ 70,000
Library Holdings: Bk Titles 30,000; Per Subs 195
Special Collections: Local Area Parenting Coll
Automation Activity & Vendor Info: (Circulation) SirsiDynix
Wireless access
Function: Doc delivery serv, ILL available, Internet access, Prog for children & young adult, Ref serv available, Summer reading prog, Telephone ref
Mem of Illinois Heartland Library System
Open Mon-Thurs 9-8, Fri 9-5, Sat 9-4
Friends of the Library Group

TUSCOLA

P TUSCOLA PUBLIC LIBRARY, 112 E Sale St, 61953. SAN 304-7067. Tel: 217-253-3812. FAX: 217-253-4599. E-mail: tuscolabibliophile@gmail.com. Web Site: www.tuscolalibrary.org. *Dir,* Devin C Black; Staff 6 (MLS 1, Non-MLS 5)
Founded 1903. Pop 4,448
Library Holdings: Bk Vols 18,000; Per Subs 45
Wireless access
Function: Homebound delivery serv, ILL available, Magnifiers for reading, Photocopying/Printing, Prog for children & young adult, Summer reading prog, Telephone ref, Wheelchair accessible
Mem of Illinois Heartland Library System
Open Mon-Thurs 10-7, Fri 10-6, Sat 10-2
Friends of the Library Group

ULLIN

J SHAWNEE COMMUNITY COLLEGE LIBRARY, 8364 Shawnee College Rd, 62992. SAN 304-7083. Tel: 618-634-3271. FAX: 618-634-3215. E-mail: library@shawneecc.edu. Web Site: www.shawneecc.edu/library. *Librn,* Tracey Johnson; E-mail: traceyj@shawneecc.edu
Founded 1969
Library Holdings: AV Mats 1,300; Bk Vols 32,400; Per Subs 41
Special Collections: Oral History
Automation Activity & Vendor Info: (Acquisitions) Innovative Interfaces, Inc. - Polaris; (Cataloging) Innovative Interfaces, Inc. - Polaris; (Circulation) Innovative Interfaces, Inc. - Polaris; (OPAC) Innovative Interfaces, Inc. - Polaris; (Serials) Innovative Interfaces, Inc. - Polaris
Wireless access
Mem of Illinois Heartland Library System
Partic in Consortium of Academic & Research Libraries in Illinois; Network of Illinois Learning Resources in Community Colleges
Open Mon-Thurs 7:45-6, Fri 7:45-4 (Spring-Fall); Mon-Fri 7:45-4 (Summer)

UNION

S ILLINOIS RAILWAY MUSEUM*, Pullman Technical Library, 7000 Olson Rd, 60180. (Mail add: PO Box 427, 60180-0427), SAN 326-4009. Tel: 815-923-2020. FAX: 815-923-2006. E-mail: pullmanlibrary@irm.org. Web Site: www.irm.org. *Curator,* Ted Anderson; *Archivist,* Al Johanson; *Historian,* Bob Webber
Founded 1974
Special Collections: Pullman Company Linen Tracings & Blueprints Coll; T-Z Company Coll, blue prints
Function: Archival coll
Restriction: Open by appt only

UNIVERSITY PARK

C GOVERNORS STATE UNIVERSITY LIBRARY*, One University Pkwy, 60466-0975. SAN 304-5315. Tel: 708-534-4111. Circulation Tel: 708-534-4112. FAX: 708-534-4564. E-mail: library@govst.edu. Web Site: www.govst.edu/library. *Tech Serv Librn,* Cynthia Morrow Romanowski; Tel: 708-534-4116, E-mail: cromanowski@govst.edu; *Ref (Info Servs),* Linda Geller; Tel: 708-534-4136, E-mail: geller@govst.edu; *Ref (Info Servs),* Paul Blobaum; Tel: 708-534-4139, E-mail: blobaum@govst.edu; Staff 29 (MLS 7, Non-MLS 22)
Founded 1969. Enrl 6,073; Fac 195; Highest Degree: Master
Library Holdings: AV Mats 26,720; CDs 356; DVDs 409; e-books 2,000; e-journals 20,165; Bk Titles 238,491; Bk Vols 263,953; Per Subs 1,917; Videos 9,008
Special Collections: Afro-American Literature (Schomberg Coll); ERIC Documents Coll, microfiche; Materials Center Coll. State Document Depository; US Document Depository
Subject Interests: Acctg, Biology, Bus & mgt, Chem, Computer sci, Counseling, Criminal law & justice, Educ, Finance, Humanities, Psychol
Automation Activity & Vendor Info: (Acquisitions) Ex Libris Group; (Cataloging) Ex Libris Group; (Circulation) Ex Libris Group; (Course Reserve) Ex Libris Group; (ILL) OCLC ILLiad; (OPAC) Ex Libris Group; (Serials) Ex Libris Group
Wireless access
Publications: Index to Non-print Materials; Information Please (Newsletter); Media Holdings List; Periodicals Holding List; Subject Guide to Indexes & Abstracts
Partic in Chicago Academic Libr Coun; Consortium of Academic & Research Libraries in Illinois; OCLC Online Computer Library Center, Inc; SMRHEC
Special Services for the Deaf - Closed caption videos
Special Services for the Blind - Assistive/Adapted tech devices, equip & products
Open Mon-Thurs 8:30am-10pm, Fri & Sat 8:30-5, Sun 1-5
Friends of the Library Group

P UNIVERSITY PARK PUBLIC LIBRARY DISTRICT*, 1100 Blackhawk Dr, 60466. SAN 304-5323. Tel: 708-534-2580. FAX: 708-534-2583. E-mail: universityparkpld@yahoo.com. Web Site: www.uppld.org. *Dir,* Tracy Ducksworth
Founded 1974. Pop 6,245; Circ 16,314
Library Holdings: Bk Vols 23,000; Per Subs 95
Automation Activity & Vendor Info: (Circulation) SirsiDynix
Wireless access
Mem of Reaching Across Illinois Library System (RAILS)
Partic in System Wide Automated Network
Open Mon-Thurs 10-8, Fri & Sat 10-5
Friends of the Library Group

URBANA

C UNIVERSITY OF ILLINOIS LIBRARY AT URBANA-CHAMPAIGN*, 1408 W Gregory Dr, 61801. SAN 340-8124. Tel: 217-333-2291. Administration Tel: 217-333-0790. E-mail: reflib@library.illinois.edu. Web Site: www.library.illinois.edu. *Dean, Libr & Univ Librn,* John P Wilkin; E-mail: jpwilkin@illinois.edu; Staff 163 (MLS 110, Non-MLS 53)
Founded 1868. Enrl 42,000; Highest Degree: Doctorate
Library Holdings: Bk Vols 13,000,000
Special Collections: 16th & 17th Century Italian Drama; 17th Century Coll; 17th Century Newsletters; 17th Century Publishing (William Bentley & Grant Richards Coll); 18th Century English Literature (Nickell Coll); Abraham Lincoln Coll; American Humor & Folklore (Franklin J Meine Coll); Aquinas; Baskette Coll on Freedom of Expression; Carl Sandburg Coll; Cobbett (Muierhead Coll); Confederate Imprints (Richard B Harwell Coll); H G Wells Coll; Hollander Library of Economic History; Incunabula including St Thomas; John Milton Coll; Political & Religious Pamphlets; Shakespeare (Ernest Ingold Coll); Shana Alexander papers; T W Baldwin Elizabethan Library; W S Merwin papers; William Maxwell papers; William Shakespeare Coll. Oral History; US Document Depository
Wireless access
Publications: Friendscript
Mem of Illinois Heartland Library System
Partic in Association of Research Libraries; Big Ten Academic Alliance; Consortium of Academic & Research Libraries in Illinois; East Central Illinois Consortium; Illinois Library & Information Network; Midwest Universities Consortium for Int Activities, Inc; OCLC Online Computer Library Center, Inc; OCLC Research Library Partnership
Open Mon-Thurs 8:30am-10pm, Fri 8:30-6, Sat 1-5, Sun 1-10
Friends of the Library Group

Departmental Libraries:

ARCHITECTURE & ART LIBRARY, 208 Architecture Bldg, 608 E Lorado Taft Dr, 61801, SAN 340-8248. Tel: 217-333-0224. E-mail: rickerlibrary@library.illinois.edu. Web Site: www.library.illinois.edu/arx. *Interim Head of Libr,* Christopher Quinn; Tel: 217-300-0224, E-mail: cquinn2@illinois.edu; *Libr Spec,* Shoshana Ruth Vegh-Gaynor; Tel: 217-300-6422, E-mail: veghgay2@illinois.edu; *Libr Spec,* Lee Margaret Whitacre; Tel: 217-300-6250, E-mail: lmw2@illinois.edu
Library Holdings: Bk Vols 58,274
Open Mon-Thurs 8:30am-10pm, Fri 8:30-5, Sat 1-5, Sun 1-10

BUSINESS INFORMATION SERVICES, 101 Main Library, 1408 W Gregory, 61801, SAN 340-8396. Tel: 217-333-3619. E-mail: bis@library.illinois.edu. Web Site: library.illinois.edu/bis. *Head Librn,* Rebecca Smith; Tel: 217-244-0388, E-mail: becky@illinois.edu; Staff 3 (MLS 3)
Library Holdings: Bk Vols 65,000; Per Subs 1,200
Open Mon-Fri 8:30-5

CHEMISTRY, 170 Noyes Lab, MC-712, 505 S Mathews Ave, 61801, SAN 340-8302. Tel: 217-333-3737. E-mail: chemlib@library.illinois.edu. Web Site: www.library.illinois.edu/chx. *Head Librn,* Mary Schlembach; Tel: 213-333-3158, E-mail: schlemba@illinois.edu
Library Holdings: Bk Vols 70,000
Open Mon-Thurs 9am-10pm, Fri 9-5, Sat 1-5, Sun 1-10

CLASSIC LIBRARY COLLECTION READING ROOM, 225 Main Library, 1408 W Gregory Dr, 61801, SAN 340-8361. Tel: 217-333-2220. E-mail: classics@library.illinois.edu. Web Site: www.library.illinois.edu/litlang/classics. *Librn,* David Morris; Tel: 217-300-5060, E-mail: dmorri9@illinois.edu. Subject Specialists: *Classical studies,* David Morris
Library Holdings: Bk Titles 54,000
Open Mon-Thurs 8:30am-10pm, Fri 8:30-6, Sat 1-5, Sun 1-10

COMMUNICATIONS, 122 Gregory Hall, MC-462, 810 S Wright St, 61801, SAN 340-8426. Tel: 217-333-2216. E-mail: comlibrarian@illinois.edu. Web Site: www.library.illinois.edu/commedia. *Head of Libr, Librn,* Lisa Romero; Tel: 217-333-6348, E-mail: l-romero@uiuc.edu
Library Holdings: AV Mats 900; Bk Vols 16,600
Open Mon-Thurs 8am-Midnight, Fri 8-5, Sat 1-5, Sun 1-Midnight

FUNK LIBRARY, AGRICULTURAL, CONSUMER & ENVIRONMENTAL SCIENCES, 1101 S Goodwin, MC-633, 61801, SAN 340-8183. Tel: 217-333-2416. Reference Tel: 217-244-2249. E-mail: aceslib@library.illinois.edu. Web Site: www.library.illinois.edu/funkaces. *Head of Libr,* Sarah C Williams; Tel: 217-333-8916, E-mail: scwillms@illinois.edu
Library Holdings: Bk Vols 119,815
Open Mon-Thurs 8:30am-2:30am, Fri 8:30am-9pm, Sat 10-9, Sun 10am-2:30am

GEOLOGY VIRTUAL LIBRARY, 1301 W Springfield Ave, 61801, SAN 340-8574. Web Site: www.library.illinois.edu/gex. *Chem Librn, Phys Sci Librn,* Mary Schlembach; Tel: 217-333-3158, E-mail: schlemba@illinois.edu; *Maps Librn,* Jenny Johnson; Tel: 217-333-3855, E-mail: jmj@illinois.edu
Library Holdings: Bk Vols 100,359

GOVERNMENT INFORMATION SERVICES, 450-F Main Library, 1408 W Gregory Dr, 61801, SAN 340-8434. Tel: 217-333-2290. E-mail: gdoclib@library.illinois.edu. Web Site: www.library.illinois.edu/govinfo. *Govt Info Coordr,* Mary Mallory; Tel: 217-244-4621, E-mail: mmallory@illinois.edu; Staff 7 (MLS 4, Non-MLS 3)
Library Holdings: Bk Vols 230,000
Open Mon-Thurs 8:30am-11pm, Fri 8:30-6

GRAINGER ENGINEERING LIBRARY INFORMATION CENTER, 1301 W Springfield Ave, MC-274, 61801, SAN 340-8485. Tel: 217-333-3576. Reference Tel: 217-244-7826. E-mail: enginlib@library.illinois.edu. Web Site: www.library.illinois.edu/enx. *Head of Libr,* William Mischo; Tel: 217-333-7497, E-mail: w-mischo@illinois.edu
Library Holdings: Bk Vols 271,625
Restriction: Badge access after hrs

HISTORY, PHILOSOPHY & NEWSPAPER, 246 Main Library, MC-522, 1408 W Gregory Dr, 61801, SAN 340-8639. Tel: 217-333-1509. E-mail: hpnl@library.illinois.edu. Web Site: www.library.illinois.edu/hpnl. *Interim Head of Libr,* Lynne Rudasill; Tel: 217-333-6879, E-mail: rudasill@illinois.edu; Staff 4 (MLS 1, Non-MLS 3)
Library Holdings: Bk Vols 40,944
Open Mon-Thurs 9-7, Fri 9-5, Sat & Sun 1-5

ILLINOIS HISTORY & LINCOLN COLLECTIONS, 324 Main Library, MC-522, 1408 W Gregory Dr, 61801, SAN 340-8728. Tel: 217-333-1777. E-mail: ihlc@library.illinois.edu. Web Site: www.library.illinois.edu/ihx. *Archives, Prog Officer,* Krista Lauren Gray; Tel: 217-333-1777, E-mail: graykr@illinois.edu; Staff 1 (MLS 1)
Library Holdings: Bk Vols 34,000
Open Mon-Fri 9-5

INFORMATION SCIENCES VIRTUAL LIBRARY, 100 Main Library, 1408 W Gregory Dr, 61801, SAN 340-8817. E-mail: lislib@library.illinois.edu. Web Site: www.library.illinois.edu/infosci. *Library Contact,* Christopher Bailey; Tel: 217-300-8365, E-mail: cbailey3@illinois.edu; Staff 1 (MLS 1)
Function: Distance learning, Electronic databases & coll, For res purposes, ILL available, Mail loans to mem, Online cat, Online info literacy tutorials on the web & in blackboard, Online ref, Orientations, Outside serv via phone, mail, e-mail & web, Ref & res, Ref serv available, Workshops

INTERNATIONAL & AREAS STUDIES LIBRARY, 321 Library, MC-522, 1408 W Gregory Dr, 61801, SAN 340-8264. Tel: 217-333-1501. Web Site: www.library.illinois.edu/ias. *Head Librn,* Steven Witt; Tel: 217-265-7518, E-mail: swwitt@illinois.edu
Founded 1965
Library Holdings: Bk Vols 420,000; Per Subs 1,250
Open Mon-Thurs 9-7, Fri 9-5, Sat & Sun 1-5

LABOR & EMPLOYMENT RELATIONS DIGITAL LIBRARY, 100 Main Library, SSHEL, MC-522, 1408 W Gregory Dr, 61801, SAN 340-8752. Tel: 217-244-1864. FAX: 217-333-2214. E-mail: sshel@library.illinois.edu. Web Site: www.library.illinois.edu/sshel/laboremployment. *Librn,* Yoo-Seong Song; Tel: 217-333-8021, E-mail: yoosong@illinois.edu
Library Holdings: Per Subs 353

CL LAW, 142 Law Bldg, MC-594, 504 E Pennsylvania Ave, Champaign, 61820, SAN 340-8787. Circulation Tel: 217-333-2915. Reference Tel: 217-244-0614. E-mail: law-refdesk@illinois.edu. Web Site: law.illinois.edu/academics/library. *Dir,* Faye Jones; Tel: 217-265-4524, E-mail: fjone@illinois.edu; Staff 9.5 (MLS 9.5)
Founded 1897
Library Holdings: Bk Vols 761,652; Per Subs 8,800
Special Collections: European Economic Commun. State Document Depository; US Document Depository
Subject Interests: Foreign law
Publications: Law Library Aids; Law Library Collection Information
Open Mon-Thurs 8am-Midnight, Fri 8am-9pm, Sat 10-9, Sun 10am-Midnight

LITERATURES & LANGUAGES, 225 Main Library, MC-522, 1408 W Gregory Dr, 61801, SAN 340-8515. Tel: 217-333-2220. E-mail: litlang@library.illinois.edu. Web Site: www.library.illinois.edu/litlang. *Head, Lit & Lang Libr,* Paula Mae Carns; Tel: 217-333-0076, E-mail: pcarns@illinois.edu; *Cinema Studies & Media Serv Spec,* Dr Robert Cagle; Tel: 217-265-0737, E-mail: cagle@illinois.edu; *Info Serv Librn, Res,* Dr David Anthony Morris; Tel: 217-996-2753, E-mail: dmorri9@illinois.edu; *Librn,* Marek Sroka; Tel: 217-265-8025, E-mail: msroka@illinois.edu. Subject Specialists: *Western European,* Paula Mae

Carns; *Comparative lit, Media,* Dr Robert Cagle; *Classical studies,* Dr David Anthony Morris; Staff 7 (MLS 5, Non-MLS 2)
Founded 2011. Fac 4
Library Holdings: Bk Vols 40,000
Subject Interests: Cinema, English lit, Fr lit, German lit, Italian, Latin Am lit, Linguistics, Medieval studies, Spanish
Function: Electronic databases & coll, For res purposes, Online info literacy tutorials on the web & in blackboard, Online ref, Outreach serv, Ref serv available, Res assist avail, Res libr
Open Mon-Thurs 8:30am-10pm, Fri 8:30-6, Sat 1-5, Sun 1-10

MAP LIBRARY, 418 Main Library, Mc-522, 1408 W Gregory Dr, 61801, SAN 340-8841. Tel: 217-333-0827. Web Site: www.library.illinois.edu/max. *Head of Libr,* Jenny Marie Johnson; Tel: 217-333-3855, E-mail: jmj@illinois.edu; Staff 2 (MLS 1, Non-MLS 1)
Library Holdings: Bk Vols 590,641
Open Mon-Fri 8:30-5

MATHEMATICS, 216 Altgeld Hall, 1409 W Green St, 61801, SAN 340-8876. Tel: 217-333-0258. E-mail: math@library.illinois.edu. Web Site: www.library.illinois.edu/mtx. *Head of Libr,* Timothy Cole; Tel: 217-244-7837, E-mail: t-cole3@illinois.edu
Library Holdings: Bk Vols 100,000
Open Mon-Thurs 9-8, Fri 9-5, Sat 1-5, Sun 1-8

MUSIC & PERFORMING ARTS, 1300 Music Bldg, MC-056, 1114 W Nevada St, 61801, SAN 340-8930. Tel: 217-333-1173. E-mail: mpal@library.illinois.edu. Web Site: www.library.illinois.edu/mpal. *Head Librn,* Kirstin Dougan; Tel: 217-244-4072, E-mail: dougan@illinois.edu
Library Holdings: CDs 34,000; DVDs 3,200; Microforms 19,000; Music Scores 520,000; Bk Vols 311,000
Open Mon-Thurs 8:30am-10pm, Fri 8:30-5, Sat 1-5, Sun 2-10

PHYSICS-ASTRONOMY VIRTUAL LIBRARY, 1301 W Springfield Ave, 61801, SAN 340-9023. Tel: 217-333-3158. Web Site: www.library.illinois.edu/phx. *Librn,* Mary Schlembach; E-mail: schlemba@illinois.edu; Staff 17 (MLS 15, Non-MLS 2)
Library Holdings: Bk Vols 47,000
Automation Activity & Vendor Info: (Acquisitions) Ex Libris Group; (Cataloging) Ex Libris Group; (Circulation) Ex Libris Group; (Course Reserve) Ex Libris Group; (OPAC) Ex Libris Group

RARE BOOK & MANUSCRIPT LIBRARY, 346 Main Library, MC-522, 1408 W Gregory Dr, 61801, SAN 340-9058. Tel: 217-333-3777. E-mail: askacurator@library.illinois.edu. Web Site: www.library.illinois.edu/rbx. *Head of Libr,* Lynn M Thomas; E-mail: lmt@illinois.edu
Library Holdings: Bk Vols 172,983
Open Mon-Fri 9-5

SOCIAL SCIENCES, HEALTH & EDUCATION LIBRARY, 100/101 Main Library, MC-522, 1408 W Gregory Dr, 61801, SAN 340-8450. Tel: 217-244-1864. E-mail: sshel@library.illinois.edu. Web Site: www.library.illinois.edu/sshel. *Head of Libr,* Nancy O'Brien; Tel: 217-333-2408, E-mail: npobrien@illinois.edu; *Librn,* Yali Feng; Tel: 217-300-6619, E-mail: yalifeng@illinois.edu; *Librn,* Cindy Ingold; Tel: 217-333-7998, E-mail: cingold@illinois.edu; *Librn,* JJ Pionke; Tel: 217-265-0002, E-mail: pionke@illinois.edu; *Librn,* Yoo-Seong Song; Tel: 217-333-8021, E-mail: yoosong@illinois.edu. Subject Specialists: *Children's lit, Curric, Educ,* Nancy O'Brien; *Behav, Sci,* Yali Feng; *Gender, Multicultural, Women's studies,* Cindy Ingold; *Health,* JJ Pionke; *Econ, Labor relations,* Yoo-Seong Song; Staff 9.4 (MLS 8, Non-MLS 1.4)
Founded 2012
Library Holdings: Bk Vols 270,000; Per Subs 747
Special Collections: Children's & Young Adult Literature (School Coll); Curriculum Coll of PreK-12 Classroom Teaching Materials; Human Relations Area Files; Instruments that Measure Intelligence (Test Coll); Occult Sciences (Mandeville Coll)
Open Mon-Thurs 8:30am-10pm, Fri 8:30-6, Sat 1-5, Sun 1-10

UNDERGRADUATE, 1402 W Gregory Dr, MC-522, 61801. Tel: 217-333-3477. Circulation E-mail: undergrad@library.illinois.edu. Web Site: www.library.illinois.edu/ugl. *Head of Libr,* David Henry Ward; Tel: 217-244-2856, E-mail: dh-ward@illinois.edu; Staff 16 (MLS 9, Non-MLS 7)
Library Holdings: Audiobooks 538; DVDs 30,000; Bk Vols 250,014; Per Subs 188
Special Collections: Gaming Resources; Graphic Novels; Loanable Technology; Popular Culture
Function: Art exhibits, Audio & video playback equip for onsite use, Bks on CD, Computers for patron use, Doc delivery serv, E-Reserves, Electronic databases & coll, Equip loans & repairs, Free DVD rentals, ILL available, Internet access, Magnifiers for reading, Online cat, Online info literacy tutorials on the web & in blackboard, Online ref, Orientations, Photocopying/Printing, Printer for laptops & handheld devices, Ref & res, Ref serv available, Scanner, Workshops

UNIVERSITY ARCHIVES, 146 Main Library, MC-522, 1408 W Gregory Dr, 61801, SAN 340-9082. Tel: 217-333-0798. E-mail: illiarch@illinois.edu. Web Site: archives.library.illinois.edu. *Univ Archivist,* William Maher; E-mail: w-maher@illinois.edu; Staff 6 (MLS 5, Non-MLS 1)
Founded 1963
Function: Archival coll
Open Mon, Tues, Thurs & Fri 8:30-12 & 1-5, Wed 10-12 & 1-5

UNIVERSITY LABORATORY HIGH SCHOOL LIBRARY, 1212 W Springfield Ave, MC-254, 61801, SAN 340-9112. Tel: 217-333-1589. Web Site: www.library.illinois.edu/uni. *Librn,* DoMonique Arnold; Tel: 217-333-1589, E-mail: darnold2@illinois.edu
Library Holdings: Bk Vols 13,700
Open Mon-Fri 7:45-4:15

CM VETERINARY MEDICINE, 1257 Veterinary Med Basic Science Bldg, 2001 S Lincoln Ave, 61802, SAN 340-9147. Tel: 217-333-8778. E-mail: vetmed@library.illinois.edu. Web Site: www.library.illinois.edu/vex. *Veterinary Med Librn,* Erin Kerby; Tel: 217-244-1295, E-mail: ekerb@illinois.edu; Staff 3 (MLS 1, Non-MLS 2)
Library Holdings: Bk Vols 52,000
Open Mon-Fri 8:30-5

P THE URBANA FREE LIBRARY, 210 W Green St, 61801. SAN 304-7164. Tel: 217-367-4057. Reference Tel: 217-367-4405. Administration Tel: 217-367-4058. FAX: 217-367-4061. Administration E-mail: administration@urbanafree.org. Web Site: urbanafreelibrary.org. *Exec Dir,* Celeste Choate; E-mail: cchoate@urbanafree.org; *Assoc Dir,* Dawn Cassady; E-mail: dcassady@urbanafree.org; *Director, Adult & Youth Services & Acquisitions,* Rachel Fuller; Tel: 217-367-4069, E-mail: rfuller@urbanafree.org; *Director, Champaign County Historical Archives,* Donica Swann; Tel: 217-367-4025, E-mail: dmartin@urbanafree.org; *Dir, Commun Engagement,* Amanda Standerfer; E-mail: astanderfer@urbanafree.org
Founded 1874. Pop 41,250
Special Collections: Champaign County Historical Archives, county records; City of Urbana Municipal Records. Municipal Document Depository; Oral History
Subject Interests: Genealogy, Local hist, Maps, Photog
Automation Activity & Vendor Info: (ILL) OCLC WorldShare Interlibrary Loan
Wireless access
Function: 24/7 Electronic res, 24/7 Online cat, 3D Printer, Adult bk club, Adult literacy prog, Archival coll, Art exhibits, Art programs, Audiobks via web, Bks on CD, Chess club, Children's prog, Computer training, Computers for patron use, E-Readers, Electronic databases & coll, Free DVD rentals, Home delivery & serv to seniorr ctr & nursing homes, Homebound delivery serv, ILL available, Internet access, Large print keyboards, Literacy & newcomer serv, Magazines, Magnifiers for reading, Mail & tel request accepted, Makerspace, Mango lang, Meeting rooms, Microfiche/film & reading machines, Movies, Museum passes, Music CDs, Notary serv, Online cat, Online ref, Orientations, Outreach serv, Outside serv via phone, mail, e-mail & web, OverDrive digital audio bks, Photocopying/Printing, Printer for laptops & handheld devices, Prog for adults, Prog for children & young adult, Ref & res, Ref serv available, Res performed for a fee, Scanner, Senior outreach, Spanish lang bks, STEM programs, Story hour, Study rm, Summer & winter reading prog, Summer reading prog, Tax forms, Teen prog, Telephone ref, Visual arts prog, Wheelchair accessible, Winter reading prog, Writing prog
Mem of Illinois Heartland Library System
Special Services for the Deaf - TTY equip
Special Services for the Blind - Low vision equip
Open Mon-Thurs 9-9, Fri & Sat 9-6, Sun 1-5
Friends of the Library Group

UTICA

P UTICA PUBLIC LIBRARY DISTRICT*, 224 Mill St, 61373. (Mail add: PO Box 367, 61373-0367), SAN 304-7172. Tel: 815-667-4509. FAX: 815-667-4140. E-mail: uticalibrary@comcast.net. *Dir,* Marlene Ernat; *Librn,* Robbyn Partain; E-mail: uticalibrary@comcast.net; *Asst Librn,* Kathy Barbee; Staff 6 (MLS 1, Non-MLS 5)
Founded 1952. Pop 2,589; Circ 115,644; Fac 5
Library Holdings: Audiobooks 350; DVDs 300; Large Print Bks 2,000; Bk Vols 50,000; Per Subs 20; Talking Bks 2,300
Special Collections: LaSalle County History Coll
Wireless access
Function: Computers for patron use, Digital talking bks, Free DVD rentals, Genealogy discussion group, Homebound delivery serv, ILL available, Internet access, Magazines, Microfiche/film & reading machines, Movies, Online cat, OverDrive digital audio bks, Photocopying/Printing, Prog for children & young adult, Story hour, Summer reading prog, Tax forms, VHS videos
Mem of Reaching Across Illinois Library System (RAILS)
Open Mon & Wed 2-8, Tues & Thurs 9-12 & 5-8, Fri 1-5, Sat 8:30-1:30
Friends of the Library Group

VALMEYER

P VALMEYER PUBLIC LIBRARY DISTRICT, 300 S Cedar Bluff, 62295. SAN 323-4495. Tel: 618-935-2626. FAX: 618-310-1127. Web Site: valmeyerlibrary.com. *Librn,* Lori Brutton; E-mail:

lbrutton@valmeyerk12.org; *Libr Asst,* Edna Gravot; *Libr Asst,* Elaine Knobloch; Staff 3 (MLS 1, Non-MLS 2)
Founded 1984. Pop 2,319
Library Holdings: Bk Titles 17,000; Bk Vols 20,000; Per Subs 2
Wireless access
Mem of Illinois Heartland Library System
Open Mon & Thurs 8-6:30, Tues, Wed & Fri 8-4

VANDALIA

P EVANS PUBLIC LIBRARY DISTRICT, 215 S Fifth St, 62471-2703. SAN 304-7180. Tel: 618-283-2824. FAX: 618-283-4705. E-mail: epldill@gmail.com. Web Site: evanspubliclibrary.org. *Libr Dir,* Jessica Blain; E-mail: eplddirector@gmail.com; Staff 1 (Non-MLS 1)
Founded 1921. Pop 11,791; Circ 84,061
Jul 2013-Jun 2014 Income $329,366, State $16,167, County $273,075, Locally Generated Income $25,498. Mats Exp $44,701, Books $31,267, Per/Ser (Incl. Access Fees) $6,025, AV Mat $6,689, Electronic Ref Mat (Incl. Access Fees) $720. Sal $152,137 (Prof $59,339)
Library Holdings: Bk Vols 32,217; Per Subs 135; Videos 1,582
Special Collections: James Hall Coll; Lincoln (Rankin Coll); Local History & Genealogy; Vandalia Authors
Automation Activity & Vendor Info: (Cataloging) Innovative Interfaces, Inc; (Circulation) Innovative Interfaces, Inc; (OPAC) Innovative Interfaces, Inc; (Serials) Innovative Interfaces, Inc
Wireless access
Function: Bks on cassette, Bks on CD, CD-ROM, Children's prog, Computers for patron use, Electronic databases & coll, Homebound delivery serv, ILL available, Magnifiers for reading, Music CDs, Online cat, Photocopying/Printing, Ref serv available, Summer reading prog, Telephone ref, VHS videos, Wheelchair accessible
Mem of Illinois Heartland Library System
Partic in Illinois Library & Information Network
Special Services for the Deaf - TDD equip; TTY equip
Special Services for the Blind - Home delivery serv; Large print bks; Magnifiers; Talking bks
Open Mon-Thurs 9-7, Fri & Sat 9-5
Friends of the Library Group

S VANDALIA CORRECTIONAL CENTER LIBRARY*, Rte 51 N, 62471. (Mail add: PO Box 500, 62471-0500), SAN 376-1193. Tel: 618-283-4170. *Libr Assoc,* Clark Phillips

VENICE

P VENICE PUBLIC LIBRARY*, 325 Broadway, 62090. SAN 304-7199. Tel: 618-877-1330. FAX: 618-877-0633. E-mail: venicepubliclibrary@gmail.com. *Dir,* Diane West
Founded 1953. Pop 1,890; Circ 10,000
Library Holdings: Bk Vols 9,218; Per Subs 10
Wireless access
Mem of Illinois Heartland Library System
Special Services for the Deaf - TTY equip
Open Tues & Thurs 10-4, Wed & Fri 9-3, Sat 10-2

VERMONT

P VERMONT PUBLIC LIBRARY*, 101 N Main St, 61484. SAN 304-7202. Tel: 309-784-6291. FAX: 309-784-6291. E-mail: vermontlibrary@sybertech.net. Web Site: vermontpubliclibrary.net. *Libr Dir,* Ashley Vance; Staff 2 (MLS 1, Non-MLS 1)
Founded 1947. Pop 806
Library Holdings: Bk Vols 5,676
Wireless access
Open Mon, Wed & Fri 2-6, Tues & Thurs 2-7, Sat 10-1

VICTORIA

P VICTORIA PUBLIC LIBRARY DISTRICT*, 227 E Main St, 61485. (Mail add: PO Box 216, 61485-0216), SAN 375-9628. Tel: 309-879-2295. FAX: 309-879-2295. E-mail: vipl@mymctc.net. *Librn,* Carol Weedman
Pop 865; Circ 10,560
Library Holdings: Bk Vols 13,420; Per Subs 10
Open Mon-Fri 10-12 & 1-5, Sat 10-12 & 1-3

VIENNA

S ILLINOIS DEPARTMENT OF CORRECTIONS*, Shawnee Correctional Center Library, 6665 State Rte 146E, 62995. SAN 371-7429. Tel: 618-658-8371, Ext 2120. Web Site: www2.illinois.gov/idoc/facilities/Pages/shawneecorrectionalcenter.aspx. *Librn,* Karin Pannier; Staff 2 (Non-MLS 2)
Founded 1985
Library Holdings: Bk Titles 16,000; Per Subs 18
Special Collections: Federal & Illinois Law
Special Services for the Blind - Talking bks
Restriction: Staff & inmates only

P VIENNA CARNEGIE PUBLIC LIBRARY*, 401 Poplar St, 62995. (Mail add: PO Box 616, 62995-0616), SAN 304-7229. Tel: 618-658-5051. FAX: 618-658-5051. E-mail: viepub@yahoo.com. *Librn,* Margaret Mathis
Founded 1910. Pop 1,420; Circ 6,000
Library Holdings: Bk Vols 9,553
Special Collections: Old Books & Literature
Mem of Illinois Heartland Library System
Open Mon-Wed, Fri & Sat 1-5

S VIENNA CORRECTIONAL CENTER LIBRARY*, 6695 State Rte 146 E, 62995. (Mail add: PO Box 200, 62995-0200), SAN 304-7210. Tel: 618-658-8371. *Librn,* Karin Pannier; Staff 2 (MLS 1, Non-MLS 1)
Founded 1972
Library Holdings: Bk Titles 17,000
Special Collections: Criminology Coll; Law Library; SW Reporter
Subject Interests: Law

VILLA GROVE

P CAMARGO TOWNSHIP DISTRICT LIBRARY*, 14 N Main St, 61956. SAN 304-7237. Tel: 217-832-5211. FAX: 217-832-7203. E-mail: camargotownshipdistlib@yahoo.com. Web Site: camargotownship.org. *Dir,* Jackie Wells; *Asst Dir,* Sarah Smith
Founded 1919. Pop 4,034; Circ 38,459
Library Holdings: AV Mats 2,007; Large Print Bks 400; Bk Vols 22,085; Per Subs 126; Talking Bks 971
Automation Activity & Vendor Info: (Cataloging) Horizon; (Circulation) Horizon
Wireless access
Mem of Illinois Heartland Library System
Partic in Association for Rural & Small Libraries
Special Services for the Blind - Talking bks
Open Mon & Thurs 9-8, Tues, Wed & Fri 9-5, Sat 9-12 & 1-5
Friends of the Library Group

VILLA PARK

P VILLA PARK PUBLIC LIBRARY, 305 S Ardmore Ave, 60181-2698. SAN 304-7245. Tel: 630-834-1164. FAX: 630-834-0489. E-mail: vppladmin@vppl.info. Web Site: www.vppl.info. *Libr Dir,* Sandra D Hill; Tel: 630-834-1164, Ext 111, E-mail: shill@vppl.info; *Head, Circ, Outreach Serv,* Kandice Krettler; E-mail: kkrettler@vppl.info; *Head, Mat Serv,* John Bradford; E-mail: jbradford@vppl.info; *Head, Pub Serv,* Sean Birmingham; Tel: 630-834-1164, Ext 109, E-mail: sbirmingham@vppl.info; *Youth Serv Mgr,* Jean Jansen; E-mail: jjansen@vppl.info; *Automation Serv Coordr,* Jeff Sand; E-mail: jsand@vppl.info; Staff 49 (MLS 9, Non-MLS 40)
Founded 1928. Pop 21,904; Circ 298,116
Library Holdings: Bk Vols 109,850; Per Subs 286
Special Collections: Local History (Early History of Villa Park), bks, clippings, microfilm, slides, tapes
Automation Activity & Vendor Info: (Acquisitions) SirsiDynix; (Circulation) SirsiDynix
Wireless access
Function: 24/7 Electronic res, 24/7 Online cat, Bks on CD, Children's prog, Computer training, E-Readers, E-Reserves, Homebound delivery serv, ILL available
Publications: The Resource (Newsletter)
Mem of Reaching Across Illinois Library System (RAILS)
Partic in System Wide Automated Network
Open Mon-Thurs 9:30-9, Fri-Sat 9:30-5, Sun (Oct-April) 1-5
Friends of the Library Group

VIOLA

P VIOLA PUBLIC LIBRARY DISTRICT, 1701 17th St, 61486. (Mail add: PO Box 479, 61486-0479), SAN 304-7253. Tel: 309-596-2620. FAX: 309-596-2822. E-mail: violapld@hotmail.com. Web Site: violapubliclibrary.webs.com. *Dir,* Lill Batson; Staff 1 (Non-MLS 1)
Founded 1948. Pop 2,246; Circ 17,929
Library Holdings: Audiobooks 951; CDs 200; DVDs 951; e-books 2,917; Bk Titles 11,115; Per Subs 33; Videos 75
Wireless access
Function: Bks on CD, Children's prog, Computer training, Computers for patron use, Free DVD rentals, ILL available, Music CDs, Online cat, OverDrive digital audio bks, Photocopying/Printing, Prog for adults, Summer reading prog, Tax forms, VHS videos, Wheelchair accessible
Mem of Reaching Across Illinois Library System (RAILS)
Open Mon-Thurs 9-12 & 2-6, Fri 9-12 & 2-5, Sat 9-12
Friends of the Library Group

VIRDEN

P GRAND PRAIRIE OF THE WEST PUBLIC LIBRARY DISTRICT*, 142 W Jackson St, 62690-1257. SAN 304-7261. Tel: 217-965-3015. FAX: 217-965-3801. *Dir,* Shirley Blankenship
Pop 5,229; Circ 28,853
Library Holdings: Bk Vols 20,000; Per Subs 36
Wireless access
Mem of Illinois Heartland Library System
Open Mon-Wed & Fri 10-4:50, Thurs 10-7:50, Sat 10-12:50

VIRGINIA

P VIRGINIA MEMORIAL PUBLIC LIBRARY*, 100 N Main St, 62691-1364. SAN 304-727X. Tel: 217-452-3846. FAX: 217-452-3846. E-mail: vmpl@casscomm.com. Web Site: virginiamemorialpubliclibrary.com. *Libr Dir,* Patty Brogdon; *Libr Asst,* Karen Long
Founded 1916. Pop 1,728; Circ 28,878
Library Holdings: AV Mats 264; Large Print Bks 838; Bk Vols 14,431; Per Subs 35; Talking Bks 70
Special Collections: Genealogy
Subject Interests: Local hist
Automation Activity & Vendor Info: (OPAC) TLC (The Library Corporation)
Publications: Illinois Libraries
Open Tues 12-5, Wed 1-6, Fri 9-4, Sat 9-Noon
Friends of the Library Group

WALNUT

P WALNUT PUBLIC LIBRARY DISTRICT*, 101 Heaton, 61376. (Mail add: PO Box 728, 61376-0728), SAN 304-7288. Tel: 815-379-2159. FAX: 815-379-4098. *Dir,* Jaclyn Trujillo; E-mail: director.wpld@yahoo.com; *ILL,* Rebecca Fritz; *Programming,* Kayla Greenwell
Founded 1939. Pop 1,894; Circ 29,700
Library Holdings: Bks on Deafness & Sign Lang 10; Bk Vols 24,218; Per Subs 40
Special Collections: Don Marquis Coll
Subject Interests: Local hist
Automation Activity & Vendor Info: (Acquisitions) Follett Software; (Cataloging) Follett Software; (Circulation) Follett Software; (ILL) OCLC
Wireless access
Mem of Reaching Across Illinois Library System (RAILS)
Open Mon & Wed 9-6, Tues & Fri 12-5, Sat 9-1

WARREN

P WARREN TOWNSHIP PUBLIC LIBRARY, 210 Burnett Ave, 61087. (Mail add: PO Box 427, 61087-0427), SAN 304-7296. Tel: 815-745-2076. FAX: 815-745-2076. E-mail: warren.township.public.library@gmail.com. Web Site: wtpl.weebly.com. *Ch, Dir,* Valerie Woodley; E-mail: warrenlibrary.childrenservices@gmail.com; *Ad,* Brandy Marsden
Founded 1886. Pop 1,601
Library Holdings: Bk Vols 13,000; Per Subs 50
Subject Interests: Local hist
Wireless access
Function: 24/7 Electronic res, 24/7 Online cat, Activity rm, Adult bk club, Children's prog, Computers for patron use, Free DVD rentals, Holiday prog, ILL available, Internet access, Magazines, Magnifiers for reading, Meeting rooms, Microfiche/film & reading machines, Movies, Museum passes, Online cat, Outside serv via phone, mail, e-mail & web, OverDrive digital audio bks, Photocopying/Printing, Prog for adults, Prog for children & young adult, Story hour, Study rm, Summer reading prog, Tax forms, Teen prog, Wheelchair accessible
Mem of Reaching Across Illinois Library System (RAILS)
Special Services for the Deaf - Assisted listening device
Open Tues & Wed 12-7, Thurs 9-12 & 1-5, Sat 9-1

WARRENSBURG

P BARCLAY PUBLIC LIBRARY DISTRICT*, 220 S Main St, 62573-9657. (Mail add: PO Box 349, 62573-0349), SAN 304-730X. Tel: 217-672-3621. FAX: 217-672-8404. E-mail: barclaylib@yahoo.com. Web Site: www.barclay.lib.il.us. *Dir,* Michelle Sawicki; E-mail: director@barclay.lib.il.us; *Ch,* Cindy Lewis; Staff 1 (Non-MLS 1)
Founded 1942. Pop 7,600; Circ 48,000
Library Holdings: Bk Titles 28,145; Bk Vols 29,000; Per Subs 135
Automation Activity & Vendor Info: (Cataloging) SirsiDynix; (Circulation) SirsiDynix; (ILL) SirsiDynix; (OPAC) SirsiDynix
Wireless access
Mem of Illinois Heartland Library System
Open Mon, Wed & Fri 9-5, Tues & Thurs 9-8, Sat 9-1
Friends of the Library Group

WARRENVILLE

S ILLINOIS YOUTH CENTER*, Warrenville Library, 30 W 200 Ferry Rd, 60555. (Mail add: PO Box 828, 60555-0828), SAN 324-0045. Tel: 630-983-6231. Reference Tel: 630-983-6231, Ext 262. Administration Tel: 630-983-6231, Ext 260. FAX: 630-983-6213. *Librn,* Shawnetta Graham; E-mail: shawnetta.graham@doc.illinois.gov; Staff 2 (MLS 1, Non-MLS 1)
Founded 1973
Library Holdings: AV Mats 300; Bk Titles 10,000; Bk Vols 11,000
Special Collections: National Geographics (1960's to Present)
Subject Interests: Romances, Young adult bks
Mem of Reaching Across Illinois Library System (RAILS)
Restriction: Not a lending libr, Not open to pub

P WARRENVILLE PUBLIC LIBRARY DISTRICT, 28 W 751 Stafford Pl, 60555. SAN 324-5144. Tel: 630-393-1171. FAX: 630-393-1688. Web Site: www.warrenville.com. *Dir,* Sandra Whitmer; E-mail: director@warrenville.com; *Syst Adminr,* Cynthia Makowski; E-mail: cynthia@warrenville.com; *Mgr, Mem Serv,* Jaime Perpich; E-mail: jaime@warrenville.com; *Pub Serv Mgr,* Paul Dobersztyn; E-mail: paul@warrenville.com; *Acq & Cat, Coordr,* Position Currently Open; Staff 7 (MLS 5, Non-MLS 2)
Founded 1979. Pop 13,551; Circ 216,000
Jul 2020-Jun 2021 Income $2,172,736. Mats Exp $1,784,169
Special Collections: Local Artist (Albright Coll), original art; Original Fine Arts Coll; Original Fine Arts Coll
Subject Interests: Local hist, Visual arts
Automation Activity & Vendor Info: (Cataloging) SirsiDynix; (Circulation) SirsiDynix; (OPAC) SirsiDynix
Wireless access
Function: 24/7 Electronic res, 24/7 Online cat, Adult bk club, Audiobks via web, Bilingual assistance for Spanish patrons, Bks on CD, Children's prog, Computer training, Computers for patron use, E-Readers, Electronic databases & coll, Free DVD rentals, Homebound delivery serv, ILL available, Internet access, Life-long learning prog for all ages, Magazines, Mango lang, Meeting rooms, Movies, Museum passes, Music CDs, Online cat, OverDrive digital audio bks, Photocopying/Printing, Preschool outreach, Printer for laptops & handheld devices, Prog for adults, Prog for children & young adult, Ref serv available, Scanner, Spanish lang bks, STEM programs, Story hour, Study rm, Summer reading prog, Teen prog, Wheelchair accessible
Publications: Newsletter (Quarterly)
Mem of Reaching Across Illinois Library System (RAILS)
Partic in System Wide Automated Network
Open Mon-Thurs 9:30-9, Fri 9:30-7, Sat 9:30-5, Sun 1-5

WARSAW

P WARSAW PUBLIC LIBRARY, 1025 Webster St, 62379. SAN 304-7326. Tel: 217-256-3417. FAX: 217-256-3154. E-mail: info@warsawlib.org. Web Site: www.warsawlib.org. *Librn,* Daniela Parish
Pop 1,793; Circ 23,658
Library Holdings: Bk Vols 18,000; Per Subs 68
Special Collections: Local History; Local Newspapers (on film from 1840-1973)
Wireless access
Open Mon-Thurs 11-6, Fri 10-5

WASHINGTON

P WASHINGTON DISTRICT LIBRARY*, Five Points Washington, 380 N Wilmor Rd, 61571. SAN 304-7334. Tel: 309-444-2241. FAX: 309-444-4711. E-mail: questions@washingtondl.org. Web Site: washington.lib.il.us. *Libr Dir,* Alexandra Walsh; E-mail: awalsh@washingtondl.org; *Ch Serv, Ref (Info Servs),* Alison Dixon; Staff 5 (MLS 2, Non-MLS 3)
Founded 1937. Pop 19,955; Circ 128,136
Library Holdings: Bk Titles 43,000; Bk Vols 65,000; Per Subs 165
Wireless access
Partic in OCLC Online Computer Library Center, Inc
Open Mon 9-6, Tues-Thurs 9-8, Fri 9-5, Sat 9-5 (9-1 June-Aug), Sun 1-5
Friends of the Library Group
Branches: 1
SUNNYLAND BRANCH, 16 Washington Plaza, 61571. Tel: 309-745-3023. FAX: 309-745-3023. *Br Mgr,* Lisa Koski
Pop 23,604
Library Holdings: Bk Titles 10,000; Per Subs 25
Open Mon & Wed 9-6, Tues 1-8, Thurs 1-6, Fri 9-5, Sat (Sept-May) 9-1
Friends of the Library Group

WATERLOO

P MORRISON-TALBOTT LIBRARY*, 215 Park St, 62298-1305. SAN 304-7342. Tel: 618-939-6232. FAX: 618-939-4974. E-mail: mtl@waterloolibrary.org. Web Site: www.waterloolibrary.org. *Dir,* Elaine Steingrubey; E-mail: elaines@waterloolibrary.org; Staff 6 (Non-MLS 6)

Founded 1892. Pop 10,134; Circ 82,889
Library Holdings: Bk Vols 32,079; Per Subs 130
Special Collections: History & Genealogy of Monroe County, Ill
Automation Activity & Vendor Info: (Acquisitions) Innovative Interfaces, Inc; (Cataloging) Innovative Interfaces, Inc; (Circulation) Innovative Interfaces, Inc; (Course Reserve) Innovative Interfaces, Inc; (ILL) Innovative Interfaces, Inc; (OPAC) Innovative Interfaces, Inc; (Serials) Innovative Interfaces, Inc
Wireless access
Mem of Illinois Heartland Library System
Partic in GateNet; OCLC-LVIS
Open Mon-Thurs 9-8:30, Fri 9-5, Sat 9-4
Friends of the Library Group

WATERMAN

P CLINTON TOWNSHIP PUBLIC LIBRARY*, 110 S Elm St, 60556. (Mail add: PO Box 299, 60556-0299), SAN 304-7350. Tel: 815-264-3339. FAX: 815-264-3814. E-mail: ctplibrary@mchsi.com. Staff 2 (Non-MLS 2)
Founded 1914. Pop 1,868
Library Holdings: Bk Vols 11,479; Per Subs 62
Subject Interests: Genealogy
Wireless access
Mem of Reaching Across Illinois Library System (RAILS)
Open Mon & Wed 1-9, Fri 1-6, Sat 9-1

WATSEKA

S IROQUOIS COUNTY GENEALOGICAL SOCIETY LIBRARY*, Old Courthouse Museum, 103 W Cherry St, 60970-1524. SAN 326-3916. Tel: 815-432-3730. Web Site: sites.rootsweb.com/~ilicgs. *Dir,* Mary Buhr; *Librn,* Ginny Lee
Founded 1969
Library Holdings: Bk Vols 930; Per Subs 20
Special Collections: Iroquois County Census (1790-1920), micro; Iroquois County Newspapers (1850-1959), micro; Probates (1833-1913) & Civil Cases
Subject Interests: Cemeteries, Census, Marriage
Wireless access
Publications: Stalker (Quarterly)
Open Mon-Fri 10-4

P WATSEKA PUBLIC LIBRARY*, 201 S Fourth St, 60970. SAN 304-7369. Tel: 815-432-4544. FAX: 815-432-4545. E-mail: watsekalibrary@yahoo.com. Web Site: www.watsekalibrary.org. *Dir,* Kim Zumwalt
Founded 1898. Pop 5,543; Circ 54,442
Library Holdings: Audiobooks 1,130; DVDs 389; Large Print Bks 1,068; Bk Vols 35,250; Per Subs 100; Videos 227
Automation Activity & Vendor Info: (Acquisitions) Horizon; (Cataloging) Horizon; (Circulation) Horizon; (Course Reserve) Horizon; (ILL) Horizon; (Media Booking) Horizon; (OPAC) Horizon; (Serials) Horizon
Wireless access
Mem of Illinois Heartland Library System
Open Mon-Thurs (Sept-May) 10-8, Fri 10-5:30, Sat 10-3; Mon & Tues (June-Aug) 10-8, Wed-Fri 10-5:30, Sat 10-3
Friends of the Library Group

WAUCONDA

P WAUCONDA AREA PUBLIC LIBRARY DISTRICT*, 801 N Main St, 60084. SAN 304-7377. Tel: 847-526-6225. FAX: 847-526-6244. TDD: 847-526-6236. E-mail: library@wauclib.org. Web Site: www.wauclib.org. *Dir,* Thomas D Kern; Tel: 847-526-6225, Ext 209, E-mail: tkern@wauclib.org; Staff 6 (MLS 6)
Founded 1939. Pop 27,246; Circ 442,037
Jul 2018-Jun 2019 Income $3,433,000
Library Holdings: Audiobooks 4,000; AV Mats 27,000; CDs 7,000; DVDs 17,000; e-books 2,700; Large Print Bks 2,000; Bk Titles 97,000; Per Subs 300
Automation Activity & Vendor Info: (Cataloging) Innovative Interfaces, Inc; (ILL) OCLC FirstSearch; (OPAC) Innovative Interfaces, Inc; (Serials) EBSCO Online
Wireless access
Function: 24/7 Electronic res, 24/7 Online cat, 3D Printer, Activity rm, Adult bk club, Adult literacy prog, After school storytime, Art exhibits, Audio & video playback equip for onsite use, Audiobks via web, AV serv, Bilingual assistance for Spanish patrons, Bk club(s), Bk reviews (Group), Bks on cassette, Bks on CD, CD-ROM, Children's prog, Citizenship assistance, Computer training, Computers for patron use, Doc delivery serv, Electronic databases & coll, Family literacy, Free DVD rentals, Holiday prog, Home delivery & serv to seniorr ctr & nursing homes, Homebound delivery serv, Homework prog, ILL available, Instruction & testing, Internet access, Literacy & newcomer serv, Museum passes, Music CDs, Notary serv, Online cat, Online info literacy tutorials on the web & in blackboard, Online ref, Orientations, Outreach serv, Outside serv via phone, mail, e-mail & web, OverDrive digital audio bks, Photocopying/Printing, Preschool outreach, Prof lending libr, Prog for adults, Prog for children & young adult, Ref & res, Ref serv available, Senior computer classes, Senior outreach, Story hour, Summer reading prog, Tax forms, Teen prog, Telephone ref, Visual arts prog, Wheelchair accessible, Workshops
Publications: Newsletter
Mem of Reaching Across Illinois Library System (RAILS)
Open Mon-Thurs 9-9, Fri 9-6, Sat 9-5, Sun 12-4

WAUKEGAN

GL WILLIAM D BLOCK MEMORIAL LAW LIBRARY*, 18 N County St, 60085-4359. SAN 304-7385. Tel: 847-377-2800. FAX: 847-984-5873. E-mail: lawlibrary@lakecountyil.gov. Web Site: www.19thcircuitcourt.state.il.us/1259/Law-Library. *Libr Dir,* Emanuel Zoberman; Tel: 847-377-2267; Staff 3 (MLS 1, Non-MLS 2)
Founded 1845
Library Holdings: Bk Vols 20,000; Per Subs 20
Special Collections: 1964-present; Illinois Appellate Court Briefs of the Second Judicial District; Illinois Legal Practice Materials; Law Books on the State of Illinois
Automation Activity & Vendor Info: (Acquisitions) Inmagic, Inc.; (Cataloging) Inmagic, Inc.; (Circulation) Inmagic, Inc.; (OPAC) Inmagic, Inc.
Wireless access
Special Services for the Blind - Reader equip
Open Mon-Fri 8-5

M VISTA HEALTH SYSTEMS, EAST SITE*, 1324 N Sheridan Rd, 60085. SAN 304-7407. Tel: 847-360-3000. FAX: 847-360-2402. Web Site: vistahealth.com. *Librn,* Position Currently Open
Founded 1969
Library Holdings: Bk Titles 1,000; Per Subs 64
Partic in Lake County Consortium
Restriction: Staff use only

P WAUKEGAN PUBLIC LIBRARY*, 128 N County St, 60085. SAN 304-7415. Tel: 847-623-2041. FAX: 847-623-2092, 847-623-2094. E-mail: wkgnref@waukeganpl.info. Web Site: www.waukeganpl.org. *Exec Dir,* Selina Gomez-Beloz; E-mail: sgbeloz@waukeganpl.info; *Children's Mgr,* Patrick Toto; *Colls Mgr,* Fran Juergensmeyer; *Customer Serv Mgr,* Marilyn McClelland; *Digital Serv Mgr, IT Mgr,* Kyle Shaub; *Educ Mgr, Mgr, Literacy Serv,* Gale Graves; *Reader Serv Mgr, Ref Mgr,* Janet Wigodner
Founded 1898. Pop 91,962; Circ 650,000
Wireless access
Open Mon-Thurs 10-8, Fri 10-6, Sat & Sun 1-5
Friends of the Library Group
Branches: 1
HINKSTON PARK BRANCH, Hinkston Field House, 800 N Baldwin Ave, 60085. Tel: 847-263-8077.
Open Mon-Thurs 11-7, Fri 1-5
Bookmobiles: 1

WAVERLY

P WAVERLY PUBLIC LIBRARY*, 291 N Pearl St, 62692. SAN 304-7423. Tel: 217-435-2051. FAX: 217-435-2051. E-mail: wavpl@yahoo.com. Web Site: www.waverlyil.com/library. *Librn,* Julie Samaras; *Asst Librn,* Kathy Pereira
Founded 1880. Pop 1,402; Circ 11,000
Library Holdings: Bk Vols 11,000; Per Subs 29
Open Tues, Thurs & Fri 1-6, Wed 1-7, Sat 9-12
Friends of the Library Group

WAYNE CITY

P WAYNE CITY PUBLIC LIBRARY*, Wayne City Kissner Public Library, 102 S Main St, 62895. (Mail add: PO Box 455, 62895-0455), SAN 304-7431. Tel: 618-895-2661. FAX: 618-895-2661. E-mail: wcilpubliclibrary@gmail.com. *Librn,* Amy Esmon
Founded 1971. Pop 1,032; Circ 4,938
Library Holdings: DVDs 243; Large Print Bks 223; Bk Vols 21,613; Per Subs 3; Videos 146
Subject Interests: Illinois
Wireless access
Function: Archival coll, Bk reviews (Group), Computers for patron use, Free DVD rentals, Genealogy discussion group, Homebound delivery serv, Photocopying/Printing, VHS videos, Wheelchair accessible
Mem of Illinois Heartland Library System
Open Tues 12-6, Wed & Thurs 12-5, Fri 12-4
Restriction: Non-resident fee

WAYNESVILLE

P WAYNESVILLE TOWNSHIP LIBRARY*, 303 E Second St, 61778. SAN 304-744X. Tel: 217-949-5111. FAX: 217-949-5111. E-mail: waytlib@hotmail.com. Web Site: waytlib.wixsite.com/website. *Librn,* Holly Murphy; *Libr Asst,* Susie Freeman
Founded 1938. Pop 768; Circ 5,191
Library Holdings: Bk Vols 14,000
Wireless access
Open Mon 2-7, Tues & Thurs 1-5, Wed 11-7, Sat 10:30-2:30

WELDON

P WELDON PUBLIC LIBRARY DISTRICT*, 505 Maple St, 61882. (Mail add: PO Box 248, 61882-0248), SAN 304-7458. Tel: 217-736-2215. FAX: 217-736-2215. Web Site: www.weldon.lib.il.us. *Libr Dir,* Lori Rich; E-mail: lrich@weldon.lib.il.us
Founded 1922. Pop 876; Circ 9,801
Library Holdings: Bk Vols 9,784; Per Subs 44
Automation Activity & Vendor Info: (Cataloging) SirsiDynix; (Circulation) SirsiDynix
Wireless access
Mem of Illinois Heartland Library System
Open Tues & Wed 1-7, Thurs 1-6, Fri 10-6, Sat 10-3

WENONA

P BOND PUBLIC LIBRARY*, 208 S Chestnut St, 61377. SAN 304-7466. Tel: 815-853-4665. FAX: 815-853-4665. E-mail: bondlibrary.il@gmail.com. Web Site: cityofwenona.org/community/library. *Librn,* Sharon Freise
Founded 1896. Pop 1,065; Circ 6,728
Library Holdings: Large Print Bks 175; Bk Titles 20,000; Per Subs 45
Special Collections: County History (Marshall, La Salle, Tazewell, Putnam, Livingston, McLean, Upper Ohio Valley, Logan); Local Newspapers, micro
Wireless access
Mem of Reaching Across Illinois Library System (RAILS)
Special Services for the Deaf - Bks on deafness & sign lang
Open Tues 10:30-7, Wed 1-6, Fri 10:30-6, Sat 9-1
Friends of the Library Group

WEST CHICAGO

P WEST CHICAGO PUBLIC LIBRARY DISTRICT, 118 W Washington St, 60185. SAN 304-7474. Tel: 630-231-1552. FAX: 630-231-1578. TDD: 630-231-5478. Web Site: wcpld.info. *Dir,* Benjamin R Weseloh; E-mail: bweseloh@wcpld.info; *Adult Serv Mgr,* Amanda Ghobrial; E-mail: aghobrial@wcpld.info; *Circ Serv Mgr,* Gabriel Cardenas; E-mail: gcardenas@wcpld.info; Staff 27 (MLS 7, Non-MLS 20)
Founded 1927. Pop 27,444; Circ 183,372
Library Holdings: Bk Vols 83,013; Per Subs 281
Special Collections: Book-plates Coll
Subject Interests: Railroads
Automation Activity & Vendor Info: (Acquisitions) SirsiDynix; (Cataloging) SirsiDynix; (Circulation) SirsiDynix; (Course Reserve) SirsiDynix; (ILL) SirsiDynix; (Media Booking) SirsiDynix; (OPAC) SirsiDynix; (Serials) SirsiDynix
Wireless access
Publications: Biblio News (Newsletter)
Mem of Reaching Across Illinois Library System (RAILS)
Partic in System Wide Automated Network
Open Mon-Thurs 9-6, Fri & Sat 9-4
Friends of the Library Group

WEST FRANKFORT

P WEST FRANKFORT PUBLIC LIBRARY*, 402 E Poplar St, 62896. SAN 304-7482. Tel: 618-932-3313. FAX: 618-932-3313. E-mail: wftplibrary@gmail.com. Web Site: westfrankfortpubliclibrary.org. *Dir,* Pam Sevenski; Staff 4 (Non-MLS 4)
Founded 1927. Pop 8,182; Circ 50,000
Library Holdings: High Interest/Low Vocabulary Bk Vols 50; Bk Vols 40,000; Per Subs 45
Subject Interests: Antiques, Art, Fine arts, Furniture, Genealogy
Automation Activity & Vendor Info: (Acquisitions) Innovative Interfaces, Inc; (Cataloging) Innovative Interfaces, Inc; (Circulation) Innovative Interfaces, Inc; (ILL) Innovative Interfaces, Inc; (OPAC) Innovative Interfaces, Inc; (Serials) Innovative Interfaces, Inc
Wireless access
Mem of Illinois Heartland Library System
Special Services for the Blind - Bks on cassette; Talking bks
Open Mon-Fri 9-6, Sat 10-4
Friends of the Library Group

WEST SALEM

P WEST SALEM PUBLIC LIBRARY*, 112 W South St, 62476-1206. (Mail add: PO Box 128, 62476-0128), SAN 304-7490. Tel: 618-456-8970. FAX: 618-456-8970. E-mail: wslibrary@yahoo.com. *Dir,* Patricia Ann Fisher
Founded 1966. Pop 1,145
Library Holdings: Bk Vols 7,000; Per Subs 10
Mem of Illinois Heartland Library System
Open Mon 9-12 & 1-7, Tues & Thurs 1-7

WEST UNION

P WEST UNION DISTRICT LIBRARY, 209 W Union St, 62477-0138. (Mail add: PO Box 138, 62477-0138), SAN 376-2769. Tel: 217-279-3556. FAX: 217-279-3556. E-mail: wudl1985@yahoo.com. *Head Librn,* Anita Dolson; Staff 1 (Non-MLS 1)
Founded 1986. Pop 785
Library Holdings: Bk Vols 24,847; Per Subs 40
Wireless access
Mem of Illinois Heartland Library System
Open Mon & Thurs 9-1, Tues 6-8, Wed 9-5, Fri 1-6, Sat 10-12
Friends of the Library Group

WESTCHESTER

P WESTCHESTER PUBLIC LIBRARY*, 10700 Canterbury St, 60154. SAN 304-7504. Tel: 708-562-3573. E-mail: wcs@westchesterpl.org. Web Site: westchesterpl.org. *Dir,* Fidencio Marbella; *Asst Dir,* Kristen Jacobson; *Ref (Info Servs),* Patrick Callaghan; *Ref Serv, Ch,* Kristen Jacobson; Staff 9 (MLS 8, Non-MLS 1)
Founded 1956. Pop 16,824; Circ 253,965
May 2019-Apr 2020 Income $1,355,671, State $40,986, County $1,274,049, Other $40,636. Mats Exp $144,317, Books $73,641, AV Mat $6,167, Electronic Ref Mat (Incl. Access Fees) $43,228. Sal $710,073 (Prof $476,138)
Library Holdings: Audiobooks 1,798; CDs 3,355; DVDs 4,974; e-books 367,220; e-journals 3,800; Electronic Media & Resources 739,044; Large Print Bks 1,889; Bk Vols 68,117; Per Subs 92
Automation Activity & Vendor Info: (Acquisitions) SirsiDynix-WorkFlows; (Cataloging) SirsiDynix-WorkFlows; (Circulation) SirsiDynix-WorkFlows; (Discovery) EBSCO Discovery Service; (ILL) SirsiDynix-WorkFlows; (OPAC) SirsiDynix-Enterprise
Wireless access
Function: 24/7 Electronic res, 24/7 Online cat, 3D Printer, Adult bk club, Bks on CD, Children's prog, Computers for patron use, Digital talking bks, Electronic databases & coll, Free DVD rentals, Homebound delivery serv, Internet access, Magazines, Mango lang, Meeting rooms, Museum passes, Music CDs, Online cat, Photocopying/Printing, Prog for adults, Prog for children & young adult, Ref serv available, Spanish lang bks, Story hour, Study rm, Summer & winter reading prog, Tax forms, Teen prog
Mem of Reaching Across Illinois Library System (RAILS)
Partic in System Wide Automated Network
Open Mon-Thurs 10-8, Fri & Sat 10-5
Friends of the Library Group

WESTERN SPRINGS

P THOMAS FORD MEMORIAL LIBRARY, Western Springs Library, 800 Chestnut St, 60558. SAN 304-7520. Tel: 708-246-0520. FAX: 708-246-0403. E-mail: info@fordlibrary.org. Web Site: www.fordlibrary.org. *Dir,* Ted Bodewes; E-mail: bodewes@fordlibrary.org; *Head, Adult Serv,* Matthew Wenslauskis; E-mail: matthew@fordlibrary.org; *Head, Circ/ILL,* Sandy Frank; E-mail: frank@fordlibrary.org; *Head, Youth Serv,* Uma Nori; E-mail: uma@fordlibrary.org; *Youth Serv Librn,* Sarah Wilson; E-mail: sarah@fordlibrary.org; *Adminr,* Kat Lewandowski; E-mail: kathleen@fordlibrary.org; Staff 10 (MLS 10)
Founded 1932. Pop 12,876; Circ 157,203
Library Holdings: CDs 2,000; DVDs 4,000; Large Print Bks 1,200; Bk Vols 72,000; Per Subs 160
Automation Activity & Vendor Info: (Cataloging) SirsiDynix; (Circulation) SirsiDynix; (ILL) OCLC WorldShare Interlibrary Loan; (OPAC) SirsiDynix
Wireless access
Publications: Quarterly Newsletter
Mem of Reaching Across Illinois Library System (RAILS)
Partic in System Wide Automated Network
Open Mon & Wed-Sat 10-6, Tues 10-8
Friends of the Library Group

WESTMONT

P WESTMONT PUBLIC LIBRARY*, 428 N Cass, 60559-1502. SAN 304-7539. Tel: 630-969-5625. FAX: 630-969-6490. E-mail: wpl@westmontlibrary.org. Web Site: westmontlibrary.org. *Dir,* Julia C Coen; E-mail: jcoen@westmontlibrary.org; *Asst Dir, Mgr, Patron Serv,* Brittany Hoornaert Smith; E-mail: bhoornaert@westmontlibrary.org; *Access*

Serv Mgr, Amy Prechel; *Adult Serv Mgr,* Alex Carlson; *Youth Serv Mgr,* Alea Perez; *Outreach Coordr,* Carmen Higgins; E-mail: carmenh@westmontlibrary.org; Staff 7 (MLS 5, Non-MLS 2)
Founded 1943. Pop 24,685; Circ 266,998
May 2016-Apr 2017 Income $1,852,754. Mats Exp $235,325. Sal $870,923
Library Holdings: AV Mats 22,963; e-books 41,136; Bk Vols 73,744; Per Subs 136
Special Collections: Spanish Lang Coll; Westmont Town Crier & Westmont Progress Newspapers, 1943-present
Automation Activity & Vendor Info: (Cataloging) SirsiDynix-WorkFlows; (Circulation) SirsiDynix-WorkFlows; (OPAC) SirsiDynix-Enterprise
Wireless access
Function: 24/7 Electronic res, 24/7 Online cat, 3D Printer, Activity rm, Adult bk club, Adult literacy prog, Art exhibits, Audiobks via web, Bilingual assistance for Spanish patrons, Bk club(s), Bks on CD, Children's prog, Computer training, Computers for patron use, Digital talking bks, Doc delivery serv, Electronic databases & coll, Family literacy, Free DVD rentals, Home delivery & serv to seniorr ctr & nursing homes, ILL available, Mail & tel request accepted, Museum passes, Music CDs, Notary serv, Online cat, Outreach serv, Outside serv via phone, mail, e-mail & web, OverDrive digital audio bks, Photocopying/Printing, Preschool outreach, Prof lending libr, Prog for adults, Prog for children & young adult, Ref serv available, Scanner, Senior computer classes, Senior outreach, Spanish lang bks, Spoken cassettes & CDs, Spoken cassettes & DVDs, Story hour, Summer & winter reading prog, Tax forms, Teen prog, Telephone ref, VHS videos, Wheelchair accessible, Writing prog
Mem of Reaching Across Illinois Library System (RAILS)
Partic in System Wide Automated Network
Special Services for the Deaf - Assistive tech; Bks on deafness & sign lang; Closed caption videos; High interest/low vocabulary bks; Sign lang interpreter upon request for prog; Staff with knowledge of sign lang
Special Services for the Blind - Audio mat; Bks on CD; Braille alphabet card; Copier with enlargement capabilities; Disability awareness prog; Home delivery serv; Large print bks; Newsletter (in large print, Braille or on cassette); Recorded bks; Ref serv; Sound rec
Open Mon-Thurs 10-9, Fri & Sat 10-5, Sun 1-5
Restriction: Non-resident fee
Friends of the Library Group

WESTVILLE

P WESTVILLE PUBLIC LIBRARY DISTRICT*, 233 S State St, 61883. SAN 304-7547. Tel: 217-267-3170. FAX: 217-267-3468. E-mail: westvillepubliclibrary@gmail.com. Web Site: www.westvillepubliclibrarydistrict.org. *Dir,* Rick Balsamello
Founded 1937. Pop 12,499
Library Holdings: Audiobooks 1,046; CDs 266; e-books 30; Large Print Bks 430; Bk Titles 22,914; Bk Vols 40,131; Per Subs 15; Videos 2,737
Special Collections: Antique & Collectibles Coll; History Coll
Wireless access
Mem of Illinois Heartland Library System
Open Mon-Fri 9:30-6, Sat 9:30-1:30

WHEATON

SR COLLEGE CHURCH IN WHEATON LIBRARY*, 332 E Seminary Ave, 60187. SAN 304-7555. Tel: 630-668-0878. FAX: 630-668-0984. Web Site: www.college-church.org/resources/library.php. *Library Contact,* Lisa Kern; Tel: 630-668-0878, Ext 138, E-mail: lkern@college-church.org
Library Holdings: Bk Vols 13,000; Per Subs 10
Subject Interests: Biblical studies, Missions & missionaries
Automation Activity & Vendor Info: (Cataloging) Follett Software; (Circulation) Follett Software
Publications: New in the Church Library (monthly)
Open Sun 9:15-12:30 & 5:45-6:15

M MARIANJOY REHABILITATION HOSPITAL, Medical Library, 26 W 171 Roosevelt Rd, 60187. SAN 324-4903. Interlibrary Loan Service Tel: 630-909-7090. FAX: 630-909-7088. Web Site: www.nm.org. *Libr Asst,* Jane Aruin; E-mail: jane.aruin@nm.org; Staff 1 (Non-MLS 1)
Founded 1974
Library Holdings: CDs 105; e-books 1,168; e-journals 6,253; Bk Titles 1,150; Per Subs 8; Spec Interest Per Sub 8
Special Collections: Rehabilitation Medicine
Subject Interests: Occupational therapy, Phys therapy, Rehabilitation, Speech therapy
Automation Activity & Vendor Info: (Acquisitions) Auto-Graphics, Inc; (Cataloging) Auto-Graphics, Inc; (Circulation) Auto-Graphics, Inc; (ILL) EBSCO Online; (OPAC) Auto-Graphics, Inc; (Serials) Auto-Graphics, Inc
Wireless access
Function: 24/7 Electronic res, 24/7 Online cat, Doc delivery serv, Health sci info serv, ILL available, Internet access, Mail loans to mem, Photocopying/Printing, Ref serv available, Wheelchair accessible
Partic in Docline; Illinois Library & Information Network
Open Mon-Fri 9-4:30
Restriction: Circulates for staff only, Employees & their associates, External users must contact libr, Hospital employees & physicians only, Open to pub upon request, Open to researchers by request, Open to staff only

S THEOSOPHICAL SOCIETY IN AMERICA*, Henry S Olcott Memorial Library, 1926 N Main St, 60187. (Mail add: PO Box 270, 60187-0270), SAN 304-758X. Tel: 630-668-1571, Ext 304. FAX: 630-668-4976. E-mail: library@theosophical.org. Web Site: www.theosophical.org/library. *Dir,* Marina Maestas; Staff 2 (MLS 1, Non-MLS 1)
Founded 1926
Library Holdings: CDs 1,200; DVDs 1,000; Bk Titles 23,000; Bk Vols 30,000; Per Subs 85; Videos 200
Special Collections: Boris de Zirkoff Coll; Mary K Neff Coll; Rare Theosophical Journals Coll, microfilm
Subject Interests: Eastern philosophy, Mysticism, Mythology, Relig, Theosophy
Automation Activity & Vendor Info: (Cataloging) SirsiDynix; (Circulation) SirsiDynix; (ILL) OCLC WorldShare Interlibrary Loan; (OPAC) SirsiDynix
Wireless access
Mem of Reaching Across Illinois Library System (RAILS)
Partic in Illinois Library & Information Network; OCLC Online Computer Library Center, Inc; System Wide Automated Network
Open Mon, Fri & Sat 10-12 & 1-5,0 Tues-Thurs 10-12 & 1-7

C WHEATON COLLEGE*, Buswell Memorial Library, 510 Irving Ave, 60187-4234. (Mail add: 501 College Ave, 60187-5501), SAN 304-7598. Tel: 630-752-5102. Circulation Tel: 630-752-5354. Interlibrary Loan Service Tel: 630-752-5843. Reference Tel: 630-752-5169. Administration Tel: 630-752-5101. FAX: 630-752-5855. Reference E-mail: circulation@wheaton.edu. Web Site: library.wheaton.edu. *Archives, Interim Dean of Libr,* Paul Erickson; E-mail: Paul.Erickson@wheaton.edu; *Head, Ref,* Gregory Morrison; Tel: 630-752-5847, E-mail: Gregory.Morrison@wheaton.edu; *Spec Coll Librn,* Keith Call; Tel: 630-752-5851, E-mail: Keith.Call@wheaton.edu; *Media Spec,* Keith Eiten; Tel: 630-752-5092, E-mail: Keith.Eiten@wheaton.edu. Subject Specialists: *Church hist, Theol,* Gregory Morrison; *Church hist, Instrul tech,* Keith Call; *Arts, Communication, Music,* Keith Eiten; Staff 14 (MLS 8, Non-MLS 6)
Founded 1860. Enrl 2,741; Fac 226; Highest Degree: Doctorate
Library Holdings: AV Mats 35,836; e-books 2,009; Bk Titles 259,664; Bk Vols 366,811; Per Subs 1,734
Special Collections: David Aikman, Frederick Buechner, John Bunyan, Anita & Peter Deyneka, Charles Dickens, Jaque Ellul, Samuel Johnson, Kenneth & Margaret Landon, Madeline L'Engle, Coleman Luck, Calvin Miller, Malcolm Muggeridge, Hans Rookmaaker, Luci Shaw, Norman Stone; Jonathan & Charles Blanchard Papers; Oswald Chambers, Senator Daniel R Coats. US Document Depository
Subject Interests: Am lit, Anthrop, English lit, Hist, Music, Philos, Polit sci, Relig
Automation Activity & Vendor Info: (Acquisitions) Ex Libris Group; (Cataloging) Ex Libris Group; (Circulation) Ex Libris Group; (Course Reserve) Ex Libris Group; (OPAC) Ex Libris Group; (Serials) Ex Libris Group
Wireless access
Mem of Reaching Across Illinois Library System (RAILS)
Partic in Association of Chicago Theological Schools; Consortium of Academic & Research Libraries in Illinois; LIBRAS, Inc; LYRASIS; OCLC Online Computer Library Center, Inc
Special Services for the Blind - Assistive/Adapted tech devices, equip & products; Computer with voice synthesizer for visually impaired persons
Open Mon-Thurs 7:30am-Midnight, Fri 7:30am-10pm, Sat 8:30am-10pm

Departmental Libraries:

MARION E WADE CENTER, 351 E Lincoln, 60187-4213. (Mail add: 501 College Ave, 60187-5501). Tel: 630-752-5908. FAX: 630-752-5459. E-mail: wade@wheaton.edu. Web Site: www.wheaton.edu/academics/academic-centers/wadecenter. *Assoc Dir,* Marjorie L Mead; E-mail: Marjorie.L.Mead@wheaton.edu; *Archivist,* Laura Schmidt; E-mail: Laura.Schmidt@wheaton.edu; Staff 2 (MLS 1, Non-MLS 1)
Founded 1965
Library Holdings: Bk Vols 13,000; Per Subs 42
Special Collections: C S Lewis Coll, ms; Charles Williams Coll, ms; G K Chesterton Coll, ms; George MacDonald & Dorothy L Sayers Coll, ms; J R R Tolkien Coll, ms; Owen Barfield Coll, ms. Oral History
Subject Interests: Children's lit, Detective fiction, Fantasy, Sci fict, Theol
Function: Audio & video playback equip for onsite use, Bk club(s), Wheelchair accessible
Publications: Seven: An Anglo-American Literary Review (Annual)
Open Mon-Fri 9-4, Sat 9-12
Restriction: Non-circulating

P WHEATON PUBLIC LIBRARY*, 225 N Cross St, 60187-5376. SAN 304-7601. Tel: 630-668-1374. Circulation Tel: 630-868-7510. Reference Tel: 630-868-7520. Administration Tel: 630-668-3097. Automation Services Tel: 630-868-7585. FAX: 630-668-8950. Administration FAX: 630-668-1465. TDD: 630-668-0256. Reference E-mail: askref@wheatonlibrary.org. Web Site: www.wheatonlibrary.org. *Dir,* Betsy Adamowski; *Dep Dir, Head, Tech Serv,* Dawn Kovacs; E-mail: dawn@wheatonlibrary.org; *Head, Adult Serv,* Dana Tieman; Tel: 630-868-7527, E-mail: dana@wheatonlibrary.org; *Head, Community Engagement,* Courtney Tedrick; Tel: 630-868-7526, E-mail: courtney@wheatonlibrary.org; *Head, Teen Serv,* Lisa Barefield; Tel: 630-868-7534, E-mail: lbarefield@wheatonlibrary.org; *Head, Youth Serv,* Rachel Weiss; Tel: 630-868-7544, E-mail: rachel@wheatonlibrary.org; *Ch Serv,* Janet Dumas; Tel: 630-868-7543, E-mail: janet@wheatonlibrary.org; *Circ,* Ann Barnfield; Tel: 630-868-7512, E-mail: annb@wheatonlibrary.org
Founded 1891. Pop 52,894; Circ 1,247,318
Library Holdings: Audiobooks 16,138; CDs 19,258; DVDs 8,524; Electronic Media & Resources 2,426; Large Print Bks 5,512; Microforms 4,768; Bk Vols 389,091; Per Subs 475; Videos 11,780
Special Collections: DuPage County History Coll
Subject Interests: Genealogy
Automation Activity & Vendor Info: (Acquisitions) Innovative Interfaces, Inc - Millennium; (Cataloging) Innovative Interfaces, Inc - Millennium; (Circulation) Innovative Interfaces, Inc - Millennium; (ILL) Innovative Interfaces, Inc; (OPAC) Innovative Interfaces, Inc - Millennium; (Serials) Innovative Interfaces, Inc - Millennium
Wireless access
Function: Audiobks via web, Bk club(s), Bks on cassette, Bks on CD, CD-ROM, Computer training, Computers for patron use, Electronic databases & coll, Free DVD rentals, Homebound delivery serv, ILL available, Magnifiers for reading, Music CDs, Online cat, Online ref, Photocopying/Printing, Prog for adults, Prog for children & young adult, Scanner, Story hour, Summer reading prog, Tax forms, Telephone ref, VHS videos, Wheelchair accessible
Publications: Adult & Children's Newsletters; Bibliographies
Mem of Reaching Across Illinois Library System (RAILS)
Partic in OCLC Online Computer Library Center, Inc
Special Services for the Deaf - TDD equip
Special Services for the Blind - Bks on cassette; Bks on CD; Closed circuit TV magnifier; Home delivery serv; Large print bks; Text reader
Open Mon-Fri 9-9, Sat 9-5, Sun 1-5
Friends of the Library Group

WHEELING

P INDIAN TRAILS PUBLIC LIBRARY DISTRICT*, 355 S Schoenbeck Rd, 60090. SAN 304-761X. Tel: 847-459-4100. FAX: 847-459-4760. TDD: 847-459-5271. Web Site: www.indiantrailslibrary.org. *Exec Dir,* Brian Shepard; E-mail: bshepard@indiantrailslibrary.org; *Dep Dir,* Ryann Uden; E-mail: ruden@itpld.org; *Adult Serv Mgr,* Christina Stoll; E-mail: cstoll@itpld.org; *Bus Off Mgr,* Susan Beal; E-mail: sbeal@indiantrailslibrary.org; *Circ Serv Mgr,* Rosa Lloyd; E-mail: rlloyd@itpld.org; *Communications Mgr,* Susan Dennison; E-mail: sdennison@itpld.org; *Human Res Mgr,* Jennifer Wonsowicz; E-mail: jwonsowicz@itpld.org; *Mgr, Info Tech,* Michael Jackiw; E-mail: mjackiw@itpld.org; *Mgr, Mat Serv,* Matt Teske; E-mail: mteske@itpld.org; *Youth Serv Mgr,* Michele Fenton; E-mail: mfenton@itpld.org; Staff 96 (MLS 15, Non-MLS 81)
Founded 1959. Pop 65,828; Circ 912,000
Library Holdings: AV Mats 33,939; e-books 500; Bk Titles 154,007; Bk Vols 213,170; Per Subs 410
Automation Activity & Vendor Info: (Acquisitions) SirsiDynix; (Cataloging) SirsiDynix; (Circulation) SirsiDynix; (OPAC) SirsiDynix; (Serials) SirsiDynix
Function: AV serv, Home delivery & serv to seniorr ctr & nursing homes, Homebound delivery serv, ILL available, Magnifiers for reading, Outside serv via phone, mail, e-mail & web, Photocopying/Printing, Prog for children & young adult, Ref serv available, Summer reading prog, Wheelchair accessible
Publications: Children's Newsletter; General Library Newsletter; ITPLD News (Newsletter); Trails Tales (Newsletter)
Special Services for the Deaf - TDD equip; TTY equip
Special Services for the Blind - Computer with voice synthesizer for visually impaired persons; Large print bks; Large screen computer & software
Open Mon-Fri 9-9, Sat 9-5, Sun 12-5
Friends of the Library Group
Bookmobiles: 1. Head, Outreach Servs, Chris Gibson. Bk titles 4,000

WHITE HALL

P WHITE HALL TOWNSHIP LIBRARY*, 119 E Sherman St, 62092. SAN 304-7636. Tel: 217-374-6014. FAX: 217-374-6554. E-mail: whtlibraryboard@gmail.com. Web Site: whitehalltownshiplibrary.org. *Head Librn,* Penny Eilers; *Asst Librn,* Janis Chapman; Staff 3 (Non-MLS 3)
Founded 1876. Pop 3,036; Circ 13,040. Sal $24,681
Library Holdings: Audiobooks 378; CDs 151; DVDs 151; Large Print Bks 100; Bk Vols 15,516; Per Subs 33; Videos 317
Special Collections: Green Prairie Press 1985-present, microfilm; Greene & Jersey History Coll; North Greene News June 7, 1979-April 1985, microfilm; White Hall Register 1869-July 1917, microfilm; White Hall Register-Republican August 1917-1979, microfilm
Wireless access
Mem of Illinois Heartland Library System
Special Services for the Deaf - Bks on deafness & sign lang
Special Services for the Blind - Bks on cassette
Open Mon, Fri & Sat 9-5, Tues-Thurs 2-8

WILLIAMSFIELD

P WILLIAMSFIELD PUBLIC LIBRARY DISTRICT*, 407 Norman Dr, 61489. SAN 376-1398. Tel: 309-639-2630. FAX: 309-639-2611. Web Site: wpld.org. *Libr Dir,* Tamara Smith; E-mail: tamara@wpld.org
Founded 1991
Library Holdings: Bk Titles 6,200; Per Subs 29
Wireless access
Open Mon-Wed & Fri 7:30-5, Thurs 7:30-7, Sat 9-Noon
Friends of the Library Group

WILLIAMSVILLE

P WILLIAMSVILLE PUBLIC LIBRARY*, 217 N Elm St, 62693. SAN 304-7644. Tel: 217-566-3520. FAX: 217-566-3481. E-mail: billtownlib@yahoo.com. Web Site: www.williamsvillelibrary.org. *Dir,* Jean Forness
Founded 1980. Pop 1,450; Circ 5,147
Library Holdings: Bk Titles 6,000
Automation Activity & Vendor Info: (Cataloging) Horizon; (Circulation) Horizon
Wireless access
Mem of Illinois Heartland Library System
Open Mon-Thurs 10-7, Sat 10-2
Friends of the Library Group

WILMETTE

SR BETH HILLEL CONGREGATION BNAI EMUNAH, David Altman Library, 3220 Big Tree Lane, 60091. SAN 376-0057. Tel: 847-256-1213, Ext 29. FAX: 847-256-3225. Web Site: www.bhbe.org/learn/library. *Librn,* Marcie Eskin; E-mail: marcie.eskin@bhbe.org; Staff 1 (MLS 1)
Library Holdings: Bk Titles 2,000
Restriction: Mem only

S WILMETTE HISTORICAL MUSEUM, Research Library, 609 Ridge Rd, 60091-2721. SAN 329-1154. Tel: 847-853-7666. E-mail: museum@wilmette.com. Web Site: www.wilmettehistory.org. *Dir,* K Hussey-Arntson; E-mail: husseyk@wilmette.com; Staff 3 (Non-MLS 3)
Founded 1951
Library Holdings: Bk Titles 450; Bk Vols 500
Special Collections: Municipal Document Depository; Oral History
Subject Interests: Local hist
Wireless access
Publications: Museum News (Newsletter)
Restriction: Non-circulating to the pub, Open by appt only
Friends of the Library Group

P WILMETTE PUBLIC LIBRARY DISTRICT*, 1242 Wilmette Ave, 60091-2558. SAN 304-7660. Tel: 847-256-5025. Circulation Tel: 847-256-6947. Interlibrary Loan Service Tel: 847-256-6955. Reference Tel: 847-256-6935. Administration Tel: 847-256-6912. FAX: 847-256-6933. TDD: 847-256-6931. Reference E-mail: wilref@wilmettelibrary.info. Web Site: www.wilmettelibrary.info. *Libr Dir,* Anthony Auston; E-mail: aauston@wilmettelibrary.info; *Head, Adult Serv,* Betty Giorgi; Tel: 847-256-6936, E-mail: blgiorgi@wilmettelibrary.info; *Bus Mgr,* Barbara Griffiths; Tel: 847-256-6910, Fax: 847-256-6911, E-mail: bgriffiths@wilmettelibrary.info; *Ch Serv,* Keren Joshi; Tel: 847-256-6940, Fax: 847-256-6943, E-mail: kjoshi@wilmettelibrary.info; *Circ Serv,* Luciano Ward; Tel: 847-256-6950, E-mail: lward@wilmettelibrary.info; *Commun Serv,* Sarah Beth Brown; Tel: 847-256-6925, E-mail: sbbrown@wilmettelibrary.info; *Tech Serv,* Gayle Rosenberg-Justman; Tel: 847-256-6920, Fax: 847-256-6944, E-mail: grjustman@wilmettelibrary.info; Staff 48 (MLS 15, Non-MLS 33)
Founded 1901. Pop 27,087; Circ 753,000. Sal $2,293,074 (Prof $1,036,754)
Library Holdings: AV Mats 45,739; e-books 34,877; Large Print Bks 6,701; Bk Titles 200,491; Bk Vols 221,719; Per Subs 538
Special Collections: Oral History
Subject Interests: Art, Cookbks, Local hist, Poetry, Travel
Automation Activity & Vendor Info: (Acquisitions) Innovative Interfaces, Inc; (Cataloging) Innovative Interfaces, Inc; (Circulation) Innovative Interfaces, Inc; (OPAC) Innovative Interfaces, Inc

Wireless access
Publications: Off the Shelf
Mem of Reaching Across Illinois Library System (RAILS)
Partic in Cooperative Computer Services - CCS
Open Mon-Fri & Sun (Sept-May) 9-9, Sat 9-5, Sun 1-9 (1-5 June-Aug)
Friends of the Library Group

WILMINGTON

P WILMINGTON PUBLIC LIBRARY DISTRICT, 201 S Kankakee St, 60481-1338. SAN 304-7679. Tel: 815-476-2834. FAX: 815-476-7805. Web Site: www.wilmingtonlibrary.org. *Dir,* Maria Meachum; E-mail: mfbmeachum@wilmingtonlibrary.org; Staff 20 (MLS 3, Non-MLS 17)
Founded 1907. Pop 9,229; Circ 96,121
Library Holdings: CDs 4,205; DVDs 3,788; e-books 4,645; Bk Titles 40,004; Per Subs 80
Subject Interests: Antiques, Genealogy, Local hist
Automation Activity & Vendor Info: (Cataloging) Innovative Interfaces, Inc - Sierra; (Circulation) Innovative Interfaces, Inc - Sierra; (ILL) Innovative Interfaces, Inc - Sierra; (OPAC) Innovative Interfaces, Inc - Sierra
Wireless access
Publications: Book Bytes (Newsletter)
Mem of Reaching Across Illinois Library System (RAILS)
Open Mon-Thurs 9-8, Fri & Sat 9-5, Sun 12-5
Friends of the Library Group

WINCHESTER

P WINCHESTER PUBLIC LIBRARY*, 215 N Main St, 62694. SAN 304-7687. Tel: 217-742-3150. E-mail: winplibrary@irtc.net. Web Site: winchesterpubliclibrary.org. *Dir, Libr Serv,* Darlene Smith; Staff 1 (Non-MLS 1)
Founded 1907. Pop 1,600; Circ 10,259
Library Holdings: Bk Vols 17,402; Per Subs 37
Subject Interests: Local hist
Automation Activity & Vendor Info: (Cataloging) SirsiDynix-WorkFlows; (Circulation) SirsiDynix-WorkFlows
Wireless access
Open Mon 1-6, Tues & Fri 1-5, Wed & Thurs 1-7, Sat 10-12

WINDSOR

P WINDSOR STORM MEMORIAL PUBLIC LIBRARY DISTRICT*, 102 S Maple, 61957. SAN 375-9342. Tel: 217-459-2498. FAX: 217-459-2499. Web Site: www.windsor.lib.il.us. *Libr Dir,* Stacey Stremming; E-mail: stremlib1@consolidated.net; *Circ,* Holly Alendorf; *Circ,* Linda Bennett
Library Holdings: CDs 28,000; Bk Titles 14,000; Per Subs 59
Wireless access
Mem of Illinois Heartland Library System
Open Mon-Thurs 9-5, Fri 9-1, Sat 9-12

WINFIELD

M NORTHWESTERN MEDICINE CENTRAL DUPAGE HOSPITAL*, Knowledge Resource Library, 25 N Winfield Rd, 60190. SAN 304-7695. Tel: 630-933-4536. Web Site: www.nm.org/locations/central-dupage-hospital. *Libraries Mgr,* Julie Stielstra; Staff 1 (MLS 1)
Founded 1974
Library Holdings: Bk Titles 2,000; Per Subs 800
Subject Interests: Med, Nursing
Automation Activity & Vendor Info: (Cataloging) LibraryWorld, Inc; (Circulation) LibraryWorld, Inc; (ILL) OCLC WorldShare Interlibrary Loan; (OPAC) LibraryWorld, Inc
Wireless access
Function: Health sci info serv
Mem of Reaching Across Illinois Library System (RAILS)
Partic in Docline; Illinois Library & Information Network; OCLC Online Computer Library Center, Inc; Regional Med Libr - Region 3
Restriction: Access at librarian's discretion, Authorized personnel only, Badge access after hrs, Circulates for staff only, Employee & client use only, Hospital employees & physicians only

P WINFIELD PUBLIC LIBRARY*, 0S291 Winfield Rd, 60190. SAN 304-7709. Tel: 630-653-7599. FAX: 630-653-7781. E-mail: wfdstaff@winfield.lib.il.us. Web Site: www.winfield.lib.il.us/winfield. *Dir,* Matthew Suddarth; E-mail: suddarth@winfield.lib.il.us; *Adult/YA Serv Librn,* Katie Clark; *Youth Serv,* Filomena Choate; Staff 7 (MLS 5, Non-MLS 2)
Founded 1968. Pop 9,820; Circ 105,809
May 2018-Apr 2019 Income $816,540. Mats Exp $79,018, Books $57,483, Per/Ser (Incl. Access Fees) $9,217, AV Mat $12,318. Sal $405,841 (Prof $255,560)
Library Holdings: AV Mats 5,451; Bk Vols 48,440; Per Subs 178
Subject Interests: Local hist
Automation Activity & Vendor Info: (Circulation) Auto-Graphics, Inc; (OPAC) Auto-Graphics, Inc
Wireless access
Function: 24/7 Electronic res, 24/7 Online cat, Adult bk club, Art programs, Audiobks on Playaways & MP3, Audiobks via web, AV serv, Bk club(s), Bks on CD, Children's prog, Computers for patron use, E-Readers, Electronic databases & coll, Free DVD rentals, Homebound delivery serv, ILL available, Internet access, Life-long learning prog for all ages, Magazines, Magnifiers for reading, Mail & tel request accepted, Mango lang, Meeting rooms, Microfiche/film & reading machines, Movies, Museum passes, Music CDs, Online cat, Online info literacy tutorials on the web & in blackboard, OverDrive digital audio bks, Photocopying/Printing, Preschool reading prog, Printer for laptops & handheld devices, Prog for adults, Prog for children & young adult, Ref & res, Ref serv available, Story hour, Summer & winter reading prog, Summer reading prog, Tax forms, Teen prog, Telephone ref, Wheelchair accessible, Winter reading prog
Publications: The Inside Page (Newsletter)
Mem of Reaching Across Illinois Library System (RAILS)
Open Mon-Thurs 9-9, Fri & Sat 9-5
Friends of the Library Group

WINNEBAGO

P WINNEBAGO PUBLIC LIBRARY DISTRICT*, 210 N Elida St, 61088. SAN 324-5756. Tel: 815-335-7050. FAX: 815-335-7049. Web Site: winnebagopubliclibrary.org. *Dir,* Katie Schmoyer; E-mail: kschmoyer@winnebagopubliclibrary.org; Staff 13 (Non-MLS 13)
Founded 1982. Pop 7,257
Library Holdings: AV Mats 3,013; Bks on Deafness & Sign Lang 30; CDs 216; DVDs 305; Large Print Bks 658; Bk Vols 31,848; Per Subs 102; Talking Bks 450; Videos 1,772
Subject Interests: Illinois, Local hist
Automation Activity & Vendor Info: (Circulation) Follett Software
Wireless access
Mem of Reaching Across Illinois Library System (RAILS)
Open Mon-Thurs 10-8, Fri 10-6, Sat 9-3
Friends of the Library Group

WINNETKA

P WINNETKA-NORTHFIELD PUBLIC LIBRARY DISTRICT*, 768 Oak St, 60093-2515. SAN 340-9171. Tel: 847-446-7220. FAX: 847-446-5085. Web Site: www.winnetkalibrary.org. *Dir,* Rebecca Wolf; E-mail: rwolf@winnetkalibrary.org; *Asst Libr Dir,* Emily Compton-Dzak; E-mail: ecompton-dzak@winnetkalibrary.org; *Head, Circ,* Katie Cangelosi; E-mail: ccangelosi@winnetkalibrary.org; *Head, Info Tech,* Mark Swenson; *Head, Youth Serv,* Sheila Cody; Staff 42 (MLS 12, Non-MLS 30)
Founded 1884. Pop 17,808; Circ 279,477
Library Holdings: AV Mats 7,244; e-books 2,622; Electronic Media & Resources 422; Bk Vols 127,028; Per Subs 146; Talking Bks 6,181; Videos 2,220
Subject Interests: Genealogy
Automation Activity & Vendor Info: (Cataloging) SirsiDynix; (Circulation) SirsiDynix; (ILL) SirsiDynix; (OPAC) SirsiDynix
Wireless access
Publications: Source (Newsletter)
Partic in Cooperative Computer Services - CCS
Open Mon-Thurs 9-9, Fri & Sat 9-5, Sun 1-5
Friends of the Library Group
Branches: 1
NORTHFIELD BRANCH, 1785 Orchard Ln, 60093. SAN 340-9201. Tel: 847-446-5990. FAX: 847-446-6586. *Br Mgr,* Kristin Carlson; E-mail: kristin@winnetkalibrary.org; Staff 3 (MLS 3)
Library Holdings: Bk Vols 16,000; Per Subs 50
Open Mon-Thurs 9-9, Fri & Sat 9-5, Sun 1-5
Friends of the Library Group

WITT

P WITT TOWNSHIP MEMORIAL LIBRARY*, 18 N Second St, 62094. (Mail add: PO Box 442, 62094-0442), SAN 304-7725. Tel: 217-594-7333. FAX: 217-594-7333. E-mail: witttownshippl@gmail.com. *Librn,* Sue Van Ostran
Founded 1953. Pop 1,391; Circ 3,791
Library Holdings: Bk Vols 10,000
Mem of Illinois Heartland Library System
Open Tues & Thurs 9-12 & 2-5, Sat 9-12

WOOD DALE

P WOOD DALE PUBLIC LIBRARY DISTRICT*, 520 N Wood Dale Rd, 60191. SAN 304-7733. Tel: 630-766-6762. FAX: 630-766-5715. E-mail: contact@wooddalelibrary.org. Web Site: www.wooddalelibrary.org. *Dir,* Yvonne Rae Bergendorf; E-mail: director@wooddalelibrary.org; *Asst Dir,* Joanna Klos; E-mail: jklos@wooddalelibrary.org; *Mgr, Pub Serv,* Karen

Stier Pulver; E-mail: kspulver@wooddalelibrary.org; *Mgr, Tech Serv,* Jim Lindt; E-mail: jlindt@wooddalelibrary.org; *Youth Serv Mgr,* Jenny Collier; E-mail: jcollier@wooddalelibrary.org; Staff 21.5 (MLS 4.5, Non-MLS 17)
Founded 1962. Pop 11,868; Circ 188,757
Library Holdings: AV Mats 2,546; CDs 1,229; DVDs 3,715; Electronic Media & Resources 24; Large Print Bks 1,281; Bk Vols 86,165; Per Subs 193; Videos 1,749
Subject Interests: Local hist
Automation Activity & Vendor Info: (Cataloging) SirsiDynix; (Circulation) SirsiDynix; (ILL) OCLC Connexion; (OPAC) SirsiDynix
Wireless access
Mem of Reaching Across Illinois Library System (RAILS)
Partic in Multitype Automation Group in Cooperation; System Wide Automated Network
Special Services for the Deaf - Closed caption videos; High interest/low vocabulary bks; Sign lang interpreter upon request for prog
Special Services for the Blind - Accessible computers; Aids for in-house use; Audio mat; Bks available with recordings; Bks on CD; Extensive large print coll; Free checkout of audio mat; Large print bks; Large screen computer & software; Playaways (bks on MP3)
Open Mon-Thurs 10-9, Fri & Sat 10-5, Sun (Sept-May) 1-5

WOOD RIVER

P WOOD RIVER PUBLIC LIBRARY*, 326 E Ferguson Ave, 62095-2098. SAN 304-775X. Tel: 618-254-4832. FAX: 618-254-4836. E-mail: info@woodriverlibrary.org. Web Site: woodriverlibrary.org. *Dir,* Mrs Lindsey Herron; E-mail: Lindsey@woodriverlibrary.org; *Asst Dir,* Holly Berrey; E-mail: holly@woodriverlibrary.org; *Cataloger, Circ Mgr,* Katie Rusell; E-mail: Katie@woodriverlibrary.org
Founded 1920. Pop 10,493; Circ 129,980
Library Holdings: Bk Vols 65,316
Automation Activity & Vendor Info: (Circulation) Innovative Interfaces, Inc
Wireless access
Mem of Illinois Heartland Library System
Partic in Coop Libr Agency for Syst & Servs
Open Mon-Thurs 9-8, Fri & Sat 9-5, Sun 12:30-4
Friends of the Library Group

WOODHULL

P CLOVER PUBLIC LIBRARY DISTRICT*, 440 N Division St, 61490. (Mail add: PO Box 369, 61490-0369), SAN 304-7768. Tel: 309-334-2680. FAX: 309-334-2378. E-mail: cv.clover.rsa@gmail.com. Web Site: www.cloverlibrarywoodhull.com. *Dir,* Rene Bramlett; E-mail: reneebramlett@hotmail.com
Founded 1965. Pop 2,398; Circ 21,000
Library Holdings: Bk Vols 22,000; Per Subs 54
Special Collections: Woodhull Hist Coll; World War II Coll
Automation Activity & Vendor Info: (Cataloging) SirsiDynix; (Circulation) SirsiDynix
Wireless access
Mem of Reaching Across Illinois Library System (RAILS)
Open Mon-Fri 9-5, Sat 9-12

WOODRIDGE

P WOODRIDGE PUBLIC LIBRARY, Three Plaza Dr, 60517-5014. SAN 304-7776. Tel: 630-964-7899. FAX: 630-968-4126. Web Site: www.woodridgelibrary.org. *Dir,* Pam Dube; Tel: 630-487-2549, E-mail: pdube@woodridgelibrary.org; *Head, Adult/Teen Serv,* George Kalinka; Tel: 630-487-2554, E-mail: gkalinka@woodridgelibrary.org; *Head, Children's Servx,* Jessica Smith; Tel: 630-487-2567, E-mail: jsmith@woodridgelibrary.org; *Head, Circ,* Julie Lombardo; Tel: 630-487-2542, E-mail: jlombardo@woodridgelibrary.org; *Head, Tech Serv,* Amy Weiss; Tel: 630-487-2547, E-mail: aweiss@woodridgelibrary.org; Staff 14 (MLS 10, Non-MLS 4)
Founded 1967. Pop 35,900; Circ 607,000
Jan 2015-Dec 2015 Income $3,784,671, State $41,214, County $3,550,957, Locally Generated Income $143,714. Mats Exp $456,000, Books $180,000, Per/Ser (Incl. Access Fees) $30,000, AV Mat $126,000, Electronic Ref Mat (Incl. Access Fees) $120,000. Sal $1,918,000 (Prof $1,100,000)
Library Holdings: Bk Vols 175,000; Per Subs 254
Automation Activity & Vendor Info: (Acquisitions) SirsiDynix; (Cataloging) SirsiDynix; (Circulation) SirsiDynix; (Course Reserve) SirsiDynix; (ILL) SirsiDynix; (OPAC) SirsiDynix; (Serials) SirsiDynix
Wireless access
Function: Adult bk club, After school storytime, Art exhibits, Audiobks via web, AV serv, Bks on cassette, Bks on CD, CD-ROM, Children's prog, Computer training, Computers for patron use, Electronic databases & coll, Free DVD rentals, Holiday prog, Homebound delivery serv, ILL available, Magnifiers for reading, Mail & tel request accepted, Museum passes, Music CDs, Notary serv, Online cat, Orientations, Outreach serv, OverDrive digital audio bks, Photocopying/Printing, Preschool outreach, Prog for adults, Prog for children & young adult, Ref serv available, Spoken cassettes & DVDs, Story hour, Summer reading prog, Tax forms, Teen prog, Telephone ref, VHS videos, Wheelchair accessible
Mem of Reaching Across Illinois Library System (RAILS)
Partic in System Wide Automated Network
Special Services for the Deaf - TDD equip
Open Mon-Fri 9-9, Sat 9-5, Sun 1-5
Friends of the Library Group

WOODSTOCK

L MCHENRY COUNTY LAW LIBRARY*, McHenry County Government Ctr, 3rd Flr, 2200 N Seminary Ave, 60098. SAN 372-1140. Tel: 815-334-4166. FAX: 815-334-1005. Web Site: www.mchenrycountyil.gov. *Librn,* Susana Huffman; E-mail: sxhuffman@22ndcircuit.illinoiscourts.gov
Library Holdings: Bk Vols 12,000
Wireless access
Open Mon-Fri 8-12 & 1-4:30

P WOODSTOCK PUBLIC LIBRARY*, 414 W Judd, 60098-3195. SAN 304-7792. Tel: 815-338-0542. FAX: 815-334-2296. E-mail: library@woodstockil.gov. Web Site: www.woodstockpubliclibrary.org. *Libr Dir,* Nicholas Weber; E-mail: nweber@woodstockil.info; Staff 11 (MLS 10, Non-MLS 1)
Founded 1891. Pop 37,384; Circ 311,119
Library Holdings: Bk Titles 151,457
Special Collections: McHenry County History & Genealogy Coll
Automation Activity & Vendor Info: (Acquisitions) Innovative Interfaces, Inc; (Cataloging) Innovative Interfaces, Inc; (Circulation) Innovative Interfaces, Inc; (ILL) Innovative Interfaces, Inc; (OPAC) Innovative Interfaces, Inc; (Serials) Innovative Interfaces, Inc
Wireless access
Function: 24/7 Electronic res, 24/7 Online cat, Activity rm, Adult bk club, Archival coll, Art exhibits, Audiobks on Playaways & MP3, Audiobks via web, AV serv, Bilingual assistance for Spanish patrons, Bk club(s), Bks on CD, Children's prog, Computer training, Computers for patron use, E-Readers, E-Reserves, Electronic databases & coll, Family literacy, Free DVD rentals, Genealogy discussion group, Holiday prog, Home delivery & serv to seniorr ctr & nursing homes, Homebound delivery serv, ILL available, Instruction & testing, Internet access, Large print keyboards, Life-long learning prog for all ages, Literacy & newcomer serv, Magazines, Magnifiers for reading, Mail & tel request accepted, Meeting rooms, Microfiche/film & reading machines, Movies, Music CDs, Notary serv, Online cat, Online ref, Outreach serv, OverDrive digital audio bks, Photocopying/Printing, Preschool outreach, Printer for laptops & handheld devices, Prog for adults, Prog for children & young adult, Ref & res, Ref serv available, Scanner, Senior computer classes, Serves people with intellectual disabilities, Spanish lang bks, Spoken cassettes & CDs, Spoken cassettes & DVDs, Story hour, Study rm, Summer & winter reading prog, Summer reading prog, Tax forms, Teen prog, Telephone ref, Visual arts prog, Wheelchair accessible, Winter reading prog, Workshops, Writing prog
Mem of Reaching Across Illinois Library System (RAILS)
Open Mon-Thurs 9-9, Fri & Sat 9-5, Sun 1-4
Friends of the Library Group

WORDEN

P WORDEN PUBLIC LIBRARY DISTRICT*, 111 E Wall St, 62097. (Mail add: PO Box 164, 62097-0164). Tel: 618-459-7171. E-mail: wordenlibrary@outlook.com. *Dir,* Gary Naglich
Library Holdings: Bk Titles 7,084; Per Subs 7
Wireless access
Mem of Illinois Heartland Library System
Open Mon-Thurs 10-12 & 1-6, Fri 10-12 & 1-3, Sat 9-1

WORTH

P WORTH PUBLIC LIBRARY DISTRICT*, 6917 W 111th St, 60482. SAN 304-7806. Tel: 708-448-2855. FAX: 708-448-9174. Web Site: www.worthlibrary.com. *Admin Librn,* Carol Hall; E-mail: hallc@worthlibrary.com; *Head, Adult Serv,* Tim White; E-mail: whitet@worthlibrary.com; *Head, Circ,* Laura Monday; *Head, Tech Serv,* Kim Hecht; *Head, Youth Serv,* Bonnie Pawlarczyk
Founded 1963. Pop 11,467; Circ 79,410
Library Holdings: Bk Titles 45,724; Per Subs 149
Automation Activity & Vendor Info: (Circulation) Infor Library & Information Solutions
Wireless access
Publications: Worth It! (triannual library newsletter)
Mem of Reaching Across Illinois Library System (RAILS)
Partic in System Wide Automated Network
Open Mon-Fri 10-6, Sat 10-2
Friends of the Library Group

WYANET

P RAYMOND A SAPP MEMORIAL TOWNSHIP LIBRARY, 103 E Main St, 61379. (Mail add: PO Box 23, 61379-0023), SAN 304-7814. Tel: 815-699-2342. FAX: 815-699-2342. E-mail: rasapplib@gmail.com. *Dir,* Jessica Wofford; Staff 2 (Non-MLS 2)
Founded 1915. Pop 1,364; Circ 5,787
Library Holdings: AV Mats 564; Bk Vols 12,660; Per Subs 23; Talking Bks 100
Special Collections: Oral History
Wireless access
Mem of Reaching Across Illinois Library System (RAILS)
Partic in Illinois Library & Information Network
Open Mon, Tues, Wed & Fri 1-6, Thurs 3-8, Sat 8-1
Friends of the Library Group

WYOMING

P WYOMING PUBLIC LIBRARY DISTRICT*, 119 N Seventh St, 61491. SAN 304-7822. Tel: 309-695-2241. FAX: 309-695-2241. E-mail: wyoming.pl.rsa@gmail.com. Web Site: www.wyomingpubliclibrary.com. *Dir,* Mary Meaker
Pop 2,367; Circ 41,000
Library Holdings: Bk Vols 15,000; Per Subs 23
Wireless access
Open Mon & Tues 1-5:30, Wed 9-5:30, Thurs 1-7, Fri 9-5, Sat 8-12

YATES CITY

P SALEM TOWNSHIP PUBLIC LIBRARY DISTRICT*, 102 N Burson St, 61572. (Mail add: PO Box 19, 61572-0019), SAN 304-7830. Tel: 309-358-1678. FAX: 309-358-1678. E-mail: salem.tl.rsa@gmail.com. Web Site: www.salemtownshiplibrary.com. *Head Libn,* Denise Hayes
Founded 1923. Pop 1,216; Circ 9,000
Library Holdings: Bk Titles 10,000; Per Subs 30
Wireless access
Open Mon-Wed 9-6, Thurs 9-8, Fri 9-5, Sat 9-1

YORKVILLE

P YORKVILLE PUBLIC LIBRARY, 902 Game Farm Rd, 60560. SAN 304-7849. Tel: 630-553-4354. FAX: 630-553-0823. Web Site: www.yorkville.lib.il.us. *Dir,* Shelley Augustine; E-mail: saugustine@yorkville.lib.il.us
Founded 1915. Circ 35,900
Library Holdings: CDs 2,288; DVDs 1,183; Bk Vols 38,880; Per Subs 119
Special Collections: Irma Hardekopf Music Coll, bks, sheet music; Kendall County Record 1864-1978 Coll, microflm
Subject Interests: Art, Local hist, Music
Mem of Reaching Across Illinois Library System (RAILS)
Open Mon-Thurs 10-7, Fri 10-5, Sat 10-4
Friends of the Library Group

ZEIGLER

P ZEIGLER PUBLIC LIBRARY*, 102 E Maryland St, 62999. SAN 304-7857. Tel: 618-596-2041. FAX: 618-596-2041. E-mail: zlibrary102@gmail.com. *Librn,* Peggy Carpenter
Pop 1,800; Circ 4,500
Library Holdings: Bk Vols 4,500; Per Subs 7
Wireless access
Function: Activity rm
Mem of Illinois Heartland Library System
Open Mon, Wed & Fri 12-5, Tues & Thurs 12-7

ZION

P ZION-BENTON PUBLIC LIBRARY DISTRICT*, 2400 Gabriel Ave, 60099. SAN 304-7873. Tel: 847-872-4680. FAX: 847-872-4942. E-mail: library@zblibrary.org. Web Site: www.zblibrary.info. *Dir,* Michael Jacobsen; E-mail: mjacobsen@zblibrary.org; *Adult Serv Coordr,* Elsie Martinez; *Tech Serv Coordr,* Kim Nevins; *Youth Serv Coordr,* Garnet Miller; Staff 29 (MLS 7, Non-MLS 22)
Founded 1937. Pop 40,526; Circ 276,000
Library Holdings: AV Mats 17,420; Bk Vols 123,350; Per Subs 152
Subject Interests: Genealogy, Local hist
Automation Activity & Vendor Info: (Acquisitions) SirsiDynix; (Cataloging) OCLC; (Circulation) SirsiDynix; (ILL) SirsiDynix; (OPAC) SirsiDynix; (Serials) SirsiDynix
Wireless access
Publications: ZB Reader (Newsletter)
Partic in Cooperative Computer Services - CCS; OCLC Online Computer Library Center, Inc
Special Services for the Deaf - TDD equip; TTY equip
Open Mon-Thurs 9-9, Sat 9-5, Sun 1-5
Friends of the Library Group

INDIANA

Date of Statistics: FY 2020
Population, 2020 U.S. Census: 6,785,528
Total Volumes in Public Libraries: 21,073,268 (print)
Digital Resources:
Total e-books: 16,964,556
Total audio items (physical & downloadable units): 5,702,341
Total video items (physical & downloadable units): 2,833,099
Total computers for use by the public: 7,183
Total annual wireless sessions: 11,203,231
Total annual visits: 12,428,650
Volumes Per Capita: (Statewide) 3.11
Income and Expenditures:
Total Public Library Income: $401,826,367
Average Income: $1,702,654
Source of Income: Local property tax, local income tax, contractual revenue received for service, financial institution tax, license vehicle excise tax, commercial vehicle excise tax, private endorsements/grants, state grants-in-aid, license excise, other state & federal income, LSTA, CARES.
Number of County Libraries: 24
Counties Served: 92 (All receive complete or partial service)
Number of Bookmobiles in State: 26
Grants-in-Aid to Public Libraries:
Federal: $1,776,065
State: $1,397,477
Information provided courtesy of: Jennifer Clifton, Library Development Office Director; Indiana State Library

AKRON

P AKRON CARNEGIE PUBLIC LIBRARY*, 205 E Rochester St, 46910. (Mail add: PO Box 428, 46910-0428), SAN 304-7881. Tel: 574-893-4113. FAX: 574-598-2213. E-mail: akronadm@akron.lib.in.us. Web Site: www.akron.lib.in.us. *Dir,* Janet Hawley
Founded 1912. Pop 2,827; Circ 19,752
Library Holdings: Bk Vols 27,622; Per Subs 68
Special Collections: Local History, bks, microfilm. Oral History
Automation Activity & Vendor Info: (Cataloging) Follett Software; (Circulation) Follett Software
Wireless access
Partic in Midwest Collaborative for Library Services
Open Mon-Fri 9-6, Sat 9-1
Friends of the Library Group

ALBION

S CHAIN OF LAKES CORRECTIONAL FACILITY LIBRARY*, 3516 E 75th S, 46701. Tel: 260-636-3114. *Library Contact,* Rhonda Thomas-Hardy
Library Holdings: Bk Vols 500

P NOBLE COUNTY PUBLIC LIBRARY*, 813 E Main St, 46701. SAN 340-9236. Tel: 260-636-7197. Toll Free Tel: 800-811-6861. FAX: 260-636-3321. E-mail: info@myncpl.us. Web Site: www.myncpl.us. *Dir,* Sandy Petrie; E-mail: spetrie@myncpl.us; Staff 13 (MLS 3, Non-MLS 10)
Founded 1914. Pop 23,102; Circ 236,073
Library Holdings: CDs 109; Large Print Bks 312; Bk Titles 86,305; Per Subs 376; Talking Bks 2,770; Videos 7,943
Special Collections: History & Genealogy (Noble County Coll); History (Albion Memories Coll)
Automation Activity & Vendor Info: (Acquisitions) Evergreen; (Cataloging) Evergreen; (Circulation) Evergreen; (ILL) Evergreen; (OPAC) Evergreen
Wireless access
Function: Adult bk club, After school storytime, CD-ROM, Computer training, Electronic databases & coll, Equip loans & repairs, ILL available, Music CDs, Photocopying/Printing, Prog for adults, Prog for children & young adult, Ref serv available, Senior computer classes, Summer reading prog, Tax forms, VHS videos, Wheelchair accessible
Partic in Evergreen Indiana Consortium; Midwest Collaborative for Library Services; Northeast Indiana Libraries Serving Communities Consortium; Northern Indiana Computer Consortium for Libraries
Open Mon, Wed & Fri 9-5, Tues & Thurs 9-6, Sat 9-1
Friends of the Library Group
Branches: 2
EAST, 104 Ley St, Avilla, 46710, SAN 340-9260. Tel: 260-897-3900. FAX: 260-994-0008. *Br Adminr,* Victoria Ferguson; E-mail: vferguson@myncpl.us; Staff 3 (Non-MLS 3)
Open Mon, Wed & Fri 9-5, Tues & Thurs 9-6
Friends of the Library Group
WEST, 120 Jefferson St, Cromwell, 46732-0555, SAN 328-6592. Tel: 260-856-2119. FAX: 260-215-4014. *Interim Branch Admin,* Jennifer Steffey; Staff 3 (Non-MLS 3)
Open Tues & Thurs 9-6, Wed & Fri 9-5
Friends of the Library Group

ALEXANDRIA

P ALEXANDRIA-MONROE PUBLIC LIBRARY*, 117 E Church St, 46001-2005. SAN 304-789X. Tel: 765-724-2196. FAX: 765-724-2204. E-mail: AskUs@alexlibrary.net. Web Site: www.alexlibrary.net. *Interim Dir,* Sarah J Wallace; E-mail: swallace@alexlibrary.net; *Circ Mgr,* Nelly DeVault; E-mail: ndevault@alexlibrary.net; *Tech Serv Mgr,* Rachael Neese; E-mail: rneese@alexlibrary.net; *Youth Serv Mgr,* Brad Sowinski; E-mail: bsowinski@alexlibrary.net; Staff 2 (MLS 1, Non-MLS 1)
Founded 1903. Pop 10,233; Circ 77,985
Library Holdings: Bk Vols 43,116; Per Subs 136
Automation Activity & Vendor Info: (Acquisitions) TLC (The Library Corporation); (Cataloging) TLC (The Library Corporation); (Circulation) TLC (The Library Corporation); (OPAC) TLC (The Library Corporation); (Serials) TLC (The Library Corporation)
Wireless access
Partic in Evergreen Indiana Consortium; Midwest Collaborative for Library Services
Open Mon-Thurs 9-7, Fri & Sat 9-5, Sun 1-5

ANDERSON

P ANDERSON CITY, ANDERSON, STONY CREEK & UNION TOWNSHIPS PUBLIC LIBRARY*, 111 E 12th St, 46016-2701. SAN 340-9295. Tel: 765-641-2456. Circulation Tel: 765-641-2441. FAX: 765-313-4759. Reference E-mail: aplref@andersonlibrary.net. Web Site: www.andersonlibrary.net. *Dir,* Sarah Later; E-mail: slater@andersonlibrary.net; *Asst Dir, Coll Serv Mgr,* Colleen Sargent; Tel: 765-641-2455, E-mail: csargent@andersonlibrary.net; *Bus Mgr,* Tonya Carman; Tel: 765-641-2197, E-mail: tcarman@andersonlibrary.net; *Info Serv Mgr,* Crystal Ward; E-mail: cward@andersonlibrary.net; *Ch Serv,* Kathi Wittkamper; Tel: 765-241-2448, E-mail: kwittkamper@andersonlibrary.net; Staff 84 (MLS 16, Non-MLS 68)
Founded 1891
Library Holdings: Per Subs 401
Special Collections: Local History & Genealogy (Indiana Room), bks & microfilm
Automation Activity & Vendor Info: (Acquisitions) SirsiDynix; (Cataloging) SirsiDynix; (Circulation) SirsiDynix
Wireless access
Function: Audiobks via web, AV serv, Bks on CD, Children's prog, Computer training, Computers for patron use, Electronic databases & coll, Free DVD rentals, Homebound delivery serv, ILL available, Internet access, Magazines, Meeting rooms, Microfiche/film & reading machines, Museum passes, Music CDs, Notary serv, Online cat, OverDrive digital audio bks, Photocopying/Printing, Preschool outreach, Printer for laptops & handheld

devices, Prog for adults, Prog for children & young adult, Ref serv available, Spanish lang bks, Story hour, Study rm, Summer & winter reading prog, Summer reading prog, Tax forms, Teen prog, Telephone ref, Wheelchair accessible, Winter reading prog
Partic in Midwest Collaborative for Library Services; OCLC Online Computer Library Center, Inc
Special Services for the Deaf - High interest/low vocabulary bks
Special Services for the Blind - Large print bks
Open Mon-Thurs 9:30-8, Fri & Sat 9:30-5:30, Sun 1-5
Friends of the Library Group
Branches: 1
LAPEL BRANCH, 610 Main St, Lapel, 46051. (Mail add: PO Box 668, Lapel, 46051-0668), SAN 340-9325. Tel: 765-313-4089. FAX: 765-313-4759.
Founded 1972
Function: Adult bk club, AV serv, ILL available, Internet access, Photocopying/Printing, Prog for adults, Prog for children & young adult, Summer reading prog, Tax forms
Open Mon-Thurs Noon-7
Friends of the Library Group

C ANDERSON UNIVERSITY, Robert A Nicholson Library, 1100 E Fifth St, 46012-3495. SAN 340-9384. Tel: 765-641-4280. Circulation Tel: 765-641-4286. Interlibrary Loan Service Tel: 765-641-4287. Administration Tel: 765-641-4272. FAX: 765-641-3850. Web Site: library.anderson.edu. *Libr Dir,* Dr Janet L Brewer; E-mail: jlbrewer@anderson.edu; *Electronic Res Librn,* Jeff Siemon; E-mail: josiemon@anderson.edu; *Pub Serv Librn,* Heather Myers; Tel: 765-641-4288, E-mail: hnmyers@anderson.edu; *Ref Librn,* James Bell; Tel: 765-641-4281, E-mail: jcbell@anderson.edu; *Metadata Serv, Ref Librn,* Christa Welty; Tel: 765-641-4276, E-mail: cjwelty@anderson.edu; *Archivist,* Nic Don Stanton-Roark; Tel: 765-641-4285, E-mail: ndroark@anderson.edu; Staff 7.8 (MLS 5, Non-MLS 2.8)
Founded 1917. Enrl 1,600; Fac 105; Highest Degree: Doctorate
Library Holdings: AV Mats 6,491; e-books 913,953; e-journals 355,445; Electronic Media & Resources 114,123; Music Scores 7,630; Bk Vols 204,508; Per Subs 5,106
Special Collections: Anderson University & Church of God Archives; Charles E Wilson Papers; Children's Literature & Modern Poetry (York Rare Books & Special Colls); Gaither Hymnal Coll. US Document Depository
Automation Activity & Vendor Info: (Acquisitions) OCLC Worldshare Management Services; (Cataloging) OCLC Connexion; (Circulation) OCLC Worldshare Management Services; (Course Reserve) OCLC Worldshare Management Services; (Discovery) OCLC Worldshare Management Services; (ILL) OCLC ILLiad; (OPAC) OCLC Worldshare Management Services; (Serials) OCLC Worldshare Management Services
Wireless access
Function: 24/7 Electronic res, 24/7 Online cat, 3D Printer, Archival coll, Audio & video playback equip for onsite use, Computers for patron use, Distance learning, Doc delivery serv, E-Reserves, Electronic databases & coll, Equip loans & repairs, For res purposes, ILL available, Internet access, Laminating, Magazines, Mail & tel request accepted, Microfiche/film & reading machines, Movies, Music CDs, Online cat, Online info literacy tutorials on the web & in blackboard, Online ref, Orientations, Photocopying/Printing, Printer for laptops & handheld devices, Ref & res, Ref serv available, Scanner, Study rm, VHS videos, Wheelchair accessible
Partic in Academic Libraries of Indiana; Private Academic Library Network of Indiana
Open Mon-Thurs 8am-11pm, Fri 8-5, Sun 1:30pm-11pm

J IVY TECH COMMUNITY COLLEGE*, Anderson Campus Library, 815 E 60th St, 46013. SAN 372-493X. Tel: 765-643-5745, Ext 2081. Toll Free Tel: 800-644-4882. FAX: 765-643-3294. Web Site: library.ivytech.edu/east-central. *Dir,* Susan Clark; Tel: 765-289-2291, Ext 1321, E-mail: jsclark@ivytech.edu; *Instrul Librn,* Steve McLaughlin; E-mail: smclaughlin@ivytech.edu; *Lead Libr Asst, Supvr,* Laurie Brough; E-mail: lbrough@ivytech.edu; Staff 2 (MLS 1, Non-MLS 1)
Enrl 392; Fac 9
Library Holdings: AV Mats 1,115; Bk Titles 1,170; Bk Vols 1,350; Per Subs 83
Wireless access
Partic in Midwest Collaborative for Library Services
Open Mon-Thurs 7:30am-9pm, Fri 7:30-4:30

ANDREWS

P ANDREWS DALLAS TOWNSHIP PUBLIC LIBRARY, 30 E Madison St, 46702. (Mail add: PO Box 367, 46702-0367), SAN 321-0502. Tel: 260-786-3574. FAX: 260-786-3574. Web Site: andrews.lib.in.us. *Dir,* Nancy Disbro; E-mail: andrewsdirector@gmail.com; Staff 1 (MLS 1)
Pop 2,116
Wireless access
Partic in Evergreen Indiana Consortium
Open Mon & Wed 10-5, Tues & Thurs 12-7, Sat 9-1
Friends of the Library Group

ANGOLA

P CARNEGIE PUBLIC LIBRARY OF STEUBEN COUNTY*, 322 S Wayne St, 46703. SAN 304-7938. Tel: 260-665-3362. FAX: 260-665-8958. E-mail: info@steuben.lib.in.us. Web Site: www.cplsc.org. *Dir,* Sonya Dintaman; E-mail: sonyad@steuben.lib.in.us; Staff 16 (MLS 1, Non-MLS 15)
Founded 1915. Pop 14,000; Circ 120,000
Library Holdings: AV Mats 4,645; Bk Vols 64,000; Per Subs 145; Talking Bks 2,680
Subject Interests: Genealogy, Local hist
Automation Activity & Vendor Info: (Cataloging) Evergreen; (Circulation) Evergreen; (OPAC) Evergreen
Partic in Association for Rural & Small Libraries; Evergreen Indiana Consortium; Midwest Collaborative for Library Services
Open Mon-Thurs 9-8, Fri 9-5, Sat 9-3
Friends of the Library Group

C TRINE UNIVERSITY*, Sponsel Library & Information Services, One University Ave, 46703. Tel: 260-665-4162, 260-665-4164. FAX: 260-665-4283. E-mail: librarians@trine.edu, library@trine.edu. Web Site: www.trine.edu/library. *Dir for Grad & Distance Library Services,* Kristina Brewer; Tel: 260-665-4161, E-mail: brewerk@trine.edu; *Dir, Academic Support, Dir, Info Serv,* Michelle Blank; Tel: 260-665-4179, E-mail: blankm@trine.edu; *Asst Dir, Info Serv,* Patrick Ridout; Tel: 260-665-4287, E-mail: ridoutp@trine.edu; *Info Serv Assoc,* Renee Vanwagner; Tel: 260-665-4282, E-mail: vanwagnerr@trine.edu; Staff 4 (MLS 3, Non-MLS 1)
Founded 2007. Enrl 5,007; Fac 250; Highest Degree: Doctorate
May 2019-Apr 2020 Income $528,869, Parent Institution $523,951, Other $4,918
Special Collections: Hershey Museum; Kostyshak Educational Media & Learning Resources Coll; University Archives
Subject Interests: Bus, Engr, Health sci, Humanities, Natural sci, Soc sci, Teacher educ
Automation Activity & Vendor Info: (Acquisitions) OCLC; (Cataloging) OCLC Connexion; (Circulation) OCLC; (Course Reserve) OCLC; (ILL) OCLC WorldShare Interlibrary Loan; (OPAC) OCLC; (Serials) OCLC
Wireless access
Function: 24/7 Electronic res, 24/7 Online cat, Archival coll, Audiobks on Playaways & MP3, Computers for patron use, Distance learning, Doc delivery serv, E-Readers, E-Reserves, Electronic databases & coll, Equip loans & repairs, ILL available, Instruction & testing, Internet access, Laminating, Learning ctr, Meeting rooms, Music CDs, Online cat, Online info literacy tutorials on the web & in blackboard, Online ref, Orientations, OverDrive digital audio bks, Photocopying/Printing, Ref & res, Scanner, Study rm, Telephone ref, Wheelchair accessible, Workshops
Publications: Triangle (School newspaper)
Partic in Academic Libraries of Indiana; Midwest Collaborative for Library Services; Private Academic Library Network of Indiana
Special Services for the Deaf - Accessible learning ctr; Assistive tech
Special Services for the Blind - Assistive/Adapted tech devices, equip & products; Bks on CD; Dragon Naturally Speaking software; Screen reader software
Open Mon-Thurs 7:30am-11pm, Fri 7:30-5, Sat 1-5, Sun 1-9

ARGOS

P ARGOS PUBLIC LIBRARY*, 142 N Michigan St, 46501. SAN 304-7954. Tel: 574-892-5818. FAX: 574-892-5818. Web Site: argospubliclibrary.com. *Dir,* Jane Hall; E-mail: jehall@argos.lib.in.us; Staff 2 (MLS 1, Non-MLS 1)
Founded 1936. Pop 3,890; Circ 45,116
Library Holdings: CDs 219; Large Print Bks 323; Bk Vols 22,550; Per Subs 86; Talking Bks 191; Videos 1,148
Subject Interests: Art & archit
Automation Activity & Vendor Info: (Cataloging) Follett Software; (Circulation) Follett Software; (OPAC) Follett Software
Wireless access
Partic in Midwest Collaborative for Library Services
Open Mon, Wed & Fri 10-6, Tues & Thurs 11:30-8, Sat 10-2
Friends of the Library Group

ATTICA

P ATTICA PUBLIC LIBRARY*, 305 S Perry St, 47918. SAN 304-7962. Tel: 765-764-4194. FAX: 765-764-0906. Web Site: www.attica.lib.in.us. *Dir,* Norma Fink; E-mail: aplibnfink@netscape.net; *Asst Librn,* Lisa Mitton; *Ch,* Katie Cropper; Staff 3 (MLS 1, Non-MLS 2)
Founded 1902. Pop 4,429; Circ 35,920
Library Holdings: Bk Titles 28,911; Bk Vols 31,112; Per Subs 101; Talking Bks 218; Videos 317

Automation Activity & Vendor Info: (Acquisitions) Evergreen; (Cataloging) Evergreen; (OPAC) Evergreen
Wireless access
Partic in Wabash Valley Area Libr Servs Authority
Open Mon & Fri 10-6, Tues-Thurs 10-8, Sat 10-2
Friends of the Library Group

AUBURN

P ECKHART PUBLIC LIBRARY*, 603 S Jackson St, 46706-2298. SAN 304-7970. Tel: 260-925-2414. FAX: 260-333-7186. Toll Free FAX: 888-241-4393. Reference E-mail: info@epl.lib.in.us. Web Site: www.epl.lib.in.us. *Dir,* Janelle Graber; Tel: 206-925-2414, Ext 701, E-mail: jhgraber@epl.lib.in.us; *Asst Dir,* Jenny Kobiela Mondor; Tel: 206-925-2414, Ext 702, E-mail: jkobielamonder@epl.lib.in.us; *Pub Serv Mgr,* Darcy Davidson Armstrong; Tel: 206-925-2414, Ext 504, E-mail: darmstrong@epl.lib.in.us; *Tech Serv Mgr,* Lisa Rigsby; Tel: 206-925-2414, Ext 503, E-mail: lrigsby@epl.lib.in.us; Staff 29 (MLS 2, Non-MLS 27)
Founded 1910. Pop 13,331; Circ 223,000
Library Holdings: Audiobooks 4,010; CDs 2,587; DVDs 621; Large Print Bks 1,474; Bk Vols 69,323; Per Subs 188; Videos 2,637
Special Collections: Willennar Genealogy Center. Oral History
Automation Activity & Vendor Info: (Cataloging) TLC (The Library Corporation); (Circulation) TLC (The Library Corporation); (OPAC) TLC (The Library Corporation)
Wireless access
Function: Adult bk club, After school storytime, Archival coll, Bi-weekly Writer's Group, Bk club(s), Bks on cassette, Bks on CD, CD-ROM, Children's prog, Computer training, Computers for patron use, Digital talking bks, Distance learning, Electronic databases & coll, Equip loans & repairs, Free DVD rentals, Genealogy discussion group, Holiday prog, Home delivery & serv to seniorr ctr & nursing homes, Homebound delivery serv, Homework prog, ILL available, Instruction & testing, Internet access, Learning ctr, Mail & tel request accepted, Museum passes, Music CDs, Online cat, Online ref, Orientations, Outreach serv, Outside serv via phone, mail, e-mail & web, Photocopying/Printing, Preschool outreach, Prog for adults, Prog for children & young adult, Ref serv available, Scanner, Senior computer classes, Senior outreach, Spoken cassettes & CDs, Spoken cassettes & DVDs, Story hour, Summer reading prog, Tax forms, Teen prog, Telephone ref, VHS videos, Wheelchair accessible, Writing prog
Partic in Midwest Collaborative for Library Services
Open Mon-Thurs 9-8, Fri 9-7, Sat 9-5
Friends of the Library Group

AURORA

P AURORA PUBLIC LIBRARY DISTRICT*, 414 Second St, 47001-1384. SAN 304-7989. Tel: 812-926-0646. FAX: 812-926-0665. Web Site: www.eapld.org. *Dir,* Peggy Dean; E-mail: peggy@eapld.org; *Bus Mgr,* Janet Hall-Louden; E-mail: janet@eapld.org; Staff 12 (MLS 2, Non-MLS 10)
Founded 1901. Pop 17,133; Circ 157,189
Library Holdings: Audiobooks 2,228; DVDs 2,000; Large Print Bks 1,000; Microforms 99; Bk Vols 53,857; Per Subs 181; Talking Bks 510; Videos 1,500
Automation Activity & Vendor Info: (Acquisitions) TLC (The Library Corporation); (Cataloging) TLC (The Library Corporation); (OPAC) TLC (The Library Corporation)
Wireless access
Partic in Midwest Collaborative for Library Services
Open Mon, Wed & Fri 10-6, Tues & Thurs 10-8, Sat 10-3
Branches: 1
DILLSBORO PUBLIC, 10151 Library Lane, Dillsboro, 47018. (Mail add: PO Box 547, Dillsboro, 47018-0547), SAN 377-7448. Tel: 812-954-4151. FAX: 812-432-5209. *Dir,* Peggy Dean; E-mail: peggy@eapld.org; Staff 3 (MLS 1, Non-MLS 2)
Founded 1997
Library Holdings: Large Print Bks 260; Bk Titles 8,390; Bk Vols 9,800; Per Subs 43; Videos 280
Automation Activity & Vendor Info: (Circulation) TLC (The Library Corporation)
Open Mon-Fri 10-6, Sat 10-3

AVON

P AVON-WASHINGTON TOWNSHIP PUBLIC LIBRARY*, 498 N Avon Ave, 46123. SAN 376-5385. Tel: 317-272-4818. FAX: 317-272-7302. Reference E-mail: awtpl@avonlibrary.net. Web Site: www.avonlibrary.net. *Dir,* Laurel Setser; Staff 35 (MLS 8, Non-MLS 27)
Pop 26,319
Library Holdings: AV Mats 13,444; Large Print Bks 1,592; Bk Titles 75,766; Bk Vols 84,632; Per Subs 206
Special Collections: Washington Township Local History Coll
Automation Activity & Vendor Info: (Acquisitions) SirsiDynix; (Cataloging) SirsiDynix; (Circulation) SirsiDynix; (OPAC) SirsiDynix; (Serials) SirsiDynix
Wireless access
Publications: The Open Book (Newsletter)
Partic in Midwest Collaborative for Library Services
Open Mon-Thurs 9-8, Fri 9-6, Sat 10-4, Sun 2-5
Friends of the Library Group

BATESVILLE

P BATESVILLE MEMORIAL PUBLIC LIBRARY, 131 N Walnut St, 47006. SAN 304-7997. Tel: 812-934-4706. FAX: 812-934-6288. E-mail: info@ebatesville.com. Web Site: ebatesville.com. *Dir,* Kim Porter; E-mail: director@ebatesville.com; *Library Systems Admin,* Cassie Nash; Staff 9 (MLS 2, Non-MLS 7)
Founded 1937. Pop 10,852; Circ 192,991
Library Holdings: Audiobooks 1,217; AV Mats 135; Bks on Deafness & Sign Lang 40; CDs 1,408; DVDs 4,450; e-books 1,500; Electronic Media & Resources 130; Large Print Bks 700; Microforms 275; Bk Vols 45,219; Per Subs 120; Talking Bks 886
Special Collections: Hillenbrand Family Coll; James N Mahle Memorial Aviation Coll, bks, DVDs, mags, videos; Mary Stewart Center for Entrepreneurship Coll, audio, bks, DVDs, mags, periodicals, videos; Miriam Mason Coll, bks, drawings, original ms. Municipal Document Depository; Oral History
Subject Interests: Astronomy, Aviation, Entrepreneurship, Genealogy, Literacy, Local hist
Automation Activity & Vendor Info: (Cataloging) Evergreen; (Circulation) Evergreen; (ILL) Evergreen; (OPAC) Evergreen; (Serials) Evergreen
Wireless access
Function: 24/7 Electronic res, 24/7 Online cat, Activity rm, After school storytime, Art exhibits, Audio & video playback equip for onsite use, Audiobks on Playaways & MP3, Audiobks via web, Bks on cassette, Bks on CD, Children's prog, Computer training, Computers for patron use, Distance learning, Electronic databases & coll, Free DVD rentals, Genealogy discussion group, Holiday prog, Home delivery & serv to seniorr ctr & nursing homes, ILL available, Internet access, Jazz prog, Magazines, Magnifiers for reading, Mail & tel request accepted, Mango lang, Meeting rooms, Microfiche/film & reading machines, Movies, Music CDs, Notary serv, Online cat, OverDrive digital audio bks, Photocopying/Printing, Preschool outreach, Preschool reading prog, Prog for adults, Prog for children & young adult, Ref serv available, Scanner, Senior computer classes, Spanish lang bks, Story hour, Study rm, Summer reading prog, Tax forms, Teen prog, Telephone ref, Wheelchair accessible, Workshops
Partic in Midwest Collaborative for Library Services
Special Services for the Deaf - Bks on deafness & sign lang
Special Services for the Blind - Audio mat; Bks on cassette; Bks on CD; Digital talking bk machines; Info on spec aids & appliances; Large print bks; Low vision equip; Magnifiers; Playaways (bks on MP3)
Open Mon-Thurs 9-8, Fri 9-5, Sat 10-3
Restriction: In-house use for visitors, Non-circulating coll, Non-circulating of rare bks, Non-resident fee
Friends of the Library Group

BEDFORD

P BEDFORD PUBLIC LIBRARY*, 1323 K St, 47421. SAN 304-8004. Tel: 812-275-4471. FAX: 812-278-5244. E-mail: bpl@bedlib.com. Web Site: www.bedlib.org. *Dir,* Susan A Miller; E-mail: smiller@bedlib.com; *Asst Dir,* Nathan Watson; E-mail: nwatson@bedlib.com; *Bus Mgr,* Shelly Fish; E-mail: sfish@bedlib.com; *Mgr, Outreach Serv,* Jennifer Flynn; E-mail: jflynn@bedlib.com; *Tech Serv Mgr,* Sarah Cody; E-mail: scody@bedlib.com; Staff 15 (MLS 5, Non-MLS 10)
Founded 1898. Pop 34,179; Circ 387,953
Library Holdings: CDs 9,980; DVDs 6,785; e-books 27,891; e-journals 102; Bk Vols 62,706; Per Subs 147
Automation Activity & Vendor Info: (Acquisitions) SirsiDynix; (Cataloging) SirsiDynix; (Circulation) SirsiDynix
Wireless access
Open Mon-Thurs 10-6, Fri & Sat 10-5

BERNE

P BERNE PUBLIC LIBRARY*, 166 N Sprunger St, 46711-1595. SAN 304-8039. Tel: 260-589-2809. FAX: 260-589-2940. E-mail: bpl@bernepl.lib.in.us. Web Site: www.bernepl.lib.in.us. *Libr Dir,* Kathryn Gerber; Staff 11 (MLS 1, Non-MLS 10)
Founded 1935. Pop 4,150
Library Holdings: Bk Titles 68,814; Bk Vols 69,814; Per Subs 128
Special Collections: Berne & Adams County Coll; Indiana History & Genealogy Coll; Mennonite History Coll
Wireless access
Open Mon 10-8, Tues-Fri 10-6, Sat 10-2

BICKNELL

P BICKNELL-VIGO TOWNSHIP PUBLIC LIBRARY*, 201 W Second St, 47512. SAN 304-8047. Tel: 812-735-2317. FAX: 812-735-2018. Web Site: bicknell-vigo.lib.in.us. *Dir,* Deborah Kean; E-mail: kean.deborah@gmail.com; Staff 4 (MLS 2, Non-MLS 2)
Founded 1926. Pop 8,000; Circ 11,891
Library Holdings: AV Mats 433; Bk Titles 63,480; Bk Vols 65,111; Per Subs 65; Talking Bks 450; Videos 139
Automation Activity & Vendor Info: (Acquisitions) Brodart; (Cataloging) Brodart; (OPAC) Brodart
Wireless access
Partic in Ind Libr Asn
Open Mon-Thurs 10-8, Fri 10-5, Sat 10-3
Friends of the Library Group
Branches: 1
SANDBORN BRANCH, 112 Anderson St, Sandborn, 47578. Tel: 812-694-8403. *Supvr,* Colleen Bowman
Automation Activity & Vendor Info: (Circulation) Winnebago Software Co
Open Mon & Thurs 2-6 (Summer 3-7), Tues, Wed & Fri 1-5, Sat 11-4

BLOOMFIELD

P BLOOMFIELD-EASTERN GREENE COUNTY PUBLIC LIBRARY*, 125 S Franklin St, 47424. SAN 304-8055. Tel: 812-384-4125. FAX: 812-384-0820. E-mail: bloomfield@bloomfield.lib.in.us. Web Site: bloomfield.lib.in.us. *Dir,* Karen Holz; E-mail: kholz@bloomfield.lib.in.us; Staff 10 (MLS 2, Non-MLS 8)
Founded 1905
Library Holdings: Bks on Deafness & Sign Lang 25; CDs 474; DVDs 450; High Interest/Low Vocabulary Bk Vols 42; Large Print Bks 1,063; Bk Vols 32,874; Per Subs 139; Talking Bks 2,117; Videos 1,445
Special Collections: Indiana Special Coll. Municipal Document Depository; State Document Depository
Automation Activity & Vendor Info: (Acquisitions) SirsiDynix; (Cataloging) SirsiDynix; (Circulation) SirsiDynix; (ILL) OCLC Online; (OPAC) SirsiDynix; (Serials) SirsiDynix
Wireless access
Function: Adult bk club, Adult literacy prog, Computer training, Family literacy, Homebound delivery serv, ILL available, Music CDs, Photocopying/Printing, Prog for adults, Prog for children & young adult, Ref & res, Spoken cassettes & CDs, Summer reading prog, Tax forms, Telephone ref, VHS videos, Wheelchair accessible, Workshops
Partic in Evergreen Indiana Consortium; Midwest Collaborative for Library Services
Open Mon & Fri 10-4, Tues-Thurs 12-8, Sat 10-2
Friends of the Library Group
Branches: 1
EASTERN, 11453 East St, Rd 54, 47424, SAN 373-8795. Tel: 812-825-2677. FAX: 812-825-2677. E-mail: easternlibrary@smithville.net. *Br Mgr,* Karen Holz; Staff 2 (MLS 1, Non-MLS 1)
Circ 10,042
Library Holdings: Bks on Deafness & Sign Lang 12; Large Print Bks 60; Bk Vols 6,159; Per Subs 32; Talking Bks 209; Videos 272
Function: Computer training, E-Reserves, ILL available, Music CDs, Photocopying/Printing, Prog for children & young adult, Tax forms, Telephone ref, VHS videos, Wheelchair accessible
Open Mon, Wed & Fri 12-5, Tues & Thurs 3-8, Sat 9-12
Restriction: Non-resident fee
Friends of the Library Group

BLOOMINGTON

INDIANA UNIVERSITY

C INDIANA INSTITUTE ON DISABILITY & COMMUNITY*, 2853 E Tenth St, 47408-2601, SAN 371-6953. Tel: 812-855-9396. FAX: 812-855-9630. TDD: 812-855-9396. E-mail: cedir@indiana.edu. Web Site: www.iidc.indiana.edu/cedir. *Librn,* Christina Wray; Tel: 812-855-0077, E-mail: ccwray@indiana.edu; *Br Coordr,* Sharon Soto; Staff 2 (MLS 1, Non-MLS 1)
Library Holdings: Large Print Bks 280; Bk Titles 9,304; Bk Vols 9,670
Special Collections: Autism; Early Childhood Special Needs
Subject Interests: Aging, Disability awareness
Publications: CeDIR Citings (Biannually)
Special Services for the Deaf - Accessible learning ctr; Bks on deafness & sign lang
Special Services for the Blind - Accessible computers
Open Mon-Fri 8-11:30 & 12:30-4

CL SCHOOL OF LAW LIBRARY*, Maurer School of Law, 211 S Indiana Ave, 47405, SAN 304-8071. Tel: 812-855-9666. Circulation Tel: 812-855-6404. Reference Tel: 812-855-2938. FAX: 812-855-7099. Web Site: www.law.indiana.edu/lawlibrary. *Dir,* Linda Fariss; E-mail: fariss@indiana.edu; *Head, Pub Serv,* Keith Buckley; Tel: 812-855-7216, E-mail: buckley@indiana.edu; *Head, Tech Serv,* Nona Watt; E-mail: wattn@indiana.edu; *Acq Librn,* Richard Vaughan; Tel: 812-855-4199, E-mail: rvaughan@indiana.edu; *Cat Librn,* Michael Maben; Tel: 812-855-1882, E-mail: mmaben@indiana.edu; *Doc Librn,* Jennifer Bryan Morgan; Tel: 812-855-4611, E-mail: jlbryan@indiana.edu; Staff 13 (MLS 9, Non-MLS 4)
Founded 1842. Enrl 645; Fac 34
Library Holdings: Bk Titles 250,000; Bk Vols 759,000
Special Collections: 7th Circuit Records & Briefs; Indiana Court of Appeals Briefs; Indiana Supreme Court Records & Briefs; Rare Books & Archives; US Government Publications; US Supreme Court Records & Briefs
Subject Interests: US Law
Partic in Association of Research Libraries; GPO Access, Ind Coop Libr Servs Authority; OCLC Online Computer Library Center, Inc
Publications: Res Ipsa Loquitur (Newsletter)
Open Mon-Wed 7:30am-1am, Thurs & Fri 7:30am-Midnight, Sat 8am-10pm, Sun 9am-Midnight

C SINOR RESEARCH INSTITUTE FOR INNER ASIAN STUDIES*, Indiana University, Goodbody Hall 144, 1011 E Third St, 47405-7005, SAN 324-3575. Tel: 812-855-1605, 812-855-9510. FAX: 812-855-7500. E-mail: SRIFIAS@indiana.edu. Web Site: www.indiana.edu/~rifias. *Dir,* Edward J Lazzerini; E-mail: elazzeri@indiana.edu; Staff 4 (MLS 2, Non-MLS 2)
Founded 1967
Library Holdings: Bk Titles 8,691; Bk Vols 8,950; Per Subs 26; Videos 34
Special Collections: Central Asian Archives/Tibetan Coll
Subject Interests: Cent Asia, Inner Asia, Mongol studies, Tibetan studies, Turkic studies, Uralic studies
Partic in Association of Research Libraries; Midwest Collaborative for Library Services
Restriction: Non-circulating, Open to pub for ref only

C INDIANA UNIVERSITY BLOOMINGTON*, Herman B Wells Library, 1320 E Tenth St, 47405. SAN 340-9538. Tel: 812-855-0100. Circulation Tel: 812-855-4673. Reference Tel: 812-855-8028. FAX: 812-855-2576. Reference E-mail: libref@indiana.edu. Administration E-mail: libadmin@indiana.edu. Web Site: libraries.indiana.edu/wells. *Dean, Univ Libr,* Carolyn Walters; Tel: 812-855-3403, E-mail: cwalters@indiana.edu; *Operations Mgr,* Elinor Okada; Tel: 812-855-7711, E-mail: eokada@indiana.edu; Staff 144 (MLS 92, Non-MLS 52)
Founded 1824. Enrl 37,821; Fac 1,823; Highest Degree: Doctorate
Library Holdings: Bk Vols 6,770,498; Per Subs 70,370
Special Collections: 19th Century British Plays; American Revolution; Aristotle Coll; Austrian History, 1790-1843; English History Coll; George Frederick Handel Coll; History of Science & Medicine (Archives of Herman Muller - Genetics & V Hlavety - Mathematics); Indiana History Coll; Lafayette Coll; Latin Americana through the Independence Period; Lilly Rare Book Library: English & American Literature, 1640- (Milton, Defoe, John Gray, Sterne, Wordsworth, Coleridge, Byron, Tennyson, Henty, Andrew Lang, Yeats, Joseph Conrad, Upton Sinclair, Sylvia Plath); Lincoln Coll; London Low Life, Early-Mid 19th Century (Sadleir Coll); Voyages & Explorations, especially Spanish, Portuguese & Dutch; War of 1812; Western Americana. State Document Depository; UN Document Depository; US Document Depository
Automation Activity & Vendor Info: (Acquisitions) SirsiDynix; (Cataloging) SirsiDynix; (Circulation) SirsiDynix; (OPAC) SirsiDynix; (Serials) SirsiDynix
Wireless access
Function: Res libr
Publications: Indiana University Bookman (Newsletter); IUL News (Newsletter); The Source (Newsletter)
Partic in Area Libr Serv Authority; Big Ten Academic Alliance; Center for Research Libraries; Digital Libr Fedn; OCLC Online Computer Library Center, Inc
Open Mon-Thurs 8am-Midnight, Fri 8am-9pm, Sat 10-9, Sun 11am-Midnight; Mon-Thurs (Summer) 8am-10pm, Fri 8-5, Sat 10-5, Sun 1-10
Friends of the Library Group
Departmental Libraries:
BUSINESS/SPEA INFORMATION COMMONS, SPEA 150, 1315 E Tenth St, 47405, SAN 340-9627. Tel: 812-855-1957. FAX: 812-855-3398. E-mail: libbus@indiana.edu. Web Site: libraries.indiana.edu/bsic. *Dept Head,* Christina Sheley; Tel: 812-855-2448, E-mail: cmwilkin@indiana.edu; Staff 8 (MLS 3, Non-MLS 5)
Highest Degree: Doctorate
Library Holdings: Bk Vols 100,000
Automation Activity & Vendor Info: (Acquisitions) SirsiDynix-WorkFlows; (Cataloging) SirsiDynix-WorkFlows; (Circulation) SirsiDynix-WorkFlows; (Course Reserve) SirsiDynix-WorkFlows; (OPAC) SirsiDynix-WorkFlows; (Serials) SirsiDynix-WorkFlows
Open Mon-Thurs 7:30am-Midnight, Fri 7:30-6, Sat 11-6, Sun 11am-Midnight

WILLIAM & GAYLE COOK MUSIC LIBRARY, Simon Music Library & Recital Ctr M160, 200 S Jordan Ave, 47405, SAN 340-9953. Tel: 812-855-2970. FAX: 812-855-3843. E-mail: libmus@indiana.edu. Web Site: libraries.indiana.edu/music. *Dir,* Philip Ponella; E-mail: pponella@indiana.edu; *Assoc Dir,* Keith Cochran; Tel: 812-855-2974, E-mail: cochran6@indiana.edu
Library Holdings: AV Mats 138,622; Music Scores 106,769; Bk Vols 377,440
Subject Interests: Music
Open Mon-Thurs 8am-11pm, Fri 8am-9pm, Sat Noon-7, Sun Noon-11pm

EDUCATION LIBRARY, Wright Education 1160, 201 N Rose St, 47405-1006, SAN 340-9686. Tel: 812-856-8590. FAX: 812-856-8593. E-mail: libeduc@indiana.edu. Web Site: libraries.indiana.edu/education-library. *Head of Libr,* Julie Marie Frye; E-mail: jmfrye@indiana.edu
Library Holdings: Bk Vols 87,871
Special Collections: Childrens Coll; ERIC Documentation Coll; Indiana Textbook Repository
Open Mon-Thurs (Winter) 7:45am-10pm, Fri 7:45-5:30, Sat Noon-5:30, Sun Noon-10; Mon-Thurs (Summer) 8-6, Fri 8-4, Sun Noon-4

LIFE SCIENCES LIBRARY, Jordan Hall A304, 1001 E Third St, 47405-7005, SAN 340-9597. Tel: 812-855-8947. E-mail: libsci@indiana.edu. Web Site: libraries.iub.edu/life. *Head of Libr,* Jennifer Laherty; Tel: 812-855-5609, E-mail: jlaherty@indiana.edu; Staff 1 (MLS 1)
Library Holdings: Bk Vols 125,785
Open Mon-Thurs 9-5, Fri 9-4

LILLY LIBRARY RARE BOOKS & MANUSCRIPTS, 1200 E Seventh St, 47405-5500, SAN 340-9899. Tel: 812-855-2452. FAX: 812-855-3143. E-mail: liblilly@indiana.edu. Web Site: www.indiana.edu/~liblilly. *Dir,* Joel Silver; Tel: 812-855-2452, E-mail: silverj@indiana.edu
Library Holdings: Bk Vols 413,781
Open Mon-Thurs 9-6, Fri 9-5, Sat 9-1
Friends of the Library Group

NEAL-MARSHALL BLACK CULTURE CENTER LIBRARY, Neal-Marshall Ctr, Rm A113, 275 N Jordan, 47405, SAN 373-5761. Tel: 812-855-3237. FAX: 812-856-4558. E-mail: bcclib@indiana.edu. Web Site: libraries.indiana.edu/NMBCC-Library. *Head of Libr,* Deloice Holliday; Tel: 812-855-4369, E-mail: dehollid@indiana.edu; *Br Coordr,* Marianna Brough; Tel: 812-855-5932, E-mail: mabrough@indiana.edu
Founded 1972
Library Holdings: Bk Vols 8,403
Subject Interests: African-Am culture, African-Am hist
Open Mon-Thurs (Winter) 9-9, Fri 9-5, Sat 1-5, Sun 1-9; Mon-Fri (Summer) 9-5
Friends of the Library Group

CM OPTOMETRY LIBRARY, Optometry 202, 800 E Atwater Ave, 47405, SAN 340-9988. Tel: 812-855-8629. E-mail: libsci@indiana.edu. Web Site: libraries.indiana.edu/optometry-library. *Head, Sci Libr,* Jennifer Laherty; Tel: 812-855-5609, E-mail: jlaherty@indiana.edu
Founded 1968
Library Holdings: Bk Vols 22,134
Partic in Association of Vision Science Librarians; Midwest Collaborative for Library Services
Open Mon-Thurs 9-5, Fri 9-4

SCIENCES LIBRARY, Chemistry C002, 800 E Kirkwood Ave, 47405-7102, SAN 340-9651. Tel: 812-855-9452. E-mail: libsci@indiana.edu. Web Site: libraries.iub.edu/sciences-library. *Head of Libr,* Jennifer Laherty; Tel: 812-855-5609, E-mail: jlaherty@indiana.edu; Staff 1 (MLS 1)
Library Holdings: Bk Vols 47,839
Open Mon-Thurs 8am-9pm, Fri 8-5, Sun 1-9

J IVY TECH COMMUNITY COLLEGE OF INDIANA*, Joan Olcott Library, 200 Daniels Way, 47404. SAN 374-5317. Tel: 812-330-6080. Toll Free Tel: 866-447-0700. FAX: 812-330-6082. E-mail: bl-library@lists.ivytech.edu. Web Site: library.ivytech.edu/bloomington. *Libr Dir,* Carol Parkinson; E-mail: cparkinson@ivytech.edu; Staff 2 (MLS 2)
Enrl 6,000; Highest Degree: Associate
Library Holdings: AV Mats 2,414; DVDs 2,414; e-books 195,000; e-journals 100,699; Bk Titles 12,148; Per Subs 100
Subject Interests: Nursing
Automation Activity & Vendor Info: (Acquisitions) Ex Libris Group; (Cataloging) Ex Libris Group; (Circulation) Ex Libris Group; (Course Reserve) Ex Libris Group; (Discovery) EBSCO Discovery Service; (ILL) OCLC; (OPAC) Ex Libris Group
Wireless access
Function: Computers for patron use, Doc delivery serv, Electronic databases & coll, Health sci info serv, ILL available, Online cat, Online info literacy tutorials on the web & in blackboard, Online ref, Orientations, Photocopying/Printing
Partic in LYRASIS; Midwest Collaborative for Library Services
Open Mon-Thurs 8am-9:30pm, Fri 8am-9pm, Sat 8-1

P MONROE COUNTY PUBLIC LIBRARY*, 303 E Kirkwood Ave, 47408. SAN 341-0072. Tel: 812-349-3050. Circulation Tel: 812-349-3090. Web Site: www.mcpl.info. *Dir,* Marilyn Wood; E-mail: mwood@mcpl.info; *Assoc Dir,* Jane Cronkhite; E-mail: jcronkhi@mcpl.info; *Coordr,* Leanne Zdravecky; E-mail: lzdravec@mcpl.info; Staff 197 (MLS 36, Non-MLS 161)
Founded 1820. Pop 120,563; Circ 2,066,065
Library Holdings: AV Mats 74,910; Electronic Media & Resources 2,346; Bk Vols 380,098; Per Subs 1,078
Special Collections: CATS - Community Access Television; Indiana & Monroe County History (Indiana Coll), bks, mag, microfilm, newsp, pamphlets, hist tapes, maps, video & audio cassettes; VITAL - Volunteers in Tutoring Adult Learners. Oral History
Automation Activity & Vendor Info: (Acquisitions) Innovative Interfaces, Inc; (Cataloging) Innovative Interfaces, Inc; (Circulation) Innovative Interfaces, Inc; (OPAC) Innovative Interfaces, Inc; (Serials) Innovative Interfaces, Inc
Wireless access
Function: Adult bk club, Art exhibits, AV serv, Home delivery & serv to seniorr ctr & nursing homes, Homebound delivery serv, Homework prog, ILL available, Internet access, Magnifiers for reading, Music CDs, Photocopying/Printing, Prog for adults, Prog for children & young adult, Ref serv available, Spoken cassettes & CDs, Spoken cassettes & DVDs, Summer reading prog, VHS videos, Wheelchair accessible
Partic in OCLC Online Computer Library Center, Inc
Open Mon-Thurs 9-9, Fri & Sat 10-6, Sun Noon-6
Friends of the Library Group
Branches: 1
ELLETTSVILLE BRANCH, 600 W Temperance St, Ellettsville, 47429, SAN 341-0102. Tel: 812-876-1272. FAX: 812-876-2515. *Br Mgr,* Mr Chris Hosler; E-mail: chosler@mcpl.info; *Ch,* Stephanie Holman; E-mail: sholman@mcpl.info; Staff 9.3 (MLS 3, Non-MLS 6.3)
Circ 268,060
Open Mon-Thurs 10-9, Fri & Sat 10-6, Sun 1-5
Friends of the Library Group
Bookmobiles: 1

BLUFFTON

P WELLS COUNTY PUBLIC LIBRARY*, 200 W Washington St, 46714-1999. SAN 304-811X. Tel: 260-824-1612. FAX: 260-824-3129. Web Site: www.wellscolibrary.org. *Dir,* Sarah MacNeill; E-mail: smacneill@wellscolibrary.org; *Ch Serv,* Cynthia Burchell; E-mail: cburchell@wellscolibrary.org; *Circ,* Teresa Dustman; E-mail: tdustman@wellscolibrary.org; *Media Serv,* Jackie Dailey; E-mail: jdailey@wellscolibrary.org; Staff 28 (MLS 5, Non-MLS 23)
Founded 1902. Pop 27,176; Circ 391,233
Library Holdings: Audiobooks 4,341; CDs 3,079; DVDs 6,932; e-books 3,329; Bk Vols 103,159; Per Subs 275
Special Collections: Compton O Rider International Doll Coll; Harry Lindstand Art Coll; Large Print Books; Literacy Coll; Local Newspaper (Bluffton News-Banner & Ossian Journal, micro); Wells County History Coll
Automation Activity & Vendor Info: (Acquisitions) SirsiDynix; (Cataloging) SirsiDynix; (Circulation) SirsiDynix; (ILL) OCLC Online; (Media Booking) SirsiDynix; (OPAC) SirsiDynix; (Serials) SirsiDynix
Wireless access
Function: Adult bk club, After school storytime, Art exhibits, Audio & video playback equip for onsite use, Audiobks via web, AV serv, Bk club(s), Bks on cassette, Bks on CD, CD-ROM, Children's prog, Computer training, Computers for patron use, Digital talking bks, Electronic databases & coll, Equip loans & repairs, Free DVD rentals, Holiday prog, Home delivery & serv to seniorr ctr & nursing homes, ILL available, Magnifiers for reading, Music CDs, Notary serv, Online cat, Outreach serv, OverDrive digital audio bks, Photocopying/Printing, Preschool outreach, Prof lending libr, Prog for adults, Prog for children & young adult, Ref serv available, Scanner, Senior computer classes, Spoken cassettes & CDs, Spoken cassettes & DVDs, Story hour, Summer & winter reading prog, Summer reading prog, Tax forms, Teen prog, Telephone ref, VHS videos, Wheelchair accessible, Workshops
Publications: Librarian's Book Report (Newsletter)
Open Mon-Thurs 9-8, Fri 9-6, Sat 9-2
Friends of the Library Group
Branches: 1
OSSIAN BRANCH, 207 N Jefferson St, Ossian, 46777, SAN 320-0892. Tel: 260-622-4691. FAX: 260-622-7030. *Br Librn,* Susan Dailey; E-mail: sdailey@wellscolibrary.org; Staff 4 (MLS 1, Non-MLS 3)
Open Mon-Thurs 9-8, Fri 9-5, Sat 9-12
Friends of the Library Group

BOONVILLE

P BOONVILLE-WARRICK COUNTY PUBLIC LIBRARY*, 611 W Main St, 47601-1544. SAN 304-8136. Tel: 812-897-1500. FAX: 812-897-1508. E-mail: bwcpl@boonvillelib.org. Web Site: boonvillelib.org. *Dir,* Brooke Bolton; E-mail: bbolton@boonvillelib.org; Staff 9 (MLS 4, Non-MLS 5)
Founded 1911. Pop 194,150
Library Holdings: CDs 88; Bk Titles 121,478; Bk Vols 123,391; Per Subs 221; Talking Bks 410; Videos 1,733
Special Collections: Indiana Coll; Lincoln Coll
Automation Activity & Vendor Info: (Acquisitions) SirsiDynix; (Cataloging) SirsiDynix; (OPAC) SirsiDynix
Publications: Between the Pages (Patrons newsletter); Book Ends (Staff newsletter)
Open Mon-Thurs 10-8, Fri 10-5, Sat 12-5
Friends of the Library Group
Branches: 3
ELBERFELD BRANCH, 175 Sycamore St, Elberfeld, 47613, SAN 377-7596. Tel: 812-983-4029.
Library Holdings: Bk Titles 21,212; Bk Vols 22,911; Per Subs 33; Videos 112
Open Mon 1-8, Wed 1-5, Sat 9-3
Friends of the Library Group
LYNNVILLE BRANCH, 211 N Main St, Lynnville, 47619, SAN 377-760X. Tel: 812-922-5409.
Library Holdings: DVDs 25; Bk Titles 15,111; Bk Vols 17,808; Per Subs 27; Videos 101
Open Tues 11-6, Wed 3-6, Thurs 3-8
Friends of the Library Group
TENNYSON BRANCH, 318 N Main St, Tennyson, 47637, SAN 377-7626. Tel: 812-567-8933.
Library Holdings: Bk Titles 18,119; Bk Vols 19,640; Per Subs 37; Videos 112
Open Mon 2-6, Tues & Thurs 12-8, Sat 10-2
Friends of the Library Group
Bookmobiles: 2

BOSWELL

P BOSWELL & GRANT TOWNSHIP PUBLIC LIBRARY*, 101 N Clinton St, 47921. (Mail add: PO Box 315, 47921-0315), SAN 304-8144. Tel: 765-869-5428. FAX: 765-869-5428. E-mail: boswelllib@hotmail.com. Web Site: boswellpubliclibrary.com. *Dir,* Marie Brown; *Asst Librn,* Elizabeth Varner
Founded 1912. Pop 1,142; Circ 16,352
Library Holdings: AV Mats 1,450; Bk Vols 15,500; Per Subs 84; Talking Bks 250
Automation Activity & Vendor Info: (Acquisitions) SirsiDynix; (Cataloging) SirsiDynix; (Circulation) SirsiDynix; (ILL) SirsiDynix; (OPAC) SirsiDynix
Wireless access
Open Mon & Tues 12-7, Wed-Fri 12-5, Sat 9-1
Friends of the Library Group

BOURBON

P BOURBON PUBLIC LIBRARY, 307 N Main St, 46504. SAN 304-8152. Tel: 574-342-5655. FAX: 574-342-5001. *Dir,* Nick Treber; E-mail: ntreber@bourbon.lib.in.us; *Children's Spec,* Tammy Tutorow; Staff 4 (MLS 1, Non-MLS 3)
Founded 1940. Pop 2,970; Circ 37,707
Library Holdings: AV Mats 1,615; CDs 27; Large Print Bks 100; Bk Titles 21,117; Bk Vols 28,580; Per Subs 103; Talking Bks 291; Videos 572
Automation Activity & Vendor Info: (Acquisitions) EOS International; (Cataloging) EOS International; (OPAC) EOS International
Wireless access
Open Mon, Tues & Thurs 10-8, Fri 10-5, Sat 10-3

BRANCHVILLE

S BRANCHVILLE CORRECTIONAL FACILITY LAW LIBRARY*, 21390 Old State Rd 37, 47514. SAN 327-9006. Tel: 812-843-5921, Ext 4328. FAX: 812-843-4262. *Librn,* Paula Mitchell
Library Holdings: Bk Titles 10,000; Per Subs 70
Open Mon-Fri 10-6

BRAZIL

P BRAZIL PUBLIC LIBRARY, 204 N Walnut St, 47834. SAN 304-8160. Tel: 812-446-1331, 812-448-1981. FAX: 812-446-3215. Web Site: www.brazil.lib.in.us. *Dir,* Jill Scarbrough; E-mail: scarbroughj@brazil.lib.in.us; Staff 9 (MLS 1, Non-MLS 8)
Founded 1879. Pop 8,612; Circ 96,248
Library Holdings: CDs 59; Large Print Bks 161; Bk Titles 33,791; Bk Vols 35,815; Per Subs 89; Talking Bks 292; Videos 2,000
Automation Activity & Vendor Info: (Acquisitions) SirsiDynix; (Cataloging) SirsiDynix; (OPAC) SirsiDynix
Wireless access
Partic in Evergreen Indiana Consortium
Open Mon-Thurs 10-8, Fri & Sat 10-5
Friends of the Library Group

BREMEN

P BREMEN PUBLIC LIBRARY*, 304 N Jackson St, 46506. SAN 304-8179. Tel: 574-546-2849. FAX: 574-546-4938. Web Site: www.bremen.lib.in.us. *Dir,* Christopher Scandling; E-mail: cscandling@bremen.lib.in.us; *Head, Communications, Head, Adult Serv,* Holly Heller; *Head, Children's Servx,* Kate Blakely; Staff 2 (Non-MLS 2)
Founded 1956. Pop 8,474; Circ 115,000
Library Holdings: Bk Titles 45,000; Bk Vols 45,325; Per Subs 220
Automation Activity & Vendor Info: (Acquisitions) Innovative Interfaces, Inc; (Cataloging) Innovative Interfaces, Inc - Millennium; (Circulation) Innovative Interfaces, Inc; (OPAC) Innovative Interfaces, Inc; (Serials) Innovative Interfaces, Inc
Wireless access
Function: Accelerated reader prog, Adult bk club, Adult literacy prog, After school storytime, Art exhibits, Bk club(s), Bks on cassette, Bks on CD, Children's prog, Computer training, Computers for patron use, E-Reserves, Electronic databases & coll, Holiday prog, Home delivery & serv to seniorr ctr & nursing homes, Homebound delivery serv, ILL available, Internet access, Large print keyboards, Mail & tel request accepted, Music CDs, Online cat, Photocopying/Printing, Preschool outreach, Prog for adults, Prog for children & young adult, Ref & res, Ref serv available, Scanner, Senior computer classes, Serves people with intellectual disabilities, Spoken cassettes & CDs, Spoken cassettes & DVDs, Story hour, Summer reading prog, Tax forms, Telephone ref, VHS videos, Wheelchair accessible, Workshops
Publications: BLT, Bremen Library Times (Newsletter)
Partic in Midwest Collaborative for Library Services
Open Mon-Thurs 9-8, Fri & Sat 9-5
Friends of the Library Group

BRISTOL

P BRISTOL-WASHINGTON TOWNSHIP PUBLIC LIBRARY*, 505 W Vistula St, 46507. SAN 304-8187. Tel: 574-848-7458. FAX: 574-848-4391. Web Site: www.youseemore.com/bristolwash. *Dir,* Carol Anderson; E-mail: carol@bristol.lib.in.us; Staff 7 (MLS 1, Non-MLS 6)
Founded 1921. Pop 7,000
Library Holdings: AV Mats 8,000; Large Print Bks 450; Bk Titles 45,000; Per Subs 80; Talking Bks 500
Special Collections: Indiana History Coll
Automation Activity & Vendor Info: (Cataloging) TLC (The Library Corporation); (Circulation) TLC (The Library Corporation)
Wireless access
Function: ILL available
Partic in Midwest Collaborative for Library Services
Open Mon-Thurs 10-8, Fri 10-5, Sat 10-3

S ELKHART COUNTY HISTORICAL SOCIETY MUSEUM, INC*, Winifred Cosbey Library, 304 W Vistula St, 46507. (Mail add: PO Box 434, 46507-0434), SAN 329-1286. Tel: 574-848-4322. FAX: 574-848-5703. E-mail: research@elkhartcountyparks.org. Web Site: www.elkhartcountyhistory.org. *Mgr,* Julie Parker; E-mail: julie@elkhartcountyhistory.org; *Curator of Coll,* Michelle Nash; E-mail: michelle@elkhartcountyhistory.org; *Educ Curator,* Patrick McGuire; E-mail: patrick@elkhartcountyhistory.org; *Research Historian,* Frank Fisher; Staff 3 (Non-MLS 3)
Founded 1968
Library Holdings: Bk Titles 2,200; Per Subs 10
Special Collections: Elkhart County from 1830, archives
Publications: Bibliographies
Open Tues, Wed & Fri 10-4
Restriction: Non-circulating

BROOK

P BROOK-IROQUOIS-WASHINGTON PUBLIC LIBRARY*, 100 W Main St, 47922. (Mail add: PO Box 155, 47922-0155), SAN 304-8195. Tel: 219-275-2471. FAX: 219-275-8471. E-mail: library@brooklib.in.us. Web Site: www.brook.lib.in.us. *Dir,* Kristine Wright; E-mail: director@brook.lib.in.us; *Asst Librn,* Heather Hood; Staff 2 (Non-MLS 2)
Founded 1910. Pop 1,389; Circ 14,123
Library Holdings: Bk Vols 28,000; Per Subs 35
Subject Interests: Indiana, Local hist
Automation Activity & Vendor Info: (Cataloging) Mandarin Library Automation; (Circulation) Mandarin Library Automation; (OPAC) Mandarin Library Automation
Wireless access
Open Mon, Tues, Wed & Fri 9-7, Sat 9-1

BROOKSTON

P BROOKSTON - PRAIRIE TOWNSHIP PUBLIC LIBRARY*, 111 W Second St, 47923. SAN 304-8209. Tel: 765-563-6511. FAX: 765-563-6833. E-mail: info@brookston.lib.in.us. Web Site: brookstonlibrary.org. *Libr Dir,* Marilyn Blessing; *Asst Librn, Youth Spec,* Jennifer Norris; Staff 2 (Non-MLS 2)
Founded 1917. Pop 3,290; Circ 31,480
Library Holdings: DVDs 1,100; Bk Titles 32,890; Bk Vols 34,481; Per Subs 62; Talking Bks 1,011; Videos 445
Special Collections: Cookbooks; Crafts, Indiana History, bks, pamphlets. Oral History
Automation Activity & Vendor Info: (Acquisitions) Evergreen; (Cataloging) Evergreen; (OPAC) Evergreen
Wireless access
Partic in Midwest Collaborative for Library Services
Open Mon-Fri 1-5, Sat 9-1
Friends of the Library Group

BROOKVILLE

P FRANKLIN COUNTY PUBLIC LIBRARY DISTRICT*, Brookville Public Library, 919 Main St, 47012-1498. SAN 304-8217. Tel: 765-647-4031. FAX: 765-647-0278. Web Site: fclibraries.org. *Dir,* Susan Knight; E-mail: susan@fclibraries.org; *Ad,* Melody Gault; E-mail: melody@fclibraries.org; *Ch,* Jennifer Hambley; E-mail: jennifer@fclibraries.org; *Teen Librn,* Deidre Schirmer; E-mail: deidre@fclibraries.org; Staff 3 (Non-MLS 3)
Founded 1912. Pop 11,070; Circ 46,121
Library Holdings: Audiobooks 702; Electronic Media & Resources 3; Bk Titles 35,690; Bk Vols 39,972; Per Subs 132; Talking Bks 320; Videos 3,050
Special Collections: Family Histories; Genealogy Items; Heritage Art Coll; Local History Coll
Automation Activity & Vendor Info: (Cataloging) SirsiDynix; (Circulation) SirsiDynix; (OPAC) SirsiDynix
Wireless access
Function: Adult literacy prog, Art exhibits, Audio & video playback equip for onsite use, CD-ROM, Home delivery & serv to seniorr ctr & nursing homes, Homebound delivery serv, ILL available, Internet access, Music CDs, Orientations, Photocopying/Printing, Prog for adults, Prog for children & young adult, Spoken cassettes & CDs, Summer reading prog, Telephone ref, VHS videos, Wheelchair accessible
Partic in Eastern Ind Area Libr Servs Authority; Evergreen Indiana Consortium; Midwest Collaborative for Library Services
Special Services for the Deaf - Adult & family literacy prog; Bks on deafness & sign lang; High interest/low vocabulary bks
Special Services for the Blind - Bks on cassette; Bks on CD; Home delivery serv; Large print bks; Large screen computer & software; Reader equip
Open Mon-Thurs 9-8, Fri 9-6, Sat 9-3
Restriction: In-house use for visitors, Non-resident fee
Friends of the Library Group
Branches: 1
LAUREL PUBLIC LIBRARY, 200 N Clay St, Laurel, 47024. Tel: 765-698-2582. FAX: 765-698-2626. *Br Mgr,* Linda Bruns; E-mail: linda@fclibraries.org; *Cataloger,* Jodie Cregar; E-mail: jodie@fclibraries.org; Staff 1 (Non-MLS 1)
Founded 1998. Pop 11,070
Automation Activity & Vendor Info: (ILL) LAC Group
Function: Adult literacy prog, Archival coll, Art exhibits, Homebound delivery serv, ILL available, Internet access, Orientations, Photocopying/Printing, Prog for adults, Prog for children & young adult, Spoken cassettes & CDs, Summer reading prog, VHS videos, Wheelchair accessible, Workshops
Publications: Whitewater Valley Community Library (Newsletter)
Special Services for the Deaf - Adult & family literacy prog; Bks on deafness & sign lang; High interest/low vocabulary bks
Special Services for the Blind - Bks on cassette; Bks on CD; Copier with enlargement capabilities; Home delivery serv; Large print bks; Large screen computer & software; Videos on blindness & physical disabilties
Open Mon-Thurs 9-8, Fri 9-6, Sat 9-3
Restriction: Non-resident fee
Friends of the Library Group

BROWNSBURG

P BROWNSBURG PUBLIC LIBRARY*, 450 S Jefferson St, 46112-1310. SAN 304-8225. Tel: 317-852-3167. FAX: 317-852-7734. E-mail: AskUs@bburglibrary.net. Information Services E-mail: AccountInfo@bburglibrary.net. Web Site: www.bburglibrary.net. *Dir,* Denise Robinson; E-mail: drobinson@bburglibrary.net; *Asst Dir,* Amie Scott; E-mail: ascott@bburglibrary.net; *Customer Serv Mgr,* Patti Kovach; E-mail: pkovach@bburglibrary.net; *Info Serv Mgr,* Robbi Caldwell; E-mail: rcaldwell@bburglibrary.net; *Tech Serv Mgr,* Kelly Hale; E-mail: khale@bburglibrary.net; Staff 18 (MLS 12, Non-MLS 6)
Founded 1917. Pop 44,208; Circ 530,116
Jan 2017-Dec 2017 Income $1,548,671, Locally Generated Income $1,486,745, Other $61,926. Mats Exp $162,550, Books $97,535, Per/Ser (Incl. Access Fees) $5,704, AV Equip $7,340, AV Mat $11,208, Electronic Ref Mat (Incl. Access Fees) $40,763. Sal $731,883
Library Holdings: Audiobooks 3,691; DVDs 4,021; e-books 7,777; e-journals 23; Bk Vols 93,093; Per Subs 211
Automation Activity & Vendor Info: (Acquisitions) Innovative Interfaces, Inc; (Cataloging) Innovative Interfaces, Inc; (Circulation) Innovative Interfaces, Inc; (ILL) Innovative Interfaces, Inc; (OPAC) Innovative Interfaces, Inc; (Serials) Innovative Interfaces, Inc
Wireless access
Function: 24/7 Electronic res, 24/7 Online cat, Adult bk club, Archival coll, Audio & video playback equip for onsite use, Audiobks via web, AV serv, Bk club(s), Bks on CD, Children's prog, Computer training, Computers for patron use, E-Reserves, Electronic databases & coll, Equip loans & repairs, Free DVD rentals, Genealogy discussion group, Govt ref serv, Holiday prog, Home delivery & serv to seniorr ctr & nursing homes, Homebound delivery serv, ILL available, Internet access, Life-long learning prog for all ages, Magazines, Mail & tel request accepted, Meeting rooms, Microfiche/film & reading machines, Movies, Music CDs, Notary serv, Online cat, Online ref, Outreach serv, Outside serv via phone, mail, e-mail & web, OverDrive digital audio bks, Photocopying/Printing, Preschool outreach, Prog for adults, Prog for children & young adult, Ref & res, Ref serv available, Scanner, Senior computer classes, Story hour, Study rm, Summer & winter reading prog, Summer reading prog, Tax forms, Teen prog, Telephone ref, Wheelchair accessible, Winter reading prog, Writing prog
Partic in Indiana Public Library Internet Consortium; Midwest Collaborative for Library Services
Special Services for the Blind - Talking bks
Open Mon-Thurs 9-8, Fri 9-6, Sat 9-5, Sun 1-5
Friends of the Library Group

BROWNSTOWN

P BROWNSTOWN PUBLIC LIBRARY*, 120 E Spring St, 47220. SAN 304-8233. Tel: 812-358-2853. Web Site: www.brownstown.lib.in.us. *Dir,* Sherri May; E-mail: slmay@brownstownpl.org; Staff 2 (Non-MLS 2)
Founded 1910. Pop 7,080; Circ 110,103
Library Holdings: Audiobooks 575; CDs 244; DVDs 8,133; Large Print Bks 555; Bk Titles 33,112; Per Subs 70
Subject Interests: Indiana
Automation Activity & Vendor Info: (Acquisitions) Evergreen; (Cataloging) Evergreen; (Circulation) Evergreen; (OPAC) Evergreen
Wireless access
Partic in Evergreen Indiana Consortium
Open Mon-Thurs 9-7, Fri 9-6, Sat 9-4

BUNKER HILL

MIAMI CORRECTIONAL FACILITY

S PHASE I LIBRARY*, 3038 W 850 S, 46914. Tel: 765-689-8920. FAX: 765-689-5964. *Librn,* Robert Moore; Tel: 765-689-8920, Ext 5344
Founded 1999
Library Holdings: Large Print Bks 33; Bk Vols 10,500; Per Subs 8
Restriction: Inmate patrons, facility staff & vols direct access. All others through ILL only

S PHASE II LIBRARY*, 3038 W 850 S, 46914. Tel: 765-689-8920. FAX: 765-689-5964. *Librn,* Dr Barbara Kasper
Library Holdings: Bk Vols 3,000

BUTLER

P BUTLER PUBLIC LIBRARY*, 340 S Broadway St, 46721. SAN 304-8241. Tel: 260-868-2351. FAX: 260-868-5491. E-mail: staff@butlerpubliclibrary.net. Web Site: www.butlerpubliclibrary.net. *Dir,* Sarah Dempsey; E-mail: sarah@butlerpubliclibrary.net; *Children & Teen Librn,* Anna VonEwegen; E-mail: anna@butlerpubliclibrary.net; Staff 3 (MLS 1, Non-MLS 2)
Founded 1906. Pop 3,905; Circ 54,718
Library Holdings: Bk Titles 46,521; Per Subs 65
Automation Activity & Vendor Info: (Cataloging) Evergreen; (Circulation) Evergreen; (OPAC) Evergreen
Wireless access
Partic in Evergreen Indiana Consortium; Morris Automated Information Network
Open Mon-Thurs 10-7, Sat 9-1
Friends of the Library Group

CAMBRIDGE CITY

P CAMBRIDGE CITY PUBLIC LIBRARY, 600 W Main St, 47327. SAN 304-825X. Tel: 765-478-3335. FAX: 765-478-6144. E-mail: info@ccitypl.org. Web Site: www.ccitypl.org. *Dir,* Karen Bay-Winslow; *Ch,* Kim Scott; Staff 2 (Non-MLS 2)

Founded 1936. Pop 5,508; Circ 65,000
Library Holdings: Bks on Deafness & Sign Lang 20; CDs 174; DVDs 622; Large Print Bks 604; Bk Titles 34,000; Per Subs 120; Talking Bks 649; Videos 1,158
Special Collections: History (Western Wayne County); Overbeck Pottery Coll
Automation Activity & Vendor Info: (Acquisitions) Evergreen; (Cataloging) Evergreen; (Circulation) Evergreen; (Course Reserve) Evergreen; (ILL) Evergreen; (OPAC) Evergreen; (Serials) EBSCO Online
Wireless access
Function: After school storytime, Homebound delivery serv, ILL available, Internet access, Music CDs, Photocopying/Printing, Prog for adults, Prog for children & young adult, Ref serv available, Spoken cassettes & CDs, Summer reading prog, Telephone ref, VHS videos
Partic in Evergreen Indiana Consortium
Open Mon & Wed 10-6, Tues & Thurs 10-5, Fri & Sat 10-2
Friends of the Library Group

CAMDEN

P CAMDEN-JACKSON TOWNSHIP PUBLIC LIBRARY*, 183 Main St, 46917. (Mail add: PO Box 24, 46917-0024), SAN 304-8268. Tel: 574-686-2120. FAX: 574-686-4420. E-mail: camlib@camden.lib.in.us. *Dir,* Tamara Gibbs; Staff 2 (MLS 1, Non-MLS 1)
Founded 1940. Pop 1,266; Circ 6,358
Library Holdings: Bk Titles 13,049; Bk Vols 15,691; Per Subs 27; Talking Bks 429; Videos 386
Wireless access
Partic in Evergreen Indiana Consortium
Open Tues-Fri 2-6:30, Sat 9-12

CARLISLE

WABASH VALLEY CORRECTIONAL FACILITY

S LEVEL FOUR LIBRARY*, 6908 S Old US Hwy 41, 47838. (Mail add: PO Box 500, 47838-0500). Tel: 812-398-5050, Ext 4573. FAX: 812-398-5032. Web Site: www.in.gov/idoc/2409.htm.
Library Holdings: Bk Titles 1,850; Bk Vols 2,060; Per Subs 42
Function: Adult literacy prog, Audio & video playback equip for onsite use, Distance learning, For res purposes, Homebound delivery serv, ILL available, Photocopying/Printing, Prog for adults, Ref serv available, Res libr, Serves people with intellectual disabilities, Spoken cassettes & CDs, Wheelchair accessible
Restriction: Circ limited

S LEVEL THREE LIBRARY*, 6908 S Old US Hwy 41, 47838. (Mail add: PO Box 500, 47838-0500). Tel: 812-398-5050, Ext 3271. FAX: 812-398-2125. Web Site: www.in.gov/idoc/2409.htm. *Librn,* Stephanie Sark; Staff 1 (Non-MLS 1)
Library Holdings: Bk Titles 5,160; Bk Vols 5,380; Per Subs 21

CARMEL

P CARMEL CLAY PUBLIC LIBRARY, 55 Fourth Ave SE, 46032-2278. SAN 304-8284. Tel: 317-814-3900. Circulation Tel: 317-844-3361. Reference Tel: 317-844-3362. Administration Tel: 317-844-6711. FAX: 317-571-4285. Web Site: carmelclaylibrary.org. *Dir,* Bob Swanay; Tel: 317-814-3901, E-mail: bswanay@carmelclaylibrary.org; Staff 46.9 (MLS 25, Non-MLS 21.9)
Founded 1904. Pop 86,293; Circ 2,025,415
Library Holdings: AV Mats 60,911; Bk Titles 226,336; Bk Vols 280,146; Per Subs 358
Automation Activity & Vendor Info: (Acquisitions) SirsiDynix; (Cataloging) SirsiDynix; (Circulation) SirsiDynix; (Discovery) BiblioCommons; (ILL) OCLC; (OPAC) SirsiDynix
Wireless access
Publications: Happenings (Newsletter)
Special Services for the Deaf - Assistive tech; Bks on deafness & sign lang; Closed caption videos; High interest/low vocabulary bks; TDD equip
Special Services for the Blind - Audio mat; Bks on cassette; Bks on CD; Large print bks; Screen enlargement software for people with visual disabilities
Open Mon-Thurs 9-9, Fri 9-7, Sat 9-5, Sun 1-5
Friends of the Library Group

CARTHAGE

P HENRY HENLEY PUBLIC LIBRARY, Carthage Library, 102 N Main St, 46115. (Mail add: PO Box 35, 46115-0035), SAN 373-8671. Tel: 765-565-8022. E-mail: hhlibrary@outlook.com. Web Site: henryhenley.lib.in.us. *Librn,* Arlene Reynolds
Founded 1890. Pop 1,100
Library Holdings: Bk Vols 6,500
Wireless access
Open Tues & Thurs 10-6, Sat 10-2
Friends of the Library Group

CENTERVILLE

P CENTERVILLE-CENTER TOWNSHIP PUBLIC LIBRARY*, 126 E Main St, 47330-1206. SAN 304-8292. Tel: 765-855-5223. FAX: 765-855-2009. E-mail: read@centervillelibrary.info. Web Site: www.centervillelibrary.info. *Dir,* Beth Treaster; E-mail: btreaster@centervillelibrary.info; *Ch,* Carol Pentecost; E-mail: cpentecost@centervillelibrary.info; *Outreach Serv Librn,* Kristie Dickens; E-mail: kdickens@centervillelibrary.info; *Tech Serv,* Kris Turner; E-mail: kturner@centervillelibrary.info; Staff 2 (MLS 1, Non-MLS 1)
Founded 1921. Pop 7,330; Circ 38,399
Library Holdings: Audiobooks 182; DVDs 3,054; Large Print Bks 2,000; Bk Vols 35,163; Per Subs 90
Special Collections: Paintings by Local Artists
Subject Interests: Genealogy, Local hist
Automation Activity & Vendor Info: (Cataloging) Evergreen; (Circulation) Evergreen; (OPAC) Evergreen
Wireless access
Function: 24/7 Online cat, Accelerated reader prog, Adult bk club, Archival coll, Art exhibits, Bk club(s), Bks on CD, Children's prog, Computer training, Computers for patron use, Free DVD rentals, Homebound delivery serv, ILL available, Internet access, Magazines, Meeting rooms, Online cat, Outreach serv, OverDrive digital audio bks, Photocopying/Printing, Preschool reading prog, Prog for adults, Prog for children & young adult, Scanner, Study rm, Summer reading prog, Tax forms, Wheelchair accessible
Partic in Evergreen Indiana Consortium
Open Mon-Thurs 10-7, Fri 10-5, Sat 10-2

CHARLESTOWN

P CHARLESTOWN-CLARK COUNTY PUBLIC LIBRARY*, 51 Clark Rd, 47111. SAN 304-8306. Tel: 812-256-3337. FAX: 812-256-3890. Web Site: www.clarkco.lib.in.us. *Dir,* June Kruer; E-mail: jkruer@clarkco.lib.in.us; *Mgr,* Abby Cyrus; Staff 27 (MLS 9, Non-MLS 18)
Founded 1966. Pop 42,817; Circ 148,091
Library Holdings: Bk Titles 122,891; Per Subs 370; Talking Bks 762; Videos 1,934
Special Collections: Lexicography (J E Schmidt, MD Coll)
Subject Interests: Genealogy, Local hist
Automation Activity & Vendor Info: (Acquisitions) TLC (The Library Corporation); (Cataloging) TLC (The Library Corporation); (OPAC) TLC (The Library Corporation)
Wireless access
Publications: Monthly Calendar of Activities
Partic in Ind Area Libr Servs Authority; Midwest Collaborative for Library Services
Open Mon-Thurs 9-8, Fri & Sat 9-5
Branches: 4
BORDEN BRANCH, 117 W Main St, Borden, 47106. Tel: 812-258-9041. FAX: 812-967-3440. *Mgr,* Carla Akers
Library Holdings: AV Mats 1,221; DVDs 280; Bk Titles 15,906; Bk Vols 16,302; Per Subs 38; Videos 290
Open Mon 11-6, Tues & Thurs 11-7, Fri 9-6, Sat 10-2
HENRYVILLE BRANCH, 214 E Main St, Henryville, 47126. Tel: 812-294-4246. FAX: 812-294-1078. *Mgr,* Lacy Rogers
Library Holdings: AV Mats 1,355; DVDs 280; Bk Titles 20,316; Bk Vols 20,943; Per Subs 34; Videos 214
Open Mon 9-6, Tues & Thurs 10-8, Wed 12-6, Fri 9-5, Sat 10-2
NEW WASHINGTON BRANCH, 210 S Poplar St, New Washington, 47162. Tel: 812-289-1142. FAX: 812-967-4577. *Mgr,* Kelly Davis
Library Holdings: AV Mats 1,834; DVDs 728; Bk Titles 14,330; Bk Vols 14,772; Per Subs 33; Videos 177
Open Mon & Fri 9-5, Tues & Thurs 12-8, Sat 9-1
SELLERSBURG BRANCH, 430 N Indiana Ave, Sellersburg, 47172. Tel: 812-246-4493. FAX: 812-246-4382. *Mgr,* Cathy Hoover
Library Holdings: AV Mats 1,964; DVDs 313; Bk Titles 38,521; Bk Vols 39,845; Per Subs 64; Videos 792
Open Mon-Thurs 9-8, Fri & Sat 9-5

CHESTERTON

P WESTCHESTER PUBLIC LIBRARY*, Thomas Library, 200 W Indiana Ave, 46304-3122. SAN 341-0137. Tel: 219-926-7696. FAX: 219-926-6424. Web Site: www.wpl.lib.in.us. *Dir,* Lisa Stamm; E-mail: lisa@wpl.lib.in.us; *Ch,* Heather Chaddock; E-mail: heather@wpl.lib.in.us; *Ref Librn,* Marta Schumacher; E-mail: marta@wpl.lib.in.us; *AV Mgr,* Tracy McDonald; E-mail: tracy@wpl.lib.in.us; *Mgr, Automation & Ser,* Rhonda Mullin; E-mail: rhonda@wpl.lib.in.us; *Circ Mgr,* Karyn Witt; E-mail: karyn@wpl.lib.in.us; *IT Mgr,* Joseph Harry; E-mail: joe@wpl.lib.in.us; *Tech Serv Mgr,* Julie Bohannon; E-mail: julie@wpl.lib.in.us; Staff 4 (MLS 4)
Founded 1972. Pop 18,341; Circ 340,000
Library Holdings: CDs 7,800; DVDs 4,200; Bk Vols 154,000; Per Subs 125; Talking Bks 950; Videos 10,900
Special Collections: Chesterton Tribune Photo Morgue; Prairie Club Archives

Subject Interests: Local hist
Automation Activity & Vendor Info: (Acquisitions) Innovative Interfaces, Inc; (Cataloging) Innovative Interfaces, Inc; (Circulation) Innovative Interfaces, Inc; (ILL) Innovative Interfaces, Inc; (OPAC) Innovative Interfaces, Inc
Wireless access
Function: Adult bk club, Adult literacy prog, After school storytime, Archival coll, AV serv, CD-ROM, ILL available, Music CDs, Photocopying/Printing, Prog for adults, Prog for children & young adult, Ref serv available, Summer reading prog, VHS videos, Wheelchair accessible
Open Mon-Fri 9-9, Sat 9-5, Sun 1-5
Friends of the Library Group
Branches: 1
HAGEMAN, 100 Francis St, Porter, 46304, SAN 341-0161. Tel: 219-926-9080. *Br Mgr,* Suzanne Chomel; E-mail: suzanne@wpl.lib.in.us
Open Mon-Fri 9-5, Sat 1-5
Friends of the Library Group

CHURUBUSCO

P CHURUBUSCO PUBLIC LIBRARY, 116 N Mulberry St, 46723. SAN 304-8322. Tel: 260-693-6466. FAX: 260-693-6466. E-mail: buscolibrary@buscolibrary.org. Web Site: buscolibrary.org. *Libr Dir,* Rachel Eyermann; Staff 2 (MLS 1, Non-MLS 1)
Founded 1914. Pop 5,327
Library Holdings: CDs 86; Bk Vols 23,383; Per Subs 55; Talking Bks 974
Wireless access
Function: 24/7 Electronic res, 24/7 Online cat, Adult bk club, Bk club(s), Bks on cassette, Bks on CD, CD-ROM, Children's prog, Computers for patron use, E-Reserves, Free DVD rentals, Holiday prog, Home delivery & serv to seniorr ctr & nursing homes, Homebound delivery serv, ILL available, Internet access, Magazines, Movies, Music CDs, Online cat, Outreach serv, Outside serv via phone, mail, e-mail & web, Photocopying/Printing, Prog for adults, Prog for children & young adult, Ref & res, Ref serv available, Scanner, Senior outreach, Spoken cassettes & CDs, Story hour, Summer reading prog, Tax forms, Teen prog, Telephone ref, VHS videos, Wheelchair accessible
Partic in Northeast Indiana Libraries Serving Communities Consortium
Open Mon-Thurs 11-7, Fri 11-6, Sat 9-2
Friends of the Library Group

CICERO

P HAMILTON NORTH PUBLIC LIBRARY*, 209 W Brinton St, 46034. SAN 340-9503. Tel: 317-984-5623. FAX: 317-984-7505. Web Site: www.hnpl.lib.in.us. *Dir,* Ann Hoehn; E-mail: ahoehn@hnpl.lib.in.us; *Asst Dir,* Kate Marshall; E-mail: kmarshall@hnpl.lib.in.us; Staff 19 (MLS 1, Non-MLS 18)
Pop 9,968
Library Holdings: AV Mats 9,090; Bks on Deafness & Sign Lang 73; CDs 1,500; DVDs 1,000; High Interest/Low Vocabulary Bk Vols 74; Large Print Bks 1,063; Bk Vols 87,600; Per Subs 200; Talking Bks 2,000; Videos 4,590
Special Collections: Local History
Automation Activity & Vendor Info: (Acquisitions) Follett Software; (Cataloging) Follett Software; (OPAC) Follett Software
Wireless access
Function: Adult literacy prog, Archival coll, Art exhibits, AV serv, Homebound delivery serv, ILL available, Music CDs, Photocopying/Printing, Prog for adults, Prog for children & young adult, Spoken cassettes & CDs, Summer reading prog, VHS videos, Wheelchair accessible
Partic in Evergreen Indiana Consortium; Midwest Collaborative for Library Services
Open Mon-Thurs 10-8, Fri 10-5, Sat 10-4, Sun 1-4
Friends of the Library Group
Branches: 1
ATLANTA BRANCH, 100 S Walnut St, Atlanta, 46031, SAN 340-9449. Tel: 317-984-5623. FAX: 765-292-2249. *Br Mgr,* Kate Marshall; E-mail: kmarshall@hnpl.lib.in.us; Staff 3 (MLS 1, Non-MLS 2)
Founded 1916. Circ 5,271
Library Holdings: Bk Vols 10,000
Function: Archival coll, Homebound delivery serv, ILL available, Music CDs, Photocopying/Printing, Prog for adults, Prog for children & young adult, Spoken cassettes & CDs, Summer reading prog, VHS videos
Open Mon, Tues & Thurs 3-7, Wed 10-7
Friends of the Library Group

CLAYTON

P CLAYTON-LIBERTY TOWNSHIP PUBLIC LIBRARY*, 5199 Iowa St, 46118-9174. SAN 304-8330. Tel: 317-539-2991. FAX: 317-539-2050. E-mail: cltpl@tds.net. Web Site: clayton.lib.in.us. *Dir,* Angie Roberts; E-mail: cltpldirector@gmail.com; Staff 5 (MLS 1, Non-MLS 4)
Founded 1929. Pop 5,072; Circ 12,308
Library Holdings: Bks on Deafness & Sign Lang 22; Large Print Bks 1,052; Bk Vols 27,000; Per Subs 78; Videos 230
Subject Interests: Local authors, Local hist
Automation Activity & Vendor Info: (Cataloging) Follett Software; (Circulation) Follett Software; (OPAC) Follett Software
Partic in Midwest Collaborative for Library Services
Special Services for the Deaf - Closed caption videos
Open Mon, Tues & Thurs 10-7, Fri 10-5, Sat 9-1

CLINTON

P CLINTON PUBLIC LIBRARY*, 313 S Fourth St, 47842-2398. SAN 304-8349. Tel: 765-832-8349. FAX: 765-832-3823. E-mail: cpl@clintonpl.lib.in.us. Web Site: www.clintonpl.lib.in.us. *Dir,* Becky Edington; E-mail: director@clintonpl.lib.in.us; *Head, Adult Serv, Head, YA,* Ashley Wolfe; E-mail: Ashley@clintonpl.lib.in.us; *Head, Children's Servx,* Harmony Harris; E-mail: Harmony@clintonpl.lib.in.us; Staff 4 (MLS 1, Non-MLS 3)
Founded 1911. Pop 9,119; Circ 87,934
Library Holdings: Audiobooks 210; AV Mats 2,690; CDs 90; DVDs 3,000; Electronic Media & Resources 20; Large Print Bks 3,000; Bk Vols 45,088; Per Subs 78; Talking Bks 40
Special Collections: Daily Clintonian on microfilm; Genealogy & Local History Coll
Automation Activity & Vendor Info: (Cataloging) Evergreen; (Circulation) Evergreen; (ILL) Evergreen; (OPAC) Evergreen
Wireless access
Function: 24/7 Electronic res, 24/7 Online cat, Accelerated reader prog, Adult bk club, Adult literacy prog, After school storytime, Archival coll, Audiobks on Playaways & MP3, Audiobks via web, AV serv, Bi-weekly Writer's Group, Bk club(s), Bk reviews (Group), Bks on CD, Children's prog, Computer training, Computers for patron use, Digital talking bks, Electronic databases & coll, Free DVD rentals, Holiday prog, Home delivery & serv to seniorr ctr & nursing homes, Homebound delivery serv, ILL available, Instruction & testing, Large print keyboards, Life-long learning prog for all ages, Magazines, Magnifiers for reading, Mail & tel request accepted, Meeting rooms, Microfiche/film & reading machines, Movies, Music CDs, Notary serv, Online cat, Outreach serv, OverDrive digital audio bks, Photocopying/Printing, Preschool outreach, Preschool reading prog, Printer for laptops & handheld devices, Prog for adults, Prog for children & young adult, Ref & res, Ref serv available, Scanner, Spoken cassettes & CDs, STEM programs, Story hour, Summer & winter reading prog, Summer reading prog, Tax forms, Teen prog, Telephone ref, Wheelchair accessible, Winter reading prog
Partic in Evergreen Indiana Consortium
Special Services for the Blind - Bks on cassette; Bks on CD; Large print bks; Talking bk serv referral
Open Mon-Thurs 9-6, Fri 9-5, Sat 9-2
Friends of the Library Group

COATESVILLE

P COATESVILLE-CLAY TOWNSHIP PUBLIC LIBRARY*, 4928 Milton St, 46121. SAN 304-8357. Tel: 765-386-2355. FAX: 765-386-6177. E-mail: cpl@ccrtc.com. Web Site: coatesvillectpl.lib.in.us. *Librn,* Cheryl Steinborn; Staff 3 (MLS 1, Non-MLS 2)
Founded 1912. Pop 2,311; Circ 8,618
Library Holdings: Bk Titles 21,890; Bk Vols 23,450; Per Subs 72; Talking Bks 115; Videos 276
Special Collections: Coatesville Herald, 1910-1961, microfilm
Wireless access
Open Mon-Fri 1-7, Sat 10-5
Friends of the Library Group

COLFAX

P COLFAX-PERRY TOWNSHIP PUBLIC LIBRARY*, 207 S Clark St, 46035. (Mail add: PO Box 308, 46035-0308), SAN 304-8365. Tel: 765-324-2915. FAX: 765-324-2689. Web Site: colfaxptpl.org. *Dir,* Brenda Kinslow; Tel: 765-324-2915, Ext 100, E-mail: bkinslow@colfaxptpl.org; *Adult & Teen Serv,* Amanda Boska; E-mail: aboska@colfaxptpl.org; Staff 2 (MLS 1, Non-MLS 1)
Founded 1917. Pop 1,507; Circ 21,210
Library Holdings: Bk Titles 14,599; Bk Vols 15,981; Per Subs 10; Videos 1,598
Subject Interests: Genealogy, Local hist
Automation Activity & Vendor Info: (Acquisitions) Follett Software; (Cataloging) Follett Software; (ILL) Follett Software; (OPAC) Follett Software
Wireless access
Publications: Periodic Newsletter
Partic in Evergreen Indiana Consortium
Open Mon & Wed 11-6, Tues & Thurs 12:30-6:30, Fri 11-5, Sat 10-3
Friends of the Library Group

COLUMBIA CITY

P PEABODY PUBLIC LIBRARY, 1160 E State Rd 205, 46725. (Mail add: PO Box 406, 46725-0406), SAN 304-8373. Tel: 260-244-5541. FAX: 260-244-5653. E-mail: librarian@ppl.lib.in.us. Web Site: ppl.lib.in.us. *Exec Dir,* Mary Hartman; E-mail: mhartman@ppl.lib.in.us; *Asst Dir,* Christie Carnahan Whitton; E-mail: cwhitton@ppl.lib.in.us; Staff 5 (MLS 4, Non-MLS 1)
Founded 1901. Pop 15,323; Circ 267,580
Library Holdings: AV Mats 1,660; Bk Vols 90,082; Per Subs 227
Special Collections: Oral History
Subject Interests: Local hist
Automation Activity & Vendor Info: (Cataloging) SirsiDynix; (Circulation) SirsiDynix; (OPAC) SirsiDynix; (Serials) SirsiDynix
Wireless access
Partic in Midwest Collaborative for Library Services
Open Mon & Fri 9-6, Tues-Thurs 9-8, Sat 9-1, Sun (Summer) 1-5
Friends of the Library Group

COLUMBUS

S BARTHOLOMEW COUNTY HISTORICAL SOCIETY*, Cline-Keller Library, 524 Third St, 2nd Flr, 47201. SAN 329-126X. Tel: 812-372-3541. FAX: 812-372-3113. Web Site: bartholomewhistory.org. *Exec Dir,* Diane Robbins; E-mail: drobbins@bartholomewhistory.org; *Educ Mgr,* Adam Rediker; E-mail: arediker@bartholomewhistory.org
Founded 1921
Library Holdings: Bk Vols 1,310
Special Collections: Pence Coll. Oral History
Subject Interests: Genealogy, Hist, Local govt, Local hist
Publications: Quarterly Connection (Newsletter)
Open Tues-Thurs 10-12 & 1-4 or by appointment

P BARTHOLOMEW COUNTY PUBLIC LIBRARY*, 536 Fifth St, 47201-6225. SAN 341-0196. Tel: 812-379-1255. FAX: 812-379-1275. Web Site: www.mybcpl.org. *Dir,* Jason Hatton; Tel: 812-379-1251, E-mail: jhatton@mybcpl.org; *Asst Dir,* Angela Eck; Tel: 812-379-1254, E-mail: aeck@mybcpl.org; *Teen Librn,* Christina Kelley; Tel: 812-379-1260, E-mail: ckelley@mybcpl.org; *Circ Supvr,* Sonya Stretshberry; Tel: 812-379-1257, E-mail: sstretshberry@mybcpl.org. Subject Specialists: *Teen serv,* Christina Kelley; Staff 15 (MLS 11, Non-MLS 4)
Founded 1899. Sal $1,547,815
Library Holdings: Audiobooks 11,519; Bks on Deafness & Sign Lang 362; CDs 6,201; DVDs 13,059; e-books 2,560; Electronic Media & Resources 1,090; Large Print Bks 6,688; Microforms 1,000; Bk Titles 160,888; Bk Vols 172,554; Per Subs 350; Talking Bks 25,000; Videos 918
Special Collections: Talking Books for Blind & Physically Handicapped, rec, cassettes, large print
Subject Interests: Am hist, Archit, Hist, Indiana
Automation Activity & Vendor Info: (Cataloging) SirsiDynix; (Circulation) SirsiDynix; (ILL) OCLC FirstSearch; (OPAC) SirsiDynix
Wireless access
Function: After school storytime, Archival coll, Audio & video playback equip for onsite use, Audiobks via web, AV serv, Bilingual assistance for Spanish patrons, Bks on CD, Children's prog, Computer training, Computers for patron use, Digital talking bks, E-Reserves, Electronic databases & coll, Free DVD rentals, Holiday prog, ILL available, Internet access, Life-long learning prog for all ages, Magazines, Magnifiers for reading, Mail & tel request accepted, Mango lang, Meeting rooms, Microfiche/film & reading machines, Movies, Music CDs, Online cat, Online info literacy tutorials on the web & in blackboard, Online ref, Orientations, Outreach serv, OverDrive digital audio bks, Photocopying/Printing, Preschool outreach, Preschool reading prog, Prof lending libr, Prog for adults, Prog for children & young adult, Ref & res, Ref serv available, Scanner, Senior computer classes, Senior outreach, Serves people with intellectual disabilities, Spanish lang bks, Spoken cassettes & CDs, Spoken cassettes & DVDs, Story hour, Summer reading prog, Tax forms, Teen prog, Telephone ref, VHS videos, Wheelchair accessible, Workshops
Partic in Midwest Collaborative for Library Services
Special Services for the Deaf - ADA equip
Special Services for the Blind - Accessible computers; Assistive/Adapted tech devices, equip & products; Bks on cassette; Bks on CD; Bks on flash-memory cartridges; Braille alphabet card; Cassette playback machines; Cassettes; Closed circuit TV magnifier; Computer with voice synthesizer for visually impaired persons; Copier with enlargement capabilities; Daisy reader; Descriptive video serv (DVS); Digital talking bk; Digital talking bk machines; Dragon Naturally Speaking software; Extensive large print coll; Home delivery serv; HP Scan Jet with photo-finish software; Internet workstation with adaptive software; Large print & cassettes; Large print bks; Large print bks & talking machines; Large screen computer & software; Newsletter (in large print, Braille or on cassette); PC for people with disabilities; Recorded bks; Screen enlargement software for people with visual disabilities; Screen reader software; Talking bk & rec for the blind cat; Talking bks; Talking bks & player equip; ZoomText magnification & reading software
Open Mon-Thurs 8:30-9, Fri & Sat 8:30-6
Friends of the Library Group
Branches: 1
HOPE BRANCH, 635 Harrison St, Hope, 47246, SAN 341-0250. Tel: 812-546-5310. *Libr Mgr,* Dave Miller; E-mail: dmiller@mybcpl.org; Staff 1 (MLS 1)
Library Holdings: Audiobooks 200; CDs 200; DVDs 200; Large Print Bks 50; Bk Titles 12,000; Bk Vols 15,000; Per Subs 45; Videos 200
Function: Audiobks via web, Bks on cassette, Bks on CD, CD-ROM, Children's prog, Computers for patron use, E-Reserves, Electronic databases & coll, Free DVD rentals, Holiday prog, ILL available, Music CDs, Online cat, Orientations, OverDrive digital audio bks, Photocopying/Printing, Preschool outreach, Prog for children & young adult, Ref serv available, Scanner, Spoken cassettes & CDs, Spoken cassettes & DVDs, Story hour, Summer reading prog, Tax forms, VHS videos, Wheelchair accessible
Special Services for the Blind - Bks on cassette; Bks on CD; Cassettes; Large print bks
Open Mon & Tues 9-8, Wed & Sat 9-4:30, Thurs & Fri 9-6
Friends of the Library Group
Bookmobiles: 1. Mgr, Valerie Baute. Bk vols 25,000

C INDIANA UNIVERSITY-PURDUE UNIVERSITY*, University Library of Columbus, 4555 Central Ave, LC 1600, 47203. SAN 341-2830. Tel: 812-314-8703. Interlibrary Loan Service Tel: 812-314-8719. Administration Tel: 812-314-8712. FAX: 812-314-8722. Web Site: www.iupuc.edu/library. *Exec Dir,* Emily A Dill; E-mail: eadill@iupuc.edu; *Librn,* Abigail Hilyard; E-mail: agardenour@ivytech.edu; Staff 6 (MLS 4, Non-MLS 2)
Founded 1970. Enrl 6,000; Fac 400; Highest Degree: Master
Library Holdings: Audiobooks 40; CDs 25; DVDs 200; e-books 30,000; e-journals 35,000; Bk Vols 45,000; Per Subs 200; Videos 600
Automation Activity & Vendor Info: (Acquisitions) SirsiDynix; (Cataloging) SirsiDynix; (Circulation) SirsiDynix; (ILL) OCLC ILLiad; (Media Booking) SirsiDynix; (OPAC) SirsiDynix; (Serials) SirsiDynix
Wireless access
Partic in Academic Libraries of Indiana; Midwest Collaborative for Library Services
Special Services for the Blind - Accessible computers; Assistive/Adapted tech devices, equip & products; Computer access aids; Computer with voice synthesizer for visually impaired persons; Premier adaptive tech software; Scanner for conversion & translation of mats; Screen reader software; Text reader
Open Mon-Thurs 8am-9pm, Fri 8-5

CONNERSVILLE

P FAYETTE COUNTY PUBLIC LIBRARY*, 828 N Grand Ave, 47331. SAN 304-839X. Tel: 765-827-0883. FAX: 765-825-4592. Web Site: www.fcplibrary.lib.in.us. *Dir,* Betsy Slavens; E-mail: betsy@fcplibrary.lib.in.us; *Asst Dir, Youth Serv Librn,* Melissa Scott; E-mail: melissa@fcplibrary.lib.in.us; Staff 16 (MLS 2, Non-MLS 14)
Pop 25,855; Circ 207,345
Library Holdings: AV Mats 5,900; Bk Vols 96,963; Per Subs 120; Talking Bks 1,623
Automation Activity & Vendor Info: (Cataloging) SirsiDynix; (Circulation) SirsiDynix; (OPAC) SirsiDynix
Special Services for the Deaf - TDD equip
Special Services for the Blind - Bks on cassette; Bks on CD; Closed circuit TV; Computer with voice synthesizer for visually impaired persons; Home delivery serv; Internet workstation with adaptive software; Large print bks; ZoomText magnification & reading software
Open Mon-Thurs 10-7, Fri 9-5:30, Sat 9-5
Friends of the Library Group
Bookmobiles: 1. Librn, Phyllis Dice. Bk titles 7,975

CONVERSE

P CONVERSE JACKSON TOWNSHIP PUBLIC LIBRARY*, 108 S Jefferson St, 46919. (Mail add: PO Box 529, 46919-0529), SAN 304-8403. Tel: 765-395-3344. FAX: 765-395-3733. E-mail: converselib@gmail.com. Web Site: www.converselib.org. *Dir,* Andrew Horner; Staff 4 (MLS 1, Non-MLS 3)
Founded 1916. Pop 2,780; Circ 21,710
Library Holdings: Bk Titles 15,000; Per Subs 59; Talking Bks 150; Videos 1,228
Open Mon-Fri 10-6
Friends of the Library Group

CORYDON

P HARRISON COUNTY PUBLIC LIBRARY*, 105 N Capitol Ave, 47112. SAN 304-8411. Tel: 812-738-4110. FAX: 812-738-5408. E-mail: hcpl@hcpl.lib.in.us. Web Site: www.hcpl.lib.in.us. *Libr Dir,* Violet Eckart; Tel: 812-738-4110, Ext 222, E-mail: vi_eckart@hcpl.lib.in.us; *Head, Youth*

Serv, Alisa Burch; E-mail: aburch@hcpl.lib.in.us; *Syst Admin,* Jessica Stroud; Staff 2 (MLS 2)
Founded 1904. Pop 34,325
Library Holdings: AV Mats 2,654; Bks on Deafness & Sign Lang 40; e-books 470; e-journals 150; Electronic Media & Resources 26; High Interest/Low Vocabulary Bk Vols 200; Large Print Bks 2,100; Bk Titles 62,644; Per Subs 137; Talking Bks 1,903
Special Collections: State Document Depository
Subject Interests: Genealogy, Indiana, Local hist, Spanish
Automation Activity & Vendor Info: (Acquisitions) Follett Software; (Cataloging) Follett Software; (Circulation) Follett Software; (OPAC) Follett Software; (Serials) Follett Software
Wireless access
Partic in Midwest Collaborative for Library Services
Open Mon-Thurs 9-8, Fri & Sat 9-5
Friends of the Library Group
Branches: 3
ELIZABETH BRANCH, 5101 Main St, Elizabeth, 47117. Tel: 812-969-2899. FAX: 812-969-2987. E-mail: elizabeth@hcpl.lib.in.us. Web Site: www.hcpl.lib.in.us/Elizabeth.htm. *Branch Lead, Circ Assoc,* Sara Deatrick
Open Mon 9-8, Tues-Thurs 12-8, Fri & Sat 9-5
LANESVILLE BRANCH, 7340 E Pennington St NE, Lanesville, 47136. Tel: 812-952-3759. FAX: 812-952-3864. E-mail: lanesville@hcpl.lib.in.us. Web Site: www.hcpl.lib.in.us/lanesville.htm. *Branch Lead, Circ Assoc,* Nancy Rosenbaum
Open Mon-Thurs 11-8, Fri & Sat 9-5
PALMYRA BRANCH, 689 Haub St, Palmyra, 47164. Tel: 812-364-6425. FAX: 812-364-6431. E-mail: palmyra@hcpl.lib.in.us. Web Site: www.hcpl.lib.in.us/palmyra.htm. *Branch Lead, Circ Assoc,* Nikki Esarey
Open Mon-Thurs 11-8, Fri & Sat 9-5

COVINGTON

P COVINGTON-VEEDERSBURG PUBLIC LIBRARY*, 622 Fifth St, 47932. SAN 341-034X. Tel: 765-793-2572. FAX: 765-793-2621. Web Site: www.c-vpl.org. *Libr Dir,* Regina George; E-mail: cvpldirector@c-vpl.org; *Circ Supvr,* Tammie Walters; E-mail: twalters@c-vpl.org; *Prog Coordr,* Kim Kalweit; E-mail: kkalweit@c-vpl.org; *Cataloger,* Carolyn Story; Staff 9 (MLS 1, Non-MLS 8)
Founded 1914. Pop 6,683; Circ 42,700
Library Holdings: CDs 617; DVDs 1,031; Large Print Bks 2,029; Bk Titles 22,879; Per Subs 36; Talking Bks 1,523; Videos 1,960
Wireless access
Function: 24/7 Electronic res, 24/7 Online cat, Audiobks on Playaways & MP3, Audiobks via web, AV serv, Bks on CD, Children's prog, Computer training, Computers for patron use, Digital talking bks, Electronic databases & coll, Free DVD rentals, Homework prog, ILL available, Laminating, Large print keyboards, Magazines, Magnifiers for reading, Meeting rooms, Microfiche/film & reading machines, Movies, Online cat, OverDrive digital audio bks, Photocopying/Printing, Preschool outreach, Preschool reading prog, Printer for laptops & handheld devices, Prog for adults, Prog for children & young adult, Ref serv available, Scanner, Serves people with intellectual disabilities, Story hour, Summer & winter reading prog, Tax forms, Teen prog, Wheelchair accessible, Writing prog
Publications: Newsletter
Partic in Midwest Collaborative for Library Services
Open Mon, Tues & Thurs 10-8, Wed & Fri 10-6, Sat 10-2
Restriction: Free to mem
Friends of the Library Group
Branches: 1
VEEDERSBURG PUBLIC, 408 N Main St, Veedersburg, 47987, SAN 341-0374. Tel: 765-294-2808. FAX: 765-294-4648. E-mail: veedersburglibrary@c-vpl.org. *Libr Dir,* Regina George; *Mgr,* Brandy Durant; *Prog Coordr,* Brittney Ziegler; E-mail: brittneyz@c-vpl.org; Staff 4 (Non-MLS 4)
Founded 1984
Library Holdings: CDs 347; DVDs 713; Large Print Bks 674; Bk Titles 16,243; Bk Vols 16,243; Per Subs 49; Talking Bks 468; Videos 923
Function: 24/7 Electronic res, 24/7 Online cat, Adult bk club, Audiobks via web, AV serv, Bks on CD, Children's prog, Computer training, Computers for patron use, Digital talking bks, Electronic databases & coll, Free DVD rentals, ILL available, Internet access, Laminating, Magazines, Online cat, OverDrive digital audio bks, Photocopying/Printing, Preschool outreach, Preschool reading prog, Prog for adults, Prog for children & young adult, Res assist avail, Scanner, Serves people with intellectual disabilities, Story hour, Summer & winter reading prog, Tax forms, Teen prog, Wheelchair accessible, Workshops
Open Mon, Tues & Thurs 10-7, Wed & Fri 10-5, Sat 10-2
Friends of the Library Group

CRAWFORDSVILLE

P CRAWFORDSVILLE DISTRICT PUBLIC LIBRARY, 205 S Washington St, 47933. SAN 304-842X. Tel: 765-362-2242. FAX: 765-362-7986. E-mail: ref@cdpl.lib.in.us. Web Site: www.cdpl.lib.in.us. *Dir, Libr Serv,* Theresa Tyner; E-mail: dir@cdpl.lib.in.us; *Asst Dir,* Jodie Steelman Wilson; Staff 37 (MLS 5, Non-MLS 32)
Founded 1897
Special Collections: Crawfordsville History bks, microfilm, pamphlets
Subject Interests: Genealogy, Local hist
Automation Activity & Vendor Info: (Cataloging) Innovative Interfaces, Inc; (Circulation) Innovative Interfaces, Inc; (OPAC) Innovative Interfaces, Inc
Wireless access
Function: Bilingual assistance for Spanish patrons, Computers for patron use, Electronic databases & coll, Homebound delivery serv, ILL available, Online cat, Spanish lang bks, Summer & winter reading prog
Partic in Midwest Collaborative for Library Services
Open Mon-Thurs 9-9, Fri & Sat 9-5, Sun 1-5

C WABASH COLLEGE, Lilly Library, 301 W Wabash Ave, 47933. (Mail add: PO Box 352, 47933-0352), SAN 304-8438. Tel: 765-361-6443. Web Site: library.wabash.edu. *Libr Dir,* Jeff Beck; Tel: 765-361-6346, E-mail: beckj@wabash.edu; *Assoc Dir,* Laura Vogler; Tel: 765-361-6215, E-mail: voglerl@wabash.edu; *Music Coll Coord, Ref & Instruction,* Diane Norton; Tel: 765-361-3660, E-mail: nortond@wabash.edu; *Spec Coll Archivist,* Elizabeth Swift; Tel: 765-361-6378, E-mail: swiftb@wabash.edu; *Metadata Librn,* Brian McCafferty; Tel: 765-361-6404, E-mail: mccaffeb@wabash.edu; *Film & Media Librn,* Susan Albrecht; Tel: 765-361-6216, E-mail: albrechs@wabash.edu; Staff 8 (MLS 3, Non-MLS 5)
Founded 1832. Enrl 843; Fac 89; Highest Degree: Bachelor
Library Holdings: Audiobooks 423; CDs 7,164; DVDs 3,582; e-books 228,949; e-journals 22,882; Electronic Media & Resources 373; Music Scores 1,579; Bk Vols 198,775; Per Subs 1,850; Videos 2,260
Special Collections: College Archives; Byrd Coll; Early Wabash; Lincolniana; O'Kieffe Coll; Price Coll; Special Coll; Special Coll (large; Special Coll (small); Thomas Riley Marshall
Subject Interests: Abraham Lincoln, Col hist
Automation Activity & Vendor Info: (Acquisitions) OCLC Worldshare Management Services; (Cataloging) OCLC Worldshare Management Services; (Circulation) OCLC Worldshare Management Services; (Course Reserve) OCLC Worldshare Management Services; (Discovery) OCLC Worldshare Management Services; (ILL) OCLC Worldshare Management Services; (Media Booking) OCLC Worldshare Management Services; (OPAC) OCLC Worldshare Management Services; (Serials) OCLC Worldshare Management Services
Wireless access
Partic in Academic Libraries of Indiana; Private Academic Library Network of Indiana; The Oberlin Group
Open Mon-Thurs 8-8, Fri 8-4:30

CROWN POINT

P CROWN POINT COMMUNITY LIBRARY*, 122 N Main St, 46307. SAN 304-8446. Tel: 219-663-0270. FAX: 219-663-0403. E-mail: cpclask@crownpointlibrary.org. Web Site: crownpointlibrary.org. *Dir,* Selina Gomez-Beloz; Tel: 219-306-8071, E-mail: sgbeloz@crownpointlibrary.org; *Head, Circ,* Laurie Kingery; *Head, Ref Serv,* Mary Harrigan; *Head, Tech Serv, Youth Serv,* Kristal Rada; Staff 5 (MLS 5)
Founded 1906. Pop 33,069; Circ 344,522
Library Holdings: Bk Vols 93,755; Per Subs 212
Subject Interests: Indiana, Local hist, State hist
Automation Activity & Vendor Info: (Cataloging) Innovative Interfaces, Inc; (Circulation) Innovative Interfaces, Inc; (OPAC) Innovative Interfaces, Inc
Wireless access
Publications: Check It Out (Newsletter)
Partic in Midwest Collaborative for Library Services
Open Mon-Thurs 9-8, Fri & Sat 9-5, Sun 1-5
Friends of the Library Group
Branches: 1
WINFIELD, 10645 Randolph St, 46307. Tel: 219-662-4039. FAX: 219-662-4068. *Br Mgr,* Diane Keeney; Staff 1 (Non-MLS 1)
Pop 20,491; Circ 21,117
Library Holdings: Bk Titles 15,691; Bk Vols 17,801; Per Subs 46
Open Mon & Wed 10-6, Tues & Thurs 10-8, Fri 9-5, Sat 10-2

M FRANCISCAN HEALTH CROWN POINT*, Health Sciences Library, 1201 S Main St, 46307. SAN 304-8462. Tel: 219-757-6345. FAX: 219-757-6161. Web Site: franciscanhealth.org/healthcare-facilities/franciscan-health-crown-point-55. *Mgr,* Monica A Nowesnick; E-mail: monica.nowesnick@franciscanalliance.org; Staff 1 (Non-MLS 1)

Library Holdings: Bk Titles 1,401; Bk Vols 1,680; Per Subs 99
Subject Interests: Med, Nursing

CULVER

P CULVER-UNION TOWNSHIP PUBLIC LIBRARY, 107 N Main St, 46511-1595. SAN 304-8470. Tel: 574-842-2941. FAX: 574-842-3441. E-mail: staff@culver.lib.in.us. Web Site: www.culver.lib.in.us. *Dir,* Erin Lawrence; E-mail: director@culver.lib.in.us; Staff 5 (MLS 1, Non-MLS 4)
Founded 1915. Pop 3,088; Circ 56,315
Automation Activity & Vendor Info: (Acquisitions) Baker & Taylor; (Cataloging) Evergreen; (Circulation) Evergreen; (Discovery) Evergreen; (OPAC) Evergreen; (Serials) EBSCO Online
Wireless access
Function: 24/7 Electronic res, 24/7 Online cat, Adult bk club, Audiobks via web, Bk club(s), Bks on CD, Children's prog, Computers for patron use, Electronic databases & coll, Free DVD rentals, Genealogy discussion group, Health sci info serv, Internet access, Life-long learning prog for all ages, Magazines, Magnifiers for reading, Mail & tel request accepted, Meeting rooms, Microfiche/film & reading machines, Movies, Museum passes, Music CDs, Online cat, Outreach serv, OverDrive digital audio bks, Photocopying/Printing, Preschool outreach, Prog for adults, Prog for children & young adult, Ref & res, Ref serv available, Res assist avail, Scanner, STEM programs, Story hour, Summer & winter reading prog, Tax forms, Teen prog, Telephone ref, Wheelchair accessible
Partic in Evergreen Indiana Consortium
Special Services for the Deaf - Bks on deafness & sign lang; Closed caption videos
Special Services for the Blind - Bks on CD; Braille bks; Large print bks
Open Mon & Wed-Fri 10-5, Tues 10-8, Sat 10-4
Friends of the Library Group

DALE

P LINCOLN HERITAGE PUBLIC LIBRARY*, 105 Wallace St, 47523-9267. (Mail add: PO Box 784, 47523-0784), SAN 376-6802. Tel: 812-937-7170. FAX: 812-937-7102. E-mail: director@lincolnheritage.lib.in.us. Web Site: www.lincolnheritage.lib.in.us. *Dir,* Rae Ann Kippenbrock; *Youth Serv Librn,* Abby Galyan; *Libr Asst,* Rebecca Rau; Staff 9 (MLS 1, Non-MLS 8)
Founded 1989. Pop 11,347; Circ 27,901
Library Holdings: Audiobooks 3,435; DVDs 5,678; e-books 42,686; Bk Titles 60,113; Per Subs 156
Subject Interests: Genealogy, Local hist
Automation Activity & Vendor Info: (Acquisitions) Evergreen; (Cataloging) Evergreen; (Circulation) Evergreen; (Serials) Evergreen
Wireless access
Function: Art exhibits, Bk club(s), Bks on CD, Children's prog, Computers for patron use, Electronic databases & coll, Free DVD rentals, Holiday prog, Home delivery & serv to seniorr ctr & nursing homes, ILL available, Instruction & testing, Microfiche/film & reading machines, Music CDs, Notary serv, Online cat, Outreach serv, Outside serv via phone, mail, e-mail & web, OverDrive digital audio bks, Photocopying/Printing, Preschool outreach, Prog for adults, Prog for children & young adult, Ref serv available, Scanner, Spanish lang bks, Spoken cassettes & CDs, Story hour, Summer reading prog, Tax forms, Teen prog, VHS videos, Wheelchair accessible
Partic in Evergreen Indiana Consortium
Open Mon, Tues & Thurs 9-8, Wed & Fri 9-6, Sat 9-1
Friends of the Library Group

DANVILLE

P DANVILLE PUBLIC LIBRARY*, 101 S Indiana St, 46122-1809. SAN 304-8489. Tel: 317-745-2604. FAX: 317-745-0756. E-mail: mail@dplindiana.org. Web Site: dplindiana.org. *Dir,* Loren Malloy; E-mail: lmalloy@dplindiana.org; *Adult Serv Mgr,* Janet Woodrum; Tel: 317-718-8008, Ext 12, E-mail: jwoodrum@dplindiana.org; Staff 15 (MLS 3, Non-MLS 12)
Founded 1903. Pop 9,744; Circ 99,602
Library Holdings: Bk Titles 55,617; Bk Vols 58,911; Per Subs 167; Talking Bks 1,206; Videos 1,371
Subject Interests: Genealogy
Automation Activity & Vendor Info: (Cataloging) Follett Software; (Circulation) Follett Software; (OPAC) Follett Software
Function: Archival coll, ILL available, Photocopying/Printing, Ref serv available, Telephone ref
Publications: "Spolight" Newsletter (6 times yr)
Partic in Midwest Collaborative for Library Services
Open Mon-Thurs 9-8, Fri & Sat 9-5, Sun 2-5
Friends of the Library Group

DARLINGTON

P DARLINGTON PUBLIC LIBRARY*, 203 W Main St, 47940. (Mail add: PO Box 248, 47940-0248), SAN 304-8497. Tel: 765-794-4813. FAX: 765-794-4813. Web Site: darlingtonlibrary.com. *Dir,* John Dale; Staff 1 (Non-MLS 1)
Founded 1915. Pop 2,332; Circ 20,000
Library Holdings: Large Print Bks 83; Bk Titles 11,900; Bk Vols 12,000; Per Subs 45; Talking Bks 60; Videos 700
Special Collections: Oral History
Partic in Midwest Collaborative for Library Services
Open Mon-Thurs 12-6, Fri 12-4, Sat 10-Noon
Friends of the Library Group

DECATUR

P ADAMS PUBLIC LIBRARY SYSTEM*, 128 S Third St, 46733-1691. SAN 304-8500. Tel: 260-724-2605. FAX: 260-724-2877. Web Site: www.apls.lib.in.us. *Dir,* Kelly A Ehinger; E-mail: ehinger@apls.lib.in.us; *Ch,* Priscilla J Webber; E-mail: pjwebber@apls.lib.in.us; *Adult Serv,* Andrea Chronister; E-mail: achronister@apls.lib.in.us; Staff 4 (MLS 2, Non-MLS 2)
Founded 1905. Pop 10,698; Circ 167,442
Jan 2017-Dec 2017 Income (Main & Associated Libraries) $876,927, State $45,320, Locally Generated Income $765,896, Other $65,711. Mats Exp $92,942. Sal $445,236
Library Holdings: Audiobooks 3,827; Bk Vols 99,944; Per Subs 200; Videos 5,787
Special Collections: Adams County Genealogy Coll; Indiana Materials (Gene Stratton Porter Coll); Large Print Coll
Automation Activity & Vendor Info: (Cataloging) Evergreen; (Circulation) Evergreen; (OPAC) Evergreen
Wireless access
Function: 24/7 Electronic res, 24/7 Online cat, 3D Printer, Adult bk club, Adult literacy prog, Art exhibits, Audio & video playback equip for onsite use, Audiobks on Playaways & MP3, Audiobks via web, AV serv, Bk club(s), Bks on cassette, Bks on CD, Children's prog, Computer training, Computers for patron use, Family literacy, Free DVD rentals, ILL available, Internet access, Laminating, Life-long learning prog for all ages, Magnifiers for reading, Makerspace, Meeting rooms, Microfiche/film & reading machines, Music CDs, Notary serv, Online cat, Online ref, Outreach serv, OverDrive digital audio bks, Photocopying/Printing, Preschool outreach, Preschool reading prog, Printer for laptops & handheld devices, Prog for adults, Prog for children & young adult, Ref & res, Ref serv available, Scanner, Story hour, Summer & winter reading prog, Summer reading prog, Tax forms, Teen prog, Telephone ref, Wheelchair accessible, Winter reading prog
Partic in Evergreen Indiana Consortium
Open Mon-Wed 9-8, Thurs & Fri 9-5, Sat 9-1, Sun 1-5
Friends of the Library Group
Branches: 1
GENEVA BRANCH, 305 E Line St, Geneva, 46740-1026, SAN 304-9116. Tel: 260-368-7270. FAX: 260-368-9776. *Br Mgr,* Laura Schwartz; E-mail: lschwartz@apls.lib.in.us; Staff 3 (MLS 1, Non-MLS 2)
Founded 1945. Pop 1,293
Library Holdings: AV Mats 1,668; Bk Titles 29,960; Bk Vols 31,415; Per Subs 62; Talking Bks 93; Videos 758
Function: 24/7 Electronic res, 24/7 Online cat, 3D Printer, Adult literacy prog, Archival coll, Audio & video playback equip for onsite use, Audiobks via web, Bk club(s), Children's prog, Computer training, Computers for patron use, Distance learning, Doc delivery serv, Electronic databases & coll, Homebound delivery serv, ILL available, Internet access, Meeting rooms, Notary serv, Outreach serv, Photocopying/Printing, Printer for laptops & handheld devices, Prog for children & young adult, Ref serv available, Res assist avail, Story hour, Summer reading prog, Tax forms, Telephone ref, Wheelchair accessible
Partic in Ind Libr Asn
Special Services for the Deaf - Bks on deafness & sign lang; Closed caption videos
Special Services for the Blind - Audio mat; Bks on cassette; Bks on CD; Home delivery serv; Large print bks; Screen enlargement software for people with visual disabilities; Talking bk & rec for the blind cat; Talking bks
Open Mon, Wed & Fri 10-5, Tues 1-5, Thurs 1-5 & 6-8:30, Sat 9-12
Friends of the Library Group

DELPHI

P DELPHI PUBLIC LIBRARY*, 222 E Main St, 46923. SAN 304-8519. Tel: 765-564-2929. FAX: 765-564-4746. E-mail: dplibrary@delphilibrary.org. Web Site: www.delphilibrary.org. *Dir,* Kelly D Currie; Tel: 765-564-2929, Ext 21, E-mail: kelly@delphilibrary.org; *Ad,* Portia Kapraun; *Ref Librn,* Jane Cruz; *Tech Serv,* Cathy Kesterson; *Youth Librn,* Jennifer Wilson; Staff 15 (MLS 2, Non-MLS 13)
Founded 1905. Pop 7,724; Circ 104,003

Jan 2017-Dec 2017 Income (Main & Associated Libraries) $869,139, State $56,852, Locally Generated Income $777,114, Other $35,173. Mats Exp $168,479, Books $103,413, Per/Ser (Incl. Access Fees) $9,618, AV Mat $27,504, Electronic Ref Mat (Incl. Access Fees) $27,212
Library Holdings: Audiobooks 2,677; DVDs 6,258; e-books 38,172; Bk Vols 57,250; Per Subs 204
Subject Interests: Indiana, Local hist
Automation Activity & Vendor Info: (Acquisitions) SirsiDynix; (Cataloging) SirsiDynix; (Circulation) SirsiDynix; (OPAC) SirsiDynix
Wireless access
Function: 24/7 Electronic res, 24/7 Online cat, Activity rm, Adult bk club, Art exhibits, Art programs, Audiobks via web, Bk club(s), Bks on CD, Children's prog, Computer training, Computers for patron use, Digital talking bks, E-Readers, Electronic databases & coll, Equip loans & repairs, Free DVD rentals, Holiday prog, Home delivery & serv to seniorr ctr & nursing homes, Homebound delivery serv, ILL available, Internet access, Laminating, Life-long learning prog for all ages, Magazines, Magnifiers for reading, Mail & tel request accepted, Mango lang, Meeting rooms, Microfiche/film & reading machines, Movies, Museum passes, Music CDs, Notary serv, Online cat, Online ref, Outreach serv, Outside serv via phone, mail, e-mail & web, OverDrive digital audio bks, Photocopying/Printing, Preschool outreach, Preschool reading prog, Printer for laptops & handheld devices, Prog for adults, Prog for children & young adult, Ref serv available, Scanner, Senior computer classes, Senior outreach, Spanish lang bks, Spoken cassettes & CDs, Spoken cassettes & DVDs, STEM programs, Story hour, Summer & winter reading prog, Summer reading prog, Tax forms, Teen prog, Telephone ref, VHS videos, Wheelchair accessible, Winter reading prog
Partic in Midwest Collaborative for Library Services
Open Mon-Thurs 9-8, Fri 10-6, Sat 10-5
Friends of the Library Group
Branches: 1
NORTHWEST CARROLL BRANCH, 164 W Forest St, Yeoman, 47997. Tel: 574-965-2382. *Br Librn,* Jane Cruz; Tel: 765-564-2929
Open Tues & Wed 10-7, Fri 10-6, Sat 10-4

DONALDSON

JR ANCILLA COLLEGE*, Gerald J Ball Library, 9601 S Union Rd, 46513. (Mail add: PO Box 1, 46513-0001), SAN 304-8527. Tel: 574-936-8898, Ext 323. Web Site: www.ancilla.edu/library. *Dir, Libr Serv,* Cassaundra Bash; E-mail: cassaundra.bash@ancilla.edu; Staff 1.5 (MLS 1, Non-MLS 0.5)
Founded 1966. Enrl 578; Fac 53; Highest Degree: Associate
Library Holdings: Bk Titles 31,340; Bk Vols 32,941; Per Subs 201; Talking Bks 91; Videos 85
Special Collections: History of the Poor Handmaids of Jesus Christ, bks, photos, slides; Old & Rare Book Coll
Subject Interests: Art, Computer sci, Educ, Energy, Hist, Indiana, Libr & info sci, Relig
Wireless access
Partic in Private Academic Library Network of Indiana
Open Mon-Thurs 7:30-6, Fri 9-4

DUBLIN

P DUBLIN PUBLIC LIBRARY*, 2249 E Cumberland, 47335. (Mail add: PO Box 188, 47335-0188), SAN 304-8535. Tel: 765-478-6206. FAX: 765-478-6206. E-mail: dublinlibrary@yahoo.com. Web Site: dublinpl.lib.in.us. *Dir,* Gary Rubendall; Staff 1 (Non-MLS 1)
Founded 1886. Pop 1,021; Circ 4,146
Library Holdings: Large Print Bks 15; Bk Titles 11,120; Bk Vols 11,800; Per Subs 25; Talking Bks 57
Special Collections: Dublin History Coll. Oral History; State Document Depository
Automation Activity & Vendor Info: (Acquisitions) TLC (The Library Corporation); (Cataloging) Evergreen
Wireless access
Function: 24/7 Electronic res, 24/7 Online cat, Audiobks on Playaways & MP3, Bks on CD, Children's prog, Computers for patron use, ILL available, Internet access, Online cat, Photocopying/Printing, Preschool reading prog, Prog for adults, Prog for children & young adult, Scanner, Summer reading prog, Tax forms, Teen prog
Partic in Evergreen Indiana Consortium
Open Tues-Thurs 3-7, Fri 1-5, Sat 10-2

DUNKIRK

P DUNKIRK PUBLIC LIBRARY*, 127 W Washington St, 47336-1218. SAN 376-5393. Tel: 765-768-6872. FAX: 765-768-6894. Web Site: www.dunkirk.lib.in.us. *Libr Dir,* Stephanie Crouch; E-mail: scrouch@dunkirk.lib.in.us; *Libr Asst,* Mary Johnson; E-mail: mjohnson@dunkirk.lib.in.us; Staff 4 (Non-MLS 4)
Founded 1917. Pop 2,693
Library Holdings: Audiobooks 485; CDs 356; DVDs 1,969; Large Print Bks 1,340; Bk Vols 21,655; Per Subs 67; Videos 751
Automation Activity & Vendor Info: (Acquisitions) Evergreen; (Cataloging) Evergreen; (Circulation) Evergreen; (Course Reserve) Evergreen; (ILL) Evergreen; (Media Booking) Evergreen
Wireless access
Function: Bks on cassette, Bks on CD, Children's prog, Computers for patron use, Holiday prog, Homebound delivery serv, ILL available, Mail & tel request accepted, Music CDs, Photocopying/Printing, Prog for children & young adult, Scanner, Summer reading prog, Tax forms, Teen prog, VHS videos, Wheelchair accessible
Special Services for the Deaf - Closed caption videos; High interest/low vocabulary bks
Special Services for the Blind - Audio mat; Bks on cassette; Bks on CD; Cassette playback machines; Copier with enlargement capabilities; Home delivery serv; Large print bks; Talking bks
Open Mon-Wed & Fri 10-5, Thurs 10-7, Sat 9-1
Friends of the Library Group

DYER

M FRANCISCAN HEATH DYER*, Health Sciences Library, 24 Joliet St, 46311. SAN 304-8543. Tel: 219-865-2141, Ext 42133. FAX: 219-864-2146. Web Site: www.franciscanhealth.org/healthcare-facilities/franciscan-health-dyer-17. *Mgr,* Monica A Nowesnick; Staff 1 (MLS 1)
Library Holdings: Bk Vols 800; Per Subs 25
Automation Activity & Vendor Info: (Cataloging) EOS International; (Circulation) EOS International; (OPAC) EOS International; (Serials) EOS International
Wireless access
Function: Doc delivery serv, Health sci info serv, ILL available
Restriction: Lending to staff only, Med staff only, Non-circulating to the pub

R MID-AMERICA REFORMED SEMINARY LIBRARY*, 229 Seminary Dr, 46311. Tel: 219-864-2400, Ext 414. FAX: 219-864-2409. Web Site: www.midamerica.edu/library. *Theological Librn,* Alan D Strange; *Assoc Librn,* Bart Voskuil; Staff 2 (MLS 1, Non-MLS 1)
Library Holdings: CDs 57; Bk Titles 38,828; Bk Vols 40,110; Per Subs 170
Automation Activity & Vendor Info: (Acquisitions) Follett Software; (Cataloging) TLC (The Library Corporation); (Circulation) TLC (The Library Corporation); (Serials) TLC (The Library Corporation)
Special Services for the Blind - Visunet prog (Canada)
Open Mon-Thurs 8am-9pm, Fri 8-4:30, Sat 10-4; Mon-Thurs (Summer) 8-4:30, Fri 8-Noon

EARL PARK

P EARL PARK-RICHLAND TOWNSHIP PUBLIC LIBRARY, 102 E Fifth St, 47942-8700. (Mail add: PO Box 97, 47942-0097), SAN 304-8551. Tel: 219-474-6932. FAX: 219-207-5859. E-mail: earlparklibrary@gmail.com. Web Site: www.earlpark.lib.in.us. *Libr Dir,* Mrs Dana J Leonard; E-mail: earlparklibrary@gmail.com; Staff 3 (Non-MLS 3)
Founded 1914. Pop 900; Circ 7,721
Library Holdings: Audiobooks 200; DVDs 1,500; Large Print Bks 1,000; Bk Titles 20,530; Bk Vols 22,651; Per Subs 20
Subject Interests: Local hist
Automation Activity & Vendor Info: (Cataloging) Mandarin Library Automation; (Circulation) Mandarin Library Automation; (OPAC) Mandarin Library Automation
Wireless access
Special Services for the Blind - Bks on CD
Open Mon, Wed & Fri Noon-5, Tues Noon-6, Sat 9-1
Friends of the Library Group

EAST CHICAGO

P EAST CHICAGO PUBLIC LIBRARY, 2401 E Columbus Dr, 46312-2998. SAN 341-0439. Tel: 219-397-2453. FAX: 219-378-1951. Circulation FAX: 219-378-1951. TDD: 219-769-6506. Web Site: www.ecpl.org. *Dir,* Marla K Spann; E-mail: mspann@ecpl.org; *Dep Dir, Finance,* Patricia Castaneda-Rocha; E-mail: pcrocha@ecpl.org; *Assoc Dir, Reference & Adult Services,* Lacey Klemm; E-mail: lklemm@ecpl.org; *Assoc Dir, Youth Services,* Pam Bartusiewicz; E-mail: pbartusiewicz@ecpl.org; Staff 12 (MLS 3, Non-MLS 9)
Founded 1909. Pop 32,414; Circ 46,078
Library Holdings: AV Mats 2,520; Electronic Media & Resources 289; Large Print Bks 1,796; Bk Titles 187,031; Bk Vols 278,129; Per Subs 157; Talking Bks 6,301; Videos 7,071
Special Collections: History of East Chicago
Subject Interests: Ethnic studies
Automation Activity & Vendor Info: (ILL) Innovative Interfaces, Inc - Millennium
Wireless access
Publications: Bibliographies; Historical Booklets
Partic in OCLC Online Computer Library Center, Inc

Special Services for the Blind - Bks available with recordings
Open Mon-Thurs 9-8, Fri & Sat 9-5
Branches: 1
ROBERT A PASTRICK BRANCH, 1008 W Chicago Ave, 46312, SAN 341-0463. Tel: 219-397-5505. FAX: 219-398-2827. *Dep Dir, Finance,* Patricia Patricia Castaneda-Rocha
Special Services for the Blind - Bks available with recordings
Bookmobiles: 1

EDINBURGH

P EDINBURGH WRIGHT-HAGEMAN PUBLIC LIBRARY*, 119 W Main Cross St, 46124-1499. SAN 304-8594. Tel: 812-526-5487. FAX: 812-526-7057. Web Site: www.edinburgh.lib.in.us. *Libr Dir,* Chris Hoffman; E-mail: choffman@edinburgh.lib.in.us; Staff 3 (MLS 1, Non-MLS 2)
Founded 1921. Pop 4,800; Circ 51,860
Library Holdings: AV Mats 1,380; Large Print Bks 178; Bk Titles 29,801; Bk Vols 30,201; Per Subs 78; Talking Bks 700; Videos 520
Subject Interests: Genealogy
Wireless access
Open Mon-Thurs 9-7, Fri 9-6, Sat 9-1

ELKHART

R ANABAPTIST MENNONITE BIBLICAL SEMINARY LIBRARY*, 3003 Benham Ave, 46517. SAN 304-8608. Tel: 574-295-3726. Toll Free Tel: 800-964-2627. Web Site: www.ambs.edu/library. *Dir,* Karl Stutzman; Tel: 574-296-6280, E-mail: kstutzman@ambs.edu; *Librn,* Brandon Board; Tel: 574-296-6211, E-mail: bboard@ambs.edu; Staff 2 (MLS 2)
Founded 1945. Enrl 100; Highest Degree: Master
Library Holdings: Bk Vols 115,000; Per Subs 486
Special Collections: Studer Bible Coll
Subject Interests: Mennonites, Relig
Automation Activity & Vendor Info: (Acquisitions) OCLC; (Cataloging) OCLC; (Circulation) OCLC; (Discovery) OCLC; (ILL) OCLC; (OPAC) OCLC
Wireless access
Partic in Academic Libraries of Indiana; American Theological Library Association; Chicago Area Theological Libr Asn; OCLC Online Computer Library Center, Inc; Private Academic Library Network of Indiana

P ELKHART PUBLIC LIBRARY*, 300 S Second St, 46516-3109. SAN 341-0587. Circulation Tel: 574-522-2665. Interlibrary Loan Service Tel: 574-522-5669. E-mail: library@myepl.org. Web Site: www.myepl.org. *Dir,* Lisa Guedea Carreno; *Br Supvr,* Kevin Kilmer; Staff 80.5 (MLS 15, Non-MLS 65.5)
Founded 1903. Pop 90,792; Circ 1,004,652
Library Holdings: AV Mats 46,788; CDs 22,647; DVDs 23,861; Large Print Bks 9,709; Bk Vols 360,457; Per Subs 1,076
Subject Interests: Local hist
Automation Activity & Vendor Info: (Acquisitions) Innovative Interfaces, Inc; (Cataloging) Innovative Interfaces, Inc; (Circulation) Innovative Interfaces, Inc; (ILL) OCLC
Wireless access
Publications: Montage (Newsletter); Monthly Calendar of Programs
Partic in Ind Area Libr Servs Authority 2
Open Mon & Wed 9-8, Tues, Thurs & Fri 9-6, Sat 9-1
Branches: 4
CLEVELAND, 53715 CR 1, 46514. Tel: 574-266-2030. E-mail: cleveland@myepl.org. *Supvr,* Mary Ann Kempa
Open Mon, Wed & Fri 9-6, Tues & Thurs 9-8, Sat 9-1
DUNLAP, 58485 E County Rd 13, 46516, SAN 373-9066. Tel: 574-875-3100. FAX: 574-875-5512. E-mail: dunlap@myepl.org. *Supvr,* Sue Eller; Staff 3 (MLS 1, Non-MLS 2)
Library Holdings: CDs 110; Bk Titles 34,891; Bk Vols 36,101; Per Subs 51; Talking Bks 88; Videos 391
Open Mon, Wed & Fri 9-6, Tues & Thurs 9-8, Sat 9-1
PIERRE MORAN BRANCH, 2400 Benham Ave, 46517, SAN 341-0641. Tel: 574-294-6418. FAX: 574-294-6419. E-mail: pmb@myepl.org. *Supvr,* Jarrett Mitchell; Staff 3 (MLS 1, Non-MLS 2)
Library Holdings: CDs 36; Large Print Bks 114; Bk Titles 31,782; Bk Vols 33,199; Per Subs 51; Talking Bks 90; Videos 201
Open Mon, Wed & Fri 9-6, Tues & Thurs 9-8, Sat 9-1
Friends of the Library Group
OSOLO, 3429 E Bristol St, 46514, SAN 328-9133. Tel: 574-264-7234. FAX: 574-264-7343. E-mail: osolo@myepl.org. *Supvr,* Donna Mitschelen; Staff 3 (MLS 1, Non-MLS 2)
Library Holdings: CDs 39; Large Print Bks 59; Bk Titles 26,781; Bk Vols 27,981; Per Subs 32; Videos 141
Open Mon, Wed & Fri 9-6, Tues & Thurs 9-8, Sat 9-1
Bookmobiles: 2

S RUTHMERE MUSEUM*, Robert B Beardsley Arts Reference Library, 302 E Beardsley Ave, 46514. SAN 374-6275. Tel: 574-264-0330. Toll Free Tel: 888-287-7696. FAX: 574-266-0474. Web Site: www.ruthmere.org. *Curator, Librn & Archivist,* Jennifer Johns; E-mail: jjohns@ruthmere.org; Staff 1 (Non-MLS 1)
Founded 1980
Library Holdings: Bk Titles 1,917; Bk Vols 2,110; Per Subs 15
Subject Interests: Archit, Art, Decorative art
Publications: Ruthmere Record (Newsletter)
Partic in Midwest Collaborative for Library Services
Restriction: Open by appt only, Open to pub for ref only

ELWOOD

P NORTH MADISON COUNTY PUBLIC LIBRARY SYSTEM*, Elwood Public Library, 1600 Main St, 46036. SAN 304-8632. Tel: 765-552-5001. FAX: 765-552-0955. Web Site: www.elwood.lib.in.us. *Dir,* Jamie Scott; E-mail: jscott@elwood.lib.in.us; *Tech Serv Mgr,* Katie Newby; E-mail: knewby@elwood.lib.in.us; Staff 7 (MLS 1, Non-MLS 6)
Founded 1898. Pop 21,031; Circ 190,363
Library Holdings: Bk Vols 86,495; Per Subs 109
Special Collections: Local History (Indiana Coll); Wendell L Willkie Coll
Automation Activity & Vendor Info: (Acquisitions) TLC (The Library Corporation); (Cataloging) TLC (The Library Corporation); (Circulation) TLC (The Library Corporation)
Wireless access
Function: Adult literacy prog, After school storytime, Art exhibits, Audio & video playback equip for onsite use, Bks on cassette, Bks on CD, Children's prog, Computer training, Computers for patron use, E-Reserves, Free DVD rentals, Holiday prog, ILL available, Music CDs, Notary serv, Online cat, Photocopying/Printing, Preschool outreach, Prog for adults, Prog for children & young adult, Ref serv available, Scanner, Senior computer classes, Spoken cassettes & CDs, Story hour, Summer reading prog, Tax forms, Teen prog, Telephone ref, VHS videos, Wheelchair accessible
Partic in Midwest Collaborative for Library Services; Northern Indiana Computer Consortium for Libraries
Open Mon-Thurs 9:30-7, Fri 9:30-6, Sat 9:30-4, Sun 1-5
Friends of the Library Group
Branches: 2
FRANKTON COMMUNITY LIBRARY, 102 S Church St, Frankton, 46044. (Mail add: PO Box 277, Frankton, 46044-0277), SAN 323-536X. Tel: 765-551-4140. FAX: 765-754-3312. *Br Mgr,* Stacey Jones; E-mail: sjones@elwood.lib.in.us; Staff 1 (Non-MLS 1)
Function: Adult bk club, Adult literacy prog, Audio & video playback equip for onsite use, AV serv, Bks on cassette, Bks on CD, Children's prog, Computer training, Computers for patron use, Free DVD rentals, ILL available, Music CDs, Online cat, Photocopying/Printing, Prog for adults, Prog for children & young adult, Scanner, Senior computer classes, Spoken cassettes & CDs, Story hour, Summer reading prog, Tax forms, VHS videos, Wheelchair accessible
Open Mon-9:30-7, Fri 9:30-5, Sat 9:30-1
Friends of the Library Group
RALPH E HAZELBAKER LIBRARY, 1013 W Church St, Summitville, 46070. (Mail add: PO Box 486, Summitville, 46070-0486), SAN 323-5386. Tel: 765-536-2335. FAX: 765-536-9050. *Br Mgr,* Jill Murray; E-mail: jmurray@elwood.lib.in.us; Staff 1 (Non-MLS 1)
Function: Accelerated reader prog, Adult literacy prog, After school storytime, Art exhibits, Bks on cassette, Bks on CD, Children's prog, Computer training, Computers for patron use, Free DVD rentals, Govt ref serv, Holiday prog, Home delivery & serv to seniorr ctr & nursing homes, ILL available, Music CDs, Online cat, Outside serv via phone, mail, e-mail & web, Photocopying/Printing, Prog for adults, Prog for children & young adult, Scanner, Senior computer classes, Spoken cassettes & CDs, Story hour, Summer reading prog, Tax forms, Teen prog, Telephone ref, VHS videos, Wheelchair accessible
Open Mon-Thurs 9:30-7, Fri 9:30-5, Sat 9:30-1

ENGLISH

P CRAWFORD COUNTY PUBLIC LIBRARY*, 203 Indiana Ave, 47118. (Mail add: PO Box 159, 47118-0159), SAN 304-8640. Tel: 812-338-2606. FAX: 812-338-3034. E-mail: ccpltech@gmail.com. Web Site: www.ccpl.lib.in.us. *Dir,* Tracy Underhill; E-mail: underhill.tracy@gmail.com; *Tech Mgr,* David Vanlaningham; E-mail: ccpltech@gmail.com; *Genealogy Serv,* Anne Hager; E-mail: ahager947@gmail.com; *ILL Serv,* Jennifer Chanley; E-mail: illccpl@gmail.com
Founded 1954. Pop 10,000; Circ 69,556
Library Holdings: Bk Vols 35,000; Per Subs 120
Automation Activity & Vendor Info: (Acquisitions) ComPanion Corp; (Cataloging) ComPanion Corp; (Circulation) ComPanion Corp; (OPAC) ComPanion Corp
Wireless access

Special Services for the Blind - Computer with voice synthesizer for visually impaired persons
Open Tues-Thurs 10-7:30, Fri & Sat 10-4
Friends of the Library Group

EVANSVILLE

M DEACONESS MIDTOWN HOSPITAL*, Grace O Hahn Health Science Library, 600 Mary St, 47747. SAN 304-8659. Tel: 812-450-3385. FAX: 812-450-7255. Web Site: www.deaconess.com/Locations/Deaconess-Midtown-Hospital. *Librn,* Gail Lee; Staff 3 (MLS 1, Non-MLS 2)
Founded 1970
Library Holdings: Bk Titles 6,356; Bk Vols 7,400; Per Subs 140
Special Collections: Archive of Nursing; Hospital History
Subject Interests: Complementary med, Consumer health, Hospital admin, Med, Nursing
Automation Activity & Vendor Info: (Cataloging) LibraryWorld, Inc; (Circulation) LibraryWorld, Inc; (OPAC) LibraryWorld, Inc; (Serials) LibraryWorld, Inc
Wireless access
Function: Archival coll, Health sci info serv, ILL available, Ref serv available, Telephone ref
Partic in Midwest Health Sci Libr Network; National Network of Libraries of Medicine Region 6
Open Mon & Wed-Fri 8-4:30, Tues 7-4:30
Restriction: Open to pub for ref & circ; with some limitations, Pub ref by request, Pub use on premises, Restricted access

S EVANSVILLE MUSEUM OF ARTS, HISTORY & SCIENCE LIBRARY*, 411 SE Riverside Dr, 47713. SAN 304-8675. Tel: 812-425-2406. FAX: 812-421-7509. Web Site: www.emuseum.org. *Exec Dir,* Mary McNamee Bower; Tel: 812-425-2406, Ext 230, E-mail: mary@emuseum.org; *Curator of Hist,* Thomas R Lonnberg; Tel: 812-425-2406, Ext 225, E-mail: lonnberg@emuseum.org; Staff 2 (Non-MLS 2)
Founded 1904
Library Holdings: Bk Titles 6,210; Bk Vols 6,481; Per Subs 31
Special Collections: Henry B Walker Jr Memorial Art Books Coll; Vanderburgh County History Coll
Subject Interests: Anthrop, Antiques, Art & archit, Astronomy, Hist, Natural hist
Open Tues-Sat 10-5
Restriction: Non-circulating to the pub

M EVANSVILLE STATE HOSPITAL*, Staff Library, 3400 Lincoln Ave, 47714. SAN 341-0919. Tel: 812-469-6800. FAX: 812-469-6801. *Develop Dir,* Angie Paul; Tel: 812-469-6800, Ext 4979, E-mail: angela.paul@fssa.in.gov; Staff 1 (Non-MLS 1)
Founded 1944
Library Holdings: DVDs 343; Bk Titles 324
Subject Interests: Nursing, Psychiat, Psychol, Soc serv, Soc work
Partic in Evansville Area Library Consortium
Open Mon-Fri 9-4
Friends of the Library Group
Branches:
PATIENT LIBRARY, 3400 Lincoln Ave, 47714. Tel: 812-469-6800, Ext 4215. FAX: 812-469-6824. *Librn,* Kelly Kissel; E-mail: kelly.kissel@fssa.in.gov; Staff 1 (Non-MLS 1)
Founded 2003
Library Holdings: Large Print Bks 203; Bk Titles 2,546
Open Mon-Fri 8-6, Sat 9-10
Friends of the Library Group

P EVANSVILLE VANDERBURGH PUBLIC LIBRARY, 200 SE Martin Luther King Jr Blvd, 47713-1604. SAN 341-0676. Tel: 812-428-8200. Circulation Tel: 812-428-8219. Administration Tel: 812-428-8204. Automation Services Tel: 812-428-8393. Administration FAX: 812-428-8397. E-mail: central@evpl.org. Web Site: www.evpl.org. *Dir/Chief Exec Officer,* Scott Kinney; E-mail: scottk@evpl.org; Staff 27 (MLS 23, Non-MLS 4)
Founded 1911. Pop 179,703; Circ 2,313,259
Jan 2015-Dec 2015 Income (Main & Associated Libraries) $11,671,532, State $634,955, Federal $71,560, County $10,615,846, Locally Generated Income $349,171. Mats Exp $1,859,400, Books $556,197, Per/Ser (Incl. Access Fees) $72,930, AV Mat $391,571, Electronic Ref Mat (Incl. Access Fees) $838,702. Sal $4,423,675
Library Holdings: Audiobooks 32,113; AV Mats 45,109; Braille Volumes 31; CDs 70,907; DVDs 81,384; e-books 104,993; Large Print Bks 18,652; Bk Titles 500,088; Bk Vols 555,491; Per Subs 1,444; Talking Bks 20,882
Special Collections: Best Seller Express, Books, DVDs; Book Discussion; Business Central; Careers; Educational Materials Center; Foreign Language & ESL; Foundation Center; Library Science; Local Authors; Local History; Online Audio Books; Online comic and graphic novels; Online eBooks; Online magazines; Science Projects; Streaming-downloadable music, movies; Survivors of the Shoah Visual History Coll; Talking Books; Test Books. Municipal Document Depository; State Document Depository; US Document Depository
Automation Activity & Vendor Info: (Acquisitions) Innovative Interfaces, Inc; (Cataloging) Innovative Interfaces, Inc; (Circulation) Innovative Interfaces, Inc; (ILL) OCLC ILLiad; (Media Booking) EnvisionWare; (OPAC) Innovative Interfaces, Inc; (Serials) Innovative Interfaces, Inc
Wireless access
Partic in LYRASIS; Midwest Collaborative for Library Services
Special Services for the Blind - Talking bks
Open Mon-Thurs 9-8, Fri 9-6, Sat 9-5, Sun 1-5
Branches: 8
CENTRAL, 200 SE Martin Luther King Jr Blvd, 47713. Circulation Tel: 812-428-8219. Interlibrary Loan Service Tel: 812-425-4721. Reference Tel: 812-428-8218. FAX: 812-428-8397. *Branch Experience Mgr,* Susan Bloom; E-mail: susanb@evpl.org
Library Holdings: CDs 27,645; DVDs 28,498; Large Print Bks 9,369; Bk Titles 219,308; Bk Vols 249,976; Per Subs 505
EAST BRANCH, 840 E Chandler Ave, 47713, SAN 341-0706. Tel: 812-428-8231. FAX: 812-436-7320. E-mail: east@evpl.org. *Branch Experience Mgr,* Linda Baker; E-mail: lindab@evpl.org
Library Holdings: CDs 2,749; DVDs 4,314; Large Print Bks 500; Bk Titles 14,896; Bk Vols 16,314; Per Subs 44
Open Mon-Thurs 9-7, Fri 9-6, Sat 9-5
MCCOLLOUGH BRANCH, 5115 Washington Ave, 47715, SAN 341-0765. Tel: 812-428-8236. FAX: 812-473-0877. E-mail: mccollough@evpl.org. *Branch Experience Mgr,* Tyler Lemar; E-mail: tylerl@evpl.org
Library Holdings: CDs 8,255; DVDs 7,838; Large Print Bks 2,284; Bk Titles 61,058; Bk Vols 67,530; Per Subs 158
Open Mon-Thurs 9-8, Fri 9-6, Sat 9-5
NORTH PARK, 960 Koehler Dr, 47710, SAN 341-079X. Tel: 812-428-8237. FAX: 812-428-8243. E-mail: northpark@evpl.org. *Branch Experience Mgr,* Nancy Higgs; E-mail: nancyh@evpl.org
Library Holdings: CDs 10,299; DVDs 11,068; Large Print Bks 2,190; Bk Titles 57,179; Bk Vols 64,058; Per Subs 174
Open Mon-Thurs 9-8, Fri 9-6, Sat 9-5
OAKLYN, 3001 Oaklyn Dr, 47711, SAN 341-0854. Tel: 812-428-8234. FAX: 812-428-8245. E-mail: oaklyn@evpl.org. *Branch Experience Mgr,* Julia Clark; E-mail: juliac@evpl.org
Library Holdings: CDs 8,011; DVDs 10,698; Large Print Bks 2,005; Bk Titles 48,185; Bk Vols 54,268; Per Subs 131
Open Mon-Thurs 9-8, Fri 9-6, Sat 9-5
RED BANK, 120 S Red Bank Rd, 47712, SAN 371-9774. Tel: 812-428-8205. FAX: 812-428-8240. E-mail: redbank@evpl.org. *Branch Experience Mgr,* Beth Hindman; E-mail: bethh@evpl.org
Library Holdings: CDs 8,283; DVDs 9,481; Large Print Bks 1,410; Bk Titles 52,278; Bk Vols 57,482; Per Subs 194
Open Mon-Thurs 9-8, Fri 9-6, Sat 9-5
STRINGTOWN, 2100 Stringtown Rd, 47711, SAN 341-082X. Tel: 812-428-8233. FAX: 812-426-9792. E-mail: stringtown@evpl.org. *Branch Experience Mgr,* Candace Bell; E-mail: candaceb@evpl.org
Library Holdings: CDs 2,379; DVDs 4,578; Large Print Bks 336; Bk Titles 13,887; Bk Vols 14,749; Per Subs 51
Open Mon-Thurs 9-7, Fri 9-6, Sat 9-5
WEST, 2000 W Franklin St, 47712, SAN 341-0889. Tel: 812-428-8232. FAX: 812-428-8230. E-mail: west@evpl.org. *Branch Experience Mgr,* Position Currently Open
Library Holdings: CDs 3,006; DVDs 4,909; Large Print Bks 409; Bk Titles 21,635; Bk Vols 22,926; Per Subs 90
Open Mon-Thurs 9-7, Fri 9-6, Sat 9-5
Bookmobiles: 1. Youth Serv Outreach Asst, Joann Burns. Bk titles 8,748

J IVY TECH COMMUNITY COLLEGE*, Carter Library, 3501 N First Ave, Rm 141, 47710-3398. SAN 304-8713. Tel: 812-429-1412. FAX: 812-429-9802. E-mail: lib-questions-r12@lists.ivytech.edu. Web Site: library.ivytech.edu/southwest. *Dir of Libr,* Lenore Engler; E-mail: lengler@ivytech.edu; Staff 2 (MLS 2)
Founded 1969. Enrl 5,119; Fac 74; Highest Degree: Associate
Library Holdings: AV Mats 2,400; e-books 48,000; Bk Vols 7,000; Per Subs 88
Subject Interests: Health, Sci tech
Automation Activity & Vendor Info: (Cataloging) Ex Libris Group; (Circulation) Ex Libris Group; (Course Reserve) Ex Libris Group; (ILL) OCLC; (OPAC) Ex Libris Group; (Serials) SerialsSolutions
Wireless access
Function: CD-ROM, Electronic databases & coll, ILL available, Photocopying/Printing
Partic in Evansville Area Library Consortium; Midwest Collaborative for Library Services
Open Mon-Thurs 7:30am-9pm, Fri 7:30-5, Sat 9-Noon
Restriction: Open to pub for ref & circ; with some limitations

GL WILLIAM H MILLER LAW LIBRARY, 207 City-County Courts Bldg, 825 Sycamore, 47708-1849. SAN 304-8764. Tel: 812-435-5175. FAX: 812-435-5438. E-mail: evvlaw@evansville.net. Web Site: www.vanderburghgov.org/lawlibrary. *Law Librn,* Kathleen Weston; E-mail: kweston@vanderburghcounty.in.gov
Library Holdings: Microforms 4,900; Bk Vols 23,000
Wireless access
Open Mon-Fri 8-4
Restriction: Non-circulating

C UNIVERSITY OF EVANSVILLE, University Libraries, 1800 Lincoln Ave, 47722. SAN 341-1036. Tel: 812-488-2376. E-mail: library@evansville.edu. Web Site: www.evansville.edu/libraries.
Founded 1872. Highest Degree: Doctorate
Special Collections: Knecht Cartoons Coll
Wireless access
Partic in Academic Libraries of Indiana
Open Mon-Thurs 7:45am-Midnight, Fri 7:45-6, Sat 10-6, Sun Noon-Midnight

C UNIVERSITY OF SOUTHERN INDIANA*, David L Rice Library, 8600 University Blvd, 47712. SAN 304-8705. Tel: 812-464-8600. Circulation Tel: 812-464-1913. Interlibrary Loan Service Tel: 812-464-1683. Reference Tel: 812-464-1907. Toll Free Tel: 800-246-6173. FAX: 812-465-1693. E-mail: libweb@usi.edu. Web Site: www.usi.edu/library. *Dir, Libr Serv,* Marna Hostetler; Tel: 812-464-1824, E-mail: mmhostetle@usi.edu; *Asst Dir, Coll Mgt, Asst Dir, Res Mgt Serv,* Dianne Grayson; Tel: 812-464-1280, E-mail: dgrayson@usi.edu; *Instrul Serv Librn,* Kate Sherrill; Tel: 812-465-1277; *Metadata Librn, Spec Coll & Archives Librn,* Mona Meyer; Tel: 812-464-1920, E-mail: mmeyer@usi.edu; *Online Learning Librn, Ref Librn,* Becca Neel; Tel: 812-461-5328; *Scholarly Communications Librn,* Peter Whiting; Tel: 812-465-1280, E-mail: pwhiting@usi.edu; *Circ Mgr,* Debbie Clark; Tel: 812-464-1922, E-mail: dclark@usi.edu; *Univ Archivist,* Jennifer Greene; Tel: 812-464-1643, E-mail: jagreene@usi.edu; *Libr Syst Coordr,* Rose Scruggs; Tel: 812-464-1828; *Libr Assoc/ILL Section,* Kirsten Williams; Staff 10 (MLS 9, Non-MLS 1)
Founded 1965. Enrl 7,821; Fac 682; Highest Degree: Doctorate
Jul 2013-Jun 2014 Income $2,828,389. Mats Exp $832,631. Sal $1,073,914 (Prof $613,567)
Library Holdings: Audiobooks 646; AV Mats 76; CDs 1,872; DVDs 2,657; e-books 208,825; e-journals 65,574; Microforms 102,387; Bk Titles 436,365; Per Subs 212
Special Collections: Communal Studies; Digital Colls; Regional Colls; University Archives. Oral History; US Document Depository
Automation Activity & Vendor Info: (Acquisitions) Ex Libris Group; (Cataloging) Ex Libris Group; (Circulation) Ex Libris Group; (Course Reserve) Ex Libris Group; (ILL) OCLC ILLiad; (OPAC) Ex Libris Group; (Serials) Ex Libris Group
Wireless access
Partic in Academic Libraries of Indiana; Midwest Libr Consortium
Open Mon-Thurs (Winter & Spring) 7am-2am, Fri 7-7, Sat 9-9, Sun Noon-2am; Mon-Thurs (Summer) 8am-10pm, Fri 8-5, Sat 9-5, Sun 1-10

P WILLARD LIBRARY OF EVANSVILLE*, 21 First Ave, 47710-1294. SAN 304-8772. Tel: 812-425-4309. FAX: 812-421-9742. E-mail: willard@willard.lib.in.us. Web Site: www.willard.lib.in.us. *Dir,* Gregory M Hager; E-mail: ghager@willard.lib.in.us; *Ad,* Arrika Dedmond; E-mail: adedmond@willard.lib.in.us; *Ch,* Rhonda Mort; E-mail: rmort@willard.lib.in.us; *Spec Coll Librn,* Lyn Martin; Fax: 812-425-4303, E-mail: lmartin@willard.lib.in.us; *Tech Serv Librn,* John Scheer; E-mail: jscheer@willard.lib.in.us; *Bus Mgr,* Emily Phillips; E-mail: ephillips@willard.lib.in.us; *Archivist,* Patricia Sides; E-mail: psides@willard.lib.in.us; Staff 19 (MLS 5, Non-MLS 14)
Founded 1885. Pop 176,000; Circ 477,765
Library Holdings: AV Mats 2,687; Bk Vols 146,151; Per Subs 207
Special Collections: Architecture (Thrall Art Book Coll); Local History & Genealogy (Regional & Family History Center), bks, microfilm, ms; Nineteenth Century Periodical Lit, bd per
Subject Interests: Arts, Humanities, Popular fiction
Automation Activity & Vendor Info: (Cataloging) EOS International; (Circulation) EOS International; (OPAC) EOS International
Wireless access
Function: 24/7 Electronic res, 24/7 Online cat, Adult bk club, After school storytime
Open Mon & Tues 9-8, Wed-Fri 9-5:30, Sat 9-5, Sun 1-5
Friends of the Library Group

FAIRMOUNT

P FAIRMOUNT PUBLIC LIBRARY*, 217 S Main St, 46928-1926. (Mail add: PO Box 27, 46928-0027), SAN 304-8780. Tel: 765-948-3177. FAX: 765-948-3194. E-mail: fairmountpl@yahoo.com. Web Site: fairmountlibrary.net. *Dir,* Linda Magers; Staff 1 (MLS 1)
Founded 1921. Pop 4,239; Circ 8,716
Jan 2018-Dec 2018. Mats Exp $103,792. Sal $54,646
Library Holdings: Audiobooks 666; DVDs 1,361; e-books 7; Bk Vols 24,865; Per Subs 47; Videos 511
Special Collections: James Dean Coll, bks, mag & newsp articles
Subject Interests: Genealogy, Local hist
Automation Activity & Vendor Info: (Acquisitions) Koha; (Cataloging) Koha; (Circulation) Koha; (OPAC) Koha
Wireless access
Function: 24/7 Electronic res, 24/7 Online cat, Activity rm, Adult bk club, Audiobks on Playaways & MP3, Bk club(s), Bks on CD, Children's prog, Computer training, Computers for patron use, Digital talking bks, Doc delivery serv, E-Readers, Free DVD rentals, Holiday prog, Homebound delivery serv, ILL available, Internet access, Laminating, Life-long learning prog for all ages, Magazines, Meeting rooms, Movies, Museum passes, Music CDs, Notary serv, Online cat, Photocopying/Printing, Prog for adults, Prog for children & young adult, Ref serv available, Res assist avail, Scanner, Senior computer classes, Story hour, Summer reading prog, Tax forms, Teen prog, VHS videos, Wheelchair accessible
Special Services for the Blind - Bks on CD; Large print bks; Playaways (bks on MP3)
Open Mon, Wed & Fri 9:30-5:30, Tues 10-8, Sat 9:30-3:30

FARMLAND

P FARMLAND PUBLIC LIBRARY*, 116 S Main St, 47340. (Mail add: PO Box 189, 47340-0189), SAN 376-6772. Tel: 765-468-7292. FAX: 765-468-7292. E-mail: farmlandlibrary@farmlandlibrary.org. Web Site: farmlandpubliclibrary.org/home. *Dir,* Carrie E Watson; E-mail: carrie@farmlandpubliclibrary.org; Staff 3 (MLS 1, Non-MLS 2)
Pop 1,780; Circ 9,291
Library Holdings: Bk Titles 11,415; Bk Vols 12,321; Per Subs 52; Talking Bks 215; Videos 152
Wireless access
Partic in Midwest Collaborative for Library Services
Open Mon & Sat 10-2, Tues & Thurs 1-7
Friends of the Library Group

FISHERS

R WESLEYAN CHURCH*, Archives & Historical Library, 13300 Olio Rd, 46037. (Mail add: PO Box 50434, Indianapolis, 46250-0434), SAN 305-0262. Tel: 317-774-3864. FAX: 317-774-7998. Web Site: www.wesleyan.org. *Librn & Archivist,* Jane Higle; E-mail: higlej@wesleyan.org; Staff 1 (MLS 1)
Founded 1968
Library Holdings: Bk Titles 6,180; Bk Vols 6,590; Per Subs 60
Open Mon-Thurs 8-4:30

FLORA

P FLORA-MONROE TOWNSHIP PUBLIC LIBRARY*, 109 N Center St, 46929-1004. SAN 304-8799. Tel: 574-967-3912. FAX: 574-967-3671. E-mail: floralib@flora.lib.in.us. Web Site: www.flora.lib.in.us. *Dir,* Rachel Ashcraft; Staff 5 (MLS 1, Non-MLS 4)
Founded 1918. Pop 3,190; Circ 33,000
Library Holdings: Bk Titles 30,884; Per Subs 62; Talking Bks 385; Videos 959
Automation Activity & Vendor Info: (Cataloging) Evergreen; (Circulation) Evergreen; (OPAC) Evergreen
Wireless access
Function: Adult bk club, Art exhibits, Audiobks via web, AV serv, Bks on CD, Chess club, Children's prog, Computer training, Computers for patron use, Free DVD rentals, Holiday prog, Homebound delivery serv, ILL available, Photocopying/Printing, Preschool outreach, Preschool reading prog, Printer for laptops & handheld devices, Prog for adults, Prog for children & young adult, Ref serv available, Scanner, Senior computer classes, Story hour, Summer & winter reading prog, Tax forms, VHS videos, Wheelchair accessible
Partic in Midwest Collaborative for Library Services; Northern Indiana Computer Consortium for Libraries
Open Mon, Wed & Fri 10-5:30, Tues & Thurs 10-7:30, Sat 10-2
Friends of the Library Group

FORT BRANCH

P FORT BRANCH-JOHNSON TOWNSHIP PUBLIC LIBRARY*, Fort Branch Public Library, 107 E Locust St, 47648. SAN 304-8802. Tel: 812-753-4212. Web Site: www.fortbranchlibrary.com. *Dir,* Laura M Happe; E-mail: laura@fortbranchlibrary.com; Staff 2 (MLS 1, Non-MLS 1)
Founded 1916. Pop 7,416; Circ 72,641
Library Holdings: Audiobooks 1,235; AV Mats 4,148; Bk Titles 58,129; Per Subs 121
Automation Activity & Vendor Info: (Cataloging) Innovative Interfaces, Inc; (Circulation) Innovative Interfaces, Inc; (Serials) Innovative Interfaces, Inc
Open Mon, Wed & Thurs 9-5, Tues 11-7, Fri & Sat 1-5

Branches: 1
HAUBSTADT PUBLIC LIBRARY, 101 W Gibson St, Haubstadt, 47639. Tel: 812-768-6005. *Dir,* Sabrina Frederick; E-mail: sabrina@fortbranchlibrary.com
Founded 1982
Open Mon & Fri 1-5, Tues 9-5, Wed 11-5, Thurs 1-7, Sat 9-1

FORT WAYNE

P ALLEN COUNTY PUBLIC LIBRARY*, 900 Library Plaza, 46802. SAN 341-1338. Tel: 260-421-1200. FAX: 260-421-1385. Web Site: acpl-cms.wise.oclc.org. *Dir,* Position Currently Open; *Asst to the Dir,* Sara Fisher; Tel: 260-421-1202, E-mail: sfisher@acpl.info; *Mgr, Access Serv,* Norm Compton; Tel: 260-421-1246, E-mail: ncompton@acpl.info; *Mgr, Art, Music & Media,* Stacy Stamas; Tel: 260-421-1211, E-mail: sstamas@acpl.info; *Bus & Tech Mgr,* Die Jia; E-mail: djia@acpl.info; *Mgr, Ch Serv,* Mary Voors; Tel: 260-421-1221, E-mail: mvoors@acpl.info; *Colls Mgr, Mgr, Info Tech,* Kim Quintrell; Tel: 260-421-1284, E-mail: kquintrell@acpl.info; *Commun Engagement Mgr,* Stephanny Smith; Tel: 260-421-1265, E-mail: ssmith@acpl.info; *Financial Mgr,* Dave Sedestrom; Tel: 260-421-1270, E-mail: dsedestrom@acpl.info; *Mgr, Human Res,* Kendra Samulak; Tel: 260-421-1234, E-mail: ksamulak@acpl.info; *Genealogist, Spec Coll,* Curt Witcher; Tel: 260-421-1226, E-mail: cwitcher@acpl.info; *Reader Serv,* Matthew Etzel; Tel: 260-421-1236, E-mail: metzel@acpl.info; *YA Serv,* Mari Hardacre; Tel: 260-421-1256, E-mail: mhardacre@acpl.info. Subject Specialists: *Radio-TV,* Norm Compton; Staff 84 (MLS 84)
Founded 1895
Jan 2017-Dec 2017. Mats Exp $3,277,010, Books $1,777,655, Per/Ser (Incl. Access Fees) $347,987, AV Mat $449,101, Electronic Ref Mat (Incl. Access Fees) $702,267. Sal $11,503,059
Library Holdings: e-books 131,541; Bk Vols 2,138,451; Per Subs 6,893; Videos 92,293
Special Collections: Fine Arts (Art & Music), bks & slides; Genealogy, Local History & Heraldry (Reynolds Historical Genealogy Coll), bks, film & micro. State Document Depository; US Document Depository
Automation Activity & Vendor Info: (Acquisitions) SirsiDynix; (Cataloging) SirsiDynix; (Circulation) SirsiDynix; (OPAC) SirsiDynix; (Serials) SirsiDynix
Wireless access
Function: 24/7 Electronic res, 24/7 Online cat, 3D Printer, Activity rm, Adult bk club, After school storytime, Archival coll, Art exhibits, Art programs, Audiobks on Playaways & MP3, Audiobks via web, AV serv, Bk club(s), Bks on CD, CD-ROM, Chess club, Children's prog, Computer training, Computers for patron use, Electronic databases & coll, For res purposes, Free DVD rentals, Genealogy discussion group, Govt ref serv, Holiday prog, Home delivery & serv to seniorr ctr & nursing homes, Homebound delivery serv, Homework prog, ILL available, Internet access, Life-long learning prog for all ages, Magazines, Mail & tel request accepted, Makerspace, Mango lang, Meeting rooms, Microfiche/film & reading machines, Movies, Music CDs, Online cat, Online ref, Outreach serv, OverDrive digital audio bks, Photocopying/Printing, Preschool outreach, Prog for adults, Prog for children & young adult, Ref & res, Ref serv available, Res assist avail, Scanner, Senior outreach, Spanish lang bks, Spoken cassettes & CDs, STEM programs, Story hour, Study rm, Summer & winter reading prog, Summer reading prog, Tax forms, Teen prog, Telephone ref, Wheelchair accessible, Winter reading prog, Writing prog
Publications: What's Happening (Calendar)
Partic in Midwest Collaborative for Library Services; OCLC Online Computer Library Center, Inc
Special Services for the Blind - Accessible computers; Assistive/Adapted tech devices, equip & products; Radio reading serv
Open Mon-Thurs 9-9, Fri & Sat 9-6, Sun 12-5
Friends of the Library Group
Branches: 13
ABOITE, 5630 Coventry Lane, 46804, SAN 370-0941. Tel: 260-421-1310. *Librn/Br Mgr,* Kris Lill; E-mail: klill@acpl.lib.in.us; Staff 5 (MLS 3, Non-MLS 2)
Library Holdings: AV Mats 17,059; Large Print Bks 2,199; Bk Vols 88,580
Open Mon-Thurs 10-9, Fri & Sat 10-6
Friends of the Library Group
DUPONT, 536 E Dupont Rd, 46825, SAN 370-095X. Tel: 260-421-1315. *Librn/Br Mgr,* Rebecca Wolfe; E-mail: rwolfe@acpl.lib.in.us; Staff 4 (MLS 3, Non-MLS 1)
Library Holdings: AV Mats 20,105; Large Print Bks 3,348; Bk Vols 120,351
Open Mon-Thurs 10-9, Fri & Sat 10-6
Friends of the Library Group
GEORGETOWN, 6600 E State Blvd, 46815, SAN 341-1397. Tel: 260-421-1320. *Librn/Br Mgr,* Stephen Platt; E-mail: splatt@acpl.lib.in.us; Staff 4 (MLS 3, Non-MLS 1)
Library Holdings: AV Mats 16,385; Large Print Bks 2,048; Bk Vols 110,731
Open Mon-Thurs 10-9, Fri & Sat 10-6
Friends of the Library Group
GRABILL BRANCH, 13521 State St, Grabill, 46741. (Mail add: PO Box 67, Grabill, 46741), SAN 341-1427. Tel: 260-421-1325. *Librn/Br Mgr,* Mindy Patterson; E-mail: mpatterson@acpl.lib.in.us; Staff 3 (MLS 2, Non-MLS 1)
Library Holdings: AV Mats 4,717; Large Print Bks 937; Bk Vols 32,427
Open Mon, Tues & Thurs 10-9, Wed, Fri & Sat 10-6
Friends of the Library Group
HESSEN CASSEL, 3030 E Paulding Rd, 46816, SAN 341-1451. Tel: 260-421-1330. *Librn/Br Mgr,* Edith Helbert; E-mail: ehelbert@acpl.lib.in.us; Staff 4 (MLS 2, Non-MLS 2)
Library Holdings: AV Mats 7,082; Large Print Bks 1,036; Bk Vols 49,966
Open Mon, Tues & Thurs 10-9, Wed, Fri & Sat 10-6
Friends of the Library Group
LITTLE TURTLE, 2201 Sherman Blvd, 46808, SAN 341-1486. Tel: 260-421-1335. *Librn/Br Mgr,* Carla Bauman; E-mail: cbauman@acpl.lib.in.us; Staff 3 (MLS 2, Non-MLS 1)
Library Holdings: AV Mats 9,559; Large Print Bks 1,832; Bk Vols 59,483
Open Mon-Wed 10-9, Thurs-Sat 10-6
Friends of the Library Group
MONROEVILLE BRANCH, 115 Main St, Monroeville, 46773, SAN 341-1516. Tel: 260-421-1340. *Librn/Br Mgr,* Christopher Wiljer; E-mail: cwiljer@acpl.lib.in.us; Staff 2 (MLS 1, Non-MLS 1)
Library Holdings: AV Mats 3,664; Large Print Bks 1,086; Bk Vols 24,565
Open Mon & Wed 12-5 & 6-9, Tues, Thurs & Fri 10-12 & 1-6, Sat 10-2
Friends of the Library Group
NEW HAVEN BRANCH, 648 Green St, New Haven, 46774, SAN 341-1540. Tel: 260-421-1345. *Librn/Br Mgr,* Rachel King; Staff 3 (MLS 2, Non-MLS 1)
Library Holdings: AV Mats 8,132; Large Print Bks 1,019; Bk Vols 50,749
Open Mon-Wed 10-9, Thurs & Fri 10-6, Sat (Sept-May) 10-6
Friends of the Library Group
PONTIAC, 2215 S Hanna St, 46803, SAN 341-1575. Tel: 260-421-1350. *Librn/Br Mgr,* Lisa Worrell; E-mail: lworrell@acpl.lib.in.us; Staff 3 (MLS 1, Non-MLS 2)
Library Holdings: AV Mats 5,502; Large Print Bks 276; Bk Vols 28,037
Open Mon, Tues & Thurs 10-9, Wed, Fri & Sat 10-6
Friends of the Library Group
SHAWNEE, 5600 Noll Ave, 46806, SAN 341-1605. Tel: 260-421-1355. *Librn/Br Mgr,* Pamela Martin-Diaz; E-mail: pmartin@acpl.lib.in.us; Staff 3 (MLS 2, Non-MLS 1)
Library Holdings: AV Mats 13,277; Large Print Bks 2,153; Bk Vols 76,736
Open Mon-Wed 10-9, Thurs-Sat 10-6
Friends of the Library Group
TECUMSEH, 1411 E State Blvd, 46805, SAN 341-163X. Tel: 260-421-1360. *Librn/Br Mgr,* Deborah L Noggle; Tel: 260-421-1361, E-mail: dnoggle@acpl.lib.in.us; Staff 3 (MLS 2, Non-MLS 1)
Library Holdings: AV Mats 7,731; Large Print Bks 907; Bk Vols 53,627
Open Mon, Tues & Thurs 10-9, Wed, Fri & Sat 10-6
Friends of the Library Group
WAYNEDALE, 2200 Lower Huntington Rd, 46819, SAN 341-1664. Tel: 260-421-1365. *Librn/Br Mgr,* Amanda Vance; E-mail: avance@acpl.lib.in.us; Staff 3 (MLS 2, Non-MLS 1)
Library Holdings: AV Mats 15,252; Large Print Bks 2,987; Bk Vols 62,283
Open Mon, Tues & Thurs 10-9, Wed, Fri & Sat 10-6
Friends of the Library Group
WOODBURN BRANCH, 4701 State Rd 101 N, Woodburn, 46797, SAN 341-1699. Tel: 260-421-1370. *Librn/Br Mgr,* Paige Shook; E-mail: pshook@acpl.lib.in.us; Staff 3 (MLS 1, Non-MLS 2)
Library Holdings: AV Mats 3,756; Large Print Bks 408; Bk Vols 24,773
Open Mon, Wed & Fri 10-12 & 1-6, Tues & Thurs 12-5 & 6-9, Sat 10-2
Friends of the Library Group

R CONCORDIA THEOLOGICAL SEMINARY*, Wayne & Barbara Kroemer Library, 6600 N Clinton St, 46825. SAN 304-8845. Tel: 260-452-2145. Interlibrary Loan Service Tel: 260-452-2144. Administration Tel: 260-452-2146. Automation Services Tel: 260-452-3148. Information Services Tel: 260-452-3149. FAX: 260-452-2126. E-mail: library@ctsfw.edu. Web Site: www.ctsfw.edu/about/kroemer-library. *Dir, Libr Serv,* Robert V Roethemeyer; E-mail: robert.roethemeyer@ctsfw.edu; *Electronic Res Librn,* Robert E Smith; E-mail: robert.smith@ctsfw.edu; *Tech Serv Librn,* Richard A Lammert; E-mail: richard.lammert@ctsfw.edu; *Asst to the Dir,* Roger A Peters; E-mail: roger.peters@ctsfw.edu; Staff 5 (MLS 3, Non-MLS 2)

Founded 1846. Enrl 295; Fac 25; Highest Degree: Doctorate
Library Holdings: Bk Vols 184,633; Per Subs 340
Special Collections: 16th & 17th Century Lutheran Orthodoxy Coll; Hermann Sasse Coll; Missions Coll
Subject Interests: Theol
Automation Activity & Vendor Info: (Cataloging) OCLC Worldshare Management Services; (Circulation) OCLC Worldshare Management Services; (Discovery) OCLC FirstSearch; (ILL) OCLC WorldShare Interlibrary Loan; (OPAC) OCLC Worldshare Management Services; (Serials) OCLC Worldshare Management Services
Wireless access
Partic in Academic Libraries of Indiana; Midwest Collaborative for Library Services; Private Academic Library Network of Indiana
Open Mon-Thurs 7:30am-8pm, Fri 7:30-5, Sun 2-8

GM DEPARTMENT OF VETERANS AFFAIRS NORTHERN INDIANA HEALTH CARE SYSTEM*, Medical Center Library, 2121 Lake Ave, 142D, 46805. SAN 304-8969. Tel: 260-426-5431, Ext 71330. FAX: 260-460-1490. Web Site: www.northernindiana.va.gov. *Librn,* Laveta Diem; Staff 1 (Non-MLS 1)
Founded 1950
Library Holdings: Bk Titles 1,250; Bk Vols 1,500; Per Subs 55
Subject Interests: Allied health, Nursing
Open Mon-Fri 8:30-4:30

S FORT WAYNE MUSEUM OF ART*, Auer Library, 311 E Main St, 46802. SAN 328-6312. Tel: 260-422-6467. FAX: 260-422-1374. Web Site: www.fwmoa.org/library. *Info Assoc,* Suzanne Slick; E-mail: suzanne.slick@fwmoa.org; Staff 1 (MLS 1)
Founded 1922
Library Holdings: Bk Titles 7,500; Per Subs 5
Automation Activity & Vendor Info: (Cataloging) LibLime; (Circulation) LibLime; (ILL) OCLC FirstSearch; (OPAC) LibLime
Open Tues-Fri 9:30-Noon
Friends of the Library Group

S FORT WAYNE NEWS-SENTINEL LIBRARY*, 600 W Main St, 46802. SAN 374-8367. Tel: 260-461-8468. FAX: 260-461-8817. Web Site: www.news-sentinel.com. *Library Contact,* Paula Beber; E-mail: pbeber@jg.net; Staff 1 (Non-MLS 1)
Library Holdings: Bk Titles 2,198; Bk Vols 2,340
Special Collections: Fort Wayne Newspaper Coll

C INDIANA TECH*, McMillen Library, Academic Ctr, West Wing, 1600 E Washington Blvd, 46803. SAN 304-8896. Tel: 260-422-5561, Ext 2215. FAX: 260-422-3189. E-mail: mcmillen@indianatech.edu. Web Site: library.indianatech.edu. *Libr Dir,* Connie Scott; Tel: 260-422-5561, Ext 2224, E-mail: cescott@indianatech.edu; *Tech Serv Librn,* Jane Feyl; Tel: 260-422-5561, Ext 2516, E-mail: jefeyl@indianatech.edu; *Tech Serv Spec,* Sarah Dennis; Tel: 260-422-5561, Ext 2223, E-mail: sndennis@indianatech.edu; Staff 6 (MLS 4, Non-MLS 2)
Founded 1932. Highest Degree: Master
Library Holdings: Bk Titles 37,911; Bk Vols 39,808; Per Subs 262
Subject Interests: Bus, Engr, Sci tech
Automation Activity & Vendor Info: (Cataloging) Follett Software; (Circulation) Follett Software
Wireless access
Partic in Midwest Collaborative for Library Services
Open Mon-Thurs 8:30am-10pm, Fri 8:30-4, Sat 8-1, Sun 4-9

C INDIANA UNIVERSITY-PURDUE UNIVERSITY FORT WAYNE*, Walter E Helmke Library, 2101 E Coliseum Blvd, 46805-1499. SAN 341-1214. Tel: 260-481-6512. Reference Tel: 260-481-6505. FAX: 260-481-6509. Web Site: library.ipfw.edu. *Dean,* Alexis Macklin, PhD; Tel: 260-481-6514, E-mail: macklina@ipfw.edu; *Dir, Info Tech, Dir, Tech Serv,* Nathan Rupp; Tel: 260-481-6086, E-mail: ruppn@ipfw.edu; *Info Serv & Instrul Librn,* Beth Boatright; Tel: 260-481-6499, E-mail: beth.boatright@ipfw.edu; *Info Serv & Instrul Librn,* Denise Buhr; Tel: 260-481-5759, E-mail: buhrd@ipfw.edu; *Info Serv & Instrul Librn,* Shannon Johnson; Tel: 260-481-6502, E-mail: johnsons@ipfw.edu; *Info Serv & Instrul Librn,* Ann Marshall; Tel: 260-481-6515, E-mail: marshala@ipfw.edu; *Info Serv & Instrul Librn,* Susan Skekloff; Tel: 260-481-6011, E-mail: skekloff@ipfw.edu; *Info Serv & Instrul Librn,* Sarah Wagner; Tel: 260-481-6511, E-mail: wagners@ipfw.edu; *Mgr Serv Desk, Circ,* Joyce Saltsman; Tel: 260-481-4137, E-mail: saltsman@ipfw.edu. Subject Specialists: *Bus, Emerging tech, Labor studies,* Beth Boatright; *Children's lit, Communication,* Denise Buhr; *Consumer & family sci, Health sci, Human serv,* Shannon Johnson; *Humanities, Linguistics, Soc sci,* Susan Skekloff; Staff 26 (MLS 10, Non-MLS 16)
Founded 1964. Enrl 8,996; Fac 819; Highest Degree: Doctorate
Jul 2013-Jun 2014. Mats Exp $835,005, Books $109,964, Per/Ser (Incl. Access Fees) $102,210, Micro $1,996, AV Mat $5,021, Electronic Ref Mat (Incl. Access Fees) $613,000, Presv $2,814. Sal $1,132,065 (Prof $769,438)
Library Holdings: AV Mats 7,745; e-books 223,907; e-journals 78,730; Microforms 280,198; Music Scores 1,492; Bk Vols 366,918
Special Collections: Faculty Publications; Sylvia Bowman Papers; University Archives. US Document Depository
Subject Interests: Bus & mgt, Sci tech
Automation Activity & Vendor Info: (Acquisitions) SirsiDynix; (Cataloging) SirsiDynix; (Circulation) SirsiDynix; (Discovery) EBSCO Discovery Service; (ILL) OCLC ILLiad; (OPAC) SirsiDynix; (Serials) SirsiDynix
Wireless access
Function: Archival coll, Audio & video playback equip for onsite use, Bks on CD, CD-ROM, Computers for patron use, Doc delivery serv, Electronic databases & coll, Microfiche/film & reading machines, Music CDs, Online cat, Online info literacy tutorials on the web & in blackboard, Photocopying/Printing, Ref serv available, VHS videos, Wheelchair accessible
Publications: Helmke Highlights (Monthly newsletter); IPFW Faculty (Online only); Library Facts (Online only); Self-Guided Tour (Online only); Tutorials (Online only)
Partic in Academic Libraries of Indiana; Midwest Collaborative for Library Services
Special Services for the Deaf - ADA equip; Closed caption videos; Deaf publ; Sign lang interpreter upon request for prog
Special Services for the Blind - ABE/GED & braille classes for the visually impaired; Bks on CD; Closed circuit TV magnifier; Computer with voice synthesizer for visually impaired persons; Copier with enlargement capabilities; Dragon Naturally Speaking software; Duplicating spec requests; Free checkout of audio mat; Internet workstation with adaptive software; Networked computers with assistive software; PC for people with disabilities; Photo duplicator for making large print; Scanner for conversion & translation of mats; Screen enlargement software for people with visual disabilities; Screen reader software
Open Mon-Thurs 8am-11pm, Fri 8-6, Sat 8:30-5:30, Sun 12-11

J IVY TECH COMMUNITY COLLEGE-NORTHEAST*, Fort Wayne Campus Library, 3800 N Anthony Blvd, 46805-1430. SAN 304-890X. Tel: 260-480-4172. Administration Tel: 260-480-4280. Web Site: library.ivytech.edu/fortwayne. *Dir,* Nicole Treesh; E-mail: ntreesh2@ivytech.edu; *Librn,* Elizabeth Metz; E-mail: ekerscher@ivytech.edu; *Librn,* Ellie Puckett; E-mail: elefand@ivytech.edu; *Librn,* Ann Spinney; E-mail: aspinney@ivytech.edu; *Lead Libr Asst,* Jonathan Puckett; E-mail: jpuckett@ivytech.edu; *Libr Asst,* Carol Gibbs; E-mail: cgibbs14@ivytech.edu; Staff 9 (MLS 4, Non-MLS 5)
Founded 1976. Enrl 7,527; Fac 281; Highest Degree: Associate
Library Holdings: AV Mats 3,950; CDs 445; DVDs 1,900; e-books 39,453; High Interest/Low Vocabulary Bk Vols 125; Large Print Bks 15; Bk Titles 21,419; Bk Vols 23,000; Per Subs 118; Spec Interest Per Sub 110
Special Collections: Family Reading Center, children's bks, per, parenting bks; Practical Nursing, bks, per; Respiratory Therapy, bks, per
Subject Interests: Child care, Children's fiction, Parenting, Puppets
Wireless access
Function: 24/7 Electronic res, 24/7 Online cat, Audiobks via web, Bks on CD, CD-ROM, Computer training, Computers for patron use, Distance learning, Doc delivery serv, Electronic databases & coll, For res purposes, Health sci info serv, ILL available, Internet access, Large print keyboards, Magazines, Magnifiers for reading, Mail & tel request accepted, Mail loans to mem, Meeting rooms, Music CDs, Online cat, Online info literacy tutorials on the web & in blackboard, Online ref, Orientations, Outside serv via phone, mail, e-mail & web, Photocopying/Printing, Printer for laptops & handheld devices, Ref & res, Ref serv available, Res assist avail, Scanner, Spoken cassettes & CDs, Spoken cassettes & DVDs, Telephone ref, Wheelchair accessible
Publications: Bibliographies (Research guide); Guide to the Library; Newsletter (Monthly); OPAC Guide (Online only); Research Guides
Partic in Academic Libraries of Indiana; Midwest Collaborative for Library Services
Special Services for the Blind - Accessible computers; Assistive/Adapted tech devices, equip & products; Audio mat; Bks on cassette; Bks on CD; Copier with enlargement capabilities; HP Scan Jet with photo-finish software; Large print bks; Large screen computer & software; PC for people with disabilities; Screen enlargement software for people with visual disabilities; ZoomText magnification & reading software
Open Mon-Thurs 7:45am-8:45pm, Fri 7:45-6:45, Sat 9-1:45
Restriction: Open to students, fac, staff & alumni

S JOURNAL GAZETTE LIBRARY*, 600 W Main St, 46802. SAN 320-6661. Tel: 260-461-8377. FAX: 260-461-8648. E-mail: jgnews@jg.net. Web Site: www.journalgazette.net. *Mgr, News Tech,* Tom Pellegrene; E-mail: tpellegrene@jg.net; *Text Librn,* Paul Wyche; Tel: 260-461-8258, E-mail: pwyche@jg.net; *Webmaster,* Mike Durbin; Tel: 260-461-8194, E-mail: mdurbin@jg.net; Staff 3 (Non-MLS 3)
Founded 1977
Library Holdings: Bk Titles 1,279; Bk Vols 1,410; Per Subs 27
Special Collections: Journal-Gazette-1885 to Present, micro
Subject Interests: News

Function: Archival coll, Res libr
Open Mon-Fri 6-6
Restriction: Private libr

M PARK CENTER PROFESSIONAL LIBRARY*, Corporate Services, 909 E State Blvd, 46805. SAN 320-183X. Tel: 260-481-2700, Ext 2148. FAX: 260-481-2885. Web Site: www.parkcenter.org. *Mgr,* Sunita Winchester; Staff 1 (Non-MLS 1)
Founded 1983
Library Holdings: CDs 10; DVDs 25; Bk Titles 1,041; Bk Vols 15; Per Subs 1; Videos 40
Subject Interests: Mental health, Psychiat, Psychol, Soc serv (soc work)
Partic in Area Libr Serv Authority; Region 3
Restriction: Staff use only

C UNIVERSITY OF SAINT FRANCIS*, Lee & Jim Vann Library, Pope John Paul II Ctr, 2701 Spring St, Rm 102 & 202, 46808. SAN 304-8942. Tel: 260-399-8060. Information Services Tel: 260-479-5001. FAX: 260-399-8166. E-mail: library@sf.edu. Web Site: library.sf.edu. *Libr Dir,* Maureen McMahan; Tel: 260-399-7700, Ext 6059, E-mail: mmcmahan@sf.edu; *Ref & Instruction Librn,* Kyle Mossman; Tel: 260-399-7700, Ext 6067, E-mail: kmossman@sf.edu; *Coordr, Teaching & Learning Librn,* Andrea Cohn; Tel: 260-399-7700, Ext 6056, E-mail: acohn@sf.edu; *Supvr, User Serv,* Mary Larsen; Tel: 260-399-7700, Ext 6069, E-mail: mredding@sf.edu; *Doc Delivery Spec, ILL,* Barbara Chen; Tel: 260-399-7700, Ext 6061, E-mail: bchen@sf.edu; *Ser Spec,* Beth Shively Wages; Tel: 260-399-7700, Ext 6068, E-mail: ewages@sf.edu; *Instrul Designer,* Nathalie Rouamba, PhD; Tel: 260-399-7700, Ext 6086, E-mail: nrouamba@sf.edu; Staff 8 (MLS 7, Non-MLS 1)
Founded 1890. Enrl 2,350; Fac 193; Highest Degree: Master
Special Collections: ERIC Document Coll
Subject Interests: Art, Counseling, Educ, Nursing, Psychol, Spec educ
Automation Activity & Vendor Info: (Acquisitions) OCLC; (Cataloging) OCLC Connexion; (Circulation) OCLC; (Course Reserve) OCLC; (ILL) OCLC ILLiad; (OPAC) OCLC; (Serials) OCLC
Wireless access
Function: Audio & video playback equip for onsite use, Electronic databases & coll, Internet access, Orientations, Photocopying/Printing, Ref serv available, Scanner, VHS videos, Wheelchair accessible
Partic in Private Academic Library Network of Indiana
Open Mon-Thurs 7:30am-10pm, Fri 7:30-5, Sat 9-5, Sun 12-10
Restriction: Limited access for the pub, Open to students, fac, staff & alumni, Restricted loan policy

FORTVILLE

P FORTVILLE-VERNON TOWNSHIP PUBLIC LIBRARY, 625 E Broadway, 46040-1549. SAN 304-8977. Tel: 317-485-6402. FAX: 317-485-4084. E-mail: fvtpl625@gmail.com. Web Site: www.fvtpl.org. *Dir,* Melissa Dragoo; Staff 3 (MLS 2, Non-MLS 1)
Founded 1918. Pop 6,894; Circ 131,673
Library Holdings: Bk Titles 36,999; Talking Bks 2,427; Videos 7,129
Wireless access
Open Mon-Wed 10-6, Thurs 12-8, Sat 10-4

FOWLER

P BENTON COUNTY PUBLIC LIBRARY*, 102 N Van Buren Ave, 47944. SAN 304-8985. Tel: 765-884-1720. FAX: 765-884-1714. E-mail: bcpl@benton.lib.in.us. Web Site: benton.lib.in.us. *Dir,* Cara Ringle; E-mail: director@benton.lib.in.us; *Ch,* Lisa Brown; Staff 2 (Non-MLS 2)
Founded 1906. Pop 5,059; Circ 42,960
Library Holdings: Bk Titles 30,000; Per Subs 32
Special Collections: Burton Berry Coll; Louis L'Amour Westerns
Subject Interests: Agr, Art & archit, Cookbks, Environ studies, Genealogy
Automation Activity & Vendor Info: (Acquisitions) Evergreen; (Cataloging) Evergreen; (Circulation) Evergreen; (OPAC) Evergreen
Wireless access
Function: Children's prog, Computers for patron use, Free DVD rentals, Home delivery & serv to seniorr ctr & nursing homes, ILL available, Internet access, Microfiche/film & reading machines, Music CDs, Online cat, Outreach serv, OverDrive digital audio bks, Photocopying/Printing, Preschool reading prog, Ref serv available, Scanner, Spoken cassettes & CDs, Story hour, Tax forms
Partic in Evergreen Indiana Consortium
Open Mon, Wed & Fri 9-5, Tues & Thurs 9-8, Sat 10-2
Restriction: Authorized patrons, Non-resident fee
Friends of the Library Group

FRANCESVILLE

P FRANCESVILLE-SALEM TOWNSHIP PUBLIC LIBRARY*, 201 W Montgomery St, 47946. (Mail add: PO Box 577, 47946-0577), SAN 304-8993. Tel: 219-567-9433. FAX: 219-567-9451. E-mail: francesvillelibrary@yahoo.com. Web Site: pulaskionline.org/fstpl. *Dir,* Sally Sharpe; Staff 1 (Non-MLS 1)
Founded 1916. Pop 1,500; Circ 31,744
Library Holdings: CDs 150; DVDs 800; Large Print Bks 122; Bk Titles 26,000; Per Subs 75; Talking Bks 220; Videos 1,000
Automation Activity & Vendor Info: (Cataloging) AmLib Library Management System; (Circulation) AmLib Library Management System
Wireless access
Open Mon, Wed & Fri 11-5, Tues & Thurs 11-7, Sat 9-1

FRANKFORT

P FRANKFORT COMMUNITY PUBLIC LIBRARY*, 208 W Clinton St, 46041. SAN 304-9000. Tel: 765-654-8746. FAX: 765-654-8747. TDD: 765-659-3047. E-mail: fcpl@myfcpl.org. Web Site: myfcpl.org. *Dir,* Gregg Williamson; E-mail: gwilliamson@myfcpl.org; *Asst Dir,* Jen Casey; *Ch,* Meave Brewer; *Tech Serv Mgr,* Maggie Pinnick; Staff 16 (MLS 5, Non-MLS 11)
Founded 1880. Pop 33,000; Circ 266,913
Library Holdings: AV Mats 8,397; CDs 3,508; DVDs 3,339; Large Print Bks 3,377; Bk Vols 141,506; Per Subs 200; Talking Bks 3,473
Special Collections: Genealogy (Fugate & Culver Coll)
Automation Activity & Vendor Info: (Acquisitions) Innovative Interfaces, Inc; (Cataloging) Innovative Interfaces, Inc; (Circulation) Innovative Interfaces, Inc; (OPAC) Innovative Interfaces, Inc
Wireless access
Publications: Library Lines (Newsletter)
Partic in Midwest Collaborative for Library Services
Special Services for the Deaf - TDD equip
Special Services for the Blind - Assistive/Adapted tech devices, equip & products
Open Mon-Thurs 9-8, Fri & Sat 9-5, Sun (Winter) 1-5
Friends of the Library Group
Branches: 3
MICHIGAN ROAD COMMUNITY LIBRARY, 2489 N St, Rd 29, Michigantown, 46057. (Mail add: PO Box 300, Michigantown, 46057-0300), SAN 376-8384. Tel: 765-249-2303. FAX: 765-249-2303. *Br Supvr,* Chylene Click; Staff 2 (Non-MLS 2)
Founded 1984
Library Holdings: AV Mats 51; CDs 209; DVDs 184; Large Print Bks 121; Bk Vols 20,630; Per Subs 25; Talking Bks 197; Videos 868
Open Mon-Wed 1-7, Thurs 9-5, Sat 10-2
Friends of the Library Group
MULBERRY COMMUNITY LIBRARY, 615 E Jackson St, Mulberry, 46058. (Mail add: PO Box 489, Mulberry, 46058-0489), SAN 376-8392. Tel: 765-296-2604. FAX: 765-296-2604. *Br Supvr,* Carol Schriefer-McClean; Staff 2 (MLS 1, Non-MLS 1)
Founded 1984
Library Holdings: AV Mats 40; CDs 341; DVDs 490; Large Print Bks 207; Bk Vols 18,931; Per Subs 37; Talking Bks 489; Videos 881
Open Mon-Thurs 1-7, Fri 9-5, Sat 10-2
Friends of the Library Group
ROSSVILLE COMMUNITY LIBRARY, 400 W Main St, Rossville, 46065. (Mail add: PO Box 567, Rossville, 46065-0567), SAN 376-8406. Tel: 765-379-2246. FAX: 765-379-2246. *Br Operations Mgr,* Kathy Scircle; Staff 3 (MLS 1, Non-MLS 2)
Founded 1984
Library Holdings: AV Mats 1,075; CDs 394; DVDs 1,000; Large Print Bks 306; Bk Vols 26,769; Per Subs 50; Talking Bks 374
Open Mon, Wed & Fri 9-5, Tues & Thurs 1-7, Sat 10-2
Friends of the Library Group
Bookmobiles: 1

FRANKLIN

C FRANKLIN COLLEGE*, B F Hamilton Library, 101 Branigin Blvd, 46131-2623. SAN 304-9019. Tel: 317-738-8164. Circulation Tel: 317-738-8162. FAX: 317-738-8787. E-mail: library@franklincollege.edu. Web Site: library.franklincollege.edu. *Dir,* Denise Shorey; E-mail: dshorey@franklincollege.edu; *Instruction & Ref Librn,* Jessica Mahoney; E-mail: jmahoney@franklincollege.edu; *Pub Serv Coordr,* Rachel Walters; E-mail: rwalters@franklincollege.edu; *Acq,* Rebecca Wallace; E-mail: rwallace@franklincollege.edu; *Archives Asst, Tech Serv,* Jared Crocker; E-mail: jcrocker@franklincollege.edu; Staff 5 (MLS 2, Non-MLS 3)
Founded 1834. Enrl 1,012; Fac 79; Highest Degree: Bachelor
Special Collections: David Demaree Banta Coll; Indiana American Baptist Coll; Roger D Branigin Papers
Automation Activity & Vendor Info: (Acquisitions) OCLC; (Cataloging) OCLC; (Circulation) OCLC; (Course Reserve) OCLC; (ILL) OCLC WorldShare Interlibrary Loan; (OPAC) OCLC; (Serials) OCLC
Wireless access
Publications: Catalog of the David Demaree Banta Collection
Partic in Academic Libraries of Indiana; Midwest Collaborative for Library Services; OCLC Online Computer Library Center, Inc; Private Academic Library Network of Indiana

P JOHNSON COUNTY PUBLIC LIBRARY*, Administration, 49 E Monroe St, 46131. SAN 304-9027. Administration Tel: 317-738-9835. Administration FAX: 317-738-9354. Web Site: www.pageafterpage.org. *Dir,* Lisa Lintner; E-mail: llintner@jcplin.org; *Asst Dir,* Sarah Taylor; E-mail: staylor@jcplin.org; *Mgr, Human Res,* Amber Turner; E-mail: aturner@jcplin.org; *Mkt & Communications Mgr,* Jody Veldkamp; E-mail: jveldkamp@jcplin.org; *Adult Learning Ctr Spec,* Wendy Preilis; E-mail: wpreilis@jcplin.org; Staff 100 (MLS 33, Non-MLS 67)
Founded 1911. Pop 95,000; Circ 1,089,000
Library Holdings: AV Mats 41,091; e-books 16; Large Print Bks 8,198; Bk Titles 296,412; Bk Vols 362,351; Per Subs 556
Special Collections: Johnson County History
Subject Interests: Careers, Consumer, Spanish, Travel
Automation Activity & Vendor Info: (Acquisitions) SirsiDynix; (Cataloging) SirsiDynix; (Circulation) SirsiDynix; (ILL) SirsiDynix; (Media Booking) SirsiDynix; (OPAC) SirsiDynix-iBistro; (Serials) SirsiDynix
Wireless access
Publications: Program Guide
Partic in Johnson County Commun Network; OCLC Online Computer Library Center, Inc
Open Mon-Fri 8-5
Friends of the Library Group
Branches: 4
CLARK PLEASANT LIBRARY, 530 Tracy Rd, Ste 250, New Whiteland, 46184-9699, SAN 376-9445. Tel: 317-535-6206. FAX: 317-535-6018. Reference E-mail: CPL_Ref@jcplin.org. *Br Mgr,* Davin Kolderup; E-mail: dkolderup@jcplin.org; *Ch Serv Librn,* Sue Salamone; E-mail: ssalamone@jcplin.org; *Circ Mgr,* Holly Kubancsek; E-mail: hkubancsek@jcplin.org; Staff 7 (MLS 4, Non-MLS 3)
Function: Adult literacy prog, Audio & video playback equip for onsite use, AV serv, Bk club(s), CD-ROM, Computer training, E-Reserves, Electronic databases & coll, Home delivery & serv to seniorr ctr & nursing homes, Homebound delivery serv, ILL available, Magnifiers for reading, Music CDs, Photocopying/Printing, Preschool outreach, Prog for adults, Prog for children & young adult, Ref serv available, Senior computer classes, Serves people with intellectual disabilities, Summer reading prog, Tax forms, Telephone ref, VHS videos, Wheelchair accessible, Workshops
Open Mon-Thurs 9-8, Fri 9-6, Sat 9-5
Friends of the Library Group
FRANKLIN BRANCH, 401 State St, 46131. Tel: 317-738-2833. E-mail: FRL_Ref@jcplin.org. *Br Mgr,* Tiffany Wilson; E-mail: twilson@jcplin.org
Friends of the Library Group
TRAFALGAR BRANCH, 424 Tower St, Trafalgar, 46181. Tel: 317-878-9560. FAX: 317-878-4093. Reference E-mail: TRA_Ref@jcplin.org. *Br Mgr,* Todd Jones; E-mail: tjones@jcplin.org; Staff 8 (MLS 4, Non-MLS 4)
Open Mon-Thurs 9-8, Fri 9-6, Sat 9-5
Friends of the Library Group
WHITE RIVER LIBRARY, 1664 Library Blvd, Greenwood, 46142, SAN 320-9539. Tel: 317-885-1330. FAX: 317-882-4117. Reference E-mail: WRL_Ref@jcplin.org. *Br Mgr,* Linda Kilbert; E-mail: lkilbert@jcplin.org; Staff 18 (MLS 8, Non-MLS 10)
Open Mon-Thurs 9-9, Fri 9-6, Sat 9-5, Sun (Sept-May) 1-5
Friends of the Library Group

FREMONT

P FREMONT PUBLIC LIBRARY*, 1004 W Toledo St, 46737. (Mail add: PO Box 616, 46737-0007), SAN 376-2653. Tel: 260-495-7157. Administration Tel: 260-495-9227. FAX: 260-495-7127. E-mail: library@fremont.lib.in.us. Web Site: www.fremont.lib.in.us. *Dir,* Gary Green; E-mail: ggreen@fremont.lib.in.us; Staff 11 (MLS 3, Non-MLS 8)
Founded 1919. Pop 7,041; Circ 80,961
Library Holdings: Audiobooks 2,701; DVDs 6,833; e-books 6,505; Large Print Bks 2,740; Bk Titles 55,487; Per Subs 134
Automation Activity & Vendor Info: (Cataloging) TLC (The Library Corporation); (Circulation) TLC (The Library Corporation); (OPAC) TLC (The Library Corporation)
Wireless access
Function: Adult bk club, Art exhibits, Bks on CD, Children's prog, Computer training, Computers for patron use, Doc delivery serv, Electronic databases & coll, Family literacy, Holiday prog, Home delivery & serv to seniorr ctr & nursing homes, ILL available, Internet access, Life-long learning prog for all ages, Magazines, Movies, Music CDs, OverDrive digital audio bks, Photocopying/Printing, Prog for adults, Prog for children & young adult, Scanner, Story hour, Summer & winter reading prog, Tax forms, Teen prog
Open Mon-Thurs 9-8, Fri 10-6, Sat 10-4
Restriction: Non-circulating coll, Non-resident fee
Friends of the Library Group

FRENCH LICK

P MELTON PUBLIC LIBRARY*, 8496 W College St, 47432-1026. SAN 304-9035. Tel: 812-936-2177. FAX: 812-936-7524. Web Site: melton.lib.in.us. *Dir,* Trista Rue; E-mail: trista@melton.lib.in.us; Staff 3 (MLS 2, Non-MLS 1)
Pop 4,767; Circ 36,400
Library Holdings: Bk Titles 31,610; Bk Vols 33,190; Per Subs 61; Talking Bks 374; Videos 1,269
Wireless access
Partic in Evergreen Indiana Consortium
Open Mon & Fri 9-5, Tues & Thurs 9-6, Sat 10-2
Friends of the Library Group

GARRETT

P GARRETT PUBLIC LIBRARY*, 107 W Houston St, 46738. SAN 304-9043. Tel: 260-357-5485. FAX: 260-357-5170. Web Site: garrettpl.org. *Dir,* Matthew Etzel; E-mail: metzel@gpl.lib.in.us; *Adult Serv,* Andrea Basinger; E-mail: abasinger@gpl.lib.in.us; *Ch Serv,* Heidi Christiansen; E-mail: achristiansen@gpl.lib.in.us; Staff 13 (MLS 1, Non-MLS 12)
Founded 1914. Pop 9,200; Circ 50,000
Library Holdings: AV Mats 3,000; Large Print Bks 650; Bk Titles 50,000
Special Collections: Cameron Park Indian Relics Coll
Automation Activity & Vendor Info: (Cataloging) Evergreen; (Circulation) Evergreen; (OPAC) Evergreen
Wireless access
Function: Homebound delivery serv, ILL available, Large print keyboards, Prog for children & young adult, Ref serv available, Summer reading prog, Wheelchair accessible
Partic in Evergreen Indiana Consortium
Special Services for the Deaf - TTY equip
Open Mon-Thurs 9-8, Fri 9-6, Sat 9-4
Friends of the Library Group

GARY

P GARY PUBLIC LIBRARY*, Administrative Office, 220 W Fifth Ave, 46402-1215. SAN 341-1729. Tel: 219-886-2484. FAX: 219-886-6829. Web Site: www.garypubliclibrary.org. *Dir,* Diana Morrow; E-mail: morrd@garypubliclibrary.org
Founded 1908
Wireless access
Friends of the Library Group
Branches: 4
BRUNSWICK BRANCH, 4030 W Fifth Ave, 46406. Tel: 219-944-9402. FAX: 219-944-9644. *Librn,* Kenneth Green
Open Mon-Thurs 12-8, Fri & Sat 10-5
W E B DU BOIS BRANCH, 1835 Broadway, 46407-2298, SAN 341-1753. Tel: 219-886-9120. FAX: 219-886-9319. *Head Librn,* Diana Morrow; Staff 2 (MLS 1, Non-MLS 1)
Founded 1979
Library Holdings: AV Mats 1,012; Large Print Bks 115; Bk Titles 71,410; Bk Vols 73,911; Per Subs 68; Videos 290
Special Collections: Afro-American Rare Book Coll, micro-fiche
Open Mon-Thurs 12-8, Fri & Sat 10-5
Friends of the Library Group
JOHN F KENNEDY BRANCH, 3953 Broadway, 46408-1799, SAN 341-1818. Tel: 219-887-8112. FAX: 219-887-5967. *Head Librn,* Brenda Moore; Staff 2 (Non-MLS 2)
Library Holdings: AV Mats 815; Large Print Bks 91; Bk Titles 74,911; Bk Vols 75,612; Per Subs 56; Videos 211
Open Mon-Thurs 12-8, Fri & Sat 10-5
Friends of the Library Group
CARTER G WOODSON BRANCH, 501 S Lake St, 46403-2408, SAN 341-1907. Tel: 219-938-3941. FAX: 219-938-8759. *Br Mgr,* Patience A Ojomo; E-mail: ojompa@garypubliclibrary.org; Staff 2 (MLS 1, Non-MLS 1)
Library Holdings: AV Mats 791; Bk Titles 58,911; Bk Vols 59,612; Per Subs 52; Videos 231
Open Mon-Thurs 12-8, Fri & Sat 10-5
Friends of the Library Group

C INDIANA UNIVERSITY NORTHWEST, John W Anderson Library, 3400 Broadway, 46408. SAN 304-9051. Tel: 219-980-6580. Circulation Tel: 219-980-6585. Interlibrary Loan Service Tel: 219-980-6932. Reference Tel: 219-980-6582. FAX: 219-980-6558. E-mail: iunlib@iun.edu. Web Site: www.iun.edu/library. *Dean of Libr,* Latrice Booker; Tel: 219-980-6547, E-mail: lbooker@iun.edu; *Head, Circ & Reserves,* Debbie Annette Curtis; Tel: 219-980-6583, E-mail: debacurt@iun.edu; *Head, Ser, Tech Serv,* Jackie Cheairs; Tel: 219-980-6935, E-mail: jcheairs@iun.edu; *Assoc Librn, Head, Tech Serv,* Cynthia Szymanski; Tel: 219-980-6521, E-mail: cszymans@iun.edu; *Asst Librn, Coordinator, Reference Servs & Emerging Technologies,* Scott Hudnall; Tel: 219-980-6931, E-mail: schudnal@iun.edu; *Asst Librn for Teaching & Learning,* Nicholas A Casas;

Tel: 219-980-6806, E-mail: ncasas@iun.edu; Staff 13 (MLS 7, Non-MLS 6)
Founded 1940. Enrl 4,200; Fac 175; Highest Degree: Master
Library Holdings: Bk Vols 264,000
Special Collections: Calumet Regional Archives; Northwest Center for Data & Analysis. US Document Depository
Automation Activity & Vendor Info: (Acquisitions) SirsiDynix; (Cataloging) SirsiDynix; (Circulation) SirsiDynix; (ILL) SirsiDynix; (OPAC) SirsiDynix; (Serials) SirsiDynix
Wireless access
Partic in Academic Libraries of Indiana; Midwest Collaborative for Library Services; OCLC Online Computer Library Center, Inc
Open Mon-Thurs 8-7, Fri 8-5, Sat 10-5

CM INDIANA UNIVERSITY SCHOOL OF MEDICINE-NORTHWEST CENTER FOR MEDICAL EDUCATION*, Steven C Beering Medical Library, 3400 Broadway, 46408-1197. SAN 320-1848. Tel: 219-980-6709. Web Site: www.medicine.iu.edu/body.cfm?id=4973. *Coordr,* Corona Wiley; E-mail: cwiley@iun.edu; Staff 2 (MLS 1, Non-MLS 1)
Library Holdings: Bk Titles 1,800; Per Subs 15
Wireless access
Open Mon-Thurs 8-5, Fri 8-4

J IVY TECH COMMUNITY COLLEGE-NORTHWEST*, Gary Campus Library, 1440 E 35th Ave, 46409-1499. SAN 304-906X. Tel: 219-981-4410. FAX: 219-981-4415. *Libr Dir,* Barb Minich; E-mail: bweaver@ivytech.edu; *Computer Lab Tech,* Linda Holcomb; E-mail: lholcomb@ivytech.edu; Staff 4 (MLS 1, Non-MLS 3)
Founded 1972. Enrl 5,000
Library Holdings: AV Mats 4,295; e-books 28,029; e-journals 14,235; Electronic Media & Resources 42; Bk Titles 13,805; Per Subs 160
Automation Activity & Vendor Info: (Cataloging) Ex Libris Group; (OPAC) Ex Libris Group
Wireless access
Partic in Duplicate Exchange Union; Midwest Collaborative for Library Services
Open Mon-Thurs 8am-8:30pm, Fri 8-5, Sat 9-1

M METHODIST HOSPITAL*, North Lake Campus-Health Science Libraries, 600 Grant St, 46402. SAN 304-9086. Tel: 219-886-4554. FAX: 219-886-4271. Web Site: www.methodisthospitals.org. *Librn,* Fannie Ilievski; Staff 2 (MLS 1, Non-MLS 1)
Founded 1950
Library Holdings: Bk Titles 3,000; Bk Vols 3,500; Per Subs 150
Subject Interests: Cardiology, Internal med, Oncology
Wireless access
Function: AV serv, ILL available, Photocopying/Printing
Restriction: Staff use only

GAS CITY

P GAS CITY-MILL TOWNSHIP PUBLIC LIBRARY, 135 E Main St, 46933-1496. SAN 304-9108. Tel: 765-674-4718. FAX: 765-674-5176. E-mail: office@gcmtpl.lib.in.us. Web Site: www.gcmtpl.lib.in.us.
Founded 1913. Pop 9,449; Circ 77,959
Library Holdings: AV Mats 4,841; Bk Vols 35,926; Per Subs 136
Automation Activity & Vendor Info: (Acquisitions) Innovative Interfaces, Inc; (Cataloging) Innovative Interfaces, Inc; (Circulation) Innovative Interfaces, Inc; (OPAC) Innovative Interfaces, Inc
Wireless access
Partic in Midwest Collaborative for Library Services
Open Mon-Thurs 10-7, Fri & Sat 10-5
Friends of the Library Group

GOODLAND

P GOODLAND & GRANT TOWNSHIP PUBLIC LIBRARY*, 111 S Newton St, 47948. (Mail add: PO Box 405, 47948-0405), SAN 304-9124. Tel: 219-297-4431. FAX: 219-297-4431. *Dir,* Steve McNelly; E-mail: smcnelly@goodland.lib.in.us; Staff 2 (Non-MLS 2)
Founded 1907. Pop 1,100; Circ 9,829
Jan 2014-Dec 2014 Income $165,000
Library Holdings: Bk Titles 16,791; Bk Vols 18,919; Per Subs 50; Talking Bks 175; Videos 1,000
Subject Interests: Indiana
Automation Activity & Vendor Info: (Acquisitions) Koha; (Cataloging) Koha; (OPAC) Koha
Wireless access
Open Mon-Wed & Fri 12-5, Thurs 12-8, Sat 9-1

GOSHEN

GOSHEN COLLEGE
C HAROLD & WILMA GOOD LIBRARY*, 1700 S Main, 46526-4794, SAN 341-1931. Tel: 574-535-7427. Interlibrary Loan Service Tel: 574-535-7430. Reference Tel: 574-535-7431. FAX: 574-535-7438. E-mail: library@goshen.edu. Web Site: www.goshen.edu/library. *Dir,* Fritz Hartman; Tel: 574-535-7423, E-mail: fritzdh@goshen.edu; *Head, Ref & Instruction,* Eric Bradley; Tel: 574-535-7424, E-mail: ebradley@goshen.edu; *Head, Tech Serv, Ser & Syst,* Andrew Shields; *Ref & Instruction Librn,* Abby Nafziger; *Day Circ Mgr,* Ruth Hochstetler; E-mail: rutheh2@goshen.edu; *Evening Circ Supvr,* Esther Guedea; E-mail: esthergg@goshen.edu; *Libr Asst,* Yoder Tillie; Tel: 574-535-7637, E-mail: matildaky@goshen.edu. Subject Specialists: *Bus, Communications, English,* Fritz Hartman; *Educ, Hist, Psychol,* Eric Bradley; Staff 3.5 (MLS 3.5)
Founded 1894. Enrl 889; Highest Degree: Master
Jul 2014-Jun 2015 Income $522,915. Mats Exp $233,507, Books $28,400, Per/Ser (Incl. Access Fees) $112,000, Micro $2,500, Electronic Ref Mat (Incl. Access Fees) $3,145. Sal $209,764 (Prof $156,464)
Library Holdings: AV Mats 3,176; e-books 8,996; Bk Vols 134,453; Per Subs 416
Special Collections: Early American Hymnody (Jesse Hartzler Coll)
Subject Interests: Peace, Relig
Automation Activity & Vendor Info: (Acquisitions) OCLC; (Cataloging) OCLC; (Circulation) OCLC; (Course Reserve) OCLC; (ILL) OCLC; (OPAC) OCLC; (Serials) OCLC
Function: Art exhibits, Computers for patron use, Electronic databases & coll, ILL available, Online cat, Online ref, Photocopying/Printing, Wheelchair accessible
Partic in Academic Libraries of Indiana; Midwest Collaborative for Library Services; OCLC Online Computer Library Center, Inc; Private Academic Library Network of Indiana
Open Mon-Thurs 7:30am-11pm, Fri 7:30-5, Sat 1-5, Sun 3-11
Restriction: In-house use for visitors, Pub use on premises

C MENNONITE HISTORICAL LIBRARY*, 1700 S Main, 46526, SAN 341-1966. Tel: 574-535-7418. FAX: 574-535-7438. E-mail: mhl@goshen.edu. Web Site: www.goshen.edu/mhl. *Dir,* Dr John D Roth; *Assoc Librn,* Victoria M Waters; *Curator,* Joe A Springer; Staff 2 (MLS 2)
Founded 1906. Enrl 1,000; Highest Degree: Master
Library Holdings: Bk Vols 77,000; Per Subs 400
Subject Interests: Amish, Anabaptists, Genealogy, Mennonite
Automation Activity & Vendor Info: (Acquisitions) Ex Libris Group; (Cataloging) Ex Libris Group; (Circulation) Ex Libris Group; (OPAC) Ex Libris Group; (Serials) Ex Libris Group
Partic in OCLC Online Computer Library Center, Inc; Private Academic Library Network of Indiana
Publications: Mennonite Quarterly Review
Open Mon-Fri 8-5
Restriction: Circ limited

P GOSHEN PUBLIC LIBRARY*, 601 S Fifth St, 46526. SAN 304-9132. Tel: 574-533-9531. FAX: 574-533-5211. Web Site: goshenpl.lib.in.us. *Dir,* Ann-Margaret Rice; E-mail: amrice@goshenpl.lib.in.us; *Head, Adult/Teen Serv,* Emily Stuckey-Weber; E-mail: estuckeyweber@goshenpl.lib.in.us; *Head, Children's Servx,* Tina Ervin; Tel: 574-537-0241, E-mail: tervin@goshenpl.lib.in.us; *Head, Ref Serv,* Linda Neff; Tel: 574-533-9531, E-mail: lneff@goshenpl.lib.in.us; *Head, Tech Serv,* Elizabeth Rinehart; E-mail: lrinehart@goshenpl.lib.in.us; *Automation Mgr,* Ross Riker; E-mail: reriker@goshenpl.lib.in.us; *Bus Mgr,* Gregory Laughlin; Tel: 574-534-3699, E-mail: glaughlin@goshenpl.lib.in.us; *AV Coordr,* Janet Showalter; E-mail: jshowalter@goshenpl.lib.in.us; *Circ,* Michael Miller; E-mail: mmiller@goshenpl.lib.in.us; Staff 14 (MLS 11, Non-MLS 3)
Founded 1901. Pop 37,608; Circ 481,931
Library Holdings: AV Mats 26,686; Bk Titles 137,306; Per Subs 299
Special Collections: Indiana History & Local Genealogy Coll; Large Print Coll; Spanish Language Coll
Automation Activity & Vendor Info: (Acquisitions) SirsiDynix; (Cataloging) SirsiDynix; (Circulation) SirsiDynix; (OPAC) SirsiDynix; (Serials) SirsiDynix
Wireless access
Partic in Midwest Collaborative for Library Services
Special Services for the Blind - Computer with voice synthesizer for visually impaired persons
Open Mon, Wed & Thurs 10-8, Tues 1-8, Fri 10-6, Sat 10-4, Sun (Winter) 1-5
Friends of the Library Group

GREENCASTLE

C DEPAUW UNIVERSITY*, Roy O West Library, 11 E Larrabee St, 46135. SAN 341-1990. Tel: 765-658-4420. FAX: 765-658-4017. Web Site: www.depauw.edu/library. *Dean,* Rick Provine; E-mail: provine@depauw.edu; *Archivist, Spec Coll Librn,* Wesley Wilson; *Cat,* Bruce Sanders; *Coll Develop,* Joyce Dixon-Fyle; Staff 19.5 (MLS 9.5, Non-MLS 10)
Founded 1837. Enrl 2,400; Fac 220; Highest Degree: Bachelor
Library Holdings: AV Mats 25,000; Bk Titles 400,000

Special Collections: Archives of DePauw University & Indiana United Methodism, doc, flm, ms; Bret Harte Library of First Editions; German (Bence Coll); Latin (Simison Coll); Pre-Law (Williams Coll), bks, per. Oral History; State Document Depository; US Document Depository
Subject Interests: Bus & mgt, Econ, Music
Automation Activity & Vendor Info: (Acquisitions) OCLC Worldshare Management Services; (Cataloging) OCLC Worldshare Management Services; (Circulation) OCLC Worldshare Management Services; (Discovery) OCLC Worldshare Management Services; (ILL) OCLC ILLiad; (OPAC) OCLC Worldshare Management Services
Wireless access
Partic in Midwest Collaborative for Library Services
Departmental Libraries:
PREVO LIBRARY, Julian Science & Math Ctr, 46135, SAN 341-2059. Tel: 765-658-4515. *Sci Librn,* Caroline Gilson; E-mail: cgilson@depauw.edu; Staff 3 (Non-MLS 3)
Automation Activity & Vendor Info: (OPAC) Ex Libris Group

P PUTNAM COUNTY PUBLIC LIBRARY*, 103 E Poplar St, 46135. (Mail add: PO Box 116, 46135-0116), SAN 304-9159. Tel: 765-653-2755. FAX: 765-653-2756. E-mail: refdesk@pcpl21.org. Web Site: pcpl21.org, www.putnam.lib.in.us. *Libr Dir,* Matt McClelland; E-mail: mmcclelland@pcpl21.org; Staff 7.6 (MLS 4.6, Non-MLS 3)
Founded 1902. Pop 37,000; Circ 248,610
Library Holdings: AV Mats 11,292; Large Print Bks 1,625; Bk Titles 63,244; Bk Vols 71,961; Per Subs 244
Special Collections: Oral History
Subject Interests: Genealogy, Local hist
Automation Activity & Vendor Info: (Acquisitions) Innovative Interfaces, Inc; (Cataloging) Innovative Interfaces, Inc; (Circulation) Innovative Interfaces, Inc; (OPAC) Innovative Interfaces, Inc
Wireless access
Function: Archival coll, Art exhibits, Bk club(s), Bks on CD, Children's prog, Computers for patron use, Free DVD rentals, Home delivery & serv to seniorr ctr & nursing homes, Jail serv, Music CDs, Online cat, Outreach serv, Photocopying/Printing, Preschool outreach, Prog for adults, Prog for children & young adult, Ref serv available, Scanner, Spoken cassettes & CDs, Spoken cassettes & DVDs, Story hour, Summer & winter reading prog, Tax forms, Telephone ref, Wheelchair accessible
Open Mon-Thurs 9-8, Fri & Sat 9-5
Friends of the Library Group
Bookmobiles: 1. Librn, Jane Glier. Bk titles 4,000

S PUTNAMVILLE CORRECTIONAL FACILITY, Recreation Library, 1946 W US 40, 46135-9275. SAN 304-9140. Tel: 765-653-8441. FAX: 765-653-4157. *Recreation Coord,* Randy M Dragan; Tel: 765-653-8441, Ext 466, E-mail: rdragan@idoc.in.gov; Staff 1 (Non-MLS 1)
Founded 1954
Library Holdings: Audiobooks 200; CDs 500; DVDs 1,300; Large Print Bks 20; Bk Titles 10,000; Bk Vols 11,000; Per Subs 24
Open Mon-Fri 7:30am-8:30pm

GREENFIELD

P HANCOCK COUNTY PUBLIC LIBRARY*, 900 W McKenzie Rd, 46140-1741. SAN 304-9167. Tel: 317-462-5141. Reference Tel: 317-467-6672. FAX: 317-462-5711. E-mail: hcpl@hcplibrary.org. Web Site: hcplibrary.org. *Dir,* Dave Gray; E-mail: dgray@hcplibrary.org; *Asst Dir,* Barbara Roark; Staff 53 (MLS 7, Non-MLS 46)
Founded 1898. Pop 48,497; Circ 634,072
Library Holdings: Bk Titles 140,000; Bk Vols 188,000; Per Subs 275
Special Collections: James Whitcomb Riley Coll, digitized
Subject Interests: Genealogy, Indiana
Automation Activity & Vendor Info: (Acquisitions) SirsiDynix; (Cataloging) SirsiDynix; (Circulation) SirsiDynix; (OPAC) SirsiDynix; (Serials) SirsiDynix
Wireless access
Function: Adult literacy prog, AV serv, Distance learning, Health sci info serv, Home delivery & serv to seniorr ctr & nursing homes, Homebound delivery serv, ILL available, Internet access, Magnifiers for reading, Photocopying/Printing, Prog for children & young adult, Ref serv available, Satellite serv, Serves people with intellectual disabilities, Summer reading prog, Telephone ref, Wheelchair accessible, Workshops
Publications: Newsletter (Monthly)
Partic in Midwest Collaborative for Library Services
Special Services for the Deaf - Bks on deafness & sign lang; High interest/low vocabulary bks
Special Services for the Blind - Audio mat; Bks on CD; Home delivery serv; Large print bks; Magnifiers; Talking bks; Volunteer serv
Open Mon-Thurs 9-9, Fri 9-6, Sat 9-5, Sun 1-4
Friends of the Library Group
Branches: 1
SUGAR CREEK BRANCH, 5087 W US 52, New Palestine, 46163. (Mail add: PO Box 262, New Palestine, 46163-8728). Tel: 317-861-6618. FAX: 317-861-2061. *Br Mgr,* Jeanette Sherfield; Tel: 317-861-6618, Ext 20
Library Holdings: Bk Vols 35,000
Open Mon-Thurs 9-8, Fri 9-6, Sat 9-5, Sun 1-4
Bookmobiles: 1

GREENSBURG

P GREENSBURG-DECATUR COUNTY PUBLIC LIBRARY*, 1110 E Main St, 47240. SAN 304-9183. Tel: 812-663-2826. FAX: 812-663-5617. E-mail: grefdesk@greensburglibrary.org. Web Site: www.greensburglibrary.org. *Libr Dir,* Vanessa Martin; E-mail: vmartin@greensburglibrary.org; *Ch,* Jill Pratt; E-mail: jpratt@greensburglibrary.org; *Pub Serv Mgr,* Lori Durbin; E-mail: ldurbin@greensburglibrary.org; Staff 8 (MLS 4, Non-MLS 4)
Founded 1905. Pop 24,555; Circ 250,594
Library Holdings: Audiobooks 5,430; AV Mats 8,699; Electronic Media & Resources 436; Bk Vols 109,701; Per Subs 206
Special Collections: Oral History
Subject Interests: Local hist
Automation Activity & Vendor Info: (Cataloging) Evergreen; (Circulation) Evergreen; (OPAC) Evergreen
Wireless access
Function: Audiobks via web, Bk club(s), Bks on cassette, Bks on CD, Children's prog, Computer training, Computers for patron use, Digital talking bks, Electronic databases & coll, Free DVD rentals, Holiday prog, Home delivery & serv to seniorr ctr & nursing homes, ILL available, Internet access, Music CDs, Notary serv, Online cat, OverDrive digital audio bks, Photocopying/Printing, Preschool outreach, Preschool reading prog, Printer for laptops & handheld devices, Prog for adults, Prog for children & young adult, Ref serv available, Scanner, Senior computer classes, Spanish lang bks, Story hour, Summer & winter reading prog, Summer reading prog, Tax forms, Teen prog
Open Mon-Thurs 9-6, Fri 9-5, Sat 9-1
Friends of the Library Group
Branches: 1
WESTPORT BRANCH, 205 W Main St, Westport, 47283-9601, SAN 371-3830. Tel: 812-591-2330. FAX: 812-591-2330. *Librn,* Deb Smith; E-mail: dsmith@greensburglibrary.org
Founded 1989. Circ 17,407
Open Mon-Thurs 2-8, Sat 9-1
Friends of the Library Group
Bookmobiles: 1

GREENTOWN

P GREENTOWN PUBLIC LIBRARY*, 421 S Harrison St, 46936. SAN 304-9191. Tel: 765-628-3534. FAX: 765-628-3759. Web Site: www.greentownlib.org. *Dir,* Mindy Hobensack; E-mail: mindy.hobensack@eastern.k12.in.us; Staff 8 (MLS 1, Non-MLS 7)
Founded 1919. Pop 6,000; Circ 123,249
Library Holdings: Bks on Deafness & Sign Lang 12; Large Print Bks 869; Bk Vols 47,575; Per Subs 170
Special Collections: Civil War Coll; Large Print Books Coll
Automation Activity & Vendor Info: (Circulation) Evergreen; (OPAC) Evergreen
Wireless access
Open Mon, Wed & Fri 8-4, Tues & Thurs 8-8, Sat 9-1

GREENWOOD

P GREENWOOD PUBLIC LIBRARY*, 310 S Meridian St, 46143-3135. SAN 304-9205. Tel: 317-881-1953. Web Site: www.greenwoodlibrary.us. *Dir,* Cheryl Dobbs; Tel: 317-883-4229, E-mail: cdobbs@greenwoodlibrary.us; *Head, Children's Servx,* Linda Oldham Messick; E-mail: lmessiak@greenwoodlibrary.us; *Head, Ref,* Emily Ellis; Tel: 317-883-4250, E-mail: eellis@greenwoodlibrary.us; *Head, Tech Serv,* Janet Buckley; E-mail: jbuckley@greenwoodlibrary.us; Staff 45 (MLS 14, Non-MLS 31)
Founded 1917. Pop 26,849; Circ 224,321
Library Holdings: AV Mats 6,000; Bk Vols 100,000; Per Subs 360
Automation Activity & Vendor Info: (Acquisitions) SirsiDynix; (Cataloging) SirsiDynix; (Circulation) SirsiDynix; (OPAC) SirsiDynix; (Serials) SirsiDynix
Wireless access
Function: Distance learning, Homebound delivery serv, ILL available, Magnifiers for reading, Prog for children & young adult, Ref serv available, Summer reading prog, Telephone ref, Wheelchair accessible
Partic in Evergreen Indiana Consortium; Ind Libr Asn; Midwest Collaborative for Library Services; Wisconsin Valley Library Service
Open Mon-Thurs 9-8, Fri & Sat 11-5
Friends of the Library Group

CR INDIANA BAPTIST COLLEGE LIBRARY*, Leon F Maurer Library, 1301 W County Line Rd, 46142. SAN 304-9612. Tel: 317-882-2327, 317-882-2345. FAX: 317-885-2960. E-mail: info@indianabaptistcollege.com. Web Site: www.indianabaptistcollege.com. *Libr Serv Mgr,* Edna Kehrt; Staff 1 (Non-MLS 1)
Founded 1955. Enrl 130; Fac 23; Highest Degree: Doctorate
Library Holdings: Bk Titles 21,116; Bk Vols 23,410; Per Subs 33
Special Collections: Carl Byrd Antiquarian Coll
Subject Interests: Relig
Open Mon-Fri 8:30-5

HAGERSTOWN

P HAGERSTOWN JEFFERSON TOWNSHIP LIBRARY, Ten W College St, 47346. SAN 304-9213. Tel: 765-489-5632. FAX: 765-489-5808. E-mail: info@hagerstownlibrary.org. Web Site: www.hagerstownlibrary.org. *Dir,* Brenda J Campbell; E-mail: director@hagerstownlibrary.org; *Adult & Teen Serv, Tech Serv,* Jennifer Taylor; E-mail: jtaylor@hagerstownlibrary.org; *Cat, Coll Develop,* Karen Stuffel; E-mail: kstuffel@hagerstownlibrary.org; *Youth Serv,* Janette Richards; E-mail: jrichards@hagerstownlibrary.org; Staff 5 (MLS 1, Non-MLS 4)
Founded 1928. Pop 3,427; Circ 73,706
Jan 2015-Dec 2015 Income $249,767. Mats Exp $49,500, Books $35,000, Per/Ser (Incl. Access Fees) $4,000, AV Mat $9,000, Electronic Ref Mat (Incl. Access Fees) $1,500. Sal $97,912 (Prof $36,858)
Library Holdings: Audiobooks 72; Bks on Deafness & Sign Lang 13; CDs 126; DVDs 1,024; Large Print Bks 502; Bk Titles 33,410; Per Subs 81; Videos 1,200
Special Collections: Indiana Coll, bks, microfilm, newspaper
Automation Activity & Vendor Info: (Cataloging) Evergreen; (Circulation) Evergreen; (OPAC) Evergreen
Wireless access
Function: 24/7 Electronic res, 24/7 Online cat, Adult bk club, Archival coll, Audio & video playback equip for onsite use, Audiobks on Playaways & MP3, Audiobks via web, AV serv, Bk club(s), Bks on CD, Children's prog, Computers for patron use, Electronic databases & coll, Equip loans & repairs, Family literacy, Free DVD rentals, Games & aids for people with disabilities, Govt ref serv, Holiday prog, Homebound delivery serv, ILL available, Internet access, Laminating, Magazines, Magnifiers for reading, Mail & tel request accepted, Museum passes, Music CDs, Notary serv, Online cat, Outreach serv, Outside serv via phone, mail, e-mail & web, OverDrive digital audio bks, Photocopying/Printing, Preschool outreach, Preschool reading prog, Prof lending libr, Prog for adults, Prog for children & young adult, Ref serv available, Scanner, Story hour, Summer & winter reading prog, Summer reading prog, Tax forms, Teen prog, Telephone ref, VHS videos, Wheelchair accessible, Winter reading prog, Writing prog
Partic in Evergreen Indiana Consortium; Midwest Collaborative for Library Services
Special Services for the Deaf - Bks on deafness & sign lang; Closed caption videos
Special Services for the Blind - Bks on cassette; Bks on CD; Large print bks
Open Mon, Tues, Thurs & Fri 10-6, Wed 10-3, Sat 10-2
Restriction: Non-resident fee
Friends of the Library Group

HAMMOND

P HAMMOND PUBLIC LIBRARY*, 564 State St, 46320-1532. SAN 341-2113. Tel: 219-931-5100. FAX: 219-931-3474. E-mail: hpl@hammond.lib.in.us. Web Site: www.hammond.lib.in.us. *Dir,* Rene L Greenleaf; Tel: 219-931-5100, Ext 305, E-mail: greenr@hammond.lib.in.us; *Asst Dir,* Carol L Williams; Tel: 219-931-5100, Ext 345, E-mail: willic@hammond.lib.in.us; *Head, Circ,* Sherri Ervin; Tel: 219-931-5100, Ext 328, E-mail: ervins@hammond.lib.in.us; *Head, Res,* Jenny Bean; Tel: 219-931-5100, Ext 329, E-mail: beanj@hammond.lib.in.us; *Head, Youth Serv,* Allison Piech; Tel: 219-931-5100, Ext 330, E-mail: piecha@hammond.lib.in.us; Staff 18 (MLS 12, Non-MLS 6)
Founded 1902. Pop 83,048; Circ 187,020
Library Holdings: AV Mats 3,461; DVDs 11,158; e-books 45,278; Bk Vols 166,824; Per Subs 66
Special Collections: Hammond Area History (Susan G Long, Local History Room), a-tapes, bks, maps, monographs, pictures, photog, videos. Oral History; US Document Depository
Automation Activity & Vendor Info: (Acquisitions) TLC (The Library Corporation); (Cataloging) TLC (The Library Corporation); (Circulation) TLC (The Library Corporation); (ILL) OCLC; (OPAC) TLC (The Library Corporation); (Serials) EBSCO Online
Wireless access
Function: 24/7 Electronic res, 24/7 Online cat, Adult bk club, Archival coll, Art exhibits, Audiobks via web, AV serv, Bk club(s), Bks on CD, Chess club, Children's prog, Computer training, Computers for patron use, E-Readers, Electronic databases & coll, For res purposes, Free DVD rentals, Genealogy discussion group, Govt ref serv, Holiday prog, Home delivery & serv to seniorr ctr & nursing homes, Homebound delivery serv, Homework prog, ILL available, Internet access, Life-long learning prog for all ages, Magazines, Mail & tel request accepted, Mango lang, Meeting rooms, Microfiche/film & reading machines, Movies, Music CDs, Online cat, Online info literacy tutorials on the web & in blackboard, Online ref, Outreach serv, OverDrive digital audio bks, Photocopying/Printing, Preschool outreach, Preschool reading prog, Printer for laptops & handheld devices, Prof lending libr, Prog for adults, Prog for children & young adult, Ref & res, Ref serv available, Scanner, Senior computer classes, Senior outreach, Spanish lang bks, STEM programs, Story hour, Study rm, Summer & winter reading prog, Summer reading prog, Tax forms, Teen prog, Telephone ref, Wheelchair accessible, Winter reading prog
Publications: Bookends
Partic in Midwest Collaborative for Library Services
Open Mon-Thurs 9-9, Fri & Sat 9-5
Friends of the Library Group

C PURDUE UNIVERSITY*, Northwest Library, 2200 169th St, 46323-2094. SAN 304-9272. Tel: 219-989-2224. Interlibrary Loan Service Tel: 219-989-2720. Toll Free Tel: 855-608-4600, Ext 2224. FAX: 219-989-2253. Web Site: library.pnw.edu. *Dir, Univ Libr,* Tammy S Guerrero; Tel: 219-989-2675, E-mail: tsguerre@pnw.edu; *Assoc Dir,* LaShawn M Jones; Tel: 219-989-2138, E-mail: joneslm@purduecal.edu; *Educ Librn,* Sheila A Rezak; Tel: 219-989-2677, E-mail: sarezak@purduecal.edu; *Sci & Bus Librn,* Sammy Chapman, Jr; Tel: 219-989-2903, E-mail: schapma@purduecal.edu; Staff 19 (MLS 6, Non-MLS 13)
Founded 1947. Enrl 9,325; Fac 531; Highest Degree: Master
Library Holdings: Bks on Deafness & Sign Lang 126; CDs 5; DVDs 412; e-books 2,993; e-journals 9,039; Electronic Media & Resources 1,058; Large Print Bks 54; Microforms 792,765; Music Scores 7; Bk Titles 256,194; Bk Vols 269,280; Per Subs 603; Videos 850
Special Collections: Archives (Non-Current University Records); Calumet Region Materials. US Document Depository
Automation Activity & Vendor Info: (Acquisitions) Ex Libris Group; (Cataloging) OCLC; (Circulation) Ex Libris Group; (Course Reserve) Ex Libris Group; (ILL) OCLC; (OPAC) Ex Libris Group; (Serials) Ex Libris Group
Wireless access
Partic in Academic Libraries of Indiana; LYRASIS; Midwest Collaborative for Library Services; OCLC Online Computer Library Center, Inc
Special Services for the Deaf - Assistive tech
Special Services for the Blind - Braille equip; Dragon Naturally Speaking software; Internet workstation with adaptive software
Open Mon-Thurs 8am-10pm, Fri 8-5, Sat 10-2, Sun 12-8

HANOVER

C HANOVER COLLEGE*, Duggan Library, 121 Scenic Dr, 47243. SAN 304-9302. Tel: 812-866-7165. Reference Tel: 812-866-7171. FAX: 812-866-7172. Web Site: library.hanover.edu. *Dir,* Kelly Joyce; Tel: 812-866-7160, E-mail: joyce@hanover.edu; *Head, Cat,* Alynza Henderson; E-mail: henderson@hanover.edu; *Access Serv Librn,* Michael Ellis; Tel: 812-866-7169; *Archivist & Curator of Rare Bks,* Jen Duplaga; Tel: 812-866-7181, E-mail: duplaga@hanover.edu; *Circ Asst,* Patricia Lawrence; Tel: 812-866-7176, E-mail: lawrence@hanover.edu; *Govt Doc,* Reiley Noe; *Info Serv,* Heather Loehr; Tel: 812-866-7170, E-mail: loehr@hanover.edu; Staff 7 (MLS 5, Non-MLS 2)
Founded 1827. Enrl 920; Fac 100; Highest Degree: Bachelor
Special Collections: Church History (Archives of the Presbyterian Church of Indiana) bks, micro; Civil War (Daugherty Coll); Hanover College Archives; Indiana History (I M Bridgman Coll); Judith Moffett Papers; Pacifica & Northwest Exploration (Dr Ronald Kleopfer Coll); Senator William E Jenner Papers. US Document Depository
Automation Activity & Vendor Info: (Acquisitions) OCLC Worldshare Management Services; (Cataloging) OCLC Worldshare Management Services; (Circulation) OCLC Worldshare Management Services; (Discovery) OCLC Worldshare Management Services; (ILL) OCLC WorldShare Interlibrary Loan; (OPAC) OCLC WorldShare Interlibrary Loan; (Serials) OCLC Worldshare Management Services
Wireless access
Function: Govt ref serv
Partic in Academic Libraries of Indiana; LYRASIS; Midwest Collaborative for Library Services; OCLC Online Computer Library Center, Inc; OCLC-LVIS; Private Academic Library Network of Indiana
Restriction: 24-hr pass syst for students only

HARTFORD CITY

P HARTFORD CITY PUBLIC LIBRARY*, 314 N High St, 47348-2143. SAN 304-9310. Tel: 765-348-1720. FAX: 765-348-5090. E-mail: info@hartfordcity.lib.in.us. Web Site: hartfordcity.lib.in.us. *Dir,* Michele Risinger; E-mail: director@hartfordcity.lib.in.us; Staff 11 (MLS 1, Non-MLS 10)
Founded 1903. Pop 7,122; Circ 166,660

Library Holdings: AV Mats 3,100; Large Print Bks 98; Bk Titles 61,914; Bk Vols 63,411; Per Subs 321; Talking Bks 71; Videos 1,040
Special Collections: Indiana Genealogy Coll; Music (George Leonard Fulton Memorial Record Library)
Subject Interests: Genealogy, Indiana
Automation Activity & Vendor Info: (ILL) Follett Software
Wireless access
Function: ILL available
Partic in Evergreen Indiana Consortium
Open Mon-Thurs 9-7, Fri 9-5:30, Sat 9-2
Friends of the Library Group

HOBART

S HOBART HISTORICAL SOCIETY, INC*, Mariam Pleak Library, 706 E Fourth St, 46342. (Mail add: PO Box 24, 46342-0024), SAN 304-9337. Tel: 219-942-0970. *Archivist, Curator,* Rita McBride
Founded 1973
Library Holdings: Bk Titles 500; Per Subs 10
Special Collections: Genealogy; Local Newspapers; Photographs
Subject Interests: Hist, Indiana, Local hist
Open Sat 10-12

HUNTINGBURG

P HUNTINGBURG PUBLIC LIBRARY*, 419 N Jackson St, 47542. SAN 304-9345. Tel: 812-683-2052. FAX: 812-683-2056. Web Site: www.huntingburg.lib.in.us. *Dir,* Lisa McWilliams; E-mail: director@huntingburg.lib.in.us; Staff 6 (Non-MLS 6)
Founded 1922. Pop 7,178; Circ 71,402
Library Holdings: Bk Vols 34,394; Per Subs 87
Automation Activity & Vendor Info: (Cataloging) SirsiDynix; (Circulation) SirsiDynix; (OPAC) SirsiDynix
Wireless access
Partic in Evergreen Indiana Consortium; Midwest Collaborative for Library Services
Open Mon-Thurs 9-8, Fri 9-6, Sat 9-2

HUNTINGTON

P HUNTINGTON CITY-TOWNSHIP PUBLIC LIBRARY*, 255 W Park Dr, 46750. SAN 304-9353. Tel: 260-356-0824. FAX: 260-356-3073. E-mail: ask@hctpl.info. Web Site: huntingtonpub.lib.in.us. *Dir,* Rebecca Lemons; E-mail: rlemons@hctpl.info
Founded 1903. Pop 23,000; Circ 167,347
Library Holdings: Bk Titles 110,640; Bk Vols 148,000; Per Subs 186; Talking Bks 3,000
Special Collections: Genealogy; Local & State History; Trains Coll
Automation Activity & Vendor Info: (Acquisitions) SirsiDynix; (Cataloging) SirsiDynix; (Circulation) SirsiDynix
Wireless access
Partic in Midwest Collaborative for Library Services
Open Mon-Thurs 9-8, Fri & Sat 9-5
Friends of the Library Group
Branches: 1
MARKLE PUBLIC LIBRARY, 197 E Morse St, Markle, 46770. (Mail add: PO Box 578, Markle, 46770-0578), SAN 376-5342. Tel: 260-758-3332. FAX: 260-758-3332. *Dir,* Kathryn Holst; Staff 5 (MLS 1, Non-MLS 4)
Founded 1937. Pop 1,259; Circ 5,689
Library Holdings: AV Mats 750; Bk Titles 8,914; Bk Vols 11,610; Per Subs 56; Talking Bks 59; Videos 359
Open Mon, Tues, Thurs & Fri 1-7, Wed 10-12 & 1-7, Sat 9-12

CR HUNTINGTON UNIVERSITY*, RichLyn Library, 2303 College Ave, 46750. SAN 304-9361. Tel: 260-359-4060. Circulation Tel: 260-359-4054. Interlibrary Loan Service Tel: 260-359-4061. FAX: 260-358-3698. Web Site: www.huntington.edu/library. *Dir, Libr Serv,* Anita L Gray; Tel: 260-359-4063, E-mail: agray@huntington.edu; *Assoc Dir, Libr Serv,* Randy Neuman; E-mail: rneuman@huntington.edu; *Info Literacy Librn, User Serv Librn,* Carrie Halquist; E-mail: chalquist@huntington.edu
Founded 1897. Enrl 950; Fac 55; Highest Degree: Master
Library Holdings: Bk Vols 180,000
Special Collections: Archives of Huntington College; Curriculum Materials Center; United Brethren in Christ Church. US Document Depository
Automation Activity & Vendor Info: (Acquisitions) Ex Libris Group; (Cataloging) Ex Libris Group; (Circulation) Ex Libris Group; (Course Reserve) Ex Libris Group; (OPAC) Ex Libris Group; (Serials) Ex Libris Group
Wireless access
Partic in Midwest Collaborative for Library Services; OCLC Online Computer Library Center, Inc; Private Academic Library Network of Indiana
Special Services for the Blind - ZoomText magnification & reading software
Open Mon-Thurs 8am-11pm, Fri 8-5, Sat 12-5, Sun 2-11

INDIANAPOLIS

SR ALL SOULS UNITARIAN CHURCH, E Burdette Backus Memorial Library, 5805 E 56th St, 46226-1526. SAN 304-937X. Tel: 317-545-6005. E-mail: office@allsoulsindy.org. Web Site: www.allsoulsindy.org. *Committee Chair,* Diane O'Brien; E-mail: robrien25@comcast.net
Library Holdings: Bk Titles 1,290; Bk Vols 1,398; Per Subs 11
Subject Interests: Comparative relig, Philos, Relig, Soc sci & issues, Unitarianism
Wireless access
Restriction: Not open to pub

S AMERICAN LEGION NATIONAL HEADQUARTERS LIBRARY*, 700 N Pennsylvania St, 4th Flr, 46204. (Mail add: PO Box 1055, 46206-1055), SAN 304-9388. Tel: 317-630-1366. FAX: 317-630-1241. E-mail: library@legion.org. Web Site: www.legion.org/library. *Dir, Libr & Mus Serv,* Howard Trace; Staff 6 (MLS 2, Non-MLS 4)
Founded 1923
Library Holdings: Microforms 1,200; Bk Vols 12,000
Special Collections: Archives of The American Legion National Organization; National Defense; Patriotism (1919-date); Veterans' Affairs; World War I & II Posters
Subject Interests: Mil hist
Automation Activity & Vendor Info: (Cataloging) Inmagic, Inc.; (Circulation) Inmagic, Inc.; (Serials) Inmagic, Inc.
Restriction: Access at librarian's discretion, Authorized scholars by appt, Circulates for staff only, Non-circulating, Restricted access

S EDWARD A BLOCK FAMILY LIBRARY*, 705 Riley Hospital Dr, Rm 1719, 46202-5109. SAN 304-9809. Tel: 317-944-1149. FAX: 317-948-1631. E-mail: rilibrary@iuhealth.org. Web Site: www.rileychildrens.org/support-services/edward-a-block-family-library. *Librn,* Dena Vincent; E-mail: dvincent@iuhealth.org; Staff 1 (MLS 1)
Founded 1922
Library Holdings: Bks on Deafness & Sign Lang 6; CDs 315; DVDs 1,519; Per Subs 179
Special Collections: Lay Medical Information for children and parents, Accelerated Reader books, Early Reader books
Wireless access
Function: 24/7 Online cat, Bks on CD, CD-ROM, Children's prog, Free DVD rentals, Magazines, Movies, Music CDs, Online cat, Ref & res, Ref serv available, Res assist avail, Story hour, Summer reading prog
Open Mon-Fri 9-5
Restriction: In-house use for visitors, Internal circ only
Friends of the Library Group

L BOSE MCKINNEY & EVANS LLP*, Knowledge & Research Services, 111 Monument Circle, Ste 2700, 46204. SAN 372-1213. Tel: 317-684-5166. FAX: 317-223-0166. Web Site: www.boselaw.com. *Dir, Knowledge & Res Serv,* Cheryl Lynn Niemeier; E-mail: cniemeier@boselaw.com; *Res Serv Spec,* Michayla Sullivan; E-mail: mssullivan@boselaw.com. Subject Specialists: *Electronic, Res,* Michayla Sullivan; Staff 2 (MLS 2)
Library Holdings: Bk Vols 27,000; Per Subs 150
Subject Interests: Bus operations, Civil rights, Intellectual property, Labor, Litigation, Securities, Tax
Automation Activity & Vendor Info: (Acquisitions) LibraryWorld, Inc; (Cataloging) OCLC Online; (Circulation) LibraryWorld, Inc; (ILL) OCLC Online; (OPAC) LibraryWorld, Inc; (Serials) LibraryWorld, Inc
Function: For res purposes, ILL available
Restriction: Co libr, Not open to pub, Private libr, Prof mat only, Staff use only

C BUTLER UNIVERSITY LIBRARIES, Irwin Library, 4600 Sunset Ave, 46208. SAN 341-2474. Tel: 317-940-9227. Interlibrary Loan Service Tel: 317-940-9677. Reference Tel: 317-940-9235. Administration Tel: 317-940-9714. FAX: 317-940-9711. Web Site: www.butler.edu/library. *Dean of Libr,* Julie R Miller; E-mail: jlmille5@butler.edu; *Assoc Dean, Colls & Digital Services,* Josh Petrusa; Tel: 317-940-9236, E-mail: jpetrusa@butler.edu; *Assoc Dean, Instruction & User Servs,* Sally Neal; Tel: 317-940-9949, E-mail: sneal@butler.edu; *Collections Strategy Librn,* Vanessa French; Tel: 317-940-6491, E-mail: vfrench@butler.edu; *Scholarly Communications Librn,* Jennifer Coronado; Tel: 317-940-9549, E-mail: jraye@butler.edu; *Spec Coll & Archives Librn,* Sally Childs-Helton; Tel: 317-940-9265, E-mail: schildsh@butler.edu; *Visual & Performing Arts Librn,* Sarah Ward; Tel: 317-940-9218, E-mail: srward@butler.edu; Staff 24 (MLS 12, Non-MLS 12)
Founded 1855. Enrl 4,246; Fac 305; Highest Degree: Master
Library Holdings: AV Mats 18,000; e-books 500,000; e-journals 35,000; Music Scores 16,000; Bk Titles 215,000; Bk Vols 359,470; Per Subs 538

Special Collections: 19th Century American Sheet Music; 20th Century American Poetry, bks, ms; Abraham Lincoln, bks, ms, pamphlets, prints; Botanical & Zoological Prints 16th-19th Century; Jean Sibelius, publ & unpubl scores, recordings & secondary sources; Kin Hubbard-Gaar Williams Coll of Original Cartoons, bks, ms, memorabilia; Mme de Stael Research Coll; National Track & Field Historical Research Library; Pacific Islands 16th-20th Century; Rare Books Coll, bks, ms, prints; USABA Archives. US Document Depository
Automation Activity & Vendor Info: (Acquisitions) Ex Libris Group; (Cataloging) Ex Libris Group; (Circulation) Ex Libris Group; (Course Reserve) Ex Libris Group; (OPAC) Ex Libris Group; (Serials) Ex Libris Group
Wireless access
Publications: Catalogues of Special Collections; New Acquisitions List
Partic in Academic Libraries of Indiana; LYRASIS; Private Academic Library Network of Indiana
Open Mon-Thurs 8am-Midnight, Fri 8-8, Sat 12-8, Sun Noon-Midnight

Departmental Libraries:

RUTH LILLY SCIENCE LIBRARY, 740 W 46th St, 46208-3485. Tel: 317-940-9401. Web Site: www.butler.edu/library/spaces/science. *Dean of Libr,* Lewis R Miller; Tel: 317-940-9714, E-mail: lmiller@butler.edu; *Science Library Assoc,* Annette Huyumba; Tel: 317-940-9415, E-mail: amuyumba@butler.edu; Staff 1 (MLS 1)
Subject Interests: Chem, Math
Open Mon-Fri 9-5

R CHRIST CHURCH CATHEDRAL*, Margaret Ridgely Memorial Library, 125 Monument Circle, 46204-2921. SAN 304-9485. Tel: 317-636-4577. FAX: 317-635-1040. Web Site: www.cccindy.org. *Library Contact,* Mathew Stevenson; E-mail: stevenson.matthew@gmail.com
Founded 1928
Library Holdings: Bk Titles 3,370; Bk Vols 3,510; Per Subs 39
Subject Interests: Relig
Publications: Acquisitions List (Quarterly)
Open Mon-Fri 9-3
Friends of the Library Group

R CHRISTIAN THEOLOGICAL SEMINARY*, CTS Library, 1000 W 42nd St, 46208. SAN 304-9507. Tel: 317-924-1331. Circulation Tel: 317-931-2361. Reference Tel: 317-931-2367. Toll Free Tel: 800-585-0108. FAX: 317-931-2363. E-mail: research@cts.edu. Web Site: cts.libguides.com/library. *Dir,* Anthony Elia; Tel: 317-931-2365, E-mail: aelia@cts.edu; *Head, Pub Serv, Ser Librn,* Cheryl Miller Maddox; E-mail: cmaddox@cts.edu; *Sysy & Acad Tech Librn,* Dr Alan R Rhoda; Tel: 317-931-2362, E-mail: arhoda@cts.edu; *Acq Mgr, Admin Serv,* Rebecca Furnish; Tel: 317-931-2370, E-mail: rfurnish@cts.edu; *Archives, Spec Coll,* Dr Scott Seay; Tel: 317-931-2347, E-mail: sseay@cts.edu; Staff 4 (MLS 3, Non-MLS 1)
Founded 1942. Enrl 200; Fac 10; Highest Degree: Doctorate
Library Holdings: Bk Vols 220,000; Per Subs 700
Special Collections: Disciples of Christ History (Literature of the Restoration Movement), bks, ms, per
Subject Interests: Culture, Hist, Music, Relig, Soc sci & issues, Theol
Automation Activity & Vendor Info: (Circulation) OCLC Worldshare Management Services; (Discovery) OCLC Worldshare Management Services
Wireless access
Publications: Encounter (Quarterly)
Partic in Academic Libraries of Indiana; Midwest Collaborative for Library Services; OCLC Online Computer Library Center, Inc; Private Academic Library Network of Indiana
Special Services for the Blind - Audio mat

M COMMUNITY HEALTH NETWORK LIBRARY*, 1500 N Ritter Ave, 46219. SAN 304-9515. Tel: 317-355-3600. Interlibrary Loan Service Tel: 317-355-5504. FAX: 317-351-7816. E-mail: library@ecommunity.com. Web Site: www.ecommunity.com/locations/community-hospital-east. *Circuit Librn,* Amy Hughes; E-mail: ahughes2@ecommunity.com; Staff 4 (MLS 3, Non-MLS 1)
Founded 1960
Library Holdings: e-books 100; e-journals 2,000; Bk Titles 2,781; Bk Vols 3,190; Per Subs 349
Subject Interests: Bus & mgt, Med, Nursing
Automation Activity & Vendor Info: (Acquisitions) LibraryWorld, Inc; (Cataloging) LibraryWorld, Inc; (Circulation) LibraryWorld, Inc; (Course Reserve) ADLiB; (OPAC) LibraryWorld, Inc; (Serials) EBSCO Online
Wireless access
Function: ILL available, Internet access, Online info literacy tutorials on the web & in blackboard, Online ref, Ref serv available
Partic in Health Sci Libr Network; Midwest Collaborative for Library Services
Open Mon-Fri 8:30-5
Restriction: 24-hr pass syst for students only, Access for corporate affiliates, Authorized patrons, Authorized scholars by appt, Badge access after hrs, Circ limited, External users must contact libr, Hospital staff & commun, ID required to use computers (Ltd hrs), Med & nursing staff, patients & families, Med staff & students

R CONGREGATION BETH-EL ZEDECK*, Alpert-Solotken Library, 600 W 70th St, 46260. SAN 329-2762. Tel: 317-253-3441. FAX: 317-259-6849. Web Site: bez613.org/learn/library. *Librn,* Mickki Ashworth; E-mail: librarian@bez613.org; Staff 1 (Non-MLS 1)
Founded 1964
Library Holdings: Bk Titles 6,200; Bk Vols 6,400; Per Subs 15
Subject Interests: Judaica
Wireless access
Restriction: Mem only

CR CROSSROADS BIBLE COLLEGE*, Kathryn Ulmer Library, 3500 Depauw Blvd, 46268. SAN 327-974X. Tel: 317-789-8268. Toll Free Tel: 800-822-3119. FAX: 317-352-9145. *Operations Assoc, User Serv,* Joshua Wagner; E-mail: Joshua.Wagner@cbshouston.edu; Staff 1 (Non-MLS 1)
Founded 1980. Enrl 150; Fac 4; Highest Degree: Bachelor
Library Holdings: Bk Vols 5,500
Special Collections: African American History & the Black Church Coll
Subject Interests: Culture, Ethics, Hist, Philos, Theol
Wireless access
Function: 24/7 Electronic res, 24/7 Online cat, Adult literacy prog, Audio & video playback equip for onsite use, Computer training, Computers for patron use, Electronic databases & coll, Internet access, Music CDs, Online cat, Online ref, Res assist avail
Open Mon-Thurs 10-8

GM DEPARTMENT OF VETERANS AFFAIRS*, Health Science Library, 1481 W Tenth St, 46202. SAN 304-985X. Tel: 317-554-0000. FAX: 317-988-4846. *Librn,* Theresa Nolley
Founded 1952
Library Holdings: AV Mats 1,500; Bk Vols 6,050; Per Subs 500
Subject Interests: Allied health, Med, Nursing
Automation Activity & Vendor Info: (Acquisitions) EOS International; (Cataloging) EOS International; (Circulation) EOS International; (OPAC) EOS International; (Serials) EOS International
Partic in National Network of Libraries of Medicine Region 6
Open Mon-Fri 8-4:30

L KRIEG DEVAULT LLP LIBRARY*, One Indiana Sq, Ste 2800, 46204-2079. SAN 323-5920. Tel: 317-636-4341. Reference Tel: 317-238-6367. FAX: 317-636-1507. Web Site: www.kriegdevault.com. *Librn,* Ann Levy; Staff 2 (MLS 1, Non-MLS 1)
Library Holdings: Bk Titles 20,108; Bk Vols 22,707; Per Subs 36
Partic in Midwest Collaborative for Library Services
Restriction: Not open to pub, Staff use only

S DOW AGROSCIENCES*, Information Management Center, 9330 Zionsville Rd, 46268. SAN 375-3972. Tel: 317-337-3517. FAX: 317-337-3245. *Mgr,* Margaret B Hentz; E-mail: mhentz@dow.com; Staff 5 (MLS 3, Non-MLS 2)
Library Holdings: Bk Titles 5,000; Per Subs 70
Subject Interests: Agr, Organic chem
Partic in Midwest Collaborative for Library Services
Restriction: Staff use only

R DOWNEY AVENUE CHRISTIAN CHURCH, Lois Leamon Library, 111 S Downey Ave, 46219. SAN 328-2015. Tel: 317-359-5304. E-mail: frontdesk@downeyavenuechristianchurch.com. Web Site: downeyavenuechristianchurch.com/.
Library Holdings: Bk Titles 1,025; Bk Vols 1,300; Per Subs 22
Open Mon-Thurs 9-3

S EITELJORG MUSEUM OF AMERICAN INDIANS & WESTERN ART*, Watanabe Family Library, 500 W Washington St, 46204-2707. SAN 325-6820. Tel: 317-636-9378, Ext 1346. FAX: 317-264-1446. Web Site: eiteljorg.org/?s=library. *Librn,* Suzanne Braun-McGee; Tel: 317-275-1347, E-mail: sbraun-mcgee@eiteljorg.com; Staff 1 (MLS 1)
Library Holdings: CDs 55; DVDs 40; Bk Vols 7,000; Per Subs 13; Videos 540
Special Collections: The Sidney & Rosalyn Wiener Coll, bks, illustrations, pers
Subject Interests: Am Western art, hist & culture, Native Am art, hist & culture
Partic in Midwest Collaborative for Library Services; OCLC Online Computer Library Center, Inc
Restriction: Open by appt only

M FRANCISCAN HEALTH INDIANAPOLIS*, Medical Library, 8111 S Emerson Ave, 46237. SAN 304-8020. Tel: 317-528-7136. FAX: 317-782-6934. Web Site:

franciscanhealth.org/healthcare-facilities/franciscan-health-indianapolis-9. *Mgr, Libr Serv,* Position Currently Open
Founded 1972
Library Holdings: Bk Vols 500; Per Subs 180
Subject Interests: Nursing
Automation Activity & Vendor Info: (Serials) LibraryWorld, Inc
Wireless access
Partic in Cent Ind Health Sci Libr Asn; Ind Health Libr Asn; Ind State Libr Asn; Medical Library Association
Open Mon-Fri 8-4:30

SR FREE METHODIST CHURCH - USA*, Marston Memorial Historical Center & Archives, 770 N High School Rd, 46214. SAN 326-5552. Tel: 317-244-3660. Toll Free Tel: 800-342-5531. FAX: 317-244-1247. E-mail: history@fmcusa.org. Web Site: fmcusa.org/historical. *Dir,* Cathy Robling; E-mail: cathy.robling@fmcusa.org; *Digital Librn,* Kyle Moran; E-mail: kyle.moran@fmcusa.org; *Archivist,* Julianne Class; E-mail: julianne.class@fmcusa.org; Staff 3 (MLS 2, Non-MLS 1)
Founded 1969
Jan 2020-Dec 2020 Income $83,000, Locally Generated Income $25,000, Parent Institution $58,000. Mats Exp $95,000. Sal $66,183
Library Holdings: AV Mats 1,901; DVDs 146; Microforms 100; Bk Titles 11,191; Bk Vols 12,470; Per Subs 2; Videos 170
Special Collections: Methodism (John Wesley Coll), Wesleyana Material, Free Methodist Memoribilia. Oral History
Wireless access
Function: Res libr
Publications: FM History Update (Online only); Free Methodist Historical Society (Newsletter)
Partic in Evergreen Indiana Consortium
Restriction: Open by appt only
Friends of the Library Group

L ICE MILLER LLP*, Law Library, One American Sq, Ste 2900, 46282-0020. SAN 321-7698. Tel: 317-236-2100. Web Site: www.icemiller.com. *Dir, Knowledge Mgt,* Ms Lynn Fogle; Tel: 317-236-2472, Fax: 317-592-4281, E-mail: lynn.fogle@icemiller.com; Staff 5 (MLS 2, Non-MLS 3)
Founded 1910
Library Holdings: Bk Titles 27,891; Bk Vols 30,000; Per Subs 71
Subject Interests: Law, State law
Automation Activity & Vendor Info: (Acquisitions) EOS International; (Cataloging) EOS International; (OPAC) EOS International; (Serials) EOS International
Wireless access
Partic in Midwest Collaborative for Library Services; OCLC Online Computer Library Center, Inc
Open Mon-Fri 8:30-5
Restriction: Clients only

S INDIANA ACADEMY OF SCIENCE, John Shepard Wright Memorial Library, Indiana State Library, 140 N Senate Ave, 46204. SAN 373-0530. Tel: 317-232-3686. FAX: 317-232-3728. Web Site: www.indianaacademyofscience.org/resource-center/john-s-wright-library. *Head Librn,* Jocelyn Lewis; E-mail: jlewis2@library.in.gov
Founded 1885
Library Holdings: Bk Vols 13,000
Subject Interests: Natural hist
Wireless access
Open Mon-Wed & Fri 8-4:30, Thurs 8-7, Sat 8-4

S INDIANA CHAMBER OF COMMERCE*, Business Research & Information Center, 115 W Washington St S, Ste 850, 46204-3497. SAN 329-1162. Tel: 317-264-3110. FAX: 317-264-6855. Web Site: www.indianachamber.com. *Head, Res Ctr,* Michelle Kavanaugh; E-mail: mkavanaugh@indianachamber.com; Staff 2 (MLS 1, Non-MLS 1)
Library Holdings: Bk Titles 200; Bk Vols 300; Per Subs 100
Special Collections: Indiana Companies & Unions
Subject Interests: Econ, Employee benefits, Employee relations, Mkt, Unions
Publications: Top 200 Indiana Employers
Restriction: Mem only, Staff use only

S INDIANA DEPARTMENT OF ENVIRONMENTAL MANAGEMENT*, Office of Legal Counsel Library, 100 N Senate Ave, IGCN 1307, 46204-2215. SAN 329-4897. Tel: 317-232-8753. FAX: 317-233-5517. Web Site: www.in.gov/idem. *Library Contact,* Karen Willever; E-mail: kwilleve@idem.in.gov
Library Holdings: Bk Titles 320; Per Subs 1
Subject Interests: Environ, Pollution
Open Mon-Fri 8:30-4

M INDIANA HAND TO SHOULDER CENTER LIBRARY*, Ruth Lilly Hand Surgery Library, 8501 Harcourt Rd, 46260-2046. SAN 372-6436. Tel: 317-471-4340. Web Site: indianahandtoshoulder.com. *Librn,* Elaine N Skopelja; E-mail: eskopelja@ihtsc.com; Staff 1 (MLS 1)
Founded 1980
Library Holdings: DVDs 100; Bk Vols 1,400; Per Subs 16; Videos 200
Special Collections: Hand Rehabilitation; Surgery of Upper Extremity
Subject Interests: Orthopedic surgery
Automation Activity & Vendor Info: (Cataloging) LibraryWorld, Inc; (OPAC) LibraryWorld, Inc
Wireless access
Function: Doc delivery serv, For res purposes, Internet access, Online cat, Online ref
Partic in National Network of Libraries of Medicine Region 6
Restriction: Staff use only

S INDIANA HISTORICAL SOCIETY LIBRARY, William Henry Smith Memorial Library, 450 W Ohio St, 46202-3269. SAN 304-9639. Tel: 317-232-0321, Ext 3. Toll Free Tel: 800-447-1830. FAX: 317-234-0168. TDD: 317-233-6615. Web Site: www.indianahistory.org/explore/our-collections/using-our-library. *VPres, Archives & Libr,* Suzanne Hahn; Tel: 317-234-0039, E-mail: shahn@indianahistory.org; Staff 13 (MLS 10, Non-MLS 3)
Founded 1934
Library Holdings: Bk Titles 45,000
Special Collections: African American History, images, papers; Agricultural History, bks, images, papers; Architectural History, papers; Business History, bks, images, papers; Ethnic History, images, papers; Indiana Mills, images, papers; Indiana Politics, images, paper; Local History, bks, images, papers; Medical History, bks, papers; Military History, images, papers; Northwest Territory & Indiana Territory, papers; Notable Hoosiers, images, papers; Social Services, papers; Transportation, images, papers (Midwestern railroads, interurbans, covered bridges)
Subject Interests: Civil War, Indiana
Wireless access
Partic in OCLC Online Computer Library Center, Inc
Open Tues-Sat 10-5
Restriction: Closed stack, Non-circulating coll

S INDIANA LANDMARKS*, Information Center, 1201 Central Ave, 46202-2660. SAN 326-8896. Tel: 317-639-4534. Toll Free Tel: 800-450-4534. FAX: 317-639-6734. E-mail: info@indianalandmarks.org. Web Site: www.indianalandmarks.org. *Dir of Educ,* Suzanne Stanis; E-mail: sstanis@indianalandmarks.org; Staff 1 (MLS 1)
Library Holdings: Bk Titles 3,000; Per Subs 90
Subject Interests: Archit
Automation Activity & Vendor Info: (Acquisitions) LibraryWorld, Inc; (Cataloging) LibraryWorld, Inc; (Circulation) LibraryWorld, Inc
Wireless access
Publications: Indiana Preservation
Partic in Midwest Collaborative for Library Services

P INDIANA STATE LIBRARY*, 315 W Ohio St, 46202. (Mail add: 140 N Senate, 46204), SAN 341-2628. Tel: 317-232-3675. Reference Tel: 317-232-3678. Administration Tel: 317-232-3692. Information Services Tel: 317-232-3697. Toll Free Tel: 866-683-0008. FAX: 317-232-0002. TDD: 317-232-3732. E-mail: ldo@library.in.gov. Web Site: www.in.gov/library. *State Librn,* Jacob Speer; E-mail: jspeer@library.in.gov; *Assoc Dir,* Wendy Knapp; E-mail: wknapp@library.in.gov; *Librn for Blind & Physically Handicapped,* Maggie Ansty; *Supvr, Libr Develop,* Jennifer Clifton; E-mail: jclifton@library.in.gov; *Cat,* Jocelyn Lewis; E-mail: jlewis2@library.in.gov; Staff 75 (MLS 37, Non-MLS 38)
Founded 1825
Special Collections: Americana (Holliday Coll); Genealogy (Darrach Coll of Indianapolis Pub Libr); Hymn Books (Levering Sunday School); Indiana Academy of Science; Indiana Newspapers; Manuscripts; Shorthand & Typewriting (Strachan Coll). State Document Depository; US Document Depository
Subject Interests: Am hist, Genealogy, Indiana, Libr & info sci, State hist
Automation Activity & Vendor Info: (Cataloging) Evergreen; (Circulation) Evergreen; (ILL) OCLC ILLiad; (OPAC) Evergreen
Wireless access
Function: Archival coll, Govt ref serv, ILL available, Prog for adults, Ref serv available, Res libr, Wheelchair accessible, Workshops
Publications: Indiana Insights (Newsletter); Wednesday Word (Current awareness service)
Partic in Evergreen Indiana Consortium; LYRASIS; OCLC Online Computer Library Center, Inc
Special Services for the Deaf - Bks on deafness & sign lang
Special Services for the Blind - Bks & mags in Braille, on rec, tape & cassette; Braille bks; Children's Braille; Screen reader software; Talking bks & player equip; Tel Pioneers equip repair group
Open Mon, Tues, Wed & Fri 8-4:30, Thurs 8-7

P INDIANA STATE LIBRARY, Indiana Talking Book & Braille Library, 140 N Senate Ave, 46204. SAN 304-9655. Tel: 317-232-3684. Toll Free Tel: 800-622-4970. FAX: 317-232-3728. E-mail: lbph@library.IN.gov, tbbl@library.in.gov. Web Site: www.in.gov/library/tbbl.htm. *Supvr, Talking Bk,* Laura Williams; E-mail: lawilliams1@library.in.gov; Staff 5 (MLS 2, Non-MLS 3)
Founded 1934
Library Holdings: Braille Volumes 42,187; Large Print Bks 24,022; Per Subs 19; Talking Bks 305,230
Special Collections: Indiana History & Literature Coll, digital talking bk cartridge
Automation Activity & Vendor Info: (Circulation) Keystone Systems, Inc (KLAS)
Wireless access
Publications: Indiana Insights (Newsletter)
Special Services for the Blind - Braille equip; Reader equip
Open Mon-Fri 8-4:30

GL INDIANA SUPREME COURT LAW LIBRARY*, State House, Rm 316, 200 W Washington St, 46204. SAN 304-968X. Tel: 317-232-2557. Web Site: www.in.gov/judiciary/library. *Dir & Librn,* Terri Ross; Staff 3 (MLS 2, Non-MLS 1)
Founded 1867
Library Holdings: Bk Titles 72,000; Per Subs 35
Special Collections: US Document Depository
Subject Interests: State law
Automation Activity & Vendor Info: (Cataloging) LibLime; (ILL) OCLC FirstSearch; (OPAC) LibLime
Wireless access
Partic in Midwest Collaborative for Library Services; OCLC Online Computer Library Center, Inc
Open Mon-Fri 8:30-4:30

INDIANA UNIVERSITY

CM RUTH LILLY MEDICAL LIBRARY*, 975 W Walnut St, IB 100, 46202, SAN 341-2741. Tel: 317-274-7182. Interlibrary Loan Service Tel: 317-274-7184. Administration Tel: 317-274-1404. FAX: 317-278-2385. Reference E-mail: medlref@iupui.edu. Web Site: library.medicine.iu.edu. *Dean,* Dr Jay L Hess; *Dir,* Gabe Rios; Tel: 317-274-1408, E-mail: grrios@iu.edu; *Asst Dir, Libr Operations,* Rick Ralston; Tel: 317-274-1409, E-mail: rralston@iu.edu; *Biomedical Librn,* Kellie Kaneshiro; Tel: 317-274-1612, E-mail: kkaneshi@iu.edu; *Knowledge Mgr, Outreach Coordr,* Elaine Skopelja; Tel: 317-274-8358, E-mail: eskopelj@iu.edu; Staff 16 (MLS 12, Non-MLS 4)
Founded 1908. Enrl 3,591; Fac 1,002; Highest Degree: Doctorate
Library Holdings: Bk Vols 191,853; Per Subs 310; Videos 115
Special Collections: History of Medicine
Subject Interests: Allied health, Med, Nursing
Automation Activity & Vendor Info: (Cataloging) NOTIS
Partic in Association of Research Libraries; National Network of Libraries of Medicine Region 6; OCLC Online Computer Library Center, Inc; Proquest Dialog

CM SCHOOL OF DENTISTRY LIBRARY*, 1121 W Michigan St, Rm 128, 46202-5186, SAN 341-2687. Tel: 317-274-7204. Interlibrary Loan Service Tel: 317-274-5203. FAX: 317-278-1256. E-mail: ds-libry@iupui.edu. Web Site: www.iusd.iupui.edu/depts/lib/default.aspx. *Head Librn,* Jan Cox; Tel: 317-274-5207, E-mail: jcox2@iupui.edu; Staff 5 (MLS 2, Non-MLS 3)
Founded 1927. Enrl 619; Fac 129; Highest Degree: Doctorate
Library Holdings: AV Mats 5,940; e-books 40; Bk Vols 26,903; Per Subs 463
Special Collections: Archives Coll
Subject Interests: Dentistry, Med
Automation Activity & Vendor Info: (Acquisitions) SirsiDynix; (Cataloging) SirsiDynix; (Circulation) SirsiDynix; (Course Reserve) SirsiDynix; (ILL) OCLC ILLiad; (OPAC) SirsiDynix; (Serials) SirsiDynix
Function: ILL available, Ref serv available
Partic in National Network of Libraries of Medicine Region 6; OCLC Online Computer Library Center, Inc
Open Mon-Thurs 7:30am-10pm, Fri 7:30-5, Sat 9-4:30, Sun 1-5

CL RUTH LILLY LAW LIBRARY*, 530 W New York St, 46202-3225, SAN 341-2717. Tel: 317-274-3884, 317-274-4028. Reference Tel: 317-274-4026. FAX: 317-274-8825. Circulation E-mail: circlawl@iupui.edu. Web Site: www.indylaw.indiana.edu/library. *Dir,* Judith Ford Anspach; E-mail: juanspac@iupui.edu; *Assoc Dir,* Miriam A Murphy; E-mail: mimurphy@iupui.edu; *Head, Info Serv,* Catherine Lemmer; *Cat Librn,* Chris Evan Long; *Cat & Govt Doc Librn,* Wendell Johnting; E-mail: wjohntin@iupui.edu; *Ref Librn,* Richard E Humphrey; E-mail: rhumphre@iupui.edu; *Res & Instrul Serv Librn,* Susan deMaine; E-mail: sdemaine@iupui.edu; *Res & Instrul Serv Librn,* Benjamin Keele; E-mail: bkeele@iupui.edu; Staff 11 (MLS 3, Non-MLS 8)
Founded 1944. Highest Degree: Doctorate
Library Holdings: Bk Titles 240,391; Bk Vols 584,622; Per Subs 6,300
Special Collections: Commonwealth Coll; Council of Europe; European Communities, law & law-related publications; International & Comparative Materials; OAS Official Records; Rare Book Coll (especially in legal history). UN Document Depository; US Document Depository
Subject Interests: State law, US Law
Partic in Academic Libraries of Indiana; Association of Research Libraries
Publications: Bibliography of Indiana Legal Materials; Recent Monthly Acquisitions Lists
Open Mon-Fri 7:30am-Midnight, Sat 9-9, Sun 10am-Midnight

C INDIANA UNIVERSITY-PURDUE UNIVERSITY INDIANAPOLIS*, University Libraries, 755 W Michigan St, 46202-5195. SAN 341-2776. Tel: 317-274-8278. Circulation Tel: 317-274-0472. Interlibrary Loan Service Tel: 317-274-0500. Reference Tel: 317-274-0483. Administration Tel: 317-274-9833. Information Services Tel: 317-274-0469. FAX: 317-278-0368. Administration FAX: 317-278-2300, Information Services FAX: 317-274-0469. Web Site: www.ulib.iupui.edu. *Interim Dean,* Kristi Palmer; Tel: 317-278-2327, E-mail: klpalmer@iupui.edu; *Assoc Dean, Admin,* Kindra Orr; Tel: 317-278-2338, E-mail: ksorr@iupui.edu; *Assoc Dean, Coll & Info Access,* Todd Daniels-Howell; Tel: 317-274-0466, E-mail: tjdaniel@iupui.edu; *Assoc Dean, Teaching, Learning & Res,* William Orme; Tel: 317-274-0485, E-mail: orme@iupui.edu. Subject Specialists: *Liberal arts, Polit sci,* William Orme; Staff 49 (MLS 30, Non-MLS 19)
Founded 1939. Enrl 26,640; Fac 3,249; Highest Degree: Doctorate
Jul 2017-Jun 2018 Income (Main Library Only) $10,356,878, Federal $5,940, Locally Generated Income $88,703, Parent Institution $10,137,841, Other $124,394. Mats Exp $9,502,133, Books $552,874, Per/Ser (Incl. Access Fees) $3,191,255, Other Print Mats $5,385. Sal $3,811,780 (Prof $2,926,270)
Library Holdings: Audiobooks 86; AV Mats 5,262; Bks on Deafness & Sign Lang 98; CDs 3,649; DVDs 5,505; e-books 374,788; e-journals 46,758; Microforms 65,441; Music Scores 544; Bk Vols 1,372,800; Per Subs 1,733; Videos 53,640
Special Collections: Archives Coll; Artists' & Fine Press Book; Digital Colls; German Americana; Philanthropy Coll. Oral History; US Document Depository
Subject Interests: Bus & mgt, Educ, Engr, Humanities, Sci tech, Soc sci & issues
Automation Activity & Vendor Info: (Acquisitions) SirsiDynix; (Cataloging) SirsiDynix; (Circulation) SirsiDynix; (Course Reserve) SirsiDynix; (Discovery) EBSCO Discovery Service; (ILL) OCLC; (OPAC) OCLC; (Serials) SirsiDynix
Wireless access
Function: 24/7 Electronic res, 24/7 Online cat, Adult bk club, Archival coll, Art exhibits, Audio & video playback equip for onsite use, AV serv, Bk club(s), Bks on cassette, Bks on CD, Bus archives, CD-ROM, Computers for patron use, Distance learning, Doc delivery serv, E-Reserves, Electronic databases & coll, Free DVD rentals, Games & aids for people with disabilities, Govt ref serv, ILL available, Instruction & testing, Internet access, Large print keyboards, Literacy & newcomer serv, Magazines, Magnifiers for reading, Meeting rooms, Microfiche/film & reading machines, Movies, Music CDs, Online cat, Online info literacy tutorials on the web & in blackboard, Online ref, Orientations, Outreach serv, Outside serv via phone, mail, e-mail & web, Photocopying/Printing, Ref serv available, Scanner, Spanish lang bks, Spoken cassettes & CDs, Spoken cassettes & DVDs, Study rm, Telephone ref, VHS videos, Wheelchair accessible, Workshops
Partic in Academic Libraries of Indiana; LYRASIS; Midwest Collaborative for Library Services; OCLC Online Computer Library Center, Inc
Special Services for the Deaf - Interpreter on staff; Sorenson video relay syst; TTY equip
Special Services for the Blind - Accessible computers; Assistive/Adapted tech devices, equip & products; Bks on CD; Blind students ctr; Braille servs; Closed caption display syst; Closed circuit TV; Closed circuit TV magnifier; Copier with enlargement capabilities; Daisy reader; Dragon Naturally Speaking software; Internet workstation with adaptive software; Large print bks; Low vision equip; Magnifiers; Networked computers with assistive software; PC for people with disabilities; Premier adaptive tech software; Reading & writing aids; Screen reader software; Text reader; ZoomText magnification & reading software
Open Mon-Thurs 7:30am-Midnight, Fri 7:30am-9pm, Sat 8-6, Sun 10am-Midnight
Restriction: Authorized patrons, Borrowing requests are handled by ILL, Circ limited, External users must contact libr, ID required to use computers (Ltd hrs), In-house use for visitors, Limited access based on advanced application, Limited access for the pub, Non-circulating coll, Non-circulating of rare bks, Open to pub for ref & circ; with some limitations, Open to students, fac, staff & alumni, Photo ID required for access, Restricted borrowing privileges, Restricted loan policy, Secured area only open to authorized personnel

Departmental Libraries:
HERRON ART LIBRARY, Herron School of Art & Design, 735 W New York St, 46202, SAN 341-2806. Tel: 317-278-9484. Reference Tel: 317-278-9461. FAX: 317-278-9497. E-mail: herron@iupui.edu. Web Site: www.ulib.iupui.edu/herron. *Dir,* Sonja Staum-Kuniej; Tel: 317-278-9417, E-mail: sstaumku@iupui.edu; *Circ Supvr,* Seth Kong; Tel: 317-278-9434, E-mail: pkong@iupui.edu; *Visual Res Spec,* Danita Davis; Tel: 317-278-9439, E-mail: dldavis@iupui.edu; Staff 4 (MLS 2, Non-MLS 2)
Founded 1970. Enrl 900; Fac 70; Highest Degree: Master
Library Holdings: Bk Vols 24,000; Per Subs 181; Videos 210
Open Mon-Thurs 8-6, Fri 8-5

S INDIANA WOMEN'S PRISON LIBRARY*, 2596 Girl's School Rd, 46201. SAN 304-9701. Tel: 317-244-3387. FAX: 317-684-9643. Web Site: www.in.gov/idoc/2412.htm.
Founded 1932
Library Holdings: Bk Titles 12,600; Bk Vols 13,900; Per Subs 44

S THE INDIANA YOUTH INSTITUTE*, Virgina Beall Ball Library, 603 E Washington St, Ste 800, 46204-2692. Tel: 317-396-2700. Toll Free Tel: 800-343-7060. FAX: 317-396-2701. E-mail: library@iyi.org. Web Site: www.iyi.org/data-library/library. *Outreach Mgr,* Lela Smith; E-mail: lsmith@iyi.org
Library Holdings: Bk Titles 7,000
Open Mon-Fri 8-5

S INDIANAPOLIS MUSEUM OF ART AT NEWFIELDS*, Stout Reference Library, 4000 Michigan Rd, 46208-3326. SAN 304-9728. Tel: 317-923-1331, Ext 547. FAX: 317-926-8931. E-mail: library@discovernewfields.org. Web Site: discovernewfields.org/research/libraries/stout-reference-library. *Head, Libr & Archives,* Alba Fernandez-Keys; E-mail: afernandez-keys@discovernewfields.org; *Assoc Archivist, Librn,* Lydia Spotts; Staff 2 (MLS 2)
Founded 1908
Library Holdings: Bk Vols 100,000; Per Subs 160
Special Collections: Contemporary Design Manufacturer's Catalogs; Indiana Artists Files; Miller House & Garden Coll; Sales & Auction Catalogs
Automation Activity & Vendor Info: (Cataloging) OCLC Connexion; (Circulation) Horizon; (ILL) OCLC ILLiad; (Serials) EBSCO Online
Wireless access
Function: 24/7 Online cat, Archival coll, Ref serv available, Res libr
Open Mon-Sun 11-4
Restriction: Non-circulating

P INDIANAPOLIS PUBLIC LIBRARY*, Library Service Center - Administrative Headquarters, 2450 N Meridian St, 46208. (Mail add: PO Box 211, 46206-4840), SAN 341-289X. Tel: 317-275-4840. Circulation Tel: 317-275-4105. FAX: 317-269-5300. Administration FAX: 317-269-5220. Web Site: www.indypl.org. *Chief Exec Officer,* Jackie Nytes; Tel: 317-275-4001, E-mail: jnytes@indypl.org; *Chief Financial Officer,* Ijeoma Dike-Young; Tel: 317-275-4850; *Dir, Human Res,* Katherine Lerg; Tel: 317-275-4806, Fax: 317-269-5248, E-mail: klerg@indypl.org; *Dir of Strategic Planning,* Christine Cairo; Tel: 317-275-4080, E-mail: ccairo@indypl.org; *Dir, Coll Mgt,* Deborah Lambert; Tel: 317-275-4721, E-mail: dlambert@indypl.org; *Dir, Facilities,* Sharon Smith; Tel: 317-275-4301, E-mail: ssmith@indypl.org; *Dir, Info Tech,* Debra Champ; E-mail: dchamp@indypl.org; *Dep Dir, Pub Serv,* John Helling; Tel: 317-275-4012, E-mail: jhelling@indypl.org; *Area Res Mgr, Cent Libr,* Michael Williams; Tel: 317-275-4302, E-mail: mwilliams@indypl.org; *Area Res Mgr, Mid-Region,* Sharon Bernhardt; Tel: 317-275-4475, E-mail: sbernhardt@indypl.org; *Mgr, Organizational Learning & Development,* Cheryl Wright; Tel: 317-275-4808, E-mail: cwright@indypl.org; *Mgr, Support Serv & Vols Res,* Nancy Stephenson; E-mail: nstephenson@indypl.org; Staff 136 (MLS 136)
Founded 1873. Pop 877,389; Circ 16,178,837
Jan 2015-Dec 2015 Income (Main & Associated Libraries) $38,042,652, State $2,771,778, Federal $219,281, County $32,368,510, Other $2,683,083. Mats Exp $6,567,573, Books $2,813,366, Per/Ser (Incl. Access Fees) $130,910, AV Mat $1,139,320, Electronic Ref Mat (Incl. Access Fees) $2,483,977. Sal $16,546,322
Library Holdings: Audiobooks 44,173; e-books 155,477; e-journals 228; Electronic Media & Resources 46,094; Bk Vols 1,539,551; Per Subs 1,855; Videos 131,627
Special Collections: Arthur H Rumpf Menu Coll; Fine Printing Coll; Foundation Coll; Illustrated Children's Books; Indianapolis Authors; James Whitcomb Riley Coll; Julia Connor Thompson Coll; Local Indianapolis History; Storytelling; Wright Marble Cookbook Coll. US Document Depository
Subject Interests: Arts, Bus, Local hist, Music, Patents
Automation Activity & Vendor Info: (Acquisitions) Horizon; (Cataloging) Horizon; (Circulation) Horizon; (ILL) OCLC; (Serials) Horizon
Wireless access
Function: 24/7 Electronic res, 24/7 Online cat, Adult bk club, After school storytime, Archival coll, Art exhibits, Audio & video playback equip for onsite use, Audiobks via web, Bilingual assistance for Spanish patrons, Bk club(s), Bks on cassette, Bks on CD, Bus archives, CD-ROM, Children's prog, Computer training, Computers for patron use, Digital talking bks, E-Reserves, Electronic databases & coll, Free DVD rentals, Govt ref serv, Holiday prog, Home delivery & serv to seniorr ctr & nursing homes, Homebound delivery serv, Homework prog, ILL available, Internet access, Jazz prog, Large print keyboards, Life-long learning prog for all ages, Magazines, Magnifiers for reading, Meeting rooms, Microfiche/film & reading machines, Movies, Music CDs, Online cat, Online ref, Orientations, Outreach serv, Outside serv via phone, mail, e-mail & web, OverDrive digital audio bks, Photocopying/Printing, Preschool outreach, Preschool reading prog, Printer for laptops & handheld devices, Prog for adults, Prog for children & young adult, Ref & res, Ref serv available, Scanner, Senior computer classes, Spanish lang bks, Spoken cassettes & CDs, Spoken cassettes & DVDs, Story hour, Study rm, Summer reading prog, Tax forms, Teen prog, Telephone ref, VHS videos, Wheelchair accessible, Workshops
Publications: A Live Thing in the Whole Town (Local historical information); Indianapolis in the World of Books (Local historical information); Stacks: A History of the Indianapolis-Marion County Public Library (Local historical information)
Partic in Midwest Collaborative for Library Services; OCLC Online Computer Library Center, Inc
Special Services for the Deaf - Assisted listening device; Assistive tech; Closed caption videos; Sign lang interpreter upon request for prog; Sorenson video relay syst; Video relay services
Special Services for the Blind - Accessible computers; Assistive/Adapted tech devices, equip & products; Bks on cassette; Bks on CD; Cassettes; Closed circuit TV magnifier; Digital talking bk; Dragon Naturally Speaking software; Home delivery serv; Internet workstation with adaptive software; Large print & cassettes; Large print bks; Lending of low vision aids; Magnifiers; PC for people with disabilities; Screen enlargement software for people with visual disabilities; Screen reader software; Text reader; ZoomText magnification & reading software
Open Mon-Fri 8-5
Friends of the Library Group
Branches: 24
BEECH GROVE BRANCH, 1102 Main St, Beech Grove, 46107, SAN 304-8012. Tel: 317-275-4560. FAX: 317-788-0489. Web Site: www.indypl.org/locations/beech-grove. *Br Mgr,* Todd Gilbert; E-mail: tgilbert@indypl.org; *Ad,* Michele Patterson; E-mail: mpatterson@indypl.org; Staff 16 (MLS 3, Non-MLS 13)
Founded 1949. Pop 14,880; Circ 129,961
Library Holdings: Bk Titles 73,891; Bk Vols 77,801; Per Subs 263; Talking Bks 391; Videos 1,123
Open Mon-Wed 10-8, Thurs & Fri 10-6, Sat 10-5
BRIGHTWOOD, 2435 N Sherman Dr, 46218-3852, SAN 341-292X. Tel: 317-275-4310. Web Site: www.indypl.org/locations/brightwood. *Br Mgr,* Rhonda Oliver; Tel: 317-275-4315, E-mail: roliver@indypl.org; Staff 2 (MLS 1, Non-MLS 1)
Founded 1901. Pop 5,457; Circ 111,736
Library Holdings: Bk Vols 14,989
Function: 24/7 Electronic res, 24/7 Online cat, Activity rm, Children's prog, Computer training, Computers for patron use, E-Reserves, Electronic databases & coll, Free DVD rentals, ILL available, Internet access, Life-long learning prog for all ages, Magazines, Mail & tel request accepted, Meeting rooms, Movies, Music CDs, Online cat, OverDrive digital audio bks, Photocopying/Printing, Preschool outreach, Printer for laptops & handheld devices, Prog for adults, Prog for children & young adult, Ref serv available, Scanner, Spoken cassettes & CDs, Spoken cassettes & DVDs, Story hour, Summer reading prog, Tax forms, Teen prog, Telephone ref, Wheelchair accessible, Workshops
Open Mon-Wed 10-8, Thurs & Fri 10-6, Sat 10-5
CENTRAL LIBRARY, 40 E Saint Clair St, 46204. Tel: 317-275-4100. Circulation Tel: 317-275-4120. Interlibrary Loan Service Tel: 317-275-4242. Interlibrary Loan Service FAX: 317-229-4510. Web Site: www.indypl.org/locations/central-library. *Area Res Mgr, Cent Libr,* Mike Williams; E-mail: mwilliams@indypl.org
Open Mon-Wed 10-8, Thurs 10-6, Fri & Sat 10-5, Sun 12-5
COLLEGE AVENUE, 4180 N College Ave, 46205, SAN 341-2989. Tel: 317-275-4320. Web Site: www.indypl.org/locations/college-avenue. *Br Mgr,* Amy Griffin; Tel: 317-275-4325, E-mail: agriffin@indypl.org; Staff 4 (MLS 2, Non-MLS 2)
Founded 2000. Pop 13,025; Circ 529,645
Library Holdings: Bk Vols 55,649
Function: 24/7 Electronic res, 24/7 Online cat, Activity rm, Adult bk club, Art exhibits, Bks on cassette, Bks on CD, Children's prog, Computer training, Computers for patron use, E-Reserves, Electronic databases & coll, Free DVD rentals, ILL available, Internet access, Magazines, Meeting rooms, Movies, Music CDs, Online cat, OverDrive digital audio bks, Photocopying/Printing, Preschool outreach, Printer for laptops & handheld devices, Prog for adults, Prog for children & young

adult, Ref serv available, Scanner, Spanish lang bks, Spoken cassettes & CDs, Spoken cassettes & DVDs, Story hour, Summer reading prog, Tax forms, Teen prog, Telephone ref, Workshops
Open Mon-Thurs 10-8, Fri 10-6, Sat 10-5
Friends of the Library Group

DECATUR, 5301 Kentucky Ave, 46221-6540, SAN 341-3195. Tel: 317-275-4330. Web Site: www.indypl.org/locations/decatur. *Br Mgr,* Josh Crain; Tel: 317-275-4335, E-mail: jcrain@indypl.org; Staff 3 (MLS 2, Non-MLS 1)
Founded 1990. Pop 14,807; Circ 350,650
Library Holdings: Bk Vols 55,101
Function: 24/7 Electronic res, 24/7 Online cat, Activity rm, Audiobks via web, Bks on cassette, Bks on CD, Children's prog, Computer training, Computers for patron use, Digital talking bks, E-Reserves, Electronic databases & coll, Free DVD rentals, ILL available, Internet access, Life-long learning prog for all ages, Magazines, Meeting rooms, Movies, Music CDs, Online cat, Outside serv via phone, mail, e-mail & web, OverDrive digital audio bks, Photocopying/Printing, Preschool outreach, Printer for laptops & handheld devices, Prog for adults, Prog for children & young adult, Ref serv available, Scanner, Spanish lang bks, Spoken cassettes & CDs, Spoken cassettes & DVDs, Story hour, Study rm, Summer reading prog, Tax forms, Teen prog, Telephone ref, Workshops
Open Mon-Wed 10-8, Thurs & Fri 10-6, Sat 10-5

EAGLE, 3905 Moller Rd, 46254, SAN 341-3047. Tel: 317-275-4340. Web Site: www.indypl.org/locations/eagle. *Br Mgr,* Mary Agnes Hylton; Tel: 317-275-4345, E-mail: mhylton@indypl.org; Staff 5 (MLS 5)
Founded 1970. Pop 16,551; Circ 277,691
Library Holdings: Bk Vols 38,972
Function: 24/7 Electronic res, 24/7 Online cat, Activity rm, Audiobks via web, Bks on cassette, Bks on CD, Children's prog, Computer training, Computers for patron use, Digital talking bks, E-Reserves, Electronic databases & coll, Free DVD rentals, ILL available, Internet access, Life-long learning prog for all ages, Magazines, Meeting rooms, Movies, Music CDs, Online cat, Outside serv via phone, mail, e-mail & web, OverDrive digital audio bks, Photocopying/Printing, Preschool outreach, Printer for laptops & handheld devices, Prog for adults, Prog for children & young adult, Ref serv available, Scanner, Spanish lang bks, Spoken cassettes & CDs, Spoken cassettes & DVDs, Story hour, Summer reading prog, Tax forms, Teen prog, Telephone ref, Wheelchair accessible, Workshops
Open Mon-Wed 10-8, Thurs & Fri 10-6, Sat 10-5

EAST THIRTY-EIGHTH STREET, 5420 E 38th St, 46218-1873, SAN 341-3101. Tel: 317-275-4350. Web Site: www.indypl.org/locations/east-38th-street. *Br Mgr,* Shanika Heyward; Tel: 317-275-4355, E-mail: sheyward@indypl.org; Staff 5 (MLS 3, Non-MLS 2)
Founded 1957. Pop 17,583; Circ 170,991
Library Holdings: Bk Vols 32,299
Function: 24/7 Electronic res, 24/7 Online cat, Activity rm, Audiobks via web, Bks on cassette, Bks on CD, Children's prog, Computer training, Computers for patron use, Digital talking bks, E-Reserves, Electronic databases & coll, Free DVD rentals, ILL available, Internet access, Life-long learning prog for all ages, Magazines, Meeting rooms, Movies, Music CDs, Online cat, OverDrive digital audio bks, Photocopying/Printing, Preschool outreach, Printer for laptops & handheld devices, Prog for adults, Prog for children & young adult, Ref serv available, Scanner, Spanish lang bks, Spoken cassettes & CDs, Spoken cassettes & DVDs, Story hour, Summer reading prog, Tax forms, Teen prog, Telephone ref, Wheelchair accessible, Workshops
Open Mon-Wed 10-8, Thurs & Fri 10-6, Sat 10-5

EAST WASHINGTON, 2822 E Washington St, 46201-4215, SAN 341-3071. Tel: 317-275-4360. Web Site: www.indypl.org/locations/east-washington. *Br Mgr,* Doriene Smither; Tel: 317-275-4365, E-mail: dsmither@indypl.org; Staff 2 (MLS 1, Non-MLS 1)
Founded 1911. Pop 8,075; Circ 101,451
Library Holdings: Bk Vols 13,930
Function: 24/7 Electronic res, 24/7 Online cat, Audiobks via web, Bks on cassette, Bks on CD, Children's prog, Computers for patron use, Digital talking bks, E-Reserves, Electronic databases & coll, Free DVD rentals, ILL available, Internet access, Life-long learning prog for all ages, Magazines, Meeting rooms, Movies, Music CDs, Online cat, OverDrive digital audio bks, Photocopying/Printing, Preschool outreach, Printer for laptops & handheld devices, Prog for adults, Prog for children & young adult, Ref serv available, Scanner, Spanish lang bks, Spoken cassettes & CDs, Spoken cassettes & DVDs, Story hour, Summer reading prog, Tax forms, Teen prog, Telephone ref, Workshops
Open Mon-Wed 10-8, Thurs & Fri 10-6, Sat 10-5

FOUNTAIN SQUARE, 1066 Virginia Ave, 46203, SAN 341-3284. Tel: 317-275-4390. Web Site: www.indypl.org/locations/fountain-square. *Br Mgr,* Peggy Wehr; Tel: 317-275-4395, E-mail: pwehr@indypl.org; Staff 2 (MLS 1, Non-MLS 1)
Pop 6,312; Circ 137,038
Library Holdings: Bk Vols 16,328
Function: 24/7 Electronic res, 24/7 Online cat, Audiobks via web, Bks on cassette, Bks on CD, Children's prog, Computers for patron use, Digital talking bks, E-Reserves, Electronic databases & coll, Free DVD rentals, ILL available, Internet access, Life-long learning prog for all ages, Magazines, Meeting rooms, Movies, Music CDs, Online cat, OverDrive digital audio bks, Photocopying/Printing, Preschool outreach, Printer for laptops & handheld devices, Prog for adults, Prog for children & young adult, Ref serv available, Scanner, Spanish lang bks, Spoken cassettes & CDs, Spoken cassettes & DVDs, Story hour, Summer reading prog, Teen prog, Telephone ref, Wheelchair accessible, Workshops
Open Mon-Wed 10-8, Thurs & Fri 10-6, Sat 10-5

FRANKLIN ROAD, 5550 S Franklin Rd, 46239, SAN 341-3403. Tel: 317-275-4380. Web Site: www.indypl.org/locations/franklin-road. *Br Mgr,* Jill Wetnight; Tel: 317-275-4385, E-mail: jwetnight@indypl.org; Staff 5 (MLS 5)
Founded 2000. Pop 20,351; Circ 798,109
Library Holdings: Bk Vols 80,884
Function: 24/7 Electronic res, 24/7 Online cat, Activity rm, Audiobks via web, Bks on cassette, Bks on CD, Children's prog, Computers for patron use, Digital talking bks, E-Reserves, Electronic databases & coll, Free DVD rentals, ILL available, Internet access, Life-long learning prog for all ages, Magazines, Movies, Music CDs, Online cat, Preschool outreach, Printer for laptops & handheld devices, Prog for adults, Prog for children & young adult, Ref serv available, Scanner, Spanish lang bks, Spoken cassettes & CDs, Spoken cassettes & DVDs, Story hour, Study rm, Summer reading prog, Tax forms, Teen prog, Telephone ref, Wheelchair accessible, Workshops
Open Mon-Wed 10-8, Thurs & Fri 10-6, Sat 10-5, Sun 12-5

GARFIELD PARK, 2502 Shelby St, 46203-4236, SAN 341-3314. Tel: 317-275-4490. Web Site: www.indypl.org/locations/garfield-park. *Br Mgr,* Michelle Sharp; Tel: 317-275-4495, E-mail: msharp@indypl.org; Staff 6 (MLS 3, Non-MLS 3)
Founded 1965. Pop 15,660; Circ 270,785
Library Holdings: Bk Vols 35,573
Function: 24/7 Electronic res, 24/7 Online cat, Audiobks via web, Bks on cassette, Bks on CD, Children's prog, Computer training, Computers for patron use, E-Reserves, Electronic databases & coll, Free DVD rentals, ILL available, Internet access, Life-long learning prog for all ages, Magazines, Movies, Music CDs, Online cat, OverDrive digital audio bks, Photocopying/Printing, Preschool outreach, Printer for laptops & handheld devices, Prog for adults, Prog for children & young adult, Ref serv available, Scanner, Spanish lang bks, Spoken cassettes & CDs, Spoken cassettes & DVDs, Story hour, Summer reading prog, Tax forms, Teen prog, Telephone ref, Wheelchair accessible, Workshops
Open Mon-Wed 10-8, Thurs & Fri 10-6, Sat 10-5

GLENDALE, Glendale Town Ctr, 6101 N Keystone Ave, 46220, SAN 341-2954. Tel: 317-275-4410. Web Site: www.indypl.org/locations/glendale. *Br Mgr,* Judy Gray; Tel: 317-275-4415, E-mail: jgray@indypl.org; Staff 7 (MLS 6, Non-MLS 1)
Founded 2000. Pop 28,537; Circ 868,776
Library Holdings: Bk Vols 107,752
Function: 24/7 Electronic res, 24/7 Online cat, Activity rm, Audiobks via web, Bks on cassette, Bks on CD, Children's prog, Computer training, Computers for patron use, Digital talking bks, E-Reserves, Electronic databases & coll, Free DVD rentals, ILL available, Internet access, Life-long learning prog for all ages, Magazines, Meeting rooms, Movies, Music CDs, Online cat, OverDrive digital audio bks, Photocopying/Printing, Preschool outreach, Printer for laptops & handheld devices, Prog for adults, Prog for children & young adult, Ref serv available, Scanner, Spanish lang bks, Spoken cassettes & CDs, Spoken cassettes & DVDs, Story hour, Summer reading prog, Tax forms, Teen prog, Telephone ref, Wheelchair accessible, Workshops
Open Mon-Wed 10-8, Thurs & Fri 10-6, Sat 10-5, Sun 12-5

HAUGHVILLE, 2121 W Michigan St, 46222-3862, SAN 341-3136. Tel: 317-275-4420. Web Site: www.indypl.org/locations/haughville. *Br Mgr,* Nancy Mobley; Tel: 317-275-4425, E-mail: nmobley@indypl.org; Staff 3 (MLS 3)
Founded 1897. Pop 11,312; Circ 193,161
Library Holdings: Bk Vols 26,191
Function: 24/7 Electronic res, 24/7 Online cat, Audiobks via web, Bks on cassette, Bks on CD, Children's prog, Computer training, Computers for patron use, Digital talking bks, E-Reserves, Electronic databases & coll, Free DVD rentals, ILL available, Internet access, Life-long learning prog for all ages, Magazines, Meeting rooms, Movies, Music CDs, Online cat, Photocopying/Printing, Preschool outreach, Printer for laptops & handheld devices, Prog for adults, Prog for children & young adult, Ref serv available, Scanner, Spanish lang bks, Spoken cassettes & CDs, Spoken cassettes & DVDs, Story hour, Summer reading prog, Tax forms, Teen prog, Wheelchair accessible, Workshops
Open Mon-Wed 10-8, Thurs & Fri 10-6, Sat 10-5

INFOZONE, The Children's Museum, 3000 N Meridian St, 46208. Tel: 317-275-4430. Web Site: www.indypl.org/locations/infozone. *Br Mgr,* Joan Emmert; Tel: 317-275-4435, E-mail: jemmert@indypl.org; Staff 4 (MLS 1, Non-MLS 3)
Founded 2000. Pop 3,473; Circ 116,426

Library Holdings: Bk Vols 10,711
Function: 24/7 Electronic res, 24/7 Online cat, Activity rm, Audiobks via web, Bks on cassette, Bks on CD, Children's prog, Computer training, Computers for patron use, Digital talking bks, E-Reserves, Electronic databases & coll, Free DVD rentals, ILL available, Internet access, Magazines, Meeting rooms, Movies, Music CDs, Online cat, OverDrive digital audio bks, Photocopying/Printing, Preschool outreach, Printer for laptops & handheld devices, Prog for adults, Prog for children & young adult, Ref serv available, Scanner, Spanish lang bks, Spoken cassettes & CDs, Spoken cassettes & DVDs, Story hour, Summer reading prog, Tax forms, Teen prog, Telephone ref, Wheelchair accessible, Workshops
Open Mon & Fri-Sun 10-5, Tues-Thurs 10-8

IRVINGTON, 5625 E Washington St, 46219-6411, SAN 341-3012. Tel: 317-275-4450. Web Site: www.indypl.org/locations/irvington. *Br Mgr,* Sue Kennedy; Tel: 317-275-4455, E-mail: skennedy@indypl.org; Staff 5 (MLS 4, Non-MLS 1)
Founded 1903. Pop 21,192; Circ 672,852
Library Holdings: Bk Vols 70,635
Function: 24/7 Electronic res, 24/7 Online cat, Activity rm, Audiobks via web, Bks on cassette, Bks on CD, Children's prog, Computer training, Computers for patron use, Digital talking bks, E-Reserves, Electronic databases & coll, Free DVD rentals, ILL available, Internet access, Life-long learning prog for all ages, Magazines, Meeting rooms, Movies, Music CDs, Online cat, OverDrive digital audio bks, Photocopying/Printing, Preschool outreach, Printer for laptops & handheld devices, Prog for adults, Prog for children & young adult, Ref serv available, Scanner, Spanish lang bks, Spoken cassettes & CDs, Spoken cassettes & DVDs, Story hour, Summer reading prog, Tax forms, Teen prog, Telephone ref, Wheelchair accessible, Workshops
Open Mon-Wed 10-8, Thurs & Fri 10-6, Sat 10-5

LAWRENCE, 7898 N Hague Rd, 46256-1754, SAN 341-3160. Tel: 317-275-4460. Web Site: www.indypl.org/locations/lawrence. *Br Mgr,* Gregory Hill; Tel: 317-275-4463, E-mail: ghill@indypl.org; Staff 6 (MLS 6)
Founded 1983. Pop 43,346; Circ 1,213,260
Library Holdings: Bk Vols 93,589
Function: 24/7 Electronic res, 24/7 Online cat, Audiobks via web, Bks on cassette, Bks on CD, Children's prog, Computer training, Computers for patron use, Digital talking bks, E-Reserves, Electronic databases & coll, Free DVD rentals, ILL available, Internet access, Life-long learning prog for all ages, Magazines, Meeting rooms, Movies, Music CDs, Online cat, OverDrive digital audio bks, Photocopying/Printing, Preschool outreach, Printer for laptops & handheld devices, Prog for adults, Prog for children & young adult, Ref serv available, Scanner, Spanish lang bks, Spoken cassettes & CDs, Spoken cassettes & DVDs, Story hour, Summer reading prog, Tax forms, Teen prog, Telephone ref, Wheelchair accessible, Workshops
Open Mon-Wed 10-8, Thurs & Fri 10-6, Sat 10-5, Sun 12-5

MICHIGAN ROAD, 6201 N Michigan Rd, 46268, SAN 341-311X. Tel: 317-275-4370. Web Site: www.indypl.org/locations/michigan-road. *Br Mgr,* Denyce Malone; Tel: 317-275-4375, E-mail: dmalone@indypl.org; Staff 1 (MLS 1)
Founded 1979. Pop 3,529; Circ 73,934
Library Holdings: Bk Vols 11,218
Function: 24/7 Electronic res, 24/7 Online cat, Audiobks via web, Bks on cassette, Bks on CD, Children's prog, Computers for patron use, Digital talking bks, E-Reserves, Electronic databases & coll, Free DVD rentals, ILL available, Internet access, Life-long learning prog for all ages, Magazines, Meeting rooms, Movies, Music CDs, Online cat, OverDrive digital audio bks, Photocopying/Printing, Preschool outreach, Printer for laptops & handheld devices, Prog for adults, Prog for children & young adult, Ref serv available, Scanner, Spanish lang bks, Spoken cassettes & CDs, Spoken cassettes & DVDs, Story hour, Summer reading prog, Tax forms, Teen prog, Telephone ref, Wheelchair accessible, Workshops
Open Mon-Wed 10-8, Thurs & Fri 10-6, Sat 10-5

NORA, 8625 Guilford Ave, 46240-1835, SAN 341-3225. Tel: 317-275-4470. Web Site: www.indypl.org/locations/nora. *Br Mgr,* Adam Todd; Tel: 317-275-4473, E-mail: atodd@indypl.org; Staff 6 (MLS 5, Non-MLS 1)
Pop 25,382; Circ 1,056,716
Library Holdings: Bk Vols 93,072
Function: 24/7 Electronic res, 24/7 Online cat, Activity rm, Audiobks via web, Bks on cassette, Bks on CD, Children's prog, Computer training, Computers for patron use, Digital talking bks, E-Reserves, Electronic databases & coll, Free DVD rentals, ILL available, Internet access, Life-long learning prog for all ages, Magazines, Meeting rooms, Movies, Music CDs, Online cat, OverDrive digital audio bks, Photocopying/Printing, Preschool outreach, Printer for laptops & handheld devices, Prog for adults, Prog for children & young adult, Ref serv available, Scanner, Spanish lang bks, Spoken cassettes & DVDs, Story hour, Summer reading prog, Tax forms, Teen prog, Telephone ref, Wheelchair accessible, Workshops
Open Mon-Wed 10-8, Thurs & Fri 10-6, Sat 10-5, Sun 12-5

PIKE, 6525 Zionsville Rd, 46268-2352, SAN 341-3527. Tel: 317-275-4480. Web Site: www.indypl.org/locations/pike. *Br Mgr,* Tia Jah Wynne Ayers; Tel: 317-275-4487, E-mail: twayers@indypl.org; Staff 6 (MLS 6)
Pop 28,526; Circ 983,206
Library Holdings: Bk Vols 83,315
Function: 24/7 Electronic res, 24/7 Online cat, Audiobks via web, Bks on cassette, Bks on CD, Children's prog, Computer training, Computers for patron use, Digital talking bks, E-Reserves, Electronic databases & coll, Free DVD rentals, ILL available, Internet access, Life-long learning prog for all ages, Magazines, Meeting rooms, Movies, Music CDs, Online cat, OverDrive digital audio bks, Photocopying/Printing, Preschool outreach, Printer for laptops & handheld devices, Prog for adults, Prog for children & young adult, Ref serv available, Scanner, Spanish lang bks, Spoken cassettes & CDs, Spoken cassettes & DVDs, Story hour, Summer reading prog, Tax forms, Teen prog, Telephone ref, Wheelchair accessible, Workshops
Open Mon-Wed 10-8, Thurs & Fri 10-6, Sat 10-5, Sun 12-5

SOUTHPORT, 2630 E Stop 11 Rd, 46227-8899, SAN 341-3349. Tel: 317-275-4510. Web Site: www.indypl.org/locations/southport. *Br Mgr,* Fiona Duke; Tel: 317-275-4517, E-mail: fduke@indypl.org; Staff 6 (MLS 6)
Founded 1974. Pop 34,957; Circ 1,066,127
Library Holdings: Bk Vols 85,968
Function: 24/7 Electronic res, 24/7 Online cat, Audiobks via web, Bks on cassette, Bks on CD, Children's prog, Computer training, Computers for patron use, Digital talking bks, E-Reserves, Electronic databases & coll, Free DVD rentals, ILL available, Internet access, Life-long learning prog for all ages, Magazines, Meeting rooms, Movies, Music CDs, Online cat, OverDrive digital audio bks, Photocopying/Printing, Preschool outreach, Printer for laptops & handheld devices, Prog for adults, Prog for children & young adult, Ref serv available, Scanner, Spanish lang bks, Spoken cassettes & CDs, Spoken cassettes & DVDs, Story hour, Summer reading prog, Tax forms, Teen prog, Telephone ref, Workshops
Open Mon-Wed 10-8, Thurs & Fri 10-6, Sat 10-5, Sun 12-5

SPADES PARK, 1801 Nowland Ave, 46201-1158, SAN 341-3373. Tel: 317-275-4520. Web Site: www.indypl.org/locations/spades-park. *Br Mgr,* Deborah Ehret; Tel: 317-275-4522, E-mail: dehret@indypl.org; Staff 2 (MLS 1, Non-MLS 1)
Founded 1912. Pop 4,513; Circ 122,872
Library Holdings: Bk Vols 15,701
Function: 24/7 Electronic res, 24/7 Online cat, Audiobks via web, Bk club(s), Bks on cassette, Bks on CD, Children's prog, Computer training, Computers for patron use, Digital talking bks, E-Reserves, Electronic databases & coll, Free DVD rentals, ILL available, Internet access, Life-long learning prog for all ages, Magazines, Meeting rooms, Movies, Music CDs, Online cat, OverDrive digital audio bks, Photocopying/Printing, Preschool outreach, Printer for laptops & handheld devices, Prog for adults, Prog for children & young adult, Ref serv available, Scanner, Spanish lang bks, Spoken cassettes & CDs, Spoken cassettes & DVDs, Story hour, Summer reading prog, Tax forms, Teen prog, Telephone ref, Wheelchair accessible, Workshops
Open Mon-Wed 10-8, Thurs & Fri 10-6, Sat 10-5

WARREN, 9701 E 21st St, 46229-1707, SAN 341-3438. Tel: 317-275-4550. Web Site: www.indypl.org/locations/warren. *Br Mgr,* Ruth Hans; Tel: 317-275-4555, E-mail: rhans@indypl.org; Staff 6 (MLS 6)
Founded 1980. Pop 28,408; Circ 760,000
Library Holdings: Bk Vols 66,877
Function: 24/7 Electronic res, 24/7 Online cat, Adult bk club, Audiobks via web, Bks on cassette, Bks on CD, Children's prog, Computer training, Computers for patron use, Digital talking bks, E-Reserves, Electronic databases & coll, Free DVD rentals, ILL available, Internet access, Life-long learning prog for all ages, Magazines, Meeting rooms, Movies, Music CDs, Online cat, OverDrive digital audio bks, Photocopying/Printing, Preschool outreach, Printer for laptops & handheld devices, Prog for adults, Prog for children & young adult, Ref serv available, Scanner, Spanish lang bks, Spoken cassettes & CDs, Spoken cassettes & DVDs, Story hour, Summer reading prog, Tax forms, Teen prog, Telephone ref, Wheelchair accessible, Workshops
Open Mon-Wed 10-8, Thurs & Fri 10-6, Sat 10-5, Sun 12-5

WAYNE, 198 S Girls School Rd, 46231-1120, SAN 341-3462. Tel: 317-275-4530. Web Site: www.indypl.org/locations/wayne. *Br Mgr,* Melinda Mullican; Tel: 317-275-4537, E-mail: mmullican@indypl.org; Staff 6 (MLS 5, Non-MLS 1)
Founded 1969. Pop 25,874; Circ 642,093
Library Holdings: Bk Vols 72,873
Function: 24/7 Electronic res, 24/7 Online cat, Audiobks via web, Bks on cassette, Bks on CD, Children's prog, Computer training, Computers for patron use, Digital talking bks, E-Reserves, Electronic databases & coll, Free DVD rentals, ILL available, Internet access, Life-long learning prog for all ages, Magazines, Meeting rooms, Movies, Music CDs, Online cat, OverDrive digital audio bks, Photocopying/Printing, Preschool outreach, Printer for laptops & handheld devices, Prog for adults, Prog for children & young adult, Ref serv available, Scanner,

Spanish lang bks, Spoken cassettes & CDs, Spoken cassettes & DVDs, Story hour, Summer reading prog, Tax forms, Teen prog, Telephone ref, Wheelchair accessible, Workshops
Open Mon-Wed 10-8, Thurs & Fri 10-6, Sat 10-5, Sun 12-5
WEST INDIANAPOLIS, 1216 S Kappes St, 46221-1540, SAN 341-3497. Tel: 317-275-4540. Web Site: www.indypl.org/locations/west-indianapolis. *Br Mgr,* Jayne Walters; Tel: 317-275-4545, E-mail: jwalters@indypl.org; Staff 1 (MLS 1)
Pop 6,246; Circ 129,432
Library Holdings: Bk Vols 17,385
Function: 24/7 Electronic res, 24/7 Online cat, Audiobks via web, Bks on cassette, Bks on CD, Children's prog, Computers for patron use, Digital talking bks, E-Reserves, Electronic databases & coll, Free DVD rentals, ILL available, Internet access, Life-long learning prog for all ages, Magazines, Meeting rooms, Movies, Music CDs, Online cat, OverDrive digital audio bks, Photocopying/Printing, Preschool outreach, Printer for laptops & handheld devices, Prog for adults, Prog for children & young adult, Ref serv available, Scanner, Spanish lang bks, Spoken cassettes & CDs, Spoken cassettes & DVDs, Story hour, Summer reading prog, Tax forms, Teen prog, Telephone ref, Wheelchair accessible, Workshops
Open Mon-Wed 10-8, Thurs & Fri 10-6, Sat 10-5
Bookmobiles: 1. Mgr, Outreach, Jesus Moya

J INTERNATIONAL BUSINESS COLLEGE LIBRARY*, 7205 Shadeland Sta, 46256. SAN 375-4456. Tel: 317-841-2310. FAX: 317-841-6419. Web Site: www.IBCIndianapolis.edu. *Actg Librn,* Holly Bales; E-mail: hbales@ibcindianapolis.edu; Staff 1 (MLS 1)
Founded 2000. Enrl 301; Fac 25; Highest Degree: Associate
Library Holdings: Bk Titles 1,297; Bk Vols 1,462; Per Subs 63
Automation Activity & Vendor Info: (Cataloging) Book Systems; (Circulation) Book Systems; (OPAC) Book Systems
Wireless access
Open Mon-Fri 8-3
Restriction: Non-circulating to the pub

M IU HEALTH MEDICAL LIBRARY*, 1701 N Senate Blvd, Rm D1422, 46206-1367. SAN 304-9760. Tel: 317-962-8021. Interlibrary Loan Service Tel: 317-962-2979. FAX: 317-962-8397. Web Site: iuhealth.org/find-locations/iu-health-methodist-hospital.
Founded 1947
Library Holdings: e-books 300; e-journals 3,000; Bk Titles 2,700
Special Collections: Audiovisuals; Health Education
Subject Interests: Med, Nursing
Automation Activity & Vendor Info: (Acquisitions) EBSCO Online; (Cataloging) EOS International; (OPAC) EOS International
Wireless access
Partic in Midwest Collaborative for Library Services; Midwest Health Sci Libr Network; Proquest Dialog
Open Mon-Thurs 7-5:30, Fri 7-4:30

J IVY TECH COMMUNITY COLLEGE, North Meridian Campus Library, 50 W Fall Creek Pkwy N Dr, 46208. SAN 304-9698. Tel: 317-921-4782. FAX: 317-917-5719. Web Site: library.ivytech.edu/indianapolis. *Libr Dir,* Jan Woodall; Tel: 317-917-5742, E-mail: jwoodall1@ivytech.edu; *Asst Dir,* Erica McFarland; Tel: 317-917-7178, E-mail: emcfarland8@ivytech.edu; *Ref & Instruction Librn,* Katrina Earle; Tel: 317-917-7993, E-mail: kearle2@ivytech.edu; *Ref & Instruction Librn,* Kim Hurson; Tel: 317-917-1602, E-mail: khurson@ivytech.edu; *Ref & Instruction Librn,* Donna Tressler; E-mail: dtressler@ivytech.edu; Staff 9 (MLS 5, Non-MLS 4)
Founded 1969
Library Holdings: Bk Titles 23,416; Bk Vols 24,911; Per Subs 80
Subject Interests: Allied health, Bus & mgt, Educ, Sci tech, Vocational educ
Wireless access
Publications: Annual Serials List; Bibliographies; LRC (Newsletter); Periodical Holdings (Annual); reading lists
Partic in OCLC Online Computer Library Center, Inc
Open Mon-Thurs 8-7, Fri 8-5, Sat 10-4

S LILLY ENDOWMENT LIBRARY*, 2801 N Meridian St, 46208. SAN 304-9744. Tel: 317-924-5471. FAX: 317-926-4431. Web Site: lillyendowment.org. *Librn,* Mary Jo Fuller; Tel: 317-916-7316, E-mail: fullerm@lei.org; Staff 1 (MLS 1)
Founded 1974
Library Holdings: Bk Titles 4,000; Bk Vols 4,050; Per Subs 100
Subject Interests: Higher educ, Philanthropy, Relig
Automation Activity & Vendor Info: (Acquisitions) Book Systems; (Cataloging) Book Systems; (Circulation) Book Systems; (OPAC) Book Systems; (Serials) Book Systems
Wireless access
Restriction: Staff use only

C MARIAN UNIVERSITY*, Mother Theresa Hackelmeier Memorial Library, 3200 Cold Spring Rd, 46222-1997. SAN 304-9752. Tel: 317-955-6090. FAX: 317-955-6418. E-mail: librarystaff@marian.edu. Web Site: www.marian.edu/current-students/library. *Dir,* Rhonda Huisman; E-mail: rhuisman@marian.edu; *Acq Librn,* Lynne Colbert; E-mail: lcolbert@marian.edu; *Info & Instrul Serv Librn,* Edward Mandity; E-mail: emandity@marian.edu; Staff 5 (MLS 3, Non-MLS 2)
Founded 1937. Enrl 1,325; Fac 96; Highest Degree: Bachelor
Library Holdings: Bk Titles 142,690; Bk Vols 145,911; Per Subs 402
Special Collections: Am far west; Archbishop Paul C Schulte, bks, papers; Monsignor Doyle Coll
Subject Interests: Educ, Nursing, Roman Catholic Church
Wireless access
Publications: Annual Report; Marian College Library Guide
Partic in Midwest Collaborative for Library Services; OCLC Online Computer Library Center, Inc; Private Academic Library Network of Indiana

S PRESIDENT BENJAMIN HARRISON RESEARCH LIBRARY*, 1230 N Delaware St, 46202. SAN 326-5064. Tel: 317-631-1888. FAX: 317-632-5488. E-mail: harrison@bhpsite.org. Web Site: www.presidentbenjaminharrison.org. *Curator,* Jennifer Capps; E-mail: jcapps@bhpsite.org
Library Holdings: Bk Titles 2,700
Special Collections: Benjamin Harrison Coll
Restriction: Open by appt only

S ROLLS-ROYCE, Library & Knowledge Services Center, 450 S Meridian St, 46254. SAN 304-9590. Tel: 317-230-4751. E-mail: englibrindy@rolls-royce.com. Web Site: www.rolls-royce.com. *Librn,* Gabriele Hysong; E-mail: gabriele.hysong@rolls-royce.com; Staff 1 (MLS 1)
Founded 1941
Library Holdings: Bk Titles 11,210; Bk Vols 12,350; Per Subs 350
Special Collections: Allison Archives
Subject Interests: Aerospace, Gas turbines, Metallurgy
Wireless access
Open Mon-Fri 9-5

M ST VINCENT HOSPITAL & HEALTH SERVICES LIBRARY*, 2001 W 86th St, 46260. SAN 304-9825. Tel: 317-338-2095. Web Site: www.stvincent.org. *Mgr, Libr Serv,* Position Currently Open
Founded 1935
Library Holdings: e-journals 1,000; Bk Vols 1,500
Special Collections: Consumer Senior Health; Hospital Archives Coll
Subject Interests: Hospital admin, Med, Nursing, Spirituality
Automation Activity & Vendor Info: (OPAC) EOS International
Function: Ref serv available
Partic in Midwest Collaborative for Library Services
Restriction: Circulates for staff only

GL UNITED STATES COURTS LIBRARY*, Southern District of Indiana, 46 E Ohio St, Rm 445, 46204. Tel: 317-229-3925. FAX: 317-229-3927. Web Site: www.lb7.uscourts.gov. *Librn,* Sonja Simpson; Tel: 317-229-3928
Library Holdings: Bk Vols 10,000; Per Subs 55
Automation Activity & Vendor Info: (Cataloging) SirsiDynix; (OPAC) SirsiDynix
Wireless access
Restriction: Staff use only

C UNIVERSITY OF INDIANAPOLIS*, Krannert Memorial Library, 1400 E Hanna Ave, 46227-3697. SAN 304-9620. Tel: 317-788-3268. Interlibrary Loan Service Tel: 317-788-3398, 317-788-3402. Reference Tel: 317-788-2100, 317-788-6124. FAX: 317-788-3275. Web Site: uindy.edu/library. *Libr Dir,* Marisa Albrecht; E-mail: albrechtm@uindy.edu; *Cat & Acq,* Lucy Fields; E-mail: lfields@uindy.edu; *Ref & Instruction Librn,* Tedra Richter; E-mail: trichter@uindy.edu; *Syst Librn,* Jeny Nugent; E-mail: nugentjm@uindy.edu; *Univ Archivist,* Mark Vopelak; E-mail: vopelakm@uindy.edu; Staff 7 (MLS 7)
Founded 1902. Enrl 5,000; Fac 225; Highest Degree: Doctorate
Library Holdings: AV Mats 4,404; e-books 30,000; e-journals 15; Bk Titles 135,031; Bk Vols 154,257; Per Subs 650
Special Collections: Evangelical United Brethren Coll; Krannert Coll (specially bd limited editions)
Subject Interests: Educ, Hist, Nursing, Phys therapy, Psychol, Relig
Automation Activity & Vendor Info: (Acquisitions) Ex Libris Group; (Cataloging) Ex Libris Group; (Circulation) Ex Libris Group; (Course Reserve) Ex Libris Group; (ILL) Ex Libris Group; (OPAC) Ex Libris Group; (Serials) Ex Libris Group
Wireless access
Function: Archival coll, For res purposes, ILL available, Magnifiers for reading, Res libr, Telephone ref, Wheelchair accessible
Partic in Academic Libraries of Indiana; Midwest Collaborative for Library Services; Private Academic Library Network of Indiana

Open Mon-Thurs 7:30am-Midnight, Fri 7:30am-9pm, Sat 10-9, Sun 10am-Midnight
Restriction: Open to students, fac & staff, Pub use on premises

JAMESTOWN

P TRI-AREA LIBRARY, Two W Main St, 46147. (Mail add: PO Box 315, 46147-0315). Tel: 765-676-6190. E-mail: triarealibrary1@centurylink.net. Web Site: www.jamestownlibrary.com. *Board Pres,* Suzy Rich
Founded 1981
Library Holdings: Bk Titles 11,500
Wireless access
Open Tues & Thurs 1-8, Wed 11-5, Fri 1-5

JASONVILLE

P JASONVILLE PUBLIC LIBRARY, 611 W Main St, 47438-0105. (Mail add: PO Box 105, 47438), SAN 304-9884. Tel: 812-665-2025. E-mail: jvillepl@att.net. Web Site: www.jasonvillepubliclibrary.org. *Dir,* Anita Lorenzo; *Librn,* Lori Caddell; Staff 2 (MLS 1, Non-MLS 1)
Founded 1924. Pop 2,560; Circ 16,890
Library Holdings: CDs 191; Bk Titles 23,411; Bk Vols 25,121; Per Subs 31; Videos 1,041
Special Collections: Indiana History Holdings
Subject Interests: Genealogy
Open Mon & Wed 1-7, Sat 9-5
Friends of the Library Group

JASPER

P JASPER-DUBOIS COUNTY PUBLIC LIBRARY*, 1116 Main St, 47546-2899. SAN 304-9892. Tel: 812-482-2712. FAX: 812-482-7123. Web Site: www.jdcpl.us. *Dir,* Christine Golden; Tel: 812-482-2712, Ext 6115, E-mail: cgolden@jdcpl.us; *Youth Serv Librn,* Christine Howard; Tel: 812-482-2712, Ext 6114, E-mail: choward@jdcpl.us; *Br Mgr,* Beth Herzog-Schmidt; Tel: 812-482-2712, Ext 6111, E-mail: bherzog@jdcpl.us; *Libr Experience Mgr,* Jordan Schuetter; Tel: 812-482-2712, Ext 6108, E-mail: jschuetter@jdcpl.us; Staff 23 (MLS 3, Non-MLS 20)
Founded 1934. Pop 32,000; Circ 390,000
Library Holdings: CDs 600; Bk Vols 95,000; Per Subs 220; Talking Bks 3,800; Videos 3,500
Subject Interests: Genealogy, Hist, Indiana
Automation Activity & Vendor Info: (Acquisitions) TLC (The Library Corporation); (Cataloging) TLC (The Library Corporation); (Circulation) TLC (The Library Corporation); (OPAC) TLC (The Library Corporation)
Wireless access
Partic in Midwest Collaborative for Library Services
Open Mon-Thurs 9-8, Fri & Sat 9-5, Sun 12-5
Restriction: Open to pub for ref & circ; with some limitations
Friends of the Library Group
Branches: 3
BIRDSEYE BRANCH, 100 S State Rd 145, Birdseye, 47513. Tel: 812-389-1030. *Br Head,* AmyJo Lytle; E-mail: alytle@jdcpl.us
Open Tues & Thurs 2-8, Sat 10-2
DUBOIS BRANCH LIBRARY, 5506 E Main St, Dubois, 47527. Tel: 812-678-2548. FAX: 812-678-2549. Web Site: www.jdcpl.us/dubois.php. *Br Mgr,* Anita Murphy; Tel: 812-678-2548, Ext 112, E-mail: amurphy@jdcpl.lib.in.us
Library Holdings: Bk Titles 10,000
Open Mon-Thurs 10-8, Fri 10-5, Sat 10-2
FERDINAND BRANCH, 112 E 16th St, Ferdinand, 47542, SAN 371-3717. Tel: 812-367-1671. FAX: 812-367-1063. Web Site: www.jdcpl.us/ferdinand.php. *Br Mgr,* Trina James; Tel: 812-367-1671, Ext 5111, E-mail: tjames@jdcpl.us; Staff 3 (Non-MLS 3)
Founded 1960. Pop 12,000
Library Holdings: Bk Vols 21,000
Automation Activity & Vendor Info: (Serials) TLC (The Library Corporation)
Function: ILL available, Prog for adults, Prog for children & young adult, Ref serv available, Summer reading prog, Telephone ref
Open Mon-Thurs 9-8, Fri & Sat 9-5

JEFFERSONVILLE

P JEFFERSONVILLE TOWNSHIP PUBLIC LIBRARY*, 211 E Court Ave, 47130. (Mail add: PO Box 1548, 47131-1548), SAN 304-9906. Tel: 812-285-5630. Administration Tel: 812-285-5632. FAX: 812-285-5639. Web Site: jefflibrary.org. *Dir,* Libby Pollard; Tel: 812-285-5633, E-mail: lpollard@jefflibrary.org; *Local Hist & Genealogy Librn,* Diane Stepro; E-mail: dstepro@jefflibrary.org; *Br Mgr,* Becky Kelien; E-mail: bkelien@jefflibrary.org; *Pub Serv Mgr,* Kimberly Jackson; E-mail: kjackson@jefflibrary.org; *Youth Serv Mgr,* Lori Morgan; E-mail: lmorgan@jefflibrary.org; Staff 9 (MLS 9)
Founded 1900. Pop 59,062; Circ 207,554
Library Holdings: Audiobooks 13,599; AV Mats 18,475; CDs 4,320; DVDs 1,587; e-books 4,956; e-journals 77; Bk Titles 146,077; Bk Vols 177,767; Per Subs 237; Talking Bks 3,656; Videos 18,475
Special Collections: Local & Indiana History (Indiana Coll)
Automation Activity & Vendor Info: (Cataloging) Innovative Interfaces, Inc; (Circulation) Innovative Interfaces, Inc; (OPAC) Innovative Interfaces, Inc
Wireless access
Function: 24/7 Electronic res, 24/7 Online cat, Activity rm, Adult bk club, After school storytime, Art exhibits, Art programs, Audiobks on Playaways & MP3, AV serv, Bk club(s), Bks on cassette, Bks on CD, Children's prog, Computer training, Computers for patron use, Digital talking bks, Electronic databases & coll, Free DVD rentals, Games & aids for people with disabilities, Genealogy discussion group, Holiday prog, ILL available, Instruction & testing, Internet access, Large print keyboards, Life-long learning prog for all ages, Magazines, Mail & tel request accepted, Makerspace, Mango lang, Meeting rooms, Microfiche/film & reading machines, Movies, Music CDs, Notary serv, Online cat, Online ref, Orientations, Outreach serv, Outside serv via phone, mail, e-mail & web, OverDrive digital audio bks, Photocopying/Printing, Preschool outreach, Printer for laptops & handheld devices, Prog for adults, Prog for children & young adult, Ref serv available, Spanish lang bks, Spoken cassettes & DVDs, STEM programs, Story hour, Study rm, Summer reading prog, Teen prog, Telephone ref, VHS videos, Wheelchair accessible, Workshops, Writing prog
Partic in Midwest Collaborative for Library Services
Open Mon-Thurs 9-8, Fri 9-5:30, Sat 9-5
Friends of the Library Group
Branches: 1
CLARKSVILLE BRANCH, 1312 Eastern Blvd, Clarksville, 47129-1704. Tel: 812-285-5640. FAX: 812-285-5642. *Br Mgr,* Becky Kelien; Tel: 812-285-5647, E-mail: bkelien@jefflibrary.org; *Pub Serv Librn,* Jennifer Harl; E-mail: jharl@jefflibrary.org. Subject Specialists: *Children's prog,* Jennifer Harl
Library Holdings: Bk Titles 45,880; Bk Vols 50,461; Per Subs 82
Automation Activity & Vendor Info: (Acquisitions) Baker & Taylor; (Serials) Infor Library & Information Solutions
Open Mon-Thurs 9-9, Fri 9-5:30, Sat 9-5
Friends of the Library Group

C MID-AMERICA COLLEGE OF FUNERAL SERVICE LIBRARY, W H Pierce Library, 3111 Hamburg Pike, 47130. Tel: 812-288-8878. Toll Free Tel: 800-221-6158. FAX: 812-288-5942. E-mail: library@mid-america.edu. Web Site: www.mid-america.edu/about/campus-facilities.
Enrl 125; Fac 9
Library Holdings: AV Mats 110; Bk Titles 1,019; Bk Vols 1,150; Per Subs 19; Spec Interest Per Sub 25
Subject Interests: Funeral serv
Automation Activity & Vendor Info: (Cataloging) Follett Software
Wireless access
Function: Res libr
Restriction: Not open to pub

JONESBORO

P JONESBORO PUBLIC LIBRARY*, 124 E Fourth St, 46938-1105. SAN 304-9914. Tel: 765-677-9080. E-mail: jonesborolibrary56@yahoo.com. *Dir,* Carol Jones; *Asst Librn,* Terry Jones; Staff 3 (MLS 1, Non-MLS 2)
Founded 1941. Pop 2,073; Circ 10,464
Library Holdings: AV Mats 1,194; DVDs 5,000; Bk Titles 12,668; Bk Vols 14,071; Per Subs 76
Wireless access
Open Mon-Fri 12-7

KENDALLVILLE

P KENDALLVILLE PUBLIC LIBRARY*, 221 S Park Ave, 46755-2248. SAN 341-3675. Tel: 260-343-2010. FAX: 260-343-2011. E-mail: info@kendallvillelibrary.org. Web Site: www.kendallvillelibrary.org. *Libr Dir,* Katie Mullins; E-mail: kmullins@kendallvillelibrary.org; *Adult Serv Mgr,* Leah Dresser; E-mail: ldresser@kendallvillelibrary.org; *Circ Mgr,* Lynette Barnett; E-mail: lbarnett@kendallvillelibrary.org; *Youth Serv Mgr,* Beth Munk; E-mail: bmunk@kendallvillelibrary.org; *Tech Serv,* Alex Leitch; E-mail: aleitch@kendallvillelibrary.org; Staff 5 (MLS 3, Non-MLS 2)
Founded 1913. Pop 17,241; Circ 207,619
Library Holdings: AV Mats 10,175; Bk Titles 66,782; Bk Vols 68,452; Per Subs 226; Videos 943
Special Collections: Gene Stratton-Porter Coll; M F Owen Scrapbook
Subject Interests: Local hist
Automation Activity & Vendor Info: (Cataloging) TLC (The Library Corporation); (Circulation) TLC (The Library Corporation); (OPAC) TLC (The Library Corporation)
Wireless access

Publications: Annual Report; Newsletter (Monthly); Topic Supplement (Quarterly)
Partic in Evergreen Indiana Consortium; Midwest Collaborative for Library Services
Open Mon-Thurs 9-8, Fri 9-5, Sat 9-3
Friends of the Library Group
Branches: 1
LIMBERLOST PUBLIC LIBRARY, 164 Kelly St, Rome City, 46784. (Mail add: PO Box 447, Rome City, 46784-0447), SAN 341-3705. Tel: 260-854-2775. FAX: 260-854-3382. *Br Mgr,* Victoria Ferguson; Staff 2 (MLS 1, Non-MLS 1)
Library Holdings: AV Mats 561; Bk Titles 12,612; Bk Vols 13,141; Per Subs 60; Videos 217
Open Mon & Thurs 9-8, Tues & Wed 9-6, Fri 9-5, Sat 9-3
Friends of the Library Group

KENTLAND

P KENTLAND-JEFFERSON TOWNSHIP PUBLIC LIBRARY*, 201 E Graham St, 47951-1233. SAN 304-9922. Tel: 219-474-5044. FAX: 219-474-5351. E-mail: kentlandpubliclibrary@gmail.com. Web Site: kentland.lib.in.us. *Dir,* Roberta Dewing; Staff 1 (Non-MLS 1)
Founded 1912. Pop 2,000; Circ 19,824
Jan 2014-Dec 2014 Income $204,153, State $7,743, Locally Generated Income $196,410. Mats Exp $43,173, Books $28,043, Per/Ser (Incl. Access Fees) $2,302, AV Mat $12,828. Sal $38,000
Library Holdings: Audiobooks 791; DVDs 1,021; Large Print Bks 2,000; Microforms 198; Bk Titles 31,593; Per Subs 50
Automation Activity & Vendor Info: (Acquisitions) Mandarin Library Automation; (Cataloging) Mandarin Library Automation; (Circulation) Mandarin Library Automation; (OPAC) Mandarin Library Automation
Wireless access
Function: Audiobks via web, Bks on CD, Children's prog, Computers for patron use, Free DVD rentals, Holiday prog, ILL available, Microfiche/film & reading machines, Online cat, OverDrive digital audio bks, Photocopying/Printing, Preschool reading prog, Prog for adults, Prog for children & young adult, Scanner, Story hour, Summer reading prog, Tax forms, Wheelchair accessible
Open Mon 9-8, Tues & Thurs 11-6, Wed 1-8, Fri 9-5, Sat 8-Noon
Friends of the Library Group

KEWANNA

P KEWANNA-UNION TOWNSHIP PUBLIC LIBRARY*, 210 E Main St, 46939-9529. (Mail add: PO Box 365, 46939-0365), SAN 304-9930. Tel: 574-653-2011. FAX: 574-653-2130. E-mail: kewannapublib@yahoo.com. Web Site: kewanna.lib.in.us. *Dir,* Charles Rude; Staff 4 (MLS 2, Non-MLS 2)
Founded 1914. Pop 1,657; Circ 13,100
Library Holdings: AV Mats 1,650; Large Print Bks 160; Bk Titles 30,000; Per Subs 311; Talking Bks 311; Videos 875
Special Collections: Fulton County; Indiana
Subject Interests: Antiques, Arts & crafts
Wireless access
Partic in Evergreen Indiana Consortium
Open Mon-Wed & Fri 10-6, Thurs 10-8, Sat 10-3

KINGMAN

P KINGMAN-MILLCREEK PUBLIC LIBRARY, 123 W State St, 47952. (Mail add: PO Box 116, 47952-0116), SAN 304-9949. Tel: 765-397-3138. FAX: 765-397-3566. E-mail: kmpl1915-web@yahoo.com. Web Site: www.kingmanlibrary.com. *Dir,* Shannon Rollins; Staff 3 (Non-MLS 3)
Founded 1916. Pop 1,610; Circ 3,849
Library Holdings: Audiobooks 100; Bks on Deafness & Sign Lang 4; DVDs 600; Large Print Bks 300; Bk Titles 13,900; Bk Vols 14,000; Per Subs 30; Videos 1,600
Subject Interests: Local hist
Automation Activity & Vendor Info: (Cataloging) Follett Software; (Circulation) Follett Software; (OPAC) Follett Software
Wireless access
Partic in Midwest Collaborative for Library Services
Special Services for the Blind - Talking bks
Open Mon & Tues 11-6, Wed & Thurs 11-5, Fri & Sat 10-2

KIRKLIN

P KIRKLIN PUBLIC LIBRARY*, 115 N Main, 46050. SAN 304-9957. Tel: 765-279-8308. FAX: 765-279-8258. Web Site: www.kirklinlibrary.com. *Libr Dir,* Heidi Turner; E-mail: hturner@kirklinlibrary.com; Staff 3 (Non-MLS 3)
Founded 1913. Pop 1,476; Circ 14,764
Library Holdings: Bk Vols 18,000; Per Subs 50
Special Collections: Kirklin History Archives
Automation Activity & Vendor Info: (Acquisitions) Follett Software; (Cataloging) Follett Software; (Serials) Follett Software
Partic in Midwest Collaborative for Library Services
Open Mon & Wed 12-7, Tues & Thurs 10-5, Fri 12-5, Sat 10-3
Friends of the Library Group

KNIGHTSTOWN

P KNIGHTSTOWN PUBLIC LIBRARY*, Five E Main St, 46148-1248. SAN 304-9965. Tel: 765-345-5095. FAX: 765-345-5377. E-mail: ktown_library@hrtc.net. Web Site: knightstown.lib.in.us. *Dir,* Linda Davis; Staff 4 (MLS 1, Non-MLS 3)
Founded 1912. Pop 2,270; Circ 15,911
Library Holdings: AV Mats 1,159; Large Print Bks 151; Bk Titles 18,711; Bk Vols 20,094; Per Subs 67; Talking Bks 65; Videos 615
Special Collections: Knightstown, Henry County & Indiana History; Local Newspaper Coll, 1908-present
Automation Activity & Vendor Info: (Acquisitions) Evergreen; (Cataloging) Evergreen; (Circulation) Evergreen; (OPAC) Evergreen; (Serials) Evergreen
Wireless access
Function: 24/7 Electronic res, 24/7 Online cat, Archival coll, Audiobks via web, Bks on CD, Butterfly Garden, Children's prog, Computer training, Computers for patron use, Distance learning, E-Reserves, Electronic databases & coll, Free DVD rentals, Govt ref serv, Holiday prog, Home delivery & serv to seniorr ctr & nursing homes, Homebound delivery serv, ILL available, Internet access, Magazines, Magnifiers for reading, Mail & tel request accepted, Microfiche/film & reading machines, Music CDs, Notary serv, Online cat, Online ref, Orientations, Outreach serv, Outside serv via phone, mail, e-mail & web, OverDrive digital audio bks, Photocopying/Printing, Preschool outreach, Preschool reading prog, Printer for laptops & handheld devices, Prog for adults, Prog for children & young adult, Ref serv available, Scanner, Senior computer classes, Senior outreach, Serves people with intellectual disabilities, Spoken cassettes & CDs, Story hour, Summer & winter reading prog, Summer reading prog, Tax forms, Teen prog, Telephone ref
Partic in Association for Rural & Small Libraries; Evergreen Indiana Consortium
Open Mon & Fri 10-5, Tues & Thurs 10-7, Sat 10-2
Restriction: Borrowing requests are handled by ILL, In-house use for visitors, Non-resident fee
Friends of the Library Group

KNOX

P STARKE COUNTY PUBLIC LIBRARY SYSTEM*, Henry F Schricker (Main Library), 152 W Culver Rd, 46534-2220. SAN 304-9973. Tel: 574-772-7323. FAX: 574-772-4207. Web Site: scpls.org, www.starkecountylibrary.org. *Libr Dir,* Kathleen Bowman; E-mail: kbowman@starkecountylibrary.org; *Syst Adminr,* Rob Pitts; *Head, Children's & Young Adult Serv,* Janine Tuttle-Gassere; *Head, Circ,* Ashley Reed; *Head, Ref,* Ellen Pitcher; *Head, Tech Serv,* Lisa Boyle; *Readers' Advisory,* Nancy Barton; Staff 12 (MLS 3, Non-MLS 9)
Founded 1919. Pop 18,569; Circ 169,497
Library Holdings: AV Mats 9,544; Electronic Media & Resources 31; Large Print Bks 2,000; Bk Vols 102,468; Per Subs 287
Subject Interests: Genealogy, Local hist
Automation Activity & Vendor Info: (Acquisitions) Innovative Interfaces, Inc; (Cataloging) Innovative Interfaces, Inc; (Circulation) Innovative Interfaces, Inc; (OPAC) Innovative Interfaces, Inc
Wireless access
Function: Activity rm, Adult literacy prog, Archival coll, Art exhibits, Bk club(s), Bks on CD, Children's prog, Computers for patron use, Electronic databases & coll, Free DVD rentals, Home delivery & serv to seniorr ctr & nursing homes, ILL available, Jail serv, Magazines, Meeting rooms, Music CDs, Notary serv, Online cat, Outreach serv, Photocopying/Printing, Preschool outreach, Prog for adults, Prog for children & young adult, Ref serv available, Scanner, Spoken cassettes & CDs, Spoken cassettes & DVDs, Story hour, Summer & winter reading prog, Summer reading prog, Tax forms, Teen prog, Telephone ref, Wheelchair accessible, Winter reading prog
Partic in Midwest Collaborative for Library Services; Northern Indiana Computer Consortium for Libraries
Special Services for the Deaf - Bks on deafness & sign lang; Closed caption videos
Special Services for the Blind - Audio mat; Bks on cassette; Bks on CD; Copier with enlargement capabilities; Large print bks; Magnifiers; Sound rec
Open Mon-Thurs 9-7, Fri & Sat 9-5
Branches: 3
HAMLET BRANCH, Six N Starke St, Hamlet, 46532. (Mail add: PO Box 8, Hamlet, 46532-0008), SAN 324-2498. Tel: 574-867-6033. FAX: 574-207-4100. *Br Mgr,* Barbara Pilger
Open Mon 9-6, Wed & Fri 9-5, Sat 9-Noon

KOONTZ LAKE BRANCH, 7954 N State Rd 23, Walkerton, 46574, SAN 321-415X. Tel: 574-586-3353. FAX: 514-586-5047. *Br Mgr,* Paulette Varga
Open Mon & Fri 9-5, Wed 9-6, Sat 8am-11am

SAN PIERRE BRANCH, 103 S Broadway, San Pierre, 46374. (Mail add: PO Box 218, San Pierre, 46374-0218), SAN 321-4168. Tel: 219-828-4352. FAX: 219-205-3502. *Br Mgr,* Carla Stoll
Open Mon & Fri 9-5, Wed 9-6, Sat 9-1

KOKOMO

C INDIANA UNIVERSITY KOKOMO LIBRARY*, 2300 S Washington St, 46904. (Mail add: PO Box 9003, 46904-9003), SAN 305-0009. Tel: 765-455-9265. Circulation Tel: 765-455-9513. Reference Tel: 765-455-9521. E-mail: iuklib@iuk.edu. Web Site: www.iuk.edu/library. *Interim Dean of Libr,* Yan He; E-mail: yh4@iuk.edu; *Digital User Experience Librn,* Angie Thorpe; E-mail: atthorpe@iuk.edu; *Archivist, Info Serv Librn,* Meg Galasso; Tel: 765-455-9345, E-mail: galasso@iuk.edu; *Tech Serv Librn,* Ria Lukes; E-mail: rlukes@iuk.edu; Staff 8 (MLS 5, Non-MLS 3)
Founded 1945. Enrl 4,000; Fac 120; Highest Degree: Master
Jul 2017-Jun 2018 Income $1,050,314. Mats Exp $418,000, Books $80,000, Per/Ser (Incl. Access Fees) $338,000. Sal $352,151 (Prof $257,822)
Library Holdings: AV Mats 856; CDs 747; DVDs 1,544; e-books 55,000; Electronic Media & Resources 99; Microforms 7,031; Bk Vols 80,000; Per Subs 25; Videos 124
Special Collections: State Document Depository; US Document Depository
Automation Activity & Vendor Info: (Acquisitions) SirsiDynix; (Cataloging) SirsiDynix; (Circulation) SirsiDynix; (Course Reserve) SirsiDynix; (ILL) OCLC ILLiad; (Media Booking) SirsiDynix; (OPAC) SirsiDynix; (Serials) SirsiDynix
Wireless access
Publications: Check It Out (Newsletter)
Partic in Academic Libraries of Indiana; LYRASIS; Midwest Collaborative for Library Services
Open Mon-Thurs (Fall-Spring) 8-9, Fri 8-5, Sat 12-5, Sun 1-7; Mon-Thurs (Summer) 8-8, Fri 8-5

P KOKOMO-HOWARD COUNTY PUBLIC LIBRARY*, 220 N Union St, 46901-4614. SAN 305-0017. Tel: 765-457-3242. Reference Tel: 765-454-4710. FAX: 765-457-3683. E-mail: khcpl@khcpl.org. Web Site: www.khcpl.org. *Dir,* Faith Brautigam; *Asst Dir,* Doug Workinger; *Head, Coll Mgt,* Tammy Keith; E-mail: tkeith@khcpl.org; *Head, Genealogy & Local Hist,* Amy Russell; E-mail: arussell@khcpl.org; *Adult Coll Develop Librn,* Dawn VanBibber; E-mail: dvanbibber@khcpl.org; *Juv Coll Develop Librn,* Debra Andrews; E-mail: dandrews@khcpl.org; *Young Adult Coll Develop Librn,* Carly Wimmer; E-mail: cwimmer@khcpl.org; *Tech Mgr,* Aaron Smith; E-mail: asmith@khcpl.org; *Children's Coordr,* Brennan Reed; E-mail: breed@khcpl.org; *Readers' Advisory Coordr,* Meliss Wheelock; E-mail: mwheelock@khcpl.org; *Adult Serv,* Trisha Shively; E-mail: tshively@khcpl.org; *AV,* Tonya McClain; E-mail: tmcclain@khcpl.org; *Circ,* Kayla Skiles; E-mail: kskiles@khcpl.org; *Outreach Serv,* Joy Rogers; E-mail: jrogers@khcpl.org; *Principal Cataloger,* Ashley Meyers; E-mail: ameyers@khcpl.org; Staff 102 (MLS 20, Non-MLS 82)
Founded 1885. Pop 76,265; Circ 822,939
Jan 2018-Dec 2018 Income $5,897,677, State $436,858, Locally Generated Income $5,272,819, Other $188,000. Mats Exp $742,524, Books $313,469, Per/Ser (Incl. Access Fees) $19,055, AV Equip $28,103, AV Mat $145,906, Electronic Ref Mat (Incl. Access Fees) $235,991. Sal $3,544,695
Library Holdings: CDs 20,285; DVDs 28,943; e-books 46,112; e-journals 163; Electronic Media & Resources 137,957; Bk Vols 251,968; Per Subs 316
Special Collections: Hoosier Art Coll; Howard County Indiana Genealogy & History
Automation Activity & Vendor Info: (Acquisitions) Innovative Interfaces, Inc; (Cataloging) Innovative Interfaces, Inc; (Circulation) Innovative Interfaces, Inc; (Discovery) BiblioCommons; (ILL) OCLC; (OPAC) BiblioCommons
Wireless access
Function: 24/7 Electronic res, 24/7 Online cat, 3D Printer, Activity rm, Adult bk club, Art exhibits, Audiobks on Playaways & MP3, Audiobks via web, AV serv, Bk club(s), Bks on CD, CD-ROM, Children's prog, Computer training, Computers for patron use, Digital talking bks, E-Readers, Electronic databases & coll, Free DVD rentals, Home delivery & serv to seniorr ctr & nursing homes, Homebound delivery serv, ILL available, Internet access, Jail serv, Life-long learning prog for all ages, Magazines, Magnifiers for reading, Mango lang, Meeting rooms, Microfiche/film & reading machines, Movies, Museum passes, Music CDs, Notary serv, Online cat, Online ref, Outreach serv, OverDrive digital audio bks, Photocopying/Printing, Printer for laptops & handheld devices, Prog for adults, Prog for children & young adult, Ref & res, Ref serv available, Res assist avail, Res performed for a fee, Scanner, STEM programs, Story hour, Study rm, Summer reading prog, Tax forms, Teen prog, Telephone ref, Wheelchair accessible, Writing prog
Publications: A Newsletter of Seasonal Events (Quarterly)
Open Mon-Thurs 9-8, Fri & Sat 9-5:30, Sun 2-5:30
Friends of the Library Group
Branches: 2
RUSSIAVILLE BRANCH, 315 Mesa Dr, Russiaville, 46979, SAN 370-0054. Tel: 765-883-5112. FAX: 765-883-5974. *Br Asst,* Trina Evans; Staff 6 (MLS 1, Non-MLS 5)
Founded 1989
Automation Activity & Vendor Info: (Circulation) Innovative Interfaces, Inc - Sierra; (OPAC) BiblioCommons
Open Mon, Tues, Thurs, 9-8, Fri & Sat 9-5:30, Sun 2-5:30
Friends of the Library Group
SOUTH BRANCH, 1755 E Center Rd, 46902-5322, SAN 321-8589. Tel: 765-453-4150. FAX: 765-453-6677. *Br Mgr,* Lori Hugley; E-mail: lhugley@khcpl.org; Staff 14 (MLS 5, Non-MLS 9)
Founded 1978
Automation Activity & Vendor Info: (Circulation) Innovative Interfaces, Inc - Sierra; (OPAC) BiblioCommons
Open Mon-Thurs 9-8, Fri & Sat 9-5:30, Sun 2-5:30
Friends of the Library Group
Bookmobiles: 2. Outreach Mgr, Joy Record. Bk vols 7,000

LA CROSSE

P LA CROSSE PUBLIC LIBRARY, 307 E Main St, 46348. SAN 376-5369. Tel: 219-754-2606. FAX: 219-754-2600. Web Site: www.lacrosse.lib.in.us. *Dir,* Karla Wilson; E-mail: karlawilson@lacrosse.lib.in.us; Staff 6 (MLS 1, Non-MLS 5)
Pop 1,128; Circ 25,000
Jun 2019-May 2020. Mats Exp $20,535, Books $11,514, Per/Ser (Incl. Access Fees) $619, AV Equip $1,500, AV Mat $5,402, Electronic Ref Mat (Incl. Access Fees) $1,500. Sal $48,398
Library Holdings: Audiobooks 410; AV Mats 3,417; Braille Volumes 1; DVDs 2,850; e-books 95; e-journals 50; Large Print Bks 450; Bk Titles 18,050; Bk Vols 18,093; Per Subs 30
Automation Activity & Vendor Info: (Acquisitions) Follett Software; (Cataloging) Follett Software; (Circulation) Follett Software
Wireless access
Function: 24/7 Online cat, Activity rm, Adult bk club, Audiobks on Playaways & MP3, Audiobks via web, Bk club(s), Bks on CD, Children's prog, Computer training, Computers for patron use, Doc delivery serv, Electronic databases & coll, Free DVD rentals, Holiday prog, ILL available, Internet access, Magazines, Meeting rooms, Movies, Online cat, OverDrive digital audio bks, Photocopying/Printing, Prog for adults, Prog for children & young adult, Ref & res, Ref serv available, Res assist avail, Scanner, Senior computer classes, STEM programs, Story hour, Summer & winter reading prog, Summer reading prog, Teen prog, Wheelchair accessible
Special Services for the Blind - Audio mat; Bks available with recordings; Bks on CD; Cassettes; Extensive large print coll; Free checkout of audio mat; Large print bks
Open Mon 12-8:30, Tues & Fri 9-5:30, Wed 9-8:30, Thurs 12-5:30, Sat 9-1

LA PORTE

P LA PORTE COUNTY PUBLIC LIBRARY*, 904 Indiana Ave, 46350. SAN 305-0033. Tel: 219-362-6156. FAX: 219-362-6158. E-mail: help@laportelibrary.org. Web Site: www.laportelibrary.org. *Dir,* Fonda Owens; E-mail: fowens@laportelibrary.org; *Coll Mgt,* Holly Trott; *Commun Engagement Mgr,* Susan Bannwart; *Tech Serv Mgr,* Michael Sheehan; Staff 62 (MLS 13, Non-MLS 49)
Founded 1897. Pop 64,696; Circ 903,285
Library Holdings: Audiobooks 12,500; Bks on Deafness & Sign Lang 50; CDs 15,000; DVDs 19,125; e-books 702; Electronic Media & Resources 250; High Interest/Low Vocabulary Bk Vols 2,000; Large Print Bks 30,000; Microforms 11,276; Bk Titles 225,000; Bk Vols 316,000; Per Subs 255; Videos 14,855
Special Collections: History of La Porte County, City of La Porte & State of Indiana
Automation Activity & Vendor Info: (Acquisitions) Innovative Interfaces, Inc; (Cataloging) Innovative Interfaces, Inc; (Circulation) Innovative Interfaces, Inc; (OPAC) Innovative Interfaces, Inc
Wireless access
Partic in Midwest Collaborative for Library Services; OCLC Online Computer Library Center, Inc
Open Mon-Thurs 9-7, Fri 9-6, Sat 9-5
Friends of the Library Group
Branches: 6
COOLSPRING, 6925 W 400 N, Michigan City, 46360, SAN 322-5798. Tel: 219-879-3272. FAX: 219-879-3333. *Br Mgr,* Rich Bukva; E-mail: rbukva@laportelibrary.org; Staff 5 (MLS 1, Non-MLS 4)
Function: Adult bk club, Bks on CD, Children's prog, Computers for patron use, Free DVD rentals, Homework prog, ILL available, Magnifiers

for reading, Music CDs, Notary serv, Online cat, Photocopying/Printing, Preschool outreach, Prog for adults, Prog for children & young adult, Ref serv available, Serves people with intellectual disabilities, Spoken cassettes & CDs, Summer reading prog, Tax forms, Teen prog, Wheelchair accessible
Open Mon-Thurs 10-7, Fri 10-6, Sat 9-5
Restriction: Restricted pub use
Friends of the Library Group

FISH LAKE, 7981 E State Rd 4, Walkerton, 46574. (Mail add: PO Box 125, Walkerton, 46574-0125), SAN 341-3764. Tel: 219-369-1337. FAX: 219-369-1337. *Br Mgr,* Agnes Thompson; Staff 1 (Non-MLS 1)
Founded 2016
Library Holdings: CDs 250; DVDs 250; Large Print Bks 100; Bk Titles 8,761; Bk Vols 9,414; Per Subs 40
Open Tues 11-7, Wed & Fri 2-6, Thurs 2-7, Sat 9-1

HANNA BRANCH, 108 E West St, Hanna, 46340. (Mail add: PO Box 78, Hanna, 46340-0078), SAN 341-3799. Tel: 219-797-4735. FAX: 219-797-4735. *Br Mgr,* Toni Kuster; E-mail: tkuster@laportelibrary.org; Staff 1 (Non-MLS 1)
Founded 2016
Library Holdings: CDs 350; DVDs 800; Bk Titles 8,156; Bk Vols 8,391; Per Subs 32
Open Mon & Wed 1-7, Thurs & Fri 1-6, Sat 9-1

KINGSFORD HEIGHTS BRANCH, 436 Evanston Rd, Kingsford Heights, 46346. (Mail add: PO Box 219, Kingsford Heights, 46346-0219), SAN 341-3829. Tel: 219-393-3280. FAX: 219-393-3280. *Br Mgr,* Agnes Thompson; E-mail: agnes.thompson@laportelibrary.org; Staff 1 (Non-MLS 1)
Library Holdings: CDs 350; DVDs 800; Bk Titles 10,158; Bk Vols 11,900; Per Subs 40
Open Mon & Fri 11-6, Tues & Thurs 12-7, Sat 9-1

ROLLING PRAIRIE BRANCH, One E Michigan St, Rolling Prairie, 46371. (Mail add: PO Box 157, Rolling Prairie, 46371-0157), SAN 341-3853. Tel: 219-778-2390. FAX: 219-778-2390. *Br Mgr,* Jennifer Monhaut; E-mail: jennifer.monhaut@laportelibrary.org; Staff 1 (Non-MLS 1)
Founded 2017
Library Holdings: CDs 350; DVDs 800; Bk Titles 19,199; Bk Vols 21,140; Per Subs 47
Open Mon & Fri 10-6, Tues & Thurs 12-7, Sat 9-1

UNION MILLS BRANCH, 3727 W 800 S, Union Mills, 46382-9672. (Mail add: PO Box 189, Union Mills, 46382-0189), SAN 341-3888. Tel: 219-767-2604. FAX: 219-767-2604. *Br Mgr,* Position Currently Open
Library Holdings: CDs 350; DVDs 800; Bk Titles 9,649; Bk Vols 10,112; Per Subs 32
Open Mon & Wed 12-7, Tues & Fri 1-6, Sat 9-1

Bookmobiles: 1

LADOGA

P LADOGA-CLARK TOWNSHIP PUBLIC LIBRARY*, 128 E Main St, 47954. (Mail add: PO Box 248, 47954-0248), SAN 373-8965. Tel: 765-942-2456. FAX: 765-942-2457. E-mail: ladoga@ladoga.lib.in.us. Web Site: www.ladoga.lib.in.us. *Dir,* Debbie Clapp; Staff 1 (Non-MLS 1)
Founded 1919. Pop 3,372; Circ 11,125
Library Holdings: AV Mats 100; CDs 65; DVDs 10; Large Print Bks 44; Bk Titles 16,500; Bk Vols 17,000; Per Subs 41; Videos 5
Special Collections: Local History & Genealogy (Maude Long Neff Coll), bks, newsps on microfilm
Automation Activity & Vendor Info: (Acquisitions) Evergreen; (Cataloging) Evergreen; (Circulation) Evergreen; (ILL) Evergreen; (OPAC) Evergreen; (Serials) Evergreen
Wireless access
Publications: Newsletter (Quarterly)
Partic in Evergreen Indiana Consortium
Special Services for the Deaf - Bks on deafness & sign lang
Special Services for the Blind - Audio mat
Open Mon 12-5, Tues & Thurs 1-7, Wed & Fri 10-5, Sat 9-1
Friends of the Library Group

LAFAYETTE

M FRANCISCAN HEALTH LAFAYETTE*, East Medical Library, 1701 S Creasy Lane, Rm 1F29 Franciscan Health Lafayette East, 47905. Tel: 765-502-4010. FAX: 765-502-4011. Web Site: www.franciscanhealth.org. *Librn,* Patricia A Lunsford; E-mail: patty.lunsford@franciscanalliance.org; Staff 1 (MLS 1)
Founded 1970
Library Holdings: Bk Titles 7,680; Bk Vols 8,000; Per Subs 350
Special Collections: Bioethics Coll
Subject Interests: Clinical med, Hospital admin
Automation Activity & Vendor Info: (Cataloging) OCLC Connexion; (Circulation) Mandarin Library Automation; (ILL) SERHOLD; (OPAC) Mandarin Library Automation; (Serials) Prenax, Inc
Wireless access
Partic in Indiana Health Sciences Librarians Association
Open Mon-Fri 6am-8pm
Restriction: Badge access after hrs

M SAINT ELIZABETH SCHOOL OF NURSING DIVISION OF FRANCISCAN HEALTH*, Sister Floriane Library, 1501 Hartford St, St Elizabeth School of Nursing, 47904-2198. SAN 341-3942. Tel: 765-423-6125. FAX: 765-423-6841. *Librn,* Patricia A Lunsford; Tel: 765-423-6347, E-mail: patty.lunsford@franciscanalliance.org; *Libr Asst,* Ana Ramirez; E-mail: ana.ramirez@franciscanalliance.org; Staff 2 (MLS 1, Non-MLS 1)
Founded 1896. Enrl 150; Fac 32; Highest Degree: Bachelor
Library Holdings: AV Mats 4,000; Bk Titles 2,600; Bk Vols 3,000; Per Subs 100
Subject Interests: Consumer health, Med ethics, Nursing, Theol
Automation Activity & Vendor Info: (Cataloging) OCLC; (Serials) OVID Technologies
Wireless access
Publications: Annual report; bibliographies
Partic in Indiana Health Sciences Librarians Association; Midwest Collaborative for Library Services
Open Mon-Thurs 7:30-7, Fri 8-4:30
Restriction: Badge access after hrs

S TIPPECANOE COUNTY HISTORICAL ASSOCIATION*, Alameda McCollough Research Library, 1001 South St, 47901. SAN 305-0068. Tel: 765-476-8411, Ext 2. FAX: 765-476-8415. E-mail: library@tippecanoehistory.org. Web Site: www.tippecanoehistory.org/research/genealogy. *Libr Coord,* Amy Harbor
Founded 1925
Library Holdings: Bk Titles 7,684; Bk Vols 8,391; Per Subs 53; Videos 28
Special Collections: Archives Coll, diaries, letters, photos; Local History Coll; Marriage & Local Court Records. Oral History
Subject Interests: Genealogy, Local hist
Wireless access
Function: Res libr
Publications: 100 Years of the TC Courthouse; Grist Mills of Tippecanoe County, Indiana; Indians & A Changing Frontier, The Art of George Winter; Lafayette Newspapers, 150 years; Old Lafayette 1811-1853; Old Lafayette 1854-1875; Recollections of the Early Settlement of the Wabash Valley; Sandford Cox, Tippecanoe Tales (pamphlets on various local subjects); The House That Moses Fowler Built
Partic in Midwest Collaborative for Library Services
Open Thurs & Fri 1-5
Restriction: Non-circulating to the pub
Friends of the Library Group

J TIPPECANOE COUNTY-IVY TECH LIBRARY*, Campus Library, 3101 S Creasy Lane, 47903. SAN 305-0041. Tel: 765-269-5380. Reference Tel: 765-269-5389. Web Site: library.ivytech.edu/lafayette, www.tcpl.lib.in.us/branch/index.htm. *Regional Libr Dir,* Cindy Mitchell; Tel: 765-269-5381, E-mail: cmitchell42@ivytech.edu; *Librn,* Evelyn Samad; Tel: 765-269-5382, E-mail: esamad@ivytech.edu; *Librn,* JoAnn Sears; Tel: 765-269-5395, E-mail: jsears42@ivytech.edu; Staff 13 (MLS 5, Non-MLS 8)
Founded 1973. Enrl 6,500; Fac 135; Highest Degree: Associate
Library Holdings: AV Mats 2,000; e-books 34,000; e-journals 7,000; Bk Titles 50,618; Bk Vols 51,000; Per Subs 250
Subject Interests: Bus & mgt, Med, Sci tech
Automation Activity & Vendor Info: (Cataloging) SirsiDynix; (Circulation) SirsiDynix; (Course Reserve) SirsiDynix; (ILL) SirsiDynix; (OPAC) SirsiDynix
Wireless access
Partic in Midwest Collaborative for Library Services
Open Mon-Thurs 8-7, Fri 8-5, Sat 9:30-1

P TIPPECANOE COUNTY PUBLIC LIBRARY*, 627 South St, 47901-1470. SAN 305-0076. Tel: 765-429-0100. FAX: 765-429-0150. Web Site: www.tcpl.lib.in.us. *County Librn,* Jos N Holman; E-mail: jholman@tcpl.lib.in.us; *Asst County Librn,* Position Currently Open; *Head, Youth Serv,* Position Currently Open; *Outreach Mgr,* Marlene Darnell; Tel: 765-429-0192, E-mail: mdarnell@tcpl.lib.in.us; Staff 24 (MLS 20, Non-MLS 4)
Founded 1882. Pop 121,891; Circ 1,143,198
Library Holdings: AV Mats 11,945; CDs 180; Large Print Bks 495; Bk Titles 301,117; Bk Vols 302,011; Per Subs 1,947; Videos 1,865
Special Collections: Indiana Coll; Large Print Books; Local Newspaper Coll, 1831-date, micro; New Reader's Coll
Subject Interests: Mental health
Automation Activity & Vendor Info: (Acquisitions) SirsiDynix; (Circulation) SirsiDynix
Wireless access
Publications: Notes & Quotes (Newsletter); The Pocket Edition (Newsletter)

Special Services for the Blind - Computer with voice synthesizer for visually impaired persons
Open Mon-Thurs 9-9, Fri & Sat 9-6, Sun 1-6
Friends of the Library Group
Branches: 3
KLONDIKE BRANCH, 3062 Lindberg Rd, West Lafayette, 47906. Tel: 765-463-5893. FAX: 765-463-5894. *Br Mgr,* Angela White; E-mail: awhite@tcpl.lib.in.us
Library Holdings: Bk Vols 35,000
Open Mon-Thurs 10-7, Fri & Sat 10-5
WEA PRAIRIE BRANCH, 4200 S 18th St, 47909. Tel: 765-588-3002. *Br Mgr,* Position Currently Open
Open Mon-Thurs 10-7, Fri & Sat 10-5
Friends of the Library Group
Bookmobiles: 1

LAGRANGE

P LAGRANGE COUNTY PUBLIC LIBRARY*, 203 W Spring St, 46761-1845. SAN 341-3977. Tel: 260-463-2841. FAX: 260-463-2843. E-mail: info@lagrange.lib.in.us. Web Site: www.lagrange.lib.in.us. *Libr Dir,* Richard Kuster; Staff 25 (MLS 2, Non-MLS 23)
Founded 1917. Pop 39,000; Circ 405,000
Library Holdings: AV Mats 5,700; CDs 2,200; DVDs 1,700; Large Print Bks 3,800; Bk Titles 65,000; Bk Vols 100,000; Per Subs 150; Videos 1,000
Special Collections: Census Records (LaGrange County: 1830-1940), microfilm; Genealogy Department (Local Hist bks, Ohio & Pennsylvania Histories); Local Newspaper (LaGrange Standard: 1863 to present), microfilm; Local Newspaper (Topeka Journal: 1905-1957), microfilm
Automation Activity & Vendor Info: (Cataloging) Evergreen; (Circulation) Evergreen; (ILL) OCLC FirstSearch; (OPAC) Evergreen
Wireless access
Function: Bk club(s), Bks on CD, Children's prog, Computers for patron use, E-Reserves, Free DVD rentals, ILL available, Internet access, Microfiche/film & reading machines, Music CDs, Online cat, Photocopying/Printing, Prog for adults, Prog for children & young adult, Ref serv available, Scanner, Story hour, Summer reading prog, Tax forms, Teen prog, Wheelchair accessible, Writing prog
Special Services for the Deaf - Bks on deafness & sign lang
Special Services for the Blind - Bks on CD; Copier with enlargement capabilities; Extensive large print coll; Large print bks; Recorded bks
Open Mon-Thurs 9-8, Fri & Sat 9-5
Friends of the Library Group
Branches: 2
SHIPSHEWANA BRANCH, 350 Depot St, Shipshewana, 46565. (Mail add: PO Box 636, Shipshewana, 46565-0636). Tel: 260-768-7444. FAX: 260-768-7290. E-mail: shipshe@lagrange.lib.in.us.
Founded 1989
Library Holdings: Bk Titles 8,000; Per Subs 20
Function: Computers for patron use, Free DVD rentals, ILL available, Music CDs, Online cat, Photocopying/Printing
Open Mon, Tues, Thurs & Fri 11:30-6, Wed & Sat 8:30-3
TOPEKA BRANCH, 133 N Main St, Topeka, 46571. (Mail add: PO Box 236, Topeka, 46571), SAN 341-406X. Tel: 260-593-3030. FAX: 260-593-3032. E-mail: topeka@lagrange.lib.in.us.
Founded 1939
Library Holdings: Bk Titles 7,000; Bk Vols 10,000; Per Subs 73
Function: Computers for patron use, Free DVD rentals, ILL available, Music CDs, Online cat, Photocopying/Printing, Teen prog
Open Mon, Tues, Thurs & Fri 11:30-6, Wed & Sat 8:30-3
Bookmobiles: 1

LAKE VILLAGE

P NEWTON COUNTY PUBLIC LIBRARY*, Lake Village Memorial Township Library, 9444 N 315 W, 46349. (Mail add: PO Box 206, 46349-0206), SAN 305-0084. Tel: 219-992-3490. FAX: 219-992-9198. E-mail: lakevillage@newton.lib.in.us. Web Site: newton.lib.in.us/services-view/classics. *Libr Dir,* Mary K Emmrich; E-mail: director@newton.lib.in.us; *Asst Dir,* Jennifer Arrenholtz; E-mail: assistantdr@newton.lib.in.us; Staff 7 (MLS 1, Non-MLS 6)
Founded 1947. Pop 9,235; Circ 85,204
Jan 2018-Dec 2018 Income (Main & Associated Libraries) $884,096, State $235,259, Locally Generated Income $630,021, Other $18,816. Mats Exp $295,306, Books $52,181, Per/Ser (Incl. Access Fees) $4,365, AV Mat $223,461, Electronic Ref Mat (Incl. Access Fees) $15,299. Sal Prof $50,000
Library Holdings: Audiobooks 1,564; Bks on Deafness & Sign Lang 48; DVDs 10,656; e-books 51,097; e-journals 44; Large Print Bks 1,880; Bk Titles 69,261; Bk Vols 92,448; Per Subs 120
Special Collections: Jennie Milk Conrad Coll; Kankakee River, Bogus Island & Beaver Lake Information
Subject Interests: Local hist
Automation Activity & Vendor Info: (Acquisitions) Evergreen; (Cataloging) Evergreen; (Circulation) Evergreen; (ILL) Auto-Graphics, Inc; (OPAC) Evergreen; (Serials) Evergreen
Wireless access
Function: 24/7 Electronic res, 24/7 Online cat, Activity rm, Art exhibits, Audiobks via web, Bks on CD, Children's prog, Computers for patron use, Electronic databases & coll, Free DVD rentals, Holiday prog, Homebound delivery serv, ILL available, Instruction & testing, Internet access, Laminating, Magazines, Magnifiers for reading, Mail & tel request accepted, Makerspace, Meeting rooms, Movies, Notary serv, Online cat, Online ref, Outreach serv, OverDrive digital audio bks, Photocopying/Printing, Preschool reading prog, Prog for adults, Prog for children & young adult, Ref serv available, Scanner, Spoken cassettes & CDs, STEM programs, Story hour, Study rm, Summer reading prog, Tax forms, Teen prog, Telephone ref, Wheelchair accessible
Partic in Midwest Collaborative for Library Services
Special Services for the Deaf - Bks on deafness & sign lang; Closed caption videos; High interest/low vocabulary bks
Special Services for the Blind - Accessible computers; Aids for in-house use; Bks on CD; Home delivery serv; Large print bks; Magnifiers; Recorded bks; Talking bk serv referral
Open Mon & Thurs 9:30-7:30, Tues, Wed & Fri 9:30-5:30, Sat 9:30-2:30
Branches: 2
MOROCCO COMMUNITY LIBRARY, 205 S West St, Morocco, 47963. (Mail add: PO Box 87, Morocco, 47963-0087), SAN 375-9008. Tel: 219-285-2664. FAX: 219-285-0009. E-mail: morocco@newton.lib.in.us. *Br Mgr,* T Jane Gulley; Staff 6 (MLS 1, Non-MLS 5)
Founded 1963
Special Collections: Carlson Family Arrohead Coll; Glenwood Perkins Arrowhead Coll; Morocco High School memorabilia
Automation Activity & Vendor Info: (Acquisitions) Evergreen; (Cataloging) Evergreen; (Circulation) Evergreen; (ILL) Auto-Graphics, Inc; (OPAC) Evergreen; (Serials) Evergreen
Function: 24/7 Electronic res, 24/7 Online cat, Activity rm, Art exhibits, Audiobks via web, AV serv, Bks on CD, Butterfly Garden, Children's prog, Computers for patron use, Electronic databases & coll, Free DVD rentals, Holiday prog, Homebound delivery serv, ILL available, Instruction & testing, Internet access, Laminating, Magazines, Magnifiers for reading, Mail & tel request accepted, Makerspace, Meeting rooms, Microfiche/film & reading machines, Movies, Notary serv, Online cat, Online ref, Outreach serv, OverDrive digital audio bks, Photocopying/Printing, Preschool reading prog, Prog for adults, Prog for children & young adult, Ref serv available, Scanner, Spoken cassettes & CDs, STEM programs, Story hour, Study rm, Summer reading prog, Tax forms, Teen prog, Telephone ref, Wheelchair accessible
Special Services for the Deaf - Bks on deafness & sign lang; Closed caption videos; High interest/low vocabulary bks
Special Services for the Blind - Bks on CD; Copier with enlargement capabilities; Extensive large print coll; Home delivery serv; Large print bks; Magnifiers
Open Mon, Tues, Thurs & Fri 9:30-5:30, Wed 9:30-7:30, Sat 9:30-1:30
ROSELAWN LIBRARY, 4421 East State Rd 10, Roselawn, 46372. (Mail add: PO Box 57, Roselawn, 46372-0057), SAN 375-9016. Tel: 219-345-2010. FAX: 219-345-2117. E-mail: roselawn@newton.lib.in.us. *Br Mgr,* Nancy Susin; E-mail: roselawn@newton.lib.in.us; Staff 6 (MLS 1, Non-MLS 5)
Founded 1962
Special Collections: Kankakee River History Coll, Lincoln Township information, Mount Ayr School yearbooks
Automation Activity & Vendor Info: (Acquisitions) Evergreen; (Cataloging) Evergreen; (Circulation) Evergreen; (ILL) Auto-Graphics, Inc; (OPAC) Evergreen; (Serials) Evergreen
Function: 24/7 Electronic res, 24/7 Online cat, Activity rm, Adult bk club, Art exhibits, Audiobks via web, Bks on CD, Children's prog, Computers for patron use, Electronic databases & coll, Free DVD rentals, Holiday prog, Homebound delivery serv, ILL available, Instruction & testing, Internet access, Laminating, Magazines, Magnifiers for reading, Mail & tel request accepted, Makerspace, Meeting rooms, Notary serv, Online cat, Online ref, Outreach serv, OverDrive digital audio bks, Photocopying/Printing, Preschool outreach, Preschool reading prog, Prog for children & young adult, Ref serv available, Scanner, Spoken cassettes & DVDs, STEM programs, Story hour, Study rm, Summer reading prog, Tax forms, Teen prog, Telephone ref, Wheelchair accessible
Special Services for the Deaf - Bks on deafness & sign lang; Closed caption videos; High interest/low vocabulary bks
Special Services for the Blind - Bks on CD; Home delivery serv; Large print bks; Magnifiers; Talking bk serv referral
Open Mon & Wed-Fri 9:30-5:30, Tues 9:30-7:30, Sat 9:30-2:30

LAWRENCEBURG

P LAWRENCEBURG PUBLIC LIBRARY DISTRICT*, 150 Mary St, 47025-1995. SAN 305-0092. Tel: 812-537-2775. FAX: 812-537-2810. E-mail: lawplib@lpld.lib.in.us. Web Site: www.lpld.lib.in.us. *Dir,* Barbara

Bonney; E-mail: bbonney@lpld.lib.in.us; *ILS Syst Mgr,* Debra Beckett; E-mail: dbeckett@lpld.lib.in.us; Staff 8 (MLS 3, Non-MLS 5)
Founded 1910. Pop 29,000; Circ 176,000
Library Holdings: Bk Titles 75,000; Bk Vols 126,000; Per Subs 310
Special Collections: Dearborn County Indiana Cemetery Records
Subject Interests: Genealogy, Local hist
Automation Activity & Vendor Info: (Cataloging) Innovative Interfaces, Inc; (Circulation) Innovative Interfaces, Inc; (OPAC) Innovative Interfaces, Inc; (Serials) Innovative Interfaces, Inc
Wireless access
Function: Archival coll, Art exhibits, Audio & video playback equip for onsite use, AV serv, Distance learning, Home delivery & serv to seniorr ctr & nursing homes, Homebound delivery serv, ILL available, Internet access, Magnifiers for reading, Music CDs, Outside serv via phone, mail, e-mail & web, Photocopying/Printing, Prog for adults, Prog for children & young adult, Ref serv available, Satellite serv, Spoken cassettes & CDs, Summer reading prog, Telephone ref, VHS videos, Wheelchair accessible
Partic in Midwest Collaborative for Library Services
Special Services for the Deaf - Bks on deafness & sign lang; Closed caption videos
Special Services for the Blind - Audio mat; BiFolkal kits; Bks on cassette; Bks on CD; Cassette playback machines; Extensive large print coll; Home delivery serv; Large print bks; Magnifiers; Talking bks
Open Mon-Thurs 9-8, Fri 9-5, Sat 10-5
Friends of the Library Group
Branches: 1
NORTH DEARBORN BRANCH, 25969 Dole Rd, West Harrison, 47060. Tel: 812-637-0777. FAX: 812-637-0797. *Br Mgr,* Phil Kuhn; E-mail: pkuhn@lpld.lib.in.us; Staff 6 (MLS 1, Non-MLS 5)
Pop 29,111; Circ 116,291
Library Holdings: Audiobooks 2,274; AV Mats 6,516; Bks on Deafness & Sign Lang 14; CDs 876; DVDs 860; e-books 208; Bk Titles 96,036; Bk Vols 149,088; Per Subs 482; Talking Bks 323; Videos 5,013
Automation Activity & Vendor Info: (Acquisitions) Innovative Interfaces, Inc; (Cataloging) Innovative Interfaces, Inc; (Circulation) Innovative Interfaces, Inc; (ILL) OCLC WorldShare Interlibrary Loan; (OPAC) Innovative Interfaces, Inc; (Serials) Innovative Interfaces, Inc
Open Mon-Thurs 10-8, Sat 10-5
Friends of the Library Group
Bookmobiles: 1. Outreach Coordr, Jim Farris. Bk titles 5,000

LEAVENWORTH

P BREEDEN MEMORIAL LIBRARY & LITERACY CENTER*, 529 West Old State Rd 62, 47137. Tel: 812-739-4092. FAX: 812-739-2143. E-mail: breedenlibrary@yahoo.com. *Librn,* Sharon A Harvey; Staff 1 (Non-MLS 1)
Founded 1997
Wireless access
Function: Bks on cassette, Bks on CD, Children's prog, Computers for patron use, Free DVD rentals, ILL available, Music CDs, Photocopying/Printing, Scanner, Story hour, Summer reading prog, Tax forms, VHS videos, Wheelchair accessible
Open Mon, Wed, Fri & Sat 10-6
Restriction: Private libr
Friends of the Library Group

LEBANON

P LEBANON PUBLIC LIBRARY*, 104 E Washington St, 46052. SAN 305-1684. Tel: 765-482-3460. FAX: 765-680-0018. Web Site: www.leblib.org. *Dir,* Beau Cunnyngham; E-mail: Beau@leblib.org; *Head, Adult Serv,* Welty Yvonne; E-mail: yvonne@leblib.org; *Bus Mgr,* Chrissy Johnson; E-mail: chrissy@leblib.org; Staff 14 (MLS 4, Non-MLS 10)
Founded 1905. Pop 18,000; Circ 215,000
Library Holdings: Bks on Deafness & Sign Lang 100; CDs 1,550; DVDs 1,400; Electronic Media & Resources 11; High Interest/Low Vocabulary Bk Vols 200; Large Print Bks 2,400; Music Scores 1,500; Bk Titles 67,015; Per Subs 234; Talking Bks 2,400; Videos 3,000
Special Collections: Abraham Lincoln; Indiana Coll
Subject Interests: Local genealogy
Wireless access
Function: Adult bk club, Archival coll, AV serv, Bi-weekly Writer's Group, Bilingual assistance for Spanish patrons, Bk club(s), Bks on cassette, Bks on CD, Children's prog, Computers for patron use, Distance learning, Electronic databases & coll, Equip loans & repairs, Free DVD rentals, Holiday prog, Home delivery & serv to seniorr ctr & nursing homes, Homebound delivery serv, Homework prog, ILL available, Instruction & testing, Internet access, Life-long learning prog for all ages, Magazines, Meeting rooms, Microfiche/film & reading machines, Movies, Music CDs, Notary serv, Online cat, Online ref, Outreach serv, OverDrive digital audio bks, Photocopying/Printing, Preschool outreach, Preschool reading prog, Prog for adults, Prog for children & young adult, Ref & res, Ref serv available, Scanner, Serves people with intellectual disabilities, Story hour, Study rm, Summer & winter reading prog, Summer reading prog, Tax forms, Teen prog, Telephone ref, Wheelchair accessible, Winter reading prog, Workshops
Open Mon-Thurs 9-8, Fri 9-6, Sat 9-5 (9-2 Summer)
Friends of the Library Group

LIBERTY

P UNION COUNTY PUBLIC LIBRARY*, Two E Seminary St, 47353-1398. SAN 305-0114. Tel: 765-458-5355, 765-458-6227. FAX: 765-458-9375. E-mail: ucplibrary@gmail.com. Web Site: ucplib.com. *Dir,* Julie Jolliff; Staff 8 (MLS 1, Non-MLS 7)
Founded 1913. Pop 7,598; Circ 67,840
Library Holdings: CDs 90; Bk Titles 27,867; Bk Vols 29,011; Per Subs 112; Talking Bks 590; Videos 2,644
Subject Interests: Genealogy, Indiana
Automation Activity & Vendor Info: (Cataloging) Evergreen; (Circulation) Evergreen
Partic in Eastern Ind Area Libr Servs Authority; Evergreen Indiana Consortium
Open Mon-Fri 9-7
Friends of the Library Group

LIGONIER

P LIGONIER PUBLIC LIBRARY*, 300 S Main St, 46767-1812. SAN 305-0122. Tel: 260-894-4511. FAX: 260-894-4509. E-mail: ligonierpubliclibrary@yahoo.com. Web Site: www.ligonier.lib.in.us. *Dir,* Jerry L Nesbitt; E-mail: jnesbitt@ligonier.lib.in.us; Staff 4 (MLS 1, Non-MLS 3)
Founded 1907. Pop 4,410; Circ 26,870
Library Holdings: Bk Titles 24,210; Bk Vols 25,681; Per Subs 102; Talking Bks 159
Special Collections: Jewish Culture (Jewish Historical)
Automation Activity & Vendor Info: (Acquisitions) Mandarin Library Automation; (Cataloging) Mandarin Library Automation; (OPAC) Mandarin Library Automation
Open Mon-Fri 10:30-6:30, Sat 8-1

LINCOLN CITY

S US NATIONAL PARK SERVICE*, Lincoln Boyhood National Memorial Library, 2916 E South St, 47552. (Mail add: PO Box 1816, 47552-1816), SAN 323-8652. Tel: 812-937-4541. FAX: 812-937-9929. Web Site: www.nps.gov/libo. *Supvr,* Mike Capps; E-mail: mike_capps@nps.gov; Staff 2 (Non-MLS 2)
Library Holdings: Bk Titles 1,210; Bk Vols 1,340; Per Subs 22
Special Collections: Abraham Lincoln
Open Mon-Sun (Dec-Feb) 8-4:30; Mon-Sun (March-Nov) 8-5
Restriction: Open to pub for ref only

LINDEN

P LINDEN-CARNEGIE PUBLIC LIBRARY, 102 S Main St, 47955. SAN 305-0130. Tel: 765-339-4239. FAX: 765-339-4239. E-mail: lindenlibrary@yahoo.com. Web Site: lindenlibrary.com. *Dir,* Kathie Watkins; Staff 3 (MLS 1, Non-MLS 2)
Founded 1915. Pop 1,321; Circ 18,591
Library Holdings: AV Mats 1,310; Bk Titles 21,211; Bk Vols 22,691; Per Subs 95; Talking Bks 98; Videos 742
Automation Activity & Vendor Info: (Acquisitions) Book Systems; (Cataloging) Book Systems; (OPAC) Book Systems
Partic in Wabash Valley Area Libr Servs Authority
Open Mon, Wed & Fri 1-5, Tues & Thurs 1-8, Sat 8:30-12:30

LINTON

P LINTON PUBLIC LIBRARY, 95 SE First St, 47441. SAN 305-0149. Tel: 812-847-7802. FAX: 812-847-4695. E-mail: lintonpl@lintonpl.lib.in.us. Web Site: www.lintonpl.lib.in.us. *Dir,* Jennifer White; E-mail: jwhite@lintonpl.lib.in.us; Staff 6 (MLS 1, Non-MLS 5)
Founded 1907. Pop 8,447; Circ 60,000
Library Holdings: Bk Vols 33,000; Per Subs 60
Automation Activity & Vendor Info: (Acquisitions) Evergreen; (Cataloging) Evergreen; (Circulation) Evergreen; (OPAC) Evergreen
Wireless access
Open Mon-Thurs 10-7, Fri 10-5, Sat 10-3 (Winter); Mon-Thurs 10-6, Fri 10-5, Sat 10-3 (Summer)
Friends of the Library Group

LOGANSPORT

J IVY TECH COMMUNITY COLLEGE OF INDIANA*, One Ivy Tech Way, 46947. SAN 372-722X. Tel: 574-753-5101, Ext 2234. FAX: 574-753-5103. Web Site: library.ivytech.edu/kokomo. *Regional Libr Dir,* Cindy Mitchell; E-mail: cmitchell42@ivytech.edu; *Assoc Dir, Support Serv, Develop,* Karen Davis; E-mail: kdavis@ivytech.edu; Staff 1 (Non-MLS 1)

Founded 1992. Enrl 500; Fac 7
Library Holdings: AV Mats 720; Bk Titles 1,110; Bk Vols 1,282; Per Subs 47
Open Mon 9-6, Tues-Thurs 9-8, Fri 8-4:30
Friends of the Library Group

P LOGANSPORT-CASS COUNTY PUBLIC LIBRARY*, 616 E Broadway, 46947-3187. SAN 341-4124. Tel: 574-753-6383. FAX: 574-722-5889. E-mail: library@logan.lib.in.us. Web Site: www.logan.lib.in.us. *Dir,* David Ivey; E-mail: dmivey@logan.lib.in.us; *Asst Dir,* Scott Pletka; *Mgr, Ch Serv,* Larina Shaffer; *Tech Serv Mgr,* Sara Borden; Staff 24 (MLS 4, Non-MLS 20)
Founded 1894. Pop 34,992; Circ 625,899
Library Holdings: AV Mats 8,688; DVDs 27,458; e-books 3,725; Bk Vols 198,856; Per Subs 290
Automation Activity & Vendor Info: (Cataloging) Innovative Interfaces, Inc; (Circulation) Innovative Interfaces, Inc; (OPAC) Innovative Interfaces, Inc
Wireless access
Function: Audio & video playback equip for onsite use, Bks on CD, Children's prog, Computers for patron use, Electronic databases & coll, Free DVD rentals, Holiday prog, ILL available, Microfiche/film & reading machines, Music CDs, Online cat, Photocopying/Printing, Prog for adults, Prog for children & young adult, Ref serv available, Spanish lang bks, Story hour, Summer & winter reading prog, Telephone ref, Wheelchair accessible, Workshops
Open Mon-Fri 9-9, Sat 9-6, Sun Noon-6
Restriction: Non-resident fee
Branches: 1
GALVESTON BRANCH, 304 E Jackson, Galveston, 46932. (Mail add: PO Box 667, Galveston, 46932), SAN 341-4159. Tel: 574-699-6170. FAX: 574-699-6171. *Librn,* Patricia Hamilton; Staff 1 (Non-MLS 1)
Library Holdings: DVDs 3,780; Bk Vols 8,250
Open Mon & Wed 10-6, Tues, Thurs & Fri 1-6, Sat 10-3

M LOGANSPORT STATE HOSPITAL*, Staff Library, 1098 S State Rd 25, 46947. Tel: 574-737-3712. FAX: 574-737-3909. TDD: 574-732-0069. Web Site: www.in.gov/fssa/dmha/3333.htm. *Librn,* Brian Newell; E-mail: brian.newell@fssa.in.gov
Founded 1938
Library Holdings: Bk Titles 1,500
Subject Interests: Forensic psychiat, Nursing, Psychiat, Psychol
Partic in Midwest Collaborative for Library Services

LOOGOOTEE

P LOOGOOTEE PUBLIC LIBRARY*, Frances L Folks Memorial Library, 106 N Line St, 47553. SAN 305-0165. Tel: 812-295-3713. FAX: 812-295-4579. Web Site: loogootee.lib.in.us. *Dir,* Darla Wagler; E-mail: dwagler@loogootee.lib.in.us; *Asst Librn,* Terri Trotter; E-mail: ttrotter@loogootee.lib.in.us; Staff 3 (MLS 2, Non-MLS 1)
Founded 1939. Pop 2,958; Circ 15,318
Library Holdings: AV Mats 1,215; Bk Vols 16,000; Per Subs 76; Videos 29
Subject Interests: Bus & mgt, Econ, Hist, Sci tech
Automation Activity & Vendor Info: (Acquisitions) Follett Software; (Cataloging) Follett Software; (Serials) Follett Software
Wireless access
Partic in Evergreen Indiana Consortium; Four Rivers Area Libr Serv Authority
Open Mon & Tues 10-7, Thurs & Fri 10-5, Sat 9-1

LOWELL

P LOWELL PUBLIC LIBRARY*, 1505 E Commercial Ave, 46356-1899. SAN 305-0173. Tel: 219-696-7704. FAX: 219-696-5280. E-mail: reference@lowellpl.lib.in.us. Web Site: www.lowellpl.lib.in.us. *Dir,* Deborah Kristoff; E-mail: dkristoff@lowellpl.lib.in.us; *Asst Dir,* Position Currently Open; *Head, Ref,* Bethany Gray; E-mail: bgray@lowellpl.lib.in.us; *Ch Prog,* Jackie Bergstrom; E-mail: jbergstrom@lowellpl.lib.in.us; *Young Adult Programming,* Hayley Mass; E-mail: hmass@lowellpl.lib.in.us; Staff 5 (MLS 3, Non-MLS 2)
Pop 20,000; Circ 250,000
Library Holdings: AV Mats 8,000; CDs 3,000; DVDs 5,000; Large Print Bks 2,000; Bk Titles 85,065; Bk Vols 87,050; Per Subs 169
Subject Interests: Genealogy, Indiana, Local hist
Automation Activity & Vendor Info: (Cataloging) Innovative Interfaces, Inc; (Circulation) Innovative Interfaces, Inc
Wireless access
Function: 24/7 Online cat, Adult bk club
Publications: Newsletters
Open Mon-Thurs 9-8, Fri & Sat 9-5
Friends of the Library Group

Branches: 2
SCHNEIDER BRANCH, 24002 Parrish Ave, Schneider, 46376. (Mail add: PO Box 19, Schneider, 46376-0019). Tel: 219-552-1000. FAX: 219-552-0137. *Br Head,* Crista Stavros; E-mail: cstavrospl@gmail.com
Library Holdings: Bk Vols 2,000
Open Mon-Thurs 3:30pm-7pm, Sat 10-Noon
SHELBY BRANCH, 23323 Shelby Rd, Shelby, 46377. (Mail add: PO Box 237, Shelby, 46377-0237). Tel: 219-552-0809. *Br Head,* Shannon Stiener; E-mail: sstiener@gmail.com
Library Holdings: Bk Vols 4,000
Open Mon 9-12 & 1-6, Tues-Thurs 3-7, Sat 9-2

LYNN

P LYNN-WASHINGTON TOWNSHIP PUBLIC LIBRARY, 107 N Main St, 47355. SAN 305-0181. Tel: 765-874-1488. FAX: 765-874-1427. E-mail: washtwplib@hotmail.com. Web Site: lynnlibrary.lib.in.us. *Dir,* Suzanne Robinson; Staff 3 (MLS 1, Non-MLS 2)
Founded 1942. Pop 4,108; Circ 93,710
Jan 2013-Dec 2013 Income $72,000. Mats Exp $9,000
Library Holdings: AV Mats 1,096; Bk Titles 20,000; Bk Vols 25,000; Per Subs 67; Talking Bks 32; Videos 112
Automation Activity & Vendor Info: (Acquisitions) Evergreen; (Cataloging) Evergreen; (OPAC) Evergreen
Wireless access
Open Mon-Fri 12-5, Sat 8-Noon

MADISON

J IVY TECH COMMUNITY COLLEGE*, Madison Campus Library, 590 Ivy Tech Dr, 47250. SAN 372-4077. Tel: 812-265-2580, Ext 4102. Toll Free Tel: 800-403-2190. FAX: 812-265-4028. Web Site: library.ivytech.edu/southeast/home. *Dir,* Tim Renners; Tel: 800-403-2190, Ext 4106, E-mail: trenners@ivytech.edu; Staff 3 (MLS 1, Non-MLS 2)
Founded 1972. Enrl 1,200; Fac 30; Highest Degree: Associate
Library Holdings: e-books 10,000; Large Print Bks 25; Bk Titles 8,000; Bk Vols 8,500; Per Subs 95
Subject Interests: Bus, Computer, Early childhood, Electronics, Nursing, Paralegal, Psychol
Wireless access
Function: Audio & video playback equip for onsite use, AV serv, CD-ROM, Digital talking bks, Distance learning, For res purposes, Health sci info serv, ILL available, Internet access, Large print keyboards, Magnifiers for reading, Mail loans to mem, Orientations, Outside serv via phone, mail, e-mail & web, Photocopying/Printing, Res libr, Satellite serv, Telephone ref, VHS videos, Wheelchair accessible
Partic in Jefferson County Libr Coop; Midwest Collaborative for Library Services; SE Ind Area Libr Servs Authority
Special Services for the Deaf - High interest/low vocabulary bks
Special Services for the Blind - Assistive/Adapted tech devices, equip & products; Braille equip; Cassette playback machines; Computer with voice synthesizer for visually impaired persons; Copier with enlargement capabilities; Dragon Naturally Speaking software; Large print bks; Reader equip; Talking bks
Open Mon-Thurs 8-8, Fri 8-4

P MADISON-JEFFERSON COUNTY PUBLIC LIBRARY*, 420 W Main St, 47250. SAN 305-019X. Tel: 812-265-2744. E-mail: contact@mjcpl.org. Web Site: www.mjcpl.org. *Dir,* Judi Terpening; E-mail: judi@mjcpl.org; Staff 5 (MLS 5)
Founded 1818. Pop 31,700; Circ 188,934
Library Holdings: AV Mats 2,551; High Interest/Low Vocabulary Bk Vols 336; Large Print Bks 6,714; Bk Titles 105,905; Per Subs 200; Talking Bks 2,211
Special Collections: Lemen Photog Coll; Local Newspapers 1840-date (Courier Coll), micro
Subject Interests: Genealogy, Local hist
Automation Activity & Vendor Info: (Cataloging) OCLC; (OPAC) LibLime
Wireless access
Publications: @ Your Library (Bimonthly)
Partic in Evergreen Indiana Consortium; Midwest Collaborative for Library Services
Open Mon-Thurs 9-8, Fri 9-6, Sat 9-5
Friends of the Library Group

MARION

C INDIANA WESLEYAN UNIVERSITY*, Lewis A Jackson Library, 4201 S Washington St, 46953. SAN 305-022X. Tel: 765-677-2184. Interlibrary Loan Service Tel: 765-677-2981. Reference Tel: 765-677-2603. FAX: 765-677-2676. Web Site: library.indwes.edu. *Dir, Libr Serv,* Sheila O Carlblom; Tel: 765-677-2191, E-mail: sheila.carlblom@indwes.edu; *Asst Libr Dir,* Alison Johnson; Tel: 765-677-2383, E-mail: alison.johnson@indwes.edu; *Off-Campus Libr Serv Dir,* Jule Kind; Tel:

765-672-2980, E-mail: jule.kind@indwes.edu; *Ref & Instruction Librn,* Laura Kelsey; Tel: 765-677-2403, E-mail: laura.kelsey@indwes.edu; *Ref Librn,* Bruce Brinkley; Tel: 765-677-2179, E-mail: bruce.brinkley@indwes.edu; *Ref Librn,* Sarah Crume; Tel: 765-677-2334, E-mail: sarah.crume@indwes.edu; *Ref Librn,* David Dial; Tel: 216-525-6171, E-mail: david.dial@indwes.edu; *Ref Librn,* Lisa Hayes; Tel: 513-881-3611, E-mail: lisa.hayes@indwes.edu; *Ref Librn,* Amy Lorson; Tel: 502-261-5019, E-mail: amy.lorson@indwes.edu; *Ref Librn,* Jaime Pitt; Tel: 765-677-2445, E-mail: jaime.painter@indwes.edu; *Ref Librn,* Curt Rice; Tel: 219-769-5173, E-mail: curt.rice@indwes.edu; *Ref Librn,* Jay Wise; Tel: 614-529-7563, E-mail: jay.wise@indwes.edu; *Syst & Web Mgt Librn,* Pam Childers; Tel: 765-677-2983, E-mail: pam.childers@indwes.edu; *Tech Serv Librn,* Stephen Brown; Tel: 765-677-2197, E-mail: steve.brown@indwes.edu; *Coordr, Acq,* Cheri Colter; Tel: 765-677-2193, E-mail: cheri.colter@indwes.edu; *Cat Tech,* Eve Grant; Tel: 765-677-2982, E-mail: eve.grant@indwes.edu; *ILL Tech,* Lynn Crawford; E-mail: lynn.crawford@indwes.edu; Staff 20 (MLS 14, Non-MLS 6)
Founded 1920. Enrl 14,730; Highest Degree: Doctorate
Jul 2016-Jun 2017. Mats Exp $964,314, Books $188,572, Per/Ser (Incl. Access Fees) $123,452, AV Mat $29,341, Electronic Ref Mat (Incl. Access Fees) $618,256, Presv $4,693. Sal $1,059,647
Library Holdings: AV Mats 2,874; CDs 1,155; DVDs 2,219; e-books 359,278; Microforms 310,878; Bk Titles 152,637; Bk Vols 183,436; Per Subs 549; Videos 732
Special Collections: Holiness; Wesleyan Church History
Subject Interests: Counseling, Educ, Nursing, Relig
Automation Activity & Vendor Info: (Acquisitions) Innovative Interfaces, Inc; (Cataloging) Innovative Interfaces, Inc; (Circulation) Innovative Interfaces, Inc; (Course Reserve) Innovative Interfaces, Inc; (ILL) OCLC ILLiad; (OPAC) Innovative Interfaces, Inc; (Serials) Innovative Interfaces, Inc
Wireless access
Partic in Academic Libraries of Indiana; Midwest Collaborative for Library Services; OCLC Online Computer Library Center, Inc
Open Mon-Thurs 7:30am-Midnight, Fri 7:30-6, Sat 11-8

M MARION GENERAL HOSPITAL*, Medical Library, 441 N Wabash Ave, 46952. SAN 328-381X. Tel: 765-660-6000, 765-662-4760. FAX: 765-662-4523. Web Site: www.mgh.net. *Mgr, Organizational Learning & Development,* Joy Reed; Staff 1 (MLS 1)
Library Holdings: Bk Titles 1,301; Per Subs 50; Talking Bks 16
Wireless access
Partic in National Network of Libraries of Medicine Region 6
Restriction: Not open to pub

P MARION PUBLIC LIBRARY*, 600 S Washington St, 46953-1992. SAN 305-0238. Tel: 765-668-2900. Circulation Tel: 765-668-2900, Ext 101. Reference Tel: 765-668-2900, Ext 126. Administration Tel: 765-668-2900, Ext 133. FAX: 765-668-2911. TDD: 765-668-2907. E-mail: mpl@marion.lib.in.us. Web Site: www.marion.lib.in.us. *Dir,* Mary Theresa Eckerle; E-mail: meckerle@marion.lib.in.us; *Head, Children's Servx,* Clare Jozwiak; *Head, Circ,* Michelle Morgan; *Head, Genealogical Serv,* Rhonda Stoffer; *Mgr, Ref Serv,* Mary Leffler; *Tech Serv,* Karen E Blinn. Subject Specialists: *Genealogy, Hist, Indiana,* Rhonda Stoffer; Staff 49 (MLS 3, Non-MLS 46)
Founded 1884. Pop 31,320; Circ 370,649
Library Holdings: AV Mats 13,179; Bk Vols 136,774; Per Subs 436
Subject Interests: Genealogy, Local hist
Automation Activity & Vendor Info: (Acquisitions) SirsiDynix; (Cataloging) SirsiDynix; (Circulation) SirsiDynix; (OPAC) SirsiDynix
Publications: Special Edition (Newsletter)
Partic in OhioNET
Open Mon-Fri 9-8, Sat 9-5, Sun (Winter) 1-4
Friends of the Library Group

GM VA NORTHERN INDIANA HEALTHCARE SYSTEMS*, Hospital Medical Library, 1700 E 38th St, 46953. SAN 305-0254. Tel: 765-677-3110. FAX: 765-677-3111. Web Site: www.northernindiana.va.gov. *Librn,* Karen A Davis; E-mail: karen.davis@va.gov; Staff 2 (Non-MLS 2)
Library Holdings: Bk Titles 5,380; Bk Vols 5,600; Per Subs 50
Subject Interests: Geriatrics & gerontology, Med, Nursing, Psychiat, Psychol
Automation Activity & Vendor Info: (Cataloging) EOS International; (Circulation) EOS International; (OPAC) EOS International
Publications: AV Catalog; Newsletter
Partic in Eastern Ind Area Libr Servs Authority; Greater Midwest Regional Medical Libr Network; Midwest Collaborative for Library Services
Open Mon-Thurs 7:30-4

MARTINSVILLE

P MORGAN COUNTY PUBLIC LIBRARY*, 110 S Jefferson St, 46151. SAN 305-0270. Tel: 765-342-3451. FAX: 765-342-9992. Web Site: morgancountylibrary.info. *Dir,* Krista Ledbetter; E-mail: kristaq@morgancountylibrary.info; *Asst Dir,* Jennifer McKinley; E-mail: jenniferm@morgancountylibrary.info; *Youth Serv Librn,* Alyssa Morgan; E-mail: alyssam@morgancountylibrary.info; Staff 11 (MLS 5, Non-MLS 6)
Founded 1906. Pop 53,198; Circ 191,669
Library Holdings: AV Mats 2,524; Large Print Bks 480; Bk Titles 119,311; Bk Vols 166,369; Per Subs 225; Videos 416
Subject Interests: Genealogy
Automation Activity & Vendor Info: (Acquisitions) Evergreen; (Cataloging) Evergreen; (OPAC) Evergreen
Wireless access
Function: 24/7 Online cat, Accelerated reader prog, Adult bk club, Adult literacy prog, After school storytime, Art exhibits, Audiobks on Playaways & MP3, Audiobks via web, Bk club(s), Bks on CD, CD-ROM, Children's prog, Computer training, Computers for patron use, Digital talking bks, Distance learning, E-Readers, E-Reserves, Electronic databases & coll, Free DVD rentals, Genealogy discussion group, Holiday prog, Home delivery & serv to seniorr ctr & nursing homes, ILL available, Instruction & testing, Internet access, Laminating, Life-long learning prog for all ages, Literacy & newcomer serv, Magazines, Mail & tel request accepted, Meeting rooms, Microfiche/film & reading machines, Movies, Museum passes, Notary serv, Online cat, Online info literacy tutorials on the web & in blackboard, Outreach serv, Outside serv via phone, mail, e-mail & web, OverDrive digital audio bks, Photocopying/Printing, Preschool reading prog, Prog for adults, Prog for children & young adult, Ref & res, Ref serv available, Scanner, Senior computer classes, Senior outreach, Spanish lang bks, Spoken cassettes & CDs, Spoken cassettes & DVDs, Story hour, Study rm, Summer & winter reading prog, Summer reading prog, Tax forms, Teen prog, Telephone ref, Wheelchair accessible, Winter reading prog, Writing prog
Publications: Audio Cassettes List; Children's Calendar (Monthly); Guide to Services; Irregular Bookmark & Handouts for Special Programs; New Book List (Monthly); Newspaper Column (Weekly); Video List
Partic in Evergreen Indiana Consortium; Midwest Collaborative for Library Services
Open Mon-Thurs 9-8:30, Fri & Sat 9-5:30, Sun 1-5
Restriction: Non-resident fee
Branches: 5
BROOKLYN BRANCH, Six E Mill St, Brooklyn, 46111. Tel: 317-834-2003. E-mail: brooklynlibrary@hotmail.com. *Br Mgr,* Laura Brzeski
Library Holdings: Bk Vols 7,777
Open Tues & Thurs 12-7, Fri & Sat 9-4:30
EMINENCE BRANCH, Eminence Lion's Club, 11604 Walters Rd, Eminence, 46125. Tel: 765-528-2117. E-mail: eminencelibrary2@hotmail.com. *Br Mgr,* Laura Brzeski
Library Holdings: Bk Vols 4,139
Open Mon & Wed 3-7
MONROVIA BRANCH, 145 S Chestnut St, Monrovia, 46157. Tel: 317-996-4307. FAX: 317-996-3439. *Br Mgr,* Cassie Jones; E-mail: cassiej@morgancountylibrary.org
Library Holdings: Bk Vols 17,444
Open Mon-Thurs 9-8:30, Fri & Sat 9-5:30, Sun 1-5
Friends of the Library Group
MORGANTOWN BRANCH, 79 W Washington St, Morgantown, 46160. Tel: 812-597-0889. E-mail: morgantownlibrary@hotmail.com. *Br Mgr,* Laura Brzeski
Library Holdings: Bk Vols 8,300
Open Mon & Thurs Noon-7, Wed & Sat 9-4
WAVERLY BRANCH, 9410 State Rd 144, 46151. Tel: 317-422-9915. FAX: 317-422-9415. E-mail: nebranch@hotmail.com. *Br Mgr,* Julie Reid
Library Holdings: Bk Vols 30,365
Open Mon-Thurs 9-8:30, Fri & Sat 9-5:30, Sun 1-5

MENTONE

P BELL MEMORIAL PUBLIC LIBRARY*, 101 W Main St, 46539. (Mail add: PO Box 368, 46539-0368), SAN 305-0289. Tel: 574-353-7234. FAX: 574-353-1307. Web Site: www.bell.lib.in.us. *Dir,* Stephen Boggs; E-mail: sboggs@bell.lib.in.us; Staff 8 (MLS 1, Non-MLS 7)
Founded 1916. Pop 4,281; Circ 59,803
Library Holdings: Bk Titles 36,391; Bk Vols 37,142; Per Subs 490; Talking Bks 1,000; Videos 798
Subject Interests: Agr, Arts & crafts, Genealogy, Hist, Indiana, Local hist, Med, Natural sci, Relig, Sci tech
Wireless access
Partic in Midwest Collaborative for Library Services
Open Mon-Thurs 9-7, Fri & Sat 9-5
Friends of the Library Group

MERRILLVILLE

P LAKE COUNTY PUBLIC LIBRARY*, 1919 W 81st Ave, 46410-5488. SAN 341-4337. Tel: 219-769-3541. FAX: 219-769-0690. Web Site: www.lcplin.org. *Dir,* Ingrid Norris; *Asst Dir, Libr Serv,* Carolyn Strickland; E-mail: cstrickland@lcplin.org; *Asst Dir, Operations,* John Brock; E-mail: jbrock@lcplin.org; *Br Mgr,* Carol Daumer Gutjahr; Tel: 219-769-3541, Ext 332, E-mail: cdaumer@lcplin.org
Founded 1952. Pop 242,837; Circ 2,588,580
Jan 2015-Dec 2015 Income (Main & Associated Libraries) $10,767,217. Mats Exp $1,609,022
Library Holdings: DVDs 104,663; Bk Vols 823,389; Per Subs 994; Talking Bks 21,342
Special Collections: Indiana Coll, bks, pamphlets; Original South Shore Art Prints
Automation Activity & Vendor Info: (Acquisitions) Innovative Interfaces, Inc; (Circulation) Innovative Interfaces, Inc
Wireless access
Function: 24/7 Electronic res, Activity rm, Adult bk club, Adult literacy prog, After school storytime, Archival coll, Art exhibits
Publications: Library Insider (Online only)
Partic in OCLC Online Computer Library Center, Inc
Special Services for the Deaf - Bks on deafness & sign lang; Captioned film dep; High interest/low vocabulary bks; Spec interest per; Videos & decoder
Open Mon-Thurs 9-9, Fri 9-6, Sat 9-5, Sun 12-4
Friends of the Library Group
Branches: 9
CEDAR LAKE BRANCH, 10010 W 133rd Ave, Cedar Lake, 46303, SAN 341-4426. Tel: 219-374-7121. FAX: 219-374-6333. *Br Mgr,* Jonathon Davis; E-mail: jdavis@lcplin.org; Staff 2 (MLS 1, Non-MLS 1)
Library Holdings: Large Print Bks 83; Bk Titles 52,340; Bk Vols 55,680; Per Subs 49; Talking Bks 81; Videos 310
Open Mon & Wed 12:30-8:30, Tues, Thurs & Fri 10-6, Sat 9-5
Friends of the Library Group
DYER-SCHERERVILLE BRANCH, 1001 W Lincoln Hwy, Schererville, 46375-1552, SAN 341-4450. Tel: 219-322-4731. FAX: 219-865-5478. *Br Mgr,* Christine Rettig; E-mail: crettig@lcplin.org; Staff 2 (MLS 2)
Library Holdings: Large Print Bks 103; Bk Titles 101,670; Bk Vols 102,700; Per Subs 88; Talking Bks 139; Videos 410
Open Mon-Thurs 10-8:30, Fri 10-6, Sat 9-5
Friends of the Library Group
GRIFFITH-CALUMET TOWNSHIP BRANCH, 1215 E. 45th Ave., Griffith, 46319-1528, SAN 341-4515. Tel: 219-838-2825. Web Site: www.lcplin.org/gr.htm. *Br Mgr,* Beth Alyea; E-mail: balyea@lcplin.org; Staff 2 (MLS 2)
Library Holdings: Audiobooks 1,450; AV Mats 10,000; CDs 2,200; DVDs 3,900; High Interest/Low Vocabulary Bk Vols 30; Large Print Bks 1,400; Bk Titles 60,000; Bk Vols 60,300; Per Subs 75; Videos 820
Function: Adult bk club, After school storytime, Bks on CD, Children's prog, Computer training, Computers for patron use, Electronic databases & coll, Free DVD rentals, Holiday prog, ILL available, Music CDs, Online cat, Outreach serv, Photocopying/Printing, Preschool outreach, Prog for adults, Prog for children & young adult, Ref serv available, Story hour, Summer reading prog, Tax forms, Wheelchair accessible
Open Mon-Thurs 10-8:30, Fri 10-6, Sat 9-5
Friends of the Library Group
HIGHLAND BRANCH, 2841 Jewett St, Highland, 46322-1617, SAN 341-454X. Tel: 219-838-2394. *Br Mgr,* Linda Johnsen; E-mail: ljohnsen@lcplin.org; Staff 3 (MLS 2, Non-MLS 1)
Library Holdings: Bk Titles 81,200; Bk Vols 83,556; Per Subs 75
Open Mon-Thurs 10-8:30, Fri 10-6, Sat 9-5
Friends of the Library Group
HOBART BRANCH, 100 Main St, Hobart, 46342-4391, SAN 341-4574. Tel: 219-942-2243. FAX: 219-947-1823. *Br Mgr,* Erika Stolarz; E-mail: estolarz@lcplin.org; Staff 3 (MLS 2, Non-MLS 1)
Pop 25,000
Library Holdings: AV Mats 1,641; Bk Titles 82,819; Bk Vols 84,202; Per Subs 107; Talking Bks 83; Videos 261
Subject Interests: Investing
Open Mon-Thurs 10-8:30, Fri 10-6, Sat 9-5
Friends of the Library Group
LAKE STATION-NEW CHICAGO BRANCH, 2007 Central Ave, Lake Station, 46405-2061, SAN 341-4698. Tel: 219-962-2409. FAX: 219-962-8460. *Mgr,* Julie Bradford; E-mail: jbradford@lcplin.org; Staff 3 (MLS 1, Non-MLS 2)
Library Holdings: Large Print Bks 62; Bk Titles 33,491; Bk Vols 35,814; Per Subs 53; Talking Bks 119; Videos 281
Open Mon-Thurs 10-8:30, Fri 10-6, Sat 9-5
Friends of the Library Group
MUNSTER BRANCH, 8701 Calumet Ave, Munster, 46321-2526, SAN 341-4663. Tel: 219-836-8450. FAX: 219-836-5694. *Br Mgr,* Susan Gempka; E-mail: sgempka@lcplin.org; Staff 3 (MLS 2, Non-MLS 1)
Library Holdings: AV Mats 1,121; Large Print Bks 84; Bk Titles 75,615; Bk Vols 78,065; Per Subs 71; Videos 219
Open Mon-Thurs 10-8:30, Fri 10-6, Sat 9-5
Friends of the Library Group
SAINT JOHN BRANCH, 9450 Wicker Dr, Saint John, 46373-9646, SAN 341-4728. Tel: 219-365-5379. FAX: 219-365-5963. *Mgr,* Hollie Koster; E-mail: hkoster@lcplin.org; Staff 2 (MLS 2)
Library Holdings: AV Mats 780; Bk Titles 33,610; Bk Vols 35,118; Per Subs 43; Talking Bks 170; Videos 281
Open Mon-Thurs 10-8:30, Fri 10-6, Sat 9-5
Friends of the Library Group

P TALKING BOOK SERVICE, 1919 W 81st Ave, 46410-5382. Tel: 219-769-3541, Ext 323. *Librn,* Carol Daumer - Gutjahr; Staff 2 (MLS 1, Non-MLS 1)
Founded 1970
Library Holdings: AV Mats 1,140; Large Print Bks 80; Bk Titles 26,450; Bk Vols 28,112; Per Subs 53; Talking Bks 78; Videos 219
Special Collections: Descriptive Videos
Open Mon-Thurs 9-9, Fri 9-6, Sat 9-5
Friends of the Library Group

MICHIGAN CITY

S INDIANA STATE PRISON*, Michael S Thomas Learning Resource Center, One Park Row, 46360. SAN 341-4787. Tel: 219-874-7258. FAX: 219-874-0335. Web Site: www.in.gov/idoc/2413.htm. *Media Spec,* Angela McGee; Staff 11 (MLS 1, Non-MLS 10)
Founded 1969
Library Holdings: AV Mats 649; Bk Titles 14,468; Bk Vols 15,212; Per Subs 27
Subject Interests: Careers, Current events, Fiction
Function: Doc delivery serv, For res purposes, Photocopying/Printing, Res libr
Restriction: Internal circ only, Non-circulating to the pub, Not open to pub, Open to students, Private libr

P MICHIGAN CITY PUBLIC LIBRARY*, 100 E Fourth St, 46360-3302. SAN 341-4906. Tel: 219-873-3044. Circulation Tel: 219-873-3042. Information Services Tel: 219-879-4561. FAX: 219-873-3067. Administration FAX: 219-873-3475. E-mail: refdesk@mclib.org. Web Site: www.mclib.org. *Dir,* Don Glossinger; Tel: 219-873-3050, E-mail: dgloss@mclib.org; *Asst Dir,* Andrew W Smith; Tel: 219-873-3056, E-mail: awsmith@mclib.org; Staff 19 (MLS 7, Non-MLS 12)
Founded 1897. Pop 40,350; Circ 478,484
Library Holdings: Bk Titles 108,527; Bk Vols 137,151; Per Subs 420
Special Collections: Genealogy Coll; Indiana Coll. Oral History
Automation Activity & Vendor Info: (Cataloging) SirsiDynix; (Circulation) SirsiDynix; (OPAC) SirsiDynix
Wireless access
Function: Homebound delivery serv, ILL available, Ref serv available
Open Mon-Thurs 9-8, Fri & Sat 9-6, Sun (Sept-May) 1-5
Friends of the Library Group

MIDDLEBURY

P MIDDLEBURY COMMUNITY PUBLIC LIBRARY*, 101 E Winslow St, 46540. (Mail add: PO Box 192, 46540-0192), SAN 375-2860. Tel: 574-825-5601. FAX: 574-825-5150. E-mail: mclib@mdy.lib.in.us. Web Site: www.middleburylibrary.org. *Dir,* Juli Wald; E-mail: juliw@middleburylibrary.org; Staff 14 (MLS 4, Non-MLS 10)
Founded 1978. Pop 22,000; Circ 219,477
Library Holdings: Audiobooks 7,198; DVDs 7,431; Electronic Media & Resources 6,249; Large Print Bks 5,375; Bk Vols 64,540; Per Subs 158
Subject Interests: Amish, Local hist, Mennonite
Automation Activity & Vendor Info: (Acquisitions) TLC (The Library Corporation); (Cataloging) TLC (The Library Corporation); (Circulation) TLC (The Library Corporation); (Course Reserve) TLC (The Library Corporation); (OPAC) TLC (The Library Corporation)
Wireless access
Function: 24/7 Electronic res, 24/7 Online cat, Adult bk club, Archival coll, Audiobks on Playaways & MP3, Audiobks via web, Bilingual assistance for Spanish patrons, Bk club(s), Bks on CD, Children's prog, Computer training, Computers for patron use, Digital talking bks, Electronic databases & coll, Free DVD rentals, Home delivery & serv to seniorr ctr & nursing homes, Homebound delivery serv, ILL available, Internet access, Laminating, Life-long learning prog for all ages, Magazines, Magnifiers for reading, Mail & tel request accepted, Microfiche/film & reading machines, Movies, Music CDs, Notary serv, Online cat, Online ref, Outreach serv, Outside serv via phone, mail, e-mail & web, Photocopying/Printing, Preschool outreach, Preschool reading prog, Printer for laptops & handheld devices, Prog for adults, Prog for children & young adult, Ref serv available, Scanner, Senior outreach, Serves people with intellectual disabilities, Story hour, Study rm, Summer & winter reading prog, Tax forms, Teen prog, Telephone ref, Wheelchair accessible
Partic in Midwest Collaborative for Library Services; Northern Indiana Computer Consortium for Libraries
Special Services for the Deaf - Bks on deafness & sign lang

Special Services for the Blind - Bks available with recordings; Bks on CD; Copier with enlargement capabilities; Home delivery serv; Large print bks; Playaways (bks on MP3)
Open Mon-Thurs 9-8, Fri 9-6, Sat 9-2
Friends of the Library Group

MIDDLETOWN

P MIDDLETOWN FALL CREEK LIBRARY, 780 High St, 47356-1399. SAN 305-0351. Tel: 765-354-4071. FAX: 765-354-9578. Web Site: middletownpubliclibrary.net. *Dir,* Teresa Dennis; E-mail: teresa@middletownpubliclibrary.net; Staff 1 (Non-MLS 1)
Founded 1929. Pop 4,811; Circ 122,354
Library Holdings: AV Mats 1,000; Large Print Bks 300; Bk Titles 65,000; Per Subs 30
Automation Activity & Vendor Info: (Circulation) Evergreen; (Serials) EBSCO Online
Wireless access
Partic in Evergreen Indiana Consortium
Open Mon-Thurs 10-7, Fri 10-5, Sat 10-3
Friends of the Library Group

MILFORD

P MILFORD PUBLIC LIBRARY*, 101 N Main St, 46542. (Mail add: PO Box 269, 46542), SAN 305-036X. Tel: 574-658-4312. FAX: 574-658-9454. E-mail: milford@milford.lib.in.us. Web Site: www.milford.lib.in.us. *Dir,* Julie Frew; E-mail: jfrew@milford.lib.in.us; Staff 3 (MLS 2, Non-MLS 1)
Founded 1907. Pop 4,597; Circ 35,690
Library Holdings: AV Mats 3,000; Bk Vols 35,000; Per Subs 80; Videos 3,500
Special Collections: PBS Video Coll; Town of Milford & Van Buren & East Jefferson Townships History
Wireless access
Open Mon & Thurs 10-8, Tues, Wed & Fri 10-6, Sat 10-2
Friends of the Library Group

MISHAWAKA

C BETHEL COLLEGE*, Otis & Elizabeth Bowen Library, 1001 Bethel Circle, 46545. SAN 305-0386. Tel: 574-807-7180. Reference Tel: 574-807-7170. FAX: 574-807-7964. Web Site: www.bethelcollege.edu/library. *Dir, Libr Serv,* Mark Root; Tel; 574-807-3389, E-mail: rootm1@bethelcollege.edu; *Acq Librn,* Dr Clyde R Root; Tel: 574-807-7219, E-mail: rootc@bethelcollege.edu; *Asst Librn, Tech Serv,* Kevin Blowers; Tel: 574-807-7720, E-mail: blowersk@bethelcollege.edu; *Educ Res Librn,* Tim Amstutz; Tel: 574-807-7001; *Archivist,* Tim Erdel; Tel: 574-807-7153, E-mail: erdelt@bethelcollege.edu. Subject Specialists: *Educ, Hist,* Mark Root; *Nursing,* Dr Clyde R Root; *Lit,* Kevin Blowers; *Humanities,* Tim Erdel; Staff 4 (MLS 4)
Founded 1947. Enrl 1,701; Fac 116; Highest Degree: Master
Library Holdings: AV Mats 8,368; Bks on Deafness & Sign Lang 325; CDs 252; Bk Titles 125,000; Bk Vols 133,241; Per Subs 457; Videos 707
Special Collections: Bethel College Archives; Dr Otis Bowen Museum & Archives; Missionary Church Archives & Historical Coll. Oral History
Subject Interests: Educ, Nursing, Relig
Automation Activity & Vendor Info: (Cataloging) Ex Libris Group; (Circulation) Ex Libris Group; (ILL) OCLC; (OPAC) Follett Software
Wireless access
Partic in Michiana Acad Libr Consortium; OCLC Online Computer Library Center, Inc; Proquest Dialog
Open Mon-Thurs 8am-Midnight, Fri 8-6, Sat Noon-6, Sun 7pm-11pm

P MISHAWAKA-PENN-HARRIS PUBLIC LIBRARY*, 209 Lincolnway E, 46544-2084. SAN 341-4965. Tel: 574-259-5277. Circulation Tel: 574-259-5277, Ext 1200. Interlibrary Loan Service Tel: 574-259-5277, Ext 1304. Reference Tel: 574-259-5277, Ext 1300. FAX: 574-254-5585, 574-255-8489. Web Site: www.mphpl.org. *Dir,* Donna Meeks; Tel: 574-259-5277, Ext 1101, E-mail: d.meeks@mphpl.org; *Asst Dir, Libr Serv,* Eric Mims; Tel: 574-259-5277, Ext 1103, E-mail: e.mims@mphpl.org; *Asst Dir, Operational Serv, Human Res,* Dena Wargo; Tel: 574-259-5277, Ext 1102, E-mail: hr@mphpl.org; *Youth Serv Coordr,* Jennifer Ludwig; Tel: 574-259-5277, Ext 1401, E-mail: j.ludwig@mphpl.org; Staff 23 (MLS 23)
Founded 1907. Pop 89,652; Circ 715,889
Jan 2013-Dec 2013 Income (Main & Associated Libraries) $4,470,383, State $306,087, Federal $41,774, County $3,917,723, Locally Generated Income $204,799. Mats Exp $676,392, Books $348,663, Per/Ser (Incl. Access Fees) $47,812, Micro $8,275, AV Equip $15,878, AV Mat $194,115, Electronic Ref Mat (Incl. Access Fees) $61,649. Sal $2,540,580
Library Holdings: Audiobooks 15,411; AV Mats 70,069; CDs 21,516; DVDs 23,925; e-books 3,429; Electronic Media & Resources 3,095; Microforms 13,360; Bk Vols 289,298; Per Subs 355; Videos 1,023
Special Collections: Heritage Center Coll
Subject Interests: Auto repair, Local hist
Automation Activity & Vendor Info: (Acquisitions) Innovative Interfaces, Inc; (Cataloging) Innovative Interfaces, Inc; (Circulation) Innovative Interfaces, Inc; (ILL) Innovative Interfaces, Inc; (Media Booking) Innovative Interfaces, Inc; (OPAC) Innovative Interfaces, Inc; (Serials) Innovative Interfaces, Inc
Wireless access
Publications: Hi-Lites (Newsletter of Friends of Library)
Partic in Midwest Collaborative for Library Services; OCLC Online Computer Library Center, Inc
Open Mon, Wed & Fri 10-6, Tues & Thurs 10-8, Sat 10-5
Branches: 2
BITTERSWEET, 602 Bittersweet Rd, 46544-4155, SAN 322-5887. Tel: 574-259-5277. FAX: 574-259-0399. *Br Mgr,* Bruce Runnels; E-mail: b.runnels@mphpl.org; *Circ Serv Supvr,* Babett McBain; E-mail: b.mcbain@mphpl.org; *Youth Serv Supvr,* Ashley Banard; E-mail: a.banard@mphpl.org; Staff 17 (MLS 5, Non-MLS 12)
Open Mon & Wed 9-7, Tues & Thurs 9-6, Sat 10-5
HARRIS, 51446 Elm Rd, Granger, 46530-7171. Tel: 574-259-5277. FAX: 574-271-3183. *Br Mgr,* Melissa Renner; E-mail: m.renner@mphpl.org; *Children's Serv Supvr,* Anne Britton; E-mail: a.britton@mphpl.org; Staff 14 (MLS 5.5, Non-MLS 8.5)
Open Mon, Tues & Thurs 10-8, Fri 10-6, Sat 10-5

MITCHELL

P MITCHELL COMMUNITY PUBLIC LIBRARY*, 804 Main St, 47446. SAN 305-0394. Tel: 812-849-2412. E-mail: info@mitchell.lib.in.us. Web Site: mitchell.lib.in.us. *Dir,* Ophelia Georgie Roop
Founded 1917. Pop 12,007; Circ 78,851
Library Holdings: AV Mats 1,796; DVDs 750; Large Print Bks 400; Bk Titles 50,000; Bk Vols 60,000; Per Subs 70
Special Collections: Local History; Virgil "Gus" Grissom
Automation Activity & Vendor Info: (Acquisitions) Evergreen; (Cataloging) Evergreen; (Circulation) Evergreen; (OPAC) Evergreen
Wireless access
Publications: Newsletter (Bimonthly)
Partic in Evergreen Indiana Consortium; Midwest Collaborative for Library Services
Open Mon, Tues & Thurs 9-8, Fri & Sat 9-5:30
Friends of the Library Group

MONON

P MONON TOWN & TOWNSHIP PUBLIC LIBRARY*, 427 N Market St, 47959. (Mail add: PO Box 305, 47959-0305), SAN 305-0408. Tel: 219-253-6517. FAX: 219-253-8373. Web Site: www.monon.lib.in.us. *Dir,* Jo Minnick; E-mail: jminnick@monon.lib.in.us; *Youth Serv Librn,* Barbara Rayburn
Founded 1914. Pop 3,272; Circ 26,388
Library Holdings: AV Mats 2,148; Bk Vols 28,296; Per Subs 120; Talking Bks 885
Automation Activity & Vendor Info: (Cataloging) SirsiDynix; (Circulation) SirsiDynix; (OPAC) SirsiDynix; (Serials) SirsiDynix
Wireless access
Partic in Midwest Collaborative for Library Services
Open Mon & Wed 10-8, Tues, Thurs & Fri 10-6, Sat 10-3

MONTEREY

P MONTEREY-TIPPECANOE TOWNSHIP PUBLIC LIBRARY*, 6260 E Main St, 46960. (Mail add: PO Box 38, 46960-0038), SAN 305-0416. Tel: 574-542-2171. FAX: 574-542-2171. Web Site: monterey-tipp.lib.in.us. *Dir,* Renita Potthoff; E-mail: renita@monterey-tipp.lib.in.us; *Asst Librn,* Ms Toni Mersch; Staff 1 (Non-MLS 1)
Founded 1918. Pop 1,031; Circ 24,218
Library Holdings: DVDs 1,241; Large Print Bks 138; Bk Titles 12,715; Bk Vols 13,015; Per Subs 30
Special Collections: Indiana Coll
Automation Activity & Vendor Info: (Acquisitions) Baker & Taylor; (Cataloging) Brodart; (Circulation) Brodart; (OPAC) Brodart
Wireless access
Function: Activity rm, Children's prog, Computers for patron use, Doc delivery serv, Holiday prog, ILL available, Internet access, Magazines, Online cat, Photocopying/Printing, Prog for adults, Prog for children & young adult, Scanner, Summer reading prog, Teen prog, Wheelchair accessible
Partic in Midwest Collaborative for Library Services
Open Mon & Wed 10-6, Tues, Thurs & Fri 11-5, Sat 9-1

MONTEZUMA

P MONTEZUMA PUBLIC LIBRARY*, 270 Crawford St, 47862. (Mail add: PO Box 70, 47862), SAN 305-0424. Tel: 765-245-2772. Web Site: www.montezuma.lib.in.us. *Dir,* Jayanne Rumple; E-mail: director@montezuma.lib.in.us
Founded 1932. Pop 1,432; Circ 16,370

Library Holdings: DVDs 2,500; Bk Vols 16,580; Per Subs 40
Automation Activity & Vendor Info: (Acquisitions) Evergreen; (Cataloging) Evergreen; (Circulation) Evergreen; (Discovery) Evergreen; (ILL) Evergreen
Wireless access
Function: 24/7 Electronic res, 24/7 Online cat, Children's prog, Computer training, Computers for patron use, Digital talking bks, Electronic databases & coll, Free DVD rentals, ILL available, Internet access, Magazines, Mail & tel request accepted, Mango lang, Movies, Online cat, Online ref, Outside serv via phone, mail, e-mail & web, Photocopying/Printing, Prog for adults, Prog for children & young adult, Ref serv available, Scanner, Summer reading prog, Teen prog
Partic in Evergreen Indiana Consortium; Midwest Collaborative for Library Services
Open Tues & Wed 12-5, Thurs 1-7, Sat 9-1

MONTICELLO

P MONTICELLO-UNION TOWNSHIP PUBLIC LIBRARY*, 321 W Broadway, 47960. SAN 305-0432. Tel: 574-583-2665. FAX: 574-583-2782. Circulation E-mail: circulationclerk@monticello.lib.in.us. Web Site: www.monticello.lib.in.us. *Libr Dir, Youth Serv,* Tina Emerick; E-mail: director@monticello.lib.in.us; *Adult Serv,* Candace Wells; E-mail: adult@monticello.lib.in.us; *Circ Serv Librn,* Scott Miller; E-mail: smiller@monticello.lib.in.us; Staff 11 (MLS 3, Non-MLS 8)
Founded 1903. Pop 11,238; Circ 127,339
Library Holdings: AV Mats 2,400; Bks on Deafness & Sign Lang 60; Large Print Bks 219; Bk Titles 61,980; Bk Vols 63,410; Per Subs 131; Videos 1,016
Automation Activity & Vendor Info: (Cataloging) Follett Software; (Circulation) Follett Software; (OPAC) Follett Software
Wireless access
Partic in Midwest Collaborative for Library Services
Open Mon-Thurs 9-8, Fri & Sat 9-5
Friends of the Library Group

MONTPELIER

P MONTPELIER HARRISON TOWNSHIP PUBLIC LIBRARY*, 301 S Main St, 47359. SAN 305-0440. Tel: 765-728-5969. FAX: 765-728-5969. E-mail: mhtpl@hotmail.com. Web Site: mhtpl.lib.in.us. *Dir,* Cathy Leas; Staff 2 (MLS 1, Non-MLS 1)
Pop 3,042; Circ 44,118
Library Holdings: AV Mats 1,038; Large Print Bks 108; Bk Titles 26,819; Bk Vols 28,100; Per Subs 79; Videos 248
Automation Activity & Vendor Info: (Acquisitions) Follett Software; (Cataloging) Follett Software; (Serials) Follett Software
Wireless access
Open Mon-Thurs 10-7, Fri 10-5, Sat 10-2

MOORESVILLE

P MOORESVILLE PUBLIC LIBRARY*, 220 W Harrison St, 46158-1633. SAN 305-0459. Tel: 317-831-7323. FAX: 317-831-7383. Web Site: www.mooresvillelib.org. *Dir,* Diane Huerkamp; E-mail: dianeh@mooresville.lib.in.us; *Dir, Prog & Youth Serv,* Casey O'Leary; *Dir, Tech Serv,* Sandra Osborn; *Circ Coordr,* Virginia Jensen; Staff 15 (MLS 4, Non-MLS 11)
Founded 1912. Pop 18,110; Circ 119,412
Library Holdings: AV Mats 2,080; Large Print Bks 180; Bk Titles 61,411; Bk Vols 63,108; Per Subs 245; Videos 411
Special Collections: Local History Coll (Clifford C Furnas, John Dillinger & Paul Hadley); Mooresville Area Obituary Database
Subject Interests: Local hist
Automation Activity & Vendor Info: (Cataloging) SirsiDynix; (Circulation) SirsiDynix; (OPAC) SirsiDynix
Wireless access
Function: ILL available
Publications: Bookmark (Newsletter)
Partic in Evergreen Indiana Consortium; Midwest Collaborative for Library Services
Open Mon-Thurs 9-8, Fri 9-5, Sat 9-4
Friends of the Library Group

MOUNT VERNON

P ALEXANDRIAN PUBLIC LIBRARY*, 115 W Fifth St, 47620. SAN 305-0467. Tel: 812-838-3286. FAX: 812-838-9639. E-mail: alexpl@evansville.net. Web Site: www.apl.lib.in.us. *Dir,* Marissa Priddis; *Head, Commun Relations,* Stan Campbell; *Head, Adult Serv,* Patty Vahey; *Head, Coll Serv,* Charles Kendall; *Head, Outreach Serv,* Jeanne Burns; *Head, Syst Admin,* Carrie Robb; *Head, Youth Serv,* Anne Cottrell; *YA Librn,* Trisha Seidensticker; Staff 20 (MLS 4, Non-MLS 16)
Founded 1895. Pop 38,505; Circ 197,008
Library Holdings: Audiobooks 2,423; DVDs 39,915; e-books 11,762; Bk Vols 149,908; Per Subs 114
Special Collections: Curriculum Enrichment
Subject Interests: Genealogy, Indiana, Local hist
Automation Activity & Vendor Info: (Acquisitions) SirsiDynix; (Cataloging) SirsiDynix; (Circulation) SirsiDynix; (OPAC) SirsiDynix; (Serials) SirsiDynix
Wireless access
Function: AV serv, Homebound delivery serv, ILL available, Photocopying/Printing, Prog for adults, Prog for children & young adult, Ref serv available, Summer reading prog, Wheelchair accessible
Publications: APL Core (Newsletter)
Partic in Midwest Collaborative for Library Services; OCLC Online Computer Library Center, Inc
Open Mon-Thurs 9-8, Fri & Sat 9-5, Sun 1-5
Friends of the Library Group
Bookmobiles: 1. Outreach Servs, Jeanne Burns. Bk titles 22,000

MUNCIE

M BALL MEMORIAL HOSPITAL*, Library & Information Center, 2401 W University Ave, 47303-3499. SAN 305-0491. Tel: 765-747-3204. FAX: 765-747-0137. *Dir, Libr Serv,* Lorna Springston; Tel: 765-747-4229, E-mail: lspringston@iuhealth.org; *Coordr,* Janelle Cunningham; E-mail: jcunningham@iuhealth.org; *Acq & Cat,* Dana Nunn; Tel: 765-747-4470, E-mail: dnunn@iuhealth.org; *Digital Serv, Ref Serv,* Barbara Hendrixson; E-mail: bhendrixson@iuhealth.org; *Doc Delivery,* Paula McCown; Tel: 765-741-1959, E-mail: pmccown@iuhealth.org; Staff 5 (MLS 1, Non-MLS 4)
Founded 1931
Library Holdings: Bk Vols 2,700; Per Subs 430
Special Collections: Clinical, Medical & Nursing Journals & Textbooks; Consumer Health Information
Subject Interests: Allied health, Commun health, Med, Nursing
Wireless access
Function: ILL available, Photocopying/Printing, Ref serv available
Open Mon-Fri 7-4:30

C BALL STATE UNIVERSITY LIBRARIES, Alexander M Bracken Library, 2000 W University Ave, 47306-1099. SAN 341-5023. Tel: 765-285-5277. Circulation Tel: 765-285-5143. Interlibrary Loan Service Tel: 765-285-1324. Reference Tel: 765-285-1101. FAX: 765-285-2008. E-mail: maincirc@bsu.edu. Web Site: bsu.edu/academics/libraries. *Dean, Univ Libr,* Matthew Shaw; E-mail: mcshaw2@bsu.edu; *Asst Dean, Coll Res Mgt,* Sharon A Roberts; Tel: 765-285-1305, E-mail: sroberts@bsu.edu; *Asst Dean for Library Data & Discovery Solutions,* Bradley D Faust; Tel: 765-285-8032, E-mail: bfaust@bsu.edu; *Asst Dean, Pub Serv,* Suzanne S Rice; Tel: 765-285-1307, E-mail: srice@bsu.edu; *Asst Dean, Special Colls & Digital Scholarships,* Michael Szajewski; Tel: 765-285-5078, E-mail: mgszajewski@bsu.edu; *Head of Acq Serv,* Rebecca Susanne Sheffield; Tel: 765-285-8031, E-mail: rsheffie@bsu.edu; *Head, Coll Develop,* Hilde M Calvert; Tel: 765-285-8033, E-mail: hcalvert@bsu.edu; *Head, Colls & Resource Acquisition Services,* Michael Twigg; Tel: 765-285-8030, E-mail: mtwigg@bsu.edu; *Head, Info Serv,* Diane L Calvin; Tel: 765-285-3327, E-mail: dcalvin@bsu.edu; *Copyright & Scholarly Comms Mgr,* Donald Williams; Tel: 758-285-5330, E-mail: dgwilliams3@bsu.edu; *Financial & Bus Serv Mgr,* Dixie D DeWitt; E-mail: ddewitt@bsu.edu; Staff 110 (MLS 40, Non-MLS 70)
Founded 1918. Enrl 18,819; Highest Degree: Doctorate
Library Holdings: AV Mats 60,123; e-books 395,622; e-journals 140,155; Bk Titles 725,274; Bk Vols 1,031,373; Per Subs 744
Special Collections: Andrew Seager Archives of the (Indiana) Built Environment; Ball State University Archives; John Steinbeck Coll; Local Muncie & Delaware County History (Stoeckel Archives); Middletown Studies Coll. State Document Depository; US Document Depository
Automation Activity & Vendor Info: (Acquisitions) Ex Libris Group; (Cataloging) Ex Libris Group; (Circulation) Ex Libris Group; (Course Reserve) Ex Libris Group; (ILL) OCLC ILLiad; (Media Booking) Ex Libris Group; (Serials) Ex Libris Group
Wireless access
Function: Doc delivery serv, E-Reserves, ILL available, Photocopying/Printing, Scanner
Partic in Academic Libraries of Indiana; Midwest Collaborative for Library Services; OCLC Online Computer Library Center, Inc
Open Mon-Thurs 7:30am-1:30am, Fri 7am-9pm, Sat 9-9, Sun 10am-1:30am
Friends of the Library Group
Departmental Libraries:
ARCHITECTURE, Architecture Bldg, Rm 116, 47306, SAN 341-5058. Tel: 765-285-5857. FAX: 765-285-2644. Web Site: www.bsu.edu/academics/libraries/research/architecture-library. *Archit Librn,* Amy E Trendler; Tel: 765-285-5858, E-mail: aetrendler@bsu.edu. Subject Specialists: *Archit, Art,* Amy E Trendler; Staff 3 (MLS 1, Non-MLS 2)
Founded 1966
Subject Interests: Archit, Landscape archit, Urban planning
Automation Activity & Vendor Info: (Acquisitions) SirsiDynix

Open Mon-Thurs 7:30am-10pm, Fri 7:30-6, Sat 12-6, Sun 1pm-10pm
Friends of the Library Group
ARCHIVES & SPECIAL COLLECTIONS, Bracken Library, Rm 210, 47306-0161, SAN 373-532X. Tel: 765-285-5078. FAX: 765-285-8149. E-mail: libarchives@bsu.edu. Web Site: www.bsu.edu/academics/libraries. *Asst Dean, Special Colls & Digital Scholarships,* Michael Szajewski; *Head of Archives User Engagement,* Sarah Allison; Tel: 765-285-3301, E-mail: smallison@bsu.edu; *Archives Specialist,* Becky Marangelli; Tel: 765-285-5078, E-mail: rlmarangelli@bsu.edu; *Archives Collections Specialist,* Lindsey Vesperry; E-mail: lmvesperry@bsu.edu; *Archivist for Electronic Records & Digital Colls,* Ely Sheinfeld; Tel: 765-285-8723, E-mail: esheinfeld@bsu.edu; *Archives Records Analyst,* Mindy Shull; Tel: 765-285-8853, E-mail: mrshull@bsu.edu; Staff 5 (MLS 3, Non-MLS 2)
Open Mon-Fri 8-6
Friends of the Library Group
EDUCATION, MUSIC & MEDIA LIBRARY, Bracken Library BL-106, 47306, SAN 341-5112. Tel: 765-285-5065. Web Site: www.bsu.edu/academics/libraries/research/education-music-and-media. *Head of Libr,* Lisa Jarrell; Tel: 765-285-5333, E-mail: ljjarrell@bsu.edu; *Libr Supvr,* Julie Nelson; Tel: 765-285-5334, E-mail: jnelson2@bsu.edu; *Libr Spec,* Addison Smith; Tel: 765-285-8188, E-mail: ajsmith5@bsu.edu; *Circ Asst,* Courtney Jackson; Tel: 765-285-3439, E-mail: cmjackson@bsu.edu; *Media Equipment Technician,* Bill McElyea; Tel: 765-285-5340, E-mail: wwmcelyea@bsu.edu; Staff 2 (MLS 1, Non-MLS 1)
Founded 1975
Special Collections: Tubists Universal Brotherhood Association Resources, scores
Friends of the Library Group

P MUNCIE PUBLIC LIBRARY*, Maring-Hunt Library, 2005 S High St, 47302. Tel: 765-747-8200. Web Site: www.munciepubliclibrary.org. *Dir,* Akilah Nosakhere; Tel: 765-747-8201, E-mail: anosakhere@munpl.org; *Asst Dir,* Beth Kroehler; E-mail: bkroehler@munpl.org; *Br Mgr,* Mary Lou Gentis; E-mail: mgentis@munpl.org
Pop 67,500; Circ 1,016,000
Library Holdings: AV Mats 45,607; CDs 16,193; DVDs 13,423; e-books 76; Electronic Media & Resources 1,146; Large Print Bks 6,575; Bk Vols 204,320; Per Subs 494; Talking Bks 4,930; Videos 21,017
Automation Activity & Vendor Info: (Acquisitions) Horizon; (Cataloging) Horizon; (Circulation) Horizon; (Course Reserve) Horizon; (OPAC) Horizon; (Serials) Brodart
Wireless access
Function: Archival coll, AV serv, CD-ROM, Digital talking bks, ILL available, Magnifiers for reading, Meeting rooms, Outside serv via phone, mail, e-mail & web, Photocopying/Printing, Prog for adults, Prog for children & young adult, Ref serv available, Spoken cassettes & CDs, Story hour, Summer reading prog, Telephone ref, VHS videos, Wheelchair accessible, Workshops
Publications: Library Connections (Online only)
Special Services for the Blind - Assistive/Adapted tech devices, equip & products; Audio mat; Bks on cassette; Bks on CD; Computer with voice synthesizer for visually impaired persons; Low vision equip; Magnifiers; Talking bks; Videos on blindness & physical disabilties
Open Mon-Thurs 10-7, Fri 9-6, Sun 1-5
Friends of the Library Group
Branches: 3
CARNEGIE LIBRARY, 301 E Jackson St, 47305, SAN 341-5171. Tel: 765-747-8208. FAX: 765-741-5156. *Br Mgr,* Sara McKinley; E-mail: smckinley@munpl.org
Founded 1875. Pop 72,465
Special Collections: Genealogy Coll; Local History Coll
Function: Meeting rooms
Open Mon, Tues & Thurs 9-6
Friends of the Library Group
CONNECTION CORNER, 1824 E Cenntennial Ave, 47303. Tel: 765-747-8216. *Br Mgr,* Tenisha Harris; E-mail: tharris@munpl.org
Friends of the Library Group
JOHN F KENNEDY BRANCH, 1700 W McGalliard Rd, 47304, SAN 341-5325. Tel: 765-741-9727. FAX: 765-747-8206. *Br Mgr,* Donna Catron; E-mail: dcatron@munpl.org
Founded 1964
Function: Meeting rooms, Story hour
Open Mon-Thurs 10-8, Fri & Sat 9-6, Sun 1-5
Friends of the Library Group

NAPPANEE

P NAPPANEE PUBLIC LIBRARY, 157 N Main St, 46550. SAN 305-0513. Tel: 574-773-7919. FAX: 574-773-7910. Web Site: www.nappaneelibrary.org. *Dir,* Jason Fields; E-mail: jfields@nappaneelibrary.org; Staff 10 (MLS 3, Non-MLS 7)
Founded 1921. Pop 10,082; Circ 183,370
Library Holdings: Bk Titles 63,880; Bk Vols 65,960; Per Subs 195
Special Collections: Heritage Center
Automation Activity & Vendor Info: (Acquisitions) Innovative Interfaces, Inc; (Cataloging) Innovative Interfaces, Inc; (Circulation) Innovative Interfaces, Inc; (OPAC) Innovative Interfaces, Inc; (Serials) Innovative Interfaces, Inc
Wireless access
Partic in Ind Libr Asn; Midwest Collaborative for Library Services
Open Mon-Thurs 9-9, Fri 9-5:30, Sat 9-5, Sun 1-5
Friends of the Library Group

NASHVILLE

P BROWN COUNTY PUBLIC LIBRARY*, 205 Locust Lane, 47448. (Mail add: PO Box 8, 47448-0008), SAN 305-0521. Tel: 812-988-2850. FAX: 812-988-8119. Web Site: browncountylibrary.info. *Dir,* Stori Snyder; E-mail: director@browncountylibrary.info; Staff 4 (MLS 4)
Founded 1919. Pop 14,080; Circ 150,870
Library Holdings: Bk Vols 60,000; Per Subs 100
Special Collections: Brown County Artists & Authors
Automation Activity & Vendor Info: (Acquisitions) Follett Software; (Cataloging) Follett Software; (OPAC) Follett Software
Wireless access
Function: Homebound delivery serv, ILL available
Publications: Annual Report
Partic in Serving Every Ohioan Library Center
Special Services for the Deaf - TDD equip
Special Services for the Blind - Aids for in-house use; Audio mat; Bks on cassette; Bks on CD; Closed circuit TV; Large print bks; Talking bks
Open Mon-Thurs 9-8, Fri & Sat 9-5, Sun 1-5
Friends of the Library Group
Branches: 1
CORDRY SWEETWATER BRANCH, 8451 Nineveh Rd, Nineveh, 46164. Tel: 317-933-9229.
Library Holdings: Bk Vols 4,743
Open Tues 2-5, Wed & Thurs 3-6, Sat (June-Aug) 10-1

NEW ALBANY

C INDIANA UNIVERSITY SOUTHEAST LIBRARY*, 4201 Grant Line Rd, 47150. SAN 305-053X. Tel: 812-941-2262. Circulation Tel: 812-941-2485. Web Site: www.ius.edu/library. *Dir, Libr Serv,* Claude Martin Rosen; E-mail: crosen@ius.edu; *Ref Librn,* Benita Mason; E-mail: bkmason@ius.edu; *Coordr, Automation & Tech Serv,* Melanie Hughes; Tel: 812-941-2145, E-mail: mehughes@ius.edu; *Head, Coll Develop & Spec Coll,* Kate B Moore; Tel: 812-941-2189, E-mail: kabmoore@ius.edu; *Coordr, Libr Instruction,* Maria Accardi; Tel: 812-941-2551, E-mail: maccardi@ius.edu; *Coordr, Pub Serv,* Gabrielle Carr; Tel: 812-941-2489, E-mail: carrg@ius.edu; *Acq Asst,* Phyllis Nachand; Tel: 812-941-2276, E-mail: pnachand@ius.edu; *Cat Asst,* Elizabeth McMahan; Tel: 812-941-2277, E-mail: emcmahan@ius.edu; *Govt Doc Asst,* Robin King; Tel: 812-941-2496, E-mail: raking@ius.edu; *ILL Asst,* Rachel Getz; Tel: 812-941-2487, E-mail: rkgetz@ius.edu; Staff 16 (MLS 6, Non-MLS 10)
Founded 1941. Enrl 6,400; Fac 241; Highest Degree: Master
Library Holdings: Bk Titles 250,000; Per Subs 1,040
Special Collections: Ars Femina Musical Scores; Baron Hill Coll (Democratic Representative, 9th Congressional District) papers 1999-2004 & 2007-2010; Center for Cultural Resources; IUS Archives; William L Simon Sheet Music. US Document Depository
Automation Activity & Vendor Info: (Acquisitions) SirsiDynix; (Cataloging) SirsiDynix; (Circulation) SirsiDynix; (Course Reserve) SirsiDynix; (ILL) SirsiDynix; (OPAC) SirsiDynix; (Serials) SirsiDynix
Wireless access
Partic in Kentuckiana Metroversity, Inc; Midwest Collaborative for Library Services
Special Services for the Blind - Assistive/Adapted tech devices, equip & products

P NEW ALBANY-FLOYD COUNTY PUBLIC LIBRARY*, 180 W Spring St, 47150. SAN 305-0548. Tel: 812-944-8464. Administration Tel: 812-949-3734. FAX: 812-949-3532. Web Site: floydlibrary.org. *Dir,* Melissa Merida; Tel: 812-949-3525, E-mail: mmerida@nafclibrary.org; *Asst Dir,* Sandra Fortner; Tel: 812-949-3730, E-mail: sfortner@nafclibrary.org; *Head, Customer Serv,* Amanda Harris; Tel: 812-949-3528, E-mail: aharris@nafclibrary.org; *Head, Pub Serv,* Teresa Moulton; E-mail: tmoulton@nafclibrary.org; *Materials Handling Coord,* Marilyn Powell; E-mail: mpowell@nafclibrary.org; *Coll Develop,* Abby Johnson; E-mail: ajohnson@nafclibrary.org; Staff 41 (MLS 9, Non-MLS 32)
Founded 1884. Pop 74,578; Circ 413,069
Library Holdings: Bk Vols 225,759; Per Subs 405
Special Collections: Oral History; State Document Depository
Subject Interests: Genealogy, Local hist
Automation Activity & Vendor Info: (Cataloging) SirsiDynix; (Circulation) SirsiDynix; (Media Booking) SirsiDynix; (OPAC) SirsiDynix
Wireless access
Function: Adult bk club, Archival coll, Art exhibits, Audiobks via web, Bk reviews (Group), Bks on cassette, Bks on CD, Children's prog,

Computer training, Computers for patron use, Electronic databases & coll, Free DVD rentals, Homebound delivery serv, ILL available, Microfiche/film & reading machines, Music CDs, Online cat, Outreach serv, OverDrive digital audio bks, Photocopying/Printing, Prog for adults, Prog for children & young adult, Scanner, Spanish lang bks, Story hour, Summer reading prog, Teen prog, Telephone ref
Partic in Midwest Collaborative for Library Services
Open Mon-Thurs 9-8:30, Fri & Sat 9-5:30
Restriction: Residents only
Friends of the Library Group

NEW CARLISLE

P NEW CARLISLE & OLIVE TOWNSHIP PUBLIC LIBRARY*, 408 S Bray St, 46552. (Mail add: PO Box Q, 46552-0837), SAN 305-0556. Tel: 574-654-3046. FAX: 574-654-8260. E-mail: questions@ncpl.lib.in.us. Web Site: www.ncpl.lib.in.us. *Dir,* Stephanie Murphy; E-mail: smurphy@ncpl.lib.in.us; *Asst Dir,* Amy Schrock; E-mail: aschrock@ncpl.lib.in.us; *Ch Serv,* Sara Audiss; E-mail: saudiss@ncpl.lib.in.us; Staff 1 (MLS 1)
Founded 1894. Pop 5,019; Circ 140,504
Library Holdings: AV Mats 7,697; Bk Titles 40,853; Bk Vols 49,905; Per Subs 105; Talking Bks 3,868
Subject Interests: Arts & crafts, Fiction, Local hist
Automation Activity & Vendor Info: (Cataloging) TLC (The Library Corporation); (Circulation) Follett Software; (OPAC) Follett Software
Partic in Midwest Collaborative for Library Services
Open Mon-Thurs 9-8, Fri & Sat 9-5, Sun 1-5
Friends of the Library Group

NEW CASTLE

P NEW CASTLE-HENRY COUNTY PUBLIC LIBRARY*, 376 S 15th St, 47362-3205. (Mail add: PO Box J, 47362-1050), SAN 305-0572. Tel: 765-529-0362. FAX: 765-521-3581. Web Site: www.nchcpl.org. *Libr Dir,* Winnie Logan; E-mail: winniel@nchcpl.lib.in.us; *Asst Dir,* Lisa Stamm; E-mail: lisas@nchcpl.lib.in.us; *Bus Off Mgr,* Brenda Martinez; E-mail: brendam@nchcpl.lib.in.us; Staff 28 (MLS 4, Non-MLS 24)
Founded 1913. Pop 39,349; Circ 324,841
Library Holdings: AV Mats 19,688; High Interest/Low Vocabulary Bk Vols 300; Bk Titles 180,291; Per Subs 384
Special Collections: Indiana History Coll; New Castle & Henry County Coll
Automation Activity & Vendor Info: (Acquisitions) SirsiDynix; (Cataloging) SirsiDynix; (Circulation) SirsiDynix; (ILL) SirsiDynix; (OPAC) SirsiDynix
Wireless access
Partic in Midwest Collaborative for Library Services
Open Mon-Thurs 9-9, Fri 9-6, Sat 9-5, Sun 1-5
Friends of the Library Group
Bookmobiles: 1

NEW HARMONY

S WORKING MEN'S INSTITUTE MUSEUM & LIBRARY*, 407 W Tavern St, 47631. (Mail add: PO Box 368, 47631-0368), SAN 305-0599. Tel: 812-682-4806. FAX: 812-682-4806. Web Site: www.workingmensinstitute.org. *Dir,* Ryan Rokicki; E-mail: director@workingmensinstitute.org; Staff 1 (MLS 1)
Founded 1838
Library Holdings: AV Mats 100; Bk Vols 32,000; Per Subs 50; Talking Bks 50
Special Collections: New Harmony History Manuscript Coll; Rare Books Coll, from 1538
Automation Activity & Vendor Info: (Cataloging) Follett Software; (Circulation) Follett Software; (OPAC) Follett Software
Wireless access
Open Tues-Thurs 10-7, Fri & Sat 10-4:30, Sun 12-4
Friends of the Library Group

NEWBURGH

P NEWBURGH CHANDLER PUBLIC LIBRARY*, Bell Road Library, 4111 Lakeshore Dr, 47630-2274. (Mail add: PO Box 850, 47629-0850), SAN 305-0602. Tel: 812-853-5468. FAX: 812-853-6377. Web Site: www.ncplibraries.org. *Dir,* Trista Smith; Tel: 812-942-9997, E-mail: tsmith@ncplibraries.org; *Br Mgr,* Renee Beard; Tel: 812-583-5468, Ext 305, E-mail: tbeard@ncplibraries.org; *Ch,* Linda Spillman Bruns; Tel: 812-589-5468, Ext 308, E-mail: lsbruns@ncplibraries.org; *Ref Librn,* Daniel Smith; Tel: 812-589-5468, Ext 303, E-mail: dsmith@ncplibraries.org; *Teen Librn,* Susan Melfi; Tel: 812-589-5468, Ext 304, E-mail: smelfi@ncplibraries.org; *Mgr, Info Tech,* Allen Tate; Tel: 812-942-9991, E-mail: atate@ncplibraries.org; *Tech Serv,* Joan Elliott Parker; Staff 43 (MLS 5, Non-MLS 38)
Founded 1897. Pop 31,002; Circ 465,074
Library Holdings: Bk Vols 104,939; Per Subs 308
Special Collections: Warrick County Families Genealogy; Warrick County History. State Document Depository; US Document Depository
Subject Interests: Local hist
Automation Activity & Vendor Info: (Acquisitions) Innovative Interfaces, Inc; (Cataloging) Innovative Interfaces, Inc; (Circulation) Innovative Interfaces, Inc; (OPAC) Innovative Interfaces, Inc
Wireless access
Function: ILL available, Prog for children & young adult, Summer reading prog
Partic in Midwest Collaborative for Library Services
Open Mon-Thurs 9-9, Fri & Sat 9-5, Sun 1-5
Friends of the Library Group
Branches: 2
CHANDLER LIBRARY, 402 S Jaycee St, Chandler, 47610, SAN 324-3079. Tel: 812-925-7179, Ext 203. FAX: 812-925-7192. *Br Mgr,* Diane Slater; E-mail: dslater@ncplibraries.org; Staff 7.5 (Non-MLS 7.5)
Library Holdings: Bk Titles 22,840; Bk Vols 25,290; Per Subs 59; Videos 310
Open Mon & Thurs 10-6, Tues & Wed 10-8, Fri 10-5, Sat 1-5
Friends of the Library Group
NEWBURGH LIBRARY, 30 W Water St, 47630, SAN 370-1069. Tel: 812-858-1437. FAX: 812-853-5622. *Br Mgr,* Renee Beard; Staff 3 (Non-MLS 3)
Library Holdings: Bk Titles 53,640; Bk Vols 56,910; Per Subs 72; Videos 314
Open Mon 11-7, Tues-Thurs 10-6, Fri & Sat 1-5
Friends of the Library Group

NEWPORT

P VERMILLION COUNTY PUBLIC LIBRARY*, 385 E Market St, 47966. (Mail add: PO Box 100, 47966), SAN 341-5384. Tel: 765-492-3555. FAX: 765-492-9588. E-mail: vermillion.library.newport@gmail.com. Web Site: www.vermillioncpl.info. *Dir,* Misty Bishop; E-mail: mistybishop.vcpln@gmail.com; *Ch,* Vanda Liesman; E-mail: vandaliesman.vcpl@gmail.com; Staff 5 (MLS 1, Non-MLS 4)
Founded 1929. Pop 7,200; Circ 45,928
Jan 2019-Dec 2019. Mats Exp $41,407, Books $18,232, Other Print Mats $800, AV Equip $7,000, AV Mat $11,000. Sal $100,956
Library Holdings: Audiobooks 561; AV Mats 12,881; Bks on Deafness & Sign Lang 11; DVDs 2,393; e-books 51,097; Large Print Bks 370; Bk Titles 19,272; Per Subs 54; Talking Bks 400; Videos 350
Subject Interests: Genealogy, Indiana
Automation Activity & Vendor Info: (Acquisitions) Evergreen; (Cataloging) Evergreen; (Circulation) Evergreen; (OPAC) Evergreen
Wireless access
Function: 24/7 Electronic res, 24/7 Online cat, After school storytime, Audio & video playback equip for onsite use, Audiobks on Playaways & MP3, Audiobks via web, AV serv, Bks on CD, Children's prog, Computers for patron use, Digital talking bks, Family literacy, Free DVD rentals, Genealogy discussion group, Holiday prog, ILL available, Internet access, Laminating, Literacy & newcomer serv, Magazines, Mail & tel request accepted, Microfiche/film & reading machines, Movies, Notary serv, Online cat, Outreach serv, OverDrive digital audio bks, Photocopying/Printing, Prog for adults, Prog for children & young adult, Res performed for a fee, Scanner, Serves people with intellectual disabilities, STEM programs, Story hour, Summer reading prog, Tax forms, Teen prog, Telephone ref
Partic in Midwest Collaborative for Library Services
Open Mon-Thurs 10-6:30, Fri 10-5, Sat 10-2
Friends of the Library Group

NOBLESVILLE

P HAMILTON EAST PUBLIC LIBRARY*, Noblesville Library, One Library Plaza, 46060. SAN 305-0610. Tel: 317-773-1384. Web Site: www.hepl.lib.in.us. *Dir,* Edra Waterman; E-mail: ewaterman@hepl.lib.in.us; *Dep Dir,* Katie Lorton; E-mail: lortonk@hepl.lib.in.us; *Mgr, Ad Serv,* Brad Howell; E-mail: howellb@hepl.lib.in.us; *Mgr, Circ Serv,* Ann Grilliot; E-mail: grilliota@hepl.lib.in.us; *Mgr, Youth Serv,* Lori Holewinski; E-mail: holewinskil@hepl.lib.in.us
Founded 1909. Pop 148,721; Circ 2,019,986
Library Holdings: Bk Titles 394,564; Bk Vols 524,957; Per Subs 799
Special Collections: Hamilton County History & Genealogy, bk & microfilm
Automation Activity & Vendor Info: (Acquisitions) SirsiDynix; (Cataloging) SirsiDynix; (Circulation) SirsiDynix; (OPAC) SirsiDynix
Wireless access
Publications: Abstracts of the Will Records of Hamilton County, Indiana 1824-1901
Partic in Midwest Collaborative for Library Services
Special Services for the Deaf - Bks on deafness & sign lang; TDD equip; Videos & decoder
Open Mon-Thurs 9-9, Fri & Sat 9-5:30, Sun 1:30-5:30
Friends of the Library Group

Branches: 1
FISHERS BRANCH, Five Municipal Dr, Fishers, 46038-1574. Tel: 317-579-0300. FAX: 317-579-0309. *Dir,* David L Cooper
Library Holdings: Bk Vols 252,830
Open Mon-Thurs 9-9, Fri & Sat 9-5:30, Sun 1:30-5:30

NORTH JUDSON

P NORTH JUDSON-WAYNE TOWNSHIP PUBLIC LIBRARY*, 208 Keller Ave, 46366. SAN 305-0629. Tel: 574-896-2841. FAX: 574-896-2892. E-mail: lib.norjud@gmail.com. Web Site: www.njwt.lib.in.us. *Dir,* Michael Booth; Staff 2 (MLS 1, Non-MLS 1)
Founded 1921. Pop 4,987; Circ 12,000
Jan 2016-Dec 2016 Income $184,529, State $18,539, Locally Generated Income $153,370, Other $12,620. Mats Exp $17,490, Books $14,887, Per/Ser (Incl. Access Fees) $2,171, AV Mat $432. Sal $96,439 (Prof $27,400)
Library Holdings: CDs 349; DVDs 497; e-books 104; Large Print Bks 39; Microforms 255; Bk Titles 20,898; Per Subs 31
Special Collections: Excalibur Coll; Mint Growing. Oral History
Automation Activity & Vendor Info: (Cataloging) Evolve; (Circulation) Evolve; (OPAC) Evolve
Wireless access
Function: 24/7 Online cat, Activity rm, Adult bk club, Art programs, Audio & video playback equip for onsite use, AV serv, Bks on CD, Children's prog, Computers for patron use, Digital talking bks, E-Reserves, Electronic databases & coll, Holiday prog, Homebound delivery serv, ILL available, Internet access, Laminating, Magazines, Mail & tel request accepted, Meeting rooms, Microfiche/film & reading machines, Movies, Online cat, Photocopying/Printing, Preschool outreach, Preschool reading prog, Prog for adults, Prog for children & young adult, Ref & res, Ref serv available, Scanner, Spoken cassettes & CDs, Spoken cassettes & DVDs, Story hour, Summer reading prog, Tax forms, Telephone ref, Wheelchair accessible
Partic in Midwest Collaborative for Library Services; Northern Indiana Computer Consortium for Libraries
Open Mon-Thurs 10-7, Fri 10-6, Sat 10-3
Friends of the Library Group

NORTH MANCHESTER

C MANCHESTER UNIVERSITY, Funderburg Library, 604 E College Ave, 46962. SAN 305-0637. Tel: 260-982-5364. FAX: 260-232-2755. E-mail: librarians@manchester.edu. Web Site: libguides.manchester.edu, www.manchester.edu/library. *Interim Dir, Tech Serv,* Darla Vornberger Haines; Tel: 260-982-5949, E-mail: dvhaines@manchester.edu; *Access Serv Librn, Instruction Librn,* Angie Fisher; Tel: 260-982-5028, E-mail: asfisher@manchester.edu; *Archivist,* Jeanine Wine; Tel: 260-982-5361, E-mail: jmwine@manchester.edu; Staff 4 (MLS 2, Non-MLS 2)
Founded 1889. Enrl 1,300; Highest Degree: Master
Library Holdings: Bk Vols 176,052
Special Collections: Church of the Brethren Coll; College Archives; Peace Studies
Automation Activity & Vendor Info: (Acquisitions) OCLC Worldshare Management Services; (Cataloging) OCLC Worldshare Management Services; (Circulation) OCLC Worldshare Management Services; (Discovery) OCLC; (ILL) OCLC WorldShare Interlibrary Loan; (OPAC) OCLC; (Serials) OCLC Worldshare Management Services
Wireless access
Function: Archival coll, Art exhibits, Audio & video playback equip for onsite use, Computers for patron use, Doc delivery serv, Electronic databases & coll, Free DVD rentals, ILL available, Online cat, Online ref, Photocopying/Printing, Ref & res, Ref serv available, Res assist avail, Scanner, Telephone ref, VHS videos, Wheelchair accessible
Partic in Academic Libraries of Indiana; Midwest Collaborative for Library Services; OCLC Online Computer Library Center, Inc; Private Academic Library Network of Indiana
Open Mon-Thurs 7:45am-Midnight, Fri 7:45-6, Sat 1-5, Sun 1pm-Midnight
Restriction: Circ limited, In-house use for visitors

P NORTH MANCHESTER PUBLIC LIBRARY*, 405 N Market St, 46962. SAN 305-0645. Tel: 260-982-4773. FAX: 260-982-6342. E-mail: nmpl@nman.lib.in.us. Web Site: www.nman.lib.in.us. *Dir,* Position Currently Open; *Children's Mgr,* Sarah Morbitzer; E-mail: smorbitzer@nman.lib.in.us; Staff 4 (MLS 1, Non-MLS 3)
Founded 1912. Pop 6,020; Circ 128,754
Library Holdings: Bk Titles 64,225; Bk Vols 67,377; Per Subs 121
Special Collections: North Manchester News-Journal, 1882-present
Subject Interests: Genealogy, Local hist
Automation Activity & Vendor Info: (Cataloging) Follett Software; (Circulation) Follett Software; (OPAC) Follett Software
Wireless access
Partic in Midwest Collaborative for Library Services; Northern Indiana Computer Consortium for Libraries
Special Services for the Deaf - Closed caption videos
Special Services for the Blind - Audio mat; Bks on cassette; Bks on CD; Copier with enlargement capabilities; Home delivery serv; Large print bks; Playaways (bks on MP3)
Open Mon-Thurs 9-8, Fri & Sat 9-5
Friends of the Library Group

NORTH VERNON

P JENNINGS COUNTY PUBLIC LIBRARY*, 2375 N State Hwy 3, 47265. SAN 305-0653. Tel: 812-346-2091. E-mail: jlibrary@seidata.com. Web Site: jenningslib.org. *Dir,* Mary Hougland; E-mail: Mary.Hougland@jenningslib.org; *Asst Dir,* Ed Kellar; E-mail: Ed.Kellar@jenningslib.org; *Ad,* Gracie Maine; E-mail: gracie.maine@jenningslib.org; Staff 10 (MLS 3, Non-MLS 7)
Founded 1813. Pop 28,510; Circ 100,000
Library Holdings: CDs 900; Large Print Bks 1,200; Bk Titles 72,000; Bk Vols 90,000; Per Subs 236; Talking Bks 1,500; Videos 5,000
Subject Interests: Genealogy, Local hist
Automation Activity & Vendor Info: (Cataloging) Auto-Graphics, Inc; (Circulation) Auto-Graphics, Inc; (OPAC) Auto-Graphics, Inc
Wireless access
Partic in Evergreen Indiana Consortium; Midwest Collaborative for Library Services
Open Mon-Thurs 9-9, Fri 9-6, Sat 9-4
Friends of the Library Group

NORTH WEBSTER

P NORTH WEBSTER COMMUNITY PUBLIC LIBRARY*, 301 N Main St, 46555. (Mail add: PO Box 825, 46555-0008). Tel: 574-834-7122. FAX: 574-834-7122. E-mail: info@nweb.lib.in.us. Web Site: www.nweb.lib.in.us. *Libr Dir,* Helen Leinbach; E-mail: hleinbach@nweb.lib.in.us; Staff 6 (MLS 2, Non-MLS 4)
Founded 2004. Pop 6,700; Circ 91,372
Jan 2017-Dec 2017 Income $598,552, County $426,928, Locally Generated Income $171,624. Mats Exp $54,871, Books $26,765, Per/Ser (Incl. Access Fees) $3,800, AV Equip $1,000, AV Mat $13,028, Electronic Ref Mat (Incl. Access Fees) $10,278. Sal $283,907 (Prof $193,437)
Library Holdings: Audiobooks 3,029; Bks on Deafness & Sign Lang 30; Braille Volumes 4; CDs 504; DVDs 7,169; e-books 220,260; e-journals 200; Electronic Media & Resources 274,370; High Interest/Low Vocabulary Bk Vols 100; Large Print Bks 2,200; Bk Titles 43,862; Per Subs 88
Subject Interests: Genealogy
Automation Activity & Vendor Info: (Acquisitions) Baker & Taylor; (Cataloging) Evergreen; (Circulation) Evergreen; (Course Reserve) Evergreen; (ILL) Evergreen; (OPAC) Evergreen
Wireless access
Function: Accelerated reader prog, Adult bk club, Art exhibits, Audiobks via web, AV serv, Bi-weekly Writer's Group, Bk club(s), Bks on cassette, Bks on CD, Children's prog, Computer training, Computers for patron use, Digital talking bks, E-Reserves, Electronic databases & coll, Free DVD rentals, Genealogy discussion group, Holiday prog, Homebound delivery serv, ILL available, Internet access, Mail & tel request accepted, Music CDs, Online cat, Online ref, Outreach serv, Outside serv via phone, mail, e-mail & web, OverDrive digital audio bks, Photocopying/Printing, Preschool outreach, Preschool reading prog, Printer for laptops & handheld devices, Prog for adults, Prog for children & young adult, Ref serv available, Scanner, Spoken cassettes & CDs, Spoken cassettes & DVDs, Story hour, Summer reading prog, Tax forms, Teen prog, VHS videos, Wheelchair accessible
Publications: Check It Out (Monthly newsletter); Local History & Genealogy Center: From the Library (Local historical information)
Partic in Evergreen Indiana Consortium; Midwest Collaborative for Library Services; Northeast Indiana Libraries Serving Communities Consortium
Special Services for the Deaf - Accessible learning ctr; Bks on deafness & sign lang; Closed caption videos; High interest/low vocabulary bks
Special Services for the Blind - Bks on cassette; Bks on CD; Braille bks; Home delivery serv; Large print & cassettes; Large print bks; Low vision equip; Magnifiers
Open Mon-Thurs 10-7, Fri 10-6, Sat 10-3
Friends of the Library Group

NOTRE DAME

C HESBURGH LIBRARIES*, 221 Hesburgh Library, University of Notre Dame, 46556. SAN 341-5414. Tel: 574-631-5252. FAX: 574-631-6772. Web Site: library.nd.edu. *Edward H Arnold Univ Librn,* Diane Parr Walker; E-mail: dwalker6@nd.edu; *Assoc Librn,* Zheng Wang; E-mail: zheng.wang@nd.edu; *Assoc Librn,* Louis Jordan; E-mail: ljordan@nd.edu
Founded 1873. Highest Degree: Doctorate
Special Collections: 1798 Irish Rebellion Coll; 17th-Early 19th Century Books from Religious Libraries Near Olmutz (Olmutz Coll); Anastos Byzantine Coll; Armed Services Editions Coll; Autographed Books (Theodore M Hesburgh Coll); Catholic Americana; Chesterton (John Bennett Shaw Coll); Dante (John A Zahm Coll); Descartes (Denisoff Coll); Early American Newspapers (Thackenbruch Coll); Early Editions of the

Works of Edmund Burke (William Todd Coll); Early Printed Books (Astrik L Gabriel Coll); Early Printed Maps of Ireland Coll; Edward Gorey Coll; Eric Gill Coll; Fundamentalist/Evangelical Magazines (Adam L Lutzweiler Coll); Garcilaso de la Vega & the History of Peru (Durand Coll); George Berkeley (A A Luce Coll); Historical Botany (Edward Greene Coll); Irish Music (Captain Francis O'Neill Coll); Jacques Maritain Coll; Jorge Luis Borges Coll; McDevitt Inquisition Coll; Medieval & Renaissance Manuscripts; Modern Manuscript Coll; Notre Dame Coll; Penguin Paperbacks, 1935-1965; R H Gore, Sr Orchid Coll; Robert H Gore Numismatic Coll; Sports (Edmund Joyce Coll); Vatican II Documents Coll; Wolf Irish Stamp Coll. US Document Depository
Wireless access
Partic in Association of Research Libraries; Center for Research Libraries; Midwest Collaborative for Library Services; Northeast Research Libraries Consortium; OCLC Online Computer Library Center, Inc; OCLC Research Library Partnership; Research Libraries Information Network
Restriction: In-house use for visitors

Departmental Libraries:

ARCHITECTURE, 150 Walsh Family Hall of Architecture, 46556-5652, SAN 341-5449. Tel: 574-631-6654. FAX: 574-631-9662. E-mail: library.archlib.1@nd.edu. Web Site: architecture.library.nd.edu. *Archit Librn,* Jennifer Parker; Tel: 574-631-9401
Founded 1931
Publications: New Acquisitions
Restriction: Circ limited

THOMAS J MAHAFFEY JR BUSINESS INFORMATION CENTER, L001 Mendoza College of Business, 46556, SAN 378-0414. Tel: 574-631-9098. FAX: 574-631-6367. E-mail: library.bic.1@nd.edu. Web Site: bic.library.nd.edu. *Bus Librn,* Barbara Pietraszewski; Tel: 574-631-9099, E-mail: bpietras@nd.edu. Subject Specialists: *Entrepreneurship,* Barbara Pietraszewski
Founded 1995. Highest Degree: Master
Function: Res libr

MEDIEVAL INSTITUTE LIBRARY, 715 Hesburgh Library, 46556-5629, SAN 341-5651. Tel: 574-631-5724, 574-631-6603. FAX: 574-631-8644. Web Site: www.nd.edu/~medvllib. *Assessment Librn, Scholarly Resources Librn,* Julia Schneider; E-mail: jschneid@nd.edu
Founded 1948
Special Collections: Ambrosiana (Frank M Folsom Microfilm & Photographic Coll); History of Medieval Universities
Subject Interests: Byzantine studies, Medieval studies

C HOLY CROSS COLLEGE*, McKenna Library, 54515 State Rd 933 N, 46556-0308. SAN 305-0661. Tel: 574-239-8391. FAX: 574-239-8323. Web Site: www.hcc-nd.edu/mckenna-library. *Dir, Libr Serv,* Mary Ellen Hegedus; Tel: 574-239-8360, E-mail: mhegedus@hcc-nd.edu; *Assoc Dir, Libr Serv,* Sarah Kolda; Tel: 574-239-8361, E-mail: skolda@hcc-nd.edu; *Libr Tech,* Paula Morrow; E-mail: pmorrow@hcc-nd.edu; Staff 4 (MLS 3, Non-MLS 1)
Founded 1966. Fac 45; Highest Degree: Bachelor
Automation Activity & Vendor Info: (Circulation) Ex Libris Group
Wireless access
Partic in Academic Libraries of Indiana; Michiana Acad Libr Consortium; Midwest Collaborative for Library Services
Open Mon-Thurs 8:30am-1am, Fri 8:30-4:30, Sat 12:30-4:30, Sun 1-1

C SAINT MARY'S COLLEGE*, Cushwa-Leighton Library, 46556-5001. SAN 305-067X. Tel: 574-284-5280. Circulation Tel: 574-284-5278. Reference Tel: 574-284-5288. FAX: 574-284-4791. Web Site: www.saintmarys.edu/library. *Dir,* Janet Fore; Tel: 219-284-5281, E-mail: jfore@saintmarys.edu; *Cat Librn,* Katherine Marschall; Tel: 574-284-4438, E-mail: marschal@saintmarys.edu; *Coll Develop Librn,* Suzanne Hinnefeld; Tel: 574-284-5289, E-mail: shinnefe@saintmarys.edu; *Mkt Librn, Outreach Librn,* Jill Hobgood; Tel: 574-284-4804, E-mail: jhobgood@saintmarys.edu; *Per Librn,* Sue Wiegand; Tel: 574-284-4789, E-mail: swiegand@saintmarys.edu; *Ref & Instruction Librn,* Catherine Pellegrino; Tel: 574-284-5286, E-mail: cpellegr@saintmarys.edu; *Circ,* Lisa Karle; Tel: 574-284-5396, E-mail: lkarle@saintmarys.edu; Staff 13 (MLS 7, Non-MLS 6)
Founded 1855. Enrl 1,602; Fac 150; Highest Degree: Bachelor
Library Holdings: AV Mats 2,657; Bk Titles 166,301; Bk Vols 229,484; Per Subs 584; Videos 210
Special Collections: Dante
Automation Activity & Vendor Info: (Acquisitions) Ex Libris Group; (Cataloging) Ex Libris Group; (Circulation) Ex Libris Group; (ILL) OCLC; (OPAC) Ex Libris Group; (Serials) Ex Libris Group
Wireless access
Function: Audio & video playback equip for onsite use, ILL available
Partic in Michiana Acad Libr Consortium; Midwest Collaborative for Library Services; OCLC Online Computer Library Center, Inc
Open Mon-Thurs 7:45am-Midnight, Fri 7:45am-8pm, Sat 9-5, Sun 11am-1am
Restriction: Open to pub for ref & circ; with some limitations

CL UNIVERSITY OF NOTRE DAME*, Kresge Law Library, Notre Dame Law School, 2345 Biolchini Hall of Law, 46556-4640. SAN 341-5562. Tel: 574-631-7024. FAX: 574-631-6371. E-mail: lawlib@nd.edu. Web Site: law.nd.edu/faculty-scholarship/kresge-law-library. *Dir,* Thomas Mills; E-mail: tmills@nd.edu; *Dir, Technology,* Daniel Manier; Tel: 574-631-3939, E-mail: manier@nd.edu; *Assoc Dir, Res & Instruction,* Dwight King; E-mail: king.1@nd.edu; *Acq/Coll Develop Librn,* Sandra Klein; Tel: 574-631-8447, E-mail: klein.26@nd.edu; *Research Librn,* Christopher O'Byrne; Tel: 574-631-5664, E-mail: cobyrne@nd.edu; Staff 21.5 (MLS 9, Non-MLS 12.5)
Founded 1869. Enrl 540; Fac 9; Highest Degree: Doctorate
Library Holdings: AV Mats 1,785; CDs 687; DVDs 1,175; e-books 7,500; e-journals 35,000; Microforms 1,807,829; Bk Titles 222,433; Bk Vols 690,000; Per Subs 4,250
Automation Activity & Vendor Info: (Acquisitions) Innovative Interfaces, Inc - Millennium; (Cataloging) Innovative Interfaces, Inc - Millennium; (Circulation) Innovative Interfaces, Inc - Millennium; (ILL) OCLC ILLiad; (OPAC) Innovative Interfaces, Inc - Millennium; (Serials) Innovative Interfaces, Inc - Millennium
Wireless access
Open Mon-Fri 8-5
Restriction: 24-hr pass syst for students only

OAKLAND CITY

P OAKLAND CITY-COLUMBIA TOWNSHIP PUBLIC LIBRARY*, 210 S Main, 47660. SAN 305-0696. Tel: 812-749-3559. FAX: 812-749-3558. E-mail: frontdesk@occtpl.lib.in.us. Web Site: occtpl.lib.in.us. *Dir,* Julie Elmore; E-mail: admin@occtpl.lib.in.us; Staff 3 (Non-MLS 3)
Founded 1917. Pop 4,149; Circ 24,211
Library Holdings: Audiobooks 500; CDs 250; DVDs 1,500; Bk Vols 23,785; Per Subs 20; Videos 10
Special Collections: History of Pike & Gibson Counties
Wireless access
Partic in Midwest Collaborative for Library Services
Open Mon-Wed & Fri 9-6, Thurs 9-7, Sat 9-1
Friends of the Library Group

C OAKLAND CITY UNIVERSITY*, Barger-Richardson LRC, 605 W Columbia St, 47660. SAN 305-0688. Tel: 812-749-1269. FAX: 812-749-1414. Web Site: www.oak.edu/library. *Dir, Libr Serv,* Dr Denise J Pinnick; Tel: 812-749-1267, E-mail: dpinnick@oak.edu; *Asst Dir,* Megan Depoister; Tel: 812-749-1268, E-mail: mdepoister@oak.edu; Staff 3 (MLS 1, Non-MLS 2)
Founded 1890. Enrl 1,668; Fac 37; Highest Degree: Doctorate
Library Holdings: Bk Titles 110,115; Bk Vols 115,340; Per Subs 301
Special Collections: General Baptist Denomination Materials
Automation Activity & Vendor Info: (Acquisitions) Ex Libris Group; (Cataloging) Ex Libris Group; (Circulation) Ex Libris Group; (Course Reserve) Ex Libris Group; (OPAC) Ex Libris Group; (Serials) Ex Libris Group
Wireless access
Function: Res libr
Partic in Academic Libraries of Indiana; Midwest Collaborative for Library Services; Private Academic Library Network of Indiana
Open Mon-Thurs 8am-10pm, Fri 8-4:30, Sat 11-3, Sun 6pm-10pm

ODON

P ODON WINKELPLECK PUBLIC LIBRARY*, 202 W Main St, 47562. SAN 305-070X. Tel: 812-636-4949. FAX: 812-636-4949. E-mail: owpl@odon.lib.in.us. Web Site: owpl.blogspot.com. *Dir,* Susan Graber; *Asst Librn,* Lynn Brown; *Asst Librn,* Hanna Caywood; Staff 3 (Non-MLS 3)
Founded 1906. Pop 2,793; Circ 19,400
Library Holdings: Audiobooks 220; AV Mats 310; CDs 95; Large Print Bks 300; Bk Titles 15,000; Bk Vols 16,250; Per Subs 40; Videos 1,750
Automation Activity & Vendor Info: (Cataloging) Evergreen; (Circulation) Evergreen; (OPAC) Evergreen
Wireless access
Function: 24/7 Electronic res, 24/7 Online cat, Audiobks via web, Bks on cassette, Bks on CD, Computers for patron use, ILL available, Internet access, Laminating, Magazines, Meeting rooms, Movies, Music CDs, Online cat, OverDrive digital audio bks, Photocopying/Printing, Scanner, Summer reading prog, Tax forms, VHS videos
Partic in Evergreen Indiana Consortium
Open Tues 1-8, Wed & Sat 9-1, Thurs 4-8, Fri 1-5
Restriction: Non-resident fee
Friends of the Library Group

ORLAND

P JOYCE PUBLIC LIBRARY*, 6035 N State Rd 327, 46776. (Mail add: PO Box 240, 46776-0240), SAN 376-5350. Tel: 260-829-6329. *Librn,* Bonnie Hollman; E-mail: bonnieh31@frontier.com; Staff 1 (Non-MLS 1)
Founded 1903. Pop 1,841; Circ 4,868

Library Holdings: CDs 15; DVDs 200; Bk Titles 13,491; Bk Vols 14,122; Per Subs 16; Talking Bks 284; Videos 157
Wireless access
Open Tues 4-8, Wed 1-5, Sat 8-12

ORLEANS

P ORLEANS TOWN & TOWNSHIP PUBLIC LIBRARY*, 174 N Maple St, 47452. (Mail add: PO Box 142, 47452-0142), SAN 305-0718. Tel: 812-865-3270. FAX: 812-865-3270. E-mail: orleanslibrary@hotmail.com. Web Site: orleans.lib.in.us. *Dir,* Deborah M Stone; E-mail: dstone@orleans.lib.in.us; Staff 1 (Non-MLS 1)
Founded 1913. Pop 2,273; Circ 15,583
Library Holdings: CDs 222; DVDs 300; Large Print Bks 122; Bk Vols 20,000; Per Subs 26; Videos 601
Automation Activity & Vendor Info: (Acquisitions) Book Systems
Wireless access
Open Mon, Tues & Thurs 10-6, Fri 10-5, Sat 10-2

OSGOOD

P OSGOOD PUBLIC LIBRARY*, 136 W Ripley St, 47037-1229. SAN 305-0726. Tel: 812-689-4011. FAX: 812-689-5062. E-mail: opl@osgoodlibrary.org. Web Site: www.osgoodlibrary.org. *Dir,* Mark Mellang; E-mail: director@osgoodlibrary.org; Staff 6 (MLS 2, Non-MLS 4)
Founded 1912. Pop 9,533; Circ 26,910
Library Holdings: AV Mats 1,590; Bk Titles 29,840; Bk Vols 32,708; Per Subs 50; Talking Bks 270; Videos 940
Special Collections: Peoples History of Ripley County; Township Geneological Papers
Automation Activity & Vendor Info: (Cataloging) Book Systems
Wireless access
Partic in SE Ind Area Libr Servs Authority
Open Mon & Thurs 10-6, Tues & Wed 10-7, Fri 10-5, Sat 10-2
Friends of the Library Group

OTTERBEIN

P OTTERBEIN PUBLIC LIBRARY*, 23 E First St, 47970. (Mail add: PO Box 550, 47970-0550), SAN 305-0734. Tel: 765-583-2107. FAX: 765-583-2337. E-mail: contact@otterbeinlibrary.org, otterbeinlibrary@hotmail.com. Web Site: opl.lib.in.us. *Dir,* Latisha Provo; *Prog Coordr,* Addalee Farmer; E-mail: addie@otterbeinpubliclibrary.org; *Adult Serv,* Chris McCallister; E-mail: cmccalli@otterbeinpubliclibrary.org; Staff 5 (MLS 1, Non-MLS 4)
Founded 1919. Pop 1,666; Circ 32,898
Library Holdings: Audiobooks 403; CDs 208; DVDs 2,536; Large Print Bks 190; Bk Titles 14,576; Per Subs 38; Videos 1,300
Special Collections: Adam Kennedy Coll; Gene Stratton Porter Coll
Subject Interests: Local hist
Automation Activity & Vendor Info: (Acquisitions) Evergreen; (Cataloging) Evergreen; (Circulation) Evergreen; (ILL) Evergreen; (OPAC) Evergreen; (Serials) Evergreen
Wireless access
Function: After school storytime, Bks on cassette, Bks on CD, CD-ROM, Children's prog, Computer training, Computers for patron use, Free DVD rentals, Holiday prog, Homebound delivery serv, ILL available, Instruction & testing, Music CDs, Online cat, Outreach serv, Photocopying/Printing, Prog for adults, Prog for children & young adult, Ref serv available, Senior computer classes, Story hour, Summer reading prog, Teen prog, VHS videos, Wheelchair accessible
Partic in Evergreen Indiana Consortium
Open Mon, Wed & Fri 11-6, Tues & Thurs 11-7, Sat 11-3

OWENSVILLE

P OWENSVILLE CARNEGIE PUBLIC LIBRARY*, 110 S Main St, 47665. (Mail add: PO Box 219, 47665-0219), SAN 305-0742. Tel: 812-724-3335. FAX: 812-724-3336. E-mail: owensvillelibrary@gmail.com. Web Site: www.owensvillelibrary.org. *Dir,* Margo English
Founded 1917. Pop 3,742
Library Holdings: CDs 1,009; DVDs 3,148; Large Print Bks 9,000; Bk Vols 27,008; Per Subs 145; Talking Bks 400
Subject Interests: Local hist
Wireless access
Partic in Midwest Collaborative for Library Services
Open Mon & Wed 10-6, Tues 10-7, Thurs & Fri 10-5, Sat 10-3

OXFORD

P OXFORD PUBLIC LIBRARY*, 201 E Smith St, 47971. (Mail add: PO Box 6, 47971-0006), SAN 305-0750. Tel: 765-385-2177. FAX: 765-385-2313. E-mail: oxfordlibrary@sbcglobal.net. Web Site: oxford.lib.in.us. *Dir,* Brittany Hays; Staff 3 (Non-MLS 3)
Founded 1917. Pop 1,694; Circ 33,880
Library Holdings: AV Mats 2,200; DVDs 400; Large Print Bks 300; Bk Titles 23,450; Bk Vols 26,100; Per Subs 70; Talking Bks 100; Videos 1,642
Automation Activity & Vendor Info: (Acquisitions) SirsiDynix; (Cataloging) SirsiDynix; (OPAC) SirsiDynix
Wireless access
Open Mon-Fri 10-6, Sat 10-2
Friends of the Library Group

PAOLI

P PAOLI PUBLIC LIBRARY*, 100 W Water St, 47454. SAN 305-0769. Tel: 812-723-3841. FAX: 812-723-5591. E-mail: paolipubliclibrary@paoli.lib.in.us. Web Site: paoli.lib.in.us. *Adult Serv, Circ,* Cynthia Webb; *Ch Serv,* Glenda Mahuron
Founded 1918. Pop 5,780; Circ 32,907
Library Holdings: AV Mats 1,103; Bks on Deafness & Sign Lang 10; Large Print Bks 100; Bk Vols 24,117; Per Subs 50; Talking Bks 382
Subject Interests: Genealogy, Local hist
Wireless access
Open Mon & Fri 11-6, Tues & Thurs 11-7, Sat 9-1
Friends of the Library Group

PENDLETON

P PENDLETON COMMUNITY LIBRARY*, 595 E Water St, 46064-1070. SAN 305-0777. Tel: 765-778-7527. FAX: 765-778-7529. Web Site: www.pendleton.lib.in.us. *Dir,* Lynn Hobbs; E-mail: lhobbs@pendleton.lib.in.us; *Adult Ref Librn,* Chris Bellessis; E-mail: cbellessis@pendleton.lib.in.us; *Ch,* Rhonda Sparks; E-mail: rsparks@pendleton.lib.in.us; *Circ Librn,* Ashley Stout; E-mail: astout@pendleton.lib.in.us; *Bus Mgr,* Julie Oswalt; E-mail: joswalt@pendleton.lib.in.us; Staff 3 (MLS 3)
Founded 1912. Pop 20,704; Circ 137,530
Library Holdings: AV Mats 7,000; Bk Vols 53,426; Per Subs 175
Special Collections: Quaker Manuscripts
Subject Interests: Genealogy, Local hist
Automation Activity & Vendor Info: (Acquisitions) Innovative Interfaces, Inc; (Cataloging) Innovative Interfaces, Inc; (Circulation) Innovative Interfaces, Inc; (OPAC) Innovative Interfaces, Inc; (Serials) Innovative Interfaces, Inc
Wireless access
Partic in Midwest Collaborative for Library Services
Open Mon-Thurs 9-8, Fri 9-6, Sat 9-5, Sun 1-5
Friends of the Library Group

S PENDLETON CORRECTIONAL FACILITY, Offender Library, 4490 W Reformatory Rd, 46064. SAN 341-5716. Tel: 765-778-2107, Ext 1221. FAX: 765-778-1431. *Library Contact,* Larry Fowler; E-mail: lfowler@idoc.in.gov; Staff 1 (Non-MLS 1)
Founded 1897
Library Holdings: Bk Titles 15,810; Bk Vols 16,900; Per Subs 48
Subject Interests: Sci fict
Open Mon-Fri 6:15-5
Branches:
LAW, 4490 W Reformatory Rd, 46064, SAN 341-5724. Tel: 765-778-2107. FAX: 765-778-3395. *Library Contact,* Larry Fowler; Staff 1 (Non-MLS 1)
Library Holdings: Bk Titles 11,290; Bk Vols 12,300; Per Subs 41
Open Mon-Fri 6:15am-8pm

PENNVILLE

P PENNVILLE TOWNSHIP PUBLIC LIBRARY, 195 N Union St, 47369. (Mail add: PO Box 206, 47369-0206), SAN 305-0785. Tel: 260-731-3333. FAX: 260-731-3333. E-mail: pennlib@hotmail.com. Web Site: penntwplib.webs.com. *Dir,* Brenda L Cash
Pop 1,236; Circ 7,045
Library Holdings: Bk Vols 12,000; Per Subs 35
Open Tues-Thurs 3-8, Sat 9-2

PERU

P PERU PUBLIC LIBRARY, 102 E Main St, 46970-2338. SAN 305-0793. Tel: 765-473-3069. FAX: 765-473-3060. E-mail: perupubliclibrary@yahoo.com. Web Site: www.peru.lib.in.us. *Dir,* Maryann Farnham; *Asst Dir,* Michelle Spangler; Staff 7 (MLS 1, Non-MLS 6)
Founded 1902. Pop 34,165; Circ 162,810
Library Holdings: DVDs 500; Large Print Bks 108; Bk Titles 37,910; Bk Vols 55,000; Per Subs 185; Talking Bks 1,500; Videos 1,200
Subject Interests: Indiana
Publications: Miami County (encyclopedia 12 vols, genealogies 9 vols); Miami County Obituaries
Open Mon-Thurs (Winter) 9-9, Fri & Sat 9-5:30; Mon-Sat (Summer) 9-6
Restriction: Residents only
Friends of the Library Group

PETERSBURG

P PIKE COUNTY PUBLIC LIBRARY*, Petersburg Branch, 1008 E Maple St, 47567-1736. SAN 305-0807. Tel: 812-354-6257. FAX: 812-354-6259. E-mail: p.clerks@pikeco.lib.in.us. Web Site: pikeco.lib.in.us. *Dir,* Stephanie Rawlins; E-mail: director@pikeco.lib.in.us; *Asst Dir,* Faye Terry; E-mail: director.asst@pikeco.lib.in.us; *Head Librn,* Dana Hughes; E-mail: dhughes@pikeco.lib.in.us; *Tech Serv,* Pat Weathers; E-mail: pweathers@pikeco.lib.in.us; Staff 1 (MLS 1)
Founded 1953. Pop 12,837; Circ 86,838
Library Holdings: AV Mats 5,022; Bk Titles 100,000; Per Subs 142
Subject Interests: Genealogy, Indiana, Local hist
Automation Activity & Vendor Info: (Cataloging) Evergreen; (Circulation) Evergreen; (OPAC) Evergreen
Wireless access
Function: Holiday prog, Home delivery & serv to seniorr ctr & nursing homes, Homebound delivery serv, ILL available, Instruction & testing, Mail loans to mem, Music CDs, Online cat, Photocopying/Printing, Preschool outreach, Prog for adults, Prog for children & young adult, Scanner, Senior computer classes, Senior outreach, Spoken cassettes & CDs, Spoken cassettes & DVDs, Summer reading prog, Tax forms, Teen prog, Telephone ref, VHS videos, Wheelchair accessible
Open Mon & Thurs 9-8, Tues, Wed, Fri & Sat 9-5
Restriction: Lending limited to county residents, Non-circulating coll, Non-resident fee, Off-site coll in storage - retrieval as requested, Use of others with permission of librn
Friends of the Library Group
Branches: 2
OTWELL BRANCH, 2301 N Spring St, Otwell, 47564. Tel: 812-380-0066. FAX: 812-380-0037. E-mail: o.clerks@pikeco.lib.in.us. *Dir,* Stephanie Rawlins
Open Tues, Wed & Fri 9-5, Thurs 11-7, Sat 10-2
Friends of the Library Group
WINSLOW BRANCH, 105 E Center St, Winslow, 47598, SAN 376-818X. Tel: 812-789-5423. FAX: 812-789-9496. E-mail: w.clerks@pikeco.lib.in.us. *Dir,* Stephanie Rawlins; Staff 3 (Non-MLS 3)
Library Holdings: Bk Titles 10,800; Bk Vols 12,000; Per Subs 23; Videos 210
Open Tues, Wed & Fri 9-5, Thurs 11-7, Sat 10-2
Friends of the Library Group

PIERCETON

P PIERCETON & WASHINGTON TOWNSHIP LIBRARY*, 101 Catholic St, 46562. (Mail add: PO Box 328, 46562-0328), SAN 305-0815. Tel: 574-594-5474. E-mail: pierceton.library@mchsi.com. *Dir,* Pamela Myers; Staff 3 (MLS 1, Non-MLS 2)
Founded 1915. Pop 4,815; Circ 6,891
Library Holdings: AV Mats 590; Bk Titles 25,930; Bk Vols 28,861; Per Subs 41; Talking Bks 120
Wireless access
Open Tues & Thurs 11:30-5, Wed & Fri 1-5, Sat 9-1

PLAINFIELD

G INDIANA LAW ENFORCEMENT ACADEMY*, Learning Resources Center, 5402 Sugar Grove Rd, 46168. (Mail add: PO Box 313, 46168-0313), SAN 305-0823. Tel: 317-837-3236. FAX: 317-839-9741. Web Site: www.state.in.us/ilea/2335.htm. *Librn,* Connie Beck; E-mail: cbeck@ilea.in.gov; Staff 2 (MLS 1, Non-MLS 1)
Founded 1975
Library Holdings: Bk Titles 6,290; Bk Vols 7,100; Per Subs 121; Videos 72
Subject Interests: Law, Law enforcement, Photog
Function: Ref serv available
Partic in Midwest Collaborative for Library Services; Nat Criminal Justice Ref Serv
Restriction: Open to others by appt

P PLAINFIELD-GUILFORD TOWNSHIP PUBLIC LIBRARY*, 1120 Stafford Rd, 46168. SAN 305-0831. Tel: 317-839-6602. Circulation Tel: 317-838-3800. Administration Tel: 317-838-3803. FAX: 317-838-3805. Web Site: www.plainfieldlibrary.net. *Dir,* Montie Manning; Tel: 317-839-6602, Ext 2111; *Coll/Libr Mgr,* Mary Glaser; Tel: 317-839-6602, Ext 2147, E-mail: mglaser@plainfieldlibrary.net; *Commun Liaison Librn,* Joanna Carter; Tel: 317-839-6602, Ext 2159, E-mail: jcarter@plainfieldlibrary.net; *Ind Rm Librn,* Reann Poray; Tel: 317-839-6602, Ext 2114, E-mail: rporay@plainfieldlibrary.net; *Tech Serv, Training Servs Mgr,* Laura Brack; Tel: 317-839-6602, Ext 2152, E-mail: lbrack@plainfieldlibrary.net; *Youth Serv Mgr,* Kristal Hellmann; Tel: 317-839-6602, Ext 2127. Subject Specialists: *Genealogy, Hist,* Reann Poray; Staff 12 (MLS 8, Non-MLS 4)
Founded 1901. Pop 22,961; Circ 274,061
Library Holdings: Bk Titles 179,443; Per Subs 282
Special Collections: Guilford Township Historical Coll
Subject Interests: Indiana, Local hist
Automation Activity & Vendor Info: (Acquisitions) Evergreen; (Cataloging) Evergreen; (Circulation) Evergreen; (OPAC) Evergreen; (Serials) Evergreen
Wireless access
Publications: Novel News (Newsletter)
Partic in Evergreen Indiana Consortium; Midwest Collaborative for Library Services
Open Mon-Thurs 9-9, Fri 9-6, Sat 9-5, Sun 1-5
Friends of the Library Group

PLYMOUTH

S MARSHALL COUNTY HISTORICAL SOCIETY LIBRARY*, Research Library, 123 N Michigan St, 46563. SAN 305-0858. Tel: 574-936-2306. FAX: 574-936-9306. Web Site: www.mchistoricalsociety.org. *Exec Dir,* Linda Rippy; E-mail: lindarippy@mchistoricalsociety.org; *Archives Mgr,* Karin Rettinger; E-mail: karinrettinger@mchistoricalsociety.org; *Asst Res Librn,* Lynita Pollack; *Archivist,* Tim Good; E-mail: timgood@mchistoricalsociety.org; *Res Spec,* Anita Kopetski; E-mail: anita@mchistoricalsociety.org
Founded 1957
Library Holdings: Bk Titles 550
Special Collections: Marshall County History Coll
Subject Interests: Genealogy
Wireless access
Open Tues-Sat 10-4

P PLYMOUTH PUBLIC LIBRARY*, 201 N Center St, 46563. SAN 305-0866. Tel: 574-936-2324. FAX: 574-936-7423. Web Site: myplymouthlibrary.org. *Libr Dir,* Steven Buras; E-mail: stevenb@myplymouthlibrary.org; Staff 30 (MLS 1, Non-MLS 29)
Founded 1910. Pop 18,609; Circ 355,000
Library Holdings: DVDs 7,000; Large Print Bks 30,000; Bk Vols 220,000; Per Subs 215; Talking Bks 3,100
Special Collections: Indiana History; Marshall County Authors
Automation Activity & Vendor Info: (Circulation) Innovative Interfaces, Inc
Open Mon-Thurs 9-8, Fri & Sat 9-5:30, Sun 1-4
Friends of the Library Group

PORTLAND

P JAY COUNTY PUBLIC LIBRARY*, 315 N Ship St, 47371. SAN 305-0874. Tel: 260-726-7890. FAX: 260-726-7317. Web Site: www.jaycpl.lib.in.us. *Dir,* Eric Hinderliter; E-mail: ehinderliter@jaycpl.lib.in.us; Staff 22 (MLS 2, Non-MLS 20)
Founded 1898. Pop 17,998; Circ 372,000
Library Holdings: CDs 1,572; DVDs 709; Large Print Bks 4,548; Bk Vols 80,949; Per Subs 210; Talking Bks 3,171; Videos 10,000
Wireless access
Function: Adult bk club, After school storytime, Art exhibits, AV serv, Bks on cassette, Bks on CD, Children's prog, Computers for patron use, Free DVD rentals, Holiday prog, Home delivery & serv to seniorr ctr & nursing homes, ILL available, Internet access, Music CDs, Online cat, Outreach serv, Photocopying/Printing, Preschool outreach, Prog for adults, Prog for children & young adult, Ref serv available, Scanner, Spoken cassettes & CDs, Spoken cassettes & DVDs, Story hour, Summer reading prog, Tax forms, VHS videos, Wheelchair accessible
Publications: Library Newsnotes (Newsletter)
Partic in Evergreen Indiana Consortium
Open Mon-Fri 8-8, Sat 8-5
Friends of the Library Group
Bookmobiles: 1

POSEYVILLE

P POSEYVILLE CARNEGIE PUBLIC LIBRARY, 55 S Cale St, 47633. SAN 305-0882. Tel: 812-874-3418. FAX: 812-874-2026. Circulation E-mail: circulation@pcpl.lib.in.us. Web Site: www.pcpl.lib.in.us. *Dir,* Heather Morlan; E-mail: director@pcpl.lib.in.us; Staff 1 (MLS 1)
Founded 1905. Pop 4,727; Circ 33,044
Library Holdings: Audiobooks 320; CDs 524; DVDs 695; Bk Titles 12,391; Per Subs 58
Automation Activity & Vendor Info: (Acquisitions) Evergreen; (Cataloging) Evergreen; (Circulation) Evergreen; (ILL) Evergreen; (OPAC) Evergreen; (Serials) Evergreen
Wireless access
Function: Adult bk club, After school storytime, Archival coll, Art exhibits, Audiobks via web, Bk club(s), Bks on CD, Chess club, Children's prog, Computers for patron use, Electronic databases & coll, Family literacy, Free DVD rentals, Holiday prog, ILL available, Magnifiers for reading, Music CDs, Online cat, Outreach serv, OverDrive digital audio bks, Photocopying/Printing, Preschool outreach, Prog for adults, Prog for children & young adult, Ref serv available, Scanner, Serves people with

intellectual disabilities, Spoken cassettes & CDs, Spoken cassettes & DVDs, Story hour, Summer & winter reading prog, Tax forms, Teen prog, Telephone ref, Wheelchair accessible, Workshops, Writing prog
Partic in Evergreen Indiana Consortium
Open Mon, Wed & Fri 9-4, Tues & Thurs 9-7, Sat 9-1

PRINCETON

P PRINCETON PUBLIC LIBRARY*, 124 S Hart St, 47670. SAN 305-0890. Tel: 812-385-4464. FAX: 812-386-1662. Web Site: www.princetonpl.lib.in.us. *Dir,* Brenda Williams; E-mail: director@princetonpl.lib.in.us; Staff 4 (MLS 1, Non-MLS 3)
Founded 1883. Pop 11,864; Circ 70,760
Library Holdings: Audiobooks 2,321; DVDs 5,028; Microforms 381; Bk Titles 53,382; Per Subs 58; Videos 242
Special Collections: History of Gibson County, North Gibson area
Subject Interests: Genealogy, Local hist
Automation Activity & Vendor Info: (Cataloging) Evergreen; (Circulation) Evergreen; (OPAC) Evergreen
Wireless access
Open Mon-Fri 9-8, Sat 9-5, Sun 1-5
Friends of the Library Group

REMINGTON

P REMINGTON-CARPENTER TOWNSHIP PUBLIC LIBRARY*, 105 N Ohio St, 47977. (Mail add: PO Box 65, 47977-0065), SAN 305-0904. Tel: 219-261-2543. FAX: 219-261-3800. E-mail: library@rctpl.lib.in.us. Web Site: rctpl.lib.in.us. *Dir,* Sue Waibel; *Asst Librn,* Agnes J Dombrowski; Staff 1 (Non-MLS 1)
Founded 1913. Pop 2,096; Circ 13,963
Library Holdings: AV Mats 2,162; Bk Titles 31,459; Per Subs 34
Special Collections: Geneology
Automation Activity & Vendor Info: (Cataloging) Follett Software; (Circulation) Follett Software
Function: Children's prog, Computer training, Computers for patron use, ILL available, Internet access, Music CDs, Online cat, Photocopying/Printing, Preschool outreach, Prog for adults, Prog for children & young adult, Senior computer classes, Summer reading prog, Tax forms, VHS videos
Partic in Northwest Ind Area Libr Servs Authority
Open Mon & Wed 10-7, Tues & Fri 10-5, Sat 9-Noon
Friends of the Library Group

RENSSELAER

P JASPER COUNTY PUBLIC LIBRARY*, Rensselaer Public, 208 W Susan St, 47978. SAN 341-5805. Tel: 219-866-5881. FAX: 219-866-7378. Web Site: www.myjcpl.org. *Dir,* Patty Stringfellow; E-mail: pstringfellow@myjcpl.org; *HQ Librn,* Linda Poortenga; E-mail: lpoortenga@myjcpl.org; *Tech Serv Librn,* Rebecca Amalong; E-mail: ramalong@myjcpl.org; *Syst Adminr,* Sheila Maxwell; E-mail: sheila@myjcpl.org; *Webmaster,* Melissa Widner; E-mail: mwidner@myjcpl.org; Staff 26 (MLS 7, Non-MLS 19)
Founded 1905. Pop 31,525; Circ 282,602
Jan 2018-Dec 2018 Income (Main & Associated Libraries) $2,474,313, State $164,217, Federal $192, County $2,209,754, Other $100,150. Mats Exp $258,061, Books $140,751, Per/Ser (Incl. Access Fees) $21,650, AV Mat $51,991, Electronic Ref Mat (Incl. Access Fees) $43,669. Sal $1,281,692
Library Holdings: Audiobooks 21,438; e-books 45,514; e-journals 50; Bk Vols 169,161; Per Subs 396; Videos 26,116
Special Collections: Mementos of Civil War (Major General Robert H Milroy Coll). Oral History
Subject Interests: Humanities, Natural sci
Automation Activity & Vendor Info: (Acquisitions) Baker & Taylor; (Cataloging) TLC (The Library Corporation); (Circulation) TLC (The Library Corporation); (ILL) Auto-Graphics, Inc; (OPAC) TLC (The Library Corporation); (Serials) TLC (The Library Corporation)
Wireless access
Function: 24/7 Electronic res, 24/7 Online cat, Accelerated reader prog, Adult bk club, After school storytime, Archival coll, Art exhibits, Art programs, Audio & video playback equip for onsite use, Audiobks on Playaways & MP3, Audiobks via web, AV serv, Bk club(s), Bks on cassette, Bks on CD, Butterfly Garden, CD-ROM, Children's prog, Computer training, Computers for patron use, Digital talking bks, E-Readers, Electronic databases & coll, Free DVD rentals, Health sci info serv, Holiday prog, Home delivery & serv to seniorr ctr & nursing homes, Homebound delivery serv, ILL available, Instruction & testing, Internet access, Large print keyboards, Life-long learning prog for all ages, Literacy & newcomer serv, Magazines, Magnifiers for reading, Mail & tel request accepted, Makerspace, Meeting rooms, Microfiche/film & reading machines, Movies, Music CDs, Online cat, Online ref, Outreach serv, Outside serv via phone, mail, e-mail & web, OverDrive digital audio bks, Photocopying/Printing, Preschool reading prog, Printer for laptops & handheld devices, Prog for adults, Prog for children & young adult, Ref & res, Ref serv available, Res assist avail, Scanner, Senior computer classes, Senior outreach, Serves people with intellectual disabilities, Spanish lang bks, Spoken cassettes & CDs, Spoken cassettes & DVDs, STEM programs, Story hour, Study rm, Summer & winter reading prog, Summer reading prog, Tax forms, Teen prog, Telephone ref, VHS videos, Wheelchair accessible, Writing prog
Publications: Community Connections (Monthly newsletter)
Partic in Midwest Collaborative for Library Services
Special Services for the Deaf - Closed caption videos
Special Services for the Blind - Aids for in-house use; Assistive/Adapted tech devices, equip & products; Bks on cassette; Bks on CD; Cassette playback machines; Cassettes; Copier with enlargement capabilities; Free checkout of audio mat; Home delivery serv; Large print & cassettes; Large print bks; Micro-computer access & training; Playaways (bks on MP3); Recorded bks; Sound rec
Open Mon-Thurs 9-8, Fri & Sat 9-5
Friends of the Library Group
Branches: 2
DEMOTTE BRANCH, 901 Birch St SW, DeMotte, 46310. (Mail add: PO Box 16, DeMotte, 46310-0016), SAN 341-583X. Tel: 219-987-2221. FAX: 219-987-2220. *Br Librn,* Debbie Kristoff; E-mail: dkristoff@myjcpl.org
Open Mon, Tues & Thurs 9-8, Wed 9-6, Fri & Sat 9-5
Friends of the Library Group
WHEATFIELD BRANCH, 350 S Bierma St, Wheatfield, 46392, SAN 341-5864. Tel: 219-956-3774. FAX: 219-956-4808. *Br Librn,* Evie Parrish; E-mail: eparrish@myjcpl.org
Open Mon, Wed & Thurs 9:30-5:30, Tues 9:30-8, Fri & Sat 9-5
Friends of the Library Group

RICHMOND

C EARLHAM COLLEGE*, Lilly Library, 801 National Rd W, 47374-4095. SAN 341-5899. Tel: 765-983-1360. Circulation Tel: 765-983-1287. Interlibrary Loan Service Tel: 765-983-1241. Information Services Tel: 765-973-2106. FAX: 765-983-1304. Web Site: library.earlham.edu. *Interim Libr Dir,* Amy Bryant; Tel: 765-983-1302, E-mail: bryanam@earlham.edu; *Archives, Dir, Spec Coll,* Jenny Freed; Tel: 765-983-1743, E-mail: freedje@earlham.edu; *Acad Outreach/Sem Librn,* Karla Fribley; Tel: 765-983-1290, E-mail: friblka@earlham.edu; *Tech Serv Librn,* Mary A Bogue; Tel: 765-983-1363, E-mail: boguema@earlham.edu; *Sci Tech Learning Spec,* Jose Ignacio Pareja; Tel: 765-983-1612, E-mail: parejjo@earlham.edu; Staff 10 (MLS 7, Non-MLS 3)
Founded 1847. Enrl 992; Fac 109; Highest Degree: Master
Jul 2019-Jun 2020. Mats Exp $509,113, Books $63,041, Per/Ser (Incl. Access Fees) $16,642, AV Mat $6,944, Electronic Ref Mat (Incl. Access Fees) $418,647, Presv $3,839. Sal $568,194 (Prof $480,850)
Library Holdings: AV Mats 20,594; CDs 3,425; DVDs 6,625; e-books 772,196; Electronic Media & Resources 124,745; Microforms 145,863; Bk Vols 362,207; Per Subs 123,686
Special Collections: East Asian Materials, bks, micro, ms; Society of Friends, bks, micro, ms
Automation Activity & Vendor Info: (Acquisitions) OCLC Worldshare Management Services; (Cataloging) OCLC Worldshare Management Services; (Circulation) OCLC Worldshare Management Services; (Course Reserve) OCLC Worldshare Management Services; (ILL) OCLC Tipasa; (OPAC) OCLC; (Serials) OCLC Worldshare Management Services
Wireless access
Partic in Academic Libraries of Indiana; OCLC Online Computer Library Center, Inc; Private Academic Library Network of Indiana
Open Mon-Thurs 8am-9pm, Fri 8-5, Sat Noon-4, Sun Noon-9

S THE S W HAYES RESEARCH FOUNDATION*, Hayes Arboretum Library, 801 Elks Rd, 47374. SAN 326-0925. Tel: 765-962-3745. FAX: 765-966-1931. Web Site: www.hayesarboretum.org. *Exec Dir,* Stephen H Hayes, Jr; E-mail: stephenhhayes@yahoo.com; Staff 2 (MLS 1, Non-MLS 1)
Library Holdings: Bk Titles 750; Bk Vols 890; Per Subs 4
Subject Interests: Flowers, Trees
Open Tues-Sat 9-5

C INDIANA UNIVERSITY EAST CAMPUS LIBRARY, Library Services, Hayes Hall, 2325 Chester Blvd, 47374. SAN 320-9113. Tel: 765-973-8311. Reference Tel: 765-973-8279. E-mail: liblearn@iue.edu. Web Site: www.iue.edu/library. *Libr Dir,* Frances Yates; Tel: 765-973-8470, E-mail: fyates@iue.edu; *Assoc Librn,* Sue McFadden; Tel: 765-973-8325, E-mail: smcfadden@iue.edu; *Asst Librn,* KT Lowe; Tel: 765-973-8434, E-mail: lowekat@iu.edu; *Archivist, Asst Librn,* Elizabeth South; Tel: 765-973-8204, E-mail: eabrockm@iue.edu; *Ref Serv Coordr,* Matthew Dilworth; Tel: 765-973-8279, E-mail: mdilwort@iue.edu; *Coord, Service Learning,* Ann Tobin; Tel: 765-973-8411, E-mail: aktobin@iue.edu; *Coordr, User Serv,* Jesse Whitton; Tel: 765-973-8309, E-mail: jewhitton@iue.edu; Staff 5 (MLS 4, Non-MLS 1)
Founded 1975

Library Holdings: AV Mats 1,080; Bk Titles 68,911; Bk Vols 71,022; Per Subs 488; Videos 319
Automation Activity & Vendor Info: (OPAC) SirsiDynix-Unicorn
Wireless access
Partic in OCLC Online Computer Library Center, Inc
Open Mon-Thurs 8-6, Fri 8-5

S RICHMOND ART MUSEUM LIBRARY, 350 Hub Etchison Pkwy, 47374-0816. SAN 305-0920. Tel: 765-966-0256. E-mail: info@richmondartmuseum.org. Web Site: www.richmondartmuseum.org. *Educ Dir,* Lance Crow; E-mail: lance@richmondartmuseum.org; Staff 2 (Non-MLS 2)
Founded 1898
Library Holdings: Bk Vols 800
Subject Interests: Art
Wireless access
Open Tues-Sat 10-5

S WAYNE COUNTY, INDIANA, HISTORICAL MUSEUM LIBRARY, 1150 North A St, 47374. SAN 305-0947. Tel: 765-962-5756. FAX: 765-939-0909. E-mail: office@wchmuseum.org. Web Site: wchmuseum.org. *Exec Dir,* Karen Shank-Chapman; E-mail: director@wchmuseum.org; Staff 3 (MLS 1, Non-MLS 2)
Founded 1929
Library Holdings: Bk Titles 1,000; Bk Vols 1,200
Special Collections: Cartoons (Gaar Williams Coll); Early Agricultural Tools & Implements Coll; Early Transportation Coll (autos & carriages); Motion Pictures & Early Television (C Francis Jenkins Coll), doc; Textile Coll
Subject Interests: Genealogy, Local authors, Local hist, State hist
Wireless access
Publications: Newsletter (Quarterly)
Open Mon-Fri 9-4, Sat 1-4

P WAYNE TOWNSHIP LIBRARY*, Morrisson-Reeves Library, 80 N Sixth St, 47374-3079. SAN 341-5988. Tel: 765-966-8291. FAX: 765-962-1318. E-mail: library@mrlinfo.org. Web Site: www.mrlinfo.org. *Libr Dir,* Paris Pegg; Tel: 765-966-8291, Ext 101, E-mail: pegg@mrlinfo.org; *Bus Mgr,* Barbara Judy; Tel: 765-966-8291, Ext 102, E-mail: bjudy@mrlinfo.org; *Human Res Mgr,* Laura I Kehlenbrink; Tel: 765-966-8291, Ext 130, E-mail: kehlenbrink@mrlinfo.org; *Info Serv Mgr,* Melissa Hunt; Tel: 765-966-8291, Ext 123, E-mail: mhunt@mrlinfo.org; *Pub Serv Mgr,* Deirdré Schirmer; Tel: 765-966-8291, Ext 116, E-mail: dschirmer@mrlinfo.org; *Youth Serv Mgr,* Kristen Kirk; Tel: 765-966-8291, Ext 127, E-mail: kkirk@mrlinfo.org; *Tech Serv Mgr,* Sarah Morey; Tel: 765-966-8291, Ext 107, E-mail: morey@mrlinfo.org; *Pub Relations,* Jenie Lahmann; Tel: 765-966-8291, Ext 103, E-mail: lahmann@mrlinfo.org; Staff 43 (MLS 8, Non-MLS 35)
Founded 1864. Pop 51,398; Circ 456,119
Jan 2017-Dec 2017. Mats Exp $1,891,976, Books $100,000, Per/Ser (Incl. Access Fees) $10,806, AV Mat $31,715, Electronic Ref Mat (Incl. Access Fees) $11,500. Sal $929,107
Library Holdings: AV Mats 11,546; Bk Titles 157,687; Bk Vols 263,000; Per Subs 313
Special Collections: Cookbooks; Large Print; Local Newspapers (1831 to date), indexed, microfilm; Popular & Semi-Popular Music (Singin' Sam), sheet music. US Document Depository
Automation Activity & Vendor Info: (Acquisitions) SirsiDynix; (Cataloging) SirsiDynix; (Circulation) SirsiDynix; (ILL) SirsiDynix; (Media Booking) SirsiDynix; (OPAC) SirsiDynix; (Serials) SirsiDynix
Wireless access
Function: Accelerated reader prog, Adult literacy prog, After school storytime, Archival coll, Art exhibits, Audio & video playback equip for onsite use, Audiobks via web, AV serv, BA reader (adult literacy), Bks on CD, Bus archives, CD-ROM, Children's prog, Computer training, Computers for patron use, Digital talking bks, Electronic databases & coll, Free DVD rentals, Govt ref serv, Holiday prog, ILL available, Internet access, Magnifiers for reading, Mail & tel request accepted, Microfiche/film & reading machines, Music CDs, Online cat, Online ref, Outside serv via phone, mail, e-mail & web, OverDrive digital audio bks, Photocopying/Printing, Preschool outreach, Preschool reading prog, Prog for adults, Prog for children & young adult, Ref & res, Ref serv available, Scanner, Spanish lang bks, Spoken cassettes & DVDs, Story hour, Summer reading prog, Tax forms, Teen prog, Telephone ref, Wheelchair accessible, Workshops, Writing prog
Partic in Midwest Collaborative for Library Services; OCLC Online Computer Library Center, Inc
Open Mon-Thurs 9:30-8, Fri 9:30-6 & Sat 9:30-4
Friends of the Library Group
Branches: 1
WAYNE COUNTY CONTRACTUAL LIBRARY, 80 N Sixth St, 47374, SAN 341-6070. Tel: 765-966-8291. FAX: 765-962-1318. *Dir,* Paris Pegg
Founded 1864
Open Mon-Thurs 9:30-8, Fri 9:30-6, Sat 9:30-4

RIDGEVILLE

P RIDGEVILLE PUBLIC LIBRARY*, 308 N Walnut St, 47380. (Mail add: PO Box 63, 47380-0063), SAN 305-0955. Tel: 765-857-2025. FAX: 765-857-2025. E-mail: rplibrary2018@gmail.com. *Librn,* Lynn Wells; Staff 2 (MLS 1, Non-MLS 1)
Founded 1912. Pop 1,539; Circ 5,000
Library Holdings: AV Mats 30; Bk Vols 15,998; Per Subs 50
Partic in Evergreen Indiana Consortium; Midwest Collaborative for Library Services
Open Mon, Tues, Thurs & Fri 1-6, Sat 10-2
Friends of the Library Group

RISING SUN

P OHIO COUNTY PUBLIC LIBRARY, 503 Second St, 47040-1022. SAN 305-0963. Tel: 812-438-2257. FAX: 812-438-2257. E-mail: contact@ocpl.lib.in.us. Web Site: ocpl.lib.in.us. *Dir,* Amy Hoffman; Staff 4 (MLS 1, Non-MLS 3)
Founded 1916. Pop 5,623; Circ 33,119
Library Holdings: AV Mats 1,281; Large Print Bks 88; Bk Titles 26,780; Bk Vols 28,818; Per Subs 51; Talking Bks 410; Videos 759
Special Collections: Local News & History (Ohio County Newspapers, 1834-1970), microfilm (1970-present), loose files
Automation Activity & Vendor Info: (Cataloging) Follett Software; (Circulation) Follett Software
Open Mon, Wed & Fri 9-5, Tues & Thurs 9-6, Sat 9-1

ROACHDALE

P ROACHDALE-FRANKLIN TOWNSHIP PUBLIC LIBRARY*, 100 E Washington St, 46172. (Mail add: PO Box 399, 46172-0399), SAN 305-0971. Tel: 765-522-1491. FAX: 765-522-4149. E-mail: roachdalepl@tds.net. Web Site: roachdale.lib.in.us. *Dir,* Jennifer Stranger; Staff 3 (MLS 1, Non-MLS 2)
Founded 1913. Pop 2,117; Circ 14,400
Library Holdings: Bk Titles 19,840; Bk Vols 21,680; Per Subs 30; Talking Bks 350; Videos 666
Wireless access
Partic in Evergreen Indiana Consortium
Open Mon-Wed 11-5:30, Thurs 11-6, Fri 11-5, Sat 11-3:30

ROANN

P ROANN PAW PAW TOWNSHIP PUBLIC LIBRARY*, 240 S Chippewa Rd, 46974. (Mail add: PO Box 248, 46974-0248), SAN 305-098X. Tel: 765-833-5231. FAX: 765-833-5231. E-mail: roannlibrary@yahoo.com. Web Site: www.roannpubliclibrary.com. *Dir,* Joy Harber; *Asst Librn,* Eleanore Draper; Staff 3 (Non-MLS 3)
Founded 1914. Pop 1,616; Circ 7,983
Library Holdings: AV Mats 450; CDs 310; Large Print Bks 45; Bk Vols 17,151; Per Subs 25; Videos 1,600
Subject Interests: Local genealogy
Wireless access
Special Services for the Blind - Bks on cassette; Talking bks
Open Mon-Wed 1-6, Thurs & Fri 9-12 & 1-6, Sat 9-Noon
Friends of the Library Group

ROANOKE

P ROANOKE PUBLIC LIBRARY*, 314 N Main St, Ste 120, 46783-1073. (Mail add: PO Box 249, 46783-0249), SAN 305-0998. Tel: 260-672-2989. FAX: 260-676-2239. Web Site: www.roanoke.lib.in.us. *Libr Dir,* Celia Bandelier; E-mail: director@roanoke.lib.in.us; Staff 1.5 (MLS 1, Non-MLS 0.5)
Founded 1910. Pop 1,720; Circ 10,111
Library Holdings: Bk Titles 14,760; Bk Vols 16,340; Per Subs 27; Talking Bks 190; Videos 633
Special Collections: Roanoke Review, 1919 to 1981, CD-ROM
Automation Activity & Vendor Info: (Cataloging) Evergreen; (Circulation) Evergreen; (ILL) Evergreen; (OPAC) Evergreen; (Serials) Evergreen
Wireless access
Function: Bks on CD, Children's prog, Computer training, Computers for patron use, Family literacy, Free DVD rentals, Govt ref serv, ILL available, Internet access, Mail & tel request accepted, Music CDs, Notary serv, Online cat, Outside serv via phone, mail, e-mail & web, OverDrive digital audio bks, Photocopying/Printing, Preschool reading prog, Prog for adults, Prog for children & young adult, Ref & res, Ref serv available, Scanner, Senior computer classes, Spanish lang bks, Story hour, Summer reading prog, Tax forms, Teen prog, Telephone ref, VHS videos, Wheelchair accessible, Workshops
Partic in Evergreen Indiana Consortium
Open Mon-Thurs 9-7, Sat 9-1
Friends of the Library Group

ROCHESTER

S FULTON COUNTY HISTORICAL SOCIETY, INC*, Museum & Library, 37 E 375 N, 46975. SAN 371-9103. Tel: 574-223-4436. FAX: 574-224-4436. E-mail: fchs@rtcol.com. Web Site: www.fultoncountyhistory.org. *Pres,* Fred A Oden; *Dir,* Melinda Clinger; Staff 3 (Non-MLS 3)
Founded 1963
Library Holdings: Bk Titles 15,000; Per Subs 100
Special Collections: Fulton County, Indiana Coll; Potawatomi Indians Trail of Death Coll; Round Barns Coll. Oral History
Wireless access
Publications: Fulton County Folk Finder; Fulton County Historical Power Association (Newsletter); Fulton County Images; Potawatomi Trail of Death Association (Newsletter)
Open Mon-Sat 9-5
Restriction: In-house use for visitors, Not a lending libr

P FULTON COUNTY PUBLIC LIBRARY*, Rochester Library, 320 W Seventh St, 46975-1332. SAN 341-6100. Tel: 574-223-2713. Circulation Tel: 574-223-1006. Interlibrary Loan Service Tel: 574-223-1004. Reference Tel: 574-223-1003. FAX: 574-223-5102. E-mail: rochester@fulco.lib.in.us. Web Site: www.fulco.lib.in.us. *Libr Dir,* Andrea Stineback; E-mail: director@fulco.lib.in.us; *AV, Dept Head,* Tami Holloway; E-mail: av@fulco.lib.in.us; *Dept Head, Tech Serv,* Janet Johnson; *Circ Mgr,* Rose Krull; *ILL,* Tami Holloway; E-mail: ill@fulco.lib.in.us; *Syst Adminr,* April Gross; E-mail: sysadmin@fulco.lib.in.us; *Youth Serv,* Erin Streeter; Staff 34 (MLS 1, Non-MLS 33)
Founded 1906. Pop 16,227; Circ 372,403
Library Holdings: CDs 9,062; DVDs 20,335; Bk Vols 135,286; Per Subs 187
Special Collections: Indiana Local & State History Coll
Subject Interests: Agr, Bus & mgt, Hist, Indiana
Automation Activity & Vendor Info: (Acquisitions) Evergreen; (Cataloging) Evergreen; (Circulation) Evergreen; (OPAC) Evergreen
Wireless access
Function: Adult literacy prog
Partic in Midwest Collaborative for Library Services
Open Mon-Thurs 10-8, Fri 10-6, Sat 9-5
Friends of the Library Group
Branches: 2
AUBBEE, 7432 Olson Rd, Leiters Ford, 46945. (Mail add: PO Box 566, Leiters Ford, 46945-0566), SAN 341-6135. Tel: 574-542-4859. FAX: 574-542-4859. E-mail: aubbee@fulco.lib.in.us. *Br Mgr,* Carol Chileen; Staff 2 (MLS 1, Non-MLS 1)
Library Holdings: AV Mats 981; Large Print Bks 190; Bk Titles 21,110; Bk Vols 22,690; Per Subs 41; Videos 210
Open Mon 10-7, Tues-Fri 10-6, Sat 9-3
Friends of the Library Group
FULTON BRANCH, 514 State Rd 25, Fulton, 46931. (Mail add: PO Box 307, Fulton, 46931-0307), SAN 341-616X. Tel: 574-857-3895. FAX: 574-857-2215. E-mail: fulton@fulco.lib.in.us. *Br Mgr,* Margaret Pendley; Staff 2 (MLS 1, Non-MLS 1)
Library Holdings: AV Mats 871; Large Print Bks 88; Bk Titles 22,112; Bk Vols 23,490; Per Subs 46; Videos 226
Open Mon & Thurs 9-6, Tues, Wed & Fri 9-5, Sat 9-12
Friends of the Library Group

ROCKPORT

P SPENCER COUNTY PUBLIC LIBRARY*, 210 Walnut St, 47635-1398. SAN 305-1005. Tel: 812-649-4866. FAX: 812-649-4018. Reference E-mail: scplreference@gmail.com. Web Site: spencercountypubliclibrary.org. *Dir,* Sherri Risse; E-mail: scplsherrir@gmail.com; *Ch,* Carol Evrard; Staff 2 (MLS 1, Non-MLS 1)
Founded 1917. Pop 9,393; Circ 177,736
Library Holdings: Bks on Deafness & Sign Lang 84; High Interest/Low Vocabulary Bk Vols 140; Large Print Bks 1,798; Bk Titles 106,025; Per Subs 153; Talking Bks 2,282; Videos 5,101
Special Collections: Lincoln Coll, bks, pamphlets, pictures, vf
Subject Interests: Genealogy, Hist, Local hist, Relig
Automation Activity & Vendor Info: (Cataloging) Evergreen; (Circulation) Evergreen
Wireless access
Open Mon & Fri 8-5, Tues-Thurs 8am-9pm, Sat 9-3
Branches: 3
GRANDVIEW BRANCH, 403 Main St, Grandview, 47615-0717. Tel: 812-649-9732. FAX: 812-649-1963. *Br Mgr,* Jennie Weatherholt
Open Mon 9-8, Tues-Fri 9-5, Sat 9-3
PARKER BRANCH, 925 N County Rd 900W, Hatfield, 47617. Tel: 812-359-4030. FAX: 812-359-4048. *Br Mgr,* Pat Lashley
Library Holdings: Bk Vols 5,000
Open Mon-Wed & Fri 9-5, Thurs 10-6, Sat 9-12
MARYLEE VOGEL BRANCH, 6014 W Division St, Richland, 47634. Tel: 812-359-4146. FAX: 812-359-4223. *Br Mgr,* Position Currently Open
Library Holdings: Bk Vols 17,000
Open Mon-Fri 9-5, Sat 9-Noon

ROCKVILLE

P PARKE COUNTY PUBLIC LIBRARY, (Formerly Rockville Public Library), 106 N Market St, 47872. SAN 305-1013. Tel: 765-569-5544. FAX: 765-569-5546. E-mail: parkecountypl@gmail.com. Web Site: parkecountypl.lib.in.us. *Dir,* Lindsey Bishop; E-mail: lindseybishop.rpl@gmail.com; Staff 3 (Non-MLS 3)
Founded 1915. Pop 15,000
Jan 2016-Dec 2016 Income $448,420. Mats Exp $70,000. Sal $126,800
Library Holdings: Bk Vols 35,000; Per Subs 81; Talking Bks 250; Videos 800
Special Collections: Census Records, including Illinois, Ohio & New York 1820-1900; County Newspapers 1871-2014, microfilm; Genealogy Coll; Indiana Coll
Automation Activity & Vendor Info: (Acquisitions) Follett Software; (Cataloging) Follett Software; (OPAC) Follett Software
Wireless access
Open Mon-Thurs 8-6:30, Fri 8-5:30, Sat 9-2
Friends of the Library Group

S ROCKVILLE CORRECTIONAL FACILITY LIBRARY*, 811 W 50 N, 47872. Tel: 765-569-3178, Ext 510. FAX: 765-569-0149. *Librn,* April Bonomo
Library Holdings: Bk Vols 9,000

ROYAL CENTER

P ROYAL CENTER-BOONE TOWNSHIP PUBLIC LIBRARY*, 203 N Chicago St, 46978. (Mail add: PO Box 459, 46978-0459), SAN 305-1021. Tel: 574-643-3185. FAX: 574-643-5003. E-mail: royalcenterlib@frontier.com. Web Site: royalcenterlib.wordpress.com. *Dir,* Stephanie Collis; Staff 3 (MLS 1, Non-MLS 2)
Founded 1915. Pop 1,581; Circ 16,439
Library Holdings: Audiobooks 341; DVDs 700; Bk Titles 32,680; Bk Vols 35,160; Per Subs 20
Subject Interests: Ethnic studies, Relig, Soc sci & issues
Wireless access
Partic in Wabash Valley Area Libr Servs Authority
Open Tues 10-5, Wed & Thurs 11-5, Fri 11-6, Sat 10-2

RUSHVILLE

P RUSHVILLE PUBLIC LIBRARY*, 130 W Third St, 46173-1899. SAN 305-103X. Tel: 765-932-3496. FAX: 765-932-4528. E-mail: info@rushvillelibrary.com. Web Site: www.rushvillelibrary.com. *Dir,* Sue Prifogle; E-mail: director@rushvillelibrary.com; *Ad,* Jan M Garrison; E-mail: janmg@rushvillelibrary.com; *Ch Serv Librn,* Pamela J Vogel; E-mail: pjvogel@rushvillelibrary.com; *Bus Mgr,* Rhonda K Albrecht; E-mail: ralbrecht@rushvillelibrary.com; *Tech Serv, YA Serv,* Rylee Gibbs; E-mail: rgibbs@rushvillelibrary.com; Staff 9 (MLS 1, Non-MLS 8)
Founded 1910. Pop 5,995; Circ 28,000
Jan 2018-Dec 2018 Income $315,086, City $300,975, Locally Generated Income $14,111. Mats Exp $318,102, Books $19,104, Per/Ser (Incl. Access Fees) $2,412, AV Mat $4,970, Electronic Ref Mat (Incl. Access Fees) $500. Sal $170,037 (Prof $54,080)
Library Holdings: AV Mats 1,876; e-books 134; Bk Titles 27,003; Per Subs 50
Special Collections: Indiana History Coll; Rush County History Coll; Wendell Wilkie File Coll
Automation Activity & Vendor Info: (Cataloging) Innovative Interfaces, Inc; (Circulation) Innovative Interfaces, Inc; (OPAC) Innovative Interfaces, Inc
Wireless access
Function: 24/7 Online cat, Accelerated reader prog, After school storytime, Bks on CD, Children's prog, Computers for patron use, Family literacy, Free DVD rentals, Homebound delivery serv, ILL available, Internet access, Laminating, Magazines, Meeting rooms, Notary serv, Online cat, Photocopying/Printing, Prog for adults, Prog for children & young adult, Ref & res, Scanner, Story hour, Summer reading prog, Tax forms
Open Mon-Thurs 8:30-6:30, Fri 8:30-5, Sat 9-3

SAINT MARY-OF-THE-WOODS

C SAINT MARY-OF-THE-WOODS COLLEGE*, The Mary & Andrew Rooney Library, 3301 Saint Mary's Rd, 47876. SAN 305-1048. Tel: 812-535-5223. FAX: 812-535-5127. E-mail: library@smwc.edu. Web Site: library.smwc.edu. *Libr Dir,* Judith Tribble; Tel: 812-535-5255, E-mail: jtribble@smwc.edu; *Dir, Learning Res Ctr,* Christina Gunderson; Staff 2 (MLS 2)
Founded 1840. Enrl 1,687; Fac 57; Highest Degree: Master

Library Holdings: Bk Titles 90,668; Bk Vols 150,000; Per Subs 150
Special Collections: Catholic Americana; Fore-edge Painting Coll; Seventeenth & Eighteenth Century French Religious Books
Wireless access
Partic in Academic Libraries of Indiana; Midwest Collaborative for Library Services; OCLC Online Computer Library Center, Inc
Open Mon-Thurs 8am-10pm, Fri 8-7, Sat 10-5, Sun 6pm-10pm

SAINT MEINRAD

R SAINT MEINRAD ARCHABBEY & SCHOOL OF THEOLOGY*, Archabbey Library, 200 Hill Dr, 47577. SAN 305-1056. Tel: 812-357-6401. Toll Free Tel: 800-987-7311. FAX: 812-357-6398. E-mail: library@saintmeinrad.edu. Web Site: www.saintmeinrad.edu/library. *Dir,* Dr Daniel Kolb; E-mail: dkolb@saintmeinrad.edu; *Acq, Circ, ILL,* Mary Ellen Seifrig; *Cat,* Fr Joseph Cox; E-mail: jcox@saintmeinrad.edu; *Electronic Res, ILL,* Kevin Clark; E-mail: kclark@saintmeinrad.edu; Staff 4 (MLS 2, Non-MLS 2)
Founded 1854. Enrl 150; Fac 24; Highest Degree: Master
Library Holdings: Bk Titles 140,449; Bk Vols 174,531; Per Subs 333
Subject Interests: Humanities, Relig, Theol
Automation Activity & Vendor Info: (Acquisitions) OCLC Worldshare Management Services; (Cataloging) OCLC; (Circulation) OCLC Worldshare Management Services; (ILL) OCLC WorldShare Interlibrary Loan; (OPAC) OCLC Worldshare Management Services; (Serials) OCLC Worldshare Management Services
Function: 24/7 Electronic res, 24/7 Online cat, Art exhibits
Partic in Academic Libraries of Indiana; American Theological Library Association; Private Academic Library Network of Indiana
Restriction: Borrowing privileges limited to fac & registered students, Borrowing requests are handled by ILL, Circ to mem only, In-house use for visitors

SALEM

P SALEM PUBLIC LIBRARY*, 212 N Main St, 47167. SAN 305-1064. Tel: 812-883-5600. FAX: 812-883-1609. E-mail: salemindianalibrary@hotmail.com. Web Site: salemlib.lib.in.us. *Dir,* Jill DuChemin; Staff 3 (MLS 2, Non-MLS 1)
Founded 1903. Pop 9,129; Circ 36,000
Library Holdings: AV Mats 780; Bk Titles 36,080; Bk Vols 37,110; Per Subs 151; Videos 1,000
Subject Interests: Local hist
Automation Activity & Vendor Info: (Cataloging) Follett Software; (Circulation) Follett Software; (OPAC) Follett Software
Partic in Chemeketa Cooperative Regional Library Service; North of Boston Library Exchange, Inc
Open Mon-Thurs 10-7, Fri & Sat 10-5, Sun 1-5
Friends of the Library Group

S WASHINGTON COUNTY HISTORICAL SOCIETY LIBRARY*, Stevens Museum - The John Hay Center, 307 E Market St, 47167. SAN 305-1072. Tel: 812-883-6495. E-mail: info@johnhaycenter.org. Web Site: www.johnhaycenter.org/the-stevens-museum. *Librn,* Kathy Wade; *Asst Librn,* Jeremy Elliott
Library Holdings: Bk Titles 5,000
Subject Interests: Genealogy
Wireless access
Open Tues-Sat 9-5

SCOTTSBURG

P SCOTT COUNTY PUBLIC LIBRARY*, Scottsburg Public, 108 S Main St, 47170. SAN 305-1080. Tel: 812-752-2751. FAX: 812-752-2878. Web Site: www.scott.lib.in.us. *Dir,* Darlene Hall; E-mail: darlene@scott.lib.in.us; Staff 12 (MLS 2, Non-MLS 10)
Founded 1921. Pop 22,718; Circ 88,111
Library Holdings: Braille Volumes 10; CDs 350; DVDs 350; Large Print Bks 150; Bk Titles 76,539; Bk Vols 79,110; Per Subs 209; Spec Interest Per Sub 20; Talking Bks 300; Videos 350
Special Collections: Carl R Bogardus Sr, MD Coll
Subject Interests: Genealogy, Local hist, State hist
Automation Activity & Vendor Info: (Cataloging) Innovative Interfaces, Inc; (Circulation) Innovative Interfaces, Inc; (OPAC) Innovative Interfaces, Inc
Wireless access
Function: After school storytime, Archival coll, Audio & video playback equip for onsite use, AV serv, Bi-weekly Writer's Group, Homebound delivery serv, ILL available, Orientations, Photocopying/Printing, Prog for adults, Prog for children & young adult, Ref serv available, Spoken cassettes & CDs, Summer reading prog, VHS videos, Wheelchair accessible, Workshops
Partic in Midwest Collaborative for Library Services
Special Services for the Deaf - Staff with knowledge of sign lang
Special Services for the Blind - Audio mat; Bks & mags in Braille, on rec, tape & cassette; Bks available with recordings; Bks on cassette; Bks on CD; Talking bks
Open Mon & Thurs 9-8, Tues, Wed & Fri 9-6, Sat 9-5
Friends of the Library Group
Branches: 2
AUSTIN BRANCH, 26 Union Ave, Austin, 47102-1344.
Library Holdings: Bk Vols 15,000
Open Mon-Fri 9:30-5:30, Sat 10-2
LEXINGTON BRANCH, 2781 Cherry St, Lexington, 47138-8620.
Library Holdings: Bk Titles 5,000
Open Mon-Fri 9:30-5:30, Sat 10-2

SELLERSBURG

J IVY TECH COMMUNITY COLLEGE*, Paul W Ogle Library, 8204 Hwy 311, 47172-1897. SAN 320-6718. Tel: 812-246-3301, Ext 4225. FAX: 812-246-9905. Web Site: library.ivytech.edu/sellersburg. *Dir,* Marie White; E-mail: mwhite@ivytech.edu; *Libr Asst,* Joyce McAdams; Staff 3 (MLS 1, Non-MLS 2)
Founded 1974. Highest Degree: Master
Library Holdings: AV Mats 838; Bk Titles 3,911; Bk Vols 4,180; Per Subs 162
Subject Interests: Med
Open Mon-Thurs 8am-9pm, Fri 7:30-4:30

SEYMOUR

P JACKSON COUNTY PUBLIC LIBRARY*, Seymour Library, 303 W Second St, 47274-2147. SAN 341-6194. Tel: 812-522-3412. Circulation Tel: 812-522-3412, Ext 1243. Interlibrary Loan Service Tel: 812-522-3412, Ext 1240. Administration Tel: 812-522-3412, Ext 1253. FAX: 812-522-5456. Administration E-mail: admin@myjclibrary.org. Web Site: www.myjclibrary.org. *Dir,* Julia Aker; Tel: 812-522-3412, Ext 1223, E-mail: jaker@myjclibrary.org; *IT Dir,* Ben Boyer; Tel: 812-522-3412, Ext 1227, E-mail: bboyer@myjclibrary.org; *Head, Adult Serv,* Julie Lingerfelt; Tel: 812-522-3412, Ext 1239, E-mail: juliel@myjclibrary.org; *Head, Youth Serv,* Lola Snyder; Tel: 812-522-3412, Ext 1231, E-mail: lola@myjclibrary.org; *Adminr,* Mary Reed; Tel: 812-522-3412, Ext 1233, E-mail: mreed@myjclibrary.org; *Circ Mgr,* Christina Hime; Tel: 812-522-3412, Ext 1238, E-mail: chime@myjclibrary.org; *Tech Serv Mgr,* Monica Boyer; Tel: 812-522-3412, Ext 1226, E-mail: monica@myjclibrary.org; *Info Serv,* Janet Hensen; Tel: 812-522-3412, Ext 1224, E-mail: janet@myjclibrary.org; *Youth & Teen Serv,* Jill Willey; E-mail: jill@myjclibrary.org. Subject Specialists: *Family hist, Local hist,* Janet Hensen; Staff 4 (MLS 4)
Founded 1905. Pop 34,423
Jan 2017-Dec 2017. Mats Exp $233,850, Books $61,257, Per/Ser (Incl. Access Fees) $9,430, AV Equip $50,000, AV Mat $39,516, Electronic Ref Mat (Incl. Access Fees) $73,647. Sal $971,391
Library Holdings: AV Mats 16,616; Bk Vols 53,610; Per Subs 140
Special Collections: Oral History
Subject Interests: Local hist
Automation Activity & Vendor Info: (Acquisitions) Evergreen; (Circulation) Evergreen; (ILL) OCLC; (OPAC) Evergreen
Wireless access
Function: 24/7 Electronic res, 24/7 Online cat, Accelerated reader prog, Adult bk club, Archival coll, Art exhibits, Audio & video playback equip for onsite use, Audiobks on Playaways & MP3, Audiobks via web, Bk club(s), Bks on CD, CD-ROM, Children's prog, Computers for patron use, Digital talking bks, E-Readers, Electronic databases & coll, Free DVD rentals, Home delivery & serv to seniorr ctr & nursing homes, Homebound delivery serv, ILL available, Internet access, Jail serv, Laminating, Life-long learning prog for all ages, Magazines, Magnifiers for reading, Meeting rooms, Microfiche/film & reading machines, Movies, Museum passes, Music CDs, Notary serv, Online cat, Outreach serv, Outside serv via phone, mail, e-mail & web, OverDrive digital audio bks, Photocopying/Printing, Prog for adults, Prog for children & young adult, Ref & res, Ref serv available, Satellite serv, Scanner, Spoken cassettes & CDs, Spoken cassettes & DVDs, Story hour, Study rm, Summer reading prog, Tax forms, Teen prog, Telephone ref, VHS videos, Wheelchair accessible, Writing prog
Publications: Program Guide (Quarterly newsletter); Wowbrary (Newsletter)
Partic in Midwest Collaborative for Library Services
Special Services for the Deaf - Bks on deafness & sign lang; Closed caption videos
Special Services for the Blind - BiFolkal kits; Bks on CD; Computer with voice synthesizer for visually impaired persons; Descriptive video serv (DVS); Large print bks; Magnifiers
Open Mon-Thurs 8:30-2:30
Restriction: Non-circulating coll, Non-resident fee
Friends of the Library Group

Branches: 2
CROTHERSVILLE LIBRARY, 120 E Main St, Crothersville, 47229, SAN 341-6224. Tel: 812-793-2927. FAX: 812-793-3721. *Br Coordr,* Cindy Huckleberry; E-mail: cindy@myjclibrary.org; Staff 3 (Non-MLS 3)
Pop 1,570
Automation Activity & Vendor Info: (Circulation) Evergreen; (ILL) OCLC; (OPAC) Evergreen; (Serials) Evergreen
Function: 24/7 Electronic res, 24/7 Online cat, Accelerated reader prog, Adult bk club, Bk club(s), Bks on CD, CD-ROM, Children's prog, Computers for patron use, E-Reserves, Electronic databases & coll, Free DVD rentals, Holiday prog, ILL available, Internet access, Laminating, Magazines, Movies, Music CDs, Online cat, OverDrive digital audio bks, Photocopying/Printing, Prog for adults, Prog for children & young adult, Spoken cassettes & DVDs, Summer reading prog, Tax forms, Teen prog, Wheelchair accessible
Open Mon-Thurs 10-8, Fri & Sat 12-5
Friends of the Library Group
MEDORA LIBRARY, 27 Main St, Medora, 47260. (Mail add: PO Box 400, Medora, 47260-0400), SAN 371-3458. Tel: 812-966-2278. FAX: 812-966-2229. *Circ Mgr,* Christina Hime; Tel: 812-405-1832, E-mail: chime@myjclibrary.org; Staff 5 (Non-MLS 5)
Founded 1992. Pop 915
Automation Activity & Vendor Info: (Circulation) Evergreen; (ILL) OCLC; (OPAC) Evergreen
Function: 24/7 Electronic res, 24/7 Online cat, Accelerated reader prog, Adult bk club, Bk club(s), Bks on CD, CD-ROM, Children's prog, Computers for patron use, Free DVD rentals, Holiday prog, ILL available, Internet access, Laminating, Magazines, Meeting rooms, Movies, Music CDs, Online cat, Photocopying/Printing, Prog for adults, Prog for children & young adult, Spoken cassettes & CDs, Spoken cassettes & DVDs, Summer reading prog, Tax forms, Telephone ref, VHS videos, Wheelchair accessible
Open Mon-Fri 2-6, Sat 12-5
Friends of the Library Group

SHELBYVILLE

P SHELBY COUNTY PUBLIC LIBRARY, 57 W Broadway, 46176. SAN 305-1099. Tel: 317-398-7121, 317-835-2653. FAX: 317-398-4430. Web Site: www.myshelbylibrary.org. *Libr Dir,* Janet Wallace; E-mail: jwallace@sscpl.lib.in.us; *Head, Adult Serv,* Amanda White; *Head, Tech Serv,* Chelsey Edwards; *Youth Serv Dept Head,* Brandy Graves; *Hist Coll Librn,* Donna Dennison; Staff 37 (MLS 4, Non-MLS 33)
Founded 1898. Pop 44,310; Circ 132,610
Library Holdings: High Interest/Low Vocabulary Bk Vols 50; Bk Titles 91,840; Bk Vols 93,210; Per Subs 267; Talking Bks 1,402; Videos 1,520
Special Collections: Oral History
Subject Interests: Local hist
Automation Activity & Vendor Info: (Cataloging) Evergreen; (Circulation) Evergreen
Wireless access
Partic in Midwest Collaborative for Library Services
Open Mon-Thurs 9-9, Fri 9-7, Sat 9-5
Friends of the Library Group
Bookmobiles: 1. Outreach Mgr, Pam Weakley

SHERIDAN

P SHERIDAN PUBLIC LIBRARY*, 103 W First St, 46069. SAN 305-1102. Tel: 317-758-5201. FAX: 317-758-0045. Web Site: www.sheridan.lib.in.us. *Dir,* Kim Riley; E-mail: kim@sheridan.lib.in.us; *Librn,* Patty Barker; *Librn,* Dorothy Bishop; *Youth Librn,* Lindsay Spencer; Staff 4 (MLS 1, Non-MLS 3)
Founded 1912. Pop 4,892; Circ 37,812
Library Holdings: AV Mats 1,290; Large Print Bks 110; Bk Titles 36,727; Bk Vols 38,910; Per Subs 54; Videos 410
Wireless access
Partic in Cent Ind Libr Asn; Chemeketa Cooperative Regional Library Service
Open Mon-Thurs 10-7, Fri 10-5:30, Sat 9-1
Friends of the Library Group

SHOALS

P SHOALS PUBLIC LIBRARY*, 404 N High St, 47581. (Mail add: PO Box 909, 47581-0909), SAN 305-1110. Tel: 812-247-3838. FAX: 812-247-3838. E-mail: shoalspubliclibrary@gmail.com. Web Site: www.spl.lib.in.us. *Dir,* Bobbi Salmon; Staff 2 (MLS 1, Non-MLS 1)
Pop 809; Circ 15,650
Library Holdings: Bk Titles 10,214; Bk Vols 11,810; Per Subs 6; Talking Bks 50; Videos 375
Wireless access
Partic in Evergreen Indiana Consortium
Open Mon, Tues & Fri 12-5, Thurs 2-8, Sat 9-1

SOUTH BEND

M BEACON HEALTH SYSTEM*, Library Services, 615 N Michigan, 46601. SAN 329-1316. Tel: 574-647-7677. *Coordr, Libr Serv,* Lori Harding; E-mail: lharding2@beaconhealthsystem.org; Staff 3 (MLS 1, Non-MLS 2)
Subject Interests: Family practice, Gen med, Healthcare, Nursing, Rehabilitation
Automation Activity & Vendor Info: (Cataloging) OCLC Worldshare Management Services
Wireless access
Partic in Midwest Collaborative for Library Services; National Network of Libraries of Medicine Region 6; OCLC Online Computer Library Center, Inc
Open Mon-Fri 8-5

C INDIANA UNIVERSITY SOUTH BEND*, Franklin D Schurz Library, 1700 Mishawaka Ave, 46615. (Mail add: PO Box 7111, 46634-7111), SAN 305-1145. Tel: 574-520-4449. Circulation Tel: 574-520-4440. Interlibrary Loan Service Tel: 574-520-4433. Reference Tel: 574-520-4441. FAX: 574-520-4472. Web Site: iusb.edu/library. *Dean, Libr Serv,* Vicki Bloom; Tel: 574-520-4448, E-mail: vdbloom@iusb.edu; *Dir, Access Support,* Scott Opasik; Tel: 574-520-4446, E-mail: sopasik@iusb.edu; *Dir, Coll Serv,* Susan Thomas; Tel: 574-520-5500, E-mail: suethoma@iusb.edu; *Dir, Res, Instruction & Outreach,* Linda Fisher; Tel: 574-520-4442, E-mail: lfisher@iusb.edu; *Head, Electronic Res,* Feng Shan; Tel: 574-520-4189, E-mail: fshan@iusb.edu; *Head, Info Literacy,* Nancy Colborn; Tel: 574-520-4321, E-mail: ncolborn@iusb.edu; *Head, Info Tech,* Kirby Cheng; Tel: 574-520-4421, E-mail: xicheng@iusb.edu; *Head, Pub Relations & Outreach,* Julie Elliott; Tel: 574-520-4410, E-mail: jmfelli@iusb.edu; *Head, Web Serv,* Vincci Kwong; Tel: 574-520-4444, E-mail: vkwong@iusb.edu; *Scholarly Communications Librn,* Stephen Craig Finlay; Tel: 574-520-4209, E-mail: scfinlay@iusb.edu; *Bus Operations Mgr,* Angela Huff; Tel: 574-520-4404, E-mail: adhuff@iusb.edu; *Circ Supvr,* Katherin Plodowski; Tel: 574-520-4380, E-mail: kplodows@iusb.edu; *Dorothy J Wiekamp Educ Res Commons Supvr,* Kimberly Parker; Tel: 574-520-5548, E-mail: kparker@iusb.edu; *ILL Supvr,* Maureen Kennedy; E-mail: maurkenn@iusb.edu. Subject Specialists: *New media, Visual arts,* Vicki Bloom; *Astronomy, Chem, Math,* Scott Opasik; *Allied health, Polit sci, Pub affairs,* Susan Thomas; *Biology, Criminal justice, Psychol,* Linda Fisher; *Communication arts, East Asian studies,* Feng Shan; *Anthrop, Educ, Sociol,* Nancy Colborn; *Computer sci, Informatics, World lang,* Kirby Cheng; *Dance, English, Theatre,* Julie Elliott; *Bus, Econ,* Vincci Kwong; *Latin Am studies, Music, Philos,* Stephen Craig Finlay; Staff 20 (MLS 10, Non-MLS 10)
Founded 1940. Enrl 8,075; Fac 300; Highest Degree: Master
Jul 2017-Jun 2018 Income $2,393,146. Mats Exp $775,570. Sal $987,363 (Prof $782,010)
Library Holdings: CDs 1,702; DVDs 2,215; e-books 251,233; e-journals 70,254; Music Scores 6,285; Bk Vols 253,872; Per Subs 303; Videos 4,670
Special Collections: Annie Belle Boss Papers; James Lewis Casaday Theatre Coll; Lincoln Coll; Torrington Company Coll. US Document Depository
Automation Activity & Vendor Info: (Acquisitions) SirsiDynix; (Cataloging) SirsiDynix; (Circulation) SirsiDynix; (Discovery) EBSCO Discovery Service; (ILL) OCLC; (OPAC) SirsiDynix; (Serials) SirsiDynix
Wireless access
Function: Archival coll, Audio & video playback equip for onsite use, AV serv, Computers for patron use, Distance learning, Doc delivery serv, Electronic databases & coll, Govt ref serv, ILL available, Learning ctr, Magnifiers for reading, Microfiche/film & reading machines, Music CDs, Online cat, Online info literacy tutorials on the web & in blackboard, Online ref, Photocopying/Printing, Printer for laptops & handheld devices, Ref & res, Ref serv available, Res libr, Scanner, Telephone ref, Wheelchair accessible
Publications: News from IU South Bend Libraries (Biannually)
Partic in Academic Libraries of Indiana; LYRASIS; Midwest Collaborative for Library Services; OCLC Online Computer Library Center, Inc
Open Mon-Thurs 8am-Midnight, Fri 8-5, Sat 10-5, Sun Noon-Midnight
Restriction: Open to pub for ref & circ; with some limitations, Open to students, fac & staff
Friends of the Library Group

J IVY TECH COMMUNITY COLLEGE*, South Bend Campus Library, 220 Dean Johnson Blvd, 46601. SAN 305-1153. Tel: 574-289-7001, Ext 5343. *Libr Dir,* John Fribley; Tel: 574-289-7001, Ext 5341, E-mail: jfribley@ivytech.edu; *Librn,* M Elizabeth Van Jacob; Tel: 574-289-7001, Ext 1125, E-mail: mvanjacob@ivytech.edu; Staff 3 (MLS 1, Non-MLS 2)
Founded 1968. Enrl 2,500; Highest Degree: Associate
Library Holdings: AV Mats 941; Bk Titles 5,280; Bk Vols 5,690; Per Subs 70
Subject Interests: Art & archit, Bus & mgt, Med, Photog, Sci tech
Automation Activity & Vendor Info: (Acquisitions) Ex Libris Group; (Cataloging) Ex Libris Group; (Circulation) Ex Libris Group; (OPAC) Ex Libris Group

Wireless access
Open Mon-Thurs 8-8, Fri 8-5, Sat 9-1

GL LIBRARY OF THE US COURTS*, Robert A Grant Courthouse, 204 S Main St, Rm 316, 46601. SAN 372-1183. Tel: 574-246-8050. FAX: 574-246-8002. Web Site: www.lb7.uscourts.gov. *Librn,* Michael Greenlee; E-mail: michael_greenlee@ca7.uscourts.gov; Staff 1 (Non-MLS 1)
Founded 1986
Automation Activity & Vendor Info: (Acquisitions) SirsiDynix; (Cataloging) SirsiDynix; (ILL) OCLC Connexion; (OPAC) SirsiDynix; (Serials) SirsiDynix
Partic in Law Library Microform Consortium
Restriction: Not open to pub

GL SAINT JOSEPH COUNTY LAW LIBRARY*, Court House, 101 S Main St, 46601. SAN 305-117X. Tel: 574-235-9657. FAX: 574-235-9905. E-mail: stjoebar@gmail.com. Web Site: stjoebar.org/. *Exec Dir,* Amy McGuire; Tel: 574-235-9657
Library Holdings: Bk Vols 15,000
Special Collections: Law Books Coll; Reporters Coll; Statutes Coll
Open Mon-Fri 9-3

P SAINT JOSEPH COUNTY PUBLIC LIBRARY*, 304 S Main St, 46601. SAN 341-6259. Tel: 574-282-4646. FAX: 574-280-2763. TDD: 574-235-4194. Web Site: sjcpl.lib.in.us. *Exec Dir,* Debra Futa; Tel: 574-282-4604, E-mail: debra.futa@sjcpl.org; *Chief Financial Officer,* Nancy Korpal; E-mail: nancy.korpal@sjcpl.org; *Chief Opearting Officer, Pub Serv,* Trish Coleman; E-mail: t.coleman@sjcpl.org; *Chief Resource Officer,* Sarah Hill; E-mail: s.hill@sjcpl.org; *Dir, Communications & Develop,* Lisa O'Brien; E-mail: l.obrien@sjcpl.org; *Dir, Br Serv,* Rona Plummer; E-mail: r.plummer@sjcpl.org; *Ch Mgr,* Theresa Horn; E-mail: t.horn@sjcpl.org; *Coll Develop Mgr,* David Heidt; E-mail: d.heidt@sjcpl.org; *Research & Tech Mgr,* Sara Maloney; E-mail: s.maloney@sjcpl.org; *Tech Serv Mgr,* Shanti Nand; E-mail: s.nand@sjcpl.org; Staff 189 (MLS 33, Non-MLS 156)
Founded 1888. Pop 167,606; Circ 2,219,748
Jan 2017-Dec 2017 Income (Main & Associated Libraries) $14,675,217, State $1,000,847, Federal $159,180, Locally Generated Income $12,658,751, Other $856,439. Mats Exp $2,366,393, Books $1,357,906, Per/Ser (Incl. Access Fees) $150,217, AV Mat $392,877, Electronic Ref Mat (Incl. Access Fees) $465,393. Sal $5,241,268
Library Holdings: CDs 56,312; DVDs 51,612; Electronic Media & Resources 32,036; Bk Vols 476,057; Per Subs 3,076
Special Collections: Local History & Genealogy Coll (necrology & clippings file)
Automation Activity & Vendor Info: (Acquisitions) Innovative Interfaces, Inc - Sierra; (Cataloging) Innovative Interfaces, Inc - Sierra; (Circulation) Innovative Interfaces, Inc - Sierra; (Discovery) BiblioCommons; (ILL) OCLC FirstSearch; (OPAC) Innovative Interfaces, Inc; (Serials) Innovative Interfaces, Inc
Wireless access
Function: 24/7 Electronic res, 24/7 Online cat, 3D Printer, Activity rm, Audiobks via web, AV serv, Bks on CD, Children's prog, Computers for patron use, Electronic databases & coll, Homebound delivery serv, ILL available, Internet access, Magazines, Meeting rooms, Museum passes, Music CDs, Online cat, Online ref, Outreach serv, OverDrive digital audio bks, Photocopying/Printing, Prog for adults, Prog for children & young adult, Ref & res, Ref serv available, Scanner, Spanish lang bks, Story hour, Study rm, Summer reading prog, Tax forms, Teen prog, Telephone ref
Special Services for the Deaf - TTY equip
Special Services for the Blind - Large print bks
Open Mon-Thurs 10-8, Fri & Sat 10-6, Sun (Winter) 1-5
Friends of the Library Group
Branches: 9
CENTRE TOWNSHIP BRANCH, 1150 E Kern Rd, 46614. Tel: 574-251-3700. *Br Mgr,* Dawn Matthews; E-mail: d.matthews@sjcpl.org
Open Mon, Wed, Fri & Sat 10-6, Tues & Thurs 10-8
ROGER B FRANCIS BRANCH, 52655 N Ironwood Rd, 46635, SAN 341-6283. Tel: 574-282-4641. *Br Mgr,* Dana Labrum; E-mail: d.labrum@sjcpl.org
Open Mon, Wed, Fri & Sat 10-6, Tues & Thurs 12-8
GERMAN TOWNSHIP BRANCH LIBRARY, 52807 Lynnewood Ave, 46628. Tel: 574-271-5144. *Br Mgr,* Scott Sinnett; E-mail: s.sinnett@sjcpl.org
Open Mon, Wed, Fri & Sat 10-6, Tues & Thurs 12-8
LAKEVILLE BRANCH, 120 N Michigan, Lakeville, 46536, SAN 370-9248. Tel: 574-784-3446. *Br Mgr,* Rachel Finch; E-mail: r.finch@sjcpl.org
Open Mon, Wed, Fri & Sat 10-6, Tues & Thurs 12-8
LASALLE BRANCH, 3232 W Ardmore Trail, 46628, SAN 341-6313. Tel: 574-282-4633. *Br Mgr,* Michael Moriconi; E-mail: m.moriconi@sjcpl.org
Open Mon, Wed, Fri & Sat 10-6, Tues & Thurs 12-8
NORTH LIBERTY BRANCH, 105 E Market St, North Liberty, 46554, SAN 329-6822. Tel: 574-656-3664. *Br Mgr,* Michele Arnette; E-mail: m.arnette@sjcpl.org
Open Mon, Wed, Fri & Sat 10-6, Tues & Thurs 12-8
RIVER PARK BRANCH, 2022 Mishawaka Ave, 46615, SAN 341-6348. Tel: 574-282-4635. *Br Mgr,* Joseph Sipocz; E-mail: j.sipocz@sjcpl.org
Open Mon, Wed, Fri & Sat 10-6, Tues & Thurs 12-8
VIRGINIA M TUTT BRANCH, 2223 S Miami St, 46613, SAN 341-6372. Tel: 574-282-4637. *Br Mgr,* Joseph Sipocz
Open Mon, Wed, Fri & Sat 10-6, Tues & Thurs 12-8
WESTERN BRANCH, 611 S Lombardy Dr, 46619, SAN 341-6402. Tel: 574-282-4639. *Br Mgr,* Karen Mann; E-mail: k.mann@sjcpl.org
Open Mon, Wed, Fri & Sat 10-6, Tues & Thurs 12-8

M SAINT JOSEPH'S REGIONAL MEDICAL CENTER*, Medical Library, 801 E LaSalle, 46617. SAN 325-7231. Tel: 574-237-7228. FAX: 574-472-6307. Web Site: www.sjmed.com/medical-library-website. *Librn,* Jennifer Helmen; Tel: 574-335-1012, E-mail: helmenj@sjrmc.com; Staff 1 (Non-MLS 1)
Library Holdings: Bk Titles 1,100; Bk Vols 1,225; Per Subs 150
Subject Interests: Med, Nursing
Open Mon-Fri 9-5

S STUDEBAKER NATIONAL MUSEUM ARCHIVES*, 201 Chapin St, 46601. SAN 325-4526. Tel: 574-235-9714. Toll Free Tel: 888-391-5600. FAX: 574-235-5522. Web Site: archives.studebakermuseum.org, www.studebakermuseum.org. *Archivist,* Andrew Beckman; E-mail: abeckman@studebakermuseum.org
Library Holdings: Bk Titles 400; Per Subs 5
Special Collections: Industrial History Transcriptions; Labor History Coll; South Bend Area Business, Labor & Industry, photogs, vf; South Bend Labor Oral History Project; Transportation History (Studebaker Coll), flms, ms, photogs, trade lit. Oral History
Subject Interests: General indust hist, Local indust hist
Open Mon-Sat 10-5, Sun 12-5
Restriction: Non-circulating to the pub

SOUTH WHITLEY

P SOUTH WHITLEY COMMUNITY PUBLIC LIBRARY, 201 E Front St, 46787-1315. SAN 305-1196. Tel: 260-723-5321. FAX: 260-723-5326. E-mail: info@swcplib.com. Web Site: www.swcplib.com. *Dir,* Vicki Builta; E-mail: vbuilta@swcplib.com
Founded 1913. Pop 5,195
Library Holdings: Bk Vols 40,057; Per Subs 140
Special Collections: Oral History
Subject Interests: Local hist
Wireless access
Open Mon 10-6, Tues-Thurs 10-8, Fri & Sat 10-4

SPEEDWAY

P SPEEDWAY PUBLIC LIBRARY*, 5633 W 25th St, 46224-3899. SAN 305-120X. Tel: 317-243-8959. FAX: 317-243-9373. Web Site: www.speedway.lib.in.us. *Dir,* Darsi Bohr; E-mail: dbohr@speedway.lib.in.us; *Adult Serv,* Ashley Bartley; E-mail: abartley@speedway.lib.in.us; *Ch Serv,* Wendy Zishka; E-mail: wzishka@speedway.lib.in.us; Staff 3 (MLS 3)
Founded 1968. Pop 11,812; Circ 122,156
Library Holdings: AV Mats 8,060; DVDs 5,000; Bk Vols 87,362; Per Subs 116; Talking Bks 5,676
Special Collections: Auto Racing (Indianapolis 500). Municipal Document Depository
Subject Interests: Genealogy
Automation Activity & Vendor Info: (Acquisitions) SirsiDynix; (Cataloging) SirsiDynix; (ILL) OCLC; (OPAC) SirsiDynix
Wireless access
Publications: Speedreader (Newsletter)
Partic in Midwest Collaborative for Library Services
Open Mon-Thurs (Winter) 9-9, Fri & Sat 9-5; Mon-Thurs (Summer) 9-8, Fri & Sat 9-5
Friends of the Library Group

SPENCER

P OWEN COUNTY PUBLIC LIBRARY*, Ten S Montgomery St, 47460-1738. SAN 305-1218. Tel: 812-829-3392. FAX: 812-829-6165. Web Site: owenlib.org. *Dir,* Ginger Rogers; E-mail: grogers@owenlib.org; *Dir, Tech Serv,* Debbie Campbell; Staff 22 (MLS 2, Non-MLS 20)
Founded 1912. Pop 21,575; Circ 140,620
Library Holdings: Bk Titles 67,391; Per Subs 122
Subject Interests: Genealogy
Automation Activity & Vendor Info: (Acquisitions) SirsiDynix; (Cataloging) SirsiDynix; (Circulation) SirsiDynix; (OPAC) SirsiDynix; (Serials) SirsiDynix
Wireless access

Function: AV serv, ILL available, Photocopying/Printing, Prog for children & young adult, Ref serv available, Summer reading prog, Wheelchair accessible
Open Mon-Fri 10-6, Sat 9-Noon
Friends of the Library Group

SPICELAND

P SPICELAND TOWN-TOWNSHIP PUBLIC LIBRARY, 106 W Main St, 47385. (Mail add: PO Box 445, 47385-0445), SAN 305-1226. Tel: 765-987-7472. E-mail: info@spicelandlibrary.com. Web Site: spicelandlibrary.com. *Dir,* Tom Pyle; Staff 2 (MLS 1, Non-MLS 1)
Pop 2,200; Circ 7,891
Library Holdings: DVDs 75; Bk Titles 25,621; Bk Vols 27,890; Per Subs 45; Talking Bks 286; Videos 737
Automation Activity & Vendor Info: (Cataloging) TLC (The Library Corporation); (Circulation) TLC (The Library Corporation)
Open Mon 1-5, Tues 3-6, Wed 11-5, Thurs 2-6, Sat 9-Noon

SULLIVAN

P SULLIVAN COUNTY PUBLIC LIBRARIES*, 100 S Crowder St, 47882. SAN 341-6437. Tel: 812-268-4957. FAX: 812-268-5370. Web Site: www.sullivan.lib.in.us. *Dir,* Jordan C Orwig; E-mail: jorwig@sullivan.lib.in.us; *Asst Dir, Ref Serv,* Melissa Rinehart; E-mail: mrinehart@sullivan.lib.in.us; *Ch,* Jenna Armstrong; E-mail: jarmstrong@sullivan.lib.in.us; Staff 13 (Non-MLS 13)
Founded 1904. Pop 21,751; Circ 125,595
Library Holdings: AV Mats 4,335; Bks on Deafness & Sign Lang 33; CDs 1,140; DVDs 144; High Interest/Low Vocabulary Bk Vols 42; Large Print Bks 2,587; Bk Titles 49,427; Bk Vols 99,211; Per Subs 346; Talking Bks 1,243; Videos 2,968
Special Collections: Indiana Coll
Subject Interests: Genealogy, Local hist
Automation Activity & Vendor Info: (Cataloging) SydneyPlus; (Circulation) SirsiDynix; (OPAC) SirsiDynix; (Serials) SirsiDynix
Wireless access
Function: AV serv, Digital talking bks, Distance learning, Home delivery & serv to seniorr ctr & nursing homes, Homebound delivery serv, ILL available, Music CDs, Online ref, Photocopying/Printing, Prog for adults, Prog for children & young adult, Serves people with intellectual disabilities, Spoken cassettes & CDs, Summer reading prog, Tax forms, VHS videos, Wheelchair accessible, Workshops
Partic in Midwest Collaborative for Library Services
Open Mon-Thurs 9-8, Fri 9-6, Sat 9-5 (Winter); Mon-Fri 9-6, Sat 9-5 (Summer)
Friends of the Library Group
Branches: 5
CARLISLE PUBLIC, 201 N Ledgerwood St, Carlisle, 47838. (Mail add: PO Box 297, Carlisle, 47838-0297). Tel: 812-398-4480. FAX: 812-398-2370. E-mail: carlislepl@sullivan.lib.in.us. *Br Mgr,* Cheryl Goodman
Founded 1965
Automation Activity & Vendor Info: (Cataloging) Innovative Interfaces, Inc; (Circulation) Innovative Interfaces, Inc; (OPAC) Innovative Interfaces, Inc
Open Tues-Fri 11-5, Sat 9-3
DUGGER PUBLIC, 8007 E Main St, Dugger, 47848. (Mail add: PO Box 277, Dugger, 47848-0277). Tel: 812-648-2822. FAX: 812-648-2078. E-mail: duggerpl@sullivan.lib.in.us. *Br Mgr,* Deborah Loveless
Founded 1928
Automation Activity & Vendor Info: (Cataloging) LibLime; (Circulation) LibLime
Open Tues-Fri 11-5, Sat 9-3
FARMERSBURG PUBLIC, 102 W Main St, Farmersburg, 47850. Tel: 812-696-2194. FAX: 812-696-0571. E-mail: farmersburgpl@sullivan.lib.in.us. *Br Mgr,* LeAnne Daniels
Automation Activity & Vendor Info: (Cataloging) LibLime; (Circulation) LibLime
Open Tues-Fri 11-5, Sat 9-3
MEROM PUBLIC, 8554 W Market St, Merom, 47861. (Mail add: PO Box 146, Merom, 47861-0146). Tel: 812-356-4612. FAX: 812-356-4310. E-mail: merompl@sullivan.lib.in.us. *Br Mgr,* Joshua Collins
Open Tues-Fri 11-5, Sat 9-3
SHELBURN PUBLIC, 17 W Griffith, Shelburn, 47879. (Mail add: PO Box 10, Shelburn, 47879-0010). Tel: 812-397-2210. FAX: 812-397-0606. E-mail: shelburnpl@sullivan.lib.in.us. *Br Mgr,* Nondus Murray
Automation Activity & Vendor Info: (Cataloging) LibLime; (Circulation) LibLime
Open Tues-Fri 11-5, Sat 9-3

SWAYZEE

P SWAYZEE PUBLIC LIBRARY*, 301 S Washington St, 46986. (Mail add: PO Box 307, 46986-0307). Tel: 765-922-7526. FAX: 765-922-4538. E-mail: swaypub@swayzee.com. Web Site: swayzeepubliclibrary.com. *Dir & Librn,* Dana Melton; *Asst Librn,* Heather Butler; Staff 1 (Non-MLS 1)
Founded 1919
Library Holdings: Audiobooks 130; DVDs 400; Bk Titles 20,650; Per Subs 20; Talking Bks 22
Wireless access
Open Mon & Wed 12-6, Tues & Fri 11-5, Sat 9-11

SYRACUSE

P SYRACUSE TURKEY CREEK TOWNSHIP PUBLIC LIBRARY, 115 E Main St, 46567. SAN 305-1242. Tel: 574-457-3022. FAX: 574-457-8971. Web Site: www.syracuse.lib.in.us. *Dir,* Kim Blaha; E-mail: kblaha@syracuse.lib.in.us; Staff 6 (MLS 3, Non-MLS 3)
Founded 1909. Pop 9,680; Circ 75,600
Library Holdings: Audiobooks 2,216; AV Mats 3,167; DVDs 3,167; Bk Vols 26,128; Per Subs 42
Special Collections: Hotspots; Local Newspaper Coll, micro; Old historical photographs & slides
Automation Activity & Vendor Info: (Acquisitions) Baker & Taylor; (Cataloging) Evergreen; (Circulation) Evergreen; (OPAC) Evergreen
Wireless access
Function: 24/7 Electronic res, 24/7 Online cat, Activity rm, Adult bk club, After school storytime, Art programs, Audio & video playback equip for onsite use, Audiobks via web, Bk club(s), Bks on CD, Children's prog, Computer training, Computers for patron use, Digital talking bks, Electronic databases & coll, Free DVD rentals, Govt ref serv, Health sci info serv, Holiday prog, Home delivery & serv to seniorr ctr & nursing homes, Homebound delivery serv, ILL available, Internet access, Life-long learning prog for all ages, Magazines, Mail & tel request accepted, Mango lang, Microfiche/film & reading machines, Notary serv, Online cat, Online ref, Outreach serv, OverDrive digital audio bks, Photocopying/Printing, Preschool outreach, Preschool reading prog, Printer for laptops & handheld devices, Prog for adults, Prog for children & young adult, Ref & res, Ref serv available, Res assist avail, Scanner, Senior outreach, Serves people with intellectual disabilities, Spanish lang bks, STEM programs, Story hour, Summer reading prog, Tax forms, Teen prog, Telephone ref, Visual arts prog, Wheelchair accessible, Workshops, Writing prog
Partic in Association for Rural & Small Libraries; Evergreen Indiana Consortium
Open Mon, Wed & Fri 10-6, Tues & Thurs 12-8, Sat 10-2
Restriction: Non-resident fee
Friends of the Library Group

TELL CITY

P PERRY COUNTY PUBLIC LIBRARY*, 2328 Tell St, 47586. SAN 305-1250. Tel: 812-547-2661. FAX: 812-547-3038. Web Site: www.tcpclibrary.org. *Dir,* John Mundy; E-mail: jmundy@tcpclibrary.org; *Dir, Children & YA,* Lisa Hammack; E-mail: lhammack@tcpclibrary.org; *Asst Dir,* Keith Kuric; E-mail: kkuric@tcpclibrary.org; Staff 9 (MLS 1, Non-MLS 8)
Founded 1905. Pop 19,558; Circ 135,000
Library Holdings: Audiobooks 4,238; DVDs 7,150; e-books 42,686; Bk Titles 62,000; Bk Vols 89,087; Per Subs 206
Subject Interests: Genealogy, Local hist
Automation Activity & Vendor Info: (Cataloging) Evergreen; (Circulation) Evergreen; (OPAC) Evergreen
Wireless access
Function: 24/7 Electronic res, 24/7 Online cat, Adult bk club, Audiobks on Playaways & MP3, Audiobks via web, AV serv, Bk club(s), Bks on CD, Chess club, Children's prog, Computers for patron use, Electronic databases & coll, Free DVD rentals, ILL available, Internet access, Laminating, Magazines, Magnifiers for reading, Meeting rooms, Microfiche/film & reading machines, Movies, Notary serv, Online cat, Outside serv via phone, mail, e-mail & web, OverDrive digital audio bks, Photocopying/Printing, Printer for laptops & handheld devices, Prog for adults, Prog for children & young adult, Ref & res, Scanner, STEM programs, Story hour, Tax forms
Partic in Evergreen Indiana Consortium; Midwest Collaborative for Library Services
Special Services for the Blind - Bks on CD; Large print & cassettes; Large print bks; Magnifiers
Open Mon-Wed 9-8, Thurs & Fri 9-5:30, Sat 9-4:30
Friends of the Library Group
Branches: 1
CANNELTON PUBLIC LIBRARY, 210 S Eighth St, Cannelton, 47520, SAN 304-8276. Tel: 812-547-6028. FAX: 812-547-8590. Web Site: www.tcpclibrary.org/cannelton-public-library. *Br Mgr,* Sally Walker; E-mail: swalker@tcpclibrary.org; Staff 2 (MLS 1, Non-MLS 1)
Founded 1893. Pop 1,209; Circ 7,890

Library Holdings: Large Print Bks 68; Bk Titles 21,068; Bk Vols 22,391; Per Subs 57; Talking Bks 99; Videos 219
Subject Interests: Indiana
Automation Activity & Vendor Info: (Acquisitions) Follett Software; (Cataloging) Follett Software; (OPAC) Follett Software
Partic in Midwest Collaborative for Library Services
Open Mon-Wed 1-6, Thurs & Fri 1-5, Sat 9-Noon
Friends of the Library Group
Bookmobiles: 1. Dir, Brandi Sanders

TERRE HAUTE

R CENTRAL PRESBYTERIAN CHURCH LIBRARY*, 125 N Seventh St, 47807-3101. SAN 305-1269. Tel: 812-232-5049. E-mail: cpcoffice@thcpc.org. *Library Contact,* Valeri Kershaw
Founded 1960
Library Holdings: Bk Vols 2,492
Special Collections: Archives on Central Presbyterian Church & Presbyterian Church in the United States
Subject Interests: Church hist, Relig
Publications: CP Annual Report; Herald & Sunday Bulletin

R IMMANUEL EVANGELICAL LUTHERAN CHURCH LIBRARY*, 645 Poplar St, 47807. SAN 305-1331. Tel: 812-232-4972. FAX: 812-234-3935. Web Site: www.immanuelevluth.org. *Library Contact,* Kristin Schulz; E-mail: kjswrites@gmail.com; Staff 1 (Non-MLS 1)
Founded 1973
Library Holdings: Bk Titles 3,100; Videos 10
Subject Interests: Relig
Restriction: Mem only, Not open to pub

C INDIANA STATE UNIVERSITY*, Cunningham Memorial Library, 510 North 6 1/2 St, 47809. SAN 341-6496. Tel: 812-237-3700. Circulation Tel: 812-237-2541. Interlibrary Loan Service Tel: 812-237-2566. Reference Tel: 812-237-2580. Toll Free Tel: 800-851-4279. FAX: 812-237-3376. Interlibrary Loan Service FAX: 812-237-2567. Web Site: library.indstate.edu. *Dean, Libr Serv,* Robin A Crumrin; E-mail: Robin.Crumrin@indstate.edu; *Assoc Dean, Libr Serv,* Gregory Youngen; E-mail: Gregory.Youngen@indstate.edu; *Chair, Systems,* Stephen Patton; E-mail: Stephen.Patton@IndState.edu; *Chair, Pub Serv,* Brian Bunnett; E-mail: Brian.Bunnett@indstate.edu; *Chair, Spec Coll Project Dir,* Cinda May; E-mail: Cinda.May@indstate.edu; *Chair, Tech Serv,* Valentine Muyumba; E-mail: Valentine.Muyumba@indstate.edu; *Data Curation Librn,* Position Currently Open; *Educ Librn, Ref & Instruction Librn,* Edith Campbell; *Electronic Res Librn,* Melissa Gustafson; E-mail: melissa.gustafson@indstate.edu; *Emerging Tech Librn,* Position Currently Open; *Metadata Librn,* Natalie Bulick; E-mail: Natalie.Bulick@indstate.edu; *Ref & Instruction Librn,* Shelley Arvin; *Ref & Instruction Librn,* Cheryl Blevens; *Ref & Instruction Librn,* Karen Evans; *Ref & Instruction Librn,* Steve Hardin; *Ref & Instruction Librn,* Rolland McGiverin; *Ref & Instruction Librn,* Marsha Miller; *Librn, Syst & Serv,* Susan Frey; E-mail: susan.frey@indstate.edu; *Univ Archivist,* Katie Sutrina-Haney; *Curator, Permanent Art Coll,* Jocelyn Krueger; Staff 20 (MLS 18, Non-MLS 2)
Founded 1870. Enrl 11,810; Fac 558; Highest Degree: Doctorate
Jul 2016-Jun 2017 Income $4,465,893. Mats Exp $1,588,705, Books $183,382, Per/Ser (Incl. Access Fees) $450,890, Electronic Ref Mat (Incl. Access Fees) $947,746, Presv $6,687. Sal $2,446,159
Library Holdings: Audiobooks 1,257; AV Mats 114,184; CDs 27,055; DVDs 14,624; e-books 920,661; e-journals 132,221; Microforms 96,433; Bk Vols 862,939
Special Collections: American Education, Classics (Cunningham Coll) & Textbooks (Walker Coll); American Labor Movement (Debs Coll); History, Culture, Travel & Literature (Rare Books Coll); Human Memory (Hermann Coll); Indiana Education (Floyd Family Coll); Indiana Federal Writers Project/Program Coll; Indiana History & Culture (Indiana Coll); Local Publishing History & Culture (Faculty Coll); Pre-1901 Dictionaries & Word Books (Cordell Coll); Sheet & Orchestra Music (Kirk Coll); US Civil War (Neff-Guttridge Coll); Wabash Valley Visions & Voices Digital Memory Project. State Document Depository; UN Document Depository; US Document Depository
Automation Activity & Vendor Info: (Acquisitions) Innovative Interfaces, Inc - Sierra; (Cataloging) Innovative Interfaces, Inc - Sierra; (Circulation) Innovative Interfaces, Inc - Sierra; (Course Reserve) Docutek; (ILL) OCLC ILLiad; (OPAC) Innovative Interfaces, Inc - Sierra; (Serials) Innovative Interfaces, Inc - Sierra
Wireless access
Publications: Floyd Family Collection: Catalog of Textbooks & Related Materials; Sycamore.net; Walker Collection: Catalog of Textbooks
Partic in Academic Libraries of Indiana; Library Consortium of Vigo County; LYRASIS; Midwest Collaborative for Library Services; OCLC Online Computer Library Center, Inc
Special Services for the Deaf - Closed caption videos
Special Services for the Blind - Accessible computers; Aids for in-house use; Audio mat; Bks & mags in Braille, on rec, tape & cassette; Bks available with recordings; Bks on CD; Closed caption display syst; Disability awareness prog; Large print bks; Large screen computer & software; Scanner for conversion & translation of mats; Sound rec; ZoomText magnification & reading software
Friends of the Library Group

J IVY TECH COMMUNITY COLLEGE*, 8000 S Education Dr, 47802. SAN 341-6550. Tel: 812-298-2307. Toll Free Tel: 800-377-4882, Ext 2307. *Libr Dir,* David Barton; E-mail: dbarton@ivytech.edu
Founded 1967. Enrl 1,600; Fac 45
Library Holdings: AV Mats 730; Bk Titles 4,680; Bk Vols 4,870; Per Subs 71
Subject Interests: Bus & mgt, Health sci, Vocational educ
Wireless access
Open Mon-Thurs 7:30am-9pm, Fri 7:30-4:30, Sat 9-1

C ROSE-HULMAN INSTITUTE OF TECHNOLOGY*, John A Logan Library, 5500 Wabash Ave, 47803. SAN 305-1374. Tel: 812-877-8200. Web Site: www.rose-hulman.edu/Library. *Sr Dir,* Bernadette Ewen; E-mail: ewen@rose-hulman.edu; Staff 4 (MLS 3, Non-MLS 1)
Founded 1874. Enrl 2,000; Fac 185; Highest Degree: Master
Special Collections: Institute Archives
Subject Interests: Sci tech
Wireless access
Open Mon-Thurs 7:45am-Midnight, Fri 7:45-5, Sat 1-6, Sun Noon-Midnight

S SHELDON SWOPE ART MUSEUM LIBRARY*, 25 S Seventh St, 47807. SAN 305-1382. Tel: 812-238-1676. FAX: 812-238-1677. Web Site: www.swope.org. *Exec Dir,* Fred Nation; E-mail: nation@swope.org
Library Holdings: Bk Titles 1,250; Bk Vols 1,575; Per Subs 23
Special Collections: Rare Books
Subject Interests: Am archit, Arts & crafts (Am)
Partic in Midwest Collaborative for Library Services
Restriction: Not a lending libr, Open by appt only

M UNION HOSPITAL*, Medical Library, 1606 N Seventh St, 47804. SAN 305-1412. Tel: 812-238-7641. FAX: 812-238-7595. Web Site: www.uhhg.org. *Library Contact,* Alexis Sutliff; Staff 3 (MLS 2, Non-MLS 1)
Founded 1976
Library Holdings: Bk Titles 335; Bk Vols 1,119; Per Subs 60
Restriction: Staff use only

S VIGO COUNTY HISTORICAL MUSEUM LIBRARY, 929 Wabash Ave, 47803. SAN 323-4398. Tel: 812-235-9717. Web Site: www.vchsmuseum.org. *Exec Dir,* Marla Flowers; *Curator,* Suzy Quick; E-mail: suzy.quick@vchsmuseum.org
Library Holdings: Bk Titles 1,500
Wireless access
Open Tues-Sun 1-4
Friends of the Library Group

P VIGO COUNTY PUBLIC LIBRARY*, One Library Sq, 47807. SAN 341-6615. Tel: 812-232-1113. Reference Tel: 812-232-1110. Administration Tel: 812-232-1113, Ext 2202. FAX: 812-232-3208. E-mail: questions@vigo.lib.in.us. Web Site: www.vigo.lib.in.us. *Exec Dir,* Kristi Howe; E-mail: khowe@vigo.lib.in.us; *Dir, Pub Serv,* Margo Wilson; Tel: 812-232-1113, Ext 2207, E-mail: mwilson@vigo.lib.in.us; *Dir, Support Serv,* Dennis Callahan; Tel: 812-232-1113, Ext 2205, E-mail: dcallahan@vigo.lib.in.us; Staff 20 (MLS 15, Non-MLS 5)
Founded 1882. Pop 105,848; Circ 877,129
Library Holdings: AV Mats 32,837; e-books 1,780; Electronic Media & Resources 661; Bk Vols 171,999; Per Subs 865
Special Collections: Adult & Family Literacy; ESL (LifeLong Learning Center Literacy Materials); Community Archives Coll; Eugene V Debs Coll; Max Ehrmann Coll; Vigo County Marriage & Obituary Databases. Oral History
Automation Activity & Vendor Info: (Acquisitions) Innovative Interfaces, Inc - Millennium; (Cataloging) Innovative Interfaces, Inc - Millennium; (Circulation) Innovative Interfaces, Inc - Millennium; (Course Reserve) Innovative Interfaces, Inc - Millennium; (ILL) Innovative Interfaces, Inc - Millennium; (OPAC) Innovative Interfaces, Inc - Millennium; (Serials) Innovative Interfaces, Inc - Millennium
Wireless access
Function: Adult bk club, Adult literacy prog, After school storytime, Archival coll, Art exhibits, Bilingual assistance for Spanish patrons, Bk club(s), Bks on cassette, Bks on CD, Bus archives, Children's prog, Citizenship assistance, Computer training, Computers for patron use, Distance learning, Electronic databases & coll, Family literacy, Free DVD rentals, Health sci info serv, Holiday prog, Home delivery & serv to seniorr ctr & nursing homes, Homebound delivery serv, Homework prog, ILL available, Instruction & testing, Internet access, Large print keyboards, Learning ctr, Literacy & newcomer serv, Magnifiers for reading, Mail & tel

request accepted, Music CDs, Online cat, Online info literacy tutorials on the web & in blackboard, Online ref, Outreach serv, Outside serv via phone, mail, e-mail & web, Photocopying/Printing, Preschool outreach, Prog for adults, Prog for children & young adult, Ref serv available, Senior computer classes, Senior outreach, Serves people with intellectual disabilities, Spoken cassettes & CDs, Spoken cassettes & DVDs, Story hour, Summer reading prog, Tax forms, Teen prog, Telephone ref, VHS videos, Wheelchair accessible, Workshops, Writing prog
Publications: History of the Public Library in Vigo County, 1816-1975 (Local historical information); Preview (Monthly); Tutortalk (Newsletter)
Partic in Econ Develop Info Network; Indiana Public Library Internet Consortium; Library Consortium of Vigo County; Midwest Collaborative for Library Services
Special Services for the Deaf - Bks on deafness & sign lang; Closed caption videos; TDD equip
Special Services for the Blind - Audio mat; BiFolkal kits; Bks on cassette; Bks on CD; Computer with voice synthesizer for visually impaired persons; Descriptive video serv (DVS); Disability awareness prog; Extensive large print coll; Home delivery serv; Videos on blindness & physical disabilties
Open Mon-Thurs 9-9, Fri 9-6, Sat 9-5, Sun 1-5
Restriction: Non-resident fee
Friends of the Library Group
Branches: 1
WEST TERRE HAUTE BRANCH, 125 N Church St, West Terre Haute, 47885, SAN 341-6763. Tel: 812-232-2121. E-mail: west@vigo.lib.in.us. *Br Mgr,* Lauri Chandler; Tel: 812-232-1113, Ext 2901, E-mail: lchandler@vigo.lib.in.us; Staff 1 (MLS 1)
Library Holdings: AV Mats 1,790; Bk Titles 11,464; Bk Vols 12,523; Talking Bks 330
Function: Adult bk club, Electronic databases & coll, Family literacy, Homebound delivery serv, ILL available, Internet access, Online ref, Photocopying/Printing, Preschool outreach, Prog for adults, Prog for children & young adult, Ref serv available, Spoken cassettes & CDs, Spoken cassettes & DVDs, Summer reading prog, Tax forms, VHS videos
Open Mon & Wed 12-8, Tues, Thurs & Fri 10-6
Friends of the Library Group

THORNTOWN

P THORNTOWN PUBLIC LIBRARY, 124 N Market St, 46071-1144. SAN 305-1455. Tel: 765-436-7348. FAX: 765-436-7011. E-mail: info@thorntownpl.org. Web Site: www.thorntownpl.org. *Dir,* Christine Sterle; E-mail: csterle@thorntownpl.org; *Syst Adminr,* Britta Dorsey; E-mail: bdorsey@thorntownpl.org; *Head, Youth Serv,* Kathy Bowen; E-mail: kbowen@thorntownpl.org; *Ch,* Barb Lebo; E-mail: blebo@thorntownpl.org; *Local Hist Libm,* Sandy Naekel; E-mail: snaekel@thorntownpl.org; Staff 6 (MLS 3, Non-MLS 3)
Founded 1914. Pop 5,105; Circ 53,818
Library Holdings: AV Mats 5,293; Bk Titles 38,000; Per Subs 105; Videos 560
Special Collections: Local Indian Coll
Subject Interests: Local hist
Automation Activity & Vendor Info: (Cataloging) Evergreen; (Circulation) Evergreen; (ILL) Evergreen; (OPAC) Evergreen
Wireless access
Function: 24/7 Electronic res, 24/7 Online cat, Accelerated reader prog, Activity rm, Adult bk club, After school storytime, Archival coll, Audio & video playback equip for onsite use, Audiobks via web, AV serv, Bk club(s), Bks on cassette, Bks on CD, Children's prog, Computer training, Computers for patron use, E-Readers, Electronic databases & coll, Free DVD rentals, Genealogy discussion group, Holiday prog, Home delivery & serv to seniorr ctr & nursing homes, Homebound delivery serv, ILL available, Internet access, Laminating, Life-long learning prog for all ages, Magazines, Mail & tel request accepted, Meeting rooms, Microfiche/film & reading machines, Movies, Museum passes, Music CDs, Notary serv, Online cat, Outreach serv, Outside serv via phone, mail, e-mail & web, OverDrive digital audio bks, Photocopying/Printing, Preschool outreach, Preschool reading prog, Prog for adults, Prog for children & young adult, Ref serv available, Scanner, Story hour, Summer & winter reading prog, Summer reading prog, Tax forms, Teen prog, Telephone ref, Wheelchair accessible, Workshops, Writing prog
Partic in Evergreen Indiana Consortium
Open Mon & Fri 9-6, Tues-Thurs 9-8, Sat 10-4
Friends of the Library Group

TIPTON

P TIPTON COUNTY PUBLIC LIBRARY*, 127 E Madison St, 46072-1993. SAN 341-6798. Tel: 765-675-8761. FAX: 765-675-4475. E-mail: tipton@tiptonpl.org. Web Site: www.tiptonpl.org. *Dir,* Cherie Spencer; E-mail: cspencer@tiptonpl.org; *Asst Dir,* Jason Fields; E-mail: jfields@tiptonpl.org; Staff 16 (MLS 4, Non-MLS 12)
Founded 1902. Pop 16,532
Library Holdings: Bk Titles 89,000; Per Subs 318
Special Collections: Tipton & Indiana, bks, clippings & newspapers
Subject Interests: Indians
Automation Activity & Vendor Info: (Acquisitions) SirsiDynix; (Cataloging) SirsiDynix; (Circulation) SirsiDynix; (OPAC) SirsiDynix
Wireless access
Partic in Midwest Collaborative for Library Services
Open Mon-Thurs 9:30-8, Fri & Sat 9:30-5
Friends of the Library Group
Branches: 1
WINDFALL BRANCH, 109 McClellen St, Windfall, 46076, SAN 341-6828. Tel: 765-945-7655. FAX: 765-945-7655. E-mail: windfall@tiptonpl.org. *Dir,* Cherie Spencer
Library Holdings: Bk Vols 3,000
Open Mon-Fri 12-5

UNION CITY

P UNION CITY PUBLIC LIBRARY*, 408 N Columbia St, 47390-1404. SAN 305-1463. Tel: 765-964-4748. FAX: 765-964-0017. E-mail: ucpublib@gmail.com. Web Site: www.unioncity.lib.in.us. *Dir,* Paige Yoder; E-mail: director@unioncity.lib.in.us; Staff 1 (MLS 1)
Founded 1904. Pop 3,622; Circ 9,315. Sal $69,207 (Prof $46,249)
Library Holdings: Microforms 570; Bk Titles 19,449; Per Subs 51; Talking Bks 140; Videos 882
Special Collections: Local Newspapers, micro
Subject Interests: Genealogy, Local hist
Wireless access
Partic in Midwest Collaborative for Library Services
Special Services for the Blind - Bks on cassette; Bks on CD
Open Mon, Tues & Thurs 11-7, Fri 11-6, Sat 11-3

UPLAND

P BARTON REES POGUE MEMORIAL LIBRARY*, 29 W Washington St, 46989. (Mail add: PO Box 488, 46989-0488), SAN 305-1471. Tel: 765-998-2971. FAX: 765-998-2961. Web Site: upland.lib.in.us. *Dir,* Barbara Dixon; E-mail: bdlibrarydirector@yahoo.com; Staff 1 (Non-MLS 1)
Founded 1934. Pop 3,800; Circ 16,800
Library Holdings: Bk Vols 15,327; Per Subs 41; Videos 112
Automation Activity & Vendor Info: (Acquisitions) Evergreen; (Cataloging) Evergreen; (Circulation) Evergreen; (ILL) Evergreen; (OPAC) Evergreen
Wireless access
Function: 24/7 Electronic res, Art exhibits, Bks on cassette, Bks on CD, Children's prog, Computers for patron use, E-Readers, Electronic databases & coll, Free DVD rentals, Homebound delivery serv, ILL available, Instruction & testing, Magazines, Music CDs, Online cat, OverDrive digital audio bks, Photocopying/Printing, Prog for adults, Prog for children & young adult, Scanner, Spoken cassettes & CDs, Story hour, Summer reading prog, Tax forms
Open Tues & Thurs 2-8, Wed & Fri 10-6, Sat 9-1

C TAYLOR UNIVERSITY*, Zondervan Library, 236 W Reade Ave, 46989-1001. SAN 305-148X. Tel: 765-998-5522. Reference Tel: 765-998-4357. E-mail: zonlib@taylor.edu. Web Site: library.taylor.edu. *Asst Dir/Res Librn, Interim Dir,* Lana J Wilson; Tel: 765-998-5267, E-mail: lnwilson@taylor.edu; *Univ Archivist,* Ashley N Chu; Tel: 765-998-5242, E-mail: aschu@taylor.edu; *Assessment & Mkt Librn, Info Serv Librn,* Shawn D Denny; Tel: 765-998-5243, E-mail: shdenny@taylor.edu; *Coll Develop Librn, Instrul Serv Librn,* Linda J Lambert; Tel: 765-998-5270, E-mail: lnlambert@taylor.edu; *Coordr, Acq,* Shari Michael; Tel: 765-998-5264, E-mail: shmichael@taylor.edu; *Circ Coordr,* Jan King; Tel: 765-998-5266, E-mail: jnking@taylor.edu; *Resource Sharing Coord,* Kara Holloway; Tel: 765-998-5530, E-mail: Kara_Holloway@taylor.edu; Staff 10 (MLS 5, Non-MLS 5)
Founded 1846. Enrl 1,925; Fac 140; Highest Degree: Master
Jun 2014-May 2015 Income $1,004,581. Mats Exp $228,000, Books $27,000, Per/Ser (Incl. Access Fees) $35,000, Other Print Mats $15,000, AV Mat $3,000, Electronic Ref Mat (Incl. Access Fees) $145,000, Presv $3,000. Sal $372,817 (Prof $278,393)
Library Holdings: AV Mats 15,841; Bk Titles 125,715; Bk Vols 202,766; Per Subs 370
Automation Activity & Vendor Info: (Acquisitions) OCLC; (Cataloging) OCLC; (Circulation) OCLC; (ILL) OCLC; (Media Booking) OCLC; (OPAC) OCLC
Wireless access
Function: 24/7 Electronic res, Electronic databases & coll, ILL available, Online cat, Online ref
Partic in Midwest Collaborative for Library Services; OCLC Online Computer Library Center, Inc; Private Academic Library Network of Indiana
Open Mon-Thurs 7:30am-Midnight, Fri 7:30am-10pm, Sat 9am-10pm, Sun 7pm-Midnight

VALPARAISO

P PORTER COUNTY PUBLIC LIBRARY SYSTEM*, 103 Jefferson St, 46383-4820. SAN 341-6852. Tel: 219-462-0524. FAX: 219-477-4866. Web Site: pcpls.org. *Dir,* James D Cline; Tel: 219-462-0524, Ext 126, E-mail: jcline@pcpls.org; *Asst Dir,* Phyllis A Nelson; Tel: 219-462-0524, Ext 103; Staff 82 (MLS 10, Non-MLS 72)
Founded 1905. Pop 128,665; Circ 1,322,429
Library Holdings: AV Mats 163,358; Bks on Deafness & Sign Lang 300; High Interest/Low Vocabulary Bk Vols 1,500; Bk Vols 434,315; Per Subs 1,199
Special Collections: Oral History
Subject Interests: Genealogy, Indiana
Automation Activity & Vendor Info: (Acquisitions) SirsiDynix; (Circulation) SirsiDynix; (OPAC) SirsiDynix
Publications: Between-the-Stacks; Calendar of Events (Bimonthly); Summer Reading Booklet, Baby Talk Bibliography
Special Services for the Deaf - High interest/low vocabulary bks; TDD equip
Special Services for the Blind - Closed circuit TV magnifier; Computer with voice synthesizer for visually impaired persons; Reader equip
Open Mon-Thurs 9-9, Fri 9-6, Sat 9-5
Friends of the Library Group

Branches: 5

HEBRON PUBLIC, 201 W Sigler St, Hebron, 46341. (Mail add: PO Box 97, Hebron, 46341-0097), SAN 371-9561. Tel: 219-996-3684. FAX: 219-996-3680. *Br Mgr,* Jacqueline Lipski; Staff 9 (MLS 2, Non-MLS 7)
Founded 1917
Library Holdings: CDs 2,802; DVDs 4,312; Bk Vols 48,051
Automation Activity & Vendor Info: (OPAC) Innovative Interfaces, Inc
Function: Bk club(s), Bks on CD, Children's prog, Computers for patron use, Electronic databases & coll, Free DVD rentals, ILL available, Magazines, Magnifiers for reading, Mango lang, Music CDs, Online cat, Photocopying/Printing, Preschool outreach, Prog for adults, Prog for children & young adult, Scanner, Story hour, Study rm, Summer reading prog, Tax forms, Teen prog, Telephone ref, Wheelchair accessible
Open Mon & Wed 10-9, Tues, Thurs & Fri 10-6, Sat 9-5
Friends of the Library Group

KOUTS PUBLIC, 101 E Daumer Rd, Kouts, 46347, SAN 341-6917. Tel: 219-766-2271. FAX: 219-766-2273. *Br Mgr,* Hayley Dwyer; Staff 7 (MLS 1, Non-MLS 6)
Founded 1969
Library Holdings: Bk Vols 33,007
Open Mon, Wed & Fri 10-6, Tues & Thurs 10-9, Sat 9-5
Friends of the Library Group

PORTAGE PUBLIC, 2665 Irving St, Portage, 46368-3504, SAN 341-6941. Tel: 219-763-1508. FAX: 219-762-0101. *Br Mgr,* Kimberly Wiseman; Staff 16 (MLS 3, Non-MLS 13)
Founded 1970
Library Holdings: Bk Vols 109,858
Special Collections: Local History Coll (Portage, Portage Township & Ogden Dunes)
Subject Interests: Careers
Open Mon-Thurs 9-9, Fri 9-6, Sat 9-5, Sun 1-5
Friends of the Library Group

SOUTH HAVEN PUBLIC, 403 W 700 N, 46385-8407, SAN 341-6976. Tel: 219-759-4474. FAX: 219-759-4454. *Br Mgr,* Sarah Geer; Staff 6 (MLS 1, Non-MLS 5)
Founded 1974
Library Holdings: Bk Vols 47,048
Open Mon & Wed 10-9, Tues, Thurs & Fri 10-6, Sat 9-5
Friends of the Library Group

VALPARAISO PUBLIC, 103 Jefferson St, 46383-4820, SAN 341-6887. Tel: 219-462-0524. FAX: 219-477-4867. TDD: 800-743-3333. *Br Mgr,* Willow Cataldo; Staff 43 (MLS 8, Non-MLS 35)
Founded 1905
Library Holdings: Bk Vols 178,247
Subject Interests: Genealogy, Local hist
Open Mon-Thurs 9-9, Fri 9-6, Sat 9-5, Sun 1-5
Friends of the Library Group

C VALPARAISO UNIVERSITY*, Christopher Center for Library & Information Resources, 1410 Chapel Dr, 46383-6493. SAN 341-700X. Tel: 219-464-5500. Circulation Tel: 219-464-5366. Interlibrary Loan Service Tel: 219-464-5363. Administration Tel: 219-464-5364. Web Site: library.valpo.edu. *Dean of Libr,* Trisha Mileham; Tel: 219-464-5693, E-mail: trisha.mileham@valpo.edu; *Prof, Libr Sci, Sci & Electronic Serv Librn,* Ruth Connell; Tel: 219-464-5360, E-mail: ruth.connell@valpo.edu; *Asst Prof, Tech & Sci Librn,* Alison Downey; Tel: 219-464-6183, E-mail: Alison.Downey@valpo.edu; *Asst Prof, Media Cat Serv Librn, Sci Librn,* Pat Hogan-Vidal; Tel: 219-464-6128, E-mail: pat.hoganvidal@valpo.edu; *Assoc Prof, Sci Res Ctr Librn,* Rachael Muszkiewicz; Tel: 219-464-5464, E-mail: rachael.muszkiewicz@valpo.edu; *Assoc Prof,* Kimberly Whalen; Tel: 219-464-5754, E-mail: kimberly.whalen@valpo.edu; *Assoc Prof, Scholarly Communications Librn, Sci Librn,* Jonathan Bull; Tel: 219-464-5771, E-mail: jon.bull@valpo.edu; *Asst Prof, Asst Prof, Sci Librn, Sci/Eng Librn,* Nora Belzowski; Tel: 219-464-5023, E-mail: nora.belzowski@valpo.edu; *Asst Prof, Spec Coll Librn,* Judith Miller; Tel: 219-464-5808, E-mail: judith.miller@valpo.edu; *Circ Mgr,* Shannon Howe; Tel: 219-464-5168, E-mail: Shannon.Howe@valpo.edu; *Circ Mgr,* Sam Simpson; E-mail: Sam.Simpson@valpo.edu; *Evening Circ Mgr,* Sidney Findley; Tel: 219-464-5129, E-mail: Sidney.Findley@valpo.edu; *ILL Mgr,* Sara Shoppa; Tel: 219-464-5363, E-mail: Sara.Shoppa@valpo.edu; *Weekend Cir Mgr,* Anne Elizabeth Wilson-Cotey; Tel: 219-464-5125; *Acq Spec,* Rachel Volk; E-mail: rachel.volk@valpo.edu; *Cat Spec,* Stacy Fellers; Tel: 219-464-5160, E-mail: Stacy.Fellers@valpo.edu; *Govt Doc/Per Spec,* Kathy Rhynard; Tel: 219-464-6121, E-mail: kathy.rhynard@valpo.edu. Subject Specialists: *Health sci,* Kimberly Whalen; Staff 11 (MLS 10, Non-MLS 1)
Founded 1859. Enrl 3,658; Fac 346; Highest Degree: Master
Library Holdings: AV Mats 16,604; e-books 125,179; e-journals 51,971; Microforms 847,858; Bk Vols 341,508
Special Collections: University Archives. US Document Depository
Subject Interests: Lutheran studies, Theol
Automation Activity & Vendor Info: (Acquisitions) Innovative Interfaces, Inc - Millennium; (Cataloging) Innovative Interfaces, Inc; (Circulation) Innovative Interfaces, Inc - Millennium; (Course Reserve) Innovative Interfaces, Inc - Millennium; (ILL) OCLC ILLiad; (OPAC) Innovative Interfaces, Inc; (Serials) SerialsSolutions
Wireless access
Partic in Academic Libraries of Indiana; LYRASIS; Midwest Collaborative for Library Services; OCLC Online Computer Library Center, Inc; Private Academic Library Network of Indiana
Special Services for the Deaf - Closed caption videos
Special Services for the Blind - Bks on CD; ZoomText magnification & reading software
Open Mon-Thurs (Winter) 7:30am-2am, Fri 7:30am-9pm, Sat 9-6, Sun 10am-2am; Mon-Thurs (Summer) 8am-10pm, Fri 8-5

Departmental Libraries:

CL SCHOOL OF LAW LIBRARY, 656 S Greenwich St, 46383, SAN 341-7034. Tel: 219-465-7827. FAX: 219-465-7917. Web Site: www.valpo.edu/law. *Assoc Dean, Educ Serv Librn, Info Serv,* Steven Probst; Tel: 219-465-7820, E-mail: steven.probst@valpo.edu; *Assoc Law Librn,* Michael Bushbaum; E-mail: michael.bushbaum@valpo.edu; *Fac Serv Librn,* Debra Denslaw; Tel: 219-465-7876, E-mail: debra.denslaw@valpo.edu; *Digital Serv Mgr, Govt Doc Coordr,* Alison Downey; Tel: 219-464-7989, E-mail: Alison.Downey@valpo.edu; *Acq Asst, Cat,* Kathleen Mance; Tel: 219-465-7874, E-mail: Kathleen.Mance@valpo.edu; Staff 12 (MLS 7, Non-MLS 5)
Founded 1879. Enrl 560; Fac 37; Highest Degree: Doctorate
Library Holdings: AV Mats 2,332; Microforms 983,622; Bk Titles 185,131; Bk Vols 349,068; Per Subs 2,458
Special Collections: Supreme Court Records & Briefs Coll. State Document Depository; US Document Depository
Automation Activity & Vendor Info: (Acquisitions) Innovative Interfaces, Inc; (Cataloging) Innovative Interfaces, Inc; (Circulation) Innovative Interfaces, Inc; (Course Reserve) Innovative Interfaces, Inc; (ILL) OCLC ILLiad; (OPAC) Innovative Interfaces, Inc; (Serials) Innovative Interfaces, Inc
Partic in Academic Libraries of Indiana
Publications: Valparaiso University Law Review
Open Mon-Thurs 7:30am-Midnight, Fri 7:30am-10pm, Sat 9am-10pm, Sun 9-Midnight

VAN BUREN

P VAN BUREN PUBLIC LIBRARY, 115 S First St, 46991. SAN 305-151X. Tel: 765-934-2171. FAX: 765-934-4926. Web Site: vbpl.lib.in.us. *Dir,* Shiloh McMullen; E-mail: director@vbpl.lib.in.us; Staff 1 (Non-MLS 1)
Founded 1917. Pop 2,046; Circ 23,000
Library Holdings: Bk Titles 23,911; Bk Vols 24,688; Per Subs 57; Talking Bks 48; Videos 1,511
Automation Activity & Vendor Info: (Cataloging) Follett Software; (Circulation) Follett Software
Function: After school storytime, Computer training, Homebound delivery serv, ILL available, Photocopying/Printing, Prog for adults, Prog for children & young adult, Summer reading prog, Tax forms, VHS videos
Open Mon, Wed & Fri 12-5, Tues & Thurs 12-7, Sat 9-1

VERSAILLES

P TYSON LIBRARY*, 325 W Tyson St, 47042. (Mail add: PO Box 769, 47042-0769), SAN 376-5326. Tel: 812-689-5894. FAX: 812-689-7401. E-mail: info@tysonlibrary.org. Web Site: tysonlibrary.org. *Dir,* Brenda Campbell; Staff 5 (MLS 1, Non-MLS 4)
Founded 1942. Pop 3,000
Library Holdings: Audiobooks 500; CDs 300; DVDs 1,000; Bk Titles 8,000; Bk Vols 10,000; Per Subs 50; Videos 1,000
Special Collections: Indiana Coll; James Tyson Coll; Ripley Coll; Versailles Coll
Subject Interests: Fiction, Hist, Lit, Relig

Automation Activity & Vendor Info: (Cataloging) Innovative Interfaces, Inc; (Circulation) Innovative Interfaces, Inc; (OPAC) Innovative Interfaces, Inc
Wireless access
Open Mon-Thurs 10-8, Fri 10-6, Sat 10-3

VEVAY

P SWITZERLAND COUNTY PUBLIC LIBRARY*, 205 Ferry St, 47043. SAN 305-1528. Tel: 812-427-3363. FAX: 812-427-3654. E-mail: information@scpl.us. Web Site: scpl.us. *Dir,* Emily Fox; E-mail: director@scpl.us; Staff 3 (MLS 1, Non-MLS 2)
Founded 1915. Pop 10,613; Circ 48,368
Library Holdings: Bk Titles 37,390; Bk Vols 39,684; Per Subs 78; Talking Bks 210; Videos 376
Special Collections: Switzerland County History, bks, VF, microfilm, a-tapes. Oral History
Automation Activity & Vendor Info: (Acquisitions) Evergreen; (Cataloging) Evergreen; (OPAC) Evergreen
Wireless access
Function: Activity rm, Adult bk club, Adult literacy prog, Audiobks via web, Bks on CD, Children's prog, Computer training, Computers for patron use, Digital talking bks, Free DVD rentals, ILL available, Internet access, Laminating, Magazines, Microfiche/film & reading machines, Music CDs, Online cat, Outreach serv, OverDrive digital audio bks, Photocopying/Printing, Preschool outreach, Prog for children & young adult, Scanner, Senior outreach, Story hour, Summer reading prog, Tax forms, Teen prog, Wheelchair accessible
Partic in Evergreen Indiana Consortium; Midwest Collaborative for Library Services
Open Mon-Thurs 9-8, Fri & Sat 9-5

VINCENNES

P KNOX COUNTY PUBLIC LIBRARY*, 502 N Seventh St, 47591-2119. SAN 305-1544. Tel: 812-886-4380. FAX: 812-886-0342. Web Site: www.kcpl.lib.in.us. *Dir,* Emily Cooper Bunyan; E-mail: ebunyan2001@yahoo.com; *Youth Librn,* Amy Blake; *Tech Mgr,* Tyler Hannah; *Circ Supvr,* Paula Smith; Staff 6 (MLS 4, Non-MLS 2)
Founded 1889. Pop 33,978; Circ 240,000
Library Holdings: Audiobooks 8,867; AV Mats 8,424; CDs 1,259; DVDs 1,452; High Interest/Low Vocabulary Bk Vols 250; Large Print Bks 3,000; Bk Titles 92,431; Bk Vols 123,895; Per Subs 253; Talking Bks 3,392; Videos 3,318
Special Collections: Daughters of the American Revolution, Francis Vigo Chapter; Early Vincennes Court Records 1532-1805; Knox County Records; Northwest Territory History; Vincennes History; Vincennes University-Lewis Library Genealogy Coll
Subject Interests: Genealogy, Hist
Automation Activity & Vendor Info: (Cataloging) Innovative Interfaces, Inc; (Circulation) Innovative Interfaces, Inc; (OPAC) Innovative Interfaces, Inc
Wireless access
Function: Archival coll, ILL available, Ref serv available, Telephone ref
Publications: Friends (Newsletter)
Partic in OCLC Online Computer Library Center, Inc
Special Services for the Deaf - TDD equip
Special Services for the Blind - Bks on cassette; Computer with voice synthesizer for visually impaired persons; Home delivery serv
Open Mon-Wed 8:30am-9pm, Thurs-Sat 8:30-5:30, Sun 1-5
Friends of the Library Group

SR OLD CATHEDRAL LIBRARY*, 205 Church St, 47591-1133. (Mail add: 106 S Third St, 47591). Tel: 812-882-5638. FAX: 812-882-4042. Toll Free FAX: 800-886-6443. Web Site: www.evdio.org/old-cathedral-library–museum.html. *Adminr,* Fr Tony Ernst; E-mail: ternst@evdio.org; Staff 1 (Non-MLS 1)
Founded 1794
Library Holdings: Bk Titles 11,000; Bk Vols 12,100
Special Collections: Brute Coll
Subject Interests: Hist, Theol
Function: Res libr
Restriction: Open by appt only

C VINCENNES UNIVERSITY, Shake Library, Shake Library, 1002 N First St, 47591. SAN 341-7069. Tel: 812-888-4165. FAX: 812-888-5471. Web Site: www.vinu.edu/web/shake-library/welcome. *Dir, Libr Serv,* Charla Gilbert; Tel: 812-888-5377, E-mail: cgilbert@vinu.edu; *Pub Serv Librn,* Jamie Cox; Tel: 812-888-4427, E-mail: JCox@vinu.edu; *Tech Serv,* Position Currently Open; Staff 12 (MLS 3, Non-MLS 9)
Founded 1959. Enrl 3,379; Fac 210; Highest Degree: Bachelor
Special Collections: Lewis Historical Coll Library
Subject Interests: Univ hist
Automation Activity & Vendor Info: (Acquisitions) OCLC Worldshare Management Services; (Cataloging) OCLC Worldshare Management Services; (Circulation) OCLC Worldshare Management Services; (Course Reserve) OCLC Worldshare Management Services; (Discovery) OCLC Worldshare Management Services; (ILL) OCLC WorldShare Interlibrary Loan; (OPAC) OCLC Worldshare Management Services; (Serials) EBSCO Online
Wireless access
Function: 24/7 Online cat, Archival coll, Computers for patron use, Electronic databases & coll, Internet access, Mail & tel request accepted, Online cat, Online ref, Outside serv via phone, mail, e-mail & web, Photocopying/Printing, Ref & res, Ref serv available, Res assist avail, Scanner, Telephone ref
Partic in Academic Libraries of Indiana; LYRASIS; Midwest Collaborative for Library Services
Open Mon-Thurs 7:30am-Midnight, Fri 7:30-6, Sat 11-6, Sun 2-Midnight
Restriction: Access at librarian's discretion, In-house use for visitors, Non-circulating of rare bks, Open to pub for ref & circ; with some limitations, Open to students, fac & staff, Pub use on premises

WABASH

P WABASH CARNEGIE PUBLIC LIBRARY*, 188 W Hill St, 46992-3048. SAN 305-1560. Tel: 260-563-2972. FAX: 260-563-0222. E-mail: general@wabash.lib.in.us. Web Site: www.wabash.lib.in.us. *Dir,* Ware W Wimberly, III; E-mail: warew@wabash.lib.in.us; *Ref (Info Servs),* Polly Howell; Staff 10 (MLS 3, Non-MLS 7)
Founded 1903. Pop 11,743; Circ 145,000
Library Holdings: AV Mats 6,755; Bk Vols 67,466; Per Subs 168
Special Collections: Gene Stratton-Porter Coll. Oral History
Subject Interests: Gardening, Genealogy, Local hist, Travel
Automation Activity & Vendor Info: (Cataloging) Innovative Interfaces, Inc; (Circulation) Innovative Interfaces, Inc; (OPAC) Innovative Interfaces, Inc
Wireless access
Open Mon-Thurs 9-8, Fri & Sat 9-5

WAKARUSA

P WAKARUSA PUBLIC LIBRARY*, Wakarusa-Olive & Harrison Township Public Library, 124 N Elkhart St, 46573. (Mail add: PO Box 485, 46573-0485), SAN 305-1579. Tel: 574-862-2465. FAX: 574-862-4156. E-mail: info@wakarusa.lib.in.us. Web Site: www.wakarusapubliclibrary.org. *Libr Dir,* Matt Bowers; E-mail: mbowers@wakarusa.lib.in.us; Staff 10 (Non-MLS 10)
Founded 1945. Pop 7,500; Circ 110,000
Library Holdings: Audiobooks 4,000; CDs 1,400; DVDs 3,800; Large Print Bks 1,300; Bk Titles 58,000; Per Subs 80
Special Collections: Local History (Wakarusa, Indiana), pictures, clippings, oral, pamphlets
Automation Activity & Vendor Info: (Acquisitions) SirsiDynix; (Cataloging) SirsiDynix; (Circulation) SirsiDynix; (OPAC) SirsiDynix
Wireless access
Partic in Midwest Collaborative for Library Services
Open Mon, Tues & Thurs 9-8, Wed & Fri 9-5:30, Sat 9-2
Friends of the Library Group

WALKERTON

P WALKERTON-LINCOLN TOWNSHIP PUBLIC LIBRARY*, Hiler Media Center, 406 Adams St, 46574. SAN 305-1587. Tel: 574-279-0177. E-mail: walkerton.lincoln.library@gmail.com. Web Site: walkerton.lib.in.us. *Dir,* Jennifer Cygert; E-mail: jennifercygert@walkerton.lib.in.us
Founded 1913. Pop 3,053; Circ 14,866
Library Holdings: Large Print Bks 500; Bk Vols 17,268; Per Subs 22; Talking Bks 681; Videos 300
Subject Interests: Local hist
Automation Activity & Vendor Info: (Cataloging) Surpass; (Circulation) Surpass
Wireless access
Partic in Midwest Collaborative for Library Services
Open Mon-Fri 10-5

WALTON

P WALTON & TIPTON TOWNSHIP PUBLIC LIBRARY*, Walton Public, 110 N Main St, 46994. (Mail add: PO Box 406, 46994), SAN 305-1595. Tel: 574-626-2234. FAX: 574-626-2234. E-mail: waltonlibrary@walton.lib.in.us. Web Site: www.walton.lib.in.us. *Dir, Ref Librn,* Karen S Troutman; E-mail: ktroutman@walton.lib.in.us; Staff 3 (Non-MLS 3)
Founded 1914. Pop 2,490; Circ 43,000
Jan 2013-Dec 2013 Income $146,273. Mats Exp $17,394, Books $7,693, Per/Ser (Incl. Access Fees) $1,200, AV Mat $7,155. Sal $80,119 (Prof $25,000)
Library Holdings: Audiobooks 172; AV Mats 732; CDs 147; DVDs 603; e-books 93; Large Print Bks 685; Bk Titles 23,884; Bk Vols 24,120; Per Subs 68; Talking Bks 62; Videos 1,908

Subject Interests: Indiana
Wireless access
Function: Accelerated reader prog, Adult bk club, Adult literacy prog, After school storytime, Art exhibits, Audio & video playback equip for onsite use, AV serv, Bilingual assistance for Spanish patrons, Children's prog, Citizenship assistance, Computer training, Computers for patron use, Home delivery & serv to seniorr ctr & nursing homes, ILL available, Photocopying/Printing, Wheelchair accessible
Publications: Newsletter (Monthly)
Open Tues-Fri 9-6:30, Sat 10-2
Restriction: Lending limited to county residents
Friends of the Library Group

WANATAH

P WANATAH PUBLIC LIBRARY*, 114 S Main St, 46390. (Mail add: PO Box 299, 46390-0299), SAN 305-1609. Tel: 219-733-9303. FAX: 219-733-2763. E-mail: wanatahl@hotmail.com. Web Site: www.wanatahlibrary.com. *Dir*, Don Parker; Staff 3 (Non-MLS 3)
Founded 1915. Pop 1,677; Circ 14,586
Library Holdings: Audiobooks 100; AV Mats 100; Bks on Deafness & Sign Lang 10; CDs 50; DVDs 2,000; e-books 1; Large Print Bks 500; Microforms 1; Bk Vols 20,000; Per Subs 35
Special Collections: Wanatah Mirror Newspaper Complete Coll 1896-1969
Subject Interests: Hist
Automation Activity & Vendor Info: (Acquisitions) Follett Software; (Cataloging) Follett Software; (Circulation) Follett Software; (OPAC) Follett Software; (Serials) Follett Software
Wireless access
Function: 24/7 Online cat, Activity rm, Adult bk club, Adult literacy prog
Special Services for the Blind - Talking bk serv referral
Open Mon 11-7, Tues 9-5, Wed 11-6, Thur & Fri 11-5, Sat 9-1
Restriction: Access at librarian's discretion, Use of others with permission of librn

WARREN

P WARREN PUBLIC LIBRARY, 123 E Third St, 46792. (Mail add: PO Box 327, 46792-0327), SAN 305-1617. Tel: 260-375-3450. FAX: 260-375-3450. E-mail: warrenpl@warren.lib.in.us. Web Site: www.warren.lib.in.us. *Dir*, Robert Neuenschwander; *Asst Dir*, Susan Mills; Staff 2 (MLS 1, Non-MLS 1)
Founded 1916. Pop 2,629; Circ 15,078
Library Holdings: Bk Titles 19,911; Bk Vols 21,112; Per Subs 89; Talking Bks 162; Videos 574
Special Collections: Local Newspaper, micro
Automation Activity & Vendor Info: (Cataloging) Evergreen; (Circulation) Evergreen; (OPAC) Evergreen; (Serials) Evergreen
Wireless access
Partic in Northern Indiana Computer Consortium for Libraries
Open Mon, Tues & Thurs 1-6, Wed 3-8, Fri 10-6, Sat 10-2
Friends of the Library Group

WARSAW

S KOSCIUSKO COUNTY HISTORICAL SOCIETY*, Research Library & Archives, 121 N Indiana St, 46581. (Mail add: PO Box 1071, 46581-1071), SAN 373-4501. Tel: 574-269-1078. E-mail: librarian@kosciuskohistory.com. Web Site: kosciuskohistory.com. *Librn*, Sharon Sucec
Library Holdings: Bk Titles 32,911; Bk Vols 34,100; Per Subs 120
Special Collections: County Newspapers (except Warsaw); County Records, 1830-present
Subject Interests: Genealogy, Local hist
Wireless access
Open Wed-Sat 10-4
Friends of the Library Group

P WARSAW COMMUNITY PUBLIC LIBRARY, 310 E Main St, 46580-2882. SAN 305-1625. Tel: 574-267-6011. FAX: 574-269-7739. E-mail: info@warsawlibrary.org. Web Site: www.warsawlibrary.org. *Dir*, Ann M Zydek; *Asst Dir, Cat*, Joni L Brookins; *Ch Serv*, Erin Streeter; *Community Outreach*, Anna Jackson; *Info Serv*, Dana L Owen; Staff 33 (MLS 6, Non-MLS 27)
Founded 1915. Pop 27,780; Circ 383,109
Library Holdings: AV Mats 17,576; DVDs 25,265; e-books 90,424; e-journals 126; Bk Vols 166,901; Per Subs 178
Special Collections: Old & Current Local Papers, microfilms
Subject Interests: Genealogy, Local hist
Automation Activity & Vendor Info: (Acquisitions) SirsiDynix; (Cataloging) SirsiDynix; (Circulation) SirsiDynix; (ILL) OCLC; (OPAC) SirsiDynix; (Serials) SirsiDynix
Wireless access
Function: 24/7 Electronic res, 24/7 Online cat, 3D Printer, Accelerated reader prog, Activity rm, Art exhibits, Audiobks on Playaways & MP3, Audiobks via web, Bks on CD, Children's prog, Computer training, Computers for patron use, Digital talking bks, E-Reserves, Electronic databases & coll, Free DVD rentals, Holiday prog, Home delivery & serv to seniorr ctr & nursing homes, Homebound delivery serv, ILL available, Internet access, Laminating, Life-long learning prog for all ages, Magazines, Mail & tel request accepted, Mango lang, Meeting rooms, Microfiche/film & reading machines, Movies, Music CDs, Online cat, Outreach serv, Outside serv via phone, mail, e-mail & web, OverDrive digital audio bks, Photocopying/Printing, Printer for laptops & handheld devices, Prog for adults, Prog for children & young adult, Ref serv available, Res assist avail, Scanner, Spanish lang bks, STEM programs, Story hour, Study rm, Summer & winter reading prog, Tax forms, Teen prog, Telephone ref, Wheelchair accessible, Workshops, Writing prog
Publications: Check It Out (Newsletter)
Partic in Midwest Collaborative for Library Services
Open Mon & Tues 10-8, Wed-Fri 10-6, Sat 10-2
Friends of the Library Group

WASHINGTON

P WASHINGTON CARNEGIE PUBLIC LIBRARY*, 300 W Main St, 47501-2698. SAN 305-1633. Tel: 812-254-4586. FAX: 812-254-4585. E-mail: info@washingtonpubliclibrary.org. Web Site: www.washingtonpubliclibrary.org. *Dir*, Teresa Heidenreich; E-mail: teresah@washingtonpubliclibrary.org; *Adult Serv Mgr, Mgr, Programming*, Rick Chambon; *Youth Serv Mgr*, Donita Mattingly. Subject Specialists: *Acctg, Admin, Human resource mgt*, Teresa Heidenreich; Staff 5 (MLS 3, Non-MLS 2)
Founded 1902. Pop 11,509; Circ 137,000
Jan 2013-Dec 2013 Income (Main & Associated Libraries) $413,604, State $24,494, Locally Generated Income $337,408, Other $51,702. Mats Exp $55,000, Books $29,000, Per/Ser (Incl. Access Fees) $6,500, AV Mat $11,000, Electronic Ref Mat (Incl. Access Fees) $8,500. Sal $216,500 (Prof $154,220)
Library Holdings: Audiobooks 1,267; Bks on Deafness & Sign Lang 16; Braille Volumes 2; CDs 543; DVDs 658; e-books 10,816; Large Print Bks 647; Bk Titles 44,105; Per Subs 75; Videos 820
Special Collections: Daviess County Indiana History
Subject Interests: Local hist
Automation Activity & Vendor Info: (Acquisitions) Follett Software; (Cataloging) Follett Software; (Circulation) Follett Software; (OPAC) Follett Software
Wireless access
Function: Ref & res
Partic in Midwest Collaborative for Library Services
Open Mon-Wed 10-7, Thurs & Fri 10-2
Restriction: Circ to mem only
Friends of the Library Group

WATERLOO

P WATERLOO-GRANT TOWNSHIP PUBLIC LIBRARY, 300 S Wayne St, 46793. (Mail add: PO Box 707, 46793-0707), SAN 305-1641. Tel: 260-837-4491. FAX: 260-837-9148. E-mail: info@waterloo.lib.in.us. Web Site: www.waterloo.lib.in.us. *Cataloger, Interim Dir*, Jennifer Hernandez; E-mail: jhernandez@waterloo.lib.in.us; *Youth Serv*, Jordan Eckert; Staff 2 (Non-MLS 2)
Founded 1913. Pop 3,100; Circ 51,000
Library Holdings: Audiobooks 1,510; AV Mats 2,030; Bk Vols 28,000; Per Subs 100
Automation Activity & Vendor Info: (Acquisitions) Evergreen; (Cataloging) Evergreen; (Circulation) Evergreen; (OPAC) Evergreen
Wireless access
Partic in Evergreen Indiana Consortium
Open Mon-Thurs 9-8, Fri 9-5, Sat 9-1
Friends of the Library Group

WAVELAND

P WAVELAND-BROWN TOWNSHIP PUBLIC LIBRARY*, 115 E Green, 47989. SAN 305-165X. Tel: 765-435-2700. FAX: 765-435-2434. *Dir*, Rick Payne; E-mail: director@waveland.lib.in.us; *Asst Librn*, Sandra L Greene; Staff 2 (Non-MLS 2)
Founded 1916. Pop 1,750; Circ 18,000
Library Holdings: AV Mats 1,500; Large Print Bks 300; Bk Vols 14,000; Per Subs 48; Talking Bks 150
Partic in Evergreen Indiana Consortium
Open Mon 9-5, Tues & Thurs 1-5 & 6:30-8, Wed & Fri 1-5, Sat 9:30-12:30

WEST LAFAYETTE

C PURDUE UNIVERSITY LIBRARIES*, 504 W State St, 47907-2058. SAN 341-7158. Tel: 765-494-2900. Interlibrary Loan Service Tel: 765-494-2800. FAX: 765-494-0156. E-mail: libinfo@purdue.edu. Web Site: www.lib.purdue.edu. *Interim Dean of Libr*, Rhonda Phillips; E-mail:

rphillips@purdue.edu; *Assoc Dean, Acad Affairs,* Donna Ferullo; Tel: 765-494-0978, E-mail: ferullo@purdue.edu; *Assoc Dean, Res,* D Scott Brandt; Tel: 765-494-2889, E-mail: techman@purdue.edu; Staff 194 (MLS 84, Non-MLS 110)
Founded 1874. Enrl 40,090; Fac 2,743; Highest Degree: Doctorate
Library Holdings: Bk Vols 2,509,158; Per Subs 40,094
Special Collections: Aviation, Women Pilots, History of Flight (The George Palmer Putnam Coll of Amelia Earhart Papers); Design of The Golden Gate Bridge (Charles A Ellis Papers); Economic History (Krannert Special Coll); English & American Literature (George Ade Manuscripts, Charles Major Manuscripts); History of Engineering (Goss Coll, Andrey A Potter Papers); Industrial Management, Home Economics, Time & Motion Studies (Frank & Lillian Gilbreth Papers); Political Cartoons (John T McCutcheon Coll); Psychedelics (Psychoactive Substances Research Coll); Space Exploration (Neil Armstrong Papers, Janice Voss Papers, Roy Bridges Papers); Typography & Book Design (Bruce Rogers Coll-Anna Embree Baker Rogers Coll). State Document Depository; UN Document Depository; US Document Depository
Wireless access
Partic in Academic Libraries of Indiana; Association of Research Libraries; Big Ten Academic Alliance; Center for Research Libraries; Midwest Collaborative for Library Services; OCLC Online Computer Library Center, Inc

Departmental Libraries:

AVIATION TECHNOLOGY, Airport Terminal, Rm 163, 1501 Aviation Dr, 47907. (Mail add: 504 W State St, 47907), SAN 341-7182. Tel: 765-494-7640. FAX: 765-494-0156. E-mail: avtlib@purdue.edu. Web Site: www.lib.purdue.edu/libraries/avtech. *Librn,* Wei S Zakharov; Tel: 765-494-2872, E-mail: wzakharov@purdue.edu
Open Mon-Thurs 8-7, Fri 8-5, Sat & Sun 1-5

JOHN W HICKS UNDERGRADUATE LIBRARY, Hicks Undergraduate Library, Ground Flr, 504 W State St, 47907-2058, SAN 341-7166. Tel: 765-494-6733. FAX: 765-494-6744. E-mail: ugrl@purdue.edu. Web Site: www.lib.purdue.edu/libraries/ugrl. *Head of Libr,* Erla P Heyns; E-mail: eheyns@purdue.edu
Open Mon-Thurs 7:30am-Midnight, Fri 7:30-5, Sat 1-5, Sun 1pm-Midnight

HUMANITIES, SOCIAL SCIENCE & EDUCATION LIBRARY, Stewart Ctr, Rm 135, 504 W State St, 47907. (Mail add: HSSE, 504 W State St, 47907-2058), SAN 341-7336. Tel: 765-494-2831. FAX: 765-494-9007. E-mail: hsselib@purdue.edu. Web Site: www.lib.purdue.edu/libraries/hsse. *Head of Libr,* Erla P Heyns; E-mail: eheyns@purdue.edu
Open Mon-Thurs 8am-Midnight, Fri 8-6, Sat 1-5, Sun 1-Midnight

MANAGEMENT & ECONOMICS, Krannert Bldg, 2nd Flr, 403 W State St, 47907. (Mail add: MGMT, 403 W State St, 47907-2058), SAN 341-7395. Tel: 765-494-2920. Circulation Tel: 765-494-2919. FAX: 765-494-2923. E-mail: parrlib@purdue.edu. Web Site: www.lib.purdue.edu/libraries/mgmt. *Head of Libr,* Erla P Heyns; E-mail: eheyns@purdue.edu
Open Mon-Thurs 8am-Midnight, Fri 8-5, Sat 1-5, Sun 1pm-Midnight

MATHEMATICAL SCIENCES, Mathematical Sciences Bldg 311, 105 N University St, 47907. (Mail add: MATH, 504 W State St, 47907-2058), SAN 341-745X. Tel: 765-494-2855. FAX: 765-494-0548. E-mail: mathlib@purdue.edu. Web Site: www.lib.purdue.edu/libraries/math. *Head of Libr,* Nastasha Johnson; Tel: 765-494-4851, E-mail: nejohnson@purdue.edu
Open Mon-Thurs 8am-10pm, Fri 8-5, Sat 1-5, Sun 1-10

CM VETERINARY MEDICAL, Lynn Hall of Veterinary Medicine 1133, 625 Harrison St, 47907. (Mail add: VETM, 504 W State St, 47907-2058), SAN 341-7603. Tel: 765-494-2853. E-mail: vetmlib@purdue.edu. Web Site: www.lib.purdue.edu/Libraries/vetmed. *Head of Libr,* Jane S Yatcilla; Tel: 765-494-2856, E-mail: janeyat@purdue.edu
Open Mon-Thurs 8am-10pm, Fri 8-5, Sat 1-5, Sun 1-10

P WEST LAFAYETTE PUBLIC LIBRARY*, 208 W Columbia St, 47906. SAN 305-1676. Tel: 765-743-2261. FAX: 765-743-0540. E-mail: refdesk@wlaf.lib.in.us. Web Site: www.westlafayettepubliclibrary.org. *Dir,* Nick Schenkel; E-mail: nick@wlaf.lib.in.us; *Asst Dir,* Scott Tracey; E-mail: stracey@wlaf.lib.in.us; *Librn,* Erica Brown; *Cat,* Jane Dolan; *Ch Serv,* Linda Klein; *Circ,* Phyllis Heath; *Patron Serv,* Ruth Cushman; Staff 12 (MLS 3, Non-MLS 9)
Founded 1922. Pop 28,787; Circ 308,613
Library Holdings: AV Mats 4,834; Bk Titles 116,421; Bk Vols 118,111; Per Subs 484; Videos 598
Special Collections: Cancer Coll; Children's Literature Award Winners (Dickey Coll); Cookbooks (Reisner Coll); ESL/English as a Second Language Coll; Foreign Language Coll (Chinese, Korean, Hindi & Other Languages); Large Print Books Coll; Young Adult & Adult Graphic Novels
Automation Activity & Vendor Info: (Acquisitions) TLC (The Library Corporation); (Cataloging) TLC (The Library Corporation); (OPAC) TLC (The Library Corporation)
Wireless access
Publications: e-Newsletter (Monthly); Friends of the West Lafayette Public Library (Newsletter)
Partic in Midwest Collaborative for Library Services; Wabash Valley Area Libr Servs Authority
Special Services for the Deaf - Staff with knowledge of sign lang; TDD equip
Open Mon-Thurs 10-8, Fri 10-6, Sat 10-5, Sun 1-5
Friends of the Library Group

WEST LEBANON

P WEST LEBANON-PIKE TOWNSHIP PUBLIC LIBRARY*, 200 N High St, 47991. (Mail add: PO Box 277, 47991-0277), SAN 376-5377. Tel: 765-893-4605. FAX: 765-893-4605. E-mail: westleblibrary@hotmail.com. Web Site: westlebanon.lib.in.us. *Dir,* Terri Wargo; Staff 1 (Non-MLS 1)
Founded 1916. Pop 1,185; Circ 6,957
Jan 2014-Dec 2014. Mats Exp $12,519, Books $9,673, Per/Ser (Incl. Access Fees) $1,127, AV Mat $1,719. Sal $49,881 (Prof $37,400)
Library Holdings: CDs 35; DVDs 924; Microforms 2; Bk Titles 12,810; Per Subs 38
Wireless access
Function: Computers for patron use, Magnifiers for reading, Notary serv, Photocopying/Printing, Summer reading prog, VHS videos
Open Mon & Wed 11-7, Tues, Thurs & Fri 11-5, Sat 9-2

WEST TERRE HAUTE

R FIRST BAPTIST CHURCH OF WEST TERRE HAUTE LIBRARY*, 205 S Fifth, 47885. (Mail add: PO Box 126, 47885), SAN 305-1293. Tel: 812-533-2016. E-mail: libraryfbcwth@gmail.com. *Librn,* Ruth Ridener; *Librn,* Stardust Watson; *Libr Tech,* Paul Watson; Staff 5 (Non-MLS 5)
Founded 1966
Library Holdings: Audiobooks 5; AV Mats 20; Bks on Deafness & Sign Lang 2; Braille Volumes 1; CDs 7; DVDs 7; Bk Titles 6,500; Bk Vols 6,605; Videos 40
Subject Interests: Christianity, Fiction, Missions & missionaries, Music, Relig
Automation Activity & Vendor Info: (Cataloging) JayWil Software Development, Inc; (Circulation) JayWil Software Development, Inc
Function: AV serv
Open Wed 6:30pm-9pm, Sun 9-12 & 5:30-7:30

WESTFIELD

P WESTFIELD WASHINGTON PUBLIC LIBRARY*, 333 W Hoover St, 46074-9283. SAN 305-1692. Tel: 317-896-9391. FAX: 317-896-3702. Web Site: www.wwpl.lib.in.us. *Dir,* Sheryl A Sollars; E-mail: ssollars@wwpl.lib.in.us; *Asst Dir,* Kerry Green; E-mail: kgreen@wwpl.lib.in.us; *Ch Mgr,* Nancy Haggard; E-mail: nhaggard@wwpl.lib.in.us; *Info/Ref Serv Mgr,* Brittany Super; E-mail: bsuper@wwpl.lib.in.us; Staff 7 (MLS 7)
Founded 1901. Pop 32,000; Circ 400,594
Library Holdings: Audiobooks 4,160; CDs 3,048; DVDs 11,003; e-books 63,103; e-journals 75; Bk Vols 94,724; Per Subs 122
Special Collections: American Quaker Genealogy Coll
Automation Activity & Vendor Info: (Cataloging) Evergreen; (Circulation) Evergreen; (OPAC) Evergreen
Wireless access
Function: 24/7 Electronic res, 24/7 Online cat, 3D Printer, Activity rm, Adult bk club, Adult literacy prog
Publications: Friends (Newsletter)
Partic in Evergreen Indiana Consortium; Midwest Collaborative for Library Services
Open Mon-Wed 10-8, Thurs & Fri 10-6, Sat 10-5, Sun 1-5
Friends of the Library Group

WESTVILLE

C PURDUE UNIVERSITY NORTHWEST*, Westville Campus Library, Library-Student-Faculty Bldg, 2nd Flr, 1401 S US Hwy 421, 46391. SAN 305-1706. Tel: 219-785-5248. Toll Free Tel: 855-608-4600, Ext 5248. FAX: 219-785-5501. Web Site: library.pnw.edu. *Dir of the Univ Libr,* Tammy Guerrero; E-mail: tsguerre@pnw.edu; *Tech Serv Librn,* Tricia Jauquet; Tel: 219-785-5234, E-mail: tjauquet@pnw.edu; Staff 6 (MLS 3, Non-MLS 3)
Founded 1967. Enrl 3,500; Fac 95; Highest Degree: Master
Library Holdings: Bk Vols 84,900; Per Subs 390
Wireless access
Friends of the Library Group

P WESTVILLE-NEW DURHAM TOWNSHIP PUBLIC LIBRARY*, 153 Main St, 46391. (Mail add: PO Box 789, 46391-0789), SAN 305-1714. Tel: 219-785-2015. FAX: 219-785-2015. Web Site: westville.lib.in.us. *Dir,* Courtney Cassler; E-mail: director@westville.lib.in.us; Staff 3 (Non-MLS 3)
Founded 1915. Pop 4,095; Circ 23,498
Library Holdings: DVDs 5,000; Large Print Bks 50; Bk Vols 18,140; Per Subs 30; Talking Bks 500

Subject Interests: Cemetery, Veterans
Wireless access
Open Mon 2-8, Tues-Thurs 1-6, Sat 10-2

WHITING

CR CALUMET COLLEGE OF SAINT JOSEPH*, Specker Memorial Library, 2400 New York Ave, 46394. SAN 304-9248. Tel: 219-473-4373. FAX: 219-473-4259. E-mail: library@ccsj.edu. Reference E-mail: reference@ccsj.edu. Web Site: www.ccsj.edu/library. *Dir, Libr Serv,* Qi Chen; Tel: 219-473-4375, E-mail: qchen@ccsj.edu; Staff 6 (MLS 3, Non-MLS 3)
Enrl 1,300; Fac 60; Highest Degree: Master
Library Holdings: AV Mats 6,580; Bk Vols 110,000; Per Subs 74
Automation Activity & Vendor Info: (Acquisitions) Ex Libris Group; (Cataloging) Ex Libris Group; (Circulation) Ex Libris Group; (ILL) Ex Libris Group; (OPAC) Ex Libris Group; (Serials) Ex Libris Group
Function: Adult bk club, Art exhibits, ILL available, Internet access, Music CDs, Orientations, Photocopying/Printing, Prog for adults, Ref serv available, Spoken cassettes & CDs, Spoken cassettes & DVDs, VHS videos, Wheelchair accessible, Workshops
Restriction: Open to pub by appt only, Open to students, fac & staff

P WHITING PUBLIC LIBRARY*, 1735 Oliver St, 46394-1794. SAN 305-1722. Tel: 219-659-0269. FAX: 219-659-5833. E-mail: wpl@whiting.lib.in.us. Web Site: whiting.lib.in.us. *Dir,* Ms Montserrat Inglada; Tel: 219-659-0269, Ext 111; *Asst Dir,* Mary Kershner; Tel: 219-659-0269, Ext 112; *Ch,* Joelle Wake; E-mail: 219-473-4700, Ext 120; *Tech Serv,* Josephine Kaiser; Tel: 219-473-4700, Ext 115; Staff 3 (MLS 3)
Founded 1906. Pop 17,000; Circ 140,000
Library Holdings: AV Mats 4,070; CDs 1,825; DVDs 336; Bk Vols 90,687; Per Subs 245; Talking Bks 1,120; Videos 3,047
Special Collections: Books on Early Settlement of Lake County, Indiana (prehistoric period to 1800's); Local City Directory 1900's; Local History Room; Whiting, Indiana (early 1900's)
Subject Interests: Consumer, Finance
Automation Activity & Vendor Info: (Acquisitions) SirsiDynix; (Cataloging) SirsiDynix; (Circulation) SirsiDynix; (ILL) OCLC; (OPAC) SirsiDynix; (Serials) SirsiDynix
Wireless access
Function: Homebound delivery serv, ILL available
Publications: The WPL Newsletter (Quarterly)
Partic in Midwest Collaborative for Library Services
Open Mon-Thurs 9-8, Fri & Sat 9-5
Friends of the Library Group

WILLIAMSPORT

P WILLIAMSPORT-WASHINGTON TOWNSHIP PUBLIC LIBRARY, 28 E Second St, 47993-1299. SAN 305-1730. Tel: 765-762-6555. FAX: 765-762-6588. Web Site: www.wwtpl.lib.in.us. *Dir,* Christopher Brown; E-mail: cbrown@wwtpl.lib.in.us; Staff 5 (MLS 1, Non-MLS 4)
Founded 1915. Pop 2,384; Circ 45,690
Jan 2021-Dec 2021 Income $279,010. Mats Exp $31,800, Books $18,800, AV Equip $1,500, AV Mat $10,000, Electronic Ref Mat (Incl. Access Fees) $1,500. Sal $129,311 (Prof $43,500)
Library Holdings: Audiobooks 2,181; AV Mats 11; Bks on Deafness & Sign Lang 23; CDs 1,610; DVDs 3,642; Large Print Bks 1,410; Bk Vols 37,610; Per Subs 4; Videos 5,495
Special Collections: Indiana Coll; Judge Allen Sharp Coll; Star Wars & Star Trek Coll
Subject Interests: Graphic novels, Westerns
Automation Activity & Vendor Info: (Acquisitions) Follett Software; (Cataloging) Follett Software; (Circulation) Follett Software; (Course Reserve) Follett Software; (Discovery) Follett Software; (OPAC) Follett Software; (Serials) Follett Software
Wireless access
Function: Bks on CD, Children's prog, Computers for patron use, Free DVD rentals, Holiday prog, Home delivery & serv to seniorr ctr & nursing homes, Homebound delivery serv, Homework prog, ILL available, Instruction & testing, Internet access, Jail serv, Laminating, Learning ctr, Life-long learning prog for all ages, Magazines, Magnifiers for reading, Movies, Music CDs, Online cat, Photocopying/Printing, Preschool outreach, Preschool reading prog, Prog for adults, Prog for children & young adult, Ref & res, Ref serv available, Scanner, Story hour, Summer & winter reading prog, Tax forms, Teen prog, Telephone ref, Wheelchair accessible
Partic in Indiana Library Federation; Midwest Collaborative for Library Services
Special Services for the Deaf - Accessible learning ctr; Closed caption videos
Special Services for the Blind - Accessible computers; Audio mat; Bks available with recordings; Bks on CD; Digital talking bk; Home delivery serv; Large print bks; Low vision equip; Playaways (bks on MP3); Recorded bks; Sound rec; Talking bks
Open Mon & Fri 10-5, Tues & Thurs 10-7, Wed 10-8, Sat 9-2
Friends of the Library Group

WINAMAC

P PULASKI COUNTY PUBLIC LIBRARY*, 121 S Riverside Dr, 46996-1596. SAN 341-7697. Tel: 574-946-3432. FAX: 574-946-6598. TDD: 574-946-6981. E-mail: info@pulaskicounty.lib.in.us. Web Site: www.pulaskicounty.lib.in.us. *Dir,* MacKenzie Inez Ledley; E-mail: director@pulaskicounty.lib.in.us; Staff 4 (MLS 1, Non-MLS 3)
Founded 1905. Pop 10,646; Circ 113,937
Library Holdings: Audiobooks 2,508; AV Mats 2,343; CDs 1,065; DVDs 2,706; Large Print Bks 935; Bk Titles 57,534; Bk Vols 47,832; Per Subs 154
Special Collections: Local Newspapers 1869-, micro. Oral History
Subject Interests: Genealogy, Indiana, Local hist
Automation Activity & Vendor Info: (Acquisitions) AmLib Library Management System
Wireless access
Function: Adult bk club, After school storytime, Art exhibits, Bk reviews (Group), Bks on cassette, Bks on CD, CD-ROM, Children's prog, Computer training, Computers for patron use, E-Reserves, Electronic databases & coll, Free DVD rentals, Genealogy discussion group, Holiday prog, Home delivery & serv to seniorr ctr & nursing homes, Homebound delivery serv, ILL available, Jail serv, Magnifiers for reading, Masonic res mat, Music CDs, Notary serv, Outreach serv, Photocopying/Printing, Preschool outreach, Prog for adults, Prog for children & young adult, Ref serv available, Senior outreach, Serves people with intellectual disabilities, Spoken cassettes & CDs, Spoken cassettes & DVDs, Story hour, Summer & winter reading prog, Tax forms, Teen prog, Telephone ref, VHS videos, Wheelchair accessible
Partic in Midwest Collaborative for Library Services
Special Services for the Deaf - TDD equip
Open Mon-Thurs 9-7, Fri 9-6, Sat 9-4

WINCHESTER

P WINCHESTER COMMUNITY LIBRARY, 125 N East St, 47394-1698. SAN 305-1757. Tel: 765-584-4824. FAX: 765-584-3624. E-mail: wincomlib@yahoo.com. Web Site: www.wincomlib.org. *Dir,* Jana Barnes; *Dir, Ch Serv,* Melissa Bruntz; Staff 2 (Non-MLS 2)
Founded 1912. Pop 8,622; Circ 99,000
Jan 2019-Dec 2019 Income $507,657. Mats Exp $35,500. Sal $223,000
Library Holdings: Audiobooks 609; DVDs 3,549; Large Print Bks 1,698; Bk Vols 46,834; Per Subs 69
Subject Interests: Abraham Lincoln
Automation Activity & Vendor Info: (Acquisitions) Baker & Taylor; (Cataloging) Evergreen; (Circulation) Evergreen; (OPAC) Evergreen
Wireless access
Function: Adult bk club, AV serv, Bks on cassette, Bks on CD, Children's prog, Computer training, Computers for patron use, Free DVD rentals, Home delivery & serv to seniorr ctr & nursing homes, Homebound delivery serv, ILL available, Magnifiers for reading, Online cat, Photocopying/Printing, Prog for adults, Prog for children & young adult, Ref & res, Ref serv available, Story hour, Summer reading prog, Tax forms, Teen prog, Telephone ref, Wheelchair accessible
Open Mon-Thurs 9-8, Fri & Sat 9-5
Friends of the Library Group

WINONA LAKE

CR GRACE COLLEGE & GRACE THEOLOGICAL SEMINARY*, Morgan Library, 200 Seminary Dr, 46590. SAN 305-1765. Tel: 574-372-5100, Ext 6294. Reference Tel: 574-372-5100, Ext 6297. FAX: 574-372-5176. E-mail: library@grace.edu. Web Site: libguides.grace.edu/homepage. *Dir, Libr Serv,* Tonya Fawcett; Tel: 574-372-5100, Ext 6291, E-mail: fawcettl@grace.edu; *Assoc Dir, Pub & Electronic Serv,* Rhoda Palmer; Tel: 574-372-5100, Ext 6293, E-mail: rfpalmer@grace.edu; Staff 3.5 (MLS 2.5, Non-MLS 1)
Founded 1939. Enrl 1,833; Fac 65; Highest Degree: Doctorate
Library Holdings: Audiobooks 25; AV Mats 4,626; CDs 1,426; e-books 174,943; e-journals 108,488; Electronic Media & Resources 77,661; Microforms 24,760; Bk Titles 106,021; Bk Vols 137,029; Per Subs 140; Videos 328
Special Collections: Billy Sunday Papers Coll; Winona Lake Historical Coll; Winona Railroad Special Coll
Subject Interests: Biblical studies
Automation Activity & Vendor Info: (Acquisitions) OCLC; (Cataloging) OCLC; (Circulation) OCLC; (Course Reserve) OCLC; (ILL) OCLC; (OPAC) OCLC; (Serials) OCLC
Wireless access
Partic in Christian Library Consortium; Midwest Collaborative for Library Services; OCLC Online Computer Library Center, Inc; Private Academic Library Network of Indiana
Open Mon-Thurs 8am-11pm, Fri 8-6, Sat 11-6, Sun 2-6

WOLCOTT

P WOLCOTT COMMUNITY PUBLIC LIBRARY*, 101 E North St, 47995. (Mail add: PO Box 376, 47995-0376), SAN 305-1773. Tel: 219-279-2695. FAX: 219-279-2692. E-mail: wolcottlibrary@mywcpl.com. Web Site: www.mywcpl.com. *Libr Dir,* Deanna Dreblow; E-mail: dpdreblow@yahoo.com; Staff 33 (Non-MLS 33)
Founded 1923. Pop 2,193; Circ 11,292
Library Holdings: Audiobooks 345; CDs 39; DVDs 1,136; e-books 63,000; Electronic Media & Resources 400; Large Print Bks 300; Bk Titles 26,000; Per Subs 22
Automation Activity & Vendor Info: (Acquisitions) Evergreen; (Cataloging) Evergreen; (Circulation) Evergreen; (Course Reserve) Evergreen; (OPAC) Evergreen
Wireless access
Function: 24/7 Online cat, Bks on CD, Children's prog, Computers for patron use, E-Readers, Free DVD rentals, Homebound delivery serv, ILL available, Internet access, Magazines, Music CDs, Online cat, OverDrive digital audio bks, Photocopying/Printing, Preschool outreach, Preschool reading prog, Prog for adults, Prog for children & young adult, Ref serv available, Senior outreach, Spoken cassettes & CDs, Story hour, Summer & winter reading prog, Summer reading prog, Tax forms, Teen prog, Wheelchair accessible, Winter reading prog
Open Mon 1-6, Tues 9-6, Thurs 10-5, Fri 9-5, Sat 9-1
Restriction: Access for corporate affiliates

WORTHINGTON

P WORTHINGTON-JEFFERSON TOWNSHIP PUBLIC LIBRARY*, 26 N Commercial St, 47471-1415. SAN 305-1781. Tel: 812-875-3815. FAX: 812-875-3815. E-mail: WJTPL@yahoo.com. Web Site: www.worthington.lib.in.us. *Dir,* Andrea Fuller; Staff 4 (MLS 2, Non-MLS 2)
Founded 1918. Pop 2,409; Circ 21,610
Library Holdings: AV Mats 1,200; Bk Vols 18,467; Per Subs 30; Videos 1,100
Automation Activity & Vendor Info: (Acquisitions) SirsiDynix; (Cataloging) SirsiDynix; (OPAC) SirsiDynix
Partic in Stone Hills Area Libr Servs Authority
Open Mon & Wed 12-5, Tues & Thurs 12-8, Fri 9-5, Sat 9-1

YORKTOWN

P YORKTOWN PUBLIC LIBRARY, 8920 W Adaline St, 47396. Tel: 765-759-9723. FAX: 765-759-7260. Web Site: yorktownlib.org. *Dir,* Liz Rozelle; E-mail: lizrozelle@yorktownlib.org; *Asst Dir,* Laurie Hogue; E-mail: lauriehogue@yorktownlib.org; Staff 7 (MLS 3, Non-MLS 4)
Founded 2000. Pop 11,415; Circ 141,700
Jan 2020-Dec 2020 Income $794,749, State $30,478, County $465,300, Locally Generated Income $67,370, Other $231,601. Mats Exp $81,558, Books $34,848, Per/Ser (Incl. Access Fees) $4,027, AV Equip $4,719, AV Mat $13,302, Electronic Ref Mat (Incl. Access Fees) $24,662. Sal $284,196
Library Holdings: Audiobooks 3,275; Bks on Deafness & Sign Lang 42; CDs 1,053; DVDs 8,109; e-books 40,866; e-journals 25; Electronic Media & Resources 80; Large Print Bks 1,266; Bk Titles 38,754; Bk Vols 40,427; Per Subs 115
Special Collections: Yorktown, Mount Pleasant Township & Delaware County Local History Coll
Automation Activity & Vendor Info: (Acquisitions) Biblionix/Apollo; (Cataloging) Biblionix/Apollo; (Circulation) Biblionix/Apollo; (ILL) Biblionix/Apollo; (OPAC) Biblionix/Apollo; (Serials) EBSCO Online
Wireless access
Function: 24/7 Electronic res, 24/7 Online cat, Activity rm, Adult bk club, Art exhibits, Audio & video playback equip for onsite use, Audiobks on Playaways & MP3, Audiobks via web, AV serv, Bks on CD, Children's prog, Computer training, Computers for patron use, Digital talking bks, E-Readers, Electronic databases & coll, Family literacy, Free DVD rentals, Holiday prog, Home delivery & serv to seniorr ctr & nursing homes, Homebound delivery serv, ILL available, Internet access, Laminating, Magazines, Magnifiers for reading, Mail & tel request accepted, Mango lang, Movies, Museum passes, Music CDs, Notary serv, Online cat, Online info literacy tutorials on the web & in blackboard, Online ref, Outreach serv, OverDrive digital audio bks, Photocopying/Printing, Printer for laptops & handheld devices, Prog for adults, Prog for children & young adult, Ref serv available, Scanner, Senior computer classes, Senior outreach, Serves people with intellectual disabilities, Spanish lang bks, Story hour, Study rm, Summer & winter reading prog, Summer reading prog, Tax forms, Teen prog, Telephone ref, VHS videos, Wheelchair accessible, Winter reading prog
Publications: Yorktown Public Library Newsletter (Online only)
Partic in Midwest Collaborative for Library Services
Special Services for the Deaf - Bks on deafness & sign lang
Special Services for the Blind - Bks on cassette; Bks on CD; Home delivery serv; Large print bks
Open Mon-Thurs 10-7, Fri 10-6, Sat 10-4
Restriction: Non-circulating of rare bks, Non-resident fee, Residents only
Friends of the Library Group

ZIONSVILLE

P HUSSEY-MAYFIELD MEMORIAL PUBLIC LIBRARY*, 250 N Fifth St, 46077-1324. (Mail add: PO Box 840, 46077-0840), SAN 305-179X. Tel: 317-873-3149. FAX: 317-873-8339. E-mail: askalib@zionsville.lib.in.us. Web Site: zionsvillelibrary.org. *Exec Dir,* Sarah Moore; E-mail: sarahm@zionsvillelibrary.org; *Asst Dir,* Mary Rueff; E-mail: maryr@zionsvillelibrary.org; *Circ Serv Dept Head,* Julie Bigler; E-mail: julieb@zionsvillelibrary.org; *Dept Head, Tech Serv,* Sarah Childs; E-mail: sarahc@zionsvillelibrary.org; *Youth Serv Dept Head,* Kelli Brooks; E-mail: kellib@zionsvillelibrary.org; Staff 46 (MLS 3, Non-MLS 43)
Founded 1989. Pop 15,924; Circ 464,508
Library Holdings: AV Mats 18,919; Bk Vols 101,480; Per Subs 260
Special Collections: Business & Investing Room
Subject Interests: Arts & crafts, Bus, Civil War, Gardening, Investment
Automation Activity & Vendor Info: (Acquisitions) OCLC Connexion; (Cataloging) Evergreen; (Circulation) Evergreen; (OPAC) Evergreen
Wireless access
Publications: Seasons (Newsletter)
Partic in Evergreen Indiana Consortium; LYRASIS; Midwest Collaborative for Library Services
Open Mon-Thurs 9:30-8:30, Fri & Sat 9:30-5, Sun 1-5
Friends of the Library Group

S SULLIVANMUNCE CULTURAL CENTER, Local History Museum & Genealogy Library, 225 W Hawthorne St, 46077. SAN 373-4528. Tel: 317-873-4900. E-mail: info@sullivanmunce.org. Web Site: sullivanmunce.org. *Exec Dir,* Cynthia Young; E-mail: cynthiayoung@sullivanmunce.org; *Mus Dir,* Kristina Huff; E-mail: kristinah@sullivanmunce.org; Staff 1 (MLS 1)
Library Holdings: Electronic Media & Resources 2; Bk Vols 4,000
Special Collections: Early Photographs of Zionsville & Boone County (Part of Archival Coll); Indiana Paintings including Portrait of William Zion (Part of Museum Coll); Local Newspapers on microfilm, locally compiled surname & family files (Part of Genealogy Library Coll)
Subject Interests: Genealogy, Local hist
Wireless access
Function: Archival coll, Computers for patron use, Electronic databases & coll, Online cat
Open Tues-Fri 10-4, Sat 10-2
Restriction: Non-circulating, Not a lending libr

IOWA

Date of Statistics: FY 2020
Population, 2020 U.S. Census: 3,190,369
Total Titles in Public Libraries: 13,181,073
Titles Per Capita: 4.1
Total Public Library Circulation: 19,748,066
Circulation Per Capita: 6.2
Digital Resources:
Total computers for use by the public: 4,884
Total programs: 82,860
Total program attendance: 1,551,660
Door Count (Visits): 11,748,322

Income and Expenditures:
Total Public Library Income (including Grants-in-Aid): $137,222,706
Average Income: $261,625
Source of Income: Mainly public funds
Expenditures Per Capita: $41.74
Number of County & Regional Libraries: 3 county libraries
State Aid, FY 2022: $2,464,823
Federal (LSTA), FY 2021: $2,030,383
Information provided courtesy of: Scott Dermont, Library Consultant; State Library of Iowa

ACKLEY

P ACKLEY PUBLIC LIBRARY, 401 State St, 50601. SAN 305-1803. Tel: 641-847-2233. FAX: 641-648-0167. E-mail: ackleylibrary@gmail.com. Web Site: www.ackley.lib.ia.us. *Co-Dir,* Sue Abbas; *Co-Dir,* Retha Starek
Founded 1902. Pop 1,809; Circ 19,643
Library Holdings: Bk Vols 13,468; Per Subs 51
Open Mon 10:30-5, Tues & Thurs 11-7, Wed & Fri 9-5, Sat 9-2

ADAIR

P ADAIR PUBLIC LIBRARY, 310 Audubon, 50002. (Mail add: PO Box 276, 50002-0276), SAN 305-1811. Tel: 641-742-3323. FAX: 641-742-3323. E-mail: adairlibrary@gmail.com. *Dir,* Annie Brincks
Founded 1936. Pop 839; Circ 6,231
Library Holdings: Bk Titles 9,300; Per Subs 25
Open Tues 1-6, Thurs 1-5, Sat 8-Noon

ADEL

P ADEL PUBLIC LIBRARY, 303 S Tenth St, 50003-1797. SAN 305-182X. Tel: 515-993-3512. FAX: 515-993-3191. E-mail: librarian@adel.lib.ia.us. Web Site: www.adelpl.org. *Dir,* Trever Jayne; E-mail: trever@adel.lib.ia.us; *Asst Dir,* Amy Linney; E-mail: amy@adel.lib.ia.us
Pop 3,435; Circ 46,000
Library Holdings: Bk Titles 28,022; Per Subs 64
Wireless access
Open Mon & Fri 10-5, Tues-Thurs 10-7, Sat 10-1:30
Friends of the Library Group

AGENCY

P AGENCY PUBLIC LIBRARY*, 104 E Main St, 52530. (Mail add: PO Box 346, 52530-0346), SAN 305-1838. Tel: 641-937-6002. FAX: 641-937-5241. E-mail: agencypubliclibrary@gmail.com. Web Site: www.agency.lib.ia.us. *Dir,* Kim Schwartz; *Libr Asst,* Heather Fellinger
Founded 1947. Pop 638; Circ 4,260
Library Holdings: Bk Vols 7,735; Per Subs 15
Special Collections: Iowa History
Wireless access
Open Mon, Tues & Thurs 4-7:30, Wed 2-8, Fri 4-6:30, Sat 9:30-12:30, Sun 2-5

AKRON

P AKRON PUBLIC LIBRARY*, 350 Reed St, 51001. (Mail add: PO Box 348, 51001-0348), SAN 305-1846. Tel: 712-568-2601. FAX: 712-568-2601. E-mail: akronialibrary@gmail.com. Web Site: www.akron.lib.ia.us. *Dir,* Lora Pierce; *Ch, Teen Librn,* Mary Campbell
Pop 1,489; Circ 33,000
Library Holdings: CDs 60; DVDs 346; Large Print Bks 531; Bk Titles 13,000; Per Subs 62; Videos 277
Automation Activity & Vendor Info: (Acquisitions) Follett Software; (Circulation) Follett Software; (ILL) Brodart
Wireless access
Function: Adult bk club, Art exhibits, Bk club(s), Bks on cassette, Bks on CD, Children's prog, Computer training, Computers for patron use, Holiday prog, Homebound delivery serv, ILL available, Photocopying/Printing, Preschool outreach, Prog for adults, Prog for children & young adult, Ref serv available, Senior computer classes, Story hour, Summer reading prog, Tax forms, Telephone ref, VHS videos, Wheelchair accessible, Workshops
Open Mon 9-6, Tues-Fri 9:30-5:30, Sat 9-3

ALBERT CITY

P ALBERT CITY PUBLIC LIBRARY*, 215 Main St, 50510. (Mail add: PO Box 368, 50510-0368), SAN 305-1854. Tel: 712-843-2012. FAX: 712-843-2058. Web Site: www.albertcity.lib.ia.us. *Dir,* Mary Johnson; E-mail: mjohnson@albertcity.lib.ia.us
Pop 709; Circ 14,833
Library Holdings: AV Mats 683; Electronic Media & Resources 31; Bk Titles 12,000; Per Subs 48; Talking Bks 144
Automation Activity & Vendor Info: (Acquisitions) Follett Software
Wireless access
Open Mon 10-1, Tues, Thurs & Fri 10-5:30, Wed 10-6:30, Sat 9-11
Friends of the Library Group

ALBIA

P CARNEGIE EVANS PUBLIC LIBRARY ALBIA PUBLIC, 203 Benton Ave E, 52531-2036. SAN 305-1862. Tel: 641-932-2469. FAX: 641-932-2469. E-mail: albialibrary@netscape.net. Web Site: www.albia.lib.ia.us. *Dir,* Marilyn Woods; *Ref Librn,* Betty Reeves; *Ch Serv,* Ruth James
Founded 1906. Pop 3,706; Circ 173,000
Library Holdings: Bk Titles 40,000; Per Subs 25
Open Mon-Fri Noon-6, Sat 10-3

ALBION

P ALBION MUNICIPAL LIBRARY*, 400 N Main St, 50005. (Mail add: PO Box 118, 50005-0118), SAN 321-8295. Tel: 641-488-2226. FAX: 641-488-2272. E-mail: albionlib@heartofiowa.net. *Libr Dir,* Julia E Ohrt; Staff 2 (Non-MLS 2)
Founded 1982. Pop 505; Circ 29,829
Library Holdings: Bk Titles 38,014; Per Subs 15
Automation Activity & Vendor Info: (Acquisitions) Biblionix
Wireless access
Function: 24/7 Electronic res, 24/7 Online cat, Activity rm, Adult bk club, Archival coll, Bks on CD, Children's prog, Computer training, Computers for patron use, Digital talking bks, Electronic databases & coll, Free DVD rentals, Games & aids for people with disabilities, Genealogy discussion group, Holiday prog, Homebound delivery serv, ILL available, Internet access, Laminating, Literacy & newcomer serv, Magazines, Magnifiers for

reading, Mail & tel request accepted, Meeting rooms, Movies, Music CDs, Online cat, Online info literacy tutorials on the web & in blackboard, Online ref, OverDrive digital audio bks, Photocopying/Printing, Preschool outreach, Printer for laptops & handheld devices, Prog for adults, Prog for children & young adult, Ref & res, Ref serv available, Scanner, Senior computer classes, STEM programs, Story hour, Summer & winter reading prog, Summer reading prog, VHS videos, Wheelchair accessible, Words travel prog, Workshops
Open Mon & Tues (Winter) 10-6, Wed & Thurs 12-6, Sat 10-12 ; Mon (Summer) 12-6,Tues, Wed & Thurs 10-6
Friends of the Library Group

ALDEN

P DR GRACE O DOANE ALDEN PUBLIC LIBRARY, 1012 Water St, 50006. (Mail add: PO Box 78, 50006). Tel: 515-859-3820. FAX: 515-859-3919. Web Site: alden.lib.ia.us. *Dir,* Lisa Liittschwager; E-mail: director@aldenlibrary.org; *Asst Librn,* Erin Smith; *Children's Prog Mgr,* Felicia Hoppen
Pop 905; Circ 18,023
Library Holdings: Bk Titles 12,000; Per Subs 72
Wireless access
Partic in Hardin County Libr Asn
Open Mon & Wed 12:30-6, Tues & Thurs 12:30-5:30, Fri 9:30-5:30, Sat 9-Noon
Friends of the Library Group

ALEXANDER

P ALEXANDER PUBLIC LIBRARY, 409 Harriman St, 50420. (Mail add: PO Box 27, 50420-0027), SAN 305-1889. Tel: 641-692-3238. FAX: 641-692-3238. Web Site: www.alexander.lib.ia.us. *Dir,* Dee Schrodt; E-mail: dee@alexander.lib.ia.us
Founded 1962. Pop 165; Circ 8,077
Library Holdings: Bk Titles 6,500; Per Subs 30
Automation Activity & Vendor Info: (Cataloging) Follett Software
Wireless access
Open Mon 8:30-12 & 1-5, Tues, Wed & Fri 2-5, Thurs 3-6, Sat 8:30-12

ALGONA

P ALGONA PUBLIC LIBRARY*, 210 N Phillips St, 50511. SAN 305-1897. Tel: 515-295-5476. FAX: 515-295-3307. Web Site: www.ci.algona.ia.us. *Dir,* Lori Walton; E-mail: lwalton@algona.lib.ia.us; *Ch,* Vera Scrivner; E-mail: vscrivner@algona.lib.ia.us; *Adult Serv Spec,* Judy Schiltz; E-mail: judys@algona.lib.ia.us; *YA Librn,* Sonya Harsha; E-mail: sonyah@algona.lib.ia.us; Staff 3 (MLS 2, Non-MLS 1)
Founded 1904. Pop 5,741; Circ 97,900
Subject Interests: Hist, Iowa, Local hist
Automation Activity & Vendor Info: (Cataloging) TLC (The Library Corporation); (Circulation) TLC (The Library Corporation); (OPAC) TLC (The Library Corporation)
Wireless access
Open Mon-Thurs 9:30-8, Fri 9:30-5, Sat 9:30-4
Friends of the Library Group

ALLERTON

P ALLERTON PUBLIC LIBRARY, 103 S Central Ave, 50008. (Mail add: PO Box 216, 50008-9760), SAN 305-1900. Tel: 641-873-4575. E-mail: alrtnlib@gmail.com. *Librn,* Position Currently Open; *Ch,* Sheryl Hefner
Pop 559
Library Holdings: Bk Titles 8,500; Per Subs 10
Open Mon-Fri 2-5, Sat 9-Noon

ALLISON

P ALLISON PUBLIC LIBRARY*, 412 Third St, 50602. (Mail add: PO Box 605, 50602-0605), SAN 305-1919. Tel: 319-267-2562. FAX: 319-267-2562. Web Site: www.allison.lib.ia.us. *Dir,* Patty Hummel; E-mail: phummel@allison.lib.ia.us
Founded 1929. Pop 1,029; Circ 24,030
Library Holdings: Bk Titles 12,921; Bk Vols 13,500; Per Subs 40
Wireless access
Open Mon 10-12 & 2-6, Tues & Thurs 2-7, Wed & Fri 2-6, Sat 9-3

ALTA

P ALTA COMMUNITY LIBRARY*, 1009 S Main St, 51002. SAN 305-1927. Tel: 712-200-1250. Administration E-mail: admin@alta.lib.ia.us. Web Site: www.alta.lib.ia.us. *Libr Dir,* Andrea Hogrefe; *Ch,* Laura Turnquist; Staff 9 (Non-MLS 9)
Founded 1911. Pop 1,865; Circ 26,134
Library Holdings: Audiobooks 349; DVDs 2,141; Large Print Bks 947; Bk Titles 23,000; Per Subs 39
Automation Activity & Vendor Info: (Cataloging) Book Systems; (Circulation) Book Systems; (OPAC) Book Systems
Wireless access
Function: 24/7 Electronic res, 24/7 Online cat, Adult literacy prog, Audiobks via web, Bks on CD, Children's prog, Computer training, Computers for patron use, Digital talking bks, E-Readers, E-Reserves, Electronic databases & coll, Family literacy, Free DVD rentals, Holiday prog, Homebound delivery serv, ILL available, Internet access, Life-long learning prog for all ages, Magazines, Movies, Online cat, Online info literacy tutorials on the web & in blackboard, Outreach serv, Outside serv via phone, mail, e-mail & web, OverDrive digital audio bks, Photocopying/Printing, Preschool outreach, Preschool reading prog, Printer for laptops & handheld devices, Prog for adults, Prog for children & young adult, Ref & res, Scanner, Senior outreach, Spanish lang bks, STEM programs, Story hour, Summer reading prog, Tax forms, Teen prog, Telephone ref, Wheelchair accessible
Special Services for the Deaf - Adult & family literacy prog; Bks on deafness & sign lang; Closed caption videos
Special Services for the Blind - Bks on CD; Copier with enlargement capabilities; Digital talking bk; Free checkout of audio mat; Home delivery serv; Large print bks; Recorded bks
Open Mon-Fri (Winter) 8:30-7, Sat 9-1; Mon, Wed, Fri & Sat (Summer) 9-1, Tues & Thurs 3-7

ALTA VISTA

P ALTA VISTA PUBLIC LIBRARY*, 203 S White Ave, 50603. (Mail add: PO Box 157, 50603-0157), SAN 376-6551. Tel: 641-364-6009. FAX: 641-364-6009. Web Site: www.altavista.lib.ia.us. *Libr Dir,* Jackie Kush
Founded 1931. Pop 286
Library Holdings: Bk Vols 7,700; Per Subs 30
Wireless access
Function: 24/7 Electronic res, 24/7 Online cat, Activity rm, Adult bk club
Open Mon, Wed & Fri 3-6, Tues & Thurs 10-7, Sat 9-Noon

ALTON

P ALTON PUBLIC LIBRARY*, 605 Tenth St, 51003. SAN 305-1943. Tel: 712-756-4516. FAX: 712-756-4140. Web Site: www.alton.lib.ia.us. *Dir,* Cheryl Hoekstra; E-mail: cherylhoekstra@alton.lib.ia.us; *Ch,* Jen Wielenga
Founded 1923. Pop 1,095; Circ 15,000
Library Holdings: Bk Vols 10,000; Per Subs 77
Special Collections: Local Newspaper (Alton Democrat, 1883-present), micro
Automation Activity & Vendor Info: (Circulation) Follett Software
Wireless access
Open Mon-Wed 10-7, Thurs 10-8:30, Fri 10-5, Sat 10-4

ALTOONA

P ALTOONA PUBLIC LIBRARY*, 700 Eighth St SW, 50009. SAN 305-1951. Tel: 515-967-3881. FAX: 515-967-6934. Web Site: www.altoona.lib.ia.us. *Dir,* Kim Kietzman; *Asst Dir,* Amy Turgasen; *Ch,* Sheila Olson
Founded 1971. Pop 15,000; Circ 120,000
Library Holdings: Bk Titles 50,000; Per Subs 75
Automation Activity & Vendor Info: (Cataloging) Innovative Interfaces, Inc
Wireless access
Open Mon-Thurs 9-9, Fri & Sat 9-5:30, Sun 2-5:30
Friends of the Library Group

AMES

P AMES PUBLIC LIBRARY*, 515 Douglas Ave, 50010. SAN 305-1978. Tel: 515-239-5646. Web Site: www.amespubliclibrary.org. *Dir,* Mary Logsdon; *Ad,* Megan Klein Hewett; E-mail: mkleinhewett@amespubliclibrary.org; *Youth Serv,* Jerri Heid; Tel: 515-239-5643, E-mail: jheid@amespubliclibrary.org; Staff 11 (MLS 9, Non-MLS 2)
Founded 1903. Pop 58,965; Circ 2,075,569
Jul 2017-Jun 2018 Income $4,301,380, State $70,780, City $3,775,333, County $148,792, Locally Generated Income $108,731, Other $197,234. Mats Exp $558,734, Books $271,185, Per/Ser (Incl. Access Fees) $15,775, AV Mat $109,709, Electronic Ref Mat (Incl. Access Fees) $162,065. Sal $2,327,718 (Prof $788,989)
Library Holdings: Audiobooks 7,782; AV Mats 11,978; Bks on Deafness & Sign Lang 111; Braille Volumes 113; CDs 12,106; DVDs 32,841; e-books 54,826; e-journals 96; Electronic Media & Resources 61; Large Print Bks 6,908; Microforms 153; Bk Titles 160,651; Bk Vols 206,469; Per Subs 355; Videos 31,100
Special Collections: Local History (Farwell T Brown Photographic Archives)
Subject Interests: Photog

Automation Activity & Vendor Info: (Acquisitions) Innovative Interfaces, Inc; (Cataloging) OCLC; (Circulation) Innovative Interfaces, Inc; (ILL) OCLC; (OPAC) Innovative Interfaces, Inc
Wireless access
Function: 24/7 Electronic res, 24/7 Online cat, Activity rm, Adult bk club, Adult literacy prog, After school storytime, Audio & video playback equip for onsite use, Audiobks on Playaways & MP3, Audiobks via web, Bk club(s), Bk reviews (Group), Bks on CD, Children's prog, Computer training, Computers for patron use, Digital talking bks, E-Readers, E-Reserves, Electronic databases & coll, For res purposes, Free DVD rentals, Genealogy discussion group, Home delivery & serv to seniorr ctr & nursing homes, Homebound delivery serv, ILL available, Internet access, Life-long learning prog for all ages, Magazines, Magnifiers for reading, Mail & tel request accepted, Mango lang, Meeting rooms, Movies, Museum passes, Music CDs, Notary serv, Online cat, Online ref, Outreach serv, OverDrive digital audio bks, Photocopying/Printing, Preschool outreach, Printer for laptops & handheld devices, Prog for adults, Prog for children & young adult, Ref & res, Ref serv available, Scanner, Senior outreach, Spanish lang bks, Spoken cassettes & CDs, Spoken cassettes & DVDs, STEM programs, Story hour, Study rm, Summer & winter reading prog, Summer reading prog, Tax forms, Teen prog, Telephone ref, Wheelchair accessible, Winter reading prog, Workshops, Writing prog
Publications: Page One (Monthly newsletter)
Special Services for the Deaf - ADA equip; Assisted listening device; Bks on deafness & sign lang; High interest/low vocabulary bks; Sign lang interpreter upon request for prog
Special Services for the Blind - Aids for in-house use; Audio mat; Bks available with recordings; Bks on CD; Braille bks; Children's Braille; Copier with enlargement capabilities; Digital talking bk; Extensive large print coll; Free checkout of audio mat; Home delivery serv; Large print bks; Low vision equip; PC for people with disabilities; Playaways (bks on MP3); Recorded bks; Ref serv; Sound rec
Open Mon-Thurs 9-9, Fri & Sat 9-6, Sun 1-5
Friends of the Library Group
Bookmobiles: 1. Mgr, Tracy Briseno. Bk vols 3,500

M MARY GREELEY MEDICAL CENTER LIBRARY*, 1111 Duff Ave, 50010. SAN 377-5623. Tel: 515-239-2154. FAX: 515-239-2020. E-mail: medicallibrary@mgmc.com. Web Site: www.mgmc.org. *Dir & Librn,* Emily H Erickson
Library Holdings: Bk Vols 3,000; Per Subs 80
Wireless access

C IOWA STATE UNIVERSITY LIBRARY*, 302 Parks Library, 701 Morrill Rd, 50011-2102. SAN 341-7751. Tel: 515-294-1442, 515-294-1443. Interlibrary Loan Service Tel: 515-294-8073. Reference Tel: 515-294-3642. FAX: 515-294-5525. Interlibrary Loan Service FAX: 515-294-1885. Web Site: www.lib.iastate.edu. *Dean, Libr Serv,* Beth McNeil; E-mail: mcneil@iastate.edu; *Assoc Dean, Res & Instruction,* Christine King; Tel: 515-294-0904, E-mail: cking1@iastate.edu; *Assoc Dean, Curator,* Hilary Seo; Tel: 515-294-3540, E-mail: hseo@iastate.edu; *Head, Metadata & Cat, Interim Assoc Dean, Coll & Serv,* Lori O Kappmeyer; Tel: 515-294-4281, E-mail: losmus@iastate.edu; *Bus Mgr, Head, Bus Serv,* Brent Swanson; Tel: 515-294-4954, E-mail: swanie@iastate.edu; *Head, Humanities & Soc Sci,* Rebecca Jackson; Tel: 515-294-9030, E-mail: rjackson@iastate.edu; *Head, Libr Human Res,* Hilary Deike; Tel: 515-294-0443, E-mail: hdeike@iastate.edu; *Head, Libr Instruction,* Susan Vega Garcia; Tel: 515-294-4052, E-mail: savega@iastate.edu; *Head, Sci & Tech,* Lorraine Pellack; Tel: 515-294-5569, E-mail: pellack@iastate.edu; *Head, Spec Coll, Univ Archivist,* Petrina Jackson; Tel: 515-294-8270, E-mail: pjackson@iastate.edu; *Digital Scholarship Librn, Scholarly Initiatives Librn,* Harrison Inefuku; Tel: 515-294-3180, E-mail: hinefuku@iastate.edu; *Circ Coordr/Access Serv,* Angie Brown; Tel: 515-294-0448, E-mail: ambrown@iastate.edu; *Digital Archivist, Digital Scholarship Librn,* Kimberly Anderson; Tel: 515-294-8590, E-mail: kda@iastate.edu; *Acq Mgr, Res Sharing Mgr,* Dawn Mick; Tel: 515-294-0728, E-mail: mickd@iastate.edu. Subject Specialists: *Kinesiology,* Christine King; *Psychol,* Rebecca Jackson; *African-Am studies, Educ, Latino studies,* Susan Vega Garcia; *Agr educ, Food & nutrition,* Lorraine Pellack; Staff 119 (MLS 50, Non-MLS 69)
Founded 1869. Enrl 35,714; Fac 1,587; Highest Degree: Doctorate
Jul 2015-Jun 2016 Income (Main & Associated Libraries) $25,539,992, State $24,268,498, Locally Generated Income $680,300, Other $591,194. Mats Exp $12,883,873, Books $927,897, Per/Ser (Incl. Access Fees) $2,138,808, Other Print Mats $142,660. Sal $7,061,720 (Prof $3,286,455)
Library Holdings: AV Mats 1,218,595; e-books 457,967; Microforms 3,534,769; Bk Vols 2,930,438
Special Collections: Archives of Women in Science & Engineering. Oral History; State Document Depository; US Document Depository
Subject Interests: Agr, Hist of sci, Soil conservation, Veterinary med
Automation Activity & Vendor Info: (Acquisitions) Ex Libris Group; (Cataloging) Ex Libris Group; (Circulation) Ex Libris Group; (Course Reserve) Ex Libris Group; (ILL) Ex Libris Group; (Media Booking) Ex Libris Group; (OPAC) Ex Libris Group; (Serials) Ex Libris Group
Wireless access
Partic in Association of Research Libraries; Center for Research Libraries; Greater Western Library Alliance; Iowa Academic Library Alliance; National Initiative for a Networked Cultural Heritage; OCLC Online Computer Library Center, Inc
Special Services for the Blind - Braille equip; Reader equip

Departmental Libraries:

CM VETERINARY MEDICAL LIBRARY, 2280 College of Veterinary Medicine, 50011. Tel: 515-294-2225. FAX: 515-294-5525. Web Site: www.lib.iastate.edu/research-tools/collections-areas/vet-med-library. *Librn,* Jeff Alger; E-mail: jalger@iastate.edu; *Supvr,* Kristi Schaaf; Tel: 515-294-5846, E-mail: kschaaf@iastate.edu; *Libr Asst,* Lana Greve; E-mail: lgreve@iastate.edu; Staff 4 (MLS 1, Non-MLS 3)
Enrl 706; Fac 171; Highest Degree: Doctorate
Library Holdings: Bk Vols 34,000; Per Subs 700
Function: Res libr
Partic in National Network of Libraries of Medicine Region 6; Polk County Biomedical Consortium

SR SAINT THOMAS AQUINAS CHURCH, Barr Memorial Library, 2210 Lincoln Way, 50014. SAN 327-9081. Tel: 515-292-3810. Web Site: library.staparish.net. *Librn,* Brenda Neppel; E-mail: brenda@staparish.net
Library Holdings: Bk Vols 5,000

ANAMOSA

P ANAMOSA PUBLIC LIBRARY & LEARNING CENTER*, 600 E First St, 52205. SAN 305-201X. Tel: 319-462-2183. FAX: 319-462-5349. Web Site: www.anamosalibrary.org. *Dir,* Rebecca Vernon; *Ch,* Position Currently Open
Founded 1902. Pop 5,494; Circ 39,120
Library Holdings: CDs 713; DVDs 176; Large Print Bks 538; Bk Vols 32,000; Per Subs 94; Talking Bks 724; Videos 1,043
Automation Activity & Vendor Info: (Acquisitions) Baker & Taylor; (Cataloging) MITINET, Inc; (Circulation) Winnebago Software Co
Wireless access
Open Mon-Thurs 10-7, Fri 10-5, Sat 10-3
Friends of the Library Group

S ANAMOSA STATE PENITENTIARY*, Men's Reformatory Library, 406 N High St, 52205. SAN 305-2028. Tel: 319-462-3504, Ext 2237. FAX: 319-462-3013. Web Site: doc.iowa.gov/about-us/about-institutions/anamosa-state-penitentiary. *Educ Coordr,* Nicole Chambers; E-mail: nicole.chambers@iowa.gov
Library Holdings: Bk Titles 10,684; Per Subs 102
Special Collections: Science Fiction Coll
Open Mon-Fri 7:50-8:45, 9:30-12 & 1-4:45, Sat & Sun 10-Noon

ANITA

P ANITA PUBLIC LIBRARY*, 812 Third St, 50020. (Mail add: PO Box 366, 50020), SAN 305-2036. Tel: 712-762-3639. FAX: 712-762-3178. E-mail: anitapl@midlands.net. Web Site: anitalibrary.org. *Dir,* Sara Young; *Asst Librn,* Carolyn Modrell; Staff 2 (Non-MLS 2)
Pop 997; Circ 13,713
Automation Activity & Vendor Info: (Cataloging) Biblionix/Apollo; (Circulation) Follett Software; (OPAC) Biblionix/Apollo
Wireless access
Open Mon 2-8, Tues, Thurs & Fri 2-6:30, Wed 10-6:30, Sat 9-1
Friends of the Library Group

ANKENY

P ANKENY KIRKENDALL PUBLIC LIBRARY, 1250 SW District Dr, 50023. SAN 305-2060. Tel: 515-965-6460. Administration Tel: 515-965-6461. FAX: 515-289-9122. E-mail: kirkendalllibrary@ankenyiowa.gov. Web Site: www.ankenyiowa.gov/library. *Dir, Libr Serv,* Sam Mitchel; E-mail: smitchel@ankenyiowa.gov; Staff 8 (MLS 7, Non-MLS 1)
Founded 1960. Pop 58,627
Library Holdings: AV Mats 7,641; Large Print Bks 3,291; Bk Vols 64,967; Per Subs 275; Talking Bks 1,849
Automation Activity & Vendor Info: (Acquisitions) Innovative Interfaces, Inc; (Cataloging) Innovative Interfaces, Inc; (Circulation) Innovative Interfaces, Inc; (OPAC) Innovative Interfaces, Inc
Wireless access
Function: 24/7 Electronic res, 24/7 Online cat, 3D Printer, Activity rm, Adult bk club
Open Mon-Thurs 9-9, Fri & Sat 9-5:30, Sun 2-5
Friends of the Library Group

J DES MOINES AREA COMMUNITY COLLEGE LIBRARY*, Ankeny Campus, 2006 S Ankeny Blvd, 50023. SAN 305-2044. Tel: 515-964-6317. Web Site: www.library.dmacc.edu. *Dir,* Rebecca Funke; E-mail: rsfunke@dmacc.edu; *Pub Serv,* Steven Johns; E-mail: sljohns@dmacc.edu; *Tech Serv,* Lindsay Healey; E-mail: ljhealey@dmacc.edu

Library Holdings: Bk Vols 40,000; Per Subs 200
Partic in Iowa Academic Library Alliance; OCLC Online Computer Library Center, Inc
Open Mon-Thurs 7:30am-9pm, Fri 7:30-4

CR FAITH BAPTIST BIBLE COLLEGE & THEOLOGICAL SEMINARY*, John L Patten Library, 1900 NW Fourth St, 50023. SAN 305-2052. Tel: 515-964-0601, Ext 253. FAX: 515-964-1638. E-mail: libstaff@faith.edu. Web Site: faith.edu/resources/library. *Dir, Libr Serv,* Dr Paul Hartog, PhD; E-mail: hartogp@faith.edu; Staff 4 (MLS 1, Non-MLS 3)
Enrl 347; Fac 33; Highest Degree: Master
Library Holdings: Bk Vols 69,621; Per Subs 358
Special Collections: Bible Coll; Theology Coll
Automation Activity & Vendor Info: (Cataloging) Follett Software; (Circulation) Follett Software; (OPAC) Follett Software
Wireless access
Partic in OCLC Online Computer Library Center, Inc; State of Iowa Libraries Online
Open Mon, Tues & Thurs 7am-10:30pm, Wed & Fri 7-5:30, Sat 10-5

ANTHON

P HAMANN MEMORIAL LIBRARY, 311 E Main, 51004. (Mail add: PO Box 293, 51004-0293), SAN 305-2079. Tel: 712-373-5275. FAX: 712-373-5275. E-mail: HamannMemorial@longlines.com. Web Site: www.anthon.lib.ia.us. *Dir,* JoLynne Reimert; *Asst Dir,* Suann Stines; Staff 2 (MLS 2)
Founded 1903. Pop 649; Circ 900
Library Holdings: Bk Titles 5,697; Per Subs 29
Automation Activity & Vendor Info: (Acquisitions) Book Systems; (OPAC) Book Systems
Wireless access
Partic in Woodbury County Libr Syst
Open Mon-Wed & Fri 12-4:30, Sat 9-12:30

APLINGTON

P APLINGTON LEGION MEMORIAL LIBRARY, 929 Parrot St, 50604. (Mail add: PO Box 38, 50604-0038), SAN 305-2087. Tel: 319-347-2432. FAX: 319-347-2432. E-mail: mail@aplington.lib.ia.us. Web Site: www.aplington.lib.ia.us. *Dir,* Alexis Karsjens
Pop 1,054; Circ 24,000
Library Holdings: Bk Vols 16,000; Per Subs 60
Automation Activity & Vendor Info: (Cataloging) Follett Software
Open Mon 10-5, Tues & Thurs 12-7, Wed & Fri 12-5, Sat 9-12
Friends of the Library Group

ARCHER

P ARCHER PUBLIC LIBRARY*, 203 Sanford St, 51231. (Mail add: PO Box 165, 51231-0165), SAN 376-5024. Tel: 712-723-5629. E-mail: archerp1@netins.net. Web Site: archer.lib.ia.us. *Co-Librn,* Kandace Poland; *Co-Librn,* Sarah Wagenaar
Founded 1979. Pop 132; Circ 3,698
Library Holdings: Audiobooks 52; Bks on Deafness & Sign Lang 3; CDs 26; DVDs 258; Large Print Bks 354; Bk Vols 5,500; Per Subs 18; Videos 134
Function: Archival coll, Art programs, Children's prog, Free DVD rentals, Holiday prog, Magazines, Prog for adults, Prog for children & young adult, Story hour, Summer & winter reading prog, Summer reading prog
Special Services for the Blind - Bks on cassette; Bks on CD; Home delivery serv; Large print bks
Open Mon-Wed 2-4, Thurs 2-6, Fri 3-6, Sat 9-1
Friends of the Library Group

ARLINGTON

P ARLINGTON PUBLIC LIBRARY*, 711 Main St, 50606. SAN 305-2095. Tel: 563-633-3475. FAX: 563-633-3475. E-mail: arlingtonlib81@gmail.com. Web Site: www.arlington.lib.ia.us. *Dir,* Sherri Seedorff
Founded 1875. Pop 429; Circ 7,909
Library Holdings: Bk Vols 7,000; Per Subs 10
Wireless access
Open Mon 4-7, Tues, Thurs & Sat 9-Noon, Wed 9-12 & 2-7

ARMSTRONG

P ARMSTRONG PUBLIC LIBRARY*, 308 Sixth St, 50514. (Mail add: PO Box 169, 50514-0169), SAN 305-2109. Tel: 712-868-3353. FAX: 712-868-3779. Web Site: www.armstrong.lib.ia.us. *Dir,* Ginger Fortescue; E-mail: gfortescue@armstrong.lib.ia.us
Founded 1945. Pop 979; Circ 15,254
Library Holdings: AV Mats 442; Bk Titles 9,657; Bk Vols 14,000; Per Subs 38; Talking Bks 150
Special Collections: Spiritual Books
Subject Interests: Art & archit, Med, Natural sci, Relig, Sci tech
Automation Activity & Vendor Info: (Cataloging) Winnebago Software Co; (Circulation) Winnebago Software Co
Special Services for the Blind - Bks on cassette; Large print bks
Open Mon & Fri 12-6, Wed 10-6, Sat 9-1
Friends of the Library Group

ARNOLDS PARK

P ARNOLDS PARK PUBLIC LIBRARY*, City Hall Bldg, 156 N Hwy 71, 51331. (Mail add: PO Box 556, 51331-0556), SAN 305-2117. Tel: 712-332-2033. FAX: 712-332-2055. E-mail: staff@arnoldspark.lib.ia.us. Web Site: arnoldsparklibrary.com. *Dir,* Kara Rice
Pop 2,032; Circ 25,043
Library Holdings: Bk Titles 20,000; Per Subs 50
Automation Activity & Vendor Info: (Cataloging) Book Systems; (Circulation) Book Systems; (OPAC) Book Systems; (Serials) Book Systems
Wireless access
Open Mon & Tues 9-6, Wed-Fri 9-5, Sat 10-12
Friends of the Library Group

ARTHUR

P ARTHUR PUBLIC LIBRARY*, 224 S Main St, 51431. (Mail add: PO Box 77, 51431-0077), SAN 305-2125. Tel: 712-367-2240. FAX: 712-367-2240. E-mail: arthurpl@netins.net. Web Site: www.arthur.lib.ia.us. *Dir,* Kailey Childers
Founded 1925. Pop 206; Circ 6,625
Library Holdings: Bk Titles 18,059; Per Subs 15
Wireless access
Open Tues 3:30-6:30, Thurs 3:30-8:30, Sat 9-2:30

ASBURY

P DUBUQUE COUNTY LIBRARY*, Asbury Branch, 5290 Grand Meadow Dr, 52002. SAN 305-3628. Tel: 563-582-0008. FAX: 563-582-0022. E-mail: library@dubcolib.lib.ia.us. Web Site: www.dubcolib.lib.ia.us. *Dir,* Michael Wright; Staff 8 (MLS 2, Non-MLS 6)
Founded 1950. Pop 29,502; Circ 141,526
Jul 2017-Jun 2018 Income (Main & Associated Libraries) $923,572. Mats Exp $136,081. Sal $595,668
Library Holdings: Audiobooks 21,393; DVDs 9,012; e-books 46,900; Bk Vols 67,135; Per Subs 137
Subject Interests: Local hist
Automation Activity & Vendor Info: (Acquisitions) TLC (The Library Corporation); (Cataloging) TLC (The Library Corporation); (Circulation) TLC (The Library Corporation); (OPAC) TLC (The Library Corporation); (Serials) TLC (The Library Corporation)
Wireless access
Function: 24/7 Electronic res, 24/7 Online cat, Activity rm, Adult bk club, Adult literacy prog, After school storytime, Art programs, Audio & video playback equip for onsite use, Audiobks via web, Bi-weekly Writer's Group, Bk club(s), Bks on CD, Chess club, Children's prog, Computer training, Computers for patron use, Digital talking bks, Electronic databases & coll, Equip loans & repairs, Free DVD rentals, Home delivery & serv to seniorr ctr & nursing homes, ILL available, Internet access, Life-long learning prog for all ages, Magazines, Mail & tel request accepted, Meeting rooms, Movies, Museum passes, OverDrive digital audio bks, Photocopying/Printing, Preschool reading prog, Ref serv available, Res assist avail, Scanner, Senior computer classes, Spanish lang bks, Spoken cassettes & CDs, Spoken cassettes & DVDs, STEM programs, Story hour, Study rm, Summer reading prog, Telephone ref, Wheelchair accessible, Writing prog
Open Mon-Thurs 9-8, Fri 1-6, Sat 9-3
Friends of the Library Group
Branches: 4
EPWORTH BRANCH, 110 Bierman Rd, Epworth, 52045. (Mail add: PO Box 50, Epworth, 52045-0050). Tel: 563-876-3388. FAX: 563-876-3388. *Librn,* Becky Heil
Library Holdings: Bk Titles 6,000; Per Subs 32
Automation Activity & Vendor Info: (Circulation) TLC (The Library Corporation)
Open Mon, Tues & Thurs 3-7, Wed 9-12 & 1-7, Sat 9-1
FARLEY BRANCH, 205 First St, NE, Farley, 52046. (Mail add: PO Box 10, Farley, 52046). Tel: 563-744-3577. FAX: 563-744-3577.
Library Holdings: Bk Vols 6,000; Per Subs 32
HOLY CROSS BRANCH, 938 Church St, Holy Cross, 52053. (Mail add: PO Box 307, Holy Cross, 52053), SAN 376-6543. Tel: 563-870-2082. *Librn,* Becky Heil
Pop 339
Library Holdings: Bk Vols 3,500; Per Subs 32
Automation Activity & Vendor Info: (Serials) TLC (The Library Corporation)
Open Mon & Thurs 4-7, Wed 1-6, Sat 9-1

ASHTON

P ASHTON PUBLIC LIBRARY*, 3029 Third St, 51232. (Mail add: PO Box 277, 51232-0277), SAN 305-2133. Tel: 712-724-6426. FAX: 712-724-6426. E-mail: ashtlib@nethtc.net. Web Site: www.ashton.lib.ia.us. *Dir,* Heather Grotluschen
Pop 461; Circ 15,870
Library Holdings: DVDs 850; Large Print Bks 85; Bk Titles 12,260; Per Subs 53; Talking Bks 298; Videos 40
Automation Activity & Vendor Info: (Cataloging) Book Systems; (Circulation) Book Systems
Wireless access
Open Mon 4-7, Wed 10-7, Fri 8-12, Sat 9-1

ATKINS

P ATKINS PUBLIC LIBRARY*, 480 Third Ave, 52206. (Mail add: PO Box 217, 52206), SAN 305-2141. Tel: 319-446-7676. FAX: 319-446-6003. Web Site: www.atkins.lib.ia.us. *Dir,* Cathy Becker; E-mail: director@atkins.lib.ia.us
Pop 1,297; Circ 14,244
Library Holdings: Bk Titles 12,000; Per Subs 23
Automation Activity & Vendor Info: (Cataloging) Book Systems
Wireless access
Open Mon-Fri 10-12 & 1-6, Sat 9-Noon
Friends of the Library Group

ATLANTIC

P ATLANTIC PUBLIC LIBRARY*, 507 Poplar St, 50022. SAN 305-215X. Tel: 712-243-5466. FAX: 712-243-5011. E-mail: atlanticpubliclibrary@gmail.com. Web Site: www.atlantic.lib.ia.us. *Dir,* Natalie Struecker; *Ad,* Jody Allumbaugh; *Ad,* Diane McFadden; E-mail: dmcfad@atlantic.lib.ia.us; *Youth Serv Librn,* Julie Tjepkes; Staff 5.5 (MLS 1, Non-MLS 4.5)
Founded 1903. Pop 7,112; Circ 90,280
Jul 2015-Jun 2016 Income $331,240, State $5,201, City $268,000, County $13,000, Locally Generated Income $5,819, Other $39,220. Mats Exp $261,798, Books $37,530, Per/Ser (Incl. Access Fees) $3,000, Micro $1,500, Electronic Ref Mat (Incl. Access Fees) $5,982. Sal $147,900 (Prof $45,500)
Library Holdings: CDs 2,441; DVDs 26,811; e-books 8,100; Large Print Bks 1,688; Bk Vols 35,600; Per Subs 84
Subject Interests: Genealogy, Local hist
Automation Activity & Vendor Info: (Cataloging) Biblionix; (Circulation) Biblionix; (OPAC) Biblionix
Wireless access
Function: 24/7 Electronic res, Activity rm, Adult bk club, Adult literacy prog, Art exhibits, Bk club(s), Bks on CD, Children's prog, Computers for patron use, Electronic databases & coll, Free DVD rentals, Home delivery & serv to seniorr ctr & nursing homes, Homebound delivery serv, ILL available, Internet access, Laminating, Life-long learning prog for all ages, Magazines, Microfiche/film & reading machines, Movies, Music CDs, Online cat, OverDrive digital audio bks, Photocopying/Printing, Preschool outreach, Preschool reading prog, Printer for laptops & handheld devices, Prog for adults, Prog for children & young adult, Ref & res, Ref serv available, Scanner, Senior outreach, Serves people with intellectual disabilities, Story hour, Summer reading prog, Tax forms, Teen prog, Telephone ref, VHS videos, Wheelchair accessible
Partic in State of Iowa Libraries Online
Special Services for the Deaf - Interpreter on staff
Open Mon & Tues 9-7, Wed, Thurs & Fri 9-6, Sat 9-2
Friends of the Library Group

AUBURN

P AUBURN PUBLIC LIBRARY, 209 Pine St, 51433. (Mail add: PO Box 40, 51433), SAN 373-7586. Tel: 712-688-2264. FAX: 712-688-2264. E-mail: auburniowapl@gmail.com. Web Site: auburn.lib.ia.us. *Dir,* Donetta Smith Stewart
Pop 322
Library Holdings: Bk Titles 11,000; Per Subs 8
Function: 24/7 Online cat, Children's prog, Computers for patron use, Free DVD rentals, ILL available, Internet access, Large print keyboards, Magazines, Notary serv, Online cat, OverDrive digital audio bks, Photocopying/Printing, Prog for adults, Prog for children & young adult, Ref serv available, Scanner, Summer reading prog
Open Mon & Wed 1-6:30, Tues & Thurs 10-12 & 1-6, Sat 9-1

AUDUBON

P AUDUBON PUBLIC LIBRARY, 401 N Park Pl, 50025-1258. SAN 305-2168. Tel: 712-563-3301. FAX: 712-563-2580. Web Site: www.audubon.lib.ia.us. *Dir,* Gail P Richardson; E-mail: gailr@metc.net; *Ch,* Sylvia Perkins
Founded 1893. Pop 2,382; Circ 31,000
Library Holdings: Bk Vols 27,000; Per Subs 128
Special Collections: Local History & Geneaology
Wireless access
Open Mon & Wed 10-6, Tues & Thurs 10-1, Fri 10-5, Sat 10-12
Friends of the Library Group

AURELIA

P AURELIA PUBLIC LIBRARY*, 232 Main St, 51005. (Mail add: PO Box 188, 51005-0188), SAN 305-2176. Tel: 712-434-5330. FAX: 712-434-5330. E-mail: aurelia.library@aurelia.lib.ia.us. Web Site: www.aurelia.lib.ia.us. *Dir,* Sherri Stevenson; *Librn,* Janet Laursen; Staff 2 (Non-MLS 2)
Founded 1917. Pop 1,062; Circ 15,000
Library Holdings: Bk Titles 15,000; Per Subs 34
Special Collections: Iowa Coll
Subject Interests: Hist, Natural sci, Relig
Automation Activity & Vendor Info: (Circulation) OCLC WorldShare Interlibrary Loan
Wireless access
Function: Prof lending libr
Open Mon-Fri 10-6, Sat 9-1
Friends of the Library Group

AURORA

P AURORA PUBLIC LIBRARY*, 401 Woodruff St, 50607. (Mail add: PO Box 7, 50607-0007), SAN 376-7396. Tel: 319-634-3960. FAX: 319-634-3960. E-mail: director@aurora.lib.ia.us. Web Site: www.aurora.lib.ia.us. *Dir,* Kim Wessels
Pop 194
Library Holdings: Bk Vols 3,000; Per Subs 12
Wireless access
Open Mon & Tues 8-11, Wed & Thurs 8-11 & 3-6, Sat 9-11

AVOCA

P AVOCA PUBLIC LIBRARY*, Edwin M Davis Memorial Library, 213 N Elm St, 51521. (Mail add: PO Box 219, 51521-0219), SAN 305-2184. Tel: 712-343-6358. FAX: 712-343-6358. E-mail: library@cityofavoca.com. Web Site: www.avoca.swilsa.lib.ia.us. *Dir,* Serena Riesgaard; *Ch,* Jeanette Bartunek
Pop 1,610; Circ 30,000
Library Holdings: DVDs 1,000; Bk Vols 20,063; Per Subs 66; Talking Bks 650
Wireless access
Open Mon, Tues, Thurs & Fri 10-5, Wed 10-8, Sat 9-Noon

BADGER

P BADGER PUBLIC LIBRARY, 211 First Ave SE, 50516. (Mail add: PO Box 255, 50516-0255), SAN 376-5229. Tel: 515-545-4793. FAX: 515-545-4440. E-mail: badgerpubliclibrary14@gmail.com. Web Site: cityofbadger.com/library. *Dir,* Tammy Jones; E-mail: director@badger.lib.ia.us; *Asst Dir,* Bridget Osborne
Founded 1991. Pop 610
Library Holdings: Audiobooks 100; DVDs 35; Bk Vols 7,000; Per Subs 21; Videos 500
Automation Activity & Vendor Info: (Cataloging) Biblionix/Apollo
Wireless access
Open Mon & Wed 12-6, Tues 9-1, Thurs 2-8, Sat 10-2
Friends of the Library Group

BAGLEY

P BAGLEY PUBLIC LIBRARY, 117 Main, 50026. (Mail add: PO Box 206, 50026-0206), SAN 305-2192. Tel: 641-427-5214. FAX: 641-427-5214. E-mail: bagleypl@windstream.net. Web Site: bagleypubliclibrary.weebly.com. *Dir,* Jeannie Solorzano; Staff 2 (Non-MLS 2)
Founded 1976. Pop 303; Circ 3,433
Library Holdings: Audiobooks 255; DVDs 430; Large Print Bks 230; Bk Titles 5,100; Per Subs 24; Talking Bks 250; Videos 100
Special Collections: Town Depository
Subject Interests: Christian fiction
Wireless access
Function: Bks on cassette, Bks on CD, Children's prog, Computers for patron use, Free DVD rentals, Homebound delivery serv, ILL available, Instruction & testing, Internet access, Laminating, Magazines, Movies, Photocopying/Printing, Story hour, Summer reading prog, Tax forms, VHS videos, Wheelchair accessible
Open Tues 1-5, Wed 11-6, Thurs & Fri 1-5, Sat 10-12
Restriction: Restricted access

BANCROFT

P BANCROFT PUBLIC LIBRARY*, 208 E Ramsey St, 50517. (Mail add: PO Box 347, 50517-0347), SAN 305-2206. Tel: 515-885-2753. FAX: 515-885-2753. Web Site: www.bancroftiowa.com/library, www1.youseemore.com/nilc/bancroft. *Dir,* Mary Richter; E-mail: m.richter@bancroft.lib.ia.us
Founded 1961. Pop 732; Circ 21,479
Library Holdings: Bk Titles 16,684; Per Subs 40
Automation Activity & Vendor Info: (Cataloging) Follett Software; (Circulation) Follett Software
Wireless access
Open Mon, Thurs & Fri 1-5:30, Tues 9-11 & 1-5:30, Wed 1-8, Sat 9-12

BATAVIA

P BATAVIA PUBLIC LIBRARY*, 902 Third St, 52533. SAN 305-2214. Tel: 641-662-2317. *Librn,* Judy Dovico
Pop 500; Circ 2,761
Library Holdings: Bk Titles 5,112; Bk Vols 5,400; Per Subs 20
Wireless access
Open Tues & Thurs 1-4:30

BATTLE CREEK

P BATTLE CREEK PUBLIC LIBRARY, 115 Main St, 51006. SAN 305-2222. Tel: 712-365-4912. FAX: 712-365-4912. E-mail: bcpublib@frontier.com. Web Site: bcpublib.weebly.com. *Dir,* Sheila Petersen
Pop 743; Circ 9,676
Library Holdings: Bk Titles 11,989; Per Subs 29
Wireless access
Open Mon & Thurs 2-7, Tues & Wed 2-6, Fri 2-5, Sat 11-3

BAXTER

P BAXTER PUBLIC LIBRARY*, 202 E State St, 50028. (Mail add: PO Box 586, 50028-0586), SAN 376-5059. Tel: 641-227-3934. FAX: 641-227-3217. E-mail: library.baxter@gmail.com. Web Site: www.baxter.lib.ia.us. *Dir,* Marie Van Beek
Pop 1,055
Library Holdings: Bk Vols 25,000; Per Subs 30
Wireless access
Open Mon-Thurs 9-12 & 3:30-7, Sat 9-12
Friends of the Library Group

BAYARD

P BAYARD PUBLIC LIBRARY*, 315 Main St, 50029. (Mail add: PO Box 338, 50029-0338), SAN 305-2230. Tel: 712-651-2238. FAX: 712-651-2238. *Dir,* Jeannie Stone; Staff 1.5 (Non-MLS 1.5)
Founded 1936. Pop 471; Circ 17,176
Library Holdings: Audiobooks 370; AV Mats 366; Bks on Deafness & Sign Lang 2; CDs 370; DVDs 656; e-books 5,607; Bk Titles 14,096; Per Subs 52
Subject Interests: Antiques, Quilting, Sports
Automation Activity & Vendor Info: (Acquisitions) Follett Software; (Cataloging) Follett Software; (Circulation) Follett Software; (Course Reserve) Follett Software; (ILL) Follett Software; (Media Booking) Follett Software; (OPAC) Follett Software; (Serials) Follett Software
Wireless access
Partic in State of Iowa Libraries Online; West/Central Iowa Libraries Building Online Resources
Open Mon, Tues, Thurs & Fri 1-5, Wed 10-8, Sat 9-Noon
Friends of the Library Group

BEAMAN

P BEAMAN COMMUNITY MEMORIAL LIBRARY*, 223 Main St, 50609. (Mail add: PO Box 135, 50609-0135), SAN 305-2249. Tel: 641-366-2912. FAX: 641-366-3141. E-mail: library@beaman.lib.ia.us. Web Site: www.beaman.lib.ia.us. *Dir,* Sarah Dougherty; *Asst Librn,* Crystal Case; Staff 2 (Non-MLS 2)
Founded 1955. Pop 191; Circ 6,978
Library Holdings: AV Mats 4; DVDs 350; Bk Titles 6,361; Per Subs 45
Subject Interests: Local hist
Automation Activity & Vendor Info: (Cataloging) Follett Software; (Circulation) Follett Software
Wireless access
Open Mon-Fri 2-6, Sat 10-Noon

BEDFORD

P BEDFORD PUBLIC LIBRARY, 507 Jefferson St, 50833-1314. SAN 305-2257. Tel: 712-523-2828. FAX: 712-523-2640. E-mail: bedfordlibrary@mchsi.com. Web Site: www.bedford.lib.ia.us. *Dir,* Tanya Wyckoff
Founded 1915. Pop 1,620; Circ 14,326
Library Holdings: Bk Titles 22,078; Per Subs 41
Special Collections: Genealogical Coll, bks, prints; Local Newspapers; Taylor County Census, microfilm
Wireless access
Partic in Midwest Collaborative for Library Services
Open Mon 2-6, Tues, Wed & Fri 2-5:30, Thurs 9-5:30, Sat 9-12:30

BELLE PLAINE

P BELLE PLAINE COMMUNITY LIBRARY*, 904 12th St, 52208-1711. SAN 305-2265. Tel: 319-444-2902. FAX: 319-444-2902. E-mail: director@belleplaine.lib.ia.us. Web Site: www.belleplaine.lib.ia.us. *Dir,* Kristi Sorensen; *Asst Librn,* Jolene Blanchard; *Asst Librn,* Shirley Cernin; *Asst Librn,* Rima Johnson; *Asst Librn,* Paula Mengler; *Asst Librn,* Bonnie Primley
Founded 1907. Pop 2,950; Circ 20,000
Library Holdings: Bk Vols 19,000; Per Subs 80
Subject Interests: Iowa
Wireless access
Open Mon-Thurs 10-7, Fri 10-4, Sat 9-Noon

BELLEVUE

P BELLEVUE PUBLIC LIBRARY, 106 N Third St, Ste 1, 52031. SAN 305-2273. Tel: 563-872-4991. FAX: 563-872-4094. E-mail: bellevuepubliclibrary@gmail.com. Web Site: www.bellevue.lib.ia.us. *Dir,* Marian L Meyer; E-mail: marianmeyer4@aol.com; *Asst Dir,* Sheila Walsh; *Ch,* Kim Bulman
Pop 2,350; Circ 51,766
Library Holdings: Bk Vols 19,000; Per Subs 55
Wireless access
Open Mon, Tues, Thurs & Fri 10-5:30, Wed 10-7, Sat 10-3
Friends of the Library Group

BELMOND

P TALBOT BELMOND PUBLIC LIBRARY, 440 E Main St, 50421-1224. SAN 305-2281. Tel: 641-444-4160. FAX: 641-444-3457. Web Site: www.youseemore.com/NILC/Belmond. *Dir,* Sonya Trager; E-mail: strager@belmond.lib.ia.us; *Ch,* Amy Bates
Founded 1917. Pop 2,560; Circ 38,000
Library Holdings: Bk Vols 20,000; Per Subs 80
Automation Activity & Vendor Info: (Cataloging) Follett Software; (Circulation) Follett Software; (OPAC) Follett Software
Wireless access
Open Mon-Thurs 10-6, Fri 10-3, Sat 10-2
Friends of the Library Group

BENNETT

P BENNETT PUBLIC LIBRARY*, 203 Main St, 52721. (Mail add: PO Box 299, 52721-0299), SAN 305-229X. Tel: 563-890-2238. FAX: 563-890-2711. E-mail: benetlib@fbcom.net. Web Site: www.bennettpubliclibrary.com. *Dir,* Mindy Williams
Founded 1942. Pop 395; Circ 800
Library Holdings: Bk Titles 5,543
Open Tues & Thurs 2-6, Wed 1-5, Fri 9-Noon, Sat 10-1, Sun 2-4

BETTENDORF

P BETTENDORF PUBLIC LIBRARY INFORMATION CENTER*, 2950 Learning Campus Dr, 52722. (Mail add: PO Box 1330, 52722-1330), SAN 305-2311. Tel: 563-344-4175. Reference Tel: 563-344-4179. Administration Tel: 563-344-4183. FAX: 563-344-4185. E-mail: info@bettendorflibrary.com. Web Site: www.bettendorflibrary.com. *Dir,* Sue Mannix; E-mail: smannix@bettendorf.org; *Asst Dir,* Maria Levetzow; Tel: 563-344-4191, E-mail: mlevetzow@bettendorf.org; *Circ Mgr,* Carina Mulcrone; Tel: 593-344-4195, E-mail: cmulcrone@bettendorf.org; *Tech Serv Mgr,* Susan Green; Tel: 593-344-4193, E-mail: sgreen@bettendorf.org; *Youth Serv Mgr,* Paul Odell; Tel: 563-344-4189, E-mail: podell@bettendorf.org; Staff 23 (MLS 10, Non-MLS 13)
Founded 1957. Pop 31,258; Circ 620,206
Library Holdings: AV Mats 19,400; e-books 7,956; Bk Vols 150,206; Per Subs 348
Special Collections: Iowa Hist Coll
Automation Activity & Vendor Info: (Acquisitions) Innovative Interfaces, Inc; (Cataloging) Innovative Interfaces, Inc; (Circulation) Innovative Interfaces, Inc; (OPAC) Innovative Interfaces, Inc; (Serials) Innovative Interfaces, Inc
Wireless access
Publications: Pages (Newsletter)
Partic in RiverShare Libraries
Open Mon-Thurs 9-9, Fri & Sat 9-5:30, Sun 1-5
Friends of the Library Group

J SCOTT COMMUNITY COLLEGE LIBRARY*, 500 Belmont Rd, 52722. SAN 305-3253. Tel: 563-441-4150. Interlibrary Loan Service Tel: 563-441-4153. Administration Tel: 563-441-4152. FAX: 563-441-4154. E-mail: scclibrary@eicc.edu. Web Site: scottcclibrary.wordpress.com. *Asst Dean of Libr,* Michelle M Bailey; E-mail: mmbailey@eicc.edu; Staff 6 (MLS 1, Non-MLS 5)
Founded 1968. Enrl 4,506; Fac 120; Highest Degree: Associate
Library Holdings: Bk Titles 39,851; Per Subs 176
Wireless access
Function: Distance learning, ILL available
Publications: Infotrac
Partic in Quad-Link Libr Consortium
Open Mon-Fri 7:30-4:30

BIRMINGHAM

P BIRMINGHAM PUBLIC LIBRARY*, 310 Main St, 52535. (Mail add: PO Box 167, 52535-0167), SAN 305-232X. Tel: 319-498-4423. E-mail: birmlibr@netins.net. *Dir,* Michele Mitchell
Pop 488; Circ 1,075
Library Holdings: AV Mats 15; Bk Titles 6,976; Per Subs 20; Videos 332
Function: Summer reading prog
Open Wed & Sat 1-4
Restriction: Pub use on premises

BLAIRSTOWN

P BLAIRSTOWN PUBLIC LIBRARY*, 305 Locust St, Ste 2, 52209. (Mail add: PO Box 187, 52209-0187), SAN 305-2338. Tel: 319-454-6497. FAX: 319-454-6495. E-mail: btown@netins.net. Web Site: www.blairstownpubliclibrary.com. *Dir,* Molly Rach; Staff 3 (MLS 1, Non-MLS 2)
Founded 1930. Pop 682
Library Holdings: Bk Titles 11,500; Per Subs 20
Wireless access
Function: 24/7 Electronic res, 24/7 Online cat, Adult bk club, Bk club(s), Bks on CD, Children's prog, Computers for patron use, Electronic databases & coll, Family literacy, Free DVD rentals, Holiday prog, Homebound delivery serv, ILL available, Instruction & testing, Internet access, Life-long learning prog for all ages, Magazines, Microfiche/film & reading machines, Movies, Notary serv, Online cat, Online ref, Outreach serv, OverDrive digital audio bks, Photocopying/Printing, Preschool outreach, Prog for adults, Prog for children & young adult, Ref serv available, Spoken cassettes & CDs, Summer reading prog, Teen prog, Telephone ref, Visual arts prog, Wheelchair accessible, Workshops
Open Mon 10-7, Tues-Fri 1-6, Sat 10-1

BLAKESBURG

P BLAKESBURG PUBLIC LIBRARY*, 407 S Wilson St, 52536. (Mail add: PO Box 87, 52536-0087), SAN 373-6954. Tel: 641-938-2834. FAX: 641-938-2834. E-mail: library@blakesburg.lib.ia.us. Web Site: www.blakesburg.lib.ia.us. *Dir,* Cheryl Talbert; *Asst Dir,* Stacey McSparen
Pop 374
Library Holdings: DVDs 200; e-books 10,000; Large Print Bks 500; Bk Titles 5,398; Per Subs 14
Wireless access
Special Services for the Blind - Large print bks
Open Mon & Wed 3:15-8, Tues & Thurs 5:30-8:30, Sat 8am-12:30pm
Friends of the Library Group

BLOOMFIELD

P BLOOMFIELD PUBLIC LIBRARY, 107 N Columbia St, 52537-1431. SAN 305-2354. Tel: 641-664-2209. FAX: 641-664-2506. E-mail: bpl@netins.net. Web Site: www.bloomfield.lib.ia.us. *Dir,* Annette Tews; E-mail: anne.tews@bloomfield.lib.ia.us
Founded 1913. Pop 2,601; Circ 41,230
Library Holdings: DVDs 113; Large Print Bks 1,194; Bk Titles 20,711; Per Subs 51; Talking Bks 871; Videos 383
Special Collections: Davis County Genealogy Society
Subject Interests: Iowa, Local hist
Wireless access
Partic in Bergen County Cooperative Library System, Inc
Open Mon, Wed & Fri 10-5, Tues & Thurs 10-7, Sat 10-2
Friends of the Library Group

BODE

P BODE PUBLIC LIBRARY, 114 Humboldt Ave, 50519. (Mail add: PO Box 122, 50519-0122), SAN 305-2362. Tel: 515-379-1258. FAX: 515-379-1486. E-mail: bodeplib1258@gmail.com. *Dir,* Orlyn Maassen
Pop 327; Circ 5,149
Library Holdings: Bk Vols 4,682; Per Subs 32
Wireless access
Open Mon 1-8, Tues & Thurs 1-5, Fri 9-5

BONAPARTE

P BONAPARTE PUBLIC LIBRARY*, 201 Washington St, 52620. (Mail add: PO Box 158, 52620-1058), SAN 305-2370. Tel: 319-592-3677. FAX: 319-592-3577. E-mail: blibrary@netins.net. *Libr Dir,* Roberta Gonterman
Pop 458; Circ 5,026
Library Holdings: Bk Titles 8,000
Wireless access
Open Tues, Wed & Thurs 1:30-6, Fri 2:30-6, Sat 9-Noon
Friends of the Library Group

BONDURANT

P BONDURANT COMMUNITY LIBRARY*, 104 Second St NE, 50035. (Mail add: PO Box 160, 50035-0160), SAN 320-4766. Tel: 515-967-4790. FAX: 515-967-2668. E-mail: library@cityofbondurant.com. Web Site: cityofbondurant.com/bondurant-community-library. *Libr Dir,* Jill Sanders; E-mail: jills@bondurant.lib.ia.us
Founded 1976. Pop 5,318; Circ 40,543
Automation Activity & Vendor Info: (Acquisitions) Follett Software; (Cataloging) Follett Software; (Circulation) Follett Software; (Course Reserve) Follett Software; (ILL) OCLC FirstSearch; (Media Booking) OCLC FirstSearch; (OPAC) Follett Software; (Serials) Follett Software
Wireless access
Open Mon-Thurs 9-7, Fri 9-5, Sat 9-4
Friends of the Library Group

BOONE

J DES MOINES AREA COMMUNITY COLLEGE*, Boone Campus Library, 1125 Hancock Dr, 50036-5326. SAN 305-2389. Tel: 515-433-5043. Web Site: www.library.dmacc.edu. *Dir,* Rebecca Funke; E-mail: rsfunke@dmacc.edu; *Librn,* Michelle Tedrow; E-mail: matedrow1@dmacc.edu; Staff 3 (MLS 1, Non-MLS 2)
Founded 1966
Library Holdings: Bk Vols 19,000; Per Subs 115
Special Collections: Iowa Fiction; Railroads
Partic in Iowa Academic Library Alliance; OCLC Online Computer Library Center, Inc
Open Mon-Thurs 7:30-6:30, Fri 7:30-4

P ERICSON PUBLIC LIBRARY*, 702 Greene St, 50036. SAN 341-7816. Tel: 515-432-3727. FAX: 515-432-1103. E-mail: ericson@boone.lib.ia.us. Web Site: www.boone.lib.ia.us. *Dir,* Jamie Williams; E-mail: jwilliams@boone.lib.ia.us; *Asst Dir,* Andrea Williams; E-mail: awilliams@boone.lib.ia.us; Staff 6 (MLS 3, Non-MLS 3)
Founded 1901. Pop 12,803; Circ 162,105
Jul 2014-Jun 2015 Income $694,434, State $8,937, City $591,623, County $51,610, Locally Generated Income $16,339, Other $25,925. Mats Exp $66,699, Books $43,296, Other Print Mats $4,336, AV Mat $13,337, Electronic Ref Mat (Incl. Access Fees) $5,730. Sal $269,313
Library Holdings: AV Mats 16,838; e-books 20,429; Bk Vols 64,548; Per Subs 81
Subject Interests: Antiques, Genealogy, Iowa, Railroads
Automation Activity & Vendor Info: (Cataloging) Innovative Interfaces, Inc; (Circulation) Innovative Interfaces, Inc; (ILL) Innovative Interfaces, Inc; (OPAC) Innovative Interfaces, Inc
Wireless access
Partic in OCLC Online Computer Library Center, Inc
Open Mon & Tues 9-8, Wed-Fri 9-6, Sat 9-1
Friends of the Library Group

BOYDEN

P BOYDEN PUBLIC LIBRARY*, 609 Webb St, 51234. (Mail add: PO Box 249, 51234-0249), SAN 305-2397. Tel: 712-725-2281. FAX: 712-725-2224. E-mail: boylib1@premieronline.net. Web Site: www.boyden.lib.ia.us. *Dir,* Shari Fedders; E-mail: sfedders@boyden.lib.ia.us
Pop 672
Library Holdings: AV Mats 2,919; Bk Vols 23,478; Per Subs 62
Open Tues & Thurs 1-5:30, Wed 1-7, Fri 10-5, Sat 9-12

BRITT

P BRITT PUBLIC LIBRARY*, 132 Main Ave S, 50423-1627. SAN 305-2400. Tel: 641-843-4245. FAX: 641-843-4402. E-mail: brittpubliclibrary@mchsi.com. Web Site: www.youseemore.com/nilc/britt. *Dir,* Linda Friedow; *Ch,* Shannon Nielsen; Staff 3 (Non-MLS 3)
Founded 1917. Pop 2,052; Circ 14,500
Library Holdings: AV Mats 1,766; Large Print Bks 400; Bk Vols 17,366; Per Subs 54
Subject Interests: Hospice
Automation Activity & Vendor Info: (Cataloging) Follett Software; (Circulation) Follett Software

Open Mon 10-6, Tues-Thurs 10-8, Fri 10-5, Sat 9-12
Friends of the Library Group

BROOKLYN

P BROOKLYN PUBLIC LIBRARY*, 306 Jackson St, 52211. SAN 305-2419. Tel: 641-522-9272. FAX: 641-522-9272. E-mail: admin@brooklyn.lib.ia.us. Web Site: www.brooklyn.lib.ia.us. *Dir,* LuAnn Jahlas
Pop 1,367
Library Holdings: Bk Titles 8,000; Per Subs 50
Wireless access
Open Mon-Fri 11-6, Sat 9-1
Friends of the Library Group

BUFFALO CENTER

P BUFFALO CENTER PUBLIC LIBRARY*, 221 N Main St, 50424. (Mail add: PO Box 350, 50424-1037), SAN 305-2427. Tel: 641-562-2546. FAX: 641-562-2546. E-mail: bclib@wctatel.net. Web Site: www.buffalocenter.lib.ia.us. *Dir,* Sharon Hippen; *Asst Librn,* Elaine Michaelson
Pop 963; Circ 8,063
Library Holdings: Bk Titles 8,000; Per Subs 20
Automation Activity & Vendor Info: (Circulation) Biblionix/Apollo
Wireless access
Open Mon, Thurs & Fri 1-5, Tues 9:30-12 & 1-5, Wed 1-5:30, Sat 9:30-Noon

BURLINGTON

P BURLINGTON PUBLIC LIBRARY*, 210 Court St, 52601. SAN 305-2443. Tel: 319-753-1647. FAX: 319-753-0789. Web Site: www.burlington.lib.ia.us. *Dir,* Rhonda J Frevert; E-mail: rfrevert@burlington.lib.ia.us; *Coll Tech Librn,* Lois J Blythe; E-mail: lblythe@burlington.lib.ia.us; *Pub Serv Librn,* Samantha Helmick; E-mail: shelmick@burlington.lib.ia.us; *Youth Serv Librn,* Amy Power; E-mail: apower@burlington.lib.ia.us
Founded 1868. Pop 26,839; Circ 445,000
Subject Interests: County hist, Genealogy, Local hist
Automation Activity & Vendor Info: (Acquisitions) SirsiDynix; (Cataloging) SirsiDynix; (Circulation) SirsiDynix; (OPAC) SirsiDynix; (Serials) SirsiDynix
Wireless access
Open Mon-Thurs 9-8, Fri & Sat 9-5
Friends of the Library Group

BURT

P BURT PUBLIC LIBRARY*, 119 Walnut St, 50522. (Mail add: PO Box 128, 50522-0128), SAN 305-2451. Tel: 515-924-3680. FAX: 515-924-3681. Web Site: www1.youseemore.com/nilc/burt. *Libr Dir,* Nikki Brewer; E-mail: nikki@burt.lib.ia.us; *Asst Librn,* Sue Chihak; E-mail: schihak@burt.lib.ia.us
Pop 556; Circ 4,474
Library Holdings: Bk Vols 6,500; Per Subs 25
Open Mon 9-12 & 1-8, Wed & Fri 1-5:30, Sat 9-Noon

BUSSEY

P BUSSEY COMMUNITY LIBRARY*, 401 Merrill St, 50044. (Mail add: PO Box 29, 50044), SAN 376-5423. Tel: 641-944-5994. Web Site: www.bussey.lib.ia.us. *Dir,* Susan Bacon
Pop 450
Library Holdings: Bk Vols 11,000
Wireless access
Open Mon 1-4, Tues 12-6, Wed 10-4, Thurs 11-5, Sat 10-12

CALLENDER

P CALLENDER HERITAGE LIBRARY*, 505 Thomas St, 50523. (Mail add: PO Box 69, 50523-0069), SAN 305-2478. Tel: 515-548-3803. FAX: 515-548-3801. E-mail: callenderlib@lvcta.com. Web Site: cityofcallenderiowa.com/LIBRARY.html. *Dir,* Kim Anderson
Founded 1903. Pop 424; Circ 9,230
Library Holdings: Bk Titles 10,000; Per Subs 40
Open Tues & Thurs 1-6, Wed 10-12 & 1-7, Fri 1-5, Sat 9-Noon

CALMAR

P CALMAR PUBLIC LIBRARY*, 101 S Washington St, 52132. (Mail add: PO Box 806, 52132-0806), SAN 305-2486. Tel: 563-562-3010. Web Site: www.calmarlibrary.com. *Libr Dir,* Linda Crossland; *Libr Asst,* Vernelle Holthaus; *Libr Asst,* Gladys Huinker
Pop 978
Library Holdings: Audiobooks 836; DVDs 333; Large Print Bks 650; Per Subs 29; Videos 140
Automation Activity & Vendor Info: (Acquisitions) Biblionix/Apollo; (Cataloging) Biblionix/Apollo; (Circulation) Biblionix/Apollo; (Course Reserve) Biblionix/Apollo; (ILL) Biblionix/Apollo; (Media Booking) Biblionix/Apollo
Wireless access
Function: 24/7 Electronic res, 24/7 Online cat, Activity rm, Adult bk club, Audiobks via web, Bk club(s), Bks on CD, Children's prog, Computer training, Computers for patron use, Distance learning, Electronic databases & coll, For res purposes, Free DVD rentals, Govt ref serv, Health sci info serv, Holiday prog, ILL available, Internet access, Life-long learning prog for all ages, Literacy & newcomer serv, Magazines, Mail & tel request accepted, Meeting rooms, Online cat, Online ref, Outreach serv, Outside serv via phone, mail, e-mail & web, OverDrive digital audio bks, Photocopying/Printing, Preschool outreach, Preschool reading prog, Prog for adults, Prog for children & young adult, Ref & res, Ref serv available, Scanner, Senior outreach, Serves people with intellectual disabilities, Study rm, Summer reading prog, Teen prog, Telephone ref, VHS videos, Wheelchair accessible, Workshops
Partic in North Eastern Iowa Bridge to Online Resource Sharing
Open Mon-Fri 12-6, Sat 10-1

J NORTHEAST IOWA COMMUNITY COLLEGE*, Calmar Campus Library, 1625 Hwy 150, 52132. (Mail add: PO Box 400, 52132-0400), SAN 305-2494. Tel: 563-562-3263. Toll Free Tel: 800-728-2256, Ext 395. E-mail: lib-cal@nicc.edu. Web Site: www.nicc.edu/library. *Coordr,* Karen Davidson; Tel: 563-562-3263, Ext 257, E-mail: davidsonk@nicc.edu; *Acq,* Heather Busta; E-mail: bustah@nicc.edu; *Cat, ILL,* Germaine Kuhn; Tel: 563-562-3263, Ext 253, E-mail: kuhng@nicc.edu; *Coll Develop,* Position Currently Open; *Mkt,* Marvin Ehm; E-mail: ehmm@nicc.edu; *Per,* Geri Elsbernd; E-mail: elsberndg492@nicc.edu; Staff 4 (MLS 1, Non-MLS 3)
Founded 1966. Enrl 1,500; Fac 140; Highest Degree: Associate
Library Holdings: Bk Vols 19,200; Per Subs 305
Special Collections: Holocaust Coll
Subject Interests: Agr, Bus & mgt, Nursing, Sci tech
Automation Activity & Vendor Info: (Cataloging) SirsiDynix; (Circulation) SirsiDynix; (Discovery) EBSCO Discovery Service; (ILL) OCLC Connexion
Wireless access
Function: 24/7 Electronic res, 24/7 Online cat
Partic in Iowa Academic Library Alliance
Open Mon-Thurs 7:30-6, Fri 7:30-5
Restriction: 24-hr pass syst for students only

CAMANCHE

P CAMANCHE PUBLIC LIBRARY, 102 12th Ave, 52730. SAN 305-2508. Tel: 563-259-1106. FAX: 563-259-0917. E-mail: CamanchePL@camanche.lib.ia.us. Web Site: www.camanchepubliclibrary.org. *Dir,* Anna Evans; E-mail: aevans@camanche.lib.ia.us; *Ch,* Nancy McDougall; *Libr Asst,* Brenda Jacobs
Founded 1965. Pop 4,215; Circ 35,780
Library Holdings: Bk Titles 24,000; Per Subs 150
Special Collections: Iowa Coll; Mississippi River Coll
Wireless access
Open Mon, Tues, Thurs & Fri 10-4, Wed 10-6
Friends of the Library Group

CAMBRIDGE

P CAMBRIDGE MEMORIAL LIBRARY*, 225 Water St, 50046. Tel: 515-220-4542. FAX: 515-220-4542. E-mail: circdesk@cambridge.lib.ia.us. Web Site: www.cambridge.lib.ia.us. *Dir,* Erin Coughlin; E-mail: erin.coughlin@cambridge.lib.ia.us
Pop 819
Library Holdings: Bk Vols 15,000
Wireless access
Open Mon 2-7, Wed 9-11 & 12-6, Fri 3-7, Sat 9-12

CANTRIL

P CANTRIL PUBLIC LIBRARY*, 104 W Third St, 52542. (Mail add: PO Box 158, 52542-0158), SAN 376-5482. Tel: 319-397-2366. FAX: 319-397-2366. E-mail: cantril@netins.net. *Dir,* Sue Burchett
Pop 257
Library Holdings: Bk Vols 11,000
Wireless access
Special Services for the Blind - Large print bks; Talking bks
Open Mon & Wed 9-11 & 3:30-5:30, Tues & Thurs 9-11

CARLISLE

P CARLISLE PUBLIC LIBRARY*, 135 School St, 50047-8702. (Mail add: PO Box S, 50047-0718), SAN 305-2532. Tel: 515-989-0909. FAX: 515-989-4328. Web Site: www.carlisle.lib.ia.us. *Dir,* Stacy Goodhue; E-mail: sgoodhue@carlisleiowa.org

Pop 3,497; Circ 29,097
Library Holdings: Bk Vols 26,466; Per Subs 28
Special Collections: Carlisle/Hartford Scrapbook Coll; Iowa Coll
Automation Activity & Vendor Info: (Cataloging) Biblionix; (Circulation) Biblionix
Wireless access
Open Mon-Thurs 10-8, Fri & Sat 10-5
Friends of the Library Group

CARROLL

P CARROLL PUBLIC LIBRARY*, 118 E Fifth St, 51401. SAN 305-2540. Tel: 712-792-3432. FAX: 712-792-0141. E-mail: info@carroll-library.org. Web Site: www.carroll-library.org. *Dir,* Rachel Van Erdewyk; E-mail: rvanerdewyk@carroll-library.org; *Ch,* Diane Tracy; Staff 1 (MLS 1)
Founded 1893. Pop 10,098; Circ 111,846
Library Holdings: Bk Vols 79,000; Per Subs 181
Subject Interests: Genealogy, Sci fict
Automation Activity & Vendor Info: (Cataloging) ComPanion Corp; (Circulation) ComPanion Corp
Wireless access
Open Mon-Thurs 9-8, Fri 10-6, Sat 10-5
Friends of the Library Group

J DES MOINES AREA COMMUNITY COLLEGE LIBRARY*, Carroll Campus Library, 906 N Grant Rd, 51401. Tel: 712-792-8317. FAX: 712-792-8500. E-mail: carrolllibrary@dmacc.edu. Web Site: www.dmacc.edu/library. *Librn,* Lisa Dreesman; E-mail: ladreesman@dmacc.edu; *Libr Asst,* Jane Riley; E-mail: jcriley@dmacc.edu; Staff 2 (MLS 1, Non-MLS 1)
Enrl 800; Fac 26; Highest Degree: Bachelor
Library Holdings: Bk Vols 6,000; Per Subs 125
Subject Interests: Bus, Educ, Nursing, Psychol
Automation Activity & Vendor Info: (Acquisitions) Innovative Interfaces, Inc; (Cataloging) Innovative Interfaces, Inc; (Circulation) Innovative Interfaces, Inc; (Course Reserve) Innovative Interfaces, Inc; (OPAC) Innovative Interfaces, Inc; (Serials) Innovative Interfaces, Inc
Wireless access
Function: Audio & video playback equip for onsite use, Audiobks via web, Bks on CD, Computers for patron use, Electronic databases & coll, ILL available, Internet access, Online cat, Photocopying/Printing
Partic in Iowa Academic Library Alliance

CARTER LAKE

P EDWARD F OWEN MEMORIAL LIBRARY, 1120 Willow Dr, 51510-1332. SAN 305-2559. Tel: 712-347-5492. FAX: 712-347-5013. E-mail: owenlibrary@cox.net. Web Site: www.carterlakelibrary.com. *Dir,* Theresa Hawkins
Founded 1977. Pop 3,248; Circ 13,292
Library Holdings: Bk Titles 14,900; Per Subs 75
Automation Activity & Vendor Info: (Cataloging) Follett Software
Wireless access
Open Mon-Thurs 10-6, Fri 9-2, Sat 10-2

CASCADE

P CASCADE PUBLIC LIBRARY, 310 First Ave W, 52033, (Mail add: PO Box 117, 52033-0117), SAN 305-2567. Tel: 563-852-3222. FAX: 563-852-6011. E-mail: cpl@netins.net. Web Site: www.cascade.lib.ia.us. *Dir,* Melissa A Kane; *Libr Asst,* Carol Cigrand; *Libr Asst,* Rebecca Johnson; *Libr Asst,* Joyce Kremer; *Libr Asst,* Jane Strang
Founded 1968. Pop 1,958; Circ 26,055
Library Holdings: Bk Vols 16,000; Per Subs 28
Automation Activity & Vendor Info: (Acquisitions) Biblionix/Apollo; (Cataloging) Biblionix/Apollo; (Circulation) Biblionix/Apollo
Wireless access
Partic in Dubuque Area Library Information Consortium
Open Mon-Thurs 10-7, Fri 10-5, Sat 9-Noon
Friends of the Library Group

CASEY

P CASEY PUBLIC LIBRARY*, 604 McPherson St, 50048. (Mail add: PO Box 178, 50048-0178), SAN 305-2575. Tel: 641-746-2670. FAX: 641-746-2670. E-mail: caseylib@netins.net. Web Site: caseypubliclibrary.weebly.com. *Dir,* Charlsie Dougherty
Founded 1941. Pop 478; Circ 3,263
Library Holdings: AV Mats 282; High Interest/Low Vocabulary Bk Vols 150; Large Print Bks 30; Bk Titles 10,000; Bk Vols 12,023; Per Subs 10; Talking Bks 155
Special Collections: A-C Yearbooks; Adair News 1951-present; Casey Obituaries; Casey School Alumni Class Pictures; Casey Vindicator on microfilm 1878-1950
Automation Activity & Vendor Info: (ILL) OCLC
Wireless access
Special Services for the Deaf - Closed caption videos
Special Services for the Blind - Bks on cassette; Bks on CD; Large print bks
Open Mon 12-5:30, Wed 12-6, Fri 12-5:30, Sat 9-Noon
Friends of the Library Group

CEDAR FALLS

S CEDAR FALLS HISTORICAL SOCIETY ARCHIVES*, 308 W Third St, 50613. SAN 325-7282. Tel: 319-266-5149. FAX: 319-268-1812. E-mail: cfhistory@cfu.net. Web Site: www.cfhistory.org. *Exec Dir,* Carrie Eilderts; *Colls Mgr,* Julie Huffman-klinkowitz; E-mail: historycollections@cfu.net; Staff 2 (Non-MLS 2)
Founded 1962
Special Collections: Local Authors
Subject Interests: Local hist
Restriction: Open by appt only

P CEDAR FALLS PUBLIC LIBRARY, 524 Main St, 50613. SAN 305-2583. Tel: 319-273-8643. FAX: 319-273-8648. E-mail: info@cedarfallslibrary.org. Web Site: cedarfallslibrary.org. *Dir,* Kelly Stern; Tel: 319-268-5541, E-mail: director@cedarfallslibrary.org; Staff 18 (MLS 4, Non-MLS 14)
Founded 1865. Pop 36,145; Circ 269,786
Library Holdings: Bk Vols 115,757; Per Subs 253; Talking Bks 2,176; Videos 5,468
Automation Activity & Vendor Info: (Acquisitions) Innovative Interfaces, Inc; (Cataloging) Innovative Interfaces, Inc; (Circulation) Innovative Interfaces, Inc; (OPAC) Innovative Interfaces, Inc
Wireless access
Function: Bk club(s), Home delivery & serv to seniorr ctr & nursing homes, Homebound delivery serv, ILL available, Magnifiers for reading, Prog for children & young adult, Ref serv available, Spoken cassettes & CDs, Spoken cassettes & DVDs, Summer reading prog, VHS videos, Wheelchair accessible
Partic in Cedar Valley Libr Consortium
Special Services for the Blind - Low vision equip
Open Mon-Wed 10-9, Thurs & Fri 9-6, Sat 9-5, Sun 1-5
Friends of the Library Group

C UNIVERSITY OF NORTHERN IOWA LIBRARY*, Rod Library, 1227 W 27th St, 50613-3675. SAN 305-2605. Tel: 319-273-2738. Circulation Tel: 319-273-2462. Interlibrary Loan Service Tel: 319-273-2912. Reference Tel: 319-273-2838. FAX: 319-273-2913. Web Site: library.uni.edu. *Dean, Libr Serv,* Theresa Westbrock; Tel: 319-273-2737, E-mail: 'Theresa.Westbrock@uni.edu'; *Interim Assoc Dean,* Katherine F Martin; Tel: 319-273-7255, E-mail: katherine.martin@uni.edu; *Asst Dir, Chief Curator,* Nathan Arndt; Tel: 319-273-2188, E-mail: Nathan.Arndt@uni.edu; *Head, Res Serv, Head, User Serv,* Jerilyn Marshall; Tel: 319-273-3721, E-mail: jerilyn.marshall@uni.edu; *Head, Learning Serv, Head, Outreach Serv,* Chris Neuhaus; Tel: 319-273-3718, E-mail: chris.neuhaus@uni.edu; *Coll Develop Librn, Libr Assessment Coordr,* Gretchen B Gould; Tel: 319-273-6327, E-mail: gretchen.gould@uni.edu; *Coll Strategist Librn,* Barbara Weeg; Tel: 319-273-3705, E-mail: barbara.weeg@uni.edu; *Digital Scholarship Librn,* Ellen Neuhaus; Tel: 319-273-3739, E-mail: ellen.neuhaus@uni.edu; *Fine Arts Librn, Performing Arts Librn,* Angela Pratesi; Tel: 319-273-6257, E-mail: Angela.Pratesi@uni.edu; *Liaison & Instruction Librn,* Angela Cox; Tel: 319-273-2839, E-mail: angela.cox@uni.edu; *Liaison & Instruction Librn,* Anne Marie Gruber; Tel: 319-273-3711, E-mail: anne.gruber@uni.edu; *Outreach Serv Librn,* Leila Rod-Welch; Tel: 319-273-3730, E-mail: Leila.Rod-Welch@uni.edu; *Youth Serv Librn,* Katelyn Browne; Tel: 319-273-6167, E-mail: Katelyn.Browne@uni.edu; *Coordr, Cat,* Susan Moore; E-mail: susan.moore@uni.edu; *Spec Coll Coordr, Univ Archivist,* Jaycie Vos; Tel: 319-273-6307, E-mail: jaycie.vos@uni.edu; *Cat,* Clint Wrede; Tel: 319-273-2781, E-mail: clint.wrede@uni.edu; Staff 29 (MLS 19, Non-MLS 10)
Founded 1876. Enrl 12,159; Fac 788; Highest Degree: Doctorate
Jul 2012-Jun 2013 Income $6,918,850, State $6,172, Locally Generated Income $40,138, Parent Institution $6,872,540. Mats Exp $2,575,750, Books $248,916, Per/Ser (Incl. Access Fees) $450,260, Other Print Mats $248,916, Micro $25,152, Electronic Ref Mat (Incl. Access Fees) $1,584,755, Presv $17,751. Sal $3,317,869 (Prof $2,116,183)
Library Holdings: AV Mats 30,668; CDs 10,346; DVDs 5,267; e-books 8,659; e-journals 59,434; Music Scores 16,630; Bk Titles 674,281; Bk Vols 784,462; Per Subs 1,126; Videos 9,203
Special Collections: American Fiction; Center for the History of Rural Iowa Education & Culture; Grassley Papers; Iowa History; Rural School Coll; University Archives. State Document Depository; US Document Depository
Subject Interests: Art, Children's lit, Educ, Music
Automation Activity & Vendor Info: (Acquisitions) Innovative Interfaces, Inc; (Cataloging) Innovative Interfaces, Inc; (Circulation) Innovative Interfaces, Inc; (Course Reserve) Innovative Interfaces, Inc; (ILL) OCLC ILLiad; (Media Booking) Innovative Interfaces, Inc; (OPAC) Innovative Interfaces, Inc; (Serials) Innovative Interfaces, Inc

Wireless access
Publications: Guide to the Library; Library User's Guide Series
Partic in Cedar Valley Libr Consortium; Iowa Academic Library Alliance; LYRASIS; OCLC Online Computer Library Center, Inc
Special Services for the Deaf - ADA equip; Assistive tech; Bks on deafness & sign lang; Closed caption videos; Coll on deaf educ; Sign lang interpreter upon request for prog; Videos & decoder
Special Services for the Blind - Accessible computers; Aids for in-house use; Assistive/Adapted tech devices, equip & products; Audio mat; Braille alphabet card; Braille equip; Cassette playback machines; Children's Braille; Closed caption display syst; Closed circuit TV magnifier; Computer access aids; Computer with voice synthesizer for visually impaired persons; Copier with enlargement capabilities; Free checkout of audio mat; HP Scan Jet with photo-finish software; IBM screen reader; Info on spec aids & appliances; Internet workstation with adaptive software; Large screen computer & software; Low vision equip; Magnifiers; Micro-computer access & training; Networked computers with assistive software; Open bk software on pub access PC; PC for people with disabilities; Photo duplicator for making large print; Playaways (bks on MP3); Rec; Ref serv; Rental typewriters & computers; Scanner for conversion & translation of mats; Screen enlargement software for people with visual disabilities; Screen reader software; Sound rec; Talking calculator; Text reader; Videos on blindness & physical disabilties; VisualTek equip; ZoomText magnification & reading software
Open Mon-Thurs 7am-Midnight, Fri 7-7, Sat 10-5, Sun 2-Midnight

CEDAR RAPIDS

S AFRICAN AMERICAN MUSEUM OF IOWA LIBRARY, 55 12th Ave SE, 52401. Tel: 319-862-2101, Ext 217. FAX: 319-862-2105. Web Site: www.blackiowa.org. *Curator,* Felicite Wolfe; Tel: 319-862-2101, E-mail: fwolfe@blackiowa.org; Staff 1 (Non-MLS 1)
Founded 1993. Sal $32,000 (Prof $32,000)
Library Holdings: Bk Vols 4,500
Special Collections: African American History; African American History in Iowa. Oral History
Subject Interests: African hist, African-Am hist
Wireless access
Open Tues-Sat 10-4

P CEDAR RAPIDS PUBLIC LIBRARY, Ladd Library, 3750 Williams Blvd SW, 52404. SAN 341-7875. Tel: 319-398-5123. FAX: 319-398-0476. Interlibrary Loan Service E-mail: ill@crlibrary.org. Information Services E-mail: info@crlibrary.org. Web Site: www.crlibrary.org. *Libr Dir,* Dara Schmidt; E-mail: schmidtd@crlibrary.org; Staff 44.6 (MLS 12.5, Non-MLS 32.1)
Founded 1896. Pop 126,326; Circ 810,115
Library Holdings: Bk Vols 103,182; Per Subs 233
Automation Activity & Vendor Info: (Acquisitions) SirsiDynix; (Cataloging) SirsiDynix; (Circulation) SirsiDynix; (OPAC) SirsiDynix; (Serials) SirsiDynix
Wireless access
Function: Bks on CD, Children's prog, Computer training, Computers for patron use, Free DVD rentals, Homebound delivery serv, ILL available, Music CDs, Notary serv, OverDrive digital audio bks, Photocopying/Printing, Preschool outreach, Prog for adults, Prog for children & young adult, Ref serv available, Story hour, Summer & winter reading prog, Tax forms, Teen prog, Telephone ref, Visual arts prog, Wheelchair accessible
Publications: News from the Cedar Rapids Public Library (Newsletter)
Partic in Metro Library Network
Open Mon-Thurs 9-8, Fri 9-5, Sun 1-5
Friends of the Library Group

C COE COLLEGE*, Stewart Memorial Library, 1220 First Ave NE, 52402-5092. SAN 305-2621. Tel: 319-399-8023. Circulation Tel: 319-399-8585. Reference Tel: 319-399-8586. Administration Tel: 319-399-8024. Web Site: www.coe.edu/library. *Dir, Libr Serv, Univ Archivist,* Jill Jack; E-mail: Jjack@coe.edu; *Head, AV,* Laura Riskedahl; Tel: 319-399-8211, E-mail: lriskedahl@coe.edu; *Head, Circ,* Sandy Blanchard; Tel: 319-399-8595, E-mail: sblancha@coe.edu; *Head, Ref & Instruction,* Elizabeth Hoover de Galvez; Tel: 319-399-8017, E-mail: egalvez@coe.edu; *Head, Tech Serv,* Hongbo Xie; Tel: 319-399-8026, E-mail: hxie@coe.edu; *ILL Supvr,* Randi Thon; Tel: 319-399-8016, E-mail: rthon@coe.edu; *Archives Asst,* Harlene Hansen; Tel: 319-399-8787, E-mail: hhansen@coe.edu; Staff 4 (MLS 4)
Founded 1900. Enrl 1,303; Fac 123; Highest Degree: Master
Jul 2013-Jun 2014 Income $1,100,000. Mats Exp $400,000. Sal $470,000 (Prof $250,000)
Library Holdings: AV Mats 15,000; CDs 4,001; DVDs 4,787; e-books 193,392; e-journals 2,924; Microforms 5,979; Music Scores 385; Bk Titles 379,276; Per Subs 6,000; Videos 2,231
Special Collections: Paul Engle Papers; William Shirer Papers
Subject Interests: Art & archit, Hist, Relig, Soc sci & issues
Automation Activity & Vendor Info: (Acquisitions) SirsiDynix; (Cataloging) SirsiDynix; (Circulation) SirsiDynix; (Course Reserve) SirsiDynix; (ILL) OCLC ILLiad; (OPAC) SirsiDynix; (Serials) SirsiDynix
Wireless access
Publications: Coe College Library Association (Newsletter)
Partic in Iowa Academic Library Alliance; OCLC Online Computer Library Center, Inc
Open Mon-Thurs 7:45am-1am, Fri 8-6, Sat 9-6, Sun 11am-1am
Friends of the Library Group

S GENEALOGICAL SOCIETY OF LINN COUNTY IOWA*, Genealogy Library, 813 First Ave SE, 52401. (Mail add: PO Box 175, 52406-0175), SAN 370-1697. Tel: 319-369-0022. E-mail: GenSocLinnCoIA@aol.com. Web Site: GenSocLinnCoIA.weebly.com. *Librn,* Eileen Kozman. Subject Specialists: *Genealogy,* Eileen Kozman
Founded 1965
Library Holdings: CDs 300; Bk Titles 12,000
Special Collections: Linn County Cemetery & Court House Records
Function: Res libr
Publications: Linn County Heritage Hunter (Newsletter)
Open Tues-Sat 10-4 or by appointment

S GRAND LODGE OF IOWA, AF & AM, Iowa Masonic Library, 813 First Ave SE, 52406. (Mail add: PO Box 279, 52406-0279), SAN 305-2613. Tel: 319-365-1438. FAX: 319-365-1439. Web Site: grandlodgeofiowa.org. *Librn,* Craig Davis; *Asst Librn,* William Kreuger; E-mail: bill.kreuger@gl-iowa.org; Staff 2 (MLS 1, Non-MLS 1)
Founded 1845
Library Holdings: Bk Titles 100,000
Special Collections: Abraham Lincoln Coll; Arthur Edward Waite Coll; Cedar Rapids Gazette, micro; Dr Erskine Medical Coll; Early Cedar Rapids, micro, paper; Prince Hall Masonic Coll; Robert Burns Coll
Subject Interests: Hist, Iowa, Poetry, Relig
Wireless access
Open Mon-Fri 8-12 & 1-5

J KIRKWOOD COMMUNITY COLLEGE*, Benton Hall Library, Cedar Rapids Main Campus, 6301 Kirkwood Blvd SW, 52404-5260. (Mail add: PO Box 2068, 52406-2068), SAN 305-2664. Tel: 319-398-5553. Circulation Tel: 319-398-5696. Reference Tel: 319-398-5697. Toll Free Tel: 866-452-8504. FAX: 319-398-4908. E-mail: library@kirkwood.edu. Web Site: www.kirkwood.edu/library. *Dean, Learning & Libr Serv,* Arron Wings; E-mail: arron.wings@kirkwood.edu; *Access Serv Librn,* Sue Miller; Tel: 319-398-5887, E-mail: sue.miller@kirkwood.edu; *Colls Librn,* Steve Sickels; *Digital Serv Librn,* Mr Ryan Strempke-Durgin; *Ref Librn,* Jim Kelly; *Ref Librn,* Julie Petersen; *Circ Coordr,* Cindy Wiese; *Technical Spec,* Shelley Schultz; Staff 15 (MLS 9, Non-MLS 6)
Founded 1967. Enrl 15,466; Fac 929; Highest Degree: Associate
Library Holdings: AV Mats 3,944; Bks on Deafness & Sign Lang 138; Bk Vols 66,153; Per Subs 594
Automation Activity & Vendor Info: (Acquisitions) OCLC; (Cataloging) OCLC; (Circulation) OCLC; (Course Reserve) OCLC; (ILL) OCLC; (OPAC) OCLC; (Serials) OCLC
Wireless access
Publications: Faculty Handbook; Student Handbook
Partic in Iowa Academic Library Alliance
Open Mon-Thurs 7:30am-11pm, Fri 7:30-5, Sat 8:30-4, Sun 3-8
Departmental Libraries:
IOWA CITY CAMPUS LIBRARY, 1816 Lower Muscatine Rd, Iowa City, 52240. Tel: 319-887-3612. FAX: 319-887-3606. E-mail: refdesk@kirkwood.edu. Web Site: www.kirkwood.edu/iclibrary. *Ref Librn,* Glenda Davis-Driggs; *Ref Librn,* David Strass; *Coordr,* Kate Hess; E-mail: khess@kirkwood.edu; *Libr Spec,* Missy Molleston; Staff 6 (MLS 3, Non-MLS 3)
Highest Degree: Associate
Open Mon-Thurs 8-8, Fri 8-5, Sat 11-4

C MOUNT MERCY UNIVERSITY*, Busse Library, 1330 Elmhurst Dr NE, 52402-4797. SAN 305-2699. Tel: 319-368-6465. FAX: 319-363-9060. E-mail: library@mtmercy.edu. Web Site: www.mtmercy.edu/busse-library. *Dir,* Kristy Raine; E-mail: kraine@mtmercy.edu; *Access Serv Librn,* Kate Johnson; E-mail: kmjohnson@mtmercy.edu; *Instruction Librn, Res,* Anna Schmall; E-mail: aschmall@mtmercy.edu; *Ref & ILL Librn,* Robyn Clark-Bridges; E-mail: rclark@mtmercy.edu; Staff 5 (MLS 5)
Founded 1958. Enrl 1,572; Fac 98; Highest Degree: Doctorate
Automation Activity & Vendor Info: (Acquisitions) OCLC Worldshare Management Services; (Cataloging) OCLC Worldshare Management Services; (Circulation) OCLC Worldshare Management Services; (Course Reserve) OCLC Worldshare Management Services; (Discovery) OCLC; (ILL) OCLC WorldShare Interlibrary Loan; (OPAC) OCLC Worldshare Management Services; (Serials) OCLC Worldshare Management Services
Wireless access
Partic in Iowa Academic Library Alliance; OCLC Online Computer Library Center, Inc

R TEMPLE JUDAH, Gasway Memorial Library, 3221 Lindsay Lane SE, 52403. SAN 305-2729. Tel: 319-362-1261. E-mail: office@templejudah.org. Web Site: templejudah.org/organizations-and-activities/gasway-memorial-library. *Library Contact,* Terri Cohen
Founded 1950
Library Holdings: Bk Titles 1,850
Subject Interests: Judaica (lit or hist of Jews)

CENTER POINT

P CENTER POINT PUBLIC LIBRARY*, 720 Main St, 52213. (Mail add: PO Box 279, 52213-0279), SAN 305-2737. Tel: 319-849-1509. FAX: 319-849-2809. E-mail: CPULIB@centerpoint.lib.ia.us. Web Site: www.centerpoint.lib.ia.us. *Dir,* Janine Walters; E-mail: jwalters@centerpoint.lib.ia.us
Pop 2,007; Circ 32,000
Library Holdings: Bk Titles 15,000; Per Subs 52
Wireless access
Open Mon, Wed & Thurs 1-8, Tues 8:30-1, Fri 8:30-5:30, Sat 10-2

CENTERVILLE

P DRAKE PUBLIC LIBRARY*, 115 Drake Ave, 52544. SAN 305-2745. Tel: 641-856-6676. FAX: 641-856-6135. E-mail: library@centerville-ia.org. Web Site: drakepubliclibrary.org. *Dir,* JeNel Barth; *Circ Librn,* Kristin Craver; Staff 8 (Non-MLS 8)
Founded 1903. Pop 5,924; Circ 108,138
Library Holdings: Bk Titles 30,478; Per Subs 105
Automation Activity & Vendor Info: (Circulation) Follett Software
Wireless access
Function: ILL available
Open Mon-Fri 10-6, Sat 10-2
Friends of the Library Group

J INDIAN HILLS COMMUNITY COLLEGE*, Centerville Library, 721 N First St, Bldg CV06, 52544. SAN 305-2753. Tel: 641-856-2143, Ext 2237. Toll Free Tel: 800-670-3641, Ext 2237. FAX: 641-856-5527. Web Site: www.indianhills.edu/library. *Dir, Libr Serv,* Cheryl Talbert; E-mail: Cheryl.Talbert@indianhills.edu; *Libr Asst,* Melissa Schultz; E-mail: Melissa.Schultz@indianhills.edu; *Pub Serv Asst,* Debra Worley; E-mail: Deb.Worley@indianhills.edu
Library Holdings: Bk Vols 24,000; Per Subs 98
Wireless access
Partic in Iowa Academic Library Alliance
Open Mon-Thurs (Winter) 7:15-6; Mon-Thurs (Summer) 7:15-4:45

CENTRAL CITY

P CENTRAL CITY PUBLIC LIBRARY*, 137 Fourth St N, Ste 2, 52214. SAN 305-2761. Tel: 319-438-6685. FAX: 319-438-6685. Web Site: www.centralcity.lib.ia.us. *Dir,* Denise Levenhagen; E-mail: dlevenhagen@centralcity.lib.ia.us; Staff 1 (MLS 1)
Founded 1895. Pop 1,157; Circ 6,793
Library Holdings: Bk Titles 8,435; Per Subs 33
Automation Activity & Vendor Info: (Circulation) Book Systems; (OPAC) Book Systems
Wireless access
Open Mon 10:30-5, Tues & Wed 9-5, Thurs 10:30-7, Fri 10:30-4:30
Friends of the Library Group

CHARITON

P CHARITON FREE PUBLIC LIBRARY*, 803 Braden Ave, 50049. SAN 305-277X. Tel: 641-774-5514. FAX: 641-774-8695. Web Site: www.chariton.lib.ia.us. *Dir,* Kris Murphy; E-mail: murphy@chariton.lib.ia.us
Founded 1898. Pop 4,573; Circ 40,517
Library Holdings: Bk Titles 35,000; Per Subs 100
Special Collections: Iowa Census Coll; Lucas County, Federal Census, micro; Newspapers (Chariton Coll)
Automation Activity & Vendor Info: (Cataloging) Follett Software
Friends of the Library Group

CHARLES CITY

P CHARLES CITY PUBLIC LIBRARY*, 106 Milwaukee Mall, 50616-2281. SAN 305-2788. Tel: 641-257-6319. FAX: 641-257-6325. Web Site: www.charles-city.lib.ia.us. *Libr Dir,* Annette R Dean; Tel: 641-257-6317, E-mail: ccdirector34@gmail.com; *Ch,* Stacey Leerhoff; E-mail: staceycclibrary@gmail.com; Staff 4 (MLS 1, Non-MLS 3)
Founded 1904. Pop 7,682; Circ 125,000
Library Holdings: Audiobooks 720; DVDs 1,000; Large Print Bks 500; Bk Titles 52,000; Per Subs 156; Videos 1,000
Special Collections: Iowa History; Mooney Art Coll
Subject Interests: Art, Genealogy
Automation Activity & Vendor Info: (Acquisitions) Biblionix/Apollo; (Cataloging) Biblionix; (OPAC) Biblionix
Function: 24/7 Electronic res, 24/7 Online cat, Activity rm, Adult bk club, After school storytime, Archival coll, Art exhibits, Audio & video playback equip for onsite use, Audiobks via web, Bk club(s), Bks on CD, Children's prog, Computer training, Computers for patron use, Digital talking bks, Electronic databases & coll, Free DVD rentals, Homebound delivery serv, ILL available, Internet access, Life-long learning prog for all ages, Magazines, Meeting rooms, Microfiche/film & reading machines, Movies, Online cat, Online info literacy tutorials on the web & in blackboard, Outreach serv, OverDrive digital audio bks, Photocopying/Printing, Preschool outreach, Prog for adults, Prog for children & young adult, Ref & res, Ref serv available, Scanner, Senior outreach, Story hour, Summer reading prog, Tax forms, Teen prog, Wheelchair accessible
Open Mon-Thurs 10-8, Fri 10-5, Sat & Sun 1-5
Friends of the Library Group

S FLOYD COUNTY HISTORICAL SOCIETY MUSEUM LIBRARY, Research Library & Reference Library, 500 Gilbert St, 50616-2738. SAN 373-4536. Tel: 641-228-1099. E-mail: fcmiowa@gmail.com. Web Site: www.floydcountymuseum.org. *Dir,* Jennifer C Thiele; *Coll Tech,* Sara Renaud; E-mail: fcmcollections@gmail.com
Library Holdings: Bk Vols 5,000; Spec Interest Per Sub 4,000; Videos 1,000
Special Collections: Floyd County Railroad Archives; Oliver Hart Parr Coll
Subject Interests: Genealogy
Publications: Floyd County Heritage (Newsletter)

CHARTER OAK

P CHARTER OAK PUBLIC LIBRARY*, 461 Railroad, 51439. (Mail add: PO Box 58, 51439), SAN 320-8249. Tel: 712-678-3425. E-mail: colibry@outlook.com. Web Site: www.charteroak.lib.ia.us. *Dir,* Carol Meyer
Pop 530
Library Holdings: Bk Vols 5,000
Wireless access
Open Wed 1-6, Sat 8:30-1:30
Friends of the Library Group

CHELSEA

P CHELSEA PUBLIC LIBRARY, St Joseph's Parish School, 201 Broad St, 52215. (Mail add: PO Box 188, 52215-0187), SAN 305-280X. Tel: 641-489-2921. FAX: 641-489-2921. E-mail: chelsealibrary@windstream.net. Web Site: www.chelsea.lib.ia.us. *Dir,* Brad Wolter
Founded 1974. Pop 267; Circ 4,767
Library Holdings: Bk Vols 7,000; Per Subs 30
Wireless access
Open Mon 10:30-4:30, Tues & Wed 1:30-5:30, Thurs 2-7, Sat 9-12

CHEROKEE

M CHEROKEE MENTAL HEALTH INSTITUTE*, Health Science Library, 1251 W Cedar Loop, 51012. SAN 375-2747. Tel: 712-225-2594. FAX: 712-225-6974. *Adminr,* Deb Koch; E-mail: dkoch1@dhs.state.ia.us
Library Holdings: Bk Vols 500; Per Subs 5
Restriction: Open to staff only

P CHEROKEE PUBLIC LIBRARY*, 215 S Second St, 51012. SAN 305-2818. Tel: 712-225-3498. FAX: 712-225-4964. E-mail: cherlib@iowatelecom.net. Web Site: www.cherokee.lib.ia.us. *Dir,* Tyler Hahn; E-mail: tyler@cherokee.lib.ia.us
Founded 1886. Pop 5,369; Circ 65,000
Library Holdings: AV Mats 125; CDs 400; DVDs 300; Large Print Bks 900; Bk Titles 32,000; Per Subs 90; Talking Bks 1,500; Videos 1,400
Automation Activity & Vendor Info: (Cataloging) Follett Software; (Circulation) Follett Software
Wireless access
Open Mon & Thurs 10-8, Tues, Wed & Fri 10-5, Sat 10-1
Friends of the Library Group

S SANFORD MUSEUM & PLANETARIUM*, Reference Library, 117 E Willow, 51012. SAN 305-2826. Tel: 712-225-3922. FAX: 712-225-0446. E-mail: sanfordmuseum@sanfordmuseum.org. Web Site: sanfordmuseum.org. *Dir,* Linda Burkhart
Founded 1951
Library Holdings: Bk Vols 5,000
Subject Interests: Anthrop, Archaeology, Astronomy, Hist, Museology, Paleontology

CHURDAN

P CHURDAN CITY LIBRARY*, 414 Sand St, 50050. (Mail add: PO Box 185, 50050-0185), SAN 305-2834. Tel: 515-389-3423. FAX: 515-389-3401. Web Site: www.churdan.lib.ia.us. *Dir,* Shari Minnehan; E-mail: shari@churdan.lib.ia.us; *Youth Serv Dir,* Marilyn Tilley
Founded 1952. Pop 386; Circ 25,016
Library Holdings: AV Mats 1,115; DVDs 700; Bk Titles 15,000; Per Subs 28; Talking Bks 1,000
Automation Activity & Vendor Info: (Acquisitions) Book Systems; (Cataloging) Book Systems; (Circulation) Book Systems
Wireless access
Open Mon, Tues, Thurs & Fri 11:30-5:30, Wed 9:30-6, Sat 9-11

CLARE

P CLARE PUBLIC LIBRARY*, 119 E Front St, 50524. (Mail add: PO Box 5, 50524-0005), SAN 376-5164. Tel: 515-546-6222. Administration Tel: 515-546-6173. FAX: 515-546-6222. E-mail: clarepl@wccta.net. Web Site: clarepubliclibrary.com. *Librn,* Kathy Allen
Founded 1980. Pop 190
Library Holdings: AV Mats 25; Large Print Bks 50; Bk Titles 8,680; Per Subs 11; Talking Bks 74; Videos 919
Special Services for the Blind - Large print bks
Open Mon 5-8, Wed 8:30-11:30 & 4-5:30, Fri 1:30-5:30, Sat 9-1

CLARENCE

P CLARENCE PUBLIC LIBRARY*, 309 Sixth Ave, 52216. SAN 305-2842. Tel: 563-452-3734. Web Site: www.clarence.lib.ia.us. *Libr Dir,* Ashley Langenberg; E-mail: alangenberg@clarence.lib.ia.us; *Asst Librn,* Tami Finley; Staff 2 (MLS 1, Non-MLS 1)
Pop 989; Circ 7,590
Library Holdings: Bk Vols 7,842; Per Subs 13
Wireless access
Open Tues 1-5, Wed & Fri 9-12 & 1-6, Thurs 1-6, Sat 9-12
Friends of the Library Group

CLARINDA

J IOWA WESTERN COMMUNITY COLLEGE-CLARINDA CAMPUS*, Edith Lisle Library, 923 E Washington, 51632. SAN 305-2869. Tel: 712-542-5117, Ext 2234. FAX: 712-542-3604. Web Site: www.iwcc.edu. *Coordr,* Shelly Anderson; E-mail: sanderson@iwcc.edu; Staff 1 (MLS 1)
Founded 1963. Enrl 350
Automation Activity & Vendor Info: (Cataloging) SirsiDynix; (Circulation) SirsiDynix; (Serials) SirsiDynix
Partic in Iowa Academic Library Alliance
Open Mon-Thurs 8-6, Fri 8-3

P LIED PUBLIC LIBRARY, 100 E Garfield St, 51632. SAN 305-2850. Tel: 712-542-2416. FAX: 712-542-3590. E-mail: info@clarindapubliclibrary.org. Web Site: www.clarindapubliclibrary.org. *Dir,* Andrew Hoppman; E-mail: dirliedlib@gmail.com; *Youth Serv Librn,* Marissa Gruber
Pop 7,500; Circ 60,000
Library Holdings: AV Mats 609; CDs 6,600; Bk Titles 36,000; Per Subs 96
Automation Activity & Vendor Info: (Acquisitions) Book Systems
Wireless access
Open Mon 9:30-8, Tues-Thurs 9:30-6, Fri 9:30-5, Sat 9:30-2
Friends of the Library Group

CLARION

P CLARION PUBLIC LIBRARY*, 302 N Main St, 50525. SAN 305-2877. Tel: 515-532-3673. FAX: 515-532-6322. Web Site: www.clarion.lib.ia.us. *Dir,* Linda Lloyd; E-mail: clariondirector@gmail.com
Pop 2,968; Circ 36,000
Library Holdings: Bk Titles 23,000; Per Subs 45
Automation Activity & Vendor Info: (Acquisitions) Follett Software; (Cataloging) Follett Software; (Circulation) Follett Software; (ILL) Follett Software; (Media Booking) Follett Software; (OPAC) Follett Software; (Serials) Follett Software
Wireless access
Open Mon 10-8, Tues-Fri 10-5, Sat 9-Noon

CLARKSVILLE

P CLARKSVILLE PUBLIC LIBRARY, 103 W Greene St, 50619-0039. SAN 305-2885. Tel: 319-278-1168. FAX: 319-278-1168. E-mail: clarksville@butler-bremer.com. Web Site: www.clarksville.lib.ia.us. *Dir,* Kristen Clark; *Asst Librn,* Patricia Calease
Founded 1929. Pop 1,441; Circ 28,000
Library Holdings: Bk Titles 17,000; Bk Vols 17,119; Per Subs 80
Wireless access
Open Mon & Wed 10-6, Tues & Thurs 10-5, Fri 10-4, Sat 10-2

CLEAR LAKE

P CLEAR LAKE PUBLIC LIBRARY*, 200 N Fourth St, 50428-1698. SAN 305-2893. Tel: 641-357-6133. FAX: 641-357-4645. E-mail: clplib@cltel.net. Web Site: www.cllibrary.org. *Libr Dir,* Jill Pannkuk; *Asst Dir,* Aaron Ruggles; Staff 16 (MLS 1, Non-MLS 15)
Founded 1889. Pop 8,161; Circ 153,585
Library Holdings: Audiobooks 1,390; CDs 395; DVDs 2,372; Large Print Bks 2,150; Bk Titles 45,182; Bk Vols 46,453; Per Subs 164
Automation Activity & Vendor Info: (Cataloging) Biblionix/Apollo; (Circulation) Biblionix/Apollo; (OPAC) Biblionix/Apollo
Wireless access
Open Mon-Thurs 10-8, Fri & Sat 10-5
Friends of the Library Group

CLEARFIELD

P CLEARFIELD PUBLIC LIBRARY*, 401 Broadway, Ste 200, 50840-0028. SAN 305-2907. Tel: 641-336-2944. E-mail: clfdlib@windstream.net. *Librn,* Suzanne Brown; Tel: 641-336-2939
Founded 1916. Pop 371; Circ 4,127
Library Holdings: Bk Vols 7,007; Talking Bks 48
Special Services for the Blind - Bks available with recordings; Large print bks
Open Tues & Fri 8-5
Bookmobiles: 1

CLEGHORN

P M-C COMMUNITY LIBRARY*, 200 W Grace St, 51014. (Mail add: PO Box 124, 51014-0124), SAN 305-2915. Tel: 712-436-2521. FAX: 712-436-2695. E-mail: mclib@netins.net. Web Site: cleghorniowa.com/library. *Libr Dir,* Lois Alquist; *Libr Dir,* Joy Nielsen
Founded 1986. Pop 250; Circ 6,000
Library Holdings: Bk Vols 14,699; Per Subs 18
Automation Activity & Vendor Info: (Cataloging) Follett Software
Open Mon (Winter) 8-11:30 & 12-7, Tues 8-11:30 & 12-6, Sat 9-12; Mon (Summer) 2-5, Tues 12-4, Wed 9-4, Thurs & Fri 10-5, Sat 9-12

CLERMONT

P CLERMONT PUBLIC LIBRARY, 503 Larabee St, 52135. (Mail add: PO Box 49, 52135-0049), SAN 305-2923. Tel: 563-423-7286. FAX: 563-423-5511. E-mail: clmtlib@acegroup.cc. Web Site: www.clermont.lib.ia.us. *Dir,* Rebecca White
Pop 716; Circ 10,230
Library Holdings: AV Mats 420; Bk Titles 6,231; Per Subs 36
Wireless access
Open Mon 1-6, Tues & Wed 11-5, Fri 9-5, Sat 9-Noon

CLINTON

S BICKELHAUPT ARBORETUM LIBRARY*, 340 S 14th St, 52732-5432. SAN 324-7813. Tel: 563-242-4771. FAX: 563-242-7373. Web Site: www.eicc.edu/bickelhaupt. *Dir,* David Horst; *Dir, Programs,* Margo Hansen; E-mail: mahansen@eicc.edu; Staff 3 (MLS 3)
Founded 1970
Library Holdings: Bk Titles 800; Bk Vols 845; Per Subs 10
Subject Interests: Hort

J CLINTON COMMUNITY COLLEGE LIBRARY*, 1000 Lincoln Blvd, 52732. SAN 305-2931. Tel: 563-244-7046. Reference Tel: 563-244-7106. FAX: 563-244-7107. Web Site: www.eicc.edu/library. *Asst Dean, Libr Serv,* Sally Myers; E-mail: smyers@eicc.edu; *Libr Spec,* Charlotte Darsidan; Staff 3 (MLS 1, Non-MLS 2)
Founded 1966. Enrl 1,300
Library Holdings: Bk Titles 17,422; Bk Vols 18,439; Per Subs 65
Automation Activity & Vendor Info: (Cataloging) SirsiDynix-WorkFlows; (Circulation) SirsiDynix-WorkFlows; (Course Reserve) SirsiDynix-iBistro; (OPAC) SirsiDynix-iBistro; (Serials) SirsiDynix-WorkFlows
Wireless access
Function: ILL available
Partic in Iowa Academic Library Alliance; Regional Med Libr - Region 3; RiverShare Libraries
Open Mon-Thurs (Winter) 7:30am-9pm, Fri 7:30-4, Sat 8-1; Mon, Tues & Thurs (Summer) 7:30-7, Wed & Fri 7:30-4

P CLINTON PUBLIC LIBRARY*, 306 Eighth Ave S, 52732. SAN 341-8022. Tel: 563-242-8441. FAX: 563-242-8162. Web Site: www.clintonpubliclibrary.us. *Dir,* Susan Mesecher; E-mail: smesecher@clintonpubliclibrary.us; Staff 27 (MLS 3, Non-MLS 24)
Founded 1904. Pop 27,772; Circ 141,500
Library Holdings: AV Mats 1,038; Bks on Deafness & Sign Lang 68; CDs 2,432; High Interest/Low Vocabulary Bk Vols 186; Large Print Bks 10,050; Bk Titles 148,725; Per Subs 266; Talking Bks 5,656; Videos 2,572

Special Collections: Clinton & Lyons Newspapers on Microfilm 1854 to date; Clinton Authors. State Document Depository
Subject Interests: Genealogy
Automation Activity & Vendor Info: (Cataloging) Innovative Interfaces, Inc; (Circulation) Innovative Interfaces, Inc; (OPAC) Innovative Interfaces, Inc
Wireless access
Function: ILL available
Partic in RiverShare Libraries
Special Services for the Deaf - TDD equip
Open Mon-Thurs 9-8, Fri 9-5, Sat 10-2
Friends of the Library Group
Branches: 1
LYONS, 105 Main Ave, 52732. (Mail add: 306 Eighth Ave S, 52732), SAN 341-8057. Tel: 563-242-5355. FAX: 563-243-6553. E-mail: lyons@clintonpubliclibrary.us. *Library Contact,* Sharon Hess; Staff 5 (Non-MLS 5)
Library Holdings: AV Mats 585; Bk Vols 17,486; Per Subs 51
Automation Activity & Vendor Info: (Circulation) Innovative Interfaces, Inc
Function: ILL available
Open Wed-Sat 9-5
Friends of the Library Group

CLIVE

P CLIVE PUBLIC LIBRARY*, 1900 NW 114th St, 50325. SAN 920-6965. Tel: 515-453-2221. FAX: 515-453-2246. Web Site: www.cityofclive.com/government/library. *Dir,* Richard Brown; E-mail: rbrown@cityofclive.com; *Libr Mgr,* Stephanie Keller; Staff 9 (MLS 3, Non-MLS 6)
Founded 2000. Pop 14,125; Circ 223,623
Library Holdings: Bk Titles 66,000; Per Subs 190
Automation Activity & Vendor Info: (Acquisitions) Innovative Interfaces, Inc; (Cataloging) Innovative Interfaces, Inc; (Circulation) Innovative Interfaces, Inc; (OPAC) Innovative Interfaces, Inc; (Serials) Innovative Interfaces, Inc
Wireless access
Open Mon-Thurs 9-8, Fri 9-6, Sat 9-5, Sun 1-5
Friends of the Library Group

CLUTIER

P CLUTIER PUBLIC LIBRARY*, 404 Main St, 52217. SAN 376-7450. Tel: 319-479-2171. FAX: 319-479-2903. E-mail: clutier_lib@fctc.coop. *Dir,* Kupka Patti
Wireless access
Open Mon 8-12 & 2-5, Tues & Thurs 12-5, Sat 9-12

COGGON

P COGGON PUBLIC LIBRARY, 202 E Main St, 52218. (Mail add: PO Box 79, 52218-0079), SAN 376-5407. Tel: 319-435-2542. FAX: 319-435-2346. Web Site: coggonpubliclibrary.org. *Dir,* Diane Knott; E-mail: director@coggonpubliclibrary.org
Founded 1938. Pop 658
Library Holdings: Bk Vols 15,000; Per Subs 15
Wireless access
Open Tues 9-6, Wed & Fri 9-5, Sat 9-Noon

COIN

P COIN PUBLIC LIBRARY*, 115 Main St, 51636. SAN 376-5202. Tel: 712-583-3684. *Adminr,* Evelyn Loghry
Founded 1981. Pop 252
Library Holdings: e-journals 14,190; Large Print Bks 33; Bk Vols 13,437; Talking Bks 53; Videos 86
Open Mon & Wed 2:30-4:30, Tues, Thurs & Fri 9am-10:30am

COLESBURG

P COLESBURG PUBLIC LIBRARY*, 220 Main St, 52035. (Mail add: PO Box 159, 52035-0159), SAN 376-5237. Tel: 563-856-5800. FAX: 563-856-5800. E-mail: carwell2019@gmail.com, colepl@iowatelecom.net. Web Site: www.colesburg.lib.ia.us. *Libr Dir,* Carol Walthart; E-mail: cwalthart@colesburg.lib.ia.us
Founded 1983. Pop 420; Circ 7,000
Library Holdings: Bks on Deafness & Sign Lang 20; Bk Vols 13,570; Per Subs 26
Automation Activity & Vendor Info: (Circulation) Biblionix/Apollo
Wireless access
Open Mon 1-6, Tues 10-8, Wed 4-8, Thurs 9-2, Fri 1-5, Sat 9-Noon
Friends of the Library Group

COLFAX

P COLFAX PUBLIC LIBRARY*, 25 W Division St, 50054. SAN 305-2966. Tel: 515-674-3625. E-mail: colfaxlib@mediacombb.net. Web Site: www.colfax.lib.ia.us. *Dir,* Jill Miller
Pop 2,223; Circ 9,000
Library Holdings: Bk Vols 7,110; Per Subs 25
Wireless access
Open Mon 2-8, Tues-Fri 2-6, Sat 9-12

COLLINS

P COLLINS PUBLIC LIBRARY*, 212 Main St, 50055. (Mail add: PO Box 79, 50055), SAN 305-2974. Tel: 641-385-2464. FAX: 641-385-2464. E-mail: collinspubliclibrary@gmail.com. Web Site: collins.lib.ia.us. *Dir,* Sara Coree
Founded 1936. Pop 499; Circ 20,033
Library Holdings: AV Mats 650; CDs 152; DVDs 889; Large Print Bks 270; Music Scores 150; Bk Titles 10,380; Per Subs 16; Talking Bks 45; Videos 378
Special Collections: Samuel Clemens Coll
Wireless access
Function: Adult bk club, Audio & video playback equip for onsite use, Bks on cassette, Bks on CD, CD-ROM, Children's prog, Computer training, Computers for patron use, Electronic databases & coll, Equip loans & repairs, Family literacy, Free DVD rentals, Govt ref serv, Holiday prog, Homebound delivery serv, Homework prog, ILL available, Magnifiers for reading, Mail & tel request accepted, Mail loans to mem, Music CDs, Outreach serv, Outside serv via phone, mail, e-mail & web, Photocopying/Printing, Preschool outreach, Prog for children & young adult, Ref serv available, Scanner, Senior computer classes, Senior outreach, Story hour, Summer reading prog, Tax forms, Teen prog, VHS videos, Wheelchair accessible
Special Services for the Deaf - Bks on deafness & sign lang; High interest/low vocabulary bks
Special Services for the Blind - Audio mat; Bks on cassette; Bks on CD; Braille alphabet card; Cassette playback machines; Cassettes; Home delivery serv; Large print & cassettes; Large print bks; Magnifiers
Open Tues 9-11 & 4-7, Wed 9-11 & 2-6, Thurs 4-7, Fri 2-6, Sat 9-Noon
Friends of the Library Group

COLO

P COLO PUBLIC LIBRARY*, 309 Main St, 50056. (Mail add: PO Box 324, 50056-0324), SAN 305-2982. Tel: 641-377-2900. FAX: 641-377-2468. E-mail: cololibrary@netins.net. Web Site: www.colo.lib.ia.us. *Dir,* Joanie Jamison; *Ch,* Mary Lou Haddock
Pop 868; Circ 21,786
Library Holdings: Bk Vols 15,000; Per Subs 40; Videos 1,100
Wireless access
Open Mon & Fri 11-6, Wed 11-8, Thurs 9-6, Sat 9-4

COLUMBUS JUNCTION

P COLUMBUS JUNCTION PUBLIC LIBRARY, 232 Second St, 52738-1028. SAN 305-2990. Tel: 319-728-7972. FAX: 319-728-2303. E-mail: columbusjunctionlibrary@gmail.com. Web Site: www.columbusjct.lib.ia.us. *Dir,* Mandy Grimm; E-mail: mandy.grimm@columbusjct.lib.ia.us; *Asst Dir,* Sue Reid; E-mail: sue.reid@columbusjct.lib.ia.us
Founded 1948. Pop 1,900; Circ 16,579
Library Holdings: AV Mats 566; Bk Titles 14,000; Per Subs 50
Special Collections: Videos, Large Print & Audiotapes
Wireless access
Open Mon-Thurs 10-6, Fri 10-4:30, Sat 9-Noon
Friends of the Library Group

CONRAD

P CONRAD PUBLIC LIBRARY*, 114 N Main St, 50621. (Mail add: PO Box 189, 50621-0189), SAN 305-3008. Tel: 641-366-2583. FAX: 641-366-3105. E-mail: conradlibrary@conrad.lib.ia.us. Web Site: www.conrad.lib.ia.us. *Ch, Dir,* Susan Blythe; E-mail: susan@conrad.lib.ia.us; *Librn,* Jana Smith; Staff 3 (Non-MLS 3)
Founded 1936. Pop 1,055
Library Holdings: Bk Vols 16,051; Per Subs 113
Subject Interests: Genealogy
Automation Activity & Vendor Info: (Cataloging) Follett Software; (Circulation) Follett Software; (OPAC) Follett Software
Wireless access
Open Mon & Wed 9-8, Tues & Thurs 2-8, Fri 2-6, Sat 9-Noon

COON RAPIDS

P COON RAPIDS PUBLIC LIBRARY*, 123 Third Ave, 50058-1601. SAN 305-3016. Tel: 712-999-5410. FAX: 712-999-5411. E-mail: crlibrary.ia@gmail.com. Web Site: www.coonrapids.lib.ia.us. *Dir,* Maura Marsh; E-mail: maura.marsh@coonrapids.lib.ia.us
Pop 1,305; Circ 19,097
Library Holdings: AV Mats 802; Bk Titles 15,074; Per Subs 60; Videos 539
Automation Activity & Vendor Info: (Acquisitions) Baker & Taylor; (Circulation) Book Systems; (OPAC) Book Systems
Wireless access
Open Mon, Tues, Thurs & Fri 11-6, Wed 11-8, Sat 8-Noon
Friends of the Library Group

CORALVILLE

P CORALVILLE PUBLIC LIBRARY, 1401 Fifth St, 52241. SAN 305-3024. Tel: 319-248-1850. FAX: 319-248-1890. Reference E-mail: reference@coralville.org. Web Site: www.coralvillepubliclibrary.org. *Dir,* Alison Ames Galstad; E-mail: agalstad@coralville.org; *Asst Dir,* Ellen Alexander; E-mail: ehampe@coralville.org; *Ch Serv Librn,* Erika Binegar; E-mail: ebinegar@coralville.org; *Youth Serv Coordr,* Sara Glenn; E-mail: sglenn@coralville.org; Staff 13.3 (MLS 7.5, Non-MLS 5.8)
Founded 1965. Pop 18,907; Circ 368,950
Jul 2014-Jun 2015 Income $1,726,438, State $52,230, City $1,512,164, County $91,029, Locally Generated Income $2,815, Other $68,200. Mats Exp $197,325. Sal $1,293,572
Library Holdings: Audiobooks 9,168; CDs 9,168; DVDs 7,886; e-books 14,957; e-journals 135; Bk Titles 93,353; Per Subs 180; Videos 10,986
Automation Activity & Vendor Info: (Acquisitions) Innovative Interfaces, Inc; (Cataloging) Innovative Interfaces, Inc; (Circulation) Innovative Interfaces, Inc; (OPAC) Innovative Interfaces, Inc; (Serials) Innovative Interfaces, Inc
Wireless access
Function: 24/7 Electronic res, 24/7 Online cat, Activity rm, Adult bk club, After school storytime
Open Mon, Wed & Fri 10-6, Tues & Thurs 10-7, Sat 10-4, Sun 12-4
Friends of the Library Group

CORNING

P CORNING PUBLIC LIBRARY*, 603 Ninth St, 50841-1304. SAN 305-3032. Tel: 641-322-3866. FAX: 641-322-3491. E-mail: cornpl@mchsi.com. Web Site: corningpubliclibraryia.weebly.com. *Dir,* Alyssa Ogburn; *Ad,* Laura Bowman; *Ch,* Denise Kester
Founded 1916. Pop 1,783; Circ 44,618
Library Holdings: AV Mats 1,800; Bk Vols 29,000; Per Subs 45
Special Collections: American Indian Literature
Partic in Iowa Libr Asn
Open Mon, Tues, Thurs & Fri 9:30-5:30, Wed 9:30-8, Sat 9:30-1

CORRECTIONVILLE

P CORRECTIONVILLE PUBLIC LIBRARY*, 532 Driftwood, 51016. (Mail add: PO Box 308, 51016), SAN 305-3040. Tel: 712-342-4203. FAX: 712-342-4203. Web Site: www.correctionville.lib.ia.us. *Dir,* Vicki Knaack; E-mail: director@correctionville.lib.ia.us
Founded 1899. Pop 821; Circ 8,047
Library Holdings: Audiobooks 58; Bks on Deafness & Sign Lang 2; DVDs 158; Large Print Bks 96; Bk Vols 15,000; Per Subs 4; Videos 324
Wireless access
Open Mon & Thurs 1-5, Tues 3-6, Wed 2-6, Sat 9-2; Mon 1-9, Tues 3-6, Thurs 1-5, Sat 9-2 (Summer)
Friends of the Library Group

CORWITH

P CORWITH PUBLIC LIBRARY*, 110 NW Elm, 50430. (Mail add: PO Box 308, 50430-0308), SAN 305-3059. Tel: 515-583-2536. FAX: 515-583-2535. E-mail: corlib@comm1net.net. Web Site: www.youseemore.com/NILC/Corwith. *Libr Dir,* Courtney Fish
Pop 309; Circ 9,072
Library Holdings: Bk Vols 7,651; Per Subs 15
Automation Activity & Vendor Info: (Acquisitions) TLC (The Library Corporation)
Wireless access
Partic in N Iowa Libr Exten
Open Mon & Fri 1-6, Wed 1-8, Thurs 6-8, Sat 9-Noon

CORYDON

P KARL MILES LECOMPTE MEMORIAL LIBRARY*, 110 S Franklin, 50060-1518. SAN 305-3067. Tel: 641-872-1621. E-mail: admin@corydon.lib.ia.us. Web Site: www.corydon.lib.ia.us. *Dir,* Leona Darrah
Pop 1,591; Circ 30,192
Library Holdings: Bk Titles 16,000; Per Subs 30
Wireless access
Open Mon, Wed & Fri 12-5, Tues 10-11 & 12-5, Thurs 3-7, Sat 9-Noon

S WAYNE COUNTY HISTORICAL SOCIETY, Prairie Trails Museum of Wayne County Iowa Genealogical Library, Hwy 2, 515 E Jefferson St, 50060. (Mail add: PO Box 104, 50060), SAN 375-1783. Tel: 641-872-2211. E-mail: ptmuseum@grm.net. Web Site: www.prairietrailsmuseum.org. *Head Librn,* Kay Milner; Staff 8 (Non-MLS 8)
Founded 1975
Library Holdings: Microforms 50; Bk Vols 750
Special Collections: County Census Records 1850-1920; Doctor's Records; Early Wills & Birth Certificates; Obituaries; Old Newspapers & Newspaper Clippings
Subject Interests: Obituary info
Wireless access
Open Mon-Sat 1-5 (April-Oct)

COULTER

P COULTER PUBLIC LIBRARY*, 111 Main St, PO Box 87, 50431-0087. SAN 305-3075. Tel: 641-866-6798. FAX: 641-866-6798. E-mail: coullib@frontiernet.net. *Dir,* Barb Gardner
Founded 1971. Pop 262; Circ 4,391
Library Holdings: Bk Titles 7,081; Per Subs 12
Automation Activity & Vendor Info: (Acquisitions) Biblionix/Apollo; (Cataloging) Biblionix/Apollo; (Circulation) Biblionix/Apollo; (ILL) Biblionix/Apollo; (Media Booking) Biblionix/Apollo; (OPAC) Biblionix/Apollo; (Serials) Biblionix/Apollo
Wireless access
Open Tues-Thurs 1-5, Fri 1-6, Sat 9-12

COUNCIL BLUFFS

P COUNCIL BLUFFS PUBLIC LIBRARY, 400 Willow Ave, 51503-9042. SAN 305-3091. Tel: 712-323-7553. Circulation Tel: 712-323-7553, Ext 4001. Interlibrary Loan Service Tel: 712-323-7553, Ext 5426. Reference Tel: 712-323-7553, Ext 4014. Administration Tel: 712-323-7553, Ext 5424. Automation Services Tel: 712-323-7553, Ext 5333. FAX: 712-323-1269. Web Site: www.councilbluffslibrary.org. *Libr Dir,* Antonia Krupicka-Smith; Tel: 712-323-7553, Ext 5423, E-mail: akrupickasmith@councilbluffslibrary.org; *Teen Librn,* Jamie Ruppert; Tel: 712-323-7553, Ext 5422, E-mail: jruppert@councilbluffslibrary.org; *Automation & Networking Mgr,* Tom Ryan; E-mail: tryan@councilbluffslibrary.org; *Circ & Adult Serv Mgr,* Bailey Adams; Tel: 712-323-7553, Ext 5418, E-mail: bhalbur@councilbluffslibrary.org; *Mgr, Ad Serv,* Andrew Bouska; Tel: 712-323-7553, Ext 5416, E-mail: abouska@councilbluffslibrary.org; *Support Serv Mgr,* Mary Carpenter; Tel: 712-323-7553, Ext 5425, E-mail: mcarp@councilbluffslibrary.org; *Youth Serv Mgr,* Anna Hartmann; Tel: 712-323-7553, Ext 5417, E-mail: ahartmann@councilbluffslibrary.org; Staff 8 (MLS 7, Non-MLS 1)
Founded 1866. Pop 61,324; Circ 217,726
Jul 2020-Jun 2021 Income $3,215,728, State $25,708, City $2,782,934, County $250,000. Mats Exp $315,429
Library Holdings: Audiobooks 8,957; DVDs 16,447; e-books 64,603; Electronic Media & Resources 4,012; Bk Vols 106,956; Per Subs 150
Special Collections: Complete Daily Nonpareil newspaper; Lewis Carroll Coll; Railroads (Grenville Mellen Dodge Coll); Woman Suffrage (Amelia Bloomer Coll)
Automation Activity & Vendor Info: (Acquisitions) SirsiDynix-Symphony; (Cataloging) SirsiDynix-Symphony; (Circulation) SirsiDynix-Symphony; (ILL) SirsiDynix-Symphony; (Media Booking) SirsiDynix-Symphony; (OPAC) SirsiDynix-Symphony; (Serials) SirsiDynix-Symphony
Wireless access
Function: 3D Printer, Accelerated reader prog, Adult bk club, Archival coll, Art exhibits, Audiobks via web, AV serv, Bilingual assistance for Spanish patrons, Bk club(s), Bks on CD, Chess club, Children's prog, Computer training, Computers for patron use, Digital talking bks, E-Reserves, Electronic databases & coll, Equip loans & repairs, Free DVD rentals, Holiday prog, Home delivery & serv to seniorr ctr & nursing homes, Homebound delivery serv, ILL available, Internet access, Laminating, Magazines, Magnifiers for reading, Mail & tel request accepted, Makerspace, Mango lang, Meeting rooms, Movies, Museum passes, Music CDs, Notary serv, Online cat, Online ref, Outside serv via phone, mail, e-mail & web, OverDrive digital audio bks, Photocopying/Printing, Preschool outreach, Printer for laptops & handheld devices, Prog for adults, Prog for children & young adult, Ref serv available, Scanner, Senior computer classes, Senior outreach, Serves people with intellectual disabilities, Spanish lang bks, Story hour, Study rm, Summer reading prog, Tax forms, Teen prog, Telephone ref, Wheelchair accessible
Special Services for the Deaf - TTY equip

Open Mon-Thurs 9-9, Fri & Sat 9-5, Sun 1-5
Friends of the Library Group

CRESCO

P CRESCO PUBLIC LIBRARY*, 320 N Elm St, 52136-1452. SAN 305-3105. Tel: 563-547-2540. FAX: 563-547-1769. Web Site: www.cresco.lib.ia.us. *Dir,* Cynthia Kay; E-mail: cbkay@cresco.lib.ia.us
Founded 1915. Pop 3,905; Circ 139,956
Library Holdings: Bk Titles 30,780; Per Subs 106
Wireless access
Open Mon-Wed 9-8, Thurs & Fri 9-5, Sat 9-Noon
Friends of the Library Group

CRESTON

P GIBSON MEMORIAL LIBRARY, 200 W Howard St, 50801-2339. SAN 305-3113. Tel: 641-782-2277. FAX: 641-782-4604. E-mail: crestonlibrary310@gmail.com. Web Site: www.creston.lib.ia.us. *Dir,* Aric Bishop; Tel: 641-782-6507, E-mail: aricbishop@gmail.com; *Asst Dir, Ch Serv,* Sue Teutsch; Staff 6 (MLS 1, Non-MLS 5)
Founded 1932
Library Holdings: Bk Titles 30,000; Per Subs 100
Subject Interests: Genealogy
Automation Activity & Vendor Info: (Cataloging) Follett Software; (Circulation) Follett Software; (OPAC) Follett Software
Wireless access
Open Mon & Wed 10-8, Tues, Thurs & Fri 10-6, Sat 10-3
Friends of the Library Group

J SOUTHWESTERN COMMUNITY COLLEGE*, Learning Resource Center, 1501 W Townline St, 50801. SAN 305-3121. Tel: 641-782-1462. FAX: 641-782-1301. Web Site: www.swcciowa.edu/library. *Dir, Libr Serv,* Ann Coulter; Tel: 641-782-1340, E-mail: coulter@swcciowa.edu; *Libr Asst,* Ruth Bolinger; E-mail: bolinger@swcciowa.edu; Staff 2.5 (MLS 1, Non-MLS 1.5)
Founded 1965. Enrl 1,600
Library Holdings: Bk Titles 14,320; Bk Vols 15,194; Per Subs 170
Automation Activity & Vendor Info: (Circulation) Innovative Interfaces, Inc; (OPAC) Innovative Interfaces, Inc
Wireless access
Function: 24/7 Electronic res, 24/7 Online cat, Audiobks via web, AV serv, Electronic databases & coll
Open Mon-Thurs (Fall & Spring) 7:30am-8pm, Fri 7:30-4; Mon-Thurs (Summer) 7:30-4:30, Fri 7:30-4

CRYSTAL LAKE

P CRYSTAL LAKE PUBLIC LIBRARY*, 225 State Ave S, 50432. (Mail add: PO Box 152, 50432), SAN 377-547X. Tel: 641-565-3325. FAX: 641-565-3325. E-mail: crystallakelibrary50432@gmail.com. Web Site: www1.youseemore.com/NILC/JEMCenterPL. *Dir,* Lisa Swingen
Pop 285
Library Holdings: AV Mats 100; Bk Titles 5,300; Per Subs 48
Automation Activity & Vendor Info: (Acquisitions) Follett Software; (Cataloging) Follett Software; (Circulation) Follett Software; (ILL) Follett Software; (OPAC) Follett Software
Open Mon 8:30-12 & 4-6, Wed & Fri 8:30-12 & 2-5, Sat 9:30-11

CUMBERLAND

P CUMBERLAND PUBLIC LIBRARY, 119 Main St, 50843-9900. (Mail add: PO Box 150, 50843-0150), SAN 305-313X. Tel: 712-774-5334. FAX: 712-774-5334. E-mail: cmblibry@netins.net. Web Site: cumberlandiowa.com/library. *Dir,* Carolyn Hartman
Pop 281; Circ 6,400
Library Holdings: AV Mats 400; Bk Vols 6,500; Per Subs 25
Wireless access
Open Tues & Wed 8:30-4:30, Fri 4-6, Sat 8:30-10:30

CUSHING

P CUSHING COMMUNITY LIBRARY*, 202 Main St, 51018. (Mail add: PO Box 13, 51018-0013). Tel: 712-384-2501. E-mail: cushinglibrary2@schallertel.net. Web Site: www.cushing.lib.ia.us. *Dir,* Elaine Droegmiller; E-mail: edroegmiller@cushing.lib.ia.us
Pop 246
Library Holdings: AV Mats 385; CDs 19; Bk Vols 4,588; Videos 255
Wireless access
Open Mon 2-7, Thurs 5-7, Sat 10-12
Friends of the Library Group

DALLAS CENTER

P ROY R ESTLE MEMORIAL LIBRARY*, 1308 Walnut St, 50063. (Mail add: PO Box 521, 50063-0521), SAN 305-3148. Tel: 515-992-3185. FAX: 515-992-4929. Web Site: www.dallascenter.lib.ia.us. *Dir,* Shelly Cory; E-mail: scory@dallascenter.lib.ia.us; Staff 4 (Non-MLS 4)
Founded 1945. Pop 1,595; Circ 38,524
Library Holdings: Audiobooks 4,676; DVDs 605; Large Print Bks 1,093; Bk Titles 18,940; Per Subs 63; Talking Bks 3,178; Videos 231
Special Collections: County Newspapers, 1890 to present, micro; Dallas County Cemetery Records; Dallas County Genealogical Coll
Subject Interests: Local hist
Automation Activity & Vendor Info: (Acquisitions) Follett Software; (Circulation) Follett Software; (OPAC) Follett Software
Wireless access
Function: Adult bk club, After school storytime, Archival coll, Bk club(s), Bks on cassette, Bks on CD, Children's prog, Computers for patron use, Free DVD rentals, Home delivery & serv to seniorr ctr & nursing homes, Homebound delivery serv, ILL available, Online cat, Photocopying/Printing, Prog for children & young adult, Ref serv available, Scanner, Spoken cassettes & CDs, Story hour, Summer reading prog, Tax forms, Telephone ref, VHS videos, Wheelchair accessible
Open Mon & Fri 9-5, Tues-Thurs 9-7, Sat 9-12
Friends of the Library Group

DAVENPORT

P DAVENPORT PUBLIC LIBRARY*, 321 Main St, 52801-1490. SAN 305-3172. Tel: 563-326-7832. Reference Tel: 563-326-7844. FAX: 563-326-7809. Web Site: www.davenportlibrary.com. *Dir,* Amy Groskopf; E-mail: agroskopf@davenportlibrary.com; *Asst Dir,* Lexie Reiling; E-mail: lreiling@davenportlibrary.com; Staff 18 (MLS 18)
Founded 1877. Pop 100,802; Circ 946,114
Library Holdings: Audiobooks 36,353; AV Mats 18,971; e-books 5,047; Bk Vols 313,042; Per Subs 889
Special Collections: Iowa Authors Coll; Patent & Trademark Resource Center. State Document Depository; US Document Depository
Subject Interests: Bus & mgt, Econ, Genealogy
Automation Activity & Vendor Info: (Acquisitions) Innovative Interfaces, Inc; (Cataloging) Innovative Interfaces, Inc; (Circulation) Innovative Interfaces, Inc; (ILL) OCLC FirstSearch
Wireless access
Function: Bks on cassette
Publications: Main Entries (Newsletter)
Partic in OCLC Online Computer Library Center, Inc; RiverShare Libraries
Special Services for the Deaf - TDD equip
Open Mon-Thurs 9:30-8, Fri & Sat 9:30-5:30, Sun (Fall-Spring) 1-4
Friends of the Library Group
Branches: 3
EASTERN AVENUE BRANCH, 6000 Eastern Ave, 52807.
FAIRMOUNT STREET, 3000 N Fairmount St, 52804-1160, SAN 324-2552.
Open Mon & Thurs-Sat 9:30-5:30, Tues & Wed 12-8
RICHARDSON-SLOANE SPECIAL COLLECTIONS CENTER, 321 Main St, 52801-1409, SAN 371-8646. Tel: 563-326-7902. FAX: 563-326-7901.
Library Holdings: Bk Titles 1,600; Per Subs 20
Open Mon 12-8, Tues-Sat 9-5:30
Friends of the Library Group

M GENESIS HEALTH SYSTEM*, Clinical Library, 1227 E Rusholme St, 52803. SAN 375-9369. Tel: 563-421-2287. FAX: 563-421-2288. E-mail: library@genesishealth.com. *Med Librn,* Karlene Campbell; E-mail: campbellka@genesishealth.com; Staff 2 (MLS 2)
Library Holdings: Bk Titles 1,500; Per Subs 100
Wireless access
Partic in Quad City Area Biomedical Consortium
Open Mon-Fri 7-4

CM PALMER COLLEGE OF CHIROPRACTIC-DAVENPORT CAMPUS*, David D Palmer Health Sciences Library, 1000 Brady St, 52803-5287. SAN 305-3202. Tel: 563-884-5641. Reference Tel: 563-884-5896. Administration Tel: 563-884-5441. FAX: 563-884-5897. Web Site: library.palmer.edu. *Sr Dir,* Christine Deines; Tel: 563-884-5442, E-mail: christine.deines@palmer.edu; *Head Librn, Tech Serv,* Sandy Lewis; E-mail: sandra.lewis@palmer.edu; *Head, Spec Coll & Archives,* Rosemary Riess; E-mail: rosemary.riess@palmer.edu; Staff 14 (MLS 3, Non-MLS 11)
Founded 1897. Enrl 1,433; Fac 101; Highest Degree: Doctorate
Library Holdings: AV Mats 24,190; e-books 10,600; e-journals 15,805; Bk Titles 30,643; Bk Vols 59,774; Per Subs 151
Special Collections: BJ Palmer Papers Coll; Gustave Dubbs Papers; Kenneth Cronk Papers; Lyndon Lee Papers Coll; Palmer College Archives Coll; Russel Gibbons Papers; Ted Shrader Papers; Walter Wardwell Papers
Subject Interests: Alternative & complimentary health care, Basic sci, Chiropractic health care, Diagnosis, Imaging

Automation Activity & Vendor Info: (Acquisitions) Innovative Interfaces, Inc - Sierra; (Cataloging) Innovative Interfaces, Inc - Sierra; (Circulation) Innovative Interfaces, Inc - Sierra; (Course Reserve) Innovative Interfaces, Inc - Sierra; (Discovery) EBSCO Discovery Service; (ILL) OCLC WorldShare Interlibrary Loan; (OPAC) Innovative Interfaces, Inc - Sierra; (Serials) Innovative Interfaces, Inc - Sierra
Wireless access
Partic in Greater Midwest Regional Medical Libr Network; Iowa Academic Library Alliance; Iowa Private Academic Library Consortium; Quad City Area Biomedical Consortium

S PUTNAM MUSEUM & SCIENCE CENTER, 1717 W 12th St, 52804. SAN 305-3229. Tel: 563-324-1933. FAX: 563-324-6638. E-mail: museum@putnam.org. Web Site: www.putnam.org. *Curator,* Christine Chandler; E-mail: cchandler@putnam.org
Founded 1867
Library Holdings: Bk Titles 20,400
Special Collections: Manuscripts (A LeClaire, I Hall, L Summers, I Wetherby, R Cram, Black Store, Putnam Family, James Grant); Steamboats, files, photog
Subject Interests: Art, Hist, Local hist, Sci tech
Restriction: Open by appt only

CR SAINT AMBROSE UNIVERSITY LIBRARY*, 518 W Locust St, 52803. SAN 305-3237. Tel: 563-333-6246. Reference Tel: 563-333-6245. FAX: 563-333-6248. Web Site: www.sau.edu/library. *Exec Dir, Info Res, Libr Dir,* Mary B Heinzman; Tel: 563-333-6241, E-mail: heinzmanmaryb@sau.edu; *Asst Libr Dir,* Julia B Salting; Tel: 563-333-6244, E-mail: saltingjuliab@sau.edu; *Head, Media Serv,* Karly Lyle; Tel: 563-333-6242, E-mail: SteeleKarlyJ@sau.edu; *Ref & Instruction Librn,* Conrad W Bendixen; Tel: 563-333-6473, E-mail: bendixenconradw@sau.edu; *Circ Supvr,* Bryan Hinds; Tel: 563-333-6475, E-mail: hindsbryant@sau.edu; *Evening Circ Supvr,* Brandi Swanson; Tel: 563-333-5813, E-mail: swansonbrandij@sau.edu; *Archivist,* Onnica F Marquez; Tel: 563-333-5868, E-mail: marquezonnicaf@sau.edu; *Ref,* Elizabeth Kunze; Tel: 563-333-6035, E-mail: kunzeelizabeths@sau.edu; *Ref (Info Servs),* Stella Herzig; Tel: 563-333-6056, E-mail: herzigstellaj@sau.edu; *Ref (Info Servs),* Leslie Ross; Tel: 563-333-6472, E-mail: rosslesliem@sau.edu; *Ref (Info Servs),* Jennifer A Smith; Tel: 563-333-6474, E-mail: smithjennifera@sau.edu. Subject Specialists: *Acctg, Bus, Gen ref,* Mary B Heinzman; *Criminal justice, Soc work, Sociol,* Julia B Salting; *Art hist, Computer sci,* Karly Lyle; *Nursing, Occupational therapy, Phys therapy,* Conrad W Bendixen; *Archives, Art hist,* Onnica F Marquez; *Kinesiology, Lang, Polit sci,* Elizabeth Kunze; *Philos, Psychol, Theol,* Stella Herzig; *Art, Music, Theatre,* Leslie Ross; *Chemistry, Engr, Environ,* Jennifer A Smith; Staff 15 (MLS 8, Non-MLS 7)
Founded 1882. Enrl 3,105; Fac 275; Highest Degree: Doctorate
Jul 2017-Jun 2018 Income $1,641,046. Mats Exp $606,750, Books $110,000, Per/Ser (Incl. Access Fees) $375,000, AV Equip $6,000, AV Mat $12,000, Electronic Ref Mat (Incl. Access Fees) $95,000, Presv $8,750. Sal $801,700 (Prof $392,900)
Library Holdings: Audiobooks 150; AV Mats 4,200; CDs 549; DVDs 1,298; e-books 150,000; e-journals 33,189; Bk Titles 172,854; Bk Vols 186,951; Per Subs 250
Subject Interests: Am Irish, Bus & mgt, Liberal arts, Occupational therapy, Phys therapy, Relig
Automation Activity & Vendor Info: (Acquisitions) Ex Libris Group; (Cataloging) Ex Libris Group; (Circulation) Ex Libris Group; (ILL) Clio; (OPAC) Ex Libris Group; (Serials) Ex Libris Group
Wireless access
Function: 24/7 Online cat, Archival coll, Computers for patron use, Electronic databases & coll, Internet access, Magazines, Online cat, Online ref, Ref serv available, Telephone ref, Wheelchair accessible
Partic in Iowa Academic Library Alliance; Iowa Private Academic Library Consortium
Special Services for the Deaf - Accessible learning ctr; Closed caption videos
Special Services for the Blind - Bks on CD; Closed circuit TV magnifier; Copier with enlargement capabilities; Internet workstation with adaptive software; Networked computers with assistive software; Reading & writing aids; Recorded bks; Screen reader software
Open Mon-Thurs 7:45-Midnight, Fri 7:45-5, Sat 10-7, Sun Noon-Midnight
Restriction: Authorized patrons, Borrowing privileges limited to fac & registered students, In-house use for visitors

DAYTON

P DAYTON PUBLIC LIBRARY*, 22 First St NW, 50530. (Mail add: PO Box 378, 50530-0378), SAN 305-3288. Tel: 515-547-2700. FAX: 515-547-2700. E-mail: dpl@lvcta.com. Web Site: www.youseemore.com/nilc/Dayton. *Dir,* Tanya E Campbell; Staff 1 (Non-MLS 1)
Founded 1900. Pop 830; Circ 14,674
Jul 2012-Jun 2013 Income $45,407, State $1,492, City $18,100, Federal $840, County $15,659, Locally Generated Income $9,316
Library Holdings: Audiobooks 237; Bks-By-Mail 99,999; DVDs 1,021; e-books 9,139; e-journals 13; Large Print Bks 564; Bk Titles 12,564; Per Subs 39; Talking Bks 237; Videos 1,036
Subject Interests: Christian fiction
Automation Activity & Vendor Info: (Cataloging) TLC (The Library Corporation); (Circulation) TLC (The Library Corporation); (Serials) EBSCO Online
Wireless access
Function: 24/7 Electronic res, Audio & video playback equip for onsite use, Audiobks via web, Bks on CD, Children's prog, Computers for patron use, Digital talking bks, Electronic databases & coll, Homebound delivery serv, ILL available, Internet access, Magazines, Movies, Online cat, Online ref, Outside serv via phone, mail, e-mail & web, OverDrive digital audio bks, Photocopying/Printing, Prog for adults, Prog for children & young adult, Ref serv available, Scanner, Summer reading prog, Tax forms, VHS videos, Wheelchair accessible
Open Mon, Wed & Fri 11-6, Sat 9-Noon
Friends of the Library Group

DE SOTO

P DE SOTO PUBLIC LIBRARY, 405 Walnut St, 50069. (Mail add: PO Box 585, 50069-0585), SAN 305-3296. Tel: 515-834-2690. FAX: 515-834-2131. E-mail: desotolibrary@mchsi.com. Web Site: www.desotopubliclibrary.com. *Dir,* Brianna Glenn; Staff 3 (MLS 3)
Pop 1,035
Library Holdings: Bk Vols 9,000; Per Subs 28
Function: Adult literacy prog, For res purposes, Home delivery & serv to seniorr ctr & nursing homes, Homebound delivery serv, ILL available, Photocopying/Printing, Prog for children & young adult, Summer reading prog, Telephone ref, Wheelchair accessible
Open Mon-Wed 10-6,Thurs 10-8, Fri 1-6, Sat 10-1

DECORAH

P DECORAH PUBLIC LIBRARY*, 202 Winnebago St, 52101. SAN 305-3318. Tel: 563-382-3717. FAX: 563-382-4524. E-mail: dpl@decorah.lib.ia.us. Web Site: www.decorah.lib.ia.us. *Dir,* Kristin Torresdal; E-mail: ktorresdal@decorah.lib.ia.us; *Ch, YA Librn,* Rachael Button; E-mail: rbutton@decorah.lib.ia.us; *Libr Asst,* Heidi Swets; E-mail: heidi@decorah.lib.ia.us; Staff 4 (Non-MLS 4)
Founded 1893. Pop 8,200; Circ 13,682
Jul 2014-Jun 2015 Income $754,226, State $38,000, City $279,148, County $49,000, Locally Generated Income $320,000, Other $68,078. Mats Exp $40,000. Sal $274,429
Library Holdings: Large Print Bks 9,942; Bk Vols 73,905; Per Subs 200; Talking Bks 3,548
Special Collections: County Historical Archives; Vera Harris Large Print Book Coll
Automation Activity & Vendor Info: (Cataloging) Biblionix/Apollo; (Circulation) Biblionix/Apollo
Wireless access
Publications: Annual Report
Special Services for the Blind - Large print bks; Talking bks
Open Mon-Thurs 10-8, Fri & Sat 10-5
Friends of the Library Group

C LUTHER COLLEGE, Preus Library, 700 College Dr, 52101. SAN 305-3326. Tel: 563-387-1166. Reference Tel: 563-387-1163. FAX: 563-387-1657. E-mail: library@luther.edu. Web Site: www.luther.edu/library. *Digital Initiatives Librn, Libr Dir,* Ryan Gjerde; Tel: 563-387-1288, E-mail: gjerdery@luther.edu; *Acq Librn, Res Mgt Librn,* Freeda Brook; Tel: 563-387-2124, E-mail: broofr01@luther.edu; *First Year Experience Librn,* Germano Streese; Tel: 563-387-2223, E-mail: strege01@luther.edu; *Instrul Tech Librn,* Holly White; Tel: 563-387-1790, E-mail: whitho01@luther.edu; *Res & Instruction Librn,* Dr Andrea Beckendorf; Tel: 563-387-1227, E-mail: beckenan@luther.edu; *Col Archivist,* Hayley Jackson; Tel: 563-387-1725, E-mail: jackha01@luther.edu
Founded 1861. Enrl 1,800; Fac 170; Highest Degree: Bachelor
Library Holdings: CDs 3,608; DVDs 2,512; e-books 13,065; e-journals 31,893; Music Scores 5,377; Bk Vols 333,314; Per Subs 823
Special Collections: Luther College Archives; Norwegian-American Newspapers
Subject Interests: Fine arts, Norwegian hist, Rare bks
Automation Activity & Vendor Info: (Acquisitions) OCLC; (Cataloging) OCLC; (Circulation) OCLC; (Course Reserve) OCLC; (ILL) OCLC ILLiad; (Media Booking) OCLC; (OPAC) OCLC WorldShare Interlibrary Loan; (Serials) OCLC
Wireless access
Partic in Iowa Academic Library Alliance; Iowa Private Academic Library Consortium; OCLC Online Computer Library Center, Inc

S VESTERHEIM NORWEGIAN-AMERICAN MUSEUM, Special Library, 502 W Water St, 52101. (Mail add: PO Box 379, 52101-0379), SAN 325-5727. Tel: 563-382-9681. FAX: 563-382-8828. E-mail:

info@vesterheim.org. Web Site: vesterheim.org. *Coll Mgr,* Jennifer Kovarik; E-mail: jkovarik@vesterheim.org
Founded 1967
Library Holdings: Bk Titles 10,000; Bk Vols 11,000; Per Subs 20
Special Collections: Norwegian Lang Works Published in America
Subject Interests: Norwegian & Norwegian-Am folk art, Norwegian-Am fine art, Norwegian-Am hist
Wireless access
Function: Archival coll, Photocopying/Printing, Ref & res, Res libr
Publications: Vesterheim (Magazine) (Biannually); Vesterheim Current (Online only)
Restriction: Non-circulating, Non-circulating coll, Non-circulating of rare bks, Not a lending libr, Open by appt only

DELHI

P DELHI PUBLIC LIBRARY*, 311 Franklin St, 52223. (Mail add: PO Box 233, 52223-0233), SAN 305-3342. Tel: 563-922-2037. FAX: 563-922-2037. E-mail: delhipubliclibrary311@gmail.com. Web Site: www.delhi.lib.ia.us. *Dir,* Arlene Chappell; E-mail: achappell@delhi.lib.ia.us; Staff 1 (Non-MLS 1)
Founded 1940. Pop 452; Circ 6,041
Library Holdings: Bk Titles 8,388; Per Subs 20
Automation Activity & Vendor Info: (Cataloging) Follett Software
Wireless access
Open Mon 9-11, Tues & Thurs 1:30-5:30, Wed 10-5:30, Sat 9-Noon (Summer); Tues & Thurs 1:30-6, Wed 10-6, Sat 9-Noon (Winter)
Friends of the Library Group

DENISON

P NORELIUS COMMUNITY LIBRARY*, 1403 First Ave S, 51442-2014. SAN 305-3350. Tel: 712-263-9355. FAX: 712-263-8578. E-mail: denlib@frontiernet.net. Web Site: www.denison.lib.ia.us. *Dir,* Monica Walley; *Asst Dir,* Sandra Haynes; Staff 8 (MLS 1, Non-MLS 7)
Founded 1904. Pop 7,339; Circ 111,376
Library Holdings: CDs 228; DVDs 107; Large Print Bks 785; Bk Vols 46,750; Per Subs 191; Talking Bks 1,854; Videos 1,512
Automation Activity & Vendor Info: (Cataloging) Book Systems; (Circulation) Book Systems
Wireless access
Open Mon-Thurs 9-8, Fri & Sat 9-5
Friends of the Library Group

DENVER

P DENVER PUBLIC LIBRARY*, 100 Washington St, 50622. (Mail add: PO Box 692, 50622-0692), SAN 305-3369. Tel: 319-984-5140. FAX: 319-984-5140. Web Site: www.denver.lib.ia.us. *Dir,* Kelly Platte; E-mail: kplatte@denver.lib.ia.us; *Asst Dir,* Kristyn Kline; E-mail: KKline@denver.lib.ia.us
Founded 1959. Pop 3,654; Circ 50,187
Library Holdings: Bk Titles 35,000; Per Subs 50
Wireless access
Open Mon 10-7, Tues & Wed 10-6, Thurs 10-8, Fri 10-5, Sat 9-12
Friends of the Library Group

DES MOINES

M BROADLAWNS MEDICAL CENTER*, Health Sciences Library, 1801 Hickman Rd, 50314. SAN 305-3385. Tel: 515-282-2200, 515-282-2394. Web Site: www.broadlawns.org. *Librn,* Rachel Sindelar
Library Holdings: Bk Vols 1,400; Per Subs 160
Subject Interests: Clinical med, Nursing, Psychiat
Wireless access
Partic in Greater Midwest Regional Medical Libr Network; Polk County Biomedical Consortium

L DAVIS BROWN LAW FIRM*, 215 Tenth St, Ste 1300, 50309. SAN 305-3504. Tel: 515-288-2500. FAX: 515-243-0654. E-mail: info@lawiowa.com. Web Site: www.lawiowa.com. *Library Contact,* Susan Prunty; E-mail: susanprunty@davisbrownlaw.com
Library Holdings: Bk Vols 11,000
Restriction: Staff use only

J DES MOINES AREA COMMUNITY COLLEGE LIBRARY*, Urban Campus, 1100 Seventh St, 50314. Tel: 515-248-7210. FAX: 515-248-7534. E-mail: urbanlibrary@dmacc.edu. Web Site: www.dmacc.edu/urban/library. *Librn,* Polly Mumma; Tel: 515-697-7739, E-mail: psmumma@dmacc.edu
Library Holdings: Bk Vols 13,000; Per Subs 50
Subject Interests: Law
Automation Activity & Vendor Info: (Acquisitions) Innovative Interfaces, Inc - Millennium; (Cataloging) Innovative Interfaces, Inc - Millennium; (Circulation) Innovative Interfaces, Inc - Millennium; (Course Reserve) Innovative Interfaces, Inc - Millennium; (OPAC) Innovative Interfaces, Inc - Millennium; (Serials) Innovative Interfaces, Inc - Millennium
Wireless access
Partic in Iowa Academic Library Alliance; Polk County Biomedical Consortium
Open Mon-Thurs 7:30am-8:30pm, Fri 7:30-1:30

S DES MOINES ART CENTER LIBRARY*, 4700 Grand Ave, 50312. SAN 305-3415. Tel: 515-277-4405. FAX: 515-271-0357. Web Site: desmoinesartcenter.org. *Assoc Curator,* Laura Burkhalter; E-mail: lburkhalter@desmoinesartcenter.org
Founded 1950
Library Holdings: AV Mats 120; Bk Titles 16,500; Per Subs 20
Subject Interests: 21st Century art, Art (19th Century), Art (20th Century)
Wireless access
Restriction: Open by appt only

P DES MOINES PUBLIC LIBRARY*, 1000 Grand Ave, 50309. SAN 341-8294. Tel: 515-283-4152. Interlibrary Loan Service Tel: 515-283-4292. FAX: 515-237-1654. Reference E-mail: reference@dmpl.org. Web Site: www.dmpl.org. *Dir,* Sue Woody; Tel: 515-283-4103, E-mail: sawoody@dmpl.org; *Dep Dir,* ; Tel: 515-283-4102; *Supv Librn, Tech Serv,* Jennifer Tormey; Tel: 515-283-4155, E-mail: jntormey@dmpl.org; *Cent Libr Mgr,* Jon T Hobbs; Tel: 515-283-4265, E-mail: jthobbs@dmpl.org; Staff 89.5 (MLS 36.8, Non-MLS 52.7)
Founded 1866. Pop 198,682; Circ 1,421,567. Sal $5,583,850
Library Holdings: Audiobooks 60,479; CDs 7,847; DVDs 26,764; e-books 3,401; Bk Vols 494,233; Per Subs 843
Special Collections: Foundation Center. Oral History; US Document Depository
Subject Interests: Iowa, Sheet music
Automation Activity & Vendor Info: (Acquisitions) Horizon; (Cataloging) Horizon; (Circulation) Horizon; (OPAC) Horizon
Wireless access
Publications: Annual Report; Engage (Library Magazine); Insight (Newsletter)
Special Services for the Blind - Bks on cassette; Bks on CD; Large print bks; Magnifiers
Open Mon-Thurs 9-8, Sat 10-5, Sun 1-5
Friends of the Library Group
Branches: 5
EAST SIDE, 2559 Hubbell Ave, 50317, SAN 341-8324. Tel: 515-283-4152. FAX: 515-248-6256. *Br Supvr,* Ashley Molzen; E-mail: armolzen@dmpl.org
Library Holdings: Bk Vols 58,393
Open Mon-Thurs 10-8, Fri 10-6, Sat 10-5
FOREST AVENUE, 1326 Forest Ave, 50314, SAN 341-8383. Tel: 515-283-4152. FAX: 515-242-2853. *Br Supvr,* Brooke Santillan; E-mail: basantillan@dmpl.org
Library Holdings: Bk Vols 43,092
Open Mon-Thurs 10-8, Fri 10-6, Sat 10-5
Friends of the Library Group
FRANKLIN AVENUE, 5000 Franklin Ave, 50310, SAN 341-8359. Tel: 515-283-4152. FAX: 515-271-8734. *Br Mgr,* Nikki Hayter; E-mail: nmhayter@dmpl.org
Library Holdings: Bk Vols 116,106
Open Mon-Thurs 10-8, Fri 10-6, Sat 10-5, Sun 1-5
Friends of the Library Group
NORTH SIDE, 3516 Fifth Ave, 50313, SAN 341-8413. Tel: 515-283-4152. FAX: 515-242-2684. *Br Supvr,* Kate Young; E-mail: keyoung@dmpl.org
Library Holdings: Bk Vols 50,369
Open Mon-Thurs 10-8, Fri 10-6, Sat 10-5
Friends of the Library Group
SOUTH SIDE, 1111 Porter Ave, 50315, SAN 341-8448. Tel: 515-283-4152. FAX: 515-256-2567. *Br Supvr,* Brenda Hall; E-mail: bkhall@dmpl.org
Library Holdings: Bk Vols 71,057
Open Mon-Thurs 10-8, Fri 10-6, Sat 10-5

C DRAKE UNIVERSITY, Cowles Library, 2725 University Ave, 50311. SAN 341-8111. Tel: 515-271-3993. Reference Tel: 515-271-2113. Information Services Tel: 515-271-2111. Toll Free Tel: 800-443-7253. FAX: 515-271-3933. E-mail: cowles-ill@drake.edu. Web Site: library.drake.edu. *Dean of Libr,* Gillian Gremmels; Tel: 515-271-1823, E-mail: gillian.gremmels@drake.edu; *Dir, Archives & Spec Coll,* Hope Bibens; Tel: 515-271-2088, E-mail: hope.bibens@drake.edu; *Librn, Digital Literacy & Gen Educ,* Carrie Dunham-LaGree; Tel: 515-271-2175, E-mail: carrie.dunham-lagree@drake.edu; *Librarian for Discovery Services & Tech,* Andrew Welch; Tel: 515-271-2862, E-mail: andrew.welch@drake.edu; *Data & Business Librarian,* Cameron Tuai; Tel: 515-271-2924, E-mail: cameron.tuai@drake.edu; *Digital Projects Librn,* Bart Schimdt; Tel: 515-271-2940, E-mail: bart.schmidt@drake.edu; *Graduate Health Professions Librn,* Priya Shenoy; Tel: 515-271-2879, E-mail: priya.shenoy@drake.edu; *Instrul Serv Librn,* Marcia Keyser; Tel: 515-271-3989, E-mail: marcia.keyser@drake.edu; *Projects Librarian,* Bruce Gilbert; Tel: 515-271-4821, E-mail: bruce.gilbert@drake.edu; *Ref Librn,*

Mark Stumme; Tel: 515-271-3192, E-mail: mark.stumme@drake.edu; *STEM Librarian,* Dan Chibnall; Tel: 515-271-2112, E-mail: dan.chibnall@drake.edu; *Admin Mgr,* Jordan Flynn; Tel: 515-271-1936, E-mail: jordan.flynn@drake.edu; *Electronic Res Mgr,* Laura Krossner; Tel: 515-271-2475, E-mail: laura.krossner@drake.edu; *Coord, Serials, Acquisitions, & Electronic Resources,* Teri Koch; Tel: 515-271-2941, E-mail: teri.koch@drake.edu; *Knowledge Mgmt & Operations Specialist,* Meredith Scherb; Tel: 515-271-2119, E-mail: meredith.scherb@drake.edu; *Electronic Rec Archivist,* Doreen Dixon; Tel: 515-271-2933, E-mail: doreen.dixon@drake.edu; *Info Serv Assoc,* Deanna Cunningham; Tel: 515-271-3993, E-mail: deanna.cunningham@drake.edu; *Library Applications Developer,* Zoie Taylor; Tel: 515-271-2975, E-mail: zoie.taylor@drake.edu. Subject Specialists: *Culture, Educ,* Gillian Gremmels; *Intl relations, Law, Politics,* Hope Bibens; *Journalism, LGBTQ Studies, Women studies,* Carrie Dunham-LaGree; *English, Lit, Theatre arts,* Andrew Welch; *Pub admin,* Cameron Tuai; *Art, Design, Hist,* Bart Schimdt; *Health, Pharm, Sci,* Priya Shenoy; *Bus, Pub admin,* Bruce Gilbert; *Music,* Laura Krossner; *Psychol,* Teri Koch; *Art, Design, World lang,* Doreen Dixon; Staff 22 (MLS 12, Non-MLS 10)
Founded 1881. Enrl 5,139; Fac 289; Highest Degree: Doctorate
Jun 2013-May 2014 Income $3,604,501. Mats Exp $1,034,624, Books $174,137, Per/Ser (Incl. Access Fees) $816,457, Micro $5,064, AV Mat $10,805, Electronic Ref Mat (Incl. Access Fees) $17,514, Presv $10,647. Sal $1,211,181 (Prof $1,059,592)
Library Holdings: AV Mats 2,969; CDs 1,342; DVDs 1,683; e-books 337,967; e-journals 32,000; Microforms 936,702; Music Scores 9,718; Bk Titles 1,177,547; Bk Vols 551,472; Per Subs 1,887; Videos 940
Special Collections: David S Kruidenier Jr Papers; Ding Darling Coll; Drake Related Materials; ERIC Documents to 2004, microfiche; eScholarShare; Gardner Cowles Jr Papers; Heritage Coll; Historic Des Moines Images; John Cowles Papers. State Document Depository; US Document Depository
Subject Interests: Health sci, Mus, Relig
Automation Activity & Vendor Info: (Acquisitions) SirsiDynix; (Cataloging) SirsiDynix; (Circulation) SirsiDynix; (Course Reserve) SirsiDynix; (ILL) OCLC ILLiad; (OPAC) SirsiDynix; (Serials) SirsiDynix
Wireless access
Partic in Iowa Academic Library Alliance; Mid-America Law Library Consortium; OCLC Online Computer Library Center, Inc; OCLC-LVIS; Polk County Biomedical Consortium; Scholarly Publ & Acad Resources Coalition
Open Mon-Thurs 7:30am-Midnight, Fri 7:30am-8pm, Sat 10-8, Sun 10am-Midnight
Restriction: Badge access after hrs

Departmental Libraries:

CL DRAKE LAW LIBRARY, Opperman Hall, 2604 Forest Ave, 50311. (Mail add: 2507 University Ave, 50311-4516), SAN 341-8146. Tel: 515-271-3189. Interlibrary Loan Service Tel: 515-271-3759. Reference Tel: 515-271-2053. FAX: 515-271-2530. E-mail: law-circulation@drake.edu. Web Site: drake.edu/law/library. *Assoc Dean, Dir,* John D Edwards; Tel: 515-271-2142, E-mail: john.edwards@drake.edu; *Circ & Ref Librarian,* Karen Wallace; Tel: 515-271-2989, E-mail: karen.wallace@drake.edu; *Coll Mgt, Metadata Librn,* David B Hanson; Tel: 515-271-2077, E-mail: david.hanson@drake.edu; *Ref & Instruction Librn,* Rebecca Lutkenhaus; E-mail: rebecca.lutkenhaus@drake.edu; *Access Services Assoc,* Joe Stouffer; Tel: 515-271-4960, E-mail: joseph.stouffer@drake.edu; *Public Services Assoc,* Elicia Ropte; Tel: 515-271-3759, E-mail: elicia.ropte@drake.edu; *Tech Serv Assoc,* Michael Spoerl; Tel: 515-271-2051, E-mail: michael.spoerl@drake.edu; Staff 8 (MLS 5, Non-MLS 3)
Founded 1865. Enrl 325; Fac 25; Highest Degree: Doctorate
Library Holdings: AV Mats 580; e-books 1,058,394; Microforms 125,923; Bk Titles 62,486; Bk Vols 363,121; Per Subs 2,703
Special Collections: Iowa Legal History. State Document Depository; US Document Depository
Automation Activity & Vendor Info: (Acquisitions) Ex Libris Group; (Cataloging) Ex Libris Group; (Circulation) Ex Libris Group; (OPAC) Ex Libris Group; (Serials) Ex Libris Group
Open Mon-Thurs 8-8, Fri 8-5:30, Sat 10-5, Sun Noon-8
Friends of the Library Group

C GRAND VIEW UNIVERSITY LIBRARY*, 1350 Morton Ave, 50316. SAN 305-3431. Tel: 515-263-2877. Reference Tel: 515-263-2949. E-mail: library@grandview.edu. Web Site: www.grandview.edu/student-life/library. *Dir,* Pam Rees; Tel: 515-263-6098, E-mail: prees@grandview.edu; *Access Serv Librn, Archivist,* Sheri Muller; Tel: 515-263-6199, E-mail: smuller@grandview.edu; *Tech Serv Asst,* Bradley Gilbert; Tel: 515-263-2936, E-mail: bgilbert@grandview.edu; Staff 6 (MLS 3, Non-MLS 3)
Founded 1896. Enrl 1,660; Fac 100; Highest Degree: Master
Library Holdings: Bk Vols 120,000; Per Subs 400
Special Collections: Iowa Danish Immigrant Archives. State Document Depository
Subject Interests: Bus, Communication, Educ, Graphic design, Liberal arts, Nursing
Automation Activity & Vendor Info: (Acquisitions) Ex Libris Group; (Cataloging) Ex Libris Group; (Circulation) Ex Libris Group; (Course Reserve) Ex Libris Group; (Discovery) Ex Libris Group; (ILL) OCLC; (OPAC) Ex Libris Group; (Serials) Ex Libris Group
Wireless access
Function: 24/7 Electronic res, 24/7 Online cat, Archival coll, Computers for patron use, Electronic databases & coll, Internet access, Magazines, Online cat, Online info literacy tutorials on the web & in blackboard, Photocopying/Printing, Ref serv available, Scanner, Telephone ref, Wheelchair accessible
Partic in Iowa Academic Library Alliance; Iowa Private Academic Library Consortium; OCLC Online Computer Library Center, Inc; Polk County Biomedical Consortium; State of Iowa Libraries Online
Special Services for the Blind - Reader equip
Open Mon-Thurs 7:45am-11pm, Fri 7:45-4:30, Sat 12-4, Sun 1-10
Restriction: Borrowing privileges limited to fac & registered students, Open to students, fac & staff, Pub use on premises

S IOWA GENEALOGICAL SOCIETY LIBRARY, 628 E Grand Ave, 50309-1924. SAN 321-5741. Tel: 515-276-0287. E-mail: igs@iowagenealogy.org. Web Site: www.iowagenealogy.org/?page_id=24. *Librn,* Anthony Cupp
Founded 1965
Library Holdings: Microforms 11,730; Bk Vols 30,000; Per Subs 70
Special Collections: Iowa Cemetery, Census & Court House Records; Iowa Pioneers; US Federal Census Microfilm; World War I Draft Records
Subject Interests: Genealogy, Hist
Wireless access
Function: Res libr
Publications: Hawkeye Heritage (Quarterly); IGS Newsletter (Bimonthly)
Open Mon, Wed, Fri & Sat 10-4, Tues & Thurs 10-9
Restriction: Non-circulating

G IOWA LEAGUE OF CITIES LIBRARY*, 500 SW Seventh St, Ste 101, 50309-4111. SAN 320-1872. Tel: 515-244-7282. FAX: 515-244-0740. Web Site: www.iowaleague.org. *Asst Dir,* Mickey Shields; E-mail: mickeyshields@iowaleague.org
Founded 1961
Library Holdings: Bk Vols 450; Per Subs 12
Special Collections: Iowa Municipal Codes Coll; League Monthly Magazine-Iowa Coll (1899-present); Local Government Subjects Coll
Subject Interests: Law, Local govt
Restriction: Pub use on premises

M IOWA METHODIST MEDICAL CENTER*, Health Sciences Library, 1200 Pleasant St, 50309. SAN 341-8235. Tel: 515-241-6490. FAX: 515-241-3383. E-mail: MLB.library@unitypoint.org. Web Site: www.unitypoint.org/desmoines/health-sciences-library.aspx. *Dir,* Nancy O'Brien; Staff 5 (MLS 2, Non-MLS 3)
Founded 1940
Library Holdings: Bk Titles 5,000; Per Subs 300
Subject Interests: Allied health, Consumer health, Health sci, Med, Nursing, Nutrition
Wireless access
Partic in Greater Midwest Regional Medical Libr Network; Polk County Biomedical Consortium
Open Mon-Fri 10-2

P IOWA REGIONAL LIBRARY FOR THE BLIND & PHYSICALLY HANDICAPPED*, 524 Fourth St, 4th Flr, 50309-2364. SAN 305-344X. Tel: 515-281-1333. Toll Free Tel: 800-362-2587, Ext 3. FAX: 515-281-1263. TDD: 515-281-1355. E-mail: library@blind.state.ia.us. Web Site: blind.iowa.gov/library. *Dir,* Sarah E Willeford; E-mail: sarah.willeford@blind.state.ia.us; Staff 24 (MLS 4, Non-MLS 20)
Founded 1960
Library Holdings: Large Print Bks 6,445; Bk Titles 94,168; Bk Vols 310,630; Per Subs 75; Talking Bks 49,897
Special Collections: Print Coll of Books about Blindness
Special Services for the Deaf - TDD equip
Special Services for the Blind - Assistive/Adapted tech devices, equip & products; Braille bks; Computer with voice synthesizer for visually impaired persons; Talking bks
Open Mon-Fri 8-4:30
Friends of the Library Group

CM MERCY COLLEGE OF HEALTH SCIENCES LIBRARY, 928 Sixth Ave, 50309-1239. SAN 377-0990. Tel: 515-643-6613. E-mail: library@mchs.edu. Web Site: mchs.edu/students/library. *Dir, Libr & Media Serv,* Jennie Ver Steeg; E-mail: jversteeg@mercydesmoines.org; *Asst Dir,* Jennifer Thompson; E-mail: jthompson@mercydesmoines.org; Staff 4 (MLS 3, Non-MLS 1)
Highest Degree: Bachelor
Library Holdings: Bk Titles 9,261; Bk Vols 10,497; Per Subs 111

Wireless access
Function: 24/7 Electronic res, 24/7 Online cat, Audio & video playback equip for onsite use, AV serv, CD-ROM, Computers for patron use, Distance learning, Doc delivery serv, Electronic databases & coll, For res purposes, ILL available, Internet access, Laminating, Magazines, Mail & tel request accepted, Mail loans to mem, Online cat, Online info literacy tutorials on the web & in blackboard, Online ref, Orientations, Photocopying/Printing, Ref & res, Ref serv available, Scanner, Spoken cassettes & CDs, Spoken cassettes & DVDs, Study rm, Telephone ref, VHS videos, Wheelchair accessible
Partic in Iowa Academic Library Alliance; OCLC Online Computer Library Center, Inc; Polk County Biomedical Consortium
Open Mon-Thurs 7:30am-9pm, Fri 7:30-5, Sat 10-2, Sun 5-9
Restriction: Badge access after hrs, Limited access for the pub

M MERCY MEDICAL CENTER*, Levitt Library, 1111 Sixth Ave, 50314-2611. SAN 305-3482. Tel: 515-247-4189. FAX: 515-643-8809. E-mail: library@mercydesmoines.org. Web Site: www.mercyone.org/desmoines/for-healthcare-professionals/levitt-medical-library. *Mgr,* Jeanette Stonebraker; E-mail: jstonebraker@mercydesmoines.org
Founded 1961
Library Holdings: Bk Vols 4,384; Per Subs 139
Automation Activity & Vendor Info: (Cataloging) TLC (The Library Corporation); (Circulation) TLC (The Library Corporation); (OPAC) OCLC
Wireless access
Open Mon-Fri 8-4:30

L PRINCIPAL FINANCIAL GROUP*, Law Library, 711 High St, 50392. SAN 375-3352. Tel: 515-247-5893. FAX: 515-248-3011. *Law Librn, Mgr, Libr Serv,* Brent Chesson
Founded 1939
Library Holdings: Bk Titles 800; Bk Vols 5,000; Per Subs 20
Subject Interests: Ins, Pensions, State law
Open Mon-Fri 9-6

S STATE HISTORICAL SOCIETY OF IOWA-DES MOINES LIBRARY*, 600 E Locust, 50319-0290. SAN 305-3466. Tel: 515-281-6200. Interlibrary Loan Service Tel: 515-281-5070. Web Site: iowaculture.gov/history/research. *State Archivist,* Anthony Jahn; Tel: 515-281-4895, E-mail: Anthony.Jahn@iowa.gov; *ILL, Ref Librn,* Shari Stelling; E-mail: Shari.Stelling@iowa.gov; *Spec Coll & Archives Librn,* Becki Plunkett; *Archivist,* Sharon Avery; *Archivist,* Jeffrey Dawson; *Archives Assoc,* Bruce Krueger; *Microfilm Presv Spec,* Delpha Musgrave; *Digital Newsp Project Asst,* Jessica Nay; Tel: 515-725-3402, E-mail: Jessica.Nay@iowa.gov; Staff 9 (MLS 2, Non-MLS 7)
Founded 1892
Special Collections: Manuscripts; Photo Archives; State Archives
Subject Interests: Genealogy, Iowa hist
Wireless access
Open Wed-Sat 9-4:30

P STATE LIBRARY OF IOWA, 1112 E Grand Ave, 50319. SAN 341-8472. Tel: 515-281-4105. Toll Free Tel: 800-248-4483. FAX: 515-281-6191. Web Site: www.statelibraryofiowa.org. *State Librn,* Michael Scott; E-mail: michael.scott@iowa.gov; *Ref Librn,* Helen Dagley; Tel: 515-281-3063, E-mail: helen.dagley@iowa.gov; *Info Spec,* Emily Bainter; Tel: 515-281-7574, E-mail: emily.bainter@lib.state.ia.us; Staff 26 (MLS 16, Non-MLS 10)
Founded 1838. Pop 2,776,755
Library Holdings: Bk Titles 370,195; Bk Vols 450,913; Per Subs 42
Special Collections: Attorney General Opinions; Bar Association Proceedings; Iowa; Iowa State Publications; Law. State Document Depository
Automation Activity & Vendor Info: (Cataloging) ByWater Solutions; (Circulation) ByWater Solutions; (ILL) OCLC; (OPAC) Koha; (Serials) EBSCO Online
Wireless access
Function: Art exhibits, Audio & video playback equip for onsite use, Computer training, Computers for patron use, Distance learning, Doc delivery serv, Electronic databases & coll, Govt ref serv, ILL available, Internet access, Legal assistance to inmates, Mail & tel request accepted, Mail loans to mem, Online cat, Online ref, Outside serv via phone, mail, e-mail & web, Photocopying/Printing, Prof lending libr, Ref serv available, Summer reading prog, Telephone ref, Wheelchair accessible, Workshops
Publications: CE Calendar; Documents Catalog & Index; Footnotes; Inservice to Iowa (Public Libraries Measures of Quality); Iowa Certification Manual for Public Libraries; Library Directory; Long Range Plan; Public Library Statistics; Summer Reading Program
Partic in Iowa Resource & Info Sharing; OCLC Online Computer Library Center, Inc; Polk County Biomedical Consortium
Open Mon-Fri 8-4:30

GL STATE LIBRARY OF IOWA*, Iowa State Law Library, State Capitol Bldg, 2nd Flr, 1007 E Grand Ave, 50319. SAN 372-1248. Tel: 515-281-5124. FAX: 515-281-6515. E-mail: Law.Library@iowa.gov. Web Site: www.statelibraryofiowa.org/services/collections/law-library. *State Librn,* Michael Scott; E-mail: Michael.Scott@iowa.gov; *Libr Consult,* Mandy Easter; E-mail: Mandy.Easter@iowa.gov; Staff 3 (MLS 2, Non-MLS 1)
Founded 1835
Library Holdings: Bk Vols 100,000
Special Collections: English law; Iowa law. State Document Depository; US Document Depository
Wireless access
Open Mon-Fri 8-4:30
Restriction: Open to pub for ref only

GL UNITED STATES COURT OF APPEALS*, Des Moines Branch Library, 110 E Court Ave, Ste 358, 50309. SAN 325-4305. Tel: 515-284-6228. FAX: 515-284-6296. E-mail: library8th@ca8.uscourts.gov. Web Site: www.lb8.uscourts.gov. *Librn,* Melissa Miller
Library Holdings: Bk Vols 17,000; Per Subs 50
Open Mon-Fri 8-4:30

DEWITT

P THE FRANCES BANTA WAGGONER COMMUNITY LIBRARY*, 505 Tenth St, 52742-1335. SAN 305-330X. Tel: 563-659-5523. FAX: 563-659-2901. E-mail: fbwclib@dewitt.lib.ia.us. Web Site: www.dewitt.lib.ia.us. *Dir,* Jillian Aschliman; E-mail: jillianaschliman@dewitt.lib.ia.us; *Ch,* Cindy Nees; *Tech Librn,* Sara Kutzli-Armstrong; E-mail: sarakutzli@dewitt.lib.ia.us; *Youth Serv Librn,* Erica Voss; E-mail: ericavoss@dewitt.lib.ia.us; *Circ/Customer Serv Mgr,* Joellyn McDonnell; E-mail: joellynmcdonnell@dewitt.lib.ia.us; Staff 5 (Non-MLS 5)
Founded 1897. Pop 5,049; Circ 111,644
Library Holdings: AV Mats 3,080; DVDs 2,832; Large Print Bks 60; Bk Vols 35,761; Per Subs 91
Subject Interests: Newsp on microfilm
Automation Activity & Vendor Info: (Acquisitions) Book Systems; (Cataloging) Book Systems; (Circulation) Book Systems; (OPAC) Book Systems
Wireless access
Function: Writing prog
Partic in Iowa Libr Asn
Open Mon, Tues & Thurs 10-8, Wed & Fri 10-5, Sat 10-4
Friends of the Library Group

DEXTER

P DEXTER PUBLIC LIBRARY, 724 Marshall St, 50070. (Mail add: PO Box 37, 50070-0037), SAN 305-3520. Tel: 515-789-4490. FAX: 515-789-4490. E-mail: dexterpl@mchsi.com. Web Site: c5.dexter.lib.ia.us. *Dir,* Mary McColloch; *Asst Dir,* Janine Nelson
Founded 1930. Pop 669; Circ 10,065
Library Holdings: AV Mats 628; Bk Vols 8,147; Per Subs 17
Open Mon-Wed & Fri 10-12 & 2-6, Thurs 2-6, Sat 9-Noon
Friends of the Library Group

DIKE

P DIKE PUBLIC LIBRARY*, 133 E Elder, 50624-9612. SAN 305-3547. Tel: 319-989-2608. FAX: 319-989-2984. E-mail: dikepubliclibrary@dike.lib.ia.us. Web Site: dikepubliclibrary.org. *Dir,* Billie Dall; *Asst City Librn,* Laura Williams; Staff 2 (Non-MLS 2)
Pop 1,025; Circ 52,146
Jul 2014-Jun 2015 Income $86,000, City $64,246, County $19,054. Mats Exp $25,551. Sal $35,000 (Prof $25,000)
Library Holdings: Large Print Bks 350; Bk Vols 18,000; Per Subs 45; Talking Bks 1,500
Automation Activity & Vendor Info: (Cataloging) Follett Software; (Circulation) Follett Software
Wireless access
Function: Homebound delivery serv, ILL available
Open Mon 10-6, Tues-Fri 10-5, Sat 9-Noon

DONNELLSON

P DONNELLSON PUBLIC LIBRARY*, 411 Main, 52625. (Mail add: PO Box 290, 52625-0290), SAN 305-3555. Tel: 319-835-5545. FAX: 319-835-5545. Web Site: www.donnellson.lib.ia.us. *Dir,* Brenda Christine Knox; E-mail: bknox@donnellson.lib.ia.us; *Asst Dir,* Gayle Austin; Staff 3 (Non-MLS 3)
Founded 1937. Pop 940; Circ 43,149
Library Holdings: AV Mats 1,020; DVDs 340; Bk Titles 15,740; Bk Vols 15,749; Per Subs 63; Talking Bks 1,600; Videos 900
Special Collections: Genealogy Coll; Local History Coll
Automation Activity & Vendor Info: (Circulation) Follett Software; (OPAC) Follett Software
Wireless access

Function: ILL available
Partic in State of Iowa Libraries Online
Open Mon-Fri 11:30-7:30, Sat 10-3:30

DOON

P DOON PUBLIC LIBRARY*, 207 Barton Ave, 51235. (Mail add: PO Box 218, 51235-0218), SAN 305-3563. Tel: 712-726-3526. FAX: 712-726-3526. E-mail: doonlib@speednet.com. Web Site: www.doon.lib.ia.us. *Dir,* Amy Zevenbergen
Founded 1930. Pop 537; Circ 6,407
Library Holdings: Bk Titles 12,000; Per Subs 22
Wireless access
Open Mon 2-5:30, Tues & Wed 11-3, Thurs 4-8, Fri 2-5, Sat 10-12

DOWS

P DOWS COMMUNITY LIBRARY*, 114 Ellsworth, 50071. (Mail add: PO Box 427, 50071-0427), SAN 305-358X. Tel: 515-852-4326. FAX: 515-852-4326. E-mail: dowslib@wmtel.net. Web Site: dows.lib.ia.us. *Dir,* Deb Olson
Founded 1925. Pop 538; Circ 8,852
Library Holdings: Bk Titles 9,000; Bk Vols 9,400; Per Subs 15
Special Collections: Newspapers 1896-present, microfilm. Oral History
Wireless access
Partic in OCLC Online Computer Library Center, Inc
Open Mon 1-6, Tues & Fri 1-5, Wed 10-12 & 1-5:30, Sat 9-12
Friends of the Library Group

DUBUQUE

P CARNEGIE-STOUT PUBLIC LIBRARY*, 360 W 11th St, 52001. SAN 305-3601. Tel: 563-589-4225. Administration Tel: 563-589-4313. FAX: 563-589-4217. Web Site: www.dubuque.lib.ia.us. *Libr Dir,* Nick Rossman; Tel: 563-589-4126, E-mail: nrossman@dubuque.lib.ia.us; *Adult Serv Mgr,* Amy Muchmore; *Circ Mgr,* Michelle Oberhoffer; Tel: 563-589-4139, E-mail: moberhoffer@dubuque.lib.ia.us; *Youth Serv Mgr,* Danielle Day; Tel: 563-589-4138, E-mail: dday@dubuque.lib.ia.us; *IT Supvr,* Michael Kerth; Tel: 563-589-4229, E-mail: mkerth@dubuque.lib.ia.us; *Commun Relations, Supvr,* Deb Stephenson; Tel: 563-589-4243, E-mail: dstephen@dubuque.lib.ia.us; Staff 53 (MLS 13, Non-MLS 40)
Founded 1902. Pop 58,646; Circ 705,000
Jul 2019-Jun 2020 Income $3,633,662, State $36,339, City $3,545,421, Other $51,902. Mats Exp $504,891, Books $243,170, Per/Ser (Incl. Access Fees) $35,886, Micro $3,407, AV Equip $1,000, AV Mat $134,946, Electronic Ref Mat (Incl. Access Fees) $86,482. Sal $1,849,266
Library Holdings: Audiobooks 18,358; DVDs 53,313; e-books 12,206; Bk Titles 193,250; Per Subs 415
Special Collections: Bike Library. Municipal Document Depository
Subject Interests: Iowa, Local hist
Automation Activity & Vendor Info: (Acquisitions) Koha; (Cataloging) Koha; (Circulation) Koha; (ILL) OCLC; (OPAC) Koha; (Serials) Koha
Wireless access
Function: 24/7 Electronic res, 24/7 Online cat, 3D Printer, Activity rm, Adult bk club, Art exhibits, Audio & video playback equip for onsite use, Audiobks via web, AV serv, Bk club(s), Bk reviews (Group), Bks on CD, Chess club, Children's prog, Computer training, Computers for patron use, Digital talking bks, E-Readers, Electronic databases & coll, Equip loans & repairs, Free DVD rentals, Holiday prog, Home delivery & serv to seniorr ctr & nursing homes, Homebound delivery serv, ILL available, Internet access, Laminating, Life-long learning prog for all ages, Magazines, Mail & tel request accepted, Makerspace, Mango lang, Meeting rooms, Microfiche/film & reading machines, Movies, Music CDs, Notary serv, Online cat, Online ref, Outreach serv, Outside serv via phone, mail, e-mail & web, OverDrive digital audio bks, Photocopying/Printing, Preschool outreach, Preschool reading prog, Printer for laptops & handheld devices, Prog for adults, Prog for children & young adult, Ref & res, Ref serv available, Res assist avail, Scanner, Senior outreach, Spanish lang bks, STEM programs, Story hour, Study rm, Summer & winter reading prog, Summer reading prog, Tax forms, Teen prog, Telephone ref, Wheelchair accessible, Winter reading prog, Workshops
Partic in Dubuque Area Library Information Consortium; State of Iowa Libraries Online
Open Mon-Wed 9-8, Thurs 12-8, Fri & Sat 9-5, Sun 1-5
Friends of the Library Group

CR CLARKE UNIVERSITY, Nicholas J Schrup Library, 1550 Clarke Dr, 52001. SAN 305-361X. Tel: 563-588-6320. Administration Tel: 563-588-6580. E-mail: library@clarke.edu. Web Site: clarke.edu/academics/library. *Libr Dir,* Sue Leibold; E-mail: susanne.leibold@clarke.edu; *Ref Librn,* Jamie Byerly; *Metadata Librn,* Jenny Parker; *Circ Desk Mgr,* Zeny Renier; E-mail: zeny.renier@clarke.edu; Staff 4 (MLS 3, Non-MLS 1)
Founded 1843. Enrl 800; Fac 105; Highest Degree: Doctorate
Jun 2021-May 2022. Mats Exp $220,500, Books $15,000, Per/Ser (Incl. Access Fees) $25,000, AV Mat $500, Electronic Ref Mat (Incl. Access Fees) $180,000. Sal $150,000 (Prof $150,000)
Library Holdings: DVDs 1,300; e-books 165,000; e-journals 10; Electronic Media & Resources 1,800; Microforms 5,000; Bk Vols 81,000; Per Subs 25
Special Collections: BVM Heritage Coll; Rare Books
Automation Activity & Vendor Info: (Acquisitions) OCLC Worldshare Management Services; (Cataloging) OCLC Worldshare Management Services; (Circulation) OCLC Worldshare Management Services; (Course Reserve) OCLC Worldshare Management Services; (Discovery) OCLC Worldshare Management Services; (ILL) OCLC WorldShare Interlibrary Loan; (OPAC) OCLC Worldshare Management Services; (Serials) OCLC Worldshare Management Services
Wireless access
Function: 24/7 Electronic res, 24/7 Online cat, Archival coll, Computers for patron use, Distance learning, Doc delivery serv, Electronic databases & coll, Equip loans & repairs, Free DVD rentals, Health sci info serv, ILL available, Instruction & testing, Internet access, Laminating, Learning ctr, Magazines, Mail & tel request accepted, Mail loans to mem, Meeting rooms, Movies, Online cat, Online info literacy tutorials on the web & in blackboard, Online ref, Orientations, Outside serv via phone, mail, e-mail & web, Photocopying/Printing, Ref serv available, Res assist avail, Scanner, Telephone ref, Wheelchair accessible, Workshops
Partic in Dubuque Area Library Information Consortium; Iowa Academic Library Alliance; Iowa Libr Asn; Iowa Private Academic Library Consortium; OCLC Online Computer Library Center, Inc
Open Mon-Thurs 7:30am-11pm, Fri 7:30-5, Sat 12-6, Sun Noon-11

CR EMMAUS BIBLE COLLEGE LIBRARY, 2570 Asbury Rd, 52001-3096. SAN 304-4998. Tel: 563-588-8000, Ext 1003. FAX: 563-588-1216. *Librn,* John Rush; E-mail: jrush@emmaus.edu; Staff 1 (MLS 1)
Founded 1941. Enrl 190; Highest Degree: Bachelor
Library Holdings: Bk Titles 110,000; Bk Vols 120,000; Per Subs 180
Special Collections: Plymouth Brethren Writings, bibliog & flm
Subject Interests: Biblical studies
Automation Activity & Vendor Info: (OPAC) Koha
Wireless access
Partic in Chicago Area Theological Libr Asn; Dubuque Area Library Information Consortium

C LORAS COLLEGE LIBRARY*, 1450 Alta Vista St, 52004-4327. (Mail add: PO Box 164, 52004-0164), SAN 305-3644. Tel: 563-588-7189. Interlibrary Loan Service Tel: 563-588-4969. Reference Tel: 563-588-7042. Administration Tel: 563-588-7164. Toll Free Tel: 800-245-6727. Web Site: library.loras.edu/home. *Libr Dir,* Position Currently Open; *Access Serv Librn, Spec Coll Librn,* Heidi Pettitt; Tel: 563-588-7873, E-mail: heidi.pettitt@loras.edu; *Assessment Librn, Instruction Coordr,* Marissa Krein; Tel: 563-588-7917, E-mail: marissa.krein@loras.edu; *E-Res & Research Serv Librn,* Kristen Smith; Tel: 563-588-7042, E-mail: kristen.smith@loras.edu; *Outreach Librn,* Position Currently Open; *Acq, ILL Coordr,* Lisa Finnegan; Tel: 563-588-4969, E-mail: lisa.finnegan@loras.edu; *Asst to the Dir, Budget Coord,* Elizabeth Busch; Tel: 563-588-7009, E-mail: elizabeth.busch@loras.edu; Staff 7 (MLS 5, Non-MLS 2)
Founded 1839. Enrl 1,440; Fac 103; Highest Degree: Master
Library Holdings: Bk Vols 278,765; Per Subs 20
Special Collections: Center for Dubuque History Coll; Dubuque County Document Depository; Horace Coll; Loras College Archives; T S Eliot Coll; Torch Press Imprints Coll; William Boyd Allison Government Document Coll. Municipal Document Depository; State Document Depository; US Document Depository
Subject Interests: Hist, Lit
Automation Activity & Vendor Info: (Acquisitions) OCLC Worldshare Management Services; (Cataloging) OCLC Worldshare Management Services; (Circulation) OCLC Worldshare Management Services; (Course Reserve) OCLC Worldshare Management Services; (OPAC) OCLC Worldshare Management Services
Wireless access
Function: 24/7 Online cat, Computers for patron use, Distance learning, Electronic databases & coll, Equip loans & repairs, For res purposes, Govt ref serv, ILL available, Internet access, Meeting rooms, Microfiche/film & reading machines, Movies, Online cat, Online info literacy tutorials on the web & in blackboard, Online ref, Orientations, Outreach serv, Printer for laptops & handheld devices, Ref & res, Ref serv available, Scanner, Study rm, VHS videos, Wheelchair accessible
Partic in Dubuque Area Library Information Consortium; Five Colleges, Inc; Iowa Academic Library Alliance; Iowa Private Academic Library Consortium; OCLC Online Computer Library Center, Inc
Restriction: Borrowing requests are handled by ILL, In-house use for visitors, Non-circulating of rare bks

M MERCY MEDICAL CENTER*, Anthony C Pfohl Health Sciences Library, 250 Mercy Dr, 52001. SAN 305-3652. Tel: 563-589-8020. FAX: 563-589-8185. Web Site: www.mercyone.org/dubuque. *Library Contact,* Kathy Hoffmann; E-mail: hoffmkf@mercyhealth.com; Staff 1 (MLS 1)
Founded 1973
Library Holdings: Bk Titles 1,144; Bk Vols 1,155; Per Subs 74
Subject Interests: Health sci
Automation Activity & Vendor Info: (Acquisitions) EOS International; (Cataloging) EOS International; (OPAC) EOS International; (Serials) EBSCO Online
Wireless access
Function: Computers for patron use, ILL available, Photocopying/Printing
Partic in Dubuque Area Library Information Consortium
Open Mon-Fri 8-4:30
Restriction: Authorized patrons, Badge access after hrs, Circ limited, Hospital employees & physicians only, In-house use for visitors, Non-circulating to the pub

S TELEGRAPH HERALD LIBRARY*, 801 Bluff St, 52001. (Mail add: PO Box 688, 52001-0688), SAN 305-3695. Tel: 563-588-5611. FAX: 563-588-5745. E-mail: thonline@wcinet.com. Web Site: www.telegraphherald.com. *Archivist, Research Librn,* Katherine Brimeyer; Tel: 563-588-5777, E-mail: kay.brimeyer@thmedia.com
Founded 1970
Library Holdings: Bk Vols 800
Special Collections: City Directories (from 1856, incomplete); History-Dubuque & area; Necrology Card File (from 1974)
Open Mon-Fri 8-5

M UNITYPOINT HEALTH-FINLEY HOSPITAL*, Resource Center, 350 N Grandview Ave, 52001. Tel: 563-589-2398. FAX: 563-557-2813. Web Site: www.unitypoint.org/dubuque/default.aspx. *Educ Mgr,* Dana O'Brien
Library Holdings: Bk Vols 2,500; Per Subs 105
Subject Interests: Consumer health, Nursing
Open Mon-Fri 8-4:30

C UNIVERSITY OF DUBUQUE LIBRARY, Charles C Myers Library, 2000 University Ave, 52001. SAN 305-3687. Tel: 563-589-3100. Interlibrary Loan Service Tel: 563-589-3559. Reference Tel: 563-589-3770. FAX: 563-589-3722. Reference E-mail: reference@dbq.edu. Web Site: www.dbq.edu/library. *Libr Dir,* Christopher Doll; Tel: 563-589-3215, E-mail: cdoll@dbq.edu; *Asst Dir, Libr Instruction & Pub Serv,* Becky Canovan; *Electronic Systems Librn,* Joseph Letriz; *Ref & Instruction Librn,* Jessica Condlin; *Ref & Instruction Librn,* Sarah Slaughter; *Circ Supvr,* Jaimie Shaffer; *Coll Mgt, ILL,* Sue Reiter; *Evening Supvr,* Kirsten Lillegard; Staff 10.3 (MLS 5, Non-MLS 5.3)
Founded 1852. Enrl 2,180; Fac 101; Highest Degree: Doctorate
Library Holdings: e-journals 310,057; Bk Vols 148,568; Per Subs 138
Special Collections: German Presbyterian Coll; Walter F Peterson Coll; William J Petersen Coll; Woodword Coll
Subject Interests: Relig
Automation Activity & Vendor Info: (Acquisitions) OCLC Worldshare Management Services; (Cataloging) OCLC Worldshare Management Services; (Circulation) OCLC Worldshare Management Services; (OPAC) OCLC Worldshare Management Services; (Serials) OCLC Worldshare Management Services
Wireless access
Partic in Dubuque Area Library Information Consortium; Iowa Academic Library Alliance; Iowa Private Academic Library Consortium
Open Mon-Thurs 7am-Midnight, Fri 7am-9pm, Sat 8:30am-9pm, Sun 10am-Midnight

SR WARTBURG THEOLOGICAL SEMINARY, Reu Memorial Library, 333 Wartburg Pl, 52004. (Mail add: PO Box 5004, 52004-5004), SAN 325-5808. Tel: 563-589-0267. FAX: 563-589-0296. E-mail: library@wartburgseminary.edu. Web Site: www.wartburgseminary.edu/academics/academic-resources/library. *Dir,* Susan J Ebertz; *Coordr, Libr Serv,* Hannah Bernhard; E-mail: hbernhard@wartburgseminary.edu; Staff 4 (Non-MLS 4)
Founded 1853. Enrl 162
Library Holdings: Bk Vols 85,148; Per Subs 246
Partic in Dubuque Area Library Information Consortium; Iowa Academic Library Alliance
Open Mon-Thurs 7:30am-10pm, Fri 7:30-4:30, Sat 10-4:30, Sun 2-10

DUMONT

P DUMONT COMMUNITY LIBRARY*, 602 Second St, 50625. (Mail add: PO Box 159, 50625-0159), SAN 305-3725. Tel: 641-857-3304. FAX: 641-857-3304. Web Site: www.dumont.lib.ia.us. *Dir,* Deb Eisentrager; *Asst Librn,* Jodi Angstman
Founded 1927. Pop 650; Circ 12,535
Library Holdings: Bk Titles 11,000; Per Subs 52
Wireless access
Function: 24/7 Electronic res, 24/7 Online cat, Adult bk club, After school storytime, Audiobks on Playaways & MP3, Audiobks via web, Bks on cassette, Bks on CD, Children's prog, Computers for patron use, Electronic databases & coll, ILL available, Internet access, Magazines, Mail & tel request accepted, Meeting rooms, Movies, Music CDs, Online cat, OverDrive digital audio bks, Photocopying/Printing, Preschool reading prog, Prog for adults, Prog for children & young adult, Story hour, Summer reading prog, VHS videos, Wheelchair accessible
Open Mon & Tues 1-5, Wed & Fri 9-12 & 1-5, Thurs Noon-7, Sat 9-12
Friends of the Library Group

DUNCOMBE

P DUNCOMBE PUBLIC LIBRARY*, 621 Prince St, 50532. (Mail add: PO Box 178, 50532-0178), SAN 376-5210. Tel: 515-543-4646. FAX: 515-543-8186. E-mail: duncpl@wccta.net. Web Site: youseemore.com/NILC/Duncombe. *Dir,* Mary Jane Kudla; Staff 2 (Non-MLS 2)
Founded 1978. Pop 410
Library Holdings: Audiobooks 99; DVDs 566; Large Print Bks 160; Bk Vols 6,084; Per Subs 44; Videos 280
Automation Activity & Vendor Info: (Acquisitions) TLC (The Library Corporation); (Cataloging) TLC (The Library Corporation); (Circulation) TLC (The Library Corporation); (Course Reserve) TLC (The Library Corporation); (ILL) TLC (The Library Corporation)
Wireless access
Open Mon 10-12 & 1-6, Tues-Thurs 1-5, Fri 1-6, Sat 9-12

DUNKERTON

P DUNKERTON PUBLIC LIBRARY*, 203 E Tower St, 50626. (Mail add: PO Box 249, 50626-0249), SAN 305-3733. Tel: 319-822-4610. FAX: 319-822-4664. E-mail: dunkpublib@dunkerton.net. Web Site: www.dunkerton.lib.ia.us. *Dir,* Michelle Wheeler
Pop 1,100; Circ 5,800
Library Holdings: Bk Titles 8,200
Automation Activity & Vendor Info: (Cataloging) Biblionix; (Circulation) Biblionix
Wireless access
Open Mon, Tues & Thurs 2-7, Wed, Fri & Sat 10-2
Friends of the Library Group

DUNLAP

P DUNLAP PUBLIC LIBRARY*, 102 S Tenth St, 51529. SAN 305-3741. Tel: 712-643-5311. FAX: 712-643-5311. *Librn,* Paula Hess; E-mail: pjhess55@hotmail.com
Pop 1,217; Circ 16,483
Library Holdings: Bk Titles 11,000; Bk Vols 13,175; Per Subs 38
Wireless access
Open Mon-Thurs 9-5:30, Fri 9-5, Sat 10-1
Friends of the Library Group

DYERSVILLE

P JAMES KENNEDY PUBLIC LIBRARY*, 320 First Ave E, 52040. SAN 305-375X. Tel: 563-875-8912. FAX: 563-875-6162. E-mail: librarian@dyersville.lib.ia.us. Web Site: www.dyersville.lib.ia.us. *Dir,* Shirley J Vonderhaar; E-mail: svonderhaar@dyersville.lib.ia.us; *Asst Libr Dir,* Dawn Schrandt; E-mail: dschrandt@dyersville.lib.ia.us; *Sr Serv,* Ann Boeckenstedt; E-mail: aboeckenstedt@dyersville.lib.ia.us; *Youth Serv,* Kimshiro Benton; E-mail: kbenton@dyersville.lib.ia.us; Staff 2.5 (MLS 1, Non-MLS 1.5)
Founded 1956. Pop 4,035; Circ 140,210
Library Holdings: Bk Titles 56,300; Per Subs 94
Automation Activity & Vendor Info: (Acquisitions) Follett Software
Wireless access
Partic in Association for Rural & Small Libraries; Dubuque Area Library Information Consortium
Open Mon-Thurs 9-8, Fri & Sat 9-5, Sun 1-4
Friends of the Library Group

DYSART

P NORMA ANDERS PUBLIC LIBRARY, 320 Main St, 52224. (Mail add: PO Box 519, 52224-0519), SAN 305-3768. Tel: 319-476-5210. FAX: 319-476-2671. E-mail: n.anders.lib@dysart.lib.ia.us. Web Site: www.dysart.lib.ia.us. *Ch, Dir,* Janene Krug; E-mail: janenekrug@dysart.lib.ia.us
Founded 1882. Pop 1,379; Circ 26,238
Library Holdings: Bk Vols 29,000; Per Subs 82
Automation Activity & Vendor Info: (Acquisitions) Biblionix; (Cataloging) Biblionix; (Circulation) Biblionix; (Course Reserve) Biblionix; (ILL) Biblionix; (Media Booking) Biblionix; (OPAC) Biblionix; (Serials) Biblionix

Wireless access
Open Mon, Wed & Thurs 10-6, Tues & Fri 1-5, Sat 9-Noon

EAGLE GROVE

P EAGLE GROVE MEMORIAL LIBRARY*, 101 S Cadwell Ave, 50533. SAN 305-3776. Tel: 515-448-4115. FAX: 515-448-5279. Web Site: www1.youseemore.com/nilc/eaglegrove. *Dir,* Jan Grandgeorge; E-mail: jgrandgeorge@eaglegrove.lib.ia.us; *Ch,* Renee Simons; *Circ,* Marilyn Schnell; Staff 1 (Non-MLS 1)
Founded 1903. Pop 6,231; Circ 58,400
Library Holdings: AV Mats 557; Large Print Bks 1,289; Bk Vols 30,000; Per Subs 75; Talking Bks 1,725
Automation Activity & Vendor Info: (Circulation) TLC (The Library Corporation); (OPAC) TLC (The Library Corporation)
Wireless access
Special Services for the Blind - Bks on CD; Large print bks
Open Mon-Thurs 10-7, Fri & Sat 10-4:30

EARLHAM

P EARLHAM PUBLIC LIBRARY*, 120 S Chestnut Ave, 50072. (Mail add: PO Box 310, 50072-0310), SAN 305-3792. Tel: 515-758-2121. FAX: 515-758-2121. E-mail: library@earlham.lib.ia.us. Web Site: www.earlham.lib.ia.us. *Dir,* Justina Wuebker; *Asst Librn,* Ellyn Reel; Staff 1.2 (Non-MLS 1.2)
Pop 1,450; Circ 14,800
Library Holdings: Audiobooks 232; DVDs 817; e-books 10,042; Bk Titles 17,900; Per Subs 38
Automation Activity & Vendor Info: (Cataloging) Biblionix
Wireless access
Function: Adult bk club, Archival coll, Audiobks via web, Bk club(s), Bks on CD, Children's prog, Computers for patron use, Electronic databases & coll, Free DVD rentals, ILL available, Online cat, Online info literacy tutorials on the web & in blackboard, OverDrive digital audio bks, Photocopying/Printing, Prog for adults, Prog for children & young adult, Scanner, Story hour, Summer reading prog
Partic in West/Central Iowa Libraries Building Online Resources
Open Mon, Tues & Thurs 10-7, Wed 9-7, Fri 10-5, Sat 9-12
Friends of the Library Group

EARLVILLE

P RUTH SUCKOW MEMORIAL LIBRARY, 122 Northern Ave, 52041. SAN 305-3806. Tel: 563-923-5235. FAX: 563-923-5235. E-mail: librarian@earlville.lib.ia.us. *Dir,* Laurie Ellen Boies
Founded 1937. Pop 812; Circ 11,293
Library Holdings: AV Mats 321; Bk Titles 12,000; Per Subs 32; Talking Bks 30
Special Collections: Ruth Suckow Coll
Wireless access
Open Mon & Fri 1-5, Wed 9-12, 1-5 & 6-8, Sat 9-12

EARLY

P EARLY PUBLIC LIBRARY, 107 Main St, 50535-5010. (Mail add: PO Box 399, 50535-0399), SAN 305-3814. Tel: 712-273-5334. FAX: 712-273-5334. E-mail: earlylibrary@gmail.com. Web Site: www.early.lib.ia.us. *Dir,* Kristine Luy
Founded 1926. Pop 800; Circ 15,228
Library Holdings: Bk Vols 24,000; Per Subs 69
Open Tues & Wed 10-12 & 1-6, Thurs 1-6, Fri 1-4, Sat 10-Noon
Friends of the Library Group

EDDYVILLE

P EDDYVILLE PUBLIC LIBRARY, 202 S Second St, 52553. (Mail add: PO Box 399, 52553-0399), SAN 305-3822. Tel: 641-969-4815. FAX: 641-969-4040. E-mail: elibrary@pcsia.net. Web Site: www.eddyville.lib.ia.us. *Dir,* Vicki Vroegh
Founded 1897. Pop 1,064; Circ 10,181
Library Holdings: AV Mats 470; Large Print Bks 66; Bk Vols 10,000; Per Subs 37
Automation Activity & Vendor Info: (Cataloging) Follett Software; (Circulation) Follett Software
Open Mon & Tues 9:30-12 & 1-5:30, Wed 9:30-12 & 1-6, Thurs 9:30-12 & 1-4, Fri 9-12:30, Sat 10:30-11:30
Friends of the Library Group

EDGEWOOD

P EDGEWOOD PUBLIC LIBRARY, 203 W Union St, 52042. (Mail add: PO Box 339, 52042-0339), SAN 305-3830. Tel: 563-928-6242. FAX: 563-928-6242. Web Site: www.edgewood.lib.ia.us. *Dir,* Cathy Shaw; E-mail: cshaw@edgewood.lib.ia.us
Founded 1933. Pop 925; Circ 23,677
Library Holdings: Bk Titles 12,000; Per Subs 52
Automation Activity & Vendor Info: (Circulation) Follett Software
Wireless access
Function: Adult bk club, Home delivery & serv to seniorr ctr & nursing homes, Homebound delivery serv, Homework prog, ILL available, Internet access, Prog for adults, Prog for children & young adult, Spoken cassettes & CDs, Summer reading prog, VHS videos, Wheelchair accessible
Open Mon 12-7, Tues 10-5, Wed 12-8, Thurs 12-6, Fri 12-4, Sat 9-1

ELBERON

P ELBERON PUBLIC LIBRARY*, 106 Main St, 52225. (Mail add: PO Box 114, 52225), SAN 377-581X. Tel: 319-439-5476. FAX: 319-439-5476. Web Site: www.elberon.lib.ia.us. *Dir,* Ivy Weber; E-mail: director@elberon.lib.ia.us
Founded 1990
Library Holdings: Bk Vols 10,593; Per Subs 24
Open Tues 1-6, Wed-Fri 12-5

ELDON

P ELDON CARNEGIE PUBLIC LIBRARY*, 608 W Elm St, 52554. (Mail add: PO Box 430, 52554-0430), SAN 305-389X. Tel: 641-652-7517. FAX: 641-652-7517. E-mail: library@eldon.lib.ia.us. Web Site: www.eldon.lib.ia.us. *Dir,* Suzanne Streeby; *Asst Librn,* Christina Albert; E-mail: calbert@eldon.lib.ia.us
Founded 1913. Pop 1,877; Circ 5,500
Library Holdings: AV Mats 510; Bk Vols 10,200; Per Subs 17
Subject Interests: Genealogy
Wireless access
Open Mon & Fri 2:30-6:30, Tues-Thurs 12-6:30, Sat 10-1
Friends of the Library Group

ELDORA

P ELDORA PUBLIC LIBRARY*, 1202 Tenth St, 50627. SAN 305-3857. Tel: 641-939-2173. FAX: 641-939-7563. Web Site: www.eldora.lib.ia.us. *Dir,* Joan Grothoff; E-mail: jgrothoff@eldora.lib.ia.us; *Asst Dir,* Susan Hassman; E-mail: shassman@eldora.lib.ia.us; Staff 2 (MLS 1, Non-MLS 1)
Pop 3,035; Circ 45,000
Library Holdings: Bk Vols 25,000; Per Subs 75
Wireless access
Open Mon 9-8, Tues-Fri 9-6, Sat 9-3
Friends of the Library Group

ELDRIDGE

P SCOTT COUNTY LIBRARY SYSTEM*, 200 N Sixth Ave, 52748. SAN 341-8561. Tel: 563-285-4794. FAX: 563-285-4743. Web Site: www.scottcountylibrary.org. *Dir,* Tricia Kane; E-mail: tkane@scottcountylibrary.org; *Ref Serv Librn, YA Librn,* Sarah Carlin; E-mail: scarlin@scottcountylibrary.org; *Youth Serv Librn,* Emily Arnold; *Circ, Tech Serv,* Connie Owings; E-mail: cowings@scottcountylibrary.org; Staff 55 (MLS 3, Non-MLS 52)
Founded 1950. Pop 27,756; Circ 310,463
Library Holdings: Bk Vols 136,491; Per Subs 645
Special Collections: Scott County History
Automation Activity & Vendor Info: (Acquisitions) SirsiDynix; (Cataloging) SirsiDynix; (Circulation) SirsiDynix; (ILL) OCLC; (OPAC) SirsiDynix; (Serials) SirsiDynix
Wireless access
Partic in Quad-Link Libr Consortium; RiverShare Libraries
Open Mon-Thurs 8-8, Fri 8-4:30, Sat 9:30-4:30
Friends of the Library Group
Branches: 5
BLUE GRASS BRANCH, 114 N Mississippi St, Blue Grass, 52726, SAN 341-8596. Tel: 563-381-2868. FAX: 563-381-2868. *Ch,* Gina Chesling
Pop 1,169
Library Holdings: Bk Vols 5,000
Open Tues, Thurs & Fri 3-7, Wed & Sat 9-1
Friends of the Library Group
BUFFALO BRANCH, 329 Dodge St, Buffalo, 52728, SAN 341-8626. Tel: 563-381-1797. FAX: 563-381-1797. *Assoc Librn,* Cindy Mosier
Pop 1,321
Library Holdings: Bk Vols 5,000
Open Mon, Tues & Thurs 2-7, Wed 9-1 & 2-7, Sat 8-12
DURANT BRANCH, 402 Sixth St, Durant, 52747, SAN 341-8650. Tel: 563-785-4725. FAX: 563-785-4725. *Assoc Librn,* Kim Olson
Library Holdings: Bk Vols 10,000
Open Mon, Wed & Fri 2-7, Thurs & Sat 9-12
PRINCETON BRANCH, 328 River Dr, Princeton, 52768, SAN 341-8804. Tel: 563-289-4282. FAX: 563-289-4282. *Librn,* Dawn McMeen; *Librn,* Penne Miller; Staff 1 (Non-MLS 1)
Library Holdings: Bk Vols 6,000
Open Mon & Sat 9-12, Tues & Fri 3-7, Thurs 4-8
Friends of the Library Group

WALCOTT BRANCH, 207 S Main St, Walcott, 52773. (Mail add: PO Box 698, Walcott, 52773-0698), SAN 341-8839. Tel: 563-284-6612. FAX: 563-284-6612. *Librn,* Sheri Roberts; E-mail: sroberts@scottcountylibrary.org
Pop 1,528
Library Holdings: Bk Vols 6,000
Open Mon & Wed 2-7, Tues 1-5, Fri 9-1, Sat 9-12
Friends of the Library Group
Bookmobiles: 1. In Charge, Cathy Zimmerman

ELGIN

P ELGIN PUBLIC LIBRARY*, 214 Main St, 52141. (Mail add: PO Box 36, 52141-0036), SAN 305-3865. Tel: 563-426-5313. FAX: 563-426-5999. Web Site: www.elgin.lib.ia.us. *Dir,* Lisa Leuck; E-mail: librarylisa@elgin.lib.ia.us
Founded 1927. Pop 702; Circ 24,603
Library Holdings: Bk Vols 15,000; Per Subs 51
Wireless access
Publications: Annual Report
Partic in OCLC Online Computer Library Center, Inc
Open Mon, Tues & Fri 1-5, Wed 12-5, Thurs 1-6, Sat 9:30-12:30
Friends of the Library Group

ELK HORN

P ELK HORN PUBLIC LIBRARY*, 2027 Washington St, 51531. (Mail add: PO Box 119, 51531-0119), SAN 305-3873. Tel: 712-764-2013. FAX: 712-764-5515. E-mail: ehlib@metc.net. Web Site: elkhornlibrary.weebly.com. *Dir,* Alissa LaCanne
Pop 875
Library Holdings: Bk Titles 3,000; Bk Vols 4,000; Per Subs 24
Wireless access
Open Mon, Tues, Thurs & Fri 12:30-4:30, Wed 12:30-6:30, Sat 9-11

ELKADER

P ELKADER PUBLIC LIBRARY*, 130 N Main St, 52043. (Mail add: PO Box 310, 52043-0310), SAN 305-3881. Tel: 563-245-1446. FAX: 563-245-1446. Web Site: www.elkader.lib.ia.us. *Dir,* Lisa Pope; E-mail: director@elkader.lib.ia.us; *Asst Librn,* Hila Garms; *Asst Librn,* Carol Hauge; *Asst Librn,* Lisa Ihde; *Asst Librn,* Katrina Moyna; Staff 2 (MLS 1, Non-MLS 1)
Founded 1926
Library Holdings: Audiobooks 585; CDs 50; DVDs 1,100; Large Print Bks 1,490; Bk Vols 17,600; Per Subs 25
Wireless access
Open Mon-Thurs 9:30-6, Fri 9:30-5, Sat 9:30-1
Friends of the Library Group

ELLIOTT

P ELLIOTT PUBLIC LIBRARY*, 401 Main St, 51532. (Mail add: PO Box 306, 51532-0306), SAN 376-5156. Tel: 712-767-2355. FAX: 712-767-2355. E-mail: elliotlib@netins.net. Web Site: www.elliott.lib.ia.us. *Dir,* Janet Weaver; *Asst Dir,* Nancy Moss; Staff 2 (Non-MLS 2)
Founded 1917. Pop 670; Circ 5,654
Library Holdings: DVDs 26; Large Print Bks 502; Bk Titles 10,000; Per Subs 23; Talking Bks 107; Videos 612
Wireless access
Function: ILL available
Open Tues & Fri 1-5, Wed 1-6, Thurs 12-4, Sat 9-Noon
Friends of the Library Group

ELLSWORTH

P ELLSWORTH PUBLIC LIBRARY*, 1549 Dewitt St, 50075. (Mail add: PO Box 338, 50075-0338), SAN 305-3903. Tel: 515-836-4852. FAX: 515-836-2162. Web Site: www.ellsworth.lib.ia.us. *Dir,* Debra Caudle Chavira; E-mail: director@ellsworth.lib.ia.us
Pop 480; Circ 6,977
Library Holdings: Bk Titles 6,000; Bk Vols 6,571; Per Subs 23
Automation Activity & Vendor Info: (Cataloging) Follett Software
Open Mon & Thurs 12-5, Tues 10-6, Wed 12-6, Fri 1-5, Sat 9-Noon

ELMA

P ELMA PUBLIC LIBRARY, 710 Busti Ave, 50628. (Mail add: PO Box 287, 50628-0287), SAN 305-3911. Tel: 641-393-8100. FAX: 641-393-8100. E-mail: elmaialibrary@gmail.com. Web Site: www.elma.lib.ia.us. *Dir,* Renee Burke; *Asst Librn,* Paula Zweibohmer
Founded 1915. Pop 1,828; Circ 13,000
Library Holdings: AV Mats 583; Bk Titles 9,085; Per Subs 45
Special Collections: Local Newspaper on microflim
Wireless access
Open Mon & Thurs 10-6, Tues 1-6, Wed 10-7, Sat 10-2

ELY

P ELY PUBLIC LIBRARY, 1595 Dows St, 52227. (Mail add: PO Box 249, 52227-0249), SAN 305-392X. Tel: 319-848-7616. FAX: 319-848-4056. Web Site: www.ely.lib.ia.us. *Dir,* Sarah L Sellon; E-mail: ssellon@ely.lib.ia.us; *Tech Serv Librn,* Paula Bradway; E-mail: pbradway@ely.lib.ia.us; *Youth Serv Librn,* Tracy Clair; E-mail: tclair@ely.lib.ia.us; Staff 119 (MLS 101, Non-MLS 18)
Founded 1974. Pop 1,992; Circ 47,350; Fac 5
Library Holdings: Audiobooks 461; DVDs 2,960; e-books 10,594; Bk Vols 17,695; Per Subs 40
Subject Interests: Czechoslovakia, Hist, Iowa
Wireless access
Open Mon & Thurs 9-8, Tues & Wed 1-8, Fri 1-5, Sat 9-4
Friends of the Library Group

EMERSON

P EMERSON PUBLIC LIBRARY*, 701 Morton Ave, 51533. (Mail add: PO Box 282, 51533-0282), SAN 328-0756. Tel: 712-824-7867. FAX: 712-824-7867. E-mail: emlib@myomnitel.com. Web Site: www.emersonia.org/your_government/library.php. *Librn,* Melody Stephens; Staff 1 (MLS 1)
Founded 1982. Pop 2,350; Circ 10,945
Library Holdings: AV Mats 577; Large Print Bks 85; Bk Titles 12,450; Per Subs 21; Talking Bks 164
Subject Interests: Local hist
Wireless access
Function: Prog for children & young adult
Open Mon 3:30-5:30, Wed 3-7, Sat 9-1
Bookmobiles: 1

EMMETSBURG

P EMMETSBURG PUBLIC LIBRARY*, 707 N Superior St, 50536. SAN 305-3938. Tel: 712-852-4009. FAX: 712-852-3785. E-mail: info@emmetsburg.lib.ia.us. Web Site: www.emmetsburg.lib.ia.us. *Dir,* Nathan Clark; E-mail: nclark@emmetsburg.lib.ia.us; *Asst Dir,* Donna Mason; *Youth Serv Dir,* Kari Gramowski; E-mail: kgramowski@iowalakes.edu; Staff 5 (Non-MLS 5)
Founded 1908. Pop 4,900; Circ 50,525
Library Holdings: Bk Titles 39,270; Per Subs 115; Talking Bks 1,252
Automation Activity & Vendor Info: (Acquisitions) TLC (The Library Corporation); (Cataloging) TLC (The Library Corporation); (Circulation) TLC (The Library Corporation); (OPAC) TLC (The Library Corporation)
Wireless access
Open Mon-Thurs 8-8, Fri 8-5:30, Sat 9:30-2:30
Friends of the Library Group

J IOWA LAKES COMMUNITY COLLEGE LIBRARIES*, Emmetsburg Campus, 3200 College Dr, 50536. Tel: 712-852-5317. Toll Free Tel: 800-242-5108. FAX: 712-852-3094. Web Site: www.iowalakes.edu/student_services/library. *Dir, Libr Serv,* Matthew Pannkuk; E-mail: mpannkuk@iowalakes.edu
Automation Activity & Vendor Info: (Cataloging) Follett Software; (Circulation) Follett Software
Wireless access
Partic in Iowa Academic Library Alliance
Open Mon-Thurs 7:30am-8pm, Fri 7:30-4

EPWORTH

CR DIVINE WORD COLLEGE*, Matthew Jacoby Memorial Library, 102 Jacoby Dr SW, 52045. (Mail add: PO Box 380, 52045), SAN 305-3946. Tel: 563-876-3353, Ext 207. Interlibrary Loan Service Tel: 563-876-3353, Ext 262. Administration FAX: 563-876-3407. Web Site: opac.dwci.edu. *Dir,* Daniel Ceabron Williams; E-mail: dwilliams@dwci.edu; *Asst Librn, ILL,* Brother Anthony Kreinus; E-mail: akreinus@dwci.edu; *Asst Librn,* Elizabeth Winter; E-mail: ewinter@dwci.edu; Staff 2 (MLS 2)
Founded 1915. Enrl 112; Fac 33; Highest Degree: Bachelor
Jul 2013-Jun 2014. Mats Exp $46,424, Books $21,560, Per/Ser (Incl. Access Fees) $15,649, Micro $137, AV Mat $5,169, Electronic Ref Mat (Incl. Access Fees) $1,861, Presv $1,585. Sal $126,415 (Prof $100,318)
Library Holdings: AV Mats 13,081; Bks on Deafness & Sign Lang 11; CDs 971; DVDs 1,486; Bk Titles 68,197; Bk Vols 89,892; Per Subs 264; Talking Bks 151; Videos 580
Special Collections: Vietnamese Literature
Subject Interests: Cross-cultural studies, Philos, Relig
Automation Activity & Vendor Info: (Cataloging) Koha; (Circulation) Koha; (Course Reserve) Koha; (OPAC) Koha; (Serials) Koha
Wireless access
Partic in Dubuque Area Library Information Consortium; Iowa Academic Library Alliance; Iowa Private Academic Library Consortium
Restriction: Open to others by appt

ESSEX

P LIED PUBLIC LIBRARY*, 508 Iowa St, 51638. (Mail add: PO Box 298, 51638-0298), SAN 305-3954. Tel: 712-379-3355. FAX: 712-379-3355. E-mail: elibrar@heartland.net. Web Site: www.essex.lib.ia.us. *Dir,* Amber Duncan
Founded 1939. Pop 1,001; Circ 13,259
Library Holdings: AV Mats 694; Bk Titles 9,321; Bk Vols 11,740; Per Subs 25
Wireless access
Open Mon & Fri 3-6, Tues & Thurs 9:30-12 & 3-6, Wed 3-8 (3-6 Summer), Sat 10-Noon

ESTHERVILLE

P ESTHERVILLE PUBLIC LIBRARY, 613 Central Ave, 51334-2294. SAN 305-3962. Tel: 712-362-7731. FAX: 712-362-3509. E-mail: info@estherville.lib.ia.us. Web Site: www.estherville.lib.ia.us. *Dir,* Tena Sunde; E-mail: tena.hanson@estherville.lib.ia.us; *Asst Dir,* Beth Reineke; E-mail: beth.reineke@estherville.lib.ia.us; Staff 5.8 (Non-MLS 5.8)
Founded 1882. Pop 6,250; Circ 64,730
Jul 2012-Jun 2013 Income $413,168, State $2,588, City $390,875, County $19,500, Other $205. Mats Exp $25,327. Sal $173,203
Library Holdings: AV Mats 232; CDs 1,101; Bk Titles 44,290; Per Subs 80; Talking Bks 1,533; Videos 576
Subject Interests: Genealogy, Iowa
Automation Activity & Vendor Info: (Acquisitions) Biblionix; (Cataloging) Biblionix; (Circulation) Biblionix; (ILL) Biblionix; (Serials) EBSCO Online
Wireless access
Publications: Friends of Library Newsletter (Quarterly)
Partic in State of Iowa Libraries Online
Special Services for the Deaf - Bks on deafness & sign lang; High interest/low vocabulary bks
Open Mon-Wed 9:30-6, Thurs 9:30-8, Fri 9:30-5, Sat 9:30-1
Friends of the Library Group

J IOWA LAKES COMMUNITY COLLEGE LIBRARIES*, Estherville Campus, 300 S 18th St, 51334. SAN 305-3970. Tel: 712-362-7936. Interlibrary Loan Service Tel: 712-362-7991. FAX: 712-362-5970. Web Site: www.iowalakes.edu/student_services/library. *Dir, Libr Serv,* Matthew Pannkuk; E-mail: mpannkuk@iowalakes.edu; Staff 2 (MLS 2)
Founded 1964. Enrl 3,100
Library Holdings: Bk Vols 30,812; Per Subs 195; Videos 1,480
Automation Activity & Vendor Info: (Cataloging) Follett Software; (Circulation) Follett Software
Wireless access
Function: Doc delivery serv, ILL available, Photocopying/Printing
Partic in Iowa Academic Library Alliance
Open Mon-Thurs 7:30am-8:30pm, Fri 7:30-4

EVANSDALE

P EVANSDALE PUBLIC LIBRARY*, 123 N Evans Rd, 50707. SAN 305-3989. Tel: 319-232-5367. FAX: 319-232-5367. E-mail: eplib@mchsi.com. Web Site: www.evansdale.lib.ia.us. *Dir,* Shannon Jensen; *Ch,* Denise Rand; E-mail: denise.rand@evansdale.lib.ia.us; Staff 2 (Non-MLS 2)
Founded 1968. Pop 5,003; Circ 9,655
Library Holdings: Bk Vols 16,396; Per Subs 35
Automation Activity & Vendor Info: (Acquisitions) Book Systems; (Cataloging) Book Systems; (Circulation) Book Systems; (Course Reserve) Book Systems; (ILL) Book Systems; (Media Booking) Book Systems; (OPAC) Book Systems; (Serials) Book Systems
Wireless access
Function: 24/7 Online cat, Activity rm, Audiobks via web, Bks on cassette, Bks on CD, Children's prog, Computers for patron use, Electronic databases & coll, Free DVD rentals, Home delivery & serv to seniorr ctr & nursing homes, ILL available, Internet access, Magazines, Movies, Music CDs, Notary serv, Online cat, Online ref, Outreach serv, Photocopying/Printing, Prog for adults, Prog for children & young adult, Ref & res, Summer reading prog, Tax forms, Teen prog, VHS videos, Wheelchair accessible
Open Mon & Thurs 11-7, Tues, Wed, Fri & Sat 11-5
Friends of the Library Group

EVERLY

P EVERLY PUBLIC LIBRARY, 308 N Main St, 51338. (Mail add: PO Box 265, 51338-0265), SAN 305-3997. Tel: 712-834-2390. FAX: 712-834-2390. E-mail: everlylibrary@gmail.com, library1@evertek.net. Web Site: library0.wixsite.com/everlypubliclibrary, www.everlyiowa.com/Amenities/Everly_Public_Library.html. *Libr Dir,* Jeannett Palmer
Founded 1917. Pop 850; Circ 4,387
Library Holdings: AV Mats 205; Bk Titles 4,866; Bk Vols 6,121; Per Subs 16
Wireless access
Partic in State of Iowa Libraries Online
Open Mon, Tues & Thurs 11-3 & 5-9, Fri 11-3
Friends of the Library Group

EXIRA

P EXIRA PUBLIC LIBRARY*, 114 W Washington St, 50076. (Mail add: PO Box 368, 50076-0368), SAN 320-8257. Tel: 712-268-5489. FAX: 712-268-5489. E-mail: exiralib@metc.net. Web Site: www.exira.lib.ia.us. *Dir,* Jessie Wheeler; *Ch,* Katie Wheeler
Pop 810; Circ 10,506
Library Holdings: Bk Vols 17,500; Per Subs 60
Wireless access
Open Mon & Thurs 9-12 & 1:30-6, Tues, Wed & Fri 2-5, Sat 9-Noon

FAIRBANK

P FAIRBANK PUBLIC LIBRARY*, 212 E Main St, 50629. (Mail add: PO Box 426, 50629-0426), SAN 305-4004. Tel: 319-635-2487. FAX: 319-635-2487. E-mail: f.library@mchsi.com. Web Site: fairbank-ia.org/library.php. *Dir,* Angela Berg; *Libr Asst,* Beth Dixon
Pop 980; Circ 12,832
Library Holdings: Bk Titles 11,000; Per Subs 36
Function: Adult bk club, Bks on CD, Children's prog, Computers for patron use, Home delivery & serv to seniorr ctr & nursing homes, Magazines, Meeting rooms, Movies, Online cat, OverDrive digital audio bks, Photocopying/Printing, Prog for children & young adult, Res libr, Wheelchair accessible
Open Mon, Tues, Thurs & Fri 1-5, Wed 9-11 & 1-5, Sat 9-12

FAIRFAX

P FAIRFAX PUBLIC LIBRARY, 313 Vanderbilt St, 52228. (Mail add: PO Box 187, 52228-0187), SAN 305-4012. Tel: 319-846-2994. FAX: 319-846-2889. E-mail: fairfax2@southslope.net. Web Site: www.fairfax.lib.ia.us. *Dir,* Cathy Bayne; E-mail: cathy.bayne@fairfax.lib.ia.us
Pop 980; Circ 20,000
Library Holdings: Bk Vols 9,000; Per Subs 21
Open Mon-Thurs 12-7, Fri 12-6, Sat 9-2

FAIRFIELD

P FAIRFIELD PUBLIC LIBRARY*, 104 W Adams Ave, 52556. SAN 305-4020. Tel: 641-472-6551. FAX: 641-472-3249. E-mail: circ@fairfield.lib.ia.us. Web Site: www.youseemore.com/fairfield. *Dir,* Rebecca Johnson; E-mail: rjohnson@fairfield.lib.ia.us; *Youth Serv Librn,* Afton Pedrick; Tel: 641-472-6551, Ext 114, E-mail: aftonp@fairfield.lib.ia.us; Staff 12 (MLS 2, Non-MLS 10)
Founded 1853. Pop 10,000
Library Holdings: Bk Titles 67,000; Per Subs 231
Automation Activity & Vendor Info: (Circulation) SirsiDynix; (OPAC) SirsiDynix
Wireless access
Function: 24/7 Electronic res, 24/7 Online cat, Activity rm, Adult literacy prog, Archival coll, Art exhibits, Art programs, Audio & video playback equip for onsite use, Audiobks on Playaways & MP3, Audiobks via web, AV serv, Bk club(s), Bks on CD, CD-ROM, Children's prog, Computer training, Computers for patron use, Digital talking bks, Distance learning, Doc delivery serv, Electronic databases & coll, Equip loans & repairs, Free DVD rentals, Games & aids for people with disabilities, Homebound delivery serv, Homework prog, ILL available, Instruction & testing, Internet access, Laminating, Learning ctr, Life-long learning prog for all ages, Literacy & newcomer serv, Magazines, Magnifiers for reading, Mail loans to mem, Meeting rooms, Microfiche/film & reading machines, Movies, Music CDs, Online cat, Online info literacy tutorials on the web & in blackboard, Online ref, Orientations, OverDrive digital audio bks, Photocopying/Printing, Preschool outreach, Preschool reading prog, Prog for adults, Prog for children & young adult, Ref & res, Res assist avail, Scanner, Senior computer classes, Senior outreach, Story hour, Study rm, Summer & winter reading prog, Summer reading prog, Tax forms, Telephone ref, Visual arts prog, Wheelchair accessible, Winter reading prog, Workshops
Open Mon, Wed, Thurs & Fri 9:30-6, Tues 9:30-8, Sat & Sun 1-5

C MAHARISHI UNIVERSITY OF MANAGEMENT LIBRARY*, 1000 N Fourth St, 52557. SAN 305-4039. Tel: 641-472-1148. Circulation Tel: 641-472-1154. Interlibrary Loan Service Tel: 641-472-7000, Ext 3334. Reference Tel: 641-472-7000, Ext 3733. FAX: 641-472-1173. E-mail: library@mum.edu. Web Site: www.mum.edu/library. *Dir,* Rouzanna Vardanyan; E-mail: rvardanyan@mum.edu; *Ref Librn,* Martin Schmidt; E-mail: mschmidt@mum.edu; *Tape Librn,* Peter Freund; E-mail: pfreund@mum.edu; *ILL Officer,* Brian Stair; E-mail: ill@mum.edu; *Acq*

Mgr, Bibiana Lamprea; E-mail: libacq@mum.edu; Staff 3 (MLS 1, Non-MLS 2)
Founded 1971. Enrl 1,420; Fac 85; Highest Degree: Doctorate
Jul 2016-Jun 2017. Mats Exp $107,000, Books $46,000, Per/Ser (Incl. Access Fees) $60,000
Library Holdings: Bk Vols 140,000; Per Subs 145
Special Collections: Maharishi Vedic Science (Maharishi Mahesh Yogi & MUM Faculty), a-tapes, bks, flm, v-tapes; Vedic Literature
Subject Interests: Am lit, Art, Computer sci, Educ, English lit, Med, Mgt, Organic gardening, Physics, Physiology
Automation Activity & Vendor Info: (Acquisitions) Mandarin Library Automation; (Cataloging) Mandarin Library Automation; (Circulation) Mandarin Library Automation; (Course Reserve) Mandarin Library Automation; (ILL) OCLC; (OPAC) Mandarin Library Automation; (Serials) Mandarin Library Automation
Wireless access
Publications: Bibliography of General Reference Works; Bibliography on WWW Sites for Business Management; Index to Modern Science & Vedic Science; Serials Holdings Lists
Partic in Iowa Academic Library Alliance; Iowa Private Academic Library Consortium; OCLC Online Computer Library Center, Inc
Friends of the Library Group

FARMERSBURG

P FARMERSBURG PUBLIC LIBRARY, 208 S Main St, 52047. (Mail add: PO Box 167, 52047-0167), SAN 305-4047. Tel: 563-536-2229. FAX: 563-536-2229. E-mail: webmaster@farmersburg.lib.ia.us. Web Site: www.farmersburg.lib.ia.us. *Dir,* Heidi Landt; *Librn,* Heather Schissel
Founded 1920. Pop 291; Circ 1,519
Library Holdings: Bk Titles 6,900
Subject Interests: Local hist
Wireless access
Open Tues & Wed 9:30-2, Thurs 1-6, Fri 9:30-2:30, Sat 9:30-10:30

FARMINGTON

P FARMINGTON PUBLIC LIBRARY*, 205 Elm St, 52626. (Mail add: PO Box 472, 52626-0472), SAN 305-4055. Tel: 319-878-3702. FAX: 319-878-3727. E-mail: farmingtonlib52626@gmail.com. *Libr Dir,* Alicia Rider; Staff 1 (MLS 1)
Pop 750; Circ 10,975
Library Holdings: Audiobooks 20; AV Mats 1; CDs 2; DVDs 560; High Interest/Low Vocabulary Bk Vols 68; Large Print Bks 485; Bk Titles 18,442; Bk Vols 26,500; Per Subs 3
Wireless access
Function: Computers for patron use, E-Readers, Free DVD rentals, ILL available, Internet access, Magazines, Meeting rooms, Photocopying/Printing, Printer for laptops & handheld devices, Summer reading prog, Wheelchair accessible
Open Tues & Thurs 1-6, Wed & Fri 1-5, Sat 9-Noon

FARNHAMVILLE

P FARNHAMVILLE PUBLIC LIBRARY*, 240 Hardin St, 50538. (Mail add: PO Box 216, 50538-0216), SAN 376-5261. Tel: 515-544-3660. FAX: 515-544-3204. E-mail: farnlib@wccta.net. Web Site: www.farnhamville.lib.ia.us. *Librn,* Kristin Fields
Founded 1927. Pop 430
Library Holdings: Bk Vols 5,903; Per Subs 28
Wireless access
Special Services for the Blind - Bks on CD; Large print bks
Open Mon, Wed & Fri 1-6, Sat 9-12

FAYETTE

P FAYETTE COMMUNITY LIBRARY*, 104 W State St, 52142. (Mail add: PO Box 107, 52142-0107), SAN 305-4071. Tel: 563-425-3344. FAX: 563-425-3344. E-mail: fayettelib@iowatelecom.net. Web Site: www.fayettelibrary.lib.ia.us. *Dir,* Annette Butikofer; E-mail: abutikofer23@gmail.com
Founded 1934. Pop 1,380; Circ 15,000
Library Holdings: Bk Vols 15,000; Per Subs 20
Automation Activity & Vendor Info: (Acquisitions) Biblionix; (Cataloging) Biblionix; (Circulation) Biblionix; (ILL) Biblionix; (Media Booking) Biblionix; (OPAC) Biblionix; (Serials) Biblionix
Wireless access
Open Mon & Fri 10-5, Tues & Wed 1-8, Thurs & Sat 1-5
Friends of the Library Group

C UPPER IOWA UNIVERSITY, Henderson-Wilder Library, 605 Washington St, 52142. (Mail add: PO Box 1857, 52142-1857), SAN 305-408X. Tel: 563-425-5261. Interlibrary Loan Service Tel: 563-425-5186. FAX: 563-425-5271. E-mail: library@uiu.edu. Web Site: uiu.edu/academics/library. *Dir,* Kelly Donovan; E-mail: donovank15@uiu.edu; *Archivist,* Janette Garcia; E-mail: garciaj26@uiu.edu; *Libr Assoc,* Katie Brooks; E-mail: brooksk20@uiu.edu; Staff 3 (MLS 2, Non-MLS 1)
Founded 1901. Enrl 3,855; Fac 125; Highest Degree: Master
Library Holdings: Bk Titles 65,550; Bk Vols 68,032; Per Subs 125
Special Collections: NASA Coll, clippings, pictures, slides; UIU University Archives, artifacts, clippings, pictures, publications. US Document Depository
Automation Activity & Vendor Info: (Acquisitions) Ex Libris Group; (Cataloging) Ex Libris Group; (Circulation) Ex Libris Group; (ILL) Ex Libris Group; (OPAC) Ex Libris Group; (Serials) Ex Libris Group
Wireless access
Partic in Iowa Academic Library Alliance; OCLC Online Computer Library Center, Inc
Open Mon-Thurs 7:30-11, Fri 7:30-5, Sat 11-3; Mon-Thurs 8-5, Fri 8-3 (Summer)

FENTON

P FENTON PUBLIC LIBRARY*, 605 Maple, 50539-0217. (Mail add: PO Box 217, 50539-0217). Tel: 515-889-2333. FAX: 515-889-2333. E-mail: flibrary@netins.net. Web Site: www.youseemore.com/NILC/FentonPL/. *Dir,* Michele Espe
Library Holdings: Bk Vols 7,766; Per Subs 24
Automation Activity & Vendor Info: (Cataloging) Follett Software; (Circulation) Follett Software; (OPAC) Follett Software
Wireless access
Open Mon 12-6, Wed 12-7, Fri 10-5, Sat 9-11

FERTILE

P FERTILE PUBLIC LIBRARY, 204 W Main St, 50434-1020. (Mail add: PO Box 198, 50434-0198), SAN 305-4101. Tel: 641-797-2787. FAX: 641-797-2787. E-mail: ferlib@wctatel.net. Web Site: www.youseemore.com/NILC/FertilePL. *Libr Dir,* Angie Thompson; Staff 2 (Non-MLS 2)
Founded 1968. Pop 360
Library Holdings: Bk Vols 10,003; Per Subs 42
Special Services for the Blind - Bks on cassette; Copier with enlargement capabilities; Large print bks
Open Mon & Wed 1-6, Tues & Thurs 3-6, Fri 9-12 & 2-6, Sat 9-Noon
Friends of the Library Group

FONDA

P FONDA PUBLIC LIBRARY*, 104 W Second St, 50540. (Mail add: PO Box 360, 50540-0360), SAN 305-411X. Tel: 712-288-4467. FAX: 712-288-6633. Web Site: www.fonda.lib.ia.us. *Dir,* Linda Mercer; E-mail: linda.mercer@fonda.lib.ia.us
Founded 1942. Pop 1,500; Circ 7,449
Library Holdings: AV Mats 1,000; Bk Titles 6,970; Per Subs 18
Wireless access
Open Mon, Thurs & Fri 1-5, Wed 10-8, Sat 9-12

FONTANELLE

P FONTANELLE PUBLIC LIBRARY*, 303 Washington St, 50846. (Mail add: PO Box 387, 50846-0387), SAN 305-4128. Tel: 641-745-4981. FAX: 641-745-3017. E-mail: fplibrary@iowatelecom.net. Web Site: fontanellepubliclibrary.weebly.com. *Dir,* Melissa Menefee; *Asst to the Dir,* Deb Bauer
Pop 805; Circ 2,833
Library Holdings: Bk Titles 9,500; Per Subs 18
Open Tues 9:30-5:30, Wed 9:30-6, Thurs 9:30-3:30, Fri 1:30-5:30, Sat 9-11

FOREST CITY

P FOREST CITY PUBLIC LIBRARY, 115 East L St, 50436. SAN 305-4136. Tel: 641-585-4542. FAX: 641-585-2939. E-mail: library@forestcityia.com. Web Site: www1.youseemore.com/nilc/forestcitypl. *Libr Dir,* Christa Cosgriff
Founded 1897. Pop 4,151; Circ 40,760
Subject Interests: Scandinavia
Automation Activity & Vendor Info: (Cataloging) TLC (The Library Corporation); (Circulation) TLC (The Library Corporation); (OPAC) TLC (The Library Corporation)
Wireless access
Open Mon-Thurs 10-7, Fri 10-5, Sat 10-2

CR WALDORF UNIVERSITY*, Luise V Hanson Library, (Formerly Waldorf College), 106 S Sixth St, 50436. SAN 305-4144. Tel: 641-585-8110. FAX: 641-585-8111. E-mail: library@waldorf.edu. Web Site: www.waldorf.edu/faculty-staff/departments/library. *Libr Dir,* Sarah Beiting; Tel: 641-585-8671; *Libr Operations,* Tricia Baker; E-mail: tricia.baker@waldorf.edu; Staff 2 (MLS 2)
Founded 1903. Enrl 513; Fac 45; Highest Degree: Bachelor
Library Holdings: Bk Vols 65,000; Per Subs 125

Special Collections: Bible Coll
Automation Activity & Vendor Info: (Cataloging) EOS International; (Circulation) EOS International; (OPAC) EOS International
Wireless access
Function: ILL available, Internet access, Photocopying/Printing, Ref serv available
Partic in Iowa Academic Library Alliance
Open Mon-Thurs 8am-11pm, Fri 8-5, Sun 4-10; Mon-Thurs (Summer) 9-5, Fri 9-3

FORT ATKINSON

P FORT ATKINSON PUBLIC LIBRARY, 302 Third St NW, 52144. (Mail add: PO Box 277, 52144-0277), SAN 305-4152. Tel: 563-534-2222. FAX: 563-534-2222. Web Site: www.fortatkinson.lib.ia.us. *Dir,* Laura Thomas; E-mail: lthomas@fortatkinson.lib.ia.us; *Ch,* Position Currently Open
Founded 1964. Pop 389; Circ 4,248
Library Holdings: Bk Titles 6,335; Per Subs 31
Automation Activity & Vendor Info: (Acquisitions) Biblionix; (Cataloging) Biblionix; (Circulation) Biblionix; (ILL) Biblionix; (Media Booking) Biblionix; (OPAC) Biblionix; (Serials) Biblionix
Wireless access
Open Mon 1:30-6, Tues-Thurs 1:30-5, Fri 10-Noon

FORT DODGE

P FORT DODGE PUBLIC LIBRARY, 424 Central Ave, 50501. SAN 341-8863. Tel: 515-573-8167. E-mail: fdplinfo@fortdodgeiowa.org. Web Site: www.fortdodgelibrary.org. *Dir,* Rita Schmidt; Tel: 515-573-8167, Ext 6229, E-mail: rschmidt@fortdodgeiowa.org; *Ch Serv Librn,* Laurie Hotz; Tel: 515-573-8167, Ext 6244, E-mail: lhotz@fortdodgeiowa.org; *Teen & Adult Librn,* Erika Earp; Tel: 515-573-8167, Ext 6231, E-mail: eearp@fortdodgeiowa.org; Staff 10 (MLS 2, Non-MLS 8)
Founded 1890. Pop 25,206; Circ 230,101
Special Collections: Iowa Coll; Webster County Coll
Subject Interests: Local hist
Automation Activity & Vendor Info: (Cataloging) TLC (The Library Corporation); (Circulation) TLC (The Library Corporation); (OPAC) TLC (The Library Corporation)
Wireless access
Function: 24/7 Electronic res, 24/7 Online cat, Adult bk club, Archival coll, Audiobks via web, Bks on CD, Children's prog, Computers for patron use, E-Readers, Electronic databases & coll, Family literacy, Free DVD rentals, Home delivery & serv to seniorr ctr & nursing homes, ILL available, Internet access, Life-long learning prog for all ages, Magazines, Mail & tel request accepted, Meeting rooms, Microfiche/film & reading machines, Music CDs, Online cat, OverDrive digital audio bks, Photocopying/Printing, Printer for laptops & handheld devices, Prog for adults, Prog for children & young adult, Ref & res, Ref serv available, Scanner, Serves people with intellectual disabilities, Story hour, Study rm, Summer & winter reading prog, Summer reading prog, Teen prog, Telephone ref, Wheelchair accessible, Writing prog
Open Mon & Tues 9-8, Wed-Fri 9-5:30, Sat 9-1
Friends of the Library Group

J IOWA CENTRAL COMMUNITY COLLEGE*, Fort Dodge Center Library, One Triton Circle, 50501. SAN 370-3177. Tel: 515-576-7201, Ext 1156. Web Site: www.iowacentral.edu/ARC/library.asp. *Dir,* Lori Walton; E-mail: walton_l@iowacentral.edu; Staff 12 (MLS 2, Non-MLS 10)
Founded 1967. Enrl 2,836
Library Holdings: Bk Vols 55,000; Per Subs 350
Subject Interests: Educ, Iowa, Local hist
Wireless access
Partic in Iowa Academic Library Alliance
Open Mon-Thurs 7:30am-Midnight, Fri 6-4:30, Sun 2pm-Midnight

FORT MADISON

P FORT MADISON PUBLIC LIBRARY*, 1920 Avenue E, 52627. SAN 305-4187. Tel: 319-372-5721. FAX: 319-372-5726. Web Site: www.fortmadison-ia.com/index.aspx?nid=269. *Dir,* Sarah Clendineng; E-mail: sarahclen@fortmadison.lib.ia.us; *Circ Supvr,* Deborah Albee
Founded 1894. Pop 10,717; Circ 55,000
Library Holdings: Bk Titles 70,000; Bk Vols 85,000; Per Subs 150
Special Collections: Black History (Dr Harry D Harper Sr Coll); Genealogy & Local History; Railroad (Chester S Gross Memorial Coll)
Wireless access
Open Mon-Wed 9:30-6, Thurs 9:30-7, Fri 9:30-5, Sat 9-1
Friends of the Library Group

FREDERICKSBURG

P UPHAM MEMORIAL LIBRARY*, 138 W Main St, 50630. (Mail add: PO Box 281, 50630-0281), SAN 305-4217. Tel: 563-237-6498. FAX: 563-237-6218. E-mail: director@fredericksburg.lib.ia.us. Web Site: www.fredericksburg.lib.ia.us. *Dir,* Katie Rich; E-mail: katie@fredericksburg.lib.ia.us; *Ch,* Kayla Wendland; E-mail: kayla@fredericksburg.lib.ia.us; Staff 3 (Non-MLS 3)
Founded 1935. Pop 931
Library Holdings: Bk Titles 11,555; Per Subs 50; Talking Bks 370
Automation Activity & Vendor Info: (Acquisitions) Biblionix; (Cataloging) Biblionix; (Circulation) Biblionix
Wireless access
Partic in State of Iowa Libraries Online
Open Tues 9-12 & 1-7, Wed 1-7, Thurs & Fri 9-12 & 1-5:30, Sat 9-Noon
Friends of the Library Group

GALVA

P GALVA PUBLIC LIBRARY*, 203 S Main St, 51020. (Mail add: PO Box 203, 51020-0203), SAN 305-4225. Tel: 712-282-4400. FAX: 712-282-4400. E-mail: bookwrm203@yahoo.com. Web Site: galvaiowa.com/library. *Dir,* Trish Niemeier
Pop 398; Circ 6,700
Library Holdings: AV Mats 340; Bk Vols 5,800; Per Subs 31
Wireless access
Open Mon, Tues & Fri 1-5, Wed 9-Noon, Thurs 1-6
Friends of the Library Group

GARDEN GROVE

P GARDEN GROVE PUBLIC LIBRARY, 103 W Main St, 50103. (Mail add: PO Box 29, 50103-0029), SAN 376-6829. Tel: 641-443-2172. *Librn,* Sarah Chrisman; E-mail: sarah.alma.chrisman@gmail.com
Pop 165; Circ 4,673
Library Holdings: Audiobooks 22; DVDs 150; Large Print Bks 280; Bk Vols 3,300
Wireless access
Open Wed 2-6, Sat 12-6

GARNAVILLO

P GARNAVILLO PUBLIC LIBRARY*, 122 Main St, 52049. (Mail add: P O Box 254, 52049), SAN 305-4241. Tel: 563-964-2119. FAX: 563-964-2119. Web Site: www.garnavillo.lib.ia.us. *Dir,* Mary Fran Nikolai; E-mail: mfnikolai@garnavillo.lib.ia.us; *Asst Librn,* Karolyn Balk; E-mail: kbalk@garnavillo.lib.ia.us; *Asst Librn,* June Wolter; E-mail: jwolter@garnavillo.lib.ia.us
Founded 1939. Pop 757; Circ 36,641
Library Holdings: Bk Vols 21,000; Per Subs 38
Special Collections: Garnavillo History & Genealogy Coll
Automation Activity & Vendor Info: (Acquisitions) Biblionix; (Cataloging) Biblionix; (Circulation) Biblionix
Wireless access
Special Services for the Blind - Large print bks; Talking bks
Open Tues 10-4, Wed 10-8, Thurs 3-8, Sat 10-2

GARNER

P GARNER PUBLIC LIBRARY*, 416 State St, 50438. (Mail add: PO Box 406, 50438-0406), SAN 305-425X. Tel: 641-923-2850. FAX: 641-923-2339. E-mail: garnerpubliclibrary@comm1net.net. Web Site: www.garnerlibrary.com. *Dir,* Ellen Petty; Staff 2 (MLS 1, Non-MLS 1)
Founded 1873. Pop 3,129; Circ 33,700
Jul 2016-Jun 2017 Income (Main Library Only) $157,449, State $2,275, City $110,861, County $26,468, Locally Generated Income $17,845. Mats Exp $35,258, Books $22,926, Per/Ser (Incl. Access Fees) $3,187, AV Mat $6,192, Electronic Ref Mat (Incl. Access Fees) $2,953. Sal $67,216 (Prof $42,385)
Library Holdings: Audiobooks 4,061; DVDs 1,361; e-books 23,278; e-journals 213; Large Print Bks 736; Bk Titles 12,372; Per Subs 60
Automation Activity & Vendor Info: (Acquisitions) TLC (The Library Corporation); (Cataloging) TLC (The Library Corporation); (Circulation) TLC (The Library Corporation); (OPAC) TLC (The Library Corporation)
Wireless access
Open Mon 10-8, Tues & Wed 10-5:30, Thurs 12-8, Fri 12-5:30, Sat 10-2
Friends of the Library Group

GARRISON

P GARRISON PUBLIC LIBRARY*, 201 E Pine St, 52229. (Mail add: PO Box 26, 52229-0026), SAN 320-8265. Tel: 319-477-5531. FAX: 319-477-5531. E-mail: gplibrary@garrison.lib.ia.us. Web Site: garrison.lib.ia.us. *Dir,* Angela Dague; E-mail: ang.dague@garrison.lib.ia.us
Founded 1975. Pop 371
Library Holdings: DVDs 531; Bk Titles 5,143; Per Subs 2
Automation Activity & Vendor Info: (Acquisitions) ResourceMATE; (Cataloging) ResourceMATE; (OPAC) ResourceMATE; (Serials) EBSCO Online
Wireless access
Function: Accelerated reader prog, Activity rm, Art programs, Children's prog, Computers for patron use, Electronic databases & coll, Free DVD

rentals, Internet access, Laminating, Life-long learning prog for all ages, Magazines, Makerspace, Notary serv, Online cat, Outside serv via phone, mail, e-mail & web, OverDrive digital audio bks, Photocopying/Printing, Printer for laptops & handheld devices, Prog for adults, Prog for children & young adult, Scanner, STEM programs, Summer reading prog, Teen prog, Wheelchair accessible, Winter reading prog, Workshops
Open Mon, Wed & Thurs 1-6, Tues 10-2, Sat 9-Noon

GARWIN

P GARWIN PUBLIC LIBRARY, 308 Fourth St, 50632. SAN 305-4268. Tel: 641-499-2024. FAX: 641-499-2024. E-mail: garwinlibrary@mediacombb.net. *Dir,* Lola Slingluff
Pop 527; Circ 5,000
Library Holdings: DVDs 400; Bk Titles 10,000; Per Subs 26; Talking Bks 100; Videos 125
Wireless access
Open Mon-Wed & Fri 1-5, Sat 9-1
Friends of the Library Group

GEORGE

P GEORGE PUBLIC LIBRARY*, 119 S Main St, 51237. (Mail add: PO Box 738, 51237-0738), SAN 305-4276. Tel: 712-475-3897. E-mail: geolibry@mtcnet.net. Web Site: george.lib.ia.us. *Dir,* Kayla Gerloff; Staff 1 (Non-MLS 1)
Founded 1937. Pop 1,051; Circ 28,356
Library Holdings: Audiobooks 287; DVDs 917; Large Print Bks 564; Bk Vols 10,782; Per Subs 44; Videos 69
Wireless access
Open Mon & Wed 1-6, Tues & Thurs 1-5, Fri 10-6, Sat 8:30am-10:30am

GILMAN

P GILMAN PUBLIC LIBRARY*, 106 N Main St, 50106. (Mail add: PO Box 383, 50106), SAN 305-4284. Tel: 641-498-2120. E-mail: gillib@partnercom.net. Web Site: www.gilman.lib.ia.us. *Dir,* Beth Crow
Pop 642; Circ 4,706
Library Holdings: Bk Vols 5,000
Wireless access
Open Mon, Wed & Fri 1-6, Tues, Thurs & Sat 9-12
Friends of the Library Group

GILMORE CITY

P GILMORE CITY PUBLIC LIBRARY, 308 S Gilmore St, 50541. (Mail add: PO Box 283, 50541-0283). Tel: 515-373-6562. E-mail: gclibrary@gilmorecityiowa.com. Web Site: www.gilmorecity.lib.ia.us. *Dir,* Lorna Naeve; *Ch,* Michelle Bissell
Pop 466
Library Holdings: AV Mats 1,100; Bk Titles 11,000; Per Subs 12
Wireless access
Open Mon, Wed & Thurs 1-5, Tues & Fri 1-6, Sat 9-Noon

GLADBROOK

P GLADBROOK PUBLIC LIBRARY*, 301 Second St, 50635. (Mail add: PO Box 399, 50635-0399), SAN 305-4306. Tel: 641-473-3236. FAX: 641-473-3236. E-mail: gladlib@windstream.net. Web Site: gladbrookpubliclibrary.com. *Dir,* Beth Heller Wegner; *Asst Librn,* Stephanie Harders; *Asst Librn,* Felichia Seda
Pop 1,015; Circ 10,394
Library Holdings: Bk Titles 11,221; Bk Vols 12,300; Per Subs 37
Automation Activity & Vendor Info: (Circulation) Biblionix/Apollo
Wireless access
Open Mon 12-5, Tues 12-8, Wed-Fri 10-5, Sat 10-12

GLENWOOD

P GLENWOOD PUBLIC LIBRARY*, 109 N Vine St, 51534. SAN 305-4314. Tel: 712-527-5252. FAX: 712-527-3872. E-mail: questions@glenwood.lib.ia.us. Web Site: www.glenwood.lib.ia.us. *Dir,* Tara Anderson Painter; E-mail: tara@glenwood.lib.ia.us; *Ad,* Linda Greenwood; E-mail: linda@glenwood.lib.ia.us; *Ch,* Jonatha Basye; E-mail: jonatha@glenwood.lib.ia.us; Staff 6 (Non-MLS 6)
Founded 1896. Pop 5,358; Circ 54,912
Jul 2014-Jun 2015 Income $213,333, State $3,873, City $141,438, County $23,820, Locally Generated Income $44,202. Mats Exp $29,287, Books $17,904, Per/Ser (Incl. Access Fees) $2,500, Micro $200, AV Mat $1,677, Electronic Ref Mat (Incl. Access Fees) $7,006. Sal $137,935
Library Holdings: CDs 800; DVDs 2,313; Bk Vols 36,770; Per Subs 100; Videos 1,100
Subject Interests: Genealogy, Local hist
Automation Activity & Vendor Info: (Cataloging) Biblionix; (Circulation) Biblionix
Wireless access
Function: Adult bk club, Art exhibits, Bks on cassette, Bks on CD, Children's prog, Computers for patron use, Free DVD rentals, Home delivery & serv to seniorr ctr & nursing homes, Homebound delivery serv, ILL available, Music CDs, Photocopying/Printing, Prog for adults, Prog for children & young adult, Ref serv available, Spoken cassettes & CDs, Spoken cassettes & DVDs, Summer reading prog, Tax forms, Telephone ref, VHS videos, Wheelchair accessible
Open Mon, Tues, Thurs & Fri 9-6, Wed 9-8, Sat 9-Noon
Friends of the Library Group

GLIDDEN

P GLIDDEN PUBLIC LIBRARY, 110 Idaho St, 51443. (Mail add: PO Box 345, 51443-0345), SAN 305-4330. Tel: 712-659-3781. FAX: 712-659-3805. E-mail: glibrary@mchsi.com. Web Site: www.glidden.lib.ia.us. *Dir,* Erin Wolf; Staff 2 (Non-MLS 2)
Founded 1924. Pop 1,100; Circ 25,073
Jul 2015-Jun 2016 Income $48,808, State $1,099, City $35,291, County $11,609, Other $809. Mats Exp Books $7,000. Sal $25,000 (Prof $20,000)
Library Holdings: Audiobooks 15; Bks-By-Mail 98; Bks on Deafness & Sign Lang 5; CDs 15; DVDs 250; Large Print Bks 150; Bk Titles 12,107; Per Subs 45
Wireless access
Function: 24/7 Electronic res, Activity rm, Adult bk club, Archival coll, Audiobks via web, Bk club(s), Bks on CD, Children's prog, Computer training, Computers for patron use, Free DVD rentals, Genealogy discussion group, Holiday prog, Home delivery & serv to seniorr ctr & nursing homes, Homebound delivery serv, ILL available, Internet access, Magazines, Mail & tel request accepted, Mail loans to mem, Meeting rooms, Microfiche/film & reading machines, Movies, Online cat, Orientations, Outreach serv, Outside serv via phone, mail, e-mail & web, OverDrive digital audio bks, Photocopying/Printing, Preschool outreach, Preschool reading prog, Prog for adults, Senior outreach, Serves people with intellectual disabilities, Story hour, Study rm, Summer & winter reading prog, Summer reading prog, Tax forms, Wheelchair accessible, Winter reading prog
Open Mon-Wed & Fri 12-5, Thurs 10-6, Sat 9-1

GOWRIE

P GOWRIE PUBLIC LIBRARY*, 1204 Market St, 50543. (Mail add: PO Box 137, 50543-0137), SAN 305-4349. Tel: 515-352-3315. FAX: 515-352-3713. E-mail: gowriepl@wccta.net. Web Site: www1.youseemore.com/nilc/Gowrie. *Dir,* Lacey Spece
Founded 1930. Pop 1,038; Circ 15,282
Library Holdings: Bk Vols 9,500; Per Subs 31
Automation Activity & Vendor Info: (Acquisitions) Follett Software; (Cataloging) Follett Software; (Circulation) Follett Software; (ILL) Follett Software; (Media Booking) Follett Software; (OPAC) Follett Software; (Serials) Follett Software
Wireless access
Open Mon, Tues, Thurs & Fri 1-5, Wed 1-7, Sat 9-Noon

GRAETTINGER

P GRAETTINGER PUBLIC LIBRARY*, 115 W Robins St, 51342. (Mail add: PO Box 368, 51342-0368), SAN 305-4357. Tel: 712-859-3592. FAX: 712-859-3592. Web Site: www.graettinger.lib.ia.us. *Libr Dir,* Debbi Harris; E-mail: dharris@graettinger.lib.ia.us
Founded 1939. Pop 844; Circ 13,136
Library Holdings: AV Mats 418; Bk Titles 12,000; Per Subs 30
Automation Activity & Vendor Info: (Acquisitions) Follett Software
Wireless access
Special Services for the Blind - Bks on cassette; Bks on CD
Open Tues, Thurs & Fri 9-5, Wed 9-6, Sat 9-12
Friends of the Library Group

GRAFTON

P GRAFTON PUBLIC LIBRARY*, 201 Fourth Ave, 50440. (Mail add: PO Box 25, 50440-0025), SAN 305-4365. Tel: 641-748-2735. FAX: 641-748-2739. E-mail: graftonlib@wctatel.net. Web Site: www.graftoniowa.com/library, www.youseemore.com/nilc/Grafton. *Dir,* Nancy Walker
Pop 300; Circ 8,425
Library Holdings: Audiobooks 112; Bks on Deafness & Sign Lang 3; CDs 5; DVDs 1,060; Large Print Bks 216; Bk Vols 11,033; Per Subs 65; Talking Bks 211; Videos 1,867
Automation Activity & Vendor Info: (Acquisitions) Winnebago Software Co; (Cataloging) Follett Software; (Circulation) Winnebago Software Co; (ILL) Winnebago Software Co
Wireless access
Open Tues-Fri 2-6:30, Sat 9-3

GRAND JUNCTION

P GRAND JUNCTION PUBLIC LIBRARY*, 106 E Main St, 50107. (Mail add: PO Box 79, 50107-0079), SAN 305-4373. Tel: 515-738-2506. Web Site: www.grandjunction.lib.ia.us. *Dir,* Diane Kafer; E-mail: diane.kafer@grandjunction.lib.ia.us; *Asst Dir,* Katherine Thomas; E-mail: kthomas@grandjunction.lib.ia.us; Staff 2 (Non-MLS 2)
Founded 1929. Pop 850; Circ 16,850
Library Holdings: Audiobooks 130; Bks on Deafness & Sign Lang 10; DVDs 410; Large Print Bks 500; Bk Titles 8,954; Per Subs 40
Automation Activity & Vendor Info: (Acquisitions) Book Systems; (Cataloging) Book Systems; (Circulation) Book Systems; (Course Reserve) Book Systems; (ILL) Book Systems; (Media Booking) Book Systems; (OPAC) Book Systems; (Serials) Book Systems
Wireless access
Open Mon, Tues & Thurs 2-6, Wed 11-5, Fri 1-5

GRANGER

P GRANGER PUBLIC LIBRARY*, 2216 Broadway, 50109. (Mail add: PO Box 399, 50109), SAN 305-4381. Tel: 515-999-2088. FAX: 515-999-9156. Web Site: www.grangeriowa.org/library. *Dir,* Harriet Peterson; E-mail: harriet.peterson@granger.lib.ia.us
Pop 619
Library Holdings: Bk Titles 6,062; Per Subs 30
Wireless access
Open Mon & Thurs 2-7, Tues & Wed 9-12 & 1-7, Sat 9:30-Noon
Friends of the Library Group

GREENE

P GREENE PUBLIC LIBRARY*, 231 W Traer St, 50636-9406. (Mail add: PO Box 280, 50636-0280), SAN 305-439X. Tel: 641-816-5642. FAX: 641-816-4838. E-mail: gpl@myomnitel.com. Web Site: www.greene.lib.ia.us. *Dir,* Cynthia Siemons; E-mail: cynthias@greene.lib.ia.us; *Ch,* Dorothy Leavens
Founded 1872. Pop 2,600; Circ 27,707
Library Holdings: AV Mats 1,227; Bk Titles 17,046; Per Subs 89
Special Collections: The Greene Recorder (1876-1996), microfilm
Automation Activity & Vendor Info: (Acquisitions) Follett Software; (Cataloging) Follett Software; (Circulation) Follett Software
Wireless access
Open Mon & Wed 9-9, Tues & Thurs Noon-5, Fri 9-5, Sat 9-3
Friends of the Library Group

GREENFIELD

P GREENFIELD PUBLIC LIBRARY*, 202 S First St, 50849. (Mail add: PO Box 328, 50849), SAN 305-4403. Tel: 641-743-6120. E-mail: greenpl@iowatelecom.net. Web Site: www.greenfieldiowapubliclibrary.com. *Dir,* Lynn Heinbuch
Founded 1916. Pop 2,129; Circ 27,531
Library Holdings: DVDs 500; Bk Vols 23,378; Per Subs 100
Subject Interests: Genealogy
Automation Activity & Vendor Info: (Acquisitions) Book Systems; (Cataloging) Book Systems; (Circulation) Book Systems; (ILL) Book Systems; (Media Booking) Book Systems; (OPAC) Book Systems; (Serials) Book Systems
Wireless access
Open Mon-Wed & Fri 10-5:30, Thurs 10-7, Sat 10-Noon
Friends of the Library Group

GRIMES

P GRIMES PUBLIC LIBRARY*, 200 N James, 50111. SAN 305-4411. Tel: 515-986-3551. FAX: 515-986-9553. E-mail: library@grimes.lib.ia.us. Web Site: www.grimes.lib.ia.us. *Libr Dir,* Cheryl Heid; E-mail: heid@grimeslibrary.org; *Asst Dir,* Karalee Kerr; E-mail: karalee@grimeslibrary.org; Staff 9 (Non-MLS 9)
Founded 1972. Pop 5,098
Library Holdings: Bk Titles 30,804; Bk Vols 33,260; Per Subs 40
Automation Activity & Vendor Info: (Cataloging) Follett Software; (Circulation) Follett Software; (OPAC) Follett Software
Wireless access
Open Mon-Thurs 9-7:30, Fri 9-5:30, Sat 9-4:30, Sun 1-4:30

GRINNELL

P DRAKE COMMUNITY LIBRARY*, 930 Park St, 50112-2016. SAN 305-4438. Tel: 641-236-2661. FAX: 641-236-2667. E-mail: library@grinnelliowa.gov. Web Site: www.grinnell.lib.ia.us. *Dir,* Marilyn Kennett; E-mail: mkennett@grinnelliowa.gov; *Syst Adminr,* Monique Shore; E-mail: mshore@grinnelliowa.gov; *Youth Serv Librn,* Karen Neal; E-mail: kneal@grinnelliowa.gov; Staff 9 (MLS 2, Non-MLS 7)
Founded 1901. Pop 9,218; Circ 85,145
Jul 2020-Jun 2021 Income $626,547, State $7,594, City $582,630, County $21,173, Locally Generated Income $15,150. Mats Exp $58,300, Books $35,100, Per/Ser (Incl. Access Fees) $6,100, Micro $500, AV Mat $4,600, Electronic Ref Mat (Incl. Access Fees) $12,000. Sal $408,976 (Prof $374,775)
Library Holdings: Audiobooks 2,645; Bks on Deafness & Sign Lang 31; CDs 422; DVDs 1,905; e-books 49,496; Large Print Bks 4,435; Bk Vols 69,326; Per Subs 150; Videos 1,994
Special Collections: State Document Depository
Subject Interests: Local hist
Automation Activity & Vendor Info: (Acquisitions) Baker & Taylor; (Cataloging) Baker & Taylor; (Circulation) Horizon; (OPAC) SirsiDynix-Enterprise; (Serials) EBSCO Discovery Service
Wireless access
Function: 24/7 Electronic res, 24/7 Online cat, Activity rm, Adult bk club, After school storytime, Archival coll, Art exhibits, Audio & video playback equip for onsite use, Audiobks via web, Bk club(s), Bks on cassette, Bks on CD, Butterfly Garden, Children's prog, Computer training, Computers for patron use, Digital talking bks, Electronic databases & coll, Equip loans & repairs, Free DVD rentals, Govt ref serv, Holiday prog, Home delivery & serv to seniorr ctr & nursing homes, Homebound delivery serv, Homework prog, ILL available, Internet access, Laminating, Life-long learning prog for all ages, Magazines, Magnifiers for reading, Mail & tel request accepted, Mango lang, Meeting rooms, Microfiche/film & reading machines, Movies, Music CDs, Notary serv, Online cat, Online info literacy tutorials on the web & in blackboard, Online ref, Outreach serv, Outside serv via phone, mail, e-mail & web, OverDrive digital audio bks, Photocopying/Printing, Preschool outreach, Preschool reading prog, Printer for laptops & handheld devices, Prog for adults, Prog for children & young adult, Ref serv available, Scanner, Senior outreach, Serves people with intellectual disabilities, Spanish lang bks, Spoken cassettes & CDs, Spoken cassettes & DVDs, Story hour, Study rm, Summer reading prog, Tax forms, Teen prog, Telephone ref, Wheelchair accessible
Open Mon-Thurs 10-8, Fri 10-6, Sat 10-5, Sun 1:30-4
Friends of the Library Group

C GRINNELL COLLEGE LIBRARIES, Burling Library, 1111 Sixth Ave, 50112-1770. SAN 305-442X. Tel: 641-269-3350. Interlibrary Loan Service Tel: 641-269-3005. Administration Tel: 641-269-3351. FAX: 641-269-4283. E-mail: query@grinnell.edu. Web Site: www.grinnell.edu/academics/libraries. *Librn of the Col,* Mark Christel; E-mail: christelmark@grinnell.edu; *Acq & Discovery Librn,* Sharon R Clayton; Tel: 641-269-3380, E-mail: claytons@grinnell.edu; *Digital Scholarship Librn,* Elizabeth Rodrigues; Tel: 641-269-3362, E-mail: rodrigue8@grinnell.edu; *Discovery, Systems & Digital Strategy Librarian,* Kayla Reed; Tel: 641-269-4775, E-mail: reedkayla@grinnell.edu; *Coordr of Res Serv, Humanities Librn,* Phillip Jones; Tel: 641-269-3355, E-mail: jonesphi@grinnell.edu; *Sci Librn,* Kevin Engel; Tel: 641-269-4234, E-mail: engelk@grinnell.edu; *Soc Studies & Data Serv Librn,* Julia Bauder; Tel: 641-269-4431; *Col Archivist & Spec Coll Librn,* Chris Jones; Tel: 641-269-3364, E-mail: joneschr@grinnell.edu; *Project Archivist,* Laura Michelson; E-mail: michelson@grinnell.edu. Subject Specialists: *Arabic lang, Art hist, Fr,* Sharon R Clayton; *Humanities,* Elizabeth Rodrigues; *Dance, Theatre,* Kayla Reed; *Col hist, Local hist,* Chris Jones; Staff 23.7 (MLS 8, Non-MLS 15.7)
Enrl 1,697; Fac 161; Highest Degree: Bachelor
Jul 2019-Jun 2020. Mats Exp $2,276,402, Books $775,822, AV Mat $21,748, Electronic Ref Mat (Incl. Access Fees) $1,465,603, Presv $13,229. Sal $1,008,588 (Prof $698,506)
Library Holdings: AV Mats 27,981; e-books 1,208,787; e-journals 148,773; Electronic Media & Resources 107,499; Microforms 26,651; Bk Titles 483,352; Bk Vols 661,077; Per Subs 147,768
Special Collections: East Asian Coll; Iowa, Local History & College Archives, bks & ms; James Norman Hall Coll, paper & ms; Pinne Coll, bks & ms; Salisbury House Coll. State Document Depository; US Document Depository
Automation Activity & Vendor Info: (Acquisitions) Ex Libris Group; (Cataloging) Ex Libris Group; (Circulation) Ex Libris Group; (Course Reserve) Atlas Systems; (ILL) OCLC ILLiad; (OPAC) Ex Libris Group; (Serials) Ex Libris Group
Wireless access
Function: Archival coll, Audio & video playback equip for onsite use, Computers for patron use, Internet access, Magazines, Online cat
Partic in Iowa Academic Library Alliance; Oberlin Group
Special Services for the Blind - Assistive/Adapted tech devices, equip & products; Computer with voice synthesizer for visually impaired persons

GRISWOLD

P GRISWOLD PUBLIC LIBRARY*, 505 Main, 51535. (Mail add: PO Box 190, 51535-0190), SAN 305-4446. Tel: 712-778-4130. FAX: 712-778-4140. E-mail: grislib@netins.net. Web Site: griswoldlibraryia.weebly.com. *Libr Dir,* Lisa Metheny; *Asst Librn,* Susan Peterson; Staff 1 (Non-MLS 1)
Founded 1977. Pop 1,039; Circ 18,482

Library Holdings: Bk Vols 10,134; Per Subs 33
Automation Activity & Vendor Info: (Acquisitions) Follett Software; (Cataloging) Follett Software; (Circulation) Follett Software; (ILL) Follett Software; (Media Booking) Follett Software; (OPAC) Follett Software; (Serials) Follett Software
Wireless access
Function: Bks on CD, Children's prog, Computers for patron use, E-Reserves, Electronic databases & coll, Free DVD rentals, Homebound delivery serv, ILL available, Online cat, Outreach serv, Photocopying/Printing, Preschool outreach, Prog for adults, Prog for children & young adult, Scanner, Story hour, Summer reading prog, Tax forms, VHS videos, Wheelchair accessible
Open Mon, Tues & Fri 10-12 & 1-5, Wed 10-12 & 1-6, Sat 10-12
Restriction: In-house use for visitors
Friends of the Library Group

GRUNDY CENTER

P KLING MEMORIAL LIBRARY*, 708 Seventh St, 50638-1430. SAN 305-4454. Tel: 319-825-3607. FAX: 319-825-5863. E-mail: library@grundycenter.lib.ia.us. Web Site: www.grundycenter.lib.ia.us. *Dir,* Lindsey Freese; *Ch Serv Librn,* Becky Bonnette; *Teen Serv Librn,* Lenah Oltman
Pop 2,596; Circ 50,000
Library Holdings: Audiobooks 1,007; AV Mats 2,000; CDs 20; DVDs 1,588; e-books 10,594; Large Print Bks 2,364; Bk Vols 27,521; Per Subs 98
Special Collections: Herbert Quick Coll
Subject Interests: Iowa
Automation Activity & Vendor Info: (Circulation) Biblionix/Apollo; (OPAC) Biblionix/Apollo
Wireless access
Open Mon, Wed & Fri 10-5, Tues & Thurs 10-7, Sat 10-Noon
Friends of the Library Group

GUTHRIE CENTER

P MARY J BARNETT MEMORIAL LIBRARY*, 400 Grand St, 50115-1439. SAN 305-4462. Tel: 641-747-8110. FAX: 641-747-8003. E-mail: mjblib@netins.net. Web Site: www.guthriecenter.lib.ia.us. *Dir,* Patricia Sleister; *Asst Dir,* Sue Hjelle; Staff 1 (MLS 1)
Founded 1902. Pop 2,000; Circ 40,000
Library Holdings: Bk Titles 30,000; Per Subs 85
Wireless access
Partic in Association for Rural & Small Libraries
Open Mon-Thurs 2-6, Fri 9-12
Friends of the Library Group

GUTTENBERG

P GUTTENBERG PUBLIC LIBRARY*, 603 S Second St, 52052. (Mail add: PO Box 130, 52052-0130), SAN 305-4470. Tel: 563-252-3108. E-mail: librarian@guttenberg.lib.ia.us. Web Site: www.guttenberg.lib.ia.us. *Dir,* Sandra Barron; *Ch,* Nancy Ruzicka
Pop 2,000; Circ 27,000
Automation Activity & Vendor Info: (Acquisitions) Biblionix/Apollo; (Cataloging) Biblionix/Apollo; (Circulation) Biblionix/Apollo; (ILL) Biblionix/Apollo; (Media Booking) Biblionix/Apollo; (OPAC) Biblionix/Apollo; (Serials) Biblionix/Apollo
Wireless access
Open Mon & Wed 10-6:30, Tues, Thurs & Fri 10-5, Sat 10-3
Friends of the Library Group

HAMBURG

P HAMBURG PUBLIC LIBRARY, 1301 Main St, 51640. SAN 305-4489. Tel: 712-382-1395. E-mail: libraryhamburg@gmail.com. Web Site: sites.google.com/site/hamburgiowalibrary. *Dir,* Ellen Longman; *Asst Librn,* Nancy Middaugh; Staff 2 (Non-MLS 2)
Founded 1919. Pop 1,187; Circ 6,000
Library Holdings: Bk Titles 11,000
Wireless access
Partic in State of Iowa Libraries Online
Open Mon 1-6, Tues-Thurs 12-5, Fri 11-5, Sat 9-12
Friends of the Library Group

HAMPTON

P HAMPTON PUBLIC LIBRARY*, Four Federal St S, 50441-1934. SAN 305-4497. Tel: 641-456-4451. FAX: 641-456-2377. E-mail: hplibrary@mchsi.com. Web Site: www.hampton.lib.ia.us. *Dir,* Kim Manning; E-mail: kim@hampton.lib.ia.us; *Asst Dir,* Suzy Knipfel; Staff 2 (MLS 2)
Founded 1889. Pop 4,133
Library Holdings: Bk Titles 35,000; Per Subs 103
Subject Interests: Genealogy, Iowa
Automation Activity & Vendor Info: (Acquisitions) TLC (The Library Corporation); (Cataloging) TLC (The Library Corporation); (Circulation) TLC (The Library Corporation); (Course Reserve) TLC (The Library Corporation); (ILL) TLC (The Library Corporation); (OPAC) TLC (The Library Corporation); (Serials) TLC (The Library Corporation)
Wireless access
Open Mon & Thurs 10-5:30, Tues & Wed 10-8, Fri & Sat 10-3
Friends of the Library Group

HANLONTOWN

P KINNEY MEMORIAL LIBRARY*, 214 Main St, 50444. (Mail add: PO Box 58, 50444-0058), SAN 305-4500. Tel: 641-896-2888. FAX: 641-896-2890. E-mail: redhawks@WCTAtel.net. Web Site: www1.youseemore.com/NILC/Kinney. *Dir,* Ramona Kinseth
Pop 193; Circ 2,975
Library Holdings: Bk Titles 5,114; Per Subs 21
Wireless access
Open Mon, Tues & Thurs 3-7, Wed & Sat 9-1

HARCOURT

P HARCOURT COMMUNITY LIBRARY*, 106 W Second St, 50544. (Mail add: PO Box 358, 50544-0358), SAN 305-4519. Tel: 515-354-5391. FAX: 515-354-5391. E-mail: harcourt@lvcta.com. Web Site: www.youseemore.com/NILC/HarcourtPL. *Dir,* Kathy Hay
Founded 1950. Pop 700; Circ 5,200
Library Holdings: Bk Vols 6,000; Per Subs 45
Open Tues 10-6, Wed 12-6, Thurs 4-8, Sat 9-Noon

HARLAN

P HARLAN COMMUNITY LIBRARY, 718 Court St, 51537. SAN 305-4527. Tel: 712-755-5934. FAX: 712-755-3952. E-mail: info@harlanlibrary.org. Web Site: www.harlan.lib.ia.us. *Libr Dir,* Amanda J Brewer; E-mail: abrewer@harlanlibrary.org; *Ad,* Elizabeth Schechinger; E-mail: eschechinger@harlanlibrary.org; *Youth Serv Librn,* Emily Kurth-Christensen; E-mail: echristensen@harlanlibrary.org; *Libr Tech,* Linda Burger; E-mail: lburger@harlanlibrary.org; Staff 6 (Non-MLS 6)
Founded 1980. Pop 5,282; Circ 102,447
Library Holdings: Bk Titles 50,000; Bk Vols 50,250; Per Subs 126
Special Collections: Iowa History Coll
Automation Activity & Vendor Info: (Cataloging) Follett Software; (Circulation) Follett Software; (OPAC) Follett Software
Wireless access
Function: 24/7 Electronic res, 24/7 Online cat, Adult bk club, Audiobks via web, Bi-weekly Writer's Group, Bk club(s), Bks on cassette, Bks on CD, Children's prog, Computers for patron use, Doc delivery serv, Electronic databases & coll, Equip loans & repairs, Free DVD rentals, ILL available, Instruction & testing, Internet access, Laminating, Magazines, Meeting rooms, Microfiche/film & reading machines, Movies, Music CDs, Outside serv via phone, mail, e-mail & web, OverDrive digital audio bks, Photocopying/Printing, Preschool outreach, Preschool reading prog, Prog for adults, Prog for children & young adult, Scanner, Serves people with intellectual disabilities, Story hour, Summer reading prog, VHS videos, Wheelchair accessible
Open Mon-Fri 9-6, Sat 9-Noon

HARPERS FERRY

P DOLORES TILLINGHAST MEMORIAL LIBRARY, 234 N Fourth St, 52146. (Mail add: PO Box 57, 52146-0057), SAN 376-5040. Tel: 563-586-2524. FAX: 563-586-2524. E-mail: dolorestillinghastmemlib@gmail.com. Web Site: harpersferryiowa.com/library. *Dir,* Jodi Delaney
Founded 1990. Pop 330
Library Holdings: Bk Vols 9,641; Per Subs 70
Wireless access
Open Mon, Tues & Sat 9-12, Wed 4-7, Thurs 5-7, Fri 2-5

S US NATIONAL PARK SERVICE*, Effigy Mounds National Monument Library, 151 Hwy 76, 52146. SAN 370-3185. Tel: 563-873-3491. Web Site: www.nps.gov/efmo. *Library Contact,* Jessica Pope; E-mail: jessica_pope@nps.gov
Library Holdings: Bk Vols 10,000
Special Collections: Ellison Orr Coll, ms
Subject Interests: Natural hist
Restriction: Non-circulating, Open to others by appt, Pub ref by request

HARTLEY

P HARTLEY PUBLIC LIBRARY*, 91 First St SE, 51346. SAN 305-4535. Tel: 712-928-2080. FAX: 712-928-2823. Web Site: www.hartley.lib.ia.us. *Dir,* Cynthia Gelderman; *Adult Coordr,* Ellen Treimer; E-mail: ellen@hartley.lib.ia.us; *Children's & Teen Serv Coordr,* Heather Grotluschen

Founded 1942. Pop 1,733
Library Holdings: AV Mats 905; Large Print Bks 82; Bk Vols 21,665; Per Subs 104; Talking Bks 574
Automation Activity & Vendor Info: (Cataloging) Follett Software; (Circulation) Follett Software
Wireless access
Function: Home delivery & serv to seniorr ctr & nursing homes, Homebound delivery serv, ILL available, Photocopying/Printing, Prog for children & young adult, Summer reading prog, Wheelchair accessible
Open Mon 1-8, Tues & Thurs 10-5, Wed & Fri 1-5, Sat 8:30-12:30
Friends of the Library Group

HAWARDEN

P HAWARDEN PUBLIC LIBRARY*, 803 Tenth St, 51023. SAN 305-456X. Tel: 712-551-2244. FAX: 712-551-1720. Web Site: hawardenpubliclibrary.com. *Dir,* Lori Juhlin; E-mail: lori.juhlin@hawarden.lib.ia.us
Founded 1901. Pop 29,000; Circ 43,990
Library Holdings: Bk Titles 26,730; Bk Vols 27,520; Per Subs 100
Special Collections: Hawarden Historical Slides; Hawarden History; Howard Olsen Map Coll; Iowa Coll
Automation Activity & Vendor Info: (Cataloging) Book Systems; (Circulation) Book Systems; (OPAC) Book Systems
Wireless access
Partic in State of Iowa Libraries Online
Open Mon-Wed 10-6, Thurs 10-7, Fri 10-5, Sat 10-2

HAWKEYE

P HAWKEYE PUBLIC LIBRARY*, 104 S Second St, 52147. SAN 305-4586. Tel: 563-427-5536. FAX: 563-427-5536. Web Site: www.hawkeye.lib.ia.us. *Dir,* Carrie Davis; E-mail: carrie@hawkeye.lib.ia.us
Pop 480; Circ 6,300
Library Holdings: Bk Titles 7,829; Per Subs 30
Subject Interests: Civil War
Automation Activity & Vendor Info: (Acquisitions) Follett Software; (Cataloging) Follett Software; (Circulation) Follett Software; (Serials) Follett Software
Wireless access
Partic in North Eastern Iowa Bridge to Online Resource Sharing
Open Tues 11:30-5:30, Wed 11:30-6:30, Thurs 9:30-3:30

HEDRICK

P HEDRICK PUBLIC LIBRARY*, 109 N Main St, 52563. (Mail add: PO Box 427, 52563-0427), SAN 305-4594. Tel: 641-653-2211. FAX: 641-653-2487. Web Site: www.hedrick.lib.ia.us. *Dir,* Jennifer Carriker; E-mail: director@hedrick.lib.ia.us
Pop 837
Library Holdings: AV Mats 185; Bk Titles 7,765; Per Subs 16; Videos 120
Open Mon & Thurs 2-6, Tues 2-5, Wed 12:30-6, Fri 2-5:30, Sat 8:30-11:30

HIAWATHA

P HIAWATHA PUBLIC LIBRARY*, 150 W Willman St, 52233. SAN 305-4608. Tel: 319-393-1414. FAX: 319-393-6005. E-mail: hpllibdesk@gmail.com. Web Site: www.hiawathapubliclibrary.org. *Dir,* Jeaneal C Weeks; E-mail: weeksj@hiawatha-iowa.com; *Ad,* Erin Zaputil; E-mail: zaputile@hiawatha-iowa.com; *Tech Serv Librn,* Deb Tobias; E-mail: tobiasd@hiawatha-iowa.com; *Youth Serv Librn,* Alicia Mangin; E-mail: mangina@hiawatha-iowa.com; Staff 12 (MLS 2, Non-MLS 10)
Founded 1960. Pop 7,024; Circ 181,401
Library Holdings: Bk Titles 38,351; Per Subs 94
Automation Activity & Vendor Info: (Cataloging) SirsiDynix; (Circulation) SirsiDynix
Wireless access
Function: 24/7 Electronic res, 24/7 Online cat, Activity rm, Adult bk club, Audiobks via web, Bk club(s), Bks on CD, Chess club, Children's prog, Citizenship assistance, Computer training, Computers for patron use, Digital talking bks, Doc delivery serv, Electronic databases & coll, Family literacy, Free DVD rentals, Holiday prog, Home delivery & serv to seniorr ctr & nursing homes, Homebound delivery serv, ILL available, Internet access, Life-long learning prog for all ages, Literacy & newcomer serv, Magazines, Magnifiers for reading, Mail & tel request accepted, Meeting rooms, Movies, Music CDs, Notary serv, Online cat, Online info literacy tutorials on the web & in blackboard, Online ref, Orientations, Outreach serv, Outside serv via phone, mail, e-mail & web, OverDrive digital audio bks, Photocopying/Printing, Preschool outreach, Preschool reading prog, Printer for laptops & handheld devices, Prog for adults, Prog for children & young adult, Ref & res, Ref serv available, Scanner, Serves people with intellectual disabilities, Spoken cassettes & CDs, Spoken cassettes & DVDs, Story hour, Study rm, Summer & winter reading prog, Summer reading prog, Tax forms, Teen prog, Telephone ref, Visual arts prog, Wheelchair accessible, Winter reading prog, Writing prog

Partic in Metro Library Network
Open Mon-Thurs 10-8, Fri & Sat 10-5, Sun 1-4
Friends of the Library Group

HILLSBORO

P HILLSBORO PUBLIC LIBRARY*, 100 W Commercial St, 52630. (Mail add: PO Box 117, 52630-0117), SAN 305-4616. Tel: 319-253-4000. FAX: 319-253-4000. E-mail: libraryhillsboro@gmail.com. Web Site: www.hillsboro.lib.ia.us. *Dir,* Position Currently Open; *Asst Dir,* Breeana Runyon
Founded 1937. Pop 180; Circ 3,120
Library Holdings: Bk Titles 8,000
Wireless access
Open Mon, Wed & Fri 3:30-5:30

HOLSTEIN

P STUBBS MEMORIAL LIBRARY, 207 E Second St, 51025. SAN 305-4624. Tel: 712-368-4563. FAX: 712-368-4483. E-mail: stubbslibrary@holstein.lib.ia.us. Web Site: www.holstein.lib.ia.us. *Dir,* Emily Todd; *Asst Librn,* Brenda Bennett
Pop 1,477; Circ 33,312
Library Holdings: Bk Titles 24,000; Per Subs 75
Wireless access
Open Mon 2-8, Tues, Thurs & Fri 2-6, Wed 10-12 & 2-6, Sat 9-1

HOPKINTON

P HOPKINTON PUBLIC LIBRARY*, 110 First St SE, 52237. (Mail add: PO Box 220, 52237-0220), SAN 305-4632. Tel: 563-926-2514. FAX: 563-926-2514. E-mail: hopkinton@hotmail.com. Web Site: hopkinton.lib.ia.us. *Dir,* Kim Ungs
Founded 1944. Pop 685; Circ 12,000
Library Holdings: Bks-By-Mail 36; CDs 110; Large Print Bks 200; Bk Titles 13,000; Per Subs 28; Talking Bks 25; Videos 890
Special Collections: Iowa Coll
Wireless access
Special Services for the Blind - Audio mat; Large print bks
Open Tues & Thurs 10-5, Wed 10-6, Fri & Sat 9-Noon

HOSPERS

P HOSPERS PUBLIC LIBRARY*, 213 Main St, 51238. (Mail add: PO Box 6, 51238-0248). Tel: 712-752-8400. FAX: 712-752-8601. E-mail: hosperslibrary@hospers.lib.ia.us. Web Site: www.hospers.lib.ia.us. *Dir,* Brenda Klaassen
Library Holdings: AV Mats 250; Bk Vols 8,000; Per Subs 20; Talking Bks 150
Special Collections: Local Artists Paintings Coll
Automation Activity & Vendor Info: (Cataloging) Book Systems; (Circulation) Book Systems; (OPAC) Book Systems
Wireless access
Open Mon & Fri 9-12 & 1-5, Tues & Thurs 9-12 & 1-8

HUBBARD

P HUBBARD PUBLIC LIBRARY*, 218 E Maple St, 50122. (Mail add: PO Box 339, 50122-0339), SAN 305-4640. Tel: 641-864-2771. FAX: 641-864-2712. E-mail: hubbardlibrary@gmail.com. Web Site: www.hubbardiowa.com/publiclibrary. *Dir,* Rachel Thompson
Founded 1930. Pop 850; Circ 20,000
Jul 2013-Jun 2014 Income $63,000, City $38,000, County $15,000, Other $10,000. Mats Exp $12,960, Books $10,000, Per/Ser (Incl. Access Fees) $1,500, AV Mat $1,000, Electronic Ref Mat (Incl. Access Fees) $460. Sal $42,000 (Prof $14,000)
Automation Activity & Vendor Info: (Acquisitions) TLC (The Library Corporation); (Cataloging) TLC (The Library Corporation); (Circulation) TLC (The Library Corporation)
Wireless access
Function: Adult bk club, After school storytime, Art exhibits, Audiobks via web, Bk club(s), Bks on CD, Children's prog, Computer training, Computers for patron use, Electronic databases & coll, Equip loans & repairs, Free DVD rentals, Genealogy discussion group, Holiday prog, Home delivery & serv to seniorr ctr & nursing homes, Homebound delivery serv, ILL available, Instruction & testing, Internet access, Large print keyboards, Magnifiers for reading, Mail & tel request accepted, Mail loans to mem, Online cat, Online info literacy tutorials on the web & in blackboard, Photocopying/Printing, Preschool outreach, Preschool reading prog, Printer for laptops & handheld devices, Prof lending libr, Prog for adults, Prog for children & young adult, Scanner, Senior computer classes, Story hour, Summer reading prog, Teen prog, Telephone ref, VHS videos, Wheelchair accessible, Workshops
Partic in Northeast Ohio Regional Library System; Ohio Public Library Information Network
Open Mon & Fri 9-6, Tues & Thurs 12:30-6, Wed 9-7, Sat 9-Noon

HUDSON

P HUDSON PUBLIC LIBRARY*, 401 Fifth St, 50643. (Mail add: PO Box 480, 50643), SAN 305-4659. Tel: 319-988-4217. E-mail: staff@hudson.lib.ia.us. Web Site: www.hudson.lib.ia.us. *Dir,* Mary L Bucy; *Asst Dir,* Zach Van Stanley; E-mail: zvansanley@hudson.lib.ia.us; Staff 3.1 (Non-MLS 3.1)
Pop 3,621; Circ 29,587
Jul 2013-Jun 2014 Income $201,000. Mats Exp $25,169. Sal $99,000
Library Holdings: Bk Titles 29,000; Per Subs 93
Automation Activity & Vendor Info: (Circulation) Follett Software; (OPAC) Follett Software
Wireless access
Function: Archival coll, AV serv, Distance learning, Homebound delivery serv, ILL available, Photocopying/Printing, Prog for adults, Prog for children & young adult, Ref serv available, Summer reading prog, Telephone ref, Wheelchair accessible
Special Services for the Blind - Large print bks; Talking bks
Open Mon, Wed & Thurs 10-8, Tues 8-8, Fri 8-6, Sat 10-5

HULL

P HULL PUBLIC LIBRARY*, 1408 Main St, 51239. (Mail add: PO Box 822, 51239), SAN 305-4667. Tel: 712-439-1321. FAX: 712-439-1534. E-mail: hulllib@premieronline.net. Web Site: www.hull.lib.ia.us. *Dir,* Matt Hoehamer; *Ch,* Marge Vander Esch; Staff 6 (Non-MLS 6)
Pop 1,960; Circ 65,000
Special Collections: Local Newspaper, 1892-, micro
Automation Activity & Vendor Info: (Acquisitions) Follett Software; (Cataloging) Follett Software; (Circulation) Follett Software
Wireless access
Open Mon & Wed 12:30-9, Tues & Thurs 9:30-5:30, Fri 12:30-5:30, Sat 9-12:30
Friends of the Library Group

HUMBOLDT

P HUMBOLDT PUBLIC LIBRARY*, 30 Sixth St N, 50548. SAN 305-4675. Tel: 515-332-1925. FAX: 515-332-1926. E-mail: office@humboldtpubliclibrary.com. Web Site: humboldtpubliclibrary.com. *Dir,* Demi Johnson; E-mail: director@humboldtpubliclibrary.com; *Ch,* Julie Larson; Staff 3 (MLS 1, Non-MLS 2)
Founded 1908. Pop 4,452; Circ 82,395
Library Holdings: AV Mats 1,967; Bk Titles 26,547; Per Subs 80
Automation Activity & Vendor Info: (Acquisitions) Follett Software; (Cataloging) Follett Software; (Circulation) Follett Software; (ILL) Follett Software; (Media Booking) Follett Software; (OPAC) Follett Software; (Serials) Follett Software
Wireless access
Open Mon, 10-8, Tues-Fri 10-5:30, Sat 9-3

HUMESTON

P HUMESTON PUBLIC LIBRARY*, 302 Broad St, 50123. (Mail add: PO Box 97, 50123-0097), SAN 305-4683. Tel: 641-877-4811. E-mail: humlib@iowatelecom.net. Web Site: www.humeston.lib.ia.us. *Libr Dir,* Jackie Gunzenhauser; *Asst Libr Dir,* Leona Darrah
Founded 1925. Pop 494; Circ 7,690
Library Holdings: Audiobooks 150; DVDs 345; Large Print Bks 200; Bk Titles 9,500; Per Subs 10
Automation Activity & Vendor Info: (Cataloging) Biblionix/Apollo; (Circulation) Biblionix/Apollo
Wireless access
Function: Bk club(s), Computers for patron use, ILL available, Preschool outreach, Story hour, Summer reading prog, Wheelchair accessible
Special Services for the Blind - Bks on CD; Large print bks
Open Mon & Fri 1-5, Tues 2-5, Wed 10-11 & 1-6, Sat 9-Noon

HUXLEY

P HUXLEY PUBLIC LIBRARY, 515 N Main Ave, 50124. (Mail add: PO Box 5, 50124-0005), SAN 305-4691. Tel: 515-597-2552. FAX: 515-597-2554. E-mail: huxleylibrary@huxleyiowa.org. Web Site: www.huxleyiowa.org/public-library. *Dir, Libr Serv,* Cathy Van Maanen; Staff 5 (Non-MLS 5)
Founded 1972. Pop 2,800; Circ 74,565
Library Holdings: AV Mats 1,253; Bk Vols 36,000; Per Subs 50; Talking Bks 581
Special Collections: Iowa History; Norwegian Language Books
Automation Activity & Vendor Info: (Cataloging) Follett Software; (Circulation) Follett Software
Open Mon-Thurs 9-7, Fri 9-5, Sat 9-1
Friends of the Library Group

IDA GROVE

P IDA GROVE PUBLIC LIBRARY*, 100 E Second St, 51445. SAN 305-4705. Tel: 712-364-2306. FAX: 712-364-3228. E-mail: librarian@idagrove.lib.ia.us. Web Site: www.idagrove.lib.ia.us. *Dir,* Angela Scales; E-mail: angela.scales@idagrove.lib.ia.us
Founded 1908. Pop 2,268
Library Holdings: Bk Titles 15,000; Per Subs 65
Wireless access
Open Mon 10-6, Tues 11-5, Wed Noon-5, Thurs Noon-7, Fri 10-7, Sat 9-2

INDEPENDENCE

P INDEPENDENCE PUBLIC LIBRARY*, 805 First St E, 50644. SAN 305-4713. Tel: 319-334-2470. FAX: 319-332-0306. E-mail: indylib@indytel.com. Web Site: independenceia.org/library. *Libr Dir,* Laura Blaker; E-mail: lblaker@indytel.com; *Asst Dir,* Amy McGraw; E-mail: amcgraw@indytel.com; Staff 7 (MLS 1, Non-MLS 6)
Founded 1857. Pop 6,000; Circ 89,611
Library Holdings: Audiobooks 1,584; DVDs 1,064; Bk Vols 32,160; Per Subs 84
Automation Activity & Vendor Info: (Cataloging) Follett Software; (Circulation) Follett Software; (OPAC) Follett Software
Wireless access
Function: Art exhibits, Audiobks via web, Bks on CD, Children's prog, Computer training, Computers for patron use, Electronic databases & coll, Free DVD rentals, Internet access, Online cat, Online ref, OverDrive digital audio bks, Photocopying/Printing, Preschool outreach, Prog for adults, Prog for children & young adult, Ref serv available, Story hour, Summer reading prog, Tax forms, Teen prog, Telephone ref, Wheelchair accessible
Partic in Chemeketa Cooperative Regional Library Service
Open Mon-Thurs 9:30-8, Fri 9:30-5, Sat 9:30-4, Sun 1-4
Restriction: Authorized patrons
Friends of the Library Group

INDIANOLA

P INDIANOLA PUBLIC LIBRARY*, 207 North B St, 50125. SAN 305-473X. Tel: 515-961-9418. FAX: 515-961-9419. E-mail: iplinfo@indianolaiowa.gov. Web Site: www.indianolaiowa.gov/Library. *Dir,* Michele Patrick; E-mail: mpatrick@indianolaiowa.gov; *Ch Serv Librn,* Janis Comer; E-mail: jcomer@indianolaiowa.gov; *Tech Serv Librn,* Jody Ross; E-mail: jross@indianolaiowa.gov; *Teen & Adult Librn,* Alison Brown; E-mail: abrown@indianolaiowa.gov; Staff 8 (MLS 2, Non-MLS 6)
Founded 1884. Pop 14,132; Circ 151,631
Library Holdings: Bk Vols 45,000; Per Subs 123
Subject Interests: Genealogy, Local hist
Automation Activity & Vendor Info: (Acquisitions) Innovative Interfaces, Inc; (Cataloging) Innovative Interfaces, Inc; (Circulation) Innovative Interfaces, Inc; (Serials) Innovative Interfaces, Inc
Function: 24/7 Electronic res, 24/7 Online cat, Activity rm, Adult bk club, Adult literacy prog, After school storytime, Archival coll, Audiobks on Playaways & MP3, Audiobks via web, Bk club(s), Bks on cassette, Bks on CD, Children's prog, Distance learning, Doc delivery serv, Free DVD rentals, Home delivery & serv to seniorr ctr & nursing homes, Homebound delivery serv, ILL available, Internet access, Life-long learning prog for all ages, Magazines, Meeting rooms, Microfiche/film & reading machines, Movies, Music CDs, Online cat, Online ref, Outreach serv, OverDrive digital audio bks, Photocopying/Printing, Preschool outreach, Preschool reading prog, Prog for adults, Prog for children & young adult, Ref serv available, Scanner, Summer reading prog, Telephone ref
Open Mon-Wed 10-8, Thurs 10-6, Fri & Sat 10-5
Friends of the Library Group

CR SIMPSON COLLEGE, Dunn Library, 508 North C St, 50125-1216. SAN 305-4748. Circulation Tel: 515-961-1663. Interlibrary Loan Service Tel: 515-961-1485. Administration Tel: 515-961-1519. Automation Services Tel: 515-961-1748. E-mail: dunnlib@simpson.edu. Web Site: www.simpson.edu/internal/dunn-library. *Col Librn/Archivist,* Cyd Dyer; E-mail: cyd.dyer@simpson.edu; *Research Librn,* Steve Duffy; E-mail: steve.duffy@simpson.edu; *Research Librn,* Liz Grimsbo; E-mail: liz.grimsbo@simpson.edu; Staff 4.1 (MLS 2.4, Non-MLS 1.7)
Founded 1860. Enrl 1,153; Fac 100; Highest Degree: Master
Jun 2020-May 2021 Income $582,123. Mats Exp $236,692, Books $30,184, Per/Ser (Incl. Access Fees) $163,563, Electronic Ref Mat (Incl. Access Fees) $42,945. Sal $227,888 (Prof $162,626)
Library Holdings: CDs 1,467; DVDs 1,985; e-books 211,769; e-journals 295,200; Microforms 8,543; Bk Vols 113,130; Per Subs 123; Videos 33,000
Special Collections: Avery O Craven Coll(antebellum South); Joseph W Walt Coll (Liechtenstein)
Automation Activity & Vendor Info: (Acquisitions) OCLC Worldshare Management Services; (Cataloging) OCLC; (Circulation) OCLC Worldshare Management Services; (Course Reserve) OCLC Worldshare Management Services; (Discovery) OCLC Worldshare Management

Services; (ILL) OCLC WorldShare Interlibrary Loan; (OPAC) OCLC Worldshare Management Services; (Serials) OCLC Worldshare Management Services
Wireless access
Publications: Annual Report; Archive Finding Guides (Online only); Bookmark
Partic in Iowa Academic Library Alliance; Iowa Private Academic Library Consortium; OCLC Online Computer Library Center, Inc
Open Mon-Thurs 7:45am-Midnight, Fri 7:45-4:30, Sat 10-2, Sun Noon-Midnight

INWOOD

P INWOOD PUBLIC LIBRARY, 103 S Main St, 51240. (Mail add: PO Box 69, 51240-0069), SAN 305-4756. Tel: 712-753-4814. Administration E-mail: admin@inwood.lib.ia.us. Web Site: www.inwood.lib.ia.us. *Dir,* Donna Bos; E-mail: donnab@inwood.lib.ia.us
Founded 1924. Pop 1,200; Circ 34,250
Library Holdings: CDs 150; DVDs 700; Large Print Bks 100; Bk Titles 16,470; Per Subs 48; Talking Bks 626; Videos 1,000
Subject Interests: Best sellers
Automation Activity & Vendor Info: (Acquisitions) Follett Software; (Cataloging) Follett Software; (Circulation) Follett Software
Open Mon & Wed 2-5:30, Tues 9-11 & 2-5:30, Thurs 2-6, Sat 9-1

IONIA

P IONIA COMMUNITY LIBRARY*, 101 W Iowa St, 50645. (Mail add: PO Box 130, 50645), SAN 305-4764. Tel: 641-394-4803. FAX: 641-394-4803. Web Site: www.ionia.lib.ia.us. *Dir,* Lydia Klinkel; E-mail: director@ionia.lib.ia.us; Staff 1 (MLS 1)
Founded 1974. Pop 350
Library Holdings: Bk Titles 6,000; Per Subs 24
Automation Activity & Vendor Info: (Acquisitions) Biblionix/Apollo; (Cataloging) Biblionix/Apollo; (Circulation) Biblionix/Apollo; (ILL) Biblionix/Apollo; (Media Booking) Biblionix/Apollo; (OPAC) Biblionix/Apollo; (Serials) Biblionix/Apollo
Wireless access
Partic in Lakeland Library Cooperative
Open Mon 1-6, Tues 10-3, Wed 4-8, Thurs & Sun 1-5

IOWA CITY

S ACT INFORMATION RESOURCE CENTER, 200 ACT Dr, 52243. (Mail add: PO Box 168, 52243-0168), SAN 305-4772. Tel: 319-337-1166. FAX: 319-337-1538. *Mgr,* Jacqueline Snider; Staff 3 (MLS 1, Non-MLS 2)
Founded 1968
Special Collections: ERIC Coll
Subject Interests: Educ
Wireless access
Function: ILL available, Ref serv available
Partic in OCLC Online Computer Library Center, Inc
Restriction: Co libr, Not open to pub

P IOWA CITY PUBLIC LIBRARY*, 123 S Linn St, 52240. SAN 305-4780. Tel: 319-356-5200. FAX: 319-356-5494. Web Site: www.icpl.org. *Dir,* Elsworth Carman; Tel: 319-356-5241, E-mail: elsworth-carman@icpl.org; *Dir of Develop,* Patty McCarthy; Tel: 319-356-5249, E-mail: pmccarthy@icpl.org; *Admin Coordr,* Elyse Miller; Tel: 319-887-6003, E-mail: emiller@icpl.org; *Adult Serv Coordr,* Maeve Clark; Tel: 319-887-6004, E-mail: maeve-clark@icpl.org; *Children's Serv Coordr,* Angela Pilkington; Tel: 319-887-6019, E-mail: angela-pilkington@icpl.org; *Coordr, Coll Serv,* Anne Mangano; Tel: 319-887-6006, E-mail: anne-mangano@icpl.org; *Commun & Access Serv Coordr,* Sam Helmick; Tel: 319-887-6007, E-mail: sam-helmick@icpl.org; *IT Coordr,* Brent Palmer; Tel: 319-887-6035, E-mail: brent-palmer@icpl.org; Staff 42 (MLS 15, Non-MLS 27)
Founded 1896. Pop 67,862; Circ 1,512,852
Library Holdings: AV Mats 40,887; Electronic Media & Resources 53; Bk Vols 195,036; Per Subs 546
Automation Activity & Vendor Info: (Acquisitions) Innovative Interfaces, Inc; (Cataloging) Innovative Interfaces, Inc; (Circulation) Innovative Interfaces, Inc; (ILL) Innovative Interfaces, Inc; (OPAC) Innovative Interfaces, Inc; (Serials) Innovative Interfaces, Inc
Wireless access
Function: Audio & video playback equip for onsite use, Audiobks via web, AV serv, Bks on cassette, Bks on CD, CD-ROM, Children's prog, Computer training, Computers for patron use, Electronic databases & coll, Free DVD rentals, Holiday prog, Home delivery & serv to seniorr ctr & nursing homes, Homebound delivery serv, Homework prog, ILL available, Internet access, Jail serv, Mail & tel request accepted, Mail loans to mem, Music CDs, Online cat, Online ref, OverDrive digital audio bks, Photocopying/Printing, Preschool outreach, Prog for adults, Prog for children & young adult, Ref serv available, Senior outreach, Spoken cassettes & CDs, Spoken cassettes & DVDs, Summer reading prog, Tax forms, Teen prog, Telephone ref, VHS videos, Wheelchair accessible, Workshops, Writing prog
Publications: Window (Newsletter)
Open Mon-Thurs 10-9, Fri 10-8, Sat 10-6, Sun 12-5

S STATE HISTORICAL SOCIETY OF IOWA*, Iowa City Library, 402 Iowa Ave, 52240-1806. SAN 305-4802. Tel: 319-335-3916. FAX: 319-335-3935. Web Site: iowaculture.gov/history. *Cat, Metadata Librn,* Allison Johnson; Tel: 319-335-3936, E-mail: allison-johnson-1@uiowa.edu; *Ref Librn,* Hang Nguyen; Tel: 319-335-3926, E-mail: hang-nguyen@uiowa.edu; *Spec Coll Librn,* Mary Bennett; Tel: 319-335-3938, E-mail: Mary-Bennett@uiowa.edu; *Libr Tech,* Charles Scott; Tel: 319-335-3911, E-mail: charles-scott@uiowa.edu; Staff 4 (MLS 3, Non-MLS 1)
Founded 1857
Special Collections: Manuscripts; Photo Archives
Subject Interests: Agr, Civil law, Genealogy, Hist, Iowa, Labor law, Maps, Women's hist
Automation Activity & Vendor Info: (Cataloging) Ex Libris Group
Wireless access
Function: Archival coll, Res libr
Publications: Annals of Iowa (Journal)
Partic in OCLC Online Computer Library Center, Inc
Open Wed-Sat 9-4:30
Restriction: Non-circulating to the pub, Not a lending libr

UNIVERSITY OF IOWA

C BLOMMERS MEASUREMENT RESOURCES LIBRARY*, 304 Lindquist Ctr, 52242-1587, SAN 322-6840. Tel: 319-335-5416. FAX: 319-335-6038. Web Site: www.education.uiowa.edu/itp/blommers. *Librn,* Anna Marie Guengerich; E-mail: anna-guengerich@uiowa.edu; Staff 2 (MLS 1, Non-MLS 1)
Founded 1973
Library Holdings: Bk Titles 4,000; Per Subs 40
Special Collections: Current Tests; Historical Tests
Subject Interests: Educ testing, Measurements, Statistics
Automation Activity & Vendor Info: (Cataloging) Follett Software; (Circulation) Follett Software; (OPAC) Follett Software; (Serials) Follett Software
Open Mon-Fri 8-12 & 1-5

C SOJOURNER TRUTH LIBRARY*, 130 N Madison, 52242, SAN 325-7304. Tel: 319-335-1486. FAX: 319-353-1985. E-mail: wrac@uiowa.edu. Web Site: www.uiowa.edu/~wrac/library. *Dir,* Linda Kroon; E-mail: linda-kroon@uiowa.edu
Library Holdings: Bk Vols 500
Subject Interests: Eating disorders, Family, Gender, Health, Money, Safety
Open Mon-Fri 9-5

CM UNIVERSITY OF IOWA HOSPITALS & CLINICS*, Patients Library, 8016 JCP, 200 Hawkins Dr, 52242-1046. SAN 305-4829. Tel: 319-356-2468. FAX: 319-353-8793. Web Site: www.uihealthcare.org/patientlibrary. *Dir,* Mindwell S Egeland; Tel: 319-384-8908, E-mail: mindwell-egeland@uiowa.edu; Staff 2 (MLS 1, Non-MLS 1)
Founded 1932
Library Holdings: Bk Titles 11,000
Special Collections: Consumer Health Information; Popular recreational materials
Subject Interests: Consumer health
Automation Activity & Vendor Info: (OPAC) Follett Software
Wireless access
Function: Telephone ref
Open Mon-Fri 9-4, Sat & Sun 1-4

C UNIVERSITY OF IOWA LIBRARIES*, 100 Main Library, 125 W Washington St, 52242-1420. SAN 341-8928. Circulation Tel: 319-335-5912. Interlibrary Loan Service Tel: 319-335-5917. Reference Tel: 319-335-5429. Information Services Tel: 319-335-5299. Reference E-mail: lib-ref@uiowa.edu. Web Site: www.lib.uiowa.edu. *Univ Librn,* John P Culshaw; E-mail: john-culshaw@uiowa.edu
Founded 1855. Highest Degree: Doctorate
Special Collections: State Document Depository; UN Document Depository; US Document Depository
Automation Activity & Vendor Info: (Acquisitions) Ex Libris Group
Wireless access
Partic in Big Ten Academic Alliance; Iowa Academic Library Alliance
Friends of the Library Group

Departmental Libraries:

ART, 235 Art Bldg W, 141 N Riverside Dr, 52242, SAN 341-8952. Tel: 319-335-3089. FAX: 319-335-5900. E-mail: lib-art@uiowa.edu. Web Site: www.lib.uiowa.edu/art. *Head Librn,* Rijn Templeton; E-mail: rijn-templeton@uiowa.edu
Library Holdings: Bk Vols 132,000
Friends of the Library Group

RITA BENTON MUSIC LIBRARY, 2006 Main Library, 52242, SAN 341-9258. Tel: 319-335-3086. E-mail: lib-mus@uiowa.edu. Web Site: www.lib.uiowa.edu/music/. *Head Librn,* Katie Buehner; E-mail: katie-buehner@uiowa.edu
Enrl 30,000; Highest Degree: Doctorate
Library Holdings: Bk Vols 99,484
Friends of the Library Group

CL COLLEGE OF LAW LIBRARY, 200 Boyd Law Bldg, 52242-1166, SAN 341-9169. Tel: 319-335-9002. Reference Tel: 319-335-9005. FAX: 319-335-9039. Reference E-mail: lawlib-ref@uiowa.edu. Web Site: www.law.uiowa.edu/library. *Assoc Dean, Res,* Arthur E Bonfield; Tel: 319-335-9020, E-mail: arthur-bonfield@uiowa.edu; *Head, Continuing Coll,* Sherri Bethke; Tel: 319-335-9041, E-mail: sherri-bethke@uiowa.edu; *Head, Pub Serv,* Ted Potter; Tel: 319-335-9017, E-mail: ted-potter@uiowa.edu; *Circ Librn, ILL Librn,* John Bergstrom; Tel: 319-335-9015, E-mail: john-bergstrom@uiowa.edu; *Conbtiuning Coll Librn,* Virginia Melroy; Tel: 319-335-9077, E-mail: virginia-melroy@uiowa.edu; *Intl Law Librn,* Don Ford; Tel: 319-335-9068, E-mail: donald-ford@uiowa.edu; *Bibliographer, Ref Librn,* Druet Cameron-Klugh; Tel: 319-335-9038, E-mail: druet-klugh@uiowa.edu; *Ref Librn,* Ellen Jones; Tel: 319-335-6829, E-mail: ellen-jones@uiowa.edu; *Collection Access Mgt,* Karen Nobbs; Tel: 319-335-9029, E-mail: karen-nobbs@uiowa.edu; Staff 14 (MLS 14)
Founded 1868. Enrl 680; Fac 44; Highest Degree: Doctorate
Library Holdings: Bk Vols 1,200,000; Per Subs 9,500
Special Collections: UN Doc (Readex Coll). US Document Depository
Subject Interests: Environ studies, Law
Partic in National Network of Libraries of Medicine Region 6; OCLC Online Computer Library Center, Inc; OCLC Research Library Partnership; Research Libraries Information Network
Publications: Law Library User's Guide; News Briefs
Open Mon-Thurs 7:30am-Midnight, Fri 7:30am-10pm, Sat 9am-10pm, Sun Noon-Midnight

ENGINEERING, 2001 Seamans Ctr, 52242-1420. Tel: 319-335-6047. FAX: 319-335-5900. E-mail: lib-engineering@uiowa.edu. Web Site: www.lib.uiowa.edu/eng.
Library Holdings: Bk Vols 109,563
Friends of the Library Group

CM HARDIN LIBRARY FOR THE HEALTH SCIENCES, 600 Newton Rd, 52242, SAN 341-9134. Tel: 319-335-9871. Interlibrary Loan Service Tel: 319-335-9874. Information Services Tel: 319-335-9151. FAX: 319-353-3752. E-mail: lib-hardin@uiowa.edu. Web Site: www.lib.uiowa.edu/hardin. *Dir,* Janna Lawrence; E-mail: janna-lawrence@uiowa.edu
Founded 1882
Library Holdings: Bk Vols 285,241
Subject Interests: Hist of med
Partic in National Network of Libraries of Medicine Region 6
Publications: Heirs of Hippocrates
Friends of the Library Group

MARVIN A POMERANTZ BUSINESS LIBRARY, Ten E Jefferson St, 52242, SAN 341-8987. Tel: 319-335-3077. FAX: 319-335-3752. E-mail: lib-bus@uiowa.edu. Web Site: www.lib.uiowa.edu/biz.
Library Holdings: Bk Vols 32,989
Friends of the Library Group

SCIENCES, 120 Iowa Ave, 52242-1325, SAN 341-9312. Tel: 319-335-3083. FAX: 319-335-2698. E-mail: lib-sciences@uiowa.edu. Web Site: www.lib.uiowa.edu/sciences/. *Head Librn,* Leo Clougherty; E-mail: leo-clougherty@uiowa.edu
Library Holdings: Bk Vols 46,541
Friends of the Library Group

IOWA FALLS

P ROBERT W BARLOW MEMORIAL LIBRARY*, 921 Washington Ave, 50126. SAN 305-4845. Tel: 641-648-2872. Web Site: www.iowafallslib.com. *Dir,* Erin Finnegan-Andrews; E-mail: erina@iowafalls.lib.ia.us; *Asst Dir,* Nancy Hoffman; E-mail: nancyh@iowafalls.lib.ia.us; *Youth Serv Librn,* Rebecca Wood; E-mail: rebeccaw@iowafalls.lib.ia.us
Founded 1896. Pop 6,100; Circ 76,000
Library Holdings: Bk Titles 52,000; Per Subs 170
Special Collections: Travel Guides
Automation Activity & Vendor Info: (Cataloging) TLC (The Library Corporation); (Circulation) TLC (The Library Corporation); (OPAC) TLC (The Library Corporation)
Wireless access
Open Mon-Fri 2-6, Sat 9-12
Friends of the Library Group

J ELLSWORTH COMMUNITY COLLEGE*, Osgood Library, 1100 College Ave, 50126-1199. SAN 305-4853. Tel: 641-648-4611, Ext 233. FAX: 641-648-3128. E-mail: ecclib@iavalley.edu. Web Site: ecc.iavalley.edu/resources-for-students/library. *Mgr,* Sandra Greufe; E-mail: Sandra.Greufe@iavalley.edu
Founded 1890. Enrl 950
Library Holdings: Bk Titles 24,689; Bk Vols 25,664; Per Subs 240
Partic in Iowa Academic Library Alliance; Iowa Higher Educ Instrul Resource Consortia
Open Mon-Thurs 7:30-9:30, Fri 7:30-3:30, Sun 5-9

IRWIN

P LIED IRWIN PUBLIC LIBRARY*, 509 Ann St, 51446. (Mail add: PO Box 255, 51446-0255), Tel: 712-782-3335. FAX: 712-782-3335. E-mail: irwinlibrarian@yahoo.com. *Dir,* Karen Plagman
Pop 372
Library Holdings: Bk Vols 2,506
Open Wed & Sat 11-1, Thurs & Fri 2-5

JAMAICA

P JAMAICA PUBLIC LIBRARY, 316 Main St, 50128. (Mail add: PO Box 122, 50128-0122), SAN 305-4861. Tel: 641-429-3362. FAX: 641-429-3362. E-mail: jampublib@netins.net. *Dir,* Alan Robinson
Founded 1948. Pop 237; Circ 3,994
Library Holdings: Bk Titles 6,500; Per Subs 12; Talking Bks 100
Subject Interests: Genealogy, Local hist
Open Mon-Fri 1-5
Friends of the Library Group

JANESVILLE

P JANESVILLE PUBLIC LIBRARY*, 227 Main St, 50647. (Mail add: PO Box 328, 50647-0328), SAN 305-487X. Tel: 319-987-2925. FAX: 319-987-2925. E-mail: janesvillelibrary@mchsi.com. Web Site: www.janesville.lib.ia.us. *Dir,* Lisa Gansen
Pop 825; Circ 15,783
Library Holdings: Audiobooks 27; DVDs 829; Bk Vols 9,898; Per Subs 53; Videos 321
Automation Activity & Vendor Info: (Acquisitions) Follett Software; (Cataloging) Follett Software; (Circulation) Follett Software; (ILL) Follett Software; (Media Booking) Follett Software; (OPAC) Follett Software; (Serials) Follett Software
Wireless access
Open Mon, Tues & Thurs 12-6, Wed 10-6, Fri 1-5, Sat 9-Noon

JEFFERSON

P JEFFERSON PUBLIC LIBRARY*, 200 W Lincoln Way, 50129-2185. SAN 305-4888. Tel: 515-386-2835. FAX: 515-386-8163. E-mail: jeflib@netins.net. Web Site: www.jefferson.lib.ia.us. *Dir,* Jane Millard; *Asst Dir, Ch,* Terry Clark
Founded 1903. Pop 4,600; Circ 80,000
Library Holdings: Bk Titles 45,000; Per Subs 60
Special Collections: Greene County. Oral History
Subject Interests: Genealogy
Automation Activity & Vendor Info: (Cataloging) Innovative Interfaces, Inc; (Circulation) Innovative Interfaces, Inc; (OPAC) Innovative Interfaces, Inc
Wireless access
Partic in Chemeketa Cooperative Regional Library Service
Open Mon & Wed 1-8, Tues & Thurs 11-8, Fri 1-5:30, Sat 9-1; Mon & Wed (Summer) 1-8, Tues & Thurs 11-5:30, Fri 1-5:30, Sat 9-1
Friends of the Library Group

JESUP

P JESUP PUBLIC LIBRARY*, 721 Sixth St, 50648. (Mail add: PO Box 585, 50648-0585), SAN 305-4896. Tel: 319-827-1533. FAX: 319-827-1580. E-mail: jesuplibrary@jesup.lib.ia.us. Web Site: www.jesup.lib.ia.us. *Dir,* Becky Burke; E-mail: bburke@jesup.lib.ia.us; *Asst Librn,* Becky Bauer-Fisher; E-mail: bbauer-fisher@jesup.lib.ia.us; Staff 3 (Non-MLS 3)
Pop 2,299; Circ 33,453
Library Holdings: Audiobooks 561; CDs 288; DVDs 150; Large Print Bks 368; Bk Titles 18,526; Per Subs 56; Videos 376
Automation Activity & Vendor Info: (Cataloging) Follett Software; (Circulation) Follett Software
Wireless access
Open Mon, Wed & Fri 10-6, Tues & Thurs 9-8, Sat 10-2
Friends of the Library Group

JEWELL

P MONTGOMERY MEMORIAL LIBRARY*, 711 Main St, 50130. (Mail add: PO Box 207, 50130-0207), SAN 305-490X. Tel: 515-827-5112. FAX: 515-827-5112. E-mail: jewell-library@globalccs.net. Web Site: www.youseemore.com/nilc/jewell/directory.asp. *Dir,* Roxie Young; *Libr Asst,* Marcia Wheeler
Founded 1947. Pop 1,200

Special Collections: History of Hamilton County, Jewell Township
Automation Activity & Vendor Info: (Cataloging) Follett Software; (Circulation) Follett Software
Wireless access
Open Mon-Wed 1-7, Thurs & Fri 10-5, Sat 10-1

JOHNSTON

S DUPONT PIONEER*, Research Library, 8325 NW 62nd Ave, 50131. (Mail add: PO Box 7062, 50131-7062), SAN 324-7120. Tel: 515-535-4818. Web Site: www.pioneer.com. *Librn*, Ken Braun; E-mail: ken.braun@pioneer.com; Staff 4 (MLS 2, Non-MLS 2)
Founded 1983
Library Holdings: Bk Titles 1,700; Per Subs 220
Subject Interests: Agr, Law, Plant genetics
Automation Activity & Vendor Info: (Acquisitions) Inmagic, Inc.; (Cataloging) Inmagic, Inc.; (Circulation) Inmagic, Inc.; (OPAC) Inmagic, Inc.; (Serials) Inmagic, Inc.
Wireless access
Function: ILL available
Restriction: Co libr

P JOHNSTON PUBLIC LIBRARY*, 6700 Merle Hay Rd, 50131-0327. SAN 376-5458. Tel: 515-278-5233. FAX: 515-278-4975. Web Site: www.johnstonlibrary.com. *Dir*, Eric Melton; E-mail: melton@johnstonlibrary.com; *Asst Dir, Circ Mgr*, Molly Guerra; E-mail: guerra@johnstonlibrary.com; *Pub Serv Librn*, Elizabeth Stevens; E-mail: stevens@johnstonlibrary.com; *Youth Serv Librn*, Megan Sockness; E-mail: sockness@johnstonlibrary.com; Staff 13.5 (MLS 2, Non-MLS 11.5)
Founded 1988. Pop 17,285; Circ 309,405
Library Holdings: Audiobooks 11,000; CDs 5,000; DVDs 4,818; Electronic Media & Resources 4,200; Bk Vols 62,609; Per Subs 198; Videos 100
Automation Activity & Vendor Info: (Cataloging) SirsiDynix; (Circulation) SirsiDynix
Wireless access
Open Mon-Thurs 9-8, Fri & Sat 9-5:30, Sun 1-5
Friends of the Library Group

JOICE

P JOICE PUBLIC LIBRARY*, 303 Keerl St, 50446. (Mail add: PO Box 183, 50446-0183), SAN 305-4918. Tel: 641-588-3330. FAX: 641-588-3330. E-mail: jhawks@wctatel.net. *Dir*, Mardene Lien
Pop 3,500; Circ 6,000
Library Holdings: Audiobooks 55; Bks on Deafness & Sign Lang 3; Large Print Bks 200; Bk Titles 7,000; Bk Vols 7,000; Per Subs 17; Videos 820
Automation Activity & Vendor Info: (Acquisitions) Follett Software; (Cataloging) Follett Software; (Circulation) Follett Software; (ILL) Follett Software; (Media Booking) Follett Software; (OPAC) Follett Software; (Serials) Follett Software
Wireless access
Open Tues 9-12 & 1-6, Wed & Thurs 1-6, Fri 2-5, Sat 9-11

KALONA

P KALONA PUBLIC LIBRARY, 510 C Ave, 52247. (Mail add: PO Box 1212, 52247-1212), SAN 305-4926. Tel: 319-656-3501. FAX: 319-656-3503. Web Site: www.kalona.lib.ia.us. *Dir*, Trevor Sherping; E-mail: director@kalonapubliclibrary.com
Pop 2,363; Circ 55,912
Library Holdings: Bk Vols 27,775; Per Subs 47
Subject Interests: Amish
Automation Activity & Vendor Info: (Cataloging) ComPanion Corp; (Circulation) ComPanion Corp
Wireless access
Open Mon-Thurs 9:30-8, Fri 9:30-5, Sat 9:30-3
Friends of the Library Group

KANAWHA

P KANAWHA PUBLIC LIBRARY*, 121 N Main, 50447. (Mail add: PO Box 148, 50447-0148), SAN 305-4934. Tel: 641-762-3595. FAX: 641-762-3966. E-mail: norby@comm1net.net. Web Site: www.youseemore.com/nilc/Kanawha. *Dir*, Christine Guthmiller; Staff 1 (Non-MLS 1)
Founded 1921. Pop 652; Circ 4,831
Library Holdings: Audiobooks 257; DVDs 937; e-books 33,725; Electronic Media & Resources 7; Bk Titles 8,924; Per Subs 39; Talking Bks 15,607
Automation Activity & Vendor Info: (Cataloging) TLC (The Library Corporation); (Circulation) TLC (The Library Corporation); (ILL) TLC (The Library Corporation); (OPAC) TLC (The Library Corporation)
Wireless access
Function: 24/7 Electronic res, 24/7 Online cat, Activity rm, Adult bk club, Audio & video playback equip for onsite use, Audiobks via web, Bk club(s), Bks on CD, Children's prog, Computers for patron use, E-Readers, Electronic databases & coll, Free DVD rentals, Health sci info serv, Home delivery & serv to seniorr ctr & nursing homes, ILL available, Internet access, Laminating, Magazines, Magnifiers for reading, Meeting rooms, Movies, Online cat, Online info literacy tutorials on the web & in blackboard, Online ref, OverDrive digital audio bks, Photocopying/Printing, Prog for adults, Prog for children & young adult, Ref serv available, Scanner, Spanish lang bks, Summer reading prog, Teen prog
Partic in State of Iowa Libraries Online
Open Mon & Fri 11-5:30, Wed 11-6, Sat 9-Noon

KENSETT

P KENSETT PUBLIC LIBRARY, 214 Fifth St, 50448. (Mail add: PO Box 55, 50448-0055), SAN 305-4942. Tel: 641-845-2222. FAX: 641-845-2222. E-mail: kensettlibrary@mchsi.com. Web Site: www.youseemore.com/nilc/kensett. *Dir*, William Hillson
Founded 1965. Pop 280; Circ 7,200
Library Holdings: DVDs 960; Bk Titles 5,000; Per Subs 27
Wireless access
Function: 24/7 Online cat, After school storytime, Children's prog, Computers for patron use, Free DVD rentals, ILL available, Internet access, Magazines, Makerspace, Movies, Online cat, Photocopying/Printing, Printer for laptops & handheld devices, Prog for children & young adult, Ref & res, Res assist avail, Serves people with intellectual disabilities, STEM programs, Story hour, Summer reading prog
Open Mon 9-2, Tues & Thurs 12-6, Sat 9-Noon

KEOKUK

P KEOKUK PUBLIC LIBRARY*, 210 N Fifth St, 52632. SAN 305-4950. Tel: 319-524-1483. FAX: 319-524-2320. E-mail: director@keokuk.lib.ia.us. Web Site: www.keokuk.lib.ia.us. *Dir*, Emily Rohlfs; E-mail: erohlfs@keokuk.lib.ia.us; Staff 7 (MLS 1, Non-MLS 6)
Founded 1893. Pop 10,511; Circ 85,279
Library Holdings: Bk Titles 70,000; Per Subs 200
Subject Interests: Local hist
Automation Activity & Vendor Info: (Circulation) Innovative Interfaces, Inc
Wireless access
Function: 24/7 Electronic res, 24/7 Online cat, Art exhibits, Audiobks on Playaways & MP3, Audiobks via web, Bks on CD, Children's prog, Computer training, Computers for patron use, Digital talking bks, Electronic databases & coll, Free DVD rentals, Holiday prog, ILL available, Internet access, Laminating, Magazines, Mango lang, Meeting rooms, Microfiche/film & reading machines, Movies, Music CDs, Online cat, Online ref, Outreach serv, Outside serv via phone, mail, e-mail & web, OverDrive digital audio bks, Photocopying/Printing, Preschool outreach, Preschool reading prog, Prog for adults, Prog for children & young adult, Ref & res, Ref serv available, Scanner, Senior computer classes, Story hour, Summer & winter reading prog, Summer reading prog, Tax forms, Teen prog, Telephone ref, Wheelchair accessible, Winter reading prog
Open Mon-Thurs 9-8 (9-7 Summer), Fri 9-5, Sat 9-3
Restriction: Non-circulating of rare bks, Non-resident fee
Friends of the Library Group

KEOSAUQUA

P KEOSAUQUA PUBLIC LIBRARY*, 608 First St, 52565. (Mail add: PO Box 160, 52565-0160), SAN 305-4977. Tel: 319-293-3766. FAX: 319-293-3766. E-mail: keolib@netins.net. Web Site: www.keosauqua.lib.ia.us. *Libr Dir*, Nicole Annis; *Asst Librn*, Shelby Filson; *Circ Librn*, Janet Herring
Founded 1910. Pop 1,020; Circ 18,450
Library Holdings: Audiobooks 25; DVDs 900; Large Print Bks 300; Bk Titles 11,000
Subject Interests: Genealogy, Iowa, Natural hist
Automation Activity & Vendor Info: (Acquisitions) Baker & Taylor; (Cataloging) Follett Software; (Circulation) Follett Software; (ILL) Follett Software
Wireless access
Special Services for the Deaf - Closed caption videos
Open Mon, Tues & Fri 1-5, Wed 1-6, Thurs 10-5, Sat 8-12

KEOTA

P WILSON MEMORIAL LIBRARY*, 109 E Washington Ave, 52248. SAN 305-4985. Tel: 641-636-3850. FAX: 641-636-3050. E-mail: wilsonlib@keota.lib.ia.us. Web Site: www.keota.lib.ia.us. *Dir*, Toni Greiner; E-mail: tgreiner@keota.lib.ia.us
Founded 1877. Pop 1,100; Circ 15,000
Library Holdings: Bk Titles 11,617; Bk Vols 11,741; Per Subs 16
Automation Activity & Vendor Info: (Cataloging) OCLC WorldShare Interlibrary Loan; (Circulation) OCLC WorldShare Interlibrary Loan;

(OPAC) OCLC WorldShare Interlibrary Loan; (Serials) OCLC WorldShare Interlibrary Loan
Wireless access
Open Mon 10-6, Tues-Fri 10-5, Sat 8-12

KEYSTONE

P SCHROEDER PUBLIC LIBRARY*, 93 Main St, 52249. (Mail add: PO Box 305, 52249-0305), SAN 305-4993. Tel: 319-442-3329. FAX: 319-442-3327. E-mail: keystnpl@netins.net. Web Site: www.keystone.lib.ia.us. *Dir,* Laura Hopper; *Asst Librn,* Joan Boudreau; *Ch,* Melissa Miller; Staff 1 (Non-MLS 1)
Founded 1975. Pop 622; Circ 12,630
Library Holdings: Audiobooks 322; CDs 115; DVDs 726; Large Print Bks 150; Bk Titles 6,773; Per Subs 64; Videos 100
Automation Activity & Vendor Info: (Acquisitions) Book Systems; (Cataloging) Book Systems; (Circulation) Book Systems; (OPAC) Book Systems
Wireless access
Open Mon & Wed 1-6, Tues & Thurs 9-12 & 1-5, Fri 1-5, Sat 9-12

KIMBALLTON

P KIMBALLTON PUBLIC LIBRARY, 118 Main St, 51543. (Mail add: PO Box 67, 51543-0067), SAN 305-5000. Tel: 712-773-3002. E-mail: kimclerk@metc.net. *Dir,* Tammy Thompson
Pop 1,000
Library Holdings: Bk Vols 7,000; Per Subs 36
Open Mon-Fri 1-5

KINGSLEY

P KINGSLEY PUBLIC LIBRARY*, 220 Main St, 51028. (Mail add: PO Box 400, 51028-0400), SAN 305-5019. Tel: 712-378-2410. E-mail: library@wiatel.net. Web Site: kingsleylibrary.com. *Librn,* Julie Culler
Founded 1966. Pop 1,500; Circ 30,804
Library Holdings: Bk Titles 17,595; Per Subs 41
Wireless access
Open Mon & Thurs 9:30-12 & 1-8, Tues, Wed & Fri 9:30-12 & 1-5, Sat 9:30-1

KLEMME

P KLEMME PUBLIC LIBRARY*, 204 E Main St, 50449. (Mail add: PO Box 275, 50449-0275), SAN 305-5027. Tel: 641-587-2369. FAX: 866-380-3876. E-mail: klemlibr@comm1net.net. Web Site: www1.youseemore.com/nilc/klemme. *Dir,* Kathy Olthoff
Founded 1967. Pop 509; Circ 4,865
Library Holdings: Bk Vols 8,000; Per Subs 60
Automation Activity & Vendor Info: (Acquisitions) Beacon - TLC (The Library Corporation); (Cataloging) Beacon - TLC (The Library Corporation); (Circulation) Beacon - TLC (The Library Corporation); (ILL) Beacon - TLC (The Library Corporation); (Media Booking) Beacon - TLC (The Library Corporation); (OPAC) Beacon - TLC (The Library Corporation); (Serials) Beacon - TLC (The Library Corporation)
Wireless access
Open Mon-Wed & Fri 10-12 & 1-5, Thurs 10-12 & 1-6, Sat 9am-11pm

KNOXVILLE

P KNOXVILLE PUBLIC LIBRARY*, 213 E Montgomery St, 50138-2296. SAN 305-5035. Tel: 641-828-0585. FAX: 641-828-0513. E-mail: knoxlib@knoxville.lib.ia.us. Web Site: www.knoxville.lib.ia.us. *Dir,* Roslin I Thompson; *Asst Dir,* Staci Stanton; E-mail: staci.stanton@knoxville.lib.ia.us; *Youth Serv Librn,* Holly A Shelford. Subject Specialists: *Elem educ,* Holly A Shelford; Staff 9 (MLS 1, Non-MLS 8)
Founded 1912. Pop 7,731; Circ 119,146
Library Holdings: AV Mats 4,404; CDs 521; DVDs 489; Large Print Bks 1,795; Bk Vols 26,544; Per Subs 123; Talking Bks 1,719; Videos 2,067
Automation Activity & Vendor Info: (Cataloging) TLC (The Library Corporation); (Circulation) TLC (The Library Corporation); (OPAC) TLC (The Library Corporation)
Wireless access
Function: Home delivery & serv to seniorr ctr & nursing homes, ILL available, Photocopying/Printing, Prog for children & young adult, Summer reading prog, Wheelchair accessible
Open Mon-Thurs 10-8, Fri 10-5, Sat 10-3, Sun (Sept-May) 2-4
Friends of the Library Group

LA PORTE CITY

P HAWKINS MEMORIAL LIBRARY*, 308 Main St, 50651. SAN 305-5051. Tel: 319-342-3025. FAX: 319-342-3025. E-mail: hawkins@laportecity.lib.ia.us. Web Site: www.laportecity.lib.ia.us. *Dir,* Jolene Kronschnabel; Staff 4 (Non-MLS 4)
Founded 1946. Pop 2,300; Circ 23,800
Library Holdings: Bk Vols 21,757; Per Subs 62
Wireless access
Function: 24/7 Electronic res, 24/7 Online cat, Accelerated reader prog, Adult bk club, Audiobks via web, Bk club(s), Bks on CD, Children's prog, Computers for patron use, E-Reserves, Free DVD rentals, Holiday prog, ILL available, Internet access, Laminating, Magazines, Microfiche/film & reading machines, Movies, Online cat, Online info literacy tutorials on the web & in blackboard, OverDrive digital audio bks, Photocopying/Printing, Preschool outreach, Preschool reading prog, Prog for adults, Prog for children & young adult, Scanner, Story hour, Summer reading prog, Tax forms, Wheelchair accessible
Open Mon 8-4, Tues, Thurs & Fri 1-6, Wed 1-7, Sat 9-1

LACONA

P LACONA PUBLIC LIBRARY*, 107 E Main, 50139. (Mail add: PO Box 75, 50139-1014), SAN 376-5466. Tel: 641-534-4400. FAX: 641-534-4430. E-mail: laconalibrary@iowatelecom.net. Web Site: www.lacona.lib.ia.us. *Dir,* Sarah Hunkele
Library Holdings: Audiobooks 60; DVDs 300; Bk Vols 7,400; Per Subs 24
Special Collections: Lacona History/Genealogy; Warren/Marion/Lucas Cty, births. marriages, obits
Wireless access
Open Tues 2-6, Wed 1-4, Thurs 1-8, Fri 3-6, Sat 9-Noon
Friends of the Library Group

LAKE CITY

P LAKE CITY PUBLIC LIBRARY*, 110 E Washington St, 51449. SAN 305-506X. Tel: 712-464-3413. FAX: 712-464-3226. Web Site: www.lakecity.lib.ia.us. *Dir,* Michele Deluhery; E-mail: director@lakecity.lib.ia.us; *Asst Dir,* Kim Olson; E-mail: ill@lakecity.lib.ia.us; *Librn, Website Mgr,* Justina Wuebker; E-mail: librarian@lakecity.lib.ia.us; *Prog Coordr,* Vicki Tasler; E-mail: programs@lakecity.lib.ia.us
Founded 1901. Pop 3,200; Circ 25,819
Library Holdings: Bk Vols 17,000; Per Subs 60
Wireless access
Function: Adult bk club, Art exhibits, Audiobks via web, Bks on CD, CD-ROM, Children's prog, Computer training, Computers for patron use, Free DVD rentals, Home delivery & serv to seniorr ctr & nursing homes, ILL available, Magnifiers for reading, Music CDs, Online cat, Photocopying/Printing, Preschool reading prog, Prog for adults, Prog for children & young adult, Scanner, Senior computer classes, Senior outreach, Spoken cassettes & CDs, Summer reading prog, Tax forms, Teen prog, Wheelchair accessible
Open Mon & Fri 12:30-5:30, Tues-Thurs 9-8, Sat 9-12
Friends of the Library Group

LAKE MILLS

P LAKE MILLS PUBLIC LIBRARY*, 102 S Lake St, 50450. SAN 305-5078. Tel: 641-592-0092. FAX: 641-592-0093. Web Site: www1.youseemore.com/NILC/LakeMills/default.asp. *Dir,* Stephanie Stevens; E-mail: director@lakemills.lib.ia.us
Pop 2,281; Circ 31,000
Library Holdings: Bk Titles 22,000; Per Subs 100
Automation Activity & Vendor Info: (Acquisitions) TLC (The Library Corporation); (Cataloging) TLC (The Library Corporation); (Circulation) TLC (The Library Corporation)
Wireless access
Function: 24/7 Electronic res, 24/7 Online cat, Adult bk club, Audiobks via web, Bks on CD, Children's prog, Computers for patron use, Electronic databases & coll, Free DVD rentals, Holiday prog, Home delivery & serv to seniorr ctr & nursing homes, ILL available, Internet access, Movies, Notary serv, Online cat, Outreach serv, OverDrive digital audio bks, Photocopying/Printing, Prog for adults, Prog for children & young adult, Story hour, Summer reading prog, Teen prog, Wheelchair accessible
Special Services for the Blind - Bks on CD; Large print bks
Open Mon-Thurs 10-12 & 1-7, Fri 10-12 & 1-6, Sat 9-1

LAKE PARK

P LAKE PARK PUBLIC LIBRARY*, 905 S Market St, 51347. (Mail add: PO Box 344, 51347). Tel: 712-832-9505. FAX: 712-832-9507. E-mail: lpplibrary@lakepark.lib.ia.us. Web Site: www.lakeparkpubliclibrary.com. *Libr Dir,* Deb Grubich
Wireless access
Function: Photocopying/Printing, Summer reading prog
Open Tues 10-6, Wed-Fri 10-5, Sat 10-Noon
Friends of the Library Group

LAKE VIEW

P LAKE VIEW PUBLIC LIBRARY*, 202 Main St, 51450. (Mail add: PO Box 20, 51450-0020), SAN 305-5094. Tel: 712-657-2310. FAX: 712-657-2310. E-mail: lvl@netins.net. Web Site: www.lakeview.lib.ia.us. *Dir,* Kay Montano
Founded 1920. Pop 1,301; Circ 25,398
Library Holdings: Audiobooks 828; Bk Titles 20,334; Per Subs 85; Videos 1,294
Special Collections: Civil War (Goffrey C Ward Coll), bk, v-tapes; Des Moines Register; Lake View Resort 1941-to-date (weekly paper); Library of America; Wall Street Journal
Wireless access
Partic in OCLC Online Computer Library Center, Inc
Special Services for the Blind - Talking bks
Open Mon 10-12 & 2-8, Tues, Thurs & Fri 2-8, Wed 10-12 & 2-8, Sat 10-3
Friends of the Library Group

LAKOTA

P LAKOTA PUBLIC LIBRARY*, 204 Third St, 50451-7084. (Mail add: PO Box 178, 50451-0178), SAN 305-5108. Tel: 515-886-2312. FAX: 515-886-2312. Web Site: www.youseemore.com/NILC/Lakota. *Dir,* Susan Kearney
Pop 281; Circ 4,200
Jul 2015-Jun 2016 Income $22,295, State $1,540, City $4,550, County $14,786, Other $1,419. Mats Exp $2,700
Library Holdings: CDs 33; DVDs 500; Bk Vols 5,090; Per Subs 25; Videos 306
Automation Activity & Vendor Info: (Acquisitions) TLC (The Library Corporation); (Cataloging) TLC (The Library Corporation); (Circulation) TLC (The Library Corporation); (ILL) TLC (The Library Corporation); (Media Booking) TLC (The Library Corporation); (OPAC) TLC (The Library Corporation); (Serials) TLC (The Library Corporation)
Wireless access
Special Services for the Blind - Large print bks
Open Tues & Thurs 1-5 & 6-8, Wed 9-2, Sat 9-12

LAMONI

C GRACELAND UNIVERSITY*, Frederick Madison Smith Library, One University Pl, 50140. SAN 305-5116. Circulation Tel: 641-784-5361. FAX: 641-784-5497. Web Site: graceland.edu/fmsmith. *Interim Dir,* Sabrina Davis; E-mail: sdavis1@graceland.edu; *Coll Mgt, Govt Doc,* Marsha Jackel; E-mail: jackel@graceland.edu; *ILL, Per,* Betsy Folkins; Tel: 641-784-5483, E-mail: folkins@graceland.edu; Staff 8.5 (MLS 3, Non-MLS 5.5)
Founded 1895. Enrl 2,103; Fac 81; Highest Degree: Master
Library Holdings: AV Mats 3,681; CDs 329; e-books 6,592; e-journals 479; Electronic Media & Resources 8,607; Microforms 131,737; Bk Titles 150,938; Bk Vols 194,765; Per Subs 558; Videos 1,352
Special Collections: Mormon History Manuscripts, bks & micro. State Document Depository; US Document Depository
Subject Interests: Allied health, Mormons, Nursing
Automation Activity & Vendor Info: (Acquisitions) Innovative Interfaces, Inc; (Cataloging) Innovative Interfaces, Inc; (Circulation) Innovative Interfaces, Inc; (Course Reserve) Innovative Interfaces, Inc; (ILL) OCLC; (OPAC) Innovative Interfaces, Inc; (Serials) Innovative Interfaces, Inc
Wireless access
Function: Archival coll, Audio & video playback equip for onsite use, AV serv, Distance learning, Doc delivery serv, E-Reserves, Electronic databases & coll, ILL available, Internet access, Outside serv via phone, mail, e-mail & web, Photocopying/Printing, Ref serv available, Telephone ref
Partic in Iowa Academic Library Alliance; OCLC Online Computer Library Center, Inc
Open Mon-Thurs (Winter) 8am-1:45am, Fri 8am-4:45pm, Sat 1pm-4:45pm, Sun 1pm-1:45am; Mon-Fri (Summer) 8-4:45

P LAMONI PUBLIC LIBRARY, 301 W Main St, 50140. SAN 305-5124. Tel: 641-784-6686, E-mail: lamonilibrary@gmail.com. Web Site: www.lamonilibrary.org. *Libr Dir,* Felicia Williams
Founded 1922. Pop 2,444; Circ 33,000
Library Holdings: AV Mats 1,513; Large Print Bks 881; Bk Titles 23,764; Bk Vols 25,000; Per Subs 36; Talking Bks 1,700
Automation Activity & Vendor Info: (Circulation) Follett Software
Wireless access
Function: Bk club(s), Bks on CD, Children's prog, Computers for patron use, Electronic databases & coll, Free DVD rentals, Games & aids for people with disabilities, Home delivery & serv to seniorr ctr & nursing homes, ILL available, Internet access, Laminating, Magazines, Meeting rooms, Online cat, OverDrive digital audio bks, Photocopying/Printing, Prog for children & young adult, Scanner, Spanish lang bks, STEM programs, Story hour, Summer reading prog, Tax forms, Teen prog
Open Mon, Wed & Fri 1-6, Tues & Thurs 10-8, Sat 10-2

LAMONT

P LAMONT PUBLIC LIBRARY*, 616 Bush St, 50650. (Mail add: PO Box 116, 50650-0116), SAN 305-5132. Tel: 563-924-3203. FAX: 563-924-3203. Web Site: www.lamont.lib.ia.us. *Dir,* Angie Happel; E-mail: ahappel@lamont.lib.ia.us
Pop 1,147; Circ 7,927
Library Holdings: Bk Titles 4,000; Per Subs 12
Open Tues 1-5, Wed 1-6, Thurs & Fri 11-3, Sat 8-11

LANSING

P MEEHAN MEMORIAL LANSING PUBLIC LIBRARY*, 515 Main St, 52151. SAN 305-5140. Tel: 563-538-4693. FAX: 563-538-4693. E-mail: library@lansing.lib.ia.us. Web Site: www.lansing.lib.ia.us. *Libr Dir,* Derva Burke; E-mail: dburke@lansing.lib.ia.us
Pop 1,207; Circ 12,211
Library Holdings: Bk Vols 10,137; Per Subs 35; Talking Bks 266
Automation Activity & Vendor Info: (Acquisitions) ComPanion Corp; (Cataloging) ComPanion Corp; (Circulation) ComPanion Corp
Wireless access
Special Services for the Blind - Large print bks; Talking bks
Open Mon & Sat 9-Noon, Tues, Thurs & Fri 11-7
Friends of the Library Group

LARCHWOOD

P LARCHWOOD PUBLIC LIBRARY*, 1020 Broadway, 51241. (Mail add: PO Box 97, 51241-0097), SAN 305-5159. Tel: 712-477-2583. FAX: 712-477-2572. E-mail: lpblib@alliancecom.net. *Dir,* Sylvia Van't Hul; *Asst Dir,* Kathy Sorlie; *Children's & Teen Serv Coordr,* Esther Knutson
Founded 1927. Pop 866
Library Holdings: Audiobooks 1,161; DVDs 1,629; e-books 16,000; Bk Titles 14,172; Per Subs 31
Automation Activity & Vendor Info: (Acquisitions) Book Systems; (Cataloging) Book Systems; (Circulation) Book Systems; (OPAC) Book Systems
Wireless access
Function: Bks on CD, Children's prog, Computers for patron use, Homebound delivery serv, Magazines, Story hour, Summer reading prog
Open Mon & Tues 9-11 & 1-6, Thurs 2-6, Sat 9-1
Restriction: Authorized personnel only
Friends of the Library Group

LAURENS

P LAURENS PUBLIC LIBRARY*, 273 N Third St, 50554. SAN 305-5167. Tel: 712-841-4612. FAX: 712-841-4612. Web Site: www.laurenspubliclibrary.com. *Dir,* Glenda Mulder; E-mail: director@laurenspubliclibrary.com; *Asst Dir,* Deb Hertz; E-mail: assistantdir@laurenspubliclibrary.com; *Ch,* Jeri Wenell; E-mail: childrens@laurenspubliclibrary.com; Staff 4 (Non-MLS 4)
Founded 1910. Pop 1,476; Circ 38,449
Library Holdings: Bk Vols 25,000; Per Subs 75
Wireless access
Open Mon-Wed 11-8, Thurs & Fri 11-5, Sat 9-1

LAWLER

P LAWLER PUBLIC LIBRARY*, 412 E Grove, 52154. (Mail add: PO Box 235, 52154-0235), SAN 305-5175. Tel: 563-238-2191. FAX: 563-238-2191. E-mail: lawlerlibrary@gmail.com. Web Site: lawlerpubliclibrary.com. *Libr Dir,* Cathy Humpal
Founded 1964. Pop 329; Circ 5,468
Library Holdings: DVDs 510; Bk Titles 6,833; Per Subs 36; Videos 24
Wireless access
Open Mon, Tues & Thurs 1-5, Wed 1-6, Sat 8:30-12

LE GRAND

P LE GRAND PIONEER HERITAGE LIBRARY*, 204 N Vine St, 50142. (Mail add: PO Box 188, 50142-0188), SAN 373-918X. Tel: 641-479-2122. FAX: 641-479-2122. Web Site: www.legrand.lib.ia.us. *Dir,* Shelley Barron; E-mail: sbarron@legrand.lib.ia.us
Pop 854; Circ 14,809
Library Holdings: Bk Titles 9,516; Bk Vols 9,581; Per Subs 42
Special Collections: Native American Legends
Automation Activity & Vendor Info: (Cataloging) Follett Software; (Circulation) Follett Software
Open Tues 10-8, Wed 9-12 & 5-8, Thurs 10-5, Sun 3-6
Friends of the Library Group

LE MARS

P LE MARS PUBLIC LIBRARY*, 46 First St SW, 51031. SAN 305-5183. Tel: 712-546-5004. FAX: 712-546-5797. E-mail: library@lemars.lib.ia.us. Web Site: www.lemars.lib.ia.us. *Dir,* Shirley Taylor; E-mail:

shirley.taylor@lemars.lib.ia.us; *Ch,* Lisa Vander Sluis; E-mail: lisa.vandersluis@lemars.lib.ia.us
Founded 1894. Pop 9,500
Library Holdings: Bk Vols 40,000; Per Subs 149
Subject Interests: Local hist
Wireless access
Open Mon-Thurs 9-8, Fri 9-6, Sat 9-1
Friends of the Library Group

LECLAIRE

P LECLAIRE COMMUNITY LIBRARY, 323 Wisconsin St, 52753. SAN 341-8685. Tel: 563-289-6007. E-mail: library@leclaireiowa.gov. Web Site: www.leclaireiowa.gov/153/Library. *Libr Dir,* Ellen A Miller; E-mail: emiller@leclaireiowa.org
Library Holdings: AV Mats 5,000; Bk Vols 23,000; Per Subs 60
Wireless access
Partic in RiverShare Libraries
Open Mon-Thurs 10-7, Fri 10-5, Sat 10-2
Friends of the Library Group

LEDYARD

P LEDYARD PUBLIC LIBRARY*, 220 Edmunds St, 50556. (Mail add: PO Box 8, 50556-0008), SAN 305-5205. Tel: 515-646-3111. FAX: 515-646-3111. E-mail: llibrary@iowatelecom.net. Web Site: www.ledyardiowa.org/ledyard-public-library. *Head Librn,* Nancy Runksmeier
Founded 1971. Pop 616; Circ 3,951
Library Holdings: Audiobooks 446; Bks on Deafness & Sign Lang 2; CDs 98; DVDs 104; Large Print Bks 94; Bk Titles 5,702; Per Subs 12; Videos 206
Special Collections: Ledyard Yearbooks; Ledyard, Connecticut Informational Books. Municipal Document Depository
Wireless access
Open Mon & Wed 1-5, Sat 8-Noon

LEHIGH

P LEHIGH PUBLIC LIBRARY*, 241 Elm St, 50557. (Mail add: PO Box 138, 50557-0138), SAN 305-5213. Tel: 515-359-2967. FAX: 515-359-2973. Web Site: www1.youseemore.com/nilc/lehighpl. *Dir,* Marcie Bass; E-mail: director@lehigh.lib.ia.us
Founded 1927. Pop 497; Circ 12,605
Library Holdings: AV Mats 910; Bk Titles 7,000; Per Subs 44
Automation Activity & Vendor Info: (Circulation) Follett Software
Wireless access
Open Mon 11-6, Tues, Wed & Fri 12:30-5:30, Sat 10-12

LENOX

P LENOX PUBLIC LIBRARY*, 101 N Main St, 50851. SAN 305-5221. Tel: 641-333-4411. FAX: 641-333-4411. E-mail: library@lenoxia.com. Web Site: www.lenox.lib.ia.us. *Dir,* Shari Burger; E-mail: shari@lenox.lib.ia.us; Staff 1 (Non-MLS 1)
Founded 1941. Pop 1,500; Circ 10,000
Library Holdings: DVDs 290; Bk Titles 4,800; Per Subs 113
Automation Activity & Vendor Info: (Cataloging) Biblionix; (Circulation) Biblionix
Wireless access
Function: Adult bk club, Archival coll, Bks on cassette, Bks on CD, Children's prog, Computer training, Computers for patron use, Free DVD rentals, ILL available, Magazines, Microfiche/film & reading machines, Movies, Online cat, Photocopying/Printing, Prog for children & young adult, Scanner, Senior computer classes, Spanish lang bks, Summer reading prog, VHS videos, Wheelchair accessible
Open Mon 10-12 & 1-6, Tues-Fri 10-12 & 1-5:30, Sat 9-12

LEON

P LEON PUBLIC LIBRARY*, 200 W First St, 50144. SAN 305-523X. Tel: 641-446-6332. FAX: 641-446-3746. Web Site: www.leon.lib.ia.us. *Dir,* Darlene Richardson; E-mail: darlene@leon.lib.ia.us
Pop 1,983; Circ 21,199
Library Holdings: Bk Vols 16,594; Per Subs 39
Wireless access
Open Mon 12:30-7:30, Tues & Thurs 10:30-5:30, Wed & Fri 12:30-5:30, Sat 10:30-1:30

LETTS

P LETTS PUBLIC LIBRARY*, 125 E Iowa St, 52754. (Mail add: PO Box B, 52754-0410), SAN 305-5248. Tel: 319-726-5121. FAX: 319-726-5121. Web Site: www.letts.lib.ia.us. *Dir,* Karen Koppe; E-mail: karenk@letts.lib.ia.us
Founded 1910. Pop 384; Circ 2,094
Library Holdings: Bk Titles 7,500; Per Subs 25
Automation Activity & Vendor Info: (Cataloging) Follett Software
Wireless access
Publications: Newsletter (Quarterly)
Open Mon, Wed & Sat 9-Noon, Tues 9-12 & 1-6, Thurs 9-12 & 1-7, Fri 1-5

LEWIS

P LEWIS PUBLIC LIBRARY & HERITAGE CENTER*, 412 W Main, 51544. (Mail add: PO Box 40, 51544), SAN 376-5172. Tel: 712-769-2228. FAX: 712-769-2228. E-mail: lewislibrary@netins.net. Web Site: lewispubliclibrary.weebly.com. *Head Librn,* Lisa Metheny; *Asst Librn,* Nancy Jones
Pop 430
Library Holdings: Audiobooks 90; DVDs 600; Large Print Bks 50; Bk Titles 3,999; Bk Vols 5,050; Per Subs 3; Videos 125
Wireless access
Open Mon & Wed 1-6, Thurs & Fri 1-5, Sat 9-12

LIME SPRINGS

P LIME SPRINGS PUBLIC LIBRARY*, 112 W Main St, 52155. (Mail add: PO Box 68, 52155-0068), SAN 305-5264. Tel: 563-566-2207. FAX: 563-566-2207. E-mail: lspublib@mchsi.com. Web Site: www.limesprings.lib.ia.us. *Dir,* Janet DeVries
Library Holdings: Audiobooks 458; DVDs 838; Bk Titles 7,550; Per Subs 49
Wireless access
Open Mon, Tues & Thurs 2-8, Wed & Sat 10-5, Fri 2-5

LINDEN

P LINDEN PUBLIC LIBRARY*, 131 S Main St, 50146. (Mail add: PO Box 18, 50146-0018), SAN 305-5272. Tel: 641-744-2124. E-mail: library@linden.lib.ia.us. Web Site: www.linden.lib.ia.us. *Dir,* Julie Bishop
Pop 264; Circ 2,072
Library Holdings: Bk Titles 6,023; Per Subs 10
Wireless access
Open Mon 2-5, Tues 2-6, Wed & Sat 8:30am-11:30am, Thurs 1-5, Fri 1-4

LINN GROVE

P LINN GROVE PUBLIC LIBRARY*, 110 Weaver St, 51033. SAN 305-5280. Tel: 712-296-3919. FAX: 712-296-3919. Web Site: linngroveiowa.org/community_library.html. *Dir,* Emily Brown; E-mail: director@linngrove.lib.ia.us
Founded 1934. Pop 145; Circ 1,200
Library Holdings: AV Mats 578; Large Print Bks 15; Bk Vols 7,389; Talking Bks 65; Videos 534
Subject Interests: Christian fiction, Iowa, Relig
Function: Accelerated reader prog, ILL available, Photocopying/Printing
Open Tues & Fri 2:30-5, Wed 11-6, Sat 12-2

LISBON

P LISBON PUBLIC LIBRARY*, 101 E Main St, 52253. (Mail add: PO Box 217, 52253-0217), SAN 305-5299. Tel: 319-455-2800. FAX: 319-455-2800. E-mail: lisbonlibraryia@gmail.com. Web Site: www.lisbon.lib.ia.us. *Dir,* Amy White; E-mail: amy@lisbon.lib.ia.us
Founded 1936. Pop 2,000; Circ 14,000
Library Holdings: Bk Titles 10,000; Per Subs 18
Special Collections: Local History
Wireless access
Open Mon 9-1 & 2-5, Tues 2-5, Wed 2-8:30, Thurs 10-5, Fri 12-5, Sat 9-1
Friends of the Library Group

LITTLE ROCK

P LITTLE ROCK PUBLIC LIBRARY*, 402 Main St, 51243. (Mail add: PO Box 308, 51243-0308), SAN 376-5288. Tel: 712-479-2298. FAX: 712-479-2298. E-mail: lrbooks@mtcnet.net. *Dir,* LeAnn Gerken
Library Holdings: Bk Vols 6,300; Per Subs 32
Wireless access
Open Tues, Thurs & Fri 2-6, Wed 2-7, Sat 9-12

LIVERMORE

P LIVERMORE PUBLIC LIBRARY*, 402 Fifth St, 50558. (Mail add: PO Box 18, 50558-0018), SAN 305-5329. Tel: 515-379-2078. FAX: 515-379-2078. Web Site: www1.youseemore.com/nilc/livermore. *Dir,* Kris Landolt; E-mail: kris@livermore.lib.ia.us
Founded 1935. Pop 515; Circ 4,056
Library Holdings: Bk Vols 7,666; Per Subs 22; Talking Bks 232; Videos 536
Function: Prog for children & young adult
Open Mon 1-6, Wed 9-12 & 1-5, Thurs & Fri 1-5, Sat 9-12

LOGAN

P LOGAN PUBLIC LIBRARY*, 121 E Sixth St, 51546. SAN 305-5337. Tel: 712-644-2551. FAX: 712-644-2551. Web Site: loganpubliclibrary.weebly.com. *Dir,* Connie Johnson; E-mail: Cjohnson@logan.lib.ia.us; *Youth Serv Librn,* JJ Angregg; E-mail: Jandregg@logan.lib.ia.us
Founded 1920. Pop 1,900; Circ 23,400
Library Holdings: Bk Vols 16,700; Per Subs 69
Automation Activity & Vendor Info: (Acquisitions) Follett Software
Wireless access
Open Mon & Wed 11-8, Tues, Thurs & Fri 11-5, Sat 11-3
Friends of the Library Group
Bookmobiles: 1

LOHRVILLE

P J J HANDS LIBRARY*, 609 Second St, 51453. (Mail add: PO Box 277, 51453-0277), SAN 305-5345. Tel: 712-465-4115. FAX: 712-465-4115. E-mail: jjhands@lohrville.lib.ia.us. Web Site: www.lohrville.lib.ia.us. *Dir,* Amber Dischler
Founded 1935. Pop 771; Circ 11,000
Library Holdings: AV Mats 512; Bk Vols 16,500; Per Subs 58
Automation Activity & Vendor Info: (Acquisitions) Book Systems; (Cataloging) Book Systems; (Circulation) Book Systems
Wireless access
Open Mon-Wed 9:30-5:30, Thurs & Sat 9:30-12, Fri 9:30-6
Friends of the Library Group

LOST NATION

P LOST NATION PUBLIC LIBRARY, 410 Main St, 52254. (Mail add: PO Box 397, 52254-0397), SAN 376-4974. Tel: 563-678-2114. FAX: 563-678-2368. E-mail: lnchlib@netins.net. Web Site: lostnation.lib.ia.us. *Libr Dir,* Heather Gilroy
Pop 467; Circ 2,346
Library Holdings: Bk Titles 9,000
Wireless access
Open Mon, Tues & Thurs 9-11 & 4-6, Wed 9-11 & 1-6, Fri & Sat 9-11

LOWDEN

P LOWDEN PUBLIC LIBRARY*, 605 Main St, 52255. (Mail add: PO Box 307, 52255-0307), SAN 320-8273. Tel: 563-941-7629. Web Site: www.lowden.lib.ia.us. *Dir,* Kendahl Goering; E-mail: kg@lowden.lib.ia.us
Pop 790; Circ 9,439
Library Holdings: Bk Titles 9,400; Per Subs 10
Wireless access
Open Mon & Wed 10-12 & 1-7, Tues & Fri 8-12 & 1-5, Sat 9-11
Friends of the Library Group

LUVERNE

P LUVERNE PUBLIC LIBRARY*, 113 DeWitt St, 50560. (Mail add: PO Box 37, 50560-0037), SAN 305-5361. Tel: 515-882-3436. FAX: 515-882-3436. Web Site: www.yousemore.com/nilc/LuVernePL/default.asp. *Dir,* Sarah Banchs; E-mail: director@luverne.lib.ia.us
Pop 418; Circ 10,200
Library Holdings: Bk Vols 10,606; Per Subs 45
Open Mon & Wed 1:30-8, Fri 1:30-5:30, Sat 10-4

LYNNVILLE

P LYNNVILLE PUBLIC LIBRARY, 404 East St, 50153. (Mail add: PO Box 96, 50153-0096), SAN 376-4982. Tel: 641-527-2590. FAX: 641-527-2592. E-mail: lynnlibrary@netins.net. Web Site: www.lynnville.lib.ia.us. *Dir,* Barb Hoogeveen
Library Holdings: AV Mats 1,958; Bk Titles 9,300; Bk Vols 11,700; Per Subs 49
Wireless access
Open Mon & Tues 11-3, Wed 3-7, Thurs 2-7, Sat 9-Noon
Friends of the Library Group

LYTTON

P LYTTON PUBLIC LIBRARY*, 118 Main St, 50561. (Mail add: PO Box 136, 50561-0136), SAN 376-5318. Tel: 712-466-2522. FAX: 712-466-2522. E-mail: lyttnlib@iowatelecom.net. *Dir,* Beth Vauble
Pop 350
Library Holdings: Bk Vols 5,000
Wireless access
Open Mon 1-6, Tues-Fri 12-5, Sat 9-12
Friends of the Library Group

MADRID

P MADRID PUBLIC LIBRARY*, 100 W Third St, 50156. SAN 305-5388. Tel: 515-795-3846. FAX: 515-795-3697. E-mail: circdesk@madrid.lib.ia.us. Web Site: madridiowa.org/library. *Dir,* Angie Strong; E-mail: angie@madrid.lib.ia.us; *Children & Teen Librn,* Stephanie Fogarty
Founded 1934. Pop 2,395; Circ 23,687
Library Holdings: Bk Vols 15,000; Per Subs 80; Talking Bks 979; Videos 868
Automation Activity & Vendor Info: (Circulation) Book Systems; (OPAC) Book Systems
Wireless access
Open Mon-Thurs 9-7, Fri 9-5:30, Sat 9-12
Friends of the Library Group

MALLARD

P MALLARD PUBLIC LIBRARY*, 605 Inman St, 50562. SAN 320-8281. Tel: 712-425-3330. FAX: 712-425-3236. E-mail: mallardl@ncn.net. Web Site: www.mallard.lib.ia.us. *Dir,* Kris Wallskog
Founded 1940. Pop 420; Circ 8,007
Library Holdings: Bk Vols 8,000; Per Subs 20
Wireless access
Open Mon 1-6, Wed 9-12 & 1-5:30, Fri 1-5:30, Sat 9-12

MALVERN

P MALVERN PUBLIC LIBRARY*, 502 Main St, 51551. (Mail add: PO Box 180, 51551-0180), SAN 305-5396. Tel: 712-624-8554. FAX: 712-624-8245. E-mail: malvernlibraryia@gmail.com. Web Site: malvernlibrary.weebly.com. *Libr Dir,* Rebecca Bassich
Founded 1914. Pop 1,200; Circ 16,424
Library Holdings: Bk Vols 13,000; Per Subs 50
Special Collections: Malvern Leader Coll
Automation Activity & Vendor Info: (Cataloging) Follett Software
Wireless access
Open Mon, Tues, Thurs & Fri 9:30-6, Wed & Sat 9:30-3
Friends of the Library Group

MANCHESTER

P MANCHESTER PUBLIC LIBRARY*, 304 N Franklin St, 52057. SAN 305-540X. Tel: 563-927-3719. FAX: 563-927-3058. E-mail: manchpl@manchester.lib.ia.us. Web Site: www.manchesterlibraryia.org. *Dir,* Kristy Folsom; *Asst Dir,* Amanda McGreal; *Ch,* Angie Shere; Staff 1 (MLS 1)
Founded 1903. Pop 5,179; Circ 101,047
Special Collections: Manchester Newspapers, 1871-2015
Subject Interests: Genealogy, Hist, Local hist
Automation Activity & Vendor Info: (Circulation) Biblionix
Wireless access
Function: 24/7 Electronic res, 24/7 Online cat, Adult bk club, Audiobks on Playaways & MP3, Audiobks via web, Bks on CD, Children's prog, Computers for patron use, Electronic databases & coll, Free DVD rentals, ILL available, Internet access, Magazines, Meeting rooms, Movies, Music CDs, Notary serv, Online cat, Outreach serv, OverDrive digital audio bks, Photocopying/Printing, Preschool reading prog, Prog for adults, Prog for children & young adult, Ref serv available, Scanner, Senior outreach, Story hour, Summer reading prog, Tax forms, Teen prog, Telephone ref, Wheelchair accessible
Open Mon-Thurs 9:30-8, Fri 9:30-5, Sat 9-3
Friends of the Library Group

MANILLA

P MANILLA PUBLIC LIBRARY*, 447 Main St, 51454. (Mail add: PO Box 459, 51454-0459), SAN 305-5418. Tel: 712-654-5192. E-mail: manillalibrarian@gmail.com. Web Site: www.manillapubliclibrary.com. *Librn,* Laurie North
Founded 1932. Pop 839; Circ 5,795
Library Holdings: Bk Titles 5,241; Bk Vols 6,200
Open Mon 3-5, Wed 3:30-6:30, Sat 9-11

MANLY

P MANLY PUBLIC LIBRARY, 127 S Grant, 50456. (Mail add: PO Box 720, 50456-0720), SAN 305-5426. Tel: 641-454-2982. FAX: 641-454-0126. Web Site: www.yousemore.com/NILC/ManlyPL. *Dir,* Connie Moretz; E-mail: director@manly.lib.ia.us; *Librn,* Sandy Aves; *Librn,* Reina Trosper; *Librn,* Lauren Schilling; *Librn,* Kathy Young; *Tech Librn,* William Hillson
Pop 1,342; Circ 25,613
Jul 2014-Jun 2015 Income $55,000. Mats Exp $15,465, Books $6,665, Per/Ser (Incl. Access Fees) $1,038, Other Print Mats $4,197, AV Mat $3,565. Sal $32,517

Library Holdings: Audiobooks 50; CDs 10; Large Print Bks 150; Bk Titles 15,202; Per Subs 47; Talking Bks 50; Videos 1,150
Automation Activity & Vendor Info: (Acquisitions) Beacon - TLC (The Library Corporation); (Circulation) Beacon - TLC (The Library Corporation); (Course Reserve) Beacon - TLC (The Library Corporation)
Wireless access
Open Mon 2-8, Tues & Wed 2-6, Thurs 10-12 & 2-8, Fri 2-5, Sat 10-4

MANNING

P MANNING PUBLIC LIBRARY, 310 Main St, 51455. SAN 305-5434. Tel: 712-655-2260. FAX: 712-655-2260. E-mail: library@manningia.com. Web Site: www.manningia.com/pview.aspx?id=21049&catid=70. *Dir,* Linda Muhlbauer
Pop 1,490; Circ 10,536
Library Holdings: AV Mats 100; Bk Titles 13,900; Per Subs 25
Wireless access
Open Mon, Wed, Thurs & Fri 10-4:30, Tues 10-6, Sat 10-Noon

MANSON

P MANSON PUBLIC LIBRARY*, 1312 10th Ave, 50563. (Mail add: PO Box 309, 50563-0309), SAN 305-5442. Tel: 712-469-3986. FAX: 712-469-3076. E-mail: mansonpl@ncn.net. Web Site: www.manson.lib.ia.us. *Dir,* Laura Koons; E-mail: lkoons@manson.lib.ia.us
Founded 1922. Pop 1,848
Library Holdings: Bk Vols 17,266; Per Subs 36
Automation Activity & Vendor Info: (Circulation) Book Systems
Wireless access
Open Mon & Fri 1-4:30, Tues & Wed 10-4:30, Thurs 1-7:30

MAPLETON

P FISHER-WHITING MEMORIAL LIBRARY, Mapleton Public Library, 609 Courtright St, 51034. SAN 305-5450. Tel: 712-881-1312. FAX: 712-881-1313. E-mail: staff@mapleton.lib.ia.us. Web Site: www.mapleton.lib.ia.us. *Dir,* Peg Gay
Pop 1,495; Circ 24,617
Library Holdings: Bk Titles 17,676; Per Subs 45
Wireless access
Function: 24/7 Electronic res, 24/7 Online cat, Activity rm, Adult bk club, After school storytime, Archival coll, Bk club(s), Children's prog, Citizenship assistance, Computer training, Computers for patron use, Equip loans & repairs, Free DVD rentals, ILL available, Instruction & testing, Internet access, Magazines, Mail loans to mem, Meeting rooms, Microfiche/film & reading machines, Movies, Online cat, Online info literacy tutorials on the web & in blackboard, Online ref, Outside serv via phone, mail, e-mail & web, OverDrive digital audio bks, Photocopying/Printing, Preschool reading prog, Printer for laptops & handheld devices, Prog for adults, Prog for children & young adult, Scanner, Wheelchair accessible
Open Mon-Fri 11-7, Sat 11-3
Friends of the Library Group

MAQUOKETA

P MAQUOKETA PUBLIC LIBRARY*, 126 S Second St, 52060. SAN 305-5469. Tel: 563-652-3874. Web Site: www.maquoketa.lib.ia.us. *Exec Dir,* Elena Lanz; E-mail: director@maquoketa.lib.ia.us
Founded 1878. Pop 6,101; Circ 72,644
Library Holdings: Bk Vols 35,000; Per Subs 92
Subject Interests: Iowa, Lit, Local hist
Automation Activity & Vendor Info: (Acquisitions) Follett Software
Wireless access
Partic in Dubuque Area Library Information Consortium
Special Services for the Deaf - Closed caption videos
Special Services for the Blind - Audio mat; Bks available with recordings; Bks on cassette; Bks on CD; Cassette playback machines; Cassettes; Home delivery serv; Large print bks; Recorded bks; Screen enlargement software for people with visual disabilities; Sound rec
Open Mon, Tues & Thurs 10-8, Wed & Fri 10-6, Sat 9-3
Friends of the Library Group

MARATHON

P MARATHON PUBLIC LIBRARY*, 306 W Attica St, 50565. SAN 305-5477. Tel: 712-289-2200. *Dir,* James Cox
Pop 234
Library Holdings: Bk Titles 9,000; Per Subs 37
Wireless access
Open Tues 10-4, Wed 10-6, Thurs 1-5, Sat 9-Noon

MARBLE ROCK

P MARBLE ROCK PUBLIC LIBRARY, 122 S Main St, 50653. (Mail add: PO Box 236, 50653-0236), SAN 305-5485. Tel: 641-315-4480. FAX: 641-315-4480. E-mail: mrlib@myomnitel.com. Web Site: www.marblerock.org. *Libr Dir,* Elaine Ott
Founded 1946. Pop 334; Circ 6,000
Library Holdings: Bk Vols 4,500; Per Subs 40
Open Mon, Tues, Thurs & Fri 1:30-5, Wed 9-11 & 1:30-6, Sat 9-12

MARCUS

P MARCUS PUBLIC LIBRARY*, 106 N Locust St, 51035. (Mail add: PO Box 528, 51035-0528), SAN 305-5493. Tel: 712-376-2328. FAX: 712-376-4628. E-mail: marcuspl@midlands.net. Web Site: www.marcus.lib.ia.us. *Dir,* Beth Kingdon; Staff 1.1 (Non-MLS 1.1)
Founded 1908. Pop 1,200; Circ 20,970
Jul 2019-Jun 2020 Income $83,218, State $1,683, City $72,160, County $8,700, Other $675. Mats Exp $17,645, Books $14,805, Per/Ser (Incl. Access Fees) $970, AV Mat $1,389, Electronic Ref Mat (Incl. Access Fees) $481. Sal $29,506
Library Holdings: Audiobooks 229; CDs 12; DVDs 1,146; e-books 27,375; Electronic Media & Resources 14; High Interest/Low Vocabulary Bk Vols 212; Large Print Bks 1,198; Bk Titles 16,968; Per Subs 29
Subject Interests: Local hist
Automation Activity & Vendor Info: (Cataloging) Book Systems; (Circulation) Book Systems; (OPAC) Book Systems
Wireless access
Function: 24/7 Electronic res, 24/7 Online cat, Adult bk club, Adult literacy prog, Archival coll, Audiobks via web, Bk club(s), Bks on CD, Children's prog, Computer training, Computers for patron use, Free DVD rentals, ILL available, Internet access, Magazines, Meeting rooms, Movies, Music CDs, Online cat, Online ref, Outside serv via phone, mail, e-mail & web, Photocopying/Printing, Prog for adults, Prog for children & young adult, Ref & res, Scanner, Serves people with intellectual disabilities, Summer & winter reading prog, Summer reading prog, Tax forms, Teen prog, Wheelchair accessible
Open Mon-Wed 12-5:30, Thurs 12-8, Fri 10-1:30
Friends of the Library Group

MARENGO

P MARENGO PUBLIC LIBRARY*, 235 E Hilton St, 52301. SAN 305-5507. Tel: 319-741-3825. FAX: 319-741-3825. Web Site: www.marengo.lib.ia.us. *Dir,* Jackie Jordan; E-mail: Director@marengo.lib.ia.us; *Librn,* Judy Madsen; Staff 3 (Non-MLS 3)
Founded 1904. Pop 2,535; Circ 35,648
Library Holdings: Audiobooks 350; AV Mats 1,016; CDs 200; DVDs 450; Large Print Bks 300; Bk Titles 20,225; Bk Vols 20,245; Per Subs 92; Videos 1,200
Special Collections: Iowa County History, bd vols, micro
Automation Activity & Vendor Info: (Acquisitions) Follett Software; (Cataloging) Follett Software; (Circulation) Follett Software; (OPAC) Follett Software
Wireless access
Open Mon-Thurs 10-7, Fri 10-5, Sat 10-1
Friends of the Library Group

MARION

P MARION PUBLIC LIBRARY*, 1095 Sixth Ave, 52302. SAN 305-5515. Tel: 319-377-3412. E-mail: info@marionpubliclibrary.org. Web Site: marionpubliclibrary.org. *Libr Dir,* Hollie Trenary; E-mail: htrenary@marionpubliclibrary.org; *Asst Dir,* Jo Pearson; E-mail: jpearson@cityofmarion.org; *Access Serv Librn,* Position Currently Open; *Ad,* Madeline Jarvis; E-mail: mjarvis@cityofmarion.org; *Ch Serv Librn,* Olivia Stoner; E-mail: ostoner@cityofmarion.org; *Teen Serv Librn,* Rachel Pollari; E-mail: rpollari@cityofmarion.org; Staff 36 (MLS 6, Non-MLS 30)
Pop 39,000; Circ 761,658
Automation Activity & Vendor Info: (Acquisitions) SirsiDynix; (Cataloging) SirsiDynix; (Circulation) SirsiDynix
Wireless access
Function: 24/7 Electronic res, 24/7 Online cat, Adult bk club, Audio & video playback equip for onsite use, Audiobks on Playaways & MP3, Audiobks via web, Bk club(s), Bks on CD, Children's prog, Computers for patron use, Digital talking bks, Doc delivery serv, E-Reserves, Electronic databases & coll, Free DVD rentals, Genealogy discussion group, Holiday prog, Home delivery & serv to seniorr ctr & nursing homes, Homebound delivery serv, ILL available, Internet access, Magazines, Mail & tel request accepted, Mail loans to mem, Meeting rooms, Movies, Music CDs, Notary serv, Online cat, Online ref, Outreach serv, Outside serv via phone, mail, e-mail & web, OverDrive digital audio bks, Photocopying/Printing, Prog for adults, Prog for children & young adult, Ref & res, Ref serv available, Scanner, Senior outreach, Story hour, Study rm, Summer reading prog, Teen prog, Telephone ref, Wheelchair accessible

Open Mon-Thurs 9:30-9, Fri-Sat 9:30-5, Sun (Sept-May) 2-5
Friends of the Library Group

MARSHALLTOWN

S EMERSON AUTOMATION SOLUTIONS INFORMATION CENTER*, 301 S First Ave, 50158. SAN 329-0557. Tel: 641-754-2161, 641-754-3111. FAX: 641-754-3159. *Mgr, Knowledge Network & Info Serv,* Mark Heindselman; E-mail: mark.heindselman@emerson.com; *Info Ctr Analyst,* Brian Herman; E-mail: brian.herman@emerson.com
Founded 1979
Library Holdings: AV Mats 3,000; Bk Titles 3,500; Per Subs 175
Automation Activity & Vendor Info: (OPAC) Inmagic, Inc.
Function: 24/7 Electronic res, 24/7 Online cat
Open Mon-Fri 7:30-4:30
Restriction: Access at librarian's discretion, Access for corporate affiliates, Badge access after hrs

S IOWA VETERAN'S HOME LIBRARY*, 1301 Summit St, 50158. SAN 305-5531. Tel: 641-753-4412. Web Site: ivh.iowa.gov. *Librn,* Sonia Hayek
Library Holdings: Bk Vols 5,000; Per Subs 37
Subject Interests: Geriatrics & gerontology
Open Mon-Fri 9-4, Sat & Sun 10-2

J MARSHALLTOWN COMMUNITY COLLEGE*, B J Harrison Library, 3700 S Center St, 50158. SAN 320-6777. Tel: 641-844-5690. FAX: 641-754-1442. E-mail: mcclibrary@iavalley.edu. Web Site: mcc.iavalley.edu/resources-for-students/library. *Libr Serv Mgr,* Emily Horner; E-mail: Emily.Horner@iavalley.edu; Staff 2 (MLS 1, Non-MLS 1)
Founded 1927. Highest Degree: Associate
Library Holdings: Bk Vols 58,000; Per Subs 1,224
Automation Activity & Vendor Info: (Cataloging) SirsiDynix-WorkFlows; (Circulation) SirsiDynix-WorkFlows; (OPAC) SirsiDynix; (Serials) SirsiDynix-WorkFlows
Wireless access
Function: Electronic databases & coll, ILL available, Music CDs, Online cat, Online ref, Orientations, Photocopying/Printing, Prof lending libr, Scanner, Wheelchair accessible
Partic in Iowa Academic Library Alliance
Open Mon-Wed 7:30am-8pm, Thurs 7:30-6, Fri 7:30-3
Restriction: Fee for pub use

P MARSHALLTOWN PUBLIC LIBRARY*, 105 W Boone St, 50158-4911. SAN 341-9347. Tel: 641-754-5738. FAX: 641-754-5708. E-mail: mtownlibrary@yahoo.com. Web Site: www.marshalltownlibrary.org. *Dir,* Sarah Rosenblum; E-mail: srosenblum@marshalltown-ia.gov; *Pub Serv Mgr, Tech Mgr,* Katie Fink; E-mail: kfink@marshalltown-ia.gov; *Youth Serv Mgr,* Joa LaVille; Staff 8 (MLS 2, Non-MLS 6)
Founded 1898. Pop 33,518; Circ 315,070
Library Holdings: Audiobooks 6,374; DVDs 8,482; Bk Vols 104,736; Per Subs 225; Talking Bks 3,676
Subject Interests: Genealogy, Local hist
Automation Activity & Vendor Info: (Cataloging) SirsiDynix; (Circulation) SirsiDynix; (OPAC) SirsiDynix
Wireless access
Open Mon-Thurs 9-8, Fri 9-6, Sat 9-4, Sun 1-4 (Fall-Winter); Mon-Thurs 9-7, Fri 9-6, Sat 9-4, Sun 1-4 (Summer)
Friends of the Library Group

MARTELLE

P MARTELLE PUBLIC LIBRARY*, 202 South St, 52305. (Mail add: PO Box 86, 52305-0086), SAN 305-5558. Tel: 319-482-4121. FAX: 319-482-4121. Web Site: www.martelle.lib.ia.us. *Dir,* Theresa Pennington; E-mail: tpennington@martelle.lib.ia.us
Founded 1950. Pop 316; Circ 3,831
Library Holdings: Bk Titles 4,600; Per Subs 18
Wireless access
Open Tues & Thurs 2-6, Wed 9-5, Sat (Sept-May) 9-1

MASON CITY

S CHARLES H MACNIDER MUSEUM LIBRARY*, 303 Second St SE, 50401. SAN 305-5566. Tel: 641-421-3666. FAX: 641-422-9612. E-mail: macniderinformation@masoncity.net. Web Site: macniderart.org. *Dir,* Edith Blanchard; E-mail: eblanchard@masoncity.net; *Assoc Curator,* Mara Linskey-Deegan; E-mail: mlinskeydeegan@masoncity.net
Founded 1966
Library Holdings: Bk Vols 1,500; Per Subs 10
Subject Interests: Art, Art hist
Open Tues & Thurs 9-8, Wed, Fri & Sat 9-5
Restriction: In-house use for visitors, Not a lending libr

P MASON CITY PUBLIC LIBRARY*, 225 Second St SE, 50401. SAN 305-5574. Tel: 641-421-3668. Reference Tel: 641-421-3670. Administration Tel: 641-421-3669. FAX: 641-423-2615. Web Site: www.mcpl.org. *Dir,* Mary Markwalter; E-mail: mammarkwalter@gmail.com; *Asst Dir,* Penny V Weitzel; E-mail: business@mcpl.org; *YA Librn,* Calista McCollough; E-mail: calista@masoncity.lib.ia.us; Staff 15 (MLS 1, Non-MLS 14)
Founded 1876. Pop 29,172; Circ 55,000
Jul 2013-Jun 2014 Income $1,001,200, State $7,200, City $881,000, Federal $1,000, County $82,000, Locally Generated Income $30,000. Mats Exp $95,000, Books $30,000, Per/Ser (Incl. Access Fees) $8,000, AV Mat $18,000, Electronic Ref Mat (Incl. Access Fees) $39,000. Sal $875,870 (Prof $76,640)
Library Holdings: Bk Titles 107,000; Bk Vols 109,000; Per Subs 325
Special Collections: Lee P Loomis Archive of Mason City History; Prairie School Architecture Coll. State Document Depository
Subject Interests: Art & archit, Civil War, Local hist
Automation Activity & Vendor Info: (Acquisitions) Innovative Interfaces, Inc; (Cataloging) Innovative Interfaces, Inc; (Circulation) Innovative Interfaces, Inc; (OPAC) Innovative Interfaces, Inc; (Serials) Innovative Interfaces, Inc
Wireless access
Publications: Annual Report
Special Services for the Blind - World Bk Encyclopedia on cassette
Open Mon-Thurs 9-8, Fri & Sat 9-5
Friends of the Library Group

M MERCY MEDICAL CENTER - NORTH IOWA*, Medical Library, 1000 Fourth St SW, 50401. SAN 305-5604. Tel: 641-428-7699. E-mail: library@mchs.com. Web Site: libguides.mccn.edu/mercy. *Regional Dir, Library Services,* Stevo Roksandic; E-mail: sroksandic@mchs.com; Staff 1 (MLS 1)
Library Holdings: Bk Titles 1,900; Per Subs 250; Videos 46
Subject Interests: Med, Nursing
Automation Activity & Vendor Info: (Acquisitions) EOS International; (Cataloging) EOS International; (OPAC) EOS International; (Serials) EOS International
Partic in Greater Midwest Regional Medical Libr Network
Open Mon-Fri 8-4:30

J NORTH IOWA AREA COMMUNITY COLLEGE LIBRARY*, 500 College Dr, 50401. SAN 305-5590. Tel: 641-422-4232. Interlibrary Loan Service Tel: 641-422-4407. FAX: 641-422-4131. E-mail: librarian@niacc.edu. Web Site: www.niacc.edu/student-life/library. *Libr Assoc,* Kim Kraus; E-mail: Kim.Kraus@niacc.edu; *ILL,* Cindy Eyeberg; E-mail: Cindy.Eyberg@niacc.edu; Staff 4 (MLS 1, Non-MLS 3)
Founded 1918. Enrl 3,181; Fac 84; Highest Degree: Associate
Library Holdings: Audiobooks 325; AV Mats 2,134; CDs 29; DVDs 274; e-books 13,631; e-journals 65; Electronic Media & Resources 71; Microforms 433; Bk Titles 19,885; Bk Vols 27,129; Per Subs 279; Videos 826
Automation Activity & Vendor Info: (Cataloging) Innovative Interfaces, Inc; (Circulation) Innovative Interfaces, Inc; (ILL) OCLC; (OPAC) Innovative Interfaces, Inc
Wireless access
Publications: NIACC Library Handbook
Partic in Iowa Academic Library Alliance; LYRASIS; OCLC Online Computer Library Center, Inc
Open Mon-Thurs 7:30am-8pm, Fri 7:30-4

MASSENA

P MASSENA PUBLIC LIBRARY*, 122 Main, 50853. (Mail add: PO Box 95, 50853-0095), SAN 305-5612. Tel: 712-779-3726. E-mail: massplib@netins.net. *Dir,* Linda Eilts
Founded 1918. Pop 350; Circ 5,281
Library Holdings: DVDs 50; Bk Titles 3,806; Per Subs 17; Videos 60
Wireless access
Function: 24/7 Electronic res, 24/7 Online cat
Partic in Association for Rural & Small Libraries; Northern New York Library Network
Open Tues 8-12 & 1-5, Wed 1-6, Fri 12-5 , Sat 9-11; Mon (Summer) 8-12 & 1-5
Friends of the Library Group

MAXWELL

P MAXWELL PUBLIC LIBRARY*, 109 Main St, 50161. (Mail add: PO Box 128, 50161-0128), SAN 305-5620. Tel: 515-387-8780. FAX: 515-387-8780. E-mail: maxwell_public_library2011@hotmail.com. *Dir,* Crystal Clair; *Libr Asst,* Anna Baldwin; *Libr Asst,* Carol Newton
Pop 800; Circ 6,977
Library Holdings: Bk Vols 5,586
Subject Interests: Iowa
Wireless access
Open Mon 9-7, Tues, Wed & Thurs 4-7, Sat 11-2

MAYNARD

P MAYNARD COMMUNITY LIBRARY*, 245 Main St W, 50655. (Mail add: PO Box 225, 50655-0225), SAN 376-5253. Tel: 563-637-2330. FAX: 563-637-2330. E-mail: maynardlibrary@mchsi.com. Web Site: www.maynard.lib.ia.us. *Dir,* Lezlie Barry
Library Holdings: Bk Vols 6,200; Per Subs 37
Automation Activity & Vendor Info: (Cataloging) Biblionix/Apollo
Wireless access
Open Mon 1-5, Tues & Wed 9-12 & 1-5, Thurs 1-7, Fri & Sat 9-12

MCGREGOR

P MCGREGOR PUBLIC LIBRARY*, 334 Main St, 52157. (Mail add: PO Box 398, 52157-0398), SAN 305-537X. Tel: 563-873-3318. FAX: 563-873-3318. E-mail: mplib@mchsi.com. Web Site: www.mcgregor.lib.ia.us. *Dir,* Michele Pettit; *Ch,* Jane Lundquist; *Asst Librn,* Pam Smalley
Pop 797; Circ 23,462
Library Holdings: Bk Titles 14,500; Per Subs 31
Subject Interests: Local hist
Open Mon & Wed 2:30-8:30, Tues & Thurs 10:30-5:30, Fri 2:30-5:30, Sat 9:30-3:30

MECHANICSVILLE

P MECHANICSVILLE PUBLIC LIBRARY*, 218 E First St, 52306. (Mail add: PO Box 370, 52306-0370), SAN 305-5647. Tel: 563-432-7135. FAX: 563-432-6612. Web Site: www.mechanicsville.lib.ia.us. *Dir,* Meredith Dehmer; E-mail: mdehmer@mechanicsville.lib.ia.us
Pop 1,146; Circ 19,424
Library Holdings: Bk Vols 16,438; Per Subs 20
Wireless access
Open Mon 10-12 & 1-3, Tues 1-5, Thurs 3-6

MEDIAPOLIS

P MEDIAPOLIS PUBLIC LIBRARY*, 128 N Orchard St, 52637. (Mail add: PO Box 39, 52637-0039), SAN 305-5655. Tel: 319-394-3895. FAX: 319-394-3916. Web Site: www.mediapolis.lib.ia.us. *Dir,* Ali Iserman; E-mail: director@mediapolis.lib.ia.us; Staff 4 (Non-MLS 4)
Founded 1915. Pop 1,650; Circ 3,500
Library Holdings: AV Mats 1,000; Bks on Deafness & Sign Lang 10; High Interest/Low Vocabulary Bk Vols 1,000; Large Print Bks 550; Bk Vols 23,000; Per Subs 73; Talking Bks 200
Automation Activity & Vendor Info: (Cataloging) Biblionix/Apollo; (Circulation) Biblionix/Apollo; (OPAC) Biblionix/Apollo
Wireless access
Function: AV serv, ILL available, Photocopying/Printing, Prog for children & young adult, Summer reading prog, Wheelchair accessible
Open Mon-Fri 10-6, Sat 10-2
Friends of the Library Group

MELBOURNE

P MELBOURNE PUBLIC LIBRARY*, 603 Main St, 50162. SAN 376-5431. Tel: 641-482-3115. Web Site: www.melbourne.lib.ia.us. *Libr Dir,* Sara Mechtel; E-mail: sara.mechtel@melbourne.lib.ia.us; Staff 2 (Non-MLS 2)
Founded 1975
Library Holdings: Large Print Bks 300; Bk Titles 14,000; Per Subs 24; Talking Bks 428
Automation Activity & Vendor Info: (Cataloging) Follett Software; (Circulation) Follett Software
Wireless access
Open Mon, Tues, Thurs & Fri & Sun 3-7, Wed 10-12 & 3-7
Friends of the Library Group

MELCHER-DALLAS

P MELCHER-DALLAS PUBLIC LIBRARY*, 111 S Main St, 50163. (Mail add: PO Box 684, 50163). Tel: 641-947-6700. FAX: 641-947-6700. E-mail: m-dpl-1@hotmail.com. Web Site: www.melcher-dallas.lib.ia.us. *Dir,* Lori Davis; E-mail: loridavis@melcher-dallas.lib.ia.us
Pop 1,298; Circ 7,580
Library Holdings: AV Mats 215; Bk Vols 8,267
Wireless access
Open Mon 9-3, Tues, Thurs & Fri 11-5, Wed 12-6, Sat 9-11
Friends of the Library Group

MELVIN

P MELVIN PUBLIC LIBRARY, 232 Main St, 51350. SAN 376-5148. Tel: 712-736-2107. E-mail: libraryinmelvin@gmail.com. *Dir,* Pauline McDougall
Pop 400; Circ 500
Library Holdings: Audiobooks 3; Bk Vols 3,853; Per Subs 40
Wireless access
Open Mon & Thurs 2-5, Sat 9-12

MENLO

P MENLO PUBLIC LIBRARY*, Menlo Community Bldg, 504 Fifth St, 50164. (Mail add: PO Box 234, 50164), SAN 305-568X. Tel: 641-524-4201. FAX: 641-524-2682. Web Site: menlopubliclibrary.weebly.com/. *Dir,* Julie O'Brien; E-mail: director@menlo.lib.ia.us
Founded 1942. Pop 365; Circ 9,996
Library Holdings: Audiobooks 15; Bks on Deafness & Sign Lang 5; Braille Volumes 1; CDs 35; DVDs 250; Electronic Media & Resources 5; High Interest/Low Vocabulary Bk Vols 50; Large Print Bks 100; Bk Vols 9,580; Per Subs 23; Videos 15
Wireless access
Special Services for the Deaf - Am sign lang & deaf culture; Bks on deafness & sign lang
Special Services for the Blind - Accessible computers; Audio mat
Open Tues & Wed 3-7, Thurs-Sat 9-2
Friends of the Library Group

MERRILL

P MERRILL PUBLIC LIBRARY*, 608 Main St, 51038. SAN 305-5698. Tel: 712-938-2503. FAX: 712-938-2402. E-mail: merrilllibrary@mtcnet.net. Web Site: merrilliowa.com/library.html. *Librn,* Val Smith; *Ch,* Julie Schultz
Pop 752; Circ 7,950
Library Holdings: Bk Vols 6,400; Per Subs 71
Wireless access
Open Mon & Wed 1:30-5, Tues & Thurs 6-8, Fri & Sat 9-12

MESERVEY

P MESERVEY PUBLIC LIBRARY*, 719 First St, 50457. (Mail add: PO Box 68, 50457), SAN 305-5701. Tel: 641-358-6274. FAX: 641-358-6274. Web Site: chelseaprice.wixsite.com/mplib. *Dir,* Chelsea Price; E-mail: chelseaprice@meservey.lib.ia.us
Founded 1965. Pop 580; Circ 5,296
Library Holdings: AV Mats 271; Bk Titles 7,844; Per Subs 22
Open Mon 4-6:30, Wed & Fri 1-5, Thurs 1-7:30, Sat 9-12

MILFORD

P MILFORD MEMORIAL LIBRARY*, 1009 Ninth St, Ste 5, 51351. SAN 305-571X. Tel: 712-338-4643. FAX: 712-338-4859. E-mail: info@milford.lib.ia.us. Web Site: milfordlibrary.weebly.com. *Dir,* Beth K Sorenson; *Asst Dir,* Gillian Anderson; *Ch,* Betty Naab
Founded 1923. Pop 2,474; Circ 86,000
Library Holdings: Audiobooks 12,639; CDs 631; DVDs 728; e-books 10,042; e-journals 73; Large Print Bks 1,479; Bk Vols 23,804; Per Subs 175
Automation Activity & Vendor Info: (Cataloging) OCLC CatExpress; (Circulation) Biblionix; (OPAC) Biblionix
Wireless access
Function: Photocopying/Printing
Open Mon, Tues, Thurs & Fri 9:30-5:30, Wed 9:30-8, Sat 10-1:30
Friends of the Library Group

MILO

P MILO PUBLIC LIBRARY, 123 Main St, 50166. SAN 305-5728. Tel: 641-942-6557. FAX: 641-942-6557. E-mail: milolibrary@windstream.net. Web Site: www.milolibrary50166.com. *Dir,* Renee Hembry
Founded 1955. Pop 839; Circ 13,657
Library Holdings: AV Mats 438; Large Print Bks 236; Bk Titles 12,474; Per Subs 78
Special Collections: Local History Coll, bks, newsp, obituaries, photogs
Wireless access
Open Mon & Thurs 2-7:30, Tues 6-8, Wed & Thurs 9-12 & 2-5:30, Fri 9-11 & 2-5:30, Sat 9-Noon

MILTON

P MILTON PUBLIC LIBRARY*, 422 N Main St, 52570. SAN 305-5736. Tel: 641-656-4611. E-mail: miltonpubliclibrary@icloud.com. *Librn,* Clint Whitmill; E-mail: clint.whitmill@icloud.com
Pop 443; Circ 1,218
Library Holdings: DVDs 10; Bk Vols 8,000
Wireless access
Open Wed & Thurs 1:30-4:30, Fri 9:30-12:30

MINBURN

P MINBURN PUBLIC LIBRARY*, 315 Baker St, 50167. (Mail add: PO Box 23, 50167-0023), SAN 305-5744. Tel: 515-677-2712. FAX: 515-677-2245. E-mail: library@minburnlibrary.com. Web Site: minburnlibrary.weebly.com. *Dir,* Nicole Connick
Pop 390; Circ 1,532
Library Holdings: Bk Vols 6,000; Per Subs 28
Wireless access
Open Mon 9-6, Wed 9-1, Thurs 1-5, Fri-3, Sat 9-12
Friends of the Library Group

MISSOURI VALLEY

P MISSOURI VALLEY PUBLIC LIBRARY*, 420 E Huron St, 51555. SAN 305-5752. Tel: 712-642-4111. FAX: 712-642-4172. E-mail: movalleypubliclibrary@gmail.com. Web Site: www.movalleypubliclibrary.org. *Libr Dir,* Bruce Kocher; *Ch,* DeAnn Kruempel
Founded 1881. Pop 2,800; Circ 33,000
Library Holdings: Bk Titles 30,900; Per Subs 50
Wireless access
Open Mon-Wed & Fri 10-5:30, Thurs 1-8, Sat 10-2
Friends of the Library Group

MITCHELLVILLE

S IOWA CORRECTIONAL INSTITUTION FOR WOMEN LIBRARY, 420 Mill St SW, 50169. SAN 305-6740. Tel: 515-725-5195. FAX: 515-967-5347. *Activity Spec,* Darcia Stepanek; Tel: 515-725-5114, E-mail: darcia.stepanek@iowa.gov; Staff 1 (Non-MLS 1)
Library Holdings: Bk Vols 19,500; Per Subs 20
Subject Interests: Ethnic studies, Feminism
Restriction: Staff & inmates only

P MITCHELLVILLE PUBLIC LIBRARY*, 205 Center Ave N, 50169. (Mail add: PO Box 727, 50169-0727), SAN 305-5779. Tel: 515-967-3339. FAX: 515-967-1868. E-mail: mplibr@mitchellville.lib.ia.us. Web Site: www.mitchellville.lib.ia.us. *Dir,* Ellen Heather; E-mail: ellen.stahl@mitchellville.lib.ia.us
Pop 2,017; Circ 20,747
Library Holdings: Bk Titles 13,096; Per Subs 45
Automation Activity & Vendor Info: (Circulation) Book Systems
Wireless access
Open Tues & Fri 10-6, Wed & Thurs 10-8, Sat 9-2
Friends of the Library Group

MODALE

P MODALE PUBLIC LIBRARY, 210 N Main St, 51556. (Mail add: PO Box 28, 51556-0028), SAN 305-5787. Tel: 712-645-2826. FAX: 712-645-2826. E-mail: modalepl@iowatelecom.net. Web Site: modalepubliclibrary.weebly.com. *Libr Dir,* Tamara Smith-Cooperrider; Tel: 402-319-6043
Circ 5,080
Library Holdings: Bk Vols 8,371; Per Subs 20; Talking Bks 100
Open Tues & Wed 2-6:30, Sat Noon-2:30
Friends of the Library Group

MONDAMIN

P MONDAMIN PUBLIC LIBRARY, 201 Maple St, 51557. (Mail add: PO Box 190, 51557-0190), SAN 305-5795. Tel: 712-646-2888. FAX: 712-646-2888. E-mail: mpl@iowatelecom.net. Web Site: www.mondamin.lib.ia.us. *Libr Dir,* Christine Hussing
Founded 1934. Pop 1,743; Circ 3,664
Library Holdings: Audiobooks 350; AV Mats 50; DVDs 3,257; Bk Titles 11,217; Per Subs 15; Videos 202
Automation Activity & Vendor Info: (Cataloging) Follett Software
Wireless access
Open Tues & Sat 9-2, Wed & Thurs 1-6

MONONA

P MURPHY HELWIG LIBRARY, 111 N Page, 52159. (Mail add: PO Box 942, 52159-0942), SAN 305-5809. Tel: 563-539-2356. FAX: 563-539-2306. E-mail: murphy@monona.lib.ia.us. Web Site: www.monona.lib.ia.us. *Dir,* Heidi Landt; *Asst Dir,* Susan Trappe
Founded 1934. Pop 1,550; Circ 15,572
Library Holdings: Bk Titles 13,500; Per Subs 65
Wireless access
Open Mon-Thurs 10-6, Fri 10-4, Sat 10-12

MONROE

P MONROE PUBLIC LIBRARY*, 416 S Buchanan St, 50170. (Mail add: PO Box 780, 50170-0780), SAN 376-5474. Tel: 641-259-3065. FAX: 641-259-3065. E-mail: admin@readmonroe.org. Web Site: www.monroe.lib.ia.us. *Dir,* Brenda Tripp-Lanser; Staff 2 (MLS 1, Non-MLS 1)
Pop 1,808
Library Holdings: Bk Vols 21,250; Per Subs 22
Subject Interests: Local hist
Automation Activity & Vendor Info: (Cataloging) Follett Software; (Circulation) Follett Software
Wireless access
Function: Adult bk club, Bks on cassette, Bks on CD, Computers for patron use, Free DVD rentals, Holiday prog, ILL available, Music CDs, Photocopying/Printing, Story hour, Summer reading prog, Tax forms, VHS videos, Wheelchair accessible
Open Mon & Wed 12-6, Tues & Thurs 10-6, Fri 12-5, Sat 9-Noon
Friends of the Library Group

MONTEZUMA

P MONTEZUMA PUBLIC LIBRARY*, 500 E Main St, 50171. (Mail add: PO Box 158, 50171-0158), SAN 305-5817. Tel: 641-623-3417. FAX: 641-623-3339. E-mail: montepl@zumatel.net. *Dir,* Diane M Kitzmann
Founded 1916. Circ 20,500
Library Holdings: Bk Vols 15,407; Per Subs 55
Wireless access
Open Mon-Wed 11:30-5:30, Thurs 11:30-6, Fri 10-4, Sat 9:30-Noon

MONTICELLO

P ROSS & ELIZABETH BATY MONTICELLO PUBLIC LIBRARY*, 205 E Grand St, 52310-1617. SAN 376-7493. Tel: 319-465-3354. FAX: 319-465-4587. Web Site: www.monticello.lib.ia.us. *Dir,* Michelle Turnis; E-mail: michelleturnis@monticello.lib.ia.us
Library Holdings: Bk Vols 19,326; Per Subs 54
Wireless access
Open Mon-Thurs 9-7, Fri 9-6, Sat 9-1
Friends of the Library Group

MONTROSE

P MONTROSE PUBLIC LIBRARY*, 200 Main St, 52639. (Mail add: PO Box 100, 52639-0100), SAN 305-5833. Tel: 319-463-5532. FAX: 319-463-5532. E-mail: montroselibrary12@yahoo.com. Web Site: www.leeco.lib.ia.us/montrose. *Dir,* Lana Clark; *Ch,* Joann Fenn
Founded 1928. Pop 957; Circ 14,334
Library Holdings: DVDs 150; Bk Titles 10,034; Per Subs 28
Subject Interests: Local hist
Wireless access
Open Mon & Wed-Fri 3-7, Sat 9-1

MOORHEAD

P MOORHEAD PUBLIC LIBRARY*, 100 Oak St, 51558. Tel: 712-886-5211. *Dir,* Carolyn Archer
Library Holdings: Bk Vols 3,500; Per Subs 11
Open Sat 1-4
Friends of the Library Group

MORAVIA

P MORAVIA PUBLIC LIBRARY*, 100 E Chariton, 52571. SAN 305-5841. Tel: 641-724-3440. FAX: 641-724-3440. E-mail: webmaster@moravia.lib.ia.us. Web Site; www.moravia.lib.ia.us. *Dir,* Ann Repp; E-mail: moravialibrary@iowatelecom.net
Founded 1941. Pop 688
Library Holdings: CDs 220; DVDs 862; Large Print Bks 315; Bk Titles 12,015; Per Subs 12; Spec Interest Per Sub 3; Talking Bks 28
Subject Interests: Genealogy, Local hist
Automation Activity & Vendor Info: (Cataloging) Follett Software; (Circulation) Follett Software
Wireless access
Open Mon & Thurs 10-6, Wed 9-2:30, Sat 9-1:30
Friends of the Library Group

MORLEY

P MORLEY PUBLIC LIBRARY*, 507 Vine St, 52312. SAN 305-585X. Tel: 319-489-9271. FAX: 319-489-9271. Web Site: www.morley.lib.ia.us. *Dir,* Leanne Ketelsen; E-mail: leanne.ketelsen@morley.lib.ia.us
Pop 95; Circ 1,600
Library Holdings: Bk Titles 7,000; Per Subs 10
Wireless access
Open Mon 10-6, Sat 8am-10am

MORNING SUN

P MELLINGER MEMORIAL LIBRARY*, 11 Division St, 52640. (Mail add: PO Box 8, 52640-0008), SAN 305-5868. Tel: 319-868-7505. FAX: 319-868-4136. E-mail: mslib@louisacomm.net. Web Site: www.morningsun.lib.ia.us. *Dir,* Arnie Herrick
Founded 1915. Pop 956; Circ 9,538
Library Holdings: Bk Titles 8,664; Per Subs 41
Wireless access
Open Mon 10-6, Tues-Fri 10-5, Sat 10-1
Friends of the Library Group

MOULTON

P GARRETT MEMORIAL LIBRARY*, 123 S Main, 52572. SAN 305-5876. Tel: 641-642-3664. FAX: 641-642-3664. Web Site: www.moulton.lib.ia.us. *Libr Dir,* Lindsey Hanes; E-mail: lindsey.hanes@moulton.lib.ia.us; *Asst Libr Dir,* Wilma Stevenson
Founded 1968. Pop 658; Circ 6,831
Library Holdings: Bk Vols 10,000; Per Subs 35
Subject Interests: Genealogy
Automation Activity & Vendor Info: (Circulation) Follett Software
Wireless access
Open Mon 1-6, Tues-Thurs 1-5, Fri & Sat 10-1

MOUNT AYR

P MOUNT AYR PUBLIC LIBRARY*, 121 W Monroe St, 50854. SAN 305-5884. Tel: 641-464-2159. FAX: 641-464-2159. E-mail: mlibrary@mchsi.com. Web Site: www.mtayr.lib.ia.us. *Dir,* Mary Kathryn Gepner; *Assoc Librn,* Bobbie Bainum; *Asst Librn,* Dorothy Main
Founded 1916. Pop 1,938; Circ 33,124
Library Holdings: Bk Vols 14,000; Per Subs 65
Subject Interests: Genealogy, Local hist
Automation Activity & Vendor Info: (Cataloging) Follett Software; (Circulation) Follett Software
Open Mon-Wed & Fri 1:30-5, Thurs 10:30-6, Sat 9:30-12

MOUNT PLEASANT

C IOWA WESLEYAN UNIVERSITY, J Raymond Chadwick Library, 107 W Broad St, 52641. SAN 305-5906. Tel: 319-385-6316. Interlibrary Loan Service Tel: 319-385-6318. FAX: 319-385-6324. Reference E-mail: reference@iw.edu. Web Site: iw.edu/library. *Dir,* Paula Wiley; E-mail: paula.wiley@iw.edu; *E-Res/Instrul Librn,* Jeff Meyer; E-mail: jeff.meyer@iw.edu; *Circ Assoc,* Brianna Enearl; E-mail: bri.enearl@iw.edu; Staff 3 (MLS 3)
Founded 1857. Enrl 834; Fac 48; Highest Degree: Master
Library Holdings: Bk Titles 74,509; Bk Vols 109,567; Per Subs 441
Special Collections: German-Americanism; Iowa Conference of the United Methodist Church Archives; Iowa History. State Document Depository
Automation Activity & Vendor Info: (Circulation) OCLC Worldshare Management Services; (Media Booking) OCLC Worldshare Management Services; (OPAC) OCLC Worldshare Management Services
Wireless access
Publications: Library Guides
Partic in Iowa Academic Library Alliance; Iowa Private Academic Library Consortium; OCLC Online Computer Library Center, Inc
Open Mon-Thurs 7:30am-11pm, Fri 7:30-5, Sun 2-11

P MOUNT PLEASANT PUBLIC LIBRARY*, 307 E Monroe, Ste 101, 52641. SAN 305-5914. Tel: 319-385-1490. FAX: 319-385-1491. Web Site: www.mountpleasantiowalibrary.com. *Dir,* Jeffrey Meyer; E-mail: mtpleasant.director@gmail.com; Staff 10 (MLS 3, Non-MLS 7)
Founded 1901. Pop 8,668; Circ 100,000
Jul 2015-Jun 2016 Income $360,279, State $6,606, City $300,000, County $25,460, Locally Generated Income $28,213. Mats Exp $97,231, Books $45,309, Per/Ser (Incl. Access Fees) $7,900, Other Print Mats $38,378, AV Mat $4,455, Electronic Ref Mat (Incl. Access Fees) $1,189. Sal $235,000 (Prof $180,000)
Library Holdings: Audiobooks 1,807; AV Mats 2,007; Bks on Deafness & Sign Lang 22; Braille Volumes 1; CDs 343; DVDs 2,007; Electronic Media & Resources 4; Large Print Bks 4,434; Microforms 5; Bk Vols 46,005; Per Subs 121; Videos 868
Special Collections: Henry County & Mt Pleasant History
Automation Activity & Vendor Info: (Acquisitions) Biblionix; (Cataloging) Biblionix; (Circulation) Biblionix; (OPAC) Biblionix
Wireless access
Special Services for the Deaf - TDD equip
Open Mon-Thurs 9-8, Fri 9-5:30, Sat 9-2
Friends of the Library Group

MOUNT VERNON

C CORNELL COLLEGE, Russell D Cole Library, 620 Third St SW, 52314-1012. SAN 305-5922. Tel: 319-895-4271. E-mail: library@cornellcollege.edu. Web Site: www.cornellcollege.edu/library. *Dir,* Gregory Cotton; Tel: 319-895-4454, E-mail: gcotton@cornellcollege.edu; Staff 5.5 (MLS 5.5)
Founded 1853. Enrl 1,050; Fac 70; Highest Degree: Master
Library Holdings: AV Mats 7,599; Bk Vols 139,670; Per Subs 600; Talking Bks 1,871
Automation Activity & Vendor Info: (Acquisitions) OCLC Worldshare Management Services; (Cataloging) OCLC Worldshare Management Services; (Circulation) OCLC Worldshare Management Services; (Course Reserve) OCLC Worldshare Management Services; (Serials) OCLC Worldshare Management Services
Wireless access
Partic in Iowa Academic Library Alliance; OCLC Online Computer Library Center, Inc
Open Mon-Thurs 8am-11pm, Fri 8-5, Sat 10-4, Sun Noon-11pm

MOVILLE

P WOODBURY COUNTY LIBRARY*, 825 Main St, 51039. (Mail add: PO Box 625, 52052), SAN 341-9401. Tel: 712-873-3322. FAX: 712-873-3744. E-mail: wcolib@wiatel.net. Web Site: www.woodburycounty.lib.ia.us. *Dir,* Donna Chapman; Staff 1 (MLS 1)
Founded 1949. Pop 12,000
Library Holdings: Bk Titles 53,000; Per Subs 40
Subject Interests: Local hist
Open Mon & Wed 8-6, Tues, Thurs & Fri 8-5, Sat 8-1
Friends of the Library Group
Branches: 3
CORD MEMORIAL LIBRARY, 215 Main St, Danbury, 51019, SAN 341-9436. Tel: 712-883-2207. E-mail: danburylib@gmail.com. *Librn,* Larraine Christensen
Pop 384
Library Holdings: Bk Vols 3,500
Open Tues & Thurs 1-4:30 & 7-9, Sat 9:30-3
Friends of the Library Group
HORNICK BRANCH, 510 Main St, Hornick, 51026. (Mail add: PO Box 26, Hornick, 51026), SAN 341-9460. Tel: 712-874-3616. E-mail: horlib@wiatel.net. *Librn,* Bobbi Moore
Library Holdings: Bk Vols 3,500
Open Mon 2-6, Wed 9-12 & 1-5:30, Fri 9-12
Friends of the Library Group
PIERSON BRANCH, 201 Main St, Pierson, 51048, SAN 341-9495. Tel: 712-375-7535. E-mail: piersonlibrary@gmail.com. *Librn,* Jane Schieuer
Library Holdings: Bk Vols 3,500
Open Mon & Wed 10-2:30, Thurs 4-7 (Summer); Mon 10-2 & 3:30-6:30, Wed 10-2, Thurs 3:30-6:30 (Winter)
Friends of the Library Group
Bookmobiles: 1. Libr Contact, Kyle Ford

MURRAY

P MURRAY PUBLIC LIBRARY, 416 Maple St, 50174. (Mail add: PO Box 186, 50174-0186), SAN 305-5930. Tel: 641-447-2711. E-mail: murray.library@grm.net. *Dir,* Brenda Reasoner
Pop 750; Circ 2,400
Library Holdings: Bk Titles 10,000; Per Subs 87
Wireless access
Open Mon & Wed 12-6, Fri 12-5, Sat 9-12

MUSCATINE

S MUSCATINE ART CENTER, Art Reference Library, 1314 Mulberry Ave, 52761. SAN 373-4544. Tel: 563-263-8282. FAX: 563-263-4702. E-mail: art@muscatineiowa.gov. Web Site: www.muscatineartcenter.org. *Coordr,* Lynn Bartenhagen; E-mail: lbartenhagen@muscatineiowa.gov
Library Holdings: Bk Vols 1,000
Subject Interests: Am fine art, Decorative art
Open Tues, Wed & Fri 10-5, Thurs 10-7, Sat & Sun 1-5

P MUSSER PUBLIC LIBRARY*, 408 E Second St, 52761. SAN 305-5965. Tel: 563-263-3065. Circulation Tel: 563-263-3065, Ext 3. Reference Tel: 563-263-3065, Ext 4. FAX: 563-264-1033. E-mail: refmus@muscatineiowa.gov. Web Site: www.musserpubliclibrary.org. *Dir,* Pam Collins; Tel: 563-263-3065, Ext 104, E-mail: pcollins@muscatineiowa.gov; *Asst Dir,* Robert Fiedler; Tel: 563-263-3065, Ext 125, E-mail: rfiedler@muscatineiowa.gov; *Youth Serv Mgr,* Betty Collins; Tel: 563-263-3065, Ext 109, E-mail: bcollins@muscatineiowa.gov; *Archivist, Youth Serv,* Jenny Howell; Tel: 563-263-3065, Ext 105, E-mail: jhowell@muscatineiowa.gov; *ILL,* Dan Chapman; E-mail: dchapman@muscatineiowa.gov; *Tech Serv,* Mallory Moffitt; Tel: 563-263-3065, Ext 122, E-mail: mmoffitt@muscatineiowa.gov; Staff 18 (MLS 4, Non-MLS 14)

Founded 1901. Pop 33,592; Circ 268,295
Library Holdings: Bk Titles 130,673; Bk Vols 135,997; Per Subs 225
Special Collections: Area Servicemen; The Little House Books by Laura Ingalls Wilder. Oral History
Subject Interests: Local hist, WWII
Automation Activity & Vendor Info: (Circulation) Innovative Interfaces, Inc
Wireless access
Partic in RiverShare Libraries
Open Mon-Fri 10-8, Sat 10-2, Sun 1-3
Friends of the Library Group

NASHUA

P NASHUA PUBLIC LIBRARY, 220 Brasher St, 50658. (Mail add: PO Box 619, 50658-0619), SAN 305-5973. Tel: 641-435-4635. FAX: 641-435-4635. E-mail: naslib@butler-bremer.com. Web Site: www.nashua.lib.ia.us. *Libr Dir,* Heather Hackman; E-mail: director@nashua.lib.ia.us
Founded 1902. Pop 2,000; Circ 17,428
Library Holdings: Large Print Bks 380; Bk Vols 13,994; Per Subs 63
Special Collections: Nashua Reporter & Weekly Nashua Post, 1872-present, micro
Wireless access
Open Mon-Wed 10-6, Thurs 10-5, Sat 10-1

NEVADA

P NEVADA PUBLIC LIBRARY, 631 K Ave, 50201. SAN 305-5981. Tel: 515-382-2628. FAX: 515-382-3552. E-mail: npl@nevada.lib.ia.us. Web Site: nevada.lib.ia.us. *Dir,* Position Currently Open; *Asst Dir, Interim Dir,* Amanda Bellis; E-mail: amanda@nevada.lib.ia.us; *Youth Librn,* Travis Landuis; E-mail: travis@nevada.lib.ia.us; Staff 6 (MLS 3, Non-MLS 3)
Founded 1876. Pop 7,000; Circ 100,000
Jul 2014-Jun 2015 Income $401,016, State $5,740, City $324,772, County $43,251, Locally Generated Income $27,253. Mats Exp $55,621, Books $38,584, Per/Ser (Incl. Access Fees) $4,000, Manu Arch $4,000, Micro $150, AV Mat $8,737, Electronic Ref Mat (Incl. Access Fees) $150. Sal $385,542
Library Holdings: Audiobooks 7,113; DVDs 4,899; e-books 28,919; Electronic Media & Resources 8,490; Large Print Bks 3,540; Bk Vols 57,751; Per Subs 142
Special Collections: Geneology (Obits)
Automation Activity & Vendor Info: (Cataloging) Baker & Taylor; (Circulation) Follett Software; (OPAC) Follett Software
Wireless access
Function: 24/7 Electronic res, Adult bk club, After school storytime, Bk club(s), Bks on CD, CD-ROM, Children's prog, Computer training, Computers for patron use, Digital talking bks, Free DVD rentals, Holiday prog, Home delivery & serv to seniorr ctr & nursing homes, Homebound delivery serv, ILL available, Internet access, Life-long learning prog for all ages, Magazines, Mail & tel request accepted, Meeting rooms, Microfiche/film & reading machines, Movies, Music CDs, Online cat, Outreach serv, OverDrive digital audio bks, Photocopying/Printing, Preschool reading prog, Prog for adults, Prog for children & young adult, Ref serv available, Scanner, Senior computer classes, Senior outreach, Serves people with intellectual disabilities, Spanish lang bks, Story hour, Study rm, Summer & winter reading prog, Summer reading prog, Tax forms, Teen prog, Telephone ref, Wheelchair accessible, Winter reading prog
Open Mon-Thurs 10-8, Fri 10-6, Sat 10-4
Friends of the Library Group

NEW ALBIN

P NEW ALBIN PUBLIC LIBRARY, 176 Elm St, 52160. (Mail add: PO Box 12, 52160-0012), SAN 305-599X. Tel: 563-544-4747. FAX: 563-544-4757. E-mail: library@acegroup.cc. Web Site: newalbinpubliclibrary.weebly.com.
Pop 534; Circ 3,821
Library Holdings: Bk Titles 5,500; Per Subs 45
Wireless access
Open Mon & Thurs 4-7, Tues, Wed & Fri 9-11 & 4-7

NEW HAMPTON

P NEW HAMPTON PUBLIC LIBRARY*, 20 W Spring St, 50659. SAN 305-6007. Tel: 641-394-2184. FAX: 641-394-5482. Web Site: www.nhpl.weebly.com. *Dir,* Carrie Becker; E-mail: director@newhampton.lib.ia.us; Staff 3 (MLS 1, Non-MLS 2)
Pop 3,660; Circ 57,100
Library Holdings: CDs 128; Bk Vols 25,000; Per Subs 75; Talking Bks 1,506; Videos 650
Automation Activity & Vendor Info: (Cataloging) Follett Software; (Circulation) Follett Software
Wireless access
Open Mon-Thurs 10-7:30, Fri 10-5, Sat 10-2
Friends of the Library Group

NEW HARTFORD

P ELIZABETH RASMUSSEN MARTIN MEMORIAL LIBRARY*, 406 Packwaukee, 50660. (Mail add: PO Box 292, 50660-0292), SAN 305-6015. Tel: 319-983-2533. FAX: 319-983-2533. Web Site: www.newhartford.lib.ia.us. *Dir,* Jill Norton; E-mail: director@newhartford.lib.ia.us
Pop 516; Circ 4,531
Library Holdings: Bk Titles 11,074; Per Subs 12
Wireless access
Open Tues-Fri 11-6, Sat 9-11
Friends of the Library Group

NEW LONDON

P H J NUGEN PUBLIC LIBRARY, 103 E Main St, 52645. SAN 305-6023. Tel: 319-367-7704. FAX: 319-367-7710. Web Site: www.newlondon.lib.ia.us. *Libr Dir,* Mrs Taelor Garza Donnolly; E-mail: tgarza@newlondon.lib.ia.us; *Asst Libr Dir,* Brittney Lerner; E-mail: blerner@newlondon.lib.ia.us; *Libr Asst,* Angelia Manning; E-mail: amanning@newlondon.lib.ia.us
Founded 1937. Pop 1,857
Library Holdings: Bk Titles 15,000; Per Subs 39
Wireless access
Open Mon & Wed 10-7, Tues & Thurs 10-6, Fri 10-5, Sat 10-2

NEW MARKET

P NEW MARKET PUBLIC LIBRARY, 407 Main St, 51646. (Mail add: PO Box 68, 51646-0116), SAN 305-6031. Tel: 712-585-3467. E-mail: nmlibrary@myfmtc.com. Web Site: newmarketia.com/library. *Librn,* Tonya Kennedy
Pop 584; Circ 1,841
Library Holdings: Bk Titles 3,474; Per Subs 20
Wireless access
Open Tues 2-4:30, Thurs 1-5, Sat 1:30-3:30

NEW SHARON

P STILWELL PUBLIC LIBRARY, (Formerly New Sharon Public Library), 107 W Maple, 50207. (Mail add: PO Box 72, 50207), SAN 305-604X. Tel: 641-637-4049. E-mail: nsstilwell72@gmail.com. Web Site: newsharon.lib.ia.us/library-information, newsharoniowa.com/library. *Dir,* Diane Klinker; E-mail: klinkerd@newsharon.lib.ia.us; *Youth Librn,* Allison Pollpeter
Pop 1,225; Circ 50,013
Library Holdings: Bk Titles 10,000; Bk Vols 15,000
Wireless access
Open Mon 12-7, Tues 3-7, Wed & Thurs 12-5, Sat 9-Noon

NEW VIRGINIA

P NEW VIRGINIA PUBLIC LIBRARY*, 504 Book Alley, 50210. (Mail add: PO Box 304, 50210-0304), SAN 305-6058. Tel: 641-449-3614. E-mail: nvlibr@windstream.net. Web Site: newvirginia.lib.ia.us. *Libr Dir,* Tracee Dembinski; *Libr Asst,* Phyllis Travis
Founded 1972. Circ 7,969
Library Holdings: Bks on Deafness & Sign Lang 25; Bk Vols 8,000; Per Subs 20
Automation Activity & Vendor Info: (Cataloging) LibraryWorld, Inc
Wireless access
Function: Adult bk club, Children's prog, Computers for patron use, Electronic databases & coll, For res purposes, ILL available, Internet access, Makerspace, Meeting rooms, Movies, Online cat, Outreach serv, OverDrive digital audio bks, Photocopying/Printing, Prog for adults, Prog for children & young adult, Ref & res, STEM programs, Story hour, Summer & winter reading prog, Summer reading prog, Teen prog, Wheelchair accessible, Winter reading prog
Open Tues & Thurs 4-8, Wed 9-11 & 1-8, Sat 9-Noon
Friends of the Library Group

NEWELL

P NEWELL PUBLIC LIBRARY*, 205 E Second St, 50568. (Mail add: PO Box 667, 50568-0667), SAN 305-6066. Tel: 712-272-4334. FAX: 712-272-4334. Web Site: www.newell.lib.ia.us. *Libr Dir,* Sherri Peterson; E-mail: sherri@newell.lib.ia.us
Founded 1883. Pop 889; Circ 7,492
Library Holdings: AV Mats 667; Bk Vols 16,113; Per Subs 47; Talking Bks 112
Automation Activity & Vendor Info: (Cataloging) Book Systems; (Circulation) Book Systems
Wireless access

Open Mon 2-8, Tues, Wed & Fri 2-5, Thurs 10-12 & 1-5, Sat 9-11
Friends of the Library Group

NEWHALL

P NEWHALL PUBLIC LIBRARY*, 109 Railroad St E, 52315. (Mail add: PO Box 348, 52315-0348), SAN 376-5415. Tel: 319-223-5510. FAX: 319-223-5510. Web Site: www.newhall.lib.ia.us. *Dir,* April Stull; E-mail: astull@newhall.lib.ia.us
Founded 1882. Pop 875; Circ 974; Fac 2
Library Holdings: Bk Vols 7,800; Per Subs 15
Automation Activity & Vendor Info: (Cataloging) Biblionix/Apollo; (Circulation) Biblionix/Apollo
Wireless access
Function: 24/7 Online cat, Accelerated reader prog, Adult bk club, Bk club(s), Bks on CD, Children's prog, Computers for patron use, E-Readers, Free DVD rentals, Internet access, Laminating, Magazines, Mail & tel request accepted, Makerspace, Meeting rooms, Movies, Notary serv, Online cat, Online ref, OverDrive digital audio bks, Preschool reading prog, Prog for adults, Prog for children & young adult, Res assist avail, Scanner, Summer & winter reading prog, Summer reading prog, Winter reading prog
Open Mon 2-7, Tues & Thurs 1-6, Wed & Fri 9-12 & 1-6, Sat 9-11
Restriction: Lending libr only via mail

NEWTON

NEWTON CORRECTIONAL FACILITY
S CORRECTIONAL RELEASE CENTER LIBRARY*, 307 S 60th Ave W, 50208. (Mail add: PO Box 218, 50208-0218). Tel: 641-792-7552, Ext 357. FAX: 641-792-9288.
Library Holdings: Bk Vols 5,000; Per Subs 40
Open Mon-Fri 7:30-4
S NCF LIBRARY*, 307 S 60th Ave W, 50208. (Mail add: PO Box 218, 50208-0218). Tel: 641-792-7552, Ext 568. FAX: 641-791-1680. *Library Contact,* Brian Pfeifer
Library Holdings: Bk Vols 5,000; Per Subs 25
Open Mon-Fri 8-10:30 & 12:30-4

P NEWTON PUBLIC LIBRARY, 100 N Third Ave W, 50208. (Mail add: PO Box 746, 50208-0746), SAN 305-6082. Tel: 641-792-4108. FAX: 641-791-0729. E-mail: newtonpl@newton.lib.ia.us. Web Site: www.newton.lib.ia.us. *Libr Dir,* Nicole Terry; E-mail: nterry@newton.lib.ia.us; *Pub Serv Librn,* Rebecca Klein; E-mail: rklein@newton.lib.ia.us; *Youth Serv Librn,* Phylis Peter; E-mail: ppeter@newton.lib.ia.us
Founded 1896. Pop 17,000; Circ 161,468
Library Holdings: Bk Vols 80,014; Per Subs 141
Special Collections: Iowa Coll; Newton Daily Newspaper. State Document Depository
Automation Activity & Vendor Info: (Acquisitions) SirsiDynix; (Cataloging) SirsiDynix; (Circulation) SirsiDynix; (OPAC) SirsiDynix; (Serials) SirsiDynix
Wireless access
Partic in OCLC Online Computer Library Center, Inc
Open Mon-Thurs 10-8, Sat 10-2
Friends of the Library Group

NORA SPRINGS

P NORA SPRINGS PUBLIC LIBRARY*, 45 N Hawkeye Ave, 50458. (Mail add: PO Box 337, 50458-0337), SAN 305-6090. Tel: 641-749-5569. E-mail: nslib1@myomnitel.com. Web Site: www.youseemore.com/nilc/NoraSprings. *Dir,* Renee Bartling
Pop 1,532; Circ 10,706
Library Holdings: Bk Vols 8,000; Per Subs 46
Automation Activity & Vendor Info: (Cataloging) Follett Software; (Circulation) Follett Software
Open Mon & Fri 9-5:30, Tues & Thurs 1:30-5:30, Wed 1:30-7, Sat 9-12

NORTH ENGLISH

P NORTH ENGLISH PUBLIC LIBRARY*, 123 S Main, 52316. (Mail add: PO Box 427, 52316-0427), SAN 305-6104. Tel: 319-664-3725. FAX: 319-664-3725. Web Site: www.northenglish.lib.ia.us. *Dir,* Annette Shannahan; E-mail: ashannahan@northenglish.lib.ia.us
Founded 1934. Pop 1,040; Circ 19,000
Library Holdings: Bk Vols 11,000
Special Collections: North English Record (paper) 1902-2004
Automation Activity & Vendor Info: (Acquisitions) Follett Software
Wireless access
Partic in Iowa Libr Asn
Open Mon, Tues & Thurs 1-5:30, Wed 1-6, Fri 9-5, Sat 9-12:30

NORTH LIBERTY

P NORTH LIBERTY LIBRARY, 520 W Cherry St, 52317-9797. (Mail add: PO Box 320, 52317-0320), SAN 323-5998. Tel: 319-626-5701. Administration Tel: 319-626-5778. E-mail: nlcl@northlibertyiowa.org. Web Site: www.northlibertylibrary.org. *Libr Dir,* Jennifer Garner; E-mail: jgarner@northlibertyiowa.org; *Asst Dir,* Jennifer Jordebrek; E-mail: jjordebrek@northlibertyiowa.org; *Ad,* Amy Golly; E-mail: agolly@northlibertyiowa.org; *Coll Develop Librn,* Andrew Frisbie; E-mail: afrisbie@northlibertyiowa.org; *Family Serv Librn,* Emily Tabor; E-mail: etabor@northlibertyiowa.org; *Pub Serv Librn,* Kellee Forkenbrock; E-mail: kforkenbrock@northlibertyiowa.org; *Youth & Teen Serv Librn,* Erin Silva; E-mail: esilva@northlibertyiowa.org; *Mkt Coordr,* Melanie Harrison; E-mail: mharrison@northlibertyiowa.org. Subject Specialists: *Literacy,* Jennifer Jordebrek; Staff 18 (MLS 8, Non-MLS 10)
Founded 1986. Pop 19,228
Library Holdings: Audiobooks 2,365; DVDs 5,068; e-books 43,202; Large Print Bks 581; Bk Titles 37,493; Bk Vols 40,550; Per Subs 69
Special Collections: Bike Locks; Cake pans; Caregiver story time kits; Speck Air Quality monitors
Subject Interests: Early childhood
Automation Activity & Vendor Info: (Acquisitions) Innovative Interfaces, Inc; (Cataloging) Innovative Interfaces, Inc; (Circulation) Innovative Interfaces, Inc; (OPAC) Innovative Interfaces, Inc; (Serials) Innovative Interfaces, Inc
Wireless access
Function: 24/7 Electronic res, 24/7 Online cat, Activity rm, Adult bk club, Art exhibits, Art programs, Audiobks on Playaways & MP3, Audiobks via web, Bk club(s), Bks on CD, Butterfly Garden, Children's prog, Computer training, Computers for patron use, Distance learning, E-Readers, Electronic databases & coll, Family literacy, Free DVD rentals, Games & aids for people with disabilities, Holiday prog, Home delivery & serv to seniorr ctr & nursing homes, Homebound delivery serv, ILL available, Internet access, Magazines, Mail loans to mem, Mango lang, Meeting rooms, Movies, Museum passes, Notary serv, Online cat, Online info literacy tutorials on the web & in blackboard, Outreach serv, OverDrive digital audio bks, Photocopying/Printing, Preschool outreach, Preschool reading prog, Printer for laptops & handheld devices, Prog for adults, Prog for children & young adult, Ref serv available, Scanner, Senior computer classes, Senior outreach, Serves people with intellectual disabilities, Spoken cassettes & CDs, STEM programs, Story hour, Study rm, Summer & winter reading prog, Summer reading prog, Teen prog, Telephone ref, Wheelchair accessible, Winter reading prog, Workshops
Publications: Brochure (Quarterly); Library Newsletter (Monthly)
Partic in Association for Rural & Small Libraries; Iowa Libr Asn; State of Iowa Libraries Online
Open Mon-Thurs 8-8, Fri 8-5, Sat 10-5, Sun 1-4
Friends of the Library Group

NORTHWOOD

P NORTHWOOD PUBLIC LIBRARY*, 906 First Ave S, 50459. (Mail add: PO Box 137, 50459-0137), SAN 305-6112. Tel: 641-324-1340. E-mail: northwoodlibrary@mchsi.com. Web Site: www.youseemore.com/NILC/Northwood. *Libr Dir,* Morgan Johnson
Pop 2,193; Circ 26,149
Library Holdings: Bk Titles 19,000; Bk Vols 22,000; Per Subs 56
Wireless access
Open Mon & Fri 1-5, Tues & Thurs 10-7, Sat 10-2
Friends of the Library Group

NORWALK

P NORWALK EASTER PUBLIC LIBRARY*, 1051 North Ave, 50211. SAN 305-6120. Tel: 515-981-0217. FAX: 515-981-4346. Web Site: norwalk.iowa.gov/government/departments/library. *Libr Dir,* Holly Sealine; E-mail: hsealine@norwalk.iowa.gov; *Asst Dir,* Annette Clark; E-mail: annettec@norwalk.iowa.gov; *Youth & Teen Serv Librn,* Mallory Inman; E-mail: malloryi@norwalk.iowa.gov; Staff 15 (MLS 3, Non-MLS 12)
Founded 1962. Pop 10,000; Circ 71,943
Automation Activity & Vendor Info: (Acquisitions) Biblionix/Apollo; (Cataloging) Biblionix/Apollo; (Circulation) Biblionix/Apollo; (OPAC) Biblionix/Apollo
Wireless access
Function: 24/7 Electronic res, 24/7 Online cat, Activity rm, Adult bk club, Adult literacy prog, Bk club(s), Bks on CD, Children's prog, Computers for patron use, Free DVD rentals, Home delivery & serv to seniorr ctr & nursing homes, Homebound delivery serv, ILL available, Internet access, Laminating, Life-long learning prog for all ages, Magazines, Notary serv, Online cat, Outreach serv, OverDrive digital audio bks, Photocopying/Printing, Preschool outreach, Prog for adults, Prog for children & young adult, Scanner, Story hour, Study rm, Summer reading prog, Teen prog, Wheelchair accessible
Special Services for the Deaf - Closed caption videos
Special Services for the Blind - Bks on CD
Open Mon-Thurs 10-8, Fri 11-6, Sat 10-5, Sun 1-4

NORWAY

P NORWAY PUBLIC LIBRARY, 108 Railroad St, 52318. (Mail add: PO Box 7, 52318-0007), SAN 320-829X. Tel: 319-227-7487. FAX: 319-227-7487. E-mail: norwaypl@southslope.net. *Dir,* Ms Sydney Kaup
Founded 1976. Pop 633; Circ 5,348
Library Holdings: Bk Titles 9,000; Per Subs 23
Wireless access
Open Tues & Thurs 2-7, Fri 10-1 & 2-6, Sat 9-12
Friends of the Library Group

OAKLAND

P ECKELS MEMORIAL LIBRARY, 207 S Hwy 6, 51560. (Mail add: PO Box 519, 51560-0519), SAN 305-6147. Tel: 712-482-6668. FAX: 712-482-6668. E-mail: eckelslibrary@gmail.com. Web Site: eckelslibrary.com. *Dir,* Kari Rose
Pop 1,700; Circ 13,027
Library Holdings: Bk Titles 26,000; Per Subs 38
Wireless access
Open Mon, Tues, Thurs & Fri 10-5, Wed 10-6, Sat 10-Noon

OCHEYEDAN

P OCHEYEDAN PUBLIC LIBRARY*, 874 Main St, 51354. (Mail add: PO Box 427, 51354-0427), SAN 305-6155. Tel: 712-758-3352. FAX: 712-758-3352. Web Site: www.ocheyedan.lib.ia.us. *Dir,* Bev Bjork; E-mail: director@ocheyedan.lib.ia.us
Founded 1912. Pop 536; Circ 13,000
Library Holdings: DVDs 1,000; Bk Vols 11,180; Per Subs 45; Talking Bks 50; Videos 200
Wireless access
Open Tues 9:30-5:30, Wed 1-6, Thurs 10-5, Fri 1-5:30, Sat 10-12

ODEBOLT

P FIELD-CARNEGIE LIBRARY*, 200 Walnut St, 51458. SAN 305-6163. Tel: 712-668-2718. FAX: 712-668-4380. E-mail: fieldcar@netins.net. Web Site: www.odebolt.lib.ia.us. *Dir,* Julie Childers
Founded 1898. Pop 1,256; Circ 17,150
Library Holdings: Bk Vols 13,922; Per Subs 53
Wireless access
Open Mon, Tues, Thurs & Fri 2-6, Wed 10-12, Sat 9-12
Friends of the Library Group

OELWEIN

P OELWEIN PUBLIC LIBRARY*, 201 E Charles St, 50662-1939. SAN 305-6171. Tel: 319-283-1515. FAX: 319-283-6646. E-mail: oelwein@oelwein.lib.ia.us. Web Site: www.oelwein.lib.ia.us. *Dir,* Susan Macken; *Asst Dir,* Catherine Harris
Founded 1909. Pop 7,564; Circ 70,842
Library Holdings: Bk Vols 44,000; Per Subs 120
Special Collections: Oral History
Automation Activity & Vendor Info: (Cataloging) Biblionix; (Circulation) Biblionix
Wireless access
Open Mon-Thurs 9:30-8, Fri 9:30-5:30, Sat 9:30-4, Sun 2-5:30
Friends of the Library Group

OGDEN

P LEONARD A GOOD COMMUNITY LIBRARY*, 208 W Mulberry St, 50212. (Mail add: PO Box 696, 50212-0696), SAN 305-618X. Tel: 515-275-4550. E-mail: ogdenlibrary@netins.net. Web Site: www.ogden.lib.ia.us. *Dir,* Lori Reutter
Founded 1947. Pop 2,000; Circ 38,911
Library Holdings: Bk Titles 12,000; Per Subs 31
Wireless access
Open Mon 10-7, Tues & Fri 1-5, Wed & Thurs 9-5, Sat 9-Noon

OLIN

P OLIN PUBLIC LIBRARY*, 301 Parkway St, 52320. (Mail add: PO Box 318, 52320-0318), SAN 305-6198. Tel: 319-484-2944. FAX: 319-484-2944. Web Site: www.olin.lib.ia.us. *Dir,* Leanne M Ketelsen; E-mail: lketelsen@olin.lib.ia.us
Pop 735; Circ 3,376
Library Holdings: Bk Titles 6,365; Per Subs 29
Open Tues, Thurs & Fri 10-5, Wed 10-7, Sat 8-Noon

ONAWA

P ONAWA PUBLIC LIBRARY*, 707 Iowa Ave, 51040. SAN 305-6201. Tel: 712-423-1733. FAX: 712-433-4622. Web Site: www.onawa.lib.ia.us. *Dir,* Amy McDermott; E-mail: amy.m@onawa.lib.ia.us; *Asst Dir,* Chris Zink; E-mail: chris.z@onawa.lib.ia.us; Staff 2 (Non-MLS 2)
Founded 1907. Pop 6,401; Circ 53,028
Library Holdings: CDs 323; DVDs 1,220; e-books 15,607; Large Print Bks 1,190; Microforms 200; Bk Titles 45,650; Bk Vols 46,840; Per Subs 40
Subject Interests: Genealogy, Local hist
Automation Activity & Vendor Info: (Cataloging) Book Systems; (Circulation) Book Systems
Wireless access
Open Mon & Wed 11-6, Tues & Thurs 11-8, Fri & Sat 11-5
Friends of the Library Group

ORANGE CITY

C NORTHWESTERN COLLEGE*, DeWitt Learning Commons & Library, 101 Seventh St SW, 51041. SAN 305-621X. Tel: 712-707-7234. FAX: 712-707-7247. E-mail: library@nwciowa.edu. Web Site: library.nwciowa.edu. *Libr Dir,* Greta Grond; Tel: 712-707-7248, E-mail: ggrond@nwciowa.edu; *Info Literacy Librn, Sr Ref Librn,* Anne Mead; Tel: 712-707-7237, E-mail: amead@nwciowa.edu; *Archivist, Ref Librn,* Dr Doug Anderson; Tel: 712-707-7402, E-mail: firth@nwciowa.edu; *Access Serv Coordr,* Sara Huyser; Tel: 712-707-7311, E-mail: sara.huyser@nwciowa.edu; *Acq & Ser Coordr,* Heather Sas; Tel: 712-707-7235, E-mail: heather.sas@nwciowa.edu; *Cataloger, Libr Syst Spec,* Sherri Langton; Tel: 712-707-7236, E-mail: slangton@nwciowa.edu; Staff 7 (MLS 4, Non-MLS 3)
Founded 1882. Enrl 1,280; Fac 65; Highest Degree: Bachelor
Library Holdings: Bk Titles 98,000; Bk Vols 108,000; Per Subs 530
Special Collections: Dutch Related-Reformed Church, bks, newsp, micro. US Document Depository
Subject Interests: Hist, Lit, Relig
Automation Activity & Vendor Info: (Acquisitions) EOS International; (Cataloging) EOS International; (Circulation) EOS International; (OPAC) EOS International
Wireless access
Partic in Christian Library Consortium; Illinois Library & Information Network; Iowa Private Academic Library Consortium; Metronet; Minitex; OCLC Online Computer Library Center, Inc
Open Mon-Thurs (Fall & Spring) 7:30am-Midnight, Fri 7:30am-10pm, Sat 8-5, Sun 1:30-Midnight; Mon-Thurs (Summer) 8am-8:30pm, Fri 8-4

P ORANGE CITY PUBLIC LIBRARY, 112 Albany Ave SE, 51041. SAN 305-6228. Tel: 712-707-4302. FAX: 712-707-4431. E-mail: info@orangecitylibrary.org. Web Site: orangecityiowa.com/residents/library. *Dir,* Lisa Johnson; Staff 6.3 (MLS 1, Non-MLS 5.3)
Founded 1915. Pop 6,004; Circ 212,292
Library Holdings: AV Mats 13,529; DVDs 5,100; Bk Vols 63,771; Per Subs 60
Special Collections: Dutch Costume Patterns for Dutch Festival in May
Automation Activity & Vendor Info: (Acquisitions) Biblionix/Apollo; (Cataloging) Biblionix/Apollo; (Circulation) Biblionix/Apollo; (OPAC) Biblionix/Apollo
Wireless access
Function: 24/7 Electronic res, 24/7 Online cat, Accelerated reader prog, Adult bk club, Art exhibits, Art programs, Bilingual assistance for Spanish patrons, Bks on CD, Butterfly Garden, Children's prog, Computer training, Computers for patron use, Electronic databases & coll, Free DVD rentals, Govt ref serv, Homebound delivery serv, ILL available, Internet access, Magazines, Magnifiers for reading, Movies, Online cat, Outreach serv, Photocopying/Printing, Prog for adults, Prog for children & young adult, Ref & res, Ref serv available, Res assist avail, Scanner, Spanish lang bks, STEM programs, Story hour, Study rm, Summer & winter reading prog, Tax forms, Teen prog, Telephone ref, Writing prog
Open Mon & Thurs 9-8, Tues, Wed & Friday 9-5, Sat 10-2

OSAGE

P OSAGE PUBLIC LIBRARY*, 406 Main St, 50461-1125. SAN 305-6236. Tel: 641-732-3323. FAX: 641-732-4419. E-mail: osagepl@osage.net. Web Site: sites.google.com/view/osagepubliclibrary. *Dir,* Syd Heimer; Staff 1 (MLS 1)
Founded 1876. Circ 98,089
Library Holdings: Bk Vols 39,741; Per Subs 47
Special Collections: Hamlin Garland Coll; Iowa Coll
Automation Activity & Vendor Info: (Circulation) Follett Software; (OPAC) Follett Software
Wireless access
Open Mon-Thurs 9-8, Fri 9-5, Sat 9-2:30

OSCEOLA

P OSCEOLA PUBLIC LIBRARY*, 300 S Fillmore St, 50213. SAN 305-6244. Tel: 641-342-2237. FAX: 641-342-6057. E-mail: osceolalib@osceola.lib.ia.us. Web Site: www.osceola.lib.ia.us. *Libr Dir,* Aric Bishop; E-mail: abishop@osceola.lib.ia.us; *Children & Teen Librn,* Krista Woodward; E-mail: kwoodard@osceola.lib.ia.us; *Adult Serv Spec, Programming,* Tessa Hall

Founded 1909. Pop 4,150; Circ 84,880
Library Holdings: Bk Vols 22,000; Per Subs 102
Automation Activity & Vendor Info: (Cataloging) Follett Software; (Circulation) Follett Software
Wireless access
Open Mon & Wed 9-7, Tues, Thurs & Fri 12-5, Sat 9-12:30

OSKALOOSA

P OSKALOOSA PUBLIC LIBRARY, 301 S Market St, 52577. SAN 305-6252. Tel: 641-673-0441. FAX: 641-673-6237. E-mail: opl@oskaloosalibrary.org. Web Site: www.oskaloosalibrary.org. *Libr Dir,* Marion Gaughan; E-mail: mgaughan@oskaloosalibrary.org; *Ch,* Kilie Steel; *Teen Librn,* Julie Dunn-McKee; *Youth Serv Librn,* Chandi Maleski; Staff 10 (MLS 2, Non-MLS 8)
Founded 1903. Pop 22,507; Circ 198,518
Library Holdings: Bk Titles 54,316; Bk Vols 55,000; Per Subs 198
Subject Interests: Hist
Automation Activity & Vendor Info: (Circulation) SirsiDynix; (OPAC) SirsiDynix
Wireless access
Function: Telephone ref
Open Mon, Tues & Thurs 10-8, Wed, Fri & Sat 10-5
Friends of the Library Group

C WILLIAM PENN UNIVERSITY, Wilcox Library, 201 Trueblood Ave, 52577. SAN 305-6260. Tel: 641-673-1096. FAX: 641-673-1098. E-mail: cwalibrarian@wmpenn.edu. Web Site: www.wmpenn.edu/library. *Instrul Serv, Interim Libr Dir, Ref Librn,* Samantha Mead; Tel: 641-673-1197, E-mail: samantha.mead@wmpenn.edu; Staff 2 (MLS 2)
Founded 1873. Highest Degree: Bachelor
Library Holdings: Bk Vols 68,291; Per Subs 349
Special Collections: Quakerism (Quaker Coll)
Subject Interests: Educ, Indust arts, Soc sci & issues
Automation Activity & Vendor Info: (Cataloging) SirsiDynix; (Circulation) SirsiDynix; (OPAC) SirsiDynix
Wireless access
Partic in Iowa Academic Library Alliance; OCLC Online Computer Library Center, Inc
Open Mon-Thurs 8am-10pm, Fri 8-5, Sun 2-10

OSSIAN

P OSSIAN PUBLIC LIBRARY*, 123 W Main, 52161. (Mail add: PO Box 120, 52161-0120), SAN 305-6279. Tel: 563-532-9461. FAX: 563-532-9461. Web Site: www.ossian.lib.ia.us. *Dir,* Kay Elsbernd; E-mail: director@ossian.lib.ia.us; Staff 1 (Non-MLS 1)
Founded 1956. Pop 842; Circ 10,502
Library Holdings: CDs 115; DVDs 15; Bk Vols 8,910; Per Subs 30; Talking Bks 150; Videos 290
Automation Activity & Vendor Info: (Cataloging) Follett Software; (Circulation) Follett Software
Wireless access
Open Mon, Tues & Thurs 2-5:30, Wed & Fri 2-7, Sat 9-12

OTTUMWA

J INDIAN HILLS COMMUNITY COLLEGE LIBRARY*, 525 Grandview Ave, 52501. SAN 305-6287. Tel: 641-683-5199. Administration Tel: 641-683-5174. Automation Services Tel: 641-683-5178. Toll Free Tel: 800-726-2585, Ext 5199. FAX: 641-683-5184. E-mail: library@indianhills.edu. Web Site: www.indianhills.edu/library. *Exec Dean,* Darlas Shockley; E-mail: Darlas.Shockley@indianhills.edu; *Librn,* Cheryl Talbert; E-mail: Cheryl.Talbert@indianhills.edu
Founded 1960. Enrl 3,500; Fac 250; Highest Degree: Associate
Library Holdings: Bk Vols 30,000; Per Subs 270
Automation Activity & Vendor Info: (Cataloging) TLC (The Library Corporation); (Circulation) TLC (The Library Corporation); (Course Reserve) TLC (The Library Corporation)
Wireless access
Publications: Monthly Acquisitions List
Partic in Iowa Academic Library Alliance
Open Mon-Thurs (Fall-Spring) 7:15am-9pm, Fri & Sat 10-5, Sun 4:30-10; Mon-Thurs (Summer) 7:15am-8pm, Fri 10-5, Sun 4:30-10

P OTTUMWA PUBLIC LIBRARY*, 102 W Fourth St, 52501. SAN 305-6295. Tel: 641-682-7563. FAX: 641-682-4970. Web Site: www.ottumwapubliclibrary.org. *Dir,* Sonja Ferrell; Tel: 641-682-7563, Ext 202, E-mail: sferrell@ottumwapubliclibrary.org; *Asst Dir,* Ron Houk; Tel: 641-682-7563, Ext 203, E-mail: rhouk@ottumwapubliclibrary.org; *Ch,* Allyson Kirking; Tel: 641-682-7563, Ext 210, E-mail: akirking@ottumwapubliclibrary.org; *Ref Librn/Genealogy,* Ashley Manning; Tel: 641-682-7563, Ext 205, E-mail: amanning@ottumwapubliclibrary.org; Staff 12 (MLS 1, Non-MLS 11)
Founded 1872. Pop 25,023
Library Holdings: AV Mats 1,500; Bk Vols 70,000; Per Subs 120; Talking Bks 400
Special Collections: Ottumwa & Wapello County History (Iowa Coll), bks, clippings, pictures
Automation Activity & Vendor Info: (Cataloging) SirsiDynix; (Circulation) SirsiDynix; (OPAC) SirsiDynix
Wireless access
Function: 24/7 Online cat, Activity rm, Adult bk club, Archival coll, Audiobks via web, Bi-weekly Writer's Group, Bk club(s), Bks on CD, Children's prog, Computer training, Computers for patron use, Digital talking bks, E-Readers, Electronic databases & coll, Free DVD rentals, Home delivery & serv to seniorr ctr & nursing homes, Homebound delivery serv, ILL available, Internet access, Magazines, Mango lang, Meeting rooms, Microfiche/film & reading machines, Movies, Music CDs, Online cat, Online info literacy tutorials on the web & in blackboard, Online ref, Outreach serv, OverDrive digital audio bks, Photocopying/Printing, Preschool outreach, Preschool reading prog, Printer for laptops & handheld devices, Prog for adults, Prog for children & young adult, Ref serv available, Scanner, Senior outreach, Spanish lang bks, Spoken cassettes & DVDs, Summer & winter reading prog, Summer reading prog, Tax forms, Teen prog, Telephone ref, Writing prog
Open Mon-Thurs 9-7, Fri & Sat 9-5
Friends of the Library Group

OXFORD

P OXFORD PUBLIC LIBRARY*, 112 Augusta Ave, 52322. (Mail add: PO Box 160, 52322-0160), SAN 376-6799. Tel: 319-828-4087. FAX: 319-828-4087. E-mail: oxfordlibrary@southslope.net. Web Site: www.oxford.lib.ia.us. *Dir,* Sarah Uthoff
Library Holdings: Bk Vols 8,047; Per Subs 18
Partic in Bibliomation Inc
Open Wed 2-5, Fri 2-6, Sat 9-11:30 & 1-4
Friends of the Library Group

OXFORD JUNCTION

P WREGIE MEMORIAL LIBRARY*, 105 W Broadway, 52323. (Mail add: PO Box 345, 52323-0345), SAN 305-6325. Tel: 563-826-2450. FAX: 563-826-2450. E-mail: library@oxfordjunction.lib.ia.us. Web Site: www.oxfordjunction.lib.ia.us. *Dir,* Stephanie Dosland
Founded 1940
Library Holdings: Bk Titles 5,891; Per Subs 24
Special Collections: Oxford Mirror 1879-1952, micro
Wireless access
Open Tues & Fri 8-11:30, Wed 12-5, Thurs 12-6, Sat 8-12

PALMER

P PALMER PUBLIC LIBRARY*, 520 Hanson Ave, 50571. (Mail add: PO Box 114, 50571-0114), SAN 320-8222. Tel: 712-359-2296. E-mail: palib@ncn.net. Web Site: www.palmer.lib.ia.us. *Dir,* Ramona Miller
Pop 230; Circ 6,457
Library Holdings: Bk Titles 11,187; Per Subs 21
Wireless access
Partic in Iowa Libr Asn
Open Mon 1-5, Wed 1:30-6, Sat 9:30-12:30

PANORA

P PANORA PUBLIC LIBRARY*, 102 N First St, 50216. SAN 305-6341. Tel: 641-755-2529. FAX: 641-755-3009. E-mail: pnralib@netins.net. Web Site: www.panoralibrary.com. *Dir,* Kimberly Finnegan
Founded 1902. Pop 1,211; Circ 16,787
Library Holdings: Bk Titles 15,000; Per Subs 78
Wireless access
Function: Bks on cassette, ILL available, Prog for children & young adult, Tax forms
Open Mon 12-7, Tues & Thurs 12-5, Wed 12-8, Fri 9:30-5, Sat 9:30-Noon
Friends of the Library Group

PARKERSBURG

P KOTHE MEMORIAL LIBRARY*, 309 Third St, 50665-1030. (Mail add: PO Box 160, 50665-0160), SAN 305-635X. Tel: 319-346-2442. FAX: 319-346-2442. E-mail: library@parkersburg.lib.ia.us. Web Site: www.parkersburg.lib.ia.us. *Dir,* Deb Decker; E-mail: deb@parkersburg.lib.ia.us
Pop 2,571; Circ 31,300
Library Holdings: AV Mats 1,300; Bk Vols 16,000; Per Subs 51
Automation Activity & Vendor Info: (Circulation) Follett Software
Wireless access
Open Mon & Wed 10-8, Tues, Thurs & Fri 10-5:30, Sat 10-1
Friends of the Library Group

PATON

P WILLIAM PATON PUBLIC LIBRARY*, 105 Main St, 50217. (Mail add: PO Box 70, 50217-0070), SAN 305-6368. Tel: 515-968-4559. FAX: 515-968-4558. Web Site: www.paton.lib.ia.us. *Dir,* Alysha Oravetz; E-mail: director@paton.lib.ia.us
Pop 255; Circ 7,270
Library Holdings: Bk Titles 13,888; Per Subs 15
Open Wed & Thurs 1-7, Fri 4-7, Sat 10-2, Sun 12-3

PAULLINA

P PAULLINA PUBLIC LIBRARY*, 113 S Mickley St, 51046. (Mail add: PO Box 60, 51046-0060), SAN 305-6376. Tel: 712-949-3941. FAX: 712-949-3866. Web Site: www.paullina.lib.ia.us. *Dir,* Dorothy Harper; E-mail: director@paullina.lib.ia.us
Founded 1908. Pop 1,056; Circ 11,500
Library Holdings: Bk Vols 21,570; Per Subs 37; Talking Bks 802; Videos 760
Automation Activity & Vendor Info: (Acquisitions) Book Systems; (Cataloging) Book Systems; (Circulation) Book Systems
Wireless access
Special Services for the Blind - Bks on cassette; Bks on CD; Large print bks
Open Mon & Thurs 2-6, Tues & Wed 10-6, Fri 1-5, Sat 9-2

PELLA

C CENTRAL COLLEGE*, Geisler Library, Campus Box 6500, 812 University St, 50219-1999. SAN 341-955X. Tel: 641-628-5219. Interlibrary Loan Service Tel: 641-628-5193. FAX: 641-628-5327. Web Site: www.central.edu/library. *Dir,* Elizabeth McMahon; Tel: 641-628-5345, E-mail: mcmahone@central.edu; *Integrated Learning Librn,* Mary Anderson; Tel: 641-628-5220, E-mail: andersonm@central.edu; *Tech Serv Librn,* Kyle Winward; Tel: 641-628-5158, E-mail: winwardk@central.edu; *Libr Office Mgr,* Sue Van Vark; E-mail: vanvarks@central.edu; *Media Ctr Mgr,* Debra Phipps; E-mail: phippsd@central.edu; *Circ Supvr,* Lana Goodrich; E-mail: goodrichl@central.edu; *ILL Coordr,* Kelly Taylor; E-mail: taylork@central.edu; Staff 6.9 (MLS 3, Non-MLS 3.9)
Founded 1853. Enrl 1,250; Fac 103; Highest Degree: Bachelor
Library Holdings: AV Mats 4,284; CDs 1,242; DVDs 2,210; e-books 11,187; e-journals 15,491; Electronic Media & Resources 26,681; Music Scores 3,916; Bk Vols 116,289; Per Subs 87; Videos 702
Special Collections: Dutch in America & Iowa (Scholte Coll), bks & letters; George Enescu Coll of Romanian Music; Helen Van Dyke Miniature Book Coll; Pella History, newsp & docs. Oral History
Automation Activity & Vendor Info: (Acquisitions) OCLC Worldshare Management Services; (Cataloging) OCLC Worldshare Management Services; (Circulation) OCLC Worldshare Management Services; (Course Reserve) OCLC Worldshare Management Services; (ILL) OCLC WorldShare Interlibrary Loan; (OPAC) OCLC; (Serials) OCLC Worldshare Management Services
Wireless access
Publications: Annual Report; Collection Guides (Online only)
Partic in Iowa Academic Library Alliance; Iowa Private Academic Library Consortium; OCLC Online Computer Library Center, Inc
Open Mon-Thurs 8am-Midnight, Fri 8-5, Sat 1-5, Sun 2-Midnight

P PELLA PUBLIC LIBRARY, 603 Main St, 50219. SAN 305-6384. Tel: 641-628-4268. FAX: 641-628-1735. E-mail: pplcirc@cityofpella.com. Web Site: www.cityofpella.com/library. *Libr Dir,* Mara Strickler; E-mail: mstrickler@cityofpella.com; *Asst Dir,* Christopher Brown; *Youth Serv Librn,* Katie Dreyer; Staff 3 (MLS 2, Non-MLS 1)
Founded 1903. Pop 11,000; Circ 268,811
Automation Activity & Vendor Info: (Acquisitions) SirsiDynix; (Cataloging) SirsiDynix; (Circulation) SirsiDynix; (Discovery) EBSCO Discovery Service; (ILL) OCLC; (OPAC) SirsiDynix; (Serials) SirsiDynix
Wireless access
Partic in OCLC Online Computer Library Center, Inc
Open Mon-Thurs 10-9, Fri 10-6, Sat 10-5, Sun 1:30-4:30
Friends of the Library Group

PEOSTA

R NEW MELLERAY LIBRARY*, 6632 Melleray Circle, 52068. SAN 375-4332. Tel: 563-588-2319, Ext 426. FAX: 563-588-4117. E-mail: mc@newmelleray.org. Web Site: newmelleray.org. *Librn,* Fr David Bock
Founded 1849
Library Holdings: Bk Titles 32,000; Per Subs 40
Subject Interests: Comparative relig, Hist, Psychol
Wireless access
Restriction: Mem only, Residents only, Restricted access

J NORTHEAST IOWA COMMUNITY COLLEGE*, Peosta Library, 8342 NICC Dr, 52068. SAN 305-3598. Tel: 563-556-5110, Ext 224. FAX: 563-557-0340. Web Site: www.nicc.edu. *Coordr,* Victor Lieberman; E-mail: liebermanv@nicc.edu; *Acq,* Phyllis Mausser; *ILL,* Julie Conolly
Founded 1971. Enrl 2,402
Library Holdings: Bk Vols 17,000; Per Subs 150
Subject Interests: Bus, Health
Automation Activity & Vendor Info: (Cataloging) SirsiDynix; (Circulation) Horizon; (OPAC) SirsiDynix; (Serials) Surpass
Wireless access
Partic in Dubuque Area Library Information Consortium; Iowa Academic Library Alliance
Open Mon-Thurs 7am-8pm, Fri 7-5

PERRY

P PERRY PUBLIC LIBRARY, 1101 Willis Ave, 50220. SAN 305-6392. Tel: 515-465-3569. FAX: 515-465-9881. E-mail: info@perry.lib.ia.us. Web Site: www.perry.lib.ia.us. *Libr Dir,* Mary Murphy; E-mail: mmurphy@perry.lib.ia.us; *Dep Libr Dir,* Misty Von Behren; *Ch,* Suzanne Kestel; Staff 4 (Non-MLS 4)
Founded 1904. Pop 10,000; Circ 75,000
Library Holdings: Bk Titles 54,000; Per Subs 91
Automation Activity & Vendor Info: (Cataloging) OCLC; (Circulation) Innovative Interfaces, Inc; (ILL) OCLC; (OPAC) Innovative Interfaces, Inc; (Serials) Innovative Interfaces, Inc
Wireless access
Function: 24/7 Electronic res, 24/7 Online cat, Activity rm, Adult bk club, Art exhibits, Audio & video playback equip for onsite use, Audiobks via web, Children's prog, Computers for patron use, E-Reserves, Electronic databases & coll, Equip loans & repairs, Free DVD rentals, ILL available, Internet access, Laminating, Life-long learning prog for all ages, Magazines, Mail & tel request accepted, Meeting rooms, Movies, Music CDs, Notary serv, Online cat, Online info literacy tutorials on the web & in blackboard, Online ref, Orientations, Outreach serv, Photocopying/Printing, Preschool reading prog, Prog for adults, Prog for children & young adult, Ref serv available, Senior computer classes, Senior outreach, Serves people with intellectual disabilities, Spanish lang bks, Spoken cassettes & CDs, Spoken cassettes & DVDs, Story hour, Study rm, Summer & winter reading prog, Tax forms, Teen prog, Telephone ref, Wheelchair accessible
Open Mon-Thurs 10-7, Fri 10-6, Sat 10-2
Restriction: Free to mem
Friends of the Library Group

PETERSON

P KIRCHNER-FRENCH MEMORIAL LIBRARY*, 101 Main St, 51047. (Mail add: PO Box 203, 51047-0203), SAN 305-6406. Tel: 712-295-6705. FAX: 712-295-6705. E-mail: kirchner@iowatelecom.net. Web Site: www.peterson.lib.ia.us. *Dir,* Gloria Terrell; E-mail: gterrell@peterson.lib.ia.us; *Asst Dir, Ch,* Joni Click; Staff 1 (Non-MLS 1)
Founded 1926. Pop 362; Circ 4,787
Library Holdings: Bk Titles 6,505; Per Subs 24; Talking Bks 94; Videos 567
Special Collections: Peterson Patriot (1869-1983)
Wireless access
Function: Bk club(s), Homebound delivery serv, ILL available, Prog for adults, Prog for children & young adult, Ref serv available, Summer reading prog, Telephone ref, VHS videos
Open Mon 9-12 & 2-5, Tues, Thurs & Fri 2-5, Wed 2-6, Sat 9-12

PLAINFIELD

P PLAINFIELD PUBLIC LIBRARY*, 723 Main St, 50666. (Mail add: PO Box 327, 50666-0327), SAN 305-6414. Tel: 319-276-4461. FAX: 319-276-4461. E-mail: bookit@butler-bremer.com. Web Site: plainfieldiowa.com/plainfieldlibrary2.htm. *Dir,* Jane Juchems
Founded 1978. Circ 9,000
Library Holdings: DVDs 600; Bk Vols 12,000; Per Subs 33
Automation Activity & Vendor Info: (Cataloging) Follett Software; (Circulation) Follett Software
Wireless access
Open Mon, Tues & Fri 12-5, Wed 10-6, Sat 10-12

PLEASANT HILL

P PLEASANT HILL PUBLIC LIBRARY*, 5151 Maple Dr, 50327-8456. SAN 376-5032. Tel: 515-266-7815. FAX: 515-266-7793. Web Site: www.pleasanthilliowa.org/114/Library. *Dir,* John Lerdal; E-mail: jlerdal@pleasanthill.lib.ia.us; Staff 5 (MLS 1, Non-MLS 4)
Founded 1982. Pop 9,000; Circ 110,000
Library Holdings: Bks on Deafness & Sign Lang 9; CDs 380; DVDs 481; High Interest/Low Vocabulary Bk Vols 15; Large Print Bks 365; Bk Titles 45,000; Bk Vols 50,000; Per Subs 62; Talking Bks 1,700; Videos 998

Automation Activity & Vendor Info: (Cataloging) Innovative Interfaces, Inc; (Circulation) Innovative Interfaces, Inc; (OPAC) Innovative Interfaces, Inc
Wireless access
Open Mon-Thurs 10-8, Fri 10-6, Sat 10-5, Sun 1-5
Friends of the Library Group

PLEASANTVILLE

P WEBB SHADLE MEMORIAL LIBRARY, 301 W Dallas, 50225. (Mail add: PO Box 338, 50225-0338), SAN 305-6422. Tel: 515-848-5617. FAX: 515-481-9078. E-mail: webbshadle@pleasantville.lib.ia.us. Web Site: webbshadle.org. *Dir*, JoEllen Glick
Founded 1955. Pop 2,000; Circ 26,000
Library Holdings: Bk Vols 15,000; Per Subs 65
Special Collections: Americana Coll
Wireless access
Open Mon, Tues & Fri 10-12 & 1-5, Wed 10-6, Sat 9am-11am
Friends of the Library Group

PLOVER

P PLOVER PUBLIC LIBRARY, 301 Main St, 50573. (Mail add: PO Box 112, 50573-0112), SAN 305-6430. Tel: 712-857-3532. E-mail: plover@ncn.net, plovercityclerk@yahoo.com. *Dir*, Ann Miller
Pop 380; Circ 2,463
Library Holdings: AV Mats 312; DVDs 75; Bk Titles 2,500; Per Subs 23; Talking Bks 50; Videos 310
Subject Interests: Local hist
Automation Activity & Vendor Info: (Cataloging) ResourceMATE; (Circulation) ResourceMATE
Wireless access
Open Mon 1-6:30, Thurs 1-6, Sat 9-Noon

POCAHONTAS

P POCAHONTAS PUBLIC LIBRARY*, 14 Second Ave NW, 50574. SAN 305-6457. Tel: 712-335-4471. FAX: 712-335-4471. E-mail: pocahontaspl@pocahontas.lib.ia.us. Web Site: www.pocahontas.lib.ia.us. *Dir*, Lola DeWall; *Librn*, Linda Ferguson; *Librn*, Jane Schott; *Ch*, Leesa Clausen; *Adult Serv*, Mona Zhorne; Staff 5 (Non-MLS 5)
Founded 1922. Pop 1,970; Circ 22,993
Library Holdings: Bk Vols 19,684; Per Subs 65
Subject Interests: Genealogy, Local hist, Railroads
Automation Activity & Vendor Info: (Cataloging) Book Systems; (Circulation) Book Systems; (OPAC) Book Systems
Wireless access
Open Mon, Tues & Fri 11-5, Wed & Thurs 11-8, Sat 9-1

POLK CITY

P POLK CITY COMMUNITY LIBRARY*, 1500 W Broadway St, 50226-2001. (Mail add: PO Box 259, 50226-0259), SAN 305-6465. Tel: 515-984-6119. FAX: 515-984-9273. E-mail: library@polkcitylibrary.org. Web Site: polkcitylibrary.com. *Interim Dir*, Pam Witt
Founded 1974. Pop 1,908; Circ 14,730
Library Holdings: Bk Titles 12,000
Automation Activity & Vendor Info: (Cataloging) Follett Software; (Circulation) Follett Software
Wireless access
Publications: Booklist
Open Mon-Thurs 10-8, Fri 10-6, Sat 10-4
Friends of the Library Group

POMEROY

P POMEROY PUBLIC LIBRARY*, 114 S Ontario St, 50575. (Mail add: Box 187, 50575-0187), SAN 305-6473. Tel: 712-468-2311. FAX: 712-468-2311. Web Site: www.pomeroy.lib.ia.us. *Dir*, Marcia Ehn; E-mail: director@pomeroy.lib.ia.us
Pop 895; Circ 10,462
Library Holdings: DVDs 45; Large Print Bks 60; Bk Vols 9,000; Per Subs 35; Talking Bks 85; Videos 150
Wireless access
Open Mon 10-12 & 1-5, Wed & Fri 1-5, Thurs 1-6, Sat 9-12

POSTVILLE

P POSTVILLE PUBLIC LIBRARY, 235 W Tilden, 52162. SAN 305-6481. Tel: 563-864-7600. FAX: 563-864-7600. E-mail: library@postville.lib.ia.us. Web Site: www.postville.lib.ia.us. *Dir*, Cindy Berns
Pop 2,200; Circ 19,594
Library Holdings: Bk Titles 18,000; Per Subs 52
Automation Activity & Vendor Info: (Cataloging) ComPanion Corp; (Circulation) ComPanion Corp
Wireless access
Open Mon & Tues 9-1, Wed-Fri 9-5, Sat 9-12

PRAIRIE CITY

P PRAIRIE CITY PUBLIC LIBRARY*, 100 E Fifth St, 50228. (Mail add: PO Box 113, 50228-0113), SAN 376-7507. Tel: 515-994-2308. E-mail: library@prairiecityiowa.us. Web Site: www.prairiecity.lib.ia.us. *Dir*, Sue Ponder
Library Holdings: Bk Vols 8,524; Per Subs 34
Wireless access
Open Mon & Fri 1-5, Tues & Thurs 4-8, Wed 9-11 & 1-5, Sat 9-Noon
Friends of the Library Group

PRESCOTT

P PRESCOTT PUBLIC LIBRARY*, 607 Second St, 50859-0177. SAN 376-5199. Tel: 641-335-2238. FAX: 641-335-2238. E-mail: prescottlibrary@windstream.net. *Dir*, Crystal Schafer
Pop 611; Circ 1,346
Library Holdings: Bk Vols 3,517; Per Subs 5
Wireless access
Open Mon & Wed 8-12, Thurs 1-6, Sat 8-10

PRESTON

P PRESTON PUBLIC LIBRARY*, One W Gillet, 52069. (Mail add: PO Box 605, 52069-0605), SAN 305-649X. Tel: 563-689-3581. FAX: 563-689-3581. Web Site: www.preston.lib.ia.us. *Dir*, Caroline M Bredekamp; E-mail: director@preston.lib.ia.us
Founded 1974. Circ 14,297
Library Holdings: Bk Vols 18,000; Per Subs 40
Automation Activity & Vendor Info: (Cataloging) Book Systems; (Circulation) Book Systems
Wireless access
Partic in Southeastern Libraries Cooperating
Open Mon & Wed 1-8, Tues 9:30-11:30 & 1-5, Thurs 1-5, Fri 10-5, Sat 10-3

PRIMGHAR

P PRIMGHAR PUBLIC LIBRARY*, 320 First St NE, 51245. (Mail add: PO Box 9, 51245-0009), SAN 305-6503. Tel: 712-957-8981. FAX: 712-957-8981. E-mail: primlib@tcaexpress.net. Web Site: www.primghar.lib.ia.us. *Dir*, Leann Langfitt
Pop 1,050; Circ 22,640
Library Holdings: Bk Titles 14,000; Per Subs 31
Wireless access
Open Tues & Wed 1-5:30, Thurs 1-6, Fri 9-12 & 1-5, Sat 9-Noon

QUIMBY

P QUIMBY PUBLIC LIBRARY, 120 N Main, 51049. (Mail add: PO Box 186, 51049-0186), SAN 305-6511. Tel: 712-445-2413. FAX: 712-445-2688. E-mail: qpl@midlands.net. Web Site: www.quimby.lib.ia.us. *Dir*, Linda Sones; E-mail: linda@quimby.lib.ia.us; *Asst Librn*, Lois Pinkerton
Pop 334; Circ 2,736
Library Holdings: Bk Titles 6,433; Per Subs 30
Wireless access
Open Mon-Wed & Fri 1-5, Thurs 3-6, Sat 9-1

RADCLIFFE

P RADCLIFFE PUBLIC LIBRARY, 210 Isabella St, 50230. (Mail add: PO Box 348, 50230-0348), SAN 305-652X. Tel: 515-899-7914. FAX: 515-899-7914. E-mail: rad_lib@netins.net. *Dir*, Marilyn Raska-Engelson
Pop 593; Circ 11,193
Library Holdings: Bk Titles 15,756; Per Subs 50
Wireless access
Open Mon & Wed 10-7, Tues, Thurs & Fri 10-5, Sat 9-Noon

RAKE

P RAKE PUBLIC LIBRARY*, 123 N Main St, 50465. (Mail add: PO Box 166, 50465-0166), SAN 305-6538. Tel: 641-566-3388. FAX: 641-566-3388. E-mail: rakelibrary@wctatel.net. *Dir*, Virginia Cooper
Founded 1962. Pop 438; Circ 5,000
Library Holdings: Bk Titles 7,000
Automation Activity & Vendor Info: (Cataloging) Follett Software
Wireless access
Open Tues, Wed & Fri 9-11:30 & 1:30-5, Thurs 9-11:30 & 1:30-6, Sat 9am-10:30am

RANDOLPH

P RANDOLPH PUBLIC LIBRARY*, 106 S Main St, 51649. (Mail add: PO Box 112, 51649-0112), SAN 305-6546. Tel: 712-625-3561. FAX: 712-625-3561. Web Site: www.randolphia.com. *Librn,* Linda Heywood; E-mail: linda@randolph.lib.ia.us
Founded 1960. Pop 820; Circ 5,000
Library Holdings: AV Mats 413; Bks on Deafness & Sign Lang 25; DVDs 450; Bk Titles 10,000; Per Subs 12
Special Collections: Randolph Enterprise Newspapers, 1895-1970
Wireless access
Open Mon & Thurs 2-5:30, Tues 1:30-6, Wed 10-12 & 2-5:30, Sat 8:30-11:30
Friends of the Library Group

READLYN

P READLYN COMMUNITY LIBRARY*, 309 Main St, 50668. (Mail add: PO Box 249, 50668-0249), SAN 305-6554. Tel: 319-279-3432. FAX: 319-279-3432. E-mail: readlynlib@gmail.com. Web Site: www.readlyn.lib.ia.us. *Dir,* Barb Sowers; Staff 4 (MLS 2, Non-MLS 2)
Founded 1965. Pop 858; Circ 17,185
Library Holdings: Bk Titles 14,000; Per Subs 73
Wireless access
Function: 24/7 Electronic res, 24/7 Online cat, Activity rm, Adult bk club
Special Services for the Blind - Audio mat
Open Mon & Thurs 10-7, Tues, Wed & Fri 10-5, Sat 9-Noon

RED OAK

P RED OAK PUBLIC LIBRARY*, 400 N Second St, 51566. SAN 305-6562. Tel: 712-623-6516. FAX: 712-623-6518. Web Site: www.redoak.lib.ia.us. *Dir,* Kathi Most; Staff 1 (Non-MLS 1)
Founded 1908. Pop 12,000; Circ 75,000
Special Collections: State & Local History
Wireless access
Open Mon & Wed 10-8, Tues & Thurs-Sat 10-5

REDFIELD

P REDFIELD PUBLIC LIBRARY, 1112 Thomas St, 50233. (Mail add: PO Box L, 50233-0911), SAN 305-6570. Tel: 515-833-2200. E-mail: r.library@mchsi.com. Web Site: redfield.lib.ia.us. *Libr Dir,* Lori Stonehocker
Pop 959; Circ 11,000
Library Holdings: Bk Titles 10,500; Per Subs 36
Wireless access
Open Mon & Wed-Fri 1-6, Tues 9-12 & 1-6, Sat 9-12 & 1-4

REINBECK

P REINBECK PUBLIC LIBRARY*, 501 Clark St, 50669. SAN 305-6589. Tel: 319-788-2652. FAX: 319-788-2826. E-mail: reinlibr@reinbeck.net. Web Site: www.reinbeck.lib.ia.us. *Dir,* Janet Slessor; *Asst Librn,* Ann Rae Billerbeck; *Asst Librn,* Cherie Eckhoff
Pop 1,664
Jul 2017-Jun 2018 Income $104,311, State $2,378, City $75,022, County $24,954, Locally Generated Income $1,707, Other $250. Mats Exp $21,566, Books $10,497, Per/Ser (Incl. Access Fees) $1,500, Other Print Mats $8,593, AV Mat $419, Electronic Ref Mat (Incl. Access Fees) $557. Sal $45,166 (Prof $36,500)
Library Holdings: Audiobooks 377; AV Mats 1,146; CDs 377; DVDs 568; Bk Vols 21,856; Per Subs 75; Videos 61
Automation Activity & Vendor Info: (Acquisitions) Follett Software; (Circulation) Follett Software
Wireless access
Function: 24/7 Electronic res, 24/7 Online cat, Adult bk club, Bks on CD, Children's prog, Computers for patron use, Electronic databases & coll, Free DVD rentals, Home delivery & serv to seniorr ctr & nursing homes, Homebound delivery serv, ILL available, Instruction & testing, Internet access, Magazines, Mail & tel request accepted, Online cat, Photocopying/Printing, Preschool outreach, Prog for adults, Prog for children & young adult, Story hour, Summer reading prog, Tax forms, VHS videos, Wheelchair accessible

REMBRANDT

P REMBRANDT PUBLIC LIBRARY*, Main St & Broadway, 50576. (Mail add: PO Box 169, 50576-0186), SAN 373-8906. Tel: 712-286-6801. FAX: 712-286-6801. E-mail: librarian@rembrandt.lib.ia.us. *Dir,* Patria Jenson
Founded 1930. Pop 380; Circ 5,450
Library Holdings: Bk Titles 5,000; Per Subs 15
Wireless access
Function: Preschool reading prog
Open Tues 10-5, Thurs 10-6:30, Sat 9-12

REMSEN

P REMSEN PUBLIC LIBRARY, 211 Fulton St, 51050. SAN 305-6600. Tel: 712-786-2911. FAX: 712-786-3255. Web Site: www.remsen.lib.ia.us. *Dir,* Janeene Klein; E-mail: jklein@midlands.net
Founded 1939
Library Holdings: DVDs 50; Large Print Bks 500; Bk Titles 16,000; Per Subs 60; Talking Bks 200; Videos 200
Automation Activity & Vendor Info: (Cataloging) Follett Software; (Circulation) Follett Software
Wireless access
Open Mon & Fri 1-5, Tues & Thurs 9-5, Wed 9-6, Sat 9am-11am

RENWICK

P RENWICK PUBLIC LIBRARY, 204 Stoddard St, 50577. (Mail add: PO Box 38, 50577-0038), SAN 305-6619. Tel: 515-824-3209. FAX: 515-824-3209. E-mail: renwickl@wmtel.net. *Dir,* Jan Thompson
Pop 280; Circ 6,814
Library Holdings: Bk Titles 4,000; Bk Vols 4,500; Per Subs 15
Wireless access
Open Tues 1-4, Wed 10-5

RICEVILLE

P RICEVILLE PUBLIC LIBRARY*, 307 Woodland Ave, 50466. SAN 305-6627. Tel: 641-985-2273. FAX: 641-985-4002. Web Site: www.ricevillepubliclibrary.com. *Dir,* Betsy Morse; E-mail: director@riceville.lib.ia.us
Founded 1928. Pop 1,300; Circ 30,535
Library Holdings: AV Mats 943; Large Print Bks 789; Bk Titles 12,000; Bk Vols 13,050; Per Subs 36; Talking Bks 560
Automation Activity & Vendor Info: (Cataloging) Follett Software; (Circulation) Follett Software; (OPAC) Follett Software
Wireless access
Open Mon 10-7, Tues-Thurs 10-6, Fri 10-5, Sat 10-3
Friends of the Library Group

RICHLAND

P RICHLAND PUBLIC LIBRARY*, 100 E Main St, 52585. (Mail add: PO Box 160, 52585), SAN 305-6635. Tel: 319-456-6541. FAX: 319-456-6541. E-mail: richlib@iowatelecom.net. Web Site: www.richland.lib.ia.us. *Dir,* Cindy McCan
Pop 1,221; Circ 9,565
Library Holdings: AV Mats 406; Bk Titles 9,000; Per Subs 15
Automation Activity & Vendor Info: (Acquisitions) Follett Software
Wireless access
Open Tues-Thurs 2:30-6:30, Fri 12-5, Sat 9-Noon

RINGSTED

P RINGSTED PUBLIC LIBRARY*, Eight W Maple St, 50578. SAN 305-6651. Tel: 712-866-0878. FAX: 712-866-0879. E-mail: rlibrary@ringtelco.com. Web Site: www.ringsted.lib.ia.us. *Dir,* Diane Jorgensen
Pop 440; Circ 3,584
Library Holdings: Bk Titles 9,674; Per Subs 16
Wireless access
Open Mon, Wed, Fri & Sat 9-12, Tues & Thurs 3-7

RIPPEY

P RIPPEY PUBLIC LIBRARY*, 224 Main St, 50235. (Mail add: PO Box 184, 50235-0184), SAN 305-666X. Tel: 515-436-7714. FAX: 515-436-7485. E-mail: rippeyli@windstream.net. Web Site: www.rippey.lib.ia.us. *Librn,* Shawneene Kenan
Wireless access
Special Services for the Blind - Large print bks
Open Mon-Fri 1-5

ROCK RAPIDS

P ROCK RAPIDS PUBLIC LIBRARY*, 102 S Greene St, 51246. SAN 305-6678. Tel: 712-472-3541. FAX: 712-472-3541. E-mail: rrlib@premieronline.net. Web Site: www.rockrapids.lib.ia.us. *Dir,* Linda McCormack
Founded 1893. Pop 2,549; Circ 51,929
Jul 2015-Jun 2016 Income $173,993, State $1,626, City $145,680, County $19,244, Locally Generated Income $2,340, Other $5,103. Mats Exp $16,072, Books $9,701, Per/Ser (Incl. Access Fees) $2,720, AV Mat $1,793, Electronic Ref Mat (Incl. Access Fees) $1,858. Sal $89,406
Library Holdings: Audiobooks 1,603; DVDs 1,376; Microforms 339; Bk Vols 42,153; Per Subs 46
Automation Activity & Vendor Info: (Cataloging) Book Systems; (Circulation) Book Systems; (OPAC) Book Systems
Wireless access

Function: 24/7 Online cat, Adult bk club, Bks on CD, Children's prog, Computers for patron use, Free DVD rentals, ILL available, Internet access, Magazines, Meeting rooms, Online cat, Summer reading prog
Open Mon & Wed Noon-8, Tues & Thurs 10-8, Fri Noon-5:30, Sat 10-3
Friends of the Library Group

ROCK VALLEY

P ROCK VALLEY PUBLIC LIBRARY*, 1531 Main St, 51247-1127. SAN 305-6686. Tel: 712-476-5651. FAX: 712-476-5261. E-mail: rvplibrary@gmail.com. Web Site: www.rockvalley.lib.ia.us. *Dir,* Nicole McCray; *YA Librn,* Nicky Hueschen
Founded 1916. Pop 3,700; Circ 115,980
Library Holdings: Bk Vols 46,000; Per Subs 50
Special Collections: Oral History
Wireless access
Open Mon & Wed 10-9, Tues & Thurs-Sat 10-5

ROCKFORD

P ROCKFORD PUBLIC LIBRARY*, 202 W Main Ave, 50468-1212. (Mail add: PO Box 496, 50468-0496), SAN 305-6694. Tel: 641-756-3725. FAX: 641-756-3725. E-mail: rkfdlib@myomnitel.com. Web Site: www.rockford.lib.ia.us. *Libr Dir,* Stacy Campbell; Staff 3 (Non-MLS 3)
Founded 1917. Pop 860; Circ 17,403
Library Holdings: AV Mats 710; Bk Titles 7,189; Per Subs 42; Talking Bks 572
Automation Activity & Vendor Info: (Acquisitions) Biblionix/Apollo; (Cataloging) Biblionix/Apollo; (Circulation) Biblionix/Apollo; (ILL) Biblionix/Apollo; (OPAC) Biblionix/Apollo; (Serials) Biblionix/Apollo
Wireless access
Function: 24/7 Electronic res, 24/7 Online cat, Adult bk club, Archival coll, Audiobks via web, Bks on CD, Children's prog, Computers for patron use, E-Readers, Electronic databases & coll, Free DVD rentals, Holiday prog, ILL available, Internet access, Magazines, Meeting rooms, Microfiche/film & reading machines, Movies, Music CDs, Online cat, OverDrive digital audio bks, Photocopying/Printing, Prog for adults, Prog for children & young adult, Summer reading prog, VHS videos, Wheelchair accessible
Partic in MOBIUS
Open Mon, Tues, Thurs & Fri 1-5:30, Wed 1-7:30, Sat 9-12

ROCKWELL

P ROCKWELL PUBLIC LIBRARY*, 307 Main St E, 50469. (Mail add: PO Box 419, 50469-0419), SAN 305-6708. Tel: 641-822-3268. FAX: 641-822-3168. E-mail: rkwlpl@netins.net. Web Site: www1.youseemore.com/nilc/Rockwell. *Dir,* Carla Dougherty; Staff 4 (Non-MLS 4)
Founded 1900. Pop 1,039; Circ 18,526
Automation Activity & Vendor Info: (Cataloging) TLC (The Library Corporation); (Circulation) TLC (The Library Corporation)
Wireless access
Function: 24/7 Electronic res, 24/7 Online cat, Adult bk club, After school storytime, Art exhibits, Audiobks via web, Bk club(s), Bks on CD, Children's prog, Computer training, Computers for patron use, Electronic databases & coll, Free DVD rentals, Holiday prog, Home delivery & serv to seniorr ctr & nursing homes, Homebound delivery serv, ILL available, Instruction & testing, Internet access, Laminating, Life-long learning prog for all ages, Magazines, Mail & tel request accepted, Meeting rooms, Online cat, Outreach serv, OverDrive digital audio bks, Photocopying/Printing, Preschool reading prog, Printer for laptops & handheld devices, Prog for adults, Prog for children & young adult, Ref serv available, Scanner, Senior outreach, Serves people with intellectual disabilities, Study rm, Summer reading prog, Teen prog, Telephone ref, Wheelchair accessible
Open Mon-Thurs 10-6, Fri 10-3, Sat 10-2

ROCKWELL CITY

S NORTH CENTRAL CORRECTIONAL FACILITY, Inmate Library, 313 Lanedale, 50579. SAN 375-3263. Tel: 712-297-7521, Ext 229. FAX: 712-297-9316. *Librn,* Joe Bush; Staff 9 (MLS 1, Non-MLS 8)
Library Holdings: Bk Titles 6,000; Per Subs 20
Subject Interests: Law
Restriction: Staff & inmates only

P ROCKWELL CITY PUBLIC LIBRARY*, 424 Main St, 50579-1415. SAN 305-6732. Tel: 712-297-8422. FAX: 712-297-8422. Web Site: www.rockwellcity.lib.ia.us. *Dir,* Denise Pohl; E-mail: director@rockwellcity.lib.ia.us; *Ch,* Sarah Weiss
Founded 1897. Pop 1,919; Circ 21,176
Library Holdings: High Interest/Low Vocabulary Bk Vols 80; Bk Titles 17,762; Bk Vols 18,178; Per Subs 72
Special Collections: Calhoun County Genealogical Society Library
Wireless access
Publications: Column Inches (Newsletter)
Open Mon 11-5, Tues 11-7, Wed-Fri 10-5, Sat 9-Noon
Friends of the Library Group

ROLAND

P ROLAND PUBLIC LIBRARY, 221 N Main St, 50236. (Mail add: PO Box 409, 50236-0409), SAN 376-544X. Tel: 515-388-4086. E-mail: rolandlib@globalccs.net. Web Site: www.roland.lib.ia.us. *Dir,* Laura Urbanek
Founded 1983
Library Holdings: Bk Vols 12,000; Per Subs 10
Wireless access
Open Mon-Fri 10-7, Sat 9-1

ROLFE

P ROLFE PUBLIC LIBRARY*, 319 Garfield St, 50581-1118. SAN 305-6759. Tel: 712-848-3143. E-mail: rplib@ncn.net. Web Site: www.rolfe.lib.ia.us. *Dir,* Terri Kipfer
Founded 1926. Pop 575; Circ 4,270
Library Holdings: Audiobooks 26; DVDs 976; Large Print Bks 136; Bk Vols 10,791; Per Subs 9
Special Collections: Local Hist Coll, pictures, papers. Oral History
Wireless access
Function: 24/7 Online cat, Adult bk club
Open Mon 2-6, Tues, Thurs & Fri 2-5, Wed 9-12 & 2-5, Sat 9-Noon
Friends of the Library Group

ROWAN

P ROWAN PUBLIC LIBRARY*, 101 Main St, 50470. (Mail add: PO Box 202, 50470-0202), SAN 305-6767. Tel: 641-853-2327. FAX: 641-853-2327. E-mail: librarystaff_rowan@yahoo.com. Web Site: www1.youseemore.com/nilc/rowanpl. *Dir,* Joyce Eriksen; E-mail: joyceeriksen@rowan.lib.ia.us
Founded 1964. Pop 180; Circ 6,300
Library Holdings: Bk Vols 11,214
Wireless access
Open Mon & Wed 10-6, Fri 10-5, Sat 9-Noon

ROYAL

P ROYAL PUBLIC LIBRARY*, 302 Main St, 51357. (Mail add: PO Box 199, 51357-0199), SAN 305-6775. Tel: 712-933-5500. E-mail: rlibrary@royaltelco.net. *Librn,* Barbara Fletcher
Pop 479; Circ 4,379
Library Holdings: Bk Vols 6,558; Per Subs 86
Open Mon, Wed & Fri 2-4:30, Tues & Sat 9:30-11:30, Thurs 4:30-6:30
Friends of the Library Group

RUDD

P RUDD PUBLIC LIBRARY*, 308 Chickasaw St, 50471. (Mail add: PO Box 305, 50471-0305), SAN 305-6783. Tel: 641-395-2385. FAX: 641-395-2385. E-mail: ruddlib@myomnitel.com. Web Site: www.rudd.lib.ia.us. *Libr Dir,* Amy Leaman; E-mail: libdirector@myomnitel.com
Founded 1956. Pop 430; Circ 16,875
Library Holdings: Bk Vols 7,000; Per Subs 48
Open Mon, Wed & Fri 12-6, Sat 9-12

RUNNELLS

P RUNNELLS COMMUNITY LIBRARY, 6575 SE 116th St, 50237-1193. Tel: 515-957-5662. E-mail: runnellsialibrary@gmail.com. Web Site: sites.google.com/view/runnellsialibrary. *Librn,* Samantha Reid; E-mail: sam.runnels.library@gmail.com
Pop 500
Library Holdings: Bk Titles 4,500
Automation Activity & Vendor Info: (Cataloging) Book Systems; (Circulation) Book Systems
Wireless access
Open Tues & Thurs 4:30-7:30, Sat 9-1 (Winter); Mon & Wed 9-12, Thurs 4-7, Sat 10-2 (Summer)
Friends of the Library Group

RUTHVEN

P RUTHVEN PUBLIC LIBRARY*, 1301 Gowrie St, 51358. (Mail add: PO Box 280, 51358-0280), SAN 305-6791. Tel: 712-837-4820. FAX: 712-837-4820. E-mail: info@ruthven.lib.ia.us. Web Site: www.ruthven.lib.ia.us. *Dir,* Kayann Rose; *Librn,* BJ Hemmingsen; *Librn,* Cheryl Sikora; *Librn,* Connie Woods; Staff 2 (Non-MLS 2)
Pop 1,408; Circ 10,000
Library Holdings: Bk Vols 14,000; Per Subs 15
Wireless access

Function: ILL available
Open Mon 8:30-6, Wed-Fri 8:30-4:30, Sat 9-12
Friends of the Library Group

SABULA

P KRABBENHOFT PUBLIC LIBRARY, 512 Elk St, 52070. (Mail add: PO Box 340, 52070-0340), SAN 305-6805. Tel: 563-687-2950. FAX: 563-687-2950. E-mail: krabbenhoftpubliclibrary@gmail.com. Web Site: www.sabula.lib.ia.us. *Librn,* Lisa Hartman
Founded 1961. Pop 670; Circ 12,724
Library Holdings: AV Mats 700; Bk Vols 15,000; Per Subs 40
Open Mon & Sat 9-1, Tues, Thurs & Fri 1-5, Wed 5-8

SAC CITY

P SAC CITY PUBLIC LIBRARY*, 1001 W Main St, 50583. SAN 305-6813. Tel: 712-662-7276. FAX: 712-662-7802. Web Site: www.saccity.lib.ia.us. *Dir,* Kim Nelsen; E-mail: knelsen@saccity.lib.ia.us; *Asst Librn,* Joyce O'Tool; E-mail: jotool@saccity.lib.ia.us; *Ch,* Cathie Hass
Founded 1913. Pop 2,460; Circ 11,000
Library Holdings: AV Mats 500; Large Print Bks 300; Bk Titles 32,000; Per Subs 78; Talking Bks 600
Special Collections: Oral History
Subject Interests: Local hist
Open Mon-Wed 9:30-5:30, Thurs 9:30-6:30, Fri 9:30-4:30
Friends of the Library Group

SAINT ANSGAR

P NISSEN PUBLIC LIBRARY*, Saint Ansgar Public Library, 217 W Fifth St, 50472. (Mail add: PO Box 40, 50472-0040), SAN 305-6821. Tel: 641-713-2218. FAX: 641-713-4716. E-mail: nissenlib@myomnitel.com. Web Site: www.youseemore.com/NILC/Nissen. *Dir,* Marsha Kuntz; *Asst Dir,* S Stohr; *Libr Asst,* J Kuntz; Staff 5 (Non-MLS 5)
Founded 1927. Pop 1,030
Library Holdings: Bk Titles 10,569; Per Subs 60; Talking Bks 541
Automation Activity & Vendor Info: (Cataloging) Follett Software; (Circulation) Follett Software; (ILL) Follett Software
Open Mon & Wed 10-11:30, 1-5:30 & 6-7, Tues, Thurs & Sat 1-5:30, Fri 9-12 & 1-5:30

SAINT CHARLES

P SAINT CHARLES PUBLIC LIBRARY*, 113 S Lumber St, 50240. (Mail add: PO Box 2, 50240-0118). Tel: 641-396-2945. E-mail: scplibrary@myomnitel.com. Web Site: stcharlesiowa.org/town-departments/library. *Dir,* Kirk Freeman
Pop 619; Circ 2,804
Library Holdings: Bk Vols 7,199; Per Subs 17
Wireless access
Partic in System Wide Automated Network
Open Mon & Tues 10-6, Thurs 10-7, Sun 2-5

SALEM

P CREW PUBLIC LIBRARY*, 107 E Cherry St, 52649. (Mail add: PO Box 117, 52649-0117), SAN 305-683X. Tel: 319-258-9007. FAX: 319-258-9007. E-mail: crew2009@iowatelecom.net. Web Site: salem.lib.ia.us. *Dir,* Kelly Patterson
Founded 1940. Pop 500; Circ 13,500
Library Holdings: Bk Titles 10,000; Per Subs 20
Wireless access
Open Mon, Tues & Thurs 1-5, Wed 1-6, Sat 9-12
Friends of the Library Group

SANBORN

P SANBORN PUBLIC LIBRARY*, 407 Main St, 51248. (Mail add: PO Box 430, 51248-0430), SAN 305-6848. Tel: 712-930-3215. FAX: 712-930-3170. E-mail: spl@tcaexpress.net. Web Site: www.sanborn.lib.ia.us. *Co-Dir,* Denise Bohnet; E-mail: dbohnet@sanborn.lib.ia.us; *Co-Dir,* Alvina Reitsma; E-mail: areitsma@sanborn.lib.ia.us
Founded 1911. Pop 1,353
Library Holdings: DVDs 378; Large Print Bks 47; Bk Vols 20,000; Per Subs 76; Talking Bks 591; Videos 425
Automation Activity & Vendor Info: (Cataloging) Follett Software; (Circulation) Follett Software
Wireless access
Function: ILL available, Prog for children & young adult, Spoken cassettes & CDs, Spoken cassettes & DVDs, Summer reading prog, VHS videos
Open Mon & Wed 11:30-7, Thurs 11:30-5:30, Fri & Sat 8:30-Noon
Restriction: Restricted loan policy
Friends of the Library Group

SCHALLER

P SCHALLER PUBLIC LIBRARY*, 103 S Main St, 51053. (Mail add: PO Box 427, 51053-0427), SAN 305-6856. Tel: 712-275-4741. E-mail: splibr@schallertel.net. *Dir,* Brenda Naberhaus
Pop 779
Library Holdings: Bk Titles 9,000; Bk Vols 11,476; Per Subs 20; Talking Bks 191
Wireless access
Partic in State of Iowa Libraries Online
Open Mon & Fri 2:30-5:30, Tues 9-11 & 2:30-5:30, Wed & Thurs 2-6, Sat 9-11

SCHLESWIG

P SCHLESWIG PUBLIC LIBRARY*, 202 Cedar St, 51461-0306. SAN 305-6864. Tel: 712-676-3470. E-mail: schleswiglibrary@gmail.com. Web Site: www.schleswig.lib.ia.us. *Dir,* Amy Hoffmeier
Founded 1940. Pop 2,000; Circ 4,810
Library Holdings: Bk Titles 11,017
Special Collections: Schleswig Leader Coll (1909 to 1981), 75th Anniversary, microflim, sound flm
Wireless access
Open Mon 3-8, Tues & Thurs 9-12, Wed & Fri 3-6, Sat 9-2
Friends of the Library Group

SCRANTON

P HF & MAUDE E MARCHANT MEMORIAL LIBRARY*, 1110 Main St, 51462. (Mail add: PO Box 68, 51462-0068), SAN 305-6872. Tel: 712-652-3453. Administration E-mail: admin@scranton.lib.ia.us. Web Site: www.scranton.lib.ia.us. *Dir,* Wendy Johnson
Founded 2014. Pop 602; Circ 15,350
Library Holdings: Bk Vols 10,000; Per Subs 44
Automation Activity & Vendor Info: (Cataloging) Book Systems; (Circulation) Book Systems
Wireless access
Open Mon 1-6, Tues-Fri 1-5, Sat 10-12
Friends of the Library Group

SEYMOUR

P SEYMOUR COMMUNITY LIBRARY*, 123 N Fifth St, 52590. SAN 305-6880. Tel: 641-898-2966. FAX: 641-898-2305. E-mail: seycomlib@lisco.net. *Librn,* Jessie Morriss
Founded 1940. Pop 1,036; Circ 7,662
Library Holdings: Bk Titles 10,000
Open Mon-Fri 1-5

SHEFFIELD

P SHEFFIELD PUBLIC LIBRARY, 123 Third St, 50475. (Mail add: PO Box 616, 50475-0616), SAN 305-6899. Tel: 641-892-4717. FAX: 641-892-4248. E-mail: shefflib@mchsi.com. Web Site: www.sheffield.lib.ia.us. *Dir,* Jessica Foreshoe
Pop 930; Circ 22,793
Library Holdings: Bk Titles 17,381; Per Subs 64
Automation Activity & Vendor Info: (Cataloging) Follett Software; (Circulation) Follett Software; (OPAC) Follett Software
Wireless access
Open Mon & Thurs 10-6, Tues, Wed & Fri 1-6, Sat 10-2

SHELDON

J NORTHWEST IOWA COMMUNITY COLLEGE LIBRARY*, 603 W Park St, 51201. SAN 305-6902. Tel: 712-324-5066. Web Site: www.nwicc.edu. *Dir,* Molly Galm; Tel: 712-324-5066, Ext 116, E-mail: mgalm@nwicc.edu
Founded 1974. Enrl 850; Fac 50
Library Holdings: Bk Titles 13,000; Bk Vols 15,000; Per Subs 250
Subject Interests: Bus & mgt, Electronics, Mechanical engr, Sci tech
Automation Activity & Vendor Info: (Cataloging) Innovative Interfaces, Inc; (Circulation) Innovative Interfaces, Inc; (OPAC) Innovative Interfaces, Inc
Wireless access
Partic in Iowa Academic Library Alliance; OCLC Online Computer Library Center, Inc; State of Iowa Libraries Online
Open Mon-Thurs 7:30-7, Fri 7:30-4:30

P SHELDON PUBLIC LIBRARY*, 925 Fourth Ave, 51201. SAN 305-6910. Tel: 712-324-2442. FAX: 712-324-5609. E-mail: sheldonpubliclibrary@gmail.com. Web Site: www.sheldon.lib.ia.us. *Dir,* Nicole Morgan; E-mail: nmorgan@sheldon.lib.ia.us; *Asst Dir,* Brenda Klaahssen; E-mail: brenda.k@sheldon.lib.ia.us
Founded 1904. Pop 5,003; Circ 94,680

Library Holdings: AV Mats 746; Bk Titles 29,802; Per Subs 100; Talking Bks 801
Special Collections: Local Newspaper 1874-1997, micro
Automation Activity & Vendor Info: (Serials) EBSCO Online
Wireless access
Open Mon 10-8, Tues-Fri 10-5, Sat 10-2
Friends of the Library Group

SHELL ROCK

P BENNY GAMBAIANI PUBLIC LIBRARY*, 104 S Cherry St, 50670. (Mail add: PO Box 320, 50670-0811), SAN 305-6929. Tel: 319-885-4345. FAX: 319-885-6209. E-mail: gambaian@butler-bremer.com. Web Site: www.shellrocklibrary.org. *Dir,* Pascale Bruns; *Asst Librn,* Sue Kaus; *Libr Assoc,* Kaylee Frost; Staff 3 (Non-MLS 3)
Pop 1,298; Circ 25,000
Library Holdings: Large Print Bks 79; Bk Titles 14,000; Per Subs 69; Talking Bks 359
Special Collections: Shell Rock Newspapers, microfilm
Automation Activity & Vendor Info: (Circulation) Follett Software
Wireless access
Function: Home delivery & serv to seniorr ctr & nursing homes, Homebound delivery serv, ILL available, Internet access, Mail loans to mem, Outside serv via phone, mail, e-mail & web, Photocopying/Printing, Prog for children & young adult, Summer reading prog, Wheelchair accessible, Workshops
Open Mon & Fri 12-5, Tues & Thurs 12-8, Wed 9-5, Sat 9am-11am

SHELLSBURG

P SHELLSBURG PUBLIC LIBRARY*, 110 Main St, 52332. (Mail add: PO Box 248, 52332-0248), SAN 305-6937. Tel: 319-436-2112. FAX: 319-436-2874. Web Site: www.shellsburg.lib.ia.us. *Dir,* Julie Kimm; E-mail: director@shellsburg.lib.ia.us; *Asst Librn,* Kathy Walton; Staff 1 (Non-MLS 1)
Founded 1970. Pop 998; Circ 21,179
Library Holdings: CDs 42; DVDs 175; Large Print Bks 72; Bk Titles 12,725; Per Subs 12; Videos 64
Automation Activity & Vendor Info: (Acquisitions) Follett Software
Wireless access
Function: Bk club(s), Bks on cassette, Bks on CD, Children's prog, Computers for patron use, Free DVD rentals, ILL available, Magnifiers for reading, Online cat, OverDrive digital audio bks, Photocopying/Printing, Summer reading prog, Tax forms, VHS videos, Wheelchair accessible
Open Mon-Wed 10-12 & 2-6, Thurs & Fri 2-6
Restriction: Authorized patrons, Borrowing requests are handled by ILL, Circ limited
Friends of the Library Group

SHENANDOAH

P SHENANDOAH PUBLIC LIBRARY, 201 S Elm St, 51601. SAN 305-6945. Tel: 712-246-2315. FAX: 712-246-5847. E-mail: libraryq@shenandoahiowa.net, shenlib@shenandoahiowa.net. Web Site: www.shenandoah.lib.ia.us. *Dir,* Carrie Falk; E-mail: spldirector@shenandoahiowa.net; *Tech Coordr,* Joy Stortdedt; *Ch Serv,* Elizabeth Trippler; *Circ,* Carole Dailey; Staff 4 (MLS 2, Non-MLS 2)
Founded 1904. Pop 5,546; Circ 65,564
Library Holdings: Bk Vols 55,000
Automation Activity & Vendor Info: (Cataloging) Biblionix/Apollo; (Circulation) Biblionix/Apollo; (OPAC) Biblionix/Apollo
Wireless access
Open Mon-Wed, Fri & Sat 10-6, Thurs 10-8
Friends of the Library Group

SIBLEY

P SIBLEY PUBLIC LIBRARY*, 406 Ninth St, 51249. SAN 305-6953. Tel: 712-754-2888. FAX: 712-754-2590. Web Site: www.sibley.lib.ia.us. *Dir,* Mary Earll; E-mail: mary.earll@sibley.lib.ia.us; *Youth Serv Coordr,* Rachel Galvin; E-mail: rachel.galvin@sibley.lib.ia.us; Staff 4 (MLS 1, Non-MLS 3)
Founded 1917. Pop 2,796; Circ 48,594
Library Holdings: Audiobooks 111; DVDs 656; Large Print Bks 48; Bk Titles 21,151; Per Subs 56
Automation Activity & Vendor Info: (Cataloging) Follett Software; (Circulation) Follett Software
Wireless access
Function: 24/7 Electronic res, 24/7 Online cat, Adult bk club, After school storytime, Audiobks on Playaways & MP3, Audiobks via web, Bilingual assistance for Spanish patrons, Bk club(s), Bks on CD, Children's prog, Computers for patron use, Electronic databases & coll, Family literacy, Free DVD rentals, Holiday prog, Home delivery & serv to seniorr ctr & nursing homes, Homebound delivery serv, ILL available, Internet access, Life-long learning prog for all ages, Magazines, Mango lang, Meeting rooms, Microfiche/film & reading machines, Movies, Online cat, Outreach serv, OverDrive digital audio bks, Photocopying/Printing, Preschool outreach, Prog for adults, Prog for children & young adult, Scanner, Spanish lang bks, Story hour, Study rm, Summer reading prog, Tax forms, Teen prog, Wheelchair accessible
Open Mon, Tues & Thurs 10-8, Wed & Fri 10-5, Sat 10-2

SIDNEY

P SIDNEY PUBLIC LIBRARY*, 1002 Illinois St, 51652. (Mail add: PO Box 479, 51652-0479), SAN 305-6961. Tel: 712-374-6203. FAX: 712-374-6303. E-mail: read@sidney.lib.ia.us. Web Site: www.sidney.lib.ia.us. *Libr Dir,* Ms Riley Moreland
Pop 1,499; Circ 8,715
Library Holdings: DVDs 175; Large Print Bks 250; Bk Vols 10,750; Per Subs 33; Talking Bks 216; Videos 845
Automation Activity & Vendor Info: (Cataloging) Follett Software
Wireless access
Open Mon 11-7, Tues & Sat 9-1, Wed 12-7, Fri 10-5

SIGOURNEY

P SIGOURNEY PUBLIC LIBRARY*, 720 E Jackson, 52591-1505. SAN 305-697X. Tel: 641-622-2890. FAX: 641-622-3391. E-mail: sigopl@lisco.com. Web Site: www.sigourney.lib.ia.us. *Dir,* Amanda Rostami
Pop 4,870; Circ 58,400
Library Holdings: Bk Vols 22,773; Per Subs 40
Automation Activity & Vendor Info: (Cataloging) Follett Software; (Circulation) Follett Software
Wireless access
Open Mon-Thurs 11-7, Fri 11-6, Sat 11-3
Friends of the Library Group

SILVER CITY

P SILVER CITY PUBLIC LIBRARY*, 408 Main St, 51571. Tel: 712-525-9053. FAX: 712-525-9053. E-mail: silvercitylibraryia@gmail.com. Web Site: www.silvercity.lib.ia.us. *Libr Dir,* Valerie Sue Garner
Library Holdings: AV Mats 608; DVDs 70; Large Print Bks 40; Bk Titles 6,030; Per Subs 21; Videos 512
Wireless access
Open Mon & Sat 8:30-1, Tues, Wed & Fri 2-6

SIOUX CENTER

CR DORDT UNIVERSITY, John & Louise Hulst Library, 700 Seventh St NE, 51250. SAN 305-6996. Tel: 712-722-6040. E-mail: library@dordt.edu. Web Site: www.dordt.edu/academics/john-and-louise-hulst-library.
Founded 1955. Enrl 1,467; Highest Degree: Master
Special Collections: Dutch History Coll
Subject Interests: Educ, Hist, Relig
Automation Activity & Vendor Info: (Acquisitions) OCLC Worldshare Management Services; (Cataloging) OCLC Worldshare Management Services; (Circulation) OCLC Worldshare Management Services; (Discovery) OCLC Worldshare Management Services; (OPAC) OCLC Worldshare Management Services; (Serials) OCLC Worldshare Management Services
Wireless access
Partic in Iowa Academic Library Alliance

P SIOUX CENTER PUBLIC LIBRARY*, 102 S Main Ave, 51250-1801. SAN 305-7003. Tel: 712-722-2138. FAX: 712-722-1235. Web Site: siouxcenterlibrary.org. *Dir,* Becky Bilby; E-mail: becky.bilby@siouxcenterlibrary.org; *Admin Serv,* Heidi Ouwinga; E-mail: Heidi.Ouwinga@siouxcenterlibrary.org; *Ch,* Twila DeGroot; *Adult Programming,* Julie Kreun; Staff 11 (MLS 2, Non-MLS 9)
Founded 1927. Pop 7,500
Library Holdings: e-books 62,487; Large Print Bks 3,300; Bk Titles 62,179; Per Subs 143
Special Collections: Genealogy of Sioux County. Oral History
Subject Interests: Genealogy, Hist, Iowa, Spanish lang mat
Automation Activity & Vendor Info: (Cataloging) Book Systems; (OPAC) Book Systems
Wireless access
Function: 24/7 Electronic res, 24/7 Online cat, Accelerated reader prog, Activity rm, Adult bk club, Adult literacy prog, After school storytime, Archival coll, Art exhibits, Art programs, Audiobks on Playaways & MP3, AV serv, Bilingual assistance for Spanish patrons, Bk club(s), Bk reviews (Group), Bks on CD, Children's prog, Computer training, Computers for patron use, Digital talking bks, Distance learning, E-Readers, E-Reserves, Electronic databases & coll, Equip loans & repairs, Family literacy, For res purposes, Free DVD rentals, Games & aids for people with disabilities, Govt ref serv, Homebound delivery serv, Homework prog, ILL available, Instruction & testing, Internet access, Magazines, Magnifiers for reading, Mail & tel request accepted, Makerspace, Meeting rooms, Movies, Music CDs, Notary serv, Online cat, Online info literacy tutorials on the web &

in blackboard, Online ref, Outreach serv, Outside serv via phone, mail, e-mail & web, OverDrive digital audio bks, Photocopying/Printing, Preschool outreach, Preschool reading prog, Printer for laptops & handheld devices, Prof lending libr, Prog for adults, Prog for children & young adult, Ref & res, Ref serv available, Res assist avail, Res libr, Scanner, Senior computer classes, Senior outreach, Serves people with intellectual disabilities, Spanish lang bks, STEM programs, Story hour, Study rm, Summer & winter reading prog, Summer reading prog, Tax forms, Teen prog, Visual arts prog, Wheelchair accessible, Winter reading prog, Workshops
Partic in State of Iowa Libraries Online
Special Services for the Deaf - Bks on deafness & sign lang; High interest/low vocabulary bks
Special Services for the Blind - Bks on CD; Copier with enlargement capabilities; Home delivery serv; Large print bks
Open Mon-Thurs 9-9, Fri 9-5, Sat 9-1

SIOUX CITY

C BRIAR CLIFF UNIVERSITY*, The Bishop Mueller Library, 3303 Rebecca St, 51104. SAN 305-7011. Tel: 712-279-5449. FAX: 712-279-1723. E-mail: library@briarcliff.edu. Web Site: www.briarcliff.edu/student-life/buildings-and-facilities/bishop-mueller-library. *Univ Librn,* Breanne Kirsch; Tel: 712-279-5451, E-mail: Breanne.Kirsch@briarcliff.edu; *Head, Pub Serv, Head, Res Serv,* Angela Houk; Tel: 712-279-5442, E-mail: angela.houk@briarcliff.edu; *ILL Librn, Tech Serv Librn,* Sister Mary Jane Koenigs; Tel: 712-279-5535, E-mail: MaryJane.Koenigs@briarcliff.edu; Staff 3.5 (MLS 1.5, Non-MLS 2)
Founded 1930. Enrl 928; Fac 64; Highest Degree: Doctorate
Library Holdings: e-books 250,000
Subject Interests: Nursing, Soc serv (soc work), Sociol, Theol
Automation Activity & Vendor Info: (Cataloging) Koha; (Circulation) Koha; (OPAC) Koha
Wireless access
Function: ILL available
Partic in Iowa Academic Library Alliance; Iowa Private Academic Library Consortium; Sioux City Library Cooperative
Open Mon-Thurs 7:45am-Midnight, Fri 7:45-5, Sat 12:30-4:30, Sun 1-Midnight
Friends of the Library Group

C MORNINGSIDE UNIVERSITY, Hickman-Johnson-Furrow Learning Center, 1501 Morningside Ave, 51106. SAN 305-7046. Tel: 712-274-5195. Reference Tel: 712-274-5193. FAX: 712-274-5224. Web Site: library.morningside.edu. *Asst Prof, Libr Dir,* Adam Fullerton; Tel: 712-274-5247, E-mail: fullertona@morningside.edu; *Ref & Instruction Librn,* Holly Schettler; Tel: 712-274-5246, E-mail: schettlerh@morningside.edu; *Circ Mgr,* Karen Wascher; Tel: 712-274-5245, E-mail: johnsonka@morningside.edu; *Tech Serv,* Susan Trisler; E-mail: trisler@morningside.edu; Staff 5 (MLS 2, Non-MLS 3)
Founded 1894. Enrl 1,369; Fac 70; Highest Degree: Doctorate
Library Holdings: AV Mats 1,200; Bk Titles 42,000; Per Subs 115
Automation Activity & Vendor Info: (Cataloging) OCLC Worldshare Management Services; (Circulation) OCLC Worldshare Management Services; (Course Reserve) OCLC Worldshare Management Services; (ILL) OCLC Worldshare Management Services; (OPAC) OCLC Worldshare Management Services; (Serials) OCLC Worldshare Management Services
Wireless access
Function: Online cat
Publications: Newsletter
Partic in Council of Independent Colleges; Iowa Academic Library Alliance; Iowa Private Academic Library Consortium; Iowa Resource & Info Sharing; OCLC Online Computer Library Center, Inc
Restriction: Open to pub for ref & circ; with some limitations

CM ST LUKE'S COLLEGE LIBRARY*, 2800 Pierce St, Ste 202, 51104. (Mail add: 2720 Stone Park Blvd, 51104). Tel: 712-279-3156. Toll Free Tel: 800-352-4660, Ext 3156. Web Site: www.stlukescollege.edu/about-st-lukes-library.aspx. *Dept Chair,* Nancy Zubrod; Tel: 712-279-4961, E-mail: nancy.zubrod@stlukescollege.edu
Library Holdings: Bk Titles 2,260; Bk Vols 2,500; Per Subs 35
Subject Interests: Family practice, Med, Nursing
Automation Activity & Vendor Info: (Cataloging) CyberTools for Libraries; (Circulation) CyberTools for Libraries; (OPAC) CyberTools for Libraries
Wireless access
Open Mon-Thurs 7:30-7, Fri 7:30-4, Sat & Sun 12-5

S SIOUX CITY ART CENTER*, Margaret Avery Heffernan Reference Library, 225 Nebraska St, 51101-1712. SAN 305-7062. Tel: 712-279-6272. Reference Tel: 712-279-6272, Ext 208. FAX: 712-255-2921. Web Site: www.siouxcityartcenter.org. *Admin Serv,* Kjersten Welch; E-mail: kwelch@sioux-city.org
Library Holdings: CDs 12; Bk Vols 1,500; Videos 63
Subject Interests: Art (20th Century)
Function: Res libr
Restriction: Non-circulating to the pub, Open by appt only

P SIOUX CITY PUBLIC LIBRARY*, Wilbur Aalfs Main Library, 529 Pierce St, 51101-1203. SAN 341-9673. Tel: 712-255-2933. E-mail: questions@siouxcitylibrary.org. Web Site: www.siouxcitylibrary.org. *Dir,* Helen Rigdon; E-mail: hrigdon@siouxcitylibrary.org; *Operations Mgr,* Sara Leiss; *Ch Serv,* Adrienne Dunn; *Circ Serv,* Marla Kerr; Staff 18 (MLS 7, Non-MLS 11)
Founded 1877. Pop 82,678; Circ 432,280
Jul 2014-Jun 2015 Income (Main & Associated Libraries) $2,830,326, State $31,326, City $2,600,000, Locally Generated Income $77,000, Other $122,000. Mats Exp $295,000, Books $203,000, Per/Ser (Incl. Access Fees) $18,000, AV Mat $38,000, Electronic Ref Mat (Incl. Access Fees) $36,000. Sal $2,057,000
Library Holdings: AV Mats 9,921; Large Print Bks 2,331; Bk Vols 127,268; Per Subs 144
Special Collections: US Document Depository
Automation Activity & Vendor Info: (Acquisitions) SirsiDynix; (Cataloging) SirsiDynix; (Circulation) SirsiDynix; (OPAC) SirsiDynix
Wireless access
Function: 24/7 Electronic res, Activity rm, Audio & video playback equip for onsite use, Audiobks via web, AV serv, Bk club(s), Bks on CD, Children's prog, Computer training, Computers for patron use, Electronic databases & coll, Family literacy, Free DVD rentals, Home delivery & serv to seniorr ctr & nursing homes, Homebound delivery serv, ILL available, Internet access, Magazines, Mango lang, Meeting rooms, Microfiche/film & reading machines, Movies, Online cat, OverDrive digital audio bks, Photocopying/Printing, Preschool outreach, Prog for children & young adult, Ref serv available, Scanner, Summer reading prog, Tax forms, Telephone ref, Wheelchair accessible
Publications: Book Remarks (Newsletter)
Open Mon-Wed 9-8, Thurs-Sat 9-5, Sun 1-5
Friends of the Library Group
Branches: 2
PERRY CREEK BRANCH LIBRARY, Plaza Professional Center, Lower B, 2912 Hamilton Blvd, 51104-2410, SAN 341-9797. Tel: 712-255-2926. *Br Supvr,* Betsy Thompson
Library Holdings: AV Mats 716; Large Print Bks 414; Bk Vols 10,369; Per Subs 25
Friends of the Library Group
SCHROEDER-MORNINGSIDE BRANCH LIBRARY, 4005 Morningside Ave, 51106-2448, SAN 341-9738. Tel: 712-255-2924. *Br Supvr,* Jennifer Delperdang
Library Holdings: AV Mats 5,007; Large Print Bks 3,075; Bk Vols 40,580; Per Subs 59
Friends of the Library Group

J WESTERN IOWA TECH COMMUNITY COLLEGE*, Western Iowa Tech Library, 4647 Stone Ave, 51106. (Mail add: PO Box 5199, 51102-5199), SAN 305-7089. Tel: 712-274-8733, Ext 1239. Administration Tel: 712-274-8733, Ext 1324. FAX: 712-274-6423. E-mail: library@witcc.edu. Web Site: www.witcc.edu/library. *Libr Mgr,* Sharon Dykshoorn; Staff 2 (MLS 1, Non-MLS 1)
Founded 1966. Enrl 5,731; Highest Degree: Associate
Jul 2017-Jun 2018 Income $72,270. Mats Exp $71,246, Books $7,000, Per/Ser (Incl. Access Fees) $56,970, AV Mat $3,000, Electronic Ref Mat (Incl. Access Fees) $4,276. Sal $113,074 (Prof $73,712)
Automation Activity & Vendor Info: (Cataloging) SirsiDynix; (Circulation) SirsiDynix; (Course Reserve) SirsiDynix; (ILL) OCLC WorldShare Interlibrary Loan; (OPAC) SirsiDynix; (Serials) EBSCO Online
Wireless access
Partic in Iowa Academic Library Alliance; Sioux City Library Cooperative
Open Mon-Thurs 7:30-6, Fri 7:30-5, Sat 8-Noon
Friends of the Library Group

SIOUX RAPIDS

P SIOUX RAPIDS MEMORIAL LIBRARY, 215 Second St, 50585. (Mail add: PO Box 445, 50585-0445), SAN 305-7100. Tel: 712-283-2064. FAX: 712-283-2064. E-mail: sxrlibrary@gmail.com. Web Site: www.siouxrapids.lib.ia.us. *Dir,* Luellen Kay Phelps
Pop 775; Circ 14,140
Library Holdings: Bk Vols 19,250; Per Subs 15
Special Collections: Sioux Rapids Bulletin Press (1800's-current), micro
Wireless access
Open Mon, Tues & Thurs 12-6, Wed 9-3, Fri & Sat 9-Noon

SLATER

P SLATER PUBLIC LIBRARY*, 105 N Tama St, 50244. (Mail add: PO Box 598, 50244-0598), SAN 305-7119. Tel: 515-228-3558. FAX: 515-228-3558. Web Site: slaterlibrary.org. *Dir,* Jennifer Gogerty; E-mail: director@slaterlibrary.org; Staff 4 (MLS 1, Non-MLS 3)

Founded 1970. Pop 2,000; Circ 22,074
Library Holdings: Bk Vols 15,000; Per Subs 40; Videos 1,000
Special Collections: Slater News & Tri County Times, 1890-present, microfilm
Automation Activity & Vendor Info: (Cataloging) Follett Software; (Serials) EBSCO Online
Wireless access
Open Mon-Thurs 10-7, Fri 10-5, Sat 10-Noon
Friends of the Library Group

SLOAN

P SLOAN PUBLIC LIBRARY*, 502 Evans St, 51055. SAN 305-7127. Tel: 712-428-4200. FAX: 712-428-6546. E-mail: slolib@longlines.com. Web Site: www.sloan.lib.ia.us. *Dir,* Tami Coil; *Libr Asst,* Victoria Eliason
Founded 1935. Pop 973; Circ 14,856
Jul 2015-Jun 2016 Income $52,075, State $1,500, City $33,675, Locally Generated Income $8,300, Other $8,600. Mats Exp $9,380, Books $5,500, Per/Ser (Incl. Access Fees) $400, AV Mat $2,480, Electronic Ref Mat (Incl. Access Fees) $1,000. Sal $26,000
Library Holdings: Audiobooks 105; DVDs 1,435; Large Print Bks 75; Bk Titles 9,135; Per Subs 32
Subject Interests: Hist, Iowa
Automation Activity & Vendor Info: (Cataloging) Book Systems
Wireless access
Function: Accelerated reader prog, Activity rm, Audiobks via web, Bks on CD, Children's prog, Computer training, Computers for patron use, E-Reserves, Electronic databases & coll, Free DVD rentals, Holiday prog, Homebound delivery serv, ILL available, Internet access, Laminating, Life-long learning prog for all ages, Magazines, Movies, Photocopying/Printing, Preschool outreach, Prog for children & young adult, Scanner, Story hour, Study rm, Summer reading prog, Teen prog, Wheelchair accessible
Special Services for the Deaf - Bks on deafness & sign lang; Captioned film dep
Open Mon & Thurs 1:30-6:30, Tues 4-7, Wed 10-6:30, Fri 1:30-5:30, Sat 9-Noon

SOLON

P SOLON PUBLIC LIBRARY*, 320 W Main St, 52333-9504. SAN 305-7135. Tel: 319-624-2678. FAX: 319-624-5034. Administration E-mail: admin@solon.lib.ia.us. Web Site: www.solon.lib.ia.us. *Dir,* Kris Brown; *Youth Serv Librn,* Cassandra Elton
Founded 1965. Pop 2,000; Circ 97,498
Library Holdings: Audiobooks 2,358; DVDs 2,556; Bk Titles 29,296; Per Subs 59
Automation Activity & Vendor Info: (Acquisitions) Auto-Graphics, Inc
Wireless access
Function: Adult bk club, Bks on CD, Children's prog, Computers for patron use, Electronic databases & coll, Free DVD rentals, Holiday prog, ILL available, Internet access, Music CDs, Online cat, Outreach serv, OverDrive digital audio bks, Photocopying/Printing, Preschool outreach, Preschool reading prog, Prog for adults, Prog for children & young adult, Scanner, Summer reading prog, Tax forms, Teen prog, Wheelchair accessible
Partic in North Eastern Iowa Bridge to Online Resource Sharing
Open Mon-Thurs 12-8, Fri & Sat 10-5
Restriction: Access at librarian's discretion
Friends of the Library Group

SOMERS

P SOMERS PUBLIC LIBRARY, 502 Sixth St, 50586. (Mail add: PO Box 114, 50586-0114), SAN 305-7143. Tel: 515-467-5522. E-mail: somersli@wccta.net. Web Site: somers.lib.ia.us. *Dir,* Helene Tsubira
Founded 1973. Pop 167; Circ 3,768
Library Holdings: Bk Titles 5,475
Open Mon-Wed 1-5, Thurs 1-6, Sat 9-Noon

SOUTH ENGLISH

P SOUTH ENGLISH PUBLIC LIBRARY*, 407 Ives St, 52335. (Mail add: PO Box 162, 52335-0162), SAN 305-7151. Tel: 319-667-2715. FAX: 319-667-4507. E-mail: slibrary@netins.net. Web Site: www.southenglish.lib.ia.us. *Dir,* Brandi Meyer; E-mail: brandi.meyer@southenglish.lib.ia.us
Founded 1936. Pop 270; Circ 2,862
Library Holdings: Bk Titles 4,637
Open Tues-Thurs 4-7, Sat 9-12

SPENCER

P SPENCER PUBLIC LIBRARY, 21 E Third St, 51301-4131. SAN 305-716X. Tel: 712-580-7290. FAX: 712-580-7468. E-mail: libraryinfo@spenceriowacity.com. Web Site: www.spencerlibrary.com. *Dir,* Mandie Roberts; *Asst Dir,* Paula Brown; *Ch,* Sarah Beth Fuchsen; *YA Librn,* Kayla Schlichte; Staff 12 (MLS 1, Non-MLS 11)
Founded 1904. Pop 11,317
Library Holdings: CDs 2,384; DVDs 691; Large Print Bks 2,843; Bk Vols 49,735; Per Subs 217; Talking Bks 1,122; Videos 447
Special Collections: Career-Related Materials; Charlotte Brett Genealogy Coll
Subject Interests: Local hist
Automation Activity & Vendor Info: (Cataloging) TLC (The Library Corporation); (Circulation) TLC (The Library Corporation); (OPAC) TLC (The Library Corporation)
Wireless access
Publications: SPLASH (Newsletter)
Special Services for the Blind - Computer with voice synthesizer for visually impaired persons
Open Mon-Thurs 9-8, Fri & Sat 9-5
Friends of the Library Group

SPILLVILLE

P SPILLVILLE PUBLIC LIBRARY*, 201 Oak St, 52168. (Mail add: PO Box 197, 52168-0197), SAN 325-2558. Tel: 563-562-3723. FAX: 563-562-4373. E-mail: libraryspillvillepublic@gmail.com. Web Site: www.spillville.lib.ia.us. *Dir,* Ruth Kuhn
Founded 1980
Library Holdings: Bks on Deafness & Sign Lang 10; CDs 109; DVDs 41; Bk Titles 5,500; Bk Vols 6,052; Per Subs 25; Talking Bks 168; Videos 428
Automation Activity & Vendor Info: (Cataloging) Follett Software; (Circulation) Follett Software
Open Mon, Tues & Fri 1:30-5:30, Wed 9-1, Thurs 1:30-6:30, Sat 9-Noon

SPIRIT LAKE

J IOWA LAKES COMMUNITY COLLEGE*, Spirit Lake Campus, 800 21st St, 51360. Tel: 712-336-3439, 712-336-6564. FAX: 712-336-1357. E-mail: slsuccess@iowalakes.edu. Web Site: www.iowalakes.edu/student-services/library. *Dir of Libr,* Shannon Motter; E-mail: smotter@iowalakes.edu; *Supvr,* Mary Maber
Wireless access
Open Mon-Thurs 8-4, Fri 8-Noon

P SPIRIT LAKE PUBLIC LIBRARY*, 702 16th St, 51360. SAN 305-7178. Tel: 712-336-2667. FAX: 712-336-0511. Administration E-mail: admin@spiritlake.lib.ia.us. Web Site: slpublib.com. *Libr Dir,* Cindy Davis; *Dir, Ch Serv,* Krista Elmquist; E-mail: kelmquist@spiritlake.lib.ia.us; Staff 4 (Non-MLS 4)
Founded 1912. Pop 4,840; Circ 111,297
Library Holdings: Audiobooks 2,333; DVDs 1,062; Bk Vols 26,242; Per Subs 231
Special Collections: Northwest Iowa History Coll. Oral History
Automation Activity & Vendor Info: (Cataloging) OCLC CatExpress; (Circulation) Book Systems; (OPAC) Book Systems
Wireless access
Open Mon-Thurs 10-7, Fri 10-5, Sat 10-3
Friends of the Library Group

SPRINGVILLE

P SPRINGVILLE MEMORIAL LIBRARY*, 264 Broadway St, 52336. (Mail add: PO Box 78, 52336-0078), SAN 305-7186. Tel: 319-854-6444. FAX: 319-854-6443. E-mail: sprlibry@netins.net. Web Site: www.springville.lib.ia.us. *Dir,* Linda K Eldred; Staff 2 (Non-MLS 2)
Founded 1949. Pop 1,091; Circ 13,487
Library Holdings: Bk Vols 14,500; Per Subs 25
Open Mon-Wed 11-6, Thurs 10-8, Fri 11-5, Sat 11-3
Friends of the Library Group

STACYVILLE

P STACYVILLE PUBLIC LIBRARY*, 106 N Broad St, 50476. SAN 305-7194. Tel: 641-710-2531. E-mail: stacylib@myomnitel.com. Web Site: www.youseemore.com/nilc/stacyville. *Dir,* Barb Klapperich
Founded 1967. Pop 494; Circ 38,000
Library Holdings: Bk Titles 16,000
Special Collections: Oral History
Automation Activity & Vendor Info: (Cataloging) TLC (The Library Corporation); (Circulation) TLC (The Library Corporation)
Wireless access
Open Mon, Tues & Fri 10-12 & 2-6:30, Wed & Thurs 2-6:30, Sat 10-2:30

STANHOPE

P STANHOPE PUBLIC LIBRARY*, 600 Main St, 50246. (Mail add: PO Box 67, 50246-0067), SAN 305-7208. Tel: 515-826-3211. FAX: 515-826-3211. E-mail: stanpl@netins.net. Web Site: www.stanhope.lib.ia.us. *Dir,* Dee Weir; E-mail: dee.weir@stanhope.lib.ia.us

Founded 1950. Pop 488; Circ 4,000
Library Holdings: Bk Vols 7,000; Per Subs 22
Wireless access
Open Mon 10-12 & 3-6, Tues-Thurs 1-6, Fri 3-6, Sat 10-Noon

STANTON

P STANTON PUBLIC LIBRARY, 501 Elliott St, Ste A, 51573. (Mail add: PO Box 130, 51573-0130). Tel: 712-829-2290. FAX: 712-829-2570. E-mail: stanlib@myfmtc.com. Web Site: www.stanton.lib.ia.us. *Dir,* Shelley Anderson
Wireless access
Open Mon 1-5, Tues 9-11 & 2-5, Wed 1-6, Thurs & Fri 2-5

STANWOOD

P STANWOOD PUBLIC LIBRARY*, 202 E Broadway, 52337. (Mail add: PO Box 234, 52337-0234), SAN 305-7224. Tel: 563-942-3531. FAX: 563-942-3531. Web Site: www.stanwood.lib.ia.us. *Libr Dir,* Judy Birely; E-mail: jbirely@stanwood.lib.ia.us
Founded 1949. Pop 705; Circ 3,366
Library Holdings: Bk Titles 7,500
Wireless access
Open Mon 2-5, Tues & Thurs 2-7, Wed 4-6, Fri 9-4, Sat 11-2
Friends of the Library Group

STATE CENTER

P GUTEKUNST PUBLIC LIBRARY*, 309 Second St SE, 50247-0550. (Mail add: PO Box 603, 50247-0550), SAN 305-7232. Tel: 641-483-2741. FAX: 641-483-2131. Web Site: www.statecenter.lib.ia.us. *Libr Dir,* Mara Edler; E-mail: maraedler.lib@gmail.com; *Librn,* Carol Driscoll; *Ch,* Linda Good
Circ 55,000
Library Holdings: Bk Titles 19,536; Bk Vols 23,283; Per Subs 90
Automation Activity & Vendor Info: (Cataloging) Biblionix/Apollo; (Circulation) Biblionix/Apollo
Open Mon-Thurs 9-12 & 2-7, Fri 9-5, Sat 10-3
Friends of the Library Group

STEAMBOAT ROCK

P STEAMBOAT ROCK PUBLIC LIBRARY*, 511 Market St, 50672. (Mail add: PO Box 416, 50672-0416), SAN 305-7240. Tel: 641-868-2300. FAX: 641-868-2345. E-mail: srocklib@heartofiowa.net. Web Site: www.youseemore.com/nilc/steamboatrock. *Libr Dir,* Michelle Andersen; E-mail: michelle@steamboatrock.lib.ia.us; Staff 3 (Non-MLS 3)
Founded 1959. Pop 310; Circ 11,586
Library Holdings: Bk Titles 2,390; Bk Vols 8,000; Per Subs 33
Wireless access
Open Tues-Thurs 1-6, Fri Noon-5, Sat 10-Noon

STOCKPORT

P STOCKPORT PUBLIC LIBRARY*, 113 E Beswick St, 52651. (Mail add: PO Box 62, 52651-0062), SAN 305-7259. Tel: 319-796-4681. FAX: 319-796-4681. E-mail: stocklib@netins.net. *Librn,* Twila Chaplin
Pop 847; Circ 1,553
Library Holdings: DVDs 200; Bk Vols 7,800; Per Subs 5
Subject Interests: Local hist, State
Wireless access
Function: After school storytime, Bks on CD, Computers for patron use, Free DVD rentals, Internet access, Masonic res mat, Photocopying/Printing, Printer for laptops & handheld devices, Summer reading prog
Open Mon & Wed 2:30-5:30, Fri 9-Noon

STORM LAKE

C BUENA VISTA UNIVERSITY LIBRARY, H W Siebens School of Business / Forum, 610 W Fourth St, 50588. Tel: 712-749-2127, 712-749-2203. Interlibrary Loan Service Tel: 712-749-2096. Toll Free Tel: 877-288-2240. FAX: 712-749-2059. E-mail: library@bvu.edu. Web Site: www.bvu.edu/library. *Libr Dir,* Jodie Morin; Tel: 712-749-2097, E-mail: morinj@bvu.edu; *Digital Res Librn, Tech Serv Librn,* Alyssa Grigsby; Tel: 712-749-2092, E-mail: grigsbya@bvu.edu; *Archivist, Ref Librn,* Joan Curbow; Tel: 712-749-2094, E-mail: curbowj@bvu.edu; *Access Serv,* Kelly Olson; Tel: 712-749-2098, E-mail: olsonk@bvu.edu; Staff 5 (MLS 4, Non-MLS 1)
Founded 1891. Enrl 1,444; Fac 81; Highest Degree: Master
Special Collections: BVU Archives
Subject Interests: Col hist
Automation Activity & Vendor Info: (Acquisitions) OCLC Worldshare Management Services; (Cataloging) OCLC Worldshare Management Services; (Circulation) OCLC Worldshare Management Services; (Course Reserve) OCLC Worldshare Management Services; (Discovery) OCLC Worldshare Management Services; (ILL) OCLC Tipasa; (OPAC) OCLC Worldshare Management Services; (Serials) OCLC Worldshare Management Services
Wireless access
Function: 24/7 Online cat, Photocopying/Printing, Ref serv available
Partic in Iowa Academic Library Alliance; Iowa Private Academic Library Consortium; OCLC-LVIS
Open Mon-Thurs 8am-9pm, Fri 8-5, Sun 1-9; Mon-Thurs 8-5, Fri 8-3 (Summer)
Restriction: Open to pub for ref & circ; with some limitations

P STORM LAKE PUBLIC LIBRARY*, 609 Cayuga St, 50588. SAN 305-7275. Tel: 712-732-8026. FAX: 712-732-7609. E-mail: stormlakepubliclibrary@gmail.com. Administration E-mail: admin@stormlake.lib.ia.us. Web Site: www.stormlake.lib.ia.us. *Libr Dir,* Elizabeth Huff; E-mail: elizabeth.huff@stormlake.lib.ia.us; Staff 7 (MLS 1, Non-MLS 6)
Founded 1905. Pop 10,600; Circ 88,287
Library Holdings: Bk Titles 42,176; Bk Vols 42,502; Per Subs 86
Special Collections: Spanish Coll
Automation Activity & Vendor Info: (Cataloging) Follett Software; (Circulation) Follett Software; (OPAC) Follett Software
Wireless access
Publications: Annual Report; Newsletter (Quarterly)
Partic in West/Central Iowa Libraries Building Online Resources
Open Mon & Fri (Winter) 9-6, Tues & Wed 9-7, Thurs 9-8, Sat 9-2; Mon-Fri (Summer) 9-6, Sat 9-2
Friends of the Library Group

STORY CITY

P BERTHA BARTLETT PUBLIC LIBRARY*, 503 Broad St, 50248-1133. SAN 305-7283. Tel: 515-733-2685. FAX: 515-733-2843. E-mail: berthab@storycity.lib.ia.us. Web Site: www.storycity.lib.ia.us. *Dir,* Kolleen Taylor; *Asst Dir,* Denise Froehlich; Staff 4 (Non-MLS 4)
Founded 1922. Pop 3,228
Library Holdings: AV Mats 1,053; Bks on Deafness & Sign Lang 14; CDs 283; DVDs 315; Large Print Bks 1,280; Bk Vols 37,019; Per Subs 53; Talking Bks 1,121; Videos 654
Automation Activity & Vendor Info: (Cataloging) ComPanion Corp; (Circulation) ComPanion Corp; (OPAC) ComPanion Corp; (Serials) EBSCO Online
Wireless access
Function: Adult bk club, After school storytime, Audiobks via web, Bilingual assistance for Spanish patrons, Bk club(s), Bks on CD, CD-ROM, Children's prog, Computer training, Computers for patron use, Free DVD rentals, Home delivery & serv to seniorr ctr & nursing homes, ILL available, Music CDs, Online cat, Photocopying/Printing, Preschool outreach, Prog for adults, Prog for children & young adult, Ref serv available, Scanner, Spanish lang bks, Spoken cassettes & CDs, Summer reading prog, Tax forms, Teen prog, VHS videos, Wheelchair accessible
Open Mon, Wed & Fri 10-5, Tues & Thurs 10-7, Sat 10-2
Friends of the Library Group
Branches: 1
GILBERT BRANCH, 207 Main St, Gilbert, 50105. Tel: 515-232-0087. E-mail: Gilbertlibrary@storycity.lib.ia.us.
Open Tues & Thurs 3:30-7:30, Sat 10-Noon

STRATFORD

P STRATFORD PUBLIC LIBRARY*, 816 Shakespeare, 50249. (Mail add: PO Box 320, 50249-0320), SAN 305-7291. Tel: 515-838-2131. FAX: 515-838-2183. E-mail: stratlib@globalccs.net. Web Site: www.youseemore.com/nilc/Stratford. *Dir,* Diana Erickson; *Asst Librn,* Deb Risen
Founded 1926. Pop 720; Circ 9,500
Library Holdings: AV Mats 370; Bk Vols 6,454; Per Subs 41; Talking Bks 165
Special Collections: Stratford Courier Newspaper 1892-1959, micro 1978-present, paper
Wireless access
Open Mon-Fri 1-6, Sat 9-12

STRAWBERRY POINT

P STRAWBERRY POINT PUBLIC LIBRARY*, 401 Commercial St, 52076. (Mail add: PO Box 340, 52076-0340), SAN 305-7305. Tel: 563-933-4340. FAX: 563-933-4340. Web Site: www.strawberrypoint.lib.ia.us. *Dir,* Patty Lincoln; E-mail: plincoln@strawberrypoint.lib.ia.us
Pop 1,115; Circ 32,872
Library Holdings: e-books 4,449; Bk Titles 25,883; Per Subs 63
Automation Activity & Vendor Info: (Media Booking) Biblionix/Apollo; (OPAC) Biblionix/Apollo
Wireless access
Open Mon & Fri 2:30-5:30, Tues 9-12 & 2:30-6:30, Wed 11-5:30, Thurs 9-5;30, Sat 9-12

STUART

P STUART PUBLIC LIBRARY, 111 E Front St, 50250. (Mail add: PO Box 220, 50250-0220), SAN 305-7313. Tel: 515-523-2152. FAX: 515-523-1484. E-mail: stuartlib@stuart.lib.ia.us. Web Site: stuartlibrary.org. *Dir,* Lisa Sherman; E-mail: lisa.sherman@stuart.lib.ia.us
Founded 1901. Pop 1,650; Circ 28,961
Library Holdings: Bk Vols 18,751; Per Subs 70
Subject Interests: Iowa
Wireless access
Function: 24/7 Electronic res, 24/7 Online cat, Activity rm, Adult bk club, After school storytime, Archival coll, Audiobks on Playaways & MP3, Audiobks via web, Bks on CD, Children's prog, Citizenship assistance, Computers for patron use, Electronic databases & coll, Family literacy, Free DVD rentals, Govt ref serv, Health sci info serv, Holiday prog, Home delivery & serv to seniorr ctr & nursing homes, Homebound delivery serv, ILL available, Internet access, Laminating, Life-long learning prog for all ages, Magazines, Magnifiers for reading, Mail & tel request accepted, Makerspace, Meeting rooms, Movies, Online cat, Online info literacy tutorials on the web & in blackboard, Online ref, Outreach serv, OverDrive digital audio bks, Photocopying/Printing, Preschool reading prog, Printer for laptops & handheld devices, Prog for adults, Prog for children & young adult, Ref & res, Ref serv available, Res assist avail, Scanner, Senior outreach, Serves people with intellectual disabilities, Spanish lang bks, Spoken cassettes & DVDs, STEM programs, Story hour, Summer & winter reading prog, Summer reading prog, Telephone ref, Wheelchair accessible
Open Mon & Wed 10-6, Tues, Thurs & Fri 8:30-4, Sat 10-2
Restriction: Non-circulating, Photo ID required for access, Restricted borrowing privileges
Friends of the Library Group

SULLY

P SULLY COMMUNITY LIBRARY*, 318 Sixth Ave, 50251. (Mail add: PO Box 227, 50251-0227), SAN 371-5434. Tel: 641-594-4148. FAX: 641-594-2978. E-mail: sullylib@netins.net. Web Site: www.sully.lib.ia.us. *Dir,* Kathy Zylstra
Library Holdings: Bk Vols 10,000
Automation Activity & Vendor Info: (Acquisitions) OCLC CatExpress; (Cataloging) Follett Software; (Circulation) Follett Software
Wireless access
Open Mon 12-7, Wed 10-7, Thurs & Sat 9-12
Friends of the Library Group

SUMNER

P SUMNER PUBLIC LIBRARY*, 206 N Railroad St, 50674. SAN 305-7321. Tel: 563-578-3324. FAX: 563-578-3324. E-mail: library@sumner.lib.ia.us. Web Site: www.sumner.lib.ia.us. *Dir,* Denise Hoins
Pop 2,100; Circ 35,000
Library Holdings: Bk Titles 25,000; Per Subs 70
Automation Activity & Vendor Info: (Cataloging) Follett Software; (Circulation) Follett Software
Wireless access
Open Mon, Wed & Thurs 9-8, Tues & Fri 1-5, Sat 9-4

SUTHERLAND

P GENERAL N B BAKER PUBLIC LIBRARY*, 315 Ash St, 51058. (Mail add: PO Box 370, 51058-0280), SAN 305-733X. Tel: 712-446-3839. FAX: 712-446-3839. E-mail: genbakrlibr@midlands.net. Web Site: nbblibrary.webs.com. *Dir,* Nancy Hill; Staff 2 (Non-MLS 2)
Founded 1875. Pop 714; Circ 9,835
Library Holdings: Bk Vols 8,142; Per Subs 54
Special Collections: Iowa Coll
Subject Interests: Hist
Open Tues & Wed 10-4, Thurs 1-6, Fri 12-4, Sat 9-Noon
Friends of the Library Group

SWALEDALE

P SWALEDALE PUBLIC LIBRARY*, 504 Main St, 50477. (Mail add: PO Box 114, 50477-0114), SAN 305-7348. Tel: 641-995-2352. FAX: 641-995-2352. E-mail: swdl@frontiernet.net. Web Site: swaledalelibrary.weebly.com. *Dir,* Sherry Hopkins; E-mail: sherry@swaledale.lib.ia.us
Founded 1972. Pop 185; Circ 1,778
Library Holdings: Bk Vols 5,818; Per Subs 38; Videos 542
Wireless access
Function: After school storytime, Children's prog, Computers for patron use, Digital talking bks, Free DVD rentals, Holiday prog, ILL available, Instruction & testing, Mail & tel request accepted, Music CDs, Photocopying/Printing, Prog for children & young adult, Scanner, Summer reading prog, Teen prog, VHS videos, Wheelchair accessible, Workshops
Special Services for the Blind - Large print bks
Open Mon & Wed 12-6, Tues 9-12 & 3:30-6, Thurs 3:30-6, Sat 9-1

SWEA CITY

P SWEA CITY PUBLIC LIBRARY*, 208 Third St N, 50590. (Mail add: PO Box 368, 50590-1013), SAN 305-7356. Tel: 515-272-4216. FAX: 515-272-4216. E-mail: sweacpl@gmail.com. *Dir,* Angie Kintzle
Founded 1900. Pop 642; Circ 19,000
Library Holdings: Bk Titles 15,988; Per Subs 35; Talking Bks 131
Wireless access
Open Mon 11-5, Wed 12-5, Fri 8-4, Sat 8-10
Friends of the Library Group

TABOR

P TABOR PUBLIC LIBRARY*, 723 Main St, 51653. (Mail add: PO Box 27, 51653-0027), SAN 305-7364. Tel: 712-629-2735. Web Site: www.tabor.lib.ia.us. *Dir,* Dawn Miller; E-mail: dawn.miller@tabor.lib.ia.us
Pop 993; Circ 3,954
Library Holdings: Bk Vols 8,286; Per Subs 13
Wireless access
Open Tues & Fri 1-5, Wed & Thurs 10-6, Sat 9-1

TAMA

P TAMA PUBLIC LIBRARY*, Louise & Lucille Hink Library, 401 Siegel St, 52339. SAN 305-7372. Tel: 641-484-4484. FAX: 641-484-4484. E-mail: tamalibrary@tama.lib.ia.us. Web Site: www.tama.lib.ia.us. *Dir,* Julie D Shook
Founded 1907. Pop 2,877
Library Holdings: Audiobooks 174; CDs 37; DVDs 326; Electronic Media & Resources 8; Large Print Bks 521; Bk Titles 28,249; Per Subs 56; Videos 1,130
Special Collections: Mesquakie Indian Coll
Automation Activity & Vendor Info: (Acquisitions) Book Systems; (Cataloging) Book Systems; (Circulation) Book Systems; (Course Reserve) Book Systems; (ILL) Book Systems; (Media Booking) Book Systems; (OPAC) Book Systems; (Serials) Book Systems
Wireless access
Open Mon & Wed (Oct-April) 12-5, Tues & Thurs 12-8, Fri 9-5, Sat 9-12, Sun 1-4; Mon & Wed (May-Sept) 12-5, Tues & Thurs 12-8, Fri 9-5

TERRIL

P TERRIL COMMUNITY LIBRARY*, 115 N State St, 51364. (Mail add: PO Box 38, 51364), SAN 305-7380. Tel: 712-853-6224. E-mail: library@terril.net. Web Site: www.terril.lib.ia.us. *Dir,* Linda Dingel; E-mail: library@terril.net
Founded 1933. Pop 400; Circ 8,001
Library Holdings: Bk Vols 8,000
Wireless access
Open Mon 3-8, Wed 10-6, Fri 11-1, Sat 9-2

THOMPSON

P THOMPSON PUBLIC LIBRARY*, 102 N Jackson St, 50478. (Mail add: PO Box 81, 50478-0081), SAN 305-7399. Tel: 641-584-2829. E-mail: thomplib@wctatel.net. Web Site: www.thompson.lib.ia.us. *Dir,* Fairy Florence; E-mail: florence@thompson.lib.ia.us
Founded 1937. Pop 668
Library Holdings: Bk Titles 4,000; Bk Vols 5,300; Per Subs 20
Wireless access
Open Tues & Thurs 9-11:30 & 2-5, Wed 2-6, Fri 2-5, Sat 9-11

THORNTON

P THORNTON PUBLIC LIBRARY, 412 Main St, 50479. (Mail add: PO Box 208, 50479), SAN 305-7402. Tel: 641-998-2261, 641-998-2416. FAX: 641-998-2470. E-mail: thorntonpl@frontiernet.net. Web Site: thornton.lib.ia.us, www.thornton-iowa.com/city_organizations?id=3. *Libr Dir,* Sibyl Jorgensen; *Board Pres,* Pam Muhlenbruch
Pop 442; Circ 19,400
Library Holdings: Bk Titles 9,000; Per Subs 20
Open Mon-Fri 2-6, Sat 9-11:30

TIFFIN

P SPRINGMIER COMMUNITY LIBRARY*, 311 W Marengo Rd, 52340-9308. Tel: 319-545-2960. FAX: 319-545-2863. E-mail: springmiercommunitylibrary@gmail.com. *Dir,* Kris Petersen
Pop 2,100; Fac 3
Library Holdings: Bk Titles 10,400
Automation Activity & Vendor Info: (Cataloging) ComPanion Corp; (Circulation) ComPanion Corp
Function: 24/7 Electronic res, 24/7 Online cat, After school storytime, Audiobks on Playaways & MP3, Audiobks via web, Chess club, Children's

prog, Computer training, Computers for patron use, Digital talking bks, Holiday prog, Home delivery & serv to seniorr ctr & nursing homes, Homework prog, ILL available, Laminating, Life-long learning prog for all ages, Magazines, Movies, Online cat, Preschool outreach, Preschool reading prog, Prog for adults, Prog for children & young adult, Senior computer classes, Story hour, Study rm, Summer & winter reading prog, Tax forms, Teen prog, Wheelchair accessible
Open Mon-Thurs 10-6, Fri & Sat 9-Noon

TIPTON

P TIPTON PUBLIC LIBRARY, 206 Cedar St, 52772-1753. SAN 305-7410. Tel: 563-886-6266. FAX: 563-886-6257. E-mail: staff@tipton.lib.ia.us. Web Site: www.tipton.lib.ia.us. *Dir,* Denise Smith; E-mail: denises@tipton.lib.ia.us
Founded 1901. Circ 40,619
Library Holdings: Bks-By-Mail 15; Large Print Bks 861; Bk Titles 21,000; Per Subs 59; Talking Bks 150
Special Collections: Cedar County Genealogical Society; Cedar County History Coll; Grant Wood Lithographs; Marvin Cone & Polly Kemp Works
Automation Activity & Vendor Info: (Cataloging) ComPanion Corp; (Circulation) ComPanion Corp
Wireless access
Open Mon-Thurs 10-8, Fri 10-5, Sat 10-1
Friends of the Library Group

TITONKA

P TITONKA PUBLIC LIBRARY*, 136 Main St N, 50480. (Mail add: PO Box 323, 50480-0323), SAN 305-7429. Tel: 515-928-2509. FAX: 515-928-2519. E-mail: tykeplib@netins.net. Web Site: www.youseemore.com/nilc/Titonka. *Dir,* Laurie Lee
Founded 1913
Library Holdings: Bk Titles 6,800; Bk Vols 7,270; Per Subs 50
Special Collections: Wood carving
Automation Activity & Vendor Info: (Cataloging) Follett Software; (Circulation) Follett Software; (OPAC) Follett Software
Function: ILL available
Special Services for the Blind - Large print bks
Open Mon 10-1 & 2-7, Tues-Thurs 10-1 & 2-6, Sat 10-Noon
Friends of the Library Group

TOLEDO

S TAMA COUNTY HISTORICAL SOCIETY & GENEALOGY LIBRARY*, 200 N Broadway, 52342. SAN 371-9200. Tel: 641-484-6767. FAX: 641-484-7677. E-mail: tamacountyhistory@gmail.com. Web Site: www.tamacountyhistory.org. *Pres,* Elizabeth Reece; Staff 6 (MLS 6)
Founded 1974
Library Holdings: Bk Titles 5,500; Per Subs 22
Open Tues-Sat 1-4:30

P TOLEDO PUBLIC LIBRARY*, 206 E High St, 52342-1617. SAN 305-7437. Tel: 641-484-3362. FAX: 641-484-2058. E-mail: tpl@toledo.lib.ia.us. Web Site: www.toledo.lib.ia.us. *Dir,* Sheri McFate; E-mail: sherim@toledo.lib.ia.us; *Asst Dir,* Brandi Harms; E-mail: brandih@toledo.lib.ia.us; *Libr Asst,* Mary Brandt
Founded 2013. Pop 2,539; Circ 23,000
Library Holdings: Bk Titles 21,000; Per Subs 74
Special Collections: Iowa Coll
Automation Activity & Vendor Info: (Cataloging) Follett Software; (Circulation) Follett Software
Open Mon-Thurs 10-6, Fri 10-5, Sat 9-Noon

TRAER

P TRAER PUBLIC LIBRARY*, 531 Second St, 50675. SAN 305-7445. Tel: 319-478-2180. FAX: 319-478-2180. Web Site: www.traer.lib.ia.us. *Dir,* Rosanne Foster; E-mail: rfoster@traer.lib.ia.us; *Asst Dir,* Sue Morrison; Staff 2 (Non-MLS 2)
Founded 1916. Pop 1,794; Circ 41,880
Library Holdings: Audiobooks 689; DVDs 2,535; Large Print Bks 1,279; Bk Vols 14,409; Per Subs 126; Videos 135
Automation Activity & Vendor Info: (Acquisitions) Biblionix; (Cataloging) Biblionix; (Circulation) Biblionix
Wireless access
Function: Accelerated reader prog, Adult bk club, Audiobks via web, Bks on cassette, Bks on CD, Children's prog, Computer training, Computers for patron use, Free DVD rentals, Home delivery & serv to seniorr ctr & nursing homes, Homebound delivery serv, ILL available, Mail & tel request accepted, Photocopying/Printing, Prog for adults, Prog for children & young adult, Senior computer classes, Spoken cassettes & CDs, Spoken cassettes & DVDs, Story hour, Summer reading prog, Tax forms, VHS videos, Wheelchair accessible
Open Mon 1-7, Tues & Fri 1-5, Wed 10-5, Thurs 10-7, Sat 10-12
Friends of the Library Group

TRIPOLI

P TRIPOLI PUBLIC LIBRARY*, 101 Fourth Ave SW, 50676. (Mail add: PO Box 430, 50676-0430), SAN 305-7453. Tel: 319-882-4807. FAX: 319-882-3580. E-mail: director@tripoli.lib.ia.us. Web Site: www.tripoli.lib.ia.us. *Dir & Librn,* Annette Martin; E-mail: Ann@tripoli.lib.ia.us; Staff 3 (MLS 1, Non-MLS 2)
Founded 1951. Pop 1,280; Circ 31,855
Library Holdings: Bk Titles 13,200; Per Subs 48
Subject Interests: Hist, Iowa
Wireless access
Open Mon 9-7, Tues 1:30-5:30, Wed 1-6, Thurs 9-5, Fri 9-3, Sat 9-12
Friends of the Library Group

TRURO

P TRURO PUBLIC LIBRARY*, 114 E Center St, 50257. (Mail add: PO Box 49, 50257), SAN 305-7461. Tel: 641-765-4220. FAX: 641-765-4220. E-mail: trurolib@myomnitel.com. Web Site: www.truro.lib.ia.us. *Dir,* Tracee Dembinski
Founded 1930. Pop 662; Circ 5,680
Library Holdings: Bk Vols 14,677; Per Subs 60
Wireless access
Open Tues 9:30-3:30, Wed 3-6, Thurs 10-6, Sat 9-12

UNION

P UNION PUBLIC LIBRARY*, 406 Commercial St, 50258. (Mail add: PO Box 146, 50258), SAN 305-747X. Tel: 641-486-5561. FAX: 641-486-2284. Web Site: www.union.lib.ia.us. *Dir,* Laura Newby; E-mail: director@union.lib.ia.us
Founded 1968. Pop 1,875; Circ 25,000
Library Holdings: Bk Vols 23,000; Per Subs 86
Wireless access
Partic in LibraryLinkNJ, The New Jersey Library Cooperative
Open Mon & Wed 1-7, Tues, Thurs & Fri 10-5, Sat 10-2

URBANDALE

P URBANDALE PUBLIC LIBRARY*, 3520 86th St, 50322. SAN 305-7496. Tel: 515-278-3945. Reference Tel: 515-331-4488. FAX: 515-278-3918. Reference FAX: 515-331-6737. E-mail: reference@urbandale.org. Web Site: www.urbandalelibrary.org. *Dir,* Nicholas Janning; E-mail: njanning@urbandale.org; *Asst Dir, Colls Mgr,* Leslie Noble; *Ref Serv Librn,* Jeanette Andrews; *Youth Serv Librn,* Carmen Epstein; E-mail: cepstein@urbandale.org; Staff 19 (MLS 6, Non-MLS 13)
Founded 1961. Pop 35,904; Circ 644,028
Library Holdings: AV Mats 15,118; DVDs 10,869; Bk Vols 130,897; Per Subs 362
Automation Activity & Vendor Info: (Cataloging) SirsiDynix; (Circulation) SirsiDynix; (ILL) OCLC; (OPAC) SirsiDynix; (Serials) SirsiDynix
Wireless access
Partic in OCLC Online Computer Library Center, Inc
Open Mon-Thurs 9-9, Fri & Sat 9-6, Sun 1-5

UTE

P UTE PUBLIC LIBRARY*, 130 Main St, 51060. (Mail add: PO Box 155, 51060-0155), SAN 376-7485. Tel: 712-885-2237. FAX: 712-885-1705. Web Site: cityofute.com/index.php/library. *Librn,* Linda Seieroe
Library Holdings: High Interest/Low Vocabulary Bk Vols 300; Bk Vols 2,500
Open Mon-Fri 8-2
Friends of the Library Group

VAN HORNE

P VAN HORNE PUBLIC LIBRARY*, 114 Main St, 52346. (Mail add: PO Box 280, 52346-0280), SAN 305-750X. Tel: 319-228-8744. FAX: 319-228-8744. Web Site: www.vanhorne.lib.ia.us. *Dir,* Mechelle Lambert; E-mail: director@vanhorne.lib.ia.us
Pop 1,400; Circ 9,760
Library Holdings: Bk Vols 9,835
Wireless access
Open Mon-Thurs 8:30-11 & 3:30-6:30, Fri & Sat 8:30-11

VAN METER

P VAN METER PUBLIC LIBRARY*, 505 Grant St, 50261. (Mail add: PO Box 160, 50261), SAN 305-7518. Tel: 515-996-2435. FAX: 515-996-2207. E-mail: library@vanmeteria.gov. Web Site: vanmeteria.gov/library. *Libr Dir,* Nancy Studebaker; E-mail: nstudebaker@vanmeteria.gov
Pop 866; Circ 9,743
Library Holdings: Bk Vols 8,000; Per Subs 21

Wireless access
Open Mon, Wed & Fri 10-5, Tues & Thurs 12-8, Sat 10-3

VENTURA

P VENTURA PUBLIC LIBRARY*, Seven W Ventura St, 50482. (Mail add: PO Box 200, 50482-0200), SAN 305-7534. Tel: 641-829-4410. FAX: 641-829-4410. E-mail: ventpl@cltel.net. Web Site: www.youseemore.com/nilc/Ventura. *Dir,* Carol Clemens
Founded 1968. Pop 614; Circ 11,000
Library Holdings: Bks on Deafness & Sign Lang 20; Bk Titles 10,500; Per Subs 50
Wireless access
Function: Homebound delivery serv
Open Mon-Thurs 11-5, Fri 1-6, Sat 9-12

VICTOR

P VICTOR PUBLIC LIBRARY*, 710 Second St, 52347. (Mail add: PO Box 686, 52347-0686), SAN 305-7542. Tel: 319-647-3646. FAX: 319-647-3646. Web Site: www.victor.lib.ia.us. *Dir,* Tiffany Lynn; E-mail: tiffany.lynn@victor.lib.ia.us
Library Holdings: Bk Vols 11,480; Per Subs 51
Wireless access
Open Mon, Wed & Fri 9-6, Sat 9-12

VILLISCA

P VILLISCA PUBLIC LIBRARY*, 204 S Third Ave, 50864. SAN 305-7550. Tel: 712-826-2452. FAX: 712-826-2686. E-mail: staff@villisca.lib.ia.us. Web Site: www.villisca.lib.ia.us. *Dir,* Martha Herzberg; *Asst Librn,* Vivian Adair; E-mail: vivian@villisca.lib.ia.us. Subject Specialists: *Ch,* Martha Herzberg
Founded 1903. Pop 2,500; Circ 13,232
Jul 2016-Jun 2017. Mats Exp $48,280
Library Holdings: Bk Vols 14,000; Per Subs 55
Special Collections: Chinese Coll, Native American Arrowhead Coll, Pitcher Coll
Automation Activity & Vendor Info: (Cataloging) Biblionix/Apollo; (Circulation) Biblionix/Apollo; (Course Reserve) Biblionix/Apollo; (ILL) Biblionix/Apollo; (Media Booking) Biblionix/Apollo; (OPAC) Biblionix/Apollo; (Serials) Biblionix/Apollo
Wireless access
Function: 24/7 Online cat, Adult bk club, Archival coll, Audiobks on Playaways & MP3, Bk club(s), Bks on CD, Children's prog, Computer training, Computers for patron use, E-Readers, Electronic databases & coll, Free DVD rentals, Holiday prog, Home delivery & serv to seniorr ctr & nursing homes, Homebound delivery serv, ILL available, Internet access, Magazines, Meeting rooms, Movies, Online cat, Outside serv via phone, mail, e-mail & web, OverDrive digital audio bks, Photocopying/Printing, Preschool outreach, Printer for laptops & handheld devices, Prog for adults, Prog for children & young adult, Ref & res, Scanner, Senior outreach, Story hour, Summer reading prog, Teen prog, Wheelchair accessible
Open Tues & Thurs 1-5, Wed 8-6, Fri 10-6, Sat 9-1
Restriction: Access at librarian's discretion, Borrowing requests are handled by ILL, Circ to mem only, External users must contact libr, Free to mem, In-house use for visitors, Open to pub upon request
Friends of the Library Group

VINTON

P VINTON PUBLIC LIBRARY*, 510 Second Ave, 52349. SAN 305-7569. Tel: 319-472-4208. FAX: 319-472-2548. E-mail: vintonpl@vintonlibrary.com. Web Site: www.vintonlibrary.com. *Dir,* Janette McMahon; *Ch,* Amy Noe
Founded 1902. Pop 5,102; Circ 78,727. Sal $114,244
Library Holdings: Audiobooks 1,141; Bks on Deafness & Sign Lang 5; DVDs 372; e-books 4,026; Large Print Bks 1,829; Bk Titles 26,828; Bk Vols 26,928; Per Subs 67; Talking Bks 868; Videos 301
Automation Activity & Vendor Info: (Cataloging) Book Systems; (Circulation) Book Systems; (OPAC) Book Systems
Wireless access
Function: Homebound delivery serv, ILL available, Photocopying/Printing, Prog for children & young adult, Ref serv available, Summer reading prog, Telephone ref, Wheelchair accessible
Open Mon-Thurs 9-6, Fri 9-4

VOLGA

P VOLGA PUBLIC LIBRARY*, 505 Washington St, 52077. (Mail add: PO Box 131, 52077-0131), SAN 305-7577. Tel: 563-767-3511. FAX: 563-767-3511. E-mail: volgalib@iowatelecom.net. *Dir,* Rebecca Spielbauer
Founded 1923. Circ 4,537
Library Holdings: CDs 110; DVDs 70; Bk Titles 5,836; Per Subs 27; Talking Bks 138; Videos 454
Automation Activity & Vendor Info: (Acquisitions) Winnebago Software Co; (Cataloging) Winnebago Software Co; (Circulation) Winnebago Software Co
Wireless access
Special Services for the Blind - Large print bks; Talking bks
Open Mon 1-6, Wed 1-8, Thurs 12-5, Sat 9-12

WADENA

P WADENA PUBLIC LIBRARY*, 136 S Mill St, 52169. (Mail add: PO Box 19, 52169-0019), SAN 305-7585. Tel: 563-774-2039. FAX: 563-774-2039. E-mail: wadenapl@windstream.net. Web Site: www.wadena.lib.ia.us. *Dir,* Mona Benson; *Ch,* Position Currently Open
Founded 1950. Pop 242; Circ 5,677
Library Holdings: Bk Titles 8,164; Per Subs 15
Subject Interests: Educ, Hist
Wireless access
Open Mon 1:30-6, Wed & Sat 9-12, Thurs 2-6

WALL LAKE

P WALL LAKE PUBLIC LIBRARY*, 116 Main St, 51466. (Mail add: PO Box 68, 51466-0068), SAN 305-7593. Tel: 712-664-2983. FAX: 712-664-2577. Web Site: www.walllake.lib.ia.us. *Dir,* Ms Jody Fischer; E-mail: jody.fischer@walllake.lib.ia.us
Founded 1909. Pop 950; Circ 7,200
Library Holdings: Bk Vols 13,000; Per Subs 28
Wireless access
Open Mon 2-6, Tues, Thurs & Fri 2-5:30, Wed 11-5, Sat 10-Noon

WALNUT

P WALNUT PUBLIC LIBRARY, 224 Antique City Dr, 51577. (Mail add: PO Box 347, 51577-0347), SAN 305-7607. Tel: 712-784-3533. FAX: 712-784-3511. E-mail: wlntlib@walnutel.net. Web Site: www.walnut.lib.ia.us. *Dir,* Margo Matthies; *Librn,* Judy Schrecengost
Pop 897; Circ 8,981
Library Holdings: Bk Vols 10,000; Per Subs 46
Open Mon, Tues, Thurs & Fri 1-5, Wed 1-6, Sat 9-12

WAPELLO

P KECK MEMORIAL LIBRARY*, 119 N Second St, 52653. SAN 305-7615. Tel: 319-523-5261. FAX: 319-523-5261. Web Site: www.wapello.lib.ia.us. *Dir,* Llewann Bryant; E-mail: lbryant@wapello.lib.ia.us
Pop 2,124; Circ 39,291
Library Holdings: Bk Vols 29,144; Per Subs 50
Wireless access
Open Mon & Wed 9-8, Tues, Thurs & Fri 9-5, Sat 9-12
Friends of the Library Group

WASHINGTON

P WASHINGTON PUBLIC LIBRARY*, 115 W Washington St, 52353. SAN 305-7623. Tel: 319-653-2726. FAX: 319-653-3095. Administration E-mail: admin@washington.lib.ia.us. Web Site: www.washington.lib.ia.us. *Dir,* Bryna Walker; E-mail: bryna.walker@washington.lib.ia.us; *Ch,* Jolisa Weidner; Staff 6.5 (MLS 1, Non-MLS 5.5)
Founded 1877. Pop 13,750; Circ 82,838
Jul 2016-Jun 2017 Income $9,000, Locally Generated Income $9,000. Mats Exp $38,734, Books $24,384, AV Mat $9,277, Electronic Ref Mat (Incl. Access Fees) $5,073. Sal $221,559 (Prof $50,440)
Library Holdings: Audiobooks 2,385; AV Mats 8,362; DVDs 986; e-books 7,956; Bk Titles 39,473; Per Subs 136
Special Collections: Art Coll (Circulating Art Coll); Board Games (Circulating Board Game Coll)
Subject Interests: Genealogy
Automation Activity & Vendor Info: (Acquisitions) Baker & Taylor; (Cataloging) ComPanion Corp; (Circulation) ComPanion Corp; (OPAC) ComPanion Corp; (Serials) EBSCO Online
Wireless access
Function: Art exhibits, Audiobks via web, Bilingual assistance for Spanish patrons, Bks on CD, CD-ROM, Children's prog, Computers for patron use, Electronic databases & coll, Free DVD rentals, Holiday prog, Home delivery & serv to seniorr ctr & nursing homes, ILL available, Magnifiers for reading, Mail & tel request accepted, Microfiche/film & reading machines, Music CDs, Notary serv, Online cat, Outreach serv, Outside serv via phone, mail, e-mail & web, OverDrive digital audio bks, Photocopying/Printing, Preschool outreach, Preschool reading prog, Prog for adults, Prog for children & young adult, Ref serv available, Spanish lang bks, Story hour, Summer reading prog, Tax forms, Teen prog, Telephone ref, Wheelchair accessible, Winter reading prog
Partic in Saint Louis Regional Library Network; State of Iowa Libraries Online
Special Services for the Deaf - Bks on deafness & sign lang

Special Services for the Blind - Bks available with recordings; Bks on CD; Extensive large print coll; Free checkout of audio mat; Home delivery serv; Large print bks; Magnifiers; Ref serv
Open Mon-Thurs 8-8, Fri 8-5, & Sat 8-1
Friends of the Library Group

WASHTA

P WASHTA PUBLIC LIBRARY*, 100 S Fifth Ave, 51061. (Mail add: PO Box 121, 51061-0121), SAN 305-7631. Tel: 712-447-6546. FAX: 712-447-6158. E-mail: washtapl@yahoo.com. *Dir,* Erin Rydgren
Pop 284
Library Holdings: Per Subs 16
Wireless access
Open Tues 2-6, Wed 8-4, Fri 4-7, Sat 3-5

WATERLOO

CM ALLEN COLLEGE*, Barrett Library, 1990 Heath St, 50703. SAN 325-5905. Tel: 319-226-2005. FAX: 319-226-2020, 319-226-2053. E-mail: Library@allencollege.edu. Web Site: www.allencollege.edu/library. *Dir, Libr Serv,* Dr Ruth Yan; Tel: 319-226-2080, E-mail: Ruth.Yan@allencollege.edu; Staff 2 (MLS 1, Non-MLS 1)
Founded 1995. Enrl 350; Fac 50; Highest Degree: Master
Library Holdings: AV Mats 40; Bk Titles 400; Per Subs 90
Automation Activity & Vendor Info: (Acquisitions) Innovative Interfaces, Inc; (Cataloging) Innovative Interfaces, Inc; (Circulation) Innovative Interfaces, Inc; (Course Reserve) Innovative Interfaces, Inc; (ILL) Innovative Interfaces, Inc; (Media Booking) Innovative Interfaces, Inc; (OPAC) Innovative Interfaces, Inc; (Serials) Innovative Interfaces, Inc
Wireless access
Function: Doc delivery serv, For res purposes, Health sci info serv, ILL available, Internet access, Ref serv available, Res libr, Telephone ref
Partic in Iowa Academic Library Alliance
Open Mon-Thurs 8-8, Fri 8-4
Restriction: Open to students, fac & staff

S GROUT MUSEUM OF HISTORY & SCIENCE, Hans J Chryst Archival Library, 503 South St, 50701. SAN 305-7666. Tel: 319-234-6357. FAX: 319-236-0500. E-mail: info@gmdistrict.org. Web Site: www.groutmuseumdistrict.org. *Archivist,* Catreva Manning; E-mail: catreva.manning@gmdistrict.org
Founded 1956
Library Holdings: Bk Titles 6,000
Special Collections: Iowa Authors Coll, clippings & memoirs; Photogs; Rare Books Coll (Indian & Iowa History)
Subject Interests: Genealogy, Local hist
Open Tues-Sat 10-4

J HAWKEYE COMMUNITY COLLEGE LIBRARY*, 1501 E Orange Rd, 50701-9014. (Mail add: PO Box 8015, 50704-8015), SAN 305-7674. Tel: 319-296-4006. E-mail: hcclibrary@hawkeyecollege.edu. Web Site: hawkeyecollege.edu/academics/library. *Dir,* Candace Havely; Tel: 319-296-4229, E-mail: candace.havely@hawkeyecollege.edu; *Digital Serv Librn, Ref & Instruction Librn,* Sarah Quin; Tel: 319-296-4006, Ext 1227, E-mail: sarah.quin@hawkeyecollege.edu; *ILL,* Eric Bryden; Tel: 319-296-4006, Ext 1716, E-mail: eric.bryden@hawkeyecollege.edu; *Libr Tech,* Megan Blackford; Tel: 319-296-4006, Ext 1231, E-mail: megan.blackford@hawkeyecollege.edu; Staff 4.5 (MLS 2, Non-MLS 2.5)
Founded 1970. Enrl 3,770; Fac 387; Highest Degree: Associate
Automation Activity & Vendor Info: (Cataloging) Ex Libris Group; (Circulation) Ex Libris Group; (Discovery) Ex Libris Group; (ILL) OCLC; (OPAC) Ex Libris Group; (Serials) Ex Libris Group
Wireless access
Partic in Cedar Valley Libr Consortium; Iowa Academic Library Alliance
Open Mon-Thurs 7am-8pm, Fri 7-4:30, Sun 12-8

P WATERLOO PUBLIC LIBRARY, 415 Commercial St, 50701-1385. SAN 341-9851. Tel: 319-291-4521. Circulation Tel: 319-291-4480. Reference Tel: 319-291-4476. Administration Tel: 319-291-4496. Automation Services Tel: 319-291-4497. FAX: 319-291-6736. Administration FAX: 319-291-9013. TDD: 319-291-3823. E-mail: askus@waterloopubliclibrary.org. Web Site: www.waterloopubliclibrary.org. *Interim Dir, Pub Serv,* Jillian Rutledge; E-mail: jrutledge@waterloopubliclibrary.org; *Youth Serv Librn,* Lori Petersen; E-mail: lpetersen@WaterlooPublicLibrary.org; Staff 41 (MLS 7, Non-MLS 34)
Founded 1896. Pop 68,747; Circ 466,903
Library Holdings: AV Mats 16,740; Bk Vols 205,960; Per Subs 376
Automation Activity & Vendor Info: (Acquisitions) SirsiDynix; (Cataloging) SirsiDynix; (Circulation) SirsiDynix; (OPAC) SirsiDynix; (Serials) SirsiDynix
Wireless access
Function: 24/7 Electronic res, 24/7 Online cat, Activity rm, Adult bk club, Adult literacy prog, Audiobks on Playaways & MP3, Audiobks via web, Bilingual assistance for Spanish patrons, Bk club(s), Bks on cassette, Bks on CD, Children's prog, Computer training, Computers for patron use, Digital talking bks, Distance learning, E-Reserves, Electronic databases & coll, Family literacy, For res purposes, Free DVD rentals, Genealogy discussion group, Govt ref serv, Health sci info serv, Holiday prog, Home delivery & serv to seniorr ctr & nursing homes, Homebound delivery serv, Homework prog, ILL available, Instruction & testing, Internet access, Learning ctr, Magazines, Magnifiers for reading, Mail & tel request accepted, Makerspace, Meeting rooms, Microfiche/film & reading machines, Movies, Music CDs, Notary serv, Online cat, Online ref, Orientations, Outreach serv, Photocopying/Printing, Preschool outreach, Preschool reading prog, Printer for laptops & handheld devices, Prof lending libr, Prog for adults, Ref & res, Ref serv available, Res assist avail, Scanner, Senior computer classes, Senior outreach, Spanish lang bks, Spoken cassettes & CDs, Spoken cassettes & DVDs, STEM programs, Story hour, Study rm, Summer reading prog, Tax forms, Teen prog, Telephone ref, Wheelchair accessible
Partic in Cedar Valley Libr Consortium
Special Services for the Deaf - TDD equip
Special Services for the Blind - Computer with voice synthesizer for visually impaired persons
Open Mon-Thurs 9-7, Fri & Sat 9-5
Friends of the Library Group

WATERVILLE

P WATERVILLE PUBLIC LIBRARY, 115 Main St, Unit 3, 52170. SAN 376-5245. Tel: 563-535-7295. Web Site: www.waterville.lib.ia.us. *Dir,* Heather Bente; E-mail: director@waterville.lib.ia.us; Staff 1 (Non-MLS 1)
Founded 1994. Pop 250; Circ 6,000
Library Holdings: DVDs 3,000; Large Print Bks 1,000; Bk Vols 6,000; Per Subs 12; Talking Bks 50; Videos 250
Wireless access
Function: Activity rm, Audiobks via web, Bks on CD, Children's prog, Computers for patron use, Free DVD rentals, Holiday prog, Home delivery & serv to seniorr ctr & nursing homes, Homebound delivery serv, ILL available, Internet access, Life-long learning prog for all ages, Mail & tel request accepted, Meeting rooms, Movies, Outreach serv, OverDrive digital audio bks, Photocopying/Printing, Printer for laptops & handheld devices, Prog for adults, Prog for children & young adult, Study rm, Summer reading prog, Workshops
Open Tues 2-6, Thurs 10-6

WAUCOMA

P WAUCOMA PUBLIC LIBRARY*, 103 First Ave SW, 52171. (Mail add: PO Box 131, 52171), SAN 321-5180. Tel: 563-776-4042. FAX: 563-776-4042. E-mail: director@waucoma.lib.ia.us. *Dir,* Angie Robbins
Founded 1978. Pop 699; Circ 5,000
Library Holdings: Bk Titles 6,000; Per Subs 10
Wireless access
Open Tues & Sat 9am-11am, Wed-Fri 3-7

WAUKEE

P WAUKEE PUBLIC LIBRARY, 950 S Warrior Lane, 50263. SAN 305-7690. Tel: 515-978-7944. FAX: 515-987-1280. Web Site: www.waukeepubliclibrary.org. *Libr Dir,* Kristine Larson; E-mail: klarson2@waukee.org; *Youth Serv Librn,* Keri Weston-Stoll; E-mail: kweston-stoll@waukee.org; Staff 16 (MLS 5, Non-MLS 11)
Founded 1929. Pop 24,000; Circ 183,190
Jul 2019-Jun 2020 Income $1,082,887, State $27,253, City $1,017,755, County $9,842, Locally Generated Income $9,971, Other $18,066. Mats Exp $75,702, Books $47,074, Per/Ser (Incl. Access Fees) $1,200, AV Mat $6,562, Electronic Ref Mat (Incl. Access Fees) $20,866. Sal $563,593
Library Holdings: Audiobooks 1,457; DVDs 4,680; e-books 59,948; Electronic Media & Resources 57; Large Print Bks 1,177; Per Subs 50; Talking Bks 44
Automation Activity & Vendor Info: (Acquisitions) TLC (The Library Corporation); (Cataloging) TLC (The Library Corporation); (Circulation) TLC (The Library Corporation); (OPAC) TLC (The Library Corporation)
Wireless access
Function: 24/7 Electronic res, 24/7 Online cat, Adult bk club, Art exhibits, Audiobks via web, Bk club(s), Bks on CD, Butterfly Garden, Children's prog, Computers for patron use, Digital talking bks, E-Reserves, Electronic databases & coll, Equip loans & repairs, Family literacy, Free DVD rentals, Holiday prog, Home delivery & serv to seniorr ctr & nursing homes, Homebound delivery serv, ILL available, Instruction & testing, Internet access, Life-long learning prog for all ages, Magazines, Meeting rooms, Movies, Online cat, Outreach serv, OverDrive digital audio bks, Photocopying/Printing, Preschool outreach, Preschool reading prog, Prog for adults, Prog for children & young adult, Scanner, Senior outreach, STEM programs, Story hour, Study rm, Summer & winter reading prog, Summer reading prog, Teen prog, Telephone ref, Wheelchair accessible, Winter reading prog
Publications: The Notice (Quarterly newsletter)

Open Mon-Thurs 9-8, Fri 9-5:30, Sat 9-4, Sun 1-4
Friends of the Library Group

WAUKON

P ROBEY MEMORIAL LIBRARY*, 401 First Ave NW, 52172. SAN 305-7704. Tel: 563-568-4424. FAX: 563-568-5026. E-mail: robeymemorial@waukon.lib.ia.us. Web Site: www.waukon.lib.ia.us. *Dir,* Cate St Clair; E-mail: cates@waukon.lib.ia.us
Founded 1920. Pop 3,897; Circ 50,948
Library Holdings: Bk Vols 25,457; Per Subs 101
Special Collections: Iowa Coll; Large Print Coll
Automation Activity & Vendor Info: (Cataloging) Follett Software; (Circulation) Follett Software
Wireless access
Open Mon-Thurs 10-8, Fri 10-6, Sat 10-4

WAVERLY

C WARTBURG COLLEGE LIBRARY, Vogel Library, 100 Wartburg Blvd, 50677-0903. SAN 305-7712. Tel: 319-352-8500. Administration Tel: 319-352-8315. FAX: 319-352-8312. Web Site: www.wartburg.edu/library. *Dir,* Susan Meyeraan; E-mail: susan.meyeraan@wartburg.edu; *Col Librn, Info Literacy Librn,* Jill Westen; E-mail: jill.westen@wartburg.edu; *Info Literacy Librn, Tech Librn,* Heidi Parker; E-mail: heidi.parker@wartburg.edu; *Info Literacy Librn,* Position Currently Open; *Archivist,* Position Currently Open; *Circ Supvr,* Meredith Borchardt; E-mail: meredith.borchardt@wartburg.edu; *ILL Supvr,* Elisa Klope; E-mail: elisa.klope@wartburg.edu; *Tech Serv Supvr,* Dennis Goodyear; E-mail: dennis.goodyear@wartburg.edu; Staff 7.4 (MLS 4, Non-MLS 3.4)
Founded 1852. Enrl 1,550; Fac 95; Highest Degree: Bachelor
Library Holdings: e-books 162,600; e-journals 54,600; Electronic Media & Resources 80,000; Microforms 8,480; Bk Titles 225,000; Bk Vols 250,000
Special Collections: Archives of Iowa Broadcasting History; College Archives
Automation Activity & Vendor Info: (Acquisitions) Ex Libris Group; (Cataloging) OCLC; (Circulation) Ex Libris Group; (Course Reserve) Ex Libris Group; (ILL) OCLC Tipasa
Wireless access
Partic in Iowa Academic Library Alliance; Iowa Private Academic Library Consortium
Open Mon-Thurs 7:30am-Midnight, Fri 7:30-5, Sat 1-5, Sun 1-Midnight

P WAVERLY PUBLIC LIBRARY*, 1500 W Bremer Ave, 50677. SAN 305-7720. Tel: 319-352-1223. FAX: 319-352-0872. E-mail: Waverly@waverly.lib.ia.us. Web Site: www.waverlyia.com/public-library. *Dir,* Sarah Meyer-Ryerson; E-mail: smeyer@waverly.lib.ia.us
Founded 1857. Pop 8,968; Circ 148,000
Library Holdings: High Interest/Low Vocabulary Bk Vols 100; Bk Titles 60,000; Bk Vols 68,000; Per Subs 162
Subject Interests: Local hist
Automation Activity & Vendor Info: (Cataloging) SirsiDynix; (Circulation) SirsiDynix; (OPAC) SirsiDynix
Wireless access
Open Mon & Tues 9-8, Wed-Fri 9-6, Sat 9-4, Sun 2-5 (Sept-May) 1-4
Friends of the Library Group

WEBB

P WEBB PUBLIC LIBRARY*, 124 Main St, 51366. (Mail add: PO Box 97, 51366-0097), SAN 305-7739. Tel: 712-838-7719. E-mail: webbialibrary@gmail.com. Web Site: cityofwebb.com/webb-public-library. *Dir,* Evonne Hinkley; Staff 1 (Non-MLS 1)
Pop 222; Circ 3,487
Library Holdings: Bk Titles 8,000; Per Subs 35
Subject Interests: Local hist
Wireless access
Open Tues-Fri 1-5

WEBSTER CITY

P KENDALL YOUNG LIBRARY*, 1201 Willson Ave, 50595-2294. SAN 305-7755. Tel: 515-832-9100. FAX: 515-832-9102. E-mail: info@kylib.org. Web Site: www.kylib.org/KendallYoung. *Dir,* Ketta Lubberstedt-Arjes; E-mail: Kettala@kylib.org; Staff 17 (MLS 3, Non-MLS 14)
Founded 1898. Pop 8,176; Circ 73,640
Library Holdings: Audiobooks 1,860; Bks on Deafness & Sign Lang 35; CDs 495; DVDs 673; Large Print Bks 1,250; Bk Vols 59,391; Per Subs 144; Videos 833
Special Collections: Clark R Mollenhoff Coll; MacKinlay Kantor Coll
Subject Interests: Genealogy, Local hist
Automation Activity & Vendor Info: (Cataloging) TLC (The Library Corporation); (Circulation) TLC (The Library Corporation)
Wireless access
Function: Adult bk club, After school storytime, Archival coll, Art exhibits, Audiobks via web, AV serv, Bks on cassette, Bks on CD, CD-ROM, Children's prog, Computer training, Computers for patron use, Digital talking bks, E-Reserves, Electronic databases & coll, Free DVD rentals, Genealogy discussion group, Holiday prog, Home delivery & serv to seniorr ctr & nursing homes, Homebound delivery serv, ILL available, Internet access, Magnifiers for reading, Mail & tel request accepted, Music CDs, Online cat, Outside serv via phone, mail, e-mail & web, OverDrive digital audio bks, Photocopying/Printing, Preschool outreach, Prog for adults, Prog for children & young adult, Ref & res, Ref serv available, Scanner, Senior computer classes, Spoken cassettes & CDs, Spoken cassettes & DVDs, Story hour, Summer reading prog, Tax forms, Teen prog, Telephone ref, VHS videos, Wheelchair accessible, Workshops
Partic in North Eastern Iowa Bridge to Online Resource Sharing
Special Services for the Deaf - Closed caption videos
Special Services for the Blind - Audio mat; Bks on cassette; Bks on CD; Copier with enlargement capabilities; Extensive large print coll; Home delivery serv; Low vision equip
Open Mon & Fri 10-6, Tues-Thurs 10-8, Sat 10-5
Friends of the Library Group

WELLMAN

P WELLMAN SCOFIELD PUBLIC LIBRARY*, 711 Fourth St, 52356. (Mail add: PO Box 420, 52356), SAN 305-7763. Tel: 319-646-6858. FAX: 319-646-6561. Web Site: www.wellman.lib.ia.us. *Dir,* Carol Wilkins; E-mail: director@wellman.lib.ia.us; Staff 2.5 (Non-MLS 2.5)
Founded 1909. Pop 1,408; Circ 24,000
Library Holdings: Bk Titles 17,756; Per Subs 25
Automation Activity & Vendor Info: (Cataloging) ComPanion Corp; (Circulation) ComPanion Corp; (OPAC) ComPanion Corp
Wireless access
Function: ILL available
Open Mon-Thurs 10-6, Fri 10-4, Sat 9-1

WELLSBURG

P WELLSBURG PUBLIC LIBRARY*, 411 N Adams St, 50680. (Mail add: PO Box 489, 50680-0489), SAN 305-7771. Tel: 641-869-5234. FAX: 641-869-5234. Web Site: www.wellsburg.lib.ia.us. *Dir,* Karen Mennenga; E-mail: Karen@wellsburg.lib.ia.us; Staff 2 (Non-MLS 2)
Pop 709
Library Holdings: Bk Titles 9,000; Per Subs 40
Special Collections: Ortssippen Books (German genealogy)
Wireless access
Open Tues, Wed & Fri 10-5, Thurs 10-7, Sat 10-12

WESLEY

P WESLEY PUBLIC LIBRARY*, 206 W Main St, 50483. (Mail add: PO Box 37, 50483-0037), SAN 305-778X. Tel: 515-679-4214. FAX: 515-679-4214. E-mail: wplbooks@yahoo.com. Web Site: www.youseemore.com/NILC/Wesley. *Dir,* Lany Mitchell
Founded 1950. Pop 467; Circ 9,849
Library Holdings: Bk Titles 6,877; Bk Vols 7,091; Per Subs 44
Wireless access
Open Mon & Wed 1-7, Thurs-Sat 9-Noon

WEST BEND

P WEST BEND PUBLIC LIBRARY*, 316 S Broadway, 50597. (Mail add: PO Box 46, 50597-0046), SAN 305-7798. Tel: 515-887-6411. FAX: 515-887-6412. E-mail: wbplib@ncn.net. Web Site: www1.youseemore.com/nilc/WestBend/default.asp. *Dir,* Lisa Riesenberg; *YA Librn,* Lou Metzger; E-mail: loumet14@gmail.com
Founded 1939. Pop 902; Circ 54,000
Library Holdings: AV Mats 800; Large Print Bks 300; Bk Titles 13,100; Bk Vols 13,380; Per Subs 70; Talking Bks 130
Automation Activity & Vendor Info: (Cataloging) Follett Software; (Circulation) Follett Software; (OPAC) Follett Software; (Serials) EBSCO Online
Wireless access
Open Mon-Wed & Fri 10-5:30, Thurs 10-6, Sat 9-12
Friends of the Library Group

WEST BRANCH

S NATIONAL ARCHIVES & RECORDS ADMINISTRATION*, Herbert Hoover Presidential Library-Museum, 210 Parkside Dr, 52358-9685. (Mail add: PO Box 488, 52358-0488), SAN 305-781X. Tel: 319-643-5301. FAX: 319-643-6045. E-mail: hoover.library@nara.gov. Web Site: hoover.archives.gov. *Dir,* Dr Thomas Schwartz
Founded 1962
Library Holdings: AV Mats 40,000; Microforms 3,000; Bk Vols 20,000; Per Subs 7

Special Collections: Bourke Hickenlooper Coll; Clark R Mollenhoff Coll; Gerald P Nye Coll; H R Gross Coll; Hanford MacNider Coll; Herbert Hoover Coll; Hugh R Wilson Coll; James P Goodrich Coll; James Westbrook Pegler Coll; Lewis L Strauss Coll; Lou Henry Hoover Coll; Nathan W MacChesney Coll; Robert E Wood Coll; Rose Wilder Lane Coll; Verne Marshall Coll; Walter Trohan Coll; William C Mullendore Coll; William P MacCracken Coll; William R Castle Coll
Subject Interests: Econ, Hist, Polit sci
Wireless access
Partic in Research Libraries Information Network
Open Mon-Fri 9-5
Friends of the Library Group

P WEST BRANCH PUBLIC LIBRARY*, 300 N Downey, 52358. (Mail add: PO Box 460, 52358-0460), SAN 305-7801. Tel: 319-643-2633. FAX: 319-643-4148. E-mail: staff@wbpl.org. Web Site: wbpl.org. *Dir,* Nick Shimmin; E-mail: nshimmin@wbpl.org; *Adult Serv, Asst Dir,* Jessica Schafer; E-mail: jschafer@wbpl.org; *Youth Serv,* Isolda Page; E-mail: ipage@wbpl.org
Pop 2,316; Circ 38,000
Library Holdings: Bk Titles 19,506; Per Subs 20
Wireless access
Function: 24/7 Online cat, Adult bk club, After school storytime, Audiobks on Playaways & MP3, Audiobks via web, Bks on CD, Children's prog, Computers for patron use, Free DVD rentals, Holiday prog, Home delivery & serv to seniorr ctr & nursing homes, Homebound delivery serv, Internet access, Laminating, Life-long learning prog for all ages, Magazines, Makerspace, Meeting rooms, Movies, Notary serv, Online cat, Online ref, Outreach serv, OverDrive digital audio bks, Photocopying/Printing, Preschool outreach, Scanner, STEM programs, Story hour, Summer & winter reading prog, Summer reading prog, Tax forms, Teen prog, Wheelchair accessible
Open Mon-Thurs 12-8, Fri 10-5, Sat 10-2, Sun 12-4
Friends of the Library Group

WEST BURLINGTON

M GREAT RIVER MEDICAL CENTER LIBRARY*, 1221 S Gear Ave, 52655-1679. SAN 305-2435. Tel: 319-768-4075. FAX: 319-768-4080. Web Site: www.greatrivermedical.org/library. *Librn,* Sarah Goff; E-mail: sgoff@grhs.net; Staff 1 (MLS 1)
Library Holdings: DVDs 100; Bk Vols 2,000; Per Subs 28
Wireless access
Open Tues-Fri 7:30-4

J SOUTHEASTERN COMMUNITY COLLEGE LIBRARY*, Yohe Memorial Library, 1500 W Agency Rd, Rm 171, 52655. (Mail add: PO Box 180, 52655-0180), SAN 341-9916. Tel: 319-752-2731, Ext 5090. FAX: 319-753-0322. Web Site: www.scciowa.edu/academics/library. *Librn,* Brian P McAtee; Tel: 319-752-2731, Ext 5091, E-mail: bmcatee@scciowa.edu; Staff 7 (MLS 3, Non-MLS 4)
Founded 1920. Enrl 2,000; Fac 80
Library Holdings: Bk Vols 30,000; Per Subs 300
Subject Interests: Anthrop, Art & archit, Environ studies
Automation Activity & Vendor Info: (Cataloging) Innovative Interfaces, Inc; (Circulation) Innovative Interfaces, Inc; (OPAC) Innovative Interfaces, Inc
Wireless access
Partic in Iowa Academic Library Alliance
Open Mon-Thurs (Winter) 7am-9pm, Fri 7-4:30; Mon-Fri (Summer) 7-4:30
Departmental Libraries:
FRED KARRE MEMORIAL LIBRARY-KEOKUK CAMPUS, 335 Messenger Rd, Rm 201, Keokuk, 52632. (Mail add: PO Box 6007, Keokuk, 52632-6007), SAN 328-9141. Tel: 319-524-3221, Ext 1960. FAX: 319-524-6433. *Librn,* Julie Meyer; Tel: 319-524-3221, Ext 1961, E-mail: jmeyer@scciowa.edu; Staff 1 (MLS 1)
Library Holdings: Bk Vols 9,500; Per Subs 75
Subject Interests: Art
Partic in SE Regional Libr Servs
Open Mon-Thurs (Winter) 7:30am-9pm, Fri 7:30-4; Mon-Thurs (Summer) 7:30-5, Fri 7:30am-11:30am

WEST DES MOINES

P WEST DES MOINES PUBLIC LIBRARY*, 4000 Mills Civic Pkwy, 50265-2049. SAN 305-7836. Tel: 515-222-3400. Circulation Tel: 515-222-3404. Reference Tel: 515-222-3403. FAX: 515-222-3401. E-mail: library@wdm.iowa.gov. Web Site: www.wdmlibrary.org. *Dir,* Darryl Eschete; *Head, Circ,* Heather Hildreth; *Head, Coll Serv,* Ann Renken; Tel: 515-222-3410, E-mail: ann.renken@wdm.iowa.gov; *Head, Pub Serv,* Shirley Houghtaling; *Commun Serv Coordr,* Ellen Smith; Tel: 515-222-3407, E-mail: ellen.smith@wdm.iowa.gov; *Tech Serv Coordr,* Louise Alcorn; Tel: 515-222-3573, E-mail: louise.alcorn@wdm.iowa.gov; Staff 7 (MLS 6, Non-MLS 1)
Founded 1940. Pop 64,560; Circ 1,223,334
Library Holdings: AV Mats 25,945; CDs 8,284; DVDs 10,989; e-books 9,910; e-journals 44; Electronic Media & Resources 25; Large Print Bks 5,674; Bk Vols 138,559; Per Subs 239; Talking Bks 5,433
Wireless access
Function: 24/7 Electronic res, 24/7 Online cat, Adult bk club, Audiobks via web, Bk club(s), Bks on CD, Children's prog, Computers for patron use, Digital talking bks, Electronic databases & coll, Home delivery & serv to seniorr ctr & nursing homes, Homebound delivery serv, ILL available, Internet access, Magazines, Notary serv, Online cat, OverDrive digital audio bks, Photocopying/Printing, Preschool outreach, Preschool reading prog, Printer for laptops & handheld devices, Prog for adults, Prog for children & young adult, Ref serv available, Scanner, Study rm, Summer & winter reading prog, Summer reading prog, Telephone ref, Wheelchair accessible
Publications: WDM (Magazine)
Open Mon-Thurs (Oct-April) 9-9, Fri 9-6, Sat 9-5, Sun 2-5; Mon-Thurs (May-Sept) 9-9, Fri 9-6, Sat 10-4
Friends of the Library Group

WEST LIBERTY

P WEST LIBERTY FREE PUBLIC LIBRARY*, 400 N Spencer St, 52776. SAN 305-7844. Tel: 319-627-2084. FAX: 319-627-2135. E-mail: wllibrary@wlpl.org. Web Site: www.wlpl.org. *Dir,* Allie Paarsmith; E-mail: apaarsmith@wlpl.org; Staff 5 (Non-MLS 5)
Founded 1904. Pop 3,300; Circ 28,000
Library Holdings: Bk Titles 18,000; Per Subs 52
Special Collections: Spanish & Laosian materials
Automation Activity & Vendor Info: (Cataloging) Follett Software; (Circulation) Follett Software
Wireless access
Open Mon-Thurs 10-7, Fri & Sun 2-5
Friends of the Library Group

WEST POINT

P WEST POINT PUBLIC LIBRARY, 317 Fifth St, 52656. (Mail add: PO Box 236, 52656-0236), SAN 305-7852. Tel: 319-837-6315. FAX: 319-837-6250. Web Site: www.westpoint.lib.ia.us. *Dir,* Dara Sanders; E-mail: dsanders@westpoint.lib.ia.us
Founded 1946. Pop 1,000; Circ 25,139
Library Holdings: Bk Titles 10,000; Per Subs 60
Wireless access
Open Mon-Fri 11-6, Sat 9-2

WEST UNION

S FAYETTE COUNTY HISTORICAL SOCIETY LIBRARY, 100 N Walnut St, 52175-1347. SAN 371-7763. Tel: 563-422-5797. E-mail: fayettehistorical@gmail.com. Web Site: www.fayettecountyiowa.org/HistoricalCenter.html. *Librn,* Phyllis Holmstrom
Founded 1975
Library Holdings: Bk Titles 250
Special Collections: Oral History

P WEST UNION COMMUNITY LIBRARY*, 210 N Vine St, 52175. SAN 305-7860. Tel: 563-422-3103. FAX: 563-422-3103. E-mail: webmaster@westunion.lib.ia.us. Web Site: www.westunion.lib.ia.us. *Dir,* Jill Clark; *Libr Asst,* Elaine Reicks; E-mail: childrenslib@westunion.lib.ia.us; Staff 5 (Non-MLS 5)
Founded 1928. Pop 2,594; Circ 49,182
Library Holdings: Bk Vols 25,638; Per Subs 73; Talking Bks 800
Special Collections: Lincoln Coll
Automation Activity & Vendor Info: (Cataloging) Follett Software; (Circulation) Follett Software; (OPAC) Follett Software
Wireless access
Partic in Association for Rural & Small Libraries
Open Mon, Wed & Fri 10-5:30, Tues & Thurs 10-7, Sat 9-12

WESTGATE

P WESTGATE PUBLIC LIBRARY*, 180 Main St, 50681. Tel: 563-578-5151. FAX: 563-578-5151. E-mail: westgatelibrary@iowatelecom.net. Web Site: www.westgate.lib.ia.us. *Dir,* Sandra Wolff
Pop 263; Circ 6,510
Library Holdings: Bk Titles 6,110; Per Subs 30
Open Mon & Thurs 1:30-7, Tues, Wed & Sat 9-12

WHAT CHEER

P WHAT CHEER PUBLIC LIBRARY*, 308 S Barnes St, 50268-0008. (Mail add: PO Box 324, 50268), SAN 321-1770. Tel: 641-634-2859. FAX: 641-634-2007. Administration E-mail: admin@whatcheer.lib.ia.us. Web Site: www.whatcheer.lib.ia.us. *Dir,* Carolyn Becker; Staff 1 (Non-MLS 1)

Founded 1897. Pop 803
Library Holdings: Bk Titles 5,000
Wireless access
Open Mon 11-6, Wed 8:30-3:30, Thurs 1:30-5:30, Sat 9-11

WHEATLAND

P CURTIS MEMORIAL LIBRARY*, 116 S Main, 52777. (Mail add: PO Box 429, 52777), SAN 320-8303. Tel: 563-374-1534. FAX: 563-374-1534. E-mail: admin@wheatland.lib.ia.us. Web Site: www.wheatland.lib.ia.us. *Libr Dir,* Amy Softa; E-mail: asofta@wheatland.lib.ia.us; *Libr Asst,* Nathan Horner
Pop 840; Circ 5,665
Special Collections: Old Local Newspaper Coll (1860-1962), microfilm
Subject Interests: Local hist
Wireless access
Open Mon 10-1 & 2-7, Tues-Thurs 10-1 & 2-6, Fri 10-1 & 2-5, Sat 10-1

WHITING

P WHITING PUBLIC LIBRARY*, 407 Whittier St, 51063. (Mail add: PO Box 288, 51063-0288), SAN 305-7917. Tel: 712-455-2612. FAX: 712-455-2612. Web Site: www.whiting.lib.ia.us. *Dir,* Margaret A Polly; *Asst Dir,* Pamela Rasmussen; *Adult Serv,* Larry Lage; *Teen Serv,* Dawn Teel; E-mail: dawn.teel@whiting.lib.ia.us; Staff 4 (MLS 1, Non-MLS 3)
Founded 1912. Pop 702; Circ 22,072
Jul 2015-Jun 2016 Income $73,391, State $2,220, City $55,875, County $5,705, Locally Generated Income $8,741, Other $850. Mats Exp $71,588, Books $12,613, Per/Ser (Incl. Access Fees) $1,500, AV Equip $840, AV Mat $2,888, Electronic Ref Mat (Incl. Access Fees) $2,428. Sal $5,709 (Prof $34,744)
Library Holdings: Audiobooks 943; DVDs 1,764; Large Print Bks 374; Bk Titles 10,969; Bk Vols 10,965; Per Subs 68
Automation Activity & Vendor Info: (Cataloging) Book Systems; (Circulation) Book Systems; (OPAC) Book Systems
Wireless access
Function: 24/7 Electronic res, 24/7 Online cat, Activity rm, Audiobks via web, Bks on CD, Children's prog, Computers for patron use, Doc delivery serv, Electronic databases & coll, Free DVD rentals, Govt ref serv, Holiday prog, Home delivery & serv to seniorr ctr & nursing homes, Homebound delivery serv, ILL available, Internet access, Laminating, Learning ctr, Life-long learning prog for all ages, Literacy & newcomer serv, Magazines, Magnifiers for reading, Mail & tel request accepted, Meeting rooms, Movies, Online cat, Online ref, Outreach serv, OverDrive digital audio bks, Photocopying/Printing, Preschool outreach, Preschool reading prog, Printer for laptops & handheld devices, Prog for adults, Prog for children & young adult, Ref & res, Ref serv available, Spoken cassettes & CDs, Story hour, Study rm, Summer reading prog, Teen prog, Telephone ref, Wheelchair accessible
Open Mon-Wed 1-7, Thurs 9-7, Fri 9-12, Sat 1-5

WHITTEMORE

P WHITTEMORE PUBLIC LIBRARY*, 405 Fourth St, 50598. (Mail add: PO Box 356, 50598-0356), SAN 305-7925. Tel: 515-884-2680. FAX: 515-884-2323. Web Site: www.youseemore.com/nilc/whittemore. *Dir,* Sandy Long; E-mail: sandyl@whittemore.lib.ia.us; *Asst Dir,* Joy Metzger; E-mail: joym@whittemore.lib.ia.us
Founded 1940. Pop 504; Circ 15,352. Sal $40,991
Library Holdings: CDs 883; DVDs 1,548; Large Print Bks 475; Bk Vols 18,657; Per Subs 55; Videos 300
Automation Activity & Vendor Info: (Acquisitions) TLC (The Library Corporation); (Cataloging) TLC (The Library Corporation); (Circulation) TLC (The Library Corporation); (OPAC) TLC (The Library Corporation)
Wireless access
Open Mon 2-6, Tues & Thurs 9-11 & 2-7:30, Wed & Fri 2-5:30, Sat 9-1
Friends of the Library Group

WILLIAMS

P WILLIAMS PUBLIC LIBRARY*, 216 Main St, 50271. (Mail add: PO Box 36, 50271-0036), SAN 305-7933. Tel: 515-854-2643. FAX: 515-854-2643. E-mail: willpl@wmtel.net. Web Site: www.williams.lib.ia.us. *Dir,* Diane Sinclair; Staff 1 (Non-MLS 1)
Founded 1948. Pop 512; Circ 5,907
Library Holdings: Audiobooks 3,305; AV Mats 715; CDs 183; DVDs 785; e-books 6,044; Electronic Media & Resources 3; High Interest/Low Vocabulary Bk Vols 58; Large Print Bks 178; Bk Titles 20,225; Per Subs 35; Videos 35
Wireless access
Function: Adult bk club, Art exhibits, Audio & video playback equip for onsite use, Bk club(s), Bks on cassette, Bks on CD, Children's prog, Computer training, Computers for patron use, Free DVD rentals, Health sci info serv, Holiday prog, ILL available, Internet access, Online cat, Online ref, Photocopying/Printing, Prog for adults, Prog for children & young adult, Scanner, Senior computer classes, Serves people with intellectual disabilities, Spoken cassettes & CDs, Spoken cassettes & DVDs, Story hour, Summer reading prog, VHS videos, Wheelchair accessible, Workshops
Open Mon 2-7:30, Tues-Fri 2-6, Sat 8:30-12:30

WILLIAMSBURG

P WILLIAMSBURG PUBLIC LIBRARY*, 300 W State St, 52361. (Mail add: PO Box 48, 52361-0048), SAN 305-7941. Tel: 319-668-1195. FAX: 319-668-9621. Web Site: www.williamsburg.lib.ia.us. *Dir,* Randall Schroeder; E-mail: rschroeder@williamsburgiowa.org; *Asst Dir,* Perla Josue; E-mail: pjosue@williamsburgiowa.org; Staff 4.5 (MLS 1, Non-MLS 3.5)
Founded 1934. Pop 3,000; Circ 42,468
Jul 2012-Jun 2013 Income $197,153, State $381, City $177,334, County $18,640, Locally Generated Income $798. Mats Exp $29,014, Books $27,164, AV Mat $600, Electronic Ref Mat (Incl. Access Fees) $1,250. Sal $118,701 (Prof $31,000)
Library Holdings: Audiobooks 1,693; DVDs 2,212; e-books 3,305; Bk Titles 19,951; Per Subs 73
Wireless access
Function: 24/7 Electronic res, 24/7 Online cat, Activity rm, Adult bk club
Partic in North Eastern Iowa Bridge to Online Resource Sharing
Open Mon & Wed 10-7, Tues & Thurs 10-5, Fri 10-6, Sat 10-1
Friends of the Library Group

WILTON

P WILTON PUBLIC LIBRARY*, 1215 Cypress, 52778. (Mail add: PO Box 447, 52778-0447), SAN 305-795X. Tel: 563-732-2583. FAX: 563-732-2593. E-mail: wplstaff@netwtc.net. Web Site: www.wilton.lib.ia.us. *Dir,* Sharon Bowers; *Librn,* Rhonda Brown
Founded 1935. Pop 2,829; Circ 28,753
Library Holdings: AV Mats 1,000; Large Print Bks 500; Bk Vols 20,000; Per Subs 85
Special Collections: Wilton Advocate (high school yearbook)
Subject Interests: Local hist
Automation Activity & Vendor Info: (Cataloging) Biblionix; (Circulation) Biblionix
Wireless access
Open Mon 11-8, Tues-Thurs 11-6, Fri 10-6, Sat 10-3, Sun 2-5
Friends of the Library Group

WINFIELD

P WINFIELD PUBLIC LIBRARY*, 112 W Ash, 52659-9511. (Mail add: PO Box 47, 52469), SAN 305-7968. Tel: 319-257-3247. FAX: 319-257-3247. Web Site: www.winfield.lib.ia.us. *Dir,* Jacque Lake; E-mail: director47@winfield.lib.ia.us; Staff 2 (MLS 1, Non-MLS 1)
Founded 1916. Pop 2,200; Circ 8,171
Jul 2012-Jun 2013 Income $55,000, State $900, City $41,800, County $9,955, Locally Generated Income $2,300, Other $50. Mats Exp $11,600. Sal $15,000
Library Holdings: Audiobooks 75; DVDs 485; e-books 10,040; Large Print Bks 375; Bk Titles 13,940; Per Subs 76
Subject Interests: Agr, Educ, Relig
Wireless access
Function: Adult bk club, Audiobks via web, Bks on CD, Children's prog, Computers for patron use, E-Reserves, Electronic databases & coll, Free DVD rentals, ILL available, Internet access, Magnifiers for reading, Mail & tel request accepted, Microfiche/film & reading machines, Online cat, OverDrive digital audio bks, Photocopying/Printing, Preschool outreach, Scanner, Senior outreach, Story hour, Summer reading prog
Open Mon, Wed & Fri 10-6, Tues & Thurs 12-6, Sat 9-12

WINTERSET

P WINTERSET PUBLIC LIBRARY, 123 N Second St, 50273-1508. SAN 305-7976. Tel: 515-462-1731. FAX: 515-462-4196. E-mail: library@winterset.lib.ia.us. Web Site: wintersetlibrary.org. *Dir,* David Hargrove; E-mail: david.hargrove@winterset.lib.ia.us; *Pub Serv Librn,* Chris Baumgarn; E-mail: chris.baumgarn@winterset.lib.ia.us; *Youth Serv Librn,* Tiffany Rohe; E-mail: tiffany.porter@winterset.lib.ia.us; Staff 5 (MLS 2, Non-MLS 3)
Founded 1891. Pop 5,130; Circ 97,508
Jul 2012-Jun 2013 Income $511,725, State $3,565, City $396,428, County $48,580, Locally Generated Income $12,999, Other $50,153. Mats Exp $495,381, Books $34,845, Per/Ser (Incl. Access Fees) $4,000, AV Mat $5,188, Electronic Ref Mat (Incl. Access Fees) $5,904. Sal $232,321 (Prof $54,432)
Library Holdings: Audiobooks 9,119; DVDs 3,590; e-books 6,989; Electronic Media & Resources 5,241; Large Print Bks 600; Microforms 300; Bk Titles 43,715; Per Subs 130
Special Collections: Antiques & Collectibles; Audio Books; Genealogy Coll; Iowa History Coll; John Wayne Videos; Large Print Coll; Madison

County Court Records; Madison County Land & Probate Records; Madison County Newspaper, microfilm
Automation Activity & Vendor Info: (Cataloging) OCLC; (Circulation) Innovative Interfaces, Inc; (ILL) OCLC; (OPAC) Innovative Interfaces, Inc
Wireless access
Function: Adult bk club, Art exhibits, Audio & video playback equip for onsite use, Audiobks via web, AV serv, Bi-weekly Writer's Group, Bk club(s), Bks on CD, Children's prog, Computer training, Computers for patron use, Digital talking bks, Doc delivery serv, Electronic databases & coll, Free DVD rentals, Genealogy discussion group, Health sci info serv, Holiday prog, Homebound delivery serv, ILL available, Instruction & testing, Mail & tel request accepted, Microfiche/film & reading machines, Music CDs, Online cat, Outside serv via phone, mail, e-mail & web, OverDrive digital audio bks, Photocopying/Printing, Preschool outreach, Prog for adults, Prog for children & young adult, Ref & res, Scanner, Senior computer classes, Serves people with intellectual disabilities, Story hour, Summer reading prog, Tax forms, Teen prog, Telephone ref, VHS videos, Wheelchair accessible
Partic in OCLC Online Computer Library Center, Inc
Open Mon-Thurs 9-6, Fri 9-5, Sat 9-1
Friends of the Library Group

WINTHROP

P WINTHROP PUBLIC LIBRARY, 354 W Madison St, 50682. (Mail add: PO Box 159, 50682-0159), SAN 305-7984. Tel: 319-935-3374. FAX: 319-935-3574. E-mail: winthroppl@winthrop.lib.ia.us. Web Site: c5.winthrop.lib.ia.us/. *Dir,* Nina Payne; E-mail: nina@winthrop.lib.ia.us; Staff 3 (Non-MLS 3)
Pop 871; Circ 12,402
Library Holdings: Bk Titles 9,250; Per Subs 30
Automation Activity & Vendor Info: (Circulation) Book Systems
Wireless access
Partic in Minitex
Open Mon-Tues, Thurs & Fri 1-5, Wed 1-8, Sat 930-1130

WODEN

P WODEN PUBLIC LIBRARY, 304 Main St, 50484. (Mail add: PO Box 156, 50484-0156), SAN 305-7992. Tel: 641-926-5716. FAX: 641-926-5716. E-mail: wodenlib@wctatel.net. Web Site: youseemore.com/NILC/WodenPL. *Dir,* Lisa Swingen
Founded 1960. Pop 240; Circ 6,895
Library Holdings: Bk Titles 5,000; Per Subs 40
Wireless access
Open Tues & Thurs 10-4, Wed 1-6, Sat 9-Noon

WOODBINE

P WOODBINE CARNEGIE PUBLIC LIBRARY*, 58 Fifth St, 51579. SAN 305-800X. Tel: 712-647-2750. FAX: 712-647-2750. Web Site: www.woodbinepubliclibrary.org. *Libr Dir,* Wendy Doyel; E-mail: wendy@woodbine.lib.ia.us
Pop 1,566; Circ 23,000
Library Holdings: Bk Titles 24,000; Per Subs 67
Wireless access
Open Tues, Thurs & Fri 10-5, Wed 10-7, Sat 9-12

WOODWARD

P WOODWARD PUBLIC LIBRARY*, 118 S Main St, 50276. (Mail add: PO Box 510, 50276-0510), SAN 305-8018. Tel: 515-438-2636. FAX: 515-438-2166. E-mail: wpublib@minburncomm.net. Web Site: www.woodwardlibrary.org. *Dir,* Myrna Griffith; E-mail: wpldirector@minburncomm.net; *Libr Asst,* Susan Lemon; Staff 1.3 (Non-MLS 1.3)
Founded 1946. Pop 1,500; Circ 18,748
Library Holdings: AV Mats 750; Bk Vols 19,000; Per Subs 68
Automation Activity & Vendor Info: (Circulation) Follett Software
Wireless access
Function: Adult bk club, Art exhibits, Audiobks via web, AV serv, Bk club(s), Bks on CD, Children's prog, Computer training, Computers for patron use, Free DVD rentals, Holiday prog, Homebound delivery serv, ILL available, Instruction & testing, Magnifiers for reading, Music CDs, Notary serv, OverDrive digital audio bks, Photocopying/Printing, Preschool outreach, Prog for adults, Prog for children & young adult, Scanner, Story hour, Summer & winter reading prog, Teen prog, Wheelchair accessible
Open Mon, Wed & Fri 9-12 & 1-5, Tues 4-7, Thurs 9-12 & 1-7, Sat 9-12
Friends of the Library Group

WYOMING

P WYOMING PUBLIC LIBRARY*, 109 Main St, 52362. (Mail add: PO Box 139, 52362-0139), SAN 305-8026. Tel: 563-488-3975. FAX: 563-488-3975. E-mail: mylibrary@wyoming.lib.ia.us. Web Site: www.wyoming.lib.ia.us. *Libr Dir,* Lucy Johnson
Founded 1947. Pop 878; Circ 16,135
Library Holdings: Bk Titles 7,000; Per Subs 24
Wireless access
Open Tues 12-6, Wed & Fri 2-6, Thurs & Sat 9-12

ZEARING

P ZEARING PUBLIC LIBRARY*, 101 E Main, 50278. (Mail add: PO Box 197, 50278-0197), SAN 305-8034. Tel: 641-487-7888. FAX: 641-487-7886. E-mail: zearing@zearing.lib.ia.us, zearinglibrary@netins.net. Web Site: www.zearing.lib.ia.us. *Dir,* Shayna Spencer
Founded 1975. Pop 630; Circ 7,270
Library Holdings: Large Print Bks 95; Bk Titles 10,636; Per Subs 20; Talking Bks 538
Subject Interests: Iowa, World War II
Automation Activity & Vendor Info: (Circulation) Follett Software
Wireless access
Open Mon, Tues, Thurs & Fri 3-7, Wed 10-7, Sat 10-3

KANSAS

Date of Statistics: Not provided.

ABILENE

P ABILENE PUBLIC LIBRARY*, 209 NW Fourth, 67410-2690. SAN 305-8042. Tel: 785-263-3082. FAX: 785-263-2274. E-mail: apl@abilenelibrary.org. Web Site: abilene.lib.nckls.org. *Dir,* Wendy Moulton; E-mail: wmoulton@abilenelibrary.org; *Assoc Dir,* Kara Cromwell; *Ch,* Sheryl Davidson; Tel: 785-263-1303
Founded 1908. Pop 7,378; Circ 93,420
Library Holdings: CDs 704; Bk Vols 61,157; Per Subs 106; Videos 1,718
Automation Activity & Vendor Info: (Acquisitions) Follett Software; (Cataloging) Follett Software; (Circulation) Follett Software; (OPAC) Follett Software
Wireless access
Mem of North Central Kansas Libraries System
Partic in Abilene Library Consortium; OCLC Online Computer Library Center, Inc
Special Services for the Deaf - TTY equip
Open Mon-Wed & Fri 9-6, Thurs 9-7, Sat 9-2
Friends of the Library Group

S MUSEUM OF INDEPENDENT TELEPHONY LIBRARY*, 412 S Campbell St, 67410. SAN 326-0984. Tel: 785-263-2681. FAX: 785-263-0380. E-mail: Heritagecenterdk@sbcglobal.net. Web Site: www.dickinsoncountyhistoricalsociety.com/museum-of-telephony. *Dir,* Position Currently Open
Founded 1973
Library Holdings: Bk Vols 600; Per Subs 10
Special Collections: Oral History
Restriction: Open by appt only, Open to pub for ref only

S NATIONAL ARCHIVES & RECORDS ADMINISTRATION, Dwight D Eisenhower Presidential Library, Museum & Boyhood Home, 200 SE Fourth St, 67410-2900. SAN 305-8050. Tel: 785-263-6700. Toll Free Tel: 877-746-4453. FAX: 785-263-6715, 785-263-6718. E-mail: eisenhower.library@nara.gov. Web Site: eisenhowerlibrary.gov. *Dir,* Dawn Hammatt; Staff 11 (MLS 1, Non-MLS 10)
Founded 1962
Library Holdings: Bk Vols 27,000; Per Subs 75
Special Collections: World War II & Eisenhower Administration Manuscript Coll
Subject Interests: Presidents (US), World War II
Wireless access
Function: Archival coll
Publications: Overview (Newsletter)
Open Mon-Fri 9-4:45
Friends of the Library Group

AGRA

P F LEE DOCTOR LIBRARY*, 222 Main St, 67621. (Mail add: PO Box 97, 67621). Tel: 785-638-2444. E-mail: agralib@gmail.com. *Librn,* Connie Gordon
Mem of Central Kansas Library System
Open Mon 7pm-9pm, Tues-Fri 3-6

ALLEN

P LYON COUNTY, LIBRARY DISTRICT ONE*, 421 Main St, 66833. (Mail add: PO Box 8, 66833), SAN 320-4774. Tel: 620-528-3451. FAX: 620-528-3451. E-mail: lyoncolibrary@gmail.com. Web Site: lyoncounty.lib.nckls.org. *Librn,* Nikki Plankinton
Founded 1976. Pop 1,104; Circ 5,774
Library Holdings: Bk Titles 9,000
Special Collections: Microfilms of Old Local Newspapers
Mem of North Central Kansas Libraries System
Open Mon 10-12 & 4-6, Tues-Fri 9-Noon, Sat 10-2

ALMENA

P ALMENA CITY LIBRARY*, 415 Main, 67622. (Mail add: PO Box 153, 67622-0153), SAN 320-1880. Tel: 785-669-2336. E-mail: almenlib@ruraltel.net. Web Site: almena.nwkls.org. *Library Contact,* Harold Rivera; Staff 1 (Non-MLS 1)
Founded 1903. Pop 373; Circ 4,313
Library Holdings: Bk Vols 4,500; Per Subs 10
Wireless access
Function: ILL available
Mem of Northwest Kansas Library System
Open Mon 3-6, Tues & Fri 1-5, Sat 9-Noon

ALTAMONT

P ALTAMONT PUBLIC LIBRARY, 407 Houston St, 67330. (Mail add: PO Box 219, 67330-0219), SAN 305-8077. Tel: 620-784-5530. E-mail: library@altamontks.com. Web Site: altamont.mykansaslibrary.org. *Dir,* Freda Edwards; Staff 1 (Non-MLS 1)
Founded 1928
Library Holdings: Bk Vols 14,372; Per Subs 50
Wireless access
Open Mon, Tues & Fri 1-5, Wed & Thurs 1-5 & 6-8

ALTON

P ALTON LIBRARY*, 516 Nicholas Ave, 67623. (Mail add: PO Box 5, 67623), *Library Contact,* Carolyn Williams
Mem of Central Kansas Library System
Open Fri 1-4

ALTOONA

P ALTOONA PUBLIC LIBRARY, 714 Main St, 66710. (Mail add: PO Box 177, 66710-0177), SAN 305-8085. Tel: 620-568-6645. E-mail: apublib@yahoo.com. Web Site: altoona.mykansaslibrary.org. *Dir,* Lacretia Colonder
Pop 564; Circ 2,970
Library Holdings: Bk Vols 5,000; Per Subs 20
Wireless access
Open Mon, Wed & Fri 1-6. Sat 8-Noon

AMERICUS

P AMERICUS TOWNSHIP LIBRARY, 710 Main St, 66835. (Mail add: PO Box 404, 66835-0404), SAN 305-8093. Tel: 620-443-5503. FAX: 620-443-5218. E-mail: americuslibrary@gmail.com. Web Site: americus.lib.nckls.org. *Dir,* Anita Westcott
Pop 1,591; Circ 33,124
Library Holdings: Bk Vols 18,000; Per Subs 28
Automation Activity & Vendor Info: (Cataloging) SirsiDynix
Mem of North Central Kansas Libraries System
Open Mon, Wed & Fri 1-5:30, Tues & Thurs 9-12 & 1-5:30, Sat 9-Noon

ANDALE

P ANDALE DISTRICT LIBRARY, 328 Main St, 67001. (Mail add: PO Box 58, 67001-0071). Tel: 316-444-2363. E-mail: andaledistlib@gmail.com. Web Site: andalelibrary.info. *Librn,* Sonya Horsch
Library Holdings: Audiobooks 29; AV Mats 291; Bk Titles 15,529; Per Subs 10
Automation Activity & Vendor Info: (Cataloging) Follett Software; (Circulation) Follett Software; (OPAC) Follett Software
Wireless access
Mem of South Central Kansas Library System
Open Tues & Thurs 9-12 & 2-6, Sat 9-Noon (Summer); Tues 2-6, Thurs 9-12 & 2-6, Sat 9-Noon (Sept-May)
Friends of the Library Group

ANDOVER

P ANDOVER PUBLIC LIBRARY*, 1511 E Central Ave, 67002. SAN 305-8107. Tel: 316-558-3500. FAX: 316-558-3503. Web Site: andoverlibrary.org. *Dir,* Tom Taylor; E-mail: tomtaylor@andoverlibrary.org; *Asst Dir,* Karyn Schemm; E-mail: kmschemm@andoverlibrary.org; *ILL,* Kathy Pyles; E-mail: kpyles@andoverlibrary.org; Staff 5 (MLS 1, Non-MLS 4)
Pop 15,000; Circ 187,354
Library Holdings: Audiobooks 2,729; Braille Volumes 3; DVDs 4,633; e-books 9,522; e-journals 10; Large Print Bks 1,010; Bk Vols 43,418; Per Subs 26
Automation Activity & Vendor Info: (Acquisitions) Baker & Taylor; (Cataloging) ByWater Solutions; (Circulation) ByWater Solutions; (ILL) Auto-Graphics, Inc; (OPAC) ByWater Solutions; (Serials) EBSCO Online
Wireless access
Function: Adult bk club, Art exhibits, Audiobks via web, Bk club(s), Bks on CD, Butterfly Garden, Children's prog, Computers for patron use, Free DVD rentals, Home delivery & serv to seniorr ctr & nursing homes, Homebound delivery serv, ILL available, Internet access, Magazines, Magnifiers for reading, Mango lang, Meeting rooms, Microfiche/film & reading machines, Movies, Museum passes, Online cat, OverDrive digital audio bks, Passport agency, Photocopying/Printing, Preschool outreach, Preschool reading prog, Prog for adults, Prog for children & young adult, Scanner, Story hour, Study rm, Summer reading prog, Tax forms, Teen prog, Wheelchair accessible
Mem of South Central Kansas Library System
Open Mon-Thurs 9-8, Fri 9-5, Sat 9-3
Friends of the Library Group

ANTHONY

P ANTHONY PUBLIC LIBRARY*, 624 E Main, 67003-2738. SAN 305-8115. Tel: 620-842-5344. Administration Tel: 620-842-5344, Ext 2. FAX: 620-842-5684. E-mail: anthonylib@gmail.com. Web Site: www.anthonykansas.org/public-library. *Dir,* Eldon Younce
Founded 1897. Pop 9,640; Circ 21,216
Library Holdings: Bk Vols 49,661; Per Subs 45
Special Collections: County Cemetery Records; County Newspaper Coll, micro; Dawes Indian Rolls (Enrollment cards for the five civilized tribes 1898-1914)
Automation Activity & Vendor Info: (Cataloging) Follett Software; (Circulation) Follett Software
Wireless access
Function: Accelerated reader prog, AV serv, Bks on cassette, Bks on CD, CD-ROM, Children's prog, Computers for patron use, Free DVD rentals, ILL available, Internet access, Music CDs, Photocopying/Printing, Prog for children & young adult, Scanner, Spoken cassettes & CDs, Spoken cassettes & DVDs, Story hour, Summer reading prog, Tax forms, Telephone ref, VHS videos, Wheelchair accessible
Mem of South Central Kansas Library System
Open Mon-Thurs 10-7, Fri 10-5, Sat 1-5

ARGONIA

P DIXON TOWNSHIP LIBRARY*, 120 W Walnut, 67004. (Mail add: PO Box 95, 67004-0095), SAN 305-8123. Tel: 620-435-6979. E-mail: dixtwplib@havilandtelco.com. *Dir,* Kim Dunn
Pop 783; Circ 7,366
Library Holdings: Audiobooks 1; Bks on Deafness & Sign Lang 5; DVDs 409; Bk Vols 5,500; Per Subs 15
Wireless access
Mem of South Central Kansas Library System
Open Mon, Tues & Thurs 1-5, Wed 1-6
Friends of the Library Group

ARKANSAS CITY

P ARKANSAS CITY PUBLIC LIBRARY, 120 E Fifth Ave, 67005-2695. SAN 305-8131. Tel: 620-442-1280. FAX: 620-442-4277. E-mail: arkcitypl@acpl.org. Web Site: arkcity.scklslibrary.info, www.acpl.org. *Dir,* Mendy Pfannenstiel; Staff 8.6 (Non-MLS 8.6)
Founded 1908. Pop 12,000; Circ 97,699
Automation Activity & Vendor Info: (Cataloging) Innovative Interfaces, Inc; (Circulation) Innovative Interfaces, Inc; (ILL) Auto-Graphics, Inc; (OPAC) Innovative Interfaces, Inc
Wireless access
Mem of South Central Kansas Library System
Open Mon & Thurs 10-8, Tues, Wed & Fri 10-6, Sat 10-2
Friends of the Library Group

J COWLEY COUNTY COMMUNITY COLLEGE*, Renn Memorial Library, 131 S Third St, 67005. SAN 305-814X. Tel: 620-441-5334. FAX: 620-441-5356. E-mail: library@cowley.edu. Web Site: www.cowley.edu/library. *Dir, Libr Serv,* Rhoda M MacLaughlin; E-mail: Rhoda.MacLaughlin@cowley.edu; *Libr Asst,* Katie Boyle; E-mail: Katie.Boyle@cowley.edu; Staff 3 (MLS 1, Non-MLS 2)
Founded 1922. Enrl 3,098; Fac 47
Library Holdings: AV Mats 200; e-books 1,200; Bk Titles 26,000; Per Subs 80
Special Collections: Kansas Room, bks & per
Automation Activity & Vendor Info: (Cataloging) Follett Software; (Circulation) Follett Software; (ILL) Auto-Graphics, Inc; (OPAC) Follett Software
Wireless access
Function: ILL available
Mem of South Central Kansas Library System
Open Mon-Thurs (Winter) 7:45am-10pm, Fri 7:45-4, Sun 2-10; Mon-Thurs (Summer) 7-8, Fri 8-Noon
Restriction: Open to pub with supv only, Open to students, fac & staff

ARLINGTON

P ARLINGTON CITY LIBRARY*, 900 W Main St, 67514. (Mail add: PO Box 396, 67514-0396), SAN 305-8158. Tel: 620-538-2471. FAX: 620-538-2471. E-mail: arllib@yahoo.com. *Dir,* Ginger Stiggins
Founded 1933. Pop 442; Circ 4,550
Library Holdings: Bk Titles 5,500; Bk Vols 6,671
Wireless access
Mem of South Central Kansas Library System
Open Mon 9-Noon, Tues & Thurs 10-6
Friends of the Library Group

ARMA

P ARMA CITY LIBRARY*, 508 E Washington, 66712. (Mail add: PO Box 822, 66712-0822), SAN 376-7671. Tel: 620-347-4811. FAX: 620-347-4977. E-mail: armalibrary@hotmail.com. Web Site: arma.mykansaslibrary.org. *Dir,* Brenda Banks; Staff 1 (Non-MLS 1)
Founded 1993. Circ 6,500
Library Holdings: Bk Vols 6,500; Per Subs 20
Special Collections: Local Newspaper, 1915-1974 microfilm
Automation Activity & Vendor Info: (Circulation) Follett Software
Wireless access
Mem of Southeast Kansas Library System
Open Mon-Wed & Fri 11-5, Thurs 12-6, Sat 10-2

ASHLAND

P ASHLAND CITY LIBRARY, 604 Main St, 67831. (Mail add: PO Box 397, 67831-0397), SAN 305-8166. Tel: 620-635-2589. FAX: 620-635-2931. E-mail: ashlib@ashlandlibrary.info. Web Site: ashlandlibrary.info. *Libr Dir,* Cara Vanderree; *Libr Asst,* Faith Tonne
Founded 1920. Pop 800

Library Holdings: Audiobooks 315; DVDs 1,294; Large Print Bks 264; Bk Titles 17,132; Per Subs 30
Special Collections: Local newspaper 1884-1989 micro
Automation Activity & Vendor Info: (Cataloging) OCLC; (Circulation) Follett Software; (ILL) Auto-Graphics, Inc
Wireless access
Mem of Southwest Kansas Library System
Open Mon, Tues, Thurs & Fri 10-5:30, Wed 10-7:30, Sat 9-1

ATCHISON

P ATCHISON PUBLIC LIBRARY*, 401 Kansas Ave, 66002. SAN 305-8174. Tel: 913-367-1902. FAX: 913-367-2717. E-mail: askus@atchisonlibrary.org. Web Site: www.atchisonlibrary.org. *Dir,* Jacque Slingsby; Tel: 913-367-1902, Ext 208, E-mail: jslingsby@atchisonlibrary.org; *Circ Supvr,* Mary Domann; Tel: 913-367-1902, Ext 214, E-mail: circulation@atchisonlibrary.org; *Adult Serv,* Jennifer George; *ILL,* Cindy Kloepper; Staff 2 (MLS 1, Non-MLS 1)
Pop 11,000; Circ 100,000
Library Holdings: Bk Vols 63,000; Per Subs 80
Special Collections: Local History Coll, microfilm, newsp & prints
Subject Interests: Hist, Music
Automation Activity & Vendor Info: (Acquisitions) SirsiDynix; (Cataloging) SirsiDynix; (Circulation) SirsiDynix; (ILL) SirsiDynix; (OPAC) SirsiDynix
Wireless access
Mem of Northeast Kansas Library System
Open Mon-Thurs 9-8, Fri 9-5, Sat 9-2
Friends of the Library Group

C BENEDICTINE COLLEGE LIBRARY, 1020 N Second St, 66002-1499. SAN 342-0000. Tel: 913-360-7608. FAX: 913-360-7622. E-mail: ill@benedictine.edu. Web Site: benedictine.libguides.com/bcexperience, www.benedictine.edu/academics/library. *Libr Dir,* Steven Gromatzky; Tel: 913-360-7511, E-mail: sgromatzky@benedictine.edu; *Asst Libr Dir,* Darla Meyer; Tel: 913-360-7516, E-mail: dmeyer@benedictine.edu; *Coordr, Ser/Govt Doc,* Wanda Adams; Tel: 913-360-7610, E-mail: wadams@benedictine.edu; *Circ Coordr,* Sister Kathleen Flanagan; Tel: 913-360-7510, E-mail: kflanagan@benedictine.edu; *ILL Coordr,* Jane Schuele; Tel: 913-360-7609, E-mail: jschuele@benedictine.edu; Staff 2 (MLS 2)
Founded 1858. Enrl 1,352; Fac 70; Highest Degree: Doctorate
Library Holdings: e-books 170,000; Electronic Media & Resources 900; Bk Vols 250,000; Per Subs 275
Special Collections: Belloc; Chesterton; Church Fathers (Abbey Coll); Gerontology (Jay Gatson Coll); Monasticism; Philosophy (Ture Snowden Coll)
Subject Interests: Agr, Educ, Hist, Relig
Automation Activity & Vendor Info: (Acquisitions) SirsiDynix; (Cataloging) SirsiDynix; (Circulation) SirsiDynix; (Course Reserve) SirsiDynix; (ILL) SirsiDynix; (OPAC) SirsiDynix; (Serials) SirsiDynix
Wireless access
Mem of Northeast Kansas Library System
Partic in Health Sciences Library Network of Kansas City, Inc; OCLC Online Computer Library Center, Inc
Open Mon-Thurs 7:45am-11pm, Fri 7:45-5, Sat 10-5, Sun Noon-11

ATTICA

P ATTICA CITY LIBRARY*, 125 N Main St, 67009. (Mail add: PO Box 137, 67009-0137), SAN 305-8190. Tel: 620-254-7767. E-mail: acl@attica.net. *Dir,* Rayedene Hughes
Founded 1900. Pop 630; Circ 5,184
Library Holdings: AV Mats 356; Bk Vols 11,779; Per Subs 45; Talking Bks 136
Mem of South Central Kansas Library System
Open Tues-Fri 1-5, Sat 9-Noon

ATWOOD

P ATWOOD PUBLIC LIBRARY*, 102 S Sixth St, 67730-1998. SAN 305-8204. Tel: 785-626-3805. FAX: 785-626-3805. E-mail: atwoodlibrary@atwoodtv.net. Web Site: atwood.nwkls.org. *Librn,* Grace Kastens
Pop 2,250; Circ 11,500
Library Holdings: Bk Titles 22,372; Per Subs 48
Automation Activity & Vendor Info: (Circulation) Follett Software; (OPAC) Follett Software
Wireless access
Mem of Northwest Kansas Library System
Open Mon, Tues, Thurs & Fri 9-5, Wed 9-6, Sat 10:30-1:30

AUGUSTA

P AUGUSTA PUBLIC LIBRARY*, 1609 State St, 67010-2098. SAN 305-8212. Tel: 316-775-2681. FAX: 316-775-2681. *Dir,* Lisa Daniels; E-mail: ldaniels@apl.kscoxmail.com; Staff 4 (Non-MLS 4)
Founded 1919. Pop 8,500; Circ 78,000
Library Holdings: Bk Vols 30,000; Per Subs 100
Automation Activity & Vendor Info: (Cataloging) Innovative Interfaces, Inc; (Circulation) Innovative Interfaces, Inc; (OPAC) Innovative Interfaces, Inc
Wireless access
Function: 24/7 Electronic res, 24/7 Online cat, Activity rm, Adult bk club, After school storytime, Audiobks on Playaways & MP3, Audiobks via web, Bk club(s), Bks on CD, Children's prog, Computer training, Computers for patron use, Electronic databases & coll, Free DVD rentals, Genealogy discussion group, Homebound delivery serv, ILL available, Internet access, Life-long learning prog for all ages, Magazines, Meeting rooms, Movies, Music CDs, Notary serv, Online cat, Outreach serv, OverDrive digital audio bks, Photocopying/Printing, Preschool outreach, Prog for adults, Prog for children & young adult, Ref & res, Ref serv available, Res performed for a fee, Scanner, Senior computer classes, Senior outreach, Serves people with intellectual disabilities, Spanish lang bks, Story hour, Study rm, Summer & winter reading prog, Summer reading prog, Tax forms, Teen prog, Wheelchair accessible, Winter reading prog, Workshops
Mem of South Central Kansas Library System
Open Mon-Thurs 9:30-8, Fri 9:30-6, Sat 9:30-3
Friends of the Library Group

AXTELL

P AXTELL PUBLIC LIBRARY*, 401 Maple, 66403. SAN 305-8220. Tel: 785-736-2858. E-mail: axtellpl@gmail.com. Web Site: lib.nckls.org/library-directory/#Axtell. *Dir,* Peggy Hasenkamp
Founded 1937. Pop 435; Circ 2,075
Library Holdings: Large Print Bks 243; Bk Vols 5,046; Per Subs 21; Talking Bks 146
Mem of North Central Kansas Libraries System
Open Tues, Wed & Fri 2-5, Sat 9-Noon

BALDWIN CITY

C BAKER UNIVERSITY*, Collins Library, 518 Eighth St, 66006. (Mail add: PO Box 65, 66006-0065), SAN 305-8239. Tel: 785-594-8414. Reference E-mail: reference@bakeru.edu. Web Site: lib.bakeru.edu. *Dir, Libr Serv,* Ray Walling; Tel: 785-594-8389, E-mail: ray.walling@bakeru.edu; *Bus Librn,* Irene Weiner; Tel: 785-594-8445, E-mail: irene.weiner@bakeru.edu; *Instruction Librn,* Carolyn Clark; Tel: 785-594-4543, E-mail: carolyn.clark@bakeru.edu; *Tech Serv Librn,* Nate Poell; Tel: 785-594-4582, E-mail: npoell@bakeru.edu; *Univ Archivist,* Sara DeCaro; Tel: 785-594-8380, E-mail: sara.decaro@bakeru.edu; Staff 6 (MLS 5, Non-MLS 1)
Founded 1858. Enrl 2,299; Fac 197; Highest Degree: Doctorate
Jul 2013-Jun 2014 Income $500,000. Mats Exp $152,000, Books $27,000, Per/Ser (Incl. Access Fees) $19,000, Manu Arch $3,000, Electronic Ref Mat (Incl. Access Fees) $103,000. Sal $230,000
Library Holdings: CDs 1,457; DVDs 560; e-books 108,000; Electronic Media & Resources 28; Microforms 18,000; Music Scores 1,270; Bk Vols 56,000; Per Subs 32; Videos 356
Special Collections: Baker University Archives; Kansas Area Archives of the United Methodist Church; Quayle Rare Bible Coll. US Document Depository
Subject Interests: Biology, Western US hist
Automation Activity & Vendor Info: (Cataloging) OCLC; (Circulation) OCLC; (Course Reserve) OCLC; (ILL) OCLC WorldShare Interlibrary Loan; (OPAC) OCLC; (Serials) OCLC
Wireless access
Function: Archival coll, Art exhibits, Computers for patron use, Electronic databases & coll, Govt ref serv, ILL available, Microfiche/film & reading machines, Online cat, Online info literacy tutorials on the web & in blackboard, Photocopying/Printing, Ref serv available, Study rm, Wheelchair accessible
Mem of Northeast Kansas Library System
Open Mon-Thurs 8am-10pm, Fri 8-4:30, Sun 2-10

P BALDWIN CITY LIBRARY*, 800 Seventh St, 66006. (Mail add: PO Box 565, 66006-0565), SAN 305-8247. Tel: 785-594-3411. FAX: 785-594-3411. E-mail: baldwinpl@baldwin.lib.ks.us. Web Site: www.baldwincitylibrary.org. *Dir,* Position Currently Open; *Asst Librn,* Phyllis Braun
Founded 1916. Pop 4,145; Circ 47,336
Library Holdings: Audiobooks 1,278; AV Mats 1,031; CDs 277; DVDs 680; Large Print Bks 288; Bk Titles 22,649; Per Subs 78; Videos 1,031
Special Collections: The Kansas Shelf Coll

Automation Activity & Vendor Info: (Cataloging) Follett Software; (Circulation) Follett Software; (ILL) Follett Software; (OPAC) Follett Software
Wireless access
Mem of Northeast Kansas Library System
Partic in Kansas Info Circuit
Open Mon & Wed 9-9, Tues, Thurs & Fri 9-5, Sat 8:30-12:30
Friends of the Library Group

BASEHOR

P BASEHOR COMMUNITY LIBRARY DISTRICT 2*, 1400 158th St, 66007. SAN 326-3967. Tel: 913-724-2828. FAX: 913-724-2898. Web Site: www.basehorlibrary.org. *Dir,* Diana Weaver; E-mail: dweaver@basehorlibrary.org; *Asst Dir,* Jenne Laytham; E-mail: jlaytham@basehorlibrary.org; Staff 11 (Non-MLS 11)
Founded 1985. Pop 8,730; Circ 138,746
Library Holdings: Audiobooks 1,565; DVDs 4,500; Bk Vols 40,000; Per Subs 136
Wireless access
Mem of Northeast Kansas Library System
Partic in NExpress Consortium
Open Mon-Thurs 9-8, Fri & Sat 9-5, Sun 1-5
Friends of the Library Group

BAXTER SPRINGS

P JOHNSTON PUBLIC LIBRARY*, 210 W Tenth St, 66713. SAN 305-8255. Tel: 620-856-5591. E-mail: johnstonpubliclibrarybsks@gmail.com. Web Site: johnston.mykansaslibrary.org. *Dir,* Andrea Bresee; Staff 1 (MLS 1)
Founded 1905. Pop 4,348; Circ 44,573
Library Holdings: Bk Vols 40,329; Per Subs 77
Subject Interests: Civil War, Kansas, Native Americans
Wireless access
Open Mon 9-6, Tues-Fri 9-5, Sat 9-12

BEATTIE

P BEATTIE PUBLIC LIBRARY, 715 Main St, 66406. Tel: 785-353-2348. Web Site: beattie.lib.nckls.org. *Dir,* Jan Studer; E-mail: jwstuder@bluevalley.net
Wireless access
Mem of North Central Kansas Libraries System
Open Tues, Thurs & Sat 10-1

BELLE PLAINE

P BELLE PLAINE CITY LIBRARY*, 222 W Fifth Ave, 67013. SAN 305-8263. Tel: 620-488-3431. E-mail: bplib@sktc.net. Web Site: belleplaine.scklslibrary.info, www.bpks.org/library. *Dir,* Loree Hisken; *Asst Librn,* Amber Warne
Founded 1915. Pop 1,800; Circ 9,411
Library Holdings: Bk Vols 11,500; Per Subs 25
Wireless access
Mem of South Central Kansas Library System
Open Mon & Thurs 1-8, Tues 1-6, Wed & Fri 10-12 & 1-6, Sat 10-Noon

BELLEVILLE

P BELLEVILLE PUBLIC LIBRARY*, 1327 19th St, 66935. SAN 305-8271. Tel: 785-527-5305. FAX: 785-527-5305. E-mail: belleville.staff@gmail.com. Web Site: www.bellevillelibrary.org. *Dir,* Leah Krotz; E-mail: belleville.director@gmail.com
Founded 1927. Pop 2,517; Circ 33,841
Library Holdings: Bk Vols 23,000; Per Subs 67
Special Collections: Republic County History Coll; Republic County New papers, 1870-1995, micro; World War II Veterans. Oral History
Automation Activity & Vendor Info: (Cataloging) Follett Software; (Circulation) Follett Software; (OPAC) Follett Software
Wireless access
Mem of Central Kansas Library System
Open Mon-Thurs 10-7, Fri 10-5, Sat 10-3
Friends of the Library Group

BELOIT

P PORT LIBRARY, 1718 N Hersey, 67420. (Mail add: PO Box 427, 67420), SAN 305-828X. Tel: 785-738-3936. E-mail: portlib@nckcn.com. Web Site: www.portlibrary.org. *Dir,* Rachel Malay; Staff 6 (MLS 1, Non-MLS 5)
Founded 1931. Pop 3,790; Circ 24,313
Jan 2020-Dec 2020 Income (Main Library Only) $258,449, State $1,072, City $242,098, Federal $998, Locally Generated Income $12,229, Other $2,052. Mats Exp $33,737, Books $22,950, Per/Ser (Incl. Access Fees) $2,983, AV Mat $7,804. Sal $122,039 (Prof $39,750)
Library Holdings: AV Mats 3,464; CDs 895; DVDs 2,569; e-books 625,833; Large Print Bks 1,393; Microforms 317; Bk Vols 22,407; Per Subs 64
Special Collections: Local Cookbooks; Local History Coll; Quilts & Quilting Coll
Automation Activity & Vendor Info: (Cataloging) Book Systems; (Circulation) Book Systems; (ILL) Auto-Graphics, Inc; (OPAC) Book Systems
Wireless access
Function: 24/7 Electronic res, 24/7 Online cat, Activity rm, Adult bk club, After school storytime, Archival coll, Art exhibits, Audio & video playback equip for onsite use, Audiobks on Playaways & MP3, Audiobks via web, Bilingual assistance for Spanish patrons, Bks on CD, Children's prog, Computer training, Computers for patron use, Digital talking bks, E-Readers, E-Reserves, Electronic databases & coll, Equip loans & repairs, Free DVD rentals, Holiday prog, Home delivery & serv to seniorr ctr & nursing homes, Homebound delivery serv, ILL available, Instruction & testing, Internet access, Large print keyboards, Magazines, Magnifiers for reading, Mail & tel request accepted, Mango lang, Meeting rooms, Microfiche/film & reading machines, Movies, Music CDs, Online cat, Orientations, Outreach serv, Outside serv via phone, mail, e-mail & web, OverDrive digital audio bks, Photocopying/Printing, Preschool outreach, Preschool reading prog, Prog for adults, Prog for children & young adult, Ref & res, Ref serv available, Res performed for a fee, Scanner, Serves people with intellectual disabilities, Spoken cassettes & CDs, Story hour, Study rm, Summer & winter reading prog, Summer reading prog, Teen prog, Telephone ref, VHS videos, Wheelchair accessible, Winter reading prog
Mem of Central Kansas Library System
Open Mon-Fri 10-5
Restriction: Circ limited, Non-circulating of rare bks, Non-resident fee

BENNINGTON

P BENNINGTON LIBRARY*, 300 N Nelson, 67422. Tel: 785-416-0097, 785-416-2102. E-mail: bennreading@gmail.com. Web Site: bennreading.wixsite.com/website-1. *Library Contact,* Vanessa Everhart
Wireless access
Mem of Central Kansas Library System
Open Tues (Winter) 3-6, Wed 3-8; Tues (Summer) 10-1

BERN

P BERN COMMUNITY LIBRARY, 405 Main St, 66408. SAN 376-5598. Tel: 785-336-3000. FAX: 785-336-3000. E-mail: librarian@bernlibrary.org. Web Site: bern.mykansaslibrary.org. *Dir,* Kathie Platt; *Asst Librn,* Heather Carroll; Staff 2 (Non-MLS 2)
Founded 1995. Pop 455; Circ 4,768
Library Holdings: Bk Vols 11,875
Wireless access
Mem of Northeast Kansas Library System
Open Mon 8-Noon, Wed 2-8, Thurs & Fri 2-5, Sat 9-Noon

BIRD CITY

P BIRD CITY PUBLIC LIBRARY*, 110 E Fourth St, 67731. (Mail add: PO Box 175, 67731-0175), SAN 305-8301. Tel: 785-734-2203. E-mail: birdcitylibrary@gmail.com. Web Site: birdcity.nwkls.org. *Librn,* Diane Burns
Pop 620; Circ 3,491
Library Holdings: Bk Vols 7,323; Per Subs 20
Wireless access
Mem of Northwest Kansas Library System
Open Mon-Fri 2-5:30

BISON

P BISON COMMUNITY LIBRARY*, 202 Main St, 67520. (Mail add: PO Box 406, 67520-0406), SAN 305-831X. Tel: 785-356-4803. FAX: 785-356-2403. E-mail: bisonlib@gbta.net. *Dir & Librn,* Kathleen Rippel; Staff 1 (MLS 1)
Founded 1964. Pop 240; Circ 1,623
Library Holdings: Audiobooks 27; CDs 6; DVDs 454; e-books 2; Electronic Media & Resources 41; Large Print Bks 110; Bk Vols 3,576; Per Subs 1
Special Collections: Local and Kansas History
Automation Activity & Vendor Info: (Cataloging) Koha; (Circulation) Koha; (ILL) Auto-Graphics, Inc; (OPAC) Koha
Wireless access
Function: 24/7 Electronic res, 24/7 Online cat, Audiobks on Playaways & MP3, Audiobks via web, Bks on CD, CD-ROM, Children's prog, Computer training, Computers for patron use, Digital talking bks, Doc delivery serv, E-Readers, Electronic databases & coll, Equip loans & repairs, Free DVD rentals, Games & aids for people with disabilities, Govt ref serv, Health sci info serv, ILL available, Internet access, Large print keyboards, Life-long learning prog for all ages, Magazines, Mail & tel

request accepted, Mango lang, Movies, Music CDs, Online cat, Orientations, OverDrive digital audio bks, Photocopying/Printing, Preschool reading prog, Printer for laptops & handheld devices, Prog for adults, Prog for children & young adult, Ref & res, Ref serv available, Res assist avail, Scanner, Senior outreach, Serves people with intellectual disabilities, Spoken cassettes & CDs, Story hour, Summer reading prog, Tax forms, Telephone ref, Wheelchair accessible
Mem of Central Kansas Library System
Open Tues 1-6, Wed 3-8, Thurs 9-2
Restriction: In-house use for visitors

BLUE MOUND

P LINN COUNTY LIBRARY DISTRICT NO 3, Blue Mound Library, 316 E Main St, 66010. (Mail add: PO Box 13, 66010-0013), SAN 305-8328. Tel: 913-756-2628. FAX: 913-756-2628. E-mail: bluemoundlibrary@yahoo.com. Web Site: bluemound.mykansaslibrary.org. *Dir & Librn,* Brenda Curtis
Founded 1964. Pop 584; Circ 6,815
Library Holdings: Bk Vols 6,000
Special Collections: Oral History
Automation Activity & Vendor Info: (Cataloging) Koha; (Circulation) Koha
Wireless access
Mem of Southeast Kansas Library System
Open Tues-Sat 11-5

BLUE RAPIDS

P BLUE RAPIDS PUBLIC LIBRARY*, 14 Public Sq, 66411. (Mail add: PO Box 246, 66411-0246), SAN 305-8336. Tel: 785-363-7709. E-mail: bluerapidslibrary@gmail.com. Web Site: bluerapids.lib.nckls.org. *Librn,* Lynne Turner
Founded 1874. Pop 1,047; Circ 4,251
Library Holdings: AV Mats 89; Bk Vols 5,577; Per Subs 24; Videos 64
Wireless access
Mem of North Central Kansas Libraries System
Open Mon & Fri 11-5, Wed 12-5, Sat 9-Noon
Friends of the Library Group

BONNER SPRINGS

P BONNER SPRINGS CITY LIBRARY*, 201 N Nettleton Ave, 66012. SAN 305-8344. Tel: 913-441-2665. FAX: 913-441-2660. E-mail: cheneylibrary@gmail.com. Web Site: bonnerlibrary.org. *Libr Dir,* Jack Granath; E-mail: jgranath@bonnerlibrary.org; *Asst Dir,* Kathleen Schram; E-mail: kschram@bonnerlibrary.org; *Teen/YA Librn,* Lesley Lard; E-mail: llard@bonnerlibrary.org; *Circ Coordr,* Katy Konovalske; E-mail: kkonovalske@bonnerlibrary.org; *Tech Coordr,* Travis Slankard; E-mail: tslankard@bonnerlibrary.org; Staff 6.2 (MLS 1, Non-MLS 5.2)
Founded 1946. Pop 10,000; Circ 100,000
Library Holdings: Bk Vols 50,000; Per Subs 65
Automation Activity & Vendor Info: (Cataloging) SirsiDynix; (Circulation) SirsiDynix; (OPAC) SirsiDynix; (Serials) SirsiDynix
Mem of Northeast Kansas Library System
Open Mon-Thurs 9-8, Fri & Sat 9-5, Sun 1-5
Friends of the Library Group

S WYANDOTTE COUNTY HISTORICAL MUSEUM, Trowbridge Research Library, 631 N 126th St, 66012. SAN 305-8352. Tel: 913-573-5002. Web Site: www.wycokck.org/departments/wyandotte-county-historical-museum. *Dir,* Amy Loch; E-mail: aloch@wycokck.org; *Curator,* David Hartman; E-mail: dhartman@wycokck.org
Founded 1956
Library Holdings: Bk Vols 2,000
Special Collections: County Cemetery Records; Early Family Records; Naturalization Records; Photographic File; Wyandotte County Materials
Wireless access
Restriction: Open by appt only

BREWSTER

S NORTHWEST KANSAS HERITAGE CENTER*, Library & Museum, 401 Kansas Ave, 67732. (Mail add: PO Box 284, 67732-0284), SAN 376-768X. Tel: 785-694-2891. *Librn,* Betty Wolfe
Mem of Northwest Kansas Library System
Open Mon & Wed 1-4, Sat 9-11

BRONSON

P BRONSON PUBLIC LIBRARY*, 509 Clay St, 66716. SAN 305-8360. Tel: 620-939-4910. FAX: 620-939-4569. E-mail: bronson_library@yahoo.com. Web Site: bronson.mykansaslibrary.org. *Dir & Librn,* Diana Huff
Founded 1935. Pop 419; Circ 5,656
Library Holdings: Bk Vols 4,600; Per Subs 19
Wireless access
Mem of Southeast Kansas Library System
Open Tues & Thurs 10-12 & 1-6:30, Sat 9-Noon

BUCKLIN

P BUCKLIN PUBLIC LIBRARY, 201 S Main St, 67834. (Mail add: PO Box 596, 67834-0596), SAN 305-8387. Tel: 620-826-3223. FAX: 620-826-3794. E-mail: bplibrary2@bucklinpubliclibrary.org. Web Site: www.bucklinpubliclibrary.org. *Dir,* Shelly Huelsman; E-mail: director@bucklinpubliclibrary.org; Staff 3 (MLS 1, Non-MLS 2)
Founded 1964. Pop 719; Circ 4,300
Library Holdings: AV Mats 602; CDs 97; DVDs 35; Large Print Bks 629; Music Scores 35; Bk Titles 18,162; Per Subs 35; Talking Bks 368; Videos 439
Special Collections: Art Coll; Kansas History Coll; Oprah's Book Club
Subject Interests: Best sellers, Inspirational reading, Mystery, Sci fict, Western
Automation Activity & Vendor Info: (Cataloging) Auto-Graphics, Inc; (Circulation) Auto-Graphics, Inc; (OPAC) Auto-Graphics, Inc
Wireless access
Function: 24/7 Online cat, Activity rm, Adult bk club, Children's prog, Computers for patron use, Electronic databases & coll, Free DVD rentals, ILL available, Internet access, Mail & tel request accepted, Online cat, Online ref, Orientations, Outreach serv, Outside serv via phone, mail, e-mail & web, Photocopying/Printing, Preschool reading prog, Printer for laptops & handheld devices, Prog for adults, Prog for children & young adult, Ref & res, Ref serv available, Res assist avail, Scanner, Story hour, Summer reading prog, Wheelchair accessible
Mem of Southwest Kansas Library System
Open Mon-Fri 12:30-5:30, Sat 10-1

BUHLER

P BUHLER PUBLIC LIBRARY*, 121 N Main St, 67522-0664. SAN 305-8395. Tel: 620-543-2241. FAX: 620-543-2241. E-mail: buhlerpubliclibrary@gmail.com. Web Site: www.buhlerks.org/city-services/library. *Dir,* Pam Fast
Pop 1,200; Circ 8,398
Library Holdings: Bk Vols 11,000; Per Subs 30
Wireless access
Mem of South Central Kansas Library System
Open Mon, Wed & Fri 12-5, Tues 10-5:30, Thurs 10-7, Sat 9-12

BURDETT

P PAWNEE HEIGHTS LIBRARY*, 603 Elm St, 67523. (Mail add: PO Box 66, 67523), SAN 305-8409. Tel: 620-525-6279. E-mail: oldbag1951@yahoo.com. *Librn,* Paula Catlin
Library Holdings: Bk Vols 2,000
Mem of Central Kansas Library System
Open Thurs 5pm-7pm, Sat 9-Noon

BURLINGAME

P BURLINGAME COMMUNITY LIBRARY*, 122 W Santa Fe Ave, 66413. SAN 305-8417. Tel: 785-654-3400. FAX: 785-654-3411. E-mail: director@burlingame.lib.ks.us. Web Site: burlingame.mykansaslibrary.org. *Dir,* Brandi Shaffer
Founded 1970. Pop 913; Circ 6,493
Library Holdings: Bk Vols 12,000
Automation Activity & Vendor Info: (Cataloging) Follett Software; (Circulation) Follett Software; (Serials) Follett Software
Wireless access
Mem of Northeast Kansas Library System
Open Mon, Tues & Fri 1-5, Wed & Thurs 10-6, Sat 9-1
Friends of the Library Group

BURLINGTON

P COFFEY COUNTY LIBRARY*, 410 Juniatta St, 66839. SAN 305-8425. Tel: 620-364-2010. FAX: 620-364-2603. Web Site: www.cclibraryks.org. *Adminr,* Darren Daugherty; E-mail: ddaugherty@cclibks.org; Staff 36 (MLS 2, Non-MLS 34)
Founded 1987. Pop 8,743; Circ 166,264
Library Holdings: Bk Vols 86,939; Per Subs 288
Subject Interests: Genealogy
Automation Activity & Vendor Info: (Cataloging) SirsiDynix; (Circulation) SirsiDynix; (OPAC) SirsiDynix
Wireless access
Mem of Southeast Kansas Library System
Open Mon-Fri 8-5

Branches: 6

BURLINGTON BRANCH, 410 Juniatta, 66839. Tel: 620-364-5333. FAX: 620-364-2603. E-mail: burlington@mail.cclibks.org. *Dir,* Monica Mader; E-mail: mmader@cclibks.org; Staff 6 (MLS 1, Non-MLS 5)
Open Mon-Thurs 9-8, Fri 9:30-5, Sat 10-3
Friends of the Library Group

GRIDLEY BRANCH, 512 Main St, Gridley, 66852, SAN 305-9316. Tel: 620-836-3905. FAX: 620-836-3401. E-mail: gridley@mail.cclibks.org. *Dir,* Janet Birk; E-mail: janetbirk23@yahoo.com; Staff 4 (Non-MLS 4)
Open Mon, Wed & Fri 9-5, Tues 9-7, Thurs 10-7, Sat 9-12

LEBO BRANCH, 327 S Ogden St, Lebo, 66856-9306, SAN 306-0012. Tel: 620-256-6452. FAX: 620-256-6301. E-mail: lebo@mail.cclibks.org. *Dir,* Mary Barker; E-mail: maryebarker@yahoo.com; Staff 4 (Non-MLS 4)
Open Mon, Wed & Fri 9-5, Tues & Thurs 9-7, Sat 9-12

LEROY BRANCH, 725 Main St, LeRoy, 66857, SAN 306-0063. Tel: 620-964-2321. FAX: 620-964-2394. E-mail: leroy@mail.cclibks.org. *Dir,* Cindy Stohs; E-mail: cjstohs1619@yahoo.com; Staff 3 (Non-MLS 3)
Library Holdings: Bk Vols 16,000
Open Mon, Tues, Thurs & Fri 8:30-5, Wed 8:30-7:30, Sat 9-12
Friends of the Library Group

NEW STRAWN BRANCH, 365 N Main St, New Strawn, 66839, SAN 373-5729. Tel: 620-364-8910. FAX: 620-364-5354. E-mail: newstrawn@mail.cclibks.org.
Open Mon & Wed-Fri 9-5, Tues 9-6, Sat 9-12

WAVERLY BRANCH, 608 Pearson, Waverly, 66871-9688, SAN 306-1760. Tel: 785-733-2400. FAX: 785-733-2474. E-mail: waverly@mail.cclibks.org. *Dir,* Marcella Chapman; E-mail: mechapman@yahoo.com; Staff 4 (Non-MLS 4)
Publications: Waverly City History Book
Open Mon 9-7, Tues-Thurs 9-5:30, Fri 9-5, Sat 9-12

BURNS

P BURNS PUBLIC LIBRARY, 104 N Washington St, 66840. (Mail add: PO Box 233, 66840-0233), SAN 305-8433. Tel: 620-726-5717. E-mail: burns.director@gmail.com. Web Site: burns.lib.nckls.org. *Libr Dir,* Sandy Jenkins
Pop 363; Circ 1,319
Library Holdings: Bk Vols 4,500
Wireless access
Mem of North Central Kansas Libraries System
Open Mon & Wed 12:30-3, Tues 12:30-3 & 4:30-6:30, Thurs 4:30-6:30, Fri 10-2

BURR OAK

P BURR OAK COMMUNITY LIBRARY, 231 Pennsylvania St, 66936. Tel: 785-647-5597. FAX: 785-647-5597. E-mail: bolibrary@ruraltel.net. *Librn,* Tonia Underwood
Pop 366; Circ 1,696
Library Holdings: AV Mats 194; DVDs 639; Bk Vols 10,373; Per Subs 17
Wireless access
Mem of Central Kansas Library System
Open Mon 4-7, Tues & Thurs 10-3, Wed 10-6

BURRTON

P RUTH DOLE MEMORIAL LIBRARY*, 121 N Burrton Ave, 67020. (Mail add: PO Box 400, 67020), SAN 305-845X. Tel: 620-463-7902. E-mail: burrlib400@gmail.com. Web Site: burrton.scklslibrary.info, burrtonkansas.com/library.htm. *Librn,* Rhonda Corwin
Pop 1,000; Circ 7,834
Library Holdings: Bk Vols 9,712; Per Subs 12
Wireless access
Mem of South Central Kansas Library System
Open Mon & Fri 1-5, Wed 9-5, Sat 9-12

BUSHTON

P FARMER TOWNSHIP COMMUNITY LIBRARY*, Main St, 460 Ave E, 67427-8825. (Mail add: PO Box 23, 67427-0023), SAN 305-8468. Tel: 620-562-3352, 620-562-3568. E-mail: ftcl@hbcomm.net. *Librn,* Nikole Orth-Smith
Pop 593; Circ 5,952
Library Holdings: Bk Vols 5,009
Special Collections: Juvenile Book of US Presidents; Kansas Coll
Mem of South Central Kansas Library System
Open Mon & Wed 1-5:30

CALDWELL

P CALDWELL PUBLIC LIBRARY*, 120 S Main St, 67022. SAN 305-8476. Tel: 620-845-6879. E-mail: librarian@readcaldwell.com. Web Site: readcaldwell.com. *Dir,* Lisa Moreland
Founded 1912. Pop 1,044
Library Holdings: Audiobooks 100; DVDs 250; Bk Vols 10,000; Per Subs 20
Wireless access
Mem of South Central Kansas Library System
Open Mon 10-6, Wed-Sat 10-2
Friends of the Library Group

CANEY

P CANEY CITY LIBRARY*, 211 W Fifth Ave, 67333. SAN 305-8484. Tel: 620-879-5341. FAX: 620-879-5828. E-mail: caneylibrary@yahoo.com. Web Site: caney.mykansaslibrary.org. *Dir,* Jennifer Rosson
Pop 2,284; Circ 13,104
Library Holdings: Audiobooks 294; DVDs 1,702; Large Print Bks 400; Bk Vols 9,435
Wireless access
Mem of Southeast Kansas Library System
Open Mon, Wed & Fri 12-6, Tues 12-7, Thurs 8-1, Sat 8-2
Friends of the Library Group

CANTON

P CANTON TOWNSHIP CARNEGIE LIBRARY, 203 N Main St, 67428. (Mail add: PO Box 336, 67428-0336), SAN 305-8492. Tel: 620-628-4349. E-mail: cantonlibrary1921@yahoo.com. Web Site: canton.scklslibrary.info. *Dir,* Treva Prieb
Founded 1909. Pop 1,187; Circ 6,012
Library Holdings: Bk Vols 4,200; Per Subs 15
Wireless access
Mem of South Central Kansas Library System
Open Mon & Wed 4-7, Thurs 10-1 & 4-7, Fri & Sat 10-1

CARBONDALE

P CARBONDALE CITY LIBRARY, 302 Main St, 66414-9635. (Mail add: PO Box 330, 66414-0330), SAN 305-8506. Tel: 785-836-7638. FAX: 785-836-7789. Web Site: www.carbondalecitylibrary.org. *Libr Dir,* Heather Garrison; E-mail: director@carbondalecitylibrary.org; *Asst Dir,* Traci Smith
Founded 1971. Pop 1,500
Library Holdings: Bk Vols 8,000; Per Subs 10
Wireless access
Mem of Northeast Kansas Library System
Open Mon 1-5, Tues & Fri 9-12 & 1-5, Wed 9-1, Thurs 9-6, Sat 9-12
Friends of the Library Group

CAWKER CITY

P CAWKER CITY PUBLIC LIBRARY*, 802 Locust, 67430. (Mail add: PO Box 136, 67430-0136), SAN 305-8514. Tel: 785-781-4925. E-mail: cawkerlib@nckcn.com. *Dir,* Kathy Bowles
Founded 1884. Pop 467; Circ 3,500
Library Holdings: Audiobooks 40; CDs 34; DVDs 216; e-books 2; Large Print Bks 129; Microforms 106; Bk Titles 9,600; Per Subs 18; Talking Bks 120
Wireless access
Function: Art exhibits, Bk reviews (Group), Bks on cassette, Bks on CD, CD-ROM, Children's prog, Computers for patron use, Free DVD rentals, Genealogy discussion group, Holiday prog, Home delivery & serv to seniorr ctr & nursing homes, ILL available, Photocopying/Printing, Prog for adults, Prog for children & young adult, Scanner, Story hour, Summer reading prog, Tax forms, VHS videos, Wheelchair accessible, Workshops
Mem of Central Kansas Library System
Open Tues 10-1, Wed 1-7, Thurs & Fri 1-5, Sat 9-Noon

CEDAR VALE

P CEDAR VALE MEMORIAL LIBRARY*, 608 Cedar St, 67024. (Mail add: PO Box 369, 67024-0369), SAN 376-5555. Tel: 620-758-2598. FAX: 620-758-2598. E-mail: cvmemlib@sktc.net. Web Site: cedarvale.mykansaslibrary.org. *Dir,* Stephanie McAdam
Pop 600
Library Holdings: Bk Vols 4,100
Wireless access
Mem of Southeast Kansas Library System
Open Mon-Wed 2-6:30, Thurs 9-Noon & 2-6:30, Fri 10-4

CENTRALIA

P CENTRALIA COMMUNITY LIBRARY*, 520 Fourth St, 66415. SAN 305-8522. Tel: 785-857-3331. E-mail: librarian@centralialibrary.com. Web Site: www.centralialibrary.com. *Libr Dir,* Dreda Smith; Staff 2 (Non-MLS 2)
Founded 1880. Pop 504; Circ 10,324
Library Holdings: DVDs 850; Bk Vols 8,430; Per Subs 10
Automation Activity & Vendor Info: (Acquisitions) LibLime; (Cataloging) LibLime; (Circulation) LibLime; (Course Reserve) LibLime; (ILL) LibLime; (Media Booking) LibLime; (OPAC) LibLime; (Serials) LibLime
Wireless access
Mem of Northeast Kansas Library System
Open Mon 10:30-7, Wed 8:30-2 & 5-8, Thurs 8:30-2, Fri 8:30-2 & 4-6, Sat 8:30-Noon

CHANUTE

P CHANUTE PUBLIC LIBRARY, 111 N Lincoln, 66720-1819. SAN 305-8530. Tel: 620-431-3820. FAX: 620-431-3848. E-mail: publiclibrary@chanute.org. Web Site: www.chanute.org/317/Public-Library. *Dir,* Kara Hale; Staff 4 (MLS 1, Non-MLS 3)
Founded 1905. Pop 16,500; Circ 120,617
Library Holdings: AV Mats 6,170; Large Print Bks 1,500; Bk Vols 59,960; Per Subs 130
Special Collections: Esther Clark Hill Coll; Nora B Cunningham Coll, letters
Subject Interests: Local hist
Automation Activity & Vendor Info: (Circulation) Follett Software; (OPAC) Follett Software
Mem of Southeast Kansas Library System
Open Mon-Thurs 9:30-8, Fri & Sat 9-5, Sun 1-5 (Winter); Mon-Thurs 9:30-6, Fri & Sat 9:30-5 (Summer)
Friends of the Library Group

S MARTIN & OSA JOHNSON SAFARI MUSEUM*, Stott Explorers Library, 111 N Lincoln Ave, 66720. SAN 325-7320. Tel: 620-431-2730. FAX: 620-431-2730. E-mail: osajohns@safarimuseum.com. Web Site: www.safarimuseum.com. *Dir,* Conrad G Froehlich
Founded 1980
Library Holdings: Bk Vols 10,000
Subject Interests: Africa, Natural hist, Pacific
Publications: Wait-A-Bit News
Open Tues-Sat 10-5, Sun 1-5
Restriction: Not a lending libr

J NEOSHO COUNTY COMMUNITY COLLEGE*, Chapman Library, 800 W 14th St, 66720-2699. SAN 305-8549. Tel: 620-432-0384, Ext 246. Interlibrary Loan Service Tel: 620-431-2820, Ext 296. Interlibrary Loan Service Toll Free Tel: 800-729-6222, Ext 296. FAX: 620-432-9841. E-mail: library@neosho.edu. Web Site: dc3.agverso.com/home?cid=dc3&lid=nc3. *Coordr, Libr Serv,* Todd Knispel; E-mail: tknispel@neosho.edu; Staff 4 (MLS 1, Non-MLS 3)
Founded 1936. Highest Degree: Associate
Library Holdings: Bk Vols 31,000; Per Subs 80
Special Collections: Genealogy
Automation Activity & Vendor Info: (Circulation) Follett Software; (OPAC) Follett Software
Wireless access
Open Mon-Thurs 8-8, Fri 8-5

CHAPMAN

P CHAPMAN PUBLIC LIBRARY*, 402 N Marshall, 67431. (Mail add: PO Box F, 67431-2644), SAN 305-8557. Tel: 785-922-6548. FAX: 785-922-6548. E-mail: library@chapmanks.com. Web Site: chapman.lib.nckls.org. *Dir,* Amanda Manning
Pop 1,428; Circ 7,798
Library Holdings: Bk Vols 14,516; Per Subs 50
Special Collections: KS History (Chapman Coll)
Automation Activity & Vendor Info: (Cataloging) Follett Software; (Circulation) Follett Software
Wireless access
Mem of North Central Kansas Libraries System
Open Tues-Fri 9-12 & 1-5:30, Sat 9-1

CHENEY

P CHENEY PUBLIC LIBRARY*, 203 N Main St, 67025. (Mail add: PO Box 700, 67025-0700), SAN 305-8565. Tel: 316-542-3331. E-mail: cheneylibrary@gmail.com. Web Site: www.cheneypubliclibrary.org. *Dir,* Susan Woodard
Founded 1940. Pop 1,800; Circ 25,363
Library Holdings: Bk Vols 13,000; Per Subs 17
Automation Activity & Vendor Info: (Cataloging) Innovative Interfaces, Inc; (Circulation) Innovative Interfaces, Inc
Wireless access
Mem of South Central Kansas Library System
Open Mon-Wed & Fri 9-1 & 2-5, Thurs 3-7, Sat 9-1
Friends of the Library Group

CHERRYVALE

P CHERRYVALE PUBLIC LIBRARY*, 329 E Main St, 67335. SAN 305-8573. Tel: 620-336-3460. FAX: 620-336-3460. Web Site: cherryvalelibrary.org/wp. *Dir,* April Read; E-mail: libdir2011@cherrypl.ks.coxmail.com
Founded 1913. Pop 2,770; Circ 20,526
Library Holdings: Large Print Bks 300; Bk Vols 16,400; Talking Bks 100
Wireless access
Mem of Southeast Kansas Library System
Open Mon-Fri 12-5
Friends of the Library Group

CHETOPA

P CHETOPA CITY LIBRARY*, 312 Maple, 67336. (Mail add: PO Box 206, 67336-0206), SAN 305-8581. Tel: 620-236-7194. E-mail: chetopacitylibrary@yahoo.com. Web Site: chetopa.mykansaslibrary.org. *Librn,* Kay Wolfe
Founded 1875. Pop 1,850; Circ 16,236
Library Holdings: Audiobooks 50; DVDs 400; Large Print Bks 1,200; Bk Vols 25,000; Per Subs 25
Subject Interests: Alaskana
Wireless access
Function: Adult bk club, Adult literacy prog, Art exhibits
Mem of Southeast Kansas Library System
Open Mon, Tues, Thurs & Fri 1-5, Wed 8-Noon
Restriction: 24-hr pass syst for students only, Access at librarian's discretion, Authorized personnel only
Friends of the Library Group

CIMARRON

P CIMARRON CITY LIBRARY*, 120 N Main, 67835. (Mail add: PO Box 645, 67835-0645), SAN 305-859X. Tel: 620-855-3808. FAX: 620-855-3884. Web Site: cimarroncitylibrary.org. *Dir,* Candis Hemel; E-mail: director@cimarroncitylibrary.org; Staff 3 (Non-MLS 3)
Founded 1934. Pop 1,934; Circ 35,286
Library Holdings: AV Mats 1,127; Electronic Media & Resources 100; Bk Vols 36,303; Per Subs 73; Talking Bks 1,448
Automation Activity & Vendor Info: (Circulation) Follett Software; (OPAC) Follett Software
Wireless access
Mem of Southwest Kansas Library System
Open Mon-Wed & Fri 10-6, Thurs 10-8, Sat 10-2
Friends of the Library Group
Branches: 2
ENSIGN BRANCH, 108 Aubrey, Ensign, 67841. (Mail add: PO Box 25, Ensign, 67841-0025). Tel: 620-865-2199. E-mail: ensignlib@yahoo.com. *Librn,* Pam Renfro
Pop 200
Library Holdings: Bk Vols 1,000
Automation Activity & Vendor Info: (Circulation) Auto-Graphics, Inc
Open Mon-Fri 3:30-5:30
INGALLS BRANCH, 220 S Main St, Ingalls, 67853. Tel: 620-335-5580. E-mail: ingallslibrary@yahoo.com. *Librn,* Debbie Milne
Library Holdings: Bk Titles 4,000
Automation Activity & Vendor Info: (Cataloging) Auto-Graphics, Inc; (Circulation) Auto-Graphics, Inc
Open Mon-Thurs 4-6, Fri 9am-11am

CLAFLIN

P INDEPENDENT TOWNSHIP LIBRARY*, 108 Main St, 67525. (Mail add: PO Box 163, 67525-0163), SAN 305-8603. Tel: 620-587-3488. FAX: 620-587-3488. *Dir,* Judy Wondra; E-mail: jwondra@hbcomm.net
Founded 1962. Pop 887; Circ 8,358
Library Holdings: AV Mats 148; DVDs 120; Large Print Bks 120; Bk Titles 9,205; Per Subs 20; Talking Bks 65; Videos 300
Special Collections: Arts & Crafts Coll; Kansas Book Title Coll; Original Claflin Clarion Newspaper Coll, dated back to 1800's, micro
Wireless access
Mem of Central Kansas Library System
Open Mon 3:30-8, Tues & Fri 9-12:30, Thurs 1-5:30, Sat 9-Noon

CLAY CENTER

P CLAY CENTER CARNEGIE LIBRARY, 706 Sixth St, 67432. SAN 305-8611. Tel: 785-632-3889. FAX: 785-630-2970. E-mail: contactus@cckslibrary.org. Web Site: claycenter.lib.nckls.org. *Libr Dir,* Shanda Cramer; E-mail: director@cckslibrary.org; *Ch,* Pixie Knepper; E-mail: kidslib@cckslibrary.org; *ILL Librn,* Janet Legg; E-mail: ccill@cckslibrary.org
Founded 1901. Pop 4,640; Circ 44,349
Library Holdings: Bk Titles 40,264; Per Subs 97
Wireless access
Mem of North Central Kansas Libraries System
Open Mon-Thurs 10-8, Fri 10-6, Sat 10-2
Friends of the Library Group

CLEARWATER

P CLEARWATER PUBLIC LIBRARY*, 109 E Ross St, 67026-7824. SAN 305-8638. Tel: 620-584-6474. FAX: 620-584-2995. Web Site: www.clearwaterkslibrary.org. *Dir,* Tina Welch; E-mail: cpldirector@sktc.net; Staff 4 (MLS 1, Non-MLS 3)
Pop 2,481; Circ 22,273
Library Holdings: Bk Vols 15,757; Per Subs 32
Automation Activity & Vendor Info: (Cataloging) Innovative Interfaces, Inc; (Circulation) Innovative Interfaces, Inc; (ILL) Auto-Graphics, Inc; (OPAC) Innovative Interfaces, Inc
Wireless access
Mem of South Central Kansas Library System
Open Tues & Thurs 10-7, Wed & Fri 10-5, Sat 10-2
Friends of the Library Group

CLIFTON

P CLIFTON PUBLIC LIBRARY*, 104 E Parallel, 66937. (Mail add: PO Box J, 66937-0310), SAN 305-8646. Tel: 785-455-2222. E-mail: clifpblib@hotmail.com. Web Site: clifton.lib.nckls.org. *Librn,* Pat Bloomfield
Founded 1954. Pop 600; Circ 400
Library Holdings: Bk Vols 3,000
Wireless access
Mem of North Central Kansas Libraries System
Open Mon & Fri 1-5, Tues 2-5, Wed 9-12 & 2-5, Sat 9-Noon

CLYDE

P CLYDE PUBLIC LIBRARY*, Randolph-Decker Library, 107 S Green St, 66938. (Mail add: PO Box 85, 66938-0085), SAN 305-8654. Tel: 785-446-3563. E-mail: rdpl@twinvalley.net. Web Site: www.clydekansas.org. *Dir,* Barb George; *Prog Dir,* Barb Bielser
Founded 1920. Pop 722; Circ 12,305
Library Holdings: Bk Vols 15,000
Wireless access
Mem of Central Kansas Library System
Open Mon-Thurs 2-6, Fri 9-1

COFFEYVILLE

J COFFEYVILLE COMMUNITY COLLEGE*, Graham Library, 400 W 11th, 67337-5064. SAN 305-8662. Tel: 620-251-7700, Ext 2032. FAX: 620-252-7366. Web Site: www.coffeyville.edu/academics/graham-library. *Dir,* Marty Evensvold; E-mail: martye@coffeyville.edu; Staff 1 (MLS 1)
Founded 1923. Enrl 1,170; Fac 45; Highest Degree: Associate
Library Holdings: Bks on Deafness & Sign Lang 12; Bk Titles 25,108; Bk Vols 27,626; Per Subs 308
Automation Activity & Vendor Info: (Acquisitions) Follett Software; (Cataloging) Follett Software; (Circulation) Follett Software; (OPAC) Follett Software; (Serials) Follett Software
Wireless access
Mem of Southeast Kansas Library System
Special Services for the Blind - ZoomText magnification & reading software
Open Mon-Thurs 8am-10pm, Fri 8-5; Mon-Fri (Summer) 8-4

P COFFEYVILLE PUBLIC LIBRARY*, 311 W Tenth St, 67337. SAN 305-8670. Tel: 620-251-1370. FAX: 620-251-1512. Web Site: www.coffeyvillepl.org. *Dir,* Lee Ann Eggers; E-mail: le@coffeyvillepl.org; *Asst Dir,* Rachel Koszalka; *Ch,* Heather Van Dyne; E-mail: hv@coffeyvillepl.org; *ILL,* Corey Kneedler; E-mail: ck@coffeyvillepl.org; Staff 6 (MLS 2, Non-MLS 4)
Founded 1906. Pop 10,517; Circ 76,287
Library Holdings: Bks on Deafness & Sign Lang 52; CDs 505; DVDs 400; Large Print Bks 1,800; Bk Titles 74,239; Per Subs 101; Talking Bks 400; Videos 1,121
Subject Interests: Genealogy
Automation Activity & Vendor Info: (Cataloging) Auto-Graphics, Inc; (Circulation) Follett Software; (ILL) Auto-Graphics, Inc; (OPAC) Follett Software
Wireless access
Mem of Southeast Kansas Library System
Special Services for the Deaf - Bks on deafness & sign lang; High interest/low vocabulary bks
Special Services for the Blind - BiFolkal kits; Bks on CD; Copier with enlargement capabilities; Extensive large print coll; Home delivery serv; Lending of low vision aids; Magnifiers; Talking bks
Open Mon-Thurs 9-8, Fri & Sat 9-5
Restriction: Non-resident fee

COLBY

J COLBY COMMUNITY COLLEGE*, H F Davis Memorial Library, 1255 S Range Ave, 67701. SAN 305-8689. Tel: 785-460-4689. Administration Tel: 785-460-5487. FAX: 785-460-4600. Web Site: www.colbycc.edu/student/library. *Dir,* Tara Schroer; E-mail: tara.schroer@colbycc.edu; *Libr Assoc,* Carol Bohme; E-mail: carol.bohme@colbycc.edu; Staff 3 (MLS 1, Non-MLS 2)
Founded 1964. Enrl 2,402; Fac 150; Highest Degree: Associate
Library Holdings: AV Mats 2,222; CDs 69; DVDs 2,937; e-books 44; Bk Titles 28,347; Per Subs 200
Special Collections: Cookbook Coll
Subject Interests: Kansas
Automation Activity & Vendor Info: (Acquisitions) EOS International; (Cataloging) EOS International; (Circulation) EOS International; (OPAC) EOS International
Wireless access
Mem of Northwest Kansas Library System
Partic in State Library of Kansas
Open Mon-Thurs 7:30am-9pm, Fri 7:30-5, Sun 1-7
Restriction: Circ privileges for students & alumni only

P PIONEER MEMORIAL LIBRARY, 375 W Fourth St, 67701-2197. SAN 305-8697. Tel: 785-460-4470. FAX: 785-460-4472. E-mail: colbykslibrary@yahoo.com. Web Site: www.colbylibrary.com. *Dir,* Melany A Wilks; E-mail: director@colbylibrary.com; *Asst Dir,* Wynn Duffey; E-mail: assistantdirector@colbylibrary.com; *Circ Supvr,* Alicia Unruh; E-mail: contactus@colbylibrary.com; *Adult Serv, ILL,* Nancy Saddler; E-mail: adult@colbylibrary.com; *Ch Serv,* Judy Kleinsorge; E-mail: child-youth@colbylibrary.com; *Asst Youth Serv,* Garrett Nemecheck; Staff 10 (MLS 1, Non-MLS 9)
Founded 1926. Pop 8,219; Circ 153,460
Jan 2020-Dec 2020 Income $9,158, State $1,633, Locally Generated Income $7,525. Mats Exp $335,029, Books $17,000, Per/Ser (Incl. Access Fees) $3,100, AV Mat $18,000. Sal $226,015
Library Holdings: Audiobooks 1,949; AV Mats 276; Bks on Deafness & Sign Lang 3; Braille Volumes 4; CDs 10; DVDs 2,184; e-books 1,028; Large Print Bks 2,701; Bk Titles 40,734; Bk Vols 45,641; Per Subs 105; Videos 263
Special Collections: Kansas Coll
Automation Activity & Vendor Info: (Acquisitions) Auto-Graphics, Inc; (Cataloging) Auto-Graphics, Inc; (Circulation) Auto-Graphics, Inc; (ILL) Auto-Graphics, Inc; (OPAC) Auto-Graphics, Inc; (Serials) Auto-Graphics, Inc
Wireless access
Function: 24/7 Online cat, 3D Printer, Activity rm, Adult bk club, Audiobks on Playaways & MP3, Bi-weekly Writer's Group, Bk club(s), Bk reviews (Group), Bks on CD, Children's prog, Computer training, Computers for patron use, Electronic databases & coll, ILL available, Instruction & testing, Internet access, Laminating, Life-long learning prog for all ages, Magazines, Makerspace, Meeting rooms, Movies, Notary serv, Online cat, Outside serv via phone, mail, e-mail & web, OverDrive digital audio bks, Photocopying/Printing, Preschool reading prog, Printer for laptops & handheld devices, Prog for adults, Prog for children & young adult, Ref & res, Ref serv available, Res assist avail, Scanner, Senior computer classes, Spanish lang bks, STEM programs, Story hour, Summer & winter reading prog, Summer reading prog, Tax forms, Teen prog, VHS videos, Wheelchair accessible, Winter reading prog, Workshops
Publications: Annual Report; The Library Link
Mem of Northwest Kansas Library System
Special Services for the Deaf - Am sign lang & deaf culture; Bks on deafness & sign lang; Closed caption videos
Special Services for the Blind - Audio mat; Bks available with recordings; Bks on cassette; Bks on CD; Cassette playback machines; Cassettes; Large print & cassettes; Large print bks; Large print bks & talking machines; Talking bks; Talking bks & player equip
Open Mon-Thurs 9-8, Fri 9-5, Sat 9-4, Sun 1-4 (Winter); Mon-Wed 9-6, Thurs 9-8, Fri 9-5, Sat 9-4 (Summer)
Friends of the Library Group

COLDWATER

P COLDWATER-WILMORE REGIONAL LIBRARY*, 221 E Main, 67029. (Mail add: PO Box 606, 67029-0606), SAN 342-006X. Tel: 620-582-2333. FAX: 620-582-2333. E-mail: coldlibrary1@gmail.com. Web Site: coldwater-wilmorelibrary.info. *Dir,* Ellen Selzer; Staff 1 (MLS 1)
Founded 1912. Pop 800
Library Holdings: Bk Vols 14,000; Per Subs 15
Wireless access
Mem of Southwest Kansas Library System
Open Mon 3:30-7:30, Tues-Sat 9-12 & 1:30-5:30
Branches: 1
WILMORE BRANCH, 100 Taft St, Wilmore, 67155, SAN 342-0094. Tel: 620-738-4464. *Librn,* Pat White
Library Holdings: Bk Titles 335
Open Tues & Fri 1-6

COLONY

P COLONY CITY LIBRARY*, 339 Cherry St, 66015. (Mail add: PO Box 85, 66015-0085), SAN 305-8719. Tel: 620-852-3530. FAX: 620-852-3107. E-mail: colonylibrary@yahoo.com. Web Site: colonycity.mykansaslibrary.org. *Librn,* Kloma Buckle
Pop 397; Circ 1,517
Library Holdings: Bks on Deafness & Sign Lang 10; DVDs 70; Large Print Bks 100; Music Scores 39; Bk Titles 4,500; Per Subs 20; Talking Bks 16; Videos 352
Wireless access
Mem of Southeast Kansas Library System
Partic in SE Kans Libr Asn
Open Mon-Fri 9-12 & 1-4

COLUMBUS

P COLUMBUS PUBLIC LIBRARY*, 205 N Kansas, 66725. SAN 305-8727. Tel: 620-429-2086. FAX: 620-429-1950. E-mail: columbuspubliclibrary@gmail.com. Web Site: columbus.mykansaslibrary.org. *Dir,* Lauren Dainty
Founded 1905. Pop 3,597; Circ 30,418
Library Holdings: Bk Vols 15,000; Per Subs 70
Automation Activity & Vendor Info: (Acquisitions) Follett Software
Wireless access
Open Mon-Fri 9-6, Sat 10-3

COLWICH

P COLWICH COMMUNITY LIBRARY*, 432 W Colwich Ave, 67030. SAN 305-8735. Tel: 316-796-1521. E-mail: colwichlibrary@gmail.com, library@colwich.kscoxmail.com. Web Site: colwichks.org/live-here/library, www.colwichlibrary.org. *Dir,* Joanna Kraus; Staff 2 (Non-MLS 2)
Founded 1961. Pop 2,257; Circ 16,821
Library Holdings: Bk Vols 14,100; Per Subs 62
Automation Activity & Vendor Info: (Circulation) Innovative Interfaces, Inc
Wireless access
Publications: Website
Mem of South Central Kansas Library System
Open Mon-Thurs 8-11 & 3-8, Fri 8-11 & 3-6, Sat 10-2

CONCORDIA

P FRANK CARLSON LIBRARY*, 702 Broadway, 66901. SAN 305-8743. Tel: 785-243-2250. E-mail: frankcarlsonlibrary@yahoo.com. Web Site: fcarlsonlib.org. *Dir,* Denise de Rochefort-Reynolds; Staff 4 (MLS 1, Non-MLS 3)
Founded 1892. Pop 5,300; Circ 75,000
Library Holdings: Bk Vols 38,000; Per Subs 131
Special Collections: Business Resources; Frank Carlson Coll; Kansas Coll; US Constitution
Automation Activity & Vendor Info: (Cataloging) LibLime Koha; (Circulation) LibLime Koha; (OPAC) LibLime Koha
Wireless access
Mem of Central Kansas Library System
Open Mon-Wed 9-5:30, Thurs 9-7, Fri 9-5, Sat 9-1

J CLOUD COUNTY COMMUNITY COLLEGE LIBRARY*, 2221 Campus Dr, 66901-5305. (Mail add: PO Box 1002, 66901-1002), SAN 305-8751. Tel: 785-243-1435, Ext 224. Toll Free Tel: 800-729-5101, Ext 226. E-mail: library@cloud.edu. Web Site: www.cloud.edu/Academics/Library. *Dir, Libr Serv,* Jennifer Schroeder; Tel: 785-243-1435, Ext 226, E-mail: jschroeder@cloud.edu; *Libr Assoc,* Krystal Richard; Tel: 785-243-1435, Ext 227, E-mail: krichard@cloud.edu; Staff 2 (MLS 1, Non-MLS 1)
Founded 1968. Enrl 1,680; Fac 139; Highest Degree: Associate
Library Holdings: AV Mats 1,666; e-books 9,151; Bk Titles 18,308; Bk Vols 21,067; Per Subs 30
Special Collections: Child Care Coll
Automation Activity & Vendor Info: (Cataloging) Auto-Graphics, Inc; (Circulation) Auto-Graphics, Inc; (ILL) Auto-Graphics, Inc; (OPAC) Auto-Graphics, Inc
Wireless access
Function: Bi-weekly Writer's Group
Open Mon-Thurs 7:45am-9pm, Fri 7:45-5, Sun 6pm-8pm

S CLOUD COUNTY HISTORICAL SOCIETY MUSEUM LIBRARY*, 635 Broadway, 66901. SAN 325-7347. Tel: 785-243-2866. E-mail: museum@cloudcountyks.org. Web Site: www.cloudcountyks.org/main/other-offices/historical-society. *Curator,* Florence Girard
Founded 1959
Library Holdings: Bk Vols 550
Special Collections: Municipal Document Depository
Open Tues-Fri 1-5, Sat 11-5

CONWAY SPRINGS

P CONWAY SPRINGS CITY LIBRARY*, 210 W Spring St, 67031. (Mail add: PO Box 183, 67031-0183), SAN 376-5563. Tel: 620-456-2859. FAX: 620-456-3294. E-mail: cwslibrary@havilandtelco.com. Web Site: www.conwayspringsks.com/departments/library. *Librn,* Marsha Harrelson; *Libr Asst,* Robyn Cooper
Library Holdings: Bk Vols 11,000; Per Subs 20
Mem of South Central Kansas Library System
Open Tues & Fri 10-1, Wed 10-1 & 2:30-6

COPELAND

P COPELAND PUBLIC LIBRARY, 109 Santa Fe St, 67837. (Mail add: PO Box 121, 67837-0121), SAN 305-8778. Tel: 620-668-5559. *Librn,* Hargett Marcia; E-mail: hargettmarcia@gmail.com
Pop 310; Circ 1,033
Library Holdings: Bk Vols 6,000
Automation Activity & Vendor Info: (Cataloging) Brodart; (Circulation) Brodart
Wireless access
Open Mon-Thurs 10-12 & 2-5; Mon-Thurs 10-12 & 1-4 (Summer)

CORNING

P CORNING CITY LIBRARY*, 6221 Fifth St, 66417-8485. SAN 305-8786. Tel: 785-868-2755. FAX: 785-868-2755. Web Site: www.corningcitylibrary.org. *Libr Dir,* Karleen Boden; E-mail: kboden@corningcitylibrary.org
Founded 1920. Pop 167; Circ 2,072
Library Holdings: DVDs 22; Large Print Bks 164; Bk Vols 7,000; Per Subs 12; Videos 462
Mem of Northeast Kansas Library System
Open Mon 12:30-5, Wed 3:30-8:30, Sat 9-1

COTTONWOOD FALLS

P BURNLEY MEMORIAL LIBRARY*, 401 N Oak, 66845. (Mail add: PO Box 509, 66845-0509), SAN 376-558X. Tel: 620-273-9119. E-mail: burnleylibrary@gmail.com. Web Site: burnley.lib.nckls.org. *Dir,* Janet Ayers
Library Holdings: Bk Vols 10,000; Per Subs 22
Automation Activity & Vendor Info: (Acquisitions) ComPanion Corp; (Cataloging) ComPanion Corp; (Circulation) ComPanion Corp; (OPAC) ComPanion Corp
Wireless access
Mem of North Central Kansas Libraries System
Open Mon, Tues, Thurs & Sat 2-5, Wed 2-5 & 7-9, Fri 12-5

COUNCIL GROVE

P COUNCIL GROVE PUBLIC LIBRARY, 829 W Main St, 66846. SAN 305-8794. Tel: 620-767-5716. FAX: 620-767-7312. E-mail: cglib@tctelco.net. Web Site: councilgrove.lib.nckls.org. *Libr Dir,* Shannon Reid-Wheat; *Asst Dir, Youth Serv Librn,* Michelle Gibson; *ILL,* Aimee Roberts; Staff 5 (Non-MLS 5)
Founded 1876. Pop 2,280; Circ 23,190
Library Holdings: Audiobooks 1,300; AV Mats 1,235; DVDs 500; Large Print Bks 834; Bk Titles 20,422; Per Subs 36
Automation Activity & Vendor Info: (Cataloging) Follett Software; (Circulation) Follett Software; (ILL) Auto-Graphics, Inc; (OPAC) Follett Software; (Serials) Follett Software
Wireless access
Function: Audio & video playback equip for onsite use, Bk club(s), Bks on cassette, Bks on CD, Children's prog, Computers for patron use, Electronic databases & coll, Free DVD rentals, ILL available, Music CDs, Online cat, OverDrive digital audio bks, Photocopying/Printing, Prog for adults, Prog for children & young adult, Scanner, Story hour, Summer reading prog, Tax forms, VHS videos, Wheelchair accessible
Mem of North Central Kansas Libraries System

Open Mon & Tues 11-6, Wed-Fri 11-4
Friends of the Library Group

COURTLAND

P COURTLAND COMMUNITY LIBRARY*, 403 Main St, 66939. (Mail add: PO Box 85, 66939-0085), SAN 305-8808. Tel: 785-374-4260. FAX: 785-374-4252. E-mail: library@courtland.net. Web Site: courtland.mykansaslibrary.org. *Libr Dir,* Barbara Langston
Founded 1922. Pop 377
Library Holdings: Bk Vols 5,000; Per Subs 21
Mem of Central Kansas Library System
Open Mon 9:30-11:30, Tues 2:30-7, Fri 2:30-6

CUBA

P HILLCREST PUBLIC LIBRARY, 804 Bristol, 66940. (Mail add: PO Box 33, 66940-0033). Tel: 785-729-3355. E-mail: hillcrestlibrary66940@yahoo.com. Web Site: hillcrestpl.blogspot.com. *Dir,* Lori Haval
Founded 2000. Pop 920
Library Holdings: Bk Vols 12,000; Per Subs 50; Talking Bks 125; Videos 200
Automation Activity & Vendor Info: (Cataloging) Follett Software; (Circulation) Follett Software
Mem of Central Kansas Library System
Open Mon & Wed 8-12 & 5-7, Tues, Thurs & Fri 8-Noon

DELPHOS

P DELPHOS PUBLIC LIBRARY*, 114 W Second, 67436. (Mail add: PO Box 284, 67436-0284), SAN 376-5679. Tel: 785-523-4668. E-mail: delphoslib@twinvalley.net. *Dir,* Sharon Snively; E-mail: s_snively@hotmail.com
Library Holdings: Bk Vols 6,000; Per Subs 10
Wireless access
Mem of Central Kansas Library System
Open Tues 10-2, Thurs 1-7, Fri 1-5, Sat 10-Noon

DERBY

P DERBY PUBLIC LIBRARY*, 1600 E Walnut Grove, 67037. SAN 305-8816. Tel: 316-788-0760. FAX: 316-788-7313. E-mail: info@derbylibrary.com. Web Site: derbylibrary.com. *Dir,* Eric Gustafson; E-mail: eric@derbylibrary.com; *Asst Dir,* Debbie Thomas; E-mail: debbie@derbylibrary.com; *ILL & Cat Coordr,* Joanne Condon; E-mail: joanne@derbylibrary.com; *Pub Support Serv Coordr,* Kristy Norman; E-mail: kristy@derbylibrary.com; *Tech Coordr,* Justin Ball; E-mail: justin@derbylibrary.com; *Youth Serv Coordr,* Carri Fry; E-mail: carri@derbylibrary.com; Staff 18.6 (MLS 1, Non-MLS 17.6)
Founded 1958. Pop 22,000; Circ 323,908
Jan 2013-Dec 2013 Income $866,652, State $13,000, City $784,652, Locally Generated Income $40,000, Other $29,000. Mats Exp $166,493, Books $79,493, Per/Ser (Incl. Access Fees) $7,000, AV Mat $45,000, Electronic Ref Mat (Incl. Access Fees) $35,000. Sal $494,000 (Prof $69,120)
Library Holdings: AV Mats 4,540; Braille Volumes 32; CDs 2,459; DVDs 4,357; Electronic Media & Resources 38; High Interest/Low Vocabulary Bk Vols 208; Large Print Bks 4,788; Bk Titles 60,000; Bk Vols 80,000; Per Subs 100
Automation Activity & Vendor Info: (Acquisitions) LibLime; (Cataloging) LibLime; (Circulation) LibLime; (ILL) Auto-Graphics, Inc; (OPAC) LibLime
Wireless access
Function: Adult bk club, After school storytime, Art exhibits, Audiobks via web, Bk club(s), Bks on CD, Children's prog, Computers for patron use, Electronic databases & coll, Free DVD rentals, Holiday prog, Home delivery & serv to seniorr ctr & nursing homes, ILL available, Internet access, Music CDs, Online cat, OverDrive digital audio bks, Photocopying/Printing, Prog for adults, Prog for children & young adult, Story hour, Summer reading prog, Tax forms, Teen prog, Wheelchair accessible
Mem of South Central Kansas Library System
Special Services for the Deaf - Closed caption videos; High interest/low vocabulary bks; Sign lang interpreter upon request for prog
Special Services for the Blind - Large print bks; PC for people with disabilities
Open Mon-Thurs 9-8:30, Fri 9-6, Sat 9-5, Sun 1-5
Friends of the Library Group

DIGHTON

P LANE COUNTY LIBRARY*, 144 South Lane, 67839. (Mail add: PO Box 997, 67839-0997), SAN 305-8824. Tel: 620-397-2808. FAX: 620-397-5937. Web Site: www.lanecolibrary.info. *Dir,* Ruby Martin; E-mail: director@lanecolibrary.info; *Asst Librn,* Mona Peck
Founded 1934. Pop 2,211; Circ 33,323
Library Holdings: Bks on Deafness & Sign Lang 18; CDs 111; DVDs 270; Large Print Bks 54; Bk Vols 20,400; Per Subs 76; Talking Bks 563; Videos 1,451
Special Collections: Our Kansas Room-Kansas Books
Subject Interests: Genealogy
Automation Activity & Vendor Info: (Acquisitions) Auto-Graphics, Inc; (Cataloging) Follett Software; (Circulation) Follett Software; (Course Reserve) Relais International; (ILL) Follett Software
Wireless access
Function: Adult bk club, Audio & video playback equip for onsite use, CD-ROM, Genealogy discussion group, Home delivery & serv to seniorr ctr & nursing homes, Homebound delivery serv, Homework prog, ILL available, Internet access, Online ref, Outside serv via phone, mail, e-mail & web, Photocopying/Printing, Preschool outreach, Prog for children & young adult, Spoken cassettes & CDs, Spoken cassettes & DVDs, Summer reading prog, Tax forms, VHS videos
Mem of Southwest Kansas Library System
Open Mon & Thurs 9-8, Tues, Wed & Fri 9-5
Friends of the Library Group
Branches: 1
HEALY EXTENSION, 2009 W Hwy 4, Healy, 67850-5088. (Mail add: PO Box 144, Healy, 67850-0144). Tel: 620-398-2267. E-mail: healylib@st-tel.net. *Dir,* Roberta Barnett
Library Holdings: Bk Vols 3,500
Open Mon 9-1, Wed 1:30-5:30
Friends of the Library Group

DODGE CITY

S BOOT HILL MUSEUM, Special Library & Archives, 500 W Wyatt Earp Blvd, 67801. SAN 373-4552. Tel: 620-227-8188. FAX: 620-227-7673. E-mail: research@boothill.org. Web Site: www.boothill.org. *Curator,* Kathie Bell; *Curator,* Karen Pankratz
Library Holdings: Bk Vols 2,000; Per Subs 7
Special Collections: Historic Photographs Coll
Partic in Dodge City Library Consortium
Restriction: Open by appt only

J DODGE CITY COMMUNITY COLLEGE LIBRARY*, 2501 N 14th, 67801. SAN 305-8840. Tel: 620-225-1321, Ext 287, 620-227-9287. Administration Tel: 620-227-9285. E-mail: library@dc3.edu. Web Site: dc3-verso.auto-graphics.com/MVC, dc3.edu/location/library. *Dir,* Shelly Huelsman; E-mail: shuelsman@dc3.edu; *Circ, ILL,* Sara Wilson; E-mail: swilson@dc3.edu; *Govt Doc,* Jolene Durler; Staff 1 (MLS 1)
Founded 1935. Enrl 2,414; Fac 85; Highest Degree: Associate
Jul 2017-Jun 2018 Income $52,950. Mats Exp $30,681, Books $12,000, Per/Ser (Incl. Access Fees) $8,500, AV Mat $181, Electronic Ref Mat (Incl. Access Fees) $10,000. Sal $89,000 (Prof $55,000)
Library Holdings: DVDs 1,082; e-books 1,000; Bk Titles 33,000; Per Subs 15
Special Collections: US Document Depository
Automation Activity & Vendor Info: (Acquisitions) Auto-Graphics, Inc; (Cataloging) Auto-Graphics, Inc; (Circulation) Auto-Graphics, Inc; (Course Reserve) Auto-Graphics, Inc; (ILL) Auto-Graphics, Inc; (OPAC) Auto-Graphics, Inc; (Serials) Auto-Graphics, Inc
Wireless access
Function: Archival coll, Computers for patron use, Distance learning, Electronic databases & coll, Free DVD rentals, Govt ref serv, ILL available, Instruction & testing, Mail & tel request accepted, Microfiche/film & reading machines, Orientations, Photocopying/Printing, Scanner, Wheelchair accessible
Mem of Southwest Kansas Library System
Partic in Dodge City Library Consortium
Open Mon-Thurs 8am-9pm, Fri 8-4, Sun 6pm-9pm

P DODGE CITY PUBLIC LIBRARY*, 1001 N Second Ave, 67801. SAN 305-8859. Tel: 620-225-0248. FAX: 620-225-2761. Interlibrary Loan Service FAX: 620-225-0868. Administration FAX: 620-225-1931. E-mail: library@dcpl.info. Web Site: www.dcpl.info. *Dir,* Brandon Hines; E-mail: brandonh@dcpl.info; *Pub Serv Librn,* Michael Biltz; E-mail: michaelb@trails.net; *Ref Librn,* Sam Shipley; *ILL Mgr,* Cindy Shipley; Staff 19 (MLS 3, Non-MLS 16)
Founded 1905. Pop 26,101; Circ 125,962
Library Holdings: AV Mats 3,949; DVDs 7,935; Electronic Media & Resources 44; Bk Vols 126,671; Per Subs 202
Special Collections: Kansas Coll. State Document Depository
Subject Interests: Gardening, Hist, Kansas, Spanish (Lang)
Automation Activity & Vendor Info: (Acquisitions) SirsiDynix; (Cataloging) SirsiDynix; (Circulation) SirsiDynix; (Media Booking) SirsiDynix; (OPAC) SirsiDynix; (Serials) SirsiDynix
Wireless access
Mem of Southwest Kansas Library System
Partic in OCLC Online Computer Library Center, Inc

Open Mon-Thurs 9-8, Fri 9-6, Sat 9-5
Friends of the Library Group

S KANSAS HERITAGE CENTER LIBRARY*, 1000 N Second Ave, 67801. (Mail add: PO Box 1207, 67801-1207), SAN 305-8832. Tel: 620-227-1616. FAX: 620-227-1701. Web Site: www.dcpl.info/kansas-heritage-center?page_id=150. *Exec Dir,* Diedre Lemon; E-mail: diedrel@dcpl.info; Staff 4 (MLS 1, Non-MLS 3)
Founded 1966
Library Holdings: Bk Titles 6,400; Bk Vols 9,000; Per Subs 45; Videos 500
Special Collections: Dodge City & Kansas Research Files; Dodge City Newspaper, 1876-present, micro
Subject Interests: Kansas
Wireless access
Publications: 399 Kansas Characters; Color Kansas Characters Poster/Coloring Book; Color Oklahoma Characters Poster/Coloring Book; Dodge City, Cowboy Capital; Kansas Symbols Coloring Book; Oklahoma Symbols Coloring Book; Santa Fe Trail Adventures; Sentinel to the Cimarron: The Frontier Experience of Fort Dodge, Kansas; West by Southwest
Open Mon-Fri 8-5

P SOUTHWEST KANSAS LIBRARY SYSTEM*, 100 Military Ave, Ste 210, 67801. SAN 342-0124. Tel: 620-225-1231. Toll Free Tel: 800-657-2533. FAX: 620-225-0252. E-mail: swkls@swkls.org. Web Site: swkls.org. *Dir,* Holly Mercer; Tel: 620-225-1231, Ext 204, E-mail: hmercer@swkls.org; *Ref & ILL Librn,* Patti Cummins; Tel: 620-225-1231, Ext 207, E-mail: pcummins@swkls.org; *Bus Mgr,* Tandy Ritchhart; Tel: 620-225-1231, Ext 200, E-mail: tritchhart@swkls.org; Staff 10 (MLS 2, Non-MLS 8)
Founded 1968. Pop 151,689
Library Holdings: Bk Vols 14,709; Per Subs 12
Special Collections: Spanish (Popular Reading)
Automation Activity & Vendor Info: (Acquisitions) Auto-Graphics, Inc; (Cataloging) Auto-Graphics, Inc; (Circulation) Auto-Graphics, Inc
Wireless access
Publications: Southwest Kansas Library System Newsletter; System Scene
Member Libraries: Ashland City Library; Brownell Public Library; Bucklin Public Library; Cimarron City Library; Coldwater-Wilmore Regional Library; Dodge City Community College Library; Dodge City Public Library; Dudley Township Public Library; Ford City Library; Fowler Public Library; Grant County Library; Greeley County Library; Hamilton County Library; Hanston City Library; Haskell Township Library; Henry Laird Library; Jetmore Public Library; Kearny County Library; Kinsley Public Library; Kismet Public Library; Lane County Library; Liberal Memorial Library; Meade Public Library; Meadowlark Library; Minneola City Library; Montezuma Township Library; Morton County Library; Ness City Public Library; Plains Community Library; Protection Township Library; Ransom Public Library; Scott County Library; Seward County Community College Library; Spearville Township Library; Stanton County Public Library; Stevens County Library; Utica Library Association; Wichita County Public Library
Partic in Association for Rural & Small Libraries; Telecommunications Libr Info Network
Special Services for the Blind - Audio mat; Bks & mags in Braille, on rec, tape & cassette; Braille equip; Digital talking bk machines; Large print bks
Open Mon-Fri 8-5
Branches: 1

P TALKING BOOKS, 100 Military Ave, Ste 210, 67801. Tel: 620-225-1231. Toll Free Tel: 800-657-2533. FAX: 620-225-0252. Web Site: swkls.org/about/services/talking-books. *Outreach Coordr, Talking Bks,* Richard Brookman; E-mail: rbrookman@skls.org; Staff 1 (Non-MLS 1)
Library Holdings: Bk Vols 500
Open Mon-Fri 8-5
Bookmobiles: 1

DOUGLASS

P DOUGLASS PUBLIC LIBRARY, 319 S Forrest St, 67039. (Mail add: PO Box 190, 67039-0190), SAN 305-8875. Tel: 316-746-2600. FAX: 316-746-3936. E-mail: douglb@sbcglobal.net. Web Site: www.douglasslibrary.com. *Dir,* Cina Shirley
Founded 1941. Pop 2,626
Library Holdings: Bk Vols 20,000; Per Subs 51
Automation Activity & Vendor Info: (Cataloging) Biblionix/Apollo; (Circulation) Biblionix/Apollo
Wireless access
Mem of South Central Kansas Library System
Open Mon-Wed 9-5, Thurs 9-6, Sat 9-2
Friends of the Library Group

DOWNS

P DOWNS CARNEGIE LIBRARY*, 504 S Morgan, 67437-2019. SAN 305-8883. Tel: 785-454-3821. FAX: 785-454-3821. E-mail: downslibrary@ruraltel.net. *Dir,* Sherry Knouf
Founded 1905. Pop 1,170; Circ 20,000
Library Holdings: Bk Vols 15,000; Per Subs 20
Subject Interests: Hist, Kansas
Automation Activity & Vendor Info: (Cataloging) Koha; (Circulation) Koha
Wireless access
Mem of Central Kansas Library System
Open Mon 1-6, Tues & Thurs 1-5, Wed 1-7, Fri 12-5, Sat 11-5

DWIGHT

P DWIGHT LIBRARY*, 637 Main, 66849. (Mail add: PO Box 278, 68849-0278), SAN 305-8891. Tel: 785-482-3804. E-mail: dwlibrary@tctelco.net. *Pres,* Marilyn Kaluhiokalani
Pop 261; Circ 1,200
Library Holdings: Bk Vols 2,305; Per Subs 6
Wireless access
Mem of North Central Kansas Libraries System
Open Mon 9-10, Wed 10-12 & 1:30-4:30, Sat 10-12 & 1-3

EDNA

P EDNA PUBLIC LIBRARY*, 105 N Delaware, 67342. (Mail add: PO Box 218, 67342-0218), SAN 305-8905. Tel: 620-922-3470. E-mail: ednalibrary@yahoo.com. Web Site: edna.mykansaslibrary.org. *Librn,* Sharon Triebel
Founded 1950. Pop 537
Library Holdings: Large Print Bks 292; Bk Vols 6,249; Per Subs 10; Talking Bks 18
Wireless access
Mem of Southeast Kansas Library System
Special Services for the Blind - Talking bks
Open Mon & Wed 9-11 & 1-6, Tues & Thurs 2:30-6, Sat 9-2

EFFINGHAM

P EFFINGHAM COMMUNITY LIBRARY, 414 Main St, 66023. (Mail add: PO Box 189, 66023-0189), SAN 305-8913. Tel: 913-833-5881. FAX: 913-833-5881. E-mail: info@effinghamlibrary.net. Web Site: www.effinghamlibrary.net. *Dir,* Scott Strine; E-mail: sstrine@effinghamlibrary.net
Founded 1927. Pop 548; Circ 600
Library Holdings: CDs 90; Electronic Media & Resources 20; Large Print Bks 120; Bk Vols 7,461; Per Subs 20; Talking Bks 36; Videos 200
Wireless access
Mem of Northeast Kansas Library System
Open Mon, Tues & Thurs 2-6, Wed 10-2, Sat 10-12

EL DORADO

P BRADFORD MEMORIAL LIBRARY*, 611 S Washington St, 67042. SAN 305-8921. Tel: 316-321-3363. E-mail: services@bradfordlibrary.info. Web Site: bradford.scklf.info. *Dir,* Kristi Jacobs; E-mail: kristi@bradfordlibrary.info; Staff 14 (MLS 2, Non-MLS 12)
Founded 1897. Pop 12,686; Circ 156,705
Library Holdings: AV Mats 8,425; Bks on Deafness & Sign Lang 64; Large Print Bks 7,971; Bk Titles 67,337; Per Subs 108
Special Collections: Mental Health Coll; Ornithology Coll
Automation Activity & Vendor Info: (Acquisitions) Follett Software; (Cataloging) Follett Software; (Circulation) Follett Software
Wireless access
Function: Adult bk club, Bks on cassette, Bks on CD, Computers for patron use, Digital talking bks, Electronic databases & coll, Equip loans & repairs, Free DVD rentals, Games & aids for people with disabilities, Home delivery & serv to seniorr ctr & nursing homes, Homebound delivery serv, ILL available, Internet access, Mail & tel request accepted, Music CDs, Online cat, Outreach serv, OverDrive digital audio bks, Photocopying/Printing, Prog for adults, Prog for children & young adult, Ref serv available, Spoken cassettes & CDs, Story hour, Summer reading prog, Tax forms, Teen prog, Telephone ref, VHS videos, Wheelchair accessible
Mem of South Central Kansas Library System
Open Mon-Thurs 9-8, Fri & Sat 9-5
Friends of the Library Group

J BUTLER COMMUNITY COLLEGE LIBRARY & ARCHIVES, L W Nixon Library, El Dorado campus, Library 600 Bldg, 901 S Haverhill Rd, 67042-3280. SAN 305-893X. Tel: 316-322-3234. Interlibrary Loan Service Tel: 316-322-6858. Administration Tel: 316-322-3168. Automation Services Tel: 316-323-6810. FAX: 316-322-3315. E-mail: lwnixon@butlercc.edu. Web Site: www.butlercc.edu/libraries. *Archives, Dir of Libr,* Judy Bastin;

Tel: 316-322-3235, E-mail: jbastin@butlercc.edu; *Lead Res & Instruction Librn,* Kim Veliz; Tel: 316-323-6845, E-mail: kveliz@butlercc.edu; *Access Serv, Instruction Librn,* Kara Price; Tel: 316-323-3102, E-mail: kprice9@butlercc.edu; *Ref & Instruction Librn,* Ruth Harries; Tel: 316-323-6846, E-mail: rharries@butlercc.edu; *Ref & Instruction Librn,* Morgan Roberts; Tel: 316-323-6843, E-mail: mroberts25@butlercc.edu; *Resource Librn, Syst Librn,* Mary Walker; E-mail: mwalker6@butlercc.edu; *Tech Serv Librn,* Teresa Mayginnes; Tel: 316-323-6842, E-mail: tmayginnes@butlercc.edu; *Archivist, Bus Mgr,* Ronald Rozzell; E-mail: rrozzell@butlercc.edu. Subject Specialists: *Admin, Copyright, Policy,* Judy Bastin; *Libr instruction,* Kara Price; *Info tech, Libr mgt syst, Statistics,* Mary Walker; *Libr mgt syst,* Teresa Mayginnes; *Archives, Financial,* Ronald Rozzell; Staff 8 (MLS 7, Non-MLS 1)
Founded 1927. Enrl 7,238; Fac 511; Highest Degree: Associate
Special Collections: Butler Community College Archives; Marianne Koke Memorial Folk Arts Coll; McCormick Pioneer Women Coll
Subject Interests: Folk art, Pioneer women
Automation Activity & Vendor Info: (Cataloging) Auto-Graphics, Inc; (Circulation) Auto-Graphics, Inc; (ILL) Auto-Graphics, Inc; (OPAC) Auto-Graphics, Inc
Wireless access
Mem of South Central Kansas Library System
Special Services for the Deaf - Bks on deafness & sign lang
Special Services for the Blind - Accessible computers; Bks on cassette; Bks on CD; Closed caption display syst; Computer access aids; Copier with enlargement capabilities; Free checkout of audio mat; IBM screen reader; Internet workstation with adaptive software; Screen enlargement software for people with visual disabilities; Screen reader software; ZoomText magnification & reading software
Open Mon-Thurs (Winter) 8am-7pm, Fri 8-5; Mon-Fri (Summer) 8-5
Departmental Libraries:
BUTLER OF ANDOVER LIBRARY, Library Rm 5012, 715 E 13th St, Andover, 67002. Tel: 316-218-6371. *Res & Instruction Librn,* Judy Bastin; *Libr Spec,* Jennifer Clark; E-mail: jclark59@butlercc.edu; Staff 2 (MLS 1, Non-MLS 1)
Founded 2007. Highest Degree: Associate
Function: 24/7 Electronic res, 24/7 Online cat, Adult bk club, Audiobks via web, Bks on CD, Computer training, Computers for patron use, Electronic databases & coll, For res purposes, Free DVD rentals, ILL available, Internet access, Mango lang, Online cat, Online ref, Outside serv via phone, mail, e-mail & web, Photocopying/Printing, Ref & res, Ref serv available, Res assist avail, Telephone ref
Open Mon-Thurs 8-7, Fri 8-1
Restriction: Circ to mem only, Free to mem, In-house use for visitors

S ROLLA A CLYMER RESEARCH LIBRARY*, Olive Clifford Stone Library, 383 E Central, 67042. SAN 326-4629. Tel: 316-321-9333. FAX: 316-321-3619. E-mail: education@kansasoilmuseum.org, research@kansasoilmuseum.org. Web Site: www.kansasoilmuseum.org/research-home. *Curator,* Suzanne Walenta; E-mail: suzanne@kansasoilmuseum.org; Staff 1 (MLS 1)
Founded 1977
Library Holdings: Bk Titles 3,902; Bk Vols 4,008
Special Collections: Walnut Valley Times, El Dorado Republican & El Dorado Times Local Newspaper Coll, 1870-present, micro; William Allen White Coll. Oral History
Subject Interests: Kansas, Local hist, Petroleum indust
Wireless access
Function: Res libr
Open Tues-Fri (Oct-May) 10-4, Sat 12-5 (9-5 Summer)
Restriction: Not a lending libr

S KANSAS DEPARTMENT OF CORRECTIONS, El Dorado Correctional Facility Library, 1737 SE Hwy 54, 67042. (Mail add: PO Box 311, 67042). Tel: 316-321-7284. FAX: 316-322-2018. Web Site: www.doc.ks.gov/facilities/edcf. *Librn,* Jeff Gauss; E-mail: jeff.gauss@ks.gov
Library Holdings: Bk Vols 10,000; Per Subs 20
Automation Activity & Vendor Info: (Cataloging) Follett Software; (Circulation) Follett Software; (OPAC) Follett Software

ELKHART

P MORTON COUNTY LIBRARY*, 410 Kansas, 67950. (Mail add: PO Box 938, 67950), SAN 305-8948. Tel: 620-697-2025. FAX: 620-697-4205. Web Site: www.mocolib.info. *Dir,* Toni Jones Bressler; E-mail: director@mocolib.info; *Asst Dir,* Mandy Dunn
Founded 1922. Pop 3,408; Circ 144,007
Library Holdings: Bk Vols 35,000; Per Subs 110
Special Collections: Doll Coll; Quilt & Cookbook Coll
Automation Activity & Vendor Info: (Cataloging) Auto-Graphics, Inc; (Circulation) Auto-Graphics, Inc; (ILL) Auto-Graphics, Inc; (Serials) EBSCO Online
Wireless access
Mem of Southwest Kansas Library System
Open Mon-Fri 9-5:30
Branches: 1
ROLLA BRANCH, 202 Third St, Rolla, 67954. (Mail add: PO Box 2, Rolla, 67954-0412). Tel: 620-593-4328. FAX: 620-593-4276. E-mail: library@usd217.org. *Dir,* Toni Jones-Bressler; Tel: 620-697-2025, E-mail: director@mocolib.info; Staff 3 (Non-MLS 3)
Founded 1970. Pop 500
Library Holdings: Audiobooks 401; CDs 75; DVDs 583; Large Print Bks 154; Bk Vols 17,896; Per Subs 36; Videos 907
Automation Activity & Vendor Info: (Acquisitions) Auto-Graphics, Inc; (OPAC) Auto-Graphics, Inc
Open Mon-Thurs 8-5
Bookmobiles: 1

ELLINWOOD

P ELLINWOOD SCHOOL & COMMUNITY LIBRARY, 210 N Schiller Ave, 67526. SAN 305-8956. Tel: 620-564-2306. FAX: 620-564-2848. Web Site: hslibrary.usd355.org. *Dir, Libr Serv,* Sheri Holmes; E-mail: sholmes@usd355.org; *Ch, ILL Librn,* Treva Paden; E-mail: tpaden@usd355.org; *Pub Serv Librn, Tech Serv Librn,* Julie Blakeslee; E-mail: jblakeslee@usd355.org; Staff 3 (MLS 1, Non-MLS 2)
Pop 2,300; Circ 21,334
Library Holdings: Bk Vols 30,000; Per Subs 85
Automation Activity & Vendor Info: (Cataloging) Follett Software; (Circulation) Follett Software; (ILL) Follett Software
Wireless access
Mem of Central Kansas Library System
Open Mon-Thurs (Winter) 8-7, Fri 8-4, Sat 10-2; Mon-Thurs (Summer) 9-7, Fri 9-Noon

SR SAINT JOHN'S LUTHERAN CHURCH LIBRARY*, 512 N Wilhelm Ave, 67526. SAN 325-5921. Tel: 620-564-2044. E-mail: info@stjohnellinwood.org. Web Site: stjohnellinwood.org. *Librn,* Paula Knop
Library Holdings: Audiobooks 40; CDs 200; DVDs 706; Electronic Media & Resources 1; Large Print Bks 135; Bk Titles 5,275; Per Subs 5; Videos 1,103

ELLIS

P ELLIS PUBLIC LIBRARY*, 907 Washington St, 67637. (Mail add: PO Box 107, 67637-0107), SAN 305-8964. Tel: 785-726-3464. FAX: 785-726-3900. E-mail: ellispubliclibrary@eaglecom.net. *Librn,* Steve Arthur; Staff 1 (Non-MLS 1)
Founded 1876. Pop 1,873
Library Holdings: CDs 30; DVDs 200; Bk Vols 1,440; Per Subs 40
Special Collections: EPL Archives, docs, oral hist; Kansas Coll. Oral History
Subject Interests: Eastern European immigration, Local hist, Railroad hist, Transportation, Westward US expansion
Automation Activity & Vendor Info: (Cataloging) Follett Software; (Circulation) Follett Software
Wireless access
Mem of Central Kansas Library System
Open Mon & Wed-Fri 10-6, Tues 10-8, Sat 10-2

ELLSWORTH

S KANSAS DEPARTMENT OF CORRECTIONS, Ellsworth Correctional Facility Inmate Library, 1607 State St, 67439. (Mail add: PO Box 107, 67439-0107). Tel: 785-472-5501, Ext 250, 785-472-6250. FAX: 785-472-4032. *Librn,* Francis J Devadason; E-mail: Francis.Devadason@ks.gov; *Libr Asst III,* Position Currently Open; Staff 2 (MLS 1, Non-MLS 1)
Library Holdings: Bks on Deafness & Sign Lang 12; Electronic Media & Resources 1; Bk Titles 12,346; Bk Vols 13,467; Per Subs 17
Automation Activity & Vendor Info: (Cataloging) Koha; (Circulation) Koha; (OPAC) Koha
Function: Electronic databases & coll, ILL available, Jail serv, Legal assistance to inmates, Magazines, Online cat, Orientations, Photocopying/Printing, Ref serv available, Spanish lang bks, Wheelchair accessible
Restriction: Staff & inmates only

P J H ROBBINS MEMORIAL LIBRARY*, 219 N Lincoln Ave, 67439-3313. SAN 305-8972. Tel: 785-472-3969. FAX: 785-472-4191. E-mail: libirobbins@yahoo.com. Web Site: jhrml.weebly.com. *Dir,* Linda Homolka
Founded 1913. Pop 3,500; Circ 48,000
Library Holdings: Bk Vols 21,941; Per Subs 69
Special Collections: Cemetery Records of Ellsworth County. Oral History
Automation Activity & Vendor Info: (Cataloging) Follett Software; (Circulation) Follett Software

Mem of Central Kansas Library System
Open Mon-Fri 10-6, Sat 10-2

EMPORIA

P EMPORIA PUBLIC LIBRARY*, 110 E Sixth Ave, 66801-3960. SAN 305-8980. Tel: 620-340-6462. Reference Tel: 620-340-6450. Administration Tel: 620-340-6464. Web Site: www.emporialibrary.org. *Dir,* Robin Newell; E-mail: newellr@emporialibrary.org; *Ch Serv,* Lori Heller; Tel: 620-340-6467, E-mail: hellerl@emporialibrary.org; *Pub Serv,* Molly Chenault; Tel: 620-340-6451, E-mail: chenaultm@emporialibrary.org; Staff 11 (MLS 7, Non-MLS 4)
Founded 1869. Pop 27,975; Circ 290,280
Jan 2019-Dec 2019 Income $1,021,609. Mats Exp $82,413. Sal $611,675
Library Holdings: Bk Vols 71,132; Per Subs 90
Subject Interests: Local hist
Automation Activity & Vendor Info: (Acquisitions) Biblionix/Apollo; (Cataloging) Biblionix/Apollo; (Circulation) Biblionix/Apollo; (Serials) EBSCO Online
Wireless access
Function: 24/7 Electronic res, 24/7 Online cat, 3D Printer, Activity rm, Adult bk club, Archival coll, Art exhibits, Art programs, Audiobks on Playaways & MP3, Audiobks via web, AV serv, Bk club(s), Bk reviews (Group), Bks on CD, Butterfly Garden, Children's prog, Computer training, Computers for patron use, Doc delivery serv, E-Readers, Electronic databases & coll, Equip loans & repairs, Family literacy, Free DVD rentals, Games & aids for people with disabilities, Holiday prog, Home delivery & serv to seniorr ctr & nursing homes, Homebound delivery serv, ILL available, Instruction & testing, Internet access, Laminating, Life-long learning prog for all ages, Magazines, Magnifiers for reading, Meeting rooms, Microfiche/film & reading machines, Movies, Online cat, Online info literacy tutorials on the web & in blackboard, Outreach serv, Outside serv via phone, mail, e-mail & web, OverDrive digital audio bks, Photocopying/Printing, Preschool outreach, Preschool reading prog, Printer for laptops & handheld devices, Prof lending libr, Prog for adults, Prog for children & young adult, Ref & res, Ref serv available, Res assist avail, Scanner, Senior computer classes, Senior outreach, Serves people with intellectual disabilities, Spanish lang bks, STEM programs, Story hour, Study rm, Summer & winter reading prog, Summer reading prog, Tax forms, Teen prog, Telephone ref, Visual arts prog, Wheelchair accessible, Winter reading prog, Workshops, Writing prog
Mem of North Central Kansas Libraries System
Partic in OCLC Online Computer Library Center, Inc
Open Mon-Thurs 9-8, Fri 9-6, Sat 11-5, Sun 2-5
Restriction: Authorized patrons
Friends of the Library Group

C EMPORIA STATE UNIVERSITY*, William Allen White Library, 1200 Commercial St, Box 4051, 66801. SAN 342-0183. Tel: 620-341-5207. Circulation Tel: 620-341-5054. Interlibrary Loan Service Tel: 620-341-5050. Administration Tel: 620-341-5040. Automation Services Tel: 620-341-5058. Toll Free Tel: 877-613-7323. FAX: 620-341-5997. Web Site: www.emporia.edu/libsv. *Dean of Libr,* Michelle Hammon; E-mail: mhammon2@emporia.edu; *Dir of Assessment,* Cynthia Kane; Tel: 620-341-5480, E-mail: ckane1@emporia.edu; *ILL Supvr,* Candy Johnson; E-mail: cjohnso1@emporia.edu; *Cat, Metadata Serv,* Sarah Johnson; Tel: 620-341-5719, E-mail: sjohns37@emporia.edu; *Res & Ref Serv,* Terri Summey; E-mail: tsummey@emporia.edu; Staff 19 (MLS 7, Non-MLS 12)
Founded 1863. Enrl 6,000; Fac 347; Highest Degree: Doctorate
Library Holdings: AV Mats 8,012; e-books 8,090; Bk Titles 566,924; Bk Vols 649,621; Per Subs 1,438
Special Collections: Children's Books (May Massee Coll), bk, orig illust; Children's Literature (Mary White Coll); Elizabeth Yates Coll; Emporia State University Materials (Normaliana); Lois Lenski Coll, mss, illust; William Allen White Coll, bks, mss, letters. State Document Depository; US Document Depository
Automation Activity & Vendor Info: (Acquisitions) Innovative Interfaces, Inc; (Cataloging) Innovative Interfaces, Inc; (Circulation) Innovative Interfaces, Inc; (Course Reserve) Innovative Interfaces, Inc; (ILL) Innovative Interfaces, Inc; (Media Booking) Innovative Interfaces, Inc; (OPAC) Innovative Interfaces, Inc; (Serials) Innovative Interfaces, Inc
Wireless access
Open Mon-Thurs 7:30am-11pm, Fri 7:30-6, Sat 9-6, Sun Noon-11

C FLINT HILLS TECHNICAL COLLEGE LIBRARY, 3301 W 18th Ave, 66801. Tel: 620-341-1323. Toll Free Tel: 800-711-6947. FAX: 620-343-4610. Web Site: fhtc.edu/academics/college-resources/library. *Dir of Info Resources & Assessment,* Denise Gilligan; E-mail: dgilligan@fhtc.edu; Staff 1 (MLS 1)
Founded 1963. Enrl 500; Fac 65; Highest Degree: Associate
Library Holdings: AV Mats 200; Bk Vols 2,500; Per Subs 40
Automation Activity & Vendor Info: (Acquisitions) Auto-Graphics, Inc; (Cataloging) Auto-Graphics, Inc; (Circulation) Auto-Graphics, Inc; (Course Reserve) Auto-Graphics, Inc; (ILL) Auto-Graphics, Inc; (OPAC) Auto-Graphics, Inc
Wireless access
Function: Computer training, Electronic databases & coll, Health sci info serv, Homework prog, ILL available, Internet access, Orientations, Outside serv via phone, mail, e-mail & web, Photocopying/Printing, Ref serv available, Telephone ref, VHS videos, Wheelchair accessible, Workshops
Mem of North Central Kansas Libraries System
Open Mon-Thurs 7:30-4:30, Fri 7:30-4

S KANSAS MASONIC LIBRARY & MUSEUM, Grande Lodge Library, 25 W Fifth Ave, 66801. Tel: 785-234-5518. Web Site: www.kansasmason.org.
Library Holdings: Bk Vols 13,000
Open Mon-Fri 9-4

P KANSAS STATE LIBRARY*, Kansas Talking Books Service, One Kellogg Circle, 66801. (Mail add: PO Box 4055, 66801), SAN 306-1515. Tel: 620-341-6280. Toll Free Tel: 800-362-0699. E-mail: KTB@ks.gov. Web Site: kslib.info/talking. *Dir,* Michael Lang; Tel: 620-341-6287, E-mail: michael.lang@ks.gov; Staff 9 (MLS 5, Non-MLS 4)
Founded 1970. Circ 260,000
Function: Digital talking bks, Mail & tel request accepted, Online cat, Outreach serv, Outside serv via phone, mail, e-mail & web, Summer reading prog, Wheelchair accessible
Publications: Newsletter
Special Services for the Blind - Braille bks; Descriptive video serv (DVS); Web-Braille
Open Mon-Fri 8-5
Friends of the Library Group

ENTERPRISE

P ENTERPRISE PUBLIC LIBRARY, 202 S Factory, 67441. (Mail add: PO Box 307, 67441-0307), SAN 305-9006. Tel: 785-263-8351. E-mail: eprisepublib@gmail.com. Web Site: enterprise.lib.nckls.org. *Librn,* Stephanie Widler
Pop 995; Circ 12,723
Library Holdings: Bk Vols 17,500; Per Subs 48
Wireless access
Publications: Readers Guide
Mem of North Central Kansas Libraries System
Open Mon 1-6, Tues-Thurs 10-3

ERIE

P ERIE CITY PUBLIC LIBRARY, 204 S Butler, 66733-1349. SAN 305-9014. Tel: 620-244-5119. FAX: 620-244-5119. E-mail: direpl66733@gmail.com. Web Site: eriecity.mykansaslibrary.org. *Dir,* Julie Kent
Pop 1,400; Circ 14,508
Library Holdings: Bk Vols 13,500; Per Subs 25
Special Collections: Kansas Coll
Automation Activity & Vendor Info: (Cataloging) Follett Software; (Circulation) Follett Software
Mem of Southeast Kansas Library System
Open Mon-Fri 8-12 & 1-5:30

EUDORA

P EUDORA PUBLIC LIBRARY, 14 E Ninth St, 66025. SAN 305-9022. Tel: 785-542-2496. FAX: 785-542-2496. E-mail: eudoralibrary@gmail.com, eudorapl@sunflower.com. Web Site: eudorapubliclibrary.org. *Libr Dir,* Carol Wohlford
Founded 1967. Pop 7,000; Circ 36,000
Library Holdings: Bk Vols 10,000; Per Subs 40
Automation Activity & Vendor Info: (Cataloging) Koha; (Circulation) Koha
Wireless access
Mem of Northeast Kansas Library System
Open Mon & Wed 9-8, Tues & Thurs 9-6, Fri 9-5, Sat 9-1
Friends of the Library Group

EUREKA

P EUREKA PUBLIC LIBRARY*, 606 N Main St, 67045. SAN 305-9030. Tel: 620-583-6222. FAX: 620-583-6222. E-mail: carnegie@fox-net.net. Web Site: www.eurekapubliclibrary.org. *Libr Dir,* Constance Mitchell; Staff 3 (MLS 1, Non-MLS 2)
Founded 1892. Pop 2,663; Circ 35,000
Jan 2013-Dec 2013 Income $114,932, State $1,052, City $74,887, Locally Generated Income $10,035, Other $28,958. Mats Exp $11,783, Books $8,937, Per/Ser (Incl. Access Fees) $1,656, AV Mat $1,190. Sal $56,912 (Prof $39,937)
Library Holdings: Audiobooks 417; DVDs 747; Large Print Bks 613; Bk Titles 17,500; Bk Vols 18,338; Per Subs 54; Talking Bks 203; Videos 978
Automation Activity & Vendor Info: (Cataloging) SirsiDynix; (Circulation) SirsiDynix; (ILL) Auto-Graphics, Inc; (OPAC) SirsiDynix
Wireless access

Mem of Southeast Kansas Library System
Open Mon 1-5:30, Tues-Fri 10-5:30, Sat 10-1
Friends of the Library Group

S GREENWOOD COUNTY HISTORICAL SOCIETY LIBRARY, 120 W Fourth, 67045-1445. (Mail add: PO Box 86, 67045), SAN 371-7941. Tel: 316-583-6682. E-mail: gwhistory@sbcglobal.net. Web Site: www.gwhistory.com. *Pres,* Mike Pitko
Library Holdings: Bk Titles 500
Special Collections: Oral History
Subject Interests: Genealogy
Open Mon-Fri 10-4

EVEREST

P BARNES READING ROOM*, 640 Main St, 66424. (Mail add: PO Box 204, 66424-0204), SAN 305-9049. Tel: 785-548-7733. FAX: 785-548-7733. E-mail: barnesreadingroom@rainbowtel.net. Web Site: everest.mykansaslibrary.org. *Dir,* Nancy Linck
Pop 433; Circ 3,134
Library Holdings: Bk Vols 7,413; Per Subs 10
Mem of Northeast Kansas Library System
Open Mon-Wed 3:30-7:30, Thurs & Fri 3:30-6:30

FALL RIVER

P FALL RIVER PUBLIC LIBRARY*, 314 Merchant Ave, 67047. SAN 376-804X. Tel: 620-658-4432. E-mail: fallriverpubliclibrary@gmail.com. *Librn,* Sue York
Library Holdings: Bk Vols 6,000
Wireless access
Open Mon & Thurs 2-6

FLORENCE

P FLORENCE PUBLIC LIBRARY*, 324 Main St, 66851. SAN 305-9057. Tel: 620-878-4649. E-mail: library.florence@gmail.com. Web Site: florence.lib.nckls.org, florenceks.com/text/city/city_library.htm. *Dir,* Mary Jane Grimmett
Pop 672; Circ 7,000
Library Holdings: Bk Vols 8,200; Per Subs 21
Mem of North Central Kansas Libraries System
Open Mon-Fri 3-5:30, Sat 10-12

FORMOSO

P FORMOSO PUBLIC LIBRARY*, 108 Main St, 66942. (Mail add: PO Box 156, 66942-0156), SAN 305-9065. Tel: 785-794-2424. E-mail: libfor@nckcn.com. *Libr Dir,* Barbara Langston
Pop 100; Circ 1,800
Library Holdings: Bk Vols 4,202
Wireless access
Mem of Central Kansas Library System
Open Mon & Wed 3-6:30, Fri 9-12

FORT LEAVENWORTH

UNITED STATES ARMY
A COMBINED ARMS RESEARCH LIBRARY*, US Army Command & General Staff College, Eisenhower Hall, 250 Gibbon Ave, 66027-2314, SAN 342-0302. Tel: 913-758-3001. Circulation Tel: 913-758-3002. Interlibrary Loan Service Tel: 913-758-3017. Reference Tel: 913-758-3053. Administration Tel: 913-758-3033. FAX: 913-758-3014. Web Site: carl.army.mil. *Dir,* Edwin B Burgess; E-mail: edwin.b.burgess.civ@mail.mil; *Dep Dir, Pub Serv Librn,* Pamela S Bennett; Tel: 913-758-3058, E-mail: pamela.bennett@us.army.mil; *Acq Librn,* Tiffany L Konczey; Tel: 913-758-3013, E-mail: tiffany.konczey@us.army.mil; *Chief Doc Librn,* Rusty P Rafferty; Tel: 913-758-3128, E-mail: russ.rafferty@us.army.mil; *Sr Ref Librn,* Joanne E Knight; E-mail: joanne.knight@us.army.mil; *Archives Chief,* Kathleen M Buker; Tel: 913-758-3161, E-mail: kathleen.buker@us.army.mil; *Circ Supvr,* Kelsey Reed; Tel: 913-758-3005, E-mail: kelsey.e.reed.civ@mail.mil; *Syst Adminr,* Patricia E Knuth; Tel: 913-758-3019, E-mail: pat.knuth@us.army.mil; Staff 29 (MLS 19, Non-MLS 10)
Founded 1882
Library Holdings: Bk Vols 320,000; Per Subs 642
Special Collections: Combined Arms & Fort Leavenworth Archives
Subject Interests: Land warfare, Leadership, Mil hist, Nat security
Automation Activity & Vendor Info: (Acquisitions) Horizon; (Cataloging) Horizon; (Circulation) Horizon; (ILL) OCLC; (OPAC) Horizon; (Serials) Horizon
Function: Bks on cassette, Bks on CD, Children's prog, Computers for patron use, Digital talking bks, Electronic databases & coll, Free DVD rentals, ILL available, Internet access, Online ref, Orientations, Outreach serv, Outside serv via phone, mail, e-mail & web, OverDrive digital audio bks, Prog for children & young adult, Ref & res, Ref serv available, Res libr, Scanner, Spoken cassettes & CDs, Spoken cassettes & DVDs, Story hour, Summer reading prog, Telephone ref, VHS videos, Workshops
Partic in MECC/LWG
Open Mon-Thurs 7-7, Fri 7-4:30, Sat & Sun 10-5
Restriction: Open to fac, students & qualified researchers, Open to pub for ref & circ; with some limitations

A UNITED STATES DISCIPLINARY BARRACKS LIBRARY*, 1301 N Warehouse Rd, 66027-2304. Tel: 913-758-3864. FAX: 913-758-3927. *Librn,* Angela Perry; E-mail: angela.e.perry@us.army.mil; Staff 2 (MLS 1, Non-MLS 1)
Library Holdings: Bk Vols 11,300; Per Subs 13
Function: Adult literacy prog, Jail serv
Restriction: Clients only, Govt use only, Inmate patrons, facility staff & vols direct access. All others through ILL only, Not a lending libr, Not open to pub

FORT RILEY

UNITED STATES ARMY
A FORT RILEY POST LIBRARY*, Bldg 5306, Hood Dr, 66442-6416, SAN 342-0337. Tel: 785-239-5305. FAX: 785-239-4422. *Librn, Project Mgr,* Terri Seaman; E-mail: terri.seaman@us.army.mil; *Cataloger/Ref Librn,* John Triplett; Tel: 785-239-9582, E-mail: john.triplett@us.army.mil; Staff 4 (MLS 1, Non-MLS 3)
Library Holdings: AV Mats 3,000; DVDs 700; Large Print Bks 45; Bk Titles 21,000; Bk Vols 22,000; Per Subs 60; Talking Bks 320; Videos 1,800
Subject Interests: Mil hist
Automation Activity & Vendor Info: (Cataloging) OCLC Connexion; (Circulation) Horizon; (OPAC) Horizon; (Serials) Horizon
Function: Electronic databases & coll, Family literacy, Prog for children & young adult, Spoken cassettes & CDs, Summer reading prog, Wheelchair accessible
Mem of North Central Kansas Libraries System
Special Services for the Blind - Bks on CD; Home delivery serv; Talking bks & player equip
Open Tues-Sat 11-6, Sun 12-5

AM IRWIN ARMY COMMUNITY HOSPITAL MEDICAL LIBRARY*, CDR USAMEDDAC-Med Libr, 600 Caisson Hill Rd, 66442-7037, SAN 320-9288. Tel: 785-239-7874. FAX: 785-239-7626. *Med Librn,* Phyllis Whiteside; E-mail: phyllis.j.whiteside.civ@mail.mil
Partic in Midcontinental Regional Med Libr Program
Open Mon-Fri 7:30-11 & 12-4:30

S US CAVALRY MUSEUM*, Museum Division Library & Archives, Bldg 263, Cameron Ave, 66442. (Mail add: Fort Riley Museum, Bldg 205, Henry Ave, 66442), SAN 329-3025. Tel: 785-239-2737. FAX: 785-239-6243. Web Site: www.fortrileyhistoricalsociety.org/us-cavalry-museum.html. *Dir,* Dr Bob Smith, PhD
Library Holdings: Bk Titles 8,000; Per Subs 34
Subject Interests: First infantry div hist, Mil hist, US cavalry hist
Restriction: Open to pub upon request

FORT SCOTT

J FORT SCOTT COMMUNITY COLLEGE LIBRARY*, 2108 S Horton, 66701. SAN 305-9073. Tel: 620-223-2700, Ext 3441. FAX: 620-223-6530. Web Site: www.fortscott.edu/library. *Dir, Libr Serv,* Susie Arvidson; E-mail: susiea@fortscott.edu; Staff 4 (MLS 2, Non-MLS 2)
Founded 1919. Enrl 2,660; Fac 48
Library Holdings: Bk Vols 10,000; Per Subs 10
Subject Interests: Kansas
Automation Activity & Vendor Info: (Cataloging) SirsiDynix; (Circulation) SirsiDynix
Wireless access
Open Mon-Fri 8-5

P FORT SCOTT PUBLIC LIBRARY*, 201 S National Ave, 66701. SAN 305-9081. Tel: 620-223-2882. E-mail: fortscottlibrary@yahoo.com. Web Site: fortscott.mykansaslibrary.org. *Dir,* Lisa Walter; *Ch Serv,* Valetta Cannon
Pop 8,893
Library Holdings: Bk Vols 38,000; Per Subs 50
Subject Interests: Kansas, Local hist
Automation Activity & Vendor Info: (Cataloging) Follett Software; (Circulation) Follett Software
Wireless access
Mem of Southeast Kansas Library System
Open Mon-Fri 9-6, Sat 9-2

FOWLER

P FOWLER PUBLIC LIBRARY*, 510 Main St, 67844. (Mail add: PO Box 226, 67844), SAN 305-909X. Tel: 620-646-5550. FAX: 620-646-5439. Web Site: www.fowlerlibrary.info. *Dir,* Ben Rogers; E-mail: director@fowlerlibrary.info
Founded 1963. Pop 650
Library Holdings: Bk Titles 11,180; Per Subs 30
Wireless access
Mem of Southwest Kansas Library System
Open Tues 9-3, Wed-Fri 12-6, Sat 9-2

FRANKFORT

P FRANKFORT CITY LIBRARY*, 104 E Second St, 66427. SAN 305-9103. Tel: 785-292-4320. E-mail: franklib@bluevalley.net. Web Site: frankfort.lib.nckls.org. *Dir,* Alice Jones
Founded 1888
Library Holdings: Bk Vols 10,000; Per Subs 25
Special Collections: Kansas History
Wireless access
Mem of North Central Kansas Libraries System
Open Mon 1-5, Tues, Thurs & Fri 9-12 & 1-5, Wed 1-8

FREDONIA

P FREDONIA PUBLIC LIBRARY, 807 Jefferson St, 66736. SAN 305-9111. Tel: 620-378-2863. FAX: 620-378-2645. E-mail: fredodir@twinmounds.com. Web Site: www.fredoniapubliclibrary.org. *Dir,* Michelle Hulse
Founded 1914. Circ 27,865
Library Holdings: Bk Vols 35,000; Per Subs 20
Automation Activity & Vendor Info: (Cataloging) Follett Software; (Circulation) Follett Software
Wireless access
Open Mon-Thurs 10-8, Fri 10-6, Sat 10-12
Friends of the Library Group

S WILSON COUNTY HISTORICAL SOCIETY MUSEUM LIBRARY, 420 N Seventh St, 66736-1315. SAN 325-5948. Tel: 620-378-3965. E-mail: wilcohisoc@twinmounds.com. Web Site: www.wilsoncountykshistoricalsociety.org. *Pres,* Joyce Garner
Founded 1968
Library Holdings: Bk Titles 1,030
Special Collections: Civil War Coll; Family Histories; History & Genealogy Coll
Subject Interests: Local hist
Wireless access
Open Tues-Fri 1-4:30, Sat 10-2

GALENA

P GALENA PUBLIC LIBRARY*, 315 W Seventh St, 66739-1293. SAN 305-912X. Tel: 620-783-5132. FAX: 620-783-5030. E-mail: galenapubliclibrary@yahoo.com. *Dir,* Nellie Hoskins
Pop 3,054; Circ 15,700
Library Holdings: Bk Vols 35,000; Per Subs 52
Special Collections: Cemetary records for Cherokee County; Genealogy Coll; Local Newspapers, 1877
Wireless access
Mem of Southeast Kansas Library System
Open Mon & Wed 1-8, Tues, Thurs & Fri 10:30-5:30, Sat 11-2
Friends of the Library Group

GARDEN CITY

P FINNEY COUNTY PUBLIC LIBRARY, 605 E Walnut St, 67846. SAN 305-9146. Tel: 620-272-3680. FAX: 620-272-3682. Web Site: finneylibrary.org. *Library Contact,* Carly Smith; E-mail: carly.smith@finneylibrary.org; Staff 13 (MLS 1, Non-MLS 12)
Founded 1897. Pop 38,000; Circ 103,000
Library Holdings: AV Mats 4,216; Bk Vols 100,000; Per Subs 300
Special Collections: Kansas Coll; Powell Coll; Spanish & Vietnamese Literature
Subject Interests: Genealogy, Kansas
Automation Activity & Vendor Info: (Cataloging) SirsiDynix; (Circulation) SirsiDynix
Wireless access
Function: 24/7 Electronic res, 24/7 Online cat, Activity rm, Adult bk club, Adult literacy prog, After school storytime
Special Services for the Blind - Internet workstation with adaptive software; Reader equip
Open Mon-Sat 9-8, Sun 1-6
Friends of the Library Group

J GARDEN CITY COMMUNITY COLLEGE*, Thomas F Saffell Library, 801 Campus Dr, 67846. SAN 305-9138. Tel: 620-276-7611. FAX: 620-276-9630. E-mail: library@gcccks.edu. Web Site: www.gc3library.wordpress.com. *Libr Dir,* Trent Smith; Tel: 620-276-9510, E-mail: trent.smith@gcccks.edu; *Libr Asst,* Kathy Winter; Tel: 620-276-9656, E-mail: kathy.winter@gcccks.edu; Staff 4 (MLS 1, Non-MLS 3)
Founded 1919. Enrl 2,233; Fac 110; Highest Degree: Associate
Library Holdings: Bk Titles 33,000; Bk Vols 47,000; Per Subs 100
Automation Activity & Vendor Info: (Cataloging) Follett Software; (Circulation) Follett Software; (OPAC) Follett Software
Function: ILL available
Open Mon-Thurs 7:15am-9pm, Fri 8-4:30, Sun 6pm-9pm

GARDEN PLAIN

P GARDEN PLAIN COMMUNITY LIBRARY, 421 W Ave B, 67050. (Mail add: PO Box 195, 67050). Tel: 316-535-2990. FAX: 316-535-2990. E-mail: gpcomlib@yahoo.com. Web Site: www.gardenplain.com/services/library. *Head Librn,* Joyce Loehr
Library Holdings: Bk Vols 7,747
Wireless access
Mem of South Central Kansas Library System
Open Mon, Tues & Fri 3-5, Wed 3-7, Sat 10-2

GARNETT

P GARNETT PUBLIC LIBRARY*, 125 W Fourth St, 66032-1350. (Mail add: PO Box 385, 66032-0385), SAN 305-9154. Tel: 785-448-3388. FAX: 785-448-3936. E-mail: garnettlibrary@yahoo.com. Web Site: garnett.mykansaslibrary.org. *Dir,* Andrea Sobba
Founded 1912. Pop 3,400; Circ 54,000
Library Holdings: Bk Vols 30,000; Per Subs 35
Special Collections: Mary Bridget McAuliffe Walker Art Coll
Automation Activity & Vendor Info: (Acquisitions) Koha; (Cataloging) Koha; (OPAC) Koha
Wireless access
Mem of Southeast Kansas Library System
Open Mon & Thurs 2-7, Tues, Wed & Fri 10-3, Sat 10-1
Friends of the Library Group

GAYLORD

P GAYLORD CITY LIBRARY*, 504 Main St, 67638-3884. SAN 376-5121. Tel: 785-697-2650. Web Site: www.gaylordkansas.com/library.html. *Vols Librn,* Donna Muck
Library Holdings: Bk Vols 3,000
Mem of Central Kansas Library System
Open Tues & Thurs 9am-11am

GENESEO

P GENESEO PUBLIC LIBRARY*, 725 Main St, 67444-9702. (Mail add: PO Box 166, 67444-0166), SAN 305-9162. Tel: 620-824-6140. E-mail: gplib@hometelco.net. *Librn,* D'Ann Dorris
Pop 521; Circ 5,350
Library Holdings: Bk Vols 3,500; Per Subs 20
Special Collections: Kansas History Coll
Wireless access
Mem of South Central Kansas Library System
Open Tues, Wed & Thurs 12-5

GIRARD

P GIRARD PUBLIC LIBRARY*, 128 W Prairie Ave, 66743-1498. SAN 305-9170. Tel: 620-724-4317. FAX: 620-724-8374. Web Site: girardpubliclibrary.net. *Dir,* Barb Bailey; E-mail: GirardPL@ckt.net; *Librn,* Sarah Goings; E-mail: GiraldPL4@ckt.net; *Ch,* April Zagonel; E-mail: GiraldPL3@ckt.net; Staff 6 (Non-MLS 6)
Founded 1899. Pop 3,160; Circ 38,859
Library Holdings: Audiobooks 2,579; AV Mats 3,508; Bks on Deafness & Sign Lang 22; e-books 99; Large Print Bks 523; Bk Titles 33,048; Per Subs 79
Special Collections: Crawford County History Coll; Halderman-Julius (Little Blue Books); Kansas Authors; The Girard Press (1869-1999), micro
Automation Activity & Vendor Info: (Circulation) ComPanion Corp; (Serials) EBSCO Online
Wireless access
Mem of Southeast Kansas Library System
Special Services for the Blind - Accessible computers; Audio mat; Bks on cassette; Bks on CD; Cassettes; Copier with enlargement capabilities; Large print bks; Playaways (bks on MP3); Radio reading serv; Recorded bks; Talking bk & rec for the blind cat
Open Mon 9:30-7, Tues-Thurs 9:30-6, Fri 9:30-5, Sat 9:30-3; Mon-Thurs (June-Aug) 9-6, Fri 9:30-5, Sat 9:30-3

GLASCO

P GLASCO CITY LIBRARY, 206 E Main St, 67445. (Mail add: PO Box 595, 67445-0595), SAN 305-9189. Tel: 785-568-2313. E-mail: gclibrary@twinvalley.net. Web Site: www.glascokansas.org/library. *Librn,* Donna Guidry
Founded 1916. Pop 600; Circ 5,700
Library Holdings: Bk Vols 10,250; Per Subs 40
Wireless access
Mem of Central Kansas Library System
Open Tues 1-5, Wed & Thurs 10-Noon

GLEN ELDER

P GLEN ELDER LIBRARY, 120 S Market St, 67446. (Mail add: PO Box 188, 67446-0188). Tel: 785-545-3632. E-mail: glellib@nckcn.com. Web Site: www.glenelder.com/city-library. *Librn,* Angie Ahlvers
Founded 1885. Pop 475; Circ 1,716
Library Holdings: Large Print Bks 100; Bk Titles 3,966; Per Subs 12; Talking Bks 10
Special Collections: Glen Elder History Coll; School History of Glen Elder Coll
Wireless access
Mem of Central Kansas Library System
Open Mon & Wed 8-1
Friends of the Library Group

GODDARD

P GODDARD PUBLIC LIBRARY*, 201 N Main St, 67052. (Mail add: PO Box 443, 67052-0443), SAN 305-9200. Tel: 316-794-8771. FAX: 316-794-3405. E-mail: staff@goddardlibrary.com. Web Site: www.goddardlibrary.com. *Dir,* April Hernandez; E-mail: director@goddardlibrary.com; *Asst Dir,* Michelle Stewart; *Outreach Specialist, Programming Spec,* Carrie Wharton; E-mail: outreach@goddardlibrary.com
Founded 1969. Pop 1,900; Circ 20,120
Library Holdings: Bk Vols 15,049; Per Subs 50
Wireless access
Mem of South Central Kansas Library System
Open Mon 9-7, Tues-Thurs 9:30-7, Fri 9:30-5, Sat 9-3, Sun 1-4
Friends of the Library Group

GOESSEL

P GOESSEL PUBLIC LIBRARY*, 101 S Cedar, 67053. (Mail add: PO Box 36, 67053-0036), SAN 305-9219. Tel: 620-367-8440. FAX: 620-367-2774. E-mail: goeslib@mtelco.net. Web Site: goessel.lib.nckls.org. *Dir,* Laura Dailey; *Librn,* Amy Rosfeld; Staff 2 (Non-MLS 2)
Founded 1968. Pop 565; Circ 3,000
Library Holdings: Large Print Bks 100; Bk Vols 700; Per Subs 20; Spec Interest Per Sub 10; Talking Bks 200; Videos 400
Automation Activity & Vendor Info: (Cataloging) Book Systems; (Circulation) Book Systems
Wireless access
Function: Computers for patron use, Free DVD rentals, ILL available, Online cat, Photocopying/Printing, Preschool reading prog, Scanner, Story hour, Summer reading prog
Mem of North Central Kansas Libraries System
Open Mon 4-8, Tues 5-7, Fri 9-1, Sat 9-12

GOODLAND

P GOODLAND PUBLIC LIBRARY, 812 Broadway, 67735. SAN 305-9227. Tel: 785-899-5461. FAX: 785-890-6744. E-mail: gplstaff@goodlandlibrary.org. Web Site: www.goodlandlibrary.org. *Adult Serv, Dir,* Karen Gillihan; E-mail: kareng@goodlandlibrary.org; *Ref Librn,* Laura McClung; *Ch Serv,* Marcy Melia; Staff 5 (Non-MLS 5)
Founded 1912. Pop 5,000; Circ 51,000
Jan 2017-Dec 2017 Income $200,000. Mats Exp $167,000, Books $18,000, Per/Ser (Incl. Access Fees) $4,500, AV Equip $4,300, Electronic Ref Mat (Incl. Access Fees) $1,000. Sal $104,000
Library Holdings: CDs 800; DVDs 345; Large Print Bks 1,717; Bk Vols 46,000; Per Subs 150; Talking Bks 1,800; Videos 1,031
Automation Activity & Vendor Info: (Cataloging) Auto-Graphics, Inc; (Circulation) Auto-Graphics, Inc; (ILL) Auto-Graphics, Inc; (OPAC) Auto-Graphics, Inc
Wireless access
Mem of Northwest Kansas Library System
Open Mon-Thurs 9-7, Fri & Sat 9-5

GOVE

P GOVE CITY LIBRARY*, 301 Sherman, 67736. (Mail add: PO Box 66, 67736-0066), SAN 305-9235. Tel: 785-938-2242. E-mail: govelib@ruraltel.net. Web Site: gove.nwkls.org. *Librn,* Rayna Kopriva
Founded 1937. Pop 148; Circ 1,964
Library Holdings: Bk Vols 3,623
Wireless access
Mem of Northwest Kansas Library System
Open Tues & Thurs 2:30-5:30, Wed 4-7

GRAINFIELD

P GRAINFIELD CITY LIBRARY, 242 Main, 67737. (Mail add: PO Box 154, 67737-0154), SAN 305-9243. Tel: 785-673-4770. E-mail: grain1lb@ruraltel.net. Web Site: grainfield.nwkls.org. *Town Librn,* Bonnie Wood
Pop 417; Circ 2,410
Library Holdings: Bk Vols 4,086
Wireless access
Mem of Northwest Kansas Library System
Open Mon-Thurs 3:30-6

GREAT BEND

J BARTON COUNTY COMMUNITY COLLEGE LIBRARY*, 245 NE 30 Rd, 67530. SAN 305-9251. Tel: 620-792-9365. FAX: 620-792-3238. E-mail: library@bartonccc.edu. Web Site: www.bartonccc.edu/library. *Libr Dir,* ReGina Reynolds; E-mail: reynoldsr@bartonccc.edu
Founded 1969
Library Holdings: Bk Vols 30,000; Per Subs 130
Special Collections: Rural Gerontology Grant Coll
Subject Interests: Nursing
Automation Activity & Vendor Info: (Cataloging) Book Systems; (Circulation) Book Systems
Wireless access
Open Mon-Thurs (Fall-Spring) 8am-8:30pm, Fri 7:30-4:30, Sun 2-8; Mon-Thurs (Summer) 7-5:30

P CENTRAL KANSAS LIBRARY SYSTEM*, 1409 Williams St, 67530-4020. SAN 305-926X. Tel: 620-792-4865. Toll Free Tel: 800-362-2642 (Kansas only). FAX: 620-792-5495. Administration FAX: 620-793-7270. Web Site: www.ckls.org. *Admin Mgr,* Steve Kummer; E-mail: skummer@ckls.org; *Asst Dir,* Maribeth Shafer; E-mail: mshafer@ckls.org; *IT Mgr,* Andy Mitchener; E-mail: amitchener@ckls.org; *Outreach Mgr,* Joy Boyd; E-mail: jboyd@ckls.org; *Youth Serv Consult,* Patty Collins; E-mail: pcollins@ckls.org. Subject Specialists: *Continuing educ,* Maribeth Shafer; Staff 9 (MLS 5, Non-MLS 4)
Founded 1968. Pop 202,000
Library Holdings: Bk Vols 30,000; Per Subs 50
Wireless access
Publications: Post (Newsletter); Trustee Handbook
Member Libraries: Alton Library; Barnard Library; Belleville Public Library; Bennington Library; Bison Community Library; Burr Oak Community Library; Cawker City Public Library; Clyde Public Library; Courtland Community Library; Delphos Public Library; Downs Carnegie Library; Ellinwood School & Community Library; Ellis Public Library; F Lee Doctor Library; Formoso Public Library; Frank Carlson Library; Gaylord City Library; Glasco City Library; Glen Elder Library; Great Bend Public Library; Gypsum Community Library; Hays Public Library; Hillcrest Public Library; Hoisington Public Library; Hunter Public Library; Independent Township Library; J H Robbins Memorial Library; Jamestown City Library; Jewell Public Library; Jordaan Memorial Library; Kanopolis Public Library; Kensington Community-School Library; Kirwin City Library; Lang Memorial Library; Lebanon-Community Library; Lincoln Carnegie Library; Logan Public Library; Long Island Community Library; Lucas Public Library; Luray City Library; Mankato City Library; McCracken Public Library; Minneapolis Public Library; Natoma Library; Osborne Public Library; Otis Community Library; Palco Public Library; Pawnee Heights Library; Phillipsburg City Library; Plainville Memorial Library; Port Library; Rae Hobson Memorial Library; Randall Public Library; Rush Center Library; Russell Public Library; Salina Public Library; Scandia City Library; Smith Center Public Library; Stockton Public Library; Sunshine City Library; Sylvan Grove Public Library; Tipton Library
Special Services for the Blind - Bks & mags in Braille, on rec, tape & cassette; Bks available with recordings; Braille music coll; Low vision equip
Open Mon-Fri 9-5
Branches: 1

P SUBREGIONAL LIBRARY FOR THE BLIND & PHYSICALLY HANDICAPPED, 1409 Williams St, 67530-4020. *Talking Bks Consult,* Cathy Rhan; E-mail: crhan@ckls.org
Founded 1973. Circ 34,000
Library Holdings: Large Print Bks 3,198; Talking Bks 20,088

Open Mon-Fri 9-5
Bookmobiles: 1. Supvr, Gail Santy

P GREAT BEND PUBLIC LIBRARY*, 1409 Williams St, 67530. SAN 305-9286. Tel: 620-792-2409. FAX: 620-792-5495, 620-793-7270. Web Site: greatbend.mykansaslibrary.org. *Dir,* Gail Santy; E-mail: gsanty@ckls.org; *Asst Dir,* Diedre Lemon; E-mail: dlemon@ckls.org; *Admin Mgr,* Vickie Herl; E-mail: vherl@ckls.org; Staff 2 (MLS 2)
Founded 1908. Pop 15,000; Circ 200,000
Library Holdings: Bk Vols 100,000; Per Subs 300
Special Collections: Petroleum Geology (American Petroleum Institute Coll). Oral History
Automation Activity & Vendor Info: (Acquisitions) Follett Software; (Cataloging) Follett Software; (Circulation) Follett Software; (OPAC) Follett Software
Mem of Central Kansas Library System
Partic in OCLC Online Computer Library Center, Inc
Open Mon-Thurs (Winter) 9-8, Fri & Sat 10-5, Sun 1-5; Mon-Wed (Summer) 8:30-6, Thurs 8:30-8, Fri & Sat 9-5
Friends of the Library Group

GREENLEAF

P GREENLEAF PUBLIC LIBRARY*, 408 Commercial St, 66943. (Mail add: PO Box 209, 66943-0209). Tel: 785-747-7232. *Dir,* Delores Laflen
Mem of North Central Kansas Libraries System
Open Wed & Fri 1-4

GREENSBURG

P KIOWA COUNTY LIBRARY*, 320 S Main, Ste 120, 67054. SAN 305-9294. Tel: 620-723-1118. E-mail: kwcolib@gmail.com. Web Site: www.facebook.com/KiowaCountyLibrary. *Head Librn,* Cassie Gamble; *Asst Librn,* Tim Morton; Staff 2 (Non-MLS 2)
Founded 1936
Library Holdings: Audiobooks 499; DVDs 1,095; Large Print Bks 344; Bk Vols 19,000; Per Subs 18
Automation Activity & Vendor Info: (Cataloging) Biblionix; (Circulation) Biblionix
Wireless access
Open Mon-Fri 9:30-5:30, Sat (Summer) 10:30-1:00
Branches: 2
HAVILAND BRANCH, 112 N Main, Haviland, 67059. (Mail add: PO Box 295, Haviland, 67059). Tel: 620-862-5350. E-mail: kwcolib@gmail.com. *Br Librn,* Liz Ballard
Founded 1936
Library Holdings: Audiobooks 69; DVDs 665; Large Print Bks 81; Bk Vols 12,262; Per Subs 12
Automation Activity & Vendor Info: (Cataloging) Biblionix; (Circulation) Biblionix
Open Mon-Fri 1:30-5
MULLINVILLE BRANCH, 115 N Main, Mullinville, 67109. (Mail add: PO Box 137, Mullinville, 67109-0137). Tel: 620-548-2630. *Br Librn,* Jodi Behee
Pop 200; Circ 2,353
Library Holdings: Audiobooks 2; DVDs 963; Per Subs 10
Open Mon-Fri 2-5

GRENOLA

P GRENOLA PUBLIC LIBRARY, 205 S Main St, 67346. (Mail add: PO Box 131, 67346-0131), SAN 305-9308. Tel: 620-358-3707. FAX: 620-358-3820. E-mail: grenlib@sktc.net. Web Site: grenola.mykansaslibrary.org. *Dir,* Tina Fullhart; Staff 1 (Non-MLS 1)
Founded 1950. Pop 347; Circ 2,082
Library Holdings: Bk Vols 5,500; Per Subs 15
Wireless access
Function: Audio & video playback equip for onsite use, Audiobks on Playaways & MP3, Bks on cassette, Bks on CD, Free DVD rentals, ILL available, Internet access, Laminating, Printer for laptops & handheld devices, Summer reading prog, VHS videos
Mem of Southeast Kansas Library System
Special Services for the Blind - Assistive/Adapted tech devices, equip & products; Bks available with recordings; Bks on CD; Large print bks
Open Mon, Wed & Thurs 3-7

GRINNELL

P MOORE FAMILY LIBRARY*, 95 S Adams, 67738. (Mail add: PO Box 159, 67738-0159), SAN 376-5512. Tel: 785-824-3885. E-mail: moorefamilylibrary@yahoo.com. Web Site: moorefamily.nwkls.org. *Dir,* Ms Pat Baalman
Founded 1985
Library Holdings: Bk Vols 5,000
Wireless access
Function: ILL available, Ref serv available, Summer reading prog
Mem of Northwest Kansas Library System
Open Mon & Wed 4:30-6:30, Sat 9:30-11:30

GYPSUM

P GYPSUM COMMUNITY LIBRARY*, 521 Maple St, 67448. (Mail add: PO Box 19, 67448-0019), SAN 305-9324. Tel: 785-536-4319. E-mail: gypsumlibrary@yahoo.com. *Librn,* Joyce Roe
Founded 1910. Pop 408; Circ 2,827
Library Holdings: Bk Vols 8,000; Per Subs 20
Wireless access
Mem of Central Kansas Library System
Open Mon & Wed 1-6, Sat 8-Noon

HALSTEAD

P HALSTEAD PUBLIC LIBRARY, 264 Main St, 67056-0285. SAN 305-9332. Tel: 316-835-2170. FAX: 316-835-2170. E-mail: halpublib@hotmail.com. Web Site: halstead.scklslibrary.info. *Dir,* Joleen Ross
Founded 1905. Pop 2,000; Circ 14,000
Library Holdings: Bk Vols 18,000; Per Subs 33
Special Collections: Halstead City History Coll; Kansas Coll
Wireless access
Mem of South Central Kansas Library System
Open Mon, Wed & Fri 10-5, Tues & Thurs 10-7, Sat 10-1

HAMILTON

P HAMILTON CITY LIBRARY, 21 E Main St, 66853. (Mail add: PO Box 128, 66853-0128), SAN 305-9359. Tel: 620-678-3646. FAX: 620-678-3646. E-mail: hclibrary66853@yahoo.com. Web Site: hamiltoncity.mykansaslibrary.org. *Dir,* Brooke Schlotterbeck
Founded 1970. Pop 380; Circ 2,213
Library Holdings: Bk Titles 7,400; Per Subs 14
Wireless access
Mem of Southeast Kansas Library System
Open Mon-Thurs 2-6, Fri 11-6

HANOVER

P HANOVER PUBLIC LIBRARY*, 205 Jackson St, 66945-8874. (Mail add: PO Box 97, 66945-0097), SAN 305-9367. Tel: 785-337-2424. E-mail: hanoverlib@gmail.com. Web Site: hanover.lib.nckls.org. *Librn,* Donna Jueneman
Founded 1954. Pop 839
Library Holdings: Bk Vols 18,000; Per Subs 50
Wireless access
Mem of North Central Kansas Libraries System
Open Tues & Thurs 12-5, Wed & Sat 8-1

HANSTON

P HANSTON CITY LIBRARY*, 105 N Logan, 67849-9409. SAN 373-8981. Tel: 620-623-2798. E-mail: hclibrary7@gmail.com. Web Site: hanston.readinks.info. *Librn,* Jaimi Burke; Staff 2 (Non-MLS 2)
Founded 1963. Pop 287; Circ 2,469
Library Holdings: AV Mats 379; Bk Vols 5,138; Per Subs 23; Talking Bks 106
Function: Homebound delivery serv, ILL available, Internet access, Photocopying/Printing, Prog for children & young adult, Summer reading prog
Mem of Southwest Kansas Library System
Open Mon 1-5, Wed 9-12 & 6-8, Sat 9-Noon

HARDTNER

P HARDTNER PUBLIC LIBRARY*, 102 E Central, 67057. (Mail add: PO Box 38, 67057-0038), SAN 305-9375. Tel: 620-296-4586. E-mail: hardlbkw@gmail.com. *Head Librn,* Susan R Cruz
Founded 1913. Pop 412; Circ 1,638
Library Holdings: Audiobooks 290; CDs 25; DVDs 5,938; e-books 98; e-journals 1; Electronic Media & Resources 12; Large Print Bks 1,962; Bk Titles 10,274; Bk Vols 25; Per Subs 20; Spec Interest Per Sub 1; Videos 11
Wireless access
Function: Activity rm, After school storytime, Audio & video playback equip for onsite use, Audiobks on Playaways & MP3, Bks on cassette, Bks on CD, CD-ROM, Children's prog, Computers for patron use, Free DVD rentals, Holiday prog, ILL available, Internet access, Laminating, Magazines, Movies, Music CDs, Prog for adults, Prog for children & young adult, Ref & res, Story hour, Summer reading prog, Teen prog, Wheelchair accessible
Mem of South Central Kansas Library System
Open Tues & Thurs 3:30-8, Sat 1-4
Friends of the Library Group

HARPER

P HARPER PUBLIC LIBRARY*, 708 W 14th St, 67058. SAN 305-9383. Tel: 620-896-2959. FAX: 620-896-2778. E-mail: harperlib@sctelcom.net. Web Site: harper.scklf.info. *Libr Dir,* Debra Olds; *Asst Librn,* Michelle Harder; Staff 2 (Non-MLS 2)
Founded 1876. Pop 1,700; Circ 16,354
Library Holdings: Bk Vols 16,800; Per Subs 62
Wireless access
Mem of South Central Kansas Library System
Open Mon & Wed 9-12 & 1:30-8, Tues & Thurs 1:30-8, Fri 9-5, Sat 9-1

HARTFORD

P ELMENDARO TOWNSHIP LIBRARY*, 224 Commercial St, 66854. (Mail add: PO Box 38, 66854-0038), SAN 305-9391. Tel: 620-392-5518. E-mail: elmlibhartford@gmail.com. Web Site: hartford.lib.nckls.org. *Dir,* Marcia Sell
Founded 1966. Pop 1,700
Library Holdings: Bk Vols 10,000; Per Subs 40
Subject Interests: Econ, Health, Soc sci & issues, Spec needs
Wireless access
Mem of North Central Kansas Libraries System
Special Services for the Blind - Talking bks
Open Mon, Wed & Thurs 2-6, Tues & Fri 9:30-2

HAVEN

P HAVEN PUBLIC LIBRARY*, 121 N Kansas Ave, 67543. (Mail add: PO Box 340, 67543-0340), SAN 373-8973. Tel: 620-465-3524. FAX: 620-465-3524. E-mail: havenlibrarian@gmail.com. Web Site: haven.scklf.info. *Dir,* Trudy Littlestar; *Ch,* Stephanie Confer; Staff 2 (Non-MLS 2)
Founded 1902. Pop 1,175; Circ 12,391
Library Holdings: Bk Vols 11,325; Per Subs 52
Wireless access
Mem of South Central Kansas Library System
Open Tues & Thurs 12-7, Wed 12-5, Fri & Sat 9-2
Friends of the Library Group

HAVILAND

C BARCLAY COLLEGE*, Worden Memorial Library, 100 E Cherry St, 67059. SAN 305-9413. Tel: 620-862-5274. Toll Free Tel: 800-862-0226, Ext 31. FAX: 620-862-5403. E-mail: library@barclaycollege.edu. Web Site: www.barclaycollege.edu/resources/library. *Libr Dir,* Jeannie Ross; E-mail: jeannie.ross@barclaycollege.edu; Staff 1 (MLS 1)
Founded 1892. Enrl 197; Fac 18; Highest Degree: Master
Library Holdings: Bk Vols 50,000; Per Subs 75
Special Collections: Quaker Rare Books
Subject Interests: Relig
Automation Activity & Vendor Info: (Cataloging) Follett Software; (Circulation) Follett Software; (Serials) Follett Software
Wireless access
Function: CD-ROM, For res purposes, ILL available, Music CDs, VHS videos
Open Mon-Fri 7:45am-11pm, Sat & Sun 2-11

HAYS

S ELLIS COUNTY HISTORICAL SOCIETY ARCHIVES*, 100 W Seventh St, 67601. SAN 329-7489. Tel: 785-628-2624. FAX: 785-628-0386. Web Site: www.elliscountyhistoricalmuseum.org. *Dir,* Ms Lee Dobratz; E-mail: director@echshays.org; *Archives Asst,* Betty Macdonald; E-mail: research@echshays.org; Staff 5 (MLS 2, Non-MLS 3)
Founded 1972
Special Collections: County; Local History, docs, photog; Volga German History, docs, photog
Function: Archival coll, Res libr
Open Tues-Sat 11-5

C FORT HAYS STATE UNIVERSITY, Forsyth Library, 502 S Campus Dr, 67601. SAN 305-9421. Tel: 785-628-4434. Interlibrary Loan Service Tel: 785-628-4351. FAX: 785-628-4096. Web Site: www.fhsu.edu/library. *Interim Dean, Libr Serv,* MaryAlice Wade; Tel: 785-628-4342, E-mail: mawade2@fhsu.edu; *Libr Operations Coordr,* Lacey Wegner; Tel: 785-628-5837, E-mail: llwegner@fhsu.edu; *Univ Archivist,* Amber Watts; Tel: 785-628-5282, E-mail: akwatts2@fhsu.edu; *Coll Spec, Resource Dev Specialist,* Karen Pfeifer; Tel: 785-628-4343, E-mail: kapfeifer@fhsu.edu; *Outreach Specialist,* Brittney Squire; Tel: 785-628-5566, E-mail: bmsquire@fhsu.edu; *Govt Doc, Spec Coll,* Brian Gribben; E-mail: b_gribben@fhsu.edu; Staff 18 (MLS 9, Non-MLS 9)
Founded 1902. Enrl 5,600; Fac 300
Library Holdings: Bk Vols 350,000; Per Subs 1,800
Special Collections: Children's Literature; History (Ethnic Coll, Volga Germans) bks, tapes; History (Western Coll, Western Kansas). Oral History; State Document Depository; US Document Depository
Automation Activity & Vendor Info: (Acquisitions) Ex Libris Group; (Cataloging) Ex Libris Group; (Circulation) Ex Libris Group; (Course Reserve) Ex Libris Group; (ILL) OCLC; (OPAC) Ex Libris Group; (Serials) Ex Libris Group
Wireless access
Partic in OCLC Online Computer Library Center, Inc
Open Mon-Thurs (Winter) 7:30am-Midnight, Fri 7:30-7, Sat 10-5, Sun 1-Midnight; Mon-Fri (Summer) 8-5

P HAYS PUBLIC LIBRARY*, 1205 Main, 67601-3693. SAN 305-943X. Tel: 785-625-9014. FAX: 785-625-8683. Web Site: www.hayspublib.org. *Libr Dir,* Brandon Hines; E-mail: bhines@hayslibrary.org; *Ad,* Samantha Dean; E-mail: sdean@hayspublib.org; *Ch,* Cathleen Kroeger; Tel: 785-625-5916, E-mail: ckroeger@hayspublib.org; *YA Serv,* Vera Haynes; Tel: 785-623-4944, E-mail: vhaynes@hayspublib.org; Staff 30 (MLS 2, Non-MLS 28)
Founded 1899. Pop 19,827
Library Holdings: AV Mats 26,000; Bks on Deafness & Sign Lang 158; High Interest/Low Vocabulary Bk Vols 105; Large Print Bks 5,700; Bk Vols 146,000; Per Subs 200
Subject Interests: Kansas, Local hist
Automation Activity & Vendor Info: (Cataloging) TLC (The Library Corporation); (Circulation) TLC (The Library Corporation); (OPAC) TLC (The Library Corporation)
Wireless access
Function: 24/7 Online cat, Activity rm, Adult bk club, After school storytime, Archival coll, Audiobks on Playaways & MP3, Bk club(s), Children's prog, Computer training, Computers for patron use, Electronic databases & coll, For res purposes, Free DVD rentals, Genealogy discussion group, Holiday prog, Homework prog, ILL available, Internet access, Laminating, Mail & tel request accepted, Mango lang, Meeting rooms, Microfiche/film & reading machines, Movies, Music CDs, Notary serv, Online cat, Outreach serv, Photocopying/Printing, Preschool outreach, Preschool reading prog, Printer for laptops & handheld devices, Prog for adults, Prog for children & young adult, Ref serv available, Scanner, Senior outreach, Serves people with intellectual disabilities, Story hour, Summer reading prog, Tax forms, Teen prog, Wheelchair accessible, Words travel prog
Publications: The Bookmark (Newsletter)
Mem of Central Kansas Library System
Special Services for the Deaf - TTY equip
Special Services for the Blind - Braille bks
Open Mon-Thurs 9-8, Fri 9-6, Sat 9-5, Sun 1-5
Friends of the Library Group

HAYSVILLE

P HAYSVILLE COMMUNITY LIBRARY*, 210 S Hays, 67060. (Mail add: PO Box 285, 67060-0285), SAN 320-4782. Tel: 316-524-5242. FAX: 316-524-0142. E-mail: hcl@haysvillecommunitylibrary.org. Web Site: www.haysvillecommunitylibrary.org. *Dir,* Ken Bell; Staff 12 (MLS 2, Non-MLS 10)
Founded 1977. Pop 9,627; Circ 75,970
Library Holdings: Bk Vols 45,000; Per Subs 132
Special Collections: Genealogy Coll; Kansas (Kansas & Local History), bks, newspapers; Quilting bks; Sports bks
Automation Activity & Vendor Info: (Cataloging) Innovative Interfaces, Inc; (Circulation) Innovative Interfaces, Inc; (OPAC) Innovative Interfaces, Inc
Wireless access
Function: Adult bk club, Art exhibits, Bks on cassette, Bks on CD, Children's prog, Computer training, Computers for patron use, Electronic databases & coll, Free DVD rentals, ILL available, Notary serv, Online cat, Photocopying/Printing, Scanner, Senior computer classes, Story hour, Summer reading prog, Tax forms, Telephone ref, VHS videos, Wheelchair accessible
Mem of South Central Kansas Library System
Open Mon-Thurs 9-8, Fri & Sat 10-5
Friends of the Library Group

HEPLER

P HEPLER CITY LIBRARY*, 105 S Prairie, 66746. (Mail add: PO Box 148, 66746-0148), SAN 305-9448. Tel: 620-368-4379. FAX: 620-368-4379. E-mail: heplerlibrary@yahoo.com. Web Site: hepler.mykansaslibrary.org. *Libr Dir,* Shirley Ann Franklin
Pop 187; Circ 2,155
Library Holdings: Bk Vols 4,126
Wireless access
Mem of Southeast Kansas Library System
Open Mon 4-8, Tues-Thurs 2-6
Friends of the Library Group

HERINGTON

P HERINGTON PUBLIC LIBRARY*, 102 S Broadway, 67449. SAN 305-9456. Tel: 785-258-2011. FAX: 785-258-3260. Web Site: herington.lib.nckls.org. *Dir,* Shelly Wirtz; E-mail: director@heringtonlib.info
Founded 1897. Pop 3,000; Circ 31,250
Library Holdings: Audiobooks 120; DVDs 1,200; Bk Vols 11,000; Per Subs 10
Automation Activity & Vendor Info: (Cataloging) Auto-Graphics, Inc
Wireless access
Mem of North Central Kansas Libraries System
Open Mon-Thurs 11-6, Fri & Sat 9-3

HESSTON

C HESSTON COLLEGE*, Mary Miller Library, 301 S Main St, 67062-8901. (Mail add: PO Box 3000, 67062-3000), SAN 342-0361. Tel: 620-327-8245. FAX: 620-327-8300. E-mail: library@hesston.edu. Web Site: www.hesston.edu/academics/library. *Libr Dir,* Margaret Wiebe; E-mail: margaret.wiebe@hesston.edu; Staff 1 (MLS 1)
Founded 1908. Enrl 435; Fac 50; Highest Degree: Associate
Library Holdings: AV Mats 3,000; Bk Titles 30,000; Per Subs 225
Automation Activity & Vendor Info: (Acquisitions) Auto-Graphics, Inc; (Cataloging) Auto-Graphics, Inc; (Circulation) Auto-Graphics, Inc; (ILL) Auto-Graphics, Inc; (OPAC) Auto-Graphics, Inc
Wireless access
Mem of South Central Kansas Library System
Open Mon-Thurs 8am-Midnight, Fri 8-5, Sat 1-5, Sun 2-Midnight

P HESSTON PUBLIC LIBRARY*, 300 N Main St, 67062. (Mail add: PO Box 640, 67062-0640), SAN 305-9472. Tel: 620-327-4666. FAX: 620-327-4459. E-mail: hesstonpubliclibrary@gmail.com. Web Site: hesston.scklf.info. *Dir,* Libby Albers; Staff 6 (MLS 1, Non-MLS 5)
Founded 1937. Pop 3,618; Circ 49,020
Jan 2013-Dec 2013 Income $204,920, State $1,499, City $178,511, County $13,003, Locally Generated Income $10,408, Other $1,499. Mats Exp $23,698, Books $17,464, Per/Ser (Incl. Access Fees) $4,019, AV Mat $1,143, Electronic Ref Mat (Incl. Access Fees) $1,072. Sal $110,450 (Prof $50,000)
Library Holdings: AV Mats 2,172; Bk Vols 36,650; Per Subs 75
Special Collections: Children's Videos; Educational Toys; Family Diversity; Sewing Patterns
Subject Interests: Aging, Amish, Ecology, Landscape archit, Lifelong wellness, Mennonites, Quilts, Spirituality, Transportation
Automation Activity & Vendor Info: (Cataloging) Follett Software; (Circulation) Follett Software; (OPAC) Follett Software
Wireless access
Function: ILL available, Photocopying/Printing, Telephone ref
Mem of South Central Kansas Library System
Open Mon-Wed & Fri 9-6, Thurs 9-8, Sat 9-2

HIAWATHA

P MORRILL PUBLIC LIBRARY*, 431 Oregon, 66434-2290. SAN 305-9480. Tel: 785-742-3831. FAX: 785-742-2054. E-mail: morrill@hiawathalibrary.org. Web Site: www.hiawathalibrary.org. *Dir,* Position Currently Open; *Outreach Serv Librn,* Susan Bryant; Staff 12 (Non-MLS 12)
Founded 1882. Pop 3,410; Circ 92,676
Library Holdings: Bk Vols 38,727; Per Subs 100
Wireless access
Function: 24/7 Electronic res, 24/7 Online cat, Activity rm, Adult bk club, After school storytime, Audiobks on Playaways & MP3, Audiobks via web, Bk club(s), Bks on CD, Children's prog, Computers for patron use, Digital talking bks, Equip loans & repairs, Free DVD rentals, ILL available, Internet access, Magazines, Mail & tel request accepted, Mango lang, Meeting rooms, Microfiche/film & reading machines, Movies, Notary serv, Online cat, Outreach serv, OverDrive digital audio bks, Photocopying/Printing, Preschool outreach, Preschool reading prog, Prog for adults, Prog for children & young adult, Scanner, Story hour, Summer reading prog, Tax forms, Telephone ref, Wheelchair accessible
Mem of Northeast Kansas Library System
Open Mon-Thurs 9-8, Fri 9-5, Sat 10-4, Sun 1-4
Friends of the Library Group

HIGHLAND

J HIGHLAND COMMUNITY COLLEGE LIBRARY*, 606 W Main, 66035. SAN 305-9499. Tel: 785-442-6054. Circulation Tel: 785-442-6053. FAX: 785-442-6101. E-mail: Library@Highlandcc.edu. Web Site: highlandcc.edu/pages/library_4. *Libr Asst,* Betty Forney; E-mail: bforney@highlandcc.edu; Staff 3 (MLS 1, Non-MLS 2)
Founded 1858. Enrl 3,500; Fac 79; Highest Degree: Associate
Library Holdings: DVDs 125; Bk Titles 22,500; Bk Vols 23,000; Per Subs 125; Videos 1,750
Special Collections: Local History, videocassettes
Subject Interests: Soc sci & issues
Automation Activity & Vendor Info: (Circulation) TLC (The Library Corporation)
Wireless access
Mem of Northeast Kansas Library System
Open Mon-Thurs (Winter) 7:30am-10pm, Fri 7:30-4, Sat 10-4, Sun 3:30-10; Mon-Fri (Summer) 7:30-4

HILL CITY

P GRAHAM COUNTY PUBLIC LIBRARY*, 414 N West St, 67642. SAN 305-9502. Tel: 785-421-2722. FAX: 785-421-5583. E-mail: gclibrary@ruraltel.net. Web Site: ghcopublib.org. *Dir,* Marcy Gansel; *Libr Asst,* Carol Nickelson; Staff 4 (Non-MLS 4)
Founded 1972. Pop 3,219
Library Holdings: Bk Vols 31,219; Per Subs 60
Special Collections: Graham County Newspapers 1879-present; Wildflowers of Graham County
Wireless access
Open Mon-Wed & Fri 9:30-5:30, Thurs 9:30-8:30, Sat 9:30-2:30
Friends of the Library Group

HILLSBORO

P HILLSBORO PUBLIC LIBRARY*, 120 E Grand Ave, 67063. SAN 305-9510. Tel: 620-947-3827. FAX: 620-947-3810. E-mail: hillsboropubliclib@gmail.com. Web Site: hillsboro.lib.nckls.org. *Libr Dir,* Jeanie Bartel; *Ch,* Rhiannon Janzen; Staff 3 (Non-MLS 3)
Founded 1926. Pop 2,833; Circ 38,430
Library Holdings: AV Mats 968; Bks on Deafness & Sign Lang 13; Large Print Bks 74; Bk Titles 20,489; Per Subs 65; Talking Bks 209
Automation Activity & Vendor Info: (Cataloging) Auto-Graphics, Inc; (Circulation) Auto-Graphics, Inc
Wireless access
Function: ILL available, Internet access, Photocopying/Printing, Prog for adults, Prog for children & young adult, Summer reading prog, Telephone ref, Wheelchair accessible
Mem of North Central Kansas Libraries System
Open Mon 10-7, Tues-Fri 10-5, Sat 10-Noon

C TABOR COLLEGE LIBRARY, 400 S Jefferson St, 67063. SAN 305-9529. Tel: 620-947-3121, Ext 1201. FAX: 620-947-2607. E-mail: library@tabor.edu. Web Site: www.tabor.edu/library. *Dir, Libr Serv,* Janet L Williams; Tel: 620-947-3121, Ext 1202, E-mail: janetw@tabor.edu; Staff 1 (MLS 1)
Founded 1908. Enrl 535; Fac 45
Jul 2019-Jun 2020. Mats Exp $58,000, Books $5,000, Per/Ser (Incl. Access Fees) $3,000, Electronic Ref Mat (Incl. Access Fees) $50,000
Library Holdings: CDs 2,175; DVDs 1,250; e-books 250,000; Music Scores 3,000; Bk Titles 25,000
Special Collections: Center for Mennonite Brethren Studies, bks, ms, per
Subject Interests: Germans from Russia, Hymnals, Kansas, Relig
Automation Activity & Vendor Info: (Acquisitions) OCLC Online; (Cataloging) OCLC Online; (Circulation) OCLC Online; (Course Reserve) OCLC Online; (ILL) OCLC WorldShare Interlibrary Loan; (OPAC) OCLC Online; (Serials) OCLC Online
Wireless access
Function: Distance learning, Doc delivery serv, ILL available, Internet access, Music CDs, Orientations, Outside serv via phone, mail, e-mail & web, Prof lending libr, Ref serv available, Wheelchair accessible, Workshops
Open Mon-Thurs 7:30am-11pm, Fri 7:30-5, Sun (Sept-May) 2-11

HOISINGTON

P HOISINGTON PUBLIC LIBRARY, 169 S Walnut, 67544. SAN 305-9537. Tel: 620-653-4128. E-mail: library@hoisingtonks.org. Web Site: hoisingtonpl.weebly.com. *Dir,* Karen LaPierre; *Staff Librn,* Melissa Hipp; E-mail: hoisington.library.staff@gmail.com
Founded 1928. Pop 2,685
Library Holdings: AV Mats 620; Large Print Bks 5,510; Bk Vols 19,320; Per Subs 93
Automation Activity & Vendor Info: (Cataloging) Book Systems; (Circulation) Book Systems
Wireless access
Mem of Central Kansas Library System
Open Mon & Wed 10-6, Tues, Thurs & Fri 12-6, Sat 12-4

HOLTON

P BECK BOOKMAN LIBRARY*, 420 W Fourth St, 66436-1572. SAN 305-9545. Tel: 785-364-3532. FAX: 785-364-5402. E-mail: holtoncitylib@gmail.com. Web Site: www.holtonks.net/library/index.html. *Dir,* Amy Austin; *Circ,* Linda Porter; *Circ,* Susan Schirmer; *Circ,* Gail Schmitz; *Tech Serv & Automation,* Helen Murphy Plankinton

Founded 1897. Pop 15,000; Circ 59,319
Library Holdings: Bk Vols 28,370; Per Subs 52
Special Collections: Campbell College Coll; Kansas Coll
Automation Activity & Vendor Info: (Cataloging) ByWater Solutions; (Circulation) ByWater Solutions
Wireless access
Mem of Northeast Kansas Library System
Open Mon-Thurs 9:30-7, Fri 9:30-6:30, Sat 9:30-2:30

HOPE

P HOPE COMMUNITY LIBRARY, 216 N Main St, 67451. SAN 376-7663. Tel: 785-366-7219. E-mail: hopelibrary@tctelco.net. Web Site: hope.lib.nckls.org. *Dir,* Nakita Hirsch; *Librn,* Vicki Gruber
Wireless access
Mem of North Central Kansas Libraries System
Open Tues & Wed 2-5, Thurs 9-1, Fri 1-4, Sat 9-12
Friends of the Library Group

HORTON

P HORTON PUBLIC LIBRARY*, 809 First Ave E, 66439-1898. SAN 305-9553. Tel: 785-486-3326. FAX: 785-486-2116. E-mail: hortonlibrary@hortonlibrary.org. Web Site: www.hortonlibrary.org. *Dir,* Jessica Buhrman; E-mail: director@hortonlibrary.org; *Librn,* Carolyn Olsen
Founded 1925. Pop 2,000; Circ 18,000
Library Holdings: Bk Vols 16,000; Per Subs 41
Special Collections: Kansas Coll
Automation Activity & Vendor Info: (Cataloging) Koha; (Circulation) Koha; (OPAC) Koha
Wireless access
Function: 24/7 Online cat, Accelerated reader prog, Activity rm, Audio & video playback equip for onsite use, Audiobks via web, Bk club(s), Bks on CD, Children's prog, Computer training, Computers for patron use, Electronic databases & coll, Home delivery & serv to seniorr ctr & nursing homes, Homebound delivery serv, ILL available, Internet access, Laminating, Magazines, Magnifiers for reading, Mail & tel request accepted, Mango lang, Meeting rooms, Microfiche/film & reading machines, Movies, Online cat, Preschool outreach, Prog for children & young adult, Scanner, Spanish lang bks, Spoken cassettes & CDs, Spoken cassettes & DVDs, Story hour, Summer reading prog, Tax forms, VHS videos, Wheelchair accessible
Mem of Northeast Kansas Library System
Open Mon, Wed, Thurs & Fri 1-7, Tues 9-1 & 4-7, Sat 9-1

HOWARD

P HOWARD CITY LIBRARY*, 126 S Wabash, 67349. SAN 305-9561. Tel: 620-374-2890. FAX: 620-374-2017. E-mail: HowCitLib@sktc.net. Web Site: howardlibrary.org. *Librn,* Karen Eshelman
Founded 1921. Pop 976; Circ 6,057
Library Holdings: Bk Vols 17,600; Per Subs 15
Special Collections: Kansas Coll
Mem of Southeast Kansas Library System
Special Services for the Blind - Large print bks
Open Mon 3-6, Tues 4-7, Wed-Fri 2-5, Sat 9-12

HOXIE

P SHERIDAN COUNTY LIBRARY, 801 Royal Ave, 67740. (Mail add: PO Box 607, 67740-0607), SAN 305-957X. Tel: 785-675-3102. E-mail: sheridanlib@ruraltel.net. Web Site: sheridancounty.nwkls.org. *Dir,* Sarah Burk
Pop 3,500; Circ 34,473
Library Holdings: Bk Vols 18,400; Per Subs 61
Subject Interests: Kansas
Automation Activity & Vendor Info: (Cataloging) Follett Software; (Circulation) Follett Software
Wireless access
Mem of Northwest Kansas Library System
Open Mon, Tues, Thurs & Fri 9-5, Wed 9-6
Friends of the Library Group

HUGOTON

P STEVENS COUNTY LIBRARY*, 500 S Monroe, 67951-2639. SAN 305-9588. Tel: 620-544-2301. FAX: 620-544-2322. E-mail: library@stevenscountylibrary.com. Web Site: www.stevenscountylibrary.com. *Dir,* Eunice M Schroeder; *Asst Dir, Youth Serv,* Stacey L Strickland; *Adult Serv,* Laurie Crawford; Staff 10 (MLS 2, Non-MLS 8)
Founded 1914. Pop 5,056; Circ 79,002
Library Holdings: CDs 3,219; DVDs 3,044; Electronic Media & Resources 48; Bk Vols 41,159; Per Subs 125
Special Collections: Art Print Coll; Kansas Room Coll; Stevens County Genealogical Society Coll
Automation Activity & Vendor Info: (Cataloging) Auto-Graphics, Inc; (Circulation) Auto-Graphics, Inc; (ILL) Auto-Graphics, Inc; (OPAC) Auto-Graphics, Inc
Wireless access
Function: Art exhibits, Audiobks via web, AV serv, Bilingual assistance for Spanish patrons, Bks on CD, CD-ROM, Children's prog, Computer training, Computers for patron use, Digital talking bks, Distance learning, E-Reserves, Electronic databases & coll, Family literacy, For res purposes, Free DVD rentals, Genealogy discussion group, Govt ref serv, Health sci info serv, Holiday prog, Home delivery & serv to seniorr ctr & nursing homes, Homebound delivery serv, Homework prog, ILL available, Instruction & testing, Internet access, Jail serv, Literacy & newcomer serv, Magnifiers for reading, Mail & tel request accepted, Masonic res mat, Music CDs, Notary serv, Online cat, Online info literacy tutorials on the web & in blackboard, Online ref, Orientations, Outreach serv, Outside serv via phone, mail, e-mail & web, OverDrive digital audio bks, Photocopying/Printing, Preschool outreach, Printer for laptops & handheld devices, Prog for adults, Prog for children & young adult, Ref & res, Ref serv available, Satellite serv, Scanner, Senior computer classes, Senior outreach, Spoken cassettes & CDs, Spoken cassettes & DVDs, Story hour, Summer & winter reading prog, Summer reading prog, Tax forms, Teen prog, Telephone ref, Wheelchair accessible, Winter reading prog, Workshops
Mem of Southwest Kansas Library System
Open Mon-Sat 9-6

HUMBOLDT

P HUMBOLDT PUBLIC LIBRARY, 916 Bridge St, 66748. SAN 305-9596. Tel: 620-473-2243. FAX: 620-473-2192. E-mail: humboldtpublibrary@gmail.com. Web Site: www.humboldtkslibrary.com. *Dir,* Melinda Herder
Founded 1939. Pop 3,500; Circ 19,000
Library Holdings: Bk Vols 19,500; Per Subs 52
Special Collections: City History; high school year bks
Subject Interests: Parenting, Photog, Relig, Sci fict
Automation Activity & Vendor Info: (Cataloging) Follett Software; (Circulation) Follett Software
Wireless access
Partic in OCLC Online Computer Library Center, Inc
Open Tues-Thurs 9:30-7, Fri 9:30-5:30, Sat 9:30-1:30

HUNTER

P HUNTER PUBLIC LIBRARY*, 109 E First St, 67452. Tel: 785-592-3010. E-mail: hunterlibrary@wilsoncom.us. *Librn,* Mary Kralicek
Mem of Central Kansas Library System
Open Wed & Sun 9am-11:30am

HUTCHINSON

J HUTCHINSON COMMUNITY COLLEGE, John F Kennedy Library, 1300 N Plum St, 67501. SAN 305-9618. Tel: 620-665-3547. Toll Free Tel: 800-289-3501, Ext 3547. FAX: 620-665-3392. E-mail: jfk@hutchcc.edu. Web Site: www.hutchcc.edu/john-f-kennedy-library. *Dir, Support Serv,* Bradley Fenwick; E-mail: fenwickb@hutchcc.edu; *Access & Tech Serv Librn,* Position Currently Open; *Pub Serv Librn,* Melissa Emo; Tel: 620 665-3548, E-mail: emom@hutchcc.edu; *Coordr, Libr Serv,* Emily Hemmerling; Tel: 620-665-3338, E-mail: hemmerlinge@hutchcc.edu; *Libr Asst,* Katie Harbold; E-mail: harboldk@hutchcc.edu; Staff 5 (MLS 3, Non-MLS 2)
Founded 1928. Enrl 5,598; Fac 314; Highest Degree: Associate
Jul 2021-Jun 2022. Mats Exp $29,000, Books $9,200, Per/Ser (Incl. Access Fees) $16,300, AV Mat $3,500
Library Holdings: AV Mats 2,453; e-books 11,000; Bk Vols 41,780; Per Subs 121
Automation Activity & Vendor Info: (Cataloging) TLC (The Library Corporation); (Circulation) TLC (The Library Corporation); (OPAC) TLC (The Library Corporation); (Serials) TLC (The Library Corporation)
Wireless access
Mem of South Central Kansas Library System
Open Mon-Thurs (Winter) 7:30am-9pm, Fri 7:30-5, Sun 5-9; Mon-Thurs (Summer) 8-7, Fri 8-4

P HUTCHINSON PUBLIC LIBRARY*, 901 N Main, 67501-4492. SAN 305-9626. Tel: 620-663-5441. FAX: 620-663-9506. Interlibrary Loan Service FAX: 620-663-1583. Reference FAX: 620-663-1583. Web Site: www.hutchpl.org. *Dir,* Gregg Wamsley; E-mail: gwamsley@hutchpl.org; *Head, Circ,* Dianna Brown; E-mail: dbrown@hutchpl.org; *Head, ILL, Head, Ref,* Cheryl Canfield; E-mail: cherylc@hutchpl.org; *Tech Serv Team Leader,* Ruth Heidebrecht; E-mail: rheidebrecht@hutchpl.org; *Ch Serv,* Terry Christner; E-mail: tchris@hutchpl.org; Staff 42 (MLS 8, Non-MLS 34)
Founded 1901. Pop 62,155; Circ 386,142
Library Holdings: Bk Titles 32,631; Bk Vols 289,081; Per Subs 396

Special Collections: State Document Depository; US Document Depository
Automation Activity & Vendor Info: (Acquisitions) Innovative Interfaces, Inc; (Cataloging) Innovative Interfaces, Inc; (Circulation) Innovative Interfaces, Inc; (OPAC) Innovative Interfaces, Inc; (Serials) Innovative Interfaces, Inc
Wireless access
Function: 24/7 Electronic res, 24/7 Online cat, Activity rm, Adult bk club, Adult literacy prog, Archival coll, Art exhibits, Audio & video playback equip for onsite use, Audiobks via web, Bilingual assistance for Spanish patrons, Bk club(s), Bks on CD, Bus archives, Children's prog, Computer training, Computers for patron use, E-Readers, Electronic databases & coll, For res purposes, Free DVD rentals, Govt ref serv, Home delivery & serv to seniorr ctr & nursing homes, Homebound delivery serv, ILL available, Internet access, Magazines, Magnifiers for reading, Mail & tel request accepted, Meeting rooms, Microfiche/film & reading machines, Music CDs, Online cat, Online ref, Outreach serv, Photocopying/Printing, Preschool outreach, Printer for laptops & handheld devices, Prog for adults, Prog for children & young adult, Ref & res, Ref serv available, Scanner, Senior outreach, Story hour, Study rm, Summer & winter reading prog, Summer reading prog, Tax forms, Teen prog, Visual arts prog, Wheelchair accessible, Workshops, Writing prog
Mem of South Central Kansas Library System
Open Mon-Thurs 9-9, Fri & Sat 9-6, Sun 1-5
Friends of the Library Group

S KANSAS DEPARTMENT OF CORRECTIONS*, Hutchinson Correctional Facility Central Library, 500 S Reformatory Rd, 67501. (Mail add: PO Box 1568, 67504-1568). Tel: 620-662-2321, Ext 4365. *Dir,* Kathryn Androski; Staff 2 (MLS 1, Non-MLS 1)
Library Holdings: Bk Vols 10,000; Per Subs 21
Automation Activity & Vendor Info: (Cataloging) Koha; (Circulation) Koha; (OPAC) Koha
Restriction: Not open to pub, Restricted access

INDEPENDENCE

J INDEPENDENCE COMMUNITY COLLEGE LIBRARY*, 1057 W College Ave, 67301. Tel: 620-331-4100, 620-332-5468. FAX: 620-331-6821. Web Site: www.indycc.edu/student-life/library. *Libr Dir,* Sarah Owen; E-mail: sowen@indycc.edu; Staff 4 (MLS 2, Non-MLS 2)
Founded 1925. Enrl 1,190; Highest Degree: Associate
Library Holdings: AV Mats 778; Bk Vols 30,098; Per Subs 54
Special Collections: William Inge Coll
Automation Activity & Vendor Info: (Acquisitions) Follett Software; (Cataloging) Follett Software; (Circulation) Follett Software; (ILL) Auto-Graphics, Inc; (Serials) Follett Software
Wireless access
Open Mon-Fri 8-5

P INDEPENDENCE PUBLIC LIBRARY*, 220 E Maple, 67301. SAN 305-9642. Tel: 620-331-3030. FAX: 620-331-4093. Web Site: www.iplks.org. *Dir,* Jeri Hopkins; E-mail: jeri@iplks.org; *Ch,* Charlene Mitchell; *Mgr, Tech Serv,* Rebecca Passaur; E-mail: becky@iplks.org; Staff 11 (MLS 2, Non-MLS 9)
Founded 1882. Pop 13,500; Circ 121,613
Library Holdings: Audiobooks 1,604; AV Mats 195; DVDs 1,625; High Interest/Low Vocabulary Bk Vols 50; Large Print Bks 899; Microforms 62; Bk Titles 37,964; Per Subs 128
Special Collections: Business Coll; Genealogy Coll; Local Newspapers, micro
Automation Activity & Vendor Info: (Acquisitions) Follett Software; (Cataloging) Follett Software; (Circulation) Follett Software; (Course Reserve) Follett Software; (ILL) Follett Software; (Media Booking) Follett Software; (OPAC) Follett Software; (Serials) Follett Software
Wireless access
Function: ILL available
Open Mon, Wed & Fri 10-6, Tues & Thurs 10-7
Friends of the Library Group

INMAN

P INMAN PUBLIC LIBRARY*, 100 N Main, 67546. (Mail add: PO Box 416, 67546-0416), SAN 305-9650. Tel: 620-585-2474. E-mail: inmankslibrary@gmail.com. Web Site: inmanlibrary.com. *Dir,* Donna Sallee
Founded 1943. Pop 1,000; Circ 10,000
Library Holdings: AV Mats 250; Bk Vols 18,000; Per Subs 30
Automation Activity & Vendor Info: (Circulation) Auto-Graphics, Inc
Wireless access
Mem of South Central Kansas Library System
Open Mon-Fri 1-7, Sat 9-12

IOLA

J ALLEN COMMUNITY COLLEGE LIBRARY*, 1801 N Cottonwood, 66749-1648. SAN 305-9669. Tel: 620-365-5116, Ext 6235. E-mail: accclib@allencc.edu. Web Site: www.allencc.edu/index.php/library. *Dir,* Sandy Moore; E-mail: moore@allencc.edu; *Learning Coordr,* Alice Williamson; E-mail: williamson@allencc.edu; *Libr Tech,* Jill Hoffman; E-mail: hoffman@allencc.edu; Staff 3 (MLS 1, Non-MLS 2)
Founded 1970. Enrl 3,128; Fac 65; Highest Degree: Associate
Library Holdings: Audiobooks 22; AV Mats 521; Bks on Deafness & Sign Lang 16; CDs 415; e-books 12,874; e-journals 8,953; Electronic Media & Resources 353; High Interest/Low Vocabulary Bk Vols 108; Large Print Bks 48; Music Scores 63; Bk Titles 38,326; Bk Vols 39,261; Per Subs 104; Videos 521
Subject Interests: Local genealogy
Automation Activity & Vendor Info: (Cataloging) Follett Software; (Circulation) Follett Software; (Course Reserve) Follett Software; (OPAC) Follett Software
Wireless access
Function: Ref serv available
Publications: Policies & Procedures Manual
Mem of Southeast Kansas Library System
Special Services for the Deaf - Assistive tech; Closed caption videos; High interest/low vocabulary bks
Special Services for the Blind - Assistive/Adapted tech devices, equip & products; Bks available with recordings; Bks on cassette; Bks on CD; Computer with voice synthesizer for visually impaired persons; Dragon Naturally Speaking software; Large print bks; Magnifiers; Music instrul cassettes; PC for people with disabilities; Reader equip; Rec of textbk mat; Screen enlargement software for people with visual disabilities; Screen reader software; ZoomText magnification & reading software
Open Mon-Thurs (Winter) 7:45am-9pm, Fri 7:45-4; Mon-Fri (Summer) 7:45-4

P IOLA PUBLIC LIBRARY*, 218 E Madison Ave, 66749. SAN 305-9677. Tel: 620-365-3262. FAX: 620-365-5137. E-mail: iolaref@sekls.org. Web Site: iola.mykansaslibrary.org. *Dir,* Roger L Carswell; E-mail: rcarswell@sekls.org; *Ch Serv,* Lesa Cole; E-mail: lcole@sekls.org; *Pub Serv,* Melissa Frantz; E-mail: mfrantz@sekls.org; Staff 3 (MLS 1, Non-MLS 2)
Founded 1884. Pop 5,312; Circ 64,321
Jan 2019-Dec 2019 Income $332,329, State $1,525, City $224,733, Other $106,071. Mats Exp $23,658, Books $13,138, Per/Ser (Incl. Access Fees) $4,077, AV Mat $5,643, Electronic Ref Mat (Incl. Access Fees) $800. Sal $170,995
Library Holdings: Audiobooks 1,523; CDs 801; DVDs 2,223; Microforms 540; Bk Vols 30,951; Per Subs 61
Special Collections: Kansas History Coll
Subject Interests: Genealogy, State hist
Automation Activity & Vendor Info: (Cataloging) ByWater Solutions; (Circulation) ByWater Solutions; (OPAC) ByWater Solutions
Wireless access
Function: 24/7 Electronic res, 24/7 Online cat, Audiobks on Playaways & MP3, Bks on CD, Children's prog, Computers for patron use, E-Readers, Electronic databases & coll, Equip loans & repairs, Free DVD rentals, Homebound delivery serv, ILL available, Internet access, Magazines, Mail & tel request accepted, Mango lang, Meeting rooms, Microfiche/film & reading machines, Movies, Music CDs, Online cat, Passport agency, Photocopying/Printing, Prog for adults, Prog for children & young adult, Ref serv available, Scanner, Story hour, Study rm, Summer reading prog, Teen prog, Telephone ref, Wheelchair accessible
Open Mon-Thurs 9:30-8, Fri & Sat 9-5
Friends of the Library Group

P SOUTHEAST KANSAS LIBRARY SYSTEM*, 218 E Madison Ave, 66749. SAN 305-9685. Tel: 620-365-5136. Toll Free Tel: 800-279-3219. FAX: 620-365-5137. Web Site: www.sekls.org. *Dir,* Roger L Carswell; E-mail: rcarswell@sekls.org; *Tech Coordr,* Melissa Geist; E-mail: mgeist@sekls.org; *Libr Consult,* Eric Green; *Youth Serv Consult,* Tammie Benham; E-mail: tbenham@sekls.org; *ILL,* Brenda Cash; E-mail: bcash@sekls.org; *Talking Bks,* Melissa Frantz; Fax: mfrantz@sekls.org; *Tech Serv,* Kim Burns; E-mail: kburns@sekls.org; Staff 17 (MLS 4, Non-MLS 13)
Founded 1966
Jan 2019-Dec 2019 Income $1,775,294, State $50,225, Federal $1,600, Other $1,723,469. Mats Exp $1,812,486, Books $46,055, Per/Ser (Incl. Access Fees) $1,426, AV Mat $3,003. Sal $646,168
Library Holdings: Audiobooks 916; DVDs 942; Microforms 2,072; Bk Vols 58,338; Per Subs 17
Special Collections: Kansas Census
Subject Interests: Genealogy
Automation Activity & Vendor Info: (Cataloging) ByWater Solutions; (Circulation) ByWater Solutions; (OPAC) ByWater Solutions
Wireless access
Publications: SEKLS Stacks of News (Newsletter)

Member Libraries: Allen Community College Library; Arma City Library; Bronson Public Library; Caney City Library; Cedar Vale Memorial Library; Chanute Public Library; Cherryvale Public Library; Chetopa City Library; Coffey County Library; Coffeyville Community College; Coffeyville Public Library; Colony City Library; Edna Public Library; Erie City Public Library; Eureka Public Library; Fort Scott Public Library; Galena Public Library; Garnett Public Library; Girard Public Library; Graves Memorial Public Library; Grenola Public Library; Hamilton City Library; Hepler City Library; Howard City Library; Kincaid Community Library; Labette Community College Library; Linn County Library District No 1; Linn County Library District No 2; Linn County Library District No 3; Linn County Library District No 5; Longton Library; Mary Sommerville Mound City Library District 4; McCune Osage Township Library; Moran Public Library; Mound Valley Public Library; Oswego Public Library; Pittsburg Public Library; Prescott City Public Library; Savonburg Public Library; Sedan Public Library; Thayer Friday Reading Club City Library; Toronto Public Library; W A Rankin Memorial Library; Weir Public Library; Yates Center Public Library

JAMESTOWN

P JAMESTOWN CITY LIBRARY*, 311 D Walnut St, 66948. (Mail add: PO Box 287, 66948-0287), SAN 305-9693. Tel: 785-439-6258. E-mail: jameslib@nckcn.com. Web Site: www.jamestowncitylibrary.com. *Librn,* Carol J Glotzbach; Staff 1 (MLS 1)
Founded 1898. Pop 325; Circ 6,928
Library Holdings: Bk Vols 8,100; Per Subs 22; Spec Interest Per Sub 10
Special Collections: Children Around the World Coll
Wireless access
Mem of Central Kansas Library System
Open Mon & Wed 4-6, Thurs 2:30-4:30, Sat 11-3

JENNINGS

P JENNINGS CITY LIBRARY*, 133 S Kansas Ave, 67643. (Mail add: PO Box 84, 67643-0084), SAN 305-9707. Tel: 785-678-2666. E-mail: jenlibsg@ruraltel.net. Web Site: jennings.nwkls.org. *Librn,* Nikki Rowlison
Pop 194; Circ 3,804
Library Holdings: Bk Vols 4,711; Per Subs 10
Subject Interests: Local hist
Wireless access
Mem of Northwest Kansas Library System
Open Mon, Wed, Fri & Sat 9-11

JETMORE

P JETMORE PUBLIC LIBRARY*, 310 Main St, 67854. SAN 305-9715. Tel: 620-357-8336. E-mail: jetpl@jetpl.info. Web Site: www.jetpl.info. *Exec Dir,* Jacque Sherrill; Staff 1 (MLS 1)
Library Holdings: Bk Titles 15,386; Per Subs 18
Special Collections: Hodgemon County Census & Newspapers, micro; Hodgemon County Genealogy Coll
Automation Activity & Vendor Info: (Acquisitions) Auto-Graphics, Inc; (Cataloging) Auto-Graphics, Inc; (Circulation) Auto-Graphics, Inc; (ILL) Auto-Graphics, Inc
Wireless access
Mem of Southwest Kansas Library System
Open Mon & Tues 9-1 & 2-7, Wed 2-7, Thurs 9-4
Friends of the Library Group

JEWELL

P JEWELL PUBLIC LIBRARY, 216 Delaware St, 66949. (Mail add: PO Box 283, 66949-0283), SAN 305-9723. Tel: 785-428-3630. FAX: 785-428-3630. E-mail: jewellpl@nckcn.com. *Head Librn,* Marsha Erikson
Founded 1926. Pop 478; Circ 5,049
Library Holdings: AV Mats 80; Bks-By-Mail 5,000; Large Print Bks 40; Bk Vols 5,060; Per Subs 15
Special Collections: Quilting Coll
Wireless access
Mem of Central Kansas Library System
Open Mon, Wed & Thurs 1-6, Tues 2-7

JOHNSON

P STANTON COUNTY PUBLIC LIBRARY, 103 E Sherman, 67855. (Mail add: PO Box 480, 67855-0480), SAN 305-9731. Tel: 620-492-2302. FAX: 620-492-2203. E-mail: library@stantoncountylib.info. Web Site: www.stantoncountylib.info. *Dir,* Colleen Kilbreath; E-mail: director@stantoncountylib.info; *Ch,* Position Currently Open
Pop 2,339; Circ 36,568
Library Holdings: AV Mats 2,000; Large Print Bks 35; Bk Vols 3,900; Per Subs 70; Talking Bks 1,700
Automation Activity & Vendor Info: (Cataloging) Follett Software; (Circulation) Follett Software
Wireless access
Publications: Library Journal (Weekly)
Mem of Southwest Kansas Library System
Open Mon-Fri 8:30-6, Sat 10-2

JUNCTION CITY

P DOROTHY BRAMLAGE PUBLIC LIBRARY*, 230 W Seventh St, 66441-3097. SAN 305-974X. Tel: 785-238-4311. FAX: 785-238-7873. E-mail: jclibrary@jclib.org. Web Site: www.jclib.org. *Dir,* Susan Moyer; E-mail: susanm@jclib.org; *Asst Dir,* Donna Porter; E-mail: donnap@jclib.org; *Head, Children's Servx, Head, Youth Serv,* Kelly Liptak; E-mail: kellyl@jclib.org
Founded 1907. Pop 31,099; Circ 139,000
Library Holdings: Bk Vols 75,000
Automation Activity & Vendor Info: (Acquisitions) Baker & Taylor; (Cataloging) Auto-Graphics, Inc; (Circulation) Auto-Graphics, Inc
Wireless access
Publications: Community Information Directory (Annual); LIFE Directory (Periodical)
Mem of North Central Kansas Libraries System
Open Mon-Thurs 9-9, Fri 9-6, Sat 9-5, Sun 1-5
Friends of the Library Group

KANOPOLIS

P KANOPOLIS PUBLIC LIBRARY*, 221 N Kansas, 67454. (Mail add: PO Box 205, 67454), SAN 376-5652. Tel: 785-472-3053. E-mail: kanopolis@eaglecom.net. *Librn,* Heather Galvan
Pop 525
Library Holdings: Bk Vols 6,100; Per Subs 25
Wireless access
Mem of Central Kansas Library System
Open Mon, Tues, Thurs & Fri 2-5, Wed 10-2

KANSAS CITY

C DONNELLY COLLEGE*, Trant Memorial Library, 608 N 18th St, 66102. SAN 305-9774. Tel: 913-621-8735. Administration Tel: 913-621-8791. FAX: 913-621-8719. Web Site: www.donnelly.edu/students/library. *Acad Librn,* Tyler Johnson; E-mail: tjohnson@donnelly.edu; Staff 6 (MLS 1, Non-MLS 5)
Founded 1949. Enrl 500; Fac 80; Highest Degree: Bachelor
Library Holdings: Bk Vols 38,000; Per Subs 75
Special Collections: African-American Heritage (Roe Coll)
Subject Interests: Biblical studies, Women's studies
Automation Activity & Vendor Info: (OPAC) SirsiDynix
Wireless access
Function: Ref serv available
Mem of Northeast Kansas Library System
Open Mon-Fri 8:30-12 & 1-4:30

J KANSAS CITY KANSAS COMMUNITY COLLEGE LIBRARY*, 7250 State Ave, 66112. SAN 305-9782. Tel: 913-288-7650. FAX: 913-288-7606. Web Site: kckcc.libguides.com/Learning_Commons/LearningServices. *Ref Librn,* Barbara Stransky; E-mail: bstransky@kckcc.edu; *Ref/Media Serv Librn,* Penny Mahon; E-mail: pmahon@kckcc.edu; Staff 11 (MLS 5, Non-MLS 6)
Founded 1923. Enrl 7,000; Fac 3; Highest Degree: Associate
Jul 2012-Jun 2013. Mats Exp $208,000, Books $30,000, Per/Ser (Incl. Access Fees) $25,000, Micro $1,000, AV Mat $12,000, Electronic Ref Mat (Incl. Access Fees) $140,000
Library Holdings: AV Mats 12,000; CDs 2,500; DVDs 2,500; e-books 49,000; Bk Titles 60,000; Bk Vols 75,000; Per Subs 100; Videos 2,500
Special Collections: US Document Depository
Subject Interests: Educ, Mortuary sci, Nursing
Automation Activity & Vendor Info: (Acquisitions) EOS International; (Cataloging) EOS International; (Circulation) EOS International; (Course Reserve) EOS International; (ILL) EOS International; (Media Booking) EOS International; (OPAC) EOS International; (Serials) EOS International
Wireless access
Mem of Northeast Kansas Library System
Partic in Kansas City Library Service Program; OCLC Online Computer Library Center, Inc
Special Services for the Deaf - Assistive tech; Closed caption videos
Special Services for the Blind - Assistive/Adapted tech devices, equip & products
Open Mon-Thurs 7:30am-9pm, Fri 7:30-4:30, Sat 9-3:30 (Winter); Mon-Thurs 7:30-2 (Summer)
Restriction: Open to pub for ref & circ; with some limitations

P KANSAS CITY, KANSAS PUBLIC LIBRARY*, 625 Minnesota Ave, 66101. SAN 342-0515. Tel: 913-295-8250, Ext 1. FAX: 913-279-2033. Web Site: www.kckpl.org. *Libr Dir,* Carol Levers; Tel: 913-295-8250, Ext 6420, E-mail: clevers@kckpl.org; *Asst Libr Dir,* Rochelle McCaully; Tel: 913-295-8250, Ext 6020, E-mail: rmccaully@kckpl.org; *Human Res Mgr,* Tammie Sharp; Tel: 913-295-8250, Ext 6400, E-mail: tsharp@kckpl.org;

Hed, Bkmobile Dept, Linda Bowman; Tel: 913-295-8250, Ext 6500, E-mail: lbowman@kckpl.org; Staff 130 (MLS 32, Non-MLS 98)
Founded 1892. Pop 150,314; Circ 959,256
Library Holdings: AV Mats 56,955; Electronic Media & Resources 2,198; Bk Vols 487,863; Per Subs 980
Special Collections: Fine Arts; Spanish Language; Wyandot Indians (Connelley Coll), bks & ms. State Document Depository
Subject Interests: Kansas
Automation Activity & Vendor Info: (Acquisitions) SirsiDynix
Wireless access
Function: Photocopying/Printing, Ref serv available
Publications: Advice from the Experts; Divulgacion; Happy Kids; Health Notes; New Ideas for Non Profits; Real Money; Taking Stock; The Fiction Connection
Mem of Northeast Kansas Library System
Partic in Mid-America Library Alliance; OCLC Online Computer Library Center, Inc
Open Mon-Thurs 8:30-8:30, Fri & Sat 8:30-5, Sun 1-5
Friends of the Library Group
Branches: 4
MR & MRS F L SCHLAGLE LIBRARY, 4051 West Dr, 66109. Tel: 913-295-8250, Ext 2. *Br Mgr,* Jessica Lawrenz; E-mail: jlawrenz@kckpl.org
Friends of the Library Group
SOUTH BRANCH, 3104 Strong Ave, 66106, SAN 342-054X. Tel: 913-295-8250, Ext 3. FAX: 913-722-7402. *Br Mgr,* Darla Brown; E-mail: dbrown@kckpl.org; Staff 13 (MLS 2, Non-MLS 11)
Library Holdings: AV Mats 9,468; Bk Vols 66,671; Per Subs 87
Special Collections: Spanish Language Coll
Open Mon-Thurs 8:30-8:30, Fri & Sat 8:30-5, Sun 1-5
Friends of the Library Group
TURNER COMMUNITY, 831 S 55th St, 66106. Tel: 913-295-8250, Ext 4. *Bus Mgr,* Aaron Froelich; E-mail: afroelich@kckpl.org
WEST WYANDOTTE, 1737 N 82nd St, 66112. Tel: 913-295-8250, Ext 5. *Br Mgr,* Linda Wolford; E-mail: lwolford@kckpl.org
Friends of the Library Group
Bookmobiles: 3

S KANSAS UNIVERSITY MEDICAL CENTER, Clendening History of Medicine Library, 1020-1030 Robinson Bldg, 3901 Rainbow Blvd, 66160-7311. (Mail add: University of Kansas Medical Ctr, MS 1024, 3901 Rainbow Blvd, 66160), SAN 375-4375. Tel: 913-588-7244. FAX: 913-588-7060. E-mail: clendening@kumc.edu. Web Site: clendening.kumc.edu. *Dir,* Dr Christopher Crenner; Tel: 913-588-7098; *Rare Bks,* Dawn McInnis; E-mail: dmcinnis@kumc.edu; Staff 1 (Non-MLS 1)
Founded 1945
Library Holdings: Bk Vols 26,000; Per Subs 40
Special Collections: Anesthesia, Roentgenology, Hemotology & Microscopy Colls; Florence Nightingale & Joseph Lister Letters; Rudolf Virchow Manuscripts; Samuel Crumbine Papers
Subject Interests: Bioethics, Hist of med
Automation Activity & Vendor Info: (Acquisitions) Ex Libris Group; (Cataloging) Ex Libris Group; (Circulation) Ex Libris Group
Wireless access
Open Mon & Wed 9-1, Tues & Thurs 12-4
Restriction: Circ limited, Closed stack
Friends of the Library Group

M PROVIDENCE MEDICAL CENTER LIBRARY*, 8929 Parallel Pkwy, 66112-0430. SAN 342-0604. Tel: 913-596-3990. FAX: 913-596-4098. Web Site: www.providencekc.com. *Librn,* Marin Goodier; E-mail: mgoodier@primehealthcare.com; Staff 1 (Non-MLS 1)
Founded 1964
Library Holdings: Bk Titles 500
Subject Interests: Consumer health, Health sci
Open Mon-Fri 8-4:30

GL UNITED STATES COURTS*, Kansas City, Kansas Branch Library, 624 US Courthouse, 500 State Ave, 66101. Tel: 913-735-2200. *Librn,* Meg Martin; Tel: 913-735-2497, E-mail: meg_martin@ca10.uscourts.gov; *Libr Tech,* Linda A Wassberg; E-mail: linda_wassberg@ca10.uscourts.gov; Staff 2 (MLS 1, Non-MLS 1)
Founded 1994
Library Holdings: Bk Vols 1,000; Per Subs 12
Automation Activity & Vendor Info: (Acquisitions) SirsiDynix; (Cataloging) SirsiDynix; (OPAC) SirsiDynix
Restriction: Not open to pub, Secured area only open to authorized personnel

CM UNIVERSITY OF KANSAS MEDICAL CENTER*, Archie R Dykes Library of Health Sciences, 2100 W 39th Ave, 66160. (Mail add: 3901 Rainbow Blvd, Mail Stop 1050, 66160), SAN 305-9812. Tel: 913-588-7166. Interlibrary Loan Service Tel: 913-588-5073. Administration Tel: 913-588-7300. Toll Free Tel: 800-332-4193. FAX: 913-588-8675. Reference E-mail: dykesref@kumc.edu. Web Site: www.library.kumc.edu. *Dir,* Crystal Cameron-Vedros; E-mail: cvedros@kumc.edu; Staff 17 (MLS 9, Non-MLS 8)
Founded 1906. Enrl 2,560; Highest Degree: Doctorate
Library Holdings: e-journals 12,000; Bk Titles 54,000; Bk Vols 62,476; Per Subs 1,000
Special Collections: History & Philosophy of Medicine (Clendening Coll)
Subject Interests: Health sci
Automation Activity & Vendor Info: (Acquisitions) Ex Libris Group; (Cataloging) Ex Libris Group; (Circulation) Ex Libris Group; (Course Reserve) Blackboard Inc
Wireless access
Function: Computer training, Doc delivery serv, E-Reserves, Electronic databases & coll, Health sci info serv, ILL available, Internet access, Photocopying/Printing
Mem of Northeast Kansas Library System
Partic in Health Sciences Library Network of Kansas City, Inc; Midcontinental Regional Med Libr Program; OCLC Online Computer Library Center, Inc
Open Mon-Thurs 7am-11pm, Fri 7am-10pm, Sat 8am-9pm, Sun 8am-11pm

GL WYANDOTTE COUNTY LAW LIBRARY*, Court House, 710 N Seventh St, Ste 500, 66101-3999. SAN 305-9820. Tel: 913-573-2899. FAX: 913-573-2892. *Librn,* Debbie Dercher
Founded 1925
Library Holdings: Bk Vols 50,000
Wireless access
Open Mon-Fri 8-5

KENSINGTON

P KENSINGTON COMMUNITY-SCHOOL LIBRARY*, 203 S Jackson, 66951. (Mail add: PO Box 188, 66951-0188), SAN 376-5660. Tel: 785-476-2219. FAX: 785-476-2215. E-mail: ktownlibrary@gmail.com. Web Site: www.kensingtonks.net/library. *Dir,* Erica L Barnes; E-mail: ebarnes@usd110.net; Staff 2 (Non-MLS 2)
Library Holdings: Bk Vols 12,000; Per Subs 70
Automation Activity & Vendor Info: (Serials) ByWater Solutions
Wireless access
Mem of Central Kansas Library System
Open Mon 8-8, Tues-Fri 8-4, Sat 9-2; Mon (Summer) 2-8, Tues-Sat 9-2

KINCAID

P KINCAID COMMUNITY LIBRARY*, 500 Fifth Ave, 66039. (Mail add: PO Box 25, 66039-0025). Tel: 620-439-5500. E-mail: kincaidcommunitylibrary@gmail.com. *Librn,* Jennifer Gum-Fowler; Staff 2 (Non-MLS 2)
Founded 2014. Pop 381; Circ 2,251
Wireless access
Function: 24/7 Electronic res, 24/7 Online cat, Bks on CD, Children's prog, Computer training, Computers for patron use, E-Readers, Free DVD rentals, Holiday prog, Home delivery & serv to seniorr ctr & nursing homes, ILL available, Internet access, Mango lang, Movies, Photocopying/Printing, Preschool reading prog, Prog for adults, Prog for children & young adult, Story hour, Summer reading prog, Workshops
Mem of Southeast Kansas Library System
Open Mon & Fri 2pm-6pm, Wed 9-12 & 2-6

KINGMAN

P KINGMAN CARNEGIE PUBLIC LIBRARY, 455 N Main St, 67068-1395. SAN 305-9839. Tel: 620-532-3061. FAX: 620-532-2528. Web Site: www.kingmanlibrary.org. *Libr Dir,* Nichole M Balkenbush; E-mail: nbalkenbush@kingmanlibrary.org; *Youth Serv Librn,* Nelda Slider; E-mail: nslider@kingmanlibrary.org
Founded 1913. Pop 3,200; Circ 56,827
Library Holdings: AV Mats 636; High Interest/Low Vocabulary Bk Vols 162; Large Print Bks 718; Bk Vols 30,235; Per Subs 68; Talking Bks 332
Subject Interests: Local newsp
Automation Activity & Vendor Info: (Acquisitions) Follett Software; (Circulation) Follett Software
Wireless access
Mem of South Central Kansas Library System
Open Mon, Tues & Thurs 10-8, Wed & Fri 10-6, Sat 10-2
Friends of the Library Group

KINSLEY

P KINSLEY PUBLIC LIBRARY*, 208 E Eighth St, 67547-1422. SAN 305-9855. Tel: 620-659-3341. Web Site: www.kinsleylibrary.info. *Dir,* Joan Weaver; E-mail: director@kinsleylibrary.info; *Librn,* Julia Butler; E-mail: ill@kinsleylibrary.info; Staff 2.1 (Non-MLS 2.1)
Founded 1904. Pop 1,200; Circ 19,100

Library Holdings: AV Mats 1,000; Large Print Bks 285; Bk Titles 23,000; Per Subs 70; Talking Bks 300
Special Collections: DAR Magazines 1914-1963; Kinsley Historical Downtown Digital Map on line; Kinsley Newspapers 1878-present, micro; Local Oral Histories. Oral History
Subject Interests: Carnivals, Genealogy, Local hist
Automation Activity & Vendor Info: (Circulation) Auto-Graphics, Inc
Wireless access
Mem of Southwest Kansas Library System
Open Mon & Wed 9-7, Tues, Thurs & Fri 9-11 & 1-5, Sat 1-5
Friends of the Library Group

KIOWA

P KIOWA PUBLIC LIBRARY*, 123 N Seventh St, 67070. SAN 305-9863. Tel: 620-825-4630. FAX: 620-825-4630. E-mail: kiowalb@sctelcom.net. *Dir,* Jamie Johnson
Founded 1950. Pop 1,160; Circ 9,000
Library Holdings: DVDs 100; Large Print Bks 1,500; Bk Vols 15,000; Per Subs 16
Automation Activity & Vendor Info: (Cataloging) Follett Software; (Circulation) Follett Software
Wireless access
Function: Accelerated reader prog, Audio & video playback equip for onsite use, Bks on cassette, Bks on CD, Computers for patron use, Free DVD rentals, Home delivery & serv to seniorr ctr & nursing homes, Homebound delivery serv, ILL available, Photocopying/Printing, Summer reading prog, Tax forms, Wheelchair accessible
Mem of South Central Kansas Library System
Special Services for the Blind - Accessible computers; Bks on cassette; Bks on CD; Cassette playback machines; Copier with enlargement capabilities; Large print bks
Open Mon 7pm-9pm, Tues 2-5 & 7-9, Wed 12-5, Sat 10-1
Friends of the Library Group

KIRWIN

P KIRWIN CITY LIBRARY*, First & Main, 67644. (Mail add: PO Box 445, 67644-0445), SAN 305-9871. Tel: 785-543-6652. FAX: 785-543-6168. E-mail: library@ruraltel.net. Web Site: cityofkirwin.com/kirwin_city_library.htm. *Librn,* Ashley Roth
Pop 267; Circ 5,000
Library Holdings: Bk Vols 7,900; Per Subs 3
Special Collections: Papers Published in Kirwin, 1889-1942
Wireless access
Publications: History of Kirwin, Kansas 1869-1969; The Saga of Fort Kirwin
Mem of Central Kansas Library System
Open Mon-Thurs 9-12 & 1-4

KISMET

P KISMET PUBLIC LIBRARY*, 503 Main St, 67859-9615. (Mail add: PO Box 66, 67859-0066), SAN 326-5536. Tel: 620-563-7357. FAX: 620-563-7143. Web Site: www.kismetlibrary.info. *Dir,* Pam Orth; E-mail: director@kismetlibrary.info
Library Holdings: Bk Vols 7,418; Per Subs 16
Wireless access
Function: AV serv, ILL available
Mem of Southwest Kansas Library System
Open Mon 1-7, Tues & Thurs 1-6, Wed 8-12 & 1-5, Sat 9-1

LA CROSSE

P BARNARD LIBRARY*, 521 Elm, 67548. (Mail add: PO Box 727, 67548-0727), SAN 305-988X. Tel: 785-222-2826. FAX: 785-222-2826. E-mail: blibrary@gbta.net. *Dir,* Bernie Reifschneider
Founded 1926. Pop 1,800
Library Holdings: Bk Titles 17,000; Per Subs 41
Special Collections: Kansas Coll
Automation Activity & Vendor Info: (Cataloging) Follett Software; (Circulation) Follett Software
Wireless access
Mem of Central Kansas Library System
Open Mon, Tues & Fri 11-4:30, Wed 1-6, Thurs 11-7, Sat 10-1

LA CYGNE

P LINN COUNTY LIBRARY DISTRICT NO 2*, 209 N Broadway, 66040. (Mail add: PO Box 127, 66040-0127), SAN 305-9898. Tel: 913-757-2151. FAX: 913-757-2405. E-mail: lacyg1lb@peoplestelecom.net, lacygnelibrary@gmail.com. Web Site: www.lacygnelibrary.org. *Dir,* Christine Waddell; *Asst Librn, Ch Serv, Tech Serv,* Janet Reynolds; *Ch Serv,* LaVeda Riggs; Staff 3 (Non-MLS 3)
Founded 1908. Pop 2,500; Circ 23,266
Library Holdings: Audiobooks 534; Bks on Deafness & Sign Lang 15; CDs 135; DVDs 1,737; High Interest/Low Vocabulary Bk Vols 600; Large Print Bks 3,588; Bk Titles 35,088; Bk Vols 35,250; Per Subs 95; Talking Bks 322; Videos 150
Special Collections: Genealogy; Kansas Books & Authors; LaCygne Journals 1870-2000, microfilm
Automation Activity & Vendor Info: (Cataloging) Follett Software; (Circulation) Follett Software; (ILL) Auto-Graphics, Inc; (OPAC) Follett Software
Wireless access
Function: After school storytime, Audiobks via web, Bk club(s), Bks on CD, Children's prog, Computer training, Computers for patron use, Electronic databases & coll, Free DVD rentals, Genealogy discussion group, Holiday prog, Laminating, Life-long learning prog for all ages, Magazines, Mail & tel request accepted, Mango lang, Microfiche/film & reading machines, Movies, Music CDs, Notary serv, Online cat, Photocopying/Printing, Preschool outreach, Preschool reading prog, Printer for laptops & handheld devices, Prog for adults, Prog for children & young adult, Scanner, Senior computer classes, Spanish lang bks, Story hour, Summer reading prog, Tax forms, Teen prog, VHS videos, Wheelchair accessible
Mem of Southeast Kansas Library System
Open Mon, Tues & Thurs 9-6, Wed 9-4, Fri 9-5, Sat 9-Noon
Friends of the Library Group

LAKIN

P KEARNY COUNTY LIBRARY, 101 E Prairie, 67860. (Mail add: PO Box 773, 67860-0773), SAN 305-9901. Tel: 620-355-6674. FAX: 620-355-6801. E-mail: kearnycolib@yahoo.com. Web Site: kearnycolib.info. *Dir,* Tammy Dickey; *Asst Dir,* Cesilia Enriquez; Staff 4 (MLS 1, Non-MLS 3)
Founded 1956. Pop 4,177; Circ 30,794
Library Holdings: Bk Titles 33,000; Per Subs 69
Special Collections: Foundation Center for Grant Writing; Graphic Novels; Native American Coll
Subject Interests: Kansas
Wireless access
Function: Photocopying/Printing
Publications: Weekly Newspaper
Mem of Southwest Kansas Library System
Open Mon, Wed, Thurs & Fri 9-5, Tues 9-7, Sat 10-1
Friends of the Library Group

LANSING

S KANSAS DEPARTMENT OF CORRECTIONS*, Lansing Correctional Facility Library, 301 E Kansas Ave, 66043. (Mail add: PO Box 2, 66043-0002). Tel: 913-727-3235. Web Site: www.doc.ks.gov/facilities/lcf. *Librn,* John Stiffin
Library Holdings: Bk Vols 20,000; Per Subs 18

P LANSING COMMUNITY LIBRARY, 730 First Terrace, Ste 1, 66043. Tel: 913-727-2929. FAX: 913-727-2969. E-mail: library@lansingks.org. Web Site: www.lansingks.org/library. *Dir,* Terri Wojtalewicz; E-mail: twojtalewicz@lansingks.org
Library Holdings: Bk Titles 32,000
Automation Activity & Vendor Info: (Cataloging) Koha; (Circulation) Koha
Wireless access
Mem of Northeast Kansas Library System
Open Mon-Fri 9-6, Sat 11-3
Friends of the Library Group

LARNED

S FORT LARNED HISTORICAL SOCIETY, INC*, Santa Fe Trail Center Library, 1349 K-156 Hwy, 67550. SAN 305-9928. Tel: 620-285-2054. FAX: 620-285-7491. E-mail: curator@santafetrailcenter.org. Web Site: www.santafetrailcenter.org. *Dir/Curator,* Anna Bassford
Founded 1974
Library Holdings: Bk Titles 3,500; Per Subs 10
Special Collections: Grand Army of the Republic Records (B F Larned Post); Official Records & Correspondence; Pawnee County, Kansas School Records; R R Smith Glass Magic Lantern Slide Coll; War of the Rebellion Coll
Subject Interests: Kansas
Function: Res libr
Restriction: Non-circulating

P JORDAAN MEMORIAL LIBRARY*, 724 Broadway St, 67550-3051. SAN 305-991X. Tel: 620-285-2876. FAX: 620-285-7275. Web Site: www.jordaanlibrary.wordpress.com. *Dir,* Debby Gore; E-mail: dgorejordaanlibrary@gmail.com; Staff 4.5 (Non-MLS 4.5)
Founded 1915. Pop 5,000; Circ 30,000

Library Holdings: Large Print Bks 3,000; Bk Vols 39,000; Per Subs 107; Talking Bks 465
Subject Interests: Hist, Kansas
Automation Activity & Vendor Info: (Cataloging) Follett Software
Mem of Central Kansas Library System
Open Mon-Fri 9-6, Sat 10-4

S KANSAS DEPARTMENT OF CORRECTIONS*, Larned Correctional Mental Health Facility Library, 1318 KS Hwy 264, 67550. Tel: 620-285-6249. FAX: 620-285-8070. *Library Contact,* Ms J Herman
Library Holdings: Bk Vols 2,000; Per Subs 52; Talking Bks 30
Restriction: Not open to pub

LARNED STATE HOSPITAL

M J T NARAMORE MEMORIAL LIBRARY*, 1301 KS Hwy 264, 67550-9365, SAN 342-0728. Tel: 620-285-4303. FAX: 620-285-4325.
Founded 1953
Library Holdings: Bk Vols 1,500; Per Subs 30
Special Collections: Dr Homer Davis Coll; J T Naramore Coll
Open Mon-Fri 8-5

M PATIENTS' LIBRARY*, 1301 KS Hwy 264, 67550-9365, SAN 342-0752. Tel: 620-285-4303. FAX: 620-285-4325.
Founded 1948
Library Holdings: Bk Vols 3,000; Per Subs 15
Subject Interests: Local hist
Special Services for the Deaf - Videos & decoder
Special Services for the Blind - Braille bks; Large print bks & talking machines
Open Mon-Fri 8-5

S US NATIONAL PARK SERVICE*, Fort Larned National Historic Site Library, 1767 KS Hwy 156, 67550. SAN 370-3150. Tel: 620-285-6911. FAX: 620-285-3571. E-mail: fols_internet@nps.gov. Web Site: www.nps.gov/fols. *Librn,* Celeste Dixon
Library Holdings: Bk Vols 1,600; Per Subs 10
Special Collections: Fort Larned Documents 1859-1878; Microfilm Coll
Function: Res libr
Open Mon-Sun 8:30-4:30

LAWRENCE

C HASKELL INDIAN NATIONS UNIVERSITY, Tommaney Library, 155 Indian Ave, 66046-4800. SAN 305-9936. Tel: 785-749-8470. FAX: 785-749-8473. Web Site: haskell.edu/library/library, haskell.libguides.com/library. *Librn,* Carrie Cornelius; Tel: 785-749-8470, Ext 211, E-mail: ccornelius@haskell.edu; *Libr Tech,* Doris Watts; E-mail: dwatts@haskell.edu; Staff 5 (MLS 1, Non-MLS 4)
Founded 1884. Enrl 900; Fac 34; Highest Degree: Bachelor
Library Holdings: DVDs 250; e-books 300,000; Bk Vols 66,000; Per Subs 250
Special Collections: Indians of North America Coll
Subject Interests: Indians
Automation Activity & Vendor Info: (Acquisitions) SirsiDynix; (Cataloging) OCLC CatExpress; (Circulation) SirsiDynix; (ILL) SirsiDynix; (OPAC) SirsiDynix
Wireless access
Function: ILL available
Publications: American Indian Periodicals & Tribal Newspapers
Mem of Northeast Kansas Library System
Partic in Kans City Pub Libr Consortium
Open Mon-Thurs 8-8, Fri 8-5, Sun 11-8
Restriction: Staff & prof res, Students only, Teacher & adminr only

G KANSAS GEOLOGICAL SURVEY LIBRARY, Core Library, 1930 Constant Ave, 66047-3726. SAN 324-0096. Tel: 785-864-4909. FAX: 785-864-5317. Web Site: www.kgs.ku.edu. *Librn,* Nikki Potter; Tel: 785-864-2098, E-mail: npotter@kgs.ku.edu
Founded 1973
Library Holdings: Bk Titles 17,000; Per Subs 55
Subject Interests: Energy, Geol, Kansas, Natural res, Water res
Publications: Bibliography of Kansas Geology; Kansas State Geological Survey Open-file Reports
Open Mon-Fri 8-5

P LAWRENCE PUBLIC LIBRARY, 707 Vermont St, 66044-2371. SAN 305-9952. Tel: 785-843-3833. FAX: 785-843-3368. E-mail: custserv@lplks.org. Web Site: www.lplks.org. *Exec Dir,* Brad Allen; Tel: 785-843-3833, Ext 102, E-mail: brad@lawrence.lib.ks.us; *Community Partnerships, Dir of Develop,* Kathleen Morgan; Tel: 785-843-3833, Ext 131, E-mail: kmorgan@lawrence.lib.ks.us; *Fac Mgr,* Jon Ratzlaff; Tel: 785-843-3833, Ext 135, E-mail: jratzlaff@lawrence.lib.ks.us; *Coll, Tech Mgr,* Tricia Karlin; Tel: 785-843-3833, Ext 109, E-mail: tkarlin@lawrence.lib.ks.us; *Accounts Coord,* Jeffrey Bergeron; Tel: 785-843-3833, Ext 145, E-mail: jbergeron@lawrence.lib.ks.us; *Diversity & Inclusion Coord,* Ms Frankie Haynes; Tel: 785-843-3833 Ext 125, E-mail: fhaynes@lawrence.lib.ks.us; *Info Serv Coordr,* Melissa Fisher Isaacs; Tel: 785-843-3833, Ext 113, E-mail: mfisherisaacs@lawrence.lib.ks.us; *Coordr, Info Tech,* Aaron Brumley; Tel: 785-843-3833, Ext 106, E-mail: abrumley@lawrence.lib.ks.us; *Mkt Coordr,* Heather Kearns; Tel: 785-843-3833, Ext 123, E-mail: hkearns@lawrence.lib.ks.us; *Outreach & Events Coord,* Kristin Soper; Tel: 785-843-3833, Ext 122, E-mail: ksoper@lawrence.lib.ks.us; *Public Technology Coord,* Jim Barnes; Tel: 785-843-3833 Ext 151, E-mail: jbarnes@lawrence.lib.ks.us; *Reader's Serv Coordr,* Polli Kenn; Tel: 785-843-3833, Ext 132, E-mail: pkenn@lawrence.lib.ks.us; *Youth Serv Coordr,* Karen Allen; Tel: 785-843-3833, Ext 121, E-mail: kallen@lawrence.lib.ks.us; Staff 85 (MLS 20, Non-MLS 65)
Founded 1904. Pop 100,000; Circ 1,300,000
Jan 2020-Dec 2020 Income $5,045,720, State $28,992, City $4,782,000, Other $234,727. Mats Exp $711,300. Sal $2,700,000
Library Holdings: AV Mats 45,000; Bk Vols 167,000; Per Subs 200
Special Collections: Osma Local History Coll
Automation Activity & Vendor Info: (Acquisitions) SirsiDynix; (Cataloging) SirsiDynix; (Circulation) SirsiDynix; (Discovery) BiblioCommons; (ILL) OCLC; (OPAC) BiblioCommons; (Serials) SirsiDynix
Wireless access
Function: 24/7 Electronic res, 24/7 Online cat, Activity rm, Adult bk club, Archival coll, Art exhibits, Art programs, Audiobks via web, AV serv, Bi-weekly Writer's Group, Bk club(s), Bk reviews (Group), Bks on CD, Children's prog, Computer training, Computers for patron use, E-Readers, Electronic databases & coll, Free DVD rentals, Home delivery & serv to seniorr ctr & nursing homes, Homebound delivery serv, Homework prog, ILL available, Internet access, Life-long learning prog for all ages, Magazines, Mail & tel request accepted, Mango lang, Meeting rooms, Microfiche/film & reading machines, Movies, Music CDs, Notary serv, Online cat, Online ref, Outreach serv, OverDrive digital audio bks, Photocopying/Printing, Printer for laptops & handheld devices, Prog for adults, Prog for children & young adult, Ref & res, Ref serv available, Res assist avail, Scanner, Senior computer classes, Senior outreach, Serves people with intellectual disabilities, Spanish lang bks, Spoken cassettes & CDs, Spoken cassettes & DVDs, STEM programs, Story hour, Study rm, Summer & winter reading prog, Summer reading prog, Tax forms, Teen prog, Telephone ref, Visual arts prog, Wheelchair accessible, Winter reading prog, Workshops, Writing prog
Mem of Northeast Kansas Library System
Open Mon-Thurs 10-8, Fri-Sun 10-6
Friends of the Library Group

P NORTHEAST KANSAS LIBRARY SYSTEM*, 4317 W Sixth St, 66049. SAN 306-1302. Tel: 785-838-4090. Toll Free Tel: 888-296-6963 (KS only). FAX: 785-838-3989. Web Site: www.nekls.org. *Syst Dir,* Laura A DeBaun; E-mail: ldebaun@nekls.org; *Asst Dir, Libr Develop Consult,* Michael McDonald; E-mail: mmcdonald@nekls.org; *Serv Consult,* Robin Hastings; E-mail: rhastings@nekls.org; *Youth & Continuing Ed Consultant,* Anna Foote; E-mail: afoote@nekls.org; Staff 10 (MLS 5, Non-MLS 5)
Founded 1966
Subject Interests: Libr sci, Tech
Automation Activity & Vendor Info: (Cataloging) ByWater Solutions; (Circulation) ByWater Solutions; (ILL) ByWater Solutions; (OPAC) ByWater Solutions
Wireless access
Publications: Directory; Librarians Report
Member Libraries: Atchison Public Library; Baker University; Baldwin City Library; Barnes Reading Room; Basehor Community Library District 2; Beck Bookman Library; Benedictine College Library; Bern Community Library; Bonner Springs City Library; Burlingame Community Library; Carbondale City Library; Centralia Community Library; Corning City Library; Delaware Township Library; Donnelly College; Effingham Community Library; Eudora Public Library; Haskell Indian Nations University; Highland Community College Library; Horton Public Library; Johnson County Library; Kansas City Kansas Community College Library; Kansas City, Kansas Public Library; Lansing Community Library; Lawrence Public Library; Leavenworth Public Library; Library District Number One, Doniphan County; Linwood Community Library; Louisburg Public Library; Lyndon Carnegie Library; Mary Cotton Public Library; McLouth Public Library; Meriden-Ozawkie Public Library; MidAmerica Nazarene University; Morrill Public Library; Nortonville Public Library; Olathe Public Library; Osage City Public Library; Osawatomie Public Library; Osawatomie State Hospital; Oskaloosa Public Library; Ottawa Library; Ottawa University; Overbrook Public Library; Paola Free Library; Perry-Lecompton Community Library; Pomona Community Library; Richmond Public Library; Rossville Community Library; Seneca Free Library; Silver Lake Library; Tonganoxie Public Library; Topeka & Shawnee County Public Library; University of Kansas Libraries; University of Kansas Medical Center; University of Saint Mary; Washburn University; Wellsville City Library; Wetmore Public Library; Williamsburg Community Library; Winchester Public Library
Open Mon-Fri 7:30-5

CR UNIVERSITY OF KANSAS, DEPARTMENT OF RELIGIOUS STUDIES*, William J Moore Reading Room, Smith Hall, Rm 109, 1300 Oread Ave, 66045-7615. SAN 305-9944. Tel: 785-864-4341. FAX: 785-864-5205. E-mail: rstudies@ku.edu. *Librn & Archivist,* Patricia Baudino Cecil; E-mail: pbcecil@ku.edu
Founded 1901. Fac 6; Highest Degree: Master
Library Holdings: Bk Titles 12,000; Bk Vols 14,000; Per Subs 46
Subject Interests: Bible studies, Buddhism, Christianity, Hinduism, Islam, Judaism
Wireless access
Restriction: Private libr

C UNIVERSITY OF KANSAS LIBRARIES, Watson Library, 1425 Jayhawk Blvd, 66045-7544. SAN 342-0787. Circulation Tel: 785-864-8983. Reference Tel: 785-864-3347. Web Site: www.lib.ku.edu. *Dean of Libr,* Kevin L Smith; Tel: 785-864-4711, E-mail: klsmith12@ku.edu; *Exec Assoc Dean,* Kent Miller; E-mail: kmiller@ku.edu; *Exec Assoc Dean,* Mary Roach; E-mail: mroach@ku.edu; Staff 67 (MLS 42, Non-MLS 25)
Founded 1866. Enrl 23,958; Highest Degree: Doctorate
Library Holdings: e-journals 157,790
Special Collections: 18th Century English History & Literature Coll; 19th Century Spanish Plays; Anglo-Saxon Types; Children's Books; Chinese Classics; Continental Renaissance Coll; Edmund Curll Coll; English Poetical Miscellanies; French Revolution Coll; Historical Cartography Coll; Irish History & Literature Coll; Joyce Coll; Kansas History Coll; Linnaeus Coll; Modern American Poetry Coll; Modern Extremist Politics Coll; Opera & Jazz Sound Recordings; Rilke Coll; Sir Robert Walpole Coll; Wilcox Coll; Yeats Coll. State Document Depository; UN Document Depository; US Document Depository
Subject Interests: Botany, Colombia, Econ, Ornithology, Sci fict, Travel, Women
Automation Activity & Vendor Info: (Acquisitions) Ex Libris Group; (Cataloging) Ex Libris Group; (Circulation) Ex Libris Group; (OPAC) Ex Libris Group; (Serials) Ex Libris Group
Wireless access
Partic in Association of Research Libraries; Center for Research Libraries; Greater Western Library Alliance; OCLC Online Computer Library Center, Inc; OCLC Research Library Partnership
Open Mon-Thurs 8am-Midnight, Fri 8-6, Sat Noon-5, Sun Noon-Midnight

Departmental Libraries:

ANSCHUTZ LIBRARY, 1301 Hoch Auditoria Dr, 66045-7537. Tel: 785-864-4928. Reference Tel: 785-864-4930. Web Site: lib.ku.edu/locations/anschutz. *Operations Mgr,* Scott Cossel; Tel: 785-864-4599, E-mail: scossel@ku.edu
Open Mon-Thurs 8am-Midnight, Fri 8-8, Sat 10-8 (Sept-May); Mon-Thurs 8am-9pm, Fri 8-5, Sat Noon-5, Sun 10-5 (June-July); Mon-Fri 8-5, Sat 1-5 (Aug)

THOMAS GORTON MUSIC & DANCE LIBRARY, 1530 Naismith Dr, 66045-3102, SAN 342-1058. Tel: 785-864-3496. *Operations Mgr,* Chris Bohling; Tel: 785-864-3397, E-mail: cbohling@ku.edu; *Performing Arts & Humanities Librn,* Sara Outhier; Tel: 785-864-0389, E-mail: southier@ku.edu
Subject Interests: Applied music, Composition, Music educ, Music theory, Music therapy
Open Mon-Thurs 8-8, Fri 8-5, Sat & Sun 12-5

MURPHY ART & ARCHITECTURE LIBRARY, 1301 Mississippi St, 66045-7500, SAN 342-0817. Tel: 785-864-3020. *Librn,* Andi Back; Tel: 785-864-3425, E-mail: aback@ku.edu
Subject Interests: Archit, Art, Art hist, Design, Photog hist
Open Mon-Thurs 8-8, Fri 8-5, Sat & Sun Noon-5

SPAHR ENGINEERING LIBRARY, 1532 W 15th St, 66045-7611, SAN 342-099X. Tel: 785-864-3866. *Librn,* Scott Cossel; Tel: 785-864-4599, E-mail: scossel@ku.edu

SPENCER RESEARCH LIBRARY, 1450 Poplar Lane, 66045-7616, SAN 342-1112. Tel: 785-864-4334. *Head of Libr,* Beth M Whittaker; Tel: 785-864-4275, E-mail: bethwhittaker@ku.edu
Open Mon-Fri 10-4, Sat 9-12:30

CL WHEAT LAW LIBRARY, Green Hall, Rm 200, 1535 W 15th St, 66045-7608, SAN 342-0930. Tel: 785-864-3025. Circulation Tel: 785-864-3026. E-mail: lawret@ku.edu. Web Site: law.ku.edu/library. *Dir,* Christopher Steadham; Tel: 785-864-9242, E-mail: csteadham@ku.edu; *Asst Dir, Instrul Serv Librn,* W Blake Wilson; E-mail: wilsonwb@ku.edu; *Asst Dir, Public & Technical Servs,* Pamela Crawford; E-mail: pcraw4d@ku.edu; *Head, Tech Serv,* Brenna Truhe; E-mail: btruhe@ku.edu; *Circ/Ser Mgr,* Jeff Montgomery; E-mail: jmontgom@ku.edu; *Libr Asst,* Melissa Doebele; E-mail: mdoebele@ku.edu; Staff 13 (MLS 8, Non-MLS 5)
Founded 1878. Highest Degree: Doctorate
Library Holdings: Bk Vols 360,139; Per Subs 3,702
Special Collections: State Document Depository; US Document Depository
Automation Activity & Vendor Info: (Course Reserve) Blackboard Inc; (ILL) OCLC
Partic in Mid-America Law Library Consortium
Mem of Northeast Kansas Library System
Open Mon-Thurs 7:30am-11pm, Fri 7:30-5, Sat 9-5, Sun 10am-11pm
Friends of the Library Group

S UNIVERSITY OF KANSAS LIFE SPAN INSTITUTE*, Research & Training Center on Independent Living Library, 4089 Dole Ctr, 1000 Sunnyside Dr, 66045-7555. SAN 375-1899. Tel: 785-864-4095. FAX: 785-864-5063. TDD: 785-864-0706. E-mail: rtcil@ku.edu. Web Site: www.rtcil.org. *Librn,* Amalia Monroe-Gulick; E-mail: almonroe@ku.edu
Library Holdings: Bk Vols 300; Per Subs 15
Open Mon-Fri 8-5

LEAVENWORTH

P LEAVENWORTH PUBLIC LIBRARY, 417 Spruce St, 66048. SAN 305-9960. Tel: 913-682-5666. FAX: 913-682-1248. E-mail: helpdesk@lvplks.org. Web Site: www.leavenworthpubliclibrary.org. *Libr Dir,* Matthew Nojonen; E-mail: mnojonen@lvplks.org; *Asst Dir,* Valarie Lamoreaux; E-mail: asstdir@lvplks.org; Staff 7 (MLS 4, Non-MLS 3)
Founded 1895. Pop 35,000
Jan 2016-Dec 2016 Income $1,164,490, City $1,026,083, Locally Generated Income $33,150, Other $105,257. Mats Exp $140,800, Books $70,700, Per/Ser (Incl. Access Fees) $7,000, Micro $5,000, AV Mat $57,500, Presv $600. Sal $622,000 (Prof $153,740)
Library Holdings: Audiobooks 2,806; AV Mats 10,644; CDs 2,397; DVDs 5,072; e-books 384; Large Print Bks 3,308; Bk Vols 69,714; Per Subs 115
Special Collections: Oral History; State Document Depository
Subject Interests: Kansas, Local hist
Automation Activity & Vendor Info: (Acquisitions) ByWater Solutions; (Cataloging) ByWater Solutions; (Circulation) ByWater Solutions; (ILL) Auto-Graphics, Inc; (OPAC) ByWater Solutions
Wireless access
Function: Activity rm, Archival coll, Art exhibits, Audiobks via web, AV serv, Bks on cassette, Bks on CD, Children's prog, Computers for patron use, E-Reserves, Electronic databases & coll, Free DVD rentals, ILL available, Internet access, Life-long learning prog for all ages, Magazines, Microfiche/film & reading machines, Movies, Music CDs, Notary serv, Online cat, Online ref, Photocopying/Printing, Preschool reading prog, Prog for adults, Prog for children & young adult, Ref serv available, Scanner, Story hour, Study rm, Summer & winter reading prog, Summer reading prog, Tax forms, Teen prog, Telephone ref, Wheelchair accessible
Publications: Leavenworth Legacy
Mem of Northeast Kansas Library System
Partic in NExpress Consortium
Open Mon-Thurs 9-9, Fri & Sat 9-5, Sun 1-5
Friends of the Library Group

C UNIVERSITY OF SAINT MARY*, De Paul Library, 4100 S Fourth St, 66048. SAN 305-9979. Tel: 913-758-6306. Administration Tel: 913-758-6111. Web Site: www.stmary.edu/depaul-library. *Dir,* Danielle Dion; E-mail: danielle.dion@stmary.edu; *Emerging Tech Librn,* Ashley Creek; Tel: 913-758-4329, E-mail: ashley.creek@stmary.edu; *Res Serv,* Dan Dorris; E-mail: dorrisd@stmary.edu; *Res Serv,* Rebecca Hall; E-mail: rebecca.hall@stmary.edu; Staff 3 (MLS 3)
Founded 1923. Enrl 1,044; Fac 52; Highest Degree: Doctorate
Library Holdings: AV Mats 1,970; e-books 5,000; Bk Titles 94,280; Bk Vols 118,566; Per Subs 205; Talking Bks 15
Special Collections: Abraham Lincoln, bks, clippings, music, pamphlets; Americana (including Ethnic Minorities), bks, doc, letters, micro; Bible, bks, incunabula, ms; Music, orchestral scores; Shakespeare, bks, microfilm
Automation Activity & Vendor Info: (Acquisitions) EOS International; (Cataloging) EOS International; (Circulation) EOS International; (OPAC) EOS International; (Serials) EOS International
Wireless access
Mem of Northeast Kansas Library System
Partic in State Library of Kansas
Open Mon-Thurs 8am-9:30pm, Fri 8-4:30, Sun 5:30-9:30

LEAWOOD

SR SAINT PAUL SCHOOL OF THEOLOGY LIBRARY, East Bldg, Library Rm C134, 13720 Roe Ave, 66224. SAN 309-0639. Tel: 913-253-5036. E-mail: splib@spst.edu. Web Site: www.spst.edu/library. *Libr Coord,* Richard Liantonio; E-mail: richard.liantonio@spst.edu; Staff 1 (MLS 1)
Founded 1958. Fac 14; Highest Degree: Doctorate
Library Holdings: Bk Titles 90,000; Bk Vols 100,000; Per Subs 550; Videos 500
Automation Activity & Vendor Info: (Cataloging) Innovative Interfaces, Inc; (Circulation) Innovative Interfaces, Inc; (Course Reserve) Innovative Interfaces, Inc; (ILL) Innovative Interfaces, Inc; (OPAC) Innovative Interfaces, Inc; (Serials) Innovative Interfaces, Inc
Wireless access
Partic in Amigos Library Services, Inc; MOBIUS; OCLC Online Computer Library Center, Inc
Open Mon-Tues 8am-9pm, Wed-Thurs 8-5

LEBANON

P LEBANON-COMMUNITY LIBRARY, 404½ Main St, 66952. (Mail add: PO Box 67, 66952-0067), SAN 306-0004. Tel: 785-389-5711. E-mail: leblibrary@ruraltel.net. *Librn,* Linda Scott; Staff 1 (Non-MLS 1)
Founded 1901
Special Collections: Kansas; Lebanon
Wireless access
Mem of Central Kansas Library System
Open Mon 4-7, Tues 12-5, Wed 11-6, Thurs 10-3

LENEXA

G US ENVIRONMENTAL PROTECTION AGENCY*, Region 7 Library, 11201 Renner Blvd, 66219. SAN 309-0302. Tel: 913-551-7979. E-mail: r7-library@epa.gov. Web Site: www.epa.gov/libraries/region-7-library-services. *Fed Libr Mgr,* Vincent Shawver; Staff 1 (MLS 1)
Founded 1970
Subject Interests: Ecology, Environ, Environ educ, Pollution control, Toxicology
Function: Computers for patron use, Mail & tel request accepted, Ref serv available, Telephone ref
Restriction: Borrowing requests are handled by ILL, Open to others by appt

LENORA

P LENORA PUBLIC LIBRARY*, 110 N Main St, 67645. (Mail add: PO Box 247, 67645-0247), SAN 306-0020. Tel: 785-567-4432. E-mail: lenoralib@ruraltel.net. Web Site: lenora.nwkls.org. *Libr Dir,* JoAnn Brooks
Founded 1930. Pop 250; Circ 4,041
Library Holdings: Bk Vols 6,500
Automation Activity & Vendor Info: (Cataloging) Gateway; (Circulation) Gateway
Wireless access
Mem of Northwest Kansas Library System
Open Tues & Thurs 11:30-5:30, Sat 10-12
Friends of the Library Group

LEON

P LEON PUBLIC LIBRARY, 711 N West St, 67074. (Mail add: PO Box 57, 67074-0057), SAN 306-0039. Tel: 316-742-3438. E-mail: leonlibrary@sktc.net. Web Site: cityofleon.org/library. *Library Contact,* Barbara Templin
Pop 667; Circ 5,409
Library Holdings: Bk Vols 4,450
Mem of South Central Kansas Library System
Open Sat 9-1

LEONARDVILLE

P LEONARDVILLE CITY LIBRARY*, 117 N Erpelding Ave, 66449. (Mail add: PO Box 141, 66449-0141), SAN 306-0047. Tel: 785-293-5606. E-mail: llibrary@twinvalley.net. Web Site: leonardville.lib.nckls.org. *Dir,* Barbara Lee
Founded 1963. Pop 348; Circ 6,144
Library Holdings: Bk Vols 5,000
Wireless access
Mem of North Central Kansas Libraries System
Open Mon 5-7:30, Tues 12:45-5, Wed 6-7:30, Thurs 2-5:30, Sat 9-11:30

LEOTI

P WICHITA COUNTY PUBLIC LIBRARY, 208 S Fourth St, 67861. (Mail add: PO Box 490, 67861-0490), SAN 306-0055. Tel: 620-375-4322. FAX: 620-375-4322. E-mail: wicolib@gmail.com. Web Site: wichitacounty.readinks.info. *Dir,* Amy Nichol
Founded 1928. Pop 2,900; Circ 18,103
Library Holdings: Bk Titles 19,605; Per Subs 81
Special Collections: Kansas Historical Library; Kansas International Portrait Gallery
Automation Activity & Vendor Info: (Acquisitions) Follett Software; (Cataloging) Follett Software; (Circulation) Follett Software; (OPAC) Follett Software
Wireless access
Mem of Southwest Kansas Library System
Open Mon 9-6:30, Tues 9-5:30, Wed-Fri 10-5:30, Sat 9-Noon

LEWIS

P MEADOWLARK LIBRARY*, 208 Main St, 67552. (Mail add: PO Box 331, 67552-0331), SAN 306-0071. Tel: 620-324-5743. E-mail: meadowlk@gmail.com. Web Site: meadowlark.readinks.info. *Librn,* Mary Cross
Founded 1925. Pop 500; Circ 4,289
Library Holdings: Bk Vols 16,000; Per Subs 23
Wireless access
Mem of Southwest Kansas Library System
Open Tues & Thurs 9-12:30 & 1-5, Sat 9-Noon

LIBERAL

P LIBERAL MEMORIAL LIBRARY, 519 N Kansas, 67901-3345. SAN 306-008X. Tel: 620-626-0180. FAX: 620-626-0182. E-mail: reference@lmlibrary.org. Web Site: www.lmlibrary.org. *Dir,* Royce Kitts; E-mail: director@lmlibrary.org; Staff 13 (MLS 1, Non-MLS 12)
Founded 1904. Pop 25,000; Circ 150,000
Library Holdings: Audiobooks 3,307; CDs 1,250; DVDs 2,510; e-books 295; Bk Titles 68,075; Per Subs 170; Videos 2,451
Special Collections: Map Coll of Southwest Kansas & Oklahoma Panhandle; Seward County Newspapers, 1886-1999 (microfiche)
Subject Interests: Local genealogy
Automation Activity & Vendor Info: (Cataloging) Auto-Graphics, Inc; (Circulation) Auto-Graphics, Inc; (ILL) Auto-Graphics, Inc
Wireless access
Publications: Novel Ideas Newsletter; Weekly Newspaper Articles
Mem of Southwest Kansas Library System
Special Services for the Deaf - Videos & decoder
Special Services for the Blind - Bks on cassette
Open Mon-Thurs 9-8, Fri 9-6, Sat 9-1
Friends of the Library Group

J SEWARD COUNTY COMMUNITY COLLEGE LIBRARY*, 1801 N Kansas, 67901. (Mail add: PO Box 1137, 67905-1137), SAN 306-0098. Tel: 620-417-1160. E-mail: library@sccc.edu. Web Site: www.sccc.edu/web/academic/library. *Libr Tech,* Deanna Martin; Tel: 620-417-1165, E-mail: deanna.martin@sccc.edu
Founded 1967
Library Holdings: Bk Titles 40,000; Per Subs 190
Automation Activity & Vendor Info: (Cataloging) EOS International; (Circulation) EOS International; (OPAC) EOS International
Wireless access
Mem of Southwest Kansas Library System
Open Mon-Thurs 7:45am-10pm, Fri 7:45am-4:45pm, Sun 1-9

LINCOLN

P LINCOLN CARNEGIE LIBRARY*, 203 S Third St, 67455. SAN 306-0101. Tel: 785-524-4034. E-mail: lincolnlibraryks@gmail.com. Web Site: www.lincolncl.blogspot.com. *Ch, Dir,* Mary Anderson
Founded 1913. Pop 1,200; Circ 12,000
Library Holdings: AV Mats 500; Large Print Bks 75; Bk Vols 17,000; Per Subs 25
Special Collections: Lincoln County Papers, 1873-present
Wireless access
Function: Bk club(s), Bks on CD, Children's prog, Computers for patron use, ILL available, Mail & tel request accepted, Online cat, Photocopying/Printing, Prog for children & young adult, Summer reading prog, Tax forms, VHS videos
Mem of Central Kansas Library System
Open Mon-Wed & Fri 10-1 & 2-5, Thurs 10-1 & 2-6, Sat 9-1 (Winter); Mon-Thurs 10-1 & 2-6 (Summer)
Friends of the Library Group

LINDSBORG

C BETHANY COLLEGE*, Wallerstedt Learning Center, 335 E Swensson St, 67456-1896. SAN 306-011X. Tel: 785-227-3380, Ext 8165. Web Site: www.bethanylb.edu/academics/learning-center. *Dir,* Denise Carson; Tel: 785-227-3380, Ext 8342, E-mail: carsond@bethanylb.edu; Staff 2 (MLS 2)
Founded 1907. Enrl 700; Fac 40
Library Holdings: Bk Vols 60,000; Per Subs 5
Automation Activity & Vendor Info: (Cataloging) OCLC Worldshare Management Services; (Circulation) OCLC Worldshare Management Services; (OPAC) OCLC Worldshare Management Services
Wireless access
Mem of South Central Kansas Library System
Partic in Associated Colleges of Central Kansas; LYRASIS
Open Mon-Thurs 7:30am-10pm, Fri 7:30-5, Sun 6pm-10pm

P LINDSBORG COMMUNITY LIBRARY*, 111 S Main St, 67456. SAN 306-0128. Tel: 785-227-2710. E-mail: lindsborgcommunitylibrary@gmail.com. Web Site: www.lindsborglibrary.org. *Dir,* Suzanna Swenson; Staff 3 (Non-MLS 3)
Circ 26,000
Library Holdings: Bk Vols 24,000; Per Subs 35
Special Collections: Civil War Coll; Swedish Heritage Coll
Subject Interests: Kansas, Scandinavia
Automation Activity & Vendor Info: (Acquisitions) Innovative Interfaces, Inc; (Cataloging) Innovative Interfaces, Inc; (Circulation) Innovative

Interfaces, Inc; (OPAC) Innovative Interfaces, Inc; (Serials) Innovative Interfaces, Inc
Wireless access
Function: Bks on cassette, Bks on CD, Children's prog, Computers for patron use, Free DVD rentals, ILL available, Online cat, Photocopying/Printing, Scanner, Serves people with intellectual disabilities, Story hour, Summer reading prog, Tax forms, VHS videos, Wheelchair accessible
Mem of South Central Kansas Library System
Open Mon 10-7, Tues-Fri 10-6, Sat 10-2
Friends of the Library Group

LINWOOD

P LINWOOD COMMUNITY LIBRARY*, 19649 Linwood Rd, 66052. (Mail add: PO Box 80, 66052-0080), SAN 320-9997. Tel: 913-723-3208. FAX: 913-301-3686. E-mail: linwoodlib@linwoodlibrary.org. Web Site: www.linwoodcommunitylibrary.org. *Dir,* Mike Washburn; E-mail: washburnm@linwoodlibrary.org; Staff 2 (Non-MLS 2)
Founded 1977. Pop 2,768; Circ 44,648
Library Holdings: CDs 284; DVDs 664; Bk Titles 15,791; Per Subs 59; Videos 674
Special Collections: Indian Coll; Kansas Coll; Reference Coll
Automation Activity & Vendor Info: (Acquisitions) Follett Software; (Cataloging) Follett Software; (Circulation) Follett Software; (OPAC) Follett Software
Wireless access
Function: Bk club(s), Computer training, Genealogy discussion group, Homework prog, ILL available, Mail & tel request accepted, Photocopying/Printing, Preschool outreach, Prog for adults, Prog for children & young adult, Ref serv available, Summer reading prog, VHS videos, Workshops
Mem of Northeast Kansas Library System
Open Mon-Wed & Fri 9-6:30,Thurs 9-9, Sat 11-3
Friends of the Library Group

LITTLE RIVER

P LITTLE RIVER COMMUNITY LIBRARY*, 125 Main St, 67457. (Mail add: PO Box 98, 67457-0098), SAN 306-0136. Tel: 620-897-6610. E-mail: lrcomlib@lrmutual.com. Web Site: littleriver.scklslibrary.info. *Librn,* Janet Crandall
Founded 1932. Pop 734; Circ 12,171
Library Holdings: Bk Titles 12,381; Per Subs 30
Subject Interests: Kansas
Wireless access
Function: ILL available, Prog for children & young adult, Ref serv available, Summer reading prog
Mem of South Central Kansas Library System
Open Mon, Tues & Fri 9-4, Thurs 9-12 & 1-4
Friends of the Library Group

LOGAN

P LOGAN PUBLIC LIBRARY, 109 W Main St, 67646. (Mail add: PO Box 356, 67646-0356), SAN 306-0144. Tel: 785-689-4333. E-mail: loganlib@ruraltel.net. *Dir & Librn,* Norma Mullen; Staff 1 (Non-MLS 1)
Founded 1900. Pop 538; Circ 3,700
Library Holdings: Bk Vols 5,065; Per Subs 25
Subject Interests: Local hist
Automation Activity & Vendor Info: (Acquisitions) ByWater Solutions; (Cataloging) ByWater Solutions
Wireless access
Function: 24/7 Electronic res, 24/7 Online cat, Accelerated reader prog, Adult bk club, Archival coll, Art exhibits, Audiobks on Playaways & MP3, Audiobks via web, Bk club(s), Bks on CD, CD-ROM, Children's prog, Computers for patron use, Digital talking bks, Electronic databases & coll, Free DVD rentals, Homebound delivery serv, ILL available, Internet access, Magazines, Mail & tel request accepted, Mango lang, Meeting rooms, Microfiche/film & reading machines, Movies, Online cat, Outreach serv, OverDrive digital audio bks, Photocopying/Printing, Preschool outreach, Preschool reading prog, Printer for laptops & handheld devices, Prog for adults, Prog for children & young adult, Scanner, Spanish lang bks, Story hour, Summer & winter reading prog, Summer reading prog, Teen prog, Wheelchair accessible, Winter reading prog, Workshops
Mem of Central Kansas Library System
Special Services for the Blind - Bks on cassette; Bks on CD; Home delivery serv; Large print & cassettes; Talking bks & player equip
Open Mon 6-8, Tues-Thurs 1:30-5:30, Sat 10-Noon

LONG ISLAND

P LONG ISLAND COMMUNITY LIBRARY*, 359 Washington Ave, 67647. (Mail add: PO Box 94, 67647), SAN 306-0152. Tel: 785-854-7474. E-mail: longipat@ruraltel.net. *Librn,* Brittanie Larison
Founded 1921. Pop 187; Circ 1,510
Library Holdings: Bk Titles 3,416; Per Subs 12
Wireless access
Mem of Central Kansas Library System
Open Mon 2-5, Tues & Thurs 3-5, Sat 8:30-11:30

LONGTON

P LONGTON LIBRARY*, 512A Kansas Ave, 67352. (Mail add: PO Box 163, 67352-0163). Tel: 620-642-6012. FAX: 620-642-6012. E-mail: longtonbooks@yahoo.com. *Librn,* Christina Friend
Library Holdings: Audiobooks 75; Bks-By-Mail 1,000; DVDs 50; Large Print Bks 500; Bk Titles 3,000; Per Subs 5; Talking Bks 600; Videos 100
Wireless access
Mem of Southeast Kansas Library System
Special Services for the Blind - Bks available with recordings; Bks on cassette; Bks on CD; Copier with enlargement capabilities; Talking bks; Talking bks & player equip
Open Tues-Fri 2-5
Friends of the Library Group

LOUISBURG

P LOUISBURG PUBLIC LIBRARY, 206 S Broadway, 66053. SAN 306-0179. Tel: 913-837-2217. FAX: 913-837-2218. Web Site: www.louisburglibrary.org. *Libr Dir,* Kiersten Allen; E-mail: kallen@louisburglibrary.org; *Adult Serv,* Holly Mclain; E-mail: hmclain@louisburglibrary.org; *Coll Develop,* Jennifer Keagle; E-mail: jkeagle@louisburglibrary.org; *ILL,* Danielle Folsom; E-mail: dfolsom@louisburglibrary.org; *Youth Serv,* Elizabeth Ellis; E-mail: eellis@louisburglibrary.org; Staff 2 (MLS 1, Non-MLS 1)
Founded 1968. Pop 8,500; Circ 52,000
Library Holdings: Bk Titles 41,614; Per Subs 85
Automation Activity & Vendor Info: (Cataloging) Follett Software; (Circulation) Follett Software; (ILL) Follett Software; (OPAC) Follett Software
Wireless access
Function: ILL available
Mem of Northeast Kansas Library System
Open Mon-Thurs 9-7, Fri 9-5, Sat 9-3, Sun 1-5
Restriction: Pub use on premises
Friends of the Library Group

LUCAS

P LUCAS PUBLIC LIBRARY*, 209 S Main, 67648-9718. (Mail add: PO Box 278, 67648-0278), SAN 306-0187. Tel: 785-525-6305. FAX: 785-525-6305. E-mail: lucas1lb@wtciweb.com. *Librn,* Mary Ann Steinle
Founded 1938. Pop 425; Circ 3,196
Library Holdings: Bk Vols 5,600; Per Subs 23
Mem of Central Kansas Library System
Open Mon & Fri 1:30-5:30, Wed 3-7, Sat 9-Noon

LURAY

P LURAY CITY LIBRARY*, 119 N Main St, 67649. (Mail add: PO Box 292, 67649-0292). Tel: 785-698-2208. E-mail: luraylib@gorhamtel.com. *Librn,* Charlene Walker
Mem of Central Kansas Library System
Open Mon 1-6, Thurs 9:30-12 & 1:3:30

LYNDON

P LYNDON CARNEGIE LIBRARY, 127 E Sixth, 66451. (Mail add: PO Box 563, 66451-0563), SAN 306-0195. Tel: 785-828-4520. FAX: 785-828-4565. E-mail: lyndonlibrary@lyndonlibrary.org. Web Site: www.lyndonlibrary.org. *Libr Dir,* Genea Reynolds; E-mail: greynolds@lyndonlibrary.org; *Asst Librn,* Sharon Culley
Pop 1,536; Circ 2,968
Library Holdings: Bk Vols 17,000; Per Subs 10
Automation Activity & Vendor Info: (Cataloging) SirsiDynix; (Circulation) SirsiDynix
Mem of Northeast Kansas Library System
Open Mon-Thurs 9-1 & 2-6, Sat 9-12
Friends of the Library Group

LYONS

P LYONS PUBLIC LIBRARY*, 201 W Main St, 67554. SAN 306-0209. Tel: 620-257-2961. E-mail: lyonslibr@hotmail.com. Web Site: lyons.scklslibrary.info. *Dir,* Becky McBeth; Staff 1 (MLS 1)
Founded 1908. Pop 3,500; Circ 12,914
Library Holdings: Bk Vols 24,092; Per Subs 75
Special Collections: Kansas Coll, bks by Kansas authors & bks about Kansas; Local Newspaper Coll; Lyons Daily News on Microfilm; Santa Fe Trail, Coronado & Quivira

Automation Activity & Vendor Info: (Cataloging) Follett Software; (Circulation) Follett Software
Wireless access
Mem of South Central Kansas Library System
Open Mon-Thurs (Winter) 10-7, Fri & Sat 10-6; Mon-Sat (Summer) 10-6

MACKSVILLE

P MACKSVILLE CITY LIBRARY*, 333 N Main St, 67557. (Mail add: PO Box 398, 67557-0398), SAN 306-0241. Tel: 620-348-3555. FAX: 620-348-3555. E-mail: macksvillecitylibrary@hotmail.com. Web Site: macksvillelibrary.com. *Libr Dir,* Jody Suiter
Founded 1935. Pop 488
Library Holdings: AV Mats 247; Bk Vols 11,601; Per Subs 15
Wireless access
Mem of South Central Kansas Library System
Open Mon & Wed 1-6, Sat 9-12

MADISON

P MADISON PUBLIC LIBRARY, 110 S First St, 66860. SAN 306-0284. Tel: 620-437-2634. FAX: 620-437-2631. E-mail: madisonks.library@gmail.com. Web Site: madison.mykansaslibrary.org. *Dir,* Christine Inman
Pop 826
Library Holdings: Bk Vols 8,234; Per Subs 47
Subject Interests: Kansas
Wireless access
Open Tues, Wed & Fri 9-4, Thurs 10-5, Sat 9-1

MANHATTAN

C KANSAS STATE UNIVERSITY LIBRARIES*, 1117 Mid-Campus Dr N, 66506. SAN 342-1201. Tel: 785-532-3014. Circulation Tel: 785-532-7423. Interlibrary Loan Service Tel: 785-532-7440. Administration Tel: 784-432-7400. FAX: 785-532-7864. E-mail: libhelp@k-state.edu. Web Site: www.lib.k-state.edu. *Dean of Libr,* Lori A Goetsch; E-mail: lgoetsch@k-state.edu; Staff 83.4 (MLS 35, Non-MLS 48.4)
Founded 1863. Enrl 22,343; Fac 1,574; Highest Degree: Doctorate
Jul 2018-Jun 2019 Income (Main & Associated Libraries) $14,288,123. Mats Exp $5,780,615, Books $148,731, Per/Ser (Incl. Access Fees) $5,486,417, Presv $16,050. Sal $7,085,845 (Prof $5,592,225)
Library Holdings: AV Mats 257,037; e-books 1,795,114; e-journals 122,195; Bk Titles 1,348,050; Bk Vols 2,134,277; Per Subs 174,701
Special Collections: Agriculture & Rural Life Coll; Clementine Paddleford Papers; Consumer Movement Coll; Cookery Coll; Dan D Casement Papers; Donald V R Drenner Papers; Gail Kubik Papers; Grain Science & Milling Coll; Historic Costume & Textiles; History of Higher Education & Land Grant Universities Coll; Kansas & Kansas State University History Coll; Kenneth S Davis Papers; L Frank Baum & The Wizard of Oz Coll; Linnaeana; Louis Zukofsky Papers; Manuscript Cookbooks, Miniature Books & Photographs; McDill "Huck" Boyd Papers; Military History Coll; Repository for Permanent Records of Kansas State University; Richard L D Morse Papers; Robert Graves Coll; Science Fiction Coll; Society for Military History Coll. State Document Depository; US Document Depository
Automation Activity & Vendor Info: (Acquisitions) Ex Libris Group; (Cataloging) Ex Libris Group; (Circulation) Ex Libris Group; (ILL) OCLC; (OPAC) Ex Libris Group; (Serials) Ex Libris Group
Wireless access
Partic in Center for Research Libraries; Greater Western Library Alliance; LYRASIS; OCLC Online Computer Library Center, Inc
Special Services for the Deaf - Assistive tech
Special Services for the Blind - Assistive/Adapted tech devices, equip & products
Friends of the Library Group

Departmental Libraries:

MATHEMATICS & PHYSICS LIBRARY, 105 Cardwell Hall, 66506, SAN 342-1295. Tel: 785-532-6827. FAX: 785-532-6806. Web Site: www.lib.k-state.edu/branches/physics. *Librn,* Barbara Steward; E-mail: drawets@k-state.edu
Subject Interests: Math, Physics
Open Mon-Thurs 8-5 & 7-9, Fri 8-5

CM VETERINARY MEDICAL LIBRARY, Veterinary Medical Complex, 408 Trotter Hall, 66506-5614, SAN 342-1325. Tel: 785-532-6006. FAX: 785-532-2838. E-mail: vetlib@vet.k-state.edu. Web Site: www.vet.ksu.edu/depts/library. *Dir,* Gayle Willard; E-mail: gwillard@vet.k-state.edu
Special Collections: Animal Nutrition; Human-Animal Relationships; Veterinary History
Subject Interests: Animals, behavior of, Health sci, Human relations, Nutrition, Veterinary med
Open Mon-Wed 8am-10pm, Thurs 8am-11pm, Fri 8-5, Sun 1-10

PAUL WEIGEL LIBRARY OF ARCHITECTURE, PLANNING & DESIGN, 323 Seaton Hall, 66506, SAN 342-1236. Tel: 785-532-5968. FAX: 785-532-6722. Web Site: www.lib.k-state.edu/branches/arch. *Libr Asst III,* Maxine Ganske; Tel: 785-532-5978, E-mail: mlganske@k-state.edu
Subject Interests: Archit, Construction, Engr, Landscape archit, Planning, Regional studies
Open Mon-Fri 8-12 & 1-5

C MANHATTAN CHRISTIAN COLLEGE LIBRARY*, 1415 Anderson Ave, 66502-4081. SAN 306-0314. Tel: 785-539-3571, Ext 113. FAX: 785-539-0832. E-mail: mcclib@mccks.edu. Web Site: www.mccks.edu/academics/library. *Dir, Libr Serv,* Caleb May; E-mail: caleb.may@mccks.edu; *Libr Asst,* Brittany Girton; E-mail: brittany.girton@mccks.edu; Staff 2 (MLS 1, Non-MLS 1)
Founded 1927. Enrl 170; Fac 10; Highest Degree: Bachelor
Library Holdings: CDs 142; DVDs 243; e-books 3,899; e-journals 11,467; Bk Titles 37,227; Bk Vols 43,123; Per Subs 80; Videos 450
Special Collections: Restoration Movement, commentaries
Subject Interests: Biblical studies, Counseling, Missions & missionaries, Music, Relig educ, Theol studies
Automation Activity & Vendor Info: (Cataloging) OCLC Connexion; (Circulation) EOS International; (Course Reserve) EOS International; (ILL) OCLC WorldShare Interlibrary Loan; (OPAC) EOS International
Wireless access
Function: Online cat, Telephone ref, VHS videos, Wheelchair accessible
Partic in OCLC Online Computer Library Center, Inc; OCLC-LVIS; Private Academic Libraries Section, Kansas Library Association; State Library of Kansas
Open Mon 7:30am-10pm, Tues-Thurs 7:30am-11pm, Fri 7:30-5, Sun 4-11
Restriction: Authorized patrons, Fee for pub use, In-house use for visitors, Open to pub for ref & circ; with some limitations, Open to students, fac, staff & alumni, Photo ID required for access

P MANHATTAN PUBLIC LIBRARY*, 629 Poyntz Ave, 66502. SAN 306-0322. Tel: 785-776-4741. FAX: 785-776-1545. E-mail: refstaff@manhattan.lib.ks.us. Web Site: www.mhklibrary.org. *Dir,* Linda Knupp; E-mail: lknupp@mhklibrary.org; *Asst Dir,* John Pecoraro; E-mail: jpecoraro@mhklibrary.org; *YA Librn,* Janene Hill; E-mail: jhill@manhattan.lib.ks.us; *Adult Serv Mgr,* Susan Withee; E-mail: swithee@manhattan.lib.ks.us; *Mgr, Ch Serv,* Jennifer Adams; E-mail: jadams@manhattan.lib.ks.us; Staff 22 (MLS 5, Non-MLS 17)
Founded 1904. Pop 44,831; Circ 547,571
Library Holdings: Bk Vols 173,954; Per Subs 325; Talking Bks 5,065
Special Collections: State Document Depository
Automation Activity & Vendor Info: (Acquisitions) SirsiDynix; (Cataloging) SirsiDynix; (Circulation) SirsiDynix; (OPAC) SirsiDynix
Wireless access
Publications: Friends Newsletter
Mem of North Central Kansas Libraries System
Partic in OCLC Online Computer Library Center, Inc
Special Services for the Blind - Assistive/Adapted tech devices, equip & products
Open Mon-Thurs 9-9, Fri 9-8, Sat 9-6, Sun 1-6
Friends of the Library Group

P NORTH CENTRAL KANSAS LIBRARIES SYSTEM*, 629 Poyntz Ave, 66502. SAN 306-0330. Tel: 785-776-4741. Toll Free Tel: 800-432-2796. FAX: 785-776-1545. Web Site: lib.nckls.org. *Dir,* Linda Knupp; Tel: 785-776-4741, Ext 101, E-mail: lknupp@MHKLibrary.org; *Asst Dir,* Carol R Barta; Tel: 785-776-4741, Ext 801, E-mail: cbarta@nckls.org; *Coll & Tech Serv Mgr,* Marcia Allen; E-mail: mallen@nckls.org; Staff 11.8 (MLS 1.3, Non-MLS 10.5)
Founded 1968. Pop 221,265
Library Holdings: Bk Vols 58,140
Automation Activity & Vendor Info: (Acquisitions) Auto-Graphics, Inc; (Cataloging) OCLC Connexion; (Circulation) Auto-Graphics, Inc; (ILL) Auto-Graphics, Inc; (OPAC) Auto-Graphics, Inc
Function: Home delivery & serv to seniorr ctr & nursing homes, ILL available, Prof lending libr, Ref & res, Summer reading prog, Workshops
Publications: North Central Kansas Libraries (Newsletter)
Member Libraries: Abilene Public Library; Americus Township Library; Axtell Public Library; Beattie Public Library; Blue Rapids Public Library; Burnley Memorial Library; Burns Public Library; Chapman Public Library; Clay Center Carnegie Library; Clifton Public Library; Council Grove Public Library; Dorothy Bramlage Public Library; Dwight Library; Elm Creek Township Library; Elmendaro Township Library; Emporia Public Library; Enterprise Public Library; Flint Hills Technical College Library; Florence Public Library; Frankfort City Library; Goessel Public Library; Greenleaf Public Library; Haddam Library; Hanover Public Library; Herington Public Library; Hillsboro Public Library; Hope Community Library; Julie Thomas Memorial Library; Leonardville City Library; Lyon County, Library District One; Manhattan Public Library; Marion City Library; Marysville Public Library; Ogden Public Library; Peabody Township Library; Pottawatomie Wabaunsee Regional Library; Riley City Library; Solomon Public Library; Talmage Public Library; United States Army; Vermillion Public Library; Wakefield Public Library; Wamego

Public Library; Washington Public Library; Waterville Public Library; White City Public Library
Partic in OCLC Online Computer Library Center, Inc
Special Services for the Blind - Assistive/Adapted tech devices, equip & products
Open Mon-Fri 8-5

S RILEY COUNTY HISTORICAL MUSEUM*, Seaton Memorial Library, 2309 Claflin Rd, 66502. SAN 306-0349. Tel: 785-565-6490. FAX: 785-565-6491. Web Site: www.rileycountyks.gov/1259/Historical-Archives-and-Research-Library. *Librn & Archivist,* Linda Glasgow; E-mail: lglasgow@rileycountyks.gov; Staff 1 (Non-MLS 1)
Founded 1916
Library Holdings: Bk Titles 4,500
Special Collections: Local History Coll, photog
Subject Interests: County hist, Frontier & pioneer life, Hist, Kansas
Publications: Architects & Buildings of Manhattan; Digging K-State; Historic Homes, Manhattan; Indices to Riley County Marriage Records 1887-1918; Land Grant Ladies: KSU Presidential Wives; Memory Lane Map 1976; Parades & Pastimes, Play & Picnics (photographs); Riley County Officials & Their Families 1855-1900 (monograph); The Churches of Manhattan & Vicinity; This Land is Our Land: The Public Domain in the Vicinity of Riley County & Manhattan, Kansas; Tracing Traditions (juvenile coloring book)
Open Tues-Fri 8:30-5 by appointment
Restriction: Non-circulating to the pub

S RILEY COUNTY KANSAS GENEALOGICAL SOCIETY LIBRARY, 2005 Claflin Rd, 66502-3415. SAN 326-2421. Tel: 785-565-6495. E-mail: info@rileycgs.com. Web Site: www.rileycgs.com. *Pres,* Barry Michie; *Libr Coord,* Marilyn Kirkelie; Staff 32 (Non-MLS 32)
Founded 1963
Library Holdings: CDs 32; Bk Titles 4,500; Per Subs 450
Special Collections: Genealogy Coll; Local Family History Coll; Pioneers of Riley County, Kansas Family Histories, 1853-1860
Subject Interests: Genealogy
Publications: Kansas Kin Newsletter (Quarterly)
Open Tues & Thurs 10-4, Wed & Sat 1-4
Restriction: Non-circulating

MANKATO

P MANKATO CITY LIBRARY*, 214 N High St, 66956-2006. SAN 306-0357. Tel: 785-378-3885. E-mail: manpl@nckcn.com. *Dir, Librn,* Crystal Fullerton
Founded 1902. Pop 1,205; Circ 15,383
Library Holdings: Bk Vols 13,265; Per Subs 44
Wireless access
Mem of Central Kansas Library System
Open Tues-Fri 10-6, Sat 10-1

MARION

P MARION CITY LIBRARY*, 101 Library St, 66861. SAN 306-0365. Tel: 620-382-2442. E-mail: mlibrary@eaglecom.net. Web Site: marion.lib.nckls.org. *Dir,* Janet Marler
Pop 1,951; Circ 19,276
Library Holdings: Bk Vols 24,000; Per Subs 60
Special Collections: Kansas Coll
Subject Interests: Genealogy
Automation Activity & Vendor Info: (Cataloging) Follett Software; (Circulation) Follett Software; (OPAC) Follett Software
Mem of North Central Kansas Libraries System
Open Mon & Thurs 10-8, Tues, Wed & Fri 10-5, Sat 9-1

MARQUETTE

P MARQUETTE COMMUNITY LIBRARY*, 121 N Washington, 67464-0389. (Mail add: PO Box 389, 67464), SAN 306-0373. Tel: 785-546-2561. E-mail: marqlib@ks-usa.net. Web Site: marquette.scklslibrary.info. *Librn,* Mary Kay Lindh
Founded 1964. Pop 768; Circ 7,622
Library Holdings: CDs 10; DVDs 185; Large Print Bks 110; Bk Vols 7,998; Per Subs 15
Wireless access
Mem of South Central Kansas Library System
Open Tues 2-7, Wed 11-6, Sat 10-1

MARYSVILLE

P MARYSVILLE PUBLIC LIBRARY, 1009 Broadway, 66508. SAN 306-0381. Tel: 785-562-2491. FAX: 785-562-4086. E-mail: maryslb@bluevalley.net. Web Site: marysville.lib.nckls.org. *Libr Dir,* Janice Lyhane; E-mail: jlyhane@bluevalley.net; Staff 3 (MLS 1, Non-MLS 2)
Founded 1935. Pop 3,140; Circ 31,525
Library Holdings: AV Mats 1,929; Bks on Deafness & Sign Lang 33; Large Print Bks 793; Bk Vols 37,138; Per Subs 156
Special Collections: Marshall County Coll
Subject Interests: Kansas
Automation Activity & Vendor Info: (Cataloging) Auto-Graphics, Inc; (Circulation) Auto-Graphics, Inc; (ILL) Auto-Graphics, Inc; (OPAC) Auto-Graphics, Inc
Wireless access
Function: Homebound delivery serv
Mem of North Central Kansas Libraries System
Special Services for the Blind - Magnifiers; Talking bks
Open Mon-Wed & Fri 10-6, Thurs 10-7:30, Sat 10-2

MCCONNELL AFB

A UNITED STATES AIR FORCE, McConnell Air Force Base Library, McConnell AFB, Robert J Dole Community Ctr, Education Ctr Wing, 53476 Wichita St, Bldg 412, 67221. SAN 342-1171. Tel: 316-759-4207. FAX: 316-759-4254. Web Site: mcconnellafblibrary.com. *Dir,* Darla Cooper; E-mail: darla.cooper@us.af.mil; Staff 7 (MLS 1, Non-MLS 6)
Founded 1953
Library Holdings: Audiobooks 2,200; DVDs 3,800; Bk Vols 22,000; Per Subs 5
Special Collections: Chief of Staff Reading List; Kansas Coll; Military Aviation History Coll
Automation Activity & Vendor Info: (Acquisitions) SirsiDynix; (Cataloging) SirsiDynix; (Circulation) SirsiDynix; (OPAC) SirsiDynix; (Serials) SirsiDynix
Wireless access
Function: ILL available
Mem of South Central Kansas Library System
Partic in OCLC Online Computer Library Center, Inc
Open Mon-Thurs 9-5, Fri 9-4

MCCRACKEN

P MCCRACKEN PUBLIC LIBRARY, 303 Main St, 67556. (Mail add: PO Box 125, 67556-0125), SAN 306-0217. Tel: 785-394-2444. FAX: 785-394-2444. E-mail: mccrpul@gbta.net. *Dir,* Krystal Lineberry
Founded 1936. Pop 200; Circ 1,964
Library Holdings: Bk Vols 8,500; Per Subs 25
Special Collections: McCracken Newspapers, 1887-1945 & 1951-1997, micro
Wireless access
Mem of Central Kansas Library System
Open Mon & Thurs 2-6, Wed 12-4

MCCUNE

P MCCUNE OSAGE TOWNSHIP LIBRARY*, 509 Sixth St, 66753. (Mail add: PO Box 73, 66753-0073), SAN 306-0225. Tel: 620-632-4112. E-mail: books@ckt.net. Web Site: mccune.mykansaslibrary.org. *Libr Dir,* Position Currently Open
Pop 423; Circ 2,300
Library Holdings: DVDs 40; Large Print Bks 400; Bk Vols 3,900; Per Subs 12; Talking Bks 40; Videos 600
Special Collections: History/Genealogy Coll
Wireless access
Mem of Southeast Kansas Library System
Open Tues & Thurs 9-6, Sat 9-1

MCDONALD

P MCDONALD PUBLIC LIBRARY*, PO Box 89, 67745-0089. SAN 306-0233. Tel: 785-538-2238. *Librn,* Melissa Dinning
Pop 238; Circ 3,100
Library Holdings: Bk Vols 4,500
Open Tues 12:30-2:30, Sat 10-12

MCLOUTH

P MCLOUTH PUBLIC LIBRARY*, 215 S Union, 66054. (Mail add: PO Box 69, 66054-0069). Tel: 913-796-2225. FAX: 913-796-2230. Web Site: mclouth.mykansaslibrary.org. *Dir,* Carolyn Knotts; E-mail: director@mclouth.lib.ks.us
Library Holdings: Bk Vols 5,000; Per Subs 10
Wireless access
Mem of Northeast Kansas Library System
Open Mon, Tues, Thurs & Fri 11-5, Wed 11-7, Sat 11-2
Friends of the Library Group

MCPHERSON

CR CENTRAL CHRISTIAN COLLEGE OF KANSAS*, Briner Library, 1200 S Main, 67460. (Mail add: PO Box 1403, 67460), SAN 306-025X. Tel: 620-241-0723, Ext 117. FAX: 620-241-6032. Web Site: library.centralchristian.edu. *Libr Dir,* Beverly Kelley; E-mail: bev.kelley@centralchristian.edu; *Assoc Dir,* Lynda Linder; Tel: 620-241-0723, Ext 359, E-mail: Lynda.Linder@centralchristian.edu; Staff 2 (MLS 1, Non-MLS 1)
Founded 1894. Enrl 548; Fac 19; Highest Degree: Master
Jul 2019-Jun 2020. Mats Exp $23,100, Books $200, Per/Ser (Incl. Access Fees) $1,000, Other Print Mats $800, AV Mat $1,000, Electronic Ref Mat (Incl. Access Fees) $20,000, Presv $100. Sal $69,000 (Prof $60,000)
Library Holdings: CDs 688; DVDs 579; e-books 29,691; e-journals 17,480; Electronic Media & Resources 57; Bk Titles 28,078; Per Subs 53
Special Collections: Free Methodist Coll; Japanese Coll
Subject Interests: Bus, Liberal studies, Psychol, Relig, Sports sci
Automation Activity & Vendor Info: (Acquisitions) Auto-Graphics, Inc; (Cataloging) Auto-Graphics, Inc; (Circulation) Auto-Graphics, Inc; (Course Reserve) Auto-Graphics, Inc; (Discovery) Auto-Graphics, Inc; (ILL) Auto-Graphics, Inc; (OPAC) Auto-Graphics, Inc; (Serials) EBSCO Online
Wireless access
Function: 24/7 Electronic res, 24/7 Online cat, Archival coll, Computers for patron use, Distance learning, Electronic databases & coll, For res purposes, Free DVD rentals, ILL available, Internet access, Laminating, Magazines, Mango lang, Music CDs, Online cat, Online ref, Orientations, Outside serv via phone, mail, e-mail & web, Photocopying/Printing, Ref & res, Ref serv available, Res assist avail, Scanner, Spanish lang bks, Study rm, Telephone ref, Wheelchair accessible
Mem of South Central Kansas Library System
Partic in Private Academic Libraries Section, Kansas Library Association
Open Mon-Thurs 8am-11pm, Fri 8-5, Sun 6pm-11pm
Restriction: Open to fac, students & qualified researchers, Open to pub for ref & circ; with some limitations, Open to students, fac, staff & alumni, Pub use on premises

C MCPHERSON COLLEGE*, Miller Library, 1600 E Euclid St, 67460. SAN 306-0268. Tel: 620-242-0487. E-mail: library@mcpherson.edu. Web Site: www.mcpherson.edu/academics/library. *Libr Asst,* Lindsey Loucks; E-mail: loucksl@mcpherson.edu; Staff 1 (MLS 1)
Founded 1887. Enrl 800; Fac 40; Highest Degree: Bachelor
Library Holdings: Bk Vols 95,000; Per Subs 300
Special Collections: Automobile Restoration Special Coll; Church of the Brethren Archives; McPherson College Archives
Automation Activity & Vendor Info: (Cataloging) Book Systems; (Circulation) Book Systems; (Course Reserve) Book Systems; (ILL) OCLC; (OPAC) Book Systems; (Serials) Book Systems
Wireless access
Function: Archival coll, Art exhibits, Audio & video playback equip for onsite use, AV serv, CD-ROM, Electronic databases & coll, Free DVD rentals, ILL available, Internet access, Laminating, Learning ctr, Literacy & newcomer serv, Magazines, Magnifiers for reading, Mango lang, Movies, Music CDs, Online cat, Online ref, Orientations, Outreach serv, Outside serv via phone, mail, e-mail & web, Photocopying/Printing, Ref & res, Ref serv available, Res assist avail, Scanner, Study rm, Telephone ref, VHS videos, Wheelchair accessible, Workshops
Mem of South Central Kansas Library System
Open Mon-Thurs 7:30am-Midnight, Fri 7:30-5, Sun 2-Midnight
Restriction: Open to pub for ref & circ; with some limitations

P MCPHERSON PUBLIC LIBRARY, 214 W Marlin, 67460-4299. SAN 306-0276. Tel: 620-245-2570. E-mail: library@macpl.org. Web Site: www.macpl.org. *Dir,* Steve Read; *Head, Adult Serv,* Jennie Hall; *Coordr, Ch & Youth Serv,* Jennifer McCulley; *Archivist,* Melissa Smith; Staff 13 (MLS 1, Non-MLS 12)
Founded 1902. Pop 13,672; Circ 190,162
Jan 2020-Dec 2020 Income $963,631, State $3,762, City $882,156, Locally Generated Income $31,900, Other $45,813. Mats Exp $83,578, Books $64,927, Per/Ser (Incl. Access Fees) $5,476, AV Mat $4,575, Electronic Ref Mat (Incl. Access Fees) $5,600, Presv $3,000. Sal $492,100
Library Holdings: Audiobooks 2,267; CDs 1,357; DVDs 3,076; Electronic Media & Resources 12; Large Print Bks 2,960; Microforms 593; Bk Vols 87,296; Per Subs 144
Special Collections: Kansas Coll; Local History. Oral History
Subject Interests: Genealogy, Local hist
Automation Activity & Vendor Info: (Acquisitions) Innovative Interfaces, Inc; (Cataloging) Innovative Interfaces, Inc; (Circulation) Innovative Interfaces, Inc; (OPAC) Innovative Interfaces, Inc; (Serials) Innovative Interfaces, Inc
Wireless access
Function: 24/7 Electronic res, 24/7 Online cat, Activity rm, Adult bk club, After school storytime, Archival coll, Art exhibits, Audiobks on Playaways & MP3, Audiobks via web, Bk club(s), Bk reviews (Group), Bks on CD, Children's prog, Computers for patron use, Doc delivery serv, Electronic databases & coll, Free DVD rentals, Homebound delivery serv, ILL available, Internet access, Magazines, Magnifiers for reading, Mail & tel request accepted, Mango lang, Meeting rooms, Microfiche/film & reading machines, Movies, Music CDs, Online cat, Online ref, Outreach serv, Photocopying/Printing, Preschool outreach, Preschool reading prog, Printer for laptops & handheld devices, Prog for adults, Prog for children & young adult, Ref & res, Ref serv available, Scanner, Spoken cassettes & CDs, Story hour, Summer & winter reading prog, Summer reading prog, Tax forms, Teen prog, Telephone ref, Wheelchair accessible, Winter reading prog, Writing prog
Mem of South Central Kansas Library System
Special Services for the Blind - Bks on CD; Closed circuit TV magnifier; Large print bks; Large screen computer & software; Talking bk serv referral
Open Mon-Thurs 9-8, Fri 9-6, Sat 1-5, Sun 2-5

MEADE

P MEADE PUBLIC LIBRARY*, 104 E West Plains, 67864. (Mail add: PO Box 609, 67864-0609), SAN 306-039X. Tel: 620-873-2522. FAX: 620-873-2522. Web Site: www.meadelibrary.info. *Dir,* Audrey Flowers; E-mail: director@meadelibrary.info
Founded 1895. Pop 1,600; Circ 30,000
Library Holdings: Bk Vols 24,000; Per Subs 60
Subject Interests: Antiques, Collectibles, Landscaping, Parenting
Automation Activity & Vendor Info: (Cataloging) Follett Software; (Circulation) Follett Software
Wireless access
Mem of Southwest Kansas Library System
Partic in OCLC Online Computer Library Center, Inc
Open Mon & Thurs 9:30-12 & 1-7, Tues, Wed & Fri 9:30-12 & 1-5, Sat 9:30-1
Friends of the Library Group

MEDICINE LODGE

P LINCOLN LIBRARY*, 201 N Main St, 67104. SAN 306-0403. Tel: 620-886-5746. FAX: 620-886-9985. E-mail: medicinelodgelibrary@gmail.com. Web Site: medicinelodge.scklf.info. *Libr Dir,* April Hernandez
Founded 1898. Pop 3,000; Circ 40,804
Library Holdings: Bk Vols 21,412; Per Subs 52
Special Collections: Indians; Kansas History
Wireless access
Mem of South Central Kansas Library System
Open Mon & Thurs 10-7, Tues, Wed & Fri 10-5:30, Sat 10-4

MERIDEN

P MERIDEN-OZAWKIE PUBLIC LIBRARY*, 7272 K4 Hwy, Ste D, 66512. SAN 306-0411. Tel: 785-484-3393. FAX: 785-484-3222. E-mail: meridencommunitylibrary@gmail.com. Web Site: meriden-ozawkie.org. *Dir,* Jerie Tichenor; E-mail: jtichenor@meriden.lib.ks.us
Founded 1968. Pop 4,492; Circ 15,250
Library Holdings: Bk Vols 14,000; Per Subs 12
Automation Activity & Vendor Info: (Cataloging) Follett Software
Wireless access
Function: 24/7 Electronic res, 24/7 Online cat, Adult bk club, Adult literacy prog, Audiobks on Playaways & MP3, Audiobks via web, Bk club(s), Bks on CD, Children's prog, Computer training, Computers for patron use, Digital talking bks, E-Readers, Electronic databases & coll, Family literacy, Free DVD rentals, Govt ref serv, Holiday prog, Homebound delivery serv, ILL available, Internet access, Literacy & newcomer serv, Magazines, Mango lang, Meeting rooms, Movies, Music CDs, Online cat, Online info literacy tutorials on the web & in blackboard, Online ref, Outreach serv, Outside serv via phone, mail, e-mail & web, OverDrive digital audio bks, Photocopying/Printing, Preschool outreach, Preschool reading prog, Prog for adults, Prog for children & young adult, Ref & res, Ref serv available, Scanner, Story hour, Summer & winter reading prog, Summer reading prog, Tax forms, Teen prog, Telephone ref, Wheelchair accessible
Mem of Northeast Kansas Library System
Open Mon & Thurs 9-6:30, Fri 9-5:30, Sat 9-2
Friends of the Library Group

MINNEAPOLIS

P MINNEAPOLIS PUBLIC LIBRARY*, 519 Delia Ave, 67467. SAN 306-0438. Tel: 785-392-3205. FAX: 785-392-2934. E-mail: mplibrary@nckcn.com. *Dir,* Ronald D Brubaker
Founded 1892. Circ 20,382
Library Holdings: Bk Vols 20,000; Per Subs 50
Automation Activity & Vendor Info: (Cataloging) ByWater Solutions; (Circulation) ByWater Solutions
Wireless access
Mem of Central Kansas Library System

Partic in Metronet; Minitex
Open Mon, Tues & Thurs 10-7, Wed-Fri 10-5, Sat 10-3

MINNEOLA

P MINNEOLA CITY LIBRARY, 112 Main St, 67865. (Mail add: PO Box 95, 67865-0095), SAN 306-0446. Tel: 620-885-4749. FAX: 620-885-4278. E-mail: minlib@minneolalibrary.info. Web Site: www.minneolalibrary.info. *Dir,* Stephanie Swonger
Founded 1930. Pop 700; Circ 10,000
Library Holdings: Bk Vols 14,000; Per Subs 25
Automation Activity & Vendor Info: (Acquisitions) Auto-Graphics, Inc; (Cataloging) Auto-Graphics, Inc; (ILL) Auto-Graphics, Inc; (OPAC) Auto-Graphics, Inc
Wireless access
Mem of Southwest Kansas Library System
Open Mon 9-5, Tues & Fri 10-2, Wed & Thurs 1-6

MOLINE

P MOLINE PUBLIC LIBRARY*, 107 N Main, 67353. (Mail add: PO Box 96, 67353-0096), SAN 306-0462. Tel: 620-647-3310. FAX: 620-647-3310. E-mail: moline_library@yahoo.com. *Librn,* Position Currently Open
Pop 553; Circ 8,128
Library Holdings: Bk Vols 5,000; Per Subs 16
Open Tues 9-Noon, Sat 9-5

MONTEZUMA

P MONTEZUMA TOWNSHIP LIBRARY*, 309 N Aztec, 67867. (Mail add: PO Box 416, 67867-0416), SAN 306-0470. Tel: 620-846-7032. FAX: 620-846-7032. E-mail: library@montelib.info. Web Site: www.montelib.info. *Libr Dir,* Shannon McGregor
Founded 1923. Pop 1,587; Circ 5,835
Library Holdings: Bk Vols 15,587
Automation Activity & Vendor Info: (Cataloging) Auto-Graphics, Inc; (Circulation) Auto-Graphics, Inc
Wireless access
Function: After school storytime, Audio & video playback equip for onsite use, Audiobks via web, Bks on cassette, Bks on CD, CD-ROM, Children's prog, Computer training, Computers for patron use, Distance learning, E-Reserves, Electronic databases & coll, Home delivery & serv to seniorr ctr & nursing homes, Homebound delivery serv, Homework prog, ILL available, Instruction & testing, Internet access, Online cat, Online ref, Outside serv via phone, mail, e-mail & web, OverDrive digital audio bks, Photocopying/Printing, Prog for children & young adult, Ref & res, Ref serv available, Scanner, Story hour, Summer reading prog, VHS videos, Wheelchair accessible
Mem of Southwest Kansas Library System
Open Mon-Wed & Fri 1-5:30, Thurs 9-11 & 1-5:30

MORAN

P MORAN PUBLIC LIBRARY, 308 N Spruce St, 66755. (Mail add: PO Box 186, 66755-0186), SAN 306-0489. Tel: 620-237-4334. E-mail: moranlibrary@yahoo.com. Web Site: moran.mykansaslibrary.org. *Librn,* Cynthia Chalker
Founded 1957. Pop 674; Circ 5,000
Library Holdings: AV Mats 500; Large Print Bks 350; Bk Titles 9,000; Per Subs 15; Talking Bks 75
Mem of Southeast Kansas Library System
Open Tues, Wed & Fri 3:30-5:30, Thurs 5-7

MORGANVILLE

P JULIE THOMAS MEMORIAL LIBRARY*, 108 Main St, 67468. (Mail add: c/o Janet Gaston, PO Box 39, 67468), *Library Contact,* Janet Gaston
Library Holdings: Bk Vols 6,000
Mem of North Central Kansas Libraries System
Open Mon 4-6, Wed 2:30-4:30

MOUND CITY

P MARY SOMMERVILLE MOUND CITY LIBRARY DISTRICT 4*, 630 Main St, 66056. SAN 306-0497. Tel: 913-795-2788. FAX: 913-795-2801. E-mail: marysommervillelibrary@yahoo.com. Web Site: marysommerville.mykansaslibrary.org. *Librn,* Ginny Clark
Pop 874; Circ 10,491
Library Holdings: DVDs 1,000; Bk Vols 14,000; Per Subs 30
Automation Activity & Vendor Info: (Cataloging) Follett Software; (Circulation) Follett Software
Mem of Southeast Kansas Library System
Open Mon-Fri 9-4:30, Sat 9-1

MOUND VALLEY

P MOUND VALLEY PUBLIC LIBRARY*, 411 Hickory, 67354. SAN 306-0500. Tel: 620-328-3282. FAX: 620-328-3341. E-mail: mound_valley_library@hotmail.com. Web Site: moundvalleyks.com/wp/library. *Dir,* Lee Stegall; Tel: 620-328-4158
Founded 1973. Pop 496; Circ 5,293
Library Holdings: Audiobooks 15; DVDs 532; Large Print Bks 200; Bk Vols 5,000; Per Subs 15
Wireless access
Mem of Southeast Kansas Library System
Open Mon-Fri 1-5, Sat 9-12

MOUNDRIDGE

P MOUNDRIDGE PUBLIC LIBRARY*, 220 S Christian, 67107. SAN 306-0519. Tel: 620-345-6355. E-mail: moundridgelib@gmail.com. Web Site: moundridge.scklslibrary.info. *Dir,* Betsy Davis; Staff 2 (MLS 1, Non-MLS 1)
Founded 1967. Pop 1,575; Circ 32,900. Sal $35,000
Library Holdings: Audiobooks 50; DVDs 500; Large Print Bks 50; Bk Vols 20,000; Per Subs 110
Automation Activity & Vendor Info: (Cataloging) Innovative Interfaces, Inc; (Circulation) Innovative Interfaces, Inc; (ILL) Innovative Interfaces, Inc
Wireless access
Mem of South Central Kansas Library System
Open Mon 9-8, Tues-Fri 9-6, Sat 9-12

MOUNT HOPE

P MOUNT HOPE PUBLIC LIBRARY*, 109 S Ohio St, 67108. (Mail add: PO Box 309, 67108-0309), SAN 306-0527. Tel: 316-667-2665. E-mail: mounthopelibrary@yahoo.com. Web Site: mthope.polarislibrary.com. *Dir,* Barbara Nowak
Pop 1,096; Circ 12,668
Library Holdings: Bk Vols 9,000; Per Subs 36
Wireless access
Mem of South Central Kansas Library System
Open Mon-Wed 2-8, Fri & Sat 9-1

MULVANE

P MULVANE PUBLIC LIBRARY, 408 N Second Ave, 67110. SAN 306-0535. Tel: 316-777-1211. FAX: 316-777-1755. Web Site: mulvane.scklslibrary.info. *Libr Dir,* Shanna Smith; E-mail: director@mulvanelibrary.org; Staff 7 (MLS 1, Non-MLS 6)
Pop 6,500; Circ 80,000; Fac 9
Library Holdings: DVDs 3,500; Bk Vols 36,000; Per Subs 71
Automation Activity & Vendor Info: (Acquisitions) Baker & Taylor; (Cataloging) Main Library Systems; (Circulation) Main Library Systems; (OPAC) Main Library Systems
Wireless access
Function: 24/7 Online cat, Activity rm, Adult bk club, After school storytime
Mem of South Central Kansas Library System
Open Mon-Thurs 10-6, Fri 10-5, Sat 10-2
Friends of the Library Group

NATOMA

P NATOMA LIBRARY*, 505 Elm St, 67651. (Mail add: PO Box 174, 67651). Tel: 785-885-4121. *Librn,* Betty Pruter; E-mail: bjp1@ruraltel.net
Mem of Central Kansas Library System
Open Tues & Thurs 10-12 & 4-6, Sat 10-2

NEODESHA

P W A RANKIN MEMORIAL LIBRARY*, 502 Indiana St, 66757. SAN 306-0543. Tel: 620-325-3275. E-mail: neodeshalibrary@hotmail.com. Web Site: neodesha.org/government/departments/library, rankin.mykansaslibrary.org. *Libr Dir,* Mary Meckley; *Asst Dir,* Rita Banta; *Ch Serv,* Kathy Botts
Founded 1912. Pop 2,837; Circ 37,000
Library Holdings: AV Mats 1,455; Large Print Bks 2,000; Bk Titles 19,046; Per Subs 88; Talking Bks 950
Special Collections: Altoona Advocate (Aug 27, 1886-1977); Neodesha Daily Sun (Mar 1891-Oct 27, 1983), micro; Neodesha Derrick (Aug 18, 1994-2004); Neodesha Register (Nov 1883-Dec 29, 1983); Neodesha Sun Register (Jan 1990-Aug 11, 1994)
Wireless access
Mem of Southeast Kansas Library System
Open Mon-Wed 9:30-6:30, Thurs & Fri 9:30-5:30, Sat 9-Noon
Friends of the Library Group

NESS CITY

P NESS CITY PUBLIC LIBRARY*, 113 S Iowa Ave, 67560-1992. SAN 306-0551. Tel: 785-798-3415. FAX: 785-798-2313. Web Site: nesscitylibrary.org. *Dir,* Laurie Petersilie; E-mail: director@nesscitylibrary.org; *Asst Librn, ILL,* Laurie Dinges; Staff 2 (Non-MLS 2)
Founded 1887. Pop 1,476; Circ 26,477
Library Holdings: Audiobooks 683; AV Mats 1,443; DVDs 1,443; Bk Titles 19,246; Per Subs 43
Subject Interests: Genealogy
Automation Activity & Vendor Info: (Circulation) Auto-Graphics, Inc; (OPAC) Auto-Graphics, Inc
Wireless access
Function: 24/7 Online cat, Bks on CD, Children's prog, Computers for patron use, Free DVD rentals, Homebound delivery serv, ILL available, Internet access, Jail serv, Laminating, Magazines, Mail & tel request accepted, Mango lang, Music CDs, Online cat, Online ref, Scanner, Story hour, Summer reading prog, Tax forms
Mem of Southwest Kansas Library System
Special Services for the Blind - Reading & writing aids; Talking bks
Open Tues 10-9, Wed-Fri 10-5:30, Sat 9-12
Restriction: Borrowing requests are handled by ILL

NEWTON

P NEWTON PUBLIC LIBRARY*, 720 N Oak, 67114. SAN 306-056X. Tel: 316-283-2890. FAX: 316-283-2916. E-mail: library@newtonplks.org. Web Site: www.newtonplks.org. *Libr Dir,* Marianne Eichelberger; E-mail: meichelb@newtonplks.org; *Adult Serv,* Daniel Eells; E-mail: deells@newtonplks.org; *Coll Develop,* Stefanie Knopp; E-mail: sknopp@newtonplks.org; *Info Tech,* Carr Nathan; *Spec Serv,* Samuel Jack; E-mail: sjack@newtonplks.org; *Youth Serv,* Amy Bayes; E-mail: abayes@newtonplks.org; *Yout Serv Asst,* Sharon Cepeda; E-mail: scepeda@newtonplks.org; Staff 9 (MLS 3, Non-MLS 6)
Founded 1886. Pop 19,000
Jan 2019-Dec 2019 Income $915,184, State $5,644, City $781,848, County $9,600, Locally Generated Income $42,292, Other $75,800. Mats Exp $142,759. Sal $400,434
Library Holdings: Audiobooks 3,994; DVDs 8,062; e-books 151,751; e-journals 80; Electronic Media & Resources 40,753; Large Print Bks 10,416; Microforms 533; Bk Vols 83,563; Per Subs 105
Special Collections: Digital Library Initiative, local interviews. Oral History
Subject Interests: Genealogy, Kansas, Spanish
Automation Activity & Vendor Info: (Acquisitions) Innovative Interfaces, Inc; (Cataloging) Innovative Interfaces, Inc; (Circulation) Innovative Interfaces, Inc; (ILL) Auto-Graphics, Inc; (OPAC) Innovative Interfaces, Inc; (Serials) Innovative Interfaces, Inc
Wireless access
Function: 24/7 Electronic res, 24/7 Online cat, Adult bk club, Art exhibits, Art programs, Audiobks on Playaways & MP3, Audiobks via web, AV serv, Bilingual assistance for Spanish patrons, Bk club(s), Bks on CD, CD-ROM, Children's prog, Computer training, Computers for patron use, Digital talking bks, Electronic databases & coll, Equip loans & repairs, Free DVD rentals, Genealogy discussion group, Holiday prog, Home delivery & serv to seniorr ctr & nursing homes, Homebound delivery serv, ILL available, Internet access, Laminating, Life-long learning prog for all ages, Magazines, Mail & tel request accepted, Mango lang, Meeting rooms, Microfiche/film & reading machines, Movies, Music CDs, Online cat, Online ref, Outreach serv, Outside serv via phone, mail, e-mail & web, OverDrive digital audio bks, Photocopying/Printing, Preschool outreach, Preschool reading prog, Printer for laptops & handheld devices, Prog for adults, Prog for children & young adult, Ref serv available, Scanner, Senior computer classes, Senior outreach, Serves people with intellectual disabilities, Spanish lang bks, Spoken cassettes & CDs, Spoken cassettes & DVDs, STEM programs, Story hour, Summer & winter reading prog, Summer reading prog, Tax forms, Teen prog, Telephone ref, Visual arts prog, Wheelchair accessible, Workshops
Mem of South Central Kansas Library System
Special Services for the Blind - Aids for in-house use; Bks available with recordings; Bks on CD; Bks on flash-memory cartridges; Digital talking bk; Digital talking bk machines; Extensive large print coll; Home delivery serv; Large print bks; Magnifiers; Micro-computer access & training; Playaways (bks on MP3); Recorded bks; Ref serv; Sound rec; Talking bks
Open Mon-Thurs 9-9, Fri & Sat 9-6
Restriction: ID required to use computers (Ltd hrs), In-house use for visitors

NICKERSON

P NICKERSON PUBLIC LIBRARY*, 23 N Nickerson, 67561. (Mail add: PO Box 368, 67561-0368), SAN 306-0578. Tel: 620-422-3361. Toll Free Tel: 800-234-0529. FAX: 620-422-3361. E-mail: nickpublib@yahoo.com. Web Site: nickerson.scklf.info. *Librn,* Ramona Getz; Tel: 620-259-3714, E-mail: ramionagetz@gmail.com
Founded 1916
Library Holdings: Bk Vols 11,500; Per Subs 25
Wireless access
Mem of South Central Kansas Library System
Open Tues-Thurs 12-6, Fri & Sat 9-3
Friends of the Library Group

NORCATUR

P NORCATUR PUBLIC LIBRARY*, 301 E Ossipee St, 67653. (Mail add: PO Box 84, 67653-0084). Tel: 785-693-3025. E-mail: norcaturlibrary@gmail.com. Web Site: norcatur.nwkls.org. *Librn,* Cathy Anthony
Wireless access
Mem of Northwest Kansas Library System
Open Mon-Fri 9-Noon

NORTH NEWTON

C BETHEL COLLEGE LIBRARY*, 300 E 27th St, 67117-0531. SAN 342-135X. Tel: 316-284-5361. E-mail: library@bethelks.edu. Web Site: www.bethelks.edu/community/library. *Co-Dir, Libr & Dir Tech Serv,* Barbara Thiesen; *Access Serv Librn,* Renae Stucky; *ILL,* Katie Hoody; Staff 3 (MLS 2, Non-MLS 1)
Founded 1891. Enrl 456; Fac 42; Highest Degree: Bachelor
Library Holdings: CDs 1,106; DVDs 559; Music Scores 1,379; Bk Titles 84,125; Bk Vols 102,219; Per Subs 291; Videos 428
Subject Interests: Music, Relig
Automation Activity & Vendor Info: (Acquisitions) Ex Libris Group; (Cataloging) Ex Libris Group; (Circulation) Ex Libris Group; (Course Reserve) Ex Libris Group; (ILL) Ex Libris Group; (Media Booking) Ex Libris Group; (OPAC) Ex Libris Group; (Serials) Ex Libris Group
Mem of South Central Kansas Library System
Partic in Associated Colleges of Central Kansas; OCLC Online Computer Library Center, Inc
Open Mon-Thurs (Winter) 8am-Midnight, Fri 8-5, Sat 1-5, Sun 1-Midnight; Mon-Thurs (Summer) 8-11

Departmental Libraries:

MENNONITE LIBRARY & ARCHIVES, 300 E 27th St, 67117-0531. Tel: 316-284-5304. FAX: 316-284-5843. E-mail: mla@bethelks.edu. Web Site: www.bethelks.edu/mla. *Archivist, Dir,* John Thiesen; *Archivist,* James Lynch; *Cat,* Barbara Thiesen
Founded 1936
Library Holdings: AV Mats 161,534; CDs 224; Bk Titles 27,054; Bk Vols 32,928; Per Subs 280; Videos 171
Special Collections: 17th Century Dutch Art Coll; Cheyenne Indian (Rodolphe Petter Coll), bk, mss & photog; Hopi Indian (H R Voth Coll), bk, mss & photog; Peace (H P Krehbiel Coll), bk & mss; Showalter Oral History Coll (numerous topics, especially World War I conscientious objectors & World War II Civilian Public Service)
Subject Interests: Biblical studies, Dutch (Lang), Genealogy, German (Lang), Hist, Mennonites, Reformation
Publications: Mennonite Life (Quarterly)
Open Mon-Thurs 10-12 & 1-5
Friends of the Library Group

NORTON

P NORTHWEST KANSAS LIBRARY SYSTEM*, Two Washington Sq, 67654-1615. SAN 306-0608. Tel: 785-877-5148. Toll Free Tel: 800-432-2858. FAX: 785-877-5697. E-mail: business@nwkls.org, consultant@nwkls.org. Web Site: www.nwkls.org. *Dir,* George Seamon; E-mail: director@nwkls.org; *Asst Librn,* Heather Frew; E-mail: ill@nwkls.org; *Acq & Cat, Asst Librn, Talking Bks,* Kama Mandl; E-mail: talk@nwkls.org; *Asst Librn,* Jennifer Mapes; E-mail: rotation@nwkls.org; *Bus Mgr,* Alice Evans; *Children's Consult, Sch Libr Consult, Talking Bks Consult,* Mary Boller; E-mail: tbook@nwkls.org; *Tech Consult,* Dave Fisher; Staff 8 (MLS 3, Non-MLS 5)
Founded 1966. Pop 38,364
Library Holdings: AV Mats 847; CDs 400; DVDs 420; Large Print Bks 5,746; Bk Vols 10,028
Special Collections: 6 by 6: Ready to Read Kits; KHC TALK Books Series; YT Kits. State Document Depository
Automation Activity & Vendor Info: (Cataloging) Auto-Graphics, Inc; (Circulation) Auto-Graphics, Inc; (ILL) Auto-Graphics, Inc; (OPAC) Auto-Graphics, Inc
Wireless access
Function: ILL available
Publications: NWKLS Exchange (Newsletter)
Member Libraries: Almena City Library; Atwood Public Library; Bird City Public Library; Colby Community College; Goodland Public Library; Gove City Library; Grainfield City Library; Jay Johnson Public Library; Jennings City Library; Lenora Public Library; Moore Family Library; Norcatur Public Library; Northwest Kansas Heritage Center; Norton Public Library; Oakley Public Library; Oberlin City Library; Pioneer Memorial

Library; Selden Public Library; Sharon Springs Public Library; Sheridan County Library; St Francis Public Library; WaKeeney Public Library
Partic in LYRASIS
Special Services for the Blind - Talking bks
Open Mon-Fri 8-5

P NORTON PUBLIC LIBRARY*, One Washington Sq, 67654. SAN 306-0616. Tel: 785-877-2481. FAX: 785-874-4404. E-mail: nortonpl2@ruraltel.net. Web Site: nortonpubliclibrary.org. *Dir,* Pat Hart; *Ch,* Patty Kleinschmidt; *Ch Serv,* Rosalie McMullen; *ILL,* Judy Fawcett; Staff 3.8 (Non-MLS 3.8)
Founded 1909. Pop 5,500; Circ 64,800
Library Holdings: Bk Vols 78,000; Per Subs 46
Special Collections: Masonic Coll
Function: Art exhibits, Chess club, Children's prog, Computer training, Computers for patron use, Digital talking bks, E-Reserves, Free DVD rentals, Home delivery & serv to seniorr ctr & nursing homes, Homebound delivery serv, ILL available, Internet access, Music CDs, Online cat, Online ref, OverDrive digital audio bks, Photocopying/Printing, Preschool outreach, Prog for children & young adult, Ref serv available, Story hour, Summer reading prog, Tax forms, Telephone ref, VHS videos, Wheelchair accessible
Mem of Northwest Kansas Library System
Partic in SAILS Library Network
Open Mon-Thurs 10-8, Fri 10-6, Sat 1-5
Friends of the Library Group

NORTONVILLE

P NORTONVILLE PUBLIC LIBRARY, 407 Main St, 66060. (Mail add: PO Box 179, 66060-0179), SAN 306-0624. Tel: 913-886-2060. FAX: 913-886-3070. Web Site: www.nortonvillelibrary.org. *Dir,* Greta Funk; E-mail: director@nortonvillelibrary.org; Staff 1 (Non-MLS 1)
Founded 1897. Pop 1,110; Circ 12,127
Jan 2015-Dec 2015 Income $66,946, State $523, Locally Generated Income $35,422. Mats Exp $10,337, Books $6,596, Per/Ser (Incl. Access Fees) $426, AV Mat $3,315
Library Holdings: Audiobooks 159; CDs 129; DVDs 3,315; Electronic Media & Resources 61; Large Print Bks 397; Bk Vols 15,952; Per Subs 38
Wireless access
Function: 24/7 Online cat, Audiobks via web, Bks on CD, Children's prog, Computer training, Computers for patron use, Electronic databases & coll, Free DVD rentals, Holiday prog, Home delivery & serv to seniorr ctr & nursing homes, Homebound delivery serv, ILL available, Internet access, Life-long learning prog for all ages, Magazines, Movies, Music CDs, Online cat, OverDrive digital audio bks, Photocopying/Printing, Preschool reading prog, Prog for adults, Prog for children & young adult, Scanner, Senior computer classes, Summer reading prog, Tax forms, Teen prog, Wheelchair accessible
Mem of Northeast Kansas Library System
Open Tues, Thurs & Fri 9-5, Wed 1-6, Sat 9-Noon

NORWICH

P NORWICH PUBLIC LIBRARY*, 209 South Pkwy, 67188-0397. (Mail add: PO Box 97, 67118-0097). Tel: 620-478-2235. *Librn,* Candace Perkins; E-mail: cperkins@knusd331.com
Founded 1923. Pop 490; Circ 4,674
Library Holdings: Bk Vols 5,422; Per Subs 16
Mem of South Central Kansas Library System
Partic in OCLC Online Computer Library Center, Inc
Open Mon, Tues, Thurs & Fri 8:30-3:30, Wed 8:30-5, Sat 9-1

OAKLEY

P OAKLEY PUBLIC LIBRARY, 700 W Third St, 67748. SAN 306-0640. Tel: 785-671-4776. FAX: 785-671-3868. E-mail: oaklib@st-tel.net. Web Site: ksoakleylibrary.org. *Dir,* Victoria Halbleib; *Asst Dir,* Patricia Keyes; *Ch,* Steve Johnson; Staff 1 (Non-MLS 1)
Founded 1923. Pop 2,029; Circ 38,019
Library Holdings: Bk Vols 17,550; Per Subs 20
Automation Activity & Vendor Info: (Acquisitions) Auto-Graphics, Inc; (Cataloging) Auto-Graphics, Inc; (Circulation) Auto-Graphics, Inc; (ILL) Auto-Graphics, Inc; (Serials) Auto-Graphics, Inc
Wireless access
Mem of Northwest Kansas Library System
Special Services for the Blind - Assistive/Adapted tech devices, equip & products; Audio mat; BiFolkal kits; Bks available with recordings; Bks on cassette; Bks on CD; Cassette playback machines; Cassettes; Copier with enlargement capabilities; Digital talking bk; Extensive large print coll; Home delivery serv; Large print & cassettes; Large print bks & talking machines; Reader equip; Rec & flexible discs; Talking bks & player equip; Videos on blindness & physical disabilties
Open Mon-Thurs 9-6, Fri 9-5, Sat 9-3

OBERLIN

P OBERLIN CITY LIBRARY*, 104 E Oak, 67749-1997. SAN 306-0659. Tel: 785-475-2412. E-mail: olibrary22@gmail.com. Web Site: oberlin.nwkls.org, www.oberlin-kansas.com/2196/Library. *Dir,* Ronda Schroer
Founded 1903. Pop 2,300; Circ 31,000
Library Holdings: Audiobooks 600; DVDs 2,000; Bk Vols 15,000; Per Subs 25
Wireless access
Mem of Northwest Kansas Library System
Open Mon-Thurs 9:30-8, Fri 9:30-5, Sat 10-3
Friends of the Library Group

OGDEN

P OGDEN PUBLIC LIBRARY, 220 Willow St, 66517. (Mail add: PO Box 366, 66517-0366). Tel: 785-537-0351. *Dir,* Lory Bullis; E-mail: lorybullis@gmail.com
Library Holdings: AV Mats 150; Bk Vols 5,000
Wireless access
Mem of North Central Kansas Libraries System
Open Mon-Fri 1-5

OLATHE

GL JOHNSON COUNTY LAW LIBRARY*, Courthouse, Rm 101, 100 N Kansas Ave, 66061. SAN 306-0667. Tel: 913-715-4153, 913-715-4154. FAX: 913-715-4152. E-mail: LAWLib@jocogov.org. Web Site: www.jocogov.org/dept/law-library/home. *Dir,* Thomas Marsh; Staff 4 (MLS 1, Non-MLS 3)
Founded 1952
Library Holdings: AV Mats 100; Bk Titles 2,200; Bk Vols 23,000; Per Subs 50
Automation Activity & Vendor Info: (Cataloging) EOS International; (Circulation) EOS International; (OPAC) EOS International; (Serials) EOS International
Wireless access
Function: Computers for patron use, Doc delivery serv, Notary serv, Online cat, Photocopying/Printing, Ref serv available, Telephone ref
Open Mon-Fri 8-5
Restriction: Circ limited, Non-circulating to the pub, Pub use on premises

C MIDAMERICA NAZARENE UNIVERSITY*, Mabee Library & Learning Resource Center, 2030 E College Way, 66062-1899. SAN 306-0683. Tel: 913-971-3485. FAX: 913-971-3285. E-mail: library@mnu.edu. Web Site: www.mnu.edu/learning-commons/library. *Libr Dir,* Dr Mark Hayse; E-mail: mahayse@mnu.edu; *Asst Libr Dir, Computer Serv Librn, Univ Archivist,* Lon Dagley; Tel: 913-971-3566, E-mail: ledagley@mnu.edu; Staff 5.5 (MLS 3, Non-MLS 2.5)
Founded 1968. Enrl 1,800; Fac 100; Highest Degree: Master
Jul 2014-Jun 2015 Income $600,000. Mats Exp $273,000, Books $5,000, Per/Ser (Incl. Access Fees) $88,000, Electronic Ref Mat (Incl. Access Fees) $180,000. Sal $330,000 (Prof $220,000)
Library Holdings: AV Mats 360,000; CDs 1,200; DVDs 80; Bk Titles 94,000; Per Subs 240
Special Collections: Church of the Nazarene Publications
Automation Activity & Vendor Info: (Acquisitions) Innovative Interfaces, Inc; (Cataloging) Innovative Interfaces, Inc; (Circulation) Innovative Interfaces, Inc; (Course Reserve) Innovative Interfaces, Inc; (ILL) Innovative Interfaces, Inc; (Media Booking) Innovative Interfaces, Inc; (OPAC) Innovative Interfaces, Inc; (Serials) Innovative Interfaces, Inc
Wireless access
Mem of Northeast Kansas Library System
Open Mon-Thurs 7am-Midnight, Fri 7-5, Sat Noon-5, Sun 3pm-Midnight
Restriction: Fee for pub use

P OLATHE PUBLIC LIBRARY*, 201 E Park St, 66061. SAN 306-0691. Tel: 913-971-6850. Interlibrary Loan Service Tel: 913-971-6854. Reference Tel: 913-971-6851. FAX: 913-971-6839. TDD: 913-971-6855. Web Site: www.olathelibrary.org. *Dir,* Emily F Baker; Tel: 913-971-6880, E-mail: ebaker@olatheks.org; *Head, Adult Serv,* Maggie Baker; Tel: 913-971-6849; *Head, Customer Serv, Human Res,* Leslie K Ellsworth; Tel: 913-971-6856, E-mail: lellsworth@olatheks.org; *Ch Serv,* Jennifer Adamson; Tel: 913-971-6869; *Teen Serv,* Angela Parks; Tel: 913-971-6881; Staff 65 (MLS 12, Non-MLS 53)
Founded 1909. Pop 128,000; Circ 1,533,000
Special Collections: Business & Automotive Reference Coll; Kansas Room; Microfilm Coll; Music & Books on CD's Coll
Automation Activity & Vendor Info: (Acquisitions) SirsiDynix; (Cataloging) SirsiDynix; (Circulation) SirsiDynix-WorkFlows; (OPAC) SirsiDynix
Wireless access
Mem of Northeast Kansas Library System
Partic in Mid-America Library Alliance
Special Services for the Deaf - TDD equip

Special Services for the Blind - Computer with voice synthesizer for visually impaired persons; Sec-Tec enlarger; ZoomText magnification & reading software
Open Mon-Thurs 9-8:30, Fri 9-6, Sat 10-5, Sun 1-5
Friends of the Library Group
Branches: 1
INDIAN CREEK, 12990 S Black Bob Rd, 66062. Tel: 913-971-5235. FAX: 913-971-5239. *Br Mgr,* Kathleen O'Leary; Tel: 913-971-5240, E-mail: koleary@olatheks.org; Staff 35 (MLS 4, Non-MLS 31)
Library Holdings: AV Mats 19,702; Bk Vols 91,608
Function: ILL available
Special Services for the Deaf - TDD equip
Special Services for the Blind - Computer with voice synthesizer for visually impaired persons; ZoomText magnification & reading software
Open Mon-Thurs 10-8:30, Fri 10-6, Sat Noon-5, Sun 1-5
Friends of the Library Group

OSAGE CITY

P OSAGE CITY PUBLIC LIBRARY*, 515 Main St, 66523. SAN 306-0705. Tel: 785-528-2620, 785-528-3727. FAX: 785-528-4502. Web Site: www.osagecitylibrary.org. *Libr Dir,* Jeanette Stromgren; E-mail: jstromgren@osagecitylibrary.org; *Libr Asst,* Mavet Cooper; E-mail: mcooper@osagecitylibrary.org; Staff 1 (MLS 1)
Founded 1922. Pop 2,667; Circ 55,359
Library Holdings: Bk Vols 22,691; Per Subs 60
Special Collections: Cake Pan Coll
Automation Activity & Vendor Info: (Cataloging) Koha; (Circulation) Koha; (OPAC) Koha
Wireless access
Function: Activity rm, Adult bk club, Art programs, Audiobks on Playaways & MP3, Bks on CD, Children's prog, Computer training, Computers for patron use, Digital talking bks, Family literacy, Free DVD rentals, Holiday prog, Home delivery & serv to seniorr ctr & nursing homes, Homebound delivery serv, ILL available, Instruction & testing, Magazines, Mail & tel request accepted, Meeting rooms, Microfiche/film & reading machines, Movies, Music CDs, Online cat, Photocopying/Printing, Preschool outreach, Prog for adults, Prog for children & young adult, Ref serv available, Scanner, STEM programs, Story hour, Summer reading prog, Tax forms, Teen prog, Telephone ref, Wheelchair accessible
Mem of Northeast Kansas Library System
Open Mon-Thurs 10-8, Fri 10-5, Sat 10-2
Friends of the Library Group

OSAWATOMIE

P OSAWATOMIE PUBLIC LIBRARY*, 527 Brown Ave, 66064. (Mail add: PO Box 37, 66064), SAN 306-0713. Tel: 913-755-2136. FAX: 913-755-2335. E-mail: osawatomiepubliclibrary@gmail.com, osawlibrary@yahoo.com. Web Site: osawatomieks.org/index.aspx?NID=87, www.osawatomie.org. *Libr Dir,* Elizabeth Trigg
Pop 4,413; Circ 28,292
Library Holdings: Bk Titles 20,221; Per Subs 60
Special Collections: Kansas Coll
Automation Activity & Vendor Info: (Cataloging) Koha; (Circulation) Koha; (ILL) Koha
Wireless access
Mem of Northeast Kansas Library System
Open Mon, Wed & Fri 9-5, Tues & Thurs 11-6:30, Sat 10-2
Friends of the Library Group

OSBORNE

P OSBORNE PUBLIC LIBRARY*, 325 W Main St, 67473-2425. SAN 306-073X. Tel: 785-346-5486. FAX: 785-346-2888. E-mail: osbor1lb@ruraltel.net. *Dir,* Karen Wallace
Founded 1913. Pop 2,120; Circ 34,226
Library Holdings: Bk Titles 22,000; Per Subs 28
Subject Interests: Genealogy, Local hist
Automation Activity & Vendor Info: (ILL) Auto-Graphics, Inc
Wireless access
Function: AV serv, Homebound delivery serv, ILL available, Prog for children & young adult, Summer reading prog, Telephone ref, Wheelchair accessible
Mem of Central Kansas Library System
Partic in Kans Libr Asn
Open Mon & Thurs 10-7, Tues, Wed & Fri 10-5, Sat 10-2

OSKALOOSA

P OSKALOOSA PUBLIC LIBRARY*, 315 Jefferson St, 66066. (Mail add: PO Box 347, 66066-0347), SAN 306-0748. Tel: 785-863-2475. FAX: 785-863-2088. E-mail: staff@oskielibrary.org. Web Site: www.oskielibrary.org. *Libr Dir,* Cheryl Sylvester; E-mail: csylvester@oskielibrary.org
Pop 1,500; Circ 18,000
Subject Interests: Kansas
Automation Activity & Vendor Info: (Cataloging) Koha; (Circulation) Koha
Wireless access
Mem of Northeast Kansas Library System
Open Mon 9-6, Tues-Fri 9-5, Sat 9-1
Friends of the Library Group

OSWEGO

P OSWEGO PUBLIC LIBRARY, 704 Fourth St, 67356. SAN 306-0756. Tel: 620-795-4921. FAX: 620-795-4921. E-mail: library@oswegolibrary.org. Web Site: oswego.mykansaslibrary.org. *Dir & Librn,* Heather Duke
Pop 1,777; Circ 21,000
Library Holdings: Audiobooks 130; CDs 125; DVDs 1,190; Bk Titles 13,000; Per Subs 25; Videos 50
Automation Activity & Vendor Info: (Cataloging) LibLime; (Circulation) LibLime; (ILL) LibLime; (OPAC) LibLime
Wireless access
Mem of Southeast Kansas Library System
Open Tues 1-6, Wed 10-5:30, Thurs & Fri 1-5:30, Sat 9-1
Friends of the Library Group

OTIS

P OTIS COMMUNITY LIBRARY*, 122 S Main St, 67565. (Mail add: PO Box 7, 67565), SAN 306-0764. Tel: 785-387-2287. E-mail: otis1lib@gbta.net. Web Site: otiscommunitylibrary.doodlekit.com. *Librn,* Aimee Kenyon
Pop 410; Circ 5,181
Library Holdings: Bk Vols 6,000; Per Subs 33
Special Collections: Children's Video Coll; Kansas Shelf
Wireless access
Mem of Central Kansas Library System
Open Mon-Wed & Fri 2-6

OTTAWA

P OTTAWA LIBRARY*, 105 S Hickory St, 66067. SAN 306-0772. Tel: 785-242-3080. FAX: 785-242-8789. Reference E-mail: ottawalibraryreference@yahoo.com. Web Site: www.ottawalibrary.org. *Exec Dir,* Terry Chartier; E-mail: terry.chartier@ottawalibrary.org; *Head, Circ, Librn,* Lori Clayton; E-mail: lori.clayton@ottawalibrary.org; *Tech Serv Mgr,* Pam Miller; *Acq, Coordr, Cat,* Heidi Van der Heuvel; *Ch Serv,* Cyndi Brewer; E-mail: cyndi.brewer@ottawalibrary.org; *ILL,* Sheryl Servatius-Brown; Staff 14 (MLS 2, Non-MLS 12)
Founded 1872. Pop 12,000; Circ 119,957
Library Holdings: AV Mats 7,635; Bk Vols 59,378; Per Subs 124
Subject Interests: Genealogy, Local hist
Automation Activity & Vendor Info: (Cataloging) Koha; (Circulation) Koha; (OPAC) Koha
Wireless access
Function: 24/7 Online cat, Adult bk club
Mem of Northeast Kansas Library System
Open Mon-Thurs 9-8, Fri 9-5, Sat 9-1
Friends of the Library Group

CR OTTAWA UNIVERSITY*, Gangwish Library, 1001 S Cedar St, 66067. SAN 306-0780. Tel: 785-248-2538. Interlibrary Loan Service Tel: 785-248-2535. Administration Tel: 785-248-2536. Toll Free Tel: 800-755-5200. FAX: 785-229-1012. E-mail: library@ottawa.edu. Web Site: myottawa.ottawa.edu/ics/Resources/Myers_Library_Online. *Dir, Libr Serv,* Gloria Creed-Dikeogu, PhD; E-mail: gloria.creeddikeogu@ottawa.edu; Staff 3 (MLS 2, Non-MLS 1)
Founded 1865. Enrl 533; Fac 44; Highest Degree: Master
Library Holdings: Audiobooks 50; AV Mats 385; CDs 1,000; DVDs 4,000; e-books 120,000; Microforms 1,123; Music Scores 300; Bk Titles 70,000; Bk Vols 71,193; Per Subs 30; Videos 300
Special Collections: Baptist Church History Coll; Chinese Art & Related Asiatic Studies; J H Kilbuck Coll; Native American Indian Artifact Coll
Automation Activity & Vendor Info: (Cataloging) EOS International; (Circulation) EOS International; (Course Reserve) EOS International; (ILL) OCLC; (OPAC) EOS International; (Serials) EOS International
Wireless access
Function: Archival coll, Art exhibits, Audiobks via web, Bks on cassette, Bks on CD, Computers for patron use, Distance learning, Electronic databases & coll, ILL available, Internet access, Music CDs, Online info literacy tutorials on the web & in blackboard, OverDrive digital audio bks, Photocopying/Printing, Ref & res, Scanner, Spoken cassettes & DVDs, VHS videos
Mem of Northeast Kansas Library System
Open Mon-Thurs (Fall & Spring) 7:45am-Midnight, Fri 7:45-5, Sun 1-Midnight; Mon-Fri (Summer) 9-5

OVERBROOK

P OVERBROOK PUBLIC LIBRARY, 317 Maple St, 66524. (Mail add: PO Box 389, 66524), SAN 306-0799. Tel: 785-862-9840. FAX: 785-836-5005. E-mail: staff@overbrook.lib.ks.us. Web Site: overbrook.mykansaslibrary.org. *Libr Dir,* Kyle Sederstrom; E-mail: ksederstrom@overbrook.lib.ks.us
Founded 1928. Pop 973; Circ 14,557
Library Holdings: Large Print Bks 910; Bk Titles 18,751; Per Subs 14
Special Collections: Kansas Coll
Wireless access
Function: Adult bk club, Bks on cassette, Bks on CD, CD-ROM, Computer training, Computers for patron use, Home delivery & serv to seniorr ctr & nursing homes, ILL available, Internet access, Music CDs, Online ref, Photocopying/Printing, Prog for children & young adult, Summer reading prog, Tax forms, VHS videos
Mem of Northeast Kansas Library System
Open Mon-Wed & Fri 10-6, Thurs 10-7, Sat 9-1
Friends of the Library Group

OVERLAND PARK

CM CLEVELAND UNIVERSITY CHIROPRACTIC & HEALTH SCIENCES*, Ruth R Cleveland Memorial Library, 10850 Lowell Ave, 66210. SAN 324-7147. Tel: 913-234-0814. FAX: 913-234-0901. E-mail: library@cleveland.edu. Web Site: www.cleveland.edu/academics/library. *Dir,* Simone Briand; E-mail: simone.briand@cleveland.edu; Staff 3 (MLS 1, Non-MLS 2)
Founded 1976. Enrl 486; Fac 53
Library Holdings: Bk Titles 13,900; Bk Vols 15,000; Per Subs 301
Special Collections: Chiropractic texts, journals
Subject Interests: Acupuncture, Chiropractic, Nutrition, Orthopedics, Radiology
Automation Activity & Vendor Info: (Cataloging) EOS International; (Circulation) EOS International
Wireless access
Publications: Library News (monthly); quarterly list of new books; Subject bibliographies
Partic in Health Sciences Library Network of Kansas City, Inc
Open Mon-Fri 8-5
Friends of the Library Group

J JOHNSON COUNTY COMMUNITY COLLEGE*, Billington Library, 12345 College Blvd, 66210. SAN 306-0802. Tel: 913-469-3871. Circulation Tel: 913-469-4484. Reference Tel: 913-469-8500. Web Site: library.jccc.edu. *Dir,* Mark Daganaar; Tel: 913-469-3882, E-mail: mdaganaar@jccc.edu; *Archives Librn,* John Russell; Tel: 913-469-8500, Ext 3284, E-mail: jrussell@jccc.edu; *Coll Develop Librn,* Judith Guzzy; Tel: 913-469-8500, Ext 3297, E-mail: jguzzy@jccc.edu; *Copyright Librn,* Mark Swails; Tel: 913-469-8500, Ext 3773, E-mail: mswails@jccc.edu; *Digital Librn,* Barry Bailey; Tel: 913-469-8500, Ext 4841, E-mail: bbaile14@jccc.edu; *Instruction Librn, Online Librn,* Jessica Tipton; Tel: 913-469-8500, Ext 3286, E-mail: jtipton4@jccc.edu; Staff 12 (MLS 7, Non-MLS 5)
Founded 1969. Enrl 30,000; Fac 800; Highest Degree: Associate
Library Holdings: Bk Titles 89,000; Bk Vols 100,000; Per Subs 80
Automation Activity & Vendor Info: (Acquisitions) SerialsSolutions; (Cataloging) SerialsSolutions; (Circulation) SerialsSolutions; (Course Reserve) SerialsSolutions; (OPAC) SerialsSolutions; (Serials) SerialsSolutions
Wireless access
Partic in Mid-America Library Alliance
Special Services for the Deaf - Bks on deafness & sign lang; Spec interest per; Staff with knowledge of sign lang
Open Mon-Thurs (Fall & Spring) 7:30am-10pm, Fri 7:30-5, Sat 10-8, Sun 12-6; Mon-Thurs (Summer) 7:30am-10pm, Fri 7:30-5, Sat 8-5

P JOHNSON COUNTY LIBRARY*, 9875 W 87th St, 66212. (Mail add: PO Box 2901, Shawnee Mission, 66201-1301), SAN 342-1627. Tel: 913-826-4600. Web Site: www.jocolibrary.org. *County Librn,* Sean Casserley; E-mail: casserleys@jocolibrary.org; *Dep County Librn,* Tricia Suellentrop; E-mail: suellentropp@jocolibrary.org; *Assoc Dir, Br Serv,* Jennifer Mahnken; Tel: 913-826-4706; *Teen Librn,* Kate McNair; *Coll Develop Mgr,* Lacie Griffen; *Communications Mgr,* Robin Carol; *Youth Serv Mgr,* Angel Tucker; Staff 280 (MLS 61, Non-MLS 219)
Founded 1952. Pop 400,600
Library Holdings: AV Mats 210,992; e-books 1,400; Bk Vols 1,196,429; Per Subs 2,851
Special Collections: State Document Depository; US Document Depository
Subject Interests: Bus, Genealogy, Local hist
Automation Activity & Vendor Info: (Acquisitions) SirsiDynix; (Cataloging) SirsiDynix; (Circulation) SirsiDynix; (OPAC) SirsiDynix; (Serials) SirsiDynix
Wireless access
Mem of Northeast Kansas Library System
Partic in Mid-America Library Alliance; OCLC Online Computer Library Center, Inc
Open Mon-Thurs 9-8, Fri 9-6, Sat 9-5, Sun 1-5
Friends of the Library Group
Branches: 14
ANTIOCH, 8700 Shawnee Mission Pkwy, Merriam, 66202, SAN 376-883X. *Br Mgr,* Tad Twidell; *Asst Br Mgr,* Sheida Bates; Staff 4 (MLS 4)
Founded 1955. Pop 38,426; Circ 557,000
Library Holdings: AV Mats 19,000; Bk Vols 111,000; Per Subs 131
Open Mon-Thurs 9-8, Fri 9-6, Sat 9-5, Sun 1-5
Friends of the Library Group
BLUE VALLEY, 9000 W 151st St, 66221, SAN 342-1678. *Br Mgr,* Stephanie Bailey; *Asst Br Mgr,* Matt Hammes; Staff 3 (MLS 3)
Founded 1982. Pop 75,712; Circ 871,815
Library Holdings: AV Mats 24,872; Bk Vols 109,687; Per Subs 123
Open Mon-Thurs 10-8, Fri 9-6, Sat 9-5, Sun 1-5
Friends of the Library Group
CEDAR ROE, 5120 Cedar St, Roeland Park, 66205, SAN 342-1686. *Br Mgr,* Terry Velasquez; *Asst Br Mgr,* Alice Pierson; Staff 1 (MLS 1)
Founded 1969. Pop 16,138; Circ 331,013
Library Holdings: AV Mats 12,379; Bk Vols 77,478
Open Mon-Thurs 9-8, Fri 9-6, Sat 10-2
Friends of the Library Group
CENTRAL RESOURCE, 9875 W 87th St, 66212. *Br Mgr,* Laura Hunt; *Asst Br Mgr,* Nancy Birmingham; *Asst Br Mgr,* Linda King; Staff 87 (MLS 20, Non-MLS 67)
Founded 1995. Circ 1,042,841
Library Holdings: AV Mats 40,697; Bk Vols 288,644; Per Subs 874
Subject Interests: Genealogy, Regional
Open Mon-Thurs 9-8, Fri 9-6, Sat 9-5, Sun 1-5
Friends of the Library Group
CORINTH, 8100 Mission Rd, Prairie Village, 66208, SAN 342-1716. *Br Mgr,* Amy Barclay; Staff 3 (MLS 3)
Founded 1963. Pop 43,102; Circ 779,534
Library Holdings: AV Mats 23,677; Large Print Bks 3,599; Bk Vols 160,635; Per Subs 170
Open Mon-Thurs 9-8, Fri 9-6, Sat 9-5, Sun 1-5
Friends of the Library Group
DE SOTO BRANCH, 33145 W 83rd St, De Soto, 66018, SAN 342-1740. *Br Mgr,* Christian Madrigal; Staff 1 (MLS 1)
Founded 1967. Pop 6,062; Circ 86,843
Library Holdings: AV Mats 5,036; Bk Vols 20,347; Per Subs 47
Open Tues, Wed & Fri 10-6, Thurs 1-8, Sat 10-2
Friends of the Library Group
EDGERTON BRANCH, 319 E Nelson St, Edgerton, 66021. *Br Mgr,* John Keogh
Founded 2000. Pop 2,062; Circ 45,337
Library Holdings: AV Mats 2,876; Bk Vols 9,998; Per Subs 23
Open Tues & Wed 1-6, Thurs 1-8, Fri 1-5, Sat 10-2
Friends of the Library Group
GARDNER BRANCH, 137 E Shawnee St, Gardner, 66030, SAN 342-1775. *Br Mgr,* John Keogh; Staff 2 (MLS 2)
Founded 1960. Pop 17,869; Circ 252,509
Library Holdings: AV Mats 10,108; Bk Vols 42,096; Per Subs 89
Open Mon-Thurs 9-8, Fri 9-6, Sat 9-5
Friends of the Library Group
LEAWOOD PIONEER BRANCH, 4700 Town Center Dr, Leawood, 66211, SAN 375-6300. *Br Mgr,* Rita Glick; Staff 2 (MLS 2)
Founded 1994. Pop 34,202; Circ 536,621
Library Holdings: AV Mats 15,190; Bk Vols 77,207; Per Subs 117
Open Mon-Thurs 9-8, Fri 9-6, Sat 9-5
Friends of the Library Group
LENEXA CITY CENTER LIBRARY, 8778 Penrose Lane, Lenexa, 66219, SAN 328-6630. *Br Mgr,* Ken Werne; Staff 3 (MLS 3)
Founded 1986. Pop 38,771; Circ 561,511
Library Holdings: AV Mats 18,185; Bk Vols 95,921; Per Subs 165
Friends of the Library Group
MONTICELLO BRANCH, 22435 W 66th St, Shawnee, 66226. Tel: 913-826-4768. Web Site: www.jocolibrary.org/locations/monticello. *Br Mgr,* Christian Madrigal
Open Mon-Thurs 9-8, Fri 9-6, Sat 9-5, Sun 1-5
OAK PARK, 9500 Bluejacket St, 66214, SAN 342-1805. *Br Mgr,* Roxanne Belcher; Staff 2 (MLS 2)
Founded 1969. Pop 34,732; Circ 615,485
Library Holdings: AV Mats 21,278; Bk Vols 121,042; Per Subs 165
Open Mon-Thurs 9-8, Fri 9-6, Sat 9-5
Friends of the Library Group
SHAWNEE BRANCH, 13811 Johnson Dr, Shawnee, 66216, SAN 371-9839. *Br Mgr,* Terry Velasquez; *Asst Br Mgr,* Alice Pierson; Staff 10 (MLS 1, Non-MLS 9)
Founded 1992. Pop 28,304; Circ 424,170
Library Holdings: AV Mats 11,792; Bk Vols 69,047; Per Subs 122

Open Mon-Thurs 9-8, Fri 9-6, Sat 9-5
Friends of the Library Group
SPRING HILL BRANCH, 109 S Webster St, Spring Hill, 66083, SAN 342-183X. *Br Mgr,* John Keogh; Staff 2 (Non-MLS 2)
Founded 1971. Pop 4,816; Circ 110,552
Library Holdings: AV Mats 4,281; Bk Vols 16,617; Per Subs 35
Open Mon-Wed 10-6, Thurs 1-8, Sat 10-2
Friends of the Library Group

C NATIONAL AMERICAN UNIVERSITY*, Learning Resource Center, 10310 Mastin St, 66212-5451. Tel: 913-981-8700. Toll Free Tel: 800-770-2959. Web Site: www.national.edu. *Campus Librn,* Marilyn Miller; E-mail: marmiller@national.edu; Staff 1 (MLS 1)
Founded 2000. Fac 25; Highest Degree: Master
Wireless access
Function: Computers for patron use, Distance learning, Electronic databases & coll, Internet access, Learning ctr, Online cat, Online ref, Orientations, Outside serv via phone, mail, e-mail & web, Photocopying/Printing, Ref serv available
Restriction: Internal circ only, Open to students, fac & staff

OXFORD

P OXFORD PUBLIC LIBRARY*, 115 S Sumner St, 67119. (Mail add: PO Box 266, 67119-0266), SAN 306-0829. Tel: 620-455-2221. FAX: 620-455-2221. E-mail: oxfordkslib@gmail.com. Web Site: www.oxfordks.org/oxford-public-library.htm. *Librn,* Karen Parsons; Staff 1.5 (Non-MLS 1.5)
Pop 1,172; Circ 6,490
Library Holdings: Audiobooks 50; Bk Vols 8,000
Subject Interests: Hist, Kansas
Automation Activity & Vendor Info: (Cataloging) Innovative Interfaces, Inc; (Circulation) Innovative Interfaces, Inc
Wireless access
Mem of South Central Kansas Library System
Open Mon, Tues, Thurs & Fri 9-12 & 1-5, Wed 9-12 & 1-7

PALCO

P PALCO PUBLIC LIBRARY*, 309 Main St, 67657. (Mail add: PO Box 218, 67657-0218), SAN 306-0837. Tel: 785-737-4286. E-mail: palcolibrary@gmail.com. *Dir & Librn,* Danielle Wells; *Librn,* Kim Eichman
Pop 550; Circ 5,637
Library Holdings: Bk Vols 7,500; Per Subs 9
Wireless access
Mem of Central Kansas Library System
Open Tues & Thurs 10-4, Sat 8-11

PAOLA

P PAOLA FREE LIBRARY*, 101 E Peoria, 66071. SAN 306-0845. Tel: 913-259-3655. FAX: 913-259-3656. Web Site: www.paolalibrary.org. *Dir,* Emily Burgdorf; E-mail: eburgdorf@cityofpaola.com; *Asst Dir, Youth Serv,* Cari Michael; E-mail: youthservices@cityofpaola.com; *Cat,* Beverly Looney; Staff 9 (MLS 1, Non-MLS 8)
Founded 1876. Pop 5,000; Circ 50,000
Library Holdings: Bks on Deafness & Sign Lang 25; Large Print Bks 480; Bk Vols 37,874; Per Subs 75; Spec Interest Per Sub 27; Talking Bks 1,355
Automation Activity & Vendor Info: (Circulation) Follett Software; (ILL) Auto-Graphics, Inc; (OPAC) Follett Software
Mem of Northeast Kansas Library System
Special Services for the Blind - Talking bks
Open Mon-Thurs 9-8, Fri 9-5, Sat 10-4
Friends of the Library Group

PARK CITY

P PARK CITY PUBLIC LIBRARY*, 2107 E 61st St N, 67219. Tel: 316-744-6318. FAX: 316-744-6319. Web Site: www.parkcitypubliclibrary.com. *Dir,* Len Warren; E-mail: lwarren@parkcitypubliclibrary.com; Staff 5 (Non-MLS 5)
Founded 2000. Pop 7,500; Circ 28,000
Library Holdings: Audiobooks 500; DVDs 1,500; Large Print Bks 500; Bk Vols 28,000; Per Subs 28
Automation Activity & Vendor Info: (Cataloging) ComPanion Corp; (Circulation) ComPanion Corp; (OPAC) ComPanion Corp
Wireless access
Function: 24/7 Electronic res, 24/7 Online cat, Adult bk club
Open Mon & Tues 9-7, Wed, Thurs & Fri 9-6, Sat 9-1
Friends of the Library Group

PARKER

P LINN COUNTY LIBRARY DISTRICT NO 1*, 234 W Main St, 66072. (Mail add: PO Box 315, 66072-0315), SAN 376-771X. Tel: 913-898-4650. FAX: 913-898-4650. E-mail: parkerlibrary@yahoo.com. Web Site: parker.mykansaslibrary.org. *Dir & Librn,* Loree K Bowman
Library Holdings: Bk Vols 10,000; Per Subs 37
Wireless access
Mem of Southeast Kansas Library System
Open Mon-Fri 10-6
Friends of the Library Group

PARSONS

J LABETTE COMMUNITY COLLEGE LIBRARY, 1230 Main S, 67357. (Mail add: 200 S 14th, 67357), SAN 306-0853. Tel: 620-820-1167. Interlibrary Loan Service Tel: 620-820-1154. Administration Tel: 620-820-1168. Toll Free Tel: 888-522-3883. FAX: 620-421-1469. Web Site: www.labette.edu/library. *Dir, Libr Serv,* Scotty M Zollars; E-mail: scottz@labette.edu; *ILL, Libr Asst,* Phylis A Coomes; E-mail: phylisc@labette.edu. Subject Specialists: *Admin, Info, Literacy,* Scotty M Zollars; Staff 3 (MLS 1, Non-MLS 2)
Founded 1923. Enrl 1,084; Fac 69; Highest Degree: Associate
Jul 2021-Jun 2022 Income (Main Library Only) $164,771, Parent Institution $164,771. Mats Exp $32,159, Books $2,400, Per/Ser (Incl. Access Fees) $10,154, Electronic Ref Mat (Incl. Access Fees) $19,605. Sal $120,845 (Prof $61,210)
Library Holdings: Bk Titles 13,547; Bk Vols 15,668; Per Subs 35
Special Collections: Carnegie Art Book Coll; Labette County & Kansas History
Subject Interests: Acad, Children's lit
Automation Activity & Vendor Info: (Cataloging) ByWater Solutions; (Circulation) ByWater Solutions; (Discovery) EBSCO Discovery Service; (ILL) Auto-Graphics, Inc; (OPAC) ByWater Solutions; (Serials) ByWater Solutions
Wireless access
Function: 24/7 Electronic res, 24/7 Online cat, Archival coll, Art exhibits, Computers for patron use, Distance learning, Electronic databases & coll, ILL available, Internet access, Magazines, Mail & tel request accepted, Microfiche/film & reading machines, Online cat, Online info literacy tutorials on the web & in blackboard, Online ref, Orientations, Photocopying/Printing, Printer for laptops & handheld devices, Ref & res, Ref serv available, Res assist avail, Telephone ref, Wheelchair accessible
Mem of Southeast Kansas Library System
Partic in Southeast Kansas Academic Librarians Council
Open Mon-Thurs (Winter) 8am-9pm, Fri 8-Noon; Mon & Tues (Summer) 7-7, Wed & Thurs 7-4:30
Restriction: 24-hr pass syst for students only, Access at librarian's discretion, Badge access after hrs, Borrowing requests are handled by ILL, Non-circulating coll, Open to students, fac & staff, Photo ID required for access, Pub access by telephone only, Pub ref by request

P PARSONS PUBLIC LIBRARY*, 311 S 17th St, 67357. SAN 306-0861. Tel: 620-421-5920. FAX: 620-421-3951. E-mail: staff@parsonslibrary.org. Web Site: www.parsonslibrary.org. *Dir,* Jean Strader; Staff 10 (MLS 1, Non-MLS 9)
Founded 1908. Pop 11,177; Circ 95,742
Library Holdings: Bk Vols 69,934; Per Subs 110
Subject Interests: Kansas
Automation Activity & Vendor Info: (Cataloging) Innovative Interfaces, Inc - Sierra; (Circulation) Innovative Interfaces, Inc - Sierra; (OPAC) Innovative Interfaces, Inc - Sierra
Wireless access
Open Mon-Thurs (Winter) 9-7:30, Fri 9-5, Sat 10-4; Mon & Thurs (Summer) 9-7:30, Tues & Wed 9-5:30, Fri 9-5, Sat 10-4

M PARSONS STATE HOSPITAL & TRAINING CENTER LIBRARY*, 2601 Gabriel Ave, 67357. SAN 342-1473. Tel: 620-421-6550, Ext 1781. Web Site: kdads.ks.gov/state-hospitals-and-institutions/parsons-state-hospital-and-training-center. *Librn,* Nancy Holding; E-mail: nancy.holding@psh.ks.gov
Founded 1956
Library Holdings: Bk Vols 6,600

PARTRIDGE

P PARTRIDGE PUBLIC LIBRARY*, 23 S Main St, 67566. SAN 306-087X. Tel: 620-567-2467. FAX: 620-567-2467. E-mail: plibrary23@gmail.com. Web Site: partridge.scklf.info. *Dir,* Keturah Delehoy
Pop 338; Circ 6,496
Library Holdings: Bk Vols 16,798; Per Subs 23
Special Collections: Kansas Author's Coll; Kansas Coll
Mem of South Central Kansas Library System
Open Mon, Tues & Thurs 1-6, Fri 9-2

PEABODY

P PEABODY TOWNSHIP LIBRARY*, 214 Walnut St, 66866. SAN 306-0896. Tel: 620-983-2502. E-mail: peabodytownshiplibrary@gmail.com. Web Site: peabody.lib.nckls.org. *Libr Dir,* Rodger L Charles
Founded 1874. Pop 1,705; Circ 10,909
Library Holdings: Bk Vols 10,000; Per Subs 26
Automation Activity & Vendor Info: (Cataloging) Auto-Graphics, Inc; (Circulation) Auto-Graphics, Inc
Wireless access
Function: 24/7 Electronic res, Accelerated reader prog, Activity rm, Adult bk club, Audio & video playback equip for onsite use, Audiobks on Playaways & MP3, Audiobks via web, Bk club(s), Children's prog, Computers for patron use, Digital talking bks, Distance learning, E-Readers, Electronic databases & coll, Free DVD rentals, ILL available, Internet access, Laminating, Magazines, Meeting rooms, Movies, Online cat, Online info literacy tutorials on the web & in blackboard, Online ref, Outside serv via phone, mail, e-mail & web, Photocopying/Printing, Ref & res, Scanner, Serves people with intellectual disabilities, Wheelchair accessible
Mem of North Central Kansas Libraries System
Open Tues 9-Noon & 2-8, Wed-Fri 2-5, Sat 9-Noon

PERRY

P PERRY-LECOMPTON COMMUNITY LIBRARY*, Highland College, Perry Center, 203 W Bridge St, 66073. Tel: 785-597-5031. E-mail: plibrary338@gmail.com. Web Site: www.facebook.com/perrylecomptoncommunitylibrary. *Dir,* Jane Barnett
Mem of Northeast Kansas Library System
Open Tues & Thurs 9-12 & 4-7, Sat 10-4

PHILLIPSBURG

P PHILLIPSBURG CITY LIBRARY*, 888 Fourth St, 67661. SAN 306-090X. Tel: 785-543-5325. FAX: 785-543-5374. E-mail: pblib1@ruraltel.net. Web Site: www.phillipsburgks.us/index.aspx?NID=136. *Dir,* Kelly Grismore
Founded 1926. Pop 2,500; Circ 53,441
Library Holdings: Bk Titles 35,137; Per Subs 75
Subject Interests: Genealogy, Kansas
Automation Activity & Vendor Info: (Acquisitions) ByWater Solutions; (Cataloging) ByWater Solutions; (Circulation) ByWater Solutions; (OPAC) ByWater Solutions
Wireless access
Function: 24/7 Electronic res, 24/7 Online cat, Activity rm, Art exhibits, Audiobks on Playaways & MP3, Audiobks via web, Bks on CD, Children's prog, Computer training, Computers for patron use, Digital talking bks, Free DVD rentals, Genealogy discussion group, Home delivery & serv to seniorr ctr & nursing homes, ILL available, Internet access, Magazines, Magnifiers for reading, Meeting rooms, Microfiche/film & reading machines, Online cat, OverDrive digital audio bks, Photocopying/Printing, Preschool reading prog, Prog for adults, Prog for children & young adult, Scanner, Story hour, Summer & winter reading prog, Summer reading prog, Tax forms, Telephone ref, Wheelchair accessible
Mem of Central Kansas Library System
Open Mon-Fri 10-6, Sat 9-2

PITTSBURG

P PITTSBURG PUBLIC LIBRARY*, 308 N Walnut, 66762-4732. SAN 306-0918. Tel: 620-231-8110. FAX: 620-232-2258. E-mail: info@pplonline.org. Web Site: pplonline.org. *Dir,* Bev Clarkson; E-mail: bclarkson@pplonline.org; *Asst Dir,* Anndee Peterson; Tel: 620-230-5567, E-mail: apeterson@pplonline.org; *Head, Adult Serv,* Carol Ann Robb; Tel: 620-230-5568, E-mail: carobb@pplonline.org; *Head, Circ,* Cindy Gier; Tel: 620-230-5512, E-mail: cgier@pittsburgpubliclibrary.org; *Head, Info Tech,* James Swafford; Tel: 620-230-5511, E-mail: jswafford@pittsburgpubliclibrary.org; *Head, Tech Serv,* Becky Galindo; Tel: 620-230-5563, E-mail: bgalindo@pittsburgpubliclibrary.org; *Head, Youth Serv,* Gail Sheppard; Tel: 620-230-5564, E-mail: gsheppard@pittsburgpubliclibrary.org; Staff 19 (MLS 2, Non-MLS 17)
Founded 1902. Pop 19,646; Circ 239,419
Library Holdings: CDs 8,641; DVDs 3,370; Bk Vols 55,777; Per Subs 142
Special Collections: Crawford County Genealogical Society Coll
Subject Interests: Local hist, Med, Relig
Automation Activity & Vendor Info: (Cataloging) SirsiDynix; (Circulation) SirsiDynix; (OPAC) SirsiDynix
Wireless access
Function: Audiobks via web, Bks on CD, Children's prog, Computer training, Computers for patron use, Electronic databases & coll, Free DVD rentals, Holiday prog, Homebound delivery serv, Homework prog, ILL available, Magnifiers for reading, Mail & tel request accepted, Music CDs, Online cat, OverDrive digital audio bks, Photocopying/Printing, Prog for adults, Prog for children & young adult, Ref serv available, Scanner, Senior computer classes, Story hour, Summer reading prog, Tax forms, Teen prog, Telephone ref, VHS videos, Wheelchair accessible
Mem of Southeast Kansas Library System
Open Mon-Thurs 9-8, Fri & Sat 9-5, Sun 1-5
Friends of the Library Group

C PITTSBURG STATE UNIVERSITY*, Leonard H Axe Library, 1605 S Joplin St, 66762-5889. (Mail add: 1701 S Broadway, 66762), SAN 306-0926. Tel: 620-235-4878. Circulation Tel: 620-235-4882. Interlibrary Loan Service Tel: 620-235-4890. Administration Tel: 620-235-4879. Automation Services Tel: 620-235-4087. Information Services Tel: 620-235-4888. FAX: 620-235-4090. Web Site: axe.pittstate.edu. *Dean, Libr Serv,* Randy Roberts; E-mail: reroberts@pittstate.edu; *Cat Librn,* Morgan McCune; Tel: 620-235-4895, E-mail: mmccune@pittstate.edu; *Per/Ref Librn,* Barbara Pope; Tel: 620-235-4884, E-mail: bpope@pittstate.edu; *Ref Librn,* Robert Lindsey; Tel: 620-235-4887, E-mail: rlindsey@pittstate.edu; *Libr Syst Mgr,* David Nance; E-mail: dnance@pittstate.edu; *Syst Coordr,* Susan Johns-Smith; Tel: 620-235-4115, E-mail: sjohnssmith@pittstate.edu; *Spec Coll,* Janette Mauk; Tel: 620-235-4883, E-mail: jmauk@pittstate.edu; Staff 21 (MLS 9, Non-MLS 12)
Founded 1903. Enrl 7,200; Fac 298; Highest Degree: Master
Jul 2012-Jun 2013 Income $1,905,143. Mats Exp $752,000, Books $175,500, Per/Ser (Incl. Access Fees) $355,239, AV Mat $500, Electronic Ref Mat (Incl. Access Fees) $118,000, Presv $10,000. Sal $1,568,000
Library Holdings: Bks on Deafness & Sign Lang 145; Bk Titles 328,745; Bk Vols 497,639; Per Subs 3,425
Special Collections: Historic Map Coll; Southeast Kansas Coll, bks, per, ms, tapes, photog; University Archives, bks, per, ms, tapes, photog. State Document Depository; US Document Depository
Automation Activity & Vendor Info: (Acquisitions) SirsiDynix; (Cataloging) SirsiDynix; (Circulation) SirsiDynix; (Course Reserve) SirsiDynix; (OPAC) SirsiDynix; (Serials) SirsiDynix
Wireless access
Special Services for the Blind - Large screen computer & software
Open Mon-Thurs (Fall-Spring) 7:30am-11pm, Fri 7:30-5, Sat 9-5, Sun Noon-Midnight; Mon-Thurs (Summer) 7:30am-8pm, Fri 7:30-5, Sun 3-8
Friends of the Library Group

PLAINS

P PLAINS COMMUNITY LIBRARY*, 500 Grand Ave, 67869. (Mail add: PO Box 7, 67869-0007), SAN 376-5571. Tel: 620-563-7326. FAX: 620-563-6114. E-mail: plainslibrary@plainslibrary.info. Web Site: www.plainslibrary.info. *Dir,* Jessica Collins; Staff 3 (Non-MLS 3)
Founded 1969. Pop 1,485; Circ 16,000
Library Holdings: Audiobooks 420; DVDs 900; Bk Titles 21,000; Per Subs 20
Automation Activity & Vendor Info: (Cataloging) Auto-Graphics, Inc; (Circulation) Auto-Graphics, Inc; (Serials) EBSCO Online
Wireless access
Function: 24/7 Electronic res, 24/7 Online cat, Accelerated reader prog, Activity rm, Audiobks on Playaways & MP3, Bks on CD, Children's prog, Computer training, Computers for patron use, Digital talking bks, Free DVD rentals, Home delivery & serv to seniorr ctr & nursing homes, Homebound delivery serv, ILL available, Internet access, Magazines, Mango lang, Movies, Music CDs, Online cat, Online ref, Outreach serv, Photocopying/Printing, Preschool outreach, Preschool reading prog, Prog for adults, Prog for children & young adult, Ref & res, Ref serv available, Scanner, Spanish lang bks, Spoken cassettes & CDs, Story hour, Summer & winter reading prog, Summer reading prog, Tax forms, Teen prog, Wheelchair accessible
Mem of Southwest Kansas Library System
Open Mon & Thurs 10-6:30, Tues & Fri 10-5, Sat 9-1
Restriction: Borrowing requests are handled by ILL, Circ limited
Friends of the Library Group

PLAINVILLE

P PLAINVILLE MEMORIAL LIBRARY*, 200 SW First St, 67663. SAN 306-0942. Tel: 785-434-2786. FAX: 785-434-2786. E-mail: pville2@ruraltel.net. Web Site: plainvillepl.blogspot.com. *Dir,* Cheryl Hageman; *Asst Librn,* Brenda Frederking
Pop 2,458; Circ 12,000
Library Holdings: Bk Vols 13,000; Per Subs 30
Automation Activity & Vendor Info: (Cataloging) Book Systems; (Circulation) Book Systems; (OPAC) Book Systems
Wireless access
Mem of Central Kansas Library System
Open Mon-Fri 9-5:30, Sat 9-12 & 1-4

PLEASANTON

P LINN COUNTY LIBRARY DISTRICT NO 5, Pleasanton Lincoln Library, 752 Main St, 66075. (Mail add: PO Box 101, 66075-0101), SAN 306-0950. Tel: 913-352-8554. FAX: 913-352-8556. E-mail:

pleaslinlib@ckt.net. Web Site: pleasanton.mykansaslibrary.org. *Libr Dir,* Wendy Morlan; *Circ Serv,* Susan Brown; *Circ Serv,* Roberta Willis; Staff 3 (Non-MLS 3)
Founded 1903. Pop 1,818
Library Holdings: Audiobooks 357; DVDs 1,993; Bk Titles 8,319; Per Subs 31
Automation Activity & Vendor Info: (Cataloging) Koha; (Circulation) Koha; (ILL) Auto-Graphics, Inc; (OPAC) ByWater Solutions
Wireless access
Function: 24/7 Electronic res, 24/7 Online cat, Audiobks via web, Bks on CD, Butterfly Garden, Children's prog, Computer training, Computers for patron use, Electronic databases & coll, Free DVD rentals, ILL available, Internet access, Laminating, Magazines, Mail & tel request accepted, Meeting rooms, Outreach serv, Outside serv via phone, mail, e-mail & web, Photocopying/Printing, Preschool outreach, Prog for adults, Prog for children & young adult, Ref serv available, Scanner, Summer reading prog, Telephone ref, Wheelchair accessible
Mem of Southeast Kansas Library System
Open Mon-Fri 10-4

S LINN COUNTY MUSEUM & GENEALOGY LIBRARY*, Dunlap Park, 307 E Park St, 66075. (Mail add: PO Box 137, 66075-0137), SAN 325-6022. Tel: 913-352-8739. FAX: 913-352-8739. E-mail: linncohist-gen@ckt.net. *Pres,* Ola May Earnest
Library Holdings: Bk Titles 500; Per Subs 135
Subject Interests: Civil War, Genealogy, Kansas, State hist
Wireless access
Open Tues & Thurs 9-4, Sat 1-5

POMONA

P POMONA COMMUNITY LIBRARY*, 115 E Franklin St, 66076. Tel: 785-566-3300. FAX: 785-566-3301. E-mail: pomonalibraryks@gmail.com. Web Site: pomona.mykansaslibrary.org. *Dir,* Judy Stratton; E-mail; directorpomona@pomonalibraryks.org
Library Holdings: Bk Vols 4,000
Mem of Northeast Kansas Library System
Open Mon & Wed 12-6, Tues & Thurs 9-6, Sat 12-4

POTWIN

P POTWIN PUBLIC LIBRARY, 126 N Randall, 67123. SAN 306-0969. Tel: 620-752-3421. FAX: 620-752-3421. E-mail: potwinlibrary@wheatstate.com.
Founded 1932
Library Holdings: Bk Vols 4,000
Wireless access
Function: Computers for patron use, Free DVD rentals, ILL available, Movies, Prog for children & young adult, Summer reading prog
Mem of South Central Kansas Library System
Open Mon-Thurs 1-7

PRAIRIE VIEW

P SUNSHINE CITY LIBRARY*, Prairie View City Library, 207 Kansas St, 67664. (Mail add: PO Box 424, 67664), SAN 306-0977. Tel: 785-973-2265. E-mail: read@ruraltel.net. *Librn,* Gloria DeWitt
Founded 1966. Pop 131; Circ 1,552
Library Holdings: Bk Vols 3,485; Per Subs 15; Talking Bks 80; Videos 125
Mem of Central Kansas Library System
Open Mon 2-6, Wed 8-11:30, Sat 8:30-11:30

PRAIRIE VILLAGE

R VILLAGE CHURCH LIBRARY*, 6641 Mission Rd, 66208-1799. SAN 306-0985. Tel: 913-262-4200. FAX: 913-262-0304. Web Site: www.villagepres.org. *Librn,* Karen Lundgrin; E-mail: karen.lundgrin@villagepres.org
Library Holdings: Large Print Bks 22; Bk Vols 3,974; Per Subs 3
Open Mon-Fri 8:30-5, Sun 8:30-1

PRATT

J PRATT COMMUNITY COLLEGE*, Linda Hunt Memorial Library, 348 NE State Rd 61, 67124. SAN 306-0993. Tel: 620-450-2172. Toll Free Tel: 800-294-3091 (Kansas only). FAX: 620-672-2288. Web Site: www.prattcc.edu/department/linda-hunt-memorial-library. *Dir, Learning Res,* Frank Stahl; Tel: 620-450-2238, E-mail: FrankS@prattcc.edu. Subject Specialists: *Computer sci, Educ,* Frank Stahl; Staff 2.5 (MLS 1, Non-MLS 1.5)
Founded 1938. Enrl 1,000; Fac 45; Highest Degree: Associate
Library Holdings: Audiobooks 98; AV Mats 2,490; e-books 1,000; Bk Titles 27,938; Bk Vols 32,351; Per Subs 250; Videos 2,000
Automation Activity & Vendor Info: (Acquisitions) Follett Software; (Cataloging) Follett Software; (Circulation) Follett Software; (Serials) EBSCO Online
Wireless access
Function: Audiobks via web, AV serv, Bks on cassette, Bks on CD, CD-ROM, Computers for patron use, Digital talking bks, Electronic databases & coll, Equip loans & repairs, ILL available, Internet access, Learning ctr, Mail & tel request accepted, Online cat, Outside serv via phone, mail, e-mail & web, Photocopying/Printing, Ref & res, Ref serv available, Scanner, Spoken cassettes & CDs, Spoken cassettes & DVDs, VHS videos, Wheelchair accessible
Open Mon-Thurs 8am-9pm, Fri 8-5

P PRATT PUBLIC LIBRARY*, 401 S Jackson St, 67124. SAN 306-1000. Tel: 620-672-3041, 620-672-5842. FAX: 620-672-5151. E-mail: staff@prattpubliclibrary.org. Web Site: www.prattpubliclibrary.org. *Libr Dir,* Rochelle A Westerhaus; E-mail: rochelle@prattpubliclibrary.org; Staff 5 (Non-MLS 5)
Founded 1910. Pop 9,745; Circ 59,132
Special Collections: Kansas History
Automation Activity & Vendor Info: (Cataloging) Biblionix/Apollo; (Circulation) Biblionix/Apollo; (ILL) Auto-Graphics, Inc
Wireless access
Function: 24/7 Online cat, Adult bk club
Special Services for the Blind - Recorded bks; ZoomText magnification & reading software
Open Mon-Thurs 10-7, Fri & Sat 10-6

PRESCOTT

P PRESCOTT CITY PUBLIC LIBRARY*, 174 W Third, 66767. (Mail add: PO Box 112, 66767), SAN 306-1019. Tel: 913-471-4593. E-mail: prescottkansaslibrary@yahoo.com. Web Site: prescott.mykansaslibrary.org. *Libr Dir,* Ginny Clark
Founded 1975. Pop 600; Circ 3,915
Library Holdings: Bk Vols 5,000; Per Subs 15
Special Collections: Kansas History
Wireless access
Mem of Southeast Kansas Library System
Open Mon-Fri 3-6

PRETTY PRAIRIE

P PRETTY PRAIRIE PUBLIC LIBRARY*, 119 W Main St, 67570. (Mail add: PO Box 68, 67570), SAN 306-1027. Tel: 620-459-6392. FAX: 620-459-7354. E-mail: cityofprettyprairie3@gmail.com. Web Site: www.prettyprairie.scklslibrary.info. *Coll Develop, Dir,* Angie Simmons; *Asst City Librn,* Jenifer Albright; Staff 3 (MLS 2, Non-MLS 1)
Founded 1945. Pop 657; Circ 7,533
Library Holdings: Bk Titles 11,000; Per Subs 40
Automation Activity & Vendor Info: (Cataloging) Auto-Graphics, Inc; (Circulation) Auto-Graphics, Inc; (OPAC) Auto-Graphics, Inc
Wireless access
Mem of South Central Kansas Library System
Open Mon-Fri 9-12 & 1-5, Sat 9-12

PROTECTION

P PROTECTION TOWNSHIP LIBRARY*, 404 N Broadway, 67127. (Mail add: PO Box 265, 67127-0265). Tel: 620-622-4886. FAX: 620-622-4492. E-mail: pclibrary@protectionlibrary.com. Web Site: www.protectionlibrary.com. *Libr Dir,* Sueann Sawyer
Founded 1934. Pop 700
Library Holdings: Bk Vols 5,000
Special Collections: Stan Herd Art Gallery
Wireless access
Function: Home delivery & serv to seniorr ctr & nursing homes, Homebound delivery serv, Homework prog, Large print keyboards, Wheelchair accessible
Mem of Southwest Kansas Library System
Open Mon-Thurs 10-4, Fri 11-5

QUINTER

P JAY JOHNSON PUBLIC LIBRARY*, 411 Main St, 67752. (Mail add: PO Box 369, 67752-0369), SAN 306-1035. Tel: 785-754-2171. E-mail: jjplquinter@gmail.com. Web Site: jjpl.nwkls.org. *Dir,* Ms Desi Rae Churchwell
Founded 1932. Pop 952; Circ 24,084
Library Holdings: Bk Vols 17,000; Per Subs 35
Special Collections: Geneaology & Community History (Heritage Room)
Automation Activity & Vendor Info: (Cataloging) Auto-Graphics, Inc
Wireless access
Mem of Northwest Kansas Library System
Open Mon, Wed & Fri 10-5, Tues & Thurs 10-7, Sat 10-1
Friends of the Library Group

RANDALL

P RANDALL PUBLIC LIBRARY*, 107 Main St, 66963. (Mail add: PO Box 101, 66963-0101), SAN 306-1043. Tel: 785-739-2380. FAX: 785-739-2331. E-mail: randallpubliclibrary@yahoo.com. *Librn,* Elisha Bolte
Pop 154; Circ 999
Library Holdings: Bk Vols 3,764; Per Subs 10
Mem of Central Kansas Library System
Open Mon & Thurs 2-6, Tues 2-4

RANSOM

P RANSOM PUBLIC LIBRARY*, 411 S Vermont Ave, 67572. (Mail add: PO Box 263, 67572-0263), SAN 306-1051. Tel: 785-731-2855. FAX: 785-731-2518. Web Site: www.ransomlibrary.info. *Dir,* Sherrill Weeks; E-mail: director@ransomlibrary.info
Pop 468; Circ 9,860
Library Holdings: Bk Vols 5,400; Per Subs 30
Automation Activity & Vendor Info: (Cataloging) Follett Software; (Circulation) Follett Software
Wireless access
Mem of Southwest Kansas Library System
Open Mon, Wed & Fri 10-6, Sat 9-12

REPUBLIC

P RAE HOBSON MEMORIAL LIBRARY*, 401 Pawnee Ave, 66964. (Mail add: PO Box 3, 66964-0003). Tel: 785-361-2481. E-mail: raehoblib@gmail.com. Web Site: raehobson.mykansaslibrary.org. *Librn,* Marilyn Aurand
Pop 300; Circ 2,301
Library Holdings: Bk Vols 4,000; Per Subs 10
Subject Interests: Fiction
Wireless access
Mem of Central Kansas Library System
Open Tues & Thurs 12:30-5:30
Friends of the Library Group

RICHMOND

P RICHMOND PUBLIC LIBRARY*, 107 E Central, 66080. (Mail add: PO Box 237, 66080-0237), SAN 306-1078. Tel: 785-835-6163. FAX: 785-835-6163. Web Site: richmond.mykansaslibrary.org. *Dir,* Connie A Weber; E-mail: cweber@richmond.lib.ks.us; Staff 2 (Non-MLS 2)
Founded 1938. Pop 500; Circ 7,707
Library Holdings: Audiobooks 25; CDs 57; DVDs 1,543; Large Print Bks 300; Bk Titles 5,330; Per Subs 10
Special Collections: Halloween Masks Coll
Wireless access
Function: Children's prog, Computers for patron use, Free DVD rentals, ILL available, Music CDs, Photocopying/Printing, Prog for adults, Prog for children & young adult, Scanner, Spoken cassettes & DVDs, Summer reading prog, VHS videos
Mem of Northeast Kansas Library System
Partic in Public Library InterLINK
Open Mon & Fri 2-6, Wed & Thurs 10-6, Sat 12-3
Friends of the Library Group

RILEY

P RILEY CITY LIBRARY*, 115 S Broadway, 66531. (Mail add: PO Box 204, 66531-0204). Tel: 785-485-2978. E-mail: rileycitylibrary@gmail.com. *Dir,* Patricia I Peterson; *Circ Librn,* Laura Gayle Coon
Library Holdings: Bk Vols 4,000
Automation Activity & Vendor Info: (ILL) Auto-Graphics, Inc
Wireless access
Mem of North Central Kansas Libraries System
Open Mon, Wed & Fri 1-6, Sat 10-2
Friends of the Library Group

ROSE HILL

P ROSE HILL PUBLIC LIBRARY*, 306 N Rose Hill Rd, 67133. (Mail add: PO Box 157, 67133-0157). Tel: 316-776-3013. Web Site: scklslibrary.info. *Dir,* Cindy Maxey; E-mail: cmaxey@cityofrosehill.com
Library Holdings: Bk Vols 2,000; Per Subs 11; Talking Bks 400
Automation Activity & Vendor Info: (Cataloging) Chancery SMS; (Circulation) Chancery SMS; (OPAC) Chancery SMS
Wireless access
Mem of South Central Kansas Library System
Open Mon-Thurs 9-7, Sat 9-1

ROSSVILLE

P ROSSVILLE COMMUNITY LIBRARY*, 407 N Main St, 66533. (Mail add: PO Box 618, 66533-0618), SAN 306-1086. Tel: 785-584-6454. FAX: 785-584-6454. Web Site: rossvillelibrary.org. *Dir,* Christi McKenzie; E-mail: director@rossvillelibrary.org; *Asst Dir,* Adena Harris; Staff 1 (MLS 1)
Pop 1,635; Circ 19,023
Library Holdings: Bk Vols 11,720; Per Subs 43
Wireless access
Mem of Northeast Kansas Library System
Open Mon, Tues & Thurs 10-6, Wed 10-7, Fri 10-5, Sat 10-12

RUSH CENTER

P RUSH CENTER LIBRARY*, 220 Washington, 2396 W Hwy 96, 67575. Tel: 785-372-4222. *Librn,* Carol Reynolds; E-mail: carolr@gbta.net
Mem of Central Kansas Library System
Open Tues & Thurs 2-4, Sat 9am-11am

RUSSELL

P RUSSELL PUBLIC LIBRARY, 126 E Sixth St, 67665. SAN 306-1108. Tel: 785-483-2742. FAX: 785-483-6254. E-mail: ruspublib@gmail.com. Web Site: www.ruspublib.org. *Dir,* Jessica McGuire; Staff 4 (Non-MLS 4)
Founded 1906. Pop 4,525; Circ 22,884
Jan 2020-Dec 2020 Income $189,362, State $1,284, Locally Generated Income $160,115, Other $27,963
Library Holdings: Audiobooks 760; DVDs 992; Large Print Bks 2,225; Bk Titles 15,772; Per Subs 20
Automation Activity & Vendor Info: (Cataloging) ByWater Solutions; (Circulation) ByWater Solutions; (OPAC) ByWater Solutions
Wireless access
Function: 24/7 Electronic res, 24/7 Online cat, Activity rm, Adult bk club, Adult literacy prog, After school storytime, Art programs, Audiobks on Playaways & MP3, Audiobks via web, AV serv, Bks on CD, Children's prog, Computers for patron use, E-Readers, Electronic databases & coll, Free DVD rentals, Holiday prog, ILL available, Internet access, Laminating, Life-long learning prog for all ages, Magazines, Magnifiers for reading, Mango lang, Meeting rooms, Microfiche/film & reading machines, Movies, Music CDs, Notary serv, Online cat, Online ref, Outreach serv, OverDrive digital audio bks, Photocopying/Printing, Preschool outreach, Preschool reading prog, Printer for laptops & handheld devices, Prog for adults, Prog for children & young adult, Res performed for a fee, Scanner, Spoken cassettes & CDs, Spoken cassettes & DVDs, STEM programs, Story hour, Study rm, Summer reading prog, Teen prog, Wheelchair accessible, Workshops
Mem of Central Kansas Library System
Open Mon-Thurs 10-6, Fri 10-5, Sat 10-3

SABETHA

P MARY COTTON PUBLIC LIBRARY, 915 Virginia, 66534-1950. (Mail add: PO Box 70, 66534-0070), SAN 306-1124. Tel: 785-284-3160. FAX: 785-284-3605. Web Site: www.sabethalibrary.org. *Dir,* Kim Priest; E-mail: kimpriest@sabethalibrary.org; Staff 3 (Non-MLS 3)
Founded 1912. Pop 2,500; Circ 56,000
Library Holdings: Audiobooks 1,000; Bks on Deafness & Sign Lang 15; DVDs 1,400; e-books 750; High Interest/Low Vocabulary Bk Vols 12,000; Large Print Bks 500; Bk Titles 30,000; Bk Vols 31,000; Per Subs 55; Talking Bks 150
Special Collections: Albany School/Town Pictures; Sabetha Herald Newspaper Coll, 1880; Sabetha High School Yearbooks 1903-2019
Subject Interests: Genealogy, Local hist
Automation Activity & Vendor Info: (Cataloging) ByWater Solutions; (Circulation) ByWater Solutions; (ILL) ByWater Solutions; (OPAC) Koha
Wireless access
Function: Home delivery & serv to seniorr ctr & nursing homes, ILL available, Magnifiers for reading, Photocopying/Printing, Prog for children & young adult, Serves people with intellectual disabilities, Summer reading prog, Wheelchair accessible
Mem of Northeast Kansas Library System
Open Mon & Wed 9:30-8, Tues, Thurs & Fri 9:30-5:30, Sat 10-4
Friends of the Library Group

SAINT FRANCIS

P ST FRANCIS PUBLIC LIBRARY*, 121 N Scott St, 67756. (Mail add: PO Box 688, 67756-0688), SAN 306-1132. Tel: 785-332-3292. E-mail: library@cityofstfrancis.net. Web Site: stfrancis.nwkls.org. *Dir,* Nathan Fiala
Founded 1988. Circ 21,202
Library Holdings: Bk Vols 15,000; Per Subs 48
Wireless access
Mem of Northwest Kansas Library System
Open Mon, Tues Thurs & Fri 10:30-5:30, Wed 10:30-7

SAINT JOHN

P IDA LONG GOODMAN MEMORIAL LIBRARY, 406 N Monroe, 67576. SAN 306-1140. Tel: 620-549-3227. FAX: 620-549-6589. E-mail: ilgml@usd350.com. Web Site: www.usd350.com/vnews/display.v/SEC/Library. *Libr Dir,* Laura Davis; E-mail: davisl@usd350.com; Staff 1 (Non-MLS 1)
Founded 1969. Pop 1,173; Circ 20,466
Library Holdings: Audiobooks 212; Bk Titles 29,171
Special Collections: Sheet Music; St John News (1880-)
Subject Interests: Educ, Genealogy, Hist, Kansas, Local hist
Automation Activity & Vendor Info: (Acquisitions) Baker & Taylor; (Circulation) ComPanion Corp; (ILL) Auto-Graphics, Inc
Wireless access
Function: Accelerated reader prog, Adult bk club, After school storytime, Audiobks via web, Bilingual assistance for Spanish patrons, Bks on cassette, Bks on CD, Children's prog, Computer training, Computers for patron use, Digital talking bks, Family literacy, Free DVD rentals, Holiday prog, Homework prog, Internet access, Microfiche/film & reading machines, Orientations, Outreach serv, Outside serv via phone, mail, e-mail & web, Photocopying/Printing, Preschool outreach, Preschool reading prog, Prog for adults, Prog for children & young adult, Scanner, Senior outreach, Spanish lang bks, Spoken cassettes & CDs, Story hour, Summer reading prog, Tax forms, VHS videos, Wheelchair accessible
Mem of South Central Kansas Library System
Open Mon-Thurs 7:30-7, Fri 7:30-5, Sat 9-Noon
Friends of the Library Group

SAINT MARYS

P POTTAWATOMIE WABAUNSEE REGIONAL LIBRARY*, St Marys Headquarters Library, 306 N Fifth St, 66536-1404. SAN 342-1503. Tel: 785-437-2778. FAX: 785-437-2778. E-mail: illpowab@gmail.com. Web Site: home.oct.net/pwrlad. *Dir,* Judith Cremer; E-mail: pwrldr@gmail.com; Staff 2 (MLS 2)
Founded 1962. Pop 25,674; Circ 59,515
Jan 2016-Dec 2016 Income (Main & Associated Libraries) $568,436, State $8,111, County $527,106, Locally Generated Income $30,226, Other $2,993. Mats Exp $60,681, Books $49,478, Per/Ser (Incl. Access Fees) $4,345, AV Mat $4,469, Electronic Ref Mat (Incl. Access Fees) $2,389. Sal $347,798
Library Holdings: Audiobooks 4,448; DVDs 3,517; e-books 97,931; e-journals 247,125; Electronic Media & Resources 66; Large Print Bks 9,789; Microforms 537; Bk Vols 105,972; Per Subs 93
Automation Activity & Vendor Info: (Cataloging) Auto-Graphics, Inc; (Circulation) Auto-Graphics, Inc; (ILL) Auto-Graphics, Inc; (OPAC) Auto-Graphics, Inc
Wireless access
Function: 24/7 Electronic res, 24/7 Online cat, Audiobks via web, Bks on cassette, Bks on CD, Children's prog, Computers for patron use, Digital talking bks, E-Reserves, Electronic databases & coll, Free DVD rentals, Homework prog, ILL available, Internet access, Magazines, Mail & tel request accepted, Mango lang, Microfiche/film & reading machines, Movies, Music CDs, Online cat, Outside serv via phone, mail, e-mail & web, OverDrive digital audio bks, Photocopying/Printing, Preschool reading prog, Prog for children & young adult, Ref & res, Ref serv available, Spoken cassettes & CDs, Story hour, Summer reading prog, Tax forms, Telephone ref, VHS videos, Wheelchair accessible
Mem of North Central Kansas Libraries System
Special Services for the Blind - Audio mat; Bks on cassette; Cassettes; Large print & cassettes; Large print bks
Open Mon, Tues & Fri 8:30-5, Wed 8:30-6, Thurs 8:30-7, Sat 9-1
Branches: 3

ALMA BRANCH, 115 W Third St, Alma, 66401. (Mail add: PO Box 420, Alma, 66401-0420), SAN 342-1538. Tel: 785-765-3647. FAX: 785-765-3647. E-mail: powabalm@gmail.com. *Br Librn,* Lori Beth Terrell; *Asst Br Librn,* Lorelie Wilson; Staff 1 (Non-MLS 1)
Founded 1962
Automation Activity & Vendor Info: (Circulation) Auto-Graphics, Inc
Function: Audiobks via web, Bks on cassette, Bks on CD, Children's prog, Computers for patron use, Digital talking bks, E-Reserves, Electronic databases & coll, Free DVD rentals, Holiday prog, Home delivery & serv to seniorr ctr & nursing homes, Homework prog, ILL available, Internet access, Life-long learning prog for all ages, Magazines, Mail & tel request accepted, Mango lang, Microfiche/film & reading machines, Music CDs, Online cat, Online info literacy tutorials on the web & in blackboard, Online ref, Orientations, Outside serv via phone, mail, e-mail & web, OverDrive digital audio bks, Photocopying/Printing, Preschool reading prog, Prog for adults, Prog for children & young adult, Ref serv available, Scanner, Story hour, Summer reading prog, Tax forms, Telephone ref, Visual arts prog, Wheelchair accessible
Special Services for the Blind - Audio mat; Bks on cassette; Cassettes; Large print & cassettes; Large print bks
Open Mon, Tues & Fri 9-12:15 & 12:45-5, Wed 9-12:15 & 12:45-7

ESKRIDGE BRANCH, 115 S Main St, Eskridge, 66423. (Mail add: PO Box 87, Eskridge, 66423-0087), SAN 342-1562. Tel: 785-449-2296. FAX: 785-449-2296. E-mail: powabesk@gmail.com. *Br Librn,* Jan Brown; *Asst Br Librn,* Judy Morton; Staff 1 (Non-MLS 1)
Founded 1962
Automation Activity & Vendor Info: (Circulation) Auto-Graphics, Inc
Function: 24/7 Electronic res, 24/7 Online cat, Art programs, Audiobks via web, Bks on cassette, Bks on CD, Children's prog, Computers for patron use, Digital talking bks, E-Reserves, Electronic databases & coll, Free DVD rentals, Holiday prog, Home delivery & serv to seniorr ctr & nursing homes, Homework prog, ILL available, Internet access, Life-long learning prog for all ages, Magazines, Mail & tel request accepted, Mango lang, Microfiche/film & reading machines, Online cat, Online info literacy tutorials on the web & in blackboard, Online ref, Orientations, Outside serv via phone, mail, e-mail & web, OverDrive digital audio bks, Photocopying/Printing, Preschool reading prog, Prog for adults, Prog for children & young adult, Ref serv available, Scanner, Story hour, Summer reading prog, Tax forms, Telephone ref, Visual arts prog, Wheelchair accessible
Special Services for the Blind - Audio mat; Bks on cassette; Cassettes; Large print & cassettes; Large print bks; Talking bk serv referral
Open Mon-Wed 8:30-12:30 & 1-6, Fri 9-12:30 & 1-4

ONAGA BRANCH, 313 Leonard St, Onaga, 66521. (Mail add: PO Box 310, Onaga, 66521-0310), SAN 342-1597. Tel: 785-889-4531. FAX: 785-889-4531. E-mail: powabona@gmail.com. *Br Librn,* Sallie Force; *Asst Br Librn,* Janet Hulinsky; Staff 1 (Non-MLS 1)
Founded 1962
Automation Activity & Vendor Info: (Circulation) Auto-Graphics, Inc
Function: 24/7 Electronic res, 24/7 Online cat, Art programs, Audiobks via web, Bks on cassette, Bks on CD, Children's prog, Computers for patron use, Digital talking bks, E-Reserves, Electronic databases & coll, Free DVD rentals, Holiday prog, Home delivery & serv to seniorr ctr & nursing homes, Homework prog, ILL available, Internet access, Life-long learning prog for all ages, Magazines, Mail & tel request accepted, Mango lang, Microfiche/film & reading machines, Music CDs, Online cat, Online info literacy tutorials on the web & in blackboard, Online ref, Outside serv via phone, mail, e-mail & web, OverDrive digital audio bks, Photocopying/Printing, Preschool reading prog, Prog for adults, Prog for children & young adult, Ref serv available, Scanner, Story hour, Summer reading prog, Tax forms, Telephone ref, Visual arts prog
Special Services for the Blind - Audio mat; Bks on cassette; Cassettes; Large print & cassettes; Large print bks; Talking bk serv referral
Open Mon 9-12:30 & 1-7, Tues & Fri 9-12:30 & 1-5, Wed 9-12:30 & 1-6:30

SAINT PAUL

P GRAVES MEMORIAL PUBLIC LIBRARY, 717 Central Ave, 66771. (Mail add: PO Box 354, 66771-0354), SAN 306-1159. Tel: 620-449-2001. FAX: 620-449-2001. Web Site: stpaul.mykansaslibrary.org. *Dir,* Sharon Blackburn; E-mail: gmpldirector@hotmail.com
Founded 1955. Pop 927; Circ 6,292
Library Holdings: Bk Vols 5,537; Per Subs 18
Special Collections: Local Newspaper 1901-1961; W W Graves, writings & bks
Wireless access
Mem of Southeast Kansas Library System
Open Mon-Fri 9-12 & 1-5
Restriction: Authorized patrons

SALINA

C KANSAS STATE UNIVERSITY AT SALINA*, Polytechnic Library, Technology Ctr Bldg, Rm 111, 2310 Centennial Rd, 67401. SAN 306-1175. Tel: 785-826-2636. FAX: 785-826-2937. E-mail: sallib@k-state.edu. Web Site: polytechnic.k-state.edu/academics/resources/library. *Dir,* Lisa Shappee; E-mail: lmccraft@k-state.edu; *Cat, Circ,* Pam Bower; E-mail: pbower@k-state.edu; Staff 4 (MLS 2, Non-MLS 2)
Founded 1965. Enrl 1,000; Fac 100; Highest Degree: Doctorate
Library Holdings: Bk Vols 30,000; Per Subs 100
Subject Interests: Aeronaut, Aviation, Bus & mgt, Computer info, Computer sci, Construction engr tech, Electronic tech, Math, Mechanical tech
Automation Activity & Vendor Info: (Acquisitions) Ex Libris Group; (Cataloging) Ex Libris Group; (Circulation) Ex Libris Group; (OPAC) Ex Libris Group; (Serials) Ex Libris Group
Wireless access
Open Mon-Thurs (Winter) 8am-9pm, Fri 8-5, Sun 6pm-10pm; Mon-Thurs (Summer) 8-8, Fri 8-5
Friends of the Library Group

C KANSAS WESLEYAN UNIVERSITY*, Memorial Library, 100 E Claflin Ave, 67401-6100. SAN 306-1183. Tel: 785-833-4395. Interlibrary Loan Service Tel: 785-833-4396. E-mail: library@kwu.edu. Web Site:

www.kwu.edu/library. *Dir, Libr Serv,* Kelley A Weber; E-mail: kelley.weber@kwu.edu; *Asst Librn,* Kate Wise; E-mail: kate.wise@kwu.edu; Staff 2 (MLS 2)
Founded 1886. Enrl 800; Fac 50; Highest Degree: Master
Library Holdings: e-books 7,500; Bk Titles 78,500; Per Subs 117
Automation Activity & Vendor Info: (Circulation) Koha; (ILL) OCLC WorldShare Interlibrary Loan; (OPAC) Koha; (Serials) Koha
Wireless access
Function: ILL available
Partic in Associated Colleges of Central Kansas; OCLC Online Computer Library Center, Inc
Open Mon-Thurs 8am-11pm, Fri 8-5, Sat 1-5, Sun 2-11 (Fall & Winter); Mon-Fri 8-5 (Summer)
Restriction: Open to pub for ref & circ; with some limitations

P SALINA PUBLIC LIBRARY*, 301 W Elm St, 67401. SAN 306-1205. Tel: 785-825-4624. FAX: 785-823-0706. Web Site: www.salinapubliclibrary.org. *Dir,* Lindsey Miller-Escarfuller; *Head of Processing,* Nick Berezovsky; E-mail: nickbere@salpublib.org; *Coll Develop, Head, Info Serv,* Angela Allen; E-mail: aallen@salpublib.org; *Head, Outreach Serv,* Lori Berezovsky; E-mail: loribere@salpublib.org; *Head, Youth Serv,* Lisa Newman; *Bus & Human Res Mgr,* Sandy Wilcox; E-mail: swilcox@salpublib.org; *Circ,* Kristi Hansen; E-mail: khansen@salpublib.org; *ILL,* Connie Hocking; E-mail: chocking@salpublib.org; *Tech Ctr Mgr,* Melanie Hedgespeth; E-mail: melanie@salpublib.org; Staff 38 (MLS 7, Non-MLS 31)
Founded 1897
Special Collections: Campbell Room of Kansas History
Subject Interests: Art, Educ, Hist
Automation Activity & Vendor Info: (Cataloging) LibLime Koha; (Circulation) LibLime Koha; (OPAC) LibLime Koha
Wireless access
Function: 24/7 Electronic res, 24/7 Online cat, Adult bk club, After school storytime, Archival coll, Art exhibits, Audiobks on Playaways & MP3, Audiobks via web, AV serv, Bk club(s), Bks on CD, Children's prog, Computer training, Computers for patron use, E-Readers, Electronic databases & coll, Free DVD rentals, Genealogy discussion group, Holiday prog, Home delivery & serv to seniorr ctr & nursing homes, Homebound delivery serv, ILL available, Instruction & testing, Internet access, Learning ctr, Life-long learning prog for all ages, Magazines, Magnifiers for reading, Mango lang, Microfiche/film & reading machines, Movies, Music CDs, Online cat, Online ref, Orientations, Outreach serv, Outside serv via phone, mail, e-mail & web, OverDrive digital audio bks, Photocopying/Printing, Preschool outreach, Preschool reading prog, Printer for laptops & handheld devices, Prog for adults, Prog for children & young adult, Ref & res, Ref serv available, Scanner, Senior computer classes, Senior outreach, Spanish lang bks, Story hour, Study rm, Summer & winter reading prog, Summer reading prog, Tax forms, Telephone ref, Wheelchair accessible, Winter reading prog, Workshops
Publications: Class Catalog; Cover to Cover (Newsletter)
Mem of Central Kansas Library System
Open Mon-Thurs 9-9, Fri & Sat 9-6, Sun 1-6
Friends of the Library Group

SATANTA

P DUDLEY TOWNSHIP PUBLIC LIBRARY, Satanta Library, 105 N Sequoyah St, 67870. (Mail add: PO Box 189, 67870-0189). Tel: 620-649-2213. FAX: 620-649-2213. E-mail: satantalibrary@gmail.com. Web Site: satanta.readinks.info. *Dir,* Suzie Boschman
Founded 1931
Special Collections: Kansas Coll
Wireless access
Mem of Southwest Kansas Library System
Open Mon-Wed & Fri 10:30-5:30, Thurs 1-8, Sat 9-Noon

SAVONBURG

P SAVONBURG PUBLIC LIBRARY*, 101A S Walnut, 66772. SAN 306-123X. Tel: 620-754-3835. E-mail: savonburglibrarian@gmail.com. *Dir,* Kathy Hale
Founded 1963. Pop 113; Circ 4,017
Library Holdings: Bk Vols 5,000; Per Subs 20
Automation Activity & Vendor Info: (Acquisitions) LibLime; (Cataloging) LibLime; (Circulation) LibLime
Wireless access
Mem of Southeast Kansas Library System
Open Tues & Thurs 2-6, Wed 4-6, Sat 10-Noon

SCANDIA

P SCANDIA CITY LIBRARY*, 318 Fourth St, 66966. (Mail add: PO Box 20, 66966-0020), SAN 306-1248. Tel: 785-335-2271. FAX: 785-335-2271. E-mail: scandiacitylibrary@gmail.com. Web Site: scandiacitylibrary.blogspot.com. *Librn,* Linda Tebow
Pop 650
Library Holdings: Bk Titles 9,000; Per Subs 40
Subject Interests: Swedish (Lang)
Wireless access
Mem of Central Kansas Library System
Open Mon-Sat 2-6

SCOTT CITY

P SCOTT COUNTY LIBRARY*, 110 W Eighth, 67871-1599. SAN 306-1256. Tel: 620-872-5341. FAX: 620-872-0248. E-mail: sclib@wbsnet.org. Web Site: www.sclibrary.info. *Libr Dir,* Lori Hawker
Founded 1923. Pop 5,582
Library Holdings: Bk Titles 45,000; Per Subs 100
Automation Activity & Vendor Info: (Cataloging) Follett Software; (Circulation) Follett Software
Wireless access
Mem of Southwest Kansas Library System
Open Mon & Thurs 10-8, Tues & Wed 10-6, Fri & Sat 10-5

SEDAN

P SEDAN PUBLIC LIBRARY, 115 N Chautauqua St, 67361. SAN 306-1264. Tel: 620-725-3405. FAX: 620-725-3405. E-mail: sedanlibrary@yahoo.com. Web Site: sedan.mykansaslibrary.org. *Dir,* Kayla Ford; Staff 2 (Non-MLS 2)
Pop 1,450
Library Holdings: Bk Vols 9,400; Per Subs 29
Mem of Southeast Kansas Library System
Open Mon & Tues 12:30-6, Wed 12:30-5:30, Thurs 2:30-7:30, Fri 9-5:30, Sat 9-2:30

SEDGWICK

P LILLIAN TEAR LIBRARY, 511 N Commercial, 67135. (Mail add: PO Box 28, 67135-0028), SAN 306-1272. Tel: 316-772-5727. E-mail: sedgwicktearlib@cityofsedgwick.org. *Libr Dir,* Chantel Rindt
Founded 1929. Pop 1,450; Circ 10,000
Library Holdings: Bk Vols 6,000; Per Subs 20
Special Collections: Sheet Music Coll
Wireless access
Mem of South Central Kansas Library System
Open Mon-Fri 10-6

SELDEN

P SELDEN PUBLIC LIBRARY*, 109 S Kansas Ave, 67757. (Mail add: PO Box 244, 67757-0244), SAN 376-513X. Tel: 785-386-4321. E-mail: seldenpl@ruraltel.net. Web Site: selden.nwkls.org. *Librn,* Marsha Rogers
Library Holdings: Audiobooks 50; AV Mats 50; CDs 10; DVDs 15; Large Print Bks 2,500; Bk Titles 5,000; Bk Vols 7,000; Videos 40
Wireless access
Mem of Northwest Kansas Library System
Open Mon & Sat 9am-11am, Wed 5-7

SENECA

P SENECA FREE LIBRARY*, 606 Main St, 66538. SAN 306-1280. Tel: 785-336-2377. FAX: 785-336-3699. E-mail: librarian@senecafreelibrary.org. Web Site: senecafreelibrary.org. *Libr Dir,* Kate Haynie; E-mail: khaynie@senecafreelibrary.org; Staff 1 (Non-MLS 1)
Founded 1917. Pop 2,000; Circ 60,000
Library Holdings: Audiobooks 900; CDs 700; DVDs 1,300; Large Print Bks 500; Bk Vols 26,000; Per Subs 54; Videos 400
Automation Activity & Vendor Info: (Acquisitions) LibLime; (Cataloging) LibLime; (Circulation) LibLime; (ILL) Auto-Graphics, Inc
Wireless access
Function: Adult bk club, Archival coll, Art exhibits, Bk club(s), Bks on cassette, Children's prog, Computer training, Computers for patron use, Family literacy, For res purposes, Free DVD rentals, Home delivery & serv to seniorr ctr & nursing homes, Homebound delivery serv, ILL available, Instruction & testing, Internet access, Mail & tel request accepted, Mail loans to mem, Online cat, Online ref, Orientations, Outreach serv, Outside serv via phone, mail, e-mail & web, OverDrive digital audio bks, Photocopying/Printing, Prof lending libr, Prog for children & young adult, Ref & res, Ref serv available, Res performed for a fee, Spoken cassettes & CDs, Story hour, Summer reading prog, Tax forms, Teen prog, VHS videos, Wheelchair accessible
Mem of Northeast Kansas Library System
Open Mon-Thurs 10-8, Fri 10-5, Sat 10-2

SHARON SPRINGS

P SHARON SPRINGS PUBLIC LIBRARY, 414 N Main St, 67758. (Mail add: PO Box 607, 67758-0607), SAN 306-1299. Tel: 785-852-4685. E-mail: sharonspringslibrary@fairpoint.net. Web Site:

sharonsprings.nwkls.org. *Head Librn,* Sharon Van Allen; E-mail: skvanallen@yahoo.com
Founded 1930. Pop 1,064; Circ 8,093
Library Holdings: AV Mats 13; Bk Vols 8,200; Per Subs 14
Subject Interests: Local hist
Automation Activity & Vendor Info: (Cataloging) Winnebago Software Co; (Circulation) Winnebago Software Co
Wireless access
Mem of Northwest Kansas Library System
Open Mon-Fri 9-5:30

SHAWNEE

R CENTRAL BAPTIST THEOLOGICAL SEMINARY LIBRARY, Shumaker Library, 6601 Monticello Rd, 66226-3513. SAN 305-9766. Tel: 913-667-5700, 913-667-5725. Administration Tel: 913-667-5729. FAX: 913-371-8110. Web Site: libguides.cbts.edu/home. *Libr Dir,* Vance M Thomas; Fax: 913-667-5789, E-mail: vmthomas@cbts.edu; *Libr Asst,* Linda Kiesling; Tel: 913-667-5733, E-mail: lkiesling@cbts.eud; Staff 2 (MLS 1, Non-MLS 1)
Founded 1901. Highest Degree: Doctorate
Library Holdings: Bk Vols 105,000; Per Subs 75
Subject Interests: Baptists, Relig
Automation Activity & Vendor Info: (Cataloging) SirsiDynix; (Circulation) SirsiDynix
Wireless access
Partic in American Theological Library Association; Amigos Library Services, Inc; Kansas City Library Service Program; Mid-America Library Alliance
Open Mon, Tues & Thurs 10-10, Wed & Fri 10-4:30 (Sept-May); Mon-Fri 10-4:30 (June-Aug)

SHAWNEE MISSION

M ADVENTHEALTH SHAWNEE MISSION MEDICAL LIBRARY, 9100 W 74th St, 66204. SAN 320-1899. Tel: 913-676-2101. Interlibrary Loan Service Tel: 913-676-2103. FAX: 913-676-2106. *Med Librn,* Melody J Senecal; E-mail: melody.senecal@AdventHealth.com; *Libr Coord,* Jeanne Bodnar; E-mail: jeanne.bodnar@AdventHealth.com; Staff 1.2 (MLS 1, Non-MLS 0.2)
Founded 1963
Library Holdings: CDs 100; DVDs 50; e-books 1,219; e-journals 3,400; Bk Vols 5,000; Per Subs 50
Automation Activity & Vendor Info: (Acquisitions) EOS International; (Cataloging) EOS International; (Circulation) EOS International; (ILL) OCLC WorldShare Interlibrary Loan; (OPAC) EOS International; (Serials) EOS International
Wireless access
Partic in OCLC Online Computer Library Center, Inc
Open Mon-Thurs 8-5, Fri 8-4:30

SILVER LAKE

P SILVER LAKE LIBRARY*, 203 Railroad St, 66539. (Mail add: PO Box 248, 66539-0248), SAN 306-1310. Tel: 785-582-5141. FAX: 785-582-0175. E-mail: library@silverlakelibrary.org. Web Site: www.silverlakelibrary.org. *Libr Dir,* Cathy Newland; E-mail: cnewland@silverlakelibrary.org; *Asst Dir,* Emily Marasco; E-mail: emarasco@silverlakelibrary.org; *Circ Librn,* Karla Bahret; *Circ Librn,* Sherry Baker; *Circ Librn,* Amber Hamilton; *Circ Librn,* Cassie Johnston; *Outreach Librn,* Patty Clark; *Youth Serv Librn,* Tracey DeShazo; Staff 2 (Non-MLS 2)
Founded 1974
Library Holdings: Bks on Deafness & Sign Lang 20; Bk Titles 8,000; Bk Vols 9,000; Per Subs 50
Special Collections: Children with Disabilities
Subject Interests: Inspirational
Automation Activity & Vendor Info: (Cataloging) SirsiDynix; (Circulation) SirsiDynix; (ILL) SirsiDynix
Wireless access
Function: Photocopying/Printing, Prog for children & young adult
Publications: Silver Lake Library Times
Mem of Northeast Kansas Library System
Special Services for the Blind - Audio mat
Open Mon & Wed-Fri 9-6, Tues 9-8, Sat 9-1
Friends of the Library Group

SMITH CENTER

P SMITH CENTER PUBLIC LIBRARY, 117 W Court St, 66967. SAN 306-1329. Tel: 785-282-3361. FAX: 785-282-6740. E-mail: smcntpl@ruraltel.net. Web Site: smithcenterpl.blogspot.com. *Libr Dir,* Joanna Runyon; *Asst Librn,* Ann Reinert; *Asst Librn,* Kay Seeman
Pop 2,100; Circ 30,603
Library Holdings: Bk Vols 17,000; Per Subs 59
Wireless access
Mem of Central Kansas Library System
Open Mon-Wed & Fri 10-5, Thurs 10-8, Sat 10-1

SOLOMON

P SOLOMON PUBLIC LIBRARY*, 108 N Walnut St, 67480. (Mail add: PO Box 246, 67480-0246), SAN 306-1337. Tel: 785-655-3521. E-mail: slibrary@eaglecom.net. Web Site: solomon.lib.nckls.org. *Dir,* Connie Avery; E-mail: connieavery48@yahoo.com
Founded 1934. Pop 1,192; Circ 9,492
Library Holdings: Bk Vols 12,500; Per Subs 35
Automation Activity & Vendor Info: (Acquisitions) Auto-Graphics, Inc; (Circulation) Auto-Graphics, Inc; (ILL) Auto-Graphics, Inc
Wireless access
Mem of North Central Kansas Libraries System
Open Mon & Wed 12-6, Tues, Thurs & Fri 3-6, Sat 10-4

SOUTH HAVEN

P SOUTH HAVEN TOWNSHIP LIBRARY, 104 W Baird, 67140. (Mail add: PO Box 227, 67140-0027), SAN 306-1345. Tel: 620-892-5268. E-mail: shtpl@kanokla.net. *Librn,* Marilyn Mitchell
Founded 1937. Pop 733; Circ 3,545
Library Holdings: Bk Vols 7,870
Mem of South Central Kansas Library System
Open Thurs-Sat 1-4:30

SOUTH HUTCHINSON

P SOUTH CENTRAL KANSAS LIBRARY SYSTEM*, 321 N Main St, 67505. SAN 342-0426. Tel: 620-663-3211. Toll Free Tel: 800-234-0529. FAX: 620-663-9797. Web Site: sckls.info. *Dir,* Paul Hawkins; E-mail: paul@sckls.info; *IT Dir,* Larry Papenfuss; E-mail: larry@sckls.info; *Human Res & Finance Coordr,* Mia Wilson; E-mail: mia@sckls.info; *Tech Coordr,* Lisa Sharbaugh; E-mail: lisa@sckls.info; *Training Coordr,* Katherine Hughes; E-mail: katherineh@sckls.info; *Libr Support Spec,* Katherine Williams; E-mail: katherine@sckls.info; *Outreach Serv Spec,* Nicole Penley; E-mail: nicole@sckls.info; *Tech Consult,* Sharon Barnes; E-mail: sharon@sckls.info; *Tech Consult,* Robyn Bravi; E-mail: robyn@sckls.info; *Tech Consult,* Tamia Taylor-Bader; E-mail: tamia@sckls.info; *Technology Spec,* Stefanie Gostautas; E-mail: stefanie@sckls.info; *Sch Libr Consult, Youth Serv Consult,* Robin Hargrave; E-mail: robin@sckls.info; Staff 12 (MLS 8, Non-MLS 4)
Founded 1967
Jan 2019-Dec 2019 Income $3,118,870, State $50,000, Locally Generated Income $2,844,087, Other $224,783. Mats Exp $83,000. Sal $496,585
Library Holdings: Bk Vols 50,000; Per Subs 20
Special Collections: Book Discussion Sets Coll; Professional Coll
Automation Activity & Vendor Info: (OPAC) Auto-Graphics, Inc
Member Libraries: Andale District Library; Andover Public Library; Anthony Public Library; Arkansas City Public Library; Arlington City Library; Attica City Library; Augusta Public Library; Belle Plaine City Library; Bethany College; Bethel College Library; Bradford Memorial Library; Buhler Public Library; Butler Community College Library & Archives; Caldwell Public Library; Canton Township Carnegie Library; Central Christian College of Kansas; Cheney Public Library; Clearwater Public Library; Colwich Community Library; Conway Springs City Library; Cowley County Community College; Derby Public Library; Dixon Township Library; Douglass Public Library; Farmer Township Community Library; Friends University; Garden Plain Community Library; Geneseo Public Library; Goddard Public Library; Halstead Public Library; Hardtner Public Library; Harper Public Library; Haven Public Library; Haysville Community Library; Hesston College; Hesston Public Library; Hutchinson Community College; Hutchinson Public Library; Ida Long Goodman Memorial Library; Inman Public Library; Kingman Carnegie Public Library; Kiowa Public Library; Leon Public Library; Lillian Tear Library; Lincoln Library; Lindsborg Community Library; Little River Community Library; Lyons Public Library; Macksville City Library; Marquette Community Library; McPherson College; McPherson Public Library; Moundridge Public Library; Mount Hope Public Library; Mulvane Public Library; Newman University; Newton Public Library; Nickerson Public Library; Nora E Larabee Memorial Library; Norwich Public Library; Oxford Public Library; Partridge Public Library; Potwin Public Library; Pretty Prairie Public Library; Rose Hill Public Library; Ruth Dole Memorial Library; South Haven Township Library; Southwestern College; Sterling College; Sterling Free Public Library; Sylvia Public Library; Towanda Public Library; Turon Community Library; Udall Public Library; United States Air Force; Valley Center Public Library; Viola Township Library; Walton Community Library; Wellington Public Library; Whitewater Memorial Library; Wichita Public Library; Wichita State University Libraries; Zenda Public Library
Partic in South Central Kansas Automation Network

SPEARVILLE

P SPEARVILLE TOWNSHIP LIBRARY*, 414 N Main St, 67876. (Mail add: PO Box 464, 67876-0464), SAN 306-1353. Tel: 620-385-2501. FAX: 620-385-2508. E-mail: slibrary@ucom.net. Web Site: www.spearvillelibrary.org. *Dir,* Leesa Shafer; Staff 1 (Non-MLS 1)
Founded 1929. Pop 1,232; Circ 14,780
Library Holdings: Bk Vols 25,000; Per Subs 70
Automation Activity & Vendor Info: (Cataloging) Auto-Graphics, Inc; (Circulation) Auto-Graphics, Inc; (ILL) Auto-Graphics, Inc; (OPAC) Auto-Graphics, Inc
Wireless access
Mem of Southwest Kansas Library System
Open Mon 1-8, Tues 10-6, Wed 1-6, Thurs 9-3 & 5-8

STAFFORD

P NORA E LARABEE MEMORIAL LIBRARY*, 108 N Union St, 67578-1339. SAN 306-1361. Tel: 620-234-5762. E-mail: larabeelibrary@gmail.com. Web Site: stafford.scklslibrary.info. *Libr Dir,* Jan McKeel
Founded 1906. Pop 1,027; Circ 35,000
Library Holdings: Bk Vols 25,000; Per Subs 50
Wireless access
Mem of South Central Kansas Library System
Open Mon-Fri 2-6, Sat 10-Noon

STERLING

C STERLING COLLEGE*, Mabee Library, 125 W Cooper, 67579. SAN 306-137X. Tel: 620-278-4234. Administration Tel: 620-278-4233. Toll Free Tel: 800-346-1017. FAX: 620-278-4414. E-mail: library@sterling.edu, mabee@sterling.edu. Web Site: www.sterling.edu/academics/mabee-library. *Dir,* Laurel Watney; E-mail: lwatney@sterling.edu; Staff 4 (MLS 1, Non-MLS 3)
Founded 1887. Enrl 600; Fac 40; Highest Degree: Bachelor
Library Holdings: Bk Titles 52,000; Per Subs 173
Automation Activity & Vendor Info: (Cataloging) LibLime Koha; (Circulation) LibLime Koha; (Course Reserve) LibLime Koha; (OPAC) LibLime Koha; (Serials) LibLime Koha
Wireless access
Function: Ref serv available
Mem of South Central Kansas Library System
Partic in OCLC Online Computer Library Center, Inc; Private Academic Libraries Section, Kansas Library Association
Open Mon-Thurs 7:30am-Midnight, Fri 7:30-5, Sat 1-5, Sun 2-5 & 8pm-Midnight

P STERLING FREE PUBLIC LIBRARY*, 138 N Broadway, 67579-2131. SAN 306-1388. Tel: 620-278-3191. FAX: 620-278-3191. E-mail: sfpl1917@gmail.com. Web Site: sterling.scklslibrary.info. *Dir,* Amy C Gard
Founded 1917. Pop 2,600; Circ 36,000
Library Holdings: AV Mats 1,200; Large Print Bks 100; Bk Titles 15,802; Bk Vols 18,716; Per Subs 100; Talking Bks 300
Automation Activity & Vendor Info: (Cataloging) Follett Software; (Circulation) Follett Software; (OPAC) Follett Software
Mem of South Central Kansas Library System
Open Mon-Thurs (Winter) 1-8, Fri & Sat 1-6; Mon-Fri (Summer) 10-7

STOCKTON

P STOCKTON PUBLIC LIBRARY*, 124 N Cedar, 67669-1636. SAN 306-1396. Tel: 785-425-6372. FAX: 785-425-6372. E-mail: stocklib@ruraltel.net. Web Site: stockton.mykansaslibrary.org. *Dir,* Christine Sander; *Librn,* Anne Williams
Pop 1,500; Circ 20,000
Library Holdings: Audiobooks 458; Bks on Deafness & Sign Lang 8; CDs 77; DVDs 111; Large Print Bks 484; Microforms 116; Music Scores 24; Bk Vols 15,944; Per Subs 32; Spec Interest Per Sub 18; Videos 824
Special Collections: Genealogy (Rooks County Record, 1878-1983)
Automation Activity & Vendor Info: (Circulation) LibLime; (ILL) Auto-Graphics, Inc; (Serials) EBSCO Online
Wireless access
Mem of Central Kansas Library System
Partic in OCLC Online Computer Library Center, Inc
Open Mon, Tues & Thurs 10-7, Wed & Fri 10-5, Sat 10-1

SUBLETTE

P HASKELL TOWNSHIP LIBRARY, 300 Easy St, 67877. SAN 306-140X. Tel: 620-675-2771. E-mail: haskelllib@gmail.com. Web Site: haskelltownshiplibrary.org. *Libr Dir,* Sara Koehn
Founded 1922. Pop 1,900; Circ 9,000
Library Holdings: Bk Vols 24,000; Per Subs 80
Automation Activity & Vendor Info: (Cataloging) Follett Software
Wireless access
Mem of Southwest Kansas Library System
Open Mon, Wed & Fri 10-5:30, Tues & Thurs 10-6, Sat 10-12

SYLVAN GROVE

P SYLVAN GROVE PUBLIC LIBRARY*, 122 S Main St, 67481. (Mail add: PO Box 96, 67481-0096), SAN 306-1426. Tel: 785-526-7188. FAX: 785-526-7189. E-mail: sylvangrovepubliclibrary@gmail.com. Web Site: livelincolncounty.com/business/sylvan-grove-public-library. *Librn,* Ramie Schulteis
Founded 1931. Pop 376; Circ 3,245
Library Holdings: Bk Vols 4,236; Per Subs 25
Wireless access
Mem of Central Kansas Library System
Open Tues 9:30-4:30, Wed 3-7, Fri 1-5

SYLVIA

P SYLVIA PUBLIC LIBRARY, 121 S Main St, 67581. (Mail add: PO Box 68, 67581-0068), SAN 306-1434. Tel: 620-486-2021. FAX: 620-615-7347. E-mail: sylvialibrary@hotmail.com. Web Site: sylvia.scklslibrary.info. *Librn,* Cheryl Eisenhour
Pop 210; Circ 550
Library Holdings: Bk Titles 4,731; Per Subs 3
Mem of South Central Kansas Library System
Open Tues & Fri 1-6

SYRACUSE

P HAMILTON COUNTY LIBRARY*, 102 W Ave C, 67878. (Mail add: PO Box 1307, 67878-1307), SAN 306-1442. Tel: 620-384-5622. FAX: 620-384-5623. Web Site: syracuselibrary.info. *Dir,* Amy Brucker; E-mail: director@syracuselibrary.info; Staff 3 (Non-MLS 3)
Founded 1931. Pop 2,474; Circ 25,198
Jan 2016-Dec 2016 Income (Main Library Only) $261,007, State $2,422, Federal $86, County $238,898, Other $19,601. Mats Exp $13,115, Books $12,659, Per/Ser (Incl. Access Fees) $456. Sal $123,927
Library Holdings: Audiobooks 17,529; DVDs 1,252; e-books 130,307; Bk Titles 22,987; Per Subs 5; Videos 1,252
Subject Interests: Genealogy
Automation Activity & Vendor Info: (Cataloging) Auto-Graphics, Inc; (Circulation) Auto-Graphics, Inc; (ILL) Auto-Graphics, Inc
Wireless access
Function: 24/7 Electronic res, 24/7 Online cat, Activity rm, Audiobks on Playaways & MP3, Audiobks via web, Bks on CD, Children's prog, Computer training, Computers for patron use, Digital talking bks, Electronic databases & coll, Family literacy, Free DVD rentals, Genealogy discussion group, Govt ref serv, Holiday prog, Home delivery & serv to seniorr ctr & nursing homes, Homebound delivery serv, ILL available, Instruction & testing, Internet access, Laminating, Life-long learning prog for all ages, Magazines, Mango lang, Meeting rooms, Microfiche/film & reading machines, Movies, Online cat, Online info literacy tutorials on the web & in blackboard, Online ref, Orientations, Outreach serv, Photocopying/Printing, Preschool outreach, Preschool reading prog, Prog for adults, Prog for children & young adult, Ref & res, Ref serv available, Scanner, Senior outreach, Story hour, Study rm, Summer & winter reading prog, Summer reading prog, Tax forms, Teen prog, Winter reading prog, Workshops
Mem of Southwest Kansas Library System
Special Services for the Deaf - Bks on deafness & sign lang; Closed caption videos
Special Services for the Blind - Aids for in-house use; Bks & mags in Braille, on rec, tape & cassette; Bks available with recordings; Bks on CD; Copier with enlargement capabilities; Digital talking bk; Digital talking bk machines; Large print bks; Large print bks & talking machines; Playaways (bks on MP3); Talking bks
Open Mon, Wed & Fri 9-5, Tues & Thurs 9-6
Friends of the Library Group

TALMAGE

P TALMAGE PUBLIC LIBRARY*, 2994 Main St, 67842. (Mail add: PO Box 807, 67842-0807). Tel: 785-643-9126. E-mail: talmagelibrary@gmail.com. Web Site: talmage.lib.nckls.org. *Board Pres,* Shawni Sheets; *Dir,* Position Currently Open
Wireless access
Mem of North Central Kansas Libraries System
Open Mon-Fri 10-4, Sat & Sun by appointment
Friends of the Library Group

THAYER

P THAYER FRIDAY READING CLUB CITY LIBRARY*, 200 W Neosho Ave, 66776. (Mail add: PO Box 37, 66776-0037), SAN 306-1450. Tel: 620-839-5646. FAX: 620-839-5646. E-mail: thayerfrc@embarqmail.com.

Web Site: thayerfriday.mykansaslibrary.org. *Librn,* Suprena Cheshier; E-mail: suprenacheshier@hotmail.com; Staff 1897 (MLS 1896, Non-MLS 1)
Pop 500; Circ 5,000
Library Holdings: Bk Vols 8,615; Per Subs 13
Wireless access
Function: 24/7 Electronic res, 24/7 Online cat, Adult bk club, Audio & video playback equip for onsite use, Audiobks via web, Bks on CD, Children's prog, Computer training, Computers for patron use, Digital talking bks, Doc delivery serv, Electronic databases & coll, Free DVD rentals, Holiday prog, Homebound delivery serv, ILL available, Internet access, Laminating, Magazines, Mango lang, Meeting rooms, Movies, Music CDs, Notary serv, Online cat, Online info literacy tutorials on the web & in blackboard, Online ref, OverDrive digital audio bks, Photocopying/Printing, Printer for laptops & handheld devices, Prog for adults, Prog for children & young adult, Ref & res, Scanner, Summer reading prog, Tax forms, Wheelchair accessible
Mem of Southeast Kansas Library System
Open Mon 2-7, Tues & Wed 2-6, Thurs 11-12 & 1-5, Fri 2-5, Sat 10-Noon

TIPTON

P TIPTON LIBRARY*, Main St, 67485. (Mail add: 313 Grasshopper, 67485-9616). Tel: 785-373-6975. *Library Contact,* Pat Allen
Library Holdings: Bk Vols 3,000
Mem of Central Kansas Library System
Open Thurs (Summer) 8:40-4:30; Thurs (Winter) 8:30-11:30 & 1-4:30

TONGANOXIE

P TONGANOXIE PUBLIC LIBRARY*, 303 S Bury St, 66086. SAN 306-1469. Tel: 913-845-3281. FAX: 913-845-2962. Web Site: www.tonganoxielibrary.org. *Dir,* Nicole Holifield; E-mail: director@tonganoxielibrary.org; Staff 9 (MLS 1, Non-MLS 8)
Founded 1899. Pop 5,000; Circ 70,000
Library Holdings: Audiobooks 1,090; CDs 1,603; DVDs 2,777; Electronic Media & Resources 573; High Interest/Low Vocabulary Bk Vols 30; Large Print Bks 1,500; Bk Vols 26,023; Per Subs 40; Spec Interest Per Sub 12; Talking Bks 110
Special Collections: Kansas Coll
Automation Activity & Vendor Info: (ILL) Auto-Graphics, Inc
Wireless access
Function: Bks on CD, Children's prog, Computer training, Computers for patron use, Free DVD rentals, ILL available, Magnifiers for reading, Microfiche/film & reading machines, Music CDs, Online cat, OverDrive digital audio bks, Photocopying/Printing, Prog for adults, Prog for children & young adult, Scanner, Senior computer classes, Senior outreach, Spanish lang bks, Story hour, Summer reading prog, Tax forms, Teen prog, Wheelchair accessible, Winter reading prog
Mem of Northeast Kansas Library System
Special Services for the Blind - Talking bks
Open Mon-Thurs 9-8, Fri & Sat 9-5, Sun 1-5
Friends of the Library Group

TOPEKA

S KANSAS DEPARTMENT OF CORRECTIONS*, Topeka Juvenile Correctional Facility Library, 1430 NW 25th St, 66618-1499. Tel: 785-354-9800. FAX: 785-354-9878. *Librn,* Chasidy Williams
Library Holdings: Bk Vols 9,000; Per Subs 12
Automation Activity & Vendor Info: (Acquisitions) Follett Software; (Cataloging) Follett Software; (Circulation) Follett Software; (OPAC) Follett Software; (Serials) Follett Software
Restriction: Not open to pub

G KANSAS DEPARTMENT OF TRANSPORTATION LIBRARY, Eisenhower Bldg, 4th Flr, 700 SW Harrison St, 66603-3745. SAN 306-1493. Tel: 785-291-3854. FAX: 785-291-3717. E-mail: KDOT#Research.Library@ks.gov. *Librn,* Marie Manthe; E-mail: marie.manthe@ks.gov; Staff 1 (MLS 1)
Founded 1962
Library Holdings: e-books 9,350; Electronic Media & Resources 400; Bk Vols 34,000
Subject Interests: Engr, Transportation
Open Mon-Fri 8-5

S KANSAS HISTORICAL SOCIETY*, Library & Archives Division, 6425 SW Sixth Ave, 66615-1099. SAN 306-1507. Tel: 785-272-8681. Reference Tel: 785-272-8681, Ext 117. FAX: 785-272-8682. TDD: 785-272-8683. Reference E-mail: reference@kshs.org. Web Site: www.kshs.org. *Dir, State Archives,* Matt Veatch; *Head, Ref,* Lin Fredricksen; E-mail: lfredericksen@kshs.org; *Cat & Acq,* Margaret Knecht; E-mail: mknecht@kshs.org; *Ref Librn,* Susan Forbes; E-mail: sforbes@kshs.org; *Curator,* Blair Tarr; E-mail: btarr@kshs.org; *Sr Archivist,* Megan Burton; E-mail: megan.burton@ks.gov; Staff 17 (MLS 6, Non-MLS 11)
Founded 1875
Library Holdings: Bk Vols 180,814; Per Subs 475
Special Collections: Kansas State Archives, AV, maps, ms, newsp & photos. Oral History; State Document Depository; US Document Depository
Subject Interests: Civil War, Genealogy, Kansas, Native Americans
Automation Activity & Vendor Info: (Cataloging) OCLC Connexion; (OPAC) Innovative Interfaces, Inc; (Serials) Innovative Interfaces, Inc
Wireless access
Function: Archival coll, ILL available
Open Tues-Sat 9-4:30
Restriction: Non-circulating

GL KANSAS SUPREME COURT, Law Library, Kansas Judicial Ctr, 301 SW Tenth Ave, 1st Flr, 66612-1502. SAN 306-1523. Tel: 785-296-3257. FAX: 785-296-1863. E-mail: lawlibrary@kscourts.org. Web Site: www.kscourts.org/kansas-courts/law-library. *Asst Dir, Ref,* Marcia Hannon; Tel: 785-368-7371, E-mail: hannonm@kscourts.org; *Libr Asst,* Marie Valdivia; Tel: 785-368-7372, E-mail: valdiviam@kscourts.org; Staff 3 (MLS 1, Non-MLS 2)
Founded 1855
Jul 2021-Jun 2022 Income $574,829, State $569,250, Locally Generated Income $5,579. Mats Exp $515,260, Books $26,852, Per/Ser (Incl. Access Fees) $396,491, Electronic Ref Mat (Incl. Access Fees) $85,690, Presv $6,227. Sal $450,376
Library Holdings: Bk Vols 132,460; Per Subs 130
Special Collections: US Document Depository
Automation Activity & Vendor Info: (Cataloging) Innovative Interfaces, Inc; (OPAC) Innovative Interfaces, Inc
Wireless access
Function: 24/7 Online cat, Computers for patron use, Electronic databases & coll, For res purposes, Notary serv, Online cat, OverDrive digital audio bks, Ref & res, Ref serv available, Res assist avail
Open Mon-Fri 8-5
Restriction: Circ limited

P STATE LIBRARY OF KANSAS*, State Capitol Bldg, Rm 312-N, 300 SW Tenth Ave, 66612. SAN 342-1864. Tel: 785-296-3296. Toll Free Tel: 800-432-3919 (KS Only). FAX: 785-368-7291. E-mail: infodesk@library.ks.gov. Web Site: www.kslib.info. *State Librn,* Eric Norris; Tel: 785-296-5466, E-mail: eric.norris@ks.gov; *Dir, Ref,* Cindy Roupe; E-mail: cindy.roupe@ks.gov; *Dir, Statewide Libr Serv,* Jeff Hixon; E-mail: jeff.hixon@ks.gov; *Cat Librn, ILL Librn,* Brett Rurode; *Res Sharing Spec,* Rhonda Machlan; *State Doc Cataloger,* Bill Sowers; Staff 27 (MLS 16, Non-MLS 11)
Founded 1855
Special Collections: Kansas Legislative Materials. State Document Depository; US Document Depository
Subject Interests: Demographics, Govt, Pub policy issues
Automation Activity & Vendor Info: (Cataloging) Evergreen; (Circulation) Evergreen; (ILL) Auto-Graphics, Inc; (OPAC) Evergreen; (Serials) Evergreen
Wireless access
Partic in OCLC Online Computer Library Center, Inc
Special Services for the Blind - Descriptive video serv (DVS)
Open Mon-Fri 8-5
Branches: 1
KANSAS TALKING BOOKS SERVICE
See Separate Entry in Emporia under Kansas State Library

M STORMONT-VAIL HEALTH*, Stauffer Health Science Library, 1500 SW Tenth Ave, 66604-1353. SAN 327-7933. Tel: 785-354-5800. FAX: 785-354-5059. E-mail: hslibemail@stormontvail.org. Web Site: stormontvail.org/stauffer-health-sciences-library. *Dir,* Lenora Kinzie; Staff 3 (MLS 1, Non-MLS 2)
Library Holdings: Bk Titles 8,000; Per Subs 200
Subject Interests: Med, Nursing
Open Mon-Fri 7-5
Restriction: Researchers only

P TOPEKA & SHAWNEE COUNTY PUBLIC LIBRARY*, 1515 SW Tenth Ave, 66604-1374. SAN 342-1929. Tel: 785-580-4400. Interlibrary Loan Service Tel: 785-580-4425. FAX: 785-580-4496. TDD: 785-580-4544. Web Site: www.tscpl.org. *Chief Exec Officer,* Gina Millsap; E-mail: gmillsap@tscpl.org; *Chief Financial Officer,* Sheryl Weller; E-mail: sweller@tscpl.org; *Chief Operating Officer,* Robert Banks; E-mail: rbanks@tscpl.org; *Digital Serv Dir,* David Lee King; E-mail: dking@tscpl.org; *Dir, Mkt & Communications,* Diana Friend; E-mail: dfriend@tscpl.org; *Pub Serv Dir,* Marie Pyko; E-mail: mpyko@tscpl.org; *Pub Serv Mgr,* Stephanie Hall; *Circ Supvr,* Ruth Rodden; E-mail: rrodden@tscpl.org; *Tech Serv Supvr,* Scarlett Fisher-Herreman; E-mail: sfherreman@tscpl.org; *Youth Serv Supvr,* LeAnne Brungardt; E-mail: lbrungardt@tscpl.org; *Cat,* Renee Patzer; E-mail: rpatzer@tscpl.org; Staff 176 (MLS 27, Non-MLS 149)
Founded 1870. Pop 167,747; Circ 2,141,520

Library Holdings: AV Mats 98,784; Large Print Bks 27,070; Bk Vols 386,435; Per Subs 1,301; Talking Bks 28,340
Special Collections: Federal Census Depository Coll; Miniature Books; Topeka, bks, photos & film
Subject Interests: Art & archit, Illustrated bks, Music
Automation Activity & Vendor Info: (Acquisitions) BiblioCommons; (Cataloging) BiblioCommons; (Circulation) BiblioCommons; (Discovery) BiblioCommons; (ILL) BiblioCommons; (OPAC) BiblioCommons; (Serials) BiblioCommons
Wireless access
Function: Archival coll, AV serv, Games & aids for people with disabilities, Home delivery & serv to seniorr ctr & nursing homes, Homebound delivery serv, ILL available, Internet access, Large print keyboards, Magnifiers for reading, Outside serv via phone, mail, e-mail & web, Photocopying/Printing, Prog for adults, Prog for children & young adult, Ref serv available, Serves people with intellectual disabilities, Summer reading prog, Wheelchair accessible, Workshops
Publications: Library Edition; Library News Update (Newsletter)
Mem of Northeast Kansas Library System
Special Services for the Deaf - Bks on deafness & sign lang; Closed caption videos; Spec interest per; Staff with knowledge of sign lang; TDD equip; TTY equip
Special Services for the Blind - Reader equip
Open Mon-Fri 9-9, Sat 9-6, Sun Noon-9
Friends of the Library Group
Bookmobiles: 3. In Charge, Sandy Hestand. Bk vols 56,100

P TOPEKA GENEALOGICAL SOCIETY LIBRARY*, 2717 SE Indiana Ave, 66605-1440. (Mail add: PO Box 4048, 66604-0048), SAN 370-7334. Tel: 785-233-5762. E-mail: library@tgstopeka.org. Web Site: tgstopeka.org/cpage.php?pt=53. *Libr Dir,* Lyn Hutchinson
Founded 1968
Library Holdings: Bk Titles 5,800; Bk Vols 6,000; Per Subs 612
Special Collections: Original Shawnee County Kansas Probate Books 1856-1920; Shawnee County Cemetery Files; Shawnee County Kansas Naturalization Records; Surname Card File
Subject Interests: Genealogy, Hist
Publications: Topeka Genealogical Society Quarterly; Topeka Society Newsletter
Open Mon, Wed & Thurs 1-4, Sat 10-3
Restriction: Circ limited

C WASHBURN UNIVERSITY*, Mabee Library, 1700 SW College Ave, 66621. SAN 342-1988. Tel: 785-670-1179. Circulation Tel: 785-670-1485. Interlibrary Loan Service Tel: 785-670-1489. Reference Tel: 785-670-1483. Toll Free Tel: 800-736-9060. FAX: 785-670-3223. Web Site: www.washburn.edu/mabee. *Dean of Libr,* Dr Alan Bearman; E-mail: alan.bearman@washburn.edu; *Assoc Dean, Univ Libr,* Sean Bird; Tel: 785-670-1550, E-mail: sean.bird@washburn.edu; *Tutoring Servs, Writing Ctr Dir,* Sean Stacey; Tel: 785-670-1484, E-mail: sean.stacey@washburn.edu; *Head, Circ/ILL,* Andrea Leon; E-mail: andrea.leon@washburn.edu; *Discovery Librn,* Angela Beatie; Tel: 785-670-1503, E-mail: angela.beatie@washburn.edu; *First Year Experience Librn,* Stephen Woody; Tel: 785-670-2507, E-mail: stephen.woody@washburn.edu; *Info Literacy Librn,* Andrea Thimesch; Tel: 785-670-1932, E-mail: andrea.thimesch@washburn.edu; *Instruction Librn,* Jean Marshall; Tel: 785-670-1276, E-mail: jean.marshall@washburn.edu; *Health Informatics Coord, Librn,* Gwen Wilson; Tel: 785-670-2609, E-mail: gwen.wilson@washburn.edu; *Pub Access Librn,* Amanda Luke; Tel: 785-670-1481, E-mail: amanda.luke@washburn.edu; *Ref Librn,* Kelly Leahy; Tel: 785-670-1982, E-mail: kelly.leahy@washburn.edu; *Spec Coll Librn,* Martha Imparato; Tel: 785-670-1981, E-mail: martha.imparato@washburn.edu; *Coll Develop Mgr,* Lori Fenton; Tel: 785-670-1984, E-mail: lori.fenton@washburn.edu; *Fac Mgr,* Lori Rognlie; Tel: 785-670-1986, E-mail: lori.rognlie@washburn.edu; *Acq Spec,* Teresa Nitcher; Tel: 785-670-1985, E-mail: teresa.nitcher@washburn.edu; *Digital Media Spec,* Jennifer Somers; Tel: 785-670-1275, E-mail: jennifer.somers@washburn.edu; *Tech Consult,* Farhan Makda; Tel: 785-670-1480, E-mail: farhan.makda@washburn.edu; Staff 18 (MLS 12, Non-MLS 6)
Founded 1865. Enrl 6,289; Fac 344; Highest Degree: Master
Library Holdings: AV Mats 1,153; CDs 569; DVDs 2,404; e-books 121,178; e-journals 89,389; Electronic Media & Resources 41,013; Microforms 3,068; Bk Vols 318,854; Per Subs 481; Videos 3,303
Special Collections: Bradbury Thompson Materials; College & University History (Washburn Archives); Thomas Fox Averill Kansas Studies Coll; Washburn University Institutional Repository; William I Koch Art History Coll
Automation Activity & Vendor Info: (Acquisitions) Innovative Interfaces, Inc - Sierra; (Cataloging) Innovative Interfaces, Inc - Sierra; (Circulation) Innovative Interfaces, Inc - Sierra; (Course Reserve) Innovative Interfaces, Inc - Sierra; (Discovery) Innovative Interfaces, Inc - Sierra; (ILL) OCLC ILLiad; (OPAC) Innovative Interfaces, Inc - Sierra; (Serials) Innovative Interfaces, Inc - Sierra
Wireless access
Publications: Among Friends (Newsletter)
Mem of Northeast Kansas Library System
Partic in Amigos Library Services, Inc; LYRASIS; Mid-America Law Library Consortium; NELLCO Law Library Consortium, Inc.; OCLC Online Computer Library Center, Inc
Special Services for the Deaf - Assistive tech
Special Services for the Blind - Assistive/Adapted tech devices, equip & products
Open Mon-Wed 7am-2am, Thurs 7am-11pm, Fri 7-6, Sat 10-5, Sun 1pm-2am
Friends of the Library Group

Departmental Libraries:

CARNEGIE EDUCATION LIBRARY, 1700 SW College Ave, 66621, SAN 342-2011. Tel: 785-670-1436. Web Site: libguides.washburn.edu/celguide.
Founded 1984
Open Mon-Fri 8:30-5:30

CL SCHOOL OF LAW LIBRARY, 1700 SW College Ave, 66621, SAN 342-2046. Tel: 785-670-1088. FAX: 785-670-3194. E-mail: lawlibrary@washburnlaw.edu. Web Site: www.washburnlaw.edu/library. *Dir,* Thomas Sneed; Tel: 785-670-1658, E-mail: thomas.sneed@washburn.edu; *Asst Dir, Head, Tech Serv,* Martin Wisneski; Tel: 785-670-1788, E-mail: martin.wisneski@washburn.edu; *Head, Access Serv,* Barbara Ginzburg; Tel: 785-670-1087, E-mail: barbara.ginzburg@washburn.edu; *Tech Adminr, User Serv,* Jason Dinkel; Tel: 785-670-1776, E-mail: jason.dinkel@washburn.edu; *Cat Librn,* Rebecca Alexander; Tel: 785-670-1040, E-mail: rebecca.alexander@washburn.edu; *Instrul Tech Librn,* Glen McBeth; Tel: 785-670-1778, E-mail: glen.mcbeth@washburn.edu; *Librn, Res & Bibliog Instruction,* Creighton Miller; Tel: 785-670-1041, E-mail: creighton.miller@washburn.edu; *Digital Projects, Spec Coll Librn,* Janet Todwong; Tel: 785-670-3191, E-mail: janet.todwong@washburn.edu; *Cat Spec, Supvr,* Leigh Ives; Tel: 785-670-1777, E-mail: leigh.ives@washburn.edu; *Tech Serv Asst,* Sylvia Hurla; Tel: 785-670-1799, E-mail: sylvia.hurla@washburn.edu
Founded 1903. Enrl 304; Fac 28; Highest Degree: Doctorate
Special Collections: Brown vs Board of Education Historic Document Coll; Kansas Supreme Court Briefs. State Document Depository; US Document Depository
Automation Activity & Vendor Info: (Acquisitions) Innovative Interfaces, Inc - Sierra; (Cataloging) Innovative Interfaces, Inc - Sierra; (Circulation) Innovative Interfaces, Inc - Sierra; (Course Reserve) Innovative Interfaces, Inc - Sierra; (Discovery) Innovative Interfaces, Inc - Sierra; (ILL) OCLC; (OPAC) Innovative Interfaces, Inc - Sierra; (Serials) Innovative Interfaces, Inc - Sierra
Partic in OCLC Online Computer Library Center, Inc

TORONTO

P TORONTO PUBLIC LIBRARY, 215 W Main St, 66777. (Mail add: PO Box 244, 66777-0244), SAN 376-7213. Tel: 620-637-2661. E-mail: torlib@embarqmail.com. Web Site: toronto.mykansaslibrary.org. *Dir,* May Damron
Library Holdings: Bk Titles 8,000; Per Subs 10
Wireless access
Mem of Southeast Kansas Library System
Open Tues-Fri 2-6:30, Sat 10-2

TOWANDA

P TOWANDA PUBLIC LIBRARY*, 620 Highland, 67144-9042. SAN 306-1604. Tel: 316-536-2464. FAX: 316-536-2847. E-mail: towandalibrary@gmail.com. Web Site: towandalibrary.info. *Libr Dir,* Cole Everhart; *Asst Libr Dir,* Joy Barron; *Storytime Dir,* Shawna Mosier; Staff 2 (Non-MLS 2)
Founded 1936. Pop 1,426; Circ 5,357
Library Holdings: High Interest/Low Vocabulary Bk Vols 50; Large Print Bks 50; Bk Titles 13,048; Bk Vols 15,048; Per Subs 35; Talking Bks 150
Subject Interests: Local hist, Reading
Automation Activity & Vendor Info: (ILL) OCLC
Wireless access
Function: Adult literacy prog, Homebound delivery serv, ILL available, Prog for children & young adult
Mem of South Central Kansas Library System
Special Services for the Blind - Bks on CD
Open Mon, Wed & Fri 10-6, Sat 10-12
Friends of the Library Group

TRIBUNE

P GREELEY COUNTY LIBRARY*, 517 Broadway, 67879. (Mail add: PO Box 300, 67879-0300). Tel: 620-376-4801. FAX: 620-376-4077. Web Site: www.greeleycolibrary.info. *Libr Dir,* Ronna Schmidt; E-mail: director@greeleycolibrary.info
Library Holdings: Bk Vols 15,000; Per Subs 20

Automation Activity & Vendor Info: (Cataloging) Auto-Graphics, Inc; (Circulation) Auto-Graphics, Inc; (ILL) Auto-Graphics, Inc; (OPAC) Auto-Graphics, Inc; (Serials) Auto-Graphics, Inc
Wireless access
Function: Computers for patron use
Mem of Southwest Kansas Library System
Open Mon, Tues, Thurs & Fri 9:30-5, Wed 1-7; Mon, Tues & Fri (Summer) 8-2:30, Wed 1-7, Thurs 8-5

TROY

P LIBRARY DISTRICT NUMBER ONE, DONIPHAN COUNTY*, 105 N Main, 66087. (Mail add: PO Box 220, 66087-0220), SAN 306-1612. Tel: 785-985-2597, 833-LIB-DIS1 (542-3471). FAX: 785-985-2602. E-mail: library@librarydistrict1.org. Web Site: www.librarydistrict1.org. *Dir,* Becky Etherton; E-mail: betherton@librarydistrict1.org; Staff 13 (MLS 1, Non-MLS 12)
Founded 1974
Special Collections: Doniphan County Hist. Oral History
Subject Interests: Genealogy, Kansas
Wireless access
Function: 24/7 Electronic res, 24/7 Online cat, Bks on CD, Children's prog, Computers for patron use, Free DVD rentals, Holiday prog, Home delivery & serv to seniorr ctr & nursing homes, Internet access, Microfiche/film & reading machines, Music CDs
Mem of Northeast Kansas Library System
Partic in NExpress Consortium
Special Services for the Deaf - Closed caption videos
Special Services for the Blind - Playaways (bks on MP3)
Open Mon-Thurs 9-7, Fri 9-5, Sat 9-1
Friends of the Library Group
Branches: 3
ELWOOD BRANCH, 410 N Ninth, Elwood, 66024. (Mail add: PO Box 208, Elwood, 66024). Tel: 913-365-5625. *Librn,* Shelley Anderson
Special Services for the Deaf - Closed caption videos
Special Services for the Blind - Large print bks
Open Tues-Fri 12-6
Friends of the Library Group
HIGHLAND BRANCH, 306 W Main, Highland, 66035. Tel: 785-442-3078. *Librn,* Betty Snyder
Library Holdings: Audiobooks 150; CDs 40; DVDs 100; Large Print Bks 20; Bk Vols 6,000; Videos 40
Open Mon-Thurs 10-6
WATHENA BRANCH, 206 St Joseph, Wathena, 66090. Tel: 785-990-2665. *Librn,* Shelley Anderson
Library Holdings: Bk Vols 2,000
Open Mon-Thurs 1-7, Fri 9-12 & 1-6, Sat 9-1
Friends of the Library Group

TURON

P TURON COMMUNITY LIBRARY*, 501 E Price, 67583-9464. (Mail add: PO Box 357, 67583-0357), SAN 306-1620. Tel: 620-497-6409. E-mail: turonlib@sctelcom.net. *Dir,* Angela Williams; Tel: 620-388-3106; Staff 1 (Non-MLS 1)
Pop 380
Library Holdings: Audiobooks 40; CDs 20; DVDs 200; Large Print Bks 100; Bk Titles 6,238; Per Subs 10; Spec Interest Per Sub 2; Videos 30
Special Collections: Local School Annuals; Local Turon News Papers; Turon History Section
Wireless access
Function: Activity rm, Adult bk club, Summer reading prog
Mem of South Central Kansas Library System
Open Tues-Thurs 4-7:30, Sat 10-1

UDALL

P UDALL PUBLIC LIBRARY*, 109 E First St, 67146. (Mail add: PO Box 135, 67146-0135), SAN 306-1639. Tel: 620-782-3435. E-mail: library@cityofudall.com. Web Site: www.cityofudall.com/udall-public-library. *Librn,* Bertha Rhoads
Pop 910; Circ 3,000
Library Holdings: Bk Vols 3,600
Mem of South Central Kansas Library System
Open Tues, Thurs & Fri 3-6, Wed & Sat 10-1

ULYSSES

P GRANT COUNTY LIBRARY, 215 E Grant Ave, 67880. SAN 306-1647. Tel: 620-356-1433. FAX: 620-356-1344. E-mail: grantcolibrary215@gmail.com. Web Site: www.grantcolib.info. *Dir,* Holly Mathes; E-mail: holly@pld.com; *Asst Librn, Spec Coll Librn,* Nidia Gallegos; *Ch,* Maribel Sandoval; *YA Serv,* M J Siebert
Founded 1915. Pop 10,000; Circ 95,000
Library Holdings: Bk Vols 50,000; Per Subs 140
Special Collections: Large Print Books; Local Newspapers (to 1989), cassettes, micro; Spanish Coll, bks, micro, per & rec. Oral History
Subject Interests: Art & archit, Frontier & pioneer life, Genealogy, Kansas, Relig, Soc sci & issues
Automation Activity & Vendor Info: (Acquisitions) Follett Software; (Cataloging) Follett Software; (Circulation) Follett Software
Wireless access
Mem of Southwest Kansas Library System
Open Mon-Fri 9-6
Friends of the Library Group

VALLEY CENTER

P VALLEY CENTER PUBLIC LIBRARY*, 314 E Clay St, 67147. SAN 306-1663. Tel: 316-755-7350. FAX: 316-755-7351. E-mail: valleycenterlibrary@yahoo.com. Web Site: www.valleycenterlibrary.org. *Dir,* Janice Sharp; E-mail: janicesharp@yahoo.com; Staff 5 (Non-MLS 5)
Founded 1923. Pop 7,313; Circ 49,573
Jan 2020-Dec 2020 Income $310,026, Locally Generated Income $276,536, Other $33,490. Mats Exp $310,026, Books $24,000, Per/Ser (Incl. Access Fees) $12,500. Sal $173,382
Library Holdings: Audiobooks 2,696; Bks-By-Mail 821; DVDs 1,863; e-books 151,751; Electronic Media & Resources 9,296; Bk Vols 40,166; Per Subs 48; Videos 77
Special Collections: Ark Valley News Coll, 1975-1998, micro; Kansas Writers Coll; Valley Center Index Coll, 1897-1975, micro; Valley Center News Coll, 1882-1890, micro
Automation Activity & Vendor Info: (Acquisitions) Biblionix/Apollo; (Cataloging) Biblionix/Apollo; (Circulation) Biblionix/Apollo; (ILL) Auto-Graphics, Inc
Wireless access
Function: 24/7 Electronic res, 24/7 Online cat, Adult bk club, Audiobks on Playaways & MP3, Bk club(s), Bks on CD, Children's prog, Computers for patron use, Digital talking bks, E-Readers, Free DVD rentals, Homebound delivery serv, ILL available, Instruction & testing, Internet access, Laminating, Magazines, Mail & tel request accepted, Microfiche/film & reading machines, Movies, Notary serv, Online cat, Online info literacy tutorials on the web & in blackboard, OverDrive digital audio bks, Photocopying/Printing, Preschool reading prog, Prog for adults, Prog for children & young adult, Scanner, Spanish lang bks, Story hour, Study rm, Summer reading prog, Tax forms, Teen prog, Wheelchair accessible, Winter reading prog
Mem of South Central Kansas Library System
Partic in South Central Kansas Automation Network
Open Mon-Wed & Fri 10-6, Thurs 10-8, Sat 9-2
Friends of the Library Group

VALLEY FALLS

P DELAWARE TOWNSHIP LIBRARY*, 421 Mary St, 66088. SAN 306-1671. Tel: 785-945-3990. Web Site: valleyfalls.mykansaslibrary.org, valleyfalls.org/library. *Dir,* Adam Doolittle; E-mail: director@valleyfalls.lib.ks.us
Founded 1945. Pop 1,200; Circ 7,024
Library Holdings: Bk Vols 12,800; Per Subs 24
Automation Activity & Vendor Info: (Acquisitions) Follett Software; (Circulation) Follett Software; (ILL) Follett Software; (Serials) Follett Software
Wireless access
Mem of Northeast Kansas Library System
Open Mon-Sat 9-12 & 1-5

VERMILLION

P VERMILLION PUBLIC LIBRARY, 102 1/2 Main St, 66544. SAN 376-5504. Tel: 785-382-6227. E-mail: verlibrary@gmail.com. Web Site: vermillion.lib.nckls.org. *Dir,* Julie Lane
Circ 2,500
Library Holdings: Bk Vols 3,500
Wireless access
Mem of North Central Kansas Libraries System
Open Mon & Tues 1:30-5:30, Wed & Sat 9-11:30
Friends of the Library Group

VIOLA

P VIOLA TOWNSHIP LIBRARY*, 100 N Grice, 67149. (Mail add: PO Box 547, 67149-0547), SAN 306-168X. Tel: 620-584-6679. E-mail: violalibrary@gmail.com. *Dir,* Jeana Bender; *Librn,* Lexi Ternes
Pop 200; Circ 604
Library Holdings: Bk Vols 5,000; Per Subs 32
Automation Activity & Vendor Info: (Cataloging) Autolib Library & Information Management Systems; (Circulation) Autolib Library & Information Management Systems; (OPAC) Autolib Library & Information Management Systems
Wireless access

Mem of South Central Kansas Library System
Open Mon 9-2, Wed 9-12 & 1-5

WAKEENEY

P WAKEENEY PUBLIC LIBRARY*, 610 Russell Ave, 67672. SAN 306-1698. Tel: 785-743-2960. FAX: 785-743-5802. E-mail: waklib@ruraltel.net. Web Site: www.tregocountyks.com/2293/Public-Library. *Dir,* Louella Kaiser
Founded 1906. Pop 1,924; Circ 23,945
Library Holdings: AV Mats 851; Bk Vols 23,922; Per Subs 61
Subject Interests: Kansas
Function: ILL available, Photocopying/Printing, Ref serv available, Telephone ref
Mem of Northwest Kansas Library System
Special Services for the Blind - Talking bks
Open Mon, Wed & Fri 1-5, Tues 9-6, Thurs 1-6, Sat 9:30-1:30

WAKEFIELD

P WAKEFIELD PUBLIC LIBRARY*, 205 Third St, 67487. (Mail add: PO Box 348, 67487-0348), SAN 306-1701. Tel: 785-461-5510. FAX: 785-461-5510. E-mail: wakefieldpubliclibrary@gmail.com. Web Site: wakefield.lib.nckls.org, wakefieldks.com/main. *Dir,* Rita Jo Braden
Founded 1914. Pop 900; Circ 3,800
Library Holdings: Bk Vols 8,500; Per Subs 30
Subject Interests: Local hist
Wireless access
Mem of North Central Kansas Libraries System
Open Mon & Wed 1-7, Fri & Sat 10-4:30

WALNUT

P WALNUT PUBLIC LIBRARY*, 511 W Robbins, 66780. SAN 306-171X. Tel: 620-354-6794. FAX: 620-354-6795. E-mail: walnutlibrary@ckt.net. Web Site: walnut.mykansaslibrary.org. *Dir, Librn,* Sierra Kirkpatrick
Library Holdings: Bk Vols 3,000; Per Subs 16
Open Mon & Wed 3-7, Tues & Thurs 5-7

WALTON

P WALTON COMMUNITY LIBRARY*, 122 Main St, 67151. (Mail add: PO Box 200, 67151-0200), SAN 306-1728. Tel: 620-837-3252. FAX: 620-837-3252. E-mail: waltoncommunitylibrary@pixius.net. *Librn,* Shannon Nickel
Pop 260; Circ 3,600
Library Holdings: Bk Vols 3,000; Per Subs 25
Mem of South Central Kansas Library System
Open Mon-Fri 8-12 & 1-4

WAMEGO

P WAMEGO PUBLIC LIBRARY, 431 Lincoln, 66547. SAN 306-1736. Tel: 785-456-9181. FAX: 785-456-8986. E-mail: info@wamegopubliclibrary.com. Web Site: wamego.lib.nckls.org. *Dir,* Darci Hildebrand; E-mail: director@wamegopubliclibrary.com; Staff 5 (Non-MLS 5)
Founded 1937. Pop 5,000; Circ 60,000
Library Holdings: Bk Titles 19,266; Per Subs 70
Subject Interests: Genealogy, Hist, Kansas
Automation Activity & Vendor Info: (Acquisitions) Follett Software; (Cataloging) Follett Software; (Circulation) Follett Software
Wireless access
Mem of North Central Kansas Libraries System
Open Mon-Thurs 10-7, Fri 10-5, Sat 9-1
Friends of the Library Group

WASHINGTON

P WASHINGTON PUBLIC LIBRARY*, 116 E Second St, 66968-1916. SAN 306-1744. Tel: 785-325-2114. E-mail: washingtonlibraryks@gmail.com. Web Site: washington.lib.nckls.org. *Libr Dir,* Janet Keller
Founded 1909. Pop 5,683; Circ 10,739
Library Holdings: Audiobooks 87; Large Print Bks 1,155; Bk Titles 18,080; Per Subs 14
Special Collections: Antique Doll Coll
Automation Activity & Vendor Info: (Acquisitions) Auto-Graphics, Inc; (Cataloging) Auto-Graphics, Inc; (Circulation) Auto-Graphics, Inc; (ILL) Auto-Graphics, Inc; (OPAC) Auto-Graphics, Inc
Wireless access
Mem of North Central Kansas Libraries System
Open Tues, Wed & Fri 10-5, Thurs 10-4, Sat 9-5
Friends of the Library Group

WATERVILLE

P WATERVILLE PUBLIC LIBRARY*, 129 E Commercial St, 66548. (Mail add: PO Box 132, 66548-0132), SAN 306-1752. Tel: 785-363-6014. FAX: 785-363-2778. E-mail: watervillelib@gmail.com. Web Site: www.waterville.lib.nckls.org. *Dir,* Lee Jones
Founded 1914. Pop 900; Circ 5,490
Library Holdings: Audiobooks 100; DVDs 450; Large Print Bks 500; Bk Titles 8,500; Per Subs 40
Automation Activity & Vendor Info: (Cataloging) Auto-Graphics, Inc; (Circulation) Auto-Graphics, Inc
Wireless access
Mem of North Central Kansas Libraries System
Open Tues 10-1 & 2-6, Wed & Fri 1-6, Thurs 5-8, Sat 9-1
Friends of the Library Group

WEIR

P WEIR PUBLIC LIBRARY, 111 E Main St, 66781. (Mail add: PO Box 248, 66781-0248), SAN 306-1779. Tel: 620-396-8899. FAX: 620-356-8889. E-mail: weirpubliclibrary@ckt.net. Web Site: weir.mykansaslibrary.org.
Founded 1896. Pop 636; Circ 6,541
Library Holdings: Audiobooks 570; DVDs 500; Large Print Bks 200; Bk Vols 9,300; Per Subs 35; Videos 1,000
Wireless access
Function: 24/7 Online cat, Bks on CD, Children's prog, Computers for patron use, Free DVD rentals, ILL available, Internet access, Magazines, Online cat, Photocopying/Printing, Preschool reading prog, Printer for laptops & handheld devices, Scanner, Summer reading prog, Wheelchair accessible
Mem of Southeast Kansas Library System
Open Mon-Fri 9:30-6

WELLINGTON

P WELLINGTON PUBLIC LIBRARY*, 121 W Seventh St, 67152. SAN 306-1787. Tel: 620-326-2011. FAX: 620-326-8193. E-mail: wpl@wellingtonpubliclibrary.org. Web Site: wellington.sckls.info. *Dir,* Jo Plumb; E-mail: jplumb@wellingtonpubliclibrary.org
Founded 1916. Pop 8,535; Circ 60,081
Library Holdings: Bk Vols 53,000; Per Subs 105
Automation Activity & Vendor Info: (Acquisitions) Horizon; (Cataloging) Horizon; (Circulation) Horizon; (OPAC) Horizon
Wireless access
Mem of South Central Kansas Library System
Open Mon & Wed 9:30-6, Tues & Thurs 9:30-8:30, Fri 9:30-5, Sat 9:30-4
Friends of the Library Group

WELLSVILLE

P WELLSVILLE CITY LIBRARY, 115 W Sixth St, 66092. (Mail add: PO Box 517, 66092-0517), SAN 306-1795. Tel: 785-883-2870. FAX: 785-883-2880. E-mail: wclibrary@wellsvillelibrary.org. *Libr Dir,* Becky Dodd; *Asst Librn,* Robin Avers; Staff 3 (Non-MLS 3)
Founded 1939. Pop 1,722; Circ 19,000
Library Holdings: Audiobooks 304; Bk Vols 18,600; Per Subs 25; Videos 3,000
Special Collections: Wellsville Globes, newsp
Automation Activity & Vendor Info: (Cataloging) Koha
Wireless access
Function: 24/7 Online cat, Activity rm, Archival coll, Art exhibits, Bks on CD, Children's prog, Computer training, Computers for patron use, ILL available, Internet access, Magazines, Meeting rooms, Online cat, Story hour, Summer reading prog, Tax forms, Wheelchair accessible
Mem of Northeast Kansas Library System
Partic in Kansas Info Circuit
Open Mon-Fri 9-6, Sat 9-1
Friends of the Library Group

WETMORE

P WETMORE PUBLIC LIBRARY*, 333 Second St, 66550. (Mail add: PO Box 126, 66550), SAN 306-1809. Tel: 785-866-2250. FAX: 785-866-2250. Web Site: www.wetmorepubliclibrary.org. *Dir,* Misty Ballenger; *Librn,* Kristina Rice
Founded 1966. Pop 375; Circ 4,350
Library Holdings: AV Mats 95; Large Print Bks 160; Bk Titles 15,500; Talking Bks 120
Wireless access
Mem of Northeast Kansas Library System
Open Mon, Tues, Thurs & Fri 12-5, Wed 3:30-6, Sat 8am-9am

WHITE CITY

P WHITE CITY PUBLIC LIBRARY, 111 E Mackenzie, 66872. (Mail add: PO Box 206, 66872-0206), SAN 306-1817. Tel: 785-349-5551. E-mail: wclib@tctelco.net. Web Site: whitecity.lib.nckls.org. *Dir,* Ciri George; E-mail: cirigeorge@yahoo.com
Founded 1933. Pop 900; Circ 7,500
Library Holdings: Bk Vols 10,000; Per Subs 30
Wireless access
Mem of North Central Kansas Libraries System
Open Tues & Thurs 10-4, Sat 10-2
Friends of the Library Group

WHITEWATER

P WHITEWATER MEMORIAL LIBRARY*, 118 E Topeka, 67154. (Mail add: PO Box 9, 67154-0009), SAN 306-1825. Tel: 316-799-2471. FAX: 316-799-1099. E-mail: whitelib@sbcglobal.net. Web Site: www.whitewaterlib.info. *Libr Dir,* Jean Thiessen
Founded 1928. Pop 713; Circ 24,782
Jan 2018-Dec 2018 Income $69,207, State $11,701, City $55,214, Other $2,292. Mats Exp $8,451, Books $6,768, Per/Ser (Incl. Access Fees) $1,663, Electronic Ref Mat (Incl. Access Fees) $20. Sal $34,642 (Prof $33,778)
Library Holdings: Audiobooks 729; Bks on Deafness & Sign Lang 10; Braille Volumes 1; CDs 292; DVDs 2,102; e-books 64; e-journals 1; High Interest/Low Vocabulary Bk Vols 100; Large Print Bks 300; Bk Vols 11,863; Per Subs 38
Special Collections: Novelty Cake Pans
Automation Activity & Vendor Info: (Acquisitions) Innovative Interfaces, Inc; (Cataloging) Innovative Interfaces, Inc; (Circulation) Innovative Interfaces, Inc; (Course Reserve) Innovative Interfaces, Inc; (OPAC) Innovative Interfaces, Inc
Wireless access
Function: 24/7 Electronic res, 24/7 Online cat, Adult bk club, Audio & video playback equip for onsite use, Audiobks on Playaways & MP3, Audiobks via web, Bks on CD, CD-ROM, Children's prog, Computer training, Computers for patron use, Digital talking bks, E-Readers, Electronic databases & coll, Free DVD rentals, Holiday prog, Home delivery & serv to seniorr ctr & nursing homes, Homebound delivery serv, ILL available, Internet access, Magazines, Mail & tel request accepted, Mail loans to mem, Mango lang, Microfiche/film & reading machines, Movies, Music CDs, Online cat, Photocopying/Printing, Preschool reading prog, Prog for adults, Prog for children & young adult, Ref serv available, Scanner, Spanish lang bks, STEM programs, Story hour, Summer & winter reading prog, Summer reading prog, Teen prog, Telephone ref, Wheelchair accessible
Mem of South Central Kansas Library System
Partic in South Central Kansas Automation Network
Special Services for the Deaf - Bks on deafness & sign lang; Closed caption videos; High interest/low vocabulary bks
Special Services for the Blind - Bks on CD; Braille bks; Large print bks; Talking bks
Open Mon & Thurs 1:30-8, Tues, Wed & Fri 10-5, Sat 10-1
Friends of the Library Group

WICHITA

C FRIENDS UNIVERSITY*, Edmund Stanley Library, 2100 W University Ave, 67213-3397. SAN 306-1868. Tel: 316-295-5880. Toll Free Tel: 800-794-6945, Ext 5880. FAX: 316-295-5080. E-mail: askalibrarian@friends.edu. Web Site: library.friends.edu, www.friends.edu/academics/library. *Dir,* Anne Crane; Tel: 316-295-5610, E-mail: annec@friends.edu; *Circ Mgr,* Kristina Sojka; E-mail: kristina_sojka@friends.edu. Subject Specialists: *Computer, Music,* Anne Crane; Staff 7 (MLS 4, Non-MLS 3)
Founded 1898. Enrl 2,222; Highest Degree: Master
Library Holdings: AV Mats 367; CDs 2,335; DVDs 1,389; e-journals 21,731; Microforms 269; Music Scores 528; Bk Titles 66,864; Bk Vols 76,940; Per Subs 816; Videos 1,520
Special Collections: Friends University Archives, bks, cassette tapes, cats, correspondence, letters, memorabilia, negatives, newsletters, reel-to-reel tapes, student newsp, yearbks; MAYM (Mid America Yearly Meeting Coll), Quaker genealogies, meeting bks & photog; Quaker Room Coll, bks, journals, newsletters, newsp, pamphlets
Automation Activity & Vendor Info: (Acquisitions) SirsiDynix; (Cataloging) SirsiDynix; (Circulation) SirsiDynix; (Course Reserve) SirsiDynix; (ILL) OCLC FirstSearch; (OPAC) SirsiDynix; (Serials) SirsiDynix
Wireless access
Function: Archival coll, Art exhibits, Computers for patron use, Electronic databases & coll, ILL available, Online cat, Orientations, Photocopying/Printing, Ref serv available
Mem of South Central Kansas Library System
Partic in OCLC Online Computer Library Center, Inc; Private Academic Libraries Section, Kansas Library Association
Open Mon-Thurs (Fall & Spring) 7:45am-10pm, Fri 7:45-4, Sat 9-5, Sun 3-10; Mon-Thurs (Summer) 8-7, Fri 8-Noon
Restriction: Limited access for the pub, Open to pub for ref & circ; with some limitations, Open to students, fac, staff & alumni

S MIDWEST HISTORICAL & GENEALOGICAL SOCIETY, INC LIBRARY, 1203 N Main St, 67203. (Mail add: PO Box 1121, 67201-1121), SAN 326-4939. Tel: 316-264-3611. E-mail: library@mhgswichita.org. Web Site: mhgswichita.org/wp. *Librn,* Julia Langel
Founded 1966
Library Holdings: Bk Titles 20,000; Per Subs 45
Subject Interests: Genealogy, Local hist
Wireless access
Publications: MHGS Register (Quarterly)
Open Tues & Sat 10-4

CR NEWMAN UNIVERSITY*, Dugan Library, 3100 McCormick Ave, 67213. SAN 306-1884. Tel: 316-942-4291. FAX: 316-942-1747. Web Site: www.newmanu.edu/campus-life/campus-services/dugan-library. *Dir,* Steven L Hamersky; Tel: 316-942-4291, Ext 2108, E-mail: hamerskys@newmanu.edu; *Ref & Instruction Librn,* Jeanette Parker; Tel: 316-942-4291, Ext 2104, E-mail: parkerj@newmanu.edu; Staff 2 (MLS 2)
Founded 1933. Enrl 2,700; Highest Degree: Master
Library Holdings: AV Mats 2,100; Bk Titles 106,429; Bk Vols 126,000; Per Subs 345
Special Collections: Cardinal Newman Coll
Subject Interests: Allied health, Catholicism, Nursing
Automation Activity & Vendor Info: (Acquisitions) Baker & Taylor; (Cataloging) EOS International; (Circulation) EOS International; (Course Reserve) EOS International; (Media Booking) EOS International; (OPAC) EOS International; (Serials) EOS International
Wireless access
Publications: Handbooks (for faculty & students); Video Catalog
Mem of South Central Kansas Library System
Partic in Amigos Library Services, Inc
Open Mon-Thurs 8am-Midnight, Fri 8-5, Sat 11-3, Sun 2-Midnight
Restriction: Open to pub for ref & circ; with some limitations

L SEDGWICK COUNTY LAW LIBRARY*, 225 N Market St, Ste 210, 67202-2023. SAN 325-6081. Tel: 316-263-2251. FAX: 316-263-0629. Web Site: www.wichitabar.org/page/SedgCoLawLibrary. *Head Librn,* John Lewallen; E-mail: JLewallen@wichitabar.org
Library Holdings: Bk Titles 1,500; Bk Vols 30,000
Wireless access
Open Mon-Thurs 8-7, Fri 8-5, Sat 11-3

C UNIVERSITY OF KANSAS - KANSAS GEOLOGICAL SURVEY, Kansas Geologic Sample Repository, 4150 W Monroe St, 67209. SAN 374-9576. Tel: 316-943-2343. FAX: 316-943-1261. E-mail: kgsr@ku.edu. Web Site: www.kgs.ku.edu/General/wichita.html. *Mgr,* Doug Louis; Tel: 316-943-2343, Ext 203; Staff 3 (MLS 1, Non-MLS 2)
Founded 1938
Library Holdings: Bk Vols 2,000
Special Collections: Oil & Gas Well Data; Rock Samples from Gas & Oil Wells
Function: Computers for patron use, Electronic databases & coll, Online ref, Photocopying/Printing, Ref & res
Open Mon-Fri 8-12 & 1-5

CM UNIVERSITY OF KANSAS SCHOOL OF MEDICINE-WICHITA, George J Farha Medical Library, 1010 N Kansas, 67214-3199. SAN 373-2770. Tel: 316-293-2629. E-mail: medref@kumc.edu. Web Site: www.kumc.edu/school-of-medicine/campuses/wichita. *Dir,* Heather Van Buren; *Coordr, ILL,* Kathryn Mann; E-mail: kmann3@kumc.edu; *Cataloger, Ref,* Susan Clark; E-mail: sclark3@kumc.edu; Staff 6 (MLS 3, Non-MLS 3)
Founded 1981. Enrl 98; Fac 94; Highest Degree: Master
Library Holdings: Bk Vols 3,800; Per Subs 367
Automation Activity & Vendor Info: (Acquisitions) Ex Libris Group; (Cataloging) Ex Libris Group; (Circulation) Ex Libris Group; (OPAC) Ex Libris Group; (Serials) Ex Libris Group
Wireless access

M VIA CHRISTI LIBRARIES*, North Saint Francis Street, 929 N Saint Francis St, 67214-1315. SAN 306-1906. Tel: 316-268-5979, 316-268-6799. FAX: 316-268-8694. Web Site: www.viachristi.org/health-professionals/via-christi-library.
Founded 1938
Library Holdings: Bk Vols 5,000
Subject Interests: Allied health, Med, Nursing
Automation Activity & Vendor Info: (Cataloging) CyberTools for Libraries; (Circulation) CyberTools for Libraries; (OPAC) CyberTools for Libraries; (Serials) CyberTools for Libraries

Wireless access
Function: Health sci info serv
Publications: Wichita Area Health Science Libraries Union List
Open Mon-Fri 8-4:30
Restriction: Circulates for staff only, Employees & their associates, Lending to staff only, Med staff only, Private libr

J WICHITA AREA TECHNICAL COLLEGE*, Southside Education Ctr, 4501 E 47th St S, 67210. Tel: 316-677-9492. Interlibrary Loan Service Tel: 316-677-1749. FAX: 316-554-2650. E-mail: library@watc.edu. *Dir,* Britten Kuckelman; E-mail: bkuckelman@watc.edu; *Libr Asst,* Elka Garcia; E-mail: egarcia1@watc.edu; *Libr Spec,* Delia Loud; E-mail: dloud@watc.edu
Function: Computers for patron use
Open Mon-Thurs 7:30am-8pm, Fri 7:30-5, Sat 8:30-Noon

S WICHITA ART MUSEUM, The Emprise Bank Research Library, 1400 W Museum Blvd, 67203-3296. SAN 306-1965. Tel: 316-268-4918. FAX: 316-268-4980. E-mail: library@wichitaartmuseum.org. Web Site: www.wichitaartmuseum.org. *Librn,* Joyce Goering Norris; Staff 1 (MLS 1)
Founded 1963
Jan 2020-Dec 2020. Mats Exp $6,000, Books $3,000, Per/Ser (Incl. Access Fees) $3,000
Library Holdings: Electronic Media & Resources 2; Bk Titles 11,854; Per Subs 22
Special Collections: Chris Paulsen Polk Papers; Elizabeth S Navas Archival Papers; Howard E Wooden Archival Papers
Automation Activity & Vendor Info: (Cataloging) Ex Libris Group; (OPAC) Ex Libris Group; (Serials) Ex Libris Group
Wireless access
Open Tues & Thurs 9:30-2:30
Restriction: Open to pub for ref only

P WICHITA PUBLIC LIBRARY*, Advanced Learning Library, 711 W Second St, 67203. SAN 342-2135. Tel: 316-261-8500. Circulation Tel: 316-261-8508. Interlibrary Loan Service Tel: 316-261-8583. FAX: 316-262-4540. Administration E-mail: admin@wichitalibrary.org. Web Site: www.wichitalibrary.org. *Dir of Libr,* Cynthia Berner; Tel: 316-261-8520, E-mail: cberner@wichita.gov; *Commun Engagement Mgr, Partnerships,* Julie Sherwood; Tel: 316-261-8590, E-mail: JSherwood@wichita.gov; *Coll Develop Mgr,* Sarah Kittrell; Tel: 316-261-8580, E-mail: skittrell@wichita.gov; *Customer Serv Mgr,* Kristi Dowell; Tel: 316-261-8530, E-mail: KDowell@wichita.gov; *Digital Serv Mgr,* Jeff Tate; Tel: 316-261-8522, E-mail: JTate@wichita.gov; *Div Mgr, Mgr, Learning Serv,* Larry Vos; Tel: 316-261-8540, E-mail: lvos@wichita.gov; *Support Serv Mgr,* Tammy Penland; Tel: 316-261-8534, Fax: 316-858-7321, E-mail: tpenland@wichita.gov; *Communications Spec,* Sean Jones; Tel: 316-261-8524, E-mail: sjones@wichita.gov; Staff 32 (MLS 31, Non-MLS 1)
Founded 1876
Jan 2018-Dec 2018 Income (Main & Associated Libraries) $10,164,368, State $349,076, City $9,469,142, Federal $15,000, Other $3,333,150. Mats Exp $852,656, Books $562,981, Per/Ser (Incl. Access Fees) $52,432, AV Mat $183,475, Electronic Ref Mat (Incl. Access Fees) $53,768. Sal $5,019,969
Library Holdings: Audiobooks 33,980; e-books 19,169; Microforms 13,950; Bk Vols 503,016; Per Subs 642; Videos 46,175
Special Collections: Motor Manuals; Mueller Philatelic Coll; Sullivan-Gagliardo Children's Literature Art Coll; Wichita Photo Archive (in cooperation with Wichita State University & the Wichita-Sedgwick County Historical Museum)
Subject Interests: Auto repair, Genealogy, Kansas, Local hist, Schematics
Automation Activity & Vendor Info: (Acquisitions) Innovative Interfaces, Inc; (Cataloging) Innovative Interfaces, Inc; (Circulation) Innovative Interfaces, Inc; (ILL) Innovative Interfaces, Inc; (OPAC) Innovative Interfaces, Inc; (Serials) Innovative Interfaces, Inc
Wireless access
Function: 24/7 Electronic res, 24/7 Online cat, 3D Printer, Adult bk club, Archival coll, Audio & video playback equip for onsite use, Audiobks on Playaways & MP3, Bilingual assistance for Spanish patrons, Bk club(s), Bks on cassette, Bks on CD, Children's prog, Computer training, Computers for patron use, Electronic databases & coll, Free DVD rentals, Genealogy discussion group, Holiday prog, ILL available, Internet access, Life-long learning prog for all ages, Magazines, Magnifiers for reading, Mail & tel request accepted, Mango lang, Meeting rooms, Microfiche/film & reading machines, Movies, Music CDs, Online cat, Photocopying/Printing, Preschool outreach, Preschool reading prog, Printer for laptops & handheld devices, Prog for adults, Prog for children & young adult, Ref & res, Ref serv available, Res assist avail, Senior computer classes, Spanish lang bks, Spoken cassettes & CDs, Spoken cassettes & DVDs, STEM programs, Story hour, Study rm, Summer & winter reading prog, Summer reading prog, Tax forms, Teen prog, Telephone ref, VHS videos, Wheelchair accessible, Winter reading prog, Writing prog
Mem of South Central Kansas Library System
Special Services for the Deaf - Sign lang interpreter upon request for prog
Special Services for the Blind - Bks on cassette; Bks on CD; Computer with voice synthesizer for visually impaired persons; Descriptive video serv (DVS); Extensive large print coll; Internet workstation with adaptive software; Large print bks; Magnifiers; Recorded bks; Talking bk serv referral; ZoomText magnification & reading software
Open Mon-Thurs 10-8, Fri & Sat 10-6, Sun 1-5
Friends of the Library Group
Branches: 6
LIONEL ALFORD REGIONAL LIBRARY, 3447 S Meridian, 67217-2151. Tel: 316-337-9119. *Br Mgr,* Robyn Belt
Founded 2003
Open Mon-Thurs 10-8, Fri & Sat 10-6, Sun (Winter) 1-5
Friends of the Library Group
MAYA ANGELOU NORTHEAST BRANCH, 3051 E 21st St, 67214, SAN 342-2283. Tel: 316-688-9580. *Br Mgr,* Anne Ethen
Open Tues 1-8, Wed-Sat 1-6
Friends of the Library Group
EVERGREEN BRANCH, 2601 N Arkansas, 67204. Tel: 316-303-8181. *Br Mgr,* Anne Ethen; E-mail: aethen@wichita.gov
Founded 2002
Open Mon-Thurs 10-8, Fri & Sat 10-6, Sun (Winter) 1-5
Friends of the Library Group
LINWOOD PARK BRANCH, 1901 S Kansas Ave, 67211, SAN 342-216X. Tel: 316-337-9125. *Br Mgr,* Robyn Belt
Open Mon 1-8, Tues-Fri 11-6
Friends of the Library Group
FORD ROCKWELL BRANCH, 5939 E Ninth St, 67208, SAN 342-2194. Tel: 316-688-9361. *Br Mgr,* Savannah Ball
Open Mon-Thurs 10-8, Fri & Sat 10-6, Sun (Winter) 1-5
Friends of the Library Group
WESTLINK BRANCH, 8515 Bekemeyer St, 67212, SAN 342-2402. Tel: 316-337-9456. *Br Mgr,* Tracie Partridge
Open Mon-Thurs 10-8, Fri & Sat 10-6, Sun (Winter) 1-5
Friends of the Library Group

S WICHITA-SEDGWICK COUNTY HISTORICAL MUSEUM LIBRARY, 204 S Main St, 67202. SAN 325-6103. Tel: 316-265-9314. E-mail: wschm@wichitahistory.org. Web Site: www.wichitahistory.org. *Dir,* Eric M Cale; E-mail: ecale@wichitahistory.org; *Curator,* Jami Frazier Tracy; E-mail: jtracy@wichitahistory.org; Staff 1 (Non-MLS 1)
Founded 1939
Library Holdings: Bk Vols 330; Per Subs 10
Subject Interests: Local hist
Function: Archival coll
Restriction: Open by appt only

C WICHITA STATE UNIVERSITY LIBRARIES*, 1845 Fairmount, 67260-0068. SAN 306-1981. Tel: 316-978-3582. Interlibrary Loan Service Tel: 316-978-3167. Reference Tel: 316-978-3584. Administration Tel: 316-978-3586. FAX: 316-978-3048. Administration FAX: 316-978-3727. Web Site: libraries.wichita.edu. *Interim Dean of Libr, Sr Assoc Dean, Univ Libr,* Kathy Downes; E-mail: kathy.downes@wichita.edu; *Coordr, Coll Develop, Interim Assoc Dean,* Cathy Moore-Jansen; Tel: 316-978-5080, E-mail: cathy.moore-jansen@wichita.edu; *Asst Dean, Tech Serv,* Nancy Deyoe; Tel: 316-978-5140, E-mail: nancy.dayoe@wichita.edu; *Instruction & Res Serv Librn,* Aaron Bowen; Tel: 316-978-5077, E-mail: aaron.bowen@wichita.edu; *Instruction & Res Serv Librn,* Nathan Filbert; Tel: 316-978-5210, E-mail: nathan.filbert@wichita.edu; *Coordr, Libr Instruction, Instruction & Res Serv Librn,* Shonn Haren; Tel: 316-978-6331, E-mail: shonn.haren@wichita.edu; *Instruction & Res Serv Librn,* Meghann Kuhlmann; Tel: 316-978-5075, E-mail: meghann.kuhlmann@wichita.edu; *Metadata & Digital Initiatives Librn,* Lizzy Walker; Tel: 316-978-5138, E-mail: lizzy.walker@wichita.edu; *Ref Librn,* Angela Paul; Tel: 316-978-5084, E-mail: angela.paul@wichita.edu; *Tech Dev Librn,* Samuel Willis; Tel: 316-978-5104, E-mail: samuel.willis@wichita.edu; *Acq, Digital Res Coordr,* Mary Walker; Tel: 316-978-5792, E-mail: mary.walker@wichita.edu; *Curator, Spec Coll & Univ Archives,* Dr Lorraine Madway; Tel: 316-978-3590, E-mail: lorraine.madway@wichita.edu; *Cat & Metadata,* Susan Matveyeva; Tel: 316-978-5139, E-mail: susan.matveyeva@wichita.edu; *Info & Res Serv,* Rachel Crane; Tel: 316-978-5078, E-mail: rachel.crane@wichita.edu. Subject Specialists: *Anthrop,* Cathy Moore-Jansen; *Fine arts, Music,* Rachel Crane; Staff 18 (MLS 17, Non-MLS 1)
Founded 1895. Enrl 14,550; Fac 515; Highest Degree: Doctorate
Library Holdings: e-books 59,000; e-journals 56,647; Music Scores 33,840; Bk Vols 2,013,870; Per Subs 57,165
Special Collections: American Anti-Slavery Movement Coll; American Civil War Sanitary Commission Papers (Kantor Coll); Aviation History of World War I Coll; Congressional Papers of Members of Congress from Kansas & Seven Other States; Gordon Parks Papers; History of Books & Printing (Aitchison Coll); Hypnotism, Mesmerism & Animal Magnetism (Tinterow Coll); Kansas & the Great Plains (Historical Map Coll); Original Editorial Cartoons of Gene Bassett; Patent & Trademark Depository; W H Auden Coll; Wichita State University Archives; William Lloyd Garrison

Papers; World War I & II Pamphlet Coll. State Document Depository; US Document Depository
Subject Interests: Engr, Hist, Manufacturing, Music, Psychol, Urban studies
Automation Activity & Vendor Info: (Acquisitions) Ex Libris Group; (Cataloging) Ex Libris Group; (Circulation) Ex Libris Group; (Course Reserve) Ex Libris Group; (ILL) OCLC ILLiad; (OPAC) Ex Libris Group; (Serials) Ex Libris Group
Wireless access
Mem of South Central Kansas Library System
Friends of the Library Group
Departmental Libraries:
CHEMISTRY, 127 McKinley Hall, 67260-0051, SAN 324-3311. Tel: 316-978-3764. FAX: 316-978-3048. Web Site: library.wichita.edu/science/chemistry/chemlib.html.
Open Mon-Thurs 8-7, Fri 8-5, Sat & Sun 1-5
MUSIC LIBRARY, C 116 DFAC, 67260-0053, SAN 324-332X. Tel: 316-978-3029. FAX: 316-978-3584. Web Site: library.wichita.edu/music/mindex.html. *Librn,* Rachel Crane; E-mail: rachel.crane@wichita.edu
Library Holdings: CDs 5,797; Music Scores 24,585
Automation Activity & Vendor Info: (Acquisitions) Ex Libris Group; (Cataloging) Ex Libris Group; (Circulation) Ex Libris Group; (Course Reserve) Ex Libris Group; (ILL) Ex Libris Group; (Media Booking) Ex Libris Group; (OPAC) Ex Libris Group; (Serials) Ex Libris Group
Open Mon & Tues 8-8, Wed-Fri 8-5

WILLIAMSBURG

P WILLIAMSBURG COMMUNITY LIBRARY, 107 S Louisa, 66095. (Mail add: PO Box 142, 66095-0142). Tel: 785-746-5407. FAX: 785-746-5490. E-mail: wmbglib@williamsburgcommunitylibrary.org. Web Site: www.williamsburgcommunitylibrary.org. *Dir,* Shae Crowley; *Libr Asst,* Amy Jones
Founded 1984
Library Holdings: DVDs 1,500; Large Print Bks 1,000; Bk Titles 15,000
Wireless access
Mem of Northeast Kansas Library System
Open Mon & Tues 9-4, Wed 9-7, Thurs 1-5, Sat 10-2

WILSEY

P ELM CREEK TOWNSHIP LIBRARY*, Wilsey Library, 213 N Fifth St, 66873-9768. SAN 306-199X. Tel: 785-497-2289. E-mail: books@tctelco.net. Web Site: elmcreek.lib.nckls.org. *Dir,* Samantha J Asebedo
Pop 300; Circ 5,200
Library Holdings: DVDs 559; Large Print Bks 208; Bk Titles 4,255
Wireless access
Function: Free DVD rentals, Holiday prog, ILL available, Internet access, Laminating, Photocopying/Printing, Printer for laptops & handheld devices, Scanner, Summer reading prog, Teen prog
Mem of North Central Kansas Libraries System
Open Wed 9-12 & 2-6, Sat 9-12

WILSON

P LANG MEMORIAL LIBRARY*, 2405 Ave F, 67490. (Mail add: PO Box 310, 67490-0310), SAN 320-4790. Tel: 785-658-3648. FAX: 785-658-3647. E-mail: langlib@wtciweb.com. Web Site: langmemoriallibrary.weebly.com. *Dir,* Doris Holzmeister-Shaw
Founded 1924. Pop 765; Circ 5,322
Library Holdings: Audiobooks 32; AV Mats 315; Bks on Deafness & Sign Lang 2; Braille Volumes 1; CDs 12; DVDs 181; Large Print Bks 75; Microforms 100; Bk Titles 3,600; Talking Bks 2; Videos 339
Automation Activity & Vendor Info: (Cataloging) Follett Software; (Circulation) Follett Software; (OPAC) Follett Software
Wireless access
Function: Adult bk club, Bk club(s), Bks on CD, Children's prog, Computers for patron use, Digital talking bks, E-Readers, Free DVD rentals, Internet access, Magazines, Microfiche/film & reading machines, Movies, Music CDs, Online cat, Photocopying/Printing, Preschool reading prog, Prog for children & young adult, Scanner, Senior computer classes, Story hour, Summer reading prog, Teen prog, Wheelchair accessible, Workshops
Mem of Central Kansas Library System
Open Mon, Wed & Fri 12:30-5:30

WINCHESTER

P WINCHESTER PUBLIC LIBRARY, 203 Fourth St, 66097. SAN 376-5490. Tel: 913-774-4967. FAX: 913-774-4967. E-mail: library@winchesterlibrary.org. Web Site: www.winchesterlibrary.org. *Libr Dir,* Position Currently Open; *Asst Librn,* Kristie Scrivner; *Libr Asst,* Molly Finley; Staff 2 (Non-MLS 2)
Pop 1,271
Library Holdings: Audiobooks 25; CDs 20; DVDs 200; Electronic Media & Resources 1; Large Print Bks 500; Bk Titles 12,500; Per Subs 3
Automation Activity & Vendor Info: (Cataloging) SirsiDynix; (Circulation) SirsiDynix; (OPAC) SirsiDynix
Wireless access
Function: 24/7 Electronic res, 24/7 Online cat, Activity rm, Adult bk club, Bk club(s), Computers for patron use, Homebound delivery serv, ILL available, Internet access, Mail & tel request accepted, Meeting rooms, Music CDs, Photocopying/Printing, Prog for children & young adult, Senior computer classes, Story hour, Summer reading prog, VHS videos, Wheelchair accessible
Mem of Northeast Kansas Library System
Partic in Kans City Mo Libr & Info Network
Special Services for the Deaf - Closed caption videos
Special Services for the Blind - Bks on cassette; Bks on CD; Home delivery serv; Large print bks
Open Mon, Wed & Fri 12-6, Tues 10-6, Thurs 10-7, Sat 10-Noon

WINFIELD

S COWLEY COUNTY HISTORICAL SOCIETY MUSEUM LIBRARY, 1011 Mansfield St, 67156-3557. SAN 306-2007. Tel: 620-221-4811. E-mail: cchsm@kans.com. Web Site: www.cchsm.com.
Founded 1967
Library Holdings: Bk Vols 750
Special Collections: Military History of the Civil War; Winfield History, photog & newsp. Oral History
Subject Interests: Family hist, Local hist
Function: Res libr
Open Tues-Sun 1pm-4pm

C SOUTHWESTERN COLLEGE*, Harold & Mary Ellen Deets Memorial Library, 100 College St, 67156. SAN 306-2031. Tel: 620-229-6225. Toll Free Tel: 866-734-1275. Web Site: resources.scdeetslibrary.org. *Libr Dir,* Marjorie Snyder; Tel: 620-229-6312, E-mail: marjorie.snyder@sckans.edu; Staff 3 (MLS 2, Non-MLS 1)
Founded 1885. Enrl 845; Fac 48; Highest Degree: Doctorate
Library Holdings: Bk Vols 55,000; Per Subs 106
Special Collections: Black History & Literature (Ludgood-Walker Afro-American Studies Coll); Center for Bellarusion Studies Coll; East Asia (Sidney DeVere Brown Coll)
Subject Interests: Liberal arts
Automation Activity & Vendor Info: (Acquisitions) Innovative Interfaces, Inc; (Cataloging) Innovative Interfaces, Inc; (Circulation) Innovative Interfaces, Inc; (ILL) OCLC; (OPAC) Innovative Interfaces, Inc; (Serials) Innovative Interfaces, Inc
Wireless access
Function: Distance learning, Doc delivery serv, For res purposes, ILL available, Photocopying/Printing
Mem of South Central Kansas Library System
Partic in Amigos Library Services, Inc; New Mexico Consortium of Academic Libraries; OCLC Online Computer Library Center, Inc
Restriction: Open to pub for ref & circ; with some limitations, Open to students, fac & staff

P WINFIELD PUBLIC LIBRARY*, 605 College St, 67156-3199. SAN 306-204X. Tel: 620-221-4470. FAX: 620-221-6135. E-mail: library@wpl.org. Web Site: www.wpl.org. *Dir,* Joan Cales; E-mail: jcales@wpl.org; *Youth Serv Librn,* Joanna Brazil; E-mail: jbrazil@wpl.org; *Adult Serv, Pub Serv Spec,* Jessica Faulk; E-mail: jfaulk@wpl.org; Staff 12 (Non-MLS 12)
Founded 1912. Pop 11,900; Circ 189,000
Library Holdings: AV Mats 2,336; Large Print Bks 3,626; Bk Titles 59,930; Bk Vols 60,658; Per Subs 168
Special Collections: Laura Ingalls Wilder letters
Subject Interests: Art, Genealogy, Kansas
Automation Activity & Vendor Info: (OPAC) Innovative Interfaces, Inc
Wireless access
Function: After school storytime, Art exhibits, Audio & video playback equip for onsite use, Audiobks via web, Bk club(s), Bks on CD, Children's prog, Computer training, Computers for patron use, Electronic databases & coll, Family literacy, Free DVD rentals, Games & aids for people with disabilities, Holiday prog, Homebound delivery serv, ILL available, Large print keyboards, Magnifiers for reading, Music CDs, Online cat, Outreach serv, OverDrive digital audio bks, Photocopying/Printing, Preschool outreach, Prog for adults, Prog for children & young adult, Ref serv available, Scanner, Senior computer classes, Senior outreach, Story hour, Summer reading prog, Tax forms, Teen prog, Telephone ref, Wheelchair accessible, Workshops, Writing prog
Publications: Newsletter (Monthly)
Open Mon-Thurs 9-8, Fri & Sat 10-6, Sun 1-5
Friends of the Library Group

YATES CENTER

P YATES CENTER PUBLIC LIBRARY, 218 N Main, 66783. SAN 306-2066. Tel: 620-625-3341. E-mail: ycpublib@yahoo.com. Web Site: yatescenter.mykansaslibrary.org. *Dir,* Janice Jones; Staff 4 (Non-MLS 4)
Founded 1908. Pop 1,998; Circ 16,667
Library Holdings: Bk Vols 15,500; Per Subs 41
Mem of Southeast Kansas Library System
Open Mon-Fri 10-5:30, Sat Noon-4

ZENDA

P ZENDA PUBLIC LIBRARY*, 215 N Main, 67159. (Mail add: PO Box 53, 67159-0053), SAN 306-2074. Tel: 620-243-5791. E-mail: zendalibrary@gmail.com. Web Site: zenda.scklslibrary.info. *Dir,* Teresa Medlock
Founded 1967. Pop 248
Library Holdings: Bk Vols 7,905; Per Subs 11
Wireless access
Function: ILL available, Prog for children & young adult, Summer reading prog
Mem of South Central Kansas Library System
Open Mon & Wed 8:30-11, Thurs 6-8, Sat 8:30-12:30
Friends of the Library Group

KENTUCKY

Date of Statistics: FY 2019-2020
Population, 2020 U.S. Census: 4,477,251
Population Served by Public Libraries & Bookmobiles: 4,475,071
Total Volumes in Public Libraries & Bookmobiles: 8,990,741
Volumes Per Capita (statewide): 2.01
Volumes Per Capita (population served): 2.01
Total Public Library Circulation (including Bookmobiles): 25,717,063
Circulation Per Capita (statewide): 5.75
Circulation Per Capita (population served): 5.75
Digital Resources:
Total e-books: 19,259,500
Total audio items (physical and downloadable units): 5,914,147
Total video items (physical and downloadable units): 4,364,335
Total computers for use by the public: 4,888
Total annual wireless sessions: 5,318,812
Income and Expenditures:
Total Public Library Income: $210,620,092
Source of Income:
Public Funds: $203,948,527
State & Federal: $6,672,240
Expenditure Per Capita (population served): $37.28
Expenditure Per Capita (statewide): $37.28
Number of (Regional) Libraries: 4
Number of Bookmobiles in State: 72
Grants-in-Aid to Public Libraries:
Federal (Library Services & Technology Act): $2,489,254
Information provided courtesy of: Jay Bank, Systems Support; Kentucky Department for Libraries

ALBANY

P CLINTON COUNTY PUBLIC LIBRARY, 302 King Dr, 42602. SAN 306-2082. Tel: 606-387-5989. FAX: 606-387-5989. E-mail: CCPLHelpDesk@outlook.com. Web Site: clintoncountypubliclibrary.org. *Dir,* Margaret England; Staff 4 (MLS 2, Non-MLS 2)
Founded 1958. Pop 9,616; Circ 87,037
Library Holdings: Bk Titles 23,234; Bk Vols 32,981; Per Subs 24
Subject Interests: Kentucky
Automation Activity & Vendor Info: (Acquisitions) Follett Software; (Circulation) Follett Software
Wireless access
Open Mon-Wed & Fri 8-5, Sat 8-Noon
Bookmobiles: 1. Librn, Deborah Sells

ASHLAND

J ASHLAND COMMUNITY & TECHNICAL COLLEGE*, Mansbach Memorial Library, 1400 College Dr, 41101. SAN 306-2090. Tel: 606-326-2169. FAX: 606-326-2186. Reference E-mail: as_library@kctcs.edu. Web Site: www.ashland.kctcs.edu/current-students/student-resources/libraries. *Dir, Libr Serv,* Pamela Klinepeter; Tel: 606-326-2254, E-mail: Pamela.Klinepeter@kctcs.edu; *Tech Serv Librn,* Bettie George Frye; Tel: 606-326-2141, E-mail: BettieGeorge.Frye@kctcs.edu; Staff 5 (MLS 3, Non-MLS 2)
Founded 1938. Enrl 2,103; Fac 90; Highest Degree: Associate
Library Holdings: Bk Titles 42,197; Bk Vols 50,466; Per Subs 102
Special Collections: Fraley Memorial; Jesse Stuart Coll; Kentucky Authors Coll; Learning Disabilities (Ashworth Coll). US Document Depository
Automation Activity & Vendor Info: (Acquisitions) Ex Libris Group; (Cataloging) Ex Libris Group; (Circulation) Ex Libris Group; (Course Reserve) Ex Libris Group; (OPAC) Ex Libris Group
Wireless access
Partic in OCLC Online Computer Library Center, Inc
Open Mon-Thurs 7:30-5:30, Fri 8-4
Departmental Libraries:
TECHNOLOGY DRIVE CAMPUS LIBRARY, 902 Technology Dr, Grayson, 41143. (Mail add: 1400 College Dr, 41101). Tel: 606-326-2000. Toll Free Tel: 800-928-4256. *Dir, Libr Serv,* Pamela Klinepeter
Library Holdings: Bk Titles 570; Bk Vols 650

P BOYD COUNTY PUBLIC LIBRARY*, 1740 Central Ave, 41101. SAN 306-2112. Tel: 606-329-0090. FAX: 606-329-0578. Administration FAX: 606-325-4574. Web Site: www.thebookplace.org. *Libr Dir,* Debbie Cosper; E-mail: dcosper@thebookplace.org; *Pub Serv Mgr,* Ben Nunley; E-mail: bnunley@thebookplace.org; *Supvr, Genealogy Serv,* James Kettel; E-mail: jkettel@thebookplace.org; *Supvr, Youth Serv,* Position Currently Open; *Tech Serv Supvr,* Kellie Nunley; E-mail: knunley@thebookplace.org; Staff 7 (MLS 5, Non-MLS 2)
Founded 1935. Pop 47,979; Circ 555,356
Jul 2018-Jun 2019 Income (Main & Associated Libraries) $3,167,313, State $72,761, Locally Generated Income $2,898,444, Other $182,094. Mats Exp $536,764, Books $110,778, Per/Ser (Incl. Access Fees) $145,000, AV Mat $177,359, Electronic Ref Mat (Incl. Access Fees) $103,627. Sal $937,423 (Prof $77,458)
Library Holdings: Audiobooks 17,458; CDs 5,283; DVDs 55,903; e-books 457,162; e-journals 124; Electronic Media & Resources 144; Bk Titles 133,635; Per Subs 385
Special Collections: Arnold Hanners Photo Coll; Genealogy & Local History (Minnie C Winder Coll), bks & micro; Ky Vital Records 1911-1995; Records from Bellefonte, Buena Vista, Princess & Amanda Furnace Operations
Automation Activity & Vendor Info: (Acquisitions) Innovative Interfaces, Inc; (Cataloging) OCLC; (Circulation) Innovative Interfaces, Inc; (ILL) OCLC Tipasa; (OPAC) Innovative Interfaces, Inc; (Serials) EBSCO Online
Wireless access
Function: 24/7 Electronic res, 24/7 Online cat, Accelerated reader prog, Adult bk club, Archival coll, Audiobks on Playaways & MP3, Audiobks via web, Bk club(s), Bks on CD, Butterfly Garden, Children's prog, Computer training, Computers for patron use, Digital talking bks, E-Reserves, Electronic databases & coll, Free DVD rentals, Holiday prog, Home delivery & serv to seniorr ctr & nursing homes, Homebound delivery serv, ILL available, Instruction & testing, Internet access, Jail serv, Life-long learning prog for all ages, Magazines, Mail & tel request accepted, Mango lang, Meeting rooms, Microfiche/film & reading machines, Movies, Music CDs, Notary serv, Online cat, Online ref, Outreach serv, Outside serv via phone, mail, e-mail & web, OverDrive digital audio bks, Photocopying/Printing, Preschool outreach, Printer for laptops & handheld devices, Prog for adults, Prog for children & young adult, Ref serv available, Res assist avail, Scanner, Senior computer classes, STEM programs, Story hour, Study rm, Summer reading prog, Tax forms, Teen prog, Telephone ref, Wheelchair accessible
Partic in OCLC Online Computer Library Center, Inc; SE Ind Area Libr Servs Authority
Special Services for the Deaf - Assisted listening device; Closed caption videos
Special Services for the Blind - Accessible computers; Audio mat; Computer access aids; Copier with enlargement capabilities; Large print bks
Open Mon-Thurs 9-8, Fri & Sat 9-5, Sun 1-5
Restriction: Borrowing requests are handled by ILL, Closed stack, Non-circulating of rare bks, Non-resident fee
Friends of the Library Group
Branches: 2
CATLETTSBURG BRANCH, 2704 Louisa St, Catlettsburg, 41129, SAN 324-296X. Tel: 606-739-8332. FAX: 606-739-5907. *Pub Serv Mgr,* Ben Nunley; Tel: 606-329-0090, E-mail: bnunley@thebookplace.org
Open Mon-Thurs 9-8, Fri 9-5, Sat 1-5
Friends of the Library Group

KYOVA BRANCH, 10699 US Rte 60, Ste 920, 41102, SAN 321-8414. Tel: 606-929-5346. FAX: 606-929-5471. *Pub Serv Mgr,* Ben Nunley; Tel: 606-329-0090, E-mail: bnunley@thebookplace.org
Open Mon-Thurs 9-8, Sun 1-5
Friends of the Library Group

R FIRST BAPTIST CHURCH LIBRARY*, 1701 Winchester Ave, 41101. (Mail add: PO Box 787, 41105-0787), SAN 306-2120. Tel: 606-324-3100. FAX: 606-324-4344. E-mail: fbcashlandky@gmail.com. Web Site: www.fbcashlandky.org. *Librn,* Lynn Hutchinson
Library Holdings: Bk Vols 8,000

AUBURN

S SOUTH UNION SHAKER VILLAGE, Julia Neal Library, 850 Shaker Museum Rd, 42206. (Mail add: PO Box 177, 42206-0177), SAN 375-0736. Tel: 270-542-4167. Web Site: www.southunionshakervillage.com/library-research. *Curator, Exec Dir,* Thomas Collier Hines; E-mail: director@southunionshakervillage.com
Founded 1986
Library Holdings: Bk Titles 1,000
Special Collections: Historic Photographs; Manuscripts; Primary Materials
Subject Interests: Kentucky
Function: Archival coll
Open Tues-Fri 10-4
Restriction: Non-circulating
Friends of the Library Group

AUGUSTA

P KNOEDLER MEMORIAL LIBRARY*, 315 Main St, 41002. SAN 306-2139. Tel: 606-756-3911. *Librn,* Karen Smithers
Founded 1928
Library Holdings: Bk Titles 12,000
Special Collections: Bracken County History; Kentuckiana (Walter Rankins Coll)
Open Mon, Tues, Thurs & Fri 11-5

BARBOURVILLE

P KNOX COUNTY PUBLIC LIBRARY*, 206 Knox St, 40906. SAN 306-2147. Tel: 606-546-5339. FAX: 606-546-3602. E-mail: knoxlibrary@barbourville.com. Web Site: www.youseemore.com/knox. *Dir,* Lana Hale; *Asst Dir,* George West; Staff 1 (Non-MLS 1)
Founded 1964. Pop 30,239; Circ 74,309
Library Holdings: Audiobooks 698; AV Mats 135; Bks on Deafness & Sign Lang 15; CDs 492; DVDs 950; Large Print Bks 350; Microforms 175; Bk Titles 49,000; Bk Vols 52,000; Per Subs 48; Spec Interest Per Sub 5; Videos 500
Special Collections: Genealogy Coll; Kentucky Coll
Automation Activity & Vendor Info: (Cataloging) TLC (The Library Corporation); (Circulation) TLC (The Library Corporation); (OPAC) TLC (The Library Corporation)
Partic in Ky Libr Asn
Open Mon-Wed & Fri 9-5, Thurs 12-7, Sat 9-1
Bookmobiles: 1

C UNION COLLEGE*, Weeks-Townsend Memorial Library, 310 College St, Campus Box D-21, 40906-1499. SAN 306-2155. Tel: 606-546-1240. Reference Tel: 606-546-1243. FAX: 606-546-1239. E-mail: library@unionky.edu. Reference E-mail: refdesk@unionky.edu. Web Site: www.unionky.edu/library. *Dir, Libr Serv,* Tara L Cooper; Tel: 606-546-1241, E-mail: tcooper@unionky.edu; *Asst Librn,* Bobbie Hamilton; Tel: 606-546-1662, E-mail: bhamilto@unionky.edu; *Pub Serv Mgr,* Billie Daniels; Tel: 606-546-1630, E-mail: bdaniels@unionky.edu; *Coordr, Tech Serv,* Quetha Boles; Tel: 606-546-1627, E-mail: qboles@unionky.edu; Staff 3 (MLS 3)
Founded 1879. Enrl 1,108; Fac 55; Highest Degree: Master
Library Holdings: e-books 103,467; e-journals 15,211; Bk Vols 138,000; Per Subs 339; Videos 907
Special Collections: US Document Depository
Subject Interests: Civil War, Educ, Genealogy, State hist
Automation Activity & Vendor Info: (Acquisitions) Innovative Interfaces, Inc; (Cataloging) Innovative Interfaces, Inc; (Circulation) Innovative Interfaces, Inc; (Course Reserve) Innovative Interfaces, Inc; (ILL) OCLC; (OPAC) Innovative Interfaces, Inc; (Serials) Innovative Interfaces, Inc
Wireless access
Function: Archival coll, Computers for patron use, E-Reserves, Govt ref serv, Online cat, Photocopying/Printing, Wheelchair accessible
Partic in Appalachian College Association; Association of Independent Kentucky Colleges & Universities; LYRASIS; OCLC Online Computer Library Center, Inc
Open Mon-Thurs 7:30-6, Fri 7:30-4:30

BARDSTOWN

S OSCAR GETZ MUSEUM OF WHISKEY HISTORY LIBRARY*, Spalding Hall, 114 N Fifth St, 40004. SAN 329-8779. Tel: 502-348-2999. E-mail: whiskeymuseum@bardstowncable.net. Web Site: www.oscargetzwhiskeymuseum.com. *Curator,* Linda McCluskey
Founded 1979
Library Holdings: Bk Vols 300
Special Collections: Oral History
Open Mon-Fri (May-Oct) 10-5, Sat 10-4, Sun 12-4; Tues-Sat (Nov-April) 10-4, Sun 12-4

P NELSON COUNTY PUBLIC LIBRARY*, 201 Cathedral Manor, 40004-1515. SAN 342-2496. Tel: 502-348-3714. FAX: 502-348-5578. E-mail: library@ncplky.org. Web Site: ncplky.org. *Dir,* Sharon Shanks; E-mail: sshanks@ncplky.org; *Asst Dir,* Michael Greenwell; E-mail: mgreenwell@ncplky.org; *Acq Librn,* Carrie McDonald; *Ch,* Stephanie King; E-mail: sking@ncplky.org; Staff 22 (MLS 3, Non-MLS 19)
Founded 1967. Pop 40,000; Circ 374,309
Jul 2016-Jun 2017 Income (Main & Associated Libraries) $2,458,132, State $89,959, Locally Generated Income $2,368,173. Mats Exp $297,684, Books $189,330, Per/Ser (Incl. Access Fees) $5,884, AV Equip $16,840, AV Mat $8,424, Electronic Ref Mat (Incl. Access Fees) $77,206. Sal $781,654 (Prof $547,158)
Library Holdings: Audiobooks 12,497; AV Mats 27,704; CDs 670; DVDs 7,357; e-books 116,574; Large Print Bks 3,798; Bk Vols 104,933; Per Subs 119
Special Collections: Genealogy Coll; Kentucky Coll
Wireless access
Function: 24/7 Electronic res, 24/7 Online cat, Accelerated reader prog, Activity rm, After school storytime, Art exhibits, Audio & video playback equip for onsite use, Audiobks via web, Bi-weekly Writer's Group, Bk club(s), Bks on cassette, Bks on CD, Children's prog, Computer training, Computers for patron use, Digital talking bks, E-Reserves, Electronic databases & coll, Family literacy, Free DVD rentals, Genealogy discussion group, Holiday prog, Home delivery & serv to seniorr ctr & nursing homes, Homebound delivery serv, ILL available, Instruction & testing, Internet access, Magnifiers for reading, Mail & tel request accepted, Microfiche/film & reading machines, Music CDs, Notary serv, Online cat, Online info literacy tutorials on the web & in blackboard, Outreach serv, Outside serv via phone, mail, e-mail & web, OverDrive digital audio bks, Photocopying/Printing, Preschool outreach, Prog for adults, Prog for children & young adult, Ref & res, Ref serv available, Scanner, Senior outreach, Spanish lang bks, Spoken cassettes & CDs, Spoken cassettes & DVDs, Story hour, Summer & winter reading prog, Tax forms, Teen prog, VHS videos, Wheelchair accessible, Workshops, Writing prog
Open Mon, Fri & Sat 9-5, Tues-Thurs 9-8, Sun 1-5
Branches: 2
BLOOMFIELD BRANCH, 114 Fairfield Hill, Bloomfield, 40008. (Mail add: PO Box 249, Bloomfield, 40008-0024), SAN 342-2526. Tel: 502-252-9129. FAX: 502-252-8255. *Br Mgr,* Rhonda Olliges; E-mail: rolliges@nelsoncopublib.org; *Br Librn,* Glenda Owens; Staff 2 (Non-MLS 2)
Pop 1,000; Circ 6,994
Open Tues & Thurs 10-8, Wed 12-6, Fri 10-3, Sat 9-3
NEW HAVEN BRANCH, 318 Center St, New Haven, 40051, SAN 342-2615. Tel: 502-549-6735. FAX: 502-549-5668. *Br Mgr,* Catherine Williams; E-mail: cwilliams@nelsoncopublib.org; Staff 3 (Non-MLS 3)
Pop 900; Circ 30,963
Library Holdings: Bk Vols 2,600
Open Mon 10-1, Tues & Thurs 9-8, Wed 9-6, Sat 9-3
Bookmobiles: 1. Librn, Eileen Peterson. Bk titles 1,290

BEATTYVILLE

P LEE COUNTY PUBLIC LIBRARY*, 255 Industrial Park Rd, 41311. (Mail add: PO Box V, 41311-2022), SAN 306-2163. Tel: 606-464-8014. FAX: 606-464-2052. E-mail: leecopublib@yahoo.com. Web Site: heartofthekentuckyriver.com/library. *Dir,* Sonya Spencer
Pop 7,916; Circ 74,832
Library Holdings: Large Print Bks 250; Bk Vols 30,000; Per Subs 60
Special Collections: Genealogical Coll; Kentucky Coll; Quilt Coll
Wireless access
Partic in Public Information Network for Electronic Services
Open Mon-Fri 9-5, Sat 9-1
Friends of the Library Group

BEDFORD

P TRIMBLE COUNTY PUBLIC LIBRARY, 35 Equity Dr, 40006. SAN 306-2171. Tel: 502-255-7362. FAX: 502-255-7491. E-mail: info@trimblelibrary.org. Web Site: www.trimblelibrary.org. *Dir,* Dena Ratliff Warren; E-mail: director@trimblelibrary.org; *Asst Dir,* Elizabeth Tweedy; E-mail: btweedy@trimblelibrary.org
Pop 7,800; Circ 41,998

Library Holdings: Bk Vols 20,000; Per Subs 50
Subject Interests: Children's fiction, Popular mat
Automation Activity & Vendor Info: (Acquisitions) TLC (The Library Corporation); (Cataloging) TLC (The Library Corporation); (Circulation) TLC (The Library Corporation); (Course Reserve) TLC (The Library Corporation); (ILL) TLC (The Library Corporation); (Media Booking) TLC (The Library Corporation); (OPAC) TLC (The Library Corporation); (Serials) TLC (The Library Corporation)
Wireless access
Open Mon, Tues & Thurs 9-7, Wed 9-1, Fri 9-5, Sat 10-4
Bookmobiles: 1

BENTON

P MARSHALL COUNTY PUBLIC LIBRARY SYSTEM*, 1003 Poplar St, 42025. SAN 342-264X. Tel: 270-527-9969. FAX: 270-527-0506. E-mail: mcpl@marshallcolibrary.org. Web Site: www.marshallcolibrary.org. *Dir,* Tammy Blackwell; Tel: 270-527-9969, Ext 124, E-mail: tblackwell@marshallcolibrary.org; *Br Mgr,* Lenisa Jones; Tel: 270-527-9969, Ext 131, E-mail: ljones@marshallcolibrary.org; *Ch,* Beth Kerrick; Tel: 270-527-9969, Ext 126, E-mail: bkerrick@marshallcolibrary.org; *ILL,* Charla Cope; Tel: 270-527-9969, Ext 129, E-mail: ccope@marshallcolibrary.org; Staff 1 (MLS 1)
Founded 1968. Pop 30,000
Special Collections: Local History. Oral History
Automation Activity & Vendor Info: (Acquisitions) Evergreen; (Cataloging) Evergreen; (Circulation) Evergreen; (OPAC) Evergreen
Wireless access
Open Mon-Sat 9-5
Branches: 2
CALVERT CITY, 23 Park Rd, Calvert City, 42029. (Mail add: PO Box 465, Calvert City, 42029), SAN 342-2704. E-mail: ccpl@marshallcolibrary.org. *Br Mgr,* Wesley Berhow; Tel: 270-527-9969, Ext 221, E-mail: wberhow@marshallcolibrary.org
Open Mon-Sat 9-5
HARDIN, 4640 Murray Hwy, Hardin, 42048, SAN 342-2674. E-mail: hbpl@marshallcolibrary.org. *Br Mgr,* Deidre Tosh; Tel: 270-527-9969, Ext 324, E-mail: dtosh@marshallcolibrary.org
Open Mon-Sat 9-5
Bookmobiles: 1. Librn, Hayden Eubanks

BEREA

C BEREA COLLEGE*, Hutchins Library, 100 Campus Dr, 40404. SAN 342-2739. Tel: 859-985-3364. Interlibrary Loan Service Tel: 859-985-3275. Reference Tel: 859-985-3109. Administration Tel: 859-985-3266. Automation Services Tel: 859-985-3274. E-mail: reference_desk@berea.edu. Web Site: libraryguides.berea.edu. *Dir,* Anne Chase; E-mail: chasea@berea.edu; *Assoc Dir, Libr Serv,* Calvin Gross; E-mail: calvin_gross@berea.edu; *Head, Spec Coll & Archives,* Rachel Vagts; Tel: 859-985-3267, E-mail: vagts@berea.edu; *Instrul Serv Librn,* Amanda Peach; Tel: 859-985-3279, E-mail: peacha@berea.edu; *Instrul Serv Librn,* Ed Poston; Tel: 859-985-3172, E-mail: postonp@berea.edu; *Acq, ILL,* Patty Tarter; E-mail: tarterp@berea.edu; *Cat,* Mary Beth Bonet; Tel: 859-985-3283, E-mail: bonetm@berea.edu; *Coll Archivist,* Lori Myers-Steele; Tel: 859-985-3253, E-mail: myers-steelel@berea.edu; *Coordr, Electronic Res,* Susan Henthorn; Tel: 859-985-3268, E-mail: susan_henthorn@berea.edu; *Coordr, Info Literacy,* Angel Rivera; Tel: 859-985-3372, E-mail: riveralopeza@berea.edu; *Res Serv Spec,* Sharyn Miller; Tel: 859-985-3892, E-mail: sharyn_miller@berea.edu; *Sound Rec Archivist,* Harry Rice; Tel: 859-985-3249, E-mail: riceh@berea.edu; *User Serv Spec,* Judy Gergen; Tel: 859-985-3285, E-mail: gergenj@berea.edu; Staff 13 (MLS 8, Non-MLS 5)
Founded 1870. Enrl 1,586; Fac 113; Highest Degree: Bachelor
Jul 2015-Jun 2016. Mats Exp $426,402, Books $41,831, Per/Ser (Incl. Access Fees) $107,583, Micro $14,722, Electronic Ref Mat (Incl. Access Fees) $247,282, Presv $4,569
Library Holdings: AV Mats 15,959; e-books 238,420; e-journals 68,520; Electronic Media & Resources 17,933; Microforms 149,822; Bk Vols 346,053; Per Subs 258
Special Collections: Appalachian Sound Archives; Berea Archives, ms; Shedd-Lincoln Coll; Weatherford-Hammond Appalachian Coll, bks & ms. Oral History
Automation Activity & Vendor Info: (Acquisitions) Ex Libris Group; (Cataloging) Ex Libris Group; (Circulation) Ex Libris Group; (Course Reserve) Ex Libris Group; (ILL) Atlas Systems; (OPAC) Ex Libris Group; (Serials) Ex Libris Group
Wireless access
Partic in Appalachian College Association; Association of Independent Kentucky Colleges & Universities; Federation of Kentucky Academic Libraries; OCLC Online Computer Library Center, Inc
Open Mon-Thurs 8am-Midnight, Fri 8-7, Sat 10-6, Sun 2-Midnight

BOONEVILLE

P OWSLEY COUNTY PUBLIC LIBRARY, 185 Hwy 11, 41314. (Mail add: PO Box 280, 41314-0280). Tel: 606-593-5700. FAX: 606-593-5708. E-mail: ocpl.owlsleycounty@aol.com. *Dir,* Lesa Marcum; Staff 3 (Non-MLS 3)
Founded 1970. Pop 4,755; Circ 17,047
Library Holdings: Bk Titles 28,000; Per Subs 130; Videos 2,500
Special Collections: Kentucky Genealogy Coll
Subject Interests: Genealogy
Wireless access
Open Mon-Fri 9-5
Friends of the Library Group

BOWLING GREEN

P WARREN COUNTY PUBLIC LIBRARY*, 1225 State St, 42101. SAN 306-2198. Tel: 270-781-4882. FAX: 270-781-3699. Web Site: www.warrenpl.org. *Dir,* Lisa R Rice; Tel: 270-781-4882, Ext 202, E-mail: lisar@warrenpl.org; *Fac & Tech Mgr,* Alex Love; E-mail: alexl@warrenpl.org; *Outreach Mgr,* Court Stevens; E-mail: courtneys@warrenpl.org; *Tech Serv,* Holly H Hedden; Staff 50 (MLS 7, Non-MLS 43)
Founded 1940. Pop 80,000; Circ 582,000
Library Holdings: Bk Vols 136,439; Per Subs 225
Automation Activity & Vendor Info: (Cataloging) SirsiDynix; (Circulation) SirsiDynix; (ILL) SirsiDynix; (OPAC) SirsiDynix
Wireless access
Function: ILL available
Partic in OCLC Online Computer Library Center, Inc
Open Mon & Wed 8-6, Tues & Thurs 8-4, Fri & Sat 9-5
Friends of the Library Group
Branches: 2
BOB KIRBY BRANCH, 175 Iron Skillet Court, 47104. Tel: 270-782-0252. *Br Mgr,* Ashley Fowlkes; Tel: 270-782-0252, Ext 207, E-mail: ashleyf@warrenpl.org
Open Mon & Wed 8-4, Tues & Thurs 8-6, Fri & Sat 9-5
Friends of the Library Group
SMITHS GROVE BRANCH, 115 Second St, Smiths Grove, 42171. Tel: 270-563-6651. FAX: 270-563-1006. *Br Mgr,* Ashley Fowkles
Library Holdings: Bk Titles 10,000; Per Subs 10
Open Mon-Thurs 8-4, Fri 9-5
Friends of the Library Group
Bookmobiles: 1

C WESTERN KENTUCKY UNIVERSITY LIBRARIES, Helm-Cravens Library Complex, 1906 College Heights Blvd, No 11067, 42101-1067. SAN 342-2852. Tel: 270-745-6125. Circulation Tel: 270-745-3951. Interlibrary Loan Service Tel: 270-745-6118. FAX: 270-745-6422. E-mail: web.reference@wku.edu. Web Site: www.wku.edu/library. *Dean, Univ Libr,* Susann deVries; Tel: 270-745-5055, E-mail: susann.devries@wku.edu; *Chair, Dept of Library Public Services,* Laura DeLancey; Tel: 270-745-3979, E-mail: laura.delancey@wku.edu; *Head, Tech Serv,* Deana Groves; Tel: 270-745-6151, E-mail: deana.groves@wku.edu; *Health Sci Librn,* Carol Watwood; Tel: 270-745-3912, E-mail: carol.watwood@wku.edu; *Humanities & Soc Sci Librn,* Sean Kinder; Tel: 270-745-6339, E-mail: sean.kinder@wku.edu; *Spec Coll Cat Librn,* Joseph Shankweiler; Tel: 270-745-6306, E-mail: joseph.shankweiler@wku.edu; *Faculty Subject Specialist,* Dan Forrest; Tel: 270-745-6164, E-mail: dan.forrest@wku.edu; *ILL Spec,* Kathy Foushee; Tel: 270-745-4241, E-mail: katherine.foushee@wku.edu; Staff 31 (MLS 31)
Founded 1907. Enrl 19,761; Fac 1,120; Highest Degree: Doctorate
Library Holdings: Bk Titles 656,517; Bk Vols 783,803; Per Subs 3,912
Special Collections: Oral History; US Document Depository
Subject Interests: Folklore, Hist, Kentucky, Law, Shakers
Automation Activity & Vendor Info: (Acquisitions) Ex Libris Group; (Cataloging) Ex Libris Group; (Circulation) Ex Libris Group; (Course Reserve) Ex Libris Group; (ILL) Ex Libris Group; (Media Booking) Ex Libris Group; (OPAC) Ex Libris Group; (Serials) Ex Libris Group
Wireless access
Partic in LYRASIS; OCLC Online Computer Library Center, Inc
Open Mon-Thurs 8am-Midnight, Fri 8-4:30, Sun 1pm-Midnight
Friends of the Library Group

BRANDENBURG

P MEADE COUNTY PUBLIC LIBRARY*, 996 Old Ekron Rd, 40108. SAN 306-2201. Tel: 270-422-2094. FAX: 270-422-3133. Web Site: www.meadereads.org. *Dir,* Margaret Benham; E-mail: margaret@meadereads.org; Staff 11 (MLS 1, Non-MLS 10)
Founded 1967. Pop 25,000
Library Holdings: Bk Vols 23,200; Per Subs 63
Special Collections: Oral History
Subject Interests: Genealogy, Local hist

Automation Activity & Vendor Info: (Acquisitions) Brodart; (Cataloging) Brodart; (Circulation) Brodart
Function: Accelerated reader prog, Adult bk club, Art exhibits, Audio & video playback equip for onsite use, Audiobks via web, Bks on cassette, Bks on CD, CD-ROM, Children's prog, Computer training, Computers for patron use, Digital talking bks, Equip loans & repairs, Free DVD rentals, Holiday prog, Home delivery & serv to seniorr ctr & nursing homes, ILL available, Internet access, Jail serv, Music CDs, Notary serv, Online cat, Photocopying/Printing, Prog for children & young adult, Scanner, Serves people with intellectual disabilities, Story hour, Summer reading prog, Tax forms, Teen prog, VHS videos, Wheelchair accessible
Partic in LYRASIS
Open Mon-Thurs 9-8, Fri 9-5, Sat 9-3
Friends of the Library Group
Bookmobiles: 1

BROOKSVILLE

P BRACKEN COUNTY PUBLIC LIBRARY*, 310 W Miami St, 41004. (Mail add: PO Box 305, 41004-0305). Tel: 606-735-3620. FAX: 606-735-3378. Web Site: www.brackenlibrary.org. *Dir,* Christian Shroll; E-mail: bcpldirector@icloud.com
Library Holdings: Bk Titles 22,000; Per Subs 78
Wireless access
Open Mon, Tues, Thurs & Fri 9-5, Wed 9-8, Sat 9-1
Bookmobiles: 1

BROWNSVILLE

P EDMONSON COUNTY PUBLIC LIBRARY*, 280 Ferguson St, 42210. (Mail add: PO Box 219, 42210-0219), SAN 306-221X. Tel: 270-597-2146. E-mail: ecplib@yahoo.com. Web Site: ecplibrary.com. *Dir,* Jeanie Munsee; Staff 6 (Non-MLS 6)
Founded 1956. Pop 11,644; Circ 50,883
Library Holdings: CDs 295; DVDs 280; Large Print Bks 600; Bk Titles 25,000; Per Subs 46; Talking Bks 378; Videos 425
Special Collections: Genealogy Coll; Local History Coll
Automation Activity & Vendor Info: (Cataloging) TLC (The Library Corporation); (Circulation) TLC (The Library Corporation); (ILL) OCLC
Wireless access
Function: Home delivery & serv to seniorr ctr & nursing homes, Homebound delivery serv, ILL available, Music CDs, Prog for children & young adult, Ref serv available, Summer reading prog, VHS videos, Wheelchair accessible
Open Mon-Thurs 9-7, Fri 9-4:30, Sat 9-1
Bookmobiles: 1. Dir, Jason Miller

BURGIN

G NORTHPOINT TRAINING CENTER*, Residents' Library, 710 Walter Reed Rd, 40310. (Mail add: PO Box 479, 40310-0479), SAN 325-0989. Tel: 859-239-7012, Ext 3095. FAX: 859-239-7173. *Librn,* James Dennis; Staff 11 (MLS 1, Non-MLS 10)
Founded 1983
Library Holdings: Bk Titles 3,000; Per Subs 130

BURKESVILLE

P CUMBERLAND COUNTY PUBLIC LIBRARY*, 114 W Hill St, 42717. (Mail add: PO Box 440, 42717-0440), SAN 306-2228. Tel: 270-864-2207. Web Site: cumberlandcountylibrary.org. *Dir,* Paige D La Grange; E-mail: paige.lagrange@cumberlandcountylibrary.org; *Circ Librn,* Vickie Staley; E-mail: vickie.staley@cumberlandcountylibrary.org
Founded 1938. Pop 7,200; Circ 57,536
Library Holdings: Bk Vols 25,000; Per Subs 25
Automation Activity & Vendor Info: (Cataloging) Book Systems; (Circulation) Book Systems
Wireless access
Open Mon-Fri 8:50-4:50, Sat 8:50-11:50
Bookmobiles: 1. Librn, Terry Staley

BURLINGTON

P BOONE COUNTY PUBLIC LIBRARY*, 1786 Burlington Pike, 41005. SAN 306-2589. Tel: 859-342-2665. FAX: 859-689-0435. E-mail: info@bcpl.org. Web Site: www.bcpl.org. *Dir,* Carrie Herrmann; E-mail: director@bcpl.org; *Asst Dir,* Shawn Fry; E-mail: sfry@bcpl.org; *Br Mgr,* Melissa Fulton; *Cat Mgr, Colls Serv Mgr,* Jennifer Gregory; *Fac Mgr,* Jeff West; *Genealogy Mgr, Local Hist Mgr,* Bridgit Striker; *Pub Relations Mgr,* Jennifer Cheek; *Human Res Coordr,* Sherri Slavey; *Info Serv Coordr,* Patricia Yannarella; *IT Coordr,* Michael Savarino; *Outreach Coordr, Youth Serv Coordr,* Jennifer Timmerman; Staff 32 (MLS 30, Non-MLS 2)
Founded 1973. Pop 130,000; Circ 1,384,041
Jul 2019-Jun 2020 Income (Main & Associated Libraries) $9,461,690, State $40,203, Federal $86,799, County $8,321,581, Other $910,886. Mats Exp $1,129,071. Sal $4,535,198
Library Holdings: e-books 170,418; Bk Vols 252,377; Per Subs 602
Special Collections: Boone County Kentucky History
Automation Activity & Vendor Info: (Acquisitions) SirsiDynix; (Cataloging) SirsiDynix; (Circulation) SirsiDynix; (ILL) Relais International; (OPAC) SirsiDynix; (Serials) SirsiDynix
Wireless access
Function: 24/7 Electronic res, 24/7 Online cat, 3D Printer, Activity rm, Adult bk club, After school storytime, Art exhibits, Audiobks on Playaways & MP3, Bi-weekly Writer's Group, Bk club(s), Bks on CD, CD-ROM, Children's prog, Computer training, Computers for patron use, Electronic databases & coll, Free DVD rentals, Govt ref serv, Holiday prog, Home delivery & serv to seniorr ctr & nursing homes, Homebound delivery serv, Homework prog, ILL available, Internet access, Magazines, Magnifiers for reading, Mail & tel request accepted, Makerspace, Mango lang, Meeting rooms, Microfiche/film & reading machines, Music CDs, Online cat, Online ref, Outreach serv, Outside serv via phone, mail, e-mail & web, OverDrive digital audio bks, Photocopying/Printing, Preschool outreach, Preschool reading prog, Prog for adults, Prog for children & young adult, Ref & res, Ref serv available, Senior outreach, Spanish lang bks, STEM programs, Story hour, Summer reading prog, Telephone ref, Visual arts prog, Wheelchair accessible, Workshops, Writing prog
Publications: Discover (Monthly newsletter)
Partic in SouthWest Ohio & Neighboring Libraries
Special Services for the Deaf - Adult & family literacy prog; Bks on deafness & sign lang; Closed caption videos; High interest/low vocabulary bks; Sign lang interpreter upon request for prog
Special Services for the Blind - Bks on CD; Copier with enlargement capabilities; Extensive large print coll; Free checkout of audio mat; Home delivery serv; Large print bks; Magnifiers; Playaways (bks on MP3); Ref serv; Screen enlargement software for people with visual disabilities
Open Mon-Fri 9-9, Sat 10-6, Sun 1-6
Branches: 5
CHAPIN MEMORIAL, 6517 Market St, Petersburg, 41080. Tel: 859-342-2665. FAX: 859-689-4313. *Br Mgr,* Patricia Yannarella
Open Mon & Thurs 12-7, Tues 12-6, Wed 10-6, Fri 12-6
FLORENCE BRANCH, 7425 US 42, Florence, 41042. Tel: 859-342-2665. FAX: 859-371-0037. *Br Mgr,* Jake Moore
Open Mon-Thurs 9-8, Fri 9-6, Sat 10-6, Sun 1-6
SCHEBEN BRANCH, 8899 US 42, Union, 41091. Tel: 859-342-2665. FAX: 859-384-5557. *Br Mgr,* Amy Foster
Open Mon-Thurs 9-8, Fri 9-6, Sat 10-6, Sun 1-6
WALTON BRANCH, 21 S Main St, Walton, 41094-1135. Tel: 859-342-2665. FAX: 859-485-7049. *Br Mgr,* Sharon Franklin
Open Mon 9-8, Tues-Fri 9-6, Sat 10-6, Sun 1-6

CADIZ

P JOHN L STREET LIBRARY*, 244 Main St, 42211-9153. Tel: 270-522-6301. FAX: 270-522-1107. E-mail: johnlstreetlibrary@yahoo.com. Web Site: www.jlslibrary.org. *Dir,* Pamela Thomas Metts
Founded 1954. Pop 12,593; Circ 110,011
Library Holdings: Bk Titles 45,000; Per Subs 120
Automation Activity & Vendor Info: (Acquisitions) Follett Software; (Cataloging) Follett Software; (Circulation) Follett Software; (Course Reserve) Follett Software; (ILL) Follett Software; (Media Booking) Follett Software; (OPAC) Follett Software; (Serials) Follett Software
Wireless access
Open Mon 9-8, Tues-Fri 9-5:30, Sat 9-12
Bookmobiles: 1. In Charge, Pam Underwood

CAMPBELLSVILLE

C CAMPBELLSVILLE UNIVERSITY*, Montgomery Library, One University Dr, 42718-2799. SAN 306-2252. Tel: 270-789-5024. FAX: 270-789-5336. Web Site: www.campbellsville.edu/academics/academic-affairs/montgomery-library. *Dean, Libr Serv,* Position Currently Open; *Pub Serv Librn,* Kay Alston; Tel: 270-789-5360, E-mail: klalston@campbellsville.edu; *Ref Librn,* Glen Taul; Tel: 270-789-5390, E-mail: getaul@campbellsville.edu; Staff 6 (MLS 2, Non-MLS 4)
Founded 1906. Enrl 1,365; Fac 92; Highest Degree: Master
Library Holdings: Bk Vols 86,000; Per Subs 900
Special Collections: College Archives
Subject Interests: Relig, US Civil War
Automation Activity & Vendor Info: (Cataloging) Ex Libris Group; (Circulation) Ex Libris Group; (OPAC) Ex Libris Group
Publications: Policies & Procedures Handbook
Partic in Appalachian College Association; Association of Independent Kentucky Colleges & Universities
Open Mon-Thurs 8am-10pm, Fri 8-5, Sat 10-4, Sun 4pm-10pm; Mon-Fri (Summer) 8-5

P TAYLOR COUNTY PUBLIC LIBRARY*, 1316 E Broadway, 42718. SAN 306-2260. Tel: 270-465-2562. FAX: 270-465-8026. E-mail: info@tcplibrary.org. Web Site: www.tcplibrary.org. *Dir,* Cherita Barlow
Founded 1974. Pop 32,000
Library Holdings: Bk Vols 58,245; Per Subs 21
Automation Activity & Vendor Info: (Cataloging) Book Systems; (Circulation) Book Systems; (OPAC) Book Systems
Wireless access
Function: 24/7 Online cat, Activity rm, Adult bk club, Adult literacy prog, After school storytime, Art exhibits, Audiobks via web, Bi-weekly Writer's Group, Bilingual assistance for Spanish patrons, Bk club(s), Bks on CD, CD-ROM, Children's prog, Citizenship assistance, Computer training, Computers for patron use, Digital talking bks, E-Reserves, Equip loans & repairs, Family literacy, Free DVD rentals, Govt ref serv, Holiday prog, Home delivery & serv to seniorr ctr & nursing homes, Homebound delivery serv, Homework prog, Internet access, Laminating, Life-long learning prog for all ages, Literacy & newcomer serv, Magazines, Magnifiers for reading, Mail & tel request accepted, Mango lang, Meeting rooms, Microfiche/film & reading machines, Movies, Music CDs, Notary serv, Online cat, Online ref, Outreach serv, OverDrive digital audio bks, Photocopying/Printing, Preschool outreach, Preschool reading prog, Prog for adults, Prog for children & young adult, Ref & res, Ref serv available, Res libr, Scanner, Senior computer classes, Spanish lang bks, Spoken cassettes & CDs, Spoken cassettes & DVDs, Story hour, Study rm, Summer & winter reading prog, Summer reading prog, Tax forms, Teen prog, Wheelchair accessible, Winter reading prog, Words travel prog, Workshops
Open Mon-Thurs 9-7, Fri 9-5, Sat 9-3
Friends of the Library Group

CAMPTON

P WOLFE COUNTY PUBLIC LIBRARY, 164 Kentucky Hwy 15 N, 41301. (Mail add: PO Box 10, 41301-0010), SAN 306-2279. Tel: 606-668-6571. FAX: 606-668-6561. E-mail: wolib@mrtc.com. Web Site: www.wcplib.org. *Dir,* Julie Hendrix
Pop 7,000; Circ 48,193
Library Holdings: Bk Vols 22,700; Per Subs 49
Special Collections: Kentucky Genealogy Coll
Wireless access
Open Mon, Wed & Fri 9-4:30, Tues & Thurs 9-6, Sat 9-1
Friends of the Library Group

CARLISLE

P NICHOLAS COUNTY PUBLIC LIBRARY, 223 N Broadway St, 40311. SAN 306-2287. Tel: 859-289-5595. FAX: 859-289-4340. Web Site: www.nicholasreads.org. *Dir,* Becky Reid; E-mail: becky@nicholascountylibrary.com; Staff 2 (Non-MLS 2)
Founded 1961. Pop 7,080
Library Holdings: Bks on Deafness & Sign Lang 31; Large Print Bks 420; Bk Vols 27,358; Per Subs 20; Talking Bks 360
Special Collections: Genealogy Reels, Census, Births, Marriages & Deaths, Bonds, Deeds, Wills from 1790
Automation Activity & Vendor Info: (Cataloging) Book Systems; (Circulation) Book Systems; (OPAC) Book Systems
Wireless access
Open Mon-Fri 9-4
Bookmobiles: 1. Librn, Susan Short

CARROLLTON

P CARROLL COUNTY PUBLIC LIBRARY*, 136 Court St, 41008. SAN 306-2295. Tel: 502-732-7020. FAX: 502-732-7122. E-mail: information@carrollcountylibrary.org. Web Site: www.youseemore.com/carroll. *Dir,* Hillary Arney; E-mail: hillary@carrollcountylibrary.org; *Asst Dir,* Patricia Hersey; E-mail: patricia@carrollcountylibrary.org; *Outreach Serv Librn,* Sue Guelda; E-mail: sue@carrollcountylibrary.org; *Circ Mgr,* Martha Noffsinger; E-mail: martha@carrollcountylibrary.org; *Tech Serv,* Rita Stangle; E-mail: rita@carrollcountylibrary.org; *Youth Serv,* Leslie Sutherland; E-mail: leslie@carrollcountylibrary.org; Staff 1 (Non-MLS 1)
Founded 1978. Pop 10,000; Circ 90,000
Library Holdings: AV Mats 4,486; Bks on Deafness & Sign Lang 10; Large Print Bks 1,282; Bk Vols 24,854; Per Subs 76
Special Collections: Kentucky Coll
Subject Interests: Genealogy, Local hist, Spanish lang mat
Automation Activity & Vendor Info: (Cataloging) TLC (The Library Corporation); (Circulation) TLC (The Library Corporation); (OPAC) TLC (The Library Corporation)
Wireless access
Partic in Pub Libr Asn of N Ky
Special Services for the Blind - Audio mat; Bks on cassette; Bks on CD; Talking bk & rec for the blind cat; Talking bks & player equip
Open Mon-Thurs 9:30-8, Fri & Sat 9:30-5

CLINTON

P HICKMAN COUNTY MEMORIAL LIBRARY*, 110 Craig Lane, 42031-1427. Tel: 270-653-2225. E-mail: hickman.co.mem.lib@gmail.com. *Librn,* Laura Poole
Founded 1917. Pop 5,146; Circ 12,481
Library Holdings: Bk Titles 11,000; Per Subs 23
Wireless access
Open Mon-Fri (Summer) 2-5, Sat 9:30-12:30; Mon-Fri (Winter) 2-4:30, Sat 9:30-12:30

COLD SPRING

P CAMPBELL COUNTY PUBLIC LIBRARY DISTRICT*, 3920 Alexandria Pike, 41076. SAN 306-3801. Tel: 859-781-6166. FAX: 859-572-5049. E-mail: csinfo@cc-pl.org. Web Site: www.cc-pl.org. *Libr Dir,* J C Morgan; E-mail: jcmorgan@cc-pl.org; *Br Mgr,* Dave Anderson; E-mail: danderson@cc-pl.org; Staff 57.5 (MLS 17.5, Non-MLS 40)
Founded 1978. Pop 90,000; Circ 853,519
Library Holdings: Bk Vols 200,000; Per Subs 300
Automation Activity & Vendor Info: (Acquisitions) Innovative Interfaces, Inc; (Cataloging) Innovative Interfaces, Inc; (Circulation) Innovative Interfaces, Inc; (OPAC) Innovative Interfaces, Inc
Wireless access
Function: Homebound delivery serv, ILL available, Prog for children & young adult, Ref serv available, Summer reading prog, Wheelchair accessible
Publications: Connections (Monthly)
Partic in LYRASIS; SouthWest Ohio & Neighboring Libraries
Open Mon-Thurs 9-9, Fri 9-7, Sat 9-5, Sun 1-5
Friends of the Library Group
Branches: 3
ALEXANDRIA BRANCH, 8333 Alexandria Pike, Alexandria, 41001. Tel: 859-572-7463. E-mail: alinfo@cc-pl.org. *Br Supvr,* Noah Bartel
Open Tues-Fri 11-7, Sat 11-5
PHILIP N CARRICO BRANCH, 1000 Highland Ave, Fort Thomas, 41075. Tel: 859-572-5033. FAX: 859-572-5038. E-mail: ftinfo@cc-pl.org. *Br Mgr,* Pam Posik; Tel: 859-572-5033, Ext 19, E-mail: pposik@cc-pl.org
Library Holdings: Bk Vols 74,000
Open Mon-Thurs 9-9, Fri 9-7, Sat 9-5, Sun 1-5
NEWPORT BRANCH, 901 E Sixth St, Newport, 41071. Tel: 859-572-5035. FAX: 859-572-5036. E-mail: nwinfor@cc-pl.org. *Asst Dir, Br Mgr,* Chantelle Bentley-Phillips; Tel: 859-572-5035, Ext 22, E-mail: cphillips@cc-pl.org
Library Holdings: Bk Vols 73,000; Per Subs 80
Open Mon-Thurs 9-9, Fri 9-7, Sat 9-5, Sun 1-5
Bookmobiles: 1

COLUMBIA

P ADAIR COUNTY PUBLIC LIBRARY*, 307 Greensburg St, 42728-1488. SAN 306-2309. Tel: 270-384-2472. FAX: 270-384-9446. E-mail: adaircountypubliclibrary@gmail.com. Web Site: www.adaircountypubliclibrary.com. *Dir,* Lee Ann Jessee; *Librn,* Jewel Kimbler; *Ch Serv,* Aleina Milligan; *Genealogist,* Ernestine Bennett
Pop 15,233; Circ 49,026
Library Holdings: Bk Vols 25,000; Per Subs 12
Special Collections: Janice Holt Giles Coll
Subject Interests: Kentucky
Automation Activity & Vendor Info: (Acquisitions) Book Systems; (Cataloging) Book Systems; (Circulation) Book Systems; (ILL) OCLC; (Media Booking) Book Systems; (OPAC) Book Systems; (Serials) Book Systems
Wireless access
Partic in OCLC Online Computer Library Center, Inc
Open Mon-Wed & Fri 8-5, Thurs 9-6, Sat 8-Noon
Bookmobiles: 1. Librn, Anita Riddle

CR LINDSEY WILSON COLLEGE*, Katie Murrell Library, 210 Lindsey Wilson St, 42728. SAN 306-2325. Tel: 270-384-8102. Administration Tel: 270-384-8250. Toll Free Tel: 800-264-6483. FAX: 270-384-4188. E-mail: library@lindsey.edu. Web Site: www.lindsey.edu/library. *Dir,* Houston Barnes; E-mail: barnesh@lindsy.edu; *Pub Serv Librn,* Tim Hopper; Tel: 270 384 8251, E-mail: hoopert@lindey.edu. Subject Specialists: *Fantasy, Mil hist, Sci fict,* Houston Barnes; *Farming, Music, Relig,* Tim Hopper; Staff 5 (MLS 2, Non-MLS 3)
Founded 1902. Enrl 2,651; Highest Degree: Doctorate
Jul 2015-Jun 2016. Mats Exp $141,776, Books $24,435, Per/Ser (Incl. Access Fees) $70,002, Other Print Mats $17,945, AV Equip $2,886, AV Mat $1,062, Electronic Ref Mat (Incl. Access Fees) $25,346, Presv $100. Sal $198,500 (Prof $134,760)
Library Holdings: Audiobooks 25; CDs 770; DVDs 1,222; e-books 278,000; e-journals 30,000; Electronic Media & Resources 97,732; Bk Titles 61,009; Bk Vols 66,069; Per Subs 154
Special Collections: Methodism on the Frontier (Methodist Coll). Oral History; US Document Depository

Subject Interests: Local hist, Methodism
Automation Activity & Vendor Info: (Acquisitions) Innovative Interfaces, Inc; (Cataloging) Innovative Interfaces, Inc; (Circulation) Innovative Interfaces, Inc; (Course Reserve) Blackboard Inc; (ILL) OCLC FirstSearch; (Media Booking) Innovative Interfaces, Inc; (OPAC) Innovative Interfaces, Inc; (Serials) EBSCO Online
Wireless access
Function: Art exhibits, Bks on CD, Computers for patron use, Digital talking bks, Distance learning, Doc delivery serv, Electronic databases & coll, Free DVD rentals, ILL available, Internet access, Laminating, Magazines, Mail & tel request accepted, Online cat, Online info literacy tutorials on the web & in blackboard, Orientations, Photocopying/Printing, Ref serv available, Spoken cassettes & DVDs, Study rm, Wheelchair accessible
Partic in Appalachian College Association; Association of Independent Kentucky Colleges & Universities; Federation of Kentucky Academic Libraries
Special Services for the Blind - Recorded bks
Open Mon-Thurs 7:30-11, Fri 7:30-5, Sat 1-5, Sun 2-10
Restriction: Open to pub by appt only

CORBIN

P CORBIN PUBLIC LIBRARY, 215 Roy Kidd Ave, 40701. SAN 306-2333. Tel: 606-528-6366. FAX: 606-523-1895. E-mail: information@corbinkylibrary.org. Web Site: www.corbinkylibrary.org. *Dir,* Donna Chadwell
Founded 1916. Pop 22,472; Circ 56,233
Library Holdings: Bk Vols 30,000; Per Subs 52
Special Collections: Corbin Time Tribune, 1917-1970, micro
Wireless access
Open Mon & Wed-Fri 10-5, Tues 10-7, Sat 10-2
Friends of the Library Group

COVINGTON

S BEHRINGER-CRAWFORD MUSEUM*, Lawrence Duba Library, 1600 Montague Rd, Devou Park, 41011. SAN 373-4579. Tel: 859-491-4003. E-mail: info@bcmuseum.org. Web Site: www.bcmuseum.org. *Exec Dir,* Laurie Risch; E-mail: lrisch@bcmuseum.org; *Educ Dir,* Kim Gehring-Cook; E-mail: education@bcmuseum.org; *Curator of Coll,* Maridith Yahl; E-mail: bcmcurator@gmail.com
Library Holdings: Bk Vols 1,250
Wireless access
Open Tues-Sat 10-5, Sun 1-5

P KENTON COUNTY PUBLIC LIBRARY*, Covington Beach, 502 Scott Blvd, 41011. SAN 342-300X. Tel: 859-962-4060. Reference Tel: 859-962-4071. FAX: 859-261-2676. E-mail: crefdesk@kentonlibrary.org. Web Site: www.kentonlibrary.org/locations/covington. *Dir,* Dave Schroeder; E-mail: dave.schroeder@kentonlibrary.org; *Br Mgr,* Paul Duryea; Tel: 859-962-4074; Staff 94 (MLS 29, Non-MLS 65)
Founded 1967. Pop 151,464; Circ 2,128,503
Library Holdings: AV Mats 107,625; Bks on Deafness & Sign Lang 251; CDs 21,250; DVDs 36,253; e-books 7,574; Electronic Media & Resources 455; Large Print Bks 548; Bk Titles 221,621; Bk Vols 457,729; Per Subs 1,069; Talking Bks 15,675; Videos 9,450
Special Collections: Northern Kentucky Newspapers Index, 1835-1931, 1984-present
Subject Interests: Kentucky, Local hist
Automation Activity & Vendor Info: (Acquisitions) SirsiDynix; (Cataloging) SirsiDynix; (Circulation) SirsiDynix; (OPAC) SirsiDynix
Wireless access
Function: Homebound delivery serv, Preschool outreach
Publications: Calendar (Monthly)
Partic in SouthWest Ohio & Neighboring Libraries
Open Mon-Fri 9-7, Sat 10-5
Friends of the Library Group
Branches: 3
ADMINISTRATION CENTER, 3095 Hulbert Ave, Erlanger, 41018. Tel: 859-341-3200. *Dir,* David E Schroeder; Tel: 859-578-3600, E-mail: dave.schroeder@kentonlibrary.org; *Human Res Dir,* Lisa Deham; Tel: 859-578-3604; *Dir, Pub Relations,* Robin Klaene; Tel: 859-578-3608, E-mail: robin.klaene@kentonlibrary.org; *Supvr, Coll Develop,* Becky Bowen; Tel: 859-578-7949; *Pub Relations Coordr,* Gina Stegner; Tel: 859-578-3609, E-mail: gina.stegner@kentonlibrary.org
WILLIAM E DURR BRANCH, 1992 Walton-Nicholson Rd, Independence, 41051. SAN 376-916X. Tel: 859-962-4030. Interlibrary Loan Service Tel: 859-962-4081. Reference Tel: 859-962-4031. FAX: 859-962-4037. Web Site: www.kentonlibrary.org/locations/william-e-durr-branch. *Br Mgr,* Faith Mulberry; Tel: 859-962-4036
Library Holdings: Bk Vols 70,000; Per Subs 100
Open Mon-Fri 9-7, Sat 10-5
Friends of the Library Group
ERLANGER BRANCH, 401 Kenton Lands Rd, Erlanger, 41018. SAN 342-3034. Tel: 859-962-4200. Reference Tel: 859-962-4002. FAX: 859-962-4010. Web Site: www.kentonlibrary.org/locations/erlanger. *Br Mgr,* Angela Payer; Tel: 859-962-4001
Library Holdings: Bk Vols 150,000; Per Subs 200
Open Mon-Fri 9-7, Sat 10-5
Friends of the Library Group
Bookmobiles: 2

SR ST WALBURG MONASTERY ARCHIVES*, 2500 Amsterdam Rd, 41017. SAN 375-6521. Tel: 859-331-6324. FAX: 859-331-2136. Web Site: www.stwalburg.org. *Communications Dir,* Sister Deborah Harmeling; Tel: 859-331-6771, E-mail: sdhosb@yahoo.com; *Archivist,* Sister Margaret Mary Gough; E-mail: nunsrus9@gmail.com; Staff 3 (MLS 1, Non-MLS 2)
Founded 1859
Restriction: Open by appt only

CRESTVIEW HILLS

C THOMAS MORE UNIVERSITY BENEDICTINE LIBRARY, 333 Thomas More Pkwy, 41017-2599. SAN 306-2597. Tel: 859-344-3300. FAX: 859-344-3342. Reference E-mail: reference@thomasmore.edu. Web Site: library.thomasmore.edu. *Libr Dir,* Michael Wells; E-mail: wellsm@thomasmore.edu; *Govt Doc Librn, Ref Librn,* Kelly Bilz; Tel: 859-344-3615, E-mail: bilzk@thomasmore.edu; *Circ Supvr, ILL,* Joyce McKinley; Staff 3 (MLS 2, Non-MLS 1)
Founded 1921. Enrl 2,011; Fac 66; Highest Degree: Master
Jun 2020-May 2021 Income $192,492. Mats Exp $171,492, Books $10,000, Per/Ser (Incl. Access Fees) $41,000, AV Mat $500, Electronic Ref Mat (Incl. Access Fees) $113,000. Sal $35,000 (Prof $90,000)
Library Holdings: AV Mats 1,298; e-books 637,644; e-journals 54; Bk Titles 75,632; Bk Vols 81,127; Per Subs 64; Videos 1,298
Special Collections: Thomas More Univ. US Document Depository
Automation Activity & Vendor Info: (Acquisitions) ByWater Solutions; (Cataloging) ByWater Solutions; (Circulation) ByWater Solutions; (Course Reserve) ByWater Solutions; (Discovery) EBSCO Discovery Service; (ILL) OCLC Online; (Media Booking) ByWater Solutions; (OPAC) ByWater Solutions; (Serials) EBSCO Online
Wireless access
Partic in American Theological Library Association; Association of Independent Kentucky Colleges & Universities; Christian Library Consortium; LYRASIS; OCLC Online Computer Library Center, Inc; SouthWest Ohio & Neighboring Libraries
Open Mon-Thurs 8-8, Fri 8-4:30, Sat 10-4, Sun 2-10

CUMBERLAND

J SOUTHEAST KENTUCKY COMMUNITY & TECHNICAL COLLEGE*, Gertrude Angel Dale Library, 207 Chrisman Hall, 700 College Rd, 40823. SAN 306-2384. Tel: 606-589-3099. FAX: 606-589-3176. Web Site: southeast.kctcs.edu/current-students/library/index.aspx. *Dir, Libr Serv,* Lynn Cox; Tel: 606-589-3073, E-mail: lynn.cox@kctcs.edu; *Campus Librn,* Lisa Ahlstedt; *Tech Serv,* Mitch Caudill; E-mail: mitch.caudill@kctcs.edu; *Tech Serv,* Mike Justice; E-mail: mike.justice@kctcs.edu; *Libr Spec,* Doris Browning; Tel: 606-589-3001; Staff 5 (MLS 2, Non-MLS 3)
Founded 1960. Enrl 1,416; Fac 69; Highest Degree: Associate
Special Collections: Kentucky Authors Coll
Subject Interests: Appalachia, Caribbean, Coal, Nursing, Pottery
Automation Activity & Vendor Info: (Cataloging) Ex Libris Group; (Circulation) Ex Libris Group; (Course Reserve) Ex Libris Group; (OPAC) Ex Libris Group
Wireless access
Function: 24/7 Electronic res, 24/7 Online cat, Doc delivery serv, E-Readers, Electronic databases & coll, For res purposes, Free DVD rentals, ILL available, Instruction & testing, Internet access, Music CDs, Notary serv, Online cat, Online ref, Orientations, Photocopying/Printing, Ref & res, Ref serv available, Scanner, Wheelchair accessible
Partic in OCLC Online Computer Library Center, Inc
Open Mon-Fri 8-4:30

CYNTHIANA

P CYNTHIANA-HARRISON COUNTY PUBLIC LIBRARY*, 104 N Main St, 41031. SAN 342-3069. Tel: 859-234-4881. FAX: 859-234-0059. E-mail: info@cynthianalibrary.org. Web Site: www.cynthianalibrary.org. *Dir,* Bessie Davis; E-mail: bdavis@cynthianalibrary.org; *Pub Relations, Youth Serv Librn,* Cindy Franklin; E-mail: cfranklin@cynthianalibrary.org; *Circ, ILL,* Terry Harris; E-mail: tharris@cynthianalibrary.org; *Tech Serv,* Starla Fields; E-mail: sfields@cynthianalibrary.org; Staff 10 (MLS 1, Non-MLS 9)
Founded 1932. Pop 18,227; Circ 108,600
Library Holdings: Bk Titles 45,000; Per Subs 97
Special Collections: Cissy Gregg Cookbook Coll; Civil War Coll; Kentucky & Local History; Whaley Photographic Coll. Oral History
Subject Interests: Econ, Genealogy, Health sci, Hist, Home econ
Wireless access

Function: After school storytime, Archival coll, Art exhibits, Audio & video playback equip for onsite use, CD-ROM, Computer training, Electronic databases & coll, Equip loans & repairs, Home delivery & serv to seniorr ctr & nursing homes, Homebound delivery serv, Homework prog, ILL available, Mail & tel request accepted, Music CDs, Photocopying/Printing, Preschool outreach, Prog for adults, Prog for children & young adult, Spoken cassettes & CDs, Summer reading prog, Tax forms, Telephone ref, VHS videos, Wheelchair accessible, Workshops
Special Services for the Blind - Web-Braille
Open Mon-Thurs 9-7, Fri 9-6, Sat 9-5
Bookmobiles: 1. Coordr, Ada Adair

DANVILLE

P BOYLE COUNTY PUBLIC LIBRARY*, 307 W Broadway, 40422. SAN 306-2406. Tel: 859-236-8466, 859-238-7323. FAX: 859-236-7692. E-mail: library@boylepublib.org. Web Site: www.boylepublib.org. *Dir,* Georgia de Araujo; E-mail: gdearaujo@boylepublib.org; *Ch,* Libby McWhorter; E-mail: lmcwhorter@boylepublib.org; *Circ Supvr,* Kathy Phillips; E-mail: kphillips@boylepublib.org; *Coordr, Info Tech,* Joseph Hurt; E-mail: jhurt@boylepublib.org; Staff 21.6 (MLS 7, Non-MLS 14.6)
Founded 1893. Pop 29,924; Circ 215,163
Jul 2017-Jun 2018 Income $1,966,701, State $126,356, County $1,701,963, Other $138,382. Mats Exp $138,786, Books $75,056, Per/Ser (Incl. Access Fees) $6,252, AV Mat $36,249, Electronic Ref Mat (Incl. Access Fees) $21,229. Sal $724,533
Library Holdings: Audiobooks 9,105; DVDs 8,097; e-books 171,014; Electronic Media & Resources 60; Microforms 754; Bk Vols 129,631; Per Subs 105
Subject Interests: Kentucky, Shakers
Automation Activity & Vendor Info: (Cataloging) Innovative Interfaces, Inc; (Circulation) Innovative Interfaces, Inc; (OPAC) Innovative Interfaces, Inc
Wireless access
Function: 24/7 Electronic res, 24/7 Online cat, Accelerated reader prog, Activity rm, Adult bk club, Adult literacy prog, After school storytime, Art exhibits, Bk club(s), Bks on CD, Chess club, Children's prog, Computer training, Computers for patron use, Free DVD rentals, Holiday prog, Homebound delivery serv, ILL available, Internet access, Magazines, Magnifiers for reading, Mail & tel request accepted, Mango lang, Microfiche/film & reading machines, Movies, Music CDs, Notary serv, Online cat, Outreach serv, OverDrive digital audio bks, Photocopying/Printing, Preschool outreach, Prog for adults, Prog for children & young adult, Ref serv available, Scanner, Senior computer classes, Senior outreach, Serves people with intellectual disabilities, Spanish lang bks, Story hour, Study rm, Summer reading prog, Tax forms, Teen prog, Telephone ref, VHS videos, Wheelchair accessible
Special Services for the Deaf - Staff with knowledge of sign lang
Special Services for the Blind - Bks on CD; Bks on flash-memory cartridges; Large print bks; Magnifiers; Talking bk serv referral
Open Mon & Thurs 9-8, Tues, Wed & Fri 9-5:30, Sat 9-5, Sun 1-5
Friends of the Library Group
Bookmobiles: 1

C CENTRE COLLEGE OF KENTUCKY*, Grace Doherty Library, 600 W Walnut St, 40422. SAN 306-2392. Tel: 859-238-5272. Circulation Tel: 859-238-5279. Reference Tel: 859-238-5277. FAX: 859-236-7925. E-mail: library@centre.edu. Web Site: library.centre.edu/home, www.centre.edu/offices/library. *Dir, Libr Serv,* Carrie Frey; Tel: 859-238-5275, E-mail: carrie.frey@centre.edu; *Instruction & Assessment Librn, Ref Librn,* Karoline Manny; E-mail: karoline.manny@centre.edu; *Acq,* Crystal Wesley; Tel: 859-238-5273, E-mail: crystal.wesley@centre.edu; *Tech Serv,* Beth Morgan; E-mail: beth.morgan@centre.edu; Staff 9 (MLS 4, Non-MLS 5)
Founded 1819. Enrl 1,130; Highest Degree: Bachelor
Library Holdings: CDs 3,334; e-books 30,757; e-journals 17,874; Bk Titles 225,841; Bk Vols 289,804; Per Subs 750
Special Collections: Centre College Archives; LeCompte Davis Coll. State Document Depository; US Document Depository
Automation Activity & Vendor Info: (Acquisitions) Innovative Interfaces, Inc; (Cataloging) Innovative Interfaces, Inc; (Circulation) Innovative Interfaces, Inc; (Course Reserve) Innovative Interfaces, Inc; (ILL) Innovative Interfaces, Inc; (OPAC) Innovative Interfaces, Inc; (Serials) Innovative Interfaces, Inc
Wireless access
Partic in Asn of Colleges of the South; Association of Independent Kentucky Colleges & Universities; LYRASIS
Open Mon-Thurs 7:30am-Midnight, Fri 7:30am-9pm, Sat 9-6, Sun 9am-Midnight

DIXON

P WEBSTER COUNTY PUBLIC LIBRARY*, 101 State Rte 132 E, 42409. SAN 342-3123. Tel: 270-639-9171. FAX: 270-639-6207. E-mail: libweb@bellsouth.net. Web Site: www.youseemore.com/webster. *Dir,* Erin Russelburg; *Cat Librn,* Heather Bentley; *Ch,* Shannon Sheridan; *Genealogy Librn,* Mandee Franklin
Founded 1954. Pop 13,955; Circ 85,552
Library Holdings: Bk Titles 24,000; Per Subs 146
Special Collections: Webster County Authors (Rice Coll)
Subject Interests: Genealogy, Hist
Automation Activity & Vendor Info: (Cataloging) TLC (The Library Corporation); (Circulation) TLC (The Library Corporation)
Wireless access
Open Mon-Wed & Fri 9-4, Thurs 9-6, Sat 9-2
Branches: 1
PROVIDENCE BRANCH, 230 Willow St, Providence, 42450, SAN 342-3158. Tel: 270-667-5658. FAX: 270-667-6368. E-mail: publi100@bellsouth.net. *Br Librn,* Misty Ashcraft
Open Mon-Wed & Fri 9-4, Thurs 9-6, Sat 9-2
Bookmobiles: 1. Librn, LuAnne Riggs

EDDYVILLE

S KENTUCKY STATE PENITENTIARY*, Inmate Library, 266 Water St, 42038. SAN 306-2430. Tel: 270-388-2211. Web Site: corrections.ky.gov/Facilities/AI/ksp. *Librn,* Position Currently Open; *Library Contact,* Dionne Hardin
Founded 1958

P LYON COUNTY PUBLIC LIBRARY*, 261 Commerce St, 42038. (Mail add: PO Box 546, 42038-0546), SAN 306-2449. Tel: 270-388-7720. FAX: 270-388-7735. E-mail: lcpl@lyonlibrary.org. Web Site: www.lyoncountylibrary.com. *Dir,* Lee Ann Cummins
Founded 1970. Pop 8,200; Circ 45,556
Library Holdings: Bk Vols 29,000; Per Subs 30
Special Collections: Genealogy Coll; Indian Arrowhead Coll; Lyon County History Coll; Stamp & Foreign Money Coll. Oral History
Automation Activity & Vendor Info: (Acquisitions) Follett Software
Wireless access
Open Mon-Fri 8-6, Sat 9-12

EDGEWOOD

J GATEWAY COMMUNITY & TECHNICAL COLLEGE*, Edgewood Campus Library, 790 Thomas More Pkwy, 41017. Tel: 859-442-4162. FAX: 859-341-6859. Web Site: gateway.kctcs.edu/current-students/student-resources/library. *Dir,* Denise Fritsch; E-mail: denise.fritsch@kctcs.edu; *Libr Coord,* Glenna Herald; E-mail: glenna.herald@kctcs.edu
Library Holdings: Bk Titles 672; Per Subs 90
Wireless access
Open Mon-Thurs 8am-9pm, Fri 8-5, Sat-Sun 8-1:30
Departmental Libraries:
BOONE CAMPUS LIBRARY, 500 Technology Way, Rm B09, Florence, 41042. Tel: 859-442-1682. *Dir, Knowledge Mgt,* Jeremy Berberich; E-mail: Jeremy.Berberich@kctcs.edu
Open Mon-Thurs 8-9, Fri 8-4:30, Sat 8-1

J URBAN CAMPUS LIBRARY, 516 Madison Ave, Technology, Innovation, and Enterprise Building, Covington, 41011. Tel: 859-442-4148. Web Site: www.gateway.kctcs.edu/Library.aspx. *Info Serv, Libr Dir,* Denise Fritsch
Open Mon-Thurs 8am-7pm, Fri 8-4:30

EDMONTON

P METCALFE COUNTY PUBLIC LIBRARY, 200 S Main St, 42129. (Mail add: PO Box 626, 42129-0626), SAN 306-2457. Tel: 270-432-4981. FAX: 270-432-5966. E-mail: metcalfelibrary@gmail.com. Web Site: metcalfepublic.com. *Libr Dir,* Kasey Warf
Founded 1940
Library Holdings: Bk Titles 33,747; Per Subs 25
Subject Interests: Agr, Genealogy
Wireless access
Open Mon 8:30-5:30, Tues, Wed & Fri 8:30-4:30, Thurs & Sat 9-1
Bookmobiles: 1

ELIZABETHTOWN

J ELIZABETHTOWN COMMUNITY & TECHNICAL COLLEGE LIBRARY, 600 College Street Rd, 42701. SAN 306-2465. Tel: 270-706-8812. Web Site: elizabethtown.kctcs.edu/current-students/student-resources/library. *Librn, Libr Dir,* Katie Meyer; Tel: 270-706-8443, E-mail: cmeyer0015@kctcs.edu; *Librn, Tech Serv,* Laurie MacKellar; E-mail: laurie.mackellar@kctcs.edu; *Acq,* Sarah Jones; E-mail: sarahs.jones@kctcs.edu; Staff 3.5 (MLS 2, Non-MLS 1.5)
Founded 1964. Enrl 3,000; Highest Degree: Associate
Library Holdings: Bk Vols 44,000; Per Subs 150
Automation Activity & Vendor Info: (Cataloging) Ex Libris Group; (Circulation) Ex Libris Group; (Course Reserve) Ex Libris Group; (ILL) Ex Libris Group; (OPAC) Ex Libris Group

Wireless access
Partic in Federation of Kentucky Academic Libraries; LYRASIS

P HARDIN COUNTY PUBLIC LIBRARY, 100 Jim Owen Dr, 42701. SAN 306-2473. Tel: 270-769-6337. FAX: 270-769-0437. Web Site: www.hcpl.info. *Dir,* Rene R Hutcheson; E-mail: director@hcpl.info; *Head, Tech Serv,* Diana Caine; E-mail: hcpldianac@gmail.com; Staff 16 (MLS 2, Non-MLS 14)
Founded 1958
Jul 2019-Jun 2020 Income $1,068,634, State $43,431, County $943,000, Locally Generated Income $82,203. Mats Exp $108,803, Books $69,222, AV Mat $19,828, Electronic Ref Mat (Incl. Access Fees) $19,828. Sal $437,048 (Prof $67,163)
Library Holdings: Audiobooks 3,269; AV Mats 6,685; CDs 216; DVDs 3,490; e-books 167,918; Electronic Media & Resources 43,961; Bk Vols 83,691; Per Subs 103
Automation Activity & Vendor Info: (Cataloging) Book Systems; (Circulation) Book Systems; (OPAC) Book Systems
Wireless access
Function: 24/7 Electronic res, 24/7 Online cat, Accelerated reader prog, Activity rm, Adult bk club, After school storytime, Art programs, Audiobks via web, Bi-weekly Writer's Group, Bk club(s), Bks on CD, Children's prog, Computer training, Computers for patron use, Digital talking bks, Electronic databases & coll, Health sci info serv, Holiday prog, Home delivery & serv to seniorr ctr & nursing homes, Homebound delivery serv, Homework prog, ILL available, Instruction & testing, Internet access, Life-long learning prog for all ages, Literacy & newcomer serv, Magnifiers for reading, Mail & tel request accepted, Mango lang, Meeting rooms, Movies, Music CDs, Online cat, Online ref, Outreach serv, Outside serv via phone, mail, e-mail & web, OverDrive digital audio bks, Photocopying/Printing, Preschool outreach, Preschool reading prog, Printer for laptops & handheld devices, Prog for adults, Prog for children & young adult, Ref & res, Ref serv available, Res assist avail, Scanner, Senior outreach, Serves people with intellectual disabilities, Spanish lang bks, Spoken cassettes & CDs, Spoken cassettes & DVDs, STEM programs, Story hour, Study rm, Summer reading prog, Teen prog, Telephone ref, Wheelchair accessible, Workshops, Writing prog
Open Mon-Thurs 9-6, Fri 9-5, Sat 9-3
Friends of the Library Group

M HARDIN MEMORIAL HOSPITAL*, William R Handley Health Sciences Library, 913 N Dixie Ave, 42701-2503. Tel: 270-706-1688. FAX: 270-706-1336. E-mail: library@hmh.net. Web Site: www.hmh.net. *Libr Coord,* Tammy Jo Waugh
Library Holdings: Bk Vols 600
Subject Interests: Allied health, Med, Nursing
Wireless access
Open Mon-Fri 8-4:30

ELKTON

P TODD COUNTY PUBLIC LIBRARY*, 302 E Main St, 42220. SAN 306-2503. Tel: 270-265-9071. FAX: 270-265-2599. E-mail: toddcountylibrary@yahoo.com. Web Site; toddcountylibrary.org. *Dir,* Audrea Clairmont
Founded 1977. Pop 12,000
Library Holdings: Bk Titles 31,000; Bk Vols 33,638; Per Subs 23
Special Collections: Robert Penn Warren Coll
Subject Interests: Genealogy, Kentucky
Automation Activity & Vendor Info: (Cataloging) Innovative Interfaces, Inc; (Circulation) Innovative Interfaces, Inc; (OPAC) Innovative Interfaces, Inc
Wireless access
Partic in LYRASIS
Open Mon 9-7, Tues-Fri 9-5, Sat 9-1
Friends of the Library Group
Bookmobiles: 1

EMINENCE

P HENRY COUNTY PUBLIC LIBRARY*, 172 Eminence Terrace, 40019-1146. SAN 306-2511. Tel: 502-845-5682. FAX: 502-845-4807. E-mail: info@henrylibrary.org. Web Site: www.henrylibrary.org. *Dir,* Tony Jones; E-mail: Tony.Jones@henrylibrary.org; *Children's & YA Librn,* Suzanne Bant; E-mail: Suzanne@henrylibrary.org; Staff 9 (Non-MLS 9)
Pop 16,000; Circ 74,000
Library Holdings: Bk Vols 35,000; Per Subs 95
Automation Activity & Vendor Info: (Cataloging) TLC (The Library Corporation); (Circulation) TLC (The Library Corporation)
Wireless access
Open Mon-Thurs 9-8, Fri & Sat 9-5
Bookmobiles: 1

FALMOUTH

P PENDLETON COUNTY PUBLIC LIBRARY*, 801 Robbins St, 41040. SAN 306-2546. Tel: 859-654-8535. FAX: 859-654-8538. Web Site: pcplibrary.org. *Dir,* Melissa Byrd; E-mail: mbyrd@pcplibrary.org
Founded 1953. Pop 14,000; Circ 99,427
Library Holdings: Bk Vols 31,000; Per Subs 36
Special Collections: E E Barton Genealogy Coll of Northern Kentucky Families; The Falmouth Outlook, microflm
Automation Activity & Vendor Info: (Cataloging) Evolve; (Circulation) Evolve; (OPAC) Evolve
Wireless access
Open Mon-Sat 9-8, Sun 1-5
Bookmobiles: 1. Outreach Servs, Sandra Florence. Bk titles 2,200

FLEMINGSBURG

P FLEMING COUNTY PUBLIC LIBRARY, 202 Bypass Blvd, 41041-1298. SAN 306-2570. Tel: 606-845-7851. FAX: 606-845-7045. E-mail: flemingcountylibrary@yahoo.com. Web Site: www2.youseemore.com/fleming. *Dir,* Mary Rushing; E-mail: mrushing@fleminglibrary.org; *Cat/ILL Spec, Tech Serv,* Paula McGraw; E-mail: pmcgraw@fleminglibrary.org; *Adult Serv,* Robyn Ramey; *Youth Serv,* Kathy Davenport; E-mail: kdavenport@fleminglibrary.org; Staff 6 (Non-MLS 6)
Founded 1962. Pop 14,000; Circ 102,000
Library Holdings: Bks on Deafness & Sign Lang 20; Bk Vols 28,000; Per Subs 70
Special Collections: Frank Sousley Coll; Harriet Dudley Grannis Coll; Henry Chittison History/Music Coll. State Document Depository
Subject Interests: Genealogy
Automation Activity & Vendor Info: (Cataloging) TLC (The Library Corporation); (Circulation) TLC (The Library Corporation); (Course Reserve) TLC (The Library Corporation); (ILL) OCLC; (OPAC) TLC (The Library Corporation); (Serials) TLC (The Library Corporation)
Wireless access
Open Mon & Wed 9-6, Tues, Thurs & Fri 9-4
Friends of the Library Group
Bookmobiles: 1. Librn, Barbara Faris

FORT CAMPBELL

A UNITED STATES ARMY*, R F Sink Memorial Library, Bldg 38, Screaming Eagle Blvd, 42223-5342. SAN 342-3182. Tel: 270-798-5729. Interlibrary Loan Service Tel: 270-956-3350. Reference Tel: 270-956-3344. Administration Tel: 270-798-1217. FAX: 270-798-0369. Web Site: campbell.armymwr.com/us/campbell/programs/robert-f-sink-memorial-library. *Librn,* James Moore; Staff 5 (MLS 5)
Founded 1941
Library Holdings: CDs 1,791; DVDs 1,146; Bk Titles 76,337; Bk Vols 88,216; Per Subs 315; Talking Bks 2,414; Videos 3,579
Special Collections: Local History, microfiche; Official Records of the Civil War; World War II Coll
Subject Interests: Mil hist
Automation Activity & Vendor Info: (Cataloging) Innovative Interfaces, Inc - Sierra; (Circulation) Innovative Interfaces, Inc - Sierra; (ILL) OCLC
Wireless access
Publications: In house bibliographies
Partic in OCLC Online Computer Library Center, Inc
Open Mon & Fri-Sun 9-5, Tues-Thurs 9-8

FORT KNOX

UNITED STATES ARMY
A BARR MEMORIAL LIBRARY*, 62 W Spearhead Division Ave, Bldg 400, 40121-5187. Tel: 502-624-1232, 502-624-4636. E-mail: usarmy.knox.imcom-atlantic.mbx.dfmwr-barr-library@mail.mil. *Librn,* Cindy Arnold; Staff 11 (MLS 3, Non-MLS 8)
Library Holdings: AV Mats 8,000; Bk Vols 84,000; Per Subs 250; Talking Bks 1,000
Subject Interests: Kentucky, Mil sci
Automation Activity & Vendor Info: (Cataloging) TLC (The Library Corporation); (Circulation) TLC (The Library Corporation); (OPAC) TLC (The Library Corporation)
Publications: In-house bibliographies
Open Mon-Thurs 9-8, Fri & Sat 9-5
A PATTON MUSEUM OF CAVALRY & ARMOR EMERT L DAVIS MEMORIAL LIBRARY*, 4554 Fayette Ave, 40121. (Mail add: PO Box 208, 40121-0208), SAN 342-3352. Tel: 502-624-6968. FAX: 502-624-2364. *Librn,* Candace L Fuller; E-mail: candy.fuller@us.army.mil
Founded 1975
Library Holdings: Bk Vols 13,000; Per Subs 20

Special Collections: General George S Patton, Jr Coll, photog; Robert J Icks' Photo & Manuscript Coll on Armored Equipment, bks, maps, photogs. Oral History
Partic in Tradoc

FRANKFORT

P KENTUCKY DEPARTMENT FOR LIBRARIES & ARCHIVES*, 300 Coffee Tree Rd, 40601. (Mail add: PO Box 537, 40602), SAN 342-3425. Tel: 502-564-8300. FAX: 502-564-5773. E-mail: kdla-referencedesk@ky.gov. Web Site: kdla.ky.gov. *State Librn,* Terry Manuel; *Dir, Libr Div,* Elizabeth Milburn; Staff 170 (MLS 85, Non-MLS 85)
Founded 1834
Library Holdings: Audiobooks 4,594; AV Mats 570; CDs 110; DVDs 1,341; Large Print Bks 17,150; Microforms 1,061; Music Scores 343; Bk Titles 76,428; Per Subs 203; Videos 4,649
Special Collections: Civil War Records (Confederate & Union in Kentucky); Confederate Pensions; Kentuckiana Coll; Kentucky Public Records, Maps & Genealogy Coll; Local Government Depository Coll; Louisville Courier-Journal (1868-to-date), micro. State Document Depository
Subject Interests: Art, Geol, Hist, Kentucky, Lit, Soc sci & issues
Automation Activity & Vendor Info: (Acquisitions) OCLC Worldshare Management Services; (Cataloging) OCLC Worldshare Management Services; (Circulation) OCLC Worldshare Management Services; (Discovery) OCLC Worldshare Management Services; (ILL) OCLC WorldShare Interlibrary Loan; (Media Booking) OCLC Worldshare Management Services; (OPAC) OCLC Worldshare Management Services; (Serials) OCLC Worldshare Management Services
Wireless access
Publications: Checklist of Kentucky State Publications; Statistical Report of Kentucky Public Libraries
Partic in OCLC Online Computer Library Center, Inc
Special Services for the Blind - Braille bks; Children's Braille; Digital talking bk; Digital talking bk machines; Local mags & bks recorded; Machine repair; Newsletter (in large print, Braille or on cassette); Talking bk & rec for the blind cat; Talking bk serv referral; Talking bks from Braille Inst
Open Mon-Fri 9-4
Branches: 1
KENTUCKY TALKING BOOK LIBRARY
See Separate Entry

S KENTUCKY HISTORICAL SOCIETY*, Martin F Schmidt Research Library, 100 W Broadway St, 40601. SAN 306-2643. Tel: 502-564-1792. Reference Tel: 502-564-1792, Ext 4460. FAX: 502-564-4701. E-mail: khsrefdesk@ky.gov. Web Site: www.history.ky.gov. *Exec Dir,* Scott Alvey; E-mail: scott.alvey@ky.gov; *Dir, Res Serv,* Louise Jones; E-mail: louise.jones@ky.gov; *Oral Hist Adminr,* Sarah Schmitt; E-mail: sarahm.schmitt@ky.gov; *Head, Ref Serv,* Cheri Daniels; E-mail: cheri.daniels@ky.gov; *Librn,* Courtney Jordan; E-mail: courtney.jordan@ky.gov; Staff 10 (MLS 5, Non-MLS 5)
Founded 1836
Library Holdings: Bk Titles 48,539; Bk Vols 101,029; Per Subs 197; Spec Interest Per Sub 47
Special Collections: Oral History; State Document Depository
Subject Interests: Genealogy, Hist, Kentucky, Manuscripts, Maps, Rare bks
Automation Activity & Vendor Info: (Cataloging) Ex Libris Group; (Circulation) Ex Libris Group
Wireless access
Publications: Chronicle (Quarterly); Kentucky Ancestors (Quarterly); The Register (Quarterly)
Open Wed-Sat 10-5
Restriction: Circulates for staff only

GL KENTUCKY STATE LAW LIBRARY*, 700 Capital Ave, Ste 200, 40601. SAN 306-2708. Tel: 502-564-4848. FAX: 502-564-5041. E-mail: statelawlibrary@kycourts.net. Web Site: courts.ky.gov/aoc/statelawlibrary. *Librn,* Jennifer Frazier; Staff 2 (MLS 1, Non-MLS 1)
Founded 1954
Library Holdings: e-journals 304; Bk Titles 10,500; Bk Vols 134,000
Special Collections: Kentucky Law
Subject Interests: Anglo-Am law
Publications: Guide to Kentucky Legal Research: A State Bibliography (1985); Index to Kentucky Legal History, 18th & 19th Centuries (1983)
Partic in OCLC Online Computer Library Center, Inc
Special Services for the Deaf - TDD equip
Open Mon-Fri 8-4:30

C KENTUCKY STATE UNIVERSITY, Paul G Blazer Library, 400 E Main St, 40601-2355. SAN 306-2678. Tel: 502-597-6852. Circulation Tel: 502-597-6851. Reference Tel: 502-597-6857. FAX: 502-597-5068. Web Site: www.kysu.edu/academics/library. *Dir, Libr Serv,* Sheila A Stuckey; E-mail: sheila.stuckey@kysu.edu; *Head, Archives & Spec Coll, Records Librn,* Sharon McGee; Tel: 502-597-6824, E-mail: sharon.mcgee@kysu.edu; *Coordr, Libr Instruction, Head, Pub Serv,* Nkechi Amadife; Tel: 502-597-6817, E-mail: nkechi.amadife@kysu.edu; *ILL, Per/Ref Librn,* Dantrea Hampton; Tel: 502-597-5946, E-mail: dantrea.hampton@kysu.edu; *Distance Educ, Ref Librn,* Bobby Walter; Tel: 502-597-6855, E-mail: bobby.walter@kysu.edu; *Acq, Cataloger, Resource Dev Librn,* Debbra Tate; Tel: 502-597-6862, E-mail: debbra.tate@kysu.edu; Staff 11 (MLS 6, Non-MLS 5)
Founded 1960. Enrl 1,785; Fac 151; Highest Degree: Doctorate
Library Holdings: Microforms 328,572
Special Collections: Black Studies, bks, flm & micro. Oral History; US Document Depository
Automation Activity & Vendor Info: (Acquisitions) OCLC Worldshare Management Services; (Cataloging) OCLC Worldshare Management Services; (Circulation) OCLC Worldshare Management Services; (Course Reserve) OCLC Worldshare Management Services; (Discovery) OCLC Worldshare Management Services; (ILL) OCLC WorldShare Interlibrary Loan; (OPAC) OCLC Worldshare Management Services; (Serials) OCLC Worldshare Management Services
Wireless access
Function: 24/7 Electronic res, 24/7 Online cat, Archival coll, Computers for patron use, Distance learning, Electronic databases & coll, Govt ref serv, ILL available, Internet access, Magazines, Online cat, Online ref, Orientations, Photocopying/Printing, Ref & res, Ref serv available, Tax forms, Telephone ref
Partic in Federation of Kentucky Academic Libraries; HBCU Library Alliance; OCLC Online Computer Library Center, Inc
Open Mon-Thurs 8am-10pm, Fri 8-5, Sat 11-3, Sun 2-9

P KENTUCKY TALKING BOOK LIBRARY, 300 Coffee Tree Rd, 40601. (Mail add: PO Box 537, 40602-0537), SAN 306-2651. Tel: 502-564-5791. Toll Free Tel: 800-372-2968. FAX: 502-564-5773. E-mail: ktbl.mail@ky.gov. Web Site: www.kdla.ky.gov/librarians/talkingbook. *Br Mgr,* Barbara Penegor; Tel: 502-564-1738; Staff 8 (MLS 4, Non-MLS 4)
Founded 1969
Library Holdings: Braille Volumes 39,160; Bk Titles 114,117; Per Subs 84; Talking Bks 91,933
Special Collections: Kentucky Digital Talking Books
Wireless access
Function: 24/7 Electronic res, Audiobks via web, Digital talking bks, E-Readers, Equip loans & repairs, ILL available, Mail & tel request accepted, Mail loans to mem, Online cat, Outside serv via phone, mail, e-mail & web
Special Services for the Blind - Audio mat; Bks on flash-memory cartridges; Braille bks; Braille equip; Braille servs; Children's Braille; Digital talking bk; Digital talking bk machines; Duplicating spec requests; Local mags & bks recorded; Newsletter (in large print, Braille or on cassette); Newsline for the Blind; Production of talking bks; Reader equip; Soundproof reading booth; Talking bk & rec for the blind cat; Talking bks; Talking bks & player equip; Web-Braille
Open Mon-Fri 8-4
Restriction: Registered patrons only

P PAUL SAWYIER PUBLIC LIBRARY*, 319 Wapping St, 40601-2605. SAN 306-2694. Tel: 502-352-2665. FAX: 502-227-2250. E-mail: director@pspl.org. Web Site: www.pspl.org. *Exec Dir,* Donna Gibson; Tel: 502-352-2665, Ext 200, E-mail: donnag@pspl.org; *Adult Serv,* Jaci West; E-mail: jaci@pspl.org; *Youth Serv,* Erinn Conness; E-mail: erinn@pspl.org; Staff 28.2 (MLS 5.6, Non-MLS 22.6)
Founded 1908. Pop 49,648; Circ 516,329
Jul 2013-Jun 2014 Income $3,104,648, State $26,663, Locally Generated Income $2,957,431, Other $120,554. Mats Exp $2,616,141. Sal $1,716,237
Library Holdings: e-books 73,905; Bk Vols 126,401; Per Subs 184
Subject Interests: Local hist
Automation Activity & Vendor Info: (Cataloging) TLC (The Library Corporation); (Circulation) TLC (The Library Corporation); (OPAC) TLC (The Library Corporation); (Serials) TLC (The Library Corporation)
Wireless access
Function: 24/7 Electronic res, Activity rm, Adult bk club, Art exhibits, Audiobks via web, Bk club(s), Bks on CD, Children's prog, Computer training, Computers for patron use, E-Readers, Free DVD rentals, Home delivery & serv to seniorr ctr & nursing homes, Homebound delivery serv, ILL available, Instruction & testing, Internet access, Magazines, Magnifiers for reading, Mango lang, Music CDs, Notary serv, Online cat, Online ref, Outreach serv, OverDrive digital audio bks, Photocopying/Printing, Preschool outreach, Printer for laptops & handheld devices, Prog for adults, Prog for children & young adult, Ref serv available, Scanner, Senior computer classes, Senior outreach, Story hour, Study rm, Summer reading prog, Teen prog, Telephone ref, Wheelchair accessible
Open Mon-Thurs 9-8, Fri 9-6, Sat 9-5, Sun 1-5
Friends of the Library Group

FRANKLIN

P GOODNIGHT MEMORIAL PUBLIC LIBRARY, 203 S Main St, 42134. SAN 306-2716. Tel: 270-586-8397. FAX: 270-586-8397. E-mail: goodmeml@bellsouth.net. Web Site: www.gmpl.org. *Dir,* Audrey Phillips; *Media/IT Mgr,* Jim Peterson; *Coordr, Prog,* Athena Richardson; *Outreach Serv,* Heather Wes-Hall; *Tech Serv,* Stephanie Hogan; Staff 2 (MLS 2)
Founded 1937. Pop 18,500; Circ 89,136
Library Holdings: Bk Vols 40,000; Per Subs 50
Automation Activity & Vendor Info: (Cataloging) TLC (The Library Corporation); (Circulation) TLC (The Library Corporation); (OPAC) TLC (The Library Corporation)
Wireless access
Open Mon & Tues 9-7, Wed-Sat 9-5:30
Friends of the Library Group
Bookmobiles: 1. Bkmobile Servs, Cheri Read

FRENCHBURG

P MENIFEE COUNTY PUBLIC LIBRARY, 1585 Main St, 40322. (Mail add: PO Box 49, 40322-0049), SAN 306-2724. Tel: 606-768-2212. FAX: 606-768-9676. E-mail: menifeelibrary@hotmail.com. *Dir,* Melissa Wells
Pop 6,000; Circ 33,303
Library Holdings: AV Mats 404; Bk Vols 26,000; Per Subs 55; Talking Bks 787
Subject Interests: Genealogy, Kentucky
Automation Activity & Vendor Info: (Cataloging) TLC (The Library Corporation); (Circulation) TLC (The Library Corporation)
Wireless access
Open Mon, Wed & Fri 9-5, Tues & Thurs 9-7, Sat 9-3

FULTON

P FULTON COUNTY PUBLIC LIBRARY*, 312 Main St, 42041. SAN 342-3573. Tel: 270-472-3439. FAX: 270-472-6241. E-mail: fultonpl@bellsouth.net. Web Site: fultoncounty.ky.gov/services/pages/fulton-county-public-library-district.aspx. *Dir,* Molly Gannon
Founded 1965. Pop 14,382; Circ 83,680
Library Holdings: Bk Vols 70,000; Per Subs 150
Special Collections: Civil War Records
Subject Interests: Antiques, Genealogy, Hist
Wireless access
Open Tues 10:30-8, Wed-Fri 9-5, Sat 9-Noon
Friends of the Library Group
Branches: 1
HICKMAN PUBLIC, 902 Moscow Ave, Hickman, 42050, SAN 342-3603. Tel: 270-236-2464. FAX: 270-236-1442. E-mail: hickmanlibrary@yahoo.com. *Librn,* Judy Reason
Open Mon & Fri 9-5, Tues-Thurs 9-6
Friends of the Library Group
Bookmobiles: 1. Librn, Laura Snyder

GEORGETOWN

C GEORGETOWN COLLEGE, Ensor Learning Resource Center, 400 E College St, 40324. SAN 306-2732. Tel: 502-863-8400. Interlibrary Loan Service Tel: 502-863-8413. Reference Tel: 502-863-8401. FAX: 502-868-7740. Web Site: libguides.georgetowncollege.edu/LRC. *Dir, Libr Serv,* Andrew Adler; Tel: 502-863-8405, E-mail: Andrew_Adler@georgetowncollege.edu; *Cat Librn, User Serv,* Sandy Baird; Tel: 502-863-8410, E-mail: Sandra_Baird@georgetowncollege.edu; *Coll Strategist Librn, User Experience Librn,* Maria Taylor; Tel: 502-863-8403, E-mail: Maria_Taylor@georgetowncollege.edu; *Evening Circ, Libr Syst Mgr,* Randall Myers; Tel: 502-863-8406, E-mail: Randall_Myers@georgetowncollege.edu; Staff 4.5 (MLS 3, Non-MLS 1.5)
Founded 1829. Enrl 1,047; Fac 77; Highest Degree: Master
Library Holdings: Audiobooks 862; CDs 2,394; DVDs 4,255; e-books 113,331; e-journals 41,701; Electronic Media & Resources 10,261; Microforms 189,600; Bk Titles 146,316; Bk Vols 185,000; Per Subs 314; Videos 2,750
Special Collections: Christianity (Thompson Coll); Georgetown News & Georgetown Times, newsp; History Coll; Law (Smith Coll); Pre-1660 English Literature, microbk; Rankin Civil War Coll; Religion
Automation Activity & Vendor Info: (Acquisitions) Ex Libris Group; (Cataloging) Ex Libris Group; (Circulation) Ex Libris Group; (Course Reserve) Ex Libris Group; (Media Booking) Ex Libris Group; (OPAC) Ex Libris Group; (Serials) Ex Libris Group
Wireless access
Function: ILL available, Microfiche/film & reading machines, Music CDs, Online cat, Wheelchair accessible
Partic in Association of Independent Kentucky Colleges & Universities; Council of Independent Colleges; Federation of Kentucky Academic Libraries; OCLC Online Computer Library Center, Inc
Open Mon-Thurs 7:45am-1am, Fri 7:45-6, Sat 10-6, Sun 1pm-1am
Restriction: ID required to use computers (Ltd hrs)

P SCOTT COUNTY PUBLIC LIBRARY*, 104 S Bradford Lane, 40324-2335. SAN 306-2740. Tel: 502-863-3566. FAX: 502-863-9621. Web Site: www.scottpublib.org. *Asst Dir,* Patti Burnside; E-mail: patti@scottpublib.org; *Adult Serv Mgr,* Melissa Gibson; E-mail: melissa@scottpublib.org; *Youth Serv Mgr,* Roseann Polashek; Staff 37 (MLS 8, Non-MLS 29)
Founded 1928
Jul 2016-Jun 2017 Income $2,795,291, County $2,675,596, Locally Generated Income $99,195, Other $20,500. Mats Exp $403,425, Books $146,796, Per/Ser (Incl. Access Fees) $17,000, AV Mat $101,174, Electronic Ref Mat (Incl. Access Fees) $135,767. Sal $1,021,799
Library Holdings: Audiobooks 8,155; CDs 2,438; DVDs 6,409; e-books 73,687; Bk Vols 99,072; Per Subs 183; Talking Bks 8,155
Subject Interests: Genealogy, Kentucky
Automation Activity & Vendor Info: (Cataloging) TLC (The Library Corporation); (Circulation) TLC (The Library Corporation); (OPAC) TLC (The Library Corporation); (Serials) TLC (The Library Corporation)
Wireless access
Function: 24/7 Electronic res, 24/7 Online cat, 3D Printer, Accelerated reader prog, Activity rm, Adult bk club, After school storytime, Archival coll, Art exhibits, Audio & video playback equip for onsite use, Audiobks on Playaways & MP3, Audiobks via web, AV serv, Bi-weekly Writer's Group, Bilingual assistance for Spanish patrons, Bk club(s), Bks on CD, Butterfly Garden, Children's prog, Computer training, Computers for patron use, Digital talking bks, Doc delivery serv, E-Reserves, Electronic databases & coll, Equip loans & repairs, Family literacy, For res purposes, Free DVD rentals, Games & aids for people with disabilities, Genealogy discussion group, Govt ref serv, Health sci info serv, Holiday prog, Home delivery & serv to seniorr ctr & nursing homes, Homebound delivery serv, Homework prog, ILL available, Instruction & testing, Internet access, Jail serv, Jazz prog, Laminating, Large print keyboards, Life-long learning prog for all ages, Literacy & newcomer serv, Magazines, Magnifiers for reading, Mail & tel request accepted, Mango lang, Meeting rooms, Microfiche/film & reading machines, Movies, Music CDs, Notary serv, Online cat, Online info literacy tutorials on the web & in blackboard, Online ref, Orientations, Outreach serv, Outside serv via phone, mail, e-mail & web, OverDrive digital audio bks, Photocopying/Printing, Preschool outreach, Preschool reading prog, Printer for laptops & handheld devices, Prof lending libr, Prog for adults, Prog for children & young adult, Ref & res, Ref serv available, Res libr, Satellite serv, Scanner, Senior computer classes, Senior outreach, Serves people with intellectual disabilities, Spanish lang bks, Spoken cassettes & CDs, Spoken cassettes & DVDs, Story hour, Study rm, Summer & winter reading prog, Summer reading prog, Tax forms, Teen prog, Telephone ref, Visual arts prog, Wheelchair accessible, Winter reading prog, Words travel prog, Workshops, Writing prog
Special Services for the Deaf - ADA equip; Adult & family literacy prog; Bks on deafness & sign lang; Sign lang interpreter upon request for prog; Staff with knowledge of sign lang
Special Services for the Blind - Accessible computers; Assistive/Adapted tech devices, equip & products; BiFolkal kits; Bks on CD; Copier with enlargement capabilities; Digital talking bk; Extensive large print coll; Home delivery serv; Internet workstation with adaptive software; Large print bks; Low vision equip; Playaways (bks on MP3); Recorded bks; Ref serv; Rental typewriters & computers
Open Mon-Thurs 9-9, Fri & Sat 9-6, Sun 1-5
Friends of the Library Group
Bookmobiles: 1. Outreach Mgr, Darlene Sargent. Bk vols 600

GLASGOW

P MARY WOOD WELDON MEMORIAL LIBRARY, 1530 S Green St, 42141. SAN 306-2759. Tel: 270-651-2824. FAX: 270-659-0367. Web Site: www.weldonpubliclibrary.org. *Dir,* Ami Sandell; E-mail: asandell@weldonpubliclibrary.org; *Mgr, Circ Serv,* Angelina Clark; *Mgr, Tech Serv,* Deloris Flowers; *Mgr, Youth Serv,* Kelly Bowles; *Coordr, Outreach Serv,* Barbara Brodt; Staff 1 (MLS 1)
Founded 1925. Pop 34,000; Circ 117,000
Library Holdings: Bk Vols 61,000; Per Subs 115
Special Collections: Genealogy (Kentucky Coll), bks, micro
Automation Activity & Vendor Info: (Cataloging) TLC (The Library Corporation); (Circulation) TLC (The Library Corporation); (OPAC) TLC (The Library Corporation)
Wireless access
Open Mon-Thurs 9-8, Fri & Sat 9-4
Friends of the Library Group
Bookmobiles: 1. Coordr, Barbara Brodt

GRAYSON

CR KENTUCKY CHRISTIAN UNIVERSITY*, Young Library, 100 Academic Pkwy, 41143. SAN 306-2767. Tel: 606-474-3240. FAX: 606-474-3123. E-mail: library@kcu.edu. Web Site: www.kcu.edu/library. *Dir,* Naulayne Enders; Tel: 606-474-3276, E-mail: nenders@kcu.edu; *Asst Librn,* Patty Greene; Tel: 606-474-3241, E-mail: pgreene@kcu.edu; *ILL & Ser,* Liz Kouns; Tel: 606-474-3292, E-mail: ekouns@kcu.edu

Enrl 430
Library Holdings: e-books 100,000; e-journals 40,000; Bk Vols 100,000; Per Subs 11,000
Special Collections: Mission Papers (1969-present); Restoration Church History
Subject Interests: Educ, Relig
Automation Activity & Vendor Info: (Acquisitions) Innovative Interfaces, Inc; (Cataloging) Innovative Interfaces, Inc; (Circulation) Innovative Interfaces, Inc; (Course Reserve) Innovative Interfaces, Inc; (ILL) Innovative Interfaces, Inc; (OPAC) Innovative Interfaces, Inc; (Serials) Innovative Interfaces, Inc
Wireless access
Publications: Library News; Search Strategy Handbook; Your Library
Partic in Appalachian College Association
Open Mon & Wed 8am-10pm, Tues & Thurs 8-9:30 & 10:30-10, Fri 8-5, Sat 9-1, Sun 3-10; Mon-Fri (Summer) 8-5

GREENSBURG

P GREEN COUNTY PUBLIC LIBRARY*, 112 W Court St, 42743. SAN 306-2775. Tel: 270-932-7081. FAX: 270-932-7081. E-mail: contact@gcpl.info. Web Site: www.gcpl.info. *Dir,* Shelley Pruitt; E-mail: shelleypruitt@kyol.net; *Ch,* Debbie Harris; *Libr Mgr,* Missy Curry; *Circ,* Kayla Bradshaw; Staff 4 (Non-MLS 4)
Founded 1966. Pop 11,510; Circ 99,469
Library Holdings: Bk Vols 35,000; Per Subs 31
Special Collections: Genealogy & History of Original Green County
Open Mon 8:30-6:30, Tues, Thurs & Fri 8:30-4:30, Sat 8:30am-12:30pm

GREENUP

P GREENUP COUNTY PUBLIC LIBRARY*, 508 Main St, 41144-1036. SAN 342-3638. Tel: 606-473-6514. FAX: 606-473-0318. E-mail: greenuplibrary@gmail.com. Web Site: www2.youseemore.com/greenup. *Dir,* Sharon Haines
Founded 1969. Pop 39,132; Circ 237,137
Library Holdings: Bk Vols 95,578; Per Subs 290
Special Collections: Jesse Stuart Coll, photogs. Oral History
Subject Interests: Genealogy, Hist, Kentucky, Local hist
Automation Activity & Vendor Info: (Cataloging) Marcive, Inc; (Circulation) Marcive, Inc; (OPAC) Marcive, Inc
Wireless access
Open Mon & Thurs 9-8, Tues, Wed & Fri 9-5, Sat 9-2
Branches: 2
FLATWOODS BRANCH, 1705 Argillite Rd, Flatwoods, 41139, SAN 342-3662. Tel: 606-836-3771. FAX: 606-836-8674. *Librn,* Sharon Haines
Founded 1969
Library Holdings: Bk Titles 35,000; Bk Vols 45,000
Subject Interests: Kentucky
Open Mon, Tues & Thurs 10-8, Wed, Fri & Sat 10-5
MCKELL PUBLIC, 22 McKell Lane, South Shore, 41175, SAN 342-3697. Tel: 606-932-4478. FAX: 606-932-4478. *Librn,* Sue Evans
Subject Interests: Kentucky
Open Mon, Tues, Thurs & Fri 9-5, Wed 9-8, Sat 9-2
Bookmobiles: 1

GREENVILLE

P MUHLENBERG COUNTY LIBRARIES*, Harbin Memorial Library, 117 S Main St, 42345. SAN 342-3727. Tel: 270-338-4760. E-mail: hmlib@mcplib.org. Web Site: www.mcplib.org. *Libr Dir,* Janet Harrison; E-mail: janet@mcplib.org; Staff 2 (Non-MLS 2)
Founded 1970. Pop 31,839; Circ 148,000
Library Holdings: Bk Vols 90,000; Per Subs 140; Talking Bks 2,200
Subject Interests: Genealogy, Local hist
Automation Activity & Vendor Info: (Cataloging) SirsiDynix; (Circulation) SirsiDynix
Wireless access
Open Mon-Wed & Fri 9-5, Thurs 9-7, Sat 9-1
Friends of the Library Group
Branches: 2
CENTRAL CITY BRANCH, 108 E Broad St, Central City, 42330, SAN 342-3786.
Open Mon 9-7, Tues-Fri 9-5, Sat 9-1
Friends of the Library Group
THISTLE COTTAGE HISTORY & GENEALOGY ANNEX, 122 S Cherry St, 42345. Web Site: mcplib.org/thistlecottage.
Closed for renovations 2020-
Open Mon-Fri 11-4

HARDINSBURG

P BRECKINRIDGE COUNTY PUBLIC LIBRARY*, 308 Old Hwy 60, 40143. (Mail add: PO Box 248, 40143-0248), SAN 342-3816. Tel: 270-756-2323. FAX: 270-756-5634. Web Site: www.bcplibrary.org. *Dir,* Sarah Flood; E-mail: sarah_flood@bellsouth.net; Staff 9.3 (MLS 2, Non-MLS 7.3)
Founded 1953. Pop 20,040; Circ 140,170
Jul 2013-Jun 2014 Income (Main & Associated Libraries) $952,675. Mats Exp $124,883, Books $74,596, Per/Ser (Incl. Access Fees) $4,760, AV Mat $30,104, Electronic Ref Mat (Incl. Access Fees) $15,423. Sal $206,756 (Prof $84,543)
Library Holdings: Audiobooks 2,783; DVDs 5,868; e-books 73,901; Large Print Bks 6,000; Bk Titles 66,520; Per Subs 131
Automation Activity & Vendor Info: (Acquisitions) Evolve; (Cataloging) Evolve; (Circulation) Evolve; (Course Reserve) Evolve; (ILL) Evolve; (OPAC) Evolve; (Serials) Evolve
Wireless access
Function: Accelerated reader prog, Activity rm, After school storytime, Bk club(s), Bks on CD, Children's prog, Computers for patron use, E-Reserves, Electronic databases & coll, Free DVD rentals, Holiday prog, Home delivery & serv to seniorr ctr & nursing homes, Homebound delivery serv, ILL available, Magazines, Online cat, Outreach serv, Photocopying/Printing, Preschool outreach, Prog for adults, Prog for children & young adult, Scanner, Serves people with intellectual disabilities, Story hour, Study rm, Summer reading prog, Tax forms, Teen prog, Wheelchair accessible
Special Services for the Blind - BiFolkal kits; Bks on cassette; Bks on CD; Large print bks; Large screen computer & software
Open Mon-Fri 8:30-6:30, Sat 9-2
Branches: 2
CLOVERPORT COMMUNITY, 301 Poplar St, Cloverport, 40111, SAN 342-3840. Tel: 270-788-3388, Ext 236. FAX: 270-788-6640. Web Site: www.bcplibrary.org/cloverport-branch.html. *Librn,* Bethaney Brent; Staff 1 (Non-MLS 1)
Function: Adult bk club, Bks on CD, Children's prog, Computers for patron use, Free DVD rentals, ILL available, Photocopying/Printing, Prog for children & young adult, Story hour, Summer reading prog, Teen prog, Wheelchair accessible
Open Mon 9:30-5:30, Tues-Fri 12:30-5:30
IRVINGTON BRANCH, 1109 West US 60, Irvington, 40146. (Mail add: PO Box 381, Irvington, 40146-0381), SAN 342-3875. Tel: 270-547-7404. FAX: 270-547-7420. *Librn,* Angie Scott
Open Mon 9-5, Tues-Fri 11:30-4:30

HARLAN

P HARLAN COUNTY PUBLIC LIBRARIES*, Bryan W Whitfield Jr Public Library, 107 N Third St, 40831. SAN 342-3905. Tel: 606-573-5220. FAX: 606-573-5220. E-mail: harlanlibrary@gmail.com. Web Site: harlancountylibraries.org. *Dir,* Richard Haynes; *Br Mgr,* Renae Shepherd; Staff 2 (MLS 1, Non-MLS 1)
Founded 1968. Pop 32,095; Circ 78,454
Library Holdings: AV Mats 5,753; DVDs 1,000; Bk Vols 67,000; Per Subs 98; Talking Bks 2,562; Videos 400
Special Collections: Coal; Genealogy; Kentucky
Automation Activity & Vendor Info: (Cataloging) Innovative Interfaces, Inc; (Circulation) Innovative Interfaces, Inc; (OPAC) Innovative Interfaces, Inc
Wireless access
Open Mon, Wed, Fri & Sat 9-5, Tues & Thurs 9-8
Branches: 2
REBECCA CAUDILL PUBLIC LIBRARY, 310 W Main St, Cumberland, 40823, SAN 342-393X. Tel: 606-589-2409. FAX: 606-589-2409. *Br Mgr,* Patricia North
Open Mon, Wed & Fri 9-5, Tues & Thurs 9-7, Sat 9-2
EVARTS PUBLIC LIBRARY, 127A Yocum St, Evarts, 40828. Tel: 606-837-9703. FAX: 606-837-9703. *Br Mgr,* Lisa Adkisson
Founded 2011
Open Tues, Wed, Fri & Sat 9-5, Thurs 11-7
Bookmobiles: Librn, Jay Moses. Bk vols 5,696

HARRODSBURG

S HARRODSBURG HISTORICAL SOCIETY, Harrodsburg Mercer County Research Library, 220 S Chiles St, 40330. (Mail add: PO Box 316, 40330-0316), SAN 375-1112. Tel: 859-734-5985. E-mail: library@harrodsburghistorical.org. Web Site: harrodsburghistorical.org. *Chmn,* Mrs Larrie Curry; *Tech Serv Librn,* Nancy Hill; E-mail: hhsboard2020@gmail.com; Staff 6 (MLS 1, Non-MLS 5)
Library Holdings: Bk Vols 2,570; Per Subs 10
Special Collections: County Historical Archives
Open Wed-Fri 1-4

P MERCER COUNTY PUBLIC LIBRARY*, 109 W Lexington St, 40330-1542. SAN 306-2805. Tel: 859-734-3680. FAX: 859-734-7524. E-mail: staff@mcplib.info. Web Site: www.mcplib.info. *Dir,* Robin Ison; *Acq Librn,* Carolyn Sue Patterson; E-mail: cwp@mcplib.info; Staff 16 (MLS 1, Non-MLS 15)
Founded 1970. Pop 20,817; Circ 177,838

Library Holdings: AV Mats 8,958; Bk Vols 62,557; Per Subs 121
Special Collections: Draper Manuscripts Coll; Joy's Toys Coll
Subject Interests: Genealogy, Kentucky
Automation Activity & Vendor Info: (Cataloging) Innovative Interfaces, Inc; (Circulation) Innovative Interfaces, Inc; (Course Reserve) Innovative Interfaces, Inc; (OPAC) Innovative Interfaces, Inc
Wireless access
Function: AV serv, Games & aids for people with disabilities, Homebound delivery serv, ILL available, Magnifiers for reading, Photocopying/Printing, Prog for children & young adult, Ref serv available, Summer reading prog, Telephone ref, Wheelchair accessible
Open Mon, Tues & Thurs 9-7:30, Wed 9-5:30, Fri & Sat 9-5, Sun 1-5
Bookmobiles: 1

S SHAKER VILLAGE OF PLEASANT HILL MUSEUM LIBRARY, 3501 Lexington Rd, 40330. SAN 373-4587. Tel: 859-734-5411. FAX: 859-734-7278. E-mail: collections@shakervillageky.org. Web Site: shakervillageky.org. *Pres & Chief Exec Officer,* Maynard Crossland; *Colls Mgr,* Rebecca Soules; E-mail: rsoules@shakervillageky.org
Founded 1968
Library Holdings: Bk Vols 3,000; Spec Interest Per Sub 5
Special Collections: Shakers & the Village at Pleasant Hill, ephemera, ms, photographs
Subject Interests: 19th Century indust, Agr, Archit, Decorative art, Hist presv, Kentucky, Mus studies, Relig studies, Shakers
Wireless access
Function: Res libr
Restriction: Open by appt only

HARTFORD

P OHIO COUNTY PUBLIC LIBRARY*, 413 Main St, 42347. SAN 306-2813. Tel: 270-298-3790. FAX: 270-298-4214. E-mail: info@ohiocountypubliclibrary.org. Web Site: www.ohiocountypubliclibrary.org. *Dir,* Melissa Acquaviva
Founded 1967. Pop 23,500; Circ 130,250
Library Holdings: Bk Vols 59,100; Per Subs 85
Special Collections: Charles C Curran Coll, prints, VF; Ohio County History. Oral History
Automation Activity & Vendor Info: (Acquisitions) Follett Software
Wireless access
Open Mon & Tues 8:30-7:30, Wed-Fri 8:30-4:30, Sat 9-3
Bookmobiles: 1

HAWESVILLE

P HANCOCK COUNTY PUBLIC LIBRARY*, 1210 Madison St, 42348. SAN 342-3964. Tel: 270-927-6760. FAX: 270-927-6847. E-mail: hcplky@gmail.com. Web Site: www.hcplky.org. *Dir,* Tina Snyder; *Ch,* Kendra Husk; *Teen Librn,* Bolin Emily; *Circ Mgr,* Sherry Hagman; *Cataloger,* Tammy Sturgeon
Founded 1954. Pop 9,000; Circ 60,000
Library Holdings: Bk Vols 32,700; Per Subs 63
Special Collections: Oral History
Automation Activity & Vendor Info: (Cataloging) TLC (The Library Corporation); (Circulation) TLC (The Library Corporation)
Wireless access
Open Mon-Wed & Fri 8:30-4:30, Thurs 8:30-7, Sat 8:30-12:30
Friends of the Library Group
Branches: 1
LEWISPORT BRANCH, 403 Second St, Lewisport, 42348, SAN 342-3999. Tel: 270-295-3765. *Br Mgr,* Kelley Richardson
Library Holdings: Bk Vols 5,000
Open Mon & Wed-Fri 8:30-4:30, Tues 8:30-7, Sat 8:30am-12:30pm
Friends of the Library Group
Bookmobiles: 1. Librn, Lana Jones

HAZARD

J HAZARD COMMUNITY & TECHNICAL COLLEGE LIBRARY*, Stephens Library, One Community College Dr, 41701. SAN 306-2821. Tel: 606-436-5721, 606-487-3145. Toll Free Tel: 800-246-7521, Ext 73304. FAX: 606-487-3603. Web Site: hazard.kctcs.edu/current-students/student-resources/library. *Dir, Libr Serv,* Cathy Branson; Tel: 606-487-3550, E-mail: cathy.branson@kctcs.edu; *Ref Librn,* Evelyn E Hudson; Tel: 606-487-3147, E-mail: ehudson0018@kctcs.edu; *Pub Serv,* Dee Dee Wells; Tel: 606-487-3145, E-mail: deirdre.campbell@kctcs.edu; *Tech Serv,* Marlene Conley; Tel: 606-487-3146, E-mail: marlene.conley@kctcs.edu; Staff 4 (MLS 2, Non-MLS 2)
Founded 1968. Highest Degree: Associate
Library Holdings: e-books 56,000; Bk Vols 42,249
Special Collections: US Document Depository
Subject Interests: Genealogy, Local hist
Automation Activity & Vendor Info: (Acquisitions) Ex Libris Group; (Cataloging) OCLC; (Circulation) Ex Libris Group; (Course Reserve) Ex Libris Group; (ILL) OCLC; (OPAC) Ex Libris Group
Wireless access
Partic in Federation of Kentucky Academic Libraries
Open Mon, Wed & Thurs 8-5, Tues 8-7:30, Fri 8-4:30

P PERRY COUNTY PUBLIC LIBRARY*, 289 Black Gold Blvd, 41701. SAN 306-2848. Tel: 606-436-2475, 606-436-4747. FAX: 606-436-0191. E-mail: library@perrylib.org. Web Site: www.perrycountylibrary.org. *Dir,* Sheila Lindsay; E-mail: slindsay@perrylib.org; *Asst Dir,* Tina Williams; *Ad,* Amy Eversole; *Youth Serv Librn,* Jessica Chandler; *Circ Desk Mgr,* Rayeanna Emery; *Human Res Mgr,* Cynthia France; *Pub Serv Mgr,* Rob Mullins; Staff 19 (Non-MLS 19)
Founded 1967. Pop 27,343; Circ 168,929
Jul 2016-Jun 2017 Income $1,919,193, State $19,032, County $1,846,682, Locally Generated Income $53,479. Mats Exp $2,007,161. Sal $657,452
Library Holdings: Audiobooks 5,096; DVDs 8,636; e-books 129,483; Electronic Media & Resources 29,310; Per Subs 136
Special Collections: Audio Books; DVD; Genealogy; Music CD
Automation Activity & Vendor Info: (Circulation) Evolve; (ILL) OCLC FirstSearch
Wireless access
Function: 24/7 Electronic res, 24/7 Online cat, Activity rm, Adult bk club, Art exhibits, Audiobks via web, Bk club(s), Bks on CD, Children's prog, Computers for patron use, E-Reserves, Electronic databases & coll, Free DVD rentals, Games & aids for people with disabilities, Holiday prog, Home delivery & serv to seniorr ctr & nursing homes, Homebound delivery serv, ILL available, Internet access, Magazines, Magnifiers for reading, Mail & tel request accepted, Mango lang, Meeting rooms, Microfiche/film & reading machines, Movies, Music CDs, Notary serv, Online cat, Online ref, Outreach serv, OverDrive digital audio bks, Photocopying/Printing, Preschool reading prog, Printer for laptops & handheld devices, Prog for adults, Prog for children & young adult, Ref serv available, Scanner, Senior outreach, Serves people with intellectual disabilities, Spanish lang bks, Story hour, Study rm, Summer reading prog, Tax forms, Teen prog, Wheelchair accessible
Special Services for the Deaf - Bks on deafness & sign lang; Closed caption videos
Special Services for the Blind - Bks on CD; Copier with enlargement capabilities; Large print bks; PC for people with disabilities; Playaways (bks on MP3); Recorded bks; Screen enlargement software for people with visual disabilities; ZoomText magnification & reading software
Open Mon-Fri 9-7, Sat 8-4
Bookmobiles: 1. Librn, Terry Delph

M SOUTHEAST KENTUCKY AREA HEALTH EDUCATION CENTER*, Library Services, 100 Medical Center Dr, 41701-9429. SAN 370-5277. Tel: 606-439-6796. FAX: 606-439-6798. Web Site: www.southeastkyahec.com/library-services. *Asst Librn,* Jaime Grace; E-mail: jgrace0036@kctcs.edu
Founded 1985
Library Holdings: Bk Titles 2,000; Bk Vols 2,200; Per Subs 350
Special Collections: US Document Depository
Subject Interests: Med, Nursing, Rural health
Automation Activity & Vendor Info: (Cataloging) Marcive, Inc
Function: Doc delivery serv
Publications: Newsletter
Partic in Bluegrass Medical Libraries; Kentucky Medical Library Association; Nat AHEC Librns; Tennessee Health Science Library Association
Open Mon & Tues 8-4:30, Fri 8-Noon

HENDERSON

J HENDERSON COMMUNITY COLLEGE*, Hartfield Library, 2660 S Green St, 42420. SAN 306-2856. Tel: 270-831-9760. FAX: 270-831-9765. E-mail: hencclibrary@kctcs.edu. Web Site: henderson.kctcs.edu/current-students/student-resources/libraries. *Dir, Libr Serv,* Michael Knecht; Tel: 270-831-9761, E-mail: mike.knecht@kctcs.edu; *Ref Librn,* Kevin Reid; Tel: 270-831-9766, E-mail: kevin.reid@kctcs.edu; *Libr Spec,* Allison Horning; E-mail: allison.horning@kctcs.edu; Staff 2 (MLS 2)
Founded 1960. Enrl 1,175; Fac 60
Library Holdings: Bk Vols 27,624; Per Subs 186
Automation Activity & Vendor Info: (Acquisitions) Ex Libris Group; (Cataloging) Ex Libris Group; (Circulation) Ex Libris Group; (Course Reserve) Ex Libris Group; (OPAC) Ex Libris Group
Wireless access
Partic in LYRASIS
Open Mon-Thurs 7:45-7, Fri 7:45-4:30

P HENDERSON COUNTY PUBLIC LIBRARY, 101 S Main St, 42420. SAN 306-2864. Tel: 270-826-3712. FAX: 270-827-4226. Web Site: www.hcpl.org. *Dir,* Shannon Sandefur; E-mail: ssandefur@hcpl.org; Staff 20 (MLS 4, Non-MLS 16)
Founded 1904. Pop 45,000; Circ 310,207
Library Holdings: AV Mats 18,006; CDs 1,692; DVDs 4,008; Large Print Bks 7,328; Bk Vols 114,000; Per Subs 60; Talking Bks 5,586; Videos 6,660
Automation Activity & Vendor Info: (Cataloging) Innovative Interfaces, Inc; (Circulation) Innovative Interfaces, Inc; (OPAC) Innovative Interfaces, Inc
Wireless access
Function: 24/7 Electronic res, 24/7 Online cat, 3D Printer, Adult bk club, Archival coll, Art exhibits, Audiobks via web, Bk club(s), Bks on CD, Children's prog, Computer training, Computers for patron use, Electronic databases & coll, Free DVD rentals, Genealogy discussion group, Holiday prog, Home delivery & serv to seniorr ctr & nursing homes, Homebound delivery serv, ILL available, Internet access, Life-long learning prog for all ages, Magazines, Makerspace, Mango lang, Meeting rooms, Microfiche/film & reading machines, Music CDs, Notary serv, Online cat, Outreach serv, OverDrive digital audio bks, Passport agency, Photocopying/Printing, Preschool outreach, Preschool reading prog, Printer for laptops & handheld devices, Prog for adults, Prog for children & young adult, Ref serv available, Scanner, Senior computer classes, Senior outreach, STEM programs, Story hour, Study rm, Summer reading prog, Tax forms, Teen prog, Telephone ref, Wheelchair accessible
Partic in LYRASIS; OCLC Online Computer Library Center, Inc
Open Mon-Thurs 9-8, Fri & Sat 9-5, Sun 1:30-5
Friends of the Library Group
Bookmobiles: 1. Librn, Juanita Daughtery. Bk vols 3,478

HIGHLAND HEIGHTS

C NORTHERN KENTUCKY UNIVERSITY*, W Frank Steely Library, University Dr, 41099. (Mail add: Nunn Dr, 41099), SAN 342-4022. Tel: 859-572-5457. Interlibrary Loan Service Tel: 859-572-6365. Automation Services Tel: 859-572-6309. FAX: 859-572-5390. Web Site: inside.nku.edu/library. *Dean of Libr,* Andrea Falcone; E-mail: falconea1@nku.edu; *Assoc Dean Coll Mgt,* Lois Schultz; Tel: 859-572-5275, E-mail: schultz@nku.edu; *Interim Head, Access Serv,* Laura Sullivan; Tel: 859-572-5724, E-mail: sullivanl@nku.edu; *Discovery Serv, E-Resources Librn, Interim Head, Coll Develop,* Donna Smith; Tel: 859-572-6140, E-mail: smithd@nku.edu; *Librn,* Perry Bratcher; E-mail: bratcher@nku.edu; *Librn,* Michael Providenti; Tel: 859-572-5936, E-mail: providenti@nku.edu; *Govt Doc Librn,* Philip Yannarella; Tel: 859-572-5455, E-mail: yannarella@nku.edu; *Intellectual Property Librn,* John Schlipp; Tel: 859-572-5723, E-mail: schlippj1@nku.edu; *Res & Instruction Librn,* Jennifer Smith, PhD; Tel: 859-572-6620, E-mail: smithjen@nku.edu; *Teaching & Learning Librn,* Mary Chesnut; Tel: 859-572-5826, E-mail: chestnut@nku.edu; *Teaching & Learning Librn,* Threasa Wesley; Tel: 859-572-5721, E-mail: wesley@nku.edu; *Univ Archivist,* Lois Hamill; Tel: 859-572-5863, E-mail: hamilll1@nku.edu; Staff 42 (MLS 22, Non-MLS 20)
Founded 1968. Enrl 15,816; Fac 530; Highest Degree: Doctorate
Jul 2014-Jun 2015. Mats Exp $1,185,910, Books $62,575, Per/Ser (Incl. Access Fees) $1,123,035, Presv $300. Sal $2,215,565
Library Holdings: AV Mats 11,834; CDs 5,328; e-books 38,665; e-journals 49,729; Microforms 599,034; Music Scores 9,992; Bk Titles 677,502; Bk Vols 773,658; Videos 5,971
Special Collections: Confederate Imprints; Kentucky One Thousand, ultra fiche; Library of American Civilization; Library of American Literature; Ohio River Materials. US Document Depository
Subject Interests: Kentucky
Automation Activity & Vendor Info: (Acquisitions) OCLC; (Cataloging) OCLC; (Circulation) OCLC; (Course Reserve) Blackboard Inc; (ILL) OCLC; (OPAC) OCLC; (Serials) EBSCO Online
Wireless access
Function: Archival coll, Art exhibits, Audio & video playback equip for onsite use, Computers for patron use, Distance learning, Doc delivery serv, E-Reserves, Electronic databases & coll, Govt ref serv, ILL available, Online cat, Online info literacy tutorials on the web & in blackboard, Online ref, Orientations, Outreach serv, Photocopying/Printing, Ref serv available, Scanner, Tax forms, Telephone ref, VHS videos, Wheelchair accessible
Partic in Federation of Kentucky Academic Libraries
Special Services for the Deaf - Assistive tech
Special Services for the Blind - Computer with voice synthesizer for visually impaired persons; PC for people with disabilities; Screen enlargement software for people with visual disabilities; Talking bks
Open Mon-Thurs 7:30am-10pm, Fri 7:30-5, Sat 10-5, Sun 2:30-10
Friends of the Library Group

CL NORTHERN KENTUCKY UNIVERSITY, Salmon P Chase College of Law Library, Nunn Dr, 41099. SAN 306-2368. Tel: 859-572-6030. FAX: 859-572-6529, 859-572-6664. Web Site: chaselaw.nku.edu/current-students/library.html. *Dir, Law Libr,* Carol Bredemeyer; Tel: 859-572-5395; *Assoc Dir, Libr Serv,* Tobe Liebert; Tel: 859-572-6485, E-mail: liebertl1@nku.edu; *Circ Supvr,* Stephanie Felty; Tel: 859-572-5715, E-mail: hunleys1@nku.edu; Staff 16 (MLS 7, Non-MLS 9)
Enrl 400; Fac 34; Highest Degree: Doctorate
Library Holdings: Bk Titles 85,000; Bk Vols 340,000; Per Subs 2,085
Automation Activity & Vendor Info: (Acquisitions) Ex Libris Group; (Cataloging) Ex Libris Group; (Circulation) Ex Libris Group; (OPAC) Ex Libris Group; (Serials) Ex Libris Group
Wireless access
Publications: Law Library Handbook
Partic in OCLC Online Computer Library Center, Inc; State Assisted Academic Library Council of Kentucky
Open Mon-Thurs 8am-10pm, Fri 8-5, Sat 9-5, Sun 2-6

HINDMAN

P KNOTT COUNTY PUBLIC LIBRARY*, 238 Hwy 160 S, 41822. (Mail add: PO Box 667, 41822-0667), SAN 306-2880. Tel: 606-785-5412. FAX: 606-785-4299. E-mail: kclib9@hotmail.com. Web Site: www.knottcountylibrary.com. *Head Librn,* Tammie Owens
Pop 17,906; Circ 38,856
Library Holdings: Bk Vols 25,000; Per Subs 44
Special Collections: Appalachian: Genealogy
Automation Activity & Vendor Info: (Cataloging) TLC (The Library Corporation); (Circulation) TLC (The Library Corporation)
Wireless access
Open Mon-Fri 8:30-5
Friends of the Library Group

HODGENVILLE

P LARUE COUNTY PUBLIC LIBRARY, 215 Lincoln Dr, 42748. SAN 306-2899. Tel: 270-358-3851. FAX: 270-358-8647. E-mail: info@laruelibrary.org. Web Site: laruelibrary.org. *Dir,* Dana Jolly; E-mail: dana@laruelibrary.org
Founded 1917. Pop 14,174; Circ 65,000
Library Holdings: AV Mats 2,400; Bks on Deafness & Sign Lang 45; CDs 200; DVDs 150; Large Print Bks 1,500; Music Scores 30; Bk Titles 41,527; Bk Vols 49,000; Per Subs 62; Talking Bks 850; Videos 900
Special Collections: Lincoln Coll
Subject Interests: Abraham Lincoln
Automation Activity & Vendor Info: (Cataloging) Book Systems; (Circulation) Book Systems; (Course Reserve) Book Systems; (ILL) OCLC; (OPAC) Book Systems; (Serials) OCLC FirstSearch
Wireless access
Special Services for the Blind - Bks on CD
Open Mon, Wed & Fri 9-5, Tues & Thurs 9-7, Sat 9-2
Friends of the Library Group
Bookmobiles: 1

HOPKINSVILLE

P HOPKINSVILLE-CHRISTIAN COUNTY PUBLIC LIBRARY*, 1101 Bethel St, 42240. SAN 306-2902. Tel: 270-887-4262, Circulation Tel: 270-887-4262, Ext 101, 270-887-4262, Ext 102. FAX: 270-887-4264. Web Site: hccpl.org. *Dir,* DeeAnna Sova; Tel: 270-887-4262, Ext 106, E-mail: director@hccpl.org; *Libr Office Mgr,* Pat Taylor; Tel: 270-887-4262, Ext 107, E-mail: pat@hccpl.org; *Outreach Librn,* Elysa Parks; Tel: 270-887-4262, Ext 124, E-mail: elysa@hccpl.org; *Youth Serv Librn,* Tiffany Luna; Tel: 270-887-4262, Ext 116, E-mail: tiffany@hccpl.org; *Cat/ILL Spec,* Laura Wildey; Tel: 270-887-4362, Ext 108, E-mail: laura@hccpl.org; Staff 4 (MLS 3, Non-MLS 1)
Founded 1874. Pop 72,351; Circ 54,166
Jul 2016-Jun 2017 Income $904,867. Mats Exp $113,580. Sal $328,860
Library Holdings: e-books 123,758; Bk Titles 102,470
Special Collections: McCarroll Genealogy Coll
Automation Activity & Vendor Info: (Acquisitions) SirsiDynix; (Cataloging) SirsiDynix; (Circulation) SirsiDynix; (OPAC) SirsiDynix
Wireless access
Function: 24/7 Electronic res, 24/7 Online cat, Audiobks via web, Bk club(s), Bks on CD, Children's prog, Computers for patron use, Electronic databases & coll, Free DVD rentals, ILL available, Internet access, Life-long learning prog for all ages, Magazines, Magnifiers for reading, Mango lang, Meeting rooms, Microfiche/film & reading machines, Movies, Music CDs, Online cat, Photocopying/Printing, Preschool outreach, Preschool reading prog, Prog for adults, Prog for children & young adult, Ref & res, Ref serv available, Res assist avail, Res performed for a fee, Spanish lang bks, Story hour, Summer reading prog, Tax forms, Teen prog, Wheelchair accessible
Open Mon, Wed & Fri 9-6, Tues & Thurs 10-7, Sat 9-5

J HOPKINSVILLE COMMUNITY COLLEGE LIBRARY, 720 North Dr, 42240. (Mail add: PO Box 2100, 42241-2100), SAN 306-2910. Tel: 270-707-3764. Interlibrary Loan Service Tel: 270-707-3763. Toll Free Tel: 866-534-2224. FAX: 270-885-6048. Web Site:

hopkinsville.kctcs.edu/current-students/student-resources/library. *Dir, Libr Serv,* Elysa Parks; E-mail: eparks0023@kctcs.edu; Staff 3 (MLS 1, Non-MLS 2)
Founded 1965. Fac 75; Highest Degree: Associate
Library Holdings: DVDs 955; e-books 49,527; Bk Vols 36,360
Special Collections: Kentucky Coll
Automation Activity & Vendor Info: (Cataloging) Ex Libris Group; (Circulation) Ex Libris Group; (Course Reserve) Ex Libris Group; (OPAC) Ex Libris Group
Wireless access
Open Mon-Fri 7:30-4:30

M WESTERN STATE HOSPITAL*, Professional Library, 2400 Russellville Rd, 42241. (Mail add: PO Box 2200, 42241-2200), SAN 306-2929. Tel: 270-889-6025, Ext 2888. FAX: 270-885-5257. Web Site: westernstatehospital.ky.gov. *Dir, Admin Serv,* Roger Westfall
Founded 1940
Library Holdings: Bk Titles 2,000
Subject Interests: Nursing, Psychiat, Soc serv (soc work)
Publications: Hospital Newsletter
Partic in Ky-Ohio-Mich Regional Med Libr
Restriction: Staff use only

HORSE CAVE

P HORSE CAVE FREE PUBLIC LIBRARY*, 111 Higbee St, 42749-1110. SAN 306-2937. Tel: 270-786-1130. FAX: 270-786-1131. E-mail: hclib@scrtc.com. Web Site: www.horsecaveky.com/free-public-library. *Dir,* Theresa Jones; *Asst Librn,* Doris Jones
Founded 1912. Pop 8,000; Circ 13,200
Library Holdings: Bk Vols 9,000; Per Subs 30
Special Collections: Kentucky Coll
Wireless access
Open Mon-Fri 8:30-5

HYDEN

C FRONTIER NURSING UNIVERSITY*, Alice E Whitman Memorial Library, 195 School St, 41749. Tel: 859-899-2953. E-mail: librarian@frontier.edu. Web Site: library.frontier.edu/home. *Dir, Libr Serv,* Billie Anne Gebb; E-mail: BillieAnne.Gebb@frontier.edu; *Asst Dir, Libr Serv,* Zach Young; E-mail: Zach.Young@frontier.edu
Library Holdings: e-journals 60; Bk Vols 1,700
Wireless access
Open Mon-Fri 8-5

P LESLIE COUNTY PUBLIC LIBRARY*, 22065 Main St, 41749. SAN 306-2945. Tel: 606-672-2460. FAX: 606-672-4213. Web Site: www2.youseemore.com/leslie. *Dir,* Clifford Hamilton; E-mail: chamilton@leslielibrary.com; *Librn,* Mason Collett; *Ch,* Leona Hamrick
Founded 1963. Pop 11,000; Circ 148,880
Library Holdings: Bk Vols 37,000; Per Subs 85
Special Collections: Genealogy (Leslie County Coll); Kentucky Coll
Automation Activity & Vendor Info: (Cataloging) TLC (The Library Corporation); (Circulation) TLC (The Library Corporation); (OPAC) TLC (The Library Corporation)
Wireless access
Special Services for the Deaf - Bks on deafness & sign lang; High interest/low vocabulary bks
Open Mon, Wed & Fri 8-5, Tues & Thurs 8-8, Sat 8-2
Bookmobiles: 1. Librn, Keith Collett

INEZ

P MARTIN COUNTY PUBLIC LIBRARY, Central Library, 180 E Main St, 41224. (Mail add: PO Box 1318, 41224-1318). Tel: 606-298-7766. FAX: 606-298-0680. E-mail: tech@martincolibrary.com. Web Site: www.martincolibrary.com. *Dir,* Tammy Jones; E-mail: tj@martincolibrary.com
Jul 2015-Jun 2016 Income $575,700. Mats Exp $37,500, Books $25,000, Per/Ser (Incl. Access Fees) $1,000, AV Mat $11,500. Sal $196,000
Library Holdings: Bk Vols 24,966; Per Subs 25
Automation Activity & Vendor Info: (Acquisitions) TLC (The Library Corporation); (Cataloging) TLC (The Library Corporation); (Circulation) TLC (The Library Corporation); (Course Reserve) TLC (The Library Corporation); (ILL) TLC (The Library Corporation); (Media Booking) TLC (The Library Corporation); (OPAC) TLC (The Library Corporation); (Serials) TLC (The Library Corporation)
Wireless access
Open Mon-Fri 9-5
Branches: 1
RUFUS M REED PUBLIC, 1442 River Front Rd, Lovely, 41231. (Mail add: PO Box 359, Lovely, 41231-0359). Tel: 606-395-6500. FAX: 606-395-6001. *Br Mgr,* Angela Begley
Library Holdings: Bk Vols 18,000; Per Subs 20
Open Mon-Fri 9-5
Bookmobiles: 1

IRVINE

P ESTILL COUNTY PUBLIC LIBRARY*, 246 Main St, 40336-1026. SAN 306-2953. Tel: 606-723-3030. FAX: 606-726-9971. E-mail: estillcolibrary@gmail.com. Web Site: www2.youseemore.com/estill. *Dir,* Kathy Watson; *Ch,* Amy Noland-Hughes; *Libr Asst,* Raymond Chaney; *Adult Serv,* Lesa Ledford
Founded 1969. Pop 14,500; Circ 81,700
Library Holdings: Bk Vols 36,500; Per Subs 86
Special Collections: Kentucky Coll
Automation Activity & Vendor Info: (Cataloging) TLC (The Library Corporation); (Circulation) TLC (The Library Corporation); (OPAC) TLC (The Library Corporation)
Wireless access
Publications: Bibliographies; Booklists; Newsletter
Open Mon, Tues & Fri 9-8, Wed 9-5, Thurs 12-8, Sat 9-2
Bookmobiles: 1. Librn, Sherri Jenkins

JACKSON

P BREATHITT COUNTY PUBLIC LIBRARY*, 1024 College Ave, 41339. SAN 306-2961. Tel: 606-666-5541. FAX: 606-666-8166. E-mail: breathitt@bellsouth.net. Information Services E-mail: bclibinfo@bellsouth.net. Web Site: www.breathittcountylibrary.com. *Dir,* Stephen Bowling; *Extended Serv,* Susan Pugh; E-mail: sgpugh@bellsouth.net
Founded 1967. Pop 17,000
Library Holdings: DVDs 1,100; Bk Vols 52,000; Per Subs 50
Special Collections: Genealogical Research Library; History & Census Records (Breathitt and surrounding counties); Surname Information Files
Automation Activity & Vendor Info: (Acquisitions) Follett Software; (Cataloging) Follett Software; (Circulation) Follett Software; (Course Reserve) Follett Software; (ILL) Follett Software; (Media Booking) Follett Software; (OPAC) Follett Software; (Serials) Follett Software
Wireless access
Open Mon, Wed & Fri 8-5, Tues & Thurs 8-7, Sat 9-4

J HAZARD COMMUNITY & TECHNICAL COLLEGE*, Lees College Campus Library, 601 Jefferson Ave, 41339. SAN 306-297X. Tel: 606-666-7521. Reference Tel: 606-487-3147. Toll Free Tel: 800-246-7521, Ext 73568. FAX: 606-487-3555. Web Site: www.hazard.kctcs.edu/current-students/student-resources/library. *Dir, Libr Serv,* Cathy Branson; Tel: 606-487-3550, E-mail: cathy.branson@kctcs.edu; *Ref & Instruction Librn,* Evelyn E Hudson; E-mail: ehudson0018@kctcs.edu; *Pub Serv & ILL,* Donna Collins; *Tech Serv,* Barbie Henson; Staff 1 (MLS 1)
Founded 1883
Library Holdings: e-books 190,000; Bk Vols 50,000
Special Collections: Appalachia & Kentuckiana, bks, flm, cassettes & per. Oral History
Subject Interests: Local hist, Relig
Automation Activity & Vendor Info: (Cataloging) OCLC; (Circulation) Ex Libris Group; (ILL) OCLC; (OPAC) Ex Libris Group
Wireless access
Partic in Federation of Kentucky Academic Libraries
Open Mon-Thurs 8-5:30, Fri 8-4:30

R KENTUCKY MOUNTAIN BIBLE COLLEGE*, Gibson Library, 855 Hwy 541, 41339-9433. SAN 306-4239. Tel: 606-693-5000. Circulation Tel: 606-693-5000, Ext 200. FAX: 606-693-4884. Web Site: www.kmbc.edu/academics/library. *Librn,* Patricia Bowen; E-mail: pbowen@kmbc.edu; Staff 1 (MLS 1)
Founded 1931. Enrl 72; Fac 17; Highest Degree: Bachelor
Library Holdings: Bk Vols 37,900; Per Subs 191
Special Collections: Holiness, Missionary, Religious Biography
Wireless access
Open Mon-Thurs 7:30am-9pm, Fri 7:30-5, Sat 2-4

JAMESTOWN

P RUSSELL COUNTY PUBLIC LIBRARY*, 535 N Main St, 42629. (Mail add: PO Box 970, 42629), SAN 306-2988. Tel: 270-343-7323. FAX: 270-343-2019. E-mail: help@russellcountylibrary.com. Web Site: www.russellcountylibrary.com. *Dir,* Lindsey B Westerfield; E-mail: lindsey@russellcountylibrary.com; *Libr Mgr,* Angie McGowan; E-mail: angie@russellcountylibrary.com; *Ref Librn,* Glenda York; E-mail: glenda@russellcountylibrary.com; *Ch,* Fillamay Cowell; E-mail: fil@russellcountylibrary.com; *Youth Serv Librn,* Kristina Daffron; E-mail: kristina@russellcountylibrary.com
Founded 1967. Pop 17,000; Circ 72,359
Library Holdings: Bk Vols 49,371; Per Subs 56
Special Collections: Westerns

Subject Interests: Easy bks, Genealogy, Juv, Kentucky, Romance langs, Sci fict, Young adult lit
Automation Activity & Vendor Info: (Circulation) TLC (The Library Corporation)
Wireless access
Open Mon-Fri 8-4:30, Sat 12-Noon

LA GRANGE

S KENTUCKY STATE REFORMATORY LIBRARY*, 3001 W Hwy 146, 40032. SAN 306-3011. Tel: 502-222-9441. FAX: 502-222-9022. Web Site: corrections.ky.gov/Facilities/AI/ksr. *Librn,* Brian Elpers; Staff 1 (MLS 1)
Founded 1938
Library Holdings: Audiobooks 148; CDs 1,675; DVDs 407; High Interest/Low Vocabulary Bk Vols 50; Large Print Bks 75; Music Scores 275; Bk Vols 23,100; Per Subs 128
Subject Interests: Fiction
Automation Activity & Vendor Info: (ILL) OCLC
Wireless access
Friends of the Library Group

S LUTHER LUCKETT CORRECTIONAL COMPLEX LIBRARY*, 1612 Dawkins Rd, 40031. (Mail add: PO Box 6, 40031-0006). Tel: 502-222-0363, Ext 3580. Web Site: corrections.ky.gov/depts/AI/LLCC. *Librn,* Mary D Morgan; E-mail: maryd.morgan@ky.gov
Library Holdings: Bk Vols 9,000; Per Subs 70
Automation Activity & Vendor Info: (Cataloging) LiBRARYSOFT; (Circulation) LiBRARYSOFT
Partic in OCLC Online Computer Library Center, Inc
Restriction: Staff & inmates only

P OLDHAM COUNTY PUBLIC LIBRARY*, 308 Yager Ave, 40031. SAN 320-1902. Tel: 502-222-9713. FAX: 502-222-1141. Web Site: www.oldhampl.org. *Dir,* Jessica Powell; E-mail: jessica.powell@oldhampl.org; *Asst Libr Dir, Librn,* Mary Mielczarek; E-mail: Marym@oldhampl.org; Staff 39 (MLS 7, Non-MLS 32)
Founded 1968. Pop 55,000; Circ 453,725
Library Holdings: AV Mats 116,008; Bk Vols 96,507; Per Subs 216
Special Collections: Census Coll; Genealogy Coll, bks & films; Kentucky Coll; Large Type Coll; Video Cassette Coll
Automation Activity & Vendor Info: (Cataloging) TLC (The Library Corporation); (Circulation) TLC (The Library Corporation); (OPAC) TLC (The Library Corporation)
Wireless access
Partic in LYRASIS
Open Mon-Thurs 9:30-8, Fri & Sat 9:30-5
Friends of the Library Group
Branches: 2
MAHAN OLDHAM COUNTY PUBLIC, 12505 Harmony Landing Lane, Goshen, 40026. (Mail add: PO Box 145, Goshen, 40026-0145), SAN 377-7324. Tel: 502-228-1852. FAX: 502-228-1896. *Br Mgr,* Susan Bunting; E-mail: Susanb@oldhampl.org
Automation Activity & Vendor Info: (Acquisitions) TLC (The Library Corporation); (Course Reserve) TLC (The Library Corporation); (ILL) TLC (The Library Corporation); (Media Booking) TLC (The Library Corporation); (Serials) TLC (The Library Corporation)
Open Mon-Thurs 10-8, Fri & Sat 10-5
Friends of the Library Group
SOUTH OLDHAM, 6720 W Hwy 146, Crestwood, 40014. (Mail add: PO Box 365, Crestwood, 40014-0365), SAN 377-7340. Tel: 502-241-1108. FAX: 502-241-9017. *Br Mgr,* Julie Wilson; E-mail: juliew@oldhampl.org
Open Mon-Thurs 10-8, Fri & Sat 10-5

LANCASTER

P GARRARD COUNTY PUBLIC LIBRARY*, 101 Lexington St, 40444. SAN 306-302X. Tel: 859-792-3424. FAX: 859-792-2366. E-mail: garrardlibrary@gmail.com. Web Site: garrardpublib.state.ky.us. *Dir,* Laura McWilliams
Pop 10,853; Circ 84,000
Library Holdings: Bk Vols 30,000; Per Subs 40
Automation Activity & Vendor Info: (Acquisitions) AmLib Library Management System; (Cataloging) AmLib Library Management System; (Circulation) AmLib Library Management System; (Course Reserve) AmLib Library Management System; (ILL) AmLib Library Management System; (Media Booking) AmLib Library Management System; (OPAC) AmLib Library Management System; (Serials) AmLib Library Management System
Wireless access
Open Mon, Wed & Fri 9-5, Tues & Thurs 9-8, Sat 9-3
Bookmobiles: 1

LAWRENCEBURG

P ANDERSON COUNTY PUBLIC LIBRARY*, 114 N Main St, 40342. SAN 306-3038. Tel: 502-839-6420. FAX: 502-839-7243. Web Site: aplkentucky.org. *Dir,* Pam Marks; E-mail: pmarks@andersonpubliclibrary.org; *Asst Dir,* Alison Morgan; *Mgr, Youth & Family Serv,* Sherry Noon; *Outreach Serv Spec,* Deborah Perry; Staff 3 (MLS 1, Non-MLS 2)
Founded 1908. Pop 20,000; Circ 60,000
Library Holdings: Bk Titles 45,000; Bk Vols 55,700; Per Subs 81
Automation Activity & Vendor Info: (Cataloging) Innovative Interfaces, Inc; (Circulation) Innovative Interfaces, Inc
Wireless access
Open Mon-Fri 9-8, Sat 9-4, Sun 1-5
Friends of the Library Group

LEBANON

P MARION COUNTY PUBLIC LIBRARY*, 201 E Main St, 40033-1133. SAN 306-3046. Tel: 270-692-4698. FAX: 270-692-9555. Web Site: www.marioncopublic.org. *Dir, Outreach Librn,* Amy Morgeson; E-mail: directormcpl@marioncopublic.org; *Asst Dir,* Sandy Nunley; E-mail: sandy.nunley@marioncopublic.org; *Ch,* Morgan Trigg; E-mail: morgan.trigg@marionpublic.org; *Genealogy Librn, Ref Librn,* Jama Watts; E-mail: jama.watts@marionpublic.org; *Adult Programming, Librn,* Stephanie Smothers; E-mail: stephanie.smothers@marionpublic.org; *Teen Librn,* Jade Appleby; E-mail: jade.appleby@marionpublic.org; *Cataloger,* Terry Brockman; E-mail: terry.brockman@marionpublic.org; *Cataloger,* Angela Selter; E-mail: angels.selter@marionpublic.org; Staff 6 (Non-MLS 6)
Founded 1966. Pop 18,812; Circ 100,186
Library Holdings: AV Mats 4,058; DVDs 1,200; Large Print Bks 1,234; Bk Titles 46,383; Per Subs 90; Talking Bks 1,149; Videos 700
Special Collections: Local Genealogy Coll
Subject Interests: Genealogy, Hist, Kentucky
Automation Activity & Vendor Info: (Cataloging) Follett Software; (Circulation) Follett Software; (ILL) OCLC; (OPAC) Follett Software
Wireless access
Special Services for the Blind - Bks on cassette; Bks on CD; Talking bks
Open Mon-Thurs 9-6, Fri 9-5, Sat 9-3
Friends of the Library Group
Bookmobiles: 1

LEITCHFIELD

P GRAYSON COUNTY PUBLIC LIBRARY*, 163 Carroll Gibson Blvd, 42754-1488. SAN 325-187X. Tel: 270-259-5455. FAX: 270-259-4552. Web Site: www.graysoncountylibrary.org. *Dir,* Lisa Jones; E-mail: jones@graysoncpl.org; *Asst Dir,* Melissa Decker; E-mail: decker@graysoncpl.org; *Genealogy & Per,* Bettie Arndell; E-mail: arndell@graysoncpl.org; *ILL,* Kevin Small; E-mail: small@graysoncpl.org; *Youth Serv,* Laura Lindsey; E-mail: lindsey@graysoncpl.org
Founded 1976. Pop 25,746; Circ 111,219
Library Holdings: AV Mats 1,894; e-books 56,752; Large Print Bks 1,615; Bk Titles 7,067; Bk Vols 40,000; Per Subs 60; Talking Bks 501; Videos 650
Subject Interests: Genealogy, Kentucky, Local hist
Automation Activity & Vendor Info: (Cataloging) TLC (The Library Corporation); (Circulation) TLC (The Library Corporation); (OPAC) TLC (The Library Corporation)
Wireless access
Function: ILL available, Photocopying/Printing, Telephone ref
Partic in OCLC Online Computer Library Center, Inc; Soline
Open Mon & Thurs 9-7, Tues, Wed, Fri & Sat 9-5
Friends of the Library Group
Bookmobiles: 1. Librn, Michelle Childress

LEXINGTON

L BINGHAM GREENEBAUM DOLL LLP*, Law Library, 300 W Vine St, Ste 1200, 40507-1622. SAN 323-7222. Tel: 859-288-4717. FAX: 859-255-2742. E-mail: bgdlibrary@bgdlegal.com. Web Site: www.bgdlegal.com. *Librn,* Lynn Fogle; E-mail: lfogle@bgdlegal.com; *Librn,* Zachary O'Connor; E-mail: zoconnor@bgdlegal.com
Library Holdings: Bk Titles 120; Bk Vols 300; Per Subs 60
Wireless access
Open Mon-Fri 9-5

S BLACKBURN CORRECTIONAL COMPLEX LIBRARY*, 3111 Spurr Rd, 40511. Tel: 859-246-2366, Ext 6271. FAX: 859-246-2376. Web Site: corrections.ky.gov/Facilities/AI/BCC/Pages/default.aspx. *Librn,* Jonathan Ashurst; E-mail: jonathan.ashurst@ky.gov
Library Holdings: Audiobooks 55; Bks on Deafness & Sign Lang 1; Bk Vols 4,000; Per Subs 55

J BLUEGRASS COMMUNITY & TECHNICAL COLLEGE*, Learning Resource Center, Oswald Bldg, 470 Cooper Dr, 40506-0235. SAN 306-3151. Tel: 859-246-6380. Interlibrary Loan Service Tel: 859-246-6388. FAX: 859-246-4675. Web Site: bluegrass.kctcs.edu/library.aspx. *Libr Dir, Tutoring Servs,* Robert Campbell; Tel: 859-246-6545, E-mail: robert.campbell@kctcs.edu; *Electronic Res Librn,* Maureen Cropper; Tel: 859-246-6394, E-mail: maureen.cropper@kctcs.edu; *Pub Serv Librn,* Steve Stone; Tel: 859-246-6387, E-mail: steve.stone@kctcs.edu; *Tech Serv Librn,* Kathleen Richardson; Tel: 859-246-6386, E-mail: kathleen.richardson@kctcs.edu; *Circ Supvr,* Maria Yosifova; E-mail: maria.yosifova@kctcs.edu; Staff 6.5 (MLS 5, Non-MLS 1.5)
Founded 1976. Enrl 8,775; Fac 654; Highest Degree: Associate
Library Holdings: AV Mats 4,052; Bk Titles 40,636; Bk Vols 42,823; Per Subs 165
Automation Activity & Vendor Info: (Acquisitions) Ex Libris Group; (Cataloging) Ex Libris Group; (Circulation) Ex Libris Group; (Course Reserve) Ex Libris Group; (ILL) OCLC FirstSearch; (OPAC) Ex Libris Group
Wireless access
Function: Art exhibits, Audio & video playback equip for onsite use, AV serv, Bks on CD, CD-ROM, Computers for patron use, Distance learning, E-Reserves, Electronic databases & coll, Equip loans & repairs, Free DVD rentals, ILL available, Internet access, Magnifiers for reading, Mail & tel request accepted, Music CDs, Online cat, Online info literacy tutorials on the web & in blackboard, Online ref, Orientations, Photocopying/Printing, Ref serv available, Scanner, VHS videos, Wheelchair accessible
Partic in LYRASIS; OCLC Online Computer Library Center, Inc
Departmental Libraries:
NEWTON LEARNING COMMONS, 120 Classroom Bldg, 500 Newton Pike, 40508. Tel: 859-246-6713. Web Site: bluegrass.kctcs.edu/library. *Pub Serv Librn,* Terry Buckner; Tel: 859-246-6397, E-mail: terry.buckner@kctcs.edu
Open Mon-Thurs 7:45-7, Fri 7:45-4:30

S CARRIAGE MUSEUM OF AMERICA LIBRARY, 4075 Iron Works Pkwy, 40511. SAN 372-7823. Tel: 859-259-2933. FAX: 859-231-0973. E-mail: cmalibrary@windstream.net. Web Site: www.carriagemuseumlibrary.org. *Dir, Operations,* John Stallard; Staff 1 (Non-MLS 1)
Founded 1978
Library Holdings: Bk Titles 3,000
Special Collections: Ken Sowles Coll; Paul Downing Coll; Richard B Harrington Coll; Thomas Ryder Coll
Subject Interests: Horse drawn transportation
Function: Archival coll, Internet access, Ref serv available
Restriction: Non-circulating, Open by appt only
Friends of the Library Group

M CENTRAL BAPTIST HOSPITAL LIBRARY*, 1740 Nicholasville Rd, 40503. Tel: 859-260-6297. FAX: 859-260-6442. *Dir,* Lonnie Wright; E-mail: lwright@bhsi.com; *Librn,* Carla Townsend; E-mail: carla.townsend@bhsi.com
Founded 1954
Library Holdings: Bks on Deafness & Sign Lang 10; Bk Titles 2,750; Bk Vols 3,000; Per Subs 275
Wireless access
Open Mon-Fri 8-4:30

R CENTRAL CHRISTIAN CHURCH LIBRARY*, 219 E Short St, 40507. SAN 306-3089. Tel: 859-233-1551. FAX: 859-252-9287. Web Site: www.centralchristianlex.org/library. *Librn,* Jeanette Knowles; Staff 1 (MLS 1)
Library Holdings: Bk Vols 8,500
Subject Interests: Bible study, Ethics, Philos, Relig, Theol

M EASTERN STATE HOSPITAL*, Resource Library, 1350 Bull Lea Rd, 40511. SAN 306-3100. Tel: 859-246-8135. FAX: 859-246-7018. *Librn,* Shane Shoemaker
Founded 1951
Library Holdings: Bk Vols 5,000; Per Subs 150
Subject Interests: Med, Psychiat, Psychol, Pub health
Open Mon-Fri 8:30-4

L FAYETTE COUNTY LAW LIBRARY*, 120 N Limestone St, Ste C-357, 3rd Flr, 40507. Tel: 859-246-2141. E-mail: fayettelawlibrary@kycourts.net. *Library Contact,* Vincent Riggs
Library Holdings: Bk Vols 6,000
Wireless access
Open Mon-Fri 8-4

S HEADLEY-WHITNEY MUSEUM LIBRARY, 4435 Old Frankfort Pike, 40510. SAN 325-545X. Tel: 859-255-6653. FAX: 859-255-8375. E-mail: education@headley-whitney.org. Web Site: www.headley-whitney.org. *Curator, Exec Dir,* Christina Bell
Library Holdings: Bk Vols 1,500; Per Subs 12
Subject Interests: Art, Ceramics, Furniture, Glassware, Jewels, Silver
Restriction: Non-circulating to the pub, Open by appt only

S KEENELAND ASSOCIATION, Keeneland Library, Keeneland Race Course, 4201 Versailles Rd, 40510. (Mail add: PO Box 1690, 40588-1690), SAN 306-3135. Tel: 859-254-3412, Ext 4223. Toll Free Tel: 800-456-3412. FAX: 859-288-4191. E-mail: library@keeneland.com. Web Site: www.keeneland.com/keeneland-library. *Libr Dir,* Becky Ryder; Tel: 859-280-4761, E-mail: bryder@keeneland.com
Founded 1939
Library Holdings: Bk Vols 30,000; Per Subs 45; Videos 1,500
Special Collections: American Racing Coll, photog negative; Peb Coll
Subject Interests: Horses
Wireless access
Open Mon-Fri 8:30-4:30
Restriction: Non-circulating to the pub

P LEXINGTON PUBLIC LIBRARY*, 140 E Main St, 40507-1376. SAN 342-4057. Tel: 859-231-5500. FAX: 859-231-5598. Web Site: www.lexpublib.org. *Exec Dir,* Heather Dieffenbach; Tel: 859-231-5533, E-mail: hdieffenbach@lexpublib.org; *Dir, Access & Strategic Initiatives,* Tonya Head; Tel: 859-231-5506, E-mail: thead@lexpublib.org; Staff 169.5 (MLS 45, Non-MLS 124.5)
Founded 1898. Pop 260,512; Circ 2,825,384. Sal $5,712,449 (Prof $2,398,158)
Library Holdings: e-books 4,344; Bk Vols 464,003
Special Collections: African-American Coll; Early Kentucky Books; Early Kentucky Newspapers; Grants Coll; Large Print Coll; Lexington Urban County Doc Coll
Automation Activity & Vendor Info: (Cataloging) TLC (The Library Corporation); (Circulation) TLC (The Library Corporation); (OPAC) TLC (The Library Corporation)
Wireless access
Special Services for the Deaf - TTY equip
Open Mon-Thurs 9-9, Fri 9-6, Sat 9-5, Sun 1-5
Friends of the Library Group
Branches: 5
BEAUMONT, 3080 Fieldstone Way, 40513, SAN 342-4146. FAX: 859-422-6878. *Br Mgr,* Jim Shoemaker; Staff 33 (MLS 8, Non-MLS 25)
Friends of the Library Group
EASTSIDE, 3000 Blake James Dr, 40509, SAN 342-4081. FAX: 859-422-6868. *Br Mgr,* Kelly Lamm; Staff 13 (MLS 6, Non-MLS 7)
Function: Audiobks via web, Bks on cassette, Bks on CD, Chess club, Children's prog, Computer training, Computers for patron use, ILL available, Music CDs, Online cat, Photocopying/Printing, Prog for adults, Prog for children & young adult, Ref & res, Senior computer classes, Spoken cassettes & CDs, Spoken cassettes & DVDs, Story hour, Summer reading prog, Tax forms, Teen prog, Telephone ref, VHS videos, Wheelchair accessible
Open Mon-Thurs 9:30-9, Fri 9:30-6, Sat 9:30-5, Sun 1-5
Friends of the Library Group
NORTHSIDE, 1733 Russell Cave Rd, 40505, SAN 322-6352. FAX: 859-422-6898. *Br Mgr,* Jenny Lewis; Staff 9.5 (MLS 4, Non-MLS 5.5)
Open Mon-Thurs 9:30-9, Fri & Sat 9:30-5, Sun 1-5
Friends of the Library Group
TATES CREEK, 3628 Walden Dr, 40517, SAN 342-4111. FAX: 859-422-6888. *Br Mgr,* Johnna Waldon; Staff 28 (MLS 9, Non-MLS 19)
Open Mon-Thurs 9:30-9, Fri & Sat 9:30-5, Sun 1-5
Friends of the Library Group
VILLAGE BRANCH, 2185 Versailles Rd, 40504. FAX: 859-422-6358. *Br Mgr,* Position Currently Open
Open Mon-Thurs 9:30-9, Fri 9:30-6, Sat 9:30-5, Sun 1-5
Friends of the Library Group

R LEXINGTON THEOLOGICAL SEMINARY*, Bosworth Memorial Library, 230 Lexington Green Circle, Ste 300, 40503. SAN 306-316X. Tel: 859-280-1229. FAX: 859-281-6042. E-mail: libraryrefdesk@lextheo.edu. Web Site: lextheo.libguides.com/. *Libr Dir,* Dolores Yilibuw; Tel: 859-280-1224, E-mail: dyilibuw@lextheo.edu; *Archival Librn,* J Charles Heaberlin; E-mail: cheaberlin@lextheo.edu; *Circ Mgr, Reserves Mgr,* Katie Wolsky; E-mail: kwolsky@lextheo.edu; Staff 3 (MLS 3)
Founded 1865. Enrl 48; Fac 5; Highest Degree: Doctorate
Aug 2017-Jul 2018. Mats Exp $105,000, Books $26,370, Per/Ser (Incl. Access Fees) $2,419, Other Print Mats $89, Electronic Ref Mat (Incl. Access Fees) $29,328. Sal $108,000
Library Holdings: AV Mats 500; e-books 28,000; Bk Vols 94,000; Per Subs 98
Special Collections: John Mason Neale, Disciples of Christ
Subject Interests: Biblical studies, Christianity, Theol
Automation Activity & Vendor Info: (Acquisitions) OCLC Worldshare Management Services; (Cataloging) OCLC Worldshare Management Services; (Circulation) OCLC Worldshare Management Services; (Course Reserve) OCLC Worldshare Management Services; (Discovery) OCLC

Worldshare Management Services; (ILL) OCLC WorldShare Interlibrary Loan; (OPAC) OCLC Worldshare Management Services; (Serials) OCLC Worldshare Management Services
Wireless access
Publications: Lexington Theological (Quarterly); Occasional Papers; The Bulletin (News Letter of Lexington Theological Seminary)
Partic in Christian Library Consortium
Open Mon-Fri 9-5

L STOLL KEENON OGDEN PLLC*, Law Library, 300 W Vine St, Ste 2100, 40507-1801. SAN 372-1205. Tel: 859-231-3000. FAX: 859-253-1093. Web Site: www.skofirm.com. *Librn,* Jeffrey L Frey; E-mail: jeffrey.frey@skofirm.com
Library Holdings: Bk Vols 10,000; Per Subs 150
Restriction: Staff use only

C TRANSYLVANIA UNIVERSITY LIBRARY*, J Douglas Gay Jr/Frances Carrick Thomas Library, 300 N Broadway, 40508. SAN 306-3194. Tel: 859-233-8225. E-mail: library@transy.edu. Web Site: libguides.transy.edu, www.transy.edu/academics/library. *Libr Dir,* Susan M Brown; Tel: 859-233-8408, E-mail: subrown@transy.edu; *Head, Pub Serv,* Helen Bischoff; E-mail: hbischoff@transy.edu; *Head, Tech Serv,* Jason Cooper; E-mail: jacooper@transy.edu; *Spec Coll Librn,* B J Gooch; E-mail: bjgooch@transy.edu; *Acq/Ser Supvr,* Ann Long; E-mail: along@transy.edu; *Evening Supvr,* Phillip Ira Walker; E-mail: piwalker@transy.edu; Staff 8 (MLS 5, Non-MLS 3)
Founded 1780. Enrl 1,100; Fac 90; Highest Degree: Bachelor
Library Holdings: AV Mats 3,100; e-books 84,000; e-journals 15,000; Microforms 61; Bk Titles 118,000; Per Subs 500
Special Collections: Horse, Sporting & Natural History (Clara S Peck Coll); Kentucky History (J Winston Coleman Kentuckiana Coll), bks, photogs; Medicine to 1850 (Transylvania Medical Library); University archives & ms
Automation Activity & Vendor Info: (Acquisitions) Ex Libris Group; (Cataloging) Ex Libris Group; (Circulation) Ex Libris Group; (Course Reserve) Ex Libris Group; (ILL) OCLC ILLiad; (OPAC) Ex Libris Group; (Serials) Ex Libris Group
Wireless access
Partic in Association of Independent Kentucky Colleges & Universities; Federation of Kentucky Academic Libraries; LYRASIS; OCLC Online Computer Library Center, Inc
Open Mon-Thurs (Winter) 8am-1:30am, Fri 8-5, Sat Noon-5, Sun Noon-1:30am; Mon-Thurs (Summer) 8:30-5, Fri 8:30-4

C UNIVERSITY OF KENTUCKY LIBRARIES*, William T Young Library, 401 Hilltop Ave, 40506. (Mail add: 500 S Limestone St, 40506-0456), SAN 342-4200. Tel: 859-218-1881. Interlibrary Loan Service Tel: 859-218-1849, 859-218-1880. Reference Tel: 859-218-2048. Administration Tel: 859-218-1939. Administration FAX: 859-257-8379. Circulation E-mail: lib.circdesk@email.uky.edu. Reference E-mail: refdesk@uky.edu. Web Site: libraries.uky.edu, libraries.uky.edu/WTYL. *Assoc Dean, Spec Coll, Interim Dean of Libr,* Deirdre Scaggs; Tel: 859-257-3653, Fax: 859-257-6311, E-mail: deirdre@uky.edu; *Assoc Dean, Acad Affairs & Res,* Stacey Greenwell; Tel: 859-218-1322, E-mail: stacey@uky.edu; *Assoc Dean, Teaching, Learning & Res,* Jennifer Bartlett; E-mail: jen.bartlett@uky.edu; *Sr Assoc Dean for Coll, Digital Scholarship & Tech Serv,* Mary Beth Thomson; Tel: 859-218-1227, E-mail: mbthomson@uky.edu; *Dir, Admin & Finance,* Melissa Barlow; Tel: 859-218-0162, E-mail: melissa.barlow@uky.edu
Founded 1909. Highest Degree: Doctorate
Library Holdings: Bk Vols 1,200,000; Per Subs 27,000
Special Collections: 17th-Century English Literature: Milton & Miltoniana; Appalachian Coll (Appalachian Regional Commission Archives, Frontier Nursing Service, archives, bks, ms); Applied Anthropology Documentation Coll; Broadcast & Audio-Visual Archives; Broadside Ballads & Chapbooks; Dime Novels; Early English Romantics: Wordsworth, Coleridge, Lamb (W Hugh Peal Coll); French English & Spanish Drama, 1600-1930; Graphic Arts; Kentuckiana (Breckinridge Family, Henry Clay, Cassius M Clay, Laura Clay, Zachary Taylor, Wickliffe-Preston Papers); Kentucky Imprints (Samuel M Wilson Coll); Medicine (Daniel Drake Coll); Modern Political Archives (incl Alben Barkley, A B Chandler, Earl Clements, John Sherman Cooper, Thruston & Rogers C B Morton, Stanley Reed, Jouett Shouse, Brent Spence, A O Stanley, Fred Vinson, Wilson Wyatt); Musicology (Alfred Cortot Library); Photographic Archives; Printing & Modern Fine Printing (King Library Press, Victor Hammer, Gravesend & Bur Presses); Spanish Manuscript Coll, 1139-1800; Urban Planning Coll; Western Travel. Canadian and Provincial; Oral History; US Document Depository
Subject Interests: Agr, Appalachia, Coal, Educ, Engr, Hist, Humanities, Law, Med, Music
Automation Activity & Vendor Info: (Acquisitions) Ex Libris Group; (Cataloging) Ex Libris Group; (Circulation) Ex Libris Group; (OPAC) Ex Libris Group
Wireless access
Partic in Association of Research Libraries; Association of Southeastern Research Libraries; Center for Research Libraries; Federation of Kentucky Academic Libraries; LYRASIS; National Network of Libraries of Medicine Region 1; State Assisted Academic Library Council of Kentucky
Departmental Libraries:
AGRICULTURAL INFORMATION CENTER, N24 Agricultural Science Bldg N, 1100 Nicholasville Rd, 40546-0091, SAN 342-4235. Tel: 859-257-2758. FAX: 859-323-4719. Web Site: libraries.uky.edu/AIC. *Head of Libr,* Valerie Perry; Tel: 859-257-8360, E-mail: vperry@uky.edu; *Agr Librn,* Jason Keinsley; Tel: 859-218-1523, E-mail: jkeinsley@uky.edu. Subject Specialists: *Agr, Biol sci,* Valerie Perry
Subject Interests: Agr, Botany, Entomology, Food indust & trade, Forestry, Hort, Landscape archit, Nutrition, Veterinary med
DESIGN LIBRARY, 200 Pence Hall, 175 Library Dr, 40506-0041, SAN 342-426X. Tel: 859-257-4305. FAX: 859-257-4305. Web Site: libraries.uky.edu/Design. *Head of Libr,* Faith Harders; E-mail: Faith.Harders@uky.edu
Special Collections: Le Corbusier
Subject Interests: Archit, Furniture, Interior design, Urban planning
EDUCATION, 227 Dickey Hall, 251 Scott St, 40506-0017, SAN 342-4413. Tel: 859-257-9692. E-mail: EducationLib@uky.edu. Web Site: libraries.uky.edu/Educ. *Acad Librn,* Sarah Vaughn; Tel: 859-218-4882, E-mail: sarah.vaughn@uky.edu
Special Collections: Economic Education Coll; KERA Coll
Subject Interests: Children's lit, Educ, Kentucky
CL LAW LIBRARY, College of Law, Bosworth Hall, 631 S Limestone St, 40506-0048, SAN 342-4502. Tel: 859-257-8686. Reference Tel: 859-257-8131. FAX: 859-323-4906. E-mail: rs_lawref@uky.edu. Reference E-mail: lawcirc@uky.edu. Web Site: library.law.uky.edu/home. *Libr Dir & Assoc Prof of Law,* James Donovan; Tel: 859-257-8351, E-mail: james.donovan@uky.edu; *Head, Tech Serv,* Patty Alvayay; Tel: 859-257-2925, E-mail: patricia.alvayay@uky.edu; *Student Serv/Outreach Librn,* Charlie Amiot; Tel: 859-257-1081; *Instrul Serv Librn,* Beau Steenken; Tel: 859-257-1578, E-mail: beau.steenken@uky.edu
Special Collections: Human Rights; International Primary & Legal Coll; Kentucky Supreme Court Briefs; US & Kentucky Legal Materials; US Supreme Court, briefs, rec
Subject Interests: Law, Legal mat
Partic in LYRASIS
Publications: Acquisitions List; Bibliographic Guides; Pathfinders
LEXMARK LIBRARY, 740 New Circle Rd NW, 40511, SAN 306-3127. Tel: 859-232-3783. FAX: 859-232-5728. E-mail: ilibrary@lexmark.com. Web Site: libraries.uky.edu/bydept.php?dept_id=38. *Libr Spec,* Mr Lynn Robertson; E-mail: lynn.robertson@uky.edu; Staff 2 (MLS 1, Non-MLS 1)
Founded 1991
Special Collections: Patents; Products Manuals; Programming Trade Literature
Subject Interests: Bus & mgt, Chem, Electronic engr, Mechanical engr, Metallurgy, Physics
Restriction: Employee & client use only
LUCILLE LITTLE FINE ARTS LIBRARY, 160 Patterson Dr, 40506-0224, SAN 342-4294. Tel: 859-257-2800. FAX: 859-257-4662. E-mail: falib@email.uky.edu. Web Site: libraries.uky.edu/FAlib. *Head of Libr, Music Librn,* Paula Hickner; Tel: 859-257-4104, E-mail: paula.hickner@uky.edu; *Visual & Performing Arts Librn,* Karyn Hinkle; Tel: 859-257-3938, E-mail: karyn.hinkle@uky.edu; *Stacks Mgr,* Chris Little; Tel: 859-257-4604, E-mail: chris.little@uky.edu. Subject Specialists: *Music,* Paula Hickner
Special Collections: Acting Editions of Plays; Early Music Treatises (Alfred Cortot Coll); Wilcox American Music Coll
Subject Interests: Art, Music, Photog
CM MEDICAL CENTER LIBRARY, William R Willard Medical Education Bldg 298, 800 Rose St, 40536-0298, SAN 342-4561. Tel: 859-323-5300. Interlibrary Loan Service Tel: 859-323-6565. FAX: 859-323-1040. E-mail: mclib@uky.edu. Web Site: libraries.uky.edu/MCL. *Libr Dir,* Rick Brewer; Tel: 859-323-5296, E-mail: rick.brewer@uky.edu; *Asst Dir, Access, Delivery & Outreach Serv,* Laura Davison; Tel: 859-323-6138, E-mail: davison@email.uky.edu; *Liaison Librn,* Frank Davis; Tel: 859-323-3983, E-mail: fldavi2@email.uky.edu. Subject Specialists: *Dentistry,* Rick Brewer
Founded 1957. Highest Degree: Doctorate
Subject Interests: Allied health, Dentistry, Med, Nursing, Pub health
Partic in OCLC Online Computer Library Center, Inc
SCIENCE & ENGINEERING LIBRARY, 211 King Bldg, 179 Funkhouser Dr, 40506-0039. Tel: 859-257-0121. FAX: 859-323-3225. E-mail: SciEngLib@uky.edu. Web Site: libraries.uky.edu/SciLib. *Head, Eng & Sci Libr,* Christie Peters; Tel: 859-218-4841, E-mail: christie.peters@uky.edu; *Cat & Ref Librn, Maps Selector,* Gwen Curtis; Tel: 859-257-1853, E-mail: gwen.curtis@uky.edu; *Pub Serv Mgr,* Rachel Combs; Tel: 859-257-6217, E-mail: rachel.combs@uky.edu; *Sr Libr Tech,* Jan Coburn; Tel: 859-257-2965, E-mail: jan.coburn@uky.edu; *Sr Libr Tech,* Alice Wasielewski; Tel: 859-257-6217, E-mail: alice.was@uky.edu; *Academic Liaison,* Jan Carver; Tel: 859-257-4074, Fax: 859-323-4988, E-mail: jbcarv1@email.uky.edu; *Academic Liaison,* Tom Hecker; Tel:

859-257-8343, E-mail: tom.hecker@uky.edu; *Academic Liaison,* Sue Smith. Subject Specialists: *Engr,* Christie Peters; *Astronomy, Chem, Physics,* Jan Carver; *German, Math, Statistics,* Tom Hecker; *Computer sci, Engr,* Sue Smith
Subject Interests: Astronomy, Chem, Geol sci, Maps, Math, Physics, Statistics

SPECIAL COLLECTIONS RESEARCH CENTER, Margaret I King Library, 179 Funkhouser Dr, 40506-0039. Tel: 859-257-1742. FAX: 859-257-6311. Reference E-mail: SCLREF@LSV.UKY.EDU. Web Site: libraries.uky.edu/SC. *Libr Dir,* Deirdre Scaggs; Tel: 859-257-3653, E-mail: deirdre@uky.edu; *Dir, Louis B Nunn Ctr for Oral Hist,* Doug Boyd; Tel: 859-257-9672, E-mail: doug.boyd@uky.edu. Subject Specialists: *Oral hist,* Doug Boyd
Special Collections: Wendell H Ford Public Policy Research Center. Oral History
Subject Interests: Appalachian coll, Archives, Kentuckiana, Modern political archives, Oral hist prog

LIBERTY

P CASEY COUNTY PUBLIC LIBRARY*, 238 Middleburg St, 42539. SAN 320-8192. Tel: 606-787-9381. FAX: 606-787-7720. E-mail: info@caseylibrary.org. Web Site: www.caseylibrary.org. *Dir,* Jan J Banks; E-mail: janbanks@caseylibrary.org; *Asst Libr Dir,* Kathy Goode; E-mail: kathygoode@caseylibrary.org; *Asst Librn,* Doree Henkman; Staff 2 (MLS 1, Non-MLS 1)
Founded 1976. Pop 15,557; Circ 124,000
Library Holdings: Bk Vols 48,000; Per Subs 50
Special Collections: Genealogy Coll; Kentucky Coll; Large Print Coll. Oral History
Automation Activity & Vendor Info: (Cataloging) Follett Software; (Circulation) Follett Software
Wireless access
Open Mon, Tues, Wed & Fri 9-6, Sat 9-3
Friends of the Library Group
Bookmobiles: 1. Librn, Jim Tucker

LONDON

P LAUREL COUNTY PUBLIC LIBRARY DISTRICT*, 120 College Park Dr, 40741. SAN 306-3224. Tel: 606-864-5759. Web Site: laurellibrary.org. *Dir,* Leah Rudder; E-mail: leah@laurellibrary.org; *Mgr, Libr Serv, Operations Mgr,* Lisa Mynatt; *IT Mgr,* Jamey Jeffrey; *Cat Supvr,* Rachel Horton; *Children's Serv Supvr,* Raina Brown; E-mail: rbrown@laurellibrary.org; Staff 32 (MLS 2, Non-MLS 30)
Founded 1915. Pop 52,790; Circ 165,000
Library Holdings: Bk Vols 162,000; Per Subs 60
Automation Activity & Vendor Info: (Cataloging) Innovative Interfaces, Inc; (Circulation) Innovative Interfaces, Inc; (OPAC) Innovative Interfaces, Inc
Wireless access
Open Mon-Sat 10-5
Friends of the Library Group

LOUISA

P LAWRENCE COUNTY PUBLIC LIBRARY*, 102 W Main St, 41230. (Mail add: PO Box 600, 41230-0600), SAN 306-3259. Tel: 606-638-4497. FAX: 606-638-1293. Web Site: www.lcplky.org. *Dir,* Carlie Pelfrey; E-mail: carlie@lcplky.org; *Ch,* Deanna Ferris; E-mail: deanna@lcplky.org; *Outreach Coordr,* Liz Parsons; E-mail: liz@lcplky.org
Pop 15,800; Circ 61,025
Library Holdings: AV Mats 410; Bk Vols 35,000; Per Subs 110; Talking Bks 361
Special Collections: Genealogy Coll; Kentucky Coll
Automation Activity & Vendor Info: (Cataloging) Brodart; (Circulation) Brodart; (OPAC) Brodart
Wireless access
Special Services for the Blind - Talking bks
Open Mon, Wed & Fri 9-5, Tues 9-6, Thurs 9-7, Sat 9-1
Bookmobiles: 1. Librn, Elizabeth Parsons. Bk vols 2,500

LOUISVILLE

S AMERICAN PRINTING HOUSE FOR THE BLIND, INC, M C Migel Library & Barr Research Library, 1839 Frankfort Ave, 40206. SAN 311-5798. Toll Free Tel: 800-223-1839, Ext 705. E-mail: resource@aph.org. Web Site: archive.org/details/aphmigel, migel.aph.org. *Spec Coll Librn,* Justin A Gardner; E-mail: jgardner@aph.org; Staff 1 (MLS 1)
Founded 1921
Library Holdings: AV Mats 7,000; Bks on Deafness & Sign Lang 1,340; CDs 143; e-books 2,789; e-journals 12; Bk Vols 18,000; Per Subs 6
Subject Interests: Blindness, Visual impairment
Automation Activity & Vendor Info: (Cataloging) OCLC; (ILL) OCLC
Function: Archival coll, Electronic databases & coll, Health sci info serv, Music CDs, Online cat, Ref serv available, Wheelchair accessible
Publications: Bibliographies
Special Services for the Blind - Assistive/Adapted tech devices, equip & products; Closed circuit TV; Computer with voice synthesizer for visually impaired persons; Photo duplicator for making large print; Reader equip; Scanner for conversion & translation of mats
Open Mon-Fri 8-4:30
Restriction: Access at librarian's discretion, Circulates for staff only, In-house use for visitors, Not a lending libr

M BAPTIST HEALTH LOUISVILLE*, Hagan-Pedigo Library, 4000 Kresge Way, 40207-4676. SAN 324-5977. Tel: 502-897-8183. FAX: 502-897-8020. *Librn,* Dina Burshteyn; E-mail: dburshteyn@bhsi.com
Founded 1978
Library Holdings: Bk Titles 1,200; Per Subs 160
Subject Interests: Med, Nursing
Automation Activity & Vendor Info: (Cataloging) EOS International
Partic in Kentucky Medical Library Association; LYRASIS; National Network of Libraries of Medicine Region 1
Open Mon-Fri 8-4:30

C BELLARMINE UNIVERSITY, W L Lyons Brown Library, 2001 Newburg Rd, 40205-0671. SAN 306-3291. Circulation Tel: 502-272-8141. Interlibrary Loan Service Tel: 502-272-8314. Reference Tel: 502-272-8317. Administration Tel: 502-272-8137. Web Site: www.bellarmine.edu/library. *Dir,* John Stemmer, PhD; Tel: 502-272-8140, E-mail: jstemmer@bellarmine.edu; *Asst Dir, Ref & Instruction Librn,* Martha Perry Lundgren; Tel: 502-272-8139, E-mail: mperry@bellarmine.edu; *Ref Librn,* Kevin Peers; Tel: 502-272-8315, E-mail: kpeers@bellarmine.edu; *Ref & ILL Librn,* John Boyd; E-mail: jboyd@bellarmine.edu; *Circ Supvr,* Tammy Uchida; Tel: 502-272-8308; *Acq,* Kat McMain; E-mail: kmcmain@bellarmine.edu; *Asst to the Dir,* Patrick Blair; E-mail: pblair@bellarmine.edu; Staff 9.5 (MLS 4.5, Non-MLS 5)
Founded 1950. Fac 176; Highest Degree: Doctorate
Library Holdings: Per Subs 176
Special Collections: E M Kelly Papers; Louisville Archdiocesan Coll, A-tapes; Louisville Historical League Coll, A-tapes; Thomas Merton Coll; William "Billy" Reed Sports Journalism Coll. Oral History
Subject Interests: Health sci
Automation Activity & Vendor Info: (Acquisitions) OCLC Worldshare Management Services; (Cataloging) OCLC Worldshare Management Services; (Circulation) OCLC Worldshare Management Services; (Discovery) OCLC Worldshare Management Services; (ILL) OCLC WorldShare Interlibrary Loan; (OPAC) OCLC Worldshare Management Services; (Serials) OCLC Worldshare Management Services
Wireless access
Partic in Coun of Independent Ky Cols & Univs; Federation of Kentucky Academic Libraries; Kentuckiana Metroversity, Inc; LYRASIS; OCLC Online Computer Library Center, Inc
Open Mon-Thurs 7am-2am, Fri 7am-7pm, Sat 8am-7pm, Sun Noon-2am

S EMBROIDERERS GUILD OF AMERICA, Dorothy Babcock Memorial Library, 1205 E Washington St, Ste 104, 40206. SAN 325-5735. Tel: 502-589-6956. FAX: 502-584-7900. E-mail: egahq@egausa.org. Web Site: egausa.org/library. *Adminr,* Cynthia Welch; E-mail: cwelch@egausa.org. Subject Specialists: *Educ, Needlework, Presv,* Cynthia Welch
Founded 1970
Library Holdings: Bk Titles 3,000
Special Collections: Clip Art Files; Needleart Videos; Rare Books
Subject Interests: Hist
Wireless access
Publications: Needle Arts Magazine & "How To" books
Open Mon-Fri 9-5

S FILSON HISTORICAL SOCIETY LIBRARY, 1310 S Third St, 40208. SAN 306-3402. Tel: 502-635-5083. E-mail: research@filsonhistorical.org. *Chief Exec Officer, Pres,* Richard Clay; *Librn,* Kathryn Bratcher; E-mail: bratcher@filsonhistorical.org; *Curator,* James Holmberg; E-mail: holmberg@filsonhistorical.org; Staff 10 (MLS 7, Non-MLS 3)
Founded 1884
Library Holdings: Bk Titles 60,000; Per Subs 100
Special Collections: Ephemera; Historical manuscripts; KY portraits; Maps; Newspapers; Photographs; Prints; Rare books; Sheet music; Silver (Kentucky Silversmiths Coll)
Subject Interests: Genealogy, Hist, Kentucky, Local hist
Automation Activity & Vendor Info: (Cataloging) OCLC Connexion
Wireless access
Function: 24/7 Electronic res, 24/7 Online cat, Archival coll, Electronic databases & coll, For res purposes, Internet access, Magnifiers for reading, Mail & tel request accepted, Microfiche/film & reading machines, Online cat, Ref & res, Ref serv available, Res assist avail, Res libr, Res performed for a fee
Publications: Ohio Valley History (Quarterly); The Filson (Quarterly newsletter)

Partic in LYRASIS
Open Mon-Fri 9-4:30
Restriction: Authorized scholars by appt, Circulates for staff only, Closed stack, Fee for pub use, Free to mem, In-house use for visitors, Internal use only, Non-circulating, Non-circulating coll, Non-circulating of rare bks, Non-circulating to the pub, Not a lending libr, Registered patrons only, Secured area only open to authorized personnel

L FROST BROWN TODD LLC, Law Library, 400 W Market St, Ste 3200, 40202-3363. SAN 372-1264. Tel: 502-589-5400. FAX: 502-581-1087. Web Site: www.frostbrowntodd.com. *Libr Mgr,* Tracie Tiegs; E-mail: ttiegs@fbtlaw.com; Staff 2 (MLS 1, Non-MLS 1)
Function: For res purposes
Restriction: Staff use only

J JEFFERSON COMMUNITY & TECHNICAL COLLEGE*, Downtown Campus - John T Smith Learning Resource Center, 109 E Broadway, 40202. SAN 342-4626. Tel: 502-213-2154. Web Site: jefferson.kctcs.libguides.com, www.jefferson.kctcs.edu/about_us/library. *Dir, Libr Serv,* Sheree Huber Williams; Tel: 502-213-2156, E-mail: sheree.williams@kctcs.edu; *Ref Librn,* Nancy Mollette; Tel: 502-213-2362, E-mail: nancy.mollette@kctcs.edu; *Ref/ILL,* Lisa Eichholtz; Tel: 502-213-2281, E-mail: lisa.eichholtz@kctcs.edu; *Tech Serv Librn,* Nina Deeley; Tel: 502-213-2373, E-mail: nina.deeley@kctcs.edu
Founded 1968. Enrl 8,431; Fac 172; Highest Degree: Associate
Library Holdings: Bk Titles 50,321; Bk Vols 53,672; Per Subs 196
Automation Activity & Vendor Info: (Acquisitions) Ex Libris Group; (Cataloging) Ex Libris Group; (Circulation) Ex Libris Group; (Course Reserve) Ex Libris Group; (OPAC) Ex Libris Group; (Serials) Ex Libris Group
Function: Ref serv available
Partic in LYRASIS

Departmental Libraries:

SOUTHWEST CAMPUS LIBRARY, 1000 Community College Dr, 40272, SAN 342-4650. Tel: 502-213-7222. FAX: 502-935-8653. *Evening Librn,* Dan Bays; *Librn,* Krista Districh-Osiecki; *Librn,* Rafe Johnson; Tel: 502-213-7210; *Circ Mgr,* Kelly O'Hara; E-mail: kelly.o'hara@kctcs.edu; *Info Spec,* Jonathan Gass; Tel: 502-213-7388
Founded 1972
Library Holdings: Bk Titles 33,200; Per Subs 50
Partic in LYRASIS
Open Mon-Thurs 8am-9pm, Fri 9-2:30, Sat 10-2

L JEFFERSON COUNTY PUBLIC LAW LIBRARY*, Old Jail Bldg, Ste 240, 514 W Liberty St, 40202. SAN 306-3429. Tel: 502-574-5943. FAX: 502-574-3483. E-mail: jcpll@bluegrass.net. Web Site: www.jcpll.net. *Dir,* Sherryl Borders; Staff 1 (MLS 1)
Founded 1839
Library Holdings: Bk Vols 90,000
Special Collections: Indiana Coll; Kentucky Coll
Wireless access
Open Mon-Fri 8:30-4:30
Friends of the Library Group

R JEWISH COMMUNITY CENTER, Israel T Naamani Library, 3600 Dutchmans Lane, 40205. SAN 306-3313. Tel: 502-459-0660. FAX: 502-459-6885. E-mail: info@jewishlouisville.org. Web Site: jewishlouisville.org.
Founded 1948
Library Holdings: Large Print Bks 50; Bk Vols 7,000; Per Subs 20
Special Collections: Jewish Music, Art, Theology, Crafts & Local Jewish History, Holocaust, Genealogy
Publications: Jewish Holiday Bibliographies; Newsletter (Monthly)
Open Mon-Sun 9-6

S KENTUCKY SCHOOL FOR THE BLIND LIBRARY, 1867 Frankfort Ave, 40206. SAN 325-1853. Tel: 502-897-1583, Ext 6301. FAX: 502-897-2850. Web Site: www.ksb.k12.ky.us. *Sch Librn,* Christi Unker; E-mail: christi.unker@ksb.kyschools.us; Staff 1 (MLS 1)
Founded 1842
Library Holdings: Audiobooks 100; Large Print Bks 1,000; Bk Titles 25,000
Special Collections: Braille, Talking Books
Subject Interests: Phys handicaps, Recreational reading
Automation Activity & Vendor Info: (Cataloging) Follett Software; (Circulation) Follett Software
Function: 24/7 Electronic res, 24/7 Online cat
Special Services for the Blind - Audio mat; Braille bks; Large print bks
Open Mon-Fri 7-2:30

P LOUISVILLE FREE PUBLIC LIBRARY*, 301 York St, 40203-2205. SAN 342-4685. Tel: 502-574-1611. Circulation Tel: 502-574-1781. Interlibrary Loan Service Tel: 502-574-1711. Reference Tel: 502-574-1616. Administration Tel: 502-574-1760. FAX: 502-574-1666, 502-574-1693. Reference FAX: 502-574-1657. Web Site: www.lfpl.org. *Dir,* Mr Lee Burchfield; E-mail: lee.burchfield@lfpl.org; *Asst Dir,* Carrick Arehart; Tel: 502-574-1712, E-mail: carrick.arehart@lfpl.org; Staff 67 (MLS 67)
Founded 1902. Pop 721,594; Circ 3,750,653
Special Collections: US Document Depository
Subject Interests: Patents
Wireless access
Open Mon-Thurs 9-9, Fri & Sat 9-5, Sun 1-5
Friends of the Library Group

Branches: 15

BON AIR REGIONAL, 2816 Del Rio Pl, 40220, SAN 342-474X. Tel: 502-574-1795. FAX: 502-454-0169. Web Site: www.lfpl.org/branches/bonair.htm. *Br Mgr,* Lisa Claybrooks; E-mail: lisa.claybrooks@lfpl.org
Founded 1965
Open Mon-Thurs 9-9, Fri & Sat 9-5, Sun 1-5
Friends of the Library Group

CRESCENT HILL, 2762 Frankfort Ave, 40206, SAN 342-4774. Tel: 502-574-1793. FAX: 502-894-8505. Web Site: www.lfpl.org/branches/crescent-hill.htm. *Br Mgr,* Laura Kelleher; E-mail: laura.kelleher@lfpl.org; *Asst Br Mgr,* Barbara Ledford; E-mail: barbara.ledford@lfpl.org
Open Mon-Thurs 10-9, Fri & Sat 10-5
Friends of the Library Group

FAIRDALE BRANCH, 10620 W Manslick Rd, Fairdale, 40118, SAN 378-0260. Tel: 502-375-2051. FAX: 502-375-2016. Web Site: www.lfpl.org/branches/fairdale.htm. *Br Mgr,* Marci Reed; E-mail: marci.reed@lfpl.org
Open Mon, Wed & Thurs 12-8, Tues 10-8, Fri & Sat 10-5
Friends of the Library Group

HIGHLANDS-SHELBY PARK, 1250 Bardstown Rd, Ste 4, 40204, SAN 342-4987. Tel: 502-574-1672. FAX: 502-451-0548. Web Site: www.lfpl.org/branches/highlands-shelbypark.htm. *Br Mgr,* Beth Nahinsky; E-mail: beth.nahinsky@lfpl.org; *Ref Librn,* Ruth Ellen Flint
Open Mon-Thurs 10-9, Fri & Sat 10-5
Friends of the Library Group

IROQUOIS, 601 W Woodlawn Ave, 40215, SAN 342-5045. Tel: 502-574-1720. FAX: 502-367-1468. Web Site: www.lfpl.org/branches/iroquois.htm. *Br Mgr,* Valerie Viers; E-mail: valerie.viers@lfpl.org
Open Mon-Thurs 10-9, Fri & Sat 10-5, Sun 1-5
Friends of the Library Group

JEFFERSONTOWN BRANCH, 10635 Watterson Trail, Jeffersontown, 40299, SAN 342-507X. Tel: 502-267-5713. FAX: 502-266-6569. Web Site: www.lfpl.org/branches/jeffersontown.htm. *Br Mgr,* Kate Leitner; E-mail: kate.leitner@lfpl.org; *Librn,* James Falkenstine; E-mail: jim.falkenstine@LFPL.org; *Ch,* Melissa McCullough; E-mail: melissa.mccullough@LFPL.org; Staff 4 (MLS 3, Non-MLS 1)
Function: 24/7 Electronic res, Adult bk club, Audiobks via web, Bks on CD, Children's prog, Computer training, Computers for patron use, E-Reserves, Electronic databases & coll, Family literacy, Free DVD rentals, ILL available, Life-long learning prog for all ages, Magazines, Music CDs, Online cat, Orientations, Outreach serv, Photocopying/Printing, Preschool outreach, Preschool reading prog, Prog for adults, Prog for children & young adult, Ref & res, Ref serv available, Spanish lang bks, Story hour, Summer reading prog, Teen prog, Wheelchair accessible
Open Mon-Thurs 10-9, Fri & Sat 10-5
Friends of the Library Group

NEWBURG, 4800 Exeter Ave, 40218. Tel: 502-479-6160. FAX: 502-479-6160. Web Site: www.lfpl.org/branches/newburg.htm. *Br Mgr,* Danera Blincoe; Tel: 502-479-6162, E-mail: danera.blincoe@lfpl.org
Open Mon-Thurs 10-9, Fri & Sat 10-5
Friends of the Library Group

NORTHEAST REGIONAL, 15 Bellevoir Circle, 40223. Tel: 502-394-0379. Web Site: www.lfpl.org/branches/northeast.html. *Br Mgr,* Rachel Smith; E-mail: rachel.smith@lfpl.org
Open Mon-Thurs 9-9, Fri & Sat 9-5, Sun 1-5

PORTLAND, 3305 Northwestern Pkwy, 40212, SAN 342-5258. Tel: 502-574-1744. FAX: 502-776-9947. Web Site: www.lfpl.org/branches/portland.htm. *Br Mgr,* Jacqueline Matthews; E-mail: jacqueline.matthews@lfpl.org
Open Mon-Wed 10-8, Thurs 12-8, Fri & Sat 12-5
Friends of the Library Group

ST MATTHEWS-ELINE BRANCH, 3940 Grandview Ave, 40207, SAN 342-4804. Tel: 502-574-1771. FAX: 502-894-8709. Web Site: www.lfpl.org/branches/stmatthews.htm. *Br Mgr,* Position Currently Open
Open Mon-Thurs 10-9, Fri & Sat 10-5, Sun 1-5
Friends of the Library Group

SHAWNEE, 3912 W Broadway, 40211, SAN 342-5282. Tel: 502-574-1722. FAX: 502-776-9983. Web Site: www.lfpl.org/branches/shawnee.htm. *Br Mgr,* Richelle Treves; E-mail: richelle.treves@lfpl.org
Open Mon-Thurs 10-9, Fri & Sat 10-5, Sun 1-5
Friends of the Library Group

SHIVELY, 3920 Dixie Hwy, 40216, SAN 342-5134. Tel: 502-574-1730. FAX: 502-449-3886. Web Site: www.lfpl.org/branches/shively.htm.
Open Mon-Thurs 10-9, Fri & Sat 10-5
SOUTH CENTRAL REGIONAL, 7300 Jefferson Blvd, 40219, SAN 342-5169. Tel: 502-964-3515. FAX: 502-964-7025. Web Site: www.lfpl.org/branches/NewSouthCentral.htm. *Br Mgr,* Raechael Robertson; E-mail: raechael.robertson@lfpl.org; *Ch,* Karen Evans; E-mail: karen.evans@lfpl.org
Open Mon-Thurs 9-9, Fri & Sat 9-5, Sun 1-5
Friends of the Library Group
SOUTHWEST REGIONAL, 9725 Dixie Hwy, 40272, SAN 328-9028. Tel: 502-933-0029. Web Site: www.lfpl.org/branches/southwest.htm. *Br Mgr,* Diane Bundy; E-mail: diane.bundy@lfpl.org; *Asst Br Mgr,* Jamia Ball; E-mail: jamia.ball@lfpl.org
Open Mon-Thurs 9-9, Fri & Sat 9-5, Sun 1-5
Friends of the Library Group
WESTERN, 604 S Tenth St, 40203, SAN 342-5401. Tel: 502-574-1779. FAX: 502-589-9937. Web Site: www.lfpl.org/branches/western.htm. *Br Mgr,* Natalie Woods; E-mail: natalie.woods@lfpl.org
Special Collections: Black History
Open Mon, Tues & Thurs 12-8, Wed 10-8, Fri & Sat 10-5
Friends of the Library Group
Bookmobiles: 1

S LOUISVILLE METRO PLANNING COMMISSION*, Louisville Metropolitan Planning Library, 444 S Fifth St, Ste 300, 40202. SAN 371-1714. Tel: 502-574-6230. FAX: 502-574-8129. Web Site: louisvilleky.gov/government/planning-design/planning-commission. *Communications Mgr,* Jessica Wethington; Tel: 502-574-5174, E-mail: jessica.wethington@louisvilleky.gov
Library Holdings: Bk Vols 400

R LOUISVILLE PRESBYTERIAN THEOLOGICAL SEMINARY*, Ernest Miller White Library, 1044 Alta Vista Rd, 40205-1798. SAN 306-3488. Tel: 502-992-9398. FAX: 502-895-1096. Circulation E-mail: circdesk@lpts.edu. Web Site: www.lpts.edu/library. *Interim Dir,* Jill Sherman; E-mail: jsherman@lpts.edu; *Assoc Libr Dir,* Angela G Morris; E-mail: amorris@lpts.edu; *Instrul Tech Adminr,* Carolyn Cardwell; Tel: 502-895-3411, Ext 422, E-mail: ccardwell@lpts.edu; *Tech Serv Librn,* Angeles Ramos-Ankrum; Tel: 502-895-3411, Ext 397, E-mail: aramosankrum@lpts.edu; Staff 5 (MLS 3, Non-MLS 2)
Founded 1853. Enrl 200; Fac 22; Highest Degree: Doctorate
Library Holdings: AV Mats 7,000; Microforms 12,000; Bk Vols 175,430; Per Subs 543
Special Collections: Reformation & Presbyterian History Coll
Subject Interests: Related disciplines, Relig, Theol
Automation Activity & Vendor Info: (Acquisitions) Ex Libris Group; (Cataloging) Ex Libris Group; (Circulation) Ex Libris Group; (OPAC) Ex Libris Group; (Serials) Ex Libris Group
Wireless access
Function: Res libr
Partic in Federation of Kentucky Academic Libraries; Kentuckiana Metroversity, Inc; LYRASIS
Special Services for the Blind - Accessible computers; Assistive/Adapted tech devices, equip & products; Computer with voice synthesizer for visually impaired persons; Internet workstation with adaptive software; Screen reader software
Open Mon-Thurs (Fall & Spring) 8am-10pm, Fri 8-5, Sat 12-5, Sun 5pm-10pm; Mon, Wed & Fri (Summer) 8:30-5, Tues & Thurs 8:30-8

S NATIONAL SOCIETY OF THE SONS OF THE AMERICAN REVOLUTION*, SAR Genealogical Research Library, 809 W Main St, 40202. Tel: 502-588-6138. E-mail: library@sar.org. Web Site: library.sar.org. *Libr Dir,* Joe Hardesty; E-mail: jhardesty@sar.org; Staff 2 (MLS 1, Non-MLS 1)
Jan 2018-Dec 2018 Income $150,000
Library Holdings: e-books 689; Microforms 5,000; Bk Vols 35,000; Per Subs 10
Special Collections: George Rogers Clark Papers; Lafayette Papers; Morristown Manuscript Coll
Subject Interests: Colonial period, Genealogy, Revolutionary war
Wireless access
Open Mon-Fri 9:30-4:30
Restriction: Non-circulating
Friends of the Library Group

M NORTON HEALTHCARE*, Medical Library, 200 E Chestnut St, 40202. (Mail add: PO Box 35070, 40232-5070), SAN 306-3526. Tel: 502-629-8125. FAX: 502-629-8138. E-mail: library@nortonhealthcare.org. Web Site: www.nortonhealthcare.com. *Med Librn,* Beth Johnson; E-mail: beth.johnson2@nortonhealthcare.org; *Med Librn,* Cecilia Railey; E-mail: cecilia.railey@nortonhealthcare.org; Staff 3 (MLS 2, Non-MLS 1)
Founded 1959
Library Holdings: Bk Titles 3,200; Per Subs 275
Special Collections: Hospitals' Archives
Subject Interests: Allied health, Consumer health, Med, Nursing, Orthopedics, Pediatrics
Automation Activity & Vendor Info: (Cataloging) Ex Libris Group; (Circulation) Ex Libris Group; (OPAC) Ex Libris Group
Partic in Kentucky Medical Library Association; OCLC Online Computer Library Center, Inc
Restriction: Staff & mem only

CR SIMMONS COLLEGE OF KENTUCKY LIBRARY*, 1000 S Fourth St, 40203. SAN 328-1221. Tel: 502-776-1443. FAX: 502-776-2227. Web Site: www.simmonscollegeky.edu/library. *Libr Dir,* Andrew Chalk; E-mail: achalk@simmonscollegeky.edu; Staff 1 (MLS 1)
Enrl 106; Highest Degree: Master
Library Holdings: Bks on Deafness & Sign Lang 3; Bk Vols 5,000
Special Collections: Oral History
Wireless access
Open Mon-Fri 9-5

R SOUTHERN BAPTIST THEOLOGICAL SEMINARY, James P Boyce Centennial Library, 2825 Lexington Rd, 40280-0294. SAN 342-5436. Circulation Tel: 502-897-4713. Interlibrary Loan Service Tel: 502-897-4553. Reference Tel: 502-897-4071. Administration Tel: 502-897-4807. Toll Free Tel: 800-626-5525. Administration FAX: 502-897-4600. Web Site: library.sbts.edu. *Dir, Libr Tech,* John Merritt; E-mail: jamerritt@sbts.edu; *Dir, Tech Serv,* Jeanne Kennedy; E-mail: jkennedy@sbts.edu; *Assoc Librn,* Laura Strickland; E-mail: lstrickland@sbts.edu; *Librn,* C Berry Driver, Jr; E-mail: bdriver@sbts.edu; *Archivist,* Adam Winters; E-mail: awinters@sbts.edu; Staff 22 (MLS 5, Non-MLS 17)
Founded 1859. Enrl 3,300; Fac 61; Highest Degree: Doctorate
Library Holdings: Bk Vols 400,000; Per Subs 914
Special Collections: Archaeology (William F Albright Coll); Evangelism (Billy Graham Coll); Gospel Music (Ingersoll Coll); Hymnology (Converse Hymnology Coll); Missions (R Pierce Beaver Coll); Music (Everett Helm Coll)
Subject Interests: Archaeology, Bible, Educ, Ethics, Hist, Music, Psychol, Relig, Theol
Automation Activity & Vendor Info: (Acquisitions) Ex Libris Group; (Cataloging) Ex Libris Group; (Circulation) Ex Libris Group; (Course Reserve) Ex Libris Group; (ILL) Ex Libris Group; (OPAC) Ex Libris Group; (Serials) Ex Libris Group
Wireless access
Partic in Kentuckiana Metroversity, Inc
Open Mon-Thurs 7:45am-7pm, Sat 9-2

C SPALDING UNIVERSITY LIBRARY, 853 Library Lane, 40203-9986. SAN 306-3585. Tel: 502-585-7130. E-mail: library@spalding.edu. Web Site: library.spalding.edu. *Libr Dir,* Brandi Duggins; E-mail: bduggins@spalding.edu; *Access Serv Librn,* Seth Cohen; E-mail: scohen01@spalding.edu; *Instruction & Learning Librn,* Leah Cover; E-mail: lcover@spalding.edu; *Access Serv, Evening/Weekend Supvr, ILL Librn,* Justin Kennedy; E-mail: jkennedy03@spalding.edu; Staff 4 (MLS 4)
Founded 1920. Enrl 1,650; Fac 128; Highest Degree: Doctorate
Special Collections: Edith Stein Coll; Kentucky Coll
Automation Activity & Vendor Info: (Acquisitions) OCLC Worldshare Management Services; (Cataloging) OCLC Worldshare Management Services; (Circulation) OCLC Worldshare Management Services; (ILL) OCLC Worldshare Management Services; (OPAC) EBSCO Discovery Service
Wireless access
Partic in Coun of Independent Ky Cols & Univs; Kentuckiana Metroversity, Inc; OCLC Online Computer Library Center, Inc

S SPEED ART MUSEUM LIBRARY*, 2035 S Third St, 40208. SAN 306-3593. Tel: 502-634-2700. FAX: 502-636-2899. Web Site: www.speedmuseum.org. *Dir of Coll,* Scott Erbes; Tel: 502-634-2740, E-mail: serbes@speedmuseum.org
Founded 1927
Library Holdings: Bk Titles 18,717; Per Subs 50; Spec Interest Per Sub 50
Special Collections: Indian (Weygold Coll); J B Speed's Lincoln Books
Subject Interests: Archit, Art, Decorative art, Films & filmmaking, Photog
Publications: Acquisitions List; Bibliographies; Gallery Publications Index; Index to the Scrapbooks; Speed Bulletin (In-house Index)
Restriction: Open by appt only

L STITES & HARBISON, Law Library, 400 W Market St, Ste 1800, 40202. SAN 372-1280. Tel: 859-226-2341. Web Site: www.stites.com. *Librn,* Elizabeth Polly; E-mail: epolly@stites.com
Library Holdings: Bk Vols 25,000
Special Collections: Historical Kentucky Statutes (back to 1800s)
Restriction: Staff use only

C SULLIVAN UNIVERSITY LIBRARY, 2222 Wendell Ave, 40205. SAN 324-1777. Tel: 502-456-6773. FAX: 502-456-0016. E-mail: liblex@sullivan.edu. Web Site: libguides.sullivan.edu/website. *Sr Dir, Libr,* Jackie Young-Lenarz; E-mail: jayoung@sullivan.edu; *Electronic Res Librn,* Judy Ford; E-mail: joford@sullivan.edu; Staff 7 (MLS 6, Non-MLS 1)
Founded 1975. Enrl 2,500; Fac 80; Highest Degree: Doctorate
Library Holdings: DVDs 500; e-journals 32,000; Bk Titles 20,000; Bk Vols 31,000; Per Subs 160
Special Collections: Culinary Coll; Julia Child Cookbook Award Nominees 1991-Present; Pharmacy Coll
Subject Interests: Acctg, Bus mgt, Computer sci, Culinary, Paralegal, Travel
Automation Activity & Vendor Info: (Cataloging) TLC (The Library Corporation); (Circulation) TLC (The Library Corporation); (OPAC) TLC (The Library Corporation)
Wireless access
Partic in Kentucky Medical Library Association
Open Mon-Thurs 8-8, Fri 8-4, Sat 8-5
Restriction: Non-circulating to the pub, Pub use on premises

Departmental Libraries:

DUPONT CIRCLE, 4000 Dupont Circle, 40207. Tel: 502-447-1000. Toll Free Tel: 800-264-1799. *Librn,* Amie Baltes; E-mail: abaltes@sullivan.edu
Library Holdings: AV Mats 251; Bk Vols 2,974; Per Subs 70
Open Mon-Thurs 8am-9:30pm, Fri 8-Noon

LEXINGTON CAMPUS, 2355 Harrodsburg Rd, Lexington, 40504. Tel: 859-514-3309. FAX: 859-224-7744. *Libr Dir,* Kandace Rogers; E-mail: krogers@sullivan.edu; Staff 2 (MLS 1, Non-MLS 1)
Founded 1892. Enrl 275; Fac 54; Highest Degree: Associate
Library Holdings: AV Mats 172; e-books 61,300; e-journals 45,000; Bk Titles 1,500; Bk Vols 3,625; Per Subs 50
Subject Interests: Allied health, Archit tech, Computer tech, Engr tech, Graphic arts
Automation Activity & Vendor Info: (Acquisitions) TLC (The Library Corporation); (Cataloging) TLC (The Library Corporation); (Circulation) TLC (The Library Corporation); (OPAC) TLC (The Library Corporation); (Serials) TLC (The Library Corporation)
Function: AV serv, CD-ROM, Computer training, Computers for patron use, Internet access, Learning ctr, Online cat, Photocopying/Printing, Ref & res, Ref serv available
Open Mon-Thurs 8-7, Fri 8-4, Sat 8-Noon
Restriction: 24-hr pass syst for students only, Access at librarian's discretion, Authorized patrons, Borrowing privileges limited to fac & registered students, Limited access for the pub

C UNIVERSITY OF LOUISVILLE LIBRARIES*, 2215 S Third St, 40208. (Mail add: Ekstrom Library, Rm 203, 40292), SAN 342-5495. Tel: 502-852-6745. FAX: 502-852-7394. Web Site: library.louisville.edu. *Dean,* Robert E Fox, Jr; E-mail: bob.fox@louisville.edu; Staff 98 (MLS 37, Non-MLS 61)
Founded 1911. Enrl 22,367; Fac 2,316; Highest Degree: Doctorate
Jul 2019-Jun 2020. Mats Exp $15,483,391. Sal $4,993,915
Library Holdings: e-books 215,800; e-journals 90,700; Bk Titles 973,229; Bk Vols 2,066,246
Special Collections: US Document Depository
Automation Activity & Vendor Info: (Acquisitions) OCLC Worldshare Management Services; (Cataloging) OCLC Worldshare Management Services; (Circulation) OCLC Worldshare Management Services; (Course Reserve) OCLC Worldshare Management Services; (Discovery) OCLC Worldshare Management Services; (ILL) OCLC ILLiad; (Media Booking) OCLC Worldshare Management Services; (OPAC) OCLC Worldshare Management Services; (Serials) OCLC Worldshare Management Services
Wireless access
Function: Art exhibits, Computers for patron use, Digital talking bks, Distance learning, Doc delivery serv, E-Reserves, Electronic databases & coll, Equip loans & repairs, Free DVD rentals, ILL available, Internet access, Microfiche/film & reading machines, Online cat, Online info literacy tutorials on the web & in blackboard, Online ref, Outreach serv, Photocopying/Printing, Printer for laptops & handheld devices, Ref & res, Ref serv available, Res libr, Telephone ref, Wheelchair accessible
Partic in Association of Research Libraries; Association of Southeastern Research Libraries; Coalition for Networked Information; Federation of Kentucky Academic Libraries; Kentuckiana Metroversity, Inc; LYRASIS; State Assisted Academic Library Council of Kentucky
Friends of the Library Group

Departmental Libraries:

DWIGHT ANDERSON MUSIC LIBRARY, 105 W Brandeis Ave, 40208. (Mail add: University of Louisville, 40292), SAN 342-5649. Tel: 502-852-5659. FAX: 502-852-7701. *Dir,* James Procell; Tel: 502-852-0528, E-mail: jjproc01@louisville.edu; Staff 6 (MLS 2, Non-MLS 4)
Founded 1947
Library Holdings: AV Mats 39,502; Music Scores 81,423; Bk Vols 165,664; Per Subs 145
Special Collections: 18th-19th Century Plorodine Music (Ricasoli Coll); 20th Century Music (Grawemeyer Coll)
Automation Activity & Vendor Info: (Acquisitions) OCLC Worldshare Management Services; (Cataloging) OCLC Worldshare Management Services; (Circulation) OCLC Worldshare Management Services; (Course Reserve) OCLC Worldshare Management Services; (Discovery) OCLC Worldshare Management Services; (ILL) OCLC WorldShare Interlibrary Loan; (OPAC) OCLC Worldshare Management Services; (Serials) OCLC Worldshare Management Services
Function: For res purposes

CL BRANDEIS SCHOOL OF LAW LIBRARY, 2301 S Third St, 40208. (Mail add: Law Library, University of Louisville, 40292), SAN 342-5584. Tel: 502-852-6392. FAX: 502-852-8906. Web Site: www.law.louisville.edu/library. *Dir,* David Ensign; E-mail: david.ensign@louisville.edu; Staff 15 (MLS 6, Non-MLS 9)
Fac 30; Highest Degree: Doctorate
Special Collections: Justice (Louis D Brandeis Coll & John M Harlan Sr Coll), ms. US Document Depository
Function: Res libr
Restriction: Circ limited

MARGARET BRIDWELL ART LIBRARY, 2301 S Third St, 40208. (Mail add: Schneider Hall, Belknap Campus, 40292). Tel: 502-852-6741. Web Site: library.louisville.edu/art/home. *Dir,* Courtney Baron; E-mail: courtney.baron@louisville.edu; Staff 3 (MLS 1, Non-MLS 2)
Founded 1956

WILLIAM F EKSTROM LIBRARY, Belknap Campus, 2215 S Third St, 40208. (Mail add: William F Ekstrom Library, University of Louisville, 40292). Tel: 502-852-6745. Circulation Tel: 502-852-6757. Reference Tel: 502-852-6747. FAX: 502-852-7394. *Assoc Dean & Dir,* Bruce L Keisling; Staff 37 (MLS 16, Non-MLS 21)
Founded 1911. Enrl 22,367; Fac 2,403; Highest Degree: Doctorate
Library Holdings: Bk Vols 1,488,195; Per Subs 1,765
Special Collections: US Document Depository
Automation Activity & Vendor Info: (Acquisitions) OCLC Worldshare Management Services; (Cataloging) OCLC Worldshare Management Services; (Circulation) OCLC Worldshare Management Services; (Course Reserve) OCLC Worldshare Management Services; (Discovery) OCLC Worldshare Management Services; (ILL) OCLC ILLiad; (OPAC) OCLC Worldshare Management Services; (Serials) OCLC Worldshare Management Services
Function: Art exhibits, Audio & video playback equip for onsite use, Audiobks via web, AV serv, Computers for patron use, Distance learning, Doc delivery serv, E-Reserves, Electronic databases & coll, Equip loans & repairs, For res purposes, Govt ref serv, ILL available, Internet access, Learning ctr, Online cat, Online info literacy tutorials on the web & in blackboard, Online ref, Orientations, Outreach serv, Photocopying/Printing, Printer for laptops & handheld devices, Ref & res, Ref serv available, Scanner, Telephone ref, VHS videos, Wheelchair accessible
Special Services for the Deaf - Assistive tech
Special Services for the Blind - Assistive/Adapted tech devices, equip & products; Web-Braille
Restriction: ID required to use computers (Ltd hrs), In-house use for visitors, Open to pub for ref & circ; with some limitations, Open to students, fac, staff & alumni, Secured area only open to authorized personnel
Friends of the Library Group

CM KORNHAUSER HEALTH SCIENCES LIBRARY, Health Sciences Ctr, 500 S Preston St, 40202. (Mail add: University of Louisville, Health Sciences Library, 40292). Tel: 502-852-5775. Circulation Tel: 502-852-5771. FAX: 502-852-1631. *Dir,* Vida Vaughn; Tel: 502-852-8540, E-mail: vmvaug01@louisville.edu; Staff 19 (MLS 6, Non-MLS 13)
Founded 1837. Highest Degree: Doctorate
Library Holdings: e-books 64; Bk Titles 92,295; Bk Vols 150,467
Special Collections: Anesthesia Coll; History Coll; Kentucky Medicine Coll; Neurology Coll; Neurosurgery Coll; Pherenology Coll; Psychiatry Coll
Subject Interests: Allied health, Dentistry, Med, Nursing
Automation Activity & Vendor Info: (Acquisitions) OCLC Worldshare Management Services; (Cataloging) OCLC Worldshare Management Services; (Circulation) OCLC Worldshare Management Services; (Course Reserve) OCLC Worldshare Management Services; (Discovery) OCLC Worldshare Management Services; (ILL) OCLC Worldshare Management Services; (OPAC) OCLC Worldshare Management Services; (Serials) OCLC Worldshare Management Services
Function: Accelerated reader prog
Partic in Greater Midwest Regional Medical Libr Network
Friends of the Library Group

GM VETERANS AFFAIRS MEDICAL CENTER LIBRARY*, 800 Zorn Ave, 40206. SAN 306-3615. Tel: 502-287-6240. FAX: 502-287-6134. Web Site: www.louisville.va.gov. *Med Librn,* Anthony Micchelli; Staff 1 (MLS 1)
Founded 1952

Library Holdings: DVDs 100; e-books 5,000; e-journals 5,000; Bk Titles 300
Automation Activity & Vendor Info: (Circulation) LibraryWorld, Inc; (OPAC) LibraryWorld, Inc; (Serials) SerialsSolutions
Wireless access
Function: ILL available, Internet access, Photocopying/Printing, Ref serv available
Partic in Kentucky Medical Library Association
Open Mon-Fri 8-4:30

MADISONVILLE

M BAPTIST HEALTH MADISONVILLE*, Medical Library, 900 Hospital Dr, 42431-1694. SAN 323-6331. Tel: 270-825-5252. FAX: 270-825-3411. *Librn,* Teresa C Ruddell; E-mail: teresa.ruddell@bhsi.com
Library Holdings: Bk Vols 1,500; Per Subs 220
Subject Interests: Consumer health info, Med
Wireless access
Partic in Ky Area Health Educ Ctr Consortium

P HOPKINS COUNTY-MADISONVILLE PUBLIC LIBRARY*, 425 E Center St, 42431. SAN 342-5762. Tel: 270-825-2680. FAX: 270-452-2451. Web Site: www.publiclibrary.org. *Dir,* Joel Meador; E-mail: director@publiclibrary.org
Founded 1974. Pop 47,300; Circ 189,714
Library Holdings: AV Mats 45; Electronic Media & Resources 16; Large Print Bks 1,000; Bk Vols 85,000; Per Subs 108; Talking Bks 800
Special Collections: Kentucky Coll; Rare Book Coll
Automation Activity & Vendor Info: (Circulation) Mandarin Library Automation
Wireless access
Open Tues-Fri 10:30-5:30, Sat 10:30-3:30
Friends of the Library Group
Branches: 1
DAWSON SPRINGS BRANCH, 103 W Ramsey St, Dawson Springs, 42408-1738, SAN 342-5797. Tel: 270-797-8990. FAX: 270-797-8998. E-mail: branchlibrary@publiclibrary.org. *Asst Dir, Br Mgr,* Angel Killough
Library Holdings: Bk Vols 30,000
Open Tues-Fri 10-5:30, Sat Noon-3
Friends of the Library Group
Bookmobiles: 1. Librn, Shanna Turner

J MADISONVILLE COMMUNITY COLLEGE*, Loman C Trover Library, Learning Resource Ctr, 2nd Flr, 2000 College Dr, 42431. SAN 306-364X. Tel: 270-824-1722. FAX: 270-824-1869. Web Site: www.madisonville.kctcs.edu/academics/library. *Interim Dir,* Colin Magee; Tel: 207-824-8674, E-mail: cmagee0002@kctcs.edu; *Librn,* Camille Richmond; Tel: 270-824-1721, E-mail: camille.richmond@kctcs.edu
Founded 1968
Library Holdings: Bk Titles 24,000; Bk Vols 28,099; Per Subs 233
Subject Interests: Nursing, Phys therapy
Automation Activity & Vendor Info: (Acquisitions) Ex Libris Group; (Cataloging) Ex Libris Group; (OPAC) Ex Libris Group
Wireless access
Partic in Federation of Kentucky Academic Libraries; State Assisted Academic Library Council of Kentucky
Open Mon, Tues & Thurs 7:30-4:30, Wed 7:30-6, Fri 8-4

MANCHESTER

P CLAY COUNTY PUBLIC LIBRARY, 211 Bridge St, 40962. SAN 306-3658. Tel: 606-598-2617. FAX: 606-598-4671. E-mail: ccplib2@yahoo.com. Web Site: www.claycountylibrary.org. *Dir,* Linda Sandlin; *Asst Dir,* Donna Gillahan; *Cat & Acq,* Olivia Dezarn
Founded 1954. Pop 24,000; Circ 53,470
Library Holdings: Bk Vols 20,000; Per Subs 67
Special Collections: Kentucky Coll; Large Print Books & Magazines; Local History Coll
Automation Activity & Vendor Info: (Cataloging) TLC (The Library Corporation); (Circulation) TLC (The Library Corporation); (OPAC) TLC (The Library Corporation)
Wireless access
Open Mon & Thurs 9-8, Tues, Wed & Fri 9-5, Sat 9-1
Friends of the Library Group
Bookmobiles: 1. Librn, Cecily Hubbard

MARION

P CRITTENDEN COUNTY PUBLIC LIBRARY, 204 W Carlisle St, 42064-1727. SAN 306-3666. Tel: 270-965-3354. FAX: 270-965-3354. Web Site: www.crittendenlibrary.org. *Dir,* Brandie Ledford; E-mail: brandie.ledford@crittendenlibrary.org; *Children & Youth Serv Librn, Teen Librn,* Melissa Vasquez; Staff 1 (Non-MLS 1)
Founded 1953. Pop 9,207; Circ 58,376
Library Holdings: Bk Vols 30,000; Per Subs 92
Special Collections: Oral History
Subject Interests: Alaskana, Local hist
Automation Activity & Vendor Info: (Cataloging) Follett Software; (Circulation) Follett Software
Wireless access
Open Mon & Tues 9-6, Wed-Fri 9-5, Sat 9-1
Friends of the Library Group
Bookmobiles: 1. Librn, Nancy Brock

MAYFIELD

P GRAVES COUNTY PUBLIC LIBRARY*, 601 N 17th St, 42066. SAN 306-3674. Tel: 270-247-2911. FAX: 270-247-2990. E-mail: gravespubliclibrary@gmail.com. Web Site: gravescountypubliclibrary.org/. *Dir,* Deana Gschwind; *Ch,* Susie Cain; *Programmer,* Elizabeth Brown
Founded 1940
Library Holdings: Bk Titles 53,934; Per Subs 108
Automation Activity & Vendor Info: (Acquisitions) Innovative Interfaces, Inc; (Circulation) Innovative Interfaces, Inc
Wireless access
Function: 24/7 Electronic res, 24/7 Online cat, Adult bk club, Audiobks via web, Bk club(s), Bks on CD, Children's prog, Computer training, Computers for patron use, Digital talking bks, E-Readers, Electronic databases & coll, Free DVD rentals, Genealogy discussion group, Holiday prog, Home delivery & serv to seniorr ctr & nursing homes, Homebound delivery serv, ILL available, Internet access, Large print keyboards, Magazines, Mango lang, Meeting rooms, Microfiche/film & reading machines, Movies, Music CDs, Online cat, Online ref, Outreach serv, Preschool outreach, Prog for adults, Prog for children & young adult, Scanner, Story hour, Study rm, Summer reading prog, Tax forms, Teen prog, Wheelchair accessible, Workshops
Open Mon, Tues, Thurs & Fri 9-8, Wed & Sat 9-5
Friends of the Library Group
Bookmobiles: 1. Librn, Sandy Hennessee

MAYSVILLE

P MASON COUNTY PUBLIC LIBRARY*, 218 E Third St, 41056. SAN 306-3690. Tel: 606-564-3286. FAX: 606-564-5408. E-mail: masoncountypubliclibrary@gmail.com. Web Site: www.masoncountylibrary.com. *Dir,* Valerie Zempter; *Asst Librn,* Pam Erskine; *Ch,* Alexa Colemire; Staff 5 (MLS 1, Non-MLS 4)
Founded 1876. Pop 17,765
Jul 2015-Jun 2016 Income $885,600, State $35,000, County $770,000, Locally Generated Income $10,600, Other $70,000. Mats Exp $572,480, Books $42,000, Per/Ser (Incl. Access Fees) $6,800, AV Equip $3,231, AV Mat $11,950, Electronic Ref Mat (Incl. Access Fees) $1,500. Sal $229,830 (Prof $55,798)
Library Holdings: Audiobooks 3,660; Bks on Deafness & Sign Lang 14; Braille Volumes 3; DVDs 4,061; e-books 116,125; Electronic Media & Resources 22,014; High Interest/Low Vocabulary Bk Vols 19,000; Bk Vols 32,000; Per Subs 58
Special Collections: Music
Subject Interests: Kentucky
Automation Activity & Vendor Info: (Cataloging) Biblionix/Apollo; (Circulation) Biblionix/Apollo; (ILL) OCLC WorldShare Interlibrary Loan; (OPAC) OCLC Worldshare Management Services
Wireless access
Partic in Ky Libr Asn
Special Services for the Blind - Accessible computers; Audio mat; Bks available with recordings
Open Mon 9-8, Tues-Fri 9-6, Sat 9-5

J MAYSVILLE COMMUNITY & TECHNICAL COLLEGE*, Maysville Campus Library, 1755 US Hwy 68, 41056. SAN 306-3682. Tel: 606-759-7141, Ext 66206. FAX: 606-759-7176. Web Site: www.maysville.kctcs.edu/Academics/library.aspx. *Dir, Libr Serv,* Sonja R Eads; Tel: 606-759-7141, Ext 66126, E-mail: sonja.eads@kctcs.edu; *Asst Prof, Librn III,* Carla Redden; Tel: 606-759-7141, Ext 66125, E-mail: carla.redden@kctcs.edu; *Libr Spec,* Garon Overley; Tel: 606-759-7141, Ext 66276, E-mail: garon.overley@kctcs.edu; *Libr Spec,* Seth Sisler; Tel: 606-759-7141, Ext 66124, E-mail: ssisler0002@kctcs.edu; Staff 7 (MLS 3, Non-MLS 4)
Founded 1968. Enrl 3,543; Fac 95; Highest Degree: Associate
Library Holdings: e-books 33,488; Bk Vols 37,423; Per Subs 32; Videos 2,939
Special Collections: Career Coll, AV, bks, micro; Kentuckiana Historical Coll; Rare Books
Subject Interests: Hist, Kentucky, Nursing, Tech subjects
Automation Activity & Vendor Info: (Cataloging) Ex Libris Group; (Circulation) Ex Libris Group; (Course Reserve) Ex Libris Group; (ILL) OCLC; (OPAC) Ex Libris Group
Wireless access
Publications: On A Roll (Monthly bulletin)

Partic in LYRASIS; OCLC Online Computer Library Center, Inc
Open Mon-Thurs (Fall & Spring) 8-7, Fri 8-4:30); Mon-Fri (Summer) 8-4:30
Departmental Libraries:
LICKING VALLEY CAMPUS LIBRARY, 319 Webster Ave, Cynthiana, 41031. Tel: 859-234-8626, Ext 66417. *Libr Spec,* Carla Keller
Automation Activity & Vendor Info: (Cataloging) Ex Libris Group; (Circulation) Ex Libris Group; (Course Reserve) Ex Libris Group; (OPAC) Ex Libris Group
Open Mon, Thurs & Fri 8-4:30, Tues & Wed 8-7
ROWAN CAMPUS LIBRARY, 609 Viking Dr, Morehead, 40351. Tel: 606-783-1538, Ext 66366. *Libr Spec,* Kathy Riddle; E-mail: kriddle0004@kctcs.edu
Automation Activity & Vendor Info: (Cataloging) Ex Libris Group; (Circulation) Ex Libris Group; (Course Reserve) Ex Libris Group; (OPAC) Ex Libris Group
Open Mon & Thurs-Fri 8-4:30, Tues & Wed 8-7

MCKEE

P JACKSON COUNTY PUBLIC LIBRARY*, 338 N Main St, 40447. (Mail add: PO Box 160, 40447-0160), SAN 306-3631. Tel: 606-287-8113. FAX: 606-287-7774. Web Site: www.jacksoncolibky.com. *Dir,* Ashley Wagers; E-mail: ashley.wagers@jcplib.org
Founded 1973. Pop 13,495; Circ 36,438
Library Holdings: Bk Vols 23,432; Per Subs 25
Automation Activity & Vendor Info: (Cataloging) Book Systems; (Circulation) Book Systems; (OPAC) Book Systems
Wireless access
Partic in Ky Libr Asn
Bookmobiles: Librn, Georgia Million

MIDDLESBORO

P MIDDLESBOROUGH-BELL COUNTY PUBLIC LIBRARY*, 126 S 20th St, 40965. (Mail add: PO Box 1677, 40965-3677), SAN 306-3704. Tel: 606-248-4812. FAX: 606-248-8766. Web Site: www.bellcpl.org. *Actg Dir,* Michele B Lawson; E-mail: director@bellcpl.org; *Youth Serv Librn,* Megan Hughes Jeffrey; Staff 6 (MLS 1, Non-MLS 5)
Founded 1912. Pop 35,000; Circ 81,867
Library Holdings: Bk Vols 88,879; Per Subs 1,600
Special Collections: Oral History
Subject Interests: Genealogy for local families, Kentucky, Local hist
Automation Activity & Vendor Info: (Cataloging) Innovative Interfaces, Inc; (Circulation) Innovative Interfaces, Inc; (OPAC) Innovative Interfaces, Inc
Open Mon-Fri 9-6, Sat 10-4
Friends of the Library Group

J SOUTHEAST KENTUCKY COMMUNITY & TECHNICAL COLLEGE*, Middlesboro Campus Library, 1300 Chichester Ave, 40965. SAN 371-957X. Tel: 606-248-0442. FAX: 606-248-3268. Web Site: southeast.kctcs.edu/library. *Campus Libr Dir,* Michael Justice; E-mail: mike.justice@kctcs.edu; *Libr Spec,* Mike Justice; Tel: 606-248-0443, E-mail: mike.justice@kctcs.edu; Staff 3 (MLS 2, Non-MLS 1)
Library Holdings: e-books 14,000; Bk Vols 25,000; Per Subs 90
Automation Activity & Vendor Info: (Cataloging) Ex Libris Group; (Circulation) Ex Libris Group; (Course Reserve) Ex Libris Group; (OPAC) Ex Libris Group
Wireless access
Open Mon-Fri 8-4:30

MIDWAY

C MIDWAY UNIVERSITY*, Little Memorial Library, 512 E Stephens St, 40347-1120. SAN 306-3712. Tel: 859-846-5316. E-mail: library@midway.edu. Web Site: www.midway.edu/library. *Instrul Tech Librn,* Dr Karoline Manny; *Instrul Tech Librn,* Jeremy Puckett; Staff 2 (MLS 2)
Founded 1847. Enrl 1,200; Fac 120; Highest Degree: Master
Library Holdings: Bk Titles 56,000
Automation Activity & Vendor Info: (Acquisitions) Ex Libris Group; (Cataloging) Ex Libris Group; (Circulation) Ex Libris Group; (ILL) OCLC FirstSearch; (OPAC) Ex Libris Group; (Serials) Ex Libris Group
Wireless access
Partic in Association of Independent Kentucky Colleges & Universities; Federation of Kentucky Academic Libraries; KLN
Restriction: Open by appt only

MONTICELLO

P WAYNE COUNTY PUBLIC LIBRARY*, 157 Rolling Hills Blvd, 42633. SAN 306-3720. Tel: 606-348-8565. FAX: 606-348-3829. E-mail: waynelib@windstream.net. Web Site: www.waynecountylibrary.org. *Libr Dir,* Anne Garner; *Asst Librn,* Barbara Sexton; *Ch,* Donna Tuggle; *YA Librn,* Marlene Bass
Founded 1949. Pop 20,969; Circ 201,237
Library Holdings: Audiobooks 2,052; CDs 259; DVDs 1,803; Bk Vols 53,189; Per Subs 146
Special Collections: Genealogy Coll
Automation Activity & Vendor Info: (Cataloging) Follett Software; (Circulation) Follett Software
Wireless access
Partic in Northeast Ohio Regional Library System; Ohio Public Library Information Network
Open Mon, Wed, Fri & Sat 9-5:30, Tues & Thurs 9-7:30
Bookmobiles: 1. Librn, Debbie Marcum

MOREHEAD

C MOREHEAD STATE UNIVERSITY*, Camden-Carroll Library, 150 University Blvd, 40351. SAN 306-3739. Tel: 606-783-2200. Circulation Tel: 606-783-5490. Interlibrary Loan Service Tel: 606-783-5107. Reference Tel: 606-783-5491. Administration Tel: 606-783-5169. Toll Free Tel: 800-423-0884. FAX: 606-783-5037. E-mail: library@moreheadstate.edu. Web Site: research.moreheadstate.edu/home. *Dean, Libr Serv,* David Gregory; Tel: 606-783-5100, E-mail: d.gregory@moreheadstate.edu; *Head, Access Serv,* Rodney Watkins; Tel: 606-783-9343, E-mail: rlwatk01@moreheadstate.edu; *Head, Cat, Head, Tech Serv,* Pamela Colyer; Tel: 606-783-5118, E-mail: p.colyer@moreheadstate.edu; *Coordr, Head, Res & Instrul Serv,* Tom Kmetz; Tel: 606-783-5111, E-mail: t.kmetz@moreheadstate.edu; *Head, Spec Coll & Archives,* Dieter Ullrich; E-mail: d.ullrich@moreheadstate.edu; *Acq Librn, Syst,* Jason Griffith; Tel: 606-783-5119, E-mail: j.griffith@moreheadstate.edu; *Distance Instruction Librn,* Bridgette Whitt; Tel: 606-783-5287, E-mail: br.whhitt@moreheadstate.edu; *Ser/Govt Doc Librn,* Mykie Howard; Tel: 606-783-5116, E-mail: my.howard@moreheadstate.edu; Staff 24 (MLS 8, Non-MLS 16)
Founded 1922. Enrl 10,584; Fac 348; Highest Degree: Doctorate
Library Holdings: Audiobooks 3; AV Mats 19,977; CDs 9,870; DVDs 9,532; e-books 191,692; e-journals 75,792; Microforms 13,166; Music Scores 11,462; Bk Titles 302,950; Bk Vols 346,287; Per Subs 103; Videos 10,104
Special Collections: Adron & Mignon Doran Coll; Appalachian Coll; James Still Coll; Jesse Stuart Coll; Roger W Barbour Coll; University Archives. US Document Depository
Subject Interests: Appalachia, Educ, Math, Music, Nursing, Philos, Phys sci, Psychol, Soc serv (soc work)
Automation Activity & Vendor Info: (Acquisitions) Ex Libris Group; (Cataloging) Ex Libris Group; (Circulation) Ex Libris Group; (Course Reserve) Ex Libris Group; (Discovery) Ex Libris Group; (ILL) OCLC ILLiad; (OPAC) Ex Libris Group; (Serials) Ex Libris Group
Wireless access
Function: 24/7 Electronic res, 24/7 Online cat, Archival coll, Art exhibits, Audiobks on Playaways & MP3, Computers for patron use, Doc delivery serv, E-Reserves, Electronic databases & coll, Free DVD rentals, ILL available, Internet access, Meeting rooms, Microfiche/film & reading machines, Music CDs, Online cat, Online info literacy tutorials on the web & in blackboard, Online ref, Photocopying/Printing, Ref & res, Wheelchair accessible
Partic in Federation of Kentucky Academic Libraries; LYRASIS; OCLC Online Computer Library Center, Inc; State Assisted Academic Library Council of Kentucky
Open Mon, Tues & Wed 7am-Midnight, Thurs 7am-11pm, Fri 7-6, Sat 11-7, Sun 1-Midnight

P ROWAN COUNTY PUBLIC LIBRARY, 175 Beacon Hill Dr, 40351-6031. SAN 306-3747. Tel: 606-784-7137. FAX: 606-784-2130. E-mail: email@rowancountylibrary.org. Web Site: rowancountylibrary.org. *Dir,* Timothy Gampp; *Pub Serv Librn,* Cynthia J Leach; *Prog Coordr,* Sandra Fleshman; Staff 11 (MLS 2, Non-MLS 9)
Founded 1952. Pop 22,872; Circ 112,000
Library Holdings: Audiobooks 5,719; AV Mats 10,500; Large Print Bks 2,605; Bk Titles 43,493; Bk Vols 49,413; Per Subs 217
Special Collections: Rowan County Cemetery Records
Subject Interests: Cemetery, Genealogy, Kentucky, Obituary info
Automation Activity & Vendor Info: (Cataloging) TLC (The Library Corporation); (Circulation) TLC (The Library Corporation); (OPAC) TLC (The Library Corporation)
Wireless access
Function: Homebound delivery serv, Photocopying/Printing, Prog for children & young adult, Ref serv available, Serves people with intellectual disabilities, Summer reading prog, Wheelchair accessible
Open Mon-Sat 10-5
Friends of the Library Group
Bookmobiles: 1. Librn, Donna Christian

M ST CLAIRE REGIONAL MEDICAL CENTER LIBRARY*, 222 Medical Circle, 40351. SAN 320-3786. Tel: 606-783-6861. FAX: 606-784-2178. Web Site: www.st-claire.org. *Libr Asst,* Alfredia Mocabee
Founded 1966

Library Holdings: Bk Titles 1,250; Per Subs 150
Wireless access
Open Mon-Fri 8-4:30

MORGANFIELD

P UNION COUNTY PUBLIC DISTRICT LIBRARY, 126 S Morgan St, 42437. SAN 342-5827. Tel: 270-389-1696. FAX: 270-389-3925. Web Site: www1.youseemore.com/unioncounty. *Dir,* Debbie McClanahan; E-mail: ucpl.debbie@gmail.com; *Asst Dir,* Shirley Mercer; Staff 6 (Non-MLS 6)
Founded 1964. Pop 15,488; Circ 38,010
Library Holdings: AV Mats 397; Bk Titles 34,000; Bk Vols 34,852; Per Subs 90; Talking Bks 264
Subject Interests: Local genealogy, Local hist
Function: ILL available
Partic in LYRASIS
Open Mon-Fri 9-4

MORGANTOWN

P BUTLER COUNTY PUBLIC LIBRARY*, 116 W Ohio St, 42261. (Mail add: PO Box 247, 42261-0247), SAN 306-3755. Tel: 270-526-4722. FAX: 270-526-9974. Web Site: www.bcplky.org. *Dir,* Kenna Martin; E-mail: kenna.martin@bcplky.org; *Asst Librn,* Position Currently Open
Founded 1954. Pop 12,938; Circ 37,959
Library Holdings: Audiobooks 386; DVDs 1,500; Bk Vols 35,000; Per Subs 41
Automation Activity & Vendor Info: (Cataloging) Evolve; (Circulation) Evolve; (OPAC) Evolve
Wireless access
Function: 24/7 Electronic res, 24/7 Online cat, Activity rm
Open Mon & Wed-Fri 8:30-4:30, Tues 8:30-7, Sat 9-2
Bookmobiles: 1. Librn, Sharon Nabours

MOUNT OLIVET

P ROBERTSON COUNTY PUBLIC LIBRARY*, 207 N Main St, 41064. (Mail add: PO Box 282, 41064-0282), SAN 320-8206. Tel: 606-724-5746. Administration Tel: 606-724-2015. FAX: 606-724-5746. E-mail: robertsoncountylibrary@yahoo.com. *Dir,* Carol Mitchell; E-mail: carolm.mitchell@ky.gov; *Ch Serv, Circ,* Christy Haywood
Founded 1979. Pop 2,266; Circ 30,737
Library Holdings: Bk Vols 15,206; Per Subs 22
Automation Activity & Vendor Info: (Cataloging) Triple B Technologies; (Circulation) Triple B Technologies
Wireless access
Special Services for the Blind - Bks on cassette
Open Mon, Tues, Thurs & Fri 9-5, Wed 9-6, Sat 9-Noon
Bookmobiles: 1. Librn, Dian Oaks

MOUNT STERLING

P MONTGOMERY COUNTY PUBLIC LIBRARY*, 328 N Maysville Rd, 40353. SAN 376-5806. Tel: 859-498-2404. FAX: 859-498-7477. E-mail: askmtsterlinglibrary@yahoo.com. Web Site: www.youseemore.com/mtsterling. *Dir,* Melissa Smathers-Barnes; *Ad,* Lori McAlister; *Ch Serv Librn,* Betty Trump; Staff 6 (MLS 1, Non-MLS 5)
Founded 1871. Pop 24,000; Circ 125,000
Library Holdings: AV Mats 2,675; Bks on Deafness & Sign Lang 25; CDs 300; DVDs 600; Electronic Media & Resources 50; Bk Vols 45,000; Per Subs 106; Talking Bks 835; Videos 1,000
Open Mon-Thurs 9-9, Fri & Sat 9-6
Branches: 1
CAMARGO BRANCH, 4406C Camargo Rd, 40353. Tel: 859-499-4244. *Ad, Br Mgr,* Lori McAlister
Open Mon-Fri 9-6
Bookmobiles: 1. Librn, Nena Donovan

MOUNT VERNON

P ROCKCASTLE COUNTY PUBLIC LIBRARY*, 60 Ford Dr, 40456. SAN 306-3763. Tel: 606-256-2388. FAX: 606-256-5460. Web Site: www.rockcastlelibrary.org. *Dir,* Pamela Chaliff; E-mail: pam@rockcastlelibrary.org
Founded 1954. Pop 13,973; Circ 81,014
Library Holdings: Bk Vols 24,155; Per Subs 40
Subject Interests: Genealogy
Automation Activity & Vendor Info: (Acquisitions) Brodart; (Cataloging) Brodart; (Circulation) Brodart
Open Mon-Fri 9:30-6, Sat 9:30-2

MUNFORDVILLE

P HART COUNTY PUBLIC LIBRARY*, 500 E Union St, 42765. SAN 306-3771. Tel: 270-524-1953. FAX: 270-524-7323. E-mail: hartcountypubliclibrary@gmail.com, hcpl@scrtc.com. Web Site: www.hartcountypubliclibrary.us. *Dir,* Vicki Logsdon
Founded 1968. Pop 17,000; Circ 93,652
Library Holdings: Per Subs 100
Special Collections: Oral History
Subject Interests: Genealogy
Automation Activity & Vendor Info: (Cataloging) Follett Software; (Circulation) Follett Software; (OPAC) Follett Software
Wireless access
Open Mon-Fri 9-5, Sat 8:30-Noon
Bookmobiles: 3

MURRAY

P CALLOWAY COUNTY PUBLIC LIBRARY, 710 Main St, 42071. SAN 306-378X. Tel: 270-753-2288. FAX: 270-753-8263. E-mail: contactccpl@callowaycountylibrary.org. Web Site: www.callowaycountylibrary.org. *Dir,* Mignon G Reed; Tel: 270-753-2288, Ext 101, E-mail: mignon.reed@callowaycountylibrary.org; *Bus Mgr,* Wyneth C Herrington; Tel: 270-753-2288, Ext 106, E-mail: wyneth.herrington@callowaycountylibrary.org; Staff 3 (MLS 3)
Founded 1967. Pop 33,000; Circ 350,000
Library Holdings: Bk Vols 63,000; Per Subs 150
Special Collections: Calloway County Antique Photographs Coll; Kentucky Authors & Titles (Kentucky Coll). Oral History
Automation Activity & Vendor Info: (Cataloging) TLC (The Library Corporation); (Circulation) TLC (The Library Corporation); (ILL) OCLC; (OPAC) TLC (The Library Corporation)
Wireless access
Publications: Pot Pouri-Calloway County
Open Mon-Fri 8-8, Sat 9-5, Sun 1-5
Friends of the Library Group

C MURRAY STATE UNIVERSITY*, Harry Lee Waterfield Library, 205 Waterfield Library, Dean's Office, 42071-3307. SAN 342-5916. Tel: 270-809-2291. Circulation Tel: 270-809-4990. Interlibrary Loan Service Tel: 270-809-4298, 270-809-4420. Reference Tel: 270-809-2053. FAX: 270-809-3736. Web Site: lib.murraystate.edu. *Dean,* Ashley Ireland; Tel: 270-809-5604, E-mail: aireland@murraystate.edu; *Asst Dean, Dir, Tech Serv,* Cris Ferguson; Tel: 270-809-5607; *Metadata Librn,* Leslie Engelson; Tel: 270-809-4818, E-mail: lengelson@murraystate.edu; Staff 13 (MLS 12, Non-MLS 1)
Founded 1923. Enrl 10,156; Fac 395; Highest Degree: Doctorate
Library Holdings: AV Mats 15,661; e-books 51,049; e-journals 64,102; Bk Titles 330,959; Bk Vols 336,205; Per Subs 1,305
Special Collections: Forrest Pogue Coll; Irvin S Cobb Coll; Jackson Purchase History & Genealogy; Jesse Stuart Coll, bks, memorabilia, ms; National, State & Regional Political Records. US Document Depository
Automation Activity & Vendor Info: (Acquisitions) Ex Libris Group; (Cataloging) Ex Libris Group; (Circulation) Ex Libris Group; (Course Reserve) Ex Libris Group; (ILL) OCLC; (OPAC) Ex Libris Group; (Serials) Ex Libris Group
Wireless access
Partic in Federation of Kentucky Academic Libraries; LYRASIS; OCLC Online Computer Library Center, Inc; State Assisted Academic Library Council of Kentucky
Special Services for the Blind - Reader equip; ZoomText magnification & reading software
Open Mon-Thurs 7am-12:30am, Fri 7am-8pm, Sat 10-8, Sun Noon-12:30am
Friends of the Library Group

NICHOLASVILLE

P JESSAMINE COUNTY PUBLIC LIBRARY*, 600 S Main St, 40356. SAN 306-3828. Tel: 859-885-3523. FAX: 859-885-5164. Circulation E-mail: information@jesspublib.org. Web Site: www.jesspublib.org. *Exec Dir,* Dr Ron Critchfield; Staff 26 (MLS 4, Non-MLS 22)
Founded 1968. Pop 40,016; Circ 386,182
Library Holdings: AV Mats 4,365; Bk Vols 60,682; Per Subs 115; Talking Bks 4,216
Special Collections: Jessamine County Genealogy; Kentucky Coll
Subject Interests: Kentucky
Automation Activity & Vendor Info: (Cataloging) SirsiDynix
Wireless access
Special Services for the Deaf - Assistive tech
Special Services for the Blind - Computer with voice synthesizer for visually impaired persons
Open Mon-Wed 9-9, Thurs 11:30-9, Fri 9-6, Sat 9-5, Sun 1-5
Friends of the Library Group
Bookmobiles: 1

OWENSBORO

CR BRESCIA UNIVERSITY, Father Leonard Alvey Library, 717 Frederica St, 42301. SAN 306-3836. Tel: 270-686-4212. Web Site: libguides.brescia.edu/home. *Dir, Libr & Info Serv,* Sister Judith N Riney; Tel: 270-686-4288, E-mail: judith.riney@brescia.edu; *Asst Librn,* Maura O'Donoghue; Tel: 270-686-4213, E-mail: maura.odonoghue@brescia.edu; *Pub Serv Mgr,* Sarah Cox; E-mail: sarah.cox@brescia.edu; *Cat, ILL,* Carol Ranburger; Tel: 270-686-4214, E-mail: carol.ranburger@brescia.edu; Staff 4 (MLS 2, Non-MLS 2)
Founded 1950. Enrl 950; Highest Degree: Master
Library Holdings: e-books 120,000; e-journals 14,000; Bk Titles 79,000; Bk Vols 86,000
Special Collections: Kentuckiana
Subject Interests: Lit, Relig
Automation Activity & Vendor Info: (Acquisitions) OCLC Worldshare Management Services; (Cataloging) OCLC Worldshare Management Services; (Circulation) OCLC Worldshare Management Services; (OPAC) OCLC Worldshare Management Services
Wireless access
Function: 24/7 Electronic res, 24/7 Online cat
Publications: Faculty Handbook; List of Acquisitions; Student Handbook
Partic in Association of Independent Kentucky Colleges & Universities; Federation of Kentucky Academic Libraries; OCLC Online Computer Library Center, Inc
Open Mon-Thurs 7:30am-10pm, Fri 7:30-4, Sun 5-10

P DAVIESS COUNTY PUBLIC LIBRARY*, 2020 Frederica St, 42301. SAN 306-3860. Tel: 270-684-0211. FAX: 270-684-0218. Administration FAX: 270-691-1890. Web Site: www.dcplibrary.org. *Dir,* Erin Waller; Tel: 270-684-0211, Ext 259; *Bus Mgr,* Debbie Young; E-mail: dyoung@dcplibrary.org; *Circ Mgr, Pub Serv,* Brandon Hagan; *Coll Develop Mgr,* Alicia Harrington; *Commun Engagement Mgr,* Shannon Sandefur; *Info Tech,* Brian Lashbrook; *ILL,* Rhonda Schell; *Ref & Info Serv,* Christy Temple; Staff 44 (MLS 6, Non-MLS 38)
Founded 1909. Pop 98,218; Circ 797,963
Jul 2013-Jun 2014 Income $4,113,216, State $109,563, Federal $9,896, Locally Generated Income $3,780,720, Other $213,037. Mats Exp $499,950, Books $237,275, Per/Ser (Incl. Access Fees) $85,710, Other Print Mats $168, AV Mat $70,475, Electronic Ref Mat (Incl. Access Fees) $106,322. Sal $1,512,880 (Prof $105,060)
Library Holdings: AV Mats 28,683; CDs 12,675; DVDs 15,591; e-books 78,343; Large Print Bks 16,353; Microforms 203; Bk Vols 215,366; Per Subs 3,615
Subject Interests: Genealogy, Hist, Kentucky, Local hist
Automation Activity & Vendor Info: (Acquisitions) Baker & Taylor; (Cataloging) OCLC; (Circulation) Innovative Interfaces, Inc; (Discovery) EBSCO Discovery Service; (ILL) OCLC; (OPAC) Innovative Interfaces, Inc
Wireless access
Open Mon-Thurs 9-9, Fri 9-8, Sat 9-6, Sun 1-5
Friends of the Library Group

C KENTUCKY WESLEYAN COLLEGE*, Howard Greenwell Library, 3000 Frederica St, 42301. SAN 306-3852. Tel: 270-852-3259. Interlibrary Loan Service Tel: 270-852-3258. FAX: 270-926-3196. Web Site: library.kwc.edu. *Dir,* Pat McFarling; E-mail: patmc@kwc.edu; *Access Serv,* Naomi Golovin; E-mail: ngolovin@kwc.edu; *Info Serv,* Deborah Russell; E-mail: drussell@kwc.edu; Staff 3 (MLS 3)
Founded 1858. Enrl 766; Fac 43; Highest Degree: Bachelor
Library Holdings: e-books 40,678; Bk Vols 80,113; Per Subs 107
Special Collections: Dan M King Architecture Coll; First Editions-American & English Literature (Dr & Mrs M David Orrahood Coll); Kentuckiana; Kentucky United Methodist Heritage Center Coll, bks, mss, pamphlets & pictures; KWC Archives; Toraichi Matsumoto Memorial Coll. US Document Depository
Automation Activity & Vendor Info: (OPAC) OCLC Worldshare Management Services
Wireless access
Publications: Catalog of the Dan M King Architecture Coll; Catalog of the Dr & Mrs M David Orrahood Coll; KWC Non-Graduates 1866-1949, Millersburg-Winchester
Partic in OCLC Online Computer Library Center, Inc

S OWENSBORO AREA MUSEUM OF SCIENCE & HISTORY LIBRARY*, 122 E Second St, 42303-4108. SAN 323-4800. Tel: 270-687-2732. FAX: 270-687-2738. E-mail: information@owensboromuseum.org. Web Site: www.owensboromuseum.org. *Chief Exec Officer,* Kathy Olson; E-mail: kolson@owensboromuseum.org
Founded 1966
Library Holdings: Bk Vols 450; Per Subs 12
Subject Interests: Kentucky, Mus studies, Native Am, Natural hist
Wireless access
Open Tues-Sat 10-5, Sun 1-5

J OWENSBORO COMMUNITY & TECHNICAL COLLEGE*, Learning Resources Center, Learning Resource Ctr Bldg, 1st Flr, 4800 New Hartford Rd, 42303. SAN 323-584X. Tel: 270-686-4590. FAX: 270-686-4594. E-mail: octc.library@kctcs.edu. Web Site: owensboro.kctcs.edu/current-students/student-resources/libraries.aspx. *Dir, Libr Serv,* Donna Abell; Tel: 270-686-4575, E-mail: donna.abell@kctcs.edu; *Pub Serv Librn,* John Lutzel; Tel: 270-686-4574, E-mail: john.lutzel@kctcs.edu; *Acq, Libr Spec,* Lora Waters; Tel: 270-686-4580, E-mail: lora.waters@kctcs.edu; Staff 6 (MLS 2, Non-MLS 4)
Founded 1986. Enrl 2,827; Fac 100; Highest Degree: Associate
Library Holdings: AV Mats 1,261; e-books 100,000; Bk Titles 21,981; Bk Vols 23,440; Per Subs 8
Automation Activity & Vendor Info: (Cataloging) Ex Libris Group; (Circulation) Ex Libris Group; (Course Reserve) Ex Libris Group; (OPAC) Ex Libris Group
Wireless access
Partic in LYRASIS; OCLC Online Computer Library Center, Inc
Open Mon-Thurs 7:45-5:30, Fri 7:45-4:30

M OWENSBORO MEDICAL HEALTH SYSTEM*, Threlkel Health Sciences Library, 1201 Pleasant Valley Rd, 42303. Tel: 270-417-2000, 270-417-6864. *Med Librn,* Virginia Marx; E-mail: virginia.marx@owensborohealth.org
Library Holdings: Bk Vols 1,000
Wireless access
Open Mon-Fri 8-4:30

OWENTON

P OWEN COUNTY PUBLIC LIBRARY*, 1370 Hwy 22 E, 40359. SAN 306-3887. Tel: 502-484-3450. FAX: 502-484-3463. Web Site: www.owencountylibrary.org. *Dir,* Cyndi Clifton; E-mail: director@owenlibrary.org
Pop 11,300; Circ 89,000
Library Holdings: Bk Vols 28,600; Per Subs 64
Subject Interests: Kentucky
Automation Activity & Vendor Info: (Cataloging) Book Systems; (ILL) OCLC WorldShare Interlibrary Loan
Wireless access
Open Mon, Tues & Thurs 9:30-8, Fri & Sat 9:30-5
Friends of the Library Group

OWINGSVILLE

P BATH COUNTY MEMORIAL LIBRARY*, 24 W Main St, 40360. (Mail add: PO Box 380, 40360-0380), SAN 306-3895. Tel: 606-674-2531. FAX: 606-336-5039. E-mail: bcml@bathlibrary.org. Web Site: www2.youseemore.com/bath. *Dir,* Michael Richter; *Cataloger,* Lois Crump; *Adult Programming,* Vicki Browning; *ILL,* Julia D Jones; Staff 4.8 (Non-MLS 4.8)
Pop 11,707; Circ 62,604
Library Holdings: AV Mats 261; CDs 211; Large Print Bks 1,060; Bk Vols 23,587; Per Subs 79; Talking Bks 733; Videos 1,586
Special Collections: Kentucky Genealogy
Automation Activity & Vendor Info: (Cataloging) TLC (The Library Corporation); (Circulation) TLC (The Library Corporation); (OPAC) TLC (The Library Corporation)
Wireless access
Function: Homebound delivery serv, ILL available, Magnifiers for reading, Photocopying/Printing, Prog for children & young adult, Spoken cassettes & CDs, Summer reading prog, Tax forms, VHS videos, Wheelchair accessible
Special Services for the Blind - Bks on cassette; Large print bks
Open Mon-Sat (Fall & Spring) 9:30-5:30; Mon, Tues, Thurs & Fri (Summer) 9:30-7, Wed & Sat 9:30-5:30
Branches: 1
SHARPSBURG BRANCH, 7781 W Tunnel Hill Rd, Sharpsburg, 40374. Tel: 606-247-2100. E-mail: bcml_sharpsburg@windstream.net. *Asst Dir, Operations,* Christi Crump
Open Mon, Wed & Sat 9:30-5:30
Bookmobiles: 1. Librn, Tom Byron

PADUCAH

P MCCRACKEN COUNTY PUBLIC LIBRARY*, 555 Washington St, 42003. SAN 306-3917. Tel: 270-442-2510. FAX: 270-443-5857. Web Site: www.mclib.net. *Libr Dir,* Susan Baier; E-mail: sbaier@mclib.net; *Adult Serv Mgr,* Sarah Pace-McGowan; E-mail: smcgowan@mclib.net; *Bus Mgr,* Kim Hunt; E-mail: khunt@mclib.net; *Tech Serv Mgr,* Brian Medlin; *Youth Serv Mgr,* Linda Bartley; E-mail: lbartley@mclib.net; *Tech Coordr,* Jay Hite; E-mail: jhite@mclib.net; Staff 4.5 (MLS 3, Non-MLS 1.5)
Founded 1901. Pop 64,950; Circ 336,367

Jul 2014-Jun 2015 Income $3,282,696, State $35,789, County $3,036,229, Locally Generated Income $177,301. Mats Exp $1,667,738, Books $311,547, Per/Ser (Incl. Access Fees) $12,500, Other Print Mats $14,500, AV Mat $215,775, Electronic Ref Mat (Incl. Access Fees) $1,074,140, Presv $39,276. Sal $937,587 (Prof $97,000)
Library Holdings: CDs 7,527; DVDs 38,672; e-books 57,093; Bk Titles 113,491; Bk Vols 127,542; Per Subs 218
Special Collections: Genealogy, bks, ms; History (Kentucky Coll), bks, ms; Literature (Irvin S Cobb Coll), bks, ms
Automation Activity & Vendor Info: (Acquisitions) SirsiDynix; (Circulation) SirsiDynix; (ILL) OCLC ILLiad
Wireless access
Function: Accelerated reader prog, Bk reviews (Group), Bks on cassette, Bks on CD, Children's prog, Computers for patron use, Free DVD rentals, Games & aids for people with disabilities, ILL available, Jail serv, Photocopying/Printing, Preschool outreach, Prog for adults, Prog for children & young adult, Tax forms, Telephone ref, Wheelchair accessible
Open Mon-Thurs 11-7, Fri & Sat 10-5, Sun 1-5
Friends of the Library Group

J WEST KENTUCKY COMMUNITY & TECHNICAL COLLEGE*, Matheson Library, 4810 Alben Barkley Dr, 42001. (Mail add: PO Box 7380, 42002-7380), SAN 306-3909. Tel: 270-534-3197. Interlibrary Loan Service Tel: 270-534-3189. FAX: 270-554-6218. Web Site: www.westkentucky.kctcs.edu > Current Students > Library. *Dir, Libr Serv,* Amy Sullivan; Tel: 270-534-3171, E-mail: amy.sullivan@kctcs.edu; *User Serv Librn,* Carol Driver; Tel: 270-534-3170, E-mail: carol.driver@kctcs.edu; Staff 4 (MLS 2, Non-MLS 2)
Founded 1932. Enrl 3,023; Fac 142; Highest Degree: Associate
Library Holdings: Audiobooks 305; AV Mats 239; DVDs 1,382; e-books 233,299; e-journals 64,719; Bk Vols 21,671; Per Subs 37; Videos 36,272
Special Collections: Kentucky & Paducah area coll
Automation Activity & Vendor Info: (Cataloging) OCLC Connexion; (Circulation) Ex Libris Group; (Discovery) Ex Libris Group; (ILL) OCLC; (OPAC) Ex Libris Group
Wireless access
Function: 24/7 Electronic res, 24/7 Online cat, AV serv, Bks on CD, Computers for patron use, Distance learning, E-Readers, Electronic databases & coll, Equip loans & repairs, Free DVD rentals, Health sci info serv, ILL available, Internet access, Large print keyboards, Magazines, Microfiche/film & reading machines, Online cat, Online info literacy tutorials on the web & in blackboard, Online ref, Orientations, Photocopying/Printing, Printer for laptops & handheld devices, Prog for adults, Ref & res, Scanner, Study rm, Wheelchair accessible
Partic in Federation of Kentucky Academic Libraries; State Assisted Academic Library Council of Kentucky
Open Mon-Thurs (Fall & Spring)7:30-5:30, Fri 7:30-4
Restriction: Limited access for the pub, Open to students, fac, staff & alumni

PAINTSVILLE

P JOHNSON COUNTY PUBLIC LIBRARY*, 444 Main St, 41240. SAN 306-3933. Tel: 606-789-4355. FAX: 606-789-6758. E-mail: johnsonlibrary@bellsouth.net. Web Site: www.johnsoncountypubliclibrary.org. *Dir,* Karen Daniel
Pop 23,827; Circ 207,863
Library Holdings: Audiobooks 1,199; AV Mats 172; DVDs 856; Microforms 120; Bk Vols 55,000; Per Subs 63; Talking Bks 973; Videos 391
Automation Activity & Vendor Info: (Cataloging) AmLib Library Management System; (Circulation) AmLib Library Management System; (Course Reserve) AmLib Library Management System; (OPAC) AmLib Library Management System
Wireless access
Open Mon, Wed & Fri 9:30-5, Tues & Thurs 9:30-8, Sat 9-2
Bookmobiles: 1. Librn, Ryan Skaggs

PARIS

P PARIS-BOURBON COUNTY LIBRARY*, 701 High St, 40361. SAN 306-395X. Tel: 859-987-4419. FAX: 859-987-2421. Web Site: www.bourbonlibrary.org. *Dir,* Mark Adler; E-mail: madler@bourbonlibrary.org; *Asst Dir,* Jenni Link; E-mail: jlink@bourbonlibrary.org; Staff 11 (MLS 3, Non-MLS 8)
Founded 1904. Pop 19,729; Circ 132,732
Library Holdings: Bk Vols 42,283; Per Subs 98
Automation Activity & Vendor Info: (Acquisitions) AmLib Library Management System; (Cataloging) AmLib Library Management System; (Circulation) AmLib Library Management System; (ILL) AmLib Library Management System; (OPAC) AmLib Library Management System
Wireless access
Open Mon-Thurs 9-8, Fri & Sat 9-5:30, Sun 1-5
Friends of the Library Group
Bookmobiles: 1

PEWEE VALLEY

S KENTUCKY CORRECTIONAL INSTITUTION FOR WOMEN LIBRARY*, 3000 Ash Ave, 40056. (Mail add: PO Box 337, 40056-0337), SAN 306-3968. Tel: 502-241-8454, Ext 2302. Web Site: corrections.ky.gov/facilities/AI/KCIW. *Librn,* Lisa Wegner; E-mail: lwegner@ky.gov; Staff 1 (MLS 1)
Founded 1973
Library Holdings: Bk Titles 33,292
Restriction: Not open to pub

PIKEVILLE

P PIKE COUNTY PUBLIC LIBRARY DISTRICT*, 119 College St, 41502-1787. (Mail add: PO Box 1197, 41502-1197), SAN 306-249X. Tel: 606-432-9977. FAX: 606-432-9908. Web Site: www.pikelibrary.org. *Dir,* Leean Allen; E-mail: allen@pikelibrary.org
Founded 1970
Library Holdings: Bk Vols 168,472; Per Subs 296
Automation Activity & Vendor Info: (Cataloging) TLC (The Library Corporation); (Circulation) TLC (The Library Corporation); (OPAC) TLC (The Library Corporation)
Open Mon-Fri 8:30-5
Branches: 6
BELFRY PUBLIC, 24371 US Hwy 119 N, Belfry, 41514. (Mail add: PO Box 340, Belfry, 41514), SAN 342-6394. Tel: 606-353-9429. FAX: 330-408-0015.
Open Tues & Thurs 10:30-7, Wed & Fri 9:30-6, Sat 9-5
ELKHORN CITY PUBLIC, 150 E Main St, Elkhorn City, 41522, SAN 375-541X. Tel: 606-754-5451. FAX: 330-248-0020.
Open Tues & Thurs 10:30-7, Wed & Fri 9:30-6, Sat 9-5
LEE AVENUE BRANCH, 126 Lee Ave, 41501. Tel: 606-437-6001. FAX: 606-945-0038.
Open Tues-Fri 10-7, Sat 9-6
PHELPS PUBLIC, 38575 State Hwy 194 E, Phelps, 41553, SAN 328-8773. Tel: 606-456-7860. FAX: 330-248-0027.
Open Tues & Thurs 10-7, Wed & Fri 9:30-6, Sat 9-5
PIKEVILLE PUBLIC, 119 College St, 41501-1787, SAN 376-9941. Tel: 606-432-1285. FAX: 330-838-0023.
Open Mon-Thurs 9-7, Fri & Sat 9-5
VESTA ROBERTS-JOHNSON MEMORIAL LIBRARY, 180 Hwy 610 W, Virgie, 41572. (Mail add: PO Box 548, Virgie, 41572-0548), SAN 321-3331. Tel; 606-639-9839. FAX: 330-247-0035.
Founded 1980
Open Tues & Thurs 10:30-7, Wed & Fri 9:30-6, Sat 9-5
Bookmobiles: 1. Librn, Brenda Griffin. Bk vols 4,000

C UNIVERSITY OF PIKEVILLE*, Frank M Allara Library, 147 Sycamore St, 41501-9118. SAN 306-3976. Tel: 606-218-5617. Web Site: www.upike.edu/Library. *Dir of Libr,* Edna M Fugate; Tel: 606-218-5606, E-mail: ednafugate@upike.edu; *Assoc Librn,* Mary A Harmon; Tel: 606-218-5610, E-mail: MaryHarmon@upike.edu; *Digital Librn, Outreach Librn,* Tyler Kroon; Tel: 606-218-5619, E-mail: tylerkroon@upike.edu; *Ref & Instruction Librn,* Haley Fannin; Tel: 606-218-5609, E-mail: HaleyFannin@upike.edu; Staff 8 (MLS 5, Non-MLS 3)
Founded 1920. Enrl 1,169; Fac 54; Highest Degree: Master
Library Holdings: Bk Titles 61,071; Bk Vols 70,883; Per Subs 357
Subject Interests: Appalachia, Genealogy, Kentucky, Optometry
Automation Activity & Vendor Info: (Acquisitions) Innovative Interfaces, Inc - Sierra; (Cataloging) Innovative Interfaces, Inc - Sierra; (Circulation) Innovative Interfaces, Inc - Sierra; (OPAC) Innovative Interfaces, Inc - Sierra
Wireless access
Partic in Appalachian College Association; Coun of Independent Ky Cols & Univs; LYRASIS; OCLC Online Computer Library Center, Inc
Open Mon-Thurs 7:30am-Midnight, Fri 7:30-5, Sat 9-5, Sun 3-11

CM UNIVERSITY OF PIKEVILLE*, Medical Library, Community Technology Ctr, 3rd Flr, 119 College St, 41501. (Mail add: Kentucky College of Osteopathic Medicine Library, 147 Sycamore St, 41501). Tel: 606-218-5150. E-mail: kycomlibrary@upike.edu. *Med Librn,* Melinda Robertson; Tel: 606-218-5157, E-mail: MelindaRobertson@upike.edu; *Acq, Libr Tech,* Michelle Elswick; E-mail: MichelleElswick@upike.edu
Open Mon-Fri 8:30-5:30

PINEVILLE

CR CLEAR CREEK BAPTIST BIBLE COLLEGE*, Carolyn Boatman Brooks Memorial Library, 300 Clear Creek Rd, 40977. Tel: 606-337-3196. FAX: 606-337-2372. E-mail: library@ccbbc.edu. Web Site: www.ccbbc.edu. *Dir, Libr Serv,* Lynn Kahkola; Staff 2 (MLS 1, Non-MLS 1)
Founded 1926. Enrl 150; Highest Degree: Bachelor
Library Holdings: e-books 22,000; Bk Titles 43,945; Per Subs 120
Automation Activity & Vendor Info: (Cataloging) TLC (The Library Corporation); (Circulation) TLC (The Library Corporation); (Course

Reserve) TLC (The Library Corporation); (ILL) OCLC; (OPAC) TLC (The Library Corporation)
Wireless access
Partic in Christian Library Consortium; KLN
Open Mon, Tues & Thurs 7:45am-10pm, Wed & Fri 7:45-4, Sat 10-2

P PINEVILLE-BELL COUNTY PUBLIC LIBRARY*, 214 Walnut St, 40977. (Mail add: PO Box 1490, 40977-1490), SAN 306-3992. Tel: 606-337-3422. FAX: 606-337-9862. E-mail: pineville@bellcpl.org. Web Site: www.bellcpl.org. *Actg Dir,* Michele Lawson; Tel: 606-248-4812, Fax: 606-248-8766, E-mail: director@bellcpl.org; *Br Mgr, Interim Asst Dir,* Elizabeth Warren; E-mail: pineville@bellcpl.org; *Youth Serv Librn,* Erica Overbay; E-mail: eoverbay@bellcpl.org; Staff 5 (Non-MLS 5)
Founded 1933. Pop 20,300
Library Holdings: Bk Vols 39,000; Per Subs 84
Special Collections: Oral History
Subject Interests: Genealogy, Hist, Local hist
Automation Activity & Vendor Info: (Cataloging) Innovative Interfaces, Inc; (Circulation) Innovative Interfaces, Inc; (ILL) Innovative Interfaces, Inc; (OPAC) Innovative Interfaces, Inc
Open Mon-Fri 10-6, Sat 10-4
Bookmobiles: 1. Librn, Marilou Johnson

PIPPA PASSES

C ALICE LLOYD COLLEGE*, McGaw Library & Learning Center, 100 Purpose Rd, 41844. SAN 306-400X. Tel: 606-368-6112. FAX: 606-368-6212. E-mail: mcgaw_library@hotmail.com. Web Site: www.alc.edu/academics/mcgaw-library-and-learning-center. *Dir,* Jeannie Galloway; Tel: 606-368-6113, E-mail: jeanniegalloway@alc.edu; *Pub Serv Librn,* William Slone; Tel: 606-368-6117, E-mail: williamslone@alc.edu; *Tech Serv Librn,* Janice Hicks; Tel: 606-368-6114, E-mail: janicehicks@alc.edu; *Evening Supvr, Spec Coll,* Jamie Holt; E-mail: jamieholt@alc.edu; Staff 2 (MLS 1, Non-MLS 1)
Founded 1923. Enrl 600; Highest Degree: Bachelor
Library Holdings: e-books 120,000; Bk Vols 74,218; Per Subs 219
Special Collections: Appalachian Oral History; Appalachian Photographic Coll; Children's Literature Coll
Automation Activity & Vendor Info: (Acquisitions) Innovative Interfaces, Inc; (Cataloging) Innovative Interfaces, Inc; (Circulation) Innovative Interfaces, Inc; (Course Reserve) Innovative Interfaces, Inc; (OPAC) Innovative Interfaces, Inc; (Serials) Innovative Interfaces, Inc
Partic in Appalachian College Association; Association of Independent Kentucky Colleges & Universities; Federation of Kentucky Academic Libraries; LYRASIS
Open Mon-Thurs (Winter) 8am-11pm, Fri 8-4:30, Sun 6pm-11pm; Mon-Fri (Summer) 8-4:30
Friends of the Library Group

PRESTONSBURG

J BIG SANDY COMMUNITY & TECHNICAL COLLEGE*, One Bert T Combs Dr, 41653. SAN 306-4034. Tel: 606-886-3863, 606-889-4834. Toll Free Tel: 855-462-7282. FAX: 606-886-8683. Web Site: www.bigsandy.kctcs.edu. *Dir,* Judy K Howell; Tel: 606-889-4750, E-mail: judy.howell@kctcs.edu; Staff 9 (MLS 3, Non-MLS 6)
Founded 1964. Enrl 4,600; Fac 120; Highest Degree: Associate
Jul 2013-Jun 2014. Mats Exp $100,000
Library Holdings: AV Mats 1,432; e-books 64,722; Bk Titles 43,273; Per Subs 178
Special Collections: Eastern Kentucky History Coll
Automation Activity & Vendor Info: (Cataloging) OCLC; (Circulation) Ex Libris Group; (Course Reserve) Ex Libris Group; (ILL) Ex Libris Group; (OPAC) Ex Libris Group
Wireless access
Function: Archival coll, Bk club(s), Computers for patron use, Distance learning, Doc delivery serv, Electronic databases & coll, ILL available, Photocopying/Printing, Wheelchair accessible
Publications: Federation of Kentucky Academic Libraries (FOKAL)
Special Services for the Blind - Magnifiers; ZoomText magnification & reading software
Open Mon-Thurs 8-8, Fri 8-4:30
Departmental Libraries:
MAYO-PAINTSVILLE CAMPUS, Bldg C, 513 Third St, Paintsville, 41240. Tel: 606-789-2831. *Libr Tech,* Carol Talbert; Tel: 606-886-7343, E-mail: carol.talbert@kctcs.edu
Library Holdings: AV Mats 191; Bk Vols 25,000; Per Subs 30
Open Mon-Fri 8-4

P FLOYD COUNTY PUBLIC LIBRARY, 161 N Arnold Ave, 41653. SAN 306-4026. Tel: 606-886-2981. FAX: 606-886-2284. E-mail: fclib.asp@gmail.com. Web Site: www.fclib.org. *Dir,* Jonathan Campbell; E-mail: jcampbell@fclib.org
Founded 1957. Pop 42,379; Circ 123,450
Library Holdings: Bk Vols 71,270; Per Subs 50
Special Collections: Kentucky Coll
Automation Activity & Vendor Info: (Cataloging) Innovative Interfaces, Inc; (Circulation) Innovative Interfaces, Inc; (OPAC) Innovative Interfaces, Inc
Wireless access
Open Mon, Wed & Fri 8:30-5, Tues & Thurs 8:30-6, Sat 8:30-1
Bookmobiles: 1

PRINCETON

P GEORGE COON PUBLIC LIBRARY*, 114 S Harrison St, 42445. (Mail add: PO Box 230, 42445-0230), SAN 306-4042. Tel: 270-365-2884. FAX: 270-365-2892. Web Site: www.georgecoonpubliclibrary.com. *Dir,* Nichelle Faughn; E-mail: nfaughn@gcplibrary.org; *Ch,* Ashley Jones; Staff 1 (Non-MLS 1)
Founded 1913. Pop 12,898; Circ 55,229
Library Holdings: AV Mats 1,786; Bk Titles 26,622; Per Subs 41; Talking Bks 504
Special Collections: Genealogy (Ira Fears Coll), microfilm, bks; Rare Book Coll. Oral History
Automation Activity & Vendor Info: (Cataloging) TLC (The Library Corporation); (Circulation) TLC (The Library Corporation)
Wireless access
Open Mon & Wed-Fri 9-5, Tues 9-7, Sat 9-Noon
Friends of the Library Group

RICHMOND

C EASTERN KENTUCKY UNIVERSITY LIBRARIES*, 103 Crabbe Library, 521 Lancaster Ave, 40475-3102. SAN 342-6068. Tel: 859-622-1790. Interlibrary Loan Service Tel: 859-622-1415. Reference Tel: 859-622-6594. FAX: 859-622-1174. Web Site: www.library.eku.edu. *Dean of Libr,* Betina Gardner; Tel: 859-622-1778, E-mail: betina.gardner@eku.edu; *Archives & Spec Coll Librn, Team Leader,* Jackie Couture; Tel: 859-622-1792, E-mail: jackie.couture@eku.edu; *Pub Serv Librn, Ref & Instruction Librn,* Karen Gilbert; Tel: 859-622-1781, E-mail: karen.gilbert@eku.edu; *Coordr, Pub Serv,* Julie George; Tel: 859-622-3071, E-mail: julie.george@eku.edu; Staff 26 (MLS 22, Non-MLS 4)
Founded 1906. Enrl 12,184; Fac 663; Highest Degree: Master
Library Holdings: Audiobooks 614; AV Mats 14,467; Bks on Deafness & Sign Lang 177; Braille Volumes 74; CDs 5,144; DVDs 714; e-books 4,436; e-journals 18,819; Large Print Bks 143; Microforms 1,330,422; Bk Titles 571,175; Bk Vols 659,342; Per Subs 1,566; Videos 4,858
Special Collections: Learning Resources Center; Madison County-Eastern Kentucky University Law Library Coll; University Archives (Kentuckiana; bks; microfiche; mss). US Document Depository
Subject Interests: Educ, Humanities, Music, Nursing, Occupational therapy
Automation Activity & Vendor Info: (Acquisitions) Ex Libris Group; (Cataloging) Ex Libris Group; (Circulation) Ex Libris Group; (Course Reserve) Ex Libris Group; (ILL) OCLC ILLiad; (OPAC) Ex Libris Group; (Serials) Ex Libris Group
Wireless access
Partic in LYRASIS; OCLC Online Computer Library Center, Inc
Special Services for the Deaf - Assistive tech; Bks on deafness & sign lang; High interest/low vocabulary bks; TDD equip
Special Services for the Blind - Assistive/Adapted tech devices, equip & products
Open Mon-Wed 7am-2am, Thurs 7am-10pm, Fri 7:30-6, Sat 11-6
Friends of the Library Group
Departmental Libraries:
THE ELIZABETH K BAKER MUSIC LIBRARY, Foster Bldg, 521 Lancaster Ave, 40475, SAN 342-6122. Tel: 859-622-1795. FAX: 859-622-1174. Web Site: www.library.eku.edu/music. *Librn,* Dr Greg Engstrom; E-mail: greg.engstrom@eku.edu; *Libr Assoc,* Trudy Conway; E-mail: trudy.conway@eku.edu
Library Holdings: AV Mats 7,064; Music Scores 9,248; Bk Vols 12,182; Per Subs 129
Subject Interests: Music
Partic in LYRASIS
Open Mon-Thurs 8-8, Fri 8-4:30

P MADISON COUNTY PUBLIC LIBRARY*, 507 W Main St, 40475. SAN 375-3093. Tel: 859-623-6704. FAX: 859-623-2032. E-mail: richmond@madisonlibrary.org. Web Site: madisonlibrary.org. *Libr Dir,* Ruthie Maslin; E-mail: rmaslin@madisonlibrary.org; *Youth Serv Librn,* Ari Barron; *Br Serv Supvr,* Paige Beichler; Staff 17 (MLS 3, Non-MLS 14)
Founded 1988. Pop 84,786; Circ 221,325
Library Holdings: CDs 2,856; DVDs 2,360; Bk Vols 94,731; Per Subs 217; Talking Bks 4,502; Videos 6,864
Subject Interests: Genealogy, Kentucky, Spanish
Automation Activity & Vendor Info: (Cataloging) SirsiDynix; (Circulation) SirsiDynix; (OPAC) SirsiDynix
Wireless access

Open Mon-Thurs 9-8, Fri & Sat 9-6, Sun 1-5
Friends of the Library Group
Branches: 1
BEREA BRANCH, 319 Chestnut St, Berea, 40403, SAN 375-3107. Tel: 859-986-7112. FAX: 859-986-7208. E-mail: berea@madisonlibrary.org. *Br Serv Supvr,* Kathy V Hamblin; E-mail: kathyh@madisonlibrary.org; *Youth Serv Librn,* Pat Acevedo; E-mail: patacevedo@madisonlibrary.org
Founded 1988. Pop 72,408
Open Mon-Thurs 9-8, Fri & Sat 9-6
Friends of the Library Group
Bookmobiles: 1. Librn, Beth Madden

RUSSELLVILLE

P LOGAN COUNTY PUBLIC LIBRARY*, 225 Armory Dr, 42276. (Mail add: PO Box 357, 42276), SAN 306-4093. Tel: 270-726-6129. FAX: 270-726-6127. E-mail: librarian@loganlibrary.org. Web Site: loganlibrary.org. *Dir,* King Simpson; E-mail: king@loganlibrary.org; *Adult Prog Coordr,* Tracy Houchens; E-mail: tracy@loganlibrary.org; *Children's Serv Coordr,* Carole Ann Faulkner; E-mail: carole@loganlibrary.org; *Acq, ILL,* Shelly Turner; E-mail: shellyf@loganlibrary.org; *Cat, Tech,* Sherryl Appling; E-mail: sherry@loganlibrary.org; *Ref Serv,* Mark Griffin; E-mail: mark@loganlibrary.org; *Ref Serv,* Ruth Mazour; E-mail: ruth@loganlibrary.org; *Ref Serv,* Beverly Terry; E-mail: beverly@loganlibrary.org; Staff 3 (MLS 1, Non-MLS 2)
Founded 1966. Pop 28,000; Circ 350,000
Library Holdings: Bk Vols 42,991; Per Subs 32
Special Collections: Oral History
Subject Interests: Census, Family hist, Genealogy, Local newsp, Photog hist
Automation Activity & Vendor Info: (Acquisitions) Evolve; (Cataloging) Evolve; (Circulation) Evolve; (Course Reserve) Evolve; (ILL) OCLC FirstSearch; (OPAC) Evolve
Wireless access
Special Services for the Blind - Bks on CD; Large print bks; Large screen computer & software
Open Mon-Thurs 9-8, Fri 9-5, Sat 10-5, Sun 2-5
Friends of the Library Group
Branches: 2
ADAIRVILLE BRANCH, 101 Church St, Adairville, 42202, SAN 320-8141. Tel: 270-539-4601. FAX: 270-539-4601. *Librn,* Sharon Fuller; E-mail: sharon@loganlibrary.org
Library Holdings: Bk Vols 2,027
Open Mon & Wed 1:30-5:30, Fri 2-5:30
Friends of the Library Group
AUBURN BRANCH, 433 W Main St, Auburn, 42206, SAN 320-8168. Tel: 270-542-8180. FAX: 270-542-8180. *Librn,* Erdene Hughes; E-mail: erdene@loganlibrary.org
Library Holdings: Bk Vols 2,129
Open Mon & Fri 12-5, Wed 9-5
Friends of the Library Group

SALYERSVILLE

P MAGOFFIN COUNTY PUBLIC LIBRARY*, 141 Church St, 41465. (Mail add: PO Box 435, 41465-0435), SAN 306-4115. Tel: 606-349-2411. FAX: 606-349-1120. E-mail: maglib@foothills.net. Web Site: www.youseemore.com/magoffinpl. *Dir,* Melanie A Cain; E-mail: melanieac@bellsouth.net
Pop 13,515; Circ 29,747
Library Holdings: Bk Vols 22,000; Per Subs 15
Wireless access
Open Mon, Wed & Fri 9-5, Tues & Thurs 9-6

SANDY HOOK

P ROCKY J ADKINS PUBLIC LIBRARY*, 207 S KY Rte 7, 41171. (Mail add: PO Box 750, 41171-0750). Tel: 606-738-5796. FAX: 606-738-4980. E-mail: ellcolib@mrtc.com. *Dir,* Belinda Smith; *Asst Dir,* Rosemary Moore; Staff 1 (Non-MLS 1)
Library Holdings: Audiobooks 463; Braille Volumes 152; CDs 476; DVDs 1,657; e-journals 31; Bk Vols 18,492; Per Subs 21
Automation Activity & Vendor Info: (Acquisitions) Follett Software; (Cataloging) Follett Software; (Circulation) Follett Software; (OPAC) Follett Software
Wireless access
Open Mon-Fri 8:30-5

SCOTTSVILLE

P ALLEN COUNTY PUBLIC LIBRARY*, 106 W Public Sq, 42164. (Mail add: PO Box 1447, 42164-1447), SAN 306-4123. Tel: 270-237-3861. FAX: 270-237-4095. E-mail: info@allencountylibrary.com. Web Site: www.allencountylibrary.com. *Dir,* Sheila Stovall; E-mail: sstovall@allencountylibrary.com; Staff 6 (Non-MLS 6)
Founded 1953. Pop 17,128; Circ 115,876
Library Holdings: Bk Vols 27,891; Per Subs 101
Special Collections: Kentucky Coll; Large Christian Fiction Coll; Large Type Books
Automation Activity & Vendor Info: (Acquisitions) TLC (The Library Corporation); (Cataloging) TLC (The Library Corporation); (Circulation) TLC (The Library Corporation); (Course Reserve) TLC (The Library Corporation); (OPAC) TLC (The Library Corporation)
Partic in Barron County Library Services
Open Mon-Thurs 9-7, Fri & Sat 9-4
Friends of the Library Group
Bookmobiles: 1

SHELBYVILLE

P SHELBY COUNTY PUBLIC LIBRARY*, 309 Eighth St, 40065. SAN 306-4131. Tel: 502-633-3803. FAX: 502-633-4025. Administration E-mail: admin@scplibrary.net. Web Site: www.youseemore.com/shelby. *Dir,* Pamela W Federspiel; *Circ,* Brooklyn Montfort; *Circ,* Whitney Stephens; *Outreach Serv,* Amanda Perry; *Ref,* Shana Shack; *Tech Serv,* Ann Blansett; Staff 5 (MLS 1, Non-MLS 4)
Founded 1899. Pop 34,000; Circ 155,000
Library Holdings: Bk Vols 52,000; Per Subs 63
Special Collections: Shelby County Historical Records, micro
Automation Activity & Vendor Info: (Cataloging) TLC (The Library Corporation); (Circulation) TLC (The Library Corporation); (OPAC) TLC (The Library Corporation)
Wireless access
Open Mon-Thurs 9-7, Fri 9-5:30, Sat 9-1:30
Friends of the Library Group
Bookmobiles: 1

SHEPHERDSVILLE

P BULLITT COUNTY PUBLIC LIBRARY*, Ridgway Memorial Library, 127 N Walnut St, 40165-6083. (Mail add: PO Box 99, 40165-0099), SAN 342-6157. Tel: 502-543-7675. Reference Tel: 502-543-7675, Ext 2002. Administration Tel: 502-543-7675, Ext 2006. FAX: 502-543-5487. E-mail: reference@bcplib.org. Web Site: www.bcplib.org. *Dir,* Joe Schweiss; E-mail: joe@bcplib.org; *Asst Dir, Mgr, Human Res,* Jennifer Nippert; E-mail: jnippert@bcplib.org; Staff 51 (MLS 1, Non-MLS 50)
Founded 1954. Pop 75,653; Circ 346,000
Library Holdings: Bk Vols 129,167; Per Subs 131
Special Collections: Oral History
Automation Activity & Vendor Info: (Cataloging) TLC (The Library Corporation); (Circulation) TLC (The Library Corporation); (OPAC) TLC (The Library Corporation)
Wireless access
Function: AV serv, ILL available, Photocopying/Printing, Prog for children & young adult, Summer reading prog, Wheelchair accessible
Open Mon-Thurs 9-8, Fri & Sat 9-5, Sun 1-5
Branches: 4
HILLVIEW BRANCH, 155 Terry Blvd, Hillview, Louisville, 40229. Tel: 502-957-5759. FAX: 502-957-0448. E-mail: hil@bcplib.org. *Br Mgr,* Mona Timberlake
Open Mon-Thurs 9-8, Fri & Sat 9-5
LEBANON JUNCTION BRANCH, 11382 S Preston Hwy, Lebanon Junction, 40150, SAN 342-6181. Tel: 502-833-4648. FAX: 502-833-9877. E-mail: ljl@bcplib.org. *Br Mgr,* Tobee Taylor
Open Mon-Thurs 9-8, Fri & Sat 9-5
MOUNT WASHINGTON BRANCH, 214 N Bardstown Rd, Mount Washington, 40047, SAN 342-6211. Tel: 502-538-7560. FAX: 502-538-2696. E-mail: mwl@bcplib.org. *Br Mgr,* Pam Rowe
Open Mon-Thurs 9-8, Fri & Sat 9-5
NICHOLS BRANCH, 10729 Hwy 44 W, West Point, 40177. Tel: 502-324-7699. FAX: 502-922-4355. E-mail: nil@bcplib.org. *Br Mgr,* Stephanie Simmons
Open Mon-Thurs 11-7, Fri & Sat 9-5

SOMERSET

P PULASKI COUNTY PUBLIC LIBRARY*, 304 S Main St, 42501. SAN 342-6270. Tel: 606-679-8401. FAX: 606-679-1779. E-mail: pulaski.library@pulaskilibrary.com. Web Site: www.pulaskipubliclibrary.org. *Dir,* Charlotte Kay Keeney; E-mail: charlotte.keeney@pulaskilibrary.com; *Ch,* Position Currently Open; *Circ Librn,* Lori Yeager; E-mail: lori.yeager@pulaskilibrary.com; *Ref Librn,* Ruth Thomas; E-mail: ruth.thomas@pulaskilibrary.com; *Teen Librn,* Shawn Spaw; E-mail: shawn.spaw@pulaskilibrary.com; Staff 3 (Non-MLS 3)
Founded 1905. Pop 61,000; Circ 386,577
Library Holdings: AV Mats 18,112; Bk Vols 98,469; Per Subs 210
Special Collections: Oral History
Subject Interests: Genealogy
Automation Activity & Vendor Info: (Cataloging) TLC (The Library Corporation); (Circulation) TLC (The Library Corporation); (OPAC) TLC (The Library Corporation)
Wireless access

Open Mon-Fri 9-7, Sat 9-5
Restriction: Borrowing requests are handled by ILL
Friends of the Library Group
Branches: 4
BURNSIDE BRANCH, 85 E French Ave, Burnside, 42519. (Mail add: PO Box 7, Burnside, 42519-0007), SAN 342-6300. Tel: 606-561-5287. FAX: 606-561-5287. E-mail: burnside.library@pulaskilibrary.com. *Br Mgr,* Katie Nichols; E-mail: katie.nichols@pulaskilibrary.com
Open Mon, Wed & Fri 10-5, Tues & Thurs 10-7, Sat 9-Noon
NANCY BRANCH, Mills Springs Plaza, Nancy, 42544. (Mail add: PO Box 88, Nancy, 42544-0088), SAN 342-6335. Tel: 606-636-4241. FAX: 606-636-4241. E-mail: nancy.library@pulaskilibrary.com. *Librn,* J Noelene Whitaker; E-mail: noelene.whitaker@pulaskilibrary.com
Open Mon, Wed & Fri 10-5, Tues & Thurs 10-7, Sat 9-Noon
SCIENCE HILL BRANCH, 215 Main St, Science Hill, 42553. (Mail add: PO Box 448, Science Hill, 42553-0448), SAN 342-636X. Tel: 606-423-4221. FAX: 606-423-4221. E-mail: sciencehill.library@pulaskilibrary.com. *Librn,* Maggie Miracle; E-mail: maggie.miracle@pulaskilibrary.com
Open Mon, Wed & Fri 10-5, Tues & Thurs 10-7, Sat 9-Noon
SHOPVILLE BRANCH, 144 Shopville Rd, 42503, SAN 377-6727. Tel: 606-274-1671. FAX: 606-274-1671. E-mail: shopville.library@newwavecomm.com. *Librn,* Melanie Taylor
Founded 1995
Open Mon, Wed & Fri 10-5, Tues & Thurs 10-7, Sat 9-Noon
Bookmobiles: 1. Librn, Lindsey Meade

J SOMERSET COMMUNITY COLLEGE LIBRARY*, Harold B Strunk Learning Resource Ctr, 808 Monticello St, 42501. SAN 306-414X. Tel: 606-451-6710. Interlibrary Loan Service Tel: 606-451-6713. Toll Free Tel: 877-629-9722. FAX: 606-679-5139. Web Site: www.somerset.kctcs.edu/academics/learning_commons. *Dir, Pub Serv,* Mary Taylor Huntsman; E-mail: mary.huntsman@kctcs.edu; Staff 7 (MLS 3, Non-MLS 4)
Founded 1965. Enrl 3,292; Fac 310; Highest Degree: Associate
Library Holdings: Audiobooks 92; CDs 389; DVDs 1,263; e-books 52,219; Bk Titles 27,087; Bk Vols 32,535; Per Subs 144
Special Collections: Local Newspaper, microfilm
Automation Activity & Vendor Info: (Cataloging) Ex Libris Group; (Circulation) Ex Libris Group; (Course Reserve) Ex Libris Group; (OPAC) Ex Libris Group
Wireless access
Partic in LYRASIS
Special Services for the Deaf - Staff with knowledge of sign lang
Open Mon-Thurs 7:45-7, Fri 7:45-4:30, Sat 10-4

SPRINGFIELD

P WASHINGTON COUNTY PUBLIC LIBRARY*, 333 W Main St, 40069. SAN 306-4158. Tel: 859-336-7655. FAX: 859-336-0256. E-mail: info@wcplky.org. Web Site: www1.youseemore.com/washingtoncountypl. *Dir,* Tara O'Hagan; E-mail: director@wcplky.org; *Outreach Coordr,* Diana Morgan; E-mail: diana.morgan@wcplky.org; Staff 11 (MLS 1, Non-MLS 10)
Founded 1964. Pop 12,063; Circ 99,435
Special Collections: Elizabeth Madox Roberts Coll. Oral History
Automation Activity & Vendor Info: (Acquisitions) TLC (The Library Corporation); (Cataloging) TLC (The Library Corporation); (Circulation) TLC (The Library Corporation); (ILL) OCLC WorldShare Interlibrary Loan; (OPAC) TLC (The Library Corporation); (Serials) TLC (The Library Corporation)
Wireless access
Function: 24/7 Online cat, Activity rm, Adult bk club, After school storytime, Archival coll, Audiobks via web, Bk club(s), Bks on CD, Chess club, Children's prog, Computer training, Computers for patron use, Electronic databases & coll, Free DVD rentals, Holiday prog, Home delivery & serv to seniorr ctr & nursing homes, Homebound delivery serv, ILL available, Internet access, Magazines, Magnifiers for reading, Mail & tel request accepted, Meeting rooms, Microfiche/film & reading machines, Movies, Music CDs, Online cat, Outreach serv, Outside serv via phone, mail, e-mail & web, OverDrive digital audio bks, Photocopying/Printing, Preschool outreach, Preschool reading prog, Prog for adults, Prog for children & young adult, Scanner, Senior computer classes, Senior outreach, Serves people with intellectual disabilities, Spoken cassettes & CDs, Spoken cassettes & DVDs, Story hour, Study rm, Summer & winter reading prog, Summer reading prog, Tax forms, Teen prog, Telephone ref, VHS videos, Wheelchair accessible, Winter reading prog
Open Mon, Tues, Wed & Thurs 10-8, Fri 10-5, Sat 10-3
Bookmobiles: 1

STANFORD

P LINCOLN COUNTY PUBLIC LIBRARY*, 201 Lancaster St, 40484. SAN 306-4174. Tel: 606-365-7513. FAX: 606-365-5566. Web Site: www.lcplinfo.org. *Dir,* Amanda Gearhart; E-mail: director@lcplinfo.org; *Asst Dir,* Angela Hensley; *Outreach Librn,* Lisa McCullough; *Children's & Teen Serv,* Amanda Wheeler
Pop 19,000; Circ 136,000
Library Holdings: Bk Vols 30,000; Per Subs 66
Automation Activity & Vendor Info: (Cataloging) Book Systems; (Circulation) Book Systems
Wireless access
Open Mon, Wed & Fri 9-6, Tues & Thurs 9-8, Sat 9-3
Bookmobiles: 1. Librn, Lisa McCullough

STANTON

P POWELL COUNTY PUBLIC LIBRARY*, 725 Breckenridge St, 40380. SAN 306-4182. Tel: 606-663-4511. FAX: 606-663-4346. Web Site: www.pcplky.org. *Dir,* Allison Vanlandingham; E-mail: avanlandingham@pcplky.org; *Adult Serv,* Elizabeth Short; *Youth Serv,* Amy Ashley
Founded 1964. Pop 13,237; Circ 92,402
Library Holdings: Bk Vols 20,000; Per Subs 64
Special Collections: Genealogy Coll (Kentucky Room); New Readers, large print
Automation Activity & Vendor Info: (Cataloging) Book Systems
Wireless access
Open Mon, Tues & Thurs 9-7, Wed & Fri 9-5, Sat 10-3
Friends of the Library Group
Bookmobiles: 1. Librn, Elizabeth Short

TAYLORSVILLE

P SPENCER COUNTY PUBLIC LIBRARY, 168 Taylorsville Rd, 40071. SAN 320-8214. Tel: 502-477-8137. FAX: 502-477-5033. E-mail: scpl@spencercolibrary.us. Web Site: www.spencercountylibrary.us. *Dir,* Debra Lawson; E-mail: lawson_director@spencercolibrary.us; *Asst Dir, Tech,* Lisa Johnson; *Adult Serv,* Stacy Tiller
Pop 17,061; Circ 48,425
Library Holdings: Audiobooks 1,120; DVDs 3,094; e-books 14,765; Large Print Bks 434; Bk Vols 43,000; Per Subs 32
Special Collections: Kentucky, Genealogy
Automation Activity & Vendor Info: (Cataloging) Book Systems; (Circulation) Book Systems; (ILL) OCLC; (OPAC) Book Systems
Wireless access
Partic in Ky Libr Asn; Midwest Collaborative for Library Services
Open Mon & Wed 10-6, Tues & Thurs 10-7, Fri 10-4, Sat 10-3
Friends of the Library Group

TOMPKINSVILLE

P MONROE COUNTY PUBLIC LIBRARY*, William B Harlan Memorial Library, 500 W Fourth St, 42167. SAN 306-4190. Tel: 270-487-5301. FAX: 270-487-5309. Web Site: www.wbhmlibrary.org. *Dir,* Monica Edwards; E-mail: monicae@wbhmlibrary.org; *Asst Dir, Ch,* Brandi Stewart; *Pub Serv Librn,* Cindy Strode; *Circ, Genealogy Serv,* Stephanie Hestand
Founded 1966. Pop 12,353
Automation Activity & Vendor Info: (Cataloging) SirsiDynix; (Circulation) SirsiDynix
Wireless access
Function: Adult bk club, Art exhibits, Bk club(s), Bks on CD, CD-ROM, Children's prog, Computers for patron use, Electronic databases & coll, Family literacy, Free DVD rentals, Holiday prog, Home delivery & serv to seniorr ctr & nursing homes, Homebound delivery serv, ILL available, Internet access, Mail & tel request accepted, Microfiche/film & reading machines, Online cat, Online ref, Outreach serv, Photocopying/Printing, Preschool outreach, Preschool reading prog, Printer for laptops & handheld devices, Prog for children & young adult, Ref serv available, Story hour, Summer reading prog, Tax forms, Telephone ref, Wheelchair accessible, Workshops
Open Mon 8:30-6, Tues-Fri 8:30-5, Sat 9-2
Friends of the Library Group
Bookmobiles: 1. Librn, Cindy Strode

TRAPPIST

SR THE ABBEY OF GETHSEMANI LIBRARY*, 3642 Monks Rd, 40051. SAN 306-4204. Tel: 502-549-3117. FAX: 502-549-4124. Web Site: www.monks.org. *Library Contact,* Fr Gaetan Blanchette; Tel: 502-549-4406
Founded 1848
Library Holdings: Bk Vols 40,000
Special Collections: Cistercian Monastic History & Liturgy, rare bks; Saint Bernard & DeRance, rare bks; Thomas Merton Coll
Subject Interests: Philos, Relig, Theol

VANCEBURG

P LEWIS COUNTY PUBLIC LIBRARY*, 27 Third St, 41179. SAN 306-4220. Tel: 606-796-2532. FAX: 606-796-0760. E-mail: lewiscountylibrary@gmail.com. Web Site: www.lewiscountylibrary.net. *Dir,*

Marilyn Conway; *Asst Dir,* Kathy Hartley; *Ch,* Alison Spangler; Staff 3 (Non-MLS 3)
Founded 1954. Pop 14,545; Circ 82,402
Library Holdings: Bk Vols 31,000; Per Subs 50
Special Collections: Oral History
Automation Activity & Vendor Info: (Acquisitions) Follett Software; (Cataloging) Follett Software; (Circulation) Follett Software; (Course Reserve) Follett Software; (ILL) OCLC WorldShare Interlibrary Loan; (OPAC) Follett Software
Wireless access
Partic in OCLC Online Computer Library Center, Inc; Tenn-Share
Open Mon & Fri 8:30-5, Tues & Thurs 8:30-6, Wed 10-2, Sat 8:30-12:30
Friends of the Library Group

VERSAILLES

S WOODFORD COUNTY HISTORICAL SOCIETY*, Genealogy Library, 121 Rose Hill, 40383-1221. Tel: 859-873-6786. E-mail: woodfordkyhs@gmail.com. Web Site: www.woodfordcountykyhistoricalsociety.com. *Curator,* Martha Martin; *Asst Curator,* Brandon Nichols
Founded 1966
Library Holdings: Bk Titles 3,500
Subject Interests: Genealogy, Hist
Publications: Woodford Heritage News (Newsletter)
Open Tues-Sat 10-4

P WOODFORD COUNTY LIBRARY*, 115 N Main St, 40383-1289. SAN 306-4247. Tel: 859-873-5191. FAX: 859-873-1542. E-mail: ref@woodfordlibrary.org. Web Site: www.woodfordcountylibrary.com. *Dir,* Karen Kasacavage; E-mail: kkasacavage@woodfordlibrary.org; *Asst Dir,* John Crawford; E-mail: jcrawford@woodfordlibrary.org; Staff 38 (MLS 10, Non-MLS 28)
Founded 1967. Pop 25,000; Circ 210,000
Library Holdings: Bk Vols 39,744; Per Subs 110
Subject Interests: Local hist
Automation Activity & Vendor Info: (Cataloging) TLC (The Library Corporation); (Circulation) TLC (The Library Corporation)
Wireless access
Open Mon-Fri 9-6, Sat 1-5
Friends of the Library Group
Branches: 1
MIDWAY BRANCH, 400 Northside Dr, Midway, 40347. Tel: 859-846-4014. FAX: 859-846-4035. *Br Mgr,* Stacy Thurman; E-mail: sthurman@woodfordlibrary.org; Staff 1 (MLS 1)
Library Holdings: AV Mats 2,000; Bk Vols 15,000; Per Subs 40
Open Mon-Fri 9-6, Sat 1-5
Friends of the Library Group

WARSAW

P GALLATIN COUNTY PUBLIC LIBRARY*, 209 W Market St, 41095. (Mail add: PO Box 848, 41095-0848), SAN 321-0510. Tel: 859-567-7323. FAX: 859-567-4750. Web Site: www.gallatincountylibrary.org. *Dir,* Shirley S Warnick; Tel: 859-567-2786, E-mail: shirley@gallatincpl.org; *Ch,* Amy Dickerson; E-mail: amy@gallatincpl.org; *Circ Librn,* Bonnie Roberts; E-mail: Bonnie@gallatincpl.org; *Genealogy Librn, Tech Librn,* Brittany Skinner; E-mail: brittany@gallatincpl.org; *Asst Ch, Circ, Teen Librn,* Emily Arnold; E-mail: emily@gallatincpl.org; *Asst Librn, Cat,* Alice Johnson; E-mail: alice@gallatincpl.org; *Circ/Per, Outreach Serv,* Jessica Gay; Tel: 859-567-2786, E-mail: jessica@gallatincpl.org; Staff 1 (Non-MLS 1)
Founded 1978. Pop 8,035; Circ 56,433
Jul 2019-Jun 2020 Income (Main Library Only) $836,575, State $11,000, Locally Generated Income $825,575. Mats Exp $73,700, Books $45,000, Per/Ser (Incl. Access Fees) $2,200, Other Print Mats $2,000, AV Mat $11,000, Electronic Ref Mat (Incl. Access Fees) $12,000, Presv $1,500. Sal $226,514 (Prof $59,462)
Library Holdings: Audiobooks 1,770; AV Mats 5,830; Bks on Deafness & Sign Lang 5; CDs 735; DVDs 3,942; e-books 442,390; Electronic Media & Resources 4; Large Print Bks 1,235; Bk Titles 30,927; Per Subs 96; Videos 2,758
Automation Activity & Vendor Info: (Acquisitions) Book Systems; (Cataloging) Book Systems; (Circulation) Book Systems; (ILL) OCLC Online; (OPAC) Book Systems
Wireless access
Function: 24/7 Electronic res, 24/7 Online cat, Accelerated reader prog, Adult bk club, Archival coll, Audiobks via web, Bi-weekly Writer's Group, Bk club(s), Bks on CD, Children's prog, Computer training, Computers for patron use, E-Readers, Equip loans & repairs, Free DVD rentals, Holiday prog, Home delivery & serv to seniorr ctr & nursing homes, Homebound delivery serv, ILL available, Instruction & testing, Internet access, Large print keyboards, Magazines, Magnifiers for reading, Meeting rooms, Movies, Music CDs, Notary serv, Online cat, Online ref, Outreach serv, Photocopying/Printing, Preschool outreach, Prog for adults, Prog for children & young adult, Scanner, Senior computer classes, Senior outreach, Story hour, Study rm, Summer reading prog, Tax forms, Teen prog, Wheelchair accessible
Special Services for the Deaf - Bks on deafness & sign lang
Special Services for the Blind - Accessible computers; Aids for in-house use; BiFolkal kits; Bks on CD; Computer access aids; Large print bks; Large screen computer & software; Magnifiers; PC for people with disabilities; Photo duplicator for making large print
Open Mon, Tues, Wed & Thurs 9-7, Fri 9-5, Sat 9-2

WEST LIBERTY

S EASTERN KENTUCKY CORRECTIONAL COMPLEX LIBRARY*, 200 Road to Justice, 41472. Tel: 606-743-2800. FAX: 606-743-2811. Web Site: corrections.ky.gov/depts/AI/EKCC. *Library Contact,* James Whitt; E-mail: jamese.whitt@ky.gov
Library Holdings: Bk Vols 18,000; Per Subs 35
Restriction: Not open to pub

P MORGAN COUNTY PUBLIC LIBRARY*, 151 University Dr, 41472. SAN 306-4255. Tel: 606-743-4151. FAX: 606-743-2170. E-mail: morgancountypubliclibrary@gmail.com. Web Site: www.youseemore.com/mcpl. *Libr Dir,* Allison Ennis; *Asst Dir, Children & Youth Serv Librn,* Aaron Gibbs; E-mail: assistantdirector@gmail.com
Founded 1965. Pop 11,406; Circ 76,576
Library Holdings: Bk Vols 30,000; Per Subs 29
Subject Interests: Genealogy
Automation Activity & Vendor Info: (Cataloging) TLC (The Library Corporation); (Circulation) TLC (The Library Corporation)
Open Mon, Tues, Thurs & Fri 9-7, Wed 9-5, Sat 10-3

WHITESBURG

P LETCHER COUNTY PUBLIC LIBRARY DISTRICT*, Harry M Caudill Memorial Library, 220 Main St, 41858. SAN 342-6459. Tel: 606-633-7547. FAX: 606-633-3407. E-mail: hmclib@lcld.org. Web Site: www.lcld.org/harry-m.-caudill.html. *Dir,* Alita Vogel; E-mail: avogel@lcld.org; *Head Librn,* Vicki Hurst; *Ch,* Tessa Caudill
Founded 1952. Pop 25,277; Circ 124,667
Jul 2012-Jun 2013 Income (Main & Associated Libraries) $1,083,093, State $27,315, Federal $1,980, County $1,037,630, Other $16,168. Mats Exp $112,307, Books $70,605, Per/Ser (Incl. Access Fees) $3,983, Other Print Mats $6,643, AV Equip $10,153, AV Mat $12,098, Electronic Ref Mat (Incl. Access Fees) $8,825. Sal $234,894 (Prof $65,605)
Library Holdings: Audiobooks 2,255; AV Mats 544; CDs 2,257; DVDs 5,938; e-books 57,093; Electronic Media & Resources 2; Large Print Bks 2,000; Bk Titles 96,000; Bk Vols 100,856; Per Subs 191; Videos 2,330
Subject Interests: Genealogy, Local hist
Automation Activity & Vendor Info: (Cataloging) TLC (The Library Corporation); (Circulation) TLC (The Library Corporation); (ILL) OCLC; (OPAC) TLC (The Library Corporation); (Serials) TLC (The Library Corporation)
Wireless access
Open Mon & Wed-Fri 9-5, Tues 9-7, Sat 9-4
Branches: 3
BLACKEY BRANCH, 295 Main St Loop, Blackey, 41804. (Mail add: PO Box 337, Blackey, 41804), SAN 374-4566. Tel: 606-633-4013. FAX: 606-632-9808. E-mail: blackeypublib@lcld.org. Web Site: www.lcld.org/blackey.html. *Head Librn,* Mary Grace Raglin; *Asst Librn,* Nettie Combs
Automation Activity & Vendor Info: (Acquisitions) TLC (The Library Corporation); (Course Reserve) TLC (The Library Corporation)
Open Mon-Fri 9-5, Sat 9-4
FLEMING NEON PUBLIC LIBRARY, 1008 Hwy 317, Neon, 41840. (Mail add: PO Box 236, Neon, 41840-0236), SAN 342-6513. Tel: 606-855-7913. FAX: 606-855-4565. E-mail: lwlib@lcld.org. Web Site: www.lcld.org/fleming-neon.html. *Head Librn,* Jenay Ellen Hall; E-mail: ejenay@bellsouth.net; *Asst Librn,* Patricia Brashear
Pop 1,600
Open Mon-Wed & Fri 9-5, Thurs 9-7, Sat 9-1
JENKINS PUBLIC, 9543 Hwy 805, Jenkins, 41537. (Mail add: PO Box 687, Jenkins, 41537-0687), SAN 342-6483. Tel: 606-832-4101. FAX: 606-832-0040. E-mail: jplib@lcld.org. Web Site: www.lcld.org/jenkins.html. *Head Librn,* Peggy Bentley; *Libr Asst,* Missy Hall
Automation Activity & Vendor Info: (Course Reserve) TLC (The Library Corporation)
Open Mon 9-7, Tues-Fri 9-5, Sat 9-1
Bookmobiles: 1. Librn, Legina Adams

J SOUTHEAST KENTUCKY COMMUNITY & TECHNICAL COLLEGE*, Whitesburg Campus Library, Two Long Ave, 41858. SAN 372-6959. Tel: 606-633-0279. FAX: 606-633-7225. Web Site: www.southeast.kctcs.edu/current-students/library. *Campus Libr Dir,* Mitchell Caudill; Staff 2 (MLS 1, Non-MLS 1)
Founded 1990

Library Holdings: Bk Vols 4,800; Per Subs 38
Automation Activity & Vendor Info: (Cataloging) Ex Libris Group; (Circulation) Ex Libris Group; (OPAC) Ex Libris Group
Wireless access
Function: For res purposes
Open Mon-Fri 8-4:30

WHITLEY CITY

P MCCREARY COUNTY PUBLIC LIBRARY DISTRICT*, Six N Main St, 42653. (Mail add: PO Box 8, 42653-0008), SAN 320-4812. Tel: 606-376-8738. FAX: 606-376-3631. E-mail: mcpl@highland.net. Web Site: www.mccrearylibrary.org. *Dir,* Kay Morrow; *Head, Circ,* Debbie Lyons; *Ch Serv,* Holly Daugherty; Staff 1 (Non-MLS 1)
Founded 1975. Pop 17,190; Circ 80,821
Jul 2013-Jun 2014 Income $404,303, State $46,303, Federal $60, County $338,627, Locally Generated Income $19,313. Mats Exp $54,023, Books $31,198, Per/Ser (Incl. Access Fees) $1,160, AV Mat $6,065, Electronic Ref Mat (Incl. Access Fees) $15,600. Sal $190,196 (Prof $49,000)
Library Holdings: Bks on Deafness & Sign Lang 10; CDs 216; DVDs 3,555; Large Print Bks 1,550; Microforms 100; Bk Titles 51,595; Bk Vols 51,850; Per Subs 35; Talking Bks 883; Videos 1,276
Special Collections: Pictorial History of McCreary County. Oral History
Automation Activity & Vendor Info: (Acquisitions) Follett Software; (Cataloging) Follett Software; (Circulation) Follett Software; (ILL) OCLC FirstSearch
Wireless access
Function: ILL available
Special Services for the Deaf - Video & TTY relay via computer
Special Services for the Blind - Audio mat
Open Mon & Thurs 9-7, Tues, Wed & Fri 9-5:30, Sat 9-4
Bookmobiles: 1

WICKLIFFE

P BALLARD-CARLISLE-LIVINGSTON COUNTY PUBLIC LIBRARY*, 257 N Fourth St, 42087. SAN 320-4804. Tel: 270-335-5059. *Head Librn,* Mary Silgals; E-mail: marysilgals@gmail.com
Founded 1981
Library Holdings: AV Mats 2,563; Bk Vols 23,421; Per Subs 54
Subject Interests: Genealogy
Wireless access
Open Thurs & Fri 9-4
Friends of the Library Group

WILLIAMSBURG

C UNIVERSITY OF THE CUMBERLANDS, Grover M Hermann Library, 821 Walnut St, 40769. SAN 306-4263. Tel: 606-539-4329. Administration Tel: 606-539-4328. FAX: 606-539-4317. Web Site: www.ucumberlands.edu/library. *Libr Dir,* Jan Wren; Tel: 606-539-4328, E-mail: jan.wren@ucumberlands.edu; *Ref & Instruction Librn,* Carrie Byrd; Tel: 606-539-4160, E-mail: carrie.byrd@ucumberlands.edu; *Tech Serv Librn,* Whitney Taylor; Tel: 606-539-4464, E-mail: whitney.taylor@ucumberlands.edu; Staff 6 (MLS 3, Non-MLS 3)
Founded 1889. Enrl 14,791; Fac 150; Highest Degree: Doctorate
Library Holdings: AV Mats 390; e-books 299,234; e-journals 103,463; Electronic Media & Resources 101; Bk Vols 75,680
Special Collections: Children's Coll; Steele-Reese Appalachian Coll. US Document Depository
Automation Activity & Vendor Info: (Cataloging) Ex Libris Group; (Circulation) Ex Libris Group; (OPAC) Ex Libris Group
Wireless access
Partic in Association of Independent Kentucky Colleges & Universities

P WHITLEY COUNTY LIBRARY*, 285 S Third St, 40769. SAN 306-4271. Tel: 606-549-0818. FAX: 606-539-9242. E-mail: whitleylib@gmail.com. Web Site: www.whitleylibrary.org. *Dir,* Greg Meadors; *Ch,* Shonna Brown; *Circ Supvr,* Betty Croley
Founded 1960. Pop 33,396; Circ 124,937
Library Holdings: Bk Vols 25,000; Per Subs 65
Automation Activity & Vendor Info: (Acquisitions) TLC (The Library Corporation); (Cataloging) TLC (The Library Corporation); (Circulation) TLC (The Library Corporation); (Course Reserve) TLC (The Library Corporation); (OPAC) TLC (The Library Corporation)
Open Mon & Thurs 9-8, Tues, Wed & Fri 9-6, Sat 9-2
Bookmobiles: 1

WILLIAMSTOWN

P GRANT COUNTY PUBLIC LIBRARY DISTRICT*, 201 Barnes Rd, 41097-9482. SAN 306-428X. Tel: 859-824-2080. FAX: 859-824-2083. E-mail: info@grantlib.org. Web Site: www.grantlib.org. *Dir,* Susan Nimersheim; E-mail: s.nimersheim@grantlib.org; *Pub Serv Librn,* Melissa Wallace; E-mail: m.wallace@grantlib.org; *Reader Serv Librn,* Angie Gabbard; E-mail: a.gabbard@grantlib.org; *Cat,* Cora Walter; E-mail: c.walter@grantlib.org; *Youth Serv,* Geneva Hoffman; E-mail: g.hoffman@grantlib.org. Subject Specialists: *Adult fiction, Illinois,* Angie Gabbard; Staff 6 (MLS 4, Non-MLS 2)
Founded 1956. Pop 24,610; Circ 124,394
Library Holdings: AV Mats 3,004; CDs 793; DVDs 1,900; Large Print Bks 310; Bk Vols 35,132; Per Subs 96; Talking Bks 600; Videos 232
Special Collections: Genealogy Coll; Kentuckiana; Pedometers
Wireless access
Function: Bk club(s), Bks on CD, Children's prog, Computers for patron use, Doc delivery serv, E-Readers, Electronic databases & coll, Free DVD rentals, Home delivery & serv to seniorr ctr & nursing homes, Homebound delivery serv, ILL available, Magazines, Mango lang, Microfiche/film & reading machines, Music CDs, Notary serv, Online cat, Outreach serv, OverDrive digital audio bks, Photocopying/Printing, Preschool outreach, Printer for laptops & handheld devices, Prog for adults, Prog for children & young adult, Satellite serv, Senior outreach, Story hour, Summer & winter reading prog, Summer reading prog, Tax forms, Teen prog, Wheelchair accessible, Winter reading prog
Open Mon-Thurs 9-8, Fri & Sat 9-6, Sun 1-6

WILMORE

R ASBURY THEOLOGICAL SEMINARY*, B L Fisher Library, 204 N Lexington Ave, 40390-1199. SAN 306-4301. Tel: 859-858-2100. FAX: 859-858-2330. E-mail: helpdesk@asburyseminary.edu. Web Site: asburyseminary.edu/academics/library/. *Dean, Libr & Info Tech,* Paul Tippey; E-mail: paul.tippey@asburyseminary.edu; *Dir, Coll Serv, Strategic Operations,* Don Butterworth; E-mail: don.butterworth@asburyseminary.edu; *Dir, Instrul Serv,* Wesley Custer; E-mail: wesley.custer@asburyseminary.edu; Staff 16 (MLS 6, Non-MLS 10)
Founded 1939. Enrl 1,300; Fac 67; Highest Degree: Doctorate
Library Holdings: Bk Vols 260,000; Per Subs 1,054
Special Collections: Healing (Alfred E Price Coll); Wesleyan/Holiness; World Council of Churches (Faith & Order Papers Coll)
Subject Interests: Biblical studies, Missions, Theol
Automation Activity & Vendor Info: (Acquisitions) Evergreen; (Cataloging) Evergreen; (Circulation) Evergreen; (OPAC) EBSCO Discovery Service
Publications: Occasional Bibliographic Papers of the B L Fisher Library
Partic in LYRASIS
Open Mon-Thurs 7:30am-10:00pm, Fri 7:30-6, Sat 8-5

C ASBURY UNIVERSITY*, Kinlaw Library, One Macklem Dr, 40390-1198. SAN 306-4298. Tel: 859-858-3511. Circulation Tel: 859-858-3511, Ext 2265. Reference Tel: 859-858-3511, Ext 2257. FAX: 859-858-3921. Reference E-mail: reference@asbury.edu. Web Site: www.asbury.edu/academics/resources/library. *Asst Dir, Head, Archives & Spec Coll,* Suzanne Gehring; Tel: 859-858-3511, Ext 2126, E-mail: suzanne.gehring@asbury.edu; *Head, Res & Distance Serv,* Jennifer Walz; Tel: 859-858-3511, Ext 2269, E-mail: jlwalz@asbury.edu; *Educ Librn,* Katrina Salley; Tel: 859-858-3511, Ext 2467, E-mail: katrina.salley@asbury.edu; *Instrul Serv Librn,* Amy Bessin; Tel: 859-858-3511, Ext 2270, E-mail: amy.bessin@asbury.edu; *ILL Mgr,* Bonnie Temple; Tel: 859-858-3511, Ext 2143, E-mail: bonnie.temple@asbury.edu; *Acq, Supvr,* Darlene Bryan; Tel: 859-858-3511, Ext 2425; *Circ Supvr,* Toni Knight; Tel: 859-858-3511, Ext 2268; Staff 11 (MLS 6, Non-MLS 5)
Founded 1890. Enrl 1,800; Fac 120; Highest Degree: Master
Special Collections: College Archives; Faculty & Alumni Publications; Missionary Coll. Oral History
Subject Interests: Holiness lit, Local hist
Automation Activity & Vendor Info: (Acquisitions) SirsiDynix; (Cataloging) SirsiDynix; (Circulation) SirsiDynix; (Course Reserve) SirsiDynix; (OPAC) SirsiDynix; (Serials) SirsiDynix
Wireless access
Publications: Collegii Asburiensis Bibliotheca
Partic in Association of Independent Kentucky Colleges & Universities; Christian Libr Network; Consortium of College & University Media Centers; OCLC Online Computer Library Center, Inc
Special Services for the Blind - Assistive/Adapted tech devices, equip & products
Open Mon-Thurs 7:30am-11:50pm, Fri 7:30-5, Sat 12-8

WINCHESTER

P CLARK COUNTY PUBLIC LIBRARY*, 370 S Burns Ave, 40391-1876. SAN 306-431X. Tel: 859-744-5661. FAX: 859-744-5993. E-mail: clarkbooks@gmail.com. Web Site: www.clarkbooks.org. *Dir,* Julie Maruskin; *Adult Serv,* John Maruskin; *Youth Serv,* Renee Wallace
Founded 1950. Pop 29,500; Circ 172,000
Library Holdings: Bk Vols 89,000; Per Subs 300
Special Collections: Heirloom Seal & Plant Materials Coll; Kentucky History (Doyle Coll & Kentucky Coll); Local Genealogy (Doyle Coll, Family File), bks, micro
Subject Interests: Out of print bks, Rare children's bks

Automation Activity & Vendor Info: (Acquisitions) TLC (The Library Corporation); (Cataloging) TLC (The Library Corporation); (Circulation) TLC (The Library Corporation)
Wireless access
Partic in LYRASIS
Open Mon-Thurs 9-8, Fri 9-5:30, Sat 9-5, Sun 1-5
Friends of the Library Group

LOUISIANA

Date of Statistics: FY 2020
Population, 2020 U.S. Census: 4,645,318
Population, 2021 Census Estimate: 4,657,757
Population Served by Public Libraries: 4,555,496
Total Volumes in Public Libraries: 22,447,124
Volumes Per Capita: 4.89
Total Public Library Circulation: 41,076,562
Circulation Per Capita: 8.94
Digital Resources:
Total e-books: 6,020,849
Total audio items (physical & downloadable units): 3,340,661
Total video items (physical & downloadable units): 2,126,176
Total computers for use by the public: 5,284
Total annual wireless sessions: 3,365,716
Income and Expenditures:
Total Public Library Income: $286,674,082
Median & Average Income: $4,278,718 (average); $1,494,273 (median)
Source of Income: Public Funds (Primarily property tax)
Expenditures Per Capita: $50.20
Number of County or Multi-county (Regional) Libraries: 67
Counties Served: 64
Information provided courtesy of: Michael Golrick, Head of Reference & Library Consultant; State Library of Louisiana

ABBEVILLE

P VERMILION PARISH LIBRARY*, Abbeville Branch, 405 E Saint Victor St, 70510-5101. (Mail add: PO Drawer 640, 70511-0640), SAN 342-6548. Tel: 337-893-2655. FAX: 337-898-0526. E-mail: abbeville@vermilion.lib.la.us. Web Site: www.vermilionparishlibrary.com. *Dir,* Charlotte Trosclair; E-mail: ctrosclair@vermilion.lib.la.us; *Admin Mgr,* Dawn Hebert; *Adult Serv Mgr, YA Mgr,* Sue Trahan; *Br Mgr,* Susan Stelly; *Bus Mgr,* Amy Stelly; *Ch Mgr,* Sara Bailey-McDaniel; *IT Mgr,* Grant Domingue; Staff 16 (MLS 1, Non-MLS 15)
Founded 1941. Pop 53,044; Circ 299,077
Library Holdings: AV Mats 6,600; Bks on Deafness & Sign Lang 81; Large Print Bks 7,755; Bk Titles 136,294; Bk Vols 174,319; Per Subs 97; Talking Bks 4,957
Special Collections: Louisiana Coll
Automation Activity & Vendor Info: (Acquisitions) Book Systems; (Cataloging) Book Systems; (Circulation) Book Systems; (Course Reserve) Book Systems; (OPAC) Book Systems
Wireless access
Partic in Loan System Helping Automate Retrieval of Knowledge
Special Services for the Blind - Bks on cassette; Bks on CD; Large print bks; Large screen computer & software; Low vision equip
Open Mon-Thurs 9-6:30, Fri 9-5:30, Sat 9-1
Friends of the Library Group
Branches: 5
DELCAMBRE BRANCH, 206 W Main St, Delcambre, 70528-2918, SAN 342-6602. Tel: 337-685-2388. FAX: 337-685-2388. E-mail: delcambre@vermilion.lib.la.us. *Br Supvr,* Bonnie Richard; Staff 2 (Non-MLS 2)
Library Holdings: AV Mats 115; Bk Vols 18,000; Per Subs 22
Open Mon-Thurs 10-5:30, Fri 10-5, Sat 9-12
ERATH BRANCH, 111 W Edwards St, Erath, 70533-4027, SAN 342-6637. Tel: 337-937-5628. FAX: 337-937-5656. E-mail: erath@vermilion.lib.la.us. *Br Supvr,* Patrice LeBlanc; Staff 1 (Non-MLS 1)
Library Holdings: AV Mats 76; Bk Vols 16,904; Per Subs 22
Function: BA reader (adult literacy), Bks on cassette, Bks on CD, CD-ROM, Children's prog, Citizenship assistance, Computer training, Computers for patron use, Distance learning, E-Reserves, Free DVD rentals, Govt ref serv, Health sci info serv, Holiday prog, Home delivery & serv to seniorr ctr & nursing homes, Homework prog, ILL available, Internet access, Large print keyboards, Literacy & newcomer serv, Magnifiers for reading, Mail & tel request accepted, Online cat, Online ref, Orientations, Outreach serv, Photocopying/Printing, Preschool outreach, Prof lending libr, Prog for adults, Prog for children & young adult, Ref & res, Ref serv available, Senior outreach, Serves people with intellectual disabilities, Spoken cassettes & CDs, Spoken cassettes & DVDs, Story hour, Summer reading prog, Tax forms, Teen prog, Telephone ref, VHS videos, Wheelchair accessible, Workshops
Open Mon-Thurs 10-5:30, Fri 10-5, Sat 9-12
GUEYDAN BRANCH, 704 Tenth St, Gueydan, 70542-3806, SAN 342-6661. Tel: 337-536-6781. FAX: 337-536-0112. E-mail: gueydan@vermilion.lib.la.us. *Br Supvr,* Angela Touchet LeBlanc; Staff 1 (Non-MLS 1)
Library Holdings: AV Mats 110; Bk Vols 18,313; Per Subs 23
Open Mon-Thurs 10-5:30, Fri 10-5, Sat 9-12
KAPLAN BRANCH, 815 N Cushing Ave, Kaplan, 70548-2614, SAN 342-6696. Tel: 337-643-7209. FAX: 337-643-7250. E-mail: kaplan@vermilion.lib.la.us. *Br Supvr,* Linda Leonard; Staff 2 (Non-MLS 2)
Library Holdings: AV Mats 75; Bk Vols 31,025; Per Subs 36
Open Mon & Wed 9-5:30, Tues & Thurs 9-6:30, Fri 9-5, Sat 9-12
MAURICE BRANCH, 8901 Maurice Ave, Maurice, 70555, SAN 342-6726. Tel: 337-893-5583. FAX: 337-385-2610. E-mail: maurice@vermilion.lib.la.us. *Br Mgr,* Lou Ella Landry; Staff 2 (Non-MLS 2)
Library Holdings: AV Mats 90; Bk Vols 14,770; Per Subs 20
Open Mon-Thurs 11:30-6, Fri 11:30-5, Sat 9-12
Bookmobiles: 1. Mgr, Angelle Briggs

ALEXANDRIA

§J CENTRAL LOUISIANA TECHNICAL COMMUNITY COLLEGE LIBRARY, Alexandria Main Campus, 516 Murray St, 71301. Tel: 318-487-5443, Ext 1137, 318-487-5443, Ext 1931. E-mail: library@cltcc.edu. Web Site: cltcclibrary.cltcc.edu. *Dir, Libr Serv,* Ms Daenel Vaughn-Tucker; E-mail: dvaughntucker@cltcc.edu
Wireless access
Function: Computers for patron use, ILL available, Photocopying/Printing, Res assist avail, Scanner
Partic in Louisiana Library Network
Open Mon-Fri 8-4:30
Restriction: Non-circulating

L GOLD, WEEMS, BRUSER, SUES & RUNDELL*, Law Library, 2001 MacArthur Dr, 71301. (Mail add: PO Box 6118, 71301-6118), SAN 372-1299. Tel: 318-445-6471. FAX: 318-445-6476. Web Site: www.goldweems.com. *Libr Asst,* Barbara Fontenot; E-mail: bfontenot@goldweems.com
Library Holdings: Bk Titles 1,287; Per Subs 77
Restriction: Not open to pub

C LOUISIANA STATE UNIVERSITY AT ALEXANDRIA*, James C Bolton Library, 8100 Hwy 71 S, 71302. SAN 306-4344. Tel: 318-473-6438. Reference Tel: 318-473-6442. FAX: 318-473-6556. E-mail: library@lsua.edu. Web Site: www.lsua.edu/library. *Interim Dir,* Rusty Gaspard; Tel: 318-473-6443, E-mail: rgaspard@lsua.edu; *Syst Librn,* Michael Waller; Tel: 318-427-0102, E-mail: mwaller@lsua.edu; *Col Archivist & Rec Mgt Coordr,* Michelle Riggs; Tel: 318-619-2960, E-mail: mriggs@lsua.edu; *Ser, Tech Serv,* Titus Belgard; Tel: 318-473-6440, E-mail: tbelgard@lsua.edu. Subject Specialists: *Hist,* Michelle Riggs; Staff 5 (MLS 5)

Founded 1960. Enrl 2,574; Fac 1; Highest Degree: Bachelor
Jul 2014-Jun 2015 Income $310,294. Mats Exp $102,000, Books $35,000, Per/Ser (Incl. Access Fees) $5,000, Electronic Ref Mat (Incl. Access Fees) $58,000, Presv $4,000. Sal $227,024 (Prof $153,998)
Library Holdings: CDs 142; DVDs 162; e-books 202,444; e-journals 90,724; Electronic Media & Resources 77; Microforms 19,000; Bk Titles 121,161; Per Subs 57
Automation Activity & Vendor Info: (Acquisitions) SirsiDynix; (Cataloging) SirsiDynix; (Circulation) SirsiDynix; (Course Reserve) SirsiDynix; (Discovery) EBSCO Discovery Service; (ILL) OCLC ILLiad; (Media Booking) SirsiDynix; (OPAC) SirsiDynix; (Serials) SirsiDynix
Wireless access
Function: Archival coll, Electronic databases & coll, ILL available, Instruction & testing, Online cat, Online info literacy tutorials on the web & in blackboard, Ref & res, Ref serv available
Partic in Louisiana Academic Library Information Network; Louisiana Library Network; LYRASIS
Open Mon-Thurs 7:45am-10pm, Fri 7:45-4:30, Sat 10-6, Sun 3-10; Mon-Fri (Summer) 8-4:30
Restriction: In-house use for visitors, Internal use only
Friends of the Library Group

P RAPIDES PARISH LIBRARY*, 411 Washington St, 71301-8338. SAN 342-6785. Tel: 318-442-2411. Circulation Tel: 318-445-2411, Ext 1020. Interlibrary Loan Service Tel: 318-445-2411, Ext 1074. Reference Tel: 318-445-1840, Ext 1032. Administration Tel: 318-445-6436. Automation Services Tel: 318-445-2411, Ext 1050. FAX: 318-445-6478. Administration FAX: 318-445-2466. TDD: 318-445-8074. E-mail: info@rpl.org. Web Site: www.rpl.org. *Dir,* Laura-Ellen Ayres; Tel: 318-445-6436, Ext 1001, E-mail: lea@rpl.org; *Asst Dir, Support Serv,* Wesley Saunders; Tel: 318-445-2412, Ext 1044, E-mail: whsaunders@rpl.org; *Bus Mgr,* Jimmy Holsomback; Tel: 318-445-6436, Ext 1004, E-mail: joh@rpl.org; *Direct Serv Coordr,* Lenna Mouton; Tel: 318-445-6436, Ext 1002; *Coordr, Outreach Serv,* Tammy DiBartolo; Tel: 318-442-2483, Ext 1906; *Officer, Pub Relations,* Jennifer Hughes; Tel: 318-445-2411,Ext 1060, E-mail: jhughes@rpl.org; Staff 27 (Non-MLS 27)
Founded 1942. Pop 134,655; Circ 659,793
Jan 2018-Dec 2018 Income (Main & Associated Libraries) $6,266,025, State $187,416, Federal $71,449, County $5,793,242, Other $213,918. Mats Exp $396,747, Books $245,291, Per/Ser (Incl. Access Fees) $22,788, AV Mat $50,647, Electronic Ref Mat (Incl. Access Fees) $66,119. Sal $2,447,833
Special Collections: Louisiana Coll; Map Coll. State Document Depository
Subject Interests: Local hist
Automation Activity & Vendor Info: (Acquisitions) Innovative Interfaces, Inc; (Cataloging) Innovative Interfaces, Inc; (Circulation) Innovative Interfaces, Inc; (ILL) Innovative Interfaces, Inc; (OPAC) Innovative Interfaces, Inc; (Serials) Innovative Interfaces, Inc
Wireless access
Function: 24/7 Electronic res, 24/7 Online cat, 3D Printer, Accelerated reader prog, Adult bk club, After school storytime, Art exhibits, Art programs, Audiobks on Playaways & MP3, Audiobks via web, AV serv, Bi-weekly Writer's Group, Bk club(s), Bk reviews (Group), Bks on cassette, Bks on CD, Children's prog, Computer training, Computers for patron use, Digital talking bks, Electronic databases & coll, Family literacy, For res purposes, Free DVD rentals, Genealogy discussion group, Govt ref serv, Holiday prog, Home delivery & serv to seniorr ctr & nursing homes, Homebound delivery serv, Homework prog, ILL available, Internet access, Jail serv, Laminating, Life-long learning prog for all ages, Magazines, Magnifiers for reading, Mail & tel request accepted, Makerspace, Meeting rooms, Microfiche/film & reading machines, Movies, Music CDs, Online cat, Online ref, Outreach serv, Outside serv via phone, mail, e-mail & web, OverDrive digital audio bks, Photocopying/Printing, Preschool outreach, Printer for laptops & handheld devices, Prog for adults, Prog for children & young adult, Ref & res, Ref serv available, Res assist avail, Scanner, Senior outreach, Serves people with intellectual disabilities, Spanish lang bks, Spoken cassettes & CDs, Spoken cassettes & DVDs, STEM programs, Story hour, Study rm, Summer & winter reading prog, Summer reading prog, Tax forms, Teen prog, Telephone ref, VHS videos, Wheelchair accessible, Winter reading prog, Workshops, Writing prog
Publications: Friends of the Rapides Library (Newsletter); Ripple (Newsletter)
Partic in Loan System Helping Automate Retrieval of Knowledge
Special Services for the Deaf - Assisted listening device; Assistive tech; Bks on deafness & sign lang
Special Services for the Blind - Accessible computers; Assistive/Adapted tech devices, equip & products; Bks & mags in Braille, on rec, tape & cassette; Bks on cassette; Bks on CD; Braille bks; Cassettes; Copier with enlargement capabilities; Free checkout of audio mat; Internet workstation with adaptive software; Large print bks; Large screen computer & software; PC for people with disabilities; Photo duplicator for making large print; Playaways (bks on MP3); Ref serv; Screen enlargement software for people with visual disabilities
Open Mon-Sat 9-7, Sun 1-5
Restriction: Circ to mem only, ID required to use computers (Ltd hrs), In-house use for visitors
Friends of the Library Group
Branches: 9
BOYCE BRANCH, 500 A Ulster Ave, Boyce, 71409. (Mail add: PO Box 792, Boyce, 71409-0792), SAN 342-6815. Tel: 318-793-2182. FAX: 318-793-2736. Circulation E-mail: bccirc@rpl.org. *Mgr,* Deborah Boerboom; E-mail: dpboerboom@rpl.org; Staff 2 (Non-MLS 2)
Open Tues 9-12 & 1-6, Wed & Fri 1-6, Thurs & Sat 9-1
Friends of the Library Group
HINESTON BRANCH, 1810 Hwy 121, Hineston, 71438, SAN 342-6882. Tel: 318-793-8461. FAX: 318-793-0691. Circulation E-mail: hncirc@rpl.org. *Mgr,* Joy Luttrell; Staff 2 (MLS 1, Non-MLS 1)
Founded 1984
Open Mon & Sat 9-1, Tues 1:30-5, Wed & Fri 9-1 & 2-6
GEORGIE G JOHNSON BRANCH, 1610 Veterans Dr, Lecompte, 71346. (Mail add: PO Box 1207, Lecompte, 71346-1207), SAN 342-6904. Tel: 318-776-5153. FAX: 318-776-6744. Circulation E-mail: jncirc@rpl.org. *Interim Mgr,* Teri Sullivan; Staff 2 (Non-MLS 2)
Open Tues & Thurs 9-5, Wed & Fri 1-5, Sat 9-1
Friends of the Library Group
MARTIN LUTHER KING, JR BRANCH, 1115 Broadway Ave, 71301. Tel: 318-445-3912. Circulation E-mail: kgcirc@rpl.org. *Br Mgr,* LaKeisha Henton; Staff 4 (Non-MLS 4)
Open Mon-Thurs 9-7, Fri & Sat 9-5
LIBUSE BRANCH, 6375 Hwy 28 E, Pineville, 71360. Tel: 318-443-7259. *Br Mgr,* Pamela Martin; Staff 5 (MLS 1, Non-MLS 4)
Open Mon-Thurs 9-7, Fri & Sat 9-5
MARTIN BRANCH, 801 W Shamrock, Pineville, 71360, SAN 342-6963. Tel: 318-442-7575. FAX: 318-449-4946. Circulation E-mail: mrcirc@rpl.org. *Librn,* Pamela Bennett; Staff 3 (Non-MLS 3)
Founded 1950
Open Mon-Sat 9-6
J W MCDONALD BRANCH, 1075 Hwy 497, Glenmora, 71433. (Mail add: PO Box 1206, Glenmora, 71433). Tel: 318-748-4848. FAX: 318-748-4851. Circulation E-mail: mccirc@rpl.org. *Mgr,* Gail Goldberg; Staff 3 (Non-MLS 3)
Open Mon & Fri 1-6, Tues 10-6, Wed 1-5, Thurs 9-6, Sat 9-1
Friends of the Library Group
J L ROBERTSON BRANCH, 809 Tioga High School Rd, Ball, 71405, SAN 342-7021. Tel: 318-640-3098. FAX: 318-640-8713. Circulation E-mail: rbcirc@rpl.org. *Mgr,* Shayne Bertrand; Staff 5 (Non-MLS 5)
Founded 1942
Open Mon-Thurs 9-7, Fri & Sat 9-5
WESTSIDE REGIONAL, 5416 Provine Pl, 71303, SAN 342-6939. Tel: 318-442-2483. FAX: 318-442-7678. Circulation E-mail: wrcirc@rpl.org. *Interim Mgr,* Pam Martin; *Presch Outreach Plus Mgr,* Keisha White; Tel: 318-442-2483, Ext 1905; *Coordr, Outreach Serv,* Tammy DiBartolo; Tel: 318-442-2483, Ext 1906, E-mail: youthservices@rpl.org; *Youth Serv - Prog,* Karla Kirby; Tel: 318-442-2483, Ext 1904, E-mail: kjkirby@rpl.org; Staff 13 (MLS 2, Non-MLS 11)
Open Mon-Thurs 9-6, Fri & Sat 9-5
Bookmobiles: 1. In Charge, Londa Price

M RAPIDES REGIONAL MEDICAL CENTER*, Medical Library, 211 Fourth St, 71301-8421. (Mail add: PO Box 30101, 71301), SAN 306-4352. Tel: 318-473-3563, 318-769-5341. Toll Free FAX: 844-766-2671. Web Site: www.rapidesregional.com. *Library Contact,* Ann Vanderlick; E-mail: ann.vanderlick@hcahealthcare.com; Staff 1 (Non-MLS 1)
Founded 1963
Library Holdings: Bk Vols 1,800; Per Subs 141
Subject Interests: Allied health, Health sci, Med, Nursing
Restriction: Staff use only

AMITE

P TANGIPAHOA PARISH LIBRARY*, Administration Office, 204 NE Central Ave, 70422. SAN 342-7110. Tel: 985-748-7559. FAX: 985-748-2812. Web Site: www.tangilibrary.com. *Dir,* Barry Bradford; E-mail: bbradford@tangilibrary.com; *Asst Dir,* Bianca Roberts; E-mail: broberts@tangilibrary.com; Staff 6 (MLS 5, Non-MLS 1)
Founded 1944. Pop 117,000; Circ 330,500
Library Holdings: AV Mats 13,688; Bk Vols 187,343; Per Subs 300
Subject Interests: Genealogy, Local hist
Wireless access
Function: 24/7 Electronic res, 24/7 Online cat, Accelerated reader prog, Adult bk club, Adult literacy prog, After school storytime, Archival coll, Art programs, Audiobks via web, Bk club(s), Bks on CD, Children's prog, Computer training, Computers for patron use, Digital talking bks, Electronic databases & coll, Family literacy, For res purposes, Free DVD rentals, Govt ref serv, Health sci info serv, Holiday prog, ILL available, Internet access, Jazz prog, Life-long learning prog for all ages, Magazines, Mail & tel request accepted, Meeting rooms, Microfiche/film & reading machines, Movies, Online cat, Online ref, Outreach serv, Outside serv via phone, mail, e-mail & web, OverDrive digital audio bks,

Photocopying/Printing, Preschool outreach, Preschool reading prog, Printer for laptops & handheld devices, Prog for adults, Prog for children & young adult, Ref & res, Ref serv available, Res assist avail, Senior computer classes, Senior outreach, Serves people with intellectual disabilities, Spanish lang bks, STEM programs, Story hour, Study rm, Summer reading prog, Tax forms, Teen prog, Telephone ref, Wheelchair accessible, Workshops, Writing prog
Partic in Loan System Helping Automate Retrieval of Knowledge
Friends of the Library Group
Branches: 6
AMITE BRANCH, 204 NE Central Ave, 70422. Tel: 985-748-7151. FAX: 985-748-5476. *Br Mgr,* Avery Smith; Staff 1 (MLS 1)
Founded 1944. Pop 5,500
Library Holdings: AV Mats 360; Bk Vols 45,000; Per Subs 86
Open Mon & Tues 8:30-8, Wed-Fri 8:30-6:30, Sat 8:30-3
HAMMOND BRANCH, 314 E Thomas, Hammond, 70401, SAN 342-7234. Tel: 985-345-0937, 985-345-3909. FAX: 985-345-2188. *Br Mgr,* Diana Riederer; Staff 1 (MLS 1)
Pop 17,639
Library Holdings: AV Mats 216; Bk Vols 48,757; Per Subs 52
Open Mon, Tues & Fri 8:30-6:30, Wed & Thurs 8:30-8, Sat 8:30-3
INDEPENDENCE BRANCH, 290 S Pine St, Independence, 70443. (Mail add: PO Box 439, Independence, 70443-0439), SAN 342-7269. Tel: 985-878-2970. FAX: 985-878-1996. *Br Mgr,* Lindsey Hines-Mayo
Pop 2,000
Library Holdings: Bk Vols 15,101; Per Subs 21
Open Mon-Fri 10-5:30, Sat 9-1
KENTWOOD BRANCH, 101 Ave F, Kentwood, 70444, SAN 342-7293. Tel: 985-229-3596. FAX: 985-229-4566. *Br Mgr,* Rachel Vaccaro; Staff 1 (MLS 1)
Pop 2,805
Library Holdings: AV Mats 207; Bk Vols 22,211; Per Subs 37
Open Mon-Fri 10-5:30, Sat 9-1
Friends of the Library Group
LORANGER BRANCH, 19451 Hwy 40, Loranger, 70446. (Mail add: PO Box 515, Loranger, 70446-0515), SAN 342-7315. Tel: 985-878-6224. FAX: 985-878-3571. *Br Mgr,* Kenyotta Zanders
Pop 3,500
Library Holdings: Bk Vols 6,235; Per Subs 21
Open Mon-Fri 10-5:30, Sat 9-1
PONCHATOULA BRANCH, 380 N Fifth St, Ponchatoula, 70454, SAN 342-7358. Tel: 985-386-6554. FAX: 985-370-5019. *Br Mgr,* Brenda Neidhamer; Staff 3 (Non-MLS 3)
Pop 5,700
Library Holdings: AV Mats 148; Bk Vols 49,544; Per Subs 72
Open Mon & Tues 8:30-8, Wed-Fri 8:30-6:30, Sat 8:30-3
Friends of the Library Group

ANGIE

S RAYBURN CORRECTIONAL CENTER LIBRARY*, 27268 Hwy 21 N, 70426. SAN 373-8574. Tel: 985-661-6300. *Librn,* Pam Ard; Tel: 985-661-6328, E-mail: pamard@corrections.state.la.us; *Libr Asst,* Sheryl Jones; E-mail: sheryljones@corrections.state.la.us
Library Holdings: Bk Vols 12,800; Per Subs 36
Mem of Washington Parish Library System
Special Services for the Deaf - Am sign lang & deaf culture; Assisted listening device
Special Services for the Blind - Audiovision-a radio reading serv
Open Mon-Sun 7am-9pm

ANGOLA

S LOUISIANA STATE PENITENTIARY LIBRARY*, Main Prison Library, A Bldg, 17544 Tunica Trace, 70712. SAN 306-4379. Tel: 225-655-2031. FAX: 225-655-2585. Web Site: www.corrections.state.la.us/contact/correctional-facilities/louisiana-state-penitentiary. *Librn,* Michele Jones
Founded 1968
Jan 2018-Dec 2018. Mats Exp $18,000, Books $5,000, Per/Ser (Incl. Access Fees) $13,000. Sal $8,000
Library Holdings: Audiobooks 329; AV Mats 298; Bks on Deafness & Sign Lang 3; CDs 78; DVDs 281; High Interest/Low Vocabulary Bk Vols 462; Bk Vols 43,161; Per Subs 116; Videos 465
Special Collections: Criminal Justice; Science Fiction
Automation Activity & Vendor Info: (Circulation) Follett Software
Open Mon-Sun 8-12, 1-3 & 6-9

ARCADIA

P BIENVILLE PARISH LIBRARY*, 2768 Maple St, 71001. SAN 306-4387. Tel: 318-263-7410. Toll Free Tel: 888-285-6750. FAX: 318-263-7428. Administration E-mail: admin.g1bv@pelican.state.lib.la.us. Web Site: www.bienvillelibrary.org. *Dir,* Peggy Walls; E-mail: pwalls@state.lib.la.us; *Asst Dir,* Ellen Butler; Staff 9 (MLS 1, Non-MLS 8)
Founded 1964. Pop 15,979; Circ 150,945
Library Holdings: AV Mats 1,280; Bk Titles 65,497; Bk Vols 88,000; Per Subs 226
Special Collections: Large print books, Louisiana material
Subject Interests: Genealogy, La
Automation Activity & Vendor Info: (Acquisitions) Innovative Interfaces, Inc; (Cataloging) Innovative Interfaces, Inc; (Circulation) Innovative Interfaces, Inc; (Course Reserve) Innovative Interfaces, Inc; (ILL) Innovative Interfaces, Inc; (OPAC) Innovative Interfaces, Inc
Partic in Association for Rural & Small Libraries; Loan System Helping Automate Retrieval of Knowledge
Open Mon & Wed-Fri 8:15-6, Tues 8:15-7, Sat 8:15-Noon
Branches: 3
CASTOR BRANCH, 1955 Hwy 507, Castor, 71016. Tel: 318-544-8451. *Br Mgr,* Shelly Hinkel
Founded 2009
Open Mon, Wed & Fri 8:15-5, Sat 8:15-Noon
RINGGOLD BRANCH, 2078 Hall St, Ringgold, 71068, SAN 324-3001. Tel: 318-894-9770. FAX: 318-894-4339. *Br Mgr,* Annette McLemore; Staff 4 (Non-MLS 4)
Library Holdings: AV Mats 80; Bk Vols 11,400; Per Subs 35
Open Mon & Wed-Fri 8:15-5, Tues 8:15-7, Sat 8:15-12
SALINE BRANCH, 1434 Fourth St, Saline, 71070. Tel: 318-576-8990. FAX: 318-576-8780. *Br Mgr,* Jeannie Basinger
Open Mon, Wed & Fri 8:15-5, Sat 8:15-12

ATLANTA

S WINN CORRECTIONAL CENTER LIBRARY*, 180 CCA Blvd, 71483. Tel: 318-628-3971. Web Site: doc.louisiana.gov/contact/correctional-facilities/winn-correctional-center.
Library Holdings: Bk Vols 6,922; Per Subs 13
Restriction: Not open to pub
Friends of the Library Group

BARKSDALE AFB

A UNITED STATES AIR FORCE*, Barksdale Air Force Base Library, 744 Douhet Dr, Bldg 4244, 71110. SAN 342-7447. Tel: 318-456-4101. Reference Tel: 318-456-5993. FAX: 318-459-7523. E-mail: 2FSS.FSDL.Library@us.af.mil. Web Site: accc.ent.sirsi.net/client/en_US/barksdale. *Dir,* Coralie Frances Morris; E-mail: coralie.morris.1@us.af.mil; *Acq,* Anthony Bellucci; *Cat,* Chris Rhodes. Subject Specialists: *Econ, Law,* Coralie Frances Morris; Staff 5 (MLS 2, Non-MLS 3)
Founded 1933
Library Holdings: AV Mats 4,200; Bk Vols 38,500; Per Subs 79
Special Collections: Chief of Staff Reading Lists; Louisiana History & Culture; Project Warrior Coll
Subject Interests: Mil hist (US)
Automation Activity & Vendor Info: (Acquisitions) SirsiDynix; (Cataloging) SirsiDynix; (Circulation) SirsiDynix; (Course Reserve) SirsiDynix; (OPAC) SirsiDynix; (Serials) SirsiDynix
Wireless access
Function: ILL available
Special Services for the Blind - Large print bks
Restriction: Open to govt employees only

BASTROP

P MOREHOUSE PARISH LIBRARY*, 524 E Madison Ave, 71220. SAN 342-7471. Tel: 318-281-3696. FAX: 318-281-3683. E-mail: tlmh@state.lib.la.us. *Dir,* Donald R Smith; E-mail: donsmith@state.lib.la.us; Staff 6.8 (MLS 1, Non-MLS 5.8)
Founded 1940. Pop 27,559; Circ 72,939
Library Holdings: Audiobooks 619; CDs 431; DVDs 4,354; e-books 2,432; Large Print Bks 2,699; Bk Vols 54,043; Per Subs 87
Subject Interests: Genealogy, Local hist
Automation Activity & Vendor Info: (Cataloging) Book Systems; (Circulation) Book Systems; (ILL) Auto-Graphics, Inc; (OPAC) Book Systems
Wireless access
Function: 24/7 Electronic res, 24/7 Online cat, Audiobks via web, Bks on CD, Children's prog, Computers for patron use, Digital talking bks, Electronic databases & coll, Holiday prog, ILL available, Internet access, Magazines, Microfiche/film & reading machines, Movies, Online cat, OverDrive digital audio bks, Photocopying/Printing, Prog for adults, Prog for children & young adult, Ref serv available, Summer reading prog
Mem of Trail Blazer Library System
Partic in Loan System Helping Automate Retrieval of Knowledge
Open Mon-Fri 8-5:30, Sat 9-1
Restriction: Circ limited, Lending limited to county residents

Branches: 4
COLLINSTON BRANCH, 4620 Main St, Collinston, 71229, SAN 342-7560. Tel: 318-874-3531. *Br Mgr,* Martha Crymes; Staff 1 (Non-MLS 1)
Library Holdings: Audiobooks 1; CDs 431; Large Print Bks 202; Bk Vols 3,960
Automation Activity & Vendor Info: (Cataloging) Book Systems; (Circulation) Book Systems; (ILL) Auto-Graphics, Inc; (OPAC) Book Systems
Open Mon & Thurs 12-3
DUNBAR, 1102 Perry St, 71220, SAN 342-7595. Tel: 318-281-1137. *Br Mgr,* Kishier Robinson; Staff 1 (Non-MLS 1)
Library Holdings: Audiobooks 226; CDs 14; DVDs 234; Large Print Bks 173; Bk Vols 6,887
Automation Activity & Vendor Info: (Cataloging) Book Systems; (Circulation) Book Systems; (ILL) Auto-Graphics, Inc; (OPAC) Book Systems
Open Mon-Fri 1-5
MER ROUGE BRANCH, 107 S 16th St, Mer Rouge, 71261, SAN 342-7625. Tel: 318-647-5639. *Br Mgr,* Sue Barthol; Staff 1 (Non-MLS 1)
Library Holdings: Audiobooks 168; CDs 9; DVDs 28; Large Print Bks 278; Bk Vols 4,050
Automation Activity & Vendor Info: (Cataloging) Book Systems; (Circulation) Book Systems; (ILL) Auto-Graphics, Inc; (OPAC) Book Systems
Open Tues 9-5
OAK RIDGE BRANCH, 106 N Oak St, Oak Ridge, 71264, SAN 342-765X. Tel: 318-244-5329. *Br Mgr,* Carolyn Files; Staff 1 (Non-MLS 1)
Library Holdings: Audiobooks 14; CDs 2; Large Print Bks 70; Bk Vols 2,697; Per Subs 16
Open Mon & Thurs 8-11

BATON ROUGE

J BATON ROUGE COMMUNITY COLLEGE*, Magnolia Library, 201 Community College Dr, 70806. Tel: 225-216-8303. Reference Tel: 225-216-8555. Administration Tel: 225-216-8186. FAX: 225-216-8712. E-mail: librarian@mybrcc.edu, library@mybrcc.edu. Web Site: www.mybrcc.edu/library. *Assoc Dean, Learning Res,* Jacqueline L Jones; Tel: 225-216-8170, E-mail: jonesjl@mybrcc.edu; *Ref Librn,* Peter Klubek; Tel: 225-216-8505, E-mail: klubekp@mybrcc.edu; *Ref Librn,* Lauren Wade McAdams; Tel: 225-216-8552, E-mail: wadel2@mybrcc.edu; *Cat Librn,* Jenny Wong; Tel: 225-216-8590, E-mail: wongj@mybrcc.edu; *Supvr, Ser,* Laddawan Kongchum; Tel: 225-216-8017, E-mail: kongchuml@mybrcc.edu. Subject Specialists: *African-Am hist,* Jacqueline L Jones; *Art, Educ,* Peter Klubek; *Biology, Chem, Nursing,* Lauren Wade McAdams; *Computer sci, Math,* Jenny Wong; *Avionics, Phys sci, Proc tech,* Laddawan Kongchum; Staff 8.5 (MLS 8.5)
Founded 1998. Enrl 7,150; Fac 293; Highest Degree: Associate
Library Holdings: Audiobooks 541; AV Mats 168; CDs 360; DVDs 2,760; e-books 59,377; Bk Titles 37,292; Bk Vols 45,601; Per Subs 215; Videos 2,356
Special Collections: Carville V Earle Coll; Multicultural Children's Resource Coll
Automation Activity & Vendor Info: (Acquisitions) SirsiDynix; (Cataloging) SirsiDynix; (Circulation) SirsiDynix; (Course Reserve) SirsiDynix; (OPAC) SirsiDynix; (Serials) SirsiDynix
Wireless access
Function: Ref serv available
Partic in Louisiana Academic Library Information Network; Louisiana Library Network; LYRASIS
Open Mon-Thurs 7:30am-8pm, Fri 7:30-5, Sat 8-12
Friends of the Library Group

M BATON ROUGE GENERAL MEDICAL CENTER*, Health Sciences Library, 3600 Florida Blvd, 70806. (Mail add: PO Box 2511, 70821-2511). Tel: 225-387-7000, 225-387-7012. FAX: 225-381-6116. E-mail: healthinformation.library@brgeneral.org. Web Site: brgeneral.org. *Librn,* Wendy Pesch
Library Holdings: Bk Vols 450; Per Subs 100
Wireless access
Open Mon-Fri 8-4:30

S CAPITAL CITY PRESS, The Advocate/The Times-Picayune Library, 10705 Rieger Rd, 70809. (Mail add: PO Box 588, 70821-0588), SAN 306-4395. Administration Tel: 225-388-0304. E-mail: refdesk@theadvocate.com. Web Site: www.theadvocate.com. *Dir,* Judy Jumonville; E-mail: jjumonville@theadvocate.com; Staff 1 (MLS 1)
Founded 1922
Library Holdings: Bk Vols 200; Per Subs 30
Wireless access
Function: Ref serv available
Partic in Merlin
Restriction: Staff use only

P EAST BATON ROUGE PARISH LIBRARY*, Main Library, 7711 Goodwood Blvd, 70806-7625. SAN 342-7684. Tel: 225-231-3700. Circulation Tel: 225-231-3740. Interlibrary Loan Service Tel: 225-231-3755. Reference Tel: 225-231-3750. Automation Services Tel: 225-231-7520. FAX: 225-231-3788. Administration E-mail: eref@ebrpl.com. Web Site: www.ebrpl.com. *Dir,* Spencer Watts; Fax: 225-231-3759, E-mail: spencerwatts@brgov.com; *Dep Libr Dir,* Kristin Edson; Tel: 225-231-3702, E-mail: kedson@ebrpl.com; *Asst Dir, Admin Serv,* Mary Stein; Tel: 225-231-3710, E-mail: mstein@ebrpl.com; *Asst Dir, Br Serv,* Patricia Husband; Tel: 225-231-3785, E-mail: phusband@ebrpl.com; *Head, YA,* Brandi Burton; Tel: 225-231-3770, E-mail: bburton@ebrpl.com; *Bus Mgr,* Rhonda Pinsonat; Tel: 225-231-3705, E-mail: rpinsonat@brgov.com; *Br Serv Coordr,* Lori Juge; Tel: 225-231-3780, E-mail: ljuge@ebrpl.com; *Children's Serv Coordr,* Tara Dearing; Tel: 225-231-3760, E-mail: tdearing@ebrpl.com; *Circ Serv Coordr,* Position Currently Open; *Coordr, Spec Projects, Literacy Prog Coordr,* Pabby Arnold; Tel: 225-924-9389, E-mail: parnold@ebrpl.com; *Computer Coordr, Tech Serv Coordr,* Bryce Tomlin; E-mail: btomlin@ebrpl.com; *Ref Coordr,* Andrew Tadman; Tel: 225-231-3735, E-mail: atadman@ebrpl.com; *Acq,* Jenny Wong; E-mail: jwong@ebrpl.com; *Coll Develop,* Mechelle Whitney; E-mail: colldev@ebrpl.com; *ILL,* Sarah Roseman; E-mail: ill@ebrpl.com; *Outreach Serv,* Tameka Roby; Tel: 225-231-3710, E-mail: troby@ebrpl.com; Staff 422 (MLS 112, Non-MLS 310)
Founded 1939. Pop 446,268; Circ 2,924,461
Jan 2017-Dec 2017 Income (Main & Associated Libraries) $45,583,238, County $44,940,322, Other $642,916. Mats Exp $5,855,367, Books $2,107,932, Per/Ser (Incl. Access Fees) $175,661, Other Print Mats $58,554, AV Mat $761,198, Electronic Ref Mat (Incl. Access Fees) $2,752,022. Sal $16,649,380
Library Holdings: Audiobooks 24,038; AV Mats 242,045; Braille Volumes 346; CDs 1,971; DVDs 163,305; e-books 160,488; Electronic Media & Resources 196,880; Large Print Bks 103,597; Microforms 1; Bk Vols 1,706,222; Per Subs 2,729; Talking Bks 25,919; Videos 163,305
Special Collections: Oral History
Subject Interests: Genealogy, Grants, La
Automation Activity & Vendor Info: (Acquisitions) Infor Library & Information Solutions; (Cataloging) Infor Library & Information Solutions; (Circulation) Infor Library & Information Solutions; (Discovery) EBSCO Discovery Service; (ILL) TLC (The Library Corporation); (OPAC) Infor Library & Information Solutions; (Serials) Infor Library & Information Solutions
Wireless access
Function: 24/7 Electronic res, 24/7 Online cat, 3D Printer, Activity rm, Adult bk club, Adult literacy prog, After school storytime, Archival coll, Art exhibits, Audiobks on Playaways & MP3, Audiobks via web, AV serv, Bk club(s), Bks on CD, Bus archives, Butterfly Garden, CD-ROM, Chess club, Children's prog, Citizenship assistance, Computer training, Computers for patron use, Digital talking bks, E-Reserves, Electronic databases & coll, Family literacy, For res purposes, Free DVD rentals, Games & aids for people with disabilities, Genealogy discussion group, Govt ref serv, Health sci info serv, Holiday prog, Home delivery & serv to seniorr ctr & nursing homes, Homework prog, ILL available, Instruction & testing, Internet access, Jail serv, Jazz prog, Life-long learning prog for all ages, Literacy & newcomer serv, Magazines, Magnifiers for reading, Mail & tel request accepted, Mango lang, Meeting rooms, Microfiche/film & reading machines, Movies, Music CDs, Online cat, Online info literacy tutorials on the web & in blackboard, Online ref, Orientations, Outreach serv, Outside serv via phone, mail, e-mail & web, OverDrive digital audio bks, Photocopying/Printing, Preschool outreach, Preschool reading prog, Printer for laptops & handheld devices, Prog for adults, Prog for children & young adult, Ref & res, Ref serv available, Res libr, Satellite serv, Scanner, Senior computer classes, Senior outreach, Serves people with intellectual disabilities, Spanish lang bks, Spoken cassettes & CDs, Spoken cassettes & DVDs, Story hour, Study rm, Summer & winter reading prog, Summer reading prog, Tax forms, Teen prog, Telephone ref, VHS videos, Visual arts prog, Wheelchair accessible, Winter reading prog, Workshops, Writing prog
Publications: Community Information Directory (Online only); The Source (Monthly newsletter)
Partic in Loan System Helping Automate Retrieval of Knowledge
Special Services for the Deaf - Adult & family literacy prog; Assisted listening device; Bks on deafness & sign lang; Closed caption videos; High interest/low vocabulary bks; Sign lang interpreter upon request for prog; Staff with knowledge of sign lang
Special Services for the Blind - Accessible computers; Aids for in-house use; Assistive/Adapted tech devices, equip & products; Audio mat; BiFolkal kits; Bks & mags in Braille, on rec, tape & cassette; Bks available with recordings; Bks on CD; Braille equip; Children's Braille; Club for the blind; Computer access aids; Computer with voice synthesizer for visually impaired persons; Copier with enlargement capabilities; Digital talking bk; Disability awareness prog; Extensive large print coll; Free

checkout of audio mat; Info on spec aids & appliances; Internet workstation with adaptive software; Large print bks; Local mags & bks recorded; Low vision equip; Magnifiers; Open bk software on pub access PC; PC for people with disabilities; Playaways (bks on MP3); Recorded bks; Screen reader software; Talking bks; Text reader; Videos on blindness & physical disabilties; ZoomText magnification & reading software

Branches: 13

BAKER BRANCH, 3501 Groom Rd, Baker, 70714, SAN 342-7714. Tel: 225-778-5940. Reference Tel: 225-778-5950. Web Site: www.ebrpl.com/LocationsandHours/bak.html. *Br Mgr,* Ashley Lightell; Tel: 225-778-5980, E-mail: alightell@ebrpl.com
Library Holdings: Bk Vols 78,243
Open Mon-Thurs 9-8, Fri & Sat 9-6, Sun 2-6

BLUEBONNET REGIONAL, 9200 Bluebonnet Blvd, 70810, SAN 373-1243. Tel: 225-763-2240. Reference Tel: 225-763-2250. Web Site: www.ebrpl.com/LocationsandHours/bbr.html. *Br Mgr,* Kelley Young; Tel: 225-763-2280, E-mail: kyoung@ebrpl.com
Library Holdings: Bk Vols 173,577
Open Mon-Thurs 9-9, Fri & Sat 9-6, Sun 2-6

CARVER, 720 Terrace St, 70802, SAN 342-7749. Tel: 225-389-7440. Reference Tel: 225-389-7450. Web Site: www.ebrpl.com/LocationsandHours/car.html. *Br Mgr,* Roblyn Honeysucker; Tel: 225-389-7480, E-mail: rhoneysucker@ebrpl.com
Library Holdings: Bk Vols 44,126
Open Mon-Thurs 9-8, Fri & Sat 9-6, Sun 2-6

CENTRAL, 11260 Joor Rd, 70818, SAN 342-7773. Tel: 225-262-2640. Reference Tel: 225-262-2650. Web Site: www.ebrpl.com/LocationsandHours/cen.html. *Br Mgr,* Heather Harrison; Tel: 225-262-2680, E-mail: hharrison@ebrpl.com
Library Holdings: Bk Vols 108,581
Open Mon-Thurs 9-8, Fri & Sat 9-6, Sun 2-6

DELMONT GARDENS, 3351 Lorraine St, 70805, SAN 342-7838. Tel: 225-354-7040. Reference Tel: 225-354-7050. Web Site: www.ebrpl.com/LocationsandHours/dgb.html. *Br Mgr,* Melissa Bradley; Tel: 225-354-7080, E-mail: mbradley@ebrpl.com
Library Holdings: Bk Vols 90,053
Open Mon-Thurs 9-8, Fri & Sat 9-6, Sun 2-6

EDEN PARK, 5131 Greenwell Springs Rd, 70806, SAN 342-7811. Tel: 225-231-3240. Reference Tel: 225-231-3250. Web Site: www.ebrpl.com/LocationsandHours/ede.html. *Br Mgr,* Letrice Davis; Tel: 225-231-3280, E-mail: ldavis@ebrpl.com
Library Holdings: Bk Vols 47,279
Open Mon-Thurs 9-8, Fri & Sat 9-6, Sun 2-6

FAIRWOOD BRANCH, 12910 Old Hammond Hwy, 70816. Tel: 225-924-9384. Reference Tel: 225-924-9385. Web Site: www.ebrpl.com/LocationsandHours/fai.html. *Br Mgr,* Leila Reilly; Tel: 225-924-9380, E-mail: lreilly@ebrpl.com
Library Holdings: Bk Vols 51,296
Open Mon-Thurs 9-8,Fri & Sat 9-6, Sun 2-6

GREENWELL SPRINGS ROAD REGIONAL, 11300 Greenwell Springs Rd, 70814, SAN 376-964X. Tel: 225-274-4440. Reference Tel: 225-274-4450. Web Site: www.ebrpl.com/LocationsandHours/gsr.html. *Br Mgr,* Brandon Reilly; Tel: 225-274-4480, E-mail: breilly@ebrpl.com
Library Holdings: Bk Vols 130,482
Open Mon-Thurs 9-9, Fri & Sat 9-6, Sun 2-6

JONES CREEK REGIONAL, 6222 Jones Creek Rd, 70817, SAN 370-1301. Tel: 225-756-1140. Reference Tel: 225-756-1150. Web Site: www.ebrpl.com/LocationsandHours/jcr.html. *Br Mgr,* Yvonne Hull; Tel: 225-756-1180, E-mail: yhull@ebrpl.com
Library Holdings: Bk Vols 181,731
Open Mon-Thurs 9-9, Fri & Sat 9-6, Sun 2-6

PRIDE-CHANEYVILLE BRANCH, 13600 Pride-Port Hudson Rd, Pride, 70770, SAN 342-7862. Tel: 225-658-1540. Reference Tel: 225-658-1550. Web Site: www.ebrpl.com/LocationsandHours/pri.html. *Br Mgr,* Ginger Cagnolatti; Tel: 225-658-1580, E-mail: gcagnolatti@ebrpl.com
Library Holdings: Bk Vols 47,250
Open Mon-Thurs 9-8, Fri & Sat 9-6, Sun 2-6

RIVER CENTER, 447 Third St, 70802, SAN 342-7803. Tel: 225-389-4967. Reference Tel: 225-389-4964. Web Site: www.ebrpl.com/LocationsandHours/rcb.html. *Br Mgr,* Allison Cooper; Tel: 225-389-4967, E-mail: acooper@ebrpl.com
Library Holdings: Bk Vols 86,189
Special Collections: Baton Rouge History Coll; Career Center; Foundation Center Cooperating Coll. Oral History
Open Mon-Thurs 8-7, Fri & Sat 9-6, Sun 2-6

SCOTLANDVILLE, 7373 Scenic Hwy, 70807, SAN 342-7897. Tel: 225-354-7540. Reference Tel: 225-354-7550. Web Site: www.ebrpl.com/LocationsandHours/sco.html. *Br Mgr,* Amy Sideris; Tel: 225-354-7580, E-mail: asideris@ebrpl.com
Library Holdings: Bk Vols 79,077
Open Mon-Thurs 9-8, Fri & Sat 9-6, Sun 2-6

ZACHARY BRANCH, 1900 Church St, Zachary, 70791, SAN 342-7927. Tel: 225-658-1840. Reference Tel: 225-658-1850. Web Site: www.ebrpl.com/LocationsandHours/zac.html. *Br Mgr,* Kimberly Reeves; Tel: 225-658-1880, E-mail: kreeves@ebrpl.com
Library Holdings: Bk Vols 109,754
Open Mon-Thurs 9-9, Fri & Sat 9-6, Sun 2-6

Bookmobiles: 1. Bk vols 51,479

C FRANCISCAN MISSIONARIES OF OUR LADY UNIVERSITY LIBRARY*, 5329 Didesse St, 70808. (Mail add: 5414 Brittany Dr, 70808), SAN 378-4533. Tel: 225-768-1730. Interlibrary Loan Service Tel: 225-490-1657. FAX: 225-761-7303. E-mail: Library@franu.edu. Web Site: www.franu.edu/offices-services/library. *Co-Dir,* Lucas Huntington; Tel: 225-768-1732, E-mail: Lucas.Huntington@franu.edu; *Co-Dir,* Maggie McCann; Tel: 225-768-1783, E-mail: Maggie.Mccann@franu.edu; *Cat Librn,* Fatima Zamin; E-mail: fzamin@franu.edu; Staff 9.5 (MLS 3.5, Non-MLS 6)
Founded 1923. Enrl 2,000; Fac 120; Highest Degree: Master
Library Holdings: CDs 300; DVDs 150; e-books 14,000; e-journals 100; Bk Titles 30,000; Per Subs 150; Videos 1,000
Special Collections: Historical Nursing Coll (Some materials date in the 1800's)
Wireless access
Function: Art exhibits, Audio & video playback equip for onsite use, CD-ROM, Computers for patron use, Electronic databases & coll, ILL available, Online cat, Online info literacy tutorials on the web & in blackboard, Online ref, Orientations, Photocopying/Printing, Ref & res, Ref serv available, Telephone ref, VHS videos
Partic in Louisiana Library Network; LYRASIS
Open Mon-Thurs 8am-9pm, Fri 8-4:30

C JIMMY SWAGGART BIBLE COLLEGE & SEMINARY LIBRARY*, 8919 World Ministry Ave, 70810-9000. (Mail add: PO Box 262550, 70826-2550). Tel: 225-768-3890. FAX: 225-768-4533. E-mail: info@jsbc.edu. Web Site: www.jsbc.edu. *Dir,* Stephanie Beauregard
Library Holdings: Bk Titles 25,000
Wireless access
Open Mon-Thurs 7:30-5, Fri 7:30-2:30

L HUEY P LONG MEMORIAL LAW LIBRARY, State Capitol, 900 N Third St, 14th Flr, 70802. (Mail add: PO Box 94183, 70804). Tel: 225-342-2414. FAX: 225-342-2725. *Law Librn,* Monica Corbett; E-mail: corbettm@legis.la.gov
Library Holdings: Bk Vols 10,000; Per Subs 50

GL LOUISIANA DEPARTMENT OF JUSTICE OFFICE OF THE ATTORNEY GENERAL*, Law Library, 1885 N Third St, 4th Flr, 70802. (Mail add: PO Box 94005, 70804-9005), SAN 327-4829. Tel: 225-326-6422. FAX: 225-326-6495. *Law Librn,* Mary Adams; E-mail: adamsm@ag.louisiana.gov; Staff 1 (MLS 1)
Library Holdings: Bk Vols 10,000; Per Subs 30
Restriction: Not open to pub

S LOUISIANA ECONOMIC DEVELOPMENT LIBRARY*, LaSalle Bldg, 617 N Third St, 11th Flr, 70802. (Mail add: PO Box 94185, 70804-9185), SAN 306-4476. Tel: 225-342-3071. Web Site: www.opportunitylouisiana.com. *Librn,* Paula Bryars; E-mail: bryars@la.gov; Staff 1 (MLS 1)
Library Holdings: Per Subs 20
Special Collections: Business Reference; Current Economic Development Material; LED Publications, Economic Development Research Studies
Subject Interests: Econ develop, La

GL LOUISIANA HOUSE OF REPRESENTATIVES, David R Poynter Legislative Research Library, 900 N Third St, 70804. (Mail add: PO Box 94012, 70804-9012), SAN 306-4468. Tel: 225-342-2430. FAX: 225-342-2431. TDD: 888-850-6489. E-mail: drplibrary@legis.la.gov. Web Site: house.louisiana.gov/H_Staff/HLS_RESEARCH_LIB. *Libr Dir,* Frances Carlson Thomas; *Librn,* Robyn Cockerham; Tel: 225-342-2434; *Librn,* Robin Boatright Stalder; Tel: 225-342-2432; *Librn,* Jenna Steward; Tel: 225-342-2433. Subject Specialists: *Govt affairs,* Robyn Cockerham; *Legal,* Robin Boatright Stalder; *Commerce,* Jenna Steward; Staff 5 (MLS 5)
Founded 1952
Library Holdings: Bk Vols 15,000; Per Subs 110
Special Collections: Legislative Archival Coll, committee reports; Legislative Documents & Research Publications, per, clippings
Automation Activity & Vendor Info: (Cataloging) Inmagic, Inc.
Publications: Membership in the Louisiana House of Representatives, 1812-2016 (Local historical information); Resume (Annual summary of enactments)
Special Services for the Deaf - TTY equip
Restriction: Not open to pub

G LOUISIANA OFFICE OF THE SECRETARY OF STATE*, Division of Archives, Records Management & History Library, 3851 Essen Lane, 70809-2137. (Mail add: PO Box 94125, 70804-9125), SAN 326-5463. Tel: 225-922-1208. FAX: 225-922-0433. E-mail: library@sos.la.gov. Web Site:

www.sos.la.gov. *Adminr,* Bill Stafford; E-mail: bstafford@sos.la.gov; Staff 1 (MLS 1)
Founded 1956
Library Holdings: Bk Titles 6,400; Bk Vols 7,000; Per Subs 50
Special Collections: Louisiana Confederate Government (Rebel Archives Coll), doc; Louisiana Death Certificates, 1912-1960; Lumber Industry (Louisiana Longleaf Lumber Co Coll); Orleans Parish Birth Certificates, 1790-1910; Orleans Parish Death Certificates, 1804-1960; Orleans Parish Marriage Certificates, 1831-1960. Oral History; US Document Depository
Subject Interests: Genealogy, Mil hist
Wireless access
Publications: Legacy (Newsletter)
Open Mon-Fri 8-4
Friends of the Library Group

C LOUISIANA STATE UNIVERSITY LIBRARIES, 295 Middleton Library, 70803. SAN 342-8133. Tel: 225-578-2217. Circulation Tel: 225-578-2058. Interlibrary Loan Service Tel: 225-578-2138. Reference Tel: 225-578-5652. FAX: 225-578-9432. Web Site: www.lib.lsu.edu. *Dean,* Stanley Wilder; E-mail: wilder@lsu.edu; *Asst Dean,* Meshelle Fargason; E-mail: mfargason1@lsu.edu; *Head, Circ,* Elissa Plank; Tel: 225-578-3216, E-mail: esp1061@lsu.edu; *Colls Librn,* Tom Diamond; Tel: 225-578-6572, E-mail: notted@lsu.edu; *Coord, Research & Instruction,* Allen LeBlanc; Tel: 225-578-2738, E-mail: aleb118@lsu.edu; *Collection Analysis Librn,* Mike Russo; Tel: 225-578-6823, E-mail: mrusso1@lsu.edu; *Head, ILL,* Jacob Fontenot; Tel: 225-578-6722, E-mail: jacob.fontenot@lsu.edu; Staff 131 (MLS 41, Non-MLS 90)
Founded 1860. Enrl 28,985; Fac 1,415; Highest Degree: Doctorate
Library Holdings: AV Mats 21,242; e-books 43,295; e-journals 17,265; Bk Vols 3,213,314; Per Subs 18,695
Special Collections: Louisiana & Lower Mississippi Coll; McIlhenny Natural History Coll; Rare Book Coll. Oral History; State Document Depository; UN Document Depository; US Document Depository
Automation Activity & Vendor Info: (Acquisitions) SirsiDynix; (Cataloging) OCLC; (Circulation) SirsiDynix; (ILL) OCLC; (Media Booking) SirsiDynix; (OPAC) SirsiDynix; (Serials) SirsiDynix
Wireless access
Publications: Guide to Oral History Collections in Louisiana; Guide to the Russell B Long Coll; Historical Collections of Louisiana (CD-ROM Edition)
Partic in Association of Southeastern Research Libraries; La Acad Libr Info Network Consortium; Louisiana Library Network; LYRASIS; National Network of Libraries of Medicine Region 3; OCLC Online Computer Library Center, Inc; OCLC Research Library Partnership; USDA SW Regional Doc Delivery Syst

Departmental Libraries:

CARTER MUSIC RESOURCES CENTER, 295 Middleton Library, Rm 202, 70803-3300, SAN 376-8538. Tel: 225-578-4674. Interlibrary Loan Service Tel: 225-578-2138. Web Site: www.lib.lsu.edu/collections/music. *Music Resources Supervisor,* Mikel LeDee; E-mail: mledee1@lsu.edu; Staff 3 (MLS 1, Non-MLS 2)
Library Holdings: CDs 208; Music Scores 20,554; Bk Vols 57,600; Per Subs 90; Videos 411
Subject Interests: Hist, Music

CARTOGRAPHIC INFORMATION CENTER, Dept of Geography & Anthropology, Howe-Russell-Kniffen Geoscience Complex, Rm 313, 70803-4100. Tel: 225-578-6247. FAX: 225-578-4420. Web Site: lsu.edu/cic. *Dir, Maps Librn,* John M Anderson; E-mail: janders@lsu.edu; Staff 1 (MLS 1)
Founded 1954
Library Holdings: CDs 1,713; Bk Vols 4,122
Special Collections: Coastal Louisiana Geomorphology (James P Morgan Coll); Richard J Russell Reprint Coll; Robert C West Coll, photog, maps, slides. US Document Depository
Subject Interests: La, Latin Am, Miss river
Function: For res purposes, Govt ref serv, Magnifiers for reading, Res libr, Wheelchair accessible
Open Mon-Fri 7:30-12 & 12:30-4
Restriction: Closed stack, Restricted borrowing privileges

CL PAUL M HEBERT LAW CENTER, One E Campus Dr, 70803-1000. Tel: 225-578-4042. Circulation Tel: 225-578-8814. FAX: 225-578-5773. TDD: 225-388-4706. E-mail: lawreference@lsu.edu. Web Site: www.law.lsu.edu/library. *Asst Dean, Dir, Libr & Info Tech,* Todd Venie; Tel: 225-578-4952, E-mail: tvenie@lsu.edu; *Asst Dir for Instructional Tech,* Will Monroe; Tel: 225-578-7838, E-mail: wmonro1@lsu.edu; *Asst Dir for Resource Mgmt,* Natalie Palermo; Tel: 225-578-6530, E-mail: palermo@lsu.edu; *Head, Access Services & Govt Info,* Melanie Sims; Tel: 225-578-8815, E-mail: notmes@lsu.edu; *Acq Librn,* Ajaye Bloomstone; Tel: 225-578-4044, E-mail: llajaye@lsu.edu; *Info Serv Librn,* Rita Parham; Tel: 225-578-4043, E-mail: llrita@lsu.edu; Staff 19 (MLS 8, Non-MLS 11)
Founded 1906. Enrl 650; Fac 36; Highest Degree: Doctorate
Library Holdings: Bk Titles 139,589; Bk Vols 850,000; Per Subs 12,229
Special Collections: Foreign, Comparative & International Law
Automation Activity & Vendor Info: (Acquisitions) SirsiDynix; (Cataloging) SirsiDynix; (Circulation) SirsiDynix; (Course Reserve) SirsiDynix; (ILL) SirsiDynix; (OPAC) SirsiDynix; (Serials) SirsiDynix
Function: Doc delivery serv, ILL available, Photocopying/Printing, Ref serv available, Res libr
Partic in Louisiana Library Network

CM LSU SCHOOL OF VETERINARY MEDICINE LIBRARY, Skip Bertman Dr, 70803-8414, SAN 342-8222. Tel: 225-578-9800. FAX: 225-578-9798. E-mail: svmlibrary@lsu.edu. Web Site: lsu.edu/vetmed/library. *Dir,* Corrie Hess; Tel: 225-578-9799, E-mail: clong2@lsu.edu; *Tech Serv Librn,* Chairity Waugh; Tel: 225-578-9796, E-mail: cwaugh3@lsu.edu; *Outreach Librn,* Brian Collins; Tel: 225-578-9794, E-mail: bcollins2@lsu.edu; *Circ Assoc,* Brenda Irvin; E-mail: birvin@lsu.edu; *Public Services & Acquisitions Assoc,* Angela Alleman; Tel: 225-578-7058, E-mail: alleman@lsu.edu; Staff 6 (MLS 2, Non-MLS 4)
Founded 1974. Enrl 350; Highest Degree: Doctorate
Library Holdings: Bk Vols 47,000; Per Subs 600
Special Collections: Reprint Coll on Parasitology, 1865-1972
Subject Interests: Veterinary med
Automation Activity & Vendor Info: (Acquisitions) SirsiDynix; (Cataloging) OCLC; (Circulation) SirsiDynix; (OPAC) SirsiDynix; (Serials) SirsiDynix

C SOUTHERN UNIVERSITY*, John B Cade Library, 167 Roosevelt Steptoe Ave, 70813-0001. SAN 342-8257. Tel: 225-771-4990. Circulation Tel: 225-771-2855. Interlibrary Loan Service Tel: 225-771-2869. Information Services Tel: 225-771-2841. FAX: 225-771-4113. Web Site: www.subr.edu/page/2441. *Dean of Libr,* Dawn Kight; E-mail: dawn_kight@subr.edu; *Head, Circ,* Linda Forsythe; E-mail: linda_forsythe@subr.edu; *Head, Ref,* Jordan Signater; E-mail: jordan_signater@subr.edu; Staff 39 (MLS 13, Non-MLS 26)
Founded 1880. Enrl 8,572; Fac 425; Highest Degree: Doctorate
Library Holdings: AV Mats 42,734; e-books 16,325; e-journals 200; Electronic Media & Resources 593; Bk Titles 308,156; Bk Vols 406,815; Per Subs 1,675
Special Collections: Archives & Shade Coll. State Document Depository; US Document Depository
Subject Interests: African-Am, Agr, Art & archit, Bus & mgt, Econ, Educ
Automation Activity & Vendor Info: (Acquisitions) SirsiDynix; (Cataloging) SirsiDynix; (Circulation) SirsiDynix; (Course Reserve) SirsiDynix; (ILL) Infotrieve; (OPAC) SirsiDynix; (Serials) SirsiDynix
Wireless access
Publications: Cade Books & Bytes (Newsletter)
Partic in Louisiana Library Network; LYRASIS; OCLC Online Computer Library Center, Inc
Open Mon-Thurs (Winter) 7:30am-Midnight, Fri 7:30-5, Sat 1-5, Sun 2-Midnight; Mon-Thurs (Summer) 7:30am-8pm, Fri 7:30-5, Sun 4pm-10pm

Departmental Libraries:

CL OLIVER B SPELLMAN LAW LIBRARY, Two Roosevelt Steptoe, 70813. (Mail add: PO Box 9294, 70813-9294). Tel: 225-771-2146. FAX: 225-771-6254. Web Site: www.sulc.edu/directory/office/law-library. *Dir,* Phebe Huderson-Poydras; E-mail: ppoydras@sulc.edu; *Ref Librn,* Marilyn French; E-mail: mfrench@sulc.edu; *Libr Spec III,* William M Lockhart, Jr; E-mail: wlockhart@sulc.edu; Staff 17 (MLS 6, Non-MLS 11)
Founded 1947. Enrl 450; Fac 45; Highest Degree: Doctorate
Library Holdings: Bk Titles 91,924; Bk Vols 475,081; Per Subs 989
Special Collections: South Africa Law. State Document Depository; US Document Depository
Subject Interests: Civil rights
Automation Activity & Vendor Info: (Acquisitions) SirsiDynix; (Cataloging) SirsiDynix; (Circulation) SirsiDynix; (Course Reserve) SirsiDynix; (OPAC) SirsiDynix; (Serials) SirsiDynix
Partic in Louisiana Library Network; LYRASIS; OCLC Online Computer Library Center, Inc; Proquest Dialog
Publications: Library Newsletter; Reflections; Southern Univ Law Review
Open Mon-Thurs (Winter) 7am-Midnight, Fri 7-5, Sat 9-5, Sun 2-10; Mon-Thurs (Summer) 8am-9pm, Fri 8-5, Sat 10-4, Sun 2-10

P STATE LIBRARY OF LOUISIANA*, 701 N Fourth St, 70802-5232. (Mail add: PO Box 131, 70821-0131), SAN 342-8044. Tel: 225-342-4923. Circulation Tel: 225-342-4915. Interlibrary Loan Service Tel: 225-342-4918. Reference Tel: 225-342-4913. Automation Services Tel: 225-342-6759. FAX: 225-219-4804. Circulation FAX: 225-342-7962. Interlibrary Loan Service FAX: 225-219-4725. TDD: 225-219-1696. Administration E-mail: admin@state.lib.la.us. Web Site: www.state.lib.la.us. *State Librn,* Rebecca Hamilton; E-mail: rhamilton@crt.state.la.us; *Dep State Librn,* Diane M Brown; E-mail: dbrown@crt.state.la.us; *Assoc State Librn,* Margaret Placke; Tel: 225-342-4951, E-mail: mplacke@crt.state.la.us; *Dir, Louisiana Ctr for the Bk,* Jim Davis; Tel: 225-342-9714, E-mail: jdavis@slol.lib.la.us; *Head, Access Serv,* Kytara Gaudin; Tel: 225-342-4920, E-mail: kgaudin@slol.lib.la.us; *Head, Acq & Ser,* Lesli Gray; Tel: 225-342-4937, E-mail: lgray@slol.lib.la.us; *Head, Info*

Tech, Troy Morris; E-mail: tmorris@slol.lib.la.us; *Head, Ref,* Michael Golrick; Tel: 225-219-4726, E-mail: mgolrick@slol.lib.la.us; *Bus Mgr,* Katie McClelland; E-mail: kmclelland@slol.lib.la.us; *Outreach Serv,* Sheila Coleman; Tel: 225-342-4942, Fax: 225-342-6817, E-mail: scoleman@slol.lib.la.us; Staff 44 (MLS 20, Non-MLS 24)
Founded 1925
Jul 2018-Jun 2019 Income $7,748,303, State $4,234,263, Federal $240,000, Locally Generated Income $90,000. Mats Exp $25,000. Sal $416,035
Library Holdings: AV Mats 28,413; Large Print Bks 21,037; Bk Vols 543,181; Per Subs 374; Talking Bks 278,381
Special Collections: Huey Long Photographs; Louisiana History, Politics, Economics, Literature. State Document Depository; US Document Depository
Subject Interests: La
Automation Activity & Vendor Info: (Acquisitions) Horizon; (Cataloging) Horizon; (Circulation) Horizon; (ILL) Auto-Graphics, Inc; (OPAC) Horizon; (Serials) Horizon
Wireless access
Publications: Library Laws of Louisiana; Louisiana Libraries-Economic Impact; Official Publications: Lists of the Public Documents of Louisiana; Public Documents; Public Libraries in Louisiana Statistical Report; Quick Facts-Louisiana Libraries; Searching for Your Louisiana Ancestors & All That Jazz
Partic in Amigos Library Services, Inc; OCLC Online Computer Library Center, Inc
Special Services for the Deaf - ADA equip; Captioned film dep; High interest/low vocabulary bks
Special Services for the Blind - Accessible computers; Bks & mags in Braille, on rec, tape & cassette; Bks on flash-memory cartridges; Braille bks; Closed circuit TV magnifier; Copier with enlargement capabilities; Descriptive video serv (DVS); Digital talking bk; Digital talking bk machines; Extensive large print coll; Home delivery serv; Integrated libr/media serv; Internet workstation with adaptive software; Large print bks; Large screen computer & software; Low vision equip; Machine repair; Newsletter (in large print, Braille or on cassette); PC for people with disabilities; Recorded bks; Screen enlargement software for people with visual disabilities; Screen reader software; Soundproof reading booth; Talking bks; Talking bks & player equip; Tel Pioneers equip repair group; Web-Braille
Open Mon-Thurs 10-2
Friends of the Library Group

P STATE LIBRARY OF LOUISIANA*, Talking Books & Braille Library, 701 N Fourth St, 70802. (Mail add: PO Box 131, 70821-0131), SAN 306-4492. Tel: 225-342-0035. Toll Free Tel: 800-543-4702. FAX: 225-342-6817. E-mail: tbbl@state.lib.la.us. Web Site: www.state.lib.la.us. *Coordr, Spec Serv, Regional Librn,* Sheila Coleman; Tel: 225-342-4942, E-mail: scoleman@slol.lib.la.us; *Readers' Advisory, Supvr,* David Rainey; Tel: 225-342-5148, E-mail: drainey@slol.lib.la.us; Staff 14 (MLS 4, Non-MLS 10)
Founded 1933
Library Holdings: Large Print Bks 18,000; Bk Titles 60,000; Talking Bks 200,000
Subject Interests: La
Publications: Louisiana Hotlines (Newsletter)
Special Services for the Blind - Cassettes; Descriptive video serv (DVS); Large print bks
Open Mon-Fri 10-2
Friends of the Library Group

R UNIVERSITY BAPTIST CHURCH LIBRARY, 5775 Highland Rd, 70808. SAN 306-4522. Tel: 225-766-9474. FAX: 225-766-9101. E-mail: communications@ubc-br.org, office@ubc-br.org. Web Site: www.ubc-br.org. *Librn,* Dr Patsy Perritt
Founded 1955
Library Holdings: Bk Titles 6,250; Bk Vols 6,500
Special Collections: Children's Literature (Jim Smith Memorial Coll)
Subject Interests: Church hist
Wireless access

M WOMAN'S HOSPITAL*, Health Sciences Library, 100 Woman's Way, 70817. (Mail add: PO Box 95009, 70895-9009). Tel: 225-924-8462. FAX: 225-924-8467. E-mail: hslibrary@womans.org. Web Site: www.womans.org. *Info Spec,* Louise McLaughlin
Library Holdings: Bk Vols 1,600; Per Subs 150
Wireless access
Restriction: Staff use only

BELLE CHASSE

P PLAQUEMINES PARISH LIBRARY*, Administration Office, Bldg 203, Ste B-11, 333 F Edward Herbert Blvd, 70037. SAN 342-8583. Tel: 504-934-6765. FAX: 504-934-6775. Web Site: plaqueminesppl.booksys.net/opac/plaqueminesppl/index.html. *Asst Libr Dir, Interim Libr Dir,* Patrisha Walker; E-mail: pwalker@ppgov.net; Staff 1 (MLS 1)
Founded 1959
Special Collections: J Ben Meyer Historical Plaquemines Parish Coll; Louisiana Census Coll, microfilm; Video Cassette Coll
Automation Activity & Vendor Info: (Cataloging) Book Systems; (Circulation) Book Systems; (OPAC) Book Systems
Wireless access
Function: Audio & video playback equip for onsite use, AV serv, Bks on cassette, Children's prog, Computers for patron use, E-Reserves, Electronic databases & coll, ILL available, Internet access, Photocopying/Printing, Preschool outreach, Prog for children & young adult, Ref & res, Scanner, Summer reading prog, Tax forms, VHS videos, Wheelchair accessible
Partic in Loan System Helping Automate Retrieval of Knowledge
Open Mon-Fri 8:30-5
Restriction: Residents only
Branches: 3
BELLE CHASSE BRANCH, 8442 Hwy 23, 70037, SAN 342-8613. Tel: 504-393-0449, 504-394-3570. FAX: 504-394-6102. *Br Librn,* Brigette Bolton; E-mail: bbolton@ppgov.net; *Br Librn,* Andrea Declouet; E-mail: adeclouet@ppgov.net; *Br Librn,* Barbara Nash; E-mail: bnash@ppgov.net; *Br Librn,* Dana Wallace; E-mail: dwallace@ppgov.net
Pop 26,049; Circ 18,546
Library Holdings: AV Mats 1,112; Bks on Deafness & Sign Lang 25; Large Print Bks 112; Bk Titles 24,121; Bk Vols 26,624; Per Subs 91; Talking Bks 62; Videos 889
Function: Audio & video playback equip for onsite use, Bks on cassette, Children's prog, Computers for patron use, E-Reserves, Electronic databases & coll, ILL available, Photocopying/Printing, Prog for children & young adult, Scanner, Spoken cassettes & CDs, Summer reading prog, Tax forms, VHS videos, Wheelchair accessible
Open Mon, Wed & Fri 8:30-5, Tues & Thurs 8:30-7
Restriction: Residents only
BURAS BRANCH, 35572 Hwy 11, Buras, 70041. Tel: 504-564-0921, 504-564-0944. *Br Librn,* Leigh Galmiche Armstrong; E-mail: larmstrong@ppgov.net; *Br Librn,* Mona Fitzmorris; E-mail: Rfitzmorris@ppgov.net; *Br Librn,* Michele Newborn; E-mail: Mnewborn@ppgov.net
Open Mon-Fri 9-4
PORT SULPHUR BRANCH, 139 Civic Dr, Port Sulphur, 70083, SAN 342-8702. Tel: 504-564-3681, 504-564-3682. FAX: 504-564-3274. *Br Librn,* Peggy Lightell; E-mail: plightell@ppgov.net
Open Mon-Fri 8:30-5
Bookmobiles: 1. Librn, Donna Pobrica

BLANCHARD

R FIRST BAPTIST CHURCH OF BLANCHARD*, FBC Media Center, 201 Attaway St, 71009. (Mail add: PO Box 65, 71009-0065), SAN 374-826X. Tel: 318-929-2346. FAX: 318-929-4680. E-mail: fbcblanchard@bellsouth.net. Web Site: www.fbcblanchard.com. *Library Contact,* Kevin Sandifer
Library Holdings: AV Mats 112; Bk Vols 2,700

BOSSIER CITY

J BOSSIER PARISH COMMUNITY COLLEGE LIBRARY*, 6220 E Texas St, Bldg A, 71111. SAN 306-4530. Tel: 318-678-6042, 318-678-6275. FAX: 318-678-6400. E-mail: refdesk@bpcc.edu. Web Site: www.bpcc.edu/bpcclibrary. *Dean, Learning Res,* Brenda Brantley; Tel: 318-678-6068, E-mail: bbrantley@bpcc.edu; *Cat Librn,* Timothy Osteen; Tel: 318-678-6543, E-mail: tosteen@bpcc.edu; *Ref Librn,* Sarah Mazur; Tel: 318-678-6077, E-mail: smazur@bpcc.edu; *Libr Coord,* Stephanie Cox; Tel: 318-678-6224, E-mail: scox@bpcc.edu; Staff 11 (MLS 5, Non-MLS 6)
Founded 1968. Enrl 4,700; Fac 111; Highest Degree: Associate
Library Holdings: AV Mats 2,600; Bk Titles 45,000; Per Subs 230
Special Collections: Local Newspaper, micro, vertical file
Subject Interests: Hist
Automation Activity & Vendor Info: (Acquisitions) Mandarin Library Automation; (Cataloging) SirsiDynix; (Circulation) SirsiDynix; (Course Reserve) SirsiDynix; (Serials) SirsiDynix
Wireless access
Function: Distance learning, Doc delivery serv, ILL available, Photocopying/Printing, Ref serv available
Partic in Louisiana Library Network
Open Mon-Thurs (Fall & Spring) 7am-8pm, Fri 7-4:30; Mon-Fri (Summer) 8-4:30
Restriction: Open to students, fac & staff

P BOSSIER PARISH LIBRARIES*, Central Library, 2206 Beckett St, 71111. SAN 342-8400. Tel: 318-746-1693. FAX: 318-746-7768. Administration E-mail: libadmin@bossierlibrary.org. Web Site: www.bossierlibrary.org. *Libr Dir,* Heather McEntee; *Ad,* Katie Millsap; *Youth Serv Librn,* Joy Creasong; *Cent Libr Mgr,* Position Currently Open; *Circ Mgr,* Tammie Crochet; Staff 2 (MLS 1, Non-MLS 1)

Founded 1940
Special Collections: Bossier Parish Police Jury Minutes, 1881-present, microfilm; County Newspaper, 1859-present, bd vols, microfilm
Subject Interests: Local hist archives
Automation Activity & Vendor Info: (Cataloging) TLC (The Library Corporation); (Circulation) TLC (The Library Corporation); (ILL) Auto-Graphics, Inc; (OPAC) TLC (The Library Corporation)
Wireless access
Function: 24/7 Electronic res, 24/7 Online cat, Accelerated reader prog, Adult bk club, After school storytime, Archival coll, Art exhibits, Audiobks on Playaways & MP3, Audiobks via web, AV serv, Bk club(s), Bks on CD, CD-ROM, Children's prog, Computer training, Computers for patron use, Electronic databases & coll, Family literacy, Free DVD rentals, Holiday prog, Home delivery & serv to seniorr ctr & nursing homes, Homebound delivery serv, ILL available, Instruction & testing, Internet access, Life-long learning prog for all ages, Magazines, Magnifiers for reading, Mail & tel request accepted, Movies, Online cat, Online ref, Outreach serv, Outside serv via phone, mail, e-mail & web, OverDrive digital audio bks, Photocopying/Printing, Preschool outreach, Preschool reading prog, Printer for laptops & handheld devices, Prog for adults, Prog for children & young adult, Ref & res, Ref serv available, Res assist avail, Scanner, Senior computer classes, Senior outreach, Spanish lang bks, STEM programs, Story hour, Study rm, Summer & winter reading prog, Summer reading prog, Tax forms, Teen prog, Telephone ref, Wheelchair accessible, Workshops, Writing prog
Mem of Green Gold Library System
Partic in Loan System Helping Automate Retrieval of Knowledge
Open Mon-Thurs 9-8, Fri 9-6, Sat 9-5, Sun 1-5
Friends of the Library Group
Branches: 7

HENRY L AULDS MEMORIAL BRANCH, 3950 Wayne Ave, 71112, SAN 342-8494. Tel: 318-742-2337. Administration Tel: 318-742-5819. FAX: 318-752-4034. *Br Mgr,* Karen Hinson; *Asst Br Mgr,* Sharon Tyson; Staff 1 (Non-MLS 1)
Founded 1971
Function: Art exhibits, Bks on CD, Children's prog, Computer training, Computers for patron use, Electronic databases & coll, ILL available, Online cat, OverDrive digital audio bks, Photocopying/Printing, Printer for laptops & handheld devices, Prog for adults, Prog for children & young adult, Ref serv available, Story hour, Summer reading prog, Tax forms, Teen prog, Wheelchair accessible
Open Mon-Thurs 9-8, Fri 9-6, Sat 9-5, Sun 1-5

BENTON BRANCH, 115 Courthouse Dr, Benton, 71006. (Mail add: PO Box 400, Benton, 71006-0400), SAN 342-8435. Tel: 318-965-2751. FAX: 318-965-4379. *Br Mgr,* Heather Smith; *Asst Br Mgr,* Charmetra Ardoin; Staff 1 (MLS 1)
Function: After school storytime, Art exhibits, Bks on CD, Children's prog, Computer training, Computers for patron use, Electronic databases & coll, ILL available, Online cat, OverDrive digital audio bks, Photocopying/Printing, Preschool outreach, Printer for laptops & handheld devices, Prog for adults, Prog for children & young adult, Ref serv available, Story hour, Summer reading prog, Tax forms, Teen prog, Wheelchair accessible, Workshops
Open Mon-Thurs 9-8, Fri 9-6, Sat 11-5, Sun 1-5

EAST 80 BRANCH, 1050 Bellevue Rd, Haughton, 71037, SAN 329-661X. Tel: 318-949-2665. FAX: 318-949-2067. *Br Mgr,* Beverly Miles; *Asst Br Mgr,* Brittainy Pope; Staff 1 (Non-MLS 1)
Function: 24/7 Electronic res, 24/7 Online cat, Adult bk club, After school storytime, Audiobks on Playaways & MP3, Bk club(s), Bks on CD, Children's prog, Computer training, Computers for patron use, Electronic databases & coll, Family literacy, Free DVD rentals, Holiday prog, Life-long learning prog for all ages, Magazines, Meeting rooms, Movies, Online cat, Photocopying/Printing, Preschool reading prog, Printer for laptops & handheld devices, Prog for adults, Prog for children & young adult, Ref & res, Ref serv available, Res assist avail, STEM programs, Story hour, Study rm, Summer & winter reading prog, Summer reading prog, Teen prog, Wheelchair accessible
Open Mon-Thurs 9-8, Fri 9-6, Sat 9-5, Sun 1-5

HAUGHTON BRANCH, 116 E McKinley Ave, Haughton, 71037, SAN 342-8524. Tel: 318-949-0196. FAX: 318-949-0195. *Br Mgr,* Audra Bartholomew; *Asst Br Mgr,* Felesha Sweeney; Staff 1 (Non-MLS 1)
Function: Bks on CD, Children's prog, Computers for patron use, Electronic databases & coll, Free DVD rentals, ILL available, Online cat, OverDrive digital audio bks, Photocopying/Printing, Preschool outreach, Printer for laptops & handheld devices, Prog for adults, Prog for children & young adult, Ref serv available, Story hour, Summer reading prog, Tax forms, Teen prog, Telephone ref, Wheelchair accessible
Open Mon-Thurs 9-8, Fri 9-6, Sat 9-5, Sun 1-5

HISTORY CENTER, 2206 Beckett St, 71111. Tel: 318-746-7717. *Mgr,* Ann Middleton; *Curator,* Marisa Richardson; *Outreach/Educ,* Pam Carlisle; Staff 3 (MLS 1, Non-MLS 2)
Special Collections: Oral History
Automation Activity & Vendor Info: (Acquisitions) TLC (The Library Corporation)
Function: Archival coll, Art exhibits, Computers for patron use, Electronic databases & coll, Outreach serv, Photocopying/Printing, Ref serv available, Scanner, Wheelchair accessible
Open Mon-Thurs 9-8, Fri 9-6, Sat 9-5, Sun 1-5
Restriction: Non-circulating coll

PLAIN DEALING BRANCH, 208 E Mary Lee St, Plain Dealing, 71064, SAN 342-8559. Tel: 318-326-4233. *Br Mgr,* Tanika Johnson; *Asst Br Mgr,* Arneshia McCullough; Staff 1 (Non-MLS 1)
Function: Art exhibits, Bks on CD, Children's prog, Computers for patron use, Electronic databases & coll, Free DVD rentals, ILL available, Online cat, OverDrive digital audio bks, Photocopying/Printing, Preschool outreach, Printer for laptops & handheld devices, Prog for children & young adult, Ref serv available, Story hour, Summer reading prog, Tax forms, VHS videos, Wheelchair accessible
Open Mon-Fri 9-6, Sat 11-5

ANNA P TOOKE MEMORIAL BRANCH, 451 Fairview Point Rd, Elm Grove, 71051, SAN 342-8508. Tel: 318-987-3915. *Br Mgr,* Mary Sanders; *Asst Br Mgr,* Melody Windham; Staff 1 (Non-MLS 1)
Founded 2015
Function: 24/7 Electronic res, 24/7 Online cat, Accelerated reader prog, Activity rm, Adult literacy prog, After school storytime, Audiobks via web, AV serv, Bks on CD, Children's prog, Computers for patron use, Digital talking bks, E-Reserves, Electronic databases & coll, Family literacy, For res purposes, Free DVD rentals, Govt ref serv, Health sci info serv, Holiday prog, Homework prog, ILL available, Internet access, Life-long learning prog for all ages, Magazines, Mail & tel request accepted, Meeting rooms, Museum passes, Online cat, Online ref, Outreach serv, OverDrive digital audio bks, Photocopying/Printing, Preschool reading prog, Prog for adults, Prog for children & young adult, Ref serv available, Story hour, Summer & winter reading prog, Summer reading prog, Tax forms, Teen prog, Telephone ref, Wheelchair accessible, Winter reading prog, Workshops
Open Mon-Fri 9-6, Sat 11-5

BRIDGE CITY

S BRIDGE CITY CORRECTIONAL CENTER FOR YOUTH*, Riverside Alternative High School Library, 3225 River Rd, 70094. (Mail add: PO Box 9098, 70094), SAN 326-4874. Tel: 504-436-4253. FAX: 504-437-3024. *Librn,* Andrea Drummond; Tel: 504-437-3091
Library Holdings: Bk Titles 2,200; Per Subs 25
Automation Activity & Vendor Info: (Acquisitions) Follett Software; (Cataloging) Follett Software; (Circulation) Follett Software; (OPAC) Follett Software
Restriction: Not open to pub

CAMERON

P CAMERON PARISH LIBRARY*, 512 Marshall St, 70631. (Mail add: PO Box 1130, 70631-1130), SAN 306-4549. Tel: 337-775-5421. Toll Free FAX: 800-861-3492. Web Site: www.cameron.lib.la.us. *Adminr,* Dede Sanders; E-mail: dsanders@cameron.lib.la.us; *Financial Admin Officer,* Tina Boudreaux; E-mail: tboudreaux@cameron.lib.la.us; Staff 3 (Non-MLS 3)
Founded 1958. Pop 6,980; Circ 76,805
Library Holdings: Bk Vols 15,000; Per Subs 20
Special Collections: Cookbooks
Subject Interests: La
Automation Activity & Vendor Info: (Cataloging) Book Systems; (Circulation) Book Systems; (OPAC) Book Systems
Wireless access
Function: Accelerated reader prog, Adult bk club, Art exhibits, Bks on CD, Children's prog, Computer training, Computers for patron use, Electronic databases & coll, Free DVD rentals, ILL available, Internet access, Music CDs, Online cat, Outreach serv, OverDrive digital audio bks, Photocopying/Printing, Preschool outreach, Prog for adults, Prog for children & young adult, Ref & res, Ref serv available, Senior outreach, Spoken cassettes & CDs, Story hour, Summer reading prog, Tax forms, Teen prog, Telephone ref, VHS videos, Wheelchair accessible, Workshops
Partic in Libraries SouthWest; Loan System Helping Automate Retrieval of Knowledge
Open Mon-Thurs 9-5, Fri 8-4, Sat 9-2
Branches: 5

GRAND CHENIER BRANCH, 2863 Grand Chenier Hwy, Grand Chenier, 70643. Tel: 337-538-2214. Toll Free FAX: 888-788-2998. *Br Mgr,* Beckie Primeaux; E-mail: bprimeaux@cameron.lib.ia.us
Library Holdings: Bk Titles 3,787
Open Mon-Thurs 9-5, Fri 8-4, Sat 9-2

GRAND LAKE, 10200 Gulf Hwy, Lake Charles, 70607. Tel: 337-598-5950. Toll Free FAX: 800-861-8035. *Br Mgr,* JoDee Roberts; E-mail: jroberts@cameron.lib.ia.us
Library Holdings: Bk Titles 10,364
Open Mon-Thurs 9-5, Fri 8-4, Sat 9-2

HACKBERRY BRANCH, 983 Main St, Hackberry, 70645. Tel: 337-762-3978. Toll Free FAX: 888-453-1296. *Br Mgr,* Penelope Courvelle; E-mail: pcourvelle@cameron.lib.ia.us
Library Holdings: Bk Titles 6,642
Open Mon-Thurs 9-5, Fri 8-4, Sat 9-2
JOHNSON BAYOU, 4586 Gulf Beach Hwy, 70631. Tel: 337-569-2892. Toll Free FAX: 888-489-7817. *Br Mgr,* Julie Carlson; E-mail: jcarlson@cameron.lib.ia.us
Library Holdings: Bk Titles 4,433
Open Mon-Thurs 9-5, Fri 8-4, Sat 9-2
LOWRY BRANCH, 454 Lowry Hwy, Lake Arthur, 70549. Tel: 337-774-3030. *Br Mgr,* Alice Duhon; E-mail: aduhon@cameron.lib.ia.us
Library Holdings: Bk Titles 227
Open Mon, Tues & Thurs 9-12 & 12:30-6
Bookmobiles: 1

CHALMETTE

J NUNEZ COMMUNITY COLLEGE LIBRARY*, 3710 Paris Rd, 70043. Tel: 504-278-6231. Web Site: www.nunez.edu/Library. *Librn,* Richard DeFoe; Tel: 504-278-6295, Ext 295, E-mail: rdefoe@nunez.edu; *Evening Librn,* Christine Todd; Tel: 504-278-6295, Ext 232, E-mail: ctodd@nunez.edu; *Libr Spec,* Rachel Monson; Tel: 504-278-6295, Ext 230, E-mail: rmonson@nunez.edu; Staff 1.5 (MLS 1.5)
Founded 1992. Enrl 2,500; Fac 50; Highest Degree: Associate
Library Holdings: Audiobooks 54; AV Mats 2,341; Bks on Deafness & Sign Lang 30; Braille Volumes 1; Bk Titles 43,567; Bk Vols 43,767; Per Subs 28
Automation Activity & Vendor Info: (Acquisitions) SirsiDynix; (Cataloging) SirsiDynix; (Circulation) SirsiDynix; (Media Booking) SirsiDynix; (OPAC) SirsiDynix; (Serials) SirsiDynix
Wireless access
Partic in Louisiana Library Network; New Orleans Educational Telecommunications Consortium
Open Mon-Thurs 7:30-7:30, Fri 8-4:30

CHAUVIN

G LOUISIANA UNIVERSITIES MARINE CONSORTIUM, Lumcon Library, 8124 Hwy 56, 70344-2124. SAN 326-4815. Tel: 985-851-2800, 985-851-2806. FAX: 985-851-2874. Web Site: www.lumcon.edu/library. *Assoc Librn,* John Conover; Tel: 985-851-2875, E-mail: jconover@lumcon.edu; Staff 2 (MLS 1, Non-MLS 1)
Founded 1979
Library Holdings: Bk Titles 7,500; Bk Vols 5,800; Per Subs 200
Subject Interests: Geochemistry, Marine biol, Oceanography
Automation Activity & Vendor Info: (Cataloging) SirsiDynix; (OPAC) SirsiDynix
Publications: Effects of Offshore Oil & Gas Development: A Current Awareness Bibliography (Annotated, quarterly); US Minerals Management Service
Partic in Louisiana Library Network; LYRASIS; OCLC Online Computer Library Center, Inc
Open Mon-Fri 7-3:30

CLINTON

P AUDUBON REGIONAL LIBRARY*, 12220 Woodville St, 70722. (Mail add: PO Box 8389, 70722-8389), SAN 342-8796. Tel: 225-683-8753. FAX: 225-683-3623. Web Site: audubonregional.org. *Dir,* Michele D Jones; E-mail: mjones@audubonregional.org; *Br Mgr,* Shana Selders; Staff 21 (MLS 1, Non-MLS 20)
Founded 1963. Pop 46,000; Circ 147,992
Library Holdings: AV Mats 1,000; Bk Vols 88,609; Per Subs 212
Subject Interests: Genealogy, Hist, La
Automation Activity & Vendor Info: (Cataloging) TLC (The Library Corporation); (Circulation) TLC (The Library Corporation); (ILL) TLC (The Library Corporation); (OPAC) TLC (The Library Corporation)
Wireless access
Partic in Loan System Helping Automate Retrieval of Knowledge
Open Mon-Thurs 9-5, Fri 9-3, Sat 9-1
Friends of the Library Group
Branches: 2
JACKSON BRANCH, 3312 College St, Jackson, 70748. (Mail add: PO Box 1830, Jackson, 70748-1830), SAN 342-8885. Tel: 225-634-7408. FAX: 225-634-5896. *Br Mgr,* Londa Matthews; Staff 3 (Non-MLS 3)
Library Holdings: AV Mats 242; Bk Vols 14,678; Per Subs 62
Open Mon-Thurs 9-5, Fri 9-3, Sat 9-1
Friends of the Library Group
ST HELENA BRANCH, 6108 Hwy 10, Greensburg, 70441, SAN 342-8850. Tel: 225-435-7135. FAX: 504-222-4335. *Br Mgr,* Jean Claxton; Staff 2 (Non-MLS 2)
Library Holdings: AV Mats 78; Bk Vols 13,055; Per Subs 32
Special Collections: St Helena Parish Information Coll, local genealogy & hist
Subject Interests: Genealogy, Local hist
Open Mon-Thurs 9-5, Fri 9-3, Sat 9-1
Friends of the Library Group

COLFAX

P GRANT PARISH LIBRARY*, 300 Main St, 71417-1830. SAN 306-4565. Tel: 318-627-9920. FAX: 318-627-9900. E-mail: checksout@grant.lib.la.us. Web Site: grantparishlibrary.org. *Dir,* Deidre Fuqua; E-mail: dfuqua@grant.lib.la.us; *Asst Dir,* Karln Vasquez; E-mail: kvasquez@grant.lib.la.us; Staff 5 (MLS 1, Non-MLS 4)
Founded 1959. Pop 17,495; Circ 90,600
Library Holdings: Bk Vols 62,137; Per Subs 131
Subject Interests: Genealogy, Hist, La
Automation Activity & Vendor Info: (Acquisitions) Auto-Graphics, Inc; (Cataloging) Auto-Graphics, Inc; (Circulation) Auto-Graphics, Inc; (Course Reserve) Auto-Graphics, Inc; (ILL) Auto-Graphics, Inc; (OPAC) Auto-Graphics, Inc; (Serials) Auto-Graphics, Inc
Wireless access
Partic in Loan System Helping Automate Retrieval of Knowledge
Open Mon 8-6, Tues-Fri 8-5, Sat 9-Noon
Branches: 4
DRY PRONG BRANCH, 603 Russell Hataway St, Dry Prong, 71423. Tel: 318-899-7588. FAX: 318-899-7588. *Br Mgr,* Jessica Wright; Staff 1 (Non-MLS 1)
Library Holdings: Bk Vols 4,650; Per Subs 20
Open Mon, Tues & Thurs 1-5, Wed 8-12 & 1-5, Fri 8-12
GEORGETOWN BRANCH, 4570 Hwy 500, Georgetown, 71432, SAN 377-7561. Tel: 318-827-9427. FAX: 318-827-9427. *Br Mgr,* Debbie Nugent; Staff 1 (Non-MLS 1)
Library Holdings: Bk Vols 2,000; Per Subs 19
Open Mon, Wed & Thurs 1-5, Tues 8-12 & 1-5, Fri 8-12
MONTGOMERY BRANCH, 940 Caddo St, Montgomery, 71454. Tel: 318-646-3660. FAX: 318-646-3660. *Br Mgr,* Pat Dubois; Staff 1 (Non-MLS 1)
Library Holdings: Bk Vols 6,520; Per Subs 11
Open Mon & Tues 1-5, Thurs 8-12, Fri 8-12 & 1-5
POLLOCK BRANCH, 1316 Pine St, Pollock, 71467. Tel: 318-765-9616. FAX: 318-765-9616. *Br Mgr,* Castidy Garrett; Staff 1 (Non-MLS 1)
Library Holdings: Bk Vols 5,580; Per Subs 16
Open Mon, Wed & Fri 1-5, Tues & Thurs 8-12
Bookmobiles: 1. Mgr, Treesnic Jones

COLUMBIA

P CALDWELL PARISH LIBRARY, 211 Jackson, 71418. (Mail add: PO Box 1499, 71418-1499), SAN 306-4573. Tel: 318-649-2259. FAX: 318-649-7768. E-mail: caldwellparishlibrary@gmail.com. Web Site: caldwell-parish-library.info. *Dir,* Tammi Hartsfield; Staff 4 (MLS 1, Non-MLS 3)
Founded 1953. Pop 9,810; Circ 53,096
Library Holdings: AV Mats 256; Bk Vols 40,275; Per Subs 160
Automation Activity & Vendor Info: (Acquisitions) Book Systems; (Cataloging) Book Systems; (Circulation) Book Systems; (OPAC) Book Systems
Wireless access
Function: 24/7 Electronic res, 24/7 Online cat, Accelerated reader prog, Activity rm
Mem of Trail Blazer Library System
Partic in Loan System Helping Automate Retrieval of Knowledge
Open Mon-Fri 8-5, Sat 8:30-Noon

COTTONPORT

S RAYMOND LABORDE CORRECTIONAL CENTER LIBRARY*, 1630 Prison Rd, 71327. Tel: 318-876-2891, Ext 350. FAX: 318-876-4220. *Library Contact,* Kelsey Osman
Founded 1990
Subject Interests: Fantasy, Fiction, Westerns
Restriction: Not open to pub, Restricted access

COUSHATTA

P RED RIVER PARISH LIBRARY*, 410 E Carroll St, 71019. (Mail add: PO Box 1367, 71019-1367), SAN 306-4581. Tel: 318-932-5614. FAX: 318-932-6747. Web Site: redriverlibrary.org. *Dir,* Trey Lewis; E-mail: mlewis@state.lib.la.us; Staff 6 (MLS 1, Non-MLS 5)
Founded 1962. Pop 10,500; Circ 84,000
Library Holdings: AV Mats 4,000; Bk Vols 24,166
Automation Activity & Vendor Info: (Cataloging) Innovative Interfaces, Inc; (Circulation) Innovative Interfaces, Inc; (OPAC) Innovative Interfaces, Inc
Wireless access
Partic in Loan System Helping Automate Retrieval of Knowledge
Open Mon-Fri 9-5, Sat 9-1

COVINGTON

P SAINT TAMMANY PARISH LIBRARY*, 1112 W 21st Ave, 70433. SAN 342-894X. Tel: 985-871-1219. Circulation Tel: 985-893-6280. Interlibrary Loan Service Tel: 985-809-5773. FAX: 985-871-1224. Circulation FAX: 985-893-6283. Web Site: www.sttammanylibrary.org. *Dir,* Kelly LaRocca; E-mail: Kelly@stpl.us; Staff 84 (MLS 14, Non-MLS 70)
Founded 1950. Pop 191,268; Circ 1,167,914
Library Holdings: Bk Titles 250,000; Bk Vols 497,202; Per Subs 1,000
Subject Interests: Local hist
Automation Activity & Vendor Info: (Acquisitions) Innovative Interfaces, Inc; (Cataloging) Innovative Interfaces, Inc; (Circulation) Innovative Interfaces, Inc; (ILL) OCLC; (OPAC) Innovative Interfaces, Inc; (Serials) Innovative Interfaces, Inc
Wireless access
Partic in Loan System Helping Automate Retrieval of Knowledge
Special Services for the Deaf - Bks on deafness & sign lang; High interest/low vocabulary bks
Open Mon-Fri 8-5
Friends of the Library Group
Branches: 11
ABITA SPRINGS BRANCH, 71683 Leveson St, Abita Springs, 70420, SAN 342-8974. Tel: 985-893-6285. FAX: 985-893-1336. E-mail: abita@stpl.us. Web Site: www.sttammanylibrary.org/locations/3. *Br Mgr,* Kay Redd
Open Mon, Tues, Thurs & Fri 10-6, Wed 12-8
BUSH BRANCH, 81597 Hwy 41, Bush, 70431, SAN 342-9008. Tel: 985-886-3588. FAX: 985-886-1054. E-mail: bush@stpl.us. Web Site: www.sttammanylibrary.org/locations/4. *Br Mgr,* Susan Taggart
Open Mon, Tues, Thurs & Fri 10-6, Wed 12-8
CAUSEWAY BRANCH, 3457 Hwy 190, Mandeville, 70471. Tel: 985-626-9779. FAX: 985-626-9783. E-mail: causeway@stpl.us. Web Site: www.sttammanylibrary.org/locations/5. *Br Mgr,* Sally McKissack; *Circ Mgr,* Adrienne Ivy
Open Mon-Thurs 9-8, Fri & Sat 9-5
COVINGTON BRANCH, 310 W 21st Ave, 70433. Tel: 985-893-6280. FAX: 985-893-1271. E-mail: covington@stpl.us. Web Site: www.sttammanylibrary.org/locations/6. *Br Mgr,* Tamie Martin; *Circ Mgr,* Melanie Sharp
Library Holdings: Bk Vols 563,786
Closed for renovation until fall of 2019
Open Mon-Thurs 9-8, Fri & Sat 9-5
FOLSOM BRANCH, 82393 Railroad Ave, Folsom, 70437, SAN 342-9091. Tel: 985-796-9728. FAX: 985-796-9304. E-mail: folsom@stpl.us. Web Site: www.sttammanylibrary.org/locations/9. *Br Mgr,* Amy Strain
Subject Interests: Gardening, Horses
Open Mon, Tues, Thurs & Fri 10-6, Wed 12-8
LACOMBE BRANCH, 28027 Hwy 190, Lacombe, 70445, SAN 342-9121. Tel: 985-882-7858. FAX: 985-882-8072. E-mail: lacombe@stpl.us. Web Site: www.sttammanylibrary.org/locations/12. *Br Mgr,* Rhonda Spiess
Open Mon, Tues, Thurs & Fri 10-6, Wed 12-8
LEE ROAD BRANCH, 79213 Hwy 40, 70435, SAN 329-6512. Tel: 985-893-6284. FAX: 985-871-1349. E-mail: leeroad@stpl.us. Web Site: www.sttammanylibrary.org/locations/13. *Br Mgr,* Lisa Haley
Open Mon, Tues, Thurs & Fri 10-6, Wed 12-8
MADISONVILLE BRANCH, 1123 Main St, Madisonville, 70447. Tel: 985-845-4819. FAX: 985-845-0473. E-mail: madisonville@stpl.us. Web Site: www.sttammanylibrary.org/locations/24. *Bus Mgr,* Sally Gill; *Circ Mgr,* Mary Thompson
Open Mon-Thurs 9-8, Fri & Sat 9-5
Friends of the Library Group
MANDEVILLE BRANCH, 844 Girod St, Mandeville, 70448, SAN 342-9180. Tel: 985-626-4293. FAX: 985-624-4621. E-mail: mandeville@stpl.us. Web Site: www.sttammanylibrary.org/locations/15. *Br Mgr,* Jennifer Mayer; *Circ Mgr,* Carra Rowland
Open Mon-Thurs 9-8, Fri & Sat 9-5
PEARL RIVER BRANCH, 64580 Hwy 41, Pearl River, 70452, SAN 342-9210. Tel: 985-863-5518. FAX: 985-863-1730. E-mail: pearlriver@stpl.us. Web Site: www.sttammanylibrary.org/locations/16. *Br Mgr,* Adele Salzer
Open Mon, Tues, Thurs & Fri 10-6, Wed 12-8
SLIDELL BRANCH, 555 Robert Blvd, Slidell, 70458, SAN 342-9245. Tel: 985-646-6470. FAX: 985-645-3553. E-mail: slidell@stpl.us. Web Site: www.sttammanylibrary.org/locations/18. *Br Mgr,* Sue Ryan; *Circ Mgr,* Carolyn Erminger
Special Collections: Bayou Bonfouca Superfund Project Documents; Genealogy Coll; Louisiana Documents; Southern Shipbuilding Corporation Superfund Project Documents
Open Mon-Thurs 9-8, Fri & Sat 9-5

CROWLEY

P ACADIA PARISH LIBRARY*, 1125 N Parkerson Ave, 70526. (Mail add: PO Box 1509, 70527-1509), SAN 342-927X. Tel: 337-788-1880, 337-788-1881. FAX: 337-788-3759. Administration E-mail: admin.b1ac@pelican.state.lib.la.us. Web Site: www.acadia.lib.la.us. *Dir,* Ted Landry; E-mail: tlandry@pelican.state.lib.la.us; *Acq, Ref Serv,* Ann Mire; Staff 29 (MLS 4, Non-MLS 25)
Founded 1945. Pop 59,600
Library Holdings: AV Mats 1,115; Bk Vols 150,000; Per Subs 310
Special Collections: Paul Freeland's Crowley Coll
Automation Activity & Vendor Info: (Cataloging) TLC (The Library Corporation); (Circulation) TLC (The Library Corporation); (OPAC) TLC (The Library Corporation)
Wireless access
Partic in Loan System Helping Automate Retrieval of Knowledge
Open Mon-Fri 8-5:30, Sat 9-1
Branches: 6
CHURCH POINT BRANCH, 311 N Vista St, Church Point, 70525, SAN 342-9334. Tel: 337-684-5774. FAX: 337-684-1593. *Bus Mgr,* Linda Wills; Staff 1 (Non-MLS 1)
Pop 4,477
Library Holdings: AV Mats 112; Bk Vols 5,290; Per Subs 52
Open Mon-Fri 8-5, Sat 9-12
ESTHERWOOD BRANCH, 116 N LeBlanc St, Estherwood, 70534. (Mail add: PO Box 230, Estherwood, 70534-0230), SAN 342-9423. Tel: 337-785-1090. *Librn,* Katrina Benoit; Staff 1 (Non-MLS 1)
Pop 900
Library Holdings: AV Mats 88; Bk Vols 1,769; Per Subs 19
Open Mon & Wed 3-5
IOTA BRANCH, 119 Duson, Iota, 70543. (Mail add: PO Box 950, Iota, 70543-0950), SAN 342-9482. Tel: 337-779-2770. FAX: 337-779-2770. *Br Mgr, Librn,* Anne Ritter; Staff 1 (Non-MLS 1)
Pop 1,256
Library Holdings: AV Mats 110; Bk Vols 5,340; Per Subs 31
Open Mon-Fri 1-5
MERMENTAU BRANCH, 107 Second St, Mermentau, 70556. (Mail add: PO Box 369, Mermentau, 70556-0369), SAN 342-9512. Tel: 318-824-0690. FAX: 318-824-0690. *Librn,* Katrina Benoit; Staff 1 (Non-MLS 1)
Pop 801
Library Holdings: AV Mats 56; Bk Vols 2,109; Per Subs 11
Open Tues & Thurs 1-5
MORSE BRANCH, 209 S Jules Ave, Morse, 70559. (Mail add: PO Box 369, Morse, 70559-0369), SAN 342-9520. Tel: 337-783-0784. FAX: 337-783-0784. *Librn,* Mary Sonnier; Staff 1 (Non-MLS 1)
Pop 782
Library Holdings: AV Mats 49; Bk Vols 2,098
Open Mon & Wed 1-5, Fri 8-12 & 1-5
RAYNE BRANCH, 109 W Perrodin, Rayne, 70578, SAN 342-9547. Tel: 337-334-3188. FAX: 337-334-1181. *Librn,* Trudy Ronkartz; Staff 5 (Non-MLS 5)
Pop 8,502
Library Holdings: AV Mats 234; Bk Vols 35,191; Per Subs 70
Open Mon-Thurs 8-5:30, Fri 8-5, Sat 9-12

DERIDDER

P BEAUREGARD PARISH LIBRARY*, 205 S Washington Ave, 70634. Tel: 337-463-6217. Toll Free Tel: 800-524-6239 (Beauregard Parish only). FAX: 337-462-5434. E-mail: help@beau.org. Web Site: library.beau.org. *Dir,* Erin Chesnutt; E-mail: admin@beau.org; Staff 5 (Non-MLS 5)
Pop 35,000; Circ 381,017
Library Holdings: AV Mats 7,771; Bk Vols 83,154; Per Subs 210; Videos 6,300
Wireless access
Partic in Association for Rural & Small Libraries; Libraries SouthWest; Loan System Helping Automate Retrieval of Knowledge
Open Mon-Wed & Fri 9-5:30, Thurs 9-7:30, Sat 9-1
Branches: 5
EAST BEAUREGARD, 7580 Hwy 26, Wye Community, Dry Creek, 70634. (Mail add: 205 S Washington Ave, 70634). Tel: 337-463-6217. FAX: 337-462-5434. *Library Contact,* Linda Harper; Staff 2 (Non-MLS 2)
Library Holdings: AV Mats 50; Bk Vols 4,000; Per Subs 16
Open Mon 1:30-5:30, Wed 9-5:30, Sat 9-1
FIELDS BRANCH, 13287 Hwy 389, Fields, 70653. Tel: 337-463-6217. FAX: 337-462-5434. Administration E-mail: admin@beau.org. *Library Contact,* Lenore Pickering; Staff 2 (Non-MLS 2)
Library Holdings: AV Mats 56; Bk Vols 4,000; Per Subs 16
Open Tues & Sat 9-1, Fri 2-5:30
MERRYVILLE BRANCH, 1007 Hwy 110, Merryville, 70653. (Mail add: 205 S Washington Ave, 70634). Tel: 337-463-6217. FAX: 337-462-5434. *Br Mgr,* Tess Yeager; Staff 1 (Non-MLS 1)
Library Holdings: AV Mats 60; Bk Vols 4,281; Per Subs 17
Open Mon & Thurs 1-5, Tues, Fri & Sat 9-1
SINGER BRANCH, 9130 Hwy 27, Singer, 70660. (Mail add: 205 S Washington Ave, 70634). Tel: 337-463-6217. FAX: 337-462-5434.
Library Holdings: AV Mats 68; Bk Vols 3,100; Per Subs 15
Open Tues 1:30-5:30, Fri & Sat 9-1

SOUTH BEAUREGARD, 6713 Hwy 12, Ragley, 70657. Tel: 337-463-6217. FAX: 337-462-5434. *Library Contact,* Stephanie Gibbs
Library Holdings: AV Mats 63; Bk Vols 3,412; Per Subs 18
Open Mon 9-5, Wed & Thurs 1-5, Sat 9-1

DESTREHAN

P SAINT CHARLES PARISH LIBRARY*, East Regional Branch, 160 W Campus Dr, 70047. (Mail add: PO Box 1029, 70047), SAN 343-1436. Tel: 985-764-2366. Administration Tel: 985-764-9643. FAX: 985-764-0447. Administration FAX: 985-764-1744. Web Site: myscpl.org. *Dir,* Leann Callahan; E-mail: leann.benedict@myscpl.org; *Asst Dir,* Amy Duke; E-mail: amy.duke@myscpl.org; *Asst Dir,* Lauren Pitz; E-mail: lauren.pitz@myscpl.org; *Librn,* Roberta August; E-mail: roberta.august@myscpl.org; *Circ Supvr,* Ashley Lay; E-mail: ashley.lay@myscpl.org; Staff 31 (MLS 7, Non-MLS 24)
Wireless access
Partic in Loan System Helping Automate Retrieval of Knowledge
Open Mon-Thurs 9-8, Fri & Sat 9-5
Friends of the Library Group
Branches: 5
HAHNVILLE BRANCH, 14996 River Rd, Ste A, Hahnville, 70057, SAN 343-1460. Tel: 985-783-2341. *Circ Supvr,* Brandy Barnes; Staff 2 (Non-MLS 2)
Open Mon-Fri 9-5
NORCO BRANCH, 590 Apple St, Norco, 70079, SAN 343-1495. Tel: 985-764-6581. *Circ Supvr,* Julia Thibodaux; Staff 2 (Non-MLS 2)
Open Mon 10-8, Tues-Thurs 10-6, Fri 9-5, Sat 10-2
PARADIS BRANCH, 307 Audubon St, Paradis, 70080. Tel: 985-758-1868. FAX: 985-758-1869. *Circ Supvr,* Anne St Pierre; Staff 2 (Non-MLS 2)
Open Mon 10-8, Tues-Thurs 10-6, Fri 9-5, Sat 10-2
SAINT ROSE BRANCH, 90 E Club Dr, Saint Rose, 70087. Tel: 504-465-0646. FAX: 504-465-0629. *Circ Supvr,* Eve Fiffie; Staff 2 (Non-MLS 2)
Open Mon 10-8, Tues-Thurs 10-6, Fri 9-5, Sat 10-2
WEST REGIONAL BRANCH, 105 Lakewood Dr, Luling, 70070, SAN 343-1401. Tel: 985-785-8471. FAX: 985-785-8499. *Circ Supvr,* Julie Cancienne; Staff 16 (MLS 1, Non-MLS 15)
Founded 1955. Pop 48,000; Circ 325,000
Subject Interests: Hist, La
Open Mon-Thurs 9-8, Fri & Sat 9-5
Bookmobiles: 1. Supvr, Claire Cermak

DONALDSONVILLE

P ASCENSION PARISH LIBRARY*, Donaldsonville Branch (Headquarters), 500 Mississippi St, 70346. SAN 342-9660. Tel: 225-473-8052. FAX: 225-473-9522. Administration E-mail: admin.c1ac@pelican.state.lib.la.us. Web Site: www.myapl.org. *Dir,* Angelle Deshautelles; E-mail: adeshaut@pelican.state.lib.la.us; *Assoc Dir,* Larie Myers; *Asst Dir,* John Stelly; *Ad,* Chriselle Henry; *Br Librn,* Dionne Laborde; *Cat Librn,* Vivian Solar; *Youth Serv Librn,* Shelly Miller; Staff 62 (MLS 12, Non-MLS 50)
Founded 1960. Pop 88,000; Circ 310,481
Library Holdings: Bk Vols 224,000; Per Subs 540
Special Collections: US Army Corps of Engineers, Lower Mississippi Valley Flood Control, doc
Automation Activity & Vendor Info: (Cataloging) TLC (The Library Corporation); (Circulation) TLC (The Library Corporation); (OPAC) TLC (The Library Corporation)
Partic in Loan System Helping Automate Retrieval of Knowledge
Open Mon, Wed & Fri 8:30-5:30, Tues & Thurs 8:30-8, Sat 8:30-12:30
Branches: 3
DUTCHTOWN BRANCH, 13278 Hwy 73, Geismar, 70734. Tel: 225-673-8699. *Br Mgr,* Jordan Signater
Open Mon, Wed & Fri 8:30-5:30, Tues & Thurs 8:30-8, Sat 8:30am-12:30pm
GALVEZ BRANCH, 40300 Hwy 42, Prairieville, 70769, SAN 325-397X. Tel: 225-622-3339. FAX: 225-622-2550. *Br Librn,* Joe Dolgos
Open Mon, Wed & Fri 8:30-5:30, Tues & Thurs 8:30-8, Sat 8:30-12:30
GONZALES BRANCH, 708 S Irma Blvd, Gonzales, 70737, SAN 342-9695. Tel: 225-647-3955. FAX: 225-644-0063. *Br Librn,* Chriselle Henry
Open Mon-Thurs 8:30-8, Fri & Sat 8:30-5:30

EUNICE

P EUNICE PUBLIC LIBRARY*, 222 S Second St, 70535. SAN 343-4826. Tel: 337-466-7077. FAX: 337-466-7077. E-mail: eunicepubliclibrary@gmail.com. *Librn,* Position Currently Open; Staff 3 (Non-MLS 3)
Library Holdings: AV Mats 130; Bk Vols 33,407; Per Subs 56
Open Mon-Fri 8-5, Sat 8-Noon

C LOUISIANA STATE UNIVERSITY AT EUNICE, LeDoux Library, 2048 Johnson Hwy, 70535. (Mail add: PO Box 1129, 70535-1129), SAN 306-4611. Tel: 337-550-1380. Interlibrary Loan Service Tel: 337-550-1384. Reference Tel: 337-550-1385. FAX: 337-550-1455. E-mail: library@lsue.edu. Web Site: www.lsue.edu/library. *Dir,* Cassie Jobe-Ganucheau; E-mail: cjobe@lsue.edu; *Ref Librn,* Mary Kate Colligan; Staff 3 (MLS 2, Non-MLS 1)
Founded 1967. Enrl 3,300; Fac 75; Highest Degree: Associate
Library Holdings: Audiobooks 100; CDs 200; DVDs 200; e-books 50,000; e-journals 200; Microforms 300; Bk Vols 74,000; Per Subs 218
Special Collections: Rare Louisiana History (Sabatier Coll)
Subject Interests: Genealogy, La
Automation Activity & Vendor Info: (Acquisitions) SirsiDynix; (Cataloging) SirsiDynix; (Circulation) SirsiDynix; (OPAC) SirsiDynix; (Serials) SirsiDynix
Wireless access
Partic in Louisiana Library Network; OCLC Online Computer Library Center, Inc
Open Mon-Thurs 7:30am-8pm, Fri 7:30-4
Friends of the Library Group

FARMERVILLE

P UNION PARISH LIBRARY*, 202 W Jackson St, 71241. SAN 306-462X. Tel: 318-368-9226, 318-368-9288. FAX: 318-368-9224. Administration E-mail: t1un@pelican.state.lib.la.us. Web Site: www.youseemore.com/unionparish. *Dir,* Stephanie Herrmann; E-mail: sherrman@state.lib.la.us
Founded 1956. Pop 20,690; Circ 62,068
Library Holdings: AV Mats 692; Large Print Bks 1,253; Bk Titles 46,876; Bk Vols 55,359; Per Subs 61; Talking Bks 856
Automation Activity & Vendor Info: (Cataloging) TLC (The Library Corporation); (Circulation) TLC (The Library Corporation); (OPAC) TLC (The Library Corporation)
Publications: Beacon Bulletin (Monthly)
Mem of Trail Blazer Library System
Partic in Loan System Helping Automate Retrieval of Knowledge
Open Mon-Fri 8-5, Sat 8-Noon
Bookmobiles: 1. Bkmobile Servs Dir, JoAnn Buggs

FERRIDAY

P CONCORDIA PARISH LIBRARY*, 1609 Third St, 71334-2298. SAN 342-975X. Tel: 318-757-3550. FAX: 318-757-1941. Web Site: www.concordialibrary.org. *Libr Dir,* Amanda Taylor; E-mail: ataylor@concordialibrary.org; Staff 5 (MLS 1, Non-MLS 4)
Founded 1928
Library Holdings: AV Mats 210; Bk Vols 85,000; Per Subs 95
Automation Activity & Vendor Info: (Cataloging) Innovative Interfaces, Inc; (Circulation) Innovative Interfaces, Inc; (OPAC) Innovative Interfaces, Inc
Wireless access
Function: 24/7 Electronic res, 24/7 Online cat, Activity rm, Adult literacy prog
Mem of Trail Blazer Library System
Partic in Loan System Helping Automate Retrieval of Knowledge
Open Mon, Tues, Wed & Thurs 8-6, Fri 8-5, Sat 8:30-Noon
Restriction: Authorized patrons
Branches: 2
CLAYTON BRANCH, 31451 Hwy 15, Clayton, 71326, SAN 342-9784. Tel: 318-757-6460. *Br Mgr,* Dorothy Davis; Staff 2 (Non-MLS 2)
Pop 750
Library Holdings: AV Mats 58; Bk Vols 15,000; Per Subs 12
Function: 24/7 Electronic res, 24/7 Online cat, Activity rm, Adult literacy prog
Open Mon-Thurs 2-5, Fri 8-5
Restriction: Authorized patrons
VIDALIA BRANCH, 408 Texas St, Vidalia, 71373, SAN 342-9814. Tel: 318-336-5043. FAX: 318-336-0904. *Br Mgr,* Hattie Neal; E-mail: hneal@concordialibrary.org; Staff 2 (Non-MLS 2)
Library Holdings: Bk Vols 20,000; Per Subs 45
Function: 24/7 Electronic res, 24/7 Online cat, Activity rm, Adult literacy prog
Open Mon & Fri 8-5, Tues, Wed & Thurs 8-6
Restriction: Authorized patrons
Bookmobiles: 1. Librn, Rhonda Dean. Bk vols 1,200

FORT POLK

S FORT POLK MILITARY MUSEUM LIBRARY*, 7881 Mississippi Ave, Bldg 927, 71459. (Mail add: PO Box 3143, 71459-3143), SAN 374-8286. Tel: 337-531-7905. Web Site: www.jrtc-polk.army.mil/museum.html. *Dir/Curator,* Richard Grant; Tel: 337-531-4840, E-mail: richard.grant33.civ@mail.mil
Founded 1972
Library Holdings: Bk Vols 500; Per Subs 100
Function: Ref serv available
Open Mon-Sat 8-4:30

UNITED STATES ARMY

A ALLEN MEMORIAL LIBRARY*, Bldg 660, 7460 Colorado Ave, 71459-5000, SAN 342-9849. Tel: 337-531-2665. FAX: 337-531-6687. *Dir,* Kelly Herbert
Library Holdings: Bk Vols 70,000; Per Subs 260
Subject Interests: La, Mil hist
Automation Activity & Vendor Info: (Cataloging) Horizon; (Circulation) Horizon; (OPAC) Horizon
Partic in OCLC Online Computer Library Center, Inc
Open Mon-Thurs 10-7, Fri 10-5, Sat 10-6, Sun 2-6

AM USA MEDDAC MEDICAL LIBRARY, FORT POLK - BAYNE-JONES ARMY COMMUNITY HOSPITAL*, 1585 Third St, Bldg 285, 71459-5110, SAN 342-9873. Tel: 337-531-3725, 337-531-3726. FAX: 337-531-3082. E-mail: usarmy.polk.medcom-bjach.mbx.library@mail.mil. *Librn,* Cecelia Higginbotham; Staff 1 (MLS 1)
Founded 1961
Library Holdings: Microforms 2,500; Bk Vols 2,000; Per Subs 63
Automation Activity & Vendor Info: (Acquisitions) OCLC; (Cataloging) OCLC; (Circulation) OCLC; (ILL) OCLC; (OPAC) OCLC WorldShare Interlibrary Loan; (Serials) OCLC
Partic in Army Medical Department - Medical Library & Information Network; National Network of Libraries of Medicine Region 3; OCLC Online Computer Library Center, Inc; S Cent Regional Libr Prog
Open Mon-Fri 8-4:30

FRANKLIN

P SAINT MARY PARISH LIBRARY*, 206 Iberia St, 70538-4906. SAN 342-9903. Tel: 337-828-1624, 337-828-1647. FAX: 337-828-2329. Web Site: stmarylibrary.org. *Dir,* Julie Champagne; E-mail: jchampag@state.lib.la.us; Staff 39 (MLS 1, Non-MLS 38)
Founded 1953. Pop 48,669; Circ 321,828
Library Holdings: Bk Vols 178,155; Per Subs 239
Subject Interests: Genealogy
Automation Activity & Vendor Info: (Cataloging) TLC (The Library Corporation); (Circulation) TLC (The Library Corporation); (OPAC) TLC (The Library Corporation)
Publications: Library Lagniappe
Partic in Loan System Helping Automate Retrieval of Knowledge
Open Mon-Fri 8-5
Friends of the Library Group
Branches: 6
AMELIA BRANCH, 625 Lake Palourde, Amelia, 70360, SAN 342-9911. Tel: 985-631-2262. FAX: 985-631-2632. *Interim Br Mgr,* Leisha Babin
Library Holdings: Bk Vols 16,138
Open Mon-Fri 8:30-5:30, Sat 9-12
BAYOU VISTA BRANCH, 1325 Bellview Dr, Bayou Vista, 70380, SAN 377-9998. Tel: 985-399-9866. FAX: 985-399-4232. *Br Mgr,* Leisha Babin
Founded 1998
Open Mon-Fri 8:30-5:30, Sat 9-12
BERWICK BRANCH, 3527 Fourth St, Berwick, 70342, SAN 342-9938. Tel: 985-385-2943. FAX: 985-385-6474. *Br Mgr,* Diane Matherne
Library Holdings: Bk Vols 31,406
Open Mon-Fri 8:30-5:30, Sat 9-12
DE GRUMMOND BRANCH, 9340 Hwy 182, Centerville, 70522. (Mail add: PO Box 185, Centerville, 70522). Tel: 337-836-1717, 337-836-1718. Web Site: stmarylibrary.org/centerville. *Libr Assoc,* Sandy Breaux; *Libr Assoc,* Eunia Gross
Open Mon-Fri 8:30-5:30, Sat 9-Noon
PATTERSON BRANCH, 529 Catherine St, Patterson, 70392, SAN 342-9997. Tel: 985-395-2777. FAX: 985-399-4469. *Br Mgr,* Lisa Wilson
Library Holdings: Bk Vols 23,415
Open Mon-Fri 8:30-5:30, Sat 9-12
WEST END, 100 Charenton Rd, Baldwin, 70514. (Mail add: PO Box 309, Baldwin, 70514-0309), SAN 374-4175. Tel: 337-923-6205. FAX: 337-923-4507. *Br Mgr,* Connie Durocher
Open Mon-Fri 8:30-5:30, Sat 9-12
Bookmobiles: 1. Bk vols 18,511

FRANKLINTON

P WASHINGTON PARISH LIBRARY SYSTEM*, Headquarters, 825 Free St, 70438. SAN 343-0022. Tel: 985-839-7805. FAX: 985-839-7807. E-mail: franklintonbranchlibrary@gmail.com. Web Site: washingtonparishlibrary.info. *Dir,* Allison B Barron; E-mail: tangilibrarian@gmail.com; Staff 5 (MLS 1, Non-MLS 4)
Founded 1946. Pop 48,185; Circ 153,776
Library Holdings: Bk Vols 109,405
Special Collections: Washington Parish & Local History
Automation Activity & Vendor Info: (Circulation) Innovative Interfaces, Inc
Wireless access
Function: Bks on cassette, Bks on CD, Computer training, Computers for patron use, Electronic databases & coll, Free DVD rentals, ILL available, Magnifiers for reading, Mail & tel request accepted, Online cat, Photocopying/Printing, Prog for adults, Prog for children & young adult, Ref serv available, Satellite serv, Scanner, Spoken cassettes & CDs, Spoken cassettes & DVDs, Summer reading prog, Tax forms, Telephone ref, VHS videos, Wheelchair accessible
Member Libraries: Rayburn Correctional Center Library
Partic in Loan System Helping Automate Retrieval of Knowledge
Open Mon-Fri 8-5
Friends of the Library Group
Branches: 4
BOGALUSA BRANCH, 304 Ave F, Bogalusa, 70427, SAN 343-0081. Tel: 985-735-1961. FAX: 985-735-1996. *Br Mgr,* Melanie Charrier; Staff 1 (Non-MLS 1)
Library Holdings: Bk Vols 40,000; Per Subs 16
Function: Art exhibits, Photocopying/Printing, Ref serv available, Summer reading prog, Tax forms
Open Mon & Tues 9-6, Wed-Fri 9-5, Sat 9-1
ENON, 14093 Hwy 16, 70438, SAN 343-0146. Tel: 985-839-9385. FAX: 985-839-9385. *Br Mgr,* Winola Holliday; Staff 1 (Non-MLS 1)
Library Holdings: Bk Vols 2,640
Function: After school storytime, AV serv, Computers for patron use, ILL available, Ref serv available, Summer reading prog, Tax forms
Open Tues-Thurs 9-5, Fri 10-5
FRANKLINTON BRANCH, 825 Free St, 70438, SAN 343-0170. Tel: 985-839-7805. FAX: 985-839-7808. *Br Mgr,* Bobbie Jones; Staff 1 (Non-MLS 1)
Library Holdings: Bk Vols 39,000; Per Subs 20
Automation Activity & Vendor Info: (Cataloging) Innovative Interfaces, Inc; (OPAC) Innovative Interfaces, Inc
Function: Bks on cassette, Bks on CD, Computers for patron use, ILL available, Photocopying/Printing, Ref serv available
Open Mon & Tues 9-6, Wed & Fri 9-5, Sat 9-1
THOMAS, 30369 Hwy 424, 70438, SAN 343-0235. Tel: 985-848-7061. FAX: 985-848-7061. *Br Mgr,* Lahoma Dawson
Library Holdings: Bk Vols 3,678
Automation Activity & Vendor Info: (Acquisitions) Innovative Interfaces, Inc; (Cataloging) Innovative Interfaces, Inc
Open Mon-Thurs 9-5

GONZALES

J RIVER PARISHES COMMUNITY COLLEGE LIBRARY, 925 W Edenborne Pkwy, Rm 141, 70737. (Mail add: PO Box 2367, 70707). Tel: 225-743-8550. FAX: 225-644-8212. E-mail: library@rpcc.edu. Web Site: rpcclibrary.stacksdiscovery.com. *Dir, Libr Serv,* Wendy Johnson; E-mail: wjohnson@rpcc.edu; *Head, Pub Serv,* Deidra Douglas; E-mail: ddouglas@rpcc.edu; *Head, Tech Serv,* Connie Chemay; E-mail: cchemay@rpcc.edu; Staff 3 (MLS 3)
Founded 1999. Enrl 3,500; Fac 125; Highest Degree: Associate
Library Holdings: AV Mats 2,800; e-books 90,000; e-journals 30,000; Bk Titles 17,000; Bk Vols 18,000; Per Subs 30
Automation Activity & Vendor Info: (Cataloging) SirsiDynix; (Circulation) SirsiDynix; (Course Reserve) SirsiDynix; (Discovery) EBSCO Discovery Service; (ILL) OCLC Online; (OPAC) SirsiDynix; (Serials) SirsiDynix
Wireless access
Function: Computers for patron use, Online cat, Photocopying/Printing, Scanner
Partic in Louisiana Library Network; OCLC Online Computer Library Center, Inc
Open Mon-Thurs 7:30-7:30, Fri 7:30-5
Restriction: Authorized patrons, Borrowing privileges limited to fac & registered students, In-house use for visitors

GRAMBLING

C GRAMBLING STATE UNIVERSITY*, A C Lewis Memorial Library, 403 Main St, 71245-2761. SAN 306-4638. Tel: 318-274-3354. Circulation Tel: 318-274-2161. Interlibrary Loan Service Tel: 318-274-7732. Reference Tel: 318-274-2227. Administration Tel: 318-274-2568. Toll Free Tel: 800-569-4714. FAX: 318-274-3268. Interlibrary Loan Service FAX: 318-274-4085. Web Site: www.gram.edu/library. *Dean,* Adrienne C Webber; E-mail: webbera@gram.edu; *Head Librn,* Cecilia Iwala-Olufarati; Tel: 318-274-7367, E-mail: iwalac@gram.edu; *Head, Acq, Ser Librn,* Dr Rosemary N Mokia; Tel: 318-274-6122, E-mail: mokiar@gram.edu; Staff 9 (MLS 8, Non-MLS 1)
Founded 1935. Enrl 5,207; Fac 248; Highest Degree: Doctorate. Sal $953,996 (Prof $483,772)
Library Holdings: Audiobooks 666; AV Mats 3,559; e-books 20,483; Electronic Media & Resources 261,704; Microforms 122,298; Bk Titles 1,614,155
Special Collections: Afro-American Rare Books, fiche; Crime & Juvenile Delinquency, fiche; Education (ERIC 1970-1980), fiche; English Literature, fiche; Housing & Urban Affairs 1965-1972, fiche; Library of American Civilization, fiche; Mary Watson Hymon Afro-American Coll; National

Woman's Party Papers, micro; Schomburg Coll (partial); Sociology (Black Culture), micro; The Adams' Papers, micro; Update, fiche
Automation Activity & Vendor Info: (Cataloging) SirsiDynix; (Circulation) SirsiDynix; (OPAC) SirsiDynix
Wireless access
Publications: Brochures; Handbooks; Newsletters
Partic in Louisiana Library Network; LYRASIS; Proquest Dialog
Open Mon-Thurs 7:30am-10pm (7:30am-9pm Summer), Fri 7:30-2, Sat 10-2, Sun 4-10

HAMMOND

C SOUTHEASTERN LOUISIANA UNIVERSITY*, Linus A Sims Memorial Library, SLU Box 10896, 1211 SGA Dr, 70402. SAN 306-4646. Tel: 985-549-2027, 985-549-3860. Circulation Tel: 985-549-3484. Interlibrary Loan Service Tel: 985-549-5318. Automation Services Tel: 985-549-3954. Web Site: www.selu.edu/library. *Dir,* Eric Johnson; E-mail: ejohnson@selu.edu; Staff 20 (MLS 19, Non-MLS 1)
Founded 1925. Enrl 15,662; Fac 715; Highest Degree: Master
Library Holdings: AV Mats 49,138; CDs 512; e-books 38,829; Bk Vols 376,894; Per Subs 2,381; Videos 5,920
Special Collections: State Document Depository; US Document Depository
Subject Interests: Genealogy
Automation Activity & Vendor Info: (Acquisitions) SirsiDynix; (Cataloging) SirsiDynix; (Circulation) SirsiDynix; (OPAC) SirsiDynix; (Serials) SirsiDynix
Wireless access
Partic in Louisiana Library Network; LYRASIS
Open Mon-Thurs (Fall & Spring) 7:30am-11pm, Fri 7:30-4:30, Sat 9-4, Sun 2-11; Mon-Wed (Summer) 7am-10pm, Thurs 7-6
Friends of the Library Group

HARRISONBURG

P CATAHOULA PARISH LIBRARY*, 300 Bushley St, 71340. (Mail add: PO Box 218, 71340-0218), SAN 343-0324. Tel: 318-744-5271. FAX: 318-744-5251. Web Site: catahoulalibrary.net. *Dir,* Wayne Spence; E-mail: wspence@state.lib.la.us; *Mgr,* Shelly McLendon; Staff 4 (MLS 1, Non-MLS 3)
Founded 1949. Pop 11,992; Circ 91,688
Library Holdings: Bk Titles 38,792; Bk Vols 39,219; Per Subs 86
Special Collections: Catahoula Parish History Coll
Subject Interests: Genealogy
Automation Activity & Vendor Info: (Cataloging) Book Systems; (Circulation) Book Systems; (OPAC) Book Systems
Wireless access
Partic in Loan System Helping Automate Retrieval of Knowledge
Open Mon-Fri 8-4:30
Branches: 2
JONESVILLE BRANCH, 205 Pond St, Jonesville, 71343, SAN 343-0359. Tel: 318-339-7070. FAX: 318-339-7073. E-mail: jonesvillelibrary@gmail.com. *Br Mgr,* Rhonda Book; Staff 2 (Non-MLS 2)
Library Holdings: Bk Vols 15,000; Per Subs 21
Open Mon-Fri 8-4:30
SICILY ISLAND BRANCH, 308 Newman St, Sicily Island, 71368, SAN 343-0383. Tel: 318-389-5804. FAX: 318-389-5804. *Br Mgr,* Vonda Ryan; Staff 1 (MLS 1)
Library Holdings: Bk Vols 19,000; Per Subs 11
Open Mon-Wed 8-4:30
Bookmobiles: 1

HOMER

P CLAIBORNE PARISH LIBRARY*, 909 Edgewood Dr, 71040. SAN 343-0413. Tel: 318-927-3845. FAX: 318-927-5349. Web Site: www.youseemore.com/claiborne. *Dir,* Pamela Suggs; E-mail: psuggs@state.lib.la.us; Staff 15 (MLS 1, Non-MLS 14)
Founded 1951. Pop 17,095; Circ 89,809
Library Holdings: AV Mats 560; Bk Titles 50,000; Per Subs 250
Subject Interests: La
Automation Activity & Vendor Info: (Cataloging) TLC (The Library Corporation); (Circulation) TLC (The Library Corporation); (OPAC) TLC (The Library Corporation)
Partic in Loan System Helping Automate Retrieval of Knowledge
Open Mon-Fri 8-6, Sat 9-1
Friends of the Library Group
Branches: 1
JOE W WEBB MEMORIAL, 1919 Main St, Haynesville, 71038, SAN 343-0448. Tel: 318-624-0364. FAX: 318-624-2624. *Br Libn,* Sandra Bower; Staff 4 (MLS 1, Non-MLS 3)
Library Holdings: AV Mats 119; Bk Vols 16,883; Per Subs 76
Open Mon-Fri 8-12 & 1-4:45
Friends of the Library Group
Bookmobiles: 1

S DAVID WADE CORRECTIONAL CENTER*, Wade Library, 670 Bell Hill Rd, 71040. Tel: 318-927-0424, Ext 227. *Library Contact,* Karen Bays
Library Holdings: Bk Vols 10,056
Restriction: Not open to pub

HOUMA

P TERREBONNE PARISH LIBRARY*, 151 Library Dr, 70360. SAN 343-0502. Tel: 985-876-5861. FAX: 985-917-0582. Administration FAX: 985-876-5864. Web Site: www.mytpl.org. *Dir,* Mary Cosper LeBoeuf; E-mail: mcleboeuf@mytpl.org; *Asst Dir,* Tracy Guyan; E-mail: tguyan@mytpl.org; *Br Mgr, Main Libr,* Gina Hebert; E-mail: ghebert@mytpl.org; *Acq Librn,* Keisa Arceneaux; E-mail: karceneaux@mytpl.org; *Children & Youth Serv Librn,* Naomi Magola; E-mail: nmagola@mytpl.org; *Ref Supvr,* Brigid Laborie; E-mail: blaborie@mytpl.org; *Commun Outreach Coordr,* Kati Callais; E-mail: kcallais@mytpl.org; *Pub Relations Coordr,* Jessi Suire; E-mail: jsuire@mytpl.org; Staff 16 (MLS 10, Non-MLS 6)
Founded 1939. Pop 113,328; Circ 416,621
Jan 2018-Dec 2018 Income (Main & Associated Libraries) $639,500, County $544,500, Locally Generated Income $79,000, Other $16,000. Mats Exp $724,870, Books $338,026, Per/Ser (Incl. Access Fees) $37,002, AV Equip $105,561, AV Mat $100,200, Electronic Ref Mat (Incl. Access Fees) $144,081. Sal $2,140,660
Library Holdings: Audiobooks 17,666; DVDs 35,037; e-books 19,856; Bk Vols 306,030; Per Subs 895
Subject Interests: Petroleum
Automation Activity & Vendor Info: (Cataloging) TLC (The Library Corporation); (Circulation) TLC (The Library Corporation); (ILL) TLC (The Library Corporation); (Serials) TLC (The Library Corporation)
Wireless access
Partic in Loan System Helping Automate Retrieval of Knowledge
Friends of the Library Group
Branches: 8
BAYOU DULARGE, 837 Bayou Dularge Rd, 70363, SAN 375-460X. Tel: 985-851-1752. FAX: 985-851-0287. E-mail: dularge@mytpl.org. *Br Mgr,* Magan LeBoeuf; E-mail: dularge@mytpl.org
Library Holdings: Bk Vols 17,399
Open Mon-Thurs 10-6, Fri 10-5
Friends of the Library Group
BOURG BRANCH, 4405 Saint Andrew St, Bourg, 70343-5431, SAN 343-0537. Tel: 985-594-4717. FAX: 985-594-8392. E-mail: bourg@mytpl.org. *Mgr,* Stephanie Mahaffey
Library Holdings: Bk Vols 12,083
Open Mon-Thurs 10-6, Fri 10-5
Friends of the Library Group
CHAUVIN BRANCH, 5500 Hwy 56, Chauvin, 70344, SAN 343-0596. Tel: 985-594-9771. FAX: 985-594-7506. E-mail: chauvin@mytpl.org. *Br Mgr,* Janet Chauvin; E-mail: jchauvin@mytpl.org
Library Holdings: Bk Vols 12,011
Open Mon-Thurs 10-6, Fri 10-5
Friends of the Library Group
DULAC BRANCH, 200 Badou Rd, Dulac, 70353. Tel: 985-563-5014. FAX: 985-563-2015. *Bus Mgr,* Candace Chauvin; Staff 1 (Non-MLS 1)
Library Holdings: Bk Vols 9,480
Open Mon-Thurs 10-6, Fri 10-5
Friends of the Library Group
EAST HOUMA, 778 Grand Caillou Rd, 70363, SAN 343-0626. Tel: 985-876-7072. FAX: 985-876-9658. E-mail: easthouma@mytpl.org. *Br Mgr,* Rhonda Madison
Founded 1968
Library Holdings: Bk Vols 48,487
Open Mon-Thurs 9-9, Fri & Sat 9-6
Friends of the Library Group
GIBSON BRANCH, 6400 Bayou Black Dr, Gibson, 70356, SAN 326-7512. Tel: 985-575-2639. FAX: 985-575-3069. E-mail: gibson@mytpl.org. *Br Mgr,* Charlotte Celestin
Library Holdings: Bk Vols 9,288
Open Mon-Thurs 10-6, Fri 10-5
Friends of the Library Group
MONTEGUT BRANCH, 1135 Hwy 55, Montegut, 70377, SAN 343-0650. Tel: 985-594-4390. FAX: 985-594-9512. E-mail: montegut@mytpl.org. *Br Mgr,* Katie Jolly
Library Holdings: Bk Vols 8,851
Open Mon-Thurs 10-6, Fri 10-5
Friends of the Library Group
NORTH TERREBONNE, 4130 W Park Ave, Gray, 70359. (Mail add: 151 Library Dr, 70360), SAN 343-0669. Tel: 985-868-3050. FAX: 985-868-9404. E-mail: north@mytpl.org. *Br Mgr,* Amy Riche'; E-mail: ariche@mytpl.org; Staff 1 (MLS 1)
Library Holdings: Bk Vols 50,593
Open Mon-Thurs 9-9, Fri & Sat 9-6, Sun 2-6
Friends of the Library Group

JACKSON

S DIXON CORRECTIONAL INSTITUTE*, Law Library, PO Box 788, 70748. Tel: 225-634-1200. FAX: 225-634-4400. *Dir,* Ivy Miller
Library Holdings: Bk Vols 3,600; Per Subs 10
Restriction: Not open to pub

EASTERN LOUISIANA MENTAL HEALTH SYSTEMS
M CHAPMAN MEMORIAL LIBRARY*, 4502 Hwy 951, 70748. (Mail add: PO Box 498, 70748-0498). Tel: 225-634-0560. FAX: 225-634-0188. E-mail: elmhs-library@la.gov. Web Site: www.dhh.louisiana.gov. *Library Contact,* Ada Lord; E-mail: alord@dhh.la.gov
Library Holdings: Bk Vols 3,000
Open Mon-Fri 8-4:30
Restriction: Access at librarian's discretion
M MEDICAL LIBRARY*, 4502 Hwy 951, 70748. (Mail add: PO Box 498, 70748), SAN 373-9031. Tel: 225-634-0560.
Library Holdings: Bk Titles 157; Bk Vols 163; Per Subs 11
Subject Interests: Psychiat
Restriction: Staff use only

JENA

P LASALLE PARISH LIBRARY*, 3108 N First St, 71342. (Mail add: PO Box 3199, 71342-3199), SAN 343-0715. Tel: 318-992-5675. FAX: 318-992-7374. Administration E-mail: admin.h1ls@state.lib.la.us. Web Site: www.lasalle.lib.la.us. *Dir,* Andrea Book; E-mail: abook@state.lib.la.us; *Outreach Serv Librn,* Becky Davidson; *Cat, Coll Develop,* Barbara Murphy; *Ch Serv, ILL & Distance Libr Serv Spec,* Donna Estis; *Circ,* Chasity Garrett; Staff 5 (Non-MLS 5)
Founded 1952. Pop 14,040
Library Holdings: AV Mats 5,436; Bks on Deafness & Sign Lang 57; Electronic Media & Resources 60; Large Print Bks 387; Bk Vols 59,175; Per Subs 109
Subject Interests: La
Automation Activity & Vendor Info: (Cataloging) Book Systems; (Circulation) Book Systems; (OPAC) Book Systems
Wireless access
Function: Internet access, Photocopying/Printing, Preschool outreach
Partic in IAC Searchbank; Loan System Helping Automate Retrieval of Knowledge
Open Mon & Wed-Fri 8-5, Tues 8-6, Sat 9-1
Friends of the Library Group
Branches: 1
OLLA BRANCH, 1449 Blake St, Olla, 71465. (Mail add: PO Box 1417, Olla, 71465-1417), SAN 343-074X. Tel: 318-495-5570. FAX: 318-495-5593. *Br Mgr,* Kristie Proffer; E-mail: kproffer@state.lib.la.us; Staff 1 (Non-MLS 1)
Library Holdings: AV Mats 300; Bks on Deafness & Sign Lang 20; Per Subs 44
Open Mon-Fri 9-5
Friends of the Library Group
Bookmobiles: 1

JENNINGS

P JEFFERSON DAVIS PARISH LIBRARY*, 118 W Plaquemine St, 70546. SAN 343-0774. Tel: 337-824-1210. FAX: 337-824-5444. Web Site: www.jefferson-davis.lib.la.us. *Dir,* Linda LeBert-Corbello, PhD; E-mail: llebert@state.lib.la.us; *Br Mgr,* Suzanne Young; E-mail: syoung@state.lib.la.us; Staff 15 (Non-MLS 15)
Founded 1968. Pop 32,000; Circ 101,878
Library Holdings: Electronic Media & Resources 760; Bk Vols 100,950; Per Subs 254; Talking Bks 2,317; Videos 2,064
Subject Interests: Indians, La
Automation Activity & Vendor Info: (Cataloging) Book Systems; (Circulation) Book Systems; (ILL) TLC (The Library Corporation); (OPAC) Book Systems
Publications: Christmas Cookbook
Partic in Libraries SouthWest
Open Mon-Fri 9-6, Sat 9-1
Branches: 4
ELTON BRANCH, 813 Main St, Elton, 70532, SAN 343-0804. Tel: 318-584-2640. FAX: 318-584-2236. *Mgr,* Kitty Marsh
Library Holdings: Bk Vols 9,034
Special Collections: Coushatta Indian Coll
Open Mon 9-6, Tues-Fri 11:30-6, Sat 9-12
JENNINGS HEADQUARTER BRANCH, 118 W Plaquemine, 70546-0356, SAN 322-5755. Tel: 318-824-1210. Toll Free Tel: 800-735-0746. FAX: 318-824-5444. *Br Mgr,* Susanne Young; Staff 1 (Non-MLS 1)
Founded 1968. Pop 31,435; Circ 68,878
Library Holdings: Bk Vols 23,564
Open Mon-Fri 9-6, Sat 9-1
LAKE ARTHUR BRANCH, 600 Fourth St, Lake Arthur, 70549, SAN 343-0839. Tel: 337-774-3661. FAX: 337-774-3657. *Br Mgr,* Deanna LeMarie
Library Holdings: Bk Vols 18,841
Open Mon & Wed-Fri 11:30-6, Tues 9-6, Sat 9-12
MCBURNEY MEMORIAL, 301 S Sarah St, Welsh, 70591, SAN 343-0863. Tel: 337-734-3262. FAX: 337-734-4540. *Mgr,* Denice Sonnier
Library Holdings: Bk Vols 15,577
Open Mon & Wed-Fri 11:30-6, Tues 9-6, Sat 9-12
Bookmobiles: 1. Bk Courier, Kathy LeJeune

P JENNINGS CARNEGIE PUBLIC LIBRARY*, 303 Cary Ave, 70546. SAN 306-4654. Tel: 337-821-5517. FAX: 337-821-5527. E-mail: crystal@jenningscarnegielibrary.com. Web Site: www.jenningscarnegielibrary.com. *Dir,* Harriet Shultz
Founded 1885. Pop 12,500; Circ 39,157
Library Holdings: Audiobooks 835; AV Mats 891; Large Print Bks 2,759; Bk Vols 54,664; Per Subs 64; Talking Bks 156; Videos 220
Automation Activity & Vendor Info: (Cataloging) Book Systems; (Circulation) Book Systems
Partic in Loan System Helping Automate Retrieval of Knowledge
Open Mon-Sat 9-5

JONESBORO

P JACKSON PARISH LIBRARY*, 614 S Polk Ave, 71251-3442. SAN 306-4662. Tel: 318-259-5697, 318-259-5698. FAX: 318-259-3374. Web Site: www.jacksonparishlib.org. *Libr Dir,* Marcie Nelson; E-mail: mnelson@state.lib.la.us; *Br Mgr,* Angela Holder; *ILL Coordr,* Vickie Yates; Staff 10 (MLS 2, Non-MLS 8)
Founded 1960. Pop 16,240; Circ 107,944
Library Holdings: AV Mats 580; Bk Vols 63,316; Per Subs 162
Special Collections: Jennifer Blake Coll
Subject Interests: La, Local hist
Automation Activity & Vendor Info: (Cataloging) TLC (The Library Corporation); (Circulation) TLC (The Library Corporation); (ILL) Auto-Graphics, Inc; (OPAC) TLC (The Library Corporation)
Wireless access
Function: Ref serv available
Mem of Trail Blazer Library System
Partic in Loan System Helping Automate Retrieval of Knowledge
Open Mon-Fri 8-5:30, Sat 8-Noon
Branches: 1
CHATHAM BRANCH, 1500 Pine St, Chatham, 71226. Tel: 318-249-2980, 318-249-2981. *Br Mgr,* Phyllis Moore
Open Mon-Thurs 8:30-6, Fri & Sat 8:30-12:30
Bookmobiles: 1. Bkmobile Coord, Amber Pagett. Bk titles 10,204

KROTZ SPRINGS

P KROTZ SPRINGS MUNICIPAL PUBLIC LIBRARY*, 216 Park St, 70570. (Mail add: PO Box 218, 70750). Tel: 337-566-8190. Web Site: krotzsprings.net/library. *Dir,* Suzanne Belleau; E-mail: b1ks@state.lib.la.us; *Librn,* Jo Anne Johnson; E-mail: b1ks@state.lib.la.us
Founded 2007
Library Holdings: Bk Titles 2,726
Automation Activity & Vendor Info: (Cataloging) Book Systems; (Circulation) Book Systems
Wireless access
Partic in Loan System Helping Automate Retrieval of Knowledge
Open Mon-Fri 9-5

LAFAYETTE

P LAFAYETTE PUBLIC LIBRARY*, 301 W Congress, 70501-6866. (Mail add: PO Box 3427, 70502), SAN 306-4700. Tel: 337-261-5784. Interlibrary Loan Service Tel: 337-261-5757. Reference Tel: 337-261-5787. Administration Tel: 337-261-5781. FAX: 337-261-5782. E-mail: compser.b1lf@state.lib.la.us. Web Site: lafayettepubliclibrary.org. *Dir,* Teresa Elberson; E-mail: teresa.elberson@lafayettepubliclibrary.org; *Br Mgr,* Linda Broussard; Tel: 337-504-5332, E-mail: linda.broussard@lafayettepubliclibrary.org; *Ch Serv,* Katherine Mulloy; Tel: 337-261-5786, E-mail: kathy.mulloy@lafayettepubliclibrary.org; *Libr Adminr,* Terry Roy; Tel: 337-261-5781, E-mail: terry.roy@lafayettepubliclibrary.org; Staff 11 (MLS 11)
Founded 1946. Pop 172,193; Circ 1,017,698
Library Holdings: AV Mats 1,011; Bk Vols 337,627; Per Subs 501
Special Collections: Adult New Readers; Dolls; Genealogy Coll; Jobs Coll; Large Print; Louisiana Coll
Automation Activity & Vendor Info: (Cataloging) SirsiDynix; (Circulation) SirsiDynix; (OPAC) SirsiDynix; (Serials) SirsiDynix
Wireless access
Function: Homebound delivery serv
Partic in Loan System Helping Automate Retrieval of Knowledge; LYRASIS

Open Mon-Thurs 8:30am-9pm, Fri 8:30-6, Sat 9-5, Sun 12-6
Friends of the Library Group
Branches: 8
BUTLER MEMORIAL & MARTIN LUTHER KING CENTER, 309 Cora St, 70501, SAN 376-981X. Tel: 337-234-0363. *Library Contact,* David Mingo; Staff 1 (Non-MLS 1)
Library Holdings: Bk Vols 1,394
Open Mon-Thurs 3-7
CHENIER CENTER, 220 W Willow St, Bldg C, 70501. Tel: 337-291-2941. *Library Contact,* David Mingo; Staff 2 (Non-MLS 2)
Library Holdings: Bk Vols 5,377; Per Subs 12
Open Mon-Thurs 9-7, Fri 9-6, Sat 11-3
DUSON BRANCH, 310 Ave au Nord, Duson, 70529, SAN 376-9836. Tel: 337-873-3521. *Library Contact,* Dominique Ducote; Staff 1 (Non-MLS 1)
Library Holdings: Bk Vols 6,995; Per Subs 11
Open Mon-Fri 9-6
EAST REGIONAL LIBRARY, 215 La Nueville Rd, Youngsville, 70592. Tel: 337-445-3168. *Library Contact,* Lisa Cotton
Open Mon-Fri 9-8, Sat 10-5, Sun 12-6
MILTON BRANCH, Cedar Village Shopping Ctr, 108 W Milton Ave, Milton, 70558, SAN 376-7353. Tel: 337-856-5261. *Library Contact,* Katie Martin
Library Holdings: Bk Vols 10,145; Per Subs 23
Open Mon-Fri 9-6
NORTH REGIONAL BRANCH, 5101 N University Ave, Carencro, 70520, SAN 376-9828. Tel: 337-896-6323. *Regional Br Mgr,* Jackie Lopez; Staff 11 (MLS 3, Non-MLS 8)
Library Holdings: Bk Vols 10,926; Per Subs 11
Open Mon-Fri 9-8, Sat 10-5, Sun 12-6
SCOTT BRANCH, 5808 W Cameron St, Scott, 70583, SAN 376-9844. Tel: 337-232-9321. *Librn,* Eloise Dotson; Staff 1 (Non-MLS 1)
Library Holdings: Bk Vols 8,331; Per Subs 16
Open Mon 10-7, Tues-Fri 9-6
SOUTH REGIONAL LIBRARY, 6101 Johnston St, 70503. Tel: 337-981-1028. *Regional Libr Mgr,* Theresa Roy; Staff 21 (MLS 6, Non-MLS 15)
Open Mon-Thurs 9-9, Fri 9-7, Sat 9-5, Sun 12-6

S LAFAYETTE SCIENCE MUSEUM*, Research Library, 433 Jefferson St, 70501-7013. SAN 374-941X. Tel: 337-291-5544. FAX: 337-291-5464. Web Site: www.lafayettesciencemuseum.org/archives/#library. *Adminr,* Kevin B Krantz; E-mail: kkrantz@lafayettela.gov; *Coll Curator,* Dr Deborah J Clifton, PhD; Tel: 337-291-5415; *Libr Assoc,* Edi Gilbert; E-mail: egilbert@lafayettela.gov. Subject Specialists: *Archives, Sci, Tech,* Dr Deborah J Clifton, PhD; *Lit,* Edi Gilbert; Staff 2 (MLS 1, Non-MLS 1)
Library Holdings: AV Mats 360; Bk Titles 5,000; Bk Vols 10,000; Spec Interest Per Sub 50
Special Collections: Archives; Rare Book Coll. Municipal Document Depository; Oral History
Subject Interests: Astronomy, Environ sci, Natural hist, Natural sci, Phys sci
Wireless access
Function: Archival coll, Ref & res
Partic in National Network of Libraries of Medicine Region 3
Restriction: Non-circulating coll, Open to pub by appt only, Open to researchers by request

L ONEBANE LAW FIRM APC*, Law Library, 1200 Camellia Blvd, Ste 300, 70508. (Mail add: PO Box 3507, 70502-3507), SAN 372-0837. Tel: 337-237-2660. FAX: 337-266-1232. E-mail: info@onebane.com. Web Site: www.onebane.com. *Human Res,* Sondra Broussard; E-mail: broussards@onebane.com; *Library Contact,* Vicky Baccus; E-mail: baccusv@onebane.com
Library Holdings: Bk Vols 13,000; Per Subs 60
Restriction: Staff use only

C REMINGTON COLLEGE LIBRARY, 4021-A Ambassador Caffery Pkwy, Ste 100A, 70503. Tel: 337-981-4010. FAX: 337-983-7130.
Enrl 400; Fac 30
Library Holdings: AV Mats 300; Bk Vols 6,600; Per Subs 65; Talking Bks 10
Automation Activity & Vendor Info: (Cataloging) Book Systems; (Circulation) Book Systems
Open Mon-Thurs 7:30am-10pm, Fri 8-4

§J SOUTH LOUISIANA COMMUNITY COLLEGE, Lafayette Campus Library, Devalcourt Bldg, 1st Flr, 1101 Bertrand Dr, 70506. Tel: 337-521-8927. E-mail: library@solacc.edu. Web Site: libguides.solacc.edu/library. *Dir, Libr Serv,* Katherine Rolfes; Tel: 337-521-8906, E-mail: katherine.rolfes@solacc.edu; *Access Serv Librn,* Bill French; Tel: 337-521-8998, E-mail: bill.french@solacc.edu; *Access Serv Librn,* Jennifer Schmidt; Tel: 337-521-8935, E-mail: jennifer.gauthier@solacc.edu
Wireless access
Function: Computers for patron use, ILL available, Photocopying/Printing, Res assist avail, Scanner
Partic in Louisiana Library Network
Open Mon-Fri 8-5

C UNIVERSITY OF LOUISIANA AT LAFAYETTE, Edith Garland Dupré Library, 400 E St Mary Blvd, 70503. (Mail add: PO Box 40199, 70504-0199), SAN 343-0898. Tel: 337-482-6396. Circulation Tel: 337-482-6025. Interlibrary Loan Service Tel: 337-482-6035. Reference Tel: 337-482-6030. E-mail: duprelibrary@louisiana.edu. Web Site: library.louisiana.edu. *Dean, Univ Libr,* Dr Brian J Doherty; E-mail: brian.doherty@louisiana.edu; *Assoc Dean,* Susan Richard; E-mail: susan.richard@louisiana.edu; *Asst Dean, Pub Serv,* Blair Stapleton; Tel: 337-482-1173, E-mail: blair.stapleton@louisiana.edu; *Asst Dean, Tech Serv,* Sherry Curry; Tel: 337-482-5704, E-mail: sheryl.curry@louisiana.edu; *Head, Cat,* Janelle Zetty; Tel: 337-482-6033, E-mail: janelle.zetty@louisiana.edu; *Head, Coll Develop,* Andrea Flockton; Tel: 337-482-6677, E-mail: andrea.flockton@louisiana.edu; *Head, Distance Learning Servs,* Ian Richardson; Tel: 337-482-6452, E-mail: ian.richardson@louisiana.edu; *Head, E-Res & Ser,* Michael Mitchell; Tel: 337-482-6197, E-mail: michael.mitchell@louisiana.edu; *Head, ILL,* Yolanda Landry; Tel: 337-482-1612, E-mail: yolanda.thomas@louisiana.edu; *Head, Instrul Serv,* Jennifer Hamilton; Tel: 337-482-1160, E-mail: jennifer.hamilton@louisiana.edu; *Head, Ref & Res Serv,* Heather Plaisance; Tel: 337-482-1172, E-mail: heather.plaisance@louisisna.edu; *Head, Spec Coll,* Zachary Stein; Tel: 337-482-6427, E-mail: zachary.stein@louisiana.edu; Staff 56 (MLS 18, Non-MLS 38)
Founded 1901. Enrl 16,450; Fac 826; Highest Degree: Doctorate
Jul 2019-Jun 2020 Income $2,259,011. Mats Exp $1,910,126, Books $6,077, Per/Ser (Incl. Access Fees) $18,699, Electronic Ref Mat (Incl. Access Fees) $1,885,350. Sal $1,840,634
Library Holdings: Bk Titles 535,208; Bk Vols 951,243; Per Subs 1,259
Special Collections: Acadian & Creole Folklore; Cajun & Creole Music Coll; Ernest J Gaines Center; Louisiana Coll; Regional Photographic Coll. US Document Depository
Automation Activity & Vendor Info: (Cataloging) SirsiDynix; (Circulation) SirsiDynix; (Course Reserve) SirsiDynix; (Discovery) EBSCO Discovery Service; (ILL) OCLC ILLiad; (OPAC) SirsiDynix; (Serials) SirsiDynix
Wireless access
Publications: Bayou State Periodical Index
Partic in Louisiana Library Network; LYRASIS
Special Services for the Deaf - ADA equip
Special Services for the Blind - Accessible computers; Audio mat; Bks on cassette; Bks on CD; Computer access aids
Open Mon-Thurs 7:30am-11:00pm, Fri 7:30-4:30, Sat 10-5, Sun 2-11

LAKE CHARLES

P CALCASIEU PARISH PUBLIC LIBRARY SYSTEM*, 301 W Claude St, 70605-3457. SAN 306-4727. Tel: 337-721-7147. Web Site: www.calcasieulibrary.org. *Dir,* Marjorie Harrison; E-mail: mharrison@calcasieulibrary.org; *Dir, Human Res,* Angela Stutes; E-mail: astutes@calcasieulibrary.org; *Assoc Librn, Coll & Computing Serv,* Loretta Gharst; E-mail: lgharst@calcasieulibrary.org; *Assoc Librn, Pub Serv,* Pamela Edwards; E-mail: pedwards@calcasieulibrary.org; *Bus Mgr,* Peggy Dupuis; E-mail: pdupuis@calcasieulibrary.org; *Fac Mgr,* Dwight Toland; E-mail: dtoland@calcasieulibrary.org; *Pub Info Officer,* Christy Comeaux; E-mail: ccomeaux@calcasieulibrary.org; Staff 143 (MLS 16, Non-MLS 127)
Founded 1944. Pop 203,436; Circ 2,118,142
Jan 2019-Dec 2019 Income (Main & Associated Libraries) $12,242,893, State $122,810, Locally Generated Income $11,654,725, Other $465,358. Mats Exp $1,566,299, Books $289,213, Per/Ser (Incl. Access Fees) $57,311, AV Mat $343,525. Sal $4,471,661
Library Holdings: Audiobooks 8,310; AV Mats 72,367; Bks on Deafness & Sign Lang 66; CDs 6,037; DVDs 43,826; e-books 450,793; e-journals 150; Electronic Media & Resources 408,399; Large Print Bks 21,000; Microforms 5,499; Bk Vols 309,531; Per Subs 804; Spec Interest Per Sub 21; Talking Bks 159
Subject Interests: Genealogy, Local hist
Automation Activity & Vendor Info: (Acquisitions) SirsiDynix; (Cataloging) SirsiDynix; (Circulation) SirsiDynix; (ILL) Auto-Graphics, Inc; (OPAC) SirsiDynix; (Serials) SirsiDynix
Wireless access
Publications: Staff Intranet (Online only)
Partic in Libraries SouthWest; Loan System Helping Automate Retrieval of Knowledge
Open Mon-Thurs 9-8, Fri 9-6, Sat 9-5, Sun 2-6
Friends of the Library Group

Branches: 12
EPPS MEMORIAL, 1320 N Simmons St, 70601, SAN 374-6933. Tel: 337-721-7090. *Br Mgr,* Felicia Oliver; E-mail: foliver@calcasieulibrary.org
Pop 17,699; Circ 26,894
Library Holdings: Audiobooks 181; AV Mats 1,393; CDs 138; DVDs 711; Bk Vols 10,472
Open Mon-Thurs 9-8, Fri 9-6, Sat 9-5
Friends of the Library Group
CARNEGIE MEMORIAL, 411 Pujo St, 70601-4254. Tel: 337-721-7084. *Br Mgr,* Brandon Shoumaker; E-mail: bshoumaker@calcasieulibrary.org
Founded 1901. Pop 8,849; Circ 28,754
Library Holdings: Audiobooks 280; AV Mats 2,021; CDs 139; DVDs 1,165; Bk Vols 9,333
Open Mon-Fri 9-6
Friends of the Library Group
CENTRAL LIBRARY, 301 W Claude St, 70605. Tel: 337-721-7116. *Br Mgr,* Carly Searcy; E-mail: csearcy@calcasieulibrary.org
Pop 58,183; Circ 399,689
Library Holdings: Audiobooks 3,605; AV Mats 21,287; CDs 2,647; DVDs 11,549; Bk Vols 91,397; Talking Bks 62
Open Mon-Thurs 9-8, Fri 9-6, Sat 9-5, Sun 2-6
Friends of the Library Group
DEQUINCY BRANCH, 102 W Harrison St, DeQuincy, 70633, SAN 374-6925. Tel: 337-721-7087. *Br Mgr,* Janet Jordy; E-mail: jjordy@calcasieulibrary.org
Pop 9,582; Circ 54,209
Library Holdings: Audiobooks 292; AV Mats 3,803; CDs 198; DVDs 2,688; Bk Vols 17,584
Open Mon-Fri 9-6
Friends of the Library Group
FONTENOT MEMORIAL, 1402 Center St, Vinton, 70668, SAN 374-6941. Tel: 337-721-7095. *Br Mgr,* Jared Lessard; E-mail: jlessard@calcasieulibrary.org
Pop 7,771; Circ 31,687
Library Holdings: Audiobooks 160; AV Mats 2,060; CDs 79; DVDs 1,099; Bk Vols 9,236
Open Mon-Fri 9-6
Friends of the Library Group
HAYES BRANCH, 7709 Perier St, Hayes, 70646, SAN 374-695X. Tel: 337-721-7098. *Br Mgr,* Angel Trahan; E-mail: atrahan@calcasieulibrary.org
Founded 2009. Pop 3,926; Circ 12,211
Library Holdings: Audiobooks 76; AV Mats 1,940; CDs 54; DVDs 1,150; Bk Vols 5,217
Open Mon-Fri 10-6
Friends of the Library Group
IOWA BRANCH, 107 First St, Iowa, 70647, SAN 374-6968. Tel: 337-721-7101. *Br Mgr,* Cornell Thomas; E-mail: cthomas@calcasieulibrary.org
Pop 10,151; Circ 38,767
Library Holdings: Audiobooks 122; AV Mats 3,211; CDs 164; DVDs 1,650; Bk Vols 13,711
Open Mon-Fri 9-6
Friends of the Library Group
MOSS BLUFF, 261 Parish Rd, 70611, SAN 374-6909. Tel: 337-721-7128. E-mail: mbstaff@calcasieulibrary.org. *Br Mgr,* Cory Bond; E-mail: cbond@calcasieulibrary.org
Pop 22,236; Circ 157,796
Library Holdings: Audiobooks 600; AV Mats 10,189; CDs 602; DVDs 6,586; Bk Vols 33,861
Open Mon-Thurs 9-8, Fri 9-6, Sat 9-5, Sun 2-6
Friends of the Library Group
SOUTHWEST LOUISIANA GENEALOGICAL & HISTORICAL LIBRARY, 411 Pujo St, 70601-4254, SAN 374-700X. Tel: 337-721-7110. *Br Mgr,* Brandon Shoumaker; E-mail: bshoumaker@calcasieulibrary.org
Pop 8,829; Circ 178
Library Holdings: DVDs 4; Microforms 5,499; Bk Vols 16,908; Spec Interest Per Sub 15
Subject Interests: Genealogy
Open Mon-Fri 9-6, Sat 9-5
Friends of the Library Group
STARKS BRANCH, 113 S HWY 109, Starks, 70661-4362, SAN 374-6992. Tel: 337-721-7107. E-mail: st@calcasieulibrary.org. *Br Mgr,* Janet Jordy; E-mail: jjordy@calcasieulibrary.org
Pop 1,953; Circ 9,879
Library Holdings: Audiobooks 83; AV Mats 1,239; CDs 61; DVDs 883; Bk Vols 6,185
Open Mon & Fri 9-1, Tues & Thurs 2-6, Wed 9-6
Friends of the Library Group
SULPHUR REGIONAL, 1160 Cypress St, Sulphur, 70663, SAN 373-7365. Tel: 337-721-7141. E-mail: sul@calcasieulibrary.org. *Br Mgr,* Sheryl Chaisson; E-mail: schaisson@calcasieulibrary.org
Pop 43,840; Circ 262,155
Library Holdings: Audiobooks 2,296; AV Mats 20,018; CDs 1,602; DVDs 12,921; Bk Vols 70,937
Open Mon-Thurs 9-8, Fri 9-6, Sat 9-5, Sun 2-6
Friends of the Library Group
WESTLAKE BRANCH, 937 Mulberry St, Westlake, 70669, SAN 374-7018. Tel: 337-721-7113. E-mail: wl@calcasieulibrary.org. *Br Mgr,* Delores Verdine; E-mail: dverdine@calcasieulibrary.org
Pop 10,416; Circ 48,020
Library Holdings: Audiobooks 397; AV Mats 3,990; CDs 274; DVDs 2,600; Bk Vols 17,229
Open Mon-Fri 9-6
Friends of the Library Group

C MCNEESE STATE UNIVERSITY*, Lether E Frazar Memorial Library, 300 S Beauregard Dr, 70609. (Mail add: PO Box 91445, 70609), SAN 306-4735. Tel: 337-475-5716. Interlibrary Loan Service Tel: 337-475-5726. Reference Tel: 337-475-5725. Toll Free Tel: 800-622-3352. FAX: 337-475-5719, 337-475-5727. TDD: 337-475-5722. Web Site: www.library.mcneese.edu. *Assoc Prof, Dir,* Debbie Delafoisse Johnson-Houston; E-mail: djohnsonhouston@mcneese.edu; *Asst Prof, Head, Acq,* Lonnie Beene; Tel: 337-475-5724, E-mail: lbeene@mcneese.edu; *Asst Prof, Head, Archives & Spec Coll,* Pati Threatt; Tel: 337-475-5731, E-mail: pthreatt@mcneese.edu; *Asst Prof, Govt Info Librn, Head, Govt Info,* Mary Jane Bloomquist; Tel: 337-475-5718, E-mail: mbloomquist@mcneese.edu; *Asst Prof, Head, Pub Serv,* Walt Fontane; Tel: 337-475-5729, E-mail: wfontane@mcneese.edu; *Cat Librn, ILL Librn,* David Guillory; E-mail: dguilroy@mcneese.edu; *Asst Prof, Info Res Librn,* Jerome Marcantel; Tel: 337-475-5728, E-mail: jmarcantel@mcneese.edu; *Asst Prof, Pub Serv Librn,* Barbara Houssiere; Tel: 337-475-5732, E-mail: bhoussie@mcneese.edu; *Instr, Pub Serv Librn,* Sandra Keirsey; Tel: 337-475-5740, E-mail: skeirsey@mcneese.edu; *Instr, Pub Serv Librn,* Shandi Thibodeaux; Tel: 337-475-5739, E-mail: sthibodeaux@mcneese.edu; Staff 16 (MLS 10, Non-MLS 6)
Founded 1939. Enrl 6,295; Fac 369; Highest Degree: Master
Library Holdings: e-books 112,202; e-journals 140,487; Microforms 269,482; Bk Vols 155,000; Per Subs 457
Special Collections: 20th Century American First Editions; Fore-Edge Paintings; Lake Charles, Southwestern Louisiana Archives. Oral History; State Document Depository; US Document Depository
Subject Interests: Educ
Automation Activity & Vendor Info: (Acquisitions) SirsiDynix; (Cataloging) SirsiDynix; (Circulation) SirsiDynix; (Course Reserve) SirsiDynix; (ILL) SirsiDynix; (Media Booking) SirsiDynix; (OPAC) SirsiDynix; (Serials) SirsiDynix
Wireless access
Function: 24/7 Electronic res, 24/7 Online cat
Publications: Friends of the Library (Online only)
Partic in Libraries SouthWest; Louisiana Library Network; LYRASIS
Friends of the Library Group
Departmental Libraries:
, 300 Beauregard Dr, 70609. Tel: 337-475-5410. FAX: 337-475-5398. *Admin Officer,* Marcella Miller; E-mail: mmiller@mcneese.edu
Founded 1970. Enrl 8,295; Fac 369
Library Holdings: Bk Vols 8,500
Special Collections: Curriculum Materials; Library Science
Restriction: Open to students, fac & staff

§J SOWELA TECHNICAL COMMUNITY COLLEGE LIBRARY, Arts & Humanities Bldg, 2000 Merganser St, 70616. Tel: 337-421-6530. E-mail: sowela.library@sowela.edu. Web Site: www.sowela.edu/student-life/library. *Libr Dir,* Mary Frances Sherwood; Tel: 337-421-6926, E-mail: mary.sherwood@sowela.edu; *Ref & Instruction Librn,* Khalil El-Bathy; Tel: 337-421-6928, E-mail: khalil.el-bathy@sowela.edu; *Tech Serv Librn,* Darren MacLennan; Tel: 337-421-6927, E-mail: darren.maclennan@sowela.edu
Wireless access
Function: Res assist avail
Partic in Louisiana Library Network
Main SOWELA library temporarily closed due to hurricane damage, 2020-
Departmental Libraries:
OAKDALE CAMPUS, 117 Hwy 1152, Oakdale, 71463. Tel: 318-335-3944. *Libr Asst,* Katelyn Warren; E-mail: katelyn.warren@sowela.edu
Open Mon-Fri 7:45-4:30
MORGAN SMITH LIBRARY, JENNINGS CAMPUS, 2110 N Sherman St, Jennings, 70546. Tel: 337-421-6567. *Libr Tech,* Holly Goodwin; Tel: 337-824-4811, Ext 4656, E-mail: holly.goodwin@sowela.edu
Function: Computers for patron use, Photocopying/Printing
Open Mon-Fri 9-2

LAKE PROVIDENCE

P EAST CARROLL PARISH LIBRARY*, 109 Sparrow St, 71254-2645. SAN 306-4751. Tel: 318-559-2615. FAX: 318-559-4635. Web Site: ecplib.org. *Libr Dir,* Krishanda Sanders; E-mail: kmayers@state,lib.la.us; Staff 6 (MLS 1, Non-MLS 5)
Founded 1954. Pop 8,166; Circ 43,085
Library Holdings: AV Mats 3,151; Bk Vols 29,861; Per Subs 48
Special Collections: Caldecott Coll; Coretta S King Coll; Newbery Coll
Subject Interests: African-Am hist, Hist, La
Automation Activity & Vendor Info: (Cataloging) Book Systems; (Circulation) Book Systems; (ILL) Book Systems; (OPAC) Book Systems
Wireless access
Function: 24/7 Electronic res, 24/7 Online cat, Accelerated reader prog, Activity rm, After school storytime, Archival coll, Art programs, Audio & video playback equip for onsite use, Audiobks on Playaways & MP3, Audiobks via web, AV serv, Bks on cassette, Bks on CD, Children's prog, Computers for patron use, Digital talking bks, E-Readers, Electronic databases & coll, Family literacy, For res purposes, Free DVD rentals, Games & aids for people with disabilities, Govt ref serv, Health sci info serv, Home delivery & serv to seniorr ctr & nursing homes, Homework prog, ILL available, Internet access, Laminating, Life-long learning prog for all ages, Literacy & newcomer serv, Magazines, Mail & tel request accepted, Makerspace, Meeting rooms, Microfiche/film & reading machines, Movies, Music CDs, Online cat, Online info literacy tutorials on the web & in blackboard, Online ref, Outreach serv, OverDrive digital audio bks, Photocopying/Printing, Preschool outreach, Preschool reading prog, Printer for laptops & handheld devices, Prog for adults, Prog for children & young adult, Ref & res, Ref serv available, Scanner, Senior outreach, STEM programs, Story hour, Summer & winter reading prog, Summer reading prog, Teen prog, Telephone ref, Wheelchair accessible
Mem of Trail Blazer Library System
Partic in Loan System Helping Automate Retrieval of Knowledge
Open Mon-Fri 8-5, Sat 8-12
Restriction: Borrowing requests are handled by ILL
Friends of the Library Group
Bookmobiles: 1. Librns, Bobbie Prine & Cynthia Devereaux-Hampton. Bk vols 6,615

LAPLACE

P SAINT JOHN THE BAPTIST PARISH LIBRARY*, Norris J Millet Sr Library, 2920 New Hwy 51, 70068. SAN 343-0952. Tel: 985-652-6857. FAX: 985-652-3689. E-mail: sjbplinfo@stjohn.lib.la.us. Web Site: stjohnlib.com. *Dir,* Andrea Tullos; E-mail: aftullos@stjohn.lib.la.us; *Asst Dir,* Amy Y. Riche; E-mail: ariche@stjohn.lib.la.us; *Info Tech, Syst Adminr,* Purnell Brewer; E-mail: pbrowner@stjohn.lib.la.us; *Ch,* Trina Smith; E-mail: tcsmith@stjohn.lib.la.us; *ILL Librn,* Regina W Burke; E-mail: rburke@stjohn.lib.la.us; *Bus Mgr,* Karen Simon; E-mail: busoffice@stjohn.lib.la.us; Staff 41 (MLS 4, Non-MLS 37)
Founded 1966. Pop 46,393
Library Holdings: Audiobooks 6,975; AV Mats 11,754; Bks on Deafness & Sign Lang 41; Braille Volumes 5; DVDs 11,712; e-books 411; e-journals 50; Electronic Media & Resources 74; High Interest/Low Vocabulary Bk Vols 131; Large Print Bks 5,059; Microforms 816; Music Scores 32; Bk Vols 171,802; Per Subs 197
Special Collections: Parish History, photos
Subject Interests: Genealogy, La, Local hist
Automation Activity & Vendor Info: (Cataloging) Innovative Interfaces, Inc; (Circulation) Innovative Interfaces, Inc; (OPAC) Innovative Interfaces, Inc
Wireless access
Function: 24/7 Electronic res, Accelerated reader prog, Adult bk club, After school storytime, Online cat, Wheelchair accessible
Partic in Loan System Helping Automate Retrieval of Knowledge
Open Mon-Thurs 10-8, Fri & Sat 10-5
Friends of the Library Group
Branches: 3
ROLAND BORNE SR MEMORIAL LIBRARY, 2979 Hwy 18, Edgard, 70049, SAN 343-0987. Tel: 985-497-3453. FAX: 985-267-1617. *Br Supvr,* JoAnn Proctor; E-mail: japroctor@stjohn.lib.la.us
Library Holdings: Bk Vols 14,684
Open Mon & Wed 9-12:30 & 1:30-7, Tues, Thurs & Fri 9-12:30 & 1:30-5:30, Sat 9-12:30
Friends of the Library Group
FRAZEE-HARRIS MEMORIAL LIBRARY, 111 Historic Front St, Garyville, 70051. Tel: 985-535-6868. FAX: 985-535-8709. *Br Supvr,* Dawn Monica; E-mail: dmonica@stjohn.lib.la.us
Library Holdings: Bk Vols 9,255
Open Mon & Thurs 10-12:30 & 1:30-7, Tues, Wed & Fri 9-12:30 & 1-5, Sat 10-2
LEROY D WILLIAMS MEMORIAL LIBRARY, 170 W Tenth St, Reserve, 70084, SAN 329-6202. Tel: 985-536-4107. FAX: 985-536-4116. *Br Supvr,* Brandy Barnes; E-mail: bbarnes@stjohn.lib.la.us
Library Holdings: Bk Vols 31,040
Open Mon, Wed, Fri & Sat 9-5, Tues & Thurs 9-8

LEESVILLE

C NORTHWESTERN STATE UNIVERSITY LIBRARIES*, Leesville Library, 3329 University Pkwy, 71446. Tel: 337-392-3126. FAX: 337-392-3184. Web Site: library.nsula.edu/leesville-library. *Libr Mgr,* Anna T MacDonald; E-mail: macdonalda@nsula.edu; *Libr Assoc,* Heather Ritter; E-mail: ritterh@nsula.edu
Library Holdings: AV Mats 989; DVDs 100; Bk Vols 24,000
Automation Activity & Vendor Info: (Cataloging) SirsiDynix; (Circulation) SirsiDynix; (OPAC) SirsiDynix
Wireless access
Open Mon-Thurs 8:30-6, Fri 8-Noon
Friends of the Library Group

P VERNON PARISH LIBRARY*, 1401 Nolan Trace, 71446. SAN 343-1010. Tel: 337-239-2027. Toll Free Tel: 800-737-2231. FAX: 337-238-0666. E-mail: w1vr@state.lib.la.us. Web Site: www1.youseemore.com/VernonParish. *Dir,* Howard L Coy, Jr; E-mail: hcoy@state.lib.la.us
Founded 1956. Pop 55,000; Circ 264,612
Library Holdings: CDs 873; DVDs 4,888; e-books 31,200; Bk Vols 92,460; Videos 4,952
Special Collections: Fishing Rods; Local History Archives; School Yearbooks. State Document Depository; US Document Depository
Subject Interests: Archives, Civil War, Genealogy, La, World War II
Automation Activity & Vendor Info: (Acquisitions) Baker & Taylor; (Cataloging) TLC (The Library Corporation); (Circulation) TLC (The Library Corporation); (ILL) TLC (The Library Corporation); (Serials) EBSCO Online
Wireless access
Function: Online cat
Partic in Loan System Helping Automate Retrieval of Knowledge
Open Mon-Thurs 9-8, Fri & Sat 9-5:30
Branches: 2
PAUL LAWRENCE DUNBAR BRANCH, 1003 N Gladys, 71446. (Mail add: 1401 Nolan Trace, 71446), SAN 343-1045. Tel: 337-239-7037. *Br Mgr,* Betty Stokes
Founded 1956
Special Collections: Archives; Federals Depository; Genealogy Coll
Open Mon, Wed & Fri 3:30-7, Sat 1:30-6
PITKIN BRANCH, 7277 Hwy 463, Pitkin, 70656, SAN 370-1190. Tel: 318-358-3294. FAX: 318-358-3294. *Br Mgr,* Donna Strother
Open Mon 2-6, Wed 9-1, Fri 1-5, Sat 9-12
Friends of the Library Group
Bookmobiles: 1

LIVINGSTON

P LIVINGSTON PARISH LIBRARY*, 13986 Florida Blvd, 70754. (Mail add: PO Box 397, 70754-0397), SAN 343-107X. Tel: 225-686-4100. FAX: 225-686-7424. Web Site: www.mylpl.info. *Dir,* Giovanni Tairov; E-mail: giovanni@mylpl.info; *Asst Dir,* Jennifer Seneca; E-mail: jseneca@mylpl.info; Staff 8 (MLS 2, Non-MLS 6)
Founded 1946. Pop 87,311; Circ 281,195
Library Holdings: AV Mats 780; Bk Titles 153,831; Per Subs 434
Automation Activity & Vendor Info: (Cataloging) TLC (The Library Corporation); (Circulation) TLC (The Library Corporation); (OPAC) TLC (The Library Corporation)
Wireless access
Publications: Free State
Partic in Loan System Helping Automate Retrieval of Knowledge
Open Mon & Wed 9-6, Tues & Thurs 9-8, Fri 9-5, Sat 9-3
Friends of the Library Group
Branches: 5
ALBANY SPRINGFIELD, 26941 Louisiana Hwy 43, Hammond, 70403. (Mail add: PO Box 1256, Albany, 70711), SAN 343-110X. Tel: 225-686-4130. FAX: 225-567-3768. E-mail: albany@mylpl.info. *Br Mgr,* Dustin Cotton; Staff 1 (Non-MLS 1)
Circ 12,705
Library Holdings: Bk Vols 40,000; Per Subs 30
Open Mon & Wed 9-6, Tues & Thurs 9-8, Fri 9-5, Sat 10-2
DENHAM SPRINGS - WALKER BRANCH, 8101 US Hwy 190, Denham Springs, 70726, SAN 343-1134. Tel: 225-686-4140. FAX: 225-791-6325. E-mail: denham@mylpl.info. *Br Mgr,* Trevor Collings
Circ 136,261
Library Holdings: AV Mats 300; Bk Vols 55,000; Per Subs 75
Open Mon-Thurs 9-9, Fri & Sat 9-5, Sun 2-6
Friends of the Library Group

MAIN BRANCH, 20390 Iowa St, 70754. Tel: 225-686-4160. FAX: 225-686-3888. E-mail: main@mylpl.info. *Br Mgr,* Holley Hughes
Open Mon & Wed 9-6, Tues & Thurs 9-8, Fri 9-5, Sat 9-3
SOUTH BRANCH, 23477 Louisiana Hwy 444, 70754. Tel: 225-686-4170. FAX: 225-686-9979. E-mail: south@mylpl.info. *Br Mgr,* Wendy Corkem
Library Holdings: Bk Vols 35,000; Per Subs 25
Open Mon & Wed 9-6, Tues & Thurs 9-8, Fri 9-5, Sat 10-2
WATSON BRANCH, 36581 Outback Rd, Denham Springs, 70706. Tel: 225-686-4180. FAX: 225-664-1949. E-mail: watson@mylpl.info. *Br Mgr,* Danielle Durr; Staff 3 (MLS 1, Non-MLS 2)
Circ 36,848
Library Holdings: Bk Vols 50,000; Per Subs 60
Open Mon-Thurs 9-8, Fri & Sat 9-5
Bookmobiles: 1

LUTCHER

P ST JAMES PARISH LIBRARY*, 1879 W Main St, 70071-5140. SAN 343-1525. Tel: 225-869-3618. FAX: 225-869-8435. Web Site: www.stjamesla.com/154/Library. *Dir,* Keri Walker; E-mail: keri.walker@stjamesla.com; Staff 8 (Non-MLS 8)
Founded 1966. Pop 22,000; Circ 85,000
Library Holdings: AV Mats 1,323; Bk Vols 86,000; Per Subs 151
Special Collections: Louisiana Coll; St James File (parish hist)
Automation Activity & Vendor Info: (Cataloging) Horizon; (Circulation) Horizon; (OPAC) Horizon; (Serials) Horizon
Wireless access
Partic in Loan System Helping Automate Retrieval of Knowledge
Open Mon-Thurs 8-6, Fri 8-4, Sat 8-Noon
Branches: 1
VACHERIE LIBRARY, 2593 Hwy 20, Vacherie, 70090-5601. (Mail add: PO Box 190, Vacherie, 70090-0190), SAN 343-155X. Tel: 225-265-9066. FAX: 225-265-4691. *Br Mgr,* Betsy Octave; E-mail: betsy.octave@stjamesla.com; Staff 2 (Non-MLS 2)
Library Holdings: Bk Vols 21,000; Per Subs 62
Special Collections: Parish History (St James Parish File), bks, clippings, microflm, newsp
Open Mon-Thurs 8-5, Fri 8-4, Sat 8-Noon
Bookmobiles: 1

MANSFIELD

P DESOTO PARISH LIBRARY*, 109 Crosby St, 71052. SAN 321-7485. Tel: 318-872-6100. FAX: 318-872-6120. Web Site: desotoparishlibrary.org, www.desotoparishlibrary.org. *Libr Dir,* Delbert Terry; E-mail: dterry@state.lib.la.us; *Asst Dir, Syst Adminr,* William Smith; E-mail: bsmith@state.lib.la.us; *Ch,* Darron Spencer; E-mail: dspencer@state.lib.la.us; *Chief Cataloger, Mgr,* Doris Ross; E-mail: dross@state.lib.la.us; *Libr Asst,* Latrishia Grant-Jackson; E-mail: ljackson@state.lib.la.us; *Libr Asst,* Peyton Guy; E-mail: pguy@state.lib.la.us; *Libr Asst,* Ms Curlie Gillyard; Tel: 318-872-6100, E-mail: cgillyard@state.lib.la.us; *Libr Asst,* Bethany Kauffman; E-mail: bmellas@state.lib.la.us; *Libr Asst,* Brian McCarty; E-mail: bmccarty@state.lib.la.us; *Libr Asst,* Marian Ponthieus; E-mail: mponthieus@state.lib.la.us; *Acq, Libr Asst,* Francis Tyler; E-mail: ftyler@state.lib.la.us. Subject Specialists: *Human resources, Info syst, Planning, Policy,* Delbert Terry; Staff 4 (MLS 1, Non-MLS 3)
Founded 1941. Pop 27,083
Special Collections: Louisiana History
Subject Interests: Civil War, World War I, World War II
Automation Activity & Vendor Info: (Acquisitions) SirsiDynix; (Cataloging) SirsiDynix; (Circulation) SirsiDynix; (Discovery) SirsiDynix; (ILL) Auto-Graphics, Inc; (OPAC) SirsiDynix; (Serials) EBSCO Discovery Service
Wireless access
Function: 24/7 Electronic res, 24/7 Online cat, Activity rm, Adult bk club, Adult literacy prog, After school storytime, Archival coll, Art exhibits, Audio & video playback equip for onsite use, Audiobks on Playaways & MP3, Audiobks via web, AV serv, Bk club(s), Bk reviews (Group), Bks on CD, CD-ROM, Children's prog, Citizenship assistance, Computer training, Computers for patron use, Digital talking bks, E-Reserves, Electronic databases & coll, Free DVD rentals, Holiday prog, Homebound delivery serv, Homework prog, ILL available, Internet access, Jail serv, Large print keyboards, Magazines, Magnifiers for reading, Meeting rooms, Microfiche/film & reading machines, Movies, Online cat, Online ref, Outreach serv, OverDrive digital audio bks, Photocopying/Printing, Preschool outreach, Preschool reading prog, Printer for laptops & handheld devices, Prog for adults, Prog for children & young adult, Ref & res, Ref serv available, Scanner, Senior computer classes, Senior outreach, Spanish lang bks, Spoken cassettes & CDs, Spoken cassettes & DVDs, Story hour, Study rm, Summer & winter reading prog, Summer reading prog, Tax forms, Teen prog, Telephone ref, Wheelchair accessible, Workshops
Publications: Turing Pages (Monthly newsletter)
Partic in Green Gold Libr Syst; Loan System Helping Automate Retrieval of Knowledge
Special Services for the Deaf - ADA equip; Assisted listening device
Special Services for the Blind - Accessible computers
Open Mon-Thurs 9-6, Fri 9-5, Sat 9-1
Friends of the Library Group
Branches: 3
LOGANSPORT BRANCH, 203 Hwy 5, Logansport, 71049. (Mail add: PO Box 970, Logansport, 71049-0970), SAN 321-7493. Tel: 318-697-2311. FAX: 318-697-4081. *Br Mgr,* Linda Foreman; *Ch Serv,* Terri Hawsey; E-mail: thawsey@state.lib.la.us; *Libr Asst,* Wesley Horton; E-mail: whorton@state.lib.la.us; *Libr Asst,* Diane Pitts; E-mail: dpitts@state.lib.la.us; *Libr Asst,* Lartoshee Edwards; E-mail: ledwards@state.lib.la.us; *Libr Asst,* Angela Toney; E-mail: atoney@state.lib.la.us; Staff 6 (MLS 1, Non-MLS 5)
Pop 1,565
Library Holdings: Bk Vols 20,900
Subject Interests: Local hist
Function: 24/7 Electronic res, 24/7 Online cat, Accelerated reader prog, Activity rm, Adult literacy prog, Art exhibits, Art programs, Audiobks on Playaways & MP3, Audiobks via web, AV serv, Bk club(s), Bks on CD, CD-ROM, Children's prog, Computer training, Computers for patron use, Digital talking bks, Electronic databases & coll, Free DVD rentals, Holiday prog, Home delivery & serv to seniorr ctr & nursing homes, Homebound delivery serv, Homework prog, ILL available, Instruction & testing, Life-long learning prog for all ages, Magazines, Magnifiers for reading, Mail & tel request accepted, Meeting rooms, Microfiche/film & reading machines, Movies, Online cat, Online ref, Outreach serv, OverDrive digital audio bks, Photocopying/Printing, Preschool outreach, Preschool reading prog, Printer for laptops & handheld devices, Prog for adults, Prog for children & young adult, Ref & res, Ref serv available, Res assist avail, Res performed for a fee, Scanner, Senior computer classes, Senior outreach, Serves people with intellectual disabilities, Spoken cassettes & CDs, Spoken cassettes & DVDs, Story hour, Study rm, Summer & winter reading prog, Summer reading prog, Tax forms, Teen prog, Telephone ref, Wheelchair accessible, Winter reading prog, Workshops
Publications: Turning Pages (Monthly newsletter)
Open Mon-Thurs 9-6, Fri 9-5, Sat 9-1
Friends of the Library Group
PELICAN BRANCH, 145 Jackson Ave, Pelican, 71063-2803. (Mail add: PO Box 109, Pelican, 71063-0109), SAN 324-2501. Tel: 318-755-2353. FAX: 318-755-2031. *Mgr,* Sarah Crump; E-mail: sabraham@state.lib.la.us; *Ch Serv,* Kriston Newsome; E-mail: knewsome@state.lib.la.us; *Libr Assoc,* Carol Crump; E-mail: ccrump@state.lib.la.us; *Libr Assoc,* Barbara Jones; E-mail: bjones@state.lib.la.us; Staff 4 (Non-MLS 4)
Automation Activity & Vendor Info: (Acquisitions) SirsiDynix-WorkFlows; (Cataloging) SirsiDynix-WorkFlows; (Circulation) SirsiDynix-WorkFlows
Function: 24/7 Electronic res, 24/7 Online cat, Accelerated reader prog, Activity rm, Adult bk club, Adult literacy prog, After school storytime, Archival coll, Art exhibits, Audiobks on Playaways & MP3, Audiobks via web, AV serv, Bk club(s), Bks on CD, Children's prog, Computer training, Computers for patron use, Digital talking bks, Electronic databases & coll, Free DVD rentals, Holiday prog, Home delivery & serv to seniorr ctr & nursing homes, Homebound delivery serv, Homework prog, ILL available, Instruction & testing, Internet access, Life-long learning prog for all ages, Magazines, Magnifiers for reading, Mail & tel request accepted, Meeting rooms, Microfiche/film & reading machines, Online cat, Online ref, Outreach serv, OverDrive digital audio bks, Photocopying/Printing, Preschool outreach, Preschool reading prog, Printer for laptops & handheld devices, Prog for adults, Prog for children & young adult, Ref & res, Ref serv available, Res assist avail, Res performed for a fee, Scanner, Senior computer classes, Senior outreach, Serves people with intellectual disabilities, Spoken cassettes & CDs, Spoken cassettes & DVDs, Story hour, Study rm, Summer & winter reading prog, Summer reading prog, Tax forms, Teen prog, Telephone ref, Wheelchair accessible, Winter reading prog, Workshops, Writing prog
Publications: Turning Pages (Monthly newsletter)
Special Services for the Blind - Accessible computers; Bks available with recordings; Bks on CD; Extensive large print coll; Large print bks
Open Mon 9-6, Tues-Fri 9-5, Sat 9-1
Friends of the Library Group
STONEWALL BRANCH, 808 Hwy 171, Stonewall, 71078, SAN 321-7507. Tel: 318-925-9191. FAX: 318-925-3392. *Br Mgr,* Tammy Overton; *Ch Serv,* Delores Cole; E-mail: dcole@state.lib.la.us; *Libr Assoc,* Sharon Bogan; Fax: 318-915-1694, E-mail: sbogan@state.lib.la.us; *Libr Assoc,* Robert Gullion; E-mail: rgullion@state.lib.la.us; *Libr Assoc,* Nell Holder; E-mail: nholder@state.lib.la.us; *Libr Assoc,* Carol Tolliver; E-mail: ktolliver@state.lib.la.us; *Libr Asst,* Beverly Grubb; E-mail: bgrubb@state.lib.la.us; Staff 7 (Non-MLS 7)
Pop 2,188
Automation Activity & Vendor Info: (Acquisitions) SirsiDynix-WorkFlows; (Cataloging) SirsiDynix-WorkFlows;

(Circulation) SirsiDynix-WorkFlows; (ILL) Auto-Graphics, Inc; (OPAC) SirsiDynix
Function: 24/7 Electronic res, 24/7 Online cat, Accelerated reader prog, Activity rm, Adult bk club, After school storytime, Art exhibits, Art programs, Audiobks via web, AV serv, Bk club(s), Bks on CD, Bus archives, Children's prog, Computer training, Computers for patron use, Digital talking bks, E-Readers, E-Reserves, Electronic databases & coll, Free DVD rentals, Holiday prog, Home delivery & serv to seniorr ctr & nursing homes, Homebound delivery serv, Homework prog, ILL available, Instruction & testing, Internet access, Magazines, Mail & tel request accepted, Mail loans to mem, Meeting rooms, Movies, Online cat, Online info literacy tutorials on the web & in blackboard, Online ref, Orientations, Outreach serv, Outside serv via phone, mail, e-mail & web, OverDrive digital audio bks, Photocopying/Printing, Preschool outreach, Preschool reading prog, Printer for laptops & handheld devices, Prof lending libr, Prog for adults, Prog for children & young adult, Ref & res, Res performed for a fee, Scanner, Senior computer classes, Senior outreach, Serves people with intellectual disabilities, Specialized serv in classical studies, Story hour, Study rm, Summer & winter reading prog, Summer reading prog, Tax forms, Teen prog, Telephone ref, Wheelchair accessible
Open Mon 9-6, Tues-Fri 9-5, Sat 9-1
Friends of the Library Group

MANY

P SABINE PARISH LIBRARY*, 705 Main St, 71449-3199. SAN 343-1649. Tel: 318-256-4150. FAX: 318-256-4154. Web Site: sabineparishlibrary.org. *Dir,* Deborah Anderson; E-mail: danderson@sabineparishlibrary.org; Staff 4 (MLS 1, Non-MLS 3)
Founded 1933. Pop 23,460; Circ 123,956
Library Holdings: AV Mats 4,048; Bk Vols 63,527; Per Subs 249
Special Collections: Sabine Parish History Coll
Automation Activity & Vendor Info: (Cataloging) TLC (The Library Corporation); (Circulation) TLC (The Library Corporation); (OPAC) TLC (The Library Corporation)
Wireless access
Partic in Loan System Helping Automate Retrieval of Knowledge
Open Mon & Tues 8-6, Wed-Fri 8-5, Sat 8-Noon
Branches: 4
CONVERSE BRANCH, 108 W Port Arthur Ave, Converse, 71419. (Mail add: PO Box 69, Converse, 71419), SAN 343-1673. Tel: 318-567-3121. *Br Mgr,* Patti Ebarb
Open Mon, Tues & Thurs 12-5
PLEASANT HILL BRANCH, 8434 Bridges St, Pleasant Hill, 71065. (Mail add: PO Box 277, Pleasant Hill, 71065-0277), SAN 343-1851. Tel: 318-796-2595. *Br Mgr,* Martha Mary
Open Mon & Thurs 12-5
TOLEDO BRANCH, 12350 Texas Hwy, 71449, SAN 328-7378. Tel: 318-256-4152. *Br Mgr,* Olivia Barnard
Open Mon-Fri 12-5
ZWOLLE BRANCH, 2218 Port Arthur St, Zwolle, 71486. (Mail add: PO Box 536, Zwolle, 71486), SAN 343-1886. Tel: 318-645-6955. *Br Mgr,* Erma Jean Martinez
Open Mon & Tues 11-5, Wed-Fri 12-5

MARKSVILLE

P AVOYELLES PARISH LIBRARY*, Marksville Branch, 606 N Main St, 71351. SAN 343-1916. Tel: 318-253-7559. FAX: 318-253-6361. Web Site: www.avoyelles.lib.la.us. *Dir,* Theresa Thevenote; E-mail: ttheveno@state.lib.la.us; *Assoc Librn,* Nealie Hale; Staff 5 (Non-MLS 5)
Founded 1949. Pop 40,801; Circ 95,608
Library Holdings: AV Mats 356; Bk Vols 79,860; Per Subs 200
Special Collections: Louisiana Room
Automation Activity & Vendor Info: (Cataloging) Book Systems; (Circulation) Book Systems; (ILL) Book Systems; (OPAC) Book Systems
Partic in Loan System Helping Automate Retrieval of Knowledge
Open Mon, Tues, Thurs & Fri 8-5, Wed 9-6, Sat 9-1
Friends of the Library Group
Branches: 6
BUNKIE BRANCH, 200 Walnut St, Bunkie, 71322. (Mail add: PO Box 80, Bunkie, 71322-0080), SAN 343-1940. Tel: 318-346-6122. FAX: 318-346-4301. *Br Mgr,* Angie Vernon; Staff 2 (Non-MLS 2)
Open Mon, Tues, Thurs & Fri 8-5, Wed 9-6, Sat 9-1
Friends of the Library Group
MONTEZ M JUNEAU BRANCH, 209 Cottonport Ave, Cottonport, 71327, SAN 343-1975. Tel: 318-876-3411. FAX: 318-876-2404. *Br Mgr,* Position Currently Open
Open Mon, Tues, Thurs & Fri 7:30-4, Wed 9:30-6, Sat 9-1
MANSURA BRANCH, 2111 Cleco Rd, Mansura, 71350. (Mail add: PO Box 448, Mansura, 71350-0448). Tel: 318-964-2118. FAX: 318-964-5701. *Br Mgr,* Annette Rabalais; Staff 2 (Non-MLS 2)
Library Holdings: AV Mats 54; Bk Vols 1,112; Per Subs 20
Open Mon-Fri 8-5
MOREAUVILLE BRANCH, Community Ctr, 343 Tassin St, Moreauville, 71355. (Mail add: PO Box 130, Moreauville, 71355-0130), SAN 343-2092. Tel: 318-985-2767. *Br Mgr,* Lauri Burke
Library Holdings: Bk Vols 4,604; Per Subs 33
Open Tues 10-5, Fri 10-3
PLAUCHEVILLE BRANCH, Town Hall, 146 Gin St, Plaucheville, 71362. (Mail add: PO Box 27, Plaucheville, 71362-0027), SAN 343-2122. Tel: 318-359-1016. *Br Mgr,* Roxanna Honea; Staff 2 (Non-MLS 2)
Library Holdings: AV Mats 91; Bk Vols 4,033; Per Subs 23
Open Tues 8-1 & 3-5, Fri 8-1
SIMMESPORT BRANCH, 461 Main St, Simmesport, 71369, SAN 343-2157. Tel: 318-941-2822. FAX: 318-941-5880. *Br Mgr,* Lorraine Chesne; Staff 2 (Non-MLS 2)
Open Mon & Fri 8-12 & 1-5, Wed 9-12 & 1-6, Sat 9-1
Friends of the Library Group

METAIRIE

P JEFFERSON PARISH LIBRARY*, East Bank Regional Library, 4747 W Napoleon Ave, 70001. SAN 343-2181. Tel: 504-838-1190. Interlibrary Loan Service Tel: 504-838-1114. Reference Tel: 504-457-4659, 504-838-1111. Administration Tel: 504-838-1100. Automation Services Tel: 504-838-1101. FAX: 504-838-1117. Interlibrary Loan Service FAX: 504-838-1121. Reference FAX: 504-849-8800. Administration FAX: 504-838-1110. Automation Services FAX: 504-457-0198. Web Site: www.jefferson.lib.la.us, www.jplibrary.net. *Dir,* Marylyn Haddican; Tel: 504-838-1133, E-mail: mhaddican@jefferson.lib.la.us
Founded 1949. Pop 436,181
Library Holdings: Bk Titles 307,991
Subject Interests: Genealogy
Wireless access
Partic in Loan System Helping Automate Retrieval of Knowledge
Open Mon-Thurs 9-9, Fri & Sat 9-5, Sun 1-5
Friends of the Library Group
Branches: 14
BELLE TERRE, 5550 Belle Terre Rd, Marrero, 70072, SAN 343-219X. Tel: 504-349-5910. *Br Mgr, Librn II,* Thomas Giroir; E-mail: tgiroir@jefferson.lib.la.us
Open Mon-Thurs 9-9, Fri & Sat 9-5
Friends of the Library Group
JANE O'BRIEN CHATELAIN WEST BANK REGIONAL, 2751 Manhattan Blvd, Harvey, 70058, SAN 370-9493. Tel: 504-364-2660. Reference Tel: 504-364-3720. FAX: 540-364-3739. *Br Mgr,* Daniel Cangelosi; E-mail: dcangelosi@jefferson.lib.la.us
Founded 1990
Open Mon-Thurs 9-9, Fri & Sat 9-5, Sun 1-5
Friends of the Library Group
GRAND ISLE BRANCH, 143 Ludwig Lane, Grand Isle, 70358, SAN 343-2211. Tel: 985-787-3450. *Br Mgr,* Thomas Giroir; E-mail: tgiroir@jefferson.lib.la.us
Open Tues & Wed 10-6, Fri & Sat 10-4
Friends of the Library Group
GRETNA BRANCH, 102 Willow Dr, Gretna, 70053, SAN 343-2246. Tel: 504-364-2716. *Br Mgr,* William McKee; E-mail: wmckee@jefferson.lib.la.us
Open Mon & Tues 12-8, Wed & Thurs 10-6, Fri & Sat 9-5
Friends of the Library Group
HARAHAN BRANCH, 219 Soniat Ave, Harahan, 70123, SAN 343-2270. Tel: 504-736-8745. FAX: 504-736-8746. *Br Mgr,* Maria Piacun; E-mail: mpiacun@jefferson.lib.la.us
Founded 1957
Open Mon-Thurs 9-9, Fri & Sat 9-5
Friends of the Library Group
LAFITTE BRANCH, 4917 City Park Dr, Ste B, Lafitte, 70067, SAN 343-236X. Tel: 504-689-5097. FAX: 504-689-3354. *Br Mgr, Librn II,* John Gallagher; E-mail: jgallaher@jefferson.lib.la.us
Founded 1982
Open Mon & Tues 12-8, Wed & Thurs 10-6, Fri & Sat 9-5
Friends of the Library Group
LAKESHORE, 1100 W Esplanade, 70005, SAN 376-9429. Tel: 504-838-4375. FAX: 504-838-4379. *Br Mgr,* Danielle Joachim; E-mail: djoachim@jefferson.lib.la.us
Open Mon-Thurs 9-9, Fri & Sat 9-5
Friends of the Library Group
EDITH S LAWSON LIBRARY (WESTWEGO BRANCH), 635 Fourth St, Westwego, 70094, SAN 343-2513. Tel: 504-349-5912. *Br Mgr,* Position Currently Open
Open Mon-Thurs 9-9, Fri & Sat 9-5
Friends of the Library Group
LIVE OAK, 125 Acadia Dr, Waggaman, 70094, SAN 329-6644. Tel: 504-736-8475. FAX: 504-431-0653. *Br Mgr,* Position Currently Open
Founded 1989
Open Mon & Tues 12-8, Wed & Thurs 10-6, Fri & Sat 9-5
Friends of the Library Group

NORTH KENNER, 630 W Esplanade Ave, Kenner, 70065, SAN 343-2335. Tel: 504-736-8730. *Br Mgr,* Allison Williams; E-mail: awilliams@jefferson.lib.la.us
Open Mon-Thurs 9-9, Fri & Sat 9-5
Friends of the Library Group
OLD METAIRIE, 2350 Metairie Rd, 70001, SAN 343-2424. Tel: 504-838-4353. FAX: 504-838-1014. *Br Mgr,* Suzanne Upshaw
Closed for Renovations April 2019-
Friends of the Library Group
ROSEDALE, 4036 Jefferson Hwy, Jefferson, 70121, SAN 329-3173. Tel: 504-838-4350. FAX: 504-838-1129. *Br Mgr,* Skye Cornelia; E-mail: scornelia@jefferson.lib.la.us
Open Mon & Tues 12-8, Wed & Thurs 10-6, Fri & Sat 9-5
Friends of the Library Group
TERRYTOWN BRANCH, 680 Heritage Ave, Terrytown, 70056, SAN 343-2459. Tel: 504-364-2717. FAX: 504-364-2718. *Br Mgr,* Smith Nathan
Closed for Renovation 2019-
Friends of the Library Group
CHARLES A WAGNER BRANCH, 6646 Riverside Dr, 70003, SAN 343-2483. Tel: 504-838-1193. *Br Mgr,* Sheila Bradford; E-mail: sbradford@jefferson.lib.la.us
Founded 1963
Open Mon & Tues 12-8, Wed & Thurs 10-6, Fri & Sat 9-5
Friends of the Library Group

MINDEN

P WEBSTER PARISH LIBRARY SYSTEM*, 521 East & West St, 71055. SAN 343-2548. Tel: 318-371-3080. Circulation Tel: 318-371-3080, Ext 110. FAX: 318-371-3081. Web Site: www.websterparishlibrary.org. *Dir,* Savannah Jones; Tel: 318-371-3080, Ext 115; Staff 3 (MLS 2, Non-MLS 1)
Founded 1929
Library Holdings: Bk Vols 85,058; Per Subs 203
Subject Interests: La
Automation Activity & Vendor Info: (Acquisitions) Innovative Interfaces, Inc; (Cataloging) Innovative Interfaces, Inc; (Circulation) Innovative Interfaces, Inc; (Course Reserve) Innovative Interfaces, Inc; (ILL) Innovative Interfaces, Inc; (OPAC) Innovative Interfaces, Inc; (Serials) Innovative Interfaces, Inc
Wireless access
Function: 24/7 Electronic res, Accelerated reader prog, Activity rm, Adult bk club, Audio & video playback equip for onsite use, Audiobks on Playaways & MP3, Audiobks via web, AV serv, Bk club(s), Bks on CD, CD-ROM, Children's prog, Computer training, Computers for patron use, E-Reserves, Electronic databases & coll, Free DVD rentals, Games & aids for people with disabilities, Genealogy discussion group, Home delivery & serv to seniorr ctr & nursing homes, Homework prog, ILL available, Internet access, Magazines, Magnifiers for reading, Mail & tel request accepted, Microfiche/film & reading machines, Movies, Music CDs, Online cat, Outside serv via phone, mail, e-mail & web, OverDrive digital audio bks, Photocopying/Printing, Preschool reading prog, Printer for laptops & handheld devices, Prog for adults, Prog for children & young adult, Scanner, Serves people with intellectual disabilities, Spoken cassettes & CDs, Story hour, Study rm, Summer & winter reading prog, Summer reading prog, Tax forms, Teen prog, Telephone ref, VHS videos, Wheelchair accessible, Winter reading prog
Partic in Loan System Helping Automate Retrieval of Knowledge
Special Services for the Deaf - Spec interest per
Open Mon-Fri 8-5
Restriction: Authorized patrons
Branches: 7
COTTON VALLEY BRANCH, 21241 Hwy 371, Cotton Valley, 71018, SAN 343-2572. Tel: 318-832-4290. FAX: 318-832-5335. *Br Mgr,* Sharlett Troquille
Library Holdings: Bk Vols 6,032
Open Mon-Fri 1-5
DOYLINE BRANCH, 333 Main St, Doyline, 71023. (Mail add: PO Box 8, Doyline, 71023-0008), SAN 343-2637. Tel: 318-745-3800. FAX: 318-745-2170. *Br Mgr,* Kelly Burge
Library Holdings: Bk Vols 6,446
Open Mon, Tues, Thurs & Fri 1-6
HEFLIN BRANCH, 7041 Hwy 531, Heflin, 71039, SAN 343-2661. Tel: 318-371-1027. FAX: 318-382-9613. *Br Mgr,* Dedra Harris
Library Holdings: Bk Vols 3,720
Open Mon, Wed & Fri 2-5
WILLIE & MARY MACK MEMORIAL BRANCH, 1000 S Arkansas St, Springhill, 71075, SAN 343-2815. Tel: 318-539-4117. FAX: 318-539-3718. *Br Mgr,* Renee McCluskey
Library Holdings: Bk Vols 21,036
Open Mon-Thurs 8:15-7, Fri & Sat 8:15-5
MINDEN MAIN, 521 East & West St, 71055, SAN 343-2726. Tel: 318-371-3080. FAX: 318-371-3081. *Br Mgr,* Shelia Phenix
Library Holdings: Bk Vols 36,686
Open Mon-Thurs 8:15-8, Fri & Sat 8:15-5
SAREPTA BRANCH, 24522 Hwy 371, Sarepta, 71071. (Mail add: PO Box 127, Sarepta, 71071-0127). Tel: 318-847-4992. FAX: 318-847-4826. *Br Mgr,* Julie Talley
Library Holdings: Bk Vols 4,855
Open Mon 1-5, Tues 8-5, Sat 9-1
SIBLEY BRANCH, 127 SE Fourth St, Sibley, 71073. Tel: 318-377-1320. *Br Mgr,* Troyanne Williamson
Founded 2006
Open Mon-Fri 1-5

MONROE

§J LOUISIANA DELTA COMMUNITY COLLEGE, Library & Learning Resource Center, 7500 Millhaven Rd, Rm 139, 71203. Tel: 318-345-9027. E-mail: library@ladelta.edu. Web Site: www.ladelta.edu/academics/library. *Dir, Libr Serv,* Amelia Brister; Tel: 318-345-9143, E-mail: ameliabrister@ladelta.edu; *Libr Spec II,* Ms Marty Davis; Tel: 318-345-9140, E-mail: mmckaskle@ladelta.edu
Wireless access
Function: ILL available, Photocopying/Printing, Res assist avail
Partic in Louisiana Library Network
Open Mon & Tues 7-6, Wed-Fri 7-4:30; Mon-Thurs 8-4:30, Fri 8am-11:30 am (Summer)
Departmental Libraries:
BASTROP CAMPUS, 6736 Airport Rd, Bastrop, 71221. Tel: 318-283-0836.
Open Mon-Thurs 8-4:30
JONESBORO CAMPUS, 236 Industrial Dr, Rm 136, Jonesboro, 71251. Tel: 318-480-5010.
Open Mon-Fri 8-4:30
LAKE PROVIDENCE CAMPUS, 156 Hwy 883-1, Rm 15, Lake Providence, 71254. Tel: 318-231-5100.
Open Mon-Thurs 10-2
TALLULAH CAMPUS, 132 Old Hwy 65 S, Rm 13, Tallulah, 71282. Tel: 318-474-5221.
Open Mon-Fri 8-4; Mon-Thurs 9-2 (Summer)
WEST MONROE CAMPUS, 609 Vocational Pkwy, Rm A249, West Monroe, 71292. Tel: 318-397-6200.
Open Mon-Thurs 8-4:30
WINNSBORO CAMPUS, 2889 Hwy 15, Rm 411, Winnsboro, 71295. Tel: 318-367-6200.
Open Mon-Thurs 8-7:30

M OCHSNER LSU HEALTH SHREVEPORT MONROE MEDICAL CENTER*, E A Conway Medical Center Library, 4864 Jackson St, 71202. (Mail add: PO Box 1881, 71210-8005), SAN 306-4778. Tel: 318-330-7644. FAX: 318-330-7649. *Dir, Libr Serv,* Lesley Arnott; E-mail: larnot@lsuhsc.edu; Staff 1 (MLS 1)
Library Holdings: e-journals 500; Bk Vols 612; Per Subs 200
Subject Interests: Clinical med
Open Mon-Fri 8-4:30

P OUACHITA PARISH PUBLIC LIBRARY*, 1800 Stubbs Ave, 71201. SAN 343-284X. Tel: 318-327-1490. FAX: 318-327-1373. Web Site: www.oplib.org. *Libr Dir,* Robin Toms; E-mail: rtoms@oplib.org; *Head, Info Tech,* Eileen R Kontrovitz; E-mail: eileenk@oplib.org; *Head, Pub Serv,* Nancy Green; E-mail: ngreen@oplib.org; *Head, Tech Serv,* Joy Davis; E-mail: jdavis@oplib.org; *Br Mgr, Main Libr,* Holly Priestley; E-mail: hpriestley@oplib.org; *Bus Mgr,* Marilyn Binford; E-mail: mbinford@oplib.org; *Youth Serv Coordr,* LaKeisha Bosworth; E-mail: lbosworth@oplib.org; Staff 120 (MLS 8, Non-MLS 112)
Founded 1940. Pop 147,898; Circ 834,964
Library Holdings: Audiobooks 16,469; AV Mats 69,854; Bks on Deafness & Sign Lang 253; CDs 7,775; DVDs 16,635; e-books 4,961; Large Print Bks 19,902; Bk Vols 377,139; Per Subs 1,209; Videos 19,376
Special Collections: Genealogy, bks, microflm, microfiche, clippings, photog, original source mat. Oral History; State Document Depository
Subject Interests: La
Automation Activity & Vendor Info: (Acquisitions) Innovative Interfaces, Inc; (Cataloging) Innovative Interfaces, Inc; (Circulation) Innovative Interfaces, Inc; (Serials) Innovative Interfaces, Inc
Wireless access
Function: After school storytime, Archival coll, Digital talking bks, Home delivery & serv to seniorr ctr & nursing homes, Homework prog, ILL available, Internet access, Music CDs, Photocopying/Printing, Preschool outreach, Prog for adults, Prog for children & young adult, Spoken cassettes & CDs, Summer reading prog, Wheelchair accessible
Mem of Trail Blazer Library System
Partic in Loan System Helping Automate Retrieval of Knowledge
Open Mon-Thurs 9-8, Fri 9-6, Sat 9-5, Sun 2-5
Friends of the Library Group

Branches: 9
OLLIE BURNS BRANCH, 5601 Hwy 165 S, Richwood, 71202. Tel: 318-327-1235. FAX: 318-329-8255. *Br Mgr,* Jade Wheeler; E-mail: jwheeler@oplib.org
Library Holdings: CDs 600; DVDs 500; Bk Vols 15,000; Per Subs 87; Talking Bks 500; Videos 100
Open Mon-Thurs 9-8, Fri 9-6, Sat 9-5
Friends of the Library Group
CARVER MCDONALD BRANCH, 2941 Renwick St, 71201, SAN 343-2874. Tel: 318-327-1477. FAX: 318-329-4061. *Br Mgr,* Joyce Powell; E-mail: jpowell@oplib.org; Staff 7 (Non-MLS 7)
Library Holdings: AV Mats 3,824; CDs 405; DVDs 846; Large Print Bks 110; Bk Titles 29,993; Bk Vols 30,634; Per Subs 110; Talking Bks 412; Videos 1,574
Open Mon-Fri 9-6, Sat 9-5
Friends of the Library Group
ANNA MEYER BRANCH, 1808 Hwy 165 S, 71202, SAN 343-2904. Tel: 318-327-1351. FAX: 318-329-4059. *Br Mgr,* Position Currently Open
Library Holdings: AV Mats 2,682; CDs 522; DVDs 753; Large Print Bks 465; Bk Titles 26,850; Bk Vols 28,231; Per Subs 42; Talking Bks 512; Videos 1,491
Open Mon-Fri 10-6, Sat 10-2
Friends of the Library Group
OUACHITA VALLEY BRANCH, 601 McMillian Rd, West Monroe, 71291, SAN 343-2939. Tel: 318-327-1470. FAX: 318-327-1473. *Br Mgr,* Nora Collins; E-mail: ncollins@oplib.og; Staff 19 (Non-MLS 19)
Library Holdings: AV Mats 12,404; CDs 1,072; DVDs 1,516; Large Print Bks 5,218; Bk Vols 79,213; Per Subs 125; Talking Bks 4,197; Videos 4,981
Open Mon-Thurs 9-8, Fri 9-6, Sat 9-5, Sun 2-5
Friends of the Library Group
CPL J R SEARCY MEMORIAL LIBRARY, 5775 Jonesboro Rd, West Monroe, 71292. Tel: 318-327-1240. FAX: 318-323-7565. *Br Mgr,* Vicky Powell; E-mail: vpowell@oplib.org
Library Holdings: CDs 327; DVDs 2,007; Bk Vols 9,896; Per Subs 76; Talking Bks 690
Open Mon-Thurs 9-8, Fri 9-6, Sat 9-5
Friends of the Library Group
STERLINGTON MEMORIAL BRANCH, 305 Keystone Rd, 71203. Tel: 318-327-1382. FAX: 318-665-9476. *Br Mgr,* Sandra Smith; E-mail: ssmith@oplib.org
Library Holdings: CDs 700; DVDs 2,600; Bk Vols 15,550; Per Subs 85; Talking Bks 1,450; Videos 450
Open Mon-Thurs 9-8, Fri 9-6, Sat 9-5
Friends of the Library Group
WEST MONROE BRANCH, 315 Cypress St, West Monroe, 71291, SAN 343-2963. Tel: 318-327-1365. FAX: 318-329-4062. *Br Mgr,* Debbie Sidders; E-mail: dsidders@oplib.org; Staff 2 (Non-MLS 2)
Library Holdings: AV Mats 4,332; CDs 332; DVDs 696; Large Print Bks 2,583; Bk Vols 52,622; Per Subs 89; Talking Bks 653; Videos 2,082
Open Mon-Fri 9-6, Sat 9-5
Friends of the Library Group
WEST OUACHITA BRANCH, 188 Hwy 546, West Monroe, 71291. Tel: 318-397-5414. FAX: 318-397-8657. *Br Mgr,* Kathleen Byrd; E-mail: kbyrd@oplib.org; Staff 9 (MLS 1, Non-MLS 8)
Library Holdings: AV Mats 5,613; CDs 638; DVDs 1,158; Large Print Bks 1,535; Bk Vols 28,778; Per Subs 42; Talking Bks 1,388; Videos 2,718
Open Mon-Thurs 9-8, Fri 9-6, Sat 9-5
Friends of the Library Group
LOUISE WILLIAMS BRANCH, 140 Bayou Oaks Dr, 71203. Tel: 318-327-5422. FAX: 318-343-3476. *Br Mgr,* Terrie Wright; E-mail: twright@oplib.org; Staff 7 (MLS 2, Non-MLS 5)
Library Holdings: AV Mats 4,120; CDs 461; DVDs 1,300; Large Print Bks 1,351; Bk Vols 18,004; Talking Bks 1,283; Videos 930
Open Mon-Thurs 9-8, Fri 9-6, Sat 9-5
Friends of the Library Group
Bookmobiles: 1. Bkmobile Mgr, Karen DeMoss. Bk titles 9,889

P TRAIL BLAZER LIBRARY SYSTEM*, c/o Ouachita Public Library, 1800 Stubbs Ave, 71201. Tel: 318-327-1490. FAX: 318-327-1373. *Libr Dir,* Robin Toms; E-mail: rtoms@oplib.org
Member Libraries: Caldwell Parish Library; Concordia Parish Library; East Carroll Parish Library; Franklin Parish Library; Jackson Parish Library; Lincoln Parish Library; Louisiana Tech University; Madison Parish Library; Morehouse Parish Library; Ouachita Parish Public Library; Richland Parish Library; Tensas Parish Library; Union Parish Library; West Carroll Parish Library
Open Mon-Thurs 9-8, Fri 9-6, Sat 9-5, Sun 2-5

C UNIVERSITY OF LOUISIANA AT MONROE LIBRARY, 700 University Ave, 71209-0720. SAN 306-4794. Tel: 318-342-1063. Interlibrary Loan Service Tel: 318-342-1067. Reference Tel: 318-342-1071. Administration Tel: 318-342-1050. FAX: 318-342-1075. E-mail: reference@ulm.edu. Web Site: www.ulm.edu/library. *Libr Dir,* Megan Lowe; Tel: 318-342-3041, E-mail: lowe@ulm.edu; *ILL Librn,* Melinda Matthews; E-mail: matthews@ulm.edu; *Libr Spec Supvr,* Virginia Allen; Tel: 318-342-1064, E-mail: allen@ulm.edu; *Ref Coordr,* Maren Williams; Tel: 318-342-1065, E-mail: mawilliams@ulm.edu; *Spec Coll Coordr,* Heather Pilcher; Tel: 318-342-1054, E-mail: pilcher@ulm.edu; *Coordr, Tech Serv,* Charles Hughes; Tel: 318-342-3051, E-mail: hughes@ulm.edu; *Acq,* Lila Jefferson; Tel: 318-342-1053, E-mail: jefferson@ulm.edu; Staff 10 (MLS 10)
Founded 1931. Enrl 8,500; Highest Degree: Doctorate
Special Collections: Civil War (Gilhula Coll); Governor James Noe Papers; Griffin Photograph Coll; Regional History (Otto E Passman Papers). State Document Depository; US Document Depository
Subject Interests: Educ, Family counseling, Gerontology, Health sci, Marriage counseling, Pharm
Automation Activity & Vendor Info: (Acquisitions) SirsiDynix; (Cataloging) SirsiDynix; (Circulation) SirsiDynix; (Course Reserve) SirsiDynix; (ILL) OCLC ILLiad; (OPAC) SirsiDynix; (Serials) SirsiDynix
Wireless access
Partic in Louisiana Academic Library Information Network; Louisiana Library Network; OCLC Online Computer Library Center, Inc
Restriction: ID required to use computers (Ltd hrs), In-house use for visitors

MORGAN CITY

P MORGAN CITY PUBLIC LIBRARY, 220 Everett St, 70380. (Mail add: PO Box 988, 70381-0988), SAN 306-4816. Tel: 985-380-4646. FAX: 985-380-4699. E-mail: info@morgancitylibrary.com. Web Site: morgancitylibrary.com. *Supvr,* Geraldine Besse; Staff 3 (Non-MLS 3)
Founded 1934. Pop 16,114; Circ 44,616
Library Holdings: AV Mats 326; Bk Vols 48,000; Per Subs 135
Automation Activity & Vendor Info: (Cataloging) Follett Software; (Circulation) Follett Software; (OPAC) Follett Software
Partic in Loan System Helping Automate Retrieval of Knowledge
Open Mon-Fri 1:30-5:30

NAPOLEONVILLE

P ASSUMPTION PARISH LIBRARY*, 293 Napoleon Ave, 70390-2123. SAN 306-4824. Tel: 985-369-7070. FAX: 985-369-6019. Web Site: www.assumptionlibrary.com. *Dir,* Lauren Bordelon; E-mail: lbordelon@assumptionlibrary.com; Staff 13 (MLS 1, Non-MLS 12)
Founded 1968. Pop 24,328; Circ 68,845
Library Holdings: AV Mats 1,000; Bk Vols 65,000; Per Subs 125
Special Collections: Assumption Pioneer (1850), micro; French Language Materials Coll (childrens & adult); Southern Louisiana Genealogy
Automation Activity & Vendor Info: (Cataloging) TLC (The Library Corporation); (Circulation) TLC (The Library Corporation); (OPAC) TLC (The Library Corporation)
Partic in Loan System Helping Automate Retrieval of Knowledge
Open Mon-Fri 8:30-5:30, Sat 8:30am-12:30pm
Friends of the Library Group
Branches: 3
BAYOU L'OURSE BRANCH, 1214 Hwy 662, Morgan City, 70380. Tel: 985-631-3200. FAX: 985-631-3200. E-mail: bayoulourselibrary@yahoo.com. *Br Mgr,* Betsy Theriot
Library Holdings: Bk Vols 6,000
Open Mon, Wed & Thurs 1-5:30, Tues 1-7, Sat 8:30-12:30
LABADIEVILLE BRANCH, 105 Cherry St, Labadieville, 70372. Tel: 985-526-7055. FAX: 985-526-0278. *Br Mgr,* Lenore Carter; Staff 2 (Non-MLS 2)
Library Holdings: AV Mats 91; Bk Vols 15,000; Per Subs 25
Open Mon & Wed-Fri 1-5:30, Tues 1-7
Friends of the Library Group
PIERRE PART BRANCH, 2800 Hwy 70 S, Pierre Part, 70390. Tel: 985-252-4220. FAX: 985-252-1476. *Br Mgr,* Alicia Aucoin; Staff 2 (Non-MLS 2)
Library Holdings: AV Mats 88; Bk Vols 10,000; Per Subs 20
Open Mon-Thurs 10-5:30, Sat 8:30-12:30
Friends of the Library Group

NATCHITOCHES

P NATCHITOCHES PARISH LIBRARY*, 450 Second St, 71457-4649. SAN 343-2998. Tel: 318-357-3280. FAX: 318-357-7073. E-mail: info@natlib.org. Web Site: www.natlib.org. *Libr Dir,* Jessica McGrath; Tel: 318-238-9225, E-mail: jessica@natlib.org; *Dir of Libr Operations,* Vallery B Washington; Tel: 318-238-9226, E-mail: vallery@natlib.org; *Ch,* Darlene Weems; Tel: 318-238-9222, E-mail: darlene@natlib.org; *Br Mgr, Main Libr,* Rosalind LaCour; Tel: 318-238-9241, E-mail: rosalind@natlib.org; *Br Mgr,* Fredricka Lacey; Tel: 318-476-3280, E-mail: fredricka@natlib.org; *Outreach Coordr,* Alan Niette; Tel: 318-238-9236, E-mail: alan@natlib.org; *IT Spec,* Marcus Richard; Tel: 318-238-9238, E-mail: marc@natlib.org; *Tech Serv Adminr,* Deborah Ransome; Tel: 318-238-9239, E-mail: deborah@natlib.org; Staff 31 (MLS 1, Non-MLS 30)
Founded 1939. Pop 39,162; Circ 142,602

Jan 2017-Dec 2017 Income (Main & Associated Libraries) $2,381,071, State $37,000, County $2,305,911, Locally Generated Income $38,160. Mats Exp $1,795,527, Books $88,000, Per/Ser (Incl. Access Fees) $11,000, AV Equip $70,000, AV Mat $43,000, Electronic Ref Mat (Incl. Access Fees) $60,000. Sal $1,324,830 (Prof $74,000)
Library Holdings: Audiobooks 14,494; e-books 39,407; Bk Vols 84,882; Per Subs 120; Videos 8,633
Special Collections: Louisiana History; Natchitoches Authors
Subject Interests: La, Local hist
Automation Activity & Vendor Info: (Cataloging) TLC (The Library Corporation); (Circulation) TLC (The Library Corporation); (ILL) TLC (The Library Corporation); (OPAC) TLC (The Library Corporation)
Wireless access
Function: 24/7 Electronic res, 24/7 Online cat, 3D Printer, Adult bk club, Adult literacy prog, Art programs, Audiobks on Playaways & MP3, Audiobks via web, Bks on CD, Chess club, Children's prog, Citizenship assistance, Computer training, Computers for patron use, Digital talking bks, Electronic databases & coll, Free DVD rentals, Holiday prog, Home delivery & serv to seniorr ctr & nursing homes, Homebound delivery serv, ILL available, Internet access, Laminating, Magazines, Magnifiers for reading, Mail & tel request accepted, Meeting rooms, Movies, Online cat, Outreach serv, OverDrive digital audio bks, Photocopying/Printing, Preschool outreach, Printer for laptops & handheld devices, Prog for adults, Prog for children & young adult, Ref & res, Ref serv available, Res assist avail, Scanner, Senior computer classes, Senior outreach, Spanish lang bks, STEM programs, Story hour, Summer reading prog, Tax forms, Teen prog, Telephone ref, Visual arts prog, Wheelchair accessible
Partic in Green Gold Libr Syst; Loan System Helping Automate Retrieval of Knowledge
Special Services for the Deaf - High interest/low vocabulary bks
Special Services for the Blind - Accessible computers; Bks on CD; Copier with enlargement capabilities; Home delivery serv; Internet workstation with adaptive software; Large print bks; Large screen computer & software; Magnifiers; Playaways (bks on MP3); Screen reader software
Open Mon-Fri 9-6, Sat 9-5
Friends of the Library Group
Branches: 1
NORTHEAST BRANCH, 3129 Hwy 71, Campti, 71411. Tel: 318-476-3280. FAX: 318-476-3284. *Br Mgr,* Fredricka Lacey; E-mail: fredricka@natlib.org; Staff 4 (Non-MLS 4)
Founded 2016. Circ 14,568
Function: 24/7 Electronic res, 24/7 Online cat, Art programs, Audiobks on Playaways & MP3, Audiobks via web, Bks on CD, Children's prog, Computer training, Computers for patron use, Electronic databases & coll, Free DVD rentals, Holiday prog, Homebound delivery serv, ILL available, Internet access, Magazines, Mail & tel request accepted, Movies, Online cat, Outreach serv, OverDrive digital audio bks, Photocopying/Printing, Preschool outreach, Prog for adults, Prog for children & young adult, Ref & res, Ref serv available, Res assist avail, Scanner, Senior computer classes, Story hour, Summer reading prog, Tax forms, Telephone ref
Open Mon-Thurs 10-6, Sat 10-2
Friends of the Library Group
Bookmobiles: 2

C NORTHWESTERN STATE UNIVERSITY LIBRARIES, Eugene P Watson Memorial Library, 913 University Pkwy, 71497. SAN 343-3234. Tel: 318-357-4477. Administration Tel: 318-357-4403. Toll Free Tel: 888-540-9657. FAX: 318-357-4470. Interlibrary Loan Service FAX: 318-357-5201. E-mail: reference@nsula.edu. Web Site: library.nsula.edu. *Dir of Libr,* Abbie Landry; E-mail: landry@nsula.edu; *Head, Access Serv,* Michael E Matthews; Tel: 318-357-4466, E-mail: maatthewsm@nsula.edu; *Head, Cat, Head, Coll Develop,* Debbie Huntington; Tel: 318-357-6947, E-mail: huntingtond@nsula.edu; *Head, Circ,* Yolanda Bobb; E-mail: ybobb@nsula.edu; *Head, Ser & Media,* Anna T MacDonald; Tel: 318-357-4407, E-mail: MacDonalda@nsula.edu; *Archivist,* Mary Linn Wernet; Tel: 318-357-4585, E-mail: wernet@nsula.edu; *ILL,* Jackie Hawkins; Tel: 318-357-5465, E-mail: jacquelinem@nsula.edu; *Ref & Libr Instruction,* Position Currently Open. Subject Specialists: *Govt doc,* Michael E Matthews; *State hist,* Mary Linn Wernet; Staff 20 (MLS 7, Non-MLS 13)
Founded 1884. Enrl 10,000; Fac 309; Highest Degree: Doctorate
Jul 2020-Jun 2021. Mats Exp $647,532, Books $88,041, Per/Ser (Incl. Access Fees) $454,536, Micro $35,508, Electronic Ref Mat (Incl. Access Fees) $60,265, Presv $9,182. Sal $889,984
Library Holdings: AV Mats 7,000; e-books 23,000; Bk Vols 312,324; Per Subs 1,271
Special Collections: Carl F Gauss (Dunnington Coll); Isthmian Canal, United States & Louisiana History (Owen Coll); Literature (Aswell Coll); Louisiana Folklore (Saucier Coll); Louisiana History & Folklore (Melrose Coll); Louisiana History (Egan, Safford, Harris & Cloutier Coll); Louisiana History, Indians & Botany (Dormon Coll); Mexican Revolution (Grass Coll); Poetry (Bancroft Coll). Oral History; State Document Depository; US Document Depository
Subject Interests: Bus, Educ, Nursing
Automation Activity & Vendor Info: (Acquisitions) SirsiDynix; (Cataloging) SirsiDynix; (Circulation) SirsiDynix; (ILL) OCLC; (OPAC) SirsiDynix; (Serials) SirsiDynix
Wireless access
Publications: Index & Abstracts of Colonial Documents in the Eugene P Watson Memorial Library; LibGuides; Library Handbook; User Guides
Partic in Louisiana Library Network
Open Mon-Thurs 7:30am-Midnight, Fri 7:30am-2am, Sun 2-Midnight
Friends of the Library Group

NEW IBERIA

P IBERIA PARISH LIBRARY*, 445 E Main St, 70560-3710. SAN 343-3269. Tel: 337-364-7024, 337-364-7074. Reference Tel: 337-364-7305. Administration Tel: 337-364-7150, 337-364-7188. FAX: 337-364-7042. Administration FAX: 337-364-7622. E-mail: newiberialib@yahoo.com. Web Site: iberialibrary.org. *Dir,* Kathleen Miles; E-mail: kmiles@iberialibrary.org; *Asst Dir,* Cheryl Braud; E-mail: cbraud@iberialibrary.org; *Ch,* Amy Bernard; E-mail: abernard@iberialibrary.org; *Circ Supvr,* Jacqui Giovinazzo; *Circ Supvr,* Charlene Judice; *Commun Relations Coordr,* Stephanie Lee; E-mail: slee@iberialibrary.org; *Cataloger,* Don Crook; E-mail: dcrook@iberialibrary.org; *ILL, Ref Serv,* Marjorie Hills; E-mail: mhills@iberialibrary.org; Staff 7 (MLS 5, Non-MLS 2)
Founded 1947. Pop 73,400; Circ 218,726
Library Holdings: Audiobooks 5,617; AV Mats 8,411; CDs 352; DVDs 2,839; e-books 4,902; Electronic Media & Resources 75; Large Print Bks 9,315; Bk Titles 174,470; Bk Vols 249,763; Per Subs 355; Talking Bks 3,161; Videos 6,499
Special Collections: Bunk Johnson Coll; I A & Carroll Martin Photo Coll. Oral History
Automation Activity & Vendor Info: (Cataloging) Innovative Interfaces, Inc; (Circulation) Innovative Interfaces, Inc; (ILL) Auto-Graphics, Inc; (OPAC) Innovative Interfaces, Inc
Wireless access
Partic in Loan System Helping Automate Retrieval of Knowledge
Open Mon-Thurs 8:30-8, Fri & Sat 8:30-5:30, Sun 1:30-5:30
Friends of the Library Group
Branches: 7
COTEAU BRANCH, 6308 Coteau Rd, 70560, SAN 375-5746. Tel: 337-364-7430. FAX: 337-364-7430. E-mail: cotlib@yahoo.com. *Br Mgr,* Jean Segura; Staff 1 (Non-MLS 1)
Founded 1992
Open Mon-Fri 1-6
Friends of the Library Group
DELCAMBRE BRANCH, 206 W Main St, Delcambre, 70528-2918. Tel: 337-685-2388. FAX: 337-685-2388. E-mail: delcambre@vermilion.lib.la.us. *Br Mgr,* Bonnie Richard; Staff 1 (Non-MLS 1)
Open Mon-Thurs 10-11:30 & 12:30-5:30, Fri 10-11:30 & 12:30-5, Sat 9-12
Friends of the Library Group
JEANERETTE BRANCH, 411 Kentucky St, Jeanerette, 70544, SAN 343-3358. Tel: 337-276-4014. FAX: 337-276-9595. E-mail: jeanerettebranch@yahoo.com. *Br Mgr,* John Braud; *Libr Asst,* Jenny Switzer; Staff 1 (Non-MLS 1)
Founded 1979
Open Mon-Fri 9-6, Sat 10-3
Friends of the Library Group
LOREAUVILLE BRANCH, 510 N Main St, Loreauville, 70552, SAN 343-3382. Tel: 337-229-6348. FAX: 337-229-6348. E-mail: loreauvillebranch@yahoo.com. *Br Mgr,* Cynthia Sherman; Staff 1 (Non-MLS 1)
Founded 1961
Open Mon-Fri 1-6, Wed 9-12 & 1-6
Friends of the Library Group
LYDIA BRANCH, 4800 Freyou Rd, 70560, SAN 343-3412. Tel: 337-364-7808. FAX: 337-364-7808. E-mail: lydia_branch@yahoo.com. *Br Co-Mgr,* JoAnn Clay; *Br Co-Mgr,* Lauren Salkowitz; Staff 2 (Non-MLS 2)
Open Mon-Fri 9-6, Sat 10-3
Friends of the Library Group
PARKVIEW BRANCH, 500 Grand Pre Blvd, 70563. Tel: 337-364-7480. FAX: 337-364-7714. E-mail: parkviewlib@yahoo.com. *Br Mgr,* Linda Thronson
Special Collections: Genealogy
Special Services for the Blind - Computer with voice synthesizer for visually impaired persons; Large print bks; Low vision equip; Magnifiers
Open Mon-Fri 9-6, Sat 10-3
ST PETER STREET BRANCH, 1111 W Saint Peter St, 70560. Tel: 337-364-7670. FAX: 337-364-7261. E-mail: stp_lib@yahoo.com. *Br Mgr,* Nancy Guidry; Staff 1 (Non-MLS 1)
Founded 2005
Open Mon-Fri 9-6, Sat 10-3
Friends of the Library Group

NEW ORLEANS

L ADAMS & REESE LLP*, Law Library, One Shell Sq, 701 Poydras St, Ste 4500, 70139. SAN 372-0888. Tel: 504-581-3234. FAX: 504-566-0210. Web Site: www.adamsandreese.com. *Dir, Libr Serv,* Catherine Filippi; E-mail: catherine.filippi@arlaw.com; Staff 1 (MLS 1)
Library Holdings: Bk Vols 15,500; Per Subs 200

S AMISTAD RESEARCH CENTER*, Tulane University, Tilton Hall, 6823 St Charles Ave, 70118. SAN 306-4840. Tel: 504-862-3222. Administration Tel: 504-862-3225. FAX: 504-862-8961. Administration FAX: 504-862-8741. Reference E-mail: reference@amistadresearchcenter.org. Web Site: www.amistadresearchcenter.org. *Exec Dir,* Dr Kara Tucina Olidge, PhD; E-mail: kolidge@tulane.edu; *Dir, Ref & Libr Serv,* Christopher Harter; Tel: 504-862-3229, E-mail: charter@tulane.edu; *Dir of Proc,* Laura Thomson; Tel: 504-314-2137, E-mail: thomsonl@tulane.edu; *Archivist,* Brenda Flora; Tel: 504-862-3221, E-mail: bflora@tulane.edu; *Ref Archivist,* Chianta Dorsey; Tel: 504-862-3228, E-mail: cdorsey3@tulane.edu; Staff 7 (MLS 5, Non-MLS 2)
Founded 1966
Library Holdings: Bk Titles 25,000; Per Subs 30
Special Collections: Aaron Douglas Coll; American Missionary Association Archives; Countee Cullen Papers; Harlem Renaissance Authors Coll
Subject Interests: African-Am, Appalachian Whites, Latino studies, Minorities
Wireless access
Function: Archival coll, Online cat
Publications: Amistad E-Newsletter (Online only)
Partic in OCLC Online Computer Library Center, Inc
Open Mon-Fri 8:30-4:30, Sat 9-1
Restriction: Closed stack, Non-circulating
Friends of the Library Group

M CHILDREN'S HOSPITAL*, Medical Library, 200 Henry Clay Ave, 70118. SAN 322-8533. Tel: 504-896-9264. FAX: 504-896-3932. Web Site: www.chnola.org/cme. *Dir, Med Libr,* Catherine Mooney; E-mail: catherine.mooney@lcmchealth.org; Staff 1 (MLS 1)
Library Holdings: Bk Titles 350; Bk Vols 2,000; Per Subs 50
Subject Interests: Abused children, Congenital, Developmental anatomy, Malformations, Pediatric emergency, Pediatric intensive care, Pediatric neonatal intensive care, Pediatric neurology, Pediatric neurosurgery, Pediatric oncology, Pediatric surgery, Pediatrics orthopedics
Partic in Health Sciences Library Association of Louisiana

J DELGADO COMMUNITY COLLEGE*, City Park Campus - Moss Memorial Library, Bldg 10, Rm 116, 615 City Park Ave, 70119. SAN 306-493X. Tel: 504-671-5317. Reference E-mail: cpcir@dcc.edu. Web Site: dcc.libguides.com/library. *Dean, Libr Serv,* Timothy Stamm; Tel: 504-671-5482, E-mail: tstamm@dcc.edu; *Acq, Coll Develop & mgt, Coordr, Librn,* Caitlin Cooper; Tel: 504-671-5327, E-mail: ccoope@dcc.edu; *Librn,* Gera J Bridgewater; E-mail: gbridg@dcc.edu; *ILL, Librn, Ref & Copyright,* Courtney Rimes Stortz; Tel: 504-671-5315, E-mail: crimes@dcc.edu; Staff 15 (MLS 6, Non-MLS 9)
Founded 1921. Enrl 16,670
Library Holdings: Bk Vols 123,000; Per Subs 981
Special Collections: State Document Depository
Subject Interests: La
Automation Activity & Vendor Info: (Cataloging) SirsiDynix; (Circulation) SirsiDynix; (Course Reserve) SirsiDynix; (ILL) OCLC; (OPAC) SirsiDynix
Wireless access
Partic in New Orleans Educational Telecommunications Consortium
Open Mon-Thurs 8-8, Fri 8-6, Sat 10-2

Departmental Libraries:

JM CHARITY SCHOOL OF NURSING LIBRARY, 450 S Claiborne Ave, Rm 301, 70112, SAN 306-4913. Tel: 504-571-1274. FAX: 504-568-5494. E-mail: CSNLibrary@dcc.edu. *Librn,* Alicia Schwarzenbach
Founded 1895. Enrl 600
Library Holdings: Bk Titles 5,105; Bk Vols 7,700; Per Subs 115
Subject Interests: Med, Nursing
Automation Activity & Vendor Info: (Cataloging) SirsiDynix; (Circulation) SirsiDynix; (OPAC) SirsiDynix
Partic in Louisiana Library Network
Open Mon-Fri 8-4:30

L DEUTSCH KERRIGAN*, Law Library, 755 Magazine St, 70130-3672. SAN 306-4948. Tel: 504-581-5141, Ext 438. FAX: 504-566-1201. E-mail: info@deutschkerrigan.com. Web Site: www.deutschkerrigan.com.
Founded 1926
Library Holdings: Bk Vols 30,000; Per Subs 25
Subject Interests: Great Britain
Restriction: Staff use only

C DILLARD UNIVERSITY*, Will W Alexander Library, 2601 Gentilly Blvd, 70122. SAN 306-4956. Tel: 504-816-4786. E-mail: dulibrary@dillard.edu. Web Site: www.dillard.edu/_academics/library. *Dir, Libr Serv,* Position Currently Open; *Coll Develop, Ref Librn,* Beverly Harris; E-mail: bharris@dillard.edu; *Info Literacy, Research Librn,* Germaine Palmer; E-mail: gpalmer@dillard.edu; *Archivist,* John Kennedy; E-mail: jkennedy@dillard.edu; *Access Serv,* Malik Bartholomew; E-mail: mbartholomew@dillard.edu. Subject Specialists: *Archives & Spec Coll,* John Kennedy; Staff 6 (MLS 4, Non-MLS 2)
Founded 1961. Enrl 1,300; Fac 140; Highest Degree: Bachelor
Library Holdings: e-books 88,000; Bk Vols 106,000; Per Subs 100
Special Collections: Howard Patton (African American Authors Coll); Literature & Architecture (McPherson Memorial Freedom Coll); Spitz (David), Beale (Howard Kennedy), Goldstein (Moise) & Richards (E V) Coll. State Document Depository
Subject Interests: African-Am studies, Humanities, Nursing, Soc sci & issues
Automation Activity & Vendor Info: (Acquisitions) Ex Libris Group; (Cataloging) Ex Libris Group; (Circulation) Ex Libris Group; (Discovery) EBSCO Discovery Service; (ILL) Ex Libris Group; (OPAC) Ex Libris Group; (Serials) Ex Libris Group
Wireless access
Publications: Acquisitions List (Quarterly); Bibliographies; Gifts & Exchange List
Partic in Louisiana Academic Library Information Network; Louisiana Library Network; LYRASIS; New Orleans Educational Telecommunications Consortium; OCLC Online Computer Library Center, Inc
Open Mon-Thurs 9-9, Fri 9-5, Sun 2-6

L GORDON, ARATA, MONTGOMERY, BARNETT, MCCOLLAM, DUPLANTIS & EAGAN, LLC*, Law Library, 201 Saint Charles Ave, Ste 4000, 70170. SAN 326-2596. Tel: 504-582-1111. FAX: 504-582-1121. Web Site: www.gamb.com. *Librn,* Eumont Jack; E-mail: jeumont@gamb.com
Library Holdings: Bk Vols 10,000; Per Subs 50
Wireless access
Restriction: Staff use only

S HERMANN-GRIMA HOUSE LIBRARY, 820 Saint Louis St, 70112. SAN 374-8324. Tel: 504-274-0746. Web Site: www.hgghh.org/imagemap_area/hermann-grima-library. *Exec Dir,* Tessa Jagger; *Chief Curator,* Katie Burlison; Tel: 504-274-0745, E-mail: katieb@hgghh.org
Library Holdings: Bk Vols 700; Per Subs 10
Special Collections: New Orleans Coll 1830-1860
Restriction: Private libr, Staff use only

S HISTORIC NEW ORLEANS COLLECTION*, William Research Center, 410 Chartres St, 70130-2102. SAN 306-4980. Tel: 504-523-4662, 504-598-7171. FAX: 504-598-7168. E-mail: wrc@hnoc.org. Web Site: www.hnoc.org/research. *Dir,* Alfred E Lemmon; Tel: 504-598-7124, E-mail: alfredl@hnoc.org; *Assoc Dir,* Jason Wiese; Tel: 504-598-7183, E-mail: jasonw@hnoc.org; *Curator, Rare Bks, Sr Librn,* Pamela D Arceneaux; Tel: 504-598-7118, E-mail: pamela@hnoc.org; *Oral Historian, Sr Curator,* Mark Cave; Tel: 504-598-7132, E-mail: markc@hnoc.org; *Cataloger,* Nina Bozak; Tel: 504-556-7131, E-mail: NinaB@hnoc.org; Staff 9 (MLS 4, Non-MLS 5)
Founded 1966
Library Holdings: Bk Vols 16,000; Per Subs 30
Special Collections: Battle of New Orleans Coll; Manuscript Coll; Maps; New Orleans broadsides, directories, imprints, sheet music, selected ephemera; Photographic Coll; Ursuline Nuns Library Coll; Vieux Carre Survey (information on property in the French Quarter of New Orleans)
Subject Interests: La
Automation Activity & Vendor Info: (OPAC) MINISIS Inc
Publications: Bibliography of New Orleans Imprints, 1764-1864; Bound to Please (Collection catalog); Charting Louisiana; Guide to Research at the Historic New Orleans Coll; Guide to the Vieux Carre Survey
Partic in LYRASIS; OCLC Online Computer Library Center, Inc
Open Tues-Sat 9:30-4:30
Friends of the Library Group

S JEAN LAFITTE NATIONAL HISTORICAL PARK & PRESERVE*, Chalmette Battlefield Library, 419 Decatur St, 70130. SAN 321-4486. Tel: 504-589-3882. FAX: 504-589-3851. Web Site: www.nps.gov/jela. *Curator,* Kathy Lang
Founded 1939
Library Holdings: DVDs 50; Bk Titles 350
Special Collections: Battle of New Orleans, bks, ms; Park archeology & research studies; War of 1812 History
Subject Interests: Cultural hist, La, State hist
Restriction: Open by appt only, Open to pub for ref only

GL LAW LIBRARY OF LOUISIANA, Louisiana Supreme Court, 2nd Flr, 400 Royal St, 70130-2104. SAN 306-5014. Tel: 504-310-2400. Reference Tel: 504-310-2515. Toll Free Tel: 800-820-3038 (LA only). FAX: 504-310-2419. E-mail: library@lasc.org. Web Site: lasc.libguides.com. *Dir, Law Libr,* Miriam Childs; Tel: 504-310-2403, E-mail: mchilds@lasc.org; *Asst Admin,* Gail Bragg; Tel: 504-310-2411, E-mail: gbragg@lasc.org; *Head, Coll Serv,* Tara Cunningham; Tel: 504-310-2402, E-mail: tcunningham@lasc.org; *Head, Pub Serv,* Sara Pic; Tel: 504-310-2412, E-mail: svpic@lasc.org; *Coll Serv Librn,* Angela Reaux; Tel: 504-310-2432, E-mail: areaux@lasc.org; *Librn,* Cynthia Jones; Tel: 504-310-2406, E-mail: cjones@lasc.org; *Researcher,* Francis Norton; Tel: 504-310-2405, E-mail: fnorton@lasc.org; *Libr Assoc,* Jenny Martin; Tel: 504-310-2401, E-mail: jmartin@lasc.org; Staff 6 (MLS 5, Non-MLS 1)
Founded 1838
Jul 2020-Jun 2021. Mats Exp $1,627,826, Books $524,121, Per/Ser (Incl. Access Fees) $11,796, Micro $887, Electronic Ref Mat (Incl. Access Fees) $221,858, Presv $8,034. Sal $496,152
Library Holdings: Bk Vols 105,858; Per Subs 50
Special Collections: 19th Century American and French Law, Louisiana Law. State Document Depository; US Document Depository
Automation Activity & Vendor Info: (Cataloging) EOS International; (Circulation) EOS International; (Discovery) EOS International; (ILL) OCLC WorldShare Interlibrary Loan; (OPAC) EOS International; (Serials) EOS International
Wireless access
Function: 24/7 Online cat, Electronic databases & coll, Magazines, Magnifiers for reading, Microfiche/film & reading machines, Online cat, Online ref, Photocopying/Printing, Ref serv available, Res libr, Telephone ref
Publications: De Novo (Newsletter)
Open Mon-Fri 9-5
Restriction: Circulates for staff only, Non-circulating of rare bks, Non-circulating to the pub, Restricted borrowing privileges

S LOUISIANA STATE MUSEUM, Louisiana Historical Center, 400 Esplanade Ave, 70116. SAN 306-5022. Tel: 504-568-3660. Toll Free Tel: 800-568-6968. Web Site: www.crt.state.la.us/louisiana-state-museum/collections/historical-center/library. *Curator,* Sarah-Elizabeth Gundlach; E-mail: sgundlach@crt.la.gov; Staff 1 (Non-MLS 1)
Founded 1930
Library Holdings: Bk Titles 28,000
Special Collections: Charity Hospital Coll, Hibernia Coll,scrapbooks, maps, newspapers, sheet music
Subject Interests: La hist, Local hist, Regional hist
Wireless access
Restriction: Non-circulating to the pub, Open by appt only

Branches:

NEW ORLEANS JAZZ CLUB COLLECTION, Old US Mint, 400 Esplanade Ave, 70176. (Mail add: PO Box 2448, 70165-2448). Tel: 504-568-6968. Toll Free Tel: 800-568-6968. FAX: 504-568-4995. Web Site: crt.state.la.us/louisiana-state-museum/collections, louisianastatemuseum.org/collections. *Dir of Coll,* Greg Lambousy; Staff 1 (Non-MLS 1)
Library Holdings: Bk Vols 28,500
Special Collections: New Orleans Jazz Club Coll. Oral History
Subject Interests: Jazz music
Function: Archival coll, For res purposes, Ref serv available
Restriction: Authorized scholars by appt, Closed stack, Not a lending libr, Pub ref by request

CM LOUISIANA STATE UNIVERSITY HEALTH SCIENCES CENTER*, John P Ische Library, 433 Bolivar St, Box B3-1, 70112-2223. SAN 343-3471. Tel: 504-568-6100. Interlibrary Loan Service Tel: 504-568-6101. Reference Tel: 504-568-6102, 504-568-8339. Administration Tel: 504-568-6105. FAX: 504-568-7718. Web Site: www.lsuhsc.edu/library/information/ische.aspx. *Dir of Libr,* J Dale Prince; E-mail: jprin2@lsuhsc.edu; *Head, Acq, Head, Coll Develop,* Marlene Bishop; Tel: 504-568-6109, E-mail: mbisho@lsuhsc.edu; *Head, ILL, Head, Info Tech,* Jennifer Lloyd; Tel: 504-568-5550, E-mail: jlloyd@lsuhsc.edu; *Ref Librn,* Wesley Lucas; Tel: 504-941-8160, E-mail: wlucas@lsuhsc.edu; *Br Coordr,* Julie Schiavo; Tel: 504-941-8162, E-mail: jschia@lsuhsc.edu; *Ref (Info Servs),* Carolyn Bridgewater; E-mail: cbridg@lsuhsc.edu; *Ref (Info Servs),* Kathryn E Kerdolff; E-mail: kkerdo@lsuhsc.edu; *Ser,* Rebecca Bealer; Tel: 504-568-6108, E-mail: rbeale@lsuhsc.edu. Subject Specialists: *Dental,* Wesley Lucas; *Dental,* Julie Schiavo; Staff 12 (MLS 11, Non-MLS 1)
Founded 1931
Library Holdings: Bk Titles 60,798; Bk Vols 254,721; Per Subs 7,375
Subject Interests: Allied health, Dentistry, Med, Nursing, Pub health
Automation Activity & Vendor Info: (Acquisitions) Innovative Interfaces, Inc; (Cataloging) Innovative Interfaces, Inc; (Circulation) Innovative Interfaces, Inc; (ILL) OCLC ILLiad; (OPAC) Innovative Interfaces, Inc; (Serials) Innovative Interfaces, Inc
Wireless access
Partic in Louisiana Library Network; SCAMeL
Restriction: Open to fac, students & qualified researchers

Departmental Libraries:

SCHOOL OF DENTISTRY LIBRARY, 1100 Florida Ave, 70119-2799, SAN 343-3501. Tel: 504-941-8158. FAX: 504-941-8161. *Head of Libr,* Elizabeth Strother; E-mail: estrot@lsuhsc.edu; *Ref (Info Servs),* Julie Schiavo; E-mail: jschia@lsuhsc.edu

C LOYOLA UNIVERSITY NEW ORLEANS*, J Edgar & Louise S Monroe Library, 6363 Saint Charles Ave, 70118. (Mail add: Campus Box 198, 6363 Saint Charles Ave, 70118), SAN 343-3536. Tel: 504-864-7111. Interlibrary Loan Service Tel: 504-864-7137. Administration Tel: 504-864-7051. Toll Free Tel: 877-614-0633. FAX: 504-864-7247. Reference E-mail: libref@loyno.edu. Web Site: library.loyno.edu. *Dean of Libr,* Deborah Poole; E-mail: poole@loyno.edu; *Assoc Dean, Tech Serv,* Laurie Phillips; *Coordr, Archives & Spec Coll,* Trish Nugent; *Digital Initiatives Librn,* Elizabeth Kelly; *Coordr, Acq,* Denise Ammons; *Circ Coordr,* Evonne Kelly Lawrence; *Coordr, Media Serv,* Susan Brower; *ILL Coordr,* Patricia Doran; *Online Serv Coordr,* Jim Hobbs; Staff 34 (MLS 14, Non-MLS 20)
Founded 1912. Enrl 5,600; Fac 300; Highest Degree: Master
Library Holdings: AV Mats 14,872; e-books 14,330; Bk Vols 342,833; Per Subs 1,339
Special Collections: History (Spanish Documents & French Documents), micro; Louisiana Coll; New Orleans Province of Society of Jesus, archives; University Archives. US Document Depository
Subject Interests: English lit, Philos
Automation Activity & Vendor Info: (Acquisitions) SirsiDynix; (Cataloging) SirsiDynix; (Circulation) SirsiDynix; (Course Reserve) SirsiDynix; (ILL) SirsiDynix; (Media Booking) SirsiDynix; (OPAC) SirsiDynix; (Serials) SirsiDynix
Wireless access
Partic in Louisiana Academic Library Information Network; Louisiana Library Network; LYRASIS; New Orleans Educational Telecommunications Consortium

Departmental Libraries:

CL LOYOLA LAW LIBRARY, School of Law, 7214 St Charles Ave, 70118, SAN 343-3625. Tel: 504-861-5539. Circulation Tel: 504-861-5545. Reference Tel: 504-861-5692. FAX: 504-861-5895. Web Site: law.loyno.edu/library. *Dir,* P Michael Whipple; E-mail: pmwhippl@loyno.edu; *Cat Librn,* Cathy Wagar; *Foreign & Intl Law Librn,* Nona Beisenherz; *Sr Ref Librn,* Brian Huddleston; *Ref Librn,* Francis X Norton; *Ref Librn,* Etheldra Scoggin; *Ser/Doc Librn,* Michele Pope. Subject Specialists: *Foreign law, Intl law,* Nona Beisenherz; Staff 7 (MLS 7)
Founded 1914. Enrl 745; Fac 59
Library Holdings: Bk Vols 195,000; Per Subs 3,574
Special Collections: GATT; US Supreme Court Records & Briefs. State Document Depository; US Document Depository
Automation Activity & Vendor Info: (Acquisitions) Innovative Interfaces, Inc; (Cataloging) Innovative Interfaces, Inc; (Circulation) Innovative Interfaces, Inc; (Course Reserve) Innovative Interfaces, Inc; (OPAC) Innovative Interfaces, Inc; (Serials) Innovative Interfaces, Inc
Partic in Louisiana Library Network; LYRASIS; OCLC Online Computer Library Center, Inc
Open Mon-Fri 7:30am-Midnight, Sat & Sun 9am-10pm

L MILLING, BENSON, WOODWARD LLP*, Law Library, 909 Poydras St, Ste 2300, 70112. SAN 326-100X. Tel: 504-569-7000. FAX: 504-569-7001. Web Site: www.millinglaw.com. *Managing Librn,* Vanessa Odems; E-mail: vodems@millinglaw.com
Library Holdings: Bk Vols 10,000; Videos 10
Subject Interests: Law
Restriction: Staff use only

CR NEW ORLEANS BAPTIST THEOLOGICAL SEMINARY*, John T Christian Library, 4110 Seminary Pl, 70126. SAN 343-365X. Tel: 504-282-4455. FAX: 504-816-8429. E-mail: library@nobts.edu. Web Site: www.nobts.edu/Library. *Dean of Libr,* Dr Jeff Griffin; Tel: 504-282-4455, Ext 3288, E-mail: jgriffin@nobts.edu; *Dir, Tech Serv,* Kyara St Amant; Tel: 504-282-4455, Ext 3227, E-mail: kstamant@nobts.edu; *Cat Librn,* Connie Pong; Tel: 504-282-4455, Ext 8454, E-mail: cpong@nobts.edu; *Coll Develop Librn, Media Librn, Music Librn,* Eric Benoy; Tel: 504-282-4455, Ext 3336, E-mail: ebenoy@nobts.edu; *Extn Serv Librn,* Helen Shin; Tel: 770-321-1606, Fax: 770-321-5363, E-mail: hshin@nobts.edu; *Circ Mgr,* Rebekah Phillips; E-mail: rphillips@nobts.edu; *Archivist,* Erin Marsh; E-mail: emarsh@nobts.edu; *Asst to the Dean of Libraries,* Michele McClellan; Tel: 504-816-8018, E-mail: circ1@nobts.edu. Subject Specialists: *Educ, Music, Theol,* Eric Benoy; *Archives,* Erin Marsh; Staff 11.5 (MLS 5.5, Non-MLS 6)
Founded 1917. Enrl 1,400; Fac 70; Highest Degree: Doctorate
Aug 2013-Jul 2014 Income (Main & Associated Libraries) $850,000. Mats Exp $318,500, Books $70,000, Per/Ser (Incl. Access Fees) $95,000, Manu Arch $500, Micro $1,000, AV Mat $2,000, Electronic Ref Mat (Incl. Access Fees) $140,000, Presv $10,000

Library Holdings: AV Mats 13,100; CDs 350; DVDs 196; e-books 127,000; Electronic Media & Resources 12; Microforms 18,824; Bk Titles 265,000; Bk Vols 344,000; Per Subs 800; Videos 2,000
Special Collections: C Penrose St Amant Coll; Institutional Archives; Pastor R G Lee Library; Rare Books, 15th-19th Century; Rare Pamphlets, 18th-19th Century; Southern Baptist Convention (SBC) Coll; V L Stanfield Papers
Automation Activity & Vendor Info: (Acquisitions) Horizon; (Cataloging) Horizon; (Circulation) Horizon; (ILL) OCLC WorldShare Interlibrary Loan; (OPAC) Horizon; (Serials) Horizon
Wireless access
Function: Archival coll, Audio & video playback equip for onsite use, Computers for patron use, Doc delivery serv, Electronic databases & coll, ILL available, Microfiche/film & reading machines, Music CDs, Online cat, Photocopying/Printing, Ref & res, VHS videos
Partic in Georgia Library Learning Online; Louisiana Academic Library Information Network; Louisiana Library Network; LYRASIS
Open Mon-Thurs 7:30am-10pm, Fri 7:30-7, Sat 10-3
Restriction: Borrowing privileges limited to fac & registered students, Borrowing requests are handled by ILL, In-house use for visitors, Non-circulating of rare bks

Departmental Libraries:

CR MARTIN MUSIC LIBRARY, 4110 Seminary Pl, 70126. Tel: 504-282-4455, Ext 3289. Administration Tel: 504-282-4455, Ext 3336. FAX: 504-816-8429. E-mail: musiclibrary@nobts.edu. Web Site: www.nobts.edu/library/martin/default.html. *Dir,* Eric Benoy; E-mail: ebenoy@nobts.edu; Staff 2 (MLS 1, Non-MLS 1)
Founded 1920. Enrl 1,400; Highest Degree: Doctorate
Library Holdings: AV Mats 6,800; CDs 3,535; DVDs 200; Electronic Media & Resources 3; Music Scores 17,400; Bk Vols 21,400; Per Subs 80; Videos 440
Special Collections: Martin & Keith Rare Hymnal Coll, 17th-20th Century
Automation Activity & Vendor Info: (Acquisitions) Horizon; (Cataloging) Horizon; (Circulation) Horizon; (ILL) OCLC WorldShare Interlibrary Loan; (OPAC) Horizon; (Serials) Horizon
Function: Archival coll, Distance learning, Doc delivery serv, Electronic databases & coll, Microfiche/film & reading machines, Music CDs, Online cat, Ref serv available, VHS videos
Open Mon-Thurs 7:30am-11pm, Fri 7:30-7:30, Sat 10-7
Restriction: Borrowing requests are handled by ILL, In-house use for visitors, Non-circulating of rare bks, Non-circulating to the pub, Open to students, fac & staff, Restricted borrowing privileges

S NEW ORLEANS-BIRMINGHAM PSYCHOANALYTIC CENTER LIBRARY, 3624 Coliseum St, 70115. SAN 371-2680. Tel: 504-899-5815. FAX: 504-899-5886. E-mail: nobpcenter@gmail.com, outreach@nobpc.org. Web Site: nobpc.org/resources/library.
Library Holdings: Bk Vols 1,600
Wireless access

S NEW ORLEANS MUSEUM OF ART*, Felix J Dreyfous Library, One Collins Diboll Circle City Park, 70124. (Mail add: PO Box 19123, 70179-0123), SAN 306-5057. Tel: 504-658-4117. FAX: 504-658-4199. Web Site: www.noma.org.
Founded 1972
Library Holdings: Bk Vols 20,000; Per Subs 70; Spec Interest Per Sub 70
Special Collections: WPA Index to New Orleans Artists, 1805-1940
Subject Interests: Art (19th Century), Art (20th Century), Glass technology, La, Oriental art, Paintings, Photog, Pottery, Pre-Columbian art, Prints
Wireless access
Function: Ref & res
Publications: Arts Quarterly; Handbook of the Collection
Restriction: Open to pub by appt only

P NEW ORLEANS PUBLIC LIBRARY*, 219 Loyola Ave, 70112-2044. SAN 343-3714. Tel: 504-529-7323, 504-596-2570. Circulation Tel: 504-596-2560. FAX: 504-596-2609. Web Site: www.nolalibrary.org. *Exec Dir & State Librn,* Gabriel Morley; E-mail: gmorley@nolalibrary.org; *Human Res Dir,* Rose Matthews; *IT Dir,* Jerry Pinkston; E-mail: JPinkston@nolalibrary.org; *Bus Mgr,* Michel Thompson; E-mail: busoffice@nolalibrary.org
Founded 1896. Pop 496,938; Circ 1,168,633
Library Holdings: Bk Vols 794,830; Per Subs 999
Special Collections: City Archives, microflm & mss; Foundation Center Coop Coll; Louisiana Division, bks, micro, audio & video tapes, news reels, slides, maps, pictures. US Document Depository
Automation Activity & Vendor Info: (Acquisitions) SirsiDynix; (Circulation) SirsiDynix
Wireless access
Partic in Loan System Helping Automate Retrieval of Knowledge; OCLC Online Computer Library Center, Inc
Open Mon-Thurs 10-8, Fri & Sat 10-5, Sun 1-5
Friends of the Library Group

Branches: 14
ALGIERS REGIONAL LIBRARY, 3014 Holiday Dr, 70131, SAN 343-3773. Tel: 504-596-2641. FAX: 504-596-2661. *Libr Mgr,* Mary Ann Marx
Founded 1966
Library Holdings: Bk Vols 55,958
Open Mon-Thurs 10-8, Fri & Sat 10-5, Sun 1-5
ALVAR LIBRARY, 913 Alvar St, 70117-5409, SAN 343-3803. Tel: 504-596-2667. FAX: 504-596-2667. *Libr Mgr,* Adrienne Johnson
Library Holdings: Bk Vols 17,957
Open Mon-Thurs 10-8, Fri & Sat 10-5
CENTRAL CITY LIBRARY, 2405 Jackson Ave, Bldg C, Rm 235, 70113. Tel: 504-596-3110. *Libr Mgr,* Maria Landrum
Open Mon-Thurs 10-7, Fri 11-4
CHILDREN'S RESOURCE CENTER LIBRARY, 913 Napoleon Ave, 70115-2862, SAN 343-3951. Tel: 504-596-2628. FAX: 504-596-2669. *Libr Mgr,* Linda Gielec
Library Holdings: Bk Vols 19,443
Open Mon-Thurs 10-8, Fri & Sat 10-5
EAST NEW ORLEANS REGIONAL LIBRARY, 5641 Read Blvd, 70127-3105, SAN 343-3862. Tel: 504-596-0200. *Libr Mgr,* Christopher Nulph
Library Holdings: Bk Vols 57,057
Open Mon-Thurs 10-8, Fri & Sat 10-5, Sun 1-5
CITA DENNIS HUBBELL LIBRARY, 725 Pelican Ave, 70114, SAN 343-3749. Tel: 504-596-3113. FAX: 504-596-2666. *Libr Mgr,* Seale Paterson
Library Holdings: Bk Vols 23,468
Open Mon-Thurs 10-8, Fri & Sat 10-5
ROSA F KELLER LIBRARY & COMMUNITY CENTER, 4300 S Broad Ave, 70125, SAN 374-6836. Tel: 504-596-2660. FAX: 504-596-2678. *Libr Mgr,* Sharon Kohl
Library Holdings: Bk Vols 37,200
Open Mon-Thurs 10-8, Fri & Sat 10-5
DR MARTIN LUTHER KING JR LIBRARY, 1611 Caffin Ave, 70117, SAN 376-9410. Tel: 504-596-2695. *Libr Mgr,* Mary Abler
Library Holdings: Bk Vols 20,000
Open Mon-Thurs 10-8, Fri & Sat 10-5
MILTON H LATTER MEMORIAL LIBRARY, 5120 St Charles Ave, 70115-4941, SAN 343-3927. Tel: 504-596-2625. FAX: 504-596-2665. *Libr Mgr,* Missy Abbott; Staff 12 (MLS 2, Non-MLS 10)
Founded 1948
Library Holdings: Bk Vols 60,000; Per Subs 20
Open Mon-Thurs 10-8, Fri & Sat 10-5, Sun 1-5
Friends of the Library Group
NORMAN MAYER LIBRARY, 3001 Gentilly Blvd, 70122, SAN 343-3897. Tel: 504-596-3100. *Libr Mgr,* Kristen Corby
Library Holdings: Bk Vols 34,653
Open Mon-Thurs 10-8, Fri & Sat 10-5, Sun 1-5
MID-CITY LIBRARY, 4140 Canal St, 70119. Tel: 504-596-2654. *Interim Libr Mgr,* Robin Goldblum
Open Mon-Thurs 10-8, Fri & Sat 10-5
NORA NAVRA LIBRARY, 1902 St Bernard Ave, 70116-1317, SAN 343-3986. Tel: 504-596-3118. *Libr Mgr,* Charles Young
Library Holdings: Bk Vols 16,842
Open Mon-Thurs 10-8, Fri & Sat 10-5
NIX LIBRARY, 1401 S Carrollton Ave, 70118-2809, SAN 343-401X. Tel: 504-596-2630. FAX: 504-596-2672. *Libr Mgr,* Damian Lambert
Library Holdings: Bk Vols 22,978
Open Mon-Thurs 10-8, Fri & Sat 10-5
ROBERT E SMITH LIBRARY, 6301 Canal Blvd, 70124-3117, SAN 343-4044. Tel: 504-596-2638. *Libr Mgr,* Sara Olivia Melton
Library Holdings: Bk Vols 51,951
Open Mon-Thurs 10-8, Fri & Sat 10-5, Sun 1-5

R NOTRE DAME SEMINARY GRADUATE SCHOOL OF THEOLOGY*, Reverend Robert J Stahl S.M. Memorial Library, 2901 S Carrollton Ave, 70118-4391. SAN 306-5065. Tel: 504-866-7426, Ext 700. FAX: 504-866-6260. E-mail: Library@nds.edu. Web Site: nds.edu/notre-dame-seminary-library. *Libr Dir,* Thomas B Bender, IV; E-mail: tbender@nds.edu; Staff 1 (MLS 1)
Founded 1923. Enrl 173; Fac 32; Highest Degree: Master
Library Holdings: AV Mats 847; e-books 22,991; Electronic Media & Resources 8; Music Scores 45; Bk Vols 88,155; Per Subs 168
Subject Interests: Philos, Theol
Automation Activity & Vendor Info: (Acquisitions) Follett Software; (Cataloging) Follett Software; (Circulation) Follett Software; (ILL) OCLC FirstSearch; (OPAC) Follett Software; (Serials) EBSCO Online
Wireless access
Function: 24/7 Electronic res, 24/7 Online cat, Electronic databases & coll
Partic in Louisiana Academic Library Information Network; Louisiana Library Network
Special Services for the Blind - Aids for in-house use; Bks & mags in Braille, on rec, tape & cassette; Braille bks; Cassette playback machines; Digital talking bk machines

Restriction: 24-hr pass syst for students only, Access at librarian's discretion, Authorized personnel only, Authorized scholars by appt, In-house use for visitors, Non-circulating of rare bks, Non-circulating to the pub, Open to fac, students & qualified researchers, Open to pub by appt only, Open to pub for ref only, Open to pub upon request, Open to pub with supv only, Open to qualified scholars, Open to researchers by request, Open to students, fac, staff & alumni, Researchers by appt only, Use of others with permission of librn, Visitors must make appt to use bks in the libr

M OCHSNER MEDICAL LIBRARY, 1514 Jefferson Hwy, 1st Flr, 70121-2429. SAN 306-5073. Tel: 504-842-3760. FAX: 504-842-5339. E-mail: medicallibrary@ochsner.org. Web Site: education.ochsner.org/medical-library. *Mgr,* Kelly Fogarty; *Med Librn,* Thomas Bell; *Med Librn,* Ben Bryant; *Archivist,* Courtney Masters; *Libr Asst,* Kathy Hawkins; *Libr Asst,* Teresha Ussin; Staff 6 (MLS 3, Non-MLS 3)
Founded 1944
Special Collections: Ochsner Historical Archives. Oral History
Automation Activity & Vendor Info: (Circulation) OPALS (Open-source Automated Library System); (ILL) OCLC ILLiad; (OPAC) OPALS (Open-source Automated Library System); (Serials) OCLC
Wireless access
Function: 24/7 Electronic res, 24/7 Online cat, Computers for patron use, Doc delivery serv, Electronic databases & coll, Health sci info serv, ILL available, Internet access, Learning ctr, Online cat, Photocopying/Printing, Res libr, Wheelchair accessible
Partic in Docline; OCLC Online Computer Library Center, Inc
Open Mon-Fri 7:30-5
Restriction: Access at librarian's discretion, Badge access after hrs, Circulates for staff only, Lending to staff only, Open to pub for ref & circ; with some limitations

L PHELPS DUNBAR LLP*, Law Library, 365 Canal St, Ste 2000, 70130-6534. SAN 372-087X. Tel: 504-566-1311, Ext 1788. FAX: 504-568-9130. *Law Librn,* Jennifer Dabbs; E-mail: dabbsj@phelps.com
Library Holdings: Bk Vols 50,000; Per Subs 75
Automation Activity & Vendor Info: (Cataloging) EOS International; (Serials) EOS International
Restriction: Staff use only

L SIMON, PERAGINE, SMITH & REDFEARN LLP*, Law Library, Energy Ctr, 1100 Poydras St, 30th Flr, 70163. SAN 372-090X. Tel: 504-569-2030. FAX: 504-569-2999. Web Site: www.spsr-law.com. *Library Contact,* Steven Jacobson; E-mail: sjacobson@spsr-law.com; Staff 1 (MLS 1)
Founded 1979
Library Holdings: e-books 2; e-journals 2; Bk Vols 300; Per Subs 15
Wireless access
Open Mon-Fri 9-5:30

C SOUTHERN UNIVERSITY IN NEW ORLEANS, Leonard S Washington Memorial Library, 6400 Press Dr, 70126. SAN 306-5111. Tel: 504-286-5225. FAX: 504-284-5490. Web Site: www.suno.edu. *Dir,* Shatiqua Wilson; E-mail: swilson@suno.edu; *Ref Librn,* Tariana Smith; E-mail: tdsmith@suno.edu; *Coordr, Pub Serv,* Erika Witt; E-mail: ewitt@suno.edu; *Coordr, Tech Serv,* Laurie Gaillard; E-mail: lgaillar@suno.edu; *Libr Spec III,* Karla Ayala; E-mail: kayala@suno.edu; *Libr Spec II,* Christopher Lewis; E-mail: clewis@suno.edu
Founded 1959. Enrl 2,146; Fac 102; Highest Degree: Master
Library Holdings: Bk Vols 231,601; Per Subs 512
Special Collections: Afro-French. State Document Depository; US Document Depository
Subject Interests: Educ, Ethnic studies, Soc sci & issues
Automation Activity & Vendor Info: (Acquisitions) SirsiDynix; (Cataloging) SirsiDynix; (Circulation) SirsiDynix; (OPAC) SirsiDynix; (Serials) SirsiDynix
Wireless access
Partic in Louisiana Library Network; New Orleans Educational Telecommunications Consortium
Open Mon-Wed 7:30am-9pm, Thurs & Fri 7:30-5, Sat 10-3

C TULANE UNIVERSITY*, Howard-Tilton Memorial Library, 7001 Freret St, 70118-5682. SAN 343-4133. Tel: 504-865-5131. Interlibrary Loan Service Tel: 504-865-5610. FAX: 504-865-6773. Web Site: library.tulane.edu/about/howard-tilton. *Dean,* David Banush; E-mail: dbanush@tulane.edu; *Assoc Dean,* Andy Corrigan; Tel: 504-865-5679, E-mail: andyc@tulane.edu; *Head, Media Serv,* Lisa Hooper; Tel: 504-314-7822, E-mail: lhooper1@tulane.edu; Staff 33 (MLS 33)
Founded 1834. Enrl 11,487; Fac 927; Highest Degree: Doctorate
Library Holdings: Bk Vols 2,330,750; Per Subs 14,141
Special Collections: Architecture Library; Latin American Library; Louisiana History Coll; Rare Books; Southeastern Architectural Archive; University Archives; William Ranson Hogan Jazz Archive. US Document Depository
Automation Activity & Vendor Info: (Acquisitions) Ex Libris Group; (Cataloging) Ex Libris Group; (Circulation) Ex Libris Group; (Course Reserve) Ex Libris Group; (ILL) OCLC; (OPAC) Ex Libris Group; (Serials) Ex Libris Group
Wireless access
Publications: The Jazz Archivist, Annual Report
Partic in Association of Research Libraries; Louisiana Library Network; LYRASIS; New Orleans Educational Telecommunications Consortium; Proquest Dialog
Open Mon-Thurs 7:30am-1:45am, Fri 7:30am-9:45pm, Sat 9am-9:45pm, Sun 9am-1:45am
Friends of the Library Group

Departmental Libraries:

ARCHITECTURE LIBRARY, Richardson Memorial Bldg, Rm 202, 6823 St Charles Ave, 70118, SAN 343-4168. Tel: 504-865-5391. FAX: 504-862-8966. E-mail: circ@tulane.edu. Web Site: library.tulane.edu/libraries/architecture. *Head Librn,* Sean Knowlton; E-mail: sean@tulane.edu
Library Holdings: Bk Vols 30,000; Per Subs 330

A H CLIFFORD MATHEMATICS RESEARCH LIBRARY, 430 Gibson Hall, 6823 St Charles Ave, 70118, SAN 343-4257. Tel: 504-862-3455. FAX: 504-865-5063. Web Site: sse.tulane.edu/math. *Librn,* Bea Calvert; E-mail: bcalvert@tulane.edu
Library Holdings: e-journals 245; Bk Vols 35,000; Per Subs 350
Special Collections: Alexander Doniphan Wallace Coll; Edward Daire Conway Coll; Frank Douglas Quigley Coll
Subject Interests: Math
Open Mon-Fri 8-5

CL LAW LIBRARY, Weinmann Hall, 3rd Flr, 6329 Freret St, 70118-6231, SAN 343-4222. Tel: 504-865-5952. Interlibrary Loan Service Tel: 504-862-8896. Reference Tel: 504-865-8872. Administration Tel: 504-865-5950. FAX: 504-865-5917. E-mail: lawlib@tulane.edu. Web Site: library.law.tulane.edu/screens/index.html. *Dir, Law Libr & Assoc Prof of Law,* James E Duggan; E-mail: duggan@tulane.edu; *Sr Ref Librn,* Kimberly Koko Glorioso; Tel: 504-865-5902, E-mail: kglorioso@tulane.edu; *Acq Librn,* Aubrey Rector; Tel: 504-862-8866, E-mail: arector@tulane.edu; *Cat Librn,* Cynthia Barrilleaux; Tel: 504-862-8867, E-mail: cbarril@tulane.edu; *Foreign, Comparative & Intl Law/Ref Librn,* Roy Sturgeon; Tel: 504-865-5953, E-mail: rsturgeo@tulane.edu; *Govt Doc/Micro Ref Librn,* Carla Pritchett; Tel: 504-865-5994, E-mail: cpritch@tulane.edu; *Instruction Coordr, Ref Librn,* Megan Garton; Tel: 504-865-5941, E-mail: mgarton@tulane.edu; Staff 16 (MLS 8, Non-MLS 8)
Founded 1847. Enrl 714; Fac 41; Highest Degree: Doctorate
Special Collections: French Civil Law Coll; Maritime Law Coll; Roman Law Coll
Automation Activity & Vendor Info: (Acquisitions) Innovative Interfaces, Inc; (Cataloging) Innovative Interfaces, Inc; (Circulation) Innovative Interfaces, Inc; (Course Reserve) Innovative Interfaces, Inc; (OPAC) Innovative Interfaces, Inc; (Serials) Innovative Interfaces, Inc
Partic in OCLC Online Computer Library Center, Inc

CM RUDOLPH MATAS LIBRARY OF THE HEALTH SCIENCES, Tulane Health Sciences Campus, 1430 Tulane Ave, SL-86, 70112-2699, SAN 343-4281. Tel: 504-988-5155. Circulation Tel: 504-988-2403. Interlibrary Loan Service Tel: 504-988-5156. FAX: 504-988-7417. Reference E-mail: medref@tulane.edu. Web Site: matas.tulane.edu. *Dir,* Neville Prendergast; Tel: 504-988-2060, E-mail: nprender@tulane.edu; *Educ & Outreach Librn,* Elaine Hicks; Tel: 504-988-2785, E-mail: ehicks2@tulane.edu; *Cataloger, Hist Librn,* Mary Holt; Tel: 504-988-2062, E-mail: maryholt@tulane.edu; *Ref & Educ Librn,* Molly Knapp; *Research Librn,* Laura Wright; Tel: 504-988-2063, E-mail: lwright7@tulane.edu; *Coordr, Res Serv,* Keith Pickett; Tel: 504-988-2406, E-mail: kpicket1@tulane.edu; *ILL Tech,* Brittani Williams; Tel: 504-988-2413, E-mail: bwilli18@tulane.edu. Subject Specialists: *Pub health,* Elaine Hicks; Staff 14 (MLS 7, Non-MLS 7)
Founded 1844. Enrl 13,486; Highest Degree: Doctorate
Library Holdings: e-books 25,000; e-journals 8,174; Bk Titles 54,601; Bk Vols 157,758
Special Collections: Louisiana Medicine & Medical Biography
Subject Interests: Med, Pub health
Automation Activity & Vendor Info: (Cataloging) OCLC Connexion; (ILL) OCLC ILLiad; (OPAC) Ex Libris Group
Function: Health sci info serv, ILL available, Outreach serv
Partic in Coop Libr Agency for Syst & Servs; SCAMEL/NLM
Publications: Library News @ TUHSC (Online only)
Open Mon-Fri 8-6
Restriction: Badge access after hrs, Open to students, fac & staff

MUSIC & MEDIA LIBRARY, 7001 Freret St, 6th Flr, 70118-5682. Tel: 504-865-5642. FAX: 504-865-6773. E-mail: mediaservices@tulane.edu. Web Site: library.tulane.edu/libraries/media-services. *Libr Assoc,* CC Chapman; E-mail: kchapma1@tulane.edu
Library Holdings: Bk Vols 21,744; Per Subs 90
Open Mon-Thurs (Winter) 8:30am-10pm, Fri 8-5, Sat 10-5, Sun 2-10; Mon-Thurs (Summer) 8:30-5, Fri 8:30-4:45, Sat 10-1

TURCHIN LIBRARY, Goldring/Woldenberg Hall I, 3rd Flr, Seven McAlister Pl, 70118, SAN 343-4370. Tel: 504-865-5376. FAX: 504-862-8953. E-mail: turchin@tulane.edu. Web Site: turchin.tulane.edu. *Head Librn,* Betsy Clementson; E-mail: betsy@tulane.edu
Library Holdings: Bk Vols 30,000; Per Subs 200
Subject Interests: Acctg, Finance, Organizational behavior
Open Mon-Thurs 8:30am-11pm, Fri 8:30-6, Sat Noon-6, Sun Noon-11

A UNITED STATES ARMY*, Corps of Engineers New Orleans District Technical Library, 7400 Leake Ave, Rm 108, 70118. SAN 343-4400. Tel: 504-862-2559. FAX: 504-862-1721. Web Site: www.mvn.usace.army.mil/library. *Librn,* Sandra Brown; E-mail: sandra.a.brown@usace.army.mil; Staff 1 (MLS 1)
Founded 1974
Library Holdings: Bk Titles 14,000; Per Subs 500
Special Collections: Environmental Impact Statements; Government Reports; Standards & Specifications
Subject Interests: Archaeology, Biology, Civil engr, Environ studies, Flood control, Navigation, Water res
Partic in OCLC Online Computer Library Center, Inc; Proquest Dialog
Open Mon-Fri 7:30-3:30
Restriction: Off-site coll in storage - retrieval as requested

GL UNITED STATES COURT OF APPEALS, Fifth Circuit Library, 600 Camp St, Rm 106, 70130. SAN 306-5154. Tel: 504-310-7797. FAX: 504-310-7578. E-mail: library_mailbox@ca5.uscourts.gov. Web Site: www.lb5.uscourts.gov. *Law Librn,* Sue Creech
Special Collections: Government Documents Coll

G UNITED STATES DEPARTMENT OF AGRICULTURE*, Southern Regional Research Center, 1100 Robert E Lee Blvd, Bldg 001 SRRC, 70124-4305. (Mail add: PO Box 19687, 70179-0687), SAN 306-5162. Tel: 504-286-4288. FAX: 504-286-4396. Web Site: www.ars.usda.gov/southeast-area/new-orleans-la/southern-regional-research-center. *Actg Dir,* K Thomas Klasson; E-mail: thomas.klasson@usda.gov
Founded 1941
Library Holdings: Bk Vols 25,000; Per Subs 500
Subject Interests: Bacteriology, Chem, Entomology, Food sci, Microbiology, Textiles
Automation Activity & Vendor Info: (Cataloging) SirsiDynix; (OPAC) SirsiDynix
Publications: Post Harvest News from the Library
Partic in OCLC Online Computer Library Center, Inc
Open Mon-Fri 8-4:30

G US DEPARTMENT OF THE INTERIOR*, Bureau of Ocean Energy Management, Gulf Coast Region, 1201 Elmwood Park Blvd, Rm 636A, 70123-2394. SAN 306-4905. Tel: 504-736-2521. FAX: 504-736-2525. *Libr Dir,* Stephen V Pomes; E-mail: stephen.pomes@boem.gov; Staff 1 (MLS 1)
Library Holdings: CDs 300; e-books 5,000; e-journals 1,000; Per Subs 30; Videos 20
Subject Interests: Environ law, Geol, Geophysics, Marine biol, Oceanography, Paleontology, Petroleum engr
Automation Activity & Vendor Info: (Cataloging) Follett Software; (Circulation) Follett Software; (ILL) OCLC; (OPAC) Follett Software
Partic in Federal Library & Information Network; OCLC Online Computer Library Center, Inc; OCLC-LVIS; Soline
Restriction: Employees only

C UNIVERSITY OF HOLY CROSS, Blaine S Kern Library, 4123 Woodland Dr, 70131. SAN 306-5081. Tel: 504-394-7744, 504-398-2145. Toll Free Tel: 800-259-7744. FAX: 504-391-2421. Web Site: uhcno.edu/library. *Libr Dir,* Diana Schaubhut; Tel: 504-398-2103, E-mail: dschaubhut@uhcno.edu; *Govt Doc Librn, Ref Serv Librn,* Jennifer Creevy; Tel: 504-398-2102, E-mail: jcreevy@uhcno.edu; *ILL, Ref Librn, Ser,* Samuel Readman; Tel: 504-398-2101, E-mail: sreadman@uhcno.edu; *Acq, Cat,* Katharine Rubin; Tel: 504-398-2119, E-mail: krubin@uhcno.edu; Staff 6.5 (MLS 4, Non-MLS 2.5)
Founded 1916. Highest Degree: Doctorate
Special Collections: US Document Depository
Automation Activity & Vendor Info: (OPAC) SirsiDynix-Enterprise
Wireless access
Partic in Call; Louisiana Library Network; LYRASIS; New Orleans Educational Telecommunications Consortium
Open Mon-Thurs 8-8, Fri 8-3
Friends of the Library Group

C UNIVERSITY OF NEW ORLEANS*, Earl K Long Library, 2000 Lakeshore Dr, 70148. SAN 306-5200. Tel: 504-280-6556. Circulation Tel: 504-280-6355. Interlibrary Loan Service Tel: 504-280-7276. Reference Tel: 504-280-6355. Administration FAX: 504-280-7277. E-mail: libref@uno.edu. Web Site: libguides.uno.edu. *Dean of Libr, Info Serv,* Ray Wang; E-mail: rwang9@uno.edu; *Assoc Dean of Libr, Info Serv,* Lora Amsberryaugier; Tel: 504-280-5563, E-mail: lamsberr@uno.edu; *Dept Chair, Resource Management, Scholarly Communications Officer,* Jeanne Pavy; Tel: 504-280-6547, E-mail: jpavy@uno.edu; *Div Head, Library Services,* Brandon Adler; Tel: 504-280-4397, E-mail: bwadler@uno.edu; Staff 19 (MLS 6, Non-MLS 13)
Founded 1958. Fac 232; Highest Degree: Doctorate
Library Holdings: Bk Vols 1,300,000; Per Subs 80,000
Special Collections: Egyptology (Judge Pierre Crabites Coll); European Community; Louisiana History; Nuclear Regulatory Commission; Orleans Parish School Board; Supreme Court of Louisiana Archives; William Faulkner (Frank A Von der Haar Coll). State Document Depository; US Document Depository
Subject Interests: Econ, Educ, Law, Natural sci, Soc sci & issues
Automation Activity & Vendor Info: (Acquisitions) SirsiDynix; (Cataloging) SirsiDynix; (Circulation) SirsiDynix; (Course Reserve) SirsiDynix; (OPAC) SirsiDynix; (Serials) SirsiDynix
Wireless access
Partic in Louisiana Library Network; LYRASIS; New Orleans Educational Telecommunications Consortium; OCLC Online Computer Library Center, Inc
Friends of the Library Group

C XAVIER UNIVERSITY OF LOUISIANA*, Library Resource Center, One Drexel Dr, 70125-1098. SAN 343-446X. Tel: 504-520-7305. Circulation Tel: 504-520-7311. FAX: 504-520-7940. E-mail: library@xula.edu. Reference E-mail: refinfo@xula.edu. Web Site: www.xula.edu/library/index.php. *Interim Libr Dir,* Tamera Hanken; E-mail: thanken@xula.edu; *Head, Circ Serv, Librn,* Teri Mojgani; E-mail: cmojgani@xula.edu; *Assoc Univ Archivist,* Irwin Lachoff; E-mail: ilachoff@xula.edu. Subject Specialists: *Southern Jewish hist,* Irwin Lachoff; Staff 11 (MLS 8, Non-MLS 3)
Founded 1925. Enrl 3,012; Fac 165; Highest Degree: Doctorate
Library Holdings: CDs 6,457; e-books 38,000; e-journals 19,156; Music Scores 500; Bk Vols 254,998; Videos 2,527
Special Collections: Black Studies (Negro History & Culture Coll); Southern & Black Catholica; Southern Writers. Oral History; State Document Depository; US Document Depository
Subject Interests: African-Am, Creative writing
Automation Activity & Vendor Info: (Acquisitions) SirsiDynix; (Cataloging) SirsiDynix; (Circulation) SirsiDynix; (Discovery) EBSCO Discovery Service; (OPAC) SirsiDynix; (Serials) SirsiDynix
Wireless access
Publications: Information Literacy: Survival Skills for the Information Age; Xavier Review (with Department of English); Xavier Review Occassional Publications Series (with Department of English)
Partic in Louisiana Library Network; LYRASIS; New Orleans Educational Telecommunications Consortium
Open Mon-Thurs 7:30am-2:00am, Fri 7:30am-8pm, Sat 12-6, Sun 12:30-Midnight

NEW ROADS

P POINTE COUPEE PARISH LIBRARY*, New Roads (Main Branch), 201 Claiborne St, 70760. SAN 343-4524. Tel: 225-638-9847. Administration Tel: 225-638-9841. FAX: 225-638-9847. E-mail: interlibloan@yahoo.com. Web Site: www.pointe-coupee.lib.la.us. *Dir,* Melissa Hymel; Staff 5 (Non-MLS 5)
Pop 22,002; Circ 149,478
Library Holdings: AV Mats 1,152; Bk Vols 80,000; Per Subs 216
Special Collections: Louisiana Studies
Subject Interests: Art & archit, Geol, Humanities
Wireless access
Partic in Loan System Helping Automate Retrieval of Knowledge
Open Mon-Thurs 8:30-7:30, Fri & Sat 8:30-5, Sun 1-5
Friends of the Library Group
Branches: 4
INNIS BRANCH, 6444 Louisiana Hwy 1, Innis, 70747, SAN 343-4559. Tel: 225-492-2632. FAX: 225-492-2632. *Br Mgr,* Ms Bennie Rice; Staff 2 (Non-MLS 2)
Library Holdings: AV Mats 150; Bk Vols 6,000; Per Subs 37
Open Mon-Fri 10-6
Friends of the Library Group
LIVONIA BRANCH, 3100 Hwy 78, Livonia, 70755, SAN 343-4583. Tel: 225-637-2987. FAX: 225-637-2987. *Br Mgr,* Ms Roye Chenevert; Staff 2 (Non-MLS 2)
Library Holdings: Bk Vols 6,000; Per Subs 27
Open Mon-Fri 1-6
Friends of the Library Group
MORGANZA BRANCH, 221 S Louisiana Hwy 1, Morganza, 70759, SAN 343-4613. Tel: 225-694-2428. FAX: 225-694-2428. *Br Mgr,* Dana Bergeron; Staff 2 (Non-MLS 2)
Library Holdings: Bk Vols 6,000; Per Subs 18
Open Mon-Fri 1-6
Friends of the Library Group

JULIAN POYDRAS BRANCH, 4985 Poydras Lane, Rougon, 70773, SAN 343-4648. Tel: 225-627-5846. FAX: 225-627-5846. *Br Mgr,* Debra Soileau; Staff 2 (Non-MLS 2)
Library Holdings: Bk Vols 6,000; Per Subs 22
Open Mon-Fri 9:30-2:30
Friends of the Library Group

OAK GROVE

P WEST CARROLL PARISH LIBRARY*, 101 Marietta St, 71263. (Mail add: PO Box 703, 71263-0703), SAN 306-5235. Tel: 318-428-4100. Administration Tel: 318-428-2697. FAX: 318-428-9887. Web Site: www.youseemore.com/wcpl. *Asst Dir,* Jan Franklin; Staff 6 (MLS 1, Non-MLS 5)
Founded 1967. Pop 12,100; Circ 75,000
Library Holdings: AV Mats 814; Large Print Bks 2,500; Bk Titles 23,000; Bk Vols 25,209; Per Subs 126; Talking Bks 200; Videos 700
Special Collections: Louisiana Coll
Automation Activity & Vendor Info: (Cataloging) TLC (The Library Corporation); (Circulation) TLC (The Library Corporation); (ILL) TLC (The Library Corporation); (OPAC) TLC (The Library Corporation)
Mem of Trail Blazer Library System
Partic in Loan System Helping Automate Retrieval of Knowledge
Open Mon-Fri 8:30-5
Bookmobiles: 1. Librn, Melody Harris. Bk titles 2,000

OBERLIN

P ALLEN PARISH LIBRARIES*, 320 S Sixth St, 70655. (Mail add: PO Box 400, 70655-0400), SAN 343-4702. Tel: 318-491-4543. Toll Free Tel: 800-960-3015 (Louisiana Only). FAX: 337-639-2654. Web Site: www.allen.lib.la.us. *Dir,* Agnes Guillory; E-mail: aguillory@state.lib.la.us; Staff 10 (MLS 1, Non-MLS 9)
Founded 1957. Pop 24,242; Circ 137,936
Library Holdings: CDs 47; Bk Vols 90,000; Per Subs 181; Talking Bks 1,886; Videos 3,393
Special Collections: Oral History
Automation Activity & Vendor Info: (Cataloging) Innovative Interfaces, Inc; (Circulation) Innovative Interfaces, Inc; (OPAC) Innovative Interfaces, Inc
Wireless access
Partic in Libraries SouthWest; Loan System Helping Automate Retrieval of Knowledge
Open Mon-Fri 8-5, Sat 9-Noon
Friends of the Library Group
Branches: 2
KINDER BRANCH, 833 Fourth Ave, Kinder, 70648. (Mail add: PO Drawer 1990, Kinder, 70648), SAN 343-4761. Tel: 318-491-4514. FAX: 337-738-4213. *Br Mgr,* Lashandalyn Bracy; Staff 1 (Non-MLS 1)
Library Holdings: Bk Vols 19,000; Per Subs 81; Talking Bks 179
Open Mon-Fri 8-5, Sat 9-12
Friends of the Library Group
OAKDALE BRANCH, 405 E Sixth Ave, Oakdale, 71463, SAN 343-4737. Tel: 318-335-2690. FAX: 318-335-4743. *Br Mgr,* Brenda Tichy; Staff 2 (MLS 1, Non-MLS 1)
Library Holdings: AV Mats 82; Bk Vols 30,000; Per Subs 56
Open Mon-Fri 8-5, Sat 9-3
Friends of the Library Group
Bookmobiles: 1. Mgr, Chalanda Duncan

OPELOUSAS

P OPELOUSAS PUBLIC LIBRARY*, 212 E Grolee St, 70570. (Mail add: PO Box 249, 70571-0249), SAN 343-4796. Tel: 337-948-3693. FAX: 337-948-5200. E-mail: opelousaspubliclibrary@gmail.com. Web Site: opelousaspubliclibrary.org. *Librn,* Angela Zachery; Staff 12 (MLS 1, Non-MLS 11)
Founded 1967. Pop 76,947
Library Holdings: AV Mats 680; Bk Vols 41,593; Per Subs 150
Special Collections: Large print bks
Subject Interests: Genealogy, Hist, La
Automation Activity & Vendor Info: (Cataloging) Book Systems; (Circulation) Book Systems; (OPAC) Book Systems
Wireless access
Partic in Loan System Helping Automate Retrieval of Knowledge
Open Mon-Fri 8-5:30, Sat 8-5

PINEVILLE

CENTRAL LOUISIANA STATE HOSPITAL
M DISTEFANO MEMORIAL LIBRARY*, 242 W Shamrock St, 71361. (Mail add: PO Box 5031, 71360-5031), SAN 343-4850. Tel: 318-484-6363. FAX: 318-484-6284. *Librn,* Deborah Boerdoom; Staff 3 (MLS 1, Non-MLS 2)
Founded 1958
Library Holdings: Bk Titles 3,000; Bk Vols 5,000; Per Subs 150
Subject Interests: Mental health, Neurology, Psychiat, Psychol, Psychotherapy, Soc serv (soc work)
Partic in S Cent Regional Med Libr Program
Restriction: Med staff only

M FOREST GLEN PATIENT'S LIBRARY*, 242 W Shamrock St, 71361. (Mail add: PO Box 5031, 71360-5031), SAN 343-4885. Tel: 318-484-6364. FAX: 318-484-6284. *Librn,* Deborah Boerdoom
Library Holdings: Bk Vols 10,000; Per Subs 20

C LOUISIANA COLLEGE*, Richard W Norton Memorial Library, 1140 College Dr, 71359. SAN 306-5243. Tel: 318-487-7201. E-mail: library@lacollege.edu. Web Site: lacollege.libguides.com/home?group_id=13470. *Libr Dir,* Dr Rusty Tryon; Tel: 318-487-7110, E-mail: rusty.tryon@lacollege.edu; *Adminr, Circ Asst,* Gayle Murrell; Tel: 318-487-7109, E-mail: gayle.murrell@lacollege.edu; *Cat Asst, Ser,* T J Norris; Tel: 318-487-7210, E-mail: toni.norris@lacollege.edu; *Coll Asst,* Joann Caples; Tel: 318-487-7143, E-mail: carolyn.caples@lacollege.edu; Staff 4 (MLS 1, Non-MLS 3)
Founded 1906. Enrl 1,236; Fac 117; Highest Degree: Master
Aug 2018-Jul 2019. Mats Exp $200,000
Library Holdings: e-books 301,231; e-journals 86,957; Electronic Media & Resources 46,569; Bk Vols 81,432; Per Subs 84
Special Collections: State Document Depository; US Document Depository
Automation Activity & Vendor Info: (Cataloging) TLC (The Library Corporation); (Circulation) TLC (The Library Corporation); (Course Reserve) TLC (The Library Corporation); (Discovery) EBSCO Discovery Service; (ILL) OCLC WorldShare Interlibrary Loan; (OPAC) TLC (The Library Corporation)
Wireless access
Partic in Christian Library Consortium; Louisiana Library Network; LYRASIS
Open Mon-Thurs 7:45am-11pm, Fri 7:45am-2pm, Sat 10am-2pm, Sun 6pm-11pm

PLAQUEMINE

P IBERVILLE PARISH LIBRARY*, 24605 J Gerald Berret Blvd, 70764. SAN 343-4915. Tel: 225-687-2520, 225-687-4397. FAX: 225-687-9719. Web Site: myipl.org. *Dir,* Michael Staton; E-mail: mstaton@state.lib.la.us; *Asst Dir,* David Hughes; Tel: 225-687-2520, Ext 101, E-mail: dhughes@myipl.org; *Head, Info Serv,* Elizabeth Haynes; E-mail: ehaynes@myipl.org; *Cat, Tech Serv Adminr,* Audrey Devillier; E-mail: adevilli@state.lib.la.us; *Circ,* Sandra Gilbert; E-mail: sgilbert@state.lib.la.us; *Ser,* Julie Simoneaux; E-mail: jsimonea@state.lib.la.us; Staff 10 (MLS 4, Non-MLS 6)
Founded 1951. Pop 33,000; Circ 242,536
Library Holdings: DVDs 380; Large Print Bks 3,855; Bk Vols 174,803; Per Subs 594; Talking Bks 2,205; Videos 4,555
Special Collections: Oral History
Subject Interests: La, Local authors, Local hist
Automation Activity & Vendor Info: (Acquisitions) TLC (The Library Corporation); (Cataloging) TLC (The Library Corporation); (Circulation) TLC (The Library Corporation); (ILL) Auto-Graphics, Inc; (OPAC) TLC (The Library Corporation); (Serials) TLC (The Library Corporation)
Wireless access
Partic in Loan System Helping Automate Retrieval of Knowledge
Open Mon-Thurs 8:30-6:30, Fri 8:30-5, Sat 9-4
Friends of the Library Group
Branches: 7
BAYOU PIGEON, 36625 Hwy 75, 70764, SAN 343-4974. Tel: 225-545-8567. FAX: 225-545-8567. E-mail: bayoupigeon.c1il@state.lib.la.us. *Br Mgr,* Joy Mullins; Staff 1 (Non-MLS 1)
Pop 33,000
Library Holdings: Bk Vols 6,441; Per Subs 12
Open Mon & Wed 12-6, Fri 10-1 & 2-5
Friends of the Library Group
BAYOU SORREL, 33415 Hwy 75, 70764. (Mail add: 32983 Gracie Lane, 70764), SAN 343-494X. Tel: 225-659-7055. FAX: 225-659-7055. E-mail: bayousorrel.c1il@pelican.state.lib.la.us. *Br Mgr,* Jo Ann Mendoza; Staff 1 (Non-MLS 1)
Library Holdings: AV Mats 30; Bk Vols 5,113; Per Subs 16
Open Mon & Wed 12-6, Fri 10-1 & 2-5
EAST IBERVILLE, 5715 Monticello St, Saint Gabriel, 70776, SAN 343-5008. Tel: 225-642-8380. FAX: 225-642-8381. E-mail: eastiberville.c1il@pelican.state.lib.la.us. *Br Mgr,* Lydia Haydel; Staff 1 (Non-MLS 1)
Pop 33,000
Library Holdings: AV Mats 160; Bk Vols 29,569; Per Subs 42
Open Mon-Wed 9-5, Thurs 9-6, Sat 8-12
Friends of the Library Group
GROSSE TETE BRANCH, 18135 Willow Rd, Grosse Tete, 70740. (Mail add: PO Box 218, Grosse Tete, 70740), SAN 343-5016. Tel: 225-648-2667. FAX: 225-648-2667. E-mail:

grossetete.c1il@pelican.state.lib.la.us. *Br Mgr,* Anna Angelloz; Staff 1 (Non-MLS 1)
Pop 33,000
Library Holdings: Bk Vols 6,124; Per Subs 10
Open Mon, Wed & Fri 10-1 & 2-5
Friends of the Library Group
MARINGOUIN BRANCH, 77175 Ridgewood Dr, Maringouin, 70757. (Mail add: PO Box 37, Maringouin, 70757), SAN 343-5032. Tel: 225-625-2743. FAX: 225-625-2743. E-mail: maringouin.c1il@pelican.state.lib.la.us. *Br Mgr,* Debra Lewis; Staff 1 (Non-MLS 1)
Pop 33,000
Library Holdings: Bk Vols 10,027; Per Subs 26
Open Mon & Wed 10-1 & 2-6:30, Fri 10-1 & 2-5
ROSEDALE BRANCH, 15695 Rosedale Rd, Rosedale, 70772. (Mail add: PO Box 410, Rosedale, 70772-0410), SAN 343-5067. Tel: 225-648-2213. FAX: 225-648-2213. E-mail: rosedale.c1il@pelican.state.lib.la.us. *Br Mgr,* Brenda Coles; Staff 1 (Non-MLS 1)
Library Holdings: Bk Vols 7,084; Per Subs 14
Open Tues 9-12 & 2-6, Thurs 9-12 & 1-5, Sat 12-4
Friends of the Library Group
WHITE CASTLE BRANCH, 32835 Bowie St, White Castle, 70788, SAN 343-5121. Tel: 225-545-8424. FAX: 225-545-4536. E-mail: whitecastle.c1il@pelican.state.lib.la.us. *Br Mgr,* Kitty Wood; Staff 1 (Non-MLS 1)
Library Holdings: AV Mats 110; Bk Vols 20,668; Per Subs 40
Open Mon, Tues & Thurs 8:30-5, Wed 8:30-6, Sat 9-1
Friends of the Library Group

PORT ALLEN

P WEST BATON ROUGE PARISH LIBRARY, 830 N Alexander Ave, 70767. SAN 306-526X. Tel: 225-342-7920. FAX: 225-342-7918. Web Site: www.wbrpl.com. *Dir,* Tamie Martin; E-mail: tmartin@wbrplibrary.us; *Ad,* Luis Interiano; *Circ Mgr,* James D Bridges; *ILL & Ser,* Cyndi Jones; Staff 4 (MLS 4)
Founded 1965. Pop 25,000; Circ 87,042
Library Holdings: AV Mats 3,000; Bk Vols 87,000; Per Subs 180; Talking Bks 1,400
Special Collections: Louisiana Material
Automation Activity & Vendor Info: (Cataloging) TLC (The Library Corporation); (Circulation) TLC (The Library Corporation); (OPAC) TLC (The Library Corporation)
Wireless access
Function: 24/7 Electronic res, 24/7 Online cat, Accelerated reader prog, Activity rm
Partic in Loan System Helping Automate Retrieval of Knowledge
Special Services for the Deaf - Accessible learning ctr
Special Services for the Blind - Accessible computers; Assistive/Adapted tech devices, equip & products; Bks on CD; Children's Braille; Closed circuit TV magnifier; Computer access aids; Computer with voice synthesizer for visually impaired persons; Digital talking bk; Extensive large print coll; IBM screen reader; Large print bks; Large screen computer & software; Low vision equip; PC for people with disabilities; Screen enlargement software for people with visual disabilities; Screen reader software; Talking bk serv referral; Talking bks
Open Mon, Wed & Fri 8:30-5:30, Tues & Thurs 8:30-8, Sat 9-1
Bookmobiles: 1. Libr Tech, Amy Hebert

RAYVILLE

P RICHLAND PARISH LIBRARY*, 1410 Louisa St, 71269. SAN 343-5156. Tel: 318-728-4806. FAX: 318-728-6108. Web Site: www.richlandparishlibrary.org. *Dir,* Amanda Stewart; E-mail: astewart@state.lib.la.us; *Asst Librn,* Sarah Brashears; Staff 3 (Non-MLS 3)
Founded 1926. Pop 21,774; Circ 110,051
Library Holdings: AV Mats 256; Bk Vols 66,281; Per Subs 118
Special Collections: 1927 Flood Coll; Literature (Ruth Hatch Coll); Reference (Innis Morris Ellis Coll). Oral History
Automation Activity & Vendor Info: (Cataloging) TLC (The Library Corporation); (Circulation) TLC (The Library Corporation); (OPAC) TLC (The Library Corporation)
Wireless access
Mem of Trail Blazer Library System
Partic in Loan System Helping Automate Retrieval of Knowledge; LYRASIS
Open Mon-Fri 8:30-7, Sat 8:30-Noon
Branches: 2
DELHI BRANCH, 520 Main St, Delhi, 71232, SAN 343-5180. Tel: 318-878-5121. FAX: 318-878-0674. *Br Mgr,* Kim Fryer; Staff 2 (Non-MLS 2)
Library Holdings: Bk Vols 19,101; Per Subs 47
Open Mon-Fri 8:30-5, Sat 8:30-Noon
MANGHAM BRANCH, 302 Hixon St, Mangham, 71259, SAN 343-5210. Tel: 318-248-2493. FAX: 318-248-3912. *Br Mgr,* Kathryn Berry; Staff 1 (Non-MLS 1)
Library Holdings: AV Mats 80; Bk Vols 7,900; Per Subs 21
Open Mon-Fri 9-5, Sat 8:30-Noon

RUSTON

P LINCOLN PARISH LIBRARY*, 910 N Trenton St, 71270. SAN 306-5286. Tel: 318-251-5030, 318-251-5031. Administration Tel: 318-513-6409. FAX: 318-251-5045. Administration FAX: 318-513-6446. Web Site: www.mylpl.org. *Dir,* Vivian McCain; E-mail: vmccain@mylpl.org; *Head, Children's Servx,* Margie Mealer; Tel: 318-513-5513, E-mail: mmealer@mylpl.org; *Head, Circ,* Sharon Hancock; Tel: 318-513-5506, E-mail: shancock@mylpl.org; *Head, Mat Mgt,* Theresa Spivey; Tel: 318-513-5526, E-mail: tspivey@mylpl.org; *Head, Pub Serv,* Jeremy Bolom; Tel: 318-513-5512, E-mail: jbolom@mylpl.org; Staff 13 (MLS 2, Non-MLS 11)
Founded 1962. Pop 42,935; Circ 378,000
Library Holdings: DVDs 13,359; Bk Vols 98,016; Per Subs 279; Talking Bks 5,004
Subject Interests: Genealogy, Local hist
Automation Activity & Vendor Info: (Cataloging) Auto-Graphics, Inc; (Circulation) Auto-Graphics, Inc; (OPAC) Auto-Graphics, Inc
Wireless access
Publications: Library Pages (Newsletter)
Mem of Trail Blazer Library System
Partic in Green Gold Libr Syst; Loan System Helping Automate Retrieval of Knowledge
Special Services for the Deaf - Assistive tech
Special Services for the Blind - Assistive/Adapted tech devices, equip & products
Open Mon-Thurs 9-8, Fri & Sat 9-6, Sun 1-5
Friends of the Library Group

C LOUISIANA TECH UNIVERSITY*, Prescott Memorial Library, Everett St at The Columns, 71272. (Mail add: PO Box 10408, 71272-0046), SAN 306-5294. Tel: 318-257-3555. Interlibrary Loan Service Tel: 318-257-2523. Administration Tel: 318-257-2577. FAX: 318-257-2579. Interlibrary Loan Service FAX: 318-257-2447. Web Site: www.latech.edu/library. *Head, Ref,* Mrs Lynell S Buckley; E-mail: nell@latech.edu; *Bus Liaison Librn,* Sue Jones McFadden; E-mail: sumac@latech.edu; *Govt Doc Librn,* Abigail DeSoto; E-mail: desoto@latech.edu; *Sci/Eng Librn,* Kevin Dominic Cuccia; E-mail: kevinc@latech.edu; *Libr Spec Supvr,* Regina Foster; E-mail: reginaf@latech.edu; *IT Spec,* William Lancaster; E-mail: lancaste@latech.edu; *Univ Archivist,* Nolan Eller; E-mail: ellern@latech.edu; Staff 27 (MLS 11, Non-MLS 16)
Founded 1895. Enrl 11,257; Fac 390; Highest Degree: Doctorate
Library Holdings: AV Mats 526; CDs 7,874; e-books 133,223; e-journals 57,419; Microforms 578,248; Bk Vols 470,872; Per Subs 2,654
Special Collections: State Document Depository; US Document Depository
Automation Activity & Vendor Info: (Acquisitions) SirsiDynix; (Cataloging) SirsiDynix; (Circulation) SirsiDynix; (OPAC) SirsiDynix; (Serials) SirsiDynix
Wireless access
Mem of Trail Blazer Library System
Partic in La Acad Libr Info Network Consortium; Louisiana Library Network; LYRASIS
Open Mon-Thurs (Fall & Spring) 7:30am-11pm, Fri 7:30-5, Sat 10-6, Sun 1-11; Mon-Thurs (Summer) 7:30am-9pm, Fri 7:30am-12:30pm, Sun 5pm-9pm

SAINT BENEDICT

CR SAINT JOSEPH SEMINARY COLLEGE*, Rouquette Library, 75376 River Rd, 70457-9900. SAN 306-5308, Tel: 985-867-2237. FAX: 985-867-2270. E-mail: rouquette@sjasc.edu. Web Site: www.sjasc.edu. *Libr Dir,* Bonnie Bess Wood; Staff 4 (MLS 2, Non-MLS 2)
Founded 1891. Enrl 160; Highest Degree: Bachelor
Library Holdings: e-books 150,000; Bk Vols 30,000; Per Subs 155
Subject Interests: Educ, Fine arts, Hist, Lit, Philos, Relig
Automation Activity & Vendor Info: (Cataloging) OCLC Worldshare Management Services; (Circulation) OCLC Worldshare Management Services; (Discovery) OCLC Worldshare Management Services; (ILL) OCLC Worldshare Management Services; (OPAC) OCLC Worldshare Management Services
Wireless access
Partic in Louisiana Library Network
Open Mon-Fri 8-6

SAINT FRANCISVILLE

P WEST FELICIANA PARISH LIBRARY*, 5114 Burnett Rd, 70775-4341. (Mail add: PO Box 3120, 70775-3120), SAN 342-8915. Tel: 225-635-3364. FAX: 225-635-4986. Web Site: www.wfplibrary.org. *Libr Dir,* Glenna

Clark Fallin; E-mail: gfallin@wfplibrary.org; *Libr Mgr,* Penny Graham; E-mail: pgraham@wfplibrary.org; Staff 5.3 (MLS 1.3, Non-MLS 4)
Founded 2003. Pop 15,000
Library Holdings: Per Subs 75
Special Collections: Genealogy (Louisiana & West Feliciana Parish)
Automation Activity & Vendor Info: (Acquisitions) Baker & Taylor; (Cataloging) TLC (The Library Corporation); (Circulation) TLC (The Library Corporation); (ILL) OCLC; (OPAC) TLC (The Library Corporation); (Serials) EBSCO Online
Wireless access
Function: 24/7 Electronic res, Activity rm, Archival coll, Art exhibits, Audiobks via web, Bk club(s), Children's prog, Computers for patron use, E-Readers, Electronic databases & coll, Family literacy, Free DVD rentals, Genealogy discussion group, Jail serv, Magazines, Magnifiers for reading, Microfiche/film & reading machines, Movies, Music CDs, Online cat, Photocopying/Printing, Preschool outreach, Preschool reading prog, Prog for children & young adult, Scanner, Senior outreach, Story hour, Study rm, Summer reading prog, Teen prog, Wheelchair accessible
Partic in Loan System Helping Automate Retrieval of Knowledge
Open Mon-Thurs 8:30-7, Fri 8:30-6, Sat 9-4
Restriction: Access at librarian's discretion, Badge access after hrs, Borrowing requests are handled by ILL, In-house use for visitors
Friends of the Library Group

SAINT GABRIEL

S LOUISIANA CORRECTIONAL INSTITUTE FOR WOMEN LIBRARY*, 7205 Hwy 74, 70776. (Mail add: PO Box 26, 70776-0026), SAN 306-5316. Tel: 225-319-2701, Ext 2369. FAX: 225-319-2757. *Librn,* Rene Matthews
Founded 1969
Library Holdings: Bk Vols 6,900; Per Subs 14
Open Mon-Fri 8-8, Sat & Sun 8-2:30
Friends of the Library Group

SAINT JOSEPH

P TENSAS PARISH LIBRARY*, 135 Plank Rd, 71366. (Mail add: PO Box 228, 71366-0228), SAN 306-5324. Tel: 318-766-3781. FAX: 318-766-0098. E-mail: tensaslibrary@gmail.com. *Dir,* Jacqueline Slang; Staff 4 (Non-MLS 4)
Founded 1952. Pop 7,200; Circ 37,453
Library Holdings: AV Mats 300; Bk Vols 25,600; Per Subs 32
Special Collections: Louisiana Section
Automation Activity & Vendor Info: (Cataloging) Book Systems
Wireless access
Mem of Trail Blazer Library System
Partic in Loan System Helping Automate Retrieval of Knowledge
Open Mon-Wed & Fri 8-5, Thurs 8-12

SAINT MARTINVILLE

P SAINT MARTIN PARISH LIBRARY*, St Martinville Branch, 201 Porter St, 70582. SAN 306-5332. Tel: 337-394-2207, Ext 223. Administration Tel: 337-394-2207, Ext 210. FAX: 337-394-2248. Web Site: stmartinparishlibrary.org. *Dir,* Charlar Brew; E-mail: cbrew@stmartinparishlibrary.org; *Br Mgr,* Kathleen Landry; Staff 19 (MLS 2, Non-MLS 17)
Founded 1955. Pop 46,262; Circ 199,003
Library Holdings: AV Mats 900; Bk Vols 142,883; Per Subs 278
Subject Interests: Genealogy, Hist, La
Automation Activity & Vendor Info: (Cataloging) TLC (The Library Corporation); (Circulation) TLC (The Library Corporation); (OPAC) TLC (The Library Corporation)
Wireless access
Publications: Genealogy catalog, microfilm catalog
Partic in Loan System Helping Automate Retrieval of Knowledge
Open Mon-Thurs 8-6, Fri 8-5, Sat 8-Noon
Friends of the Library Group
Branches: 3
BREAUX BRIDGE BRANCH, 205 N Main St, Breaux Bridge, 70517, SAN 329-6962. Tel: 337-332-2733. FAX: 337-332-2733. *Br Mgr,* Mona Trosclair; Staff 2 (Non-MLS 2)
Library Holdings: AV Mats 310; Bk Vols 25,000; Per Subs 46
Open Mon-Thurs 8-6, Fri 8-5, Sat 8-Noon
Friends of the Library Group
CECILIA BRANCH, 2460 Cecilia Sr High School Hwy, Cecilia, 70521, SAN 329-6989. Tel: 337-667-7411. FAX: 337-667-7411. *Br Mgr,* Rachel Dugan; Staff 2 (Non-MLS 2)
Library Holdings: Bk Vols 11,000; Per Subs 27
Open Mon-Thurs 8-6, Fri 8-5, Sat 8-Noon
Friends of the Library Group
PARKS BRANCH, 1012 Martin St, Parks, 70582, SAN 377-614X. Tel: 337-342-2690. FAX: 337-342-2690. *Br Mgr,* Mary Jones; Staff 2 (Non-MLS 2)
Library Holdings: Bk Vols 16,000; Per Subs 29
Open Mon-Thurs 10-6, Fri 9-5, Sat 8-Noon
Friends of the Library Group

SCHRIEVER

§J FLETCHER TECHNICAL COMMUNITY COLLEGE LIBRARY, 1407 Hwy 311, Rm 128, 70395. Tel: 985-448-7910. E-mail: library@fletcher.edu. Web Site: library.fletcher.edu. *Director of Library & Academic Support,* Jodi Duet; Tel: 985-448-7946, E-mail: jodi.duet@fletcher.edu; *Outreach & Instruction Librn,* Marian Mays; *Tech Serv Librn,* K C Celestine; Tel: 985-488-7963, E-mail: kcelestine@fletcher.edu
Wireless access
Function: Computers for patron use, ILL available, Res assist avail, Study rm
Partic in Louisiana Library Network
Open Mon-Fri 8-4

SHREVEPORT

S AMERICAN ROSE SOCIETY, Schorr Rose Horticulture & Research Library, Klima Rose Hall, 8877 Jefferson Paige Rd, 71119. (Mail add: PO Box 30000, 71130-0030), SAN 327-4616. Tel: 318-938-5402. FAX: 318-938-5405. Web Site: www.rose.org/schorr-library. *Dir of Publ(s),* Beth Smiley; Tel: 318-383-3570, Ext 107, E-mail: beth@rose.org
Library Holdings: Bk Titles 710
Subject Interests: Flowers, Gardening
Restriction: Not a lending libr, Open by appt only

C CENTENARY COLLEGE OF LOUISIANA*, John F Magale Memorial Library, 2834 Woodlawn St, 71104. (Mail add: 2911 Centenary Blvd, PO Box 41188, 71134-1188), SAN 306-5367. Tel: 318-869-5047. FAX: 318-869-5690. Reference E-mail: ref@centenary.edu. Web Site: www.centenary.edu/library. *Dir, Libr Serv,* Christy Jordan Wrenn; Tel: 318-869-5057, E-mail: cwrenn@centenary.edu; *Asst Dir, Libr Serv,* Ashley E Rulo; Tel: 318-869-5058, E-mail: arulo@centenary.edu; *Dir, Hurley Music Libr,* Thomas Hundemer; E-mail: thundemer@centenary.edu; *Circ, ILL Librn,* Sharon K Chevalier; Tel: 318-869-5047, E-mail: schevali@centenary.edu; *Ser Coll Mgr & Acq,* Marcia M Alexander; E-mail: malexand@centenary.edu; *Col Archivist,* Chris Brown; Tel: 318-869-5462, E-mail: cbrown@centenary.edu. Subject Specialists: *Music hist,* Thomas Hundemer; *Doc delivery,* Sharon K Chevalier; Staff 6 (MLS 3, Non-MLS 3)
Founded 1825. Enrl 550; Fac 57; Highest Degree: Master
Library Holdings: AV Mats 29,789; Bks-By-Mail 1,766; Bks on Deafness & Sign Lang 10; CDs 3,186; DVDs 3,875; e-books 155,940; e-journals 962; Electronic Media & Resources 461,090; Microforms 362,406; Music Scores 9,307; Bk Titles 151,971; Bk Vols 342,040; Per Subs 130; Videos 7,470
Special Collections: Bill Corrington Papers & Personal Library; Centenary College Archives; Jack London Papers; Louisiana United Methodist Church Archives; North Louisiana Historical Association Archives; Pierce Cline Archive; Rare Books; Religious Studies Coll. State Document Depository
Subject Interests: Am lit, Geol, Music educ, Relig
Automation Activity & Vendor Info: (Acquisitions) SirsiDynix-WorkFlows; (Cataloging) SirsiDynix-WorkFlows; (Circulation) SirsiDynix-WorkFlows; (Course Reserve) SirsiDynix-WorkFlows; (Discovery) EBSCO Discovery Service; (ILL) OCLC ILLiad; (Media Booking) SirsiDynix-WorkFlows; (OPAC) SirsiDynix-Enterprise; (Serials) SirsiDynix-WorkFlows
Wireless access
Function: Art exhibits, ILL available
Publications: Archives & Special Coll (Archives guide); Information Literacy Handbook (Research guide); Magale Library Annual Report (Research guide); Magale Library Welcomes Centernary College Alumni (Reference guide); Online Information Literacy Subject Research Guides; Student Worker Guidelines & Evaluation (Reference guide); The Magale Message (Monthly newsletter); Welcome to John F Magale Memorial Library (Research guide); Welcome to Non-Centenary College Patrons (Reference guide)
Partic in Associated Colleges of the South; Louisiana Library Network; OCLC Online Computer Library Center, Inc; OCLC-LVIS
Special Services for the Deaf - Bks on deafness & sign lang
Special Services for the Blind - Screen reader software
Open Mon-Thurs 7:30am-10pm, Fri 7:30-4:30, Sat 1-5, Sun 2-10
Restriction: Authorized patrons, Authorized scholars by appt, Borrowing privileges limited to fac & registered students, Circ limited, ID required to use computers (Ltd hrs), In-house use for visitors, Lending libr only via mail, Limited access based on advanced application, Open evenings by appt, Private libr

R FIRST UNITED METHODIST CHURCH, Bliss Memorial Library, 500 Common St, 71101. (Mail add: PO Box 1567, 71165-1567), SAN 306-5375. Tel: 318-424-7771. FAX: 318-429-6888. E-mail: info@firstshreveport.org. Web Site: www.fumcshreveport.org.

Founded 1946
Library Holdings: Large Print Bks 75; Bk Titles 12,000; Bk Vols 12,500
Subject Interests: Fiction, Relig
Wireless access
Special Services for the Blind - Large print bks
Restriction: Mem only, Not open to pub

C LOUISIANA STATE UNIVERSITY*, Noel Memorial Library, One University Pl, 71115-2399. SAN 306-5405. Tel: 318-798-5069. Interlibrary Loan Service Tel: 318-797-5225. Reference Tel: 318-798-5068. Administration Tel: 318-798-4131. FAX: 318-797-5156. Administration FAX: 318-798-4138. E-mail: librefdesk@lsus.edu. Web Site: www.lsus.edu/library. *Dean, Head, Access Serv & Syst,* Brian Sherman; Tel: 318-798-4117, E-mail: Brian.Sherman@LSUS.edu; *Head, Res Serv,* Dr Julienne Wood; Tel: 318-797-5072, E-mail: Julienne.Wood@LSUS.edu; *Head, Tech Serv,* James Evans; Tel: 318-797-5070, E-mail: James.Evans2@LSUS.edu; *Govt Doc, Ref Librn,* Rachael Green; Tel: 318-798-4158, E-mail: Rachael.Green@LSUS.edu; *Ref Librn,* Kay Slattery; Tel: 318-798-4152, E-mail: Kay.Stebbins@LSUS.edu; *Acq,* Becky Dean; Tel: 318-798-4157, E-mail: Becky.Dean@LSUS.edu; *Archivist,* Dr Laura McLemore; Tel: 318-797-5378, E-mail: Laura.McLemore@LSUS.edu; *Curator, James Smith Noel Coll,* Dr Robert Leitz; Tel: 318-798-4161, E-mail: Robert.Leitz@LSUS.edu; *Cataloger,* Martha Lawler; Tel: 318-798-4163, E-mail: Martha.Lawler@LSUS.edu; Staff 11 (MLS 8, Non-MLS 3)
Founded 1967. Enrl 4,000; Fac 160; Highest Degree: Doctorate
Jul 2014-Jun 2015 Income $1,387,933. Sal $731,570 (Prof $443,757)
Library Holdings: AV Mats 4,550; e-books 254,056; e-journals 73,943; Microforms 413,534; Bk Vols 396,348; Per Subs 298
Special Collections: James Smith Noel Coll; Northwest Louisiana & Lower Red River Region (Archives & Special Coll). Oral History; State Document Depository; US Document Depository
Automation Activity & Vendor Info: (Acquisitions) SirsiDynix; (Cataloging) SirsiDynix; (Circulation) SirsiDynix; (Course Reserve) SirsiDynix; (Discovery) EBSCO Discovery Service; (ILL) OCLC; (OPAC) SirsiDynix; (Serials) SirsiDynix
Wireless access
Function: 24/7 Electronic res, Online cat
Partic in Amigos Library Services, Inc; Louisiana Library Network; OCLC Online Computer Library Center, Inc
Open Mon-Thurs 7:30am-10pm, Fri 7:30-4:30, Sun 1-10
Friends of the Library Group

CM LOUISIANA STATE UNIVERSITY HEALTH SCIENCES CENTER*, Health Sciences Library, 1501 Kings Hwy, 71130. (Mail add: PO Box 33932, 71130-3932), SAN 306-5413. Tel: 318-675-5445. FAX: 318-675-5442. Web Site: lib-sh.lsuhsc.edu. *Interim Dir,* Will Olmstadt; Tel: 318-675-6487, E-mail: wolmst@lsuhsc.edu; *Asst Dir, Syst,* Mararia Adams; Tel: 318-675-5448, E-mail: madams@lsuhsc.edu; *Asst Dir, Tech Serv,* Betty Tucker; Tel: 318-675-5457, E-mail: btucke@lsuhsc.edu; *Head, User Access Serv,* Montie Dobbins; Tel: 318-675-5664, E-mail: mdobbi@lsuhsc.edu; *Head, User Educ/Outreach,* Julie Esparza; Tel: 318-675-54179, E-mail: jespar@lsuhsc.edu; *Cat Librn, Digitization Librn,* Locrecia Amber; Tel: 318-675-5458, E-mail: labne2@lsuhsc.edu; *ILL Librn,* Barbara Reilly; Tel: 318-675-5452, E-mail: breill@lsuhsc.edu; *Libr Assoc,* Katrina Bell; Tel: 318-675-5393, E-mail: kbell@lsuhsc.edu; Staff 22 (MLS 16, Non-MLS 6)
Founded 1968. Enrl 400; Highest Degree: Doctorate
Library Holdings: Bk Vols 190,623; Per Subs 325
Special Collections: Archives; History of Medicine; Medical Fiction
Subject Interests: Allied health, Med, Nursing
Automation Activity & Vendor Info: (Acquisitions) Innovative Interfaces, Inc; (Cataloging) Innovative Interfaces, Inc; (Circulation) Innovative Interfaces, Inc; (OPAC) Innovative Interfaces, Inc; (Serials) Innovative Interfaces, Inc
Wireless access
Function: Doc delivery serv
Publications: Library Bulletin (Bimonthly); Library Newsletter; LSUMC Faculty Publications (ann)
Partic in Louisiana Library Network; South Central Academic Medical Libraries Consortium
Open Mon-Fri 7:30am-11pm, Sat 9am-11pm, Sun Noon-11

M NORTHWESTERN STATE UNIVERSITY COLLEGE OF NURSING & ALLIED HEALTH - LIBRARY*, Shreveport Nursing Library, 1800 Line Ave, Rm 101, 71101. (Mail add: 1800 Line Ave, Mail Stop 101, 71101). Administration Tel: 318-677-3007. E-mail: nursinglibrary@nsula.edu. *Head of Libr,* SherriLynn Voebel; E-mail: voebels@nsula.edu; *Admin Assoc,* Sandra Rufty; E-mail: ruftys@nsula.edu. Subject Specialists: *Med,* SherriLynn Voebel; Staff 2 (MLS 1, Non-MLS 1)
Founded 1998. Enrl 2,000; Fac 42; Highest Degree: Doctorate
Automation Activity & Vendor Info: (Cataloging) SirsiDynix; (Circulation) SirsiDynix; (Course Reserve) SirsiDynix-WorkFlows; (Discovery) SirsiDynix; (ILL) OCLC; (OPAC) SirsiDynix; (Serials) SirsiDynix
Wireless access
Function: 24/7 Electronic res, 24/7 Online cat
Restriction: Authorized patrons, Borrowing requests are handled by ILL, Not open to pub

S R W NORTON ART GALLERY*, Reference & Research Library, 4747 Creswell Ave, 71106. SAN 306-543X. Tel: 318-865-4201. FAX: 318-869-0435. E-mail: gallery@rwnaf.org. Web Site: www.rwnaf.org. *Librn,* Melisa Elrod
Founded 1966
Library Holdings: Bk Titles 10,000; Per Subs 10
Special Collections: Early US, State & Local History, especially Virginia (James M Owens Memorial)
Subject Interests: Fine arts, Genealogy, Ornithology
Open Wed & Thurs 10-5, Fri & Sat 10-7, Sun 1-5
Restriction: Non-circulating to the pub

P SHREVE MEMORIAL LIBRARY*, 424 Texas St, 71101. SAN 343-5245. Tel: 318-226-5897. FAX: 318-226-4780. E-mail: publicmain@shreve-lib.org. Web Site: www.shreve-lib.org. *Exec Dir,* John Tuggle; E-mail: jtuggle@shreve-lib.org; *Br Mgr,* Chris Kirkley; E-mail: ckirkley@shreve-lib.org; Staff 48 (MLS 18, Non-MLS 30)
Founded 1923. Pop 254,969; Circ 73,205
Jan 2015-Dec 2015 Income (Main & Associated Libraries) $15,833,165, State $389,852, Locally Generated Income $14,988,860, Other $454,453. Mats Exp $1,272,480, Books $600,970, Per/Ser (Incl. Access Fees) $125,622, AV Mat $284,296, Electronic Ref Mat (Incl. Access Fees) $261,592. Sal $6,557,327 (Prof $125,000)
Library Holdings: Audiobooks 1,860; AV Mats 10,622; Bks on Deafness & Sign Lang 24; CDs 3,932; DVDs 5,789; e-books 24,810; Large Print Bks 2,582; Bk Titles 73,217; Bk Vols 89,514; Per Subs 365
Special Collections: Census Info; Louisiana Coll (History, Authors, Cookbooks, LA Magazines); Law Coll; The Selective Federal Depository Coll; US Gov't Manual; Federal Register; Stat Abstracts of U.S.; Public Papers of the Pres of the U.S.. State Document Depository; US Document Depository
Subject Interests: Geol, Petroleum
Automation Activity & Vendor Info: (Acquisitions) SirsiDynix; (Cataloging) SirsiDynix; (Circulation) SirsiDynix; (ILL) TLC (The Library Corporation); (OPAC) SirsiDynix
Wireless access
Function: 24/7 Electronic res, Adult bk club, Adult literacy prog, Archival coll, Audio & video playback equip for onsite use, Audiobks via web, AV serv, Bks on CD, Bus archives, Computer training, Computers for patron use, Doc delivery serv, Electronic databases & coll, Free DVD rentals, Home delivery & serv to seniorr ctr & nursing homes, ILL available, Internet access, Magazines, Meeting rooms, Microfiche/film & reading machines, Movies, Music CDs, Outside serv via phone, mail, e-mail & web, OverDrive digital audio bks, Photocopying/Printing, Prog for children & young adult, Ref serv available, Res libr, Study rm, Summer reading prog, Tax forms, Telephone ref, VHS videos, Wheelchair accessible
Publications: Area Agencies & Organizations Directory (Annual); Creating Literacy: Literacy Specialist Training Manual (Library handbook); LITstART: The Art of Family Literacy; Magazine List (Serials catalog); PALS Club: Peer Advocates for Learning & Success (Library handbook); Read for Your Life: Early Childhood Literacy & Family Learning Initiative (Library handbook)
Partic in Green Gold Libr Syst; Loan System Helping Automate Retrieval of Knowledge
Special Services for the Blind - Assistive/Adapted tech devices, equip & products; Audio mat; Bks on cassette; Bks on CD; Copier with enlargement capabilities; Large print bks; Ref serv; Screen enlargement software for people with visual disabilities; Screen reader software; Talking bks; VIEW (Visually Impaired Educational Workstation)
Open Mon-Thurs 9-9, Fri & Sat 9-6, Sun 1-5
Friends of the Library Group
Branches: 20
ATKINS BRANCH, 3704 Greenwood Rd, 71109, SAN 343-527X. Tel: 318-635-6222. FAX: 318-635-6912. E-mail: publicatkins@shreve-lib.org. *Br Mgr,* Sonja Pruitt-Kirksey; E-mail: skirksey@shreve-lib.org; Staff 1 (Non-MLS 1)
Founded 1965. Pop 254,969; Circ 30,367
Library Holdings: Audiobooks 512; AV Mats 3,967; Bks on Deafness & Sign Lang 1; CDs 1,296; DVDs 2,535; Large Print Bks 973; Bk Titles 18,099; Bk Vols 18,828; Per Subs 128
Function: 24/7 Online cat, Audio & video playback equip for onsite use, Audiobks on Playaways & MP3, Audiobks via web, AV serv, Bks on CD, Children's prog, Computer training, Computers for patron use, Electronic databases & coll, For res purposes, Free DVD rentals, ILL available, Instruction & testing, Internet access, Life-long learning prog for all ages, Magazines, Meeting rooms, Movies, Music CDs, OverDrive digital audio bks, Photocopying/Printing, Prog for adults, Prog for children & young adult, Senior computer classes, Spoken cassettes & CDs, Spoken cassettes & DVDs, Study rm, Summer reading prog, Teen prog, Wheelchair accessible

Special Services for the Blind - BC CILS
Open Mon-Wed 9-8, Thurs-Sat 9-6
Friends of the Library Group
BELCHER-WYCHE BRANCH, 409 Charles St, Belcher, 71004, SAN 343-530X. Tel: 318-378-4567. FAX: 318-378-4281. E-mail: publicbelcher@shreve-lib.org. *Br Mgr,* Lesa Miller; E-mail: lmiller@shreve-lib.org; Staff 1 (Non-MLS 1)
Pop 254,969; Circ 6,906
Library Holdings: Audiobooks 156; AV Mats 2,566; CDs 189; DVDs 2,315; Large Print Bks 93; Bk Titles 4,703; Bk Vols 4,853; Per Subs 34
Special Collections: Louisana Fiction & Nonfiction Coll
Function: 24/7 Electronic res, Audiobks via web, Bks on CD, Children's prog, Free DVD rentals, ILL available, Internet access, Music CDs, Photocopying/Printing, Summer reading prog, Wheelchair accessible
Open Tues 1-7, Thurs 3-6, Fri 10-12 & 1-5
Friends of the Library Group
BLANCHARD BRANCH, 344 Alexander St, Blanchard, 71009. (Mail add: PO Box 779, Blanchard, 71009), SAN 343-5334. Tel: 318-929-3163. FAX: 318-929-1930. *Br Mgr,* Grace Harr; E-mail: gharr@shreve-lib.org; Staff 1 (Non-MLS 1)
Founded 1933. Pop 254,969; Circ 15,240
Library Holdings: Audiobooks 144; AV Mats 1,468; CDs 211; DVDs 1,190; Large Print Bks 45; Bk Titles 4,546; Bk Vols 4,630; Per Subs 49
Function: 24/7 Electronic res, Audiobks via web, Bks on CD, Children's prog, Free DVD rentals, ILL available, Internet access, Music CDs, Photocopying/Printing, Summer reading prog, Wheelchair accessible
Open Mon & Wed 11:30-5, Tues & Thurs 11:30-6, Fri 11:30-4:30
Friends of the Library Group
BROADMOOR BRANCH, 1212 Captain Shreve Dr, 71105, SAN 343-5369. Tel: 318-869-0120. FAX: 318-868-9464. E-mail: publicbroadmoor@shreve-lib.org. *Br Mgr,* Ariel Stewart; E-mail: astewart@shreve-lib.org; Staff 5 (MLS 3, Non-MLS 2)
Founded 1948. Pop 254,969; Circ 288,567
Library Holdings: Audiobooks 1,794; AV Mats 10,436; Bks on Deafness & Sign Lang 25; CDs 3,800; DVDs 6,147; Large Print Bks 3,179; Bk Titles 53,893; Bk Vols 80,221; Per Subs 270
Special Collections: Louisiana Coll; Genealogy Coll; Shreveport City Directories; Census Info
Subject Interests: Genealogy
Function: 24/7 Electronic res, Adult bk club, Adult literacy prog, Audio & video playback equip for onsite use, Audiobks via web, AV serv, Bks on CD, Children's prog, Computer training, Computers for patron use, Digital talking bks, Electronic databases & coll, Free DVD rentals, Genealogy discussion group, Holiday prog, ILL available, Instruction & testing, Internet access, Life-long learning prog for all ages, Literacy & newcomer serv, Magazines, Magnifiers for reading, Meeting rooms, Microfiche/film & reading machines, Movies, Music CDs, Outside serv via phone, mail, e-mail & web, OverDrive digital audio bks, Photocopying/Printing, Prog for adults, Prog for children & young adult, Ref serv available, Res libr, Study rm, Summer reading prog, Tax forms, Teen prog, Telephone ref, Wheelchair accessible
Special Services for the Blind - Accessible computers; Assistive/Adapted tech devices, equip & products; Bks on CD; Reader equip; Screen reader software; Talking bks
Open Mon-Thurs 9-9, Fri & Sat 9-6, Sun 1-5
Friends of the Library Group
CEDAR GROVE-LINE AVENUE BRANCH, 8303 Line Ave, 71106, SAN 343-5393. Tel: 318-868-3890. FAX: 318-868-2071. E-mail: publiccgla@shreve-lib.org. *Br Mgr,* Linda Young; E-mail: lyoung@shreve-lib.org; Staff 1 (MLS 1)
Founded 1929. Pop 254,969; Circ 73,755
Library Holdings: Audiobooks 819; AV Mats 6,043; Bks on Deafness & Sign Lang 9; CDs 1,648; DVDs 4,138; Large Print Bks 1,101; Bk Titles 23,056; Bk Vols 23,844; Per Subs 114
Function: 24/7 Electronic res, Adult bk club, Adult literacy prog, Audiobks via web, AV serv, Bks on CD, Children's prog, Computer training, Free DVD rentals, ILL available, Instruction & testing, Internet access, Meeting rooms, Movies, Museum passes, Music CDs, OverDrive digital audio bks, Photocopying/Printing, Prog for adults, Prog for children & young adult, Ref & res, Study rm, Summer reading prog, Teen prog, Wheelchair accessible
Open Mon-Wed 9-8, Thurs-Sat 9-6
Friends of the Library Group
GILLIAM BRANCH, 12797 Main St, Gilliam, 71029, SAN 343-5407. Tel: 318-296-4227. FAX: 318-296-0025. E-mail: publicgilliam@shreve-lib.org. *Br Mgr,* Carrie Nichols-Tucker; E-mail: ctucker@shreve-lib.org; Staff 1 (Non-MLS 1)
Founded 1931. Pop 254,969; Circ 2,528
Library Holdings: Audiobooks 171; AV Mats 2,089; CDs 296; DVDs 1,717; Large Print Bks 71; Bk Titles 4,520; Bk Vols 4,691; Per Subs 42
Function: 24/7 Electronic res, Audiobks via web, Bks on CD, Children's prog, Computers for patron use, Free DVD rentals, ILL available, Internet access, Movies, Music CDs, OverDrive digital audio bks, Photocopying/Printing, Summer reading prog, Wheelchair accessible
Open Mon & Thurs 12-5, Tues 11-5
Friends of the Library Group
HAMILTON/SOUTH CADDO BRANCH, 2111 Bert Kouns Industrial Loop, 71118, SAN 343-5423. Tel: 318-687-6824. FAX: 318-686-0971. E-mail: publichsc@shreve-lib.org. *Br Mgr,* Hanna Hoang; E-mail: hhoang@shreve-lib.org; Staff 1 (Non-MLS 1)
Founded 1961. Pop 254,969; Circ 159,985
Library Holdings: Audiobooks 1,841; AV Mats 9,726; Bks on Deafness & Sign Lang 16; CDs 3,066; DVDs 6,090; Large Print Bks 2,469; Bk Titles 52,177; Bk Vols 55,804; Per Subs 256
Function: 24/7 Electronic res, Adult bk club, Adult literacy prog, Art exhibits, Audiobks on Playaways & MP3, Audiobks via web, AV serv, Bks on CD, Children's prog, Computer training, Computers for patron use, Electronic databases & coll, Free DVD rentals, Holiday prog, ILL available, Internet access, Laminating, Literacy & newcomer serv, Magazines, Magnifiers for reading, Mail & tel request accepted, Meeting rooms, Movies, Music CDs, Outside serv via phone, mail, e-mail & web, Photocopying/Printing, Prog for adults, Prog for children & young adult, Ref & res, Ref serv available, Res libr, Scanner, Study rm, Summer reading prog, Tax forms, Teen prog, VHS videos, Wheelchair accessible
Special Services for the Blind - Audio mat; Bks on cassette; Bks on CD; Large print bks; Large print bks & talking machines; Large screen computer & software; Magnifiers; Screen enlargement software for people with visual disabilities; Talking bks
Open Mon-Thurs 9-9, Fri & Sat 9-6, Sun 1-5
Friends of the Library Group
HIGGINBOTHAM/BRYSON BRANCH, 9359 Greenwood Rd, Greenwood, 71033, SAN 343-5458. Tel: 318-938-1451. FAX: 318-938-5007. E-mail: publichigg@shreve-lib.org. *Br Mgr,* Cathy Key; E-mail: ckey@shreve-lib.org; Staff 1 (Non-MLS 1)
Founded 1930. Pop 254,969; Circ 5,497
Library Holdings: Audiobooks 187; AV Mats 1,767; Bks on Deafness & Sign Lang 1; CDs 315; DVDs 1,370; Large Print Bks 264; Bk Titles 4,858; Bk Vols 4,946; Per Subs 45
Subject Interests: Genealogy, Local hist
Function: 24/7 Electronic res, Adult bk club, Adult literacy prog, Archival coll, Audiobks via web, Bks on CD, Children's prog, Computers for patron use, Electronic databases & coll, ILL available, Internet access, Magazines, Music CDs, Photocopying/Printing, Senior outreach, Summer reading prog, Wheelchair accessible
Open Mon, Fri & Sat 9-1, Tues & Thurs 3-7, Wed 1-5
Friends of the Library Group
HOLLYWOOD/UNION AVENUE, 2105 Hollywood Ave, 71108, SAN 328-8986. Tel: 318-636-5520. FAX: 318-636-5720. E-mail: publichua@shreve-lib.org. *Br Mgr,* Tenisha Edwards; E-mail: tedwards@shreve-lib.org; Staff 1 (Non-MLS 1)
Founded 1965. Pop 254,969; Circ 35,128
Library Holdings: Audiobooks 547; AV Mats 3,195; Bks on Deafness & Sign Lang 7; CDs 1,129; DVDs 1,912; Large Print Bks 1,677; Bk Titles 16,193; Bk Vols 16,987; Per Subs 65; Videos 1
Function: 24/7 Electronic res, Audio & video playback equip for onsite use, Audiobks via web, Bks on CD, Children's prog, Free DVD rentals, Home delivery & serv to seniorr ctr & nursing homes, Homebound delivery serv, ILL available, Internet access, Movies, Music CDs, OverDrive digital audio bks, Photocopying/Printing, Prog for adults, Prog for children & young adult, Study rm, Summer reading prog, Teen prog, VHS videos, Wheelchair accessible
Open Mon-Wed 9-8, Thurs-Sat 9-6
Friends of the Library Group
HOSSTON BRANCH, 15487 US Hwy 71, Hosston, 71043, SAN 343-5482. Tel: 318-287-3265. FAX: 318-287-3324. E-mail: publichosston@shreve-lib.org. *Br Mgr,* Mindi Broussard; E-mail: mbroussard@shreve-lib.org; Staff 1 (Non-MLS 1)
Founded 1931. Pop 254,969; Circ 2,866
Library Holdings: Audiobooks 117; AV Mats 1,922; CDs 259; DVDs 1,591; Large Print Bks 224; Bk Titles 3,557; Bk Vols 3,670; Per Subs 43
Function: 24/7 Electronic res, Audiobks via web, Bks on CD, Children's prog, Computers for patron use, Free DVD rentals, ILL available, Internet access, Magazines, Music CDs, Photocopying/Printing, Summer reading prog, Wheelchair accessible
Open Mon, Wed & Fri 10-5
Friends of the Library Group
MEANS BRANCH, 7016 E Magnolia Lane, Ida, 71044, SAN 343-5547. Tel: 318-284-3416. FAX: 318-284-3274. E-mail: publicmeans@shreve-lib.org. *Br Mgr,* Lois Carter; E-mail: lcarter@shreve-lib.org; Staff 1 (Non-MLS 1)
Founded 1930. Pop 254,969; Circ 4,425
Library Holdings: Audiobooks 50; AV Mats 1,732; CDs 147; DVDs 1,581; Large Print Bks 196; Bk Titles 2,763; Bk Vols 2,881; Per Subs 24
Special Collections: Local Genealogy, Local Cemetery List
Function: 24/7 Electronic res, Art exhibits, Audio & video playback equip for onsite use, Audiobks via web, AV serv, Bks on CD, Children's prog, Computer training, Computers for patron use, Electronic databases & coll, Free DVD rentals, ILL available, Internet access, Life-long learning prog for all ages, Magazines, Meeting rooms, Music CDs,

Outside serv via phone, mail, e-mail & web, OverDrive digital audio bks, Photocopying/Printing, Summer reading prog, Telephone ref, Wheelchair accessible
Open Tues, Wed & Fri 12-5
Friends of the Library Group
MOORETOWN BRANCH, 4360 Hollywood Ave, 71109. Tel: 318-636-5524. FAX: 318-636-6438. E-mail: publicmooretown@shreve-lib.org. *Br Mgr,* Rose Davis; E-mail: rosed@shreve-lib.org; Staff 1 (MLS 1)
Founded 2003. Pop 254,969; Circ 22,422
Library Holdings: Audiobooks 695; AV Mats 5,441; Bks on Deafness & Sign Lang 5; CDs 1,483; DVDs 3,660; Large Print Bks 275; Bk Titles 14,453; Bk Vols 15,187; Per Subs 73
Function: 24/7 Electronic res, Audio & video playback equip for onsite use, Audiobks via web, AV serv, Bks on CD, Children's prog, Computers for patron use, Electronic databases & coll, Free DVD rentals, ILL available, Internet access, Magazines, Meeting rooms, Movies, Music CDs, Photocopying/Printing, Prog for children & young adult, Wheelchair accessible
Open Mon-Wed 9-8, Thurs-Sat 9-6
Friends of the Library Group
MOORINGSPORT BRANCH, 603 Latimer St, Mooringsport, 71060, SAN 343-5571. Tel: 318-996-6720. FAX: 318-996-7900. E-mail: publicmspt@shreve-lib.org. *Br Mgr,* Cynthia Clark; E-mail: cclark@shreve-lib.org; Staff 1 (Non-MLS 1)
Founded 1930. Pop 254,969; Circ 8,302
Library Holdings: Audiobooks 185; AV Mats 2,483; Bks on Deafness & Sign Lang 2; CDs 315; DVDs 2,053; Large Print Bks 167; Bk Titles 6,611; Bk Vols 6,693; Per Subs 71
Function: 24/7 Electronic res, Audiobks via web, Bks on CD, Children's prog, Computers for patron use, Electronic databases & coll, Free DVD rentals, ILL available, Internet access, Magazines, Movies, Music CDs, Photocopying/Printing, Prog for children & young adult, Summer reading prog, Wheelchair accessible
Open Mon-Fri 11-6
Friends of the Library Group
NORTH CADDO BRANCH, 615 N Pine St, Vivian, 71082, SAN 343-5601. Tel: 318-375-3975. FAX: 318-375-4597. E-mail: publicnc@shreve-lib.org. *Br Mgr,* Bernice Bradshaw; E-mail: bbradshaw@shreve-lib.org; Staff 1 (Non-MLS 1)
Founded 1930. Pop 254,969; Circ 32,632
Library Holdings: Audiobooks 997; AV Mats 6,855; Bks on Deafness & Sign Lang 14; CDs 1,932; DVDs 4,691; Large Print Bks 2,989; Bk Titles 30,093; Bk Vols 31,213; Per Subs 205
Special Collections: Louisiana Coll
Function: 24/7 Electronic res, Adult literacy prog, Audio & video playback equip for onsite use, Audiobks on Playaways & MP3, Audiobks via web, AV serv, Bks on CD, Children's prog, Computer training, Computers for patron use, Electronic databases & coll, Family literacy, For res purposes, Free DVD rentals, ILL available, Instruction & testing, Internet access, Learning ctr, Life-long learning prog for all ages, Literacy & newcomer serv, Magazines, Magnifiers for reading, Meeting rooms, Music CDs, Outreach serv, OverDrive digital audio bks, Photocopying/Printing, Preschool reading prog, Prog for adults, Prog for children & young adult, Ref & res, Senior outreach, Study rm, Summer reading prog, VHS videos, Wheelchair accessible
Special Services for the Blind - Magnifiers; Screen enlargement software for people with visual disabilities
Open Mon-Wed 9-8, Thurs-Sat 9-6
Friends of the Library Group
NORTH SHREVEPORT BRANCH, 4844 N Market St, 71107. Tel: 318-674-8172. FAX: 318-674-8175. E-mail: publicns@shreve-lib.org. *Br Mgr,* Position Currently Open
Founded 2003. Pop 254,969; Circ 59,672
Library Holdings: Audiobooks 759; AV Mats 5,594; Bks on Deafness & Sign Lang 16; CDs 1,294; DVDs 3,917; Large Print Bks 1,412; Bk Titles 22,405; Bk Vols 22,894; Per Subs 179
Function: 24/7 Electronic res, Adult literacy prog, Audio & video playback equip for onsite use, Audiobks on Playaways & MP3, Audiobks via web, AV serv, Computer training, Computers for patron use, Electronic databases & coll, Free DVD rentals, ILL available, Instruction & testing, Internet access, Life-long learning prog for all ages, Magazines, Meeting rooms, Movies, Music CDs, Online cat, OverDrive digital audio bks, Photocopying/Printing, Prog for adults, Prog for children & young adult, Ref & res, Summer reading prog, Teen prog, Telephone ref, VHS videos, Wheelchair accessible
Open Mon-Wed 9-8, Thurs-Sat 9-6
Friends of the Library Group
OIL CITY BRANCH, 102 Allen St, Oil City, 71061, SAN 343-5636. Tel: 318-995-7975. FAX: 318-995-0401. E-mail: publicoc@shreve-lib.org. *Br Mgr,* Sherri Baca; E-mail: sbaca@shreve-lib.org; Staff 1 (Non-MLS 1)
Founded 1932. Pop 254,969; Circ 7,492
Library Holdings: Audiobooks 146; AV Mats 2,736; Bks on Deafness & Sign Lang 1; CDs 285; DVDs 2,408; Large Print Bks 495; Bk Titles 5,197; Bk Vols 5,334; Per Subs 43
Special Collections: Old School Yearbooks(Oil City & Vivian); Older Large Print Romances
Function: 24/7 Electronic res, Audiobks on Playaways & MP3, Audiobks via web, AV serv, Bks on CD, Children's prog, Computers for patron use, Electronic databases & coll, Free DVD rentals, ILL available, Instruction & testing, Internet access, Magazines, Meeting rooms, Movies, Music CDs, Photocopying/Printing, Prog for adults, Prog for children & young adult, Summer reading prog, Teen prog, VHS videos, Wheelchair accessible
Open Mon, Tues & Thurs 11-6
Friends of the Library Group
DAVID RAINES BRANCH, 2855 Martin Luther King Jr Dr, 71107, SAN 343-5660. Tel: 318-222-0824. FAX: 318-222-9154. E-mail: publicraines@shreve-lib.org. *Br Mgr,* Sharon Samuel-Wade; E-mail: swade@shreve-lib.org; Staff 1 (MLS 1)
Founded 1972. Pop 254,969; Circ 26,937
Library Holdings: Audiobooks 496; AV Mats 4,894; Bks on Deafness & Sign Lang 8; CDs 1,108; DVDs 3,531; Large Print Bks 830; Bk Titles 14,907; Bk Vols 16,394; Per Subs 142
Function: 24/7 Electronic res, Audiobks on Playaways & MP3, Audiobks via web, AV serv, Bks on CD, Computer training, Computers for patron use, Electronic databases & coll, Free DVD rentals, ILL available, Internet access, Magazines, Meeting rooms, Movies, Music CDs, Online cat, Outside serv via phone, mail, e-mail & web, OverDrive digital audio bks, Photocopying/Printing, Prog for adults, Prog for children & young adult, Ref & res, Study rm, Summer reading prog, VHS videos, Wheelchair accessible
Open Mon-Wed 9-8, Thurs-Sat 9-6
Friends of the Library Group
RODESSA BRANCH, 10093 Main St, Rodessa, 71069, SAN 343-5695. Tel: 318-223-4336. FAX: 318-223-4298. E-mail: publicrodessa@shreve-lib.org. *Br Mgr,* Laura Carroll; E-mail: lcarroll@shreve-lib.org; Staff 1 (Non-MLS 1)
Founded 1936. Pop 254,969; Circ 5,400
Library Holdings: Audiobooks 102; AV Mats 1,947; CDs 242; DVDs 1,643; Large Print Bks 50; Bk Titles 4,221; Bk Vols 4,331; Per Subs 57
Function: 24/7 Electronic res, Audiobks on Playaways & MP3, Audiobks via web, Bks on CD, Computers for patron use, Electronic databases & coll, Free DVD rentals, ILL available, Instruction & testing, Internet access, Magazines, Movies, Music CDs, OverDrive digital audio bks, Photocopying/Printing, Prog for adults, Prog for children & young adult, Summer reading prog, VHS videos, Wheelchair accessible
Open Mon-Thurs 11-5
Friends of the Library Group
WALLETTE BRANCH, 363 Hearne Ave, 71103, SAN 343-5512. Tel: 318-425-3630. FAX: 318-226-8311. E-mail: publicwallette@shreve-lib.org. *Br Mgr,* Wyolanda Hall; E-mail: whall@shreve-lib.org; Staff 1 (Non-MLS 1)
Founded 1951. Pop 254,969; Circ 20,564
Library Holdings: Audiobooks 617; AV Mats 5,224; Bks on Deafness & Sign Lang 21; CDs 1,353; DVDs 3,648; Large Print Bks 959; Bk Titles 18,283; Bk Vols 19,764; Per Subs 185
Special Collections: State Library Database; Community Resource Directory; Literacy programs with Bossier Parish Community College
Function: 24/7 Electronic res, Adult literacy prog, Audiobks on Playaways & MP3, Audiobks via web, AV serv, Bks on CD, Children's prog, Computer training, Computers for patron use, Electronic databases & coll, Family literacy, Free DVD rentals, ILL available, Instruction & testing, Internet access, Literacy & newcomer serv, Magazines, Music CDs, Photocopying/Printing, Preschool reading prog, Prog for adults, Prog for children & young adult, Ref & res, Scanner, Senior computer classes, Study rm, Summer reading prog, Teen prog, VHS videos, Wheelchair accessible
Open Mon-Wed 9-9, Thurs-Sat 9-6
Friends of the Library Group
WEST SHREVEPORT BRANCH, 4380 Pines Rd, 71119, SAN 370-4491. Tel: 318-635-0883. FAX: 318-621-1056. E-mail: publicws@shreve-lib.org. *Br Mgr,* Jennifer Fleming; E-mail: jfleming@shreve-lib.org; Staff 1 (Non-MLS 1)
Founded 1989. Pop 254,969; Circ 20,564
Library Holdings: Audiobooks 1,127; AV Mats 7,775; Bks on Deafness & Sign Lang 16; CDs 2,239; DVDs 5,251; Large Print Bks 3,080; Bk Titles 33,065; Bk Vols 34,092; Per Subs 164
Function: 24/7 Electronic res, Adult literacy prog, Audio & video playback equip for onsite use, Audiobks via web, AV serv, Bks on CD, Children's prog, Computer training, Computers for patron use, Electronic databases & coll, Free DVD rentals, ILL available, Internet access, Life-long learning prog for all ages, Magazines, Meeting rooms, Music CDs, OverDrive digital audio bks, Photocopying/Printing, Prog for children & young adult, Study rm, Summer reading prog, VHS videos, Wheelchair accessible
Open Mon-Wed 9-9, Thurs-Sat 9-6
Friends of the Library Group
Bookmobiles: 2

J SOUTHERN UNIVERSITY AT SHREVEPORT*, Shreveport Campus Library, 3050 Martin Luther King Jr Dr, 71107. SAN 306-5480. Tel: 318-670-6392. FAX: 318-674-3403. Web Site: www.susla.edu/university-library. *Libr Dir,* Jane O'Riley; Tel: 318-670-9401, E-mail: joriley@susla.edu; *Libr Spec II,* Tawana Henderson; E-mail: thenderson@susla.edu; *Cataloger,* Rose M Powell; E-mail: rmpowell@susla.edu; Staff 9 (MLS 3, Non-MLS 6)
Founded 1967. Enrl 2,538; Fac 168
Library Holdings: e-books 11,079; Bk Titles 36,140; Bk Vols 51,421; Per Subs 240
Special Collections: Black Studies, bks, pictures; Louisiana Coll
Subject Interests: Ethnic studies, Natural sci
Automation Activity & Vendor Info: (Cataloging) SirsiDynix; (Circulation) SirsiDynix; (OPAC) SirsiDynix; (Serials) EBSCO Online
Wireless access
Partic in Louisiana Library Network
Open Mon-Thurs 8-9, Fri 8-Noon, Sat 9-1

L UNITED STATES COURTS LIBRARY*, 300 Fannin St, Rm 5012, 71101-6305. SAN 372-0934. Tel: 318-676-3230. FAX: 318-934-4866. E-mail: 5satlib-Shreveport@ca5.uscourts.gov. Web Site: www.lb5.uscourts.gov/Directory/?Shreveport. *Librn,* Marian Drey; Staff 1 (MLS 1)
Founded 1989
Library Holdings: Bk Vols 10,000; Per Subs 40
Automation Activity & Vendor Info: (OPAC) SirsiDynix
Open Mon-Fri 9-5

SUNSET

P SOUTH ST LANDRY COMMUNITY LIBRARY*, 235 Marie St, 70584. SAN 373-7659. Tel: 337-662-3442. FAX: 337-662-3475. Web Site: www.southstlandrylibrary.com. *Dir,* Barbara A Malbrue; E-mail: bmalbrue2@pelican.state.lib.la.us; Staff 7 (Non-MLS 7)
Founded 1989. Pop 8,500
Library Holdings: Bks on Deafness & Sign Lang 54; CDs 144; DVDs 350; Large Print Bks 150; Bk Vols 31,672; Per Subs 65; Talking Bks 163; Videos 1,569
Special Collections: The Louisiana Coll
Automation Activity & Vendor Info: (Acquisitions) Book Systems; (Cataloging) Book Systems; (Circulation) Book Systems; (OPAC) Book Systems
Function: CD-ROM, ILL available, Music CDs, Photocopying/Printing, Prog for adults, Prog for children & young adult, Summer reading prog, VHS videos, Workshops
Publications: Library Log (Quarterly)
Partic in Loan System Helping Automate Retrieval of Knowledge
Open Tues 10-8, Wed-Fri 10-6, Sat 10-4
Friends of the Library Group

TALLULAH

P MADISON PARISH LIBRARY*, 403 N Mulberry St, 71282. SAN 343-575X. Tel: 318-574-4308. FAX: 318-574-4312. E-mail: admin.t1md@pelican.state.lib.la.us. *Dir,* Kizzy Bynum; E-mail: bynumkim@yahoo.com; Staff 4 (MLS 1, Non-MLS 3)
Founded 1945. Pop 12,930; Circ 19,625
Library Holdings: Bk Titles 26,800; Bk Vols 28,000; Per Subs 80
Subject Interests: Art & archit, Econ, Hort, Music, Relig, World War II
Automation Activity & Vendor Info: (Cataloging) Book Systems; (Circulation) Book Systems; (OPAC) Book Systems
Mem of Trail Blazer Library System
Partic in Loan System Helping Automate Retrieval of Knowledge
Open Mon 11:30-8, Tues-Fri 8:30-5:30, Sat 8:30-12:30

THIBODAUX

P LAFOURCHE PARISH PUBLIC LIBRARY, 314 Saint Mary St, 70301. SAN 343-5814. Tel: 985-446-1163. FAX: 985-446-3848. E-mail: headquarters@lafourche.org. Web Site: www.lafourche.org. *Dir,* Laura Sanders; E-mail: lsanders@lafourche.org; Staff 51 (MLS 3, Non-MLS 48)
Founded 1947. Pop 92,157; Circ 338,480
Library Holdings: Bk Titles 124,220; Bk Vols 234,403; Per Subs 400
Subject Interests: Genealogy, La
Automation Activity & Vendor Info: (Acquisitions) TLC (The Library Corporation); (Cataloging) TLC (The Library Corporation); (Circulation) TLC (The Library Corporation); (ILL) TLC (The Library Corporation); (OPAC) TLC (The Library Corporation); (Serials) TLC (The Library Corporation)
Wireless access
Partic in Loan System Helping Automate Retrieval of Knowledge
Open Mon-Fri 9-4:30
Friends of the Library Group
Branches: 10
BAYOU BLUE BRANCH, 198 Mazerac St, Houma, 70364. Tel: 985-580-0634. FAX: 985-580-9640. E-mail: bayoublue@lafourche.org. *Br Mgr,* Tangella Bergeron
Open Mon-Thurs 8:30-5:30
CHOCTAW BRANCH, 1887 Choctaw Rd, 70301. Tel: 985-633-6453. FAX: 985-633-8873. E-mail: choctaw@lafourche.org. *Br Mgr,* Luticia Cortez
Library Holdings: Bk Titles 12,000
Open Mon-Thurs 8:30-5:30
GHEENS BRANCH, 153 N Leon Dr, Gheens, 70355. Tel: 985-532-2288. FAX: 985-532-2288. E-mail: gheens@lafourche.org. *Br Mgr,* Jessica Cassell
Library Holdings: Bk Titles 9,000
Open Mon & Wed 10-6, Tues & Thurs 2-6
GOLDEN MEADOW BRANCH BIBLIOTECA HISPANA BRANCH, 1403 N Bayou Dr, Golden Meadow, 70357-2513, SAN 343-5903. Tel: 985-475-5660. FAX: 985-475-4517. E-mail: GoldenMeadow@lafourche.org. *Br Librn,* Katina Gaudet; Staff 2 (Non-MLS 2)
Pop 18,200; Circ 226,953
Library Holdings: Bk Titles 19,776; Per Subs 43
Open Mon-Thurs 8:30-5:30
Friends of the Library Group
LAROSE BRANCH, 305 E Fifth St, Larose, 70373, SAN 343-5938. Tel: 985-693-3336. FAX: 985-693-3978. E-mail: larose@lafourche.org. *Br Mgr,* Sally Guidroz; Staff 4 (Non-MLS 4)
Founded 1947. Pop 9,000
Library Holdings: Bk Titles 20,199; Per Subs 50
Function: Accelerated reader prog, After school storytime, Art exhibits, Children's prog, Computer training, Computers for patron use, Free DVD rentals, Holiday prog, Home delivery & serv to seniorr ctr & nursing homes, Music CDs, Photocopying/Printing, Preschool outreach, Prog for adults, Prog for children & young adult, Story hour, Summer reading prog, Teen prog, VHS videos
Open Mon-Thurs 8:30-5:30
Friends of the Library Group
LOCKPORT BRANCH, 720 Crescent Ave, Lockport, 70374, SAN 343-5997. Tel: 985-532-3158. FAX: 985-532-0270. E-mail: lockport@lafourche.org. *Br Mgr,* Brenda Bascle; Staff 6 (Non-MLS 6)
Library Holdings: Bk Titles 21,859; Per Subs 49
Open Mon-Thurs 9-7, Fri & Sat 9-1
Friends of the Library Group
RACELAND BRANCH, 177 Recreation Dr, Raceland, 70394-2915, SAN 343-6020. Tel: 985-537-6875. FAX: 985-537-2292. E-mail: raceland@lafourche.org. *Supvr,* Meryl Foret; Staff 3 (Non-MLS 3)
Library Holdings: Bk Titles 21,804; Per Subs 53
Open Mon-Thurs 8:30-5:30
Friends of the Library Group
SOUTH LAFOURCHE PUBLIC LIBRARY, 16241 East Main St, CutOff, 70345, SAN 343-5873. Tel: 985-632-7140. FAX: 985-632-4963. E-mail: southlafourche@lafurche.org. *Br Mgr,* Tammi Blanchard; Staff 7 (Non-MLS 7)
Library Holdings: Bk Titles 31,250; Per Subs 50
Subject Interests: Genealogy, La
Open Mon-Thurs 9-7, Fri & Sat 9-1
Friends of the Library Group
THIBODAUX BRANCH, 705 W Fifth St, 70301. Tel: 985-447-4119. FAX: 985-449-4128. E-mail: thibodaux@lafourche.org. *Br Mgr,* Sandra Lirette
Function: 3D Printer, Computers for patron use, Microfiche/film & reading machines, Photocopying/Printing, Scanner
Open Mon-Thurs 9-7, Fri & Sat 9-1
MARTHA SOWELL UTLEY MEMORIAL (ADMINISTRATIVE OFFICE), 314 St Mary St, 70301-2620, SAN 343-6055. Tel: 985-447-4119. FAX: 985-449-4128. *Br Mgr,* Patricia Boatman; Staff 14 (MLS 7, Non-MLS 7)
Library Holdings: Bk Titles 46,670; Per Subs 145
Subject Interests: Genealogy, La
Open Mon-Fri 9-4:30
Friends of the Library Group

C NICHOLLS STATE UNIVERSITY*, Allen J Ellender Memorial Library, 906 E First St, 70310. (Mail add: PO Box 2028, 70310), SAN 306-5529. Tel: 985-448-4646, 985-448-4660. Interlibrary Loan Service Tel: 985-448-4654. Reference Tel: 985-448-4625. FAX: 985-448-4925. Web Site: www.nicholls.edu/library. *Head, Archives, Interim Dir,* Clifton Theriot; Tel: 985-448-4621, E-mail: clifton.theriot@nicholls.edu; *Head, Access Serv,* Van P Viator; E-mail: van.viator@nicholls.edu; *Head, Govt Info,* Hayley Johnson; E-mail: hayley.johnson@nicholls.edu; *Head, Tech Serv,* Michael Arseneau; E-mail: michael.arseneau@nicholls.edu; Staff 29 (MLS 10, Non-MLS 19)
Founded 1948. Enrl 7,345; Fac 301; Highest Degree: Master
Library Holdings: Bk Titles 301,477; Bk Vols 532,948; Per Subs 1,650

Special Collections: Cajun & Zydeco Music Heritage; Center for Traditional Louisiana Boat Building; Local History (Historic Thibodaux & Historic Lafourche Parish); Sugar Cane Plantations (J Wilson Lepine Coll & Laurel Valley Coll), diaries, ms; United States Senators' Papers (Allen J Ellender Archives). State Document Depository; US Document Depository
Subject Interests: Agr, Bus & mgt, Culinary arts, Econ, Educ, Marine biol, Nursing
Automation Activity & Vendor Info: (Acquisitions) SirsiDynix; (Cataloging) SirsiDynix; (Circulation) SirsiDynix; (OPAC) SirsiDynix; (Serials) SirsiDynix
Wireless access
Partic in La Acad Libr Info Network Consortium
Open Mon-Thurs 7:30am-11pm, Fri 7:30-4:30, Sun 3pm-11pm

VILLE PLATTE

P EVANGELINE PARISH LIBRARY*, 916 W Main St, 70586. SAN 306-5537. Tel: 337-363-1369. FAX: 337-363-2353. Web Site: evangelinelibrary.org. *Interim Libr Dir,* Yvonne Lavergne; E-mail: ylavergne@evangelinelibrary.org; Staff 12 (MLS 2, Non-MLS 10)
Founded 1948. Pop 33,274; Circ 131,715
Library Holdings: AV Mats 3,979; Bk Vols 64,871; Per Subs 655
Special Collections: Louisiana, Cajuns & Cajun Music Coll
Subject Interests: Genealogy
Automation Activity & Vendor Info: (Cataloging) Innovative Interfaces, Inc; (Circulation) Innovative Interfaces, Inc; (OPAC) Innovative Interfaces, Inc
Wireless access
Partic in Libraries SouthWest; Loan System Helping Automate Retrieval of Knowledge
Open Mon, Thurs & Fri 8-6, Tues 8-8, Wed 10-6, Sat 8-Noon
Friends of the Library Group
Branches: 5
BASILE BRANCH, 3036 Stagg Ave, Basile, 70515. (Mail add: PO Box 369, Basile, 70515). Tel: 337-432-6794. FAX: 337-432-6794. *Br Mgr,* Sherry Bergeron; Staff 2 (Non-MLS 2)
Library Holdings: Bk Titles 3,000; Per Subs 22
Open Mon-Fri 8-5
CHATAIGNIER BRANCH, 111 N First St, Chataignier, 70524. Tel: 337-885-2028. *Br Mgr,* Emily Fontenot; Staff 1 (Non-MLS 1)
Founded 1995
Library Holdings: AV Mats 50; Bk Titles 2,936; Bk Vols 2,949; Per Subs 44
Open Tues & Thurs 9-5, Wed 10-5
Friends of the Library Group
FATHER LESLIE T H PRESCOTT BRANCH, 111 Walnut St, Pine Prairie, 70576. (Mail add: PO Box 680, Pine Prairie, 70576-0680). Tel: 337-599-3179. FAX: 337-599-3188. *Br Mgr,* Angie Henry; Staff 2 (Non-MLS 2)
Founded 2000
Open Mon-Fri 8-5
Friends of the Library Group
MAMOU BRANCH, 317 Second St, Ste A, Mamou, 70554. Tel: 337-468-5750. FAX: 337-468-5750. *Br Mgr,* Gigi Fontenot; Staff 1 (Non-MLS 1)
Founded 1976
Library Holdings: Bk Titles 5,000; Per Subs 33
Open Mon-Fri 8-5
Friends of the Library Group
TURKEY CREEK, 13951 Veterans Memorial Hwy, Turkey Creek, 70586. Tel: 337-461-2304. FAX: 337-461-2304. *Br Mgr,* Tina King; *Asst Br Mgr,* Ruth Stanley
Founded 2005
Library Holdings: Bk Vols 3,000
Open Wed 10-5, Thurs 8-5

WASHINGTON

P WASHINGTON MUNICIPAL LIBRARY*, 418 N Main St, 70589. (Mail add: PO Box 249, 70589-0249). Tel: 337-826-7336. FAX: 337-826-7521. Web Site: townofwashington.la/washington-library. *Dir,* Delilah Jackson; E-mail: delimore@bellsouth.net
Library Holdings: Bk Vols 8,051
Automation Activity & Vendor Info: (Cataloging) Book Systems; (Circulation) Book Systems
Partic in Loan System Helping Automate Retrieval of Knowledge
Open Tues & Wed 10-6, Thurs 9-5, Fri & Sat 9-1

WINNFIELD

P WINN PARISH LIBRARY*, 200 N St John St, 71483-2718. SAN 343-608X. Tel: 318-628-4478. FAX: 318-628-9820. Web Site: www.winn.lib.la.us. *Libr Dir,* Mona Bamburg; E-mail: mbamburg@state.lib.la.us; Staff 10 (Non-MLS 10)
Founded 1937. Pop 16,397; Circ 101,995
Library Holdings: AV Mats 460; Bk Vols 98,000; Per Subs 250
Subject Interests: Genealogy, La
Automation Activity & Vendor Info: (Acquisitions) Auto-Graphics, Inc; (Cataloging) Auto-Graphics, Inc; (Circulation) Auto-Graphics, Inc; (ILL) Auto-Graphics, Inc; (OPAC) Auto-Graphics, Inc
Wireless access
Partic in Loan System Helping Automate Retrieval of Knowledge
Special Services for the Blind - Large screen computer & software
Open Mon-Fri 8:30-5:30, Sat 8:30-12:30
Friends of the Library Group
Branches: 4
ATLANTA BRANCH, 110 School Rd, Atlanta, 71404. (Mail add: PO Box 231, Atlanta, 71404-0231), SAN 343-611X. Tel: 318-628-7657. *Br Mgr,* Carolyn Washington; Staff 1 (Non-MLS 1)
Library Holdings: AV Mats 40; Bk Vols 3,200; Per Subs 10
Open Mon-Thurs 9-4
CALVIN BRANCH, 255 Second St, Calvin, 71410. (Mail add: PO Box 150, Calvin, 71410-0150), SAN 343-6144. Tel: 318-727-9644. FAX: 318-727-9644. *Br Mgr,* Jan Collins; Staff 1 (Non-MLS 1)
Library Holdings: AV Mats 30; Bk Vols 3,600; Per Subs 10
DODSON BRANCH, 206 E Gresham, Dodson, 71422, SAN 343-6179. Tel: 318-628-2821. *Br Mgr,* Tonya LeBaron; Staff 1 (Non-MLS 1)
Library Holdings: AV Mats 45; Bk Vols 3,600; Per Subs 10
Open Mon-Thurs 8-4
SIKES BRANCH, 125 Fifth St, Sikes, 71473-0125. (Mail add: PO Box 60, Sikes, 71473-0060), SAN 343-6209. Tel: 318-628-2824. *Br Mgr,* Angella Wilson; Staff 1 (Non-MLS 1)
Library Holdings: AV Mats 30; Bk Vols 3,600; Per Subs 12
Open Mon, Wed & Thurs 9-4

WINNSBORO

P FRANKLIN PARISH LIBRARY, 705 Prairie St, 71295. SAN 343-6233. Tel: 318-435-4336. FAX: 318-435-1990. Web Site: www.franklinparishlibrary.org. *Libr Dir,* Onie Parker; E-mail: onie@franklinparishlibrary.org; Staff 6 (MLS 1, Non-MLS 5)
Founded 1950. Pop 22,387; Circ 74,046
Library Holdings: AV Mats 3,000; Bk Vols 80,000; Per Subs 87
Special Collections: Louisiana Coll
Automation Activity & Vendor Info: (Cataloging) Innovative Interfaces, Inc; (Circulation) Innovative Interfaces, Inc; (OPAC) Innovative Interfaces, Inc
Wireless access
Mem of Trail Blazer Library System
Partic in Loan System Helping Automate Retrieval of Knowledge
Open Mon-Fri 8:30-5:30, Sat 8-12:30
Friends of the Library Group
Branches: 1
WISNER BRANCH, 129 Fort Scott St, Wisner, 71378. (Mail add: PO Box 260, Wisner, 71378-0260), SAN 343-6268. Tel: 318-724-7399. FAX: 318-724-7399. *Br Mgr,* Jan Roberts; Staff 2 (Non-MLS 2)
Library Holdings: AV Mats 88; Bk Vols 10,010; Per Subs 52
Open Tues & Thurs 8-12:30 & 1:30-5

MAINE

Date of Statistics: FY 2020
Population, 2020 U.S. Census: 1,362,359
Population Served by Public Libraries Reporting: 1,318,844
Total Volumes in Public Libraries Reporting: 6,101,463
Volumes Per Capita: 4.63
Total Public Library Circulation: 6,073,640
Circulation Per Capita: 4.61
Digital Resources:
Total e-books: 4,997,220
Total audio items (physical and downloadable units): 2,994,109
Total video items (physical and downloadable units): 878,905
Total computers for use by the public: 1,924
Total computer use: 360,860
Total annual wireless sessions: 801,784
Income and Expenditures:
Total Public Library Expenditures: $51,381,003
Expenditures Per Capita: $38.96
Number of Regional Districts: 1
Information provided courtesy of: Jenny Melvin, State Data Coordinator ; Maine State Library.

ACTON

P ACTON PUBLIC LIBRARY*, 35 H Rd, 04001. SAN 306-5545. Tel: 207-636-2781. E-mail: actonpublib@gmail.com. Web Site: acton.lib.me.us. *Dir,* Elise Miller
Founded 1920. Pop 2,400; Circ 3,000
Library Holdings: Audiobooks 164; CDs 50; DVDs 436; Large Print Bks 146; Bk Vols 7,115; Per Subs 5
Wireless access
Mem of Maine State Library, Region 1
Open Tues 11-4, Wed & Fri 9-2, Thurs 4-7, Sat 9-Noon
Friends of the Library Group

ALBION

P ALBION PUBLIC LIBRARY*, 18 Main St, 04910. (Mail add: PO Box 355, 04910-0355), SAN 376-3803. Tel: 207-437-2220. E-mail: albion@albion.lib.me.us. *Librn,* Martha M Doore
Pop 8,000
Library Holdings: AV Mats 260; Bk Vols 10,450
Automation Activity & Vendor Info: (Cataloging) Book Systems; (Circulation) Book Systems; (OPAC) Book Systems
Wireless access
Open Mon & Thurs 2-8, Wed & Sat 9-11
Friends of the Library Group

ALFRED

P PARSONS MEMORIAL LIBRARY, 27 Saco Rd, 04002. SAN 306-5561. Tel: 207-324-2001. E-mail: alflib@roadrunner.com. Web Site: parsonsmemoriallibrary.com, www.alfredme.gov/about_alfred/parsons_memorial_library.php. *Libr Dir,* Isabel Turk; E-mail: iturk@alfredme.gov; *Ch,* Caley Mackenzie; E-mail: cmackenzie@alfredme.gov; Staff 1 (Non-MLS 1)
Pop 1,850; Circ 5,417
Library Holdings: Bk Vols 24,000; Per Subs 25
Wireless access
Mem of Maine State Library, Region 1
Open Mon & Wed 11-6, Tues 10-4, Sat 10-3
Friends of the Library Group

ANDOVER

P ANDOVER PUBLIC LIBRARY, 46 Church St, 04216. (Mail add: PO Box 393, 04216-0393), SAN 306-557X. Tel: 207-392-4841. E-mail: andover@andover.lib.me.us. Web Site: www.andover.lib.me.us. *Dir,* Janet Farrington; E-mail: janetf@andover.lib.me.us; Staff 1 (Non-MLS 1)
Pop 971; Circ 7,014
Library Holdings: Bk Vols 11,000; Per Subs 24
Automation Activity & Vendor Info: (Cataloging) Readerware
Wireless access
Open Tues, Wed & Sat 1-4:30, Thurs 1-4:30 & 6-8

APPLETON

P MILDRED STEVENS WILLIAMS MEMORIAL LIBRARY*, Appleton Library, 2916 Sennebec Rd, 04862. SAN 306-5588. Tel: 207-785-5656. Web Site: www.appletonlibraryme.org. *Libr Coord,* Julie Sells; E-mail: appletonlibraryjulie@gmail.com; Staff 1 (Non-MLS 1)
Founded 1946. Pop 1,316; Circ 1,000
Library Holdings: Bk Vols 6,500
Special Collections: Maine Coll
Wireless access
Function: Prog for children & young adult
Open Tues 12-8, Wed 3-6, Thurs 10-3 & 6-8, Sat 10-1
Friends of the Library Group

ASHLAND

P ASHLAND COMMUNITY LIBRARY*, 57 Exchange St, 04732. (Mail add: PO Box 639, 04732-0639), SAN 306-5596. Tel: 207-435-6532. Web Site: townofashland.org/departments/library. *Librn,* Cynthia Morton; E-mail: cmorton@ashland.lib.me.us; Staff 1 (Non-MLS 1)
Founded 1960. Pop 2,248; Circ 9,561
Library Holdings: DVDs 800; Large Print Bks 100; Bk Vols 2,354
Special Collections: Aroostook. Oral History
Wireless access
Function: Computers for patron use, Free DVD rentals, Internet access, Laminating, Magazines, Meeting rooms, Photocopying/Printing, Tax forms, Wheelchair accessible
Open Mon, Wed & Fri 9-6

AUBURN

S ANDROSCOGGIN HISTORICAL SOCIETY*, Clarence E March Library, Two Turner St, Unit 8, 04210-5978. SAN 306-5618. Tel: 207-784-0586. E-mail: info@androhist.org. Web Site: www.androhist.org, www.rootsweb.ancestry.com/~meandrhs. *Pres,* Elizabeth Young; *Library Contact,* David Colby Young
Founded 1923
Library Holdings: Bk Vols 3,900; Per Subs 15; Spec Interest Per Sub 15
Special Collections: Historical Diaries & Photographs (Local Coll); Local Maps; Local Vital & Church Record Coll
Subject Interests: Genealogy, Local hist
Function: Archival coll, For res purposes, Photocopying/Printing, Ref serv available, Res libr, Telephone ref
Publications: Androscoggin History (Newsletter)
Open Wed & Thurs 1-4:30, Fri 1-4
Restriction: Not a lending libr, Open to pub for ref only, Open to pub with supv only, Pub use on premises
Friends of the Library Group

P AUBURN PUBLIC LIBRARY*, 49 Spring St, 04210. SAN 306-5626. Tel: 207-333-6640. FAX: 207-333-6644. E-mail: email@auburnpubliclibrary.org. Web Site: www.auburnpubliclibrary.org,

www.libraryla.org. *Dir,* Mamie Anthoine Ney; Tel: 207-333-6640, Ext 2020, E-mail: mmaney@auburnpubliclibrary.org; *Asst Dir, Head, Coll Serv,* Suzanne Sullivan; *Head, Children's Servx,* Debbie Cleveland; *Head, Ref & Adult Serv,* Martin Gagnon; *Ref & Teen Librn,* Donna Wallace; *Info Syst Coordr,* Brian Usher; *Libr Develop Coordr,* Susuan Raymond Geismar. Subject Specialists: *Develop, Grant writing,* Susuan Raymond Geismar; Staff 24 (MLS 3, Non-MLS 21)
Founded 1890. Pop 25,591; Circ 233,036
Jul 2017-Jun 2018 Income $1,200,000
Library Holdings: Audiobooks 2,886; CDs 1,922; DVDs 2,446; Bk Vols 72,113; Per Subs 150
Subject Interests: Genealogy, Local hist
Automation Activity & Vendor Info: (Acquisitions) Baker & Taylor; (Cataloging) Innovative Interfaces, Inc - Sierra; (Circulation) Innovative Interfaces, Inc - Sierra; (Discovery) Innovative Interfaces, Inc - Sierra; (ILL) Innovative Interfaces, Inc - Sierra; (OPAC) Innovative Interfaces, Inc - Sierra
Wireless access
Function: 24/7 Electronic res, 24/7 Online cat, 3D Printer, Activity rm, Adult bk club, Art exhibits, Art programs, Audio & video playback equip for onsite use, Audiobks on Playaways & MP3, Audiobks via web, Bk club(s), Bks on cassette, Bks on CD, Bus archives, Butterfly Garden, Children's prog, Computer training, Computers for patron use, E-Readers, Electronic databases & coll, Family literacy, For res purposes, Games & aids for people with disabilities, Holiday prog, Home delivery & serv to seniorr ctr & nursing homes, Homework prog, ILL available, Instruction & testing, Internet access, Large print keyboards, Life-long learning prog for all ages, Literacy & newcomer serv, Magazines, Magnifiers for reading, Mail & tel request accepted, Makerspace, Mango lang, Meeting rooms, Microfiche/film & reading machines, Movies, Museum passes, Music CDs, Online cat, Online info literacy tutorials on the web & in blackboard, Orientations, Outreach serv, OverDrive digital audio bks, Photocopying/Printing, Preschool outreach, Preschool reading prog, Printer for laptops & handheld devices, Prof lending libr, Prog for adults, Prog for children & young adult, Ref & res, Ref serv available, Res assist avail, Res performed for a fee, Scanner, Senior computer classes, Senior outreach, Serves people with intellectual disabilities, Spoken cassettes & CDs, STEM programs, Story hour, Study rm, Summer & winter reading prog, Summer reading prog, Tax forms, Teen prog, Telephone ref, VHS videos, Visual arts prog, Wheelchair accessible, Winter reading prog, Workshops, Writing prog
Publications: News from the Auburn Public Library (Newsletter)
Special Services for the Blind - Accessible computers; Aids for in-house use; Assistive/Adapted tech devices, equip & products
Open Mon & Thurs 9-8, Tues, Wed & Fri 9-6, Sat 9-5; Mon (Summer) 9-8, Tues-Fri 9-6, Sat 9-1

CM CENTRAL MAINE COMMUNITY COLLEGE LIBRARY*, Jalbert Hall, Main Flr, 1250 Turner St, 04210. SAN 377-9785. Tel: 207-755-5218. Interlibrary Loan Service Tel: 207-755-5335. FAX: 207-755-5494. E-mail: reference@cmcc.edu. Web Site: www.cmcc.edu/library. *Dir, Learning Commons,* Judith Moreno; Tel: 207-755-5266, E-mail: jmoreno@cmcc.edu; *Pub Serv Librn,* Judi H Moreno; Tel: 207-755-5265, E-mail: jmoreno@cmcc.edu; Staff 3 (MLS 2, Non-MLS 1)
Library Holdings: e-books 300; Bk Vols 14,100; Per Subs 130
Automation Activity & Vendor Info: (Acquisitions) Innovative Interfaces, Inc; (Cataloging) Innovative Interfaces, Inc; (Circulation) Innovative Interfaces, Inc; (Course Reserve) Innovative Interfaces, Inc; (ILL) OCLC FirstSearch; (OPAC) Innovative Interfaces, Inc; (Serials) Innovative Interfaces, Inc
Wireless access
Partic in LYRASIS; Maine Health Sci Librs & Info Consortium
Open Mon-Thurs (Summer) 8-6, Fri 8-4:30; Mon-Thurs (Fall & Spring) 8-7, Fri 8-4:30

AUGUSTA

GM DEPARTMENT OF VETERANS AFFAIRS*, Learning Resources Center, Togus VA Medical Ctr, One VA Center, 04330. SAN 306-5758. Tel: 207-623-5279. FAX: 207-623-5766. *Librn,* Christine Fleuriel; Staff 1 (MLS 1)
Founded 1943
Library Holdings: Bk Vols 1,300; Per Subs 200
Subject Interests: Health sci
Automation Activity & Vendor Info: (Acquisitions) CyberTools for Libraries; (Cataloging) CyberTools for Libraries; (Circulation) CyberTools for Libraries; (OPAC) CyberTools for Libraries; (Serials) CyberTools for Libraries
Partic in Health Sci Libr & Info Coop
Open Mon-Fri 7:30-4

P LITHGOW PUBLIC LIBRARY, 45 Winthrop St, 04330-5599. SAN 306-5669. Tel: 207-626-2415. Web Site: www.lithgowlibrary.org. *Dir,* Sarah Schultz-Nielsen; E-mail: sarah@lithgowlibrary.org; *Syst Librn,* Chris Gibson; E-mail: chris.gibson@lithgowlibrary.org; Staff 4 (MLS 4)
Founded 1896. Pop 19,136; Circ 173,440
Jul 2014-Jun 2015 Income $661,121, City $647,121, Other $14,000. Mats Exp $62,200, Books $48,000, AV Mat $14,200. Sal $454,928
Library Holdings: Audiobooks 3,181; DVDs 3,139; e-books 2,241; Electronic Media & Resources 63; Bk Vols 58,756; Per Subs 105
Automation Activity & Vendor Info: (Cataloging) Innovative Interfaces, Inc; (Circulation) Innovative Interfaces, Inc; (OPAC) Innovative Interfaces, Inc
Wireless access
Partic in Maine InfoNet
Open Mon-Thurs 9-8, Fri 9-5, Sat 9-12
Friends of the Library Group

S MAINE DEPARTMENT OF TRANSPORTATION LIBRARY, Transportation Headquarters Bldg, 1st Flr, 24 Child St, 04330. (Mail add: 16 State House Sta, 04333-0016). Tel: 207-624-3000, 207-624-3230. FAX: 207-624-3221. E-mail: maine.dot@maine.gov. Web Site: www.maine.gov/mdot/library, www.maine.gov/msl/libs/directories/displaysp.shtml?id=45929. *Pub Info Officer,* Paul Merrill; E-mail: paul.merrill@maine.gov; Staff 1 (MLS 1)
Library Holdings: CDs 200; DVDs 10; Bk Vols 12,000; Per Subs 60; Videos 340
Subject Interests: Transportation
Automation Activity & Vendor Info: (Cataloging) Inmagic, Inc.
Open Mon-Fri 7:30-3:30

M MAINE GENERAL MEDICAL CENTER*, Alfond Center for Health Library, 35 Medical Center Pkwy, 04330. SAN 343-6322. Tel: 207-626-1325. FAX: 207-626-1537. E-mail: library@mainegeneral.org. *Librn,* Janet Bolduc; Staff 2 (MLS 1, Non-MLS 1)
Library Holdings: Bk Vols 3,000; Per Subs 52
Subject Interests: Consumer health, Hist of med
Automation Activity & Vendor Info: (Acquisitions) Innovative Interfaces, Inc; (Cataloging) Innovative Interfaces, Inc; (Circulation) Innovative Interfaces, Inc; (OPAC) Innovative Interfaces, Inc; (Serials) Innovative Interfaces, Inc
Function: Archival coll, Health sci info serv
Open Mon-Fri 8-4:30
Restriction: Access at librarian's discretion, Badge access after hrs, Circulates for staff only

GL MAINE STATE LAW & LEGISLATIVE REFERENCE LIBRARY, 43 State House Sta, 04333-0043. SAN 306-5731. Tel: 207-287-1600. FAX: 207-287-6467. Reference E-mail: Lawlib.Reference@legislature.maine.gov. Web Site: legislature.maine.gov/lawlibrary. *Dir,* John R Melendez-Barden; E-mail: john.melendez-barden@legislature.maine.gov; *Dep Dir,* Jessica Van Buren; *Sr Law Librn,* Alex Burnett; *Sr Law Librn,* Jessica Lundgren; *Assoc Law Librn,* Ryan Jones; *Assoc Law Librn,* Andrew Roache; *Libr Assoc,* Susan Beane; *Libr Assoc,* Jennifer Locke; *Libr Assoc,* Amanda Ouellette; *Libr Asst,* Gianine Lupo; *Libr Tech II,* Dylan Sinclair; Staff 12 (MLS 6, Non-MLS 6)
Founded 1971
Jul 2014-Jun 2015 Income $1,508,482. Mats Exp $380,116
Library Holdings: Bk Vols 114,035; Per Subs 120
Special Collections: Law & Legislative Digital Library; Legislative Committee Master Files (111th Legislative to present). State Document Depository; US Document Depository
Automation Activity & Vendor Info: (Acquisitions) Innovative Interfaces, Inc; (Cataloging) Innovative Interfaces, Inc; (Circulation) Innovative Interfaces, Inc; (ILL) OCLC; (OPAC) Innovative Interfaces, Inc; (Serials) Innovative Interfaces, Inc
Wireless access
Publications: Legislative Reference Bibliographies
Open Mon-Fri 8-5

P MAINE STATE LIBRARY*, Talking Books Plus/Library for the Blind & Physically Handicapped, 230 State St, 04333. (Mail add: 64 State House Sta, 04333-0064). Tel: 207-287-5650. Toll Free Tel: 800-762-7106. FAX: 207-287-5654. Web Site: www.maine.gov/msl/outreach/lbph. *State Librn,* James Ritter; E-mail: James.Ritter@maine.gov; Staff 3 (MLS 3)
Founded 1972
Library Holdings: Bk Vols 135,000
Special Collections: French Language, cassette
Wireless access
Publications: Talking Books (Newsletter); Talking Books Borrower's Handbook
Special Services for the Blind - Audio mat; Bks & mags in Braille, on rec, tape & cassette; Digital talking bk machines; Home delivery serv; Large print bks & talking machines; Newsline for the Blind
Open Mon, Wed & Thurs 9-6, Tues 9-7, Fri 9-5, Sat 9-2
Friends of the Library Group

P MAINE STATE LIBRARY*, State House Complex, Cultural Bldg, 230 State St, 04333. (Mail add: State House Complex, Cultural Bldg, 64 State House Sta, 04333-0064), SAN 343-6357. Tel: 207-287-5600. Interlibrary

Loan Service Tel: 207-287-5641. Reference Tel: 207-287-5608. Administration Tel: 207-287-5620. FAX: 207-287-5615. Administration FAX: 207-287-5624. Web Site: www.maine.gov/msl. *State Librn,* James Ritter; E-mail: James.Ritter@maine.gov; *Dir of Coll, Dir, Digital Initiatives, Dir, Promotion,* Adam Fisher; Tel: 207-287-5629, E-mail: Adam.C.Fisher@maine.gov; *Dir of Develop,* Janet McKenney; E-mail: Janet.Mckenney@maine.gov; *Dir, Innovations, Dir, Pub Serv & Outreach, Dir, Res,* Alison Maxell; E-mail: Alison.L.Maxell@maine.gov; Staff 19 (MLS 17, Non-MLS 2)
Founded 1839. Circ 188,768
Jul 2012-Jun 2013 Income $4,826,978, State $2,882,776, Federal $1,254,225, Other $689,977. Mats Exp $346,500, Books $55,000, Per/Ser (Incl. Access Fees) $55,000, Manu Arch $1,500, AV Equip $5,000, AV Mat $5,000, Electronic Ref Mat (Incl. Access Fees) $225,000. Sal $2,182,068
Library Holdings: Audiobooks 1,071; AV Mats 1,445; Bks-By-Mail 43,818; Bks on Deafness & Sign Lang 4; Large Print Bks 222,480; Bk Vols 349,948; Per Subs 410; Talking Bks 92,893; Videos 1,890
Special Collections: Maine Authors; Maine Counties, Towns, Boundaries & Rivers (Map Coll); Maine Genealogy Coll; Maine Government, Baxter State Park & Conservation (Baxter Coll), letters, scrapbks, personal rec; Mt Katahdin, Lumbering in Northern Maine 1876-1936 & the Appalachian Trail (Avery Coll). Oral History; State Document Depository
Subject Interests: Genealogy, Hist
Automation Activity & Vendor Info: (Acquisitions) Innovative Interfaces, Inc; (Cataloging) Innovative Interfaces, Inc; (Circulation) Innovative Interfaces, Inc; (ILL) Innovative Interfaces, Inc; (OPAC) Innovative Interfaces, Inc; (Serials) Innovative Interfaces, Inc
Wireless access
Partic in Association for Rural & Small Libraries; OCLC Online Computer Library Center, Inc
Special Services for the Deaf - Bks on deafness & sign lang; Video & TTY relay via computer
Special Services for the Blind - Bks on CD; Extensive large print coll; Large print bks & talking machines; Machine repair; Rec & flexible discs; Talking bk & rec for the blind cat; Talking bks & player equip; Tel Pioneers equip repair group
Open Mon, Wed & Thurs 9-6, Tues 9-7, Fri 9-5, Sat 9-2
Branches: 1
LIBRARY FOR THE BLIND & PHYSICALLY IMPAIRED
See Separate Entry

C UNIVERSITY OF MAINE AT AUGUSTA LIBRARIES*, Bennett D Katz Library, 46 University Dr, 04330-9410. SAN 306-574X. Tel: 207-621-3349. Toll Free Tel: 877-862-1234, Ext 3349. FAX: 207-621-3311. E-mail: uma.library@maine.edu. Web Site: www.uma.edu/academics/libraries. *Libr Dir,* Stacey Brownlie; Tel: 207-621-3186, E-mail: stacey.brownlie@maine.edu; *Asst Dir, Libr Serv, Coll Develop,* Brenda Sevigny-Killen; Tel: 207-621-3351, E-mail: brenda.sevigny@maine.edu; *Acad Librn, Ref & Instruction,* Donna Maher; Tel: 207-621-3161, E-mail: donna.maher@maine.edu. Subject Specialists: *Copyright,* Brenda Sevigny-Killen; Staff 7 (MLS 3.5, Non-MLS 3.5)
Founded 1965. Enrl 4,361; Fac 242; Highest Degree: Bachelor
Library Holdings: Bk Vols 57,176; Per Subs 120; Videos 1,887
Special Collections: Maine Related Materials; Research Materials
Subject Interests: Archit, Art, Bus, Liberal arts, Maine, Nursing
Automation Activity & Vendor Info: (Acquisitions) Innovative Interfaces, Inc; (Cataloging) Innovative Interfaces, Inc; (Circulation) Innovative Interfaces, Inc; (Course Reserve) Innovative Interfaces, Inc; (ILL) Innovative Interfaces, Inc; (Media Booking) Innovative Interfaces, Inc; (OPAC) Innovative Interfaces, Inc; (Serials) Innovative Interfaces, Inc
Wireless access
Partic in Central Maine Libr District; OCLC Online Computer Library Center, Inc; OCLC-LVIS
Open Mon-Thurs (Winter) 8-8, Fri 8-5, Sun 1-5; Mon-Fri (Summer) 8-5

BAILEYVILLE

P WOODLAND PUBLIC LIBRARY*, 169 Main St, 04694. (Mail add: PO Box 549, 04694-0549), SAN 306-7912. Tel: 207-427-3235. FAX: 207-427-3673. Web Site: baileyvillemaine.com. *Librn,* Sylvia Brown; *Librn,* Jeanne Goggin
Founded 1912. Pop 2,200; Circ 2,365
Library Holdings: CDs 10; Large Print Bks 400; Bk Vols 19,998; Per Subs 25; Talking Bks 400; Videos 40
Special Collections: Maine Authors Coll
Wireless access
Open Tues-Thurs 12:30-5:30, Fri 11:30-4:30

BANGOR

S BANGOR HISTORICAL SOCIETY LIBRARY*, 159 Union St, 04401. SAN 371-6651. Tel: 207-942-1900. E-mail: info@bangorhistoricalsociety.org. Web Site: www.bangorhistoricalsociety.org. *Exec Dir,* Michael Melochick; E-mail: director@bangorhistoricalsociety.org; *Curator, Operations Mgr,* Matt Bishop; E-mail: curator@bangorhistoricalsociety.org; Staff 5 (Non-MLS 5)
Founded 1864
Library Holdings: Bk Titles 1,000
Subject Interests: Local hist
Wireless access
Function: Archival coll, Art exhibits
Restriction: Non-circulating coll, Not a lending libr

P BANGOR PUBLIC LIBRARY*, 145 Harlow St, 04401-1802. SAN 343-6470. Tel: 207-947-8336. Toll Free Tel: 800-427-8336. FAX: 207-945-6694. E-mail: info@bangorpubliclibrary.org. Web Site: www.bangorpubliclibrary.org. *Libr Dir,* Ben Treat; E-mail: ben.treat@bangorpubliclibrary.org; *Head, Children's Dept,* Christine Erickson; E-mail: cerick@bangorpubliclibrary.org; Staff 34 (MLS 10, Non-MLS 24)
Founded 1883. Pop 31,903; Circ 150,674
Library Holdings: Bk Vols 475,000; Per Subs 275
Special Collections: Aroostook War of 1839; Genealogy & Town History; Jewish communities of eastern Maine; Mountaineering; Ornithology; Penobscot Expedition of 1779; World War II Unit History. State Document Depository; US Document Depository
Subject Interests: Hist
Automation Activity & Vendor Info: (Acquisitions) Innovative Interfaces, Inc; (Cataloging) Innovative Interfaces, Inc; (Circulation) Innovative Interfaces, Inc; (ILL) Innovative Interfaces, Inc; (OPAC) Innovative Interfaces, Inc; (Serials) Innovative Interfaces, Inc
Wireless access
Function: 24/7 Electronic res, Adult literacy prog, Archival coll, Art exhibits, ILL available, Meeting rooms, Ref & res
Partic in Maine School & Library Network; OCLC Online Computer Library Center, Inc
Open Mon-Thurs 10-8, Fri & Sat 10-5; Mon-Thurs (Summer) 10-7, Fri 10-5
Friends of the Library Group

J BEAL COLLEGE LIBRARY*, 99 Farm Rd, 04401-6831. SAN 306-5774. Tel: 207-947-4591. FAX: 207-947-0208. Web Site: www.beal.edu/library. *Librn,* Donna Bancroft; E-mail: dbancroft@beal.edu; *Librn,* Tegan Mills; Staff 1 (Non-MLS 1)
Founded 1965. Enrl 350; Fac 25; Highest Degree: Associate
Library Holdings: Bk Vols 10,000; Per Subs 20
Subject Interests: Allied med professions, Bus, Law enforcement
Automation Activity & Vendor Info: (Cataloging) Book Systems; (Circulation) Book Systems; (OPAC) Book Systems
Wireless access
Function: 24/7 Electronic res, 24/7 Online cat, Audiobks via web, Computers for patron use, Free DVD rentals, ILL available, Internet access, Online cat, OverDrive digital audio bks, Photocopying/Printing, Ref serv available, VHS videos
Partic in Maine InfoNet
Restriction: Access at librarian's discretion, Borrowing requests are handled by ILL, Open to students, fac & staff

M DOROTHEA DIX PSYCHIATRIC CENTER LIBRARY, Patient Library, 656 State St, 04402. (Mail add: PO Box 926, 04402-0926). Tel: 207-941-4226. FAX: 207-941-4228. Web Site: www.maine.gov/dhhs/DDPC. *Librn,* Ruth Mare; E-mail: ruth.mare@maine.gov
Library Holdings: Bk Titles 7,000; Per Subs 20
Partic in National Network of Libraries of Medicine Region 7
Open Mon-Fri 1-4

J EASTERN MAINE COMMUNITY COLLEGE LIBRARY*, Katahdin Hall, 354 Hogan Rd, 04401. SAN 306-5782. Tel: 207-974-4640. Reference Tel: 207-974-4740. Administration Tel: 207-974-4606. FAX: 207-974-4641. E-mail: library@emcc.edu. Web Site: emcc.libguides.com/emcclibrary. *Libr Dir,* William Cook; E-mail: wcook@emcc.edu. Subject Specialists: *Hist, Med, Spec coll,* William Cook; Staff 1.5 (MLS 1, Non-MLS 0.5)
Founded 1968. Enrl 1,365; Fac 173; Highest Degree: Associate
Library Holdings: AV Mats 235; e-books 300; Electronic Media & Resources 42; Bk Titles 16,211; Bk Vols 16,274; Per Subs 212; Videos 235
Special Collections: American Welding Society-Reference Coll
Subject Interests: Automotive engr, Construction, Electronics, Nursing, Radiology
Automation Activity & Vendor Info: (Acquisitions) Innovative Interfaces, Inc; (Cataloging) Innovative Interfaces, Inc; (Circulation) Innovative Interfaces, Inc; (Course Reserve) Innovative Interfaces, Inc; (ILL) Innovative Interfaces, Inc; (OPAC) Innovative Interfaces, Inc; (Serials) Innovative Interfaces, Inc
Wireless access
Function: 24/7 Electronic res, 24/7 Online cat, Art exhibits, Computers for patron use, Distance learning, Doc delivery serv, Electronic databases & coll, Internet access, Online cat, Online ref, Orientations, Outside serv via

phone, mail, e-mail & web, Photocopying/Printing, Ref & res, Scanner, Telephone ref
Partic in NE Libr Network
Special Services for the Deaf - Bks on deafness & sign lang
Special Services for the Blind - Magnifiers
Open Mon-Thurs (Winter) 8am-9pm, Fri 8-5; Mon-Fri (Summer) 9-3
Restriction: Open to pub for ref only, Open to students, fac & staff, Pub ref by request
Friends of the Library Group

C HUSSON UNIVERSITY*, W Tom & Bonnie Sawyer Library, One College Circle, 04401-2999. SAN 306-5790. Tel: 207-941-7187, 207-941-7188. Web Site: www.husson.edu/library. *Univ Librn,* Susanna Pathak; E-mail: pathaks@husson.edu; *Resource Discovery & Access Librn,* Diane Hanscom; E-mail: hanscomd@husson.edu; Staff 2 (MLS 2)
Founded 1947. Highest Degree: Doctorate
Library Holdings: Bk Vols 40,000; Per Subs 500
Automation Activity & Vendor Info: (Cataloging) Innovative Interfaces, Inc; (Circulation) Innovative Interfaces, Inc; (Course Reserve) Innovative Interfaces, Inc; (OPAC) Innovative Interfaces, Inc; (Serials) Innovative Interfaces, Inc
Wireless access
Partic in LYRASIS; National Network of Libraries of Medicine Region 7
Open Mon-Thurs 8am-Midnight, Fri 8-7, Sat 10-7, Sun 10am-Midnight; Mon-Thurs (Summer) 8-6, Fri 8-4:30

M NORTHERN LIGHT EASTERN MAINE MEDICAL CENTER*, Hadley Parrot Health Sciences Library, 489 State St, 04401. (Mail add: PO Box 404, 04402-0404), SAN 320-4502. Tel: 207-973-8228. FAX: 207-973-8233. E-mail: libraryemmc@emhs.org. Web Site: northernlighthealth.org/Eastern-Maine-Medical-Center. *Med Librn,* Linda Kerecman; E-mail: lkerecman@emhs.org; Staff 4 (MLS 3, Non-MLS 1)
Founded 1892
Library Holdings: e-books 50; e-journals 1,000; Bk Titles 7,541; Per Subs 100
Special Collections: Hospital Annual Reports & Archives
Subject Interests: Consumer health, Med, Nursing
Automation Activity & Vendor Info: (Cataloging) Innovative Interfaces, Inc; (Circulation) Innovative Interfaces, Inc; (OPAC) Innovative Interfaces, Inc; (Serials) Innovative Interfaces, Inc
Wireless access
Function: Bks on cassette, Computers for patron use, Electronic databases & coll, Health sci info serv, ILL available, Internet access, Online cat, Orientations, Photocopying/Printing, Ref serv available, Scanner
Partic in Health Sci Libr & Info Coop; Maine School & Library Network
Open Mon-Fri 8-4:30
Restriction: Badge access after hrs, Open to staff, patients & family mem

C UNIVERSITY OF MAINE AT AUGUSTA*, Nottage Library (Bangor Campus), 85 Texas Ave, Belfast Hall, 04401. SAN 306-5812. Tel: 207-262-7900. Administration Tel: 207-262-7902. Web Site: uma.edu/library. *Asst Dir,* Senta Sellers; Tel: 207-262-7905, E-mail: senta.sellers@maine.edu; *Libr Spec II,* Catherine Geren; *Libr Spec II,* Nathan Green; Staff 3 (MLS 1, Non-MLS 2)
Founded 1968. Enrl 950; Fac 30; Highest Degree: Bachelor
Library Holdings: Bk Vols 25,000; Per Subs 180
Subject Interests: Dental health, Veterinary tech
Wireless access
Function: AV serv, Children's prog, Distance learning, Doc delivery serv, Electronic databases & coll, For res purposes, ILL available, Microfiche/film & reading machines, Online cat, Online info literacy tutorials on the web & in blackboard, Online ref, Scanner
Open Mon-Thurs 8-7, Fri 8-4:30, Sat & Sun 12:30-4:30
Restriction: Authorized patrons

BAR HARBOR

C COLLEGE OF THE ATLANTIC*, Thorndike Library, 105 Eden St, 04609-1198. SAN 306-5820. Tel: 207-801-5665. Web Site: www.coa.edu/library. *Libr Dir,* Jane Hultberg; Tel: 207-801-5660, E-mail: jhultberg@coa.edu; *Assoc Dir,* Patricia Cantwell; Tel: 207-801-5661, E-mail: tcantwell@coa.edu; *Archivist/Librn,* Hannah Stevens; Tel: 207-801-5662, E-mail: hstevens@coa.edu; *Coordr, Libr Asst,* Catherine Preston-Schreck; Tel: 207-801-5664, E-mail: cpreston-schreck@coa.edu; *AV Tech Spec,* Zach Soares; Tel: 207-801-5663, E-mail: zsoares@coa.edu; Staff 4 (MLS 3, Non-MLS 1)
Founded 1972. Enrl 325; Fac 26; Highest Degree: Master
Library Holdings: Bk Vols 45,000; Per Subs 250
Automation Activity & Vendor Info: (Cataloging) Evergreen; (Circulation) Evergreen; (ILL) OCLC; (OPAC) Evergreen; (Serials) SerialsSolutions
Wireless access
Partic in Westchester Academic Library Directors Organization
Open Mon-Thurs 7:30am-11pm, Fri 7:30am-10pm, Sat 10-10, Sun 10am-Midnight

M JACKSON LABORATORY*, Joan Staats Library, 600 Main St, 04609-1500. SAN 306-5839. Tel: 207-288-6146. FAX: 207-288-6079. E-mail: ill@jax.org, library@jax.org. Web Site: www.jax.org/research-and-faculty/resources/joan-staats-library-at-the-jackson-laboratory (www.jax.org/research-and-faculty/resources/joan-staats-library-at-the-jackson-laboratory). *Librn,* Douglas Macbeth; E-mail: douglas.macbeth@jax.org; *Info Analyst,* Ann Jordan; Tel: 207-288-6241, E-mail: ann.jordan@jax.org; Staff 4 (MLS 2, Non-MLS 2)
Founded 1929
Library Holdings: Bk Titles 4,000; Per Subs 310
Special Collections: Historical archives of the Jackson Laboratory
Subject Interests: Biology, Cancer
Wireless access
Partic in NRML; OCLC Online Computer Library Center, Inc; Proquest Dialog
Open Mon-Fri 7:30-4

P JESUP MEMORIAL LIBRARY*, 34 Mount Desert St, 04609-1727. SAN 306-5847. Tel: 207-288-4245. E-mail: info@jesuplibrary.org. Web Site: www.jesuplibrary.org. *Libr Dir,* Ruth A Eveland; E-mail: reveland@jesuplibrary.org; *Youth Serv Librn,* Mae Corrion; E-mail: mcorrion@jesuplibrary.org; Staff 8 (MLS 1, Non-MLS 7)
Founded 1911. Pop 5,235; Circ 64,877
Jan 2017-Dec 2017 Income $454,183, City $47,672, Locally Generated Income $194,817, Other $211,694. Mats Exp $29,650. Sal $330,696
Library Holdings: Bk Vols 31,000; Per Subs 50
Special Collections: Genealogy Coll; Local Newspapers from 1881-1968, microfilm and digital
Automation Activity & Vendor Info: (Cataloging) Innovative Interfaces, Inc; (Circulation) Innovative Interfaces, Inc; (OPAC) Innovative Interfaces, Inc
Wireless access
Function: 24/7 Electronic res, 24/7 Online cat, Archival coll, Art exhibits, Audio & video playback equip for onsite use, Audiobks via web, Bi-weekly Writer's Group, Bks on cassette, Bks on CD, Children's prog, Computer training, Computers for patron use, E-Reserves, Electronic databases & coll, Equip loans & repairs, Free DVD rentals, Home delivery & serv to seniorr ctr & nursing homes, ILL available, Internet access, Large print keyboards, Life-long learning prog for all ages, Magazines, Mail & tel request accepted, Mango lang, Microfiche/film & reading machines, Music CDs, Online cat, Photocopying/Printing, Prog for adults, Prog for children & young adult, Ref & res, Ref serv available, Scanner, Serves people with intellectual disabilities, Spoken cassettes & CDs, Spoken cassettes & DVDs, Story hour, Summer reading prog, Tax forms, Telephone ref, VHS videos, Workshops, Writing prog
Partic in Maine Libr Asn
Open Tues, Fri & Sat 10-5, Wed & Thurs 10-8

BAR MILLS

P BERRY MEMORIAL LIBRARY*, 93 Main St, 04004. (Mail add: PO Box 25, 04004-0025), SAN 306-5855. Tel: 207-929-5484. E-mail: berrylibrary93@gmail.com. Web Site: www.berrylibrary.com. *Dir,* Kat Sovetsky; Staff 1 (Non-MLS 1)
Founded 1929. Pop 8,000
Library Holdings: Bk Titles 6,500; Per Subs 12
Special Collections: Genealogy (Downeast Ancestry; Histories of Several Maine Towns; Maine Authors (Kate D Wiggin Coll); Narragansett & Buxton Town Histories; Saco Valley Settlements & Families
Wireless access
Mem of Maine State Library, Region 1
Open Tues 11-5, Thurs 4-8, Sat 9-11

BATH

S MAINE MARITIME MUSEUM*, Library Archives, 243 Washington St, 04530. SAN 306-5863. Tel: 207-443-1316, Ext 328. Reference Tel: 207-443-1316, Ext 336. FAX: 207-443-1665. E-mail: library@maritimeme.org. Web Site: www.mainemaritimemuseum.org/research/library. *Chief Curator,* Chris Timm; E-mail: ctimm@maritimeme.org; Staff 2 (Non-MLS 2)
Founded 1964
Library Holdings: Bk Titles 10,000; Bk Vols 14,000; Per Subs 25; Videos 482
Special Collections: Bath, Maine Built Vessels (Photograph Coll); Ship Logs Coll, original doc in bk form; Ship Papers (Sewall Coll), original doc
Subject Interests: Maritime hist
Partic in Maine InfoNet
Open Tues & Thurs 9:30-3
Restriction: Closed stack, Fee for pub use, Non-circulating coll, Not a lending libr

P PATTEN FREE LIBRARY*, 33 Summer St, 04530. SAN 306-5871. Tel: 207-443-5141. FAX: 207-443-3514. Web Site: www.patten.lib.me.us. *Dir,* Lesley Dolinger; Tel: 207-443-5141, Ext 15, E-mail: lesley.dolinger@patten.lib.me.us; *Develop Dir,* Samantha Ricker; Tel: 207-443-5141, Ext 19, E-mail: slricker@patten.lib.me.us; *Head, Tech Serv,* Deborah Tamaras; Tel: 207-443-5141, Ext 14, E-mail: dtomaras@patten.lib.me.us; *Outreach & Instruction Librn,* Roberta Jordan; Tel: 207-443-5141, Ext 25, E-mail: rjordan@patten.lib.me.us; *Ref Librn,* Laurel Cox; Tel: 207-443-5141, Ext 12, E-mail: laurel@patten.lib.me.us; *Adult Serv Mgr,* Leslie Mortimer; Tel: 207-443-5141, Ext 21, E-mail: lmortimer@patten.lib.me.us; *ILL Coordr,* Mary Ellen Wilson; Tel: 207-443-5141, Ext 24, E-mail: mewilson@patten.lib.me.us; *Ch Serv,* Carol McFadden; Tel: 207-443-5141, Ext 17, E-mail: ccmcfadden@patten.lib.me.us; Staff 10 (MLS 6, Non-MLS 4)
Founded 1847. Pop 17,500; Circ 143,259
Library Holdings: Bk Vols 56,165; Per Subs 243
Special Collections: Historic Preservation (Sagadahoc Preservation Inc Coll); Maine History & Genealogy Coll; Maritime (Whitmore, Stevens, Bath Iron Works Colls); Native American (Staton Coll)
Subject Interests: Genealogy, Local hist, Maritime hist
Wireless access
Publications: Good Times & Hard Times in Bath, 1936-1986; I Am Now a Soldier: The Civil War Diaries of Lorenzo Vanderhoeff; Maine Odyssey; Pattens of Bath, a Seagoing Dynasty
Open Tues & Wed 10-8, Thurs & Fri 10-5, Sat 10-4
Friends of the Library Group

BELFAST

P BELFAST FREE LIBRARY*, 106 High St, 04915. SAN 306-588X. Tel: 207-338-3884. FAX: 207-338-3895. E-mail: info@belfastlibrary.org. Web Site: belfastlibrary.org. *Libr Dir,* Steve Norman; E-mail: snorman@belfastlibrary.org; *Youth Serv Librn,* Erica Rubin Irish; E-mail: erirish@belfastlibrary.org; *Adult Prog Coordr,* Brenda Harrington; E-mail: bharrington@belfastlibrary.org; *Ref, Spec Coll,* BJ Jamieson; E-mail: bjjamieson@belfastlibrary.org; Staff 9 (MLS 5, Non-MLS 4)
Founded 1887. Pop 8,188; Circ 131,311
Jul 2013-Jun 2014 Income $626,529, City $534,769, Locally Generated Income $91,760. Mats Exp $46,535, Books $34,200, Per/Ser (Incl. Access Fees) $5,000, Manu Arch $500, AV Mat $4,500, Electronic Ref Mat (Incl. Access Fees) $2,335. Sal $354,455
Library Holdings: AV Mats 9,257; e-books 7,310; Bk Vols 48,252; Per Subs 117
Subject Interests: Genealogy, Local hist
Automation Activity & Vendor Info: (Cataloging) Innovative Interfaces, Inc; (Circulation) Innovative Interfaces, Inc; (ILL) Innovative Interfaces, Inc; (OPAC) Innovative Interfaces, Inc
Wireless access
Function: Archival coll, Art exhibits, Audiobks via web, Bk club(s), Bks on CD, Children's prog, Computers for patron use, Genealogy discussion group, ILL available, Microfiche/film & reading machines, OverDrive digital audio bks, Photocopying/Printing, Story hour, Summer reading prog, Wheelchair accessible
Special Services for the Blind - Large print bks; Talking bks
Open Mon 9:30-8, Tues, Thurs & Fri 9:30-6, Wed 12-8, Sat 10-2
Friends of the Library Group

M WALDO COUNTY GENERAL HOSPITAL, Health Sciences Library, 118 Northport Ave, 04915. SAN 377-9246. Tel: 207-338-2500, Ext 4154. FAX: 207-338-6029. E-mail: librarys@wchi.com. Web Site: mainehealth.org/waldo-county-general-hospital. *Education Coord, Librn,* Lois Dutch
Library Holdings: Per Subs 5
Wireless access

BELGRADE

P BELGRADE PUBLIC LIBRARY*, 124 Depot Rd, 04917. Tel: 207-495-3508. FAX: 207-495-3508. E-mail: Belgrade@belgrade.lib.me.us. Web Site: www.townofbelgrade.com/library. *Librn,* Megan Aube; *Asst Librn,* Debra Balberchak; *Asst Librn,* Jared Bond
Founded 2000. Pop 3,124; Circ 10,522
Library Holdings: Audiobooks 219; AV Mats 50; CDs 137; DVDs 383; e-books 7,514; Large Print Bks 229; Bk Titles 7,200; Bk Vols 7,806; Per Subs 30; Videos 141
Special Collections: Local History Coll
Automation Activity & Vendor Info: (Cataloging) LibraryWorld, Inc; (Circulation) LibraryWorld, Inc; (OPAC) LibraryWorld, Inc
Wireless access
Function: ILL available, Ref serv available
Special Services for the Blind - Audio mat; Large print bks
Open Tues & Thurs 10-7, Wed & Fri 2-6, Sat 10-2
Friends of the Library Group

BERNARD

P BASS HARBOR MEMORIAL LIBRARY*, 89 Bernard Rd, 04612. (Mail add: PO Box 99, 04612-0099), SAN 376-351X. Tel: 207-244-3798. E-mail: librarian@bassharborlibrary.com. Web Site: bassharborlibrary.com. *Dir,* Lisa Taplin Murray; E-mail: lisa.murray@bassharborlibrary.com; *Librn,* Amanda Crafts; E-mail: acrafts@bassharborlibrary.com; Staff 1 (Non-MLS 1)
Library Holdings: Bk Titles 8,700; Per Subs 30
Wireless access
Open Tues-Thurs 11-4, Sat 11-1
Friends of the Library Group

BERWICK

P BERWICK PUBLIC LIBRARY*, 103 Old Pine Hill Rd, 03901. (Mail add: PO Box 838, 03901-0838), SAN 376-3889. Tel: 207-698-5737. FAX: 207-698-5737. Web Site: www.berwick.lib.me.us. *Dir,* Sharon Kelly; E-mail: skelly@berwickpubliclibrary.org; *Asst Dir,* Alaina Goodnough; E-mail: agoodnough@berwickpubliclibrary.org; Staff 4 (MLS 1, Non-MLS 3)
Founded 1987. Pop 7,676
Library Holdings: Audiobooks 470; AV Mats 1,841; Bk Titles 23,755; Per Subs 21; Talking Bks 200
Special Collections: Local History Coll; Maine Coll
Automation Activity & Vendor Info: (Cataloging) Innovative Interfaces, Inc - Sierra
Wireless access
Function: 24/7 Electronic res, 24/7 Online cat, Adult bk club, Art exhibits, Bk club(s), Bks on CD, Children's prog, Computer training, Computers for patron use, Electronic databases & coll, Free DVD rentals, Genealogy discussion group, Holiday prog, Homebound delivery serv, ILL available, Internet access, Magazines, Mail & tel request accepted, Makerspace, Meeting rooms, Movies, Museum passes, Music CDs, Online cat, Photocopying/Printing, Prog for adults, Prog for children & young adult, Ref serv available, Senior outreach, Spoken cassettes & CDs, Spoken cassettes & DVDs, Story hour, Summer & winter reading prog, Summer reading prog, Tax forms, Telephone ref, VHS videos, Wheelchair accessible
Mem of Maine State Library, Region 1
Partic in Maine School & Library Network
Special Services for the Blind - Talking bks
Open Tues & Wed 9:30-7:30, Fri & Sat 9:30-1:30
Restriction: Authorized patrons, Circ to mem only, In-house use for visitors
Friends of the Library Group

BETHEL

P BETHEL LIBRARY ASSOCIATION, Six Broad St, 04217. (Mail add: PO Box 130, 04217-0130), SAN 306-5898. Tel: 207-824-2520. E-mail: bethellibrarymaine@gmail.com. Web Site: www.bethellibraryassociation.org. *Libr Dir,* Michelle Conroy; E-mail: mconroy@bethel.lib.me.us; Staff 1 (Non-MLS 1)
Pop 6,000; Circ 20,000
Library Holdings: AV Mats 1,000; Bk Titles 19,000; Bk Vols 20,000; Per Subs 56; Talking Bks 1,000
Special Collections: Maine History Coll
Automation Activity & Vendor Info: (Cataloging) Winnebago Software Co; (Circulation) Winnebago Software Co; (OPAC) Winnebago Software Co
Wireless access
Open Mon & Wed 9-1, Tues & Thurs 12-5

BIDDEFORD

P MCARTHUR PUBLIC LIBRARY*, 270 Main St, 04005. (Mail add: PO Box 346, 04005-0346), SAN 306-591X. Tel: 207-284-4181. Reference E-mail: reference@mcarthur.lib.me.us. Web Site: www.mcarthurpubliclibrary.org. *Dir,* Jeff Cabral; E-mail: jcabral@mcarthur.lib.me.us; Staff 13.6 (MLS 4, Non-MLS 9.6)
Founded 1863. Pop 21,386; Circ 131,732. Sal $475,320 (Prof $167,735)
Library Holdings: AV Mats 7,059; e-books 2,370; Bk Vols 55,319; Per Subs 114
Automation Activity & Vendor Info: (Cataloging) Innovative Interfaces, Inc; (Circulation) Innovative Interfaces, Inc; (ILL) Innovative Interfaces, Inc; (OPAC) Innovative Interfaces, Inc; (Serials) Innovative Interfaces, Inc
Wireless access
Function: Adult bk club, Archival coll, Art exhibits, Audiobks via web, Bk club(s), Bks on CD, Bus archives, Children's prog, Computer training, Computers for patron use, Digital talking bks, E-Reserves, Electronic databases & coll, Equip loans & repairs, Family literacy, Free DVD rentals, Games & aids for people with disabilities, Govt ref serv, Holiday prog, ILL available, Internet access, Literacy & newcomer serv, Magnifiers for reading, Mail & tel request accepted, Microfiche/film & reading machines, Museum passes, Music CDs, Online cat, Online ref, Orientations, Outreach

serv, Outside serv via phone, mail, e-mail & web, OverDrive digital audio bks, Photocopying/Printing, Preschool outreach, Preschool reading prog, Printer for laptops & handheld devices, Prog for adults, Prog for children & young adult, Ref & res, Ref serv available, Story hour, Summer & winter reading prog, Tax forms, Teen prog, Telephone ref, VHS videos, Wheelchair accessible, Workshops
Mem of Maine State Library, Region 1
Partic in Maine School & Library Network
Special Services for the Blind - Aids for in-house use; Bks available with recordings; Bks on cassette; Bks on CD; Large print bks; Magnifiers; Talking bks
Open Mon-Thurs 9:30-8, Fri 9:30-5, Sat 9:30-3:30

C UNIVERSITY OF NEW ENGLAND LIBRARIES*, Jack S Ketchum Library, 11 Hills Beach Rd, 04005. SAN 322-8142. Tel: 207-602-2361. Interlibrary Loan Service Tel: 207-602-2386. Reference Tel: 207-602-2363. Administration Tel: 207-602-2319. FAX: 207-602-5922. E-mail: library@une.edu. Web Site: library.une.edu. *Interim Dean, Libr Serv,* Elizabeth Dyer; *Assoc Dean, Digital Serv Librn, Syst Librn,* Stew MacLehose; Tel: 207-221-4535, E-mail: smaclehose@une.edu; *Research & Teaching Librn,* Cadence Atchinson; Tel: 207-602-2497, E-mail: catchinson@une.edu; *Research & Teaching Librn,* Barbara Swartzlander; Tel: 207-602-2315, E-mail: bswartzlander@une.edu; *Archivist, New England Osteopathic Heritage Ctr,* Zachary Enright; Tel: 207-602-2131, E-mail: zenright@une.edu; Staff 17 (MLS 16, Non-MLS 1)
Founded 1831. Enrl 5,789; Highest Degree: Doctorate
Library Holdings: e-books 1,500,000; e-journals 160,000; Bk Vols 135,000; Videos 60,000
Special Collections: Maine Women Writers Coll; New England Osteopathic Heritage Center
Subject Interests: Allied health, Educ, Life sci, Marine biol, Med
Automation Activity & Vendor Info: (Acquisitions) Innovative Interfaces, Inc; (Cataloging) Innovative Interfaces, Inc; (Circulation) Innovative Interfaces, Inc; (ILL) Innovative Interfaces, Inc
Wireless access
Mem of Maine State Library, Region 1
Partic in National Network of Libraries of Medicine Region 7; OCLC Online Computer Library Center, Inc
Departmental Libraries:
JOSEPHINE S ABPLANALP LIBRARY, Portland Campus, 716 Stevens Ave, Portland, 04103, SAN 306-7262. Tel: 207-221-4330. Reference Tel: 207-221-4363. FAX: 207-221-4893. *Dean, Libr Serv,* Andrew J Golub; Tel: 207-602-2319, E-mail: agolub@une.edu; *Access Serv Librn,* Bethany Kenyon; Tel: 207-221-4325, E-mail: bkenyon@une.edu; *Pub Serv Librn,* Elizabeth Dyer; Tel: 207-221-4333, E-mail: edyer@une.edu; *Pub Serv Librn,* Roberta Gray; Tel: 207-221-4323, E-mail: rgray@une.edu; *Acq,* Chris McKinnon; Tel: 207-221-4327, E-mail: cmckinnon@une.edu; *Cat,* Robin Sanford; Tel: 207-221-4328, E-mail: rsanford@une.edu; *Curator,* Cally Gurley; Tel: 207-221-4324, E-mail: cgurley@une.edu; Staff 15 (MLS 11, Non-MLS 4)
Founded 1831. Enrl 1,373; Fac 66; Highest Degree: Master
Library Holdings: e-books 130,000; e-journals 75,000; Bk Vols 135,000
Special Collections: George & Barbara Bush Legacy Coll; Maine Women Writers Coll; New England Osteopathic Heritage Center; UNE Art Gallery; Westbrook College History Coll
Subject Interests: Anesthesiology, Nursing
Automation Activity & Vendor Info: (OPAC) Innovative Interfaces, Inc

BLUE HILL

S BAGADUCE MUSIC LENDING LIBRARY*, 49 South St, 04614. SAN 373-0573. Tel: 207-374-5454. FAX: 207-374-2733. E-mail: library@bagaducemusic.org. Web Site: www.bagaducemusic.org. *Exec Dir,* Teresa Myrwang; E-mail: teresa@bagaducemusic.org; *Operations Dir,* Lynette Woods; E-mail: lynette@bagaducemusic.org; *Spec Events Coordr,* Cheri Robbins; E-mail: cheri@bagaducemusic.org; *Cataloger,* Ellen Lamerson; Staff 4 (Non-MLS 4)
Founded 1983
Library Holdings: Music Scores 250,000; Bk Titles 215,000
Special Collections: State of Maine Music Coll. State Document Depository
Subject Interests: Music, Music scores, Sheet music
Wireless access
Function: 24/7 Online cat, Archival coll, Art exhibits, Children's prog, Computers for patron use, Electronic databases & coll, For res purposes, Internet access, Mail & tel request accepted, Mail loans to mem, Meeting rooms, Online cat, Prog for adults, Prog for children & young adult, Ref & res, Res libr, Scanner, Wheelchair accessible, Workshops
Publications: Collection Catalogs (Quarterly newsletter)
Open Mon-Fri 10-4
Restriction: Access at librarian's discretion, Authorized patrons, Circ to mem only
Friends of the Library Group

P BLUE HILL PUBLIC LIBRARY*, Five Parker Point Rd, 04614. SAN 306-5944. Tel: 207-374-5515. FAX: 207-374-5254. E-mail: library@bhpl.net. Web Site: www.bhpl.net. *Dir,* Richard Boulet; Tel: 207-374-5515, Ext 13, E-mail: rboulet@bhpl.net; *Asst Dir,* Hannah Cyrus; Tel: 207-374-5515, Ext 11, E-mail: hannah.cyrus@bhpl.net; *Youth Serv Librn,* Claire Malina; Tel: 207-374-5515, Ext 15, E-mail: claire.malina@bhpl.net; Staff 7.3 (MLS 1.3, Non-MLS 6)
Founded 1796. Pop 2,599; Circ 105,000
Library Holdings: Bk Titles 39,000; Bk Vols 41,500; Per Subs 100
Special Collections: Large Print Books; Maine Local History Coll
Automation Activity & Vendor Info: (Cataloging) Follett Software; (Circulation) Follett Software; (OPAC) Follett Software
Wireless access
Open Mon-Wed & Fri 9-6, Thurs 9-8, Sat 9-5
Friends of the Library Group

BOOTHBAY HARBOR

P BOOTHBAY HARBOR MEMORIAL LIBRARY, Four Oak St, 04538. SAN 306-5952. Tel: 207-633-3112. E-mail: ahoy@bbhlibrary.org. Web Site: bbhlibrary.org. *Exec Dir,* Joanna Breen; E-mail: director@bbhlibrary.org; *Asst Dir,* Harolyn Hylton; E-mail: harolyn@bbhlibrary.org; Staff 4 (MLS 1, Non-MLS 3)
Founded 1924. Pop 6,000; Circ 45,000
Library Holdings: Bk Vols 27,000; Per Subs 45
Special Collections: Maine (Osgood Coll); Military History (Farmer Coll)
Automation Activity & Vendor Info: (Cataloging) Innovative Interfaces, Inc; (Circulation) Innovative Interfaces, Inc; (ILL) Innovative Interfaces, Inc; (OPAC) Innovative Interfaces, Inc
Wireless access
Function: 24/7 Electronic res, 24/7 Online cat, 3D Printer, Activity rm, Adult bk club, Art exhibits, Audiobks via web, AV serv, Bk club(s), Bks on CD, Butterfly Garden, Children's prog, Computer training, Computers for patron use, Digital talking bks, Doc delivery serv, E-Readers, Electronic databases & coll, Equip loans & repairs, For res purposes, Free DVD rentals, Health sci info serv, Holiday prog, Home delivery & serv to seniorr ctr & nursing homes, Homebound delivery serv, ILL available, Internet access, Laminating, Life-long learning prog for all ages, Literacy & newcomer serv, Magazines, Magnifiers for reading, Meeting rooms, Movies, Museum passes, Online cat, Online ref, Orientations, Outreach serv, Outside serv via phone, mail, e-mail & web, Photocopying/Printing, Preschool outreach, Preschool reading prog, Printer for laptops & handheld devices, Prog for adults, Prog for children & young adult, Ref & res, Ref serv available, Res assist avail, Satellite serv, Scanner, Senior outreach, Serves people with intellectual disabilities, Spoken cassettes & CDs, STEM programs, Story hour, Summer & winter reading prog, Summer reading prog, Tax forms, Teen prog, Telephone ref, Wheelchair accessible, Workshops, Writing prog
Partic in Maine InfoNet
Special Services for the Deaf - Bks on deafness & sign lang
Special Services for the Blind - Aids for in-house use; Bks on CD; Large print bks
Open Tues, Thurs & Fri 9:30-4:30, Wed 9:30-7, Sat 10-4
Friends of the Library Group

BOWDOINHAM

P BOWDOINHAM PUBLIC LIBRARY*, 13A School St, 04008. SAN 306-5960. Tel: 207-666-8405. Web Site: www.bowdoinhamlibrary.org. *Dir,* Kate Cutko; E-mail: kcutko@bowdoinham.lib.me.us; Staff 1 (Non-MLS 1)
Founded 1929. Pop 2,800; Circ 12,808
Library Holdings: Bk Titles 13,000; Bk Vols 13,676; Per Subs 25
Special Collections: Maine Coll
Wireless access
Open Tues 10-12, 2-5 & 7-8, Wed 2-6, Fri 2-5, Sat 10-3
Friends of the Library Group

BRADFORD

P JOHN B CURTIS FREE PUBLIC LIBRARY, 435 Main Rd, 04410. (Mail add: 187 Wilder Davis Rd, 04410-3428), SAN 378-1283. Tel: 207-327-2111. Web Site: www.facebook.com/jbcurtislibrary. *Dir,* Brenda S Mowdy; E-mail: olibird1@gmail.com
Founded 1913. Pop 1,200; Circ 3,331
Library Holdings: Large Print Bks 25; Bk Vols 11,100; Per Subs 3
Wireless access
Open Mon & Wed 5-7, Sat 10-3 (Winter); Mon 5-7, Wed 9-11 & 5-7, Sat 10-3 (Winter)

BREMEN

P BREMEN LIBRARY, 204 Waldoboro Rd, 04551. (Mail add: PO Box 163, 04551-0163), SAN 376-379X. Tel: 207-529-5572. E-mail: bremenmainelibrary@gmail.com. Web Site: bremenlibrary.org. *Librn,* Kristen Budlong; Staff 1 (Non-MLS 1)
Library Holdings: Bk Vols 11,000

Wireless access
Function: Computers for patron use, ILL available, Photocopying/Printing, Story hour
Open Wed & Fri 10-3, Thurs 10-7, Sat 10-1

BREWER

P BREWER PUBLIC LIBRARY*, 100 S Main St, 04412. SAN 306-5979. Tel: 207-989-7943. FAX: 207-989-8426. E-mail: public-library@brewermaine.gov. Web Site: www.brewermaine.gov/library. *Dir,* Darren French; Staff 4 (Non-MLS 4)
Founded 1908. Pop 9,200; Circ 61,000
Library Holdings: AV Mats 3,400; Bk Vols 41,000; Per Subs 67
Special Collections: Fannie Hardy Eckstorm Coll, 1865-1946; Joshua Chamberlain Coll
Automation Activity & Vendor Info: (Cataloging) Follett Software; (Circulation) Follett Software; (OPAC) Follett Software
Wireless access
Open Mon & Wed 9-7, Tues, Thurs & Fri 9-5

BRIDGTON

P BRIDGTON PUBLIC LIBRARY*, One Church St, 04009. SAN 306-5987. Tel: 207-647-2472. FAX: 207-647-5660. E-mail: bpldirector@bridgton.lib.me.us. Web Site: bridgtonlibrary.org. *Dir,* Amy Stone; E-mail: amys@bridgton.lib.me.us; Staff 2 (MLS 1, Non-MLS 1)
Founded 1895. Pop 5,400; Circ 28,000
Library Holdings: AV Mats 2,500; Bk Vols 27,000; Per Subs 65
Special Collections: Local History Coll
Automation Activity & Vendor Info: (Cataloging) Follett Software; (Circulation) Follett Software
Wireless access
Mem of Maine State Library, Region 1
Open Tues 9-6, Wed & Fri 9-5, Sat 9-3
Friends of the Library Group

S LAKES ENVIRONMENTAL ASSOCIATION*, Environmental Resource Library, Bradley Lakes Center, 230 Main St, 04009. Tel: 207-647-8580. E-mail: lakes@leamaine.org. Web Site: www.mainelakes.org/lea-facilities. *Library Contact,* Mary Jewett; E-mail: mary@mainelakes.org
Mem of Maine State Library, Region 1
Open Mon-Fri 8-4

BROOKLIN

P FRIEND MEMORIAL PUBLIC LIBRARY*, One Reach Rd, 04616. (Mail add: PO Box 57, 04616-0057), SAN 306-6010. Tel: 207-359-2276. E-mail: staff@friend.lib.me.us. Web Site: www.friendml.org. *Dir,* Stephanie Atwater; E-mail: director@friend.lib.me.us; Staff 3 (MLS 1, Non-MLS 2)
Founded 1912. Circ 18,200
Library Holdings: Audiobooks 646; DVDs 1,320; Large Print Bks 475; Bk Vols 17,000; Per Subs 58
Wireless access
Open Tues, Wed, Fri & Sat (Winter) 10-4, Thurs 10-6; Tues-Sat (Summer) 10-6
Friends of the Library Group

BROOKSVILLE

P BROOKSVILLE FREE PUBLIC LIBRARY, INC*, Townhouse Bldg, One Townhouse Rd, 04617-3647. (Mail add: PO Box 38, 04617-0038), SAN 306-6029. Tel: 207-326-4560. FAX: 207-326-4560. E-mail: info@brooksvillelibrary.org. Web Site: www.brooksvillelibrary.org. *Libr Dir,* Brook Minner; Staff 2 (MLS 1, Non-MLS 1)
Founded 1953. Pop 753; Circ 3,960
Library Holdings: Bk Vols 12,500; Per Subs 37
Subject Interests: Genealogy, Local hist
Wireless access
Publications: Newsletter
Partic in Scoop Purchasing Coop
Open Mon & Wed 9-5, Thurs 6pm-8pm, Sat 9-12
Friends of the Library Group

BROWNFIELD

P BROWNFIELD PUBLIC LIBRARY, 216 Main St, 04010. (Mail add: PO Box 215, 04010-0215), SAN 374-5473. Tel: 207-935-3003. E-mail: info@brownfieldpubliclibrary.org. Web Site: www.brownfieldpubliclibrary.org. *Libr Dir,* Judi Tordo; Staff 1 (Non-MLS 1)
Founded 1908. Pop 1,643; Circ 2,784
Library Holdings: Audiobooks 112; DVDs 525; Large Print Bks 20; Bk Vols 7,044; Per Subs 2
Wireless access
Mem of Maine State Library, Region 1
Open Tues 2-6, Wed & Sat 10-2

BROWNVILLE

P BROWNVILLE FREE PUBLIC LIBRARY*, 27 Church St, 04414-3235. (Mail add: PO Box 687, 04414-0687), SAN 321-513X. Tel: 207-965-8334. E-mail: brownvillelibrary@trcmaine.org. Web Site: www.trcmaine.org/brownvillelibrary. *Librn,* Autumn Chadwick
Pop 1,540
Library Holdings: Large Print Bks 10; Bk Vols 15,000; Per Subs 16; Spec Interest Per Sub 5
Open Tues & Thurs Noon-6

BRUNSWICK

C BOWDOIN COLLEGE LIBRARY*, 3000 College Sta, 04011-8421. SAN 306-6037. Circulation Tel: 207-725-3280. Interlibrary Loan Service Tel: 207-725-3283. Reference Tel: 207-725-3227. Administration Tel: 207-725-3155. Administration FAX: 207-725-3083. Web Site: library.bowdoin.edu. *Col Librn,* Marjorie Hassen; E-mail: mhassen@bowdoin.edu; *Dir, Archives & Spec Coll,* Kat Stefko; E-mail: kstefko@bowdoin.edu; *Head, Cat,* Mary Macul; *Art Librn,* Anne Haas; *Colls Librn,* Joan Campbell; Tel: 207-725-3285; *Digital Tech Integration Librn,* Mike McDermott; *Humanities Librn, Media Librn,* Carmen Greenlee; Tel: 207-725-3286; *Coord, Research & Instruction, Music & Res Librn,* Karen Jung; *Res & Instruction Librn, Soc Sci Librn,* Beth Hoppe; Tel: 207-725-3260, E-mail: ehoppe@bowdoin.edu; *Res & Instruction Librn,* Barbara Levergood; *Sci Librn,* Sue O'Dell; *Syst & Digital Initiatives Librn,* Karl Fattig; *Web Technologies Librn,* Carr Ross; *Assoc Librn, Research, Instruction & Outreach,* Erin Valentino; Tel: 207-725-3749, E-mail: evalenti@bowdoin.edu; *ILL Supvr,* Guy Saldanha; *Archivist,* Caroline Moseley; E-mail: cmoseley@bowdoin.edu; *Archivist, Res Serv,* Roberta Schwartz; Tel: 207-725-3134. Subject Specialists: *Humanities,* Carmen Greenlee; *Soc sci,* Beth Hoppe; Staff 32 (MLS 16.1, Non-MLS 15.9)
Founded 1794. Enrl 1,773; Fac 185; Highest Degree: Bachelor
Library Holdings: AV Mats 29,864; e-books 299,661; e-journals 29,543; Bk Vols 1,034,168; Per Subs 1,275
Special Collections: Abbot Coll; Arctic Coll; Carlyle Coll; Hawthorne Coll; Huguenot Coll; Longfellow Coll; Maine Coll; Senator George J Mitchell Papers. US Document Depository
Automation Activity & Vendor Info: (Acquisitions) Innovative Interfaces, Inc - Millennium; (Cataloging) Innovative Interfaces, Inc - Millennium; (Circulation) Innovative Interfaces, Inc - Millennium; (Course Reserve) Innovative Interfaces, Inc - Millennium; (OPAC) Innovative Interfaces, Inc - Millennium; (Serials) Innovative Interfaces, Inc - Millennium
Wireless access
Publications: From the Library (Newsletter)
Partic in LYRASIS; OCLC Online Computer Library Center, Inc
Special Services for the Deaf - TDD equip
Departmental Libraries:
BECKWITH MUSIC LIBRARY, Gibson Hall, 1st Flr, 9201 College Sta, 04011. Tel: 207-725-3570. *Coord, Research & Instruction, Music Librn,* Karen Jung; Tel: 207-725-3311, E-mail: kjung@bowdoin.edu
Open Mon-Thurs 9am-Midnight, Fri 9-5, Sat 11-5, Sun Noon-Midnight
HATCH SCIENCE LIBRARY, Hatch Science Bldg, 2nd Flr, 3100 College Sta, 04011. Tel: 207-725-3004. FAX: 207-725-3095. *Sci Librn,* Sue O'Dell; Tel: 207-725-3265, E-mail: sodell@bowdoin.edu
Open Mon-Thurs 8:30am-Midnight, Fri 8:30-8, Sat Noon-8, Sun Noon-Midnight
PIERCE ART LIBRARY, Visual Arts Ctr, 9300 College Sta, 04011-8493. Tel: 207-725-3690. *Art Librn,* Anne Haas; E-mail: ahaas@bowdoin.edu
Open Mon-Thurs 9am-11pm, Fri 9-5, Sat 12-5, Sun Noon-11

P CURTIS MEMORIAL LIBRARY*, 23 Pleasant St, 04011-2295. SAN 306-6045. Tel: 207-725-5242. FAX: 207-725-6313. Web Site: www.curtislibrary.com. *Dir,* Elisabeth Doucett; E-mail: edoucett@curtislibrary.com; *Asst Libr Dir, Youth Serv Mgr,* Pamela Jenkins; E-mail: pjenkins@curtislibrary.com; Staff 20 (MLS 11, Non-MLS 9)
Founded 1883. Pop 26,000; Circ 359,695
Library Holdings: Bk Vols 146,625
Wireless access
Function: Art exhibits, Bks on cassette, Bks on CD, Children's prog, Computers for patron use, Digital talking bks, E-Reserves, Electronic databases & coll, Free DVD rentals, Health sci info serv, Homebound delivery serv, Homework prog, ILL available, Internet access, Magnifiers for reading, Mail & tel request accepted, Museum passes, Music CDs, Photocopying/Printing, Prog for children & young adult, Ref & res, Ref serv available, Summer reading prog, Tax forms, Telephone ref, VHS videos, Wheelchair accessible, Writing prog
Publications: Cornerstones of Science Newlsetter (Biannually); Library Newsletter
Mem of Maine State Library, Region 1
Special Services for the Blind - Assistive/Adapted tech devices, equip & products; Bks on cassette; Bks on CD; Closed circuit TV magnifier; Home delivery serv; Internet workstation with adaptive software; Large print bks;

Low vision equip; Magnifiers; Open bk software on pub access PC; Volunteer serv; ZoomText magnification & reading software
Open Mon-Thurs 9:30-8, Fri 9:30-6, Sat 9:30-5, Sun Noon-4
Friends of the Library Group

S PEJEPSCOT HISTORY CENTER, Research Library, 159 Park Row, 04011. SAN 306-6053. Tel: 207-729-6606. E-mail: info@pejepscothistorical.org. Web Site: pejepscothistorical.org. *Exec Dir,* Larissa Vigue Picard; E-mail: director@pejepscothistorical.org; Staff 3 (Non-MLS 3)
Founded 1888
Library Holdings: Bk Titles 500; Bk Vols 700
Special Collections: History of Brunswick Coll, 1803-59 Lincoln, Isaac, LC MS 65-20001, papers; Joshua Lawrence Chamberlain Coll; Local Franco-American History, Local Industrial History Coll. Oral History
Subject Interests: Local hist
Wireless access
Function: Archival coll, Prog for adults, Prog for children & young adult, Ref & res, Res assist avail, Res libr, Res performed for a fee
Open Wed-Fri 10-12 & 1-4 (Winter); Tues-Sat 10-12 & 1-4 (Summer)
Restriction: Access at librarian's discretion, By permission only, External users must contact libr, Fee for pub use, Free to mem, Internal use only, Non-circulating, Not a lending libr, Open to pub for ref only, Open to pub with supv only

BRYANT POND

P WHITMAN MEMORIAL LIBRARY*, 28 S Main St, 04219. (Mail add: PO Box 307, 04219-0307), SAN 306-7920. Tel: 207-665-2505. E-mail: whitmanlibrary@roadrunner.com. *Librn,* Althea Hathaway; Staff 1 (Non-MLS 1)
Founded 1908. Pop 1,194; Circ 2,456
Library Holdings: AV Mats 50; Bk Vols 11,219; Per Subs 21
Automation Activity & Vendor Info: (Cataloging) Follett Software; (Circulation) Follett Software
Wireless access
Open Tues & Thurs 1-5

BUCKFIELD

P ZADOC LONG FREE LIBRARY*, Five Turner St, 04220. (Mail add: PO Box 179, 04220-0158). Tel: 207-336-2171. E-mail: zadoc@zadoc.lib.me.us. Web Site: zadoc0.wixsite.com/zadoc. *Dir,* Katie Clukey; *Dep Libr Dir,* Kathy Hladik; Staff 1 (Non-MLS 1)
Founded 1901. Pop 3,944; Circ 3,002
Library Holdings: Audiobooks 190; DVDs 30; Large Print Bks 60; Bk Titles 6,000; Per Subs 15; Videos 150
Special Collections: 23rd Maine Company C Reports; Long Diaries; Long Family Photos
Automation Activity & Vendor Info: (Cataloging) JayWil Software Development, Inc; (Circulation) JayWil Software Development, Inc
Wireless access
Function: Adult bk club
Open Mon & Wed 1-7, Tues 9-7, Sat 9-3
Friends of the Library Group

BUCKSPORT

P BUCK MEMORIAL LIBRARY, 47 Main St, 04416. (Mail add: PO Box DD, 04416), SAN 306-607X. Tel: 207-469-2650. E-mail: info@bucklibrary.org. Web Site: bucklibrary.org. *Dir,* Lisa Ladd
Founded 1887. Pop 4,345; Circ 10,233
Library Holdings: Bk Vols 27,000; Per Subs 20
Wireless access
Open Mon-Fri 10-5, Sat 10-12

BUXTON

P WEST BUXTON PUBLIC LIBRARY*, State Rd 112, 34 River Rd, 04093-0348. (Mail add: PO Box 348, 04093-0348), SAN 306-6088. Tel: 207-727-5898. Web Site: www.westbuxtonpubliclibrary.org. *Libr Dir,* Cherise Feser; E-mail: director@westbuxtonpubliclibrary.org; Staff 1 (Non-MLS 1)
Founded 1925. Pop 9,300
Library Holdings: AV Mats 150; Bks-By-Mail 30; CDs 10; DVDs 25; Large Print Bks 30; Bk Titles 6,350; Per Subs 5; Videos 50
Wireless access
Function: Art exhibits, Bks on cassette, Bks on CD, Computers for patron use, E-Reserves, Free DVD rentals, Games & aids for people with disabilities, Holiday prog, ILL available, Magnifiers for reading, Music CDs, Notary serv, Photocopying/Printing, Prof lending libr, Prog for adults, Prog for children & young adult, Summer reading prog, Tax forms, VHS videos, Wheelchair accessible
Mem of Maine State Library, Region 1
Open Tues & Thurs 4-8, Sat 9-1

CALAIS

P CALAIS FREE LIBRARY*, Nine Union St, 04619. SAN 306-6096. Tel: 207-454-2758. Web Site: www.calaisfreelibrary.com. *Dir,* Joyce M Garland; E-mail: jgarlandCFL@gmail.com; Staff 5 (MLS 2, Non-MLS 3)
Founded 1892. Pop 3,963; Circ 49,420
Library Holdings: AV Mats 350; Bk Vols 33,000; Per Subs 49
Special Collections: Champlain Coll; James S Pike Coll; Maine & Genealogy Coll, microfiche; State of Maine Coll
Automation Activity & Vendor Info: (Cataloging) Innovative Interfaces, Inc; (Circulation) Innovative Interfaces, Inc; (OPAC) Innovative Interfaces, Inc
Wireless access
Open Tues-Sat 10-6
Friends of the Library Group

J WASHINGTON COUNTY COMMUNITY COLLEGE LIBRARY*, One College Dr, 04619. SAN 322-8452. Tel: 207-454-1051. FAX: 207-454-1053. Web Site: www.wccc.me.edu/academics/support/library-sub-page. *Dir, Libr Serv,* Elizabeth Phillips; Tel: 207-454-1050, E-mail: ephillips@wccc.me.edu; *Librn,* John Leavitt; E-mail: johnleavitt@wccc.me.edu; Staff 2 (MLS 1, Non-MLS 1)
Enrl 375; Fac 27; Highest Degree: Associate
Library Holdings: Bk Vols 11,000; Per Subs 140
Automation Activity & Vendor Info: (Acquisitions) Innovative Interfaces, Inc; (Cataloging) Innovative Interfaces, Inc; (Circulation) Innovative Interfaces, Inc; (Course Reserve) Innovative Interfaces, Inc; (ILL) Innovative Interfaces, Inc; (OPAC) Innovative Interfaces, Inc; (Serials) Innovative Interfaces, Inc
Wireless access
Partic in Maine InfoNet; Maine State Libr Network
Open Mon-Thurs 8-7, Fri 8-4:30

CAMDEN

P CAMDEN PUBLIC LIBRARY*, 55 Main St, 04843-1703. SAN 306-610X. Tel: 207-236-3440. FAX: 207-236-6673. E-mail: info@librarycamden.org. Web Site: www.librarycamden.org. *Dir,* Nikki Maounis; *Asst Dir,* Ken Gross; *Ch,* Amy Hand; Staff 10 (MLS 2, Non-MLS 8)
Founded 1896. Pop 5,050; Circ 257,786
Library Holdings: AV Mats 6,354; e-books 890; Large Print Bks 686; Bk Vols 60,186; Per Subs 114
Special Collections: Edna St Vincent Millay Coll. Oral History
Automation Activity & Vendor Info: (Acquisitions) Innovative Interfaces, Inc; (Cataloging) Innovative Interfaces, Inc; (Circulation) Innovative Interfaces, Inc; (OPAC) Innovative Interfaces, Inc; (Serials) Innovative Interfaces, Inc
Wireless access
Function: 24/7 Electronic res, 24/7 Online cat, 3D Printer, Adult bk club, Archival coll, Art exhibits, Art programs, Audiobks via web, Bi-weekly Writer's Group, Bk club(s), Bks on CD, Chess club, Children's prog, Computer training, Digital talking bks, E-Readers, E-Reserves, Electronic databases & coll, Free DVD rentals, Holiday prog, Home delivery & serv to seniorr ctr & nursing homes, Homebound delivery serv, ILL available, Internet access, Life-long learning prog for all ages, Magazines, Mail & tel request accepted, Mango lang, Meeting rooms, Microfiche/film & reading machines, Movies, Music CDs, Online cat, Online ref, Outreach serv, Photocopying/Printing, Preschool outreach, Preschool reading prog, Printer for laptops & handheld devices, Prog for adults, Prog for children & young adult, Ref & res, Res assist avail, Senior outreach, STEM programs, Story hour, Summer reading prog, Tax forms, Teen prog, Telephone ref, Wheelchair accessible
Publications: Library Underground (Newsletter)
Partic in Maine InfoNet
Open Mon, Wed, Fri & Sat 9-6, Tues & Thurs 9-9, Sun 1-5

CANAAN

P CANAAN PUBLIC LIBRARY, 22 Hinckley Rd, 04924. (Mail add: PO Box 280, 04924-0280). Tel: 207-474-2149. E-mail: canplib@canaan.lib.me.us. Web Site: canaanpubliclibrary.com. *Dir,* Dixie Ring
Founded 1878. Pop 2,400
Library Holdings: AV Mats 10; Bk Vols 12,000; Per Subs 14; Talking Bks 150
Special Collections: Maine Coll
Automation Activity & Vendor Info: (Cataloging) ComPanion Corp; (Circulation) ComPanion Corp
Wireless access
Open Tues 12-5, Wed 10-6, Fri 10-5
Friends of the Library Group

CAPE ELIZABETH

P THOMAS MEMORIAL LIBRARY, Six Scott Dyer Rd, 04107. SAN 322-6786. Tel: 207-799-1720. Web Site: www.thomasmemoriallibrary.org. *Dir,* Rachel Davis; E-mail: rdavis@thomas.lib.me.us; *Asst Dir, Ch Serv, YA Serv,* Megan Smith; E-mail: msmith@thomas.lib.me.us; Staff 12 (MLS 4, Non-MLS 8)
Founded 1919. Pop 9,130; Circ 123,373
Library Holdings: Electronic Media & Resources 1; Large Print Bks 678; Bk Vols 48,303; Per Subs 86; Talking Bks 2,110; Videos 1,814
Special Collections: Gabriel A Zimpritch Coll; Maine Coll
Subject Interests: Contemporary lit, Contemporary poetry
Automation Activity & Vendor Info: (Cataloging) Innovative Interfaces, Inc; (Circulation) Innovative Interfaces, Inc; (OPAC) Innovative Interfaces, Inc
Wireless access
Mem of Maine State Library, Region 1
Open Mon, Wed, Fri & Sat 10-5, Tues & Thurs 10-7
Friends of the Library Group

CAPE PORPOISE

P CAPE PORPOISE LIBRARY, Kennebunkport, Atlantic Hall, 173 Main St, 04014. (Mail add: PO Box 7714, 04014-7714). Tel: 207-967-5668. FAX: 207-967-5668. E-mail: cplibrary@cape-porpoise.lib.me.us. Web Site: atlantichall.org/library. *Dir,* Mary Giknis; Staff 1 (Non-MLS 1)
Pop 4,054; Circ 24,173
Library Holdings: Bk Titles 6,500
Wireless access
Mem of Maine State Library, Region 1
Open Tues & Thurs 1-4, Fri & Sat 9-12

CARIBOU

P CARIBOU PUBLIC LIBRARY*, 30 High St, 04736. SAN 306-6126. Tel: 207-493-4214. FAX: 207-493-4654. Web Site: www.cariboupubliclibrary.org. *Libr Dir,* Hope Rumpca-Shafer; E-mail: LibraryDirector@cariboumaine.org; *Ch,* Erin Albers; *Asst Librn,* Mary Anderson; *Asst Librn, Cataloger,* Kim Ezzy; *Asst Librn,* Amy Garcia; *Asst Librn, ILL,* Liza Guerrette; *Asst Librn,* Pat Karpen; Staff 6 (MLS 1, Non-MLS 5)
Founded 1911. Pop 8,000; Circ 65,700
Library Holdings: Bk Vols 48,000; Per Subs 105
Special Collections: Local History Coll; Local Newspapers 1887-1976, microfilm. Oral History
Automation Activity & Vendor Info: (Cataloging) Book Systems; (Circulation) Book Systems; (Course Reserve) Book Systems; (OPAC) Book Systems
Wireless access
Function: 24/7 Electronic res, 24/7 Online cat, Activity rm, Adult bk club, After school storytime, Archival coll, Art exhibits, Art programs, Audio & video playback equip for onsite use, Audiobks on Playaways & MP3, Audiobks via web, Bi-weekly Writer's Group, Bk club(s), Bks on CD, Butterfly Garden, CD-ROM, Children's prog, Computer training, Computers for patron use, Digital talking bks, E-Reserves, Electronic databases & coll, For res purposes, Free DVD rentals, Genealogy discussion group, Health sci info serv, Holiday prog, Home delivery & serv to seniorr ctr & nursing homes, ILL available, Internet access, Laminating, Learning ctr, Life-long learning prog for all ages, Magazines, Mail & tel request accepted, Meeting rooms, Microfiche/film & reading machines, Movies, Music CDs, Online cat, Online info literacy tutorials on the web & in blackboard, Online ref, Outreach serv, Photocopying/Printing, Preschool outreach, Preschool reading prog, Printer for laptops & handheld devices, Prog for adults, Prog for children & young adult, Ref & res, Ref serv available, Res assist avail, Scanner, Senior computer classes, Senior outreach, Spanish lang bks, Spoken cassettes & CDs, Spoken cassettes & DVDs, STEM programs, Story hour, Study rm, Summer & winter reading prog, Summer reading prog, Tax forms, Teen prog, Telephone ref, Visual arts prog, Wheelchair accessible, Winter reading prog, Workshops, Writing prog
Open Mon-Thurs 10-7, Fri 10-6, Sat 10-2
Friends of the Library Group

CARMEL

P SIMPSON MEMORIAL LIBRARY*, Eight Plymouth Rd, 04419. (Mail add: PO Box 186, 04419-0186), SAN 376-3544. Tel: 207-848-7145. FAX: 207-848-7145. Web Site: www.simpsonmemorial.org. *Dir,* Becky Ames; E-mail: bames@simpson.lib.me.us; Staff 1 (Non-MLS 1)
Pop 2,850; Circ 4,005
Library Holdings: Audiobooks 192; Bks-By-Mail 30; Bks on Deafness & Sign Lang 5; CDs 96; DVDs 92; Large Print Bks 200; Bk Titles 6,068; Per Subs 11; Videos 315
Wireless access
Function: Bks on cassette, Bks on CD, Children's prog, Computer training, Computers for patron use, Family literacy, Free DVD rentals, ILL available, Internet access, Music CDs, Photocopying/Printing, Ref serv available, Story hour, Summer reading prog, VHS videos, Wheelchair accessible
Open Tues & Thurs 11-7, Sat 9-1
Restriction: Access at librarian's discretion

CARRABASSETT

P CARRABASSETT VALLEY PUBLIC LIBRARY, 3209 Carrabassett Dr, 04947. Tel: 207-237-3535. FAX: 207-237-3536. Web Site: www.carrabassettvalley.org/public-library. *Dir,* Andrea DeBiase; E-mail: adebiase@carrabassett.lib.me.us
Founded 1989
Library Holdings: Bk Vols 10,000
Wireless access
Open Tues-Fri 10-5, Sat 10-3

CASCO

P CASCO PUBLIC LIBRARY, Five Leach Hill Rd, 04015. (Mail add: PO Box 420, 04015-0420), SAN 306-6142. Tel: 207-627-4541. E-mail: cascolibrarian@gmail.com. Web Site: cascopubliclibrary.org. *Dir,* Michelle Brenner; E-mail: cascolibdirector@gmail.com; *Libr Asst,* Wanda Vaughn-Carr; Staff 3 (Non-MLS 3)
Founded 1946. Pop 3,450; Circ 28,000
Library Holdings: Audiobooks 2,241; CDs 231; DVDs 1,928; e-books 5,388; Large Print Bks 116; Bk Vols 17,280; Per Subs 17
Wireless access
Function: 24/7 Online cat, Adult bk club, Audiobks via web, Bks on CD, Children's prog, Computers for patron use, Free DVD rentals, ILL available, Internet access, Meeting rooms, Movies, Music CDs, Online cat, OverDrive digital audio bks, Photocopying/Printing, Prog for adults, Story hour, Workshops
Mem of Maine State Library, Region 1
Partic in Maine School & Library Network
Special Services for the Deaf - Adult & family literacy prog
Open Tues 10-7, Wed & Sun 12-5, Thurs 10-5

CASTINE

C MAINE MARITIME ACADEMY*, Nutting Memorial Library, Pleasant St, Box C-1, 04420. SAN 306-6150. Tel: 207-326-2263. E-mail: library@mma.edu. Web Site: mainemaritime.edu/nutting-memorial-library. *Head Librn,* Lauren Gargani; Tel: 207-326-2260, E-mail: lauren.gargani@mma.edu; *Pub Serv Librn,* Ann Dyer; Tel: 207-326-2264, E-mail: ann.dyer@mma.edu; *Tech Serv Librn,* Sarah Danser; Tel: 207-326-2262, E-mail: sarah.danser@mma.edu; Staff 5 (MLS 3, Non-MLS 2)
Founded 1941. Enrl 820; Fac 65; Highest Degree: Master
Library Holdings: Bk Titles 66,000; Per Subs 250
Special Collections: Federal Maritime Commission Papers (Kanuk Coll); Military History (Schieffelin Coll); Oceanography (Gilmartin Coll). US Document Depository
Subject Interests: Marine tech, Maritime hist, Mil hist
Automation Activity & Vendor Info: (Acquisitions) Innovative Interfaces, Inc; (Cataloging) Innovative Interfaces, Inc; (Circulation) Innovative Interfaces, Inc; (Course Reserve) Innovative Interfaces, Inc; (ILL) OCLC; (OPAC) Innovative Interfaces, Inc; (Serials) Innovative Interfaces, Inc
Wireless access
Function: ILL available
Partic in LYRASIS

P WITHERLE MEMORIAL LIBRARY*, 41 School St, 04421. (Mail add: PO Box 202, 04421), SAN 306-6169. Tel: 207-326-4375. E-mail: refdesk@witherle.lib.me.us. Web Site: www.witherle.lib.me.us. *Libr Dir,* Anne Romans; E-mail: afr@witherle.lib.me.us; *Asst Dir, Youth Serv,* Irene Hall; E-mail: irene@witherle.lib.me.us; Staff 4 (MLS 1, Non-MLS 3)
Founded 1801. Pop 1,012; Circ 20,208
Jul 2019-Jun 2020 Income $188,188, City $84,688, Locally Generated Income $1,800, Other $101,700. Mats Exp $25,596, Books $18,675, Per/Ser (Incl. Access Fees) $1,421, AV Mat $5,250, Electronic Ref Mat (Incl. Access Fees) $250. Sal $107,260 (Prof $50,335)
Library Holdings: Audiobooks 1,173; Bks on Deafness & Sign Lang 11; Braille Volumes 5; CDs 598; DVDs 2,829; e-books 19,298; Electronic Media & Resources 60; Large Print Bks 386; Microforms 20; Bk Titles 12,604; Bk Vols 12,604; Per Subs 41
Special Collections: Castine Coll, local history materials; Castine Newspapers on Microfilm 1800s & 1900s
Automation Activity & Vendor Info: (Acquisitions) Innovative Interfaces, Inc; (Cataloging) Innovative Interfaces, Inc; (Circulation) Innovative Interfaces, Inc; (ILL) Innovative Interfaces, Inc; (Media Booking) Innovative Interfaces, Inc; (OPAC) Innovative Interfaces, Inc; (Serials) Innovative Interfaces, Inc
Wireless access
Function: 24/7 Electronic res, 24/7 Online cat, Activity rm, Adult bk club, Archival coll, Art exhibits, Art programs, Audiobks on Playaways & MP3,

Audiobks via web, AV serv, Bk club(s), Bks on CD, Children's prog, Computer training, Computers for patron use, Electronic databases & coll, Equip loans & repairs, Free DVD rentals, Holiday prog, Homebound delivery serv, Homework prog, ILL available, Internet access, Life-long learning prog for all ages, Magazines, Mail & tel request accepted, Microfiche/film & reading machines, Movies, Music CDs, Online cat, Orientations, Outreach serv, Outside serv via phone, mail, e-mail & web, Photocopying/Printing, Printer for laptops & handheld devices, Prog for adults, Prog for children & young adult, Ref & res, Ref serv available, Res assist avail, Scanner, Senior computer classes, Senior outreach, Spoken cassettes & CDs, Spoken cassettes & DVDs, STEM programs, Story hour, Summer & winter reading prog, Summer reading prog, Telephone ref, Wheelchair accessible, Winter reading prog, Workshops, Writing prog
Special Services for the Deaf - Bks on deafness & sign lang; Closed caption videos
Special Services for the Blind - Large print bks; Talking bks
Open Mon-Fri 10-5, Sat 10-3
Friends of the Library Group

CENTER LOVELL

P LEWIS DANA HILL MEMORIAL LIBRARY*, 2079 Main St, 04231-9702. (Mail add: PO Box 92, 04016-0092), SAN 376-3757. Tel: 207-928-2301. E-mail: ldhill2079@gmail.com. *Head Librn,* Nancy Wilson; Staff 1 (Non-MLS 1)
Pop 3,000
Library Holdings: DVDs 200; Large Print Bks 50; Bk Titles 9,000; Bk Vols 10,000; Per Subs 15; Talking Bks 100; Videos 400
Wireless access
Open Tues & Thurs 5-7, Sat 9-12

CHARLESTON

S MAINE DEPARTMENT OF CORRECTIONS*, Charleston Correctional Facility Library, 1202 Dover Rd, 04422. Tel: 207-285-0876. FAX: 207-285-0815. *Librn,* Gary Gray
Founded 1980
Library Holdings: Bk Vols 3,000; Per Subs 15
Restriction: Not open to pub, Restricted access

S MOUNTAIN VIEW CORRECTIONAL FACILITY LIBRARY, 1182 Dover Rd, 04422. Tel: 207-285-0880. FAX: 207-285-0836. *Librn,* Matthew Dever
Library Holdings: Bk Titles 5,674; Per Subs 15

CHEBEAGUE ISLAND

P CHEBEAGUE ISLAND LIBRARY, 247 South Rd, Unit 3, 04017-3200. SAN 306-6207. Tel: 207-846-4351. FAX: 207-846-4358. E-mail: cheblib@hotmail.com. Web Site: cheblib.wixsite.com/chebeaguelibrary. *Dir,* Chloe Dyer
Founded 1965. Pop 2,000; Circ 13,450
Library Holdings: AV Mats 2,000; Large Print Bks 180; Bk Vols 16,000; Per Subs 32; Talking Bks 584
Subject Interests: Genealogy, Local hist, Maine
Wireless access
Mem of Maine State Library, Region 1
Open Tues & Thurs 4-8, Wed, Fri & Sat 10-1 (Winter); Mon 6-8, Wed, Fri & Sat 10-1 (Summer)
Friends of the Library Group

CHERRYFIELD

P CHERRYFIELD FREE PUBLIC LIBRARY, 35 Main St, 04622. (Mail add: PO Box 121, 04622-4201), SAN 321-5989. Tel: 207-546-4228. E-mail: cherryfieldpubliclibrary@gmail.com. Web Site: cherryfieldlibrary.com. *Dir,* Cara Elizabeth Sawyer; Staff 1 (MLS 1)
Founded 1837. Pop 1,320; Circ 2,106
Library Holdings: DVDs 1,766; Large Print Bks 350; Bk Titles 7,000; Talking Bks 320
Wireless access
Open Tues-Fri 2-6, Sat 11-3

CHINA

P ALBERT CHURCH BROWN MEMORIAL LIBRARY*, 37 Main St, 04358. (Mail add: PO Box 6146, China Village, 04926-0146), SAN 376-687X. Tel: 207-968-2926. E-mail: chinalibraryacb@gmail.com. *Librn,* Mary Grow; Staff 1 (Non-MLS 1)
Pop 4,328
Library Holdings: AV Mats 110; Bk Vols 16,500; Per Subs 13
Wireless access
Open Tues 2-6:30, Thurs 2-5:30, Sat 10-Noon

CLIFF ISLAND

P CLIFF ISLAND LIBRARY*, 119 Sunset Ave, 04019. (Mail add: PO Box 117, 04019-0119). E-mail: library@cliffisland.com. *Dir,* Amy Lent
Wireless access
Mem of Maine State Library, Region 1
Open Mon, Wed & Fri (Summer) 10-Noon, Sat 1-3

CLINTON

P BROWN MEMORIAL LIBRARY*, 53 Railroad St, 04927. SAN 376-7434. Tel: 207-426-8686. FAX: 207-426-8686. E-mail: brownmemorial@roadrunner.com. Web Site: www.clinton-me.us. *Libr Dir,* Cheryl Dickey-Whitish; *Asst Dir,* Cindy Lowell
Pop 3,636; Circ 5,840
Library Holdings: AV Mats 171; Bk Vols 13,478; Per Subs 36; Videos 100
Open Mon (Winter) 10-5, Tues & Wed 10-6, Thurs 12-8, Sat 9-1; Mon & Wed (Summer) 9-4, Tues 10-6, Thurs 12-8, Fri 9-3, Sat 9-1
Friends of the Library Group

CORINNA

P STEWART FREE LIBRARY*, Eight Levi Stewart Dr, 04928. SAN 306-6185. Tel: 207-278-2454. FAX: 207-278-5200. Web Site: www.corinna.govoffice.com. *Dir,* Jamie Irving; E-mail: stewartdirector@stewart.lib.me.us; Staff 1 (Non-MLS 1)
Pop 2,196; Circ 7,228
Library Holdings: AV Mats 402; Large Print Bks 70; Bk Titles 12,516; Per Subs 18; Talking Bks 160
Special Collections: Abraham Lincoln, Napoleon & Civil War (Levi Stewart Private Library Room)
Wireless access
Open Tues 9-2, Wed & Thurs 1-7, Sat 9-Noon

CORINTH

P ATKINS MEMORIAL LIBRARY, 360 Main St, 04427. Tel: 207-285-7226. E-mail: atkinslibrary@aol.com. *Dir,* Christina Bean
Founded 1937. Pop 2,793; Circ 1,615
Library Holdings: AV Mats 25; Bk Vols 12,000
Special Collections: Annuals (Academy Rocket, Central High School Rocket); Local Interest
Function: Archival coll, Children's prog, Computers for patron use
Open Thurs 12:30-6
Restriction: Non-circulating of rare bks, Residents only

CORNISH

P BONNEY MEMORIAL LIBRARY*, 36 Main St, 04020. (Mail add: PO Box 857, 04020-0857), SAN 306-6193. Tel: 207-625-8083. FAX: 207-625-8083. Web Site: www.bonney.lib.me.us, www.bonneylib.org. *Dir,* Cheryl Hevey; E-mail: chevey@bonney.lib.me.us; Staff 1 (MLS 1)
Founded 1928. Pop 1,403
Library Holdings: Audiobooks 532; CDs 160; DVDs 85; Bk Titles 14,758; Per Subs 15; Videos 310
Automation Activity & Vendor Info: (Cataloging) LibraryWorld, Inc; (Circulation) LibraryWorld, Inc; (OPAC) LibraryWorld, Inc
Wireless access
Mem of Maine State Library, Region 1
Open Mon & Wed 10-7, Tues & Thurs 12-6, Sat (Sept-June) 10-1
Friends of the Library Group

CRANBERRY ISLES

P GREAT CRANBERRY LIBRARY*, 251 Cranberry Rd, 04625. (Mail add: PO Box 89, 04625-0013). Tel: 207-244-7358. FAX: 207-244-7358. E-mail: greatcranberrylibrary@yahoo.com. Web Site: www.cranberryisles.com. *Dir,* Ingrid Gaither; Staff 1 (Non-MLS 1)
Founded 1977. Circ 2,402
Library Holdings: Large Print Bks 20; Bk Vols 7,556; Per Subs 16; Talking Bks 80
Special Collections: Municipal Document Depository
Wireless access
Open Tues & Fri (Oct-May) 10-2; Mon-Fri (June-Aug) 10-2

CUMBERLAND

P PRINCE MEMORIAL LIBRARY*, 266 Main St, 04021-9754. SAN 306-6215. Tel: 207-829-2215. FAX: 207-829-2221. E-mail: library@cumberlandmaine.com. Web Site: www.princememorial.lib.me.us/researcher. *Dir,* Thomas C Bennett; Tel: 207-829-2216, E-mail: tbennett@cumberlandmaine.com; *Circ Librn,* Arabella Eldredge; E-mail: aeldredge@cumberlandmaine.com; *Ref Librn,* Elizabeth Tarasevich; E-mail: etarasevich@cumberlandmaine.com; *Youth Serv Librn,* Lauren Isele; E-mail: lisele@cumberlandmaine.com; Staff 3 (MLS 1, Non-MLS 2)

Founded 1923. Pop 10,300; Circ 94,000
Library Holdings: Audiobooks 1,353; DVDs 3,561; Large Print Bks 1,870; Bk Titles 47,000; Per Subs 98
Special Collections: Maine Coll
Automation Activity & Vendor Info: (Cataloging) ComPanion Corp; (Circulation) ComPanion Corp; (OPAC) ComPanion Corp
Wireless access
Mem of Maine State Library, Region 1
Open Mon-Thurs 9-8, Fri 9-5, Sat 9-2
Friends of the Library Group

CUSHING

P CUSHING PUBLIC LIBRARY*, 39 Cross Rd, 04563. (Mail add: PO Box 25, 04563-0025). Tel: 207-354-8860. E-mail: cushinglibrary@cushing.lib.me.us. Web Site: www.cushing.lib.me.us. *Dir,* Rebecca Dinces
Founded 1995. Pop 1,400
Library Holdings: AV Mats 200; Bk Vols 3,000; Talking Bks 200
Wireless access
Open Mon & Fri 10-2, Wed 10-4, Sat 10-Noon
Friends of the Library Group

DAMARISCOTTA

P SKIDOMPHA PUBLIC LIBRARY, 184 Main St, 04543. (Mail add: PO Box 70, 04543-0070), SAN 306-6223. Tel: 207-563-5513. Circulation Tel: 207-563-1058. FAX: 207-563-1941. Web Site: www.skidompha.org. *Exec Dir,* Matthew Graff; E-mail: director@skidompha.org; Staff 3 (Non-MLS 3)
Founded 1905. Pop 9,000; Circ 68,000
Library Holdings: Large Print Bks 250; Bk Vols 30,000; Per Subs 20
Subject Interests: Genealogy, Local hist
Automation Activity & Vendor Info: (Acquisitions) Innovative Interfaces, Inc; (Cataloging) Innovative Interfaces, Inc; (Circulation) Innovative Interfaces, Inc; (ILL) Innovative Interfaces, Inc
Wireless access
Open Tues, Wed & Fri 10-4, Sat 10-1
Friends of the Library Group

DANFORTH

P DANFORTH PUBLIC LIBRARY*, 46 Central St, 04424. (Mail add: PO Box 66, 04424-0066). Tel: 207-448-2055. Web Site: www.danforth.lib.me.us. *Library Contact,* Elizabeth Wilson
Pop 600
Library Holdings: DVDs 100; Large Print Bks 95; Bk Vols 2,500
Wireless access
Open Tues & Sat (Summer) 10-2; Sat (Winter) 10-12:30

DEER ISLE

S DEER ISLE-STONINGTON HISTORICAL SOCIETY LIBRARY, ARCHIVES & MUSEUM, Rte 15A/416 Sunset Rd, 04627. (Mail add: PO Box 652, 04627-0652), SAN 370-2162. Tel: 207-348-6400. E-mail: DISHS.info@gmail.com. Web Site: dis-historicalsociety.org. *Pres,* Susan Greenlaw
Founded 1959
Library Holdings: Bk Vols 789
Special Collections: Oral History
Subject Interests: Genealogy, Island Indians, Marine hist, Marine vessels, Steamboats, Yachts
Open Wed-Fri (Summer) 1-4; Wed & Fri (Winter) 1-4 or by appointment

P CHASE EMERSON MEMORIAL LIBRARY*, 17 Main St, 04627. (Mail add: PO Box 9, 04627-0009), SAN 306-6231. Tel: 207-348-2899. E-mail: deerislelibrary@gmail.com. Web Site: www.deerislelibrary.org. *Dir,* Valerie Messana; Staff 1 (Non-MLS 1)
Founded 1922. Pop 1,985; Circ 5,552
Library Holdings: Bk Titles 24,000; Per Subs 12; Talking Bks 500; Videos 300
Special Collections: Merchant Sail (William A Fairburn Coll); Official Records of the Union & Confederate Armies (War of the Rebellion Coll)
Wireless access
Open Mon 2-6, Wed 10-4, Sat 9-12

DENMARK

P DENMARK PUBLIC LIBRARY*, 121 E Main St, 04022. (Mail add: PO Box 50, 04022-0050), SAN 376-3811. Tel: 207-452-2200. E-mail: denmarklib@denmark.lib.me.us. Web Site: denmarklibrary3.wixsite.com/denmarklibrary. *Librn,* Robin Gosbee; Staff 1 (Non-MLS 1)
Founded 1987. Pop 2,008
Library Holdings: Bk Vols 6,500
Wireless access
Open Tues & Thurs 2-7, Wed 9-Noon, Sat 9-1
Friends of the Library Group

DENNYSVILLE

P LINCOLN MEMORIAL LIBRARY, 17 King St, 04628. (Mail add: PO Box 53, 04628-0053). Tel: 207-726-4750. FAX: 207-726-4751. E-mail: lincmem@lincolnd.lib.me.us. Web Site: www.facebook.com/TheLincolnMemorialLibrary. *Dir,* Dr Colin Windhorst
Library Holdings: AV Mats 66; Large Print Bks 10; Bk Vols 5,000; Per Subs 10; Talking Bks 26
Special Collections: Local History & Genealogy Coll
Wireless access
Open Mon 4-7, Tues & Fri 1:30-4, Wed 2-4
Friends of the Library Group

DETROIT

P ANNA FIELD FERNALD LIBRARY*, 35 S Main St, 04929-3252. Tel: 207-257-4488. FAX: 207-257-2434. E-mail: townofdetroit@roadrunner.com. *Co-Dir,* Elsie Kelley; *Co-Dir,* Carol McCarron
Founded 1988. Pop 833; Circ 219
Library Holdings: Bk Vols 2,500

DEXTER

P ABBOTT MEMORIAL LIBRARY, One Church St, 04930. SAN 306-6258. Tel: 207-924-7292. Web Site: abbott-library.com. *Dir,* Liz Breault; E-mail: liz@abbott-library.com; Staff 1 (MLS 1)
Founded 1894. Pop 3,580; Circ 24,764
Library Holdings: AV Mats 1,780; Bk Titles 19,225; Bk Vols 26,217; Per Subs 72
Special Collections: Maine History Coll, bks, cht, maps
Automation Activity & Vendor Info: (Cataloging) Winnebago Software Co; (Circulation) Winnebago Software Co
Wireless access
Open Tues-Fri 9:30-6, Sat 9:30-2:30

DIXFIELD

P LUDDEN MEMORIAL LIBRARY*, 42 Main St, 04224. (Mail add: PO Box 805, 04224-0805), SAN 306-6266. Tel: 207-562-8838. FAX: 207-562-4311. Web Site: www.dixfield.org/library.html. *Dir,* Peggy Malley; E-mail: peggy.malley@ludden.lib.me.us; Staff 1 (Non-MLS 1)
Founded 1939. Pop 5,000; Circ 28,663
Jul 2018-Jun 2019. Mats Exp $145,000
Library Holdings: Bk Vols 20,000; Per Subs 33
Special Collections: Maine Town Histories & Geneologies
Automation Activity & Vendor Info: (Cataloging) Innovative Interfaces, Inc; (Circulation) Innovative Interfaces, Inc; (ILL) Innovative Interfaces, Inc; (OPAC) Innovative Interfaces, Inc
Wireless access
Function: 24/7 Online cat, Activity rm, Audio & video playback equip for onsite use, Audiobks via web, Bks on cassette, Bks on CD, Children's prog, Computers for patron use, Electronic databases & coll, Free DVD rentals, Games & aids for people with disabilities, Homebound delivery serv, ILL available, Internet access, Learning ctr, Life-long learning prog for all ages, Magazines, Mail & tel request accepted, Meeting rooms, Movies, Online cat, Outside serv via phone, mail, e-mail & web, OverDrive digital audio bks, Photocopying/Printing, Prog for children & young adult, Ref serv available, Scanner, Serves people with intellectual disabilities, Spoken cassettes & CDs, Spoken cassettes & DVDs, Story hour, Study rm, Summer reading prog, Tax forms, VHS videos, Wheelchair accessible
Special Services for the Blind - Large print bks
Open Mon-Fri 9:30-5:30, Sat 9-12

DOVER-FOXCROFT

P THOMPSON FREE LIBRARY*, 186 E Main St, 04426. SAN 306-6274. Tel: 207-564-3350. FAX: 207-564-3531. E-mail: thompsonfreelibrary@gmail.com. Web Site: www.thompson.lib.me.us. *Dir,* Greta Schroeder; Staff 3 (MLS 1, Non-MLS 2)
Founded 1898. Pop 4,200; Circ 60,000
Library Holdings: CDs 21; DVDs 70; Bk Vols 30,365; Per Subs 30; Talking Bks 1,300; Videos 1,700
Special Collections: Maine Town Histories
Subject Interests: Gardening, Genealogy, Hist
Automation Activity & Vendor Info: (Cataloging) Evergreen; (Circulation) Evergreen; (OPAC) Evergreen
Wireless access
Open Tues & Thurs 9-7, Wed & Fri 9-5, Sat 9-1
Friends of the Library Group

DRESDEN

P BRIDGE ACADEMY PUBLIC LIBRARY, 44 Middle Rd, 04342. Tel: 207-737-8810. FAX: 207-737-8810. E-mail: bridge.academy.library@gmail.com. Web Site: www.bapl.us. *Dir,* Amalia Farel; Staff 1 (Non-MLS 1)
Pop 1,750; Circ 1,400
Library Holdings: Large Print Bks 25; Bk Titles 8,000; Per Subs 12; Talking Bks 150
Special Collections: Maine Books
Automation Activity & Vendor Info: (Acquisitions) LibraryWorld, Inc
Wireless access
Function: Electronic databases & coll, Online ref, Photocopying/Printing, Prog for adults, Prog for children & young adult
Partic in Maine State Libr Network
Special Services for the Deaf - Assisted listening device; Bks on deafness & sign lang
Open Tues & Thurs 2-7, Sat 9-Noon

EAST BALDWIN

P BROWN MEMORIAL LIBRARY*, Two Norton Pl, 04024. (Mail add: PO Box 24, 04024-0024), SAN 372-7548. Tel: 207-787-3155. E-mail: bml@brown.lib.me.us. Web Site: www.brown.lib.me.us. *Librn,* Janet Fricker; Staff 1 (MLS 1)
Founded 1906. Pop 1,300; Circ 3,500
Library Holdings: Bks on Deafness & Sign Lang 10; CDs 90; DVDs 25; Electronic Media & Resources 4; Large Print Bks 50; Bk Vols 10,000; Videos 450
Special Collections: Baldwin History, bks, photogs; Baldwin Town Records
Automation Activity & Vendor Info: (Acquisitions) Baker & Taylor; (Cataloging) Koha; (Circulation) Koha; (OPAC) Koha
Wireless access
Mem of Maine State Library, Region 1
Special Services for the Deaf - Bks on deafness & sign lang
Open Mon 9-11:30, Wed 2-6, Fri 3-6, Sat 9-1

EAST MACHIAS

P STURDIVANT PUBLIC LIBRARY, 514 Main St, 04630. (Mail add: PO Box 117, 04630), SAN 306-6290. Tel: 207-255-0070. E-mail: sturdivantpubliclibrary@gmail.com. Web Site: www.sturdivant.lib.me.us. *Dir,* Joyce Holway
Founded 1934. Pop 1,200
Library Holdings: Bk Vols 7,500
Wireless access
Open Tues & Sat 10-2, Wed 12-7

EAST MILLINOCKET

P EAST MILLINOCKET PUBLIC LIBRARY, 53 Main St, 04430. SAN 306-6304. Tel: 207-746-3554. FAX: 207-746-3550. Web Site: eastmillinocket.org/public-library.aspx. *Library Contact,* Angela Cote; E-mail: acote@gwi.net; Staff 1 (Non-MLS 1)
Library Holdings: Large Print Bks 300; Bk Titles 22,700
Automation Activity & Vendor Info: (Cataloging) LS 2000; (Circulation) LS 2000
Open Mon & Fri 9-Noon, Tues-Thurs 1-4

EAST VASSALBORO

P VASSALBORO PUBLIC LIBRARY*, 930 Bog Rd, 04935. (Mail add: PO Box 62, 04935-0062), SAN 306-6312. Tel: 207-923-3233. E-mail: vplibrary@gmail.com. *Libr Dir,* Donna Lambert; *Asst Librn,* Brian Stanley; Staff 2 (Non-MLS 2)
Founded 1910. Pop 4,000; Circ 23,031
Library Holdings: Bk Titles 27,584; Bk Vols 37,000; Per Subs 20
Subject Interests: Local hist
Wireless access
Open Mon & Wed 12:30-8, Sat 10-6

EAST WATERBORO

P WATERBORO PUBLIC LIBRARY, 187 Main St, 04030. SAN 376-3854. Tel: 207-247-3363. FAX: 207-247-3363. E-mail: librarian@waterborolibrary.org. Web Site: www.waterborolibrary.org. *Dir,* Julie Hoyle; E-mail: julie@waterborolibrary.org; *Asst Librn,* Pauline Keith
Founded 1985. Pop 7,500
Library Holdings: DVDs 50; Bk Titles 21,000; Per Subs 20; Talking Bks 800; Videos 650
Automation Activity & Vendor Info: (Cataloging) Follett Software; (Circulation) Follett Software; (OPAC) Follett Software
Wireless access
Function: 24/7 Electronic res, 24/7 Online cat, Adult bk club, Audiobks via web, Bks on CD, Children's prog, Computers for patron use, Free DVD rentals, Holiday prog, ILL available, Internet access, Life-long learning prog for all ages, Magazines, Mail & tel request accepted, Meeting rooms, Online cat, Photocopying/Printing, Preschool reading prog, Printer for laptops & handheld devices, Prog for adults, Prog for children & young adult, Scanner, Story hour, Summer & winter reading prog, Summer reading prog, Tax forms, Telephone ref, Wheelchair accessible, Writing prog
Mem of Maine State Library, Region 1
Open Mon, Tues & Thurs 2-8, Wed 9-3, Sat 9-2
Friends of the Library Group

EASTPORT

P PEAVEY MEMORIAL LIBRARY*, 26 Water St, 04631-1599. SAN 306-6320. Tel: 207-853-4021. FAX: 207-853-4021. E-mail: peaveymemoriallibrary@yahoo.com. *Dir,* Dana Chevalier
Founded 1893. Pop 4,100; Circ 7,384
Library Holdings: CDs 400; Bk Vols 33,000; Per Subs 40; Talking Bks 450; Videos 1,000
Special Collections: Civil War Coll; Genealogy Coll; Local Artists Coll, paintings, prints; Local Authors Coll; Local History Coll; Maine Coll; Newspaper, 1819-1915 (Eastport Sentinel Coll), micro & bd vols
Wireless access
Special Services for the Blind - Braille bks; Large print bks; Talking bks
Open Mon 10-8, Tues-Fri 10-5, Sat 10-3, Sun Noon-3
Friends of the Library Group

ELIOT

P WILLIAM FOGG LIBRARY*, 116 Old Rd, 03903. (Mail add: PO Box 359, 03903-0359), SAN 306-6339. Tel: 207-439-9437. FAX: 207-439-1580. Web Site: williamfogglibrary.org. *Adult Serv, Dir,* Lydia P Goodwin; E-mail: goodwinl@williamfogglibrary.org; *Asst Dir, Ch Serv,* Maureen Flanagan; E-mail: childrensservices@williamfogglibrary.org; Staff 5 (MLS 2, Non-MLS 3)
Founded 1907. Pop 6,000; Circ 20,000
Library Holdings: Bk Titles 22,000; Bk Vols 23,000; Per Subs 40
Subject Interests: Genealogy, Local hist
Automation Activity & Vendor Info: (Cataloging) Follett Software; (Circulation) Follett Software; (OPAC) Follett Software
Wireless access
Mem of Maine State Library, Region 1
Special Services for the Blind - Large print & cassettes
Open Mon & Wed 11-6, Tues, Thurs & Sat 10-5
Friends of the Library Group

ELLSWORTH

P ELLSWORTH PUBLIC LIBRARY*, 20 State St, 04605. SAN 306-6347. Tel: 207-667-6363. FAX: 207-667-4901. Web Site: www.ellsworth.lib.me.us. *Libr Dir,* Amy Wisehart; E-mail: director@ellsworthlibrary.net; *Asst Dir,* Sandy Abbott; *Commun Engagement Librn,* Abby Morrow; *Youth Serv Librn,* Keli Gancos; *Circ Tech,* Mary McKillop; *Youth Serv,* Cheryl Flanders; Staff 10.5 (MLS 2, Non-MLS 8.5)
Founded 1897. Pop 24,000; Circ 174,000
Library Holdings: AV Mats 2,640; Bk Vols 37,929; Per Subs 140; Talking Bks 1,450; Videos 1,329
Special Collections: Whitmore Genealogy Coll
Subject Interests: Local hist
Automation Activity & Vendor Info: (Acquisitions) Biblionix/Apollo; (Cataloging) Biblionix/Apollo; (Circulation) Biblionix/Apollo; (OPAC) Biblionix/Apollo
Wireless access
Open Mon, Tues & Fri 9-5, Wed & Thurs 9-8, Sat 9-2
Friends of the Library Group

ENFIELD

P COLE MEMORIAL LIBRARY*, 789 Hammett Rd, 04493-4347. SAN 325-2698. Tel: 207-732-4270. FAX: 207-732-5335. E-mail: colelibrary@colemem.lib.me.us. Web Site: www.colemem.lib.me.us. *Dir,* Susan Kramer
Founded 1974. Pop 1,664
Library Holdings: AV Mats 296; Large Print Bks 61; Bk Titles 3,072; Bk Vols 3,098
Special Collections: Genealogy Coll
Wireless access
Open Mon-Thurs 7-5

FAIRFIELD

J KENNEBEC VALLEY COMMUNITY COLLEGE*, Lunder Library, 92 Western Ave, 04937-1367. SAN 321-5636. Tel: 207-453-5004. Interlibrary Loan Service Tel: 207-453-5195. FAX: 207-453-5194. E-mail: library@kvcc.me.edu. Web Site: www.kvcc.me.edu/pages/library. *Dir,*

Stephen LaRochelle; E-mail: slarochelle@kvcc.me.edu; *Pub Serv Librn,* Barbara Bartley; E-mail: bbartley@kvcc.me.edu; Staff 3 (MLS 3)
Founded 1979. Enrl 2,000; Fac 50; Highest Degree: Associate
Library Holdings: Bk Vols 17,000; Per Subs 30; Videos 2,500
Subject Interests: Allied health, Bus, Computers, Nursing
Wireless access
Partic in LYRASIS; OCLC Online Computer Library Center, Inc
Open Mon-Thurs 9-4, Fri 9-1

P LAWRENCE PUBLIC LIBRARY*, 33 Lawrence Ave, 04937. SAN 306-6355. Tel: 207-453-6867. E-mail: library@fairfieldme.com. Web Site: www.fairfieldme.com/library. *Dir,* Louella Bickford; Staff 1 (Non-MLS 1)
Founded 1901. Pop 6,113; Circ 15,597
Library Holdings: Bk Titles 26,000; Per Subs 60
Special Collections: Fairfield Historical Society Coll
Automation Activity & Vendor Info: (Cataloging) Winnebago Software Co; (Circulation) Winnebago Software Co; (OPAC) Winnebago Software Co
Wireless access
Open Mon 12-6, Tues, Wed & Fri 10-5, Thurs 12-8, Sat 9-2
Friends of the Library Group

FALMOUTH

P FALMOUTH MEMORIAL LIBRARY, Five Lunt Rd, 04105. SAN 306-6363. Tel: 207-781-2351. FAX: 207-781-4094. E-mail: staff@falmouthmemoriallibrary.org. Web Site: falmouthmemoriallibrary.org. *Libr Dir,* Jenna Mayotte; E-mail: jmayotte@falmouthmemoriallibrary.org; *Asst Dir, Cataloger,* Ellen Conway; E-mail: econway@falmouth.lib.me.us; Staff 5 (MLS 5)
Founded 1944. Pop 12,000; Circ 172,000
Library Holdings: CDs 1,106; DVDs 700; Large Print Bks 320; Bk Titles 42,588; Per Subs 90; Talking Bks 1,189; Videos 1,200
Special Collections: Crafts & Needlepoint Coll; Gardening Coll; Maine Coll
Subject Interests: Local hist
Automation Activity & Vendor Info: (Cataloging) Innovative Interfaces, Inc; (Circulation) Innovative Interfaces, Inc; (OPAC) Innovative Interfaces, Inc
Wireless access
Function: Adult bk club, Art exhibits, Bk club(s), Home delivery & serv to seniorr ctr & nursing homes, Homebound delivery serv, ILL available, Internet access, Magnifiers for reading, Music CDs, Photocopying/Printing, Prog for adults, Prog for children & young adult, Ref serv available, Spoken cassettes & CDs, Spoken cassettes & DVDs, Summer reading prog, VHS videos, Wheelchair accessible
Mem of Maine State Library, Region 1
Open Mon, Tues & Thurs-Sat 9:30-5, Wed 9:30-7
Friends of the Library Group

S MAINE EDUCATION CENTER FOR THE DEAF & HARD OF HEARING, Governor Baxter School for the Deaf Library, One Mackworth Island, 04105-1951. SAN 328-1973. Tel: 207-781-3165. FAX: 207-781-6240. Web Site: www.mecdhh.org. *Library Contact,* Leona Anderson
Library Holdings: Bk Titles 9,000; Per Subs 30
Subject Interests: Am sign lang, Audiology, Deaf culture, Deaf educ, Deafness
Automation Activity & Vendor Info: (Cataloging) Follett Software; (Circulation) Follett Software; (Course Reserve) Follett Software
Wireless access
Function: ILL available, Outside serv via phone, mail, e-mail & web, Photocopying/Printing, Prof lending libr, Telephone ref
Special Services for the Deaf - Am sign lang & deaf culture; Coll on deaf educ; Staff with knowledge of sign lang; TTY equip
Open Mon, Tues, Thurs & Fri 12:30-2:30
Restriction: Circ limited

M MAINEHEALTH*, Falmouth Learning Resource Center, Five Bucknam Rd, Ste 1A, 04105. Tel: 207-781-1732. Toll Free Tel: 866-609-5183. FAX: 207-781-1546. E-mail: LC-LRCLibrary@mainehealth.org, LEARNINGCENTER@mainehealth.org. Web Site: www.mainehealthlearningcenter.org. *Dir,* Ward Peck; E-mail: peckw@mainehealth.org
Mem of Maine State Library, Region 1
Open Mon-Fri 8:30-4:30
Branches:
SCARBOROUGH LEARNING RESOURCE CENTER, 100 Campus Dr, Ste 122, Scarborough, 04074. E-mail: learningcenter@mainehealth.org. *Dir,* Ward Peck; E-mail: peckw@mainehealth.org
Open Mon-Fri 8:30-4:30

FARMINGTON

P FARMINGTON PUBLIC LIBRARY, 117 Academy St, 04938. SAN 306-6371. Tel: 207-778-4312. E-mail: desk@farmington.lib.me.us, farmingtonpubliclibrary@farmington.lib.me.us. Web Site: www.farmington.lib.me.us. *Dir,* Jessica Casey; Staff 6 (MLS 1, Non-MLS 5)
Founded 1890. Pop 7,597; Circ 53,000
Library Holdings: Audiobooks 2,000; DVDs 2,300; e-books 15,000; Large Print Bks 1,800; Bk Titles 62,000; Per Subs 75
Special Collections: Genealogy Coll; History Coll
Automation Activity & Vendor Info: (Cataloging) Biblionix/Apollo; (Circulation) Biblionix/Apollo; (ILL) Biblionix/Apollo; (OPAC) Biblionix/Apollo
Wireless access
Function: 24/7 Electronic res, 24/7 Online cat, Adult bk club
Partic in Maine State Libr Network
Open Tues 10-6, Wed & Thurs 10-7, Fri 10-5, Sat 10-2

C UNIVERSITY OF MAINE AT FARMINGTON*, Mantor Library, 116 South St, 04938-1990. SAN 306-638X. Tel: 207-778-7210. FAX: 207-778-7223. Web Site: www2.umf.maine.edu/library. *Dir,* Bryce D Cundick; E-mail: bryce.cundick@maine.edu; *Ref (Info Servs),* Laurie MacWhinnie; Staff 4 (MLS 4)
Founded 1933. Enrl 1,750; Fac 110; Highest Degree: Master
Library Holdings: Bk Vols 55,000; Per Subs 56
Special Collections: University of Maine at Farmington Archives
Automation Activity & Vendor Info: (Acquisitions) Innovative Interfaces, Inc; (Cataloging) Innovative Interfaces, Inc; (Circulation) Innovative Interfaces, Inc; (Course Reserve) Innovative Interfaces, Inc; (ILL) Innovative Interfaces, Inc; (Media Booking) Innovative Interfaces, Inc; (OPAC) Innovative Interfaces, Inc; (Serials) Innovative Interfaces, Inc
Wireless access
Partic in OCLC Online Computer Library Center, Inc
Open Mon-Thurs (Winter) 7:45am-11pm, Fri 7:45-5, Sat 12-5, Sun 11-11; Mon-Fri (Summer) 8-4:30
Friends of the Library Group

FAYETTE

P UNDERWOOD MEMORIAL LIBRARY, 2006 Main St, 04349. SAN 306-6398. Tel: 207-685-3778. E-mail: faylib@fayette.lib.me.us. Web Site: fayettemaine.org/underwood-library. *Libr Dir,* Michele Briggs
Founded 1953. Pop 1,155; Circ 4,393
Library Holdings: Audiobooks 112; DVDs 484; Large Print Bks 50; Bk Titles 6,950; Per Subs 5
Subject Interests: Maine
Automation Activity & Vendor Info: (Acquisitions) Baker & Taylor; (Circulation) LibraryWorld, Inc
Wireless access
Function: 24/7 Online cat, Bks on CD, Computers for patron use, Free DVD rentals, Homebound delivery serv, ILL available, Internet access, Magazines, Mail & tel request accepted, Online cat, Photocopying/Printing, Printer for laptops & handheld devices, Prog for adults, Prog for children & young adult, Story hour, Wheelchair accessible
Open Wed 1-7, Thurs 10-4

FORT FAIRFIELD

P FORT FAIRFIELD PUBLIC LIBRARY*, 339 Main St, 04742-1199. SAN 306-6401. Tel: 207-472-3880. E-mail: library@fortfairfield.org. Web Site: www.fortfairfieldlibrary.org. *Librn,* Jennifer Gaenzle; Staff 1 (Non-MLS 1)
Founded 1895. Pop 3,880; Circ 20,869
Library Holdings: Audiobooks 226; Bks on Deafness & Sign Lang 10; Braille Volumes 10; DVDs 954; Large Print Bks 728; Microforms 3,796; Bk Titles 27,990; Per Subs 50
Special Collections: Civil War (Drew Coll); County History; Genealogy Coll; Obituary Archive; State History; Town History; Town Newspaper Archive. Oral History
Subject Interests: County genealogy, County hist, Local genealogy, Local hist, State genealogy, State hist
Automation Activity & Vendor Info: (Acquisitions) Book Systems; (Cataloging) Book Systems; (Circulation) Book Systems
Wireless access
Partic in Maine InfoNet
Open Tues-Fri 10-5:30, Sat 10-4
Friends of the Library Group

FORT KENT

P FORT KENT PUBLIC LIBRARY, One Monument Sq, 04743. SAN 306-641X. Tel: 207-834-3048. FAX: 207-834-2630. Web Site: www.fort-kent.lib.me.us. *Head Librn,* Michelle Raymond; E-mail: mray@fort-kent.lib.me.us
Founded 1936. Pop 4,268; Circ 22,596
Library Holdings: Bk Vols 22,000

Wireless access
Open Mon, Tues & Thurs 12-5, Wed & Fri 11-7

C UNIVERSITY OF MAINE AT FORT KENT, Blake Library, 23 University Dr, 04743. SAN 306-6428. Tel: 207-834-7525. Reference Tel: 207-834-7527. FAX: 207-834-7518. Web Site: www.umfk.edu/library. *Exec Dir, Academic Support Services,* Leslie Kelly; Tel: 207-834-7522, E-mail: lesliek@maine.edu; *Libr Dir, Ref Librn,* Sofia Birden; E-mail: sbirden@maine.edu; *Acq, Ser,* Brenda Pelletier; Tel: 207-834-7523, E-mail: brenda.m.pelletier@maine.edu; *Circ & ILL,* Debra Durkin; Tel: 207-834-7526, E-mail: debra.durkin@maine.edu; Staff 4 (MLS 2, Non-MLS 2)
Founded 1878. Enrl 1,100; Fac 30; Highest Degree: Bachelor
Library Holdings: Audiobooks 200; DVDs 1,007; Bk Vols 48,280; Per Subs 183; Videos 1,763
Special Collections: Aroostook Coll; Maine Coll; University Coll
Automation Activity & Vendor Info: (Cataloging) Innovative Interfaces, Inc; (Circulation) Innovative Interfaces, Inc; (Serials) Innovative Interfaces, Inc
Wireless access
Function: Art exhibits, Audio & video playback equip for onsite use, Audiobks via web, Bks on cassette, Bks on CD, Computers for patron use, E-Reserves, Electronic databases & coll, Free DVD rentals, ILL available, Music CDs, Online cat, Online info literacy tutorials on the web & in blackboard, Online ref, Orientations, Outside serv via phone, mail, e-mail & web, OverDrive digital audio bks, Photocopying/Printing, Printer for laptops & handheld devices, Ref serv available, Scanner, Tax forms, VHS videos, Wheelchair accessible
Open Mon-Thurs 8am-9pm, Fri 8-8, Sat 11-8, Sun 11-9 (Fall & Spring); Mon-Fri 8-4:30 (Summer)

FREEPORT

P FREEPORT COMMUNITY LIBRARY*, Ten Library Dr, 04032. SAN 306-6436. Tel: 207-865-3307. FAX: 207-865-1395. E-mail: fcl@freeportmaine.com. Web Site: freeportlibrary.com. *Dir,* Arlene Arris; E-mail: aarris@freeportmaine.com; Staff 7 (MLS 1, Non-MLS 6)
Founded 1904. Pop 8,200; Circ 150,440
Library Holdings: Audiobooks 3,343; DVDs 3,914; Large Print Bks 552; Bk Titles 54,270; Bk Vols 55,547; Per Subs 157; Talking Bks 1,965; Videos 2,688
Special Collections: Maine (State & Local Historical Records); Sportman's Coll
Automation Activity & Vendor Info: (Acquisitions) Follett Software
Wireless access
Mem of Maine State Library, Region 1
Open Mon & Wed 10-8, Tues & Thurs 10-5, Fri 12-5, Sat 10-2
Friends of the Library Group

FRENCHBORO

P FRENCHBORO LIBRARY, 21 High St, 04635. E-mail: frenchborolibrary@gmail.com. Web Site: www.frenchboro.lib.me.us. *Libr Dir,* Jan Keiper
Founded 1850. Pop 65
Library Holdings: DVDs 20; Bk Vols 6,000; Talking Bks 60; Videos 300
Special Collections: Biographies Coll; Crafts Coll; Maine Coll; Sea Stories
Wireless access

FRIENDSHIP

P FRIENDSHIP PUBLIC LIBRARY*, Three Main St, 04547. (Mail add: PO Box 39, 04547-0039). Tel: 207-832-5332. *Librn,* Alice Benner
Founded 1915. Circ 2,982
Library Holdings: Large Print Bks 150; Bk Vols 17,000; Per Subs 23; Talking Bks 75
Special Collections: Oral History
Wireless access
Open Wed (Winter) 2-6, Sat 9-12; Wed (Summer) 2-8, Fri 1-4, Sat 9-12

FRYEBURG

P FRYEBURG PUBLIC LIBRARY*, 515 Main St, 04037. SAN 306-6452. Tel: 207-935-2731. FAX: 207-935-7217. E-mail: library@fryeburgmaine.org. *Librn,* Jennifer Spofford; Staff 1 (Non-MLS 1)
Founded 1903. Pop 3,398; Circ 9,759
Library Holdings: Bk Titles 10,440; Per Subs 5
Special Collections: Clarence E Mulford Coll
Automation Activity & Vendor Info: (Acquisitions) LiBRARYSOFT
Wireless access
Open Mon, Wed & Thurs 9-4, Tues 12-6, Sat 9-Noon
Friends of the Library Group

GARDINER

P GARDINER PUBLIC LIBRARY, 152 Water St, 04345. SAN 306-6460. Tel: 207-582-3312. FAX: 207-583-8305. Web Site: www.gpl.lib.me.us. *Libr Dir,* Justin Hoenke; E-mail: j.hoenke@gardinermaine.com; *Asst Dir,* Scott Handville; E-mail: shandville@gpl.lib.me.us; *Ch,* Ginni Nichols; E-mail: gnichols@gpl.lib.me.us; *Spec Coll Librn, Youth Serv Librn,* Dawn Thistle; E-mail: archive@gpl.lib.me.us; *Tech Librn,* Ann Russell; E-mail: arussell@gpl.lib.me.us; *Libr Asst,* Audrey Littlefield; Staff 4 (Non-MLS 4)
Founded 1881. Pop 16,588; Circ 141,882
Library Holdings: Bk Vols 42,364; Per Subs 89
Special Collections: E A Robinson Coll; Laura E Richards Coll; The Yellow House Papers
Wireless access
Publications: Who Reads What List (Annual)
Open Mon, Wed & Thurs 10:30-5:30, Tues 10:30-7:30, Fri 9:30-5, Sat 9:30-12:30
Friends of the Library Group

GEORGETOWN

P LAURA E RICHARDS LIBRARY, 863 Five Islands Rd, 04548. (Mail add: PO Box 222, 04548-0222), SAN 372-6339. Tel: 207-371-9995. E-mail: lauraerichardslibrary@gmail.com. *Dir,* Karen MacGillivary
Founded 1937. Pop 1,020; Circ 2,905
Library Holdings: Bk Vols 4,900
Special Collections: Maine Coll
Wireless access
Function: Spoken cassettes & CDs
Mem of Maine State Library, Region 1
Open Mon & Wed 3-6, Fri & Sat 9-Noon

GORHAM

P BAXTER MEMORIAL LIBRARY*, 71 South St, 04038. SAN 306-6479. Tel: 207-222-1190. FAX: 207-839-7749. Web Site: baxterlibrary.org. *Dir,* James Rathbun; E-mail: jrathbun@msln.net; *Pub Serv Librn,* Julia Hoisington; E-mail: jhoisington@msln.net; *Youth Serv Librn,* Heidi Whelan
Founded 1908. Pop 14,141; Circ 106,518
Library Holdings: Bk Vols 33,000; Per Subs 87
Automation Activity & Vendor Info: (Cataloging) Innovative Interfaces, Inc; (Circulation) Innovative Interfaces, Inc; (OPAC) Innovative Interfaces, Inc
Wireless access
Mem of Maine State Library, Region 1
Open Mon & Fri 9-4, Tues-Thurs 9-7, Sat 9-1
Friends of the Library Group

P NORTH GORHAM PUBLIC LIBRARY, Two Standish Neck Rd, 04038-2469. Tel: 207-892-2575. E-mail: libng@north-gorham.lib.me.us. Web Site: www.north-gorham.lib.me.us. *Libr Coord,* Jennifer Plummer
Founded 1897
Library Holdings: AV Mats 250; Bk Vols 9,500; Per Subs 13; Talking Bks 350
Automation Activity & Vendor Info: (Cataloging) LibraryWorld, Inc; (Circulation) LibraryWorld, Inc
Wireless access
Mem of Maine State Library, Region 1
Open Mon & Thurs 3-5:30, Wed 6-8, Sat 10-1

GRAY

P GRAY PUBLIC LIBRARY*, Five Hancock St, 04039. SAN 306-6495. Tel: 207-657-4110. FAX: 207-657-4138. E-mail: graylib@gray.lib.me.us. Web Site: www.gray.lib.me.us. *Dir,* Joshua Tiffany; *Ch,* Kathy George; *Circ Mgr,* Darcel Devou; Staff 4 (MLS 2, Non-MLS 2)
Founded 1906. Pop 7,850; Circ 80,630
Library Holdings: Bk Titles 32,352; Per Subs 20
Special Collections: Maine Coll
Subject Interests: Agr, Humanities, Med, Natural sci
Automation Activity & Vendor Info: (Cataloging) Innovative Interfaces, Inc - Millennium; (Circulation) Innovative Interfaces, Inc - Millennium; (OPAC) Innovative Interfaces, Inc - Millennium
Wireless access
Mem of Maine State Library, Region 1
Open Tues & Wed 10-8, Thurs 10-6, Fri 10-5, Sat 10-3
Friends of the Library Group

GREENE

P JULIA ADAMS MORSE MEMORIAL LIBRARY*, 105 Main St, 04236. (Mail add: PO Box 597, 04236-0597), SAN 306-6509. Tel: 207-946-5544. Web Site: www.morse.lib.me.us. *Librn,* Steven Bouchard; E-mail: sbouchard.jamm.library@gmail.com; Staff 1 (MLS 1)
Founded 1955. Pop 4,356; Circ 16,411
Library Holdings: Audiobooks 392; DVDs 1,258; Bk Vols 13,667

Wireless access
Function: 24/7 Electronic res, 24/7 Online cat, Audiobks via web, Bks on CD, Children's prog, Computers for patron use, Electronic databases & coll, Free DVD rentals, ILL available, Internet access, Museum passes, Online cat, Photocopying/Printing, Printer for laptops & handheld devices, Ref serv available, Story hour, Summer reading prog, Wheelchair accessible
Open Mon, Tues & Thurs 12-7, Wed & Sat 9-3
Friends of the Library Group

GREENVILLE

P SHAW PUBLIC LIBRARY, Nine Lily Bay Rd, 04441. (Mail add: PO Box 510, 04441-0510), SAN 306-6517. Tel: 207-695-3579. E-mail: shawpublic2@yahoo.com. Web Site: sites.google.com/site/shawpubliclibrary, www.greenvilleme.com/library. *Libr Dir,* Laura Nederhoff
Pop 2,037; Circ 15,379
Library Holdings: Bk Vols 20,000; Per Subs 50
Wireless access
Open Tues & Fri 10-2, Wed & Thurs 10-5, Sat 10-1

GUILFORD

P GUILFORD MEMORIAL LIBRARY*, Four Library St, 04443. (Mail add: PO Box 177, 04443-0177), SAN 306-6525. Tel: 207-876-4547. E-mail: info@guilfordmemoriallibrary.org. Web Site: www.guilfordmemoriallibrary.org. *Dir,* Andrea Koltai-Price; E-mail: director@guilfordmemoriallibrary.org; Staff 3 (MLS 1, Non-MLS 2)
Founded 1903
Library Holdings: Large Print Bks 1,500; Bk Vols 16,000; Per Subs 27; Talking Bks 350
Wireless access
Partic in Maine Balsam Library Consortium
Open Tues-Thurs 10-5, Fri 9-4

HAMPDEN

P EDYTHE L DYER COMMUNITY LIBRARY*, 269 Main Rd N, 04444. SAN 306-6541. Tel: 207-862-3550. Web Site: www.edl.lib.me.us. *Dir, Libr Serv,* Debora Lozito; E-mail: debbie.lozito@edythedyer.lib.me.us; *Youth Serv,* Mary Beckett; E-mail: mbeckett@edythedyer.lib.me.us; Staff 5 (MLS 2, Non-MLS 3)
Founded 1982. Pop 7,257; Circ 71,957
Jul 2015-Jun 2016 Income $266,143, City $249,608, Locally Generated Income $5,535, Other $11,000. Mats Exp $27,762, Books $16,917, Per/Ser (Incl. Access Fees) $1,692, AV Mat $8,853, Electronic Ref Mat (Incl. Access Fees) $300. Sal $150,124 (Prof $53,389)
Library Holdings: Audiobooks 246; CDs 1,792; DVDs 1,492; e-books 1,650; Large Print Bks 1,239; Bk Titles 20,713; Bk Vols 23,357; Per Subs 62
Automation Activity & Vendor Info: (Cataloging) Innovative Interfaces, Inc; (Circulation) Innovative Interfaces, Inc; (ILL) Innovative Interfaces, Inc; (OPAC) Innovative Interfaces, Inc; (Serials) Innovative Interfaces, Inc
Wireless access
Function: 24/7 Electronic res, 24/7 Online cat, Adult bk club, Art exhibits, Audiobks on Playaways & MP3, Audiobks via web, Bk club(s), Bks on CD, Children's prog, Computers for patron use, Digital talking bks, E-Reserves, Electronic databases & coll, Free DVD rentals, ILL available, Internet access, Life-long learning prog for all ages, Magazines, Mail & tel request accepted, Music CDs, Online cat, Photocopying/Printing, Preschool reading prog, Prog for adults, Prog for children & young adult, Story hour, Summer reading prog, Tax forms, Telephone ref, Wheelchair accessible, Writing prog
Special Services for the Blind - Bks on CD
Open Mon & Wed 9-8, Tues, Thurs & Fri 9-5; Sat (Fall-Spring) 9-2
Friends of the Library Group

HARPSWELL

P CUNDY'S HARBOR LIBRARY, 935 Cundy's Harbor Rd, 04079-4511. Tel: 207-725-1461. Web Site: www.cundysharbor.me. *Dir,* Heather Logan; E-mail: chldirector@cundysharbor.me
Founded 1953
Library Holdings: AV Mats 100; Bk Vols 5,321
Special Collections: Maine, Local History Coll
Wireless access
Mem of Maine State Library, Region 1
Open Tues & Thurs 10-4, Sat 10-3
Friends of the Library Group

HARRINGTON

P GALLISON MEMORIAL LIBRARY*, 1292 Main St, 04643. (Mail add: PO Box 176, 04643-0176). Tel: 207-483-4547. E-mail: gallisonlibrary@gallison.lib.me.us. Web Site: www.gallison.lib.me.us. *Dir,* Gweneth Strout
Pop 1,000
Library Holdings: Bk Vols 6,000; Talking Bks 60; Videos 120
Special Collections: Antiquarian Books & Novels; Local History Coll; Maine Coll
Wireless access
Open Mon-Fri 2-5; Mon-Fri (Summer) 2-6

HARRISON

P BOLSTERS MILLS VILLAGE LIBRARY*, 659 Bolsters Mills Rd, 04040-6827. Tel: 207-583-6421. *Librn,* Charna Katz
Founded 1859
Library Holdings: Large Print Bks 35; Bk Vols 9,702; Talking Bks 70; Videos 49
Special Collections: Children's Biographies Coll; Local History Coll; Maine Coll
Wireless access
Mem of Maine State Library, Region 1
Open Wed 7pm-9pm, Sat 2-4
Friends of the Library Group

P HARRISON VILLAGE LIBRARY*, Four Front St, 04040. (Mail add: PO Box 597, 04040-0597), SAN 306-6568. Tel: 207-583-2970. Web Site: www.harrison.lib.me.us. *Librn,* Kathleen Kramer; E-mail: kkramer@harrison.lib.me.us; Staff 1 (Non-MLS 1)
Founded 1908. Pop 2,315; Circ 7,469
Library Holdings: Bk Vols 7,500; Per Subs 15
Automation Activity & Vendor Info: (Cataloging) Follett Software; (Circulation) Follett Software
Wireless access
Mem of Maine State Library, Region 1
Open Mon & Wed 1-7, Thurs 11-5, Sat 10-2
Friends of the Library Group

HARTLAND

P HARTLAND PUBLIC LIBRARY*, 16 Mill St, 04943. SAN 306-6576. Tel: 207-938-4702. Web Site: hartlandpubliclibrary.org. *Librn,* Nicholas Berry; E-mail: nickb@hartland.lib.me.us; Staff 1 (MLS 1)
Founded 1902. Pop 5,700; Circ 24,000
Library Holdings: Audiobooks 600; CDs 1,250; DVDs 6,000; Large Print Bks 730; Bk Titles 23,500; Bk Vols 24,000; Per Subs 62
Special Collections: Local History Coll
Automation Activity & Vendor Info: (Acquisitions) Evergreen; (Cataloging) Evergreen; (Circulation) Evergreen; (OPAC) Evergreen
Wireless access
Function: Adult bk club, Bks on cassette, Bks on CD, Computers for patron use, Free DVD rentals, ILL available, Music CDs, Online cat, Photocopying/Printing, Serves people with intellectual disabilities, Wheelchair accessible
Partic in Maine Balsam Library Consortium
Open Tues-Thurs 10-6, Fri 10-5, Sat 10-1

HIRAM

P SOLDIERS MEMORIAL LIBRARY*, 85 Main St, 04041. (Mail add: PO Box 281, 04041-0281), SAN 372-7696. Tel: 207-625-4650. E-mail: hiramlibrary@soldiers.lib.me.us. Web Site: www.soldiers.lib.me.us. *Libr Dir,* Pamela Slattery-Thomas; Staff 1 (Non-MLS 1)
Founded 1915. Pop 1,260; Circ 1,818
Library Holdings: Bk Titles 10,000
Special Collections: Maine Coll
Subject Interests: Fiction, Genealogy, Local hist
Automation Activity & Vendor Info: (Cataloging) LEX Systems Inc; (Circulation) LEX Systems Inc
Special Services for the Deaf - Bks on deafness & sign lang
Special Services for the Blind - Audio mat; Bks on cassette; Bks on CD; Cassettes; Copier with enlargement capabilities; Large print bks; Talking bk & rec for the blind cat
Open Tues 2-5, Wed & Thurs 10-5, Sat 9:30-12:30

HOLLIS

P SALMON FALLS LIBRARY*, 322 Old Alfred Rd, 04042. SAN 376-6489. Tel: 207-929-3990. FAX: 207-929-3990. *Librn,* Mary Weyer; E-mail: mweyer1@gmail.com; Staff 1 (Non-MLS 1)
Library Holdings: Bk Vols 10,000; Per Subs 17
Mem of Maine State Library, Region 1
Open Mon 3-6, Wed 4-7, Thurs 3-8, Sat 9-Noon
Friends of the Library Group

HOLLIS CENTER

P HOLLIS CENTER PUBLIC LIBRARY*, 14 Little Falls Rd, 04042. (Mail add: PO Box 119, 04042), SAN 343-6594. Tel: 207-929-3911. E-mail: director@holliscenterpubliclibrary.org. Web Site: www.holliscenterpubliclibrary.org/. *Libr Dir,* Caroline Nickerson; Staff 1 (MLS 1)
Founded 1918. Pop 4,000
Jul 2018-Jun 2019. Mats Exp $7,850, Books $7,500, Electronic Ref Mat (Incl. Access Fees) $350
Library Holdings: Audiobooks 72; DVDs 989; Large Print Bks 8; Bk Titles 17,000; Per Subs 16
Automation Activity & Vendor Info: (Circulation) Biblionix
Wireless access
Function: 24/7 Online cat, Audiobks via web, Bks on CD, Children's prog, Computers for patron use, Free DVD rentals, ILL available, Internet access, Magazines, Movies, Museum passes, Online cat, Photocopying/Printing, Printer for laptops & handheld devices, Scanner, Story hour, Summer & winter reading prog, Tax forms
Mem of Maine State Library, Region 1
Open Mon 9:30-12:30 & 3-7, Wed 2-7, Fri 10-2, Sat 10-4

HOULTON

P CARY LIBRARY*, 107 Main St, 04730. SAN 343-6659. Tel: 207-532-1302. FAX: 207-532-4350. E-mail: library@cary.lib.me.us. Web Site: www.cary.lib.me.us. *Dir,* Linda Faucher; E-mail: faucherl@cary.lib.me.us; *Ch,* Shelley Murchie; E-mail: murchies@cary.lib.me.us; *Libr Office Mgr,* Barbara Ek; E-mail: ekb@cary.lib.me.us; *Circ/Adult Serv,* Donna Meek; E-mail: meekd@cary.lib.me.us; Staff 4 (Non-MLS 4)
Founded 1903. Pop 14,000; Circ 83,841
Library Holdings: Bk Vols 50,000; Per Subs 92
Special Collections: Aroostook County Oral History; Aroostook Newspapers (1859-1938), micro. Oral History
Automation Activity & Vendor Info: (Cataloging) Follett Software; (Circulation) Follett Software; (OPAC) Follett Software
Wireless access
Open Mon-Wed & Fri 9-5, Thurs 9-8, Sat 9-1

ISLAND FALLS

P KATAHDIN PUBLIC LIBRARY, 20 Library St, 04747. (Mail add: PO Box 148, 04747-0148), SAN 306-6592, *Librn,* Rebecca J Drew; Tel: 207-463-2372, E-mail: rdrew@katahdin.lib.me.us; Staff 1 (Non-MLS 1)
Founded 1866. Pop 1,100; Circ 1,200
Jan 2021-Dec 2021 Income $12,900, City $11,000, Locally Generated Income $1,500, Other $400. Mats Exp $3,820, Books $3,120, Other Print Mats $700. Sal $2,400
Library Holdings: Bks on Deafness & Sign Lang 11; CDs 24; DVDs 164; Large Print Bks 240; Bk Vols 17,260; Per Subs 9; Talking Bks 164
Special Collections: Oral History
Subject Interests: Town hist
Automation Activity & Vendor Info: (Acquisitions) DEMCO
Wireless access
Function: For res purposes, ILL available, Internet access, Magazines, Tax forms, Wheelchair accessible
Partic in Maine State Libr Network
Special Services for the Blind - Talking bks
Open Tues & Thurs 9-12 & 1-4

ISLE AU HAUT

P REVERE MEMORIAL LIBRARY*, Revere Memorial Hall, Ten Main St, 04645. SAN 374-4876. Tel: 207-335-5001. FAX: 207-335-5001. E-mail: revere@revere.lib.me.us. Web Site: www.revere.lib.me.us. *Librn,* Brenda Clark; E-mail: bjordan.clark@gmail.com
Founded 1906. Pop 300
Library Holdings: CDs 30; DVDs 20; Bk Vols 2,500; Per Subs 10; Talking Bks 25; Videos 200
Special Collections: Founding Families & Isle Au Haut Oral History Coll. Oral History
Wireless access
Open Wed (Winter) 10-1; Mon, Wed & Fri (Summer) 10-1

ISLESBORO

P ALICE L PENDLETON LIBRARY, 309 Main Rd, 04848. (Mail add: PO Box 77, 04848-0077), SAN 306-6606. Tel: 207-734-2218. Web Site: alplibrary.org. *Libr Dir,* Melissa Olson; E-mail: librarydir@townofislesboro.com; Staff 1 (Non-MLS 1)
Founded 1918. Pop 599; Circ 8,962
Library Holdings: AV Mats 200; Bk Vols 20,000; Per Subs 54; Talking Bks 500
Special Collections: Local Authors Coll; Maine Genealogy Books; Oil Paintings; Ship Models
Automation Activity & Vendor Info: (Cataloging) Follett Software; (Circulation) Follett Software
Wireless access
Special Services for the Blind - Bks on cassette; Descriptive video serv (DVS)
Open Tues-Sat 10:30-4:30
Friends of the Library Group

JACKMAN

P JACKMAN PUBLIC LIBRARY*, 604 Main St, 04945. (Mail add: PO Box 8, 04945-0008), SAN 321-0383. Tel: 207-668-2110. *Dir,* Carolyn Talpey; E-mail: ctalpey@gmail.com; Staff 2 (Non-MLS 2)
Founded 1917. Pop 1,100
Library Holdings: Large Print Bks 35; Bk Vols 6,520; Talking Bks 167
Special Collections: Maine Authors Coll
Wireless access
Open Wed & Sat 2-4

JEFFERSON

P JEFFERSON PUBLIC LIBRARY*, 48 Washington Rd, 04348. (Mail add: PO Box 226, 04348-0226). Tel: 207-549-7491. E-mail: jplmaine@gmail.com. *Librn,* Kathleen Stone
Founded 1984. Pop 2,400
Library Holdings: Bk Vols 4,000; Talking Bks 30
Open Tues & Thurs 4-7

JONESPORT

P PEABODY MEMORIAL LIBRARY*, 162 Main St, 04649. (Mail add: PO Box 210, 04649-0210), SAN 376-3536. Tel: 207-497-3003. E-mail: peabodylibrarian@peabody.lib.me.us. Web Site: www.peabody.lib.me.us. *Librn,* Heidi Lynn Hinkley; Staff 1 (Non-MLS 1)
Founded 1915. Pop 1,800
Automation Activity & Vendor Info: (Acquisitions) Biblionix; (Cataloging) Biblionix; (Circulation) Biblionix
Wireless access
Open Tues-Thurs 10-4, Sat 10-2
Friends of the Library Group

KENDUSKEAG

P CASE MEMORIAL LIBRARY, 911 Stetson Rd E, 04450. (Mail add: PO Box 124, 04450-0124), SAN 306-6622. Tel: 207-884-8598. FAX: 207-884-3043. E-mail: casememoriallibrary@gmail.com, ktown@ne.twcbc.com. *Dir,* Wendy Cousins; *Asst Librn,* Stephanie Clark
Pop 1,210; Circ 1,300
Library Holdings: Bk Vols 6,000
Wireless access
Function: Children's prog, Summer reading prog
Partic in Maine Balsam Library Consortium
Open Tues & Thurs 2-6, Sat 10-2
Friends of the Library Group

KENNEBUNK

S THE BRICK STORE MUSEUM*, Edith Cleaves Barry Library, 117 Main St, 04043. SAN 326-615X. Tel: 207-985-4802. E-mail: info@brickstoremuseum.org. Web Site: www.brickstoremuseum.org. *Exec Dir,* Cynthia Walker; E-mail: edirector@brickstoremuseum.org
Library Holdings: Bk Vols 3,000
Special Collections: Oral History; State Document Depository
Subject Interests: Archit, Decorative art, Local hist
Function: Archival coll, For res purposes, Homebound delivery serv, Photocopying/Printing, Ref serv available, Wheelchair accessible
Restriction: Non-circulating, Open to pub by appt only, Open to pub with supv only

P KENNEBUNK FREE LIBRARY*, 112 Main St, 04043. SAN 306-6649. Tel: 207-985-2173. FAX: 207-985-4730. E-mail: kfl@kennebunk.lib.me.us. Web Site: www.kennebunklibrary.org. *Libr Dir,* Michelle Conners; *Asst Dir, Head, Adult Serv,* Allison Atkins; *Ch, Head, Youth Serv,* Maria Richardson; Staff 12 (MLS 2, Non-MLS 10)
Founded 1882. Pop 10,000; Circ 121,436
Library Holdings: Bks on Deafness & Sign Lang 25; Large Print Bks 1,700; Bk Titles 38,655; Bk Vols 41,097; Per Subs 130; Talking Bks 1,250
Special Collections: Bolton Travel Library; Kenneth Joy Photographic Coll; Walker Diaries. Oral History
Automation Activity & Vendor Info: (Cataloging) Follett Software; (Circulation) Follett Software; (OPAC) Follett Software
Wireless access
Function: Home delivery & serv to seniorr ctr & nursing homes, Homebound delivery serv, ILL available, Internet access, Large print keyboards, Photocopying/Printing, Prog for adults, Prog for children &

young adult, Ref serv available, Summer reading prog, Wheelchair accessible
Publications: History of Kennebunk
Mem of Maine State Library, Region 1
Open Mon & Tues 9:30-8, Wed 12:30-8, Thurs-Sat 9:30-5
Friends of the Library Group

KENNEBUNKPORT

P LOUIS T GRAVES MEMORIAL PUBLIC LIBRARY, 18 Maine St, 04046. (Mail add: PO Box 391, 04046-0391), SAN 306-6657. Tel: 207-967-2778. Web Site: www.graveslibrary.org. *Libr Dir,* Mary-Lou Boucouvalas; E-mail: ml@graves.lib.me.us; Staff 3 (MLS 1, Non-MLS 2)
Founded 1921. Pop 3,500; Circ 6,000
Library Holdings: CDs 100; DVDs 30; Bk Vols 33,000; Per Subs 105; Talking Bks 1,422; Videos 1,282
Special Collections: Booth Tarkington Coll; Kenneth Roberts Coll; Margaret Deland Coll. Oral History
Automation Activity & Vendor Info: (OPAC) Follett Software
Wireless access
Mem of Maine State Library, Region 1
Partic in OCLC Online Computer Library Center, Inc
Open Mon-Fri 10-4, Sat 9:30-12

S THE NEW ENGLAND ELECTRIC RAILWAY HISTORICAL SOCIETY*, Seashore Trolley Museum Library, 195 Log Cabin Rd, 04046. (Mail add: PO Box A, 04046), SAN 377-4503. Tel: 207-967-2712. FAX: 207-967-0867. Web Site: www.trolleymuseum.org. *Exec Dir,* Katie Orlando; Tel: 207-967-2800, E-mail: director@neerhs.org; *Librn,* Karen Dooks
Library Holdings: Bk Vols 10,000
Subject Interests: Electric railway, Motor bus, Transit
Wireless access
Restriction: Open by appt only
Friends of the Library Group

KINGFIELD

P WEBSTER FREE LIBRARY, 22 Depot St, 04947. (Mail add: PO Box 518, 04947-0518), SAN 306-6673. Tel: 207-265-2052. E-mail: websterlibrary2@gmail.com. Web Site: websterlibrarykingfield.org, www.kingfieldme.org/webster-library. *Libr Dir,* Julia Bouwsma
Pop 1,083; Circ 7,610
Library Holdings: Bk Vols 13,000; Per Subs 22
Wireless access
Special Services for the Blind - Audio mat; Large print bks
Open Mon & Thurs 2:30-6, Wed 10-2, Sat 9-1

KITTERY

S OLD YORK HISTORICAL SOCIETY RESEARCH CENTER, 22 Shapleigh Rd, 03904. (Mail add: PO Box 312, York, 03909-0312), SAN 306-7947. Tel: 207-361-3556. E-mail: research@oldyork.org. Web Site: www.oldyork.org/archives-library. *Archivist,* Marlane Bottino; Staff 1 (MLS 1)
Library Holdings: Bk Titles 6,000
Special Collections: Local Photographs & Genealogies; Rare Books & Manuscripts from Local 18th Century Private Libraries & the York Social Library, estab 1796
Subject Interests: Am folk art, Decorative art, Genealogy, Local hist
Wireless access
Publications: Old York Occasional Papers (Local historical information)
Mem of Maine State Library, Region 1
Restriction: Open by appt only

P RICE PUBLIC LIBRARY, Eight Wentworth St, 03904. SAN 306-6681. Tel: 207-439-1553. FAX: 207-439-1765. E-mail: arabella@rice.lib.me.us. Web Site: www.rice.lib.me.us. *Dir,* Lee Perkins; E-mail: perkinse@rice.lib.me.us; Staff 8 (MLS 1, Non-MLS 7)
Founded 1875. Pop 9,687; Circ 99,246
Library Holdings: AV Mats 2,900; Bks on Deafness & Sign Lang 34; Large Print Bks 712; Bk Titles 54,041; Bk Vols 57,500; Per Subs 123
Special Collections: Kittery History & Genealogy, bks, photog
Automation Activity & Vendor Info: (Cataloging) Innovative Interfaces, Inc; (Circulation) Innovative Interfaces, Inc; (ILL) Innovative Interfaces, Inc; (OPAC) Innovative Interfaces, Inc
Wireless access
Function: Home delivery & serv to seniorr ctr & nursing homes, Homebound delivery serv, ILL available, Photocopying/Printing, Prog for adults, Prog for children & young adult, Spoken cassettes & CDs, Summer reading prog, VHS videos
Mem of Maine State Library, Region 1
Special Services for the Deaf - Bks on deafness & sign lang; High interest/low vocabulary bks
Open Tues & Fri 10-5, Wed & Thurs 12-8, Sat 10-2
Friends of the Library Group

LEBANON

P MARTHA SAWYER COMMUNITY LIBRARY*, 53 Upper Guinea Rd, 04027. Tel: 207-457-1299, Ext 5. E-mail: mscl@msad60.org. Web Site: mscl.msad60.org, www.lebanon-me.org/library. *Librn,* Mary Polletta
Mem of Maine State Library, Region 1
Open Mon, Wed & Thurs 3:30-7:30, Sat 10-1; Tues & Wed (Summer) 11-3, Thurs 11-2 & 5-8

LEWISTON

C BATES COLLEGE*, George & Helen Ladd Library, 48 Campus Ave, 04240. SAN 306-6703. Tel: 207-786-6263. Reference Tel: 207-786-6271. FAX: 207-786-6055. Web Site: www.bates.edu/library. *Assoc Col Librn, Res Serv,* Courtney Seymour; Tel: 207-786-8324, E-mail: cseymour@bates.edu; *Art Librn, Music Librn,* Christopher Schiff; Tel: 207-786-6274, E-mail: cschiff@bates.edu; *Humanities Librn,* Christina Bell; Tel: 207-786-8323, E-mail: cbell@bates.edu; *Soc Sci Librn,* Christine Murray; Tel: 207-786-6268, E-mail: cmurray2@bates.edu; Staff 24 (MLS 12.5, Non-MLS 11.5)
Founded 1855. Enrl 1,773; Fac 187; Highest Degree: Bachelor
Jul 2014-Jun 2015. Mats Exp $1,920,116, Books $467,371, Per/Ser (Incl. Access Fees) $1,249,355
Library Holdings: AV Mats 35,783; e-journals 73,002; Bk Vols 522,993
Special Collections: Bates College Archives Coll; Books from the Library of Marsden Hartley; Dorothy Freeman Coll; Edmund S Muskie Coll; Freewill Baptist Coll; Jonathan Stanton Natural History Coll; Judaica (Berent Coll); Nineteenth Century Works in French & German (Rice Coll); Signed First Editions (Phelps Coll). Oral History; US Document Depository
Automation Activity & Vendor Info: (Acquisitions) Innovative Interfaces, Inc; (Cataloging) Innovative Interfaces, Inc; (Circulation) Innovative Interfaces, Inc; (ILL) OCLC ILLiad; (OPAC) Innovative Interfaces, Inc; (Serials) Innovative Interfaces, Inc
Wireless access
Partic in CBB Librs; Maine InfoNet; NExpress Consortium

M CENTRAL MAINE MEDICAL CENTER*, Gerrish-True Health Sciences Library, 300 Main St, 04240. (Mail add: PO Box 4500, 04240), SAN 306-6711. Tel: 207-795-5956. FAX: 207-795-2569. E-mail: library@cmhc.org. Web Site: www.cmhc.org/health-professionals. *Librn,* Sarah Hudson; E-mail: hudsonsa@cmhc.org; Staff 2 (MLS 2)
Library Holdings: Bk Vols 2,500; Per Subs 280
Special Collections: Health Information Coll
Automation Activity & Vendor Info: (Cataloging) Evergreen; (Circulation) Evergreen; (ILL) Innovative Interfaces, Inc - Millennium; (OPAC) Evergreen; (Serials) Evergreen
Wireless access
Partic in National Network of Libraries of Medicine Region 7; North Atlantic Health Sciences Libraries, Inc
Open Mon-Fri 8-4
Restriction: Badge access after hrs

P LEWISTON PUBLIC LIBRARY*, 200 Lisbon St, 04240. SAN 343-6713. Tel: 207-513-3004. Circulation Tel: 207-513-3134. Reference Tel: 207-513-3135. FAX: 207-784-3011. TDD: 207-513-3007. Reference E-mail: lplreference@lewistonmaine.gov. Web Site: lplonline.org. *Libr Dir,* Marcela Peres; E-mail: mperes@lewistonmaine.gov; *Ad,* Steven Bouchard; E-mail: sgbouchard@lewistonmaine.gov; *Ch,* Sara Groves; E-mail: sgroves@lewistonmaine.gov; *Coll Serv Librn,* Karen Jones; E-mail: kjones@lewistonmaine.gov; *Lending Serv Supvr,* Katherine Webber; E-mail: kwebber@lewistonmaine.gov; Staff 19.2 (MLS 4, Non-MLS 15.2)
Founded 1902. Pop 36,000; Circ 223,500
Library Holdings: AV Mats 5,400; Bk Vols 128,300; Per Subs 292
Special Collections: Bates Manufacturing Company Coll; Franklin Company Coll; French Literature (Dr Eustache N Giguere Memorial); Lewiston History Coll; W S Libbey Company Coll
Automation Activity & Vendor Info: (Cataloging) Innovative Interfaces, Inc; (Circulation) Innovative Interfaces, Inc; (ILL) Innovative Interfaces, Inc; (OPAC) Innovative Interfaces, Inc; (Serials) Innovative Interfaces, Inc
Wireless access
Open Mon-Thurs 10-7, Fri 10-5, Sat 10-2
Friends of the Library Group

LIBERTY

P LIBERTY LIBRARY, 59 Main St, 04949. (Mail add: PO Box 280, 04949-0280). Tel: 207-589-3161. Web Site: liberty.lib.me.us. *Libr Dir,* Barb Rehmeyer; E-mail: brehmeyer@liberty.lib.me.us
Founded 1995. Pop 2,500
Library Holdings: Audiobooks 299; AV Mats 1,454; Bk Vols 10,155
Automation Activity & Vendor Info: (Cataloging) Innovative Interfaces, Inc - Sierra; (Circulation) Innovative Interfaces, Inc - Sierra

Wireless access
Open Mon 10-7, Tues-Thurs 10-4

LIMERICK

P LIMERICK PUBLIC LIBRARY, 55 Washington St, 04048-3500. SAN 376-3870. Tel: 207-793-8975. FAX: 207-793-8443. E-mail: ll-cs@limerick.lib.me.us. Web Site: limerickme.org/library.html, limerickme.org/library_1. *Dir,* Cynthia Smith; Staff 2 (Non-MLS 2)
Library Holdings: Bk Vols 21,000; Per Subs 20
Wireless access
Mem of Maine State Library, Region 1
Open Mon & Fri 1-5, Tues 9-6, Wed 9-12 & 3-8, Sat 9-1
Friends of the Library Group

LIMESTONE

P ROBERT A FROST MEMORIAL LIBRARY*, 42 Main St, 04750. SAN 306-672X. Tel: 207-325-4706. FAX: 207-325-3035. E-mail: rfrostml@gmail.com. *Librn,* Robin Thurston; *Asst Librn,* Kelly Johndro
Founded 1899. Pop 3,000; Circ 20,000
Library Holdings: Audiobooks 270; AV Mats 78; CDs 169; DVDs 871; Large Print Bks 207; Bk Titles 24,542; Bk Vols 27,312; Per Subs 31
Special Collections: Aroostook History, bks, pamphlets; State & Local History, bks, maps, pamphlets, scrapbks. Oral History
Wireless access
Function: 24/7 Online cat, Activity rm, Adult bk club, Audio & video playback equip for onsite use, Audiobks on Playaways & MP3, Bks on CD, CD-ROM, Children's prog, Computers for patron use, E-Readers, Free DVD rentals, Holiday prog, Homebound delivery serv, ILL available, Internet access, Laminating, Magazines, Meeting rooms, Movies, Music CDs, Online cat, OverDrive digital audio bks, Photocopying/Printing, Prog for adults, Prog for children & young adult, Ref & res, Scanner, Spoken cassettes & CDs, Study rm, Summer reading prog, Wheelchair accessible
Publications: Booklist
Open Mon-Wed & Fri Noon-5, Thurs Noon-6
Friends of the Library Group

LIMINGTON

P DAVIS MEMORIAL LIBRARY, 928 Cape Rd, 04049. SAN 306-6738. Tel: 207-637-2422. E-mail: librarian@davismemoriallibrary.com. Web Site: www.davismemoriallibrary.com. *Libr Dir,* Mariah Machado; Staff 2 (Non-MLS 2)
Founded 1912. Pop 3,400; Circ 13,900
Library Holdings: AV Mats 400; Large Print Bks 25; Bk Vols 12,500; Per Subs 40; Talking Bks 360
Special Collections: Town Histories & Genealogy
Wireless access
Function: Adult bk club, Bk club(s), ILL available, Mail & tel request accepted, Music CDs, Photocopying/Printing, Prog for children & young adult, Summer reading prog, VHS videos
Publications: Davis Memorial Library Newsletter (Monthly)
Mem of Maine State Library, Region 1
Partic in Maine School & Library Network
Special Services for the Deaf - Bks on deafness & sign lang; High interest/low vocabulary bks
Special Services for the Blind - Bks on cassette; Bks on CD; Copier with enlargement capabilities; Large print bks
Open Mon & Tues 2-8, Thurs 10-6, Fri 2-6, Sat 10-1
Friends of the Library Group

LINCOLN

P LINCOLN MEMORIAL LIBRARY*, 21 W Broadway, 04457. SAN 306-6746. Tel: 207-794-2765. FAX: 207-794-2606. Web Site: lincolnmaine.org/library. *Dir,* Linda Morrill; E-mail: Linda.Morrill@lincolnmaine.org; *Ch Serv,* Sandy Michaud; Staff 2 (Non-MLS 2)
Founded 1879. Pop 5,221
Library Holdings: Bks on Deafness & Sign Lang 10; Bk Vols 30,000; Per Subs 30
Automation Activity & Vendor Info: (Cataloging) Follett Software; (Circulation) Follett Software
Wireless access
Function: Adult bk club, After school storytime, Archival coll, Art exhibits, Bks on cassette, Bks on CD, Children's prog, Computer training, Computers for patron use, Free DVD rentals, Holiday prog, Home delivery & serv to seniorr ctr & nursing homes, ILL available, Music CDs, Photocopying/Printing, Preschool outreach, Prog for adults, Prog for children & young adult, Ref & res, Ref serv available, Spoken cassettes & CDs, Spoken cassettes & DVDs, Story hour, Summer reading prog, Tax forms, Teen prog, VHS videos, Wheelchair accessible
Open Mon-Fri 10-5
Friends of the Library Group

LISBON FALLS

P LISBON FALLS COMMUNITY LIBRARY*, 28 Main St, 04252-0028. SAN 306-6762. Tel: 207-353-6564. E-mail: lisbonlibrary@lisbonme.org. Web Site: www.lisbonme.org/library. *Dir,* Diane Nadeau; Staff 3 (MLS 1, Non-MLS 2)
Founded 1920. Pop 13,000; Circ 32,621
Library Holdings: Bks on Deafness & Sign Lang 60; Bk Vols 41,000; Per Subs 45
Special Collections: Maine Coll
Wireless access
Publications: Newsletter
Open Mon & Sat 8:30-12:30, Tues 12-6, Wed-Fri 8:30-4
Friends of the Library Group

LIVERMORE

P LIVERMORE PUBLIC LIBRARY, 22 Church St, 04253-3699. (Mail add: PO Box 620, 04253-0620). Tel: 207-897-7173. Web Site: www.livermore.lib.me.us. *Librn,* Amanda Barton; E-mail: amanda@livermore.lib.me.us; Staff 1 (Non-MLS 1)
Founded 1913. Circ 2,322
Library Holdings: Bk Vols 9,785
Automation Activity & Vendor Info: (Cataloging) Biblionix
Wireless access
Open Tues & Thurs 1-6, Sat 10-Noon

LIVERMORE FALLS

P TREAT MEMORIAL LIBRARY, 56 Main St, 04254. SAN 306-6770. Tel: 207-897-3631. Web Site: www.treat.lib.me.us. *Libr Dir,* Myra Rosenbaum; E-mail: treatdirector@treat.lib.me.us; Staff 2 (Non-MLS 2)
Founded 1900. Pop 3,572; Circ 24,100
Library Holdings: CDs 70; DVDs 50; Large Print Bks 200; Bk Titles 19,000; Per Subs 30; Talking Bks 75; Videos 400
Automation Activity & Vendor Info: (Cataloging) Winnebago Software Co; (Circulation) Winnebago Software Co; (OPAC) Winnebago Software Co
Wireless access
Open Tues & Thurs 1-7, Wed 10-3, Fri 1-5, Sat 10-2

LONG ISLAND

P LONG ISLAND COMMUNITY LIBRARY*, Seventh Gorham Ave, 04050. Tel: 207-766-2530. FAX: 207-766-2530. Web Site: library.long-island.lib.me.us. *Libr Dir,* Annie Donovan; *Libr Dir,* Paula Johnson
Founded 1986
Library Holdings: AV Mats 200; CDs 60; Bk Vols 8,300
Special Collections: Maine Authors; Maine Coll
Automation Activity & Vendor Info: (Cataloging) Follett Software; (Circulation) Follett Software; (OPAC) Follett Software
Wireless access
Mem of Maine State Library, Region 1
Open Mon, Fri, Sat & Sun 11:30-1:30, Tues 6:30pm-8pm, Wed 9:30-1:30 & 6:30-8, Thurs 3-5

LOVELL

P CHARLOTTE E HOBBS MEMORIAL LIBRARY*, 227 Main St, 04051. (Mail add: PO Box 105, 04051-0105), SAN 306-6789. Tel: 207-925-3177. FAX: 207-925-1209. Web Site: www.hobbslibrary.org. *Libr Dir,* Deanna Wilson; E-mail: dwilson@hobbslibrary.org; *Libr Asst,* Marie Baker; Staff 3 (Non-MLS 3)
Founded 1900. Pop 1,900; Circ 18,800
Library Holdings: Large Print Bks 145; Bk Vols 16,155; Per Subs 20
Special Collections: Children's Room; Maine Books
Wireless access
Function: Adult bk club, After school storytime, Home delivery & serv to seniorr ctr & nursing homes, ILL available, Photocopying/Printing, Prog for adults, Prog for children & young adult, Summer reading prog, VHS videos
Open Mon 9-8, Wed, Thurs & Fri 9-4, Sat 9-1; Mon & Thurs (July-Aug) 9-8, Tues, Wed & Fri 9-4, Sat 9-1
Friends of the Library Group

LUBEC

P LUBEC MEMORIAL LIBRARY*, 55 Water St, 04652-1122. SAN 324-8097. Tel: 207-733-2491. E-mail: lubecmemlib@lubec.lib.me.us. Web Site: www.lubec.lib.me.us. *Librn,* Suzanne Plaut; Staff 3 (MLS 2, Non-MLS 1)
Founded 1946. Pop 1,345; Circ 16,154
Library Holdings: Bk Titles 22,000; Per Subs 30
Special Collections: Maine Description & Travel; Maine History
Subject Interests: Local hist

Function: 24/7 Online cat, Activity rm, Art exhibits, Audiobks via web, Bks on CD, Children's prog, Computers for patron use, Free DVD rentals, Holiday prog, ILL available, Magazines, Makerspace, Meeting rooms, Movies, Music CDs, Online cat, Photocopying/Printing, Preschool outreach, Preschool reading prog, Prog for adults, Prog for children & young adult, Story hour, Summer reading prog, Tax forms
Partic in LYRASIS; OCLC Online Computer Library Center, Inc
Open Mon, Tues & Fri 10-4, Wed 10-8, Sat 10-2
Friends of the Library Group

LYMAN

P COMMUNITY LIBRARY*, Ten John St, 04002-7312. Tel: 207-499-7114. E-mail: librarian@lymanlibrary.org. Web Site: www.lymanlibrary.org. *Head Librn,* Leila Roy; Staff 2 (Non-MLS 2)
Pop 6,642; Circ 12,661
Library Holdings: Bk Vols 16,000; Per Subs 32
Wireless access
Mem of Maine State Library, Region 1
Open Tues & Wed 12-8, Thurs & Fri 9-5, Sat 10-1

MACHIAS

P PORTER MEMORIAL LIBRARY*, 92 Court St, 04654-2102. SAN 306-6797. Tel: 207-255-3933. E-mail: librarian@porter.lib.me.us. Web Site: www.porter.lib.me.us. *Dir,* Lee Downing; *Ch,* Stephen Copel Parsons; Staff 2 (Non-MLS 2)
Founded 1891. Pop 2,458; Circ 17,300
Library Holdings: Bk Titles 17,500; Per Subs 10
Special Collections: Maine Coll
Automation Activity & Vendor Info: (Acquisitions) Biblionix; (Cataloging) Biblionix; (Circulation) Biblionix
Wireless access
Function: 24/7 Electronic res, 24/7 Online cat, Activity rm, After school storytime, Archival coll, Art exhibits, Audiobks via web, Bks on CD, Butterfly Garden, Children's prog, Computers for patron use, Free DVD rentals, Holiday prog, Home delivery & serv to seniorr ctr & nursing homes, Homebound delivery serv, ILL available, Internet access, Magazines, Movies, Online cat, Photocopying/Printing, Preschool outreach, Preschool reading prog, Prog for adults, Prog for children & young adult, Story hour, Workshops
Open Tues-Fri 10-5, Sat 10-1
Friends of the Library Group

C UNIVERSITY OF MAINE AT MACHIAS, Merrill Library, 116 O'Brien Ave, 04654. SAN 306-6800. Tel: 207-255-1234. Administration Tel: 207 255-1254. FAX: 207-255-1356. Web Site: machias.edu/library. *Dir,* Marianne Thibodeau; E-mail: mthibod@maine.edu; *Asst Librn,* Ben Noeske; Tel: 207-255-1356, E-mail: ben.noeske@maine.edu; *Libr Asst,* Jeanne Vose; E-mail: jeannep@maine.edu; Staff 3 (MLS 2, Non-MLS 1)
Founded 1909. Enrl 670; Fac 30; Highest Degree: Bachelor
Automation Activity & Vendor Info: (Acquisitions) Innovative Interfaces, Inc; (Cataloging) Innovative Interfaces, Inc; (Circulation) Innovative Interfaces, Inc; (Course Reserve) Innovative Interfaces, Inc; (ILL) OCLC ILLiad; (OPAC) Innovative Interfaces, Inc; (Serials) Innovative Interfaces, Inc
Wireless access
Function: ILL available, Online cat
Partic in Maine InfoNet
Restriction: Open to pub for ref & circ; with some limitations, Open to qualified scholars, Open to students, fac & staff

MADAWASKA

P MADAWASKA PUBLIC LIBRARY*, 393 Main St, 04756-1126. SAN 306-6819. Tel: 207-728-3606. E-mail: madawaska_library@yahoo.com. Web Site: www.townofmadawaska.com/public-library.html. *Dir,* Ken Theriault
Founded 1939. Pop 4,800; Circ 22,622
Library Holdings: Bk Vols 20,000; Per Subs 40
Special Collections: Local Census (including US Census of the Madawaska Settlement of the St John Valley, 1820 & 1830; New Brunswick Family & Crop Enumeration of 1833; US Census of Aroostook County, 1840-1900; Canadian Census of Madawaska & Victoria Counties, 1851-1901); Local History (Family Genealogies-St John Valley & Canada, Photographic Coll & Oral History Coll, 1972); Marriage Registers/Repertoires (Leon Guimond Extracts of Marriages for St John Valley; Langlois Repertoire, mid 1600's-mid 1900's; Poitras Marriages of Northwest New Brunswick, 1792-2001)
Subject Interests: Genealogy
Wireless access
Open Mon-Fri 10-7, Sat 10-2

MADISON

P MADISON PUBLIC LIBRARY*, 12 Old Point Ave, 04950. SAN 306-6827. Tel: 207-696-5626. E-mail: madison@madison.lib.me.us. Web Site: www.madison.lib.me.us. *Head Librn,* Julie Forbus; E-mail: julie@madison.lib.me.us; *Asst Librn,* Margot Rushton; *Asst Librn,* Jane Shaw; Staff 3 (Non-MLS 3)
Founded 1906. Pop 9,900; Circ 15,500
Library Holdings: Large Print Bks 125; Bk Titles 16,415; Per Subs 9; Talking Bks 65
Automation Activity & Vendor Info: (Acquisitions) Follett Software; (Cataloging) Follett Software; (Circulation) Follett Software
Wireless access
Function: Homebound delivery serv, ILL available, Photocopying/Printing, Prog for children & young adult, Summer reading prog, Tax forms, Wheelchair accessible
Open Mon-Wed 10-7:30, Thurs & Fri 10-5:30, Sat 10-3

MARS HILL

P WALTER T A HANSEN MEMORIAL LIBRARY, Ten Hansen St, 04758. SAN 306-6843. Tel: 207-429-9625. E-mail: info@wtahansenlibrary.org. Web Site: wtahansenlibrary.org. *Librn,* Parker Smith
Pop 2,898; Circ 5,543
Library Holdings: Bk Vols 18,500; Per Subs 35
Special Collections: Local History Coll
Automation Activity & Vendor Info: (Cataloging) Follett Software; (Circulation) Follett Software
Wireless access
Open Mon, Tues & Thurs 12:30-8, Fri & Sat 9-1

MATTAWAMKEAG

P MATTAWAMKEAG PUBLIC LIBRARY*, 327 Main St, 04459. (Mail add: PO Box 260, 04459-0260), SAN 306-6851. Tel: 207-736-7013. FAX: 207-736-2545. *Librn,* Jane Panté; *Librn,* Priscilla York; Staff 1 (Non-MLS 1)
Pop 1,000; Circ 8,725
Library Holdings: Bk Titles 14,317; Bk Vols 15,000; Per Subs 27
Special Collections: Indian Arrowhead Coll
Open Mon & Wed 1-4 & 6:30-8:30, Fri 6:30-8:30

MECHANIC FALLS

P MECHANIC FALLS PUBLIC LIBRARY*, 108 Lewiston St, Third Flr, 04256. SAN 306-686X. Tel: 207-345-9450. E-mail: mechanicfallslibrary@gmail.com. Web Site: www.mechanicfalls.govoffice.com. *Dir,* Nancy Petersons
Founded 1897
Library Holdings: Bk Vols 11,000
Wireless access
Open Mon & Wed 9-5:30, Tues & Thurs 3-7, Sat 9-2

MERCER

P SHAW LIBRARY*, Mercer Community Center, 1015 Beach Hill Rd, Ste B, 04957. Tel: 207-779-3977. FAX: 207-587-2529. E-mail: mercershawlibrary@gmail.com. Web Site: mercershawlibrary.weebly.com. *Libr Dir,* Mary Chouinard
Founded 1875. Pop 700
Library Holdings: Bk Vols 7,397
Open Mon & Wed 5-8, Tues 9-Noon, Thurs & Sat 1-5

MEXICO

P MEXICO FREE PUBLIC LIBRARY, 134 Main St, 04257. SAN 306-6886. Tel: 207-364-3281. FAX: 207-364-5685. E-mail: library@mexicomaine.net. Web Site: www.mexico.lib.me.us. *Libr Dir,* Marilla Couch
Founded 1926. Pop 3,344; Circ 11,019
Library Holdings: AV Mats 720; Large Print Bks 175; Bk Vols 14,000; Per Subs 20; Talking Bks 200
Special Collections: Maine Coll
Wireless access
Open Wed 10-7, Thurs 8-6, Fri 9-3, Sat 9-Noon
Friends of the Library Group

MILBRIDGE

P MILBRIDGE PUBLIC LIBRARY, 18 School St, 04658. (Mail add: PO Box 128, 04658), SAN 376-3552. Tel: 207-546-3066. E-mail: milbridge-library@milbridge.lib.me.us. Web Site: sites.google.com/site/milbridgepubliclibrary. *Librn,* Amanda Fickett; Staff 1 (Non-MLS 1)
Founded 1977
Library Holdings: DVDs 500; Large Print Bks 160; Bk Titles 6,500; Bk Vols 7,000; Videos 75
Wireless access

Special Services for the Blind - Bks on cassette; Large print bks
Open Mon-Fri 8-4
Friends of the Library Group

MILLINOCKET

P MILLINOCKET MEMORIAL LIBRARY*, Five Maine Ave, 04462. SAN 306-6894. Tel: 207-723-7020. FAX: 207-723-7020. Web Site: millinocketmemoriallibrary.org. *Dir,* Matt DeLaney; E-mail: matt@millinocketmemoriallibrary.org; Staff 1 (MLS 1)
Founded 1919. Pop 4,698; Circ 25,000
Library Holdings: CDs 375; DVDs 35; Large Print Bks 1,250; Bk Vols 30,000; Per Subs 60; Talking Bks 350; Videos 560
Special Collections: Millinocket & Northern Maine History Coll, Oral History
Automation Activity & Vendor Info: (Cataloging) Innovative Interfaces, Inc; (Circulation) Innovative Interfaces, Inc; (ILL) Innovative Interfaces, Inc
Wireless access
Function: 24/7 Electronic res, Activity rm, Adult bk club, Archival coll, Art exhibits, Art programs, Audio & video playback equip for onsite use, AV serv, Doc delivery serv, Govt ref serv, Homebound delivery serv, ILL available, Internet access, Music CDs, Outside serv via phone, mail, e-mail & web, Photocopying/Printing, Prog for children & young adult, Ref serv available, Spoken cassettes & CDs, Summer reading prog, Telephone ref, VHS videos, Wheelchair accessible, Workshops
Open Mon, Wed, Thurs & Fri 10-5, Tues 12-7, Sat 10-1
Restriction: Non-resident fee
Friends of the Library Group

MILO

P MILO FREE PUBLIC LIBRARY, Four Pleasant St, 04463. SAN 306-6908. Tel: 207-943-2612. E-mail: milolibrary@trcmaine.org. Web Site: threeriverscommunity.me/milolibrary. *Libr Dir,* Annette Banker; *Asst Librn,* Kathy Doore; Staff 2 (Non-MLS 2)
Founded 1921. Pop 2,650; Circ 7,000
Library Holdings: Large Print Bks 80; Bk Vols 18,000; Per Subs 25
Subject Interests: Gardening, Genealogy, Hist
Wireless access
Function: Ref serv available
Publications: Library News & Book Reviews Published in a Local Paper
Open Mon, Wed & Fri 1-7, Sat (Sept-May) 10-Noon

MONHEGAN

P MONHEGAN MEMORIAL LIBRARY, One Library Lane, 04852. Tel: 207-596-0549. E-mail: monheganmemoriallibrary@gmail.com. Web Site: monheganlibrary.com. *Librn,* Mia Boynton; *Librn,* Matthew Holtzman; Staff 2 (Non-MLS 2)
Founded 1926. Pop 500
Library Holdings: Bk Vols 11,000; Per Subs 10
Special Collections: Archival Local History Coll; Monhegan History Coll

MONMOUTH

P CUMSTON PUBLIC LIBRARY, 796 Main St, 04259. SAN 306-6916. Tel: 207-933-4788. FAX: 207-933-3413. E-mail: cumstonpubliclibrary@gmail.com. Web Site: monmouthme.govoffice2.com. *Librn,* Julie Sawtelle; *Children's Prog Dir,* Sarah Pedersen-Faria; Staff 4 (Non-MLS 4)
Founded 1900. Pop 3,800; Circ 23,473
Library Holdings: AV Mats 1,754; Electronic Media & Resources 54; High Interest/Low Vocabulary Bk Vols 50; Large Print Bks 519; Bk Titles 16,497; Per Subs 70; Talking Bks 702
Special Collections: Maine (Biographies, History, Authors)
Automation Activity & Vendor Info: (Cataloging) Mandarin Library Automation; (Circulation) Mandarin Library Automation
Wireless access
Partic in Solar-net
Open Mon & Wed 1-8, Tues 10-1, Fri 1-5, Sat 9-1
Friends of the Library Group

MONROE

P MONROE COMMUNITY LIBRARY*, Eight Swan Lake Ave, 04951. Tel: 207-525-3515. FAX: 207-525-6602. Web Site: monroemainelibrary.wordpress.com/. *Librn,* Marge Sheridan; E-mail: sheridanmarge9@gmail.com
Pop 890
Library Holdings: CDs 45; DVDs 200; Bk Vols 4,500; Talking Bks 35; Videos 75
Open Mon & Fri 10-1, Wed 4-7

MONSON

P MONSON FREE PUBLIC LIBRARY*, 35 Greenville Rd, 04464-6432. (Mail add: PO Box 282, 04464-0282), SAN 321-5040. Tel: 207-997-3476. E-mail: monsonmelibrary@gmail.com. *Dir, Librn,* Thomas Dallamora; *Asst Librn,* Joanne Tardy; Staff 2 (Non-MLS 2)
Founded 1909. Pop 600
Library Holdings: Large Print Bks 35; Bk Titles 3,400; Bk Vols 3,678; Talking Bks 51; Videos 67
Special Collections: Berenice Abbot Coll
Wireless access
Function: Adult bk club, Bks on CD, Computers for patron use, Free DVD rentals, ILL available, Internet access, Magazines, Music CDs, Photocopying/Printing, Wheelchair accessible
Partic in Maine Balsam Library Consortium
Open Mon, Wed & Fri 12:30-4:30

MOUNT DESERT

P SOMESVILLE LIBRARY ASSOCIATION, 1116 Main St, 04660. (Mail add: PO Box 280, 04660-0280). Tel: 207-244-7404. E-mail: info@somesvillelibrary.org. Web Site: www.somesvillelibrary.org. *Dir,* Thomas Lange
Founded 1884
Library Holdings: Bk Vols 5,000
Wireless access
Open Mon 1-4 (July-Aug), Wed 1-6, Sat 9-2

MOUNT VERNON

P DR SHAW MEMORIAL LIBRARY*, 344 Pond Rd, 04352. SAN 322-8592. Tel: 207-293-2565. E-mail: DrShaw@shaw.lib.me.us. Web Site: drshawlibrary.org, www.mtvernonme.org/Library.html. *Librn,* Alice Olson; Staff 3 (MLS 2, Non-MLS 1)
Founded 1943. Pop 1,083; Circ 12,000. Sal $6,000
Library Holdings: Audiobooks 635; CDs 100; DVDs 100; Large Print Bks 50; Bk Titles 12,000; Per Subs 25; Videos 1,000
Wireless access
Partic in Maine State Libr Network
Open Mon 3-6, Wed 9-12 & 3-7, Sat 10-3
Friends of the Library Group

NAPLES

P NAPLES PUBLIC LIBRARY*, 940 Roosevelt Trail, 04055. SAN 306-6932. Tel: 207-693-6841. FAX: 207-693-7098. Web Site: www.naples.lib.me.us. *Dir,* Dani Longley; E-mail: npldirector@naples.lib.me.us; *Ch,* Kate Johnston; E-mail: childrenslib@naples.lib.me.us; *Libr Asst,* Regina Tremblay; E-mail: libassist@naples.lib.me.us; Staff 3 (Non-MLS 3)
Founded 1907. Pop 3,149; Circ 19,331
Library Holdings: Audiobooks 432; Bks on Deafness & Sign Lang 24; DVDs 1,241; Large Print Bks 1,016; Music Scores 155; Bk Titles 39,000; Bk Vols 41,000; Per Subs 32
Special Collections: Maine Historical Coll
Automation Activity & Vendor Info: (Cataloging) ByWater Solutions; (Circulation) ByWater Solutions; (OPAC) ByWater Solutions
Wireless access
Function: Bk club(s), Prog for adults, Prog for children & young adult, Workshops
Publications: Booklist
Mem of Maine State Library, Region 1
Partic in Maine State Libr Network
Open Tues & Thurs 10-7, Wed 2-7, Sat 9-1, Fri (Summer) 9-1

NEW GLOUCESTER

P NEW GLOUCESTER PUBLIC LIBRARY, 379 Intervale Rd, 04260. SAN 306-6940. Tel: 207-926-4840. Web Site: www.newgloucesterlibrary.org. *Libr Dir,* Mr Lee Shaw; E-mail: librarydirector@newgloucester.org; *Asst Librn,* Emily Martin; E-mail: assistantlibrarian@newgloucester.org; Staff 3 (Non-MLS 3)
Founded 1897. Pop 3,180; Circ 14,400
Library Holdings: Bk Titles 20,415; Bk Vols 20,500; Per Subs 27
Automation Activity & Vendor Info: (Cataloging) Follett Software; (Circulation) Follett Software
Wireless access
Mem of Maine State Library, Region 1
Open Tues, Wed & Fri 11-4, Thurs 12-7, Sat 10-3
Friends of the Library Group

R SHAKER LIBRARY*, 707 Shaker Rd, 04260. SAN 306-7149. Tel: 207-926-4597. E-mail: shakerlibrary@shaker.lib.me.us. Web Site: www.shaker.lib.me.us/library.html. *Dir,* Michael S Graham; E-mail: usshakers@aol.com; *Librn & Archivist,* Charles E. Rand; E-mail: shakerlibrary@shaker.lib.me.us

Founded 1882
Library Holdings: AV Mats 29,196; CDs 105; DVDs 100; Bk Titles 15,632; Videos 222
Special Collections: The Koreshan Unity; The Religious Society of Friends & Other Radical & Communal Groups; Thomsonian Medicine
Subject Interests: Shakers
Wireless access
Function: Archival coll, Ref & res, Ref serv available
Mem of Maine State Library, Region 1
Restriction: Non-circulating coll, Not a lending libr, Open to pub by appt only

NEW PORTLAND

P NEW PORTLAND COMMUNITY LIBRARY*, 899 River Rd, 04961. Tel: 207-628-6561. FAX: 207-628-6561. E-mail: newportlandcl@gmail.com. *Libr Dir,* Sheila Atwood
Pop 800; Circ 363
Library Holdings: Bk Vols 3,500; Per Subs 2
Automation Activity & Vendor Info: (Acquisitions) LibraryWorld, Inc; (Cataloging) LibraryWorld, Inc; (Circulation) LibraryWorld, Inc; (ILL) LibraryWorld, Inc; (Media Booking) LibraryWorld, Inc; (OPAC) LibraryWorld, Inc
Wireless access
Function: Adult bk club, Audio & video playback equip for onsite use, Bks on cassette, Bks on CD, CD-ROM, Computers for patron use, Electronic databases & coll, Free DVD rentals, ILL available, Internet access, Music CDs, Online cat, Tax forms, VHS videos
Open Tues & Sat (Winter) 9-12, Wed & Thurs 4-6; Tues & Sat (Summer) 10-12, Wed & Thurs 4-6, Sun 1-3
Friends of the Library Group

NEW SHARON

P NEW SHARON JIM DITZLER MEMORIAL LIBRARY, 37 Library Rd, 04955. (Mail add: PO Box 61, 04955-0061), SAN 376-7426. Tel: 207-779-1128. Web Site: www.newsharon.lib.me.us. *Librn,* Diana Oliver; E-mail: nsl-do@newsharon.lib.me.us; Staff 1 (Non-MLS 1)
Pop 1,250; Circ 2,863
Library Holdings: Bk Vols 8,500
Wireless access
Open Tues & Wed 2-6, Thurs & Sat 10-2

NEW VINEYARD

P NEW VINEYARD PUBLIC LIBRARY, 20 Lake St, 04956. (Mail add: PO Box 255, 04956-0255), SAN 306-6959. Tel: 207-652-2250. E-mail: newvineyardlibrary@gmail.com. Web Site: www.newvineyardlibrary.com. *Librn,* Mina Miller; Staff 1 (Non-MLS 1)
Pop 607
Library Holdings: Bk Titles 3,631; Bk Vols 4,200; Per Subs 11
Wireless access
Open Mon 5-8, Tues & Sat 10-12; Thurs 2-5
Friends of the Library Group

NEWPORT

P NEWPORT CULTURAL CENTER*, Public Library & Historical Society Museum, 154 Main St, 04953-1139. SAN 306-6967. Tel: 207-368-5074. Web Site: newportculturalcenter.org. *Ch, Dir, Libr Serv,* Joanne Elwell; E-mail: jelwell@newport.lib.me.us; *Librn,* Lee McCartin; E-mail: lmccartin@newport.lib.me.us
Founded 1899. Pop 20,701
Library Holdings: Bk Vols 14,500; Per Subs 20
Automation Activity & Vendor Info: (Cataloging) Evergreen; (Circulation) Evergreen; (OPAC) Evergreen
Open Tues-Fri 9:30-5:30, Sat 9:30-1:30

NORRIDGEWOCK

P NORRIDGEWOCK PUBLIC LIBRARY*, 40 Mercer Rd, 04957. (Mail add: PO Box 7, 04957-0007), SAN 306-6975. Tel: 207-634-2828. E-mail: library@townofnorridgewock.com. Web Site: townofnorridgewock.com/library. *Librn,* Robin Wilson; *Asst Librn,* Sallie Wilder
Pop 3,105; Circ 4,007
Library Holdings: Bks on Deafness & Sign Lang 10; Large Print Bks 200; Bk Titles 15,000; Per Subs 12; Talking Bks 150
Special Services for the Deaf - Bks on deafness & sign lang
Special Services for the Blind - Bks on cassette; Large print bks
Open Tues & Thurs 10-6, Sat 10-2

NORTH ANSON

P STEWART PUBLIC LIBRARY*, 37 Elm St, 04958. (Mail add: PO Box 177, 04958-0177). Tel: 207-635-3212. E-mail: stewlib@stewartpub.lib.me.us. Web Site: www.stewartpub.lib.me.us. *Librn,* Emily Quint
Founded 1899. Pop 2,014
Library Holdings: Bk Vols 15,474; Per Subs 20
Wireless access
Partic in Northwest Library Federation
Open Wed 2:30-6, Sat 2:30-4:30 or by appointment

NORTH BERWICK

P D A HURD LIBRARY*, 41 High St, 03906. SAN 306-6983. Tel: 207-676-2215. FAX: 207-676-7976. E-mail: hurdlibrarian@msln.net. Web Site: www.da-hurd.lib.me.us. *Dir,* Beth Sweet; E-mail: hurddirector@msln.net; *Adult Serv,* Kim Parker; *Ch Serv,* Corinne Feehan; E-mail: hurdchild@da-hurd.lib.me.us; Staff 2 (Non-MLS 2)
Founded 1927. Pop 8,475
Library Holdings: AV Mats 78; Bks-By-Mail 50; CDs 140; Large Print Bks 1,426; Bk Vols 26,892; Per Subs 81; Talking Bks 861; Videos 1,067
Special Collections: Local Genealogy, town reports, maps, regional history
Automation Activity & Vendor Info: (Cataloging) Winnebago Software Co; (Circulation) Winnebago Software Co
Wireless access
Mem of Maine State Library, Region 1
Open Mon, Wed & Fri 9:30-5, Tues & Thurs 1-7, Sat 9:30-1

NORTH BRIDGTON

S BRIDGTON ACADEMY LEARNING COMMONS*, 11 Academy Lane, 04057. (Mail add: PO Box 292, 04057-0292). Tel: 207-647-2121. FAX: 207-647-3146. Web Site: www.bridgtonacademy.org. *Dean of Academic Services,* Binaca MacDonald; E-mail: bmacdonald@bridgtonacademy.org
Library Holdings: Bk Vols 8,000
Wireless access

NORTH HAVEN

P NORTH HAVEN LIBRARY, 33 Main St, 04853. (Mail add: PO Box 486, 04853-0486), SAN 306-6991. Tel: 207-867-9797. FAX: 207-867-9797. E-mail: info@northhavenlibrary.org. *Librn,* Kathryn Quinn; E-mail: kquinn@sad7.k12.me.us; Staff 1 (Non-MLS 1)
Pop 352; Circ 4,942
Library Holdings: AV Mats 400; Bk Titles 14,000; Bk Vols 28,607; Per Subs 20
Automation Activity & Vendor Info: (Cataloging) ComPanion Corp; (Circulation) ComPanion Corp; (ILL) ComPanion Corp; (Serials) ComPanion Corp
Wireless access
Open Wed (Winter) 2-5, Sat 10-12 & 2-5; Mon-Sat (Summer) 1-5
Friends of the Library Group

NORTH JAY

P JAY-NILES MEMORIAL LIBRARY, 983 Main St, 04262. (Mail add: PO Box 5008, 04262-5008), SAN 306-6614. Tel: 207-645-4062. E-mail: info@jaynileslibrary.com. Web Site: www.jaynileslibrary.com. *Dir,* Tamara Hoke; E-mail: thoke@jaynileslibrary.com; *Ch,* Priscilla Pineau; Staff 1 (Non-MLS 1)
Founded 1917. Pop 5,086
Library Holdings: AV Mats 180; Bk Titles 33,000; Per Subs 71
Automation Activity & Vendor Info: (Cataloging) Winnebago Software Co; (Circulation) Winnebago Software Co
Wireless access
Open Mon-Wed 3-8, Thurs & Fri 12-5, Sat (Sept-June) 10-3

NORTHEAST HARBOR

P NORTHEAST HARBOR LIBRARY*, One Joy Rd, 04662. (Mail add: PO Box 279, 04662-0279), SAN 306-7017. Tel: 207-276-3333. FAX: 207-276-3315. E-mail: talktous@nehlibrary.org. Web Site: www.nehlibrary.org. *Dir,* Elly Andrews; E-mail: eandrews@nehlibrary.org; Staff 5 (MLS 1, Non-MLS 4)
Pop 2,063; Circ 42,000
Library Holdings: Bk Vols 55,000; Per Subs 62
Special Collections: Architectural Drawings of Local Structures (Gerrish Coll); Collected Works of Samuel Eliot Morison; Horticulture (R Gwynne Stout Coll); Local History (I T Moore Coll), photog. Oral History
Automation Activity & Vendor Info: (Cataloging) Winnebago Software Co; (Circulation) Winnebago Software Co
Wireless access
Function: Art exhibits, AV serv, ILL available, Prog for adults, Prog for children & young adult, Ref serv available, Summer reading prog
Open Mon, Tues, Thurs & Fri 9-6, Wed 9-7, Sat 9-5

NORWAY

P NORWAY MEMORIAL LIBRARY*, 258 Main St, 04268. SAN 306-7025. Tel: 207-743-5309. Circulation Tel: 207-743-5309, Ext 3. Reference Tel: 207-743-5309, Ext 1. Administration Tel: 207-743-5309, Ext 2. FAX: 207-744-0111. E-mail: norlib@norway.lib.me.us. Web Site: www.norway.lib.me.us. *Libr Dir,* Beth Kane; E-mail: nordir@norway.lib.me.us
Founded 1885. Pop 4,042; Circ 37,539
Library Holdings: Bk Vols 40,000; Per Subs 35
Automation Activity & Vendor Info: (Cataloging) Innovative Interfaces, Inc; (Circulation) Innovative Interfaces, Inc; (OPAC) Innovative Interfaces, Inc
Wireless access
Open Mon, Tues & Fri 10-5, Thurs 12-5, Wed 10-8, Sat 10-3
Friends of the Library Group

OAKLAND

P OAKLAND PUBLIC LIBRARY*, 18 Church St, 04963. SAN 306-7033. Tel: 207-465-7533, 207-465-9554. FAX: 207-465-9554. E-mail: staff@oaklandpubliclibrarymaine.org. Web Site: oaklandpubliclibrarymaine.org. *Head Librn,* Sarah P Roy; *Asst Librn,* Lisa Stevens; *Ch,* Gene Roy; Staff 4 (MLS 1, Non-MLS 3)
Founded 1913. Pop 6,071; Circ 26,878
Library Holdings: Large Print Bks 600; Bk Vols 23,272; Per Subs 49
Special Collections: Maine Coll, bks on tape
Subject Interests: Hist
Automation Activity & Vendor Info: (Cataloging) Follett Software; (Circulation) Follett Software
Wireless access
Open Tues 10-7, Wed-Fri 10-6
Friends of the Library Group

OCEAN PARK

P OCEAN PARK MEMORIAL LIBRARY*, 11 Temple Ave, 04063. (Mail add: PO Box 7248, 04063-7248). Tel: 207-934-9068. FAX: 207-934-2823. E-mail: opa@oceanpark.org. Web Site: www.oceanpark.org/programs/education/library/library.html. *Librn,* Lori Littlefield; Staff 2 (Non-MLS 2)
Library Holdings: Bk Vols 10,000
Mem of Maine State Library, Region 1

OGUNQUIT

P OGUNQUIT MEMORIAL LIBRARY*, 166 Shore Rd, 03907. (Mail add: PO Box 753, 03907-0753), SAN 306-7769. Tel: 207-646-9024. E-mail: ogunquitlibrary@myfairpoint.net. Web Site: ogunquitlibrary.com. *Dir,* Mary W Littlefield; *Asst Librn,* Terri Neill; *Asst Librn,* Jane Staples; Staff 3 (Non-MLS 3)
Founded 1897. Pop 3,000; Circ 15,000
Library Holdings: Bks on Deafness & Sign Lang 10; CDs 100; DVDs 75; Large Print Bks 350; Bk Vols 10,000; Per Subs 25; Talking Bks 400; Videos 40
Special Collections: Municipal Document Depository
Wireless access
Function: Bks on CD, Free DVD rentals, ILL available, Internet access, Magazines, Museum passes, Music CDs, VHS videos
Mem of Maine State Library, Region 1
Open Mon-Sat (Summer) 9-12 & 2-5; Tues-Sat (Winter)9-12 & 2-5

OLD ORCHARD BEACH

P LIBBY MEMORIAL LIBRARY, 27 Staples St, 04064. SAN 306-7041. Tel: 207-934-4351. Web Site: www.ooblibrary.org. *Dir,* Ms Lee Koenigs; E-mail: director@ooblibrary.org; *Ch,* Kim McLaughlin; E-mail: juvenileservices@ooblibrary.org; *ILL, Libr Asst,* Johannah Cushing; E-mail: circ2@ooblibrary.org; Staff 3 (Non-MLS 3)
Founded 1942. Pop 10,071; Circ 36,344
Library Holdings: Bk Titles 27,000; Per Subs 58
Special Collections: Chess Book Coll; Foreign Language films; Local History Coll
Automation Activity & Vendor Info: (Cataloging) Follett Software; (Circulation) Follett Software
Wireless access
Function: 24/7 Online cat, Activity rm, Adult bk club, Archival coll, Art exhibits, Audio & video playback equip for onsite use, Audiobks via web, AV serv, Bks on CD, Children's prog, Computer training, Computers for patron use, Doc delivery serv, E-Readers, Electronic databases & coll, Equip loans & repairs, Family literacy, For res purposes, Free DVD rentals, Games & aids for people with disabilities, Govt ref serv, Holiday prog, Home delivery & serv to seniorr ctr & nursing homes, Homebound delivery serv, ILL available, Internet access, Laminating, Life-long learning prog for all ages, Magazines, Mango lang, Meeting rooms, Movies, Museum passes, Music CDs, Online cat, Online info literacy tutorials on the web & in blackboard, Outreach serv, OverDrive digital audio bks, Photocopying/Printing, Preschool reading prog, Printer for laptops & handheld devices, Prog for adults, Prog for children & young adult, Ref & res, Ref serv available, Scanner, Senior computer classes, Senior outreach, Serves people with intellectual disabilities, Spoken cassettes & CDs, Story hour, Study rm, Summer reading prog, Tax forms, Teen prog, Telephone ref, Visual arts prog, Wheelchair accessible, Workshops
Mem of Maine State Library, Region 1
Special Services for the Deaf - Bks on deafness & sign lang; Closed caption videos
Special Services for the Blind - Bks on CD; Large print bks; Text reader
Open Tues-Fri 10-7, Sat 10-3
Restriction: Circ to mem only, Non-resident fee
Friends of the Library Group

OLD TOWN

P OLD TOWN PUBLIC LIBRARY, 46 Middle St, 04468. SAN 306-705X. Tel: 207-827-3972. FAX: 207-827-3978. E-mail: otpl@old-town.lib.me.us. Web Site: old-town.lib.me.us. *Libr Dir,* Cassandra Pool; E-mail: cpool@old-town.org; *Ch,* Cindy Seger; E-mail: cseger@old-town.org; *Circ Librn, ILL,* Samantha Ryan; E-mail: sryan@old-town.org
Founded 1904. Pop 10,487; Circ 76,135
Library Holdings: Audiobooks 1,562; DVDs 3,137; e-books 9,548; Electronic Media & Resources 5,309; Bk Vols 31,907; Per Subs 48
Special Collections: Local Newspaper, microfilm (100 yrs)
Wireless access
Function: 24/7 Electronic res, 24/7 Online cat, Activity rm, Adult bk club, After school storytime, Audiobks via web, Bk club(s), Bks on CD, Children's prog, Computers for patron use, Electronic databases & coll, Free DVD rentals, ILL available, Magazines, Meeting rooms, Movies, Museum passes, Music CDs, Online cat, Photocopying/Printing, Prog for adults, Prog for children & young adult, Ref & res, Scanner, Story hour, Summer reading prog, Tax forms
Publications: Booklist; Bulletin (for the Center for children's books); Hornbook; The Web
Open Mon & Tues 10-7, Wed-Fri 10-5, Sat 10-1
Friends of the Library Group

ORONO

P ORONO PUBLIC LIBRARY, 39 Pine St, 04473. SAN 306-7068. Tel: 207-866-5060. Web Site: www.orono.org/778/Public-Library. *Dir,* Laurie Carpenter; Tel: 207-866-5060, Ext 300, E-mail: lcarpenter@orono.org; *Youth Serv Librn,* Lindsay Varnum; E-mail: lvarnum@orono.org; *Circ Mgr,* Louise Jolliffe; E-mail: ljolliffe@orono.org; Staff 3 (Non-MLS 3)
Founded 1880. Pop 10,573; Circ 43,017
Library Holdings: Bk Vols 40,000; Per Subs 100
Automation Activity & Vendor Info: (Cataloging) Innovative Interfaces, Inc; (Circulation) Innovative Interfaces, Inc; (OPAC) Innovative Interfaces, Inc
Wireless access
Open Mon & Fri 10-5, Tues & Thurs 10-7, Wed 12-5, Sat 10-3
Friends of the Library Group

C UNIVERSITY OF MAINE, Raymond H Fogler Library, 5729 Fogler Library, 04469-5729. SAN 306-7076. Tel: 207-581-1661. Circulation Tel: 207-581-1666. Interlibrary Loan Service Tel: 207-581-1671. Reference Tel: 207-581-1673. Administration Tel: 207-581-1655. FAX: 207-581-1653. E-mail: foglerlibrary.web@maine.edu. Web Site: library.umaine.edu. *Dean of Libr,* Joyce Rumery; E-mail: rumery@maine.edu; *Dept Head, Head, Content Org,* Greg Curtis; Tel: 207-581-1681, E-mail: gregory.t.curtis@maine.edu; *Head, Coll Serv,* Deborah Rollins; Tel: 207-581-1659, E-mail: drollins@maine.edu; *Head, Ref (Info Serv),* Nancy Lewis; Tel: 207-581-3613, E-mail: lewis@maine.edu; *Head, Spec Coll,* Richard Hollinger; Tel: 207-581-1688, E-mail: richard.hollinger@maine.edu; Staff 21 (MLS 18, Non-MLS 3)
Founded 1865. Enrl 11,561; Highest Degree: Doctorate
Special Collections: Abolition & Antislavery (O'Brien Coll); Cole Maritime Coll; Hannibal Hamlin Family Papers; Indian Lore & Etymology (Eckstorm Coll); Senator William S Cohen Coll; State of Maine Coll, University Archives. State Document Depository; US Document Depository
Subject Interests: Can Am studies, Maine studies
Automation Activity & Vendor Info: (Serials) Innovative Interfaces, Inc
Wireless access
Partic in LYRASIS; Maine InfoNet; Northeast Research Libraries Consortium; OCLC Online Computer Library Center, Inc; Westchester Academic Library Directors Organization
Friends of the Library Group

ORRINGTON

P ORRINGTON PUBLIC LIBRARY*, 15 School St, 04474. SAN 376-3528. Tel: 207-825-4938. E-mail: orringtonlibrary@orrington.lib.me.us. Web Site: orringtonlibrary.wordpress.com. *Dir,* Kelly Bay; Staff 1 (Non-MLS 1)
Founded 1978. Pop 3,309

Library Holdings: Bk Titles 14,400; Per Subs 25
Automation Activity & Vendor Info: (Circulation) Follett Software
Wireless access
Open Mon 9-12 & 12:30-5, Tues, Wed & Fri 2-5, Thurs 11-12 & 12:30-7

ORR'S ISLAND

P ORR'S ISLAND LIBRARY, 1699 Harpswell Islands Rd, 04066. (Mail add: PO Box 175, 04066-0175), SAN 376-3846. Tel: 207-833-7811. E-mail: librarian@orrsislandlibrary.org. Web Site: oilblogcom.com. *Librn,* Joanne Rogers; Staff 1 (Non-MLS 1)
Pop 3,013
Library Holdings: AV Mats 1,300; Bk Titles 10,000; Per Subs 3; Talking Bks 1,000; Videos 1,300
Wireless access
Mem of Maine State Library, Region 1
Open Mon & Wed 1-4, Sat 9-3
Friends of the Library Group

OWLS HEAD

S OWLS HEAD TRANSPORTATION MUSEUM*, The Lang Education Center & Library, 117 Museum St, 04854. (Mail add: PO Box 277, 04854-0277). Tel: 207-594-4418. FAX: 207-594-4410. Web Site: owlshead.org, owlshead.org/education/the-lang-center. *Coll Mgr,* Sarah Dunne; E-mail: sd@ohtm.org; Staff 1 (MLS 1)
Library Holdings: CDs 30; DVDs 25; Music Scores 81; Bk Titles 5,327; Bk Vols 88,511; Per Subs 15; Spec Interest Per Sub 15; Videos 525
Wireless access
Function: Res libr
Publications: Strut & Axle (Quarterly)
Open Tues & Thurs 10-4
Restriction: Non-circulating

OXFORD

P FREELAND HOLMES LIBRARY*, 109 Pleasant St, 04270-4206. (Mail add: PO Box 197, 04270-0197), SAN 376-382X. Tel: 207-539-4016. E-mail: freeland@freeland-holmes.lib.me.us. Web Site: www.freeland-holmes.lib.me.us. *Librn,* Glenda Drapeau; Staff 1 (Non-MLS 1)
Library Holdings: Bk Vols 37,000
Wireless access
Open Tues & Thurs 1-5, Wed 6-8, Fri & Sat 9-Noon

PALERMO

P PALERMO COMMUNITY LIBRARY, 2789 Rte 3, 04354. (Mail add: PO Box 102, 04354-0102). Tel: 207-993-6088. E-mail: palermo@palermo.lib.me.us. Web Site: www.palermo.lib.me.us. *Library Contact,* Sharon Nichols
Founded 2000
Library Holdings: AV Mats 55; DVDs 55; Bk Vols 7,000; Talking Bks 90
Special Collections: Maine Coll
Wireless access
Function: ILL available
Open Mon 10-Noon, Tues & Thurs 3-6, Wed 6pm-7:30pm, Sat 10-2

PARKMAN

P HARVEY MEMORIAL LIBRARY, 771 State Hwy 150, 04443-3201. Tel: 207-876-3730. E-mail: townofparkman@yahoo.com. *Librn,* Brenda Hartford
Founded 1963. Pop 840
Library Holdings: AV Mats 10; Bk Vols 400; Talking Bks 10
Wireless access
Open Mon & Fri 9-5, Tues-Thurs 9-1

PARSONSFIELD

P KEZAR FALLS CIRCULATING LIBRARY*, Two Wadleigh St, 04047. (Mail add: PO Box 11, 04047-0011). Tel: 207-625-2424. E-mail: kezarfallscirclibrary@gmail.com. Web Site: www.maine.gov/msl/libs/directories/displaypub.shtml?id=41021. *Dir,* Silvia Wilson
Pop 3,280; Circ 2,899
Library Holdings: AV Mats 75; Bk Vols 11,375; Talking Bks 60
Special Collections: Local Genealogy Coll
Wireless access
Mem of Maine State Library, Region 1
Open Tues 2:30-7, Wed 10-4, Thurs 2:30-5, Sat 10-12

PATTEN

P VETERANS MEMORIAL LIBRARY, 30 Main St, 04765. (Mail add: PO Box 695, 04765-0695), SAN 306-7106. Tel: 207-528-2164. E-mail: vetmemlib@yahoo.com. Web Site: www.veterans-memorial.lib.me.us. *Librn,* Doris DeRespino
Pop 1,368; Circ 14,600
Library Holdings: Large Print Bks 150; Bk Titles 17,000; Bk Vols 18,000; Per Subs 30; Talking Bks 100
Automation Activity & Vendor Info: (Cataloging) Follett Software; (Circulation) Follett Software; (OPAC) Follett Software
Wireless access
Special Services for the Blind - Bks on cassette
Open Mon & Tues 10-12 & 1-4, Thurs 10-12, 1-4 & 6-8

PEMAQUID

P BRISTOL AREA LIBRARY, 619 Old County Rd, Rte 130, 04458. (Mail add: PO Box 173, New Harbor, 04554-0173), SAN 376-3773. Tel: 207-677-2115. E-mail: libra@msln.net. Web Site: bal.tidewater.net. *Dir,* Jackie Bennett; *Asst Librn,* Catherine Lyons; Staff 1 (Non-MLS 1)
Library Holdings: Bk Titles 10,000; Bk Vols 17,000; Per Subs 10
Wireless access
Open Mon, Wed & Fri 10-5, Thurs 2-5, Sat 10-12
Friends of the Library Group

PEMBROKE

P PEMBROKE LIBRARY*, 221 Old County Rd, 04666. (Mail add: 857 Leighton Point Rd, 04666-4507). Tel: 207-726-4745. FAX: 207-726-4745. E-mail: pemlib@pembroke.lib.me.us. *Dir,* Frederick Gralenski
Founded 2005. Pop 883; Circ 4,500
Library Holdings: Bk Vols 9,000
Wireless access
Open Tues 9-12 & 3-5, Wed 3-8, Thurs 3-5, Fri 3-6, Sat 9-12
Friends of the Library Group

PHILLIPS

P PHILLIPS PUBLIC LIBRARY, 96 Main St, 04966. (Mail add: PO Box O, 04966-1514), SAN 306-7114. Tel: 207-639-2665. FAX: 207-639-2665. Web Site: www.phillips.lib.me.us. *Librn,* Hedy Langdon; E-mail: hlangdon@phillips.lib.me.us; Staff 2 (Non-MLS 2)
Founded 1910. Pop 1,885; Circ 2,975
Library Holdings: Bk Titles 12,000; Per Subs 14
Special Collections: Local History Coll; Maine Coll
Wireless access
Open Wed 10-7, Thurs & Fri 10-5, Sat 10-2
Friends of the Library Group

PHIPPSBURG

P ALBERT F TOTMAN PUBLIC LIBRARY*, 28 Parker Head Rd, 04562. Tel: 207-389-2309. FAX: 207-389-2309. Web Site: www.totmanlibrary.org. *Dir,* Michele Morong; E-mail: director@totmanlibrary.org; Staff 1 (Non-MLS 1)
Founded 1929. Pop 2,106
Library Holdings: AV Mats 700; CDs 60; DVDs 536; Large Print Bks 85; Bk Vols 10,100; Per Subs 23; Talking Bks 325; Videos 750
Automation Activity & Vendor Info: (Acquisitions) Book Systems; (Cataloging) Book Systems; (Circulation) Book Systems; (OPAC) Book Systems
Wireless access
Function: Audiobks via web
Open Mon-Fri 10-5, Sat 10-1

PITTSFIELD

P PITTSFIELD PUBLIC LIBRARY, 110 Library St, 04967. SAN 306-7122. Tel: 207-487-5880. E-mail: bat@pittsfield.lib.me.us. Web Site: www.pittsfield.lib.me.us. *Libr Dir,* Holly Williams; Staff 4 (MLS 1, Non-MLS 3)
Founded 1904. Pop 4,200; Circ 41,697
Library Holdings: Large Print Bks 300; Bk Vols 21,000; Per Subs 70
Subject Interests: Local hist
Automation Activity & Vendor Info: (Cataloging) Follett Software; (Circulation) Follett Software
Wireless access
Open Mon-Fri 10-6, Sat (Sept-May) 10-1
Friends of the Library Group

POLAND

P ALVAN BOLSTER RICKER MEMORIAL LIBRARY, 1211 Maine St, 04274. SAN 306-7130. Tel: 207-998-4390. FAX: 207-998-2120. Web Site: www.rickerlibrary.org. *Adminr,* Joanne Messer; E-mail:

jmesser@rickerlibrary.org; *Asst Librn,* Terri LaClaire; E-mail: tlaclaire@rickerlibrary.org; Staff 7 (MLS 1, Non-MLS 6)
Founded 1963. Pop 4,866; Circ 22,000
Library Holdings: Bk Titles 25,000; Per Subs 35
Special Collections: Local History Coll; Maine Coll
Automation Activity & Vendor Info: (Cataloging) Follett Software; (Circulation) Follett Software
Wireless access
Partic in Maine InfoNet; Maine State Libr Network
Open Mon & Tues 9-8, Wed-Fri 9-5, Sat 10-2
Friends of the Library Group

PORTLAND

L BERNSTEIN SHUR LAW LIBRARY*, 100 Middle St, 04104. (Mail add: PO Box 9729, 04104-5029), SAN 329-1251. Tel: 207-228-7281. FAX: 207-774-1127. Web Site: www.bernsteinshur.com. *Librn,* Christine Bertsch; E-mail: cbertsch@bernsteinshur.com; Staff 1 (MLS 1)
Founded 1981
Library Holdings: Bk Vols 4,500; Per Subs 200
Wireless access
Mem of Maine State Library, Region 1
Restriction: Private libr

L NATHAN & HENRY B CLEAVES LAW LIBRARY, 142 Federal St, 04101. SAN 306-7165. Tel: 207-773-9712. Toll Free FAX: 866-894-9612. E-mail: info@cleaves.org. Web Site: www.cleaves.org. *Librn,* Nancy Rabasca; Staff 2 (MLS 1, Non-MLS 1)
Founded 1811
Library Holdings: Bk Vols 30,000
Special Collections: Legal Photography Archives; oral histories; Records & Briefs of the Supreme Judicial Court of the State of Maine
Wireless access
Mem of Maine State Library, Region 1
Open Mon-Fri 9-4

S GREATER PORTLAND LANDMARKS, INC*, Frances W Peabody Research Library, 93 High St, 04101. SAN 306-7181. Tel: 207-774-5561. FAX: 207-774-2509. E-mail: info@portlandlandmarks.org. Web Site: www.portlandlandmarks.org. *Exec Dir,* Hilary Bassett; E-mail: hbassett@portlandlandmarks.org; Staff 3 (MLS 1, Non-MLS 2)
Founded 1971
Library Holdings: Bk Titles 1,250; Per Subs 5
Special Collections: Biography of Architects in Maine; Buildings & Architectural Detail, microprint; Scientific American Building Monthly, 1885-1905
Subject Interests: Local hist
Wireless access
Restriction: Open to pub by appt only

S MAINE CHARITABLE MECHANIC ASSOCIATION, Mechanics' Hall Library, 519 Congress St, 04101. SAN 306-7203. Tel: 207-773-8396. E-mail: library@mainemechanics.org. Web Site: mainemechanics.org/library. *Librn,* Julie Olson; E-mail: julieolson@mainemechanics.org; Staff 1 (MLS 1)
Founded 1815
Wireless access
Mem of Maine State Library, Region 1
Partic in Maine Balsam Library Consortium
Open Tues-Thurs 10-4:30
Restriction: Mem only

S MAINE COLLEGE OF ART*, Joanne Waxman Library, 522 Congress St, 04101. SAN 321-0391. Tel: 207-775-5153. Toll Free Tel: 800-639-4808. FAX: 207-772-5069. E-mail: library@meca.edu. Web Site: www.meca.edu/academics/joanne-waxman-library. *Libr Dir,* Shiva Darbandi; Tel: 207-699-5090, E-mail: sdarbandi@meca.edu; Staff 3 (MLS 1, Non-MLS 2)
Founded 1973. Enrl 330; Fac 50; Highest Degree: Master
Library Holdings: CDs 35; DVDs 500; e-journals 53; Bk Titles 33,000; Bk Vols 43,000; Per Subs 108
Special Collections: Bill Caldwell Rare Book Room, artist bks & rare bks; Visual Resource Coll
Subject Interests: Applied arts, Art hist, Design, Fine arts, Liberal arts
Automation Activity & Vendor Info: (Acquisitions) Innovative Interfaces, Inc - Sierra; (Cataloging) Innovative Interfaces, Inc - Sierra; (Circulation) Innovative Interfaces, Inc - Sierra; (OPAC) Innovative Interfaces, Inc - Sierra; (Serials) Innovative Interfaces, Inc - Sierra
Wireless access
Function: Archival coll, Art exhibits, CD-ROM, Computers for patron use, ILL available, Online cat, Photocopying/Printing, Ref serv available, Scanner, VHS videos, Wheelchair accessible
Mem of Maine State Library, Region 1
Partic in LYRASIS; OCLC Online Computer Library Center, Inc
Open Tues-Fri 10-2 & 4-7
Restriction: Fee for pub use, In-house use for visitors, Limited access for the pub, Non-circulating of rare bks

S MAINE HISTORICAL SOCIETY*, Brown Research Library, 489 Congress St, 04101. SAN 306-7211. Tel: 207-774-1822. Reference Tel: 207-774-1822, Ext 230. FAX: 207-775-4301. E-mail: collections@mainehistory.org, research@mainehistory.org. Web Site: www.mainehistory.org. *Director, Collections & Research,* Jamie Kingman Rice; E-mail: jrice@mainehistory.org; *Research Librn,* Tiffany Link; E-mail: tlink@mainehistory.org; Staff 9 (MLS 5, Non-MLS 4)
Founded 1822
Library Holdings: Bk Titles 65,000
Special Collections: Fogg Autograph Coll; Northeast Boundary Coll; Papers of Governor William King; Portland Company Records; Records of Kennebec & Pejepscot Proprietors
Subject Interests: Early New England, Genealogy, Maine hist
Automation Activity & Vendor Info: (Cataloging) Innovative Interfaces, Inc - Sierra
Wireless access
Function: 24/7 Online cat, Archival coll, Electronic databases & coll, Ref & res, Ref serv available, Res assist avail, Res libr, Res performed for a fee
Publications: CIRCA (Newsletter); Maine History (Journal)
Mem of Maine State Library, Region 1
Partic in Maine InfoNet
Open Tues-Sat (May-Oct) 10-4; Wed-Sat (Nov-April) 10-4
Restriction: Non-circulating, Not a lending libr, Off-site coll in storage - retrieval as requested
Friends of the Library Group

S MAINE IRISH HERITAGE CENTER LIBRARY*, 34 Gray St, 04102. (Mail add: PO Box 7588, 04112-0118). Tel: 207-780-0118. E-mail: librarian@maineirish.com, maineirish@maineirish.com. Web Site: www.maineirish.com. *Librn,* Susan Flaherty; Tel: 207-210-0657, E-mail: suejflaherty@gmail.com
Library Holdings: Bk Vols 3,000
Open Mon 5-7, Fri 10-2 or by appointment

M MAINE MEDICAL CENTER LIBRARY & KNOWLEDGE SERVICES*, 22 Bramhall St, 5th Flr, 04102. SAN 306-722X. Tel: 207-662-2202. FAX: 207-761-3027. E-mail: library@mmc.org. Web Site: www.mainehealth.org/maine-medical-center/healthcare-professionals/mmc-library. *Libr Mgr,* Dina McKelvy; Staff 4 (MLS 3, Non-MLS 1)
Founded 1874
Subject Interests: Hospital admin, Med, Nursing
Automation Activity & Vendor Info: (OPAC) Innovative Interfaces, Inc - Sierra
Wireless access
Mem of Maine State Library, Region 1
Partic in Health Sci Libr & Info Coop; National Network of Libraries of Medicine Region 7; North Atlantic Health Sciences Libraries, Inc
Open Mon-Fri 8-4:30
Restriction: Badge access after hrs, Hospital staff & commun

P MAINE STATE LIBRARY, REGION 1*, Portland Office, Five Monument Sq, 04101. SAN 306-7238. Tel: 207-871-1766. Toll Free Tel: 800-649-7696. FAX: 202-871-1703. Web Site: www.maine.gov/msl/libs/districts/councils/smldboard.htm. *Libr Develop,* Elaine Bissonnette; E-mail: Elaine.M.Bissonnette@maine.gov; Staff 2 (MLS 1, Non-MLS 1)
Founded 1974. Pop 62,686; Circ 629,789
Library Holdings: Bk Vols 200; Per Subs 3
Subject Interests: Libr & info sci
Publications: News Notes
Member Libraries: Acton Public Library; Baxter Memorial Library; Bernstein Shur Law Library; Berry Memorial Library; Berwick Public Library; Bolsters Mills Village Library; Bonney Memorial Library; Bridgton Public Library; Brown Memorial Library; Brownfield Public Library; Cape Porpoise Library; Casco Public Library; Chebeague Island Library; Cliff Island Library; Community Library; Cundy's Harbor Library; Curtis Memorial Library; D A Hurd Library; Davis Memorial Library; Dorothy Fish Coastal Resource Library at Wells Reserve; Dyer Library; Falmouth Memorial Library; Freeport Community Library; Gray Public Library; Harrison Village Library; Hollis Center Public Library; Kennebunk Free Library; Kezar Falls Circulating Library; Lakes Environmental Association; Laura E Richards Library; Libby Memorial Library; Limerick Public Library; Long Island Community Library; Louis B Goodall Memorial Library; Louis T Graves Memorial Public Library; Maine Charitable Mechanic Association; Maine College of Art; Maine Historical Society; Maine Medical Center Library & Knowledge Services; MaineHealth; Martha Sawyer Community Library; McArthur Public Library; Merrill Memorial Library; Naples Public Library; Nathan & Henry B Cleaves Law Library; New England Bible College Library; New Gloucester Public Library; North Gorham Public Library; Ocean Park

Memorial Library; Ogunquit Memorial Library; Old York Historical Society Research Center; Orr's Island Library; Parsons Memorial Library; Pierce Atwood LLP; Portland Public Library; Preti Flaherty Beliveau & Pachios; Prince Memorial Library; Raymond Village Library; Rice Public Library; Richville Library; Saint Joseph's College; Salmon Falls Library; Sappi North America; Scarborough Public Library; Shaker Library; Shapleigh Community Library; South Berwick Public Library; South Portland Public Library; Southern Maine Community College Library; Spaulding Memorial Library; Springvale Public Library; Steep Falls Public Library; Thomas Memorial Library; University of Maine School of Law; University of New England Libraries; Walker Memorial Library; Waterboro Public Library; Wells Public Library; West Buxton Public Library; William Fogg Library; Windham Public Library; York County Community College Library; York Public Library

L PIERCE ATWOOD LLP*, Law Library, 254 Commercial St, 04101. SAN 372-0969. Tel: 207-791-1142. FAX: 207-791-1350. Web Site: www.pierceatwood.com. *Mgr, Libr Serv,* Kami Bedard; Tel: 207-791-1100, E-mail: kbedard@pierceatwood.com; Staff 2 (MLS 2)
Library Holdings: Bk Vols 20,000; Per Subs 120
Automation Activity & Vendor Info: (Acquisitions) Inmagic, Inc.; (Cataloging) Inmagic, Inc.; (Circulation) Inmagic, Inc.
Wireless access
Mem of Maine State Library, Region 1
Restriction: Staff use only

P PORTLAND PUBLIC LIBRARY*, Five Monument Sq, 04101. SAN 343-6802. Tel: 207-871-1700. Circulation Tel: 207-871-1700, Ext 730. Reference Tel: 207-871-1700, Ext 725. Administration Tel: 207-871-1700, Ext 757. Toll Free Tel: 800-649-7696. FAX: 207-871-1703. E-mail: reference@portlandpubliclibrary.org. Web Site: www.portlandlibrary.com. *Exec Dir,* Sarah Campbell; Tel: 207-871-1700, Ext 755, E-mail: campbell@portlib.org; *Assoc Dir,* Jessica Goodwin; Tel: 207-871-1700, Ext 736, E-mail: goodwin@portlib.org; *Dir, Adult Serv,* Sarah Skawinski; Tel: 207-871-1700, Ext 726, E-mail: skawinski@portlib.org; *Dir of Finance,* Marianne Sensale-Guerin; Tel: 207-871-1700, Ext 760, E-mail: guerin@portlib.org; *Dir, Access Serv,* Kathleen Spahn; Tel: 207-871-1700, Ext 709, E-mail: spahn@portlib.org; *Asst to the Exec Dir, Dir, External Relations,* Kristin Forester; Tel: 207-871-1700, Ext 759, E-mail: forester@portlib.org; *Dir, Youth Serv,* Mary Peverada; Tel: 207-871-1700, Ext 707, E-mail: peverada@portlib.org; *Outreach Librn, Tech Librn,* Casey Grant; Tel: 207-871-1700, Ext 729, E-mail: grant@portlib.org; Staff 59 (MLS 14, Non-MLS 45)
Founded 1867. Pop 70,080; Circ 742,779
Library Holdings: AV Mats 38,967; Bk Titles 295,337; Bk Vols 311,069; Per Subs 1,700
Special Collections: Hugh Thomson (Antique Children's Books); Jacob Abbott Coll; Jewish Bi-Centennial Oral History Program; Music by Maine Composers; Newspapers from 1785; Portland Coll; Press Books (Dun Emer, Mosher, Southworth-Anthoensen, Cuala Shagbark); Sarah Orne Jewett Coll; State of Maine (Maine Authors, Maine & Portland Imprints). Oral History; State Document Depository; US Document Depository
Subject Interests: Art, Consumer health, Ireland
Automation Activity & Vendor Info: (Acquisitions) Innovative Interfaces, Inc; (Circulation) Innovative Interfaces, Inc; (OPAC) Innovative Interfaces, Inc; (Serials) Innovative Interfaces, Inc
Wireless access
Function: 24/7 Electronic res, 24/7 Online cat, Adult bk club, Archival coll, Audio & video playback equip for onsite use, Audiobks via web, Bk club(s), Bks on cassette, Bks on CD, CD-ROM, Children's prog, Computer training, Computers for patron use, E-Readers, Electronic databases & coll, Free DVD rentals, Govt ref serv, Holiday prog, Home delivery & serv to seniorr ctr & nursing homes, ILL available, Instruction & testing, Internet access, Magazines, Magnifiers for reading, Mail & tel request accepted, Mango lang, Meeting rooms, Microfiche/film & reading machines, Movies, Museum passes, Music CDs, Online cat, Online ref, Orientations, Outreach serv, OverDrive digital audio bks, Photocopying/Printing, Preschool outreach, Printer for laptops & handheld devices, Prog for adults, Prog for children & young adult, Ref & res, Ref serv available, Scanner, Senior computer classes, Senior outreach, Story hour, Summer reading prog, Tax forms, Teen prog, Telephone ref, VHS videos, Wheelchair accessible, Workshops, Writing prog
Publications: Annual Report; Seasonal Newsletter; Services Guide
Mem of Maine State Library, Region 1
Partic in LYRASIS
Special Services for the Deaf - Bks on deafness & sign lang; High interest/low vocabulary bks; TDD equip
Special Services for the Blind - Closed circuit TV
Open Mon-Fri 11-4
Friends of the Library Group
Branches: 3
BURBANK, 377 Stevens Ave, 04103, SAN 376-1096. Tel: 207-774-4229. E-mail: burbank@portlandpubliclibrary.org. *Mgr,* Jim Charette; Staff 1 (Non-MLS 1)
Founded 1940. Circ 214,672
Library Holdings: Bk Vols 11,604; Per Subs 34
Open Tues-Thurs 2-6, Fri & Sat 10-2
Friends of the Library Group
PEAKS ISLAND BRANCH, 129 Island Ave, Peaks Island, 04108, SAN 343-6926. Tel: 207-766-5540. E-mail: peaks@portland.lib.me.us. *Mgr,* Jerri Blatt; Staff 2 (Non-MLS 2)
Founded 1978. Circ 36,872
Library Holdings: Bk Vols 22,299; Per Subs 35
Open Tues 2-6, Fri 10-1
Friends of the Library Group
RIVERTON, 1600 Forest Ave, 04103-1399, SAN 343-6985. Tel: 207-797-2915. E-mail: riverton@portlandpubliclibrary.org. *Mgr,* Catherine Curran; Staff 3 (MLS 1, Non-MLS 2)
Founded 1977. Circ 54,788
Library Holdings: Bk Vols 32,327; Per Subs 20
Open Mon & Sat 10-1, Wed & Fri 3-6
Friends of the Library Group
Bookmobiles: 1. Librn, Steve Weigle

L PRETI FLAHERTY BELIVEAU & PACHIOS*, One City Ctr, 04112. (Mail add: PO Box 9546, 04112-9546). Tel: 207-791-3000. FAX: 207-791-3111. Web Site: www.preti.com. *Law Librn,* Nicole Moss; E-mail: nmoss@preti.com
Library Holdings: Bk Vols 1,500; Per Subs 15
Wireless access
Mem of Maine State Library, Region 1
Restriction: Staff use only

CL UNIVERSITY OF MAINE SCHOOL OF LAW*, Donald L Garbrecht Law Library, 246 Deering Ave, 04102. SAN 306-7254. Tel: 207-780-4829. Circulation Tel: 207-780-4350. Interlibrary Loan Service Tel: 207-780-4818. Reference Tel: 207-780-4351. FAX: 207-780-4913. E-mail: lawlibrary@maine.edu. Web Site: mainelaw.maine.edu/library. *Law Libr Dir/Law Librn,* Christine Iaconeta; Tel: 207-780-4827, E-mail: christine.iaconeta@maine.edu; *Cat Librn, Ser,* Stephen R Salhany; Tel: 207-780-4832, E-mail: stephen.salhany@maine.edu; *Govt Doc Law Librn, Ref Serv,* Maureen P Quinlan; Tel: 207-780-4835, E-mail: maureen.quinlan@maine.edu; *Ref Law Librn,* Cindy Hirsch; Tel: 207-780-4830, E-mail: cindy.hirsch@maine.edu; *Coll Develop,* Suzanne Parent; Tel: 207-780-4353, E-mail: parent@maine.edu; Staff 10 (MLS 6, Non-MLS 4)
Founded 1962. Enrl 300; Fac 16; Highest Degree: Doctorate
Library Holdings: Bk Vols 325,000; Per Subs 1,175
Special Collections: US Document Depository
Automation Activity & Vendor Info: (Acquisitions) Innovative Interfaces, Inc; (Cataloging) Innovative Interfaces, Inc; (Circulation) Innovative Interfaces, Inc; (Course Reserve) Innovative Interfaces, Inc; (ILL) Innovative Interfaces, Inc; (Media Booking) Innovative Interfaces, Inc
Publications: Law Library Guide
Mem of Maine State Library, Region 1
Partic in NELLCO Law Library Consortium, Inc.; OCLC Online Computer Library Center, Inc
Open Mon-Fri 8-5
Friends of the Library Group

C UNIVERSITY OF SOUTHERN MAINE*, University Libraries, 314 Forest Ave, 04104. (Mail add: PO Box 9301, 04104-9301), SAN 306-6487. Tel: 207-780-4270. Interlibrary Loan Service Tel: 207-228-8449. Reference Tel: 207-780-4272. FAX: 207-780-4042. TDD: 207-780-5646. Web Site: library.usm.maine.edu. *Dir, Univ Librn,* David J Nutty; Tel: 207-780-4276, E-mail: david.nutty@maine.edu; *Coordr, Access Serv,* Bill Sargent; Tel: 207-780-8154, E-mail: william.sargent@maine.edu; *Coordr, Cat,* Elizabeth Phipps; Tel: 207-780-4990, E-mail: ephipps@usm.maine.edu; *Ref & Instruction Coordr,* Bill Grubb; Tel: 207-780-4672, E-mail: william.grubb@maine.edu; *Coordr, Spec Coll,* Susie Bock; Tel: 207-780-4269, E-mail: bocks@usm.maine.edu; Staff 33 (MLS 15, Non-MLS 18)
Founded 1878. Fac 345; Highest Degree: Doctorate
Library Holdings: AV Mats 7,349; e-books 373,571; Microforms 24,284; Music Scores 1,637; Bk Vols 385,818; Per Subs 5,470; Videos 2,522
Special Collections: Antique Cartographic Materials; Jean Byers Sampson Center for Diversity; Maine Nursing Association Archives; Osher Map Library & Smith Center for Cartographic Education
Subject Interests: Interdisciplinary
Automation Activity & Vendor Info: (Acquisitions) Innovative Interfaces, Inc; (Cataloging) Innovative Interfaces, Inc; (Circulation) Innovative Interfaces, Inc; (Course Reserve) Innovative Interfaces, Inc; (Discovery) ProQuest; (ILL) Innovative Interfaces, Inc; (Media Booking) Innovative Interfaces, Inc; (OPAC) Innovative Interfaces, Inc; (Serials) Innovative Interfaces, Inc
Wireless access
Function: Doc delivery serv, For res purposes, Govt ref serv, ILL available, Photocopying/Printing, Ref serv available, Wheelchair accessible
Publications: Reference LibGuides

Partic in Maine InfoNet; OCLC Online Computer Library Center, Inc
Open Mon-Thurs 7:45am-11pm, Fri 7:45am-8pm, Sat 10-8, Sun 10am-11pm
Departmental Libraries:
GORHAM LIBRARY & LEARNING COMMONS, 37 College Ave, Gorham, 04038. Tel: 207-780-5345. *Coordr, Learning Commons,* Ed Moore; Tel: 207-780-5346, E-mail: edward.moore@maine.edu
Open Mon-Thurs 7:45am-11pm, Fri 7:45am-8pm, Sat 11-7, Sun Noon-11
LEWISTON-AUBURN COLLEGE LIBRARY, 51 Westminster St, Lewiston, 04240. (Mail add: PO Box 1937, Lewiston, 04241-1937), SAN 377-9432. Tel: 207-753-6540. Interlibrary Loan Service Tel: 207-753-6526. FAX: 207-753-6543. *Head of Libr,* Evelyn Greenlaw; Tel: 207-753-6541, E-mail: evelyng@maine.edu; *Circ, ILL,* Dale Kuczinski; E-mail: dalek@usm.maine.edu; *Ref Serv,* Maureen Perry; E-mail: mperry@usm.maine.edu; Staff 2 (MLS 2)
Founded 1988. Enrl 1,600; Fac 45; Highest Degree: Master
Library Holdings: Bk Titles 18,000; Per Subs 210
Special Collections: Franco-American Heritage Coll
Subject Interests: Behav sci, Franco-Am hist, Interdisciplinary, Leadership mgt, Occupational therapy
Automation Activity & Vendor Info: (Circulation) Innovative Interfaces, Inc; (Course Reserve) Innovative Interfaces, Inc; (ILL) Innovative Interfaces, Inc; (OPAC) Innovative Interfaces, Inc; (Serials) Innovative Interfaces, Inc
Partic in ARIEL; Maine Health Sci Librs & Info Consortium; OCLC Online Computer Library Center, Inc
Open Mon-Fri 8-8

L VERRILL DANA LIBRARY*, One Portland Sq, 04112. (Mail add: PO Box 586, 04112-0586), SAN 328-4417. Tel: 207-774-4000, Ext 4856. FAX: 207-774-7499. Web Site: www.verrilldana.com. *Head Librn,* Anne M Reiman; Tel: 207-253-4856, E-mail: areiman@verrilldana.com; Staff 1 (Non-MLS 1)
Library Holdings: Bk Titles 13,000; Per Subs 100
Wireless access
Partic in Cas; LexisNexis; LOIS
Friends of the Library Group

PRESQUE ISLE

J NORTHERN MAINE COMMUNITY COLLEGE LIBRARY, 33 Edgemont Dr, 04769. SAN 306-7289. Tel: 207-768-2718. FAX: 207-768-2823. Web Site: www.nmcc.edu/academics/support/library. *Dir,* Ann Morrison Spinney; E-mail: naspinne@nmcc.edu; Staff 1 (MLS 1)
Founded 1968. Fac 45; Highest Degree: Associate
Library Holdings: e-books 198,000; e-journals 1,700; Bk Titles 6,200
Subject Interests: Bus, Computer, Med
Automation Activity & Vendor Info: (Acquisitions) Innovative Interfaces, Inc; (Cataloging) Innovative Interfaces, Inc; (Circulation) Innovative Interfaces, Inc; (Course Reserve) Innovative Interfaces, Inc; (ILL) Innovative Interfaces, Inc; (Media Booking) Innovative Interfaces, Inc; (OPAC) Innovative Interfaces, Inc; (Serials) Innovative Interfaces, Inc
Wireless access
Publications: Acquisition List
Partic in LYRASIS; OCLC Online Computer Library Center, Inc
Open Mon-Wed (Winter) 8-6, Thurs 8-4, Fri 8-3; Mon-Fri (Summer) 8-4

P MARK & EMILY TURNER MEMORIAL LIBRARY, 39 Second St, 04769. SAN 306-7297. Tel: 207-764-2571. Toll Free Tel: 866-758-4480. FAX: 207-768-5756. Web Site: pimainelibrary.org. *Libr Dir,* Sonja Plummer Eyler; E-mail: sonjaplummer@presqueisle.lib.me.us; Staff 10 (MLS 1, Non-MLS 9)
Founded 1908. Pop 10,000; Circ 97,000
Library Holdings: Bk Vols 65,000; Per Subs 98; Talking Bks 1,400
Special Collections: Local History Coll; Local Newspapers, microfilm, archives. Oral History
Automation Activity & Vendor Info: (Cataloging) Follett Software; (Circulation) Follett Software; (OPAC) Follett Software
Wireless access
Function: ILL available
Special Services for the Blind - Closed circuit TV magnifier
Open Mon-Thurs 9-7, Fri 9-5:30, Sat 9-2

C UNIVERSITY OF MAINE AT PRESQUE ISLE LIBRARY*, 181 Main St, 04769-2888. SAN 306-7300. Tel: 207-768-9595. FAX: 207-768-9644. Web Site: www.umpi.edu/library. *Dir, Libr Serv,* Roger Getz; E-mail: roger.getz@maine.edu; *Access Serv,* Angelita Hernandez; Tel: 207-768-9611, E-mail: angelita.hernandez@maine.edu; *Cat/Circ, ILL,* Michelle Greene; Tel: 207-768-9593, E-mail: michelle.greene@maine.edu; Staff 3 (MLS 1, Non-MLS 2)
Founded 1903. Enrl 1,344; Fac 50; Highest Degree: Bachelor
Library Holdings: CDs 21; DVDs 158; e-books 165,432; e-journals 68,000; Electronic Media & Resources 45,000; Bk Titles 66,147; Bk Vols 69,776; Per Subs 6
Special Collections: Aroostook County History Coll; Maine Coll; Rare bks. State Document Depository; US Document Depository
Subject Interests: Archives, Local hist
Automation Activity & Vendor Info: (Acquisitions) Innovative Interfaces, Inc; (Cataloging) Innovative Interfaces, Inc; (Circulation) Innovative Interfaces, Inc; (Course Reserve) Innovative Interfaces, Inc; (ILL) OCLC; (OPAC) Innovative Interfaces, Inc; (Serials) Innovative Interfaces, Inc
Wireless access
Function: 24/7 Online cat, Archival coll, Art exhibits, Doc delivery serv, E-Reserves, Electronic databases & coll, For res purposes, Free DVD rentals, Govt ref serv, ILL available, Internet access, Laminating, Meeting rooms, Movies, Music CDs, Online cat, Online ref, Orientations, OverDrive digital audio bks, Photocopying/Printing, Printer for laptops & handheld devices, Ref & res, Ref serv available, Res assist avail, Res libr, Scanner, Telephone ref
Publications: Faculty Staff Guide; Library Resources & Services Guide
Partic in LYRASIS; OCLC Online Computer Library Center, Inc
Open Mon-Thurs 7:30am-10pm, Fri 7:30-4:30, Sun 2-10; Mon-Fri (Winter & Summer) 8-4:30

PRINCETON

P PRINCETON PUBLIC LIBRARY*, 40 Main St, 04668. (Mail add: PO Box 408, 04668-0408). Tel: 207-796-5333. E-mail: library@princetonme.com. *Libr Dir,* Heidi Potter; Staff 1 (Non-MLS 1)
Circ 2,976
Library Holdings: Bk Vols 11,049; Per Subs 16
Wireless access
Open Mon 10-2, Tues & Thurs 10-4, Wed 12-6
Friends of the Library Group

PROSPECT HARBOR

P DORCAS LIBRARY*, 28 Main St, 04669. (Mail add: PO Box 167, 04669-0167), SAN 376-3501. Tel: 207-963-4027. E-mail: dorcas@dorcas.lib.me.us. Web Site: www.dorcas.lib.me.us. *Libr Dir,* Faith Lane; Staff 1 (MLS 1)
Pop 1,600
Library Holdings: Audiobooks 800; Bks-By-Mail 112; DVDs 1,200; Electronic Media & Resources 10,000; Bk Titles 10,364; Bk Vols 15,000; Per Subs 28
Automation Activity & Vendor Info: (Acquisitions) LibraryWorld, Inc
Wireless access
Open Tues & Thurs 1-7, Sat 10-4; Mon (Nov-March) 1-4
Friends of the Library Group

RANGELEY

P RANGELEY PUBLIC LIBRARY, Seven Lake St, 04970. (Mail add: PO Box 1150, 04970-1150), SAN 306-7319. Tel: 207-864-5529. FAX: 207-864-2523. Web Site: www.rangeleylibrary.org. *Dir,* Janet Wilson; E-mail: director@rangeleylibrary.org
Founded 1909. Pop 6,400; Circ 21,407
Library Holdings: Bk Vols 21,830; Per Subs 35
Special Collections: Wilhelm Reich Coll
Subject Interests: Lit
Automation Activity & Vendor Info: (Cataloging) Follett Software; (Circulation) Follett Software; (OPAC) Follett Software
Wireless access
Open Tues-Fri 10-4:30, Sat 10-2
Friends of the Library Group

RAYMOND

P RAYMOND VILLAGE LIBRARY*, Three Meadow Rd, 04071-6461. (Mail add: PO Box 297, 04071-0297), SAN 306-7327. Tel: 207-655-4283. Web Site: www.raymondvillagelibrary.org. *Dir,* Allison Griffin; E-mail: allison.griffin@raymondvillagelibrary.org; Staff 1 (Non-MLS 1)
Founded 1914. Pop 4,299; Circ 24,866
Library Holdings: Bk Vols 18,167; Per Subs 20; Talking Bks 608; Videos 1,200
Special Collections: Maine Coll
Wireless access
Mem of Maine State Library, Region 1
Open Mon & Wed 9-7, Sat 9-4

READFIELD

P READFIELD COMMUNITY LIBRARY, 1151 Main St, 04355. (Mail add: PO Box 246, 04355-0246), SAN 374-6267. Tel: 207-685-4089. E-mail: librarian@readfieldmaine.org. Web Site: readfieldlibrary.wordpresss.com. *Librn,* Melissa Small; Staff 1 (Non-MLS 1)
Pop 2,033; Circ 10,898
Library Holdings: Bk Vols 10,000; Per Subs 13
Wireless access

Open Mon 3-7, Tues & Sat 10-4, Wed 1-7
Friends of the Library Group

RICHMOND

P ISAAC F UMBERHINE LIBRARY, 86 Main St, 04357. SAN 306-7343. Tel: 207-737-2770. E-mail: isaac@umberhine.lib.me.us. Web Site: richmondmaine.com/umberhine-library.aspx, www.umberhine.lib.me.us. *Librn,* Donna McCluskey; Staff 1 (Non-MLS 1)
Pop 3,100; Circ 16,000
Library Holdings: AV Mats 600; Bk Vols 23,000; Per Subs 16; Talking Bks 600
Wireless access
Function: Homebound delivery serv, Prog for children & young adult
Open Tues & Thurs 2-8, Wed 9-2, Sat 9-Noon

ROCKLAND

S WILLIAM A FARNSWORTH LIBRARY AT THE FARNSWORTH ART MUSEUM*, 16 Museum St, 04841. SAN 306-7351. Tel: 207-596-6457. Web Site: farnsworthmuseum.org. *Assoc Curator,* Jane Bianco; Tel: 207-390-6012, E-mail: jbianco@farnsworthmuseum.org; Staff 3 (MLS 1, Non-MLS 2)
Founded 1948
Special Collections: Artist File; Jonathan Fisher; Kosti Ruohomaa-Robert Indiana Archives; Louise Nevelson Biographical Material Coll; N C Wyeth Memorabilia
Subject Interests: Art hist, Decorative art, Fine arts, Local hist, Rare bks, Victorian archit
Function: Ref serv available
Open Mon, Tues & Thurs-Sun (Summer) 10-5, Wed 10-7; Tues-Sun (Winter) 10-5
Restriction: Non-circulating to the pub

P ROCKLAND PUBLIC LIBRARY, 80 Union St, 04841. SAN 306-7378. Tel: 207-594-0310. FAX: 207-594-0333. E-mail: library@rocklandmaine.gov. Web Site: rocklandmaine.gov/municipal/departments/library. *Dir,* Amy Levine; E-mail: alevine@rocklandmaine.gov; *Dep Dir,* Patricia King; E-mail: pking@ci.rockland.me.us; Staff 7 (MLS 1, Non-MLS 6)
Founded 1892. Pop 12,500; Circ 180,000
Library Holdings: AV Mats 8,410; Bk Vols 51,868; Per Subs 79; Videos 2,300
Special Collections: Children's Coll; Literacy Volunteers Coll; Maine Coll
Automation Activity & Vendor Info: (Cataloging) Innovative Interfaces, Inc; (Circulation) Innovative Interfaces, Inc; (OPAC) Innovative Interfaces, Inc
Wireless access
Open Mon, Wed & Fri 10-5, Tues & Thurs 10-5:30, Sat 10-1
Friends of the Library Group

ROCKPORT

M PEN BAY MEDICAL CENTER*, Niles Perkins Health Science Library, Six Glen Cove Dr, 04856. SAN 377-9459. Tel: 207-921-8456. FAX: 207-921-5281. Web Site: www.mainehealth.org/Pen-Bay-Medical-Center. *Librn,* Ashley Duguay; E-mail: aduguay@mmc.org; Staff 1 (MLS 1)
Library Holdings: Bk Titles 2,000; Per Subs 224
Wireless access
Partic in Basic Health Sciences Library Network; Maine Health Sci Librs & Info Consortium; Medical Library Association; North Atlantic Health Sciences Libraries, Inc
Open Tues-Thurs 9-4

P ROCKPORT PUBLIC LIBRARY*, 485 Commercial St, 04856. (Mail add: PO Box 8, 04856-0008), SAN 306-7386. Tel: 207-236-3642. E-mail: rpl@rockport.lib.me.us. Web Site: www.rockport.lib.me.us. *Libr Dir,* Ben Blackmon; *Ad, Dep Dir,* Keith Drago; *Circ, Tech Serv Librn,* Laura Meservey; *Youth Serv Librn,* Ben Odgren; Staff 3 (Non-MLS 3)
Founded 1914. Pop 2,854; Circ 63,000
Library Holdings: AV Mats 2,500; Bk Vols 30,000; Per Subs 52
Subject Interests: Maritime hist
Automation Activity & Vendor Info: (Cataloging) Innovative Interfaces, Inc; (Circulation) Innovative Interfaces, Inc; (OPAC) Innovative Interfaces, Inc
Wireless access
Function: ILL available, Photocopying/Printing, Ref serv available
Open Mon, Tues & Thurs-Sat 9-5:30, Wed 11-8
Friends of the Library Group

RUMFORD

P RUMFORD PUBLIC LIBRARY*, 56 Rumford Ave, 04276-1919. SAN 306-7394. Tel: 207-364-3661. FAX: 207-364-7296. E-mail: rplweb@rumford.lib.me.us. Web Site: www.rumford.lib.me.us. *Dir,* Tamara Butler; E-mail: tbutler@rumford.lib.me.us; *Ch,* Sue Marshall; E-mail: smarshall@rumford.lib.me.us; *Circ Supvr,* Christy Bates; E-mail: cbates@rumford.lib.me.us; Staff 8 (MLS 1, Non-MLS 7)
Founded 1903. Pop 9,439; Circ 62,000
Library Holdings: AV Mats 403; Large Print Bks 700; Bk Vols 38,000; Per Subs 68; Talking Bks 300
Special Collections: Maine History & Fiction
Automation Activity & Vendor Info: (Cataloging) Innovative Interfaces, Inc; (Circulation) Innovative Interfaces, Inc; (OPAC) Innovative Interfaces, Inc
Wireless access
Open Mon & Sat 8-2, Tues & Thurs 9-8, Wed & Fri 9-5
Friends of the Library Group

SACO

P DYER LIBRARY, 371 Main St, 04072. SAN 306-7408. Tel: 207-283-3861. FAX: 207-283-0754. Web Site: www.dyerlibrarysacomuseum.org. *Exec Dir,* Leslie L Rounds; E-mail: lrounds@dyer.lib.me.us; *Automation/Pub Serv Librn,* Chris Rounds; E-mail: dyerref@dyer.lib.me.us; *Children's Coordr,* Brook Palmer; E-mail: bpalmer@dyer.lib.me.us; *Circ Coordr,* Cheryl Spaulding; E-mail: cspaulding@dyer.lib.me.us; Staff 1 (Non-MLS 1)
Founded 1881. Pop 20,700; Circ 117,896
Library Holdings: Bk Titles 60,000; Per Subs 120
Special Collections: Bureau of the Census; History (Maine Coll), bks, newspapers & photos (18th & 19th centuries), pamphlets, doc, town hist rec
Automation Activity & Vendor Info: (Cataloging) Follett Software; (Circulation) Follett Software; (OPAC) Follett Software
Wireless access
Function: Archival coll, Art exhibits, Electronic databases & coll, Family literacy, Home delivery & serv to senior ctr & nursing homes, ILL available, Internet access, Music CDs, Orientations, Photocopying/Printing, Preschool outreach, Prog for adults, Prog for children & young adult, Summer reading prog, Tax forms, Telephone ref, VHS videos, Workshops
Publications: Newsletter
Mem of Maine State Library, Region 1
Open Mon, Wed & Fri 9:30-5, Tues & Thurs 9:30-8, Sat 9:30-12:30

M SWEETSER CHILDREN'S SERVICES*, Professional Library, 50 Moody St, 04072-0892. SAN 378-0864. Tel: 207-294-4945. Toll Free Tel: 800-434-3000. FAX: 207-294-4940. *Librn,* Jan Wertheim
Library Holdings: Bk Titles 2,500; Per Subs 25
Open Mon-Fri 8-3:30

SANFORD

P LOUIS B GOODALL MEMORIAL LIBRARY*, 952 Main St, 04073. SAN 343-7078. Tel: 207-324-4714. FAX: 207-324-5982. E-mail: info@lbgoodall.org. Web Site: www.lbgoodall.org. *Dir,* Jackie McDougal; *Asst Dir,* Jean Collins; *Head, Children's Servx,* Deidre Walsh; *Ref Librn,* Jason Fenimore; Staff 3 (MLS 2, Non-MLS 1)
Founded 1898. Pop 18,040; Circ 125,067
Library Holdings: Bk Vols 69,984; Per Subs 127
Special Collections: US Document Depository
Automation Activity & Vendor Info: (Cataloging) Follett Software; (Circulation) Follett Software
Wireless access
Mem of Maine State Library, Region 1
Open Mon-Thurs 10-8, Fri 10-5, Sat 10-4

SANGERVILLE

P SANGERVILLE PUBLIC LIBRARY*, One Town Hall Ave, 04479. (Mail add: PO Box 246, 04479-0246), SAN 376-7582. Tel: 207-876-3491. Web Site: www.sangerville.lib.me.us. *Librn,* Leslie Steeg; E-mail: ljsteeg@msln.net
Founded 1923. Pop 700; Circ 3,760
Library Holdings: Bk Vols 11,200; Per Subs 10
Wireless access
Partic in Scoop Coop
Open Mon-Thurs 2-7, Fri 11-4

SARGENTVILLE

P SARGENTVILLE LIBRARY ASSOCIATION*, 653 Reach Rd, 04673. (Mail add: PO Box 233, Sedgwick, 04676). Tel: 207-359-8086. E-mail: sargentvillelibraryarchive@gmail.com. Web Site: www.sedgwickmaine.org/sargentville-library-association. *Librn,* Kay Grover
Founded 1905. Pop 1,300
Library Holdings: Bk Vols 3,000
Subject Interests: Sargentville hist & genealogy
Wireless access
Function: Archival coll, Ref & res, Scanner
Open Sat (June-Sept) 10-Noon, Tues (July-Aug) 6-8

SCARBOROUGH

P SCARBOROUGH PUBLIC LIBRARY, 48 Gorham Rd, 04074. SAN 306-7432. Tel: 207-883-4723. FAX: 207-883-9728. E-mail: askspl@scarboroughlibrary.org. Web Site: www.scarboroughlibrary.org. *Libr Dir,* Nancy E Crowell; Tel: 207-396-6266, E-mail: ncrowell@scarboroughlibrary.org; *Adult Serv Mgr, Asst Dir,* Catherine Morrison; Tel: 207-396-6270, E-mail: cmorrison@scarboroughlibrary.org; *Syst Librn,* Thomas B Corbett; Tel: 207-396-6271, E-mail: tcorbett@scarboroughlibrary.org; *Circ Mgr,* Michael Windsor; Tel: 207-396-6268, E-mail: mwindsor@scarboroughlibrary.org; *Youth Serv Mgr,* Louise Capizzo; Tel: 207-396-6278, E-mail: lcapizzo@scarboroughlibrary.org; *Cataloger,* Denise M Menard; Tel: 207-396-6274, E-mail: dmenard@scarboroughlibrary.org; Staff 20 (MLS 7, Non-MLS 13)
Founded 1899. Pop 19,500; Circ 215,770
Automation Activity & Vendor Info: (Circulation) Innovative Interfaces, Inc - Millennium; (ILL) Innovative Interfaces, Inc - Millennium; (OPAC) Innovative Interfaces, Inc - Millennium
Wireless access
Function: 24/7 Electronic res, Adult bk club, Adult literacy prog, Audio & video playback equip for onsite use, Audiobks via web, AV serv, Bks on CD, Children's prog, Computer training, Computers for patron use, E-Readers, Electronic databases & coll, Free DVD rentals, Home delivery & serv to seniorr ctr & nursing homes, Homebound delivery serv, ILL available, Magazines, Magnifiers for reading, Movies, Museum passes, Music CDs, Online cat, Online ref, Outreach serv, OverDrive digital audio bks, Photocopying/Printing, Preschool outreach, Preschool reading prog, Printer for laptops & handheld devices, Prog for adults, Prog for children & young adult, Ref serv available, Serves people with intellectual disabilities, Spoken cassettes & CDs, Story hour, Study rm, Summer reading prog, Tax forms, Teen prog, VHS videos, Wheelchair accessible
Publications: Footnotes (Newsletter)
Mem of Maine State Library, Region 1
Open Mon, Tues, Thurs & Fri 10-5, Wed 10-6, Sat 10-2
Restriction: Non-resident fee
Friends of the Library Group

SEARSMONT

P SEARSMONT TOWN LIBRARY*, 37 Main St S, 04973. (Mail add: PO Box 56, 04973-0105), SAN 374-7069. Tel: 207-342-5549. FAX: 207-342-3495. E-mail: stlme@searsmont.lib.me.us. *Libr Dir,* Steven Brown; Staff 1 (Non-MLS 1)
Founded 1990. Pop 1,250; Circ 4,000
Library Holdings: AV Mats 292; Bk Titles 8,860; Per Subs 30
Special Collections: Oral History
Wireless access
Special Services for the Deaf - High interest/low vocabulary bks
Open Tues 9-7, Thurs 3-7, Fri 1-5, Sat 10-2
Friends of the Library Group

SEARSPORT

P CARVER MEMORIAL LIBRARY*, 12 Union St, 04974. (Mail add: PO Box 439, 04974), SAN 306-7440. Tel: 207-548-2303. E-mail: cml@carver.lib.me.us. Web Site: www.carver.lib.me.us. *Dir,* Katie Hessler; E-mail: khessler@carver.lib.me.us
Founded 1910. Pop 2,800
Library Holdings: Audiobooks 700; Large Print Bks 200; Bk Vols 10,000; Per Subs 25; Videos 1,400
Special Collections: Maine Coll; Maritime Coll
Automation Activity & Vendor Info: (Cataloging) Biblionix; (Circulation) Biblionix
Wireless access
Open Mon-Fri 10-5:30, Sat 10-1

S PENOBSCOT MARINE MUSEUM*, Stephen Phillips Memorial Library, Nine Church St, 04974. (Mail add: PO Box 498, 04974-0498), SAN 306-7459. Tel: 207-548-2529, Ext 212. FAX: 207-548-2520. E-mail: libraryresearcher@pmm-maine.org. Web Site: www.penobscotmarinemuseum.org. *Colls Mgr, Curator,* Cipperly Good; Tel: 207-548-2529, Ext 212, E-mail: cgood@pmm-maine.org; Staff 1 (Non-MLS 1)
Founded 1936
Library Holdings: Bk Titles 12,000; Per Subs 10
Special Collections: Maritime (Logbooks, Journals, Maritime Navigation & Law, Ship Registers)
Subject Interests: Genealogy, Local hist, Maritime hist
Function: Res libr
Partic in Maine Libr Asn
Open Tues-Fri 9-1
Restriction: Non-circulating to the pub

SEBAGO

P SPAULDING MEMORIAL LIBRARY*, 282 Sebago Rd, 04029. (Mail add: PO Box 300, 04029-0300), SAN 306-7467. Tel: 207-787-2321. E-mail: directors@spaulding.lib.me.us. Web Site: www.spaulding.lib.me.us. *Dir,* Susan Newton; Staff 2 (Non-MLS 2)
Founded 1925. Pop 1,700; Circ 6,000
Library Holdings: Bk Titles 8,000
Subject Interests: Maine
Automation Activity & Vendor Info: (Cataloging) LibLime Koha; (Circulation) LibLime Koha
Wireless access
Function: Adult bk club, Bks on CD, Computer training, Computers for patron use, Free DVD rentals, ILL available, Magazines, Mail & tel request accepted, Online cat, OverDrive digital audio bks, Photocopying/Printing, Prog for adults, Prog for children & young adult, Scanner, Summer reading prog, Tax forms, VHS videos, Wheelchair accessible
Mem of Maine State Library, Region 1
Open Mon & Wed 8:30-7, Sat 9-1, Sun 2-4

SEDGWICK

P SEDGWICK LIBRARY ASSOCIATION*, 45 Main St, 04676. Tel: 207-359-2177. Web Site: www.sedgwickmaine.org/sedgwick-library-association. *Librn,* Mary Ellen Ashman
Pop 1,300
Library Holdings: AV Mats 100; Bk Vols 4,000; Talking Bks 100; Videos 40
Special Collections: Genealogy & Mystery (Maine Coll)
Open Thurs (Winter) 3-5, Sat 10-Noon; Wed (Summer) 5-7, Thurs 3-5, Sat 10-Noon

SHAPLEIGH

P SHAPLEIGH COMMUNITY LIBRARY*, 607 Shapleigh Corner Rd, 04076. (Mail add: PO Box 97, 04076-0097). Tel: 207-636-3630. E-mail: shapleighlibrary@gmail.com. Web Site: www.shapleigh.net/library.cfm. *Dir,* Katie Richards
Founded 1980. Pop 2,400; Circ 5,000
Library Holdings: AV Mats 400; Bks on Deafness & Sign Lang 4; CDs 150; DVDs 260; Large Print Bks 100; Bk Vols 18,000; Per Subs 19; Videos 30
Special Collections: Genealogy Coll; Local History Coll
Wireless access
Mem of Maine State Library, Region 1
Open Tues 3-6, Thurs & Sat 10-2 (Winter); Tues 3-8, Thurs 9-2 & 6-8, Sat 9-1 (Summer)

SHERMAN

P SHERMAN PUBLIC LIBRARY*, Nine Church St, 04776. (Mail add: 36 School St, Ste 3, 04776-3428), SAN 306-7475. Tel: 207-365-4882. Interlibrary Loan Service Tel: 207-947-8336. FAX: 207-365-4143. E-mail: shermanpl276@yahoo.com. *Dir,* Denise Tapley; Staff 1 (Non-MLS 1)
Pop 1,021; Circ 2,549
Library Holdings: Bk Vols 9,810
Special Collections: Local History Coll. Oral History
Wireless access
Open Mon-Fri 1:30-3:30
Friends of the Library Group

SKOWHEGAN

M REDINGTON-FAIRVIEW GENERAL HOSPITAL*, Health Sciences Library, 46 Fairview Ave, 04976. (Mail add: PO Box 468, 04976-0468), SAN 377-984X. Tel: 207-474-5121, Ext 419. FAX: 207-858-2314. *Librn,* Rebecca Jordan; E-mail: rjordan@rfgh.net
Library Holdings: Bk Titles 200; Per Subs 160
Partic in Maine Health Sci Librs & Info Consortium
Open Mon, Wed & Fri 7:30-4

P SKOWHEGAN PUBLIC LIBRARY*, Nine Elm St, 04976. SAN 306-7483. Tel: 207-474-9072. FAX: 207-474-9072. E-mail: skowlib@skowhegan.lib.me.us. Web Site: www.skowhegan.lib.me.us. *Dir,* Dale Jandreau; *Ch,* Angie Herrick; Staff 3 (Non-MLS 3)
Founded 1889. Pop 10,121; Circ 51,700
Library Holdings: AV Mats 1,200; Bk Vols 27,000; Per Subs 22
Wireless access
Function: Art exhibits, Audiobks via web, Bks on cassette, Bks on CD, Children's prog, Computer training, Computers for patron use, Electronic databases & coll, Free DVD rentals, Genealogy discussion group, Holiday prog, Homebound delivery serv, ILL available, Internet access, Jazz prog, Mail & tel request accepted, Microfiche/film & reading machines, Online cat, Online ref, OverDrive digital audio bks, Photocopying/Printing, Preschool outreach, Prog for adults, Prog for children & young adult, Ref

& res, Scanner, Story hour, Summer reading prog, Tax forms, Telephone ref, VHS videos, Workshops
Open Mon-Fri 10-6, Sat (Winter) 10-2
Restriction: Authorized patrons, Circ to mem only, Non-resident fee
Friends of the Library Group

C MARGARET CHASE SMITH LIBRARY, 56 Norridgewock Ave, 04976. Tel: 207-474-7133. E-mail: mcsl@mcslibrary.org. Web Site: www.mcslibrary.org. *Dir,* Dr David L Richards, PhD; E-mail: davidr@mcslibrary.org; *Curator of Coll,* Nicole Potter; E-mail: npotter@mcslibrary.org; Staff 4.5 (MLS 1, Non-MLS 3.5)
Founded 1982
Jul 2020-Jun 2021 Income $335,000. Mats Exp $1,150, Books $550, Per/Ser (Incl. Access Fees) $600. Sal $202,000 (Prof $46,000)
Library Holdings: AV Mats 473; CDs 8; DVDs 7; Bk Vols 3,300; Per Subs 2; Videos 342
Special Collections: Congressional Library of Senator Margaret Chase Smith's Career from 1940 to 1973; Scrapbooks, early 1900s to date; Statements & Speeches; Syndicated Column, Washington & You, 1941-1954
Subject Interests: Polit sci, Political hist
Wireless access
Function: 24/7 Online cat, Adult bk club, Archival coll, Res libr
Publications: Friends of the Library (Newsletter)
Open Mon-Fri 10-4
Restriction: Internal use only, Non-circulating, Not a lending libr, Open to pub by appt only, Open to qualified scholars, Open to researchers by request, Open to students

SOLON

P COOLIDGE LIBRARY, 17 S Main St, 04979. (Mail add: PO Box 238, 04979-0238), SAN 306-7491. Tel: 207-643-2562. E-mail: books@coolidge.lib.me.us. Web Site: solon.maine.gov. *Librn,* Megan Myers; Staff 1 (Non-MLS 1)
Pop 966; Circ 1,524
Library Holdings: Bk Vols 5,000; Per Subs 10
Wireless access
Open Tues 1-6:30, Thurs 10-6

SOUTH BERWICK

P SOUTH BERWICK PUBLIC LIBRARY, 27 Young St, 03908. SAN 306-7505. Tel: 207-384-3308. E-mail: sbpl@southberwicklibrary.org. Web Site: www.southberwicklibrary.org. *Libr Dir,* Karen McCarthy Eger; *Ch,* Jane Cowen Fletcher
Founded 1971. Pop 7,000; Circ 41,436
Library Holdings: Bk Vols 32,000; Per Subs 9
Automation Activity & Vendor Info: (Cataloging) Follett Software; (Circulation) Follett Software
Wireless access
Function: 24/7 Electronic res, 24/7 Online cat, Activity rm, Adult bk club, Audio & video playback equip for onsite use, Audiobks via web, Bk club(s), Bks on CD, Children's prog, Computer training, Computers for patron use, E-Readers, E-Reserves, Electronic databases & coll, Free DVD rentals, Homebound delivery serv, ILL available, Internet access, Magazines, Mail & tel request accepted, Movies, Museum passes, Online cat, OverDrive digital audio bks, Photocopying/Printing, Preschool reading prog, Prog for adults, Story hour, Study rm, Summer reading prog, Wheelchair accessible
Mem of Maine State Library, Region 1
Partic in Maine InfoNet
Open Tues 10-5, Wed 10-7, Fri 1-5, Sat 10-1
Friends of the Library Group

SOUTH BRISTOL

P RUTHERFORD LIBRARY*, 2000 State Rte 129, 04568. (Mail add: PO Box 145, 04568-0145). Tel: 207-644-1882. *Dir,* Ellen Shew; E-mail: ellenshaw@gmail.com
Founded 1903. Pop 900; Circ 5,719
Library Holdings: AV Mats 786; DVDs 20; Large Print Bks 75; Bk Vols 14,000; Per Subs 17; Talking Bks 419
Special Collections: Local History Coll
Wireless access
Open Tues-Sat 2-5

SOUTH CHINA

P SOUTH CHINA PUBLIC LIBRARY, 247 Village St, 04358. (Mail add: PO Box 417, 04358-0417), SAN 376-3765. Tel: 207-445-3094. E-mail: southchinalibrary@gmail.com. Web Site: www.southchinalibrary.org. *Librn,* Cheryl Baker
Founded 1830
Library Holdings: Bk Vols 11,100; Per Subs 14
Special Collections: Quaker (Rufus Jones Coll)
Automation Activity & Vendor Info: (Cataloging) LibraryWorld, Inc; (Circulation) LibraryWorld, Inc; (OPAC) LibraryWorld, Inc
Wireless access
Open Wed 10-12 & 1-3, Sat 10-12

SOUTH PARIS

P HAMLIN MEMORIAL LIBRARY & MUSEUM*, 16 Hannibal Hamlin Dr, 04281. (Mail add: PO Box 43, Paris, 04271-0043), SAN 306-7092. Tel: 207-743-2980. E-mail: hamlinstaff@hamlin.lib.me.us. Web Site: www.hamlin.lib.me.us. *Librn,* Jennifer Lewis; Staff 1 (Non-MLS 1)
Founded 1902. Pop 300; Circ 1,700
Library Holdings: Bk Titles 5,900; Bk Vols 6,000; Per Subs 2
Special Collections: Hamlin Family Records; Town of Paris History
Wireless access
Open Tues 8:30-5, Thurs 8:30-6, Sat 10-2

P PARIS PUBLIC LIBRARY, 37 Market Sq, 04281. SAN 306-7513. Tel: 207-743-6994. E-mail: paris.public.library@msln.net. Web Site: www.paris.lib.me.us. *Dir,* Michael F Dignan; E-mail: mdignan@paris.lib.me.us; Staff 6 (MLS 1, Non-MLS 5)
Founded 1926. Pop 5,100; Circ 57,000
Jul 2019-Jun 2020 Income $200,000, City $179,000, Locally Generated Income $11,000. Mats Exp $37,000, Books $32,000, AV Mat $4,000, Electronic Ref Mat (Incl. Access Fees) $1,000. Sal $101,000 (Prof $40,000)
Library Holdings: Audiobooks 1,913; DVDs 4,941; Large Print Bks 1,781; Bk Vols 45,000; Per Subs 10
Special Collections: Advertiser-Democrat Newspaper Coll; Town Histories; Youth's Companion Magazine Coll
Automation Activity & Vendor Info: (Cataloging) Innovative Interfaces, Inc - Sierra; (Circulation) Innovative Interfaces, Inc - Sierra; (OPAC) Innovative Interfaces, Inc - Sierra
Wireless access
Function: 24/7 Online cat, Adult bk club, Audiobks via web, Bk club(s), Bks on CD, Children's prog, Computers for patron use, Free DVD rentals, Holiday prog, Homebound delivery serv, ILL available, Internet access, Magazines, Mail & tel request accepted, Meeting rooms, Online cat, Prog for children & young adult, Res assist avail, Story hour, Summer reading prog, Teen prog
Partic in Maine InfoNet
Open Mon-Fri 9-6, Sat 9-3
Friends of the Library Group

SOUTH PORTLAND

S MAINE DEPARTMENT OF CORRECTIONS*, Long Creek Youth Development Center Library, 675 Westbrook St, 04106. SAN 321-5075. Tel: 207-822-2679. *Librn,* Matthew Dever; E-mail: matthew.dever@maine.gov
Library Holdings: Bk Titles 8,000; Per Subs 23
Automation Activity & Vendor Info: (Acquisitions) Follett Software; (Cataloging) Follett Software; (Circulation) Follett Software; (Course Reserve) Follett Software; (ILL) Follett Software; (Media Booking) Follett Software; (OPAC) Follett Software; (Serials) Follett Software
Restriction: Internal circ only

CR NEW ENGLAND BIBLE COLLEGE LIBRARY*, 879 Sawyer St, 04116. (Mail add: 502 Odlin Rd, Bangor, 04401). Tel: 207-947-1665. E-mail: info@nebc.edu. Web Site: www.nebc.edu/academics.
Founded 1979
Library Holdings: Bk Titles 13,058; Bk Vols 15,489; Per Subs 16
Wireless access
Mem of Maine State Library, Region 1
Open Mon-Wed 9-Noon

P SOUTH PORTLAND PUBLIC LIBRARY*, 482 Broadway, 04106. SAN 343-7132. Tel: 207-767-7660. FAX: 207-767-7626. Web Site: southportlandlibrary.com. *Dir,* Kevin Davis; E-mail: kdavis@southportland.org; Staff 16 (MLS 4, Non-MLS 12)
Founded 1965. Pop 25,000; Circ 228,806
Library Holdings: Bk Titles 73,228; Bk Vols 80,000; Per Subs 50
Special Collections: Cape Elizabeth Historical Records; Early American Children's Books (James Otis Kaler Coll); South Portland
Automation Activity & Vendor Info: (Cataloging) Innovative Interfaces, Inc; (Circulation) Innovative Interfaces, Inc; (OPAC) Innovative Interfaces, Inc
Wireless access
Function: 24/7 Electronic res, 24/7 Online cat, Activity rm, Adult bk club, AV serv, BA reader (adult literacy), Bk club(s), Bks on cassette, Bks on CD, Children's prog, Computers for patron use, Electronic databases & coll, For res purposes, Free DVD rentals, Genealogy discussion group, Home delivery & serv to seniorr ctr & nursing homes, Homebound delivery serv, ILL available, Internet access, Life-long learning prog for all ages, Literacy & newcomer serv, Magazines, Museum passes, Music CDs,

Online cat, Outreach serv, Photocopying/Printing, Preschool outreach, Preschool reading prog, Printer for laptops & handheld devices, Prog for adults, Prog for children & young adult, Ref & res, Ref serv available, Res assist avail, Senior outreach, Serves people with intellectual disabilities, Spoken cassettes & CDs, Spoken cassettes & DVDs, Story hour, Summer & winter reading prog, Summer reading prog, Tax forms, Teen prog, Wheelchair accessible, Workshops, Writing prog
Mem of Maine State Library, Region 1
Open Tues-Thurs 10-8, Fri & Sat 10-6
Restriction: Non-resident fee
Friends of the Library Group
Branches: 1
MEMORIAL BRANCH, 155 Wescott Rd, 04106, SAN 343-7167. Tel: 207-775-1835. FAX: 207-773-1036. *Dir,* Kevin M Davis
Circ 32,000
Library Holdings: Bk Vols 20,000; Per Subs 10
Open Mon 10-8, Wed & Fri 2-6, Sun 12-5
Friends of the Library Group

J SOUTHERN MAINE COMMUNITY COLLEGE LIBRARY*, Two Fort Rd, 04106. SAN 306-7521. Tel: 207-741-5521. E-mail: library@smccme.edu. Web Site: www.smccme.edu. *Dir, Learning Commons,* Holly Gurney; *Head, Access & Coll Serv,* Carin Dunay; *Outreach & Instruction Librn,* Meghan Hardison; *Ref & Instrul Serv Librn,* Bryan Strniste; *Patron Serv,* Joanne Langerman; Staff 5 (MLS 4, Non-MLS 1)
Founded 1964. Enrl 6,734; Fac 110; Highest Degree: Associate
Library Holdings: Audiobooks 195; CDs 158; DVDs 1,026; Bk Vols 20,586; Per Subs 190
Automation Activity & Vendor Info: (Cataloging) Innovative Interfaces, Inc; (Circulation) Innovative Interfaces, Inc; (OPAC) Innovative Interfaces, Inc; (Serials) Innovative Interfaces, Inc
Wireless access
Mem of Maine State Library, Region 1
Partic in Health Science Library Information Consortium; Maine Libr Asn; OCLC Online Computer Library Center, Inc
Open Mon-Thurs 8-8, Fri 8-5, Sun 4-8

SOUTH THOMASTON

P SOUTH THOMASTON PUBLIC LIBRARY*, Eight Dublin Rd S, 04858. (Mail add: PO Box 3, 04858-0003). Tel: 207-596-0022. FAX: 207-596-7529. E-mail: library@south-thomaston.lib.me.us. Web Site: www.south-thomaston.lib.me.us. *Dir,* Pennie Alley; Staff 1 (MLS 1)
Library Holdings: Bk Vols 5,000; Per Subs 12
Automation Activity & Vendor Info: (Acquisitions) LibraryWorld, Inc; (Circulation) LibraryWorld, Inc; (OPAC) LibraryWorld, Inc
Wireless access
Function: Adult bk club, Audiobks via web, Bks on CD, Children's prog, Computers for patron use, ILL available, Internet access, Online cat, OverDrive digital audio bks, Photocopying/Printing, Preschool outreach, Prog for adults, Prog for children & young adult, Story hour, Wheelchair accessible
Open Mon 11-4, Wed 2-7, Sat 10-2

SOUTHPORT

P SOUTHPORT MEMORIAL LIBRARY, 1032 Hendricks Hill Rd, 04576-3309. (Mail add: PO Box 148, 04576-0148), SAN 376-3781. Tel: 207-633-2741. E-mail: librarian1@southport.lib.me.us. Web Site: www.southportlibrary.org. *Librn,* Jen Britton; *Asst Librn,* Ann Thompson Mayer; Staff 3 (Non-MLS 3)
Founded 1906. Pop 3,000; Circ 13,500
Library Holdings: Bk Vols 32,000; Per Subs 30
Special Collections: Butterfly Coll. Oral History
Automation Activity & Vendor Info: (Acquisitions) LibraryWorld, Inc
Wireless access
Open Tues & Sat 9-4, Thurs 9-4 & 6-8, Wed (Summer) 9-4
Friends of the Library Group

SOUTHWEST HARBOR

P SOUTHWEST HARBOR PUBLIC LIBRARY, 338 Main St, 04679. (Mail add: PO Box 157, 04679-0157), SAN 306-7556. Tel: 207-244-7065. FAX: 207-244-3616. E-mail: circulation@swhplibrary.org. Web Site: www.swhplibrary.org. *Dir,* Erich Reed; E-mail: ereed@swhplibrary.org; *Asst Dir,* Kate Pickup McMullin; E-mail: kpmcmullin@swhplibrary.org
Founded 1895. Pop 1,752; Circ 65,000
Library Holdings: Bk Vols 41,500; Per Subs 125
Special Collections: Genealogy; Historic Photo Coll; Maine History. Oral History
Subject Interests: Oral hist tapes
Wireless access
Function: 24/7 Electronic res, 24/7 Online cat, Activity rm, Adult bk club, After school storytime, Archival coll, Art exhibits, Audiobks on Playaways & MP3, Audiobks via web, AV serv, Bk club(s), Bks on CD, Children's prog, Computer training, Computers for patron use, Distance learning, E-Readers, Electronic databases & coll, Equip loans & repairs, Free DVD rentals, Holiday prog, ILL available, Instruction & testing, Internet access, Magazines, Meeting rooms, Music CDs, Notary serv, Online cat, Online info literacy tutorials on the web & in blackboard, Online ref, OverDrive digital audio bks, Photocopying/Printing, Preschool outreach, Preschool reading prog, Printer for laptops & handheld devices, Prog for adults, Prog for children & young adult, Ref & res, Ref serv available, Scanner, Senior computer classes, Spoken cassettes & CDs, Spoken cassettes & DVDs, Story hour, Study rm, Summer & winter reading prog, Summer reading prog, Tax forms, Wheelchair accessible, Workshops
Partic in Maine InfoNet
Open Mon-Fri 10-5, Sat 10-1

SPRINGVALE

P SPRINGVALE PUBLIC LIBRARY*, 443 Main St, 04083. SAN 306-7424. Tel: 207-324-4624. E-mail: spl@springvalelibrary.org. Web Site: www.springvalelibrary.org. *Actg Dir,* Dawn M Brown; *Youth Serv Librn,* Sheila Dube; Staff 7 (MLS 1, Non-MLS 6)
Founded 1906. Pop 20,000; Circ 84,635
Library Holdings: Bk Vols 33,852; Per Subs 65
Special Collections: Genealogy & Local History Room
Subject Interests: Genealogy
Automation Activity & Vendor Info: (Cataloging) Follett Software; (Circulation) Follett Software; (OPAC) Follett Software
Wireless access
Function: Homebound delivery serv, ILL available, Photocopying/Printing, Prog for children & young adult, Ref serv available, Serves people with intellectual disabilities, Summer reading prog, Telephone ref, Wheelchair accessible
Mem of Maine State Library, Region 1
Partic in Maine School & Library Network
Special Services for the Blind - Audio mat
Open Mon, Thurs & Fri 9:30-5, Tues & Wed 9:30-7, Sat 9-2

STANDISH

P RICHVILLE LIBRARY*, 743 Richville Rd, 04084. Tel: 207-776-4698. E-mail: richvillelibrary@gmail.com. Web Site: sites.google.com/site/richvillelibrary/home. *Dir,* Karen McNutt
Library Holdings: AV Mats 400; Bk Vols 4,000
Wireless access
Mem of Maine State Library, Region 1
Open Thurs 2-5, Sat 9-Noon
Friends of the Library Group

CR SAINT JOSEPH'S COLLEGE, Wellehan Library, 278 Whites Bridge Rd, 04084-5263. SAN 306-7009. Tel: 207-893-7725. Toll Free Tel: 800-343-5498, Ext 4. FAX: 207-893-7883. Web Site: www.sjcme.edu/academics/library. *Sr Dir, Learning Commons,* Shelly Davis; Tel: 207-893-7726, E-mail: sdavis@sjcme.edu; *Head, Ref, Info Literacy,* Lynn Bivens; Tel: 207-893-7724, E-mail: lbivens@sjcme.edu; Staff 5.8 (MLS 3, Non-MLS 2.8)
Founded 1912. Highest Degree: Master
Automation Activity & Vendor Info: (Cataloging) OCLC; (Circulation) Innovative Interfaces, Inc - Millennium; (OPAC) Innovative Interfaces, Inc; (Serials) Innovative Interfaces, Inc - Millennium
Wireless access
Mem of Maine State Library, Region 1

STEEP FALLS

P STEEP FALLS PUBLIC LIBRARY*, 1128 Pequawket Trail, 04085. (Mail add: PO Box 140, 04085-0140), SAN 306-7572. Tel: 207-675-3132. E-mail: info@steepfallslibrary.org. Web Site: steepfallslib.mainememory.net/page/2601/display.html. *Dir,* Paula Paul; E-mail: paula.paul.usc@gmail.com; Staff 1 (Non-MLS 1)
Founded 1916. Pop 7,500; Circ 23,208
Library Holdings: Bk Vols 24,000; Per Subs 2
Special Collections: Hobson Coll; Pierce & Maine Colls
Subject Interests: Hist
Automation Activity & Vendor Info: (Cataloging) LibraryWorld, Inc
Wireless access
Mem of Maine State Library, Region 1
Open Mon-Wed 10-7, Sat 9-1
Friends of the Library Group

STETSON

P STETSON PUBLIC LIBRARY*, 70 Village Rd, 04488. (Mail add: PO Box 154, 04488-0154), SAN 376-3498. Tel: 207-296-2020. E-mail: volunteer@stetson.lib.me.us. Web Site: www.stetson.lib.me.us. *Librn,* Laura Ward; Staff 1 (Non-MLS 1)
Founded 1980

Library Holdings: Audiobooks 8; Bks on Deafness & Sign Lang 6; Large Print Bks 70; Music Scores 4; Bk Titles 7,300; Per Subs 8
Subject Interests: Maine, New England
Automation Activity & Vendor Info: (Cataloging) LibraryWorld, Inc; (Circulation) LibraryWorld, Inc
Wireless access
Function: 24/7 Electronic res, 24/7 Online cat, After school storytime, Children's prog, Computer training, Computers for patron use, Doc delivery serv, Holiday prog, ILL available, Internet access, Life-long learning prog for all ages, Magazines, Mail & tel request accepted, Museum passes, Music CDs, Online cat, Photocopying/Printing, Preschool reading prog, Prog for adults, Prog for children & young adult, Ref & res, Ref serv available, Res assist avail, Scanner, Story hour, Summer reading prog, Wheelchair accessible
Special Services for the Blind - Bks on CD; Large print bks
Open Tues & Sat 9-11, Wed 3-5, Thurs 5-7
Restriction: Free to mem
Friends of the Library Group

STEUBEN

P HENRY D MOORE PARRISH HOUSE & LIBRARY, 22 Village Rd, 04680. (Mail add: PO Box 127, 04680-0127), SAN 325-2183. Tel: 207-546-7301. E-mail: hdmoorelibrary@gmail.com. Web Site: www.moorelibrary.org. *Dir,* Jeanne Benedict; Staff 1 (Non-MLS 1)
Pop 1,084; Circ 7,500
Library Holdings: Bk Vols 13,000
Wireless access
Open Mon 4-7, Tues-Thurs 10-4, Sat 10-12

STOCKTON SPRINGS

P STOCKTON SPRINGS COMMUNITY LIBRARY*, Six Station St, 04981. (Mail add: PO Box 293, 04981-0293). Tel: 207-567-4147. FAX: 207-567-4147. E-mail: stocktonstaff@stocktonsprings.lib.me.us. Web Site: stocktonspringslibrary.org. *Dir,* Patricia Curley
Founded 2001
Library Holdings: Bk Vols 7,000; Per Subs 10
Automation Activity & Vendor Info: (Cataloging) Follett Software; (Circulation) Follett Software
Wireless access
Open Mon & Wed 3-5, Tues 4-7, Thurs 9-12 & 6:30-8:30, Sat 9-3

STONINGTON

P STONINGTON PUBLIC LIBRARY, 64 Main St, 04681. (Mail add: PO Box 441, 04681-0441). Tel: 207-367-5926. E-mail: stonington.public.library@gmail.com. Web Site: www.stoningtonlibrary.org. *Libr Dir,* Christopher Ross
Founded 1955. Pop 1,500
Library Holdings: Bk Vols 10,000; Talking Bks 50; Videos 100
Special Collections: Art Coll; Local & State Authors (Maine Coll); Ocean & Sea Related Fiction & Non-Fiction (Sea Coll)
Wireless access
Open Tues & Fri 10-4, Thurs 12-6, Sat 10-12
Friends of the Library Group

STRATTON

P STRATTON PUBLIC LIBRARY, 88 Main St, 04982. (Mail add: PO Box 350, 04982-0350), SAN 372-6711. Tel: 207-246-4401. FAX: 207-246-3267. E-mail: strattonpubliclibrary@gmail.com. Web Site: www.stratton.lib.me.us. *Librn,* Wendy Boyle; Staff 1 (Non-MLS 1)
Founded 1921. Pop 777; Circ 1,723
Jan 2020-Dec 2020 Income $45,617, City $37,500, Locally Generated Income $7,698, Other $419. Mats Exp $3,856, Books $3,621, Per/Ser (Incl. Access Fees) $235. Sal $38,703 (Prof $25,819)
Library Holdings: Audiobooks 440; Braille Volumes 1; DVDs 924; Large Print Bks 203; Bk Vols 6,516; Per Subs 13
Wireless access
Partic in Maine School & Library Network
Open Mon, Wed & Fri 10-5, Tues & Thurs 1-5, Sat 9-1

STRONG

P STRONG PUBLIC LIBRARY*, 14 S Main St, 04983. (Mail add: PO Box 629, 04983-0629), SAN 376-7825. Tel: 207-684-4003. E-mail: stronglibrary@strong.lib.me.us. Web Site: www.strong.lib.me.us. *Libr Dir,* Erika Ouellette; Staff 1 (Non-MLS 1)
Pop 1,200
Library Holdings: AV Mats 88; Bk Titles 7,000; Bk Vols 7,300
Open Tues 1-7, Thurs 1-5, Sat 10-2
Friends of the Library Group

SULLIVAN

P FRENCHMAN'S BAY LIBRARY*, 1776 US Hwy, No 1, 04664. (Mail add: PO Box 215, 04664-0215). Tel: 207-422-2307. E-mail: fbaylibrary2017@gmail.com. Web Site: fredurban.wix.com/fb-library-web-site. *Libr Adminr,* Cynthia Stanley; *Librn,* Christina McGowan
Founded 1952. Pop 100; Fac 2
Library Holdings: Audiobooks 164; DVDs 478; Large Print Bks 74; Bk Vols 6,721; Per Subs 1; Videos 209
Wireless access
Function: 24/7 Electronic res, 24/7 Online cat, Activity rm, After school storytime
Open Mon 5-8, Tues & Thurs 1-5, Sat 10-2
Friends of the Library Group

SWANS ISLAND

P SWANS ISLAND EDUCATIONAL SOCIETY*, Swans Island Public Library, 451 Atlantic Rd, 04685. (Mail add: PO Box 12, 04685-0012). Tel: 207-526-4330. Web Site: swansislandeducationalsociety.org/library/library-home. *Dir,* Jeanne Hoyle; E-mail: siesdirector@gmail.com; Staff 1 (Non-MLS 1)
Founded 1965. Pop 350; Circ 3,433
Library Holdings: AV Mats 50; CDs 25; DVDs 300; Large Print Bks 100; Music Scores 7; Bk Vols 10,000; Per Subs 11; Talking Bks 300; Videos 500
Special Collections: Maine Coll
Wireless access
Function: Archival coll, Art exhibits, Bks on cassette, Bks on CD, Children's prog, Computers for patron use, Distance learning, E-Reserves, Free DVD rentals, Genealogy discussion group, ILL available, Online cat, Photocopying/Printing, Preschool outreach, Scanner, Story hour, Summer reading prog, Tax forms, VHS videos
Open Tues 1-6, Wed, Fri & Sun 1-4, Thurs 10-6

TENANTS HARBOR

P JACKSON MEMORIAL LIBRARY*, 71 Main St, 04860. (Mail add: PO Box 231, 04860-0231), SAN 306-7416. Tel: 207-372-8961. E-mail: administrator@jacksonmemoriallibrary.org. Web Site: www.jacksonmem.lib.me.us. *Co-Dir,* Beckie Delaney; *Co-Dir,* Sharon Moskowitz; Staff 2 (MLS 2)
Founded 1935
Library Holdings: DVDs 100; Large Print Bks 1,000; Bk Vols 15,000; Per Subs 50; Talking Bks 600; Videos 200
Wireless access
Function: 24/7 Online cat, Activity rm, Art exhibits, Audiobks via web, Bk club(s), Children's prog, Computers for patron use, Doc delivery serv, E-Readers, Electronic databases & coll, ILL available, Internet access, Magazines, Mail & tel request accepted, Meeting rooms, Museum passes, Online cat, Photocopying/Printing, Preschool outreach, Printer for laptops & handheld devices, Prog for adults, Prog for children & young adult, Story hour, Wheelchair accessible
Open Tues-Thurs 10-6, Fri 12-5, Sat 9-2
Friends of the Library Group

THOMASTON

P THOMASTON PUBLIC LIBRARY, 60 Main St, 04861. SAN 306-7599. Tel: 207-354-2453. E-mail: library@thomastonmaine.gov. Web Site: www.thomaston.lib.me.us. *Head Librn,* Caroline Ward-Nesbit; E-mail: cwardnesbit@thomastonmaine.gov
Founded 1898. Pop 7,901; Circ 89,382
Library Holdings: Bks-By-Mail 500; CDs 400; DVDs 500; Large Print Bks 400; Music Scores 150; Bk Vols 34,000; Per Subs 20; Talking Bks 500; Videos 924
Special Collections: Municipal Document Depository; Oral History; State Document Depository
Subject Interests: Maine
Automation Activity & Vendor Info: (Acquisitions) Surpass; (Cataloging) Surpass; (Circulation) Surpass; (Course Reserve) Surpass; (ILL) Surpass
Wireless access
Partic in Maine School & Library Network
Special Services for the Blind - Talking bks
Open Mon & Fri 11-7, Tues, Wed & Thurs 11-5, Sat 9-1
Friends of the Library Group
Bookmobiles: 1

TOPSHAM

P TOPSHAM PUBLIC LIBRARY, 25 Foreside Rd, 04086. SAN 306-7602. Tel: 207-725-1727. Web Site: www.topshamlibrary.org. *Dir,* Susan M Preece; E-mail: director@topshamlibrary.org; Staff 5 (MLS 1, Non-MLS 4)
Founded 1931. Pop 10,000; Circ 58,000
Library Holdings: Bk Vols 42,000; Per Subs 60

Automation Activity & Vendor Info: (Cataloging) Innovative Interfaces, Inc; (Circulation) Innovative Interfaces, Inc; (OPAC) Innovative Interfaces, Inc
Wireless access
Function: ILL available
Open Mon & Fri 9-5, Tues-Thurs 9-8, Sat 9-4
Friends of the Library Group

TURNER

P TURNER PUBLIC LIBRARY*, 98 Matthews Way, 04282-3930. SAN 306-7610. Tel: 207-225-2030. E-mail: info@turnerpubliclibrary.org. Web Site: www.turnerpubliclibrary.org. *Libr Dir,* Kelli Burnham; *Libr Asst,* Ellen Bradley; Staff 3 (Non-MLS 3)
Library Holdings: Bk Vols 12,000
Wireless access
Open Tues & Thurs Noon-7, Fri 2-6, Sat 9:30-Noon
Friends of the Library Group

UNION

P VOSE LIBRARY*, 392 Common Rd, 04862-4249. (Mail add: PO Box 550, 04862-0550), SAN 306-7629. Tel: 207-785-4733. E-mail: librarian@voselibrary.org. Web Site: www.voselibrary.org. *Dir,* Sue McClintock; Staff 1 (Non-MLS 1)
Founded 1932. Pop 2,400; Circ 9,000
Library Holdings: AV Mats 15; Bk Vols 15,000; Per Subs 40; Talking Bks 750; Videos 150
Automation Activity & Vendor Info: (Cataloging) ComPanion Corp
Wireless access
Function: ILL available, Photocopying/Printing
Open Tues 10-8, Wed & Fri 10-6, Sat 9-12
Friends of the Library Group

UNITY

C UNITY COLLEGE*, Dorothy Webb Quimby Library, 90 Quaker Hill Rd, 04988. (Mail add: PO Box 167, 04988-0167), SAN 306-7637. Tel: 207-509-7110. Reference Tel: 207-509-7234. FAX: 207-512-1218. E-mail: library@unity.edu. Web Site: library.unity.edu. *Dir,* Kate Russell; E-mail: krussell@unity.edu; *Coll Develop Librn, Ref Librn,* Sandra Abbott-Stoud; E-mail: sstout@unity.edu; Staff 4 (MLS 1, Non-MLS 3)
Founded 1966. Enrl 650; Highest Degree: Bachelor
Library Holdings: AV Mats 1,760; Bk Titles 49,600; Bk Vols 61,000; Per Subs 325
Subject Interests: Environ sci, Natural hist, Wildlife
Automation Activity & Vendor Info: (Cataloging) Innovative Interfaces, Inc - Sierra; (Circulation) Innovative Interfaces, Inc; (ILL) OCLC; (OPAC) Innovative Interfaces, Inc
Wireless access
Partic in LYRASIS
Open Mon-Thurs 7:45am-10pm, Fri 7:45-5, Sat 10-5, Sun 10-10 (Winter); Mon 9-7, Tues-Thurs 9-4 (Summer)

VAN BUREN

P ABEL J MORNEAULT MEMORIAL LIBRARY*, 153 Main St, 04785. SAN 306-7645. Tel: 207-868-5076. Web Site: www.morneault.lib.me.us. *Dir,* Justin Martin; E-mail: jrm@morneault.lib.me.us
Founded 1974. Pop 3,000; Circ 13,500
Library Holdings: Bks on Deafness & Sign Lang 10; CDs 300; DVDs 250; Large Print Bks 350; Bk Titles 20,000; Per Subs 40; Talking Bks 200; Videos 600
Special Collections: Oral History
Subject Interests: Genealogy
Automation Activity & Vendor Info: (Acquisitions) Follett Software; (Cataloging) Follett Software; (Circulation) Follett Software; (ILL) Follett Software
Wireless access
Open Tues-Thurs 10-6, Fri 10-5, Sat 11-2
Friends of the Library Group

VINALHAVEN

P VINALHAVEN PUBLIC LIBRARY*, Six Carver St, 04863. (Mail add: PO Box 384, 04863-0384), SAN 306-7653. Tel: 207-863-4401. E-mail: vpl@vhaven.lib.me.us. Web Site: www.vinalhavenpubliclibrary.org. *Librn,* Scott Candage; *Asst Librn,* Linda Whittington; Staff 2 (Non-MLS 2)
Founded 1887. Pop 1,225; Circ 19,902
Library Holdings: Bks on Deafness & Sign Lang 10; Large Print Bks 278; Bk Vols 18,759; Per Subs 22; Talking Bks 510
Automation Activity & Vendor Info: (Cataloging) Follett Software; (Circulation) Follett Software
Wireless access
Function: Prog for children & young adult
Special Services for the Blind - Audio mat; Home delivery serv; Large print bks
Open Tues & Thurs 1-5, Wed & Fri 9-12 & 1-5, Sat 9-4
Friends of the Library Group

WALDOBORO

P WALDOBORO PUBLIC LIBRARY*, 958 Main St, 04572. (Mail add: PO Box 768, 04572), SAN 306-7661. Tel: 207-832-4484. FAX: 207-832-4484. E-mail: info@waldoboro.lib.me.us. Web Site: www.waldoborolibrary.org. *Dir,* Cathrina Skov
Founded 1916. Pop 5,000; Circ 22,642
Library Holdings: AV Mats 2,000; Bk Vols 15,000; Per Subs 20
Automation Activity & Vendor Info: (Cataloging) LibraryWorld, Inc; (Circulation) LibraryWorld, Inc
Wireless access
Function: ILL available
Publications: Newsletter (Quarterly)
Special Services for the Blind - Large print & cassettes
Open Mon & Thurs Noon-7, Wed & Fri 10-5, Sat 9-1
Friends of the Library Group

WALPOLE

C UNIVERSITY OF MAINE*, Darling Marine Center Louise Dean Library, 193 Clarks Cove Rd, 04573. SAN 306-767X. Tel: 207-563-8193. Web Site: dmc.umaine.edu/facilities/library. *Libr Asst II,* Randy Lackovic; E-mail: randy.lackovic@maine.edu; Staff 1 (Non-MLS 1)
Founded 1966. Fac 12; Highest Degree: Doctorate
Library Holdings: Bk Titles 10,000; Per Subs 300
Special Collections: Darling Marine Center History Coll; Reprint Coll; Sea Grant Coll
Subject Interests: Aquaculture, Marine biol, Marine geol, Marine zool, Oceanography
Wireless access
Partic in Maine InfoNet
Open Mon 9-4

WARREN

MAINE DEPARTMENT OF CORRECTIONS
S BOLDUC CORRECTIONAL FACILITY LIBRARY*, 516 Cushing Rd, 04864. Tel: 207-273-2036. FAX: 207-273-5124. *Actg Librn,* Brent Elwell
Library Holdings: Bk Vols 2,500; Per Subs 20
Open Mon, Tues & Fri 11:15-12:15 & 2-3, Wed & Thurs 11:15-12:15, 2-3 & 7-8, Sat & Sun 5:15-6:15

S MAINE STATE PRISON LIBRARY*, 807 Cushing Rd, 04864, SAN 306-7688. Tel: 207-273-5300. *Librn,* Jackie Weddle
Library Holdings: Bk Vols 7,000; Per Subs 20
Special Collections: State & Federal Criminal Law
Subject Interests: Art hist, Natural hist, Vocational info
Open Mon-Fri 8-11 & 1-4

P WARREN FREE PUBLIC LIBRARY*, 282 Main St, 04864. (Mail add: 167 Western Rd, 04864), SAN 306-7696. Tel: 207-273-2900. E-mail: warrenlibrary@warrenfreepubliclibrary.org. Web Site: www.warrenfreepubliclibrary.org. *Dir,* Cindy Norwood; *Librn,* Jane Waltz; *Asst Librn,* Sara Davis; Staff 1 (Non-MLS 1)
Founded 1927. Pop 4,694; Circ 11,981
Library Holdings: DVDs 502; Large Print Bks 245; Bk Vols 15,335; Per Subs 6; Talking Bks 100
Automation Activity & Vendor Info: (Cataloging) LibraryWorld, Inc; (Circulation) LibraryWorld, Inc
Wireless access
Open Mon, Tues & Thurs 4-8, Wed 12-6, Fri 10-6, Sat 9-3
Friends of the Library Group

WASHBURN

P WASHBURN MEMORIAL LIBRARY, 1290 Main St, 04786. SAN 306-770X. Tel: 207-455-4814. E-mail: wlm.me.1290@gmail.com. Web Site: washburnlibrary.com. *Libr Dir,* Tim Whiton; Staff 2 (Non-MLS 2)
Pop 2,240; Circ 17,643
Library Holdings: Audiobooks 713; DVDs 395; Bk Titles 22,480; Per Subs 20; Talking Bks 800; Videos 529
Special Collections: Aroostook County Coll. Oral History
Wireless access
Function: 24/7 Online cat, Activity rm, Bks on CD, Children's prog, Computer training, Free DVD rentals, ILL available, Magazines, Meeting rooms, Online cat, OverDrive digital audio bks, Senior computer classes, Summer reading prog, VHS videos, Wheelchair accessible
Open Tues 1-7, Wed-Fri 10-4:30, Sat 9-Noon

WASHINGTON

P GIBBS LIBRARY*, 40 Old Union Rd, 04574. (Mail add: PO Box 348, 04574-0348), SAN 376-348X. Tel: 207-845-2663. E-mail: info@gibbslibrary.org. Web Site: www.gibbslibrary.org. *Librn,* Julie Madden; *Libr Mgr,* Kate Nichols
Founded 1993. Pop 1,500; Circ 1,200
Library Holdings: Bk Titles 10,000
Special Collections: College Level Great Courses, CDs, DVDs; Stephen & Tabitha King Language Arts Audios
Automation Activity & Vendor Info: (Acquisitions) Follett Software; (Cataloging) Follett Software; (Circulation) Follett Software
Wireless access
Function: Senior computer classes
Partic in Maine School & Library Network
Open Mon 4-7, Tues 9-12 & 4-7, Wed & Thurs 3-6, Sat 9-3
Friends of the Library Group

WATERFORD

P WATERFORD LIBRARY ASSOCIATION*, 663 Waterford Rd, 04088. (Mail add: PO Box 176, 04088-0176). Tel: 207-583-2050. E-mail: wla@waterford.lib.me.us. Web Site: www.waterfordmainelibrary.org. *Librn,* Nancy Eaton; Staff 1 (Non-MLS 1)
Founded 1911. Pop 1,500
Library Holdings: Audiobooks 60; DVDs 790; Large Print Bks 30; Bk Vols 5,000; Talking Bks 100
Subject Interests: Fiction, Gardening, Maine, Non-fiction
Wireless access
Function: 24/7 Online cat, Activity rm, Adult bk club, Archival coll, Bk club(s), Bks on CD, Computers for patron use, Free DVD rentals, Homebound delivery serv, Internet access, Photocopying/Printing, Printer for laptops & handheld devices, Prog for adults, Res assist avail, Senior outreach, Wheelchair accessible
Open Wed 4-6, Sat 10-2
Friends of the Library Group

WATERVILLE

C COLBY COLLEGE LIBRARIES*, Miller Library, 5100 Mayflower Hill, 04901. SAN 343-7191. Tel: 207-859-5100. Interlibrary Loan Service Tel: 207-859-5125. Administration Tel: 207-859-5108. FAX: 207-859-5105. E-mail: libraries@colby.edu. Web Site: www.colby.edu/libraries, www.colby.edu/miller. *Dir of Libr,* Lareese M Hall; Tel: 207-859-5117, E-mail: lareese.hall@colby.edu; *Head, Coll,* Ana Noriega; Tel: 207-859-5142, E-mail: ana.noriega@colby.edu; *Head, Digital Initiatives,* Darylyne Provost; Tel: 207-859-5117, E-mail: darylyne.provost@colby.edu; *Head, Spec Coll,* Patricia Burdick; Tel: 207-859-5151, E-mail: patricia.burdick@colby.edu; *Digital Coll Librn,* Martin Kelly; Tel: 207-859-5162, E-mail: martin.kelly@colby.edu; *Humanities Librn,* Karen Gillum; Tel: 207-859-5123, E-mail: karen.gillum@colby.edu; *Humanities & Soc Sci Librn,* Marilyn R Pukkila; Tel: 207-859-5145, E-mail: marilyn.pukkila@colby.edu; *Electronic Res Mgr,* Michael C McGuire; Tel: 207-859-5161, E-mail: mike.mcguire@colby.edu; Staff 27 (MLS 12, Non-MLS 15)
Founded 1813. Enrl 1,850; Fac 175; Highest Degree: Bachelor
Jul 2012-Jun 2013 Income (Main & Associated Libraries) $4,708,494. Mats Exp $2,646,643, Books $400,000, Per/Ser (Incl. Access Fees) $1,125,000, Electronic Ref Mat (Incl. Access Fees) $475,000, Presv $16,000. Sal $1,354,845 (Prof $892,290)
Library Holdings: Audiobooks 1,264; DVDs 9,319; e-books 503,925; e-journals 86,472; Music Scores 9,848; Bk Titles 469,252; Per Subs 400; Videos 4,000
Special Collections: A E Housman Coll; Colby Archives; Contemporary Letters (Bern Porter Coll); Henry James Coll; Maine Authors (Jacob Abbot, Sarah Orne Jewett, Edna St Vincent Millay, Kenneth Roberts, Ben Ames Williams, Edwin Arlington Robinson); Modern Irish Literature (Lord Dunsany, Lady Gregory, Seamus Heaney, James Joyce, Cuala Press, J M Synge, William Trevor, W B Yeats); Thomas Hardy Coll; Thomas Mann Coll; Violet Paget Coll (Vernon Lee). US Document Depository
Automation Activity & Vendor Info: (Acquisitions) Innovative Interfaces, Inc - Millennium; (Cataloging) Innovative Interfaces, Inc - Millennium; (Circulation) Innovative Interfaces, Inc - Millennium; (Course Reserve) Innovative Interfaces, Inc - Millennium; (ILL) OCLC ILLiad; (Media Booking) Innovative Interfaces, Inc - Millennium; (OPAC) Innovative Interfaces, Inc - Millennium; (Serials) Innovative Interfaces, Inc - Millennium
Wireless access
Function: Archival coll, ILL available, Internet access, Photocopying/Printing, Ref serv available
Partic in Amigos Library Services, Inc
Open Mon-Fri 8am-1am, Fri & Sat 10am-1am
Restriction: Open to pub for ref & circ; with some limitations, Open to students, fac & staff

Departmental Libraries:
BIXLER ART & MUSIC LIBRARY, 5660 Mayflower Hill, 04901. Tel: 207-859-5660. FAX: 207-859-5105. Web Site: www.colby.edu/bixler. *Art Librn, Librn,* Margaret D Ericson; Tel: 207-859-5662, E-mail: margaret.ericson@colby.edu; *Libr Coord,* Robin Duperry; Tel: 207-859-5661, E-mail: robin.duperry@colby.edu. Subject Specialists: *Arts, Music,* Robin Duperry; Staff 1 (MLS 1)
Library Holdings: AV Mats 12,000; Bk Vols 53,000; Per Subs 100
Open Mon-Thurs 8am-Midnight, Fri 8-8, Sat 10-8, Sun 10am-Midnight
OLIN SCIENCE LIBRARY, 5790 Mayflower Hill, 04901-4799. Tel: 207-859-5790. FAX: 207-859-5105. Web Site: www.colby.edu/olin. *Head, Res & Instruction, Sci Librn,* Kara Kugelmeyer; Tel: 207-859-5791, E-mail: kara.kugelmeyer@colby.edu; Staff 1 (MLS 1)
Library Holdings: CDs 460; Microforms 1,300; Bk Vols 41,000; Videos 604
Automation Activity & Vendor Info: (OPAC) Innovative Interfaces, Inc
Open Mon-Thurs (Winter) 8am-Midnight, Fri 8am-10pm, Sat 10-10, Sun 10am-Midnight; Mon-Fri (Summer) 9-4

M INLAND HOSPITAL*, Medical Library, 200 Kennedy Memorial Dr, 04901. SAN 378-0619. Tel: 207-861-3018. FAX: 207-861-3025.
Library Holdings: Bk Titles 250; Bk Vols 310; Per Subs 40
Subject Interests: Osteopathy
Partic in Health Sci Libr Info Consortium
Restriction: Open by appt only

M MAINE GENERAL MEDICAL CENTER*, Health Sciences Library, Thayer Center for Health, 149 North St, 04901-1000. SAN 320-1929. Tel: 207-626-1325. FAX: 207-872-1460. E-mail: library@mainegeneral.org. *Librn,* Janet Bolduc
Library Holdings: e-journals 1,000; Bk Titles 1,000; Bk Vols 3,000
Subject Interests: Allied health, Lit, Med
Automation Activity & Vendor Info: (Cataloging) Innovative Interfaces, Inc - Sierra; (Circulation) Innovative Interfaces, Inc - Sierra; (ILL) Innovative Interfaces, Inc - Sierra; (OPAC) Innovative Interfaces, Inc - Sierra; (Serials) Innovative Interfaces, Inc - Sierra
Open Mon-Fri 8-4:30

C THOMAS COLLEGE LIBRARY, 180 W River Rd, 04901. SAN 306-7718. Tel: 207-859-1204. Web Site: www.thomas.edu/library. *Assoc Dir, Libr Serv,* David Smith; Tel: 207-859-1235, E-mail: david.smith@thomas.edu; *Academic Support & Services Desk Mgr,* Jeff Ferguson; *Instrul Designer,* Marilyn Hudzina; Staff 3 (MLS 1, Non-MLS 2)
Founded 1894. Enrl 650; Fac 30; Highest Degree: Master
Library Holdings: Bk Vols 5,000
Subject Interests: Bus & mgt, Criminal justice, Educ, Liberal arts
Wireless access
Open Mon-Thurs 7:30am-11pm, Fri 7:30-5, Sat 12-5, Sun 10am-11pm

S WATERVILLE HISTORICAL SOCIETY LIBRARY*, 62 Silver St, Unit B, 04901. SAN 306-7726. Tel: 207-872-9439. E-mail: info@redingtonmuseum.org. Web Site: www.redingtonmuseum.org. *Pres,* James Violette, Jr; Tel: 207-872-6286, E-mail: jviolette@redingtonmuseum.org; *Librn,* Tina Serdjenian; E-mail: tserdjenian@redingtonmuseum.org; *Curator,* Bryan Finnemore
Founded 1903
Library Holdings: Bk Titles 2,500
Special Collections: Coll of Waterville Mail (Newspaper Printed 1846-1906
Subject Interests: Civil War, Local hist
Wireless access
Restriction: Open by appt only

P WATERVILLE PUBLIC LIBRARY*, 73 Elm St, 04901-6078. SAN 306-7734. Tel: 207-872-5433. FAX: 207-873-4779. E-mail: librarian@watervillelibrary.org. Web Site: www.watervillelibrary.org. *Dir,* Sarah Sugden; *Assoc Dir, Bus & Career Ctr Coordr,* Tammy Rabideau; E-mail: trabideau@watervillelibrary.org; *Head, Patron Serv,* Larry Dodge; E-mail: ldodge@watervillelibrary.org; *Ch Serv,* Kathleen Kenny; E-mail: kkenny@watervillelibrary.org; *Cat, Tech Serv,* Cathy Perkins
Founded 1896. Pop 15,605; Circ 98,765
Library Holdings: AV Mats 6,438; Large Print Bks 1,599; Bk Vols 92,000; Per Subs 76
Special Collections: Franco-Americans & Lebanese-Americans in Waterville; Waterville-Area Genealogy & Local History. Oral History
Automation Activity & Vendor Info: (Cataloging) Innovative Interfaces, Inc; (Circulation) Innovative Interfaces, Inc; (ILL) Innovative Interfaces, Inc; (OPAC) Innovative Interfaces, Inc
Wireless access
Open Mon-Fri 10-7, Sat 10-3

WAYNE

P CARY MEMORIAL LIBRARY*, 17 Old Winthrop Rd, 04284. (Mail add: PO Box 127, 04284-0127), SAN 306-7742. Tel: 207-685-3612. Web Site: www.cary-memorial.lib.me.us. *Librn*, Janet H Adelberg; E-mail: jadelbergCML@gmail.com; Staff 1 (Non-MLS 1)
Pop 1,100; Circ 14,500
Library Holdings: Bk Vols 12,280; Per Subs 40
Special Collections: Annie Louise Cary Memorabilia (Opera Star 1841-1921); Bookplates
Wireless access
Open Mon (Winter) 9-1 & 3-6, Tues & Thurs 3-6, Wed 2-7, Sat 9-3; Mon (Summer) 9-1 & 3-6, Tues & Thurs 3-8, Wed 1-8, Sat 9-3
Friends of the Library Group

WELD

P WELD FREE PUBLIC LIBRARY*, 25 Church St, 04285. (Mail add: PO Box 120, 04285-0120), SAN 306-7750. Tel: 207-585-2439. FAX: 207-585-2439. E-mail: weldlibrary@weld.lib.me.us. *Librn*, Wendy Ames
Founded 1905. Pop 400; Circ 4,848
Library Holdings: AV Mats 350; Large Print Bks 55; Bk Vols 10,000; Per Subs 15; Talking Bks 50
Open Tues & Thurs 2-7

WELLS

S DOROTHY FISH COASTAL RESOURCE LIBRARY AT WELLS RESERVE*, Wells Reserve Library, 342 Laudholm Farm Rd, 04090. Tel: 207-646-1555, Ext 133. Administration Tel: 207-646-1555, Ext 118. FAX: 207-646-2930. Web Site: www.wellsreserve.org/visit/facilities/library. *Educ Dir*, Suzanne Kahn Eder; Tel: 207-646-1555, Ext 116, E-mail: suzanne@wellsnerr.org
Founded 1986
Library Holdings: AV Mats 150; Bk Vols 3,500
Subject Interests: Ecology, Estuary studies, Mgt
Wireless access
Mem of Maine State Library, Region 1
Open Tues 10-1 or by appointment

P WELLS PUBLIC LIBRARY, 1434 Post Rd, 04090-4508. SAN 372-6320. Tel: 207-646-8181. FAX: 207-646-5636. E-mail: libstaff@wellstown.org. Web Site: www.wellslibrary.org. *Dir*, Cindy Appleby; Tel: 207-646-8181, Ext 206, E-mail: cappleby@wellstown.org; *Asst Dir, Head, Youth Serv*, Allison Herman; *Ad*, Stefanie Claydon; *Cataloger*, Nina Kostic; Staff 9 (MLS 3, Non-MLS 6)
Founded 1979. Pop 11,500; Circ 61,000
Library Holdings: e-books 15,000; Bk Titles 35,000; Bk Vols 44,000; Per Subs 91
Automation Activity & Vendor Info: (Cataloging) Innovative Interfaces, Inc; (Circulation) Innovative Interfaces, Inc; (OPAC) Innovative Interfaces, Inc
Wireless access
Mem of Maine State Library, Region 1
Open Mon, Wed & Fri 10-6, Tues & Thurs 1-8, Sat 10-1
Friends of the Library Group

J YORK COUNTY COMMUNITY COLLEGE LIBRARY*, 112 College Dr, 04090. Tel: 207-646-9282. E-mail: library@yccc.edu. Web Site: www.yccc.edu/support-services/public/library. *Assoc Dean, Acad*, Amber Tatnall; E-mail: yatatnall@yccc.edu; *Librn*, Annette Tanguay; E-mail: yatanguay@yccc.edu; Staff 2 (MLS 2)
Founded 1998
Library Holdings: Bk Vols 8,300
Automation Activity & Vendor Info: (Acquisitions) Innovative Interfaces, Inc; (Cataloging) Innovative Interfaces, Inc; (Circulation) Innovative Interfaces, Inc; (ILL) Innovative Interfaces, Inc; (OPAC) Innovative Interfaces, Inc; (Serials) Innovative Interfaces, Inc
Wireless access
Mem of Maine State Library, Region 1
Open Mon-Thurs 8-8, Fri 9-4

WEST BOOTHBAY HARBOR

G MAINE DEPARTMENT OF MARINE RESOURCES*, Bigelow Laboratory for Ocean Sciences Library, 180 McKown Point Rd, 04575. (Mail add: PO Box 475, 04575-0475), SAN 306-7777. Tel: 207-633-9551, 207-633-9600. FAX: 207-633-9579. E-mail: library@bigelow.org. Web Site: www.bigelow.org/science/library. *Librn*, Pamela Shephard
Founded 1957
Library Holdings: Bk Titles 3,500; Per Subs 252
Special Collections: Fishing gear; Foreign Countries Documents; State & Federal Government Publications
Subject Interests: Biochem, Botany, Environ studies, Marine biol, Oceanography, Zoology
Publications: Department of Marine Resources, Scientific & Technical Publications Index 1946-1983
Partic in OCLC Online Computer Library Center, Inc; Proquest Dialog
Open Mon-Fri 8:30-4:30

WEST NEWFIELD

P NEWFIELD VILLAGE LIBRARY & READING ROOM*, 637 Water St, 04095. SAN 376-3862. Tel: 207-809-7014. E-mail: newfieldlibrary@yahoo.com. Web Site: newfieldlibrary.weebly.com. *Librn*, Cheryl Cause; Staff 1 (Non-MLS 1)
Founded 1886. Circ 700
Library Holdings: Audiobooks 300; Bks on Deafness & Sign Lang 1; Braille Volumes 1; DVDs 500; Electronic Media & Resources 49; Bk Titles 5,244
Wireless access
Function: Bks on CD, Computers for patron use, Free DVD rentals, Internet access, Magazines, Magnifiers for reading, Photocopying/Printing, Printer for laptops & handheld devices, Scanner, VHS videos
Open Tues & Thurs 9-12 & 1-4:45, Wed 12-7

WEST PARIS

P WEST PARIS PUBLIC LIBRARY, Arthur L Mann Memorial Library, 226 Main St, 04289. (Mail add: PO Box 307, 04289-0307), SAN 321-0529. Tel: 207-674-2004. E-mail: librarian@westparislibrary.org. Web Site: www.westparislibrary.org. *Dir*, Brenda Lynn Gould
Pop 2,498
Library Holdings: Audiobooks 180; DVDs 1,700; Large Print Bks 470; Bk Vols 14,620
Wireless access
Open Mon & Fri 1:30-6, Wed 1:30-7, Sat 10-2
Friends of the Library Group

WESTBROOK

S SAPPI NORTH AMERICA, Technology Center Library, 300 Warren Ave, 04092. (Mail add: PO Box 5000, 04098-5000), SAN 306-7785. Tel: 207-856-3805. FAX: 207-856-3770. Web Site: sappi.com. *Info Spec*, Lynne Palmer; E-mail: lynne.palmer@sappi.com
Library Holdings: Bk Titles 3,000; Per Subs 40
Subject Interests: Chem, Engr, Papermaking, Physics, Printing
Wireless access
Mem of Maine State Library, Region 1
Restriction: Not open to pub

P WALKER MEMORIAL LIBRARY*, 800 Main St, 04092. SAN 306-7793. Tel: 207-854-0630. FAX: 207-854-0629. E-mail: walkerlibrary@westbrook.me.us. Web Site: www.westbrookmaine.com/681/Library. *Dir*, Rosemary Bebris; E-mail: rbebris@westbrook.me.us; *Youth Serv Librn*, Kara Reiman; E-mail: kreiman@westbrook.me.us; Staff 12 (MLS 4, Non-MLS 8)
Founded 1894. Pop 16,142; Circ 118,153
Library Holdings: AV Mats 3,647; Large Print Bks 2,701; Bk Vols 54,218; Per Subs 93
Special Collections: Large Print Coll; Local History Coll. Oral History
Automation Activity & Vendor Info: (Cataloging) Innovative Interfaces, Inc; (Circulation) Innovative Interfaces, Inc; (OPAC) Innovative Interfaces, Inc
Wireless access
Publications: Monthly Calendar; Monthy e-newsletter
Mem of Maine State Library, Region 1
Open Mon, Wed & Fri 9-5, Tues & Thurs 10-7, Sat 9-1
Friends of the Library Group

WHITNEYVILLE

P WHITNEYVILLE LIBRARY ASSOCIATION, INC*, Six Cross St, 04654. SAN 306-7815. Tel: 207-255-8077. E-mail: whitstaff@msln.net. Web Site: www.whitneyville.lib.me.us. *Chief Librn, Ch, ILL Librn*, Patricia Brightly; *Asst Cat Librn, Asst Librn*, Renee Brightly; Staff 1 (Non-MLS 1)
Founded 1966. Pop 900; Circ 13,165
Library Holdings: Bk Titles 17,530; Per Subs 4
Special Collections: All Newberry & Caldecott Medal Winners 1928-97; Children's Books (Lucy Stanton Bodger Coll); Memorial Children's Book Coll (1956-1963)
Subject Interests: Art & archit, Biology, Fiction, Hist, Lit, Music, Sports
Wireless access
Function: Children's prog
Open Mon-Sat 10-4
Friends of the Library Group

WILTON

P WILTON FREE PUBLIC LIBRARY, Six Goodspeed St, 04294. (Mail add: PO Box 454, 04294-0454), SAN 306-7823. Tel: 207-645-4831. FAX: 207-645-9417. Web Site: www.wilton-free.lib.me.us. *Dir,* Jennifer Scott; E-mail: director@wilton-free.lib.me.us; *Ch,* Cassandra Savage; *Adult Serv, ILL,* Lynne Hunter; E-mail: lynne@wilton-free.lib.me.us; Staff 4 (MLS 1, Non-MLS 3)
Founded 1901. Pop 4,242; Circ 35,000
Library Holdings: AV Mats 1,615; Bks-By-Mail 375; Bks on Deafness & Sign Lang 10; CDs 427; DVDs 345; Electronic Media & Resources 60; Large Print Bks 504; Bk Titles 20,596; Bk Vols 21,000; Per Subs 63; Talking Bks 644; Videos 318
Special Collections: Genealogy Coll
Automation Activity & Vendor Info: (Acquisitions) Main Library Systems; (Cataloging) Main Library Systems; (Circulation) Main Library Systems
Wireless access
Function: Homebound delivery serv, ILL available, Photocopying/Printing, Prog for children & young adult, Summer reading prog
Special Services for the Deaf - Bks on deafness & sign lang; Staff with knowledge of sign lang
Special Services for the Blind - Large print & cassettes
Open Tues & Fri 10-5, Wed Noon-7, Thurs 10-7, Sat 10-1
Friends of the Library Group

WINDHAM

S MAINE DEPARTMENT OF CORRECTIONS*, Maine Correctional Center Library, 17 Mallison Falls Rd, 04062. Tel: 207-893-7000. FAX: 207-893-7001. *Librn,* Position Currently Open
Library Holdings: Bk Vols 11,500; Per Subs 30; Talking Bks 25
Special Collections: Law Coll
Automation Activity & Vendor Info: (Cataloging) Follett Software; (Circulation) Follett Software; (ILL) OCLC
Restriction: Not open to pub

P WINDHAM PUBLIC LIBRARY, 217 Windham Center Rd, 04062. SAN 306-784X. Tel: 207-892-1908. FAX: 207-892-1915. Web Site: www.windham.lib.me.us. *Libr Dir,* Jennifer Alvino; E-mail: jaalvino@windhammaine.us; *Ad, Cataloger,* Sally Bannen; *Ch,* Samantha Cote; *Ref/Info Tech Serv Librn,* Ray Marcotte; Staff 13 (MLS 5, Non-MLS 8)
Founded 1971. Pop 18,500; Circ 94,500
Automation Activity & Vendor Info: (Cataloging) Innovative Interfaces, Inc - Sierra; (Circulation) Innovative Interfaces, Inc - Sierra; (OPAC) Innovative Interfaces, Inc - Sierra
Wireless access
Function: 24/7 Electronic res, 24/7 Online cat, Activity rm, Adult bk club, Art exhibits, Art programs, Audiobks on Playaways & MP3, Audiobks via web, Bks on CD, Butterfly Garden, Children's prog, Computer training, Electronic databases & coll, Free DVD rentals, Holiday prog, Home delivery & serv to seniorr ctr & nursing homes, Homebound delivery serv, ILL available, Internet access, Magazines, Movies, Museum passes, Music CDs, Online cat, Photocopying/Printing, Prog for adults, Prog for children & young adult, Ref serv available, Story hour, Summer reading prog, Tax forms, Teen prog, Wheelchair accessible
Mem of Maine State Library, Region 1
Partic in Maine InfoNet
Open Mon & Wed 10-7, Tues & Thurs 10-6, Fri & Sat 9-4
Friends of the Library Group

WINSLOW

P WINSLOW PUBLIC LIBRARY*, 136 Halifax St, 04901. SAN 372-6347. Tel: 207-872-1978. FAX: 207-872-1979. Web Site: www.winslow-me.gov/departments/library. *Libr Dir,* Pamela Fesq Bonney; E-mail: pbonney@winslow-me.gov; *Tech Librn, Youth Serv,* Samantha Cote; E-mail: scote@winsolow-me.gov; Staff 2 (MLS 1, Non-MLS 1)
Founded 1905. Pop 8,000; Circ 45,000
Library Holdings: Audiobooks 1,500; AV Mats 3,500; Bks on Deafness & Sign Lang 60; CDs 775; DVDs 930; Electronic Media & Resources 4; High Interest/Low Vocabulary Bk Vols 1,050; Large Print Bks 1,587; Bk Titles 43,379; Per Subs 67; Videos 2,360
Automation Activity & Vendor Info: (Acquisitions) Winnebago Software Co; (Cataloging) Winnebago Software Co; (Circulation) Winnebago Software Co; (OPAC) Winnebago Software Co
Wireless access
Partic in Maine State Libr Network
Special Services for the Deaf - Accessible learning ctr; Adult & family literacy prog; Bks on deafness & sign lang; High interest/low vocabulary bks
Special Services for the Blind - Home delivery serv; Large print & cassettes; Large print bks
Open Mon, Tues & Fri 9-7, Wed & Thurs 1-7, Sat (Sept-June) 9-1
Friends of the Library Group

WINTER HARBOR

P WINTER HARBOR PUBLIC LIBRARY*, 18 Chapel Lane, 04693. (Mail add: PO Box 326, 04693-0326), SAN 306-7866. Tel: 207-963-7556. E-mail: winterharbor@winterharbor.lib.me.us. Web Site: www.winterharbor.lib.me.us. *Libr Dir,* Ruth Mapleton; E-mail: 963whpl@gmail.com
Founded 1918. Pop 1,120; Circ 4,185
Library Holdings: Audiobooks 200; DVDs 75; Bk Titles 4,991; Bk Vols 6,000; Videos 200
Special Collections: Maine Room
Subject Interests: Local hist, Maine, Schoodic Peninsula
Wireless access
Partic in Maine State Libr Network
Open Wed & Sat 1-4, Fri 10-4

WINTERPORT

P WINTERPORT MEMORIAL LIBRARY*, 229 Main St, 04496. (Mail add: PO Box 650, 04496-0650), SAN 306-7874. Tel: 207-223-5540. FAX: 207-223-5540. Web Site: www.winterportlibrary.org. *Librn,* Mary Lester; E-mail: mlester@winterport.lib.me.us; Staff 1 (Non-MLS 1)
Pop 2,675; Circ 8,506
Library Holdings: Bk Titles 11,244; Bk Vols 12,000; Per Subs 40
Wireless access
Open Tues & Thurs 2-7, Wed 9-2, Fri 9-4, Sat (Sept-May) 9-Noon

WINTHROP

P CHARLES M BAILEY PUBLIC LIBRARY*, 39 Bowdoin St, 04364. SAN 306-7882. Tel: 207-377-8673. Web Site: www.baileylibrary.org. *Dir,* Richard Fortin; E-mail: director@baileylibrary.org; *Ad,* Shane Malcolm Billings; E-mail: smbillings@baileylibrary.org; *Ch,* Cindy Hinkley; E-mail: chinkley@baileylibrary.org; Staff 10 (MLS 5, Non-MLS 5)
Founded 1916. Pop 6,500; Circ 65,000
Jul 2019-Jun 2020 Income $320,000, City $305,000, Other $15,000. Mats Exp $33,000, Books $25,000, Per/Ser (Incl. Access Fees) $1,500, AV Mat $5,000, Electronic Ref Mat (Incl. Access Fees) $1,500. Sal $205,000 (Prof $173,000)
Library Holdings: Audiobooks 1,400; AV Mats 2,000; Bks on Deafness & Sign Lang 50; CDs 1,000; DVDs 2,000; e-books 1,000; Electronic Media & Resources 65; High Interest/Low Vocabulary Bk Vols 250; Large Print Bks 600; Bk Titles 26,575; Bk Vols 27,181; Per Subs 25; Talking Bks 1,400
Automation Activity & Vendor Info: (Acquisitions) Baker & Taylor; (Cataloging) Innovative Interfaces, Inc - Millennium; (Circulation) Innovative Interfaces, Inc - Millennium; (ILL) Innovative Interfaces, Inc - Millennium; (OPAC) Innovative Interfaces, Inc - Millennium; (Serials) Innovative Interfaces, Inc - Millennium
Wireless access
Function: 24/7 Electronic res, 24/7 Online cat, Accelerated reader prog, Activity rm, Adult bk club, Adult literacy prog, After school storytime, Audiobks via web, Bk club(s), Bk reviews (Group), Bks on cassette, Bks on CD, CD-ROM, Children's prog, Computers for patron use, Electronic databases & coll, Free DVD rentals, Holiday prog, ILL available, Internet access, Museum passes, Music CDs, Online cat, Online ref, Orientations, OverDrive digital audio bks, Photocopying/Printing, Prog for adults, Prog for children & young adult, Ref & res, Ref serv available, Story hour, Summer reading prog, Tax forms, Teen prog, Telephone ref, VHS videos, Wheelchair accessible
Partic in Central Maine Libr District; Maine InfoNet
Special Services for the Deaf - Adult & family literacy prog
Special Services for the Blind - Accessible computers
Open Mon-Wed 10-6, Thurs 3-8, Fri & Sat 10-3
Friends of the Library Group

WISCASSET

P WISCASSET PUBLIC LIBRARY*, 21 High St, 04578-4119. SAN 306-7904. Tel: 207-882-7161. FAX: 207-882-6698. E-mail: wpl@wiscasset.lib.me.us. Web Site: www.wiscasset.lib.me.us. *Dir,* Pamela Dunning; E-mail: pdunning@wiscasset.lib.me.us; *Ch,* Laurie Ridgway; E-mail: lridgway@wiscasset.lib.me.us; *Asst Librn,* David Cherry; *Asst Librn,* Karen Delano
Founded 1920. Pop 5,865. Sal $104,137
Library Holdings: AV Mats 1,648; CDs 270; DVDs 97; Large Print Bks 356; Bk Vols 30,777; Per Subs 77; Talking Bks 748; Videos 533
Special Collections: Art Coll; Local History Archives
Automation Activity & Vendor Info: (Cataloging) Innovative Interfaces, Inc - Sierra; (Circulation) Innovative Interfaces, Inc - Sierra; (OPAC) Innovative Interfaces, Inc - Sierra
Wireless access

Function: Archival coll, Art exhibits, Audiobks via web, Bks on cassette, Bks on CD, Children's prog, Computers for patron use, Distance learning, Electronic databases & coll, Home delivery & serv to seniorr ctr & nursing homes, ILL available, Museum passes, Music CDs, Notary serv, Online cat, OverDrive digital audio bks, Passport agency, Photocopying/Printing, Prog for adults, Summer reading prog, Tax forms
Open Tues, Thurs & Fri 10-5, Wed 10-7, Sat 10-2
Friends of the Library Group

YARMOUTH

P MERRILL MEMORIAL LIBRARY, 215 Main St, 04096. SAN 306-7939. Tel: 207-846-4763. FAX: 207-846-2422. E-mail: mmlinfo@yarmouthlibrary.org. Web Site: yarmouthlibrary.org. *Dir,* Heidi Grimm; *Asst Dir, Circ Librn,* Judy Clark; *Syst/Tech Serv,* Andi Jackson-Darling; Staff 1 (Non-MLS 1)
Founded 1904. Pop 7,400; Circ 68,541
Library Holdings: Bk Vols 44,000; Per Subs 96
Subject Interests: Genealogy, Hist
Automation Activity & Vendor Info: (Cataloging) Koha; (Circulation) Koha; (OPAC) Koha
Wireless access
Publications: Monthly Newsletter
Mem of Maine State Library, Region 1
Partic in OCLC Online Computer Library Center, Inc
Open Mon, Thurs & Fri 11-5, Tues & Wed 11-6, Sat (Sept-June) 10-1
Friends of the Library Group

YORK

P YORK PUBLIC LIBRARY*, 15 Long Sands Rd, 03909. SAN 306-7955. Tel: 207-363-2818. FAX: 207-363-7250. E-mail: ypl@york.lib.me.us. Web Site: www.york.lib.me.us. *Dir,* Michelle Sampson; E-mail: msampson@york.lib.me.us; *Asst Dir,* Kim Myers; *Ch,* Kathleen Whalin; *Circ,* Position Currently Open; Staff 8 (MLS 4, Non-MLS 4)
Founded 1912. Pop 15,000
Library Holdings: AV Mats 1,699; Large Print Bks 1,500; Bk Titles 39,000; Bk Vols 40,017; Per Subs 50; Talking Bks 599
Automation Activity & Vendor Info: (Cataloging) Innovative Interfaces, Inc; (Circulation) Innovative Interfaces, Inc; (ILL) Innovative Interfaces, Inc; (OPAC) Innovative Interfaces, Inc; (Serials) Innovative Interfaces, Inc
Wireless access
Function: 24/7 Electronic res, 24/7 Online cat, Activity rm, Adult bk club, Art exhibits, Art programs, Audio & video playback equip for onsite use, Audiobks on Playaways & MP3, Audiobks via web, AV serv, Bks on CD, Computers for patron use, Electronic databases & coll, For res purposes, Free DVD rentals, Holiday prog, Home delivery & serv to seniorr ctr & nursing homes, Homebound delivery serv, ILL available, Internet access, Magazines, Magnifiers for reading, Mail & tel request accepted, Meeting rooms, Movies, Museum passes, Online cat, Online ref, Outreach serv, Outside serv via phone, mail, e-mail & web, Photocopying/Printing, Preschool reading prog, Prog for adults, Prog for children & young adult, Ref & res, Ref serv available, Res assist avail, STEM programs, Story hour, Study rm, Summer & winter reading prog, Summer reading prog, Tax forms, Teen prog, Telephone ref, Wheelchair accessible, Winter reading prog, Workshops, Writing prog
Mem of Maine State Library, Region 1
Partic in Maine InfoNet
Special Services for the Blind - Bks on CD; Home delivery serv; Large print bks; Low vision equip; Magnifiers
Open Tues-Thurs 10-7, Fri 10-5, Sat 10-2
Restriction: Non-resident fee
Friends of the Library Group

MARYLAND

Date of Statistics: FY 2017
Population, 2020 U.S. Census: 6,055,802
Population Served: 3,720,843
Total Volumes in Public Libraries: 18,425,879
Volumes Per Capita: 3.11
Book Holdings: 16,49,368
Total Public Library Circulation: 56,980,368
Circulation Per Capita: 9.53
Digital Resources:
Total e-books: 1,741,796
Total terminals available: 5,191
Total users per year: 5,604,327
Total annual wireless sessions: 15,122,526
Total databases: 1,053
Income and Expenditures:
Public library per capita funding statewide: $50.34
Capital revenue: $80,123,617
Capital expenditure: $47,149,459
Number of Bookmobiles: 19
Information derived from public sources.

ABERDEEN PROVING GROUND

UNITED STATES ARMY

A ABERDEEN AREA GARRISON LIBRARY*, Bldg 3326, 21005-5001, SAN 370-0992. Tel: 410-278-3417. FAX: 410-278-5684. *Librn,* Mike Lacomb
Library Holdings: Bk Titles 30,000; Per Subs 70
Subject Interests: Mil hist, World War II
Automation Activity & Vendor Info: (Cataloging) SirsiDynix; (Circulation) SirsiDynix
Function: ILL available, Ref serv available
Open Mon-Fri 11-6, Sat 9-2

A ORDNANCE CENTER & ORDNANCE MUSEUM LIBRARY*, 2221 Adams Bldg 5020, Fort Lee, 23801, SAN 343-7345. Tel: 804-734-4878. FAX: 410-278-7473. E-mail: usarmy.lee.tradoc.mbx.ordnance-museum@mail.mil. Web Site: www.ordmusfound.org.
Founded 1973
Library Holdings: Bk Vols 1,460
Special Collections: US Army Technical Manuals Coll
Subject Interests: Mat culture
Restriction: Not a lending libr

A PUBLIC HEALTH COMMAND LIBRARY*, 5158 Blackhawk Rd, BLDG E-5158, 21010-5403, SAN 343-7434. Tel: 410-436-4236. FAX: 410-436-4602. *Libr Tech,* Claudia A Coleman; *Libr Tech,* Letitia M Matthews
Founded 1945
Library Holdings: Bk Titles 13,000; Bk Vols 21,000; Per Subs 200
Subject Interests: Chem, Engr, Med, Occupational safety, Physics, Pub health, Toxicology
Partic in OCLC Online Computer Library Center, Inc; Proquest Dialog; US National Library of Medicine
Publications: Journal Holdings List
Restriction: Access for corporate affiliates

AM UNITED STATES ARMY MEDICAL RESEARCH INSTITUTE OF CHEMICAL DEFENSE*, Wood Technical Library, 8350 Ricketts Point Rd, 21010. SAN 343-7396. Tel: 410-436-4135. FAX: 410-436-3176. *Libr Dir,* Elisia George; E-mail: elisia.a.george.civ@mail.mil; Staff 2 (MLS 1, Non-MLS 1)
Founded 1979
Library Holdings: e-journals 25; Bk Vols 5,258; Per Subs 76
Subject Interests: Pharmacology, Toxicology
Automation Activity & Vendor Info: (Cataloging) Ex Libris Group; (Circulation) Ex Libris Group; (OPAC) Ex Libris Group; (Serials) TDNet
Function: ILL available, Res libr
Partic in National Network of Libraries of Medicine Region 1; OCLC Online Computer Library Center, Inc
Open Mon-Fri 7:30-4
Restriction: Restricted access

ACCOKEEK

S ACCOKEEK FOUNDATION LIBRARY*, 3400 Bryan Point Rd, 20607. SAN 371-2826. Tel: 301-283-2113. E-mail: info@accokeek.org. Web Site: www.accokeek.org. *Educ Mgr,* Ashley Thompson
Library Holdings: Bk Vols 2,600; Per Subs 20
Restriction: Authorized personnel only

ADELPHI

S UNITED STATES ARMY RESEARCH LABORATORY*, Technical Library, 2800 Powder Mill Rd, 20783-1197. SAN 306-7963. Tel: 301-394-2536. FAX: 301-394-1465. E-mail: libraryALC@arl.army.mil. *Tech Serv,* Louise McGovern; Staff 5 (MLS 1, Non-MLS 4)
Library Holdings: Bk Vols 36,000; Per Subs 800
Special Collections: DOD Publications
Subject Interests: Chem, Econ, Electrical engr, Electronics, Mechanical engr
Automation Activity & Vendor Info: (Acquisitions) SirsiDynix; (Cataloging) SirsiDynix; (Circulation) SirsiDynix; (OPAC) SirsiDynix; (Serials) SirsiDynix
Partic in OCLC Online Computer Library Center, Inc; Proquest Dialog; SDC Info Servs
Special Services for the Deaf - Staff with knowledge of sign lang
Open Mon-Fri 9-4

ANNAPOLIS

GL ANNE ARUNDEL COUNTY CIRCUIT COURT, Anne Arundel County Public Law Library, Seven Church Circle, Ste 303, 21401. (Mail add: PO Box 2395, 21404-2395), SAN 321-7701. Tel: 410-222-1387. FAX: 410-268-9762. E-mail: AALawLibrarian@mdcourts.gov. Web Site: www.circuitcourt.org. *Librn,* Joan Bellistri; Staff 2 (MLS 1, Non-MLS 1)
Library Holdings: Bk Titles 2,157; Bk Vols 20,263; Per Subs 30
Special Collections: Law (Maryland Coll)
Partic in Law Libr Asn of Md
Open Mon-Fri 9-4:30
Restriction: Open to pub for ref only

P ANNE ARUNDEL COUNTY PUBLIC LIBRARY*, Headquarters, Five Harry S Truman Pkwy, 21401. SAN 343-7469. Tel: 410-222-7371. FAX: 410-222-7188. Web Site: www.aacpl.net. *Exec Dir,* Hampton Auld; Tel: 410-222-7234, E-mail: sauld@aacpl.net; *Chief Financial Officer,* Scott Sedmak; Tel: 410-222-7236, E-mail: ssedmak@aacpl.net; *Chief, Human Res,* Terry Bowen; *Branch Management, Chief, Pub Serv,* Catherine Hollerbach; Tel: 410-222-7287, E-mail: chollerbach@aacpl.net; *Chief, Support Serv,* Rudy Rodela; *Head, Mat Mgt,* Roberta McGaughran; E-mail: rmcgaughran@aacpl.net; *Mgr, Info Tech,* Quinten Wilson; E-mail: qwilson@aacpl.net; *Mkt & Communications Mgr,* Christine Feldmann; *Found Dir,* Ann Glenn; Staff 261 (MLS 53, Non-MLS 208)
Founded 1936
Library Holdings: Bk Vols 1,225,198

Subject Interests: Maryland
Automation Activity & Vendor Info: (Circulation) SirsiDynix
Wireless access
Function: 24/7 Electronic res, 24/7 Online cat, 3D Printer, Adult bk club, Bilingual assistance for Spanish patrons, Bk club(s), Children's prog, Computer training, Computers for patron use, E-Readers, Homework prog, ILL available, Internet access, Magazines, Mail loans to mem, Meeting rooms, Movies, Online cat, Outreach serv, Photocopying/Printing, Preschool outreach, Prog for adults, Prog for children & young adult, Story hour, Summer reading prog, Wheelchair accessible
Publications: Library Happenings (Quarterly newsletter); Small Business Handbook; Staff Newsletter
Open Mon-Thurs 9-9, Fri & Sat 9-5, Sun 1-5
Branches: 15
BROADNECK LIBRARY, 1275 Green Holly Dr, 21401, SAN 343-7507. Tel: 410-222-1905. FAX: 410-222-1908. E-mail: bdn@aacpl.net. Web Site: www.aacpl.net/location/broadneck. *Br Mgr,* Heather Ravanbakhsh; E-mail: hravanbakhsh@aacpl.net
Open Mon-Thurs 9-9, Fri & Sat 9-5
BROOKLYN PARK LIBRARY, One E 11th Ave, Baltimore, 21225, SAN 343-7523. Tel: 410-222-6260. FAX: 410-222-6263. E-mail: bpk@aacpl.net. Web Site: www.aacpl.net/location/brooklynpark. *Br Mgr,* Ms Kt Zawodny; E-mail: kzawodny@aacpl.net
Open Mon-Thurs 9-9, Fri & Sat 9-5
MICHAEL E BUSCH ANNAPOLIS LIBRARY, 1410 West St, 21401, SAN 343-7493. Tel: 410-222-1750. FAX: 410-222-1116. E-mail: ann@aacpl.net. Web Site: www.aacpl.net/location/annapolis. *Br Mgr,* Diane Benner; E-mail: dbenner@aacpl.net
Library Holdings: Bk Vols 162,800
Open Mon-Thurs 9-9, Fri & Sat 9-5, Sun 1-5
CROFTON LIBRARY, 1681 Riedel Rd, Crofton, 21114, SAN 343-7558. Tel: 410-222-7915. FAX: 410-222-7269. Web Site: www.aacpl.net/location/crofton. *Br Mgr,* Joanie Bradford; E-mail: jbradford@aacpl.net
Open Mon-Thurs 9-9, Fri & Sat 9-5, Sun (Sept-May) 1-5
DEALE LIBRARY, 5940 Deale-Churchton Rd, Deale, 20751, SAN 343-7825. Tel: 410-222-1925, 410-867-4164. FAX: 410-222-1910. E-mail: sco@aacpl.net. Web Site: www.aacpl.net/location/deale. *Br Mgr,* Liz Saniga; E-mail: msaniga@aacpl.net
Open Mon-Thurs 9-9, Fri & Sat 9-5
EASTPORT-ANNAPOLIS NECK LIBRARY, 269 Hillsmere Dr, 21403, SAN 343-7582. Tel: 410-222-1770. FAX: 410-222-1973. Web Site: www.aacpl.net/location/eastport. *Br Mgr,* Michele Noble; E-mail: mnoble@aacpl.net
Open Mon-Thurs 9-9, Fri & Sat 9-5
EDGEWATER LIBRARY, 25 Stepneys Lane, Edgewater, 21037, SAN 371-9758. Tel: 410-222-1538. FAX: 410-222-1543. E-mail: edg@aacpl.net. Web Site: www.aacpl.net/location/edgewater. *Br Mgr,* Anne Pusey; E-mail: apusey@aacpl.net
Open Mon-Thurs 9-9, Fri & Sat 9-5
GLEN BURNIE LIBRARY, 1010 Eastway, Glen Burnie, 21061, SAN 343-7701. Tel: 410-222-6270. FAX: 410-222-6276. E-mail: nco@aacpl.net. Web Site: www.aacpl.net/location/glenburnie. *Br Mgr,* Catherine McNamara; E-mail: cmcnamara@aacpl.net
Open Mon-Thurs 9-9, Fri & Sat 9-5, Sun (Sept-May) 1-5
LINTHICUM LIBRARY, 400 Shipley Rd, Linthicum, 21090, SAN 343-7647. Tel: 410-222-6265. FAX: 410-222-6269. E-mail: lin@aacpl.net. Web Site: www.aacpl.net/location/linthicum. *Br Mgr,* Kate Boeree-Kline; E-mail: kboeree-kline@aacpl.net
Open Mon-Thurs 9-9, Fri & Sat 9-5
MARYLAND CITY AT RUSSETT LIBRARY, 3501 Russett Common, Laurel, 20724, SAN 343-7671. Tel: 301-725-2390. FAX: 301-498-5749. E-mail: mdc@aacpl.net. Web Site: www.aacpl.net/location/marylandcity. *Br Mgr,* Darnice Jasper; E-mail: djasper@aacpl.net
Open Mon-Thurs 9-9, Fri & Sat 9-5
MOUNTAIN ROAD LIBRARY, 4730 Mountain Rd, Pasadena, 21122, SAN 374-5260. Tel: 410-222-6699. FAX: 410-222-6705. E-mail: mtr@aacpl.net. Web Site: www.aacpl.net/location/mountainroad. *Br Mgr,* Veronica Lathroum; E-mail: vlathroum@aacpl.net
Open Mon-Thurs 9-9, Fri & Sat 9-5
ODENTON LIBRARY, 1325 Annapolis Rd, Odenton, 21113. Tel: 410-222-6277. FAX: 410-222-6279. E-mail: wco@aacpl.net. Web Site: www.aacpl.net/location/odenton. *Br Mgr,* Tim Van Fleet; E-mail: tvanfleet@aacpl.net
Founded 2004
Open Mon-Thurs 9-9, Fri & Sat 9-5, Sun (Sept-May) 1-5
RIVIERA BEACH LIBRARY, 8485A Fort Smallwood Rd, Pasadena, 21122, SAN 343-7760. Tel: 410-222-6285. FAX: 410-222-6287. E-mail: riv@aacpl.net. Web Site: www.aacpl.net/location/rivierabeach. *Br Mgr,* Dan Ramirez; E-mail: dramirez@aacpl.net
Open Mon-Thurs 9-9, Fri & Sat 9-5
SEVERN LIBRARY, 2624 Annapolis Rd, Rte 175, Severn, 21144, SAN 328-6673. Tel: 410-222-6280. FAX: 410-222-6283. E-mail: pro@aacpl.net. Web Site: www.aacpl.net/location/severn. *Br Mgr,* Ashley Rogers; E-mail: arogers@aacpl.net
Open Mon-Thurs 9-9, Fri & Sat 9-5
SEVERNA PARK LIBRARY, 45 McKinsey Rd, Severna Park, 21146, SAN 343-7795. Tel: 410-222-6290. FAX: 410-222-6297. E-mail: spk@aacpl.net. Web Site: www.aacpl.net/location/severnapark. *Br Mgr,* Samantha Zline; E-mail: szline@aacpl.net
Open Mon-Thurs 9-9, Fri & Sat 9-5, Sun (Sept-May) 1-5

M ANNE ARUNDEL MEDICAL CENTER LIBRARY*, 2001 Medical Pkwy, 21401. SAN 306-7998. Tel: 443-481-4877. Web Site: www.aahs.org. *Med Librn,* Joyce Cortright Miller; E-mail: jmiller@aahs.org
Founded 1970
Automation Activity & Vendor Info: (Acquisitions) EBSCO Online; (Cataloging) OVID Technologies; (Circulation) OVID Technologies
Wireless access
Function: 24/7 Electronic res
Partic in US National Library of Medicine
Restriction: Authorized patrons, Badge access after hrs, Employees only

L THURGOOD MARSHALL STATE LAW LIBRARY*, Courts of Appeals Bldg, 361 Rowe Blvd, 21401. SAN 306-8064. Tel: 410-260-1430. Toll Free Tel: 888-216-8156 (MD Only). FAX: 410-260-1572. E-mail: lawlibrary@mdcourts.gov. Web Site: mdcourts.gov/lawlib. *Dir,* Steven P Anderson; E-mail: steven.anderson@mdcourts.gov; *Dep Dir,* James Durham; *Head, Ref & Outreach,* Catherine McGuire; *Head, Coll Mgt,* Jessica Mundy; *Head, Tech Serv,* Jessie Tam; *Colls Librn,* Deborah Judy; *Ref Librn,* Tanya Thomas; *Research Librn,* Elizabeth Simmons; *Coll Mgt Spec,* Cindy Terry; *Ref Asst,* Maureen Della Barba; *Tech Serv Asst,* Scott Ashlin; Staff 10.5 (MLS 10.5)
Founded 1826
Jun 2014-May 2015 Income $3,111,659. Mats Exp $1,017,770, Books $775,315, Electronic Ref Mat (Incl. Access Fees) $242,455
Library Holdings: Bk Titles 77,750; Bk Vols 400,000; Per Subs 150
Special Collections: Audubon's Birds of America Original Havell Edition Prints; Historic Legal Materials. State Document Depository; US Document Depository
Subject Interests: Govt, Law, State hist
Automation Activity & Vendor Info: (Acquisitions) Innovative Interfaces, Inc - Sierra; (Cataloging) Innovative Interfaces, Inc - Sierra; (ILL) OCLC; (OPAC) Innovative Interfaces, Inc - Sierra; (Serials) Innovative Interfaces, Inc - Sierra
Wireless access
Function: Art exhibits, Audio & video playback equip for onsite use, AV serv, Computer training, Computers for patron use, Doc delivery serv, Electronic databases & coll, Govt ref serv, ILL available, Online cat, Outreach serv, Photocopying/Printing, Scanner
Publications: Maryland State Law Library Annual Highlights (Annual report); Maryland State Selected New Booklist (Acquisition list); The People's Law Library (Online only)
Partic in Law Library Microform Consortium; Legal Information Preservation Alliance; OCLC Online Computer Library Center, Inc
Open Mon, Wed & Fri 8-4:30, Tues & Thurs 8am-9pm, Sat 9-4
Restriction: Non-circulating to the pub

GL MARYLAND DEPARTMENT OF LEGISLATIVE SERVICES LIBRARY*, B-00 Legislative Services Bldg, 90 State Circle, 21401. SAN 306-8048. Tel: 410-946-5400. FAX: 410-946-5405. E-mail: libr@mlis.state.md.us. Web Site: dls.state.md.us. *Dir, Libr & Info Serv,* Johanne Greer; *Acq Mgr,* Cynthia Stiverson; *Cat Mgr,* Elizabeth Keyser; Staff 11 (MLS 11)
Founded 1966
Library Holdings: Bk Titles 30,000; Bk Vols 100,000; Per Subs 150
Special Collections: Codes of Fifty States; Maryland County Codes Coll; Maryland History Coll; State Publications. State Document Depository
Subject Interests: State govt
Automation Activity & Vendor Info: (Acquisitions) SirsiDynix; (Cataloging) SirsiDynix; (Circulation) SirsiDynix; (OPAC) SirsiDynix; (Serials) SirsiDynix
Publications: Maryland Documents
Partic in OCLC Online Computer Library Center, Inc
Special Services for the Deaf - TTY equip
Open Mon-Fri 8-5
Restriction: Open to pub for ref only

A THE NAVAL INSTITUTE*, History Collection Library, 291 Wood Rd, 21402-5035. SAN 324-1033. Tel: 410-295-1022. FAX: 410-295-1091. E-mail: research@usni.org. Web Site: www.usni.org/archives/about. *Mgr,* Janis Jorgensen; E-mail: jjorgensen@usni.org
Library Holdings: Bk Titles 5,000
Special Collections: Photograph Archives. Oral History
Subject Interests: Mil hist

Wireless access
Open Mon-Fri 8-4:30

C ST JOHN'S COLLEGE LIBRARY*, Greenfield Library, 60 College Ave, 21401. SAN 306-8080. Tel: 410-626-2548. Web Site: www.sjc.edu/academic-programs/libraries/greenfield-library. *Libr Dir,* Catherine Dixon; Tel: 410-626-2550, E-mail: catherine.dixon@sjc.edu; *Assoc Libr Dir,* Cara Sabolcik; Tel: 410-295-6927, E-mail: cara.sabolcik@sjc.edu; *Mgr, Tech Serv,* Emily Connell Rafferty; E-mail: emily.rafferty@sjc.edu; *Circ Asst,* Scott Chevaillier; Tel: 410-972-4117, E-mail: sfchevaillier@sjc.edu; Staff 4 (MLS 3, Non-MLS 1)
Founded 1793. Enrl 500; Highest Degree: Master
Library Holdings: CDs 200; DVDs 800; Bk Vols 115,000; Per Subs 120
Special Collections: Annapolitan Library (Bray Coll, Rev Thomas); Douglas Allanbrook Coll, musical scores; Prettyman Coll of Inscribed Books
Subject Interests: Classical studies, Hist of sci, Philos
Automation Activity & Vendor Info: (Cataloging) SirsiDynix; (Circulation) SirsiDynix; (OPAC) SirsiDynix
Wireless access
Partic in OCLC Online Computer Library Center, Inc
Open Mon & Thurs 8:30-7:30, Tues & Wed 8:30-Midnight, Fri 8:30-5:30, Sat Noon-6, Sun Noon-Midnight

C UNITED STATES NAVAL ACADEMY*, Nimitz Library, 589 McNair Rd, 21402-5029. SAN 321-3404. Tel: 410-293-6945. Reference Tel: 410-293-2420. FAX: 410-293-6909. E-mail: askref@usna.edu. Web Site: www.usna.edu/library. *Assoc Dean, Info Resources, Libr Dir,* Lawrence E Clemens; E-mail: clemens@usna.edu; *Assoc Dir, User Serv,* Catherine R Johnson; E-mail: cjohnson@usna.edu; *Head, Acq,* Margaret J Danchik; E-mail: danchik@usna.edu; *Head, Cat,* Laura R Nauta; E-mail: nauta@usna.edu; *Head, Circ,* Nicholas W Brown; E-mail: nbrown@usna.edu; *Head, Ref & Instruction,* Amanda R Click; E-mail: click@usna.edu; *Head, Spec Coll & Archives,* Jennifer A Bryan, PhD; E-mail: bryan@usna.edu; *Head, Syst,* William G Murray; E-mail: murray@usna.edu; Staff 36 (MLS 20, Non-MLS 16)
Founded 1845. Enrl 4,526; Fac 549; Highest Degree: Bachelor
Oct 2014-Sept 2015 Income $4,430,899, Federal $4,418,175, Other $12,724. Mats Exp $2,021,208, Books $266,700, Per/Ser (Incl. Access Fees) $1,548,718, Manu Arch $11,934, Other Print Mats $7,512, Micro $2,549, AV Mat $22,000, Presv $13,372. Sal $2,172,400
Library Holdings: Audiobooks 707; AV Mats 7,664; CDs 713; DVDs 5,006; e-books 4,222,709; e-journals 6,169; Electronic Media & Resources 6,772; Microforms 836; Bk Titles 972,377; Bk Vols 1,137,555; Per Subs 1,441; Talking Bks 707; Videos 1,112
Special Collections: Albert A Michelson Coll; Electricity & Magnetism (Benjamin Coll); Naval Academy Archives; Naval History & Seapower; Paine Submarine Coll; Somers Submarine Coll; Steichen Photography Coll, bks & photogs; United States Navy Manuscript Colls. Oral History; US Document Depository
Subject Interests: Mil sci, Naval hist, Naval sci
Automation Activity & Vendor Info: (Acquisitions) Innovative Interfaces, Inc; (Cataloging) Innovative Interfaces, Inc; (Circulation) Innovative Interfaces, Inc; (OPAC) Innovative Interfaces, Inc; (Serials) Innovative Interfaces, Inc
Wireless access
Partic in National Research Library Alliance; OCLC Online Computer Library Center, Inc

ARNOLD

J ANNE ARUNDEL COMMUNITY COLLEGE*, Andrew G Truxal Library, 101 College Pkwy, 21012-1895. SAN 306-8110. Tel: 410-777-2211. Circulation Tel: 410-777-2238. Interlibrary Loan Service Tel: 410-777-2536. Reference Tel: 410-777-2456. FAX: 410-777-2652. E-mail: library@aacc.edu. Web Site: www.aacc.edu/library. *Dir,* Cynthia Steinhoff; Tel: 410-777-2483, E-mail: cksteinhoff@aacc.edu; *Automation Librn,* Michelle Robertson; *Instrul Serv Librn,* Brandy Whitlock; *Access Serv,* Kim Kraus; *Distance Educ,* Sophie Reverdy; *Ref (Info Servs),* Janice Lathrop; Staff 18 (MLS 6, Non-MLS 12)
Founded 1961. Enrl 9,000; Fac 198; Highest Degree: Associate
Library Holdings: AV Mats 8,000; Bk Vols 140,000; Per Subs 375
Automation Activity & Vendor Info: (Cataloging) SirsiDynix; (Circulation) SirsiDynix; (ILL) OCLC; (OPAC) SirsiDynix; (Serials) SirsiDynix
Wireless access
Partic in Maryland Community College Library Consortium; OCLC Online Computer Library Center, Inc
Open Mon-Thurs 8am-9:45pm, Fri 8-5:45, Sat 9-4:45, Sun 12-4:45
Friends of the Library Group

BALTIMORE

S ALTERNATIVE PRESS CENTER LIBRARY*, 2239 Kirk Ave, 21218. (Mail add: PO Box 13127, 21203). Tel: 312-451-8133. E-mail: altpress@altpress.org. Web Site: www.altpress.org. *Exec Coordr,* Charles D'Adamo; E-mail: cdadamo@altpress.org; *Head Cataloger, Librn,* Kevin Jones; E-mail: kjones@altpress.org; *Indexer,* Kathleene Kunkle. Subject Specialists: *Humanities, Soc sci,* Charles D'Adamo; *Humanities,* Kathleene Kunkle; Staff 4 (MLS 3, Non-MLS 1)
Library Holdings: Bk Vols 2,000
Function: Archival coll
Restriction: Open by appt only

GL ATTORNEY GENERAL'S OFFICE*, Law Library, 200 Saint Paul Pl, 18th Flr, 21202. SAN 306-8641. Tel: 410-576-6400. FAX: 410-576-7002. Web Site: www.oag.state.md.us. *Librn,* Carly Roché; E-mail: croche@oag.state.md.us; Staff 1 (MLS 1)
Founded 1917
Library Holdings: Bk Vols 25,000; Per Subs 25
Automation Activity & Vendor Info: (Acquisitions) Inmagic, Inc.; (Cataloging) Inmagic, Inc.; (ILL) Inmagic, Inc.; (Serials) Inmagic, Inc.

L BAKER DONELSON*, 100 Light St, Ste B2, 21202-1643. SAN 327-8204. Tel: 410-230-7181, 410-685-1120. FAX: 410-547-0699. Web Site: www.bakerdonelson.com/baltimore-maryland. *Dir,* Kumar H Jayasuriya
Library Holdings: Bk Vols 3,500; Per Subs 300
Automation Activity & Vendor Info: (Cataloging) EOS International; (Circulation) EOS International; (OPAC) EOS International
Partic in Dow Jones News Retrieval; Proquest Dialog
Restriction: Staff use only

J BALTIMORE CITY COMMUNITY COLLEGE*, Bard Library, 2901 Liberty Heights Ave, 21215. SAN 343-7973. Tel: 410-462-8400. Circulation Tel: 410-462-8022. Reference Tel: 410-462-8240. FAX: 410-462-8233. Web Site: www.bccc.edu/Page/62. *Dir, Libr Serv,* David Jin; E-mail: djin@bccc.edu; Staff 7 (MLS 5, Non-MLS 2)
Founded 1947. Enrl 4,460; Fac 120; Highest Degree: Associate
Library Holdings: Bk Vols 75,000; Per Subs 150
Special Collections: Baltimore Coll; Black History Coll; Maryland Coll. Oral History
Subject Interests: Allied health, Electronics, Ethnic studies, Nursing
Automation Activity & Vendor Info: (Cataloging) SirsiDynix-Unicorn; (OPAC) SirsiDynix-Unicorn; (Serials) SirsiDynix-Unicorn
Wireless access
Publications: Baltimore Is Best
Partic in Maryland Community College Library Consortium
Open Mon-Thurs 7:45am-9pm, Fri 7:45-6, Sat 8-4:30

G BALTIMORE CITY DEPARTMENT OF LEGISLATIVE REFERENCE LIBRARY, City Hall, Rm 626, 100 N Holliday St, 21202. SAN 306-8196. Tel: 410-396-4730. FAX: 410-396-8483. Web Site: legislativereference.baltimorecity.gov. *Library Contact,* Anita Evans; E-mail: Anita_Evans@baltimorecity.gov; Staff 8 (MLS 4, Non-MLS 4)
Founded 1874
Library Holdings: Bk Vols 500
Special Collections: Baltimore City Directories 1796-1964; Baltimore City Ordinances 1774-current; Court Proceedings (Maryland Reports 1780-current); Laws of Maryland 1692-current; Niles Register 1811-1848
Publications: Baltimore Charter; Baltimore City Building & Fire Codes; Baltimore City Code; Baltimore Municipal Handbook; Book Beat (Newsletter); Public Local Laws
Open Mon-Fri 8:30-4:30
Restriction: Open to pub for ref only

S BALTIMORE METROPOLITAN COUNCIL*, Regional Information Center, 1500 Whetstone Way, Ste 300, 21230. SAN 306-8692. Tel: 410-732-9570. FAX: 410-732-9488. E-mail: ric@baltometro.org. Web Site: www.baltometro.org/information-center/regional-information-center. *Mgr,* Ms Aryn Dagirmanjian; Staff 1 (MLS 1)
Founded 1963
Library Holdings: Bk Titles 8,000; Bk Vols 10,000; Per Subs 100
Subject Interests: Demographics, Econ, Environ studies, Finance, Govt, Transportation, Urban planning
Function: Ref serv available
Publications: Acquisitions List
Partic in Maryland Interlibrary Loan Organization
Restriction: Open by appt only

S BALTIMORE MUSEUM OF ART*, E Kirkbride Miller Art Research Library, Ten Art Museum Dr, 21218-3898. SAN 306-8218. Tel: 443-573-1778. FAX: 443-573-1781. E-mail: bmalibrary@artbma.org. Web Site: artbma.org/collections/library.archive.html. *Archivist, Head Librn,* Sarah Dansberger; Tel: 443-573-1780; Staff 1 (MLS 1)
Founded 1929

Library Holdings: Bk Vols 80,000; Per Subs 75
Special Collections: Claribel Cone and Etta Cone Library and Papers; Dunton Quilting Coll; George A. Lucas Library and Papers; Henry Barton and Mary Frick Jacobs Papers; Saidie A. May Papers; Virginia White Papers
Subject Interests: Africa, Art, Decorative art, Modern art, Photog, Prints
Automation Activity & Vendor Info: (Cataloging) SirsiDynix; (OPAC) SirsiDynix; (Serials) SirsiDynix
Wireless access
Function: 24/7 Online cat, Bus archives, Computers for patron use, Electronic databases & coll, For res purposes, Magazines, Ref serv available, Res libr
Partic in OCLC Online Computer Library Center, Inc
Restriction: Non-circulating, Open by appt only

S BALTIMORE MUSEUM OF INDUSTRY, Archives & Library, 1415 Key Hwy, 2nd Flr, 21230. (Mail add: 1919A Annapolis Rd, 21230), SAN 371-8581. Tel: 410-727-4808, Ext 112. Reference E-mail: archives@thebmi.org. Web Site: www.thebmi.org/exhibitions-collections/archives-library. *Archivist,* Maggi Marzolf; E-mail: mmarzolf@thebmi.org; *Research Coordr,* Ken Jones; E-mail: archives@thebmi.org; Staff 1 (MLS 1)
Founded 1977
Special Collections: Archival & Manuscript Colls; Business & Industry in Baltimore & Environs, AV, bks, flm, negatives, per, photogs, rare bks, tapes, trade cats, vf; Non-Current Periodicals. Oral History
Subject Interests: Indust hist, Soc hist, Urban studies
Wireless access
Function: 24/7 Online cat, Archival coll, Audio & video playback equip for onsite use, AV serv, Bus archives, Computers for patron use, Electronic databases & coll, For res purposes, Internet access, Magazines, Magnifiers for reading, Mail & tel request accepted, Microfiche/film & reading machines, Museum passes, Online cat, Online ref, Orientations, Outreach serv, Outside serv via phone, mail, e-mail & web, Photocopying/Printing, Printer for laptops & handheld devices, Prog for adults, Ref & res, Ref serv available, Res assist avail, Res libr, Res performed for a fee, Scanner, Serves people with intellectual disabilities, Study rm, Telephone ref, Wheelchair accessible, Workshops
Publications: Research Center Brochure
Restriction: Non-circulating, Open by appt only, Open to pub by appt only, Open to researchers by request, Researchers by appt only, Restricted borrowing privileges, Visitors must make appt to use bks in the libr

SR CARMELITE MONASTERY, Library & Archives, 1318 Dulaney Valley Rd, 21286-1399. SAN 327-5922. Tel: 410-823-7415. FAX: 410-823-7418. E-mail: info@baltimorecarmel.org. Web Site: www.baltimorecarmel.org. *Archivist,* Sister Constance Fitzgerald; E-mail: Connie@baltimorecarmel.org
Library Holdings: Bk Titles 30,000
Special Collections: Archives of Oldest Community of Religious Women in 13 Original Colonies (1649-); Durham Coll - Maryland Law Suit (1820-1830); Rare Books from 1582
Subject Interests: Theol
Automation Activity & Vendor Info: (Cataloging) Mandarin Library Automation
Restriction: Mem only

C COPPIN STATE COLLEGE, Parlett Moore Library, 2500 W North Ave, 21216-3698. SAN 306-8331. Tel: 410-951-3400. Circulation Tel: 410-951-3424. Reference Tel: 410-951-3425. FAX: 410-951-3430. Web Site: www.coppin.edu/library. *Dir,* Mary Wanza; Tel: 410-951-3405, E-mail: mwanza@coppin.edu; *Ref Librn,* LaTrice Istance-Curtis; E-mail: lcurtis@coppin.edu; Staff 8 (MLS 2, Non-MLS 6)
Founded 1900. Enrl 2,400; Fac 111
Library Holdings: Bk Titles 79,281; Bk Vols 97,412; Per Subs 224
Special Collections: Black Studies; Maryland
Subject Interests: Biology, Educ, Nursing, Soc sci & issues
Automation Activity & Vendor Info: (Acquisitions) Ex Libris Group; (Cataloging) Ex Libris Group; (Circulation) Ex Libris Group; (Course Reserve) Ex Libris Group; (ILL) Ex Libris Group; (Media Booking) Ex Libris Group; (OPAC) Ex Libris Group; (Serials) Ex Libris Group
Wireless access
Partic in OCLC Online Computer Library Center, Inc; Univ Syst of Md
Open Mon-Thurs 8am-11pm, Fri 8-5, Sat 10-4, Sun 1-6

S CYLBURN ARBORETUM FRIENDS LIBRARY, 4915 Greenspring Ave, 21209. SAN 328-1493. Tel: 410-367-2217, Ext 2. E-mail: info@cylburn.org. Web Site: bcrp.baltimorecity.gov/cylburn, cylburn.org. *Exec Dir,* Patricia Foster
Founded 1955
Library Holdings: Bk Titles 2,000
Special Collections: Japanese Maple Coll; Magnolia Coll; Small Tree Coll
Subject Interests: Hort
Wireless access
Restriction: Mem only

GM DEPARTMENT OF VETERANS AFFAIRS - VA MARYLAND HEALTH CARE SYSTEM*, Baltimore Medical Center Library, Ten N Greene St, 21201. SAN 306-8889. Tel: 410-605-7092. Administration Tel: 410-605-7093. *Librn,* Joanna Lin; Staff 2 (MLS 1, Non-MLS 1)
Founded 1952
Library Holdings: AV Mats 700; Bk Vols 12,000; Per Subs 300
Subject Interests: Educ, Hospital admin, Med, Nursing, Psychiat, Psychol, Soc serv (soc work)
Partic in Valpac
Open Mon-Fri 9-3

L DLA PIPER US LLP*, Law Library, 6225 Smith Ave, 21209-3600. SAN 306-8668. Tel: 410-580-3010. FAX: 410-580-3261. Web Site: www.dlapiper.com. *Mgr, Libr Serv,* Rebecca Miller; E-mail: rebecca.miller@dlapiper.com; *Mgr, Tech Serv,* Brian Baxter; Tel: 410-580-4653, E-mail: brian.baxter@dlapiper.com; Staff 6 (MLS 2, Non-MLS 4)
Library Holdings: Bk Vols 27,800; Per Subs 70
Subject Interests: Admin law, Banks & banking, Labor, Securities
Wireless access
Restriction: Not open to pub

P ENOCH PRATT FREE LIBRARY*, 400 Cathedral St, 21201. SAN 343-8570. Tel: 410-396-5430. Administration Tel: 410-396-5395. FAX: 410-396-1441. Administration FAX: 410-396-1321. TDD: 410-396-3761. E-mail: info@prattlibrary.org. Web Site: www.prattlibrary.org. *Chief Exec Officer,* Heidi Daniel; E-mail: hdaniel@prattlibrary.org; *Chief of Programs & Outreach,* Kelli Shimabukuro; E-mail: kshimabukuro@prattlibrary.org; *Chief Operating Officer,* Gordon Krabbe; E-mail: gkrabbe@prattlibrary.org; *Chief, Neighborhood Libr Serv,* Herbert Malveaux; E-mail: hmalveaux@prattlibrary.org; *Dir, Mkt & Communications,* Megan McCorkell; E-mail: mccorkell@prattlibrary.org
Founded 1886
Jul 2012-Jun 2013 Income (Main & Associated Libraries) $38,698,100
Library Holdings: Audiobooks 33,945; AV Mats 125,402; CDs 35,483; DVDs 32,064; e-books 12,758; Electronic Media & Resources 83; Large Print Bks 12,212; Microforms 547; Music Scores 21,912; Bk Titles 1,141,436; Bk Vols 1,899,421; Per Subs 3,447; Videos 23,910
Special Collections: Adalbert Volck Civil War Etchings; African-American Rare Books Coll; African-American Sheet Music Coll; Baltimore Artist (Aaron Sopher Coll), drawings & prints; Baltimore Food & Wine Society Archives & Manuscripts; Baltimore Sculptor (Reuben Kramer Archives & Manuscripts); Baltimore Views, 1752-1930 (George Cator Coll); Bevan Bookplate Coll; Broadside Verses; Cookery, Gastronomy & Wines (Steiff Coll); Edgar Allen Poe Archives & Manuscripts; H L Mencken Archives & Manuscripts; Maryland Election/Campaign Literature Coll; Maryland Ephemera Coll; Maryland Imprints; Maryland Sheet Music Coll; Mencken's Saturday Night Club Sheet Music Coll; Richard Malcolm Johnston Archives & Manuscripts; Theater/Opera/Music Programs; United States Department Stores Mail Order Catalogs; Woman's Suffrage in Maryland Archives & Manuscripts; World War I & World War II Posters. State Document Depository; US Document Depository
Automation Activity & Vendor Info: (Acquisitions) SirsiDynix; (Cataloging) SirsiDynix; (Circulation) SirsiDynix; (ILL) SirsiDynix; (OPAC) SirsiDynix; (Serials) SirsiDynix
Wireless access
Publications: Cator Prints; Literacy Resources Bibliography; Menckeniana; Menckeniana; Reference Books; Selection Policies
Special Services for the Deaf - Bks on deafness & sign lang; Spec interest per; Staff with knowledge of sign lang; TTY equip
Special Services for the Blind - Reader equip; VisualTek equip
Open Mon-Thurs 10-7, Fri & Sat 10-5, Sun 1-5
Friends of the Library Group
Branches: 21
BROOKLYN BRANCH, 300 E Patapsco Ave, 21225-1828, SAN 343-8724. Tel: 410-396-1120. Toll Free Tel: 866-580-3191. E-mail: BRK@prattlibrary.org. *Mgr,* Ms Kinshasa Vargas-Pile; Tel: 443-984-4947
Open Mon & Thurs 10-8, Tues & Wed 10-5:30, Fri & Sat 10-5
CANTON BRANCH, 1030 S Ellwood Ave, 21224-4930, SAN 343-902X. Tel: 410-396-8548. E-mail: CNT@prattlibrary.org. *Mgr,* Ms Morgan Stanton; Tel: 443-984-4959
Library Holdings: Bk Vols 15,000
Open Mon & Thurs 10-8, Tues & Wed 10-5:30, Fri & Sat 10-5
Friends of the Library Group
CHERRY HILL BRANCH, 606 Cherry Hill Rd, 21225, SAN 343-947X. Tel: 410-396-1168. Toll Free Tel: 866-362-7449. E-mail: CHR@prattlibrary.org. *Br Mgr,* Ms Lynn Scott; Tel: 443-984-4932
Open Mon & Thurs 10-8, Tues & Wed 10-5:30, Fri & Sat 10-5
CLIFTON BRANCH, 2001 N Wolfe St, 21213-1477, SAN 343-950X. Tel: 410-396-0984. Toll Free Tel: 866-200-2943. E-mail: CLF@prattlibrary.org. *Br Mgr,* Ms Neelam Prasad; Tel: 443-984-4973
Open Mon & Thurs 10-8, Tues & Wed 10-5:30, Fri & Sat 10-5

EDMONDSON AVENUE BRANCH, 4330 Edmondson Ave, 21229-1615, SAN 343-9232. Tel: 410-396-0946. E-mail: EDM@prattlibrary.org. *Br Mgr,* Ms Ashley Mitchell; Tel: 443-984-4930
Open Mon & Thurs 10-8, Tues & Wed 10-5:30, Fri & Sat 10-5
Friends of the Library Group

FOREST PARK BRANCH, 3023 Garrison Blvd, 21216, SAN 343-9267. Tel: 410-396-0942. E-mail: FRS@prattlibrary.org. *Br Mgr,* Anjanette Wiggins; Tel: 443-984-4936
Open Mon & Thurs 10-8, Tues & Wed 10-5:30, Fri & Sat 10-5
Friends of the Library Group

GOVANS BRANCH, 5714 Bellona Ave, 21212-3508, SAN 343-8813. Tel: 410-396-6098. FAX: 410-396-6291. E-mail: GVN@prattlibrary.org. *Br Mgr,* Poonam Pukherjee; Tel: 443-984-4941
Open Mon & Thurs 10-8, Tues & Wed 10-5:30, Fri & Sat 10-5
Friends of the Library Group

HAMILTON BRANCH, 5910 Harford Rd, 21214-1845, SAN 343-8848. Tel: 410-396-6088. E-mail: HML@prattlibrary.org. *Br Mgr,* Laura Millay; Tel: 443-984-4935
Open Mon & Thurs 10-8, Tues & Wed 10-5:30, Fri & Sat 10-5

HAMPDEN BRANCH, 3641 Falls Rd, 21211-1815, SAN 343-9119. Tel: 410-396-6043. E-mail: HMP@prattlibrary.org. *Br Mgr,* Devon Ellis; Tel: 443-984-4949
Open Mon & Thurs 10-8, Tues & Wed 10-5:30, Fri & Sat 10-5

HERRING RUN BRANCH, 3801 Erdman Ave, 21213-2099, SAN 343-8872. Tel: 410-396-0996. E-mail: HRR@prattlibrary.org. *Br Mgr,* Gregory Fromme; Tel: 443-984-4940
Open Mon & Thurs 10-8, Tues & Wed 10-5:30, Fri & Sat 10-5
Friends of the Library Group

LIGHT STREET BRANCH, 1251 Light St, 21230-4305, SAN 343-8902. Tel: 410-396-1096. Toll Free FAX: 866-362-7449. E-mail: LGH@prattlibrary.org. *Br Mgr,* Ms Jan Westervelt; Tel: 443-984-4926
Open Mon & Thurs 10-8, Tues & Wed 10-5:30, Fri & Sat 10-5
Friends of the Library Group

NORTHWOOD BRANCH, 4420 Loch Raven Blvd, 21218-1553, SAN 343-8937. Tel: 410-396-6076. E-mail: NRT@prattlibrary.org. *Br Mgr,* Will Johnson; Tel: 443-984-3910
Open Mon & Thurs 10-8, Tues & Wed 10-5:30, Fri & Sat 10-5
Friends of the Library Group

ORLEANS STREET BRANCH, 1303 Orleans St, 21231, SAN 343-9208. Tel: 410-396-0970. E-mail: orl@prattlibrary.org. *Br Mgr,* Justin Switzer; Tel: 443-984-3914; Staff 5 (MLS 1, Non-MLS 4)
Open Mon & Thurs 10-8, Tues & Wed 10-5:30, Fri & Sat 10-5

PATTERSON PARK BRANCH, 158 N Linwood Ave, 21224-1255, SAN 343-8961. Tel: 410-396-0983. E-mail: PTT@prattlibrary.org. *Br Mgr,* Rebecca Box; Tel: 443-984-4946
Open Mon & Thurs 10-8, Tues & Wed 10-5:30, Fri & Sat 10-5
Friends of the Library Group

PENNSYLVANIA AVENUE BRANCH, 1531 W North Ave, 21217-1735, SAN 343-9321. Tel: 410-396-0399. E-mail: PNN@prattlibrary.org. *Br Mgr,* Zandra Campbell; Tel: 443-984-4939
Subject Interests: Statistics
Open Mon & Thurs 10-8, Tues & Wed 10-5:30, Fri & Sat 10-5

REISTERSTOWN ROAD BRANCH, 6310 Reisterstown Rd, 21215-2301, SAN 343-9380. Tel: 410-396-0948. E-mail: RST@prattlibrary.org. *Br Mgr,* Vera Fattah; Tel: 443-984-3918
Open Mon & Thurs 10-8, Tues & Wed 10-5:30, Fri & Sat 10-5
Friends of the Library Group

ROLAND PARK BRANCH, 5108 Roland Ave, 21210-2132, SAN 343-8996. Tel: 410-396-6099. E-mail: RLN@prattlibrary.org. *Br Mgr,* Julie Johnson; Tel: 443-984-3911; Staff 5 (MLS 2, Non-MLS 3)
Open Mon & Thurs 10-8, Tues & Wed 10-5:30, Fri & Sat 10-5
Friends of the Library Group

SOUTHEAST ANCHOR LIBRARY, 3601 Eastern Ave, 21224-4109, SAN 343-9143. Tel: 410-396-1580. E-mail: sel@prattlibrary.org. *Br Mgr,* Ms Lynne Distance; Tel: 410-396-4401
Open Mon-Thurs 10-8, Fri & Sat 10-5

WALBROOK BRANCH, 3203 W North Ave, 21216-3015, SAN 343-9410. Tel: 410-396-0935. E-mail: WLB@prattlibrary.org. *Br Mgr,* LaTrisha Milton; Tel: 443-984-4934
Open Mon & Thurs 10-8, Tues & Wed 10-5:30, Fri & Sat 10-5

WASHINGTON VILLAGE BRANCH, 856 Washington Blvd, 21230, SAN 377-6824. Tel: 410-396-1099. E-mail: WSH@prattlibrary.org. *Br Mgr,* Jessica Faulkner; Tel: 410-396-1568
Library Holdings: Bk Titles 10,000; Bk Vols 15,000
Open Mon & Thurs 10-8, Tues & Wed 10-5:30, Fri & Sat 10-5

WAVERLY BRANCH, 400 E 33rd St, 21218-3401, SAN 343-9445. Tel: 410-396-6053. E-mail: WVR@prattlibrary.org. *Br Mgr,* Anne Marie Harvey; Tel: 443-984-3913
Open Mon & Thurs 10-8, Tues & Wed 10-5:30, Fri & Sat 10-5
Friends of the Library Group

Bookmobiles: 1

L GORDON FEINBLATT LLC*, Law Library, 233 E Redwood St, 21202. SAN 372-1019. Tel: 410-576-4255. FAX: 410-576-4246. Web Site: www.gfrlaw.com. *Dir, Libr & Info Serv,* Sara Witman; E-mail: switman@gfrlaw.com; Staff 3 (MLS 2, Non-MLS 1)
Library Holdings: AV Mats 20; Bk Titles 2,000; Bk Vols 10,000; Per Subs 100
Automation Activity & Vendor Info: (Cataloging) Inmagic, Inc.
Function: For res purposes
Publications: Newsletter (Monthly)
Restriction: Co libr

M FRIEDENWALD-ROMANO LIBRARY*, Johns Hopkins Hospital, Woods Res Bldg, 600 N Wolfe St, Rm 3B-50, 21287-9105. SAN 343-8309. Tel: 410-955-3127. Web Site: www.medicalarchives.jhmi.edu/archives.html. *Librn,* Michael Piorunski; E-mail: mprunski@jhmi.edu. Subject Specialists: *Ophthalmology,* Michael Piorunski; Staff 2 (Non-MLS 2)
Founded 1925
Library Holdings: AV Mats 1,000; Bk Titles 12,000; Bk Vols 22,000; Per Subs 25
Special Collections: History of Medicine (Wilmer Coll), rare bks; Ophthalmological Drawings (Annette Burgess Art Coll), original art
Subject Interests: Hist of med, Ophthalmology
Automation Activity & Vendor Info: (Cataloging) SirsiDynix; (Circulation) SirsiDynix; (Serials) SirsiDynix
Wireless access
Function: Archival coll, For res purposes, Photocopying/Printing, Res libr, Telephone ref
Open Mon-Fri 9-4:30
Restriction: In-house use for visitors, Non-circulating to the pub, Open to pub with supv only

C GOUCHER COLLEGE LIBRARY, 1021 Dulaney Valley Rd, 21204. SAN 307-059X. Tel: 410-337-6360. Interlibrary Loan Service Tel: 410-337-6031. Reference Tel: 410-337-6212. Administration Tel: 410-337-5039. Automation Services Tel: 410-337-6370. E-mail: gcl@goucher.edu. Web Site: www.goucher.edu/library. *Asst VP, Library & Learning Commons,* Bella Gerlich; E-mail: bella.gerlich@goucher.edu; *Dir, Presv & Conserv,* Melissa Straw; E-mail: melissa.straw@goucher.edu; *Archives & Spec Coll Librn, Curator,* Kristen Welzenbach; E-mail: kristen.welzenbach@goucher.edu; *Coll Serv Librn,* Stephanie Sopka; E-mail: stephanie.sopka@goucher.edu; *Teaching & Learning Librn,* Elizabeth Johns; E-mail: emjohns@goucher.edu; *User Serv Librn,* Miranda Phair; E-mail: miranda.phair@goucher.edu; *Circ Mgr,* Tom Minnema; E-mail: tminnema@goucher.edu; *ILL Mgr,* Thomasin LaMay; E-mail: tlamay@goucher.edu; *Pub Serv Archivist,* Debbie Harner; E-mail: deborah.harner@goucher.edu. Subject Specialists: *Educ,* Debbie Harner; Staff 9 (MLS 7, Non-MLS 2)
Founded 1885. Enrl 1,402; Fac 96; Highest Degree: Master
Library Holdings: AV Mats 3,945; e-books 1,410; e-journals 25,000; Electronic Media & Resources 100; Bk Vols 301,792; Per Subs 300
Special Collections: BS Corrin & CI Winslow Political Memorablia & Political Humor Coll; Goucher College Archives; H L & Sara Haardt Mencken Coll; History of Costume; HL Mencken Coll; Jane Austen (Alberta H Burke Coll); JW Bright Coll; Mark Twain (Eugene Oberdorfer Coll); Southern Women During the Civil War (Passano Coll)
Automation Activity & Vendor Info: (Acquisitions) OCLC Worldshare Management Services; (Cataloging) OCLC Worldshare Management Services; (Circulation) OCLC Worldshare Management Services; (Discovery) OCLC; (ILL) OCLC WorldShare Interlibrary Loan; (OPAC) OCLC Worldshare Management Services; (Serials) OCLC
Wireless access
Publications: Focus (Newsletter)
Partic in Baltimore Acad Libr Consortium; LYRASIS; OCLC Online Computer Library Center, Inc
Special Services for the Deaf - ADA equip
Restriction: Open to fac, students & qualified researchers
Friends of the Library Group

M GREATER BALTIMORE MEDICAL CENTER*, John E Savage Medical Library, 6701 N Charles St, 21204. SAN 306-8420. Tel: 443-849-2530. FAX: 443-849-2664. E-mail: library@gbmc.org. Web Site: www.gbmc.org. *Dir,* Deborah Thomas; E-mail: dthomas@gbmc.org; Staff 2 (MLS 1, Non-MLS 1)
Founded 1965
Library Holdings: DVDs 50; e-journals 1,000; Bk Titles 3,000; Per Subs 165
Subject Interests: Consumer health, Obstetrics & gynecology, Ophthalmology, Otolaryngology
Automation Activity & Vendor Info: (Acquisitions) LibraryWorld, Inc; (Cataloging) LibraryWorld, Inc; (Circulation) LibraryWorld, Inc; (OPAC) LibraryWorld, Inc
Wireless access
Restriction: Staff use only

S JEWISH MUSEUM OF MARYLAND*, Library & Archives, 15 Lloyd St, 21202. SAN 326-6028. Tel: 410-732-6400. FAX: 410-732-6451. E-mail: research@jewishmuseummd.org. Web Site: www.jewishmuseummd.org. *Dir of Coll,* Joanna Church; Tel: 410-500-5349; *Archivist,* Maggie Hoffman; E-mail: mahoffman@jewishmuseummd.org; Staff 2 (Non-MLS 2)
Founded 1960
Library Holdings: Bk Titles 3,000
Special Collections: Genealogy & Family History (Robert L Weinberg Family History Center); Organization, Business, Congregational & Personal Papers of the Maryland Jewish Community. Oral History
Wireless access
Function: Archival coll, Internet access, Online cat, Res performed for a fee
Restriction: Non-circulating, Not a lending libr, Open by appt only, Researchers by appt only

JOHNS HOPKINS UNIVERSITY LIBRARIES
C JOHN WORK GARRETT LIBRARY*, Evergreen House, 4545 N Charles St, 21210, SAN 343-8066. Tel: 410-516-0889. FAX: 410-516-7202. Web Site: archives.mse.jhu.edu.
Library Holdings: Bk Vols 28,670
Special Collections: 17th Century Maryland (Books Printed Before 1700 Relating to Maryland); Architecture (Laurence H Fowler Coll); Bibles (Hoffmann Coll); Incunabula; Literature, Travel & Exploration, Natural History
Subject Interests: Rare bks
Partic in Association of Research Libraries
Restriction: Open by appt only
CM CAROL J GRAY NURSING INFORMATION RESOURCE CENTER*, 525 N Wolfe St, Rm 313, 21202. Tel: 410-955-7559. E-mail: jhuson@son.jhmi.edu. Web Site: www.welch.jhu.edu/about/nirc.html. *Assoc Dir,* Anne Seymour; E-mail: seymoura@jhmi.edu; *Librn,* Holly Harden
Library Holdings: Bk Titles 500
Partic in Maryland Interlibrary Loan Organization
Open Mon-Thurs 8am-9pm, Fri 8-4:30, Sat 10-4, Sun 1-7
C ADOLF MEYER LIBRARY*, 600 N Wolfe St, 21205. (Mail add: 1900 E Monument St, 21205-2113). Tel: 410-955-5819. FAX: 410-955-0860. Web Site: www.welch.jhu.edu/about/meyer.html. *Librn,* Ivy Garner; E-mail: ilg@jhmi.edu; *Librn,* James Tucker
Library Holdings: Bk Titles 21,300; Per Subs 104
Open Mon-Fri 8-5:30
C GEORGE PEABODY LIBRARY*, 17 E Mount Vernon Pl, 21202, SAN 343-8635. Tel: 410-659-8179. FAX: 410-659-8137. Web Site: archives.mse.jhu.edu:8000.
Founded 1857
Library Holdings: Bk Vols 252,310; Per Subs 20; Spec Interest Per Sub 30
Special Collections: Cervantes: Editions of Don Quixote; General reference coll 19th Century Art & Architecture
Subject Interests: British hist, Decorative art, Geog, Maps, Relig, Travel
Partic in Association of Research Libraries
Open Mon-Fri 9-3
Restriction: Circ limited
C SCHOOL OF PROFESSIONAL STUDIES IN BUSINESS & EDUCATION*, Ten N Charles St, 21201. Tel: 410-516-0700. FAX: 410-659-8210. *Librn,* Michael Houck
Library Holdings: Bk Titles 600
Open Mon-Fri 8:30-9, Sat 8:30-5
C THE SHERIDAN LIBRARIES*, 3400 N Charles St, 21218, SAN 343-8031. Tel: 410-516-8325. Circulation Tel: 410-516-8370. Reference Tel: 410-516-8335. FAX: 410-516-5080. Web Site: www.library.jhu.edu. *Dean,* Winston Tabb; Tel: 410-516-8328; *Assoc Dean,* Sayeed Choudhury; *Assoc Dir,* Kenneth Flower; E-mail: ken.flower@jhu.edu; *Assoc Dir,* Deborah Slingluff; Tel: 410-516-8254, E-mail: slingluff@jhu.edu; *Head, Coll Mgt,* Elizabeth Mengel; Staff 51 (MLS 39, Non-MLS 12)
Founded 1876. Enrl 17,881; Highest Degree: Doctorate
Library Holdings: AV Mats 6,000; e-journals 7,000; Bk Vols 2,619,190; Per Subs 17,757
Special Collections: 17th Century English Literature; 19th & 20th Century American; Economic Classics (Hutzler Coll); Edmund Spenser (Tudor & Stuart Club Coll); French Drama (Couet Coll); German Literature (Kurrelmeyer Coll); Lord Byron; Louis Zukofsky; Manuscripts, including Sidney Lanier, Francis Lieber, D C Gilman, John Banister Tabb, Edward Lucas White, Arthur O Lovejoy Coll; Modern German Drama (Loewenberg Coll); Sheet Music (Levy Coll); Slavery (Birney Coll); Southey (Havens Coll); Trade Unions (Barnett Coll). US Document Depository
Automation Activity & Vendor Info: (Acquisitions) SirsiDynix; (Cataloging) SirsiDynix; (Circulation) SirsiDynix
Function: Res libr
Partic in Association of Research Libraries; Baltimore Acad Libr Consortium; Chesapeake Information & Research Library Alliance; Digital Libr Fedn; Md Independent Cols & Univs Alliance; Md Libr Asn
Publications: Ex Libris
Open Mon-Thurs 8-2, Fri & Sat 8-12, Sun 10-2
Friends of the Library Group
CM WILLIAM H WELCH MEDICAL LIBRARY*, 1900 E Monument St, 21205, SAN 343-8090. Tel: 410-955-3028. FAX: 410-955-0200. Web Site: www.welch.jhu.edu. *Mgr,* Donna D Hesson; E-mail: dhesson@jhmi.edu; *Librn,* Susan Rohner
Founded 1963
Library Holdings: Bk Vols 32,000; Per Subs 174
Automation Activity & Vendor Info: (Circulation) Horizon
Partic in Association of Research Libraries; OCLC Online Computer Library Center, Inc; Research Libraries Information Network
Publications: Library Bulletin (Quarterly)
Open Mon-Thurs 8am-9pm, Fri 8-6:30, Sat 10-5, Sun 1-7
Friends of the Library Group

S JOHNS HOPKINS UNIVERSITY-PEABODY CONSERVATORY OF MUSIC*, Arthur Friedheim Library, 21 E Mount Vernon Pl, 21202-2397. SAN 343-8511. Tel: 667-208-6655. E-mail: friedheimlibrary@jhu.edu. Web Site: musiclibrary.peabody.jhu.edu. *Head Librn,* Katherine DeLaurenti; Tel: 667-208-6656, E-mail: kdelaurenti@jhu.edu; *Resource Librn,* Kirk-Evan Billet; Tel: 667-208-6659, E-mail: billet@peabody.jhu.edu; Staff 4 (MLS 3, Non-MLS 1)
Founded 1866. Enrl 575; Fac 70; Highest Degree: Doctorate
Library Holdings: AV Mats 41,000; Bk Vols 114,000; Per Subs 205
Special Collections: Asgar Hamerik & Gustav Strube Coll, ms, published works; Barringer Jazz Coll; Brick Fleagle/Luther Henderson Jazz Recordings Coll; Franz Bornschein, George Boyle, Louis Cheslock, Robert L Paul, Ronald Roxbury, Bernhard Scholz, Howard Thatcher, Timothy Spelman, Vladimir Padwa & W L Hubbard Colls; Friedman Record Coll; John Charles Thomas & Enrico Caruso Coll; Joseph Schillinger Papers
Subject Interests: Dance, Music
Automation Activity & Vendor Info: (Circulation) Horizon
Wireless access
Partic in Maryland Interlibrary Loan Organization
Friends of the Library Group

L LIBRARY COMPANY OF THE BALTIMORE BAR*, Baltimore Bar Library, 100 N Calvert St, Rm 618, 21202-1723. SAN 306-8455. Tel: 410-727-0280. FAX: 410-685-4791. Web Site: www.barlib.org. *Libr Dir,* Joseph W Bennett; E-mail: jwbennett@barlib.org; Staff 2 (MLS 2)
Founded 1840
Library Holdings: Bk Vols 200,000; Per Subs 314
Subject Interests: Law
Automation Activity & Vendor Info: (Cataloging) SirsiDynix; (OPAC) SirsiDynix; (Serials) SirsiDynix
Wireless access
Publications: Bar Library Advance Sheet
Open Mon-Thurs 8:30-7, Fri 8:30-5, Sat 10-5 (Sept-June); Mon-Thurs 8:30-6, Fri 8:30-5, Sat 10-1 (July-Aug)
Restriction: Mem only

C LOYOLA-NOTRE DAME LIBRARY, INC, 200 Winston Ave, 21212. SAN 306-8463. Tel: 410-617-6801. Interlibrary Loan Service Tel: 410-617-6804. Reference Tel: 410-617-6802. Administration Tel: 410-617-6814. Administration FAX: 410-617-6895. E-mail: askemail@loyola.edu. Web Site: www.lndl.org. *Dir,* Katy O'Neill; E-mail: mconeill@loyola.edu; *Asst Dir, Colls & Access Services,* Melissa Laytham; E-mail: cmlaytham@loyola.edu; *Asst Dir, Research & Tech Services,* Matthew Treskon; E-mail: mtreskon@loyola.edu; *Head, Archives & Spec Coll,* Jenny Kinniff; E-mail: jkinniff@loyola.edu; *Access Serv Librn,* Amanda Kramer; E-mail: akramer2@loyola.edu; *Acquisitions & Cataloging Operations Supervisor,* Laura O'Hanlon; E-mail: lohanlon@loyola.edu; *Digital Technology & Web Supervisor,* Youlanda Halterman; E-mail: yhalterman@loyola.edu; Staff 24 (MLS 15, Non-MLS 9)
Founded 1973. Enrl 5,858; Fac 514; Highest Degree: Doctorate
Library Holdings: DVDs 7,906; e-books 479,210; e-journals 137,713; Bk Titles 286,197; Bk Vols 320,002; Per Subs 57; Videos 10,076
Special Collections: American & British Literature; Fore-Edge Painted Books; Theatre Playbills; University Archive
Automation Activity & Vendor Info: (Acquisitions) Ex Libris Group; (Cataloging) Ex Libris Group; (Circulation) Ex Libris Group; (Course Reserve) Ex Libris Group; (ILL) Ex Libris Group; (Media Booking) Ex Libris Group; (OPAC) Ex Libris Group; (Serials) Ex Libris Group
Wireless access
Publications: Gator & Greyhound Gazette (Online only)
Partic in Baltimore Acad Libr Consortium; University System of Maryland & Affiliated Institutions
Open Mon-Thurs 8am-Midnight, Fri 8-6, Sat 9-8, Sun Noon-Midnight
Friends of the Library Group

S MARYLAND CENTER FOR HISTORY & CULTURE LIBRARY, H Furlong Baldwin Library, (Formerly Maryland Historical Society Library), 610 Park Ave, 21201. SAN 321-4508. Tel: 410-685-3750. Reference Tel:

410-685-3750, Ext 359. E-mail: specialcollections@mdhistory.org. Web Site: www.mdhistory.org. *Libr Dir,* Catherine Mayfield; E-mail: cmayfield@mdhistory.org; *Sr Ref Librn,* Francis O'Neill; E-mail: foneill@mdhistory.org. Subject Specialists: *Genealogy, Local hist,* Francis O'Neill; Staff 6 (MLS 5, Non-MLS 1)
Founded 1844
Library Holdings: Bk Titles 60,000; Per Subs 250
Special Collections: Historic Prints & Photographs, Manuscripts, Maps, Ephemera & Broadsides. Oral History
Subject Interests: Maryland
Wireless access
Open Wed-Sat 10-5
Restriction: Non-circulating, Photo ID required for access

G MARYLAND DEPARTMENT OF PLANNING LIBRARY*, 301 W Preston St, Rm 1101, 21201-2365. SAN 306-8498. Tel: 410-767-4500. FAX: 410-767-4480. *Library Contact,* Oumy Kande; E-mail: oumy.kande1@maryland.gov
Founded 1959
Library Holdings: Bk Titles 9,550; Per Subs 140
Special Collections: Maryland Counties & Municipalities Central Depository of Plans. State Document Depository
Subject Interests: Census, Housing, Land use, Planning, Zoning
Publications: Acquisitions list (bi-monthly)
Open Mon-Fri 8-4:30

C MARYLAND INSTITUTE COLLEGE OF ART, Decker Library, 1401 W Mount Royal Ave, 21217. (Mail add: 1300 W Mount Royal Ave, 21217), SAN 306-851X. Tel: 410-225-2304, 410-225-2311. Circulation Tel: 410-225-2272. Reference Tel: 410-225-2273. FAX: 410-225-2316. Circulation E-mail: circ@mica.edu. Reference E-mail: refer@mica.edu. Web Site: www.mica.edu/libraries/decker-library. *Dir,* Heather Slania; *Coll Serv Librn,* Deidre Thompson; *Digital Initiatives Librn,* Position Currently Open; *Info Literacy, Instrul Design Librn,* Siân Evans; *Research Servs Librn,* Chris Drolsum; *Spec Coll Librn,* Kathy Cowan; *Access Serv Mgr,* Aaron Blickenstaff; *Acq Mgr, Mgr, Ser,* Deborah Viles; *Resource Description Mgr,* Mary Alessi; *Resource Sharing Coord,* Sidney Champagne; *Digital Curation & A-V Archives Specialist,* Meredith Moore; *Sr Sys Specialist,* Sherri Faaborg; *Digital Projects, Spec,* Arthur Soontornsaratool; *Access Serv Asst,* Position Currently Open; *Coll Maint & Preservation Tech,* Raven Warner; Staff 13 (MLS 5, Non-MLS 8)
Founded 1826. Enrl 2,050; Highest Degree: Master
Library Holdings: DVDs 6,000; Per Subs 414
Special Collections: Artists' Book Coll; Erotic Coll; MICA Graduate Theses Coll; MICA Mades Audiovisual Coll; Morris Louis Study Coll; S.C. Malone Penmanship Coll; Sophia L. Crownfield Textile Design Coll; Virginia West Fiber Art Study Coll; William Henry Jackson Photochromes; Zine Coll
Subject Interests: Archit, Art, Design
Automation Activity & Vendor Info: (Acquisitions) Ex Libris Group; (Cataloging) Ex Libris Group; (Circulation) Ex Libris Group; (Discovery) Ex Libris Group; (ILL) OCLC; (OPAC) Ex Libris Group
Wireless access
Function: 24/7 Electronic res, 24/7 Online cat, Art exhibits, Audio & video playback equip for onsite use, Computers for patron use, Electronic databases & coll, Photocopying/Printing, Ref & res, Scanner
Partic in Association of Independent Colleges of Art & Design; LYRASIS
Open Mon-Thurs 8:30am-9pm, Fri 8:30-4:30, Sat & Sun Noon-6; Mon, Tues, Thurs & Fri 8:30-4:30, Wed 1-4:30 (Summer)
Friends of the Library Group

P MARYLAND STATE LIBRARY*, 25 S Charles St, Ste 1310, 21201. SAN 343-8392. Tel: 667-219-4800. FAX: 667-219-4798. Web Site: marylandlibraries.org. *State Librn,* Irene Padilla; Tel: 667-219-4801, E-mail: irene.padilla@maryland.gov; *Chief Financial Officer,* Donna Liberto; Tel: 667-219-4799, E-mail: donna.liberto1@maryland.gov; *Dir,* John Owen; Tel: 410-230-2452, E-mail: john.owen@maryland.gov; *Dir,* Tamar Sarnoff; Tel: 667-219-4802, E-mail: tamar.sarnoff@maryland.gov; *Prog Mgr,* Renee Croft; Tel: 410-713-2414, E-mail: renee.croft@maryland.gov; *Project Coordr,* Nini Beegan; Tel: 443-340-7853, E-mail: nini.beegan@maryland.gov; Staff 16 (MLS 10, Non-MLS 6)
Wireless access
Open Mon-Fri 8-5
Branches: 1
LIBRARY FOR THE BLIND & PHYSICALLY HANDICAPPED
See Separate Entry under Maryland State Library for the Blind & Physically Handicapped

P MARYLAND STATE LIBRARY FOR THE BLIND & PRINT DISABLED, (Formerly Maryland State Library for the Blind & Physically Handicapped), 415 Park Ave, 21201-3603. SAN 306-8544. Tel: 410-230-2424. Toll Free Tel: 800-964-9209 (Baltimore Metro Area). FAX: 410-333-2095. TDD: 410-333-8679, 800-934-2541. E-mail: reference.desk@maryland.gov. Web Site: www.marylandlibraries.org/Pages/Maryland-Library-for-the-Blind-and-Print-Disabled.aspx. *Libr Dir,* John Owen; E-mail: john.owen@maryland.gov; *Asst Dir,* Mary Ramos; E-mail: mary.ramos@maryland.gov; *Coll Develop Librn,* Jordan Farinelli; E-mail: jordan.farinelli@maryland.gov; *Mkt, Outreach Librn,* Ashley Biggs; E-mail: ashley.biggs1@maryland.gov; *Patron Serv Librn, Ref Librn,* Amanda Gonzalez; E-mail: amanda.gonzalez@maryland.gov; *Youth Librn,* LaShawn Myles; E-mail: lashawn.miles@maryland.gov; *Prog Coordr,* Joseph Beckett; E-mail: joseph.beckett@maryland.gov; Staff 22 (MLS 6, Non-MLS 16)
Founded 1967
Library Holdings: Large Print Bks 12,992; Bk Titles 96,018; Bk Vols 362,944; Talking Bks 362,944; Videos 856
Special Collections: Marylandia, in-house produced a-tapes
Wireless access
Function: 24/7 Electronic res, 24/7 Online cat, Adult bk club, Audiobks on Playaways & MP3, Audiobks via web, Children's prog, Computer training, Computers for patron use, Digital talking bks, Electronic databases & coll, Equip loans & repairs, Free DVD rentals, Games & aids for people with disabilities, Home delivery & serv to seniorr ctr & nursing homes, Homebound delivery serv, Internet access, Jail serv, Large print keyboards, Life-long learning prog for all ages, Literacy & newcomer serv, Mail & tel request accepted, Mail loans to mem, Meeting rooms, Online cat, Online ref, Outreach serv, Outside serv via phone, mail, e-mail & web, Prog for adults, Prog for children & young adult, Ref & res, Ref serv available, Senior computer classes, Senior outreach, Serves people with intellectual disabilities, Summer & winter reading prog, Summer reading prog, Teen prog, Telephone ref, Wheelchair accessible, Winter reading prog
Publications: Adult Newsletter (Quarterly); Annual Report; Bibliographies; Children's Newsletter (Biannually)
Special Services for the Deaf - TDD equip; Videos & decoder
Special Services for the Blind - Braille bks; Braille equip; Children's Braille; Computer access aids; Digital talking bk; Digital talking bk machines; Textbks on audio-cassettes
Restriction: Authorized patrons, Authorized personnel only, Closed stack, Open to authorized patrons, Registered patrons only
Friends of the Library Group

M MCGLANNAN HEALTH SCIENCES LIBRARY*, Mercy Medical Ctr, 301 Saint Paul Pl, 21202. SAN 343-8457. Tel: 410-332-9189. E-mail: mmclibrarymail@mdmercy.com. Web Site: mdmercy.com/about-mercy/patient-friendly-environment. *Libr Tech,* Roy Hatch; Staff 2 (MLS 1, Non-MLS 1)
Founded 1874
Library Holdings: e-books 50; e-journals 3,000; High Interest/Low Vocabulary Bk Vols 200; Bk Titles 5,000; Per Subs 65
Special Collections: Consumer Health Coll; Medicine, Nursing & Allied Health Coll
Wireless access
Function: Archival coll, Doc delivery serv, ILL available, Mail loans to mem, Ref serv available, Telephone ref
Partic in National Network of Libraries of Medicine Region 1
Open Mon-Fri 8-4:30
Restriction: Access at librarian's discretion, In-house use for visitors, Lending to staff only, Non-circulating to the pub, Open to pub with supv only

M MEDSTAR FRANKLIN SQUARE MEDICAL CENTER*, Health Sciences Library, 9000 Franklin Square Dr, 21237. SAN 306-8390. Tel: 443-777-7363. Administration Tel: 443-777-7463. FAX: 410-687-1742. E-mail: fshc_medical_library@medstar.net. *Librn,* Lynne Peters; Staff 2 (MLS 1, Non-MLS 1)
Subject Interests: Nursing, Obstetrics & gynecology
Automation Activity & Vendor Info: (Acquisitions) EOS International; (Cataloging) EOS International; (Circulation) EOS International; (ILL) TDNet; (OPAC) EOS International; (Serials) EOS International
Wireless access
Function: Computer training, Computers for patron use, Electronic databases & coll, Health sci info serv, ILL available, Instruction & testing, Internet access, Learning ctr, Mail & tel request accepted, Mail loans to mem, Online cat, Photocopying/Printing, Printer for laptops & handheld devices, Ref & res, Ref serv available, Res libr, Scanner, Serves people with intellectual disabilities, Spoken cassettes & CDs, Spoken cassettes & DVDs, Telephone ref, VHS videos, Wheelchair accessible
Open Mon-Fri 8-5
Restriction: Badge access after hrs, Hospital employees & physicians only, Open to researchers by request, Open to staff, patients & family mem, Open to students, Photo ID required for access

M MEDSTAR HARBOR HOSPITAL*, Health Sciences Library, S Main Bldg, Rm 112, 3001 S Hanover St, 21225-1290. SAN 306-8781. Tel: 410-350-3419. FAX: 410-350-2032. *Dir, Libr Serv,* Karen Jennings; Tel: 410-554-2817, E-mail: karen.l.jennings@medstar.net; Staff 2 (MLS 1, Non-MLS 1)
Founded 1913

Library Holdings: Bk Vols 3,000; Per Subs 155
Special Collections: Education Media Coll
Subject Interests: Internal med, Obstetrics & gynecology, Surgery
Wireless access
Publications: Newsletter (Quarterly)
Restriction: Staff use only
Friends of the Library Group

M MEDSTAR UNION MEMORIAL HOSPITAL*, Medical Library, 201 E University Pkwy, 21218. SAN 343-9801. Tel: 410-554-2294. FAX: 410-554-2166. *Dir, Libr Serv,* Karen Jennings; Tel: 410-554-2817, E-mail: karen.l.jennings@medstar.net; Staff 2 (MLS 1, Non-MLS 1)
Founded 1935
Library Holdings: Bk Vols 3,000; Per Subs 300
Subject Interests: Clinical med, Med, Orthopedics, Sports, Surgery
Wireless access
Partic in National Network of Libraries of Medicine Region 1
Restriction: Not open to pub

S METROPOLITAN TRANSITION CENTER LIBRARY*, 954 Forrest St, 21202. Tel: 410-230-1566. Web Site: www.dpscs.state.md.us/locations/mtc.shtml. *Librn,* Felecia Tyler; E-mail: feleciatyler@yahoo.com
Library Holdings: Bk Vols 8,299; Per Subs 22
Automation Activity & Vendor Info: (Cataloging) Follett Software; (Circulation) Follett Software

L MILES & STOCKBRIDGE PC*, Research & Information Center, 100 Light St, 21202. SAN 325-4887. Tel: 410-385-3671. FAX: 410-385-3700. Web Site: www.mslaw.com/office-locations/baltimore-maryland. *Dir, Res & Info Serv,* Rachel Englander; E-mail: renglander@milesstockbridge.com; *Mgr, Competitive Intelligence & Knowledge,* Elizabeth Kenderdine; *Research & Training Mgr,* Rachel Englander; *Res Spec,* Patricia Lesley; Staff 5 (MLS 4, Non-MLS 1)
Jan 2017-Dec 2017. Mats Exp $2,000,000, Books $4,000,000, Other Print Mats $60,000, Electronic Ref Mat (Incl. Access Fees) $5,000,000. Sal $340,000
Library Holdings: CDs 50; e-books 150; e-journals 25; Bk Titles 7,500; Bk Vols 10,000; Per Subs 150
Subject Interests: Bus, Law, Med
Automation Activity & Vendor Info: (Acquisitions) Sydney Enterprise; (Cataloging) Sydney Enterprise; (Circulation) Sydney Enterprise; (ILL) Sydney Enterprise; (OPAC) Sydney Enterprise; (Serials) Sydney Enterprise
Wireless access
Function: 24/7 Electronic res, 24/7 Online cat, Electronic databases & coll
Publications: A Guide to the Miles & Stockbridge Library
Restriction: Access at librarian's discretion, Access for corporate affiliates, Authorized personnel only, Borrowing requests are handled by ILL

C MORGAN STATE UNIVERSITY*, Earl S Richardson Library, 1700 E Cold Spring Lane, 21251. SAN 306-8579. Tel: 443-885-3477. Interlibrary Loan Service Tel: 443-885-1722. Reference Tel: 443-885-3450. Administration Tel: 443-885-3488. Administration FAX: 443-885-8246. Web Site: www.morgan.edu/library. *Dir, Libr Serv,* Dr Richard Bradberry; E-mail: richard.bradberry@morgan.edu; *Assoc Dir, Pub Serv,* Chris Iweha; Tel: 443-885-3478, E-mail: chris.iweha@morgan.edu; *Assoc Dir, Tech Serv,* Xiaoli Cheng; Tel: 443-885-1709, E-mail: xiaoli.cheng@morgan.edu; *Asst Dir, Info Tech,* Raul Valdez; Tel: 443-885-3930, E-mail: raul.valdez@morgan.edu; *Head, Access Serv, Syst Librn,* Renise Johnson; Tel: 443-885-1723, E-mail: renise.johnson@morgan.edu; *E-Res Mgt, Head, Acq, Ser,* Dr Fanuel Chirombo; Tel: 443-885-1712, E-mail: fanuel.chirombo@morgan.edu; *Instruction Librn,* Marcus Ladd; Tel: 443-885-1706, E-mail: marcus.ladd@morgan.edu; *Ref/Fed Doc Librn,* Bryan Fuller; Tel: 443-885-1705, E-mail: bryan.fuller@morgan.edu; *Univ Archivist,* Dr Ida Jones; Tel: 443-885-4294, E-mail: ida.jones@morgan.edu. Subject Specialists: *Bus, Educ, Info literacy, Nursing,* Chris Iweha; *Computer sci, Engr,* Raul Valdez; *Archives, Hist,* Dr Ida Jones; Staff 29 (MLS 7, Non-MLS 22)
Founded 1867. Enrl 7,700; Fac 450; Highest Degree: Doctorate
Jul 2019-Jun 2020 Income $78,000, Federal $78,000. Mats Exp $154,895,300. Sal $188,178,000
Library Holdings: AV Mats 18,300; Bks on Deafness & Sign Lang 223; e-journals 5,245; Electronic Media & Resources 110; Bk Vols 504,000; Per Subs 400
Special Collections: African-American History & Life (Beulah M Davis Special Colls Room); Correspondence of Late Poet & Editor (W S Braithwaite Coll), letters; Negro Employment in WWII (Emmett J Scott Coll), letters; Papers of Emeritus President (D O W Holmes Papers, Martin D Jenkins Papers), letters; Quaker & Slavery (Forbush Coll), bk, ms. US Document Depository
Subject Interests: Educ, Ethnic studies
Automation Activity & Vendor Info: (Acquisitions) Ex Libris Group; (Cataloging) Ex Libris Group; (Circulation) Ex Libris Group; (Course Reserve) Ex Libris Group; (Discovery) EBSCO Discovery Service; (ILL) OCLC; (OPAC) Ex Libris Group; (Serials) Ex Libris Group
Wireless access
Function: 24/7 Electronic res, 24/7 Online cat, Activity rm, Archival coll
Partic in University System of Maryland & Affiliated Institutions
Special Services for the Deaf - Am sign lang & deaf culture; Assisted listening device; Assistive tech; Bks on deafness & sign lang
Special Services for the Blind - Accessible computers; Aids for in-house use; Assistive/Adapted tech devices, equip & products
Open Mon-Thurs 8am-Midnight, Fri 8am-9pm; Sat 9-6, Sun 1-Midnight
Restriction: Access at librarian's discretion

S NATURAL HISTORY SOCIETY OF MARYLAND, INC LIBRARY*, 6908 Belair Rd, 21206. (Mail add: PO Box 18750, 21206), SAN 326-0194. Tel: 410-882-5376. E-mail: nhsm@marylandnature.org. Web Site: marylandnature.org. *Pres,* McSharry Joe; *Library Contact,* Patty Dowd; Staff 1 (MLS 1)
Founded 1929
Library Holdings: Bk Titles 20,200
Subject Interests: Natural hist
Wireless access

L NILES, BARTON & WILMER LAW LIBRARY*, 111 S Calvert St, Ste 1400, 21202. SAN 327-8182. Tel: 410-783-6300. FAX: 410-783-6363. Web Site: www.nilesbarton.com. *Librn,* Thea Warner; Staff 1 (Non-MLS 1)
Library Holdings: Bk Vols 10,000
Wireless access
Restriction: Staff use only

CR SAINT MARY'S SEMINARY & UNIVERSITY*, Knott Library, 5400 Roland Ave, 21210-1994. SAN 306-8722. Tel: 410-864-3626. FAX: 410-435-8571. E-mail: library@stmarys.edu. Web Site: www.stmarys.edu/the-knott-library. *Libr Dir,* Thomas Raszewski; Tel: 410-864-3621, E-mail: traszewski@stmarys.edu; *Tech Serv Librn,* Anita Prien; Tel: 410-864-3622, E-mail: aprien@stmarys.edu; Staff 3 (MLS 3)
Founded 1791. Enrl 157; Fac 25; Highest Degree: Master
Library Holdings: Bk Vols 140,000; Per Subs 403
Special Collections: Early Catholic Americana; Scripture/Orientalia (Arbez Coll); Semitics
Subject Interests: Relig, Theol
Automation Activity & Vendor Info: (Acquisitions) TLC (The Library Corporation); (Cataloging) TLC (The Library Corporation); (Circulation) TLC (The Library Corporation); (OPAC) TLC (The Library Corporation); (Serials) TLC (The Library Corporation)
Wireless access
Partic in OCLC Online Computer Library Center, Inc
Open Mon-Thurs 8am-10pm, Fri 8-4:30, Sat 8:30-5, Sun 2-10

L SAUL EWING LLP*, 500 E Pratt St, 9th Flr, 21202. SAN 306-8900. Tel: 410-332-8832. FAX: 410-332-8862. Web Site: www.saul.com. *Libr Dir,* Stacey Digan; E-mail: sdigan@saul.com; Staff 1 (MLS 1)
Library Holdings: Bk Vols 10,000; Per Subs 40
Subject Interests: Banks & banking, Commercial law, Corporate law, Labor, Litigation, Real estate, Securities
Function: For res purposes, ILL available, Internet access
Restriction: Staff use only

L SEMMES, BOWEN & SEMMES LIBRARY*, 25 S Charles St, Ste 1400, 21201. SAN 306-8757. Tel: 410-385-3936. FAX: 410-539-5223. *Dir,* Katriel Jacobs; E-mail: kjacobs@semmes.com
Subject Interests: Gen law
Automation Activity & Vendor Info: (Acquisitions) Inmagic, Inc.; (Cataloging) Inmagic, Inc.; (Serials) Inmagic, Inc.
Wireless access

M SHEPPARD PRATT HEALTH SYSTEMS*, Lawrence S Kubie Medical Library, 6501 N Charles St, 21204. (Mail add: PO Box 6815, 21285-6815), SAN 344-4694. Tel: 410-938-4595. FAX: 410-938-4596. E-mail: info@sheppardpratt.org. Web Site: www.sheppardpratt.org. *Archivist, Libr Coord,* Lisa Illum; E-mail: LIllum@sheppardpratt.org
Founded 1891
Library Holdings: Bk Vols 3,000; Per Subs 17
Subject Interests: Psychiat, Psychotherapy, Soc serv (soc work)
Partic in Proquest Dialog
Open Mon-Thurs 8-4, Fri 8-2
Restriction: Staff use only

M SINAI HOSPITAL OF BALTIMORE*, Eisenberg Medical Library, Hecht Bldg, 1st Flr, 2435 W Belvedere, 21215. SAN 306-8765. Tel: 410-601-5015, Ext 25015. FAX: 410-664-7432. Web Site: www.lifebridgehealth.org/research/theeisenbergmedicallibrary.aspx. *Med Librn,* Vaishali Jahagirdar; E-mail: vjahagirdar@lifebridgehealth.org; Staff 4 (MLS 2, Non-MLS 2)
Library Holdings: Bk Vols 4,100; Per Subs 300
Special Collections: Jewish Medicine & Health Coll; Management Coll

Subject Interests: Med, Nursing
Wireless access
Partic in National Network of Libraries of Medicine Region 1
Open Mon, Tues & Thurs 8-4:30

S SPACE TELESCOPE SCIENCE INSTITUTE LIBRARY, 3700 San Martin Dr, 21218. SAN 323-7729. Tel: 410-338-4961. E-mail: library@stsci.edu. Web Site: www.stsci.edu/scientific-community/stsci-library-and-institutional-archive. *Chief Librn,* Jenny Novacescu; E-mail: jnovacescu@stsci.edu; Staff 3 (MLS 2, Non-MLS 1)
Founded 1983
Library Holdings: Bk Titles 7,769; Bk Vols 8,863; Per Subs 207
Special Collections: Sky Survey Photographs
Subject Interests: Astrophysics
Automation Activity & Vendor Info: (Acquisitions) SirsiDynix; (Cataloging) SirsiDynix; (Circulation) SirsiDynix; (OPAC) SirsiDynix; (Serials) SirsiDynix
Wireless access
Publications: Acquisitions List; STEPsheet (preprint listing)
Restriction: Open by appt only

C STRATFORD UNIVERSITY*, Learning Resource Center, 210 S Central Ave, 2nd Flr, 21202. SAN 373-658X. Tel: 443-873-5415. FAX: 410-327-7365. E-mail: libraryba@stratford.edu. Web Site: www.stratford.edu/services/library-resource-center. *Librn,* Joanne Helouvry; Staff 4 (MLS 3, Non-MLS 1)
Founded 1987. Enrl 800; Fac 45; Highest Degree: Master
Library Holdings: AV Mats 50; DVDs 100; Bk Vols 5,000; Per Subs 5
Special Collections: Culinary/Hospitality Coll
Automation Activity & Vendor Info: (Cataloging) Koha; (Circulation) Koha; (Course Reserve) Koha; (OPAC) Koha
Wireless access
Function: Res libr
Partic in Maryland Interlibrary Consortium; Md Independent Cols & Univs Alliance
Open Mon-Thurs 7:30am-8:30pm, Fri 7:30-7
Restriction: Authorized patrons

S TRIBUNE PUBLISHING, Baltimore Sun Library, (Formerly tronc), 501 N Calvert St, 21202-3604. SAN 306-8242. Tel: 410-332-6933. Toll Free Tel: 800-829-8000, Ext 6933. FAX: 410-332-6918. Web Site: www.baltimoresun.com, www.tribpub.com. *Research Librn,* Paul McCardell; E-mail: paul.mccardell@baltsun.com; Staff 1 (MLS 1)
Founded 1837
Library Holdings: Bk Vols 7,000; Per Subs 10
Special Collections: A Aubrey Bodine Coll, black & white photogs; H L Mencken Clipping Coll; Index to The Evening Sun, 1910-1951, flm; Index to The Sun & Sunday Sun, 1891-1951, flm; John F Kennedy Memorial Coll, flm; Maryland Laws Coll
Subject Interests: Hist, Journalism
Automation Activity & Vendor Info: (Cataloging) Inmagic, Inc.; (Serials) Inmagic, Inc.
Function: 24/7 Electronic res, 24/7 Online cat, Archival coll, Res libr
Restriction: Authorized personnel only, Employees only, Internal circ only

L TYDINGS & ROSENBERG LLP*, Law Library, One E Pratt St, 9th Flr, 21202. SAN 372-0993. Tel: 410-752-9700, 410-752-9804. FAX: 410-727-5460. Web Site: tydingslaw.com. *Dir,* Jean Hessenauer; E-mail: jhessenauer@tydingslaw.com; Staff 1 (MLS 1)
Library Holdings: Bk Vols 1,000; Per Subs 25
Wireless access
Restriction: Staff use only

SR UNITED METHODIST HISTORICAL SOCIETY*, Lovely Lane Museum & Archives, 2200 St Paul St, 21218-5805. SAN 306-8838. Tel: 410-889-4458. FAX: 410-889-1501. E-mail: archives-history@bwcumc.org. Web Site: www.lovelylanemuseum.com/library.html. *Dir,* James E Reaves; *Assoc Dir,* Wanda B Hall. Subject Specialists: *Genealogy,* Wanda B Hall; Staff 2 (Non-MLS 2)
Founded 1855
Library Holdings: Bk Vols 4,857; Spec Interest Per Sub 15
Special Collections: Archives of Baltimore-Washington Conference; Journals of Preachers
Subject Interests: Hist
Publications: Methodist Union Catalog; Union List of Methodist Serials
Open Thurs & Fri 10-4
Restriction: Fee for pub use, Non-circulating
Friends of the Library Group

L UNITED STATES COURTS LIBRARY*, US Courthouse, Rm 3625, 101 W Lombard St, 21201. SAN 372-1000. Tel: 410-962-0997. FAX: 410-962-9313. Web Site: www.mdb.uscourts.gov/content/maryland's-public-law-libraries. *Law Librn,* Charmaine Metallo; E-mail: charmaine_metallo@ca4.uscourts.gov
Library Holdings: Bk Vols 38,000; Per Subs 125
Automation Activity & Vendor Info: (Acquisitions) SirsiDynix; (Cataloging) SirsiDynix; (Circulation) SirsiDynix; (ILL) SirsiDynix; (OPAC) SirsiDynix; (Serials) SirsiDynix
Open Mon-Fri 8:30-5

C UNIVERSITY OF BALTIMORE*, Langsdale Library, 1420 Maryland Ave, 21201. SAN 343-9925. Tel: 410-837-4260. Reference Tel: 410-837-4274. Administration Tel: 410-837-4290. Toll Free Tel: 888-526-4733. FAX: 410-837-4330. Circulation E-mail: langcirc@ubalt.edu. Reference E-mail: langref@ubalt.edu. Web Site: langsdale.ubalt.edu. *Dean of Libr,* Lucy Holman; Tel: 410-837-4333, E-mail: lholman@ubalt.edu; *Assoc Dir,* Jeffrey Hutson; Tel: 410-837-4298, E-mail: jhutson@ubalt.edu; *Head, Access Serv,* Sean Hogan; Tel: 410-837-4283, E-mail: shogan@ubalt.edu; *Head, Ref,* Michael Shochet; Tel: 410-837-4277, E-mail: mshochet@ubalt.edu; *Head, Spec Coll,* Aiden Faust; Tel: 410-837-4334, E-mail: afaust@ubalt.edu; *Circ Supvr,* Tammy Taylor; Tel: 410-837-4263, E-mail: ttaylor@ubalt.edu; *Archivist,* Fatemeh Rezaei; Tel: 410-837-5047, E-mail: frezaei@ubalt.edu; Staff 15 (MLS 13, Non-MLS 2)
Founded 1926. Enrl 6,265; Fac 123; Highest Degree: Doctorate
Library Holdings: Bk Vols 181,000; Per Subs 450
Special Collections: Society of Colonial Wars Archives; WMAR-TV Film Archives. Oral History; State Document Depository; US Document Depository
Automation Activity & Vendor Info: (Acquisitions) Ex Libris Group; (Cataloging) Ex Libris Group; (Circulation) Ex Libris Group; (ILL) OCLC ILLiad; (Media Booking) Ex Libris Group; (OPAC) Ex Libris Group; (Serials) Ex Libris Group
Wireless access
Publications: Langsdale Library Link
Partic in Baltimore Acad Libr Consortium; LYRASIS; OCLC Online Computer Library Center, Inc; Univ Syst of Md
Special Services for the Deaf - ADA equip; Assisted listening device; Closed caption videos
Special Services for the Blind - Assistive/Adapted tech devices, equip & products; Audio mat; Computer with voice synthesizer for visually impaired persons; Dragon Naturally Speaking software; Internet workstation with adaptive software; Large print & cassettes; Magnifiers
Open Mon-Thurs 8am-10pm, Fri 8-6, Sat & Sun 10-7

Departmental Libraries:

CL LAW LIBRARY, Angelos Law Center, 7th thru 12th Flrs, 1401 N Charles St, 21201. (Mail add: 1420 N Charles St, 21201), SAN 343-995X. Tel: 410-837-4554. Interlibrary Loan Service Tel: 410-837-4578. Reference Tel: 410-837-4559. Web Site: law.ubalt.edu/library. *Dir, Law Libr,* Adeen Postar; Tel: 410-837-4562, E-mail: apostar@ubalt.edu; *Assoc Dir, Coll, Database/Network Serv Librn,* Harvey Morrell; Tel: 410-837-4657, E-mail: hmorrell@ubalt.edu; *Assoc Dir, Pub Serv,* Joanne Dugan Colvin; Tel: 410-837-4373, E-mail: jcolvin@ubalt.edu; *Govt Doc,* Pat Behles; Tel: 410-837-4583, E-mail: pbehles@ubalt.edu; Staff 17 (MLS 10.5, Non-MLS 6.5)
Founded 1925. Enrl 1,000; Fac 45; Highest Degree: Master
Library Holdings: Bk Titles 27,130; Bk Vols 305,000; Per Subs 3,500
Special Collections: State Document Depository; US Document Depository
Automation Activity & Vendor Info: (ILL) OCLC
Partic in Cap Area Libr Consortium; Maryland Interlibrary Loan Organization; OCLC Online Computer Library Center, Inc
Publications: Anglo-American law (Research guide)
Open Mon-Thurs 8-8, Fri 8-5, Sat 9-5, Sun 12-5

UNIVERSITY OF MARYLAND, BALTIMORE

CM HEALTH SCIENCES & HUMAN SERVICES LIBRARY*, 601 W Lombard St, 21201, SAN 344-001X. Tel: 410-706-7545. Circulation Tel: 410-706-7928, 410-706-7995. Interlibrary Loan Service Tel: 410-706-3239. Information Services Tel: 410-706-7996. FAX: 410-706-3101. Web Site: www.hshsl.umaryland.edu/. *Exec Dir,* M J Tooey; E-mail: mjtooey@hshsl.umaryland.edu; *Assoc Dir, Libr Admin,* Aphrodite Bodycomb; Tel: 410-706-8853, E-mail: abodycomb@hshsl.umaryland.edu; *Exec Dir, NN/LM SE/ARMLS,* Janice Kelly; Tel: 410-706-2855; *Assoc Dir, Libr Applications & Knowledge Sys,* Ms Bohyun Kim; Tel: 410-706-0405, E-mail: bkim@hshsl.umaryland.edu; *Assoc Dir, Resources,* Beverly Gresehover; Tel: 410-706-1784, E-mail: bgreseho@hshsl.umaryland.edu; *Assoc Dir, Serv, Pub Serv,* Alexa Mayo; Tel: 410-706-1316, E-mail: amayo@hshsl.umaryland.edu. Subject Specialists: *Consulting, Educ,* Alexa Mayo; Staff 66 (MLS 29, Non-MLS 37)
Founded 1813. Enrl 5,875; Fac 1,600; Highest Degree: Doctorate
Library Holdings: Bk Vols 365,000; Per Subs 2,400
Special Collections: History of Dentistry (Grieves Coll), bks, pictures; History of Medicine (Crawford, Cordell Coll); History of Nursing; History of Pharmacy
Subject Interests: Dentistry, Med, Nursing, Pharm, Soc serv (soc work)

Automation Activity & Vendor Info: (Acquisitions) Ex Libris Group; (Cataloging) Ex Libris Group; (Circulation) Ex Libris Group; (Course Reserve) Docutek; (OPAC) Ex Libris Group; (Serials) Ex Libris Group
Partic in LYRASIS; NELLCO Law Library Consortium, Inc.; OCLC Online Computer Library Center, Inc; Univ Syst of Md
Open Mon-Fri 8am-10:30pm, Sat 8-5, Sun 11-8
Friends of the Library Group

CL THURGOOD MARSHALL LAW LIBRARY*, 501 W Fayette St, 21201-1768, SAN 344-0044. Tel: 410-706-7270. Interlibrary Loan Service Tel: 410-706-3240. Reference Tel: 410-706-6502. FAX: 410-706-8354. Interlibrary Loan Service FAX: 410-706-0554. Web Site: www.law.umaryland.edu/marshall. *Assoc Dean,* Barbara Gontrum; E-mail: bgontrum@law.umaryland.edu; *Dir, Info Policy & Mgt,* Nathan Robertson; Tel: 410-706-1213, E-mail: nrobertson@law.umaryland.edu; *Actg Dir,* Camilla Tubbs; Tel: 410-706-0792, E-mail: ctubbs@law.umaryland.edu; *Assoc Dir,* David Grahek; Tel: 410-706-2025, E-mail: dgrahek@law.umaryland.edu; *Digital Legal Res & Syst Librn,* Joseph Neumann; Tel: 410-706-2736, E-mail: jneumann@law.umaryland.edu; *Research Librn,* Maxine Grosshans; Tel: 410-706-0791, E-mail: mgross@law.umaryland.edu; *Research Librn,* Jason Hawkins; Tel: 410-706-0735, E-mail: jhawkins@law.umaryland.edu; *Research Librn,* Susan Herrick; Tel: 410-706-3213, E-mail: sherrick@law.umaryland.edu; *Research Librn,* Charles Pipins; Tel: 410-706-9784, E-mail: cpipins@law.umaryland.edu; *Research Librn,* Jenny Rensler; Tel: 410-706-2466, E-mail: jrensler@law.umaryland.edu; *Res Acq & Metadata Serv Librn,* Stephanie Bowe; Tel: 410-706-0783, E-mail: sbowe@law.umaryland.edu; Staff 24 (MLS 11, Non-MLS 13)
Founded 1843
Special Collections: East Asian Legal Studies Coll; German & French Civil Law Coll. US Document Depository
Automation Activity & Vendor Info: (Acquisitions) Ex Libris Group; (Cataloging) Ex Libris Group; (Circulation) Ex Libris Group; (ILL) Ex Libris Group; (OPAC) Ex Libris Group; (Serials) Ex Libris Group
Partic in LYRASIS; OCLC Online Computer Library Center, Inc; University System of Maryland & Affiliated Institutions
Open Mon-Thurs 7:30am-Midnight, Fri 7:30-6, Sat 9am-10pm, Sun 10am-11pm

C UNIVERSITY OF MARYLAND, BALTIMORE COUNTY, Albin O Kuhn Library & Gallery, 1000 Hilltop Circle, 21250. SAN 306-8854. Tel: 410-455-2356. Circulation Tel: 410-455-2354. Interlibrary Loan Service Tel: 410-455-2234. Reference Tel: 410-455-2346. Circulation FAX: 410-455-1153. Interlibrary Loan Service FAX: 410-455-1061. Reference FAX: 410-455-1906. Administration FAX: 410-455-1078. E-mail: aok@umbc.edu. Web Site: www.umbc.edu/library. *Dir,* Patrick Dawson; E-mail: pdawson@umbc.edu; *Assoc Dir, Library Tech & Digital Strategies,* Carolyn Sheffield; E-mail: csheffield@umbc.edu; *Assoc Dir, Pub Serv,* Timothy Hackman; E-mail: moskal@umbc.edu; *Assoc Dir, Tech Serv,* Lynda Aldana; E-mail: laldana@umbc.edu; *Head, Circ,* Paula Langley; E-mail: plangley@umbc.edu; *Head, Ref Serv,* Kathryn Sullivan; E-mail: sullivan@umbc.edu; *Head, Spec Coll,* Beth Saunders; E-mail: bethsaunders@umbc.edu; *Cat Librn,* Aimee Plaisance; E-mail: amplais@umbc.edu; *Digital Scholarship Librn,* Michelle Flinchbaugh; E-mail: flinchba@umbc.edu; *Ref & Instruction Librn,* Drew Alfgren; E-mail: alfgren@umbc.edu; *Ref & Instruction Librn,* Erin Durham; E-mail: edurham@umbc.edu; *Ref & Instruction Librn,* Joanna Gadsby; E-mail: gadsby@umbc.edu; *Ref & Instruction Librn,* Jasmine Shumaker; E-mail: jshumaker@umbc.edu; *Sci Librn,* Semhar Yohannes; E-mail: semhar@umbc.edu; *Spec Coll Librn,* Susan Graham; Fax: 410-455-1567, E-mail: sgraha1@umbc.edu; *Bus Mgr,* Shawn Parker; E-mail: sjparker@umbc.edu; *IT Serv Mgr,* Stephen Jones; E-mail: stjones@umbc.edu; *Website Mgr,* Jim Doran; E-mail: doran@umbc.edu; *Archivist,* Lindsey Loeper; E-mail: lloepe1@umbc.edu; *Archivist,* Laurianne Ojo-Ohikuare; E-mail: lojoohi1@umbc.edu; *Curator,* Emily Cullen; E-mail: emilyh2@umbc.edu; Staff 20 (MLS 16, Non-MLS 4)
Founded 1966. Enrl 13,497; Fac 931; Highest Degree: Doctorate
Jul 2021-Jun 2022 Income $9,127,348. Mats Exp $3,799,040, Books $503,088, Per/Ser (Incl. Access Fees) $3,295,952. Sal $3,900,831 (Prof $2,415,448)
Library Holdings: CDs 7,888; DVDs 7,282; e-books 61,548; e-journals 2,285; Microforms 1,018,693; Bk Vols 654,758; Per Subs 4,917; Videos 4,064
Special Collections: 19th Century English Graphic Satire (Merkle Coll); American Society for Microbiology Archives, bks, pers, ms; Baltimore Sun Photo Archives; Children's Science Books; Marylandia (Howard Coll); Photography, bks, pers, photo apparatus; Popular Culture; Tissue Culture Association Archives; University Archives, photog. Oral History; State Document Depository; US Document Depository
Automation Activity & Vendor Info: (Acquisitions) Ex Libris Group; (Cataloging) Ex Libris Group; (Circulation) Ex Libris Group; (Course Reserve) Ex Libris Group; (ILL) OCLC ILLiad; (Media Booking) Ex Libris Group; (Serials) Ex Libris Group
Wireless access
Function: 24/7 Electronic res, 24/7 Online cat
Publications: Exhibition Catalogs; From the Stacks (Newsletter)
Partic in ARIEL; OCLC Online Computer Library Center, Inc; Univ of Md Libr Info Mgt Syst; Univ Syst of Md; University System of Maryland & Affiliated Institutions
Open Mon-Thurs 7:30am-Midnight, Fri 7:30-7, Sat 10-6, Sun Noon-Midnight
Restriction: 24-hr pass syst for students only, Badge access after hrs
Friends of the Library Group

L VENABLE LLP LIBRARY*, 750 E Pratt St, 9th Flr, 21202. SAN 306-8870. Tel: 410-244-7502. Administration Tel: 410-244-7689. FAX: 410-244-7742. E-mail: lib01@venable.com. Web Site: www.venable.com. *Dir,* Barbara Folensbee-Moore; E-mail: bfolensbee-moore@venable.com; *Ref Librn,* Katherine Bare; E-mail: kbare@venable.com; Staff 4 (MLS 3, Non-MLS 1)
Founded 1900
Library Holdings: e-journals 20; Electronic Media & Resources 100; Bk Vols 30,000; Per Subs 25
Subject Interests: Bankruptcy, Banks & banking, Corporate law, Employee benefits, Employment law, Environ law, Estates, Finance, Govt, Law, Litigation, Real property, Securities, Taxation, Transportation, Trusts
Automation Activity & Vendor Info: (Cataloging) Sydney; (Circulation) Sydney; (OPAC) Sydney; (Serials) Sydney
Wireless access
Restriction: By permission only
Branches:
DC OFFICE
See Separate Entry in Washington, DC
TOWSON OFFICE, 210 W Pennsylvania Ave, Ste 500, Towson, 21204, SAN 370-9388. Tel: 410-494-6200. FAX: 410-821-0147. E-mail: lib01@venable.com. *Dir,* Barbara Folensbee-Moore
Founded 1962
Library Holdings: Bk Vols 1,250
Subject Interests: Civil litigation, Construction law, Govt, Law, Real estate law
VIRGINIA OFFICE
See Separate Entry in Vienna, Virginia

S WALTERS ART MUSEUM LIBRARY*, 600 N Charles St, 21201-5185. SAN 306-8897. Tel: 410-547-9000, Ext 297. FAX: 410-752-4797. E-mail: info@thewalters.org. Web Site: www.thewalters.org. *Archivist/Librn,* Anna Clarkson; E-mail: curatorial@thewalters.org; Staff 1 (Non-MLS 1)
Founded 1934
Library Holdings: Bk Vols 120,000; Per Subs 100
Special Collections: Art Auction Catalogs
Subject Interests: Hist
Automation Activity & Vendor Info: (Acquisitions) SirsiDynix; (Cataloging) SirsiDynix; (OPAC) SirsiDynix; (Serials) SirsiDynix
Wireless access
Function: Res libr
Partic in OCLC Online Computer Library Center, Inc
Restriction: Closed stack, Non-circulating, Not a lending libr, Open by appt only

L WHITEFORD, TAYLOR & PRESTON, LLP*, Law Library, Seven St Paul St, Ste 1500, 21202-1636. SAN 372-0616. Tel: 410-347-8700. FAX: 410-752-7092. Web Site: www.wtplaw.com. *Librn,* Mary Longchamp; E-mail: mlongchamp@wtplaw.com; Staff 4 (MLS 1, Non-MLS 3)
Library Holdings: Bk Vols 8,000; Per Subs 125
Automation Activity & Vendor Info: (Acquisitions) TLC (The Library Corporation); (Cataloging) TLC (The Library Corporation)
Restriction: Staff use only

BEL AIR

J HARFORD COMMUNITY COLLEGE LIBRARY*, 401 Thomas Run Rd, 21015. SAN 306-8935. Tel: 443-412-2131. E-mail: referenc@harford.edu. Web Site: www.harford.edu/academics/library.aspx. Staff 10 (MLS 9, Non-MLS 1)
Founded 1957. Enrl 8,145; Fac 103; Highest Degree: Associate
Library Holdings: Per Subs 79
Special Collections: Maryland Constitutional Convention File; Maryland History; Rosenburg Report. US Document Depository
Automation Activity & Vendor Info: (Acquisitions) ProQuest; (Circulation) ProQuest; (Course Reserve) ProQuest; (Discovery) EBSCO Discovery Service; (OPAC) ProQuest; (Serials) ProQuest
Wireless access
Partic in Maryland Community College Library Consortium
Special Services for the Deaf - ADA equip; Assistive tech
Special Services for the Blind - Accessible computers; Assistive/Adapted tech devices, equip & products; Screen reader software
Open Mon-Thurs 7:30am-10pm, Fri 7:30-4:30, Sat 10-5, Sun 12-4

BELCAMP

P HARFORD COUNTY PUBLIC LIBRARY*, Administrative Branch, 1221-A Brass Mill Rd, 21017-1209. SAN 344-0079. Administration Tel: 410-273-5600, 410-575-6761, 410-838-3749. FAX: 410-273-5606. Web Site: www.hcplonline.org. *Chief Exec Officer,* Mary L Hastler; Tel: 410-273-5703, E-mail: hastler@hcplonline.org; *Chief Financial Officer,* Kathy Cogar; Tel: 410-273-5646, E-mail: cogar@hcplonline.org; *Chief Operations Officer,* Daria A Parry; Tel: 410-273-5702, E-mail: parry@hcplonline.org; *Found Dir,* Jenny Dombeck; Tel: 410-273-5600, Ext 6513, E-mail: dombeck@hcplonline.org; *Human Res Dir,* Charles Ross; Tel: 410-273-5704, E-mail: ross@hcplonline.org; *Dir, Info Tech,* Ryan A Rickels; Tel: 410-273-5600, Ext 6528, E-mail: rickels@hcplonline.org; *Sr Adminr, Pub Serv,* Beth LaPenotiere; Tel: 410-273-5706, E-mail: lapenotiere@hcplonline.org; *Mkt & Communications Adminr,* Leslie Greenly Smith; Tel: 410-273-5707, E-mail: smithl@hcplonline.org; *Mat Mgt Adminr,* Jennifer Ralston; Tel: 410-273-5600, Ext 6539, E-mail: ralston@hcplonline.org
Founded 1946
Wireless access
Publications: Harford County Public Library (Annual report); Headlines & Happenings (Newsletter)
Partic in Marynet
Open Mon-Fri 8:30-5
Branches: 11
ABERDEEN BRANCH, 21 Franklin St, Aberdeen, 21001-2495, SAN 344-0109. Tel: 410-273-5608. FAX: 410-273-5610. *Br Mgr,* Jennifer Jones; E-mail: jonesj@hcplonline.org
Special Collections: African-American Coll; Parent-Teacher Coll; Ripken Literacy Center
Subject Interests: Maryland
Open Mon-Thurs 10-8, Fri & Sat 10-5, Sun (Oct-Apr) 1-5
Friends of the Library Group
ABINGDON BRANCH, 2510 Tollgate Rd, Abingdon, 21009. Tel: 410-638-3990. FAX: 410-638-3996. *Br Mgr,* Lisa Mittman; E-mail: mittman@hcplonline.org
Founded 2003
Open Mon-Thurs 10-8, Fri & Sat 10-5, Sun (Oct-Apr) 1-5
Friends of the Library Group
BEL AIR BRANCH, 100 E Pennsylvania Ave, Bel Air, 21014-3799, SAN 344-0133. Tel: 410-638-3151. FAX: 410-638-3155. *Br Mgr,* Annie Kovach; E-mail: kovach@hcplonline.org
Special Collections: Juvenile Historical Coll; LSC Coll; Parent-Teacher Coll
Subject Interests: Maryland
Special Services for the Deaf - TTY equip
Open Mon-Thurs 10-8, Fri & Sat 10-5, Sun (Oct-Apr) 1-5
Friends of the Library Group
DARLINGTON BRANCH, 1134 Main St, Darlington, 21034-1418, SAN 344-0168. Tel: 410-638-3750. FAX: 410-638-3752. *Br Mgr,* Cindy Scarpola; E-mail: scarpola@hcplonline.org
Special Collections: Parent-Teacher Coll
Subject Interests: Maryland
Open Mon-Wed 3-8, Thurs 12-5, Fri 1-5, Sat 10-2
Friends of the Library Group
EDGEWOOD BRANCH, 629 Edgewood Rd, Edgewood, 21040-2607, SAN 344-0192. Tel: 410-612-1600. FAX: 410-612-1602. *Br Mgr,* Melissa Hepler; E-mail: hepler@hcplonline.org
Special Collections: AF-AM Coll; Parent-Teacher Coll
Subject Interests: Maryland
Open Mon-Thurs 8-7:30, Fri 8-4:30, Sat 9-4:30
Friends of the Library Group
FALLSTON BRANCH, 1461 Fallston Rd, Fallston, 21047-1699, SAN 326-7059. Tel: 410-638-3003. FAX: 410-638-3005. *Br Mgr,* Tracy Miller; E-mail: millert@hcplonline.org
Special Collections: Parent-Teacher Coll
Subject Interests: Maryland
Open Mon-Thurs 10-8, Fri & Sat 10-5
Friends of the Library Group
HAVRE DE GRACE BRANCH, 120 N Union Ave, Havre de Grace, 21078-3000, SAN 344-0222. Tel: 410-939-6700. FAX: 410-939-6702. *Br Mgr,* Jamie Reilly; E-mail: reillyj@hcplonline.org
Special Collections: African-American Coll; Learn to Earn; Parent-Teacher Coll
Subject Interests: Maryland
Open Mon-Thurs 10-8, Fri & Sat 10-5
Friends of the Library Group
JARRETTSVILLE BRANCH, 3722 Norrisville Rd, Jarrettsville, 21084. Tel: 410-692-7887. FAX: 410-692-7886. *Br Mgr,* Elizabeth Bowker; E-mail: bowker@hcplonline.org
Open Mon-Thurs 10-8, Fri & Sat 10-5, Sun (Oct-Apr) 1-5
Friends of the Library Group
JOPPA BRANCH, 655 Towne Center Dr, Joppa, 21085-4497, SAN 344-0214. Tel: 410-612-1660. FAX: 410-612-1662. *Br Mgr,* Pam Taylor; E-mail: taylor@hcplonline.info
Special Collections: Parent-Teacher Coll
Subject Interests: Maryland
Open Mon-Thurs 10-8, Fri & Sat 10-5
Friends of the Library Group
NORRISVILLE BRANCH, 5310 Norrisville Rd, White Hall, 21161-8924, SAN 328-7661. Tel: 410-692-7850. FAX: 410-692-7851. *Br Mgr,* Joyce Wemer; E-mail: wemer@hcplonline.org
Open Mon-Thurs 10-8, Fri & Sat 10-5
Friends of the Library Group
WHITEFORD BRANCH, 2407 Whiteford Rd, Whiteford, 21160-1218, SAN 344-0249. Tel: 410-452-8831, 410-638-3608. FAX: 410-638-3610. *Br Mgr,* Deidrah Reeves; E-mail: reeves@hcplonline.org
Special Collections: Parent-Teacher Coll
Subject Interests: Maryland
Open Mon-Thurs 10-8, Fri & Sat 10-5
Friends of the Library Group
Bookmobiles: 2

BELTSVILLE

G UNITED STATES BUREAU OF ALCOHOL, TOBACCO, FIREARMS & EXPLOSIVES*, National Laboratory Center Library, 6000 Ammendale Rd, 20705-1250. SAN 371-1315. Tel: 202-648-6074. FAX: 202-648-6073. *Librn,* Jason Long; E-mail: jason.long@atf.gov; Staff 1 (MLS 1)
Oct 2016-Sept 2017. Mats Exp $37,000, Books $5,000, Per/Ser (Incl. Access Fees) $32,000
Library Holdings: AV Mats 25; Bk Titles 3,200; Bk Vols 4,041; Per Subs 60
Subject Interests: Analytical chem, Forensic sci
Automation Activity & Vendor Info: (Acquisitions) Ex Libris Group; (Cataloging) Ex Libris Group; (Circulation) Ex Libris Group; (ILL) OCLC WorldShare Interlibrary Loan; (OPAC) Ex Libris Group
Restriction: Staff use only

G UNITED STATES DEPARTMENT OF AGRICULTURE*, National Agricultural Library, 10301 Baltimore Ave, 20705-2351. SAN 344-0257. Tel: 301-504-5755. Administration Tel: 301-504-5248. Information Services Tel: 301-504-5788. Web Site: www.nal.usda.gov. *Dir,* Paul Wester; E-mail: Paul.Wester@ARS.USDA.GOV; *Dep Dir,* Stan Kosecki; E-mail: stan.kosecki@ars.usda.gov
Founded 1862
Library Holdings: Bk Vols 2,455,950; Per Subs 17,299
Automation Activity & Vendor Info: (Acquisitions) Ex Libris Group; (Cataloging) Ex Libris Group; (Circulation) Ex Libris Group; (ILL) Ex Libris Group; (OPAC) Ex Libris Group; (Serials) Ex Libris Group
Partic in Association of Research Libraries; OCLC Online Computer Library Center, Inc
Open Mon-Fri 9-4:30

BETHESDA

S AMERICAN OCCUPATIONAL THERAPY FOUNDATION*, Wilma L West Occupational Therapy Library, 4720 Montgomery Ln, Ste 200, 20824. Tel: 240-292-1079. FAX: 240-396-6188. E-mail: wlwlib@aotf.org. Web Site: www.aotf.org/resourceswlwlibrary. *Dir, Libr & Info Res,* Mindy Hecker; Tel: 240-292-1045, E-mail: mhecker@aotf.org; Staff 1.5 (MLS 1.5)
Founded 1980
Library Holdings: AV Mats 1,005; Bk Vols 5,466; Per Subs 60
Special Collections: A Jean Ayres Coll; AOTA Archives Coll; Gail Fidler Coll; Mary Reilly Coll
Subject Interests: Human occupation, Occupation sci, Occupational therapy, Rehabilitation
Wireless access
Function: 24/7 Online cat
Publications: Occupational Therapy Library Brochure
Partic in District of Columbia Area Health Science Libraries; National Network of Libraries of Medicine Region 1
Restriction: Authorized patrons, Open by appt only, Restricted pub use

M AMERICAN SOCIETY OF HEALTH-SYSTEM PHARMACISTS (ASHP)*, ASHP Library, 4500 East-West Hwy, Ste 900, 20814. SAN 377-1636. Tel: 301-657-3000. Web Site: www.ashp.org. *Librn,* Position Currently Open; Staff 1 (MLS 1)
Library Holdings: Bk Vols 1,200; Per Subs 500
Function: Archival coll
Restriction: By permission only, Circulates for staff only, Visitors must make appt to use bks in the libr

R BETHESDA UNITED METHODIST CHURCH LIBRARY*, 8300 Old Georgetown Rd, 20814. SAN 306-8978. Tel: 301-652-2990. FAX: 301-652-1965. E-mail: bethesdaumc@washmorefeet.org.
Founded 1956
Library Holdings: Bk Vols 4,000
Subject Interests: Biblical studies, Child welfare, Church hist, Relig
Publications: Library News (Newsletter)
Open Mon-Fri 10-5, Sun 12-2
Friends of the Library Group

S EDITORIAL PROJECTS IN EDUCATION LIBRARY*, Education Week Library, 6935 Arlington Rd, 20814. SAN 377-1237. Tel: 301-280-3100. FAX: 301-280-3200. E-mail: library@epe.org. Web Site: www.edweek.org/info/library. *Libr Dir,* Holly Peele; E-mail: hpeele@epe.org; Staff 2 (MLS 1, Non-MLS 1)
Founded 1995
Library Holdings: Bk Titles 3,898; Per Subs 223
Wireless access

SR FOURTH PRESBYTERIAN CHURCH*, Media Center, 5500 River Rd, 20816-3399. SAN 371-7321. Tel: 301-320-3600. FAX: 301-320-6315. Web Site: 4thpres.org. *Library Contact,* Jennifer Horst; Staff 5 (Non-MLS 5)
Library Holdings: Bk Titles 10,000; Per Subs 50
Automation Activity & Vendor Info: (Cataloging) Book Systems; (Circulation) Book Systems; (OPAC) Book Systems
Open Mon-Thurs 9-5, Sun 9-12:30

L LERCH, EARLY & BREWER*, Law Library, 7600 Wisconsin Ave, Ste 700, 20814. SAN 372-1035. Tel: 301-986-1300. Toll Free Tel: 800-264-8906. FAX: 301-986-0332. Web Site: www.lerchearly.com. *Librn,* Janet Camillo; E-mail: jhcamillo@lerchearly.com
Library Holdings: Bk Vols 5,000; Per Subs 35
Open Mon-Fri 8:30-6

L LINOWES & BLOCHER LLP*, Law Library, 7200 Wisconsin Ave, Ste 800, 20814. SAN 372-0608. Tel: 301-654-0504, 301-961-5163. FAX: 301-654-2801. Web Site: www.linowes-law.com. *Librn,* Donna Starkey; E-mail: dstarkey@linowes-law.com; Staff 2 (MLS 1, Non-MLS 1)
Library Holdings: Bk Vols 3,000; Per Subs 35
Subject Interests: Real estate
Automation Activity & Vendor Info: (Cataloging) Inmagic, Inc.; (Serials) Inmagic, Inc.
Restriction: Staff use only

G NATIONAL INSTITUTE OF ARTHRITIS & MUSCULOSKELETAL & SKIN DISEASES INFORMATION CLEARINGHOUSE, One AMS Circle, 20892. Tel: 301-495-4484. Toll Free Tel: 877-226-4267. FAX: 301-718-6366. TDD: 301-565-2966. E-mail: niamsinfo@mail.nih.gov. Web Site: www.niams.nih.gov.
Subject Interests: Arthritis, Bone diseases, Dermatology, Orthopedic, Osteoporosis, Rheumatology, Skin diseases, Sports
Publications: Booklets; Health topic web pages
Special Services for the Deaf - TTY equip
Restriction: Staff use only

GM NATIONAL INSTITUTES OF HEALTH LIBRARY, Ten Center Dr, Rm 1L25A, 20892. SAN 344-0400. Tel: 301-496-1080. E-mail: nihlibrary@nih.gov. Web Site: nihlibrary.nih.gov. *Actg Dir,* John Doyle; Tel: 301-827-3839, E-mail: john.doyle@nih.gov; *Br Chief,* Nancy Muir; Tel: 301-827-3839, E-mail: Nancy.Muir@nih.gov; Staff 50 (MLS 40, Non-MLS 10)
Founded 1903
Library Holdings: e-books 700; e-journals 8,500; Electronic Media & Resources 50; Bk Titles 63,000; Per Subs 8,620
Subject Interests: Biology, Chem, Health sci, Med, Physiology, Pub health
Automation Activity & Vendor Info: (Acquisitions) Innovative Interfaces, Inc; (Cataloging) Innovative Interfaces, Inc; (Circulation) Innovative Interfaces, Inc; (ILL) Relais International; (OPAC) Innovative Interfaces, Inc; (Serials) Innovative Interfaces, Inc
Wireless access
Partic in Federal Library & Information Network; OCLC Online Computer Library Center, Inc; Ser Holdings Network
Open Mon-Thurs 7:45am-8pm, Fri 7:45-6, Sat 1-5
Restriction: Non-circulating to the pub, Pub use on premises

GM NATIONAL LIBRARY OF MEDICINE*, Bldg 38, Rm 2E-17B, 8600 Rockville Pike, 20894. SAN 306-9079. Tel: 301-496-6308. Interlibrary Loan Service Tel: 301-496-5511. Toll Free Tel: 888-346-3656. FAX: 301-496-4450. E-mail: custserv@nlm.nih.gov. Web Site: www.nlm.nih.gov. *Dir,* Patricia Flatley Brennan; E-mail: patti.brennan@nih.gov; *Communications Dir,* Kathleen Cravedi; E-mail: cravedik@nlm.nih.gov
Founded 1836
Library Holdings: Bk Vols 2,500,000; Per Subs 22,500
Special Collections: Manuscripts. Oral History; US Document Depository
Subject Interests: Health sci, Med
Partic in Association of Research Libraries; National Network of Libraries of Medicine Region 1; US National Library of Medicine
Open Mon-Fri 8:30-5, Sat 8:30-12:30
Friends of the Library Group

CM UNIFORMED SERVICES UNIVERSITY OF THE HEALTH SCIENCES*, James A Zimble Learning Resource Center, 4301 Jones Bridge Rd, 20814-4799. SAN 324-2226. Tel: 301-295-3350. Circulation Tel: 301-295-3189. FAX: 301-295-3795. E-mail: lrc.services@usuhs.edu. Web Site: www.lrc.usuhs.edu. *Dir,* Alison Rollins; E-mail: alison.rollins@usuhs.edu; Staff 15 (MLS 4, Non-MLS 11)
Founded 1976. Enrl 1,100; Fac 1,000; Highest Degree: Doctorate
Library Holdings: e-books 17,000; e-journals 9,900; Bk Vols 28,000
Special Collections: US Document Depository
Subject Interests: Mil med
Automation Activity & Vendor Info: (Acquisitions) Innovative Interfaces, Inc; (Circulation) Innovative Interfaces, Inc; (Course Reserve) Innovative Interfaces, Inc; (OPAC) Innovative Interfaces, Inc; (Serials) Innovative Interfaces, Inc
Wireless access
Publications: Learning Resource Center Guides; Research Guide Series
Partic in National Network of Libraries of Medicine Region 1
Special Services for the Deaf - Staff with knowledge of sign lang
Open Mon-Thurs 7am-8pm, Fri 7-5
Friends of the Library Group

G UNITED STATES CONSUMER PRODUCT SAFETY COMMISSION LIBRARY*, 4330 East W Hwy, Rm 519, 20814. SAN 306-9001. Tel: 301-504-7570. FAX: 301-504-0124. E-mail: library@cpsc.gov. Web Site: www.cpsc.gov. *Chief Librn,* Deborah C Inyamah; Staff 2 (MLS 2)
Founded 1973
Library Holdings: Bk Titles 3,000; Per Subs 20
Special Collections: Indexed Documents Coll; Technical Standards (Standards Coll), doc, bk & micro
Subject Interests: Admin law, Bus & mgt, Econ, Engr, Health sci, Law, Med, Safety, Standards (government), Toxicology
Publications: Information Update (Newsletter); New Accessions List; User's Guide to Library & Information Services
Partic in Dun & Bradstreet Info Servs; LexisNexis; OCLC-LVIS
Open Mon-Fri 10-2
Restriction: Restricted access

BOWIE

C BOWIE STATE UNIVERSITY, Thurgood Marshall Library, 14000 Jericho Park Rd, 20715. SAN 306-9141. Tel: 301-860-3870. Circulation Tel: 301-860-3871. Reference Tel: 301-860-3862. Administration Tel: 301-860-3850. FAX: 301-860-3848. Web Site: www.bowiestate.edu/library. *Interim Dean,* Marian Rucker-Shamu; *Cataloger, Librn,* Fusako Ito; Tel: 301-860-3867, E-mail: fito@bowiestate.edu
Founded 1937
Library Holdings: Bk Vols 244,000; Per Subs 732
Special Collections: Afro-American Experience, Slave Doc; Maryland subject; Rare books; University history
Subject Interests: Art
Automation Activity & Vendor Info: (Acquisitions) OCLC ILLiad; (Cataloging) OCLC ILLiad; (Circulation) OCLC ILLiad; (Course Reserve) OCLC ILLiad; (ILL) OCLC ILLiad; (OPAC) OCLC ILLiad
Wireless access
Partic in OCLC Online Computer Library Center, Inc; Proquest Dialog
Open Mon-Thurs 8am-11pm, Fri 8-5, Sat 9-6, Sun 1-10

CAMBRIDGE

GL DORCHESTER COUNTY CIRCUIT COURT, Law Library, 206 High St, 21613. Tel: 410-228-6300. FAX: 410-221-5003. Web Site: msa.maryland.gov/msa/mdmanual/36loc/do/html/doj.html. *Law Librn,* Missy M Gallagher; E-mail: missy.gallagher@mdcourts.gov
Library Holdings: Bk Titles 40; Bk Vols 3,000
Open Mon-Fri 8:30-4:30

P DORCHESTER COUNTY PUBLIC LIBRARY*, 303 Gay St, 21613. SAN 344-0524. Tel: 410-228-7331. FAX: 410-228-6313. TDD: 410-228-0454. E-mail: dcpl@dorchesterlibrary.org. Information Services E-mail: infodesk@dorchesterlibrary.org. Web Site: www.dorchesterlibrary.org. *Dir,* Frances Cresswell; E-mail: fcresswell@dorchesterlibrary.org; Staff 7 (MLS 3, Non-MLS 4)
Founded 1922. Pop 30,400; Circ 88,657
Library Holdings: AV Mats 2,944; Electronic Media & Resources 37; Bk Titles 74,329; Bk Vols 97,329; Per Subs 153
Special Collections: Dorchester County History & Genealogy; Drama Coll; Maryland Coll

Automation Activity & Vendor Info: (Acquisitions) Innovative Interfaces, Inc - Millennium; (Cataloging) Innovative Interfaces, Inc - Millennium; (Circulation) Innovative Interfaces, Inc - Millennium; (ILL) Relais International; (OPAC) Innovative Interfaces, Inc - Millennium
Wireless access
Partic in Eastern Shore Regional Library
Special Services for the Deaf - Sign lang interpreter upon request for prog; Video relay services
Special Services for the Blind - Assistive/Adapted tech devices, equip & products; Bks on CD; Children's Braille; Copier with enlargement capabilities; Large print bks; Recorded bks; Text reader
Open Mon, Wed & Fri 10-6, Tues & Thurs 10-8, Sat 9-5
Friends of the Library Group
Branches: 1
HURLOCK BRANCH, 222 S Main St, Hurlock, 21643. (Mail add: PO Box 114, Hurlock, 21643), SAN 344-0559. Tel: 410-943-4331. FAX: 410-943-0293. *Br Mgr,* Tyvonnia Braxton; E-mail: tbraxton@dorchesterlibrary.org; Staff 3 (Non-MLS 3)
Founded 1900. Circ 37,000
Special Collections: Maryland History Coll
Function: 24/7 Electronic res, 24/7 Online cat
Special Services for the Blind - Audio mat; Children's Braille; Large print bks
Open Mon, Wed & Fri 10-6, Tues & Thurs 10-8, Sat 9-12
Friends of the Library Group

M EASTERN SHORE HOSPITAL CENTER PROFESSIONAL LIBRARY*, 5262 Woods Rd, 21613-3796. (Mail add: PO Box 800, 21613-0800), SAN 306-915X. Tel: 410-221-2385, 410-221-2485. Toll Free Tel: 888-216-8110. *Supvr, Libr Serv,* Position Currently Open
Founded 1953
Library Holdings: Bk Titles 1,000; Bk Vols 2,669; Per Subs 39
Subject Interests: Med, Nursing, Psychiat, Psychol
Wireless access
Function: ILL available
Partic in SE-Atlantic Regional Med Libr Servs; US National Library of Medicine
Restriction: Med staff only, Not open to pub

C UNIVERSITY OF MARYLAND, Center for Environmental Science, Horn Point Library, 2020 Horns Point Rd, 21613. (Mail add: PO Box 775, 21613-0775). Tel: 410-221-8450, 410-228-8200. E-mail: hpl-librarian@umces.edu. Web Site: www.umces.edu/hpl. *Chief Info Officer,* Kurt Florez; Tel: 410-221-2021, E-mail: kflorez@umces.edu; Staff 1 (MLS 1)
Founded 1972. Fac 25; Highest Degree: Doctorate
Library Holdings: Bk Titles 3,000; Bk Vols 3,350; Per Subs 97
Subject Interests: Aquaculture, Marine biol, Oceanography, Wetland ecology
Automation Activity & Vendor Info: (Serials) EBSCO Online
Wireless access
Function: ILL available
Partic in Maryland Interlibrary Loan Organization; Univ Syst of Md

CAMP SPRINGS

S TRANSPORTATION INSTITUTE*, Information Resources Center, 5201 Auth Way, 5th Flr, 20746. SAN 302-7902. Tel: 301-423-3335. FAX: 301-423-0634. Web Site: transportationinstitute.org. *Mgr,* Robyn Farrell
Founded 1968
Library Holdings: AV Mats 82; Bk Titles 1,289; Per Subs 34
Subject Interests: Water transportation
Open Mon-Fri 9-5

CAPITOL HEIGHTS

C MAPLE SPRINGS BAPTIST BIBLE COLLEGE & SEMINARY LIBRARY*, Instructional Resources Center, 4130 Belt Rd, 20743. Tel: 301-736-3631. FAX: 301-735-6507. *Dir,* Darren Jones; E-mail: darren.jones@msbbcs.edu; *Librn,* Valerie Foster; E-mail: vnfoster@hotmail.com; *Cat,* Geraldine Nelson
Founded 1986. Enrl 253; Highest Degree: Doctorate
Library Holdings: Bk Titles 6,000
Partic in OCLC Online Computer Library Center, Inc
Open Mon-Fri 8:30-5:30

CATONSVILLE

J COMMUNITY COLLEGE OF BALTIMORE COUNTY*, Catonsville Library, Y Bldg, 800 S Rolling Rd, 21228. SAN 343-7949. Circulation Tel: 443-840-2710. Reference Tel: 443-840-2730. FAX: 410-455-6436. E-mail: crefdesk@ccbcmd.edu. Web Site: library.ccbcmd.edu. *Dir, Libr Serv,* Cynthia Roberts; Tel: 443-840-4589, E-mail: croberts@ccbcmd.edu; Staff 22 (MLS 7, Non-MLS 15)
Founded 1957. Enrl 10,500; Fac 200; Highest Degree: Associate
Library Holdings: e-books 187; Bk Titles 105,246; Bk Vols 110,481; Per Subs 450
Subject Interests: Automotive tech, Computer graphics, Construction mgt, Construction tech, Criminal justice, Environ sci, Info tech, Mortuary sci, Network tech, Nursing, Teacher educ, Visual communications
Automation Activity & Vendor Info: (Acquisitions) Innovative Interfaces, Inc; (Cataloging) Innovative Interfaces, Inc; (Circulation) Innovative Interfaces, Inc; (Course Reserve) Innovative Interfaces, Inc; (ILL) Innovative Interfaces, Inc; (Media Booking) Innovative Interfaces, Inc; (OPAC) Innovative Interfaces, Inc; (Serials) Innovative Interfaces, Inc
Wireless access
Function: Computers for patron use, Doc delivery serv, Electronic databases & coll, ILL available, Magnifiers for reading, Online cat, Photocopying/Printing, Ref & res, VHS videos
Partic in Maryland Community College Library Consortium
Special Services for the Deaf - Videos & decoder
Special Services for the Blind - Audio mat; Reader equip; Talking bk & rec for the blind cat; Variable speed audiotape players; VisualTek equip
Restriction: Open to pub upon request
Departmental Libraries:
DUNDALK LIBRARY, Sollers Point Rd, COMM Bldg 7200, Baltimore, 21222, SAN 306-834X. Circulation Tel: 443-840-2591. Reference Tel: 443-840-2592. FAX: 443-840-3559. E-mail: dlibrary@ccbcmd.edu. *Dir, Libr Serv,* Cynthia Roberts; E-mail: croberts@ccbcmd.edu
Founded 1971. Enrl 1,600; Fac 125; Highest Degree: Associate
Library Holdings: Bk Vols 36,000; Per Subs 125
Subject Interests: Chem dependency, Criminal justice, Dental hygiene, Nursing, Sustainable horticulture
Automation Activity & Vendor Info: (Acquisitions) Innovative Interfaces, Inc - Millennium; (Cataloging) Innovative Interfaces, Inc - Millennium; (Circulation) Innovative Interfaces, Inc - Millennium; (Course Reserve) Innovative Interfaces, Inc - Millennium; (Discovery) EBSCO Discovery Service; (Media Booking) Innovative Interfaces, Inc - Millennium; (OPAC) Innovative Interfaces, Inc - Millennium; (Serials) Innovative Interfaces, Inc - Millennium
Partic in Maryland Interlibrary Loan Organization
Open Mon-Thurs (Fall & Spring) 7:45am-10pm, Fri 7:45-4:30, Sat 10-3; Mon-Thurs (Summer) 8:30-7:30, Fri 8:30-4:30

M SPRING GROVE HOSPITAL CENTER*, Staff Library, Tuerk Bldg, 55 Wade Ave, 21228. SAN 306-9168. Tel: 410-402-7040. FAX: 410-402-7732. Web Site: health.maryland.gov/springgrove/Pages/Department_LearningResources.aspx. *Dir,* Karima Orpia; E-mail: karima.orpia@maryland.gov
Founded 1938
Library Holdings: Bk Titles 2,100; Per Subs 26
Special Collections: American Journal of Insanity, 1846-1921; Hospital Reports from 1897
Restriction: Staff use only

CENTREVILLE

P QUEEN ANNE'S COUNTY FREE LIBRARY*, Centerville Branch, 121 S Commerce St, 21617. SAN 306-9176. Tel: 410-758-0980. FAX: 410-758-0614. E-mail: info@qaclibrary.org. Web Site: www.qaclibrary.org. *Dir,* Janet Salazar; E-mail: janet@qaclibrary.org; *Asst Dir,* Kim Baklarz; E-mail: kim@qaclibrary.org; Staff 21 (MLS 7, Non-MLS 14)
Founded 1909. Pop 47,000; Circ 400,000
Library Holdings: Bk Vols 100,305; Per Subs 10
Subject Interests: Local hist
Automation Activity & Vendor Info: (Circulation) SirsiDynix
Wireless access
Partic in Eastern Shore Regional Library; Maryland Interlibrary Loan Organization
Open Mon-Thurs 9-8, Fri & Sat 9-5, Sun 1-4
Friends of the Library Group
Branches: 1
KENT ISLAND BRANCH, 200 Library Circle, Stevensville, 21666-4026, SAN 376-9860. Tel: 410-643-8161. FAX: 410-643-7098. *Mgr,* Peggy Ranson; E-mail: pransom@quan.lib.md.us
Automation Activity & Vendor Info: (Circulation) SirsiDynix
Open Mon-Thurs 10-8, Fri & Sat 9-5

CHARLOTTE HALL

P SOUTHERN MARYLAND REGIONAL LIBRARY ASSOCIATION, INC*, 37600 New Market Rd, 20622-3041. (Mail add: PO Box 459, 20622-0459), SAN 306-9826. Tel: 301-843-3634, 301-884-0436, 301-934-9442. FAX: 301-884-0438. E-mail: smrla@somd.lib.md.us. Web Site: cosmos.somd.lib.md.us. *Chief Exec Officer,* Sharan D Marshall; E-mail: smarshall@smrla.org; *Head, Info Serv,* Jennifer Falkowski; E-mail: jfalkowski@somd.lib.md.us; *Head, Tech Serv,* Susan Grant; E-mail: sgrant@somd.lib.md.us; *Communications Mgr,* Victoria Falcon; E-mail: vfalcon@somd.lib.md.us; *Training Coordr,* Jennifer Hopwood; E-mail: jhopwood@somd.lib.md.us; Staff 16 (MLS 4, Non-MLS 12)

Founded 1959. Circ 355,742
Special Collections: State Document Depository
Automation Activity & Vendor Info: (Acquisitions) Innovative Interfaces, Inc; (Cataloging) Innovative Interfaces, Inc; (Circulation) Innovative Interfaces, Inc; (ILL) Innovative Interfaces, Inc; (OPAC) Innovative Interfaces, Inc
Wireless access
Function: 24/7 Electronic res, 24/7 Online cat, ILL available
Member Libraries: Calvert Library; Charles County Public Library; Saint Mary's County Library
Open Mon-Fri 8:30-4:30

CHESTERTOWN

P KENT COUNTY PUBLIC LIBRARY*, 408 High St, 21620-1312. SAN 306-9184. Tel: 410-778-3636. FAX: 410-778-6756. E-mail: referencedesk@kent.lib.md.us. Web Site: www.kentcountylibrary.org. *Dir,* Jackie Adams; E-mail: jadams@kent.lib.md.us; Staff 12 (MLS 4, Non-MLS 8)
Founded 1961. Pop 19,200; Circ 140,000
Automation Activity & Vendor Info: (Acquisitions) Evergreen; (Cataloging) Evergreen; (Circulation) Evergreen; (ILL) Relais International; (OPAC) Evergreen; (Serials) Evergreen
Wireless access
Partic in Eastern Shore Regional Library; Maryland Interlibrary Loan Organization
Open Mon, Tues & Thurs 9-6, Wed 9-8, Fri 9-5, Sat 9-3
Friends of the Library Group
Branches: 2
NORTH COUNTY, 111-B1 N Main St, Galena, 21635. Tel: 410-648-5380. *Mgr,* Jeanne Geibel
Open Tues & Thurs 10-6, Fri 10-5, Sat 10-2
Friends of the Library Group
ROCK HALL, Rock Hall Municipal Bldg, 5585 Main St, Rock Hall, 21661, SAN 376-8090. Tel: 410-639-7162. *Mgr,* Jeanne Geibel
Open Mon 9-3, Wed 12-6, Fri 9-4, Sat 9-1
Friends of the Library Group

C WASHINGTON COLLEGE*, Clifton M Miller Library, 300 Washington Ave, 21620. SAN 306-9192. Tel: 410-778-7280. FAX: 410-778-7288. Web Site: www.washcoll.edu/academics/library-and-academic-technology. *Dean of Libr,* Mary Alice Ball; E-mail: mball2@washcoll.edu; *Chief Academic Tech Officer,* Sharon Sledge; E-mail: ssledge2@washcoll.edu; Staff 10 (MLS 4, Non-MLS 6)
Founded 1782. Enrl 1,180; Fac 116; Highest Degree: Bachelor
Library Holdings: e-books 2,000; e-journals 15,076; Bk Titles 157,263; Bk Vols 171,830; Per Subs 602
Special Collections: Maryland Coll. US Document Depository
Automation Activity & Vendor Info: (Acquisitions) Innovative Interfaces, Inc; (Cataloging) Innovative Interfaces, Inc; (Circulation) Innovative Interfaces, Inc; (Course Reserve) Docutek; (ILL) OCLC WorldShare Interlibrary Loan; (Media Booking) Innovative Interfaces, Inc; (OPAC) Innovative Interfaces, Inc; (Serials) Innovative Interfaces, Inc
Wireless access
Publications: Miller Library (Newsletter); Reference Guide Brochures
Partic in OCLC Online Computer Library Center, Inc
Special Services for the Blind - Assistive/Adapted tech devices, equip & products
Open Mon-Thurs 8am-Midnight, Fri 8-6:30, Sat 10-6, Sun 10am-Midnight
Friends of the Library Group

CHEVERLY

M UNIVERSITY OF MARYLAND PRINCE GEORGE'S HOSPITAL CENTER*, Saul Schwartzbach Memorial Library, 3001 Hospital Dr, 20785-1193. SAN 306-9206. Tel: 301-618-2000, Ext 82490, 301-618-2490. FAX: 301-618-2493. *Library Contact,* Jane Ogora; E-mail: jane.ogora@dimensionshealth.org
Founded 1944
Library Holdings: Bk Titles 1,500; Bk Vols 5,500; Per Subs 160
Automation Activity & Vendor Info: (Acquisitions) CyberTools for Libraries; (Cataloging) CyberTools for Libraries; (ILL) CyberTools for Libraries
Partic in National Network of Libraries of Medicine Region 1
Restriction: Staff use only

CHEVY CHASE

R OHR KODESH CONGREGATION*, Salzberg Library, 8300 Meadowbrook Lane, 20815. SAN 373-059X. Tel: 301-589-3880. FAX: 301-495-4801. Web Site: ohrkodesh.org/library. *Librn,* Brenda Sislen Bergstein; E-mail: brenda.bergstein@gmail.com
Library Holdings: DVDs 200; Bk Vols 2,000
Subject Interests: Jewish hist, Judaica
Wireless access
Open Mon-Fri 8-5, Sat 12-1, Sun 9-11

CLARKSBURG

S FOI SERVICES INC LIBRARY*, 23219 Stringtown Rd, #240, 20871-9363. SAN 329-8744. Tel: 301-975-9400. FAX: 301-975-9400. E-mail: infofoi@foiservices.com. Web Site: www.foiservices.com. *Pres,* Marlene S Bobka; E-mail: mbobka@foiservices.com
Founded 1975
Special Collections: FDA Records
Subject Interests: Approval of pharmaceuticals, Regulation of pharmaceuticals
Open Mon-Fri 9-5

CLINTON

S MARYLAND NATIONAL CAPITAL PARK & PLANNING COMMISSION, James O Hall Research Center Library, 9118 Brandywine Rd, 20735. SAN 371-8697. Tel: 301-868-1121. Administration Tel: 301-868-6185. FAX: 301-868-8177. Web Site: www.surrattmuseum.org/. *Dir,* Laurie Verge; E-mail: laurie.verge@pgparks.com; *Research Librn,* Colleen Puterbaugh; E-mail: colleen.puterbaugh@pgparks.com; Staff 1 (Non-MLS 1)
Founded 2002
Library Holdings: Bk Vols 2,000
Special Collections: Andrew Jampoler Papers; Constance Young Papers; Dyer Freedom Papers; General William Tidwell Papers; James O. Hall Papers; John C. Brennan Papers; Surratt Museum Papers; William C. Davis Papers
Subject Interests: Civil War
Wireless access
Function: Archival coll, For res purposes, Microfiche/film & reading machines, Ref & res, Res assist avail, Res libr, Wheelchair accessible
Restriction: Access at librarian's discretion, Closed stack, Not a lending libr, Open by appt only
Friends of the Library Group

COLLEGE PARK

S AMERICAN INSTITUTE OF PHYSICS*, Niels Bohr Library, One Physics Ellipse, 20740-3843. SAN 311-5844. Tel: 301-209-3177. FAX: 301-209-3144. E-mail: nbl@aip.org. Web Site: aip.org/history-programs/niels-bohr-library. *Dir,* Melanie Mueller; *Asst Dir,* Allison Rein; *Photo Librn,* Audrey Lengel; *Archivist,* Chip Calhoun; *Archivist,* Amanda Nelson; *Asst Archivist,* Sarah Cochrane; Staff 8 (MLS 6, Non-MLS 2)
Founded 1962
Library Holdings: Bk Titles 16,400; Per Subs 75
Special Collections: History of Astronomy, 1850-1960, misc; History of Physics, 1850-1950, archives, autobiog, bks, dissertations, ms, notebks, oral hist mat, per, photog
Subject Interests: Astronomy, Hist of physics, Physics
Automation Activity & Vendor Info: (Acquisitions) SirsiDynix; (Cataloging) SirsiDynix; (OPAC) SirsiDynix; (Serials) SirsiDynix
Publications: Guide to the Archival Collection of the AIP Niels Bohr Library; National Catalog of Sources for History of Physics; Newsletter
Open Mon-Fri 8:30-5
Friends of the Library Group

G NATIONAL ARCHIVES & RECORDS ADMINISTRATION, Archives Library Information Center, 8601 Adelphi Rd, Rm 2500, 20740. SAN 336-9064. Tel: 301-837-2000, 301-837-3415. FAX: 301-837-0459. E-mail: alic@nara.gov. Web Site: www.archives.gov/research/alic. *Dir,* Jeffery Hartley; Tel: 301-837-1795; Staff 1 (MLS 1)
Founded 1934
Library Holdings: Bk Titles 102,200; Bk Vols 170,000; Per Subs 300
Special Collections: Archival Record Set of Publications of the United States Government; Archives & Records Management Literature; Federal Government Publications Issued by the Government Printing Office; United States History, bks, per
Automation Activity & Vendor Info: (Acquisitions) Cuadra Associates, Inc; (Cataloging) Cuadra Associates, Inc; (Circulation) Cuadra Associates, Inc
Wireless access
Partic in Federal Library & Information Network; OCLC Online Computer Library Center, Inc; OCLC Research Library Partnership
Open Mon-Fri 9-4

C UNIVERSITY OF MARYLAND LIBRARIES*, 20742. SAN 344-0583. Tel: 301-405-9128. FAX: 301-314-9408. Web Site: www.lib.umd.edu. *Interim Dean of Libr,* Babak Hamidzadeh; E-mail: babak1@umd.edu; Staff 207 (MLS 78, Non-MLS 129)
Founded 1813. Enrl 37,631; Fac 4,248; Highest Degree: Doctorate
Library Holdings: AV Mats 289,839; e-books 599,198; e-journals 22,497; Bk Vols 4,094,341; Per Subs 12,808

Special Collections: Books in Many Scholarly Fields; Broadcast Pioneers Library; East Asia Coll, misc; Gordon W Prange Coll, archives & ms; International Piano Archives at Maryland; Katherine Anne Porter Coll, bks, ms, memorabilia; Maryland State Documents; Marylandia, bks, ms; Music Educators' National Conference Historical Center Coll, misc; National & International Music Organizations Coll; National Public Broadcasting Archives; National Trust for Historic Preservation Library Coll; Official Records & Publications of the University of Maryland at College Park; Oral History Records, memorabilia; Personal Papers & Textual Manuscripts of American & English Authors of the Modern Period; Personal/Family Papers; Rare Bks; Records of Organizations, photog; Special Coll of Papers of Maryland Political Figures. Oral History; State Document Depository; US Document Depository
Automation Activity & Vendor Info: (Acquisitions) Ex Libris Group; (Cataloging) Ex Libris Group; (Circulation) Ex Libris Group; (ILL) Ex Libris Group; (OPAC) Ex Libris Group; (Serials) Ex Libris Group
Wireless access
Function: Archival coll
Publications: Library Bulletin; Library Issues
Partic in Association of Research Libraries; Association of Southeastern Research Libraries; Big Ten Academic Alliance; Center for Research Libraries; Chesapeake Information & Research Library Alliance; Northeast Research Libraries Consortium; OCLC Research Library Partnership
Open Mon-Thurs 8am-11pm, Fri 8-8, Sat 10-8, Sun Noon-11
Friends of the Library Group

Departmental Libraries:

ARCHITECTURE LIBRARY, Bldg 145, Rm 1102, 3835 Campus Dr, 20742. Tel: 301-405-6317. FAX: 301-314-9583. Web Site: www.lib.umd.edu/architecture. *Head of Libr,* Cynthia Frank; Tel: 301-405-6321, E-mail: cfrank@umd.edu
Founded 1967
Library Holdings: Bk Vols 41,294; Per Subs 158
Special Collections: World Expositions from 1851-1937
Subject Interests: Archit, Landscape archit
Automation Activity & Vendor Info: (Cataloging) Ex Libris Group; (Circulation) Ex Libris Group; (OPAC) Ex Libris Group
Open Mon-Thurs 11-4

ART LIBRARY, Art/Sociology Bldg, 2nd Flr, 2213 Parren Mitchell, 20742. Tel: 301-405-9061. Interlibrary Loan Service Tel: 301-405-9178. Interlibrary Loan Service FAX: 301-314-9416. Web Site: www.lib.umd.edu/art. *Art Librn,* Patricia Kosco Cossard; Tel: 301-405-9065, E-mail: pcossard@umd.edu. Subject Specialists: *Art hist, Studio art,* Patricia Kosco Cossard; Staff 2 (MLS 1, Non-MLS 1)
Founded 1979. Highest Degree: Doctorate
Library Holdings: Bk Vols 84,441; Per Subs 394
Special Collections: Art Exhibition Catalog Coll; Decimal Index Art of Low Countries; Emblem Books; Index Photographique de l'art de France; Marburg Index
Automation Activity & Vendor Info: (Acquisitions) Ex Libris Group; (Cataloging) Ex Libris Group; (Circulation) Ex Libris Group; (OPAC) Ex Libris Group

BROADCAST PIONEERS LIBRARY OF AMERICAN BROADCASTING, Hornbake Library, 20742, SAN 302-6000. Tel: 301-405-9160. FAX: 301-314-2634. E-mail: labcast@umd.edu. Web Site: www.lib.umd.edu/special/collections/massmedia. *Curator,* Laura Schnitker; E-mail: lschnitk@umd.edu; *Ref,* Michael Henry; E-mail: mlhenry@umd.edu; Staff 4 (MLS 3, Non-MLS 1)
Founded 1971
Library Holdings: Bk Titles 5,768; Bk Vols 9,550; Per Subs 382
Special Collections: "Wisdom" Coll; Alois Havrilla Coll, photog; Arthur Godfrey Coll; BMI Coll, a-tapes; Edythe J Meserand Coll; Elmo Neale Pickerill Coll; Jane Barton Coll, photog; Joseph E Baudino Coll; National Association of Broadcasters Coll; Peter H Bontsema Coll; Radio Advertising Bureau Coll, recording; Ray Stanich Coll; Robert E Lee Coll; Rod E Phillips Coll; St Louis Post-Dispatch Coll, photog; Westinghouse Broadcasting News Coll, a-tapes; William S Hedges Coll. Oral History
Subject Interests: Radio, Television
Open Mon, Tues, Thurs & Fri 10-5, Wed 10-8, Sat 12-5

ENGINEERING & PHYSICAL SCIENCES LIBRARY, William E Kirwan Hall, Rm 1403, 4176 Campus Dr, 20742. Tel: 301-405-9157. Interlibrary Loan Service Tel: 301-405-9178. Interlibrary Loan Service FAX: 301-314-9416. Web Site: www.lib.umd.edu/stem. *Head of Libr,* Nevenka Zdravkovska; Tel: 301-405-9144, E-mail: nevenka@umd.edu; *Agr & Natural Res Librn,* Stephanie Ritchie; Tel: 301-405-9153, E-mail: sritchie@umd.edu; Staff 7 (MLS 3, Non-MLS 4)
Founded 1953
Library Holdings: Bk Vols 397,125; Per Subs 1,450
Special Collections: Rand Corp Coll; Technical Reports (NASA & NACA, its predecessor); US Patent & Trademark Coll
Subject Interests: Engr, Phys sci

R LEE HORNBAKE LIBRARY, 0300 Hornbake Library Bldg, North Wing, 20742-7011, SAN 344-0788. Tel: 301-405-9236. FAX: 301-314-9419. E-mail: nonprint@umd.edu. Web Site: www.lib.umd.edu/lms. *Head, Nonprint Media Serv,* Carleton L Jackson; Tel: 301-405-9226, E-mail: carleton@umd.edu. Subject Specialists: *Media, Tech,* Carleton L Jackson
Special Collections: Public Television Archives Colls include: Maryland Public Television, Corporation for Public Broadcasting & NAEB Radio Programs
Function: AV serv, Computers for patron use, Electronic databases & coll, Spoken cassettes & CDs, Spoken cassettes & DVDs, VHS videos
Restriction: Borrowing privileges limited to fac & registered students

THEODORE R MCKELDIN LIBRARY, 7649 Library Lane, 20742-7011. Tel: 301-314-9046. Circulation Tel: 301-405-9095. Interlibrary Loan Service Tel: 301-405-9178. FAX: 301-314-9408. Interlibrary Loan Service FAX: 301-314-9416. Web Site: www.lib.umd.edu/mckeldin. *Interim Dean of Libr,* Babak A Hamidzadeh; E-mail: babak1@umd.edu; *Head, Spec Coll,* Kathy Glennan; E-mail: kglennan@umd.edu; *Acq,* Sudesh Angie Bhagat; Tel: 301-405-9306, E-mail: sbhagat1@umd.edu; *Terrapin Learning Commons & Student Support Serv,* Kevin Hammett; E-mail: hammett@umd.edu
Special Collections: Delaware, DC & Maryland Regional Document Depository; East Asia (Chinese, Japanese & Korean Language Publications); Gordon W Prange Coll; Katherine Ann Porter Room, bks, memorabilia, photogs; Marylandia; National Trust for Historic Preservation
Subject Interests: Rare bks
Special Services for the Deaf - TDD equip

MICHELLE SMITH PERFORMING ARTS LIBRARY, 8270 Alumni Dr, 20742-1630. Tel: 301-405-9217. Reference Tel: 301-314-1316 (Theatre & Dance), 301-405-9256 (Music). FAX: 301-314-7170. Web Site: www.lib.umd.edu/mspal. *Head of Libr, Music Librn,* Stephen Henry; E-mail: shenry@umd.edu; *Theatre, Dance & Performance Studies Librn,* Drew Baker; Tel: 301-314-0535, E-mail: dbaker@umd.edu; *Circ & Reserves Supvr,* Mary Scott; Tel: 301-405-9223, E-mail: mscott1@umd.edu; *Evening/Weekend Supvr,* Bruce Tennant; Tel: 301-405-9218, E-mail: btennant@umd.edu; *Curator,* Vincent J Novara; Tel: 301-405-9220, E-mail: vnovara@umd.edu; *Curator, Intl Piano Archives at Maryland,* Donald Manildi; Tel: 301-405-9224, E-mail: godowsky@umd.edu. Subject Specialists: *Music,* Stephen Henry; *Spec coll,* Vincent J Novara; Staff 4 (MLS 2, Non-MLS 2)
Founded 1982. Fac 4; Highest Degree: Doctorate
Library Holdings: Bk Vols 101,162; Per Subs 345
Special Collections: Arts Education (Charles Fowler Papers); Handeliana (Jacob Coppersmith Coll); International Piano Archives at Maryland; Musical Americana (Irving & Magery Lowens Coll); National & International Music Organization Coll

WHITE MEMORIAL CHEMISTRY LIBRARY, 4176 Campus Dr, 20742. Tel: 301-405-9078. Reference Tel: 301-405-9080. FAX: 301-405-9164. Web Site: www.lib.umd.edu/chem/stem. *Head Librn,* Svetla Baykoucheva; E-mail: sbaykouc@umd.edu; Staff 4 (MLS 2, Non-MLS 2)
Founded 1975
Library Holdings: Bk Vols 85,380; Per Subs 455
Subject Interests: Biochem, Chem, Microbiology, Molecular genetics
Friends of the Library Group

COLUMBIA

J HOWARD COMMUNITY COLLEGE LIBRARY*, 10901 Little Patuxent Pkwy, 2nd Flr, 21044. SAN 306-9338. Tel: 443-518-1460. FAX: 443-518-4993. Web Site: www.howardcc.edu/services-support/library. *Dir, Libr & Learning Commons,* Nana Owusu-Nkwantabisa; Tel: 443-518-4634, E-mail: nowusunkwantabisa@howardcc.edu; *Asst Dir, Information Literacy Coord,* Gail Hollander; Tel: 443-518-4633, E-mail: ghollander@howardcc.edu; *Digital Res Librn,* Amy Krug; Tel: 443-518-4788, E-mail: akrug@howardcc.edu; *Ref Librn,* Robert Garber; Tel: 443-518-1450, E-mail: rgarber@howardcc.edu; *Access Serv, Syst Librn,* Apichart Chalungsooth; Tel: 443-518-4683, E-mail: chalungsooth@howardcc.edu; Staff 13 (MLS 6, Non-MLS 7)
Founded 1970. Enrl 2,932; Fac 730; Highest Degree: Associate
Jul 2012-Jun 2013 Income $882,462. Mats Exp $267,117, Books $47,494, Per/Ser (Incl. Access Fees) $3,100, Electronic Ref Mat (Incl. Access Fees) $216,066. Sal $577,079 (Prof $413,389)
Library Holdings: AV Mats 5,281; CDs 1,457; DVDs 751; e-books 2,406; e-journals 51,602; Bk Titles 39,260; Bk Vols 45,776; Per Subs 51,669; Videos 1,875
Subject Interests: Art, Nursing
Automation Activity & Vendor Info: (Acquisitions) SirsiDynix; (Cataloging) SirsiDynix; (Circulation) SirsiDynix; (Course Reserve) SirsiDynix; (OPAC) SirsiDynix; (Serials) SirsiDynix
Wireless access
Function: Archival coll, Audio & video playback equip for onsite use, Bk club(s), Computers for patron use, E-Reserves, Electronic databases & coll, ILL available, Internet access, Magnifiers for reading, Music CDs, Online cat, Online ref, Orientations, Photocopying/Printing, Ref & res, Ref serv available, Telephone ref, VHS videos, Wheelchair accessible
Partic in LYRASIS; Maryland Community College Library Consortium; OCLC Online Computer Library Center, Inc

Special Services for the Blind - Accessible computers; Aids for in-house use; ZoomText magnification & reading software
Open Mon-Thurs 8am-11pm, Fri 8-5, Sat & Sun 1-5

C JOHNS HOPKINS UNIVERSITY LIBRARIES*, School of Professional Studies in Business & Education Library, 6740 Alexander Bell Dr, 21040. Tel: 410-516-9700, 410-516-9709. Web Site: www.library.jhu.edu. *Librn,* Michael Houck; E-mail: michael.houck@jhu.edu
Library Holdings: Bk Titles 500; Per Subs 51
Open Mon-Thurs 8:30am-10pm, Fri & Sat 8:30-5

S MARYLAND PHARMACISTS ASSOCIATION LIBRARY*, 9115 Guilford Rd, Ste 200, 21046. SAN 327-814X. Tel: 443-583-8000. FAX: 443-583-8006. E-mail: admin@mdpha.com. Web Site: www.marylandpharmacist.org. *Exec Dir,* Aliyah Horton; E-mail: aliyah.horton@mdpha.com
Library Holdings: Bk Titles 1,200; Per Subs 40
Restriction: Open by appt only

CUMBERLAND

J ALLEGANY COLLEGE OF MARYLAND LIBRARY*, Donald L Alexander Library, 12401 Willowbrook Rd SE, 21502. SAN 306-9354. Tel: 301-784-5269. Interlibrary Loan Service Tel: 301-784-5241. Reference Tel: 301-784-5138. FAX: 301-784-5017. Web Site: www.allegany.edu/library. *Dir, Learning Commons,* Julie Rando; E-mail: jrando@allegany.edu; *Coordr, Libr Serv/Libr Instruction/Ref,* Teresa Wilmes; Tel: 301-784-5294, E-mail: twilmes@allegany.edu; *Cat/Ref/Libr Instruction,* Barbara Browning; Tel: 301-784-5240; *Cat/Ref/Libr Instruction,* Matthew Hay; Tel: 301-784-5366; Staff 4 (MLS 4)
Founded 1961. Enrl 3,905; Fac 227; Highest Degree: Associate
Library Holdings: Bk Titles 49,081; Bk Vols 56,554; Per Subs 182
Special Collections: Local Hist (Appalachian Coll). Oral History; US Document Depository
Subject Interests: Allied health, Criminal law & justice, Soc sci & issues
Automation Activity & Vendor Info: (Acquisitions) Infor Library & Information Solutions; (Cataloging) Infor Library & Information Solutions; (Circulation) Infor Library & Information Solutions; (Course Reserve) Infor Library & Information Solutions; (OPAC) Infor Library & Information Solutions; (Serials) Infor Library & Information Solutions
Wireless access
Function: Audio & video playback equip for onsite use, CD-ROM, Computers for patron use, Electronic databases & coll, ILL available, Online cat, Photocopying/Printing, Ref serv available, Telephone ref, VHS videos, Wheelchair accessible
Publications: Bibliographies & User Guides; Western Maryland Materials Union List
Partic in Maryland Community College Library Consortium
Open Mon-Thurs 8am-9pm, Fri 8:30-4:30, Sat 11-5

L ALLEGANY COUNTY CIRCUIT COURT LAW LIBRARY*, Allegany County Circuit Courthouse, 30 Washington St, 21502. SAN 306-9362. Tel: 301-777-5925. FAX: 301-777-2055. *Court Adminr,* Anne M SanGiovanni
Subject Interests: Law
Wireless access
Open Mon-Fri 8:30-4:30

P ALLEGANY COUNTY LIBRARY SYSTEM*, 31 Washington St, 21502. SAN 344-0974. Tel: 301-777-1200. FAX: 301-777-7299. E-mail: washingtonstlibrary@alleganycountylibrary.info. Web Site: www.alleganycountylibrary.info. *Exec Dir,* John Taube; E-mail: jtaube@alleganycountylibrary.info; *IT Dir,* Jason Armstrong; E-mail: jarmstrong@alleganycountylibrary.info; *Libr Serv Dir,* Lisa McKenney; E-mail: lmckenney@alleganycountylibrary.info; *Programming Dir,* Jennifer Howell; E-mail: jhowell@alleganycountylibrary.info; *Br Mgr,* Laura Deneen
Founded 1924. Pop 73,000; Circ 450,000
Jul 2015-Jun 2016. Mats Exp $210,000. Sal $1,341,000
Library Holdings: Bk Vols 56,179; Per Subs 144
Special Collections: Western Maryland (Maryland History & Genealogy)
Automation Activity & Vendor Info: (Cataloging) TLC (The Library Corporation); (Circulation) TLC (The Library Corporation); (ILL) Relais International; (OPAC) TLC (The Library Corporation)
Wireless access
Function: 24/7 Electronic res, 24/7 Online cat, Activity rm, Adult bk club
Mem of Western Maryland Regional Library
Open Mon & Thurs 1-8, Tues, Wed, Fri & Sat 10-5
Friends of the Library Group
Branches: 5
FROSTBURG PUBLIC, 65 E Main St, Frostburg, 21532, SAN 344-1008. Tel: 301-687-0790. FAX: 301-687-0791. E-mail: frostburglibrary@alleganycountylibrary.info. *Br Mgr,* Connie Wilson
Open Mon, Tues, Fri & Sat 10-5, Wed &Thur 1-8
Friends of the Library Group
GEORGE'S CREEK, 76 Main St, Lonaconing, 21539. Tel: 301-463-2629. FAX: 301-463-2485. E-mail: gcreeklibrary@alleganycountylibrary.info. *Br Mgr,* Regina Spiker
Open Mon-Tues 10-5, Wed-Thu 1-8, Sat 9-5
Friends of the Library Group
LAVALE BRANCH, 815 National Hwy, LaVale, 21502, SAN 344-1032. Tel: 301-729-0855. FAX: 301-729-3490. E-mail: lavalelibrary@alleganycountylibrary.info. *Br Mgr,* Elizabeth Sell
Closed for renovation 2021-
Friends of the Library Group
SOUTH CUMBERLAND LIBRARY, 100 Seymour St, 21502, SAN 344-1067. Tel: 301-724-1607. FAX: 301-724-1504. E-mail: southlibrary@alleganycountylibrary.info. *Br Mgr,* Sarah McGuire
Open Mon, Thurs, Fri & Sat 10-5, Tues & Wed 1-8
Friends of the Library Group
WESTERNPORT LIBRARY, 66 Main St, Westernport, 21562, SAN 344-1091. Tel: 301-359-0455. FAX: 301-359-0046. E-mail: westernportlibrary@alleganycountylibrary.info. *Br Mgr,* Kathy Murphy
Open Tues 1-8, Wed-Sat 10-5
Friends of the Library Group

§S NORTH BRANCH CORRECTIONAL INSTITUTION LIBRARY, 14100 McMullen Hwy, 21502. Tel: 301-729-7602. FAX: 301-729-7603. Web Site: www.dpscs.state.md.us/locations/nbci.shtml. *Librn,* Rebecca Hammons; E-mail: rebecca.hammons@maryland.gov
Restriction: Not open to pub

S WESTERN CORRECTIONAL INSTITUTION LIBRARY*, 13800 McMullen Hwy SW, 21502. Tel: 301-729-7184. FAX: 301-729-7150. Web Site: www.dpscs.state.md.us/locations/wci.shtml. *Librn,* Liam Kennedy; E-mail: liam.kennedy@maryland.gov; Staff 1 (MLS 1)
Founded 1996
Library Holdings: Bk Vols 9,500; Per Subs 26
Automation Activity & Vendor Info: (Cataloging) Follett Software; (Circulation) Follett Software
Function: Bk club(s), Computers for patron use, Electronic databases & coll, For res purposes, Homebound delivery serv, Jail serv, Legal assistance to inmates, Magazines, Magnifiers for reading, Photocopying/Printing, Ref & res, Ref serv available, Spanish lang bks
Restriction: Inmate patrons, facility staff & vols direct access. All others through ILL only

DENTON

P CAROLINE COUNTY PUBLIC LIBRARY*, 100 Market St, 21629. SAN 344-1121. Tel: 410-479-1343. Administration Tel: 410-479-2254. FAX: 410-479-1443. Administration FAX: 410-479-4935. E-mail: info@carolib.org. Web Site: www.carolib.org. *Exec Dir,* Deborah A Bennett; E-mail: dbennett@carolib.org; *Br Mgr,* Ann M Reinecke; E-mail: areinecke@carolib.org; *IT Mgr,* John Courie; E-mail: jcourie@carolib.org; *Mgr, Youth Serv,* Amanda M Courie; E-mail: acourie@carolib.org; Staff 20 (MLS 4, Non-MLS 16)
Founded 1961. Pop 32,579; Circ 201,798
Jul 2016-Jun 2017 Income (Main & Associated Libraries) $1,840,934, State $285,527, County $1,202,435, Other $352,972. Sal $864,301
Library Holdings: Bk Vols 79,080; Per Subs 170
Special Collections: Caroline County Genealogy Coll
Automation Activity & Vendor Info: (Cataloging) Innovative Interfaces, Inc; (Circulation) Innovative Interfaces, Inc; (OPAC) Innovative Interfaces, Inc; (Serials) Innovative Interfaces, Inc
Wireless access
Function: 24/7 Electronic res, 24/7 Online cat, 3D Printer, Bks on CD, Children's prog, Computer training, Computers for patron use, Digital talking bks, Electronic databases & coll, Free DVD rentals, ILL available, Internet access, Life-long learning prog for all ages, Magazines, Meeting rooms, Microfiche/film & reading machines, Online cat, OverDrive digital audio bks, Photocopying/Printing, Preschool reading prog, Printer for laptops & handheld devices, Prog for adults, Prog for children & young adult, Ref & res, Story hour, Summer reading prog, Tax forms, Telephone ref, Wheelchair accessible
Partic in Eastern Shore Regional Library; Maryland Interlibrary Loan Organization
Open Mon-Wed, Fri 10-6, Thurs 10-8, Sat 10-3
Friends of the Library Group
Branches: 2
FEDERALSBURG BRANCH, 123 Morris Ave, Federalsburg, 21632, SAN 344-1156. Tel: 410-754-8397. FAX: 410-754-3058. *Br Mgr,* Jeanne Trice; E-mail: jtrice@carolib.org
Library Holdings: Bk Titles 5,000; Bk Vols 6,000
Open Mon, Wed & Thurs 10-6, Tues 12-8
NORTH COUNTY BRANCH, 101 Cedar Lane, Greensboro, 21639. (Mail add: PO Box 336, Greensboro, 21639-0336), SAN 377-7421. Tel: 410-482-2173. FAX: 410-482-2634. *Br Mgr,* Tara Hill-Coursey; E-mail: thill-coursey@carolib.org
Open Mon, Tues & Thurs 10-6, Wed 12-8

EASTON

S ACADEMY ART MUSEUM*, Art Resource Center & Library, 106 South St, 21601. SAN 306-9397. Tel: 410-822-2787. FAX: 410-822-5997. E-mail: academy@academyartmuseum.org. Information Services E-mail: info@academyartmuseum.org. Web Site: academyartmuseum.org. *Dir,* Ben Simons; *Chief Curator,* Anke Van Wagenberg, PhD; E-mail: avanwagenberg@academyartmuseum.org
Founded 1958
Library Holdings: Bk Vols 3,000; Per Subs 10
Special Collections: Fine Art Books
Subject Interests: Art & archit, Arts & crafts, Music, Photog
Restriction: Mem only

P TALBOT COUNTY FREE LIBRARY*, 100 W Dover St, 21601-2620. SAN 306-9419. Tel: 410-822-1626. FAX: 410-820-8217. TDD: 410-822-1916. E-mail: askus@tcfl.org. Web Site: www.tcfl.org. *Dir,* Dana Newman; E-mail: dNewman@tcfl.org; *Asst Dir,* Scott Oliver; *Acq Librn,* Karen Collier; E-mail: kcollier@tcfl.org; *Ch & Youth Librn,* Laura Powell; E-mail: lpowell@tcfl.org; *Info Serv Librn,* Jo Powers; E-mail: jpowers@tcfl.org; *Circ Mgr,* Mia Y Clark; E-mail: mclark@tcfl.org; *Coordr, ILL,* Ellen Walko; E-mail: ewalko@tcfl.org; *IT Coordr,* Robert Long; E-mail: rlong@tcfl.org; Staff 34 (MLS 14, Non-MLS 20)
Founded 1925. Pop 32,400; Circ 320,000
Library Holdings: AV Mats 6,900; Large Print Bks 1,600; Bk Titles 78,517; Bk Vols 107,127; Per Subs 150
Subject Interests: Maryland
Automation Activity & Vendor Info: (Circulation) SirsiDynix
Wireless access
Publications: Talbot County Free Library's Weathervane
Partic in Eastern Shore Regional Library
Special Services for the Deaf - TTY equip
Open Mon & Thurs 9-8, Tues & Wed 9-6, Fri & Sat 9-5
Friends of the Library Group
Branches: 1
SAINT MICHAELS BRANCH, 106 N Fremont St, Saint Michaels, 21663, SAN 376-8198. Tel: 410-745-5877. FAX: 410-745-6937. *Br Mgr,* Shauna Beulah; E-mail: sbeulah@tcfl.org
Library Holdings: Bk Titles 5,000; Bk Vols 10,000; Per Subs 105
Open Mon & Thurs 9-8, Tues & Wed 9-6, Fri & Sat 9-5
Friends of the Library Group

ELKTON

GL CECIL COUNTY CIRCUIT COURT LAW LIBRARY*, Cecil County Circuit Courthouse, 2nd Flr, 129 E Main St, 21921. Tel: 410-996-1021.
Library Holdings: Bk Titles 150; Bk Vols 5,000
Automation Activity & Vendor Info: (Circulation) Ex Libris Group; (ILL) Ex Libris Group; (Serials) Ex Libris Group
Restriction: Not open to pub

P CECIL COUNTY PUBLIC LIBRARY*, Administrative Offices, 301 Newark Ave, 21921-5441. SAN 344-1180. Tel: 410-996-1055. FAX: 410-996-5604. TDD: 410-996-5609. Web Site: www.cecilcountylibrary.org. *Exec Dir,* Morgan Miller; Tel: 410-996-1055, Ext 122, E-mail: mmiller@cecilcountylibrary.org; *Assoc Dir,* Rachel Wright; Tel: 410-996-1055, Ext 138, E-mail: rwright@cecilcountylibrary.org; *Operations Dir,* Adele Cruise; Tel: 510-996-1055, Ext 104, E-mail: acruise@cecilcountylibrary.org; *Communications Mgr, Develop Mgr,* Frazier Walker; Tel: 410-996-1055, Ext 129, E-mail: fwalker@cecilcountylibrary.org; Staff 45 (MLS 11, Non-MLS 34)
Founded 1947. Circ 1,050,893
Library Holdings: AV Mats 45,386; Bk Vols 266,938; Per Subs 694
Automation Activity & Vendor Info: (Cataloging) OCLC Connexion; (Circulation) SirsiDynix; (ILL) SirsiDynix; (OPAC) SirsiDynix-iBistro
Wireless access
Publications: Library Link (Newsletter)
Partic in Maryland ILL Org
Open Mon-Thurs 10-9, Fri & Sat 10-5
Friends of the Library Group
Branches: 7
CECILTON BRANCH, 215 E Main St, Cecilton, 21913-1000, SAN 344-1210. Tel: 410-275-1091. FAX: 410-275-1092. *Br Mgr,* Tracy Miller; E-mail: tmiller@cecilcountylibrary.org
Open Mon & Tues 10-8, Wed & Thurs 10-6, Sat 10-5
Friends of the Library Group
CHESAPEAKE CITY BRANCH, 2527 Augustine Herman Hwy, Chesapeake City, 21915, SAN 344-1229. Tel: 410-996-1134. *Br Mgr,* Allison Holbrook; E-mail: aholbrook@cecilcountylibrary.org
Open Mon & Tues 10-8, Wed & Thurs 10-6, Fri & Sat 10-5
Friends of the Library Group
ELKTON CENTER LIBRARY, 301 Newark Ave, 21921. Tel: 410-996-5600. *Br Mgr,* Jamie McCloskey; E-mail: jmccloskey@cecilcountylibrary.org
Open Mon-Thurs 10-7, Fri & Sat 10-5
Friends of the Library Group
NORTH EAST BRANCH, 485 Mauldin Ave, North East, 21901, SAN 344-1245. Tel: 410-996-6269. FAX: 410-996-6268. *Br Mgr,* Matthew Lowder; E-mail: mlowder@cecilcountylibrary.org
Library is under construction due to open 2021
Open Mon & Tues 10-8, Wed & Thurs 10-6, Fri & Sat 10-5
Friends of the Library Group
PERRYVILLE BRANCH, 500 Coudon Blvd, Perryville, 21903, SAN 344-1253. Tel: 410-996-6070. *Bus Mgr,* Madison Griffitts; E-mail: mgriffits@cecilcountylibrary.org
Open Mon-Thurs 10-9, Fri & Sat 10-5
Friends of the Library Group
PORT DEPOSIT BRANCH, 13 S Main St, Port Deposit, 21904, SAN 328-7963. Tel: 410-996-6055. FAX: 410-996-1047. *Br Mgr,* Madison Griffitts
Open Mon-Wed 12-6, Sat 10-2
Friends of the Library Group
RISING SUN BRANCH, 111 Colonial Way, Rising Sun, 21911, SAN 344-127X. Tel: 410-398-2706, 410-658-4025. FAX: 410-658-4024. *Br Mgr,* Jennifer Carter; E-mail: jcarter@cecilcountylibrary.org
Open Mon-Thurs 10-8, Fri & Sat 10-5
Friends of the Library Group

ELLICOTT CITY

P HOWARD COUNTY LIBRARY SYSTEM*, Administrative Offices, 9411 Frederick Rd, 21042. SAN 344-0850. Tel: 410-313-7750. FAX: 410-313-7742. TDD: 410-313-7883. Web Site: www.hclibrary.org. *Pres & Chief Exec Officer,* Tonya Aikens; E-mail: tonya.aikens@hclibrary.org; *Dir, Human Res,* Stacey Fields; E-mail: stacey.fields@hclibrary.org; *Data Mgt, Dir, IT,* Ben H Sfanos; E-mail: ben.sfanos@hclibrary.org; *Dir, Communications, Partnerships,* Christie P Lassen; E-mail: christie.lassen@hclibrary.org; *Chief Opearting Officer, Pub Serv,* Lew Belfont; E-mail: lew.belfont@hclibrary.org; *Chief Operating Officer, Support Serv,* Angela Brade; E-mail: angela.brade@hclibrary.org; *Head, Children's & Teen Curric,* Cari A Gast; E-mail: cari.gast@hclibrary.org; *Events & Seminars Mgr,* Alli Jessing; E-mail: alli.jessing@hclibrary.org
Founded 1940. Pop 282,000; Circ 7,439,154
Special Collections: Adult Basic Education Materials; Toys
Subject Interests: Health educ
Automation Activity & Vendor Info: (Acquisitions) Innovative Interfaces, Inc; (Cataloging) Innovative Interfaces, Inc; (Circulation) Innovative Interfaces, Inc; (OPAC) Innovative Interfaces, Inc; (Serials) Innovative Interfaces, Inc
Wireless access
Function: Wheelchair accessible
Publications: Source (Newsletter)
Special Services for the Deaf - High interest/low vocabulary bks; Staff with knowledge of sign lang; TDD equip; TTY equip
Special Services for the Blind - Screen enlargement software for people with visual disabilities
Open Mon-Thurs 10-9, Fri & Sat 10-6, Sun 1-5
Friends of the Library Group
Branches: 6
CENTRAL BRANCH, 10375 Little Patuxent Pkwy, Columbia, 21044-3499, SAN 344-0915. Tel: 410-313-7800. FAX: 410-313-7864. TDD: 410-313-7883. *Br Mgr,* Nina Krzysko; E-mail: nina.krzysko@hclibrary.org; *Adult Literacy Coordr,* Emma Ostendorp; Tel: 410-313-7900, E-mail: emma.ostendorp@hclibrary.org
Special Services for the Deaf - TDD equip
EAST COLUMBIA, 6600 Cradlerock Way, Columbia, 21045-4912, SAN 374-647X. Tel: 410-313-7700. TDD: 410-313-7740. *Br Mgr,* Suki Lee; E-mail: suki.lee@hclibrary.org
Library Holdings: Bk Vols 166,664
Special Services for the Deaf - TDD equip
ELKRIDGE BRANCH + DIY EDUCATION CENTER, 6540 Washington Blvd, Elkridge, 21075, SAN 328-5049. Tel: 410-313-5077. FAX: 410-313-5090. *Br Mgr,* Phil Lord; E-mail: phil.lord@hclibrary.org
Special Services for the Deaf - TDD equip
GLENWOOD BRANCH, 2350 State Rte 97, Cooksville, 21723. Tel: 410-313-5575. *Br Mgr,* Mary Brosenne; E-mail: mary.brosenne@hclibrary.org
MILLER BRANCH & HISTORICAL CENTER, 9421 Frederick Rd, 21042-2119, SAN 344-0885. Tel: 410-313-1950. FAX: 410-313-1999. TDD: 410-313-1957. *Br Mgr,* Susan Stonesifer; Tel: 410-313-1978, E-mail: susan.stonesifer@hclibrary.org
Special Services for the Deaf - TDD equip

SAVAGE BRANCH & STEM EDUCATION CENTER, 9125 Durness Lane, Laurel, 20723-5991, SAN 328-5022. Tel: 410-880-5975. FAX: 410-880-5999. TDD: 410-880-5979. *Br Mgr,* Diane Li; E-mail: diane.li@hclibrary.org
Special Services for the Deaf - TDD equip

EMMITSBURG

C MOUNT SAINT MARY'S UNIVERSITY, Hugh J Phillips Library, 16300 Old Emmitsburg Rd, 21727. SAN 306-9435. Tel: 301-447-5244. Web Site: libguides.msmary.edu/phillipslibrary. *Libr Dir,* Jessica J Boyer; Tel: 301-447-5426, E-mail: boyer@msmary.edu; *IT Librn,* Michael Belmont; Tel: 301-447-5591, E-mail: m.a.belmont@msmary.edu; *Student Success Librn,* Emily Holland; Tel: 301-447-5430, E-mail: e.m.holland@msmary.edu; *Evening Mgr,* Francis Lukban; Tel: 301-447-5245, E-mail: f.j.lukban@msmary.edu; *Purchasing & Accounting Mgr,* Daniel Lewis; Tel: 301-447-5253, E-mail: dlewis@msmary.edu; Staff 9 (MLS 5, Non-MLS 4)
Enrl 1,710; Fac 120; Highest Degree: Master
Library Holdings: Bk Vols 210,875; Per Subs 910
Special Collections: 16th & 17th Century Religions; Early Catholic Americana (Rhoads Memorial Archives)
Automation Activity & Vendor Info: (Acquisitions) Ex Libris Group; (Cataloging) Ex Libris Group; (Circulation) Ex Libris Group; (Course Reserve) Ex Libris Group; (ILL) Ex Libris Group; (Media Booking) Ex Libris Group; (OPAC) Ex Libris Group; (Serials) Ex Libris Group
Wireless access
Partic in OCLC Online Computer Library Center, Inc
Friends of the Library Group

G US FIRE ADMINISTRATION*, National Emergency Training Center Learning Resource Center, 16825 S Seton Ave, 21727. SAN 325-8939. Tel: 301-447-1030. Toll Free Tel: 800-638-1821. FAX: 301-447-3217. E-mail: FEMA-NETCLibrary@fema.dhs.gov. Web Site: www.usfa.fema.gov/data/library. *Head Librn,* Edward J Metz; E-mail: Edward.Metz@fema.dhs.gov; Staff 10.5 (MLS 5, Non-MLS 5.5)
Library Holdings: AV Mats 800; CDs 350; DVDs 100; Bk Titles 48,000; Bk Vols 85,000; Per Subs 300; Videos 4,377
Subject Interests: Arson, Disaster mgt, Emergency med care, Emergency response, Fire prevention, Fire serv admin, Homeland security
Automation Activity & Vendor Info: (Acquisitions) Cuadra Associates, Inc; (Cataloging) Cuadra Associates, Inc; (Circulation) Cuadra Associates, Inc; (ILL) OCLC; (OPAC) Cuadra Associates, Inc; (Serials) Cuadra Associates, Inc
Function: ILL available, Ref serv available
Partic in Federal Library & Information Network
Restriction: Not open to pub, Open to students, fac & staff

FORT GEORGE G MEADE

G SSG PAUL D SAVANUCK MEMORIAL LIBRARY, Defense Information School (DINFOS), 6500 Mapes Rd, Ste 5620, 20755-5620. Tel: 301-677-4692. FAX: 301-677-4697. E-mail: dma.meade.dinfos.list.library@mail.mil. Web Site: www.dinfos.dma.mil/Library.aspx. *Librn,* Hayward Karen; Staff 2 (MLS 1, Non-MLS 1)
Founded 1975
Library Holdings: Audiobooks 800; DVDs 1,800; Electronic Media & Resources 450; Bk Vols 15,000; Per Subs 100
Special Collections: Photography & Photojournalism (Savanuck Coll
Subject Interests: Broadcasting, Graphic arts, Journalism, Multimedia, Photog, Pub affairs, Videography
Automation Activity & Vendor Info: (Acquisitions) SirsiDynix-Symphony; (Cataloging) SirsiDynix-Symphony; (Circulation) SirsiDynix-Symphony; (OPAC) SirsiDynix-Symphony; (Serials) SirsiDynix-Symphony
Wireless access
Partic in Federal Library & Information Network; OCLC Online Computer Library Center, Inc
Restriction: Authorized patrons, Mil only, Not a lending libr, Not open to pub, Open to students, fac & staff, Photo ID required for access, Use of others with permission of librn

UNITED STATES ARMY
AM KIMBROUGH AMBULATORY CARE CENTER MEDICAL LIBRARY*, 2480 Llewellyn Ave, Ste 5800, 20755-5800, SAN 344-1326. Tel: 301-677-8228. FAX: 301-677-8108. *Library Contact,* Patricia L Passaro
Library Holdings: Bk Titles 2,057; Per Subs 140
Subject Interests: Nursing, Primary health care, Surgery
Automation Activity & Vendor Info: (Acquisitions) Ex Libris Group; (Cataloging) Ex Libris Group; (Circulation) Ex Libris Group; (Course Reserve) Ex Libris Group; (ILL) Ex Libris Group; (Serials) Ex Libris Group
Partic in SE-Atlantic Regional Med Libr Servs
Open Mon-Fri 9-5

A THE MEDAL OF HONOR MEMORIAL LIBRARY*, 4418 Llewellyn Ave, Ste 5068, 20755-5068, SAN 344-130X. Tel: 301-677-4509, 301-677-5522. Administration Tel: 301-677-3594. FAX: 301-677-2694. E-mail: ftmeade.lib@us.army.mil. Web Site: www.ftmeademwr.com/library.htm. *Supvry Librn,* Karen L Hayward; E-mail: karen.hayward@us.army.mil; Staff 3 (MLS 1, Non-MLS 2)
Founded 1952
Library Holdings: Bk Vols 25,000; Per Subs 100
Automation Activity & Vendor Info: (Acquisitions) Baker & Taylor; (Cataloging) OCLC; (Circulation) Innovative Interfaces, Inc - Millennium; (ILL) OCLC; (OPAC) Innovative Interfaces, Inc - Millennium; (Serials) Innovative Interfaces, Inc - Millennium
Partic in OCLC Online Computer Library Center, Inc
Open Tues & Thurs 11-7, Wed & Fri 11-6, Sat 10-2

G US ENVIRONMENTAL PROTECTION AGENCY*, Environmental Science Center Library, 701 Mapes Rd, 20755-5350. SAN 306-8005. Tel: 410-305-3031. FAX: 410-305-3092. E-mail: library-reg3@epa.gov. Web Site: www.epa.gov/libraries/environmental-science-center-library-services. *Librn,* Kathleen Monti; Staff 1 (MLS 1)
Founded 1964
Library Holdings: AV Mats 87; Bk Titles 6,000; Per Subs 40
Special Collections: Chesapeake Bay Coll; Delaware Coll; District of Columbia Coll; EPA Region 3 Coll; Maryland Coll; Pennsylvania Coll; Virginia Coll; West Virginia Coll
Subject Interests: Analytical chem, Environ
Automation Activity & Vendor Info: (ILL) OCLC FirstSearch
Open Mon-Thurs 9:30-12:30 & 1-4
Restriction: External users must contact libr, In-house use for visitors

FREDERICK

J FREDERICK COMMUNITY COLLEGE, Gladhill Learning Commons, 7932 Opossumtown Pike, 21702. SAN 306-946X. Tel: 301-846-2444. Administration Tel: 301-846-2446. FAX: 301-624-2877. Web Site: www.frederick.edu/student-resources/gladhill-learning-commons.aspx. *Dir, Libr Serv,* Colleen McKnight; E-mail: cmcknight@frederick.edu; Staff 5.5 (MLS 3.5, Non-MLS 2)
Founded 1957. Enrl 1,750; Fac 450; Highest Degree: Associate
Library Holdings: Bks on Deafness & Sign Lang 20; DVDs 1,076; e-books 45,800; Electronic Media & Resources 27; High Interest/Low Vocabulary Bk Vols 200; Bk Titles 12,073; Per Subs 20
Subject Interests: Nursing
Automation Activity & Vendor Info: (Acquisitions) Innovative Interfaces, Inc; (Cataloging) Innovative Interfaces, Inc; (Circulation) Innovative Interfaces, Inc; (Course Reserve) Innovative Interfaces, Inc; (ILL) OCLC; (OPAC) Innovative Interfaces, Inc
Wireless access
Partic in Maryland Community College Library Consortium; OCLC Online Computer Library Center, Inc
Open Mon-Thurs 8am-9pm, Fri 8-4, Sat 10-4

S FREDERICK COUNTY HISTORICAL SOCIETY, Heritage Frederick Library & Archives, (Formerly Frederick County Archives & Research Center Library), 24 E Church St, 21701. SAN 371-778X. Tel: 301-663-1188. Web Site: frederickhistory.org. *Archivist,* Anita Hoffman; E-mail: archivist@frederickhistory.org; Staff 1 (MLS 1)
Founded 1984
Library Holdings: Bk Titles 5,000; Bk Vols 7,000; Per Subs 30; Spec Interest Per Sub 30
Special Collections: History of Frederick County Coll, Manuscripts, Diaries, Ephemera, Periodicals, Books, Photographs, Glass Negatives, Slides, Post Cards, DVDs, CDs, Tapes, VHS, Ledgers, Newspapers, Microfilm, Lithographs, Maps, Ad Cards, Yearbooks, City Directories,etc.. Oral History
Subject Interests: Genealogy
Wireless access
Function: 24/7 Online cat, Archival coll, Audio & video playback equip for onsite use, CD-ROM, Electronic databases & coll, For res purposes, Mail & tel request accepted, Museum passes, Music CDs, Online cat, Outreach serv, Outside serv via phone, mail, e-mail & web, Photocopying/Printing, Prog for adults, Ref & res, Ref serv available, Res assist avail, Res libr, Res performed for a fee, Scanner, VHS videos, Workshops
Publications: Historical Society of Frederick County (Newsletter); Journal
Restriction: Fee for pub use, Free to mem, Non-circulating, Not a lending libr

P FREDERICK COUNTY PUBLIC LIBRARIES*, 110 E Patrick St, 21701. SAN 306-9494. Tel: 301-600-1613. FAX: 301-600-3789. Web Site: www.fcpl.org. *Dir,* James Kelly; E-mail: jkelly@frederickcountymd.gov; *Mgr, Ch & Youth Serv,* Leslie Gincley; E-mail: lgincley@frederickcountymd.gov; *Mgr, Ch & Youth Serv,* Cathy Link; Staff 157 (MLS 2, Non-MLS 155)
Founded 1937. Pop 225,721; Circ 2,325,040

Library Holdings: AV Mats 41,227; e-books 12,868; Bk Vols 445,677; Per Subs 923
Special Collections: Maryland Hist (Maryland Coll), bks, micro
Automation Activity & Vendor Info: (Cataloging) CARL.Solution (TLC); (Circulation) CARL.Solution (TLC); (OPAC) CARL.Solution (TLC); (Serials) CARL.Solution (TLC)
Wireless access
Special Services for the Deaf - Staff with knowledge of sign lang
Open Mon-Fri 8:30-4:30
Friends of the Library Group
Branches: 9
C BURR ARTZ PUBLIC LIBRARY, 110 E Patrick St, 21701, SAN 374-7506. Tel: 301-600-1630. FAX: 301-600-2905. *Br Adminr,* Beth Heltebridle; Tel: 301-600-1337, E-mail: bheltebridle@frederickcountymd.gov
Open Mon-Thurs 10-9, Fri & Sat 10-5, Sun 1-5
Friends of the Library Group
BRUNSWICK BRANCH, 915 N Maple Ave, Brunswick, 21716, SAN 320-2844. Tel: 301-600-7250. FAX: 301-834-8763. *Br Adminr,* Jennifer Diaz; Tel: 301-600-7251, E-mail: jdiaz@frederickcountymd.gov
Open Mon-Thurs 10-8, Fri & Sat 10-5
Friends of the Library Group
EMMITSBURG BRANCH, 300-A S Seton Ave, Unit 2 J, Emmitsburg, 21727, SAN 320-2852. Tel: 301-600-6329. FAX: 301-600-6330. *Br Adminr,* Amy Whitey; Tel: 301-600-7201, E-mail: awhitney@frederickcountymd.gov
Open Mon & Wed 10-6, Tues & Thurs 10-8, Sat 10-5
Friends of the Library Group
EDWARD F FRY LIBRARY, 1635 Ballenger Creek Pike, Point of Rocks, 21777. Tel: 301-874-4560.
Open Mon, Tues & Sat 10-3, Wed 3-8
Friends of the Library Group
MIDDLETOWN BRANCH, 101 Prospect, Middletown, 21769, SAN 320-2860. Tel: 301-600-7560. *Br Adminr,* Beau Bradley; E-mail: bbradley@frederickcountymd.gov
Open Mon-Thurs 10-8, Fri & Sat 10-5
Friends of the Library Group
MYERSVILLE COMMUNITY LIBRARY, Eight Harp Pl, Myersville, 21773. *Br Adminr,* Marian Currens; Tel: 301-600-8350, E-mail: mcurrens@frederickcountymd.gov
Open Mon & Wed 10-6, Tues & Thurs 10-8, Sat 10-5
THURMONT REGIONAL LIBRARY, 76 E Moser Rd, Thurmont, 21788, SAN 320-2879. Tel: 301-600-7200. *Br Adminr,* Amy Whitney; Tel: 301-600-7201, E-mail: awhitney@frederickcountymd.gov
Open Mon-Thurs 10-9, Fri & Sat 10-5, Sun 1-5
Friends of the Library Group
URBANA REGINAL LIBRARY, 9020 Amelung St, 21704. Tel: 301-600-7000. *Br Adminr,* Tara Lebherz; Tel: 301-600-7012, E-mail: tlebherz@frederickcountymd.gov
Open Mon-Thurs 10-9, Fri & Sat 10-5, Sun 1-5
Friends of the Library Group
WALKERSVILLE BRANCH, Two S Glade Rd, Walkersville, 21793, SAN 329-6024. Tel: 301-600-8200. *Br Adminr,* Robin Bowers; E-mail: rbowers@frederickcountymd.gov
Open Mon-Thurs 10-8, Fri & Sat 10-5
Friends of the Library Group
Bookmobiles: 2

M FREDERICK MEMORIAL HOSPITAL*, Walter F Prior Medical Library, 400 W Seventh St, 21701. SAN 306-9508. Tel: 240-566-3459. FAX: 240-566-3650. E-mail: medlib@fmh.org. Web Site: www.fmh.org. *Librn,* Lucy Koscielniak; Staff 1 (Non-MLS 1)
Founded 1962
Library Holdings: Bk Vols 1,000; Per Subs 50
Subject Interests: Med, Nursing, Obstetrics & gynecology, Ophthalmology, Orthopedics, Pediatrics, Psychiat, Radiology, Surgery
Automation Activity & Vendor Info: (Serials) EBSCO Online
Partic in National Network of Libraries of Medicine Region 1
Restriction: Staff use only

C HOOD COLLEGE*, Beneficial-Hodson Library, 401 Rosemont Ave, 21701. SAN 306-9524. Tel: 301-696-3909. Circulation Tel: 301-696-3709. Interlibrary Loan Service Tel: 301-696-3695. Reference Tel: 301-696-3915. FAX: 301-696-3796. Web Site: www.hood.edu/library. *Dir,* Toby Peterson; Tel: 301-696-3924, E-mail: peterson@hood.edu; *Coll Develop Librn,* Elfie Chang; Tel: 301-695-3911, E-mail: elfchang@hood.edu; *Ref & Educ Librn,* Emily Hampton; Tel: 301-696-3858, E-mail: hampton@hood.edu; *Access Services Tech,* Janet Kalinowski; Tel: 301-696-3902, E-mail: kalinowski@hood.edu; *Access Services Tech,* Melissa Wright; E-mail: wrightm@hood.edu; *Archivist, Coll Develop,* Mary Atwell; Tel: 301-696-3873, E-mail: atwell@hood.edu; *Access Serv Mgr, ILL,* Kaitlyn May; E-mail: may@hood.edu; Staff 12 (MLS 7, Non-MLS 5)
Founded 1893. Enrl 2,500; Fac 107; Highest Degree: Master. Sal $469,477
Library Holdings: Audiobooks 400; AV Mats 5,500; e-books 310,000; e-journals 24,500; Bk Vols 211,000; Per Subs 305
Special Collections: Landauer Civil War Coll; Sylvia Meagher (Kennedy Assassination Archives); Weisberg Kennedy Assassination Archives Coll
Subject Interests: Biology, Civil War, Thanatology
Automation Activity & Vendor Info: (Acquisitions) Ex Libris Group; (Cataloging) Ex Libris Group; (Circulation) Ex Libris Group; (Discovery) EBSCO Discovery Service; (ILL) OCLC; (OPAC) Ex Libris Group; (Serials) Ex Libris Group
Wireless access
Function: Archival coll, Art exhibits, Audio & video playback equip for onsite use, Bks on CD, Computers for patron use, Doc delivery serv, E-Readers, Free DVD rentals, ILL available, Magazines, Microfiche/film & reading machines, Movies, Music CDs, Online cat, Online ref, Orientations, Photocopying/Printing, Ref & res, Ref serv available, Scanner, Spoken cassettes & CDs, Study rm, Telephone ref, Wheelchair accessible, Workshops
Partic in LYRASIS; Maryland Interlibrary Loan Organization
Special Services for the Deaf - Bks on deafness & sign lang; Closed caption videos; Coll on deaf educ; Deaf publ; Spec interest per
Special Services for the Blind - Bks on CD; Reader equip; Ref serv
Open Mon-Thurs 8-8, Fri & Sat 8-4, Sun 2-8
Restriction: Authorized patrons, In-house use for visitors, Limited access for the pub, Non-circulating of rare bks, Pub use on premises, Restricted pub use

S NATIONAL CANCER INSTITUTE AT FREDERICK SCIENTIFIC LIBRARY, Bldg 549, Sultan St, 21702-8255. (Mail add: PO Box B, 21702-1124), SAN 306-9451. Tel: 301-846-1093. Interlibrary Loan Service Tel: 301-846-5843. FAX: 301-846-6332. E-mail: NCIFredlibrary@mail.nih.gov. Web Site: ncifrederick.cancer.gov/ScientificLibrary. *Libr Dir,* Tracie Frederick; E-mail: fredericktt@mail.nih.gov
Founded 1972
Subject Interests: Biological physics, Biology, Cancer, Chem
Automation Activity & Vendor Info: (Acquisitions) Ex Libris Group; (Cataloging) Ex Libris Group; (Circulation) Ex Libris Group; (Discovery) Ex Libris Group; (ILL) OCLC FirstSearch; (OPAC) Ex Libris Group; (Serials) Ex Libris Group
Wireless access
Open Mon-Fri 8:30-5

UNITED STATES ARMY
A FORT DETRICK POST LIBRARY*, Fort Detrick, 1520 Freedman Dr, 21702, SAN 324-2331. Tel: 301-619-7519. FAX: 301-619-2884. *Librn,* Doug Markin
Library Holdings: Bk Vols 32,857; Per Subs 90
Automation Activity & Vendor Info: (Cataloging) Ex Libris Group; (Circulation) Ex Libris Group; (OPAC) Ex Libris Group
Partic in OCLC Online Computer Library Center, Inc
Open Mon-Fri 9-5
AM MEDICAL RESEARCH INSTITUTE OF INFECTIOUS DISEASES LIBRARY*, Fort Detrick, 1425 Porter, 21702-5011. Tel: 301-619-2717. FAX: 301-619-6059. *Dir,* Denise Lupp; E-mail: denise.lupp@us.army.mil; Staff 3 (MLS 2, Non-MLS 1)
Library Holdings: Bk Titles 4,000; Bk Vols 10,000; Per Subs 220
Subject Interests: Communicable diseases
Partic in OCLC Online Computer Library Center, Inc; Proquest Dialog; US National Library of Medicine
Restriction: Not open to pub

FROSTBURG

C FROSTBURG STATE UNIVERSITY*, Lewis J Ort Library, One Susan Eisel Dr, 21532. SAN 306-9532. Tel: 301-687-4396. Circulation Tel: 301-687-4395. Interlibrary Loan Service Tel: 301-687-4886. Reference Tel: 301-687-4424. FAX: 301-687-7069. Interlibrary Loan Service FAX: 301-687-3009. Web Site: www.frostburg.edu/lewis-ort-library/. *Libr Dir,* Dr Lea Messman-Mandicott; E-mail: lmessman@frostburg.edu; *Access Serv Librn,* Amanda L Bena; Tel: 301-687-7012, E-mail: albena@frostburg.edu; *Acq, Coll Develop & Ser,* Randall A Lowe; Tel: 301-687-4313, E-mail: rlowe@frostburg.edu; *Spec Coll Librn,* MaryJo Price; Tel: 301-687-4889, E-mail: mprice@frostburg.edu; *Coordr of First Year Libr Instruction,* Theresa M Mastrodonato; Tel: 301-687-4425, E-mail: tmmastrodonato@frostburg.edu; *Coordr, Libr Instruction, Webmaster,* Dr Sean Henry; Tel: 301-687-4888, E-mail: shenry@frostburg.edu; *Govt Doc Coordr,* Lisa A Hartman; Tel: 301-687-4734; *Cat,* Virginia Williams; Tel: 301-687-4884, E-mail: vwilliams@frostburg.edu. Subject Specialists: *Humanities,* MaryJo Price; *Computer,* Theresa M Mastrodonato; *German,* Dr Sean Henry; *Maps,* Virginia Williams; Staff 20 (MLS 11, Non-MLS 9)
Founded 1898. Enrl 5,756; Fac 247; Highest Degree: Doctorate
Jul 2015-Jun 2016 Income $2,576,726. Mats Exp $504,256, Books $89,976, Per/Ser (Incl. Access Fees) $387,144, Other Print Mats $27,136, Electronic Ref Mat (Incl. Access Fees) $48,397, Presv $13,497. Sal $1,280,086 (Prof $694,946)
Library Holdings: AV Mats 100,000; CDs 1,398; DVDs 1,568; e-books 112,176; e-journals 95; Electronic Media & Resources 196,508;

Microforms 612,889; Bk Titles 231,109; Bk Vols 380,815; Per Subs 306; Videos 3,453
Special Collections: George Meyers American Communist Party & Labor Materials Coll; Railroad Photography (William Price Coll); Selected US Survey Maps; Senator J Glenn Beall Papers. State Document Depository; US Document Depository
Automation Activity & Vendor Info: (Acquisitions) Ex Libris Group; (Cataloging) Ex Libris Group; (Circulation) Ex Libris Group; (Course Reserve) Ex Libris Group; (ILL) OCLC ILLiad; (OPAC) Ex Libris Group; (Serials) Ex Libris Group
Wireless access
Publications: LibGuides; Library Blog; Library Handouts; Library Newsletter
Partic in LYRASIS; OCLC Online Computer Library Center, Inc; Univ Syst of Md; University System of Maryland & Affiliated Institutions
Open Mon-Thurs 7:30am-Midnight, Fri 7:30-6, Sat 11-6, Sun 1-Midnight

GAITHERSBURG

G NATIONAL INSTITUTE OF STANDARDS & TECHNOLOGY LIBRARY*, NIST Research Library, 100 Bureau Dr, Stop 2500, 20899-2500. SAN 306-9567. Tel: 301-975-2784. Circulation Tel: 301-975-2793. Interlibrary Loan Service Tel: 301-975-3060. Reference Tel: 301-975-3052. FAX: 301-869-8071. Interlibrary Loan Service FAX: 301-869-6787. E-mail: library@nist.gov. Web Site: www.nist.gov/nist-research-library. *Librn,* Keith Martin; Tel: 301-975-2789, E-mail: keith.martin@nist.gov; Staff 13 (MLS 8, Non-MLS 5)
Founded 1901
Library Holdings: Per Subs 1,500
Special Collections: Artifacts of the National Bureau of Standards (Historical Museum Coll), congressional mats, legal refs; Biographical Files on NBS & NIST Scientists & Managers; National Bureau of Standards Personalities; Old & Rare 17th & 18th Century Scientific Meterology Treaties (Historical Coll), bks, ms, tech rpts; Significant Compilations of Atomic & Molecular Properties, Chemical Kinetics (Colloid & Surface), Fundamental Particles, Mechanical, Nuclear, Solid State, Thermodynamic & Transport Properties (National Standard Reference Data Coll); Weights & Measures Historical Coll. Oral History
Subject Interests: Chem, Computer sci, Engr, Libr & info sci, Math, Physics, Statistics
Automation Activity & Vendor Info: (Acquisitions) SirsiDynix; (Circulation) SirsiDynix; (Serials) SirsiDynix
Wireless access
Publications: Abstract & Index Collection in the NIST Research Library of the National Institute of Standards & Technology; An Annotated List of Historically & Scientifically Important Works Published Before 1900 in the Library of the National Bureau of Standards; Data Bases Available at the National Institute of Standards & Technology Research Library (Annual); Foundations of Metrology: Important Early Works on Weights & Measures in the Library of the National Bureau of Standards; National Institute of Standards & Technology Research Library Handbook; National Institute of Standards & Technology, Research Library Serial Holdings (Annual); Science-Technology Information, OIS (Monthly bulletin)
Partic in Federal Library & Information Network; Nat Res Libr Alliance; OCLC Online Computer Library Center, Inc; Upcounty Libraries Roundtable
Restriction: Authorized scholars by appt, In-house use for visitors, Lending to staff only, Non-circulating to the pub, Open to researchers by request

GLEN ECHO

S UNITED STATES NATIONAL PARK SERVICE*, Clara Barton National Historic Site Library, 5801 Oxford Rd, 20812. SAN 373-1561. Tel: 301-320-1410. FAX: 301-320-1415. Web Site: www.nps.gov/clba. *Curator,* Kim Robinson; Tel: 301-320-1411
Library Holdings: Bk Vols 500
Restriction: Open by appt only

GREENBELT

G NASA*, Goddard Space Flight Center Library, Library, Bldg 21, Code 272, 20771. (Mail add: Bldg 21, Rm L200, 8800 Greenbelt Rd, 20771), SAN 306-9648. Tel: 301-286-7218. Interlibrary Loan Service Tel: 301-286-7217. FAX: 301-286-1755. E-mail: gsfc-library@lists.nasa.gov. Web Site: library.gsfc.nasa.gov. *Br Head,* Robin Miller Dixon; Tel: 301-286-9230, E-mail: robin.m.dixon@nasa.gov; *Acq Librn,* John Grunwell; Tel: 301-286-6245; *Electronic Res Mgt Librn,* Mitzi Cole; Tel: 301-286-9348; *Curator,* Patrick Healey; Tel: 301-286-0884; *Tech Info Spec,* Gordon Bonholzer; Tel: 301-286-6244; Staff 14 (MLS 12, Non-MLS 2)
Founded 1959
Library Holdings: CDs 1,574; Bk Titles 83,846; Bk Vols 103,933; Per Subs 2,371; Videos 1,279
Subject Interests: Astrophysics, Communications & navigation systs, Earth sci, Exploration systs, Heliophysics, Solar syst exploration
Automation Activity & Vendor Info: (Acquisitions) SirsiDynix; (Cataloging) SirsiDynix; (Circulation) SirsiDynix; (ILL) OCLC; (OPAC) SirsiDynix
Wireless access
Partic in NASA Library Network; National Research Library Alliance
Special Services for the Deaf - TDD equip
Restriction: Govt use only

HAGERSTOWN

GL CIRCUIT COURT FOR WASHINGTON COUNTY LAW LIBRARY*, Circuit Courthouse, 24 Summit Ave, 21740. SAN 306-9702. Tel: 240-313-2570. E-mail: mdlaw.library@mdcourts.gov. Web Site: www.courts.state.md.us.
Library Holdings: Bk Vols 20,000; Per Subs 10
Open Mon-Fri 8:30-4:30

J HAGERSTOWN COMMUNITY COLLEGE LIBRARY, William M Brish Library, Learning Resource Center, #200B, 11400 Robinwood Dr, 21742-6590. SAN 306-9664. Tel: 240-500-2237. Administration Tel: 240-500-2551. E-mail: library@hagerstowncc.edu. Web Site: www.hagerstowncc.edu/library. *Coord, Libr & Learning Support Services,* Kendra Perry; E-mail: kkperry@hagerstowncc.edu; *Digital Res Librn,* LuAnn Fisher; E-mail: lefisher@hagerstowncc.edu; *Archives, Ref Librn,* Sarah Conrad; E-mail: slconrad@hagerstowncc.edu; *Library Services,* Gayle Johnson; E-mail: grjohnson@hagerstowncc.edu; Staff 3.8 (MLS 3, Non-MLS 0.8)
Founded 1946. Enrl 2,600; Highest Degree: Associate
Automation Activity & Vendor Info: (Cataloging) SirsiDynix; (Circulation) SirsiDynix; (Course Reserve) SirsiDynix; (Discovery) EBSCO Discovery Service; (ILL) OCLC WorldShare Interlibrary Loan; (OPAC) SirsiDynix
Wireless access
Function: 24/7 Electronic res, 24/7 Online cat, Archival coll, Computers for patron use, Distance learning, Electronic databases & coll, For res purposes, Free DVD rentals, ILL available, Internet access, Meeting rooms, Movies, Online cat, Online info literacy tutorials on the web & in blackboard, Online ref, Orientations, Outreach serv, Ref & res, Ref serv available, Scanner, Study rm, Telephone ref
Partic in Maryland Community College Library Consortium
Open Mon-Thurs 8-6, Fri 8:30-4:30
Restriction: External users must contact libr, ID required to use computers (Ltd hrs), Non-circulating of rare bks, Open to pub for ref & circ; with some limitations, Open to students, fac, staff & alumni

S MARYLAND CORRECTIONAL INSTITUTION-HAGERSTOWN LIBRARY, 18601 Roxbury Rd, 21746. Tel: 240-420-1000, Ext 2347, 240-420-1340, 301-733-2800, Ext 2347. FAX: 301-797-8448. Web Site: dpscs.maryland.gov/locations/mcih.shtml. *Librn,* Michael Shaffer; E-mail: michael.shaffer@maryland.gov; Staff 1 (MLS 1)
Library Holdings: Bk Vols 11,000; Per Subs 10
Automation Activity & Vendor Info: (Cataloging) Follett Software; (Circulation) Follett Software
Restriction: Not open to pub

S MARYLAND CORRECTIONAL TRAINING CENTER LIBRARY*, 18800 Roxbury Rd, 21746. Tel: 240-420-1607. FAX: 301-797-7567. Web Site: www.dpscs.state.md.us/locations/mctc.shtml. *Librn,* Kari Patrick; E-mail: kari.patrick@maryland.gov; Staff 1 (Non-MLS 1)
Library Holdings: Bk Vols 7,542; Per Subs 30
Automation Activity & Vendor Info: (Cataloging) Follett Software; (Circulation) Follett Software
Open Mon-Fri 8:20-11 & 12:10-2:40

S NATIONAL PARK SERVICE*, Chesapeake & Ohio Canal National Historical Park Library, 1850 Dual Hwy, Ste 100, 21740. SAN 371-6228. Tel: 301-739-4200. Web Site: www.nps.gov/choh. *Historian,* Kevin Brandt
Library Holdings: Bk Titles 500
Restriction: Open by appt only

S ROXBURY CORRECTIONAL INSTITUTION LIBRARY*, 18701 Roxbury Rd, 21746. Tel: 240-420-3000, Ext 5290. FAX: 301-733-2672. Web Site: www.dpscs.state.md.us/locations/rci.shtml. *Librn,* Stefanie Cicero; E-mail: stefanie.cicero@maryland.gov; Staff 1 (MLS 1)
Library Holdings: Bk Vols 10,399; Per Subs 39
Automation Activity & Vendor Info: (Cataloging) Follett Software; (Circulation) Follett Software

P WASHINGTON COUNTY FREE LIBRARY*, 100 S Potomac St, 21740. SAN 344-1458. Tel: 301-739-3250. FAX: 301-739-7603. Web Site: www.washcolibrary.org. *Exec Dir,* Jenny Bakos; E-mail: jbakos@washcolibrary.org; *Assoc Dir, Pub Serv,* Kathleen Mary O'Connell; E-mail: ko01@washcolibrary.org; *Head, Tech Proc,* William Taylor; E-mail: wtaylor@washcolibrary.org; *Hed, Bkmobile Dept,* Laura Schnackenberg; E-mail: lschnackenberg@washcolibrary.org; *Head,*

Children's Servx, Jeff Ridgeway; E-mail: pr01@washcolibrary.org; *Head, Circ,* Delissa Key; E-mail: lk01@washcolibrary.org; *Head, County Serv,* Janlee Viands; E-mail: jv01@washcolibrary.org; *Adult Ref,* Shannon Kraushaar; E-mail: skraushaar@washcolibrary.org; *Coll Develop,* Barbara Kronewitter; E-mail: bkronewitter@washcolibrary.org
Founded 1898. Pop 147,050; Circ 946,291
Library Holdings: Bks on Deafness & Sign Lang 200; High Interest/Low Vocabulary Bk Vols 500; Large Print Bks 5,000; Bk Vols 329,105; Per Subs 580; Talking Bks 3,000
Special Collections: Government Reference Service; Historical Lectures, video; Western Maryland (Western Maryland Rm), bks, AV. Oral History; State Document Depository
Subject Interests: Bus, Genealogy, Govt, Local hist
Automation Activity & Vendor Info: (Acquisitions) Innovative Interfaces, Inc; (Cataloging) Innovative Interfaces, Inc; (Circulation) Innovative Interfaces, Inc
Wireless access
Function: Art exhibits, Audio & video playback equip for onsite use, Audiobks via web, AV serv, BA reader (adult literacy), Bi-weekly Writer's Group, Bilingual assistance for Spanish patrons, Bk club(s), Bk reviews (Group), Bks on cassette, Bks on CD, Bus archives, CD-ROM, Chess club, Children's prog, Citizenship assistance, Computer training, Computers for patron use, Digital talking bks, Distance learning, Doc delivery serv, E-Reserves, Electronic databases & coll, Equip loans & repairs, Family literacy, For res purposes, Free DVD rentals, Games & aids for people with disabilities, Genealogy discussion group, Govt ref serv, Health sci info serv, Holiday prog, Home delivery & serv to seniorr ctr & nursing homes, Homebound delivery serv, Homework prog, ILL available, Instruction & testing, Internet access, Jail serv, Jazz prog, Large print keyboards, Learning ctr, Legal assistance to inmates, Literacy & newcomer serv, Magnifiers for reading, Mail & tel request accepted, Mail loans to mem, Masonic res mat, Microfiche/film & reading machines, Museum passes, Music CDs, Notary serv, Online cat, Online info literacy tutorials on the web & in blackboard, Online ref, Orientations, Outreach serv, Outside serv via phone, mail, e-mail & web, OverDrive digital audio bks, Passport agency, Photocopying/Printing, Preschool outreach, Preschool reading prog, Printer for laptops & handheld devices, Prof lending libr, Prog for adults, Prog for children & young adult, Ref & res, Ref serv available, Res libr, Res performed for a fee, Satellite serv, Scanner, Senior computer classes, Senior outreach, Serves people with intellectual disabilities, Spanish lang bks, Specialized serv in classical studies, Spoken cassettes & CDs, Spoken cassettes & DVDs, Story hour, Summer & winter reading prog, Summer reading prog, Tax forms, Teen prog, Telephone ref, VHS videos, Visual arts prog, Wheelchair accessible, Winter reading prog, Words travel prog, Workshops
Publications: A Newspaper History of Washington County; Index to Hagerstown Newspapers
Mem of Western Maryland Regional Library
Special Services for the Deaf - Assistive tech; Bks on deafness & sign lang; Captioned film dep; Closed caption videos; Deaf publ
Special Services for the Blind - Assistive/Adapted tech devices, equip & products; Audio mat; Bks available with recordings; Bks on cassette; Bks on CD; Braille alphabet card; Braille bks; Closed circuit TV magnifier; Copier with enlargement capabilities; Home delivery serv; Large print & cassettes; Large print bks; Large screen computer & software; Low vision equip; Magnifiers; Reading & writing aids; Talking bks; Videos on blindness & physical disabilties; Volunteer serv; Web-Braille
Friends of the Library Group
Branches: 7
BOONSBORO FREE LIBRARY, 401 Potomac St, Boonsboro, 21713, SAN 344-1482. Tel: 301-432-5723. *Br Mgr,* Jennifer Ross; E-mail: jross@washcolibrary.org
Library Holdings: Bk Vols 12,350
HANCOCK WAR MEMORIAL, 231 Hancock Veterans Pkwy, Hancock, 21750, SAN 344-1512. Tel: 301-678-5300. *Br Mgr,* Pamela Mann; E-mail: pmann@washcolibrary.org
Library Holdings: Bk Vols 16,197
KEEDYSVILLE BRANCH, 22 Taylor Dr, Keedysville, 21756, SAN 373-8094. Tel: 301-432-6641. *Br Mgr,* Jennifer Ross
SHARPSBURG PUBLIC, 106 E Main St, Sharpsburg, 21782, SAN 344-1547. Tel: 301-432-8825. *Br Mgr,* Barb Twigg; E-mail: btwigg@washcolibrary.org
Library Holdings: Bk Vols 10,790
SMITHSBURG BRANCH, 66 W Water St, Smithsburg, 21783-1604, SAN 344-1571. Tel: 301-824-7722. *Br Mgr,* Tammy Gantz; E-mail: tgantz@washcolibrary.org
Library Holdings: Bk Vols 21,500
Open Mon-Fri 10-7, Sat 10-2
Friends of the Library Group
LEONARD P SNYDER MEMORIAL, 12624 Broadfording Rd, Clear Spring, 21722. Tel: 301-842-2730. *Br Mgr,* Marcella Whitmore; E-mail: mwhitmore@washcolibrary.org
WILLIAMSPORT MEMORIAL, 104 E Potomac St, Williamsport, 21795, SAN 344-1601. Tel: 301-223-7027. *Br Mgr,* Hannah Cobb; E-mail: hcobb@washcolibrary.org
Library Holdings: Bk Vols 17,512
Open Mon-Fri 10-7, Sat 10-3
Bookmobiles: 1

S WASHINGTON COUNTY HISTORICAL SOCIETY, kinship Family Heritage Research Center, 135 W Washington St, 21740. SAN 371-5183. Tel: 301-797-8782. FAX: 240-625-9498. E-mail: info@washcohistory.org. Web Site: www.washcohistory.org. *Exec Dir,* Robyn Sumner; E-mail: exdir@washcohistory.org; *Genealogist,* Jean Conte; E-mail: genealogist@washcohistory.org
Founded 1962
Library Holdings: Bk Vols 1,200
Subject Interests: Genealogy, Local hist
Wireless access
Open Tues-Fri 9-4
Restriction: Non-circulating to the pub

S WASHINGTON COUNTY MUSEUM OF FINE ARTS LIBRARY, 401 Museum Dr, 21740. (Mail add: PO Box 423, 21741-0423), SAN 325-8858. Tel: 301-739-5727. FAX: 301-745-3741. E-mail: info@wcmfa.org. Web Site: www.wcmfa.org. *Exec Dir,* Sarah J Hall; *Curator,* Daniel Fulco
Library Holdings: Bk Vols 5,000
Subject Interests: Art
Open Tues-Fri 10-5, Sat 10-4, Sun 1-5
Restriction: Non-circulating

P WESTERN MARYLAND REGIONAL LIBRARY*, 100 S Potomac St, 21740. SAN 306-9729. Tel: 301-739-3250. FAX: 301-739-7603. Web Site: www.wmrl.info. *Dir,* Elizabeth Hulett; Tel: 301-739-3250, Ext 550, E-mail: ehulett@wmrl.info; Staff 4 (MLS 4)
Founded 1967. Pop 251,064
Library Holdings: Bk Vols 61,743
Automation Activity & Vendor Info: (Cataloging) Innovative Interfaces, Inc; (Circulation) Innovative Interfaces, Inc
Publications: Western Maryland Public Libraries Sign System Manual
Member Libraries: Allegany County Library System; Ruth Enlow Library of Garrett County; Washington County Free Library
Open Mon-Fri 8-4:30

HUNT VALLEY

S BALTIMORE COUNTY HISTORICAL SOCIETY LIBRARY*, 9811 Van Buren Lane, 21030. SAN 371-9979. Tel: 410-666-1878. FAX: 410-666-5276. E-mail: info@hsobc.org. Web Site: www.hsobc.org. *Librn,* Sally Riley; Staff 1 (MLS 1)
Founded 1959
Library Holdings: Bk Titles 3,500
Special Collections: Tombstone Inscriptions, bks & ms. Oral History
Subject Interests: Genealogy, Local hist
Publications: History Trails (Quarterly)
Open Fri 12-4, Sat 10-2
Restriction: Not a lending libr

HYATTSVILLE

SR FIRST UNITED METHODIST CHURCH LIBRARY, 6201 Belcrest Rd, 20782. SAN 306-9753. Tel: 301-927-6133. FAX: 301-927-7368. E-mail: church@fumchy.org. Web Site: www.fumchy.org. *Library Contact,* Position Currently Open
Founded 1949
Library Holdings: Bk Vols 2,500

INDIAN HEAD

UNITED STATES NAVY
A ALBERT T CAMP TECHNICAL LIBRARY*, Naval Surface Warfare Ctr IHD-Technical Library, 4171 Fowler Rd, Bldg 299, Ste 101, 20640-5110. Tel: 301-744-4742. FAX: 301-744-4192. E-mail: ihdivtechnicallibrary@navy.mil. Web Site: www.ih.navy.mil. *Tec Data Librn,* Eugene Bruce; Staff 2 (Non-MLS 2)
Library Holdings: Bk Titles 5,000; Bk Vols 12,150; Per Subs 50
Special Collections: Ordnance; Research; Rocketry; Test & Evaluation Reports
Subject Interests: Chem, Engr
Function: Doc delivery serv, Electronic databases & coll, Govt ref serv, ILL available, Internet access, Online ref, Outside serv via phone, mail, e-mail & web, Photocopying/Printing, Ref serv available, Res libr, Scanner, Telephone ref
Partic in OCLC Online Computer Library Center, Inc
Restriction: Authorized personnel only, Borrowing requests are handled by ILL, Circ limited, Employee & client use only, Employees & their associates, External users must contact libr, Not open to pub, Open to mil & govt employees only, Private libr

A GENERAL LIBRARY*, Naval Support Facility-S Potomac, Strauss Ave, Bldg 620, 20640, SAN 344-2322. Tel: 301-744-4747. FAX: 301-744-4386. Web Site: www.ih.navy.mil. *Library Contact,* Janet Ferrell; E-mail: janetferrell@navy.mil; Staff 1 (Non-MLS 1)
Library Holdings: Bk Titles 7,000; Per Subs 116
Special Collections: Maryland & Charles County History Books; Navy Biographical & Historical Books
Open Mon-Fri 8-4

A MWR GENERAL LIBRARY*, Bldg 620, 4163 N Jackson Rd, 20640. Tel: 301-744-4850. Web Site: www.navylibraryindianhead.org, www.navymwrindianhead.com/recreation. *Head Librn,* Kendra Harris; E-mail: Kendra.Harris@navy.mil
Library Holdings: Bk Vols 10,000
Open Mon, Tues & Fri 6am-6pm, Wed & Thurs 6am-8pm, Sat 10-3

A NAVAL EXPLOSIVE ORDNANCE DISPOSAL TECHNOLOGY DIVISION TECHNICAL LIBRARY*, 2008 Stump Neck Rd, Code 2011, 20640-5070, SAN 344-2381. Tel: 301-744-6817. FAX: 301-744-6902. *Br Head,* William Wilson; E-mail: william.r.wilson@navy.mil; Staff 6 (MLS 1, Non-MLS 5)
Founded 1956
Library Holdings: Bk Titles 120,000; Per Subs 100
Partic in Consortium of Naval Libraries
Publications: Accession List
Restriction: Closed stack, Not open to pub, Secured area only open to authorized personnel

JESSUP

§S DORSEY RUN CORRECTIONAL FACILITY LIBRARY, 2020 Toulson Rd, 20794. Tel: 410-379-6021. Web Site: www.dpscs.state.md.us/locations/drc.shtml. *Librn,* Beatrice McTernan; E-mail: beatrice.mcternan@maryland.gov
Restriction: Not open to pub

S JESSUP CORRECTIONAL INSTITUTE, 7803 House of Corrections Rd, 20794. (Mail add: PO Box 534, 20794). Tel: 410-540-6412, 410-799-7610. Web Site: www.dpscs.state.md.us/locations/jci.shtml. *Librn,* Jeanne Lauber; E-mail: jeanne.lauber1@maryland.gov; Staff 1 (MLS 1)
Library Holdings: Bk Vols 8,800; Per Subs 38
Automation Activity & Vendor Info: (Cataloging) Follett Software; (Circulation) Follett Software
Restriction: Not open to pub

S MARYLAND CORRECTIONAL INSTITUTION FOR WOMEN LIBRARY*, 7943 Brock Bridge Rd, 20794. Tel: 410-379-3800, 410-379-3828. FAX: 410-799-8867. Web Site: www.dpscs.state.md.us/locations/mciw.shtml. *Librn,* Hananya Cohen; E-mail: hananya.cohen@maryland.gov; Staff 1 (MLS 1)
Library Holdings: Bk Vols 7,686; Per Subs 25
Automation Activity & Vendor Info: (Cataloging) Follett Software; (Circulation) Follett Software
Open Mon, Wed & Fri-Sun 9-2:30, Tues 5-8

S MARYLAND CORRECTIONAL INSTITUTION-JESSUP LIBRARY*, 7803 House of Corrections Rd, Rte 175, 20794. (Mail add: PO Box 549, 20794). Tel: 410-799-2859, 410-799-7610. FAX: 410-799-7539. Web Site: www.dpscs.state.md.us/locations/mcij.shtml. *Librn,* Position Currently Open
Library Holdings: Bk Vols 4,000; Per Subs 25
Automation Activity & Vendor Info: (Cataloging) Follett Software; (Circulation) Follett Software
Open Mon-Fri 8:30-10:30 & 1-2:15

S PATUXENT INSTITUTION LIBRARY*, 7555 Waterloo Rd, 20794. (Mail add: PO Box 700, 20794). Tel: 410-799-3400, Ext 4226. FAX: 410-799-1137. Web Site: www.dpscs.state.md.us/locations/pat.shtml. *Librn,* William Katzenberger; E-mail: william.katzenberger@maryland.gov; Staff 1 (MLS 1)
Library Holdings: Bk Vols 5,466; Per Subs 23
Automation Activity & Vendor Info: (Cataloging) Follett Software; (Circulation) Follett Software
Restriction: Not open to pub

LA PLATA

L CHARLES COUNTY CIRCUIT COURT*, Charles County Public Law Library, 200 Charles St, 20646-9602. SAN 329-8574. Tel: 301-932-3322. E-mail: ccpll@mdcourts.gov. Web Site: www.mdcourts.gov/clerks/charles/lawlibrary. *Law Librn,* Mary Jo Lazun; E-mail: mjlazun@mdcourts.gov; Staff 1 (MLS 1)
Jul 2019-Jun 2020 Income County $60,000
Library Holdings: Bk Vols 8,000
Subject Interests: Law
Automation Activity & Vendor Info: (Cataloging) LibraryWorld, Inc
Wireless access
Function: Computers for patron use, Doc delivery serv, Electronic databases & coll, For res purposes, Govt ref serv, Mail & tel request accepted, Meeting rooms, Online ref, Outside serv via phone, mail, e-mail & web, Ref & res, Ref serv available, Res assist avail, Res libr, Scanner, Serves people with intellectual disabilities
Open Mon-Fri 8-4:30
Restriction: Non-circulating, Not a lending libr, Restricted borrowing privileges, Restricted loan policy

P CHARLES COUNTY PUBLIC LIBRARY*, La Plata Branch, Two Garrett Ave, 20646. SAN 344-2411. Tel: 301-934-9001. E-mail: laplataref@ccplonline.org. Web Site: www.ccplonline.org. *Exec Dir,* Kenneth Wayne Thompson; E-mail: kthompson@ccplonline.org; *Dep Dir,* Lloyd Jansen; E-mail: ljansen@ccplonline.org; *Br Mgr,* Daniel Rheingrover; *Executive Asst,* Brenda Wendell; E-mail: bwendell@ccplonline.org; Staff 42 (MLS 11, Non-MLS 31)
Founded 1923. Pop 146,551; Circ 799,110
Library Holdings: Audiobooks 8,312; DVDs 18,644; Bk Titles 134,787; Bk Vols 201,125; Per Subs 195
Subject Interests: Local genealogy, Spanish
Automation Activity & Vendor Info: (Acquisitions) Innovative Interfaces, Inc; (Cataloging) Innovative Interfaces, Inc; (Circulation) Innovative Interfaces, Inc; (ILL) Relais International; (OPAC) Innovative Interfaces, Inc
Wireless access
Function: Adult bk club, Bk club(s), Bks on cassette, Bks on CD, Children's prog, Computer training, Computers for patron use, Electronic databases & coll, Holiday prog, Home delivery & serv to seniorr ctr & nursing homes, Homebound delivery serv, ILL available, Online cat, Online ref, Outreach serv, Outside serv via phone, mail, e-mail & web, OverDrive digital audio bks, Photocopying/Printing, Preschool outreach, Prog for adults, Prog for children & young adult, Ref serv available, Senior outreach, Spanish lang bks, Spoken cassettes & CDs, Story hour, Summer reading prog, Tax forms, Teen prog, Telephone ref, VHS videos, Wheelchair accessible
Mem of Southern Maryland Regional Library Association, Inc
Special Services for the Deaf - TDD equip
Special Services for the Blind - Audio mat
Open Mon-Thurs 9-8, Fri 1-5, Sat 9-5
Friends of the Library Group
Branches: 3
P D BROWN MEMORIAL, 50 Village St, Waldorf, 20602, SAN 344-2500. Tel: 301-645-2864. FAX: 301-843-4869. Reference E-mail: pdbrownref@ccplonline.org. *Br Mgr,* Cecelia Thomas
Open Mon-Thurs 9-8, Fri 1-5, Sat 9-5
Friends of the Library Group
POTOMAC BRANCH, 3225 Ruth B Swann Dr, Indian Head, 20640. Tel: 301-375-7375. E-mail: potomacref@ccplonline.org. *Br Mgr,* DauVeen Walker
Open Mon-Thurs 9-8, Fri 1-5, Sat 9-5
Friends of the Library Group
WALDORF WEST BRANCH, 10405 O'Donnell Pl, Waldorf, 20603. Tel: 301-645-1395. E-mail: waldorfref@ccplonline.org. *Br Mgr,* Shannon Bland
Open Mon-Thurs 9-8, Fri 1-5, Sat 9-5
Friends of the Library Group
Bookmobiles: 1. Mgr, Megan Burroughs

J COLLEGE OF SOUTHERN MARYLAND LIBRARY*, 8730 Mitchell Rd, 20646. (Mail add: PO Box 910, 20646-0910), SAN 306-9818. Tel: 301-934-7626. Toll Free Tel: 800-933-9177, Ext 7626. FAX: 301-934-7699. E-mail: library@csmd.edu. Web Site: www.csmd.edu/student-services/library-services. *Dir,* Position Currently Open; *Ref (Info Servs),* Vince Doblos; Staff 4 (MLS 3, Non-MLS 1)
Founded 1958. Enrl 11,211; Fac 204; Highest Degree: Associate
Library Holdings: AV Mats 13,615; Bk Titles 37,260; Bk Vols 45,430; Per Subs 73; Talking Bks 229
Special Collections: Southern Maryland Manuscripts & Genealogy. Oral History
Subject Interests: Local hist
Automation Activity & Vendor Info: (Cataloging) TLC (The Library Corporation); (Circulation) Follett Software; (Course Reserve) Docutek; (OPAC) Follett Software
Wireless access
Partic in Maryland Community College Library Consortium

LANDOVER

R FIRST BAPTIST CHURCH OF HIGHLAND PARK LIBRARY*, 6801 Sheriff Rd, 20785. Tel: 301-773-6655. FAX: 301-773-1347. Web Site: www.fbhp.org/library-ministry. *Libr Dir,* Ruby Alexander; *Asst Libr Dir,* Denise Dunn; Staff 2 (MLS 2)
Founded 1998
Library Holdings: Bk Titles 2,100; Per Subs 25
Subject Interests: Children's lit, Christianity

Automation Activity & Vendor Info: (Cataloging) Book Systems; (Circulation) Book Systems; (OPAC) Book Systems
Function: Ref serv available
Restriction: Mem only

S NATIONAL REHABILITATION INFORMATION CENTER, 8400 Corporate Dr, Ste 500, 20785. SAN 371-263X. Tel: 301-459-5900. Toll Free Tel: 800-346-2742. FAX: 301-459-4263. E-mail: naricinfo@heitechservices.com. Web Site: www.naric.com. *Dir,* Mark X Odum; Staff 9 (MLS 1, Non-MLS 8)
Founded 1977
Library Holdings: Bks on Deafness & Sign Lang 5,120; Bk Vols 20,000; Per Subs 108
Subject Interests: Disability, Rehabilitation, Spec educ
Function: Archival coll, Doc delivery serv, Electronic databases & coll, Govt ref serv, Internet access, Wheelchair accessible
Special Services for the Deaf - TTY equip
Special Services for the Blind - Braille servs
Open Mon-Fri 8:30-5:30
Restriction: Non-circulating to the pub

LARGO

C PRINCE GEORGE'S COMMUNITY COLLEGE LIBRARY*, 301 Largo Rd, 20774-2199. SAN 306-9842. Tel: 301-546-0462. Circulation Tel: 301-546-0475. Interlibrary Loan Service Tel: 301-546-0470. Reference Tel: 301-546-0476. E-mail: librefdesk@pgcc.edu. Web Site: pgcc.libguides.com/library. *Dir,* Priscilla Thompson; Tel: 301-546-0466, E-mail: thompspc@pgcc.edu; *Cat & Syst Librn,* John D Bartles; Tel: 301-546-0469, E-mail: jbartles@pgcc.edu; *Coll Develop Librn,* Robert Fernandez; Tel: 301-546-7566, E-mail: fernanrm@pgcc.edu; *Electronic Res Librn,* Maria Bonet; Tel: 301-546-0471, E-mail: bonetmd@pgcc.edu; *Outreach & Instruction Librn,* Jeffrey Potter; Tel: 301-546-0468, E-mail: potterjl@pgcc.edu; *Ref & Instruction Librn,* Marianne Giltrud; Tel: 301-546-0467, E-mail: giltrumx@pgcc.edu; Staff 15 (MLS 7, Non-MLS 8)
Founded 1958. Fac 216; Highest Degree: Associate
Automation Activity & Vendor Info: (Acquisitions) Ex Libris Group; (Cataloging) Ex Libris Group; (Circulation) Ex Libris Group; (Course Reserve) Ex Libris Group; (Discovery) Ex Libris Group; (ILL) OCLC; (OPAC) Ex Libris Group; (Serials) SerialsSolutions
Wireless access
Function: 24/7 Electronic res, 24/7 Online cat, Audio & video playback equip for onsite use, Bk club(s), Computers for patron use, Electronic databases & coll, ILL available, Internet access, Online cat, Online info literacy tutorials on the web & in blackboard, Online ref, Orientations, Outreach serv, Outside serv via phone, mail, e-mail & web, Photocopying/Printing, Prog for adults, Ref & res, Ref serv available, Res assist avail, Workshops
Partic in Maryland Community College Library Consortium
Open Mon-Thurs 8-8, Fri 8-5, Sat 10-3
Restriction: Restricted borrowing privileges

P PRINCE GEORGE'S COUNTY MEMORIAL LIBRARY SYSTEM*, 9601 Capital Lane, 20774. SAN 344-1636. Tel: 301-699-3500. FAX: 301-985-5494. TDD: 301-808-2061. Web Site: www.pgcmls.info. *Chief Exec Officer,* Roberta Phillips; E-mail: roberta.phillips@pgcmls.info; *Chief Opearting Officer, Pub Serv,* Michelle Hamiel; E-mail: michelle.hamiel@pgcmls.info; *Chief Operating Officer, Support Serv,* Michael Gannon; E-mail: michael.gannon@pgcmls.info; *Financial Dir,* Dejare Salehudres; *Dir, Human Res,* Jeffrey Naftal
Founded 1946. Pop 890,081; Circ 5,105,120
Library Holdings: Bk Titles 2,248,189; Per Subs 559
Special Collections: American Blacks (Sojourner Truth Room); Horses & Horse Racing (Selima Room); Maryland Room; Planned Communities & Consumers Cooperatives (Rexford G Tugwell Room)
Automation Activity & Vendor Info: (Acquisitions) Innovative Interfaces, Inc; (Circulation) Innovative Interfaces, Inc; (Discovery) EBSCO Discovery Service; (OPAC) Innovative Interfaces, Inc
Wireless access
Publications: Friends Handbook; Selection Policy for Library Materials; Service Code for Information Services; Volunteer's Handbook
Special Services for the Deaf - TTY equip
Open Mon-Fri 8:30-5
Friends of the Library Group
Branches: 19
ACCOKEEK BRANCH, 15773 Livingston Rd, Accokeek, 20607-2249, SAN 344-1660. Tel: 301-292-2880. FAX: 301-292-0984. *Area Mgr,* Melanie Townsend-Diggs; E-mail: melanie.townsend-diggs@pgcmls.info
Special Services for the Deaf - TTY equip
Open Mon & Wed 1-9, Tues & Thurs 10-6, Sat 10-5
Friends of the Library Group
BADEN BRANCH, 13603 Baden-Westwood Rd, Brandywine, 20613-8167, SAN 344-1695. Tel: 301-888-1152. *Area Mgr,* Melanie Townsend-Diggs
Open Mon-Fri 10-6
Friends of the Library Group
BELTSVILLE BRANCH, 4319 Sellman Rd, Beltsville, 20705-2543, SAN 344-1725. Tel: 301-937-0294. FAX: 301-595-3455. *Area Mgr,* Luis Labra; E-mail: luis.labra@pgcmls.info
Special Services for the Deaf - TTY equip
Open Mon & Tues 1-9, Wed-Fri 10-6, Sat 10-5
Friends of the Library Group
BLADENSBURG BRANCH, 4820 Annapolis Rd, Bladensburg, 20710-1250, SAN 344-175X. Tel: 301-927-4916. FAX: 301-454-0324. *Area Mgr,* Heather Jackson; E-mail: heather.jackson@pgcmls.info
Special Services for the Deaf - TTY equip
Open Mon-Thurs 11-7, Fri 10-6, Sat 10-5
Friends of the Library Group
BOWIE BRANCH, 15210 Annapolis Rd, Bowie, 20715, SAN 344-1784. Tel: 301-262-7000. FAX: 301-809-2792. *Area Mgr,* Luis Labra
Special Collections: Selima Room (horses & horse racing)
Special Services for the Deaf - TTY equip
Open Mon-Wed 10-9, Thurs & Fri 10-6, Sat 10-5
Friends of the Library Group
FAIRMOUNT HEIGHTS BRANCH, 5904 Kolb St, Fairmount Heights, 20743-6595, SAN 344-1873. Tel: 301-883-2650. FAX: 301-925-7936. *Area Mgr,* Lunden Gillespie; E-mail: lunden.gillespie@pgcmls.info
Special Services for the Deaf - TTY equip
Open Mon-Thurs 11-7, Sat 10-5, Sun 1-5
Friends of the Library Group
GLENARDEN BRANCH, 8724 Glenarden Pkwy, Glenarden, 20706-1646, SAN 344-1903. Tel: 301-772-5477. FAX: 301-322-3410. *Area Mgr,* Lunden Gillespie
Open Mon & Tues 12-8, Wed & Thurs 10-6, Sat 10-5
Friends of the Library Group
GREENBELT BRANCH, 11 Crescent Rd, Greenbelt, 20770-1898, SAN 344-1938. Tel: 301-345-5800. FAX: 301-982-5018. *Area Mgr,* Luis Labra
Special Collections: Tugwell Room (Planned Communities & Consumers Cooperatives)
Special Services for the Deaf - TTY equip
Open Mon & Tues 1-9, Wed & Fri 10-6, Thurs 10-9, Sat 10-5, Sun 1-5
Friends of the Library Group
HILLCREST HEIGHTS BRANCH, 2398 Iverson St, Temple Hills, 20748-6850, SAN 344-1962. Tel: 301-630-4900. *Area Mgr,* Lunden Gillespie
Special Services for the Deaf - TTY equip
Open Mon & Wed 12-8, Tues & Thurs 10-6, Sat 10-5
Friends of the Library Group
HYATTSVILLE BRANCH, 6502 America Blvd, Hyattsville, 20782, SAN 344-1997. Tel: 301-985-4690. *Area Mgr,* Heather Jackson
Special Collections: Maryland Room (Maryland & Prince George's County History)
Special Services for the Deaf - TTY equip
Open Mon-Wed 10-9, Thurs & Fri 10-6, Sat 10-5
Friends of the Library Group
LARGO-KETTERING, 9601 Capital Lane, 20774, SAN 329-6431. Tel: 301-336-4044. FAX: 301-333-8857. *Area Mgr,* Megan Jones; E-mail: megan.jones@pgcmls.info
Special Services for the Deaf - TTY equip
Open Mon & Tues 1-9, Wed-Fri 10-6, Sat 10-5
Friends of the Library Group
LAUREL BRANCH, 507 Seventh St, Laurel, 20707-4013, SAN 344-2020. Tel: 301-776-6790. *Area Mgr,* Luis Labra
Special Services for the Deaf - TTY equip
Open Mon-Thurs 10-9, Fri 10-6, Sat 10-5, Sun 1-5
Friends of the Library Group
MOUNT RAINIER BRANCH, 3409 Rhode Island Ave, Mount Rainier, 20712-2073, SAN 344-211X. Tel: 301-864-8937. FAX: 301-779-6207. *Area Mgr,* Heather Jackson
Special Services for the Deaf - TTY equip
Open Mon-Thurs 11-7, Fri 10-6, Sat 10-5
Friends of the Library Group
NEW CARROLLTON BRANCH, 7414 Riverdale Rd, New Carrollton, 20784-3799, SAN 344-2144. Tel: 301-459-6900. FAX: 301-577-5085. *Area Mgr,* Heather Jackson
Special Services for the Deaf - TTY equip
Open Mon-Thurs 10-9, Fri 10-6, Sat 10-5, Sun 1-5
Friends of the Library Group
OXON HILL BRANCH, 6200 Oxon Hill Rd, Oxon Hill, 20745-3091, SAN 344-2179. Tel: 301-839-2400. *Area Mgr,* Melanie Townsend-Diggs
Special Collections: Sojourner Truth Room (African American Hist)
Special Services for the Deaf - TTY equip
Open Mon-Wed 10-9, Thurs & Fri 10-6, Sat 10-5, Sun 1-5
Friends of the Library Group
SOUTH BOWIE BRANCH, 15301 Hall Rd, Bowie, 20721. Tel: 301-850-0475. FAX: 240-206-8047. *Area Mgr,* Megan Jones
Open Mon 10-9, Tues & Thurs 1-9, Wed & Fri 10-6, Sat 10-5, Sun 1-5
Friends of the Library Group

SPAULDINGS BRANCH, 5811 Old Silver Hill Rd, District Heights, 20747-2108, SAN 328-7513. Tel: 301-817-3750. FAX: 301-967-7087. *Area Mgr,* Lunden Gillespie
Special Services for the Deaf - TTY equip
Open Mon-Wed 10-9, Thurs & Fri 10-6, Sat 10-5, Sun 1-5
Friends of the Library Group

SURRATTS-CLINTON BRANCH, 9400 Piscataway Rd, Clinton, 20735-3632, SAN 344-2268. Tel: 301-868-9200. FAX: 301-856-9369. *Area Mgr,* Melanie Townsend-Diggs
Special Services for the Deaf - TTY equip
Open Mon-Wed 10-9, Thurs & Fri 10-6, Sat 10-5
Friends of the Library Group

UPPER MARLBORO BRANCH, 14730 Main St, Upper Marlboro, 20772-3053, SAN 344-208X. Tel: 301-627-9330. FAX: 301-627-9332. *Area Mgr,* Megan Jones
Special Services for the Deaf - TTY equip
Open Mon-Thurs 11-7, Sat 10-5
Friends of the Library Group

LAUREL

C CAPITOL TECHNOLOGY UNIVERSITY, John G & Beverly A Puente Library, 11301 Springfield Rd, 20708. SAN 306-9796. Tel: 301-369-2553. E-mail: library@captechu.edu. Web Site: www.captechu.edu/current-students/puente-library. *Dir, Libr Serv,* Allen Exner; Staff 1 (Non-MLS 1)
Founded 1966. Enrl 680; Fac 22; Highest Degree: Master
Library Holdings: Bk Titles 10,000; Per Subs 90
Subject Interests: Archives, Computer sci, Electronics, Engr, Info tech
Automation Activity & Vendor Info: (Acquisitions) EOS International; (Cataloging) EOS International; (Circulation) EOS International; (OPAC) EOS International; (Serials) EOS International
Wireless access
Open Mon-Thurs 9am-10pm, Fri-9-5, Sat 10-4 (Fall-Spring); Mon-Thurs 9-5 (Summer)

S NEWSEUM LIBRARY*, 9893 Brewers Ct, 20723. SAN 375-5193. Tel: 301-957-3217. *Dir, Res,* Rick Mastroianni; E-mail: rmastroianni@newseum.org; Staff 1 (MLS 1)
Founded 1990
Library Holdings: Bk Titles 15,000; Per Subs 15
Special Collections: First Amendment & Journalism Coll
Automation Activity & Vendor Info: (Cataloging) EOS International
Restriction: Access at librarian's discretion, Internal circ only, Open to pub by appt only

LEONARDTOWN

S ST MARY'S COUNTY HISTORICAL SOCIETY*, Research Center, 41680 Tudor Pl, 20650. (Mail add: PO Box 212, 20650-0212), SAN 306-9885. Tel: 301-475-2467. FAX: 301-475-2467. Web Site: www.stmaryshistory.org. *Exec Dir,* Peter LaPorte; E-mail: director@stmaryshistory.org; Staff 2 (MLS 1, Non-MLS 1)
Founded 1951
Library Holdings: AV Mats 45; CDs 20; DVDs 3; Electronic Media & Resources 3; Music Scores 2; Bk Titles 2,000; Bk Vols 3,500; Per Subs 35
Special Collections: Chronicles of St Mary's Coll; Early Maryland & English History Coll; Local Authors Coll. Oral History
Subject Interests: Genealogy, Local hist, Relig
Wireless access
Restriction: Non-circulating to the pub

P SAINT MARY'S COUNTY LIBRARY*, Leonardtown Library (Headquarters), 23250 Hollywood Rd, 20650. SAN 344-2535. Tel: 301-475-2846. FAX: 301-884-4415. Web Site: www.stmalib.org. *Dir,* Michael Blackwell; Tel: 301-475-2846, Ext 1013, E-mail: mblackwell@stmalib.org; *Dep Dir,* Mary Anne Bowman; Tel: 301-475-2846, Ext 1015, E-mail: mabowman@stmalib.org; *Br Mgr,* Marylee Russell; Tel: 301-475-2846, Ext 1006, E-mail: stma.manager@stmalib.org
Founded 1950. Pop 110,000
Library Holdings: Bk Vols 176,958; Per Subs 444
Automation Activity & Vendor Info: (Cataloging) SirsiDynix; (Circulation) SirsiDynix; (OPAC) SirsiDynix
Wireless access
Function: Wheelchair accessible
Mem of Southern Maryland Regional Library Association, Inc
Partic in Maryland Interlibrary Loan Organization
Open Mon-Thurs 9-8, Fri & Sat 9-5
Friends of the Library Group
Branches: 2
CHARLOTTE HALL BRANCH, 37600 New Market Rd, Charlotte Hall, 20622, SAN 344-2543. Tel: 301-884-2211. FAX: 301-884-2113. *Br Mgr,* Kathy Faubion; Tel: 301-884-2211, Ext 1006, E-mail: kfaubion@stmalib.org
Open Mon-Thurs 9-8, Fri & Sat 9-5
LEXINGTON PARK BRANCH, 21677 FDR Blvd, Lexington Park, 20653, SAN 344-256X. Tel: 301-863-8188. FAX: 301-863-2550. *Br Mgr,* Amy Ford; Tel: 301-863-8188, Ext 1012, E-mail: lexi.manager@stmalib.org
Open Mon-Thurs 9-8, Fri & Sat 9-5, Sun 1-5
Bookmobiles: 1

MCHENRY

J GARRETT COLLEGE, Library & Learning Commons, 687 Mosser Rd, 21541. SAN 306-9923. Tel: 301-387-3009. FAX: 301-387-3720. E-mail: reference@garrettcollege.edu. Web Site: garrettcollege.libguides.com. *Dir,* Jenny Meslener; Tel: 301-387-3022, E-mail: jennifer.meslener@garrettcollege.edu; *Tech Serv Librn,* Stephanie Miller; E-mail: stephanie.miller@garrettcollege.edu; *eCampus/Library Circulation Mgr,* Lois Anderson; E-mail: lois.anderson@garrettcollege.edu; Staff 4 (MLS 2, Non-MLS 2)
Founded 1971. Enrl 600; Fac 18; Highest Degree: Associate
Library Holdings: Bk Titles 24,803; Bk Vols 27,592; Per Subs 70
Special Collections: Coal Talk Oral Hist; Western Maryland. Oral History
Subject Interests: Natural res
Automation Activity & Vendor Info: (Cataloging) Follett Software; (Circulation) Follett Software; (OPAC) Follett Software
Wireless access
Partic in Maryland Community College Library Consortium

NEW WINDSOR

P CARROLL COUNTY PUBLIC LIBRARY*, Headquarters, 1100 Green Valley Rd, 21776. SAN 344-4759. Tel: 410-386-4500. Reference Tel: 410-386-4488. FAX: 410-386-4509. Web Site: library.carr.org. *Exec Dir,* Andrea Berstler; E-mail: aberstler@carr.org; *Outreach Serv Librn, Prog Serv,* Dorothy Stoltz; E-mail: dstoltz@carr.org; *Mgr, Info Tech, Web Librn,* Robert Kuntz; *Coll Develop,* Concetta Pisano; E-mail: cpisano@carr.org; *ILL,* Mallory Duff; *Tech Serv,* Elaine Adkins; Staff 144 (MLS 22, Non-MLS 122)
Founded 1958. Pop 165,000; Circ 3,579,244
Library Holdings: AV Mats 80,558; Bk Vols 584,167; Per Subs 1,461
Subject Interests: Local hist
Automation Activity & Vendor Info: (Acquisitions) Innovative Interfaces, Inc; (Cataloging) Innovative Interfaces, Inc; (Circulation) Innovative Interfaces, Inc; (OPAC) Innovative Interfaces, Inc; (Serials) Innovative Interfaces, Inc
Wireless access
Publications: Directory of Community Services for Carroll County, Maryland; Ghosts & Legends of Carroll County, Maryland
Special Services for the Deaf - TTY equip
Open Mon-Fri 9-5
Branches: 6
ELDERSBURG BRANCH, 6400 W Hemlock Dr, Eldersburg, 21784-6538, SAN 344-4872. Tel: 410-386-4460. FAX: 410-386-4466. *Br Mgr,* Nadine Rosendale
Open Mon-Thurs 9-8:45, Fri & Sat 9-5, Sun 12-5
Friends of the Library Group
FINKSBURG BRANCH, 2265 Old Westminster Pike, Finksburg, 21048. *Br Mgr,* Heather Owings
MOUNT AIRY BRANCH, 705 Ridge Ave, Mount Airy, 21771-3911, SAN 344-4813. Tel: 410-386-4470. FAX: 410-386-4477. *Br Mgr,* Patty Sundberg
Open Mon-Thurs 9-8:45, Fri & Sat 9-5
NORTH CARROLL, 2255 Hanover Pike, Greenmount, 21074, SAN 344-4783. Tel: 410-386-4480. FAX: 410-386-4486. *Br Mgr,* Darrell Robertson; E-mail: Drobertson@carr.org
Open Mon-Thurs 9-8:45, Fri & Sat 9-5
TANEYTOWN BRANCH, Ten Grand Dr, Taneytown, 21787-2421, SAN 344-4848. Tel: 410-386-4510. FAX: 410-386-4515. *Br Mgr,* Jillian Dittrich; E-mail: jdittrich@carr.org; Staff 8 (MLS 2, Non-MLS 6)
Circ 383,570
Automation Activity & Vendor Info: (OPAC) Innovative Interfaces, Inc
Open Mon-Thurs 9-8:45, Fri 9-5, Sat 9-5
WESTMINSTER BRANCH, 50 E Main St, Westminster, 21157-5097, SAN 375-6297. Tel: 410-386-4490. FAX: 410-386-4487. *Br Mgr,* Christina Kuntz; E-mail: cogle@carr.org
Special Services for the Deaf - TTY equip
Open Mon-Thurs 9-8:45, Fri & Sat 9-5, Sun 12-5
Bookmobiles: 3. In Charge, Kristin Bodvin. Bk vols 11,000

NORTH EAST

J CECIL COLLEGE*, Cecil County Veterans Memorial Library, One Seahawk Dr, 21901-1904. SAN 306-9931. Tel: 410-287-1005. E-mail: library@cecil.edu. Web Site: www.cecil.edu/student-resources/library. *Libr Dir,* Amanda Demers; Tel: 410-287-1030, E-mail: ADemers@cecil.edu; *Instrul Librn,* Melissa A D'Agostino; Tel: 443-674-1492, E-mail: dago7559@cecil.edu; Staff 4.5 (MLS 2.5, Non-MLS 2)
Founded 1968. Enrl 1,916; Fac 40; Highest Degree: Associate
Library Holdings: Audiobooks 32; e-books 57,982; Bk Titles 26,130; Per Subs 39; Videos 554
Special Collections: Bridges of Cecil County (Photographs from the depression era)
Subject Interests: Genealogy, Maryland
Automation Activity & Vendor Info: (Acquisitions) SirsiDynix; (Cataloging) SirsiDynix; (Circulation) SirsiDynix; (Course Reserve) SirsiDynix; (ILL) SirsiDynix; (OPAC) SirsiDynix; (Serials) SirsiDynix
Wireless access
Partic in Maryland Community College Library Consortium
Open Mon-Fri 7:30am-8pm, Sat 11-4

OAKLAND

P RUTH ENLOW LIBRARY OF GARRETT COUNTY*, Six N Second St, 21550. SAN 344-2659. Tel: 301-334-3996. FAX: 301-334-4152. E-mail: info@relib.net. Web Site: www.relib.net. *Dir,* Thomas Vote; E-mail: thomas@relib.net; *Asst Dir, Br Mgr,* Ann Leighton; E-mail: ann@relib.net; Staff 2 (MLS 2)
Founded 1946. Pop 29,250; Circ 225,000
Special Collections: Garrett County; Garrett County Families; Western Maryland
Subject Interests: Local hist
Automation Activity & Vendor Info: (Cataloging) Innovative Interfaces, Inc; (Circulation) Innovative Interfaces, Inc; (OPAC) Innovative Interfaces, Inc; (Serials) EBSCO Online
Wireless access
Mem of Western Maryland Regional Library
Partic in Maryland Interlibrary Loan Organization
Special Services for the Deaf - TDD equip
Open Mon & Wed 9:15-8, Tues, Thurs & Fri 9:15-5:30, Sat 9-4
Friends of the Library Group
Branches: 4
ACCIDENT BRANCH, 106 S North St, Accident, 21520. (Mail add: PO Box 189, Accident, 21520), SAN 344-2683. Tel: 301-746-8792. FAX: 301-746-8399. *Br Mgr,* Kimberly Cecil
Founded 1977. Pop 349
Open Mon, Tues, Thurs & Fri 11-5:30, Wed 11-7, Sat 9-1
Friends of the Library Group
FRIENDSVILLE BRANCH, 315 Chestnut St, Friendsville, 21531. (Mail add: PO Box 57, Friendsville, 21531-0057), SAN 344-2748. Tel: 301-746-5663. FAX: 301-334-8075. *Br Mgr,* Michele Liston; Staff 1 (Non-MLS 1)
Open Mon & Wed 2-8, Tues & Thurs 1:30-5:30, Sat 9-2
Friends of the Library Group
GRANTSVILLE BRANCH, 102 Parkview Dr, Grantsville, 21536, SAN 344-2772. Tel: 301-895-5298. FAX: 301-245-4411. *Br Mgr,* Kimberly Lishia
Open Mon 11-8, Tues-Thurs 11-5:30, Sat 9-1
Friends of the Library Group
KITZMILLER BRANCH, 288 W Main St, Kitzmiller, 21538. (Mail add: PO Box 100, Kitzmiller, 21538-0100), SAN 344-2802. Tel: 301-334-8091. FAX: 301-453-3368. *Br Mgr,* Diane Kisner
Open Mon & Wed 3-7, Tues, Thurs & Fri 9:30-Noon
Friends of the Library Group

GL GARRETT COUNTY CIRCUIT COURT LIBRARY*, Courthouse, Rm 107B, 203 S Fourth St, 21550. Tel: 301-334-1934. FAX: 301-334-5042. *Library Contact,* Timothy Miller
Library Holdings: Bk Vols 500
Restriction: Not open to pub

OXFORD

G OXFORD MARINE LIBRARY*, Cooperative Oxford Laboratory Library NOAA/NOS, 904 S Morris St, 21654-9724. SAN 306-9966. Tel: 443-258-6080. FAX: 410-226-5925. Web Site: mrl.cofc.edu/oxford. *Librn,* Position Currently Open; *Library Contact,* Dr Shawn McLaughlin; E-mail: shawn.mclaughlin@noaa.gov
Founded 1961
Library Holdings: Bk Vols 13,500; Per Subs 45
Subject Interests: Ecology, Marine biol
Publications: Annual Publications List; Dissertations; Serial & Journal Holdings; Theses List
Partic in NOAA Libraries Network; OCLC Online Computer Library Center, Inc; Proquest Dialog

PATUXENT RIVER

A UNITED STATES NAVY*, NAVAIR Scientific & Technical Library, 22269 Cedar Point Rd B407, 20670-1120. SAN 344-2837. Tel: 301-342-1927. FAX: 301-342-1933. E-mail: technical.library@navy.mil. *Supvr,* Anna Zelinski-Gafford; Staff 6 (MLS 3, Non-MLS 3)
Founded 1952
Library Holdings: Bk Vols 15,113; Per Subs 30
Special Collections: NAVAIR Technical Manuals & Directives; NAWCAD Technical Reports; Technical Coll. US Document Depository
Subject Interests: Aeronaut, Computer sci, Engr, Phys sci
Automation Activity & Vendor Info: (Cataloging) SirsiDynix; (Circulation) SirsiDynix; (ILL) OCLC; (OPAC) SirsiDynix
Wireless access
Function: Art exhibits, Bks on CD, Computers for patron use, Doc delivery serv, Electronic databases & coll, Govt ref serv, ILL available, Internet access, Online cat, Online ref, Orientations, Outreach serv, Ref & res, Ref serv available, Res libr, Tax forms
Partic in Consortium of Naval Libraries
Open Mon-Thurs 7:30-4:30, Fri 10-2
Restriction: Open to mil & govt employees only, Photo ID required for access

PIKESVILLE

R NER ISRAEL RABBINICAL COLLEGE LIBRARY*, 400 Mount Wilson Lane, 21208. SAN 306-8609. Tel: 410-484-7200. FAX: 410-484-3060. E-mail: nirc@nirc.edu. *Librn,* Avrohom S Shnidman; Tel: 443-548-8014
Founded 1933
Library Holdings: Bk Vols 23,000; Per Subs 18
Special Collections: Biblical Commentaries; Hebrew Newspapers of European Communities 1820-1937; Responsa; Talmudic Laws
Open Mon-Thurs & Sun 9-5, Fri 9-Noon

PRINCE FREDERICK

P CALVERT LIBRARY*, 850 Costley Way, 20678. SAN 307-000X. Tel: 301-855-1862, 410-535-0291. FAX: 410-535-3022. Web Site: calvertlibrary.info. *Dir,* Carrie Willson; E-mail: cwillson@calvertlibrary.info; *Pub Relations Coordr,* Robyn Truslow; E-mail: rtruslow@calvertlibrary.info; *Youth Serv Coordr,* Beverly Izzi; E-mail: bizzi@calvertlibrary.info; Staff 8 (MLS 8)
Founded 1959. Pop 84,000; Circ 962,246
Library Holdings: AV Mats 27,293; e-books 1,000; Bk Vols 153,443; Per Subs 221
Subject Interests: Maryland
Automation Activity & Vendor Info: (Acquisitions) SirsiDynix; (Circulation) SirsiDynix; (OPAC) SirsiDynix
Wireless access
Function: Adult bk club, Adult literacy prog, After school storytime, Computer training, E-Reserves, Electronic databases & coll, Family literacy, Homebound delivery serv, ILL available, Magnifiers for reading, Online ref, Photocopying/Printing, Preschool outreach, Prog for adults, Prog for children & young adult, Ref serv available, Spoken cassettes & CDs, Spoken cassettes & DVDs, Summer reading prog, Tax forms, Telephone ref, VHS videos, Workshops
Mem of Southern Maryland Regional Library Association, Inc
Special Services for the Deaf - TTY equip
Special Services for the Blind - Bks on cassette; Bks on CD; Large print bks
Open Mon-Thurs 12-5, Fri 1-5, Sat 10-2
Friends of the Library Group
Branches: 3
FAIRVIEW, 8120 Southern Maryland Blvd, Owings, 20736, SAN 321-9585. Tel: 410-257-2101. FAX: 410-257-0662. *Br Mgr,* Lisa Tassa; E-mail: ltassa@calvertlibrary.info
Open Mon-Thurs 9-9, Fri 12-5, Sat 9-5
SOUTHERN BRANCH, 13920 HG Trueman Rd, Solomons, 20688. (Mail add: PO Box 599, Lusby, 20657-0599), SAN 329-5516. Tel: 410-326-5289. FAX: 410-326-8370. *Br Mgr,* Patti McConnell; E-mail: pmcconnell@calvertlibrary.info
Open Mon-Thurs 9-9, Fri 12-5, Sat 9-5
TWIN BEACHES BRANCH, 3819 Harbor Rd, Chesapeake Beach, 20732, SAN 321-9593. Tel: 410-257-2411. FAX: 410-257-0663. *Br Mgr,* Joan Kilmon; E-mail: jkilmon@calvertlibrary.info
Open Mon-Thurs 9-9, Fri 12-5, Sat 9-5
Bookmobiles: 1. Librns, Rachel Gordon & Lisa Wieland

PRINCESS ANNE

GL SOMERSET COUNTY CIRCUIT COURT LIBRARY, Courthouse, 30512 Prince William St, 21853. (Mail add: PO Box 279, 21853-0279). Tel: 410-621-7581. FAX: 410-621-7595. Web Site: www.mdcourts.gov/circuit/somerset. *Law Librn,* Sarah Grangier; E-mail: sarah.grangier@mdcourts.gov

Library Holdings: Bk Vols 1,500
Wireless access

P SOMERSET COUNTY LIBRARY SYSTEM*, 11767 Beechwood St, 21853. SAN 344-2861. Tel: 410-651-0852. FAX: 410-651-1388. Web Site: www.somelibrary.org. *Libr Dir,* Ed Goyda; E-mail: ed.goyda@somelibrary.org; *Br Mgr,* Kayla Hodgson; E-mail: khodgson@somelibrary.org; *Tech Serv Coordr,* Michele Henry; E-mail: mhenry@somelibrary.org; *Youth Serv Coordr,* Becky Pratte; E-mail: rpratte@somelibrary.org
Founded 1967. Pop 26,500
Library Holdings: Bk Vols 104,672; Per Subs 67
Subject Interests: Hist, Maryland
Automation Activity & Vendor Info: (Acquisitions) Innovative Interfaces, Inc; (Cataloging) Innovative Interfaces, Inc; (Circulation) Innovative Interfaces, Inc; (Discovery) Innovative Interfaces, Inc; (OPAC) Innovative Interfaces, Inc; (Serials) Innovative Interfaces, Inc
Wireless access
Partic in Eastern Shore Regional Library
Open Mon-Thurs 10-7, Fri & Sat 10-5
Friends of the Library Group
Branches: 2
CRISFIELD PUBLIC, 100 Collins St, Crisfield, 21817, SAN 344-2896. Tel: 410-968-0955. *Br Mgr,* Jamie Bradshaw
Open Mon, Wed & Fri 1-7, Tues & Thurs 11-7, Sat 10-5
EWELL BRANCH, 20910 Caleb Jones Rd, Ewell, 21824, SAN 320-5282. Tel: 410-425-5141. *Br Mgr,* Christina Marshall

C UNIVERSITY OF MARYLAND-EASTERN SHORE, Frederick Douglass Library, 11868 Academic Oval, 21853. SAN 344-2926. Tel: 410-651-6621. Circulation Tel: 410-651-7691. Interlibrary Loan Service Tel: 410-651-6609. Reference Tel: 410-651-7937. Automation Services Tel: 410-651-6612. FAX: 410-651-6269. E-mail: refuser@umes.edu. Web Site: wwwcp.umes.edu/fdl. *Actg Dir, Libr Serv, Media Librn,* Sharon D Brooks; Tel: 410-651-6275, E-mail: sdbrooks@umes.edu; *Head, Access Serv,* Joseph D Bree; Tel: 410-651-6270, E-mail: jdbree@umes.edu; *Ref Librn,* Janet Dewey Eke; Tel: 410-651-7540, E-mail: jdeke@umes.edu; Staff 10 (MLS 10)
Founded 1968. Enrl 4,443; Fac 220; Highest Degree: Doctorate
Library Holdings: Audiobooks 797; DVDs 192; e-books 36,939; e-journals 5,889; Electronic Media & Resources 44,015; Microforms 500,000; Bk Titles 199,508; Bk Vols 271,310; Per Subs 937
Special Collections: African American History (Black Coll), out-of-print, rare & first editions; Maryland Eastern Shore Coll (Somerset, Wicomico & Worcester Counties), bks, clippings, correspondence, maps, photog, reports; University Archives. State Document Depository
Subject Interests: Agr, Allied health, Arts, Bus, Golf course mgt, Hospitality, Sci, Tourism
Automation Activity & Vendor Info: (Acquisitions) Ex Libris Group; (Cataloging) Ex Libris Group; (Circulation) Ex Libris Group; (Course Reserve) Ex Libris Group; (ILL) Ex Libris Group; (OPAC) Ex Libris Group; (Serials) Ex Libris Group
Wireless access
Publications: A Mini Guide; Departmental Brochures (Reference guide); Douglass Notes (Newsletter); Library Aides (Research guide); New Acquisitions List; Periodical Holdings (Union list of serials)
Partic in HBCU Library Alliance; OCLC Online Computer Library Center, Inc; University System of Maryland & Affiliated Institutions
Open Mon-Fri 7:30-5

RANDALLSTOWN

S NORTHWEST HOSPITAL CENTER, Health Sciences Library, 5401 Old Court Rd, 21133. SAN 325-8815. Tel: 410-521-2200, Ext 55682. Web Site: www.lifebridgehealth.org/northwest/northwest1.aspx. *Med Librn,* Vaishali Jahagirdar; E-mail: vjahagirdar@lifebridgehealth.org; Staff 1 (MLS 1)
Library Holdings: Bk Vols 500
Wireless access
Restriction: Med staff only, Open to others by appt

ROCKVILLE

S AMERICAN RED CROSS HOLLAND LABORATORY, Ann I Harnsberger Biomedical Sciences Library, 15601 Crabbs Branch Way, 20855-2743. SAN 377-1725. Tel: 240-314-3453. FAX: 866-814-5544. *Med Librn,* Shali Y Jiang; E-mail: shali.jiang@redcross.org; Staff 1 (Non-MLS 1)
Founded 1987
Library Holdings: Bk Vols 5,000; Per Subs 37
Automation Activity & Vendor Info: (Acquisitions) SirsiDynix; (Cataloging) SirsiDynix; (Circulation) SirsiDynix; (Course Reserve) SirsiDynix; (OPAC) SirsiDynix; (Serials) SirsiDynix
Wireless access
Partic in Medical Library Association; National Network of Libraries of Medicine Region 1
Restriction: Not open to pub, Staff use only

R BENDER JEWISH COMMUNITY CENTER OF GREATER WASHINGTON, Kass Judaic Library, 6125 Montrose Rd, 20852. SAN 307-0085. Tel: 301-881-0100. FAX: 301-881-5512. Web Site: www.benderjccgw.org.
Founded 1970
Library Holdings: DVDs 70; Bk Vols 2,000; Per Subs 15
Wireless access

J MONTGOMERY COLLEGE LIBRARY*, 51 Mannakee St, Macklin Tower, 20850. Tel: 240-567-7915. FAX: 240-567-7141. Web Site: www.montgomerycollege.edu/library. *Dir, Libr & Info Serv,* Tanner Wray; Tel: 240-567-7101, E-mail: tanner.wray@montgomerycollege.edu; *Access Serv, Assoc Dir,* Brynne Norton; Tel: 240-567-5679, E-mail: brynne.norton@montgomerycollege.edu; *Assoc Dir, Res & Teaching Assoc,* Jessame Ferguson; Tel: 240-567-7137, E-mail: jessame.ferguson@montgomerycollege.edu; *Assoc Dir, Coll, Assoc Dir, Resources,* Kari Schmidt; Tel: 240-567-4135, E-mail: kari.schmidt@montgomerycollege.edu
Highest Degree: Associate
Automation Activity & Vendor Info: (Acquisitions) Ex Libris Group; (Cataloging) Ex Libris Group; (Circulation) Ex Libris Group; (Course Reserve) Atlas Systems; (Discovery) EBSCO Discovery Service; (ILL) Atlas Systems; (OPAC) Ex Libris Group; (Serials) Ex Libris Group
Wireless access
Partic in LYRASIS; Maryland Community College Library Consortium; Maryland Interlibrary Loan Organization; OCLC Online Computer Library Center, Inc
Special Services for the Deaf - ADA equip; Closed caption videos; Sorenson video relay syst; TTY equip
Special Services for the Blind - Accessible computers; Assistive/Adapted tech devices, equip & products; Computer with voice synthesizer for visually impaired persons; Copier with enlargement capabilities; Large screen computer & software; Low vision equip; Magnifiers; PC for people with disabilities; Reader equip; Screen reader software; ZoomText magnification & reading software
Open Mon-Thurs 8am-10pm, Fri 8-5, Sat 9-5
Departmental Libraries:
GERMANTOWN CAMPUS LIBRARY, 20200 Observation Dr, Humanities Bldg (HS 110), Germantown, 20876, SAN 321-0804. Tel: 240-567-7858. Administration Tel: 240-567-7915.
Founded 1978. Highest Degree: Associate
Open Mon-Thurs 8-10, Fri 8-5, Sat 9-5
ROCKVILLE CAMPUS LIBRARY, 51 Mannakee St, Macklin Tower, 20850, SAN 307-0093. Tel: 240-567-7117. Administration Tel: 240-567-7915.
Founded 1965. Highest Degree: Associate
Open Mon-Thurs 8-10, Fri 8-5, Sat 9-5
TAKOMA PARK/SILVER SPRING CAMPUS LIBRARY, 7600 Takoma Ave, Resource Center 215, Takoma Park, 20912, SAN 307-0506. Tel: 240-567-1540. Administration Tel: 240-567-7915.
Founded 1946. Highest Degree: Associate
Open Mon-Thurs 8-10, Fri 8-5, Sat 9-5

GL MONTGOMERY COUNTY CIRCUIT COURT*, Law Library, Judicial Ctr, 50 Maryland Ave, Ste 3420, 20850. SAN 307-0107. Tel: 240-777-9120. FAX: 240-777-9126. E-mail: lawlibrary@mcccourt.com. Web Site: montgomerycountymd.gov/cct/law-library.html. *Law Librn,* Julia Viets; Tel: 240-777-9122, E-mail: jviets@mcccourt.com; *Asst Librn,* Willa Broughton. Subject Specialists: *Legal res,* Julia Viets; *Legal ref, Legal res,* Willa Broughton; Staff 3 (MLS 2.5, Non-MLS 0.5)
Library Holdings: Bk Vols 80,000; Per Subs 110
Special Collections: How To Books for self-represented patrons; Maryland, DC & Virginia Legal & Federal Materials
Subject Interests: Continuing educ, Legal
Automation Activity & Vendor Info: (Cataloging) EOS International; (OPAC) EOS International
Wireless access
Function: 24/7 Online cat, Archival coll, Audio & video playback equip for onsite use, CD-ROM, Electronic databases & coll, ILL available, Legal assistance to inmates, Notary serv, Online cat, Orientations, Outreach serv, Outside serv via phone, mail, e-mail & web, Photocopying/Printing, Ref & res, Wheelchair accessible
Open Mon-Fri 8-5:30
Restriction: Non-circulating, Open to pub for ref only

P MONTGOMERY COUNTY PUBLIC LIBRARIES*, Central Offices, 21 Maryland Ave, Ste 310, 20850. SAN 344-2985. Tel: 240-777-0002. FAX: 240-777-0014. Web Site: www.montgomerycountymd.gov/library. *Interim Dir,* Anita Vassallo; E-mail: anita.vassallo@montgomerycountymd.gov; *Interim Asst Dir,* James Donaldson; Tel: 240-777-0030, E-mail:

james.donaldson@montgomerycountymd.gov; *Bus Mgr,* Lennadene Bailey; E-mail: lennadene.bailey@montgomerycountymd.gov
Founded 1951
Special Collections: Business Resource Center (Rockville); Health Information Center (Wheaton). Oral History; US Document Depository
Subject Interests: Govt
Automation Activity & Vendor Info: (Cataloging) SirsiDynix
Wireless access
Partic in Md State Libr Network; OCLC Online Computer Library Center, Inc
Special Services for the Deaf - TTY equip
Special Services for the Blind - Newsline for the Blind; SNL for registered users
Open Mon-Fri 8:30-5
Friends of the Library Group
Branches: 22

ASPEN HILL LIBRARY, 4407 Aspen Hill Rd, 20853-2899, SAN 344-3019. Tel: 240-773-9410. FAX: 301-871-0443. TDD: 301-871-2097. *Br Mgr,* David Payne; Tel: 240-773-9401
Special Collections: Foreign Language (Spanish) Coll; Literacy Coll
Special Services for the Deaf - TTY equip
Special Services for the Blind - Closed circuit TV; Computer with voice synthesizer for visually impaired persons; Copier with enlargement capabilities; Large print bks; Magnifiers; Screen enlargement software for people with visual disabilities
Open Mon-Thurs 10-8, Fri & Sat 10-6, Sun 1-5
Friends of the Library Group

CHEVY CHASE LIBRARY, 8005 Connecticut Ave, Chevy Chase, 20815-5997, SAN 344-3078. Tel: 240-773-9590. TDD: 301-657-0830. *Br Mgr,* Christopher Borawski; Tel: 240-773-9581; Staff 16 (MLS 7, Non-MLS 9)
Special Collections: Glass Coll
Function: Wheelchair accessible
Special Services for the Deaf - TTY equip
Special Services for the Blind - Computer with voice synthesizer for visually impaired persons; Copier with enlargement capabilities; Large print bks; Screen enlargement software for people with visual disabilities
Open Mon-Thurs 10-8, Fri & Sat 10-6
Friends of the Library Group

DAMASCUS LIBRARY, 9701 Main St, Damascus, 20872, SAN 344-3108. Tel: 240-773-9444. *Br Mgr,* Ann Stillman; Tel: 240-773-9440; Staff 11.5 (MLS 4, Non-MLS 7.5)
Special Collections: Damascus Local History
Special Services for the Deaf - Video & TTY relay via computer
Special Services for the Blind - Audio mat; Computer with voice synthesizer for visually impaired persons; Copier with enlargement capabilities; Large print bks; Magnifiers; Screen enlargement software for people with visual disabilities
Open Mon & Tues 10-8, Wed 1-8, Thurs-Sat 10-6, Sun 1-5
Friends of the Library Group

DAVIS LIBRARY, 6400 Democracy Blvd, Bethesda, 20817-1638, SAN 344-3132. Tel: 240-777-0922. FAX: 301-564-5055. *Br Mgr,* Steve Warrick; Tel: 240-777-0916
Founded 1964
Special Services for the Deaf - TTY equip
Special Services for the Blind - Audio mat; Computer with voice synthesizer for visually impaired persons; Copier with enlargement capabilities; Large print bks; Screen enlargement software for people with visual disabilities
Open Mon-Thurs 10-8, Fri & Sat 10-6
Friends of the Library Group

GAITHERSBURG LIBRARY, 18330 Montgomery Village Ave, Gaithersburg, 20879, SAN 344-3191. Tel: 240-773-9490. *Br Mgr,* Cindy Schweinfest; Tel: 240-773-9494
Special Collections: Foreign Language Coll (Chinese, French, German, Korean, Spanish, Vietnamese); Literacy Coll
Special Services for the Deaf - TTY equip
Special Services for the Blind - Computer with voice synthesizer for visually impaired persons; Copier with enlargement capabilities; Large print bks; Magnifiers; Screen enlargement software for people with visual disabilities
Open Mon-Thurs 9-9, Fri & Sat 10-6, Sun 1-5
Friends of the Library Group

GERMANTOWN LIBRARY, 19840 Century Blvd, Germantown, 20874, SAN 328-9966. Tel: 240-777-0110. FAX: 240-777-0129. *Br Mgr,* Jan Baird-Adams; Tel: 240-773-0126
Special Collections: Foreign Language (Spanish) Coll
Special Services for the Deaf - TTY equip
Special Services for the Blind - Audio mat; Computer with voice synthesizer for visually impaired persons; Copier with enlargement capabilities; Large print bks; Magnifiers; Screen enlargement software for people with visual disabilities
Open Mon-Thurs 9-9, Fri & Sat 10-6, Sun 1-5
Friends of the Library Group

KENSINGTON PARK LIBRARY, 4201 Knowles Ave, Kensington, 20895-2408, SAN 344-3221. Tel: 240-773-9515. FAX: 301-897-2238. *Br Mgr,* Karen Miller; Tel: 240-773-9505; Staff 7 (MLS 4, Non-MLS 3)
Special Services for the Deaf - TTY equip
Special Services for the Blind - Audio mat; Computer with voice synthesizer for visually impaired persons; Copier with enlargement capabilities; Large print bks; Screen enlargement software for people with visual disabilities
Open Mon-Thurs 10-8, Fri & Sat 10-6
Friends of the Library Group

LITTLE FALLS LIBRARY, 5501 Massachusetts Ave, Bethesda, 20816, SAN 344-3256. Tel: 240-773-9520. FAX: 301-320-0164. *Br Mgr,* Carolyn Bogardus; Tel: 240-773-9526
Special Services for the Deaf - TTY equip
Special Services for the Blind - Computer with voice synthesizer for visually impaired persons; Copier with enlargement capabilities; Large print bks; Magnifiers; Screen enlargement software for people with visual disabilities
Open Mon-Thurs 10-8, Fri & Sat 10-6
Friends of the Library Group

LONG BRANCH LIBRARY, 8800 Garland Ave, Silver Spring, 20901. Tel: 240-777-0910. TDD: 301-565-7662. *Br Mgr,* Nathan Chadwick; Tel: 240-773-9526
Open Mon & Wed 10-8, Tues & Thurs 1-8, Fri & Sat 10-6, Sun 1-5

MONTGOMERY COUNTY CORRECTIONAL FACILITY, 22880 Whelan Lane, Boyds, 20841, SAN 344-3000. Tel: 240-773-9914. FAX: 240-773-9939. *Librn,* Lori Kebetz
Restriction: Not open to pub

CONNIE MORELLA LIBRARY, 7400 Arlington Rd, Bethesda, 20814, SAN 344-3043. Tel: 240-777-0970. FAX: 301-657-0841. *Br Mgr,* Nancy Benner; Tel: 240-773-0934
Circ 550,000
Special Services for the Deaf - TTY equip
Open Mon-Thurs 9-9, Fri & Sat 10-6, Sun 1-5
Friends of the Library Group

MAGGIE NIGHTINGALE LIBRARY, 19633 Fisher Ave, Poolesville, 20837-2071, SAN 344-3493. Tel: 240-773-9550. TDD: 301-972-7825. *Br Mgr,* Elizabeth Bowen; Tel: 240-773-9552
Special Services for the Deaf - TTY equip
Special Services for the Blind - Computer with voice synthesizer for visually impaired persons; Copier with enlargement capabilities; Large print bks; Screen enlargement software for people with visual disabilities
Open Mon-Wed 2-9, Thurs 10-9, Fri & Sat 10-6

NOYES LIBRARY FOR YOUNG CHILDREN, 10237 Carroll Pl, Kensington, 20895-3361, SAN 344-3310. Tel: 240-773-9570. FAX: 301-929-5470. *Br Mgr,* Christine Freeman; Tel: 240-777-0105
Special Services for the Blind - Computer with voice synthesizer for visually impaired persons; Screen enlargement software for people with visual disabilities
Open Tues, Thurs & Sat 9-5, Wed 1-8

OLNEY LIBRARY, 3500 Olney-Laytonsville Rd, Olney, 20832-1798, SAN 344-340X. Tel: 240-773-9545. *Actg Br Mgr,* Christine Freeman; Tel: 240-773-9540
Special Services for the Deaf - TTY equip
Special Services for the Blind - Computer with voice synthesizer for visually impaired persons; Copier with enlargement capabilities; Large print bks; Screen enlargement software for people with visual disabilities
Open Mon-Thurs 9-9, Fri & Sat 10-6, Sun 1-5
Friends of the Library Group

POTOMAC LIBRARY, 10101 Glenolden Dr, Potomac, 20854-5052, SAN 344-3345. Tel: 240-777-0690. FAX: 301-983-4479. TDD: 301-765-4083. *Actg Br Mgr,* David Payne; Tel: 240-777-0696
Special Collections: Chinese Language Coll
Special Services for the Deaf - TTY equip
Special Services for the Blind - Audio mat; Computer with voice synthesizer for visually impaired persons; Copier with enlargement capabilities; Large print bks; Screen enlargement software for people with visual disabilities
Open Mon-Thurs 10-8, Fri & Sat 10-6
Friends of the Library Group

MARILYN J PRAISNER LIBRARY, 14910 Old Columbia Pike, Burtonsville, 20866, SAN 374-7964. Tel: 240-773-9460. FAX: 301-421-5407. *Br Mgr,* Tina Deifallah; Tel: 240-773-9450
Special Collections: Foreign Language (Chinese & Korean Coll)
Special Services for the Deaf - TTY equip
Special Services for the Blind - Audio mat; Computer with voice synthesizer for visually impaired persons; Copier with enlargement capabilities; Large print bks; Screen enlargement software for people with visual disabilities
Open Mon-Thurs 9-9, Fri & Sat 10-6, Sun 1-5
Friends of the Library Group

QUINCE ORCHARD LIBRARY, 15831 Quince Orchard Rd, Gaithersburg, 20878. Tel: 240-777-0200. FAX: 240-777-0202. *Br Mgr,* James Stewart; Tel: 240-777-0212
Special Collections: Foreign Language (Chinese) Coll

Special Services for the Deaf - TTY equip
Special Services for the Blind - Audio mat; Computer with voice synthesizer for visually impaired persons; Copier with enlargement capabilities; Large print bks; Screen enlargement software for people with visual disabilities
Open Mon-Thurs 9-9, Fri & Sat 10-6
Friends of the Library Group

ROCKVILLE MEMORIAL LIBRARY, 21 Maryland Ave, 20850-2371, SAN 344-337X. Tel: 240-777-0140. FAX: 240-777-0157. *Br Mgr,* Patrick Fromm; Tel: 240-777-0277
Special Collections: Business Resource Center (Business Counselling); Children's Resource Center; County Government Archives; Foreign Language Coll (Chinese, Korean & Vietnamese); Local. US Document Depository
Special Services for the Deaf - TTY equip
Special Services for the Blind - Computer with voice synthesizer for visually impaired persons; Copier with enlargement capabilities; Large print bks; Screen enlargement software for people with visual disabilities
Open Mon-Thurs 9-9, Fri & Sat 10-6, Sun 1-5
Friends of the Library Group

SILVER SPRING LIBRARY, 900 Wayne Ave, Silver Spring, 20910-4339, SAN 344-3434. Tel: 240-773-9420. *Br Mgr,* Uzoma Onyemaechi; Tel: 240-777-9416
Special Collections: Chinese Language Coll; Literacy Coll; Spanish Language Coll
Special Services for the Deaf - TTY equip
Special Services for the Blind - Computer with voice synthesizer for visually impaired persons; Copier with enlargement capabilities; Large print bks; Screen enlargement software for people with visual disabilities
Open Mon-Thurs 9-9, Fri & Sat 10-6, Sun 1-5
Friends of the Library Group

TWINBROOK LIBRARY, 202 Meadow Hall Dr, 20851-1551, SAN 344-3469. Tel: 240-777-0240. FAX: 240-777-0258. *Br Mgr,* Eric Carzon; Tel: 240-777-0249
Special Collections: Foreign Language Coll (Chinese, Korean, Spanish, Vietnamese)
Special Services for the Deaf - TTY equip
Special Services for the Blind - Computer with voice synthesizer for visually impaired persons; Copier with enlargement capabilities; Large print bks; Screen enlargement software for people with visual disabilities
Open Mon-Thurs 10-8, Fri & Sat 10-6
Friends of the Library Group

WHEATON LIBRARY, 11701 Georgia Ave, Silver Spring, 20902, SAN 344-3523. Tel: 240-777-0678. Interlibrary Loan Service Tel: 240-777-0061. FAX: 301-929-5525. *Br Mgr,* Dianne Whitaker; Tel: 240-777-0686
Special Collections: Foreign Language (Chinese, French, German, Korean, Spanish & Vietnamese) Coll; Health Information Center; Literacy Coll; Science & Technology
Special Services for the Deaf - TTY equip
Special Services for the Blind - Audio mat; Closed circuit TV; Computer with voice synthesizer for visually impaired persons; Copier with enlargement capabilities; Large print bks; Magnifiers; Screen enlargement software for people with visual disabilities
Open Mon-Thurs 9-9, Fri & Sat 10-6, Sun 1-5

WHITE OAK LIBRARY, 11701 New Hampshire Ave, Silver Spring, 20904-2898, SAN 344-3558. Tel: 240-773-9555. FAX: 301-989-1921. *Br Mgr,* Kathie Meizner; Tel: 240-777-9558
Special Collections: Foreign Language (Spanish) Coll; Literacy Coll
Special Services for the Deaf - TTY equip
Special Services for the Blind - Computer with voice synthesizer for visually impaired persons; Copier with enlargement capabilities; Large print bks; Magnifiers; Screen enlargement software for people with visual disabilities
Open Mon-Thurs 10-8, Fri & Sat 10-6, Sun 1-5
Friends of the Library Group

S MONTGOMERY HISTORY*, Jane C Sween Research Library & Special Collections, 42 W Middle Lane, 20850. (Mail add: 111 W Montgomery Ave, 20850), SAN 326-0402. Tel: 301-340-2974. E-mail: archive@montgomeryhistory.org. Information Services E-mail: info@montgomeryhistory.org. Web Site: montgomeryhistory.org/jane-c-sween-library. *Librn & Archivist,* Sarah Hedlund; E-mail: shedlund@montgomeryhistory.org; Staff 5 (MLS 1, Non-MLS 4)
Founded 1965
Library Holdings: Bk Titles 4,100; Per Subs 10
Special Collections: Oral History
Subject Interests: Family papers, Genealogy, Local bus, Local hist, Local newsp, Manuscripts, Organization, Regional hist
Wireless access
Publications: Montgomery County Story (Biannually)
Open Wed-Fri 10-4, Sat 12-4
Restriction: Open to pub for ref only

M SHADY GROVE ADVENTIST HOSPITAL*, Medical Library, 9901 Medical Center Dr, 20850. SAN 377-4589. Tel: 240-826-6101. FAX: 240-826-6500. Web Site: extranetapps.adventisthealthcare.com/librarysgah. *Lead Librn,* Jane Ogora; E-mail: jogora@ahm.com; Staff 1 (MLS 1)
Library Holdings: e-books 1,000; e-journals 500; Bk Titles 1,700; Per Subs 230
Automation Activity & Vendor Info: (Acquisitions) CyberTools for Libraries; (Cataloging) CyberTools for Libraries; (Circulation) CyberTools for Libraries; (OPAC) CyberTools for Libraries; (Serials) CyberTools for Libraries
Wireless access
Function: ILL available
Open Mon-Thurs 8-Noon, Fri 3-7

UNITED STATES DEPARTMENT OF HEALTH & HUMAN SERVICES

GM NATIONAL CENTER FOR HEALTH STATISTICS STAFF RESEARCH LIBRARY*, 3311 Toledo Rd, Rm 2403, Hyattsville, 20782, SAN 306-9788. Tel: 301-458-4775. FAX: 301-458-4019. Web Site: www.library.psc.gov. *ILL,* Charlene Brock; *Ref (Info Servs),* Harnethia Cousar; Staff 3 (MLS 1, Non-MLS 2)
Founded 1977
Library Holdings: Bk Vols 1,500; Per Subs 120
Subject Interests: Epidemiology, Health statistics, Pub health
Automation Activity & Vendor Info: (Acquisitions) EBSCO Online; (Circulation) EBSCO Online; (OPAC) EBSCO Online; (Serials) EBSCO Online
Function: Res libr
Partic in OCLC Online Computer Library Center, Inc; Proquest Dialog
Publications: Guide to Library Resources; Recent Acquisitions List
Open Mon-Fri 9-5
Restriction: Pub use on premises

GM FDA LIBRARY*, WO2, Rm 3302, 10903 New Hampshire Ave, Silver Spring, 20993, SAN 344-3760. Reference Tel: 301-796-2039. Interlibrary Loan Service FAX: 301-796-9852. Reference FAX: 301-796-9756. *Dir,* Kathrin L McConnell; Tel: 301-796-2387, E-mail: kathrin.mcconnell@fda.hhs.gov; *Div Dir, Tech Serv,* Colleen Pritchard; Tel: 301-796-2373, E-mail: colleen.pritchard@fda.hhs.gov; Staff 23 (MLS 17, Non-MLS 6)
Founded 1948
Library Holdings: e-books 1,200; e-journals 3,000; Bk Vols 10,000; Per Subs 850
Special Collections: Adverse Drug Effects; FDA Publications
Subject Interests: Biologics, Chem, Drug laws & legislation, Drug safety, Food safety, Med device, Nutrition, Pharm, Pharmacology, Pub health, Radiology, Toxicology, Veterinary med
Restriction: Non-circulating to the pub, Open to mil & govt employees only, Open to others by appt, Photo ID required for access, Pub by appt only

UNITED STATES NUCLEAR REGULATORY COMMISSION

G LAW LIBRARY*, 11555 Rockville Pike, 20852. (Mail add: MS 0-15D21, Washington, 20555), SAN 377-4260. Tel: 301-415-1526. FAX: 301-415-3725. *Law Librn,* Bertus Lee; E-mail: bert.lee@nrc.gov; *Legis Spec,* Anne Frost; Tel: 301-415-1613, E-mail: Anne.Frost@nrc.gov.
Subject Specialists: *Admin, Environ law, Nuclear energy,* Bertus Lee
Library Holdings: Bk Vols 5,000; Per Subs 50
Function: ILL available
Restriction: Staff use only

G TECHNICAL LIBRARY*, 11545 Rockville Pike, T2C8, 20852-2738, SAN 320-6300. Tel: 301-415-6239, 301-415-7204. FAX: 301-415-5365. E-mail: library.resource@nrc.gov. *Chief, User Serv Br,* Anna Therese McGowan; E-mail: anna.mcgowan@nrc.gov; Staff 5 (MLS 3, Non-MLS 2)
Founded 1975
Library Holdings: Bk Titles 25,000; Per Subs 700
Special Collections: International Atomic Energy Agency Publications
Subject Interests: Energy, Nuclear sci, Radiation
Partic in Federal Library & Information Network; OCLC Online Computer Library Center, Inc
Restriction: Open to pub by appt only
Friends of the Library Group

S WESTAT, INC LIBRARY*, 1600 Research Blvd, 20850. SAN 307-0190. Tel: 301-251-1500. FAX: 301-294-2034. *Info Res Mgr,* Maureen Stawick
Library Holdings: Bk Vols 10,000; Per Subs 250
Subject Interests: Econ, Educ, Health sci, Labor, Mkt, Psychol, Soc sci & issues, Statistics
Open Mon-Fri 9-5

SAINT MARY'S CITY

S HISTORIC SAINT MARY'S CITY*, Research Library, 18751 Hogaboom Ln, 20686. (Mail add: PO Box 39, 20686-0039), SAN 329-3920. Tel: 240-895-4974. Administration Tel: 240-895-4960. FAX: 240-895-4968.

E-mail: archaeology@digshistory.org, Info@HSMCdigsHistory.org. Web Site: hsmcdigshistory.org. *Exec Dir,* Regina Faden, PhD; E-mail: ReginaF@DigsHistory.org; *Director, Collections & Research,* Travis Parno
Library Holdings: Bk Vols 375; Per Subs 10
Restriction: Open by appt only

C SAINT MARY'S COLLEGE OF MARYLAND LIBRARY*, 47645 College Dr, 20686-3001. SAN 307-0204. Tel: 240-895-4256. Circulation Tel: 240-895-4264. Interlibrary Loan Service Tel: 240-895-4437. Reference Tel: 240-895-4272. FAX: 240-895-4914. Circulation FAX: 240-895-4400. Interlibrary Loan Service FAX: 240-895-4492. E-mail: ask@smcm.libanswers.com. Web Site: www.smcm.edu/library. *Interim Libr Dir,* Katherine H Ryner; Tel: 240-895-4260, E-mail: khryner@smcm.edu; *Col Archivist/Ref Librn,* Kent Randell; Tel: 240-895-4196, E-mail: kdrandell@smcm.edu; *Ref & Instruction Librn,* Pamela Mann; Tel: 240-895-4285, E-mail: pemann@smcm.edu; *Ref & Instruction Librn,* Amanda VerMeulen; Tel: 240-895-4268, E-mail: aavermeulen@smcm.edu; *Patron Serv Librn,* Conrad Helms; Tel: 240-895-3214, E-mail: cahelms@smcm.edu; *Customer Serv Supvr,* Melissa Johnson; E-mail: majohnson2@smcm.edu; *Coll Tech,* Cheryl Colson; E-mail: clcolson@smcm.edu; *ILL Tech,* Brenda Rodgers; Tel: 240-895-4437, E-mail: blrodgers@smcm.edu. Subject Specialists: *Archives, Hist, Maryland,* Kent Randell; *Art, English, Media studies,* Pamela Mann; *Environ studies, Math, Sciences,* Amanda VerMeulen; Staff 15 (MLS 7, Non-MLS 8)
Founded 1840. Enrl 1,812; Fac 190; Highest Degree: Master
Jul 2015-Jun 2016. Mats Exp $683,693, Books $75,311, Per/Ser (Incl. Access Fees) $351,609, AV Mat $5,469, Electronic Ref Mat (Incl. Access Fees) $254,304, Presv $8,043. Sal $846,595 (Prof $347,189)
Library Holdings: CDs 1,433; DVDs 3,287; e-books 100,679; e-journals 67,806; Bk Titles 121,122; Bk Vols 146,194
Special Collections: College Archives; Maryland History (especially Saint Mary's County). Oral History
Automation Activity & Vendor Info: (Acquisitions) Ex Libris Group; (Cataloging) Ex Libris Group; (Circulation) Ex Libris Group; (Course Reserve) Ex Libris Group; (Discovery) EBSCO Discovery Service; (ILL) OCLC ILLiad; (Media Booking) Ex Libris Group; (OPAC) Ex Libris Group; (Serials) Ex Libris Group
Wireless access
Partic in LYRASIS; OCLC Online Computer Library Center, Inc; University System of Maryland & Affiliated Institutions
Open Mon-Wed 8am-1pm, Thurs 8-Midnight, Fri 8am-9pm, Sat 9-9, Sun 11am-1am

SAINT MICHAELS

S CHESAPEAKE BAY MARITIME MUSEUM LIBRARY, 213 N Talbot St, 21663. SAN 307-0212. Tel: 410-745-2916. FAX: 410-745-6088. E-mail: library@cbmm.org. Web Site: cbmm.org. *Chief Curator,* Pete Lesher; Tel: 410-745-4971, E-mail: plesher@cbmm.org; *Assoc Curator,* Jenifer G Dolde; Tel: 410-745-4996, E-mail: jdolde@cbmm.org; *Registrar,* Katelyn Kean; Tel: 410-745-4972, E-mail: kkean@cbmm.org; Staff 2 (Non-MLS 2)
Founded 1967
Library Holdings: Bk Vols 10,500; Per Subs 17
Special Collections: Chesapeake Bay (Constance Stuart Larrabee Coll), photog; Howard I Chapelle Papers; Manuscript Coll, 1800-; Photograph Coll, 1880-; Ships Plans (Chesapeake Indigenous Watercraft, circa 1880-). Oral History
Subject Interests: Hist, Maritime hist, Maryland, Va
Wireless access
Restriction: Open by appt only

SALISBURY

C SALISBURY UNIVERSITY*, Blackwell Library, 1101 Camden Ave, 21801-6863. SAN 307-0239. Tel: 410-543-6130. Interlibrary Loan Service Tel: 410-543-6077. Reference Tel: 410-548-5988. FAX: 410-543-6203. Web Site: www.salisbury.edu/library. *Dean of Libr, Instrul Res,* Dr Beatriz B Hardy; *Assoc Dean, Dir, Coll Mgt,* Martha Zimmerman; *Dir, External Libr Serv,* Moushumi Chakraborty; *Bus Instrul Librn,* Steve Roane; *Res & Instruction Librn,* Angeline Prichard; *Res & Instruction Librn,* Gaylord Robb; *Res & Instruction Librn,* Caroline Eckardt; *Res & Instruction Librn/Chair, Ref,* Susan Brazer; *Scholarly Communications Librn,* Position Currently Open; *Tech Librn,* Christopher Woodall; *Coordr, Curric Res Ctr,* Stephen Ford; *Info Literacy/Instruction Coordr,* James Parrigin; *Cat,* Audrey Schadt; *Cat,* Jennifer Martin; *E-Resources Librn,* Fanuel Chirombo; Staff 21 (MLS 15, Non-MLS 6)
Founded 1925. Enrl 8,671; Fac 637; Highest Degree: Doctorate
Jul 2015-Jun 2016 Income $3,028,977. Mats Exp $889,931, Books $105,095, Per/Ser (Incl. Access Fees) $455,007, Micro $4,093, Electronic Ref Mat (Incl. Access Fees) $312,729, Presv $13,007. Sal $1,188,197 (Prof $777,332)
Library Holdings: CDs 148; DVDs 1,002; e-books 225; Microforms 646,036; Bk Vols 263,449; Per Subs 722
Special Collections: Civil War (Les Callette Memorial Coll); Movie Press Kits; Special Colls Room, bks, press kits; Teacher Education (Educational Resources Coll), AV, bks, micro. State Document Depository; US Document Depository
Automation Activity & Vendor Info: (Acquisitions) Ex Libris Group; (Cataloging) Ex Libris Group; (Circulation) Ex Libris Group; (Course Reserve) Ex Libris Group; (ILL) OCLC; (OPAC) Ex Libris Group; (Serials) Ex Libris Group
Wireless access
Partic in LYRASIS; Maryland Interlibrary Loan Organization; OCLC Online Computer Library Center, Inc; Univ Syst of Md

P WICOMICO PUBLIC LIBRARIES*, 122 S Division St, 21801. SAN 307-0247. Tel: 410-749-3612. FAX: 410-548-2968. E-mail: askus@wicomico.org. Web Site: www.wicomicolibrary.org. *Libr Dir,* Position Currently Open; *Adult Serv Mgr,* Scott Mahler; Tel: 410-749-3612, Ext 138, E-mail: smahler@wicomico.org; *Circ Mgr,* Bernadette Cannady; Tel: 410-749-3612, Ext 133, E-mail: bcannady@wicomico.org; *Mkt Mgr,* Cindy Morgan Chambers; E-mail: cmorgan@wicomico.org; *Prog & Events Coordr,* Courtney Hastings; Tel: 410-749-3612, Ext 114, E-mail: chastings@wicomico.org; *Tech Serv Mgr,* Charlotte Hotton; Tel: 410-749-3612, Ext 118, E-mail: chotton@wicomico.org; Staff 9 (MLS 4, Non-MLS 5)
Founded 1927. Pop 91,987
Library Holdings: Audiobooks 8,217; DVDs 13,134; e-books 124; Bk Vols 138,911; Per Subs 217
Automation Activity & Vendor Info: (Acquisitions) Innovative Interfaces, Inc; (Cataloging) Innovative Interfaces, Inc; (Circulation) Innovative Interfaces, Inc; (OPAC) Innovative Interfaces, Inc
Wireless access
Function: Art exhibits, Audiobks via web, Bks on CD, CD-ROM, Children's prog, Citizenship assistance, Computer training, Computers for patron use, Electronic databases & coll, Free DVD rentals, ILL available, Mail & tel request accepted, Music CDs, Online cat, Online ref, Outreach serv, Outside serv via phone, mail, e-mail & web, OverDrive digital audio bks, Photocopying/Printing, Preschool outreach, Prog for adults, Prog for children & young adult, Ref & res, Ref serv available, Story hour, Summer reading prog, Tax forms, Teen prog, Wheelchair accessible
Partic in Eastern Shore Regional Library; Lower Shore Library Consortium
Special Services for the Deaf - Sign lang interpreter upon request for prog; Video & TTY relay via computer
Special Services for the Blind - Bks on CD; Computer with voice synthesizer for visually impaired persons; Large print bks
Open Mon, Wed, Fri & Sat 10-5, Tues & Thurs 10-8, Sun 1-5
Friends of the Library Group
Branches: 2
CENTRE BRANCH, N Salisbury Blvd, 21801. Tel: 410-546-5397. *Outreach Serv Librn,* Linda Parry; E-mail: lparry@wicomico.org
Library Holdings: Audiobooks 106; DVDs 55; Bk Vols 3,898; Per Subs 8
Automation Activity & Vendor Info: (Circulation) Innovative Interfaces, Inc; (OPAC) Innovative Interfaces, Inc - Millennium
Open Mon & Wed 10-9, Fri & Sat 10-6, Sun 12-6
PITTSVILLE BRANCH, 34372 Old Ocean City Rd, Pittsville, 21850-2008. Tel: 410-835-2353. *Outreach Librn,* Linda Parry
Library Holdings: Bk Titles 1,000
Open Mon & Wed 10-6, Tues & Thurs 2-8, Sat 10-4
Bookmobiles: 1. Bkmobile Mgr, Barbara Prevento

E WOR-WIC COMMUNITY COLLEGE*, Library Services, 32000 Campus Dr, 21804. Tel: 410-334-2884, 410-334-2888. FAX: 410-334-2956. Web Site: www.worwic.edu/students/learningresources/libraryresources.aspx. *Dir, Libr Serv,* Cheryl Michael; E-mail: cmichael@worwic.edu; Staff 5 (MLS 1, Non-MLS 4)
Founded 1994. Highest Degree: Associate
Library Holdings: Electronic Media & Resources 72
Wireless access
Partic in Maryland Community College Library Consortium

SANDY SPRING

S SANDY SPRING MUSEUM, Ladson Research Library & Archives, 17901 Bentley Rd, 20860. SAN 375-6807. Tel: 301-774-0022. FAX: 301-774-8149. E-mail: info@sandyspringmuseum.org. Web Site: www.sandyspringmuseum.org. *Exec Dir,* Allison Weiss; *Archivist, Digitization Projects Mgr,* Lydia Fraser; E-mail: lfraser@sandyspringmuseum.org
Library Holdings: Bk Titles 150; Bk Vols 400
Special Collections: Local African American History; Underground Railroad. Oral History
Subject Interests: Genealogy, Quakers
Wireless access
Publications: Sandy Spring Legacy, 1999
Open Wed-Sat 10-5

SEVERNA PARK

R WOODS MEMORIAL PRESBYTERIAN CHURCH LIBRARY*, 611 Baltimore-Annapolis Blvd, 21146. SAN 307-0255. Tel: 410-647-2550. FAX: 410-647-2781. E-mail: info@woodschurch.org. Web Site: www.acswebnetworks.com/woods/library.
Library Holdings: Bk Vols 2,400
Subject Interests: Children's lit, Marriage, Relig, Women's studies
Open Mon-Fri 9am-9:30pm

SHARPSBURG

S NATIONAL PARK SERVICE, Antietam National Battlefield Library, 302 E Main St, 21782. (Mail add: PO Box 158, 21782), SAN 307-0263. Tel: 301-432-5124, 301-432-8767. FAX: 301-432-4590. Web Site: www.nps.gov/anti/planyourvisit/researchers.htm. *Curator,* Susan Trail; E-mail: susan_trail@nps.gov
Founded 1940
Library Holdings: Bk Titles 3,500
Special Collections: Battle of Antietam Coll; Civil War Regimental Histories; Civil War Soldiers' Letters & Diaries; Info on Civil War Artillery; National Tribune on microfilm; Park History; Research Reports; War of the Rebellion, Official Records of the Union & Confederate Armies
Subject Interests: Civil War, Local hist
Restriction: Open by appt only

SILVER SPRING

S AMERICAN INSTITUTES FOR RESEARCH LIBRARY*, 10720 Columbia Pike, Ste 500, 20901. Tel: 301-592-3347. FAX: 301-592-8602. *Librn,* Liz Scalia; E-mail: escalia@air.org; Staff 1 (MLS 1)
Subject Interests: Educ, Health, Psychol, Soc sci
Restriction: Co libr, Employee & client use only, Not open to pub

S RACHEL CARSON COUNCIL, INC/RACHEL CARSON LANDMARK ALLIANCE*, Historic Library, 11701 Berwick Rd, 20904-2767. SAN 327-0467. Tel: 301-593-4900. FAX: 301-593-4500. E-mail: rachelcarsonlandmark@verizon.net. Web Site: rachelcarsonlandmarkalliance.org. *Pres,* Dr Diana Post
Founded 1965
Library Holdings: Bk Vols 1,500
Special Collections: Rachel Carson Coll
Subject Interests: Low-risk pest mgt, Pesticides, Rachel Carson
Restriction: Open by appt only

SR GENERAL CONFERENCE OF SEVENTH-DAY ADVENTISTS, Rebok Memorial Library, 12501 Old Columbia Pike, 20904. SAN 325-5115. Tel: 301-680-5020, 301-680-6495. FAX: 301-680-5038. E-mail: rebok@gc.adventist.org. Web Site: adventistarchives.org. *Libr Dir,* Ashlee Chism
Founded 1983
Library Holdings: Bk Vols 14,000
Special Collections: Christian Theology; Religion (Seventh-Day Adventists)
Automation Activity & Vendor Info: (Cataloging) Lucidea; (OPAC) Lucidea
Wireless access
Restriction: Open to researchers by request

M HOLY CROSS HOSPITAL OF SILVER SPRING*, Medical Library, 1500 Forest Glen Rd, 20910. SAN 325-8734. Tel: 301-754-7987. FAX: 301-754-7247. Web Site: www.holycrosshealth.org/resources-for-physicians/clinical-resources/medical-library. *Coordr,* Evyan Roberts; E-mail: Evyan.J.Roberts@holycrosshealth.org
Library Holdings: Bk Vols 1,000; Per Subs 185
Restriction: Med staff only

G NATIONAL GEODETIC SURVEY LIBRARY*, 1315 East West Hwy, N/NGS12, SSMC III, No 8200, 20910-3282. SAN 328-1876. Tel: 301-713-3249, Ext 138. FAX: 301-713-4327. *Chief Librn,* David Grosh; E-mail: david.grosh@noaa.gov
Founded 1970
Library Holdings: Bk Vols 500; Per Subs 1,500
Special Collections: 3500 Technical Papers
Subject Interests: Geodesy
Automation Activity & Vendor Info: (Cataloging) TLC (The Library Corporation); (Circulation) TLC (The Library Corporation); (ILL) TLC (The Library Corporation)
Publications: C & GS Special Publication; FGCC Publication; NOAA Manual; NOAA Professional Paper; NOAA Technical Memorandum; NOAA Technical Report
Restriction: Open by appt only

G NATIONAL OCEANIC & ATMOSPHERIC ADMINISTRATION*, NOAA Central & Regional Libraries, 1315 East West Hwy, SSMC 3, 2nd Flr, 20910. SAN 344-3582. Tel: 301-713-2607, Ext 157. FAX: 301-713-4599. TDD: 301-713-2779. Reference E-mail: library.reference@noaa.gov. Web Site: library.noaa.gov. *Libr Dir,* Deirdre Clarkin; E-mail: deirdre.clarkin@noaa.gov; *Head, Pub Serv,* Trevor Riley; E-mail: trevor.riley@noaa.gov; *Acq Librn,* Steven Quillen; E-mail: steve.quillen@noaa.gov
Founded 1809
Library Holdings: Bk Vols 1,500,000
Special Collections: Climatology (Daily Weather Maps), bks, flm; Coast & Geodetic Survey Coll; Marine Fisheries Technical Reports, micro. US Document Depository
Subject Interests: Atmospheric sci, Climatology, Ecosystems, Marine biol, Nautical charting, Ocean engr, Oceanography, Rare bks
Automation Activity & Vendor Info: (Cataloging) SirsiDynix; (Circulation) SirsiDynix; (OPAC) SirsiDynix; (Serials) SirsiDynix
Partic in Federal Library & Information Network; NOAA Libraries Network; OCLC Online Computer Library Center, Inc; Proquest Dialog
Open Mon-Fri 8:30-4:30
Friends of the Library Group
Branches:
BETTY PETERSEN MEMORIAL LIBRARY, NOAA Center for Weather & Climate Control Prediction, 5830 University Research Court, Rm 1650 E/0C4, College Park, 20740. Tel: 301-683-1307. FAX: 301-683-1308. Web Site: www.lib.ncep.noaa.gov. *Librn,* Jan Thomas; E-mail: jan.thomas@noaa.gov
Library Holdings: Bk Vols 7,000
Partic in NOAA Libraries Network
Open Mon-Fri 8:30-5

SR PRESBYTERIAN CHURCH OF THE ATONEMENT LIBRARY, 10613 Georgia Ave, 20902. SAN 327-0505. Tel: 301-649-4131. FAX: 301-649-9633. E-mail: info@atonementlife.org. Web Site: www.atonementlife.org/church-library.html. *Library Contact,* Rick Plasterer; E-mail: plastererf@yahoo.com
Founded 1953
Library Holdings: Bk Titles 4,500; Bk Vols 4,800; Per Subs 11
Subject Interests: Relig
Automation Activity & Vendor Info: (OPAC) TinyCat
Partic in Churchline Coun; Prof Libr Asn

R SILVER SPRING UNITED METHODIST CHURCH LIBRARY*, 8900 Georgia Ave, 20910. SAN 307-0441. Tel: 301-587-1215. FAX: 301-589-6338. Administration E-mail: admin@silverspringumc.org. Web Site: www.silverspringumc.org. *Librn,* Position Currently Open
Founded 1962
Library Holdings: Bk Vols 1,200
Open Mon-Fri 4-8

S US DEPARTMENT OF DEFENSE ARMED FORCES PEST MANAGEMENT BOARD*, Information Services Division, US Army Garrison - Forest Glen, Bldg 172, 2460 Linden Lane, 20910. SAN 370-2561. Tel: 301-295-7476. FAX: 301-295-7473. E-mail: osd.pentagon.ousd-atl.mbx.afpmb@mail.mil. Web Site: www.acq.osd.mil/eie/afpmb. *Chief Librn,* Terry Carpenter; E-mail: terry.l.carpenter1.civ@mail.mil; Staff 9 (MLS 9)
Library Holdings: Bk Titles 1,550; Bk Vols 2,000; Per Subs 261
Subject Interests: Med entomology, Natural res, Parasitology, Pest control, Pub health
Function: Ref serv available
Publications: Disease Vector Ecology Profiles; Technical Guides
Open Mon-Fri 6-6

SNOW HILL

P WORCESTER COUNTY LIBRARY*, 307 N Washington St, 21863. SAN 344-3884. Tel: 410-632-2600. FAX: 410-632-1159. E-mail: contact@worcesterlibrary.org. Web Site: www.worcesterlibrary.org. *Dir,* Jennifer Ranck; E-mail: jranck@worcesterlibrary.org; *Asst Dir,* Rachael Stein; E-mail: rstein@worcesterlibrary.org; *Mgr, Support Serv,* Nick Barnes; E-mail: nbarnes@worcesterlibrary.org; *Youth Serv Mgr,* Kathy Breithut; Staff 18 (MLS 2, Non-MLS 16)
Founded 1959. Pop 49,274; Circ 543,522
Subject Interests: Real estate
Automation Activity & Vendor Info: (Cataloging) Innovative Interfaces, Inc; (Circulation) Innovative Interfaces, Inc; (OPAC) Innovative Interfaces, Inc
Wireless access
Function: Audiobks via web, Bks on cassette, Bks on CD, Children's prog, Computer training, Computers for patron use, Digital talking bks, Free DVD rentals, ILL available, Music CDs, OverDrive digital audio bks, Photocopying/Printing, Prog for adults, Prog for children & young adult, Ref serv available, Senior computer classes, Summer reading prog, Tax forms, Wheelchair accessible

Publications: Agriculture Directory Program Resources Handbook; Program Schedules (Quarterly)
Partic in Eastern Shore Regional Library; Maryland Interlibrary Loan Organization
Open Mon-Fri 8-4:30
Friends of the Library Group
Branches: 5
BERLIN BRANCH, 13 Harrison Ave, Berlin, 21811, SAN 344-3914. Tel: 410-641-0650. E-mail: berlin@worcesterlibrary.org. *Br Mgr,* Alice Paterra
Open Mon & Wed 10-8, Tues, Thurs & Fri 10-6, Sat 9-1
Friends of the Library Group
OCEAN CITY BRANCH, 10003 Coastal Hwy, Ocean City, 21842, SAN 344-3949. Tel: 410-524-1818. FAX: 410-524-1143. E-mail: oceancity@worcesterlibrary.org. *Br Mgr,* Tyvonnia Braxton
Open Mon & Wed-Fri 10-6, Tues 10-7, Sat 10-3
Friends of the Library Group
OCEAN PINES BRANCH, 11107 Cathell Rd, Berlin, 21811. Tel: 410-208-4014. FAX: 410-208-4017. E-mail: oceanpines@worcesterlibrary.org. *Br Mgr,* Harry Burkett
Open Mon & Thurs 10-8, Tues, Wed & Fri 10-6, Sat 9-3
Friends of the Library Group
POCOMOKE CITY BRANCH, 301 Market St, Pocomoke City, 21851, SAN 344-3973. Tel: 410-957-0878. FAX: 410-957-4773. E-mail: pocomoke@worcesterlibrary.org. *Br Mgr,* Dawn Mackes
Open Mon, Wed & Fri 10-6, Tues & Thurs 10-8, Sat 9-1
SNOW HILL BRANCH, 307 N Washington St, 21863, SAN 344-4007. Tel: 410-632-3495. FAX: 410-632-1159. E-mail: snowhill@worcesterlibrary.org. *Br Mgr,* Betsy Gravenor-Stacey
Open Mon & Wed 10-8, Tues, Thurs & Fri 10-6, Sat 9-1

SOLOMONS

S CALVERT MARINE MUSEUM LIBRARY*, 14150 Solomons Island Rd, 20688. (Mail add: PO Box 97, 20688-0097), SAN 324-1122. Tel: 410-326-2042, Ext 14. FAX: 410-326-6691. TDD: 410-535-6355. Web Site: www.calvertmarinemuseum.com/189/Library-Archive. *Registrar,* Robert Hurry; E-mail: robert.hurry@calvertcountymd.gov
Founded 1970
Jul 2017-Jun 2018 Income $800, County $500, Locally Generated Income $300. Mats Exp $1,000, Books $500, Per/Ser (Incl. Access Fees) $300, Manu Arch $100, Presv $100
Library Holdings: AV Mats 5; CDs 50; DVDs 125; Bk Titles 8,000; Bk Vols 8,250; Per Subs 35; Videos 200
Special Collections: B B Wills Steamboat Research Files; Bernie Fowler Coll; Boat Building (M M Davis & Son Coll), blueprints, clippings, correspondence; Center for the Chesapeake Story (Chestory) Coll, Tom Wisner Archives, AV mats, artwork, docs, mats, journals, photog; Chesapeake Bay History (M V Brewington Research Coll); History of Solomons Island (Patuxent River Seafood Industries); Seafood Processing (J C Lore & Sons Coll & Warren Denton Oysterhouse Coll); Tobacco Culture in Calvert County. Oral History
Subject Interests: Ecology, Local hist, Maritime hist, Paleontology
Function: Res libr
Special Services for the Deaf - TDD equip
Restriction: Not a lending libr

C UNIVERSITY OF MARYLAND CENTER FOR ENVIRONMENTAL SCIENCE*, Chesapeake Biological Laboratory Library, Farren Ave, 146 Williams St, 20688. (Mail add: PO Box 38, 20688-0038), SAN 328-8625. Tel: 410-326-4281, 410-326-7287. FAX: 410-326-7430. E-mail: librarian@umces.edu. Interlibrary Loan Service E-mail: ill@cbl.umces.edu. Web Site: www.umces.edu/cbl. *Coordr,* Helen Cummings; Staff 1 (MLS 1)
Founded 1927. Enrl 42; Fac 20; Highest Degree: Doctorate
Jul 2012-Jun 2013 Income $100,000. Mats Exp $103,500, Books $1,000, Per/Ser (Incl. Access Fees) $60,000, Manu Arch $500, Electronic Ref Mat (Incl. Access Fees) $40,000, Presv $2,000. Sal $75,000
Library Holdings: CDs 10; DVDs 5; e-journals 24,000; Bk Titles 12,000; Bk Vols 18,000; Per Subs 500
Special Collections: Chesapeake Bay; Shellfish, early reprints
Subject Interests: Aquatic biol, Chem, Ecology, Fisheries, Marine biol
Automation Activity & Vendor Info: (Acquisitions) Ex Libris Group; (Cataloging) Ex Libris Group; (Circulation) Ex Libris Group; (Discovery) EBSCO Discovery Service; (ILL) OCLC ILLiad; (OPAC) Ex Libris Group; (Serials) Ex Libris Group
Wireless access
Function: Computers for patron use, Electronic databases & coll, ILL available, Photocopying/Printing, Ref serv available, Scanner
Partic in Maryland Interlibrary Loan Organization; OCLC-LVIS; Univ Syst of Md
Open Mon-Fri 8-5
Restriction: Authorized patrons, Authorized scholars by appt, Borrowing privileges limited to fac & registered students, Circ to mem only, In-house use for visitors, Non-circulating to the pub, Open to fac, students & qualified researchers, Open to pub for ref only, Pub use on premises

STEVENSON

C STEVENSON UNIVERSITY LIBRARY*, Greenspring Campus Library, Learning Resource Ctr, 1525 Greenspring Valley Rd, 21153-0641. SAN 307-0468. Tel: 443-334-2233. FAX: 410-486-7329. Web Site: stevenson.libguides.com/stevensonlibrary. *Dir, Libr Serv,* Susan H Bonsteel; Tel: 443-334-2320, E-mail: shbonsteel@stevenson.edu; *Coll Develop Librn, Tech Serv,* Shannon M Williams; Tel: 443-334-2346, E-mail: smwilliams@stevenson.edu; *Discovery Librn, Pub Serv Librn,* Don Osborn; *Instruction Librn, Learning Librn,* Sara Godbee; Tel: 443-334-2688, E-mail: sgodbee@stevenson.edu; *Pub Serv Librn,* Sandra A Marinaro; Tel: 443-334-2317, E-mail: smarinaro@stevenson.edu; *Cat, Ser Librn,* Christina J Hipsley; Tel: 443-334-2766, E-mail: chipsley@stevenson.edu; *Syst Librn,* Robin A Findeisen; Tel: 443-334-2218, E-mail: rfindeisen@stevenson.edu; *Historian, Univ Archivist,* Dr Glenn T Johnston; Tel: 443-334-2196, E-mail: gjohnston@stevenson.edu; Staff 12 (MLS 8, Non-MLS 4)
Founded 1953. Enrl 1,820; Fac 120; Highest Degree: Master
Library Holdings: Bk Titles 65,000; Bk Vols 75,000; Per Subs 689
Subject Interests: Educ, Nursing, Paralegal
Automation Activity & Vendor Info: (Acquisitions) Ex Libris Group; (Cataloging) Ex Libris Group; (Circulation) Ex Libris Group; (Course Reserve) Docutek; (ILL) OCLC Connexion; (OPAC) Ex Libris Group; (Serials) Ex Libris Group
Wireless access
Partic in Baltimore Acad Libr Consortium; LYRASIS
Special Services for the Blind - ZoomText magnification & reading software
Open Mon-Thurs (Summer) 8-7, Fri 8-5, Sat 11-5
Departmental Libraries:
BRADLEY T MACDONALD LEARNING COMMONS, Manning Academic Ctr S 329, 3rd Flr, 11200 Gundry Lane (Ted Herget Way), Owings Mills, 21117. Tel: 443-394-9807. Web Site: stevenson.libguides.com/c.php?g=542528. *Res & Instruction Librn,* Elizabeth Fields; Tel: 443-394-9941, E-mail: efields2@stevenson.edu
Open Mon & Fri 8:30-4:30, Tues-Thurs 8:30-7
OWNINGS MILLS CAMPUS - SCHOOL OF BUSINESS LIBRARY, Howard S Brown School of Business Leadership, 100 Campus Dr, 1st Flr, Owings Mills, 21117-7804. Tel: 443-351-4234. Web Site: stevenson.libguides.com/c.php?g=542510. *Pub Serv/Instruction Librn,* Regina G Rose; Tel: 443-352-4233, E-mail: rrose2@stevenson.edu; *Libr Asst,* Bria Sinnott; Tel: 443-352-4232, E-mail: bsinnott@stevenson.edu

STEVENSVILLE

S HISTORICAL EVALUATION & RESEARCH ORGANIZATION*, Hero Library, 1407 Love Point Rd, 21666. SAN 324-1297. Tel: 410-643-8807. FAX: 410-643-8469. E-mail: hero_library@msn.com. *Dir,* Charles Hawkins
Founded 1962
Library Holdings: Bk Titles 4,350
Special Collections: Military Law (Wiener Coll)
Subject Interests: Mil hist
Restriction: Open by appt only

SYKESVILLE

§S CENTRAL MARYLAND CORRECTIONAL FACILITY LIBRARY, 7301 Buttercup Rd, 21784. Tel: 410-481-4444. Web Site: www.dpscs.state.md.us/locations/cmcf.shtml. *Librn,* Beatrice McTernan; E-mail: beatrice.mcternan@maryland.gov
Restriction: Not open to pub

M THE LIBRARY AT SPRINGFIELD HOSPITAL CENTER*, 6655 Sykesville Rd, 21784. SAN 307-0484. Tel: 410-970-7000, Ext 3481. FAX: 410-970-7197. Staff 2.5 (Non-MLS 2.5)
Founded 1953
Library Holdings: AV Mats 300; Bks on Deafness & Sign Lang 60; High Interest/Low Vocabulary Bk Vols 57; Large Print Bks 20; Bk Titles 6,000; Per Subs 34; Spec Interest Per Sub 100; Talking Bks 20
Subject Interests: Addictions, Art therapy, Dance movement therapy, Deafness, Dietary, Forensic sci, Gerontology, Mental health, Mental illness, Music therapy, Neurology, Nursing, Occupational therapy, Phys therapy, Psychiat, Psychol, Recreational therapy, Rehabilitation, Soc serv (soc work), Speech therapy
Automation Activity & Vendor Info: (Cataloging) SirsiDynix
Function: ILL available, Photocopying/Printing
Special Services for the Blind - Bks & mags in Braille, on rec, tape & cassette
Open Mon-Fri 9-12 & 1-5

TAKOMA PARK

P TAKOMA PARK MARYLAND LIBRARY*, 101 Philadelphia Ave, 20912. SAN 307-0514. Tel: 301-891-7259. FAX: 301-270-0814. Web Site: www.takomapark.info/library. *Dir,* Ellen Arnold-Robbins; E-mail: ellenr@takomaparkmd.gov; *Pub Serv Coordr,* Rebecca Brown; *Tech Serv*

Coordr, Nic Fontem; *Children's & Youth Serv,* Karen MacPherson; Staff 8.5 (MLS 4.5, Non-MLS 4)
Founded 1935. Pop 17,299; Circ 143,898
Library Holdings: Bk Vols 63,242; Per Subs 201
Automation Activity & Vendor Info: (Cataloging) Auto-Graphics, Inc; (Circulation) ByWater Solutions; (OPAC) ByWater Solutions
Wireless access
Function: 24/7 Electronic res, 24/7 Online cat, Adult bk club, Adult literacy prog, Bilingual assistance for Spanish patrons, Bk club(s), Bk reviews (Group), Bks on CD, Children's prog, Computer training, Computers for patron use, E-Reserves, Holiday prog, Home delivery & serv to seniorr ctr & nursing homes, ILL available, Internet access, Large print keyboards, Magnifiers for reading, Music CDs, Online cat, Photocopying/Printing, Preschool outreach, Prog for adults, Prog for children & young adult, Ref serv available, Senior computer classes, Story hour, Summer reading prog, Tax forms, Teen prog, Telephone ref, Wheelchair accessible, Workshops
Partic in Maryland Interlibrary Loan Organization
Open Mon & Wed 12-9, Tues & Thurs 10-9, Fri 12-6, Sat 10-5, Sun 12-5
Friends of the Library Group

CR WASHINGTON ADVENTIST UNIVERSITY, Theofield G Weis Library, 7600 Flower Ave, 20912-7796. SAN 307-0492. Tel: 301-891-4217. Circulation Tel: 301-891-4220. Interlibrary Loan Service Tel: 301-891-4223. Administration Tel: 301-891-4222. FAX: 301-891-4204. E-mail: library@wau.edu. Web Site: www.wau.edu/academics/library. *Libr Dir,* Don Essex; E-mail: dessex@wau.edu; *Cataloger,* Genevieve Singh; Tel: 301-891-4221, E-mail: gsingh@wau.edu; *Circ Tech,* Kathy Hecht; E-mail: khecht@wau.edu; Staff 3 (MLS 1, Non-MLS 2)
Founded 1942. Enrl 968; Fac 30; Highest Degree: Master
Jul 2020-Jun 2021. Mats Exp $138,229, Books $840, Per/Ser (Incl. Access Fees) $4,491, Electronic Ref Mat (Incl. Access Fees) $132,898. Sal $112,003
Library Holdings: AV Mats 1,389; CDs 662; Per Subs 40; Videos 727
Special Collections: Adventist Heritage Room, bks, rare bks, pers; Curriculum Library, text bks, resource guides, children's bks; Music Library, music scores, media
Automation Activity & Vendor Info: (Acquisitions) OCLC Worldshare Management Services; (Cataloging) OCLC Worldshare Management Services; (Circulation) OCLC Worldshare Management Services; (Course Reserve) OCLC Worldshare Management Services; (Discovery) OCLC Worldshare Management Services; (ILL) OCLC WorldShare Interlibrary Loan; (OPAC) OCLC Worldshare Management Services; (Serials) OCLC Worldshare Management Services
Wireless access
Function: 24/7 Electronic res, 24/7 Online cat, Computers for patron use, Electronic databases & coll, ILL available, Internet access, Online cat, Photocopying/Printing, Ref serv available
Partic in Adventist Librs Info Coop; OCLC Online Computer Library Center, Inc
Open Mon-Thurs 8:30am-10pm, Fri 8:30-1, Sun 1-10
Restriction: Authorized patrons, Authorized scholars by appt, Borrowing privileges limited to fac & registered students, Borrowing requests are handled by ILL

TOWSON

GL BALTIMORE COUNTY CIRCUIT COURT LIBRARY, 401 Bosley Ave, 21204. SAN 307-0565. Tel: 410-887-3086. FAX: 410-887-4807. Web Site: www.baltimorecountymd.gov/go/lawlibrary. *Libr Dir,* Scott Stevens; E-mail: sstevens@baltimorecountymd.gov; *Asst Librn,* Kate Hobner; E-mail: khobner@baltimorecountymd.gov; Staff 3 (MLS 3)
Library Holdings: CDs 60; DVDs 100; Bk Titles 2,800; Bk Vols 50,000; Per Subs 30
Automation Activity & Vendor Info: (Acquisitions) Inmagic, Inc.; (Cataloging) Inmagic, Inc.
Wireless access
Open Mon-Fri 8:30-4:30

P BALTIMORE COUNTY PUBLIC LIBRARY*, 320 York Rd, 21204-5179. SAN 344-4031. Tel: 410-887-6100. FAX: 410-887-6103. TDD: 410-284-0160. Web Site: www.bcpl.info. *Dir,* Paula Miller; E-mail: DirectorMiller@bcpl.net; *Asst Dir,* James Cooke; E-mail: ADCooke@bcpl.net; *Asst Dir,* Natalie Edington; E-mail: ADEdington@bcpl.net; *Fiscal Serv Mgr,* Helen Rowe; *Mgr, Human Res,* Cindy Pol; *Mkt & Develop,* Linda Frederick; *Media Support Serv Mgr,* Carl Birkmeyer; *Planning & Projects Mgr,* Emily Gamertsfelder; *Coord, Ad Serv,* Julie Brophy; *Coordr, Coll Develop,* Jamie Watson; *Coordr, Tech Serv,* Jody Sharp; *Coordr, Youth Serv,* Conni L Strittmatter; Staff 184.4 (MLS 82, Non-MLS 102.4)
Founded 1948. Pop 805,029; Circ 11,287,133
Jul 2017-Jun 2018 Income (Main & Associated Libraries) $45,686,042. Mats Exp $7,581,058. Sal $21,485,847
Library Holdings: AV Mats 212,744; DVDs 114,960; e-books 45,342; Bk Vols 1,433,343; Per Subs 4,290
Special Collections: African-American Coll; Children's Picture Book Spanish Language Coll; Historical Coll; Historical Photograph Coll; Korean Coll; Local History Coll; Maryland Coll; Russian Coll; Spanish Coll
Automation Activity & Vendor Info: (Acquisitions) Innovative Interfaces, Inc; (Cataloging) Innovative Interfaces, Inc; (Circulation) Innovative Interfaces, Inc; (ILL) OCLC FirstSearch
Wireless access
Publications: Baltimore County Directory of Organizations; Branching Out; Day By Day; Your Library Programs & News
Special Services for the Deaf - TDD equip
Open Mon-Fri 8:30-5
Friends of the Library Group
Branches: 19
ARBUTUS BRANCH, 855 Sulphur Spring Rd, Baltimore, 21227, SAN 344-4066. Tel: 410-887-1451. FAX: 410-536-0328. Web Site: www.bcpl.info/locations/arbutus. *Mgr,* Robert Maranto
Circ 476,840
Library Holdings: Bk Vols 99,142
Open Mon-Thurs 9-9, Fri & Sat 9-5:30, Sun 1-5
Friends of the Library Group
CATONSVILLE BRANCH, 1100 Frederick Rd, Baltimore, 21228, SAN 344-4090. Tel: 410-887-0951. FAX: 410-788-8166. Web Site: www.bcpl.info/locations/catonsville. *Mgr,* Joanie Bradford
Circ 774,523
Library Holdings: Bk Vols 136,598
Open Mon-Thurs 9-9, Fri & Sat 9-5:30, Sun 1-5
Friends of the Library Group
COCKEYSVILLE BRANCH, 9833 Greenside Dr, Cockeysville, 21030-2188, SAN 344-4120. Tel: 410-887-7750. FAX: 410-666-0325. Web Site: www.bcpl.info/locations/cockeysville. *Mgr,* Darcy Cahill
Circ 1,511,568
Library Holdings: Bk Vols 178,752
Open Mon-Thurs 9-9, Fri & Sat 9-5:30, Sun 1-5
ESSEX BRANCH, 1110 Eastern Blvd, Baltimore, 21221, SAN 344-421X. Tel: 410-887-0295. FAX: 410-687-0075. Web Site: www.bcpl.info/locations/essex. *Mgr,* Yvette May
Circ 383,074
Library Holdings: Bk Vols 82,640
Open Mon-Thurs 9-9, Fri & Sat 9-5:30, Sun 1-5
HEREFORD BRANCH, 16940 York Rd, Monkton, 21111, SAN 378-0473. Tel: 410-887-1919. FAX: 410-329-8203. Web Site: www.bcpl.info/locations/hereford. *Mgr,* Samantha O'Heren
Circ 287,505
Library Holdings: Bk Vols 47,961
Open Mon-Thurs 9-9, Fri & Sat 9-5:30, Sun 1-5
Friends of the Library Group
LANSDOWNE BRANCH, 500 Third Ave, Baltimore, 21227. Tel: 410-887-5602. FAX: 410-887-5633. Web Site: www.bcpl.info/locations/lansdowne. *Mgr,* Cindy Swanson-Farmarco
Circ 68,012
Library Holdings: Bk Vols 19,979
Open Mon-Thurs 9-9, Fri & Sat 9-5:30, Sun 1-5
LOCH RAVEN BRANCH, 1046 Taylor Ave, 21286, SAN 378-049X. Tel: 410-887-4444. FAX: 410-296-4339. Web Site: www.bcpl.info/locations/loch-raven. *Mgr,* Hannah Wilkes
Circ 123,782
Library Holdings: Bk Vols 21,057
Open Mon-Thurs 9-9, Fri & Sat 9-5:30, Sun 1-5
Friends of the Library Group
NORTH POINT BRANCH, 1716 Merritt Blvd, Baltimore, 21222, SAN 344-4368. Tel: 410-887-7255. FAX: 410-282-3272. Web Site: www.bcpl.info/locations/north-point. *Mgr,* Elizabeth Storms
Circ 570,085
Library Holdings: Bk Vols 116,486
Open Mon-Thurs 9-9, Fri & Sat 9-5:30, Sun 1-5
OWINGS MILLS BRANCH, County Campus Metro Center, 10302 Grand Central Ave, Owings Mills, 21117. Tel: 410-887-2092. FAX: 410-356-5935. Web Site: www.bcpl.info/locations/owings-mills. *Mgr,* Anna White
Circ 593,721
Library Holdings: Bk Vols 118,340
Open Mon-Thurs 9-9, Fri & Sat 9-5:30, Sun 1-5
PARKVILLE-CARNEY BRANCH, 9509 Harford Rd, Baltimore, 21234, SAN 344-4392. Tel: 410-887-5353. FAX: 410-668-3678. Web Site: www.bcpl.info/locations/parkville-carney. *Mgr,* Position Currently Open
Circ 525,058
Library Holdings: Bk Vols 82,071
Open Mon-Thurs 9-9, Fri & Sat 9-5:30, Sun 1-5
PERRY HALL BRANCH, 9685 Honeygo Blvd, Baltimore, 21128, SAN 344-4422. Tel: 410-887-5195. FAX: 410-529-9430. Web Site: www.bcpl.info/locations/perry-hall. *Mgr,* Cynthia Kleback
Circ 714,487
Library Holdings: Bk Vols 119,510

Open Mon-Thurs 9-9, Fri & Sat 9-5:30, Sun 1-5
Friends of the Library Group
PIKESVILLE BRANCH, 1301 Reisterstown Rd, Baltimore, 21208, SAN 344-4457. Tel: 410-887-1234. FAX: 410-486-2782. Web Site: www.bcpl.info/locations/pikesville. *Mgr,* Melissa Gotsch
Circ 1,421,998
Library Holdings: Bk Vols 159,508
Open Mon-Thurs 9-9, Fri & Sat 9-5:30, Sun 1-5
Friends of the Library Group
RANDALLSTOWN BRANCH, 8604 Liberty Rd, Randallstown, 21133-4797, SAN 344-4481. Tel: 410-887-0770. FAX: 410-521-3614. Web Site: www.bcpl.info/locations/randallstown. *Mgr,* Sarah Smith
Circ 383,301
Library Holdings: Bk Vols 87,648
Open Mon-Thurs 9-9, Fri & Sat 9-5:30, Sun 1-5
Friends of the Library Group
REISTERSTOWN BRANCH, 21 Cockeys Mill Rd, Reisterstown, 21136-1285, SAN 344-4511. Tel: 410-887-1165. FAX: 410-833-8756. Web Site: www.bcpl.info/locations/reisterstown. *Mgr,* Jana Koman
Circ 451,234
Library Holdings: Bk Vols 83,597
Open Mon-Thurs 9-9, Fri & Sat 9-5:30, Sun 1-5
ROSEDALE BRANCH, 6105 Kenwood Ave, Baltimore, 21237, SAN 344-4546. Tel: 410-887-0512. FAX: 410-866-4299. Web Site: www.bcpl.info/locations/rosedale. *Mgr,* Justin Hartzell
Circ 328,903
Library Holdings: Bk Vols 73,563
Open Mon-Thurs 9-9, Fri & Sat 9-5:30, Sun 1-5
SOLLERS POINT BRANCH, 323 Sollers Point Rd, Baltimore, 21222-6169. Tel: 410-887-2485. FAX: 410-288-3125. Web Site: www.bcpl.info/locations/sollers-point. *Mgr,* Elizabeth Stack
Circ 29,399
Library Holdings: Bk Vols 17,033
Open Mon-Thurs 9-9, Fri & Sat 9-5:30, Sun 1-5
TOWSON BRANCH, 320 York Rd, 21204-5179, SAN 344-4570. Tel: 410-887-6166. FAX: 410-887-3170. Web Site: www.bcpl.info/locations/towson. *Mgr,* Tyler Wolfe
Circ 1,052,145
Library Holdings: Bk Vols 179,017
Open Mon-Thurs 9-9, Fri & Sat 9-5:30, Sun 1-5
Friends of the Library Group
WHITE MARSH BRANCH, 8133 Sandpiper Circle, Baltimore, 21236-4973, SAN 329-6725. Tel: 410-887-5097. FAX: 410-931-9229. Web Site: www.bcpl.info/locations/white-marsh. *Mgr,* Sandra Lombardo
Circ 590,394
Library Holdings: Bk Vols 100,653
Open Mon-Thurs 9-9, Fri & Sat 9-5:30, Sun 1-5
WOODLAWN BRANCH, 1811 Woodlawn Dr, Baltimore, 21207-4074, SAN 344-466X. Tel: 410-887-1336. FAX: 410-281-9584. Web Site: www.bcpl.info/locations/woodlawn. *Mgr,* Zeke White
Circ 374,995
Library Holdings: Bk Vols 85,355
Open Mon-Thurs 9-9, Fri & Sat 9-5:30, Sun 1-5
Bookmobiles: 2

C TOWSON UNIVERSITY*, Albert S Cook Library, 8000 York Rd, 21252. SAN 307-0611. Tel: 410-704-2456. Interlibrary Loan Service Tel: 410-704-3292. Reference Tel: 410-704-2462. Administration Tel: 410-704-2450. FAX: 410-704-3760. Web Site: libraries.towson.edu. *Dean, Univ Libr,* Suzanna Conrad; E-mail: sconrad@towson.edu; *Assoc Univ Librn, Admin Serv,* Mary Ranadive; Tel: 410-704-2618, E-mail: mranadive@towson.edu; *Asst Univ Librn, Coll Mgt,* Mary Gilbert; Tel: 410-704-4926, E-mail: mgilbert@towson.edu; *Asst Univ Librn, Develop/Communications,* Joyce Garczynski; E-mail: jgarczynski@towson.edu; *Asst Univ Librn, Pub Serv,* Claire Holmes; Tel: 410-704-3795, E-mail: cholmes@towson.edu; *IT Librn,* William Helman; Tel: 410-704-5748, E-mail: whelman@towson.edu; Staff 31 (MLS 22, Non-MLS 9)
Enrl 22,499; Fac 872; Highest Degree: Doctorate
Jul 2013-Jun 2014 Income $5,928,624. Mats Exp $2,262,646, Books $162,056, Per/Ser (Incl. Access Fees) $2,063,175, Electronic Ref Mat (Incl. Access Fees) $37,415. Sal $2,636,938 (Prof $1,978,152)
Library Holdings: AV Mats 1,548; CDs 66; DVDs 2,498; e-books 285,861; e-journals 53,028; Microforms 401,222; Bk Vols 624,709; Per Subs 8,579; Videos 8,014
Special Collections: Baltimore Hebrew Institute Coll
Subject Interests: Art, Educ, Ethnic studies, Fine arts, Health professions, Music, Women's studies
Automation Activity & Vendor Info: (Acquisitions) Ex Libris Group; (Cataloging) Ex Libris Group; (Circulation) Ex Libris Group; (Course Reserve) Docutek; (ILL) OCLC ILLiad; (OPAC) Ex Libris Group; (Serials) Ex Libris Group
Wireless access
Function: Archival coll, AV serv, Bk club(s), Computers for patron use, Distance learning, Doc delivery serv, E-Reserves, Electronic databases & coll, ILL available, Jazz prog, Online cat, Online info literacy tutorials on the web & in blackboard, Online ref, Orientations, Outreach serv, Photocopying/Printing, Ref & res, Ref serv available, Telephone ref, VHS videos
Partic in LYRASIS; OCLC Online Computer Library Center, Inc; Univ Syst of Md
Special Services for the Deaf - Assistive tech
Special Services for the Blind - Assistive/Adapted tech devices, equip & products
Open Mon-Thurs 7:30am-2am, Fri 8-8, Sat 12-8, Sun Noon-2am

UPPER MARLBORO

GL PRINCE GEORGE'S COUNTY*, Law Library, 14735 Main St, Rm M1400, 20772. (Mail add: PO Box 1696, 20773-1696), SAN 307-062X. Tel: 301-952-3438. FAX: 301-952-2770. Web Site: www.princegeorgescourts.org/285/law-library. *Law Librn,* Tonya Baroudi; E-mail: tebaroudi@co.pg.md.us; Staff 2 (MLS 1, Non-MLS 1)
Founded 1900
Library Holdings: Bk Titles 37,000; Per Subs 50
Subject Interests: Criminal law & justice, Law, Maryland
Wireless access
Publications: Acquisitions list
Open Mon-Fri 8:30-4:30
Friends of the Library Group

WEST BETHESDA

G NAVAL SURFACE WARFARE CENTER, Carderock Division Technical Information Center, 9500 MacArthur Blvd, 20817-5700. SAN 337-2065. Tel: 301-227-1319. FAX: 301-227-5307. *Br Head,* Ken Myers; E-mail: kenneth.l.myers@navy.mil
Library Holdings: Bk Vols 38,500; Per Subs 150
Partic in Proquest Dialog
Restriction: Not open to pub, Staff use only

WESTMINSTER

J CARROLL COMMUNITY COLLEGE*, Library & Media Center, 1601 Washington Rd, 21157-6944. SAN 373-2827. Tel: 410-386-8330. Reference Tel: 410-386-8340. Toll Free Tel: 888-221-9748. FAX: 410-386-8331. E-mail: ref_desk@carrollcc.edu. Web Site: www.carrollcc.edu/library. *Libr Dir, Media Serv,* Jeremy Green; Tel: 410-386-8335, E-mail: jgreen@carrollcc.edu; *Head, Tech Serv,* Robert Krzanowski; Tel: 410-386-8337, E-mail: rkrzanowski@carrollcc.edu; *Pub Serv Librn,* Wanda Meck; Tel: 410-386-8342, E-mail: wmeck@carrollcc.edu; *Electronic Res,* Elizabeth Beere; Tel: 410-386-8333, E-mail: ebeere@carrollcc.edu; Staff 5 (MLS 5)
Founded 1976. Enrl 3,661; Fac 300; Highest Degree: Associate
Jul 2015-Jun 2016. Mats Exp $176,000, Books $64,000, Per/Ser (Incl. Access Fees) $12,000, AV Mat $10,000, Electronic Ref Mat (Incl. Access Fees) $90,000. Sal $430,000 (Prof $351,000)
Library Holdings: CDs 372; DVDs 2,000; e-books 110,000; Electronic Media & Resources 40; Music Scores 85; Bk Titles 44,000; Per Subs 175; Videos 1,266
Automation Activity & Vendor Info: (Acquisitions) Innovative Interfaces, Inc; (Cataloging) Innovative Interfaces, Inc; (Circulation) Innovative Interfaces, Inc; (Course Reserve) Innovative Interfaces, Inc; (OPAC) Innovative Interfaces, Inc; (Serials) Innovative Interfaces, Inc
Wireless access
Function: Audio & video playback equip for onsite use, AV serv, Bks on CD, Computers for patron use, Electronic databases & coll, ILL available, Music CDs, Online info literacy tutorials on the web & in blackboard, Online ref, Orientations, Photocopying/Printing, Ref serv available
Partic in Maryland Community College Library Consortium
Open Mon-Thurs 7:30am-10pm, Fri & Sat 8:30-4:30

GL CIRCUIT COURT FOR CARROLL COUNTY*, Law Library, Historic Courthouse, 200 Willis St, 21157. SAN 307-0638. Tel: 410-386-2672. FAX: 410-751-5240. E-mail: lawlib@ccg.carr.org. Web Site: ccgovernment.carr.org/ccg/circuit-court/law-lib.aspx. *Law Librn,* Florence J Barnes; E-mail: fbarnes@ccg.carr.org
Open Mon-Fri 9-4:30

S HISTORICAL SOCIETY OF CARROLL COUNTY LIBRARY, 210 E Main St, 21157. SAN 371-6694. Tel: 410-848-6494, Ext 204. FAX: 410-848-3596. E-mail: library@hsccmd.org. Web Site: www.hsccmd.org. *Interim Exec Dir,* Kristen McMaster; E-mail: execdirector@hsccmd.org; *Curator,* Catherine Baty; E-mail: cathy@hsccmd.org; Staff 2 (Non-MLS 2)
Founded 1939
Library Holdings: Bk Titles 750; Bk Vols 1,100; Per Subs 15
Special Collections: Carroll County History, bks, ms, maps, newsp, photos; Family Files (Genealogy Typescripts, Monographs & Special Research); Land Patent Records (Tracey Coll); Taneytown Community History (Crapster Coll)

Subject Interests: Local hist
Wireless access
Open Wed-Sun 10-4

C MCDANIEL COLLEGE*, Hoover Library, Two College Hill, 21157. SAN 307-0646. Tel: 410-857-2281. Circulation Tel: 410-857-2744. Interlibrary Loan Service Tel: 410-857-2288. Reference Tel: 410-857-2282. FAX: 410-857-2748. Web Site: lib.hoover.mcdaniel.edu. *Libr Dir,* Jessame Ferguson; E-mail: jferguson@mcdaniel.edu; *Head, Pub Serv,* Mildred Elizabeth Davidson; Tel: 410-857-2278, E-mail: edavidson@mcdaniel.edu; *E-Resources Librn, Head, Tech Serv,* David Brennan; Tel: 410-857-2284, E-mail: dbrennan@mcdaniel.edu; *Evening Librn, Outreach Librn,* Samantha Schultz; Tel: 410-857-2287, E-mail: sschultz@mcdaniel.edu; *Res & Instruction Librn/Sci & Online Tech,* Janet Hack; Tel: 410-857-2283, E-mail: jhack@mcdaniel.edu; *Acq Mgr,* Linda Garber; Tel: 410-857-2285, E-mail: lgarber@mcdaniel.edu; *Circ & Reserves Mgr,* Peggy Klinge; E-mail: pklinge@mcdaniel.edu; *Cat Supvr,* Roxane Brewer; Tel: 410-857-2847, E-mail: mbrewer@mcdaniel.edu; *ILL Supvr,* Lisa Russell; Tel: 410-857-2788, E-mail: lmrussel@mcdaniel.edu; *Coordr, Info Literacy,* Jessica Gutacker; Tel: 410-386-4679, E-mail: jgutacker@mcdaniel.edu; *Coordr,* Deborah Green; Tel: 410-386-4822, E-mail: dgreen@mcdaniel.edu; *Col Archivist,* Andrea Briggs; Tel: 410-857-2793, E-mail: abriggs@mcdaniel.edu; *Ser & Govt Doc Spec,* Lorri Pickett; Tel: 410-857-2789, E-mail: lpickett@mcdaniel.edu. Subject Specialists: *Spec coll,* Andrea Briggs; Staff 13 (MLS 7, Non-MLS 6)
Founded 1867. Enrl 3,187; Fac 110; Highest Degree: Master
Library Holdings: AV Mats 14,214; e-books 177,580; Bk Titles 179,112; Bk Vols 210,549; Per Subs 66,068; Videos 59,846
Special Collections: Nora Roberts American Romance Coll. US Document Depository
Automation Activity & Vendor Info: (Acquisitions) Innovative Interfaces, Inc; (Cataloging) Innovative Interfaces, Inc; (Circulation) Innovative Interfaces, Inc; (Course Reserve) Innovative Interfaces, Inc; (Discovery) EBSCO Discovery Service; (ILL) OCLC ILLiad; (OPAC) Innovative Interfaces, Inc; (Serials) Innovative Interfaces, Inc
Wireless access
Partic in Carroll Librs in Partnership; LYRASIS; OCLC Online Computer Library Center, Inc
Special Services for the Deaf - Bks on deafness & sign lang; Spec interest per
Open Mon-Thurs 8am-Midnight, Fri 8-7, Sat 11-7, Sun Noon-Midnight

WESTOVER

EASTERN CORRECTIONAL INSTITUTION

S EAST LIBRARY*, 30420 Revells Neck Rd, 21890. Tel: 410-845-4000, Ext 6227. FAX: 410-845-4208. Web Site: www.dpscs.state.md.us/locations/eci.shtml. *Librn,* John Paul Mahofski; E-mail: john.mahofski@maryland.gov; *Evening Librn,* Sharon Brooks; Staff 1 (MLS 1)
Library Holdings: Bk Vols 5,565; Per Subs 40
Automation Activity & Vendor Info: (Cataloging) Follett Software; (Circulation) Follett Software
Open Mon-Fri 7-3:30

S WEST LIBRARY*, 30420 Revells Neck Rd, 21890. Tel: 410-845-4000, Ext 6423. FAX: 410-845-4206. Web Site: www.dpscs.state.md.us/locations/eci.shtml. *Librn,* Britney Herz; E-mail: brittney.herz@maryland.gov; *Evening Librn,* Carolee Greenwood; E-mail: carolee.greenwood1@maryland.gov; Staff 1 (MLS 1)
Founded 1989
Library Holdings: CDs 30; High Interest/Low Vocabulary Bk Vols 45; Large Print Bks 25; Bk Vols 9,262; Per Subs 21; Talking Bks 20
Automation Activity & Vendor Info: (Cataloging) Follett Software; (Circulation) Follett Software
Restriction: Staff & inmates only

WYE MILLS

C CHESAPEAKE COLLEGE, Learning Resource Center, 1000 College Circle, 21679. (Mail add: PO Box 8, 21679-0008). Tel: 410-827-5860. FAX: 410-827-5257. E-mail: lrcdesk@chesapeake.edu. Web Site: libguides.chesapeake.edu/home. *Dean for Teaching & Learning,* Chandra Gigliotti; E-mail: cgigliotti@chesapeake.edu; *Director of Library & Academic Support,* Ann Reinecke; E-mail: areinecke@chesapeake.edu; *Pub Serv Librn,* Nicole Rioux; E-mail: nrioux@chesapeake.edu; *Tech Serv Librn,* Kristy Floyd; E-mail: kfloyd@chesapeake.edu; *Cat/Circ,* Kim Green; E-mail: kgreen@chesapeake.edu
Founded 1967
Library Holdings: Bk Titles 30,000; Bk Vols 35,000
Special Collections: Eastern Shore Literature (Chesapeake Room)
Automation Activity & Vendor Info: (Cataloging) Innovative Interfaces, Inc; (Circulation) Innovative Interfaces, Inc; (Discovery) EBSCO Discovery Service; (OPAC) Innovative Interfaces, Inc
Wireless access
Partic in Maryland Community College Library Consortium
Open Mon-Thurs 8-7, Fri 8-4:30, Sun 1-5

MASSACHUSETTS

Date of Statistics: FY 2020
Population, 2020 U.S. Census: 6,893,574
Population Served by Public Libraries: 6,901,924
Unserved: 225
Number of Cities & Towns: 351
Total Holdings: 73,524,509
Holdings Per Capita: 10.65
Digital Resources:
Total e-books: 19,847,732
Total audio items (physical & downloadable units): 7,586,091
Physical: 1,228,073
Downloadable: 6,358,018
Total video items (physical & downloadable units): 2,099,826
Physical: 1,686,765
Downloadable: 413,061
Total computers for use by the public: 7,070
Income and Expenditures:
Total Operating Income: $348,958,464
Source of Income: Municipal appropriation: $314,179,792
Expenditures Per Capita: $45.67
Number of Regional Library Systems: 1
Counties Served: All 351 cities & towns (systems not developed on county basis)
Grants-in-Aid to Public Libraries: 344
State Aid: $10,059,081
State Funding for one Regional Library System & Library of The Commonwealth: $11,516,000
State Expenditures for Public Library Construction: $20 million
Information provided courtesy of: Aparna Ramachandran, Data Analyst and Technology Specialist; Massachusetts Board of Library Commissioners

ABINGTON

P ABINGTON PUBLIC LIBRARY, 600 Gliniewicz Way, 02351. SAN 307-5737. Tel: 781-982-2139. FAX: 781-878-7361. E-mail: ablib@ocln.org. Web Site: abingtonpl.org. *Dir,* Deborah Grimmett; *Asst Librn,* Sandy Bumpus; *Asst Librn,* Susan Durand; *Asst Librn,* Linda Sampson; *Ch,* Amy Hindle; *Ref Librn,* Sarah Roberts; Staff 6 (MLS 2, Non-MLS 4)
Founded 1878. Pop 16,351; Circ 87,643
Library Holdings: AV Mats 3,268; Bk Vols 61,206; Per Subs 88
Special Collections: Civil War (Arnold Coll); Large Print Coll
Wireless access
Function: Computer training
Mem of Massachusetts Library System
Partic in Old Colony Libr Network
Open Mon 1-8:30, Tues & Wed 10-5, Thurs 10-8:30
Friends of the Library Group

ACTON

P ACTON MEMORIAL LIBRARY*, 486 Main St, 01720. SAN 307-0670. Tel: 978-929-6655. FAX: 978-635-0073. TDD: 978-635-0072. Web Site: www.actonmemoriallibrary.org. *Dir,* Marcia Rich; *Asst Dir,* Danielle Savin; E-mail: dsavin@acton-ma.gov; *Head, Children's Servx,* Lee Donohue; *Head, Circ,* Sue Callahan; *Head, Ref,* Susan Paju; Staff 34 (MLS 10, Non-MLS 24)
Founded 1890. Pop 20,300; Circ 595,000
Library Holdings: AV Mats 5,400; DVDs 5,900; Electronic Media & Resources 137; Bk Vols 128,000; Per Subs 215
Special Collections: Arthur Davis Paintings; Civil War Artifacts; Literacy Coll. Municipal Document Depository; Oral History
Subject Interests: Local hist
Automation Activity & Vendor Info: (Cataloging) Innovative Interfaces, Inc; (Circulation) Innovative Interfaces, Inc; (OPAC) Innovative Interfaces, Inc
Wireless access
Publications: Good Word (Newsletter)
Special Services for the Deaf - Bks on deafness & sign lang
Special Services for the Blind - Accessible computers; Assistive/Adapted tech devices, equip & products; Audio mat; Bks on cassette; Bks on CD; Closed circuit TV magnifier; Copier with enlargement capabilities; Home delivery serv; Large print bks; Talking bks
Open Mon-Thurs 9-9, Fri & Sat 9-5, Sun (Winter) 2-5
Friends of the Library Group

ACUSHNET

P ACUSHNET PUBLIC LIBRARY*, 232 Middle Rd, 02743. SAN 307-0700. Tel: 508-998-0270. FAX: 508-998-0271. Web Site: www.acupl.org, www.sailsinc.org/acushnet. *Libr Dir,* Dina Brasseur; E-mail: dbrasseur@sailsinc.org; Staff 2 (MLS 1, Non-MLS 1)
Founded 1930. Pop 10,582; Circ 62,670
Library Holdings: Bk Vols 19,000; Per Subs 115
Automation Activity & Vendor Info: (Cataloging) SirsiDynix; (Circulation) SirsiDynix; (OPAC) SirsiDynix
Wireless access
Function: 24/7 Electronic res, 24/7 Online cat, Adult bk club, Bk club(s), Bks on CD, Children's prog, Computers for patron use, Electronic databases & coll, Free DVD rentals, Internet access, Magazines, Meeting rooms, Movies, Museum passes, Music CDs, Online cat, Photocopying/Printing, Teen prog
Mem of Massachusetts Library System
Partic in SAILS Library Network
Open Mon & Wed 10-8, Tues & Thurs 1-8, Fri 1-5, Sat 9-3
Friends of the Library Group

ADAMS

P ADAMS FREE LIBRARY, 92 Park St, 01220. SAN 307-0719. Tel: 413-743-8345. Web Site: adamslibraryma.org, town.adams.ma.us/adams-free-library. *Libr Dir,* Holli Jayko; E-mail: hjayko@town.adams.ma.us; Staff 5.5 (MLS 1.5, Non-MLS 4)
Founded 1883. Pop 9,311; Circ 70,089
Library Holdings: Audiobooks 1,174; DVDs 1,905; Large Print Bks 605; Bk Titles 29,059; Per Subs 51
Subject Interests: Genealogy, Local hist
Automation Activity & Vendor Info: (Cataloging) Evergreen; (Circulation) Evergreen; (ILL) Evergreen; (OPAC) Evergreen
Wireless access
Function: Adult bk club, Bk club(s), Bks on CD, Children's prog, Computers for patron use, Electronic databases & coll, For res purposes, Free DVD rentals, Home delivery & serv to seniorr ctr & nursing homes, Homebound delivery serv, ILL available, Internet access, Magazines, Magnifiers for reading, Mail & tel request accepted, Movies, Museum passes, Music CDs, Photocopying/Printing, Prog for adults, Prog for children & young adult, Ref & res, Story hour, Summer reading prog, Tax forms, Wheelchair accessible
Partic in Central & Western Massachusetts Automated Resource Sharing
Special Services for the Deaf - ADA equip; Assisted listening device; Assistive tech; Bks on deafness & sign lang; TTY equip; Videos & decoder
Special Services for the Blind - Aids for in-house use; Assistive/Adapted tech devices, equip & products; Audio mat; Bks on cassette; Bks on CD; Cassette playback machines; Cassettes; Large print & cassettes; Large print bks; Large print bks & talking machines; Magnifiers; Recorded bks; Talking bks & player equip
Open Mon 10-6, Tues & Thurs 12-8, Wed & Sat 12-1, Fri 12-5 (Summer); Mon 10-6, Tues & Thurs 12-8, Wed 12-1, Fri 12-5 (Fall-Spring)
Friends of the Library Group

AGAWAM

P AGAWAM PUBLIC LIBRARY*, 750 Cooper St, 01001. SAN 307-0727. Tel: 413-789-1550. FAX: 413-789-1552. Web Site: www.agawamlibrary.org. *Libr Dir,* Nancy Siegel; E-mail:

nsiegel@agawamlibrary.org; *Asst Dir,* Jolene Mercadante; E-mail: jmercadante@agawamlibrary.org; *Ad,* Cher Collins; E-mail: ccollins@agawamlibrary.org; *Ref Librn,* Jerome Walczak; E-mail: jwalczak@agawamlibrary.org; *Circ Supvr,* Laura Paul; E-mail: lpaul@agawamlibrary.org; *ILL,* Maria Yacovone; E-mail: myacovone@agawamlibrary.org; Staff 5 (MLS 5)
Pop 29,000; Circ 324,198
Library Holdings: AV Mats 18,276; Bk Vols 124,078; Per Subs 243
Automation Activity & Vendor Info: (Acquisitions) Innovative Interfaces, Inc; (Cataloging) Innovative Interfaces, Inc; (Circulation) Innovative Interfaces, Inc; (OPAC) Innovative Interfaces, Inc; (Serials) Innovative Interfaces, Inc
Wireless access
Partic in Central & Western Massachusetts Automated Resource Sharing
Open Mon-Thurs 9-9, Fri 10-6
Friends of the Library Group

AMESBURY

P AMESBURY PUBLIC LIBRARY*, 149 Main St, 01913. SAN 307-0743. Tel: 978-388-8148. E-mail: reference@amesburylibrary.org. Web Site: www.amesburylibrary.org. *Libr Dir,* Erin Matlin; E-mail: ematlin@amesburylibrary.org; *Asst Dir,* Aimie Westphal; E-mail: awestphal@amesburylibrary.org; *Head, Circ,* Michaela Pelletier; E-mail: mpelletier@amesburylibrary.org; *Head, Tech Serv,* Kerry Ann Remillard; E-mail: kremillard@amesburylibrary.org; *Ref Librn,* Dorothy Purdy; E-mail: dpurdy@amesburylibrary.org; *Ch Serv,* Clare Dombrowski; E-mail: cdombrowski@amesburylibrary.org; Staff 4 (MLS 4)
Founded 1856. Pop 16,429; Circ 146,240
Library Holdings: Audiobooks 3,250; CDs 104; DVDs 2,470; Microforms 1,026; Bk Vols 70,127; Per Subs 110
Special Collections: Amesbury Carriage History Material; Charles H Davis Painting Coll; John Greenleaf Whittier Material
Automation Activity & Vendor Info: (Cataloging) Horizon; (Circulation) Horizon; (ILL) Horizon; (OPAC) Horizon
Wireless access
Function: Adult bk club, Archival coll, Art exhibits, Audiobks via web, Bk club(s), Bks on CD, CD-ROM, Children's prog, Computer training, Computers for patron use, Electronic databases & coll, Free DVD rentals, Holiday prog, Home delivery & serv to seniorr ctr & nursing homes, Homebound delivery serv, ILL available, Museum passes, Music CDs, Online cat, Online ref, OverDrive digital audio bks, Photocopying/Printing, Preschool outreach, Prog for adults, Prog for children & young adult, Ref & res, Ref serv available, Senior outreach, Story hour, Summer reading prog, Tax forms, Teen prog, Telephone ref, Writing prog
Partic in Merrimack Valley Library Consortium
Open Mon-Wed 9:30-8, Thurs-Sat 9:30-5 (Sat 9:30-1 July & Aug)
Friends of the Library Group

AMHERST

C AMHERST COLLEGE*, Robert Frost Library, 61 Quadrangle Dr, 01002. SAN 344-4902. Circulation Tel: 413-542-2373. Interlibrary Loan Service Tel: 413-542-2215. Reference Tel: 413-542-2319. Administration Tel: 413-542-2212. FAX: 413-542-2662. E-mail: library@amherst.edu. Web Site: www.amherst.edu/library. *Dir,* Martin Garnar; *Head, Archives & Spec Coll,* Mike Kelly; *Head, Cat,* Jane Beebe; *Head, Info Tech,* Jan Jourdain; *Head, Pub Serv,* Missy Roser; *Head, Ser,* Paul Trumble; *Head, Tech Serv,* Susan Sheridan; *Access Serv Librn, Sci & Electronic Serv Librn,* Susan Kimball; *Cat Librn,* Kate Gerrity; *Cat Librn,* Rebecca Henning; *Digital Res Librn,* Catherine Winston; *Coordr, Coll Develop, Ref Librn,* Michael Kasper; *Tech Serv Librn,* Erin Loree; Staff 17 (MLS 15, Non-MLS 2)
Enrl 1,648; Fac 201; Highest Degree: Bachelor
Library Holdings: Bk Vols 1,078,161; Per Subs 5,798
Special Collections: Augustine Daly Coll; Clyde Fitch Coll; Dylan Thomas Coll; Emily Dickinson Coll; John J McCloy Coll; Richard Mann Coll; Richard Wilbur Coll; Robert Frost Coll; Rolfe Humphreys Coll; Walt Whitman Coll; William Wordsworth Coll. US Document Depository
Automation Activity & Vendor Info: (Acquisitions) Ex Libris Group; (Cataloging) Ex Libris Group; (Circulation) Ex Libris Group; (Course Reserve) Ex Libris Group; (ILL) OCLC ILLiad; (Media Booking) Ex Libris Group; (OPAC) Ex Libris Group; (Serials) Ex Libris Group
Wireless access
Publications: Friends of the Amherst College Library (Newsletter)
Restriction: Open to fac, students & qualified researchers
Friends of the Library Group
Departmental Libraries:
KEEFE SCIENCE LIBRARY, 01002. Tel: 413-542-2076. Reference Tel: 413-542-8112. Web Site: www.amherst.edu/library/depts/science. *Sci Librn,* Kristen Greenland; Staff 2 (MLS 1, Non-MLS 1)
Founded 1996
Library Holdings: Bk Vols 52,518

VINCENT MORGAN MUSIC LIBRARY, 01002. Tel: 413-542-2387. Web Site: www.amherst.edu/library/depts/music. *Music Librn,* Jane Beebe; Tel: 413-542-2667, E-mail: jabeebe@amherst.edu
Library Holdings: CDs 14,105; Music Scores 20,880; Bk Vols 30,962

C HAMPSHIRE COLLEGE LIBRARY*, Harold F Johnson Library Center, 893 West St, 01002. SAN 307-0751. Tel: 413-559-5440. Interlibrary Loan Service Tel: 413-559-5475. Reference Tel: 413-559-5758. Administration Tel: 413-559-6691. FAX: 413-559-5419. E-mail: library@hampshire.edu. Web Site: www.hampshire.edu/library/harold-f-johnson-library. *Access & Art Librn, Interim Dir,* Rachel Beckwith; E-mail: rbeckwith@hampshire.edu; *Col Archivist,* Jessica Neal; E-mail: jcnLO@hampshire.edu; Staff 8 (MLS 6, Non-MLS 2)
Founded 1970. Enrl 1,396; Fac 140; Highest Degree: Bachelor
Jul 2014-Jun 2015 Income $1,683,011. Mats Exp $349,374, Books $58,500, Per/Ser (Incl. Access Fees) $270,950, AV Equip $19,011, Presv $913. Sal $833,093 (Prof $388,681)
Library Holdings: AV Mats 42,100; e-books 64,469; Microforms 99; Bk Vols 134,544; Per Subs 56,041
Subject Interests: Environ studies, Films & filmmaking, Gender studies, Pub policy, Sustainable agr, Third World
Automation Activity & Vendor Info: (Acquisitions) Ex Libris Group; (Cataloging) OCLC Connexion; (Circulation) Ex Libris Group; (Course Reserve) Ex Libris Group; (ILL) OCLC FirstSearch; (Media Booking) Ex Libris Group; (OPAC) Ex Libris Group; (Serials) Ex Libris Group
Wireless access
Function: Art exhibits, Audio & video playback equip for onsite use, Computers for patron use, E-Reserves, Electronic databases & coll, Internet access, Music CDs, Online cat, Photocopying/Printing, Ref serv available, Spoken cassettes & CDs
Mem of Massachusetts Library System
Partic in Five Colleges, Inc; LYRASIS; OCLC Online Computer Library Center, Inc
Open Mon-Fri 8:30am-Midnight, Sat & Sun 10am-Midnight

P JONES LIBRARY, INC*, 43 Amity St, 01002-2285. SAN 344-502X. Tel: 413-259-3090. Circulation Tel: 413-259-3091. Reference Tel: 413-259-3096. Administration Tel: 413-259-3106. FAX: 413-256-4096. E-mail: info@joneslibrary.org. Web Site: www.joneslibrary.org. *Dir,* Sharon A Sharry; E-mail: sharrys@joneslibrary.org; *Head, Prog & Outreach,* Janet Ryan; Tel: 413-259-3223, E-mail: ryanj@joneslibrary.org; *Head, Borrower Serv,* Amy Anaya; Tel: 413-259-3132, E-mail: anayaa@joneslibrary.org; *Head, Coll,* Linda Wentworth; Tel: 413-259-3168, E-mail: wentworthl@joneslibrary.org; *Head, Info Serv,* Matthew Berube; Tel: 413-259-3195, E-mail: berubem@joneslibrary.org; *Head, Tech Serv,* Carolyn Platt; Tel: 413-259-3214; *Head, Youth Serv,* Mia Cabana; Tel: 413-259-3219, E-mail: cabanam@joneslibrary.org; *Facilities Supvr,* George Hicks; Tel: 413-259-3174, E-mail: hicksg@joneslibrary.org; *Curator, Spec Coll,* Cynthia Harbeson; Tel: 413-259-3182, E-mail: harbesonc@joneslibrary.org; Staff 56 (MLS 11, Non-MLS 45)
Founded 1919. Pop 38,000; Circ 500,000
Library Holdings: AV Mats 24,400; Bk Vols 209,300; Per Subs 316
Special Collections: Early Textbooks & Children's Books (Clifton Johnson Coll); Emily Dickinson Coll; Genealogy (Boltwood Coll); Harlan Fiske Stone Coll; Julius Lester Coll; Local History; Ray Stannard Baker Coll; Robert Frost Coll; Sidney Waugh Coll
Subject Interests: English (Lang)
Automation Activity & Vendor Info: (Acquisitions) Evergreen; (Cataloging) OCLC CatExpress; (Circulation) Evergreen; (OPAC) Evergreen
Wireless access
Function: 24/7 Electronic res, 24/7 Online cat, Activity rm, Adult bk club, After school storytime
Publications: Annual Report
Partic in Central & Western Massachusetts Automated Resource Sharing
Special Services for the Deaf - TDD equip; TTY equip
Special Services for the Blind - Closed circuit TV magnifier; Descriptive video serv (DVS)
Open Mon 1-5:30, Tues & Thurs 9am-9:30pm, Wed, Fri & Sat 9-5:30, Sun 1-5
Friends of the Library Group
Branches: 2
MUNSON MEMORIAL, 1046 S East St, South Amherst, 01002, SAN 344-5089. Tel: 413-259-3095. *Br Head,* Susan Hugus; E-mail: huguss@joneslibrary.org
Partic in Central & Western Massachusetts Automated Resource Sharing
Open Mon, Tues & Thurs 2-5:30, Wed 2-7:30, Sat 9-1
NORTH AMHERST BRANCH, Eight Montague Rd, 01002, SAN 344-5054. Tel: 413-259-3099. *Br Head,* Maggie Spiegel; E-mail: spiegelm@joneslibrary.org
Partic in Central & Western Massachusetts Automated Resource Sharing
Open Mon 10-1:30, Tues 2-7:30, Wed-Fri 2-5:30, Sat 10-2

S NATIONAL YIDDISH BOOK CENTER, Yiddish Book Center, Harry & Jeanette Weinberg Bldg, 1021 West St, 01002-3375. SAN 370-5056. Tel: 413-256-4900. FAX: 413-256-4700. E-mail: info@yiddishbookcenter.org, yiddish@yiddishbookcenter.org. Web Site: www.yiddishbookcenter.org. *Bibliographer,* David Mazower; E-mail: dmazower@yiddishbookcenter.org; Staff 1 (Non-MLS 1)
Library Holdings: e-books 11,000; Bk Titles 20,000; Bk Vols 1,500,000
Special Collections: Oral History
Automation Activity & Vendor Info: (Cataloging) OCLC WorldShare Interlibrary Loan
Wireless access
Publications: Steven Spielberg Digital Yiddish Library

C UNIVERSITY OF MASSACHUSETTS AMHERST LIBRARIES*, W E B Du Bois Library, 154 Hicks Way, University of Massachusetts, 01003-9275. SAN 344-5119. Tel: 413-545-2623. Circulation Tel: 413-545-2622. Interlibrary Loan Service Tel: 413-545-0553. Reference Tel: 413-545-0150. Interlibrary Loan Service FAX: 413-577-1536. Administration FAX: 413-545-6873. Web Site: www.library.umass.edu. *Dean of Libr,* Simon J Neame; Tel: 413-545-0284, E-mail: sneame@library.umass.edu; *Assoc Dean, Res & Learning Serv,* Leslie Horner Button; Tel: 413-545-6845, E-mail: button@library.umass.edu; *Dir of Libr Develop & Communications,* Carol Connare; Tel: 413-545-0995, E-mail: cconnare@library.umass.edu; *Head, Access Serv,* Kathryn Leigh; Tel: 413-577-0175, E-mail: kathrynr@library.umass.edu; *Head, Digital Scholarship Serv,* Brian Shelburne; Tel: 413-545-4061, E-mail: bps@library.umass.edu; *Head, Res Serv,* Jennifer Friedman; Tel: 413-545-6890, E-mail: jfriedman7@lumass.edu; *Head, Sci & Eng,* Rebecca Reznik-Zellen; Tel: 413-545-6739, E-mail: rreznik@library.umass.edu; *Head, Spec Coll & Archives,* Robert Cox; Tel: 413-545-6842, E-mail: rscox@library.umass.edu; *Head, Undergrad Teaching & Learning Serv,* Sarah Hutton; Tel: 413-545-6740, E-mail: shutton@library.umass.edu; *Scholarly Communications Librn,* Marilyn Billings; Tel: 413-545-6891, E-mail: mbillings@library.umass.edu; *Mgr, Circ Serv,* Thomas Paige; Tel: 413-577-2103, E-mail: tpaige@library.umass.edu; *Coordr, Learning Commons,* Carol Will; Tel: 413-545-6795, E-mail: cwill@library.umass.edu; *Curator of Coll,* Danielle Kovacs; Tel: 413-545-2784, E-mail: dkovacs@library.umass.edu; Staff 124 (MLS 42, Non-MLS 82)
Founded 1865. Enrl 24,000; Fac 1,182; Highest Degree: Doctorate
Library Holdings: Bk Vols 5,900,000; Per Subs 15,427
Special Collections: Benjamin Smith Lyman Papers & Japanese Coll; Broadside Press; County Atlases of New England, New York & New Jersey (Farm Credit Bank's Coll); French Revolution (Binet Coll); Harvey Swados Papers; Horace Mann Bond Papers; Massachusetts Government Publications; Massachusetts Labor & Business Records; Massachusetts Social Action & Peace Organizations; Massachusetts Social Service Agencies Records; Robert Francis Coll; Silvio O Conte Congressional Papers; Slavery & Anti-Slavery Pamphlets 1725-1911; Travel & Tourism in the Northeast; W B Yeats (R K Alspach Coll); W E B Du Bois Papers; Wallace Stevens Coll. State Document Depository; US Document Depository
Subject Interests: African-Am, Agr, Ethnic studies, Geog, Latin Am, Massachusetts, Natural hist, New England
Automation Activity & Vendor Info: (Acquisitions) Ex Libris Group; (Cataloging) Ex Libris Group; (Circulation) Ex Libris Group; (Course Reserve) Ex Libris Group; (OPAC) Ex Libris Group; (Serials) Ex Libris Group
Wireless access
Open Mon-Thurs 8am-Midnight, Fri 8-6, Sat 10-6, Sun 1-Midnight
Friends of the Library Group

ANDOVER

S ANDOVER CENTER FOR HISTORY & CULTURE LIBRARY*, Caroline M Underhill Research Center, 97 Main St, 01810. SAN 325-8696. Tel: 978-475-2236. E-mail: info@andoverhistoryandculture.org. *Exec Dir,* Elaine Clements; E-mail: eclements@andoverhistorical.org; *Dir of Develop,* Marilyn Helmers; E-mail: mhelmers@andoverhistorical.org; *Dir, Programs, Dir, Social Media,* Lauren Kosky-Stamm; E-mail: lkosky-stamm@andoverhistorical.org; *Colls Mgr,* Angela McBrien; E-mail: amcbrien@andoverhistoryandculture.org; Staff 3 (Non-MLS 3)
Founded 1911
Library Holdings: Bk Vols 3,240
Special Collections: 19th & 20th Century Photographs of Andover People, Events, Buildings & Sites; Andover Imprints
Subject Interests: Decorative art
Wireless access
Publications: Andover Century of Change 1896-1996; Andover Townswomen by Bessie Goldsmith; Historical Sketches of Andover

CL MASSACHUSETTS SCHOOL OF LAW LIBRARY*, Information Resource Center, 500 Federal St, 01810. SAN 371-5892. Tel: 978-681-0800. FAX: 978-681-6330. Web Site: msl.library.net, mslaw.edu. *Dir, Info Serv, Libr Dir,* Daniel Harayda; E-mail: harayda@mslaw.edu; *Dir, Technology,* Mick Coyne; E-mail: mick@mslaw.edu; *Reserves Mgr,* Anne Hemingway; E-mail: hemingway@mslaw.edu; *Tech Serv,* Shukla Biswas; E-mail: biswas@mslaw.edu; Staff 5 (MLS 4, Non-MLS 1)
Enrl 600; Fac 17; Highest Degree: Doctorate
Library Holdings: Bk Titles 11,529; Bk Vols 81,627; Per Subs 276
Automation Activity & Vendor Info: (Acquisitions) OCLC; (Cataloging) OCLC; (Circulation) OCLC
Wireless access
Mem of Massachusetts Library System
Partic in LYRASIS
Open Mon-Fri 8am-11pm, Sat 8-6:30, Sun 11-6:30

P MEMORIAL HALL LIBRARY, Two N Main St, 01810. SAN 344-5208. Tel: 978-623-8400. FAX: 978-623-8497. E-mail: rdesk@mhl.org. Web Site: mhl.org. *Dir,* Barbara McNamara; E-mail: bmcnamara@mhl.org; *Asst Dir, Circ,* Kim Lynn; E-mail: klynn@mhl.org; *Asst Dir, Tech Serv,* Clare Curran-Ball; E-mail: ccball@mhl.org; *Ch Serv,* Beth Kerrigan; *Commun Serv,* Stefani Traina; E-mail: straina@mhl.org; *Ref (Info Servs),* Dean Baumeister; E-mail: dbaumeister@mhl.org; Staff 16 (MLS 15, Non-MLS 1)
Founded 1873. Circ 472,034
Jul 2021-Jun 2022 Income $2,982,397. Mats Exp $370,000. Sal $2,321,710
Automation Activity & Vendor Info: (Acquisitions) SirsiDynix; (Cataloging) SirsiDynix; (Circulation) SirsiDynix; (ILL) SirsiDynix; (OPAC) SirsiDynix; (Serials) SirsiDynix
Wireless access
Function: 24/7 Electronic res, 24/7 Online cat, 3D Printer, Activity rm, Adult bk club, Adult literacy prog, Audiobks on Playaways & MP3, Bks on CD, Children's prog, Citizenship assistance, Computers for patron use, Electronic databases & coll, Equip loans & repairs, Free DVD rentals, Genealogy discussion group, Homebound delivery serv, ILL available, Internet access, Magazines, Makerspace, Meeting rooms, Microfiche/film & reading machines, Museum passes, Music CDs, Notary serv, Online cat, Online ref, OverDrive digital audio bks, Photocopying/Printing, Preschool outreach, Printer for laptops & handheld devices, Prog for adults, Prog for children & young adult, Ref serv available, Scanner, Spanish lang bks, Story hour, Summer & winter reading prog, Tax forms, Teen prog, Telephone ref, Wheelchair accessible
Mem of Massachusetts Library System
Partic in Merrimack Valley Library Consortium
Open Mon-Thurs 9-9, Fri & Sat 9-5, Sun 1-5
Friends of the Library Group

S PHILLIPS ACADEMY, Robert S Peabody Museum of Archaeology, 180 Main St, 01810. Tel: 978-749-4490. FAX: 978-749-4495. Web Site: www.andover.edu/learning/peabody. *Dir,* Ryan J Wheeler; E-mail: rwheeler@andover.edu
Founded 1901
Library Holdings: Bk Vols 6,000; Per Subs 15
Wireless access
Restriction: Non-circulating to the pub, Open by appt only

AQUINNAH

P AQUINNAH PUBLIC LIBRARY*, One Church St, 02535. SAN 375-4367. Tel: 508-645-2314. FAX: 508-645-2188. Web Site: www.aquinnahlibrary.org. *Actg Dir,* Rosa Parker; *Libr Assoc,* Jennifer Burkin; Staff 2 (MLS 1, Non-MLS 1)
Founded 1901. Pop 311; Circ 11,584
Library Holdings: AV Mats 1,340; Bk Vols 7,319; Per Subs 34
Automation Activity & Vendor Info: (Cataloging) Follett Software; (Circulation) Follett Software
Wireless access
Partic in Cape Libraries Automated Materials Sharing Network
Open Tues & Thurs 2-7, Sat 10-4
Friends of the Library Group

ARLINGTON

S ARMENIAN CULTURAL FOUNDATION LIBRARY*, 441 Mystic St, 02474-1108. SAN 373-0654. Tel: 781-646-3090. FAX: 781-646-3090. E-mail: armeniancultural.fdn@gmail.com. Web Site: www.armenianculturalfoundation.org. *Curator,* Ara Ghazarian
Founded 1945
Library Holdings: CDs 10; Music Scores 186; Bk Vols 55,000; Per Subs 10
Open Mon-Fri 9-2
Restriction: Non-circulating
Friends of the Library Group

P PUBLIC LIBRARY OF ARLINGTON*, Robbins Library, 700 Massachusetts Ave, 02476. SAN 344-5267. Tel: 781-316-3200, 781-316-3233. Administration Tel: 781-316-3201. FAX: 781-316-3209. Web Site: www.robbinslibrary.org. *Dir,* Andrea Nicolay; E-mail: anicolay@minlib.net; Staff 15 (MLS 15)

Founded 1807. Pop 44,028; Circ 735,796
Jul 2015-Jun 2016 Income $1,934,610, State $56,803, City $1,734,462, Federal $9,815, Locally Generated Income $133,530. Mats Exp $275,893, Books $179,691, Per/Ser (Incl. Access Fees) $16,988, Other Print Mats $6,410, Micro $10,269, AV Mat $44,791, Electronic Ref Mat (Incl. Access Fees) $17,744
Library Holdings: AV Mats 23,377; Electronic Media & Resources 223; Bk Vols 205,351; Per Subs 296
Special Collections: Robbins Print Coll, etchings, lithographs, prints. Oral History
Automation Activity & Vendor Info: (Cataloging) Innovative Interfaces, Inc; (Circulation) Innovative Interfaces, Inc; (OPAC) Innovative Interfaces, Inc
Wireless access
Partic in Minuteman Library Network
Open Mon-Wed 9-9, Thurs 1-9, Fri 9-5, Sat 9-5 (9-12 July-Aug), Sun (Oct-May) 2-5
Friends of the Library Group
Branches: 1
EDITH M FOX BRANCH LIBRARY, 175 Massachusetts Ave, 02474, SAN 344-5321. Tel: 781-316-3198. Web Site: www.robbinslibrary.org/about/fox_branch. *Librn,* Anna Litten; Tel: 781-316-3196, E-mail: alitten@minlib.net; Staff 2.5 (MLS 1, Non-MLS 1.5)
Library Holdings: Bk Vols 27,483
Open Tues, Thurs & Fri 9-5, Wed 12-8
Friends of the Library Group

ASHBURNHAM

P STEVENS MEMORIAL LIBRARY*, 20 Memorial Dr, 01430. SAN 307-0808. Tel: 978-827-4115. FAX: 978-827-4116. E-mail: library@ashburnham-ma.gov. Web Site: ashburnhamlibrary.org. *Libr Dir,* Terri Anstiss; E-mail: tanstiss@ashburnham-ma.gov; Staff 4 (MLS 1, Non-MLS 3)
Pop 5,733; Circ 27,000
Library Holdings: Bk Vols 35,000; Per Subs 35
Wireless access
Open Mon & Wed 10-8, Tues & Thurs 10-5, Fri 10-4, Sat 10-2
Friends of the Library Group

ASHBY

P ASHBY FREE PUBLIC LIBRARY, 812 Main St, 01431. SAN 307-0816. Tel: 978-386-5377. E-mail: ashbylibrary@gmail.com. Web Site: www.ashbylibrary.org. *Dir,* Tiffany Call; E-mail: tcall@cwmars.org
Pop 2,740; Circ 18,500
Library Holdings: Bk Vols 25,000
Wireless access
Mem of Massachusetts Library System
Partic in Central & Western Massachusetts Automated Resource Sharing
Open Tues & Wed 10-5, Thurs 1-8, Sat (Sept-June) 9:30-1:30
Friends of the Library Group

ASHFIELD

P BELDING MEMORIAL LIBRARY*, 344 Main St, 01330. (Mail add: PO Box 407, 01330-0407), SAN 307-0824. Tel: 413-628-4414. E-mail: bmlashfield@gmail.com. Web Site: beldingmemoriallibrary.org. *Libr Dir,* Sarah Hertel-Fernandez; E-mail: sfernandez@cwmars.org; Staff 3 (MLS 1, Non-MLS 2)
Founded 1914. Pop 1,733; Circ 32,335
Library Holdings: Audiobooks 547; DVDs 1,406; e-books 68,157; Large Print Bks 250; Bk Titles 10,436; Per Subs 37
Wireless access
Function: 24/7 Electronic res, 24/7 Online cat, Activity rm, Archival coll
Partic in Central & Western Massachusetts Automated Resource Sharing
Open Mon & Wed 2-8, Sat 10-3
Friends of the Library Group

ASHLAND

S ASHLAND HISTORICAL SOCIETY LIBRARY*, Two Myrtle St, 01721. (Mail add: PO Box 145, 01721-0145), SAN 329-8698. Tel: 508-881-8183. E-mail: ashlandhistsoc@msn.com. *Pres,* Cliff Wilson
Founded 1909
Library Holdings: Bk Vols 500
Subject Interests: Genealogy, Hist, Local hist
Restriction: Non-circulating, Open by appt only

P ASHLAND PUBLIC LIBRARY*, 66 Front St, 01721. SAN 307-0832. Tel: 508-881-0134. FAX: 508-881-0162. E-mail: library@ashlandmass.com. Web Site: www.ashlandmass.com/184/Ashland-Public-Library. *Dir,* Meena Jain; E-mail: mjain@ashlandmass.com; *Ch Serv,* Lois McAuliffe; *Tech Serv & ILL Asst,* Linda Beckwith
Pop 11,604; Circ 48,500
Library Holdings: Bk Vols 30,808; Per Subs 70
Automation Activity & Vendor Info: (Cataloging) Innovative Interfaces, Inc; (Circulation) Innovative Interfaces, Inc; (Media Booking) Innovative Interfaces, Inc
Partic in Minuteman Library Network; Northeast Ohio Regional Library System; Ohio Public Library Information Network
Open Tues-Thurs 10-8, Fri 10-6, Sat 10-5
Friends of the Library Group

ATHOL

P ATHOL PUBLIC LIBRARY*, 568 Main St, 01331. SAN 307-0840. Tel: 978-249-9515. FAX: 978-249-7636. E-mail: info@athollibrary.org. Web Site: athollibrary.org. *Dir,* Jean Shaughnessy; E-mail: jshaughnessy@cwmars.org; *Asst Dir,* Robin Shtulman; E-mail: rshtulman@cwmars.org; *ILL & Distance Libr Serv Spec,* Marie Lehmann; *Cat, Webmaster,* Kelsey Matthews; *Genealogy Serv,* Robin Brzozowski; Staff 7 (MLS 2, Non-MLS 5)
Founded 1882. Pop 11,584; Circ 147,869
Library Holdings: Bk Vols 53,497; Per Subs 58; Talking Bks 1,843; Videos 3,371
Special Collections: Local Art Originals; Local History Archives
Automation Activity & Vendor Info: (Cataloging) Evergreen; (Circulation) Evergreen; (ILL) Evergreen; (OPAC) Evergreen
Wireless access
Function: 24/7 Online cat, Activity rm, Adult bk club, Adult literacy prog, Archival coll, Art exhibits, Bk club(s), Bks on CD, Butterfly Garden, Chess club, Children's prog, Computers for patron use, Doc delivery serv, Electronic databases & coll, Equip loans & repairs, Free DVD rentals, Games & aids for people with disabilities, Home delivery & serv to seniorr ctr & nursing homes, Homebound delivery serv, ILL available, Internet access, Magazines, Magnifiers for reading, Mail & tel request accepted, Meeting rooms, Microfiche/film & reading machines, Movies, Museum passes, Music CDs, Notary serv, Online cat, Online ref, Outreach serv, OverDrive digital audio bks, Photocopying/Printing, Preschool outreach, Preschool reading prog, Prog for adults, Prog for children & young adult, Ref & res, Senior outreach, Serves people with intellectual disabilities, Spanish lang bks, STEM programs, Story hour, Study rm, Summer & winter reading prog, Tax forms, Teen prog, Telephone ref, Wheelchair accessible
Mem of Massachusetts Library System
Partic in Central & Western Massachusetts Automated Resource Sharing
Open Mon & Wed 9:30-6, Tues 9:30-8, Fri 9:30-5:30, Sat (Winter) 9:30-1
Friends of the Library Group

ATTLEBORO

P ATTLEBORO PUBLIC LIBRARY*, 74 N Main St, 02703. SAN 344-5356. Tel: 508-222-0157. Reference Tel: 508-222-0157, Ext 14. FAX: 508-226-3326. Reference E-mail: apl_ref@sailsinc.org. Web Site: attleborolibrary.org. *Dir,* Christine Johnson; *Asst Dir,* Amy Rhilinger; *Ch,* Krystal Brown; *Circ Supvr,* Katie Redfearn; *Ref (Info Servs),* Carrie Sylvia; *Tech Serv,* Heidi Cauley
Founded 1885. Pop 42,185
Library Holdings: Bk Vols 90,000; Per Subs 120
Special Collections: Attleboro History Coll, bks, ms & papers
Subject Interests: Genealogy, Local hist
Automation Activity & Vendor Info: (Cataloging) SirsiDynix; (Circulation) SirsiDynix; (OPAC) SirsiDynix
Wireless access
Partic in SAILS Library Network
Open Mon & Wed 8:30-8:30, Tues & Fri 8:30-4:30, Thurs 12:30-8:30, Sat 8:30-4:30 (8:30-1:30 Summer)
Friends of the Library Group

AUBURN

P AUBURN PUBLIC LIBRARY*, 369 Southbridge St, 01501. SAN 307-0867. Tel: 508-832-7790. FAX: 508-832-7792. Web Site: www.auburnlibrary.org. *Dir,* Jean E Collins; E-mail: jcollins@town.auburn.ma.us; Staff 8 (MLS 3, Non-MLS 5)
Founded 1872. Pop 15,870; Circ 182,080
Library Holdings: CDs 6,140; DVDs 4,594; e-books 9,754; Electronic Media & Resources 3,999; Microforms 2,900; Bk Vols 82,542; Per Subs 111
Special Collections: Local History Coll
Automation Activity & Vendor Info: (Cataloging) Evergreen; (Circulation) Evergreen; (OPAC) Evergreen
Wireless access
Mem of Massachusetts Library System
Partic in Central & Western Massachusetts Automated Resource Sharing
Open Mon-Thurs 9:30-8:30, Fri 9:30-6, Sat 9-1
Friends of the Library Group

R FIRST CONGREGATIONAL CHURCH LIBRARY*, 128 Central St, 01501. SAN 307-0875. Tel: 508-832-2845. FAX: 508-721-2539. E-mail: Library@AuburnFirstUCC.org. Web Site: www.auburnfirstucc.org.
Founded 1959
Library Holdings: Large Print Bks 60; Bk Titles 3,300
Subject Interests: Arts, Drama, Family, Fiction, Health, Hist, Nature, Non-fiction, Poetry, Travel
Restriction: Not open to pub

AVON

P AVON PUBLIC LIBRARY*, 280 W Main St, 02322. SAN 307-0905. Tel: 508-583-0378. FAX: 508-580-2757. E-mail: avlib@ocln.org. *Actg Dir, Asst Libr*n, Ann Marie Fogg; E-mail: afogg@ocln.org; Staff 6 (Non-MLS 6)
Founded 1892. Pop 4,300; Circ 42,693
Jul 2014-Jun 2015 Income $324,264. Mats Exp $85,000
Library Holdings: High Interest/Low Vocabulary Bk Vols 100; Bk Vols 31,000; Per Subs 103; Talking Bks 1,358
Special Collections: Childrens' Coll
Subject Interests: Antiques, Restoration
Automation Activity & Vendor Info: (Acquisitions) SirsiDynix; (Cataloging) SirsiDynix; (Circulation) SirsiDynix; (OPAC) SirsiDynix
Wireless access
Function: ILL available, Prog for children & young adult, Ref serv available, Summer reading prog, Wheelchair accessible
Mem of Massachusetts Library System
Partic in Old Colony Libr Network
Special Services for the Blind - Audio mat; Bks on CD
Open Mon & Wed 10-5, Tues & Thurs 10-7:30, Fri 10-3, Sat 10-2
Friends of the Library Group

AYER

P AYER LIBRARY*, 26 E Main St, 01432. SAN 307-0913. Tel: 978-772-8250. FAX: 978-772-8251. E-mail: ayerlibrary@cwmars.org. Web Site: www.ayerlibrary.org. *Libr Dir,* Tim Silva; E-mail: tsilva@ayer.ma.us; *Asst Dir,* Samantha Benoit; E-mail: sbenoit@cwmars.org
Pop 7,000; Circ 24,000
Library Holdings: Bk Vols 50,000; Per Subs 70
Automation Activity & Vendor Info: (Cataloging) Evergreen; (Circulation) Evergreen; (OPAC) Evergreen
Wireless access
Mem of Massachusetts Library System
Partic in Central & Western Massachusetts Automated Resource Sharing
Open Tues-Thurs 10-8, Fri 10-5, Sat 10-2
Friends of the Library Group

BABSON PARK

C BABSON COLLEGE*, Horn Library, 231 Forest St, 02457-0310. SAN 307-0921. Tel: 781-239-4596. Interlibrary Loan Service Tel: 781-239-4574. FAX: 781-239-5226. E-mail: library@babson.edu. Web Site: www.babson.edu/Academics/library/Pages/home.aspx. *Libr Dir,* Emily Miles; E-mail: emiles@babson.edu; *Assoc Dir, Access Serv,* Dee Stonberg; Tel: 781-239-4391, E-mail: stonberg@babson.edu; *Cat Librn,* Claire Gosselin; Tel: 781-239-4472, E-mail: cgosselin@babson.edu; *Electronic Res Librn,* Jeanne Hebard; Tel: 781-239-6405, E-mail: jhebard@babson.edu; *Instrul Serv Librn,* Samantha H Porter; Tel: 781-239-4471, E-mail: sporter1@babson.edu. Subject Specialists: *Mgt,* Dee Stonberg; Staff 18 (MLS 16, Non-MLS 2)
Founded 1919. Enrl 2,723; Fac 208; Highest Degree: Master
Library Holdings: AV Mats 4,153; e-books 57,578; e-journals 217; Bk Titles 91,488; Bk Vols 114,006; Per Subs 409
Special Collections: Sailing & Transportation (Hinckley Coll); Sir Isaac Newton Coll
Subject Interests: Bus & mgt, Econ
Automation Activity & Vendor Info: (Acquisitions) SirsiDynix; (Cataloging) SirsiDynix; (Circulation) SirsiDynix; (Course Reserve) SirsiDynix; (ILL) SirsiDynix; (OPAC) SirsiDynix; (Serials) SirsiDynix
Wireless access
Publications: Infobits (Consumer guide); ITSD Update (Newsletter)
Mem of Massachusetts Library System
Partic in LYRASIS; OCLC Online Computer Library Center, Inc; WEBnet Libr Consortium
Open Mon-Thurs 7:30am-Midnight, Fri 7:30-7:30, Sat 8:30-5:30, Sun 9am-Midnight

BARNSTABLE

L MASSACHUSETTS TRIAL COURT LAW LIBRARIES, Barnstable Law Library, First District Court House, 3195 Main St, 02630. (Mail add: PO Box 398, 02630), SAN 325-8653. Tel: 508-362-8539. FAX: 508-362-1374. E-mail: barnstablelawlibrary@gmail.com. Web Site: www.mass.gov/locations/barnstable-law-library. *Head Law Librn,* Suzanne Hoey; E-mail: suzanne.hoey@jud.state.ma.us; *Law Libr Asst,* Martha Krueger; E-mail: martha.krueger@jud.state.ma.us
Automation Activity & Vendor Info: (Cataloging) SirsiDynix; (Circulation) SirsiDynix; (ILL) OCLC WorldShare Interlibrary Loan; (OPAC) SirsiDynix; (Serials) SirsiDynix
Wireless access
Open Mon-Fri 8:30-12 & 1-3:30

P STURGIS LIBRARY*, 3090 Main St, 02630. (Mail add: PO Box 606, 02630-0606), SAN 307-093X. Tel: 508-362-6636. FAX: 508-362-5467. E-mail: sturgislibrary@comcast.net. Web Site: www.sturgislibrary.org. *Libr Dir,* Lucy E Loomis; Tel: 508-362-8448; *Ad, Asst Dir,* Corey Farrenkopf; E-mail: sturgisreference@comcast.net; *Tech Serv,* Lisa MacDonald; Staff 10 (MLS 2, Non-MLS 8)
Founded 1863. Pop 48,000; Circ 74,000
Library Holdings: Bk Titles 65,000; Bk Vols 68,000; Per Subs 55
Special Collections: Cape Cod Authors; Cape Cod Families; Early Cape Cod Land Deeds, Some Indian (Stanley W Smith Coll); Genealogy & Cape Cod History (Hooper Room); Maritime History
Subject Interests: Genealogy, Geog, Hist, Maritime hist
Automation Activity & Vendor Info: (Acquisitions) Innovative Interfaces, Inc; (Cataloging) Innovative Interfaces, Inc; (Circulation) Innovative Interfaces, Inc; (Course Reserve) Innovative Interfaces, Inc; (ILL) Innovative Interfaces, Inc; (Media Booking) Innovative Interfaces, Inc; (OPAC) Innovative Interfaces, Inc; (Serials) Innovative Interfaces, Inc
Wireless access
Mem of Massachusetts Library System
Partic in Cape Libraries Automated Materials Sharing Network
Open Mon-Sat 10-3

BARRE

P WOODS MEMORIAL LIBRARY*, 19 Pleasant St, 01005. (Mail add: PO Box 489, 01005-0489), SAN 307-0948. Tel: 978-355-2533. E-mail: barrelibrary@gmail.com. Web Site: www.barrelibrary.org. *Libr Dir,* Carol Witt; *Youth Serv Librn,* Julia Palmer; Staff 5 (MLS 1, Non-MLS 4)
Founded 1857. Pop 5,200; Circ 35,967
Library Holdings: Bks on Deafness & Sign Lang 20; Bk Titles 32,000; Per Subs 55
Special Collections: Local History Coll
Automation Activity & Vendor Info: (Cataloging) Follett Software; (Circulation) Follett Software
Wireless access
Mem of Massachusetts Library System
Partic in Central & Western Massachusetts Automated Resource Sharing
Open Tues 2-8, Wed & Thurs 10-8, Fri 2-5, Sat 10-1

BECKET

P BECKET ATHENAEUM, INC LIBRARY*, 3367 Main St, 01223. SAN 307-0956. Tel: 413-623-5483. E-mail: info@bwlibrary.org. Web Site: www.BecketAthenaeum.org. *Dir,* Jodi Shafiroff; *Librn,* Ellen Manley; *Cat Spec,* Dawn Greene; Staff 3 (Non-MLS 3)
Founded 1888. Pop 2,350
Library Holdings: Audiobooks 485; CDs 360; DVDs 2,100; Bk Titles 18,000; Per Subs 15
Automation Activity & Vendor Info: (Cataloging) Follett Software; (Circulation) Follett Software; (ILL) OCLC
Wireless access
Function: Adult bk club, Audiobks via web, Bk club(s), Bks on CD, Children's prog, Computer training, Computers for patron use, Electronic databases & coll, For res purposes, Free DVD rentals, Homework prog, ILL available, Internet access, Large print keyboards, Life-long learning prog for all ages, Magazines, Movies, Museum passes, Music CDs, Online cat, Online ref, OverDrive digital audio bks, Photocopying/Printing, Prog for adults, Prog for children & young adult, Scanner, STEM programs, Summer reading prog, Tax forms, Wheelchair accessible, Workshops
Open Tues 1-7, Wed 3-7 (10-2 Summer), Thurs 1-7, Sat 10-4

BEDFORD

P BEDFORD FREE PUBLIC LIBRARY*, Seven Mudge Way, 01730. SAN 307-0980. Tel: 781-275-9440. FAX: 781-275-3590. E-mail: bedford@minlib.net. Web Site: www.bedfordlibrary.net. *Dir,* Richard Callaghan; *Asst Dir,* Noreen O'Gara; *Head, Children's Servx,* Bethany Templeton Klem; *Head, Circ,* Jennifer Dalrymple; *Head, Ref & Adult Serv,* Rand Hall; *Head, Tech Serv,* Kathleen Ruggeri; *Teen Librn,* Dee Clarke; Staff 16 (MLS 6, Non-MLS 10)
Founded 1876. Pop 12,571; Circ 284,622
Library Holdings: CDs 2,892; DVDs 1,437; Electronic Media & Resources 144; Large Print Bks 1,022; Bk Titles 94,497; Per Subs 261; Talking Bks 2,684; Videos 2,314
Special Collections: Local History (Bedford Coll), multi-media; Parent's Coll. Oral History
Automation Activity & Vendor Info: (Acquisitions) Innovative Interfaces, Inc; (Cataloging) Innovative Interfaces, Inc; (Circulation) Innovative Interfaces, Inc; (OPAC) Innovative Interfaces, Inc
Wireless access

Function: Art exhibits, Digital talking bks, Electronic databases & coll, ILL available, Magnifiers for reading, Mail & tel request accepted, Music CDs, Photocopying/Printing, Prog for adults, Prog for children & young adult, Ref serv available, Spoken cassettes & CDs, Spoken cassettes & DVDs, Summer reading prog, Tax forms, Telephone ref, VHS videos, Wheelchair accessible
Publications: Bedford Flag Unfurled; History of the Town of Bedford
Mem of Massachusetts Library System
Partic in Minuteman Library Network
Special Services for the Blind - Bks on cassette; Bks on CD; Copier with enlargement capabilities; Digital talking bk; Magnifiers
Open Mon-Thurs 9-9, Fri 9-6, Sat 9-5, Sun 1-5
Friends of the Library Group

GM DEPARTMENT OF VETERANS AFFAIRS*, Medical Library Service, 200 Springs Rd, 01730. SAN 344-5410. Tel: 781-687-2504. FAX: 781-687-2507. *Clinical Librn,* Sarah Carnes
Founded 1928
Library Holdings: Large Print Bks 300; Bk Vols 5,500; Per Subs 245
Subject Interests: Med, Nursing, Psychol, Soc serv (soc work)
Wireless access
Open Mon-Fri 8-4:30

J MIDDLESEX COMMUNITY COLLEGE*, Bedford Campus Library, Academic Resources Bldg 1A, 591 Springs Rd, 01730. SAN 307-1014. Tel: 781-280-3708. Reference Tel: 781-280-3706. Reference E-mail: mcclibrary@middlesex.mass.edu. Web Site: libguides.middlesex.mass.edu, www.middlesex.mass.edu. *Asst Dean, Libr Serv,* Mary Ann Niles; *Dir of Libr,* Donna Maturi; E-mail: maturid@middlesex.mass.edu; *Ref Librn,* Joanna Gray; E-mail: grayjo@middlesex.mass.edu; *Circ Librn,* Kim Robbins; E-mail: robbinsk@middlesex.mass.edu
Founded 1970. Enrl 3,810; Fac 181; Highest Degree: Associate
Library Holdings: Bk Vols 53,000; Per Subs 300
Automation Activity & Vendor Info: (Cataloging) Innovative Interfaces, Inc
Wireless access
Publications: Annual Reports; Film & Video List (Annual); MCC Libraries Newsletter (Occasional); Middlesex Community College Library Periodicals

S THE MITRE CORPORATION, Information Services, 202 Burlington Rd, 01730-1420. SAN 317-3399. Tel: 781-271-7667. E-mail: infodesk@mitre.org. Web Site: www.mitre.org. *Dept Head,* Deanna D West; E-mail: dwest@mitre.org; Staff 16 (MLS 15, Non-MLS 1)
Founded 1959
Subject Interests: Aviation, Civil info systs, Communications, Cyber security, Data analysis, Defense communications, Energy, Healthcare
Wireless access
Restriction: Authorized personnel only, Co libr, Internal use only, Not open to pub

BELCHERTOWN

P CLAPP MEMORIAL LIBRARY*, 19 S Main St, 01007. (Mail add: PO Box 627, 01007-0627), SAN 307-1057. Tel: 413-323-0417. Administration Tel: 413-323-0478. FAX: 413-323-0453. E-mail: clapp@cwmars.org. Web Site: www.clapplibrary.org. *Dir,* Sheila McCormick; E-mail: smccormick@cwmars.org; *Head, Automated Libr Serv,* Nancy Bronner; *Head, Circ & Ref,* Ann Kuchieski; *Head, Children's Servx,* Jennifer Whitehead; *Libr Tech,* Keri Kelly; *Libr Tech,* Mary Senecal; Staff 8 (MLS 1, Non-MLS 7)
Founded 1887. Pop 14,000; Circ 138,333
Library Holdings: Bk Titles 22,729; Bk Vols 25,000; Per Subs 82; Talking Bks 2,000; Videos 3,000
Automation Activity & Vendor Info: (Circulation) Innovative Interfaces, Inc
Wireless access
Partic in Central & Western Massachusetts Automated Resource Sharing
Open Mon & Fri 10-6, Tues-Thurs 10-7, Sat 9-1
Friends of the Library Group

BELLINGHAM

P BELLINGHAM PUBLIC LIBRARY*, 100 Blackstone St, 02019. SAN 307-1065. Tel: 508-966-1660. FAX: 508-966-3189. E-mail: library@bellinghamlibrary.org. Web Site: www.bellinghamlibrary.org. *Dir,* Bernadette D Rivard; E-mail: brivard@bellinghamma.org; *Ref Librn,* Cecily Christensen; *YA Librn,* Amanda Maclure; *Youth Serv Librn,* Steven Fowler; Staff 8 (MLS 3, Non-MLS 5)
Founded 1894. Pop 16,675; Circ 106,836
Jul 2015-Jun 2016 Income $576,018, State $20,574, City $548,629, Other $6,825. Mats Exp $89,014. Sal $359,842
Library Holdings: Bk Titles 63,226; Per Subs 60
Automation Activity & Vendor Info: (Cataloging) Evergreen; (Circulation) Evergreen; (OPAC) Evergreen
Wireless access
Function: 24/7 Electronic res, 24/7 Online cat, Adult bk club, Audiobks on Playaways & MP3, Bk club(s), Bks on CD, Children's prog, Computers for patron use, Electronic databases & coll, Free DVD rentals, Homebound delivery serv, Internet access, Magazines, Mango lang, Meeting rooms, Museum passes, Music CDs, Online cat, OverDrive digital audio bks, Photocopying/Printing, Prog for adults, Prog for children & young adult, Ref & res, Ref serv available, Scanner, Story hour, Study rm, Summer reading prog, Tax forms, Teen prog, VHS videos, Wheelchair accessible
Mem of Massachusetts Library System
Partic in Central & Western Massachusetts Automated Resource Sharing
Open Mon & Thurs 10-8, Tues & Wed 10-6, Fri 10-5, Sat (Sept-June) 10-5
Friends of the Library Group

BELMONT

P BELMONT PUBLIC LIBRARY*, 336 Concord Ave, 02478-0904. (Mail add: PO Box 125, 02478-0125), SAN 344-547X. Tel: 617-489-2000, 617-993-2850. Circulation Tel: 617-993-2855. Reference Tel: 617-993-2870. Administration Tel: 617-993-2851. FAX: 617-993-2893. E-mail: belmontpubliclibrary@gmail.com. Web Site: belmontpubliclibrary.net. *Dir,* Peter Struzziero; Tel: 617-489-2000, Ext 2852, E-mail: pstruzziero@minlib.net; *Head, Circ,* Lisa Cassidy; *Commun Serv Librn,* Mary Carter; E-mail: mcarter@minlib.net; Staff 11 (MLS 9, Non-MLS 2)
Founded 1868. Pop 24,762; Circ 566,872
Library Holdings: AV Mats 14,419; e-books 261; Bk Vols 131,065; Per Subs 273
Automation Activity & Vendor Info: (Cataloging) Innovative Interfaces, Inc; (Circulation) Innovative Interfaces, Inc; (OPAC) Innovative Interfaces, Inc
Wireless access
Partic in Minuteman Library Network
Open Mon-Thurs 9-9, Fri & Sat 9-5, Sun 1-5
Friends of the Library Group

P EVERETT C BENTON LIBRARY*, 75 Oakley Rd, 02478-0125. (Mail add: PO Box 425, 02478), SAN 344-550X. Tel: 617-484-0988. E-mail: ecbentonlibrary@gmail.com. Web Site: www.ecbentonlibrary.org. *Pres,* Elizabeth Gibson; *Vols Coordr,* Brooks F Bard; E-mail: brooksfb@gmail.com
Library Holdings: Bk Vols 7,500
Wireless access
Open Tues & Fri 10-1, Wed & Thurs 2-7
Friends of the Library Group

R BETH EL TEMPLE CENTER, Carl Kales Memorial Library, Two Concord Ave, 02478-4075. SAN 307-1073. Tel: 617-484-6668. FAX: 617-484-6020. E-mail: library@betheltemplecenter.org. Web Site: www.betheltemplecenter.org/education/library. *Library Contact,* Liane Weber
Library Holdings: Bk Vols 2,400
Wireless access

M MCLEAN HOSPITAL, Mental Health Sciences Library, 115 Mill St, Mail Stop 203, 02478. SAN 307-109X. Tel: 617-855-2460. E-mail: mcleanlibrary@partners.org. *Med Librn & Coordr Med Educ,* Chris Vaillancourt; E-mail: cvaillan@nebh.org; Staff 1 (MLS 1)
Founded 1836
Library Holdings: e-books 200; e-journals 129; Bk Titles 6,000; Per Subs 130; Videos 15
Subject Interests: Drug dependence, Mental health, Psychiat, Psychoanalysis, Psychol, Psychopharmacology, Psychotherapy, Soc sci & issues
Automation Activity & Vendor Info: (Cataloging) OCLC; (Circulation) CyberTools for Libraries; (ILL) OCLC WorldShare Interlibrary Loan; (OPAC) CyberTools for Libraries; (Serials) TDNet
Wireless access
Partic in Association of Mental Health Libraries; Massachusetts Health Sciences Library Network; North Atlantic Health Sciences Libraries, Inc; OCLC Online Computer Library Center, Inc; Partners Library Network
Open Mon-Fri 8:30-4:45
Friends of the Library Group

BERKLEY

P BERKLEY PUBLIC LIBRARY*, Two N Main St, 02779. SAN 307-1103. Tel: 508-822-3329. FAX: 508-824-2471. E-mail: berpl@sailsinc.org. *Libr Dir,* Vicki Dawson; *Ch,* Cynthia Quinn; *Cat,* Carol Buote; *Libr Tech,* Ann Almeida; Staff 3 (Non-MLS 3)
Founded 1893. Circ 20,000
Library Holdings: Bk Vols 16,000; Per Subs 30
Automation Activity & Vendor Info: (Acquisitions) SirsiDynix-WorkFlows; (Cataloging) SirsiDynix-WorkFlows; (Circulation)

SirsiDynix-WorkFlows; (ILL) SirsiDynix-WorkFlows; (OPAC) SirsiDynix-iBistro
Wireless access
Function: 24/7 Electronic res, 24/7 Online cat, 3D Printer, Adult bk club
Mem of Massachusetts Library System
Partic in SAILS Library Network
Open Tues 9-5, Wed & Thurs 1-8, Fri 9-12, Sat 9-2
Friends of the Library Group

BERLIN

P BERLIN PUBLIC LIBRARY*, 23 Carter St, 01503-1219. SAN 307-1111. Tel: 978-838-2812. FAX: 978-838-2812. Web Site: www.townofberlin.com/library. *Dir,* Bob Hodge; E-mail: rhodge@cwmars.org; Staff 3 (MLS 1, Non-MLS 2)
Pop 2,700; Circ 18,000
Library Holdings: Bk Vols 16,000; Per Subs 60
Automation Activity & Vendor Info: (Cataloging) Evergreen; (Circulation) Evergreen; (OPAC) Evergreen
Wireless access
Partic in Central & Western Massachusetts Automated Resource Sharing
Open Mon-Thurs 11-6:30, Sat 10-1
Friends of the Library Group

BERNARDSTON

P CUSHMAN LIBRARY*, 28 Church St, 01337. (Mail add: PO Box 248, 01337-0248), SAN 307-112X. Tel: 413-648-5402. FAX: 413-648-0168. E-mail: cushmanlibrary@gmail.com. Web Site: sites.google.com/site/cushmanlibrary. *Dir,* Karen Stinchfield; *Asst Librn,* Bonnie Delcamp
Founded 1863. Pop 2,800; Circ 15,600
Library Holdings: AV Mats 1,035; Bk Titles 14,384; Bk Vols 18,000; Per Subs 28
Special Collections: Oral History
Wireless access
Partic in Central & Western Massachusetts Automated Resource Sharing
Open Mon 2-6, Wed 10-7:30, Sat 10-3:30
Friends of the Library Group

BEVERLY

S BEVERLY HISTORICAL SOCIETY*, Charles W Galloupe Memorial Library, 117 Cabot St, 01915-5107. SAN 307-1138. Tel: 978-922-1186, Ext 202. FAX: 978-922-7387. E-mail: research@beverlyhistory.org. Web Site: www.historicbeverly.net. *Assoc Dir, Coll,* Abby Battis
Founded 1891
Library Holdings: Bk Vols 2,000
Special Collections: 17th Century Essex County Settlement History; New England History (Charles W Galloupe Memorial Library); Salem & Beverly Ship Logs, 1750's to late early 20th Century; Walker Transportation Coll, photog
Subject Interests: Genealogy, Maritime, New England, Transportation
Publications: Beverly High Football in the 20th Century; Beverly Men in the War of Independence; History of Beverly; North Beverly Remembered; Reflections of Mid-20th Century Beverly; Ryal Side From Early Days of Salem Colony; Thieves, Cow Beaters & Other True Tales of Colonial Beverly; Treasures of a Seaport Town
Open Tues & Sat 9:30-4, Wed 1-9
Restriction: Non-circulating to the pub

M BEVERLY HOSPITAL MEDICAL LIBRARY*, 85 Herrick St, 01915. SAN 344-5569. Tel: 978-922-3000, Ext 2920. *Librn,* Ann M Tomes; E-mail: atomes@nhs-healthlink.org
Founded 1900
Library Holdings: Bk Vols 1,000; Per Subs 100
Special Collections: Medical Incunabula (Beverly Hospital Historical Library)
Partic in Northeastern Consortium for Health Information
Restriction: Staff use only

P BEVERLY PUBLIC LIBRARY*, 32 Essex St, 01915-4561. SAN 344-5593. Tel: 978-921-6062. FAX: 978-922-8329. E-mail: bev@noblenet.org. Web Site: beverlypubliclibrary.org. *Dir,* Anna L Langstaff; E-mail: langstaff@noblenet.org; *Head, Children's Servx,* Margie McClory; *Head, Ref,* Lisa Ryan; *Head, Tech Serv,* Laurie Formichella; Staff 19 (MLS 14, Non-MLS 5)
Founded 1855. Pop 40,235; Circ 288,380
Library Holdings: Bk Vols 180,058; Per Subs 125
Special Collections: Original Lithographs (Will Barnet Coll)
Automation Activity & Vendor Info: (Circulation) Innovative Interfaces, Inc
Wireless access
Publications: Beverly Public Library (Newsletter)
Mem of Massachusetts Library System
Partic in North of Boston Library Exchange, Inc
Open Mon-Thurs 9-9, Fri & Sat 9-5, Sun 1-5
Friends of the Library Group
Branches: 1
BEVERLY FARMS, 24 Vine St, 01915-2208, SAN 344-5623. Tel: 978-921-6066. FAX: 978-927-9239. E-mail: beverlyfarms_library@noblenet.org. *Librn,* Kate Ingalls; *Librn,* Brenda Wettergreen
Library Holdings: Bk Vols 20,756; Per Subs 30
Open Mon & Wed 10-6, Tues & Thurs 10-9, Fri 10-5, Sat 9-5
Friends of the Library Group
Bookmobiles: 1. Librn, Linda Caravaggio

C ENDICOTT COLLEGE LIBRARY*, Diane M Halle Library, 376 Hale St, 01915. SAN 307-1146. Tel: 978-232-2279. Reference Tel: 978-232-2268. Administration Tel: 978-232-2278. FAX: 978-232-2700. E-mail: end@noblenet.org. Web Site: www.endicott.edu. *Libr Dir,* Brian Courtemanche; E-mail: bcourtem@endicott.edu; *Ref Librn,* Bridget Cunio; Tel: 978-232-2285, E-mail: bcunio@endicott.edu; *Ref Librn,* Melissa Natale; Tel: 978-232-2244, E-mail: menatale@endicott.edu; *Ref Librn,* Eleanor Rogers; Tel: 978-232-2293, E-mail: erogers@endicott.edu; *Ref Librn,* Bethany Wright; E-mail: bwright@endicott.edu; *Coordr, Libr User Serv,* Laurie Souza; Tel: 978-232-2276, E-mail: lsouza@endicott.edu; *Circ Asst,* Abby Barre; E-mail: abarre@endicott.edu; *Circ Asst,* Thera Driscoll; E-mail: tdriscol@endicott.edu; *Tech Serv Asst,* Sarah Tarr; Tel: 978-232-2277, E-mail: starr@endicott.edu; Staff 9 (MLS 5, Non-MLS 4)
Founded 1939. Enrl 5,093; Fac 590; Highest Degree: Doctorate
Library Holdings: Audiobooks 6,325; AV Mats 1,185; e-books 205,434; e-journals 142,167; Microforms 6,978; Bk Titles 101,458; Bk Vols 111,066; Per Subs 29
Automation Activity & Vendor Info: (Cataloging) Evergreen; (Circulation) Evergreen; (Course Reserve) Evergreen; (ILL) Evergreen; (OPAC) Evergreen
Wireless access
Partic in North of Boston Library Exchange, Inc
Open Mon-Thurs 7:30am-Midnight, Fri 7:30am-8pm, Sat Noon-6, Sun Noon-Midnight

C MONTSERRAT COLLEGE OF ART, Paul M Scott Library, 23 Essex St, 01915. SAN 328-6231. Circulation Tel: 978-921-4242, Ext 1203. FAX: 978-922-4268. E-mail: library@montserrat.edu. Web Site: www.montserrat.edu/library. *Col Librn,* Eileen Fitzgerald; Tel: 978-921-4242, Ext 1208, E-mail: eileen.fitzgerald@montserrat.edu
Founded 1979
Library Holdings: Bk Titles 11,000; Bk Vols 12,000; Per Subs 75
Special Collections: Paul M Scott Archives
Automation Activity & Vendor Info: (Circulation) Evergreen
Wireless access
Mem of Massachusetts Library System
Partic in North of Boston Library Exchange, Inc
Open Mon-Thurs 8-8, Fri 8-5, Sun 12-4

BILLERICA

S AERODYNE RESEARCH, INC*, Technical Information Center, 45 Manning Rd, 01821-3976. SAN 307-0964. Tel: 978-663-9500. FAX: 978-663-4918. Web Site: www.aerodyne.com. *Info Spec,* Susan B Mast; E-mail: mast@aerodyne.com; Staff 1 (MLS 1)
Founded 1975
Library Holdings: Bk Vols 2,000; Per Subs 210
Subject Interests: Atmospheric chem, Optics
Publications: Journal List; Technical Information Center Bytes
Partic in SLA
Open Mon-Fri 9-5

P BILLERICA PUBLIC LIBRARY*, 15 Concord Rd, 01821. SAN 307-1189. Tel: 978-671-0948. Web Site: www.billericalibrary.org. *Head, Children's Servx, Interim Dir,* Jan Hagman; E-mail: jhagman@billericalibrary.org; *Asst Dir,* Greg McClay; E-mail: greg.maclay@billericalibrary.org
Pop 38,000; Circ 232,000
Library Holdings: AV Mats 8,000; Large Print Bks 1,500; Bk Vols 120,000; Per Subs 230
Special Collections: Oral History
Automation Activity & Vendor Info: (Cataloging) SirsiDynix; (Circulation) SirsiDynix; (OPAC) SirsiDynix
Wireless access
Partic in Merrimack Valley Library Consortium
Open Mon-Thurs 9-9, Fri & Sat 9-5, Sun 1-5
Friends of the Library Group

BLACKSTONE

P BLACKSTONE PUBLIC LIBRARY, 86 Main St, 01504. SAN 307-1200. Tel: 508-883-1931. FAX: 508-883-1531. Web Site: www.blackstonepubliclibrary.org. *Libr Dir,* Lisa Cheever; E-mail: lcheever@cwmars.org; *Asst Dir, Ch,* Tressy Collier; E-mail: tcollier@cwmars.org; *Head, Circ, Sr Libr Tech,* Donna Ansell; E-mail: dansell@cwmars.org; Staff 9 (MLS 1, Non-MLS 8)
Founded 1889. Pop 8,804
Library Holdings: Audiobooks 1,421; Braille Volumes 4; CDs 393; DVDs 2,452; Electronic Media & Resources 1; Large Print Bks 1,718; Bk Vols 36,510; Per Subs 79; Videos 2,443
Automation Activity & Vendor Info: (Cataloging) Innovative Interfaces, Inc; (Circulation) Innovative Interfaces, Inc; (ILL) Innovative Interfaces, Inc - Millennium; (OPAC) Innovative Interfaces, Inc
Wireless access
Function: Adult bk club, Computers for patron use, Electronic databases & coll, Family literacy, Free DVD rentals, Home delivery & serv to seniorr ctr & nursing homes, Homebound delivery serv, ILL available, Museum passes, Music CDs, Notary serv, Online cat, OverDrive digital audio bks, Photocopying/Printing, Prog for adults, Prog for children & young adult, Spoken cassettes & CDs, Story hour, Summer reading prog, Tax forms, Telephone ref, VHS videos, Wheelchair accessible
Mem of Massachusetts Library System
Partic in Central & Western Massachusetts Automated Resource Sharing
Open Mon 9-8, Tues & Thurs 12-8, Fri & Sat 10-2
Friends of the Library Group

BLANDFORD

P PORTER MEMORIAL LIBRARY*, 87 Main St, 01008. SAN 307-1219. Tel: 413-848-2853. E-mail: library@blandford.ma.us. Web Site: townofblandford.com/town-departments/library, www.portermemoriallibrary.org. *Dir,* Nicole Daviau; Staff 3 (Non-MLS 3)
Founded 1892. Pop 1,264; Circ 10,399
Library Holdings: Bk Vols 9,000; Per Subs 10
Subject Interests: Genealogy
Wireless access
Partic in Central & Western Massachusetts Automated Resource Sharing
Open Mon-Fri 2-6, Sat 10-4
Friends of the Library Group

BOLTON

P BOLTON PUBLIC LIBRARY, 738 Main St, 01740. (Mail add: PO Box 188, 01740-0188), SAN 307-1227. Tel: 978-779-2839. FAX: 978-779-2293. E-mail: library@townofbolton.com. Web Site: www.boltonpubliclibrary.org, www.townofbolton.com/library. *Dir,* Kelly Collins; E-mail: kcollins@cwmars.org; Staff 7 (MLS 1, Non-MLS 6)
Founded 1856. Pop 4,500; Circ 38,500
Library Holdings: Bk Vols 25,000; Per Subs 75
Subject Interests: Local hist
Automation Activity & Vendor Info: (Cataloging) Innovative Interfaces, Inc; (Circulation) Innovative Interfaces, Inc; (ILL) Innovative Interfaces, Inc; (OPAC) Innovative Interfaces, Inc
Wireless access
Mem of Massachusetts Library System
Partic in Central & Western Massachusetts Automated Resource Sharing
Open Tues-Thurs 10-8, Fri 10-5, Sat 10-2
Friends of the Library Group

BOSTON

SR AMERICAN CONGREGATIONAL ASSOCIATION*, Congregational Library & Archives, 14 Beacon St, 2nd Flr, 02108-9999. SAN 307-1235. Tel: 617-523-0470. FAX: 617-523-0491. E-mail: ref@14beacon.org. Web Site: www.congregationallibrary.org. *Exec Dir,* Stephen Butler Murray; E-mail: smurray@14beacon.org; *Libr Dir,* Tom Clark; E-mail: tclark@14beacon.org; *Librn,* Sara Belmonte; E-mail: sbelmonte@14beacon.org; *Archivist,* Zachary Bodnar; E-mail: zbodnar@14beacon.org; Staff 6 (MLS 4, Non-MLS 2)
Founded 1853
Library Holdings: Bk Titles 225,000; Per Subs 40
Special Collections: Church Records, micro, ms, rec; Mather Family Coll, ms, printed; Monographs, ms & printed; Newspapers & Periodicals, printed originals & micro; Theology & Sermons, 17th-19th centuries
Automation Activity & Vendor Info: (Cataloging) Softlink America; (OPAC) Softlink America; (Serials) Softlink America
Wireless access
Function: Mail & tel request accepted, Ref serv available, Workshops
Publications: Bulletin
Open Mon-Fri 9-5 & by appointment
Restriction: Closed stack

J BAY STATE COLLEGE LIBRARY*, 31 Saint James, 2nd Flr, 02116. (Mail add: 122 Commonwealth Ave, 02116), SAN 307-1278. Tel: 617-217-9449. FAX: 617-236-8023. E-mail: library@baystate.edu. Web Site: www.baystate.edu/library. *Col Librn,* Megan Rupe; E-mail: mrupe@baystate.edu; Staff 1 (MLS 1)
Founded 1946
Library Holdings: Bk Titles 5,300; Per Subs 100
Subject Interests: Acctg, Allied health, Bus, Early childhood, Educ, Fashion, Hotel admin, Legal, Occupational therapy, Phys therapy, Tourism, Travel
Automation Activity & Vendor Info: (Circulation) EOS International
Partic in LYRASIS
Open Mon-Thurs 8am-10pm

C BENJAMIN FRANKLIN INSTITUTE OF TECHNOLOGY*, Lufkin Memorial, Franklin Union Bldg, Rm U108, 41 Berkeley St, 02116. SAN 307-1707. Tel: 617-423-4630. Web Site: www.bfit.edu/academics/library. *Dir, Libr Serv,* Sharon B Bonk; Tel: 617-588-1356, E-mail: sbonk@bfit.edu; Staff 2 (MLS 2)
Founded 1908. Enrl 400
Library Holdings: e-books 15,000; Bk Titles 23,000; Per Subs 120
Special Collections: Benjamin Franklin Coll; Photographic Science (Dr Leonard E Ravich Coll)
Subject Interests: Archit, Civil engr, Computer sci, Electronic engr, Mechanical engr
Automation Activity & Vendor Info: (Circulation) LibraryWorld, Inc; (OPAC) LibraryWorld, Inc
Wireless access
Publications: Guide to the Library
Partic in Boston Library Consortium, Inc; LYRASIS; Mass Libr & Info Network
Open Mon-Thurs 7:30am-9pm, Fri 7:30-6

C BERKLEE COLLEGE OF MUSIC LIBRARY*, Stan Getz Media Center & Library, 150 Massachusetts Ave, 02115. (Mail add: 1140 Boylston St, MS150-Lib, 02215), SAN 307-1286. Tel: 617-747-2258. Reference Tel: 617-747-8002. FAX: 617-747-2050. E-mail: library@berklee.edu. Web Site: library.berklee.edu. *Dean, Learning Res,* Heather Reid; Tel: 617-747-2603, E-mail: hreid@berklee.edu; *Libr Dir,* Jennifer Hunt; E-mail: jhunt3@berklee.edu; *Assoc Dir, Libr Serv,* Yamil Suarez; Tel: 617-747-2617, E-mail: ysuarez@berklee.edu; *Acq Librn, Cat Librn, ILL Librn,* Reg Didham; E-mail: rdidham@berklee.edu; *Metadata Serv Mgr,* Jenee Morgan Force; Tel: 617-747-8684, E-mail: jmforce@berklee.edu; *Mgr, User Serv,* Ralph Rosen; Tel: 617-747-8338, E-mail: rrosen@berklee.edu; Staff 13 (MLS 7, Non-MLS 6)
Founded 1964. Enrl 4,200; Fac 500; Highest Degree: Master
Library Holdings: AV Mats 5,100; CDs 34,545; e-books 10,000; Music Scores 24,009; Bk Titles 27,072; Per Subs 217
Special Collections: Jazz & Rock Music Coll, scores with matching recordings
Subject Interests: Humanities, Music
Automation Activity & Vendor Info: (Cataloging) Evergreen; (Circulation) Evergreen; (OPAC) Evergreen
Wireless access
Open Mon-Thurs 9am-11:45pm, Fri 9am-9:45pm, Sat 10-9:45, Sun 1-11:45
Friends of the Library Group

C BOSTON ARCHITECTURAL COLLEGE*, Shaw & Stone Library, 320 Newbury St, 02115. SAN 307-1324. Tel: 617-585-0155. E-mail: library@the-bac.edu. Web Site: www.the-bac.edu/library. *Libr Dir,* Susan Lewis; Tel: 617-585-0234, E-mail: susan.lewis@the-bac.edu; *Assoc Dir,* Kris Liberman; Tel: 617-585-7337, E-mail: kris.liberman@the-bac.edu; *Ref Librn, Visual Res,* Sheri L Rosenzweig; Tel: 617-585-0257, E-mail: sheri.rosenzweig@the-bac.edu; *Syst Librn,* Jenny Jing; E-mail: jenny.jing@the-bac.edu; *Outreach & Coll Develop Mgr,* Robert Adams; Tel: 617-585-0232, E-mail: robert.adams@the-bac.edu; *Archivist,* Kris Kobialka; Tel: 617-585-0133, E-mail: kris.kobialka@the-bac.edu; *Cataloger,* Chris Leshock. Subject Specialists: *Spec coll,* Susan Lewis; *Archit, Design,* Robert Adams; Staff 7 (MLS 6, Non-MLS 1)
Founded 1966. Enrl 680; Fac 250; Highest Degree: Master
Library Holdings: e-journals 5,000; Bk Vols 50,000; Per Subs 120; Videos 150
Special Collections: Architectural History (Memorial Library Coll)
Subject Interests: Archit, Energy, Interior archit, Landscape archit
Automation Activity & Vendor Info: (Acquisitions) Ex Libris Group; (Cataloging) OCLC Connexion; (Circulation) Ex Libris Group; (Course Reserve) Ex Libris Group; (OPAC) Ex Libris Group; (Serials) Ex Libris Group
Wireless access
Function: 24/7 Online cat, Computers for patron use, Distance learning, E-Reserves, Electronic databases & coll, Online cat, Photocopying/Printing, Ref serv available, Scanner
Open Mon-Thurs 10-10:30, Fri & Sat 10-5, Sun 12-7

Restriction: Non-circulating of rare bks, Non-circulating to the pub, Open to pub for ref only, Open to qualified scholars, Pub use on premises
Friends of the Library Group

S BOSTON ATHENAEUM*, Ten 1/2 Beacon St, 02108-3777. SAN 307-1332. Tel: 617-227-0270. Circulation Tel: 617-227-0270, Ext 301. Interlibrary Loan Service Tel: 617-227-0270, Ext 280. E-mail: reference@bostonathenaeum.org. Web Site: www.bostonathenaeum.org. *Chief of Staff,* Emily Cure; Tel: 617-720-7661, E-mail: cure@bostonathenaeum.org; *Interim Dir,* Amy E Ryan; *Dir, Finance & Operations,* Christopher Boudrot; E-mail: boudrot@bostonathenaeum.org; *Head, Circ,* James Feeney, Jr; E-mail: feeney@bostonathenaeum.org; *Head, Reader Serv,* Mary Warnement; E-mail: warnement@bostonathenaeum.org; *Chief Librn, Tech Serv,* Will Evans; E-mail: evans@bostonathenaeum.org; Staff 40 (MLS 11, Non-MLS 29)
Founded 1807
Library Holdings: Bk Vols 603,000; Per Subs 450
Special Collections: 18th & 19th Century Tracts; American 19th Century Photographs; American Prints & Drawings; Books from the Library of George Washington; Byroniana; Confederate Imprints, bk, micro; European & American 19th Century paintings & sculpture; General Henry Knox Library; Gypsy Literature; Henry Rowe Schoolcraft Coll; John Fowles; John Masefield; Merrymount Press Coll; TS Eliot
Subject Interests: Archives, Fine arts, Hist, Manuscripts
Automation Activity & Vendor Info: (Acquisitions) Ex Libris Group; (Cataloging) Ex Libris Group; (Circulation) Ex Libris Group; (ILL) OCLC WorldShare Interlibrary Loan
Wireless access
Function: For res purposes, ILL available, Mail loans to mem, Ref serv available, Res libr, Telephone ref
Partic in LYRASIS
Open Tues 12-8, Wed-Sat 10-4

CR BOSTON BAPTIST COLLEGE LIBRARY*, 950 Metropolitan Ave, 02136. Tel: 617-364-3510, Ext 216. Web Site: www.boston.edu. *Dir,* Fred Tatro; E-mail: ftatro@boston.edu; Staff 1 (MLS 1)
Founded 1976. Enrl 120; Highest Degree: Bachelor
Library Holdings: Bk Vols 250,000
Automation Activity & Vendor Info: (Cataloging) Follett Software; (Circulation) Follett Software; (OPAC) Follett Software
Wireless access
Open Mon-Thurs 7am-10pm, Fri 7-5, Sun 9pm-11pm

M BOSTON CHILDREN'S HOSPITAL MEDICAL LIBRARY*, 300 Longwood Ave, 02115. SAN 377-9173. Tel: 617-355-7232. E-mail: library@childrens.harvard.edu. Web Site: childrenshospital.org/about-us/libraries. *Mgr, Libr Serv,* Chloe Rotman; E-mail: chloe.rotman@childrens.harvard.edu; Staff 2.3 (MLS 2, Non-MLS 0.3)
Founded 1994
Library Holdings: e-journals 2,000; Bk Titles 3,000
Subject Interests: Pediatrics
Automation Activity & Vendor Info: (OPAC) Softlink America
Wireless access
Function: Health sci info serv, ILL available, Internet access, Photocopying/Printing, Ref serv available, Wheelchair accessible
Partic in National Network of Libraries of Medicine Region 7
Open Mon-Fri 8-5
Restriction: Circulates for staff only, Non-circulating to the pub

C THE BOSTON CONSERVATORY*, Albert Alphin Music Library, Eight Fenway, 2nd Flr, 02215-4099. SAN 307-1359. Tel: 617-912-9131. FAX: 617-912-9101. E-mail: library@bostonconservatory.edu. Web Site: bostonconservatory.berklee.edu/offices-and-services/albert-alphin-library. *Dir,* Jennifer Hunt; E-mail: jhunt@bostonconservatory.edu; *Archivist, Pub Serv Librn,* Brenda Higgins; E-mail: bhiggins@bostonconservatory.edu; *Acq, Cat,* Reginald A Didham; E-mail: rdidham@bostonconservatory.edu
Founded 1867. Highest Degree: Master
Library Holdings: Bk Vols 40,000; Per Subs 85
Special Collections: James Pappoutsakis Memorial Coll; Jan Veen - Katrine Amory Hooper Memorial Art Coll
Subject Interests: Dance, Drama, Music, Opera
Automation Activity & Vendor Info: (Cataloging) Follett Software; (Circulation) Follett Software; (ILL) OCLC; (OPAC) Follett Software
Wireless access
Partic in OCLC Online Computer Library Center, Inc
Open Mon-Wed 8am-11pm, Thurs 8am-10pm, Fri 8-8, Sat 10-8, Sun 12-11

P BOSTON PUBLIC LIBRARY*, 700 Boylston St, 02116. SAN 344-5712. Tel: 617-536-5400. FAX: 617-236-4306. E-mail: ask@bpl.org. Web Site: www.bpl.org. *Pres,* David Leonard; Tel: 617-859-2034, E-mail: dleonard@bpl.org; *Dir, Libr Serv,* Michael Colford; Tel: 617-859-2389, E-mail: mcolford@bpl.org; Staff 425 (MLS 150, Non-MLS 275)
Founded 1852. Pop 574,283; Circ 3,116,540
Library Holdings: Audiobooks 65,948; AV Mats 113,633; Electronic Media & Resources 9,177; Microforms 6,943,617; Bk Vols 8,895,168; Per Subs 4,673
Special Collections: Albert H Wiggin Print Coll; American & English History & Biography incl Fine Editions (Thayer Coll), Spanish & Portuguese (Ticknor Coll); American & English History & Literature, Jurists, Artists, Men of Letters, Anti-slavery; American & Foreign Authors & Rare Editions incl Longfellow Memorial known as Artz Coll; American Accounting to 1900 (Bentley Coll); Astronomy, Mathematics & Navigation (Bowditch Coll); Books By & About Women (Galatea Coll); Books Printed in England before 1640, Newspapers, City of Boston Records & Government Documents, microfilm; Christian Science (Works of Mary Baker Eddy); Dance (Lilla Viles Wyman Coll); Defoe & Defoeana (Trent Coll); Drama (Barton, Gilbert & Ticknor Colls); Early & Important Children's Books; Early Boston Imprints (John A Lewis Coll); English & American Literature; Engravings & Early Rare Impressions (Tosti Coll); Frankliniana; Fred Allen Papers; Genealogy (New England Families, English Parish Records); German 18th & 19th Century Poetry (Sears-Freiligrath Coll); Government Documents; Great Britain, Ireland, Scotland & United States Colls; Heraldry Coll; Imprints before 1850 (Charlotte Harris Coll); James Brendan Connolly Coll (First Editions); Joan of Arc Coll; Landscape Architecture (Codman Coll); Literature Coll; Manuscript Coll; Maps & Atlases; Medieval Manuscripts; Military Science & History & Civil War (20th Regiment); Music (Brown Coll); Newspapers (Early American & Current from all over the World); Patents (Early American to present, British, German); Periodicals & Serials (Boston Imprints, Learned Societies, Literary, Foreign Language); Photographs, Early & Civil War, Baseball Players (Michael T McGreevy Coll); Picture Coll; President John Adams Library; Prince Coll; Printing Coll, 16th Century to Present; Religion & Theology Coll; Robert & Elizabeth Browning Coll; Sacco-Vanzetti Papers; Statistics; The Book of Common Prayer (Benton Coll); Theatre (Brown Coll); Theodore Parker Library; Walt Whitman Coll; Washingtoniana (Lewisson Coll); West Indies (Benjamin P Hunt Coll); Wilfred Beaulieu Papers; William Peterson Trent Coll; Works Printed by John Baskerville (Benton Coll); World War I (Mary Boyle O'Reilly Coll). UN Document Depository; US Document Depository
Automation Activity & Vendor Info: (Acquisitions) Horizon; (Cataloging) Horizon; (Circulation) Horizon
Wireless access
Function: Adult bk club, Adult literacy prog, After school storytime, Archival coll, Art exhibits, Audiobks via web, AV serv, Bk club(s), Bks on cassette, Bks on CD, Bus archives, Chess club, Children's prog, Computers for patron use, E-Reserves, Electronic databases & coll, Family literacy, Govt ref serv, Homework prog, ILL available, Internet access, Museum passes, Music CDs, Online cat, Online ref, OverDrive digital audio bks, Photocopying/Printing, Prog for adults, Ref & res, Ref serv available, Story hour, Summer reading prog, Teen prog, Telephone ref, Wheelchair accessible
Publications: Armstrong & Co Artistic Lithographers; BPL Press/Catalogue of Publications; Catalog of the Large Print Collection; Childs Gallery, Boston, 1937-1980; Evolution of a Catalogue: From Folio to Fiche; Irwin D Hoffman, an Artist's Life; Small Talk About Great Books (Bromsen lecture VII); The Sacco-Vanzetti Case: Developments & Reconsiderations, 1979; The Society of Arts & Crafts: Boston Exhibition Record, 1897-1928
Partic in Boston Library Consortium, Inc; LYRASIS; Metro Boston Libr Network
Open Mon-Thurs 9-9, Fri & Sat 9-5, Sun 1-5
Friends of the Library Group

Branches: 26

ADAMS STREET, 690 Adams St, Dorchester, 02122, SAN 344-5836. Tel: 617-436-6900. E-mail: adams@bpl.org. Web Site: www.bpl.org/locations/13. *Br Librn,* Kate Brown; E-mail: kbrown@bpl.org
Founded 1951. Circ 96,323
Library Holdings: Bk Vols 30,000; Per Subs 35
Open Mon & Wed 12-8, Tues & Thurs 10-6, Fri & Sat 9-5
Friends of the Library Group

BRIGHTON BRANCH, 40 Academy Hill Rd, Brighton, 02135, SAN 344-5895. Tel: 617-782-6032. E-mail: brighton@bpl.org. Web Site: www.bpl.org/locations/15. *Br Librn,* Uma Murthy; E-mail: umurthy@bpl.org
Founded 1969. Circ 71,539
Library Holdings: Bk Vols 75,000; Per Subs 50
Open Mon & Thurs 12-8, Tues & Wed 10-6, Fri & Sat 9-5
Friends of the Library Group

CHARLESTOWN BRANCH, 179 Main St, Charlestown, 02129, SAN 344-5925. Tel: 617-242-1248. E-mail: charlestown@bpl.org. Web Site: www.bpl.org/locations/16. *Br Librn,* Maureen S Marx; E-mail: mmarx@bpl.org
Founded 1970. Circ 83,574
Library Holdings: Bk Vols 43,000; Per Subs 71
Open Mon & Thurs 12-8, Tues & Wed 10-6, Fri 9-5, Sat 9-2
Friends of the Library Group

CHINATOWN BRANCH, Two Boylston St, 02116. Tel: 617-807-8176. E-mail: chinatown@bpl.org. Web Site: www.bpl.org/locations/83. *Br Librn,* Yan Wang
Open Mon-Thurs 10-6, Fri 9-5

CODMAN SQUARE, 690 Washington St, Dorchester, 02124, SAN 344-595X. Tel: 617-436-8214. E-mail: codman@bpl.org. Web Site: www.bpl.org/locations/17. *Br Librn,* Janice Knight; E-mail: jknight@bpl.org
Founded 1978. Circ 55,117
Library Holdings: Large Print Bks 800; Bk Vols 84,390; Per Subs 70; Talking Bks 1,500; Videos 500
Open Mon & Thurs 12-8, Tues & Wed 10-6, Fri & Sat 9-5
Friends of the Library Group

CONNOLLY, 433 Centre St, Jamaica Plain, 02130, SAN 344-5984. Tel: 617-522-1960. E-mail: connolly@bpl.org. Web Site: www.bpl.org/locations/18. *Br Librn,* Emily Todd; E-mail: etodd@bpl.org
Founded 1932. Circ 77,651
Library Holdings: Bk Vols 30,000; Per Subs 42
Open Mon 12-8, Tues-Thurs 10-6, Fri 9-5, Sat 9-2
Friends of the Library Group

DUDLEY BRANCH, 149 Dudley St, Roxbury, 02119. Tel: 617-442-6186. E-mail: dudley@bpl.org. Web Site: www.bpl.org/locations/19. *Br Librn,* Allen Knight
Founded 1978. Circ 48,859
Library Holdings: Bk Vols 11,000
Closed for renovations 2019 until Spring of 2020

EAST BOSTON, 365 Bremen St, East Boston, 02128, SAN 344-6042. Tel: 617-569-0271. E-mail: eastboston@bpl.org. Web Site: www.bpl.org/locations/21. *Br Librn,* Margaret Kelly; E-mail: mkelly@bpl.org
Founded 1914. Circ 79,150
Library Holdings: Bk Vols 39,000; Per Subs 50
Open Mon & Thurs 12-8, Tues & Wed 10-6, Fri & Sat 9-5
Friends of the Library Group

EGLESTON SQUARE, 2044 Columbus Ave, Roxbury, 02119, SAN 344-6077. Tel: 617-445-4340. E-mail: egleston@bpl.org. Web Site: www.bpl.org/locations/22. *Br Librn,* Guy Harris; E-mail: gharris@bpl.org
Founded 1953. Circ 27,800
Library Holdings: Bk Vols 24,426
Open Mon, Tues & Thurs 10-6, Wed 12-8, Fri 9-5, Sat 9-2
Friends of the Library Group

FANEUIL, 419 Faneuil St, Brighton, 02135, SAN 344-6107. Tel: 617-782-6705. E-mail: faneuil@bpl.org. Web Site: www.bpl.org/locations/23. *Br Librn,* Amy Manson; E-mail: amanson@bpl.org
Founded 1932. Circ 125,604
Library Holdings: Bk Vols 22,416; Per Subs 15
Open Mon, Wed & Thurs 10-6, Tues 12-8, Fri 9-5, Sat 9-2
Friends of the Library Group

FIELDS CORNER, 1520 Dorchester Ave, Dorchester, 02122, SAN 344-6131. Tel: 617-436-2155. E-mail: fieldscorner@bpl.org. Web Site: www.bpl.org/locations/24. *Br Librn,* Kimberly McCleary; E-mail: kmccleary@bpl.org
Founded 1969. Circ 72,518
Library Holdings: Bk Vols 33,000; Per Subs 20; Videos 400
Open Mon, Wed & Thurs 10-6, Tues 12-8, Fri 9-5, Sat 9-2
Friends of the Library Group

GROVE HALL, 41 Geneva Ave, Dorchester, 02121-3109, SAN 344-6166. Tel: 617-427-3337. E-mail: grovehall@bpl.org. Web Site: www.bpl.org/locations/25. *Br Librn,* Paul Edwards; E-mail: pedwards@bpl.org
Library Holdings: Bk Vols 32,167
Open Mon-Wed 10-6, Thurs 12-8, Fri & Sat 9-5
Friends of the Library Group

HONAN-ALLSTON BRANCH, 300 N Harvard St, Allston, 02134. Tel: 617-787-6313. E-mail: honanallston@bpl.org. Web Site: www.bpl.org/locations/26. *Br Librn,* Carin O'Connor; E-mail: coconnor@bpl.org
Founded 2001. Circ 140,007
Library Holdings: Large Print Bks 200; Bk Vols 50,000; Per Subs 65; Talking Bks 300
Open Mon & Wed 12-8, Tues & Thurs 10-6, Fri & Sat 9-5
Friends of the Library Group

HYDE PARK BRANCH, 35 Harvard Ave, Hyde Park, 02136, SAN 344-6190. Tel: 617-361-2524. E-mail: hydepark@bpl.org. Web Site: www.bpl.org/locations/27. *Br Librn,* Mary Margaret Pitts; E-mail: mmpitts@bpl.org
Founded 1912. Circ 106,476
Library Holdings: Large Print Bks 1,000; Bk Vols 50,000; Per Subs 100
Open Mon & Thurs 12-8, Tues & Wed 10-6, Fri & Sat 9-5
Friends of the Library Group

JAMAICA PLAIN BRANCH, 30 Main St, Jamaica Plain, 02130, SAN 344-6220. Tel: 617-524-2053. E-mail: jamaicaplain@bpl.org. Web Site: www.bpl.org/locations/28. *Br Librn,* Laura Pattison; E-mail: lpattison@bpl.org
Founded 1911. Circ 152,254
Library Holdings: Bk Vols 40,000; Per Subs 50
Open Mon-Wed 10-6, Thurs 12-8, Fri & Sat 9-5
Friends of the Library Group

KIRSTEIN BUSINESS, 700 Boylston St, Lower Level, 02117, SAN 344-5771. Tel: 617-536-5400, Ext 4142. Web Site: www.bpl.org/services-central-library/kblic. *Curator,* Gregor Smart; E-mail: gsmart@bpl.org
Founded 1930. Circ 39,092
Library Holdings: Bk Vols 40,000; Per Subs 480
Open Mon-Thurs 9-9, Fri & Sat 9-5, Sun 1-5

LOWER MILLS, 27 Richmond St, Dorchester, 02124-5610, SAN 344-6255. Tel: 617-298-7841. E-mail: lowermills@bpl.org. Web Site: www.bpl.org/locations/29. *Br Librn,* Margaret Phillibert
Founded 1981. Circ 59,614
Library Holdings: Large Print Bks 500; Bk Vols 45,000; Per Subs 30; Talking Bks 300
Open Mon & Thurs 12-8, Tues & Wed 10-6, Fri 9-5, Sat 9-2
Friends of the Library Group

MATTAPAN, 1350 Blue Hill Ave, Mattapan, 02126, SAN 344-628X. Tel: 617-298-9218. E-mail: mattapan@bpl.org. Web Site: www.bpl.org/locations/30. *Br Librn,* Maurice Gordon; E-mail: mgordon@bpl.org
Founded 1931. Circ 58,901
Library Holdings: AV Mats 200; Large Print Bks 200; Bk Vols 23,000; Per Subs 35
Open Mon & Wed 10-6, Tues & Thurs 12-8, Fri & Sat 9-5
Friends of the Library Group

NORTH END, 25 Parmenter St, 02113-2306, SAN 344-631X. Tel: 617-227-8135. E-mail: northend@bpl.org. Web Site: www.bpl.org/locations/31. *Br Librn,* Jennifer Hawes; E-mail: jhawes@bpl.org
Founded 1965. Circ 70,099
Library Holdings: Bk Vols 30,000; Per Subs 34
Open Mon, Tues & Thurs 10-6, Wed 12-8, Fri 9-5, Sat 9-2
Friends of the Library Group

PARKER HILL, 1497 Tremont St, Roxbury, 02120, SAN 344-6379. Tel: 617-427-3820. E-mail: parkerhill@bpl.org. Web Site: www.bpl.org/locations/34. *Interim Librn,* Allen Knight; E-mail: aknight@bpl.org
Library Holdings: Bk Vols 29,000; Per Subs 46
Open Mon-Wed 10-6, Thurs 12-8, Fri 9-5, Sat 9-2
Friends of the Library Group

ROSLINDALE BRANCH, 4246 Washington St, Roslindale, 02131, SAN 344-6409. Tel: 617-323-2343. E-mail: roslindale@bpl.org. Web Site: www.bpl.org/locations/35. *Br Librn,* Rebecca Manos; E-mail: rmanos@bpl.org
Founded 1961. Circ 90,165
Library Holdings: Bk Vols 45,000; Per Subs 70; Talking Bks 200
Open Mon-Wed 10-6, Thurs 12-8, Fri 9-5, Sat 9-2
Friends of the Library Group

SOUTH BOSTON, 646 E Broadway, 02127-1502, SAN 344-6433. Tel: 617-268-0180. E-mail: southboston@bpl.org. Web Site: www.bpl.org/locations/36. *Br Librn,* Jane Bickford; E-mail: jbickford@bpl.org
Founded 1957. Circ 90,159
Library Holdings: Bk Vols 39,000; Per Subs 45; Talking Bks 300
Open Mon & Thurs 12-8, Tues & Wed 10-6, Fri & Sat 9-5
Friends of the Library Group

SOUTH END, 685 Tremont St, 02118, SAN 344-6468. Tel: 617-536-8241. E-mail: southend@bpl.org. Web Site: www.bpl.org/locations/37. *Br Librn,* Anne Smart; E-mail: asmart@bpl.org
Founded 1971. Circ 86,452
Library Holdings: Bk Vols 50,000; Per Subs 20; Talking Bks 300
Open Mon, Wed & Thurs 10-6, Tues 12-8, Fri 9-5, Sat 9-2
Friends of the Library Group

UPHAMS CORNER, 500 Columbia Rd, Dorchester, 02125, SAN 344-6492. Tel: 617-265-0139. E-mail: uphams@bpl.org. Web Site: www.bpl.org/locations/38. *Br Librn,* Georgia Titonis; E-mail: gtitonis@bpl.org
Founded 1907. Circ 32,298
Library Holdings: Bk Vols 32,000; Per Subs 25
Open Mon-Wed 10-6, Thurs 12-8, Fri 9-5, Sat 9-2
Friends of the Library Group

WEST END, 151 Cambridge St, 02114, SAN 344-6522. Tel: 617-523-3957. E-mail: westend@bpl.org. Web Site: www.bpl.org/locations/39. *Br Librn,* Helen Bender; E-mail: hbender@bpl.org
Founded 1968. Circ 143,588
Library Holdings: Bk Vols 25,000; Per Subs 25; Talking Bks 100

Open Mon-Wed 10-6, Thurs 12-8, Fri 9-5, Sat 9-2
Friends of the Library Group

WEST ROXBURY BRANCH, 1961 Centre St, West Roxbury, 02132, SAN 344-6557. Tel: 617-325-3147. E-mail: westroxbury@bpl.org. Web Site: www.bpl.org/locations/40. *Br Librn,* Sheila Scott; E-mail: sscott@bpl.org
Founded 1922. Circ 155,565
Library Holdings: Bk Vols 105,000; Per Subs 50
Open Mon & Thurs 12-8, Tues & Wed 10-6, Fri & Sat 9-5
Friends of the Library Group

BOSTON UNIVERSITY LIBRARIES

C AFRICAN STUDIES LIBRARY*, 771 Commonwealth Ave, 02215, SAN 344-6611. Tel: 617-353-3726. FAX: 617-358-1729. Web Site: www.bu.edu/library/asl/index.html. *Librn,* David Westley; E-mail: dwestley@bu.edu; Staff 5 (MLS 3, Non-MLS 2)
Library Holdings: Bk Titles 150,000; Bk Vols 200,000; Per Subs 425
Special Collections: African Government Documents; African Studies
Partic in NELLCO Law Library Consortium, Inc.; OCLC Research Library Partnership
Open Mon-Fri 9-5

CM ALUMNI MEDICAL LIBRARY*, 715 Albany St L-12, 02118-2394, SAN 344-6670. Tel: 617-638-4232. Circulation Tel: 617-638-4244. Interlibrary Loan Service Tel: 617-638-4270. Reference Tel: 617-638-4228. Automation Services Tel: 617-638-4230. FAX: 617-638-4233. Administration FAX: 617-638-4478. Web Site: medlib.bu.edu. *Dir,* David S Ginn, PhD; E-mail: dginn@bu.edu; Staff 18 (MLS 7, Non-MLS 11)
Founded 1848
Library Holdings: AV Mats 256; e-books 190; Bk Titles 150,000; Bk Vols 160,000; Per Subs 4,000
Subject Interests: Dentistry, Med, Mental health, Pub health
Automation Activity & Vendor Info: (Acquisitions) Innovative Interfaces, Inc; (Cataloging) Innovative Interfaces, Inc; (Circulation) Innovative Interfaces, Inc; (Course Reserve) Innovative Interfaces, Inc; (ILL) Innovative Interfaces, Inc; (Media Booking) Innovative Interfaces, Inc; (OPAC) Innovative Interfaces, Inc; (Serials) Innovative Interfaces, Inc
Open Mon-Thurs 7:30am-Midnight, Fri 7:30am-10pm, Sat 10-10, Sun 10am-Midnight

C GEORGE H BEEBE COMMUNICATIONS LIBRARY*, College of Communication, 640 Commonwealth Ave, Rm B31, 02215, SAN 325-8025. Tel: 617-353-9240. Web Site: www.bu.edu/library/beebe. *Coordr,* Diane D'Almeida; E-mail: dalmeida@bu.edu; Staff 1 (Non-MLS 1)
Library Holdings: Bk Titles 45; Bk Vols 96; Per Subs 85
Special Collections: Boston Herald Newspaper Clippings, late 19th century-mid 1970's
Subject Interests: Advertising, Films & filmmaking, Journalism, Mass communications
Partic in Association of Research Libraries
Open Mon-Fri 10-5

C MUGAR MEMORIAL LIBRARY*, 771 Commonwealth Ave, 02215, SAN 344-6581. Tel: 617-353-3710. Circulation Tel: 617-353-3708. Interlibrary Loan Service Tel: 617-353-3706. Reference Tel: 617-353-3704. FAX: 617-353-2084. Web Site: www.bu.edu/library. *Univ Librn,* Robert Hudson; E-mail: rehuds@bu.edu; *Assoc Univ Librn, Digital Initiatives & Open Access,* Jackie Ammerman; E-mail: jwa@bu.edu; *Assoc Univ Librn, Grad & Res Serv,* Linda Plunket; E-mail: plunket@bu.edu; *Assoc Univ Librn, Undergrad & Distance Serv,* Thomas Casserly; E-mail: casserly@bu.edu; *Institutional Repository Librn,* Vika Zafrin; E-mail: vzafrin@bu.edu; Staff 89 (MLS 89)
Founded 1839. Enrl 29,000; Fac 2,312; Highest Degree: Doctorate
Library Holdings: Bk Vols 2,396,362; Per Subs 34,214; Talking Bks 52,224
Special Collections: African Studies; Americana to 1920 (Mark & Llora Bortman Coll); Art of the Printed Book; Browning Coll; Endowment for Biblical Research; G B Shaw Coll; H G Wells Coll; History of Nursing; Lincolniana (Edward C Stone & F Lauriston Bullard Colls); Liszt Coll; Military History; Mystery & Suspense Novel Coll; Nineteenth Century English Literature; Pascal Coll; Paul C Richards Literary & Hi Manuscript Holdings in Contemporary Literature; Private Press Books; Public Affairs, Theater, Film, Music, Journalism; Robert Frost Coll; Theodore Roosevelt Coll; Whitman Coll. Oral History
Subject Interests: Art & archit, Bus & mgt, Law, Med, Music, Relig, Soc sci & issues
Automation Activity & Vendor Info: (Acquisitions) Innovative Interfaces, Inc; (Cataloging) Innovative Interfaces, Inc; (Circulation) Innovative Interfaces, Inc; (OPAC) Innovative Interfaces, Inc; (Serials) Innovative Interfaces, Inc
Open Mon-Thurs 8am-Midnight, Fri & Sat 8am-11pm, Sun 10am-Midnight
Friends of the Library Group

C MUSIC LIBRARY*, 771 Commonwealth Ave, 02215, SAN 325-3279. Tel: 617-353-3705. FAX: 617-353-2084. E-mail: musiclib@bu.edu. Web Site: www.bu.edu/library/music. *Head Librn,* Holly E Mockovak; *Asst Head, Music Libr,* Sarah P Hunter; *Instrul & Reserves Coordr,* Anya Brodrick; *Pub Serv, Student Asst Coordr,* Donald Denniston; *Cat, Metadata Serv,* Marc Benador; Staff 5 (MLS 2, Non-MLS 3)
Highest Degree: Doctorate
Automation Activity & Vendor Info: (Cataloging) Ex Libris Group

CL PAPPAS LAW LIBRARY*, 765 Commonwealth Ave, 02215. Tel: 617-353-3151. FAX: 617-353-5995. Web Site: www.bu.edu/lawlibrary. *Libr Dir,* Marlene Alderman; Tel: 617-353-8870, E-mail: alderman@bu.edu; *Assoc Dir,* Russell Sweet; Tel: 617-353-8877; *Asst Dir,* Stefanie Weigmann; Tel: 617-358-4997, E-mail: sweig@bu.edu
Founded 1872
Library Holdings: Bk Vols 650,000
Subject Interests: Anglo-Am law, Banking & financial law, Health law, Intellectual property, Intl law, Tax law
Automation Activity & Vendor Info: (Acquisitions) Innovative Interfaces, Inc - Millennium; (Cataloging) Innovative Interfaces, Inc - Millennium; (Circulation) Innovative Interfaces, Inc - Millennium; (Course Reserve) Innovative Interfaces, Inc - Millennium; (ILL) OCLC; (OPAC) Innovative Interfaces, Inc - Millennium; (Serials) Innovative Interfaces, Inc - Millennium
Partic in Boston Library Consortium, Inc
Publications: Law Review Table of Contents; Recent Acquisitions
Open Mon-Thurs 8am-11:30pm, Fri 8am-10pm, Sat 9-9, Sun 10am-11:30pm

C FREDERIC S PARDEE MANAGEMENT LIBRARY*, Boston University School of Management, 595 Commonwealth Ave, 02215, SAN 377-8126. Tel: 617-353-4301. Reference Tel: 617-353-4303, 617-353-4304. FAX: 617-353-4307. Web Site: www.bu.edu/library/management. *Head of Libr,* Arlyne Ann Jackson; Tel: 617-353-4310, E-mail: ajac@bu.edu; *Asst Librn, Access Serv,* Brock Edmunds; Tel: 617-353-4311, E-mail: edmundsb@bu.edu; *Asst Librn, Info serv,* Kathleen M Berger; Tel: 617-353-4312, E-mail: bergerkm@bu.edu; Staff 13 (MLS 5, Non-MLS 8)
Founded 1997. Highest Degree: Doctorate
Library Holdings: e-journals 50,000; Bk Vols 60,000
Subject Interests: Acctg, Advertising, Bus, Econ, Human resources, Mgt, Mkt
Automation Activity & Vendor Info: (Acquisitions) Ex Libris Group; (Cataloging) Ex Libris Group; (Circulation) Ex Libris Group; (Course Reserve) Ex Libris Group; (ILL) OCLC ILLiad; (OPAC) Ex Libris Group; (Serials) Ex Libris Group
Function: Computers for patron use, Electronic databases & coll, ILL available, Photocopying/Printing, Scanner
Partic in Boston Library Consortium, Inc; Northeast Research Libraries Consortium
Open Mon-Thurs 8am-11pm, Fri 8-8, Sat 10-6, Sun 10am-11pm

C PICKERING EDUCATIONAL RESOURCES LIBRARY*, Two Sherborn St, 02215, SAN 344-6646. Tel: 617-353-3734. FAX: 617-353-6105. Web Site: www.bu.edu/library/education. *Librn,* Linda Plunket; Tel: 617-353-3735, E-mail: plunket@bu.edu; Staff 1 (MLS 1)
Library Holdings: Bk Vols 20,000; Per Subs 100; Videos 90
Special Collections: Curriculum Guides; Standardized Psychological and Educational Tests
Subject Interests: Educ
Partic in Association of Research Libraries; OCLC Online Computer Library Center, Inc
Open Mon-Thurs 8:30am-9pm, Fri 8:30-5, Sat 10-5

CR SCHOOL OF THEOLOGY LIBRARY*, 745 Commonwealth Ave, 2nd Flr, 02215, SAN 344-676X. Tel: 617-353-3034. Reference Tel: 617-353-5357. FAX: 617-358-0699. E-mail: sthlib@bu.edu. Web Site: www.bu.edu/sth/sthlibrary. *Head Librn,* Amy Limpitlaw; E-mail: ael23@bu.edu; *Head, Pub Serv,* James R Skypeck; *Access Serv Librn,* Stacey Battles De Ramos; *Acq Librn,* Olga Potap; *Archivist & Spec Coll Librn,* Kara Jackman; *Cat Librn,* Janet Russell; Tel: 617-353-1353, E-mail: janetr@bu.edu. Subject Specialists: *Bus,* Olga Potap; *Methodist hist,* Kara Jackman; Staff 7 (MLS 5, Non-MLS 2)
Founded 1839. Enrl 450; Fac 24; Highest Degree: Doctorate
Library Holdings: Bk Vols 145,576; Per Subs 545
Special Collections: American Guild of Organists Library; History of Christian Missions Coll; Hymnals (Metcalf-Nutter Coll); Kimball Bible Coll; Liturgy and Worship Coll; Massachusetts Bible Society Coll; New England Methodist Hist Soc Coll; Nutter-Metcalf Hymnal Coll; Oriental Art Objects (Woodward Coll)
Subject Interests: Biblical studies, Music, Philos, Relig hist, Theol
Partic in Association of Research Libraries
Open Mon-Thurs (Winter) 8am-9pm, Fri 8-5, Sat 10-6; Mon-Fri (Summer) 8:30-4:30

C SCIENCE & ENGINEERING LIBRARY*, 38 Cummington St, 02215, SAN 325-3716. Tel: 617-353-3733. Reference Tel: 617-353-9474. FAX: 617-353-3470. E-mail: selill@bu.edu. Web Site: www.bu.edu/library/sel. *Ref Librn,* Paula Carey; Tel: 617-358-3963, E-mail: pac@bu.edu; Staff 18 (MLS 4, Non-MLS 14)
Founded 1983. Enrl 25,000; Highest Degree: Doctorate
Library Holdings: Bk Titles 80,000; Bk Vols 85,000; Per Subs 1,800

Subject Interests: Aerospace sci, Biology, Chem, Cognitive sci, Computer engr, Computer sci, Earth sci, Electrical engr, Manufacturing engr, Math, Mechanical engr, Physics
Automation Activity & Vendor Info: (Circulation) Innovative Interfaces, Inc; (Course Reserve) Innovative Interfaces, Inc; (OPAC) Innovative Interfaces, Inc; (Serials) Innovative Interfaces, Inc
Function: Res libr
Partic in LYRASIS; National Network of Libraries of Medicine Region 7; Northeast Research Libraries Consortium
Open Mon-Thurs 8am-Midnight, Fri 8-7, Sat 11-7
Restriction: Open to pub for ref only

C STONE SCIENCE LIBRARY*, 771 Commonwealth Ave, 02215, SAN 370-6451. Tel: 617-353-5679. FAX: 617-353-5358. *Head Librn,* Nasim Parveen; E-mail: momen@bu.edu; Staff 2 (MLS 2)
Founded 1988. Enrl 35,000
Library Holdings: Bk Titles 10,000; Per Subs 225
Special Collections: Balloon Aerial Photographs; Geography (George K Lewis Coll); Math (Brad Washburn Coll)
Subject Interests: Archaeology, Geog, Geol, Remote sensing
Open Mon-Thurs 9-9, Fri 9-5, Sun Noon-8

M BRIGHAM & WOMEN'S HOSPITAL*, Kessler Health Education Library, 75 Francis St, 02115. SAN 377-9157. Tel: 617-732-6636. FAX: 617-582-6130. E-mail: ptrelations@partners.org. Web Site: www.brighamandwomens.org/patients-and-families/kessler-library/kessler-health-education-library.
Library Holdings: Bk Vols 1,000; Per Subs 300
Automation Activity & Vendor Info: (Cataloging) Inmagic, Inc.; (Circulation) Inmagic, Inc.; (Serials) EBSCO Online
Wireless access
Function: ILL available, Res libr
Partic in Massachusetts Health Sciences Library Network; North Atlantic Health Sciences Libraries, Inc
Open Mon-Fri 9-5:30

L BROWN, RUDNICK LLP*, Research Services, One Financial Ctr, 02111. SAN 372-0748. Tel: 617-856-8213. Reference Tel: 617-856-8111. FAX: 617-856-8201. E-mail: research@brownrudnick.com. Web Site: www.brownrudnick.com. *Dir,* Kathleen Gerwatowski; E-mail: KGerwatowski@brownrudnick.com; Staff 4 (MLS 3, Non-MLS 1)
Library Holdings: Bk Vols 10,000; Per Subs 400
Automation Activity & Vendor Info: (Cataloging) Inmagic, Inc.; (Circulation) Inmagic, Inc.; (OPAC) Inmagic, Inc.
Wireless access
Restriction: Staff use only

J BUNKER HILL COMMUNITY COLLEGE*, Library & Learning Commons, E Bldg, 3rd Flr, Rm E300, 250 New Rutherford Ave, 02129-2925. SAN 307-1456. Tel: 617-228-2213. Reference Tel: 617-228-3479. FAX: 617-228-3288. E-mail: BHCCLibrary@bhcc.mass.edu. Web Site: www.bhcc.mass.edu/library. *Dir, Libr & Learning Commons,* Vivica Smith Pierre, PhD; Tel: 617-228-3240, E-mail: vdpierre@bhcc.mass.edu; *Res Support & Instruction Librn,* Bethany Croteau; Tel: 617-936-1916, E-mail: bethany.croteau@bhcc.mass.edu; *Res Support & Instruction Librn,* Kelsy Martinez; Tel: 617-228-2211, E-mail: kelsy.martinez@bhcc.mass.edu; *Access Serv, Coordr, Libr Serv,* Wesley A Fiorentino; Tel: 617-228-2423, E-mail: wafioren@bhcc.mass.edu; *Coordr, Libr Serv,* Andrew McCarthy; Tel: 617-228-2323, E-mail: ajmccart@bhcc.mass.edu; *Acq & Coll, Coordr, Libr Serv,* Andrew E McLaughlin; Tel: 617-936-1959, E-mail: amclaugh@bhcc.mass.edu.
Subject Specialists: *Assessment, Info literacy,* Bethany Croteau; *Assessment, Info literacy,* Kelsy Martinez; *Archives, Hist,* Wesley A Fiorentino; *Acad, Assessment, Tech,* Andrew McCarthy; *Assessment,* Andrew E McLaughlin; Staff 16.5 (MLS 5.6, Non-MLS 10.9)
Founded 1973. Enrl 12,780; Fac 151; Highest Degree: Associate
Library Holdings: Audiobooks 21; AV Mats 161; CDs 150; DVDs 456; e-books 55,590; e-journals 37; Electronic Media & Resources 49,264; Large Print Bks 36; Music Scores 80; Bk Titles 44,486; Per Subs 29
Subject Interests: Allied health, Bus, Careers, Citizenship, Criminal justice, Diversity, Econ, Educ, Engr, Legal studies, Math, Nursing, Paralegal studies, Sci, Tech
Automation Activity & Vendor Info: (Acquisitions) Innovative Interfaces, Inc; (Cataloging) Innovative Interfaces, Inc; (Circulation) Innovative Interfaces, Inc; (ILL) Innovative Interfaces, Inc; (OPAC) Innovative Interfaces, Inc; (Serials) Innovative Interfaces, Inc
Wireless access
Function: ILL available, Photocopying/Printing
Partic in Massachusetts Commonwealth Consortium of Libraries in Public Higher Education Institutions
Special Services for the Blind - Talking bks & player equip
Open Mon-Thurs 8am-10pm, Fri 8-8, Sat & Sun 8-4
Restriction: Open to pub for ref & circ; with some limitations, Open to students, fac & staff

L BURNS & LEVINSON*, Law Library, 125 Summer St, 02110-1624. SAN 372-073X. Tel: 617-345-3000. FAX: 617-345-3299. Web Site: www.burnslev.com. *Mgr, Libr Serv,* Abbi Maher; E-mail: amaher@burnslev.com
Library Holdings: Bk Vols 7,000; Per Subs 50
Open Mon-Fri 9-5

S CDM SMITH INFOCENTER*, 75 State St, 02109. SAN 307-1472. Tel: 617-452-6778. E-mail: infocenter@cdmsmith.com. Web Site: www.cdmsmith.com. *Librn,* Alex Lumb; Tel: 617-452-6822; *Librn,* Cohen B Stacie; Tel: 617-452-6824; Staff 2 (MLS 2)
Founded 1963
Library Holdings: Bk Vols 1,000; Per Subs 52
Subject Interests: Environ engr, Wastewater treatment
Automation Activity & Vendor Info: (Acquisitions) EOS International; (Cataloging) EOS International; (Circulation) EOS International; (OPAC) EOS International; (Serials) EOS International
Wireless access
Function: Res libr
Mem of Massachusetts Library System
Partic in LYRASIS

L CHOATE, HALL & STEWART LLP LIBRARY*, Two International Pl, 02110. SAN 307-1510. Tel: 617-248-5000, 617-248-5202. FAX: 617-248-4000. Web Site: choate.com. *Mgr, Libr Serv,* David Goldman; E-mail: dgoldman@choate.com; Staff 5 (MLS 2, Non-MLS 3)
Library Holdings: Bk Vols 15,000
Subject Interests: Law
Restriction: Private libr

L DECHERT LAW LIBRARY*, One International Pl, 40th Flr, 100 Oliver St, 02110-2605. SAN 372-0659. Tel: 617-728-7100, Ext 7198. FAX: 617-426-6567. Web Site: www.dechert.com.
Library Holdings: Bk Vols 6,000; Per Subs 68

S THE MARY BAKER EDDY LIBRARY, Research & Reference Services, 210 Massachusetts Ave, P04-10, 02115-3017. SAN 326-3525. Tel: 617-450-7000. Reference Tel: 617-450-7218. E-mail: librarymail@mbelibrary.org. Web Site: www.marybakereddylibrary.org/research. *Exec Mgr,* Dr Michael Hamilton; Tel: 617-450-7400, E-mail: hamiltonm@mbelibrary.org; *Coll, Res, Sr Mgr,* Allyson Lazar; E-mail: lazara@mbelibrary.org; *Sr Mgr,* Stephen Graham; E-mail: grahams@mbelibrary.org; *Mgr,* Jonathon Eder; Tel: 617-450-7131, E-mail: ederj@mbelibrary.org; *Mgr, Res,* Dorothy Rivera; Tel: 617-450-7002, E-mail: riverad@mbelibrary.org; *Sr Res Archivist,* Judith Huenneke; Tel: 617-450-7111, E-mail: huennekej@mbelibrary.org; *Mgr, Spec Coll,* Alison Kobierski; Tel: 617-450-7907, E-mail: kobierskia@mbelibrary.org
Founded 2002
Library Holdings: CDs 25; DVDs 100; Bk Titles 10,000; Bk Vols 18,000; Per Subs 25; Spec Interest Per Sub 15; Videos 75
Special Collections: Organizational Records for The First Church of Christ, Scientist; The life and works of Mary Baker Eddy; The Mary Baker Eddy Archive (Includes letters, manuscripts, photographs, artifacts, books, periodicals, and other materials)
Subject Interests: 19th Century hist, Bible studies, Contemporary, Cultural studies, Relig hist, Spirituality, Women in lit, Women in theol
Automation Activity & Vendor Info: (Acquisitions) Re:discovery Software, Inc; (Cataloging) OCLC Connexion; (Circulation) Re:discovery Software, Inc; (ILL) OCLC Online; (OPAC) Re:discovery Software, Inc
Wireless access
Function: Archival coll, Art exhibits, Doc delivery serv, ILL available, Internet access, Orientations, Outside serv via phone, mail, e-mail & web, Photocopying/Printing, Ref serv available, Res libr, Spoken cassettes & CDs
Mem of Massachusetts Library System
Partic in LYRASIS; OCLC-LVIS
Open Mon–Thurs 12-4
Restriction: Open to pub for ref & circ; with some limitations, Res pass required for non-affiliated visitors

C EMERSON COLLEGE*, Iwasaki Library, 120 Boylston St, 02116-4624. SAN 307-1588. Tel: 617-824-8668. Interlibrary Loan Service Tel: 617-824-8333. Administration Tel: 617-824-8328. Automation Services Tel: 617-824-8339. Information Services Tel: 617-824-8675. FAX: 617-824-7817. Circulation E-mail: reference@emerson.edu. Web Site: www.emerson.edu/library. *Exec Dir,* Cheryl McGrath; E-mail: cheryl_mcgrath@emerson.edu; *Asst Dir,* Christina Dent; Tel: 617-824-8364, E-mail: christina_dent@emerson.edu; *Asst Dir, Syst & Tech,* Elena O'Malley; E-mail: elena_omalley@emerson.edu; *Assoc Dir, Res & Coll,* Beth Joress; Tel: 617-824-8331, E-mail: beth_joress@emerson.edu; *Head, Archives & Spec Coll,* Jennifer Williams; Tel: 617-824-8679, E-mail: jennifer_williams@emerson.edu; *Digital Initiatives Librn,* Amy Bocko; Tel: 617-824-8338, E-mail: amy_bocko@emerson.edu; *Online Learning Librn,*

Mr Lindsay Nichols; Tel: 617-824-8334, E-mail: lindsay_nichols@emerson.edu; *Coordr, Electronic Res, Ref Librn,* Daniel Crocker; Tel: 617-824-8939, E-mail: daniel_crocker@emerson.edu; *Media Res Coordr,* Maureen Tripp; Tel: 617-824-8407, E-mail: maureen_tripp@emerson.edu; *Coordr, Outreach Serv,* Cate Hirschbiel; Tel: 617-824-8340, E-mail: mary_Hirschbiel@emerson.edu; Staff 22 (MLS 12, Non-MLS 10)
Founded 1880. Enrl 4,376; Fac 267; Highest Degree: Master
Library Holdings: AV Mats 15,214; e-books 87,130; e-journals 57,126; Bk Vols 144,059; Per Subs 381
Special Collections: American Comedy Archives; Bill Dana papers; Jan Murray papers; Janis Paige papers; Variety Vaudeville Protection Agency Coll. Oral History
Subject Interests: Comedy, Mass communications, Performing arts
Automation Activity & Vendor Info: (Acquisitions) Ex Libris Group; (Cataloging) Ex Libris Group; (Circulation) Ex Libris Group; (Course Reserve) Ex Libris Group; (ILL) OCLC; (Media Booking) Dymaxion; (OPAC) Ex Libris Group; (Serials) Ex Libris Group
Wireless access
Partic in Fenway Library Consortium; Fenway Library Organization
Open Mon-Thurs 7:45am-11pm, Fri 7:45am-9pm, Sat 10-6, Sun Noon-11

C EMMANUEL COLLEGE*, Cardinal Cushing Library, 400 The Fenway, 02115. SAN 307-1596. Tel: 617-735-9927. FAX: 617-735-9763. Web Site: library.emmanuel.edu. *Assoc Dean, Learning Res,* Karen Storin Linitz; Tel: 617-975-9324, E-mail: linitzk@emmanuel.edu; *Cat Librn, Head, Access Serv,* Jennifer Woodall; Tel: 617-264-7653, E-mail: woodall@emmanuel.edu; *Assoc Librn, Electronic Res,* Catherine Tuohy; Tel: 617-264-7658, E-mail: tuohyc@emmanuel.edu; *Assoc Librn, Ref & Instruction, Outreach Serv,* Diane Zydlewski; Tel: 617-264-7654, E-mail: zydlewsd@emmanuel.edu; Staff 6.8 (MLS 4.8, Non-MLS 2)
Founded 1919. Enrl 2,802; Fac 76; Highest Degree: Master
Library Holdings: AV Mats 800; Bk Vols 96,000; Per Subs 800
Special Collections: Church History
Subject Interests: Art, Art therapy, Lit, Theol, Women's studies
Automation Activity & Vendor Info: (Acquisitions) Ex Libris Group; (Cataloging) Ex Libris Group; (Circulation) Ex Libris Group; (Course Reserve) Ex Libris Group; (ILL) Ex Libris Group; (OPAC) Ex Libris Group; (Serials) Ex Libris Group
Wireless access
Partic in Fenway Library Consortium; Fenway Library Organization
Special Services for the Deaf - Assistive tech; Bks on deafness & sign lang
Special Services for the Blind - Aids for in-house use
Open Mon-Thurs 7:30am-1am, Fri 7:30am-8pm, Sat 9-8, Sun Noon-1am

R EPISCOPAL DIOCESE OF MASSACHUSETTS*, Diocesan Library & Archives, 138 Tremont St, 02111. SAN 307-1618. Tel: 617-482-4826, Ext 488. FAX: 617-482-4826. E-mail: archivist@diomass.org. Staff 9 (MLS 2, Non-MLS 7)
Founded 1884
Special Collections: 18th & 19th Century Americana, pamphlets & SPG publications; Books of Common Prayer
Subject Interests: Church hist
Wireless access
Publications: Guide to the Parochial Archives of the Episcopal Church in Boston, 1981; Littera Scripta Manet (Newsletter)
Restriction: By permission only, Closed stack, Non-circulating coll, Not a lending libr
Friends of the Library Group

S FEDERAL RESERVE BANK OF BOSTON*, Research Library, 600 Atlantic Ave, 02210-2204. SAN 307-1634. Tel: 617-973-3397. Circulation Tel: 617-973-3396. Interlibrary Loan Service Tel: 617-973-3668. FAX: 617-973-4221. E-mail: boston.library@bos.frb.org. Web Site: www.bos.frb.org/about-the-boston-fed/business-areas/research. *Dir, Res, Exec VPres,* Geoffrey M B Tootell; E-mail: Geoff.Tootell@bos.frb.org; *Sr Res Asst,* Joshua Ballance; E-mail: Joshua.Ballance@bos.frb.org; *Sr Res Asst,* Jianlin Wang; E-mail: Jianlin.wang@bos.frb.org; Staff 5.5 (MLS 3, Non-MLS 2.5)
Founded 1921
Library Holdings: Bk Vols 70,000
Special Collections: Federal Reserve System Materials
Subject Interests: Econ, Finance
Publications: Booknews (Newsletter)
Mem of Massachusetts Library System
Open Mon-Fri 10-4
Restriction: Access at librarian's discretion, Borrowing requests are handled by ILL

C FISHER COLLEGE LIBRARY, 118 Beacon St, 02116. SAN 307-1677. Tel: 617-236-8875. E-mail: library@fisher.edu. Web Site: www.fisher.edu/library. *Col Librn, Libr Dir,* Joshua Van Kirk McKain; E-mail: jmckain@fisher.edu; *Assoc Col Librn,* Cara Parkoff; E-mail: cparkoff@fisher.edu; Staff 2 (MLS 2)
Founded 1903. Enrl 874; Fac 104; Highest Degree: Master
Jul 2020-Jun 2021. Mats Exp $171,992, Books $1,819, Per/Ser (Incl. Access Fees) $4,665, AV Mat $3,075, Electronic Ref Mat (Incl. Access Fees) $162,433. Sal $146,759
Library Holdings: DVDs 3,809; e-books 9,782; Large Print Bks 2; Bk Titles 22,169; Per Subs 24; Videos 26
Automation Activity & Vendor Info: (Acquisitions) Innovative Interfaces, Inc; (Cataloging) Innovative Interfaces, Inc; (Circulation) Innovative Interfaces, Inc; (Course Reserve) Innovative Interfaces, Inc; (ILL) OCLC FirstSearch; (OPAC) Innovative Interfaces, Inc
Wireless access
Function: 24/7 Online cat, Electronic databases & coll, Free DVD rentals, ILL available, Instruction & testing, Museum passes, Online info literacy tutorials on the web & in blackboard, Orientations, Photocopying/Printing, Ref serv available, VHS videos
Partic in LYRASIS; Metro Boston Libr Network
Open Mon-Thurs 8-10, Fri 8-4, Sun 12-5
Restriction: Open to pub for ref & circ; with some limitations, Open to students, fac, staff & alumni

L FOLEY & HOAG LLP LIBRARY*, 155 Seaport Blvd, 02210. SAN 307-1685. Tel: 617-832-7070. Reference Tel: 617-832-7098. FAX: 617-832-7000. Web Site: www.foleyhoag.com. *Dir, Libr Serv,* Sarah Bennett; E-mail: sbennett@foleyhoag.com; Staff 5 (MLS 4, Non-MLS 1)
Library Holdings: Bk Vols 50,000; Per Subs 250
Subject Interests: Corporate law, Environ law, Intellectual property, Labor, Litigation
Wireless access
Restriction: Authorized personnel only

S ISABELLA STEWART GARDNER MUSEUM LIBRARY, 25 Evans Way, 02115. SAN 328-6134. Tel: 617-264-6003, 617-566-1401. E-mail: collection@isgm.org. Web Site: www.gardnermuseum.org. *Archivist,* Shana McKenna; E-mail: archives@isgm.org; Staff 1 (Non-MLS 1)
Founded 1903
Library Holdings: Bk Titles 2,300; Per Subs 10
Special Collections: Isabella Stewart Gardner Coll, bks, binding, ms, letters, autographs, music scores, archives
Subject Interests: Art hist, Conserv
Wireless access
Function: Archival coll
Restriction: Non-circulating, Open by appt only

L GOODWIN PROCTER*, Law Library, 100 Northern Ave, 02210. SAN 328-4654. Tel: 617-570-1000, 617-570-1994. FAX: 617-523-1231. Web Site: www.goodwinprocter.com. *Managing Dir,* Anne Stemlar; E-mail: astemlar@goodwinlaw.com
Library Holdings: Bk Vols 40,000; Per Subs 2,500
Partic in Proquest Dialog

L GOULSTON & STORRS PC*, Library Services, 400 Atlantic Ave, 02110. SAN 372-0772. Tel: 617-574-4054. FAX: 617-574-7675. Web Site: www.goulstonstorrs.com. *Mgr, Libr Serv,* Robert DeFabrizio; E-mail: rdefabrizio@goulstonstorrs.com; Staff 2.5 (MLS 1.5, Non-MLS 1)
Library Holdings: Bk Vols 2,000; Per Subs 175
Subject Interests: Health, Law, Real estate, Tax
Automation Activity & Vendor Info: (Cataloging) SirsiDynix; (OPAC) SirsiDynix; (Serials) SirsiDynix
Wireless access
Function: ILL available
Restriction: Co libr, Employee & client use only, Not open to pub

S GRAND LODGE OF MASONS IN MASSACHUSETTS*, Samuel Crocker Lawrence Library, 186 Tremont St, 2nd Flr, 02111. SAN 307-1774. Tel: 617-426-6040, Ext 4221. FAX: 617-426-6115. E-mail: library@massfreemasonry.org. Web Site: www.massfreemasonry.org. *Dir,* Walter H Hunt; E-mail: whunt@massfreemasonry.org; Staff 3 (MLS 1, Non-MLS 2)
Founded 1814
Library Holdings: Bk Vols 50,000; Per Subs 60
Special Collections: Freemasonry (John Paul Jones Coll), ms; Histories; New England Towns & Cities
Function: Res libr
Open Mon-Fri 9:30-4

S HALEY & ALDRICH INC, LIBRARY, 465 Medford St, Ste 2200, 02129. SAN 373-0670. Tel: 617-886-7400. FAX: 617-886-7726. Web Site: www.haleyaldrich.com. *Library Contact,* Aubrey Denson Harrison; E-mail: adensonharrison@haleyaldrich.com
Library Holdings: Bk Titles 5,000; Bk Vols 5,500; Per Subs 15
Subject Interests: Environ engr, Geotechnical
Automation Activity & Vendor Info: (Acquisitions) Inmagic, Inc.; (Cataloging) Inmagic, Inc.; (Circulation) Inmagic, Inc.

Wireless access
Restriction: Clients only, Open by appt only, Staff use only

S HARVARD MUSICAL ASSOCIATION LIBRARY, 57A Chestnut St, 02108. SAN 307-1812. Tel: 617-523-2897. FAX: 617-523-2897. E-mail: info@hmaboston.org. Web Site: www.hmaboston.org. *Adminr,* Jim McDonald
Founded 1837
Library Holdings: Music Scores 15,000; Bk Titles 5,000
Special Collections: Chamber Music Parts; Two-Piano Music

L HEMENWAY & BARNES*, Law Library, 75 State St, 16th Flr, 02109. SAN 372-0667. Tel: 617-227-7940. FAX: 617-227-0781. Web Site: hembar.com. *Librn,* Maureen Kearney; Staff 1 (Non-MLS 1)
Founded 1863
Special Collections: Massachusetts Statutes Back to 1694
Restriction: Not open to pub

S HISTORIC NEW ENGLAND, Library & Archives, 141 Cambridge St, 02114-2702. SAN 307-1928. Tel: 617-227-3956. FAX: 617-227-9204. E-mail: archives@historicnewengland.org. Web Site: historicnewengland.org/explore/library-archives. *Librn & Archivist,* Julie Solz; E-mail: jsolz@historicnewengland.org; *Libr & Archives Spec,* Jeanne Gamble; E-mail: jgamble@historicnewengland.org; *Mus Historian,* Jennifer Pustz; E-mail: jpustz@historicnewengland.org; *Sr Curator, Libr & Archives,* Lorna Condon; E-mail: lcondon@historicnewengland.org; Staff 4 (MLS 2, Non-MLS 2)
Founded 1910
Library Holdings: Bk Titles 15,000; Bk Vols 19,000
Special Collections: Architectural Drawings, 19th & 20th Centuries (Asher Benjamin, Luther Briggs, Frank Chouteau Brown, Herbert Browne, George Clough, Ogden Codman, Jr, Robert Allen Cook, Arland Dirlam, Halfdan Hanson, Arthur Little, J Luippold, Richard Upjohn); Architecture & Design (Rare Books Coll); Builders Guides & Account Books, 19th & 20th Centuries; Edwin Whitefield Coll, sketchbks, watercolors; Ephemera Coll, advertisements, billheads, trade cards, trade cats; Family Papers & Manuscripts (Casey, Codman, Jewett, Marrett, Rundlet-May & Sayward Families); Harrison Gray Otis Business Papers; Historic American Buildings Survey, Massachusetts; Historic New England/SPNEA Institutional Records; New England Maps & Atlases; New England/Regional & Boston, pamphlets; Photographic Colls (Boston & Albany Railroad, Boston Elevated Railroad & Boston Transit Commission, Emma Coleman, Baldwin Coolidge, Alfred Cutting, Domestic Interiors, Geographic, Halliday Historic Photograph, Arthur Haskell, Mary Northend, Wallace Nutting, Henry Peabody, Fred Quimby, Soule Art Photo Company, N L Stebbins, Thompson & Thompson/New England News, Yankee Magazine)
Subject Interests: Archit, Decorative art, Photog
Wireless access
Function: Archival coll
Restriction: Open by appt only
Friends of the Library Group

S INSURANCE LIBRARY ASSOCIATION OF BOSTON*, 156 State St, 02109. SAN 307-1855. Tel: 617-227-2087. FAX: 617-723-8524. Web Site: www.insurancelibrary.org. *Exec Dir,* Glenn Cryan; Tel: 617-227-2087, ext 201, E-mail: gcryan@insurancelibrary.org; *Ref Librn,* Sarah Hart; Tel: 617-227-2087, Ext 202, E-mail: shart@insurancelibrary.org; *Educ Coordr, Ref Librn,* Meagan Stefanow; Tel: 617-227-2087, Ext 203, E-mail: mstefanow@insurancelibrary.org
Founded 1887
Library Holdings: Bk Titles 15,000; Bk Vols 30,000; Per Subs 200
Special Collections: Sanborn Fire Maps
Publications: Membership Newsletter (Quarterly)
Open Mon-Fri 9-5

L K&L GATES LLP*, Law Library, State Street Financial Ctr, One Lincoln St, 02111-2950. SAN 327-6082. Tel: 617-951-9160. FAX: 617-261-3175. Web Site: www.klgates.com. *Libr Mgr,* Elizabeth Labedz; E-mail: betsy.labedz@klgates.com. Subject Specialists: *Law,* Elizabeth Labedz; Staff 1 (MLS 1)
Library Holdings: Bk Vols 8,000; Per Subs 100
Automation Activity & Vendor Info: (Acquisitions) SirsiDynix; (Cataloging) SirsiDynix; (Circulation) SirsiDynix
Restriction: Not open to pub

GL LAW LIBRARY OF THE MASSACHUSETTS ATTORNEY GENERAL*, Francis X. Bellotti Law Library, One Ashburton Pl, 02108. SAN 307-1537. Tel: 617-963-2060, 617-963-2098. *Law Librn,* Kevin Coakley-Welch; E-mail: kevin.coakley-welch@mass.gov; Staff 2 (MLS 1, Non-MLS 1)
Founded 1975
Library Holdings: Bk Titles 2,000; Bk Vols 7,500; Per Subs 135
Special Collections: Opinions of the Attorney General; Attorney General by-law approval letters (Historical)
Subject Interests: Fed law, State law
Wireless access
Publications: Index to Opinions of Attorney General
Mem of Massachusetts Library System
Restriction: By permission only

L LIBERTY MUTUAL GROUP*, Law Library, 175 Berkeley St, 7th Flr, 02116-5066. SAN 344-6883. Tel: 617-357-9500. FAX: 617-574-5830. *Legal Info Librn,* Christina McKennerney, III; E-mail: Christina.McKennerney@@LibertyMutual.com; Staff 4 (MLS 2, Non-MLS 2)
Founded 1918
Library Holdings: Bk Vols 130,000; Per Subs 120
Subject Interests: Admin law, Ethics, Ins
Automation Activity & Vendor Info: (Acquisitions) Softlink America; (Cataloging) Softlink America; (Circulation) Softlink America; (ILL) Softlink America; (OPAC) Softlink America; (Serials) Softlink America
Wireless access
Restriction: Authorized personnel only

S THE LIBRARY OF THE FRENCH CULTURAL CENTER ALLIANCE FRANCAISE OF BOSTON*, 53 Marlborough St, 02116-2099. SAN 307-1715. Tel: 617-912-0400, Ext 419. Circulation Tel: 617-912-0417. FAX: 617-912-0450. E-mail: librarian@frenchculturalcenter.org. Web Site: www.frenchculturalcenter.org. *Librn,* Ingrid Marquardt; Staff 2 (MLS 1, Non-MLS 1)
Founded 1945
Library Holdings: Audiobooks 400; CDs 1,500; DVDs 1,050; e-books 570; Music Scores 20; Bk Vols 21,200; Per Subs 30; Videos 650
Special Collections: Children's Literature Coll; Cultures and literature of the francophone world; Films; Francophone Music & Books on CD; French Culture Coll; French language; History & Literature of France & French-Speaking Countries
Subject Interests: Humanities
Automation Activity & Vendor Info: (Cataloging) ByWater Solutions; (Circulation) ByWater Solutions; (OPAC) ByWater Solutions; (Serials) ByWater Solutions
Wireless access
Function: Adult bk club, Bks on CD, Electronic databases & coll, ILL available, Internet access, Music CDs, Online cat, Outside serv via phone, mail, e-mail & web, Ref serv available, VHS videos
Special Services for the Blind - Bks on CD
Open Tues & Thurs 10-7, Fri & Sat 10-5
Restriction: Circ to mem only

S LYMAN LIBRARY*, Educator Resource Center, Museum of Science, One Science Park, 02114. SAN 307-2150. Tel: 617-589-0170, 617-723-2500. FAX: 617-589-0494. E-mail: library@mos.org. Web Site: www.mos.org/educator-resource-center. *Coordr,* Patricia Ahl; *Instr,* Jeff Mehigan; Staff 2 (MLS 2)
Founded 1831
Library Holdings: Bk Vols 17,000; Per Subs 75
Special Collections: 19th Century Natural History, bk, journal & ms; Archives of the Boston Society of Natural History founded 1830, the predecessor of the Museum of Science; Technology & Engineering Curriculum
Subject Interests: Educ
Wireless access

S MASSACHUSETTS BOARD OF LIBRARY COMMISSIONERS, 90 Canal St, Ste 500, 02114. SAN 307-1952. Tel: 617-725-1860. Toll Free Tel: 800-952-7403 (MA only). FAX: 617-725-0140. Web Site: mblc.state.ma.us. *Dir,* James L Lonergan; E-mail: james.lonergan@state.ma.us; *Head, Libr Advisory & Dev,* Robert Favini; E-mail: robert.favini@state.ma.us; *Head, Operations & Budget,* Tracey Dimant; E-mail: tracey.dimant@state.ma.us; *Head, State Programs & Gov Liaison,* Mary Rose Quinn; E-mail: maryrose.quinn@state.ma.us; Staff 26 (MLS 13, Non-MLS 13)
Founded 1890
Library Holdings: Bk Vols 3,000
Special Collections: Agency Archival Coll
Publications: Annual Report of Board of Library Commissioners; Data for Massachusetts Series (Public Library Statistics & Personnel Data); Directory of Free Public Libraries in Massachusetts; Library Services & Technology Act Massachusetts Long Range Plan 2018-2022; MBLC Strategic Plan 2021-2025
Partic in North of Boston Library Exchange, Inc

C MASSACHUSETTS COLLEGE OF ART & DESIGN*, Morton R Godine Library, 621 Huntington Ave, 02115-5882. SAN 307-1960. Tel: 617-879-7150. Interlibrary Loan Service Tel: 617-879-7113. FAX: 617-879-7110. E-mail: library@massart.edu. Web Site: www.massart.edu/library. *Chair, Tech Serv Librn,* Rachel Resnik; Tel: 617-879-7115, E-mail: rresnik@massart.edu; *Access Serv Librn,* Gabrielle

Reed; Tel: 617-879-7102, E-mail: gabrielle.reed@massart.edu; *Instrul Serv Librn, Ref Librn,* Greg Wallace; E-mail: greg.wallace@massart.edu; *Acq, Ser Librn,* Kathryn Riel; Tel: 617-879-7112, E-mail: kriel@massart.edu; *Visual Res Librn,* Pereira Caitlin; *Reserves Mgr,* Abigail Sweeney; Tel: 617-879-7104, E-mail: abigail.sweeney@massart.edu; *Tech Serv Asst,* Denis Sullivan; Tel: 617-879-7111, E-mail: dsullivan@massart.edu; *Circ, Computer Serv,* Chrissy Hartman; E-mail: chartman@massart.edu; Staff 12 (MLS 4, Non-MLS 8)
Founded 1873. Enrl 2,000; Highest Degree: Master
Library Holdings: Bk Titles 85,000; Per Subs 280; Videos 3,100
Special Collections: Art Educ; College Archives; Design
Subject Interests: Art, Art hist, Design, Films & filmmaking
Automation Activity & Vendor Info: (Cataloging) Ex Libris Group; (Circulation) Ex Libris Group
Wireless access
Partic in Fenway Library Consortium; Fenway Library Organization; LYRASIS; OCLC Online Computer Library Center, Inc
Open Mon-Thurs 8am-9pm, Fri 8-6, Sat & Sun 11-5

CM MASSACHUSETTS COLLEGE OF PHARMACY & HEALTH SCIENCES*, Henrietta DeBenedictis Library, Matricaria Bldg, 2nd Flr, 179 Longwood Ave, 02115. SAN 307-1979. Tel: 617-732-2252. Reference Tel: 617-732-2813. FAX: 617-278-1566. Web Site: www.mcphs.edu/academics/academic-support-and-resources/libraries. *Dean, Libr & Learning Res, Dir of Libr,* Richard Kaplan; Tel: 617-732-2808, E-mail: richard.kaplan@mcphs.edu; *Assoc Dir,* Joanne Doucette; Tel: 617-732-2805, E-mail: joanne.doucette@mcphs.edu; *Data Librn, Informatics Librn, Research Librn,* Sarah McCord; Tel: 617-735-1439, E-mail: sarah.mccord@mcphs.edu; Staff 15 (MLS 7, Non-MLS 8)
Founded 1823. Highest Degree: Doctorate
Library Holdings: Bk Titles 15,000; Bk Vols 20,000; Per Subs 700
Subject Interests: Med, Pharmacology
Automation Activity & Vendor Info: (Acquisitions) Ex Libris Group; (Cataloging) Ex Libris Group; (Circulation) Ex Libris Group
Wireless access
Publications: Acquisitions List (Quarterly); Annual Report; Current Serials; Library Guide
Partic in Fenway Library Consortium; LYRASIS
Open Mon-Thurs 7:30am-11pm, Fri 7:30-7, Sat 11-9, Sun Noon-11

M MASSACHUSETTS EYE & EAR INFIRMARY LIBRARIES, 243 Charles St, 02114. SAN 328-400X. Tel: 617-573-3196. Reference Tel: 617-573-3664. FAX: 617-573-3370. Web Site: www.masseyeandear.org/education/library-resources. *Dir,* Louise Collins; E-mail: louise_collins@meei.harvard.edu; *Ref Librn,* Deborah Goss; E-mail: deborah_goss@meei.harvard.edu
Library Holdings: Bk Vols 5,500; Per Subs 150
Automation Activity & Vendor Info: (Acquisitions) Innovative Interfaces, Inc; (Cataloging) Innovative Interfaces, Inc; (Circulation) Innovative Interfaces, Inc
Partic in Asn for Vision Sci Librns; Massachusetts Health Sciences Library Network; Medical Library Association
Open Mon-Thurs 8:30-7, Fri 8:30-5
Friends of the Library Group

MASSACHUSETTS GENERAL HOSPITAL

M TRACY BURR MALLORY MEMORIAL LIBRARY*, Dept of Pathology, 55 Fruit St, 02114. SAN 344-6948. Tel: 617-726-8892. FAX: 617-726-7474. *Dir,* Dr Robert H Young; Staff 2 (MLS 1, Non-MLS 1)
Founded 1952
Library Holdings: Bk Titles 400; Bk Vols 500; Per Subs 20
Subject Interests: Pathology
Open Mon-Fri 9-5

M TREADWELL LIBRARY*, Bartlett Hall Ext-I, 55 Fruit St, 02114-2696, SAN 344-6972. Tel: 617-726-8600. Reference Tel: 617-726-8605. FAX: 617-726-6784. E-mail: treadwellqanda@partners.org. Web Site: www.massgeneral.org/library. *Dir,* Elizabeth Schneider; *Ref (Info Servs),* Martha Stone; Staff 20 (MLS 9, Non-MLS 11)
Founded 1858
Library Holdings: Bk Titles 15,000; Bk Vols 50,000; Per Subs 1,600
Subject Interests: Biochem, Biology, Med, Nursing
Automation Activity & Vendor Info: (Acquisitions) SydneyPlus; (Cataloging) SydneyPlus; (Circulation) SydneyPlus; (Course Reserve) SydneyPlus; (Serials) SydneyPlus
Partic in LYRASIS; OCLC Online Computer Library Center, Inc; Proquest Dialog
Restriction: Staff & patient use

M WARREN LIBRARY*, 55 Fruit St, 02114-2622, SAN 344-7006. Tel: 617-726-2253. *Librn,* Nancy Marshall
Founded 1841
Library Holdings: Bk Vols 10,000; Per Subs 25
Open Mon-Fri 9:30-4:15

S MASSACHUSETTS HISTORICAL SOCIETY LIBRARY, 1154 Boylston St, 02215. SAN 307-2037. Tel: 617-646-0532. FAX: 617-859-0074. E-mail: library@masshist.org. Web Site: www.masshist.org/library. *Libr Dir,* Elaine Heavey; Tel: 617-646-0509, E-mail: eheavey@masshist.org; *Ref Librn,* Anna Clutterbuck-Cook; Tel: 617-646-0561, E-mail: acook@masshist.org; *Ref Librn,* Daniel Hinchen; Tel: 617-646-0571, E-mail: dhinchen@masshist.org; Staff 18 (MLS 13, Non-MLS 5)
Founded 1791
Library Holdings: Bk Vols 200,000; Per Subs 160
Special Collections: Historical Coll, broadsides, maps, ms, photos, prints, rare bks
Subject Interests: Colonial period, Massachusetts, New England, Revolutionary period
Automation Activity & Vendor Info: (Acquisitions) Ex Libris Group; (Cataloging) Ex Libris Group
Wireless access
Function: Archival coll, Ref serv available
Publications: Massachusetts Historical Review (Journal); Miscellany (Newsletter)
Partic in OCLC Online Computer Library Center, Inc
Open Mon-Fri 10-4:45
Restriction: Closed stack, Non-circulating, Photo ID required for access

S MASSACHUSETTS SOCIETY FOR THE PREVENTION OF CRUELTY TO ANIMALS LIBRARY, 350 S Huntington Ave, 02130. SAN 327-3253. Tel: 617-522-7400. FAX: 617-522-4885. Web Site: www.mspca.org. *Archives,* Raffaela Torchia; E-mail: rtorchia@mspca.org
Library Holdings: Bk Titles 1,000; Bk Vols 1,500; Per Subs 65
Special Collections: Archives of George Angel I
Wireless access
Restriction: Researchers by appt only

S MASSACHUSETTS TAXPAYERS FOUNDATION LIBRARY, 333 Washington St, Ste 853, 02108. SAN 307-2088. Tel: 617-720-1000. FAX: 617-720-0799. E-mail: mtf_info@masstaxpayers.org. Web Site: www.masstaxpayers.org. *Pres,* Eileen McAnneny
Founded 1948
Library Holdings: Bk Vols 100; Per Subs 4
Special Collections: Massachusetts Taxpayers Foundation Archives
Publications: Annual Report; Ballot Questions (Annual); Budget Analysis (Annual); Library List (Quarterly); Massachusetts Legislative Directory; Municipal Financial Data (Annual)
Restriction: Staff use only

L MINTZ, LEVIN, COHN, FERRIS, GLOVSKY & POPEO*, Law Library, One Financial Ctr, 02111. SAN 307-2118. Tel: 617-542-6000. Circulation Tel: 617-348-4846. FAX: 617-542-2241. Web Site: www.mintz.com. *Dir, Libr Serv,* Mary E Woodruff; Tel: 617-348-1682, E-mail: MEWoodruff@mintz.com
Library Holdings: Bk Vols 5,000; Per Subs 600
Partic in Proquest Dialog

L MORRISON, MAHONEY LLP*, Law Library, 250 Summer St, 02210. SAN 372-0780. Tel: 617-439-7507. FAX: 617-439-7590. Web Site: www.morrisonmahoney.com. *Librn,* Mary Boudreau; E-mail: mboudrea@morrisonmahoney.com
Library Holdings: Bk Titles 500; Per Subs 25
Wireless access
Restriction: Staff use only

S MUSEUM OF FINE ARTS, BOSTON*, William Morris Hunt Memorial Library, 300 Massachusetts Ave, 02115. (Mail add: 465 Huntington Ave, 02115), SAN 307-2126. Tel: 617-369-3385. Interlibrary Loan Service Tel: 617-369-3971. Web Site: www.mfa.org. *Dir,* Maureen Melton; *Head Librn,* Deborah Barlow Smedstad; E-mail: dbarlowsmedstad@mfa.org; *Head, Tech Serv,* Lee-Anne Famolare; Staff 4 (MLS 3, Non-MLS 1)
Founded 1879
Library Holdings: Bk Titles 256,000; Bk Vols 423,261; Per Subs 1,000
Subject Interests: Archaeology, Egypt, Fine arts, Museology
Automation Activity & Vendor Info: (Acquisitions) Ex Libris Group; (Cataloging) Ex Libris Group; (Circulation) Ex Libris Group; (Discovery) EBSCO Discovery Service; (ILL) OCLC WorldShare Interlibrary Loan; (OPAC) Ex Libris Group; (Serials) Ex Libris Group
Wireless access
Partic in Fenway Library Consortium; Fenway Library Organization
Open Mon-Fri 1-5
Restriction: Closed stack, Open to pub for ref only

S MUSEUM OF NATIONAL CENTER OF AFRO-AMERICAN ARTISTS*, Slide Library, 300 Walnut Ave, 02119. SAN 307-2142. Tel: 617-442-8614. Web Site: www.ncaaa.org. *Chief Curator, Exec Dir,* Edmund B Gaither; E-mail: bgaither@mfa.org
Founded 1969
Library Holdings: Bk Vols 450
Open Tues-Sun 1-5

S NATIONAL ARCHIVES & RECORDS ADMINISTRATION, John F Kennedy Presidential Library & Museum, Columbia Point, 02125. SAN 307-7438. Tel: 617-514-1600. Administration Tel: 617-514-1541. Toll Free Tel: 866-535-1960. FAX: 617-514-1593. TDD: 617-514-1573. E-mail: kennedy.library@nara.gov. Web Site: www.jfklibrary.org. *Dir,* Alan Price; *Dep Dir,* James Roth; *Dir, Archives,* Karen Adler Abramson; *Dir, Educ & Pub Serv,* Nancy McCoy; *Curator,* Janice Hodson; Staff 45 (MLS 18, Non-MLS 27)
Founded 1963
Library Holdings: Bk Titles 32,000; Bk Vols 35,000; Per Subs 19
Special Collections: Ernest Hemingway Coll, film, mss, photog, printed mat; Mid-Twentieth Century American Politics & Government,; The Life & Times of John F Kennedy. Oral History
Wireless access
Publications: Historical Materials in the John F Kennedy Library
Restriction: Open by appt only
Friends of the Library Group

M NEW ENGLAND BAPTIST HOSPITAL*, Paul E Woodard Health Sciences Library, 125 Parker Hill Ave, 3rd Flr, 02120. SAN 344-7030. Tel: 617-754-5155. FAX: 617-754-6414. Web Site: nebh.org/health-professionals. *Librn,* Chris Vaillancourt; E-mail: cvaillan@nebh.org; Staff 1 (MLS 1)
Founded 1963
Library Holdings: Bk Titles 2,200; Per Subs 150
Special Collections: Orthopaedics & History of Medicine (Morton Smith-Petersen Coll); Otto Aufranc Coll
Subject Interests: Orthopedics
Wireless access
Partic in Massachusetts Health Sciences Library Network; National Network of Libraries of Medicine Region 7
Open Mon-Fri 7-4

CM NEW ENGLAND COLLEGE OF OPTOMETRY LIBRARY*, 424 Beacon St, 02115. SAN 307-2185. Tel: 617-587-5589. E-mail: library@neco.edu. Web Site: library.neco.edu. *Dir, Libr Serv,* Heather Edmonds; Tel: 617-587-5579, E-mail: edmondsh@neco.edu; *Research Librn, Support Serv,* Melissa Lydston; Tel: 617-587-5657, E-mail: lydstonm@neco.edu; *Libr Asst,* Ralph Holley; Tel: 617-587-5623, E-mail: holleyr@neco.edu; Staff 4 (MLS 2, Non-MLS 2)
Founded 1894. Enrl 500; Fac 120; Highest Degree: Doctorate
Special Collections: History of Optometry
Subject Interests: Ophthalmology, Optometry
Automation Activity & Vendor Info: (Discovery) EBSCO Discovery Service
Wireless access
Mem of Massachusetts Library System
Partic in Association of Vision Science Librarians; Basic Health Sciences Library Network; OCLC-LVIS
Open Mon-Fri 9-5, Sat 9-4

S NEW ENGLAND CONSERVATORY OF MUSIC*, Blumenthal Family Library, 255 St Butolph St, 02115. SAN 344-712X. Tel: 617-585-1250. FAX: 617-585-1245. Web Site: necmusic.edu/library. *Co-Dir,* Hannah Spence; E-mail: hannah.spence@necmusic.edu; *Co-Dir,* Richard Vallone; Tel: 617-585-1247, E-mail: richard.vallone@necmusic.edu; *Asst to the Dir,* Jason Coleman; E-mail: jason.coleman@necmusic.edu; *Archivist,* Maryalice Perrin-Mohr; Tel: 617-585-1252; *ILL,* Mary Jane Loizou; Tel: 617-585-1248, E-mail: mariajane.loizou@necmusic.edu; Staff 10 (MLS 6, Non-MLS 4)
Founded 1867
Library Holdings: CDs 65,000; Music Scores 65,000; Bk Vols 30,000; Per Subs 295
Special Collections: Firestone Hour Music Coll, rec, v-tapes; New England Composers, ms; Preston Coll of Musicians' Letters; Vaughn Monroe Coll of Camel Caravan, scores
Automation Activity & Vendor Info: (Acquisitions) Ex Libris Group; (Cataloging) Ex Libris Group; (Circulation) Ex Libris Group; (Course Reserve) Ex Libris Group; (OPAC) Ex Libris Group; (Serials) Ex Libris Group
Wireless access
Mem of Massachusetts Library System
Partic in Fenway Library Consortium; Fenway Library Organization; LYRASIS; OCLC Online Computer Library Center, Inc
Open Mon-Fri 10-4

S NEW ENGLAND HISTORIC GENEALOGICAL SOCIETY LIBRARY*, 99-101 Newbury St, 02116-3007. SAN 307-2193. Tel: 617-226-1239, 617-536-5740. Reference Tel: 617-226-1233. Toll Free Tel: 888-296-3447. FAX: 617-536-7307. E-mail: library@nehgs.org. Web Site: www.americanancestors.org. *Libr Dir,* Jean Maguire; Tel: 617-226-1229, E-mail: jmaguire@nehgs.org; *Chief Genealogist,* David Allen Lambert; Tel: 617-226-1222, E-mail: dalambert@nehgs.org; *Archivist,* Judith Lucey; Tel: 617-226-1223, E-mail: jlucey@nehgs.org; Staff 14 (MLS 5, Non-MLS 9)
Founded 1845
Library Holdings: CDs 500; Bk Titles 100,000; Bk Vols 200,000; Per Subs 700
Special Collections: Manuscripts of Family Histories; town & church records, diaries, heraldry, census records, probate records & deeds of New England states; Microtext: Census records, vital records
Subject Interests: Genealogy, Heraldry, Local hist
Automation Activity & Vendor Info: (Acquisitions) Innovative Interfaces, Inc; (Cataloging) Innovative Interfaces, Inc; (Circulation) Innovative Interfaces, Inc; (OPAC) Innovative Interfaces, Inc; (Serials) Innovative Interfaces, Inc
Wireless access
Function: CD-ROM, Electronic databases & coll, Online ref, Orientations, Photocopying/Printing, Prog for adults, Ref serv available, Wheelchair accessible
Publications: New England Ancestors Magazine; New England Historical & Genealogical Register
Partic in LYRASIS
Special Services for the Blind - Closed circuit TV magnifier
Open Tues & Thurs-Sat 9-5, Wed 9-9
Restriction: Fee for pub use, Limited access for the pub, Non-circulating

CL NEW ENGLAND LAW*, Boston Law Library, 154 Stuart St, 02116-5687. SAN 307-2231. Tel: 617-422-7288. Interlibrary Loan Service Tel: 617-422-7416. Reference Tel: 617-422-7299. Administration Tel: 617-422-7282. FAX: 617-422-7303. E-mail: refstaff@nesl.edu. Web Site: www.nesl.edu/library. *Dir,* Kristin McCarthy; Tel: 617-422-7418, E-mail: kmccarthy@nesl.edu; *Sr Ref Librn,* Barry Stearns; Tel: 617-422-7332, E-mail: bstearns@nesl.edu; *Coll Develop, Ref Librn,* Helen Litwack; Tel: 617-422-7436, E-mail: hlitwack@nesl.edu; *Acq, Electronic Res Librn,* Karen Green; Tel: 617-422-7293, E-mail: kgreen@nesl.edu; *Tech Serv Librn,* Kyle Kelly; Tel: 617-422-7214, E-mail: kkelly@nesl.edu; *Acq, Ser Spec,* James Gage; Tel: 617-422-7310, E-mail: jgage@nesl.edu; *ILL,* Connie Sellers; E-mail: csellers@nesl.edu; Staff 11 (MLS 9, Non-MLS 2)
Founded 1917. Enrl 1,100; Fac 76; Highest Degree: Doctorate
Library Holdings: Bk Vols 340,000; Per Subs 3,100
Special Collections: Standard American Law Library Coll, bks, micro, AV & on line resources
Automation Activity & Vendor Info: (Acquisitions) Innovative Interfaces, Inc; (Cataloging) Innovative Interfaces, Inc; (Circulation) Innovative Interfaces, Inc; (Serials) Innovative Interfaces, Inc
Wireless access
Publications: Library Guide; Library Newsletter; Selected List of Recent Acquisitions
Partic in LYRASIS; NELLCO Law Library Consortium, Inc.
Special Services for the Deaf - TTY equip
Open Mon-Fri 8am-10:30pm, Sat 9-7, Sun 10am-10:30pm

S NICHOLS HOUSE MUSEUM*, 55 Mount Vernon St, 02108. SAN 377-516X. Tel: 617-227-6993. FAX: 617-723-8026. E-mail: info@nicholshousemuseum.org. Web Site: nicholshousemuseum.org. *Exec Dir,* Linda Marshall
Founded 1961
Library Holdings: Bk Vols 1,000
Special Collections: Nichols Family Papers; Nichols Family Photograph Coll; Rose Standish Nichols Postcard Coll. Oral History
Subject Interests: European, Gardens
Restriction: Open by appt only

L NIXON PEABODY LLP*, Law Library, 100 Summer St, 02110-2131. SAN 372-0721. Tel: 617-345-1000. FAX: 617-345-1300. Web Site: www.nixonpeabody.com. *Libr Mgr,* Joanne Santino; E-mail: jsantino@nixonpeabody.com
Library Holdings: Bk Vols 8,500; Per Subs 150
Open Mon-Fri 9-5

C NORTHEASTERN UNIVERSITY LIBRARIES*, Snell Library, 360 Huntington Ave, 02115. SAN 344-7243. Tel: 617-373-8778. Reference Tel: 617-373-2356. Administration Tel: 617-373-5001. Web Site: library.northeastern.edu. *Dean, Univ Libr,* Dan M Cohen; E-mail: d.cohen@northeastern.edu; *Assoc Dean, Res & Learning Serv,* Evan Simpson; Tel: 617-373-4920, E-mail: e.simpson@northeastern.edu; *Assoc Dean, Content & Discovery,* Amira Aaron; Tel: 617-373-4961, E-mail: a.aaron@northeastern.edu; *Assoc Dean, Digital Strategies & Serv,* Patrick Yott; E-mail: p.yott@northeastern.edu; *Dir, Admin & Finance,* Tracy Harik; Tel: 617-373-4924, E-mail: t.harik@northeastern.edu; *Syst Adminr,* Karl Yee; Tel: 617-373-4904, E-mail: k.yee@northeastern.edu; *Head of Arts, & Social Sciences,* Gayane Karen Merguerian; Tel: 617-373-2747, E-mail: g.merguerian@northeastern.edu; *Head, Access Serv,* Brian Greene; Tel: 617-373-2401, E-mail: br.greene@northeastern.edu; *Head, Archives & Spec Coll,* Giordana Mecagni; Tel: 617-373-8318, E-mail: gmecagni@northeastern.edu; *Head, Libr Tech,* Ernesto Valencia; Tel: 617-373-3398, E-mail: e.valencia@northeastern.edu; *Head, Res Mgt,* Janet Belanger Morrow; Tel: 617-373-4959, E-mail: j.morrow@northeastern.edu;

Head, STEM, Alissa Link; Tel: 617-373-2458, E-mail: a.link@northeastern.edu; *Access & Delivery Librn, Access & Info Serv Librn,* Nicole Thomas; Tel: 617-373-4970, E-mail: ni.thomas@northeastern.edu; *Coll Develop Librn,* Amy Lewontin; Tel: 617-373-2001, E-mail: a.lewontin@northeastern.edu; *Digital Repository Librn,* Sarah Sweeney; Tel: 617-373-5062, E-mail: sj.sweeney@northeastern.edu; *Experiential Learning Librn,* Regina Pagani; Tel: 617-373-3197, E-mail: r.pagani@northeastern.edu; *Health Sci Librn,* Sandra Dunphy; Tel: 617-373-5322, E-mail: s.dunphy@northeastern.edu; *Metadata Librn,* Ms Drew Facklam; Tel: 617-373-7102, E-mail: d.facklam@northeastern.edu; *Res & Instruction Librn,* Brooke Williams; Tel: 617-373-2363, E-mail: b.williams@northeastern.edu; *Sci Librn,* Katherine Herrlich; Tel: 617-373-5305, E-mail: k.herrlich@northeastern.edu; *Res & Instruction Librn,* Roxanne B Palmatier; Tel: 617-373-4968, E-mail: r.palmatier@northeastern.edu; *Resources & Licensing Mgr,* Stacy Maubourquette; Tel: 617-373-4974, E-mail: s.maubourquette@northeastern.edu. Subject Specialists: *Jewish studies,* Amira Aaron; *Philos, Relig,* Brian Greene; *Children's lit,* Janet Belanger Morrow; *Computer sci,* Amy Lewontin; *Art, Humanities,* Regina Pagani; *Allied health fields, Med, Nursing,* Sandra Dunphy; *Chem, Pharmacology, Psychol,* Katherine Herrlich; *Criminal justice, Mil sci, Polit sci,* Roxanne B Palmatier; Staff 39.3 (MLS 31, Non-MLS 8.3)
Founded 1898. Enrl 26,761; Fac 2,313; Highest Degree: Doctorate
Library Holdings: AV Mats 18,210; e-books 365,520; e-journals 58,559; Electronic Media & Resources 43,769; Bk Titles 677,357; Bk Vols 896,213; Per Subs 69,468
Special Collections: Boston Historical Coll; Digital Repository Service; Northeastern University Archives & Historical Coll, audio, course cats, doctoral dissertations, master theses, newsp, photog, publs, rare bks, videos, yearbks. Oral History; US Document Depository
Subject Interests: Allied health, Biology, Bus, Computer sci, Criminal law & justice, Econ, Educ, Humanities, Pharmacology
Automation Activity & Vendor Info: (Acquisitions) Innovative Interfaces, Inc; (Cataloging) Innovative Interfaces, Inc; (Circulation) Innovative Interfaces, Inc; (Course Reserve) Innovative Interfaces, Inc; (ILL) OCLC ILLiad; (Media Booking) Innovative Interfaces, Inc; (OPAC) Innovative Interfaces, Inc; (Serials) TDNet
Wireless access
Function: Archival coll, Computers for patron use, Electronic databases & coll, ILL available, Online cat, Ref serv available, Wheelchair accessible
Partic in Boston Library Consortium, Inc; LYRASIS; NExpress Consortium; Northeast Research Libraries Consortium; OCLC Online Computer Library Center, Inc; OCLC Research Library Partnership
Special Services for the Deaf - Bks on deafness & sign lang; Closed caption videos; Sign lang interpreter upon request for prog
Special Services for the Blind - Assistive/Adapted tech devices, equip & products; Computer with voice synthesizer for visually impaired persons; Digital talking bk machines; Dragon Naturally Speaking software; Magnifiers; Scanner for conversion & translation of mats; Screen enlargement software for people with visual disabilities; Screen reader software; Text reader; Videos on blindness & physical disabilties
Open Mon-Thurs 7:45am-Midnight, Fri 7:45-9, Sat 9am-10pm, Sun 10-Midnight
Friends of the Library Group

CL NORTHEASTERN UNIVERSITY SCHOOL OF LAW LIBRARY*, 416 Huntington Ave, 02115. SAN 344-7367. Tel: 617-373-3332. Reference Tel: 617-373-3594. FAX: 617-373-8705. E-mail: LawResearchHelp@northeastern.edu. Web Site: www.northeastern.edu/law/library. *Libr Dir,* Sharon Persons; E-mail: s.persons@neu.edu; *Coll Develop, Sr Law Librn,* Scott Akehurst-Moore; Tel: 617-373-3331, E-mail: s.akehurstmoore@neu.edu; *Sr Law Librn,* Craig Eastland; E-mail: c.eastland@neu.edu; *Sr Law Librn,* Elliot Hibbler; Tel: 617-373-3716, E-mail: l.hibbler@neu.edu; *Acq, Supvr, Res Mgr,* Rachel Bates; Tel: 617-373-3553, E-mail: ra.bates@neu.edu; *Coordr, Coll Serv, Media Coordr, Syst Coordr,* Warren Yee; Tel: 617-373-3350, E-mail: w.yee@neu.edu; *Budget Analyst/Journal Ed,* Joseph Miranda; Tel: 617-373-3552, E-mail: j.miranda@neu.edu; Staff 16 (MLS 8, Non-MLS 8)
Founded 1898. Enrl 600; Fac 30; Highest Degree: Doctorate
Library Holdings: Bk Vols 397,000
Special Collections: Pappas Public Interest Law Coll
Automation Activity & Vendor Info: (Acquisitions) Innovative Interfaces, Inc; (Cataloging) Innovative Interfaces, Inc; (Circulation) Innovative Interfaces, Inc; (Course Reserve) Innovative Interfaces, Inc; (ILL) Innovative Interfaces, Inc; (OPAC) Innovative Interfaces, Inc; (Serials) Innovative Interfaces, Inc
Wireless access
Function: Res libr
Partic in Boston Library Consortium, Inc; LYRASIS; NELLCO Law Library Consortium, Inc.; NExpress Consortium
Open Mon-Thurs 6am-1am, Fri 6am-10pm, Sat & Sun 9-9
Restriction: Badge access after hrs, Open to students, fac & staff, Pub use on premises

L NUTTER MCCLENNEN & FISH LLP*, Law Library, Seaport West, 155 Seaport Blvd, 02210. SAN 307-2266. Tel: 617-439-2000. FAX: 617-310-9000. E-mail: librarian@nutter.com. Web Site: www.nutter.com. *Dir, Libr Serv,* Nuchine Nobari; Tel: 617-439-2492; *Sr Ref Librn,* Lila J Abraham; E-mail: labraham@nutter.com; Staff 4 (MLS 3, Non-MLS 1)
Wireless access

S PAYETTE ASSOCIATES*, David J Rowan Library, 290 Congress St, 02210. SAN 327-3458. Tel: 617-895-1000. FAX: 617-895-1002. E-mail: info@payette.com. Web Site: www.payette.com. *Librn,* Amanda Holmen; E-mail: aholmen@payette.com
Founded 1979
Library Holdings: Bk Titles 4,000; Per Subs 75
Special Collections: Healthcare
Subject Interests: Archit
Partic in Proquest Dialog
Restriction: Not open to pub

L PEABODY & ARNOLD LLP*, Law Library, Federal Reserve Plaza, 600 Atlantic Ave, 02110. SAN 372-0713. Tel: 617-951-2100. FAX: 617-951-2125. Web Site: www.peabodyarnold.com.
Library Holdings: Bk Vols 12,000

L RACKEMANN, SAWYER & BREWSTER LIBRARY*, 160 Federal St, 02110-1700. SAN 323-7478. Tel: 617-542-2300. Administration Tel: 617-897-2287. FAX: 617-542-7437. E-mail: Library@rackemann.com. Web Site: www.rackemann.com. *Law Librn,* Jennifer Valentine; E-mail: jvalentine@accufile.com; Staff 2 (MLS 1, Non-MLS 1)
Founded 1886
Library Holdings: Bk Vols 12,000; Per Subs 100
Special Collections: Zoning Coll
Subject Interests: Estates, Real estate, Trusts
Open Mon, Wed & Fri 10-4:30

S RITTNERS SCHOOL OF FLORAL DESIGN LIBRARY*, Augusta Rittner Floral Library, 345 Marlborough St, 02115. SAN 328-2198. Tel: 617-267-3824. FAX: 617-267-3824. Web Site: www.floralschool.com/library-new.htm. *Librn,* Stephen Rittner; E-mail: steve@floralschool.com
Library Holdings: Bk Vols 4,800
Subject Interests: Floral design, Mgt

L ROPES & GRAY LLP LIBRARY*, Prudential Tower, 800 Boylston St, 02199. SAN 329-0468. Tel: 617-951-7000. FAX: 617-951-7050. *Libr Mgr,* Andrea Rasmussen; E-mail: andrea.rasmussen@ropesgray.com; *Sr Res Librn,* Kimberly Sweet; Staff 9 (MLS 7, Non-MLS 2)
Library Holdings: Bk Titles 10,000; Bk Vols 40,000; Per Subs 300
Subject Interests: Law
Automation Activity & Vendor Info: (Acquisitions) Softlink America; (OPAC) Softlink America; (Serials) Softlink America
Wireless access
Restriction: Staff use only

J ROXBURY COMMUNITY COLLEGE LIBRARY*, Academic Bldg, Rm 211, 1234 Columbus Ave, 02120-3423. SAN 307-6466. Tel: 617-541-5323. FAX: 617-933-7476. E-mail: library1@rcc.mass.edu. Web Site: www.rcc.mass.edu/library. *Dir,* William Hoag; E-mail: whoag@rcc.mass.edu; Staff 3 (MLS 3)
Founded 1973. Enrl 2,368; Fac 45; Highest Degree: Associate
Library Holdings: Bk Titles 30,389; Bk Vols 38,210; Per Subs 115
Special Collections: Black United Front Archives; Mel King Papers
Automation Activity & Vendor Info: (Cataloging) SirsiDynix; (Circulation) SirsiDynix; (Course Reserve) SirsiDynix; (ILL) SirsiDynix; (OPAC) SirsiDynix
Wireless access
Mem of Massachusetts Library System
Partic in LYRASIS; OCLC Online Computer Library Center, Inc
Open Mon-Thurs 7:30am-9pm, Fri 7:30-4:30, Sat 8:30-3

M ST ELIZABETH'S MEDICAL CENTER*, Stohlman Library, 736 Cambridge St, 02135. Tel: 617-789-2177. FAX: 617-789-5081. Web Site: www.semc.org. *Librn,* Catherine Guarcello; E-mail: cguarcel@semc.org; Staff 2 (MLS 2)
Library Holdings: Bk Titles 2,000; Per Subs 200
Automation Activity & Vendor Info: (Cataloging) CyberTools for Libraries; (Circulation) CyberTools for Libraries
Partic in Massachusetts Health Sciences Library Network; North Atlantic Health Sciences Libraries, Inc
Restriction: Circulates for staff only

C SIMMONS UNIVERSITY*, Beatley Library, 300 The Fenway, 02115-5898. SAN 307-2312. Tel: 617-521-2000. Circulation Tel: 617-521-2786. Interlibrary Loan Service Tel: 617-521-2746. Reference Tel: 617-521-2784. Administration Tel: 617-521-2741. Administration FAX:

617-521-3093. E-mail: library@simmons.edu. Web Site: www.simmons.edu/library. *Libr Dir,* Vivienne Piroli; Tel: 617-521-2752, E-mail: vivienne.piroli@simmons.edu; *Dep Libr Dir, Univ Archivist,* Jason Wood; Tel: 617-521-2441, E-mail: jason.wood@simmons.edu; Staff 18 (MLS 12, Non-MLS 6)
Founded 1899. Enrl 3,982; Fac 310; Highest Degree: Doctorate
Jul 2016-Jun 2017 Income $3,090,836. Mats Exp $1,132,004, Books $204,000, Per/Ser (Incl. Access Fees) $275,000, Manu Arch $36,000, Electronic Ref Mat (Incl. Access Fees) $617,004. Sal $1,239,102 (Prof $972,038)
Library Holdings: AV Mats 7,122; e-books 378,000; e-journals 270,000; Electronic Media & Resources 131; Bk Vols 160,000; Per Subs 13
Special Collections: Career Resource Materials; Children's Literature (Knapp Coll); Simmons College Archives; Zines Coll
Subject Interests: Libr & info sci, Soc serv (soc work), Women's studies
Automation Activity & Vendor Info: (Acquisitions) Innovative Interfaces, Inc - Millennium; (Cataloging) Innovative Interfaces, Inc - Millennium; (Circulation) Innovative Interfaces, Inc - Millennium; (Course Reserve) Innovative Interfaces, Inc - Millennium; (ILL) OCLC ILLiad; (OPAC) Innovative Interfaces, Inc - Millennium; (Serials) Innovative Interfaces, Inc - Millennium
Wireless access
Function: Museum passes
Partic in Fenway Library Organization; Oberlin Group

M JOHN SNOW, INC*, JSI Research & Training Institute Library, 44 Farnsworth St, 02210-1211. SAN 377-9130. Tel: 617-482-9485. FAX: 617-482-0617. E-mail: jsinfo@jsi.com. Web Site: www.jsi.com. *Librn,* John Carper; Staff 1 (MLS 1)
Library Holdings: Bk Vols 2,000; Per Subs 10
Subject Interests: Pub health
Automation Activity & Vendor Info: (Acquisitions) Inmagic, Inc.; (Cataloging) Inmagic, Inc.
Wireless access
Restriction: Staff use only

P THE STATE LIBRARY OF MASSACHUSETTS*, George Fingold Library, State House, Rm 341, 24 Beacon St, 02133. SAN 307-2339. Tel: 617-727-2590. FAX: 617-727-9730. E-mail: Reference.Department@mass.gov. Web Site: www.mass.gov/orgs/state-library-of-massachusetts. *State Librn,* Elvernoy Johnson; Tel: 617-727-2592, E-mail: Elvernoy.Johnson@mass.gov; *Head, Ref, Info Res,* Dava Davanis; Tel: 617-727-2403, E-mail: dave.davanis@mass.gov; *Head, Spec Coll,* Beth Carroll-Horacks; Tel: 617-727-2595, E-mail: elizabeth.carroll-horacks@mass.gov; *Head, Tech Serv,* Judith Carlstrom; E-mail: judith.carlstrom@mass.gov; Staff 14 (MLS 13, Non-MLS 1)
Founded 1826
Library Holdings: Bk Vols 500,000; Per Subs 1,845
Special Collections: Americana, early Massachusetts imprints; Massachusetts History & Biography, atlases, city directories, ms, maps; Massachusetts Legislators' Private Papers; Massachusetts State House Coll, doc, photog & prints; New England History; Revolutionary War Broadsides. State Document Depository; US Document Depository
Subject Interests: Law, Legis hist, Polit sci
Automation Activity & Vendor Info: (Cataloging) Innovative Interfaces, Inc; (Circulation) Innovative Interfaces, Inc; (OPAC) Innovative Interfaces, Inc; (Serials) Innovative Interfaces, Inc
Wireless access
Function: Res libr
Publications: Annual Checklist of State Publications; Quarterly Checklist of State Publications
Partic in Boston Library Consortium, Inc; Central & Western Massachusetts Automated Resource Sharing; LYRASIS
Special Services for the Deaf - TTY equip
Open Mon-Fri 9-5
Restriction: Lending to staff only
Friends of the Library Group

C SUFFOLK UNIVERSITY*, Mildred F Sawyer Library, 73 Tremont St, 02108. SAN 344-7391. Tel: 617-573-8535. Reference Tel: 617-573-8532. Administration Tel: 617-573-8536. FAX: 617-573-8756. E-mail: sawlib@suffolk.edu. Web Site: www.suffolk.edu/sawlib. *Dir,* Sarah Griffis; E-mail: sgriffis@suffolk.edu; *Asst Dir, Head, Tech Serv,* Beata Panagopoulos; E-mail: bpanagopoulos@suffolk.edu; *Sr Ref Librn,* Sonia Didriksson; E-mail: sdidriksson@suffolk.edu; *Sr Ref Librn,* Sarah Griffis; E-mail: sgriffis@suffolk.edu; *Sr Ref Librn,* Connie Sellers; *Sr Ref Librn,* Ellen Yen; E-mail: eyen@suffolk.edu; *Electronic Res Librn,* Dennis Flanders; E-mail: dflanders@suffolk.edu; *Ref Librn,* Sarah Smith; E-mail: shmith@suffolk.edu; Staff 9 (MLS 9)
Founded 1936. Enrl 6,573; Highest Degree: Doctorate
Library Holdings: e-books 93,175; e-journals 21,709; Bk Vols 142,047; Per Subs 756
Special Collections: Afro-American Literature Coll
Automation Activity & Vendor Info: (Acquisitions) Innovative Interfaces, Inc - Millennium; (Cataloging) OCLC WorldShare Interlibrary Loan; (Circulation) Innovative Interfaces, Inc - Millennium; (OPAC) Innovative Interfaces, Inc - Millennium; (Serials) Innovative Interfaces, Inc - Millennium
Wireless access
Publications: Help & Research Guides
Partic in Fenway Library Consortium; LYRASIS; NELLCO Law Library Consortium, Inc.; Northeast Research Libraries Consortium
Open Mon-Thurs 8am-11pm, Fri & Sat 8-8, Sun 11-11
Restriction: Mem organizations only, Open to students, fac & staff

Departmental Libraries:

CL JOHN JOSEPH MOAKLEY LAW LIBRARY, 120 Tremont St, 02108-4977, SAN 344-7421. Tel: 617-573-8177. Interlibrary Loan Service Tel: 617-305-1614. Web Site: www.law.suffolk.edu/library. *Dir,* Elizabeth McKenzie; *Assoc Dir,* Susan Sweetgall; *Tech Serv,* Larry Flynn; Staff 26 (MLS 12, Non-MLS 14)
Enrl 1,671; Fac 61; Highest Degree: Doctorate
Library Holdings: Bk Titles 78,431; Bk Vols 210,690; Per Subs 6,620
Special Collections: Congressman J Joseph Moakley Archives
Automation Activity & Vendor Info: (Acquisitions) Innovative Interfaces, Inc; (Cataloging) Innovative Interfaces, Inc; (Circulation) Innovative Interfaces, Inc; (Course Reserve) Innovative Interfaces, Inc; (ILL) Innovative Interfaces, Inc; (OPAC) Innovative Interfaces, Inc; (Serials) Innovative Interfaces, Inc
Partic in OCLC Online Computer Library Center, Inc
Publications: Browsing The Library; Faculty Research Materials; Law Library Research Series
Open Mon-Fri 8am-11pm, Sat & Sun 9am-11pm

L SULLIVAN & WORCESTER, LLP*, Law Library, One Post Office Sq, 02109. SAN 372-0675. Tel: 617-338-2800. FAX: 617-338-2880. Web Site: www.sullivanlaw.com. *Dir, Libr Serv,* Christopher Laut; E-mail: claut@sullivanlaw.com; Staff 3 (MLS 2, Non-MLS 1)
Founded 1943
Library Holdings: Bk Titles 3,000; Bk Vols 25,000; Per Subs 100
Subject Interests: Corporate law
Automation Activity & Vendor Info: (Cataloging) Softlink America; (Circulation) Softlink America; (OPAC) Softlink America; (Serials) Softlink America
Publications: Brochures; Newsletter
Restriction: Not open to pub

R TEMPLE ISRAEL LIBRARY*, Beit Midrash Library-Dr Arnold L Segel Library Center, 477 Longwood Ave, 02215. SAN 307-2371. Tel: 617-566-3960. FAX: 617-731-3711. Web Site: www.tisrael.org/library. *Librn,* Ann Abrams; Tel: 617-566-3960, Ext 116, E-mail: aabrams@tisrael.org
Library Holdings: Bk Titles 10,000; Per Subs 12
Subject Interests: Judaica (lit or hist of Jews)
Friends of the Library Group

GL UNITED STATES COURT OF APPEALS*, First Circuit Library, John Joseph Moakley US Courthouse, Ste 9400, One Courthouse Way, 02210. SAN 307-2401. Tel: 617-748-9044. FAX: 617-748-9358. E-mail: circ1_lib_gen@ca1.uscourts.gov. Web Site: www.ca1.uscourts.gov/circuit-library. *Actg Circuit Librn,* Susan Lee; Staff 11 (MLS 8, Non-MLS 3)
Library Holdings: Bk Vols 40,000; Per Subs 170
Special Collections: US Document Depository
Subject Interests: Law
Automation Activity & Vendor Info: (Acquisitions) SirsiDynix; (Cataloging) SirsiDynix; (ILL) OCLC
Partic in OCLC Online Computer Library Center, Inc
Open Mon-Fri 9-4

C UNIVERSITY OF MASSACHUSETTS AT BOSTON*, Joseph P Healey Library, 100 Morrissey Blvd, 02125-3300. SAN 344-7456. Tel: 617-287-5900. Interlibrary Loan Service Tel: 617-287-5953. Circulation E-mail: library.circulation@umb.edu. Administration E-mail: library.admin@umb.edu. Web Site: www.umb.edu/library. *Interim Dean of Libr,* Joanne Riley; Tel: 617-287-5927, E-mail: joanne.riley@umb.edu; *Discovery Serv, Head, Libr Syst,* Yueqing Chen; Tel: 617-287-5167, E-mail: yueqing.chen@umb.edu; *Instrul Serv Librn,* Jenny Moyryla; Tel: 617-287-5905, E-mail: jenny.moyryla@umb.edu; *Ref Librn,* Iris Jahng; Tel: 617-287-5754, E-mail: iris.jahng@umb.edu; *Ref Librn,* Christina Mullins; Tel: 617-287-5933, E-mail: tina.mullins@umb.edu; *Ref Librn,* Cecilia Sirigos; Tel: 617-287-4071, E-mail: cecilia.sirigos@umb.edu; *Circ Mgr,* Robert Conway; Tel: 617-287-5948, E-mail: robert.conway@umb.edu; *Curator, Spec Coll, Interim Univ Archivist,* Andrew Elder; Tel: 617-287-5944, E-mail: andrew.elder@umb.edu; Staff 17 (MLS 11, Non-MLS 6)
Founded 1965. Enrl 13,232; Fac 462; Highest Degree: Doctorate
Library Holdings: Bk Vols 586,667
Wireless access

Function: Archival coll, Computers for patron use, Distance learning, Doc delivery serv, E-Reserves, Electronic databases & coll, ILL available, Internet access, Online cat, Ref & res
Partic in Boston Library Consortium, Inc; Fenway Library Consortium; Massachusetts Commonwealth Consortium of Libraries in Public Higher Education Institutions
Open Mon-Thurs 7:30am-10pm, Fri 7:30-6, Sat 9-3, Sun 11-5

C WENTWORTH INSTITUTE OF TECHNOLOGY, Douglas D Schumann Library & Learning Commons, 550 Huntington Ave, 02115-5998. SAN 307-2460. Tel: 617-989-4040. FAX: 617-989-4091. E-mail: circdesk@wit.edu, ref@wit.edu. Web Site: library.wit.edu. *Interim Libr Dir,* Dan Neal; Tel: 617-989-4790, E-mail: neald@wit.edu; *Admin Serv Coordr,* Malissa Redmond; Tel: 617-989-4299, E-mail: redmondm2@wit.edu; *Access Serv Librn, Archivist,* Ashley Bryan; Tel: 617-989-4681, E-mail: bryana2@wit.edu; *Acquisitions & Resource Sharing Librn,* Paul Engelberg; Tel: 617-989-4887, E-mail: engelbergp@wit.edu; *Ref & Instruction Librn,* Dan O'Connell; Tel: 617-989-4096, E-mail: oconnolld@wit.edu; *Ref & Instruction Librn,* Pia Romano; Tel: 617-989-4043, E-mail: romanop@wit.edu; *Cataloger,* Kurt Oliver; Tel: 617-989-4094, E-mail: oliverk@wit.edu; Staff 9.5 (MLS 6, Non-MLS 3.5)
Founded 1904. Enrl 4,000; Highest Degree: Master
Library Holdings: Bk Vols 75,000; Per Subs 500
Special Collections: Archives Coll; ASEE/ET Archives; Edward Kingman Coll; Mechanical Engineering (Richard H Lufkin Coll), bks, per
Subject Interests: Archit, Electrical engr, Electronics, Manufacturing, Mechanical engr
Automation Activity & Vendor Info: (Circulation) Ex Libris Group
Wireless access
Publications: Accessions List; Library Handbooks (Student, staff & faculty); Research Guide
Partic in Fenway Library Consortium; Fenway Library Organization; LYRASIS
Open Mon-Thurs 7am-Midnight, Fri 7-6, Sat 8-4, Sun 11am-Midnight

C WHEELOCK COLLEGE LIBRARY*, 132 Riverway, 02215-4815. SAN 307-2479. Tel: 617-879-2220. Reference Tel: 617-879-2222. FAX: 617-879-2408. Reference E-mail: reference@wheelock.edu. Web Site: www.wheelock.edu/library. *Dir, Acad Res, Dir, Libr Serv,* Ann Glannon; Tel: 617-879-2251, E-mail: aglannon@wheelock.edu; *Access Serv,* Dorothy Hibbard; Tel: 617-879-2092, E-mail: dhibbard@wheelock.edu; *Colls Librn, Resources Librn,* Rachel Gravel; Tel: 617-879-2279, E-mail: rgravel@wheelock.edu; *Digital Serv Librn,* Louisa Choy; Tel: 617-879-2213, E-mail: lchoy@wheelock.edu; Staff 7.5 (MLS 6.5, Non-MLS 1)
Founded 1889. Enrl 1,069; Fac 65; Highest Degree: Master
Library Holdings: AV Mats 3,596; e-books 10,309; e-journals 10,345; Bk Vols 92,000; Per Subs 536
Special Collections: Early Childhood Curriculum Resource Coll; History of Kindergarten in the United States; Rare & Historical Children's Literature (US & Great Britian)
Subject Interests: Early childhood educ, Educ, Soc serv (soc work), Spec educ
Automation Activity & Vendor Info: (Acquisitions) Ex Libris Group; (Cataloging) Ex Libris Group; (Circulation) Ex Libris Group; (Course Reserve) Ex Libris Group; (ILL) Ex Libris Group; (OPAC) Ex Libris Group; (Serials) Ex Libris Group
Wireless access
Publications: Bibliographies; Information Handbook; Library Guide (Library handbook)
Partic in Fenway Library Consortium; Fenway Library Organization; OCLC Online Computer Library Center, Inc
Open Mon-Thurs 7:30am-11pm, Fri 7:30-5, Sat 12-5, Sun Noon-11

L WILMERHALE LIBRARY*, 60 State St, 02109. SAN 307-1782. Tel: 617-526-6000. FAX: 617-526-5000. *Dir, Libr & Res Serv,* Donna Lombardo
Library Holdings: Bk Vols 21,000
Subject Interests: Govt, Law
Restriction: Not open to pub

BOURNE

P JONATHAN BOURNE PUBLIC LIBRARY*, 19 Sandwich Rd, 02532. SAN 344-7545. Tel: 508-759-0644. FAX: 508-759-0647. Web Site: www.bournelibrary.org. *Interim Dir,* Irja Finn; E-mail: ifinn@bournelibrary.org; *Asst Dir,* Diane M Ranney; Tel: 508-759-0644, Ext 103, E-mail: dranney@bournelibrary.org; *Ch,* Terry Johnson; Tel: 508-759-0644, Ext 106, E-mail: tjohnson@bournelibrary.org; Staff 9 (MLS 3, Non-MLS 6)
Founded 1896. Pop 18,873
Library Holdings: AV Mats 8,000; Bks on Deafness & Sign Lang 15; Large Print Bks 5,600; Bk Titles 46,000; Bk Vols 53,000; Per Subs 107
Special Collections: Army National Guard Base (Otis) Hazardous Waste Cleanup; Cape Cod Coll; EPA Materials on Massachusetts; Genealogy Coll; Large Print Coll; Young Adult Coll
Automation Activity & Vendor Info: (Acquisitions) Innovative Interfaces, Inc; (Cataloging) Innovative Interfaces, Inc; (Circulation) Innovative Interfaces, Inc; (Course Reserve) Innovative Interfaces, Inc; (ILL) Innovative Interfaces, Inc; (OPAC) Innovative Interfaces, Inc; (Serials) Innovative Interfaces, Inc
Wireless access
Mem of Massachusetts Library System
Partic in Cape Libraries Automated Materials Sharing Network
Special Services for the Deaf - Bks on deafness & sign lang; High interest/low vocabulary bks; TTY equip
Special Services for the Blind - Bks on cassette
Open Tues-Thurs 9-8, Fri & Sat 9-5:30
Friends of the Library Group

BOXBOROUGH

P SARGENT MEMORIAL LIBRARY*, 427 Massachusetts Ave, 01719. SAN 307-2487. Tel: 978-263-4680. FAX: 978-263-1275. *Libr Dir,* Peishan Bartley; E-mail: pbartley@cwmars.org; Staff 7 (MLS 1, Non-MLS 6)
Founded 1891
Library Holdings: Bk Vols 40,000; Per Subs 85
Automation Activity & Vendor Info: (Cataloging) Evergreen; (Circulation) Evergreen; (OPAC) Evergreen
Wireless access
Function: 24/7 Electronic res, 24/7 Online cat, Adult bk club, Art exhibits, Art programs, Audiobks on Playaways & MP3, Audiobks via web, Bk club(s), Bks on CD, Children's prog, Computers for patron use, Electronic databases & coll, Free DVD rentals, ILL available, Internet access, Magazines, Meeting rooms, Movies, Museum passes, Music CDs, Online cat, OverDrive digital audio bks, Preschool outreach, Prog for adults, Prog for children & young adult, Ref serv available, Senior outreach, Story hour, Summer reading prog, Tax forms
Partic in Central & Western Massachusetts Automated Resource Sharing
Open Mon-Thurs 10-8, Sat (Sept-June) 10-3
Friends of the Library Group

BOXFORD

P BOXFORD TOWN LIBRARY*, Seven-A Spofford Rd, 01921. SAN 344-7669. Tel: 978-887-7323. FAX: 978-887-6352. Web Site: www.boxfordlibrary.org. *Dir,* Kevin Bourque; E-mail: kbourque@boxfordlibrary.org; *Head, Ref,* Beth Safford; *Ch,* Joshua Kennedy
Founded 1966. Pop 8,550; Circ 85,963
Library Holdings: AV Mats 16,839; DVDs 3,371; Electronic Media & Resources 7; Bk Vols 54,617; Per Subs 311
Automation Activity & Vendor Info: (Cataloging) SirsiDynix; (Circulation) SirsiDynix; (OPAC) SirsiDynix
Wireless access
Function: Art exhibits, Bks on cassette, Bks on CD, Children's prog, Computers for patron use, E-Reserves, Electronic databases & coll, Genealogy discussion group, Holiday prog, ILL available, Museum passes, Music CDs, Online cat, OverDrive digital audio bks, Photocopying/Printing, Prog for adults, Prog for children & young adult, Ref serv available, Story hour, Summer reading prog, Tax forms, Teen prog, Telephone ref, VHS videos
Mem of Massachusetts Library System
Partic in Merrimack Valley Library Consortium
Open Mon-Thurs 10-8, Fri & Sat 10-3
Friends of the Library Group

BOYLSTON

P BOYLSTON PUBLIC LIBRARY*, 695 Main St, 01505. SAN 307-2495. Tel: 508-869-2371. FAX: 508-869-6195. Web Site: www.boylstonlibrary.org. *Dir,* Jennifer Bruneau; E-mail: jbruneau@boylston-ma.gov; *Asst Dir,* Lynn Clermont; E-mail: lclermont@boylston-ma.gov; *Ch,* Judy Friebert; E-mail: jmfriebert1@hotmail.com; Staff 2.3 (MLS 0.7, Non-MLS 1.6)
Founded 1880. Pop 4,200; Circ 24,227
Library Holdings: AV Mats 4,037; Bk Vols 26,848; Per Subs 77
Automation Activity & Vendor Info: (Acquisitions) Innovative Interfaces, Inc; (Cataloging) Innovative Interfaces, Inc; (Circulation) Innovative Interfaces, Inc; (ILL) Innovative Interfaces, Inc
Publications: Binder (Newsletter)
Mem of Massachusetts Library System
Partic in Central & Western Massachusetts Automated Resource Sharing
Open Tues & Wed 10-8, Thurs 2-8, Fri 2-5, Sat 10-2
Friends of the Library Group

S TOWER HILL BOTANIC GARDEN*, Worcester County Horticultural Society Library, 11 French Dr, 01505. (Mail add: PO Box 598, 01505-0598), SAN 307-8337. Tel: 508-869-6111, Ext 116. FAX:

508-869-0314. E-mail: librarian@towerhillbg.org. Web Site: www.towerhillbg.org/library. Staff 1 (MLS 1)
Founded 1842
Library Holdings: Bk Vols 8,700; Per Subs 26
Subject Interests: Fruit, Garden hist, Hort, Landscape design
Automation Activity & Vendor Info: (Cataloging) OCLC; (Circulation) CyberTools for Libraries; (OPAC) CyberTools for Libraries
Wireless access
Function: Archival coll, Prof lending libr
Mem of Massachusetts Library System
Partic in Council on Botanical & Horticultural Libraries, Inc
Restriction: Circ to mem only

BRAINTREE

S BRAINTREE HISTORICAL SOCIETY, INC LIBRARY & RESOURCE CENTER*, Mary Bean Cunningham Resource Center, Gilbert Bean Barn & Mary Bean Cunningham Resource Ctr, 31 Tenney Rd, 02184-4416. SAN 327-5523. Tel: 781-848-1640. FAX: 781-380-0731. E-mail: Braintreehistoricalevents@gmail.com. Web Site: braintree-historical.org. *Librn,* Claudia Shutter; *Librn,* Claudette Newhall
Founded 1930
Library Holdings: Bk Vols 3,000
Special Collections: Military History Archive; Photo Archive
Subject Interests: Antiques, Genealogy, Local hist, Shipbuilding
Wireless access
Function: Adult bk club
Restriction: Free to mem, In-house use for visitors, Not a lending libr, Open to others by appt, Open to pub by appt only, Private libr

P THAYER PUBLIC LIBRARY, 798 Washington St, 02184. SAN 344-7723. Tel: 781-848-0405. Circulation Tel: 781-848-0405, Ext 4410. Reference Tel: 781-848-0405, Ext 4417. Administration Tel: 781-848-0405, Ext 4420. FAX: 781-356-5447. Administration FAX: 781-356-0672. E-mail: referencedesk@braintreema.gov. Web Site: www.thayerpubliclibrary.org. *Dir,* Terri Stano; *Asst Dir,* Jada Maxwell; E-mail: jmaxwell@braintreema.gov; *Ch,* Elisabeth Strachan; Tel: 781-848-0405, Ext 4426; *Ref Librn,* Moira Cavanagh; Tel: 781-848-0405, Ext 4434, E-mail: mcavanagh@braintreema.gov; *Ref Librn,* Priscilla Crane; Tel: 781-848-0405, Ext 4407; Staff 25 (MLS 8, Non-MLS 17)
Founded 1874. Pop 34,598
Special Collections: Braintree Historical Coll
Automation Activity & Vendor Info: (Acquisitions) SirsiDynix; (Cataloging) SirsiDynix; (Circulation) SirsiDynix
Wireless access
Partic in Old Colony Libr Network
Open Mon-Thurs 9-9, Fri & Sat 9-5, Sun 1-5
Friends of the Library Group

BREWSTER

P BREWSTER LADIES' LIBRARY*, 1822 Main St, 02631. SAN 307-2509. Tel: 508-896-3913. FAX: 508-896-9372. E-mail: bll@brewsterladieslibrary.org. Web Site: www.brewsterladieslibrary.org. *Libr Dir,* Cindy St Amour; E-mail: cstamour@brewsterladieslibrary.org; *Asst Dir, Youth Serv Librn,* Nori Morganstein; E-mail: nmorganstein@brewsterladieslibrary.org; *Adult Serv, Ref Librn,* Mary Fecteau; E-mail: mfecteau@brewsterladieslibrary.org; *Circ Mgr,* Nina Gregson; E-mail: ngregson@brewsterladieslibrary.org; Staff 5 (MLS 3, Non-MLS 2)
Founded 1852. Pop 9,800; Circ 181,000
Library Holdings: AV Mats 48,951; Bk Titles 89,126; Per Subs 166
Special Collections: Brewster History Coll; Cape Cod Coll; Joseph Lincoln Novels; Plays. Oral History
Automation Activity & Vendor Info: (Acquisitions) Innovative Interfaces, Inc; (Cataloging) Innovative Interfaces, Inc; (Circulation) Innovative Interfaces, Inc; (ILL) Innovative Interfaces, Inc; (OPAC) Innovative Interfaces, Inc; (Serials) EBSCO Online
Wireless access
Function: Adult bk club, Archival coll, Art exhibits, Bks on cassette, Bks on CD, Children's prog, Computer training, Computers for patron use, Electronic databases & coll, Free DVD rentals, Home delivery & serv to seniorr ctr & nursing homes, Homebound delivery serv, ILL available, Internet access, Magnifiers for reading, Museum passes, Music CDs, Online cat, Photocopying/Printing, Prog for adults, Prog for children & young adult, Ref serv available, Summer reading prog, Tax forms, Teen prog, Telephone ref, VHS videos, Wheelchair accessible, Writing prog
Publications: Library Update (Newsletter)
Partic in Cape Libraries Automated Materials Sharing Network
Special Services for the Deaf - Assisted listening device
Special Services for the Blind - Large print bks
Open Tues & Thurs 10-8, Wed, Fri & Sat 10-5
Friends of the Library Group

BRIDGEWATER

P BRIDGEWATER PUBLIC LIBRARY, 15 South St, 02324. SAN 307-2525. Tel: 508-697-3331. FAX: 508-279-1467. E-mail: bwpl@sailsinc.org. Web Site: www.bridgewaterpubliclibrary.org. *Exec Dir,* Jed T Phillips; E-mail: jphillips@sailsinc.org; *Asst Dir,* Ann Gerald; E-mail: agerald@sailsinc.org; *Head, Youth Serv,* Christine Stefani; E-mail: cstefani@sailsinc.org; Staff 5 (MLS 4, Non-MLS 1)
Founded 1881. Pop 25,802; Circ 96,436
Library Holdings: Bk Vols 139,459; Per Subs 110
Automation Activity & Vendor Info: (Acquisitions) SirsiDynix; (Cataloging) SirsiDynix; (Circulation) SirsiDynix; (Media Booking) SirsiDynix; (OPAC) SirsiDynix; (Serials) SirsiDynix
Wireless access
Function: Art exhibits, Computers for patron use, E-Reserves, Electronic databases & coll, Free DVD rentals, Internet access, Museum passes, Music CDs, Online ref, OverDrive digital audio bks, Photocopying/Printing, Prog for adults, Prog for children & young adult, Ref serv available, Story hour, Summer reading prog, Tax forms, Wheelchair accessible
Partic in SAILS Library Network
Special Services for the Deaf - TDD equip
Special Services for the Blind - Assistive/Adapted tech devices, equip & products
Open Mon-Fri 10-5, Sat 9-3:30
Friends of the Library Group

C BRIDGEWATER STATE UNIVERSITY*, Clement C Maxwell Library, Ten Shaw Rd, 02325. SAN 307-2533. Tel: 508-531-1392. Interlibrary Loan Service Tel: 508-531-1706. FAX: 508-531-1349, 508-531-6103. E-mail: libraryweb@bridgew.edu. Web Site: library.bridgew.edu. *Interim Dir,* Stephen Weiter; E-mail: weiters@bridgew.edu; *Head, Educ Res Ctr,* Christine Brown; Tel: 508-531-2023, E-mail: c4brown@bridgew.edu; *Head, Ref Serv,* Position Currently Open; *Archivist, Head, Spec Coll,* Orson Kingsley; Tel: 508-531-1389, E-mail: orson.kingsley@bridgew.edu; *Head, Tech Serv,* Kumiko Reichert; Tel: 508-531-2665, E-mail: kreichert@bridgew.edu; *Ref Librn,* Pamela Hayes-Bohanan; Tel: 508-531-2893, E-mail: phayesboh@bridgew.edu; *Circ,* Kevin Manning; Tel: 508-531-2005, E-mail: kmanning@bridgew.edu; *Ref (Info Servs), Ref Serv, Ad,* Cynthia Svoboda; Tel: 508-531-1256. Subject Specialists: *Educ res,* Christine Brown; Staff 27 (MLS 10, Non-MLS 17)
Founded 1840. Enrl 11,500; Highest Degree: Master
Library Holdings: Bk Titles 280,000; Bk Vols 304,000; Per Subs 1,100
Special Collections: Abraham Lincoln Coll; Albert G Boyden Coll of Early American Textbooks; Bridgewaterana; Children's Coll; Dicken's Coll; Educational Resources Information Center, micro; Library of American Civilization, micro; Library of English Literature, micro; Standardized Tests; Tests in Microfiche; Theodore Roosevelt Coll. State Document Depository; US Document Depository
Subject Interests: Art, Educ
Automation Activity & Vendor Info: (Acquisitions) Ex Libris Group; (Cataloging) Ex Libris Group; (Circulation) Ex Libris Group; (Course Reserve) Ex Libris Group; (OPAC) Ex Libris Group; (Serials) Ex Libris Group
Wireless access
Publications: SE Mass Cooperating Libraries Union List of Serials
Partic in LYRASIS

MASSACHUSETTS DEPARTMENT OF CORRECTIONS
S INSTITUTIONAL LIBRARY AT MASSACHUSETTS TREATMENT CENTER*, One Administration Rd, 02324. Tel: 508-279-8100, Ext 8443. *Librn,* Natalya Pushkina
Library Holdings: Bk Vols 9,250; Per Subs 31
Open Mon, Tues & Fri 8-4, Wed & Thurs 8-4 & 7-9
S INSTITUTIONAL LIBRARY AT OLD COLONY CORRECTIONAL CENTER*, One Administration Rd, 02324. Tel: 508-279-6006, Ext 6803. *Librn,* Ann Cowell
Library Holdings: Bk Vols 5,000; Per Subs 38
Automation Activity & Vendor Info: (Circulation) Follett Software
Mem of Massachusetts Library System
S STATE HOSPITAL LIBRARY*, 20 Administration Rd, 02324, SAN 307-2541. Tel: 508-279-4500, Ext 4600. FAX: 508-279-4502. *Librn,* Kurt Eichner; Staff 1 (MLS 1)
Founded 1975
Library Holdings: Bk Titles 9,000; Per Subs 23
Subject Interests: Law
Restriction: Staff & inmates only

BRIMFIELD

P BRIMFIELD PUBLIC LIBRARY*, 25 Main St, 01010. (Mail add: PO Box 377, 01010), SAN 307-2584. Tel: 413-245-3518. FAX: 413-245-3468. E-mail: library@brimfieldma.org. Web Site: www.brimfieldpubliclibrary.org. *Dir,* Rebecca Wells
Founded 1877. Pop 3,136; Circ 20,179

Library Holdings: Bk Vols 15,000; Per Subs 70
Special Collections: Oral History
Subject Interests: Genealogy, Local hist
Automation Activity & Vendor Info: (Cataloging) Innovative Interfaces, Inc; (Circulation) Innovative Interfaces, Inc; (OPAC) Innovative Interfaces, Inc
Wireless access
Mem of Massachusetts Library System
Partic in Central & Western Massachusetts Automated Resource Sharing
Open Mon 9-1 & 4-8, Tues & Thurs 3-8, Wed 12-6, Sat 9-1
Friends of the Library Group

BROCKTON

P BROCKTON PUBLIC LIBRARY*, 304 Main St, 02301-5390. SAN 344-7812. Tel: 508-580-7890. Circulation Tel: 508-580-7890, Ext 107. Reference Tel: 508-580-7890, Ext 201. Administration Tel: 508-580-7890, Ext 102. FAX: 508-580-7898. E-mail: btlib@ocln.org. Web Site: www.brocktonpubliclibrary.org. *Dir,* Paul Engle; E-mail: pengle@cobma.us; *Asst Dir,* Keith Choquette; E-mail: kchoquette@cobma.us; *Head, Tech Serv,* Michelle Poor; E-mail: mpoor@ocln.org; *Ch Serv,* Tammy Campbell; E-mail: tcampbell@cobma.us; *ILL,* Kathy Donahue; E-mail: btill@ocln.org; *Ref (Info Servs),* Paula Jones; E-mail: pjones@cobma.us; Staff 45 (MLS 7, Non-MLS 38)
Founded 1867. Pop 95,672; Circ 183,000
Library Holdings: Audiobooks 4,473; CDs 6,827; DVDs 14,086; e-books 154,582; Microforms 6,881; Bk Vols 188,738; Per Subs 120
Automation Activity & Vendor Info: (Cataloging) SirsiDynix; (Circulation) SirsiDynix; (OPAC) SirsiDynix
Wireless access
Function: 24/7 Online cat, Adult bk club, Adult literacy prog, Art exhibits, Art programs, Audiobks via web, Bilingual assistance for Spanish patrons, Bk club(s), Bks on CD, Chess club, Children's prog, Citizenship assistance, Computer training, Computers for patron use, Doc delivery serv, Electronic databases & coll, Free DVD rentals, Holiday prog, Home delivery & serv to seniorr ctr & nursing homes, Homebound delivery serv, ILL available, Internet access, Magazines, Magnifiers for reading, Makerspace, Mango lang, Microfiche/film & reading machines, Movies, Museum passes, Music CDs, Online cat, Photocopying/Printing, Printer for laptops & handheld devices, Prog for adults, Prog for children & young adult, Ref & res, Ref serv available, Res assist avail, Res performed for a fee, Senior computer classes, Spanish lang bks, STEM programs, Story hour, Study rm, Summer reading prog, Tax forms, Teen prog, Wheelchair accessible
Partic in Old Colony Libr Network
Open Mon & Tues 12-9, Wed 9-9, Thurs, Fri & Sat 9-5
Friends of the Library Group
Branches: 2
EAST, 54 Kingman St, 02302, SAN 344-7871. Tel: 508-580-7892. FAX: 508-580-7861. E-mail: bteast@ocln.org. *Asst Dir,* Keith Choquette; E-mail: keithc@ocln.org; *Br Supvr,* Meagan Perry; E-mail: mperry@cobma.us; *Asst Br Supvr,* Rima Tamule; E-mail: rtamule@cobma.us; Staff 2 (Non-MLS 2)
Founded 1969. Pop 95,672; Circ 10,634
Library Holdings: Audiobooks 321; CDs 523; DVDs 4,229; Large Print Bks 471; Bk Vols 7,822; Per Subs 30
Automation Activity & Vendor Info: (Acquisitions) SirsiDynix-WorkFlows; (Circulation) SirsiDynix-WorkFlows; (OPAC) SirsiDynix-iBistro; (Serials) SirsiDynix-WorkFlows
Function: 24/7 Electronic res, 24/7 Online cat
Open Tues 9-5, Thurs 10-8
Friends of the Library Group
WEST, 540 Forest Ave, 02301, SAN 344-7936. Tel: 508-580-7894. FAX: 508-580-7863. E-mail: btwest@ocln.org. *Asst Dir,* Keith Choquette; Tel: 508-580-7890, Ext 105, E-mail: keithc@ocln.org; *Br Supvr,* Meagan Perry; E-mail: mperry@cobma.us; *Asst Br Supvr,* Rima Tamule; E-mail: rtamule@cobma.us; Staff 2 (Non-MLS 2)
Founded 1969
Library Holdings: Audiobooks 625; CDs 130; DVDs 3,165; Large Print Bks 362; Bk Vols 9,137; Per Subs 16
Automation Activity & Vendor Info: (Circulation) SirsiDynix-WorkFlows; (ILL) SirsiDynix-WorkFlows; (OPAC) SirsiDynix-iBistro; (Serials) SirsiDynix-WorkFlows
Function: 24/7 Electronic res, 24/7 Online cat, Computers for patron use, Free DVD rentals, Internet access, Summer reading prog, Tax forms
Open Mon 9-5, Wed 10-8
Friends of the Library Group

GL COMMONWEALTH OF MASSACHUSETTS - TRIAL COURT, Brockton Law Library, 72 Belmont St, 02301. SAN 307-2630. Tel: 508-586-7110. FAX: 508-580-3329. E-mail: brocklaw72@hotmail.com. Web Site: www.mass.gov/locations/brockton-law-library. *Head Law Librn,* Alexandria Bernson; E-mail: alexandra.bernson@jud.state.ma.us; *Asst Law Librn,* Lisa Ledwith; Staff 2 (MLS 1, Non-MLS 1)
Library Holdings: Bk Vols 24,532
Automation Activity & Vendor Info: (Cataloging) SirsiDynix; (Circulation) SirsiDynix; (OPAC) SirsiDynix; (Serials) SirsiDynix
Wireless access
Partic in NELLCO Law Library Consortium, Inc.
Open Mon-Fri 8:30-12 & 12:30-4

J MASSASOIT COMMUNITY COLLEGE*, Brockton Campus Library, One Massasoit Blvd, 02302. SAN 307-2622. Tel: 508-588-9100, Ext 1941. FAX: 508-427-1265. Web Site: www.massasoit.edu/library. *Dir of Libr,* Vincent Livoti; E-mail: vlivoti@massasoit.mass.edu; *Ref Librn,* Kay Neary; E-mail: kneary@massasoit.mass.edu; *Coordr, Pub Serv & Instruction,* Erin McCoy; E-mail: emccoy@massasoit.mass.edu
Founded 1966
Library Holdings: Bk Vols 63,764; Per Subs 175
Special Collections: Allied Health Resources; New York Times, 1851-date
Automation Activity & Vendor Info: (Acquisitions) SirsiDynix; (Cataloging) SirsiDynix; (Circulation) SirsiDynix
Wireless access
Open Mon-Thurs 8am-9pm, Fri 8-7, Sat 10-2
Departmental Libraries:
CANTON CAMPUS LIBRARY, 900 Randolph St, Canton, 02021. Tel: 508-588-9100, Ext 2942. *Coordr, Libr Serv,* Pauline Aiello; Tel: 508-588-9100, Ext 2945, E-mail: paiello@massasoit.mass.edu; *Libr Assoc,* Rachel Gammon; E-mail: rgammon@massasoit.mass.edu; *Libr Assoc,* Denise Seymour; E-mail: dseymour@massasoit.mass.edu
Open Mon-Thurs 8-8, Fri 8-4

M SIGNATURE HEALTHCARE - BROCKTON HOSPITAL LIBRARY*, 680 Centre St, 02302. SAN 371-2028. Tel: 508-941-7000. E-mail: library@signature-healthcare.org. Web Site: www.brocktonhospital.com. *Librn,* Catherine Moore; Staff 4 (MLS 1, Non-MLS 3)
Library Holdings: e-journals 45; Bk Titles 2,500; Bk Vols 9,000; Per Subs 268
Subject Interests: Med, Nursing
Publications: Brochures
Partic in Basic Health Sciences Library Network; Southeastern Massachusetts Consortium of Health Science
Open Mon-Fri 9-5:30

BROOKFIELD

P MERRICK PUBLIC LIBRARY*, Two Lincoln St, 01506. SAN 307-2657. Tel: 508-867-6339. FAX: 508-867-2981. E-mail: brookfieldlibrary@gmail.com. Web Site: www.merrickpubliclibrary.org. *Libr Dir,* Brenda Metterville
Pop 3,100; Circ 13,355
Library Holdings: Bk Vols 20,000; Per Subs 50
Subject Interests: Local hist
Automation Activity & Vendor Info: (Cataloging) Follett Software; (Circulation) Follett Software
Mem of Massachusetts Library System
Partic in Central & Western Massachusetts Automated Resource Sharing
Open Tues & Thurs 1-8, Wed & Fri 11-5, Sat 10-1
Friends of the Library Group

BROOKLINE

S LARZ ANDERSON AUTO MUSEUM LIBRARY & ARCHIVES*, Larz Anderson Park, 15 Newton St, 02445. SAN 375-1538. Tel: 617-522-6547. FAX: 617-524-0170. E-mail: info@larzanderson.org. Web Site: larzanderson.org. *Educ Mgr,* Anne Marie Goguen; E-mail: education@larzanderson.org; Staff 1 (Non-MLS 1)
Founded 1948
Library Holdings: Bk Vols 2,000; Per Subs 12
Special Collections: Larry Wineman Coll (GM); Larz and Isabel Anderson Coll; Roderick Blood Coll (Packard)
Subject Interests: Automobiles
Function: Res libr
Publications: Carriage House Notes (Newsletter)
Restriction: Non-circulating, Open by appt only

SR CONGREGATION MISHKAN TEFILA*, Harry & Anna Feinberg Library, 384 Harvard St, 02446. SAN 326-033X. Tel: 617-332-7770. FAX: 617-332-2871. E-mail: info@mishkantefila.org. Web Site: www.mishkantefila.org/library. *Dir, Innovations, Library Contact,* Yael Hurwitz-Lange; E-mail: yael@mishkantefila.org; Staff 1 (MLS 1)
Library Holdings: Bk Vols 5,000; Per Subs 10
Mem of Massachusetts Library System
Special Services for the Deaf - Accessible learning ctr

CR HELLENIC COLLEGE-HOLY CROSS GREEK ORTHODOX SCHOOL OF THEOLOGY*, Archbishop Iakovos Library, 50 Goddard Ave, 02445-7496. SAN 307-2673. Tel: 617-850-1223. Web Site: www.hchc.edu/library. *Dir,* Fr Joachim Cotsonis; Tel: 617-850-1243,

E-mail: jcotsonis@hchc.edu; *Circ, ILL, Per,* Hilary Rogler; Tel: 617-850-1244, E-mail: hrogler@hchc.edu; Staff 2 (MLS 2)
Founded 1937. Enrl 117; Fac 16; Highest Degree: Master
Library Holdings: AV Mats 2,343; CDs 680; DVDs 288; e-books 5,299; Microforms 885; Music Scores 310; Per Subs 307; Videos 757
Special Collections: Archbishop Iakovos Coll, rare bks; Archive
Subject Interests: Archival, Greek, Hist, Orthodox theol
Automation Activity & Vendor Info: (Acquisitions) SirsiDynix; (Cataloging) SirsiDynix; (Circulation) SirsiDynix; (ILL) OCLC Connexion; (OPAC) SirsiDynix-Enterprise; (Serials) EBSCO Online
Wireless access
Publications: Archbishop Iakovos Library Acquisitions List (Quarterly)
Mem of Massachusetts Library System
Partic in American Theological Library Association; Boston Theological Interreligious Consortium; OCLC Online Computer Library Center, Inc; Statewide California Electronic Library Consortium
Open Mon-Fri 9-5 & 7-12, Sat 10-4, Sun 7-12

P PUBLIC LIBRARY OF BROOKLINE*, 361 Washington St, 02445. SAN 344-7960. Tel: 617-730-2370. FAX: 617-730-2160. Web Site: www.brooklinelibrary.org. *Dir,* Sara F Slymon; Tel: 617-730-2360, E-mail: sslymon@minlib.net; *Asst Dir, Admin,* Anne Reed; E-mail: areed@minlib.net; *Asst Dir/Tech Librn,* Callan Bignoli; E-mail: cbignoli@minlib.net; Staff 22 (MLS 22)
Founded 1857. Pop 54,700; Circ 729,718
Library Holdings: Bk Vols 319,779; Per Subs 820
Automation Activity & Vendor Info: (Cataloging) Innovative Interfaces, Inc; (Circulation) Innovative Interfaces, Inc; (OPAC) Innovative Interfaces, Inc
Wireless access
Partic in Minuteman Library Network
Open Mon-Thurs 10-9, Fri & Sat 10-5, Sun (Fall & Winter) 1-5
Friends of the Library Group
Branches: 2
COOLIDGE CORNER, 31 Pleasant St, 02446, SAN 344-7995. Tel: 617-730-2380. FAX: 617-734-4565. *Br Supvr,* Ryan Brennan; Tel: 617-730-2380, E-mail: rbrennan@minlib.net; *Asst Br Supvr,* Amanda Troha; Tel: 617-730-2380, E-mail: atroha@minlib.net
Library Holdings: Bk Vols 93,984
Open Mon & Wed 10-6, Tues & Thurs 10-9, Fri & Sat 9:30-5, Sun (Fall & Winter) 1-5
Friends of the Library Group
PUTTERHAM, 959 W Roxbury Pkwy, Chestnut Hill, 02467, SAN 344-8029. Tel: 617-730-2385. FAX: 617-469-3947. *Br Supvr,* Batia Bloomenthal; E-mail: bbloomenthal@minlib.net
Library Holdings: Bk Vols 40,997
Open Mon & Wed 1-9, Tues & Thurs 10-6, Fri & Sat (Fall & Winter) 10-5

R TEMPLE SINAI LIBRARY*, 50 Sewall Ave, 02446. SAN 307-2703. Tel: 617-277-5888. FAX: 617-277-5842. E-mail: office@sinaibrookline.org. Web Site: www.sinaibrookline.org. *Exec Dir,* Linda Katz; E-mail: executivedirector@sinaibrookline.org
Library Holdings: Bk Vols 1,000
Subject Interests: Israel, Judaica (lit or hist of Jews), Middle East
Wireless access

BUCKLAND

P BUCKLAND PUBLIC LIBRARY*, 30 Upper St, 01338. (Mail add: PO Box 149, 01338-0149), SAN 307-2711. Tel: 413-625-9412. E-mail: bucklandpubliclibrary@cwmars.org. Web Site: www.bucklandpubliclibrary.org. *Dir,* Jane Buchanan; E-mail: jbuchanan@cwmars.org
Pop 2,165; Circ 13,820
Library Holdings: Bk Vols 9,000; Per Subs 15
Automation Activity & Vendor Info: (Cataloging) Evergreen; (Circulation) Evergreen; (OPAC) Evergreen
Wireless access
Partic in Central & Western Massachusetts Automated Resource Sharing
Open Tues 2-8, Fri 1-6, Sat 9-1

BURLINGTON

P BURLINGTON PUBLIC LIBRARY*, 22 Sears St, 01803. SAN 307-2738. Tel: 781-270-1690. FAX: 781-229-0406. Web Site: www.burlington.org/departments/library/index.php. *Dir,* Michael Wick; E-mail: mwick@burlington.org; *Asst Dir,* Marnie Smith; E-mail: msmith@burlington.org; *Circ,* Cara Enos; E-mail: cenos@burlington.org; Staff 10 (MLS 7, Non-MLS 3)
Founded 1857. Pop 23,694; Circ 240,515
Library Holdings: Bk Vols 89,000; Per Subs 168
Subject Interests: Bus & mgt, Law
Automation Activity & Vendor Info: (Cataloging) Evergreen; (Circulation) Evergreen; (OPAC) Evergreen
Wireless access
Function: ILL available, Photocopying/Printing
Partic in Merrimack Valley Library Consortium
Open Mon-Thurs 10-9, Fri 10-6, Sat 10-5, Sun 1-5
Friends of the Library Group

M LAHEY HOSPITAL & MEDICAL CENTER, Cattell Memorial Library, 41 Mall Rd, 01805. SAN 320-5827. Tel: 781-744-2409. Web Site: lahey.tdnetdiscover.com. *Med Librn,* Carol Spencer; E-mail: carol.spencer@lahey.org; Staff 1 (MLS 1)
Founded 1965
Library Holdings: e-books 73; e-journals 550; Bk Titles 400; Bk Vols 5,000
Subject Interests: Med
Automation Activity & Vendor Info: (Discovery) TDNet; (Serials) Prenax, Inc
Wireless access
Function: For res purposes
Partic in Massachusetts Health Sciences Library Network; National Network of Libraries of Medicine Region 7
Open Mon-Fri 8:30-5
Restriction: Hospital staff & commun, Non-circulating to the pub

BUZZARDS BAY

S MASSACHUSETTS MARITIME ACADEMY*, ABS Information Commons, ABS IC-123, 101 Academy Dr, 02532. SAN 307-2878. Tel: 508-830-5308. FAX: 508-830-5074. E-mail: library@maritime.edu. Web Site: www.maritime.edu/library. *Dir, Libr Serv,* Susan S Berteaux; Tel: 508-830-5035, E-mail: sberteaux@maritime.edu; Staff 4 (MLS 2, Non-MLS 2)
Founded 1970. Enrl 1,200; Highest Degree: Master
Library Holdings: e-books 120,000; e-journals 51,000; Bk Vols 44,000; Per Subs 48
Subject Interests: Emergency response, Law, Maritime studies, Nautical hist, Ocean engr, Oceanography
Automation Activity & Vendor Info: (Acquisitions) SirsiDynix; (Cataloging) SirsiDynix; (Circulation) SirsiDynix; (Course Reserve) SirsiDynix; (Discovery) SerialsSolutions; (OPAC) SirsiDynix; (Serials) SerialsSolutions
Wireless access
Function: Archival coll, Art exhibits, Wheelchair accessible
Publications: Annual Report; What's New (Acquisition list)
Partic in LYRASIS; SAILS Library Network
Open Mon-Thurs 7:30am-10pm, Fri 7:30-4, Sat 10-4, Sun 2-10
Restriction: Borrowing privileges limited to fac & registered students, Borrowing requests are handled by ILL, Circ privileges for students & alumni only

BYFIELD

P NEWBURY TOWN LIBRARY*, Zero Lunt St, 01922-1232. SAN 307-5605. Tel: 978-465-0539. Web Site: newburylibrary.org. *Dir,* Jean Ackerly; E-mail: jackerly@newburylibrary.org; *Asst Dir,* Erin Eouimet; E-mail: eouimet@newburylibrary.org; *Circ Librn,* Jane Wolff; E-mail: jwolff@newburylibrary.org; *Youth Serv Librn,* Kati Bourque; E-mail: cbourque@newburylibrary.org; Staff 9 (MLS 1, Non-MLS 8)
Founded 1926. Pop 6,900; Circ 76,901
Library Holdings: AV Mats 1,737; Electronic Media & Resources 188; Bk Vols 44,030; Per Subs 89; Videos 2,854
Automation Activity & Vendor Info: (Cataloging) SirsiDynix; (Circulation) SirsiDynix; (OPAC) SirsiDynix
Wireless access
Partic in Merrimack Valley Library Consortium
Open Tues & Thurs 10-7, Wed & Fri 10-5, Sat 10-2
Friends of the Library Group

CAMBRIDGE

S CAMBRIDGE HISTORICAL COMMISSION ARCHIVE, 831 Massachusetts Ave, 2nd Flr, 02139. SAN 329-0905. Tel: 617-349-4683. TDD: 617-349-6112. E-mail: histcomm@cambridgema.gov. Web Site: www.cambridgema.gov/historic. *Exec Dir,* Charles M Sullivan; *Archivist,* Emily Gonzalez; E-mail: egonzalez@cambridgema.gov; Staff 3 (MLS 3)
Founded 1964
Library Holdings: Bk Titles 500
Special Collections: Building Permits Index, 1886-1937; Cambridge City Directories, 1848-1972; Cambridge Historical Commission Photo Coll; Cambridge Historical Society Proceedings; Cambridge Subway Construction, photos 1909-1912; Maps & Atlases, 1830-1997; Survey of Architectural History in Cambridge, inventory with photo of every Cambridge building 1965-present. Oral History
Subject Interests: Archit, Local hist, Photog
Wireless access
Special Services for the Deaf - TDD equip

Open Mon 4-7, Tues-Thurs 9:30-11:30 & 2-4
Restriction: Non-circulating

M CAMBRIDGE HOSPITAL-CAMBRIDGE HEALTH ALLIANCE*, Bor Medical Library, 1493 Cambridge St, 02139. SAN 372-6274. Tel: 617-665-1439. FAX: 617-665-1424. *Dir,* Trish Reid; E-mail: preid@challiance.org; Staff 2 (MLS 1, Non-MLS 1)
Library Holdings: Bk Titles 1,000; Bk Vols 1,200; Per Subs 40
Subject Interests: Med, Med humanities, Podiatry, Psychiat
Wireless access
Publications: Blog/Newsletter (Online only)
Mem of Massachusetts Library System
Partic in Massachusetts Health Sciences Library Network; Medical Library Association; Northeastern Consortium for Health Information
Friends of the Library Group

P CAMBRIDGE PUBLIC LIBRARY*, 449 Broadway, 02138. SAN 344-8053. Tel: 617-349-4041. Circulation Tel: 617-349-4040. Reference Tel: 617-349-4044. Administration Tel: 617-349-4032. FAX: 617-349-4028. Web Site: www.cambridgema.gov/cpl. *Dir of Libr,* Marie McCauley; *Dep Dir,* Joy Kim; *Asst Dir, Human Res,* Shira Gubb; *Bus Mgr, Fac Mgr,* William Courier; *Circ Mgr,* Rebecca Rowlands; *Mgr, Youth Serv,* Julie Roach. Subject Specialists: *Finance,* William Courier; Staff 97 (MLS 42, Non-MLS 55)
Pop 105,000; Circ 1,397,593
Library Holdings: AV Mats 18,539; DVDs 27,415; Bk Vols 298,758; Per Subs 1,387
Wireless access
Mem of Massachusetts Library System
Partic in Minuteman Library Network
Special Services for the Deaf - TTY equip
Special Services for the Blind - Bks on CD
Open Mon-Thurs 9-9, Fri & Sat 9-5, Sun (Oct-April) 1-5
Restriction: Circ limited
Friends of the Library Group

Branches: 6

BOUDREAU (OBSERVATORY HILL) BRANCH, 245 Concord Ave, 02138, SAN 344-8231. Tel: 617-349-4017. FAX: 617-349-4424. *Br Mgr,* Jennifer Costa; E-mail: jcosta@cambridgema.gov; Staff 2 (MLS 1, Non-MLS 1)
Circ 83,818
Library Holdings: AV Mats 3,011; Bk Vols 80,807
Open Mon, Wed & Fri 10-6, Tues 10-8
Friends of the Library Group

CENTRAL SQUARE BRANCH, 45 Pearl St, 02139, SAN 344-8118. Tel: 617-349-4010. FAX: 617-349-4418.
Circ 16,640
Library Holdings: AV Mats 4,450; Bk Vols 35,356
Open Mon, Wed & Fri 10-6, Tues & Thurs 10-9, Sat (Sept-June) 10-2
Friends of the Library Group

COLLINS BRANCH, 64 Aberdeen Ave, 02138, SAN 344-8177. Tel: 617-349-4021. FAX: 617-349-4423. *Br Mgr,* Jane Philbrick; E-mail: jphilbrick@cambridgema.gov; Staff 2 (MLS 1, Non-MLS 1)
Founded 1940
Library Holdings: AV Mats 2,076; Bk Vols 45,283
Open Mon, Tues & Fri 10-6, Thurs 1-8
Friends of the Library Group

O'CONNELL BRANCH, 48 Sixth St, 02141, SAN 344-8142. Tel: 617-349-4019. FAX: 617-349-4420. *Br Mgr,* Ingrid Nowak; E-mail: inowak@cambridgema.gov; Staff 2 (MLS 2)
Circ 63,584
Library Holdings: AV Mats 1,723; Bk Vols 12,840
Open Mon-Wed 10-8, Thurs & Fri 10-6
Friends of the Library Group

O'NEILL BRANCH, 70 Rindge Ave, 02140, SAN 344-8207. Tel: 617-349-4023. FAX: 617-349-4422. *Br Mgr,* Rebecca Sexton; E-mail: rsexton@cambridgema.gov; Staff 2 (MLS 2)
Circ 106,840
Library Holdings: AV Mats 2,624; Bk Vols 22,922
Open Mon & Wed 10-8, Thurs & Fri 10-6
Friends of the Library Group

VALENTE BRANCH, 826 Cambridge St, 02141, SAN 344-8088. Tel: 617-349-4015. FAX: 617-349-4416. ; Staff 2 (MLS 1, Non-MLS 1)
Circ 55,570
Library Holdings: AV Mats 2,447; Bk Vols 23,107
Friends of the Library Group

S CENTER FOR ASTROPHYSICS LIBRARY / HARVARD & SMITHSONIAN LIBRARY, John G Wolbach Library, 60 Garden St, MS-56, 02138. SAN 307-3122. Tel: 617-496-5769. E-mail: library@cfa.harvard.edu. Web Site: library.cfa.harvard.edu. *Head Librn,* Daina Bouquin; *Librn, Collaborative Pojects,* Nico Carver; *Coll Develop Librn,* Eric Brownell; *ILL, Ref Librn,* Maria McEachern; *Asst Head Librn,* Katie Frey; Staff 6 (MLS 4, Non-MLS 2)
Founded 1959
Library Holdings: Per Subs 850
Special Collections: Astronomical Institutes Coll: Early Observatory Publications from Around the World; Early Observatory Publications (Al Coll)
Subject Interests: Astronomy, Astrophysics, Space sci
Automation Activity & Vendor Info: (Cataloging) Ex Libris Group; (Circulation) Ex Libris Group; (OPAC) Ex Libris Group; (Serials) Ex Libris Group
Wireless access
Open Mon-Fri 9-5
Restriction: Open to others by appt, Open to students, fac & staff

S GRADIENT*, Information Resource Center, 20 University Ave, 02138. SAN 370-8764. Tel: 617-395-5000. FAX: 617-395-5001. Web Site: gradientcorp.com. *Mgr,* Marcia Olson; Tel: 617-395-5562, E-mail: molson@gradientcorp.com; Staff 5 (MLS 4, Non-MLS 1)
Founded 1986
Subject Interests: Environ sci, Risk assessment, Toxicology
Automation Activity & Vendor Info: (OPAC) Inmagic, Inc.
Restriction: Co libr, Employee & client use only, Not open to pub, Staff use only

C HARVARD LIBRARY*, Wadsworth House, 1341 Massachusetts Ave, 02138. SAN 344-8266. Tel: 617-495-3650. Circulation Tel: 617-495-2413. Interlibrary Loan Service Tel: 617-495-2972. Reference Tel: 617-495-2411. FAX: 617-495-0370. Circulation FAX: 617-496-3692. E-mail: Library_Admin@Harvard.edu. Web Site: library.harvard.edu. *Univ Librn,* Martha Whitehead; E-mail: martha_whitehead@harvard.edu
Founded 1638. Enrl 25,778; Fac 2,520; Highest Degree: Doctorate
Library Holdings: Bk Vols 15,943,078
Automation Activity & Vendor Info: (Acquisitions) Ex Libris Group; (Cataloging) Ex Libris Group; (Circulation) Ex Libris Group; (Serials) Ex Libris Group
Wireless access
Publications: Harvard Librarian; Harvard Library Bulletin; HUL Notes
Partic in Association of Research Libraries; Center for Research Libraries; Coun of Libr Info Resources; Digital Libr Fedn; NELLCO Law Library Consortium, Inc.; Northeast Research Libraries Consortium; OCLC Online Computer Library Center, Inc
Special Services for the Deaf - Bks on deafness & sign lang; Spec interest per
Friends of the Library Group

Departmental Libraries:

CR ANDOVER-HARVARD THEOLOGICAL LIBRARY, Divinity School, 45 Francis Ave, 02138, SAN 344-8622. Tel: 617-495-5788. Reference Tel: 617-496-2485. Administration Tel: 617-495-5770. FAX: 617-496-4111. Web Site: library.hds.harvard.edu. *Librn,* Douglas Gragg; E-mail: douglas_gragg@harvard.edu; *Head, Spec Coll,* Maureen Jennings; E-mail: mjennings@hds.harvard.edu; Staff 7 (MLS 7)
Founded 1816. Enrl 550; Fac 41; Highest Degree: Doctorate
Library Holdings: Bk Vols 485,000; Per Subs 2,000
Special Collections: Religion of Liberal Churches
Partic in OCLC Online Computer Library Center, Inc
Open Mon-Thurs 8:30am-10pm, Fri 8:30-6 Sat 10-6, Sun Noon-10

ARNOLD ARBORETUM HORTICULTURAL LIBRARY, 125 Arborway, Jamaica Plain, 02130, SAN 344-8657. Tel: 617-522-1086. FAX: 617-524-1418. E-mail: hortlib@arnarb.harvard.edu. Web Site: arboretum.harvard.edu/library. *Head of Libr & Archives,* Lisa E Pearson; E-mail: lpearson@oeb.harvrd.edu; *Libr Asst,* Larissa Elaine Glasser; E-mail: lglasser@oeb.harvard.edu; Staff 2.3 (MLS 2, Non-MLS 0.3)
Founded 1872
Library Holdings: Bk Vols 40,000
Subject Interests: Botany, Dendrology, Garden hist, Hort, Landscape design
Function: Archival coll, Computers for patron use, Internet access, Online cat, Photocopying/Printing, Ref & res, Ref serv available, Res libr, Scanner
Open Mon-Sat 10-4
Restriction: Circ limited

BAKER LIBRARY & SPECIAL COLLECTIONS, Harvard Business School, Bloomberg Ctr, Ten Soldiers Field Rd, Boston, 02163, SAN 344-8681. Tel: 617-495-6040. FAX: 617-496-6909. Web Site: www.library.hbs.edu. *Exec Dir,* Debra Wallace; E-mail: dwallace@hbs.edu; Staff 56 (MLS 27, Non-MLS 29)
Founded 1908. Enrl 1,994; Fac 217; Highest Degree: Doctorate
Library Holdings: Bk Vols 649,142; Per Subs 2,056
Special Collections: Adam Smith (Vanderblue Coll); Business & Economics from 1484 to 1850 (Kress Coll); Credit Reports from 1840's to 1880's (R G Dun & Co Coll); Harvard Business School Archives; Historical Corporate Reports; South Sea Bubble
Partic in Research Libraries Information Network
Publications: Baker Books (Online only); HBS Working Knowledge (Online only)
Open Mon-Fri 8am-Midnight, Sat & Sun Noon-Midnight

BELFER CENTER FOR SCIENCE & INTERNATIONAL AFFAIRS LIBRARY, John F Kennedy School of Government, Rm L-369, 79 John F Kennedy St, 02138, SAN 345-0600. Tel: 617-495-1408. FAX: 617-495-8963. E-mail: bcsia_library@ksg.harvard.edu. Web Site: www.belfercenter.org/about/overview/belfer-center-library.
Founded 1973
Library Holdings: Bk Vols 4,500; Per Subs 250
Subject Interests: Environ sci, Security
Publications: Aquisitions List
Restriction: Open by appt only

BIOCHEMICAL SCIENCES TUTORIAL LIBRARY, Seven Divinity Ave, 02138-2092, SAN 344-9947. Tel: 617-495-4106. FAX: 617-496-6148. E-mail: biochsci@mcb.harvard.edu.
Library Holdings: Bk Vols 946

GEORGE DAVID BIRKHOFF MATHEMATICAL LIBRARY, Science Ctr 337, One Oxford St, 02138, SAN 344-9971. Tel: 617-495-2171. FAX: 617-495-5132. Web Site: www.math.harvard.edu/library. *Head Librn,* Nancy Miller; E-mail: nancy@math.harvard.edu; Staff 1 (Non-MLS 1)
Library Holdings: Bk Vols 13,000; Per Subs 40
Open Mon-Fri 9-5
Restriction: Non-circulating

GODFREY LOWELL CABOT SCIENCE LIBRARY, Science Ctr, One Oxford St, 02138, SAN 344-8355. Tel: 617-495-5355. Reference E-mail: cablib@fas.harvard.edu. Web Site: library.harvard.edu/libraries/cabot. *Dir of Science & Engineering Services,* Amy S Van Epps; E-mail: amy_vanepps@harvard.edu; *Head, Coll Develop,* Michael Leach; E-mail: mrleach@fas.harvard.edu; *Chem & Biol Librn,* Tina Qin; E-mail: na_qin@harvard.edu; *Eng Librn,* Robyn Rosenberg; E-mail: robyn_rosenberg@harvard.edu
Library Holdings: Bk Vols 400,000
Special Collections: Applied Mathematics, Applied Physics, Bioengineering, Computer Science, Data Science, Decision & Control, (Gordon McKay Coll), mats; Atmospheric & Earth Sciences, Climatology, Geophysics, Meteorology & Oceanography, (Blue Hill Coll), mats; Chemistry & Biology Coll; Gardner Coll of New England Landscape, photogs; Physics Research Coll, mats
Open Mon-Thurs 9am-Midnight, Fri 9-6, Sat Noon-10, Sun 10am-Midnight

CENTER FOR HELLENIC STUDIES LIBRARY, 3100 Whitehaven St NW, Washington, 20008. Tel: 202-745-4414. Interlibrary Loan Service Tel: 202-745-4416. FAX: 202-797-1540. Web Site: chs.harvard.edu. *Acq & Ref, Librn, Ser Mgt,* Erika Bainbridge; E-mail: bainbrid@chs.harvard.edu; *Acq Librn, Ref Serv,* Temple Wright
Founded 1961
Library Holdings: Bk Vols 61,000; Per Subs 300
Subject Interests: Ancient Greek lang & lit, Archaeology, Classical art, Classical hist, Classical Latin lit, Classical philos, Hellenic civilization
Automation Activity & Vendor Info: (ILL) OCLC
Restriction: By permission only, Not open to pub

CHILD MEMORIAL & ENGLISH TUTORIAL LIBRARY, Widener Library, 3rd Flr, Harvard Yard, 02138, SAN 344-9556. Tel: 617-495-4681. Web Site: projects.iq.harvard.edu/childlibrary/library-information. *Library Contact,* Michael Allen; E-mail: michaelpatrickallen@g.harvard.edu
Library Holdings: Bk Vols 17,319
Open Mon-Thurs 9am-10pm, Fri 9-7, Sat 12-5, Sun 12-8
Restriction: Non-circulating

CM FRANCIS A COUNTWAY LIBRARY OF MEDICINE, Ten Shattuck St, Boston, 02115, SAN 344-8835. Tel: 617-432-2136. Web Site: www.countway.harvard.edu. *Chief Admin Officer, Dir,* Elaine Martin; E-mail: eleaine_martin@hms.harvard.edu; *Assoc Dir of Finance & Admin,* Alison Richardson; E-mail: alison_richarson@hms.harvard.edu; *Ref & Educ Librn,* Paul Bain, PhD; E-mail: paul_bain@hms.harvard.edu. Subject Specialists: *Educ,* Paul Bain, PhD; Staff 21 (MLS 14, Non-MLS 7)
Founded 1964
Library Holdings: DVDs 23; e-books 177; e-journals 2,247; Bk Titles 246,951; Bk Vols 694,701; Per Subs 2,428
Special Collections: Americana (before 1821), Emphasis on Items Bearing New England Imprints; Chinese & Japanese Medicine, 1650-1850; Dissertations, 1498-; English & Other Foreign Imprints before 1701; Incunabula of Medical Interest (William Norton Bullard Coll); Jewish Medicine (Solomon M Hymans Coll); Legal Medicine; Medical Medals (Horatio Robinson Storer Coll); Medieval & Renaissance Manuscripts of Medical Interest; Oliver Wendell Holmes Coll; Paintings of Boston Physicians; Physicians' Account Books & Case Books, 1729-1850; Spanish Imprints, including Mexico & South America before 1826
Subject Interests: Anatomy, Biochem, Biology, Cytology (study of cells), Dermatology, Genetics, Geriatrics & gerontology, Immunology, Microscopy, Molecular biol, Obstetrics & gynecology, Oncology, Pediatrics, Pharmacology, Physiology, Psychiat, Pub health, Radiology, Statistics
Open Mon-Thurs 8am-11pm, Fri 8-8, Sat Noon-7, Sun Noon-11
Friends of the Library Group

DAVIS CENTER FOR RUSSIAN & EURASIAN STUDIES FUNG LIBRARY, Knafel Bldg, Concourse Level, 1737 Cambridge St, 02138, SAN 344-9408. Tel: 617-496-8421. FAX: 617-496-0091. Web Site: library.harvard.edu/libraries/fung. *Librn,* Svetlana K Rukhelman; E-mail: srukhelman@fas.harvard.edu
Library Holdings: Bk Vols 20,000; Per Subs 115
Function: Archival coll, CD-ROM, Electronic databases & coll, ILL available, Orientations, Ref & res, VHS videos
Open Mon-Thurs 9-9, Fri 9-5, Sun 1-9

DUMBARTON OAKS LIBRARY & ARCHIVES, 1703 32nd St NW, Washington, 20007, SAN 344-886X. Tel: 202-339-6400, Ext 6968. FAX: 202-625-0279. E-mail: library@doaks.org. Web Site: www.doaks.org/research/library-archives. *Dir,* Daniel Boomhower; E-mail: boomhowerD@doaks.org; *Acq/Ser Librn,* Sarah Pomerantz; *ILL Librn,* Ingrid Gibson; *Head Cataloger,* Sandra Parker Provenzano; *Cataloger,* Kimball Clark; Staff 15 (MLS 11, Non-MLS 4)
Founded 1936
Library Holdings: Bk Vols 222,000; Per Subs 1,130
Subject Interests: Byzantine studies, Garden design, Garden hist, Landscape archit, Medieval studies, Pre-Columbian studies
Automation Activity & Vendor Info: (ILL) OCLC; (OPAC) Ex Libris Group
Restriction: By permission only, Not open to pub

FACULTY OF ARTS & SCIENCES OFFICE OF CAREER SERVICES LIBRARY, 54 Dunster St, 02138, SAN 345-0007. Tel: 617-495-2595. FAX: 617-495-3584. Web Site: www.ocs.fas.harvard.edu. *Dir,* Robin Mount; E-mail: rmount@fas.harvard.edu
Subject Interests: Career develop
Restriction: Not open to pub

FINE ARTS LIBRARY, Littauer Ctr, 1805 Cambridge St, 02138, SAN 344-838X. Tel: 617-495-3374. Reference Tel: 617-496-3592. FAX: 617-496-4889. E-mail: falibcirc@fas.harvard.edu. Web Site: library.harvard.edu/libraries/fine-arts. *Colls Librn, Research Librn,* Jessica Evans Brady; E-mail: jevansbrady@fas.harvard.edu; *Coll Develop Librn,* Jessica Aberle; E-mail: jessica_aberle@fas.harvard.edu; *Admin Coordr,* Naoe Suzuki; E-mail: naoe_suzuki@fas.harvard.edu
Library Holdings: Bk Vols 330,000
Open Mon-Thurs 9am-10pm, Fri 9-6, Sat 10-5, Sun1-6
Friends of the Library Group

FUNG LIBRARY, Knafel Bldg, Concourse Level, 1737 Cambridge St, 02138, SAN 345-0120. Tel: 617-495-5753. FAX: 617-495-9976. Web Site: library.harvard.edu/libraries/fung. *Head of Libr,* Hugh Truslow; E-mail: truslow@fas.harvard.edu
Library Holdings: Bk Vols 40,000; Per Subs 200
Subject Interests: Chinese lang, English (Lang)
Open Mon-Thurs 9-9, Fri 9-5, Sun 1-9
Restriction: Non-circulating

HAMILTON A R GIBB ISLAMIC SEMINAR LIBRARY, Widener Library, Rm Q, Harvard University, 02138, SAN 344-9580. Tel: 617-495-2437, 617-495-4310. FAX: 617-496-2902. *Head Librn,* Michael Hopper; E-mail: mhopper@fas.harvard.edu
Founded 1981
Library Holdings: Bk Vols 7,656
Open Mon-Thurs 9am-Midnight, Fri 9-7, Sat 9-5, Sun 12-8

GUTMAN LIBRARY-RESEARCH CENTER, Graduate School of Educ, Six Appian Way, 02138, SAN 344-9041. Tel: 617-495-3453. Administration Tel: 617-495-4225. FAX: 617-495-0540. Web Site: www.gse.harvard.edu/library. *Dir & Librn,* Alex Hodges; E-mail: alex_hodges@gse.harvard.edu; *Head, Pub Serv,* Marcella Flaherty; E-mail: marcella_flaherty@gse.harvard.edu; *Head, Res & Instruction,* Position Currently Open
Library Holdings: Bk Vols 202,000; Per Subs 1,300
Special Collections: Action for Children's Television Coll; Curriculum Materials; Early American Textbooks; Educational Software; Jeanne Chall Coll; Private School Catalogs; Public School Reports
Subject Interests: Educ
Partic in OCLC Online Computer Library Center, Inc; Proquest Dialog
Open Mon-Thurs 8am-11pm, Fri 8-7, Sat 9-7, Sun 12-9

HARVARD COLLEGE LIBRARY (HEADQUARTERS), Harry Elkins Widener Memorial Library, Rm 110, 02138. Tel: 617-495-2413. Reference Tel: 617-495-2425. Web Site: library.harvard.edu/libraries/widener. *Librn,* Steven Brzozowski; E-mail: steven_brzozowski@harvard.edu
Library Holdings: Bk Vols 10,000,000
Special Collections: Author Coll: Achebe, Alcott Family, Ariosto, Aristophanes, Bacon, Beerbohm, Blake, Bossuet, Byron, Caldecott, Camoes, Carlyle, Carman, Carroll, Cervantes, Chaucer, Coleridge, Walter Crane, Cruikshank, E E Cummings, Dante, Dickens, Emily Dickinson, Donne, Dryden, T S Eliot, Emerson, Erasmus, Faulkner, Fielding, Galsworthy, John Gay, Goethe, Hearn, Heine, Herbert, Hofmannsthal, Horace, Henry James, William James, Johnson, Kipling, T E Lawrence, Lear, Levi, Longfellow, Amy Lowell, Masefield, Melville, Milton, Moliere, Montaigne, Nabokov, Persius, Petrach, Alexander Pope, Rilke, Rousseau, Schiller, Shakespeare, Shelley, Robert E Sherwood, Soyinka, Steinbeck, Stevenson, Strindberg, Tasso, Thackeray, Trotsky, Updike,

Villard Family, Gilbert White, Thomas Wolfe; Farnsworth Recreational Reading Room Coll; Harry Elkins Widener Memorial Coll; John Keats & His Circle Coll; John Keats Coll; Printing & Graphic Arts Coll; The Science Fiction Coll; Theatre Coll; Theodore Roosevelt Coll; Winsor Memorial Map Room Coll; Woodberry Poetry Room Coll. UN Document Depository; US Document Depository

Subject Interests: Am hist, Arabic lang, Art, Canadiana, Cartography, Church hist, Dutch (Lang), Educ, European hist, Folklore, German (Lang), Hist, Hist of sci, Italian (Lang), Judaica (lit or hist of Jews), Latin (Lang), Lit, Local hist, Maps, Mormons, Music, New England, Numismatics, Persian (Lang), Photog, Portuguese (Lang), Quakers, Siam, Slavic hist & lit, Spanish (Lang), Typography, Yiddish (Lang)

Partic in OCLC Online Computer Library Center, Inc; Research Libraries Information Network

Friends of the Library Group

HARVARD FOREST LIBRARY, 324 N Main St, Petersham, 01366, SAN 344-9076. Tel: 978-724-3302, Ext 229. FAX: 978-724-3595. E-mail: hflib@fas.harvard.edu. Web Site: harvardforest.fas.harvard.edu/library. *Res Asst,* Elaine D Doughty; E-mail: doughty@fas.harvard.edu

Founded 1907

Library Holdings: Bk Vols 29,326

Subject Interests: Ecology, Forestry

Restriction: Non-circulating

CL HARVARD LAW SCHOOL LIBRARY, Langdell Hall, 1545 Massachusetts Ave, 02138, SAN 344-919X. Tel: 617-495-3416, 617-495-3455. Interlibrary Loan Service Tel: 617-495-3176. Administration Tel: 617-495-3170. FAX: 617-495-4449. Web Site: hls.harvard.edu/library. *Vice Dean, Libr & Info Res,* Jonathan Zittrain; E-mail: zittrain@law.harvard.edu; *Exec Dir,* Jocelyn Kennedy; E-mail: jokennedy@law.harvard.edu; *Assoc Dir, Coll, Assoc Dir, Libr Admin,* Kevin Garewal; E-mail: kgarewal@law.harvard.edu; Staff 50 (MLS 28, Non-MLS 22)

Founded 1817. Enrl 2,000; Fac 150; Highest Degree: Doctorate

Library Holdings: Bk Titles 723,096; Bk Vols 868,619; Per Subs 49,070

Special Collections: English Common Law (Dunn Coll); French Legal History (Violett Coll); International Law (Olivart Coll); Japanese Law (de Becker Coll)

Partic in LYRASIS; OCLC Online Computer Library Center, Inc

Open Mon-Thurs 8am-Midnight, Fri 8am-9pm, Sat 9-9, Sun 9am-Midnight

HARVARD-MIT DATA CENTER, CGIS Knafel Bldg, 1737 Cambridge St, 02138, SAN 345-0279. Tel: 617-495-4734. FAX: 617-496-5149. E-mail: help@iq.harvard.edu. Web Site: projects.iq.harvard.edu. *Dir,* Gary King; E-mail: king@harvard.edu

Open Mon-Fri 9-5

Restriction: Open to students, fac & staff

HARVARD-YENCHING LIBRARY, Two Divinity Ave, 02138, SAN 344-8444. Tel: 617-495-2756. FAX: 617-496-6008. E-mail: hylpub@fas.harvard.edu. Web Site: library.harvard.edu/libraries/yenching, projects.iq.harvard.edu/yenchinglib. *Head of Libr,* James Cheng; E-mail: jkcheng@fas.harvard.edu; *Pub Serv Librn,* Sharon Li-shiuan Yang; E-mail: yang8@fas.harvard.edu; *Librn,* Phan Thi Ngoc Chan; *Librn,* Mikyung Kang; *Librn,* Xiao-He Ma; *Librn,* Kuniko McVey; *Cat,* James K Lin. Subject Specialists: *Vietnamese,* Phan Thi Ngoc Chan; *Korean,* Mikyung Kang; *Chinese,* Xiao-He Ma; *Japanese,* Kuniko McVey

Library Holdings: Bk Vols 952,000; Per Subs 5,000

Subject Interests: Japanese (Lang), Tibetan (Lang), Vietnam

Publications: Harvard-Yenching Library Bibliographical Services; Harvard-Yenching Library Occasional Reference Notes

Open Mon-Thurs 9am-10pm, Fri 9-7, Sat 9-5, Sun 12-5

Friends of the Library Group

HISTORY DEPARTMENT LIBRARY, Robinson Hall, 35 Quincy St, 02138, SAN 345-0368. Tel: 617-495-2556. FAX: 617-496-3425. E-mail: history@fas.harvard.edu. Web Site: history.fas.harvard.edu. *Library Contact,* Mary McConnell

Library Holdings: Bk Vols 9,623; Per Subs 33

Open Mon-Fri 10-6

Restriction: Non-circulating

HISTORY OF SCIENCE LIBRARY - CABOT SCIENCE LIBRARY, Science Ctr, Rm 371, One Oxford St, 02138. Tel: 617-495-5355. FAX: 617-495-5324. Reference E-mail: hslib@lists.hcs.harvard.edu. Web Site: histsci.fas.harvard.edu/history-science-library. *Research Librn,* Fred Burchsted; E-mail: burchst@fas.harvard.edu

Founded 1973

Library Holdings: Bk Vols 24,312

HOUGHTON LIBRARY-RARE BOOKS & MANUSCRIPTS, Houghton Library, Harvard Yard, 02138. Tel: 617-495-2440. FAX: 617-495-1376. E-mail: houghton_library@harvard.edu. Web Site: library.harvard.edu/libraries/houghton. *Dir,* Thomas Hyry; E-mail: hyry@fas.harvard.edu; *Assoc Librn, Pub Serv,* Kate Donovan; E-mail: kate.donovan@fas.harvard.edu; *Assoc Librn, Tech Serv,* Susan Pyzinski; E-mail: pyzynski@fas.harvard.edu

Library Holdings: AV Mats 50,000; Bk Vols 600,000; Per Subs 200

Open Mon-Thurs 9-7, Fri & Sat 9-5

JOHN F KENNEDY SCHOOL OF GOVERNMENT LIBRARY, 79 John F Kennedy St, 02138, SAN 344-8924. Tel: 617-495-1300. Reference Tel: 617-495-1302. FAX: 617-495-1972. E-mail: library_research@hks.harvard.edu. Web Site: www.hks.harvard.edu/library. *Dir, Libr & Knowledge Serv,* Leslie Donnell; E-mail: leslie_donnell@hks.harvard.edu; *Assoc Dir,* Christina Sirois; E-mail: christina.sirois@hks.harvard.edu; *Mgr, User Serv,* Keely Wilczek; E-mail: keely_wilczek@hks.harvard.edu; Staff 5 (MLS 5)

Library Holdings: Bk Vols 60,000; Per Subs 1,500

Subject Interests: Govt, Nonprofit mgt, Pub policy

Open Mon-Thurs 8am-10:45pm, Fri 8-6, Sat 12-5, Sun Noon-10:45

LAMONT LIBRARY-UNDERGRADUATE, Harvard Yard, Harvard University, 02138. Tel: 617-495-2450. Circulation Tel: 617-495-2452. FAX: 617-496-3692. Reference E-mail: lamcirc@fas.harvard.edu. Web Site: library.harvard.edu/libraries/lamont. *Head Librn,* Martin Schreiner; E-mail: schrein@fas.harvard.edu

Library Holdings: Bk Vols 200,000

Friends of the Library Group

EDA KUHN LOEB MUSIC LIBRARY, Music Bldg, Three Oxford St, 02138. Tel: 617-495-2794. FAX: 617-496-4636. E-mail: muslib@fas.harvard.edu. Web Site: library.harvard.edu/libraries/loeb-music. *Librn,* Sarah Adams; E-mail: sjadams@fas.harvard.edu; *Access Serv Librn,* Andrew Wilson; *Coll Develop Librn,* Sandi-Jo Malmon; *Music Librn, Ref, Research Servs Librn,* Liz Berndt-Morris; Staff 20 (MLS 6, Non-MLS 14)

Founded 1956. Enrl 100; Fac 21; Highest Degree: Doctorate

Library Holdings: CDs 60,000; DVDs 1,900; e-journals 110; Electronic Media & Resources 30; Microforms 40,000; Music Scores 200,000; Bk Vols 90,000; Per Subs 1,000; Videos 700

Special Collections: Archive of World Music, sound rec; Isham Memorial Library

Subject Interests: Music

Automation Activity & Vendor Info: (ILL) OCLC; (OPAC) Ex Libris Group

Function: Audio & video playback equip for onsite use, Music CDs, Ref serv available

Special Services for the Deaf - ADA equip

Special Services for the Blind - Aids for in-house use

Open Mon-Thurs 9am-10pm, Fri 9-5, Sat 1-5, Sun 1-10

Restriction: Open to fac, students & qualified researchers

FRANCES LOEB LIBRARY, Harvard Graduate School of Design, 48 Quincy St, Gund Hall, 02138, SAN 344-922X. Tel: 617-495-9163. E-mail: circ_desk@gsd.harvard.edu. Web Site: www.gsd.harvard.edu/frances-loeb-library. *Dir,* Ann Whiteside; E-mail: awhiteside@gsd.harvard.edu; *Ref Librn, Spec Coll Archivist,* Ines Zalduendo; E-mail: izalduendo@gsd.harvard.edu; *Digital Initiatives Librn,* Alix Reiskind; E-mail: areiskind@gsd.harvard.edu; *Research Librn, Support Serv Librn,* Sarah Dickinson; E-mail: sdickenson@gsd.harvard.edu; *Mgr, Instrul Tech,* Kevin Lau; E-mail: klau@gsd.harvard.edu; Staff 7 (MLS 5, Non-MLS 2)

Founded 1900. Enrl 550; Fac 100; Highest Degree: Doctorate

Library Holdings: Bk Vols 282,000; Per Subs 1,650

Special Collections: Le Corbusier Coll; Papers of Charles Eliot II, Daniel Kiley, J C Olmsted, Josep L Luis Sert, Arthur Shurcliff, Hugh Stubbins

Subject Interests: Archit, Landscape archit, Urban planning

Open Mon-Thurs 9am-10pm, Fri 9-6, Sat 12-4, Sun 12-8

NIEMAN FOUNDATION-BILL KOVACH COLLECTION OF CONTEMPORARY JOURNALISM LIBRARY, One Francis Ave, 02138, SAN 345-0481. Tel: 617-495-2237. FAX: 617-495-8976. E-mail: niemanweb@harvard.edu. Web Site: www.nieman.harvard.edu, www.niemanwatchdog.org.

Library Holdings: AV Mats 1,000; Bk Vols 2,500; Per Subs 30

Special Collections: Financial Files of PM; Herman Obermeyer American Nazi Party Coll; Herman Obermeyer Rape & Sexual Assault Coll; Nieman Alumni Coll; Roland Steel Walter Lippmann Coll

Subject Interests: Journalism

Open Mon-Fri 10-4

MILMAN PARRY COLLECTION OF ORAL LITERATURE, Widener, Rm C, 02138. Tel: 617-496-2499. *Curator,* David Elmer; E-mail: delmer@fas.harvard.edu

Library Holdings: Bk Vols 1,200; Talking Bks 3,700

Restriction: Open by appt only

PHYSICS READING ROOM, 450 Jefferson Laboratory, 17 Oxford St, 02138, SAN 344-9343. Tel: 617-495-2878. FAX: 617-495-0416. E-mail: library@physics.harvard.edu. Web Site: www.physics.harvard.edu/library. *Librn,* Marina D Werbeloff; E-mail: werbeloff@fas.harvard.edu; Staff 2 (MLS 1, Non-MLS 1)

Founded 1931. Fac 63; Highest Degree: Doctorate

Library Holdings: Bk Vols 29,340

Restriction: Non-circulating, Open to students, fac & staff

ROBBINS LIBRARY OF PHILOSOPHY, Emerson Hall 211, Harvard University, Dept of Philosophy, 25 Quincy St, 02138, SAN 345-0570. Administration Tel: 617-495-2194. FAX: 617-495-2192. Web Site:

philosophy.fas.harvard.edu/robbins-library. *Librn,* Eric Johnson-DeBaufre; E-mail: ejohnsondebaufre@fas.harvard.edu; Staff 1 (MLS 1)
Founded 1905. Fac 30; Highest Degree: Doctorate
Library Holdings: Bk Vols 10,000; Per Subs 51
Special Collections: Kierkegaard Coll in Danish
Subject Interests: Aesthetics, Analytical philos, Ethics, Hist of philosophy, Logic, Philos of mind, Philos of sci, Pragmatism, Psychol
Function: For res purposes, Online ref, Orientations, Photocopying/Printing, Ref & res, Ref serv available, Telephone ref
Restriction: Non-circulating, Open to fac, students & qualified researchers, Open to pub for ref only

ARTHUR & ELIZABETH SCHLESINGER LIBRARY ON THE HISTORY OF WOMEN IN AMERICA, Three James St, 02138-3766. (Mail add: Ten Garden St, 02138), SAN 307-3106. Tel: 617-495-8647. FAX: 617-496-8340. Reference E-mail: slref@radcliffe.harvard.edu. Web Site: www.radcliffe.edu/schlesinger-library. *Exec Dir,* Marilyn Dunn; E-mail: mdunn@radcliffe.harvard.edu; *Dir,* Jane Kamensky; E-mail: kamensky@radcliffe.harvard.edu; *Head, Res Serv,* Ellen Shea; E-mail: ellen_shea@radcliffe.harvard.edu; *Curator,* Marylene Altieri; E-mail: maltieri@radcliffe.harvard.edu; *Lea Archivist,* Jennifer Gotwals; E-mail: jgotwals@radcliffe.harvard.edu; Staff 28 (MLS 15, Non-MLS 13)
Founded 1943
Library Holdings: Bk Vols 80,000; Per Subs 230; Videos 50
Special Collections: Culinary History; Women's Studies. Oral History
Subject Interests: Women's hist, Women's rights
Partic in OCLC Online Computer Library Center, Inc; Research Libraries Information Network
Publications: 40th Anniversary Report; A Bibliography for Culinary Historians; Annual Newsletters; Innocent Documents; New Viewpoints in Women's History: Working Papers from the Schlesinger Library 50th Anniversary Conference; The Black Women Oral History Project, A Guide to the Transcripts; Women of Courage Exhibition Catalogue
Open Mon-Sat 9-5
Restriction: Non-circulating to the pub
Friends of the Library Group

HERBERT WEIR SMYTH CLASSICAL LIBRARY, Widener, Rm E, 02138. Tel: 617-495-4027. FAX: 617-496-6720. *Librn,* Kathleen Coleman
Library Holdings: Bk Vols 8,000
Open Mon-Thurs 9am-10pm, Fri 9-7, Sat 9-5, Sun 12-8
Restriction: Non-circulating, Restricted access

SOCIAL SCIENCES PROGRAM, Lamont Library, Level B, Harvard University, 02138, SAN 344-8479. Tel: 617-495-2106. FAX: 617-496-5570. Web Site: socialstudies.fas.harvard.edu. *Environ Res Librn/Govt Info Serv Mgr,* George Clark; E-mail: clark5@fas.harvard.edu
Library Holdings: Bk Vols 427,707; Per Subs 894
Special Collections: Manpower & Industrial Relations
Open Mon-Thurs 10-8, Fri 10-6, Sat 12-5, Sun 12-8

STATISTICS LIBRARY, Science Ctr, Rm 300F, One Oxford St, 02138-2901. (Mail add: Science Ctr, Rm 703, One Oxford St, 02138), SAN 345-066X. Tel: 617-496-1402. FAX: 617-496-8057. Web Site: www.stat.harvard.edu.
Highest Degree: Doctorate
Library Holdings: Bk Vols 2,000; Per Subs 19; Spec Interest Per Sub 24
Open Mon-Fri 9-5
Restriction: Circ limited, In-house use for visitors, Internal circ only, Open to fac, students & qualified researchers

TOZZER LIBRARY, 21 Divinity Ave, 02138, SAN 344-8568. Tel: 617-495-1481, 617-495-2253. FAX: 617-496-2741. E-mail: tozcirc@fas.harvard.edu. Web Site: library.harvard.edu/libraries/tozzer. *Head Librn,* Susan Gilman; E-mail: sgilman@fas.harvard.edu; Staff 4 (MLS 4)
Library Holdings: Bk Vols 272,275; Per Subs 1,521
Subject Interests: Anthrop, Archaeology
Automation Activity & Vendor Info: (Course Reserve) Ex Libris Group; (ILL) Ex Libris Group; (OPAC) Ex Libris Group
Publications: Anthropological Literature (Online only)
Open Mon-Thurs 9-8, Fri 9-5, Sat & Sun 1-5

UKRAINIAN RESEARCH INSTITUTE REFERENCE LIBRARY, 34 Kirkland St, 02138, SAN 345-0724. Tel: 617-496-5891. Administration Tel: 617-495-4053. FAX: 617-495-8097. E-mail: huri@fas.harvard.edu. Web Site: www.huri.harvard.edu/library. *Archivist, Bibliographer,* Olha Aleksic; E-mail: oaleksic@fas.harvard.edu. Subject Specialists: *Ukraine,* Olha Aleksic; Staff 2 (MLS 1, Non-MLS 1)
Founded 1973
Library Holdings: Bk Vols 3,500; Per Subs 145
Special Collections: Archives of Ukrainian Cultural Institutions & Ukrainian Civic, Cultural & Political Figures
Subject Interests: Ukraine, Ukrainian diaspora
Function: Ref serv available
Open Mon-Fri 9-5

C LESLEY UNIVERSITY, Sherrill Library, South Campus, 89 Brattle St, 02138-2790. (Mail add: 29 Everett St, 02138-2790), SAN 307-3025. Tel: 617-349-8850. Interlibrary Loan Service Tel: 617-349-8845. Reference Tel: 617-349-8872. E-mail: library@lesley.edu. Web Site: research.lesley.edu/library. *Interim Dean of Libr,* Constance Vrattos; E-mail: constance.vrattos@lesley.edu; *Head of Moriarty Library,* Ms Micki Harrington; *Electronic Res Librn,* Alexis Dhembe; *Res & Instruction Librn,* Abigail Mancini; *Univ Archivist,* Position Currently Open; Staff 8 (MLS 4, Non-MLS 4)
Founded 1909. Highest Degree: Doctorate
Special Collections: Curriculum Materials; Educational Test
Subject Interests: Art, Educ, Feminism, Psychol, Spec educ, Therapy
Automation Activity & Vendor Info: (Acquisitions) Ex Libris Group; (Cataloging) Ex Libris Group; (Circulation) Ex Libris Group; (Course Reserve) Ex Libris Group; (Discovery) EBSCO Discovery Service; (ILL) OCLC ILLiad; (OPAC) Ex Libris Group; (Serials) Ex Libris Group
Wireless access
Partic in Fenway Library Consortium; Fenway Library Organization; LYRASIS; OCLC Online Computer Library Center, Inc

C LONGY SCHOOL OF MUSIC OF BARD COLLEGE*, Bakalar Music Library, 27 Garden St, 02138. SAN 324-2846. Tel: 617-876-0956, Ext 1762. Administration Tel: 617-876-0956, Ext 1778. FAX: 617-354-8841. Web Site: longy.edu/academics/library. *Libr Dir,* Roy Rudolph; E-mail: rrudolph@longy.edu; Staff 1 (MLS 1)
Founded 1915. Enrl 210; Fac 117; Highest Degree: Master
Library Holdings: CDs 9,747; DVDs 216; Electronic Media & Resources 5; Bk Titles 4,807; Bk Vols 5,378; Spec Interest Per Sub 32
Special Collections: Baroque Dance (Margaret Daniels-Girard Coll); Nadia Baulanger, E Power Biggs & other 20th Century Longy Faculty (Longy Archives Coll), correspondence, photogs
Subject Interests: Dance, Music
Automation Activity & Vendor Info: (Cataloging) OCLC Connexion; (Circulation) ByWater Solutions; (Course Reserve) ByWater Solutions; (Discovery) ByWater Solutions; (ILL) OCLC Connexion; (OPAC) ByWater Solutions
Wireless access
Mem of Massachusetts Library System
Open Mon-Thurs 9-9, Fri 9-5, Sat 1-5, Sun 1-9; Mon-Fri (Summer) 12-5
Restriction: Open to students, fac & staff, Use of others with permission of librn

C MASSACHUSETTS INSTITUTE OF TECHNOLOGY LIBRARIES*, Office of the Director, Bldg NE36-6101, 77 Massachusetts Ave, 02139-4307. SAN 345-0783. Tel: 617-253-5651, 617-253-5655. Interlibrary Loan Service Tel: 617-253-5668. Reference Tel: 617-324-2275. FAX: 617-253-8894. E-mail: diroff-lib@mit.edu. Web Site: libraries.mit.edu. *Dir of Libr,* Dr Chris Bourg; Tel: 617-253-5297, E-mail: cbourg@mit.edu; *Dep Dir,* Tracy Gabridge; Tel: 617-253-8971, E-mail: tag@mit.edu; *Dir of Develop,* Kaija Langley; Tel: 617-452-2123, E-mail: klangley@mit.edu; *Dir, Res,* Micah Altman; Tel: 617-324-8475, E-mail: escience@mit.edu; *Assoc Dir, Tech,* Heather Yager; Tel: 617-253-3839, E-mail: hyager@mit.edu; Staff 191 (MLS 96, Non-MLS 95)
Founded 1862. Enrl 9,998; Fac 974; Highest Degree: Doctorate
Library Holdings: AV Mats 31,546; Bk Vols 2,741,944; Per Subs 22,312
Special Collections: 19th Century Glass Manufacture in US (Gaffield Coll); Architecture & Planning, photostats, slides, pamphlets; Charles Bulfinch & Benjamin Latrobe Coll, drawings; Civil Engineering (Baldwin Coll); Early History of Aeronautics (Vail Coll); Early Works in Mathematics & Physics (Louis Derr Coll); Linguistics (Roman Jakobson Coll); Maps; Microscopy, 17th-19th Century (Melville Eastham Coll); Spectroscopy (Kayser Coll). Oral History; UN Document Depository; US Document Depository
Automation Activity & Vendor Info: (Acquisitions) Ex Libris Group
Wireless access
Publications: Bibliotech (Newsletter)
Partic in Association of Research Libraries; Boston Library Consortium, Inc; LYRASIS; Proquest Dialog; Research Libraries Information Network; SDC Search Serv

Departmental Libraries:

BARKER ENGINEERING, Bldg 10-500, 77 Massachusetts Ave, 02139-4307, SAN 345-0937. Tel: 617-253-0968. FAX: 617-258-5623. Web Site: libraries.mit.edu/barker. *Dep Dir,* Tracy Gabridge; Tel: 617-253-8971, E-mail: tag@mit.edu; *Access Serv Mgr,* Jeremiah Graves; Tel: 617-253-2208, E-mail: jgraves@mit.edu; Staff 15 (MLS 8, Non-MLS 7)
Subject Interests: Applied math, Bio engr, Civil, Computer sci, Energy, Engr electrical, Environ, Mechanical, Ocean, Transportation
Function: ILL available, Res libr

DEWEY LIBRARY FOR MANAGEMENT & SOCIAL SCIENCES, MIT Bldg, Rm E53-100, 30 Wadsworth St, 02139. (Mail add: 77 Massachusetts Ave, 02139), SAN 345-0872. Tel: 617-253-5676. FAX: 617-253-0642. Web Site: libraries.mit.edu/dewey. *Access Serv Mgr,* Gregory Padilla; Tel: 617-253-2722, E-mail: gpadilla@mit.edu
Founded 1938

Special Collections: Historical Corporate Financial Reports; Industrial Relation Historical Documents; OECD Publications; United Nations Historical Documents; World Bank Publications. UN Document Depository; US Document Depository
Subject Interests: Econ, Law, Mgt & finance, Polit sci, Psychol, Sociol
Function: Bus archives, ILL available, Res libr

DISTINCTIVE COLLECTIONS, Bldg 14N-118, Hayden Library, 160 Memorial Dr, 02139-4307. (Mail add: Bldg 14N-118, 77 Massachusetts Ave, 02139-4307), SAN 345-102X. Tel: 617-253-5690. FAX: 617-258-7305. E-mail: distinctivecollections@mit.edu. Web Site: libraries.mit.edu/distinctive-collections. *Head of Libr,* Emilie Hardman; Tel: 617-875-2317, E-mail: ehardman@mit.edu; *Archivist, Res Serv,* Nora Murphy; Tel: 617-253-8066; Staff 8 (MLS 7, Non-MLS 1)
Founded 1961. Highest Degree: Doctorate
Special Collections: Animal Magnetism, Chemistry, Electricity, Engineering & Other Branches of Science & Technology (Rare Book Coll); Books & Periodicals About or By MIT Alumni, Staff; MIT & Science & Technology in the 19th & 20th Centuries (Archival & Manuscript Colls). Oral History
Function: Archival coll
Restriction: Non-circulating, Open by appt only, Open to researchers by request

HAYDEN LIBRARY - HUMANITIES & SCIENCE, Bldg 14S-100, 77 Massachusetts Ave, 02139-4307, SAN 345-0996. Tel: 617-253-5683. Circulation Tel: 617-253-5671. FAX: 617-253-3109. Interlibrary Loan Service FAX: 617-253-1690. Web Site: libraries.mit.edu/hayden. ; Staff 28 (MLS 10, Non-MLS 18)
Highest Degree: Doctorate
Subject Interests: Anthrop, Archaeology, Educ, Foreign lang, Hist, Hist of sci & tech, Libr & info sci, Linguistics, Lit, Media studies, Philos, Psychol, Relig, Women's & men's studies
Function: ILL available, Res libr
Closed for renovations until fall of 2020

LEWIS MUSIC LIBRARY, Bldg 14E-109, 77 Massachusetts Ave, 02139-4307, SAN 345-1054. Tel: 617-253-5689. Interlibrary Loan Service Tel: 617-253-5668. Reference Tel: 617-253-5636. FAX: 617-253-3109. Interlibrary Loan Service FAX: 617-253-1690. Web Site: libraries.mit.edu/music. *Actg Music Librn,* Nina Davis-Mills; E-mail: ninadm@mit.edu
Special Collections: Music & Recordings of Composers Associated with MIT
Function: ILL available

ROTCH LIBRARY-ARCHITECTURE & PLANNING, Bldg 7-238, 77 Massachusetts Ave, 02139-4307, SAN 345-0848. Tel: 617-258-5592. FAX: 617-253-9331. Web Site: libraries.mit.edu/rotch.
Special Collections: Architecture; Art; Geographic Information Systems; Housing; Islamic Architecture; Real Estate; Regional Planning & Development; Urban Planning

S SCHLUMBERGER-DOLL RESEARCH CENTER*, One Hampshire St, 02139. SAN 302-3354. Tel: 617-768-2110. Web Site: www.slb.com/about/rd/research/sdr.aspx. *VPres,* Yi-Qiao P M Song; E-mail: ysong@slb.com
Founded 1947
Library Holdings: Bk Titles 30,000; Per Subs 75
Subject Interests: Geochemistry, Geophysics, Math, Nuclear sci, Petroleum, Physics
Automation Activity & Vendor Info: (Cataloging) SirsiDynix; (Circulation) SirsiDynix; (ILL) OCLC; (Serials) SirsiDynix
Wireless access
Partic in LYRASIS; OCLC Online Computer Library Center, Inc
Restriction: Staff use only

S TIBETAN BUDDHIST RESOURCE CENTER, INC*, 1430 Massachusetts Ave, 5th Flr, 02138. Tel: 617-354-7900. FAX: 617-354-7911. E-mail: info@tbrc.org. Web Site: tbrc.org. *Exec Dir,* Jeff Wallman; Staff 6 (MLS 1, Non-MLS 5)
Founded 1998
Library Holdings: Bk Vols 26,000; Spec Interest Per Sub 40
Special Collections: Tibetan Literature
Function: Ref serv available
Open Mon-Fri 9-5
Restriction: Access at librarian's discretion
Friends of the Library Group

G JOHN A VOLPE NATIONAL TRANSPORTATION SYSTEMS CENTER*, Technical Resource Center, Kendall Sq, 55 Broadway, 02142-1093. SAN 307-3149. Tel: 617-494-2117. E-mail: VolpeTechnicalResourceCenter@dot.gov. Web Site: www.volpe.dot.gov/library. *Dir,* Susan C Dresley; E-mail: susan.dresley@dot.gov; Staff 1 (MLS 1)
Founded 1970
Library Holdings: Bk Titles 16,000; Per Subs 25
Special Collections: Volpe Center Technical Reports
Automation Activity & Vendor Info: (Circulation) EOS International; (OPAC) EOS International; (Serials) EOS International
Wireless access
Partic in Federal Library & Information Network; OCLC Online Computer Library Center, Inc
Open Mon-Fri 8:30-4:30
Restriction: Open to pub by appt only

M WHITEHEAD INSTITUTE FOR BIOMEDICAL RESEARCH*, Elizabeth Augustus Whitehead Library, 455 Main St, 02142. SAN 377-9076. Tel: 617-258-5132. FAX: 617-324-0266. Web Site: web.wi.mit.edu/library/pub/index.html. *Librn, Mgr, Libr Serv,* David Richardson; E-mail: richardson@wi.mit.edu
Founded 1984
Library Holdings: Bk Titles 300; Per Subs 30
Wireless access
Partic in National Network of Libraries of Medicine Region 7
Open Mon-Fri 9-5

CANTON

S CANTON HISTORICAL SOCIETY LIBRARY*, 1400 Washington St, 02021. SAN 375-2615. Tel: 781-821-4546. E-mail: historical@canton.org. Web Site: www.cantonhistorical.org. *Pres,* Paul Mitcheroney; *Curator,* George T Comeau; E-mail: geocomeau@gmail.com; *Curator,* James Roache
Founded 1893
Library Holdings: Bk Vols 500
Restriction: Open by appt only

P CANTON PUBLIC LIBRARY*, 786 Washington St, 02021. SAN 307-3173. Tel: 781-821-5027. FAX: 781-821-5029. E-mail: caill@ocln.org. Web Site: library.canton.ma.us. *Dir,* Andrea Capone; E-mail: acapone@ocln.org; *Sr Librn,* Lisa Quinn; E-mail: lquinn@ocln.org; Staff 6 (MLS 6)
Founded 1902. Pop 21,306; Circ 230,136
Library Holdings: AV Mats 6,422; Electronic Media & Resources 388; Bk Vols 98,770; Per Subs 147
Special Collections: Municipal Document Depository
Subject Interests: Art & archit
Automation Activity & Vendor Info: (Cataloging) SirsiDynix; (Circulation) SirsiDynix; (OPAC) SirsiDynix
Wireless access
Function: Audio & video playback equip for onsite use, Homebound delivery serv, Prog for children & young adult, Wheelchair accessible
Partic in Old Colony Libr Network
Open Mon 1-9, Tues-Thurs 10-9, Fri & Sat 10-5:30
Friends of the Library Group

M PAPPAS REHABILITATION HOSPITAL FOR CHILDREN*, Dr Paul L Norton Medical Library, Three Randolph St, 02021. SAN 326-1085. Tel: 781-830-8441. FAX: 781-830-8498. *Vols Librn,* Position Currently Open
Library Holdings: Bk Titles 500
Partic in Southeastern Massachusetts Consortium of Health Science
Restriction: Non-circulating to the pub

CARLISLE

P GLEASON PUBLIC LIBRARY*, 22 Bedford Rd, 01741-1857. SAN 307-3181. Tel: 978-369-4898. E-mail: info@gleasonlibrary.org. Web Site: gleasonlibrary.org. *Dir,* Martha Feeney-Patten; E-mail: mpatten@gleasonlibrary.org
Founded 1872. Pop 5,245; Circ 103,525
Library Holdings: AV Mats 5,066; Bk Vols 42,847; Per Subs 187
Special Collections: Local History (Wilkins Coll)
Automation Activity & Vendor Info: (Cataloging) SirsiDynix-WorkFlows; (Circulation) SirsiDynix-WorkFlows; (OPAC) SirsiDynix-Enterprise
Wireless access
Function: Ref serv available
Mem of Massachusetts Library System
Partic in Merrimack Valley Library Consortium
Open Mon, Tues & Thurs 10-9, Wed 1-9, Fri 10-5, Sat 10-5 (10-1 Summer)
Friends of the Library Group

CARVER

P CARVER PUBLIC LIBRARY*, Two Meadowbrook Way, 02330. SAN 307-319X. Tel: 508-866-3415. FAX: 508-866-3416. Web Site: www.carverpl.org. *Dir,* Carole A Julius; E-mail: cjulius@carverpl.org; *Asst Dir,* Amy Sheperdson; E-mail: asheperd@sailsinc.org; *Ch Serv,* Melissa MacLeod; E-mail: mmacleod@sailsinc.org; Staff 10 (MLS 2, Non-MLS 8)
Founded 1895. Pop 11,500; Circ 80,000
Library Holdings: Large Print Bks 300; Bk Vols 54,000; Per Subs 100; Talking Bks 300
Special Collections: Local Genealogy

Automation Activity & Vendor Info: (Acquisitions) SirsiDynix; (Cataloging) SirsiDynix; (Circulation) SirsiDynix; (Course Reserve) SirsiDynix; (ILL) SirsiDynix; (Media Booking) SirsiDynix; (OPAC) SirsiDynix; (Serials) SirsiDynix
Partic in SAILS Library Network
Open Mon & Wed 10-6, Tues & Thurs 10-8, Fri & Sat 10-4
Friends of the Library Group

CENTERVILLE

P CENTERVILLE PUBLIC LIBRARY, 585 Main St, 02632. SAN 307-3203. Tel: 508-790-6220. FAX: 508-790-6218. E-mail: centervillelibrary@yahoo.com. Web Site: www.centervillelibrary.org. *Libr Dir,* Victoria Allard; E-mail: vallard@clamsnet.org; *Youth Serv Dir,* Megan McClelland; E-mail: mmcclelland@clamsnet.org
Circ 49,937
Library Holdings: Bk Vols 32,000; Per Subs 75
Special Collections: Walter Lippmann Coll, non-fiction bks
Automation Activity & Vendor Info: (Cataloging) Innovative Interfaces, Inc; (Circulation) Innovative Interfaces, Inc; (OPAC) Innovative Interfaces, Inc
Wireless access
Partic in Cape Libraries Automated Materials Sharing Network
Open Mon, Wed & Fri 9:30-5, Tues & Thurs 9:30-7, Sat 9:30-2
Friends of the Library Group

CHARLEMONT

P TYLER MEMORIAL LIBRARY, Town Hall, 157 Main St, 01339. (Mail add: PO Box 518, 01339-0518), SAN 307-3211. Tel: 413-339-4335. FAX: 413-339-0320. E-mail: library@charlemont-ma.us. Web Site: charlemont-ma.us/index.cfm?p=p.25. *Libr Dir,* Kim Gabert; Staff 1 (MLS 1)
Pop 1,250; Circ 12,274
Library Holdings: Bk Vols 9,700; Per Subs 12
Special Collections: Local History Coll
Wireless access
Mem of Massachusetts Library System
Partic in Central & Western Massachusetts Automated Resource Sharing
Open Tues 1-5, Thurs 3-7, Sat 10-2

CHARLESTOWN

C MGH INSTITUTE OF HEALTH PROFESSIONS LIBRARY, Charlestown Navy Yard, 38 Third Ave, 4th Flr, 02129. (Mail add: Charlestown Navy Yard, 36 First Ave, 02129). E-mail: librarian@mghihp.edu. Web Site: library.mghihp.edu. *Dir, Instrul Design, Libr Dir,* Jessica Bell; Tel: 617-643-5714, E-mail: jbell@mghihp.edu; *Asst Dir, Libr Serv,* Amanda Tarbet; Tel: 617-643-6085, E-mail: atarbet@mghihp.edu; *Ref Librn,* Lindsey Nichols; Staff 3 (MLS 3)
Founded 2007. Enrl 1,636; Fac 127; Highest Degree: Doctorate
Subject Interests: Commun health
Automation Activity & Vendor Info: (Cataloging) Koha; (Circulation) Koha; (Discovery) EBSCO Discovery Service; (OPAC) Koha
Restriction: Open to others by appt, Open to students, fac & staff

CHARLTON

P CHARLTON PUBLIC LIBRARY*, 40 Main St, 01507. SAN 307-322X. Tel: 508-248-0452. FAX: 508-248-0456. Web Site: www.charltonlibrary.org. *Dir,* Cheryl Hansen; E-mail: chansen@cwmars.org; *Asst Dir, Head, Youth Serv,* Molly Garlick; E-mail: mgarlick@cwmars.org; *Head, Tech Serv,* Kathryn Webber
Founded 1905. Pop 11,400; Circ 100,000
Library Holdings: Bk Vols 40,000; Per Subs 100
Automation Activity & Vendor Info: (Cataloging) Innovative Interfaces, Inc - Millennium; (Circulation) Innovative Interfaces, Inc - Millennium
Wireless access
Mem of Massachusetts Library System
Partic in Central & Western Massachusetts Automated Resource Sharing
Open Mon, Wed & Fri 9:30-5, Tues & Thurs 9:30-8, Sat (Winter) 9:30-3
Friends of the Library Group

CHATHAM

P ELDREDGE PUBLIC LIBRARY*, 564 Main St, 02633-2296. SAN 307-3238. Tel: 508-945-5170. FAX: 508-945-5173. Web Site: www.eldredgelibrary.org. *Dir,* Amy Andreasson; E-mail: amyandreasson@clamsnet.org; Staff 4 (MLS 3, Non-MLS 1)
Founded 1895. Pop 6,700; Circ 163,000
Library Holdings: Audiobooks 4,468; DVDs 3,902; e-books 562; Electronic Media & Resources 194; Microforms 123; Bk Titles 48,338; Per Subs 126
Special Collections: Genealogy (Edgar Francis Waterman Coll)
Wireless access
Mem of Massachusetts Library System
Partic in Cape Libraries Automated Materials Sharing Network
Special Services for the Deaf - Assistive tech
Special Services for the Blind - Closed circuit TV magnifier; Copier with enlargement capabilities; Home delivery serv; Large print bks; Lending of low vision aids; Playaways (bks on MP3); Recorded bks; Text reader; ZoomText magnification & reading software
Open Mon, Wed, Fri & Sat 10-5, Tues & Thurs 1-9
Friends of the Library Group

CHELMSFORD

P CHELMSFORD PUBLIC LIBRARY*, 25 Boston Rd, 01824. SAN 345-1208. Tel: 978-256-5521. Circulation Tel: 978-256-5521, Ext 1210. Reference Tel: 978-256-5521, Ext 1211. Administration Tel: 978-256-5521, Ext 1100. FAX: 978-256-8511. Web Site: www.chelmsfordlibrary.org. *Libr Dir,* Becky Herrmann; E-mail: bherrmann@chelmsfordlibrary.org; *Asst Libr Dir,* Maria Palacio; *Asst Dir, Support Serv,* Vickie Turcotte; *Head, Borrower Serv,* Sean Smith; *Head, Reader Serv,* Jessica FitzHanso; *Head, Ref,* Danny Lykansion; *Head, Youth Serv,* Sara Dempster; *Commun Relations Spec, Marketing Specialist,* Jeffrey Hartman. Subject Specialists: *Programs,* Jessica FitzHanso; Staff 19 (MLS 10, Non-MLS 9)
Founded 1894. Pop 32,383; Circ 380,313
Library Holdings: Bk Titles 111,244; Bk Vols 117,885; Per Subs 238
Subject Interests: Local hist
Automation Activity & Vendor Info: (Cataloging) Horizon; (Circulation) Horizon; (OPAC) Horizon
Wireless access
Publications: Handbook of Chelmsford Organizations; Library Lines (Newsletter); Poetry: Community Connections
Partic in Merrimack Valley Library Consortium
Open Mon-Thurs 9:30-9, Fri & Sat 9:30-5:30, Sun (Winter) 1-5
Friends of the Library Group
Branches: 1
MACKAY, 43 Newfield St, North Chelmsford, 01863-1799, SAN 345-1232. Tel: 978-251-3212. FAX: 978-251-8782. Web Site: www.chelmsfordlibrary.org/mackay/index.html. *Ch Serv,* Bonnie Rankin
Library Holdings: Bk Vols 30,000; Per Subs 60
Open Mon & Wed 10-8, Fri 10-5, Sat 10-3
Friends of the Library Group

CHELSEA

P CHELSEA PUBLIC LIBRARY*, 569 Broadway, 02150. SAN 307-3254. Tel: 617-466-4350. Administration Tel: 617-466-4355. FAX: 617-466-4359. E-mail: coclibrary@chelseama.gov. Web Site: www.chelseama.gov/public-library. *Dir,* Sarah Gay Jackson; *Ch,* Martha Boksenbaun; Staff 4 (MLS 1, Non-MLS 3)
Founded 1870. Pop 35,100; Circ 61,000
Library Holdings: AV Mats 6,000; Large Print Bks 1,000; Bk Titles 74,000; Bk Vols 75,000; Per Subs 75
Subject Interests: Local hist archives, Spanish
Automation Activity & Vendor Info: (Acquisitions) SirsiDynix; (Cataloging) SirsiDynix; (Circulation) SirsiDynix; (OPAC) SirsiDynix; (Serials) SirsiDynix
Wireless access
Partic in Metro Boston Libr Network
Open Mon-Thurs 9-8, Fri 9-5, Sat 10-1
Friends of the Library Group

G MASSACHUSETTS WATER RESOURCES AUTHORITY LIBRARY*, Two Griffin Way, 02150. SAN 371-7682. Tel: 617-305-5583, 617-305-5584. E-mail: mwralib@mwra.state.ma.us. Web Site: www.mwra.state.ma.us. *Librn,* Karen Graham; E-mail: karen.graham@mwra.com; Staff 3 (MLS 1, Non-MLS 2)
Founded 1986
Library Holdings: Bk Titles 4,000; Bk Vols 5,000; Per Subs 75
Special Collections: Massachusetts Water Resources Authority Publications; Water System Hist
Restriction: Open by appt only

CHESHIRE

P CHESHIRE PUBLIC LIBRARY*, 23 Depot St, 01225. (Mail add: PO Box 740, 01225-0740), SAN 307-3262. Tel: 413-743-4746. E-mail: cheshire@cwmars.org. Web Site: cheshirepubliclibrary.wordpress.com, www.cheshire-ma.net/library. *Dir,* Amy Emerson-Inhelder; Staff 1 (MLS 1)
Pop 3,418; Circ 15,000
Library Holdings: Bk Vols 7,000; Per Subs 30
Wireless access
Partic in Central & Western Massachusetts Automated Resource Sharing
Open Mon 9-3, Tues 11-2 & 5-8, Thurs 3:30-6:30

CHESTER

P HAMILTON MEMORIAL LIBRARY*, 195 Rte 20, 01011. (Mail add: 15 Middlefield Rd, 01011), SAN 307-3270. Tel: 413-354-7808. E-mail: chesterlibrary@gmail.com. Web Site: townofchester.net/library. *Libra,* Hollie Jacob
Pop 1,337; Circ 5,269
Library Holdings: Bk Vols 6,000; Per Subs 22
Wireless access
Open Mon, Wed & Fri (Summer) 1-7 (12-6 Winter)
Friends of the Library Group

CHESTERFIELD

P CHESTERFIELD PUBLIC LIBRARY*, 408 Main Rd, 01012-9708. (Mail add: PO Box 305, 01012-0305), SAN 307-3289. Tel: 413-296-4735. E-mail: chesterfieldpubliclibrary@gmail.com. Web Site: www.townofchesterfieldma.com/library. *Dir,* Cynthia Squier-Klein
Pop 1,138; Circ 9,757
Library Holdings: Bk Vols 6,154; Per Subs 20
Special Collections: Hampshire County & Chesterfield
Subject Interests: Local hist
Wireless access
Partic in Central & Western Massachusetts Automated Resource Sharing
Open Mon 2-7, Wed 10-4, Sat 9-1
Friends of the Library Group

CHESTNUT HILL

C BOSTON COLLEGE LIBRARIES, 140 Commonwealth Ave, 02467. SAN 345-1267. Circulation Tel: 617-552-8038. Interlibrary Loan Service Tel: 617-552-3209. Reference Tel: 617-552-4472. Administration Tel: 617-552-4470. Interlibrary Loan Service FAX: 617-552-2600. Administration FAX: 617-552-0599. Web Site: library.bc.edu. *Univ Librn,* Thomas Wall; E-mail: thomas.wall.2@bc.edu; *Assoc Dir, Human Resources & Admin Servs,* Lyn Goode; Tel: 617-552-0160, E-mail: marilyn.goode@bc.edu; *Burns Librn & Assoc Univ Librn, Spec Coll,* Christian Dupont; Tel: 617-552-0105, E-mail: christian.dupont@bc.edu; *Assoc Univ Librn, Digital Initiatives & Serv,* Kimberly Kowal; Tel: 617-552-0841, E-mail: kimberly.kowal@bc.edu; *Assoc Univ Librn, Pub Serv,* Scott Britton; Tel: 617-552-3155, E-mail: scott.britton@bc.edu; *Assoc Univ Librn, Systems & Technology,* Emily Singley; Tel: 617-552-2918, E-mail: emily.singley@bc.edu; *Fiscal & Administrative Specialist,* Shatoya Gay; Tel: 617-552-4470, E-mail: shatoya.gay@bc.edu; Staff 141 (MLS 72, Non-MLS 69)
Founded 1863. Enrl 13,214; Fac 814; Highest Degree: Doctorate
Jun 2015-May 2016. Mats Exp $11,697,021. Sal $9,563,101 (Prof $5,949,244)
Library Holdings: e-books 494,112; Bk Titles 2,191,660; Bk Vols 3,072,624
Special Collections: Balkan Studies; Bookbuilders of Boston Archives, 1938-; Boston History; British Catholic Authors; Caribbeana; Catholic Liturgy & Life in America, 1925-1975; Eire Society of Boston Archives; Flann O'Brien Papers; Francis Thomson Coll, 1859-1907; Gilbert Keith Chesterton Coll, 1874-1936; Graham Greene Library & Archive; Hillaire Belloc Coll & Archives; Irish Coll; Irish Music Center; Jane Jacobs Coll; Jesuitica Coll, 1540-1773; Rex Stout Coll & Archives; S J Papers; Samuel Beckett Coll; Seamus Heaney Coll; The Honorable Margaret Heckler Papers; The Reverend Robert F Drinan; Theodore Dreiser Coll; Thomas Merton Coll; William Butler Yeats Coll. US Document Depository
Automation Activity & Vendor Info: (Acquisitions) Ex Libris Group; (Cataloging) Ex Libris Group; (Circulation) Ex Libris Group; (Course Reserve) Ex Libris Group; (ILL) OCLC ILLiad; (OPAC) Ex Libris Group; (Serials) Ex Libris Group
Wireless access
Partic in Boston Library Consortium, Inc; Greater NE Regional Med Libr Program; Northeast Research Libraries Consortium; OCLC Research Library Partnership

Departmental Libraries:

BAPST LIBRARY, 140 Commonwealth Ave, 02467-3810, SAN 323-5297. Tel: 617-552-3200. E-mail: bapst@bc.edu. Web Site: libguides.bc.edu/bapst.
Open Mon-Thurs 8am-Midnight, Fri 8-5, Sat 10-6, Sun 11am-Midnight

JOHN J BURNS LIBRARY OF RARE BOOKS & SPECIAL COLLECTIONS, 140 Commonwealth Ave, 02467. Tel: 617-552-3282. Circulation Tel: 617-552-4861. FAX: 617-552-2465. Web Site: libguides.bc.edu/burns. *Burns Librn & Assoc Univ Librn, Spec Coll,* Christian Dupont; Tel: 617-552-0105, E-mail: christian.dupont@bc.edu; *Head Archivist,* Amy Braitsch; Tel: 617-552-3249, E-mail: amy.braitsch@bc.edu
Special Collections: Balkan Coll; British Catholic Authors Coll; Burns & Oates Coll; Congregationalism (1629-1829); Congressional Archives (Edward P Boland, Robert F Drinan, Margaret Heckler, Thomas P O'Neill Jr); Coventry Kersy Dighton Patmore (1823-1896); David Jones (1895-1973); DeFacto School Segregation; Detective Fiction Coll; Eire Society of Boston; Ethnology; Evelyn Waugh (1903-1966); Fallon Funeral Home; Fatherless Children of France (WW I); Fine Print Coll; Flann O'Brien Papers; Folklore, Jamaica & West Africa; Foulis Press; Freemasons; Golden Cockerel Press; Graham Greene (1904); Graham Greene Coll; Hibernia Bank; Hilaire Belloc Coll; Irish Authors; Irish Coll (Samuel Becket, William Butler Yeats, Seamus Heaney); Irish Land League; Irish Literature; Irish Music Center; Jamaica; Japanese Prints; Jesuitica Coll; John Henry Newman (1801-1890); Judaica; Liturgy & Life Coll; Nativism; Nero Wolfe Attractions; New England Theology; Nicholas M Williams Ethnological Coll; Nicholas M Williams Ethnological Coll; Nonesuch Press (London); Nursing; Oriole Press; Peppercannister Press; Playbills; Publishers & Publishing; Rare Books; Rita P Kelleher Nursing Coll; Salem Divines Coll; Samuel Beckett; St Dominic's Press; St Vincent DePaul Society; Stanbrook Abbey Press; Theater Programs; Thomas P O'Neill Jr Papers; Type Designers; Union Warren Savings Bank Archives; US Congressional Archives; Viola (Dallyn) Meynell (1886-1956); West Indies; William Butler Yeats (1865-1939); Women's History (Janet Wilson James Coll); World War I & II
Subject Interests: Nursing
Publications: Art of the Book (Collection catalog); Catalogue of Books, Manuscripts, etc in the Caribbeana Section of the Nicholas M Williams Memorial Ethnological Collection; Jesuitana at Boston College
Open Mon 1-5, Tues-Fri 9:30-5
Restriction: Non-circulating

EDUCATIONAL RESOURCE CENTER, 140 Commonwealth Ave, 02467, SAN 323-5319. Tel: 617-552-4920. FAX: 617-552-0599. E-mail: erc@bc.edu. Web Site: libguides.bc.edu/erc. *Head Librn,* Tiffeni Fontno; Tel: 617-552-1172, E-mail: fontno@bc.edu
Subject Interests: Educ K-12, Psychol
Open Mon-Thurs 9am-10pm, Fri 9-5, Sat 10-6, Sun Noon-8

CATHERINE B O'CONNOR LIBRARY, Weston Observatory, 381 Concord Rd, Weston, 02193-1340, SAN 307-7934. Tel: 617-552-8300. FAX: 617-552-8388. E-mail: weston.observatory@bc.edu. Web Site: libguides.bc.edu/oconnor. *Sr Res Librn,* Enid Karr; Tel: 617-552-4477, E-mail: enid.karr@bc.edu
Subject Interests: Geol, Geophysics
Function: Res libr
Restriction: Open to fac, students & qualified researchers, Open to pub by appt only

CR THOMAS P O'NEILL JR LIBRARY (MAIN LIBRARY), 140 Commonwealth Ave, 02467. Circulation Tel: 617-552-8038. Interlibrary Loan Service Tel: 617-552-3209. Reference Tel: 617-552-4472. Administration Tel: 617-552-4470. Interlibrary Loan Service FAX: 617-552-2600. Administration FAX: 617-552-0599. Web Site: libguides.bc.edu/oneill. *Head, Access Serv,* Position Currently Open; *Head, Coll,* Stephen Sturgeon; Tel: 617-552-4470; *Head, Continuing & E-Res,* Young Moon; Tel: 617-552-3207, E-mail: young.moon.2@bc.edu; *Head, Digital Production Servs,* Andrew Weidner; Tel: 617-552-0131, E-mail: andrew.weidner@bc.edu; *Head, Libr Syst & Applications,* Luke Gaudreau; Tel: 617-552-6361, E-mail: luke.gaudreau@bc.edu; *Head, Metadata Creation & Mgt, Special Colls Technical Head,* Amy Brown; Tel: 617-552-8124, E-mail: amy.brown.3@bc.edu; *Scholarly Communications Librn,* Elliott Hibbler; E-mail: elliott.hibbler@bc.edu; *ILL Mgr,* Anne Kenny; Tel: 617-552-6937, E-mail: ann.kenny@bc.edu

SOCIAL WORK LIBRARY, McGuinn Hall B38, 140 Commonwealth Ave, 02467-3810, SAN 345-147X. Tel: 617-552-3233. Circulation Tel: 617-552-0109. E-mail: swlib@bc.edu. Web Site: libguides.bc.edu/socialwork. *Head Librn,* Hannah Ha; Tel: 617-552-3234, E-mail: hannah.ha@bc.edu; *Ref & Instruction Librn,* Adam Williams; Tel: 617-552-0792, E-mail: adam.williams2@bc.edu; *Libr Supvr,* Abigail Heingartner; Tel: 617-552-3204, E-mail: heingara@bc.edu
Subject Interests: Child welfare, Geriatrics & gerontology
Open Mon-Thurs 8am-10pm, Fri 8-5, Sat 10-6, Sun 1-9

THEOLOGY & MINISTRY LIBRARY, 117 Lake St, Brighton, 02135. (Mail add: 140 Commonwealth Ave, 02467). Tel: 617-552-0549. Web Site: libguides.bc.edu/tml. *Head Librn,* Steve Dalton; Tel: 617-552-6541, E-mail: stephen.dalton@bc.edu

S LONGYEAR MUSEUM LIBRARY*, 1125 Boylston St, 02467. SAN 370-1506. Tel: 617-278-9000. Toll Free Tel: 800-277-8943. FAX: 617-278-9003. E-mail: research@longyear.org. Web Site: www.longyear.org/learn/research-materials. *Pres,* Sandra J Houston; E-mail: shouston@longyear.org
Library Holdings: Bk Vols 6,000
Special Collections: History of Christian Science 1821-1910; Life of Mary Baker Eddy & Her Early Followers, diaries, journals, letters, logbks, photog
Subject Interests: Christian sci
Wireless access
Open Mon & Thurs-Sat 10-4, Sun 1-4
Restriction: Non-circulating

C PINE MANOR COLLEGE*, Annenberg Library & Communications Center, 400 Heath St, 02467. SAN 307-3297. Tel: 617-731-7081. Web Site: www.pmc.edu/library. *Head, Ref, Libr Dir,* Sarah Woolf; Tel:

617-731-7083, E-mail: swoolf@pmc.edu; *Head, Access Serv,* Mackenzie Davidson; E-mail: mdavidson@pmc.edu; *Info Literacy Librn,* Erin Kelley; Tel: 617-731-7082, E-mail: ekelley@pmc.edu; Staff 8 (MLS 5, Non-MLS 3)
Founded 1911. Enrl 400; Fac 59; Highest Degree: Bachelor
Library Holdings: Bk Titles 55,967; Bk Vols 63,000; Per Subs 250
Special Collections: First Editions of Noted American Women Authors
Subject Interests: Educ, Psychol
Automation Activity & Vendor Info: (Acquisitions) SirsiDynix; (Cataloging) SirsiDynix; (Circulation) SirsiDynix; (Course Reserve) SirsiDynix; (OPAC) SirsiDynix; (Serials) SirsiDynix
Wireless access
Mem of Massachusetts Library System
Partic in LYRASIS; OCLC Online Computer Library Center, Inc; Webnet
Open Mon-Thurs 8am-9:45pm, Fri 8-5, Sun 1-5

CHICOPEE

P CHICOPEE PUBLIC LIBRARY, 449 Front St, 01013. SAN 345-150X. Tel: 413-594-1800. FAX: 413-594-1819. E-mail: cpl@chicopeepubliclibrary.org. Web Site: www.chicopeepubliclibrary.org. *Libr Dir,* Laura Bovee; E-mail: lbovee@cwmars.org; *Sr Ref Librn,* Carol Lynne Bagley; E-mail: cbagley@cwmars.org; *Acq Librn,* Maureen Geoffrey; E-mail: mgeoffro@cwmars.org; *Commun Serv Librn,* Anne Gancarz; E-mail: agancarz@cwmars.org; *Electronic Res Librn,* Brigitte Bisaillon; E-mail: bbisaillon@chicopeelibrary.org; *Syst Librn,* Diane Robillard; E-mail: drobilla@cwmars.org; *Youth Serv Coordr,* Erin Daly; E-mail: edaly@cwmars.org; *Cataloger,* Crystal Lanucha; E-mail: clanucha@cwmars.org; Staff 32 (MLS 12, Non-MLS 20)
Founded 1853. Pop 55,000; Circ 431,806
Jul 2015-Jun 2016 Income (Main & Associated Libraries) $1,642,339. Mats Exp $197,081. Sal $1,276,665
Library Holdings: AV Mats 13,168; Bk Vols 90,819; Per Subs 211
Subject Interests: Local hist, Polish (Lang)
Automation Activity & Vendor Info: (Acquisitions) Evergreen; (Cataloging) Evergreen; (Circulation) Evergreen; (OPAC) Evergreen; (Serials) Evergreen
Wireless access
Function: Activity rm, Adult bk club, After school storytime, Art exhibits, Audiobks via web, Bk club(s), Bks on CD, Children's prog, Computer training, Computers for patron use, Electronic databases & coll, Genealogy discussion group, Holiday prog, Home delivery & serv to seniorr ctr & nursing homes, ILL available, Internet access, Life-long learning prog for all ages, Magazines, Mango lang, Meeting rooms, Microfiche/film & reading machines, Movies, Museum passes, Music CDs, Online cat, Online ref, Outreach serv, OverDrive digital audio bks, Photocopying/Printing, Preschool reading prog, Prog for adults, Prog for children & young adult, Ref serv available, Senior outreach, Spanish lang bks, Story hour, Study rm, Summer & winter reading prog, Summer reading prog, Tax forms, Teen prog, Telephone ref, Wheelchair accessible
Partic in Central & Western Massachusetts Automated Resource Sharing
Open Mon-Thurs 9-8, Fri 9-5, Sat 9-4
Friends of the Library Group
Branches: 1
FAIRVIEW, 402 Britton St, 01020, SAN 345-1593. Tel: 413-533-8218. *Libr Dir,* Laura Bovee; Staff 2 (Non-MLS 2)
Founded 1910. Circ 19,552
Library Holdings: Bk Vols 8,659
Function: Computers for patron use, Wheelchair accessible
Open Mon, Wed & Fri 10-5, Tues 1-8, Thurs 4-8
Friends of the Library Group
Bookmobiles: 1

C COLLEGE OF OUR LADY OF THE ELMS*, Alumnae Library, 291 Springfield St, 01013-2839. SAN 307-3300. Tel: 413-265-2280. Reference Tel: 413-265-2297. FAX: 413-594-7418. E-mail: library@elms.edu. Web Site: www.elms.edu/library. *Archivist, Dir,* Anthony Fonseca; E-mail: fonsecaa@elms.edu; *Assoc Dir, Libr Systems & Tech,* Debra Gomes; *Head, Circ, ILL,* Holly Reynolds; E-mail: reynoldsh@elms.edu; *Head, Ref,* Michael Smith; E-mail: smithm@elms.edu; *Acq, Cat,* Lynn Gamble; E-mail: gamblel@elms.edu; Staff 7 (MLS 5, Non-MLS 2)
Founded 1928. Enrl 750; Highest Degree: Master
Library Holdings: AV Mats 8,324; Bk Vols 11,947; Per Subs 823
Special Collections: 18th Century Editions of English Authors; Ecclesiology, 16th & 17th Century Editions; Sir Walter Scott Coll, First Editions. US Document Depository
Subject Interests: Irish, Philos, Relig, Theatre
Automation Activity & Vendor Info: (Cataloging) Innovative Interfaces, Inc; (Circulation) Innovative Interfaces, Inc; (Course Reserve) Innovative Interfaces, Inc; (ILL) Innovative Interfaces, Inc; (OPAC) Innovative Interfaces, Inc; (Serials) Innovative Interfaces, Inc
Publications: Barry Collection Catalog; Serials Catalog
Partic in Cooperating Libraries of Greater Springfield
Open Mon-Thurs 8am-11pm, Fri 8-7, Sat 9-5, Sun Noon-11

CHILMARK

P CHILMARK FREE PUBLIC LIBRARY, 522 South Rd, 02535. (Mail add: PO Box 180, 02535-0180), SAN 307-3319. Tel: 508-645-3360. Administration Tel: 508-645-3360, Ext 103. FAX: 508-645-3737. E-mail: chil_mail@comcast.net. Web Site: www.chilmarkma.gov/chilmark-library. *Libr Dir,* Ebba Hierta; E-mail: ehierta@clamsnet.org; *Asst Dir, Youth Serv Librn,* Rizwan Malik; Staff 2 (Non-MLS 2)
Founded 1882. Pop 948
Library Holdings: AV Mats 7,607; Bk Vols 29,080; Per Subs 92
Special Collections: Brickner Poetry Corner; Martha's Vineyard Room
Automation Activity & Vendor Info: (Cataloging) Follett Software; (Circulation) Follett Software
Wireless access
Mem of Massachusetts Library System
Partic in Cape Libraries Automated Materials Sharing Network
Open Mon & Sat 10:30-5:30, Tues 9:30-12:30, Wed 11-7:30, Thurs 3:30-6:30
Friends of the Library Group

CLARKSBURG

P CLARKSBURG TOWN LIBRARY, 711 W Cross Rd, 01247. SAN 376-7124. Tel: 413-664-6050. FAX: 413-664-6384. E-mail: clarksburgtownlibrary@gmail.com, library@claksburgma.gov. Web Site: clarksburgma.us/library. *Dir,* Megan Peters; Staff 3 (MLS 1, Non-MLS 2)
Founded 1898. Pop 1,650; Circ 17,000
Library Holdings: AV Mats 2,000; Bk Titles 14,000; Per Subs 53; Talking Bks 92
Automation Activity & Vendor Info: (Cataloging) Innovative Interfaces, Inc; (Circulation) Innovative Interfaces, Inc; (OPAC) Innovative Interfaces, Inc
Wireless access
Partic in Central & Western Massachusetts Automated Resource Sharing
Open Mon, Thurs & Fri 9-2, Wed 3-7:30, Sat 9-Noon
Friends of the Library Group

CLINTON

P BIGELOW FREE PUBLIC LIBRARY*, 54 Walnut St, 01510. SAN 307-3335. Tel: 978-365-4160. FAX: 978-365-4161. E-mail: info@bigelowlibrary.org. Web Site: www.bigelowlibrary.org. *Dir,* Marie Letarte; E-mail: mmueller@cwmars.org; *Head, Adult Serv,* Melissa Fournier; E-mail: mfournier@cwmars.org; *Head, Youth Serv,* Deborah Maypother-Marini; E-mail: dmarini@cwmars.org
Founded 1873. Pop 13,640; Circ 43,256
Library Holdings: Bk Vols 63,536; Per Subs 30
Wireless access
Function: 24/7 Electronic res, 24/7 Online cat, Adult bk club, Art programs, Audiobks on Playaways & MP3, Audiobks via web, Bk club(s), Bks on CD, Children's prog, Computers for patron use, Doc delivery serv, Electronic databases & coll, Family literacy, Free DVD rentals, Health sci info serv, Holiday prog, Home delivery & serv to seniorr ctr & nursing homes, ILL available, Internet access, Life-long learning prog for all ages, Magazines, Mail & tel request accepted, Mango lang, Meeting rooms, Movies, Museum passes, Online cat, Outreach serv, Outside serv via phone, mail, e-mail & web, OverDrive digital audio bks, Photocopying/Printing, Preschool outreach, Prog for adults, Prog for children & young adult, Ref & res, Ref serv available, Scanner, Spanish lang bks, STEM programs, Story hour, Summer reading prog, Tax forms, Teen prog, Telephone ref, Wheelchair accessible, Workshops
Mem of Massachusetts Library System
Partic in Central & Western Massachusetts Automated Resource Sharing
Open Tues & Fri 9-6, Wed & Thurs 9-8, Sat 9-2
Friends of the Library Group

COHASSET

P PAUL PRATT MEMORIAL LIBRARY*, 35 Ripley Rd, 02025. SAN 307-3343. Tel: 781-383-1348. FAX: 781-383-1698. E-mail: library@cohassetlibrary.org. Web Site: www.cohassetlibrary.org. *Libr Dir,* Meaghan James; E-mail: mjames@ocln.org; *Head, Circ,* Kristin Norton; *Ch,* Sharon Moody; E-mail: smoody@ocln.org; *Ref Librn,* Gayle Walsh; E-mail: gwalsh@ocln.org; Staff 9 (MLS 3, Non-MLS 6)
Founded 1879. Pop 7,823; Circ 85,500
Library Holdings: Bk Vols 54,428; Per Subs 164
Automation Activity & Vendor Info: (Acquisitions) SirsiDynix; (Cataloging) SirsiDynix; (Circulation) SirsiDynix
Wireless access
Partic in Old Colony Libr Network
Open Mon-Thurs 10-8, Fri & Sat 10-5, Sun (Winter) 2-5
Friends of the Library Group

COLRAIN

P GRISWOLD MEMORIAL LIBRARY, 12 Main St, 01340. (Mail add: PO Box 33, 01340-0033), SAN 307-3351. Tel: 413-624-3619. E-mail: griswold@colrain-ma-gov. Web Site: colrain-ma.gov/p/27/Griswold-Memorial-Library. *Libr Dir,* Chelsea Jordan-Makely; *Asst Libr Dir,* Kate Barrows; Staff 2 (Non-MLS 2)
Founded 1908. Pop 1,650
Library Holdings: Large Print Bks 200; Bk Vols 9,000; Per Subs 15
Automation Activity & Vendor Info: (Cataloging) Evergreen; (Circulation) Evergreen; (ILL) Evergreen; (OPAC) Evergreen
Wireless access
Function: 24/7 Online cat, Adult bk club
Mem of Massachusetts Library System
Partic in Central & Western Massachusetts Automated Resource Sharing
Open Mon -Wed 10-8, Fri 10-5, Sat 10-3
Friends of the Library Group

CONCORD

S LOUISA MAY ALCOTT MEMORIAL ASSOCIATION LIBRARY, 399 Lexington Rd, 01742. (Mail add: PO Box 343, 01742-0343), SAN 371-1552. Tel: 978-369-4118. FAX: 978-369-1367. E-mail: info@louisamayalcott.org. Web Site: www.louisamayalcott.org. *Exec Dir,* Jan Turnquist; E-mail: jturnquist@louisamayalcott.org
Library Holdings: Bk Vols 550
Special Collections: The Alcott Coll
Function: Res libr
Restriction: Not open to pub, Open by appt only

P CONCORD FREE PUBLIC LIBRARY*, 129 Main St, 01742-2494. SAN 345-1658. Tel: 978-318-3300. Reference Tel: 978-318-3347. FAX: 978-318-3344. E-mail: concord@minlib.net. Web Site: www.concordlibrary.org. *Libr Dir,* Kerry Cronin; Tel: 978-318-3377, E-mail: kcronin@concordma.gov; *Asst Libr Dir,* Deborah Ervin; *Dir of Develop,* Susan Gladstone; *Head, Children's Servx, Head, Teen Serv,* Karen Ahearn; Tel: 978-318-3358, E-mail: KAhearn@minlib.net; *Head, Circ,* Robin Demas; Tel: 978-318-3363, E-mail: rdemas@minlib.net; *Head, Ref Serv,* Barbara Gugluizza; E-mail: bgugluizza@minlib.net; *Head, Tech Serv,* Caroline Nie; Tel: 978-318-3368, E-mail: cnie@minlib.net; *Ch, YA Librn,* Fayth Chamberland; *Curator, Spec Coll Librn,* Leslie Wilson; Tel: 978-318-3342, E-mail: LWilson@minlib.net; *Staff Librn,* Jane Misslin
Founded 1873. Pop 15,551; Circ 400,000
Library Holdings: AV Mats 16,462; Bks on Deafness & Sign Lang 30; Large Print Bks 3,331; Bk Titles 225,300; Bk Vols 232,395; Per Subs 570
Special Collections: Alcott Family; Concord History; Henry David Thoreau Coll; Nathaniel Hawthorne Coll; Ralph Waldo Emerson Coll. Oral History
Subject Interests: Am lit, Hist
Automation Activity & Vendor Info: (Acquisitions) Innovative Interfaces, Inc - Millennium; (Cataloging) Innovative Interfaces, Inc - Millennium; (Circulation) Innovative Interfaces, Inc - Millennium
Wireless access
Publications: Library eNewsletter (Monthly)
Partic in Minuteman Library Network
Special Services for the Deaf - TTY equip
Open Mon-Thurs 9-9, Fri 9-6, Sat 9-5, Sun (June) 1-5
Friends of the Library Group
Branches: 1
FOWLER MEMORIAL, 1322 Main St, 01742, SAN 345-1682. Tel: 978-318-3350. FAX: 978-318-0906. *Librn,* Sharon McCarrell; *Librn,* Pat Pluskal
Library Holdings: Bk Titles 30,000
Open Mon 9-7, Tues & Wed 9-6, Thurs 1-6, Fri & Sat 9-5; Mon (Summer) 9-7, Tues & Wed 9-6, Thurs 1-6, Fri 9-5

S CONCORD MUSEUM LIBRARY*, 53 Cambridge Tpk, 01742. (Mail add: PO Box 146, 01742-0146), SAN 373-1677. Tel: 978-369-9763. FAX: 978-369-9660. E-mail: cm1@concordmuseum.org. Web Site: www.concordmuseum.org. *Mkt & Pub Relations Dir,* Carol Thistle; *Curator,* David Wood
Library Holdings: Bk Vols 950; Per Subs 12
Special Collections: Concord History Coll
Subject Interests: Decorative art
Function: Res libr
Restriction: Open by appt only

M EMERSON HOSPITAL MEDICAL LIBRARY*, 133 Old Rd to Nine Acre Corner, 01742. SAN 307-3378. Tel: 978-287-3090. *Dir, Libr Serv,* Melinda Marchand; E-mail: mmarchand@emersonhosp.org
Library Holdings: e-books 30; e-journals 532; Bk Vols 700; Per Subs 150
Wireless access
Open Mon-Fri 8:30-4:30

S MASSACHUSETTS DEPARTMENT OF CORRECTIONS*, Institution Library at MCI-Concord, 965 Elm St, 01742. (Mail add: PO Box 9106, 01742-9106), SAN 307-3386. Tel: 978-369-3220, Ext 292. FAX: 978-405-6108. *Librn,* Joshua Tetreau
Library Holdings: Large Print Bks 300; Bk Vols 8,000; Per Subs 20
Special Collections: Spanish Coll
Subject Interests: Law
Automation Activity & Vendor Info: (Acquisitions) Follett Software; (Cataloging) Follett Software; (Circulation) Follett Software
Open Mon-Fri 9-4

A UNITED STATES ARMY*, Corps of Engineers New England District Library, 696 Virginia Rd, 01742-2751. SAN 345-7206. Tel: 978-318-8349. Interlibrary Loan Service Tel: 978-318-8349. FAX: 978-318-8693. E-mail: Library@usace.army.mil. Web Site: www.nae.usace.army.mil/Contact/Library. *Chief Librn,* Timothy Hays; E-mail: timothy.p.hays@usace.army.mil; Staff 1 (MLS 1)
Founded 1947
Oct 2014-Sept 2015 Income Federal $150,000. Mats Exp $150,000, Books $5,000, Per/Ser (Incl. Access Fees) $15,000, Presv $10,000
Library Holdings: CDs 1,000; e-books 3,000; e-journals 5,000; Microforms 5,000; Bk Titles 4,400; Bk Vols 4,500; Per Subs 10
Special Collections: New England District Documents
Subject Interests: Civil engr, Ecology, Natural sci, Real estate, Soil mechanics, Structural engr, Water res
Automation Activity & Vendor Info: (Acquisitions) OCLC Connexion; (Cataloging) OCLC FirstSearch; (ILL) OCLC FirstSearch; (OPAC) OCLC
Wireless access
Partic in OCLC Online Computer Library Center, Inc; Proquest Dialog
Open Mon-Fri 9-4:30

CONWAY

P FIELD MEMORIAL LIBRARY*, One Elm St, 01341. SAN 307-3394. Tel: 413-369-4646. *Dir,* Carol Jean Baldwin; E-mail: ConwayFMLDir@gmail.com; Staff 3 (MLS 1, Non-MLS 2)
Founded 1901. Pop 1,897; Circ 12,050
Library Holdings: Bk Vols 15,500; Per Subs 20
Wireless access
Mem of Massachusetts Library System
Partic in Central & Western Massachusetts Automated Resource Sharing
Open Mon 4-7, Wed 2-7, Sat 10-2
Friends of the Library Group

COTUIT

S CAHOON MUSEUM OF AMERICAN ART*, American Painting Research Library, 4676 Falmouth Rd, 02635. (Mail add: PO Box 1853, 02635-1853), SAN 375-8338. Tel: 508-428-7581. FAX: 508-420-3709. Web Site: www.cahoonmuseum.org. *Dir,* Sarah Johnson; E-mail: sjohnson@cahoonmuseum.org
Founded 1984
Library Holdings: Bk Titles 2,000
Function: Res libr
Open Tues-Sat 10-4
Restriction: Staff use only

P COTUIT LIBRARY*, 871 Main St, 02635. (Mail add: PO Box 648, 02635-0648), SAN 307-3408. Tel: 508-428-8141. FAX: 508-428-4636. E-mail: cotuitlibrarian@gmail.com, librarian@cotuitlibrary.org. Web Site: www.cotuitlibrary.org. *Dir,* Antonia Stephens; E-mail: astephens@clamsnet.org; *Youth Serv Librn,* Lisa Nagel; E-mail: lanagel@clamsnet.org; *Circ Supvr,* Melissa Cavill; *Cat,* Kathleen Pratt; Staff 8 (MLS 3, Non-MLS 5)
Founded 1874. Circ 56,365
Jul 2012-Jun 2013 Income $306,953, State $3,125, City $144,394, Locally Generated Income $159,434. Mats Exp $36,420, Books $29,171, Per/Ser (Incl. Access Fees) $2,717, Electronic Ref Mat (Incl. Access Fees) $4,532. Sal $144,005
Library Holdings: Bk Titles 48,322; Per Subs 90
Special Collections: Art Books; Classic Mysteries; Kirkman Coll of Fine Books
Automation Activity & Vendor Info: (Acquisitions) Innovative Interfaces, Inc; (Cataloging) Innovative Interfaces, Inc; (Circulation) Innovative Interfaces, Inc; (Course Reserve) Innovative Interfaces, Inc; (ILL) Innovative Interfaces, Inc; (Media Booking) Innovative Interfaces, Inc; (OPAC) Innovative Interfaces, Inc; (Serials) Innovative Interfaces, Inc
Wireless access
Mem of Massachusetts Library System
Partic in Cape Libraries Automated Materials Sharing Network
Special Services for the Blind - Assistive/Adapted tech devices, equip & products; Home delivery serv
Open Mon & Wed 1:30-8, Tues, Thurs & Fri 9:30-5, Sat 9:30-4
Friends of the Library Group

CUMMINGTON

P BRYANT FREE LIBRARY*, 455 Berkshire Trail, Rte 9, 01026-9610. SAN 307-3416. Tel: 413-634-0109. E-mail: cummingtonlibrary@gmail.com. Web Site: www.cummington-ma.gov/Boards.php?97. *Chair,* John Maruskin; *Librn,* Mark DeMaranville
Founded 1872. Pop 994; Circ 5,857
Library Holdings: Bk Vols 7,700; Per Subs 11
Open Mon & Wed 6-9, Sat 8:30-12:30

DALTON

P DALTON FREE PUBLIC LIBRARY, 462 Main St, 01226. SAN 307-3424. Tel: 413-684-6112. FAX: 413-684-4752. E-mail: dalton@cwmars.org. Web Site: www.daltonlibrary.org. *Libr Dir,* Robert DiFazio; *Asst Dir,* Kimberly Gwilt; Staff 1 (MLS 1)
Founded 1861. Pop 6,874; Circ 42,754. Sal $118,694 (Prof $54,518)
Library Holdings: Audiobooks 1,055; DVDs 1,831; e-books 7,573; Electronic Media & Resources 31; Microforms 18; Bk Titles 37,845; Per Subs 77
Special Collections: Dalton Education Plan
Subject Interests: Local hist
Automation Activity & Vendor Info: (Circulation) Evergreen; (ILL) Evergreen; (OPAC) Evergreen
Wireless access
Function: Adult bk club, Bks on CD, Computers for patron use, Distance learning, Electronic databases & coll, Museum passes, Online cat, OverDrive digital audio bks, Photocopying/Printing, Story hour, Summer reading prog, Tax forms, Wheelchair accessible
Mem of Massachusetts Library System
Partic in Central & Western Massachusetts Automated Resource Sharing
Special Services for the Deaf - Bks on deafness & sign lang
Special Services for the Blind - Bks on CD; Copier with enlargement capabilities; Large print bks; Playaways (bks on MP3); Recorded bks
Open Mon, Thurs & Fri 12-5, Tues 10-5, Wed 12-8
Friends of the Library Group

DANVERS

J NORTH SHORE COMMUNITY COLLEGE LIBRARY*, Danvers Campus Library, One Ferncroft Rd, Danvers Campus Library, 01923-4093. SAN 307-1154. Tel: 978-762-4000. Circulation Tel: 978-739-5526. Administration E-mail: libadmin@northshore.edu. Web Site: library.northshore.edu. *Dir, Libr & Learning Res,* Rex Krajewski; Tel: 978-462-5524, E-mail: rkrajews@northshore.edu; *Access Serv Librn,* Erin D'Agostino; Tel: 978-739-5523, E-mail: edagosti@northshore.edu; *Ref & Instruction Librn,* Sarah Tremblay; Tel: 978-739-5540, E-mail: strembla@northshore.edu; *Coordr, Libr Serv,* Christine Goodchild; Tel: 978-739-5532, E-mail: cgoodchi@northshore.edu; *Coordr, Tech Serv,* John Koza; Tel: 978-739-5413, E-mail: jkoza@northshore.edu; *Libr Asst,* Phanary Auk; Tel: 978-739-5426, E-mail: pauk@northshore.edu; *Libr Asst,* Jonathan Morales; Tel: 978-462-5443, E-mail: jmorales@northshore.edu; *Libr Asst,* Judith Schena; Tel: 978-739-5412, E-mail: jschena@northshore.edu; Staff 5 (MLS 5)
Highest Degree: Associate
Automation Activity & Vendor Info: (Acquisitions) ByWater Solutions; (Cataloging) ByWater Solutions; (Circulation) ByWater Solutions; (Course Reserve) ByWater Solutions; (Discovery) EBSCO Discovery Service; (OPAC) ByWater Solutions; (Serials) ByWater Solutions
Wireless access
Function: 24/7 Electronic res, 24/7 Online cat, Art exhibits, Computers for patron use, Distance learning, E-Reserves, Electronic databases & coll, ILL available, Internet access, Magazines, Magnifiers for reading, Online cat, Online ref, Photocopying/Printing, Ref & res, Ref serv available, Res assist avail, Scanner, Telephone ref, Wheelchair accessible
Mem of Massachusetts Library System
Partic in Fenway Library Consortium; Higher Educ Libr Info Network; Massachusetts Commonwealth Consortium of Libraries in Public Higher Education Institutions
Open Mon-Thurs 8-8, Fri 8-4
Restriction: Borrowing privileges limited to fac & registered students, In-house use for visitors

P PEABODY INSTITUTE LIBRARY*, 15 Sylvan St, 01923. SAN 345-1712. Tel: 978-774-0554. FAX: 978-762-0251. E-mail: dan@noblenet.org. Web Site: www.danverslibrary.org. *Dir,* Alex Lent; *Asst Dir,* Jennifer McGeorge; *Head, Circ Serv,* Drew Meger; *Head, Ref (Info Serv),* Jim Roirdan; *Head, Tech Serv,* Chris Amorosi; *Head, Youth Serv,* Michelle Deschene-Warren; *Archivist,* Richard Trask; Staff 4 (MLS 4)
Founded 1866. Pop 25,000; Circ 204,826
Library Holdings: AV Mats 8,966; Large Print Bks 1,674; Bk Vols 119,169; Per Subs 240
Special Collections: Anti Slavery (Parker Pillsbury Coll), bks, pamphlets; Danvers (Town Records Coll), ms; Witchcraft (Ellerton J Brehart Coll), bks, pamphlets, photog, ms
Automation Activity & Vendor Info: (Cataloging) Innovative Interfaces, Inc; (Circulation) Innovative Interfaces, Inc; (ILL) Innovative Interfaces, Inc
Wireless access
Partic in North of Boston Library Exchange, Inc
Open Mon-Thurs 9-9, Fri 12-5, Sat 9-5, Sun (Sept-May) 1-5
Friends of the Library Group

DARTMOUTH

P DARTMOUTH PUBLIC LIBRARIES*, Southworth Library, 732 Dartmouth St, 02748. SAN 345-5971. Tel: 508-999-0726. FAX: 508-992-9914. E-mail: southworth@sailsinc.org. Web Site: www.town.dartmouth.ma.us/library. *Dir of Libr,* Lynne Antunes; E-mail: lantunes@town.dartmouth.ma.us; *Ch,* Christie Phillips; E-mail: cphillips@sailsinc.org; *Ref Librn,* Sharani Robins; E-mail: srobins@sailsinc.org; *Ref Librn,* Brian Walsh; E-mail: bwalsh@sailsinc.org
Pop 32,000; Circ 246,903
Library Holdings: Bk Vols 118,339; Per Subs 200
Automation Activity & Vendor Info: (Acquisitions) SirsiDynix; (Cataloging) SirsiDynix; (Circulation) SirsiDynix; (OPAC) SirsiDynix; (Serials) SirsiDynix
Wireless access
Partic in SAILS Library Network
Open Mon-Thurs 9-8, Fri & Sat 9-5
Friends of the Library Group
Branches: 1
NORTH DARTMOUTH, 1383 Tucker Rd, 02747, SAN 345-6005. Tel: 508-999-0728. FAX: 508-999-0795. *Dir of Libr,* Lynne Antunes; Tel: 508-999-0726, E-mail: lantunes@town.dartmouth.ma.us
Jul 2018-Jun 2019 Income $1,285,200, State $50,000, City $1,235,200
Library Holdings: Bk Vols 24,000
Open Mon, Wed & Fri 5-8, Tues & Thurs 9-1, Sat 9-5

DEDHAM

S DEDHAM HISTORICAL SOCIETY, 612 High St, 02026. (Mail add: PO Box 215, 02027-0215), SAN 327-3482. Tel: 781-326-1385. E-mail: library@dedhamhistorical.org. Web Site: dedhamhistorical.org/research. *Dir,* Johanna McBrien; E-mail: Society@dedhamhistorical.org; *Archivist,* Kathryn Ostrofsky; E-mail: library@dedhamhistorical.org; Staff 2 (MLS 1, Non-MLS 1)
Founded 1859
Library Holdings: Bk Titles 20,000; Per Subs 5
Special Collections: Ames Family Coll; Church Records 1638-1890; Mann Family Coll; Original Dedham Grant Area Residents & Artifacts (incl Nathaniel Ames-father & son); Records of Firms & Associations
Subject Interests: Genealogy, Town hist
Wireless access
Restriction: Open by appt only

P DEDHAM PUBLIC LIBRARY*, 43 Church St, 02026. SAN 345-1771. Tel: 781-751-9284. Reference Tel: 781-751-9287. FAX: 781-751-9289. E-mail: Dedham@minlib.net. Web Site: www.dedham-ma.gov/departments/library, www.dedhamlibrary.com. *Dir,* Ryan Brennan; E-mail: rbrennan@minlib.net; Staff 6 (MLS 6)
Founded 1872. Pop 24,729; Circ 140,195
Library Holdings: AV Mats 6,648; CDs 9,590; DVDs 32,159; e-books 1,449; Bk Vols 88,477
Special Collections: Dedham Historical Coll
Subject Interests: Archit, Art, Bus & mgt, Hist, Soc sci & issues
Automation Activity & Vendor Info: (Acquisitions) Innovative Interfaces, Inc; (Cataloging) Innovative Interfaces, Inc; (Circulation) Innovative Interfaces, Inc; (ILL) Innovative Interfaces, Inc; (OPAC) Innovative Interfaces, Inc; (Serials) Innovative Interfaces, Inc
Wireless access
Function: Adult bk club, Bks on cassette, Bks on CD, Children's prog, Computers for patron use, Homebound delivery serv, ILL available, Internet access, Museum passes, Music CDs, Photocopying/Printing, Prog for children & young adult, Ref serv available, Summer reading prog, Tax forms, Telephone ref, VHS videos, Wheelchair accessible
Partic in Minuteman Library Network
Open Mon-Thurs 9:30-8:30, Fri 9-5
Friends of the Library Group
Branches: 1
ENDICOTT BRANCH, 257 Mount Vernon St, 02026, SAN 345-1801. Tel: 781-751-9178. *Br Supvr,* Lisa Stakutis; Staff 1 (MLS 1)
Founded 1970. Circ 47,282
Library Holdings: Bk Vols 22,000
Open Mon-Thurs 9:30-8:30, Fri 9-5
Friends of the Library Group

GL MASSACHUSETTS TRIAL COURT*, Norfolk Law Library, 649 High St, Ste 210, 02026-1831. SAN 307-3459. Tel: 781-329-1401, Ext 2. FAX: 781-329-1404. E-mail: norfolklawlibrary@hotmail.com. Web Site:

www.mass.gov/locations/norfolk-law-library. *Head Librn,* Carol Ewing; *Head Law Librn,* Agnes Leathe
Founded 1898
Library Holdings: Bk Vols 40,000
Special Collections: Legal Videos for Laypeople
Subject Interests: State law
Wireless access
Mem of Massachusetts Library System
Partic in NELLCO Law Library Consortium, Inc.
Open Mon-Fri 8:30-4:30
Restriction: Non-circulating coll
Friends of the Library Group

DEERFIELD

S HISTORIC DEERFIELD INC & POCUMTUCK VALLEY MEMORIAL, Six Memorial St, 01342-9736. (Mail add: PO Box 53, 01342-0053), SAN 371-6058. Tel: 413-775-7125. E-mail: library@historic-deerfield.org. Web Site: library.historic-deerfield.org, www.historic-deerfield.org/libraries. *Librn,* Jeanne Solensky; Tel: 413-775-7126, E-mail: jsolensky@historic-deerfield.org; *Assoc Librn,* Heather Harrington; E-mail: hharrington@historic-deerfield.org; Staff 2 (MLS 2)
Founded 1970
Library Holdings: CDs 10; Bk Titles 50,350; Per Subs 40; Videos 20
Special Collections: History & Application of Color (Stephen L Wolf Coll)
Subject Interests: Archit, Decorative art, Genealogy, Hist of color, Local hist, Mat culture
Automation Activity & Vendor Info: (Cataloging) Evergreen; (Circulation) Evergreen; (OPAC) Evergreen
Wireless access
Publications: Brochure; Research at Deerfield
Partic in OCLC Online Computer Library Center, Inc
Open Tues-Fri 9-12 & 1-5

DENNIS

P DENNIS MEMORIAL LIBRARY ASSOCIATION*, 1020 Old Bass River Rd, 02638. SAN 307-3475. Tel: 508-385-2255. E-mail: dennismemorial@gmail.com. Web Site: www.dennismemoriallibrary.org. *Dir,* Nancy Symington; E-mail: nsymington@clamsnet.org; *Cataloger, Ch,* Susan Parker; *Ref Librn,* Barbara Wells; *Libr Asst,* Alice Halvorsen
Founded 1924. Pop 14,000; Circ 60,000
Library Holdings: Large Print Bks 300; Bk Vols 15,000; Per Subs 27; Talking Bks 2,500; Videos 1,500
Automation Activity & Vendor Info: (Cataloging) Innovative Interfaces, Inc; (Circulation) Innovative Interfaces, Inc; (OPAC) Innovative Interfaces, Inc
Wireless access
Partic in Cape Libraries Automated Materials Sharing Network
Open Mon-Thurs 1-8, Fri & Sat 1-5

DENNISPORT

P DENNIS PUBLIC LIBRARY*, Five Hall St, 02639. Tel: 508-760-6219. FAX: 508-760-6101. E-mail: den_mail@clamsnet.org. *Dir,* Cindy Cullen; *Asst Dir, Ref Serv,* Nicole Kramer; *Ch Serv, Tech Serv,* Lisa Cunningham; Staff 7 (MLS 2, Non-MLS 5)
Wireless access
Partic in Cape Libraries Automated Materials Sharing Network
Open Tues-Thurs 10-8, Fri & Sat 10-2
Friends of the Library Group

DIGHTON

S DIGHTON HISTORICAL SOCIETY MUSEUM LIBRARY*, 1217 Williams St, 02715-1013. (Mail add: PO Box 655, 02715-0655), SAN 372-6738. Tel: 508-669-5514. E-mail: info@dightonhistoricalsociety.org. Web Site: dightonhistoricalsociety.org. *Pres,* Christine Pacheco
Founded 1962
Library Holdings: Bk Titles 100
Special Collections: Dighton Area Pictures & Scrapbooks; Indian Artifacts; Military & Children's Clothing; Old School Books

P DIGHTON PUBLIC LIBRARY*, 395 Main St, 02715. SAN 307-3483. Tel: 508-669-6421. FAX: 508-669-6963. E-mail: di@sailsinc.org. Web Site: www.dightonlibrary.org. *Dir,* Jocelyn Tavares; E-mail: jtavares@sailsinc.org; *Ch,* Lorie Van Hook; E-mail: landrews@sailsinc.org; *Tech Serv Librn,* Phyllis Haskell; E-mail: phaskell@sailsinc.org; Staff 4 (MLS 1, Non-MLS 3)
Founded 1894. Pop 7,030; Circ 35,000
Library Holdings: CDs 200; e-books 661; Bk Vols 22,200; Per Subs 62; Talking Bks 1,200; Videos 1,500
Special Collections: Births & Deaths; Town Documents
Automation Activity & Vendor Info: (Acquisitions) SirsiDynix; (Cataloging) SirsiDynix; (Circulation) SirsiDynix; (OPAC) SirsiDynix
Wireless access
Function: Audio & video playback equip for onsite use, AV serv, Doc delivery serv, Homebound delivery serv, ILL available, Internet access, Magnifiers for reading, Photocopying/Printing, Prog for adults, Prog for children & young adult, Ref serv available, Summer reading prog, Workshops
Publications: Friend's (Newsletter)
Mem of Massachusetts Library System
Partic in SAILS Library Network
Open Mon & Fri 10-4, Tues-Thurs 12-8, Sat (Sept-May) 10-2
Friends of the Library Group

DORCHESTER

M CARNEY HOSPITAL*, Colpoys Library, 2100 Dorchester Ave, 02124. SAN 307-3513. Tel: 617-296-4000, Ext 2050. FAX: 617-474-3861. Web Site: www.carneyhospital.org. *Librn,* Charles Severens; Staff 1 (MLS 1)
Founded 1953
Library Holdings: Bk Titles 2,300; Per Subs 125
Subject Interests: Med
Automation Activity & Vendor Info: (Serials) EBSCO Online
Function: Res libr
Partic in Massachusetts Health Sciences Library Network; North Atlantic Health Sciences Libraries, Inc
Restriction: Not open to pub

DOVER

P DOVER TOWN LIBRARY*, 56 Dedham St, 02030-2214. (Mail add: PO Box 669, 02030-0669), SAN 307-3521. Tel: 508-785-8113. FAX: 508-785-0138. Web Site: dovertownlibrary.org. *Dir,* Cheryl Abdullah; E-mail: cabdullah@doverma.org; *Head, Adult Serv,* James Westen; *Head, Children's Servx,* Nancy Tegeler; *Head, Circ,* Moira Mills; *Head, Tech Serv,* Joan Campbell; *YA Librn,* Lauren Berghman; Staff 11 (MLS 5, Non-MLS 6)
Founded 1894. Pop 5,797
Automation Activity & Vendor Info: (Cataloging) Innovative Interfaces, Inc; (Circulation) Innovative Interfaces, Inc
Wireless access
Function: 24/7 Electronic res, 24/7 Online cat, Adult bk club, Art exhibits, Audiobks via web, Bk club(s), Computer training, Computers for patron use, Instruction & testing, Mail loans to mem, Museum passes, OverDrive digital audio bks, Photocopying/Printing, Prog for adults, Prog for children & young adult, Senior computer classes, Story hour, Summer reading prog, Tax forms, Teen prog, Wheelchair accessible
Mem of Massachusetts Library System
Partic in Minuteman Library Network
Open Mon-Wed 10-8, Thurs & Fri 10-6, Sat 10-4
Friends of the Library Group

DRACUT

P MOSES GREELEY PARKER MEMORIAL LIBRARY*, 28 Arlington St, 01826. SAN 307-3548. Tel: 978-454-5474. FAX: 978-454-9120. Web Site: www.dracutlibrary.org. *Libr Dir,* Nanci Milone Hill; E-mail: nhill@dracutlibrary.org; *Libr Office Mgr,* Carole Hamlton; E-mail: chamilton@dracutlibrary.org; *Ch,* Joan Powers; E-mail: jpowers@dracutlibrary.org
Founded 1922. Pop 28,000; Circ 155,000
Library Holdings: Bk Vols 80,000; Per Subs 105
Subject Interests: Local hist
Automation Activity & Vendor Info: (Cataloging) Evergreen; (Circulation) Evergreen; (OPAC) Evergreen
Wireless access
Partic in Merrimack Valley Library Consortium
Open Mon & Wed 8:30-6:30, Tues, Thurs & Fri 8:30-4:30
Friends of the Library Group

DUDLEY

P PEARLE L CRAWFORD MEMORIAL LIBRARY*, 40 Schofield Ave, 01571. SAN 307-3556. Tel: 508-949-8021. FAX: 508-949-8026. E-mail: pearle@cwmars.org. Web Site: crawfordlibrary.org. *Dir,* Karen E Wall; *Ch,* Kathryn Dunton; Staff 6 (MLS 1, Non-MLS 5)
Founded 1897. Pop 10,057; Circ 82,150
Library Holdings: Bk Vols 21,000; Per Subs 16
Wireless access
Mem of Massachusetts Library System
Partic in Central & Western Massachusetts Automated Resource Sharing
Open Mon & Thurs 10-8, Tues, Wed & Fri 10-5
Friends of the Library Group

C NICHOLS COLLEGE*, Conant Library, 127 Center Rd, 01571. (Mail add: PO Box 5000, 01571-5000), SAN 307-3564. Tel: 508-213-2334. E-mail: circulation@nichols.edu. Web Site: www.nichols.edu/about/offices-and-services/conant-library. *Libr Dir,* Carrie

Grimshaw; E-mail: carrie.grimshaw@nichols.edu; *Patron Serv Librn,* Rosalba Onofrio; Tel: 508-213-2234, E-mail: rosalba.onofrio@nichols.edu; *Syst Instruction Librn,* Matthew Haggard; Tel: 508-213-2437, E-mail: matthew.haggard@nichols.edu; Staff 6 (MLS 2, Non-MLS 4)
Founded 1815. Enrl 877; Fac 53; Highest Degree: Master
Library Holdings: Bk Vols 43,495; Per Subs 211
Special Collections: History of Dudley, Webster & Nichols Academy
Subject Interests: Econ, Finance, Mgt
Automation Activity & Vendor Info: (Cataloging) Follett Software; (Circulation) Follett Software; (OPAC) Follett Software
Wireless access
Publications: Newsletter (Biannually)
Mem of Massachusetts Library System
Partic in LYRASIS; OCLC Online Computer Library Center, Inc
Open Mon-Thurs 7:30am-12:30am, Fri 7:30-7, Sat 10-6, Sun 10am-12:30am

DUNSTABLE

P DUNSTABLE FREE PUBLIC LIBRARY, 588 Main St, 01827. (Mail add: PO Box 219, 01827-0219), SAN 307-3572. Tel: 978-649-7830. FAX: 978-649-4215. Web Site: www.dunstable-ma.gov/dunstable-free-public-library. *Dir,* Mary Beth Pallis; E-mail: mpallis@dunstablepl.org; *Ch,* Karen Debreceni; E-mail: kdebreceni@dunstablepl.org
Pop 3,000; Circ 30,000
Library Holdings: Bk Vols 26,000; Per Subs 56
Automation Activity & Vendor Info: (Cataloging) SirsiDynix; (Circulation) SirsiDynix; (OPAC) SirsiDynix
Publications: Dunstable Village; Nason's History of Dunstable, Massachusetts
Partic in Merrimack Valley Library Consortium
Open Tues 3-8, Wed-Sat 10-2; Tues & Thurs 3-8, Fri & Sat 10-2 (Summer)
Friends of the Library Group

DUXBURY

S ART COMPLEX MUSEUM*, Carl A Weyerhaeuser Library, 189 Alden St, 02331. (Mail add: PO Box 2814, 02331-2814), SAN 325-318X. Tel: 781-934-6634, Ext 35. Administration Tel: 781-934-6634, Ext 10. Web Site: artcomplex.org/carl-a-weyerhaeuser-library. *Coll Curator,* Julia Courtney; E-mail: julia.courtney@artcomplex.org; Staff 1 (MLS 1)
Library Holdings: Bk Vols 6,000; Per Subs 15
Special Collections: American Art Coll; Asian Art (Japanese Prints & Pottery Coll); Prints; Shaker Furniture
Subject Interests: Art hist
Publications: Acquisition List; Museum Catalogues; Shaped with a Passion
Closed for renovation 2021-2023
Open Wed-Sun 1-4
Restriction: Non-circulating, Open to pub for ref only
Friends of the Library Group

P DUXBURY FREE LIBRARY*, 77 Alden St, 02332. SAN 307-3599. Tel: 781-934-2721. FAX: 781-934-0663. Web Site: www.town.duxbury.ma.us/duxbury-free-library. *Dir,* Denise Garvin; E-mail: dgarvin@ocln.org; *Head, Children's Servx,* Jessica Phillips; E-mail: jphillips@ocln.org; *Head, Circ,* Suzanne Gunnerson; E-mail: sgunnerson@ocln.org; *Head, Ref,* Larissa DuBois; E-mail: ldubois@ocln.org; Staff 19 (MLS 9, Non-MLS 10)
Founded 1889. Pop 14,248; Circ 235,680
Library Holdings: AV Mats 8,000; CDs 1,000; Bk Vols 105,581; Per Subs 250; Talking Bks 3,600; Videos 4,600
Subject Interests: Local hist
Automation Activity & Vendor Info: (Cataloging) SirsiDynix; (Circulation) SirsiDynix; (OPAC) SirsiDynix
Wireless access
Mem of Massachusetts Library System
Partic in Old Colony Libr Network
Open Mon 2-8, Tues-Thurs 10-8, Fri & Sat 10-5, Sun (Winter) 1-5
Friends of the Library Group

EAST BRIDGEWATER

P EAST BRIDGEWATER PUBLIC LIBRARY*, 32 Union St, 02333. SAN 307-3602. Tel: 508-378-1616. FAX: 508-378-1617. E-mail: ebpl@sailsinc.org. Web Site: eastbridgewaterlibrary.org. *Dir, Libr Serv,* Virginia Johnson; E-mail: vjohnson@sailsinc.org; *Tech Serv Librn,* Janice Allman; E-mail: jallman@sailsinc.org; *Children's Serv Supvr,* Anne Vantran; E-mail: avantran@sailsinc.org; Staff 13 (MLS 2, Non-MLS 11)
Pop 13,526; Circ 93,205
Library Holdings: CDs 1,398; DVDs 544; e-books 361; Electronic Media & Resources 142; Large Print Bks 673; Bk Vols 50,840; Per Subs 105; Talking Bks 1,106; Videos 1,992
Special Collections: F D Millet Archive
Subject Interests: Local hist
Automation Activity & Vendor Info: (Cataloging) SirsiDynix; (Circulation) SirsiDynix; (OPAC) SirsiDynix
Wireless access
Mem of Massachusetts Library System
Partic in SAILS Library Network
Special Services for the Blind - Scanner for conversion & translation of mats
Open Mon & Tues 9-8, Wed-Fri 9-5, Sat (Winter) 9-2
Friends of the Library Group

EAST BROOKFIELD

P EAST BROOKFIELD PUBLIC LIBRARY*, Memorial Town Complex, 122 Connie Mack Dr, 01515. SAN 307-3610. Tel: 508-867-7928. FAX: 508-867-4181. Web Site: eastbrookfieldlibrary.org. *Dir,* Wendy Payette; *Ch,* Louise Meyerdierks
Pop 2,000; Circ 18,343
Jul 2012-Jun 2013 Income $69,500. Mats Exp $14,000
Library Holdings: Audiobooks 375; CDs 100; DVDs 1,228; Large Print Bks 250; Bk Vols 16,347; Per Subs 18
Automation Activity & Vendor Info: (Acquisitions) Follett Software; (Cataloging) Follett Software; (Circulation) Follett Software
Wireless access
Function: ILL available
Mem of Massachusetts Library System
Partic in Central & Western Massachusetts Automated Resource Sharing
Open Mon 2-8, Tues & Thurs 9:30-12:30 & 1:30-5:30, Wed 1:30-5:30, Sat 9-1
Friends of the Library Group

EAST DENNIS

P JACOB SEARS MEMORIAL LIBRARY*, 23 Center St, 02641. (Mail add: PO Box 782, 02641-0782), SAN 307-3629. Tel: 508-385-8151. FAX: 508-385-8151. Web Site: www.jacobsearslibrary.org. *Dir,* Phillip Inman; Staff 1 (Non-MLS 1)
Founded 1896. Pop 4,000; Circ 27,000
Library Holdings: DVDs 3,000; Large Print Bks 1,500; Bk Vols 14,500
Subject Interests: Antiques, Hist, Natural sci
Automation Activity & Vendor Info: (Acquisitions) Innovative Interfaces, Inc; (Cataloging) Innovative Interfaces, Inc; (Circulation) Innovative Interfaces, Inc; (Course Reserve) Innovative Interfaces, Inc; (OPAC) Innovative Interfaces, Inc; (Serials) Innovative Interfaces, Inc
Wireless access
Partic in Cape Libraries Automated Materials Sharing Network
Open Mon-Sat 9-1
Friends of the Library Group

EAST DOUGLAS

P SIMON FAIRFIELD PUBLIC LIBRARY*, 290 Main St, 01516. (Mail add: PO Box 607, 01516-0607), SAN 307-3637. Tel: 508-476-2695. FAX: 508-476-2695. E-mail: douglasmapubliclibrary@gmail.com. Web Site: mysfpl.org. *Dir,* Justin Snook; E-mail: jsnook@cwmars.org; Staff 1 (Non-MLS 1)
Founded 1903. Pop 5,021; Circ 20,315
Library Holdings: Bk Titles 25,000; Per Subs 52
Special Collections: Douglas History Coll
Automation Activity & Vendor Info: (Cataloging) Follett Software; (Circulation) Follett Software
Wireless access
Mem of Massachusetts Library System
Partic in Central & Western Massachusetts Automated Resource Sharing
Open Mon 12-5, Tues & Thurs 12-8, Wed 10-5, Sat 9-1
Friends of the Library Group

EAST FREETOWN

P JAMES WHITE MEMORIAL LIBRARY*, Five Washburn Rd E, 02717-1220. SAN 307-3645. Tel: 508-763-5344. E-mail: library@freetownma.gov. Web Site: www.freetownma.gov/public-libraries. *Dir,* Dorothy L Stanley-Ballard; E-mail: dstanleyballard@sailsinc.org; *Sr Librn,* Nicole Davignon; *Libr Tech,* Brittany Normandin; Staff 4 (Non-MLS 4)
Circ 18,003
Library Holdings: Bk Vols 24,524; Per Subs 121
Subject Interests: Local hist
Automation Activity & Vendor Info: (Acquisitions) SirsiDynix; (Cataloging) SirsiDynix; (Circulation) SirsiDynix
Function: Doc delivery serv, Homebound delivery serv, ILL available, Photocopying/Printing, Prog for children & young adult, Ref serv available, Summer reading prog, Telephone ref, Wheelchair accessible
Partic in SAILS Library Network

Open Tues & Thurs 10-7, Fri 10-3, Sat 1-3
Friends of the Library Group
Branches: 1
G H HATHAWAY LIBRARY, Six N Main St, Assonet, 02702, SAN 307-4013. Tel: 508-644-2385. *Librn,* Nicole Davignon
Pop 8,600
Subject Interests: Local hist
Open Mon & Wed 3-7, Fri 1-5, Sat 10-12
Friends of the Library Group

EAST LONGMEADOW

P EAST LONGMEADOW PUBLIC LIBRARY, 60 Center Sq, 01028-2459. SAN 307-3653. Tel: 413-525-5400. Circulation Tel: 413-525-5400, Ext 1511. Information Services Tel: 413-525-5400, Ext 1508. FAX: 413-525-0344. Web Site: eastlongmeadowlibrary.org. *Dir,* Layla Johnston; E-mail: layla.johnston@eastlongmeadowma.gov; *Ch,* Michele Lemire; *Tech Serv,* Kristen Savaria; Staff 13 (MLS 3, Non-MLS 10)
Founded 1896. Pop 15,300; Circ 232,688
Library Holdings: Bk Vols 82,217; Per Subs 106
Automation Activity & Vendor Info: (Cataloging) Evergreen; (Circulation) Evergreen; (ILL) Evergreen; (OPAC) Evergreen
Wireless access
Function: Audiobks via web, Bks on cassette, Bks on CD, Children's prog, Computers for patron use, Electronic databases & coll, Free DVD rentals, Museum passes, Music CDs, Online cat, OverDrive digital audio bks, Photocopying/Printing, Prog for adults, Prog for children & young adult, Story hour, Summer reading prog, Tax forms, Teen prog, Wheelchair accessible
Partic in Central & Western Massachusetts Automated Resource Sharing
Open Mon-Wed 9:30-8, Thurs & Fri 9:30-5, Sat (Sept-May) 9:30-4
Friends of the Library Group

EAST SANDWICH

S ROBERT S SWAIN NATURAL HISTORY LIBRARY, Green Briar Nature Center, Six Discovery Hill Rd, 02537. SAN 329-7845. Tel: 508-888-6870. FAX: 508-888-1919. E-mail: info@thorntonburgess.org. Web Site: www.thorntonburgess.org.
Founded 1979
Library Holdings: Bk Vols 1,800; Per Subs 10
Subject Interests: Natural hist
Function: Archival coll
Special Services for the Deaf - Spec interest per
Open Tues-Sat 10-4 (Jan-March); Mon-Sat 10-4, Sun 1-4 (April-Dec)
Restriction: Circ limited
Friends of the Library Group

EASTHAM

P EASTHAM PUBLIC LIBRARY*, 190 Samoset Rd, 02642. SAN 307-3661. Tel: 508-240-5950. FAX: 508-240-0786. Web Site: www.easthamlibrary.org. *Dir,* Debra DeJonker-Berry; E-mail: ddejonkerberry@clamsnet.org; *Ad,* Karen MacDonald; E-mail: kmacdonald@clamsnet.org; *Youth Serv Librn,* Fran McLoughlin; E-mail: fmcloughlin@clamsnet.org; *Tech Serv,* Connie Wells; Staff 6 (MLS 3, Non-MLS 3)
Founded 1878. Pop 5,646; Circ 101,779
Jul 2014-Jun 2015 Income $327,115, State $5,182, City $304,233, Other $17,700. Mats Exp $69,100, Books $32,700, Per/Ser (Incl. Access Fees) $6,400, AV Mat $13,000, Electronic Ref Mat (Incl. Access Fees) $16,500, Presv $500. Sal $226,500
Library Holdings: Audiobooks 4,344; DVDs 3,671; Large Print Bks 1,300; Bk Vols 40,714; Per Subs 118
Special Collections: Cape Cod Coll. Oral History
Subject Interests: Genealogy, Local hist
Automation Activity & Vendor Info: (Acquisitions) Innovative Interfaces, Inc; (Cataloging) Innovative Interfaces, Inc; (Circulation) Innovative Interfaces, Inc; (ILL) Innovative Interfaces, Inc; (OPAC) Innovative Interfaces, Inc; (Serials) Innovative Interfaces, Inc
Wireless access
Function: Adult bk club, Art exhibits, Bks on CD, Children's prog, Computers for patron use, Digital talking bks, Free DVD rentals, ILL available, Magazines, Museum passes, Music CDs, Online cat, OverDrive digital audio bks, Photocopying/Printing, Preschool reading prog, Prog for adults, Prog for children & young adult, Scanner, Story hour, Summer reading prog, Tax forms, Wheelchair accessible
Publications: History of the Eastham Library
Mem of Massachusetts Library System
Partic in Cape Libraries Automated Materials Sharing Network
Open Tues & Thurs 10-8, Wed 10-6, Fri & Sat 10-4
Friends of the Library Group

EASTHAMPTON

P EMILY WILLISTON MEMORIAL LIBRARY*, Nine Park St, 01027. SAN 307-367X. Tel: 413-527-1031. FAX: 413-527-3765. Web Site: www.ewmlibrary.org. *Dir,* Nora Blake; E-mail: nblake@ewmlibrary.org; *Ad,* Stephanie Levine; E-mail: slevine@ewmlibrary.org; *Youth Serv Supvr,* Jonathan Schmidt; E-mail: jschmidt@ewmlibrary.org
Founded 1869. Pop 16,000; Circ 124,000
Library Holdings: Audiobooks 2,000; CDs 929; DVDs 2,056; Large Print Bks 586; Bk Vols 58,736; Per Subs 100; Videos 1,067
Special Collections: Local History (Museum Coll), area city & town directories, photog & print archives
Automation Activity & Vendor Info: (Cataloging) Innovative Interfaces, Inc; (Circulation) Innovative Interfaces, Inc; (OPAC) Innovative Interfaces, Inc
Wireless access
Partic in Central & Western Massachusetts Automated Resource Sharing
Open Mon 10-8, Tues & Wed 9-8, Thurs & Fri 9-6, Sat 9-1
Friends of the Library Group

EASTON

C STONEHILL COLLEGE*, MacPhaidin Library, 320 Washington St, 02357. SAN 307-5958. Tel: 508-565-1313. Interlibrary Loan Service Tel: 508-565-1538. E-mail: librarydeskgroup@stonehill.edu. Web Site: www.stonehill.edu/library. *Assoc Dir, Info Syst, Interim Dir,* Jennifer Macaulay; Tel: 508-565-1238, E-mail: jmacaulay@stonehill.edu; *Dir, Archives, Hist Coll Dir,* Nicole Casper; Tel: 508-565-1396, E-mail: ncasper@stonehill.edu; *Asst Dir, Res,* Kelly Faulkner; Tel: 508-565-1329, E-mail: kfaulkner@stonehill.edu; *Interim Assoc Dir,* Allison Keaney; Tel: 508-565-1289, E-mail: akeaney@stonehill.edu; *Asst Dir, Archives,* Jon Green; Tel: 508-565-1110, E-mail: jgreen2@stonehill.edu; *Head, Ref,* Joseph Middleton; Tel: 508-565-1433, E-mail: jmiddleton@stonehill.edu; *Coll Develop Librn,* Heather O'Leary; Tel: 508-565-1318, E-mail: holeary@stonehill.edu; *Info Literacy Librn, Instrul Design Librn,* Patricia McPherson; Tel: 508-565-1844, E-mail: pmcpherson@stonehill.edu; *ILS LIbrn, Metadata Librn,* Cheryl Brigante; Tel: 505-565-1151, E-mail: cbrigante@stonehill.edu; *ILL, Ref Serv,* Heather Perry; Tel: 508-565-1538, E-mail: hperry@stonehill.edu; *Ref Serv,* Jane Swiszcz; Tel: 508-565-1452, E-mail: jswiszcz@stonehill.edu; *Syst Tech,* Kathleen C Brenner; Tel: 508-565-1213, E-mail: kbrenner@stonehill.edu. Subject Specialists: *Historical Coll,* Jon Green; Staff 20 (MLS 10, Non-MLS 10)
Founded 1948. Enrl 2,410; Fac 192; Highest Degree: Master
Library Holdings: CDs 3,093; DVDs 447; e-journals 1,282; Bk Vols 225,300; Per Subs 928; Videos 3,045
Special Collections: Michael Novak Papers; Rep Joseph W Martin Jr Papers & Memorabilia; Tofias Business Archives
Subject Interests: Bus & mgt, Relig
Automation Activity & Vendor Info: (Acquisitions) Innovative Interfaces, Inc; (Cataloging) Innovative Interfaces, Inc; (Circulation) Innovative Interfaces, Inc; (Course Reserve) Innovative Interfaces, Inc; (OPAC) Innovative Interfaces, Inc; (Serials) Innovative Interfaces, Inc
Wireless access
Mem of Massachusetts Library System
Partic in LYRASIS; OCLC Online Computer Library Center, Inc
Special Services for the Deaf - Assistive tech; Closed caption videos
Special Services for the Blind - Assistive/Adapted tech devices, equip & products
Open Mon-Thurs 8am-1am, Fri 8am-10pm, Sat 10-9, Sun 10am-1am

EDGARTOWN

L DUKES LAW LIBRARY*, Dukes County Courthouse, 81 Main St, 02539. (Mail add: PO Box 1267, 02539), SAN 373-1650. Tel: 508-627-4668. Web Site: www.dukescounty.org/Pages/DukesCountyMA_Intentions/library.
Library Holdings: Bk Vols 2,000; Per Subs 20
Open Mon-Fri 8:30-4

P EDGARTOWN FREE PUBLIC LIBRARY*, 26 W Tisbury Rd, 02539. SAN 307-3688. Tel: 508-627-4221. FAX: 508-627-9534. E-mail: edgartownlibrary@gmail.com. Information Services E-mail: info@edgartownlibrary.org. Web Site: www.edgartownlibrary.org. *Dir,* Lisa Sherman; *Asst Dir,* Deborah A MacInnis
Founded 1892. Pop 4,297; Circ 85,856
Library Holdings: Bk Vols 40,000; Per Subs 150
Automation Activity & Vendor Info: (Cataloging) Innovative Interfaces, Inc; (Circulation) Innovative Interfaces, Inc; (OPAC) Innovative Interfaces, Inc
Wireless access
Partic in Cape & Islands Interlibrary Asn; Cape Libraries Automated Materials Sharing Network
Open Mon & Thurs-Sat 10-5, Tues & Wed 10-8
Friends of the Library Group

ERVING

P ERVING PUBLIC LIBRARY, Two Care Dr, 01344. SAN 307-3696. Tel: 413-423-3348. Web Site: www.erving-ma.org/library. *Libr Dir,* Natane Halasz; E-mail: natane.halasz@erving-ma.gov
Pop 1,800; Circ 19,416
Library Holdings: Bk Vols 9,452; Per Subs 20
Wireless access
Mem of Massachusetts Library System
Partic in Central & Western Massachusetts Automated Resource Sharing
Open Mon-Thurs & Sun 1pm-7pm
Friends of the Library Group

ESSEX

P T O H P BURNHAM PUBLIC LIBRARY*, 30 Martin St, 01929. SAN 307-370X. Tel: 978-768-7410. FAX: 978-768-3370. E-mail: mes@essexpl.org. Web Site: www.essexpubliclibrary.org. *Dir,* Deborah M French; E-mail: dfrench@essexpl.org
Founded 1894. Pop 3,400; Circ 26,500
Library Holdings: Audiobooks 1,214; CDs 125; DVDs 1,685; e-books 14,457; Electronic Media & Resources 4,897; Large Print Bks 145; Bk Titles 13,486; Per Subs 24
Wireless access
Mem of Massachusetts Library System
Partic in Merrimack Valley Library Consortium
Open Mon & Wed 1-7, Tues & Fri 1-5, Thurs 10-5, Sat 10-Noon
Friends of the Library Group

EVERETT

P EVERETT PUBLIC LIBRARIES, Frederick E Parlin Memorial Library, 410 Broadway, 02149. SAN 345-1895. Tel: 617-394-2300. Reference Tel: 617-394-2302. Web Site: www.noblenet.org/everett. *Dir,* Matt Lattanzi; E-mail: Matt.Lattanzi@ci.everett.ma.us; *Ad,* Kathleen Slipp; E-mail: slipp@noblenet.org; *Tech Serv Librn,* Mark Parisi; Tel: 617-394-2305, E-mail: parisi@noblenet.org; Staff 35 (MLS 9, Non-MLS 26)
Founded 1879. Circ 111,239
Library Holdings: Per Subs 175
Subject Interests: City hist
Automation Activity & Vendor Info: (Acquisitions) Evergreen; (Cataloging) Evergreen; (Circulation) Evergreen; (ILL) Evergreen; (OPAC) Evergreen; (Serials) Evergreen
Wireless access
Function: Activity rm, Adult bk club, Online cat
Publications: Children's Brochure; General Brochure; Young Adult Brochure
Mem of Massachusetts Library System
Partic in North of Boston Library Exchange, Inc
Special Services for the Deaf - TDD equip
Special Services for the Blind - Accessible computers; Aids for in-house use; Internet workstation with adaptive software
Open Mon-Thurs 9-9, Fri & Sat 9-5
Friends of the Library Group
Branches: 1
SHUTE MEMORIAL, 781 Broadway, 02149, SAN 307-3742. Tel: 617-394-2308. *Br Librn,* Trisha To; E-mail: To@noblenet.org; Staff 5 (MLS 2, Non-MLS 3)
Library Holdings: Bk Vols 30,000; Per Subs 30
Publications: Shute Memorial Library: A Short History (Local historical information)
Open Mon-Thurs 10-6, Fri 10-5
Friends of the Library Group

FAIRHAVEN

P MILLICENT LIBRARY*, 45 Centre St, 02719. (Mail add: PO Box 30, 02719-0030), SAN 307-3769. Tel: 508-992-5342. FAX: 508-993-7288. E-mail: millicent@sailsinc.org. Web Site: www.millicentlibrary.org. *Libr Dir,* Kyle DeCicco-Carey; E-mail: kdecicco-carey@sailsinc.org; *Archivist,* Debbie Charpentier; E-mail: dcharpentier@sailsinc.org; *Youth Serv,* Jane Murphy; E-mail: jmurphy@sailsinc.org; Staff 10 (MLS 3, Non-MLS 7)
Founded 1893. Pop 16,279; Circ 124,025
Library Holdings: AV Mats 7,334; Bk Vols 64,785; Per Subs 175
Special Collections: Manjiro Nakahama (Journal of His Voyages 1840); Mark Twain (Letters to the Rogers Family)
Subject Interests: Art & archit
Automation Activity & Vendor Info: (Cataloging) SirsiDynix; (Circulation) SirsiDynix; (OPAC) SirsiDynix
Wireless access
Publications: Booklets on Fairhaven's History; Henry Huttleson Rogers; Mark Twain & Henry Huttleson Rogers, An Odd Couple; Mark Twain Letter to the Rogers Family
Partic in SAILS Library Network
Open Mon & Wed 9-8, Tues, Thurs & Fri 9-6, Sat 9-3
Friends of the Library Group

FALL RIVER

J BRISTOL COMMUNITY COLLEGE*, Eileen T Farley Learning Resources Center, 777 Elsbree St, 02720. SAN 307-3777. Tel: 508-678-2811. FAX: 508-730-3270. E-mail: libreq@bristolcc.edu. Web Site: libguides.bristolcc.edu/. *Assoc Dean, Libr Serv,* Robert Rezendes; Tel: 508-678-2811, Ext 2106, E-mail: robert.rezendes@bristolcc.edu; *Res & Instruction Librn,* James Emond; Tel: 508-678-2811, Ext 2316, E-mail: james.emond@bristolcc.edu; *Res & Instruction Librn,* Lisa Richter; Tel: 508-678-2811, Ext 3231, E-mail: Lisa.Richter@bristolcc.edu; *Res & Instruction Librn,* Susan Souza-Mort; Tel: 508-678-2811, Ext 2183, E-mail: susan.souza-mort@bristolcc.edu; *Coordr, Cat,* Patricia Hiscock; Tel: 508-678-2811, Ext 2109, E-mail: Patricia.Hiscock@bristolcc.edu; *Coord, Research & Instruction,* Emily Brown; Tel: 508-678-2811, Ext 3040, E-mail: emil.brown@bristolcc.edu; *ILL & Ser,* Melanie Johnson; Tel: 508-678-2811, Ext 2458, E-mail: melanie.johnson@bristolcc.edu; Staff 8 (MLS 6, Non-MLS 2)
Founded 1966. Enrl 5,789; Fac 138; Highest Degree: Associate
Library Holdings: Audiobooks 888; Bks on Deafness & Sign Lang 215; CDs 1,537; DVDs 923; e-books 395; Electronic Media & Resources 17; Microforms 12,640; Bk Titles 54,800; Bk Vols 63,200; Per Subs 220; Videos 4,946
Special Collections: Lizzie Borden Coll
Automation Activity & Vendor Info: (Cataloging) SirsiDynix; (Circulation) SirsiDynix; (Course Reserve) SirsiDynix; (OPAC) SirsiDynix; (Serials) SirsiDynix
Wireless access
Function: ILL available
Mem of Massachusetts Library System
Partic in Massachusetts Commonwealth Consortium of Libraries in Public Higher Education Institutions
Special Services for the Blind - Computer with voice synthesizer for visually impaired persons; Screen enlargement software for people with visual disabilities
Open Mon-Thurs 7:30am-9pm, Fri 7:30-5, Sat 10-6, Sun 11-6

S FALL RIVER HISTORICAL SOCIETY MUSEUM, Archives & Research, 451 Rock St, 02720. SAN 370-8500. Tel: 508-679-1071. Web Site: www.lizzieborden.org. *Curator,* Michael Martins; E-mail: curator@fallriverhistorical.org; *Asst Curator,* Dennis Binette
Library Holdings: Bk Vols 7,500
Wireless access
Partic in SAILS Library Network
Restriction: Open by appt only

P FALL RIVER PUBLIC LIBRARY, 104 N Main St, 02720. SAN 345-2018. Tel: 508-324-2700. Web Site: www.fallriverlibrary.org. *Adminr,* Mrs Liane Verville; E-mail: lverville@sailsinc.org; *Asst Admin,* Kathryn Kulpa; E-mail: kkkulpa@sailsinc.org; *Ch Serv,* David Mello; E-mail: dmello@sailsinc.org; *Ad,* Fellisha Desmarais; E-mail: fdasmarais@sailsinc.org; *Ref Librn,* Elizabeth Washburn; E-mail: bwashburon@sailsinc.org; *YA Librn,* Taylor Silva; E-mail: tsilva@sailsinc.org; Staff 20 (MLS 5, Non-MLS 15)
Founded 1860. Pop 88,945; Circ 206,114
Jul 2017-Jun 2018 Income (Main & Associated Libraries) $1,379,129, State $138,637, City $1,139,367, Federal $101,125. Mats Exp $136,323, Books $61,385, Per/Ser (Incl. Access Fees) $9,857, Other Print Mats $8,520, AV Mat $18,693, Electronic Ref Mat (Incl. Access Fees) $37,868. Sal $725,418
Library Holdings: Audiobooks 8,984; AV Mats 6,009; CDs 1,912; DVDs 6,980; e-books 119,985; Electronic Media & Resources 360; Large Print Bks 6,000; Bk Titles 152,227; Bk Vols 200,235; Per Subs 51; Talking Bks 3,000; Videos 3,200
Special Collections: Estes Coll of Books by Individuals Born & Who Have Lived in Fall River; Lizzie Borden Coll; Portuguese Language Materials Coll
Subject Interests: Local hist
Automation Activity & Vendor Info: (Acquisitions) SirsiDynix; (Cataloging) SirsiDynix; (Circulation) SirsiDynix; (OPAC) SirsiDynix
Wireless access
Function: 24/7 Electronic res, 24/7 Online cat, Adult bk club, Archival coll, Art programs, Bk club(s), Bks on CD, Children's prog, Digital talking bks, Electronic databases & coll, Free DVD rentals, Holiday prog, ILL available, Internet access, Magazines, Mail & tel request accepted, Meeting rooms, Microfiche/film & reading machines, Movies, Museum passes, Music CDs, Online ref, OverDrive digital audio bks, Passport agency, Photocopying/Printing, Preschool outreach, Prog for adults, Ref & res, Scanner, Story hour, Study rm, Summer reading prog, Tax forms, Teen prog, Telephone ref, Wheelchair accessible
Mem of Massachusetts Library System
Partic in SAILS Library Network
Special Services for the Blind - Audio mat; Bks on cassette; Bks on CD
Open Mon-Thurs 9-9, Fri 9-5, Sat (Sept-June) 9-5
Friends of the Library Group

S MARITIME MUSEUM AT BATTLESHIP COVE, Research Library, (Formerly Marine Museum at Fall River Library), 70 Water St, 02721. SAN 307-3807. Tel: 508-674-3533. FAX: 508-674-3534. E-mail: director@marinemuseumfr.org. Web Site: www.battleshipcove.org/maritime-museum.
Founded 1968
Library Holdings: Bk Vols 2,000
Wireless access
Restriction: Open by appt only

GL MASSACHUSETTS TRIAL COURT LAW LIBRARIES*, Fall River Law Library, Superior Courthouse, 186 S Main St, 02721. SAN 307-3793. Tel: 508-491-3475. FAX: 508-491-3482. E-mail: fallriver.lawlib@verizon.net. Web Site: www.mass.gov/locations/fall-river-law-library. *Head Librn,* Madlyn Correa; E-mail: madlyn.mc@verizon.net; *Asst Librn,* Robin Perry
Library Holdings: Bk Vols 31,000; Per Subs 37
Wireless access
Partic in NELLCO Law Library Consortium, Inc.; OCLC Online Computer Library Center, Inc
Open Mon-Fri 8:30-4:30

R TEMPLE BETH EL*, Ziskind Memorial Library, 385 High St, 02720. SAN 307-3823. Tel: 508-674-3529. FAX: 508-674-3058. E-mail: templebethel@comcast.net. Web Site: www.frtemplebethel.org. *Librn,* Robin Fielding
Founded 1955
Library Holdings: Bk Vols 6,500; Per Subs 35

S USS MASSACHUSETTS MEMORIAL COMMITTEE, INC*, Archives & Technical Library, Battleship Cove, Five Water St, 02721-1540. SAN 370-3258. Tel: 508-678-1100. Toll Free Tel: 800-533-3194 (New England only). FAX: 508-674-5597. E-mail: battleship@battleshipcove.org, curator@battleshipcove.org. Web Site: battleshipcove.org. *Curator,* Donald R Shannon; Tel: 508-678-1100, Ext 116, E-mail: dshannon@battleshipcove.org
Library Holdings: Bk Vols 2,000
Special Collections: Blue Prints of Ships & Equipment, Machinery of US Navy
Subject Interests: World War II
Wireless access
Restriction: Open by appt only

FALMOUTH

S FALMOUTH HISTORICAL SOCIETY & MUSEUMS ON THE GREEN*, History & Genealogy Archives & Library, 65 Palmer Ave, 02540. (Mail add: PO Box 174, 02541-0174), SAN 326-5080. Tel: 508-548-4857. E-mail: info@museumsonthegreen.org. Web Site: museumsonthegreen.org/archives. *Exec Dir,* Mark Schmidt; E-mail: mark@museumsonthegreen.org; *Mgr, Res,* Meg Costello; E-mail: meg@museumsonthegreen.org; Staff 1 (Non-MLS 1)
Founded 1900
Library Holdings: AV Mats 304; CDs 65; DVDs 239; Bk Vols 1,458; Spec Interest Per Sub 1
Special Collections: Katharine Lee Bates Coll; Ship's Log Coll
Subject Interests: Genealogy, Local hist, Maritime, Whaling
Wireless access
Publications: A Guide to the Manuscripts & Special Collections in the Falmouth Historical Society (Archives guide); Arnold W Dyer Hotels & Inns of Falmouth (1993) (Local historical information); Arnold W Dyer Residential Falmouth: an 1897 Souvenir brought up-to-date (c1897, 1992) (Local historical information); Theodate Geoffrey Suckanesset: Reprint with index (c1928, 1992) (Local historical information)
Open Tues & Thurs 10-2

M FALMOUTH HOSPITAL*, Medical Library, 100 Ter Heun Dr, 02540. SAN 377-9092. Tel: 508-457-3521. FAX: 508-457-3997. *Librn,* Susan Hanley
Library Holdings: Bk Vols 800; Per Subs 150
Partic in Massachusetts Health Sciences Library Network; National Network of Libraries of Medicine Region 7; Southeastern Massachusetts Consortium of Health Science

P FALMOUTH PUBLIC LIBRARY*, 300 Main St, 02540. SAN 345-2107. Tel: 508-457-2555. FAX: 508-457-2559. E-mail: info@falmouthpubliclibrary.org. Web Site: www.falmouthpubliclibrary.org. *Dir,* Linda Collins; E-mail: lcollins@falmouthpubliclibrary.org; *Asst Dir,* Jennifer Woodward; E-mail: jwoodward@falmouthpubliclibrary.org; *Ad, Head, Ref,* Jill Erickson; E-mail: jerickson@falmouthpubliclibrary.org; *Head, Syst,* Peter Cook; E-mail: pcook@falmouthpubliclibrary.org; *Ch,* Laura Ford; E-mail: lford@falmouthpubliclibrary.org; *Circ Librn,* Tammy Amon; E-mail: tamon@falmouthpubliclibrary.org; *Tech Serv Librn,* Kim DeWall; E-mail: kcdewall@falmouthpubliclibrary.org; Staff 35 (MLS 10, Non-MLS 25)
Founded 1901. Pop 33,123; Circ 452,535
Library Holdings: Audiobooks 7,602; CDs 7,602; DVDs 11,516; e-books 20,317; Electronic Media & Resources 135; Microforms 7,183; Bk Titles 128,993; Per Subs 417; Spec Interest Per Sub 18
Special Collections: Genealogy Coll; Local Author (Katharine Lee Bates Coll); Local History Coll
Subject Interests: Local hist, Poetry
Automation Activity & Vendor Info: (Acquisitions) Innovative Interfaces, Inc; (Cataloging) Innovative Interfaces, Inc; (Circulation) Innovative Interfaces, Inc; (Course Reserve) Innovative Interfaces, Inc; (ILL) Innovative Interfaces, Inc; (Media Booking) Innovative Interfaces, Inc; (OPAC) Innovative Interfaces, Inc; (Serials) Innovative Interfaces, Inc
Wireless access
Function: Summer reading prog
Mem of Massachusetts Library System
Partic in Cape Libraries Automated Materials Sharing Network
Special Services for the Deaf - Bks on deafness & sign lang; Closed caption videos; High interest/low vocabulary bks; Sign lang interpreter upon request for prog; TTY equip
Special Services for the Blind - Accessible computers; Bks available with recordings; Bks on cassette; Bks on CD; Cassettes; Computer with voice synthesizer for visually impaired persons; Copier with enlargement capabilities; Descriptive video serv (DVS); Extensive large print coll; Home delivery serv; Internet workstation with adaptive software; Large print & cassettes; Large print bks; Magnifiers; PC for people with disabilities; Recorded bks; Screen enlargement software for people with visual disabilities; Screen reader software; Sound rec; ZoomText magnification & reading software
Open Mon, Thurs & Fri 9:30-5:30, Tues & Wed 10-8:30, Sat 9:30-5, Sun 1-5
Friends of the Library Group
Branches: 2
EAST FALMOUTH BRANCH, 310 E Falmouth Hwy, East Falmouth, 02536, SAN 345-2131. Tel: 508-548-6340. FAX: 508-543-6340. *Librn,* Margaret Borden; E-mail: mborden@falmouthpubliclibrary.org
Library Holdings: Bk Vols 20,000
Open Mon & Tues 9-5, Wed 9-1, Thurs 1-7
Friends of the Library Group
NORTH FALMOUTH BRANCH, Six Chester St, North Falmouth, 02556-2408, SAN 345-2166. Tel: 508-563-2922. *Librn,* Laurie McNee; E-mail: lmcnee@falmouthpubliclibrary.org
Open Mon & Fri 2-7, Wed 10-2
Friends of the Library Group

FITCHBURG

P FITCHBURG PUBLIC LIBRARY*, 610 Main St, 01420-3146. SAN 307-3866. Tel: 978-829-1780. FAX: 978-345-9631. Reference E-mail: fplref@cwmars.org. Web Site: www.fitchburgpubliclibrary.org. *Dir,* Sharon A Bernard; E-mail: sbernard@fitchburgma.gov; *Supvr, Pub Serv,* Ashley Kenney; E-mail: kenneya@cwmars.org; Staff 24 (MLS 8, Non-MLS 16)
Founded 1859. Pop 42,000; Circ 142,687
Jul 2020-Jun 2021 Income $918,152, City $898,152, Other $20,000. Mats Exp $219,593. Sal $261,766 (Prof $317,193)
Library Holdings: Audiobooks 9,666; AV Mats 7,030; DVDs 9,520; e-books 17,026; Bk Vols 118,369; Per Subs 53
Automation Activity & Vendor Info: (Cataloging) Evergreen; (Circulation) Evergreen; (ILL) Evergreen; (OPAC) Evergreen; (Serials) Evergreen
Wireless access
Function: 24/7 Electronic res, 24/7 Online cat, 3D Printer, Activity rm, Adult bk club, Adult literacy prog, Archival coll, Art exhibits, Audiobks via web, AV serv, Bilingual assistance for Spanish patrons, Bk club(s), Bks on CD, CD-ROM, Chess club, Children's prog, Computer training, Computers for patron use, Doc delivery serv, Electronic databases & coll, Equip loans & repairs, For res purposes, Free DVD rentals, Genealogy discussion group, Health sci info serv, Home delivery & serv to seniorr ctr & nursing homes, Homework prog, ILL available, Instruction & testing, Internet access, Learning ctr, Life-long learning prog for all ages, Magazines, Magnifiers for reading, Mail & tel request accepted, Meeting rooms, Microfiche/film & reading machines, Movies, Museum passes, Music CDs, Online cat, Online ref, Outside serv via phone, mail, e-mail & web, OverDrive digital audio bks, Photocopying/Printing, Preschool reading prog, Printer for laptops & handheld devices, Prof lending libr, Prog for adults, Prog for children & young adult, Ref & res, Ref serv available, Res assist avail, Scanner, Serves people with intellectual disabilities, Spanish lang bks, Spoken cassettes & CDs, Spoken cassettes & DVDs, Story hour, Study rm, Summer reading prog, Tax forms, Teen prog, Telephone ref, Visual arts prog, Wheelchair accessible, Workshops, Writing prog
Partic in Central & Western Massachusetts Automated Resource Sharing
Special Services for the Deaf - Bks on deafness & sign lang; Closed caption videos; TTY equip
Special Services for the Blind - Magnifiers; Talking bks
Open Mon-Thurs 10-8, Fri 10-5, Sat 10-4
Friends of the Library Group

C FITCHBURG STATE UNIVERSITY*, Amelia V Galucci-Cirio Library, 160 Pearl St, 01420. SAN 307-3874. Tel: 978-665-3196. Circulation Tel: 978-665-3063. Interlibrary Loan Service Tel: 978-665-3065. Reference Tel: 978-665-3223. FAX: 978-665-3069. Circulation E-mail: circulation@fitchburgstate.edu. Web Site: library.fitchburgstate.edu. *Dean of Libr,* Jacalyn Kremer; E-mail: jkremer@fitchburgstate.edu; *Instruction Librn,* Linda LeBlanc; Tel: 978-665-3062, E-mail: lileblanc@fitchburgstate.edu; *Tech Serv Librn,* Nancy Turnbull; Tel: 978-665-4338, E-mail: nturnbu1@fitchburgstate.edu; Staff 12 (MLS 6, Non-MLS 6)
Founded 1894. Enrl 6,768; Fac 177; Highest Degree: Master
Library Holdings: AV Mats 2,455; e-journals 47,000; Electronic Media & Resources 140; Microforms 130,860; Bk Vols 220,018; Per Subs 1,861; Spec Interest Per Sub 8
Special Collections: College Archives; John van Cortland Moon Coll; Rice Art Coll; Robert Cormier Coll; Robert Salvatore Coll
Subject Interests: Bus, Communications, Computer sci, Media, Nursing
Automation Activity & Vendor Info: (Acquisitions) Ex Libris Group; (Cataloging) Ex Libris Group; (Circulation) Ex Libris Group; (Course Reserve) Docutek; (ILL) OCLC; (OPAC) Ex Libris Group; (Serials) Ex Libris Group
Wireless access
Publications: Annual Reports; Directories; LibGuides (Library instruction); Newsletter
Partic in LYRASIS; OCLC Online Computer Library Center, Inc; Proquest Dialog
Open Mon-Thurs 7:30am-11:30pm, Fri 7:30-7, Sat Noon-5, Sun 1-11:30

FLORENCE

P LILLY LIBRARY, 19 Meadow St, 01062. SAN 322-7626. Tel: 413-587-1500. FAX: 413-587-1504. E-mail: lillylibrary@cwmars.org. Web Site: www.lillylibrary.org. *Dir,* Adam Novitt; *Asst Dir,* Charlotte Carver; *Ch Serv,* Kimberly Evans-Perez; Staff 10 (MLS 1, Non-MLS 9)
Founded 1890. Pop 30,000; Circ 79,000
Library Holdings: AV Mats 812; DVDs 182; Large Print Bks 174; Bk Vols 22,185; Per Subs 109; Talking Bks 364; Videos 798
Automation Activity & Vendor Info: (Cataloging) Follett Software; (Circulation) Follett Software; (OPAC) Follett Software
Function: 24/7 Electronic res, 24/7 Online cat, Activity rm, Adult bk club, Archival coll, Audiobks via web, Bks on CD, Chess club, Children's prog, Computers for patron use, Electronic databases & coll, ILL available, Internet access, Magazines, Magnifiers for reading, Mango lang, Meeting rooms, Movies, Museum passes, Music CDs, Online cat, OverDrive digital audio bks, Photocopying/Printing, Prog for children & young adult, Ref serv available, Spanish lang bks, Story hour, Study rm, Summer reading prog, Teen prog, Wheelchair accessible
Partic in Central & Western Massachusetts Automated Resource Sharing
Open Mon, Fri & Sat 10-5, Tues & Thurs 10-8, Sat 10-5
Friends of the Library Group

FLORIDA

P FLORIDA FREE LIBRARY, 56 N County Rd, 01247-9614. SAN 307-3890. Tel: 413-664-0153. FAX: 413-663-3593. E-mail: floridafreelibrary@gmail.com. *Actg Dir,* Terry Ilene Green
Pop 779; Circ 14,965
Library Holdings: DVDs 25; Bk Titles 9,000; Per Subs 36; Videos 400
Wireless access
Partic in Central & Western Massachusetts Automated Resource Sharing
Open Mon & Fri 11:15-3:30, Tues & Thurs 10-8

FOXBOROUGH

P BOYDEN LIBRARY*, Ten Bird St, 02035. SAN 307-3904. Tel: 508-543-1245. FAX: 508-543-1193. Web Site: www.boydenlibrary.org. *Libr Dir,* Manuel Leite; E-mail: mleite@sailsinc.org; *Adult Serv, Ref (Info Servs),* Tim Golden; *Cat,* Kathy Bell-Harney; *Ch Serv,* Margaret Rossetti; E-mail: mrossett@sailsinc.org; Staff 6 (MLS 6)
Founded 1870. Pop 16,693; Circ 196,042
Library Holdings: AV Mats 10,642; Bk Vols 91,066; Per Subs 194
Special Collections: Genealogy & Local History Coll
Automation Activity & Vendor Info: (Cataloging) SirsiDynix; (Circulation) SirsiDynix; (ILL) SirsiDynix; (OPAC) SirsiDynix
Mem of Massachusetts Library System
Partic in SAILS Library Network
Open Mon-Thurs 10-8, Fri 10-6, Sat 10-5
Friends of the Library Group

FRAMINGHAM

P FRAMINGHAM PUBLIC LIBRARY*, 49 Lexington St, 01702-8278. SAN 345-2344. Tel: 508-532-5570. FAX: 508-820-7210. Web Site: framinghamlibrary.org. *Dir,* Mark Contois; Tel: 508-879-5570, Ext 4358, E-mail: mcontois@minlib.net; *Asst Dir,* Lena Kiburn; E-mail: lkilburn@minlib.net; *Coll Develop Librn,* Christine Pratt; Tel: 508-879-5570, Ext 4359, E-mail: CPratt@minlib.net; *Ch Serv,* Lucy Loveridge; Tel: 508-879-5570, Ext 4336, E-mail: lloveridge@minlib.net; *Circ,* Kelly Sprague; Tel: 508-879-5570, Ext 4345, E-mail: ksprague@minlib.net; *Commun Serv, Outreach Serv,* Amy Sadkin; Tel: 508-879-5570, Ext 4347, E-mail: asadkin@minlib.net; *Tech Serv,* Linda Benjaminsen; Tel: 508-879-5570, Ext 4319, E-mail: lbenjaminsen@minlib.net; Staff 87 (MLS 26, Non-MLS 61)
Founded 1855. Pop 64,462; Circ 872,067
Library Holdings: Bk Titles 239,718; Per Subs 394
Subject Interests: Educ, Employment, Local hist, Portuguese (Lang), Spanish (Lang)
Automation Activity & Vendor Info: (Acquisitions) Innovative Interfaces, Inc; (Cataloging) Innovative Interfaces, Inc; (Circulation) Innovative Interfaces, Inc; (OPAC) Innovative Interfaces, Inc; (Serials) Innovative Interfaces, Inc
Wireless access
Mem of Massachusetts Library System
Partic in Minuteman Library Network
Special Services for the Deaf - TTY equip
Open Mon-Thurs 9-9, Fri & Sat 9-5, Sun 1-5
Friends of the Library Group
Branches: 1
CHRISTA CORRIGAN MCAULIFFE BRANCH, Ten Nicholas Rd, 01701-3469, SAN 345-2409. Tel: 508-532-5636. FAX: 508-788-1930. *Br Mgr,* Jane Peck; E-mail: jpeck@minlib.net; *Ch Serv,* Robin Frank
Open Mon-Thurs 9-9, Fri & Sat 9-5
Friends of the Library Group

C FRAMINGHAM STATE UNIVERSITY*, Henry Whittemore Library, 100 State St, 01701. (Mail add: PO Box 9101, 01701-9101), SAN 307-3955. Tel: 508-626-4651. Circulation Tel: 508-626-4650. Reference Tel: 508-626-4654. Reference E-mail: reference@framingham.edu. Web Site: www.framingham.edu/henry-whittemore-library. *Dean of Libr,* Bonnie Mitchell; E-mail: bmitchell@framingham.edu; *Head, Scholarly Res, Head, Coll,* Shin Freedman; Tel: 508-626-4666, E-mail: sfreedman@framingham.edu; *Head, Tech Serv,* Richard Clare; E-mail: rclare@framingham.edu; *Access Serv Librn,* Karen Medin; Tel: 508-626-4027, E-mail: kmedin@framingham.edu; *Curric Librn,* Samantha Westall; Tel: 508-626-4657, E-mail: swestall@framingham.edu; *Metadata Librn,* Suzanne Meunier; Tel: 508-626-4656, E-mail: smeunier@framingham.edu; *Ref Librn,* Marion Slack; E-mail: mslack@framingham.edu; *Archivist, Spec Coll Librn,* Colleen Previte; Tel: 508-626-4648, E-mail: cprevite@framingham.edu; *Ref & Instruction Coordr,* Sandra Rothenberg; Tel: 508-626-4083, E-mail: srothenberg@framingham.edu; Staff 11 (MLS 10, Non-MLS 1)
Founded 1969. Enrl 3,445; Fac 221; Highest Degree: Master
Library Holdings: Bk Titles 169,000; Bk Vols 205,000; Per Subs 400
Special Collections: College & Local History Coll; Curriculum Materials; Eric Documents Coll; Faculty Publications; Modern American Poetry
Subject Interests: Biology, Chem, Computer sci, Educ, Natural sci, Nursing, Phys sci, Psychol, Soc sci & issues
Automation Activity & Vendor Info: (Acquisitions) Innovative Interfaces, Inc; (Cataloging) Innovative Interfaces, Inc; (Circulation) Innovative Interfaces, Inc; (ILL) Innovative Interfaces, Inc; (OPAC) Innovative Interfaces, Inc; (Serials) Innovative Interfaces, Inc
Wireless access
Publications: Staff Newsletter; Student & Faculty Handbooks; Student Employee Manual
Partic in LYRASIS; Minuteman Library Network; OCLC Online Computer Library Center, Inc
Open Mon-Thurs 8am-11pm, Fri 8-5, Sat 9-5, Sun 1-1

M METROWEST MEDICAL CENTER - FRAMINGHAM UNION HOSPITAL*, Tedeschi Library & Information Center, 115 Lincoln St, 01702. SAN 307-3963. Tel: 508-383-1590. FAX: 508-879-0471. E-mail: Library-FRA@MWMC.com. Web Site: www.mwmc.com/health-professionals. *Libr Tech,* Marian MacMaster; Staff 3 (MLS 1, Non-MLS 2)
Founded 1960
Library Holdings: Bk Vols 3,200; Per Subs 126
Subject Interests: Clinical med, Hospital admin, Nursing
Wireless access
Partic in Massachusetts Health Sciences Library Network; National Network of Libraries of Medicine Region 7; OCLC Online Computer Library Center, Inc; Proquest Dialog
Restriction: Staff use only

FRANKLIN

C DEAN COLLEGE*, E Ross Anderson Library, 99 Main St, 02038-1994. SAN 307-3998. Tel: 508-541-1771. FAX: 508-541-1918. E-mail: library@dean.edu. Web Site: www.dean.edu/academics/library.cfm. *Dir,* Ted Burke; *Librn,* Judy Tobey; *Circ,* Karline Wild; *Instrul Librn,* Michele Chapin; Staff 4 (MLS 3, Non-MLS 1)
Founded 1865. Enrl 1,400

Library Holdings: Bk Titles 32,500; Per Subs 110
Automation Activity & Vendor Info: (Cataloging) Innovative Interfaces, Inc; (Circulation) Innovative Interfaces, Inc; (Course Reserve) Innovative Interfaces, Inc; (OPAC) Innovative Interfaces, Inc; (Serials) Innovative Interfaces, Inc
Wireless access
Mem of Massachusetts Library System
Partic in Minuteman Library Network; SE Asn of Coop Higher Educ Mass Consortium

P FRANKLIN PUBLIC LIBRARY*, 118 Main St, 02038. SAN 307-4005. Tel: 508-520-4941. E-mail: franklin@minlib.net. Web Site: www.franklinma.gov/franklin-public-library. *Dir,* Felicia Oti; E-mail: foti@minlib.net; *Asst Dir,* Kim Shipala; E-mail: kshipala@minlib.net; *Head, Ref,* Vicki Earls; E-mail: vbuchanio@minlib.net; *Youth Serv Librn,* Carleigh Keating; E-mail: ckeating@minlib.net; Staff 18 (MLS 4, Non-MLS 14)
Founded 1790. Pop 29,560
Library Holdings: Bk Vols 87,000; Per Subs 230
Special Collections: Benjamin Franklin Special Coll; First Books of the Franklin Library
Subject Interests: Local hist
Wireless access
Publications: History of the Franklin Library
Open Mon-Thurs 9-8, Fri & Sat 9-5, Sun (Sept-May) 1:30-5
Friends of the Library Group

GARDNER

P LEVI HEYWOOD MEMORIAL LIBRARY*, 55 W Lynde St, 01440. SAN 307-4021. Tel: 978-632-5298. FAX: 978-630-2864. Web Site: leviheywoodmemlib.org. *Libr Dir,* Kathleen Leslie; E-mail: kleslie@cwmars.org; *Asst Dir,* Tammy Caissie; E-mail: tcaissie@cwmars.org; Staff 9 (MLS 2, Non-MLS 7)
Founded 1886. Pop 19,000
Library Holdings: Bk Vols 100,000; Per Subs 155
Subject Interests: Furniture
Automation Activity & Vendor Info: (Cataloging) Innovative Interfaces, Inc; (Circulation) Innovative Interfaces, Inc; (OPAC) Innovative Interfaces, Inc
Wireless access
Mem of Massachusetts Library System
Partic in Central & Western Massachusetts Automated Resource Sharing
Open Mon, Tues & Thurs 9-5, Wed 10-7, Fri & Sat 9-1
Friends of the Library Group

S MASSACHUSETTS DEPARTMENT OF CORRECTIONS, North Central Correctional Institution Library at Gardner, 500 Colony Rd, 01440. SAN 372-4913. Tel: 978-632-2000, Ext 325. FAX: 978-630-6044. *Librn,* Carolyn Murphy; E-mail: carolyn.murphy@massmail.state.ma.us
Library Holdings: Bk Vols 8,000; Per Subs 100

J MOUNT WACHUSETT COMMUNITY COLLEGE LIBRARY*, LaChance Library, 444 Green St, 01440. SAN 307-403X. Tel: 978-630-9125. Reference Tel: 978-630-9338. E-mail: library@mwcc.mass.edu. Web Site: library.mwcc.edu. *Asst Dean, Libr,* Jess Mynes; Tel: 978-630-9195, E-mail: j_mynes@mwcc.mass.edu; *Ref & Instrul Serv Librn,* Brooke Gilmore; *Ref & Instruction Librn,* Ellen Pratt; Tel: 978-630-9285, E-mail: e_pratt@mwcc.mass.edu; *Acq,* Jess Mynes; *Cat,* Christine Levitt; *Circ,* Carla Morrissey; Staff 5.5 (MLS 3.5, Non-MLS 2)
Founded 1964. Enrl 4,500; Fac 65; Highest Degree: Associate
Library Holdings: AV Mats 2,000; Bk Vols 45,000; Per Subs 10
Automation Activity & Vendor Info: (Acquisitions) Evergreen; (Cataloging) Evergreen; (Circulation) Evergreen; (Course Reserve) Evergreen; (ILL) Auto-Graphics, Inc; (OPAC) Evergreen; (Serials) Evergreen
Wireless access
Mem of Massachusetts Library System
Partic in Academic & Research Collaborative; Central & Western Massachusetts Automated Resource Sharing; Massachusetts Commonwealth Consortium of Libraries in Public Higher Education Institutions; OCLC Online Computer Library Center, Inc
Special Services for the Deaf - Assistive tech
Special Services for the Blind - Assistive/Adapted tech devices, equip & products
Open Mon-Thurs (Sept-June) 7:30-6, Fri 7:30-4; Mon-Thurs (July & Aug) 8-5, Fri 8-4

GEORGETOWN

P GEORGETOWN PEABODY LIBRARY, Two Maple St, 01833. SAN 307-4056. Tel: 978-352-5728. FAX: 978-352-7415. Web Site: www.georgetownpl.org. *Libr Dir,* Sarah Cognata; E-mail: scognata@georgetownpl.org; *Cat & Ref Librn,* Michele Augeri; E-mail: maugeri@georgetownpl.org; *Ch,* Catherine DeWitt; E-mail: cdewitt@georgetownpl.org; *YA Librn,* Haley Hart; E-mail: hhart@georgetownpl.org; *Circ, Sr Libr Tech,* Ruth Shores; E-mail: rshores@georgetownpl.org; *Libr Tech,* Deanna Keevan; *Ch Serv, Libr Tech,* Sharon Broll; E-mail: sbroll@georgetownpl.org; *Ch Serv, Libr Tech,* Jodi Slomsky; *Circ, Libr Tech,* Mary McHugh; Staff 9 (MLS 2, Non-MLS 7)
Founded 1869. Pop 8,517; Circ 56,493
Jul 2020-Jun 2021 Income $401,667. Mats Exp $76,317. Sal $237,035
Special Collections: Historical Newspapers; Local Town Reports
Automation Activity & Vendor Info: (Cataloging) SirsiDynix-WorkFlows; (Circulation) SirsiDynix-WorkFlows; (OPAC) SirsiDynix-Enterprise
Wireless access
Function: 24/7 Electronic res, 24/7 Online cat, Activity rm, Adult bk club, After school storytime, Archival coll, Art exhibits, Audiobks on Playaways & MP3, Audiobks via web, Bk club(s), Bks on CD, Children's prog, Computers for patron use, Electronic databases & coll, Free DVD rentals, Genealogy discussion group, Holiday prog, Homebound delivery serv, ILL available, Internet access, Magazines, Mango lang, Meeting rooms, Microfiche/film & reading machines, Movies, Museum passes, Music CDs, Online cat, Outside serv via phone, mail, e-mail & web, OverDrive digital audio bks, Photocopying/Printing, Prog for adults, Prog for children & young adult, Ref & res, Ref serv available, Scanner, Senior outreach, Story hour, Summer reading prog, Tax forms, Teen prog, Wheelchair accessible, Workshops
Partic in Merrimack Valley Library Consortium
Open Mon & Wed 2-8, Tues 10-8, Fri 10-5, Sat 9-1
Friends of the Library Group

GILL

P SLATE MEMORIAL LIBRARY*, 332 Main Rd, 01376. SAN 376-7515. Tel: 413-863-2591. FAX: 413-863-7775. E-mail: gill.slate.library@gmail.com. Web Site: gillmass.org/p/31/Slate-Memorial-Library. *Dir,* Jocelyn Castro-Santos
Pop 1,392; Circ 5,314
Library Holdings: Bk Titles 2,500; Bk Vols 3,000; Per Subs 10
Open Tues 2-6, Wed 3-7, Thurs 2-8, Sat 10-2
Friends of the Library Group

GLOUCESTER

S CAPE ANN MUSEUM LIBRARY/ARCHIVES*, 27 Pleasant St, 01930. SAN 307-4080. Tel: 978-283-0455. FAX: 978-283-4141. E-mail: library@capeannmuseum.org. Web Site: www.capeannmuseum.org. *Dir,* Oliver Barker; Tel: 978-283-0455, Ext 121; *Librn & Archivist,* Trenton Carls; Tel: 978-283-0455, Ext 119; Staff 2 (MLS 1, Non-MLS 1)
Founded 1875
Library Holdings: Bk Titles 3,800; Per Subs 25; Videos 54
Special Collections: Manuscript Coll; Rare Book Coll; Turn of the Century Documentary Photography. Municipal Document Depository
Subject Interests: Decorative art, Fine arts, Genealogy, Local hist, Maritime hist, Photog
Wireless access
Open Wed & Thurs 1:30-5, Fri & Sat 10-1
Restriction: Open to pub for ref only

M ADDISON GILBERT HOSPITAL*, Medical Library, 298 Washington St, 01930. SAN 377-9114. Tel: 978-283-4001, Ext 608. FAX: 978-281-1129. Web Site: www.beverlyhospital.org. *Librn,* Ann Tomes
Library Holdings: Bk Titles 800; Per Subs 54
Partic in Massachusetts Health Sciences Library Network; Medical Library Association; Northeastern Consortium for Health Information

P GLOUCESTER, LYCEUM & SAWYER FREE LIBRARY*, Two Dale Ave, 01930. SAN 345-2468. Tel: 978-325-5500. Web Site: www.sawyerfreelibrary.org. *Libr Dir,* Jenny Benedict; E-mail: director@sawyerfreelibrary.org; *Asst Dir,* Beth Peacock; Tel: 978-325-5555, E-mail: asstdirector@sawyerfreelibrary.org; *Ch,* Christy Rosso; Tel: 978-325-5506; *Tech Serv Librn,* Helen Freeman; Tel: 978-325-5556; *Circ Supvr,* Gail Mondello; *Sr Libr Asst,* Cynthia Williams; Tel: 978-325-5557; Staff 17 (MLS 5, Non-MLS 12)
Founded 1830. Pop 30,000; Circ 202,100
Library Holdings: Bk Vols 118,369; Per Subs 194
Special Collections: Charles Olson Coll; T S Eliot Coll; US Census. Oral History
Subject Interests: Art & archit
Automation Activity & Vendor Info: (Cataloging) Innovative Interfaces, Inc; (Circulation) Innovative Interfaces, Inc; (OPAC) Innovative Interfaces, Inc
Wireless access
Publications: Annual Report; Newsletter (Monthly)
Mem of Massachusetts Library System
Special Services for the Deaf - TTY equip
Open Mon & Wed 8:30-6, Tues & Thurs 8:30-8, Fri & Sat 8:30-5

Friends of the Library Group
Bookmobiles: 1. Librn, Sharon Cohen

P MAGNOLIA LIBRARY & COMMUNITY CENTER, One Lexington Ave, 01930. (Mail add: PO Box 5552, 01930-0007), SAN 307-4099. Tel: 978-335-8475. E-mail: magnolialibrarycommunitycenter@gmail.com. Web Site: www.magnolialibrary.org. *Head Librn,* Vignette-Noelle Lammott
Founded 1886. Pop 27,209
Library Holdings: Bk Vols 1,500
Wireless access
Open Mon-Wed (Winter) 2-4, Sat 10-12; Mon-Fri (Summer) 10-12
Friends of the Library Group

GOSHEN

P GOSHEN FREE PUBLIC LIBRARY, 42 Main St, 01032. (Mail add: 40 Main St, 01032), SAN 307-4110. Tel: 413-268-8236, Ext 111. FAX: 413-268-8237. E-mail: goshenfreelibrary@gmail.com. Web Site: www.goshen-ma.us/departments/library. *Dir & Librn,* Martha Noblick; Staff 1 (MLS 1)
Founded 1910. Pop 1,054; Circ 1,351
Library Holdings: Bk Titles 7,500; Bk Vols 8,000; Per Subs 15
Wireless access
Open Tues & Wed 11-2, Sat 11-3

GRAFTON

P GRAFTON PUBLIC LIBRARY, 35 Grafton Common, 01519. (Mail add: PO Box 387, 01519), SAN 345-2557. Tel: 508-839-4649. FAX: 508-839-7726. E-mail: info@graftonlibrary.org. Web Site: www.graftonlibrary.org. *Libr Dir,* Beth Gallaway; Tel: 508-839-4649, Ext 1105, E-mail: gallawayb@graftonlibrary.org; *Head, Children's Servx,* Sarah Banister; Tel: 508-839-4649, Ext 1107; *Head, Circ,* Susan Leto; Tel: 508-839-4649, Ext 1108, E-mail: letos@graftonlibrary.org; *Head, Ref Serv,* Heidi Fowler; Tel: 508-839-4649, Ext 1102, E-mail: fowlerh@graftonlibrary.org; *Head, Tech Serv,* Donna Bates-Tarrant; Tel: 508-839-4649, Ext 1106, E-mail: batesd@graftonlibrary.org; *Head, Teen Serv,* Allison Cusher; Tel: 508-839-4649, Ext 1104, E-mail: cushera@graftonlibrary.org; *Liaison Librn,* Kristin Pliakas; E-mail: pliakask@graftonlibrary.org; *Ref Librn,* Position Currently Open; *Teen Librn,* Position Currently Open; *Accounts Mgr,* Eileen LeBlanc; Tel: 508-839-4649, Ext 1109, E-mail: leblance@graftonlibrary.org; *Circ Asst,* Allison Picone; E-mail: piconea@graftonlibrary.org; *Circ Asst,* Sandhya Shenoy; E-mail: shenoys@graftonlibrary.org; *Library Asst, Children's,* Jennifer McNeil; Tel: 508-839-4649, Ext 1103, E-mail: mcneilj@graftonlibrary.org; *Library Asst, Children's,* Marilyn Wilcox; E-mail: wilcoxm@graftonlibrary.org; *Library Asst, Children's,* Cyndi Zarriello; E-mail: zarrielloc@graftonlibrary.org; *Library Asst, Children's,* Position Currently Open; Staff 8 (MLS 4, Non-MLS 4)
Founded 1858. Pop 17,765; Circ 150,162
Library Holdings: Audiobooks 3,596; AV Mats 6,446; DVDs 3,429; Electronic Media & Resources 491; Bk Vols 45,036; Per Subs 106
Special Collections: Grafton Mass History Coll
Automation Activity & Vendor Info: (Circulation) Evergreen; (ILL) Clio; (OPAC) Evergreen
Wireless access
Function: 24/7 Electronic res, 24/7 Online cat, Activity rm, Adult bk club, Archival coll, Audiobks on Playaways & MP3, Audiobks via web, Bk club(s), Bks on CD, Butterfly Garden, Children's prog, Computers for patron use, Electronic databases & coll, Free DVD rentals, Homebound delivery serv, ILL available, Internet access, Life-long learning prog for all ages, Magazines, Magnifiers for reading, Mail & tel request accepted, Microfiche/film & reading machines, Museum passes, Music CDs, Notary serv, Online cat, Online ref, Outreach serv, Outside serv via phone, mail, e-mail & web, Passport agency, Photocopying/Printing, Printer for laptops & handheld devices, Prog for adults, Prog for children & young adult, Ref & res, Ref serv available, Res assist avail, Scanner, STEM programs, Story hour, Summer & winter reading prog, Summer reading prog, Tax forms, Teen prog, Telephone ref, Wheelchair accessible, Winter reading prog, Workshops, Writing prog
Mem of Massachusetts Library System
Partic in Cent Mass Automated Resource Sharing Network, Inc; Central & Western Massachusetts Automated Resource Sharing
Open Mon & Tues 10-2, Wed & Thurs 2-8, Fri & Sat 10-2
Friends of the Library Group

GRANBY

P GRANBY FREE PUBLIC LIBRARY, 297 E State St, 01033. SAN 307-4137. Tel: 413-467-3320. E-mail: granbypubliclibrary@gmail.com. Web Site: www.granbylibrary.org. *Dir,* Jennifer Crosby; E-mail: jennrcrosby@gmail.com; *Youth Serv Librn,* Janice McArdle; E-mail: jmcardle302@yahoo.com; *Cataloger, Circ Asst,* Jeanne Crosby; E-mail: jcrosby@cwmars.org; Staff 3 (MLS 1, Non-MLS 2)
Founded 1891. Pop 6,221; Circ 35,500
Library Holdings: Audiobooks 1,550; DVDs 3,768; e-books 171,635; Bk Titles 39,245; Per Subs 42
Special Collections: Church Records (microfiche); Town Records
Subject Interests: Genealogy, Local hist, Math
Automation Activity & Vendor Info: (Cataloging) Innovative Interfaces, Inc; (Circulation) Innovative Interfaces, Inc; (OPAC) Innovative Interfaces, Inc
Wireless access
Function: 24/7 Online cat, Activity rm, Adult bk club, Art exhibits, Audiobks on Playaways & MP3, Audiobks via web, Bk club(s), Bks on CD, Children's prog, Computers for patron use, E-Readers, Electronic databases & coll, Family literacy, Free DVD rentals, Holiday prog, ILL available, Internet access, Life-long learning prog for all ages, Magazines, Magnifiers for reading, Mail & tel request accepted, Meeting rooms, Microfiche/film & reading machines, Movies, Museum passes, Music CDs, Online cat, Online ref, Outside serv via phone, mail, e-mail & web, OverDrive digital audio bks, Photocopying/Printing, Preschool outreach, Preschool reading prog, Prog for adults, Prog for children & young adult, Ref & res, Serves people with intellectual disabilities, STEM programs, Story hour, Study rm, Summer reading prog, Tax forms, Teen prog, Telephone ref, Wheelchair accessible, Workshops
Partic in Cent Mass Automated Resource Sharing Network, Inc; Central & Western Massachusetts Automated Resource Sharing
Open Tues, Wed & Fri 10:30-5:30, Thurs 1-8, Sat 10:30-1:30
Friends of the Library Group

GRANVILLE

P GRANVILLE PUBLIC LIBRARY, Two Granby Rd, 01034-9539. SAN 307-4153. Tel: 413-357-8531. FAX: 413-357-8531. E-mail: granvill@cwmars.org. Web Site: Granvillepubliclibrary.org. *Libr Dir,* Lise LeTellier
Founded 1902. Pop 1,183; Circ 11,707
Library Holdings: Bk Vols 8,900
Wireless access
Function: 24/7 Online cat, Bks on CD, Children's prog, Computers for patron use, Electronic databases & coll, Free DVD rentals, ILL available, Laminating, Magazines, Meeting rooms, Online cat, Online ref, OverDrive digital audio bks, Printer for laptops & handheld devices, Prog for adults, Prog for children & young adult, Story hour, Summer reading prog, Tax forms
Partic in Central & Western Massachusetts Automated Resource Sharing
Open Mon 10-12 & 3-8, Wed 3-8, Thurs 10-12 3-6, Sat 10-Noon
Restriction: Borrowing requests are handled by ILL
Friends of the Library Group

GREAT BARRINGTON

S AMERICAN INSTITUTE FOR ECONOMIC RESEARCH*, E C Harwood Library, 250 Division St, 01230-1119. (Mail add: PO Box 1000, 01230-1000), SAN 322-7928. Tel: 413-528-1216. FAX: 413-528-0103. E-mail: library@aier.org. Information Services E-mail: info@aier.org. Web Site: www.aier.org. *Librn,* Suzanne Hermann; E-mail: suzanne.hermann@aier.org; Staff 1 (MLS 1)
Founded 1962
Library Holdings: Bk Titles 15,000; Per Subs 70
Special Collections: AIER's Economic Education Bulletins 1961-present; AIER'S Research Reports 1934-present; Commercial & Financial Chronicle, 1923-1974; File of E C Harwood's Papers; The Annalist, 1923-1940
Subject Interests: Bus, Econ, Finance
Automation Activity & Vendor Info: (Cataloging) Inmagic, Inc.; (OPAC) Inmagic, Inc.; (Serials) Inmagic, Inc.
Wireless access
Publications: Business Cycle Monthly; Inflation Report (Monthly)

C BARD COLLEGE AT SIMON'S ROCK*, Alumni Library, 84 Alford Rd, 01230. SAN 307-417X. Tel: 413-528-7370. FAX: 413-528-7380. E-mail: library@simons-rock.edu. Web Site: library.simons-rock.edu. *Dir,* Brian Mikesell; Tel: 413-528-7274, E-mail: bmikesell@simons-rock.edu; *Colls Librn,* William McHenry; Tel: 413-528-7361, E-mail: wmchenry@simons-rock.edu; *Outreach Librn,* KellyAnne McGuire; Tel: 413-528-7356, E-mail: kmcguire@simons-rock.edu; *Coordr, Electronic Res,* Dana Cummings; Tel: 413-528-7284, E-mail: cummings@simons-rock.edu; Staff 4 (MLS 4)
Founded 1966. Enrl 440; Fac 45; Highest Degree: Bachelor
Special Collections: Artist Book Coll; Early Music Scores (Bernard Krainis Coll); Social Movement Pamphlets; W E B DuBois Coll on the Black Experience
Automation Activity & Vendor Info: (Acquisitions) SirsiDynix; (Cataloging) SirsiDynix; (Circulation) SirsiDynix; (ILL) OCLC; (OPAC) SirsiDynix; (Serials) SirsiDynix
Wireless access
Restriction: Open to pub for ref & circ; with some limitations

P GREAT BARRINGTON LIBRARIES*, Mason Library, 231 Main St, 01230. SAN 307-4161. Tel: 413-528-2403. Web Site: gblibraries.org. *Dir,* Amanda DeGiorgis; E-mail: adegiorgis@townofgb.org; *Asst Dir,* Donna Brown; E-mail: dbrown@townofgb.org; *Ch,* Laurie Harrison; E-mail: lharrison@townofgb.org; Staff 13 (MLS 3, Non-MLS 10)
Founded 1861. Pop 6,907; Circ 137,931
Jul 2020-Jun 2021 Income (Main & Associated Libraries) $589,000, State $10,000, City $559,000, Locally Generated Income $20,000. Mats Exp $115,077, Books $79,181, AV Mat $35,896
Library Holdings: Audiobooks 9,500; DVDs 9,500; Bk Vols 63,758
Subject Interests: Genealogy
Automation Activity & Vendor Info: (Cataloging) Evergreen; (Circulation) Evergreen
Wireless access
Function: 24/7 Online cat, Adult bk club, Archival coll, Art programs, Audiobks via web, Bks on CD, Children's prog, Computer training, Computers for patron use, Free DVD rentals, ILL available, Internet access, Magazines, Meeting rooms, Microfiche/film & reading machines, Museum passes, Online cat, OverDrive digital audio bks, Prog for adults, Prog for children & young adult, STEM programs, Story hour, Study rm, Summer reading prog, Tax forms, Wheelchair accessible
Partic in Central & Western Massachusetts Automated Resource Sharing
Open Mon-Wed 10-7, Thurs & Fri 10-6, Sat 10-3
Friends of the Library Group
Branches: 1
RAMSDELL PUBLIC LIBRARY, 1087 Main St, Housatonic, 01236-9730. (Mail add: PO Box 568, Housatonic, 01236-0568), SAN 307-4498. Tel: 413-274-3738. *Libr Dir,* Amanda DeGiorgis; E-mail: adegiorgis@townofgb.org
Circ 15,000
Library Holdings: Bk Vols 19,323; Per Subs 20
Open Mon-Wed 1-6, Sat 9-3, Sun 1-4
Friends of the Library Group

GREENFIELD

J GREENFIELD COMMUNITY COLLEGE*, Nahman-Watson Library, Core Bldg, 3rd Flr, One College Dr, 01301-9739. SAN 307-4196. Tel: 413-775-1830. Circulation Tel: 413-775-1837. FAX: 413-775-1838. Reference E-mail: reference@gcc.mass.edu. Web Site: www.gcc.mass.edu/library. *Libr Dir,* Deborah Chown; Tel: 413-775-1832, E-mail: chown@gcc.mass.edu; *Librn,* Tim Dolan; Tel: 413-775-1872, E-mail: dolant@gcc.mass.edu; *Archivist, Distance Learning Librn,* Claire Lobdell; Tel: 413-775-1834, E-mail: lobdell@gcc.mass.edu; *Coordr, Libr Serv,* Liza Harrington; Tel: 413-775-1836, E-mail: harringtonl@gcc.mass.edu; Staff 6 (MLS 3.5, Non-MLS 2.5)
Founded 1962. Enrl 1,500; Highest Degree: Associate
Library Holdings: Electronic Media & Resources 60; Bk Vols 50,000; Per Subs 176
Special Collections: Archibald MacLeish Coll
Automation Activity & Vendor Info: (Cataloging) Innovative Interfaces, Inc; (Circulation) Innovative Interfaces, Inc; (OPAC) Innovative Interfaces, Inc; (Serials) Innovative Interfaces, Inc
Wireless access
Partic in Central & Western Massachusetts Automated Resource Sharing; LYRASIS; OCLC Online Computer Library Center, Inc
Special Services for the Deaf - Assistive tech
Open Mon-Thurs 8-8, Fri 8-4

P GREENFIELD PUBLIC LIBRARY*, 402 Main St, 01301. SAN 307-420X. Tel: 413-772-1544. E-mail: librarian@greenfieldpubliclibrary.org. Web Site: www.greenfieldpubliclibrary.org. *Libr Dir,* Ellen Boyer; *Asst Libr Dir, Head, Info Serv,* Lisa Prolman; *Head, Borrower Serv,* Marjorie Curtis; *Head, Youth Serv,* Kay Lyons; *Tech Serv,* Cynthia Clifford; Staff 13 (MLS 4, Non-MLS 9)
Founded 1881. Pop 17,400; Circ 305,159
Library Holdings: AV Mats 3,692; DVDs 3,850; e-books 56,291; Electronic Media & Resources 2,046; Microforms 693; Bk Vols 35,844; Per Subs 64
Special Collections: Genealogy Coll; Town Histories-Franklin County
Subject Interests: Local hist
Automation Activity & Vendor Info: (Cataloging) Evergreen; (Circulation) Evergreen; (OPAC) Evergreen
Wireless access
Function: 24/7 Electronic res, 24/7 Online cat, Audiobks via web, AV serv, Bks on CD, Chess club, Children's prog, Computers for patron use, E-Readers, Electronic databases & coll, Free DVD rentals, Homebound delivery serv, ILL available, Internet access, Magazines, Meeting rooms, Movies, Museum passes, Music CDs, Online cat, Online ref, Photocopying/Printing, Prog for adults, Prog for children & young adult, Ref & res, Ref serv available, Scanner, Story hour, Summer reading prog, Tax forms, Teen prog, Telephone ref, Writing prog
Mem of Massachusetts Library System
Partic in Central & Western Massachusetts Automated Resource Sharing
Open Mon, Tues & Wed 9:30-8, Thurs & Fri 9:30-5, Sat 9:30-2
Friends of the Library Group

GL MASSACHUSETTS TRIAL COURT LAW LIBRARIES*, Franklin Law Library, Court House, 43 Hope St, 01301. SAN 307-4188. Tel: 413-775-7482. FAX: 413-772-0743. E-mail: franklinlawlib@hotmail.com. Web Site: www.mass.gov/locations/franklin-law-library. *Law Librn,* Kathleen Ludwig; E-mail: kathleen.ludwig@jud.state.ma.us; Staff 1 (MLS 1)
Founded 1812
Library Holdings: Bk Titles 1,600; Bk Vols 20,000; Per Subs 50
Subject Interests: Fed law, State law
Automation Activity & Vendor Info: (Cataloging) SirsiDynix; (Circulation) SirsiDynix; (ILL) OCLC; (OPAC) SirsiDynix; (Serials) SirsiDynix
Wireless access
Function: Archival coll, ILL available, Online ref, Photocopying/Printing, Ref serv available, Telephone ref
Partic in LYRASIS
Open Mon-Fri 8:30-4:30

GROTON

P GROTON PUBLIC LIBRARY*, 99 Main St, 01450. SAN 307-4218. Tel: 978-448-1167. FAX: 978-448-1169. E-mail: info@gpl.org. Web Site: www.gpl.org. *Dir,* Vanessa Abraham; E-mail: director@gpl.org; *Ch Serv,* Lauren Sanchez; Tel: 978-448-1168, Ext 1319, E-mail: kids@gpl.org; *Circ Serv, ILL,* Lisa Baylis; Tel: 978-448-1167, Ext 1318, E-mail: circulation@gpl.org; *Ref, Webmaster,* Susanne Olson; Tel: 978-448-8000, Ext 1316, E-mail: solson@gpl.org; *Ref, Syst Tech,* Jeffrey Pike; Tel: 978-448-8000, Ext 1316, E-mail: jpike@gpl.org; *YA Serv,* Deborah Dowson; Tel: 978-448-1167, Ext 1325, E-mail: teens@gpl.org; Staff 14 (MLS 3, Non-MLS 11)
Founded 1854. Pop 10,013; Circ 202,710
Jul 2015-Jun 2016 Income $642,134. Mats Exp $108,600. Sal $345,696 (Prof $151,921)
Library Holdings: AV Mats 8,460; Large Print Bks 386; Bk Titles 52,629; Bk Vols 57,260; Per Subs 147; Talking Bks 1,833
Automation Activity & Vendor Info: (Cataloging) Evergreen; (Circulation) Evergreen; (OPAC) Evergreen
Wireless access
Partic in Merrimack Valley Library Consortium
Open Tues-Sat 10-5

GROVELAND

P LANGLEY-ADAMS LIBRARY*, 185 Main St, 01834-1314. SAN 307-4226. Tel: 978-372-1732. FAX: 978-374-6590. Web Site: www.langleyadamslib.org. *Libr Dir,* Darcy Lepore; E-mail: dlepore@langleyadamslib.org; *Adult Serv & Outreach Coordr,* Sue Nakanishi; E-mail: snakanishi@langleyadamslib.org; Staff 4 (MLS 1, Non-MLS 3)
Pop 6,700
Library Holdings: Bk Vols 27,488; Per Subs 35
Automation Activity & Vendor Info: (Acquisitions) Horizon; (Cataloging) Horizon; (Circulation) Horizon; (OPAC) SirsiDynix
Wireless access
Partic in Merrimack Valley Library Consortium
Open Mon & Wed 1-8, Tues & Thurs 10-5:30, Fri 10-5, Sat 10-2
Friends of the Library Group

HADLEY

P GOODWIN MEMORIAL LIBRARY*, 50 Middle St, 01035. SAN 307-4234. Tel: 413-584-7451. FAX: 413-584-9137. E-mail: goodwinlibrary@hadleyma.org. Web Site: www.hadleyma.org/pages/HadleyMA_Library/index. *Dir,* Patrick Borezo; *Ch Serv Librn,* Luna Greenwood; Staff 3 (MLS 2, Non-MLS 1)
Pop 5,000; Circ 23,000
Library Holdings: Audiobooks 200; CDs 150; Bk Vols 26,808; Per Subs 70; Videos 2,100
Wireless access
Partic in Central & Western Massachusetts Automated Resource Sharing
Open Mon & Fri 2-7, Tues & Thurs 10-5, Wed 2-8, Sat 10-3
Friends of the Library Group

HALIFAX

P HOLMES PUBLIC LIBRARY*, 470 Plymouth St, 02338. SAN 307-4242. Tel: 781-293-2271. FAX: 781-294-8518. E-mail: hfxpl@sailsinc.org. Web Site: holmespubliclibrary.org, www.sailsinc.org/member-libraries/halifax. *Dir,* Jean Gallant; E-mail: jgallant@sailsinc.org; *Asst Dir, Tech Coordr,* Marie Coady; E-mail: mcoady@sailsinc.org; *Ref Librn,* Joanne Harris; E-mail: jharris@sailsinc.org; *Adult Serv,* Maria Bumpus; E-mail: mbumpus@sailsinc.org; *Ch Serv, YA Serv,* Stacey Beshers; E-mail: sbeshers@sailsinc.org; Staff 7 (MLS 1, Non-MLS 6)

Founded 1876. Pop 7,781; Circ 55,000
Library Holdings: Bk Titles 35,000; Per Subs 40
Automation Activity & Vendor Info: (Cataloging) SirsiDynix; (Circulation) SirsiDynix; (OPAC) SirsiDynix
Wireless access
Partic in SAILS Library Network
Special Services for the Blind - Large print bks; Talking bks & player equip
Open Mon & Wed (Summer) 10-8, Tues, Thurs & Fri 10-5; Mon & Wed (Winter) 12-8, Tues, Thurs & Fri 10-5, Sat 10-2
Friends of the Library Group

HANCOCK

P TAYLOR MEMORIAL LIBRARY*, 155 Main St, 01237. (Mail add: PO Box 1155, 01267-1155), SAN 307-4269. Tel: 413-738-5326. Interlibrary Loan Service FAX: 413-738-5310. E-mail: Taylormemoriallibraryhancock@gmail.com. Web Site: tmlhancock.weebly.com. *Chair,* Connie Chase
Pop 1,012; Circ 2,064
Library Holdings: Large Print Bks 200; Bk Vols 7,525; Talking Bks 20
Wireless access
Partic in Central & Western Massachusetts Automated Resource Sharing
Open Mon & Thurs 2-6, Sat 12-2
Friends of the Library Group

HANOVER

P JOHN CURTIS FREE LIBRARY*, 534 Hanover St, 02339. SAN 307-4277. Tel: 781-826-2972. FAX: 781-826-3130. E-mail: halib@ocln.org. Web Site: www.hanovermass.com/library. *Dir,* Virginia Johnson; E-mail: vjohnson@ocln.org; *Ch,* Lynne Campbell; E-mail: lcampbell@ocln.org; *Ref Librn,* Liz MacNeil; E-mail: emacneil@ocln.org; Staff 8 (MLS 3, Non-MLS 5)
Founded 1907. Pop 13,472; Circ 149,169
Library Holdings: CDs 3,277; DVDs 4,371; Electronic Media & Resources 42; Bk Titles 56,023; Per Subs 119
Special Collections: Historical Coll
Automation Activity & Vendor Info: (Cataloging) SirsiDynix; (Circulation) SirsiDynix; (OPAC) SirsiDynix; (Serials) SirsiDynix
Wireless access
Publications: New Books at JCFL
Partic in Old Colony Libr Network
Open Mon & Wed 10-8, Tues 1-8, Thurs-Sat 10-5
Friends of the Library Group

HANSON

P HANSON PUBLIC LIBRARY*, 132 Maquan St, 02341. SAN 307-4285. Tel: 781-293-2151. FAX: 781-293-6801. Reference E-mail: hansonref@sailsinc.org. Web Site: hansonlibrary.org. *Libr Dir,* Karen Stolfer; E-mail: kstolfer@hansonlibrary.org; *Acq, Cat,* Sue Olsen; E-mail: solsen@sailsinc.org; *Circ,* John Carrozza; E-mail: jcarrozza@sailsinc.org; *Circ,* Ann Marie Ross; E-mail: amross@sailsinc.org; *Syst Serv, Tech Serv,* Antonia Leverone; E-mail: aleveron@sailsinc.org; *Youth Serv,* Kathryn Godwin; E-mail: kgodwin@sailsinc.org; *Youth Serv,* Jessica Schneider; E-mail: jschneider@sailsinc.org
Pop 9,690; Circ 58,052
Library Holdings: Bk Titles 50,125; Per Subs 45
Subject Interests: Local hist
Wireless access
Function: Children's prog, Homework prog, ILL available, Meeting rooms, Photocopying/Printing
Partic in SAILS Library Network
Open Mon & Fri 9-5, Tues & Thurs 12-8, Wed 9-1, Sat 9-3
Friends of the Library Group

HARDWICK

P PAIGE MEMORIAL LIBRARY*, 87 Petersham Rd, 01037. (Mail add: PO Box 413, 01037), SAN 307-4293. Tel: 413-477-6704. Web Site: www.paigelibrary.com. *Dir,* Julie Bullock; E-mail: director.paige.library@gmail.com
Pop 2,379; Circ 3,592
Library Holdings: Bk Vols 12,000; Per Subs 20
Automation Activity & Vendor Info: (Cataloging) Koha; (Circulation) Koha
Wireless access
Partic in Central & Western Massachusetts Automated Resource Sharing
Open Tues & Thurs 2-7, Wed 10-4, Sat 9-1
Friends of the Library Group

HARVARD

P HARVARD PUBLIC LIBRARY*, Four Pond Rd, 01451-1647. SAN 307-4315. Tel: 978-456-4114. Circulation Tel: 978-456-4114, Ext 221. Reference Tel: 978-456-4114, Ext 225. FAX: 978-456-4115. Reference E-mail: reference@harvardpubliclibrary.org. Web Site: www.harvardpubliclibrary.org. *Dir,* Mary Wilson
Founded 1886. Pop 5,400
Library Holdings: Bk Vols 56,000; Per Subs 158
Subject Interests: Local hist, Shakers
Automation Activity & Vendor Info: (Cataloging) Innovative Interfaces, Inc; (Circulation) Innovative Interfaces, Inc; (OPAC) Innovative Interfaces, Inc
Mem of Massachusetts Library System
Partic in Central & Western Massachusetts Automated Resource Sharing
Open Mon, Tues & Thurs 10-9, Wed 10-5, Fri 10-2, Sat 10-4; Mon, Tues & Thurs 10-9, Wed 10-5, Sat 10-2 (Summer)
Friends of the Library Group

HARWICH

P BROOKS FREE LIBRARY*, 739 Main St, 02645. SAN 307-4323. Tel: 508-430-7562. FAX: 508-430-7564. E-mail: brooksfreelibrary@clamsnet.org. Web Site: www.brooksfreelibrary.org. *Dir,* Virginia A Hewitt; E-mail: vhewitt@clamsnet.org; *Asst Dir,* Emily Milan; E-mail: emilan@clamsnet.org; *Ref Librn,* Jennifer Pickett; E-mail: jpickett@clamsnet.org; *Staff Librn,* Suzanne Martell; E-mail: smartell@clamsnet.org; *Youth Serv Librn,* Ann Carpenter; E-mail: acarpenter@clamsnet.org; Staff 3 (MLS 3)
Founded 1885. Pop 12,858; Circ 145,212
Library Holdings: AV Mats 2,665; Bk Titles 50,398; Per Subs 174; Talking Bks 1,848
Special Collections: Local History Room
Automation Activity & Vendor Info: (Acquisitions) Innovative Interfaces, Inc; (Cataloging) Innovative Interfaces, Inc; (Circulation) Innovative Interfaces, Inc; (ILL) Innovative Interfaces, Inc; (OPAC) Innovative Interfaces, Inc; (Serials) Innovative Interfaces, Inc
Wireless access
Function: Homebound delivery serv, Ref serv available
Mem of Massachusetts Library System
Partic in Cape Libraries Automated Materials Sharing Network
Special Services for the Blind - Braille equip; Reader equip; Screen reader software; Vera Arkenstone
Open Mon-Thurs 10-7, Fri & Sat 10-4
Friends of the Library Group

HARWICH PORT

P HARWICH PORT LIBRARY ASSOCIATION*, 49 Lower Bank St, 02646. (Mail add: PO Box 175, 02646-0175), SAN 307-4331. Tel: 508-432-3320. E-mail: hptlibrary@verizon.net. Web Site: harwichportlibrary.org. *Dir,* Maryanne Desmareis
Founded 1923. Pop 12,000; Circ 31,632
Library Holdings: Bk Titles 14,000
Special Collections: Mystery Coll
Mem of Massachusetts Library System
Open Mon & Fri 10-5

HATFIELD

P HATFIELD PUBLIC LIBRARY*, 39 Main St, 01038. SAN 307-434X. Tel: 413-247-9097. FAX: 413-247-9237. E-mail: hatfieldpubliclibrary@gmail.com. Web Site: hatfieldpubliclibrary.org. *Dir,* Eliza Langhans; *Ch,* Hannah Paessel; Staff 1 (MLS 1)
Founded 1874. Pop 3,600; Circ 21,000
Library Holdings: AV Mats 1,249; Large Print Bks 100; Bk Titles 22,254; Per Subs 50; Talking Bks 224
Subject Interests: Local hist, Poland
Automation Activity & Vendor Info: (Cataloging) Innovative Interfaces, Inc; (ILL) Innovative Interfaces, Inc; (OPAC) Innovative Interfaces, Inc
Wireless access
Partic in Central & Western Massachusetts Automated Resource Sharing
Open Tues & Thurs 10-5, Wed & Fri 2-8, Sat 9-1
Friends of the Library Group

HAVERHILL

P HAVERHILL PUBLIC LIBRARY*, 99 Main St, 01830-5092. SAN 345-2700. Tel: 978-373-1586. Reference Tel: 978-373-1586, Ext 608. Automation Services Tel: 978-373-1586, Ext 619. FAX: 978-372-8508. Reference FAX: 978-373-8466. Web Site: www.haverhillpl.org. *Dir,* Sarah Moser; Tel: 978-373-1586, Ext 621, E-mail: smoser@haverhillpl.org; *Asst Dir,* Ricky Sirois; Tel: 978-373-1586, Ext 641, E-mail: rsirois@haverhillpl.org; *Head, Circ,* Emily Giguere; Tel: 978-373-1586, Ext 603, E-mail: egiguere@haverhillpl.org; *Head, Info Serv, Head, Ref,* Elizabeth Rieur; E-mail: erieur@haverhillpl.org; *Head, Youth Serv,* Nancy

Chase; Tel: 978-373-1586, Ext 626, E-mail: nchase@haverhillpl.org; Staff 21 (MLS 7, Non-MLS 14)
Founded 1873. Pop 60,176; Circ 459,286
Library Holdings: Electronic Media & Resources 170; Bk Titles 170,535; Per Subs 390; Talking Bks 13,366; Videos 11,608
Special Collections: Fine Arts Coll; Genealogy Coll; Haverhill & New England Towns History Coll; John Greenleaf Whittier Coll; New England States Coll; US Topo Maps
Automation Activity & Vendor Info: (Cataloging) SirsiDynix; (Circulation) SirsiDynix; (ILL) SirsiDynix; (OPAC) SirsiDynix
Wireless access
Publications: Architectural Heritage of Haverhill; Holdings of the HPL-J G Whittier Collection; HPL Technical Services Department-Procedures Manual; Internet Information; Northeast Early Childhood Resource News Center
Partic in Merrimack Valley Library Consortium
Special Services for the Blind - Computer with voice synthesizer for visually impaired persons
Open Mon, Tues & Thurs 9-9, Wed, Fri & Sat 9-5, Sun 1-5
Friends of the Library Group

J NORTHERN ESSEX COMMUNITY COLLEGE*, Bentley Library, 100 Elliott St, 01830. SAN 307-4390. Tel: 978-556-3401. FAX: 978-556-3738. Web Site: www.necc.mass.edu/library. *Dir, Libr Serv,* Mike Hearn; Tel: 978-556-3423, E-mail: mhearn@necc.mass.edu; *Ref Serv,* Liz Teoli; Tel: 978-556-3426, E-mail: eteoli@necc.mass.edu; *Circ,* Louise Bevilacqua; Tel: 978-556-3422, E-mail: lbevilacqua@necc.mass.edu; *Tech Serv,* Helen Mansur; Tel: 978-556-3425, E-mail: hmansur@necc.mass.edu; Staff 7 (MLS 5, Non-MLS 2)
Founded 1961. Enrl 3,200; Highest Degree: Associate
Library Holdings: Bk Vols 64,000; Per Subs 350
Automation Activity & Vendor Info: (Cataloging) Innovative Interfaces, Inc; (Circulation) Innovative Interfaces, Inc; (Course Reserve) Innovative Interfaces, Inc; (ILL) Innovative Interfaces, Inc; (OPAC) Innovative Interfaces, Inc
Wireless access
Publications: NECC Periodicals Holdings List
Mem of Massachusetts Library System
Partic in LYRASIS; North of Boston Library Exchange, Inc
Special Services for the Deaf - Bks on deafness & sign lang; Spec interest per
Open Mon-Thurs 8am-9pm, Fri 8-5, Sat 9-1
Departmental Libraries:
LAWRENCE CAMPUS LIBRARY, 45 Franklin St, Lawrence, 01841, SAN 376-0308. Tel: 978-738-7400. FAX: 978-738-7114. Web Site: www.necc.mass.edu/departments/library/index.htm. *Dir, Libr Serv,* Linda Hummel-Shea; Tel: 978-556-3423, E-mail: lshea@necc.mass.edu; *Coordr, Libr Serv,* Mike Hearn; E-mail: mhearn@necc.mass.edu; Staff 2 (MLS 2)
Library Holdings: Bk Vols 6,736; Per Subs 87
Subject Interests: Law, Nursing
Open Mon-Wed 9-8, Thurs 9-5, Fri 9-3, Sat 9-1

CR NORTHPOINT BIBLE COLLEGE LIBRARY*, 320 S Main St, 01835. SAN 320-7358. Tel: 978-478-3417. Administration Tel: 978-478-3416. Toll Free Tel: 800-356-4014. Web Site: northpoint.edu/academics-programs/academic-support. *Librn,* Ginger R McDonald; E-mail: gmcdonald@northpoint.edu; Staff 1 (MLS 1)
Founded 1956. Enrl 350; Fac 35; Highest Degree: Master
May 2019-Apr 2020 Income $250,000. Mats Exp $26,000, Books $7,000, Per/Ser (Incl. Access Fees) $19,000. Sal $60,000 (Prof $45,000)
Library Holdings: AV Mats 2,957; DVDs 584; Bk Vols 46,000; Per Subs 75
Subject Interests: Rare bks
Automation Activity & Vendor Info: (Acquisitions) EOS International; (Cataloging) EOS International; (Circulation) EOS International; (ILL) OCLC; (OPAC) EOS International
Wireless access
Partic in Asn of Christian Librs; LYRASIS
Open Mon-Thurs 9am-10:45pm, Fri 9-8, Sat 9-11 & 12-8, Sun 6:45pm-10:45pm

HEATH

P HEATH PUBLIC LIBRARY*, One E Main St, 01346. (Mail add: PO Box 38, 01346), SAN 307-4404. Tel: 413-337-4934, Ext 7. FAX: 413-337-8542. E-mail: heath.library@gmail.com. Web Site: www.heathlibrary.org. *Dir,* Donald Purington; E-mail: dpurington@cwmars.org; *Asst Librn,* Lyra Johnson-Fuller
Founded 1894. Pop 706; Circ 10,151
Library Holdings: AV Mats 15,000; Large Print Bks 200; Bk Titles 12,000; Per Subs 35
Wireless access
Partic in Central & Western Massachusetts Automated Resource Sharing
Open Mon 3-7, Wed 12-7, Sat 9:30-1:30
Friends of the Library Group

HINGHAM

P HINGHAM PUBLIC LIBRARY*, 66 Leavitt St, 02043. SAN 307-4412. Tel: 781-741-1405. FAX: 781-749-0956. Reference E-mail: hilib@ocln.org. Web Site: hinghamlibrary.org. *Dir,* Linda Harper; Tel: 781-741-1405, Ext 2600, E-mail: lharper@ocln.org; *Asst Dir,* Anna Byrne; Tel: 781-741-1405, Ext 2604, E-mail: abyrne@ocln.org; *Head, Tech Serv,* Jill Blair; Tel: 781-741-1405, Ext 2602, E-mail: jblair@ocln.org; *Circ Supvr,* Mary Beth Keif; Tel: 781-741-1405, Ext 1402, E-mail: mbkeif@ocln.org; Staff 29 (MLS 6, Non-MLS 23)
Founded 1869. Pop 19,500; Circ 402,062
Library Holdings: Bk Vols 174,519; Per Subs 348
Special Collections: Typography (W A Dwiggins Coll)
Subject Interests: Local hist
Automation Activity & Vendor Info: (Cataloging) SirsiDynix; (Circulation) SirsiDynix; (OPAC) SirsiDynix
Wireless access
Partic in Old Colony Libr Network
Open Mon-Thurs 10-9, Sat 9-5, Sun 1-5

HINSDALE

P HINSDALE PUBLIC LIBRARY*, 58 Maple St, 01235. (Mail add: PO Box 397, 01235-0397), SAN 307-4420. Tel: 413-655-2303. FAX: 413-655-2303. E-mail: hinsdalelibraryma@gmail.com. Web Site: www.hinsdalemass.com/library. *Dir,* Thomas A Butler, Jr; *Ch,* Lauren Paro; *Adult Serv,* Mary Lunsford; *Cat, Reader Serv,* Sue Shelsy
Founded 1866. Pop 1,780; Circ 29,745
Library Holdings: Bk Vols 10,000; Per Subs 52
Special Collections: First Congregational Church Records (1790-1980); Handwritten records of Burials of Maple Street Cemetary (1790-1912); Israel Bissell Coll; Local Newspaper Clippings (1890-to date)
Wireless access
Open Mon & Sat 9-1, Tues & Fri 2-6, Wed & Thurs 4-8
Friends of the Library Group

HOLBROOK

P HOLBROOK PUBLIC LIBRARY*, Two Plymouth St, 02343. SAN 307-4439. Tel: 781-767-3644. FAX: 781-767-5721. E-mail: holib@ocln.org. Web Site: holbrookpubliclibrary.org. *Dir,* Donald Colon; E-mail: dcolon@ocln.org; *Asst Dir,* Katrina Early; E-mail: kealy@ocln.org; *Ref Assoc,* Laura Williams; E-mail: lwilliams@ocln.org; *Circ Supvr,* Ann Gerstenecker; E-mail: agerstenecker@ocln.org; *Tech Serv Supvr,* Janet Johnson; E-mail: jjohnson@ocln.org; Staff 2 (MLS 2)
Founded 1872. Pop 10,785; Circ 70,455
Library Holdings: Bk Vols 38,820
Automation Activity & Vendor Info: (Cataloging) SirsiDynix; (Circulation) SirsiDynix; (OPAC) SirsiDynix; (Serials) SirsiDynix
Wireless access
Mem of Massachusetts Library System
Partic in Old Colony Libr Network
Open Mon 12-5, Tues & Thurs 12-8, Wed, Fri & Sat 9-5
Friends of the Library Group

HOLDEN

P GALE FREE LIBRARY*, 23 Highland St, 01520. SAN 307-4447. Tel: 508-210-5560. FAX: 508-829-0232. Web Site: www.galefreelibrary.org. *Dir,* Susan Scott; Tel: 508-210-5566, E-mail: sscott@cwmars.org; *Asst Dir,* Jennifer Rhodes; *Head, Circ,* Rachel Mimms; *Ch Serv,* Beverly Dinneen; *Tech Serv,* Veronica BeJune; Staff 16 (MLS 4, Non-MLS 12)
Founded 1888. Pop 16,000; Circ 302,000
Library Holdings: Bk Titles 65,000; Per Subs 142
Special Collections: Local Newspapers, micro. Oral History
Automation Activity & Vendor Info: (Cataloging) Evergreen; (Circulation) Evergreen; (OPAC) Evergreen
Wireless access
Mem of Massachusetts Library System
Partic in Central & Western Massachusetts Automated Resource Sharing
Special Services for the Blind - Bks on CD; Large print bks; Magnifiers; ZoomText magnification & reading software
Open Mon & Fri 9:30-5:30, Tues-Thurs 9:30-8, Sat 9-4
Friends of the Library Group

HOLLAND

P HOLLAND PUBLIC LIBRARY*, 27 Sturbridge Rd, Unit 9, 01521. SAN 307-6873. Tel: 413-245-3607. Web Site: town.holland.ma.us/library. *Dir,* Tracie Scott; E-mail: tscott@cwmars.org
Founded 1912. Pop 2,185; Circ 8,384
Library Holdings: Bk Vols 8,000
Partic in Central & Western Massachusetts Automated Resource Sharing
Open Mon-Wed 3-8, Thurs 12-5, Fri 10-2 ,Sat 10-4

HOLLISTON

P HOLLISTON PUBLIC LIBRARY*, 752 Washington St, 01746. SAN 307-4455. Tel: 508-429-0617. FAX: 508-429-0625. Web Site: www.hollistonlibrary.org. *Dir,* Leslie McDonnell; E-mail: lmcdonnell@minlib.net; *Asst Dir, Ref, YA Librn,* Jennifer Keen; E-mail: jkeen@minlib.net; *Head, Circ,* Tammy Page; E-mail: tpage@minlib.net; *Ch,* Tracy Alexander; E-mail: talexander@minlib.net
Founded 1879. Pop 14,000; Circ 176,000
Library Holdings: Bk Titles 65,032; Per Subs 109
Automation Activity & Vendor Info: (Cataloging) Innovative Interfaces, Inc; (Circulation) Innovative Interfaces, Inc; (OPAC) Innovative Interfaces, Inc
Wireless access
Open Mon-Thurs 10-8, Fri 10-6, Sat 10-4
Friends of the Library Group

HOLYOKE

J HOLYOKE COMMUNITY COLLEGE LIBRARY*, Donahue Bldg, 2nd Flr, 303 Homestead Ave, 01040-1099. SAN 307-4463. Tel: 413-538-7000, Ext 2261. Circulation Tel: 413-552-2372. Reference Tel: 413-552-2424. FAX: 413-552-2729. E-mail: library@hcc.edu. Web Site: hcc.edu/library. *Dean, Libr Serv,* Mary Dixey; Tel: 413-552-2260, E-mail: mdixey@hcc.edu; *Ref Librn,* Patricia Mangan; E-mail: pmangan@hcc.edu; *Libr Serv Coordr,* Jennifer Adams; Tel: 413-552-2733, E-mail: jadams@hcc.edu; Staff 3 (MLS 3)
Founded 1946. Highest Degree: Associate
Library Holdings: AV Mats 7,000; Bk Vols 75,000; Per Subs 400
Special Collections: Library of English Literature, ultrafiche
Automation Activity & Vendor Info: (Cataloging) OCLC; (ILL) OCLC
Wireless access
Partic in LYRASIS; OCLC Online Computer Library Center, Inc
Open Mon-Thurs 8am-8:30pm, Fri 8-4:30, Sat 10-2

P HOLYOKE PUBLIC LIBRARY*, 250 Chestnut St, 01040-4858. SAN 345-276X. Tel: 413-420-8101. Interlibrary Loan Service Tel: 413-420-8111. Reference Tel: 413-420-8106. FAX: 413-532-4230. E-mail: library@holyoke.org. Web Site: www.holyokelibrary.org. *Dir,* Maria G Pagan
Founded 1870. Pop 39,947; Circ 100,000
Library Holdings: Bk Vols 76,500; Per Subs 110
Automation Activity & Vendor Info: (Cataloging) Evergreen; (Circulation) Evergreen; (ILL) Evergreen; (OPAC) Evergreen
Wireless access
Function: Adult bk club, Bilingual assistance for Spanish patrons, Bk club(s), Bks on cassette, Bks on CD, Children's prog, Computer training, Computers for patron use, Electronic databases & coll, Free DVD rentals, ILL available, Museum passes, Music CDs, Online cat, Outside serv via phone, mail, e-mail & web, OverDrive digital audio bks, Photocopying/Printing, Preschool outreach, Prog for adults, Prog for children & young adult, Ref & res, Ref serv available, Spoken cassettes & CDs, Spoken cassettes & DVDs, Story hour, Summer reading prog, Tax forms, Teen prog, VHS videos
Partic in Central & Western Massachusetts Automated Resource Sharing
Open Mon-Thurs (Winter) 8:30-8:30, Fri & Sat 8:30-4; Mon-Wed (Summer) 8:30-6, Thurs & Fri 8:30-5
Friends of the Library Group

HOPEDALE

P BANCROFT MEMORIAL LIBRARY, 50 Hopedale St, 01747-1799. SAN 307-4471. Tel: 508-634-2209. FAX: 508-634-8095. Web Site: www.hopedale-ma.gov/bancroft-memorial-library. *Libr Dir,* Patricia Perry; E-mail: tperry@cwmars.org; *Youth Serv Librn,* Elaine Kraimer; E-mail: ekraimer@cwmars.org; Staff 3.6 (MLS 1, Non-MLS 2.6)
Founded 1898. Pop 6,142; Circ 36,351
Jul 2012-Jun 2013 Income $244,072, State $5,620, City $237,242, Locally Generated Income $1,210. Mats Exp $43,526, Books $25,866, Per/Ser (Incl. Access Fees) $2,724, AV Mat $8,255, Electronic Ref Mat (Incl. Access Fees) $6,681. Sal $137,458 (Prof $54,101)
Library Holdings: AV Mats 3,622; DVDs 1,765; Bk Vols 28,965; Per Subs 51
Special Collections: Adin Ballou Coll; Draper Corporation Coll
Automation Activity & Vendor Info: (Cataloging) Evergreen; (Circulation) Evergreen; (ILL) Evergreen; (OPAC) Evergreen
Wireless access
Mem of Massachusetts Library System
Partic in Central & Western Massachusetts Automated Resource Sharing
Open Mon & Wed 1-8, Tues & Thurs 10-5, Fri 1-5, Sat 10-2
Friends of the Library Group

HOPKINTON

P HOPKINTON PUBLIC LIBRARY*, 13 Main St, 01748. SAN 307-448X. Tel: 508-497-9777. FAX: 508-497-9778. E-mail: hopkintonlibrary@hopkintonma.gov. Web Site: www.hopkintonlibrary.org. *Dir,* Heather Backman; E-mail: nbackman@hopkintonma.gov; *Ad, Ref Librn,* Jessi McCarthy; E-mail: jmccarthy@hopkinton.ma.gov; *Youth Serv Librn,* Andrea Conboy; E-mail: asconboy@hopkintonma.gov
Founded 1890
Library Holdings: AV Mats 4,000; Large Print Bks 200; Bk Vols 35,000; Per Subs 224
Special Collections: Local History Vital Records Coll
Automation Activity & Vendor Info: (Cataloging) Innovative Interfaces, Inc; (Circulation) Innovative Interfaces, Inc; (OPAC) Innovative Interfaces, Inc
Wireless access
Mem of Massachusetts Library System
Partic in Central & Western Massachusetts Automated Resource Sharing
Open Mon-Thurs 10-9, Fri 10-6, Sat 10-4
Friends of the Library Group

HUBBARDSTON

P HUBBARDSTON PUBLIC LIBRARY*, Seven Main St, Unit 8, 01452. SAN 307-4501. Tel: 978-928-4775. FAX: 978-928-1273. E-mail: library@hubbardstonma.us. Web Site: www.hubbardstonpubliclibrary.org. *Interim Libr Dir,* Ms Chris Barbera; E-mail: cbarbera@cwmars.org
Founded 1872. Pop 2,400; Circ 11,612
Library Holdings: DVDs 300; Large Print Bks 100; Bk Vols 10,000; Per Subs 30; Videos 500
Wireless access
Mem of Massachusetts Library System
Partic in Central & Western Massachusetts Automated Resource Sharing
Open Mon & Thurs 1-7, Wed 10-4, Sat 9-Noon
Friends of the Library Group

HUDSON

P HUDSON PUBLIC LIBRARY*, Three Washington St at The Rotary, 01749-2499. SAN 307-451X. Tel: 978-568-9644. FAX: 978-568-9646. Web Site: hudsonpubliclibrary.com. *Libr Dir,* Aileen Sanchez-Himes; E-mail: asanchez-himes@cwmars.org; *Asst Dir, Tech Serv,* Deborah Kane; E-mail: dkane@cwmars.org; *Circ Mgr, ILL,* Nancy DelVecchio; E-mail: ndelvecc@cwmars.org; *Circ,* Susan Ramsbottom; E-mail: sramsbot@cwmars.org; *Circ, Ch,* Tina Craig; E-mail: tcraig@cwmars.org; *Ref (Info Servs),* Nicole Kramer; E-mail: nkramer@cwmars.org; Staff 8 (MLS 3, Non-MLS 5)
Founded 1868. Pop 19,063; Circ 237,456
Jul 2013-Jun 2014 Income $703,483. Mats Exp $104,400. Sal $506,895
Library Holdings: CDs 1,513; Electronic Media & Resources 47; Large Print Bks 850; Bk Vols 65,000; Per Subs 149; Talking Bks 2,000; Videos 4,061
Automation Activity & Vendor Info: (Acquisitions) Evergreen; (Cataloging) Evergreen; (Circulation) Evergreen
Wireless access
Function: ILL available, Prog for children & young adult, Ref serv available, Summer reading prog
Publications: Library Newsletter (Bimonthly)
Mem of Massachusetts Library System
Partic in Central & Western Massachusetts Automated Resource Sharing
Open Mon-Thurs 9-8:30, Fri 9-6, Sat 9-5
Friends of the Library Group

HULL

P HULL PUBLIC LIBRARY*, Nine Main St, 02045. SAN 307-4528. Tel: 781-925-2295. FAX: 781-925-0867. E-mail: hucirc@ocln.org. Web Site: www.hullpubliclibrary.org. *Libr Dir,* Diane Costagliola; E-mail: dcostagliola@ocln.org; *Ch,* Anne Masland; E-mail: amasland@ocln.org
Founded 1913. Pop 9,600; Circ 32,000
Library Holdings: Bk Vols 30,000; Per Subs 100
Special Collections: Local History Hull & Boston Harbor Islands
Automation Activity & Vendor Info: (Cataloging) SirsiDynix; (Circulation) SirsiDynix; (OPAC) SirsiDynix
Open Mon & Thurs 10-8, Tues & Wed 10-5, Fri 2-5, Sat 10-3
Friends of the Library Group

HUNTINGTON

P HUNTINGTON PUBLIC LIBRARY*, Seven E Main St, 01050. (Mail add: PO Box 597, 01050-0597), SAN 307-4536. Tel: 413-512-5206. FAX: 413-667-0088. E-mail: Huntingtonpubliclib@gmail.com. Web Site: thehuntingtonpubliclibrary.wordpress.com. *Libr Dir,* Heather Dunfee; Staff 3 (Non-MLS 3)
Pop 2,095; Circ 10,295
Library Holdings: Bk Vols 12,000; Per Subs 50

Wireless access
Function: Adult bk club, Art exhibits, Bk club(s), Bks on CD, Computers for patron use, Free DVD rentals, Magazines, Museum passes, Photocopying/Printing, Story hour, Summer reading prog, Wheelchair accessible
Open Mon & Tues 2-5, Wed 4-8, Thurs & Fri 2-8, Sat 10-3

HYANNIS

M CAPE COD HOSPITAL*, Medical Library, 27 Park St, 02601-5230. (Mail add: PO Box 640, 02601-0640), SAN 377-9122. Tel: 508-862-5443. FAX: 774-552-6904. E-mail: medlib@capecodhealth.org. *Dir, Med Libr,* Jeanie M Vander Pyl; Tel: 508-862-5866, E-mail: jvanderpyl@capecodhealth.org; *Cat,* Deborah Tustin; *ILL & Ser,* June Bianchi; Tel: 508-862-5867; Staff 3 (MLS 2, Non-MLS 1)
Oct 2017-Sept 2018. Mats Exp $105,000, Books $3,000, Per/Ser (Incl. Access Fees) $47,000, Electronic Ref Mat (Incl. Access Fees) $55,000
Library Holdings: AV Mats 720; e-journals 195; Bk Titles 7,977; Per Subs 147
Automation Activity & Vendor Info: (Cataloging) LibLime; (OPAC) LibLime; (Serials) SERHOLD
Wireless access
Function: ILL available
Mem of Massachusetts Library System
Partic in Massachusetts Health Sciences Library Network; North Atlantic Health Sciences Libraries, Inc; Southeastern Massachusetts Consortium of Health Science
Open Mon-Fri 8:30-4:30

P HYANNIS PUBLIC LIBRARY, 401 Main St, 02601. SAN 307-4544. Tel: 508-775-2280. FAX: 508-790-0087. E-mail: hpl_mail@clamsnet.org. Web Site: www.hyannislibrary.org. *Dir,* Antonio Stephens; *Acq Librn, Colls Librn,* Sherry Evans; *Tech Serv Librn,* Kate Howes-Joseph; *Youth Serv Librn,* Mary Bianco
Founded 1865. Pop 12,000; Circ 150,000
Library Holdings: Bk Vols 60,000; Per Subs 175
Automation Activity & Vendor Info: (Cataloging) Innovative Interfaces, Inc; (Circulation) Innovative Interfaces, Inc; (OPAC) Innovative Interfaces, Inc
Wireless access
Partic in Cape Libraries Automated Materials Sharing Network
Open Mon, Thurs & Fri 9:30-5, Tues & Wed 2-7

IPSWICH

P IPSWICH PUBLIC LIBRARY*, 25 N Main St, 01938. SAN 307-4560. Tel: 978-356-6648. FAX: 978-356-6647. E-mail: ipswich@mvlc.org. Web Site: www.ipswichlibrary.org. *Asst Dir,* Lilly Sundell-Thomas; E-mail: lthomas@ipswichlibrary.org; *Ad, Tech Librn,* Nathalie Harty; E-mail: nharty@ipswichlibrary.org; *Ch,* Laurie Collins; Tel: 978-412-8713, E-mail: lcollins@ipswichlibrary.org; *Ref Librn, Teen Serv Librn,* Katy Wuerker; E-mail: kwuerker@ipswichlibrary.org; Staff 4.3 (MLS 3.4, Non-MLS 0.9)
Founded 1868. Pop 13,175; Circ 166,503
Jul 2013-Jun 2014 Income $604,220, State $10,620, City $593,600. Mats Exp $104,430, Books $62,991, Per/Ser (Incl. Access Fees) $18,563, AV Mat $13,107, Electronic Ref Mat (Incl. Access Fees) $9,769
Library Holdings: AV Mats 9,634; Microforms 283; Bk Vols 96,782; Per Subs 216
Subject Interests: Genealogy, Local hist
Automation Activity & Vendor Info: (Cataloging) Evergreen; (Circulation) Evergreen; (ILL) Evergreen; (OPAC) Evergreen
Wireless access
Function: Adult bk club, Adult literacy prog, Archival coll, Audiobks via web, AV serv, Bks on cassette, Bks on CD, CD-ROM, Chess club, Children's prog, Computers for patron use, Electronic databases & coll, Free DVD rentals, Holiday prog, Homebound delivery serv, ILL available, Internet access, Magnifiers for reading, Museum passes, Music CDs, Online cat, Online ref, OverDrive digital audio bks, Photocopying/Printing, Preschool outreach, Prog for adults, Prog for children & young adult, Ref serv available, Summer reading prog, Tax forms, Teen prog, Telephone ref, VHS videos, Wheelchair accessible
Publications: Ipswich Public Library: The Newsletter
Partic in Merrimack Valley Library Consortium
Open Mon-Thurs 10-8, Fri 10-5:30, Sat 9-4, Sun 1-4 (Winter); Mon-Wed 9-8, Thurs & Fri 9-5, Sun 1-4 (Summer)
Friends of the Library Group

JAMAICA PLAIN

GM MASSACHUSETTS STATE LABORATORY INSTITUTE LIBRARY*, Dept of Public Health, 305 South St, 02130. SAN 377-922X. Tel: 617-983-6290. FAX: 617-983-6292. *Librn,* Jennifer D Yeaple Mann; E-mail: jennifer.mann@state.ma.us; Staff 1 (MLS 1)
Library Holdings: Bk Titles 750; Per Subs 110
Subject Interests: Clinical labs, Infectious diseases, Laboratory med, Med, Pub health med
Function: ILL available
Partic in National Network of Libraries of Medicine Region 7; OCLC Online Computer Library Center, Inc
Open Mon-Fri 8:30-5

M LEMUEL SHATTUCK HOSPITAL, Bettencourt Medical Library, 170 Morton St, 02130. SAN 345-2859. Tel: 617-971-3225. FAX: 617-971-3850. *Dir, Libr Serv,* Kathryn Noonan; E-mail: kathryn.noonan@state.ma.us; Staff 2 (MLS 1, Non-MLS 1)
Founded 1954
Library Holdings: Bk Titles 500; Per Subs 110
Wireless access
Function: ILL available
Mem of Massachusetts Library System
Partic in Massachusetts Health Sciences Library Network; National Network of Libraries of Medicine Region 7
Open Mon-Fri 8:30-5

KINGSTON

P KINGSTON PUBLIC LIBRARY*, Six Green St, 02364. SAN 307-4617. Tel: 781-585-0517. Circulation Tel: 781-585-0517, Ext 6271. Reference Tel: 781-585-0517, Ext 6272. FAX: 781-585-0521. Circulation E-mail: kicirc@kingstonpubliclibrary.org. Reference E-mail: kiref@kingstonpubliclibrary.org. Web Site: www.kingstonpubliclibrary.org. *Dir,* Sia Stewart; Tel: 781-831-6286, E-mail: sstewart@kingstonpubliclibrary.org; Staff 4 (MLS 4)
Founded 1898. Pop 12,204; Circ 192,333
Library Holdings: e-books 1,648; Bk Vols 62,216
Special Collections: History of Kingston; History of Plymouth County
Automation Activity & Vendor Info: (Cataloging) SirsiDynix; (Circulation) SirsiDynix; (OPAC) SirsiDynix
Wireless access
Open Mon 1-8, Tues-Thurs 10-8, Fri & Sat 10-5
Friends of the Library Group

LAKEVILLE

P LAKEVILLE PUBLIC LIBRARY*, Four Precinct St, 02347. SAN 307-4625. Tel: 508-947-9028. FAX: 508-923-9934. Web Site: www.lakevillelibrary.org. *Dir,* Jayme Viveiros; E-mail: jviveiros@sailsinc.org; *Youth Serv Librn,* Teresa Mirra
Founded 1914. Pop 10,639; Circ 112,000
Library Holdings: e-books 500; Large Print Bks 500; Bk Titles 28,000; Per Subs 55
Automation Activity & Vendor Info: (Cataloging) SirsiDynix; (Circulation) SirsiDynix; (OPAC) SirsiDynix
Wireless access
Partic in SAILS Library Network
Open Mon 12-8, Tues & Thurs 10-8, Wed 10-6, Sat 10-2
Friends of the Library Group

LANCASTER

P THAYER MEMORIAL LIBRARY*, 717 Main St, 01523-2248. SAN 307-4633. Tel: 978-368-8928. FAX: 978-368-8929. E-mail: tml12345678@gmail.com. Web Site: www.thayermemoriallibrary.org. *Dir,* Joseph J Mule; Staff 7 (MLS 1, Non-MLS 6)
Founded 1862. Pop 7,380; Circ 58,369
Library Holdings: AV Mats 3,228; e-books 6,548; Bk Vols 51,071; Per Subs 55
Subject Interests: Botany, Civil War, Local hist, Native Americans, Rare bks
Automation Activity & Vendor Info: (Cataloging) Innovative Interfaces, Inc; (Circulation) Innovative Interfaces, Inc; (ILL) Innovative Interfaces, Inc; (OPAC) Innovative Interfaces, Inc
Wireless access
Mem of Massachusetts Library System
Partic in Central & Western Massachusetts Automated Resource Sharing
Open Mon, Wed & Thurs 10-8, Tues 12-8, Fri 10-5, Sat 10-2
Friends of the Library Group

LANESBOROUGH

P LANESBOROUGH PUBLIC LIBRARY*, Town Hall, 83 N Main St, 01237. (Mail add: PO Box 352, 01237-0352), SAN 307-4641. Tel: 413-442-0222. FAX: 413-443-5811. Web Site: lanesboroughlibrary.weebly.com, www.lanesborough-ma.gov/lanesborough-public-library. *Dir,* Sheila Parks; E-mail: library.director@lanesborough-ma.gov
Founded 1871. Pop 2,900
Library Holdings: Bk Titles 15,000
Wireless access
Partic in Central & Western Massachusetts Automated Resource Sharing

Open Mon, Wed & Thurs 2-7, Tues 10-5, Sat 10-1
Friends of the Library Group

LAWRENCE

L LAWRENCE LAW LIBRARY*, Two Appleton St, 01840-1525. SAN 307-4668. Tel: 978-687-7608. FAX: 978-688-2346. E-mail: lawrencelawlibrary@yahoo.com. Web Site: www.mass.gov/locations/lawrence-law-library. *Head Law Librn,* Laurie Paszko
Founded 1905
Library Holdings: Bk Vols 30,000
Automation Activity & Vendor Info: (Cataloging) OCLC; (Circulation) OCLC
Wireless access
Open Mon-Fri 8:30-4:15
Friends of the Library Group

P LAWRENCE PUBLIC LIBRARY*, 51 Lawrence St, 01841. SAN 345-2913. Tel: 978-620-3600. Administration Tel: 978-620-3621. FAX: 978-688-3142. Web Site: www.lawrencefreelibrary.org. *Dir,* Jessica V Vilas Novas; E-mail: JVilasNovas@cityoflawrence.com; *Asst Dir,* Cassandra Abou-Farah; *Spec Coll Librn,* Louise Sandberg; *Children's Coordr,* Jacqueline Delacruz; *Head, Tech Serv,* Giselle Encarnacion; *Circ Coordr,* Elvin Fabian; *Teen Coordr,* Allan Zapata; Staff 24 (MLS 3, Non-MLS 21)
Founded 1872. Pop 80,000; Circ 150,000
Library Holdings: Large Print Bks 2,000; Bk Vols 150,000; Per Subs 300
Special Collections: Adult Basic Education; Career Opportunity Center Computerized Info & Referral; Funding Resources Center; Literacy; Local Historical Archives (1912 Labor Strike - Lawrence Historical Materials); Old Radio Shows (Kelly Tape Coll); Spanish Language Materials
Automation Activity & Vendor Info: (Cataloging) SirsiDynix; (Circulation) SirsiDynix; (ILL) SirsiDynix; (OPAC) SirsiDynix
Wireless access
Function: 24/7 Electronic res, 24/7 Online cat, Adult bk club, Adult literacy prog, Archival coll, Art exhibits, Art programs, Audiobks via web, AV serv, Bilingual assistance for Spanish patrons, CD-ROM, Chess club, Children's prog, Citizenship assistance, Computer training, Computers for patron use, Distance learning, Electronic databases & coll, Family literacy, Free DVD rentals, Holiday prog, Home delivery & serv to seniorr ctr & nursing homes, Homebound delivery serv, Homework prog, ILL available, Internet access, Life-long learning prog for all ages, Literacy & newcomer serv, Magazines, Magnifiers for reading, Notary serv, Orientations, Photocopying/Printing, Prog for adults, Prog for children & young adult, Ref serv available, Res assist avail, Scanner, Spanish lang bks, Spoken cassettes & CDs, STEM programs, Story hour, Summer reading prog, Tax forms, Teen prog, Telephone ref, VHS videos, Wheelchair accessible, Workshops, Writing prog
Mem of Massachusetts Library System
Partic in Merrimack Valley Library Consortium
Open Mon-Thurs 9-8, Fri 9-5
Friends of the Library Group
Branches: 1
SOUTH LAWRENCE BRANCH, 135 Parker St, South Lawrence, 01843, SAN 345-2948. Tel: 978-620-3560. FAX: 978-688-3142. *Dir,* Maureen Nimmo; Tel: 978-682-1727
Function: AV serv, CD-ROM, Electronic databases & coll, Internet access, Photocopying/Printing, Preschool outreach, Prog for children & young adult, Spoken cassettes & CDs, Summer reading prog, Telephone ref, VHS videos
Open Mon, Wed & Sat 10-5
Friends of the Library Group

LEE

P LEE LIBRARY ASSOCIATION*, 100 Main St, 01238-1688. SAN 307-4676. Tel: 413-243-0385. FAX: 413-243-0381. E-mail: lee@cwmars.org. Web Site: www.leelibrary.org. *Dir, Libr Serv,* Amanda Mark; *Pub Serv,* Rosemarie Borsody; *Tech Serv,* Jose Garcia; Staff 10 (MLS 1, Non-MLS 9)
Founded 1874. Pop 5,865; Circ 42,280
Library Holdings: Audiobooks 617; DVDs 245; e-books 1,145; Bk Titles 50,410; Per Subs 101; Videos 494
Special Collections: Oral History
Subject Interests: Local hist
Automation Activity & Vendor Info: (Cataloging) Innovative Interfaces, Inc; (Circulation) Innovative Interfaces, Inc; (OPAC) Innovative Interfaces, Inc
Wireless access
Partic in Central & Western Massachusetts Automated Resource Sharing
Open Mon, Tues & Thurs 10-8, Wed & Fri 10-5, Sat 10-2

LEEDS

GM DEPARTMENT OF VETERANS AFFAIRS*, Medical Center Library, VA Central Western Massachusetts Healthcare System, 421 N Main St, 01053-9764. SAN 307-5923. Tel: 413-584-4040, Ext 2432. FAX: 413-582-3039. *Librn,* Deanna Williams
Library Holdings: Bk Vols 5,000; Per Subs 75
Special Collections: Patient Health Coll
Subject Interests: Psychiat, Psychol
Open Mon-Fri 7:30-4
Restriction: Open to pub for ref only

LEICESTER

C BECKER COLLEGE*, Paul R Swan, 13 Washburn Sq, 01524. (Mail add: William F Ruska Library, 61 Sever St, Worcester, 01609), SAN 307-4684. Tel: 508-373-9710. E-mail: library@becker.edu. Web Site: www.becker.edu/academics/libraries-2. *Dir of Libr Operations,* Donna M Sibley; Tel: 508-373-9712, E-mail: donna.sibley@becker.edu
Enrl 1,800
Library Holdings: Bk Vols 31,000; Per Subs 104
Special Collections: Samuel May Coll
Automation Activity & Vendor Info: (Cataloging) Innovative Interfaces, Inc - Millennium; (Circulation) Innovative Interfaces, Inc - Millennium; (Course Reserve) Innovative Interfaces, Inc - Millennium; (ILL) OCLC FirstSearch; (Media Booking) Innovative Interfaces, Inc; (OPAC) Innovative Interfaces, Inc; (Serials) EBSCO Online
Wireless access
Mem of Massachusetts Library System
Partic in OCLC Online Computer Library Center, Inc
Open Mon-Thurs 8am-9pm, Fri 8-4, Sun 4-9

P LEICESTER PUBLIC LIBRARY & LOCAL HISTORY MUSEUM, 1136 Main St, 01524. SAN 345-2972. Tel: 508-892-7020. E-mail: library@leicesterma.org. Web Site: www.leicesterma.org/leicester-public-library. *Libr Dir,* Suzanne Hall; E-mail: halls@leicesterma.org; *Cat,* Donna Johnson; *Ch Serv,* Kaeleigh Hart; E-mail: khart@cwmars.org; Staff 2 (MLS 1, Non-MLS 1)
Founded 1861. Pop 10,000; Circ 35,655
Library Holdings: AV Mats 2,500; Bk Vols 37,000; Per Subs 55; Talking Bks 763
Subject Interests: Local hist
Automation Activity & Vendor Info: (Cataloging) Follett Software; (Circulation) Follett Software
Function: 24/7 Electronic res, 24/7 Online cat, Adult bk club, Archival coll, Art exhibits, Audiobks on Playaways & MP3, Audiobks via web, Bks on CD, Children's prog, E-Readers, Electronic databases & coll, Free DVD rentals, ILL available, Internet access, Magazines, Mail & tel request accepted, Meeting rooms, Museum passes, Music CDs, Online cat, Online ref, Outside serv via phone, mail, e-mail & web, OverDrive digital audio bks, Photocopying/Printing, Printer for laptops & handheld devices, Prog for adults, Prog for children & young adult, Ref & res, Ref serv available, Res assist avail, Scanner, Spanish lang bks, Story hour, Study rm, Summer reading prog, Tax forms, Teen prog, Telephone ref, Wheelchair accessible
Mem of Massachusetts Library System
Partic in Central & Western Massachusetts Automated Resource Sharing
Open Tues & Thurs 9:30-8, Wed & Fri 9:30-5, Sat (Winter) 10-2
Friends of the Library Group

LENOX

P LENOX LIBRARY ASSOCIATION*, 18 Main St, 01240. SAN 307-4706. Tel: 413-637-0197. FAX: 413-637-2115. Web Site: lenoxlib.org. *Libr Dir,* Amy Lafave; E-mail: alafave@lenoxlib.org; *Coll Develop Librn,* JoAnn Spaulding; E-mail: jspaulding@lenoxlib.org; Staff 19 (MLS 5, Non-MLS 14)
Founded 1856. Pop 5,070; Circ 93,418
Library Holdings: Bk Vols 67,289; Per Subs 137
Special Collections: Art Exhibits; Elizabeth MacKinstry Coll; Fanny Kemble Coll; Historic Photographs; Judge Julius Rockwell Coll; Music Study Scores; Thomas Egelston Coll
Subject Interests: Local hist, Music
Wireless access
Function: ILL available
Publications: Photographs by Edwin Hale Lincoln (Local historical information); Pride of Palaces (Local historical information)
Partic in Central & Western Massachusetts Automated Resource Sharing
Open Tues 10-8, Wed-Fri 10-6, Sat 10-5

LEOMINSTER

P LEOMINSTER PUBLIC LIBRARY, 30 West St, 01453. SAN 307-4730. Tel: 978-534-7522. Circulation Tel: 978-534-7522, Ext 4. Information Services Tel: 978-534-7522, Ext 3. FAX: 978-840-3357. Reference E-mail: leomref@cwmars.org, leomref@leominster-ma.gov. Web Site: www.leominsterlibrary.org. *Dir,* Alexander Lent; Tel: 978-534-7522, Ext

3505, E-mail: alent@leominster-ma.gov; *Asst Dir,* Nicole Piermarini; Tel: 978-534-7522, Ext 3507, E-mail: npiermarini@leominster-ma.gov; *Head, Adult Serv,* Tracey Graham; Tel: 978-534-7522, Ext 3598, E-mail: tgraham@leominster-ma.gov; *Head, Children's Servx,* Sarah Chapdelaine; Tel: 978-534-7522, Ext 3600, E-mail: schapdelaine@leominster-ma.gov; *Head, Tech Serv,* May Lee Tom; Tel: 978-534-7522, Ext 3599, E-mail: mltom@leominster-ma.gov; *Local Hist & Genealogy Librn,* Diane Sanabria; Tel: 978-534-7522, Ext 3605, E-mail: dsanabria@leominster-ma.gov; *Teen Serv Librn,* Nadia Friedler; Tel: 978-534-7522, Ext 3616, E-mail: mfriedler@leominster-ma.gov; *Circ Supvr,* Kathryn Pellerite; Tel: 978-534-7522, Ext 3603, E-mail: kpellerite@leominster-ma.gov; *Coordr, Spec Serv, ILL,* Ann Finch; Tel: 978-534-7522, Ext 3593, E-mail: afinch@leominster-ma.gov
Founded 1856. Pop 41,000; Circ 234,965
Library Holdings: Bk Vols 105,486; Per Subs 203
Special Collections: Career Information Center; Local Historical & Genealogical Coll; Parent Resource Center
Automation Activity & Vendor Info: (Cataloging) Innovative Interfaces, Inc; (Circulation) Innovative Interfaces, Inc; (OPAC) Innovative Interfaces, Inc
Wireless access
Publications: Between Friends (Newsletter)
Mem of Massachusetts Library System
Partic in Central & Western Massachusetts Automated Resource Sharing
Open Mon-Thurs 10-7, Fri 10-5, Sat 10-1
Friends of the Library Group

LEVERETT

P LEVERETT LIBRARY, 75 Montague Rd, 01054. (Mail add: PO Box 250, 01054-0250), SAN 307-4749. Tel: 413-548-9220. FAX: 413-548-9034. E-mail: leverettlibrary@gmail.com. Web Site: www.leverettlibrary.org. *Libr Dir,* Misha Storm
Pop 1,900; Circ 38,000
Library Holdings: Bk Vols 9,500; Per Subs 24
Automation Activity & Vendor Info: (Cataloging) Evergreen; (Circulation) Evergreen
Wireless access
Partic in Cent Mass Automated Resource Sharing Network, Inc; Central & Western Massachusetts Automated Resource Sharing
Open Tues & Thurs 3-8, Wed & Sat 10-3, Sun 12-5
Friends of the Library Group

LEXINGTON

P CARY MEMORIAL LIBRARY, 1874 Massachusetts Ave, 02420. SAN 345-3030. Tel: 781-862-6288. FAX: 781-862-7355. Web Site: www.carylibrary.org. *Libr Dir,* Koren Stembridge; Tel: 781-862-6288, Ext 84401, E-mail: kstembridge@lexingtonma.gov; *Dep Dir, Head, Tech,* Emily Smith; Tel: 781-862-6288, Ext 84402, E-mail: esmith@minlib.net; *Head, Adult Serv,* Cathie Ghorbani; Tel: 781-862-6288, Ext 84411, E-mail: cghorbani@minlib.net; *Head, Youth Serv,* Alissa Lauzon; Tel: 781-862-6288, Ext 84431, E-mail: alauzon@minlib.net; Staff 61 (MLS 26, Non-MLS 35)
Founded 1868. Pop 32,272; Circ 814,678
Library Holdings: Bk Vols 207,013; Per Subs 225
Special Collections: American Revolutionary War Coll; Cary Library Art Coll; Lexington History (Worthen Coll); The Edwin B Worthen Coll; The Fred Spider Coll; The Lexington Authors Coll. Oral History
Subject Interests: Local hist
Automation Activity & Vendor Info: (Acquisitions) Innovative Interfaces, Inc; (Cataloging) Innovative Interfaces, Inc; (Circulation) Innovative Interfaces, Inc; (Course Reserve) Innovative Interfaces, Inc; (ILL) Innovative Interfaces, Inc; (Media Booking) Innovative Interfaces, Inc; (OPAC) Innovative Interfaces, Inc; (Serials) Innovative Interfaces, Inc
Wireless access
Partic in Minuteman Library Network
Open Tues & Thurs 10-6, Wed 10-7, Fri & Sat 10-5
Friends of the Library Group

S LEXINGTON HISTORICAL SOCIETY*, 1332 Massachusetts Ave, 02420-3809. (Mail add: PO Box 514, 02420-0005), SAN 375-1015. Tel: 781-862-1703. Web Site: www.lexingtonhistory.org. *Dir,* Erica McAvoy; E-mail: director@lexingtonhistory.org; *Archives Mgr,* Elizabeth M Mubarek; Tel: 781-862-0928, E-mail: EMubarek@lexingtonhistory.org; *Colls Mgr,* Stacey Fraser; Tel: 781-862-3763, E-mail: sfraser@lexingtonhistory.org
Founded 1886
Library Holdings: Bk Titles 200

S MASSACHUSETTS INSTITUTE OF TECHNOLOGY*, Lincoln Laboratory Knowledge Services, 244 Wood St, 02420-9176. SAN 307-482X. Tel: 781-981-5500. E-mail: library@ll.mit.edu. Web Site: www.ll.mit.edu. *Sector Mgr,* Suellen Green; Tel: 781-981-3221, Fax: 781-981-0345, E-mail: sgreen@LL.MIT.EDU; *Archives Team Lead,* Nora Zaldivar; Tel: 781-981-3985, E-mail: nzaldivar@LL.MIT.EDU; *Info Mgt & Metadata Team Lead,* Bobb Menk; Tel: 781-981-5354, E-mail: bmenk@LL.MIT.EDU; Staff 23 (MLS 18, Non-MLS 5)
Founded 1952
Library Holdings: e-books 10,000; e-journals 4,000; Bk Titles 127,000; Bk Vols 130,000; Per Subs 963
Subject Interests: Aerospace sci, Electronics, Engr, Optics, Solid state physics
Automation Activity & Vendor Info: (Acquisitions) SirsiDynix; (Cataloging) SirsiDynix; (Circulation) SirsiDynix; (OPAC) SirsiDynix; (Serials) SirsiDynix
Function: Archival coll, Bus archives, Doc delivery serv, For res purposes, Govt ref serv, ILL available, Internet access, Res libr
Publications: DoD Update; Management Focus; Scanner; Technical Reports Announcement
Partic in OCLC Online Computer Library Center, Inc
Restriction: Not open to pub

S SCOTTISH RITE MASONIC MUSEUM & LIBRARY, INC*, Van Gorden-Williams Library & Archives (National Heritage Museum), 33 Marrett Rd, 02421. Tel: 781-457-4125. Web Site: www.srmml.org/library-archives. *Dir, Libr & Archives,* Jeff Croteau; E-mail: jcroteau@srmml.org; *Archivist,* John Coelho; Tel: 781-457-4116, E-mail: jcoelho@srmml.org; Staff 2 (MLS 2)
Founded 1975
Library Holdings: Bk Vols 60,000; Per Subs 50
Special Collections: Archives of Scottish Rite Northern Masonic Supreme Council
Subject Interests: Am Revolution, Americana, Freemasonry
Automation Activity & Vendor Info: (Cataloging) TLC (The Library Corporation); (Circulation) TLC (The Library Corporation); (OPAC) TLC (The Library Corporation); (Serials) TLC (The Library Corporation)
Wireless access
Function: Archival coll, Art exhibits, For res purposes, ILL available, Online cat, Ref serv available, Res libr, Telephone ref, Wheelchair accessible
Mem of Massachusetts Library System
Open Wed-Sat 10-4
Restriction: Closed stack, Open to pub for ref only, Restricted borrowing privileges

LEYDEN

P ROBERTSON MEMORIAL LIBRARY*, 849 Greenfield Rd, 01301-9419. SAN 307-4862. Tel: 413-773-9334. FAX: 413-772-0146. E-mail: leydenLibrary@gmail.com. *Head Librn,* Karin Parks
Founded 1913. Pop 720; Circ 8,850
Library Holdings: AV Mats 150; Bk Titles 3,762
Open Mon & Wed 1-6, Sat 10-Noon
Friends of the Library Group

LINCOLN

P LINCOLN PUBLIC LIBRARY, Three Bedford Rd, 01773. SAN 307-4889. Tel: 781-259-8465. Circulation Tel: 781-259-8465, Ext 203. Reference Tel: 781-259-8465, Ext 204. FAX: 781-259-1056. E-mail: lincoln@minlib.net. Web Site: www.lincolnpl.org. *Dir,* Barbara Myles; Tel: 781-259-8465, Ext 201, E-mail: bmyles@minlib.net; *Asst Dir,* Lisa Acker Rothenberg; Tel: 781-259-8465, Ext 202, E-mail: lrothenberg@minlib.net; *Ch,* Sarah Feather; Tel: 781-259-8465, Ext 205; *Ref Librn,* Robin Rappoport; *Ref Librn,* Janet Spiller; E-mail: jspiller@minlib.net; *Ref Librn,* Kate Tranquada; E-mail: ktranquada@minlib.net; *Tech Serv Librn,* Alyssa Freden; Tel: 781-259-8465, Ext 206, E-mail: afreden@minlib.net; *ILL,* Victoria Black; Tel: 781-259-8465, Ext 207; Staff 7 (MLS 6, Non-MLS 1)
Founded 1883. Pop 8,056; Circ 157,781
Library Holdings: Bk Vols 95,854; Per Subs 216
Subject Interests: Local hist
Automation Activity & Vendor Info: (Acquisitions) Innovative Interfaces, Inc; (Cataloging) Innovative Interfaces, Inc; (Circulation) Innovative Interfaces, Inc; (ILL) Innovative Interfaces, Inc; (OPAC) Innovative Interfaces, Inc
Wireless access
Partic in Minuteman Library Network
Open Mon, Wed & Thurs 1-7:30, Tues & Fri 10-6, Sat 10-5
Friends of the Library Group

LITTLETON

P REUBEN HOAR LIBRARY*, 41 Shattuck St, 01460-4506. SAN 307-4900. Tel: 978-540-2600. FAX: 978-952-2323. E-mail: info@littletonlibrary.org, mli@mvlc.org. Web Site: www.littletonlibrary.org. *Libr Dir,* Samuel Alvarez; E-mail: salvarez@littletonlibrary.org; *Asst Dir,* Helen Graham; E-mail: hgraham@littletonlibrary.org; *Sr Librn,* Andrea Curran; E-mail: acurran@littletonlibrary.org; *Sr Librn,* Diann Haduch; E-mail: dhaduch@littletonlibrary.org; Staff 15 (MLS 2, Non-MLS 13)
Founded 1887. Pop 8,000; Circ 180,583

Library Holdings: DVDs 4,995; Microforms 116; Bk Titles 75,843; Per Subs 183
Subject Interests: Local hist, Sci fict
Automation Activity & Vendor Info: (Cataloging) SirsiDynix; (Circulation) SirsiDynix; (OPAC) SirsiDynix
Wireless access
Function: After school storytime, Art exhibits, Audiobks via web, Bks on cassette, Bks on CD, Children's prog, Computers for patron use, Electronic databases & coll, Free DVD rentals, Home delivery & serv to seniorr ctr & nursing homes, Homebound delivery serv, ILL available, Mail & tel request accepted, Museum passes, Music CDs, Notary serv, Online cat, Online ref, OverDrive digital audio bks, Photocopying/Printing, Preschool outreach, Prog for children & young adult, Ref serv available, Story hour, Summer reading prog, Tax forms, Teen prog, Telephone ref, VHS videos, Wheelchair accessible
Publications: Reuben's Notes (Newsletter)
Mem of Massachusetts Library System
Partic in Merrimack Valley Library Consortium
Open Mon & Sat 10-4, Tues & Thurs 2-9, Wed 10-9, Fri 10-1
Friends of the Library Group

LONGMEADOW

C BAY PATH COLLEGE*, Hatch Library, 539 Longmeadow St, 01106. (Mail add: 588 Longmeadow St, 01106), SAN 307-4927. Tel: 413-565-1376. FAX: 413-567-8345. Web Site: library.baypath.edu. *Asst Dean, Exec Dir,* Peter Testori; Tel: 413-565-1058, E-mail: ptestori@baypath.edu; *Libr Coord,* Peter Brunette; E-mail: pbrunette@baypath.edu; *Access Serv Librn,* Miriam Neiman; E-mail: mneiman@baypath.edu; Staff 5 (MLS 5)
Founded 1897. Enrl 1,689; Fac 175; Highest Degree: Master
Library Holdings: Audiobooks 26; AV Mats 4,451; CDs 201; DVDs 612; e-books 11,894; e-journals 52; Electronic Media & Resources 85; Microforms 4,380; Bk Titles 50,958; Bk Vols 69,987; Per Subs 140; Videos 2,810
Subject Interests: Bus, Info tech, Legal, Occupational therapy, Psychol
Automation Activity & Vendor Info: (Cataloging) SirsiDynix; (OPAC) SirsiDynix
Wireless access
Partic in Cooperating Libraries of Greater Springfield; LYRASIS; OCLC-LVIS
Open Mon & Wed 9-9, Tues & Thurs 9-6, Fri & Sat 9-5, Sun 1-6

P RICHARD SALTER STORRS LIBRARY*, 693 Longmeadow St, 01106. SAN 307-4935. Tel: 413-565-4181. FAX: 413-565-4143. E-mail: richard.salterstorrs@gmail.com. Web Site: www.longmeadowlibrary.org. *Libr Dir,* Jean Maziarz; E-mail: jmaziarz@longmeadow.org; *Coll Develop Librn, Programming,* Rebecca Vitkauskas; E-mail: rvitkauskas@longmeadow.org; *Adult Serv,* Andrea Puglisi; E-mail: apuglisi@longmeadow.org; *Youth Serv,* Katie McGonigle; E-mail: kmcgonigle@longmeadow.org
Founded 1907. Pop 16,000; Circ 213,216
Library Holdings: Bk Vols 100,000; Per Subs 130
Special Collections: Genealogy Coll; Local History Coll
Automation Activity & Vendor Info: (Cataloging) Innovative Interfaces, Inc; (Circulation) Innovative Interfaces, Inc; (OPAC) Innovative Interfaces, Inc
Wireless access
Mem of Massachusetts Library System
Partic in Central & Western Massachusetts Automated Resource Sharing
Open Mon-Thurs 9-8, Fri 9-5, Sat (Sept-May) 9-4
Friends of the Library Group

LOWELL

L MASSACHUSETTS TRIAL COURT*, Lowell Law Library, Superior Court House, 360 Gorham St, 01852. SAN 307-496X. Tel: 978-452-9301. FAX: 978-970-2000. E-mail: lowlaw@meganet.net. Web Site: www.mass.gov/locations/lowell-law-library. *Head Law Librn,* Catherine Mello Alves; E-mail: catherine.alves@jud.state.ma.us; *Libr Asst,* Janet Haouchine; Staff 2 (MLS 1, Non-MLS 1)
Founded 1815
Library Holdings: Bk Vols 35,000; Per Subs 53
Special Collections: Law books - Legal Periodicals Statutes, Case Reporters, Digests, Legal Treatises
Automation Activity & Vendor Info: (Cataloging) SirsiDynix; (Circulation) Horizon; (ILL) OCLC FirstSearch; (OPAC) Horizon; (Serials) Horizon
Wireless access
Open Mon-Fri 8:30-4:15
Friends of the Library Group

J MIDDLESEX COMMUNITY COLLEGE*, City Campus Library, Federal Bldg, E Merrimack St, 01852. (Mail add: 33 Kearney Sq, 01852-1987), SAN 372-4093. Tel: 978-656-3005. Circulation Tel: 978-656-3004. FAX: 978-656-3031. E-mail: mcclibrary@middlesex.mass.edu. Web Site: libguides.middlesex.mass.edu/library. *Dir of Libr,* Donna G Maturi; E-mail: maturid@middlesex.mass.edu; *Circ Librn,* Kim Robbins; E-mail: robbinsk@middlesex.mass.edu; *Student Success Librn,* Kim Money; E-mail: moneyk@middlesex.mass.edu
Library Holdings: Bk Vols 16,000; Per Subs 200
Automation Activity & Vendor Info: (Acquisitions) Innovative Interfaces, Inc; (Cataloging) Innovative Interfaces, Inc; (Circulation) Innovative Interfaces, Inc
Wireless access
Open Mon-Thurs (Winter) 8:30-8, Fri 8:30-4:30, Sat 9-1; Mon-Fri (Summer) 8:30-4:30

P POLLARD MEMORIAL LIBRARY*, 401 Merrimack St, 01852. SAN 307-4943. Tel: 978-674-4120. FAX: 978-970-4117. E-mail: adultref@LowellLibrary.org. Web Site: www.pollardml.org. *Dir,* Victoria B Woodley; E-mail: vwoodley@LowellLibrary.org; *Asst Dir, Head, Ref,* Susan Fougstedt; E-mail: sfougstedt@lowellma.org; *Literacy Prog Dir,* Carolyn Thompson; E-mail: cthompson@lowelllibrary.org; *Head, Circ,* Elizabeth Manning; E-mail: emanning@lowelllibrary.org; *Ch,* Lauren Eldred; E-mail: leldred@lowelllibrary.org; *Commun Planning Librn,* Bridget Cooley; E-mail: bcooley@lowelllibrary.org; *Ref Librn,* Pam Colt; E-mail: pcolt@lowelllibrary.org; *Ref Librn,* Monica McDermott; E-mail: mmcdermott@lowelllibrary.org; *YA Librn,* Beth Brassel; E-mail: ebrassel@lowelllibrary.org; *Coordr, Automation & Tech Serv,* Dory Lewis; E-mail: dlewis@lowelllibrary.org; *Commun Planning Coordr,* Sean Thibodeau; E-mail: sthibodeau@lowelllibrary.org; *Coordr, Youth Serv,* Molly Hancock; E-mail: mhancock@lowelllibrary.org; *IT Spec,* Mary Ann Kearns; E-mail: mkearns@lowelllibrary.org; Staff 12 (MLS 11, Non-MLS 1)
Founded 1844. Pop 105,167; Circ 212,401
Library Holdings: AV Mats 3,981; Bk Vols 166,217; Per Subs 580
Special Collections: History of Lowell Coll
Subject Interests: Genealogy
Automation Activity & Vendor Info: (Cataloging) Evergreen; (Circulation) Evergreen; (OPAC) Evergreen
Wireless access
Function: Activity rm, Adult bk club, Adult literacy prog, Archival coll, Audiobks via web, BA reader (adult literacy), Bks on CD, CD-ROM, Children's prog, Citizenship assistance, Computer training, Computers for patron use, Digital talking bks, E-Reserves, Electronic databases & coll, Free DVD rentals, Holiday prog, ILL available, Large print keyboards, Magazines, Magnifiers for reading, Microfiche/film & reading machines, Movies, Museum passes, Music CDs, Online cat, OverDrive digital audio bks, Photocopying/Printing, Prog for adults, Prog for children & young adult, Ref serv available, Res performed for a fee, Spanish lang bks, Spoken cassettes & CDs, Story hour, Study rm, Summer reading prog, Tax forms, Teen prog, Telephone ref, Wheelchair accessible
Mem of Massachusetts Library System
Partic in Merrimack Valley Library Consortium
Special Services for the Deaf - TTY equip
Special Services for the Blind - Accessible computers; Assistive/Adapted tech devices, equip & products; Bks on CD; Computer access aids; Computer with voice synthesizer for visually impaired persons; Copier with enlargement capabilities
Open Mon-Thurs 9-9, Fri & Sat 9-5
Friends of the Library Group
Branches: 1
SENIOR CENTER BRANCH, 276 Broadway St, 01854. *Dir,* Victoria Woodley
Library Holdings: Bk Vols 2,200
Function: Computers for patron use, Photocopying/Printing
Open Mon-Fri 9-4

C UNIVERSITY OF MASSACHUSETTS LOWELL LIBRARY*, O'Leary Library, 61 Wilder St, 01854-3098. SAN 345-312X. Tel: 978-934-4550, 978-934-4551. Circulation Tel: 978-934-4585. Interlibrary Loan Service Tel: 978-934-4573. Reference Tel: 978-934-4554. Administration Tel: 978-934-4575. Automation Services Tel: 978-923-4570. FAX: 978-934-3015. Web Site: www.uml.edu/library. *Dir of Libr,* George Hart; E-mail: George_Hart@uml.edu; *Head, Access Serv,* Ellen Keane; Tel: 978-934-4594, E-mail: Ellen_Keane@uml.edu; *Ref Librn,* Sara Marks; Tel: 978-934-4581, E-mail: Sara_Marks@uml.edu; *Coordr, Access Serv,* Deborah Friedman; Tel: 978-934-4572, E-mail: Deborah_Friedman@uml.edu; Staff 24 (MLS 14, Non-MLS 10)
Enrl 8,125; Fac 453; Highest Degree: Doctorate
Library Holdings: AV Mats 7,656; e-books 4,289; e-journals 12,498; Bk Vols 397,652; Per Subs 520; Videos 6,168
Special Collections: ERIC Microfiche Coll (1972-2002). US Document Depository
Subject Interests: Allied health, Educ, Fine arts, Humanities, Nursing
Automation Activity & Vendor Info: (Acquisitions) Ex Libris Group; (Cataloging) Ex Libris Group; (Circulation) Ex Libris Group; (Course Reserve) Ex Libris Group; (ILL) OCLC; (OPAC) Ex Libris Group; (Serials) Ex Libris Group

Wireless access
Function: AV serv, Health sci info serv, ILL available, Music CDs, Orientations, Photocopying/Printing, Ref serv available, Telephone ref, VHS videos, Wheelchair accessible
Mem of Massachusetts Library System
Partic in Boston Library Consortium, Inc; LYRASIS
Special Services for the Blind - Assistive/Adapted tech devices, equip & products
Open Mon-Thurs (Winter) 7:30am-Midnight, Fri 7:30-5, Sat 10-6, Sun 1-Midnight; Mon-Thurs (Summer) 7:30am-10pm, Fri 7:30-5
Friends of the Library Group
Departmental Libraries:
CENTER FOR LOWELL HISTORY, Patrick J Mogan Cultural Ctr, 40 French St, 01852, SAN 329-6369. Tel: 978-934-4997. FAX: 978-934-4995. *Dir, Spec Coll,* Martha Mayo; Tel: 978-934-4998, E-mail: martha_mayo@uml.edu; *Archives Mgr,* Janine Whitcomb; E-mail: janine_whitcomb@uml.edu; Staff 2 (MLS 1, Non-MLS 1)
Founded 1971
Special Collections: Boston & Maine Railroad Historical Society Coll; Lowell Historical Society Coll; Lowell Museum Coll; Manning Family Coll; Middlesex Canal Assoc Coll; Proprietors of the Locks Canal Co Coll; Senator Paul E Tsongas Coll, papers; Textiles (Olney Coll); University of Lowell Archives. Oral History
Function: ILL available
Open Mon, Wed-Fri 9-5, Tues 9-9, Sat 10-3
Restriction: Non-circulating coll
LYDON LIBRARY, 84 University Ave, 01854-2896, SAN 345-309X. Tel: 978-934-3205. Interlibrary Loan Service Tel: 978-934-3206. Reference Tel: 978-934-3213. Administration Tel: 978-934-3216. FAX: 978-934-3014. *Head, Access Serv,* Ellen Keane; Tel: 978-934-3203, E-mail: ellen_keane@uml.edu; *Ref Librn,* Margaret Manion; Tel: 978-934-3211, E-mail: margaret_manion@uml.edu; *Ref Librn,* Marion Muskiewicz; Tel: 978-934-3209, E-mail: marion_muskiewicz@uml.edu; *Coordr, Access Serv,* Judith Barnes-Long; Tel: 978-934-3552, E-mail: judith_barnes@uml.edu; *Access Serv,* Denise Chandonnet; Tel: 978-934-3215, E-mail: denise_chandonnet@uml.edu; *Access Serv,* Donna Tanguay; Tel: 978-934-3204, E-mail: donna_tanguay@uml.edu. Subject Specialists: *Engr,* Margaret Manion; Staff 5 (MLS 4, Non-MLS 1)
Special Collections: University of Lowell Archives. Oral History
Subject Interests: Bus & mgt, Chem, Computer sci, Electrical engr, Engr, Environ studies, Indust engr, Nuclear engr, Physics, Software engr
Function: AV serv, Govt ref serv, ILL available, Orientations, Ref serv available, Wheelchair accessible
Open Mon-Thurs 7:30am-Midnight, Fri 7:30-5, Sat 10-6, Sun 1-Midnight

LUDLOW

P HUBBARD MEMORIAL LIBRARY*, 24 Center St, 01056-2795. SAN 307-4986. Tel: 413-583-3408. FAX: 413-583-5646. E-mail: library@ludlow.ma.us. Web Site: www.hubbardlibrary.org. *Dir,* Patrick McGowan; E-mail: pmcgowan@cwmars.org; Staff 8 (MLS 2, Non-MLS 6)
Founded 1891. Pop 22,000; Circ 107,657
Library Holdings: AV Mats 4,255; Bk Vols 56,862; Per Subs 95
Special Collections: Jack Alves Vietnam Coll
Subject Interests: World War II
Automation Activity & Vendor Info: (Circulation) Innovative Interfaces, Inc; (ILL) Innovative Interfaces, Inc; (OPAC) Innovative Interfaces, Inc
Wireless access
Partic in Central & Western Massachusetts Automated Resource Sharing
Open Mon, Wed & Fri 9-5, Tues & Thurs 9-8, Sat (Sept-June) 9-1
Friends of the Library Group

LUNENBURG

P LUNENBURG PUBLIC LIBRARY*, 1023 Massachusetts Ave, 01462. SAN 307-4994. Tel: 978-582-4140. FAX: 978-582-4141. E-mail: lunenburglibrary@gmail.com. Web Site: www.lunenburglibrary.org. *Dir,* Muir Haman; E-mail: mhaman@cwmars.org; *Ch,* Debra Laffond; E-mail: dlaffond@cwmars.org; *Digital Serv Librn,* Heather Buiwit; E-mail: hbuiwit@cwmars.org; *YA Librn,* Nicole Piermarini; E-mail: npiermarini@cwmars.org. Subject Specialists: *Communications, Info tech, Mkt,* Heather Buiwit; Staff 10 (MLS 3, Non-MLS 7)
Founded 1909. Pop 10,000
Library Holdings: Bk Titles 29,643; Per Subs 80
Automation Activity & Vendor Info: (Cataloging) Evergreen; (Circulation) Evergreen; (ILL) Evergreen; (OPAC) Evergreen
Wireless access
Function: 24/7 Electronic res, Activity rm, Adult bk club, Art exhibits, Art programs, Audio & video playback equip for onsite use, Audiobks on Playaways & MP3, Audiobks via web, Bk club(s), Bks on CD, Children's prog, Computer training, Computers for patron use, Doc delivery serv, E-Readers, E-Reserves, Electronic databases & coll, Homework prog, ILL available, Internet access, Magazines, Mail & tel request accepted, Makerspace, Meeting rooms, Movies, Museum passes, Music CDs, Online cat, Wheelchair accessible
Partic in Central & Western Massachusetts Automated Resource Sharing
Open Mon-Thurs 10-8, Sat 10-2
Restriction: Authorized patrons, Staff & customers only
Friends of the Library Group

LYNN

P LYNN PUBLIC LIBRARY*, Five N Common St, 01902. SAN 345-3154. Tel: 781-595-0567. FAX: 781-592-5050. E-mail: lynnq@noblenet.org. Web Site: www.noblenet.org/lynn. *Chief Librn,* Theresa Hurley; E-mail: hurley@noblenet.org; *Bus & Finance Mgr,* Paula Joyal; *Adult Serv,* Lindsey Robert; *Ch Serv,* Susan Cronin; *Ref (Info Servs),* Lisa Bourque; Staff 5 (MLS 2, Non-MLS 3)
Founded 1815. Pop 89,050
Library Holdings: Bk Titles 110,000; Per Subs 210
Special Collections: Shoe Industry Coll
Subject Interests: Civil War, Genealogy, Hist, Law
Automation Activity & Vendor Info: (Cataloging) Innovative Interfaces, Inc; (Circulation) Innovative Interfaces, Inc; (OPAC) Innovative Interfaces, Inc
Wireless access
Function: After school storytime, Archival coll, CD-ROM, E-Reserves, Electronic databases & coll, Home delivery & serv to seniorr ctr & nursing homes, Homework prog, ILL available, Magnifiers for reading, Mail & tel request accepted, Music CDs, Photocopying/Printing, Prog for adults, Prog for children & young adult, Ref serv available, Spoken cassettes & CDs, Spoken cassettes & DVDs, Summer reading prog, Tax forms, Telephone ref, VHS videos, Wheelchair accessible
Partic in North of Boston Library Exchange, Inc
Special Services for the Deaf - Assisted listening device; Interpreter on staff; TTY equip
Special Services for the Blind - Audiovision-a radio reading serv; Bks on cassette; Bks on CD
Open Mon-Thurs (Winter) 9-9, Fri & Sat 9-5; Mon & Wed-Fri (Summer) 9-5, Tues 9-9
Friends of the Library Group

J NORTH SHORE COMMUNITY COLLEGE LIBRARY*, Lynn Campus Library, McGee Bldg, LE127, 300 Broad St, 01901. (Mail add: One Ferncroft Rd, Lynn Campus Library, Danvers, 01923). Tel: 781-593-6722. Administration E-mail: libadmin@northshore.edu. Web Site: library.northshore.edu. *Dir, Libr & Learning Res,* Rex Krajewski; Tel: 978-462-5524, E-mail: rkrajews@northshore.edu; *Access Serv Librn,* Erin D'Agostino; Tel: 978-762-4000, Ext 6248, E-mail: edagosti@northshore.edu; *Ref Librn,* Torrey Dukes; Tel: 978-762-4000, Ext 6244, E-mail: tdukes@northshore.edu; *Coordr, Pub Serv,* Dava Davainis; Tel: 978-762-4000, Ext 6245, E-mail: ddavaini@northshore.edu; *Coordr, Tech Serv,* John Koza; Tel: 978-739-5413, E-mail: jkoza@northshore.edu; *Libr Asst,* Indira Leisba; Tel: 978-762-4000, Ext 6611, E-mail: ileisb@northshore.edu; *Libr Asst,* Edie Saranteas; Tel: 978-762-4000, Ext 6251, E-mail: esarante@northshore.edu; Staff 5 (MLS 5)
Highest Degree: Associate
Automation Activity & Vendor Info: (Acquisitions) ByWater Solutions; (Circulation) ByWater Solutions; (Course Reserve) ByWater Solutions; (Discovery) EBSCO Discovery Service; (OPAC) ByWater Solutions
Wireless access
Function: 24/7 Electronic res, 24/7 Online cat, Art exhibits, Audio & video playback equip for onsite use, Computers for patron use, E-Reserves, Electronic databases & coll, ILL available, Internet access, Online cat, Online ref, Photocopying/Printing, Printer for laptops & handheld devices, Ref & res, Scanner, Study rm, Telephone ref, Wheelchair accessible
Mem of Massachusetts Library System
Partic in Fenway Library Consortium; Higher Educ Libr Info Network; Massachusetts Commonwealth Consortium of Libraries in Public Higher Education Institutions
Open Mon-Thurs 8-8, Fri 8-4
Restriction: Borrowing privileges limited to fac & registered students, In-house use for visitors

LYNNFIELD

P LYNNFIELD PUBLIC LIBRARY*, 18 Summer St, 01940-1837. SAN 345-3278. Tel: 781-334-5411, 781-334-6404. FAX: 781-334-2164. E-mail: lfd@noblenet.org. Web Site: www.lynnfieldlibrary.org. *Dir,* Jennifer Inglis; E-mail: jinglis@noblenet.org; *Asst Dir, Head, Adult Serv,* Abigail Porter; E-mail: aporter@noblenet.org; *Head, Circ,* Katherine Decker; E-mail: decker@noblenet.org; *Head, Ref Serv,* Patricia Kelly; E-mail: kelly@noblenet.org; *Head, Tech Serv,* Nicole Goolishian; E-mail: goolishian@noblenet.org; *Head, Youth Serv,* Lauren Fox; E-mail: lfox@noblenet.org; Staff 19 (MLS 4, Non-MLS 15)
Founded 1892. Pop 11,903; Circ 113,229
Library Holdings: AV Mats 4,494; Bk Vols 55,281; Per Subs 173
Special Collections: Oral History
Subject Interests: Local hist

Automation Activity & Vendor Info: (Acquisitions) Evergreen; (Cataloging) Evergreen; (Circulation) Evergreen; (ILL) Evergreen; (OPAC) Evergreen; (Serials) Evergreen
Wireless access
Function: Homebound delivery serv, ILL available, Photocopying/Printing, Prog for children & young adult, Ref serv available, Summer reading prog, Telephone ref, Wheelchair accessible
Publications: Library Link
Mem of Massachusetts Library System
Partic in North of Boston Library Exchange, Inc
Open Mon, Tues & Thurs 9-7, Wed & Fri 9-5, Sat 9-1
Friends of the Library Group

MALDEN

P MALDEN PUBLIC LIBRARY*, 36 Salem St, 02148-5291. SAN 345-3332. Tel: 781-324-0218. Interlibrary Loan Service Tel: 781-324-0220. FAX: 781-324-4467. E-mail: info@maldenpubliclibrary.org. Web Site: www.maldenpubliclibrary.org. *Dir,* Dora St Martin; E-mail: dstmartin@maldenpubliclibrary.org; *Asst Dir,* Caron Guigli; E-mail: cguigli@maldenpubliclibrary.org; Staff 10 (MLS 10)
Founded 1879. Pop 53,313; Circ 168,328
Library Holdings: Bk Titles 194,740; Per Subs 200
Special Collections: Abraham Lincoln (Pierce Coll)
Subject Interests: Art & archit, Hist, Local hist, Relig
Automation Activity & Vendor Info: (Cataloging) SirsiDynix; (Circulation) SirsiDynix; (ILL) SirsiDynix; (OPAC) SirsiDynix; (Serials) SirsiDynix
Wireless access
Publications: Annual Report; Booklet
Partic in Metro Boston Libr Network
Open Mon-Fri 10-6
Friends of the Library Group

MANCHESTER-BY-THE-SEA

P MANCHESTER-BY-THE-SEA PUBLIC LIBRARY*, 15 Union St, 01944. SAN 307-5036. Tel: 978-526-7711. Reference Tel: 978-526-2017. FAX: 978-526-2018. E-mail: info@manchesterpl.org. Web Site: www.manchesterpl.org. *Dir,* Sara Collins; E-mail: scollins@manchesterpl.org; *Head, Circ Serv,* Lori Dumont; E-mail: ldumont@manchesterpl.org; Staff 4 (MLS 3, Non-MLS 1)
Founded 1886. Pop 5,305; Circ 55,509
Library Holdings: AV Mats 5,047; Bk Titles 45,000; Per Subs 125
Automation Activity & Vendor Info: (Cataloging) SirsiDynix; (Circulation) SirsiDynix; (OPAC) SirsiDynix
Wireless access
Mem of Massachusetts Library System
Partic in Merrimack Valley Library Consortium
Open Mon & Wed 10-8, Tues & Thurs 1-8, Fri & Sat 10-5
Friends of the Library Group

S MANCHESTER HISTORICAL MUSEUM, Ten Union St, 01944. SAN 329-7403. Tel: 978-526-7230. E-mail: archives@manchesterhistoricalmuseum.org. Information Services E-mail: info@manchesterhistoricalmuseum.org. Web Site: manchesterhistoricalmuseum.org. *Archivist,* Christine Virden
Library Holdings: Bk Titles 500
Special Collections: Local Deeds Depository Coll
Subject Interests: Doc, Genealogy, Local hist, Manuscripts, Photog
Restriction: Open by appt only

MANSFIELD

P MANSFIELD PUBLIC LIBRARY, 255 Hope St, 02048-2353. SAN 307-5044. Tel: 508-261-7380. FAX: 508-261-7422. Web Site: www.mansfieldlibraryma.com, www.sailsinc.org/mansfield. *Dir,* Catherine Coyne; E-mail: ccoyne@sailsinc.org; *Asst Dir, Head, Ref,* Whitney Brown; *Head, Tech Serv,* Katherine Schacht; *Ch,* Mary Plumer; *Youth Serv Librn,* Zebulon Wimsatt; *Circ Supvr,* Darcy Bramley; *Ref (Info Servs),* Kristen Lyle; Staff 5 (MLS 5)
Founded 1884. Pop 22,400
Subject Interests: Local hist
Automation Activity & Vendor Info: (Acquisitions) SirsiDynix-Unicorn
Wireless access
Function: 24/7 Electronic res, 24/7 Online cat, Adult bk club, Archival coll, Bks on CD, Children's prog, Computer training, Computers for patron use, Electronic databases & coll, Free DVD rentals, ILL available, Internet access, Large print keyboards, Life-long learning prog for all ages, Magazines, Magnifiers for reading, Meeting rooms, Microfiche/film & reading machines, Museum passes, Music CDs, Notary serv, Online cat, Online ref, OverDrive digital audio bks, Photocopying/Printing, Printer for laptops & handheld devices, Prog for adults, Prog for children & young adult, Ref serv available, Scanner, STEM programs, Story hour, Summer reading prog, Tax forms, Teen prog, Telephone ref, Wheelchair accessible
Mem of Massachusetts Library System
Special Services for the Deaf - Assistive tech; Bks on deafness & sign lang; Closed caption videos
Special Services for the Blind - Assistive/Adapted tech devices, equip & products; Computer with voice synthesizer for visually impaired persons
Open Mon-Thurs 10-8, Fri 10-5, Sat 10-4
Friends of the Library Group

MARBLEHEAD

P ABBOT PUBLIC LIBRARY*, 235 Pleasant St, 01945. SAN 307-5052. Tel: 781-631-1481. Reference Tel: 781-631-1481, Ext 213. FAX: 781-639-0558. E-mail: mar@noblenet.org. Web Site: www.abbotlibrary.org. *Dir,* Patricia J Rogers; E-mail: rogers@noblenet.org; *Asst Dir,* Ann E Connolly; *Ad, ILL Librn,* Jonathan Randolph; *Ch,* Karen Nee; *YA Librn,* Mary Farrell; *Tech Serv,* Christine Evans; E-mail: evans@noblenet.org; Staff 24 (MLS 6, Non-MLS 18)
Founded 1878. Pop 19,971; Circ 219,458
Library Holdings: Bk Vols 115,895; Per Subs 258
Special Collections: Yachts & Yachting
Automation Activity & Vendor Info: (Cataloging) Innovative Interfaces, Inc; (Circulation) Innovative Interfaces, Inc; (Course Reserve) Innovative Interfaces, Inc; (OPAC) Innovative Interfaces, Inc; (Serials) Innovative Interfaces, Inc
Wireless access
Mem of Massachusetts Library System
Partic in North of Boston Library Exchange, Inc
Friends of the Library Group

S MARBLEHEAD MUSEUM & HISTORICAL SOCIETY LIBRARY*, 170 Washington St, 01945-3340. SAN 320-8613. Tel: 781-631-1069. FAX: 781-631-0917. E-mail: info@marbleheadmuseum.org. Web Site: www.marbleheadmuseum.org. *Curator,* Lauren McCormack; Staff 1 (Non-MLS 1)
Founded 1898
Library Holdings: Bk Vols 1,000
Special Collections: Diary & Genealogy Coll; Ledger & Log Book Coll; Unbound Document Coll
Open Tues-Fri 10-4

MARION

P ELIZABETH TABER LIBRARY, Eight Spring St, 02738. SAN 307-5060. Tel: 508-748-1252. FAX: 508-748-0939. E-mail: ETLibrary@sailsinc.org. Web Site: www.elizabethtaberlibrary.org. *Dir,* Elisabeth Sherry; E-mail: esherry@sailsinc.org; *Ch,* Rosemary Grey; E-mail: rgrey@sailsinc.org; Staff 4 (MLS 2, Non-MLS 2)
Founded 1872. Pop 8,000
Library Holdings: AV Mats 2,500; Large Print Bks 200; Bk Titles 37,000
Special Collections: Maritime History Coll, Marion History Coll
Automation Activity & Vendor Info: (Cataloging) SirsiDynix; (Circulation) SirsiDynix; (ILL) SirsiDynix; (OPAC) SirsiDynix; (Serials) SirsiDynix
Wireless access
Publications: Newsletter
Partic in SAILS Library Network
Open Mon, Wed & Fri 10-5, Tues & Thurs 10-8, Sat 10-3, Sun (Oct-April) 1-4

MARLBOROUGH

P MARLBOROUGH PUBLIC LIBRARY*, 35 W Main St, 01752-5510. SAN 307-5095. Tel: 508-624-6900. Administration Tel: 508-624-6901. FAX: 508-485-1494. Web Site: marlboroughpubliclibrary.org. *Dir,* Margaret Cardello; Tel: 508-624-6901, E-mail: mcardello@marlborough-ma.gov; *Asst Dir, Head, Ref,* Morgan Manzella; E-mail: mmanzella@cwmars.org; *Head, Circ, Head, Tech,* Annie Glater; E-mail: aglater@cwmars.org; *Head, Tech Serv,* Kerry Carlucci; E-mail: kcarlucci@cwmars.org; *Ch,* Jennie Simopoulos; E-mail: jsimopoulos@cwmars.org; *Libr Office Mgr,* Barbara Virgil; Tel: 508-624-6996, E-mail: bvirgil@marlborough-ma.gov; *YA Serv,* Christine Amatrudo; E-mail: camatrudo@cwmars.org; Staff 33 (MLS 5, Non-MLS 28)
Founded 1871. Pop 39,415
Library Holdings: Bk Vols 130,000; Per Subs 275
Special Collections: Horatio Alger Coll
Automation Activity & Vendor Info: (Cataloging) Evergreen; (Circulation) Evergreen; (OPAC) Evergreen
Wireless access
Partic in Central & Western Massachusetts Automated Resource Sharing
Open Mon-Thurs 9-8:30, Fri & Sat 9-5, Sun 1-5
Friends of the Library Group

P MASSACHUSETTS LIBRARY SYSTEM*, 225 Cedar Hill St, Ste 229, 01752. Tel: 508-357-2121. Toll Free Tel: 866-627-7228 (MA Only). FAX: 908-357-2122. E-mail: info@masslibsystem.org. Web Site:

www.masslibsystem.org. *Interim Exec Dir,* Sara Sogigian; E-mail: sarah@masslibsystem.org
Wireless access
Member Libraries: Abbot Public Library; Abington Public Library; Acushnet Public Library; Albany International Research Co Library; American Antiquarian Society Library; American International College; Ames Free Library; Andover Newton Theological School; Anna Maria College; Ashby Free Public Library; Associated Grant Makers; Assumption University; Athol Public Library; Auburn Public Library; Avon Public Library; Ayer Library; Babson College; Bancroft Memorial Library; Beals Memorial Library; Beaman Memorial Public Library; Becker College; Bedford Free Public Library; Bellingham Public Library; Berkley Public Library; Beverly Public Library; Bigelow Free Public Library; Blackstone Public Library; Bolton Public Library; Boxford Town Library; Boyden Library; Boylston Public Library; Boynton Public Library; Brandeis University; Brimfield Public Library; Bristol Community College; Brooks Free Library; Cambridge Hospital-Cambridge Health Alliance; Cambridge Public Library; Cape Cod Community College; Cape Cod Hospital; Caritas Norwood Hospital; CDM Smith InfoCenter; Central Massachusetts Regional Library System; Charlton Memorial Hospital; Charlton Public Library; Chilmark Free Public Library; Clark University; Conant Public Library; Congregation Mishkan Tefila; Cotuit Library; Curry College; Dalton Free Public Library; Dean College; Dighton Public Library; Dover Town Library; Duxbury Free Library; East Bridgewater Public Library; East Brookfield Public Library; Eastern Nazarene College; Eastham Public Library; Eldredge Public Library; Episcopal Divinity School - Sherrill Library; Erving Public Library; Everett Public Libraries; Fall River Public Library; Falmouth Public Library; Federal Reserve Bank of Boston; Field Memorial Library; First Parish Church of Norwell; Flint Memorial Library; Flint Public Library; Fobes Memorial Library; Forbush Memorial Library; Framingham Public Library; G A R Memorial Library; Gale Free Library; Gleason Public Library; Gloucester, Lyceum & Sawyer Free Library; Gordon College; Grafton Public Library; Greenfield Public Library; Griswold Memorial Library; Hamilton-Wenham Public Library; Hampshire College Library; Harvard Public Library; Harwich Port Library Association; Haston Free Public Library; Hazen Memorial Library; Hellenic College-Holy Cross Greek Orthodox School of Theology; Holbrook Public Library; Hopkinton Public Library; Hubbardston Public Library; Hudson Public Library; J V Fletcher Library; Jacob Edwards Library; Jonathan Bourne Public Library; Joshua Hyde Public Library; Law Library of the Massachusetts Attorney General; Lawrence Library; Lawrence Public Library; Leicester Public Library & Local History Museum; Lemuel Shattuck Hospital; Leominster Public Library; Leroy Pollard Memorial Library; Levi Heywood Memorial Library; Longy School of Music of Bard College; Lucius Beebe Memorial Library; Lyman & Merrie Wood Museum of Springfield History; Lynnfield Public Library; Manchester-by-the-Sea Public Library; Mansfield Public Library; Marian Court College; Marine Biological Laboratory; Marstons Mills Public Library; Mashpee Public Library; Massachusetts Department of Corrections; Massachusetts Horticultural Society Library; Massachusetts School of Law Library; Massachusetts Trial Court; Mattapoisett Free Public Library; Medway Public Library; Memorial Hall Library; Merrick Public Library; Merrimack College; Middlesex Law Library; Milford Regional Medical Center; Milford Town Library; Millbury Public Library; Millis Public Library; Millville Free Public Library; Montague Public Libraries; Montserrat College of Art; Morse Institute Library; Mount Wachusett Community College Library; Nahant Public Library; National Fire Protection Association; Needham Free Public Library; Nevins Memorial Library; New England College of Optometry Library; New England Conservatory of Music; Newbury College Library; Newburyport Public Library; Newton Free Library; Nichols College; Norman Rockwell Museum; North Adams Public Library; North Shore Community College Library; Northborough Free Library; Northern Essex Community College; Norwell Public Library; Oxford Free Library; Pearle L Crawford Memorial Library; Pelham Library; Perkins School for the Blind; Petersham Memorial Library; Phillipston Free Public Library; Phinehas S Newton Library; Pine Manor College; Plympton Public Library; Pollard Memorial Library; Pope John XXIII National Seminary; Princeton Public Library; Provincetown Public Library; Quinsigamond Community College; Raynham Public Library; Reading Public Library; Regis College Library; Reuben Hoar Library; Richard Salter Storrs Library; Richard Sugden Library; Rockport Public Library; Rowley Public Library; Roxbury Community College Library; Rutland Free Public Library; Saint Vincent Hospital; Salem Athenaeum; Scottish Rite Masonic Museum & Library, Inc; Sharon Public Library; Sherborn Library; Shrewsbury Public Library; Simon Fairfield Public Library; Somerville Public Library; South Dennis Free Public Library; South Hadley Public Library; Southborough Public Library; Springfield Technical Community College Library; Stevens Memorial Library; Stoneham Public Library; Stonehill College; Sturgis Library; Sutton Free Public Library; T O H P Burnham Public Library; Taunton Public Library; Tewksbury Public Library; Thayer Memorial Library; The Mary Baker Eddy Library; Thomas Crane Public Library; Topsfield Town Library; Tower Hill Botanic Garden; Townsend Public Library; Truro Public Library; Tufts University; Tyler Memorial Library; Tyngsborough Public Library; University of Massachusetts Lowell Library; Upton Town Library; Uxbridge Free Public Library; Warren Public Library; Wayland Free Public Library; Wellfleet Public Library; Wenham Museum; West Bridgewater Public Library; West Warren Library; Westborough Public Library; Westport Free Public Library; Whitinsville Social Library; Wilmington Memorial Library; Woburn Public Library; Woods Hole Public Library; Woods Memorial Library; Worcester Art Museum Library; Worcester Polytechnic Institute; Worcester Public Library
Partic in Association for Rural & Small Libraries

S RAYTHEON CO*, IDS Research Library, 1001 Boston Post Rd, 2-2-2964, 01752-3789. SAN 329-112X. Tel: 508-490-2288. FAX: 508-490-2017. Web Site: www.raytheon.com. *Sr Res Librn,* Steve McCulloch; E-mail: steven_mcculloch@raytheon.com
Founded 1988
Automation Activity & Vendor Info: (Cataloging) EOS International; (Circulation) EOS International; (Discovery) ProQuest; (ILL) OCLC WorldShare Interlibrary Loan; (OPAC) EOS International; (Serials) EOS International
Wireless access
Partic in OCLC Online Computer Library Center, Inc
Restriction: Staff use only

MARSHFIELD

P VENTRESS MEMORIAL LIBRARY*, 15 Library Plaza, 02050. SAN 307-5117. Tel: 781-834-5535. FAX: 781-837-8362. Web Site: www.ventresslibrary.org. *Libr Dir,* Cyndee Marcoux; E-mail: cmarcoux@ocln.org; *Asst Dir, Head, Ref Serv,* Christine Woods; E-mail: cwoods@ocln.org; *Cat, Head, Tech Serv,* Nancy Kelly; E-mail: nkelly@ocln.org; *Adult Serv, Ref Librn,* Nancy Hickey; E-mail: nhickey@ocln.org; *Ref Librn, YA Serv,* Charlie Grosholz; E-mail: cgrosholz@ocln.org; *Circ Supvr,* Nikole Kelleher; E-mail: nkelleher@ocln.org; *Youth Serv,* Kelsey Socha; E-mail: ksocha@ocln.org; Staff 7 (MLS 6, Non-MLS 1)
Founded 1895. Pop 21,531; Circ 200,000
Jul 2018-Jun 2019 Income $767,884
Library Holdings: Bk Titles 81,539; Per Subs 200
Special Collections: Local History, prints, photogs
Subject Interests: New England
Wireless access
Function: 24/7 Electronic res, 24/7 Online cat, 3D Printer, Adult bk club, Adult literacy prog, Art exhibits, Audiobks via web, Bi-weekly Writer's Group, Bk club(s), Bks on CD, Children's prog, Computers for patron use, E-Readers, Electronic databases & coll, Equip loans & repairs, Free DVD rentals, Genealogy discussion group, Holiday prog, Homebound delivery serv, ILL available, Internet access, Life-long learning prog for all ages, Makerspace, Meeting rooms, Microfiche/film & reading machines, Movies, Museum passes, Music CDs, Notary serv, Online cat, Outreach serv, OverDrive digital audio bks, Photocopying/Printing, Preschool outreach, Prog for adults, Prog for children & young adult, Ref serv available, Res assist avail, Scanner, Senior outreach, STEM programs, Story hour, Summer reading prog, Tax forms, Teen prog, Telephone ref, Wheelchair accessible, Workshops, Writing prog
Partic in Old Colony Libr Network
Open Mon-Thurs 9-8, Fri & Sat 9-4:30
Friends of the Library Group

MARSTONS MILLS

P MARSTONS MILLS PUBLIC LIBRARY, 2160 Main St, 02648. (Mail add: PO Box 9, 02648-0009), SAN 307-5125. Tel: 508-428-5175. FAX: 508-420-5194. E-mail: help@mmpl.org. Web Site: www.mmpl.org. *Dir,* Stacie Hevener; E-mail: shevener@clamsnet.org; *Youth Serv Librn,* Lindsey Hughes; *Cataloger,* Joan Sullivan; Staff 2 (Non-MLS 2)
Founded 1891. Pop 9,500; Circ 47,000
Library Holdings: Bks on Deafness & Sign Lang 10; CDs 65; DVDs 250; Large Print Bks 250; Bk Vols 19,639; Per Subs 53; Talking Bks 748; Videos 1,100
Special Collections: Cape Cod Coll; Contemporary American Women Poets Coll
Subject Interests: Landscape design, Mysteries
Automation Activity & Vendor Info: (Acquisitions) Innovative Interfaces, Inc - Millennium; (Cataloging) Innovative Interfaces, Inc; (Circulation) Innovative Interfaces, Inc; (ILL) Innovative Interfaces, Inc; (OPAC) Innovative Interfaces, Inc
Wireless access
Function: ILL available, Prog for children & young adult, Spoken cassettes & CDs, Summer reading prog, Telephone ref, VHS videos, Wheelchair accessible
Publications: Marstons Mills Public Library Newsletter (Quarterly)
Mem of Massachusetts Library System
Partic in Cape Libraries Automated Materials Sharing Network
Special Services for the Blind - Bks on cassette; Bks on CD; Large print bks

Open Mon & Thurs-Sat 10-2, Tues 1-7, Wed 8-12
Friends of the Library Group

MASHPEE

P MASHPEE PUBLIC LIBRARY*, 64 Steeple St, 02649. (Mail add: PO Box 657, 02649-0657), SAN 376-7868. Tel: 508-539-1435. Reference Tel: 508-539-1435, Ext 3003. FAX: 508-539-1437. E-mail: mpl_mail@clamsnet.org. Web Site: mashpeepubliclibrary.org. *Dir,* Kathleen Mahoney; Tel: 508-539-1435, Ext 3010, E-mail: kmahoney@clamsnet.org; *Asst Dir, Ref Librn,* Carolyn Savage; Tel: 508-539-1435, Ext 3005, E-mail: csavage@clamsnet.org; *Youth Serv Librn,* Janet Burke; Tel: 508-539-1435, Ext 3007, E-mail: jburke@clamsnet.org; Staff 4 (MLS 3, Non-MLS 1)
Pop 14,300; Circ 220,000
Jul 2015-Jun 2016 Income $610,000, State $20,000, City $540,000, Locally Generated Income $50,000
Special Collections: Native American Coll
Automation Activity & Vendor Info: (Acquisitions) Innovative Interfaces, Inc; (Cataloging) Innovative Interfaces, Inc; (Circulation) Innovative Interfaces, Inc; (ILL) Innovative Interfaces, Inc; (OPAC) Innovative Interfaces, Inc; (Serials) Innovative Interfaces, Inc
Wireless access
Mem of Massachusetts Library System
Partic in Cape Libraries Automated Materials Sharing Network
Open Mon, Wed, Fri & Sat 10-5, Tues & Thurs 12-7
Friends of the Library Group

MATTAPOISETT

P MATTAPOISETT FREE PUBLIC LIBRARY*, Seven Barstow St, 02739-0475. (Mail add: PO Box 475, 02739). Tel: 508-758-4171. FAX: 508-758-4783. E-mail: mfpl@sailsinc.org. Web Site: www.mattapoisettlibrary.org. *Libr Dir,* Susan E Pizzolato; E-mail: spizzolo@sailsinc.org; *Ad,* Liz Sherry; E-mail: esherry@sailsinc.org; *Ch Serv,* Jeanne McCullough; E-mail: jmccullough@sailsinc.org; Staff 4 (MLS 4)
Founded 1882
Library Holdings: AV Mats 9,942; Bks on Deafness & Sign Lang 10; Bk Vols 30,000; Per Subs 94
Automation Activity & Vendor Info: (Acquisitions) SirsiDynix; (Cataloging) SirsiDynix; (Circulation) SirsiDynix
Wireless access
Function: 24/7 Electronic res, 24/7 Online cat, 3D Printer, Accelerated reader prog, Activity rm, Adult bk club, Adult literacy prog
Mem of Massachusetts Library System
Partic in SAILS Library Network
Open Tues & Wed 10-8, Thurs & Fri 10-5, Sat 10-4, Sun 1-4
Friends of the Library Group

MAYNARD

P MAYNARD PUBLIC LIBRARY*, 77 Nason St, 01754-2316. SAN 307-515X. Tel: 978-897-1010. FAX: 978-897-9884. E-mail: mayill@minlib.net. Web Site: www.maynardpubliclibrary.org. *Dir,* Stephen Weiner; E-mail: sweiner@minlib.net; *Asst Dir,* Cynthia C Howe; E-mail: chowe@minlib.net; *Asst Admin,* Carol Casey; E-mail: ccasey@minlib.net; *Circ Librn,* Sally Thurston; E-mail: sthurston@minlib.net; *YA Librn,* Casey Petipas-Haggerty; E-mail: cpetipas-haggerty@minlib.net; *Children's & Youth Serv,* Mark A Malcolm; E-mail: mmalcolm@minlib.net; *ILL, Ref,* Jeremy Robichaud; E-mail: jrobichaud@minlib.net; *Tech Serv,* Karen Weir; E-mail: kweir@minlib.net; Staff 5.5 (MLS 3, Non-MLS 2.5)
Founded 1881. Pop 10,305; Circ 45,000
Library Holdings: AV Mats 7,000; Bk Vols 50,000; Per Subs 126
Special Collections: Maynard History
Automation Activity & Vendor Info: (Cataloging) Innovative Interfaces, Inc; (Circulation) Innovative Interfaces, Inc; (ILL) Auto-Graphics, Inc; (OPAC) Innovative Interfaces, Inc
Wireless access
Function: 24/7 Electronic res, Bk club(s), Bks on CD, Computer training, Computers for patron use, Electronic databases & coll, Free DVD rentals, Homebound delivery serv, ILL available, Magazines, Magnifiers for reading, Microfiche/film & reading machines, Movies, Museum passes, Music CDs, Online cat, OverDrive digital audio bks, Photocopying/Printing, Prog for adults, Prog for children & young adult, Ref serv available, Scanner, Story hour, Study rm, Summer reading prog, Tax forms, Teen prog, Telephone ref, Workshops
Partic in Minuteman Library Network
Open Mon, Fri & Sat 10-5, Tues & Thurs 2-9, Wed 10-6
Friends of the Library Group

MEDFIELD

S MEDFIELD HISTORICAL SOCIETY LIBRARY*, Six Pleasant St, 02052. (Mail add: PO Box 233, 02052-0233), SAN 375-152X. Tel: 508-613-6606. E-mail: medfieldhistoricalsociety@gmail.com. Web Site: medfieldhistoricalsociety.org. *Librn,* Cheryl O'Malley
Founded 1891
Library Holdings: Bk Titles 200
Subject Interests: Genealogy, Local hist

P MEDFIELD PUBLIC LIBRARY*, 468 Main St, 02052-2008. SAN 307-5168. Tel: 508-359-4544. FAX: 508-359-8124. E-mail: medfield@minlib.net. Web Site: www.medfieldpubliclibrary.org. *Libr Dir,* Pam Gardner; E-mail: pgardner@minlib.net; *Head, Children's Servx,* Bernadette Foley; E-mail: bfoley@minlib.net; *Teen & Ref Serv Librn,* Erica Cote; E-mail: ecote@minlib.net; *Circ Supvr,* Moira Mills; E-mail: mmills.mld@minlib.net; Staff 8.5 (MLS 4, Non-MLS 4.5)
Founded 1872. Pop 12,275; Circ 213,178
Library Holdings: CDs 7,631; DVDs 8,801; e-books 261; e-journals 1; Bk Vols 60,271; Per Subs 125
Automation Activity & Vendor Info: (Acquisitions) Innovative Interfaces, Inc; (Cataloging) Innovative Interfaces, Inc; (Circulation) Innovative Interfaces, Inc; (ILL) Innovative Interfaces, Inc; (Media Booking) Innovative Interfaces, Inc; (OPAC) Innovative Interfaces, Inc; (Serials) Innovative Interfaces, Inc
Wireless access
Function: Adult bk club, Bk club(s), Bks on CD, Children's prog, Computer training, Computers for patron use, Electronic databases & coll, Free DVD rentals, ILL available, Museum passes, Music CDs, Online cat, Outside serv via phone, mail, e-mail & web, OverDrive digital audio bks, Photocopying/Printing, Prog for adults, Prog for children & young adult, Ref serv available, Story hour, Summer reading prog, Tax forms, Teen prog, Telephone ref, Wheelchair accessible, Workshops
Partic in Minuteman Library Network
Open Mon-Thurs 10-6, Fri & Sat 10-2
Friends of the Library Group

MEDFORD

P MEDFORD PUBLIC LIBRARY*, 200 Boston Ave, Ste G-350, 02155. SAN 307-5184. Tel: 781-395-7950. FAX: 781-391-2261. E-mail: medford@minlib.net. Web Site: www.medfordlibrary.org. *Dir,* Barbara E Kerr; E-mail: bkerr@minlib.net; *Ref (Info Servs),* Victoria Schneiderman; *YA Serv,* Nicole Perrault; *Youth Serv,* Sam Sednek; Staff 12 (MLS 9, Non-MLS 3)
Founded 1825. Pop 58,076; Circ 283,115
Library Holdings: AV Mats 1,000; Large Print Bks 500; Bk Vols 150,000; Per Subs 250
Special Collections: Medford History. Oral History
Automation Activity & Vendor Info: (Cataloging) Innovative Interfaces, Inc; (Circulation) Innovative Interfaces, Inc; (OPAC) Innovative Interfaces, Inc
Wireless access
Publications: This Month at Medford Public Library
Partic in Minuteman Library Network
Special Services for the Deaf - High interest/low vocabulary bks; TTY equip
Open Mon-Thurs 9-9, Fri 9-6, Sat (Sept-June) 9-5, Sat (July-Aug) 9-1
Friends of the Library Group

C TUFTS UNIVERSITY*, Tisch Library, 35 Professors Row, 02155-5816. SAN 345-3545. Tel: 617-627-3345. Circulation Tel: 617-627-3347. Reference Tel: 617-627-3460. FAX: 617-627-3002. Reference E-mail: tischref@tufts.edu. Web Site: tischlibrary.tufts.edu. *Dir,* Dorothy Meaney; E-mail: Dorothy.meaney@tufts.edu; *Asst Dir,* Martha Kelehan; E-mail: martha.kelehan@tufts.edu; *Asst Dir,* Alicia Morris; E-mail: alicia.morris@tufts.edu; *Univ Archivist,* Daniel Santamaria; Tel: 617-627-2696, E-mail: Daniel.Santamaria@tufts.edu; Staff 51.4 (MLS 21.6, Non-MLS 29.8)
Founded 1852. Enrl 6,923; Fac 877; Highest Degree: Doctorate
Library Holdings: Per Subs 610
Special Collections: Asa Alfred; Tufts Center for Health, Environment & Justice (Love Canal); Confederate Archives; Edwin Bolles Coll; Henri Gioiran Coll; Hosea Ballou Coll; John Holmes Coll; Musicology Coll; P T Barnum Coll; Ritter Coll; Ryder Coll; Stearus Coll; University Archives; William Bentley Sermon Coll. US Document Depository
Automation Activity & Vendor Info: (Acquisitions) Ex Libris Group; (Cataloging) Ex Libris Group; (Circulation) Ex Libris Group; (Course Reserve) Ex Libris Group; (Discovery) Ex Libris Group; (ILL) Ex Libris Group; (OPAC) Ex Libris Group; (Serials) Ex Libris Group
Wireless access
Function: ILL available, Music CDs, Online cat, Online info literacy tutorials on the web & in blackboard, Online ref, Orientations, Photocopying/Printing, Ref & res, Scanner, VHS videos, Wheelchair accessible, Workshops
Mem of Massachusetts Library System
Partic in OCLC Online Computer Library Center, Inc; OCLC Research Library Partnership
Restriction: In-house use for visitors

Departmental Libraries:

W VAN ALAN CLARK LIBRARY, SCHOOL OF THE MUSEUM OF FINE ARTS AT TUFTS, 230 The Fenway, Boston, 02115. *Head of Libr,* Darin Murphy; E-mail: darin.murphy@tufts.edu; Staff 3 (MLS 2, Non-MLS 1)

CL EDWIN GINN LIBRARY, Mugar Bldg, 1st Flr, 160 Packard St, 02155-7082, SAN 345-3669. Tel: 617-627-3273. Circulation Tel: 617-627-3852. Interlibrary Loan Service Tel: 617-627-6421. Reference Tel: 617-627-5021. FAX: 617-627-3736. Reference E-mail: ginnref@tufts.edu. Web Site: www.library.tufts.edu/ginn. *Dir,* Cynthia Rubino; Tel: 617-627-2175; *Assoc Dir,* LeRoy LaFleur; Tel: 617-627-2974; *Circ/Reserves,* Paula Cammarata; *Ref (Info Servs),* Ellen McDonald; Tel: 617-627-3858
Founded 1933. Enrl 320
Library Holdings: Bk Vols 113,741; Per Subs 900
Special Collections: Ambassador John Moors Cabot Papers; Ambassador Phillip K Crowe Papers; Edward R Murrow Papers; International Labor Office; League of Nations; Permanent Court of International Justice; United Nations Coll
Subject Interests: Intl law
Partic in Boston Library Consortium, Inc; LYRASIS

CM HIRSH HEALTH SCIENCES LIBRARY, 145 Harrison Ave, Boston, 02111, SAN 307-238X. Tel: 617-636-6705. Administration Tel: 617-636-2481. FAX: 617-636-3805. E-mail: hhsl@tufts.edu. Web Site: hirshlibrary.tufts.edu. *Dir,* Eric Albright; E-mail: Eric.Albright@tufts.edu; *Assoc Dir,* Debra Berlanstein; E-mail: Debra.Berlanstein@tufts.edu; *Head, Coll Mgt,* Frances Foret; Tel: 617-636-2448, E-mail: frances.foret@tufts.edu; *Circ Librn, Res & Instruction Librn,* Amy Lapidow; E-mail: amy.lapidow@tufts.edu; *E-Res & Ser Librn,* Jane Natches; Tel: 617-636-2452, E-mail: jane.natches@tufts.edu; *Admin Coordr,* Katherine Morley; E-mail: katherine.morley@tufts.edu; *ILL Coordr,* Connie Wong; Tel: 617-636-3787, E-mail: connie.wong@tufts.edu; Staff 31 (MLS 18, Non-MLS 13)
Founded 1906. Enrl 1,500; Highest Degree: Doctorate
Library Holdings: Bk Titles 52,128; Bk Vols 158,400; Per Subs 972
Subject Interests: Dentistry, Hist of med, Med, Nutrition, Veterinary med
Automation Activity & Vendor Info: (Acquisitions) SirsiDynix; (Cataloging) SirsiDynix; (Circulation) SirsiDynix; (ILL) SirsiDynix; (OPAC) SirsiDynix; (Serials) SirsiDynix
Function: Doc delivery serv
Partic in OCLC Online Computer Library Center, Inc; UCMP
Publications: Bibliographies; Brochures; Health Science Link (Newsletter); Online Library Guide
Open Mon-Thurs 7:45am-11pm, Fri 7:45-7, Sat & Sun 10-10
Friends of the Library Group

LILLY MUSIC LIBRARY, Granoff Music Ctr, Rm M030 Lower Level, 20 Talbot Ave, 02155, SAN 328-7726. Tel: 617-627-3594. FAX: 617-627-3002. Web Site: tischlibrary.tufts.edu/use-library/music-library. *Music Librn,* Position Currently Open; Staff 2 (MLS 1, Non-MLS 1)
Highest Degree: Master
Library Holdings: CDs 19,100; DVDs 80; Electronic Media & Resources 20; Music Scores 16,300; Bk Titles 14,500

MEDWAY

P MEDWAY PUBLIC LIBRARY*, 26 High St, 02053. SAN 345-3693. Tel: 508-533-3217. FAX: 508-533-3219. Web Site: medwaylib.org. *Dir,* Margaret Y Perkins; E-mail: mperkins@minlib.net; *Youth Serv Librn,* Lucy Anderson; E-mail: landerson@minlib.net; Staff 3 (MLS 2, Non-MLS 1)
Founded 1860. Pop 13,053; Circ 98,178
Library Holdings: AV Mats 7,460; e-books 37,830; Electronic Media & Resources 10,037; Bk Vols 59,764; Per Subs 101
Special Collections: Medway Coll. Oral History
Automation Activity & Vendor Info: (Cataloging) Innovative Interfaces, Inc; (Circulation) Innovative Interfaces, Inc; (OPAC) Innovative Interfaces, Inc
Wireless access
Function: 24/7 Electronic res, 24/7 Online cat, 3D Printer, Activity rm, Adult bk club
Mem of Massachusetts Library System
Partic in Minuteman Library Network
Open Mon-Thurs 10-8, Fri & Sat 10-2
Friends of the Library Group

MELROSE

R FIRST BAPTIST CHURCH LIBRARY*, 561 Main St, 02176. SAN 307-5192. Tel: 781-665-4470. FAX: 781-665-3050. E-mail: Melrose1BC@gmail.com.
Library Holdings: Bk Titles 1,025
Subject Interests: Art, Educ, Relig

P MELROSE PUBLIC LIBRARY*, 69 W Emerson St, 02176. SAN 345-3758. Tel: 781-665-2313. FAX: 781-662-4229. E-mail: mel@noblenet.org. Web Site: www.melrosepubliclibrary.org. *Dir,* Linda C W Gardener; *Asst Dir, Tech Serv Librn,* Diane R Wall; *Circ Librn, YA Serv,* Jill Connolly; *Ch Serv,* Marianne J Stanton; *Circ,* Erin Lewis; *Ref Serv,* Shelley O'Brien; *Ref Librn,* Christine Morrissey; Staff 21 (MLS 5, Non-MLS 16)
Founded 1871. Pop 27,503; Circ 257,500
Library Holdings: Bk Titles 109,000; Bk Vols 110,000; Per Subs 95
Special Collections: Fine Arts (Felix A Gendrot Coll); Sadie & Alex Levine Coll
Subject Interests: Art, Genealogy, Local hist
Automation Activity & Vendor Info: (Acquisitions) Innovative Interfaces, Inc; (Cataloging) Innovative Interfaces, Inc; (Circulation) Innovative Interfaces, Inc
Publications: Newsletter
Partic in North of Boston Library Exchange, Inc
Open Mon-Thurs 10-9, Fri & Sat 10-5, Sun 2-5
Friends of the Library Group

MENDON

P TAFT PUBLIC LIBRARY*, 29 North Ave, 01756. (Mail add: PO Box 35, 01756-0035), SAN 307-5214. Tel: 508-473-3259. FAX: 508-473-7049. Web Site: www.taftpubliclibrary.org. *Dir,* Andrew Jenrich; E-mail: librarydirector@mendonma.gov
Founded 1881. Pop 5,876; Circ 34,076
Library Holdings: Bk Vols 34,577; Per Subs 82
Special Collections: History Coll
Automation Activity & Vendor Info: (Cataloging) Evergreen; (Circulation) Evergreen
Wireless access
Partic in Central & Western Massachusetts Automated Resource Sharing
Open Tues & Wed 10-7, Thurs 3-7, Fri 12-5, Sat 9-Noon
Friends of the Library Group

MERRIMAC

P MERRIMAC PUBLIC LIBRARY*, 86 W Main St, 01860. SAN 307-5222. Tel: 978-346-9441. FAX: 978-346-8272. E-mail: contact@merrimaclibrary.org. Web Site: merrimaclibrary.org. *Dir,* Kelly Unsworth; E-mail: kunsworth@merrimaclibrary.org; *Youth Serv Librn,* Cathy Hornig; E-mail: chornig@merrimaclibrary.org
Founded 1930. Pop 5,400; Circ 36,008
Library Holdings: Bk Vols 28,000; Per Subs 67
Special Collections: Local History (Thomas H Hoyt Family Coll), bks & papers. State Document Depository
Automation Activity & Vendor Info: (Cataloging) Evergreen; (Circulation) Evergreen; (OPAC) Evergreen
Wireless access
Partic in Merrimack Valley Library Consortium
Open Mon & Wed 10-5, Tues & Thurs 10-7, Fri & Sat 10-2
Friends of the Library Group

METHUEN

P NEVINS MEMORIAL LIBRARY*, 305 Broadway, 01844-6898. SAN 307-5249. Tel: 978-686-4080. FAX: 978-686-8669. E-mail: contactcirc@nevinslibrary.org. Web Site: www.nevinslibrary.org. *Dir,* Krista I McLeod; E-mail: kmcleod@nevinslibrary.org; *Head, Children's Servx,* Kathleen Moran-Wallace; E-mail: kmoranwallace@nevinslibrary.org; *Head, Reader Serv,* Sarah Sullivan; E-mail: ssullivan@nevinslibrary.org; *Head, Ref,* Kirsten Underwood; E-mail: kunderwood@nevinslibrary.org; *Head, Tech Serv,* Beverly Winn; E-mail: bwinn@nevinslibrary.org; *Head, Teen Serv,* Amy Fowler; E-mail: afowler@nevinslibrary.org; Staff 45 (MLS 8, Non-MLS 37)
Founded 1883. Pop 44,000; Circ 189,000
Library Holdings: AV Mats 6,600; Bk Titles 85,024; Per Subs 182
Special Collections: Elise Nevins Morgan Meditation Series, ms & bks
Automation Activity & Vendor Info: (Cataloging) SirsiDynix; (Circulation) SirsiDynix
Wireless access
Mem of Massachusetts Library System
Partic in Merrimack Valley Library Consortium
Open Mon-Thurs 9-9, Fri & Sat 9-5; Mon-Thurs (Summer) 9-9, Fri 9-5
Friends of the Library Group

MIDDLEBOROUGH

S THE MASSACHUSETTS ARCHAEOLOGICAL SOCIETY RESEARCH LIBRARY*, 17 Jackson St, 02346-2413. (Mail add: PO Box 700, 02346-0700), SAN 370-1573. Tel: 508-947-9005. E-mail: info@massarchaeology.org. Web Site: www.massarchaeology.org. *Library Contact,* David Burbine
Founded 1939
Jul 2013-Jun 2014 Income $200

Library Holdings: High Interest/Low Vocabulary Bk Vols 40; Bk Titles 5,000; Per Subs 50; Spec Interest Per Sub 50; Videos 40
Subject Interests: Anthrop, Archaeology, Ethnography, Local hist
Function: Children's prog, Photocopying/Printing, Res libr, Wheelchair accessible
Publications: Bulletin of the Massachusetts Archaelogical Society; Newsletter; 'Round Robbins'
Open Wed 10-4, Sat 10-2
Restriction: Access at librarian's discretion, Closed stack, Not a lending libr
Friends of the Library Group

P MIDDLEBOROUGH PUBLIC LIBRARY, 102 N Main St, 02346. SAN 307-5257. Tel: 508-946-2470. FAX: 508-946-2473. E-mail: midlib@sailsinc.org. Web Site: www.midlib.org. *Dir,* Randy Gagne; E-mail: rgagne@sailsinc.org; *Asst Dir, Syst Librn,* John Walsh; E-mail: jwalsh@sailsinc.org; *YA Librn,* Christine Dargelis; E-mail: cdargeli@sailsinc.org; *Libr Tech,* Marilyn Thayer; Staff 5 (MLS 3, Non-MLS 2)
Founded 1875. Pop 21,085; Circ 130,549
Library Holdings: Bk Vols 77,308; Per Subs 214
Special Collections: Cranberry Culture Coll
Automation Activity & Vendor Info: (Acquisitions) SirsiDynix; (Cataloging) SirsiDynix; (Circulation) SirsiDynix; (OPAC) SirsiDynix
Wireless access
Partic in SAILS Library Network
Special Services for the Blind - Bks on cassette
Open Mon, Wed & Thurs 10-7, Tues 10-5, Sat 9-2
Friends of the Library Group

MIDDLEFIELD

P MIDDLEFIELD PUBLIC LIBRARY*, 188 Skyline Trail, 01243. (Mail add: PO Box 128, 01243-0128), SAN 307-5265. Tel: 413-623-6421. E-mail: library@middlefieldma.net. Web Site: middlefieldma.net/?page_id=172. *Librn,* Maryann Walsh
Library Holdings: Bk Vols 12,000
Open Mon 2-6, Wed 1:30-3, Sat 9-Noon

MIDDLETON

P FLINT PUBLIC LIBRARY*, One S Main St, 01949. SAN 307-5273. Tel: 978-774-8132. FAX: 978-777-3270. E-mail: flint3@comcast.net. Web Site: www.flintlibrary.org. *Dir,* Melissa Gaspar; E-mail: mgaspar@flintpublib.org; *Asst Dir,* Judy Gallerie; E-mail: jgallerie@flintpublib.org; *Ch,* Lisa Rundquist; E-mail: lrundquist@flintpublib.org; Staff 11 (MLS 1, Non-MLS 10)
Founded 1891. Pop 7,744; Circ 55,624
Library Holdings: AV Mats 1,473; Electronic Media & Resources 59; Large Print Bks 400; Bk Vols 38,068; Per Subs 161; Talking Bks 1,045
Special Collections: Local Author Coll
Automation Activity & Vendor Info: (Cataloging) SirsiDynix; (Circulation) SirsiDynix; (ILL) SirsiDynix; (OPAC) SirsiDynix
Wireless access
Function: Homebound delivery serv, ILL available, Photocopying/Printing, Prog for adults, Prog for children & young adult, Ref serv available, Summer reading prog, Telephone ref
Mem of Massachusetts Library System
Partic in Merrimack Valley Library Consortium
Open Mon-Thurs (Winter) 10-8, Fri 10-5, Sun 1-5; Tues-Thurs (Summer) 10-8, Fri 10-2, Sun 1-5
Friends of the Library Group

MILFORD

P MILFORD TOWN LIBRARY, 80 Spruce St, 01757. SAN 307-5281. Tel: 508-473-0651, 508-473-2145. FAX: 508-473-8651. Reference E-mail: milfordreference@cwmars.org. Web Site: www.milfordtownlibrary.org. *Dir,* Susan Edmonds; Tel: 508-473-2145, Ext 210, E-mail: sedmonds@cwmars.org; *Asst Dir,* Michael Conboy; Tel: 508-473-2145, Ext 211, E-mail: conboymj@cwmars.org; *YA Librn,* Jacque Gorman; Tel: 508-473-2145, Ext 223; *Circ Supvr,* Kathie Kirchner; Tel: 508-473-2145, Ext 218; Staff 20 (MLS 4, Non-MLS 16)
Founded 1986. Pop 27,033; Circ 204,315
Library Holdings: AV Mats 6,086; e-books 6,547; Electronic Media & Resources 4,364; Large Print Bks 2,814; Bk Vols 107,019; Per Subs 147; Talking Bks 3,053
Special Collections: Local History (Milford Room)
Automation Activity & Vendor Info: (Acquisitions) Innovative Interfaces, Inc; (Cataloging) Innovative Interfaces, Inc; (Circulation) Innovative Interfaces, Inc; (OPAC) Innovative Interfaces, Inc; (Serials) Innovative Interfaces, Inc
Wireless access
Function: AV serv, Homebound delivery serv, ILL available, Magnifiers for reading, Photocopying/Printing, Prog for children & young adult, Ref serv available, Summer reading prog, Wheelchair accessible
Mem of Massachusetts Library System
Partic in Central & Western Massachusetts Automated Resource Sharing
Special Services for the Blind - Assistive/Adapted tech devices, equip & products; Audio mat; Bks & mags in Braille, on rec, tape & cassette; Large print bks; Large screen computer & software; Low vision equip; Magnifiers; Ref serv; Talking bks & player equip
Open Mon-Thurs 9-9, Fri 9-6, Sat 9-5
Friends of the Library Group

MILL RIVER

P NEW MARLBOROUGH TOWN LIBRARY*, One Mill River Great Barrington Rd, 01244-0239. (Mail add: PO Box 239, 01244), SAN 318-1375. Tel: 413-229-6668. FAX: 413-229-6668. E-mail: newmarlborough@gmail.com. Web Site: www.newmarlboroughlibrary.org. *Dir,* Debora O'Brien
Pop 1,078; Circ 8,456
Library Holdings: Bk Vols 17,000; Per Subs 30
Wireless access
Partic in Central & Western Massachusetts Automated Resource Sharing
Open Mon, Wed & Sat (Winter) 10-5:30, Tues & Thurs 1:30-5, Fri 1:30-7:30; Mon, Wed & Sat (Summer) 10-5:30, Tues & Fri 1:30-7:30, Thurs 1:30-5:30
Friends of the Library Group

MILLBURY

P MILLBURY PUBLIC LIBRARY, 128 Elm St, 01527. SAN 307-5311. Tel: 508-865-1181. FAX: 508-865-0795. Web Site: www.millburylibrary.org. *Libr Dir,* Ann Dallair; Staff 9 (MLS 2, Non-MLS 7)
Founded 1869. Pop 13,934; Circ 70,000
Library Holdings: AV Mats 6,668; Large Print Bks 400; Bk Vols 40,000; Per Subs 100
Automation Activity & Vendor Info: (Cataloging) Follett Software; (Circulation) Follett Software
Wireless access
Mem of Massachusetts Library System
Partic in Central & Western Massachusetts Automated Resource Sharing
Open Mon 11-6, Tues-Thurs 10-8, Fri 10-6, Sat 9-2
Friends of the Library Group

MILLIS

P MILLIS PUBLIC LIBRARY*, 961 Main St, 02054. SAN 307-5338. Tel: 508-376-8282. FAX: 508-376-1278. Web Site: www.millislibrary.org. *Libr Dir,* Kim Tolson; E-mail: ktolson@minlib.net; *Youth Serv Librn,* Rachel Silverman; E-mail: rsilverman@minlib.net; *Colls Mgr,* Donna Brooks; E-mail: dbrooks@minlib.net; *Adult Serv Coordr,* Esther Davis; E-mail: edavis@minlib.net; Staff 8 (MLS 2, Non-MLS 6)
Founded 1887. Pop 8,000; Circ 188,801
Library Holdings: Audiobooks 1,285; AV Mats 2,413; Bks on Deafness & Sign Lang 6; Braille Volumes 2; CDs 1,967; DVDs 2,426; Large Print Bks 786; Bk Titles 44,189; Per Subs 95; Talking Bks 10; Videos 446
Automation Activity & Vendor Info: (Cataloging) Innovative Interfaces, Inc - Sierra; (Circulation) Innovative Interfaces, Inc - Sierra; (OPAC) Innovative Interfaces, Inc - Sierra
Wireless access
Mem of Massachusetts Library System
Partic in Minuteman Library Network
Special Services for the Deaf - Bks on deafness & sign lang; Closed caption videos; Spec interest per; Staff with knowledge of sign lang
Special Services for the Blind - Audio mat; Bks available with recordings; Bks on cassette; Bks on CD; Braille alphabet card; Braille bks; Cassette playback machines; Copier with enlargement capabilities; Descriptive video serv (DVS); Disability awareness prog; Large print bks; Sub-lending agent for Braille Inst Libr; Talking bks & player equip
Open Mon-Wed 10-8, Thurs & Fri 10-4, Sat 10-3
Friends of the Library Group

MILLVILLE

P MILLVILLE FREE PUBLIC LIBRARY*, 169 Main St, 01529. (Mail add: PO Box 726, 01529-0726), SAN 376-7736. Tel: 508-883-1887. FAX: 508-883-1887. E-mail: librarian@millvillema.org. *Libr Dir,* Colleen Anderson; *Asst Librn,* Mary Gauvin; Staff 3 (MLS 1, Non-MLS 2)
Library Holdings: Large Print Bks 150; Bk Titles 12,500; Per Subs 20
Mem of Massachusetts Library System
Partic in Central & Western Massachusetts Automated Resource Sharing
Open Mon & Wed 6-8, Tues & Thurs 1:30-5:30, Sat 10-2

MILTON

C CURRY COLLEGE*, Louis R Levin Memorial Library, 1071 Blue Hill Ave, 02186-9984. SAN 307-5346. Tel: 617-333-2177. FAX: 617-333-2164. Web Site: www.curry.edu/academics/academic-student-resources/levin-library. *Dir,*

Garrett Eastman; E-mail: garrett.eastman@curry.edu; *Head, Coll Serv,* Mary Ryan; Tel: 617-333-2937, E-mail: mryan@curry.edu; *Head, Ref,* Benjamin Brudner; Tel: 617-333-2170; *Head, Tech Serv,* David Miller; Tel: 617-333-2101; *Circ Supvr,* Leslie Becker; Tel: 617-333-2102, E-mail: lbecker@curry.edu; Staff 12 (MLS 7, Non-MLS 5)
Founded 1952. Enrl 1,880; Fac 100; Highest Degree: Master
Library Holdings: AV Mats 1,114; Bks on Deafness & Sign Lang 48; Bk Vols 94,300; Per Subs 725; Talking Bks 60
Special Collections: US Document Depository
Subject Interests: Learning disabilities
Automation Activity & Vendor Info: (Acquisitions) Innovative Interfaces, Inc; (Cataloging) Innovative Interfaces, Inc; (Circulation) Innovative Interfaces, Inc; (OPAC) Innovative Interfaces, Inc; (Serials) Innovative Interfaces, Inc
Wireless access
Function: For res purposes, ILL available, Telephone ref, Wheelchair accessible
Mem of Massachusetts Library System
Partic in LYRASIS
Open Mon-Thurs 8am-Midnight, Fri 8-8, Sat 10-6, Sun 10am-Midnight

CL LABOURE COLLEGE*, Helen Stubblefield Law Library, 303 Adams St, 02186. SAN 307-191X. Tel: 617-322-3584. FAX: 617-296-7947. E-mail: library@laboure.edu. Web Site: www.laboure.edu/students/library. *Dir, Libr Serv,* Anicia Kuchesky; Tel: 613-322-3513, E-mail: anicia_kuchesky@laboure.edu; Staff 1 (MLS 1)
Founded 1971. Enrl 600
Library Holdings: Bk Vols 4,000; Per Subs 130
Subject Interests: Nursing
Wireless access
Partic in Massachusetts Health Sciences Library Network
Open Mon-Fri 7am-9pm, Sat 9-5:30, Sun 12-5:30
Friends of the Library Group

P MILTON PUBLIC LIBRARY*, 476 Canton Ave, 02186-3299. SAN 345-3847. Tel: 617-698-5757. FAX: 617-698-0441. Reference E-mail: miref@ocln.org. Web Site: miltonlibrary.org. *Dir,* William Adamcyk; E-mail: wadamczyk@ocln.org; *Asst Dir, Head, Children's Servx,* Sara Truog; E-mail: struog@ocln.org; *Head, Adult Serv, Head, Ref Serv,* Jean Hlady; E-mail: jhlady@ocln.org; *Head, Circ,* Sylvia Mitchell; E-mail: sylviam@ocln.org; *Head, Tech Serv,* Chris Callaghan; E-mail: ccallaghan@ocln.org; *Ch,* Jennifer Struzziero; E-mail: jstruzziero@ocln.org; *Asst Ch,* Elaine Weischedel; *Ref & Tech Librn,* Regan Mulcahy; E-mail: rmulcahy@ocln.org; Staff 8 (MLS 8)
Founded 1871. Pop 26,062; Circ 292,301
Jul 2012-Jun 2013 Income $1,142,354, State $22,000, City $1,050,354, Locally Generated Income $70,000. Mats Exp $155,000. Sal $804,939
Library Holdings: CDs 8,666; DVDs 10,364; Bk Vols 93,306
Subject Interests: Local hist
Automation Activity & Vendor Info: (Cataloging) SirsiDynix; (Circulation) SirsiDynix; (OPAC) SirsiDynix; (Serials) SirsiDynix
Wireless access
Partic in Old Colony Libr Network
Open Mon-Wed 9-9, Thurs 1-9, Fri 9-5:30, Sat 9-5 , Sun (Oct-May) 1-5
Friends of the Library Group

MONROE BRIDGE

P MONROE PUBLIC LIBRARY*, 3B School St, 01350. (Mail add: PO Box 35, 01350-0035), SAN 307-5362. Tel: 413-424-5272. E-mail: monroelibrary01350@yahoo.com. *Librn,* Carla Davis-Little; E-mail: cj7173@verizon.net
Pop 120; Circ 1,581
Library Holdings: Bk Vols 3,000
Open Mon 6-7

MONSON

P MONSON FREE LIBRARY, Two High St, 01057-1095. SAN 307-5370. Tel: 413-267-3866. FAX: 413-267-5496. E-mail: monsonfl@cwmars.org. Web Site: www.monsonlibrary.com. *Libr Dir,* Hope Bodwell; Tel: 413-267-9035, E-mail: hbodwell@cwmars.org; *Youth Serv Librn,* Sandy Courtney; E-mail: scourtney@cwmars.org
Founded 1878. Pop 8,700; Circ 50,000
Library Holdings: Bk Vols 40,000; Per Subs 144
Automation Activity & Vendor Info: (Cataloging) Evergreen; (Circulation) Evergreen; (OPAC) Evergreen
Wireless access
Partic in Central & Western Massachusetts Automated Resource Sharing
Open Tues-Thurs 10-7, Fri & Sat 10-2
Friends of the Library Group

MONTEREY

P MONTEREY LIBRARY*, 452 Main Rd, 01245. (Mail add: PO Box 172, 01245-0172), SAN 307-5397. Tel: 413-528-3795. E-mail: montereylibrary@gmail.com. Web Site: www.montereymasslibrary.org. *Dir,* Mark Makuc
Founded 1890. Pop 970
Library Holdings: Bk Titles 8,000; Per Subs 14
Subject Interests: Local hist
Automation Activity & Vendor Info: (Cataloging) Innovative Interfaces, Inc; (Circulation) Innovative Interfaces, Inc
Wireless access
Function: 24/7 Electronic res, 24/7 Online cat, Adult bk club, Art exhibits, Audiobks via web, Bks on CD, Children's prog, Computer training, Computers for patron use, Electronic databases & coll, Free DVD rentals, Holiday prog, Home delivery & serv to seniorr ctr & nursing homes, Homebound delivery serv, ILL available, Internet access, Magazines, Museum passes, Online cat, Online ref, OverDrive digital audio bks, Photocopying/Printing, Prog for adults, Prog for children & young adult, Spoken cassettes & CDs, Spoken cassettes & DVDs, Summer reading prog
Partic in Central & Western Massachusetts Automated Resource Sharing
Open Mon 7am-9pm, Tues 9-12:30, Wed 2-5, Thurs 4-6, Fri 4-8, Sat 9:30-12:30 & 7-9
Friends of the Library Group

MONTGOMERY

P GRACE HALL MEMORIAL LIBRARY*, 161 Main Rd, 01085-9525. SAN 307-5400. Tel: 413-862-3894. E-mail: montgomerylibrary@yahoo.com. Web Site: mblc.state.ma.us/directories/libraries/library.php?record_id=646. *Librn,* Paula Stipek-Long
Pop 780
Library Holdings: Bk Vols 10,000; Per Subs 6
Automation Activity & Vendor Info: (Cataloging) Baker & Taylor; (Circulation) Baker & Taylor
Wireless access
Open Tues 10-5:30, Thurs 12-8, Sat 9:30-12:30
Friends of the Library Group

MOUNT WASHINGTON

P MOUNT WASHINGTON PUBLIC LIBRARY*, Town Hall, 118 East St, 01258. SAN 307-5419. Tel: 413-528-1798, 413-528-2839. FAX: 413-528-2839. E-mail: mtwashlibrary@townofmtwashington.com. Web Site: townofmtwashington.com/mt-washington-library. *Librn,* Lesliann Furcht
Pop 130; Circ 1,860
Library Holdings: Bk Titles 2,500; Videos 26
Open Mon, Wed & Thurs 8:30-1:30, Tues 1-6

NAHANT

P NAHANT PUBLIC LIBRARY*, 15 Pleasant St, 01908. SAN 307-5427. Tel: 781-581-0306. E-mail: nahant.circ@gmail.com. Web Site: www.nahantlibrary.org. *Dir,* Sharon Hawkes; E-mail: shawkes@nahant.org; *Ch Serv,* Position Currently Open; Staff 3.3 (MLS 2, Non-MLS 1.3)
Founded 1819. Pop 3,900
Library Holdings: Bk Titles 42,000; Per Subs 22
Special Collections: Nahant Historical
Wireless access
Function: 24/7 Electronic res, 24/7 Online cat, Archival coll, Art exhibits, Bks on CD, Children's prog, Computers for patron use, Distance learning, E-Reserves, Electronic databases & coll, For res purposes, Free DVD rentals, Health sci info serv, Home delivery & serv to seniorr ctr & nursing homes, Homebound delivery serv, ILL available, Internet access, Life-long learning prog for all ages, Magazines, Mail & tel request accepted, Meeting rooms, Movies, Museum passes, Online cat, Online ref, Photocopying/Printing, Preschool outreach, Prog for adults, Prog for children & young adult, Story hour, Summer reading prog, Winter reading prog
Publications: Newsletter (Occasionally)
Mem of Massachusetts Library System
Open Tues & Thurs 10-7, Wed & Fri 10-5, Sat 12-4
Friends of the Library Group

NANTUCKET

P NANTUCKET ATHENEUM, One India St, 02554-3519. (Mail add: PO Box 808, 02554-0808), SAN 307-5435. Tel: 508-228-1110. Circulation Tel: 508-228-1110, Ext 101. Reference Tel: 508-228-1110, Ext 110. FAX: 508-228-1973. E-mail: info@nantucketatheneum.org. Web Site: www.nantucketatheneum.org. *Exec Dir,* Ann Scott; Tel: 508-228-1974, E-mail: ascott@nantucketatheneum.org; *Operations Mgr,* Cheryl Creighton; E-mail: ccreighton@nantucketatheneum.org; Staff 7 (MLS 6, Non-MLS 1)
Founded 1834. Circ 113,068

Library Holdings: AV Mats 2,126; Bk Vols 38,864; Per Subs 194
Special Collections: 19th Century American Coll; Nantucket Coll
Automation Activity & Vendor Info: (Cataloging) Innovative Interfaces, Inc; (Circulation) Innovative Interfaces, Inc; (OPAC) Innovative Interfaces, Inc
Wireless access
Partic in Cape Libraries Automated Materials Sharing Network
Open Mon-Sat 9-2
Friends of the Library Group

S NANTUCKET HISTORICAL ASSOCIATION*, Research Library, Seven Fair St, 02554-3737. (Mail add: PO Box 1016, 02554-1016), SAN 327-3091. Tel: 508-228-1894. E-mail: library@nha.org. Web Site: www.nha.org. *Libr Dir,* Amelia Holmes; Tel: 508-228-1894, Ext 301, E-mail: aholmes@nha.org; Staff 2 (MLS 1, Non-MLS 1)
Founded 1894
Library Holdings: Bk Titles 5,000
Special Collections: Log Books & Account Books; Manuscript & Audio-Visual Colls; Maps. Oral History
Subject Interests: City hist, Maritime hist, Quaker hist, Rare bks, Whaling
Wireless access
Function: 24/7 Online cat, Archival coll, Art exhibits, Bus archives, Electronic databases & coll, For res purposes, Online cat, Online ref, Ref & res, Ref serv available, Res libr, Study rm, Telephone ref
Open Tues–Fri 10–4
Restriction: Closed stack, In-house use for visitors, Non-circulating

S NANTUCKET MARIA MITCHELL ASSOCIATION, Maria Mitchell Special Collections & Archives, Two Vestal St, 02554-2699. (Mail add: Four Vestal St, 02554), SAN 307-5443. Tel: 508-228-9198. FAX: 508-228-1031. Web Site: www.mariamitchell.org. *Curator, Dep Dir,* Jascin Leonardo Finger; E-mail: jfinger@mariamitchell.org
Founded 1902
Library Holdings: Bk Titles 9,000
Special Collections: Maria Mitchell Association Archives; Original Notebooks & Papers (Maria Mitchell Memorabilia Coll), journals, lecture notes, micro
Subject Interests: Astronomy, Biology, Botany, Chem, Geol, Oceanography, Ornithology, Physics, Zoology
Wireless access
Function: Archival coll, Res libr
Restriction: Non-circulating, Open by appt only

NATICK

P BACON FREE LIBRARY*, 58 Eliot St, 01760. SAN 372-7602. Tel: 508-653-6730. E-mail: bfl@minlib.net. Web Site: www.baconfreelibrary.org. *Dir,* Amy Sadkin; E-mail: asadkin@minlib.net; *Asst Dir, Children's Librn,* Fran Daneault; E-mail: fdaneault@minlib.net; *Libr Asst,* Karen Kassel; E-mail: kkassel@minlib.net; *Libr Asst,* Maria King; E-mail: mking@minlib.net; *Libr Asst,* Graziella Lesellier; E-mail: glesellier@minlib.net; *Libr Asst,* Casey Stirling; E-mail: cstirling@minlib.net; Staff 5 (MLS 2, Non-MLS 3)
Founded 1870. Pop 9,000
Special Collections: Early Christian Native Americans of South Natick; Natick Historical Coll
Automation Activity & Vendor Info: (Circulation) Innovative Interfaces, Inc
Wireless access
Function: Adult bk club, After school storytime, Archival coll, Art exhibits, Audiobks via web, Bk club(s), Bk reviews (Group), Bks on CD, CD-ROM, Children's prog, Computer training, Computers for patron use, E-Readers, Electronic databases & coll, Family literacy, Free DVD rentals, Holiday prog, ILL available, Internet access, Life-long learning prog for all ages, Literacy & newcomer serv, Magazines, Movies, Museum passes, Music CDs, Online cat, Online ref, Outreach serv, Outside serv via phone, mail, e-mail & web, OverDrive digital audio bks, Photocopying/Printing, Preschool outreach, Preschool reading prog, Prog for adults, Prog for children & young adult, Ref serv available, Scanner, Senior outreach, Serves people with intellectual disabilities, Spoken cassettes & CDs, Spoken cassettes & DVDs, Story hour, Summer reading prog
Partic in Minuteman Library Network
Open Mon & Wed-Fri 9:30-5:30, Tues 9:30-8:30, Sat (Sept-May) 9-1
Friends of the Library Group

P MORSE INSTITUTE LIBRARY*, 14 E Central St, 01760. SAN 307-5451. Tel: 508-647-6520. Reference Tel: 508-647-6521. FAX: 508-647-6527. Web Site: www.morseinstitute.org. *Libr Dir,* Jason B Homer; E-mail: jhomer@minlib.net; *Asst Dir,* Amy Sadkin; Tel: 508-647-6526; *Head, Circ,* Paula Welch; E-mail: pwelch@minlib.net; *Head, Knowledge & Community Servs,* Kate Sawisch; Tel: 508-647-6400, Ext 1527; *Head, Mat Mgt,* Karen Mattes; Tel: 508-647-6400, Ext 1534; *Commun Relations Coordr,* Anna Litten; Tel: 508-647-6524, E-mail: alitten@minlib.net; *AV,* Susan Barnicle; Tel: 508-647-6522; *Ch Serv,* Dale Smith; E-mail: dsmith@minlib.net; *Literacy Serv,* Laurie Christie; Tel: 508-647-6400, Ext 1583, E-mail: lchristie@minlib.net; Staff 30.8 (MLS 10.4, Non-MLS 20.4)
Founded 1873. Pop 33,006; Circ 567,076
Library Holdings: Audiobooks 12,146; AV Mats 19,213; e-books 27,071; Bk Vols 210,310; Per Subs 386
Special Collections: Natick Historical Coll
Automation Activity & Vendor Info: (Cataloging) Innovative Interfaces, Inc; (Circulation) Innovative Interfaces, Inc; (OPAC) Innovative Interfaces, Inc
Wireless access
Publications: Off the Shelf (Newsletter)
Mem of Massachusetts Library System
Partic in LYRASIS; Minuteman Library Network
Special Services for the Blind - Extensive large print coll; Screen enlargement software for people with visual disabilities; Talking bk serv referral; Talking bks; ZoomText magnification & reading software
Open Mon-Thurs 10-9, Fri & Sat 10-5, Sun 2-5
Friends of the Library Group
Bookmobiles: 1. Bkmobile Coordr, Rose Huling. Bk titles 2,000

S NATICK HISTORICAL SOCIETY*, 58 Eliot St, 01760. SAN 371-2567. Tel: 508-647-4841. E-mail: info@natickhistoricalsociety.org. Web Site: www.natickhistoricalsociety.org. *Exec Dir,* Aaron M Dougherty; E-mail: director@natickhistoricalsociety.org; Staff 1 (Non-MLS 1)
Founded 1870
Library Holdings: Bk Vols 2,500; Per Subs 34
Special Collections: Indian Artifacts; Vice-President Henry Wilson
Subject Interests: Local hist
Wireless access
Function: Archival coll, For res purposes, Mail & tel request accepted, Photocopying/Printing, Prog for adults, Ref & res, Wheelchair accessible
Publications: From Many Backgrounds: The Heritage of the Eliot Church of South Natick (Local historical information); Images of America-Natick-Arcadia Pub Co (Local historical information); The Arrow (Newsletter)
Open Tues (Winter) 4-8, Wed 10-2, Sat 10-1; Tues (Summer) 4-7, Wed & Sat 10-2
Restriction: Open to pub for ref only

NEEDHAM

P NEEDHAM FREE PUBLIC LIBRARY*, 1139 Highland Ave, 02494-3298. SAN 345-3960. Tel: 781-455-7559. FAX: 781-455-7591. TDD: 781-453-5617. E-mail: neemail1@minlib.net. Web Site: www.needhamma.gov/library. *Dir,* Ann C MacFate; Tel: 781-455-7559, Ext 202, E-mail: amacfate@minlib.net; *Asst Dir,* Demetri Kyriakis; Tel: 781-455-7559, Ext 203, E-mail: dkyriakis@minlib.net; *Children's Serv Supvr,* Paula A Dugan; Tel: 781-455-7559, Ext 219, E-mail: pdugan@minlib.net; *Ref Supvr,* Stefanie Claydon; Tel: 781-455-7559, E-mail: sclaydon@minlib.net; *Archivist, Tech,* Danielle Tawa; Tel: 781-455-7559, Ext 215, E-mail: dtawa@minlib.net; *Tech Serv,* Diane Browne; Tel: 781-455-7559, Ext 214, E-mail: dbrowne@minlib.net; Staff 17 (MLS 17)
Founded 1888. Pop 32,000; Circ 501,063
Jul 2016-Jun 2017 Income $1,594,282. Mats Exp $222,484, Books $122,741, Per/Ser (Incl. Access Fees) $25,438, Micro $315, AV Mat $44,073, Electronic Ref Mat (Incl. Access Fees) $29,917. Sal $1,212,043
Library Holdings: AV Mats 32,018; e-books 47,732; Large Print Bks 6,800; Bk Vols 142,272; Per Subs 207
Special Collections: Benjamin Franklin Coll; N C Wyeth Art Coll; Needham Archives; Needham History Coll
Subject Interests: Bus & mgt
Automation Activity & Vendor Info: (Cataloging) Innovative Interfaces, Inc; (Circulation) Innovative Interfaces, Inc; (ILL) Innovative Interfaces, Inc; (OPAC) Innovative Interfaces, Inc
Wireless access
Mem of Massachusetts Library System
Partic in Minuteman Library Network
Special Services for the Deaf - TTY equip
Open Mon-Thurs 9-9, Fri 9-5:30, Sat 9-5, Sun 1-7 (1-5 Summer)
Friends of the Library Group

NEW BEDFORD

P NEW BEDFORD FREE PUBLIC LIBRARY*, 613 Pleasant St, 02740-6203. SAN 345-4029. Tel: 508-991-6275. Interlibrary Loan Service Tel: 508-991-6280. FAX: 508-991-6368. Reference E-mail: nbmref@sailsinc.org. Web Site: www.newbedford-ma.gov/library. *Dir,* Olivia Melo; E-mail: omelo@sailsinc.org; *Youth Serv Coordr,* Bethany Coito; E-mail: bcoito@sailsinc.org; Staff 43 (MLS 7, Non-MLS 36)
Founded 1852. Pop 99,922; Circ 240,178
Library Holdings: AV Mats 18,559; Electronic Media & Resources 843; Bk Titles 407,132; Per Subs 762; Spec Interest Per Sub 28,504
Special Collections: Melville Whaling Room, ms, microfilm; Portuguese Coll. Oral History; US Document Depository

Subject Interests: Genealogy
Automation Activity & Vendor Info: (Cataloging) SirsiDynix; (Circulation) SirsiDynix; (OPAC) SirsiDynix
Wireless access
Partic in SAILS Library Network
Special Services for the Deaf - TDD equip
Open Mon-Thurs 9-9, Fri & Sat 9-5
Friends of the Library Group
Branches: 4
CASA DA SAUDADE BRANCH, 58 Crapo St, 02740, SAN 345-4088. Tel: 508-991-6218. FAX: 508-979-1705. *Dir,* Olivia Melo; E-mail: omelo@sailsinc.org; *Br Mgr,* Daniela Moutinho Ferreira; E-mail: dferreira@sailsinc.org; Staff 4 (MLS 1, Non-MLS 3)
Founded 1971
Library Holdings: Bk Vols 34,000; Per Subs 40
Open Mon & Wed 10-6, Tues & Thurs 12-8, Sat 9-5
Friends of the Library Group
HOWLAND-GREEN BRANCH, Three Rodney French Blvd, 02744, SAN 345-4118. Tel: 508-991-6212. FAX: 508-979-1774. *Br Mgr,* George Ripley; E-mail: gripley@sailsinc.org; Staff 3 (MLS 1, Non-MLS 2)
Founded 1964
Library Holdings: Bk Vols 24,000
Special Collections: Spanish Language Coll
Automation Activity & Vendor Info: (Acquisitions) SirsiDynix-WorkFlows; (Cataloging) SirsiDynix-WorkFlows
Open Mon & Fri 10-6, Tues & Thurs 12-8, Sat 9-5
Friends of the Library Group
FRANCIS J LAWLER BRANCH, 745 Rockdale Ave, 02740, SAN 345-4053. Tel: 508-991-6216. FAX: 508-961-3077. *Br Mgr,* Denise Plaskon; E-mail: dplaskon@sailsinc.org
Founded 1960
Library Holdings: Large Print Bks 120; Bk Vols 40,000
Open Mon & Fri 10-6, Tues & Thurs Noon-8, Sat 9-5
Friends of the Library Group
WILKS BRANCH, 1911 Acushnet Ave, 02746, SAN 345-4142. Tel: 508-991-6214. FAX: 508-998-6039. *Br Mgr,* Karen Stefanik; E-mail: kstefanik@sailsinc.org
Founded 1958
Library Holdings: Bk Vols 24,000
Open Mon & Wed 10-6, Tues & Thurs 12-8, Sat 9-5
Friends of the Library Group
Bookmobiles: 1. Librn, Karen Stefanik

S OLD DARTMOUTH HISTORICAL SOCIETY*, New Bedford Whaling Museum Research Library, 18 Johnny Cake Hill, 02740. SAN 307-5540. Tel: 508-997-0046, Ext 134. E-mail: research@whalingmuseum.org. Web Site: www.whalingmuseum.org/explore/library. *Librn,* Mark Procknik; E-mail: mprocknik@whalingmuseum.org; *Chief Curator,* Christina Connett, PhD; *Maritime Curator,* Michael Dyer; Tel: 508-997-0046, Ext 137, E-mail: mdyer@whalingmuseum.org; Staff 3 (MLS 1, Non-MLS 2)
Founded 1956
Library Holdings: Bk Vols 20,000; Spec Interest Per Sub 10
Special Collections: International Marine Archives, micro; Maritime History (Charles A Goodwin Coll); Whaling (Charles F Batchelder Coll); Whaling Museum Logbook Coll. Oral History
Subject Interests: Fine arts, Hist, Manuscripts, Navigation, Voyages, Whaling
Wireless access
Publications: 100 Highlights; 100 Years, 100 Curiosities; American Landscape & Seascape Paintings; Fifty States: America's Whaling Heritage; Kendall Whaling Museum Monograph Series; The Africa Connection; The Kendall Whaling Museum (Newsletter)
Open Tues-Fri 10-4

M SOUTHCOAST HEALTH MEDICAL LIBRARY, 101 Page St, 02740. SAN 307-5559. Tel: 508-973-5267. FAX: 508-973-5263. E-mail: SouthcoastMedLib@southcoast.org. Web Site: www.southcoast.org/for-health-professionals/library. *Med Librn,* Diana Ragas; Staff 1 (MLS 1)
Founded 1954
Library Holdings: e-journals 45; Bk Vols 650; Per Subs 45
Subject Interests: Allied health, Med, Nursing, Patient educ
Wireless access
Partic in Massachusetts Health Sciences Library Network
Open Mon, Tues, Thurs & Fri 8-4
Restriction: Authorized personnel only, Restricted borrowing privileges

NEW BRAINTREE

P LEROY POLLARD MEMORIAL LIBRARY*, 45 Memorial Dr, 01531. SAN 307-5583. Tel: 508-867-7650. FAX: 508-867-7650. E-mail: nbraintreelibrary@gmail.com. Web Site: www.newbraintreema.us. *Dir,* Joan Haynes
Pop 834; Circ 5,814
Library Holdings: Bk Vols 11,000
Mem of Massachusetts Library System
Partic in Central & Western Massachusetts Automated Resource Sharing
Open Mon 12-8:30, Thurs 12-4, Sat 9-Noon
Friends of the Library Group

NEW SALEM

P NEW SALEM PUBLIC LIBRARY, 23 S Main St, 01355. SAN 307-5591. Tel: 978-544-6334. FAX: 978-544-6334. E-mail: n_salem@cwmars.org. Web Site: www.newsalempubliclibrary.org. *Dir,* Diana Smith; *Circ Librn,* Jo Ann Tresback
Founded 1890. Pop 920; Circ 14,820
Library Holdings: Audiobooks 792; DVDs 1,968; Bk Vols 9,535; Per Subs 38; Videos 22
Automation Activity & Vendor Info: (Cataloging) Evergreen
Wireless access
Partic in Central & Western Massachusetts Automated Resource Sharing
Open Tues 12-8, Thurs 10-6, Sat 10-2
Friends of the Library Group

NEWBURYPORT

S MUSEUM OF OLD NEWBURY LIBRARY*, Cushing House Museum, 98 High St, 01950. SAN 328-2813. Tel: 978-462-2681. E-mail: info@newburyhistory.org. Web Site: newburyhistory.org/research-appointments-and-requests. *Exec Dir,* Susan Edwards; E-mail: sedwards@newburyhistory.org
Library Holdings: Bk Vols 2,500
Special Collections: Local History; Newbury, Newburyport & West Newbury
Restriction: Open by appt only

P NEWBURYPORT PUBLIC LIBRARY*, 94 State St, 01950-6619. SAN 307-5621. Tel: 978-465-4428. Circulation Tel: 978-465-4428, Ext 236. Reference Tel: 978-465-4428, Ext 226. Administration Tel: 978-465-4428, Ext 221. FAX: 978-463-0394. E-mail: npl@mvlc.org. Web Site: www.newburyportpl.org. *Head Librn,* Giselle Stevens; Tel: 978-465-4428, Ext 224, E-mail: gstevens@newburyportpl.org; *Circ Mgr,* Lynn Marks; Tel: 978-465-4428, Ext 243; *Archivist,* Sharon Spieldenner; Tel: 978-465-4428, Ext 229; *Ch Serv,* Allison Driscoll; Tel: 978-465-4428, Ext 235; *Info Serv,* Jessica Atherton; *Tech Serv,* Jane Lemuth; Tel: 978-465-4428, Ext 230; *YA Serv,* Emely MacIntosh; Tel: 978-465-4428, Ext 228; Staff 21 (MLS 7, Non-MLS 14)
Founded 1854. Pop 17,500; Circ 345,000
Library Holdings: AV Mats 9,668; Large Print Bks 1,900; Bk Vols 101,661; Per Subs 174
Special Collections: Genealogy Coll; Newburyport History, bks, doc, maps, photog
Automation Activity & Vendor Info: (Cataloging) SirsiDynix; (Circulation) SirsiDynix; (OPAC) SirsiDynix-Enterprise
Wireless access
Function: 24/7 Electronic res, 24/7 Online cat, Activity rm, Adult bk club, Archival coll, Audiobks on Playaways & MP3, Audiobks via web, Bk club(s), Bks on CD, Children's prog, Computer training, Computers for patron use, Digital talking bks, Electronic databases & coll, Free DVD rentals, Games & aids for people with disabilities, Homebound delivery serv, ILL available, Internet access, Life-long learning prog for all ages, Magazines, Magnifiers for reading, Mail & tel request accepted, Mango lang, Meeting rooms, Microfiche/film & reading machines, Movies, Museum passes, Music CDs, Online cat, Outreach serv, OverDrive digital audio bks, Photocopying/Printing, Prog for adults, Prog for children & young adult, Ref & res, Ref serv available, Scanner, Senior outreach, Story hour, Study rm, Summer & winter reading prog, Summer reading prog, Tax forms, Teen prog, Telephone ref, Wheelchair accessible
Mem of Massachusetts Library System
Partic in Merrimack Valley Library Consortium
Open Mon-Thurs 9-9, Fri & Sat 9-5, Sun (Oct-April) 1-5
Friends of the Library Group

NEWTON

S BOSTON PSYCHOANALYTIC SOCIETY & INSTITUTE, INC*, The Hanns Sachs Medical Library, 141 Herrick Rd, 1st Flr, 02459. SAN 307-1391. Tel: 617-266-0953, Ext 104. FAX: 857-255-3253. E-mail: library@bpsi.org. Web Site: www.bpsi.org/library. *Librn & Archivist,* Olga Umansky; Staff 1 (MLS 1)
Founded 1933
Library Holdings: Bk Titles 9,000; Per Subs 95
Special Collections: Archives (History of Psychoanalysis)
Subject Interests: Psychoanalysis
Automation Activity & Vendor Info: (Acquisitions) Mandarin Library Automation; (Cataloging) Mandarin Library Automation; (Circulation) Mandarin Library Automation; (Course Reserve) Mandarin Library Automation; (ILL) Mandarin Library Automation; (Media Booking) Mandarin Library Automation; (OPAC) Mandarin Library Automation; (Serials) Mandarin Library Automation

Open Mon-Fri 9-5
Friends of the Library Group

C WILLIAM JAMES COLLEGE LIBRARY, (Formerly Massachusetts School of Professional Psychology Library), One Wells Ave, 1st Flr, 02459. Tel: 617-327-6777, Ext 1221. FAX: 617-327-4447. E-mail: library@williamjames.edu. Web Site: www.williamjames.edu/student-life/services-resources/library.cfm. *Head Librn,* Julia Clement; Tel: 617-564-9405, E-mail: julia_clement@williamjames.edu; Staff 1 (MLS 1)
Founded 1974. Enrl 300; Highest Degree: Doctorate
Library Holdings: AV Mats 100; e-books 175,000; e-journals 60,000; Bk Vols 1,000; Per Subs 25
Special Collections: School Archives; Testing Kits
Subject Interests: Assessment, Clinical psychol, Counseling, Psychopharmacology, Psychotherapy, Sch psychol
Automation Activity & Vendor Info: (Circulation) Koha; (ILL) OCLC; (OPAC) Koha
Open Mon-Thurs 8am-9pm, Fri 8-5, Sat 8-3

C LASELL COLLEGE, Brennan Library, 80 A Maple Ave, 02466. SAN 307-0891. Tel: 617-243-2244. FAX: 617-243-2458. E-mail: library@lasell.edu. Web Site: www.lasell.edu/academics/academic-centers/brennan-library. *Dir,* Anna Sarneso; Tel: 617-243-2243, E-mail: asarneso@lasell.edu; *Ref (Info Servs),* Jill Shoemaker; E-mail: jshoemaker@lasell.edu; *Tech Serv,* Dev Singer; Tel: 617-243-2207, E-mail: dsinger@lasell.edu; Staff 5 (MLS 5)
Founded 1851. Enrl 1,200; Fac 120; Highest Degree: Master
Library Holdings: AV Mats 1,888; Bk Titles 55,928; Bk Vols 58,000; Per Subs 193
Special Collections: Lasell Historical Coll
Subject Interests: Bus, Child studies, Educ, Fashion, Hotel admin, Phys therapy, Physiology, Retailing, Travel
Automation Activity & Vendor Info: (Cataloging) Innovative Interfaces, Inc; (Circulation) Innovative Interfaces, Inc
Wireless access
Function: ILL available, Photocopying/Printing
Partic in Minuteman Library Network
Open Mon-Thurs 7:30am-Midnight, Fri 7:30-5, Sat 12-5, Sun Noon-Midnight

MOUNT IDA COLLEGE

J NATIONAL CENTER FOR DEATH EDUCATION LIBRARY*, 777 Dedham St, 02459, SAN 325-4836. Tel: 617-928-4552. FAX: 617-928-4713. Reference E-mail: reference@mountida.edu. Web Site: www.mountida.edu. *Head Librn,* Irene Good; E-mail: igood@mountida.edu; Staff 1 (MLS 1)
Founded 1984
Library Holdings: Bk Titles 3,000; Per Subs 47
Partic in Minuteman Library Network

J WADSWORTH LIBRARY*, 777 Dedham St, 02459, SAN 307-5699. Tel: 617-928-4552. FAX: 617-928-4038. Reference E-mail: reference@mountida.edu. Web Site: www.mountida.edu. *Dean, Info Tech & Learning Res,* Marge Lippincott; Tel: 617-928-4596, E-mail: mmlippincott@mountida.edu; *Assoc Dir, Libr Serv,* Judy Harding; E-mail: jharding@mountida.edu; *Ref Librn,* Tim Gerolami; E-mail: tgerolami@mountida.edu; *Asst Librn,* Sarah Dolan; E-mail: sdolan@mountida.edu; *Asst Librn,* Diane Post; E-mail: dpost@mountida.edu; *Asst Librn, Tech Serv,* Donna Dodson; E-mail: ddodson@mountida.edu; *Coordr, Tech Serv,* Clemencia Aramburo; E-mail: caramburo@mountida.edu; Staff 11 (MLS 11)
Founded 1939. Enrl 18; Fac 47
Library Holdings: Bk Titles 60,000; Per Subs 530
Special Collections: History of Mount Ida College Archives; National Center for Death Education Library
Subject Interests: Art, Fashion, Literary criticism, Med, Veterinary med
Automation Activity & Vendor Info: (Cataloging) Innovative Interfaces, Inc
Open Mon-Thurs 7:30am-11pm, Fri 7:30-5, Sat 10-5, Sun 2-Midnight

S NEWTON HISTORY MUSEUM AT THE JACKSON HOMESTEAD*, Manuscript & Photograph Collection Library, 527 Washington St, 02458. SAN 307-5656. Tel: 617-796-1450. Web Site: www.historicnewton.org. *Dir,* Lisa Dady; E-mail: ldady@newtonma.gov; *Curator,* Sara Goldberg; E-mail: sgoldberg@newtonma.gov; Staff 1 (MLS 1)
Founded 1950
Library Holdings: Bk Vols 1,000
Special Collections: Manuscript & Photograph Coll
Subject Interests: Abolitionism, African-Am (ethnic), Archit hist, Decorative art, Genealogy, Local hist, Slavery, State hist for genealogy
Function: Ref serv available
Open Wed-Fri 11-5, Sat & Sun 10-5

NEWTON CENTRE

CL BOSTON COLLEGE, Law Library, 885 Centre St, 02459. SAN 345-1321. Tel: 617-552-4434. Reference Tel: 617-552-2971. FAX: 617-552-2889. E-mail: lawcir@bc.edu. Web Site: www.bc.edu/bc-web/schools/law/sites/students/library. *Assoc Dean for Libr & Tech Serv,* Filippa Marullo Anzalone; Tel: 617-552-6809, E-mail: filippa.anzalone@bc.edu; *Assoc Dir, Admin & Tech Serv,* Alexander Barton; Tel: 617-552-4475, E-mail: alexander.barton@bc.edu; *Assoc Law Librn, Coll Serv, Digital Initiatives,* Helen Lacouture; Tel: 617-552-8609, E-mail: helen.lacouture@bc.edu; *Assoc Law Librn,* Mary Ann Neary; Tel: 617-552-8612, E-mail: maryann.neary@bc.edu; *Access Serv Librn,* Lily Dyer; Tel: 617-552-8610, E-mail: lily.dyer@bc.edu; *Coll Serv Librn,* Deena Frazier; Tel: 617-552-4409, E-mail: deena.frazier@bc.edu; *Legal Info Librn,* Karen S Breda; Tel: 617-552-4407, E-mail: karen.breda@bc.edu; *Legal Info Librn,* Xin Sherry Chen; Tel: 617-552-2897, E-mail: sherry.xin.chen@bc.edu; *Curator, Spec Coll, Legal Info Librn,* Laurel Davis; Tel: 617-552-4410, E-mail: laurel.davis.2@bc.edu; *Legal Info Librn,* Stephanie Farne; Tel: 617-552-8607, E-mail: stephanie.farne@bc.edu; *Legal Info Librn,* Joan A Shear; Tel: 617-552-2895, E-mail: joan.shear@bc.edu; *Digital Initiatives & Scholarly Communication Specialist,* Avi Bauer; Tel: 617-552-8602, E-mail: abraham.bauer@bc.edu. Subject Specialists: *Advan legal res, Art law,* Filippa Marullo Anzalone; Staff 17.2 (MLS 12.2, Non-MLS 5)
Founded 1929. Enrl 710; Fac 56; Highest Degree: Doctorate
Library Holdings: Bk Vols 501,875; Per Subs 2,482
Automation Activity & Vendor Info: (Acquisitions) Ex Libris Group; (Cataloging) Ex Libris Group; (Circulation) Ex Libris Group; (Course Reserve) Ex Libris Group; (ILL) OCLC ILLiad; (OPAC) Ex Libris Group; (Serials) Ex Libris Group
Wireless access
Function: Archival coll, Art exhibits, CD-ROM, Computers for patron use, E-Reserves, Electronic databases & coll, Govt ref serv, ILL available, Online cat, Online ref, Photocopying/Printing, Wheelchair accessible
Partic in Association of Jesuit Colleges & Universities; Legal Information Preservation Alliance; NELLCO Law Library Consortium, Inc.
Open Mon-Thurs 7:30am-11:45pm, Fri 7:30am-10pm, Sat 9am-10pm, Sun 10am-11:45pm
Restriction: Borrowing privileges limited to fac & registered students, Non-circulating coll, Non-circulating of rare bks, Non-circulating to the pub, Restricted access, Restricted borrowing privileges

CR HEBREW COLLEGE*, The Rae & Joseph Gann Library, 160 Herrick Rd, 02459. SAN 307-2665. Tel: 617-559-8750. FAX: 617-559-8751. E-mail: library@hebrewcollege.edu. Web Site: www.hebrewcollege.edu/library. *Libr Dir,* Harvey Sukenic; E-mail: hsukenic@hebrewcollege.edu; Staff 1 (MLS 1)
Founded 1918. Enrl 250; Fac 66; Highest Degree: Doctorate
Library Holdings: Braille Volumes 8; CDs 264; DVDs 286; Bk Vols 90,000; Per Subs 180
Subject Interests: Jewish educ, Jewish lit, Judaica, Rabbinics
Automation Activity & Vendor Info: (Cataloging) OPALS (Open-source Automated Library System); (Circulation) OPALS (Open-source Automated Library System); (OPAC) OPALS (Open-source Automated Library System)
Wireless access
Function: Distance learning, Doc delivery serv, For res purposes, ILL available, Ref serv available, Wheelchair accessible
Partic in Boston Theological Interreligious Consortium
Special Services for the Blind - Large print bks
Open Mon & Thurs 9-5, Tues & Wed 9-7, Fri 9-1, Sun 9-2
Restriction: Open to fac, students & qualified researchers, Open to pub for ref & circ; with some limitations, Photo ID required for access

P NEWTON FREE LIBRARY*, 330 Homer St, 02459-1429. SAN 345-4231. Tel: 617-796-1360. E-mail: newtonpublicservices@minlib.net. Web Site: newtonfreelibrary.net. *Dir,* Jill Mercurio; E-mail: admin@newtonfreelibrary.net; Staff 123 (MLS 44, Non-MLS 79)
Founded 1870. Pop 88,817; Circ 1,585,158
Jul 2017-Jun 2018 Income $5,939,183, City $5,644,490, Federal $9,000, Other $285,693. Mats Exp $5,585,846, Books $363,487, Per/Ser (Incl. Access Fees) $30,559, AV Mat $159,156, Electronic Ref Mat (Incl. Access Fees) $111,620. Sal $3,603,479
Library Holdings: AV Mats 79,456; CDs 40,004; DVDs 39,452; e-books 55,314; e-journals 50; Electronic Media & Resources 1,654; Bk Vols 396,043; Per Subs 445
Special Collections: Newton Historical Coll. Oral History
Automation Activity & Vendor Info: (Acquisitions) Innovative Interfaces, Inc - Sierra; (Cataloging) Innovative Interfaces, Inc - Sierra; (Circulation) Innovative Interfaces, Inc - Sierra; (Discovery) Innovative Interfaces, Inc; (OPAC) Innovative Interfaces, Inc; (Serials) Innovative Interfaces, Inc
Wireless access
Function: 24/7 Electronic res, 24/7 Online cat, 3D Printer, Activity rm, Adult bk club, Adult literacy prog, Archival coll, Art exhibits, Art programs, Audiobks on Playaways & MP3, Audiobks via web, Bk club(s),

Bks on CD, Chess club, Children's prog, Citizenship assistance, Computer training, Computers for patron use, Digital talking bks, E-Readers, E-Reserves, Electronic databases & coll, Equip loans & repairs, Family literacy, Free DVD rentals, Games & aids for people with disabilities, Genealogy discussion group, Holiday prog, Home delivery & serv to seniorr ctr & nursing homes, Homebound delivery serv, ILL available, Internet access, Magazines, Magnifiers for reading, Makerspace, Meeting rooms, Movies, Museum passes, Music CDs, Online cat, Orientations, Outreach serv, Photocopying/Printing, Preschool outreach, Preschool reading prog, Prog for adults, Prog for children & young adult, Ref & res, Ref serv available, Scanner, Senior outreach, Serves people with intellectual disabilities, Spanish lang bks, STEM programs, Story hour, Study rm, Summer reading prog, Tax forms, Teen prog, Telephone ref, Wheelchair accessible
Publications: Newsletter (Monthly)
Mem of Massachusetts Library System
Partic in Minuteman Library Network
Special Services for the Deaf - Bks on deafness & sign lang; Captioned film dep; Spec interest per; TTY equip
Special Services for the Blind - Assistive/Adapted tech devices, equip & products; Audio mat; BiFolkal kits; Bks & mags in Braille, on rec, tape & cassette; Closed circuit TV magnifier; Computer with voice synthesizer for visually impaired persons; Large print bks; Large screen computer & software; Magnifiers; Playaways (bks on MP3); Reader equip; Talking bks
Open Mon-Thurs 9-9, Fri 9-6, Sat 9-5, Sun (Sept-June) 1-5
Friends of the Library Group

NORFOLK

P NORFOLK PUBLIC LIBRARY*, Two Liberty Lane, 02056. SAN 307-5729. Tel: 508-528-3380. FAX: 508-528-6417. E-mail: norfolkpl@sailsinc.org. Web Site: norfolkpl.org. *Libr Dir,* Libby O'Neill; E-mail: eoneill@sailsinc.org; *Assoc Dir,* Sarah Ward; E-mail: sward@sailsinc.org; *Sr Librn/Youth Serv,* Courtney Allen; E-mail: callen@sailsinc.org; *Electronic Res, Ref Serv,* John Spinney; E-mail: jspinney@sailsinc.org; Staff 10 (MLS 4, Non-MLS 6)
Founded 1880. Pop 10,000
Library Holdings: Bk Titles 49,000; Per Subs 150
Automation Activity & Vendor Info: (Acquisitions) SirsiDynix; (Cataloging) SirsiDynix
Partic in SAILS Library Network
Open Mon-Thurs 10-7:30, Fri & Sat 10-4
Friends of the Library Group

NORTH ADAMS

C MASSACHUSETTS COLLEGE OF LIBERAL ARTS*, Eugene L Freel Library, 375 Church St, Ste 9250, 01247. SAN 307-5753. Tel: 413-662-5321. Reference Tel: 413-662-5325. E-mail: library@mcla.edu. Web Site: library.mcla.edu/freel_library. Staff 10 (MLS 3, Non-MLS 7)
Founded 1894. Enrl 1,000; Fac 92; Highest Degree: Master
Library Holdings: Bk Vols 135,000
Special Collections: Hoosac Valley Coll for Local History; Teacher Resources Coll. Oral History
Subject Interests: Educ, Liberal arts
Automation Activity & Vendor Info: (Cataloging) Koha; (Circulation) Koha; (Course Reserve) Koha; (Discovery) EBSCO Discovery Service; (ILL) OCLC WorldShare Interlibrary Loan; (OPAC) Koha
Wireless access
Partic in Massachusetts Commonwealth Consortium of Libraries in Public Higher Education Institutions; OCLC-LVIS

P NORTH ADAMS PUBLIC LIBRARY*, 74 Church St, 01247. SAN 307-3327. Tel: 413-662-3133. FAX: 413-662-3039. E-mail: reference@northadams-ma.gov. Web Site: www.naplibrary.com. *Dir,* Mindy Hackner; E-mail: mhackner@northadams-ma.gov; *Asst Dir, Ref & Adult Serv, Youth Serv Librn,* Kim DiLego; Staff 11 (MLS 3, Non-MLS 8)
Founded 1884. Pop 13,500; Circ 100,000
Jul 2016-Jun 2017. Mats Exp $73,100, Books $30,127, Per/Ser (Incl. Access Fees) $5,775, Micro $150, AV Mat $5,000, Electronic Ref Mat (Incl. Access Fees) $8,000. Sal Prof $249,253
Library Holdings: Bks on Deafness & Sign Lang 27; CDs 2,200; DVDs 5,740; e-books 24,552; High Interest/Low Vocabulary Bk Vols 1,070; Large Print Bks 3,500; Microforms 1,137; Music Scores 21; Bk Vols 47,561; Per Subs 180; Spec Interest Per Sub 21; Talking Bks 3,920
Special Collections: Drury High year books (digital); Hoosac Tunnel
Automation Activity & Vendor Info: (Acquisitions) Evergreen; (Cataloging) Evergreen; (Circulation) Evergreen; (ILL) Evergreen; (OPAC) Evergreen; (Serials) Evergreen
Wireless access
Function: 24/7 Electronic res, 24/7 Online cat, Activity rm, Adult bk club, Archival coll, Art exhibits, Audiobks via web, Bks on cassette, Bks on CD, Children's prog, Citizenship assistance, Computer training, Computers for patron use, E-Reserves, Electronic databases & coll, Free DVD rentals, Holiday prog, Homebound delivery serv, Internet access, Magazines, Mail & tel request accepted, Microfiche/film & reading machines, Museum passes, Music CDs, Online cat, Online ref, Photocopying/Printing, Preschool outreach, Prog for adults, Prog for children & young adult, Ref serv available, Scanner, Serves people with intellectual disabilities, Spoken cassettes & CDs, Spoken cassettes & DVDs, Story hour, Summer reading prog, Tax forms, Teen prog, Telephone ref, Wheelchair accessible, Workshops
Mem of Massachusetts Library System
Partic in Central & Western Massachusetts Automated Resource Sharing
Special Services for the Deaf - Bks on deafness & sign lang; Coll on deaf educ; High interest/low vocabulary bks
Special Services for the Blind - Accessible computers; Audio mat; Bks on CD; Home delivery serv; Large print bks; Low vision equip; PC for people with disabilities; Recorded bks; Screen enlargement software for people with visual disabilities
Open Mon-Wed & Fri 9-5, Thurs 12-8, Sat 10-1
Restriction: In-house use for visitors
Friends of the Library Group

NORTH ANDOVER

C MERRIMACK COLLEGE*, McQuade Library, 315 Turnpike St, 01845. SAN 307-580X. Tel: 978-837-5215. E-mail: mcquade@merrimack.edu. Web Site: www.merrimack.edu/library. *Dir,* Kathryn Geoffrion Scannell; Tel: 978-837-5211, E-mail: geoffrionsck@merrimack.edu; *Dir, Media Instrul Serv,* Kevin Salemme; Tel: 978-837-5377, E-mail: Kevin.Salemme@merrimack.edu; *Head, Access Serv,* Christina Condon; Tel: 978-837-5994, E-mail: Christina.Condon@merrimack.edu; *Head, Instruction & Outreach,* Lyena Chavez; Tel: 978-837-5045, E-mail: lyena.chavez@merrimack.edu; *Head, Res Mgt,* Frances Nilsson; Tel: 978-837-5064, E-mail: nilssonf@merrimack.edu
Founded 1947. Highest Degree: Master
Special Collections: Augustinian Studies; Education Resource Coll
Automation Activity & Vendor Info: (Acquisitions) Evergreen; (Cataloging) Evergreen; (Circulation) Evergreen; (Course Reserve) Evergreen; (Discovery) EBSCO Discovery Service; (ILL) OCLC WorldShare Interlibrary Loan; (OPAC) Evergreen; (Serials) Evergreen
Wireless access
Function: 24/7 Online cat, For res purposes, Internet access, Magnifiers for reading, Outside serv via phone, mail, e-mail & web, Ref & res, Wheelchair accessible
Mem of Massachusetts Library System
Special Services for the Blind - Aids for in-house use; Assistive/Adapted tech devices, equip & products
Restriction: 24-hr pass syst for students only, Access at librarian's discretion, Borrowing requests are handled by ILL, ID required to use computers (Ltd hrs), Limited access for the pub, Restricted pub use

S NORTH ANDOVER HISTORICAL SOCIETY LIBRARY*, 153 Academy Rd, 01845. SAN 373-1626. Tel: 978-686-4035. E-mail: archives.nahistory@gmail.com. Web Site: www.northandoverhistoricalsociety.org. *Exec Dir,* Carol Majahad; E-mail: director.nahistory@gmail.com; *Curator,* Inga C Larson; Staff 2 (Non-MLS 2)
Founded 1913
Library Holdings: Bk Vols 1,500
Special Collections: Local Architectural History Coll, doc, maps & photog
Subject Interests: Genealogy
Wireless access
Function: Magnifiers for reading
Restriction: Non-circulating, Open by appt only

P STEVENS MEMORIAL LIBRARY*, 345 Main St, 01845. SAN 307-5826. Tel: 978-688-9505. FAX: 978-688-9507. E-mail: smlrefservices@northandoverma.gov. Web Site: www.stevensmemlib.org. *Libr Dir,* Kathleen Keenan; Tel: 978-688-9505, Ext 42021, E-mail: kkeenan@northandoverma.gov; *Head, Children's Servx,* Charlotte Arredondo; E-mail: carredondo@northandoverma.gov; *Head, Circ,* Erin Wolff; E-mail: ewolff@northandoverma.gov; *Head, Ref, Head, YA,* Marie McAndrew-Taylor; E-mail: mmcandrew-taylor@northandoverma.gov; Staff 15 (MLS 5, Non-MLS 10)
Founded 1907. Pop 27,196; Circ 201,961
Jul 2013-Jun 2014 Income $887,066, State $23,379, City $863,687. Mats Exp $157,722, Books $87,415, Per/Ser (Incl. Access Fees) $7,000, AV Mat $31,915, Electronic Ref Mat (Incl. Access Fees) $31,392. Sal $611,300
Library Holdings: CDs 4,285; DVDs 3,903; e-books 11,843; Bk Vols 86,857
Special Collections: Essex County, Massachusetts; Poetry (Anne Bradstreet Coll)
Automation Activity & Vendor Info: (Cataloging) Evergreen; (Circulation) Evergreen; (OPAC) Evergreen; (Serials) EBSCO Online
Wireless access
Mem of Massachusetts Library System
Partic in Central & Western Massachusetts Automated Resource Sharing; Merrimack Valley Library Consortium

Special Services for the Blind - Accessible computers; Bks available with recordings; Closed circuit TV magnifier; Extensive large print coll
Open Mon-Thurs (Winter) 10-9, Fri 10-6, Sat 10-5, Sun 1-5; Mon-Thurs (Summer) 10-9, Fri 10-6
Friends of the Library Group

NORTH ATTLEBORO

P RICHARDS MEMORIAL LIBRARY*, 118 N Washington St, 02760. SAN 307-5834. Tel: 508-699-0122. FAX: 508-699-8075. Web Site: www.rmlonline.org. *Dir,* Frank Ward; E-mail: fward@sailsinc.org; *Dir of Circ,* Ellen Casaccio; *Adult Serv,* Maggie Holmes; *Ref, Tech Serv,* David Lockhart
Founded 1878. Pop 28,000; Circ 103,000
Library Holdings: AV Mats 2,565; Bk Vols 45,113; Per Subs 137; Talking Bks 1,075
Automation Activity & Vendor Info: (Cataloging) SirsiDynix; (Circulation) SirsiDynix; (OPAC) SirsiDynix
Wireless access
Partic in SAILS Library Network
Open Mon-Thurs (Winter) 9:30-8:30, Fri & Sat 9-5; Mon & Thurs (Summer) 9-8, Tues, Wed, Fri & Sat 9-5
Friends of the Library Group

NORTH BROOKFIELD

P HASTON FREE PUBLIC LIBRARY*, North Brookfield Library, 161 N Main St, 01535. SAN 307-5842. Tel: 508-867-0208. FAX: 508-867-0216. Web Site: northbrookfieldlibrary.org. *Libr Dir,* Dawn L Thistle; E-mail: dthistle@cwmars.org; *Asst Librn,* Dawn Thistle; E-mail: dthistle@cwmars.org; *Ch Serv,* Rosemary Mackenzie; E-mail: rmackenzie@cwmars.org; *Libr Asst,* Regina Allen-Davis; *Libr Asst,* Lori Buckley; Staff 3 (MLS 1, Non-MLS 2)
Founded 1879. Pop 4,817; Circ 36,554
Jul 2017-Jun 2018 Income $10,052, Locally Generated Income $9,911, Other $141. Mats Exp $22,549, Books $13,586, Per/Ser (Incl. Access Fees) $1,479, Other Print Mats $52, AV Mat $6,272, Electronic Ref Mat (Incl. Access Fees) $1,160. Sal $61,273
Library Holdings: Audiobooks 1,125; Braille Volumes 2; DVDs 1,889; e-books 55,766; Electronic Media & Resources 3; Microforms 49; Bk Vols 23,175; Per Subs 30
Special Collections: Local History (North Brookfield Journals)
Automation Activity & Vendor Info: (Cataloging) Evergreen; (Circulation) Evergreen; (ILL) Evergreen; (OPAC) Evergreen
Wireless access
Function: 24/7 Electronic res, 24/7 Online cat, Activity rm, Adult bk club, After school storytime, Art exhibits, Audio & video playback equip for onsite use, Audiobks via web, Bk club(s), Bks on CD, Children's prog, Computer training, Computers for patron use, Electronic databases & coll, Equip loans & repairs, Free DVD rentals, Holiday prog, Home delivery & serv to seniorr ctr & nursing homes, Homebound delivery serv, ILL available, Internet access, Life-long learning prog for all ages, Magazines, Meeting rooms, Microfiche/film & reading machines, Movies, Museum passes, Music CDs, Online cat, Online ref, Orientations, OverDrive digital audio bks, Photocopying/Printing, Preschool reading prog, Printer for laptops & handheld devices, Prog for adults, Prog for children & young adult, Ref serv available, Scanner, Spanish lang bks, Spoken cassettes & CDs, Story hour, Study rm, Summer reading prog, Tax forms, Teen prog, Telephone ref, Wheelchair accessible, Workshops, Writing prog
Mem of Massachusetts Library System
Partic in Central & Western Massachusetts Automated Resource Sharing
Special Services for the Blind - Bks on cassette; Bks on CD; Home delivery serv; Large print & cassettes; Low vision equip; Magnifiers; Videos on blindness & physical disabilties
Open Mon & Wed 1-7, Tues 10-5, Thurs 1-6, Sat 9-Noon
Friends of the Library Group

NORTH DARTMOUTH

C UNIVERSITY OF MASSACHUSETTS DARTMOUTH LIBRARY*, Claire T Carney Library, 285 Old Westport Rd, 02747-2300. SAN 307-5850. Tel: 508-999-8678. Circulation Tel: 508-999-8750. Interlibrary Loan Service Tel: 508-999-6951. Administration Tel: 508-999-8157. FAX: 508-999-8987. Interlibrary Loan Service FAX: 508-999-9142. Reference FAX: 508-999-9240. E-mail: libweb@umassd.edu. Web Site: www.lib.umassd.edu. *Interim Dean, Libr Serv,* Dawn Gross; Tel: 508-999-8665, E-mail: dgross1@umassd.edu; *Chair, Info Serv,* Lorraine Heffernan; Tel: 508-999-8670, E-mail: lheffernan@umassd.edu; *Chair, Libr Serv,* Matt Sylvain; Tel: 508-999-8682, E-mail: msylvain@umassd.edu; *Archives Librn, Spec Coll Librn,* Judith Farrar; Tel: 508-999-8686, E-mail: jfarrar@umassd.edu; *Fine Arts Librn, Humanities Librn,* Olivia Miller; Tel: 508-999-8526, E-mail: omiller@umassd.edu; *Coll Develop, Tech Serv,* Susan Raidy-Klein; Tel: 508-999-8666, E-mail: sraidyklein@umassd.edu; Staff 15 (MLS 14, Non-MLS 1)
Founded 1960. Enrl 8,299; Fac 350; Highest Degree: Doctorate
Library Holdings: AV Mats 9,699; e-books 243; Bk Titles 271,274; Bk Vols 468,216; Per Subs 2,754
Special Collections: Alfred Lewis manuscripts and papers; American Imprints Coll; Archives of the Center for Jewish Culture; Archives of the Franco American League of Fall River; Can; Franco-American Coll; Hansard Parliamentary Debates; Portuguese-American Historical Coll; Robert Kennedy Assassination Archives. US Document Depository
Subject Interests: Lit, Portuguese (Lang)
Automation Activity & Vendor Info: (Cataloging) Ex Libris Group; (Circulation) Ex Libris Group; (Course Reserve) Ex Libris Group; (Media Booking) Ex Libris Group; (OPAC) Ex Libris Group
Wireless access
Function: Archival coll, AV serv, Distance learning, ILL available, Photocopying/Printing, Wheelchair accessible
Publications: Library News (Newsletter)
Partic in Boston Library Consortium, Inc; LYRASIS; Southeastern Massachusetts Consortium of Health Science
Special Services for the Blind - Assistive/Adapted tech devices, equip & products
Open Mon-Thurs (Feb-May) 7:30am-11pm, Fri 7:30-5, Sat 9:30-5, Sun 12-9; Mon-Thurs (June-Aug) 7:30am-10pm, Fri 7:30-5
Friends of the Library Group

L UNIVERSITY OF MASSACHUSETTS SCHOOL OF LAW LIBRARY*, 333 Faunce Corner Rd, 02747. SAN 372-0314. Tel: 508-985-1121. Reference Tel: 508-985-1127. E-mail: lawlib@umassd.edu. Web Site: www.umassd.edu/law/library. *Dir, Law Libr,* Spencer Clough; E-mail: sclough@umassd.edu; *Asst Dean of Libr,* Misty Peltz-Steele; E-mail: mpeltzsteele@umassd.edu; *Asst Librn, Pub Serv,* Emma Wood; E-mail: emma.wood@umassd.edu; Staff 4 (MLS 4)
Automation Activity & Vendor Info: (Serials) Auto-Graphics, Inc
Wireless access
Partic in LYRASIS; OCLC Online Computer Library Center, Inc
Open Mon-Thurs 9am-9:30pm, Fri & Sat 9-5, Sun Noon-6

NORTH EASTON

P AMES FREE LIBRARY*, Easton's Public Library, 53 Main St, 02356. SAN 307-594X. Tel: 508-238-2000. FAX: 508-238-2980. Web Site: amesfreelibrary.org. *Exec Dir,* Dr Uma Hiremath; E-mail: uhiremath@amesfreelibrary.org; *Asst Dir,* Ian Dunbar; E-mail: idunbar@amesfreelibrary.org; *Head, Youth Serv,* Jessica Block; E-mail: jblock@amesfreelibrary.org; *Ref & Ad Serv Librn,* Megan Tully; *Ref/Info Tech Serv Librn,* Kate Kazlauskas; *Circ Supvr,* Mary Silva; Staff 11 (MLS 5, Non-MLS 6)
Founded 1883. Pop 23,908; Circ 144,173
Jul 2019-Jun 2020 Income $1,534,472, State $32,629, City $561,606, Locally Generated Income $940,237. Mats Exp $76,803. Sal $697,462
Library Holdings: Audiobooks 2,743; AV Mats 12,527; DVDs 4,364; e-books 48,635; Electronic Media & Resources 4,629; Bk Titles 42,927; Per Subs 161
Special Collections: Easton Journal, bd; H H Richardson Materials; Massachusetts Town Reports
Automation Activity & Vendor Info: (Acquisitions) SirsiDynix; (Cataloging) SirsiDynix; (Circulation) SirsiDynix; (ILL) SirsiDynix; (OPAC) SirsiDynix; (Serials) SirsiDynix
Wireless access
Function: 24/7 Electronic res, 24/7 Online cat, Activity rm, Adult bk club, Adult literacy prog, Art exhibits, Audiobks via web, AV serv, Bk club(s), Bk reviews (Group), Bks on CD, Children's prog, Computer training, Computers for patron use, E-Readers, Electronic databases & coll, Equip loans & repairs, Free DVD rentals, Genealogy discussion group, Holiday prog, Homebound delivery serv, ILL available, Instruction & testing, Internet access, Laminating, Large print keyboards, Life-long learning prog for all ages, Magazines, Magnifiers for reading, Mail & tel request accepted, Makerspace, Mango lang, Meeting rooms, Movies, Museum passes, Music CDs, Online cat, Online info literacy tutorials on the web & in blackboard, Outreach serv, OverDrive digital audio bks, Photocopying/Printing, Preschool outreach, Preschool reading prog, Printer for laptops & handheld devices, Prog for adults, Prog for children & young adult, Ref serv available, Scanner, Senior computer classes, Senior outreach, Serves people with intellectual disabilities, Spoken cassettes & DVDs, STEM programs, Story hour, Study rm, Summer reading prog, Tax forms, Teen prog, Telephone ref, Visual arts prog, Wheelchair accessible, Workshops, Writing prog
Publications: The First Century (A Centennial History of Ames Free Library of Easton, Inc)
Mem of Massachusetts Library System
Partic in SAILS Library Network
Special Services for the Deaf - Bks on deafness & sign lang
Special Services for the Blind - Bks on CD; Computer access aids; Home delivery serv; Large print bks; Large screen computer & software; Low vision equip; Magnifiers; ZoomText magnification & reading software
Open Mon-Thurs 10-8, Fri & Sat 10-5

Restriction: Ref only, Staff & prof res
Friends of the Library Group

NORTH READING

P FLINT MEMORIAL LIBRARY*, 147 Park St, 01864. SAN 307-5869. Tel: 978-664-4942. FAX: 978-664-0812. E-mail: mnr@mvlc.org. Web Site: www.flintmemoriallibrary.org. *Dir,* Sharon Kelleher; E-mail: skelleher@northreadingma.gov; *Asst Dir,* Dan Tremblay; E-mail: dtremblay@northreadingma.gov; *Head, Circ,* Teresa Penney; E-mail: tpenney@northreadingma.gov; *Ref Librn,* Debra Hindes; E-mail: dhindes@northreadingma.gov; *Youth Serv Librn,* Danielle Masterson; E-mail: dmasterson@morthreadingma.gov; Staff 4 (MLS 4)
Founded 1872. Pop 14,518; Circ 100,836
Library Holdings: Bk Vols 78,000; Per Subs 200
Special Collections: Genealogy & History (Clara Burnham, North Reading & George Root Colls) bks, ms, maps. Oral History
Subject Interests: Local hist
Automation Activity & Vendor Info: (Cataloging) SirsiDynix; (Circulation) SirsiDynix; (OPAC) SirsiDynix
Wireless access
Mem of Massachusetts Library System
Partic in Merrimack Valley Library Consortium
Open Mon 1-8, Tues & Thurs 10-8, Wed 1-5, Fri 11-5, Sat (Sept-May) 10-5
Friends of the Library Group

NORTH TRURO

P TRURO PUBLIC LIBRARY*, Seven Standish Way, 02652. (Mail add: PO Box 357, 02652-0357), SAN 307-5877. Tel: 508-487-1125. FAX: 508-487-3571. E-mail: tpl_mail@clamsnet.org. Web Site: www.trurolibrary.org. *Dir,* Ford Patricia; E-mail: tford@truro-ma.gov; *Asst Dir, Youth Serv,* Maggie Hanelt; E-mail: mhanelt@clamsnet.org
Founded 1894. Pop 2,000; Circ 28,000
Library Holdings: Bk Titles 25,300; Per Subs 98
Special Collections: Oral History
Automation Activity & Vendor Info: (Acquisitions) Innovative Interfaces, Inc; (Cataloging) Innovative Interfaces, Inc; (Circulation) Innovative Interfaces, Inc; (ILL) Innovative Interfaces, Inc; (OPAC) Innovative Interfaces, Inc
Wireless access
Function: Adult literacy prog, Homebound delivery serv, ILL available, Internet access, Large print keyboards, Magnifiers for reading, Music CDs, Orientations, Photocopying/Printing, Prog for adults, Prog for children & young adult, Ref serv available, Spoken cassettes & CDs, Summer reading prog, Telephone ref, VHS videos, Wheelchair accessible, Workshops
Mem of Massachusetts Library System
Partic in Cape Libraries Automated Materials Sharing Network
Special Services for the Deaf - Closed caption videos
Special Services for the Blind - Assistive/Adapted tech devices, equip & products; Audio mat; Bks available with recordings; Bks on cassette; Bks on CD; Computer with voice synthesizer for visually impaired persons; Copier with enlargement capabilities; Descriptive video serv (DVS); Home delivery serv; Large print bks; Large screen computer & software; Low vision equip; Magnifiers; Talking bks
Open Tues & Wed 9:30-8, Thurs 9:30-6, Fri & Sat 9:30-4
Friends of the Library Group

NORTHAMPTON

P FORBES LIBRARY*, 20 West St, 01060-3798. SAN 307-5885. Tel: 413-587-1011. Circulation Tel: 413-587-1011, Ext 2. Reference Tel: 413-587-1012. Administration Tel: 413-587-1017. FAX: 413-587-1015. E-mail: reference@forbeslibrary.org. Web Site: www.forbeslibrary.org. *Libr Dir,* Lisa Downing; E-mail: ldowning@forbeslibrary.org; Staff 37 (MLS 12, Non-MLS 25)
Founded 1894. Pop 30,000; Circ 396,808
Library Holdings: Audiobooks 6,250; Braille Volumes 25; CDs 6,250; DVDs 12,370; e-books 17,026; Large Print Bks 4,000; Music Scores 3,000; Bk Vols 156,063; Per Subs 1,809; Videos 12,370
Special Collections: Calvin Coolidge; Connecticut Valley History; Genealogy Coll
Subject Interests: Art & archit, Music
Automation Activity & Vendor Info: (Acquisitions) Evergreen; (Cataloging) Evergreen; (Circulation) Evergreen; (ILL) Evergreen; (OPAC) Evergreen; (Serials) Evergreen
Wireless access
Function: Adult bk club, Archival coll, Art exhibits, Audio & video playback equip for onsite use, Audiobks via web, Bk club(s), Bks on CD, Chess club, Children's prog, Computer training, Computers for patron use, Digital talking bks, E-Reserves, Electronic databases & coll, Free DVD rentals, Games & aids for people with disabilities, Genealogy discussion group, Home delivery & serv to seniorr ctr & nursing homes, Homebound delivery serv, ILL available, Internet access, Magnifiers for reading, Mail & tel request accepted, Microfiche/film & reading machines, Museum passes, Music CDs, Online cat, Online ref, Outside serv via phone, mail, e-mail & web, OverDrive digital audio bks, Photocopying/Printing, Prog for adults, Prog for children & young adult, Ref & res, Ref serv available, Scanner, Senior computer classes, Spanish lang bks, Spoken cassettes & CDs, Spoken cassettes & DVDs, Story hour, Summer reading prog, Tax forms, Teen prog, Telephone ref, Visual arts prog, Wheelchair accessible, Workshops, Writing prog
Partic in Central & Western Massachusetts Automated Resource Sharing
Special Services for the Deaf - Assistive tech; Closed caption videos
Special Services for the Blind - Reader equip
Open Mon & Wed 9-9, Tues & Thurs 1-5, Fri & Sat 9-5
Friends of the Library Group

S HISTORIC NORTHAMPTON, Archives & Library, 46 Bridge St, 01060. SAN 329-9112. Tel: 413-584-6011. FAX: 413-584-7956. Web Site: www.historic-northampton.org. *Co-Executive Dir,* Laurie Sanders; E-mail: lsanders@historicnorthampton.org; *Co-Executive Dir,* Elizabeth Sharpe; E-mail: emsharpe@historicnorthampton.org
Founded 1905
Library Holdings: Bk Titles 2,500
Special Collections: Anne Laura Clark Coll; Charles C Burleigh Jr Coll; Coolidge Family Coll; Daguerreotype, Ambrotype & Tintype Coll; Howes Brothers Photograph Coll; Main Street, Northampton Photograph Coll; Needlework Coll; Photographs by Edgar T Scott, Frederick N Kneeland & Harvey J Finison; Pro Brush Co Coll. Oral History
Subject Interests: Local hist
Publications: History of Northampton; Newsletters; Weathervane Series (Booklets on local subjects)
Restriction: Authorized scholars by appt
Friends of the Library Group

GL MASSACHUSETTS TRIAL COURT*, Hampshire Law Library, Courthouse, 99 Main St, Ste 1, 01060. SAN 307-5893. Tel: 413-586-2297. FAX: 413-584-0870. E-mail: hampshirelawlibrary@hotmail.com. Web Site: www.mass.gov/orgs/trial-court-law-libraries. *Head Law Librn,* Susan Wells; Staff 1 (MLS 1)
Founded 1894
Library Holdings: CDs 372; e-books 100; e-journals 1,500; Bk Titles 3,000; Bk Vols 16,000; Per Subs 20
Special Collections: Massachusetts Legislative Documents (paper 1871-1988, online 1994-present)
Automation Activity & Vendor Info: (Cataloging) SirsiDynix; (Circulation) SirsiDynix; (ILL) OCLC FirstSearch; (OPAC) SirsiDynix
Wireless access
Partic in LYRASIS; OCLC Online Computer Library Center, Inc
Open Mon-Fri 8:30-4:30

C SMITH COLLEGE LIBRARIES*, Neilson William Allan Library, Four Tyler Dr, 01063. SAN 345-4657. Tel: 413-585-2910. Interlibrary Loan Service Tel: 413-585-2962. Web Site: libraries.smith.edu. *Dean of Libr,* Susan Fliss; E-mail: sfliss@smith.edu; Staff 60 (MLS 33, Non-MLS 27)
Founded 1878. Enrl 2,850; Fac 293; Highest Degree: Doctorate
Library Holdings: Bk Vols 1,338,734
Special Collections: College Archives; Mortimer Rare Book Coll; Sophia Smith Coll of Women's History
Subject Interests: Women's hist
Automation Activity & Vendor Info: (Acquisitions) Ex Libris Group; (Cataloging) Ex Libris Group; (Circulation) Ex Libris Group; (Course Reserve) Ex Libris Group; (Discovery) EBSCO Discovery Service; (ILL) OCLC ILLiad; (OPAC) Ex Libris Group; (Serials) Ex Libris Group
Wireless access
Partic in LYRASIS; OCLC Online Computer Library Center, Inc
Under construction 2019-
Friends of the Library Group

Departmental Libraries:

HILLYER ART LIBRARY, Brown Fine Arts Ctr, 20 Elm St, 01063, SAN 345-4681. Tel: 413-585-2940. FAX: 413-585-6975. E-mail: hillinfo@smith.edu. Web Site: libraries.smith.edu/spaces-technology/all-spaces-technology/hillyer-art-library. *Digital Humanities Librn,* Nimisha Bhat; Tel: 413-585-2941, E-mail: mbhat@smith.edu; *Tech Serv/Circ Assoc,* Matthew Durand; Tel: 413-585-2943, E-mail: mdurand@smith.edu; Staff 3 (MLS 1, Non-MLS 2)
Library Holdings: CDs 275; DVDs 150; Microforms 1,025; Bk Titles 105,600; Bk Vols 119,000; Per Subs 200
Subject Interests: Archit, Art, Art hist, Landscaping
Automation Activity & Vendor Info: (Acquisitions) Ex Libris Group; (Cataloging) Ex Libris Group; (Circulation) Ex Libris Group; (Course Reserve) Ex Libris Group; (Discovery) EBSCO Discovery Service; (ILL) OCLC ILLiad; (OPAC) Ex Libris Group
Partic in Five Colleges, Inc
Open Mon-Thurs (Fall-Spring) 9am-11pm, Fri 9-9, Sat 10-9, Sun Noon-Midnight; Mon-Fri (Summer) 9-4
Friends of the Library Group

WERNER JOSTEN PERFORMING ARTS LIBRARY, Mendenhall Ctr for the Performing Arts, 122 Green St, 01063, SAN 345-4711. Tel: 413-585-2930, 413-585-2935. E-mail: josinfo@smith.edu. Web Site: libraries.smith.edu/spaces-technology/all-spaces-technology/josten-performing-arts-library. *Head Librn,* Marlene M Wong; Tel: 413-585-2931, E-mail: mmwong@email.smith.edu; *Circ Coordr,* Janet Spongberg; Tel: 413-585-2932, E-mail: jspongbe@email.smith.edu; Staff 1 (MLS 1)
Special Collections: Einstein Coll (music of the 16th & 17th Centuries copied in score by Alfred Einstein); Music & correspondence of Werner Josten
Subject Interests: Dance, Music
Open Mon-Thurs (Fall-Spring) 8am-11pm, Fri 8am-9pm, Sat 10am-9pm, Sun Noon-11; Mon-Fri (Summer) 10-4
Friends of the Library Group

YOUNG LIBRARY, Four Tyler Dr, 01063, SAN 345-4746. E-mail: libraryhelp@smith.edu. Web Site: libraries.smith.edu/services/locations-study-spaces/young-library. *Dean of Libr,* Susan Fliss; *Dir, Res, Teaching & Learning,* Brendan O'Connell; E-mail: boconnell@smith.edu; Staff 1 (MLS 1)
Founded 1966
Library Holdings: Bks on Deafness & Sign Lang 100; Bk Titles 154,560; Per Subs 707
Special Collections: Maps, printed, mss, wall, raised relief & gazetteers
Subject Interests: Astronomy, Biology, Chem, Computer sci, Engr, Environ sci, Exercise, Geol, Hist of sci, Math, Physics, Psychol, Sci hist, Sports
Open Mon-Thurs (Fall-Spring) 7:45am-Midnight, Fri 7:45am-11pm, Sat 10am-11pm, Sun 10am-Midnight; Mon-Fri (Summer) 8-5, Sat 10-6
Friends of the Library Group

NORTHBOROUGH

P NORTHBOROUGH FREE LIBRARY, 34 Main St, 01532-1942. SAN 307-5931. Tel: 508-393-5025. FAX: 508-393-5027. Web Site: www.northboroughlibrary.org. *Dir,* Jennifer Bruneau; E-mail: jbruneau@town.northborough.ma.us; *Ch Serv Librn,* Katrina Ireland-Bilodeau; E-mail: kireland@cwmars.org; *Ref & Ad Serv Librn,* Deborah Hersh; E-mail: reference@northboroughlibrary.org; *Teen Serv Librn,* Bonny Krantz; E-mail: bkrantz@cwmars.org; *Supvr, Circ,* Kristen Bartolomeo; E-mail: kbartolomeo@cwmars.org; Staff 4.9 (MLS 4.9)
Founded 1868. Pop 14,632; Circ 224,073
Library Holdings: Bks on Deafness & Sign Lang 10; DVDs 3,745; Electronic Media & Resources 290; Microforms 16,017; Per Subs 111
Automation Activity & Vendor Info: (Cataloging) Evergreen; (Circulation) Evergreen; (ILL) Evergreen; (OPAC) Evergreen
Wireless access
Function: 24/7 Electronic res, 24/7 Online cat, Activity rm, Adult bk club, Adult literacy prog, Archival coll, Audiobks via web, Bk club(s), Bks on CD, Children's prog, Computers for patron use, E-Reserves, Electronic databases & coll, Free DVD rentals, ILL available, Internet access, Magnifiers for reading, Mail & tel request accepted, Museum passes, Music CDs, Online cat, OverDrive digital audio bks, Photocopying/Printing, Preschool reading prog, Prog for adults, Prog for children & young adult, Ref serv available, Spoken cassettes & CDs, Story hour, Summer reading prog, Tax forms, Teen prog, Telephone ref, Wheelchair accessible
Publications: Gale Forecast (Newsletter)
Mem of Massachusetts Library System
Partic in Central & Western Massachusetts Automated Resource Sharing
Special Services for the Blind - Magnifiers; Talking bks
Open Mon 12-8:30, Tues & Wed 9:30-8:30, Thurs, Fri & Sat 9:30-5
Friends of the Library Group

NORTHFIELD

P DICKINSON MEMORIAL LIBRARY*, 115 Main St, 01360. SAN 307-5966. Tel: 413-498-2455. FAX: 413-498-5111. E-mail: dmemlib@gmail.com. Web Site: northfieldpubliclibrary.org. *Dir,* Deb Kern; E-mail: dkern@cwmars.org
Founded 1878. Pop 3,000; Circ 33,000
Library Holdings: Bk Vols 19,000; Per Subs 40
Automation Activity & Vendor Info: (Cataloging) Evergreen; (Circulation) Evergreen; (OPAC) Evergreen
Wireless access
Partic in Central & Western Massachusetts Automated Resource Sharing
Open Tues 1-8, Wed & Thurs 1-6, Fri 10-6, Sat 10-3
Friends of the Library Group

P FIELD LIBRARY*, 243 Millers Falls Rd, 01360. SAN 307-5974. Tel: 413-225-3038. *Librn,* Linda Chapin
Pop 457; Circ 1,950
Library Holdings: AV Mats 399; Bk Vols 9,448; Per Subs 60; Videos 66
Open Wed 5-7

NORTON

P NORTON PUBLIC LIBRARY, L G & Mildred Balfour Memorial, 68 E Main St, 02766. SAN 307-5982. Tel: 508-285-0265. Administration Tel: 508-286-2694. Information Services Tel: 508-286-2695. FAX: 508-285-0266. E-mail: nortonlibrary@sailsinc.org. Web Site: www.nortonlibrary.org. *Libr Dir,* Lee Parker; E-mail: lparker@sailsinc.org; *Asst Dir, Info Serv Librn,* Amanda Viana; E-mail: amanda.viana@sailsinc.org; *Youth Serv Librn,* Leah Labrecque; E-mail: leah@sailsinc.org; Staff 14 (MLS 3, Non-MLS 11)
Founded 1886. Pop 18,036; Circ 116,000
Library Holdings: Bk Vols 54,246; Per Subs 137
Subject Interests: Local hist
Wireless access
Open Mon & Wed-Fri 9:30-2:30, Tues 9:30-7:30
Friends of the Library Group

C WHEATON COLLEGE LIBRARY*, Madeleine Clark Wallace Library, 26 E Main St, 02766-2322. SAN 345-4770. Tel: 508-286-8224. Interlibrary Loan Service Tel: 508-286-3701. Web Site: wheatoncollege.edu/academics/library. *Dean of Libr,* Megan Brooks; E-mail: brooks_megan@wheatoncollege.edu; Staff 8 (MLS 8)
Founded 1840. Enrl 1,625; Fac 152; Highest Degree: Bachelor
Special Collections: History of Women; Lucy Larcom Coll; Wheaton Family Coll
Automation Activity & Vendor Info: (Acquisitions) OCLC Worldshare Management Services; (Cataloging) OCLC Worldshare Management Services; (Circulation) OCLC Worldshare Management Services; (Course Reserve) Docutek; (Discovery) OCLC Worldshare Management Services; (ILL) OCLC Tipasa; (OPAC) OCLC Worldshare Management Services; (Serials) OCLC Worldshare Management Services
Wireless access
Function: Audio & video playback equip for onsite use, Computers for patron use, E-Reserves, Electronic databases & coll, Equip loans & repairs, ILL available, Internet access, Magnifiers for reading, Online cat, Online ref, Photocopying/Printing, Ref serv available, Wheelchair accessible
Partic in Helin
Special Services for the Deaf - ADA equip
Special Services for the Blind - Accessible computers; Low vision equip; Optolec clearview video magnifier; Reader equip; Scanner for conversion & translation of mats
Open Mon-Thurs 8am-2am, Fri 8am-10pm, Sat 10-10, Sun 10am-2am
Restriction: Open to fac, students & qualified researchers, Pub use on premises

NORWELL

SR FIRST PARISH CHURCH OF NORWELL*, The James Library Center for the Arts, 24 West St, 02061. (Mail add: PO Box 164, 02061). Tel: 781-659-7100. E-mail: jameslibrary@verizon.net. Web Site: www.jameslibrary.org. *Exec Dir,* Megan Ward; *Asst Dir,* Tracey Kelly; Staff 1 (MLS 1)
Founded 1874
Library Holdings: Bk Titles 9,000
Special Collections: First Parish Church, Norwell; Local History; North River Ship Building
Mem of Massachusetts Library System
Open Tues-Fri 1-5, Sat (Sept-June) 10-1
Friends of the Library Group

P NORWELL PUBLIC LIBRARY*, 64 South St, 02061-2433. SAN 321-0812. Tel: 781-659-2015. FAX: 781-659-6755. Reference E-mail: noref@ocln.org. Web Site: www.norwellpubliclibrary.org. *Dir,* Judy McConarty; E-mail: jmcconarty@ocln.org; *Asst Dir,* Emily Goodwin; E-mail: egoodwin@ocln.org; *Ad,* Diane Rodriguez; E-mail: drodriguez@ocln.org; *Ch Serv,* Nancy Perry; E-mail: nperry@ocln.org; *Tech Serv Librn,* Pamela Achille; E-mail: pachille@ocln.org; Staff 7 (MLS 3, Non-MLS 4)
Pop 10,166; Circ 127,569
Library Holdings: Bk Vols 62,000; Per Subs 115
Automation Activity & Vendor Info: (Acquisitions) SirsiDynix; (Cataloging) SirsiDynix; (Circulation) SirsiDynix
Wireless access
Function: 24/7 Electronic res, 24/7 Online cat, Accelerated reader prog, Adult bk club, Art exhibits, Audiobks via web, Bk club(s), Bks on CD, Children's prog, Computer training, Computers for patron use, E-Reserves, Electronic databases & coll, Free DVD rentals, Games & aids for people with disabilities, Holiday prog, Home delivery & serv to seniorr ctr & nursing homes, Homebound delivery serv, Homework prog, ILL available, Instruction & testing, Large print keyboards, Magnifiers for reading, Mail & tel request accepted, Museum passes, Music CDs, Notary serv, Online cat, Orientations, Outreach serv, Photocopying/Printing, Preschool outreach, Prof lending libr, Prog for adults, Prog for children & young adult, Ref serv available, Senior computer classes, Spoken cassettes & CDs, Spoken

cassettes & DVDs, Story hour, Summer reading prog, Tax forms, Teen prog, VHS videos, Workshops, Writing prog
Mem of Massachusetts Library System
Partic in Old Colony Libr Network
Open Mon 10-8, Tues & Wed Noon-8, Thurs & Fri 10-5, Sat 10-3
Friends of the Library Group

NORWOOD

S FM GLOBAL, Technical Information Center, 1151 Boston-Providence Tpk, 02062. SAN 307-6008. Tel: 781-762-4300. Web Site: www.fmglobal.com. *Mgr,* Paul Crosby; E-mail: paul.crosby@fmglobal.com; Staff 5 (MLS 3, Non-MLS 2)
Founded 1968
Library Holdings: e-journals 120; Bk Titles 20,000; Per Subs 120
Special Collections: Corporate Historical Coll, docs, rare bks, visual mats
Subject Interests: Engr, Fire res, Loss prevention
Automation Activity & Vendor Info: (Acquisitions) Inmagic, Inc.; (Cataloging) Inmagic, Inc.; (OPAC) Inmagic, Inc.; (Serials) Inmagic, Inc.
Wireless access
Function: Bus archives, Doc delivery serv, For res purposes, Govt ref serv, Res libr
Restriction: Access for corporate affiliates, Circulates for staff only, Co libr, Open to researchers by request, Restricted access

P MORRILL MEMORIAL LIBRARY*, 33 Walpole St, 02062-1206. (Mail add: PO Box 220, 02062-0220), SAN 345-486X. Tel: 781-769-0200. Circulation Tel: 781-769-0200, Ext 224. Reference Tel: 781-769-0200, Ext 223. Information Services Tel: 781-769-0200, Ext 111. FAX: 781-769-6083. E-mail: norwood@minlib.net. Web Site: www.norwoodlibrary.org. *Libr Dir,* Clayton Cheever; E-mail: ccheever@minlib.net; *Ch,* Kate Tigue; E-mail: ktigue@minlib.net; *Literacy Coordr,* Norma Logan; E-mail: nlogan@minlib.net; *Adult Serv,* Elizabeth Reed; E-mail: lreed@minlib.net; *Ch Serv,* Jean Todesca; E-mail: jtodesca@minlib.net; *Literacy Serv,* Bonnie Wyler; E-mail: bwyler@minlib.net; *Outreach Serv,* Nancy Ling; E-mail: nling@minlib.net; *Ref Serv,* April Cushing; E-mail: acushing@minlib.net; *Tech Serv,* Diane Phillips; E-mail: dphillips@minlib.net; *Tech Serv,* Allison Palmgren; E-mail: apalmgren@minlib.net; Staff 48 (MLS 18, Non-MLS 30)
Founded 1873. Pop 29,000; Circ 300,000
Library Holdings: AV Mats 12,176; Electronic Media & Resources 12,135; Bk Vols 98,916; Per Subs 1,064
Special Collections: Norwood Coll
Automation Activity & Vendor Info: (Acquisitions) Innovative Interfaces, Inc; (Cataloging) Innovative Interfaces, Inc; (Circulation) Innovative Interfaces, Inc; (ILL) Innovative Interfaces, Inc; (OPAC) Innovative Interfaces, Inc
Function: 24/7 Electronic res, 24/7 Online cat, Activity rm, Adult bk club, Adult literacy prog, After school storytime, Audio & video playback equip for onsite use, Audiobks on Playaways & MP3, Audiobks via web, BA reader (adult literacy), Bk club(s), Bks on CD, CD-ROM, Children's prog, Citizenship assistance, Computer training, Computers for patron use, Digital talking bks, E-Readers, Electronic databases & coll, Equip loans & repairs, Free DVD rentals, Games & aids for people with disabilities, Govt ref serv, Holiday prog, Home delivery & serv to seniorr ctr & nursing homes, Homebound delivery serv, ILL available, Internet access, Large print keyboards, Life-long learning prog for all ages, Literacy & newcomer serv, Magazines, Magnifiers for reading, Mail loans to mem, Mango lang, Meeting rooms, Microfiche/film & reading machines, Movies, Museum passes, Music CDs, Notary serv, Online cat, Outreach serv, OverDrive digital audio bks, Passport agency, Photocopying/Printing, Preschool reading prog, Printer for laptops & handheld devices, Prog for adults, Prog for children & young adult, Ref & res, Ref serv available, Scanner, Senior computer classes, Senior outreach, Spoken cassettes & CDs, Spoken cassettes & DVDs, Story hour, Study rm, Summer & winter reading prog, Summer reading prog, Tax forms, Wheelchair accessible, Workshops
Publications: Calendar (Monthly); New At Your Library
Partic in Minuteman Library Network
Special Services for the Blind - Computer with voice synthesizer for visually impaired persons
Open Mon-Thurs 9-9, Fri 10-5, Sat 9-5, Sun 2-5
Friends of the Library Group

OAK BLUFFS

P OAK BLUFFS PUBLIC LIBRARY*, 56R School St, 02557. (Mail add: PO Box 2039, 02557-2039), SAN 307-6032. Tel: 508-693-9433. FAX: 508-693-5377. E-mail: oakbluffslibrary@gmail.com. Web Site: oakbluffslibrary.org. *Libr Dir,* Allyson Malik; Tel: 508-693-9433, Ext 141, E-mail: amalik@clamsnet.org; *Head, Circ,* Andrea Figaratto; Tel: 508-693-9433, Ext 140, E-mail: afigaratto@clamsnet.org; *Ch,* Sonja Drotar; Tel: 568-693-9433, Ext 126, E-mail: sdrotar@clamsnet.org; *Adult Serv, Tech Serv,* Nina Ferry; Tel: 508-693-9433, Ext 145, E-mail: nferry@clamsnet.org; Staff 3 (MLS 3)
Founded 1906. Pop 3,713; Circ 110,934
Library Holdings: CDs 1,682; Bk Vols 26,052; Per Subs 80; Videos 4,518
Automation Activity & Vendor Info: (Acquisitions) Innovative Interfaces, Inc - Millennium; (Cataloging) Innovative Interfaces, Inc - Millennium; (Circulation) Innovative Interfaces, Inc - Millennium; (ILL) Innovative Interfaces, Inc - Millennium; (OPAC) Innovative Interfaces, Inc
Wireless access
Partic in Cape Libraries Automated Materials Sharing Network
Open Tues & Thurs 10-8, Wed & Fri 10-5, Sat 10-4
Friends of the Library Group

OAKHAM

P FOBES MEMORIAL LIBRARY*, Four Maple St, Unit 9, 01068. SAN 307-6040. Tel: 508-882-3372. FAX: 508-882-3372. E-mail: library@oakham-ma.gov. Web Site: fobesmemoriallibrary.org. *Dir,* Samantha Bodine
Pop 1,079; Circ 14,000
Library Holdings: Bk Vols 15,885; Per Subs 20
Wireless access
Mem of Massachusetts Library System
Partic in Central & Western Massachusetts Automated Resource Sharing
Open Tues-Thurs 10-7, Sat 9-Noon
Friends of the Library Group

ORANGE

P WHEELER MEMORIAL LIBRARY*, 49 E Main St, 01364-1267. SAN 307-6067. Tel: 978-544-2495. FAX: 978-544-1116. Web Site: www.orangelib.org. *Dir,* Jessica Magelaner; Tel: 978-544-2495, Ext 101, E-mail: director@orangelib.org; *Coordr, ILL,* Riana Freytag; Staff 7 (MLS 2, Non-MLS 5)
Founded 1847. Pop 7,312; Circ 43,820
Library Holdings: Bk Vols 42,698; Per Subs 30
Special Collections: Local History Coll
Automation Activity & Vendor Info: (Cataloging) Evergreen; (Circulation) Evergreen; (OPAC) Evergreen
Wireless access
Partic in Central & Western Massachusetts Automated Resource Sharing
Open Mon & Tues 10-6, Wed & Thurs 1-8, Sat 10-2
Friends of the Library Group

ORLEANS

P SNOW LIBRARY*, 67 Main St, 02653-2413. SAN 307-6075. Tel: 508-240-3760. FAX: 508-255-5701. Web Site: www.snowlibrary.org. *Libr Dir,* Tavi M Prugno; E-mail: tprugno@clamsnet.org; *Asst Libr Dir,* Kaimi Rose Lum; E-mail: klum@clamsnet.org; *Circ Librn,* Jenny Fulcher; *Ref Librn,* Linda Huntington; E-mail: lhuntington@clamsnet.org; *Tech Serv Librn,* Cheryl Bergeron; E-mail: cbergeron@clamsnet.org; *Youth Serv Librn,* Ann Foster; E-mail: afoster@clamsnet.org; Staff 15 (MLS 2, Non-MLS 13)
Founded 1877. Pop 5,868; Circ 168,928
Library Holdings: AV Mats 4,632; Bk Vols 56,020; Per Subs 124; Talking Bks 4,438
Special Collections: H K Cummings Coll of Historical Photographs (1870-1900's)
Automation Activity & Vendor Info: (Acquisitions) Innovative Interfaces, Inc; (Cataloging) Innovative Interfaces, Inc; (Circulation) Innovative Interfaces, Inc; (ILL) Innovative Interfaces, Inc; (OPAC) Innovative Interfaces, Inc; (Serials) Innovative Interfaces, Inc
Function: 24/7 Electronic res, 24/7 Online cat, Adult bk club, Adult literacy prog, Archival coll, Art exhibits, Bk club(s), Bks on CD, Children's prog, Computers for patron use, Electronic databases & coll, Holiday prog, Homebound delivery serv, ILL available
Partic in Cape Libraries Automated Materials Sharing Network
Open Mon, Thurs & Fri 10-5, Tues & Wed 10-8, Sat 10-4
Friends of the Library Group

OSTERVILLE

§P OSTERVILLE VILLAGE LIBRARY, 43 Wianno Ave, 02655. Tel: 508-428-5757. E-mail: ofl_mail@clamsnet.org. Web Site: ostervillefreelibrary.org. *Exec Dir,* Cyndy Cotton; E-mail: cyndycotton@clamsnet.org
Founded 1873
Library Holdings: Per Subs 54
Wireless access
Function: Bk club(s), Children's prog, Computers for patron use, Meeting rooms, Photocopying/Printing, Teen prog
Partic in Cape Libraries Automated Materials Sharing Network
Open Mon, Wed & Fri 9-5, Tues & Thurs 10-5, Sat 9-4, Sun Noon-4

OTIS

§P OTIS LIBRARY & MUSEUM, 48 N Main Rd, 01253. (Mail add: PO Box 126, 01253). Tel: 413-269-0100, Ext 117, 413-269-0109. E-mail: info@otislibraryma.org. Web Site: otislibraryma.org, townofotisma.com/commissions-councils/library-and-museum. *Dir,* Kathleen Bort; E-mail: kbort@otislibraryma.org; *Asst Dir,* Lois Hall; *Asst Librn,* Kerry Bean
Wireless access
Partic in Central & Western Massachusetts Automated Resource Sharing
Open Wed & Fri 11-5, Thurs 12-6, Sat 9-1 (Winter); Mon 10-4, Tues 12-6, Wed & Fri 10-5, Thurs 1-7, Sat 9-1 (Summer)

OXFORD

P OXFORD FREE LIBRARY*, Charles Larned Memorial Library, 339 Main St, 01540. SAN 345-4924. Tel: 508-987-6003. FAX: 508-987-3896. Web Site: oxfordmapubliclibrary.org. *Dir,* Brittany McDougal; E-mail: bmcdougal@town.oxford.ma.us; Staff 12 (MLS 3, Non-MLS 9)
Founded 1903. Pop 13,100; Circ 125,322
Library Holdings: AV Mats 4,221; Large Print Bks 555; Bk Vols 53,000; Per Subs 111; Talking Bks 1,084
Special Collections: Local History (Records to 1850)
Automation Activity & Vendor Info: (Circulation) Innovative Interfaces, Inc
Wireless access
Mem of Massachusetts Library System
Partic in Central & Western Massachusetts Automated Resource Sharing
Special Services for the Blind - Computer with voice synthesizer for visually impaired persons; Reader equip
Friends of the Library Group

PALMER

P PALMER PUBLIC LIBRARY*, 1455 N Main St, 01069. SAN 307-6091. Tel: 413-283-3330. FAX: 413-283-9970. Web Site: www.palmer.lib.ma.us. *Dir,* Benjamin Hood; E-mail: bhood@palmer.lib.ma.us; *Borrower Serv Librn,* Richard Clark, Jr; E-mail: rclark@palmer.lib.ma.us; *Cat Librn,* Ashley Ngan; E-mail: angan@palmer.lib.ma.us; *Coll Develop Librn,* Helene O'Connor; E-mail: hoconnor@palmer.lib.ma.us; *Libr Tech, Outreach Serv Librn,* Sandra Burke; E-mail: sburke@palmer.lib.ma.us; *YA Librn,* Matthew DeCara; E-mail: mdecara@palmer.lib.ma.us; *Youth Serv Librn,* Stephanie Maher; E-mail: smaher@palmer.lib.ma.us
Founded 1878. Pop 12,112; Circ 201,398
Library Holdings: Bk Vols 111,245
Special Collections: Palmer Coll; Palmer Journal-Register
Subject Interests: Genealogy, Local hist
Automation Activity & Vendor Info: (Acquisitions) Evergreen; (Cataloging) Evergreen; (Circulation) Evergreen; (ILL) Evergreen; (OPAC) Evergreen
Wireless access
Partic in Central & Western Massachusetts Automated Resource Sharing
Special Services for the Deaf - TTY equip
Open Mon 10-5, Tues-Thurs 10-8, Fri & Sat 10-2
Friends of the Library Group

PAXTON

CR ANNA MARIA COLLEGE, Mondor-Eagen Library, 50 Sunset Lane, 01612-1198. SAN 307-6105. Tel: 508-849-3405. Interlibrary Loan Service Tel: 508-849-3407. Reference Tel: 508-849-3473. FAX: 508-849-3408. E-mail: library@annamaria.edu. Web Site: annamaria.edu/campus-life/mondor-eagen-library. *Dir,* Position Currently Open; *Electronic Res Librn,* Rebecca Crockett; E-mail: rcrockett@annamaria.edu; *Ref & Instruction Librn,* Rebecca Pac; E-mail: rpac@annamaria.edu; *Evening Supvr,* Carla Morrissey; E-mail: cmorrissey@annamaria.edu; *Tech Serv,* Jan McNamara; Tel: 508-849-3321; *Libr Asst,* Aubree Dunbar; E-mail: adunbar@annamaria.edu; Staff 6 (MLS 3, Non-MLS 3)
Founded 1946. Enrl 933; Fac 165; Highest Degree: Master
Library Holdings: Bk Vols 75,000; Per Subs 290
Subject Interests: Art, Bus, Criminal justice, Educ, English lit, Music, Psychol, Relig, Sociol
Automation Activity & Vendor Info: (Acquisitions) Innovative Interfaces, Inc - Millennium; (Cataloging) Innovative Interfaces, Inc - Millennium; (Circulation) Innovative Interfaces, Inc - Millennium; (OPAC) Innovative Interfaces, Inc; (Serials) Innovative Interfaces, Inc - Millennium
Wireless access
Function: Ref serv available
Publications: Introduction to the Library; Library Guides
Mem of Massachusetts Library System
Partic in Central & Western Massachusetts Automated Resource Sharing; LYRASIS
Open Mon-Thurs 8am-11pm, Fri 8-4:30, Sat 12-5, Sun 1-11

P RICHARDS MEMORIAL LIBRARY*, 44 Richards Ave, 01612. SAN 307-6113. Tel: 508-754-0793. FAX: 508-754-0793. Web Site: www.rmlpaxton.org. *Dir,* Deborah Bailey; E-mail: dbailey@cwmars.org; *Ch,* Kim Cooke; E-mail: kcooke@cwmars.org; Staff 1 (Non-MLS 1)
Founded 1926. Pop 4,400; Circ 51,000
Library Holdings: Bk Vols 25,795; Per Subs 70
Automation Activity & Vendor Info: (Cataloging) Follett Software; (Circulation) Follett Software
Function: Computers for patron use
Partic in Central & Western Massachusetts Automated Resource Sharing
Open Tues & Thurs 1-8, Wed & Fri 9-5, Sat (Winter) 10-4
Friends of the Library Group

PEABODY

S PEABODY HISTORICAL SOCIETY & MUSEUM, Ruth Hill Library & Archives, 31 Washington St, 01960-5520. SAN 329-8892. Tel: 978-531-0805. FAX: 978-531-7292. E-mail: info@peabodyhistorical.org. Web Site: www.peabodyhistorical.org. *Curator,* Kelly Daniell; E-mail: kelly.daniell@peabodyhistorical.org; *Asst Curator,* Nora Bigelow; E-mail: nora.bigelow@peabodyhistorical.org
Founded 1896
Library Holdings: Bk Titles 420
Special Collections: Historical Documents
Subject Interests: Genealogy
Restriction: Open by appt only

P PEABODY INSTITUTE LIBRARY*, 82 Main St, 01960-5553. SAN 345-4983. Tel: 978-531-0100. Web Site: www.peabodylibrary.org. *Dir,* Cate Merlin; Tel: 951-531-0100, Ext 16, E-mail: merlin@noblenet.org; *Asst Dir,* Alysa Hayden; Tel: 951-531-0100, Ext 25, E-mail: hayden@noblenet.org; *Pub Programming Librn, Sr Librn, Ad Serv,* Gabriela Rae Toth; Tel: 951-531-0100, Ext 17, E-mail: gtoth@noble.net; *Ref (Info Servs),* Michael Wick; Staff 55 (MLS 6, Non-MLS 49)
Founded 1852. Pop 48,000; Circ 251,665
Library Holdings: Bk Vols 162,703; Per Subs 331
Wireless access
Publications: Annual Report; Library News (Monthly); Special Pamphlets
Special Services for the Blind - Reader equip
Open Mon-Thurs & Sat 9-5
Friends of the Library Group
Branches: 2
SOUTH, 78 Lynn St, 01960, SAN 345-5017. Tel: 978-531-3380. FAX: 978-531-9113. *Sr Librn,* Jillian Parsons; Tel: 978-535-3380, Ext 11, E-mail: jparsons@noblenet.org
Library Holdings: Bk Vols 22,277
Friends of the Library Group
WEST, 603 Lowell St, 01960, SAN 345-5041. Tel: 978-535-3354. FAX: 978-535-0147. *Sr Librn,* Kristi Bryant; Tel: 978-535-3354, Ext 11, E-mail: kbryant@noblenet.org
Library Holdings: Bk Vols 24,143
Open Mon & Wed 9-6, Tues & Thurs 12-9, Sat 9-5
Friends of the Library Group

PELHAM

P PELHAM LIBRARY*, Two S Valley Rd, 01002. SAN 307-6121. Tel: 413-253-0657. FAX: 413-253-0594. E-mail: library.pelham@gmail.com. Web Site: www.pelham-library.org. *Dir,* Jodi Levine; *Librn,* Sally Goldin; *Libr Asst, Patron Serv,* Ashley Rodkey; Staff 4 (MLS 1, Non-MLS 3)
Founded 1893. Pop 1,310
Library Holdings: AV Mats 3,000; Bk Vols 29,000; Per Subs 76
Special Collections: Local Historical Books & Pamphlets. Oral History
Wireless access
Function: 24/7 Electronic res, 24/7 Online cat, Adult bk club, Archival coll, Art exhibits, Art programs, Audiobks on Playaways & MP3, Audiobks via web, AV serv, Bk club(s), Bks on CD, Children's prog, Computers for patron use, Digital talking bks, E-Readers, E-Reserves, Electronic databases & coll, Free DVD rentals, Holiday prog, ILL available, Internet access, Jazz prog, Life-long learning prog for all ages, Magazines, Mail & tel request accepted, Meeting rooms, Movies, Museum passes, Music CDs, Online cat, OverDrive digital audio bks, Photocopying/Printing, Preschool reading prog, Prog for adults, Prog for children & young adult, Ref serv available, Spoken cassettes & CDs, STEM programs, Story hour, Study rm, Summer reading prog, Tax forms, Teen prog, Telephone ref, Wheelchair accessible
Mem of Massachusetts Library System
Special Services for the Deaf - Bks on deafness & sign lang
Special Services for the Blind - Talking bks
Open Mon, Tues & Thurs 3-8, Wed 1-8, Fri 10-12, Sat 10-2
Friends of the Library Group

PEMBROKE

P PEMBROKE PUBLIC LIBRARY, 142 Center St, 02359. SAN 307-613X. Tel: 781-293-6771. FAX: 781-294-0742. E-mail: feedback@pembrokepubliclibrary.org. Web Site: www.pembrokepubliclibrary.org. *Dir,* Deborah Wall; Tel: 781-293-6771, Ext 26, E-mail: dwall@sailsinc.org; Staff 8 (MLS 2, Non-MLS 6)
Founded 1878. Pop 18,000; Circ 145,445
Library Holdings: Large Print Bks 8,540; Bk Vols 69,000; Per Subs 117; Talking Bks 22
Wireless access
Special Services for the Deaf - Closed caption videos
Special Services for the Blind - Bks & mags in Braille, on rec, tape & cassette; Bks available with recordings; Bks on cassette; Bks on CD; Talking bks
Open Mon-Thurs 10-7, Fri 10-4, Sat 10-5
Friends of the Library Group

PEPPERELL

P LAWRENCE LIBRARY, 15 Main St, 01463. SAN 307-6148. Tel: 978-433-0330. FAX: 978-433-0317. Web Site: lawrencelibrary.org. *Dir,* Debra Spratt; E-mail: dspratt@cwmars.org; *Asst Dir, Dir, Adult Serv,* Tina McEvoy; E-mail: tmcevoy@cwmars.org; *Circ,* Sherrill Burgess; E-mail: sburgess@cwmars.org; *Youth Serv,* Shannon Brittain; E-mail: sbrittain@cwmars.org; Staff 7 (MLS 4, Non-MLS 3)
Founded 1901. Pop 12,002; Circ 91,994
Library Holdings: Audiobooks 5,570; Bks on Deafness & Sign Lang 16; DVDs 5,598; e-books 323; Large Print Bks 720; Bk Vols 595,041; Per Subs 61; Talking Bks 3,695
Special Collections: Shattuck Bird Coll
Subject Interests: Genealogy, Local hist
Automation Activity & Vendor Info: (Acquisitions) Evergreen; (Cataloging) Evergreen; (Circulation) Evergreen; (ILL) Evergreen; (OPAC) Evergreen; (Serials) Evergreen
Wireless access
Function: 24/7 Electronic res, 24/7 Online cat, Activity rm, Adult bk club, Archival coll, Art exhibits, Art programs, Audiobks on Playaways & MP3, Audiobks via web, Bilingual assistance for Spanish patrons, Bk club(s), Bks on CD, Chess club, Children's prog, Computer training, Computers for patron use, Distance learning, E-Readers, E-Reserves, Electronic databases & coll, Free DVD rentals, Genealogy discussion group, Holiday prog, Home delivery & serv to seniorr ctr & nursing homes, Homebound delivery serv, ILL available, Instruction & testing, Internet access, Jazz prog, Laminating, Large print keyboards, Life-long learning prog for all ages, Magazines, Magnifiers for reading, Mail & tel request accepted, Meeting rooms, Microfiche/film & reading machines, Movies, Museum passes, Music CDs, Online cat, Online ref, Outreach serv, Outside serv via phone, mail, e-mail & web, OverDrive digital audio bks, Photocopying/Printing, Preschool outreach, Preschool reading prog, Printer for laptops & handheld devices, Prog for adults, Prog for children & young adult, Ref serv available, Res assist avail, Scanner, Senior computer classes, Senior outreach, STEM programs, Story hour, Study rm, Summer & winter reading prog, Summer reading prog, Tax forms, Teen prog, Telephone ref, Visual arts prog, Wheelchair accessible, Winter reading prog, Workshops, Writing prog
Publications: Friend of the Library (Monthly newsletter)
Mem of Massachusetts Library System
Partic in Central & Western Massachusetts Automated Resource Sharing
Friends of the Library Group

PERU

P PERU LIBRARY INC*, Six W Main Rd, 01235-9254. (Mail add: PO Box 1190, Hinsdale, 01235-1190), SAN 376-7531. Tel: 413-655-8650. FAX: 413-655-2041. E-mail: perulibrary@gmail.com. *Dir,* Ruth Calaycay
Library Holdings: Bk Vols 3,800; Talking Bks 100; Videos 1,250
Wireless access
Open Wed 1-7, Sat 9-1

PETERSHAM

P PETERSHAM MEMORIAL LIBRARY*, 23 Common St, 01366. SAN 307-6172. Tel: 978-724-3405. FAX: 978-724-0089. Web Site: www.petershamlibrary.net. *Dir,* Jayne Arata; *Asst Dir,* Jeanne Forand; Staff 2 (MLS 1, Non-MLS 1)
Founded 1890. Pop 1,100; Circ 9,170
Library Holdings: DVDs 218; Bk Titles 12,000; Per Subs 42; Videos 535
Subject Interests: Local hist
Automation Activity & Vendor Info: (Circulation) Innovative Interfaces, Inc; (ILL) Innovative Interfaces, Inc; (OPAC) Innovative Interfaces, Inc
Wireless access
Mem of Massachusetts Library System
Partic in Central & Western Massachusetts Automated Resource Sharing
Open Tues 10-5, Wed 2-7, Fri 2-5, Sat 9-1

PHILLIPSTON

P PHILLIPSTON FREE PUBLIC LIBRARY*, 25 Templeton Rd, 01331-9704. SAN 307-6180. Tel: 978-249-1734. E-mail: phillipstonlibrary@comcast.net. Web Site: www.phillipston-ma.gov/phillips-free-public-library. *Dir,* Jacqueline Prime
Pop 962; Circ 6,325
Library Holdings: Bk Vols 9,000
Wireless access
Mem of Massachusetts Library System
Partic in Central & Western Massachusetts Automated Resource Sharing
Open Tues 9-2, Wed 5pm-7pm, Sat 9-1
Friends of the Library Group

PITTSFIELD

P BERKSHIRE ATHENAEUM*, Pittsfield's Public Library, One Wendell Ave, 01201-6385. SAN 345-5076. Tel: 413-499-9480. Circulation Tel: 413-399-9480, Ext 201. Reference Tel: 413-499-9480, Ext 202. Administration Tel: 413-499-9480, Ext 205. FAX: 413-499-9489. E-mail: info@pittsfieldlibrary.org. Web Site: www.pittsfieldlibrary.org. *Libr Dir,* Alex Reczkowski; Tel: 413-499-9480, Ext 102, E-mail: alex@pittsfieldlibrary.org; *Local Hist & Genealogy Librn,* Kathleen Reilly; E-mail: kathleen@pittsfieldlibrary.org; *Ch Serv,* Samantha Cesario; E-mail: samantha@pittsfieldlibrary.org; *Circ,* Catherine Congelosi; E-mail: cathy@pittsfieldlibrary.org; *Ref,* Madeline Kelly; E-mail: madeline@pittsfieldlibrary.org; *Tech Serv,* Rebecca McDole; E-mail: becky@pittsfieldlibrary.org; Staff 9 (MLS 9)
Founded 1871. Pop 46,437; Circ 224,359
Library Holdings: AV Mats 6,825; e-books 76,596; Electronic Media & Resources 20,737; Microforms 70,128; Bk Vols 137,808; Per Subs 200; Videos 6,228
Special Collections: Berkshire Authors Room; Herman Melville Memorial Room; Morgan Ballet Coll
Subject Interests: Genealogy
Automation Activity & Vendor Info: (Acquisitions) Evergreen; (Cataloging) Evergreen; (Circulation) Evergreen; (OPAC) Evergreen; (Serials) Evergreen
Wireless access
Function: 24/7 Electronic res, 24/7 Online cat, 3D Printer, Activity rm, Adult literacy prog, Archival coll, Art exhibits, Audiobks via web, Bks on CD, Children's prog, Computer training, Computers for patron use, Digital talking bks, E-Readers, E-Reserves, Electronic databases & coll, Equip loans & repairs, For res purposes, Free DVD rentals, Games & aids for people with disabilities, Genealogy discussion group, Holiday prog, Homebound delivery serv, ILL available, Internet access, Jazz prog, Large print keyboards, Life-long learning prog for all ages, Magazines, Magnifiers for reading, Mail & tel request accepted, Meeting rooms, Microfiche/film & reading machines, Movies, Museum passes, Music CDs, Online cat, Outreach serv, OverDrive digital audio bks, Photocopying/Printing, Printer for laptops & handheld devices, Prog for adults, Prog for children & young adult, Ref & res, Scanner, Story hour, Summer reading prog, Tax forms, Wheelchair accessible
Partic in Central & Western Massachusetts Automated Resource Sharing
Special Services for the Blind - Aids for in-house use; Assistive/Adapted tech devices, equip & products; Bks on CD; Bks on flash-memory cartridges; Copier with enlargement capabilities; Digital talking bk; Digital talking bk machines; Large print bks; Large screen computer & software; Lending of low vision aids; Magnifiers; Networked computers with assistive software; Screen enlargement software for people with visual disabilities; Screen reader software; ZoomText magnification & reading software
Open Mon-Thurs (Winter) 9-9, Fri 9-5, Sat 10-5; Mon, Wed & Fri (Summer) 9-5, Tues & Thurs 9-9, Sat 10-5
Friends of the Library Group
Bookmobiles: 1

J BERKSHIRE COMMUNITY COLLEGE*, Jonathan Edwards Library, 1350 West St, 01201. SAN 307-6199. Tel: 413-236-2150, 413-236-2157. Circulation Tel: 413-236-2156. FAX: 413-448-2700. Web Site: www.berkshirecc.edu/about-bcc/library. *Dir,* Richard A Felver; Tel: 413-236-2151, E-mail: rfelver@berkshirecc.edu; *Coordr, Libr Serv,* Karen Carreras-Hubbard; Tel: 413-236-2153, E-mail: khubbard@berkshirecc.edu; Staff 1 (MLS 1)
Founded 1960. Enrl 1,551; Fac 100
Library Holdings: Bk Vols 58,400; Per Subs 350
Subject Interests: Art, Environ studies, Soc sci & issues
Automation Activity & Vendor Info: (Acquisitions) Innovative Interfaces, Inc; (Cataloging) Innovative Interfaces, Inc; (Circulation) Innovative Interfaces, Inc
Wireless access
Open Mon-Thurs 8-8, Fri 8-4

M BERKSHIRE MEDICAL CENTER*, Health Science Library, 725 North St, 01201. SAN 307-6202. Tel: 413-447-2734. *Librn,* Danielle Chretien; *Librn,* Martha Prescott; Staff 2 (MLS 1, Non-MLS 1)
Founded 1968
Library Holdings: Bk Titles 1,000; Bk Vols 1,800; Per Subs 100
Subject Interests: Med
Wireless access
Partic in Basic Health Sciences Library Network; Cooperating Libraries of Greater Springfield; Western Mass Health Info Consortium
Open Mon-Fri 9-3

L MASSACHUSETTS TRIAL COURT, Berkshire Law Library, Court House, 76 East St, 01201. SAN 324-346X. Tel: 413-442-5059. FAX: 413-448-2474. E-mail: berkshirelawlib@hotmail.com. *Head Law Librn,* Gary Smith; *Law Libr Asst,* Cassandra Wood; Staff 2 (MLS 2)
Founded 1842
Library Holdings: Bk Titles 10,000; Per Subs 40
Subject Interests: Law for layman, Mass legal mat
Automation Activity & Vendor Info: (Cataloging) OCLC Connexion; (Circulation) Horizon; (OPAC) Horizon
Wireless access
Open Mon-Fri 8:30-4:30

PLAINFIELD

P SHAW MEMORIAL LIBRARY*, 312 Main St, 01070-9709. SAN 307-6245. Tel: 413-634-5406. FAX: 413-634-5683. E-mail: plainfieldsml@gmail.com. *Librn,* Denise Sessions
Founded 1926. Pop 609; Circ 9,000
Library Holdings: Bk Titles 9,000; Per Subs 14
Wireless access
Open Tues 2-8, Thurs 5-8, Sat 9-12
Friends of the Library Group

PLAINVILLE

P PLAINVILLE PUBLIC LIBRARY*, 198 South St, 02762-1512. SAN 307-6253. Tel: 508-695-1784. FAX: 508-695-6359. E-mail: info@plainvillepubliclibrary.org. Web Site: www.plainvillepubliclibrary.org. *Dir,* Melissa M Campbell; E-mail: mcampbel@sailsinc.org; *Head, Circ,* Susan Rolfe; *Tech Serv,* Keely Penny; Staff 4.5 (MLS 1, Non-MLS 3.5)
Pop 8,200; Circ 85,000
Library Holdings: AV Mats 4,900; Bk Vols 33,376; Per Subs 74; Talking Bks 2,000
Wireless access
Function: Free DVD rentals
Partic in SAILS Library Network
Open Mon & Wed 10-8, Tues 10-5, Thurs & Sat 10-2 Fri 1-5
Friends of the Library Group

PLYMOUTH

S GENERAL SOCIETY OF MAYFLOWER DESCENDANTS*, Mayflower Society Library, Four Winslow St, 02360. (Mail add: PO Box 3297, 02361-3297), SAN 373-1669. Tel: 508-746-3188, Ext 11. FAX: 508-746-2488. E-mail: library@themayflowersociety.org. Web Site: www.themayflowersociety.org/visit/gsmd-library. *Librn/Head, Ref Coll Develop,* Carolyn Freeman Travers. Subject Specialists: *Genealogy, Hist,* Carolyn Freeman Travers; Staff 5 (MLS 1, Non-MLS 4)
Founded 1897
Library Holdings: Bk Titles 2,500; Bk Vols 3,400; Per Subs 70
Special Collections: Pilgrims Coll
Subject Interests: Genealogy, Hist, Massachusetts
Wireless access
Open Mon-Fri 10-3:30
Restriction: Non-circulating to the pub

M JORDAN HOSPITAL*, Daryl A Lima Memorial Library, 275 Sandwich St, 02360. SAN 377-9319. Tel: 508-830-2157. FAX: 508-830-2887. *Librn,* Marian A De la Cour; E-mail: mdelacour@jordanhospital.org; Staff 1 (MLS 1)
Library Holdings: Bk Titles 100; Per Subs 84
Wireless access
Function: Telephone ref
Partic in Massachusetts Health Sciences Library Network; National Network of Libraries of Medicine Region 7; North Atlantic Health Sciences Libraries, Inc; Southeastern Massachusetts Consortium of Health Science
Restriction: Non-circulating

S PILGRIM SOCIETY*, Pilgrim Hall Museum, 75 Court St, 02360. SAN 307-6261. Tel: 508-746-1620. FAX: 508-746-3396. E-mail: curator@pilgrimhall.org. Web Site: www.pilgrimhall.org/ce_library_archives.htm. *Exec Dir,* Donna D Curtin; E-mail: donna.curtin@pilgrimhall.org; Staff 8 (MLS 1, Non-MLS 7)
Founded 1820
Library Holdings: Bk Titles 6,000
Special Collections: Manuscript Coll; Plymouth, Massachusetts & Pilgrim History Coll
Subject Interests: Decorative art, Hist
Publications: Pilgrim Society News
Restriction: Open by appt only

S PLIMOTH PLANTATION*, Research Library, 137 Warren Ave, 02360. (Mail add: PO Box 1620, 02362-1620), SAN 327-3199. Tel: 508-746-1622, Ext 8379. FAX: 508-746-4978. E-mail: collections@plimoth.org. Web Site: www.plimoth.org. *Dep Dir,* Richard Pickering; *Curator of Coll,* Dr Jade W Luiz; E-mail: jluiz@plimoth.org. Subject Specialists: *Archaeology,* Dr Jade W Luiz
Founded 1968
Library Holdings: e-journals 1; Bk Titles 6,000; Bk Vols 6,400; Per Subs 50
Subject Interests: 17th Century, Anthrop, Indigenous studies
Wireless access
Function: Res libr
Restriction: Non-circulating, Open by appt only

GL PLYMOUTH LAW LIBRARY, 52 Obery St, Ste 0117, 02360. Tel: 508-747-4796. FAX: 508-746-9788. E-mail: plymouthlawlibrary@hotmail.com. Web Site: www.mass.gov/locations/plymouth-law-library. *Head Law Librn,* Louise Hoagland
Library Holdings: Bk Vols 25,000; Per Subs 7
Automation Activity & Vendor Info: (OPAC) SirsiDynix
Wireless access
Partic in NELLCO Law Library Consortium, Inc.
Open Mon-Fri 8:30-4:30

P PLYMOUTH PUBLIC LIBRARY, 132 South St, 02360. SAN 345-522X. Tel: 508-830-4250. FAX: 508-830-4258. TDD: 508-747-5882. E-mail: plref@ocln.org. Web Site: www.plymouthpubliclibrary.org. *Libr Dir,* Kelsey Casey; E-mail: kcasey@plymouth-ma.gov; Staff 31 (MLS 9, Non-MLS 22)
Founded 1857. Pop 56,000; Circ 392,739
Library Holdings: Audiobooks 1,083; AV Mats 415; CDs 9,726; e-books 2; Microforms 114,863; Bk Titles 271,866; Per Subs 294; Videos 10,814
Special Collections: Irish Coll; Plymouth Coll
Subject Interests: Genealogy
Automation Activity & Vendor Info: (Acquisitions) SirsiDynix; (Cataloging) SirsiDynix; (Circulation) SirsiDynix; (ILL) SirsiDynix; (OPAC) SirsiDynix
Wireless access
Function: Adult literacy prog
Publications: Connections
Partic in Old Colony Libr Network
Special Services for the Deaf - Assisted listening device; TTY equip
Special Services for the Blind - Talking bk serv referral
Open Mon & Wed 1-8, Tues 10-8, Thurs 10-6, Fri & Sat 1-5
Branches: 1
MANOMET BRANCH, 12 Strand Ave, 02360, SAN 345-5254. Tel: 508-830-4185. E-mail: plmlib@ocln.org. *Librn,* Margaret McGrath
Open Mon, Wed & Sat 9-5, Thurs 1-9
Friends of the Library Group

PLYMPTON

P PLYMPTON PUBLIC LIBRARY*, 248 Main St, 02367-1114. SAN 307-627X. Tel: 781-585-4551. FAX: 781-585-7660. Web Site: sails.ent.sirsi.net/client/en_US/plympton. *Dir,* Debra L Batson; E-mail: dbatson@sailsinc.org; Staff 1.8 (Non-MLS 1.8)
Founded 1894. Pop 2,800; Circ 20,450
Library Holdings: Bk Vols 24,000; Per Subs 35
Automation Activity & Vendor Info: (Cataloging) SirsiDynix; (Circulation) SirsiDynix; (OPAC) SirsiDynix
Wireless access
Function: Adult bk club, Bks on CD, Story hour
Mem of Massachusetts Library System
Partic in SAILS Library Network
Open Tues & Thurs 10-8, Sat 10-4

PRINCETON

P PRINCETON PUBLIC LIBRARY*, Two Town Hall Dr, 01541. SAN 307-6288. Tel: 978-464-2115. FAX: 978-464-2116. E-mail: library@town.princeton.ma.us. Web Site: www.princetonpubliclibrary.org. *Dir,* Mary Barroll; Staff 5 (Non-MLS 5)
Founded 1884. Pop 3,700; Circ 33,956. Sal $97,985
Library Holdings: AV Mats 1,184; CDs 5; DVDs 1,314; e-books 4,318; Electronic Media & Resources 2,460; Bk Vols 16,601; Per Subs 68
Subject Interests: Arts, Cookery, Gardening, Hist

Automation Activity & Vendor Info: (Acquisitions) Innovative Interfaces, Inc; (Cataloging) Innovative Interfaces, Inc; (Circulation) Innovative Interfaces, Inc - Millennium
Wireless access
Function: Adult bk club, After school storytime, Bk club(s), Bks on cassette, Bks on CD, Children's prog, Computers for patron use, Electronic databases & coll, Free DVD rentals, Holiday prog, Home delivery & serv to seniorr ctr & nursing homes, Homebound delivery serv, ILL available, Museum passes, Music CDs, Online cat, OverDrive digital audio bks, Photocopying/Printing, Preschool outreach, Prog for adults, Prog for children & young adult, Spoken cassettes & CDs, Story hour, Summer reading prog, VHS videos, Wheelchair accessible
Mem of Massachusetts Library System
Open Tues & Thurs 10-8, Wed 10-5, Fri (Sept-June) 12-5, Sat 10-3 (10-1 Summer)
Restriction: Authorized patrons
Friends of the Library Group

PROVINCETOWN

P PROVINCETOWN PUBLIC LIBRARY, 356 Commercial St, 02657-2209. SAN 307-6296. Tel: 508-487-7094. FAX: 508-487-7096. Web Site: www.provincetownlibrary.org. *Libr Dir,* Amy Raff; Tel: 508-487-7094 Ext 216, E-mail: araff@clamsnet.org; *Lead Librn,* Nan Cinnater; Tel: 508-487-7094 Ext 217, E-mail: ncinnater@clamsnet.org; Staff 5 (MLS 2, Non-MLS 3)
Founded 1873. Pop 3,741; Circ 56,387
Library Holdings: AV Mats 3,495; Bks on Deafness & Sign Lang 20; Bk Vols 26,886; Per Subs 176
Subject Interests: Am art, Local hist, Modern art, Paintings
Automation Activity & Vendor Info: (Acquisitions) Innovative Interfaces, Inc; (Cataloging) Innovative Interfaces, Inc; (Circulation) Innovative Interfaces, Inc; (ILL) Innovative Interfaces, Inc; (OPAC) Innovative Interfaces, Inc; (Serials) Innovative Interfaces, Inc
Wireless access
Mem of Massachusetts Library System
Partic in Cape Libraries Automated Materials Sharing Network
Special Services for the Blind - Closed circuit TV
Open Mon & Fri 10-5, Tues-Thurs 10-8, Sat & Sun 1-5
Friends of the Library Group

QUINCY

P THOMAS CRANE PUBLIC LIBRARY*, 40 Washington St, 02269-9164. SAN 345-5289. Tel: 617-376-1300. Reference Tel: 617-376-1316. FAX: 617-376-1313. Reference E-mail: quref@ocln.org. Web Site: thomascranelibrary.org. *Dir,* Megan Allen; Tel: 617-376-1331, E-mail: mallen@ocln.org; *Asst Dir,* Clayton Cheever; E-mail: ccheever@ocln.org; *Head, Circ, Reader Serv,* Jessie Thuma; E-mail: jthuma@ocln.org; *Head, Info & Outreach Serv,* Position Currently Open; *Head, Tech Serv,* Therese Mosorjak; E-mail: tmosorjak@ocln.org; *Coll Develop Librn,* Deirdre Sullivan; Tel: 617-376-1306, E-mail: dsullivan@ocln.org; *Coordr, Ch Serv,* Julie M Rines; Tel: 617-376-1332, E-mail: jrines@ocln.org; *Coordr, Info Tech,* Rory O'Brien; Tel: 617-376-1319, E-mail: robrien@ocln.org. Subject Specialists: *Local hist,* Therese Mosorjak; Staff 28 (MLS 16, Non-MLS 12)
Founded 1871. Pop 92,271; Circ 737,906. Sal $1,940,610
Library Holdings: Audiobooks 14,685; e-books 3,633; Electronic Media & Resources 1,936; Microforms 8,089; Bk Vols 240,159; Per Subs 442; Videos 16,189
Subject Interests: Art, Local hist
Automation Activity & Vendor Info: (Acquisitions) SirsiDynix; (Cataloging) SirsiDynix; (Circulation) SirsiDynix; (ILL) SirsiDynix; (OPAC) SirsiDynix; (Serials) SirsiDynix
Wireless access
Mem of Massachusetts Library System
Special Services for the Deaf - TDD equip
Special Services for the Blind - Assistive/Adapted tech devices, equip & products
Open Mon-Thurs 9-9, Fri & Sat 9-5, Sun 1-5
Friends of the Library Group
Branches: 3
ADAMS SHORE BRANCH, 519 Sea St, 02169, SAN 345-5319. Tel: 617-376-1325, 617-376-1326. FAX: 617-376-1437. Circulation E-mail: quacirc@ocln.org. *Br Librn, Ch,* Lori Seegraber; E-mail: loris@ocln.org; Staff 1 (MLS 1)
Founded 1970. Circ 34,354
NORTH QUINCY BRANCH, 381 Hancock St, 02171, SAN 345-5408. Tel: 617-376-1320, 617-376-1321. FAX: 617-376-1432. Circulation E-mail: quncirc@ocln.org. *Br Librn,* Cathy deVeer; E-mail: cdeveer@ocln.org; *Adult/YA Serv Librn,* Dorothy Cronin; E-mail: dcronin@ocln.org; Staff 2 (MLS 2)
Founded 1963. Circ 53,277
WOLLASTON BRANCH, 41 Beale St, 02170, SAN 345-5491. Tel: 617-376-1330. FAX: 617-376-1430. Circulation E-mail: quwcirc@ocln.org. *Br Librn,* Amanda Pegg-Wheat; E-mail: apegg@ocln.org; Staff 1 (MLS 1)
Founded 1923. Circ 29,452

C EASTERN NAZARENE COLLEGE, Nease Library, 23 E Elm Ave, 02170. SAN 307-8159. Tel: 617-745-3850. Web Site: libguides.enc.edu. *Dir, Libr Serv, Electronic Res,* Amy Hwang; E-mail: Amy.hwang@enc.edu; Staff 1.7 (MLS 1, Non-MLS 0.7)
Enrl 699; Fac 42; Highest Degree: Master
Library Holdings: AV Mats 1,913; DVDs 815; Bk Vols 88,104; Per Subs 17
Special Collections: Theology Coll
Automation Activity & Vendor Info: (Cataloging) SirsiDynix; (Circulation) SirsiDynix; (Discovery) EBSCO Discovery Service; (ILL) OCLC WorldShare Interlibrary Loan; (OPAC) SirsiDynix-Enterprise
Wireless access
Mem of Massachusetts Library System
Partic in Christian Library Consortium; OCLC Online Computer Library Center, Inc; Old Colony Libr Network
Open Mon-Thurs 7:30am-11pm, Fri 7:30-5, Sat Noon-4, Sun 4-11
Restriction: Badge access after hrs

S NATIONAL FIRE PROTECTION ASSOCIATION, Research Library & Archives, One Batterymarch Park, 02169-7471. SAN 307-2169. Tel: 617-984-7445. FAX: 617-984-7060. E-mail: library@nfpa.org. Web Site: www.nfpa.org/library.
Founded 1945
Special Collections: National Fire Codes, 1896-present; National Fire Protection Association Published Archives Coll; US Fire History (FIDO Coll)
Subject Interests: Codes & standards, Fires & fire protection, Safety
Automation Activity & Vendor Info: (Cataloging) Inmagic, Inc.; (OPAC) Inmagic, Inc.; (Serials) Inmagic, Inc.
Wireless access
Function: CD-ROM, Doc delivery serv, ILL available, Online cat, Photocopying/Printing, Res libr, Scanner, VHS videos, Wheelchair accessible
Mem of Massachusetts Library System
Open Mon-Fri 8:30-4:30
Restriction: Circulates for staff only, Non-circulating coll, Open to pub for ref only

J QUINCY COLLEGE*, Anselmo Learning Commons and Library, 1250 Hancock St, Rm 347, 02169. SAN 307-6326. Tel: 617-984-1680. FAX: 617-984-1782. E-mail: help@quincycollegelibrary.org. Web Site: www.quincycollegelibrary.org. *Dir of Libr,* Susan Whitehead; *Fac Librn, Tech Serv Coordr,* Janet Lanigan; *Fac Librn,* Elizabeth Do; E-mail: edo@quincycollege.edu; *Fac Librn, Instruction Coordr,* Sarah Dolan; E-mail: sdolan@quincycollege.edu; *Fac Librn, Syst Coordr,* Ruth Perez; E-mail: rperez@quincycollege.edu; Staff 7 (MLS 5, Non-MLS 2)
Founded 1958. Enrl 3,700; Fac 75; Highest Degree: Associate
Subject Interests: Allied health, Computer sci, Criminal law & justice, Environ studies, Nursing, Psychol
Automation Activity & Vendor Info: (Acquisitions) SirsiDynix-WorkFlows; (Cataloging) SirsiDynix-WorkFlows; (Circulation) SirsiDynix-WorkFlows; (Course Reserve) SirsiDynix-WorkFlows; (OPAC) SirsiDynix-WorkFlows
Wireless access
Partic in Old Colony Libr Network
Open Mon-Thurs 7:30am-8pm, Fri 8-4, Sat 8:30-1

S QUINCY HISTORICAL SOCIETY LIBRARY*, Adams Academy Bldg, Eight Adams St, 02169. SAN 328-1256. Tel: 617-773-1144. FAX: 617-773-1872. E-mail: quincyhistory@verizon.net. Web Site: www.quincyma.gov/govt/depts/library.htm. *Exec Dir,* Edward Fitzgerald, PhD
Founded 1893
Library Holdings: Bk Titles 5,000; Per Subs 14
Special Collections: Adams Family Coll, bks; Shipbuilding Coll, bks, ms & photog
Function: Res libr
Open Mon-Fri 9-Noon
Restriction: Non-circulating

RANDOLPH

P TURNER FREE LIBRARY*, Two N Main St, 02368. SAN 307-6342. Tel: 781-961-0932. Web Site: www.turnerfreelibrary.org. *Libr Dir,* Meaghan Thompson; E-mail: mthompson@ocln.org; *Asst Dir,* Elizabeth Murphy; E-mail: emurphy@ocln.org; *Head, Adult Serv,* Sharon Parrington-Wright; E-mail: sparrington-wright@ocln.org; *Head, Children's Dept,* Monica Brennan; E-mail: mbrennan@ocln.org; Staff 18 (MLS 4, Non-MLS 14)

Founded 1874. Pop 35,000; Circ 236,567
Library Holdings: Bk Vols 59,400; Per Subs 110; Talking Bks 2,300; Videos 6,970
Automation Activity & Vendor Info: (Cataloging) SirsiDynix; (Circulation) SirsiDynix
Partic in Old Colony Libr Network
Open Mon-Thurs 9-8, Fri & Sat 9-5
Friends of the Library Group

RAYNHAM

P RAYNHAM PUBLIC LIBRARY*, 760 S Main St, 02767. SAN 307-6350. Tel: 508-823-1344. FAX: 508-824-0494. Web Site: raynhampubliclibrary.org. *Dir,* Eden Fergusson; E-mail: efergusson@sailsinc.org; Staff 10 (MLS 1, Non-MLS 9)
Founded 1888
Jul 2017-Jun 2018 Income $413,458, State $16,526, City $369,932, Locally Generated Income $27,000
Library Holdings: CDs 2,020; DVDs 3,815; e-books 14,395; e-journals 50; Per Subs 44
Wireless access
Function: 24/7 Electronic res, 24/7 Online cat, Activity rm, Adult bk club, Art exhibits, Audiobks via web, Bk club(s), Bks on CD, Chess club, Children's prog, Computers for patron use, Digital talking bks, Electronic databases & coll, Free DVD rentals, Home delivery & serv to seniorr ctr & nursing homes, ILL available, Internet access, Life-long learning prog for all ages, Magazines, Meeting rooms, Museum passes, Music CDs, Online cat, OverDrive digital audio bks, Photocopying/Printing, Printer for laptops & handheld devices, Prog for adults, Prog for children & young adult, Scanner, Story hour, Summer reading prog, Tax forms, Teen prog, Workshops
Mem of Massachusetts Library System
Partic in SAILS Library Network
Open Mon-Wed 10-8, Thurs & Sat 10-2, Fri 10-5, Sun (Oct-May) Noon-4
Friends of the Library Group

READING

P READING PUBLIC LIBRARY*, 64 Middlesex Ave, 01867-2550. SAN 307-6377. Tel: 781-944-0840. FAX: 781-942-9106. E-mail: rdg@noblenet.org. Web Site: www.readingpl.org. *Dir,* Amy Lannon; Tel: 781-942-6711, Fax: 781-942-9113, E-mail: rdgadmin@noblenet.org; *Asst Dir,* Ashley Waring; *Head, Borrower Serv,* Michelle Filleul; Tel: 781-942-6702, E-mail: rdgcirc@noblenet.org; *Head, Children's Servx,* Corinne Fisher; Tel: 781-942-6705, E-mail: rdgchild@noblenet.org; *Head, Reader Serv, Head, Res Serv,* Lorraine Barry; Tel: 781-942-6703, E-mail: barry@noblenet.org; *Head, Tech Serv,* Jamie Penney; Fax: 781-942-6704, E-mail: jamie@noblenet.org; *Ad,* Andrea Fiorillo; E-mail: fiorillo@noblenet.org; *Ch,* Brenda Wettergreen; E-mail: wettergreen@noblenet.org; *Ch,* Cate Zannino; E-mail: zannino@noblenet.org; *Local Hist Librn,* Eileen Barrett; E-mail: rdghist@noblenet.org; *Teen Serv Librn,* Susan Beauregard; E-mail: beauregard@noblenet.org; Staff 38 (MLS 15, Non-MLS 23)
Founded 1867. Pop 25,000; Circ 484,610
Library Holdings: CDs 9,134; DVDs 12,700; e-books 8,302; Electronic Media & Resources 3,023; Microforms 2,507; Bk Titles 85,703; Per Subs 363
Subject Interests: Local hist
Automation Activity & Vendor Info: (OPAC) Evergreen
Wireless access
Publications: Off the Shelf (Newsletter)
Mem of Massachusetts Library System
Open Mon-Wed 9-9, Thurs 1-9, Fri & Sat 9-5
Friends of the Library Group

REHOBOTH

P BLANDING FREE PUBLIC LIBRARY, 124 Bay State Rd, 02769. SAN 307-6385. Tel: 508-252-4236. Web Site: www.rehobothantiquarian.org/blanding-library. *Dir,* Whitney Pape; E-mail: wpape@sailsinc.org; *Head, Circ,* Susan Robert; E-mail: srobert@sailsinc.org; *Ch,* Catherine Charbonneau; E-mail: ccharbonneau@sailsinc.org
Founded 1886. Pop 12,008
Library Holdings: AV Mats 1,200; Large Print Bks 60; Bk Titles 14,000; Per Subs 20; Talking Bks 200
Subject Interests: Art & archit, Hist, Music
Automation Activity & Vendor Info: (Cataloging) SirsiDynix; (Circulation) SirsiDynix; (OPAC) SirsiDynix
Wireless access
Function: 24/7 Electronic res, 24/7 Online cat, Adult bk club, Bks on CD, Butterfly Garden, Children's prog, Computers for patron use, Free DVD rentals, ILL available, Internet access, Magazines, Meeting rooms, Movies, Museum passes, Music CDs, Online cat, OverDrive digital audio bks, Photocopying/Printing, Printer for laptops & handheld devices, Prog for adults, Prog for children & young adult, Ref serv available, Story hour, Summer reading prog, Tax forms, Teen prog, Wheelchair accessible
Partic in SAILS Library Network
Open Mon-Thurs 10-8, Fri & Sat 10-4
Friends of the Library Group

REVERE

P REVERE PUBLIC LIBRARY*, 179 Beach St, 02151. SAN 307-6393. Tel: 781-286-8380. FAX: 781-286-8382. E-mail: rev@noblenet.org. Web Site: www.reverepubliclibrary.org. *Dir,* Kevin Sheehan; E-mail: ksheehan@revere.org; Staff 12 (MLS 3, Non-MLS 9)
Founded 1880. Circ 30,223
Library Holdings: Bk Vols 54,500; Per Subs 70
Special Collections: Horatio Alger Coll
Subject Interests: Local hist
Automation Activity & Vendor Info: (Cataloging) Innovative Interfaces, Inc; (Circulation) Innovative Interfaces, Inc; (OPAC) Innovative Interfaces, Inc
Wireless access
Partic in North of Boston Library Exchange, Inc
Open Mon-Thurs 8-7, Fri 9-5
Friends of the Library Group

RICHMOND

P RICHMOND FREE PUBLIC LIBRARY*, 2821 State Rd, 01254-9472. SAN 307-6407. Tel: 413-563-7795. E-mail: richmondfreepubliclibrary@gmail.com. Web Site: www.richmondfreepubliclibrary.org. *Dir,* Kristin Smith; E-mail: k.smith@richmondma.org
Pop 1,689; Circ 10,000
Library Holdings: Bk Vols 12,100; Per Subs 24
Automation Activity & Vendor Info: (Cataloging) Innovative Interfaces, Inc; (Circulation) Innovative Interfaces, Inc; (OPAC) Innovative Interfaces, Inc
Partic in Central & Western Massachusetts Automated Resource Sharing
Open Tues & Thurs 10-8, Sat 10-2
Friends of the Library Group

ROCHESTER

P JOSEPH H PLUMB MEMORIAL LIBRARY*, 17 Constitution Way, 02770. (Mail add: PO Box 69, 02770-0069), SAN 307-6415. Tel: 508-763-8600. FAX: 508-763-9593. E-mail: info@plumblibrary.com. Web Site: www.plumblibrary.com. *Libr Dir,* Gail Roberts; E-mail: groberts@sailsinc.org
Pop 5,000; Circ 53,000
Library Holdings: AV Mats 938; Bk Vols 17,849
Special Collections: Rochester Historical Coll
Automation Activity & Vendor Info: (Cataloging) SirsiDynix; (Circulation) SirsiDynix; (OPAC) SirsiDynix
Wireless access
Partic in SAILS Library Network
Open Mon & Thurs 1-8, Tues & Wed 10-6, Fri 10-5, Sat 10-2
Friends of the Library Group

ROCKLAND

P ROCKLAND MEMORIAL LIBRARY*, 20 Belmont St, 02370-2232. SAN 307-6423. Tel: 781-878-1236. FAX: 781-878-4013. E-mail: info@rocklandmemoriallibrary.org. Web Site: www.rocklandmemoriallibrary.org. *Dir,* Elizabeth MacNeil; E-mail: emacneil@ocln.org; *Circ Chief,* Tammy Gennest; *Ref Librn,* Elizabeth MacNeil; *Youth Serv Librn,* Erin Puleio; *Cataloger,* Nancy Slack; Staff 3 (MLS 3)
Founded 1878. Pop 17,632; Circ 74,879
Jul 2018-Jun 2019 Income $646,186, State $23,451, City $596,054, Locally Generated Income $26,681. Mats Exp $89,357, Books $58,708, Per/Ser (Incl. Access Fees) $9,354, AV Mat $10,368, Electronic Ref Mat (Incl. Access Fees) $6,553. Sal $395,725 (Prof $166,961)
Library Holdings: DVDs 3,119; e-books 55,554; e-journals 152; Electronic Media & Resources 6; Microforms 393; Bk Vols 48,923; Per Subs 95
Special Collections: Municipal Document Depository
Subject Interests: Local hist
Automation Activity & Vendor Info: (Cataloging) SirsiDynix-WorkFlows; (Circulation) SirsiDynix-WorkFlows; (Discovery) SirsiDynix-Enterprise; (OPAC) SirsiDynix-iBistro; (Serials) SirsiDynix-WorkFlows
Wireless access
Function: 24/7 Electronic res, 24/7 Online cat, Adult bk club, Archival coll, Art exhibits, Audiobks via web, Bk club(s), Bks on CD, Children's prog, Computers for patron use, Electronic databases & coll, Free DVD rentals, Holiday prog, ILL available, Internet access, Magazines, Magnifiers for reading, Microfiche/film & reading machines, Museum passes, Music CDs, Online cat, OverDrive digital audio bks, Photocopying/Printing, Prog

for adults, Prog for children & young adult, Ref serv available, Scanner, Summer reading prog, Tax forms, Teen prog, Telephone ref, Wheelchair accessible
Partic in Old Colony Libr Network
Special Services for the Deaf - Bks on deafness & sign lang
Special Services for the Blind - Large print bks; Magnifiers
Open Mon-Wed 9:30-8, Thurs-Sat 9:30-5
Friends of the Library Group

ROCKPORT

L EDWIN T HOLMES LAW LIBRARY*, 146 South St, 01966. SAN 372-0330. Tel: 978-546-3478. FAX: 978-546-6785. *Librn,* Edwin Holmes
Library Holdings: Bk Vols 800

P ROCKPORT PUBLIC LIBRARY, 17 School St, 01966. SAN 307-6431. Tel: 978-546-6934. FAX: 978-546-1011. E-mail: info@rockportlibrary.org. Web Site: www.rockportlibrary.org. *Libr Dir,* Cindy Grove; E-mail: cgrove@rockportlibrary.org; *Info Serv Librn, Outreach Serv Librn,* Brian Audano; E-mail: baudano@rockportlibrary.org; *Tech Serv Librn,* Dede McManus; E-mail: dmcmanus@rockportlibrary.org; *Youth Serv Librn,* K L Pereira; E-mail: kpereira@rockportlibrary.org; Staff 12 (MLS 2, Non-MLS 10)
Founded 1871. Pop 7,000
Library Holdings: Per Subs 969
Subject Interests: Art, Local hist
Automation Activity & Vendor Info: (Cataloging) Evergreen; (Circulation) Evergreen; (ILL) Clio; (OPAC) Evergreen
Wireless access
Mem of Massachusetts Library System
Partic in Merrimack Valley Library Consortium
Open Mon, Wed & Thurs 1-8, Tues & Sun 1-5, Sat 10-5
Friends of the Library Group

S SANDY BAY HISTORICAL SOCIETY & MUSEUMS LIBRARY*, 40 King St, 01966. (Mail add: PO Box 63, 01966-0063), SAN 329-0913. Tel: 978-546-9533. E-mail: info@rockporthistory.org. Web Site: rockporthistory.org.
Founded 1926
Library Holdings: Bk Vols 1,000
Special Collections: Cape Ann Hist; Genealogical Coll by Family
Subject Interests: Massachusetts
Function: Res libr
Publications: Quarterly Bulletin, Ad Hoc Brochures, Pamphlets
Open Mon 9-1
Restriction: Fee for pub use, Mem only, Non-circulating

ROWE

P ROWE TOWN LIBRARY*, 318 Zoar Rd, 01367. SAN 307-644X. Tel: 413-339-4761. FAX: 413-339-4713. E-mail: rowelibrary@gmail.com. Web Site: rowe-ma.gov/index.cfm?p=p.48. *Dir,* Lane A Molly; Staff 1 (MLS 1)
Founded 1787. Pop 380; Circ 12,000
Library Holdings: Bk Vols 12,069; Per Subs 51
Subject Interests: Local hist
Automation Activity & Vendor Info: (Cataloging) Follett Software; (Circulation) Follett Software
Partic in Central & Western Massachusetts Automated Resource Sharing
Open Tues & Sat 10-5, Wed 10-8

ROWLEY

S PEABODY ESSEX MUSEUM, Phillips Library, 306 Newburyport Tpk, 01969. Tel: 978-745-9500, Ext 3053. Reference Tel: 978-542-1553. Toll Free Tel: 800-745-4054, Ext 3053. FAX: 978-741-9012. TDD: 978-740-3649. E-mail: research@pem.org. Web Site: www.pem.org/library. *Libr Dir,* Dan Lipcan; Tel: 978-542-1536, E-mail: dan_lipcan@pem.org; *Ref & Access Serv Librn,* Jennifer Hornsby; *Tech Serv Librn,* Catherine Robertson; Staff 8.6 (MLS 8, Non-MLS 0.6)
Founded 1799
Library Holdings: Bk Vols 400,000; Per Subs 200
Special Collections: Archival & Manuscript Coll; Chinese History (Frederick Townsend Ward Coll); Hawthorniana (C E Fraser Clark Coll); Japanese & Korean Art & Culture (Edward Sylvester Morse Coll); Modern & Contemporary Indian Art (Chester & Davida Herwitz Coll); Phillips Library Ship Logbooks & Journals, 1729-1961; Salem Witch Trials Documents, 1692
Subject Interests: Am folk art, Archit, Asian art, China, Decorative art, Fashion, Fine arts, India, Indigenous art, Japan, Korea, Maritime hist, Massachusetts, Natural hist, New England, Oceania, Photog, S Asia, Textiles
Automation Activity & Vendor Info: (Cataloging) Ex Libris Group; (Circulation) Atlas Systems; (OPAC) Ex Libris Group
Wireless access
Function: 24/7 Online cat, Archival coll, Computers for patron use, Electronic databases & coll, Internet access, Microfiche/film & reading machines, Orientations, Res assist avail
Partic in Digital Libr Fedn
Restriction: Closed stack, Non-circulating, Open by appt only
Friends of the Library Group

P ROWLEY PUBLIC LIBRARY*, 141 Main St, 01969. SAN 307-6458. Tel: 978-948-2850. FAX: 978-948-2266. E-mail: info@rowleylibrary.org. Web Site: www.rowleylibrary.org. *Dir,* Pamela Jacobson; E-mail: director@rowleylibrary.org; *Ad, Asst Dir,* Amy Roderick; E-mail: aroderick@rowleylibrary.org; *Youth Serv Librn,* Teri Bennett; Staff 11 (MLS 1, Non-MLS 10)
Founded 1894. Pop 5,393
Library Holdings: AV Mats 6,330; Bk Vols 22,000; Per Subs 50
Subject Interests: Genealogy
Automation Activity & Vendor Info: (Cataloging) Follett Software; (Circulation) Follett Software; (OPAC) SirsiDynix
Wireless access
Mem of Massachusetts Library System
Partic in Merrimack Valley Library Consortium
Special Services for the Blind - Audio mat; Bks on CD; Home delivery serv; Talking bks
Open Mon-Thurs 10-8, Sat 10-2
Friends of the Library Group

ROXBURY

S METROPOLITAN COUNCIL FOR EDUCATIONAL OPPORTUNITY LIBRARY*, 40 Dimock St, 02119. SAN 328-4077. Tel: 617-427-1545. FAX: 617-541-0550. E-mail: information@metcoinc.org. Web Site: www.metcoinc.org. *Bus Mgr,* Kim Houston; E-mail: khouston@metcoinc.org
Library Holdings: Bk Vols 10,000; Per Subs 50
Open Mon-Fri 8-8

ROYALSTON

P PHINEHAS S NEWTON LIBRARY*, 19 On the Common, 01368. (Mail add: PO Box 133, 01368-0133), SAN 307-6474. Tel: 978-249-3572. FAX: 978-249-3572. E-mail: royalstonlibrary@gmail.com. Web Site: www.royalstonlibrary.org. *Dir,* Katherine Morris; *Asst Dir,* Gina Verrilli
Pop 1,012; Circ 2,326
Library Holdings: Bk Vols 9,400
Wireless access
Mem of Massachusetts Library System
Open Mon 10-8:30, Thurs 1-5 & 6:30-8:30, Sat 9-Noon
Friends of the Library Group

RUSSELL

P RUSSELL PUBLIC LIBRARY*, 162 Main St, 01071. (Mail add: PO Box 438, 01071-0438), SAN 307-6482. Tel: 413-862-6221. FAX: 413-862-3106. E-mail: russellpubliclib@gmail.com. Web Site: www.townofrussell.us/library.html. *Libr Dir,* Jodie Paradis; E-mail: rpldirector@russellma.net; *Ch,* Carol Duda; E-mail: russellpubliclib@gmail.com; Staff 3 (Non-MLS 3)
Pop 1,713; Circ 5,405
Library Holdings: Bk Vols 6,255
Open Mon, Wed & Fri 3-8, Tues & Thurs 10-2
Friends of the Library Group

RUTLAND

P RUTLAND FREE PUBLIC LIBRARY*, 280 Main St, 01543. SAN 307-6490. Tel: 508-886-4108. FAX: 508-886-4141. E-mail: contact@rutlandlibrary.org. Web Site: www.rutlandlibrary.org. *Dir,* Kerry J Remington; *Asst Dir,* Susan Liimatainen; *Ch,* Maureen Lynch; Staff 3 (Non-MLS 3)
Founded 1866. Pop 6,591; Circ 58,623
Library Holdings: Bk Vols 50,000; Per Subs 100
Automation Activity & Vendor Info: (Cataloging) Follett Software; (Circulation) Follett Software
Mem of Massachusetts Library System
Open Tues & Wed 10-8, Thurs 1-8, Sat (Sept-May) 10-1
Friends of the Library Group

SALEM

GL ESSEX LAW LIBRARY, J Michael Ruane Judicial Ctr, 56 Federal St, 01970. SAN 307-6512. Tel: 978-741-0674. FAX: 978-745-7224. E-mail: essexlawlibrary@hotmail.com. Web Site: www.mass.gov/locations/essex-law-library. *Head Law Librn,* Robin W Bates; Staff 2 (MLS 1, Non-MLS 1)
Founded 1856
Library Holdings: Bk Vols 30,000; Per Subs 200

Wireless access
Open Mon-Fri 8-4
Friends of the Library Group

M NORTH SHORE MEDICAL CENTER, SALEM HOSPITAL*, Health Sciences Library, 81 Highland Ave, 01970. SAN 324-6647. Tel: 978-354-4950. FAX: 978-744-9110. E-mail: nsmcsalemlibrary@partners.org. Web Site: nsmc.partners.org/for_healthcare_professionals/medical_libraries. *Dir, Libr Serv,* Deborah Almquist; Staff 3 (MLS 2, Non-MLS 1)
Founded 1928
Library Holdings: Bk Titles 4,400; Per Subs 250
Subject Interests: Med
Publications: Newsletter
Partic in National Network of Libraries of Medicine Region 7; Proquest Dialog
Open Mon-Fri 9-3:30
Restriction: Employees & their associates, Med staff only, Staff & patient use

S SALEM ATHENAEUM*, 337 Essex St, 01970. SAN 371-8344. Tel: 978-744-2540. FAX: 978-744-7536. E-mail: info@salemathenaeum.net. Web Site: www.salemathenaeum.net. *Exec Dir,* Jean Marie Procious; Staff 1 (MLS 1)
Founded 1760
Library Holdings: Bk Titles 54,202; Per Subs 31
Special Collections: Personal Library of Dr Edward Holyoke, 18th to early 19th century; Philosophical Library 1781; Social Library of 1760
Wireless access
Function: Bi-weekly Writer's Group, Children's prog, ILL available, Prog for adults, Ref serv available
Mem of Massachusetts Library System
Open Tues-Fri 1-6, Sat 10-2
Restriction: Circ to mem only, Open to researchers by request, Private libr, Pub use on premises

P SALEM PUBLIC LIBRARY*, 370 Essex St, 01970-3298. SAN 345-5521. Tel: 978-744-0860. FAX: 978-745-8616. E-mail: sal@noblenet.org. Web Site: www.noblenet.org/salem. *Dir,* Tara Mansfield; E-mail: mansfield@noblenet.org; *Asst Dir,* Brian Hodgdon; E-mail: hodgdon@noblenet.org; *Ch Serv,* Laura Brosnan; *Circ,* Teresa Lucey; *Ref (Info Servs),* Marie Hviding
Founded 1888. Pop 40,407; Circ 490,204
Library Holdings: Bk Vols 128,569; Per Subs 150
Wireless access
Open Mon-Thurs 9-9, Fri & Sat 9-5, Sun 1-5

C SALEM STATE UNIVERSITY*, Frederick E Berry Library, 352 Lafayette St, 01970-5353. SAN 307-6547. Tel: 978-542-6230. Interlibrary Loan Service Tel: 978-542-6501. Reference Tel: 978-542-6766. Administration Tel: 978-542-6232. Automation Services Tel: 978-542-6813. FAX: 978-542-6596. Administration FAX: 978-542-2132. Web Site: www.salemstate.edu/library. *Dean of Libr,* Elizabeth McKeigue; E-mail: elizabeth.mckeigue@salemstate.edu; *Chairperson, Res & Instruction Librn,* Carol Zoppel; Tel: 978-542-6811, E-mail: carol.zoppel@salemstate.edu; *Archivist, Librn,* Susan Edwards; Tel: 978-542-6781, E-mail: susan.edwards@salemstate.edu; *Cat Librn,* Stephen C Pew; Tel: 978-542-6769, E-mail: stephen.pew@salemstate.edu; *Electronic Res Librn,* Nancy George; Tel: 978-542-7182, E-mail: nancy.george@salemstate.edu; *Res & Instruction Librn,* Nancy Dennis; Tel: 978-542-6218, E-mail: nancy.dennis@salemstate.edu; *Res & Instruction Librn,* Cathy Fahey; Tel: 978-542-7203, E-mail: cathy.fahey@salemstate.edu; *Res & Instruction Librn,* Tara Fitzpatrick; Tel: 978-542-6765, E-mail: tara.fitzpatrick@salemstate.edu; *Res & Instruction Librn,* Jason Soohoo; Tel: 978-542-6967, E-mail: jason.soohoo@salemstate.edu; *Access Serv Coordr,* Thomas Neenan; Tel: 978-542-6368, E-mail: thomas.neenan@salemstate.edu. Subject Specialists: *Nursing,* Nancy George; *Communications, English,* Cathy Fahey; *Criminal justice, Psychol, Sociol,* Tara Fitzpatrick; *Educ,* Jason Soohoo; Staff 15 (MLS 13, Non-MLS 2)
Founded 1854. Enrl 10,125; Fac 566; Highest Degree: Master. Sal $1,490,555
Library Holdings: Audiobooks 483; AV Mats 6,739; e-books 308,454; e-journals 57,642; Electronic Media & Resources 10,931; Microforms 584,195; Bk Vols 299,210; Per Subs 400
Special Collections: Historic Geography; History of Education (19th Century Normal School Texts Coll); Music Coll; North Shore Political Archives; Salem History
Subject Interests: Bus, Educ, Humanities, Nursing, Soc sci
Automation Activity & Vendor Info: (Acquisitions) Evergreen; (Cataloging) Evergreen; (Circulation) Evergreen; (Course Reserve) Evergreen; (ILL) Evergreen; (OPAC) Evergreen; (Serials) Evergreen
Wireless access
Function: Archival coll, Audio & video playback equip for onsite use, Bks on cassette, Bks on CD, Computers for patron use, E-Reserves, Electronic databases & coll, Microfiche/film & reading machines, Online cat, Online ref, Photocopying/Printing, Ref serv available, Wheelchair accessible
Publications: Bookmark (Biannually); Brochure (Biannually); Periodical List; Research Guides (Online only)
Partic in Massachusetts Commonwealth Consortium of Libraries in Public Higher Education Institutions; North of Boston Library Exchange, Inc; Northeastern Consortium for Health Information; OCLC Online Computer Library Center, Inc
Special Services for the Deaf - ADA equip; Assisted listening device; Assistive tech
Special Services for the Blind - Assistive/Adapted tech devices, equip & products
Open Mon-Thurs 7:45am-2am, Fri 7:45-7, Sat Noon-4, Sun 2-11
Restriction: In-house use for visitors, Lending limited to county residents, Non-circulating of rare bks, Off-site coll in storage - retrieval as requested

G US NATIONAL PARK SERVICE, Salem Maritime National Historic Site Library, 160 Derby St, 01970. SAN 323-7451. Tel: 978-740-1650. Web Site: www.nps.gov/sama. *Hist Coll Librn, Ref Serv,* Emily Murphy; E-mail: emily_murphy@nps.gov; Staff 1 (Non-MLS 1)
Founded 1937
Library Holdings: Bk Titles 975; Bk Vols 1,150
Special Collections: Essex County Coll; New England Maritime History Coll; Salem History Coll
Subject Interests: Maritime hist
Function: Res libr
Restriction: Authorized personnel only, Govt use only, Internal use only, Non-circulating, Open to govt employees only, Staff use only

SALISBURY

P SALISBURY PUBLIC LIBRARY*, 17 Elm St, 01952. SAN 307-6555. Tel: 978-465-5071. Web Site: www.salisburylibrary.org. *Dir,* Terry Kyrios; E-mail: tkyrios@Salisburylibrary.org; *Asst Dir,* Corinn Flaherty; E-mail: cflaherty@salisburylibrary.org
Founded 1895. Pop 7,170; Circ 27,284
Library Holdings: Bk Titles 23,839; Per Subs 90
Subject Interests: Genealogy, Local hist
Automation Activity & Vendor Info: (Cataloging) Evergreen; (Circulation) Evergreen; (OPAC) Evergreen
Wireless access
Partic in Merrimack Valley Library Consortium
Open Mon, Wed & Fri 10-6, Tues 12-8, Thurs 10-8, Sat 10-2
Friends of the Library Group

SANDISFIELD

P SANDISFIELD FREE PUBLIC LIBRARY, 23 Sandisfield Rd, 01255. SAN 307-6563. Tel: 413-258-4966. FAX: 413-258-4225. E-mail: sandisfieldlibrary@gmail.com. *Dir,* Sadie O'Rourke; *Librn,* Theresa Spohalotz
Pop 660; Circ 3,040
Library Holdings: AV Mats 24; Bk Titles 3,750; Per Subs 12
Publications: Fact sheet for town
Open Mon & Tues 9-12:30, Wed 2-5, Thurs 5-7, Sat 10-1
Friends of the Library Group

SANDWICH

S THE SANDWICH GLASS MUSEUM LIBRARY*, 129 Main St, 02563-2233. (Mail add: PO Box 103, 02563-0103), SAN 323-8679. Tel: 508-888-0251. FAX: 508-888-4941. Web Site: www.sandwichglassmuseum.org. *Exec Dir,* Katie Campbell; E-mail: katie.campbell@sandwichglassmuseum.org; *Curator,* Dorothy Schofield; E-mail: dorothy.schofield@sandwichglassmuseum.org
Founded 1907
Library Holdings: Bk Titles 1,700; Per Subs 2
Special Collections: B & S Correspondence, Deming Jarves Letters, archival doc; Town of Sandwich Families, archival doc, letters
Subject Interests: Antiques
Restriction: Non-circulating to the pub, Open by appt only

P SANDWICH PUBLIC LIBRARY*, 142 Main St, 02563. SAN 307-658X. Tel: 508-888-0625. FAX: 508-833-1076. E-mail: spllib@comcast.net. Web Site: www.sandwichpubliclibrary.com. *Dir,* Joanne Lamothe; E-mail: jlamothe@ocln.org; *Head, Circ,* Karen Ostiguy; E-mail: kostiguy@ocln.org; *Ch,* Stu Parsons; E-mail: sparsons@ocln.org; *Ref Librn,* Brian Meneses; E-mail: bmeneses@ocln.org; *Ref Librn,* Lauren Robinson; E-mail: lrobinson@ocln.org; *Acq,* Melissa Frye; E-mail: mfrye@ocln.org; Staff 5 (MLS 5)
Founded 1891. Pop 20,000; Circ 214,000. Sal $708,463
Library Holdings: Bk Titles 58,000; Per Subs 288
Special Collections: Glass Books

Subject Interests: Glass technology
Partic in Old Colony Libr Network
Open Tues-Thurs 9:30-8:30, Fri & Sat 9:30-4, Sun (Oct-April) 12-4
Friends of the Library Group

SAVOY

P SAVOY HOLLOW LIBRARY*, Town Off Bldg, 720 Main Rd, 01256-9387. SAN 307-6598. Tel: 413-743-3573. FAX: 413-743-4292. *Dir,* Ronna Tynan; *Chair,* Susan O'Grady
Founded 1890. Pop 720; Circ 3,669
Library Holdings: Bk Vols 520
Open Mon, Wed & Thurs 8-Noon, Tues 8-12 & 7-9

SCITUATE

S SCITUATE HISTORICAL SOCIETY LIBRARY*, 43 Cudworth Rd, 02066-3802. (Mail add: PO Box 276, 02066-0276), SAN 326-7814. Tel: 781-545-1083. Web Site: scituatehistoricalsociety.org. *Archivist,* Mary Porter; E-mail: portermary@comcast.net; Staff 1 (MLS 1)
Founded 1984
Library Holdings: Bk Titles 700
Special Collections: Thomas W Lawson Coll
Subject Interests: Genealogy, Hist
Function: Res libr
Open Mon, Tues, Thurs & Fri 10-4, Sat 10-2
Restriction: Pub use on premises

P SCITUATE TOWN LIBRARY, 85 Branch St, 02066. SAN 307-6601. Tel: 781-545-8727. Web Site: www.scituatema.gov/library. *Dir,* Jessica Finnie; E-mail: jfinnie@ocln.org; *Asst Dir,* Toni Snee; E-mail: tsnee@ocln.org; *Head, Adult Serv,* Ann Lattinville; E-mail: alattinville@ocln.org; *Head, Children's Servx,* Kate Jasinski; E-mail: kjasinski@ocln.org
Founded 1893. Pop 17,829; Circ 137,466
Library Holdings: Bk Vols 74,948; Per Subs 121
Special Collections: Oral History
Automation Activity & Vendor Info: (Cataloging) SirsiDynix; (Circulation) SirsiDynix; (OPAC) SirsiDynix
Open Mon, Wed, Fri & Sat 10-5, Tues & Thurs 12-7
Friends of the Library Group

SEEKONK

P SEEKONK PUBLIC LIBRARY, 410 Newman Ave, 02771. SAN 345-570X. Tel: 508-336-8230. FAX: 508-336-6437. Web Site: www.seekonkpl.org. *Dir,* Kathleen Hibbert; Tel: 508-336-8230, Ext 56110, E-mail: khibbert@seekonkpl.org; *Assoc Dir,* Debra Clifton; Tel: 508-336-8230, Ext 56101, E-mail: dclifton@seekonkpl.org; *Admin Librn,* Vanessa Mota; Tel: 508-336-8230, Ext 56100, E-mail: vmota@seekonkpl.org; *Ad,* Katie Corrigan; Tel: 508-336-8230, Ext 56143, E-mail: kcorrigan@seekonkpl.org; *Ad,* Michelle Gario; Tel: 508-336-8230, Ext 56132, E-mail: mgario@seekonkpl.org; *Ad,* Amy Greil; Tel: 508-336-8230, Ext 56141, E-mail: agreil@seekonkpl.org; *Youth Librn,* Sharon Clarke; Tel: 508-336-8230, Ext 56142, E-mail: sclarke@seekonkpl.org; *Computer Support Spec,* Sharon Fredette; Tel: 508-336-8230, Ext 56150, E-mail: sfredette@seekonkpl.org; Staff 21 (MLS 8, Non-MLS 13)
Founded 1899. Pop 18,525; Circ 267,543
Automation Activity & Vendor Info: (Acquisitions) SirsiDynix; (Cataloging) SirsiDynix; (Circulation) SirsiDynix; (Course Reserve) SirsiDynix; (ILL) SirsiDynix; (Media Booking) SirsiDynix; (OPAC) SirsiDynix; (Serials) SirsiDynix
Wireless access
Function: 24/7 Electronic res, 24/7 Online cat, Accelerated reader prog, Activity rm, Adult bk club, Art exhibits, Audiobks via web, Bks on CD, CD-ROM, Children's prog, Computer training, Computers for patron use, Digital talking bks, E-Readers, E-Reserves, Electronic databases & coll, Family literacy, Holiday prog, Homebound delivery serv, ILL available, Internet access, Magazines, Magnifiers for reading, Mail & tel request accepted, Meeting rooms, Movies, Museum passes, Music CDs, Notary serv, Online cat, OverDrive digital audio bks, Photocopying/Printing, Preschool reading prog, Printer for laptops & handheld devices, Prog for adults, Prog for children & young adult, Ref & res, Ref serv available, Senior computer classes, Senior outreach, Serves people with intellectual disabilities, Spoken cassettes & CDs, Story hour, Tax forms, Teen prog, Telephone ref, Visual arts prog, Wheelchair accessible, Writing prog
Partic in SAILS Library Network
Open Mon-Thurs 9-8, Fri & Sat 9-5
Restriction: Non-resident fee
Friends of the Library Group

SHARON

P SHARON PUBLIC LIBRARY*, 11 N Main St, 02067-1299. SAN 307-6628. Tel: 781-784-1578. Circulation Tel: 781-784-1578, Ext 1420. Reference Tel: 781-784-1578, Ext 1422. Administration Tel: 781-784-1578, Ext 1425. Web Site: www.sharonpubliclibrary.org. *Dir,* Lee Ann Amend; E-mail: lamend@ocln.org; *Asst Dir, Head, Adult Serv,* Mikaela Wolfe; E-mail: mwolfe@ocln.org; *Head, Youth Serv,* Jessica Henderson; E-mail: jhenderson@ocln.org; *Info Serv Librn,* Hilary Umbreit; Staff 19 (MLS 5, Non-MLS 14)
Pop 17,000; Circ 223,000
Library Holdings: Bk Vols 90,000; Per Subs 125
Special Collections: Deborah Sampson Coll
Subject Interests: Local hist
Automation Activity & Vendor Info: (Acquisitions) SirsiDynix; (Cataloging) SirsiDynix; (Circulation) SirsiDynix; (Serials) SirsiDynix
Wireless access
Function: Telephone ref
Publications: News @ 11 N Main St (Newsletter)
Mem of Massachusetts Library System
Partic in Old Colony Libr Network
Open Mon & Fri 10-6, Tues-Thurs 10-8, Sat 10-5
Friends of the Library Group

SHEFFIELD

P BUSHNELL-SAGE LIBRARY, 48 Main St, 01257. SAN 307-6644. Tel: 413-229-7004. FAX: 413-229-7003. E-mail: bushnellsage@gmail.com. Web Site: www.bushnellsagelibrary.org. *Dir,* Deena Caswell; E-mail: bushnellsagedirector@gmail.com
Founded 1892. Pop 3,200; Circ 38,000
Library Holdings: Bk Vols 38,000; Per Subs 70
Automation Activity & Vendor Info: (Cataloging) Evergreen; (Circulation) Evergreen; (OPAC) Evergreen; (Serials) EBSCO Discovery Service
Wireless access
Function: 24/7 Electronic res, 24/7 Online cat, Activity rm, Archival coll, Art exhibits, Audiobks via web, Bi-weekly Writer's Group, Bks on CD, Chess club, Children's prog, Computers for patron use, Electronic databases & coll, Free DVD rentals, ILL available, Internet access, Large print keyboards, Magazines, Magnifiers for reading, Museum passes, Music CDs, Online cat, Prog for adults, Prog for children & young adult, Story hour, Study rm, Summer reading prog, Wheelchair accessible, Workshops
Partic in Central & Western Massachusetts Automated Resource Sharing
Open Tues-Thurs & Sat 10-5, Fri 10-8, Sun 2-5
Restriction: Borrowing requests are handled by ILL
Friends of the Library Group

SHELBURNE FALLS

P ARMS LIBRARY, 60 Bridge St, 01370. SAN 307-6652. Tel: 413-625-0306. E-mail: armslibrary@gmail.com. Web Site: www.armslibrary.org. *Dir,* Laurie Wheeler
Founded 1854
Library Holdings: Bk Vols 22,840; Per Subs 48
Wireless access
Partic in Central & Western Massachusetts Automated Resource Sharing
Open Mon & Wed 1-5:30, Sat 10-2:30
Friends of the Library Group

P SHELBURNE FREE PUBLIC LIBRARY*, 233 Shelburne Center Rd, 01370. SAN 307-6660. Tel: 413-625-0307. FAX: 413-625-0307. E-mail: sfplibrary@cwmars.org. Web Site: www.shelburnefreepubliclibrary.org. *Libr Dir,* Elizabeth Antaya; E-mail: eantaya@cwmars.org
Pop 8,000; Circ 8,648
Library Holdings: Bk Vols 12,000; Per Subs 33
Automation Activity & Vendor Info: (Cataloging) Innovative Interfaces, Inc; (Circulation) Innovative Interfaces, Inc; (OPAC) Innovative Interfaces, Inc
Partic in Central & Western Massachusetts Automated Resource Sharing
Open Tues & Thurs 3-7, Sat 10-Noon

SHERBORN

P SHERBORN LIBRARY*, Four Sanger St, 01770-1499. SAN 307-6679. Tel: 508-653-0770. FAX: 508-650-9243. E-mail: sherborn@minlib.net. Web Site: sherbornlibrary.org. *Dir,* Elizabeth Johnston; E-mail: ejohnston@minlib.net; *Asst Dir, Pub Serv Librn,* Liz Anderson; E-mail: eanderson@minlib.net; *Ch,* Cheryl Stern Ouellette; E-mail: couelette@minlib.net; Staff 9 (MLS 4, Non-MLS 5)
Founded 1860. Pop 4,493; Circ 54,743
Library Holdings: Bk Titles 52,725; Per Subs 169
Wireless access
Publications: First Search
Mem of Massachusetts Library System
Partic in Minuteman Library Network; OCLC Online Computer Library Center, Inc
Open Mon-Thurs 10-8, Fri & Sat 10-5 (Sept-June); Mon 10-5, Tues & Wed 10-8, Thurs 10-6, Fri 10-4, Sat 10-1 (July-Aug)
Friends of the Library Group

SHIRLEY

P HAZEN MEMORIAL LIBRARY, Three Keady Way, 01464. SAN 307-6687. Tel: 978-425-2620. FAX: 978-425-2621. E-mail: shirley@cwmars.org. Web Site: www.shirleylibrary.org. *Dir,* Debra J Roy; E-mail: droy@shirley-ma.gov; *Ad,* Spencer Stevens; E-mail: stevenss@cwmars.org; *Youth Serv Librn,* Kathleen R Buretta; E-mail: kburetta@shirley-ma.gov; Staff 3 (MLS 1, Non-MLS 2)
Founded 1893. Pop 6,373; Circ 33,929
Library Holdings: Bk Vols 36,000; Per Subs 94
Subject Interests: Local hist
Automation Activity & Vendor Info: (Cataloging) Evergreen; (Circulation) Evergreen; (OPAC) Evergreen
Wireless access
Function: 24/7 Electronic res, 24/7 Online cat, Activity rm, Adult bk club, Audiobks via web, Bk club(s), Bks on CD, Children's prog, Computers for patron use, Electronic databases & coll, Free DVD rentals, ILL available, Internet access, Magazines, Meeting rooms, Museum passes, Online cat, OverDrive digital audio bks, Photocopying/Printing, Prog for adults, Prog for children & young adult, Story hour, Study rm, Summer reading prog, Tax forms, Teen prog, Telephone ref
Mem of Massachusetts Library System
Partic in Central & Western Massachusetts Automated Resource Sharing
Open Mon, Wed & Thurs 10-6, Tues 11-7, Sat 9-1
Friends of the Library Group

SHREWSBURY

P SHREWSBURY PUBLIC LIBRARY*, 609 Main St, 01545. SAN 307-6695. Tel: 508-841-8609. Circulation Tel: 508-841-8609, Ext 3. Reference Tel: 508-841-8609, Ext 2. FAX: 508-841-8542. Web Site: www.shrewsburyma.gov/344/Library. *Libr Dir,* Priya Rathnam; E-mail: prathnam@shrewsburyma.gov; *Head, Children's Dept,* Sonja Drotar; E-mail: sdrotar@cwmars.org; *Head, Circ,* Melissa Wentworth; E-mail: mwentworth@cwmars.org; *YA Librn,* Annie Lee King; E-mail: aking@cwmars.org; Staff 51 (MLS 11, Non-MLS 40)
Founded 1872. Pop 36,805; Circ 482,373
Library Holdings: AV Mats 19,323; e-books 96,115; Bk Vols 102,342; Per Subs 175
Special Collections: Early New England History & Biography (Artemas Ward Coll)
Automation Activity & Vendor Info: (Acquisitions) Evergreen; (Cataloging) Evergreen; (Circulation) Evergreen; (ILL) Evergreen; (OPAC) Evergreen; (Serials) Evergreen
Wireless access
Function: 24/7 Electronic res, 24/7 Online cat, 3D Printer, Activity rm, Adult bk club, Art exhibits, Audiobks on Playaways & MP3, Audiobks via web, Bk club(s), Bks on CD, Computers for patron use, E-Readers, Electronic databases & coll, Equip loans & repairs, Free DVD rentals, Genealogy discussion group, Holiday prog, Home delivery & serv to seniorr ctr & nursing homes, ILL available, Internet access, Magazines, Mango lang, Meeting rooms, Museum passes, Notary serv, Online cat, Online info literacy tutorials on the web & in blackboard, Outreach serv, OverDrive digital audio bks, Photocopying/Printing, Prog for adults, Prog for children & young adult, Ref & res, Spoken cassettes & CDs, Story hour, Study rm, Summer reading prog, Telephone ref, Wheelchair accessible, Workshops
Publications: Newsletter (Quarterly)
Mem of Massachusetts Library System
Partic in Central & Western Massachusetts Automated Resource Sharing
Open Mon-Thurs 9-9, Fri 10-5, Sat 9-5, Sun (Oct-May) 1-5
Friends of the Library Group

SHUTESBURY

P MN SPEAR MEMORIAL LIBRARY*, Ten Cooleyville Rd, 01072-9766. (Mail add: PO Box 256, 01072-0256), SAN 307-6717. Tel: 413-259-1213. FAX: 413-259-1107. Web Site: sites.google.com/site/mnspearmemoriallibrary. *Dir,* Mary Anne Antonellis; E-mail: library.director@shutesbury.org
Pop 1,800; Circ 29,000
Library Holdings: DVDs 4,000; Bk Vols 8,000; Per Subs 31
Automation Activity & Vendor Info: (Cataloging) Follett Software; (Circulation) Follett Software
Partic in Central & Western Massachusetts Automated Resource Sharing
Open Mon & Wed 11-1 & 3-6, Tues & Thurs 3-7:30, Fri & Sun 3-6, Sat 10-1
Friends of the Library Group

SOMERSET

P SOMERSET PUBLIC LIBRARY, 1464 County St, 02726. SAN 345-5769. Tel: 508-646-2829. E-mail: somersetpl@sailsinc.org. Web Site: www.somersetpubliclibrary.org. *Libr Dir,* Joanne Nichting; E-mail: jnichting@sailsinc.org; *Ref Librn,* Marybeth Rua-Larsen; E-mail: mrua-larsen@sailsinc.org; *Circ Supvr,* Michelle Gagnon; E-mail: mgagnon@sailsinc.org; *Cataloger,* Susan Cordeiro; E-mail: scordeir@sailsinc.org; *Ch Serv,* Diane White; E-mail: dwhite@sailsinc.org
Founded 1897. Pop 18,165; Circ 140,745
Special Collections: Local History Coll
Automation Activity & Vendor Info: (Cataloging) SirsiDynix; (Circulation) SirsiDynix; (OPAC) SirsiDynix-Enterprise
Wireless access
Function: 24/7 Electronic res, 24/7 Online cat, Activity rm, Adult bk club, Archival coll, Audiobks via web, Bk club(s), Bks on CD, Chess club, Children's prog, Computer training, Computers for patron use, E-Readers, Electronic databases & coll, For res purposes, Free DVD rentals, Genealogy discussion group, ILL available, Internet access, Life-long learning prog for all ages, Magazines, Magnifiers for reading, Meeting rooms, Microfiche/film & reading machines, Movies, Museum passes, Music CDs, Online cat, Online info literacy tutorials on the web & in blackboard, Outside serv via phone, mail, e-mail & web, OverDrive digital audio bks, Photocopying/Printing, Printer for laptops & handheld devices, Prog for adults, Prog for children & young adult, Ref & res, Ref serv available, Res assist avail, Scanner, STEM programs, Story hour, Summer & winter reading prog, Summer reading prog, Tax forms, Teen prog, Telephone ref, Wheelchair accessible, Workshops, Writing prog
Partic in SAILS Library Network
Special Services for the Blind - Aids for in-house use
Open Mon 12-8, Tues & Wed 9-8, Thurs 9-5, Fri & Sat 9-3
Friends of the Library Group

SOMERVILLE

P SOMERVILLE PUBLIC LIBRARY*, 79 Highland Ave, 02143. SAN 345-5882. Tel: 617-623-5000. Circulation Tel: 617-623-5000, Ext 2900. Reference Tel: 617-623-5000, Ext 2955. FAX: 617-628-4052. Web Site: www.somervillepubliclibrary.org. *Dir,* Cathy Piantigini; Tel: 617-623-5000, Ext 2910, E-mail: cpiantigini@somervillema.gov; *Head, Ref,* Kevin O'Kelly; E-mail: kokelly@minlib.net; Staff 36 (MLS 18, Non-MLS 18)
Founded 1873. Pop 78,385; Circ 383,006
Library Holdings: AV Mats 14,846; Electronic Media & Resources 237; Bk Vols 217,286; Per Subs 819
Special Collections: New England & Somerville History Coll. Oral History
Subject Interests: Art, Genealogy, Travel, Women's studies
Automation Activity & Vendor Info: (Acquisitions) Innovative Interfaces, Inc; (Cataloging) Innovative Interfaces, Inc; (Circulation) Innovative Interfaces, Inc; (OPAC) Innovative Interfaces, Inc
Wireless access
Function: AV serv, Homebound delivery serv, ILL available
Mem of Massachusetts Library System
Partic in Minuteman Library Network
Open Mon-Thurs 9-9, Fri 9-6, Sat 9-5, Sun 1-5
Friends of the Library Group
Branches: 2
EAST, 115 Broadway, 02145, SAN 345-5912. Tel: 617-623-5000, Ext 2970. FAX: 617-623-9403. *Mgr,* Marita Coombs; Staff 3 (MLS 2, Non-MLS 1)
Founded 1918. Circ 25,919
Library Holdings: Bk Vols 17,207
Open Mon & Thurs 10-9, Tues 2-6, Wed & Fri 10-6
Friends of the Library Group
WEST, 40 College Ave, 02144, SAN 345-5947. Tel: 617-623-5000, Ext 2975. *Mgr,* Karen Kramer; E-mail: kkramer@minlib.net; Staff 3.4 (MLS 1.4, Non-MLS 2)
Founded 1909. Circ 75,450
Function: Adult bk club, Audiobks via web, Bks on cassette, Bks on CD, Children's prog, Computers for patron use, Electronic databases & coll, Free DVD rentals, ILL available, Museum passes, Music CDs, Online cat, Photocopying/Printing, Prog for adults, Ref serv available, Story hour, Summer reading prog, Tax forms, VHS videos
Open Mon & Thurs 10-9, Tues & Wed 9-6, Fri 2-6
Friends of the Library Group

SOUTH CHATHAM

P SOUTH CHATHAM PUBLIC LIBRARY*, 2559 Main St, 02659. (Mail add: PO Box 218, 02659-0218), SAN 307-6725. Tel: 508-430-7989. *Head Librn,* Elayne Perlstein; E-mail: elfrperl@prodigy.net
Founded 1874. Pop 5,000
Library Holdings: Bk Vols 4,500
Open Tues & Fri 1-4 (1-4:30 Summer)

SOUTH DEERFIELD

P TILTON LIBRARY, 75 N Main St, 01373. SAN 345-1860. Tel: 413-665-4683. FAX: 413-665-9118. E-mail: tiltonlibrary@cwmars.org. Web Site: www.tiltonlibrary.org. *Dir,* Candace Bradbury-Carlin; E-mail: cbradbury-carlin@cwmars.org; *Ch,* Julie Cavacco; E-mail: jcavacco@cwmars.org; Staff 1 (MLS 1)
Founded 1916. Pop 5,089; Circ 50,987

Library Holdings: Audiobooks 1,173; DVDs 1,851; e-books 174,052; e-journals 131; Bk Titles 17,537; Per Subs 79
Automation Activity & Vendor Info: (Cataloging) Evergreen; (Circulation) Evergreen; (OPAC) Evergreen
Wireless access
Function: 24/7 Electronic res, Adult bk club, Art exhibits, Audiobks via web, Children's prog, Computers for patron use, E-Readers, Electronic databases & coll, Free DVD rentals, Homebound delivery serv, ILL available, Magazines, Mail & tel request accepted, Museum passes, Music CDs, Online cat, OverDrive digital audio bks, Photocopying/Printing, Preschool outreach, Preschool reading prog, Prog for adults, Prog for children & young adult, Ref serv available, Serves people with intellectual disabilities, Story hour, Summer reading prog, Tax forms, Telephone ref, Wheelchair accessible, Workshops
Partic in Central & Western Massachusetts Automated Resource Sharing
Open Mon, Wed & Sat 11-4, Tues 1-5, Thurs 1-7
Friends of the Library Group

SOUTH DENNIS

P SOUTH DENNIS FREE PUBLIC LIBRARY*, 389 Main St, 02660. (Mail add: PO Box 304, 02660), SAN 307-6733. Tel: 508-394-8954. FAX: 508-394-4392. Web Site: www.southdennislibrary.org. *Libr Dir,* Veronica Hernandez; E-mail: vhernandez@clamsnet.org; Staff 2 (MLS 1, Non-MLS 1)
Founded 1900
Library Holdings: AV Mats 400; Large Print Bks 100; Bk Titles 6,365; Per Subs 14
Wireless access
Mem of Massachusetts Library System
Partic in Cape Libraries Automated Materials Sharing Network
Open Mon-Wed 10-4, Sat 10-12
Friends of the Library Group

SOUTH EGREMONT

P EGREMONT FREE LIBRARY*, One Buttonball Lane, 01258. (Mail add: PO Box 246, 01258-0246), SAN 307-6741. Tel: 413-528-1474. FAX: 413-528-6416. E-mail: EGRLibrary@egremont-ma.gov. Web Site: www.egremont-ma.gov/library.html. *Librn,* Lesliann Furcht
Founded 1882. Pop 1,200; Circ 6,530
Library Holdings: Large Print Bks 100; Bk Vols 9,204; Per Subs 30; Talking Bks 131
Automation Activity & Vendor Info: (Cataloging) Evergreen; (Circulation) Evergreen; (OPAC) Evergreen
Wireless access
Partic in Central & Western Massachusetts Automated Resource Sharing
Open Mon, Tues & Thurs 2-6, Sat 9-12
Friends of the Library Group

SOUTH HADLEY

C MOUNT HOLYOKE COLLEGE LIBRARY*, Library, Information & Technology Services, 50 College St, 01075. SAN 307-675X. Tel: 413-538-2225. Circulation Tel: 413-538-2230. Interlibrary Loan Service Tel: 413-538-2423. Reference Tel: 413-538-2212. FAX: 413-538-2370. Web Site: www.mtholyoke.edu/lits. *Chief Info Officer, Exec Dir,* Alex R Wirth-Cauchon, PhD; E-mail: awirthca@mtholyoke.edu; *Dir, Discovery & Access,* Erin Stalberg; Tel: 413-538-2228, E-mail: estalber@mtholyoke.edu; *Head, Archives & Spec Coll,* Leslie Fields; Tel: 413-538-2441, E-mail: lfields@mtholyoke.edu; *Coll Develop,* Kathleen Norton; Tel: 413-538-2158, E-mail: knorton@mtholyoke.edu; Staff 21 (MLS 16, Non-MLS 5)
Founded 1837. Enrl 2,100; Fac 200; Highest Degree: Master
Library Holdings: AV Mats 7,206; e-books 4,598; e-journals 1,536; Bk Titles 477,668; Bk Vols 721,223; Per Subs 3,805
Special Collections: Alumnae Letters & Diaries; Faculty Papers; Illustrated Editions of Dante's Divine Comedy (Giamatti Dante Coll); Women's Education 1920
Subject Interests: Econ, Feminism, Hist, Natural sci
Automation Activity & Vendor Info: (Acquisitions) Ex Libris Group; (Cataloging) Ex Libris Group; (Circulation) Ex Libris Group; (Course Reserve) Ex Libris Group; (Media Booking) Ex Libris Group; (OPAC) Ex Libris Group; (Serials) Ex Libris Group
Wireless access
Function: Computers for patron use
Restriction: Open to pub for ref & circ; with some limitations, Open to students, fac & staff, Pub use on premises

P SOUTH HADLEY PUBLIC LIBRARY, Two Canal St, 01075. SAN 345-6064. Tel: 413-538-5045. FAX: 413-539-9250. Web Site: www.shadleylib.org. *Dir,* Joseph Rodio; E-mail: jrodio@cwmars.org; *Head, Circ,* Rena Stromgren; E-mail: rstromgren@cwmars.org; *Br Librn,* Amber Ladley; E-mail: aladley@cwmars.org; *Ref & Ad Serv Librn,* Desiree Smelcer; E-mail: dsmelcer@cwmars.org; *Teen Prog Coordr,* Bethany Roberts; E-mail: broberts@cwmars.org; *Youth Serv,* Meg Clancy; E-mail: mclancy@cwmars.org; Staff 10.5 (MLS 5, Non-MLS 5.5)
Founded 1897. Pop 17,000; Circ 194,000
Jul 2020-Jun 2021 Income $768,944. Mats Exp $95,000. Sal $516,819
Subject Interests: Local hist
Automation Activity & Vendor Info: (Circulation) Evergreen; (ILL) Evergreen; (OPAC) Evergreen
Wireless access
Function: 24/7 Electronic res, 24/7 Online cat, Adult bk club, Archival coll, Art exhibits, Audio & video playback equip for onsite use, Audiobks on Playaways & MP3, Audiobks via web, Bi-weekly Writer's Group, Bk club(s), Bks on CD, Children's prog, Computers for patron use, Electronic databases & coll, Free DVD rentals, ILL available, Internet access, Life-long learning prog for all ages, Magazines, Meeting rooms, Museum passes, Online cat, OverDrive digital audio bks, Photocopying/Printing, Preschool reading prog, Prog for adults, Prog for children & young adult, Ref serv available, Story hour, Study rm, Summer reading prog, Tax forms, Teen prog, Wheelchair accessible
Mem of Massachusetts Library System
Partic in Central & Western Massachusetts Automated Resource Sharing
Open Mon-Wed 9:30-8, Thurs & Fri 9:30-6, Sat 9:30-1
Friends of the Library Group
Branches: 1
GAYLORD MEMORIAL LIBRARY, 47 College St, 01075. Tel: 413-538-5047. Web Site: gaylordlibrary.org. *Libr Dir,* Joe Rodio; E-mail: jrodio@cwmars.org; *Ad,* Amber Ladley; E-mail: aladley@cwmars.org; *Youth Serv Coordr,* Janet Shea; E-mail: jshea@cwmars.org
Founded 1904
Subject Interests: Local hist
Function: Homebound delivery serv, ILL available
Open Thurs 1-8, Fri 10-5, Sat 10-Noon
Friends of the Library Group

SOUTH HAMILTON

R GORDON-CONWELL THEOLOGICAL SEMINARY*, Burton L Goddard Library, 130 Essex St, 01982-2317. SAN 307-6776. Tel: 978-646-4074. Administration Tel: 978-646-4004. FAX: 978-646-4567. E-mail: glibrary@gcts.edu. Reference E-mail: reference@gcts.edu. Web Site: library.gordonconwell.edu/hamilton. *Dir,* James Darlack; E-mail: jdarlack@gcts.edu; *Asst Librn, Pub Serv, Asst Librn, Ref,* Robert McFadden; E-mail: rmcfadden@gcts.edu; *Acq, Asst Librn, Tech Support,* Pamela Gore; Tel: 978-646-4078, E-mail: pgore@gcts.edu; *Access Serv, Libr Asst,* Elizabeth Coffey. Subject Specialists: *Biblical studies,* James Darlack; Staff 7 (MLS 5, Non-MLS 2)
Founded 1970. Highest Degree: Doctorate
Library Holdings: CDs 400; Electronic Media & Resources 250; Bk Vols 174,090; Per Subs 700; Videos 1,694
Special Collections: Assyro-Babylonian (Mercer Coll); Aston Coll-Judaism, Christianity 1615-1691 (Richard Babson Coll); John Bunyan Coll; Millerite-Adventual Coll; Rare Bibles (Babson Coll); Washburn Baptist Coll
Automation Activity & Vendor Info: (Acquisitions) OCLC Worldshare Management Services; (Cataloging) OCLC Worldshare Management Services; (Circulation) OCLC Worldshare Management Services; (Course Reserve) OCLC; (Discovery) OCLC Worldshare Management Services; (ILL) OCLC; (OPAC) OCLC; (Serials) OCLC
Wireless access
Function: Audio & video playback equip for onsite use, AV serv, CD-ROM, Computers for patron use, Distance learning, Doc delivery serv, Electronic databases & coll, Free DVD rentals, ILL available, Internet access, Mail loans to mem, Microfiche/film & reading machines, Music CDs, Online cat, Online ref, Orientations, Photocopying/Printing, Printer for laptops & handheld devices, Prof lending libr, Ref & res, Ref serv available, Res libr, Satellite serv, Scanner, Spoken cassettes & CDs, Telephone ref, VHS videos, Wheelchair accessible
Partic in Christian Library Consortium
Open Mon-Thurs 7:45am-11pm, Fri 7:45-5, Sat 9-9
Restriction: Non-circulating of rare bks, Non-resident fee, Open to pub for ref & circ; with some limitations, Open to students, fac, staff & alumni

P HAMILTON-WENHAM PUBLIC LIBRARY*, 14 Union St, 01982. SAN 307-7691. Tel: 978-468-5577. FAX: 978-468-5535. E-mail: info@hwlibrary.org. Web Site: hwlibrary.org. *Libr Dir,* Kim Butler; Tel: 978-468-5577, Ext 21, E-mail: kbutler@hwlibrary.org; *Asst Dir,* Rob Pondelli; Tel: 978-468-5577, Ext 16, E-mail: rpondelli@hwlibrary.org; *Head, Circ, Head, Reader Serv,* Amy Dziewit; Tel: 978-468-5577, Ext 10, E-mail: adziewit@hwlibrary.org; *Head, Ref,* Sarah Lauderdale; Tel: 978-468-5577, Ext 19, E-mail: slauderdale@hwlibrary.org; *Head, Tech Serv,* Lewis Parsons; Tel: 978-468-5577, Ext 23, E-mail: lparsons@mvlc.org; *Ch,* Lorraine Der; Tel: 978-468-5577, Ext 13, E-mail: lder@mvlc.org; Staff 13 (MLS 1, Non-MLS 12)
Founded 2001. Pop 12,390; Circ 150,000
Library Holdings: Large Print Bks 8,000; Bk Vols 84,750; Per Subs 161
Subject Interests: Genealogy, Local hist

Automation Activity & Vendor Info: (Circulation) SirsiDynix
Wireless access
Mem of Massachusetts Library System
Partic in Merrimack Valley Library Consortium
Open Mon-Thurs 10-8, Fri 10-5, Sat 10-4
Friends of the Library Group

SOUTH WALPOLE

S MASSACHUSETTS DEPARTMENT OF CORRECTIONS*, Institution Library at MCI Cedar Junction, PO Box 100, 02071-0100. SAN 307-7330. Tel: 508-668-2100, Ext 161.
Founded 1956
Library Holdings: Bk Titles 4,300; Bk Vols 10,000
Special Collections: Law Library Coll

SOUTH WEYMOUTH

M SOUTH SHORE HOSPITAL*, Medical Library, 55 Fogg Rd, 02190. Tel: 781-340-8000, 781-624-8528. FAX: 781-331-0834. E-mail: lrmedlibrary@gmail.com. Web Site: www.southshorehospital.org. *Librn,* Laurie Regan; E-mail: laurie_regan@sshosp.org
Library Holdings: Bk Titles 500; Per Subs 135
Automation Activity & Vendor Info: (Cataloging) Auto-Graphics, Inc
Restriction: Med staff only

SOUTH YARMOUTH

P YARMOUTH TOWN LIBRARIES*, 312 Old Main St, 02664. SAN 307-8450. Tel: 508-760-4820. Circulation Tel: 508-760-4820, Ext 1313. Administration Tel: 508-760-4820, Ext 1312. Web Site: www.yarmouth.ma.us/818/Town-Libraries. *Libr Dir,* Jane Cain; E-mail: jcain@yarmouth.ma.us; *Dir of Circ,* Mitzi Krueger; Staff 10 (MLS 2, Non-MLS 8)
Founded 1866. Pop 23,793; Circ 263,776
Library Holdings: CDs 3,466; DVDs 6,170; Electronic Media & Resources 612; Bk Vols 88,000; Per Subs 337
Automation Activity & Vendor Info: (Acquisitions) Innovative Interfaces, Inc; (Cataloging) Innovative Interfaces, Inc; (Circulation) Innovative Interfaces, Inc; (OPAC) Innovative Interfaces, Inc; (Serials) Innovative Interfaces, Inc
Wireless access
Partic in Cape Libraries Automated Materials Sharing Network
Friends of the Library Group
Branches: 2
SOUTH YARMOUTH BRANCH, 312 Old Main St, 02664, SAN 307-6822. Tel: 508-760-4820. FAX: 508-760-2699.
Founded 1866
Library Holdings: Audiobooks 3,305; AV Mats 535; e-books 24,904; Bk Titles 52,377; Per Subs 337; Talking Bks 1,831; Videos 6,580
Special Collections: Joseph C Lincoln Coll
Subject Interests: Hist
Open Mon & Wed 10-8, Tues, Thurs & Fri 10-5, Sat 10-4, Sun (Sept-May) 12-4
Friends of the Library Group
WEST YARMOUTH BRANCH, 391 Main St, Rte 28, West Yarmouth, 02673, SAN 307-7853. Tel: 508-775-5206.
Founded 1891
Open Mon, Wed & Fri 11-4, Tues & Thurs 3-8, Sat (July-Sept) 11-4
Friends of the Library Group

SOUTHAMPTON

P EDWARDS PUBLIC LIBRARY*, 30 East St, 01073. SAN 307-6830. Tel: 413-527-9480. FAX: 413-527-9480. E-mail: edwards@cwmars.org. Web Site: www.southamptonlibrary.org. *Dir,* Barbara Goldin; E-mail: bgoldin@cwmars.org; *Ch Serv,* Johanna Douglass; E-mail: jdouglass@cwmars.org; *Circ,* Lisa Shea; *Tech Serv,* Carol Goulet; E-mail: cgoulet@cwmars.org; Staff 1 (MLS 1)
Founded 1904. Pop 5,736; Circ 33,044
Library Holdings: AV Mats 2,188; e-books 796; Bk Titles 30,026; Per Subs 49
Special Collections: Local History Coll; Vocal Music Coll
Automation Activity & Vendor Info: (Cataloging) Innovative Interfaces, Inc; (Circulation) Innovative Interfaces, Inc; (OPAC) Innovative Interfaces, Inc
Wireless access
Partic in Central & Western Massachusetts Automated Resource Sharing
Open Mon & Wed 10-4, Tues & Thurs 10-8, Fri 1-4, Sat 10-1
Friends of the Library Group

SOUTHBOROUGH

P SOUTHBOROUGH PUBLIC LIBRARY*, 25 Main St, 01772. SAN 307-6849. Tel: 508-485-5031. FAX: 508-229-4451. Web Site: www.southboroughlib.org. *Libr Dir,* Ryan Donovan; E-mail: rdonovan@southboroughma.com; *Sr Librn,* Patricia Ellis; *Sr Librn,* Heidi Lindsey; *Ch Serv,* Kimberley Ivers; E-mail: kivers@southboroughma.com
Founded 1852. Pop 6,326; Circ 76,156
Library Holdings: Bk Vols 63,000; Per Subs 100
Automation Activity & Vendor Info: (Cataloging) Innovative Interfaces, Inc; (Circulation) Innovative Interfaces, Inc; (OPAC) Innovative Interfaces, Inc
Wireless access
Mem of Massachusetts Library System
Partic in Central & Western Massachusetts Automated Resource Sharing
Open Mon, Fri & Sat 10-5, Tues-Thurs 10-9
Friends of the Library Group

SOUTHBRIDGE

P JACOB EDWARDS LIBRARY*, 236 Main St, 01550-2598. SAN 307-6865. Tel: 508-764-5426. Interlibrary Loan Service Tel: 508-764-5426, Ext 103. Reference Tel: 508-764-5426, Ext 105. Administration Tel: 508-764-5426, Ext 101. FAX: 508-764-5428. Web Site: www.jacobedwardslibrary.org. *Libr Dir,* Margaret Morrissey; Tel: 508-764-5426, Ext 101, E-mail: mmorriss@cwmars.org; *Ad,* Stephanie Cyr; E-mail: scyr@cwmars.org; *Ch,* Elizabeth Gendreau; Tel: 508-764-5427, E-mail: egendrea@cwmars.org; *Circ Librn,* Debrah Gendreau; Tel: 508-764-5426, Ext 103, E-mail: dgendreau@cwmars.org; Staff 3 (MLS 2, Non-MLS 1)
Founded 1914. Pop 16,793; Circ 76,667
Jul 2015-Jun 2016 Income $537,796, Locally Generated Income $2,304. Mats Exp $82,077, Books $48,556, Per/Ser (Incl. Access Fees) $5,494, Other Print Mats $3,307, AV Mat $18,036, Electronic Ref Mat (Incl. Access Fees) $6,684. Sal $357,568 (Prof $147,937)
Library Holdings: Audiobooks 4,217; DVDs 3,972; e-books 30,858; Electronic Media & Resources 229; Microforms 504; Bk Vols 78,303; Per Subs 114
Special Collections: Local Newspaper (Southbridge Evening News 1923 to present, micro) & earlier local titles too
Subject Interests: Local hist
Automation Activity & Vendor Info: (Cataloging) Evergreen; (Circulation) Evergreen; (OPAC) Evergreen
Wireless access
Function: 24/7 Electronic res, 24/7 Online cat, Activity rm, Adult bk club, Adult literacy prog, Archival coll, Art exhibits, Audiobks on Playaways & MP3, Audiobks via web, Bilingual assistance for Spanish patrons, Bks on CD, Children's prog, Citizenship assistance, Computer training, Computers for patron use, Doc delivery serv, Electronic databases & coll, ILL available, Magnifiers for reading, Mango lang, Meeting rooms, Microfiche/film & reading machines, Movies, Museum passes, Music CDs, Photocopying/Printing, Preschool reading prog, Prog for adults, Prog for children & young adult, Ref serv available, Spanish lang bks, Story hour, Tax forms, Wheelchair accessible
Publications: eNewsletter (Monthly)
Mem of Massachusetts Library System
Partic in Central & Western Massachusetts Automated Resource Sharing
Open Mon & Thurs 9-8, Tues, Wed & Fri 9-5, Sat (Sept-May) 9-1
Friends of the Library Group

SOUTHWICK

P SOUTHWICK PUBLIC LIBRARY*, 95 Feeding Hills Rd, 01077-9683. SAN 307-6881. Tel: 413-569-1221. FAX: 413-569-0440. E-mail: southwicklibrary@comcast.net. Web Site: www.southwicklibrary.com. *Dir,* Lynn Blair; E-mail: lynngblair@comcast.net; Staff 5 (Non-MLS 5)
Founded 1892. Pop 8,835; Circ 9,686
Library Holdings: Bk Titles 45,806
Wireless access
Publications: Links (Newsletter)
Partic in Central & Western Massachusetts Automated Resource Sharing
Special Services for the Blind - Talking bks
Open Mon & Tues 10-8, Wed 1-8, Thurs & Fri 10-5, Sat 10-1
Friends of the Library Group

SPENCER

SR SAINT JOSEPH'S ABBEY*, Monastic Library, 167 N Spencer Rd, 01562-1233. SAN 328-1302. Tel: 508-885-8700, Ext 521. FAX: 508-885-8701. *Adminr,* Timothy Scott; E-mail: timothy@spencerabbey.org
Library Holdings: Bk Titles 45,000; Per Subs 25
Automation Activity & Vendor Info: (Acquisitions) L4U Library Software; (Cataloging) L4U Library Software; (Circulation) L4U Library Software; (OPAC) L4U Library Software; (Serials) L4U Library Software

P RICHARD SUGDEN LIBRARY*, Eight Pleasant St, 01562. SAN 307-689X. Tel: 508-885-7513. FAX: 508-885-7523. Web Site: www.spencerpubliclibrary.org. *Dir,* Cheryl Donahue; E-mail: cdonahue@cwmars.org
Pop 11,500; Circ 60,000

Library Holdings: Audiobooks 1,600; CDs 1,600; DVDs 4,000; e-books 47,000; Bk Titles 42,000; Bk Vols 54,600; Per Subs 100
Special Collections: Historical Materials of Spencer & Massachusetts
Automation Activity & Vendor Info: (Cataloging) Evergreen; (Circulation) Evergreen; (ILL) Evergreen; (OPAC) Evergreen
Wireless access
Mem of Massachusetts Library System
Partic in Central & Western Massachusetts Automated Resource Sharing
Open Mon & Thurs 10-7, Tues & Wed 10-5
Friends of the Library Group

SPRINGFIELD

C AMERICAN INTERNATIONAL COLLEGE*, James J Shea Sr Memorial Library, 1000 State St, 01109. SAN 307-6903. Tel: 413-205-3225. Reference Tel: 413-205-3206. FAX: 413-205-3904. Web Site: www.aic.edu/library. *Dir, Libr Serv,* Heidi Spencer; Tel: 413-205-3461, E-mail: estelle.spencer@aic.edu; *Head, Circ,* Amy Schack; *Day Circ Supvr,* Michael Forrest; *Evening Circ,* Robert Taskey; *Info Literacy,* Ronald Breggia; *Info Literacy,* Nancy Little; *Info Literacy,* Katie Beth Ryan; *Circ,* Christopher Laudani; *Tech Serv,* Martin Cleaver. Subject Specialists: *Bus,* Ronald Breggia; *Health sci,* Nancy Little; *Educ,* Katie Beth Ryan; Staff 8.5 (MLS 5, Non-MLS 3.5)
Founded 1885. Enrl 3,400; Fac 120; Highest Degree: Doctorate
Library Holdings: DVDs 24; e-books 174,160; e-journals 962; Bk Titles 47,574; Bk Vols 56,511; Per Subs 195
Special Collections: Oral History
Automation Activity & Vendor Info: (Cataloging) Evergreen; (Circulation) Evergreen; (Course Reserve) Evergreen; (ILL) OCLC WorldShare Interlibrary Loan; (OPAC) Evergreen; (Serials) Evergreen
Wireless access
Mem of Massachusetts Library System
Partic in Central & Western Massachusetts Automated Resource Sharing; Cooperating Libraries of Greater Springfield
Open Mon-Thurs 7:45am-Midnight, Fri 7:45-7, Sat 10-6, Sun 10am-Midnight

M BAYSTATE MEDICAL CENTER*, Health Sciences Library, 759 Chestnut St, 01199. SAN 345-6153. Tel: 413-794-1865. FAX: 413-794-1974. E-mail: library@bhs.org. Web Site: libraryinfo.bhs.org. *Dir,* Ellen Brassil; Tel: 413-794-1866, E-mail: ellen.brassil@baystatehealth.org; Staff 8 (MLS 4, Non-MLS 4)
Library Holdings: Bk Titles 10,700; Per Subs 500
Subject Interests: Anesthesiology, Cardiology, Hist of med, Lit, Med, Nursing, Obstetrics & gynecology, Oncology, Orthopedics, Pediatrics, Surgery
Wireless access
Publications: What's New (Quarterly)
Open Mon-Fri 7-5

GL MASSACHUSETTS TRIAL COURT*, Hampden Law Library, 50 State St, 01103-2021. (Mail add: PO Box 559, 01102-0559), SAN 307-692X. Tel: 413-748-7923. FAX: 413-734-2973. E-mail: hampdenlawlibrary@yahoo.com. Web Site: www.mass.gov/courts/case-legal-res/law-lib/libraries/locations/hampden.html. *Head Librn,* Nicholas Wolowitz; Staff 5 (MLS 2, Non-MLS 3)
Founded 1890
Library Holdings: Bk Vols 61,489; Per Subs 389
Special Collections: Massachusetts Law
Subject Interests: Fed law
Partic in Cooperating Libraries of Greater Springfield; LYRASIS; OCLC Online Computer Library Center, Inc
Open Mon-Fri 8-4
Friends of the Library Group

S NAISMITH MEMORIAL BASKETBALL HALL OF FAME*, Edward J & Gena G Hickox Library, 1000 Hall of Fame Ave, 01105. SAN 307-6954. Tel: 413-781-6500. FAX: 413-781-1939. Web Site: www.hoophall.com. *Curator,* Matt Zeysing
Founded 1968
Library Holdings: Bk Titles 2,300; Per Subs 23
Special Collections: Basketball (William G Mokray Coll); Complete Set of Basketball Rule Books (Spalding Coll)
Restriction: Open by appt only

P SPRINGFIELD CITY LIBRARY*, Central Branch, 220 State St, 01103. SAN 345-6218. Tel: 413-263-6828. Circulation Tel: 413-263-6828, Ext 218. Interlibrary Loan Service Tel: 413-263-6828, Ext 200. Reference Tel: 413-263-6828, Ext 213. FAX: 413-263-6817. TDD: 413-263-6835. Web Site: www.springfieldlibrary.org. *Dir,* Molly Fogarty; Tel: 413-263-6828, Ext 290, Fax: 413-263-6825, E-mail: lfogarty@springfieldlibrary.org; *Asst Dir, Pub Serv,* Jean Canosa-Albano; Tel: 413-263-6828, Ext 291, E-mail: jcanosa@springfieldlibrary.org; *Mgr, Borrower Serv,* Patti D'Amario; Tel: 413-263-6828, Ext 220; *Mgr, Info Serv,* Mary Frederick; Tel: 413-263-6828, Ext 202; *Prog Coordr,* Matthew Jaquith; Tel: 413-263-6828, Ext 221, E-mail: mjaquith@springfieldlibrary.org; Staff 65.5 (MLS 25.5, Non-MLS 40)
Founded 1857. Pop 150,000; Circ 569,199
Library Holdings: Electronic Media & Resources 3,980; Bk Vols 645,944; Talking Bks 3,549; Videos 34,456
Special Collections: American Wood Engravings (Aston Coll); Economics (David A Wells Coll); Holacaust Coll. US Document Depository
Automation Activity & Vendor Info: (Acquisitions) Evergreen; (Cataloging) Evergreen; (Circulation) Innovative Interfaces, Inc
Wireless access
Partic in Central & Western Massachusetts Automated Resource Sharing
Special Services for the Deaf - Bks on deafness & sign lang; Captioned film dep; High interest/low vocabulary bks; Spec interest per; TDD equip
Open Mon, Tues & Thurs-Sat 9-5, Wed 10-6, Sun (Nov-Dec) 12-5
Friends of the Library Group
Branches: 8
BRIGHTWOOD BRANCH, 359 Plainfield St, 01107, SAN 345-6242. Tel: 413-263-6805. FAX: 413-263-6810. *Mgr,* David Meeks; *Supvr,* Haydee Hodis; E-mail: hhodis@springfieldlibrary.org
Library Holdings: Bk Vols 51,039
Open Mon, Tues, Thurs & Fri 9-5, Wed 10-6
Friends of the Library Group
EAST FOREST PARK BRANCH, 136 Surrey Rd, 01118. Tel: 413-263-6836. FAX: 413-263-6838. *Mgr,* Grace Larochelle; E-mail: glarochelle@springfieldlibrary.org; *Asst Mgr,* Maeleah Gorman
Library Holdings: Bk Vols 40,070
Open Mon, Tues, Thurs & Fri 9-5, Wed 10-6, Sat 9-3
Friends of the Library Group
EAST SPRINGFIELD BRANCH, 21 Osborne Terrace, 01104, SAN 345-6277. Tel: 413-263-6840. FAX: 413-263-6842. *Mgr,* Reggie Wilson; *Supvr,* Lee Moonan
Library Holdings: Bk Vols 29,833
Open Mon, Tues, Thurs & Fri 9-5, Wed 10-6, Sat 9-3
Friends of the Library Group
FOREST PARK BRANCH, 380 Belmont Ave, 01108, SAN 345-6307. Tel: 413-263-6843. *Mgr,* Grace Larochelle; E-mail: glarochelle@springfieldlibrary.org
Library Holdings: Bk Vols 68,035
Open Mon, Tues, Thurs & Fri 9-5, Wed 10-6, Sat 9-3
Friends of the Library Group
INDIAN ORCHARD BRANCH, 44 Oak St, Indian Orchard, 01151, SAN 345-6331. Tel: 413-263-6846. *Mgr,* David Meeks; *Supvr,* Peggy Dialysis
Library Holdings: Bk Vols 40,515
Open Mon, Tues, Thurs & Fri 9-5, Wed 10-6, Sat 9-3
Friends of the Library Group
LIBRARY EXPRESS AT PINE POINT, 204 Boston Post Rd, 01109, SAN 345-6390. Tel: 413-263-6855. *Mgr,* David Meeks
Library Holdings: Bk Vols 62,279
Open Mon & Fri 9-5, Wed 10-6
Friends of the Library Group
MASON SQUARE BRANCH, 765 State St, 01109, SAN 345-6455. Tel: 413-263-6853. *Mgr,* Diane Houle; *Supvr,* Sara Deignan
Library Holdings: Bk Vols 35,570
Open Mon, Tues, Thurs & Fri 9-5, Wed 10-6, Sat 9-3
Friends of the Library Group
SIXTEEN ACRES BRANCH, 1187 Parker St, 01129, SAN 345-6420. Tel: 413-263-6858. *Mgr,* Reggie Wilson; *Supvr,* Lori Chasen
Founded 1966
Library Holdings: Bk Vols 71,291
Open Mon, Tues, Thurs & Fri 9-5, Wed 10-6, Sat 9-3
Friends of the Library Group

C SPRINGFIELD COLLEGE, Library Services, 263 Alden St, 01109-3797. SAN 307-6997. Tel: 413-748-3315. Interlibrary Loan Service Tel: 413-748-3559. Administration Tel: 413-748-3308. Web Site: www.springfield.edu/library. *Dir,* Andrea S Taupier; E-mail: ataupier@springfieldcollege.edu; *Asst Dir, Coll,* Patrick Hartsfield; Tel: 413-748-3360, E-mail: jhartsfield@springfield.edu; *Asst Dir, Res,* John Brady; Tel: 413-748-3505, E-mail: jbrady2@springfield.edu; *ILL,* Lynn Martin; E-mail: lmartin@springfield.edu; Staff 16 (MLS 9, Non-MLS 7)
Founded 1885. Enrl 3,900; Fac 200; Highest Degree: Doctorate
Automation Activity & Vendor Info: (Acquisitions) OCLC Worldshare Management Services; (Cataloging) OCLC Worldshare Management Services; (Circulation) OCLC Worldshare Management Services; (Discovery) OCLC Worldshare Management Services; (ILL) OCLC Tipasa; (OPAC) OCLC Worldshare Management Services; (Serials) OCLC Worldshare Management Services
Wireless access
Open Mon-Thurs & Sun 8am-Midnight, Fri & Sat 8am-9pm

J SPRINGFIELD TECHNICAL COMMUNITY COLLEGE LIBRARY*, One Armory Sq, Bldg 27, Ste 1, 01105. (Mail add: PO Box 9000, 01102-9000), SAN 307-7012. Tel: 413-755-4532, 413-755-4845. Reference Tel: 413-755-4549. FAX: 413-755-6315. E-mail: stcclibrary@stcc.edu. Web

Site: libguides.stcc.edu. *Dean, Libr Serv,* Erica Eynouf; Tel: 413-755-4064, E-mail: eweynouf@stcc.edu; *Ref & Coll Develop Librn,* Marko Packard; Tel: 413-755-4565, E-mail: mpackard@stcc.edu; *Syst Librn,* Dan Paquette; Tel: 413-755-4550, E-mail: djpaquette@stcc.edu; *Mgr, Access Serv, Mgr, Circ Serv,* Kim Noel; Tel: 413-755-4564, E-mail: knoel@stcc.edu; *Coordr, Instruction & Ref,* Eric Warren; Tel: 413-755-4555, E-mail: ewarren@stcc.edu; Staff 6.5 (MLS 6.5)
Founded 1969. Enrl 4,400; Fac 255; Highest Degree: Associate
Jul 2014-Jun 2015. Mats Exp $103,317, Books $18,558, Per/Ser (Incl. Access Fees) $22,115, AV Mat $1,800, Electronic Ref Mat (Incl. Access Fees) $60,444, Presv $400. Sal $628,101 (Prof $441,173)
Library Holdings: AV Mats 9,435; e-books 36,588; Electronic Media & Resources 93; Bk Vols 53,000; Per Subs 209
Subject Interests: Allied health, Dental hygiene, Med, Nursing
Automation Activity & Vendor Info: (Acquisitions) Evergreen; (Cataloging) OCLC Connexion; (Circulation) Evergreen; (Course Reserve) Evergreen; (ILL) OCLC Online; (OPAC) Evergreen; (Serials) SerialsSolutions
Wireless access
Function: Art exhibits, Internet access, Magazines, Mango lang, Music CDs, Online cat, Online info literacy tutorials on the web & in blackboard, OverDrive digital audio bks, Photocopying/Printing, Ref serv available, Scanner, Study rm, Workshops
Publications: STCC Library Home Page
Mem of Massachusetts Library System
Partic in Cooperating Libraries of Greater Springfield; LYRASIS; Massachusetts Commonwealth Consortium of Libraries in Public Higher Education Institutions; OCLC Online Computer Library Center, Inc; Western Massachusetts Health Information Consortium
Open Mon-Thurs (Fall & Spring) 7:45-7:30, Fri 7:45-4, Sat 8:30-2

C WESTERN NEW ENGLAND UNIVERSITY*, D'Amour Library, 1215 Wilbraham Rd, 01119. SAN 345-648X. Tel: 413-782-1535. Interlibrary Loan Service Tel: 413-782-1654. Reference Tel: 413-782-1655. Administration Tel: 413-782-1532. Toll Free Tel: 800-325-1122, Ext 1535. FAX: 413-796-2011. Web Site: libraries.wne.edu. *Dir,* Priscilla L Perkins; E-mail: pperkins@wne.edu; *Head, Access Serv & Electronic Res,* Lindsay Roberts; E-mail: lindsay.roberts@wne.edu; *Head, Info Literacy & Instruction Serv,* Mary Jane Sobinski-Smith; Tel: 413-782-1533, E-mail: msobinsk@wne.edu; *Cat Librn,* Damian Biagi; Tel: 413-782-1635, E-mail: damian.biagi@wne.edu; *Coll Develop Librn, Ref Coordr,* Vicky Ludwig; Tel: 413-796-2265, E-mail: vludwig@wne.edu; *Health Sci Librn,* Michael Mannheim; Tel: 413-782-1534; *Info Literacy Librn,* Emily Porter-Fyke; Tel: 413-782-1537; *Archivist,* Tracey Kry; Tel: 413-782-1514, E-mail: theresa.kry@wne.edu; Staff 8 (MLS 8)
Founded 1951. Enrl 3,500; Fac 355; Highest Degree: Doctorate
Library Holdings: Audiobooks 247; CDs 3,207; DVDs 4,158; e-books 31,912; Electronic Media & Resources 10,228; Microforms 119,369; Bk Vols 106,438
Special Collections: Jennings Music Coll
Subject Interests: Arts, Bus, Criminal justice, Educ, Engr
Automation Activity & Vendor Info: (Acquisitions) Innovative Interfaces, Inc; (Cataloging) Innovative Interfaces, Inc; (Circulation) Innovative Interfaces, Inc; (Course Reserve) Innovative Interfaces, Inc; (Discovery) EBSCO Discovery Service; (ILL) OCLC; (OPAC) Innovative Interfaces, Inc; (Serials) Innovative Interfaces, Inc
Wireless access
Publications: Course Guides (Research guide); Subject Guides (Research guide)
Partic in Cooperating Libraries of Greater Springfield; LYRASIS; NELLCO Law Library Consortium, Inc.; OCLC Online Computer Library Center, Inc
Open Mon-Thurs 7:45am-Midnight, Fri 7:45am-8pm, Sat 9-5, Sun Noon-Midnight; Mon-Thurs (Summer) 8:30am-9pm, Fri 8:30-4, Sun Noon-6

CL WESTERN NEW ENGLAND UNIVERSITY*, School of Law Library, 1215 Wilbraham Rd, 01119-2689. SAN 345-651X. Tel: 413-782-1457. Web Site: www1.wne.edu/law/library. *Assoc Dean, Libr & Info Serv,* Pat Newcombe; Tel: 413-782-1616, E-mail: pnewcombe@law.wne.edu; *Assoc Dir,* Nicole Belbin; Tel: 413-782-1484, E-mail: nbelbin@law.wne.edu; *Cataloging & Metadata Librn,* Kathy Layer; Tel: 413-782-1309, E-mail: kathy.layer@law.wne.edu; *Res/Emerging Tech Librn,* Artie Berns; Tel: 413-782-1454, E-mail: artie.berns@law.wne.edu; Staff 8 (MLS 8)
Founded 1973. Enrl 517; Fac 35; Highest Degree: Doctorate
Special Collections: Government Documents; Massachusetts Continuing Legal Education Material
Subject Interests: Estate planning, Health law, Labor, Tax
Automation Activity & Vendor Info: (Acquisitions) Innovative Interfaces, Inc; (Cataloging) Innovative Interfaces, Inc; (Circulation) Innovative Interfaces, Inc; (Course Reserve) Innovative Interfaces, Inc; (ILL) OCLC WorldShare Interlibrary Loan; (Media Booking) Innovative Interfaces, Inc; (OPAC) Innovative Interfaces, Inc; (Serials) Innovative Interfaces, Inc
Wireless access
Publications: Cybercites; Library Guide (Library handbook); Research Guides & Pathfinders; Self Guided Tour

S LYMAN & MERRIE WOOD MUSEUM OF SPRINGFIELD HISTORY*, Genealogy & Local History Library, 21 Edwards St, 01103. SAN 307-6911. Tel: 413-263-6800, Ext 230. Web Site: springfieldmuseums.org/about/museum-of-springfield-history. *Pres,* Kay Simpson; E-mail: ksimpson@springfieldmuseums.org; *VPres,* Heather Haskell; E-mail: hhaskell@springfieldmuseums.org; *Curator, Archives & Libr,* Margaret Humberston; Tel: 413-314-6411, E-mail: mhumberston@springfieldmuseums.org; *Archivist,* Cliff McCarthy; Tel: 413-263-6800, Ext 308, E-mail: cmccarthy@springfieldmuseums.org; Staff 2 (MLS 1, Non-MLS 1)
Founded 1876
Library Holdings: Microforms 6,000; Bk Titles 24,000; Bk Vols 30,000; Per Subs 50
Subject Interests: Fr Can studies, Genealogy, Local hist, Massachusetts, New England genealogy
Function: Res libr
Mem of Massachusetts Library System
Open Tues-Fri 12-4
Restriction: Not a lending libr

STERLING

P CONANT PUBLIC LIBRARY, Four Meetinghouse Hill Rd, 01564. SAN 307-7039. Tel: 978-422-6409. FAX: 978-422-6643. Web Site: www.sterlinglibrary.org. *Dir,* Patricia Campbell; E-mail: pcampbell@cwmars.org; Staff 6 (MLS 3, Non-MLS 3)
Founded 1871. Pop 6,659
Library Holdings: Bk Titles 28,000; Per Subs 83
Automation Activity & Vendor Info: (Cataloging) Innovative Interfaces, Inc; (Circulation) Innovative Interfaces, Inc; (OPAC) Innovative Interfaces, Inc
Wireless access
Publications: Sterling Business Directory (Biennial); Sterling Factsheet: A Guide To Community Resources & Services (Irregular)
Mem of Massachusetts Library System
Partic in Central & Western Massachusetts Automated Resource Sharing
Open Mon-Thurs 10-8, Sat 10-3 (10-1 Summer)
Friends of the Library Group

STOCKBRIDGE

G BERKSHIRE BOTANICAL GARDEN LIBRARY, PO Box 826, 01262-0826. SAN 373-174X. Tel: 413-298-3926. FAX: 413-298-4897. Web Site: www.berkshirebotanical.org. *Dir of Educ,* Bridgette Stone; E-mail: bstone@berkshirebotanical.org
Library Holdings: Bk Vols 3,000; Per Subs 20
Restriction: Open to pub upon request

S NORMAN ROCKWELL MUSEUM, Archives & Library, Nine Rte 183, 01262. (Mail add: PO Box 308, 01262-0308), SAN 328-6177. Tel: 413-298-4100, 413-931-2251. FAX: 413-298-4145. Web Site: www.nrm.org/collections-2/archives-and-library. *Archivist,* Venus Van Ness; Tel: 413-298-4100, Ext 251, E-mail: venus@nrm.org
Founded 1969
Library Holdings: Bk Vols 1,337; Per Subs 7; Videos 270
Special Collections: American Illustration (Norman Rockwell Coll); The Norman Rockwell Archive
Wireless access
Function: Photocopying/Printing, Res assist avail
Mem of Massachusetts Library System
Restriction: Open by appt only

P STOCKBRIDGE LIBRARY ASSOCIATION*, 46 Main St, 01262. (Mail add: PO Box 119, 01262-0119), SAN 307-7055. Tel: 413-298-5501. FAX: 413-298-0218. E-mail: info@stockbridgelibrary.org. Web Site: stockbridgelibrary.org. *Libr Dir,* Wendy Pearson; E-mail: wpearson@cwmars.org
Founded 1868. Pop 2,312; Circ 59,441
Library Holdings: Bk Vols 27,000; Per Subs 70
Special Collections: Historical Coll
Partic in Central & Western Massachusetts Automated Resource Sharing
Open Tues & Fri 9-8, Wed & Thurs 9-5, Sat 9-2

STONEHAM

P STONEHAM PUBLIC LIBRARY*, 431 Main St, 02180. SAN 307-7063. Tel: 781-438-1324. FAX: 781-279-3836. E-mail: sto@noblenet.org. Web Site: stonehamlibrary.org. *Dir,* Nicole Langley; E-mail: langley@noblenet.org; *Asst Dir,* Mary Forkin; E-mail: forkin@noblenet.org; *Ref Librn,* Maureen Saltzman; E-mail: saltzman@noblenet.org; *Youth Serv Librn,* Janice L Chase; E-mail:

chase@noblenet.org; *Circ Supvr,* Deborah Cunningham; E-mail: dcunning@noblenet.org; Staff 6 (MLS 6)
Founded 1859. Pop 22,203; Circ 115,000
Library Holdings: Bk Titles 80,592; Per Subs 226
Special Collections: 18th-20th Century (Stoneham Coll), docs on micro. Oral History
Automation Activity & Vendor Info: (Acquisitions) Innovative Interfaces, Inc; (Cataloging) Innovative Interfaces, Inc; (Circulation) Innovative Interfaces, Inc; (Course Reserve) Innovative Interfaces, Inc; (ILL) Innovative Interfaces, Inc; (Media Booking) Innovative Interfaces, Inc; (OPAC) Innovative Interfaces, Inc; (Serials) Innovative Interfaces, Inc
Wireless access
Mem of Massachusetts Library System
Partic in North of Boston Library Exchange, Inc
Special Services for the Deaf - TTY equip
Open Mon, Tues & Thurs 10-9, Wed & Fri 10-5, Sat 10-2; Mon 1-9, Tues-Thurs 10-6, Fri 10-5, Sat 10-2
Friends of the Library Group

STOUGHTON

M NEW ENGLAND SINAI HOSPITAL & REHABILITATION CENTER*, Medical Library, 150 York St, 02072. SAN 377-9181. Tel: 781-344-0600. FAX: 781-344-0128. TDD: 781-341-2395. Web Site: www.newenglandsinai.org.
Library Holdings: Bk Vols 600; Per Subs 20
Wireless access
Partic in Basic Health Sciences Library Network; Massachusetts Health Sciences Library Network; North Atlantic Health Sciences Libraries, Inc; Southeastern Massachusetts Consortium of Health Science

P STOUGHTON PUBLIC LIBRARY, 84 Park St, 02072-2974. SAN 345-6544. Tel: 781-344-2711. FAX: 781-344-7340. E-mail: stlib@ocln.org. Web Site: www.stoughton.org/library-0. *Dir,* Patricia Basler; E-mail: pbasler@ocln.org; *Tech Librn, YA Serv,* Lauren Berghman; E-mail: lberghman@ocln.org; *Adult Serv, Ref Serv,* Josh Olshin; E-mail: jolshin@ocln.org; *Ch Serv,* Amy Dean; E-mail: adean@ocln.org; Staff 4 (MLS 4)
Founded 1874. Pop 25,605; Circ 143,185
Library Holdings: Bk Vols 101,767; Per Subs 196
Special Collections: Stoughton Coll
Wireless access
Publications: Stoughton Houses: 100 Years; Stoughton Public Library: 100 Years
Partic in Old Colony Libr Network
Open Mon-Thurs 9-9, Fri & Sat 9-5
Friends of the Library Group

STOW

P RANDALL LIBRARY, 19 Crescent St, 01775. SAN 307-7071. Tel: 978-897-8572. FAX: 978-897-7379. E-mail: randalllibrary@gmail.com. Web Site: www.stow-ma.gov/randall-library. *Dir,* Tina McAndrew; E-mail: tmcandrew@minlib.net; *Circ & Tech Serv Librn,* Jael Gorham; E-mail: jgorham@minlib.net; *Youth Serv Librn,* Christine Morrison; E-mail: cmorrison@minlib.net; Staff 3 (MLS 1, Non-MLS 2)
Founded 1892. Pop 6,000; Circ 126,038
Library Holdings: Audiobooks 2,371; DVDs 2,368; Large Print Bks 248; Bk Vols 42,422; Per Subs 63; Videos 329
Subject Interests: Local hist
Automation Activity & Vendor Info: (Cataloging) Innovative Interfaces, Inc; (Circulation) Innovative Interfaces, Inc; (OPAC) Innovative Interfaces, Inc
Wireless access
Function: After school storytime, Audiobks via web, Bks on cassette, Bks on CD, Children's prog, Computers for patron use, Doc delivery serv, Electronic databases & coll, Free DVD rentals, ILL available, Museum passes, Online cat, OverDrive digital audio bks, Photocopying/Printing, Ref serv available, Spoken cassettes & CDs, Spoken cassettes & DVDs, Story hour, Summer reading prog, Tax forms, Telephone ref, VHS videos, Wheelchair accessible
Partic in Minuteman Library Network
Open Tues-Thurs 9-8, Fri 9-2, Sat (Sept-June) 9-5
Friends of the Library Group

STURBRIDGE

P JOSHUA HYDE PUBLIC LIBRARY, 306 Main St, 01566-1242. SAN 307-708X. Tel: 508-347-2512. FAX: 508-347-2872. E-mail: sturbridgejhpl@cwmars.org. Web Site: www.sturbridgelibrary.org. *Dir,* Becky Plimpton; E-mail: bplimpton@cwmars.org; *Ad,* Cheryl Zelazo; E-mail: czelazo@cwmars.org; *Ch,* Patricia Lalli; E-mail: plalli@cwmars.org; Staff 12 (MLS 3, Non-MLS 9)
Founded 1896. Pop 9,000; Circ 135,000
Library Holdings: AV Mats 2,128; Bk Titles 36,830; Per Subs 91; Talking Bks 2,512
Subject Interests: Local hist
Automation Activity & Vendor Info: (Cataloging) Innovative Interfaces, Inc; (Circulation) Innovative Interfaces, Inc; (ILL) Innovative Interfaces, Inc
Wireless access
Mem of Massachusetts Library System
Partic in Central & Western Massachusetts Automated Resource Sharing
Open Mon 1:30-5, Tues-Thurs 10:30-9, Fri & Sat 10:30-5; Sun (Oct-May)1:30-5
Friends of the Library Group

SUDBURY

P GOODNOW LIBRARY, 21 Concord Rd, 01776-2383. SAN 307-7101. Tel: 978-443-1035. Reference Tel: 978-440-5520. E-mail: goodnow@sudbury.ma.us. Web Site: goodnowlibrary.org. *Libr Dir,* Esme Green; Tel: 978-440-5515, E-mail: greene@sudbury.ma.us; *Asst Dir,* Karen Tobin; Tel: 978-440-5525, E-mail: tobink@sudbury.ma.us; *Head, Ref Serv,* Joanne Lee; Tel: 978-440-5524, E-mail: jlee@minlib.net; *Head, Tech Serv,* Olivia Sederlund; Tel: 978-440-5555, E-mail: osederlund@minlib.net; *Ch,* Amy Stimac; Tel: 978-443-5545, E-mail: astimac@minlib.net; *Teen Librn,* Lily Nicolazzo; E-mail: lnicolazzo@minlib.net; *Libr Office Mgr,* Emelia Thibeault; Tel: 978-440-5511, E-mail: thibeaulte@sudbury.ma.us; *Circ,* Michael Briody; Tel: 978-440-5535, E-mail: mbriody@minlib.net; Staff 11 (MLS 11)
Founded 1862. Pop 18,000; Circ 387,059
Library Holdings: Bk Vols 93,000; Per Subs 130
Subject Interests: Genealogy, Local hist
Automation Activity & Vendor Info: (Cataloging) Innovative Interfaces, Inc; (Circulation) Innovative Interfaces, Inc; (OPAC) Innovative Interfaces, Inc
Wireless access
Function: 24/7 Electronic res, 24/7 Online cat, 3D Printer, Activity rm, Adult bk club, After school storytime, Archival coll, Art exhibits, Art programs, Audio & video playback equip for onsite use, Audiobks on Playaways & MP3, Audiobks via web, AV serv, Bk club(s), Bks on CD, Chess club, Children's prog, Computers for patron use, Digital talking bks, Doc delivery serv, E-Readers, Electronic databases & coll, Equip loans & repairs, For res purposes, Free DVD rentals, Holiday prog, Home delivery & serv to seniorr ctr & nursing homes, Homebound delivery serv, ILL available, Internet access, Large print keyboards, Life-long learning prog for all ages, Magazines, Magnifiers for reading, Mail & tel request accepted, Makerspace, Mango lang, Meeting rooms, Microfiche/film & reading machines, Movies, Museum passes, Music CDs, Online cat, Online ref, Outreach serv, OverDrive digital audio bks, Passport agency, Photocopying/Printing, Preschool outreach, Preschool reading prog, Printer for laptops & handheld devices, Prog for adults, Prog for children & young adult, Ref & res, Ref serv available, Res assist avail, Scanner, Senior outreach, Serves people with intellectual disabilities, Spoken cassettes & CDs, Spoken cassettes & DVDs, STEM programs, Story hour, Study rm, Summer & winter reading prog, Summer reading prog, Tax forms, Teen prog, Telephone ref, Wheelchair accessible, Workshops, Writing prog
Partic in Minuteman Library Network
Special Services for the Deaf - Assisted listening device; Staff with knowledge of sign lang
Special Services for the Blind - Accessible computers; Assistive/Adapted tech devices, equip & products; Large print bks; Magnifiers
Open Mon-Thurs 9-9, Fri 9-5, Sat 10-5, Sun 1-5
Friends of the Library Group

SUNDERLAND

P SUNDERLAND PUBLIC LIBRARY*, 20 School St, 01375. SAN 307-7136. Tel: 413-665-2642. FAX: 413-665-1435. Web Site: www.sunderlandpubliclibrary.org. *Dir,* Katherine Hand; E-mail: director@sunderlandpubliclibrary.org; *Head, Adult Serv,* Aaron Falbel; *Head, YA,* Heather McGuirk; *Head, Youth Serv,* Kelly Daniels Baker; *Circ,* Vanessa Ryder; Staff 4 (MLS 1, Non-MLS 3)
Founded 1869. Pop 3,777; Circ 62,000
Library Holdings: AV Mats 2,815; Bk Titles 19,340; Per Subs 99
Automation Activity & Vendor Info: (Cataloging) Innovative Interfaces, Inc; (Circulation) Innovative Interfaces, Inc; (OPAC) Innovative Interfaces, Inc
Wireless access
Function: Art exhibits, Audiobks via web, Bks on cassette, Bks on CD, Children's prog, Computers for patron use, Electronic databases & coll, Free DVD rentals, Homebound delivery serv, ILL available, Museum passes, Online cat, OverDrive digital audio bks, Photocopying/Printing, Prog for adults, Prog for children & young adult, Story hour, Summer reading prog, VHS videos, Wheelchair accessible
Partic in Central & Western Massachusetts Automated Resource Sharing
Open Mon 10-8, Tues & Wed 1-8, Fri 10-7, Sat 10-5
Friends of the Library Group

SUTTON

P SUTTON FREE PUBLIC LIBRARY*, Four Uxbridge Rd, 01590. (Mail add: PO Box 544, 01590), SAN 345-6609. Tel: 508-865-8752. FAX: 508-865-8751. Web Site: www.suttonpubliclibrary.org. *Dir,* Betsy Perry; E-mail: bperry@cwmars.org; *Youth Serv Librn,* Shannon Duffy; E-mail: sduffy@cwmars.org; *Circ Spec, ILL Spec,* Pamela Johnson; E-mail: pamelaj@cwmars.org; Staff 3 (MLS 2, Non-MLS 1)
Pop 9,800
Library Holdings: Audiobooks 306; AV Mats 3,638; CDs 720; DVDs 2,102; Electronic Media & Resources 106; Large Print Bks 532; Bk Vols 30,000; Per Subs 54; Videos 2,102
Automation Activity & Vendor Info: (Circulation) Evergreen
Wireless access
Function: Adult bk club, Archival coll, Bk club(s), Bks on CD, CD-ROM, Children's prog, Computers for patron use, Genealogy discussion group, Holiday prog, ILL available, Mango lang, Movies, Museum passes, Music CDs, Online cat, Online ref, OverDrive digital audio bks, Photocopying/Printing, Prog for adults, Prog for children & young adult, Story hour, Summer reading prog, Teen prog, Writing prog
Mem of Massachusetts Library System
Partic in Central & Western Massachusetts Automated Resource Sharing
Open Mon, Wed & Fri 10-6, Tues & Thurs 10-8, Sat 10-3
Friends of the Library Group

SWAMPSCOTT

P SWAMPSCOTT PUBLIC LIBRARY, 61 Burrill St, 01907. SAN 307-7144. Tel: 781-596-8867. FAX: 781-596-8826. E-mail: swa@noblenet.org. Web Site: www.swampscottlibrary.org. *Dir,* Alyce Deveau; E-mail: deveau@noblenet.org; *Asst Dir, Head, Tech,* Susan Conner; E-mail: conner@noblenet.org; *Head, Adult Serv, Head, Circ,* Caroline Margolis; E-mail: cmargolis@noblenet.org; *Head, Children's Servx,* Israela Abrams; *Head, Children's Servx,* Lisa Julien-Hayes; *Head, Ref (Info Serv), Head, YA,* Janina Majeran; E-mail: majeran@noblenet.org; Staff 19 (MLS 5, Non-MLS 14)
Founded 1853. Pop 14,412; Circ 172,360
Library Holdings: Bk Vols 92,488; Per Subs 100
Special Collections: Railroads & Model Railroads (Albert W Lalime Coll); Town History (Henry Sill Baldwin Coll)
Wireless access
Partic in North of Boston Library Exchange, Inc
Open Mon-Wed 10-8:30, Thurs 1-8:30, Fri 10-1, Sat 10-2:30
Friends of the Library Group

SWANSEA

P SWANSEA FREE PUBLIC LIBRARY*, 69 Main St, 02777. SAN 345-6668. Tel: 508-674-9609. FAX: 508-675-5444. Web Site: www.swansealibrary.org. *Libr Dir,* Eileen Dyer; E-mail: edyer@sailsinc.org; *Youth Serv Librn,* Carol Gafford; *Circ,* Persephone Alves; *Circ,* Kaija Gallucci; *Circ,* MaryBeth Rodiquez; *Circ,* Maire Shea
Founded 1896. Pop 16,000; Circ 82,226
Library Holdings: Bk Titles 52,000; Per Subs 117
Subject Interests: Genealogy, Hist
Wireless access
Partic in SAILS Library Network
Open Mon-Thurs 10-8, Fri 10-5, Sat 10-4
Friends of the Library Group

TAUNTON

GL BRISTOL LAW LIBRARY*, Superior Court House, Nine Court St, 02780. SAN 307-7152. Tel: 508-824-7632. FAX: 508-824-4723. E-mail: bristollawlibrary@yahoo.com. Web Site: www.mass.gov/courts/case-legal-res/law-lib/libraries/locations/bristol.html. *Actg Adminr,* Cynthia Campbell; *Interim Head Librn,* Debra O'Donnell
Founded 1858
Library Holdings: Bk Vols 28,000; Per Subs 24
Special Collections: Complete Massachusetts Laws, cases, regulations
Wireless access
Open Tues & Thurs 8-4
Friends of the Library Group

S OLD COLONY HISTORY MUSEUM*, Hurley Library, 66 Church Green, 02780. SAN 307-7160. Tel: 508-822-1622. FAX: 508-880-6317. E-mail: info@oldcolonyhistorymuseum.org. Web Site: www.oldcolonyhistorymuseum.org. *Curator of Coll,* Bronson Michaud; Staff 3 (Non-MLS 3)
Founded 1853
Library Holdings: Bk Titles 8,000; Spec Interest Per Sub 25
Special Collections: Original Manuscripts, Letters & Records
Subject Interests: Civil War, Genealogy, Local hist
Wireless access
Function: Archival coll, Bk club(s), Computers for patron use, Internet access, Magnifiers for reading, Microfiche/film & reading machines, Museum passes, Photocopying/Printing, Prog for adults, Ref & res, Ref serv available, Res libr, Res performed for a fee, Scanner, Workshops
Open Tues-Sat 10-4
Restriction: Fee for pub use, Free to mem, Non-circulating
Friends of the Library Group

P TAUNTON PUBLIC LIBRARY, 12 Pleasant St, 02780. SAN 345-6722. Tel: 508-821-1410. Circulation Tel: 508-821-1412. Reference Tel: 508-821-1413. FAX: 508-821-1414. E-mail: tplreference@sailsinc.org. Web Site: www.tauntonlibrary.org. *Dir,* Daisy Delano; E-mail: ddelano@sailsinc.org; *Adult Serv Supvr, Ref Supvr,* Virginia Johnson; *Circ Supvr,* Robyn Bryant; *Tech Serv Supvr,* Gail Coelho; *Info Tech,* Stephen Vermette; Staff 19 (MLS 6, Non-MLS 13)
Founded 1866. Pop 50,962; Circ 180,511
Library Holdings: CDs 302; DVDs 1,652; Electronic Media & Resources 92; Bk Vols 201,055; Per Subs 167; Talking Bks 3,829; Videos 2,485
Special Collections: American-Portuguese Genealogical Coll; History of Taunton File Reference Coll; Literacy Center; Portuguese Coll; Young Adult Coll
Subject Interests: Am lit, Art & archit, Genealogy, Hist, Local hist, World War II
Automation Activity & Vendor Info: (Acquisitions) SirsiDynix; (Cataloging) SirsiDynix; (Circulation) SirsiDynix; (Course Reserve) SirsiDynix; (ILL) SirsiDynix; (Media Booking) LAC Group; (OPAC) SirsiDynix; (Serials) SirsiDynix
Wireless access
Publications: Newsletter (Monthly)
Mem of Massachusetts Library System
Partic in SAILS Library Network
Special Services for the Deaf - TDD equip
Open Mon-Fri 9-8
Friends of the Library Group

TEMPLETON

P BOYNTON PUBLIC LIBRARY*, 27 Boynton Rd, 01468-1412. (Mail add: PO Box 296, 01468-0296), SAN 345-6846. Tel: 978-939-5582. FAX: 978-939-8755. Web Site: www.templeton1.org/boynton-public-library. *Dir,* Jacqueline Prime; E-mail: jprime@cwmars.org; *Asst Librn,* Karen Johnson
Pop 6,079
Library Holdings: AV Mats 335; Bk Vols 13,000; Per Subs 25
Automation Activity & Vendor Info: (Acquisitions) Horizon; (Cataloging) Horizon
Wireless access
Mem of Massachusetts Library System
Partic in Central & Western Massachusetts Automated Resource Sharing
Open Mon 10-7, Wed 9-5, Thurs 9-7, Sat 11:30-2:30
Friends of the Library Group

TEWKSBURY

P TEWKSBURY PUBLIC LIBRARY*, 300 Chandler St, 01876. SAN 307-7195. Tel: 978-640-4490. Web Site: www.tewksburypl.org. *Dir,* Diane Giarrusso; E-mail: dgiarrusso@tewksbury-ma.gov; Staff 22 (MLS 5, Non-MLS 17)
Founded 1877. Pop 29,500; Circ 35,000
Library Holdings: Bk Vols 90,000; Per Subs 175
Mem of Massachusetts Library System
Partic in Merrimack Valley Library Consortium
Open Mon-Wed 10-9, Thurs & Fri 10-5, Sat 9-5, Sun 1-5
Friends of the Library Group

TOLLAND

P TOLLAND PUBLIC LIBRARY*, 22 Clubhouse Rd, 01034. SAN 376-7108. Tel: 413-258-4201, 413-258-4794, Ext 109. E-mail: tplibrary@tolland-ma.com. Web Site: www.tolland-ma.gov/Public_Documents/TollandMA_Library/index. *Libr Dir,* Jessica Kelmelis
Pop 295; Circ 2,771
Library Holdings: Audiobooks 201; DVDs 982; Bk Vols 3,964
Wireless access
Partic in Central & Western Massachusetts Automated Resource Sharing
Open Mon & Wed 3-6, Thurs 11-4, Sat 10-Noon

TOPSFIELD

P TOPSFIELD TOWN LIBRARY*, One S Common St, 01983. SAN 307-7217. Tel: 978-887-1528. FAX: 978-887-0185. E-mail: ask@topsfieldlibrary.org. Web Site: topsfieldtownlibrary.org. *Dir,* Laura Zalewski; E-mail: lzalewski@topsfieldlibrary.org; *Asst Dir, Head, Ref & ILL Serv,* Wendy Thatcher; E-mail: wthatcher@topsfieldlibrary.org; *Head, Children's & Young Adult Serv,* Lindsey Recka; E-mail: lrecka@topsfieldlibrary.org; *Head, Adult Serv,* Christine Manning; E-mail: cmanning@topsfieldlibrary.org; *Head, Tech Serv,* Sibyl Hezlett; E-mail: shezlett@topsfieldlibrary.org; Staff 13 (MLS 2, Non-MLS 11)

Founded 1794. Pop 6,140; Circ 161,489
Library Holdings: AV Mats 3,617; Bk Titles 49,273; Per Subs 170; Talking Bks 3,557
Automation Activity & Vendor Info: (Cataloging) SirsiDynix; (Circulation) SirsiDynix
Wireless access
Mem of Massachusetts Library System
Partic in Merrimack Valley Library Consortium
Open Mon & Thurs 10-8, Tues & Sat 10-5, Wed & Fri 12-5
Friends of the Library Group

TOWNSEND

P TOWNSEND PUBLIC LIBRARY, 12 Dudley Rd, 01469. SAN 307-7225. Tel: 978-597-1714. FAX: 978-597-2779. E-mail: townsendlibrary@cwmars.org. Web Site: www.townsendlibrary.org. *Dir,* Stacy Schuttler; E-mail: sschuttler@cwmars.org; *Ch,* Molly Benevides; E-mail: mbenevides@cwmars.org; Staff 7 (MLS 1, Non-MLS 6)
Founded 1929. Pop 9,158
Library Holdings: Bk Vols 29,210; Per Subs 29
Subject Interests: Genealogy, Local hist
Wireless access
Mem of Massachusetts Library System
Partic in Central & Western Massachusetts Automated Resource Sharing
Open Tues & Wed 10-9, Thurs 2-9, Fri 10-5, Sat 10-2, Sun (Jan-April) 1-5
Friends of the Library Group

TURNERS FALLS

P MONTAGUE PUBLIC LIBRARIES*, Carnegie Library-Main Branch, 201 Ave A, 01376-1989. SAN 307-7233. Tel: 413-863-3214. FAX: 413-863-3227. Web Site: montaguepubliclibraries.org. *Dir,* Linda Hickman; Tel: 413-863-3214, Ext 101, E-mail: librarydir@montague-ma.gov; *Ch,* Angela Rovatti-Leonard; Tel: 413-863-3214, Ext 102, E-mail: arovatti-leonard@cwmars.org; Staff 7 (MLS 2, Non-MLS 5)
Library Holdings: Bk Vols 35,000; Per Subs 100
Special Collections: Local History Materials
Automation Activity & Vendor Info: (Cataloging) Innovative Interfaces, Inc; (Circulation) Innovative Interfaces, Inc; (OPAC) Innovative Interfaces, Inc
Wireless access
Mem of Massachusetts Library System
Partic in Central & Western Massachusetts Automated Resource Sharing
Open Mon & Tues 1-8, Wed 10-8, Thurs 1-5, Fri 10-5, Sat 10-2
Friends of the Library Group
Branches: 2
MILLERS FALLS BRANCH, 23 Bridge St, Millers Falls, 01349, SAN 307-532X. Tel: 413-659-3801.
Pop 1,000; Circ 11,753
Special Collections: Early Town Histories, photogs
Open Tues & Thurs 2-7
Friends of the Library Group
MONTAGUE CENTER BRANCH, 17 Center St, Montague, 01351. (Mail add: PO Box 157, Montague, 01351-0157), SAN 307-5389. Tel: 413-367-2852.
Circ 9,870
Special Collections: Early Massachusetts Historical Information
Open Mon & Wed 2-7
Friends of the Library Group

TYNGSBORO

P TYNGSBOROUGH PUBLIC LIBRARY*, 25 Bryants Lane, 01879-1003. SAN 307-7241. Tel: 978-649-7361. FAX: 978-649-2578. E-mail: circdesk@tynglib.org. Web Site: www.tynglib.org. *Dir,* Susanna Arthur; E-mail: sarthur@tynglib.org; Staff 9 (MLS 2, Non-MLS 7)
Founded 1878. Pop 11,600; Circ 84,000
Library Holdings: Audiobooks 1,755; CDs 6,000; DVDs 8,324; e-books 4,377; High Interest/Low Vocabulary Bk Vols 200; Large Print Bks 465; Bk Titles 32,000; Bk Vols 47,890; Per Subs 130
Special Collections: Puppets
Automation Activity & Vendor Info: (Cataloging) Evergreen; (Circulation) Evergreen; (ILL) Evergreen; (OPAC) Evergreen
Wireless access
Function: Archival coll, Bi-weekly Writer's Group, ILL available, Photocopying/Printing, Prog for children & young adult, Ref serv available, Summer reading prog, Telephone ref, Wheelchair accessible
Mem of Massachusetts Library System
Partic in Merrimack Valley Library Consortium
Open Mon & Wed 10:30-8, Tues & Thurs 9-5, Sat (Sept-May) 9-2
Friends of the Library Group

TYRINGHAM

P TYRINGHAM FREE PUBLIC LIBRARY*, 118 Main Rd, 01264-9700. (Mail add: PO Box 440, 01264-0440), SAN 307-725X. Tel: 413-243-1373. Web Site: www.tyringham-ma.gov/Pages/TyringhamMA_Library/index. *Librn,* Mary Garner; E-mail: mcgarn16@gmail.com
Founded 1891. Circ 355
Library Holdings: Bk Vols 7,000
Partic in Central & Western Massachusetts Automated Resource Sharing
Open Tues 3-5, Sat 10-Noon

UPTON

P UPTON TOWN LIBRARY*, Two Main St, 01568-1608. (Mail add: PO Box 1196, 01568-1196), SAN 307-7276. Tel: 508-529-6272. Web Site: www.uptonlibrary.org. *Dir,* Matthew Bachtold; E-mail: mbachtol@cwmars.org; *Ch Serv, YA Serv,* Lee Ann Murphy; E-mail: lmurphy@cwmars.org
Founded 1871. Pop 3,884; Circ 24,000
Library Holdings: Bk Vols 24,000; Per Subs 105
Automation Activity & Vendor Info: (Cataloging) Innovative Interfaces, Inc; (Circulation) Innovative Interfaces, Inc; (OPAC) Innovative Interfaces, Inc
Wireless access
Mem of Massachusetts Library System
Partic in Central & Western Massachusetts Automated Resource Sharing
Open Tues-Thurs 10-8, Fri & Sat 10-4
Friends of the Library Group

UXBRIDGE

P UXBRIDGE FREE PUBLIC LIBRARY*, 15 N Main St, 01569-1822. SAN 307-7284. Tel: 508-278-8624. FAX: 508-278-8618. E-mail: uxbridgelibrary01569@gmail.com. Web Site: www.uxbridgelibrary.org. *Libr Dir,* Deborah Hinkle; E-mail: dhinkle@cwmars.org; Staff 2 (MLS 1, Non-MLS 1)
Founded 1894. Pop 13,100; Circ 61,000
Library Holdings: Bk Vols 111,499; Per Subs 39
Special Collections: Local History & Genealogy Coll
Automation Activity & Vendor Info: (Cataloging) Evergreen; (Circulation) Evergreen; (OPAC) Evergreen
Wireless access
Mem of Massachusetts Library System
Partic in Central & Western Massachusetts Automated Resource Sharing
Open Mon & Thurs (Winter) 10-8, Tues & Wed 10-5:30, Sat 9-2; Mon & Thurs (Summer) 10-8, Tues & Wed 10-5:30, Fri 9-2
Friends of the Library Group

VINEYARD HAVEN

S MARTHA'S VINEYARD MUSEUM LIBRARY, 151 Lagoon Pond Rd, 02568. SAN 321-0731. Tel: 508-627-4441, Ext 115. FAX: 508-627-4436. Web Site: www.mvmuseum.org/research.php. *Research Librn,* A Bowdoin Van Riper; E-mail: bvanriper@mvmuseum.org; Staff 1 (Non-MLS 1)
Founded 1922
Library Holdings: Bk Titles 5,000; Per Subs 30
Special Collections: Account Books from Island Businesses & Individuals; Logbooks; Martha's Vineyard Genealogy; Photographs; Wampanoag Indian History & Genealogy. Oral History
Subject Interests: Agr, Archit, Fishing, Geol, Hist of Martha's Vineyard, Methodist histl mat, Oral hist, Seafaring, Steamboats, Whaling
Wireless access
Publications: MV Museum Quarterly (Local historical information)
Open Tues-Fri 10-5
Restriction: Open to pub for ref only

P VINEYARD HAVEN PUBLIC LIBRARY*, 200 Main St, 02568. SAN 375-3719. Tel: 508-696-4211. FAX: 508-696-7495. E-mail: vhpl_questions@clamsnet.org. Web Site: www.vhlibrary.org. *Dir,* Amy Ryan; Tel: 508-696-4211, Ext 111, E-mail: amyryan@clamsnet.org; *Ch,* Libby Mueller; Tel: 508-696-4211, Ext 114, E-mail: lmueller@clamsnet.org; *Ref Librn,* Cecily Greenaway; Tel: 508-696-4211, Ext 115; *YA Librn,* Jennifer Rapuano; Tel: 508-696-4211, Ext 118, E-mail: jrapuano@clamsnet.org; *Adult Programs,* Betty Burton; Tel: 508-696-4211, Ext 116, E-mail: bburton@clamsnet.org; *Circ & ILL,* Lagan Treischmann; Tel: 508-696-4211, Ext 112; *Circ/Ser,* Anne McDonough; Staff 7 (MLS 3, Non-MLS 4)
Founded 1878. Pop 10,000; Circ 127,000
Library Holdings: CDs 1,918; DVDs 3,761; Bk Vols 33,902; Per Subs 150
Special Collections: Vineyard Coll
Automation Activity & Vendor Info: (Acquisitions) Innovative Interfaces, Inc - Millennium; (Cataloging) Innovative Interfaces, Inc - Millennium; (Circulation) Innovative Interfaces, Inc - Millennium; (Course Reserve) Innovative Interfaces, Inc - Millennium; (ILL) Innovative Interfaces, Inc - Millennium; (Media Booking) Innovative Interfaces, Inc - Millennium;

(OPAC) Innovative Interfaces, Inc - Millennium; (Serials) Innovative Interfaces, Inc - Millennium
Wireless access
Function: Adult bk club, Art exhibits, Audiobks via web, Bks on CD, Children's prog, Computer training, Computers for patron use, Electronic databases & coll, Free DVD rentals, ILL available, Literacy & newcomer serv, Magnifiers for reading, Microfiche/film & reading machines, Museum passes, Music CDs, OverDrive digital audio bks, Photocopying/Printing, Preschool outreach, Preschool reading prog, Prog for adults, Prog for children & young adult, Ref serv available, Scanner, Spoken cassettes & CDs, Spoken cassettes & DVDs, Story hour, Summer reading prog, Tax forms, Teen prog, Wheelchair accessible
Partic in Cape Libraries Automated Materials Sharing Network
Open Mon, Wed & Sat 10-5:30, Tues & Thurs 10-8, Fri 1-5:30
Friends of the Library Group

P WEST TISBURY FREE PUBLIC LIBRARY*, 1042 State Rd, 02568. Tel: 508-693-3366. FAX: 508-696-0130. E-mail: wt_mail@clamsnet.org. Web Site: westtisburylibrary.org. *Libr Dir,* Alexandra Pratt; E-mail: apratt@clamsnet.org; *Asst Librn,* Laura Coit; Staff 5 (MLS 1, Non-MLS 4)
Founded 1893. Pop 5,700; Circ 173,000
Library Holdings: Audiobooks 2,000; Bks on Deafness & Sign Lang 50; DVDs 4,000; Large Print Bks 200; Bk Titles 54,000; Bk Vols 55,000; Per Subs 115; Talking Bks 1,371
Special Collections: Vineyard Authors
Automation Activity & Vendor Info: (Cataloging) Innovative Interfaces, Inc - Millennium; (Circulation) Innovative Interfaces, Inc - Millennium
Wireless access
Function: 24/7 Electronic res, 24/7 Online cat, Activity rm, Adult bk club, After school storytime, Art exhibits, Bk reviews (Group), Children's prog, Computers for patron use, Digital talking bks, Doc delivery serv, E-Reserves, Free DVD rentals, Health sci info serv, Holiday prog, Home delivery & serv to seniorr ctr & nursing homes, ILL available, Instruction & testing, Internet access, Jazz prog, Magnifiers for reading, Mail & tel request accepted, Online cat, Outreach serv, Passport agency, Photocopying/Printing, Prog for adults, Prog for children & young adult, Scanner, Senior computer classes, Senior outreach, Spoken cassettes & CDs, Spoken cassettes & DVDs, Story hour, Summer reading prog, Tax forms, Wheelchair accessible, Workshops
Partic in Cape Libraries Automated Materials Sharing Network
Open Mon 10-9, Tues-Thurs 10-6, Fri & Sat 10-5, Sun (Winter) 1-5
Friends of the Library Group

WAKEFIELD

P LUCIUS BEEBE MEMORIAL LIBRARY*, 345 Main St, 01880-5093. SAN 345-6900. Tel: 781-246-6334. FAX: 781-246-6385. E-mail: email@wakefieldlibrary.org. Web Site: www.wakefieldlibrary.org. *Dir,* Catherine McDonald; E-mail: cmcdonal@noblenet.org; *Asst Dir,* Jackie Powers; E-mail: powers@noblenet.org; *Head, Circ,* Meaghan Kinton; E-mail: kinton@noblenet.org; *Head, Info Serv,* Jeffrey M Klapes; E-mail: klapes@noblenet.org; *Head, Tech Serv,* Alyssa Staples; E-mail: staples@noblenet.org; *Head, Youth Serv,* Nancy Sheehan; E-mail: sheehan@noblenet.org; Staff 12 (MLS 12)
Founded 1856. Pop 25,000; Circ 300,000
Library Holdings: Bk Vols 112,000
Special Collections: Rifles, Riflery & Target Shooting (Keough Coll); Wakefield Authors
Subject Interests: Local hist
Automation Activity & Vendor Info: (Acquisitions) Evergreen; (Cataloging) Evergreen; (Circulation) Evergreen; (OPAC) Evergreen; (Serials) Evergreen
Wireless access
Mem of Massachusetts Library System
Partic in North of Boston Library Exchange, Inc
Open Mon-Thurs 9-9, Fri 9-6, Sat 9-5, Sun (Sept-June) 1-5
Friends of the Library Group

WALES

P WALES PUBLIC LIBRARY*, 77 Main St, 01081. (Mail add: PO Box 243, 01081-0243), SAN 307-7322. Tel: 413-245-9072. FAX: 413-245-9098. Web Site: www.townofwales.net/library. *Dir,* Nancy Baer; *Librn,* Carol Gruszka; *Librn,* Safia Rodriquez
Pop 1,700; Circ 6,805
Library Holdings: Bk Vols 10,000; Per Subs 12
Wireless access
Partic in Central & Western Massachusetts Automated Resource Sharing
Open Mon, Tues & Thurs 3-7, Wed 10-12 & 3-7, Sat 10-1
Friends of the Library Group

WALPOLE

P WALPOLE PUBLIC LIBRARY, 143 School St, 02081. SAN 345-6994. Tel: 508-660-7340. E-mail: info@walpolelibrary.org. Web Site: www.walpolelibrary.org. *Dir,* Salvatore Genovese; Tel: 508-660-7334, E-mail: sgenovese@walpole-ma.gov; *Asst Dir,* Molly Riportella; Tel: 508-660-6358, E-mail: mriportella@ocln.org; *Ref Librn,* Warren Smith; Tel: 508-660-7341, E-mail: wsmith@ocln.org; *Youth Serv Librn,* Kara Dean; Tel: 508-660-7384, E-mail: kdean@ocln.org; Staff 4 (MLS 4)
Founded 1876. Pop 24,818; Circ 221,762
Library Holdings: AV Mats 4,864; DVDs 8,001; Microforms 99; Bk Vols 79,596; Per Subs 127
Automation Activity & Vendor Info: (Cataloging) SirsiDynix; (Circulation) SirsiDynix; (OPAC) SirsiDynix
Wireless access
Function: 24/7 Electronic res, 24/7 Online cat, Adult bk club, Art exhibits, Audiobks via web, Bks on CD, Computers for patron use, Electronic databases & coll, Free DVD rentals, ILL available, Internet access, Magazines, Magnifiers for reading, Meeting rooms, Microfiche/film & reading machines, Museum passes, Music CDs, Online cat, OverDrive digital audio bks, Photocopying/Printing, Ref serv available, Scanner, Spoken cassettes & CDs, Story hour, Study rm, Summer reading prog, Tax forms, Telephone ref
Partic in Old Colony Libr Network
Open Mon-Thurs 9:30-9, Fri 9:30-5, Sat 9:30-3
Friends of the Library Group

WALTHAM

C BENTLEY UNIVERSITY*, Solomon R Baker Library, 175 Forest St, 02452-4705. SAN 307-7381. Tel: 781-891-2168. Interlibrary Loan Service Tel: 781-891-2301. Reference Tel: 781-891-2304. FAX: 781-891-2830. E-mail: library@bentley.edu. Web Site: library.bentley.edu. *Libr Dir,* Hope Houston; Tel: 781-891-2450, E-mail: hhouston@bentley.edu; *Mgr, Access Serv,* Anne Jorgensen; E-mail: ajorgensen@bentley.edu; *Mgr, Ref Serv,* Stephen Tracey; *Mgr, Tech Serv,* Donna Bacchiocchi; Staff 18.5 (MLS 10.5, Non-MLS 8)
Founded 1917. Enrl 5,543; Fac 291; Highest Degree: Doctorate
Special Collections: Business Histories
Subject Interests: Acctg, Bus, Econ, Finance, Mgt, Mkt
Automation Activity & Vendor Info: (Acquisitions) Innovative Interfaces, Inc - Sierra; (Cataloging) Innovative Interfaces, Inc - Sierra; (Circulation) Innovative Interfaces, Inc - Sierra; (Course Reserve) Innovative Interfaces, Inc - Sierra; (Discovery) Innovative Interfaces, Inc; (ILL) OCLC Tipasa; (Serials) SerialsSolutions
Wireless access
Partic in Boston Library Consortium, Inc; LYRASIS; Midwest Collaborative for Library Services; Westchester Academic Library Directors Organization

C BRANDEIS UNIVERSITY*, Goldfarb & Farber Libraries, 415 South St, Mailstop 045, 02454-9110. SAN 345-7087. Tel: 781-736-5626. Interlibrary Loan Service Tel: 781-736-4676. FAX: 781-736-4719. E-mail: library@brandeis.edu. Web Site: www.brandeis.edu/library. *Univ Librn,* Matthew Sheehy; E-mail: sheehy@brandeis.edu
Founded 1948. Enrl 5,311; Fac 511; Highest Degree: Doctorate
Library Holdings: e-journals 33,137; Bk Vols 1,207,217
Special Collections: Louis D Brandeis Coll. US Document Depository
Subject Interests: Judaica
Automation Activity & Vendor Info: (Acquisitions) Ex Libris Group; (Cataloging) Ex Libris Group; (Circulation) Ex Libris Group; (Course Reserve) Ex Libris Group; (ILL) OCLC ILLiad; (OPAC) Ex Libris Group; (Serials) Ex Libris Group
Wireless access
Function: Res libr
Mem of Massachusetts Library System
Partic in Boston Library Consortium, Inc; Coalition for Networked Information; OCLC Online Computer Library Center, Inc; OCLC Research Library Partnership; Scholarly Publ & Acad Resources Coalition
Open Mon-Thurs (Fall) 8:30am-2am, Fri 8:30-6, Sat Noon-6, Sun 12pm-2am; Mon-Fri (Winter) 8:30-5:30
Friends of the Library Group

S CHARLES RIVER MUSEUM OF INDUSTRY LIBRARY, 154 Moody St, 02453. SAN 375-7102. Tel: 781-893-5410. FAX: 781-891-4536. Web Site: www.charlesrivermuseum.org. *Exec Dir,* Bob Perry; E-mail: director@charlesrivermuseum.org
Founded 1980
Library Holdings: Bk Titles 3,000

S GORE PLACE SOCIETY, INC LIBRARY*, 52 Gore St, 02453. SAN 327-3210. Tel: 781-894-2798. FAX: 781-894-5795. E-mail: goreplace@goreplace.org. Web Site: www.goreplace.org. *Dir,* Susan Robertson; E-mail: susanrobertson@goreplace.org
Library Holdings: Bk Vols 2,000

S SIMPSON, GUMPERTZ & HEGER, INC LIBRARY*, 480 Totten Pond Rd, 02451. SAN 373-0662. Tel: 781-907-9000. FAX: 781-907-9009. Web Site: www.sgh.com. *Mgr,* Joan Cunningham; Staff 3 (MLS 3)
Library Holdings: Bk Vols 20,000; Per Subs 30

Subject Interests: Structural engr
Automation Activity & Vendor Info: (Cataloging) Inmagic, Inc.
Restriction: Staff use only

S THE WALTHAM MUSEUM INC LIBRARY, 25 Lexington St, 02452. SAN 373-0689. Tel: 781-893-9020. E-mail: info@walthammuseum.org. Web Site: www.walthammuseum.org. *Actg Dir,* Tom Arena
Subject Interests: City hist, Engr, Watchmaking
Wireless access
Restriction: Non-circulating, Open by appt only

P WALTHAM PUBLIC LIBRARY, 735 Main St, 02451. SAN 345-7230. Tel: 781-314-3425. Web Site: www.waltham.lib.ma.us. *Dir,* Kelly Linehan; E-mail: klinehan@minlib.net; *Asst Dir,* Deb Fasulo; E-mail: dfasulo@minlib.net; *Head, Children's Dept,* Position Currently Open; *Head, Circ,* Kim Hewitt; *Head, Ref,* Laura Bernheim; *Head, Tech Serv,* Kate Spalding; *Head, Tech,* Todd Strauss; *Head, Teen Serv,* Luke Kirkland
Founded 1865. Pop 63,000; Circ 642,884
Library Holdings: Bk Vols 195,860; Per Subs 417
Partic in Minuteman Library Network
Open Mon-Thurs 9-9, Fri & Sat 9-5, Sun 1-4
Friends of the Library Group

WARE

P YOUNG MEN'S LIBRARY ASSOCIATION LIBRARY, 37 Main St, 01082-1317. SAN 307-7535. Circulation Tel: 413-967-4858. FAX: 413-967-6060. Web Site: www.warelibrary.org. *Libr Dir,* Heidi Reed; Tel: 413-967-5491, E-mail: hreed@cwmars.org; *Ch,* Cathy Rezendes; *Circ Librn,* Kathy Nowak; Staff 4 (MLS 1, Non-MLS 3)
Founded 1872. Pop 9,824; Circ 40,532
Library Holdings: AV Mats 2,784; Bk Vols 43,962; Per Subs 91
Subject Interests: Local hist
Automation Activity & Vendor Info: (Cataloging) Evergreen; (Circulation) Evergreen; (OPAC) Evergreen
Wireless access
Function: Art exhibits, Audiobks via web, Bks on CD, Children's prog, Computers for patron use, Free DVD rentals, ILL available, Magnifiers for reading, Museum passes, Music CDs, OverDrive digital audio bks, Photocopying/Printing, Printer for laptops & handheld devices, Story hour, Summer reading prog, Tax forms, Telephone ref
Partic in Central & Western Massachusetts Automated Resource Sharing
Open Mon & Fri 1-8, Tues & Thurs 10-8, Sat 9-Noon

WAREHAM

P WAREHAM FREE LIBRARY*, 59 Marion Rd, 02571. SAN 307-7543. Tel: 508-295-2343. Circulation Tel: 508-295-2343, Ext 1011. Reference Tel: 508-295-2343, Ext 1012. FAX: 508-295-2678. Web Site: www.warehamfreelibrary.org. *Dir,* George Ripley; Tel: 508-295-2343, Ext 1010, E-mail: gripley@sailsinc.org; *Ch Serv,* Marcia Hickey; Tel: 508-295-2343, Ext 1014, E-mail: mhickey@sailsinc.org; *Tech Serv,* Kathy Murphy; Tel: 508-295-2343, Ext 1015, E-mail: kmurphy@sailsinc.org; Staff 3 (MLS 1, Non-MLS 2)
Founded 1891. Pop 22,000; Circ 70,000
Jul 2015-Jun 2016. Mats Exp $20,000
Library Holdings: Bk Vols 101,000; Per Subs 110
Special Collections: Wareham Coll. Municipal Document Depository; Oral History
Automation Activity & Vendor Info: (Cataloging) SirsiDynix; (Circulation) SirsiDynix; (OPAC) SirsiDynix
Wireless access
Function: 24/7 Electronic res, 24/7 Online cat, Activity rm, Adult bk club, Adult literacy prog, After school storytime, Archival coll, Art exhibits, Audio & video playback equip for onsite use, Audiobks on Playaways & MP3, Audiobks via web, AV serv, Bk club(s), Bk reviews (Group), Bks on cassette, Bks on CD, CD-ROM, Children's prog, Computer training, Computers for patron use, E-Readers, E-Reserves, Electronic databases & coll, Free DVD rentals, Holiday prog, Instruction & testing, Internet access, Magazines, Magnifiers for reading, Meeting rooms, Microfiche/film & reading machines, Movies, Museum passes, Music CDs, Online cat, Online info literacy tutorials on the web & in blackboard, Outreach serv, OverDrive digital audio bks, Photocopying/Printing, Preschool outreach, Prog for adults, Prog for children & young adult, Ref & res, Ref serv available, Senior computer classes, Story hour, VHS videos
Partic in SAILS Library Network
Open Tues & Thurs 10-7, Sat 9-2
Friends of the Library Group

WARREN

P WARREN PUBLIC LIBRARY*, 934 Main St, 01083-0937. SAN 307-7551. Tel: 413-436-7690. FAX: 413-436-7690. E-mail: warrenpubliclibrary@hotmail.com. Web Site: warrenpubliclibrary.org. *Dir,* Kim Kvaracein; E-mail: kkvarace@cwmars.org; Staff 1.4 (Non-MLS 1.4)
Founded 1879. Pop 5,000; Circ 23,357
Library Holdings: AV Mats 3,148; Electronic Media & Resources 26; Bk Titles 22,663; Per Subs 69
Special Collections: Genealogy Coll; Local History Coll
Wireless access
Mem of Massachusetts Library System
Partic in Central & Western Massachusetts Automated Resource Sharing
Open Tues & Thurs 11-7, Wed & Sat 11-3
Friends of the Library Group

WARWICK

P WARWICK FREE PUBLIC LIBRARY*, Four Hotel Rd, 01378-9311. SAN 307-6059. Tel: 978-544-7866. FAX: 978-544-7866. E-mail: warwick@cwmars.org. *Librn,* Ivan Ussach
Founded 1870. Pop 780
Library Holdings: Bk Titles 8,000; Per Subs 22
Partic in Central & Western Massachusetts Automated Resource Sharing
Open Mon 10-4, Tues 1-8, Thurs 5-8, Sat 10-12:30

WATERTOWN

S ARMENIAN MUSEUM OF AMERICA, INC, Mesrob G Boyajian Library, Mugar Bldg, 4th Flr, 65 Main St, 02472. SAN 325-8963. Tel: 617-926-2562, Ext 111. FAX: 617-926-0175. E-mail: info@almainc.org, info@armenianmuseum.org. Web Site: www.armenianmuseum.org/library. *Exec Dir,* Jason Sohigian; *Dir of Finance,* Berj Chekijian; E-mail: berjc@armenianmuseum.org; *Colls Mgr,* Zoe Quinn; E-mail: zquinn@armenianmuseum.org; *Curator,* Gary Lind-Sinanian; E-mail: gary@armenianmuseum.org; *Curator,* Susan Lind-Sinanian; E-mail: Susans@armenianmuseum.org; Staff 6 (Non-MLS 6)
Founded 1971
Library Holdings: AV Mats 3,000; CDs 200; DVDs 300; Music Scores 400; Bk Titles 30,000
Special Collections: Oral History
Automation Activity & Vendor Info: (Cataloging) Follett Software
Wireless access
Function: Res libr
Restriction: Open by appt only
Friends of the Library Group

P PERKINS SCHOOL FOR THE BLIND*, Perkins Library, 175 N Beacon St, 02472. SAN 345-732X. Tel: 617-972-7240. Reference Tel: 617-972-7245. Toll Free Tel: 800-852-3133. FAX: 617-972-7363. TDD: 617-972-7610. E-mail: library@perkins.org. Web Site: www.perkinslibrary.org. *Dir,* Kim L Charlson; E-mail: kim.charlson@perkins.org; *Dep Dir,* James E Gleason; *Mkt, Outreach Coordr,* Erin Fragola; E-mail: erin.fragola@perkins.org; Staff 24 (MLS 5, Non-MLS 19)
Founded 1829. Pop 25,000; Circ 511,047
Library Holdings: DVDs 1,500
Special Collections: Foreign Language, digital and cassettes; French, German, Italian, Polish, Portuguese & Massachusetts,cassettes and digital; Reference Material on Blindness & Other Physical Handicaps
Automation Activity & Vendor Info: (Acquisitions) Keystone Systems, Inc (KLAS); (Cataloging) Keystone Systems, Inc (KLAS); (Circulation) Keystone Systems, Inc (KLAS); (OPAC) Keystone Systems, Inc (KLAS)
Wireless access
Function: Adult bk club, Bk club(s), Computers for patron use, Digital talking bks, Internet access, Magnifiers for reading, Mail & tel request accepted, Museum passes, Online cat, Online ref, Ref serv available, Summer reading prog, Wheelchair accessible
Publications: Dots & Decibels (Newsletter); El Narrador (Newsletter); PerKids (Newsletter)
Mem of Massachusetts Library System
Special Services for the Deaf - TTY equip
Special Services for the Blind - Accessible computers; Assistive/Adapted tech devices, equip & products; Bks on flash-memory cartridges; Braille alphabet card; Braille bks; Braille equip; Braille servs; Cassette playback machines; Cassettes; Children's Braille; Closed circuit TV magnifier; Computer with voice synthesizer for visually impaired persons; Descriptive video serv (DVS); Digital talking bk; Digital talking bk machines; Duplicating spec requests; Extensive large print coll; Home delivery serv; Internet workstation with adaptive software; Large print bks; Local mags & bks recorded; Machine repair; Mags & bk reproduction/duplication; Newsletter (in large print, Braille or on cassette); Newsline for the Blind; Scanner for conversion & translation of mats; Screen enlargement software for people with visual disabilities; Screen reader software; Sound rec; Soundproof reading booth; Spanish Braille mags & bks; Talking bks & player equip; Variable speed audiotape players; Web-Braille; ZoomText magnification & reading software
Open Mon, Wed & Fri 8:30-5
Restriction: Authorized patrons, Circ limited
Friends of the Library Group

Branches: 1
SAMUEL P HAYES RESEARCH LIBRARY, 175 N Beacon St, 02472. Tel: 617-972-7250. FAX: 617-923-8076. E-mail: hayeslibrary@perkins.org. Web Site: www.perkins.org/researchlibrary. *Librn,* Jan Seymour-Ford; E-mail: jan.seymour-ford@perkins.org; Staff 2 (MLS 1, Non-MLS 1)
Founded 1880
Library Holdings: Bks on Deafness & Sign Lang 30; CDs 95; DVDs 90; e-books 20; Microforms 1,700; Bk Titles 8,000; Bk Vols 33,000; Per Subs 150
Special Collections: Correspondence Between Henney, Anne Sullivan & Helen Keller (Nella Braddy Henney Coll); Institutional History; International Music Braille (Bettye Krolick Coll); Laura Bridgman Coll, artifacts, journals, papers
Subject Interests: Blindness, Spec educ
Automation Activity & Vendor Info: (Cataloging) Inmagic, Inc.; (OPAC) Inmagic, Inc.; (Serials) EBSCO Online
Function: Res libr
Special Services for the Blind - Assistive/Adapted tech devices, equip & products; Closed circuit TV; Computer with voice synthesizer for visually impaired persons; Reader equip
Restriction: Non-circulating

S SASAKI ASSOCIATES, INC LIBRARY*, 64 Pleasant St, 02472. SAN 307-7578. Tel: 617-923-5336. FAX: 617-924-2748. Web Site: www.sasaki.com. *Librn & Archivist,* Sarah Bush; E-mail: sbush@sasaki.com; Staff 1 (MLS 1)
Founded 1966
Library Holdings: Bk Vols 5,000; Per Subs 150
Special Collections: Company Archives
Subject Interests: Archit, Civil engr, Graphics, Landscape archit, Planning
Restriction: Staff use only

P WATERTOWN FREE PUBLIC LIBRARY*, 123 Main St, 02472. SAN 345-7508. Tel: 617-972-6431. Reference Tel: 617-972-6436. FAX: 617-926-5471. TDD: 617-600-1154. Web Site: www.watertownlib.org. *Dir,* Leone Cole; Tel: 617-972-6434, E-mail: lcole@watertown-ma.gov; Staff 19 (MLS 19)
Founded 1868. Pop 33,284; Circ 378,518
Library Holdings: AV Mats 15,728; Bk Titles 129,204; Per Subs 346
Special Collections: Armenian Materials (in English & Armenian); Art of 19th Century Watertown Women Artists. Oral History
Subject Interests: Art & archit, Genealogy, Local hist
Automation Activity & Vendor Info: (Acquisitions) Innovative Interfaces, Inc; (Cataloging) Innovative Interfaces, Inc; (Circulation) Innovative Interfaces, Inc; (OPAC) Innovative Interfaces, Inc; (Serials) Innovative Interfaces, Inc
Publications: Crossroads on the Charles; Images of America-Watertown
Partic in Minuteman Library Network
Special Services for the Deaf - Spec interest per
Open Mon-Thurs 9-9, Fri 9-7, Sat 9-5, Sun 1-5
Friends of the Library Group

WAYLAND

P WAYLAND FREE PUBLIC LIBRARY*, Five Concord Rd, 01778. SAN 345-7621. Tel: 508-358-2311. FAX: 508-358-5249. E-mail: info@waylandlibrary.org. Web Site: www.waylandlibrary.org. *Libr Dir,* Ms Sandy Raymond; E-mail: sraymond@minlib.net; *Asst Dir,* Sandra Raymond; E-mail: sraymond@minlib.net; *Head, Circ,* Jan Demeo; E-mail: jdemeo@minlib.net; *Bibliog Serv Librn,* Marjanneke Wright; E-mail: mwright@minlib.net; *Ref Librn,* Andrew Moore; *Youth Serv Librn,* Pamela McCuen; E-mail: pmccuen@minlib.net; Staff 13 (MLS 6, Non-MLS 7)
Founded 1848. Pop 13,800; Circ 237,141
Library Holdings: AV Mats 16,265; DVDs 8,768; Bk Titles 76,791; Per Subs 224
Special Collections: Wayland Local History Coll
Subject Interests: Gardening
Automation Activity & Vendor Info: (Acquisitions) Innovative Interfaces, Inc; (Cataloging) Innovative Interfaces, Inc - Millennium; (Circulation) Innovative Interfaces, Inc - Millennium; (OPAC) Innovative Interfaces, Inc
Wireless access
Function: Adult literacy prog, Homebound delivery serv, ILL available, Internet access, Magnifiers for reading, Photocopying/Printing, Prog for adults, Prog for children & young adult, Ref serv available, Summer reading prog, Telephone ref, Wheelchair accessible
Publications: Wayland Public Library Update (Newsletter)
Mem of Massachusetts Library System
Partic in Minuteman Library Network
Open Mon-Thurs 9-9, Fri 9-6, Sat 10-1
Friends of the Library Group

WEBSTER

P CHESTER C CORBIN PUBLIC LIBRARY*, Two Lake St, 01570. SAN 307-7594. Tel: 508-949-3880. FAX: 508-949-0537. Web Site: www.corbinlibrary.org. *Libr Dir,* Amanda Grenier; E-mail: agrenier@cwmars.org; *Ad,* Peter Arsenault; *Circ Serv Librn,* Evan Hale; *Youth Serv Librn,* Andrew Tai; Staff 4 (MLS 3, Non-MLS 1)
Founded 1920. Pop 16,000; Circ 35,263
Special Collections: Historical Coll
Automation Activity & Vendor Info: (Cataloging) Evergreen; (Circulation) Evergreen; (OPAC) Evergreen
Wireless access
Function: Adult bk club, Archival coll, Audiobks via web, Bk club(s), Bks on cassette, Bks on CD, CD-ROM, Children's prog, Computer training, Computers for patron use, Electronic databases & coll, Free DVD rentals, Home delivery & serv to seniorr ctr & nursing homes, ILL available, Mail & tel request accepted, Microfiche/film & reading machines, Museum passes, Music CDs, Online cat, Online ref, OverDrive digital audio bks, Photocopying/Printing, Prog for adults, Prog for children & young adult, Ref & res, Ref serv available, Spoken cassettes & CDs, Spoken cassettes & DVDs, Story hour, Summer reading prog, Tax forms, Teen prog, Telephone ref, VHS videos, Wheelchair accessible, Workshops
Partic in Central & Western Massachusetts Automated Resource Sharing
Open Mon, Tues & Thurs 9-8, Wed 9-1, Fri 9-5, Sat 9-2
Friends of the Library Group

WELLESLEY

S MASSACHUSETTS HORTICULTURAL SOCIETY LIBRARY, 900 Washington St, Rte 16, 02482. SAN 307-2045. Tel: 617-933-4900, 617-933-4912. FAX: 617-933-4901. E-mail: library@masshort.org. Web Site: masshort.org/the-library. *Librn & Archivist,* Maureen O'Brien; E-mail: mobrien@masshort.org. Subject Specialists: *Hort, Landscape design,* Maureen O'Brien
Founded 1829
Library Holdings: Bk Vols 20,000; Per Subs 10
Special Collections: Print Coll; Rare Book Coll; Seed & Nursery Catalogs
Subject Interests: Art, Hist, Hort
Mem of Massachusetts Library System
Partic in Council on Botanical & Horticultural Libraries, Inc; LYRASIS
Open Thurs 9-Noon

J MASSBAY COMMUNITY COLLEGE*, Perkins Library, 50 Oakland St, 02481. SAN 307-7616. Tel: 781-239-2610. FAX: 781-239-3621. Web Site: www.massbay.edu/library. *Dir, Learning Serv,* Timothy Rivard; Tel: 781-239-2631, E-mail: trivard@massbay.edu; *Ref Librn,* Leigh Rudikoff; Tel: 781-239-2622, E-mail: lrudikoff@massbay.edu
Founded 1961. Highest Degree: Associate
Automation Activity & Vendor Info: (Acquisitions) ProQuest; (Cataloging) Koha; (Circulation) Koha; (Course Reserve) Koha; (OPAC) Koha; (Serials) EBSCO Online
Wireless access
Partic in Fenway Library Consortium; Massachusetts Commonwealth Consortium of Libraries in Public Higher Education Institutions
Open Mon-Thurs 7:45am-9pm, Fri 7:45-5, Sat 8-Noon
Departmental Libraries:
LEARNING RESOURCE CENTER, 19 Flagg Dr, Framingham, 01702-5928, SAN 373-2916. Tel: 508-270-4210. FAX: 508-270-4216. *Libr Coord,* Karen Delorey; Tel: 508-270-4215, E-mail: kdelorey@massbay.edu; Staff 2 (MLS 2)
Highest Degree: Associate
Library Holdings: Bk Vols 11,000
Open Mon-Thurs 8am-10pm, Fri 8-5, Sat 8-Noon

C WELLESLEY COLLEGE, Margaret Clapp Library, 106 Central St, 02481. SAN 345-7680. Tel: 781-283-2166. Interlibrary Loan Service Tel: 781-283-2101. FAX: 781-283-3690. Web Site: www.wellesley.edu/lts. *Assoc Provost, Chief Info Officer,* Ravi Ravishanker; E-mail: gravishanker@wellesley.edu; *Dir, Libr Coll,* Karen Bohrer; Tel: 781-283-2127, E-mail: kbohrer@wellesley.edu; *Spec Coll Librn,* Ruth Rogers; Tel: 781-283-3592, E-mail: rrogers@wellesley.edu; Staff 33 (MLS 22, Non-MLS 11)
Founded 1875. Enrl 2,280; Fac 285; Highest Degree: Bachelor
Library Holdings: Bk Vols 728,366; Per Subs 313
Special Collections: Book Arts; First & Rare Editions of English & American Poetry; Italian Renaissance (Plimpton Coll), bks & ms; Ruskin; Slavery (Elbert Coll). US Document Depository
Automation Activity & Vendor Info: (Acquisitions) Innovative Interfaces, Inc; (Circulation) Innovative Interfaces, Inc; (Serials) Innovative Interfaces, Inc
Wireless access
Partic in Boston Library Consortium, Inc; LYRASIS; Northeast Research Libraries Consortium; Oberlin Group; OCLC Online Computer Library Center, Inc

Open Mon-Thurs 8:15am-Midnight, Fri 8:15am-10pm, Sat 8:30-7, Sun 8:30-Midnight
Friends of the Library Group
Departmental Libraries:
ART LIBRARY, Jewett Arts Ctr, 106 Central St, 02481, SAN 345-7699. Tel: 781-283-2049. Reference Tel: 781-283-3258. *Art Librn,* Brooke Henderson; E-mail: bhenders@wellesley.edu
Restriction: Non-circulating to the pub
Friends of the Library Group
MUSIC LIBRARY, Jewett Arts Ctr, Rm 208, 106 Central St, 02481-8203, SAN 345-7702. Tel: 781-283-2075. *Music Librn,* Carol Lubkowski; Tel: 781-283-2076, E-mail: clubkows@wellesley.edu; Staff 1 (MLS 1)
Friends of the Library Group
WELLESLEY CENTERS FOR WOMEN, Cheever House, Rm 107, 106 Central St, 02481, SAN 374-9886. Tel: 781-283-2500. FAX: 781-283-2504. E-mail: wcw@wellesley.edu. Web Site: www.wellesley.edu/academics/centers/wcw. *Exec Dir,* Dr Layli Maparyan; Tel: 781-283-2503, E-mail: lmaparya@wellesley.edu
Library Holdings: Bk Vols 1,000
Restriction: Open to pub for ref only

P WELLESLEY FREE LIBRARY*, 530 Washington St, 02482. SAN 345-7745. Tel: 781-235-1610. Reference Tel: 781-235-1610, Ext 1117. FAX: 781-235-0495. Web Site: www.wellesleyfreelibrary.org. *Dir,* Jamie Jurgensen; *Asst Dir,* Elise MacLennan; Tel: 781-235-1610, Ext 1107, E-mail: emaclennan@minlib.net; *IT Dir,* Inna Ivers; Tel: 781-235-1610, Ext 1130, E-mail: iivers@minlib.net; *Head, Circ,* Pearl Der; Tel: 781-235-1610, Ext 1131, E-mail: pder@minlib.net; *Head, Ref,* Sue Hamilos; Tel: 781-235-1610, Ext 1110, E-mail: shamilos@minlib.net; *Acq,* Elaine Schicitano; *Ch Serv,* Emma Weiler; Tel: 781-235-1610, Ext 1109, E-mail: eweiler@minlib.net; Staff 65 (MLS 15, Non-MLS 50)
Founded 1883. Pop 27,982; Circ 740,077
Library Holdings: Bk Titles 230,024; Per Subs 326
Subject Interests: Bus
Automation Activity & Vendor Info: (Acquisitions) Innovative Interfaces, Inc - Sierra; (Cataloging) Innovative Interfaces, Inc - Sierra; (Circulation) Innovative Interfaces, Inc - Sierra; (OPAC) Innovative Interfaces, Inc - Sierra; (Serials) Innovative Interfaces, Inc - Sierra
Wireless access
Function: 24/7 Electronic res, 24/7 Online cat, Adult bk club, Art exhibits, Audiobks on Playaways & MP3, Audiobks via web, Bk club(s), Children's prog, Computer training, Computers for patron use, Electronic databases & coll, Free DVD rentals, Homebound delivery serv, ILL available, Internet access, Magazines, Mango lang, Meeting rooms, Microfiche/film & reading machines, Museum passes, Music CDs, Online cat, Online ref, Orientations, Outreach serv, OverDrive digital audio bks, Photocopying/Printing, Preschool outreach, Prog for adults, Prog for children & young adult, Ref & res, Ref serv available, Scanner, Senior computer classes, Study rm, Telephone ref, Workshops, Writing prog
Partic in Minuteman Library Network
Open Mon-Thurs 9-9, Fri 9-6, Sat 9-5, Sun (Sept-June) 1-5
Friends of the Library Group
Branches: 2
FELLS BRANCH, 308 Weston Rd, 02482, SAN 345-777X. Tel: 781-237-0485. *Dir,* Janice G Coduri; Tel: 781-235-1610, Ext 1129, Fax: 781-235-0495; Staff 5 (MLS 1, Non-MLS 4)
Founded 1923
Library Holdings: Bk Titles 4,783
Friends of the Library Group
WELLESLEY HILLS BRANCH, 210 Washington St, Wellesley Hills, 02481, SAN 345-780X. Tel: 781-237-0381.
Founded 1928
Library Holdings: Bk Vols 7,292
Open Tues, Wed, Fri & Sat 10-5, Thurs 10-8
Friends of the Library Group

WELLFLEET

S US NATIONAL PARK SERVICE, Cape Cod National Seashore Library, 99 Marconi Site Rd, 02667. SAN 370-3061. Tel: 508-771-2144. FAX: 508-349-9052. Web Site: www.nps.gov/caco.
Library Holdings: Bk Titles 2,500; Per Subs 10
Function: Ref serv available
Restriction: Non-circulating

P WELLFLEET PUBLIC LIBRARY, 55 W Main St, 02667. SAN 307-7659. Tel: 508-349-0310. FAX: 508-349-0312. E-mail: wpl@wellfleet-ma.gov. Web Site: www.wellfleetlibrary.org. *Dir,* Jennifer Wertkin; E-mail: jennifer.wertkin@wellfleet-ma.gov; Staff 7 (MLS 1, Non-MLS 6)
Founded 1893. Pop 3,200; Circ 97,000
Library Holdings: CDs 2,310; DVDs 1,500; Bk Vols 43,316; Per Subs 100; Videos 1,500
Special Collections: Cape Cod Coll
Subject Interests: Aquaculture, Art
Wireless access
Mem of Massachusetts Library System
Partic in Cape Libraries Automated Materials Sharing Network
Open Mon, Wed & Thurs 2-8, Tues 10-8, Fri & Sat 10-5, Sun (Nov-April) 2-5
Friends of the Library Group

WENDELL

P WENDELL FREE LIBRARY, Seven Wendell Depot Rd, 01379. (Mail add: PO Box 236, 01379-7910), SAN 307-7667. Tel: 978-544-3559. FAX: 978-544-3559. Web Site: www.wendellmass.us/index.php/wendell-free-library. *Dir,* Anna Lawrence; Staff 1 (MLS 1)
Founded 1894. Pop 886; Circ 17,415
Library Holdings: AV Mats 100; Bks on Deafness & Sign Lang 15; DVDs 500; Bk Titles 14,000; Per Subs 40; Videos 200
Wireless access
Function: Adult bk club, Art exhibits, Art programs, Audiobks via web, Bk club(s), Bks on CD, Children's prog, Computers for patron use, Free DVD rentals, ILL available, Internet access, Life-long learning prog for all ages, Magazines, Movies, Museum passes, Online cat, OverDrive digital audio bks, Photocopying/Printing, Prog for adults, Prog for children & young adult, Res assist avail, Summer reading prog, Tax forms, Teen prog
Partic in Central & Western Massachusetts Automated Resource Sharing
Open Tues 12-7, Wed 10-7, Thurs 3-7, Sat 9:30-3:30, Sun 11:30-3:30
Friends of the Library Group

WENHAM

C GORDON COLLEGE*, Jenks Library, 255 Grapevine Rd, 01984-1899. SAN 307-7675. Tel: 978-867-4878. Interlibrary Loan Service Tel: 978-867-4416. Reference Tel: 978-867-4342. FAX: 978-867-4660. E-mail: library@gordon.edu. Web Site: www.gordon.edu/library/. *Dir, Libr Serv,* Dr Myron Schirer-Suter; Tel: 978-867-4083, E-mail: myron.schirer-suter@gordon.edu; *Asst Dir, Pub Serv,* Randall Gowman; E-mail: randy.gowman@gordon.edu; *Instruction & Ser Librn,* Erica Sheet; Tel: 978-867-4345, E-mail: erica.sheet@gordon.edu; *Acq, Cat, Tech Serv Librn,* Alec Li; Tel: 978-867-4341, E-mail: alec.li@gordon.edu; *ILL,* Lori Franz; E-mail: lori.franz@gordon.edu; Staff 5 (MLS 5)
Founded 1889. Enrl 1,530; Fac 100; Highest Degree: Master
Library Holdings: CDs 1,730; DVDs 1,300; e-books 397; Microforms 31,736; Music Scores 2,008; Bk Vols 150,379; Per Subs 327; Videos 2,994
Special Collections: American Linguistics; Bibles; Global Circumnavigation; Northwest Exploration; Shakespeare (Vining Coll). US Document Depository
Subject Interests: Educ, Fine arts, Humanities, Natural sci, Soc sci & issues
Automation Activity & Vendor Info: (Acquisitions) Innovative Interfaces, Inc; (Cataloging) Innovative Interfaces, Inc; (Circulation) Innovative Interfaces, Inc; (Course Reserve) Innovative Interfaces, Inc; (ILL) Innovative Interfaces, Inc; (Media Booking) Innovative Interfaces, Inc; (OPAC) Innovative Interfaces, Inc; (Serials) Innovative Interfaces, Inc
Wireless access
Function: ILL available, Ref serv available
Mem of Massachusetts Library System
Partic in LYRASIS; North of Boston Library Exchange, Inc; OCLC Online Computer Library Center, Inc
Open Mon-Thurs 7:45am-Midnight, Fri 7:45am-9pm, Sat 10-9, Sun 2pm-Midnight

S WENHAM MUSEUM, Colonel Timothy Pickering Library, 132 Main St, 01984. SAN 307-7683. Tel: 978-468-2377. FAX: 978-468-1763. E-mail: info@wenhammuseum.org. Web Site: www.wenhammuseum.org. *Exec Dir,* Kristin Z Noon; E-mail: kristin.noon@wenhammuseum.org
Founded 1953
Library Holdings: Bk Titles 1,400
Special Collections: Historical Association, account bks, deeds, diaries, papers; Massachusetts Society for Promoting Agriculture, medals, mementoes, paintings, publications
Subject Interests: Agr, Costume design, Genealogy, Hist
Function: Res libr
Publications: Annual Report of Museum; History of Claflin-Richards House, Allens History of Wenham
Mem of Massachusetts Library System
Restriction: Non-circulating, Open by appt only

WEST ACTON

P WEST ACTON CITIZEN'S LIBRARY*, 21 Windsor Ave, 01720. SAN 307-0697. Tel: 978-929-6654. E-mail: wacl@acton-ma.gov. Web Site: www.acton-ma.gov/115/Citizens-Library. *Dir,* Jennifer Friedman; E-mail: jfriedman@acton-ma.gov
Library Holdings: Bk Vols 11,700; Per Subs 25
Wireless access
Open Tues-Fri 9:30-5, Sat (Sept-June) 9:30-12:30, Sun (Nov-May) 10-1
Friends of the Library Group

WEST BARNSTABLE

J CAPE COD COMMUNITY COLLEGE*, Wilkens Library, 2240 Iyannough Rd, 02668-1599. SAN 307-7705. Tel: 508-362-2131. Circulation Tel: 508-362-2131, Ext 4342, 508-362-2131, Ext 4480. Interlibrary Loan Service Tel: 508-362-2131, Ext 4448. Reference Tel: 508-362-2131, Ext 4343. Toll Free Tel: 877-846-3672. FAX: 508-375-4020. E-mail: refdesk@capecod.edu. Web Site: www.capecod.edu/library. *Dir,* Tim Gerolami; Tel: 508-362-2131, Ext 4351, E-mail: tgerolami@capecod.edu; *Spec Coll Librn,* Rebekah Ambrose-Dalton; Tel: 508-362-2131, Ext 4445, E-mail: rambrosedalton@capecod.edu; *Tech Serv Librn,* Jessica Jordan; Tel: 508-362-2131, Ext 4617, E-mail: jjordan@capecod.edu; *Circ Mgr,* Eileen Redfield; E-mail: ekearns@capecod.edu. Subject Specialists: *Archives, Hist,* Rebekah Ambrose-Dalton; *Illinois,* Eileen Redfield; Staff 7.7 (MLS 4, Non-MLS 3.7)

Founded 1961. Enrl 2,500; Fac 75; Highest Degree: Associate

Library Holdings: AV Mats 3,581; e-books 265,507; e-journals 76,068; Electronic Media & Resources 28,690; Bk Vols 46,555; Per Subs 75

Special Collections: Cape Cod History Coll; FC Cooperating Coll. Oral History

Automation Activity & Vendor Info: (Acquisitions) Innovative Interfaces, Inc - Sierra; (Cataloging) Innovative Interfaces, Inc - Sierra; (Circulation) Innovative Interfaces, Inc - Sierra; (Course Reserve) Innovative Interfaces, Inc - Sierra; (ILL) Innovative Interfaces, Inc - Sierra; (Media Booking) Innovative Interfaces, Inc - Sierra; (OPAC) Innovative Interfaces, Inc - Sierra; (Serials) Innovative Interfaces, Inc - Sierra

Wireless access

Function: Archival coll, Computers for patron use, Doc delivery serv, Electronic databases & coll, Equip loans & repairs, ILL available, Internet access, Learning ctr, Microfiche/film & reading machines, Online cat, Online info literacy tutorials on the web & in blackboard, Orientations, Photocopying/Printing, Ref & res, Ref serv available, Scanner, Telephone ref, Wheelchair accessible

Mem of Massachusetts Library System

Partic in Cape Libraries Automated Materials Sharing Network; Massachusetts Commonwealth Consortium of Libraries in Public Higher Education Institutions; Westchester Academic Library Directors Organization

Open Mon-Thurs 8-8, Fri 8-4:30, Sat 9-1, Sun 1-5

Restriction: Non-circulating of rare bks

P WHELDEN MEMORIAL LIBRARY*, 2401 Meetinghouse Way, 02668. (Mail add: PO Box 147, 02668-0147), SAN 307-7713. Tel: 508-362-2262. FAX: 508-362-1344. E-mail: whelden@comcast.net. Web Site: www.wheldenlibrary.org. *Dir,* Victoria Allard; E-mail: vallard@clamsnet.org; Staff 4 (Non-MLS 4)

Founded 1899. Pop 2,206; Circ 25,249

Library Holdings: AV Mats 3,709; Bk Vols 16,921; Per Subs 22

Special Collections: Finnish History Coll

Subject Interests: Local hist

Wireless access

Partic in Cape Libraries Automated Materials Sharing Network

Open Mon & Wed 2-8, Tues & Thurs-Sat 9-2

Friends of the Library Group

WEST BOYLSTON

P BEAMAN MEMORIAL PUBLIC LIBRARY*, Eight Newton St, 01583. SAN 307-7721. Tel: 508-835-3711. FAX: 508-835-4770. E-mail: beaman@cwmars.org. Web Site: beamanlibrary.org. *Dir,* Anna Shaw; E-mail: ashaw@cwmars.org; *Asst Dir,* Lauren Espe; E-mail: lespe@cwmars.org; *Ch,* Susan Smith; E-mail: ssmith@cwmars.org; Staff 4.5 (MLS 0.8, Non-MLS 3.7)

Founded 1878. Pop 7,669; Circ 73,736

Jul 2014-Jun 2015 Income $384,848, State $9,000, City $365,848, Locally Generated Income $10,000. Mats Exp $54,800, Books $31,400, Per/Ser (Incl. Access Fees) $6,000, AV Mat $5,000, Electronic Ref Mat (Incl. Access Fees) $12,400. Sal $237,085 (Prof $139,918)

Library Holdings: Bk Vols 77,754; Per Subs 89

Automation Activity & Vendor Info: (Cataloging) Evergreen; (Circulation) Evergreen; (OPAC) Evergreen

Wireless access

Function: Bk club(s), Bks on cassette, Bks on CD, Children's prog, Computers for patron use, Electronic databases & coll, Home delivery & serv to seniorr ctr & nursing homes, ILL available, Magnifiers for reading, Museum passes, Music CDs, Notary serv, Photocopying/Printing, Prog for adults, Prog for children & young adult, Story hour, Tax forms, VHS videos, Wheelchair accessible

Publications: Beaman Browser (Newsletter)

Mem of Massachusetts Library System

Partic in Central & Western Massachusetts Automated Resource Sharing

Open Tues, Wed & Thurs 10-8, Fri & Sat 10-5

Friends of the Library Group

WEST BRIDGEWATER

P WEST BRIDGEWATER PUBLIC LIBRARY*, 80 Howard St, 02379-1710. SAN 307-773X. Tel: 508-894-1255. FAX: 508-894-1258. Web Site: www.westbpl.org. *Libr Dir,* Ellen Snoeyenbos; E-mail: ellens@sailsinc.org; *Head, Children's Servx,* Nanette Ryan; *Head, Tech Serv,* Apryl Edlund; *Circ Supvr,* Michelle Sheehan; Staff 5 (MLS 1, Non-MLS 4)

Founded 1879. Pop 6,742; Circ 64,059

Library Holdings: Audiobooks 500; AV Mats 457; Bks on Deafness & Sign Lang 30; Braille Volumes 2; CDs 1,294; DVDs 1,000; e-books 893; Electronic Media & Resources 20; High Interest/Low Vocabulary Bk Vols 200; Large Print Bks 2,000; Microforms 1; Music Scores 250; Bk Titles 61,402; Per Subs 180; Videos 500

Special Collections: West Bridgewater History Coll; World War II Autobiographies & Accounts. Oral History

Subject Interests: Local genealogy, W Bridgewater hist

Automation Activity & Vendor Info: (Acquisitions) SirsiDynix; (Cataloging) SirsiDynix; (Circulation) SirsiDynix; (Course Reserve) SirsiDynix; (OPAC) SirsiDynix; (Serials) SirsiDynix

Wireless access

Publications: Heddalines (Newsletter)

Mem of Massachusetts Library System

Partic in SAILS Library Network

Open Mon, Thurs & Fri 10-5, Tues & Wed 10-8, Sat 10-2

Friends of the Library Group

WEST BROOKFIELD

P MERRIAM-GILBERT PUBLIC LIBRARY*, Three W Main St, 01585. (Mail add: PO Box 364, 01585-0364), SAN 307-7748. Tel: 508-867-1410. FAX: 508-867-1409. Web Site: www.westbrookfieldlibrary.org. *Dir,* MaryAnne Pelletier; E-mail: mapelletier@cwmars.org; *Adult Serv, Asst Librn,* Holly Takorian; *Ch Serv,* Mary Beth Jackson; E-mail: mjackson@cwmars.org; Staff 3 (Non-MLS 3)

Founded 1880. Pop 4,646; Circ 34,865

Jul 2014-Jun 2015 Income $217,978. Mats Exp $38,103. Sal $117,223

Library Holdings: Audiobooks 455; CDs 1,062; DVDs 1,577; Bk Titles 13,592; Per Subs 424

Special Collections: Massachusetts Genealogy Coll

Subject Interests: Archives, Local hist, Manuscripts

Wireless access

Function: 24/7 Electronic res, 24/7 Online cat, Activity rm, Adult bk club, Archival coll, Art exhibits, Art programs, Audio & video playback equip for onsite use, Audiobks on Playaways & MP3, Audiobks via web, Bks on CD, Chess club, Children's prog, Computer training, Computers for patron use, Digital talking bks, E-Readers, Free DVD rentals, Holiday prog, Home delivery & serv to seniorr ctr & nursing homes, ILL available, Internet access, Magazines, Magnifiers for reading, Mail & tel request accepted, Mail loans to mem, Meeting rooms, Museum passes, Music CDs, Online cat, Photocopying/Printing, Printer for laptops & handheld devices, Prog for adults, Prog for children & young adult, Story hour, Summer reading prog, Tax forms, Teen prog, Telephone ref, Wheelchair accessible

Partic in Central & Western Massachusetts Automated Resource Sharing

Open Mon & Wed 9-5, Tues & Thurs 2-8, Sat 9-Noon

Friends of the Library Group

WEST DENNIS

P WEST DENNIS FREE PUBLIC LIBRARY, 260 Main St, Rte 28, 02670. (Mail add: PO Box 158, 02670-0158), SAN 307-7764. Tel: 508-398-2050. FAX: 508-394-6279. E-mail: den_w_mail@clamsnet.org. Web Site: www.westdennislibrary.org. *Libr Dir,* Hollin Elizabeth Pagos; E-mail: hpagos@clamsnet.org; *Cataloger,* Belva Dudac

Pop 5,000; Circ 15,183

Library Holdings: Bk Vols 14,000; Per Subs 42

Wireless access

Partic in Cape Libraries Automated Materials Sharing Network

Open Sun-Fri 10-2

Friends of the Library Group

WEST FALMOUTH

P WEST FALMOUTH LIBRARY*, 575 W Falmouth Hwy, 02574. (Mail add: PO Box 1209, 02574-1209), SAN 307-7772. Tel: 508-548-4709. FAX: 508-457-9534. E-mail: wfal_mail@clamsnet.org. Web Site: www.westfalmouthlibrary.org. *Libr Dir,* Lois Hiller

Pop 2,500; Circ 39,785

Library Holdings: Bk Vols 12,500; Per Subs 28

Automation Activity & Vendor Info: (Acquisitions) Innovative Interfaces, Inc - Millennium; (Cataloging) Innovative Interfaces, Inc - Millennium; (Circulation) Innovative Interfaces, Inc - Millennium

Wireless access

Partic in Cape Libraries Automated Materials Sharing Network

Open Tues, Wed & Fri 10-5, Thurs 2-8, Sat 10-1

WEST HARWICH

P CHASE LIBRARY*, Seven Main St, 02671-1041. (Mail add: PO Box 457, 02671-0457), SAN 307-7780. Tel: 508-432-2610. E-mail: chase.lib@verizon.net. *Dir,* Claire Gradone
Founded 1907. Circ 10,000
Library Holdings: Bk Vols 20,000
Wireless access
Function: ILL available
Open Tues 10-4, Sat 10-2
Friends of the Library Group

WEST NEWBURY

P G A R MEMORIAL LIBRARY*, 490 Main St, 01985-1115. SAN 307-7799. Tel: 978-363-1105. FAX: 978-363-1116. Web Site: www.westnewburylibrary.org. *Libr Dir,* Corinn Flaherty; E-mail: cflaherty@westnewburylibrary.org; Staff 7 (MLS 1, Non-MLS 6)
Founded 1819. Pop 4,605; Circ 77,143
Jul 2017-Jun 2018 Income $356,680, State $7,281, City $349,399. Mats Exp $65,950, Books $32,696, Per/Ser (Incl. Access Fees) $7,646, AV Mat $10,135, Electronic Ref Mat (Incl. Access Fees) $15,473. Sal $250,899
Library Holdings: Audiobooks 2,164; DVDs 3,173; Electronic Media & Resources 305; Large Print Bks 164; Bk Titles 41,012; Per Subs 171
Automation Activity & Vendor Info: (Cataloging) SirsiDynix; (Circulation) SirsiDynix; (ILL) Clio
Wireless access
Function: 24/7 Electronic res, 24/7 Online cat, Adult bk club
Mem of Massachusetts Library System
Partic in Merrimack Valley Library Consortium
Open Mon-Thurs 10-8, Fri 10-5, Sat 9-1
Friends of the Library Group

WEST ROXBURY

GM VA MEDICAL CENTER*, Medical Library, 1400 Veterans of Foreign Wars Pkwy, 02132. SAN 307-7802. Tel: 617-323-7700, Ext 35142. FAX: 857-203-5532. *Chief, Libr Serv,* Elaine Alligood; Staff 2 (MLS 1, Non-MLS 1)
Library Holdings: Bk Vols 3,850; Per Subs 300
Subject Interests: Allied health, Cardiology, Med, Surgery
Open Mon-Fri 8:30-4:30

WEST SPRINGFIELD

S STORROWTON VILLAGE MUSEUM LIBRARY, 1305 Memorial Ave, 01089. SAN 373-1758. Tel: 413-205-5051. E-mail: storrow@thebige.com. Web Site: www.storrowtonvillage.com. *Dir,* Jessica K Fontaine; E-mail: jfontaine@thebige.com
Library Holdings: Bk Vols 750
Subject Interests: Local hist
Restriction: Non-circulating, Open by appt only

P WEST SPRINGFIELD PUBLIC LIBRARY*, 200 Park St, 01089. SAN 307-7810. Tel: 413-736-4561. FAX: 413-736-6469. Web Site: www.wspl.org. *Dir,* Antonia Golinski-Foisy; Tel: 413-736-4561, Ext 102, E-mail: agolinsk@cwmars.org; *Asst Dir,* Nancy D Siegel; Tel: 413-736-4561, Ext 1112, E-mail: nsiegel@cwmars.org; *YA Librn,* Mare Alos; Tel: 413-736-4561, Ext 6, E-mail: malos@cwmars.org; *Adult Serv, Ref (Info Servs),* Christopher Franks; Tel: 413-736-4561, Ext 3, E-mail: cfranks@cwmars.org; *Cat, Tech Serv Supvr,* Eileen Chapman; E-mail: echapman@cwmars.org; *Youth Serv,* Terri Mitus; Tel: 413-736-4561, Ext 4, E-mail: tmitus@cwmars.org; Staff 24 (MLS 10, Non-MLS 14)
Founded 1854. Pop 25,876; Circ 198,517
Library Holdings: Bk Vols 102,154; Per Subs 196
Automation Activity & Vendor Info: (Acquisitions) Evergreen; (Cataloging) Evergreen; (Circulation) Evergreen; (OPAC) Evergreen
Wireless access
Partic in Central & Western Massachusetts Automated Resource Sharing
Special Services for the Deaf - Assisted listening device; Closed caption videos
Special Services for the Blind - Bks on cassette; Bks on CD; Copier with enlargement capabilities; Descriptive video serv (DVS); Large print bks; Magnifiers
Open Mon-Wed (Winter) 9-9, Thurs, Fri & Sat 9-5; Mon-Thurs (Summer) 9-8, Fri 9-5
Friends of the Library Group

WEST STOCKBRIDGE

P WEST STOCKBRIDGE PUBLIC LIBRARY*, 21 State Line Rd, 01266. (Mail add: PO Box 60, 01266-0060), SAN 307-7829. Tel: 413-232-0300, Ext 308. E-mail: weststockbridgelibrary@gmail.com. Web Site: www.weststockbridgelibrary.org/home. *Dir,* Rachel Alter; *Asst Librn,* Helen Cooper; *Asst Librn,* Brad Havill
Founded 1890. Pop 1,400
Library Holdings: Bk Titles 7,500; Per Subs 15
Wireless access
Partic in Central & Western Massachusetts Automated Resource Sharing
Open Tues 10-5, Wed-Fri 2-6, Sat 10-2
Friends of the Library Group

WEST WARREN

P WEST WARREN LIBRARY*, 2370 Main St, 01092. (Mail add: PO Box 369, 01092-0369), SAN 307-7845. Tel: 413-436-9892. FAX: 413-436-5086. E-mail: wwpl@comcast.net. Web Site: sites.google.com/view/westwarrenlibrary. *Co-Dir,* Christy McCann; *Co-Dir,* Susan Tower
Circ 5,390
Library Holdings: Bk Vols 9,000; Per Subs 18
Wireless access
Mem of Massachusetts Library System
Partic in Central & Western Massachusetts Automated Resource Sharing
Open Mon & Wed (Winter) 10-7, Fri 10-5; Mon-Sat (Summer) 10-5, Sat 11-5
Friends of the Library Group

WESTBOROUGH

P WESTBOROUGH PUBLIC LIBRARY, 55 W Main St, 01581. SAN 307-787X. Tel: 508-366-3050. FAX: 508-366-3049. E-mail: westboro@cwmars.org. Web Site: www.westboroughlib.org. *Libr Dir,* Maureen Amyot; E-mail: mamyot@town.westborough.ma.us; *Asst Dir,* Lynne Soukup; E-mail: lsoukup@town.westborough.ma.us; *Ad,* Megan Balbresky; E-mail: mbalbresky@cwmars.org; *Ch,* Hannah Gavalis; E-mail: hgavalis@cwmars.org; *Local Hist Librn,* Anthony Vaver; E-mail: avaver@town.westborough.ma.us; *Teen Librn,* Jen McGrath; E-mail: jmcgrath@cwmars.org; *Circ Supvr,* Lisa Zani; E-mail: lzani@cwmars.org; Staff 17 (MLS 5, Non-MLS 12)
Founded 1908. Pop 18,000
Jul 2021-Jun 2022 Income $1,125,144, State $30,095, City $1,050,858, Federal $3,098, Locally Generated Income $41,093. Mats Exp $153,011, Books $78,253, Per/Ser (Incl. Access Fees) $8,605, Other Print Mats $5,832, AV Mat $19,418, Electronic Ref Mat (Incl. Access Fees) $40,903
Library Holdings: Audiobooks 4,933; DVDs 4,689; e-books 84,627; e-journals 34; Electronic Media & Resources 242; Bk Titles 67,756; Per Subs 142
Special Collections: Local History (Reed Coll). Oral History
Automation Activity & Vendor Info: (Cataloging) Evergreen; (Circulation) Evergreen; (OPAC) Evergreen; (Serials) Evergreen
Wireless access
Function: 24/7 Electronic res, 24/7 Online cat, Adult bk club, Archival coll, Art exhibits, Audiobks on Playaways & MP3, Audiobks via web, Bk club(s), Bks on CD, CD-ROM, Children's prog, Computer training, Computers for patron use, Electronic databases & coll, Equip loans & repairs, Family literacy, Free DVD rentals, Holiday prog, Home delivery & serv to seniorr ctr & nursing homes, Homebound delivery serv, ILL available, Internet access, Magazines, Meeting rooms, Microfiche/film & reading machines, Movies, Museum passes, Music CDs, Online cat, OverDrive digital audio bks, Photocopying/Printing, Preschool reading prog, Printer for laptops & handheld devices, Prog for adults, Prog for children & young adult, Ref & res, Ref serv available, Scanner, Story hour, Summer reading prog, Tax forms, Teen prog, Telephone ref, Wheelchair accessible
Mem of Massachusetts Library System
Partic in Central & Western Massachusetts Automated Resource Sharing
Open Mon-Thurs 9-7, Sat 9-1, Sun (Oct-May) 1-5
Friends of the Library Group

WESTFIELD

P WESTFIELD ATHENAEUM, Six Elm St, 01085-2997. SAN 345-7834. Tel: 413-568-7833. Circulation Tel: 413-568-7833, Ext 3. Administration Tel: 413-568-0638, Ext 83. Information Services Tel: 413-562-0716, Ext 4. FAX: 413-568-0988. Web Site: www.westath.org. *Dir,* Guy McLain; E-mail: gmclain@westath.org; *Head, Adult Serv,* Kelsey Socha; Tel: 413-568-7833, Ext 113, E-mail: ksocha@westath.org; *Head, Youth Serv,* Olivia Eberli; Tel: 413-568-7833, Ext 7, E-mail: oeberli@westath.org; Staff 18 (MLS 6, Non-MLS 12)
Founded 1864. Pop 41,000; Circ 327,211
Jul 2020-Jun 2021. Mats Exp $112,350, Books $57,000, Per/Ser (Incl. Access Fees) $8,000, Manu Arch $5,000, Micro $750, AV Equip $5,000, AV Mat $21,000, Electronic Ref Mat (Incl. Access Fees) $10,600, Presv $5,000. Sal $972,674 (Prof $733,014)
Library Holdings: Audiobooks 6,931; DVDs 8,433; e-books 30,858; Bk Vols 146,236; Per Subs 120
Special Collections: Local Coll, archives; Museum Coll
Automation Activity & Vendor Info: (Cataloging) Innovative Interfaces, Inc; (Circulation) Innovative Interfaces, Inc; (OPAC) Innovative Interfaces, Inc
Wireless access

Function: 24/7 Electronic res, 24/7 Online cat, Activity rm, Adult bk club, Adult literacy prog, After school storytime, Archival coll, Art exhibits, Art programs, Audiobks via web, AV serv, Bks on CD, Bus archives, Children's prog, Citizenship assistance, Computer training, Computers for patron use, Digital talking bks, Doc delivery serv, Electronic databases & coll, Family literacy, Free DVD rentals, Homebound delivery serv, ILL available, Internet access, Life-long learning prog for all ages, Mail & tel request accepted, Meeting rooms, Microfiche/film & reading machines, Museum passes, Music CDs, Online cat, Online info literacy tutorials on the web & in blackboard, Online ref, Outside serv via phone, mail, e-mail & web, Photocopying/Printing, Preschool outreach, Preschool reading prog, Printer for laptops & handheld devices, Prog for adults, Prog for children & young adult, Ref & res, Ref serv available, Res assist avail, Senior outreach, Story hour, Study rm, Summer & winter reading prog, Summer reading prog, Tax forms, Teen prog, Telephone ref, Visual arts prog, Wheelchair accessible, Winter reading prog
Partic in Central & Western Massachusetts Automated Resource Sharing
Open Mon-Thurs 9-8, Fri & Sat 9-5
Restriction: 24-hr pass syst for students only
Friends of the Library Group

C WESTFIELD STATE UNIVERSITY*, Ely Library, 577 Western Ave, 01085-2580. (Mail add: PO Box 1630, 01086-1630), SAN 307-7896. Circulation Tel: 413-572-5231. Interlibrary Loan Service Tel: 413-572-5655. Reference Tel: 413-572-5234. Administration Tel: 413-572-5639. FAX: 413-572-5520. Web Site: lib.westfield.ma.edu. *Assoc Librn, Head, Ref & Info Serv,* Brian Hubbard; E-mail: bhubbard@westfield.ma.edu; *Head, Res,* Corinne Ebbs; E-mail: cebbs@westfield.ma.edu; *Assoc Librn,* Oliver Zeff; E-mail: ozeff@westfield.ma.edu. Subject Specialists: *Educ,* Corinne Ebbs; Staff 13 (MLS 8, Non-MLS 5)
Founded 1839. Enrl 4,871; Fac 222; Highest Degree: Master
Library Holdings: Bk Titles 120,685; Bk Vols 159,126; Per Subs 638
Subject Interests: Criminal law & justice, Educ
Automation Activity & Vendor Info: (Acquisitions) Ex Libris Group; (Cataloging) Ex Libris Group; (Circulation) Ex Libris Group; (Course Reserve) Ex Libris Group; (ILL) Ex Libris Group; (Media Booking) Ex Libris Group; (OPAC) Ex Libris Group; (Serials) Ex Libris Group
Wireless access
Publications: Student Guide
Partic in Cooperating Libraries of Greater Springfield; LYRASIS; OCLC Online Computer Library Center, Inc
Special Services for the Deaf - Assisted listening device; Assistive tech
Special Services for the Blind - Accessible computers; Assistive/Adapted tech devices, equip & products; Copier with enlargement capabilities; Duplicating spec requests; Networked computers with assistive software; Scanner for conversion & translation of mats; Screen enlargement software for people with visual disabilities; Screen reader software
Open Mon-Thurs (Fall & Spring) 8am-Midnight, Fri 8-5, Sat 10-6, Sun 1-Midnight; Mon & Tues (Summer) 9-9, Wed & Thurs 9-6, Fri 9-5

WESTFORD

P J V FLETCHER LIBRARY, 50 Main St, 01886-2599. SAN 307-790X. Tel: 978-692-5555. FAX: 978-692-4418. E-mail: westfordlibrary@westfordma.gov. Web Site: www.westfordlibrary.org. *Dir,* Ellen Rainville; Tel: 978-399-2312, E-mail: erainville@westfordma.gov; *Asst Dir,* Kristina Leedberg; Tel: 978-399-2311, E-mail: kleedberg@westfordma.gov; *Head, Automation & Tech Serv, Head, Syst,* Dina Kanabar; Tel: 978-399-2308, E-mail: dkanabar@westfordma.gov; *Head, Circ,* Holly Sheridan; Tel: 978-399-2313; *Head, Info Serv,* Sarah Regan; Tel: 978-399-2309, E-mail: sregan@westfordma.gov; *Head, Youth Serv,* Nancy Boutet; Tel: 978-399-2307, E-mail: nboutet@westfordma.gov; Staff 20.2 (MLS 9, Non-MLS 11.2)
Founded 1797. Pop 21,951; Circ 322,509. Sal $1,083,226 (Prof $384,414)
Library Holdings: Audiobooks 8,149; CDs 1,560; DVDs 8,165; e-books 3,856; Electronic Media & Resources 2,688; Microforms 19,208; Bk Vols 99,393; Per Subs 342
Special Collections: Chinese Foreign Language Titles; Genealogical Data Coll; Merrimack Valley Historic Document Coll; Textile Mill Histories Coll
Automation Activity & Vendor Info: (Cataloging) Evergreen; (Circulation) Evergreen
Wireless access
Function: Adult bk club, Adult literacy prog, After school storytime, Archival coll, Audiobks via web, AV serv, Bk club(s), Bks on cassette, Bks on CD, CD-ROM, Computer training, Computers for patron use, Distance learning, Doc delivery serv, Electronic databases & coll, Homebound delivery serv, ILL available, Internet access, Microfiche/film & reading machines, Museum passes, Music CDs, Online cat, Online ref, Outside serv via phone, mail, e-mail & web, OverDrive digital audio bks, Photocopying/Printing, Preschool reading prog, Prog for adults, Prog for children & young adult, Ref serv available, Spoken cassettes & CDs, Summer reading prog, Telephone ref, VHS videos, Wheelchair accessible, Workshops
Publications: Bi-Annual Town Wide Mailing of Programs & Events; J V Fletcher Library e-News; Library Latest Byline; Online Library Website
Mem of Massachusetts Library System
Partic in Merrimack Valley Library Consortium
Open Mon-Thurs 10-9, Fri 1-5, Sat 10-5; Sun (Jan-April) 2-5
Friends of the Library Group

WESTHAMPTON

P WESTHAMPTON PUBLIC LIBRARY, One North Rd, 01027. SAN 307-7918. Tel: 413-527-5386. E-mail: westhampton@cwmars.org. Web Site: www.westhampton-ma.com/westhampton-public-library. *Dir,* Meaghan Schwelm
Founded 1866. Pop 1,750; Circ 24,000
Automation Activity & Vendor Info: (Cataloging) Innovative Interfaces, Inc; (Circulation) Innovative Interfaces, Inc; (OPAC) Innovative Interfaces, Inc
Wireless access
Partic in Basic Health Sciences Library Network; Central & Western Massachusetts Automated Resource Sharing
Open Mon & Thurs 2-8, Tues & Wed 9-12 & 1-5, Sat 10-1
Friends of the Library Group

WESTMINSTER

P FORBUSH MEMORIAL LIBRARY*, Westminster Public Library, 118 Main St, 01473. (Mail add: PO Box 468, 01473-0468), SAN 307-7926. Tel: 978-874-7416. FAX: 978-874-7424. Web Site: www.forbushlibrary.org. *Dir,* Nick Langhart; E-mail: nlanghart@westminster-ma.gov; *Ch,* Amy D Kuilema; E-mail: akuilema@westminster-ma.gov; *Ref Librn,* Jason Cavanaugh; Staff 3 (MLS 2, Non-MLS 1)
Founded 1868. Pop 7,600; Circ 40,383
Jul 2020-Jun 2021 Income $444,831, State $11,000, City $432,731, Locally Generated Income $600, Other $500. Mats Exp $87,260, Books $54,000, Per/Ser (Incl. Access Fees) $2,000, Other Print Mats $2,245, AV Mat $26,000, Electronic Ref Mat (Incl. Access Fees) $3,015. Sal $296,741 (Prof $180,000)
Library Holdings: Audiobooks 22,541; CDs 4,070; DVDs 3,850; e-books 47,500; Electronic Media & Resources 106,015; Large Print Bks 2,000; Microforms 3; Bk Vols 40,383; Per Subs 75; Videos 4,109
Special Collections: Local History & Genealogy Coll
Automation Activity & Vendor Info: (Acquisitions) Evergreen; (Cataloging) Evergreen; (Circulation) Evergreen; (ILL) Evergreen; (OPAC) Evergreen; (Serials) EBSCO Online
Wireless access
Function: 24/7 Electronic res, 24/7 Online cat, Adult bk club
Mem of Massachusetts Library System
Partic in Central & Western Massachusetts Automated Resource Sharing
Special Services for the Blind - Assistive/Adapted tech devices, equip & products
Open Tues-Thurs 10-8, Fri 10-6, Sat 9-1
Friends of the Library Group

S WESTMINSTER HISTORICAL SOCIETY LIBRARY*, 110 Main St, 01473. (Mail add: PO Box 177, 01473-0177), SAN 375-1872. Tel: 978-874-5569. E-mail: westminsterhistoricalsociety@gmail.com. Web Site: testwhs.westminsterhistoricalsociety.org. *Coll Develop, Curator,* Betsy Hannula; E-mail: betsyhannula@gmail.com
Founded 1921
Library Holdings: Bk Titles 1,000
Special Collections: General Nelson A Miles Coll
Subject Interests: Local hist
Open Mon 7pm-9pm, Wed 9-11, Fri 9-12

WESTON

R POPE JOHN XXIII NATIONAL SEMINARY*, Learning Center, 558 South Ave, 02493. SAN 307-7950. Tel: 781-810-1931, Ext 138. FAX: 781-899-9057. Web Site: www.psjs.edu/learning-center. *Librn,* Barbara Mullen-Neem; E-mail: bneem@psjs.edu
Founded 1963. Enrl 62; Fac 20; Highest Degree: Doctorate
Library Holdings: Bk Titles 65,904
Special Collections: Comprehensive English Language Theology, 1958 to date
Mem of Massachusetts Library System

C REGIS COLLEGE LIBRARY*, 235 Wellesley St, 02493. SAN 307-7969. Tel: 781-768-7300. Reference Tel: 781-768-7303. FAX: 781-768-7323. Web Site: www.regiscollege.edu/academics/regis-college-library. *Libr Dir,* Jane Peck; Tel: 781-768-7307, E-mail: jane.peck@regiscollege.edu; *Dir, Info Serv,* Tricia Reinhart; Tel: 781-768-7378, E-mail: tricia.reinhart@regiscollege.edu; *Ref Librn,* Amy Howard; E-mail: amy.howard@regiscollege.edu; *Ref Librn,* Silvia Mejia-Suarez; E-mail: silvia.mejia-suarez@regiscollege.edu; *Circ Supvr,* Benjamin Nyquist; Tel: 781-768-7302, E-mail: benjamin.nyquist@regiscollege.edu; *ILL,* Armine

Bagdasarian; Tel: 781-768-7306, E-mail: armine.bagdasarian@regiscollege.edu; Staff 11 (MLS 5, Non-MLS 6)
Founded 1927. Enrl 1,590; Fac 129; Highest Degree: Doctorate
Library Holdings: e-journals 19,140; Bk Titles 113,108; Bk Vols 135,458; Per Subs 607
Special Collections: Cardinal Newman Coll; Madeleine Doran Coll
Subject Interests: Art, Econ, Hist, Lit, Music, Natural sci, Nursing, Women's studies
Automation Activity & Vendor Info: (Acquisitions) Innovative Interfaces, Inc - Sierra; (Cataloging) Innovative Interfaces, Inc - Sierra; (Circulation) Innovative Interfaces, Inc - Sierra; (Course Reserve) Innovative Interfaces, Inc - Sierra; (ILL) Clio; (OPAC) Innovative Interfaces, Inc - Sierra; (Serials) EBSCO Online
Wireless access
Mem of Massachusetts Library System
Partic in Minuteman Library Network; OCLC Online Computer Library Center, Inc

S SPELLMAN MUSEUM OF STAMPS & POSTAL HISTORY LIBRARY*, 241 Wellesley St, 02493. SAN 307-7942. Tel: 781-768-8367. E-mail: info@spellman.org. Web Site: www.spellmanmuseum.org/library. *Curator,* George Norton; E-mail: george.norton@spellman.org
Founded 1960
Library Holdings: Bk Titles 15,000; Per Subs 20
Subject Interests: Philately
Open Thurs-Sun 12-5
Restriction: Non-circulating

P WESTON PUBLIC LIBRARY, 87 School St, 02493. SAN 307-7977. Tel: 781-786-6150. FAX: 781-786-6159. E-mail: wsnmail2@minlib.net. Web Site: www.westonlibrary.org. *Dir,* Jennifer Warner; E-mail: jwarner@minlib.net; *Asst Dir,* Allison Palmgren; E-mail: apalmgren@minlib.net; Staff 8 (MLS 8)
Founded 1857. Pop 11,469; Circ 222,463
Library Holdings: Bk Vols 91,500; Per Subs 221
Special Collections: Local History
Wireless access
Partic in Minuteman Library Network
Open Mon-Thurs 10-9, Sat 10-5, Sun 12-5
Friends of the Library Group

WESTPORT

P WESTPORT FREE PUBLIC LIBRARY*, 408 Old County Rd, 02790. SAN 307-7985. Tel: 508-636-1100. FAX: 508-636-1102. Web Site: www.sailsinc.org/member-libraries/westport, www.westport-ma.com/westport-free-public-library. *Dir,* Susan R Branco; E-mail: sbranco@sailsinc.org; *Asst Dir,* Linda R Cunha
Founded 1891. Pop 14,594; Circ 57,521
Library Holdings: Bk Titles 38,965; Per Subs 73
Wireless access
Mem of Massachusetts Library System
Partic in SAILS Library Network
Open Mon & Thurs 12:30-8:30, Tues, Wed & Fri 10-5, Sat 9-4
Friends of the Library Group

WESTWOOD

P WESTWOOD PUBLIC LIBRARY*, 660 High St, 02090. SAN 345-7893. Tel: 781-326-7562. Circulation Tel: 781-320-1048. Reference Tel: 781-320-1045. Administration Tel: 781-320-1041. FAX: 781-326-5383. Web Site: www.westwoodlibrary.org. *Dir,* Tricia Perry; E-mail: tperry@minlib.net; *Head, Adult Serv,* Molly Riportella; Tel: 718-320-1004; *Head, Children's Servx,* Elizabeth McGovern; Tel: 781-320-1043; *Head, Circ,* Karen Gallagher; Tel: 781-320-1049; *Head, Tech Serv,* June Tulikangas; Tel: 781-320-1047; Staff 31 (MLS 9, Non-MLS 22)
Founded 1898. Pop 16,055; Circ 277,870
Library Holdings: Audiobooks 8,146; AV Mats 9,791; Electronic Media & Resources 341; Bk Vols 108,342; Per Subs 275
Special Collections: Sautter Art Coll
Wireless access
Function: 24/7 Electronic res, 24/7 Online cat, Activity rm, Adult bk club, After school storytime, Art exhibits, Art programs, Audiobks on Playaways & MP3, AV serv, Bi-weekly Writer's Group, Bk club(s), Bks on CD, Children's prog, Computer training, Computers for patron use, E-Readers, Electronic databases & coll, Free DVD rentals, Genealogy discussion group, Health sci info serv, Holiday prog, Home delivery & serv to seniorr ctr & nursing homes, Homebound delivery serv, ILL available, Instruction & testing, Internet access, Life-long learning prog for all ages, Magazines, Magnifiers for reading, Mango lang, Meeting rooms, Microfiche/film & reading machines, Movies, Museum passes, Music CDs, Notary serv, Online cat, Online ref, Outreach serv, Outside serv via phone, mail, e-mail & web, OverDrive digital audio bks, Photocopying/Printing, Preschool outreach, Preschool reading prog, Printer for laptops & handheld devices, Prog for adults, Prog for children & young adult, Ref & res, Ref serv available, Scanner, Senior computer classes, Senior outreach, Serves people with intellectual disabilities, Spanish lang bks, Spoken cassettes & CDs, Spoken cassettes & DVDs, STEM programs, Story hour, Study rm, Summer reading prog, Tax forms, Teen prog, Telephone ref, Visual arts prog, Wheelchair accessible, Winter reading prog, Workshops, Writing prog
Partic in Minuteman Library Network
Open Mon-Wed 10-9, Thurs 1-9, Fri 10-6, Sat 10-5, Sun 2-5
Friends of the Library Group
Branches: 1
ISLINGTON, 280 Washington St, 02090, SAN 345-7923. Tel: 781-326-5914. *Librn,* Claire Connors
Library Holdings: Bk Vols 16,000; Per Subs 75
Open Tues & Thurs 10-5, Wed 1-8, Sat (Sept-June) 10-1
Friends of the Library Group

WEYMOUTH

P WEYMOUTH PUBLIC LIBRARIES*, Tufts Library, 46 Broad St, 02188. SAN 345-7958. Tel: 781-338-5994. E-mail: wecontact@ocln.org. Web Site: www.weymouth.ma.us/weymouth-public-libraries. *Dir,* Robert MacLean; Staff 11 (MLS 11)
Founded 1879. Pop 55,137; Circ 215,006
Library Holdings: Bk Vols 155,151; Per Subs 400
Special Collections: Local History Coll; Teachers' Professional Library. Oral History
Automation Activity & Vendor Info: (Acquisitions) SirsiDynix; (Cataloging) SirsiDynix; (Circulation) SirsiDynix; (ILL) SirsiDynix; (OPAC) SirsiDynix; (Serials) SirsiDynix
Wireless access
Open Mon-Thurs 9-9, Fri & Sat 9-5
Friends of the Library Group
Branches: 3
FOGG LIBRARY, One Columbian St, South Weymouth, 02190, SAN 345-7982. Tel: 781-340-5002. *Dir, Libr Serv,* Robert MacLean
Library Holdings: Bk Vols 25,000
Open Mon-Wed 9-9, Thurs & Fri 9-5, Sat (Sept-May) 9-5
NORTH BRANCH, 220 North St, 02191, SAN 375-2968.
Open Mon, Wed & Thurs 9-5, Tues 1-5
Friends of the Library Group
FRANKLIN N PRATT LIBRARY, 1400 Pleasant St, East Weymouth, 02189, SAN 345-8016.
Library Holdings: Bk Vols 14,000
Open Mon, Wed & Thurs 9-9, Tues & Fri 9-5, Sat (Sept-May) 9-5

WHATELY

P S WHITE DICKINSON MEMORIAL LIBRARY*, 202 Chestnut Plain Rd, 01093. (Mail add: PO Box 187, 01093-0187), SAN 307-8000. Tel: 413-665-2170. FAX: 413-665-9560. E-mail: library@whately.org. Web Site: www.whately.org/library. *Dir,* Cyndi Steiner; E-mail: csteiner@cwmars.org
Founded 1951. Pop 1,400; Circ 9,380
Library Holdings: Bk Vols 11,000
Special Collections: New England History of towns, Genealogy books - gift of Stuart Waite
Subject Interests: Local hist
Wireless access
Partic in Central & Western Massachusetts Automated Resource Sharing
Open Mon 10-5, Tues & Wed 1-8, Sat 10-3
Friends of the Library Group

WHITINSVILLE

P WHITINSVILLE SOCIAL LIBRARY*, 17 Church St, 01588. SAN 345-8075. Tel: 508-234-2151. E-mail: books@northbridgemass.org. Web Site: www.northbridgemass.org/WSL/wslhome.htm. *Dir,* Rebecca Sasseville; E-mail: rsasseville@cwmars.org; *Youth Serv Librn,* Helen O'Hara
Founded 1844. Pop 16,556
Wireless access
Function: 24/7 Online cat, Bk club(s), Bks on CD, Children's prog, Computers for patron use, Electronic databases & coll, Free DVD rentals, ILL available, Internet access, Magazines, Museum passes, Online cat, OverDrive digital audio bks, Photocopying/Printing, Prog for adults, Prog for children & young adult, Summer reading prog, Teen prog, Wheelchair accessible
Mem of Massachusetts Library System
Partic in Central & Western Massachusetts Automated Resource Sharing

WHITMAN

P WHITMAN PUBLIC LIBRARY*, 100 Webster St, 02382. SAN 307-8019. Tel: 781-447-7613. FAX: 781-447-7678. E-mail: info@whitmanpubliclibrary.org. Web Site: www.whitmanpubliclibrary.org. *Dir,* Marcie Walsh-O'Connor; E-mail: mwalsh-oconnor@ocln.org; *Asst Dir,*

Tyler Vachon; *Youth Serv Librn,* Stephanie Young; *Supvr, Circ,* Barbara Bryant; *Sr Libr Tech,* Mary Casey; Staff 5 (MLS 2, Non-MLS 3)
Founded 1879. Pop 14,381; Circ 71,078
Library Holdings: AV Mats 4,787; Bk Vols 45,536; Per Subs 113
Subject Interests: Local hist
Automation Activity & Vendor Info: (Cataloging) SirsiDynix; (Circulation) SirsiDynix; (OPAC) SirsiDynix
Wireless access
Partic in Old Colony Libr Network
Open Mon-Thurs 10-8, Fri 1-5, Sat (Sept-June) 10-4
Friends of the Library Group

WILBRAHAM

P WILBRAHAM PUBLIC LIBRARY, 25 Crane Park Dr, 01095-1799. SAN 307-8027. Tel: 413-596-6141. FAX: 413-596-5090. Reference E-mail: reference@wilbrahamlibrary.org. Web Site: www.wilbrahamlibrary.org. *Libr Dir,* Karen Demers; E-mail: karendemers@wilbrahamlibrary.org; *Ad,* Caroline Welch; *Ch,* Heidi Kane; E-mail: hkane@wilbrahamlibrary.org; Staff 17 (MLS 4, Non-MLS 13)
Founded 1892. Pop 13,500; Circ 165,262
Library Holdings: Audiobooks 4,623; AV Mats 7,775; Bk Vols 48,059; Per Subs 1,733; Videos 3,749
Special Collections: Local History (Wilbraham Coll)
Automation Activity & Vendor Info: (Acquisitions) Evergreen; (Cataloging) Evergreen; (Circulation) Evergreen; (OPAC) Evergreen
Wireless access
Function: ILL available, Outside serv via phone, mail, e-mail & web, Photocopying/Printing, Telephone ref
Publications: Library News (Newsletter)
Partic in Central & Western Massachusetts Automated Resource Sharing
Open Mon-Wed 9-8, Thurs & Fri 9-5, Sat 9-2, Sun (Sept-May) 12-5
Friends of the Library Group

WILLIAMSBURG

P MEEKINS LIBRARY*, Two Williams St, 01096. (Mail add: PO Box 772, 01096-0772), SAN 307-8035. Tel: 413-268-7472. FAX: 413-268-7488. E-mail: meekins@cwmars.org. Web Site: www.meekins-library.org. *Dir,* Beverly Bullock; E-mail: bbullock@cwmars.org
Pop 2,500; Circ 97,500
Library Holdings: Bk Titles 66,000; Per Subs 209
Automation Activity & Vendor Info: (Cataloging) Innovative Interfaces, Inc; (Circulation) Innovative Interfaces, Inc; (OPAC) Innovative Interfaces, Inc
Wireless access
Publications: Abridged Readers Guide to Periodical Literature
Partic in Central & Western Massachusetts Automated Resource Sharing
Open Tues 12-5, Wed 10-8, Thurs 3-6, Sat 10-2
Friends of the Library Group

WILLIAMSTOWN

P DAVID & JOYCE MILNE PUBLIC LIBRARY*, 1095 Main St, 01267-2627. SAN 345-813X. Tel: 413-458-5369. FAX: 413-458-3085. E-mail: milnelibrary@williamstownma.gov. Web Site: www.milnelibrary.org. *Dir,* Patricia McLeod; E-mail: pmcleod@williamstownma.gov; *Asst Dir,* Roz Broch; E-mail: rbroch@williamstownma.gov; *Ch,* Kirsten Rose; E-mail: krose@williamstownma.gov; *Ref Librn,* Kira Bingemann; E-mail: kbingemann@williamstownma.gov; *Circ Mgr,* Juliana Haubrich; E-mail: jhaubrich@williamstownma.gov; Staff 16 (MLS 3, Non-MLS 13)
Founded 1876. Pop 8,220; Circ 212,923
Library Holdings: CDs 5,599; DVDs 5,229; e-books 5,448; Large Print Bks 2,419; Bk Titles 76,081; Per Subs 268; Talking Bks 2,970
Subject Interests: Local hist
Automation Activity & Vendor Info: (Cataloging) Evergreen; (Circulation) Evergreen; (OPAC) Evergreen
Wireless access
Function: Adult bk club, Adult literacy prog, Art exhibits, Audiobks via web, Chess club, Children's prog, Computers for patron use, E-Reserves, Free DVD rentals, Home delivery & serv to seniorr ctr & nursing homes, ILL available, Museum passes, Online cat, OverDrive digital audio bks, Photocopying/Printing, Prog for adults, Ref serv available, Spoken cassettes & CDs, Summer reading prog, Tax forms, Telephone ref, Wheelchair accessible, Workshops, Writing prog
Publications: Biblio-File (Newsletter)
Partic in Central & Western Massachusetts Automated Resource Sharing
Open Mon, Tues, Thurs & Fri 10-5:30, Wed 10-8, Sat 10-4
Friends of the Library Group

S STERLING & FRANCINE CLARK ART INSTITUTE LIBRARY*, 225 South St, 01267. SAN 307-8043. Tel: 413-458-0532. FAX: 413-458-9542. E-mail: library@clarkart.edu. Web Site: www.clarkart.edu/library. *Dir,* Susan Roeper; Tel: 413-458-0551, E-mail: sroeper@clarkart.edu; *Coll Mgt Librn,* Andrea Puccio; Tel: 413-458-0535, E-mail: apuccio@clarkart.edu; *Coll & Access Serv Librn, Ref Librn,* Karen Bucky; Tel: 413-458-0532, E-mail: kbucky@clarkart.edu; *Coll Develop Librn,* Terri Boccia; Tel: 413-458-0437, E-mail: tboccia@clarkart.edu; Staff 7 (MLS 3, Non-MLS 4)
Founded 1962
Library Holdings: Bk Vols 230,000; Per Subs 650
Special Collections: Auction Catalogues; History of Photomechanical Reproduction (David A Hanson Coll); Mary Ann Beinecke Decorative Arts Coll; Robert Sterling Clark Coll of Rare & Illustrated Books
Subject Interests: Contemporary art, European art, Medieval art
Automation Activity & Vendor Info: (Acquisitions) Innovative Interfaces, Inc - Millennium; (Cataloging) Innovative Interfaces, Inc - Millennium; (Circulation) Innovative Interfaces, Inc - Millennium; (ILL) OCLC ILLiad; (OPAC) Innovative Interfaces, Inc - Millennium; (Serials) Innovative Interfaces, Inc - Millennium
Wireless access
Function: Res libr
Partic in LYRASIS; OCLC Research Library Partnership
Open Mon-Fri 9-5
Restriction: Non-circulating

C WILLIAMS COLLEGE*, Sawyer Library, 26 Hopkins Hall Dr, 01267. SAN 345-8199. Tel: 413-597-2501. Interlibrary Loan Service Tel: 413-597-2005. FAX: 413-597-4106. Web Site: library.williams.edu. *Dir of Libr,* Jonathan Miller; Tel: 413-597-2502, E-mail: jm30@williams.edu; *Head, Access Serv,* Nadine F Nance; Tel: 413-597-2920, E-mail: nfn1@williams.edu; *Head, Coll Mgt,* M Robin Kibler; Tel: 413-597-3047, E-mail: rkibler@williams.edu; *Head, Libr Syst,* Walter Komorowski; Tel: 413-597-2084, E-mail: wkomorow@williams.edu; *Head, Res Serv,* Christine Menard; Tel: 413-597-2515, E-mail: cmenard@williams.edu; *Head, Sci Libr,* Helena Warburg; Tel: 413-597-3085, E-mail: hwarburg@williams.edu; *Cat Librn,* Karen Gorss Benko; Tel: 413-597-4322, E-mail: kbenko@williams.edu; *Cat Librn,* Christine Blackman; Tel: 413-597-4403, E-mail: cblackma@williams.edu; *Chapin Librn,* Wayne Hammond; Tel: 413-597-2462, E-mail: whammond@williams.edu; *Instrul & Ref Librn,* Lori DuBois; Tel: 413-597-4614, E-mail: ldubois@williams.edu; *Ref, Web Develop Librn,* Emery Shriver; Tel: 413-597-4716, E-mail: mes4@williams.edu; *Digital Archivist/Rec Mgr,* Jessika Drmacich; Tel: 413-597-4725, E-mail: jdg1@williams.edu; *Archivist,* Sylvia Brown; Tel: 413-597-2596, E-mail: skennick@williams.edu; Staff 18 (MLS 15, Non-MLS 3)
Founded 1793. Enrl 2,099; Fac 346; Highest Degree: Master
Library Holdings: AV Mats 36,462; CDs 438; DVDs 6,570; e-books 140,954; e-journals 94,410; Microforms 418,017; Bk Vols 993,243; Per Subs 763
Special Collections: Chesterwood Archives (sculptor Daniel Chester French and family), photos, ms; Herman Rosse Coll, bks, ms, art; Paul Breman Coll (Black literature and culture), bks, ms, photos; Paul Whiteman Coll, ms, rec & scores; Pauline Baynes Coll, bks, ms, art; Samuel Butler (1835-1902) Coll, bks, ms, art, music; Shaker Coll, bks, ms & pamphlets; Walt Whitman Coll, bks, ms, ephemera; William Cullen Bryant Coll, bks & ms. US Document Depository
Subject Interests: African-Am studies, Art, Humanities, Natural sci, Performing arts
Automation Activity & Vendor Info: (OPAC) Ex Libris Group
Wireless access
Partic in Boston Library Consortium, Inc; Center for Research Libraries; OCLC Online Computer Library Center, Inc
Open Mon-Thurs 8am-2:30am, Fri 8am-10pm, Sat 9am-10pm, Sun 9am-2:30am

S WILLIAMSTOWN HISTORICAL MUSEUM, 32 New Ashford Rd, 01267. SAN 373-1995. Tel: 413-458-2160. E-mail: info@williamstownhistoricalmuseum.org. Web Site: www.williamstownhistoricalmuseum.org. *Dir,* Ellen Faeney; E-mail: ellen@williamstownhistoricalmuseum.org; Staff 1 (Non-MLS 1)
Founded 1941
Library Holdings: Bk Vols 1,805
Subject Interests: Genealogy, Local hist
Wireless access
Function: Res libr
Publications: Newsletter

WILMINGTON

P WILMINGTON MEMORIAL LIBRARY*, 175 Middlesex Ave, 01887-2779. SAN 307-8086. Tel: 978-658-2967. Reference Tel: 978-694-2099. FAX: 978-658-9699. E-mail: mwlinfo@mvlc.org. Web Site: www.wilmlibrary.org. *Dir,* Christina A Stewart; E-mail: tstewart@wilmlibrary.org; *Asst Libr Dir,* Charlotte Wood; E-mail: cwood@wilmlibrary.org; *Adult Serv, Head, Ref,* Kimberly Blakely; E-mail: kblakely@wilmlibrary.org; *Mkt Librn,* Danielle Ward; E-mail: dward@wilmlibrary.org; *Tech Librn,* Bradley McKenna; E-mail: bmckenna@wilmlibrary.org; *Ch Serv,* Barbara Raab; E-mail: braab@wilmlibrary.org; *Circ,* Linda Pavluk; E-mail:

lpavluk@wilmlibrary.org; *YA Serv,* Brittany Tuttle; E-mail: btuttle@wilmlibrary.org; Staff 10 (MLS 7, Non-MLS 3)
Founded 1871
Jul 2016-Jun 2017 Income $1,142,522. Mats Exp $147,560, Books $68,822, Per/Ser (Incl. Access Fees) $8,474, AV Mat $19,606, Electronic Ref Mat (Incl. Access Fees) $50,658. Sal $892,678 (Prof $797,802)
Library Holdings: AV Mats 8,755; Bk Vols 38,249
Automation Activity & Vendor Info: (Acquisitions) SirsiDynix; (Cataloging) SirsiDynix; (Circulation) SirsiDynix; (ILL) SirsiDynix; (OPAC) SirsiDynix; (Serials) SirsiDynix
Wireless access
Function: Adult bk club, Art exhibits, Audiobks via web, Bk club(s), Bks on cassette, Bks on CD, Children's prog, Computer training, Computers for patron use, Digital talking bks, E-Readers, E-Reserves, Electronic databases & coll, Holiday prog, Home delivery & serv to seniorr ctr & nursing homes, Homebound delivery serv, ILL available, Internet access, Life-long learning prog for all ages, Magazines, Meeting rooms, Museum passes, Music CDs, Online cat, Online ref, OverDrive digital audio bks, Photocopying/Printing, Printer for laptops & handheld devices, Prog for adults, Prog for children & young adult, Scanner, Spoken cassettes & CDs, Spoken cassettes & DVDs, STEM programs, Story hour, Summer reading prog, Tax forms, Teen prog, Telephone ref, Wheelchair accessible
Mem of Massachusetts Library System
Partic in Merrimack Valley Library Consortium
Special Services for the Deaf - Bks on deafness & sign lang; Closed caption videos
Special Services for the Blind - Audio mat; Bks on CD; Copier with enlargement capabilities; Home delivery serv; Large print bks; Photo duplicator for making large print
Open Mon-Thurs 9-9, Fri & Sat (Winter) 9-5
Friends of the Library Group

WINCHENDON

P BEALS MEMORIAL LIBRARY*, 50 Pleasant St, 01475. SAN 307-8094. Tel: 978-297-0300. FAX: 978-297-7144. Web Site: www.bealslibrary.org. *Dir,* Manuel King; E-mail: mking@townofwinchendon.com
Founded 1867. Pop 10,000; Circ 43,000
Library Holdings: Bk Vols 40,000; Per Subs 80
Subject Interests: Local hist
Automation Activity & Vendor Info: (Cataloging) Innovative Interfaces, Inc; (Circulation) Innovative Interfaces, Inc; (OPAC) Innovative Interfaces, Inc
Wireless access
Mem of Massachusetts Library System
Partic in Central & Western Massachusetts Automated Resource Sharing
Open Mon-Thurs 1-8, Fri 9-5, Sat (Sept-May) 9-1
Friends of the Library Group

WINCHESTER

G UNITED STATES FOOD & DRUG ADMINISTRATION DEPARTMENT OF HEALTH & HUMAN SERVICES*, Winchester Engineering & Analytical Center Library, 109 Holton St, 01890. SAN 307-8108. Tel: 781-756-9700. FAX: 781-729-3593.
Founded 1961
Library Holdings: Bk Titles 1,500; Per Subs 50
Subject Interests: Electronics, Engr, Med, Physics
Restriction: Staff use only

P WINCHESTER PUBLIC LIBRARY*, 80 Washington St, 01890. SAN 307-8116. Tel: 781-721-7171. Administration Tel: 781-721-7177. FAX: 781-721-7170. Administration FAX: 781-721-7101. Web Site: winpublib.org. *Dir,* Ann Wirtanen; Tel: 781-721-7171, Ext 310, E-mail: awirtanen@minlib.net; *Asst Dir,* Theresa Maturevich; Tel: 781-721-7171, Ext 318, E-mail: tmaturevich@minlib.net; *Head, Children's Servx,* Stephanie K Wolflink; Tel: 781-721-7171, Ext 322, E-mail: swolflink@minlib.net; *Head, Circ,* Melissa Roderick; Tel: 781-721-7171, Ext 316, E-mail: mroderick@minlib.net; *Head, Ref (Info Serv),* Julie A Kinchla; Tel: 781-721-7171, Ext 323, E-mail: jkinchla@minlib.net; *Head, Tech Serv,* Geraldine Pothier; Tel: 781-721-7171, Ext 327, E-mail: gpothier@minlib.net; *Ad, Ch Serv Librn,* Jenny Arch
Founded 1858. Pop 20,652; Circ 511,244
Special Collections: Civil War History (Lincoln & Lee Coll)
Automation Activity & Vendor Info: (Circulation) Innovative Interfaces, Inc
Publications: Art in the Library; Guide to Winchester Public Library
Partic in Minuteman Library Network
Special Services for the Blind - Aids for in-house use; Closed circuit TV magnifier
Open Mon-Thurs 9:30-9, Fri & Sat 9:30-5:30, Sun 2-5
Friends of the Library Group

WINDSOR

P WINDSOR FREE PUBLIC LIBRARY*, 1890 Rte 9, 01270. (Mail add: PO Box 118, 01270-0118), SAN 376-7094. Tel: 413-684-3811. FAX: 413-684-3806. E-mail: windsorma@gmail.com. Web Site: www.windsormass.com/windsor-public-library. *Dir,* Margaret Birchfield; Staff 1 (MLS 1)
Library Holdings: Audiobooks 140; CDs 150; DVDs 1,100; Bk Vols 4,350; Videos 380
Wireless access
Partic in Central & Western Massachusetts Automated Resource Sharing
Open Mon 5-7:30, Fri 12-5, Sat 10-12:30
Friends of the Library Group

WINTHROP

P WINTHROP PUBLIC LIBRARY & MUSEUM, Two Metcalf Sq, 02152-3157. SAN 307-8124. Tel: 617-846-1703. FAX: 617-846-7083. Web Site: www.winthroppubliclibrary.org. *Dir,* Greg McClay; E-mail: gmcclay@noblenet.org; *Asst Dir,* Mary Lou Osborne; E-mail: osborne@noblenet.org; Staff 6 (MLS 3, Non-MLS 3)
Founded 1885. Pop 18,263
Library Holdings: Audiobooks 3,031; CDs 52; e-books 114; Electronic Media & Resources 12; Microforms 100; Bk Vols 89,898; Per Subs 47; Videos 2,906
Special Collections: Lincoln Memorabilia; Local History (Museum Coll), bks, postcards, artifacts, pamphlets
Subject Interests: Local hist
Automation Activity & Vendor Info: (Cataloging) Evergreen; (Circulation) Evergreen; (ILL) Evergreen
Wireless access
Function: Adult bk club, Archival coll, Art exhibits, Audiobks via web, Bks on cassette, Bks on CD, Children's prog, Computers for patron use, Digital talking bks, Electronic databases & coll, Free DVD rentals, ILL available, Magnifiers for reading, Museum passes, Music CDs, Online cat, OverDrive digital audio bks, Photocopying/Printing, Prog for adults, Prog for children & young adult, Ref serv available, Spoken cassettes & CDs, Spoken cassettes & DVDs, Story hour, Summer reading prog, VHS videos
Partic in North of Boston Library Exchange, Inc
Open Mon-Thurs 10-6, Fri & Sat 10-5
Friends of the Library Group

WOBURN

GL MIDDLESEX LAW LIBRARY*, Superior Courthouse, 200 TradeCenter, 3rd Flr, 01801. SAN 307-3068. Tel: 781-939-2920. FAX: 781-939-0874. E-mail: midlawlib@yahoo.com. Web Site: www.mass.gov/locations/middlesex-law-library. *Head Law Librn,* Linda W Hom; E-mail: linda.hom@jud.state.ma.us; *Law Librn,* Position Currently Open; Staff 5 (MLS 2, Non-MLS 3)
Founded 1815
Library Holdings: e-journals 1,000; Bk Titles 4,250; Bk Vols 90,000; Per Subs 250
Special Collections: Massachusetts, United States & Federal Law. State Document Depository
Automation Activity & Vendor Info: (Acquisitions) SirsiDynix; (Cataloging) SirsiDynix; (Circulation) SirsiDynix; (ILL) SirsiDynix; (Serials) SirsiDynix
Wireless access
Mem of Massachusetts Library System
Partic in LYRASIS; OCLC Online Computer Library Center, Inc
Open Mon-Fri 9-4:30
Friends of the Library Group

P WOBURN PUBLIC LIBRARY*, 36 Cummings Park, 01801. (Mail add: PO Box 298, 01801-0298), SAN 307-8140. Tel: 781-933-0148. E-mail: woburn@minlib.net. Web Site: www.woburnpubliclibrary.org. *Dir,* Andrea Bunker; E-mail: abunker@minlib.net; *Asst Dir,* Rebecca Meehan; E-mail: rmeehan@minlib.net; *Archivist,* Thomas Doyle; E-mail: tdoyle@minlib.net; *Circ,* Patricia Daley; E-mail: pdaley@minlib.net; *Ch Serv,* Dorrie Kardin; E-mail: dkarlin@minlib.net; *Tech Serv,* Beverly Thompson; E-mail: bthompson@minlib.net; *Ref Serv, YA,* Christi Showman Farrar; *ILL, Ref,* Gregg Bouley; E-mail: gbouley@minlib.net
Founded 1856
Library Holdings: AV Mats 7,000; DVDs 1,500; Large Print Bks 1,800; Bk Vols 80,000; Per Subs 152; Videos 2,000
Subject Interests: Genealogy
Automation Activity & Vendor Info: (Acquisitions) Innovative Interfaces, Inc; (Cataloging) Innovative Interfaces, Inc; (Circulation) Innovative Interfaces, Inc; (ILL) Innovative Interfaces, Inc; (OPAC) Innovative Interfaces, Inc; (Serials) Innovative Interfaces, Inc
Wireless access
Mem of Massachusetts Library System
Partic in Minuteman Library Network

Special Services for the Blind - Aids for in-house use; Bks on cassette; Bks on CD; Closed circuit TV magnifier; Descriptive video serv (DVS); Home delivery serv; Large print bks; Magnifiers
Open Mon-Thurs 9-9, Fri & Sat 9-5:30
Friends of the Library Group

WOODS HOLE

S MARINE BIOLOGICAL LABORATORY*, Woods Hole Oceanographic Institution Data Library & Archives, McLean MS 8, 360 Woods Hole Rd, 02543-1539. SAN 345-8288. Tel: 508-289-2269. FAX: 508-457-2156. E-mail: archives@whoi.edu. Web Site: dla.whoi.edu. *Co-Dir,* Lisa Raymond; E-mail: lraymond@whoi.edu; Staff 6 (MLS 2, Non-MLS 4)
Founded 1956
Special Collections: Institution Archives, charts, data, instruments, logs, maps. Oral History
Subject Interests: Chem, Geol, Geophysics, Meteorology, Ocean engr, Oceanography
Wireless access
Restriction: Open by appt only

G NORTHEAST FISHERIES SCIENCE CENTER*, Woods Hole Laboratory Library, 166 Water St, 02543-1097. SAN 307-8175. Tel: 508-495-2000, 508-495-2260. FAX: 508-495-2258. E-mail: NEFSC.Information@noaa.gov. Web Site: www.nefsc.noaa.gov/libraries/WH-library.html. *Librn,* Jackie Riley; E-mail: Jacqueline.Riley@noaa.gov
Founded 1885
Library Holdings: Bk Vols 1,000; Per Subs 20
Special Collections: Laboratory Research (Archives 1871-1979)
Subject Interests: Biology, Ecology
Automation Activity & Vendor Info: (Cataloging) SirsiDynix; (OPAC) SirsiDynix
Partic in NOAA Libraries Network; OCLC Online Computer Library Center, Inc; Proquest Dialog
Open Mon-Fri 7-3
Restriction: Lending to staff only

P WOODS HOLE PUBLIC LIBRARY*, 581 Woods Hole Rd, 02543. (Mail add: PO Box 185, 02543-0185), SAN 307-8183. Tel: 508-548-8961. FAX: 508-540-1969. E-mail: whpl_mail@clamsnet.org. Web Site: woodsholepubliclibrary.org. *Dir,* Margaret McCormick; E-mail: mmccormick@clamsnet.org; Staff 2 (Non-MLS 2)
Founded 1910. Pop 5,000; Circ 37,000
Library Holdings: Bk Vols 29,000; Per Subs 50
Special Collections: Oral History
Subject Interests: Local hist
Automation Activity & Vendor Info: (Cataloging) Innovative Interfaces, Inc; (Circulation) Innovative Interfaces, Inc; (OPAC) Innovative Interfaces, Inc
Wireless access
Function: Computers for patron use, ILL available, Museum passes, Music CDs, Online cat, OverDrive digital audio bks, Photocopying/Printing, Preschool outreach, Prog for adults, Prog for children & young adult, Spoken cassettes & CDs, Story hour, Summer & winter reading prog, Summer reading prog, Workshops
Mem of Massachusetts Library System
Partic in Cape Libraries Automated Materials Sharing Network
Open Mon 12-5:30 & 7-9, Tues, Thurs & Fri 3-5:30, Wed 10-5:30 & 7-9, Sat 12-5:30

WORCESTER

S AMERICAN ANTIQUARIAN SOCIETY LIBRARY*, 185 Salisbury St, 01609-1634. SAN 307-8191. Tel: 508-755-5221. FAX: 508-754-9069. E-mail: library@americanantiquarian.org. Web Site: www.americanantiquarian.org. *Pres,* Ellen S Dunlap; Tel: 508-471-2161, E-mail: edunlap@mwa.org; *Head, Reader Serv,* Kimberly Toney; Tel: 508-471-2171, E-mail: ktoney@mwa.org
Founded 1812
Library Holdings: Bk Vols 690,000; Per Subs 1,200
Special Collections: Manuscripts relating to the history of the American book trades & New England families; Pre-1877 American & Canadian bks, pamphlets, almanacs, directories, children's lit, cook bks, genealogies, broadsides, graphic arts, printed ephemera, local & state histories, songsters, hymnals, sheet music, bibliographies, newspapers, & periodicals. US Document Depository
Subject Interests: Am hist, Lit
Automation Activity & Vendor Info: (Acquisitions) Ex Libris Group; (Cataloging) Ex Libris Group; (OPAC) Ex Libris Group; (Serials) Ex Libris Group
Wireless access
Publications: Bibliographies; Proceedings; Source Materials
Mem of Massachusetts Library System
Partic in Academic & Research Collaborative; OCLC Research Library Partnership
Open Mon, Tues, Thurs & Fri 10-5, Wed 10-7

C ASSUMPTION UNIVERSITY*, Emmanuel D'Alzon Library, 500 Salisbury St, 01609. SAN 307-8205. Tel: 508-767-7135. Reference Tel: 508-767-7273. FAX: 508-767-7374. E-mail: library@assumption.edu. Web Site: library.assumption.edu. *Dir, Libr Serv,* Robin Maddalena; Tel: 508-767-7272, E-mail: r.maddalena@assumption.edu; *Head, Access Serv,* Nancy O'Sullivan; Tel: 508-767-7271, E-mail: naosullivan@assumption.edu; *Head, Libr Syst & Tech,* Mary Brunelle; Tel: 508-767-7002, E-mail: mbrunelle@assumption.edu; *Head, Spec Coll, Head, Tech Serv, Interim Archivist,* Elizabeth Maisey; Tel: 508-767-7384, E-mail: emaisey@assumption.edu; *Res & Instruction Librn,* Kate Bejune; Tel: 508-767-7020, E-mail: ke.bejune@assumption.edu; *Res & Instruction Librn,* Barrie Mooney; Tel: 508-767-7035, E-mail: bmooney@assumption.edu; *Evening Supvr,* Paul Johnson; Tel: 508-767-7084, E-mail: pjohnson@assumption.edu; *Cat Asst, Coordr, Acq,* Joan O'Rourke; Tel: 508-767-7076, E-mail: jorourke@assumption.edu; *Access Serv, ILL Coordr,* Vivienne Anthony; Tel: 508-767-7291, E-mail: vanthony@assumption.edu; Staff 12.3 (MLS 8, Non-MLS 4.3)
Founded 1904. Enrl 2,754; Fac 156; Highest Degree: Master
Jun 2013-May 2014 Income $1,556,650. Mats Exp $1,371,460, Books $71,800, Per/Ser (Incl. Access Fees) $306,000, Electronic Ref Mat (Incl. Access Fees) $224,450, Presv $20,000. Sal $836,650 (Prof $673,398)
Library Holdings: Audiobooks 100; DVDs 2,323; e-books 8,518; e-journals 51,050; Electronic Media & Resources 114; Microforms 23,416; Bk Titles 152,791; Bk Vols 227,234; Per Subs 1,076; Videos 2,323
Subject Interests: Fr Can, Franco-Am, Hist, Lit, Theol
Automation Activity & Vendor Info: (Acquisitions) Ex Libris Group; (Cataloging) Ex Libris Group; (Circulation) Ex Libris Group; (Course Reserve) Ex Libris Group; (ILL) OCLC ILLiad; (OPAC) Ex Libris Group; (Serials) Ex Libris Group
Wireless access
Mem of Massachusetts Library System
Partic in OCLC Online Computer Library Center, Inc; Westchester Academic Library Directors Organization
Open Mon-Thurs 8am-1am, Fri 8-6, Sat 10-8, Sun 1-1

C BECKER COLLEGE*, William F Ruska Library, 61 Sever St, 01609. SAN 345-8377. Tel: 508-373-9710. Web Site: www.becker.edu/academics/libraries-2. *Dir of Libr,* Donna Sibley; Tel: 508-373-9712, E-mail: donna.sibley@becker.edu; *Asst Dir, Operations,* Eric Cruze; Tel: 508-373-9714, E-mail: eric.cruze@becker.edu
Enrl 1,900
Library Holdings: Bk Vols 40,000; Per Subs 117
Subject Interests: Criminal law & justice, Nursing, Philos, Psychol
Automation Activity & Vendor Info: (Acquisitions) Innovative Interfaces, Inc; (Circulation) Innovative Interfaces, Inc; (Course Reserve) Innovative Interfaces, Inc; (OPAC) Innovative Interfaces, Inc
Wireless access
Publications: Acquisitions List; Faculty Handbook
Partic in Academic & Research Collaborative
Open Mon-Thurs 7:30am-11pm, Fri 7:30-6, Sat 12-5, Sun 2-11

L BOWDITCH & DEWEY*, Law Library, 311 Main St, 01608. (Mail add: PO Box 15156, 01615-0156), SAN 372-0349. Tel: 508-926-3331. FAX: 508-929-3140. Web Site: www.bowditch.com. *Librn,* Carolyn Rofechild; E-mail: crofechild@bowditch.com
Library Holdings: Bk Vols 5,000
Partic in NELLCO Law Library Consortium, Inc.

C CLARK UNIVERSITY*, Robert Hutchings Goddard Library, 950 Main St, 01610-1477. SAN 345-8407. Tel: 508-793-7711. Interlibrary Loan Service Tel: 508-793-7578. Reference Tel: 508-793-7579. Administration Tel: 508-793-7573. FAX: 508-793-8871. Web Site: www.clarku.edu/research/goddard. *Univ Librn,* Gwen Arthur; Tel: 508-793-7384, E-mail: garthur@clarku.edu; *Head, Cat,* Randi Rousseau; Tel: 508-793-7156, E-mail: rrousseau@clarku.edu; *Head, Coll Develop,* Mott Linn; Tel: 508-753-7572, E-mail: mlinn@clarku.edu; *Syst Librn,* Edward McDermott; Tel: 508-793-7651, E-mail: emcdermott@clarku.edu; Staff 30 (MLS 12, Non-MLS 18)
Founded 1889. Enrl 2,700; Fac 163; Highest Degree: Doctorate
Library Holdings: Bk Vols 613,000; Per Subs 1,303
Special Collections: Rare Books (Robert H Goddard Coll & G Stanley Hall Papers). US Document Depository
Automation Activity & Vendor Info: (Acquisitions) Ex Libris Group; (Cataloging) Ex Libris Group; (Circulation) Ex Libris Group; (Course Reserve) Ex Libris Group; (OPAC) Ex Libris Group; (Serials) Ex Libris Group
Wireless access
Mem of Massachusetts Library System
Partic in LYRASIS; OCLC Online Computer Library Center, Inc
Open Mon-Thurs 8am-Midnight, Fri 8-8, Sat 10-8, Sun Noon-Midnight
Friends of the Library Group

Departmental Libraries:

ARCHIVES & SPECIAL COLLECTIONS, Downing & Woodland Sts, 01610-1477. (Mail add: 950 Main St, 01610-1477). Tel: 508-793-7572. FAX: 508-793-8871. E-mail: archives@clarku.edu. Web Site: www.clarku.edu/research/archives. *Archivist,* Mott Linn; E-mail: mlinn@clarku.edu
Open Mon-Fri 9:30-4

GUY H BURNHAM MAP & AERIAL PHOTOGRAPHY LIBRARY, 950 Main St, 01610-1477. Tel: 508-793-7322. FAX: 508-793-8881. Web Site: www.clarku.edu/research/maplibrary. *Librn,* Beverly Presley; Tel: 508-793-7706, E-mail: bpresley@clarku.edu
Open Mon-Fri 12:30-4:30

SCIENCE, 950 Main St, 01610. Tel: 508-793-7712. FAX: 508-793-8871. Web Site: www.clarku.edu/research/sciencelibrary. *Sci Librn,* Andy Dzaugis; E-mail: adzaugis@clarku.edu
Open Mon-Thurs 8am-10pm, Fri 8-5, Sat 9-5, Sun Noon-10

CR COLLEGE OF THE HOLY CROSS*, Dinand Library, One College St, 01610. SAN 345-8466. Tel: 508-793-3372. Circulation Tel: 508-793-2642. Interlibrary Loan Service Tel: 508-793-2639. Reference Tel: 508-793-2259. FAX: 508-793-2372. Web Site: www.holycross.edu/support-and-resources/holy-cross-libraries. *Dir,* Mark Shelton; Tel: 508-793-3371, E-mail: mshelton@holycross.edu; *Assoc Dir,* Karen Reilly; Tel: 508-793-2520, E-mail: kreilly@holycross.edu; *Head, Access & Discovery Serv,* Eileen Cravedi; Tel: 508-793-2672, E-mail: ecravedi@holycross.edu; *Head, Archives & Spec Coll,* Abigail Stambach; Tel: 508-793-2506, E-mail: astambac@holycross.edu; *Head Research, Teaching & Learning,* Alicia Hansen; Tel: 508-793-3533, E-mail: ahansen@holycross.edu; *Assessment Librn, Teaching & Learning Librn,* Monica Locker; Tel: 508-793-3473, E-mail: mlocker@holycross.edu; *Cat Librn,* Theresa Huaman; Tel: 508-793-2638, E-mail: thuaman@holycross.edu; *Digital Scholarship Librn,* Lisa Villa; Tel: 508-793-2767, E-mail: lvilla@holycross.edu; *Res, Instruction & Outreach Librn,* Laura Wilson; Tel: 508-793-3886, E-mail: lwilson@holycross.edu; *Visual Literacy & Arts Librn,* Janis DesMarais; Tel: 508-793-2453, E-mail: jdesmara@holycross.edu; *Coord, Research & Instruction,* Jennifer Whelan; Tel: 508-793-2254, E-mail: jwhelan@holycross.edu; *Asst Archivist,* Sarah Campbell; Tel: 508-793-2575, E-mail: scampbel@holycross.edu; *Content Strategist, Electronic Res, Ser,* Judith Nagata; E-mail: jnagata@holycross.edu; *Sr Content Strategist,* Mary Moran; Tel: 508-793-2478, E-mail: mjmoran@holycross.edu; *Syst,* Robert Scheier; Tel: 508-793-3495, E-mail: rscheier@holycross.edu; Staff 18 (MLS 18)
Founded 1843. Enrl 2,904; Fac 301; Highest Degree: Bachelor
Jul 2017-Jun 2018 Income (Main & Associated Libraries) $4,524,630. Mats Exp $1,684,540, Books $226,760, Per/Ser (Incl. Access Fees) $1,227,498, Electronic Ref Mat (Incl. Access Fees) $203,254, Presv $27,028. Sal $1,844,649 (Prof $1,215,207)
Library Holdings: e-books 166,984; Bk Titles 456,901; Bk Vols 646,531; Per Subs 6,936
Special Collections: Americana up to 1840, Holocaust, bks; Early Christian Iberia (Roman-Visigothic-Hispania Coll, 50-711AD), bks, maps; History (David I Walsh Coll, 1872-1947), correspondence, papers, scrapbks; History (James M Curley Coll, 1874-1958), photog, scrapbks; Irish in Worcester, 1880-1890 (Richard O'Flynn Coll); Literature (Louise I Guiney Coll, 1861-1920), bks, letters, ms; Rare Books 16th-17th Century (Jesuitana Coll)
Automation Activity & Vendor Info: (Acquisitions) Innovative Interfaces, Inc; (Cataloging) Innovative Interfaces, Inc; (Circulation) Innovative Interfaces, Inc; (Course Reserve) Innovative Interfaces, Inc; (Discovery) EBSCO Discovery Service; (ILL) OCLC ILLiad; (OPAC) Innovative Interfaces, Inc; (Serials) Innovative Interfaces, Inc
Wireless access
Publications: Handbook; Recent Acquisitions; Subject Reference Guides
Open Mon-Sun 8:30am-11pm

Departmental Libraries:

FENWICK MUSIC LIBRARY, Fenwick Bldg, 01610-2394, SAN 345-8482. Tel: 508-793-2295. *Librn,* Jared Rex; E-mail: jrex@holycross.edu; Staff 2 (MLS 1, Non-MLS 1)
Founded 1978
Library Holdings: Bk Vols 25,310; Per Subs 86

O'CALLAHAN SCIENCE LIBRARY, Swords Bldg, 01610, SAN 345-8490. Tel: 508-793-2643. Circulation Tel: 508-793-2739. *Sci Librn,* Barbara Merolli; E-mail: bmerolli@holycross.edu. Subject Specialists: *Biology, Chem, Physics,* Barbara Merolli; Staff 2 (MLS 1, Non-MLS 1)
Library Holdings: Bk Vols 101,972; Per Subs 3,962
Subject Interests: Astronomy, Biology, Chem, Computer sci, Hist of sci, Math, Med, Physics

GL MASSACHUSETTS COURT SYSTEM*, Worcester Law Library, 184 Main St, 01608. SAN 307-8345. Tel: 508-831-2525. FAX: 508-754-9933. E-mail: worcesterlaw@yahoo.com. Web Site: www.mass.gov/courts/case-legal-res/law-lib/libraries/locations/worcester.html. *Head Law Librn,* Peter Anderegg; Staff 3.5 (MLS 1.5, Non-MLS 2)
Founded 1842
Special Collections: History of Worcester County & its Cities & Towns; Legal Textbooks (Major Coll on General Law); Massachusetts & Federal Law Coll
Automation Activity & Vendor Info: (Acquisitions) SirsiDynix; (Cataloging) SirsiDynix; (Circulation) SirsiDynix
Wireless access
Open Mon-Fri 8-4
Friends of the Library Group

L MIRICK O'CONNELL*, Law Library, 100 Front St, 01608-1477. SAN 372-0357. Tel: 508-860-1505, 508-860-8500. FAX: 508-983-6259. E-mail: library@mirickoconnell.com. Web Site: www.mirickoconnell.com. *Law Librn,* Kathryn Tucker
Library Holdings: Bk Vols 5,000; Per Subs 50
Restriction: Staff use only

J QUINSIGAMOND COMMUNITY COLLEGE*, George I Alden Library, 670 W Boylston St, 01606-2092. SAN 307-8272. Tel: 508-854-4366. Administration Tel: 508-854-7472. FAX: 508-854-4204. Web Site: www.qcc.mass.edu/library. *Interim Dean of Libr,* Carey Morse; E-mail: csmorse@qcc.mass.edu; *Coll Develop Librn,* Michael Stevenson; Tel: 508-854-2793, E-mail: mstevenson@qcc.mass.edu; *Ref & Instruction Librn,* Tiger Swan; Tel: 508-854-4210, E-mail: tswan@qcc.mass.edu; *Tech Serv & Syst Librn,* Denise Cross; Tel: 508-854-4480, E-mail: dcross@qcc.mass.edu; *Mgr, Circ Serv, Mgr, ILL,* Paula McDonald; E-mail: paulam@qcc.mass.edu; Staff 7 (MLS 4, Non-MLS 3)
Founded 1963. Enrl 5,282; Fac 350; Highest Degree: Associate
Library Holdings: AV Mats 2,899; Bk Titles 45,641; Per Subs 294
Subject Interests: Bus, Criminal justice, Early childhood educ, Health sci
Automation Activity & Vendor Info: (Acquisitions) Innovative Interfaces, Inc; (Cataloging) Innovative Interfaces, Inc; (Circulation) Innovative Interfaces, Inc; (Course Reserve) Innovative Interfaces, Inc; (ILL) OCLC Online; (OPAC) Innovative Interfaces, Inc; (Serials) Innovative Interfaces, Inc
Wireless access
Function: ILL available, Internet access, Photocopying/Printing, Ref serv available, Telephone ref, Wheelchair accessible
Mem of Massachusetts Library System
Partic in LYRASIS; OCLC Online Computer Library Center, Inc
Special Services for the Deaf - TTY equip
Open Mon-Thurs (Fall & Spring) 8am-9pm, Fri 8-5, Sat 9-3; Mon-Thurs (Summer) 8am-9pm, Fri 8-5; Mon-Thurs (Winter) 8-7, Fri 8-5
Restriction: Open to students, fac & staff, Pub ref by request

M SAINT VINCENT HOSPITAL*, John J Dumphy Memorial Library, 123 Summer St, 01608. SAN 307-8280. Tel: 508-363-6117. E-mail: svh-library@stvincenthospital.com. Web Site: www.stvincenthospital.com. *Regional Dir, Library Services,* Joan Yanicke; Staff 2 (MLS 1, Non-MLS 1)
Founded 1900
Library Holdings: e-books 100; e-journals 6,000; Bk Titles 1,000; Per Subs 175
Special Collections: St Vincent Hospital History
Subject Interests: Med, Nursing
Automation Activity & Vendor Info: (Serials) TDNet
Wireless access
Mem of Massachusetts Library System
Partic in Docline; National Network of Libraries of Medicine Region 7

CM UNIVERSITY OF MASSACHUSETTS MEDICAL SCHOOL*, Lamar Soutter Library, 55 Lake Ave N, 01655-0002. SAN 307-8310. Administration Tel: 508-856-2206. FAX: 508-856-5899. Web Site: library.umassmed.edu. *Dir,* Mary Piorun; E-mail: Mary.Piorun@umassmed.edu; *Assoc Dir,* Regina Raboin; Tel: 508-856-2099, E-mail: regina.raboin@umassmed.edu; *Mgr,* Javier Crespo; Tel: 508-856-7633, E-mail: javier.crespo@umassmed.edu
Founded 1973. Highest Degree: Doctorate
Special Collections: Graphic Medicine Coll; Humanities in Medicine Coll; Massachusetts Medical History (Worcester Medical Library). US Document Depository
Automation Activity & Vendor Info: (Acquisitions) Ex Libris Group; (Cataloging) Ex Libris Group; (Circulation) Ex Libris Group; (Course Reserve) Ex Libris Group; (ILL) OCLC ILLiad; (OPAC) Ex Libris Group; (Serials) Ex Libris Group
Wireless access
Partic in Academic & Research Collaborative; Boston Library Consortium, Inc; LYRASIS; OCLC Online Computer Library Center, Inc
Special Services for the Deaf - Assistive tech

S WORCESTER ART MUSEUM LIBRARY*, 55 Salisbury St, 01609. SAN 307-8329. Tel: 508-793-4382. FAX: 508-798-5646. E-mail: library@worcesterart.org. Web Site: www.worcesterart.org. *Head Librn,* Rebecca Morin; E-mail: RebeccaMorin@worcesterart.org; Staff 3 (MLS 2, Non-MLS 1)
Founded 1909

Library Holdings: Bk Vols 45,000
Subject Interests: Asian art, European art, Prints
Mem of Massachusetts Library System
Open Wed & Fri 11-5, Thurs 11-8, Sat 10-5
Restriction: Non-circulating
Friends of the Library Group

S WORCESTER HISTORICAL MUSEUM, Research Library, 30 Elm St, 01609. SAN 307-8361. Tel: 508-753-8278, Ext 105. FAX: 508-753-9070. E-mail: library@worcesterhistory.net. Web Site: www.worcesterhistory.org/library. *Exec Dir,* William D Wallace; Tel: 508-753-8278, Ext 106; *Archives Mgr, Libr Mgr,* Wendy Essery; Staff 6 (MLS 3, Non-MLS 3)
Founded 1875
Library Holdings: Bk Titles 6,000; Bk Vols 10,000; Per Subs 20
Special Collections: Anti-Slavery (Kelley-Foster Coll), ms; Architectural Drawings Coll; City of Worcester, ms; Diner Industry; Howland Valentines; Local Information (Worcester Pamphlet Files); Out-of-Print Worcester Newspaper & Periodicals; Photographic & Graphic Coll
Subject Interests: Local hist
Open Wed-Sat 10-4

C WORCESTER POLYTECHNIC INSTITUTE, George C Gordon Library, 100 Institute Rd, 01609-2280. SAN 307-8396. Tel: 508-831-5410. Interlibrary Loan Service Tel: 508-831-6499. FAX: 508-831-5829. TDD: 508-831-6700. E-mail: library@wpi.edu. Web Site: www.wpi.edu/academics/library. *Univ Librn,* Anna K Gold; Tel: 508-831-6161, E-mail: akgold@wpi.edu; *Electronic Res Librn,* Martha Gunnarson; Staff 19 (MLS 15, Non-MLS 4)
Founded 1867. Enrl 3,600; Fac 324; Highest Degree: Doctorate
Library Holdings: e-books 38,000; e-journals 35,000; Bk Vols 270,000; Per Subs 900
Special Collections: Charles Dickens (The Robert Fellman Coll); History of Science & Technology; NASA; Theo Brown Diaries
Subject Interests: Environ studies, Safety
Wireless access
Publications: Brochure; Calendar of Library Hours; Handbook; Monthly Acquisitions; Specialized Bibliographic Instruction Material
Mem of Massachusetts Library System
Partic in LYRASIS; OCLC Online Computer Library Center, Inc; Westchester Academic Library Directors Organization
Open Mon-Thurs 8am-1am, Fri 8am-11pm, Sat 11-9, Sun 11am-1am

P WORCESTER PUBLIC LIBRARY*, Three Salem Sq, 01608. SAN 345-8644. Tel: 508-799-1655. Interlibrary Loan Service Tel: 508-799-1697. FAX: 508-799-1652. Web Site: www.mywpl.org. *Exec Dir,* Jason Homer; Tel: 508-799-1726, E-mail: jhomer@mywpl.org; Staff 27 (MLS 27)
Founded 1859. Pop 175,966; Circ 597,175
Library Holdings: AV Mats 33,014; e-books 796; Electronic Media & Resources 23,472; Bk Vols 588,958; Per Subs 1,148
Special Collections: US History (Library of American Civilization), micro. US Document Depository
Automation Activity & Vendor Info: (Acquisitions) Innovative Interfaces, Inc; (Cataloging) Innovative Interfaces, Inc; (Circulation) Innovative Interfaces, Inc; (ILL) Innovative Interfaces, Inc; (OPAC) Innovative Interfaces, Inc; (Serials) Innovative Interfaces, Inc
Wireless access
Publications: Your Library (Quarterly)
Mem of Massachusetts Library System
Partic in Academic & Research Collaborative; Central & Western Massachusetts Automated Resource Sharing; LYRASIS
Special Services for the Deaf - TTY equip
Friends of the Library Group
Branches: 7
BURNCOAT BRANCH, 526 Burncoat St, 01606. Tel: 508-799-8328.
Open Tues-Fri 4-6:30, Sat 2:30-5:30
GODDARD BRANCH, 14 Richards St, 01603. Tel: 508-799-8330.
Open Mon-Fri 3-6:30, Sat 9-Noon
GREAT BROOK VALLEY, 89 Tacoma St, 01605-3518, SAN 345-8725. Tel: 508-799-1729. *Librn,* Marilyn Rudolph; E-mail: mrudolph@worcpublib.org
Founded 1981
Library Holdings: Bk Vols 7,000
Open Mon-Fri 2-5
Friends of the Library Group
FRANCES PERKINS BRANCH, 470 W Boylston St, 01606-3226, SAN 345-8733. Tel: 508-799-1687. *Br Supvr,* Frank Sestokas
Founded 1914
Library Holdings: Bk Vols 48,000
Partic in Central & Western Massachusetts Automated Resource Sharing
Open Mon 9-9, Tues & Wed 9-5:30, Thurs & Fri 1-9
Friends of the Library Group
ROOSEVELT BRANCH, 1006 Grafton, 01604. Tel: 508-799-8327.
Open Tues-Fri 3-6:30, Sat 2:30-5:30
TATNUCK MAGNET BRANCH, 1083 Pleasant St, 01602. Tel: 508-799-8329.
Open Mon-Fri 3-6:30, Sat 9-Noon

P WORCESTER TALKING BOOK LIBRARY, Three Salem Sq, 01608-2015, SAN 345-8679. Tel: 508-799-1655, 508-799-1730. Toll Free Tel: 800-762-0085 (Mass only). FAX: 508-799-1676, 508-799-1734. TDD: 508-799-1731. E-mail: talkbook@worcpublib.org. Web Site: www.worcpublib.org/talkingbook. *Librn,* James Izatt; Staff 2 (MLS 2)
Founded 1973
Automation Activity & Vendor Info: (Cataloging) Keystone Systems, Inc (KLAS); (Circulation) Keystone Systems, Inc (KLAS); (Media Booking) Keystone Systems, Inc (KLAS); (OPAC) Keystone Systems, Inc (KLAS)
Function: Bks on cassette, Digital talking bks, Home delivery & serv to seniorr ctr & nursing homes, Homebound delivery serv, Online cat, Senior outreach, VHS videos, Wheelchair accessible
Special Services for the Blind - Braille equip; Braille servs; Magnifiers; Reader equip; Web-Braille
Open Tues-Thurs 9-9, Fri & Sat 9-5:30, Sun (Jan-May) 1:30-5:30
Friends of the Library Group

S WORCESTER RECOVERY CENTER & HOSPITAL LIBRARY*, 309 Belmont St, 01604. SAN 345-8881. Tel: 508-368-0733, 508-368-3300. Web Site: www.mass.gov/locations/worcester-recovery-center-and-hospital-wrch. *Library Contact,* Robert Gorman; Staff 2 (MLS 1, Non-MLS 1)
Founded 1956
Library Holdings: Bk Titles 4,000; Per Subs 75

C WORCESTER STATE UNIVERSITY, Learning Resource Center, 486 Chandler St, 01602. SAN 307-840X. Tel: 508-929-8027. E-mail: library@worcester.edu. Web Site: www.worcester.edu/library. *Exec Dir,* Matt Bejune; E-mail: mbejune@worcester.edu; Staff 13 (MLS 6, Non-MLS 7)
Founded 1874. Enrl 6,471; Fac 210; Highest Degree: Master
Automation Activity & Vendor Info: (Acquisitions) EBSCO Online; (Cataloging) Koha; (Circulation) Koha; (Course Reserve) Koha; (Discovery) EBSCO Discovery Service; (ILL) OCLC; (OPAC) Koha; (Serials) Prenax, Inc
Wireless access
Partic in Fenway Library Organization; Massachusetts Commonwealth Consortium of Libraries in Public Higher Education Institutions; Westchester Academic Library Directors Organization
Open Mon-Thurs 7:30am-1am, Fri 7:30-5, Sat 9-5, Sun 11am-1am

WORTHINGTON

P WORTHINGTON LIBRARY*, Frederick Sargent Huntington Memorial Library, One Huntington Rd, 01098. (Mail add: PO Box 598, 01098-0598), SAN 307-8434. Tel: 413-238-5565. E-mail: theworthingtonlibrary@gmail.com. Web Site: www.theworthingtonlibrary.org. *Dir,* Leona Arthen; Staff 1 (Non-MLS 1)
Founded 1915. Pop 1,210
Library Holdings: Large Print Bks 81; Bk Vols 8,467; Per Subs 50; Talking Bks 467; Videos 780
Special Collections: Russell H Conwell Coll
Wireless access
Open Tues 3-7, Thurs 10-12 & 3-7, Sat 10-4
Friends of the Library Group

WRENTHAM

P FISKE PUBLIC LIBRARY*, 110 Randall Rd, 02093. SAN 307-8442. Tel: 508-384-5440. FAX: 508-384-5443. E-mail: fiskepl@hotmail.com. Web Site: www.fiskelib.org. *Dir,* Mary Tobichuk; E-mail: mtobichuk@sailsinc.org; *Ref Librn,* Claudia Schumacher; E-mail: clschu@sailsinc.org; *Ch Serv,* Elizabeth Nadow; E-mail: nadow.fiskelibrary@gmail.com; *Circ,* Nancy Daniels
Founded 1892. Pop 9,166; Circ 51,500
Library Holdings: Bk Vols 55,000; Per Subs 110; Talking Bks 2,446; Videos 2,304
Automation Activity & Vendor Info: (Cataloging) SirsiDynix; (Circulation) SirsiDynix; (OPAC) SirsiDynix
Wireless access
Partic in SAILS Library Network
Open Tues-Thurs 10-8, Fri 10-5, Sat (Sept-June) 10-4
Friends of the Library Group

YARMOUTH PORT

S HISTORICAL SOCIETY OF OLD YARMOUTH LIBRARY*, 11 Strawberry Lane, 02675. (Mail add: PO Box 11, 02675-0011), SAN 373-2002. Tel: 508-362-3021. E-mail: hsoy@comcast.net. Web Site: hsoy.org. *Librn,* Daryl Marty
Library Holdings: Bk Vols 2,500

Subject Interests: Local hist
Open Tues & Thurs 10-3:30

P YARMOUTH PORT LIBRARY, 297 Main St, Rte 6A, 02675. Tel: 508-362-3717. FAX: 508-362-6739. E-mail: yarp_mail@clamsnet.org. Web Site: www.yarmouthportlibrary.org. *Librn, Adult Serv,* Leslie Altman; E-mail: laltman@clamsnet.org; *Asst Librn, Ch Serv,* Carrie Bearse; E-mail: cbearse@clamsnet.org; *Circ Asst,* Carol Riley; E-mail: criley@clamsnet.org; Staff 3 (Non-MLS 3)
Founded 1866. Circ 46,831
Special Collections: Genealogy (New England Historic General Register & Amos Otis Papers); Histories of Cape Cod
Wireless access
Function: 24/7 Electronic res, 24/7 Online cat, Adult bk club, Audiobks on Playaways & MP3, Audiobks via web, Bk club(s), Bks on CD, Computers for patron use, Electronic databases & coll, Free DVD rentals, Homebound delivery serv, ILL available, Internet access, Magazines, Mail & tel request accepted, Microfiche/film & reading machines, Museum passes, Music CDs, Online cat, OverDrive digital audio bks, Photocopying/Printing, Prog for adults, Prog for children & young adult, Story hour, Tax forms, Telephone ref, Wheelchair accessible
Partic in Cape Libraries Automated Materials Sharing Network
Open Tues, Wed & Fri 10-3, Thurs 10-6, Sat 10-Noon

MICHIGAN

Date of Statistics: FY 2021
Population, 2020 U.S. Census: 10,077,331
STATE LIBRARY ACTIVITIES
Total Number State Aid Grants Awarded: 378
Other State Grants (not as state aid): 0
Other Grants Reviewed (not as state aid): 0
STATE LIBRARY GRANT ACTIVITIES
State Aid Grants to Public Libraries: $8,413,687
State Aid Grants to Library Cooperatives: $4,614,344
State Aid to Sub-regionals (Blind/Handicapped): $0
Federal Grants Awarded: 443
Federal Library Services & Technology Act (LSTA): $4,597,286
PUBLIC LIBRARY ACTIVITIES
Reference Requests: 3,457,747
Circulation: 51,300,869
Interlibrary Loan Transactions: 2,334,543
Digital Resources:
Total audio items (physical and downloadable units): Physical 1,741,564
Total video items (physical and downloadable units): Physical 2,837,152
Total library computer use by the public: 1,485,328
Total annual wireless sessions: 6,544,885
Income and Expenditures:
Total Income Reported by Public Libraries: $491,698,584
Average Income Per Capita: $48.79
Source of Income: Mainly local (approximately 97% local, 3% state & federal)
Expenditures Per Capita: $41.20
Total Number Public Library Employees: 7,672
Total Volumes Reported by Public Libraries: 30,265,753
Average Volumes Per Capita: 3.0
Total Items Available:
Total Circulation Reported by Public Libraries: 51,300,869
Average Circulation Per Capita: 5.09
Total Physical AV Resources Available: 4,578,716
Information provided courtesy of: Joseph Hamlin, Library Data Coordinator; Library of Michigan

ADRIAN

C ADRIAN COLLEGE*, Shipman Library, 110 S Madison St, 49221. SAN 345-8911. Tel: 517-264-3828. FAX: 517-264-3748. Web Site: www.adrian.edu/library. *Electronic Res Librn,* David Cruse; Tel: 517-265-5161, Ext 4241, E-mail: dcruse@adrian.edu; *Ref Librn,* Richard Geyer; Tel: 517-265-5161, Ext 4220, E-mail: rgeyer@adrian.edu; *Tech Serv Librn,* Noelle Keller; Tel: 517-265-5161, Ext 4229; Staff 3 (MLS 3)
Founded 1859. Enrl 1,828; Fac 194; Highest Degree: Master
Jul 2019-Jun 2020. Mats Exp $273,541, Books $4,995, Per/Ser (Incl. Access Fees) $182,318, AV Mat $819, Electronic Ref Mat (Incl. Access Fees) $85,409
Library Holdings: CDs 1,352; e-books 15,890; Bk Titles 111,864; Bk Vols 121,305; Per Subs 2,794; Videos 2,252
Special Collections: Lincolniana (Piotrowski-Lemke); United Methodist (Detroit Conference Archives)
Subject Interests: Liberal arts
Automation Activity & Vendor Info: (Acquisitions) SirsiDynix; (Cataloging) SirsiDynix; (Circulation) SirsiDynix; (Course Reserve) SirsiDynix; (Discovery) EBSCO Discovery Service; (ILL) OCLC WorldShare Interlibrary Loan; (OPAC) SirsiDynix; (Serials) EBSCO Discovery Service
Wireless access
Partic in Midwest Collaborative for Library Services

P ADRIAN DISTRICT LIBRARY*, 143 E Maumee St, 49221-2773. SAN 307-8469. Tel: 517-265-2265. FAX: 517-759-3195. E-mail: adriandistrictlibrary@adrian.lib.mi.us. Web Site: www.adrian.lib.mi.us. *Dir,* Jennifer A Wrzesinski; E-mail: JWrzesinski@adrian.lib.mi.us; *Asst Dir,* Chelsey Boss; E-mail: cboss@adrian.lib.mi.us; *Youth Serv Librn,* Cathy Chesher; E-mail: cchesher@adrian.lib.mi.us; Staff 14 (MLS 3, Non-MLS 11)
Founded 1868. Pop 21,333
Jul 2016-Jun 2017. Mats Exp $116,955, Books $99,893, Electronic Ref Mat (Incl. Access Fees) $17,062. Sal $349,455
Library Holdings: Audiobooks 6,511; e-books 540; Bk Vols 92,388; Per Subs 196
Special Collections: Local History Coll
Automation Activity & Vendor Info: (Cataloging) Book Systems; (Circulation) Book Systems; (ILL) Mel Cat; (OPAC) Book Systems
Wireless access
Function: 24/7 Electronic res, 24/7 Online cat, Activity rm, Adult bk club, Archival coll, Art exhibits, Audiobks on Playaways & MP3, Audiobks via web, Bks on CD, Children's prog, Citizenship assistance, Computer training, Computers for patron use, Electronic databases & coll, Free DVD rentals, Holiday prog, Home delivery & serv to seniorr ctr & nursing homes, Homebound delivery serv, ILL available, Internet access, Large print keyboards, Life-long learning prog for all ages, Magazines, Magnifiers for reading, Mango lang, Meeting rooms, Microfiche/film & reading machines, Movies, Music CDs, Notary serv, Online cat, Outreach serv, OverDrive digital audio bks, Photocopying/Printing, Preschool outreach, Printer for laptops & handheld devices, Prog for adults, Prog for children & young adult, Ref & res, Scanner, Spanish lang bks, Story hour, Summer reading prog, Tax forms, Teen prog, Telephone ref
Mem of Woodlands Library Cooperative
Partic in Midwest Collaborative for Library Services
Open Mon, Tues, Wed & Thurs 10-8, Fri 10-5:30, Sat 10-3
Restriction: Non-resident fee
Friends of the Library Group

P LENAWEE DISTRICT LIBRARY*, 4459 W US Hwy 223, 49221-1294. SAN 345-8970. Tel: 517-263-1011. FAX: 517-263-7109. E-mail: lovemylibrary@gmail.com. Web Site: lenawee.lib.mi.us. *Dir,* Trevor Van Valkenburg; E-mail: trevor.vanvalkenburg@monroe.lib.mi.us; Staff 3 (MLS 3)
Founded 1935. Pop 42,000; Circ 180,000
Library Holdings: Bk Vols 100,000; Per Subs 144
Automation Activity & Vendor Info: (Acquisitions) Innovative Interfaces, Inc; (Cataloging) Innovative Interfaces, Inc; (Circulation) Innovative Interfaces, Inc; (OPAC) Innovative Interfaces, Inc
Wireless access
Mem of Woodlands Library Cooperative
Open Mon-Thurs 9:30-8, Fri & Sat 9:30-5:30
Branches: 5
ADDISON BRANCH, 102 S Talbot St, Addison, 49220. (Mail add: 4459 W US 223, 49221-1246), SAN 345-9004. Tel: 517-547-3414. FAX: 517-547-3414. *Librn,* Karen Swanburg
Open Mon & Wed-Fri 1-6, Sat 9:30-1
Friends of the Library Group
BRITTON BRANCH, 120 College Ave, Britton, 49229-9705. (Mail add: 4459 W US 223, 49221-1246), SAN 345-9039. Tel: 517-451-2860. FAX: 517-451-8260. *Librn,* Laura Binns
Open Mon & Fri 12-6, Wed 10-4, Sat 10-1
Friends of the Library Group
CLAYTON BRANCH, 3457 State St, Clayton, 49235-9205. (Mail add: 4459 W US 223, 49221-1246), SAN 345-9063. Tel: 517-445-2619. FAX: 517-445-2619. *Librn,* Liz Fergus
Open Mon & Wed 2-7, Fri 2-6, Sat 11-2
Friends of the Library Group
DEERFIELD BRANCH, 170 Raisin St, Deerfield, 49238-9717. (Mail add: 4459 W US 223, 49221-1246), SAN 345-9152. Tel: 517-447-3400. FAX: 517-447-3400. *Librn,* Rebecca Bizonet
Open Mon & Fri 2-6, Wed 2-8, Thurs 10-3, Sat 10-1
Friends of the Library Group
ONSTED BRANCH, 261 S Main St, Onsted, 49265-9749. (Mail add: 4459 W US 223, 49221-1246), SAN 345-9098. Tel: 517-467-2623. FAX: 517-467-6298. *Librn,* Dorothy Giroux
Open Mon & Wed 1-6, Thurs & Fri 10-4, Sat 9:30-12:30
Friends of the Library Group
Bookmobiles: 1. Librn, Nicole Cogley

M PROMEDICA BIXBY HOSPITAL*, Medical Staff Library, 818 Riverside Ave, 49221. SAN 327-6481. Tel: 517-265-0236, 517-265-0429. *Med Librn/CME Coordr,* Kathy Raines
Library Holdings: Bk Titles 100
Restriction: Staff use only

C SIENA HEIGHTS UNIVERSITY LIBRARY*, 1247 E Siena Heights Dr, 49221-1796. SAN 307-8485. Tel: 517-264-7150. Interlibrary Loan Service Tel: 517-264-7155. Reference Tel: 517-264-7205. FAX: 517-264-7711. Web Site: sienaheights.edu/library.aspx. *Dir,* Jennifer Dean; Tel: 517-264-7152, E-mail: jdean@sienaheights.edu; *Pub Serv Librn,* Melissa M Sissen; E-mail: msissen@sienaheights.edu; *Circ Serv Coordr,* Renee M Bracey; E-mail: rbracey@sienaheights.edu; *Coordr, Ser,* Peggy Hlavka; Tel: 517-264-7153, E-mail: phlavka@sienaheights.edu; Staff 4 (MLS 2, Non-MLS 2)
Founded 1919. Enrl 1,000; Fac 65; Highest Degree: Master
Library Holdings: Bk Vols 112,895; Per Subs 352
Subject Interests: Archit, Art
Automation Activity & Vendor Info: (Acquisitions) SirsiDynix; (Cataloging) SirsiDynix; (Circulation) SirsiDynix; (Course Reserve) SirsiDynix; (OPAC) SirsiDynix; (Serials) SirsiDynix
Wireless access
Partic in Midwest Collaborative for Library Services
Open Mon-Wed (Fall & Winter) 8:30am-11pm, Thurs 8:30am-9pm, Fri 8:30-5, Sat 12-5, Sun 1-11; Mon-Thurs (Summer) 8:30-8

ALANSON

P ALANSON AREA PUBLIC LIBRARY*, 7631 Burr Ave, Hwy 31, 49706. (Mail add: PO Box 37, 49706-0037), SAN 376-7744. Tel: 231-548-5465. FAX: 231-548-5465. E-mail: alanson@racc2000.com. Web Site: joomla.uproc.lib.mi.us/alanson. *Dir,* Anna LaRue
Library Holdings: Bk Titles 5,000
Wireless access
Partic in Northland Library Cooperative; Upper Peninsula Region of Library Cooperation, Inc
Open Mon-Wed 10-6, Thurs 10-7, Fri 12-5, Sat 10-2 (1-5 Summer)
Friends of the Library Group

ALBION

C ALBION COLLEGE*, Stockwell-Mudd Libraries, 602 E Cass St, 49224-1879. (Mail add: Kellog Ctr 4692, 611 E Porter St, 49224), SAN 307-8507. Circulation Tel: 517-629-0489. Interlibrary Loan Service Tel: 517-629-0383. Reference Tel: 517-629-0382. Automation Services Tel: 517-629-0270. FAX: 517-629-0504. E-mail: library@albion.edu. Web Site: library.albion.edu. *Co-Dir,* Claudia C Diaz; Tel: 517-629-0386, E-mail: cdiaz@albion.edu; *Co-Dir,* Mike Van Houten; Tel: 517-629-0293, E-mail: mvanhouten@albion.edu; *Assoc Dir, Head, Libr Syst & Tech,* Jill Marie Mason; Tel: 517-629-0270, E-mail: jmason@albion.edu; *Research Librn,* Cheryl Blackwell; E-mail: cblackwell@albion.edu; *Archivist, Spec Coll Librn,* Elizabeth Palmer; E-mail: epalmer@albion.edu; *Tech Serv Librn,* Erin Smith; E-mail: ecsmith@albion.edu; *Circ Serv Coordr,* Becky Markovich; E-mail: rmarkovich@albion.edu; *Coordr, Ser,* Marion Meilaender; E-mail: mmeilaender@albion.edu; Staff 12.2 (MLS 5.7, Non-MLS 6.5)
Founded 1835. Enrl 1,500; Fac 105; Highest Degree: Bachelor
Library Holdings: AV Mats 7,780; Bks on Deafness & Sign Lang 40; CDs 1,500; DVDs 2,000; e-books 6,331; e-journals 1,357; Music Scores 2,500; Bk Titles 278,967; Bk Vols 368,060; Per Subs 2,091; Videos 3,000
Special Collections: Albion Americana; Albion College Archives; Bible Coll; M F K Fisher; Modern Literary First Editions; Western Michigan Conference of United Methodist Church Archives, bks, letters. US Document Depository
Subject Interests: Liberal arts
Automation Activity & Vendor Info: (Acquisitions) Innovative Interfaces, Inc; (Cataloging) Innovative Interfaces, Inc; (Circulation) Innovative Interfaces, Inc; (Course Reserve) Innovative Interfaces, Inc; (ILL) Innovative Interfaces, Inc; (OPAC) Innovative Interfaces, Inc; (Serials) Innovative Interfaces, Inc
Wireless access
Function: Archival coll, Art exhibits, Audio & video playback equip for onsite use, Computers for patron use, Doc delivery serv, E-Reserves, Electronic databases & coll, Free DVD rentals, Govt ref serv, ILL available, Internet access, Learning ctr, Music CDs, Online cat, Online info literacy tutorials on the web & in blackboard, Online ref, Photocopying/Printing, Ref & res, Ref serv available, Scanner, Wheelchair accessible
Publications: Ex Libris (Newsletter)
Partic in Midwest Collaborative for Library Services; Oberlin Group; OCLC Online Computer Library Center, Inc; Woodlands Interlibrary Loan
Special Services for the Deaf - Assisted listening device; Assistive tech; Bks on deafness & sign lang; Deaf publ
Special Services for the Blind - ABE/GED & braille classes for the visually impaired; Assistive/Adapted tech devices, equip & products; Audio mat; Braille bks; Braille equip; Braille servs; Computer with voice synthesizer for visually impaired persons; Large screen computer & software; Reader equip; Talking bks
Open Mon-Thurs 8:30am-2am, Fri 8am-9pm, Sat 9-9, Sun Noon-2am
Restriction: Open to pub for ref & circ; with some limitations, Open to students, fac & staff
Friends of the Library Group

P ALBION DISTRICT LIBRARY*, 501 S Superior St, 49224. SAN 307-8515. Tel: 517-629-3993. FAX: 517-629-5354. E-mail: info@albionlibrary.org. Web Site: www.albionlibrary.org. *Dir,* Cynthia Stanczak; E-mail: director@albionlibrary.org; *Head, Youth Serv,* Jamie Bernard; E-mail: youth@albionlibrary.org; *Archivist,* Jennifer Wood; E-mail: history@albionlibrary.org; Staff 7 (MLS 2, Non-MLS 5)
Founded 1919. Pop 11,465
Library Holdings: Audiobooks 1,244; DVDs 7,356; e-books 14,544; Bk Vols 87,802; Per Subs 34
Subject Interests: Local hist
Automation Activity & Vendor Info: (Cataloging) Biblionix/Apollo; (Circulation) Biblionix/Apollo; (ILL) Innovative Interfaces, Inc; (OPAC) Biblionix/Apollo
Wireless access
Function: 24/7 Electronic res, 24/7 Online cat, Adult bk club, Adult literacy prog, Archival coll, Art programs, Audiobks via web, Bk club(s), Bks on CD, Chess club, Children's prog, Computer training, Computers for patron use, Digital talking bks, Electronic databases & coll, Family literacy, Free DVD rentals, Holiday prog, ILL available, Instruction & testing, Internet access, Life-long learning prog for all ages, Magazines, Meeting rooms, Microfiche/film & reading machines, Movies, Museum passes, Online cat, Outreach serv, Photocopying/Printing, Preschool outreach, Preschool reading prog, Prog for adults, Prog for children & young adult, Ref & res, Ref serv available, Res assist avail, Senior computer classes, Story hour, Study rm, Summer reading prog, Tax forms, Teen prog, Telephone ref, Wheelchair accessible, Workshops
Publications: A Michigan Childhood
Mem of Woodlands Library Cooperative
Partic in Association for Rural & Small Libraries; Midwest Collaborative for Library Services
Open Mon-Thurs 10-8, Sat & Sun 1-5
Friends of the Library Group

P WOODLANDS LIBRARY COOPERATIVE, PO Box 1048, 49224. SAN 307-8523. Tel: 517-629-9469. FAX: 517-629-3812. Web Site: woodlands.lib.mi.us. *Dir,* Kate Pohjola Andrade; E-mail: kate@woodlands.lib.mi.us; Staff 2 (MLS 1, Non-MLS 1)
Founded 1978. Pop 831,014
Oct 2020-Sept 2021 Income $899,029. Sal $113,547 (Prof $80,923)
Wireless access
Publications: Woodlands Wanderings (Online only)
Member Libraries: Adrian District Library; Albion District Library; Athens Community Library; Bath Township Public Library; Bellevue Township Library; Branch District Library; Burr Oak Township Library; Camden Township Library; Charlotte Community Library; Clinton Township Public Library; Colon Township Library; Constantine Township Library; Delta Township District Library; Delton District Library; DeWitt District Library; Dorothy Hull Library - Windsor Charter Township; Dowling Public Library; East Lansing Public Library; Eaton Rapids Area District Library; George W Spindler Memorial Library; Grand Ledge Area District Library; Hillsdale Community Library; Homer Public Library; Hudson Carnegie District Library; Jackson District Library; Jonesville District Library; Lenawee District Library; Litchfield District Library; Lyons Township District Library; Marshall District Library; Mendon Township Library; Milan Public Library; Monroe County Library System; Mulliken District Library; North Adams Community Memorial Library; Nottawa Township Library; Pittsford Public Library; Portland District Library; Potterville Benton Township District Library; Putnam District Library; Reading Community Library; Schoolcraft Community Library; Schultz-Holmes Memorial Library; Spring Arbor University; Stair Public Library; Sunfield District Library; Tecumseh District Library; Tekonsha Public Library; Vermontville Township Library; Waldron District Library; White Pigeon Township Library
Open Mon-Fri 8-4:30

ALDEN

P ALDEN DISTRICT LIBRARY*, 8751 Helena Rd, 49612. SAN 307-8531. Tel: 231-331-4318. FAX: 231-331-4245. E-mail: aldenlib@torchlake.com. Web Site: www.aldenlib.info. *Dir,* Sue Riegler; *Asst Dir,* Diane Nemeth
Circ 22,580
Library Holdings: Bk Vols 18,000; Per Subs 35
Wireless access
Partic in Mid-Michigan Library League
Open Mon & Wed-Fri 9-5, Tues 9-8, Sat 9-Noon
Friends of the Library Group

ALLEGAN

P ALLEGAN DISTRICT LIBRARY*, 331 Hubbard St, 49010. SAN 307-854X. Tel: 269-673-4625. FAX: 269-673-8661. E-mail: apl@alleganlibrary.org. Web Site: www.alleganlibrary.org. *Dir,* Ryan Deery; Tel: 269-673-4625, E-mail: rdeery@alleganlibrary.org; *Asst Dir, Ref Serv,* Devin Erlandson; Tel: 269-673-4625, E-mail: derlandson@alleganlibrary.org; *AV Serv Librn, ILL, Tech Coordr,* PJ Wilson; Tel: 269-673-4625, E-mail: pjwilson@alleganlibrary.org; *Network Adminr,* Alan Smith; Tel: 269-673-4625, E-mail: asmith@alleganlibrary.org; *Adult Programmer,* Aleesha Dedrich; Tel: 269-673-4625, E-mail: adedrich@alleganlibrary.org; *Children's Programmer,* Billie Spicer; Tel: 269-673-4625, E-mail: bspicer@alleganlibrary.org. Subject Specialists: *AV,* PJ Wilson; *Networking,* Alan Smith; Staff 7 (MLS 2, Non-MLS 5)
Founded 1843. Pop 16,165; Circ 86,892
Jul 2016-Jun 2017 Income $420,300, State $7,500, City $249,000, Locally Generated Income $133,100, Other $17,700. Mats Exp $38,900, Books $29,900, Per/Ser (Incl. Access Fees) $3,000, AV Mat $6,000. Sal $303,840
Library Holdings: Audiobooks 920; AV Mats 4,391; Bks on Deafness & Sign Lang 21; CDs 1,521; DVDs 614; e-books 1,932; Large Print Bks 1,708; Bk Titles 68,000; Per Subs 150; Talking Bks 920; Videos 843
Special Collections: Civil War Coll; Michigan Coll
Automation Activity & Vendor Info: (Acquisitions) ComPanion Corp; (Cataloging) ComPanion Corp; (Circulation) ComPanion Corp; (Course Reserve) ComPanion Corp; (ILL) Innovative Interfaces, Inc - Millennium; (OPAC) ComPanion Corp; (Serials) EBSCO Online
Wireless access
Function: 24/7 Electronic res, 24/7 Online cat, Adult bk club, Audiobks via web, Bk club(s), Bks on CD, Children's prog, Computers for patron use, Digital talking bks, Electronic databases & coll, Equip loans & repairs, Free DVD rentals, ILL available, Internet access, Laminating, Magazines, Mail & tel request accepted, Microfiche/film & reading machines, Music CDs, Online cat, OverDrive digital audio bks, Photocopying/Printing, Prog for adults, Prog for children & young adult, Ref serv available, Scanner, Spoken cassettes & CDs, Story hour, Summer reading prog, Tax forms, Teen prog, Wheelchair accessible
Partic in Association for Rural & Small Libraries; Southwest Michigan Library Cooperative
Open Mon-Thurs 10-9, Fri & Sat 9-5:30
Restriction: Authorized patrons, In-house use for visitors, Non-resident fee
Friends of the Library Group

ALLEN PARK

P ALLEN PARK PUBLIC LIBRARY*, 8100 Allen Rd, 48101. SAN 307-8558. Tel: 313-381-2425. FAX: 313-381-2124. Web Site: www.allenparklibrary.org. *Dir,* Sandi Blakney; E-mail: sblakney@allenparklibrary.org; *Youth Librn,* Brandi Winehart; E-mail: bswinehart@allenparklibrary.org; *Circ Supvr,* Kim Oakley; E-mail: koakley@allenparklibrary.org; Staff 5 (MLS 2, Non-MLS 3)
Founded 1927. Pop 34,169; Circ 88,045
Library Holdings: Bk Vols 80,000; Per Subs 220
Special Collections: Local Newspapers, 1921-present
Automation Activity & Vendor Info: (Cataloging) SirsiDynix; (Circulation) SirsiDynix; (OPAC) SirsiDynix
Wireless access
Open Mon, Tues & Thurs (Fall-Spring) 10-8, Wed, Fri & Sat 10-5; Mon-Fri (Summer) 10-8
Friends of the Library Group

C BAKER COLLEGE OF ALLEN PARK LIBRARY*, 4500 Enterprise Dr, 48101. Tel: 313-425-3711. FAX: 313-425-3777. E-mail: library@baker.edu. Web Site: my.baker.edu/ICS/My_Services/Department_Resources/Academic_Resource_Center/Library. *Coordr of Info & Tech Res,* Diane Childress; Tel: 810-766-4235, E-mail: dchild02@baker.edu
Founded 1911. Highest Degree: Doctorate
Library Holdings: AV Mats 50; Bk Titles 5,000; Per Subs 50
Wireless access
Partic in PALnet
Open Mon-Thurs 8:30am-9pm, Fri 8:30-5

R DETROIT BAPTIST THEOLOGICAL SEMINARY LIBRARY*, 4801 Allen Rd, 48101. SAN 373-2010. Tel: 313-381-0111, Ext 412. E-mail: library@dbts.edu. Web Site: library.dbts.edu. *Dir, Libr Serv,* Dr Mark Snoeberger; E-mail: msnoeberger@dbts.edu; *Acq Librn,* Dr John Aloisi; E-mail: jaloisi@dbts.edu; Staff 2 (MLS 1, Non-MLS 1)
Founded 1976. Enrl 120; Highest Degree: Master
Library Holdings: Bk Titles 40,000; Bk Vols 45,000; Per Subs 300
Subject Interests: Biblical studies, Church hist, Theol
Automation Activity & Vendor Info: (Acquisitions) LibLime; (Cataloging) LibLime; (Circulation) LibLime; (Course Reserve) LibLime; (ILL) LibLime; (Media Booking) LibLime; (OPAC) LibLime; (Serials) LibLime
Wireless access
Open Mon-Fri 8-4

ALLENDALE

P ALLENDALE TOWNSHIP LIBRARY*, 6175 Library Ln, 49401. SAN 307-8574. Tel: 616-895-4178. FAX: 616-895-5178. E-mail: all@llcoop.org. Web Site: www.allendalelibrary.org. *Libr Dir,* Mary Cook; Tel: 616-895-4178, Ext 2, E-mail: maryc@allendale-twp.org; *Youth Serv Librn,* Ashley Johnson; Tel: 616-895-4178, Ext 3, E-mail: ashleyjohnson@allendale-twp.org; Staff 10.2 (MLS 1.2, Non-MLS 9)
Founded 1966. Pop 14,072
Automation Activity & Vendor Info: (Cataloging) Innovative Interfaces, Inc; (Circulation) Innovative Interfaces, Inc; (OPAC) Innovative Interfaces, Inc
Wireless access
Function: Adult bk club, Audiobks via web, Bk club(s), Bks on cassette, Bks on CD, CD-ROM, Children's prog, Computer training, Computers for patron use, Electronic databases & coll, Free DVD rentals, Holiday prog, Home delivery & serv to seniorr ctr & nursing homes, Homebound delivery serv, ILL available, Instruction & testing, Internet access, Mail & tel request accepted, Music CDs, Online cat, Online ref, Orientations, Outreach serv, Photocopying/Printing, Prog for adults, Prog for children & young adult, Ref serv available, Senior computer classes, Senior outreach, Spoken cassettes & CDs, Spoken cassettes & DVDs, Story hour, Summer reading prog, Tax forms, Teen prog, Telephone ref, VHS videos, Wheelchair accessible, Workshops
Partic in Lakeland Library Cooperative
Open Mon, Tues & Thurs 9-9, Wed 1-9, Fri & Sat 9-5

C GRAND VALLEY STATE UNIVERSITY LIBRARIES*, One Campus Dr, 49401-9403. SAN 307-8582. Tel: 616-331-3500. Toll Free Tel: 800-879-0581. E-mail: library@gvsu.edu. Web Site: www.gvsu.edu/library. *Dean, Univ Libr,* Annie Belanger; E-mail: belange1@gvsu.edu; *Curator, Rare Bks,* Robert Beasecker; Tel: 616-331-8556, E-mail: beaseckr@gvsu.edu
Founded 1960. Enrl 24,541; Highest Degree: Doctorate
Special Collections: Limited Edition Series; Lincoln & the Civil War Coll; Michigan Novels; US Geological Survey Maps
Wireless access

ALMA

C ALMA COLLEGE LIBRARY*, 614 W Superior St, 48801. SAN 307-8590. Tel: 989-463-7229. FAX: 989-463-8694. Web Site: www.alma.edu/library. *Dir,* Carol A Zeile; Tel: 989-463-7342, E-mail: zeile@alma.edu; *Head, Ref & Res Serv,* Steven Vest; Tel: 989-463-7344, E-mail: vest@alma.edu; *Access Serv Librn,* Angie Kelleher; Tel: 989-463-7345, E-mail: kelleher@alma.edu; *Tech Serv Librn,* Marcus Richter; Tel: 989-463-7409, E-mail: richtermj@alma.edu; *Circ Mgr,* Melissa Hovey; E-mail: hovey@alma.edu; Staff 9 (MLS 4, Non-MLS 5)
Founded 1889. Enrl 1,261; Fac 102; Highest Degree: Bachelor
Library Holdings: AV Mats 8,377; Bk Titles 204,051; Bk Vols 251,641; Per Subs 1,200
Special Collections: College Archives
Automation Activity & Vendor Info: (Acquisitions) Innovative Interfaces, Inc; (Cataloging) Innovative Interfaces, Inc; (Circulation) Innovative Interfaces, Inc; (OPAC) Innovative Interfaces, Inc; (Serials) Innovative Interfaces, Inc
Wireless access
Partic in Midwest Collaborative for Library Services
Open Mon-Thurs (Winter) 8am-Midnight, Fri 8-8, Sat 10-8, Sun 12:30-Midnight; Mon-Fri (Summer) 8-5

P ALMA PUBLIC LIBRARY*, 500 E Superior St, 48801-1999. SAN 307-8604. Tel: 989-463-3966. FAX: 989-466-5901. Interlibrary Loan Service E-mail: ill@alma.lib.mi.us. Web Site: www.youseemore.com/alma. *Dir & Librn,* Bryan E Dinwoody; Tel: 989-463-3966, Ext 9853; *Youth/Young Adult Librn,* Marla Drudy; Tel: 989-463-3966, Ext 9581, E-mail: mdrudy@alma.lib.mi.us; *Circ Mgr,* Lorrie Taylor; Tel: 989-463-3966, Ext 9580, E-mail: ltaylor@alma.lib.mi.us; *Cataloger, Tech Serv,* Diana Simpson; Tel: 989-463-3966, Ext 9582, E-mail: dsimpson@alma.lib.mi.us; Staff 3 (MLS 1, Non-MLS 2)
Founded 1909. Circ 126,514
Library Holdings: Large Print Bks 354; Bk Vols 69,000; Per Subs 158; Talking Bks 2,061
Special Collections: Republic Truck Photography Coll
Automation Activity & Vendor Info: (Cataloging) SirsiDynix; (Circulation) SirsiDynix; (OPAC) SirsiDynix
Wireless access
Publications: Annual Report; Subject Bibliographies
Partic in White Pine Library Cooperative
Open Mon & Fri 12-9, Tues-Thurs 9:30-9, Sat 9:30-5:30
Friends of the Library Group

ALMONT

P ALMONT DISTRICT LIBRARY, Henry Stephens Memorial Library, 213 W St Clair St, 48003-8476. (Mail add: PO Box 517, 48003-0517), SAN 307-8620. Tel: 810-798-3100. FAX: 810-798-2208. Web Site: www.adlmi.org. *Dir,* Kay Hurd; E-mail: director@adlmi.org; *Coordr, Patron Serv, ILL,* Linda Clouse
Founded 1916. Pop 6,041; Circ 22,950
Library Holdings: Bk Titles 28,000
Wireless access
Function: ILL available, Photocopying/Printing, Telephone ref
Partic in Mideastern Mich Libr Coop
Open Mon-Thurs 10-7, Fri 10-5, Sat 10-2

ALPENA

J ALPENA COMMUNITY COLLEGE*, Stephen H Fletcher Library, Newport Center Bldg, Rm 111, 665 Johnson St, 49707. SAN 307-8639. Tel: 989-358-7252. FAX: 989-358-7556. E-mail: acclrc@alpenacc.edu. Web Site: discover.alpenacc.edu/admissions/current_students/library_services.php. *Dean, Learning Res, Media Serv,* Wendy Brooks; Tel: 989-358-7249, E-mail: brooksw@alpenacc.edu
Founded 1952. Enrl 1,200; Fac 85; Highest Degree: Associate
Library Holdings: AV Mats 1,667; Large Print Bks 67; Bk Titles 37,748; Bk Vols 42,169; Per Subs 134; Talking Bks 199
Automation Activity & Vendor Info: (Cataloging) Follett Software; (Circulation) Follett Software; (ILL) Auto-Graphics, Inc; (Media Booking) Follett Software; (OPAC) Follett Software; (Serials) Follett Software
Wireless access
Publications: Guide to Library
Partic in Midwest Collaborative for Library Services
Open Mon-Wed 7:30am-8pm, Thurs 7:30-5, Fri 7:30-4, Sat & Sun 12-4

P ALPENA COUNTY LIBRARY*, George N Fletcher Public Library, 211 N First St, 49707. SAN 307-8647. Tel: 989-356-6188. FAX: 989-356-2765. E-mail: contactus@alpenalibrary.org. Web Site: www.alpenalibrary.org. *Dir,* Eric Magness-Eubank; Tel: 989-356-6188, Ext 11, E-mail: emeacl@alpenalibrary.org; *Asst Dir,* Jessica Luther; Tel: 989-356-6188, Ext 25; *Children & Youth Serv Librn,* Mary Clute; Tel: 989-356-6188, Ext 13, E-mail: mclute@alpenalibrary.org; Staff 21 (MLS 2, Non-MLS 19)
Founded 1967. Pop 35,000; Circ 307,000
Library Holdings: AV Mats 3,800; Large Print Bks 750; Bk Titles 85,000; Per Subs 240
Special Collections: 19th Century Great Lakes Maritime Materials (Thunder Bay National Marine Sanctuary Research Coll); Adult Literacy Coll; Cooperating Coll for the Foundation of New York; Genealogy Center; Michigan Coll. State Document Depository; US Document Depository
Automation Activity & Vendor Info: (Cataloging) SirsiDynix; (Circulation) SirsiDynix; (OPAC) SirsiDynix; (Serials) SirsiDynix
Wireless access
Function: Adult bk club, Adult literacy prog, Archival coll, Art exhibits, Bks on cassette, Bks on CD, Children's prog, Computer training, Computers for patron use, Electronic databases & coll, Family literacy, Holiday prog, ILL available, Music CDs, Photocopying/Printing, Prog for adults, Prog for children & young adult, Ref & res, Wheelchair accessible
Partic in Midwest Collaborative for Library Services; Northland Library Cooperative; Upper Peninsula Region of Library Cooperation, Inc
Open Mon-Thurs 9:30-9, Fri & Sat 9:30-5, Sun 1-5
Friends of the Library Group

AMASA

P AMASA COMMUNITY LIBRARY*, 109 W Pine St, 49903. SAN 307-8663. Tel: 906-822-7291. *Librn,* Judy Cornelia
Pop 1,020; Circ 1,174
Library Holdings: AV Mats 23; Bk Vols 5,000
Wireless access
Open Mon-Sun 11-1:30 & 5-7:30

ANN ARBOR

P ANN ARBOR DISTRICT LIBRARY*, 343 S Fifth Ave, 48104. SAN 345-9217. Tel: 734-327-4200. Circulation Tel: 734-327-4219. Reference Tel: 734-327-4525. Administration Tel: 734-327-4263. Web Site: aadl.org. *Libr Dir,* Josie Parker; E-mail: parkerj@aadl.org; Staff 144 (MLS 21, Non-MLS 123)
Founded 1856. Pop 163,590; Circ 8,805,859
Jul 2012-Jun 2013 Income (Main & Associated Libraries) $12,056,184. Mats Exp $1,848,599. Sal $5,695,993
Library Holdings: Audiobooks 27,575; CDs 58,241; DVDs 99,202; Bk Vols 410,125
Special Collections: Ann Arbor News Archive; Art Prints; Bi-Folkal Kits; Black Studies Coll; Book Clubs to Go (Youth & Adult); Energy Meters; Language Learning Coll; Music Tools; Musical Scores; Paperback Plays; Science to Go (Interactive Science Materials); Science Tools; Stories to Go (Storytime Kits); Telescopes; World Language Coll; Youth Kits (Print Book/Audio Book Pairs, Brainquest Cards, Fandex Cards)
Subject Interests: Art, Local hist, Music
Automation Activity & Vendor Info: (Acquisitions) Innovative Interfaces, Inc; (Cataloging) Innovative Interfaces, Inc; (Circulation) Innovative Interfaces, Inc; (OPAC) Innovative Interfaces, Inc; (Serials) Innovative Interfaces, Inc
Wireless access
Function: Archival coll, Art exhibits, Audiobks via web, Bks on cassette, Bks on CD, Computer training, Computers for patron use, Doc delivery serv, Electronic databases & coll, Free DVD rentals, Holiday prog, Home delivery & serv to seniorr ctr & nursing homes, Homebound delivery serv, Homework prog, ILL available, Large print keyboards, Magnifiers for reading, Museum passes, Music CDs, Online cat, Online ref, Outreach serv, OverDrive digital audio bks, Photocopying/Printing, Preschool outreach, Prog for adults, Prog for children & young adult, Ref serv available, Scanner, Senior computer classes, Senior outreach, Spoken cassettes & CDs, Story hour, Summer reading prog, Tax forms, Telephone ref, VHS videos, Wheelchair accessible
Publications: AADL News (Newsletter); Axis: Stuff for Teens Grades 6-12 (Newsletter); Jump: Fun Stuff Just for Kids (Newsletter); WLBPD@AAADL News (Newsletter)
Partic in Midwest Collaborative for Library Services; OCLC Online Computer Library Center, Inc
Special Services for the Blind - Accessible computers; Assistive/Adapted tech devices, equip & products; BiFolkal kits; Bks on cassette; Bks on CD; Closed circuit TV magnifier; Descriptive video serv (DVS); Digital talking bk; Internet workstation with adaptive software; Large print bks; Magnifiers; Networked computers with assistive software; Newsletter (in large print, Braille or on cassette); PC for people with disabilities; Recorded bks; Ref serv; Scanner for conversion & translation of mats; Screen enlargement software for people with visual disabilities; Screen reader software; Talking bk serv referral; Talking bks; Talking bks & player equip; Variable speed audiotape players
Open Mon 10-9, Tues-Fri 9-9, Sat 9-6, Sun 12-6
Friends of the Library Group
Branches: 5
MALLETTS CREEK BRANCH, 3090 E Eisenhower Pkwy, 48108.
Special Services for the Blind - Accessible computers; Bks on CD; Large print bks; Magnifiers; Networked computers with assistive software
Open Mon 10-9, Tues-Fri 9-9, Sat 9-6, Sun 12-6
PITTSFIELD BRANCH, 2359 Oak Valley Dr, 48103.
Special Services for the Blind - Accessible computers; Bks on CD; Large print bks; Magnifiers; Networked computers with assistive software
Open Mon 10-9, Tues-Fri 9-9, Sat 10-6, Sun 12-6
TRAVERWOOD, 3333 Traverwood Dr, 48105.
Special Services for the Blind - Accessible computers; Bks on CD; Large print bks; Magnifiers; Networked computers with assistive software
Open Mon 10-9, Tues-Fri 9-9, Sat 9-6, Sun 12-6

P WASHTENAW LIBRARY FOR THE BLIND & PHYSICALLY DISABLED, 343 S Fifth Ave, 48104. Tel: 734-327-4224. E-mail: wlbpd@aadl.org. Web Site: wlbpd.aadl.org.
Library Holdings: DVDs 335; Large Print Bks 4,622; Talking Bks 14,220
Special Services for the Blind - Accessible computers; Assistive/Adapted tech devices, equip & products; Bks on CD; Bks on flash-memory cartridges; Closed caption display syst; Computer with voice synthesizer for visually impaired persons; Copier with enlargement capabilities; Descriptive video serv (DVS); Digital talking bk; Digital talking bk machines; Extensive large print coll; Free checkout of audio mat; Home delivery serv; Internet workstation with adaptive software; Large print bks; Large print bks & talking machines; Large screen computer & software; Low vision equip; Magnifiers; Networked computers with assistive software; PC for people with disabilities; Scanner for conversion & translation of mats; Screen enlargement software for people with visual disabilities; Screen reader software; Talking bks; Talking bks & player equip
Open Mon 10-9, Tues-Fri 9-9, Sat 9-6, Sun 12-6
WEST BRANCH, 2503 Jackson Rd, 48103, SAN 345-9276.
Special Services for the Blind - Accessible computers; Bks on CD; Large print bks; Magnifiers; Networked computers with assistive software
Open Mon 10-9, Tues-Fri 9-9, Sat 10-6, Sun 12-6

C CONCORDIA UNIVERSITY*, Zimmerman Library, 4090 Geddes Rd, 48105-2797. SAN 307-8698. Tel: 734-995-7454. Reference Tel: 734-995-7320. Administration Tel: 734-995-7314. Web Site: www.cuaa.edu/academics/library. *Dir, Libr Serv,* Christian R Himsel; E-mail: christian.himsel@cuw.edu
Founded 1963. Enrl 750; Fac 46; Highest Degree: Master
Library Holdings: e-journals 14,411; Bk Titles 95,000; Bk Vols 113,000; Per Subs 146
Special Collections: Classics; ERIC depository; French Language & Literature (Denkinger); History of Science (Annual Volumes & Backfile Bound Periodicals for Creation Research Society Quarterly, vols 1 to date & Journal of Victoria Institute, 1861-1975). US Document Depository

Subject Interests: Educ, Hist, Music, Natural sci, Theol
Automation Activity & Vendor Info: (Cataloging) SirsiDynix; (Circulation) SirsiDynix; (Course Reserve) SirsiDynix; (OPAC) SirsiDynix
Wireless access
Partic in Midwest Collaborative for Library Services
Open Mon-Thurs (Fall & Spring) 8am-Midnight, Fri 8-5, Sat 9-4, Sun 2-Midnight

GM DEPARTMENT OF VETERANS AFFAIRS*, VA Ann Arbor Healthcare System Medical Center Library, 2215 Fuller Rd, 48105. SAN 346-0207. Tel: 734-845-5408. FAX: 734-845-3110. Web Site: www.annarbor.va.gov. *Libr Mgr,* Sara Peth; Staff 1 (MLS 1)
Library Holdings: AV Mats 323; Bk Titles 3,300; Per Subs 185
Subject Interests: Med, Nursing, Psychol
Automation Activity & Vendor Info: (Acquisitions) EOS International; (Cataloging) EOS International; (Circulation) EOS International; (OPAC) EOS International; (Serials) EOS International
Function: Doc delivery serv, Ref serv available
Partic in Midwest Collaborative for Library Services
Open Mon-Fri 8-4:30
Restriction: Circ limited, External users must contact libr, Restricted pub use

G ENVIRONMENTAL PROTECTION AGENCY*, National Vehicle & Fuel Emissions Laboratory Library, 2000 Traverwood Dr, 48105. SAN 307-8701. Tel: 734-214-4311. FAX: 734-214-4525. E-mail: AALibrary@epa.gov. Web Site: www.epa.gov/libraries/national-vehicle-and-fuel-emissions-laboratory-library-services. *Librn,* Robin Swanson; Tel: 734-214-4136, E-mail: swanson.robin@epa.gov; *Web Librn,* Shan Liao; Tel: 734-214-4435, E-mail: liao.shan@epa.gov; Staff 2 (MLS 2)
Founded 1975
Library Holdings: Bk Vols 3,000; Per Subs 90
Special Collections: EPA Report Coll; Legislative Materials, Documents & Reports; Society of Automotive Engineers Papers, 1962-present
Subject Interests: Air pollution, Automotive engr, Fuel
Automation Activity & Vendor Info: (Cataloging) OCLC Connexion
Wireless access
Function: CD-ROM, Doc delivery serv, Govt ref serv, ILL available, Internet access, Orientations, Photocopying/Printing, Ref serv available, Telephone ref
Open Mon-Fri 9-4
Restriction: Circulates for staff only, In-house use for visitors, Lending to staff only, Non-circulating to the pub, Open to pub upon request, Open to researchers by request, Pub use on premises, Restricted borrowing privileges

G MICHIGAN DEPARTMENT OF NATURAL RESOURCES, INSTITUTE FOR FISHERIES, Fisheries Division Library, NIB G250, 400 N Ingalls St, 48109-5480. SAN 307-8779. Tel: 734-356-1934. Web Site: www.michigan.gov/dnr/0,4570,7-350-79136_79236_85892—,00.html. *Librn,* Tina M Tincher; E-mail: tinchert@michigan.gov; Staff 1 (MLS 1)
Founded 1930
Library Holdings: Bk Vols 800; Per Subs 15
Subject Interests: Fisheries
Restriction: Non-circulating to the pub, Open by appt only

S NATIONAL ARCHIVES & RECORDS ADMINISTRATION, Gerald R Ford Presidential Library, 1000 Beal Ave, 48109. SAN 321-6497. Tel: 734-205-0555. FAX: 734-205-0571. E-mail: ford.library@nara.gov. Web Site: www.fordlibrarymuseum.gov. *Dir,* Brooke Clement; E-mail: brooke.clement@nara.gov; *Supvry Archivist,* Geir Gundersen; Tel: 734-205-0556; *Archivist,* Stacy Davis; Tel: 734-205-0563; *Archivist,* Elizabeth Druga; Tel: 734-205-0554; *Archive Spec,* Tim Holtz; Tel: 734-205-0592; *Archives, Tech,* John O'Connell; Tel: 734-205-0559; *Computer Syst Adminr,* John Hurley; Tel: 734-205-0553; *Spec Events Coordr,* Position Currently Open. Subject Specialists: *Digitization,* Stacy Davis; Staff 11 (MLS 6, Non-MLS 5)
Founded 1977
Library Holdings: Bk Titles 6,550; Bk Vols 9,618; Per Subs 25
Special Collections: Personal Papers of Gerald Ford & of His Associates in Politics & Government, 1950-2000; Presidential Papers & Government Records, 1974-77 (includes Archives of President Ford, White House Staff, & National Security Council). Oral History
Subject Interests: Cold War, Foreign affairs, Politics, Presidential elections, US domestic policy
Wireless access
Function: Archival coll, Distance learning, For res purposes, Govt ref serv, Mail & tel request accepted, Online ref, Photocopying/Printing, Ref serv available, Telephone ref
Open Mon-Sat 10-5, Sun Noon-5
Restriction: Non-circulating coll
Friends of the Library Group

G NATIONAL OCEANIC & ATMOSPHERIC ADMINISTRATION*, Great Lakes Environmental Research Laboratory Library, 4840 S State Rd, 48108-9719. SAN 307-8787. Tel: 734-741-2225. FAX: 734-741-2055. Web Site: www.glerl.noaa.gov/library. *Br Chief, Info Serv,* Margaret Lansing; Tel: 734-741-2210, E-mail: margaret.lansing@noaa.gov; Staff 1 (MLS 1)
Founded 1975
Library Holdings: Bk Vols 8,655; Per Subs 213
Subject Interests: Climatology, Geophysics, Great Lakes, Limnology, Meteorology, Oceanography
Automation Activity & Vendor Info: (Cataloging) SirsiDynix; (Circulation) SirsiDynix; (OPAC) SirsiDynix
Partic in NOAA Libraries Network; OCLC Online Computer Library Center, Inc
Open Mon-Fri 9-4

M ST JOSEPH MERCY HOSPITAL*, Riecker Memorial Library, 5301 E Huron River Dr, Rm 1712, 48106. (Mail add: PO Box 995, 48106-0995), SAN 307-8809. Tel: 734-712-3045. FAX: 734-712-2679. *Librn,* Jillah Biza; E-mail: jillah.biza@stjoeshealth.org; Staff 2 (MLS 1, Non-MLS 1)
Subject Interests: Consumer health info, Med, Nursing
Wireless access
Partic in Medical Library Association; Metrop Detroit Med Libr Group; Michigan Health Sciences Libraries Association; Midwest Collaborative for Library Services; OWLSnet
Restriction: Private libr

G UNITED STATES GEOLOGICAL SURVEY, GREAT LAKES SCIENCE CENTER*, John Van Oosten Library, 1451 Green Rd, 48105-2807. SAN 307-8817. Tel: 734-214-7210. FAX: 734-994-8780. E-mail: gs-mwr-glsc_library@usgs.gov. Web Site: www.glsc.usgs.gov/library. *Tech Info Spec,* Tara Bell; E-mail: tbell@usgs.gov; Staff 1 (MLS 1)
Founded 1966
Subject Interests: Biology, Environ studies, Great Lakes
Partic in Federal Library & Information Network; Midwest Collaborative for Library Services; OCLC Online Computer Library Center, Inc
Restriction: Borrowing requests are handled by ILL, Visitors must make appt to use bks in the libr

UNIVERSITY OF MICHIGAN

C BENTLEY HISTORICAL LIBRARY*, 1150 Beal Ave, 48109-2113, SAN 345-9489. Tel: 734-764-3482. FAX: 734-936-1333. Reference E-mail: bentley.ref@umich.edu. Web Site: bentley.umich.edu. *Dir,* Terrence J McDonald; E-mail: tmcd@umich.edu; *Assoc Dir,* Nancy Bartlett; E-mail: nbart@umich.edu; Staff 22 (MLS 12, Non-MLS 10)
Founded 1935
Library Holdings: Bk Vols 60,000; Per Subs 110
Special Collections: Architectural Coll; Papers of Frank Murphy, George Romney, Arthur Vandenburg, G Mennen Williams, Gerald L K Smith, William G Milliken, Detroit Urban League; Records of University of Michigan; Temperance & Prohibition (Women's Christian Temerance Union), ms, micro, printed; US & China Coll; US & Philippines Coll
Subject Interests: Mich
Partic in Big Ten Academic Alliance; Center for Research Libraries; National Network of Libraries of Medicine Region 6; OCLC Research Library Partnership; Research Libraries Information Network
Publications: Asn of Res Librs
Open Mon-Fri 9-5
Friends of the Library Group

C WILLIAM L CLEMENTS LIBRARY*, 909 S University Ave, 48109-1190, SAN 326-4343. Tel: 734-764-2347. FAX: 734-647-0716. Web Site: www.clements.umich.edu. *Dir,* J Kevin Graffagnino; E-mail: jkgraff@umich.edu; *Assoc Dir,* Brian Leigh Dunnigan; E-mail: briand@umich.edu; *Head, Reader Serv,* Clayton D Lewis; E-mail: clayclem@umich.edu; *Curator,* Barbara DeWolfe; E-mail: bdewolfe@umich.edu. Subject Specialists: *Manuscripts,* Barbara DeWolfe; Staff 8 (MLS 7, Non-MLS 1)
Founded 1923
Library Holdings: Bk Vols 77,000; Per Subs 34
Partic in Research Libraries Information Network
Publications: Exhibit Bulletins; The Quarto
Open Mon-Wed & Fri (Winter) 9-4:45, Thurs 9-7:45; Mon-Thurs (Summer) 9-5:45, Fri 9am-11:45am
Restriction: Non-circulating
Friends of the Library Group

C SUMNER & LAURA FOSTER LIBRARY*, 265 Lorch Hall, 48109-1220, SAN 345-9519. Tel: 734-763-6609. FAX: 734-764-2769. E-mail: foster.library@umich.edu. Web Site: www.lib.umich.edu/foster-library. *Mgr,* Brenda Fischer; E-mail: bsfische@umich.edu; *Econ Librn,* Pamela MacKintosh; E-mail: pmackin@umich.edu; Staff 2 (MLS 1, Non-MLS 1)
Founded 1986
Library Holdings: Bk Vols 2,500; Per Subs 100
Special Collections: Working Papers & Research Reports from other Universities & Research Institute
Subject Interests: Econ

Partic in Association of Research Libraries
Open Mon-Thurs (Fall & Winter) 10-7, Fri 10-5

C KRESGE LIBRARY SERVICES*, Stephen M Ross School of Business, 701 Tappan St, 48109-1234, SAN 345-9306. Circulation Tel: 734-764-1375. Reference Tel: 734-764-9464. E-mail: kresge_library@umich.edu. Web Site: www.bus.umich.edu/kresgelibrary. *Dir,* Corey Seeman; Tel: 734-764-9969, E-mail: cseeman@umich.edu; *Fac Res Serv/Ref Serv Librn,* Laura Berdish; Tel: 734-763-9360, E-mail: berdish@umich.edu; *Fac Res Serv/Ref Serv Librn,* Danguole Kviklys; Tel: 734-764-8424, E-mail: dkviklys@umich.edu; *Fac Res Serv/Ref Serv Librn,* Celia Ross; Tel: 734-763-5452, E-mail: caross@umich.edu; *Instrul Serv Librn,* Sally Ziph; Tel: 734-764-5532, E-mail: sweston@umich.edu; *Digital Serv,* Jennifer Lammers Zimmer; Tel: 734-764-6845; *Tech Serv,* John Sterbenz; Tel: 734-764-5746, E-mail: jsterben@umich.edu. Subject Specialists: *Acctg, Finance,* Celia Ross; Staff 19 (MLS 8, Non-MLS 11)
Founded 1925. Enrl 3,400; Fac 189; Highest Degree: Doctorate
Library Holdings: Bk Titles 150; Bk Vols 200; Per Subs 2,500
Subject Interests: Bus, Career info
Automation Activity & Vendor Info: (Acquisitions) Innovative Interfaces, Inc; (Cataloging) Innovative Interfaces, Inc; (Circulation) Innovative Interfaces, Inc; (Course Reserve) Innovative Interfaces, Inc; (ILL) Innovative Interfaces, Inc; (Media Booking) Innovative Interfaces, Inc; (OPAC) Innovative Interfaces, Inc; (Serials) Innovative Interfaces, Inc
Function: Doc delivery serv, Electronic databases & coll, ILL available, Mail & tel request accepted, Online cat, Ref & res, Ref serv available
Partic in Association of Research Libraries; OCLC Online Computer Library Center, Inc
Restriction: Not open to pub

CL LAW LIBRARY*, 801 Monroe St, 48109-1210, SAN 345-942X. Tel: 734-764-9324. Circulation Tel: 734-764-4252. Interlibrary Loan Service Tel: 734-763-7940. FAX: 734-615-0178. Circulation FAX: 734-936-3884. Reference FAX: 734-764-5863. Web Site: www.law.umich.edu/library/info/pages/default.aspx. *Dir,* Margaret A Leary; Tel: 734-764-9322, E-mail: mleary@umich.edu; *Asst Dir,* Barbara Garavaglia; Tel: 734-764-9338, E-mail: bvaccaro@umich.edu; *Asst Dir,* Barbara Snow; Tel: 734-763-3767, E-mail: barbsnow@umich.edu; Staff 57 (MLS 12, Non-MLS 45)
Founded 1859. Enrl 1,150; Fac 60; Highest Degree: Doctorate
Library Holdings: Bk Titles 305,352; Bk Vols 941,237; Per Subs 9,733
Automation Activity & Vendor Info: (Acquisitions) Innovative Interfaces, Inc; (Cataloging) Innovative Interfaces, Inc; (Circulation) Innovative Interfaces, Inc; (Course Reserve) Innovative Interfaces, Inc; (ILL) Innovative Interfaces, Inc; (OPAC) Innovative Interfaces, Inc; (Serials) Innovative Interfaces, Inc
Partic in Law Library Microform Consortium; Midwest Collaborative for Library Services; Research Libraries Information Network
Restriction: Internal circ only, Restricted access

C TRANSPORTATION RESEARCH INSTITUTE LIBRARY*, 2901 Baxter Rd, 48109-2150, SAN 345-939X. Tel: 734-764-2171. FAX: 734-936-1081. E-mail: umtri-lib@umich.edu. Web Site: www.umtri.umich.edu. *Mgr,* Bob Sweet; Tel: 734-936-1073, E-mail: bsweet@umich.edu; Staff 5 (MLS 2, Non-MLS 3)
Founded 1965
Library Holdings: Bk Titles 110,000; Per Subs 300
Subject Interests: Automotive engr
Automation Activity & Vendor Info: (Circulation) Inmagic, Inc.
Partic in Proquest Dialog
Publications: UMTRI Bibliography (cumulative); UMTRI Current Acquisitions - A Selected List (weekly - electronic & printed editions)
Open Mon-Fri 8-12 & 1-5

C UNIVERSITY OF MICHIGAN*, University Library, 818 Hatcher Graduate Library South, 913 S University Ave, 48109-1190. SAN 345-9578. Tel: 734-764-0400. Circulation Tel: 734-764-0401. Interlibrary Loan Service Tel: 734-764-8584. Reference Tel: 734-764-9373. FAX: 734-763-5080. Circulation FAX: 734-647-9557. Interlibrary Loan Service FAX: 734-936-3630. E-mail: contact-mlibrary@umich.edu. Web Site: www.lib.umich.edu. *Univ Librn & Dean of Libr,* James Hilton; E-mail: hilton@umich.edu; *Assoc Univ Librn, Dir of the Taubman Health Sci Libr,* Nancy Allee; E-mail: nallee@umich.edu; *Assoc Univ Librn, Coll Develop,* Bryan Skib; E-mail: bskib@umich.edu; *Assoc Univ Librn, Info Tech,* Bohyun Kim; *Assoc Univ Librn, Learning & Teaching,* Laurie Alexander; E-mail: lauriea@umich.edu; *Assoc Univ Librn, Libr Operations,* Rebecca Dunkle; E-mail: rdunkle@umich.edu; Staff 488 (MLS 158, Non-MLS 330)
Founded 1817. Enrl 58,947; Fac 6,941; Highest Degree: Doctorate
Library Holdings: Bk Titles 12,803,468; Per Subs 63,329
Special Collections: American Society of Information Sciences, ms; Food & Agriculture Organizations; Human Relations Area Files; Organization of American States; World Health Organizations. Canadian and Provincial; State Document Depository; UN Document Depository; US Document Depository
Subject Interests: Astronomy, Bibliographies, Botany, E Asia, English, Geog, Hist, Hist of sci, Hist of transportation, Math, Near East, Netherlands, S Asia, Slavic (Lang), Zoology
Automation Activity & Vendor Info: (Acquisitions) Ex Libris Group; (OPAC) Ex Libris Group
Partic in OCLC Online Computer Library Center, Inc

Departmental Libraries:

ART, ARCHITECTURE & ENGINEERING LIBRARY, Duderstadt Ctr, 2281 Bonnisteel Blvd, 48109-2094, SAN 345-9667. Tel: 734-647-5747. FAX: 734-764-4487. E-mail: aael.circ@umich.edu. Web Site: www.lib.umich.edu/art-architecture-engineering-library. *Eng Librn,* Paul Grochowski; *Eng Librn,* Leena Lalwani; *Visual Res Librn,* Rebecca Price. Subject Specialists: *Archit, Urban planning,* Rebecca Price; Staff 27 (MLS 7, Non-MLS 20)
Library Holdings: Bk Vols 663,460
Special Collections: Charles Sawyer Papers; D H Burnham Papers; Geo Bringham Papers; Leonard Eaton Papers; Michigan Reports; Walter Sanders Papers. US Document Depository
Subject Interests: Archit, Art, Design, Engr, Urban planning
Function: Audio & video playback equip for onsite use, For res purposes, ILL available, Ref serv available, Res libr, Wheelchair accessible
Restriction: Open to pub for ref only, Open to students, fac & staff

ASIA LIBRARY, Harlen Hatcher Graduate Library, 913 S University Ave, 48109-1190, SAN 345-987X. Tel: 734-764-0406. FAX: 734-647-2885. E-mail: asialibrary@umich.edu. Web Site: www.lib.umich.edu/asia-library. *Head of Libr,* Dawn Lawson; Tel: 734-936-2353, E-mail: delawson@umich.edu; *Tech Serv,* Yunah Sung; Tel: 734-936-2408, E-mail: yunahs@umich.edu; Staff 11 (MLS 6, Non-MLS 5)
Founded 1948
Library Holdings: Bk Vols 689,508
Special Collections: Ch'ing Archives; Gaimosho Archives; GB PRO Files on China; Hussey Papers; Japanese Diet Proceedings; URI Files
Subject Interests: China, Far East, Japan, Korea
Publications: The Catalogs of the Asia Library, G K Hall, 1979

ASKWITH MEDIA LIBRARY, Shapiro Library, 919 S University Ave, 48109-1185, SAN 370-3533. Tel: 734-764-5360. E-mail: askwithmedia@umich.edu. Web Site: www.lib.umich.edu/askwith-media-library. *Assoc Librn,* Jeffrey Pearson; Tel: 734-763-3758, E-mail: jwpearso@umich.edu; Staff 4 (MLS 1, Non-MLS 3)
Founded 1939
Library Holdings: AV Mats 9,476; Bk Titles 40,000; Talking Bks 135; Videos 19,413
Subject Interests: Film, Media, Video
Function: Audio & video playback equip for onsite use, AV serv, Digital talking bks

FINE ARTS LIBRARY, 260 Tappan Hall, 2nd Flr, 855 S University Ave, 48109-1357, SAN 345-9934. Tel: 734-764-5405. FAX: 734-764-5408. E-mail: fineartslibrary@umich.edu. Web Site: www.lib.umich.edu/fine-arts-library. *Librn,* Deirdre Spencer; Tel: 734-763-8963, E-mail: deirdres@umich.edu. Subject Specialists: *Hist of art,* Deirdre Spencer; Staff 4 (MLS 1, Non-MLS 3)
Library Holdings: Bk Vols 96,161
Subject Interests: Art hist

HARLAN HATCHER GRADUATE LIBRARY, 913 S University Ave, 48109-1190, SAN 371-4810. Tel: 734-764-0400. Web Site: www.lib.umich.edu/hatcher-graduate-library. *Assoc Univ Librn, Learning & Teaching,* Laurie Alexander; Tel: 734-763-2381, E-mail: lauriea@umich.edu
Founded 1838
Library Holdings: Bk Vols 3,605,791
Special Collections: UN Document Depository; US Document Depository
Subject Interests: Humanities

MUSEUMS LIBRARY, Research Museums Ctr, 3600 Varsity Dr, 48108, SAN 346-0118. Tel: 734-764-0467. FAX: 734-764-3829. E-mail: museums.library@umich.edu. Web Site: www.lib.umich.edu/museums. *Biological Sci Librn,* Scott Martin; Tel: 734-764-8196, E-mail: samarti@umich.edu; *Supvr,* Charlene Stachnik; E-mail: sta@umich.edu
Library Holdings: Bk Vols 129,293
Subject Interests: Anthrop, Botany, Natural hist, Paleontology, Zoology

MUSIC LIBRARY, Earl V Moore Bldg, 3rd Flr, 1100 Baits Dr, 48109-2085, SAN 345-9756. Tel: 734-764-2512. FAX: 734-764-5097. E-mail: music.library@umich.edu. Circulation E-mail: music.circ@umich.edu. Web Site: www.lib.umich.edu/music. *Music Librn,* Jason Imbesi; E-mail: imbesij@umich.edu; *Operations Supvr,* Karin Stratton; E-mail: kstratt@umich.edu; Staff 5 (MLS 2, Non-MLS 3)
Founded 1940
Library Holdings: Bk Vols 145,732
Special Collections: American Sheet Music; Ivan Galamin Coll; Michael Rabin Coll; Radio Canada Int; Scores (Ignaz Brüll Coll); Women Composers Coll
Subject Interests: Dance, Music, Music educ, Musicology
Function: Audio & video playback equip for onsite use, Photocopying/Printing, Ref serv available

SHAPIRO SCIENCE LIBRARY, Shapiro Library Bldg, 3rd & 4th Flrs, 919 S University Ave, 48109-1185, SAN 345-9993. Circulation Tel: 734-764-7490. Reference Tel: 734-936-2327. FAX: 734-763-9813. E-mail: sciencelibrary@umich.edu. Web Site: www.lib.umich.edu/science/. *Physics & Astronomy Librn,* Jacob Glenn; Tel: 734-936-2339, E-mail: jkglenn@umich.edu; *Supvr,* Charlene M Stachnick; E-mail: sta@umich.edu; Staff 16 (MLS 7, Non-MLS 9)
Library Holdings: Bk Vols 484,030
Special Collections: Astronomical Maps; Rare Book Coll
Subject Interests: Astronomy, Biology, Chem, Geol, Math, Natural res, Physics, Statistics
Publications: Newsletter

SHAPIRO UNDERGRADUATE LIBRARY, 919 S University Ave, 48109-1185. Tel: 734-764-7490. FAX: 734-764-6849. Web Site: www.lib.umich.edu/shapiro-undergraduate-library. *Assoc Univ Librn, Learning & Teaching,* Laurie Alexander; E-mail: lauriea@umich.edu; *Coord, Libr Coll,* Pamela J MacKintosh; E-mail: pmackin@umich.edu; Staff 17 (MLS 8, Non-MLS 9)
Library Holdings: Bk Vols 150,000

SPECIAL COLLECTIONS RESEARCH CENTER, Harlan Hatcher Graduate Library South, 913 S University Ave, 48109-1190, SAN 346-0002. Tel: 734-764-9377. E-mail: special.collections@umich.edu. Web Site: www.lib.umich.edu/special-collections-library. *Dir,* Martha O'Hara Conway; Tel: 734-647-8151, E-mail: moconway@umich.edu

CM TAUBMAN HEALTH SCIENCES LIBRARY, 1135 E Catherine St, 48109-2038, SAN 345-9721. Tel: 734-764-1210. E-mail: thlibrary@umich.edu. Web Site: www.lib.umich.edu/taubman-health-sciences-library. *Dir,* Nancy Allee; Tel: 734-936-1403, E-mail: nallee@umich.edu
Founded 1920
Library Holdings: Bk Vols 398,829
Special Collections: US Document Depository
Subject Interests: Dentistry, Homeopathy, Med, Nursing, Pharm, Pub health

J WASHTENAW COMMUNITY COLLEGE*, Richard W Bailey Library, 4800 E Huron River Dr, 48105-4800. SAN 307-8841. Tel: 734-973-3379. Circulation Tel: 734-973-3741. Interlibrary Loan Service Tel: 734-973-3734. Reference Tel: 734-973-3431. FAX: 734-973-3446. Circulation E-mail: circdesk@wccnet.edu. Web Site: www.wccnet.edu/resources/library. *Dean, Learning Res,* Victor Liu; E-mail: vliu@wccnet.edu; *Dir, Access Serv,* Bethany Kennedy; Tel: 734-477-8723, E-mail: bakennedy@wccnet.edu; *Librn,* Molly Ledermann; Tel: 734-973-3313, E-mail: mledermann@wccnet.edu; *Librn,* Amy Lee; Tel: 734-677-5294, E-mail: amjlee@wccnet.edu; *Librn,* Sandy McCarthy; Tel: 734-677-5293, E-mail: mccarthy@wccnet.edu; *Librn,* Maureen Perault; Tel: 734-973-3407, E-mail: mperault@wccnet.edu; *Librn,* Meghan Rose; Tel: 734-973-3430, E-mail: mrrose@wccnet.edu; *Librn,* Martha Stuit; Tel: 734-973-5464, E-mail: mstuit@wccnet.edu; *Libr Asst,* Position Currently Open; *Access Serv Tech-ILL,* Brooke Regensburg; E-mail: bregensburg@wccnet.edu; *Access Serv Tech-Operation,* Michelle Toth; Tel: 734-477-8710, E-mail: matoth@wccnet.edu; *Access Serv Tech-Reserves,* Catherine Karain; Tel: 734-477-8709, E-mail: ckarain@wccnet.edu; *Acq Asst,* Irene Brock; Tel: 734-973-3399, E-mail: ibrock@wccnet.edu; *Acq Asst,* Heather Bertke; Tel: 734-973-3402, E-mail: hbertke@wccnet.edu; *Cataloger,* Laura Zimbleman; Tel: 734-973-3401, E-mail: laurazim@wccnet.edu; Staff 14 (MLS 5.5, Non-MLS 8.5)
Founded 1965. Enrl 8,300; Fac 400; Highest Degree: Associate
Jul 2015-Jun 2016 Income $1,480,078. Mats Exp $240,970, Books $69,970, Per/Ser (Incl. Access Fees) $44,000, Other Print Mats $4,150, AV Mat $10,000, Electronic Ref Mat (Incl. Access Fees) $112,850. Sal $1,138,654
Library Holdings: AV Mats 3,452; CDs 228; DVDs 2,351; e-books 160,538; e-journals 74,329; Bk Titles 64,658; Bk Vols 69,151; Per Subs 134; Videos 3,215
Automation Activity & Vendor Info: (Acquisitions) SirsiDynix; (Cataloging) SirsiDynix; (Circulation) SirsiDynix; (Course Reserve) Blackboard Inc; (Discovery) EBSCO Discovery Service; (ILL) Mel Cat; (OPAC) SirsiDynix; (Serials) SirsiDynix
Wireless access
Partic in Midwest Collaborative for Library Services; OCLC Online Computer Library Center, Inc
Special Services for the Deaf - Assistive tech
Special Services for the Blind - Assistive/Adapted tech devices, equip & products

S WILSON ORNITHOLOGICAL SOCIETY*, Josselyn Van Tyne Memorial Library, Univ of Michigan Museum of Zoology, 1109 Geddes Ave, 48109-1079. SAN 327-4799. Tel: 734-764-0457. FAX: 734-763-4080. Web Site: www.wilsonsociety.org/library. *Librn,* Janet Hinshaw; E-mail: jhinshaw@umich.edu; Staff 1 (Non-MLS 1)
Founded 1930
Library Holdings: Bk Titles 3,000; Spec Interest Per Sub 210
Subject Interests: Ornithology
Wireless access
Function: Mail loans to mem

ARMADA

P ARMADA FREE PUBLIC LIBRARY*, 73930 Church St, 48005. SAN 307-885X. Tel: 586-784-5921. Web Site: www.armadalib.org. *Dir,* Margaret Smith; Staff 4 (MLS 1, Non-MLS 3)
Founded 1901. Pop 5,334; Circ 44,610
Library Holdings: Bk Titles 27,799; Per Subs 82
Automation Activity & Vendor Info: (Acquisitions) SirsiDynix; (Cataloging) SirsiDynix; (Circulation) SirsiDynix; (ILL) SirsiDynix; (OPAC) SirsiDynix; (Serials) SirsiDynix
Wireless access
Open Mon & Tues 12-8, Wed & Thurs 9-8, Fri 9-5, Sat 10-2

ASHLEY

P ASHLEY DISTRICT LIBRARY, 104 N New St, 48806. (Mail add: PO Box 6, 48806-0006). Tel: 989-847-4283, Ext 1007. FAX: 989-847-5000. Web Site: www.ashleyschools.net/library. *Dir,* Lynne Clark; E-mail: lclark@ashleyschools.net; *Dir,* Mrs Shannon Lord; Tel: 989-847-4000, Ext 1007, E-mail: slord@ashleyschools.net; Staff 2 (Non-MLS 2)
Founded 1998
Library Holdings: Audiobooks 44; AV Mats 373; e-books 4,577; Bk Vols 9,839; Per Subs 23
Automation Activity & Vendor Info: (Cataloging) Follett Software; (Circulation) Follett Software
Wireless access
Function: 24/7 Electronic res, 24/7 Online cat, Accelerated reader prog
Partic in White Pine Library Cooperative
Open Mon-Fri 8:30-7; Mon (Winter) 8:30-3; (Summer) Tues & Thurs 9-7

ATHENS

P ATHENS COMMUNITY LIBRARY*, 106 E Burr Oak St, 49011-9793. (Mail add: PO Box 216, 49011-0216), SAN 307-8868. Tel: 269-729-4479. FAX: 269-729-4479. E-mail: athens_library@sbcglobal.net. Web Site: woodlands.lib.mi.us/athens. *Dir,* Diane Garlets
Founded 1922. Circ 3,237
Library Holdings: Audiobooks 305; Bk Titles 8,366; Bk Vols 8,417; Per Subs 34
Automation Activity & Vendor Info: (Cataloging) Follett Software; (Circulation) Follett Software; (ILL) Mel Cat
Wireless access
Function: Adult bk club, Bk club(s), Bks on CD, Children's prog, Computers for patron use, ILL available, Internet access, Magazines, Online cat, OverDrive digital audio bks, Photocopying/Printing, Prog for adults, Prog for children & young adult, Scanner, Story hour, Summer reading prog, Wheelchair accessible
Mem of Woodlands Library Cooperative
Open Mon 9-6, Tues & Thurs 12-8, Wed & Fri 12-6, Sat 9-1

ATLANTA

P MONTMORENCY COUNTY PUBLIC LIBRARIES*, Atlanta Headquarters, 11901 Haymeadow Rd, 49709. (Mail add: PO Box 438, 49709-0438). Tel: 989-785-3941. FAX: 989-785-3941. Web Site: www.montmorencylibrary.com. *Dir,* Lori Haas; E-mail: director@montmorencylibrary.com; *Librn,* Andrea Mellingen
Library Holdings: Bk Vols 12,196; Per Subs 15
Automation Activity & Vendor Info: (Cataloging) SirsiDynix; (Circulation) SirsiDynix
Wireless access
Function: Photocopying/Printing
Partic in Northland Library Cooperative
Open Mon & Tues 10-6, Wed-Fri 10-5, Sat 9-Noon
Branches: 2

LEWISTON PUBLIC, 2851 Kneeland St, Lewiston, 49756. (Mail add: PO Box 148, Lewiston, 49756-0148). Tel: 989-786-2985. FAX: 989-786-2985. E-mail: lewistonlibrary@montmorencylibrary.com. *Librn,* Wendy Rieck
Library Holdings: Bk Vols 10,025; Per Subs 20
Open Mon & Tues 10-6, Wed-Fri 10-5, Sat 9-Noon
Friends of the Library Group

HILLMAN WRIGHT BRANCH, 121 W Second St, Hillman, 49746-9024. (Mail add: PO Box 247, Hillman, 49746-0247). Tel: 989-742-4021. FAX: 989-742-4021. E-mail: hillmanlib@yahoo.com. *Librn,* Kim Wade
Library Holdings: Bk Vols 10,000; Per Subs 24
Special Services for the Blind - Computer with voice synthesizer for visually impaired persons; Large print bks
Open Tues, Wed & Fri 10-5, Thurs 10-7, Sat 10-2

AUBURN HILLS

P AUBURN HILLS PUBLIC LIBRARY*, 3400 E Seyburn Dr, 48326-2759. SAN 329-1332. Tel: 248-370-9466. FAX: 248-370-9364. Web Site: www.ahplibrary.org. *Dir,* Lawrence Marble; E-mail: marblel@ahplibrary.org; *Head, Adult Serv,* Renee Holden; *Head, Support Serv,* Minni Shetty; *Head, Youth Serv,* Erin Look; *Tech Coordr,* Connor McNamara; Staff 25 (MLS 5, Non-MLS 20)
Founded 1986. Pop 21,410
Library Holdings: Bk Vols 60,380
Automation Activity & Vendor Info: (Acquisitions) CARL.Solution (TLC); (Cataloging) CARL.Solution (TLC); (Circulation) CARL.Solution (TLC)
Wireless access
Function: Bk club(s), Bks on CD, Butterfly Garden, Children's prog, Computer training, Electronic databases & coll, Holiday prog, Homebound delivery serv, Magazines, Magnifiers for reading, Meeting rooms, Movies, Music CDs, Outreach serv, Photocopying/Printing, Preschool reading prog, Prog for adults, Prog for children & young adult, Scanner, Senior outreach, STEM programs, Story hour, Study rm, Summer reading prog, Tax forms, Teen prog, Writing prog
Publications: Auburn Hills Highlights (quarterly newsletter)
Open Mon-Thurs 10-9, Fri & Sat 10-6

C BAKER COLLEGE OF AUBURN HILLS*, Academic Resource Center, 1500 University Dr, 48326-2642. Tel: 248-276-8290. Toll Free Tel: 888-429-0410. FAX: 248-276-8273. E-mail: library@baker.edu. Web Site: my.baker.edu/ICS/My_Services/Department_Resources/Academic_Resource_Center/Library/. *Coordr of Info & Tech Res,* Diane Childress; Tel: 810-766-4235, E-mail: dchild02@baker.edu
Automation Activity & Vendor Info: (Cataloging) Koha; (Circulation) Koha; (Discovery) EBSCO Discovery Service; (OPAC) Koha
Wireless access
Partic in PALnet
Open Mon-Thurs 8-8, Fri 8-5

OAKLAND COMMUNITY COLLEGE

J AUBURN HILLS CAMPUS LIBRARY*, 2900 Featherstone Rd, Bldg D, 48326, SAN 320-9121. Tel: 248-232-4125. Information Services Tel: 248-232-4128. FAX: 248-232-4136. Web Site: www.oaklandcc.edu/library. *Librn,* Johnna M Balk; Tel: 248-232-4131, E-mail: jmbalk@oaklandcc.edu; Staff 4 (MLS 1, Non-MLS 3)
Founded 1965. Fac 75; Highest Degree: Associate
Jul 2019-Jun 2020. Mats Exp $90,359, Books $54,860, Per/Ser (Incl. Access Fees) $35,499. Sal $339,025 (Prof $225,025)
Library Holdings: Audiobooks 660; AV Mats 3,912; Bks on Deafness & Sign Lang 98; CDs 208; DVDs 1,706; e-journals 5; Microforms 8,464; Per Subs 138; Videos 1,338
Automation Activity & Vendor Info: (Acquisitions) Ex Libris Group; (Cataloging) Ex Libris Group; (Circulation) Ex Libris Group; (Course Reserve) Ex Libris Group; (Discovery) Ex Libris Group; (ILL) OCLC; (OPAC) Ex Libris Group; (Serials) Ex Libris Group
Function: 24/7 Electronic res, 24/7 Online cat, Art exhibits, Audio & video playback equip for onsite use, Bks on CD, CD-ROM, Computers for patron use, Digital talking bks, Distance learning, Doc delivery serv, Electronic databases & coll, Free DVD rentals, ILL available, Instruction & testing, Internet access, Magazines, Magnifiers for reading, Mail & tel request accepted, Meeting rooms, Microfiche/film & reading machines, Music CDs, Online cat, Online info literacy tutorials on the web & in blackboard, Online ref, Orientations, Outreach serv, Photocopying/Printing, Ref & res, Ref serv available, Scanner, Spanish lang bks, Spoken cassettes & CDs, Spoken cassettes & DVDs, Study rm, Telephone ref, Wheelchair accessible, Workshops
Special Services for the Deaf - Accessible learning ctr; ADA equip; Assistive tech; Bks on deafness & sign lang
Special Services for the Blind - Closed circuit TV magnifier; Computer with voice synthesizer for visually impaired persons; Copier with enlargement capabilities; Dragon Naturally Speaking software; Free checkout of audio mat; Internet workstation with adaptive software; Large print bks; Ref serv; Screen reader software
Open Mon-Thurs (Sept-June) 8am-9pm, Fri 8-5, Sat 10-2; Mon-Thurs (July-Aug) 8-8, Fri 8-4

J LIBRARY SYSTEMS*, 2900 Featherstone Rd, MTEC A210, 48326, SAN 307-8876. Tel: 248-232-4478. Interlibrary Loan Service Tel: 248-232-4479. Administration Tel: 248-232-4476. FAX: 248-232-4089. Web Site: www.oaklandcc.edu/library. *Dean,* Mary Ann Sheble; Tel: 248-341-2053, E-mail: masheble@oaklandcc.edu; *Mgr, Tech Serv,* Elizabeth A Lindley; E-mail: ealindle@oaklandcc.edu; *Coordr, Electronic Res,* Jeffrey Zachwieja; Tel: 248-522-3488, E-mail: jxzachwi@oaklandcc.edu; *Tech Serv,* Susan Appelt; Tel: 248-232-4480, E-mail: smappelt@oaklandcc.edu; *Tech Serv,* Marianne Calunas; E-mail: mxcaluna@oaklandcc.edu; Staff 5 (MLS 3, Non-MLS 2)
Founded 1965. Enrl 28,984; Highest Degree: Associate
Library Holdings: e-books 15,802
Automation Activity & Vendor Info: (Acquisitions) SirsiDynix; (Cataloging) SirsiDynix; (Circulation) SirsiDynix; (ILL) OCLC; (OPAC) SirsiDynix; (Serials) SirsiDynix
Partic in Detroit Area Library Network
Open Mon-Fri 7:30-5:30
Restriction: Restricted pub use

AUGUSTA

P MCKAY LIBRARY*, 105 S Webster St, 49012-9601. (Mail add: PO Box 308, 49012-0308), SAN 307-8884. Tel: 269-731-4000. FAX: 269-731-5323. E-mail: info@mckaylibrary.org. Web Site: www.mckaylibrary.org. *Dir,* Anne Rapp; E-mail: anne@mckaylibrary.org; *Librn,* Robin Burgamy; E-mail: robin@mckaylibrary.org
Pop 7,095; Circ 25,830
Library Holdings: Large Print Bks 200; Bk Vols 27,000; Per Subs 55
Special Collections: Local Newspaper Coll, Augusta Beacon 1902-1964, micro
Automation Activity & Vendor Info: (Cataloging) Follett Software; (Circulation) Follett Software
Wireless access
Partic in Southwest Michigan Library Cooperative
Open Mon & Tues 9-5, Wed 10-7, Thurs & Fri 10-5, Sat 10-2
Friends of the Library Group

BAD AXE

P BAD AXE AREA DISTRICT LIBRARY*, 200 S Hanselman, 48413. SAN 307-8892. Tel: 989-269-8538. FAX: 989-269-2411. Web Site: www.badaxelibrary.org. *Dir,* Mimi Herrington; E-mail: mherrington@badaxelibrary.org; Staff 8 (Non-MLS 8)
Founded 1913. Pop 6,100; Circ 65,000
Library Holdings: Bk Vols 23,000; Per Subs 110
Special Collections: Huron Daily Tribune 1860's-present; Local History Coll
Automation Activity & Vendor Info: (Cataloging) Auto-Graphics, Inc; (Circulation) Auto-Graphics, Inc; (OPAC) Auto-Graphics, Inc
Wireless access
Function: 24/7 Electronic res, 24/7 Online cat, Accelerated reader prog, Activity rm, Adult bk club, After school storytime, Archival coll, Audiobks via web, Bk club(s), Bks on CD, CD-ROM, Children's prog, Computer training, Computers for patron use, Digital talking bks, Distance learning, Electronic databases & coll, Home delivery & serv to seniorr ctr & nursing homes, Homebound delivery serv, Jail serv, Laminating, Magazines, Magnifiers for reading, Microfiche/film & reading machines, Movies, Music CDs, Notary serv, Online cat, Online info literacy tutorials on the web & in blackboard, Online ref, OverDrive digital audio bks, Photocopying/Printing, Preschool outreach, Prog for adults, Prog for children & young adult, Scanner, Senior computer classes, Story hour, Summer & winter reading prog, Summer reading prog, Tax forms, Teen prog, VHS videos, Wheelchair accessible, Winter reading prog
Partic in White Pine Library Cooperative
Open Mon-Fri 10-8, Sat 10-4
Friends of the Library Group

L HURON COUNTY LAW LIBRARY*, 250 E Huron Ave, 2nd Flr, 48413. Tel: 989-269-7112. FAX: 989-269-0005. *Library Contact,* Sarah McNames; E-mail: mcnames@co.huron.mi.us
Library Holdings: Bk Vols 2,950

BALDWIN

P PATHFINDER COMMUNITY LIBRARY, 812 Michigan Ave, 49304. (Mail add: PO Box 880, 49304-0880), SAN 307-8906. Tel: 231-745-4010. FAX: 231-745-7681. E-mail: pathfinderlibrary123@gmail.com. Web Site: pathfinderlibrary.org. *Dir,* Bonnie Povilaitis
Founded 1953. Pop 4,200; Circ 14,500
Library Holdings: Bk Vols 26,000; Per Subs 50
Wireless access
Partic in Mid-Michigan Library League
Open Mon-Sat 10-3

BARAGA

S MICHIGAN DEPARTMENT OF CORRECTIONS, Baraga Correctional Facility Library, 13924 Wadaga Rd, 49908. Tel: 906-275-5100. FAX: 906-353-7957. Web Site: www.michigan.gov/corrections. *Librn,* Regina Kemp; E-mail: kempr1@michigan.gov
Library Holdings: Bk Vols 6,000; Per Subs 8
Restriction: Not open to pub

§P OJIBWA COMMUNITY LIBRARY, 409 S Superior Ave, 49908. Tel: 906-353-8163. E-mail: oclib@up.net. Web Site: kbic-nsn.gov/index.php/departments/library. *Librn,* Angela Badke
Founded 2002
Special Collections: Native American Coll, audiobks, bks, movies, pers

Wireless access
Function: Computers for patron use, ILL available, Photocopying/Printing
Partic in Upper Peninsula Region of Library Cooperation, Inc
Open Mon & Fri 9-4, Tues-Thurs 9-5

BARRYTON

P BARRYTON PUBLIC LIBRARY*, 198 Northern Ave, 49305. (Mail add: PO Box 215, 49305-0215), SAN 307-8914. Tel: 989-382-5288. FAX: 989-382-9073. E-mail: barrytonlibrary@frontier.com. Web Site: barrytonlibrary.com. *Dir,* Marcia Laughlin
Founded 1930. Pop 3,107; Circ 20,000
Library Holdings: Bk Vols 17,000; Per Subs 25
Wireless access
Partic in Mid-Michigan Library League
Open Tues-Fri 9-6, Sat 9-1

BATH

P BATH TOWNSHIP PUBLIC LIBRARY*, 14033 Webster Rd, 48808. (Mail add: PO Box 368, 48808). Tel: 517-641-7111. FAX: 517-641-7112. E-mail: info@bathtownshippubliclibrary.org. Web Site: www.bathtownshippubliclibrary.org. *Dir,* Kristina Reynolds; E-mail: kreynolds@bathtownshippubliclibrary.org; *Cat Librn,* Derek Barth; E-mail: dbarth@bathtownshippubliclibrary.org; *Youth Librn,* Carrie Frazer; E-mail: cfrazer@bathtownshippubliclibrary.org
Mem of Woodlands Library Cooperative
Open Mon-Thurs 10-8, Fri & Sat 10-4

BATTLE CREEK

S ART CENTER OF BATTLE CREEK LIBRARY*, 265 E Emmett St, 49017. SAN 307-8922. Tel: 269-962-9511. FAX: 269-969-3838. E-mail: info@artcenterofbattlecreek.org. Web Site: www.artcenterofbattlecreek.org. *Exec Dir,* Linda Holderbaum; E-mail: director@artcenterofbattlecreek.org
Library Holdings: Bk Vols 500
Special Collections: Michigan Art Coll & Archival Library
Subject Interests: Art, Art hist
Open Tues-Fri 10-5, Sat 11-3

GM DEPARTMENT OF VETERANS AFFAIRS, Medical Center Library, Bldg 9, Rm 104, 5500 Armstrong Rd, 49015. SAN 307-8981. Tel: 269-223-6490. FAX: 269-660-6031. *Chief Librn,* Linda S Polardino; Tel: 269-223-6491, E-mail: linda.polardino@va.gov; Staff 2 (MLS 1, Non-MLS 1)
Library Holdings: Bk Vols 3,000; Per Subs 180
Subject Interests: Psychiat
Automation Activity & Vendor Info: (Cataloging) LibraryWorld, Inc; (Circulation) LibraryWorld, Inc; (OPAC) LibraryWorld, Inc
Partic in Veterans Affairs Library Network

J KELLOGG COMMUNITY COLLEGE*, Emory W Morris Library, 450 North Ave, 49017-3397. SAN 307-8965. Tel: 269-965-4122. Reference Tel: 269-965-4122, Ext 2373. FAX: 269-965-4133. TDD: 269-962-0898. Web Site: www.kellogg.edu/library. *Dean,* Dr Michele Reid; Tel: 269-660-2380, E-mail: reidm2@kellogg.edu; *Instruction Librn, Student Success Librn,* Rebekah Love; Tel: 269-565-7882, E-mail: lover@kellogg.edu; *Faculty Coordr, Library Services,* Kassie Dunham; Tel: 269-565-2613, E-mail: dunhamk@kellogg.edu; *Tech Serv Spec,* Patricia Halder; Tel: 269-565-7887, E-mail: halderp@kellogg.edu; Staff 3 (MLS 3)
Founded 1956. Enrl 3,451; Fac 400; Highest Degree: Associate
Library Holdings: e-books 21,000; Bk Vols 51,500; Per Subs 210
Automation Activity & Vendor Info: (Acquisitions) Innovative Interfaces, Inc; (Cataloging) Innovative Interfaces, Inc; (Circulation) Innovative Interfaces, Inc; (Course Reserve) Innovative Interfaces, Inc; (ILL) Innovative Interfaces, Inc; (OPAC) Innovative Interfaces, Inc; (Serials) Innovative Interfaces, Inc
Wireless access
Partic in Midwest Collaborative for Library Services; OCLC Online Computer Library Center, Inc
Special Services for the Deaf - TDD equip
Open Mon-Thurs (Winter) 7:45am-9pm, Fri 8-5, Sat 11-3; Mon-Thurs (Summer) 7:45-8

P WILLARD LIBRARY*, Seven W Van Buren St, 49017-3009. SAN 307-899X. Tel: 269-968-8166. FAX: 269-968-3284. Web Site: willardlibrary.org. *Dir,* Cathy Lucas; E-mail: clucas@willardlibrary.org; *Dep Dir,* April Dillinger
Founded 1840. Pop 90,804; Circ 1,045,517
Library Holdings: Bk Vols 180,362
Subject Interests: Local hist
Wireless access
Partic in Southwest Michigan Library Cooperative
Open Mon-Thurs 9-9, Fri 9-6, Sat 9-5, Sun (Sept-April) 1-5

Branches: 1
HELEN WARNER BRANCH, 36 Minges Creek Pl, 49015. FAX: 269-979-8072. *Br Mgr,* Melissa McPherson
Library Holdings: Bk Vols 43,251
Open Mon-Thurs 9-8, Fri & Sat 9-5, Sun (Sept-April) 1-5

BAY CITY

S BAY COUNTY HISTORICAL SOCIETY*, Butterfield Memorial Research Library, 321 Washington Ave, 48708. SAN 327-0246. Tel: 989-893-5733. FAX: 989-893-5741. Web Site: www.bchsmuseum.org/id19.html. *Libr Mgr,* Jamie Kramer; E-mail: jkramer@bchsmusuem.org
Founded 1919
Library Holdings: Bk Titles 8,000
Special Collections: Corporate Archives (Monitor Sugar Co); Patrol Craft Sailors Assoc Archives - military, WWII; Research Materials on Bay County, 1830-present, photos. Municipal Document Depository; Oral History
Subject Interests: Agr, Archit, Genealogy, Great Lakes maritime hist, Local hist, Manufacturing, Politics, WWII
Function: Res libr
Open Mon-Thurs 1-5
Restriction: Non-circulating

P BAY COUNTY LIBRARY SYSTEM*, 500 Center Ave, 48708. SAN 346-0290. Tel: 989-894-2837. FAX: 989-894-2021. TDD: 989-893-7052. Web Site: www.baycountylibrary.org. *Dir,* Trish Burns; E-mail: tburns@baycountylibrary.org; *Asst Dir,* Kevin Ayala; E-mail: kayala@baycountylibrary.org; Staff 17 (MLS 14, Non-MLS 3)
Founded 1974. Pop 107,517; Circ 880,000
Library Holdings: Bk Vols 304,554; Per Subs 781
Special Collections: Local History (Michigan Coll). State Document Depository
Subject Interests: Local hist
Automation Activity & Vendor Info: (Acquisitions) OCLC Connexion; (Circulation) Horizon; (OPAC) OCLC WorldShare Interlibrary Loan
Wireless access
Publications: Library Tidings (Newsletter)
Partic in Mideastern Michigan Library Cooperative; OCLC Online Computer Library Center, Inc; Valley Libr Consortium
Special Services for the Deaf - TDD equip
Open Mon-Fri 8-5
Friends of the Library Group
Branches: 4
AUBURN AREA BRANCH LIBRARY, 235 W Midland Rd, Auburn, 48611, SAN 346-0320. Tel: 989-662-2381. FAX: 989-662-2647. *Managing Librn,* Linda Austin; E-mail: laustin@baycountylibrary.org
Founded 1973
Library Holdings: Bk Vols 36,103
Open Tues-Thurs 10-8, Fri & Sat 9-5
PINCONNING BRANCH LIBRARY, 218 S Kaiser St, Pinconning, 48650, SAN 346-041X. Tel: 989-879-3283. FAX: 989-879-5669. *Managing Librn,* Linda Austin
Founded 1947
Library Holdings: Bk Vols 29,692
Open Tues-Thurs 10-8, Fri & Sat 9-5
SAGE BRANCH LIBRARY, 100 E Midland St, 48706, SAN 346-0444. Tel: 989-892-8555. FAX: 989-892-1516. *Managing Librn,* Jeanette Marks; E-mail: jmarks@baycountylibrary.org
Founded 1884. Pop 107,517
Open Mon, Tues & Fri 9-5, Wed & Thurs 12-8
Friends of the Library Group
ALICE & JACK WIRT PUBLIC LIBRARY, 500 Center Ave, 48708, SAN 346-0355. Tel: 989-893-9566. FAX: 989-893-9799. *Managing Librn,* Kristen Wellnitz; E-mail: kwellnitz@baycountylibrary.org
Founded 1974. Pop 107,517
Library Holdings: Bk Vols 94,471
Open Mon-Thurs 10-8, Fri & Sat 9-5, Sun (Sept-May) 1-5
Friends of the Library Group
Bookmobiles: 1

M MCLAREN BAY REGION HEALTH SCIENCES LIBRARY, Orlen J Johnson Health Sciences Library, (Formerly Bay Regional Medical Center Library), 1900 Columbus Ave, 48708-6880. SAN 307-9015. Tel: 989-894-3783. FAX: 989-894-4862. Web Site: www.mclaren.org/main/health-sciences-library-bay-region. *Med Librn/CME Coordr,* Alee Hill; E-mail: alee.hill@mclaren.org
Founded 1958
Library Holdings: Bk Titles 2,780; Per Subs 320
Subject Interests: Allied health
Function: 24/7 Electronic res, Doc delivery serv, For res purposes, Health sci info serv, ILL available, Internet access, Photocopying/Printing, Prof lending libr, Ref serv available, Scanner, Telephone ref
Publications: Union List of Serials

Partic in Greater Midwest Regional Medical Libr Network; Michigan Health Sciences Libraries Association; National Network of Libraries of Medicine Region 6
Restriction: Circulates for staff only, Pub use on premises

BEAVER ISLAND

P BEAVER ISLAND DISTRICT LIBRARY, 26400 Donegal Bay Rd, 49782. (Mail add: PO Box 246, 49782-0246). Tel: 231-448-2701. FAX: 231-448-2801. E-mail: island.library@gmail.com. Web Site: www.beaverisland.michlibrary.org. *Dir,* Patrick S McGinnity; *Librn,* Jacqueline LaFreniere; *Librn,* Merry Roe
Library Holdings: Bk Vols 17,000; Per Subs 14
Wireless access
Open Mon-Fri 9-5, Sat 10-5
Friends of the Library Group

BELDING

P ALVAH N BELDING MEMORIAL LIBRARY*, 302 E Main St, 48809-1799. SAN 307-9031. Tel: 616-794-1450. FAX: 616-794-3510. TDD: 800-649-3777. E-mail: bel@llcoop.org. Web Site: www.belding.michlibrary.org. *Dir,* Britney K Dillon; E-mail: belbd@llcoop.org; *Youth Serv,* Stephanie Reed; E-mail: belys@llcoop.org; Staff 1 (Non-MLS 1)
Founded 1890. Pop 11,000; Circ 40,484
Library Holdings: Bk Titles 54,000; Per Subs 74
Special Collections: Michigan Coll
Subject Interests: Antiques, Arts & crafts, Genealogy, Local hist
Automation Activity & Vendor Info: (Circulation) Innovative Interfaces, Inc
Wireless access
Partic in Lakeland Library Cooperative
Open Mon & Wed 9-8, Tues & Thurs 1-5, Fri 9-5, Sat 9-1
Friends of the Library Group

BELLAIRE

P BELLAIRE PUBLIC LIBRARY*, 111 S Bridge St, 49615-9566. (Mail add: PO Box 477, 49615-0477), SAN 307-904X. Tel: 231-533-8814. E-mail: bellairelibrary@torchlake.com. Web Site: www.bellairelibrary.org. *Dir,* Jane Gyulveszi; *Head Librn,* Leigh Carpenter
Pop 3,054; Circ 23,440
Library Holdings: AV Mats 1,258; Bk Vols 19,356; Per Subs 60
Wireless access
Partic in Mid-Michigan Library League
Open Tues-Thurs 10-6, Fri 10-5, Sat 10-2
Friends of the Library Group

BELLEVILLE

P BELLEVILLE AREA DISTRICT LIBRARY*, 167 Fourth St, 48111. SAN 307-9058. Tel: 734-699-3291. FAX: 734-699-6352. E-mail: fredcfischerlibrary@gmail.com. Web Site: www.belleville.lib.mi.us. *Dir,* Mary Jo Suchy; E-mail: mjsuchy@belleville.lib.mi.us; *Asst Dir,* Hilary Savage; E-mail: hsavage@belleville.lib.mi.us; Staff 9.5 (MLS 5.5, Non-MLS 4)
Founded 1920. Pop 42,000; Circ 192,000
Library Holdings: AV Mats 8,631; e-books 10,755; Bk Vols 82,967; Per Subs 171
Automation Activity & Vendor Info: (Acquisitions) SirsiDynix; (Cataloging) SirsiDynix; (Circulation) SirsiDynix; (OPAC) SirsiDynix
Wireless access
Partic in The Library Network
Open Mon-Thurs 10-9, Fri & Sat 10-5
Friends of the Library Group

BELLEVUE

P BELLEVUE TOWNSHIP LIBRARY, 212 N Main St, 49021. SAN 307-9066. Tel: 269-763-3369. FAX: 269-763-3369. E-mail: bellvu@monroe.lib.mi.us. Web Site: bellevuetownship.org/library. *Librn,* Lynn Etson
Circ 5,948
Library Holdings: Bk Vols 15,000
Automation Activity & Vendor Info: (Cataloging) Auto-Graphics, Inc; (Circulation) Auto-Graphics, Inc; (OPAC) Auto-Graphics, Inc
Wireless access
Publications: Monthly Bulletin on Libr Activities
Mem of Woodlands Library Cooperative
Open Mon-Fri 1-5 (1-6 Summer)

BENTON HARBOR

P BENTON HARBOR PUBLIC LIBRARY*, 213 E Wall St, 49022-4499. SAN 346-0509. Tel: 269-926-6139. FAX: 269-926-1674. E-mail: bentonharborlibrary@yahoo.com. Web Site: www.bentonharborlibrary.com. *Dir,* Kate Boyer; *Cat, Tech Serv,* Sharon Holloway; *Ch Serv,* Sue Kading; *Doc, Ref (Info Servs),* Jill Rauh; Staff 16 (MLS 3, Non-MLS 13)
Founded 1898. Pop 27,586; Circ 88,158
Library Holdings: Bk Vols 100,510; Per Subs 80
Special Collections: Biological Sciences (Don Farnum Coll); Black Studies (Martin Luther King Jr Coll); Civil War (Randall Perry Coll); Indian Coll; Israelite House of David Coll; Judaica (Lillian Faber Coll); Theater (Helen Polly Klock Coll). State Document Depository; US Document Depository
Subject Interests: Ethnic studies
Wireless access
Partic in Midwest Collaborative for Library Services; Southwest Michigan Library Cooperative
Open Mon & Fri 9-5:30, Tues-Thurs 9-8 (9-7 Fall)

J LAKE MICHIGAN COLLEGE, William Hessel Library, 2755 E Napier Ave, 49022. SAN 307-9074. Tel: 269-927-8605. Interlibrary Loan Service Tel: 269-927-6281. Reference Tel: 269-927-6287. Automation Services Tel: 269-927-8100. FAX: 269-927-6656. E-mail: library@lakemichigancollege.edu. Web Site: www.lakemichigancollege.edu/lib. *Ref Librn,* Diane Baker; E-mail: baker@lakemichigancollege.edu; *Circ & Ref Asst,* Vickie Semrinec; E-mail: vsemrinec@lakemichigancollege.edu; Staff 2.5 (MLS 1, Non-MLS 1.5)
Founded 1946. Enrl 3,961; Fac 66; Highest Degree: Associate
Library Holdings: Audiobooks 8; AV Mats 42; CDs 435; DVDs 800; e-books 25,000; e-journals 24,450; Large Print Bks 5; Microforms 1; Bk Vols 62,809; Per Subs 122; Videos 2,683
Special Collections: Lake Michigan College Archives
Automation Activity & Vendor Info: (Cataloging) OCLC Connexion; (Circulation) Auto-Graphics, Inc; (ILL) OCLC FirstSearch; (OPAC) Auto-Graphics, Inc
Wireless access
Function: Art exhibits, ILL available, Internet access, Online cat, Online ref, Orientations, Photocopying/Printing
Partic in Midwest Collaborative for Library Services; OCLC Online Computer Library Center, Inc
Open Mon-Thurs (Winter) 8am-9pm, Fri 8-4, Sat 10-2; Mon-Thurs (Spring & Summer) 8-6:30, Fri 8-4
Restriction: Borrowing privileges limited to fac & registered students, Limited access for the pub

BENZONIA

P BENZONIA PUBLIC LIBRARY*, 891 Michigan Ave, 49616-9784. (Mail add: PO Box 445, 49616-0445), SAN 307-9090. Tel: 231-882-4111. FAX: 231-882-4111. E-mail: benzonialibraryconnect@gmail.com. Web Site: www.benzonialibrary.org. *Dir,* Amanda McLaren; *Asst Dir,* Michelle Leines
Founded 1925. Pop 4,158; Circ 20,000
Library Holdings: CDs 100; Large Print Bks 600; Bk Vols 16,900; Per Subs 5; Talking Bks 600; Videos 300
Special Collections: Benzie Banner-Record Patriot Local Newspapers, 1888-Present; Bruce Catton Coll, bks & mat
Subject Interests: Art & archit, Hist, Local hist, Relig
Wireless access
Function: Computers for patron use, Free DVD rentals, ILL available, Literacy & newcomer serv, Mail & tel request accepted, Prog for adults, Prog for children & young adult, Ref serv available, Spoken cassettes & CDs, Story hour, Summer & winter reading prog, Summer reading prog, Tax forms, Telephone ref, Wheelchair accessible
Publications: Newsletter
Partic in Mid-Michigan Library League
Open Mon & Wed 10-7, Tues, Thurs & Fri 10-5, Sat 10-3
Friends of the Library Group

BERKLEY

P BERKLEY PUBLIC LIBRARY*, 3155 Coolidge Hwy, 48072. SAN 307-9104. Tel: 248-658-3440. FAX: 248-658-3441. E-mail: library@berkley.lib.mi.us. Web Site: www.berkleymich.org/departments/library. *Dir,* Matt Church; E-mail: mchurch@berkley.lib.mi.us; Staff 5 (MLS 4, Non-MLS 1)
Founded 1928. Pop 14,970; Circ 149,803
Jul 2013-Jun 2014 Income $673,968, State $8,111, City $609,064, Federal $3,113, County $20,000, Locally Generated Income $33,680. Mats Exp $69,050, Books $35,654, Per/Ser (Incl. Access Fees) $9,862, AV Mat $19,334, Electronic Ref Mat (Incl. Access Fees) $4,200. Sal $338,982 (Prof $199,014)
Library Holdings: Audiobooks 2,500; CDs 3,293; DVDs 5,500; e-books 10,761; Electronic Media & Resources 4,224; High Interest/Low

Vocabulary Bk Vols 250; Large Print Bks 2,974; Bk Vols 67,223; Per Subs 142
Automation Activity & Vendor Info: (Acquisitions) SirsiDynix; (Cataloging) SirsiDynix; (Circulation) SirsiDynix; (OPAC) SirsiDynix; (Serials) SirsiDynix
Wireless access
Partic in The Library Network
Open Mon-Thurs 10-8, Fri 10-6, Sat 10-3
Friends of the Library Group

BERRIEN SPRINGS

C ANDREWS UNIVERSITY*, James White Library, 4190 Administration Dr, 49104-1400. SAN 346-0568. Tel: 269-471-3264, 269-471-3275. Circulation Tel: 269-471-3267. Interlibrary Loan Service Tel: 269-471-3506. Reference Tel: 269-471-3283. FAX: 269-471-6166. Web Site: www.andrews.edu/library. *Dean of Libr,* Lawrence Onsager; Tel: 269-471-3379, E-mail: lonsager@andrews.edu; *Head, Patron Serv,* Jason St. Clair; E-mail: jasons@andrews.edu; *Head, Bibliog Serv,* Norma Greenidge; Tel: 269-471-3270, E-mail: greenidg@andrews.edu; *Head, Info Serv, Online Serv,* Cynthia Helms; Tel: 269-471-6260, E-mail: helmsc@andrews.edu; *Head, Syst & Media Serv,* Steve Sowder; Tel: 269-471-6242, E-mail: sowder@andrews.edu; *Database Librn, Off-Campus Librn, Ref & Info Serv,* Silas Oliveira; Tel: 269-471-6263, E-mail: silas@andrews.edu; *Info Serv & Instrul Librn,* Lauren Matacio; Tel: 269-471-6062, E-mail: matacio@andrews.edu; *Bibliog Serv, Per/Acq Librn,* Bernard Helms; Tel: 269-471-3208, E-mail: helms@andrews.edu; *Sem Coll Librn,* Terry Robertson; Tel: 269-471-3269, E-mail: trobtsn@andrews.edu; *Patron Serv Mgr,* Mildred McGrath; Tel: 269-471-3976, E-mail: mcgrath@andrews.edu; *Multimedia, Syst Mgr,* Josip Horonic; Tel: 269-471-3865, E-mail: horonic@andrews.edu; *Bibliog Serv, Sr Cataloger,* Felipe Tan; Tel: 269-471-6262, E-mail: tan@andrews.edu; *Bibliog Serv, Cataloger,* Xiaoming Xu; Tel: 269-471-6125, E-mail: xu@andrews.edu; *Bibliog Serv, Cat Spec,* Nancy Sheppler; Tel: 269-471-3033, E-mail: nriemann@andrews.edu; *Circ Asst, Patron Serv,* Jami Milien; Tel: 269-471-3156, E-mail: jami@andrews.edu; *Bibliog Serv, Per,* Lilly Williams; Tel: 269-471-3330, E-mail: williaml@andrews.edu; Staff 24 (MLS 15, Non-MLS 9)
Founded 1874. Enrl 2,350; Fac 240; Highest Degree: Doctorate
Library Holdings: Bk Vols 750,000; Per Subs 2,800
Special Collections: Environmental Design Research (EDRA); Seventh Day Adventist Church History (Center for Adventist Research), bks, ms, personal papers. Oral History
Subject Interests: Art, Biology, Relig
Wireless access
Partic in Adventist Librs Info Coop; OCLC Online Computer Library Center, Inc; Southwest Michigan Library Cooperative
Open Mon-Thurs 8am-10:30pm, Fri 8-3, Sun 1-10:30
Friends of the Library Group
Departmental Libraries:
ARCHITECTURAL RESOURCE CENTER, 8435 E Campus Circle Dr, 49104-0450. Tel: 269-471-2417, 616-471-3027. FAX: 269-471-6261. *Assoc Prof, Dir,* Kathleen M Demsky; Tel: 269-471-2418, E-mail: demskyk@andrews.edu; Staff 1 (MLS 1)
Founded 1986
Library Holdings: CDs 202; DVDs 254; Electronic Media & Resources 44,000; Bk Titles 30,000; Per Subs 78; Videos 505
Special Collections: Archival Coll; Human Factor in Built & Unbuilt Environment - EDRA
Subject Interests: Archit
Open Mon-Thurs 8:30am-10:30pm, Fri 8:30-1:30, Sun 5:30-10:30
MUSIC MATERIALS CENTER, 10230 Hamel Hall Rd, 49104-0230. Tel: 269-471-6217. Web Site: www.andrews.edu/library/mmcindex.html. *Asst Prof, Dir,* Marianne Kordas; Tel: 269-471-3114, E-mail: kordas@andrews.edu. Subject Specialists: *Music hist,* Marianne Kordas; Staff 1 (MLS 1)
Library Holdings: Bk Titles 12,500
Open Mon-Wed 8:25am-8:30pm, Thurs 8:25-7:30, Fri 9-2, Sun 1:30-6:30

S BERRIEN COUNTY HISTORICAL ASSOCIATION LIBRARY*, 313 N Cass St, 49103-1038. (Mail add: PO Box 261, 49103-0261), SAN 373-2029. Tel: 269-471-1202. FAX: 269-471-7412. E-mail: bcha@berrienhistory.org. Web Site: www.berrienhistory.org. *Exec Dir,* Rhiannon Cizon; E-mail: rcizon@berrienhistory.org; *Curator,* Position Currently Open
Founded 1967
Library Holdings: Bk Vols 200
Special Collections: Clark Equipment Archives
Subject Interests: Local hist
Open Sun-Sat 10-5

P BERRIEN SPRINGS COMMUNITY LIBRARY, 215 W Union St, 49103-1077. SAN 307-9112. Tel: 269-471-7074. FAX: 269-471-4433. E-mail: bsclibrary@comcast.net. Web Site: bsclibrary.org. *Dir,* Kristina Knezic; *Asst Dir,* Irene Jones; Staff 7 (Non-MLS 7)
Founded 1906. Pop 9,197; Circ 95,600
Library Holdings: Audiobooks 3,373; AV Mats 4,600; Bks on Deafness & Sign Lang 171; CDs 966; DVDs 3,227; High Interest/Low Vocabulary Bk Vols 110; Large Print Bks 1,395; Bk Titles 43,659; Bk Vols 45,334; Per Subs 120; Talking Bks 3,373
Subject Interests: Local hist
Automation Activity & Vendor Info: (Cataloging) Biblionix/Apollo; (Circulation) Biblionix/Apollo; (OPAC) Biblionix/Apollo
Function: 24/7 Online cat, Activity rm, Adult bk club, Audiobks via web, Bk club(s), Bks on CD, Children's prog, Computer training, Computers for patron use, Digital talking bks, E-Reserves, Free DVD rentals, ILL available, Internet access, Magazines, Music CDs, Notary serv, Online cat, OverDrive digital audio bks, Photocopying/Printing, Preschool reading prog, Printer for laptops & handheld devices, Prog for adults, Prog for children & young adult, Ref serv available, Scanner, Spanish lang bks, Story hour, Summer reading prog, Tax forms, Teen prog
Partic in Southwest Michigan Library Cooperative
Open Mon-Thurs 10-8, Fri 10-6, Sat 10-4

BESSEMER

P BESSEMER PUBLIC LIBRARY, 411 S Sophie St, 49911. SAN 307-9120. Tel: 906-667-0404. FAX: 906-667-0442. Web Site: joomla.uproc.lib.mi.us/bessemer. *Libr Dir,* Melissa Lupino; E-mail: melissa@uproc.lib.mi.us
Library Holdings: Audiobooks 1,328; DVDs 377; Large Print Bks 1,609; Bk Titles 20,963; Per Subs 54; Videos 1,391
Automation Activity & Vendor Info: (Cataloging) Follett Software; (Circulation) Follett Software
Wireless access
Partic in Superiorland Library Cooperative; Upper Peninsula Region of Library Cooperation, Inc
Open Mon, Tues, Thurs & Fri 9-12 & 12:30-5, Wed 10-12 & 12:30-6, Sat 9-Noon

BEULAH

P DARCY LIBRARY OF BEULAH*, 7238 Commercial Ave, 49617. (Mail add: PO Box 469, 49617-0469), SAN 307-9139. Tel: 231-882-4037. E-mail: info@darcylibraryofbeulah.org. Web Site: www.darcylibraryofbeulah.org. *Dir,* Karen Simpkins; E-mail: director@darcylibraryofbeulah.org
Library Holdings: Bk Vols 12,000; Per Subs 27
Wireless access
Partic in Mid-Michigan Library League
Open Mon, Wed & Fri 12-5, Tues & Thurs 3-7, Sat 9-1
Friends of the Library Group

BIG RAPIDS

P BIG RAPIDS COMMUNITY LIBRARY*, 426 S Michigan Ave, 49307. SAN 307-9147. Tel: 231-796-5234. FAX: 231-796-1078. E-mail: librarian@bigrapids.lib.mi.us. Web Site: www.bigrapids.lib.mi.us. *Dir,* Miriam Andrus; Staff 6 (MLS 1, Non-MLS 5)
Automation Activity & Vendor Info: (Cataloging) Innovative Interfaces, Inc; (Circulation) Innovative Interfaces, Inc; (OPAC) Innovative Interfaces, Inc
Wireless access
Partic in Association for Rural & Small Libraries; Mid-Michigan Library League
Open Mon, Wed & Fri 10-5, Tues & Thurs 11-7, Sat 9-Noon
Friends of the Library Group

C FERRIS STATE UNIVERSITY LIBRARY*, Ferris Library for Information, Technology & Education, 1010 Campus Dr, 49307-2279. SAN 307-9155. Tel: 231-591-3500. Circulation Tel: 231-591-2669. Interlibrary Loan Service Tel: 231-591-3641. Reference Tel: 231-591-3602. Administration Tel: 231-591-3728. FAX: 231-591-3724. Interlibrary Loan Service FAX: 231-591-2662. Reference TDD: 231-591-3603. Reference E-mail: ask@ferris.libanswers.com. Web Site: www.ferris.edu/library. *Dean,* Scott Garrison; *Asst Dean, Coll & Access,* Leah Monger; *Assessment Librn,* Stacy Anderson; *Colls Librn,* Fran Rosen; *Electronic Res Mgt Librn, Metadata Librn,* Dejah Rubel; *Govt Doc Librn,* Paul Kammerdiner; *Spec Coll & Archives Librn,* Melinda Isler; *Web Serv Librn,* Sela Constan-Wahl; *Libr Instruction Coordr,* Kristen Motz; Staff 20 (MLS 15, Non-MLS 5)
Founded 1884. Enrl 14,187; Fac 952; Highest Degree: Doctorate
Jul 2016-Jun 2017 Income $4,421,679, Locally Generated Income $59,790, Parent Institution $4,154,304, Other $207,585. Mats Exp $939,478, Books $49,894, Per/Ser (Incl. Access Fees) $103,940, Electronic Ref Mat (Incl. Access Fees) $780,775, Presv $4,869. Sal $1,900,053 (Prof $1,435,061)
Library Holdings: CDs 377; DVDs 1,043; e-books 236,047; e-journals 160,936; Microforms 3,089,581; Bk Titles 193,063; Bk Vols 233,334; Per Subs 556; Videos 558
Special Collections: Michigan Coll; University Archives; US Patents & Trademarks; Woodbridge N Ferris Papers. US Document Depository

Subject Interests: Criminal justice, Educ, Health sci, Law, Optometry, Pharm, Tech
Automation Activity & Vendor Info: (Acquisitions) Innovative Interfaces, Inc; (Cataloging) Innovative Interfaces, Inc; (Circulation) Innovative Interfaces, Inc; (Course Reserve) Innovative Interfaces, Inc; (Discovery) Ex Libris Group; (ILL) OCLC ILLiad; (Media Booking) Innovative Interfaces, Inc; (OPAC) Innovative Interfaces, Inc; (Serials) Innovative Interfaces, Inc
Wireless access
Function: 24/7 Electronic res, 24/7 Online cat, Archival coll, Audio & video playback equip for onsite use, Computers for patron use, Distance learning, Doc delivery serv, E-Reserves, Electronic databases & coll, Govt ref serv, Health sci info serv, ILL available, Internet access, Magnifiers for reading, Microfiche/film & reading machines, Online cat, Online info literacy tutorials on the web & in blackboard, Online ref, Photocopying/Printing, Ref & res, Scanner, Study rm, Tax forms, Telephone ref, Wheelchair accessible
Partic in OCLC Online Computer Library Center, Inc
Special Services for the Blind - Assistive/Adapted tech devices, equip & products; Braille equip; Closed circuit TV; Computer with voice synthesizer for visually impaired persons; Dragon Naturally Speaking software; Reader equip; Talking calculator; ZoomText magnification & reading software
Open Mon-Thurs 7:30am-Midnight, Fri 7:30-6, Sat 10-6, Sun 1-12

BIRCH RUN

P THOMAS E FLESCHNER MEMORIAL LIBRARY*, 11935 Silver Creek Dr, 48415-9767. (Mail add: PO Box 152, 48415-0152), SAN 325-2655. Tel: 989-624-5171. FAX: 989-624-0120. E-mail: birchrunlibrary@birchruntwp.com. Web Site: www.birchruntwp.com/fleschner-memorial-library. *Libr Dir,* Jeanette F Morrish; Tel: 989-624-9759; Staff 3 (MLS 1, Non-MLS 2)
Founded 1979. Pop 6,033; Circ 41,150
Apr 2016-Mar 2017 Income $111,176, State $3,552, County $24,062, Locally Generated Income $78,840, Other $4,722. Mats Exp $9,125, Books $4,514, AV Mat $1,046, Electronic Ref Mat (Incl. Access Fees) $3,565. Sal Prof $63,980
Library Holdings: AV Mats 2,100; DVDs 1,844; Electronic Media & Resources 10,592; Large Print Bks 800; Bk Titles 33,921; Per Subs 7; Talking Bks 2,100
Automation Activity & Vendor Info: (Acquisitions) Book Systems; (Cataloging) Book Systems; (Circulation) Book Systems; (OPAC) SirsiDynix
Wireless access
Partic in White Pine Library Cooperative
Open Mon (Winter) 10-6, Tues & Thurs 12-8, Wed 1-6, Fri 9-5, Sat 10-3; Mon (Summer) 10-6, Tues & Thurs 12-8, Wed 1-6, Fri 9-5
Friends of the Library Group

BIRMINGHAM

P BALDWIN PUBLIC LIBRARY*, 300 W Merrill St, 48009-1483. SAN 307-9163. Tel: 248-647-1700. Circulation Tel: 248-554-4630. Administration Tel: 248-647-7339. FAX: 248-647-6393. Circulation E-mail: bplcirc@baldwinlib.org. Web Site: www.baldwinlib.org. *Dir,* Douglas Koschik; E-mail: doug.koschik@baldwinlib.org; *Assoc Dir,* Rebekah Craft; E-mail: rebekah.craft@baldwinlib.org; Staff 87 (MLS 42, Non-MLS 45)
Founded 1869. Pop 35,350; Circ 430,638
Jul 2018-Jun 2019 Income $4,453,438, State $28,333, Locally Generated Income $4,425,105. Mats Exp $568,553, Books $230,405, AV Mat $118,366, Electronic Ref Mat (Incl. Access Fees) $219,782. Sal $2,211,687
Library Holdings: AV Mats 31,438; e-books 10,507; Bk Vols 100,115; Per Subs 274
Subject Interests: Genealogy, Local hist, Mich hist
Automation Activity & Vendor Info: (Acquisitions) Innovative Interfaces, Inc; (Cataloging) Innovative Interfaces, Inc; (Circulation) Innovative Interfaces, Inc; (ILL) Mel Cat; (Media Booking) Innovative Interfaces, Inc; (OPAC) Innovative Interfaces, Inc; (Serials) Innovative Interfaces, Inc
Wireless access
Function: 24/7 Electronic res, 24/7 Online cat, Adult bk club, Audiobks on Playaways & MP3, Audiobks via web, Bk club(s), Bks on CD, CD-ROM, Children's prog, Computer training, Computers for patron use, Digital talking bks, Doc delivery serv, E-Reserves, Electronic databases & coll, Free DVD rentals, Holiday prog, Home delivery & serv to seniorr ctr & nursing homes, Homebound delivery serv, Homework prog, ILL available, Instruction & testing, Internet access, Life-long learning prog for all ages, Magazines, Magnifiers for reading, Mail & tel request accepted, Mango lang, Meeting rooms, Microfiche/film & reading machines, Movies, Museum passes, Music CDs, Online cat, Outside serv via phone, mail, e-mail & web, OverDrive digital audio bks, Photocopying/Printing, Preschool outreach, Printer for laptops & handheld devices, Prog for adults, Prog for children & young adult, Ref & res, Ref serv available, Scanner, Story hour, Study rm, Summer reading prog, Tax forms, Teen prog, Telephone ref, Wheelchair accessible
Publications: Learn Connect Discover (Newsletter)
Partic in Metro Net Libr Consortium; OCLC Online Computer Library Center, Inc
Special Services for the Blind - Audio mat; Bks on CD; Large print bks; Magnifiers
Open Mon-Thurs 9:30-9, Fri & Sat 9:30-5:30, Sun 12-5
Friends of the Library Group

BLISSFIELD

P SCHULTZ-HOLMES MEMORIAL LIBRARY*, 407 S Lane St, 49228-1232. Tel: 517-486-2858. FAX: 517-486-3565. E-mail: info@blissfieldlibrary.org. Web Site: www.blissfieldlibrary.org. *Dir,* Bob Barringer; E-mail: director@blissfieldlibrary.org
Library Holdings: Bk Vols 30,000
Mem of Woodlands Library Cooperative
Open Mon, Wed, Fri & Sat 10:30-5, Tues & Thurs 1-8

BLOOMFIELD HILLS

S CRANBROOK ACADEMY OF ART LIBRARY*, 39221 Woodward Ave, 48304. (Mail add: PO Box 801, 48303-0801), SAN 307-9201. Tel: 248-645-3355. FAX: 248-645-3464. Web Site: www.cranbrookart.edu/library. *Dir, Academic Programs, Libr Dir,* Judy Dyki; Tel: 248-645-3364, E-mail: JDyki@cranbrook.edu; *Cataloger, Librn,* Autumn Diaz; Tel: 248-645-3363, E-mail: adiaz@cranbrook.edu; *Librn,* Mary Beth Kreiner; Tel: 248-645-3477, E-mail: MKreiner@cranbrook.edu; *Libr Asst,* Rachel Pontious; E-mail: RPontious@cranbrook.edu; Staff 4 (MLS 3, Non-MLS 1)
Founded 1928. Enrl 150; Fac 11; Highest Degree: Master
Library Holdings: DVDs 1,600; Bk Titles 30,000; Per Subs 190; Videos 1,400
Special Collections: Artist's Books; Booth Coll of Fine Arts Folios; Cranbrook Press Books; Exhibition Catalogs; Faculty Lectures, tapes; Fine Bindings; Folios; Theses
Subject Interests: Art & archit
Automation Activity & Vendor Info: (Cataloging) SirsiDynix; (Circulation) SirsiDynix; (ILL) OCLC; (OPAC) SirsiDynix
Wireless access
Partic in Midwest Collaborative for Library Services; OCLC Online Computer Library Center, Inc; Southeastern Michigan League of Libraries
Open Mon-Thurs 9-8, Fri 9-5, Sat & Sun 1-5

L PLUNKETT & COONEY*, Law Library, 38505 Woodward Ave, 48304. SAN 371-4101. Tel: 248-901-4099. FAX: 248-901-4040. Web Site: www.plunkettcooney.com. *Libr Mgr,* Kevin Barry; Tel: 248-901-4094, E-mail: kbarry@plunkettcooney.com; Staff 4 (MLS 2, Non-MLS 2)
Library Holdings: Bk Vols 10,000
Wireless access

R TEMPLE BETH EL, Prentis Memorial Library, 7400 Telegraph Rd, 48301-3876. SAN 307-918X. Tel: 248-851-1100. Web Site: tbeonline.org/library. *Librn,* Laura Gottlieb; E-mail: lgottlieb@tbeonline.org
Founded 1878
Library Holdings: Bk Vols 10,000
Special Collections: 16th-19th Century Judaica (Leonard Simons Coll of Rare Judaica)
Subject Interests: Jewish hist & lit, Judaica (lit or hist of Jews)
Automation Activity & Vendor Info: (Acquisitions) OPALS (Open-source Automated Library System); (Cataloging) OPALS (Open-source Automated Library System); (Circulation) OPALS (Open-source Automated Library System)
Wireless access
Open Mon-Fri 1-5
Friends of the Library Group

BLOOMFIELD TOWNSHIP

P BLOOMFIELD TOWNSHIP PUBLIC LIBRARY*, 1099 Lone Pine Rd, 48302-2410. SAN 307-9198. Tel: 248-642-5800. FAX: 248-258-2555. Web Site: btpl.org. *Dir,* Carol Mueller; *Asst Dir,* Tera Moon; *Head, Adult Serv,* Ann M Williams; *Head, Circ,* Anna Pelepchuk; *Head, Fac & Receiving,* Joel Dion; *Head, Syst,* Joan Wu; *Head, Tech Serv,* Marianne Abdoo; *Head, Youth Serv,* Marian Rafal; Staff 90 (MLS 23, Non-MLS 67)
Founded 1964. Pop 41,070; Circ 781,244
Apr 2016-Mar 2017. Mats Exp $5,986,358
Special Collections: Special Needs (Games, toys, and assistive devices for adult and young users with special needs and their caregivers.)
Automation Activity & Vendor Info: (Acquisitions) Innovative Interfaces, Inc; (Cataloging) Innovative Interfaces, Inc; (Circulation) Innovative Interfaces, Inc; (ILL) Mel Cat; (Media Booking) Innovative Interfaces, Inc; (OPAC) Innovative Interfaces, Inc; (Serials) Innovative Interfaces, Inc
Wireless access
Function: 24/7 Electronic res, 24/7 Online cat, Activity rm, Adult bk club, Archival coll, Art exhibits, Audio & video playback equip for onsite use, Audiobks on Playaways & MP3, Audiobks via web, AV serv, Bi-weekly Writer's Group, Bk club(s), Bks on CD, Butterfly Garden, CD-ROM,

Children's prog, Computer training, Computers for patron use, Digital talking bks, Distance learning, Doc delivery serv, E-Reserves, Electronic databases & coll, Family literacy, Free DVD rentals, Games & aids for people with disabilities, Holiday prog, Home delivery & serv to seniorr ctr & nursing homes, Homebound delivery serv, Homework prog, ILL available, Internet access, Large print keyboards, Life-long learning prog for all ages, Magazines, Magnifiers for reading, Mail & tel request accepted, Mail loans to mem, Mango lang, Meeting rooms, Microfiche/film & reading machines, Movies, Museum passes, Music CDs, Online cat, Outreach serv, Outside serv via phone, mail, e-mail & web, OverDrive digital audio bks, Photocopying/Printing, Preschool outreach, Preschool reading prog, Printer for laptops & handheld devices, Prog for adults, Prog for children & young adult, Ref & res, Ref serv available, Scanner, Senior computer classes, Senior outreach, Serves people with intellectual disabilities, Spanish lang bks, Spoken cassettes & CDs, Story hour, Study rm, Summer reading prog, Tax forms, Teen prog, Telephone ref, Wheelchair accessible, Workshops, Writing prog
Publications: Newsletter (Quarterly)
Partic in Metro Net Libr Consortium; Midwest Collaborative for Library Services; The Library Network
Special Services for the Deaf - TTY equip
Special Services for the Blind - Accessible computers; Aids for in-house use; Assistive/Adapted tech devices, equip & products; Bks on CD; Large print bks; Lending of low vision aids; Low vision equip; Magnifiers
Open Mon-Thurs 9:30-9, Fri 9:30-6, Sat 9:30-5:30, Sun 12-5:30
Friends of the Library Group

BOYNE CITY

P BOYNE DISTRICT LIBRARY*, 201 E Main St, 49712. SAN 307-9236. Tel: 231-582-7861. FAX: 231-582-2998. E-mail: info@boynelibrary.org. Web Site: www.boynelibrary.org. *Libr Dir,* Monica Peck; E-mail: peckm@boynelibrary.org; *Asst Dir,* Monica Kroondyk; E-mail: kroondykm@boynelibrary.org; *Head, Youth Serv,* Alexa Wright; E-mail: wrighta@boynelibrary.org; Staff 8 (Non-MLS 8)
Founded 1918. Pop 7,031; Circ 41,096
Library Holdings: Bk Titles 20,115; Bk Vols 20,175; Per Subs 75
Subject Interests: Local hist
Automation Activity & Vendor Info: (Circulation) SirsiDynix; (OPAC) SirsiDynix
Partic in Northland Library Cooperative
Open Mon-Thurs 9-8, Fri & Sat 9-5, Sun 1-5

BRECKENRIDGE

P HOWE MEMORIAL LIBRARY, 128 E Saginaw St, 48615. (Mail add: PO Box 398, 48615-0398), SAN 307-9244. Tel: 989-842-3202. FAX: 989-842-3202. E-mail: brecklib128@gmail.com. Web Site: www.howemempl.michlibrary.org. *Dir,* Sunday Ostrander
Founded 1938. Pop 6,180; Circ 23,756
Library Holdings: AV Mats 980; Bks on Deafness & Sign Lang 20; Large Print Bks 300; Bk Vols 16,997; Per Subs 81; Talking Bks 686
Automation Activity & Vendor Info: (Cataloging) Auto-Graphics, Inc; (Circulation) Auto-Graphics, Inc; (ILL) Auto-Graphics, Inc
Wireless access
Partic in White Pine Library Cooperative
Open Mon 9:30-8, Tues-Thurs 9:30-5
Friends of the Library Group

BRIDGEPORT

P BRIDGEPORT PUBLIC LIBRARY*, 3399 Williamson Rd, 48601. SAN 376-6144. Tel: 989-777-6030. FAX: 989-777-6880. E-mail: info@bridgeportlibrary.org. Web Site: www.bridgeportlibrary.org. *Dir,* Amber Hughey; E-mail: a.hughey@bridgeportlibrary.org; *Children's Coordr,* Cindy Hix; E-mail: c.hix@bridgeportlibrary.org
Library Holdings: Bk Vols 45,000; Per Subs 170
Automation Activity & Vendor Info: (Cataloging) SirsiDynix; (Circulation) SirsiDynix; (ILL) SirsiDynix; (OPAC) SirsiDynix; (Serials) SirsiDynix
Wireless access
Partic in White Pine Library Cooperative
Open Mon-Thurs 9-8, Fri 9-5, Sat 9-2

BRIDGMAN

P BRIDGMAN PUBLIC LIBRARY*, 4460 Lake St, 49106-9510. SAN 307-9252. Tel: 269-465-3663. FAX: 269-465-3249. E-mail: Bpl@brigmanlibrary.com. Web Site: bridgmanlibrary.org. *Dir,* Dennis Kreps
Founded 1966. Pop 5,576; Circ 58,754
Library Holdings: Bk Vols 31,623; Per Subs 106
Special Collections: Oral History
Wireless access
Partic in Southwest Michigan Library Cooperative
Open Mon-Thurs 10-8, Fri 10-5, Sat 10-4
Friends of the Library Group

BRIGHTON

P BRIGHTON DISTRICT LIBRARY, 100 Library Dr, 48116. SAN 307-9260. Tel: 810-229-6571. Administration Tel: 810-229-6571, Ext 206. Automation Services Tel: 810-229-6571, Ext 205. FAX: 810-229-3161. Web Site: brightonlibrary.info. *Dir,* Cindy J Mack; Tel: 810-229-6571, Ext 203, E-mail: cindy@brightonlibrary.info; *Asst Dir,* Ed Rutkowski; Tel: 810-229-6571, Ext 222, E-mail: erutkowski@brightonlibrary.info; *Head, Adult Serv,* Jennifer Osborne; Tel: 810-229-6571, Ext 225, E-mail: josborne@brightonlibrary.info; *Head, Circ Serv,* Diane Pierce; Tel: 810-229-6571, Ext 216, E-mail: dpierce@brightonlibrary.info; *Head, Coll, Head, Pub Serv,* Sarah Neidert; Tel: 810-229-6571, Ext 213, E-mail: sarah@brightonlibrary.info; *Head, Youth Serv,* Carla Sharp; Tel: 810-229-6571, Ext 209, E-mail: csharp@brightonlibrary.info; *Teen Serv Librn,* Kate Wheeler; E-mail: kate@brightonlibrary.info; Staff 19 (MLS 11, Non-MLS 8)
Founded 1992. Pop 39,594; Circ 463,768
Special Collections: Career Coll
Subject Interests: Genealogy, Local hist
Automation Activity & Vendor Info: (Cataloging) SirsiDynix; (Circulation) SirsiDynix; (OPAC) SirsiDynix
Wireless access
Publications: Brighton District Library Newsletter
Partic in The Library Network
Open Mon-Thurs 10-9, Fri & Sat 10-5
Friends of the Library Group

BRIMLEY

J BAY MILLS COMMUNITY COLLEGE*, Library & Heritage Center, 12214 W Lakeshore Dr, 49715-9320. Tel: 906-248-3354, Ext 4202. Toll Free Tel: 800-844-2622. E-mail: library@bmcc.edu. Web Site: www.bmcc.edu/student-services/library. *Dir, Libr Serv,* Megan Clarke; Tel: 906-248-3354, Ext 8435, E-mail: mclarke@bmcc.edu; *Asst Dir, Libr Serv,* Patty Croad; Tel: 906-248-3354, Ext 8418, E-mail: pteeple@bmcc.edu
Library Holdings: Bk Vols 8,000; Per Subs 30
Wireless access
Partic in Upper Peninsula Region of Library Cooperation, Inc
Open Mon-Thurs 8-6, Fri 8-4:30, Sat 10-2

BROWN CITY

P BROWN CITY PUBLIC LIBRARY*, 4207 Main St, 48416. (Mail add: PO Box 58, 48416-0058), SAN 307-9279. Tel: 810-346-2511. FAX: 810-346-2511. E-mail: bclibrary48416@yahoo.com. Web Site: www.browncitylibrary.org. *Librn,* Shirley K Wood
Circ 18,475
Library Holdings: Bk Vols 14,200; Per Subs 70
Wireless access
Partic in White Pine Library Cooperative
Open Tues & Thurs 10-5:30, Wed 12-9, Fri 11-5:30, Sat 9:30-1

BUCHANAN

P BUCHANAN DISTRICT LIBRARY*, 128 E Front St, 49107. SAN 307-9287. Tel: 269-695-3681. FAX: 269-695-0004. Web Site: www.buchananlibrary.org. *Dir,* Meg Paulette; E-mail: m.paulette@buchananlibrary.com; *Asst Dir,* Pam Salo; E-mail: p.salo@buchananlibrary.com; *Circ Mgr,* Laura Hauch; E-mail: laura.hauch@buchananlibrary.com; *Youth Serv Coordr,* Sarah Gault; E-mail: s.gault@buchananlibrary.com; *Cataloger,* Debbie VerValin; E-mail: d.vervalin@buchananlibrary.com; Staff 7 (Non-MLS 7)
Founded 1929. Pop 9,285; Circ 105,682
Library Holdings: Bk Vols 52,000; Per Subs 100
Special Collections: Local History Coll
Automation Activity & Vendor Info: (Cataloging) Follett Software; (Circulation) Follett Software; (ILL) Auto-Graphics, Inc; (OPAC) Follett Software
Partic in Southwest Michigan Library Cooperative
Open Mon, Tues & Fri 9-6, Wed & Thurs 9-8, Sat 9-2

BURLINGTON

P BURLINGTON TOWNSHIP LIBRARY*, 135 Elm St, 49029. (Mail add: PO Box 39, 49029-0039), SAN 307-9309. Tel: 517-765-2702. FAX: 517-765-2702. *Dir,* Nathaniel Mottinger; *Librn,* Susan VanWormer; Staff 1 (Non-MLS 1)
Founded 1935. Pop 1,941; Circ 4,988
Library Holdings: CDs 26; DVDs 150; Bk Titles 10,488; Talking Bks 25; Videos 100
Wireless access
Function: 24/7 Electronic res, Archival coll, Bks on CD, Computers for patron use, Free DVD rentals, ILL available, Internet access, Music CDs,

Photocopying/Printing, Spoken cassettes & DVDs, Summer reading prog, Tax forms
Open Mon 1-5, Wed & Thurs 12-5, Sat 9-1

BURNIPS

P SALEM TOWNSHIP LIBRARY*, 3007 142nd Ave, 49314. (Mail add: PO Box 58, 49314-0058), SAN 346-3532. Tel: 616-896-8170. FAX: 616-896-8035. E-mail: bur@llcoop.org. Web Site: www.burnips.llcoop.org. *Dir,* Sharon Engelsman; *Asst Librn,* Wanda Mesbergem
Library Holdings: AV Mats 1,800; Bk Vols 22,000; Per Subs 82
Automation Activity & Vendor Info: (Cataloging) Innovative Interfaces, Inc; (Circulation) Innovative Interfaces, Inc
Wireless access
Partic in Lakeland Library Cooperative
Open Mon, Wed & Thurs 10-8, Tues & Fri 1-5, Sat 10-1

BURR OAK

P BURR OAK TOWNSHIP LIBRARY, 220 S Second St, 49030-5133. (Mail add: PO Box 309, 49030-0309), SAN 307-9317. Tel: 269-489-2906. FAX: 269-489-2906. Web Site: www.burroaklibrary.michlibrary.org. *Dir,* Mary Anne Kennedy; E-mail: makdirector@burroaklibrary.com
Founded 1905. Pop 2,500; Circ 9,919
Library Holdings: Bk Vols 17,919; Per Subs 29
Automation Activity & Vendor Info: (Cataloging) Follett Software; (Circulation) Follett Software; (OPAC) Follett Software
Wireless access
Mem of Woodlands Library Cooperative
Open Mon 3-7, Tues 9-7, Thurs 12-6, Fri 12-5, Sat 9-12
Friends of the Library Group

BURT

P TAYMOUTH TOWNSHIP LIBRARY*, 2361 E Burt Rd, 48417-9426. (Mail add: PO Box 158, 48417-0158), SAN 376-706X. Tel: 989-770-4651. FAX: 989-401-5851. Interlibrary Loan Service E-mail: bur_ill@yahoo.com. Web Site: www.taymouthtwplibrary.org. *Dir,* Kathleen Naegele
Founded 1979. Pop 4,624; Circ 12,438
Library Holdings: Large Print Bks 257; Bk Titles 19,248; Per Subs 38; Talking Bks 668
Subject Interests: Local hist
Partic in White Pine Library Cooperative
Open Mon & Thurs 2-9, Tues 10-6, Fri 9-4
Friends of the Library Group

CADILLAC

C BAKER COLLEGE OF CADILLAC LIBRARY*, 9600 E 13th St, 49601-9169. Tel: 231-876-3165. Toll Free Tel: 888-313-3463. FAX: 231-775-6187. E-mail: library@baker.edu. Web Site: my.baker.edu/ICS/My_Services/Department_Resources/Academic_Resource_Center/Library. *Coordr of Info & Tech Res,* Diane Childress; Tel: 810-766-4235, E-mail: dchild02@baker.edu
Automation Activity & Vendor Info: (Cataloging) Koha; (Circulation) Koha; (Discovery) EBSCO Discovery Service; (OPAC) Koha
Wireless access
Partic in PALnet
Open Mon-Thurs 8-6, Fri 8-5

P CADILLAC-WEXFORD PUBLIC LIBRARY*, 411 S Lake St, 49601. SAN 346-0622. Tel: 231-775-6541. FAX: 231-775-6778. E-mail: liedekea@cadillaclibrary.org. Web Site: www.cadillaclibrary.org. *Dir,* Tracy Logan-Walker; E-mail: logant@cadillaclibrary.org; Staff 12 (MLS 3, Non-MLS 9)
Founded 1906. Pop 30,265; Circ 203,540
Library Holdings: Bk Vols 147,000; Per Subs 275
Automation Activity & Vendor Info: (Cataloging) Auto-Graphics, Inc; (Circulation) Auto-Graphics, Inc; (OPAC) Auto-Graphics, Inc
Wireless access
Partic in Mid-Michigan Library League; MLC
Open Mon-Thur 9-7, Fri 9-6, Sat 11-3
Friends of the Library Group
Branches: 4
BUCKLEY BRANCH, 305 S First St, Buckley, 49620-9526. Tel: 231-269-3325, Ext 3020. FAX: 231-269-3625. *Br Mgr,* Susan Utter
Automation Activity & Vendor Info: (Cataloging) Brodart; (Circulation) Brodart
Open Mon-Thurs 3:30-6:30
Friends of the Library Group
MANTON BRANCH, 404 W Main St, Manton, 49663. SAN 346-0681. Tel: 231-824-3584. FAX: 231-824-3584. *Br Mgr,* Debra Letts; Staff 2 (Non-MLS 2)
Open Mon-Fri 11-6, Sat 10-1
Friends of the Library Group
MESICK BRANCH, 105 W Mesick Ave, Mesick, 49668, SAN 346-0657. Tel: 231-885-1120. FAX: 231-885-1120. *Br Mgr,* Karen Rickard
Open Mon-Fri 11-6, Sat 11-3
Friends of the Library Group
TUSTIN BRANCH, 310 S Neilson St, Tustin, 49688. Tel: 231-829-3012. *Libr Mgr,* Sandy Leach
Open Mon, Tues & Thurs 9-5, Wed 10-5 & 6-8, Fri 1-5, Sat 9-Noon

CAMDEN

P CAMDEN TOWNSHIP LIBRARY*, 119 S Main St, 49232. (Mail add: PO Box 189, 49232-0189), SAN 307-9341. Tel: 517-368-5554. FAX: 517-368-5554. E-mail: camden@monroe.lib.mi.us. Web Site: www.camdenlibrary.org. *Dir,* Carol Love
Circ 13,947
Library Holdings: Bk Vols 8,000; Per Subs 15
Wireless access
Mem of Woodlands Library Cooperative
Open Mon & Thurs 10-5, Tues 1-7, Fri 1-5, Sat 9-1
Friends of the Library Group

CANTON

P CANTON PUBLIC LIBRARY, 1200 S Canton Center Rd, 48188-1600. SAN 321-2645. Tel: 734-397-0999. FAX: 734-397-1130. Web Site: www.cantonpl.org. *Dir,* Eva Davis; Tel: 734-397-0999, Ext 1065, E-mail: davise@cantonpl.org; *Head, Commun Relations,* Laurie Golden; E-mail: goldenl@cantonpl.org; *Head, Bus Serv,* Marian Nicholson; E-mail: nicholsonm@cantonpl.org; *Head, Circ Serv,* Kat Bounds; E-mail: boundsk@cantonpl.org; *Head, Info Serv,* Dave Ewick; E-mail: ewickd@cantonpl.org; *Head, Info Tech,* Rudie Noble; E-mail: nobler@cantonpl.org; Staff 88 (MLS 26, Non-MLS 62)
Founded 1980. Pop 93,000; Circ 837,614
Library Holdings: AV Mats 25,717; DVDs 50,644; e-books 38,550; Electronic Media & Resources 123,634; Bk Vols 213,248; Per Subs 477
Automation Activity & Vendor Info: (Acquisitions) Innovative Interfaces, Inc; (Cataloging) Innovative Interfaces, Inc; (Circulation) Innovative Interfaces, Inc; (ILL) Innovative Interfaces, Inc; (OPAC) Innovative Interfaces, Inc; (Serials) Innovative Interfaces, Inc
Wireless access
Function: 24/7 Electronic res, 24/7 Online cat, Activity rm, Adult bk club, Adult literacy prog, Audiobks via web, AV serv, Bk club(s), Bks on CD, Butterfly Garden, Children's prog, Computer training, Computers for patron use, Digital talking bks, Electronic databases & coll, Family literacy, Free DVD rentals, Home delivery & serv to seniorr ctr & nursing homes, Homebound delivery serv, ILL available, Internet access, Large print keyboards, Life-long learning prog for all ages, Magazines, Magnifiers for reading, Mango lang, Meeting rooms, Movies, Museum passes, Music CDs, Online cat, Online ref, Outreach serv, Outside serv via phone, mail, e-mail & web, OverDrive digital audio bks, Photocopying/Printing, Preschool outreach, Printer for laptops & handheld devices, Prog for adults, Prog for children & young adult, Ref serv available, Scanner, Senior outreach, STEM programs, Story hour, Study rm, Summer reading prog, Tax forms, Teen prog, Telephone ref, Wheelchair accessible
Publications: Connections
Partic in Metro Net Libr Consortium; Midwest Collaborative for Library Services; The Library Network
Open Mon-Thurs 9-9, Fri & Sat 9-6, Sun 12-6
Friends of the Library Group

CARO

P CARO AREA DISTRICT LIBRARY*, 840 W Frank St, 48723. SAN 307-935X. Tel: 989-673-4329. FAX: 989-673-4777. E-mail: info@carolibrary.org. Web Site: www.carolibrary.org. *Dir,* Erin Schmandt; Tel: 989-673-4329, Ext 102, E-mail: erin@carolibrary.org; *Asst Dir,* Melissa Armstrong; Tel: 989-673-4329, Ext 107; Staff 6 (MLS 2, Non-MLS 4)
Founded 1904. Pop 11,837
Library Holdings: AV Mats 6,020; Bks on Deafness & Sign Lang 90; Braille Volumes 13; Electronic Media & Resources 1; High Interest/Low Vocabulary Bk Vols 139; Large Print Bks 2,037; Bk Vols 62,714; Per Subs 162; Talking Bks 1,527
Subject Interests: Genealogy, Local hist
Automation Activity & Vendor Info: (Cataloging) Horizon; (Circulation) Horizon; (ILL) Horizon; (OPAC) Horizon; (Serials) Horizon
Wireless access
Publications: Indianfields Public Library History 1904-1975
Partic in Association for Rural & Small Libraries; Valley Library Consortium; White Pine Library Cooperative
Open Mon-Fri 9-8, Sat 9-5
Friends of the Library Group

CARSON CITY

P CARSON CITY PUBLIC LIBRARY*, 102 W Main St, 48811-0699. SAN 307-9376. Tel: 989-584-3680. FAX: 989-584-3680. E-mail: car@llcoop.org. Web Site: www.carsoncity.michlibrary.org. *Dir,* Beth O'Grady; E-mail: carbo@llcoop.org
Founded 1900. Pop 9,681; Circ 39,900
Library Holdings: Bk Vols 35,000; Per Subs 65
Subject Interests: Genealogy
Automation Activity & Vendor Info: (Cataloging) Innovative Interfaces, Inc; (Circulation) Innovative Interfaces, Inc; (OPAC) Innovative Interfaces, Inc
Wireless access
Partic in Lakeland Library Cooperative
Open Mon-Fri 10-6, Sat 10-2
Branches: 1
CRYSTAL COMMUNITY, 221 W Lake St, Crystal, 48818, SAN 376-9232. Tel: 989-235-6111. FAX: 989-235-6111. *Br Librn,* Brenda Geselman
Open Mon-Fri 11-6, Sat 10-2

MICHIGAN DEPARTMENT OF CORRECTIONS

S ERNEST C BROOKS CORRECTIONAL FACILITY LIBRARY*, 2500 S Sheridan Rd, Muskegon, 49444. Tel: 231-773-9200, Ext 1916. *Librn,* Elisia Hardiman; E-mail: hardimane@michigan.gov; *Libr Tech,* Geraldine Harris
Library Holdings: Bk Vols 20,000; Per Subs 15
Open Mon & Sun 12-4, Tues-Thurs 7am-9pm, Fri & Sat 7-4

S CARSON CITY CORRECTIONAL FACILITY LIBRARY*, PO Box 5000, 48811-5000. Tel: 989-584-3941, Ext 6332. FAX: 989-584-6535. *Libr Tech,* Amy Platte; Tel: 989-548-3941, Ext 6331, E-mail: plattea1@michigan.gov; Staff 3 (MLS 1, Non-MLS 2)
Founded 1987
Library Holdings: Bk Vols 10,000
Function: Audio & video playback equip for onsite use, Bks on cassette, Legal assistance to inmates, Photocopying/Printing, VHS videos
Restriction: Staff & inmates only

CASS CITY

P RAWSON MEMORIAL DISTRICT LIBRARY, 6495 Pine St, 48726-1462. SAN 307-9384. Tel: 989-872-2856. FAX: 989-872-4073. Web Site: www.rawsonlibrary.org. *Dir,* Ruth Steele; E-mail: director@rawsonlibrary.org; *Asst Libr Dir,* Jesika Struve; E-mail: librarian@rawsonlibrary.org; Staff 5 (MLS 1, Non-MLS 4)
Founded 1910. Pop 8,589; Circ 70,648
Library Holdings: Bk Vols 34,800; Per Subs 86
Automation Activity & Vendor Info: (Acquisitions) Auto-Graphics, Inc; (Cataloging) Auto-Graphics, Inc; (Circulation) Auto-Graphics, Inc; (ILL) Auto-Graphics, Inc; (OPAC) Auto-Graphics, Inc
Wireless access
Partic in White Pine Library Cooperative
Open Mon, Wed & Fri 9-8, Tues & Thurs 9-5:30, Sat 9-4
Friends of the Library Group

CASSOPOLIS

P CASS DISTRICT LIBRARY*, 319 M-62 N, 49031. SAN 346-0711. Toll Free Tel: 866-808-7323. FAX: 269-357-7824. Web Site: cassdistrictlibrary.org. *Dir,* Barbara Gordon; Tel: 269-216-7088, Ext 101, E-mail: bgordon@cass.lib.mi.us; *Tech Proc Mgr,* Brandi Roberts; Tel: 269-533-4793, Ext 104, E-mail: broberts@cass.lib.mi.us; Staff 11 (MLS 1, Non-MLS 10)
Founded 1940. Pop 39,204
Wireless access
Partic in Southwest Michigan Library Cooperative
Open Mon-Thurs 9-8, Fri 9-6, Sat 9-3
Friends of the Library Group
Branches: 4
EDWARDSBURG BRANCH, 26745 Church St, Edwardsburg, 49112, SAN 346-0746. Tel: 269-487-9215. FAX: 269-663-6215. *Br Mgr,* Cindy Casper; Tel: 269-467-0649, Ext 303, E-mail: ccasper@cawsllib.mi.us
Founded 1932
Open Mon-Thurs 9-8, Fri 9-6, Sat 9-1
HOWARD, 2341 Yankee St, Niles, 49120, SAN 346-0770. Tel: 269-487-9214. FAX: 269-684-1680. *Br Mgr,* April Hughes; Tel: 269-351-1091, Ext 202, E-mail: hughes@cass.lib.mi.us
Founded 1966
Open Mon-Thurs 11-7, Fri 10-5, Sat 10-2
Friends of the Library Group
LOCAL HISTORY, 145 N Broadway St, 49031, SAN 373-7233. Tel: 269-357-7823. FAX: 269-445-8795. *Br Mgr,* Jon Wuepper; Tel: 269-357-7823, Ext 500, E-mail: jwuepper@cass.lib.mi.us
Founded 1994
Open Mon-Thurs 9-4, Sat 10-2
MASON-UNION, 17049 US 12 E, Edwardsburg, 49112, SAN 346-0800. Tel: 269-357-7821. FAX: 269-641-7674. *Br Mgr,* Holly Nelson; Tel: 269-357-7821, Ext 400, E-mail: hnelson@cass.lib.mi.us
Founded 1973
Open Mon-Thurs 11-7, Sat 9-1
Friends of the Library Group

CEDAR SPRINGS

P CEDAR SPRINGS PUBLIC LIBRARY*, 107 N Main St, 49319. (Mail add: PO Box 280, 49319), SAN 307-9406. Tel: 616-696-1910. FAX: 616-439-3149. E-mail: ced@llcoop.org. Web Site: cedarspringslibrary.org. *Dir,* Donna Clark; E-mail: ceddc@llcoop.org
Founded 1936
Library Holdings: Bk Vols 23,000; Per Subs 15
Automation Activity & Vendor Info: (Cataloging) SirsiDynix; (Circulation) SirsiDynix; (OPAC) SirsiDynix
Wireless access
Partic in Lakeland Library Cooperative
Open Mon-Fri 10-6, Sat 9-Noon
Friends of the Library Group

CENTER LINE

P CENTER LINE PUBLIC LIBRARY*, 7345 Weingartz St, 48015-1462. SAN 307-9422. Tel: 586-758-8274. Web Site: www.centerline.gov/202/library. *Librn,* Wesleyann Johnson; E-mail: wjohnson@centerline.gov
Founded 1929. Pop 8,257; Circ 40,000
Jul 2012-Jun 2013 Income $249,293. Mats Exp $30,000. Sal $110,000
Library Holdings: Bk Vols 53,000; Per Subs 25
Automation Activity & Vendor Info: (Acquisitions) SirsiDynix; (Cataloging) SirsiDynix; (Circulation) SirsiDynix; (OPAC) SirsiDynix; (Serials) SirsiDynix
Wireless access
Partic in Suburban Library Cooperative
Open Mon & Wed 10-5, Tues & Thurs 10-7, Fri & Sat 12-5
Friends of the Library Group

CENTRAL LAKE

P CENTRAL LAKE DISTRICT LIBRARY*, 7900 Maple St, 49622. (Mail add: PO Box 397, 49622-0397), SAN 307-9430. Tel: 231-544-2517. FAX: 231-544-5016. Web Site: www.centrallakelibrary.com. *Dir,* Patti S Dawson; E-mail: director@centrallakelibrary.com; Staff 1 (Non-MLS 1)
Pop 3,839; Circ 26,106
Library Holdings: Audiobooks 1,469; Bks on Deafness & Sign Lang 12; CDs 240; DVDs 1,408; Large Print Bks 1,172; Bk Titles 22,589; Per Subs 20
Special Collections: Michigan Coll
Automation Activity & Vendor Info: (Acquisitions) Baker & Taylor; (Cataloging) Biblionix/Apollo; (Circulation) Biblionix/Apollo; (ILL) Mel Cat
Wireless access
Function: 24/7 Electronic res, 24/7 Online cat, Accelerated reader prog, Activity rm, Adult bk club, Audiobks on Playaways & MP3, Audiobks via web, AV serv, Bks on CD, Computers for patron use, E-Reserves, Electronic databases & coll, Free DVD rentals, ILL available, Internet access, Magazines, Magnifiers for reading, Mail & tel request accepted, Meeting rooms, Music CDs, Online cat, Online info literacy tutorials on the web & in blackboard, Online ref, Outside serv via phone, mail, e-mail & web, OverDrive digital audio bks, Photocopying/Printing, Prog for children & young adult, Scanner, Spoken cassettes & DVDs, Story hour, Summer reading prog, Tax forms, Telephone ref, Wheelchair accessible
Partic in Mid-Michigan Library League
Special Services for the Deaf - Bks on deafness & sign lang
Special Services for the Blind - Aids for in-house use; Bks available with recordings; Bks on CD; Large print bks; Magnifiers; Playaways (bks on MP3)
Open Mon-Fri 10-6, Sat 10-3
Restriction: Non-resident fee
Friends of the Library Group

CENTREVILLE

J GLEN OAKS COMMUNITY COLLEGE LEARNING COMMONS*, E J Shaheen Library, 62249 Shimmel Rd, 49032-9719. SAN 307-9449. Tel: 269-294-4295, 269-467-9945. Toll Free Tel: 888-994-7818. FAX: 269-467-4114. E-mail: learningcommons@glenoaks.edu, library@glenoaks.edu. Web Site: www.glenoaks.edu/academics/learning-commons. *Dir, Learning Commons,* Trista Nelson; Tel: 269-294-4293, E-mail: tnelson@glenoaks.edu; *Asst Dir, Learning Commons,* Shapan Lavinghouse; Tel: 269-294-4372; Staff 4 (MLS 1, Non-MLS 3)
Founded 1966. Enrl 1,000; Fac 71; Highest Degree: Associate

Jul 2014-Jun 2015 Income $318,776. Mats Exp $55,237, Books $9,378, Per/Ser (Incl. Access Fees) $10,069, Other Print Mats $2,671, AV Mat $242, Electronic Ref Mat (Incl. Access Fees) $7,158. Sal $166,855 (Prof $64,217)
Library Holdings: AV Mats 9,073; CDs 424; DVDs 77; e-books 2,067; Microforms 2,354; Bk Titles 42,421; Bk Vols 47,431; Per Subs 105; Videos 2,084
Automation Activity & Vendor Info: (Cataloging) OCLC Connexion; (Circulation) SirsiDynix-WorkFlows; (ILL) OCLC WorldShare Interlibrary Loan; (OPAC) SirsiDynix-iBistro
Wireless access
Function: AV serv, CD-ROM, Computers for patron use, Distance learning, Doc delivery serv, Electronic databases & coll, Homework prog, ILL available, Instruction & testing, Laminating, Magazines, Online cat, Photocopying/Printing, Prof lending libr, Ref serv available, Wheelchair accessible
Partic in Midwest Collaborative for Library Services; Southwest Michigan Library Cooperative
Special Services for the Deaf - Bks on deafness & sign lang
Special Services for the Blind - Accessible computers; ZoomText magnification & reading software
Open Mon-Thurs 8-8, Fri 8-4 (Fall-Winter); Mon-Thurs 8-4 (Spring-Summer)
Restriction: Lending limited to county residents, Non-circulating of rare bks, Open to students, fac & staff

P NOTTAWA TOWNSHIP LIBRARY*, 685 E Main St, 49032-9603. SAN 307-9457. Tel: 269-467-6289. FAX: 269-467-4422. Web Site: nottawatownshiplibrary.com. *Libr Dir,* Carrie Brueck; E-mail: carrie.brueck@monroe.lib.mi.us; *Asst Dir,* Harmony Miller; *Ch,* Karen Peterson; Staff 4 (Non-MLS 4)
Founded 1871. Pop 6,394; Circ 62,384
Jul 2015-Jun 2016 Income $245,600, State $2,600, Locally Generated Income $189,000, Other $54,000. Mats Exp $32,000. Sal $99,000
Library Holdings: AV Mats 1,528; Bks on Deafness & Sign Lang 12; CDs 73; DVDs 616; Large Print Bks 280; Bk Titles 24,894; Bk Vols 26,252; Per Subs 48; Talking Bks 1,248; Videos 912
Special Collections: Amish Religion Coll
Automation Activity & Vendor Info: (Acquisitions) Follett Software; (Cataloging) Follett Software; (Circulation) Follett Software
Wireless access
Function: 24/7 Electronic res, 24/7 Online cat, Activity rm, Adult bk club, Archival coll, Audiobks via web, AV serv, Bk club(s), Bks on CD, Children's prog, Computers for patron use, Electronic databases & coll, Equip loans & repairs, Free DVD rentals, Holiday prog, Home delivery & serv to seniorr ctr & nursing homes, Homebound delivery serv, ILL available, Internet access, Laminating, Learning ctr, Magazines, Meeting rooms, Movies, Museum passes, Music CDs, Online cat, Online ref, Outreach serv, OverDrive digital audio bks, Photocopying/Printing, Preschool reading prog, Prog for adults, Prog for children & young adult, Scanner, Spoken cassettes & CDs, Story hour, Study rm, Summer & winter reading prog, Summer reading prog, Tax forms, Teen prog, VHS videos, Wheelchair accessible, Winter reading prog, Workshops, Writing prog
Mem of Woodlands Library Cooperative
Open Mon & Wed-Fri 9-5, Tues 11-7, Sat 9-12
Friends of the Library Group

CHARLEVOIX

P CHARLEVOIX PUBLIC LIBRARY, 220 W Clinton St, 49720. SAN 307-9465. Tel: 231-547-2651. Interlibrary Loan Service Tel: 231-237-7340. FAX: 231-547-0678. E-mail: reference@charlevoixlibrary.org. Web Site: www.charlevoixlibrary.org. *Dir,* Ryan Deery; Tel: 231-237-7360, E-mail: rdeery@charlevoixlibrary.org; Staff 13.5 (MLS 5, Non-MLS 8.5)
Founded 1907. Pop 9,405; Circ 120,000
Jul 2012-Jun 2013 Income $975,480, State $3,950, County $46,000, Locally Generated Income $925,530. Mats Exp $71,600, Books $42,500, Per/Ser (Incl. Access Fees) $7,500, AV Mat $14,500, Electronic Ref Mat (Incl. Access Fees) $7,100. Sal $434,000 (Prof $171,000)
Library Holdings: Audiobooks 3,700; CDs 1,893; DVDs 3,050; e-books 1,000; Large Print Bks 1,099; Bk Vols 41,109; Per Subs 130
Special Collections: Local History. Oral History
Automation Activity & Vendor Info: (Cataloging) SirsiDynix; (Circulation) SirsiDynix; (OPAC) SirsiDynix-iBistro
Wireless access
Function: Adult bk club, Art exhibits, Audiobks via web, Bi-weekly Writer's Group, Bk club(s), Bks on cassette, Bks on CD, CD-ROM, Children's prog, Computer training, Computers for patron use, E-Reserves, Electronic databases & coll, Family literacy, Free DVD rentals, Genealogy discussion group, Home delivery & serv to seniorr ctr & nursing homes, Homebound delivery serv, ILL available, Jazz prog, Magnifiers for reading, Mail & tel request accepted, Microfiche/film & reading machines, Music CDs, Notary serv, Online cat, Online ref, Outreach serv, Outside serv via phone, mail, e-mail & web, OverDrive digital audio bks, Photocopying/Printing, Preschool outreach, Preschool reading prog, Printer for laptops & handheld devices, Prog for adults, Prog for children & young adult, Ref & res, Ref serv available, Scanner, Senior computer classes, Senior outreach, Spoken cassettes & CDs, Spoken cassettes & DVDs, Story hour, Summer reading prog, Tax forms, Teen prog, Telephone ref, VHS videos, Wheelchair accessible, Workshops
Partic in Midwest Collaborative for Library Services; Northland Library Cooperative; OCLC Online Computer Library Center, Inc; PAC2 Consortium
Open Mon-Thurs 10-8, Fri & Sat 10-5, Sun 1-5
Friends of the Library Group

CHARLOTTE

P CHARLOTTE COMMUNITY LIBRARY*, 226 S Bostwick St, 48813-1801. SAN 307-9473. Tel: 517-543-8859. FAX: 517-543-8868. Web Site: www.charlottelibrary.org. *Libr Dir,* Position Currently Open; *Dir, Finance & Gen Serv,* Marlena Arras; E-mail: marlenaarras@ameritech.net; *Head, Circ, Human Res,* Ann Goeman; E-mail: goemana@charlottelibrary.org; *Youth Serv Librn,* Christina Stuck; *ILL Spec,* Bridget Gregus; *Adult Serv,* Chiara Genovese; E-mail: genovesec@charlottelibrary.org; Staff 14 (MLS 2, Non-MLS 12)
Founded 1895. Pop 23,157; Circ 120,627
Library Holdings: Bk Titles 70,000; Per Subs 113
Special Collections: Local History Coll
Automation Activity & Vendor Info: (Acquisitions) Auto-Graphics, Inc; (Cataloging) Auto-Graphics, Inc; (Circulation) Auto-Graphics, Inc; (ILL) Mel Cat; (Media Booking) Auto-Graphics, Inc; (OPAC) Auto-Graphics, Inc; (Serials) Auto-Graphics, Inc
Wireless access
Function: Adult bk club, Adult literacy prog, Art exhibits, AV serv, Bk club(s), Bks on cassette, Bks on CD, CD-ROM, Children's prog, Computer training, Computers for patron use, Digital talking bks, E-Reserves, Home delivery & serv to seniorr ctr & nursing homes, Homebound delivery serv, ILL available, Magnifiers for reading, Music CDs, Notary serv, Online cat, Photocopying/Printing, Prog for adults, Prog for children & young adult, Ref & res, Ref serv available, Spoken cassettes & CDs, Spoken cassettes & DVDs, Summer reading prog, Tax forms, Teen prog, VHS videos, Wheelchair accessible
Mem of Woodlands Library Cooperative
Open Mon-Fri 9-8, Sat 9-2
Friends of the Library Group

CHASE

P CHASE TOWNSHIP PUBLIC LIBRARY*, Chase Library, 8400 E North St, 49623. (Mail add: PO Box 24, 49623), SAN 307-9481. Tel: 231-832-9511. FAX: 231-832-9511. E-mail: chaselibrary@yahoo.com. *Librn,* Roxanne Ware
Circ 1,906
Library Holdings: Bk Vols 11,044; Per Subs 12
Partic in Mid-Michigan Library League
Open Mon, Wed & Thurs 10-6, Tues 9-5, Fri 9-Noon

CHEBOYGAN

P CHEBOYGAN AREA PUBLIC LIBRARY*, 100 S Bailey St, 49721-1661. SAN 307-949X. Tel: 231-627-2381. FAX: 231-627-9172. E-mail: contactus@cheboyganlibrary.org. Web Site: cheboyganlibrary.org. *Dir,* Mark C Bronson
Pop 14,624
Library Holdings: Bk Vols 41,000; Per Subs 150
Automation Activity & Vendor Info: (Cataloging) SirsiDynix; (Circulation) SirsiDynix; (OPAC) SirsiDynix
Wireless access
Function: Digital talking bks, Magnifiers for reading, Music CDs, Photocopying/Printing, Prog for adults, Prog for children & young adult, Spoken cassettes & CDs, Summer reading prog, VHS videos, Wheelchair accessible
Partic in Northland Library Cooperative
Open Mon-Wed 10-8, Thurs 8-7, Fri 8-5, Sat 10-3, Sun 1-5
Restriction: Non-resident fee
Friends of the Library Group

CHELSEA

P CHELSEA DISTRICT LIBRARY*, 221 S Main St, 48118-1267. SAN 307-9503. Tel: 734-475-8732. FAX: 734-475-6190. Web Site: chelseadistrictlibrary.org. *Libr Dir,* Lori Coryell; Tel: 734-475-8732, Ext 206, E-mail: lcoryell@chelseadistrictlibrary.org; *Asst Dir,* Linda Ballard; Tel: 734-475-8732, Ext 202; *Head of Mkt,* Elaine Medrow; *Head, Circ,* Terri Lancaster; *Head, Info Serv,* Shannon Powers; *Head, Tech,* Scott Rakestraw; *Ad,* Laura Brown; *Ad,* Gabrielle Hopkins; *Ad,* Catherine Sossi; *Youth & Teen Serv Librn,* Stacey Comfort; *Youth & Teen Serv Librn,* Edith Donnell; *Youth & Teen Serv Librn,* Jessica Zubik; Staff 23 (MLS 8, Non-MLS 15)
Founded 1998. Pop 15,000

Library Holdings: Bk Vols 42,549; Per Subs 98
Special Collections: Chelsea History, bk, ms, microfilm, pictures; Wastenaw County History Coll, pictures
Automation Activity & Vendor Info: (Acquisitions) TLC (The Library Corporation); (Cataloging) TLC (The Library Corporation); (Circulation) TLC (The Library Corporation); (OPAC) TLC (The Library Corporation); (Serials) TLC (The Library Corporation)
Wireless access
Function: Adult bk club, Archival coll, Art exhibits, Bk club(s), CD-ROM, Chess club, Computer training, Digital talking bks, E-Reserves, Electronic databases & coll, Family literacy, Health sci info serv, Home delivery & serv to seniorr ctr & nursing homes, Homebound delivery serv, Homework prog, ILL available, Internet access, Music CDs, Photocopying/Printing, Preschool outreach, Prog for adults, Prog for children & young adult, Ref serv available, Senior computer classes, Summer reading prog, Telephone ref, Wheelchair accessible, Workshops
Partic in TLN
Open Mon-Thurs (Winter) 10-9, Fri 10-6, Sat 10-5, Sun 1-5; Mon-Thurs (Summer) 10-8, Fri 10-6, Sat 10-3, Sun 1-5
Friends of the Library Group

CHESANING

P RIVER RAPIDS DISTRICT LIBRARY, 227 E Broad St, 48616. SAN 307-9511. Tel: 989-845-3211. FAX: 989-845-2166. Web Site: www.riverrapidslibrary.org. *Dir,* Lynne Clark; E-mail: rrdl.director@vlc.lib.mi.us; Staff 2.8 (MLS 1, Non-MLS 1.8)
Founded 1936. Pop 4,861; Circ 29,600
Library Holdings: Bk Vols 43,392; Per Subs 60
Special Collections: Genealogy; Local History. Oral History
Automation Activity & Vendor Info: (Cataloging) Horizon; (Circulation) Horizon; (OPAC) Horizon
Wireless access
Function: Adult bk club, Audiobks via web, AV serv, Bk club(s), Bks on cassette, Bks on CD, Bus archives, Children's prog, Computer training, Computers for patron use, Digital talking bks, ILL available, Microfiche/film & reading machines, Museum passes, Music CDs, Online cat, OverDrive digital audio bks, Photocopying/Printing, Preschool outreach, Preschool reading prog, Prog for adults, Prog for children & young adult, Ref serv available, Scanner, Senior computer classes, Spoken cassettes & CDs, Spoken cassettes & DVDs, Story hour, Summer & winter reading prog, Summer reading prog, Tax forms, Teen prog, Telephone ref, VHS videos, Winter reading prog
Partic in Valley Library Consortium; White Pine Library Cooperative
Open Mon 10-6, Tues & Thurs 10-8, Sat 10-2 (Winter); Mon & Tues 10-6, Thurs 10-8, Fri 10-2 (Summer)
Restriction: Pub use on premises
Friends of the Library Group

CHESTERFIELD

P CHESTERFIELD TOWNSHIP LIBRARY*, 50560 Patricia Ave, 48051-3804. SAN 377-7537. Tel: 586-598-4900. FAX: 586-598-7900. E-mail: chesterfieldlibrary@chelibrary.org. Web Site: www.chelibrary.org. *Libr Dir,* Elizabeth Madson; E-mail: emadson@chelibrary.org; *Head, Outreach Serv, Info Serv,* Holly Kirsten; E-mail: hollykirsten@chelibrary.org; *Syst Librn, Tech Serv Supvr,* Breck McCrory; *Circ Supvr,* Shane Stewart; E-mail: shanestewart@chelibrary.org; Staff 7 (MLS 6, Non-MLS 1)
Founded 1994. Circ 314,629
Library Holdings: Audiobooks 3,534; CDs 2,515; DVDs 7,206; e-books 29,371; Bk Vols 73,474; Per Subs 194
Automation Activity & Vendor Info: (Acquisitions) SirsiDynix; (Cataloging) SirsiDynix; (Circulation) SirsiDynix; (Discovery) SirsiDynix; (ILL) SirsiDynix; (OPAC) SirsiDynix; (Serials) SirsiDynix
Wireless access
Function: 24/7 Electronic res, 24/7 Online cat, 3D Printer, Activity rm, Adult bk club, Adult literacy prog, After school storytime, Archival coll, Art exhibits, Art programs, Audiobks on Playaways & MP3, Audiobks via web, Bk club(s), Bks on CD, Children's prog, Computer training, Computers for patron use, E-Readers, Electronic databases & coll, Family literacy, Free DVD rentals, Holiday prog, Homework prog, ILL available, Internet access, Life-long learning prog for all ages, Magazines, Magnifiers for reading, Meeting rooms, Movies, Museum passes, Music CDs, Notary serv, Online cat, Outreach serv, OverDrive digital audio bks, Photocopying/Printing, Preschool outreach, Preschool reading prog, Prof lending libr, Prog for adults, Prog for children & young adult, Ref & res, Ref serv available, Scanner, Senior computer classes, Senior outreach, Serves people with intellectual disabilities, STEM programs, Story hour, Summer & winter reading prog, Summer reading prog, Teen prog, Telephone ref, Wheelchair accessible, Winter reading prog, Workshops
Partic in Suburban Library Cooperative
Open Mon-Thurs 10-8, Fri 10-5, Sat 10-4
Friends of the Library Group

CLARE

P PERE MARQUETTE DISTRICT LIBRARY*, 185 E Fourth St, 48617. SAN 307-952X. Tel: 989-386-7576. FAX: 989-386-3576. E-mail: pmdl@cityofclare.org. Web Site: www.pmdl.org. *Dir,* Sheila Bissonnette; Tel: 989-386-7576, Ext 2, E-mail: sbissonnette@cityofclare.org; *Pub Serv Librn,* Pamela McKnight; Tel: 989-386-7576, Ext 4, E-mail: pmcknight@cityofclare.org; Staff 3 (MLS 1, Non-MLS 2)
Founded 1962. Pop 10,801; Circ 27,000
Library Holdings: Bk Vols 36,000; Per Subs 80
Automation Activity & Vendor Info: (Cataloging) TLC (The Library Corporation); (Circulation) TLC (The Library Corporation); (OPAC) TLC (The Library Corporation)
Wireless access
Function: After school storytime, Homebound delivery serv, ILL available, Internet access, Magnifiers for reading, Music CDs, Photocopying/Printing, Prog for children & young adult, Ref serv available, Spoken cassettes & CDs, Summer reading prog, Telephone ref, VHS videos
Partic in Mideastern Mich Libr Coop
Open Mon-Fri 10-6, Sat 10-2
Friends of the Library Group

CLARKSTON

P CLARKSTON INDEPENDENCE DISTRICT LIBRARY*, 6495 Clarkston Rd, 48346. SAN 307-9546. Tel: 248-625-2212. Automation Services Tel: 248-625-4633. FAX: 248-625-8852. E-mail: askus@cidlibrary.org. Web Site: www.indelib.org. *Dir,* Julie Meredith; *Head, Children's & Teen Serv,* Tracy Bedford; *Head, Adult Serv,* Lawrence Marble; *Head, Circ, IT Mgr,* Bill Bowman; *Head, Tech Serv,* Bradley Reuter; Staff 4 (MLS 4)
Founded 1955. Pop 34,000; Circ 230,000
Library Holdings: High Interest/Low Vocabulary Bk Vols 200; Bk Vols 100,000; Per Subs 250
Wireless access
Partic in Metronet
Open Mon-Wed 10-9, Thurs-Sat 10-6, Sun 1-6
Friends of the Library Group

CLAWSON

P BLAIR MEMORIAL LIBRARY, 416 N Main St, 48017-1599. SAN 307-9554. Tel: 248-588-5500. FAX: 248-588-3114. Web Site: www.clawson.lib.mi.us. *Libr Dir,* Jenni Gannod; E-mail: jgannod@tln.lib.mi.us; *Youth Serv Librn,* Kristin Church
Founded 1929. Pop 12,732; Circ 105,891
Library Holdings: AV Mats 122,288; Bk Titles 64,464; Per Subs 94
Automation Activity & Vendor Info: (Cataloging) CARL.Solution (TLC); (Circulation) CARL.Solution (TLC); (ILL) CARL.Solution (TLC); (OPAC) CARL.Solution (TLC)
Wireless access
Partic in The Library Network
Open Mon & Wed Noon-8, Tues & Thurs 10-6, Sat 9-5
Friends of the Library Group

CLIMAX

P LAWRENCE MEMORIAL PUBLIC LIBRARY*, 107 N Main St, 49034-9638. (Mail add: PO Box 280, 49034-0280), SAN 307-9562. Tel: 269-746-4125. FAX: 269-746-4125. *Dir,* Ralph Weessies
Founded 1882. Pop 2,881; Circ 5,470
Library Holdings: Large Print Bks 147; Bk Vols 17,300; Per Subs 19
Special Collections: Historical Society Coll
Partic in Southwest Michigan Library Cooperative
Open Mon-Thurs 1-6, Sat 9-12

CLINTON

P CLINTON TOWNSHIP PUBLIC LIBRARY, 100 Brown St, 49236. (Mail add: PO Box 530, 49236-0530), SAN 307-9570. Tel: 517-456-4141. FAX: 517-456-4142. E-mail: clintonlibrary@clinton.lib.mi.us. Web Site: www.clintontownshiplibrary.org. *Dir,* Tamara Denby; E-mail: tdenby@clinton.lib.mi.us
Founded 1937. Pop 3,557; Circ 33,085
Library Holdings: Bk Vols 25,000; Per Subs 100
Automation Activity & Vendor Info: (Cataloging) Evolve; (Circulation) Evolve
Wireless access
Mem of Woodlands Library Cooperative
Open Mon-Thurs 11-7, Fri 11-6, Sat 10-2
Friends of the Library Group

CLINTON TOWNSHIP

C BAKER COLLEGE OF CLINTON TOWNSHIP LIBRARY, 34950 Little Mack Ave, 48035-4701. Tel: 586-790-9584. Toll Free Tel: 888-272-2842. FAX: 586-791-0967. E-mail: library-ct@baker.edu. Web Site:

www.baker.edu. *Coordr, Libr Serv,* Kim Webster; E-mail: kim.webster@baker.edu
Library Holdings: Bk Vols 20,000; Per Subs 120
Automation Activity & Vendor Info: (Cataloging) Koha; (Circulation) Koha; (OPAC) Koha
Wireless access
Partic in MeLCat; PALnet
Open Mon-Thurs 8-8, Fri 9-5, Sat 8-1

P CLINTON-MACOMB PUBLIC LIBRARY*, 40900 Romeo Plank Rd, 48038-2955. SAN 375-4251. Tel: 586-226-5000. FAX: 586-226-5008. E-mail: info@cmpl.org. Web Site: www.cmpl.org. *Libr Dir,* Larry Neal; Tel: 586-226-5011, E-mail: lneal@cmpl.org; *Head, Info Res,* Terri Dedischew; Tel: 586-226-5017; *Head, Youth Serv,* Lisa Mulvenna; Tel: 586-226-5031; *Customer Serv Mgr,* Katie LeBlanc; Tel: 586-226-5024; Staff 35 (MLS 20, Non-MLS 15)
Founded 1992. Pop 170,000; Circ 1,676,552
Library Holdings: AV Mats 77,665; Bk Vols 277,684
Automation Activity & Vendor Info: (Acquisitions) Innovative Interfaces, Inc; (Cataloging) Innovative Interfaces, Inc; (Circulation) Innovative Interfaces, Inc; (ILL) Innovative Interfaces, Inc; (OPAC) Innovative Interfaces, Inc; (Serials) Innovative Interfaces, Inc
Wireless access
Function: Accelerated reader prog, Adult bk club, Adult literacy prog, After school storytime, Art exhibits, AV serv, Bk club(s), Bks on CD, CD-ROM, Children's prog, Computer training, Computers for patron use, Digital talking bks, Electronic databases & coll, Free DVD rentals, Holiday prog, Homework prog, ILL available, Large print keyboards, Magnifiers for reading, Mail & tel request accepted, Museum passes, Music CDs, Online cat, Online ref, Orientations, OverDrive digital audio bks, Photocopying/Printing, Prog for adults, Prog for children & young adult, Ref serv available, Scanner, Serves people with intellectual disabilities, Spanish lang bks, Story hour, Summer & winter reading prog, Telephone ref, Wheelchair accessible
Publications: Library Matters (Newsletter); Library Matters (Monthly newsletter)
Special Services for the Deaf - Assisted listening device; Closed caption videos; TDD equip; TTY equip
Special Services for the Blind - Accessible computers; Assistive/Adapted tech devices, equip & products; BiFolkal kits; Bks & mags in Braille, on rec, tape & cassette; Bks available with recordings; Bks on CD; Bks on flash-memory cartridges; Blind students ctr; Closed circuit TV; Closed circuit TV magnifier; Computer with voice synthesizer for visually impaired persons; Descriptive video serv (DVS); Digital talking bk; Digital talking bk machines; Disability awareness prog; Free checkout of audio mat; Large print bks; Large print bks & talking machines; Lending of low vision aids; Low vision equip; Magnifiers; Newsletter (in large print, Braille or on cassette); Playaways (bks on MP3); Screen enlargement software for people with visual disabilities; Screen reader software; Talking bks; Talking bks & player equip
Open Mon-Thurs 9-9, Fri & Sat 9-6, Sun (Sept-May) 1-6
Friends of the Library Group
Branches: 3

P MACOMB LIBRARY FOR THE BLIND & PHYSICALLY HANDICAPPED, 40900 Romeo Plank Rd, 48038-2955, SAN 324-2250. Tel: 586-286-1580. FAX: 586-286-0634. E-mail: MLBPH@cmpl.org. Web Site: www.cmpl.org/MLBPH. *Coordr, Ch Serv, Spec Serv Librn,* Anne Mandel; E-mail: amandel@cmpl.org; Staff 4 (MLS 2, Non-MLS 2)
Founded 1983. Pop 1,200; Circ 40,350
Library Holdings: Bks on Deafness & Sign Lang 250; Large Print Bks 7,500; Talking Bks 41,698; Videos 710
Special Collections: Bi-Folkal Kits; Descriptive Videos; Matchingbook & Tape Kits
Subject Interests: Handicaps
Function: Bks on cassette, Computer training, Computers for patron use, Magnifiers for reading, Mail & tel request accepted, Mail loans to mem, Summer reading prog, Wheelchair accessible
Partic in Suburban Library Cooperative
Publications: LBPH (Newsletter)
Special Services for the Deaf - TDD equip
Special Services for the Blind - Aids for in-house use; Assistive/Adapted tech devices, equip & products; BiFolkal kits; Bks on cassette; Braille equip; Braille servs; Cassette playback machines; Closed circuit TV; Computer with voice synthesizer for visually impaired persons; Internet workstation with adaptive software; Large print bks; Large screen computer & software; Newsletter (in large print, Braille or on cassette); Open bk software on pub access PC; Screen enlargement software for people with visual disabilities; ZoomText magnification & reading software
Open Mon-Thurs 9-9, Fri & Sat 9-6, Sun (Sept-May) 1-6
Restriction: Restricted access
Friends of the Library Group

NORTH, 16800 24 Mile Rd, Macomb Township, 48042. Tel: 586-226-5082. FAX: 586-226-5088. *Br Mgr,* Gretchen Krug; Tel: 586-226-5081, E-mail: gkrug@cmpl.org; Staff 7 (MLS 4, Non-MLS 3)
Library Holdings: AV Mats 13,601; Bk Vols 52,923
Open Mon-Thurs 9-9, Fri & Sat 9-6
Friends of the Library Group

SOUTH, 35679 S Gratiot Ave, 48035. Tel: 586-226-5072. *Br Mgr,* Margaret Dekovich; Tel: 586-226-5071; Staff 7 (MLS 4, Non-MLS 3)
Library Holdings: AV Mats 9,663; Bk Vols 34,494
Open Mon-Thurs 9-9, Fri & Sat 9-6
Friends of the Library Group

COLDWATER

P BRANCH DISTRICT LIBRARY*, Coldwater Branch Library (Main), Ten E Chicago St, 49036-1615. SAN 346-086X. Tel: 517-278-2341. Circulation Tel: 517-278-2341, Ext 100. Web Site: www.branchdistrictlibrary.org. *Libr Dir,* John Rucker; Tel: 517-278-2341, Ext 115, E-mail: ruckerj@branchdistrictlibrary.org; *Br Mgr, Dir, Pub Serv,* Kimberly Feltner; Tel: 517-278-2341, Ext 123, E-mail: feltnerk@branchdistrictlibrary.org; *Teen Serv Librn,* Jessica Tefft; Tel: 517-278-2341, Ext 122, E-mail: tefftj@branchdistrictlibrary.org; Staff 38 (MLS 5, Non-MLS 33)
Founded 1991. Pop 43,664; Circ 144,023
Library Holdings: Bk Titles 71,464; Per Subs 95
Special Collections: Genealogical Research Materials
Automation Activity & Vendor Info: (Cataloging) Evergreen; (Circulation) Evergreen; (ILL) Mel Cat
Wireless access
Function: 24/7 Electronic res, 24/7 Online cat, Adult literacy prog, Audiobks via web, Bks on CD, Children's prog, Computer training, Computers for patron use, Electronic databases & coll, Free DVD rentals, Holiday prog, ILL available, Internet access, Life-long learning prog for all ages, Magazines, Mango lang, Meeting rooms, Music CDs, Notary serv, Online cat, OverDrive digital audio bks, Photocopying/Printing, Preschool reading prog, Printer for laptops & handheld devices, Prof lending libr, Prog for adults, Prog for children & young adult, Ref serv available, Scanner, Story hour, Summer reading prog, Tax forms, Teen prog, Telephone ref, Visual arts prog, Wheelchair accessible
Mem of Woodlands Library Cooperative
Open Mon 10-8, Tues-Thurs 9-8, Fri 9-5, Sat 9-3, Sun 1-5
Restriction: Free to mem, Non-resident fee
Friends of the Library Group
Branches: 5

ALGANSEE BRANCH, 580-B S Ray Quincy Rd, Quincy, 49082-9530, SAN 346-0894. Tel: 517-639-9830. FAX: 517-639-9830. *Br Mgr,* Janice Clark; Staff 2 (Non-MLS 2)
Founded 1938
Library Holdings: Bk Vols 1,700
Open Tues 12-6, Wed 1-6, Fri 10-6, Thurs 9-1, Sat 9-Noon
Friends of the Library Group

BRONSON BRANCH, 207 N Matteson St, Bronson, 49028-1308, SAN 346-0924. Tel: 517-369-3785. FAX: 517-369-3785. E-mail: bronson@branchdistrictlibrary.org. *Br Mgr,* Lynnell Eash; Staff 2 (Non-MLS 2)
Founded 1888
Library Holdings: Bk Vols 4,750
Open Mon-Fri 10-6, Sat 9-12
Friends of the Library Group

LUCILLE E DEARTH UNION TOWNSHIP BRANCH, 195 N Broadway, Union City, 49094-1153, SAN 346-1017. Tel: 517-741-5061. FAX: 517-741-5061. E-mail: union@branchdistrictlibrary.org. *Br Mgr,* Judy Gottschalk; E-mail: gottschalkj@branchdistrictlibrary.org; Staff 2 (Non-MLS 2)
Founded 1870
Open Tues & Wed 9:30-5, Fri 9:30-4:30, Sat 9-Noon
Friends of the Library Group

QUINCY BRANCH, 11 N Main St, Quincy, 49082-1163, SAN 346-0959. Tel: 517-639-4001. FAX: 517-639-4001. E-mail: quincy@branchdistrictlibrary.org. *Br Mgr,* Lisa Wood; Staff 2 (Non-MLS 2)
Founded 1870
Open Tues & Fri 9-5, Wed & Thurs 12-5, Sat 9-Noon
Friends of the Library Group

SHERWOOD BRANCH, 118 E Sherman St, Sherwood, 49089, SAN 346-0983. Tel: 517-741-7976. FAX: 517-741-7976. *Br Mgr,* Traci Counterman; E-mail: countermant@branchdistrictlibrary.org; Staff 2 (Non-MLS 2)
Founded 1947
Open Tues 2-6, Wed 9-2, Thurs 1-5, Sat 9-Noon
Friends of the Library Group

COLEMAN

P COLEMAN AREA LIBRARY*, 111 First St, 48618. (Mail add: PO Box 515, 48618-0515), SAN 307-9589. Tel: 989-465-6398. FAX: 989-465-1861. E-mail: staff@colemanlibrary.org. Web Site: www.colemanlibrary.org. *Dir,* Gale L Nelson; E-mail: library@tm.net
Founded 1968. Pop 4,594; Circ 13,340
Library Holdings: Bk Vols 19,000; Per Subs 54; Videos 812
Automation Activity & Vendor Info: (Cataloging) TLC (The Library Corporation); (Circulation) TLC (The Library Corporation); (OPAC) TLC (The Library Corporation)
Wireless access
Function: 24/7 Online cat, Bks on CD, Children's prog, Computers for patron use, ILL available, Internet access, Magazines, Meeting rooms, Movies, Online cat, Online ref, OverDrive digital audio bks, Photocopying/Printing, Prog for adults, Prog for children & young adult, Summer reading prog
Partic in Mideastern Michigan Library Cooperative
Open Tues, Wed & Fri 9-5, Thurs 12:30-8:30 Sat 8-Noon

COLOMA

P COLOMA PUBLIC LIBRARY*, 151 W Center St, 49038. (Mail add: PO Box 430, 49038-0430), SAN 307-9597. Tel: 269-468-3431. FAX: 269-468-8077. Web Site: www.colomapubliclibrary.net. *Dir,* Charles Dickinson; Staff 2 (MLS 1, Non-MLS 1)
Founded 1963. Pop 13,835; Circ 82,441
Library Holdings: Bk Vols 55,000; Per Subs 204
Subject Interests: Mich
Automation Activity & Vendor Info: (Cataloging) Follett Software; (Circulation) Follett Software; (ILL) Auto-Graphics, Inc; (OPAC) Auto-Graphics, Inc
Wireless access
Partic in Southwest Michigan Library Cooperative
Open Mon & Fri 10-5:30, Tues-Thurs 10-8, Sat 10-2

COLON

P COLON TOWNSHIP LIBRARY*, 128 S Blackstone Ave, 49040. (Mail add: PO Box 9, 49040-0009), SAN 307-9600. Tel: 269-432-3958. FAX: 269-432-4554. E-mail: colon@monroe.lib.mi.us. Web Site: www.colonlibrary.org. *Dir,* Julie Censke; E-mail: julie.censke@monroe.lib.mi.us; Staff 2 (MLS 1, Non-MLS 1)
Founded 1897. Pop 3,901; Circ 23,521
Library Holdings: Audiobooks 1,022; CDs 48; DVDs 399; Large Print Bks 228; Bk Vols 17,926; Per Subs 42; Videos 383
Automation Activity & Vendor Info: (Cataloging) Auto-Graphics, Inc; (Circulation) Auto-Graphics, Inc; (ILL) Innovative Interfaces, Inc - Millennium; (OPAC) Auto-Graphics, Inc
Wireless access
Function: Adult bk club, Bks on CD, Children's prog, Computers for patron use, ILL available, Online cat, OverDrive digital audio bks, Photocopying/Printing, Prog for children & young adult, Senior outreach, Spoken cassettes & CDs, Summer reading prog, Tax forms, Wheelchair accessible, Workshops
Mem of Woodlands Library Cooperative
Open Tues & Thurs 9-7, Wed 9-5, Fri & Sat 9-1
Friends of the Library Group

COMMERCE TOWNSHIP

P COMMERCE TOWNSHIP COMMUNITY LIBRARY*, 180 E Commerce, 48382. SAN 760-8241. Tel: 248-669-8108. FAX: 248-325-5047. Web Site: www.commercelibrary.info. *Libr Dir,* Connie Jo Ozinga; Tel: 248-669-8101, Ext 101, E-mail: cjozinga@commercelibrary.info; *Dir, Technology,* Ben Sebrowski; Tel: 248-669-8101, Ext 107, E-mail: bsebrowski@commercelibrary.info; *Head, Circ & Tech Serv,* Bill Wines; Tel: 248-669-8101, Ext 102, E-mail: bwines@commercelibrary.info; *Ad,* José Argandoña; Tel: 248-669-8101, Ext 110, E-mail: jargandona@commercelibrary.info; *Ad,* Dustin Brown; Tel: 248-669-8101, Ext 115, E-mail: dbrown@commercelibrary.info; *Teen Serv Librn,* Elizabeth Norton; Tel: 248-669-8101, Ext 109, E-mail: enorton@commercelibrary.info; *Youth Serv Librn,* Trista Reno; E-mail: treno@commercelibrary.info; *Youth Serv Librn,* Ashley Rosetto; E-mail: arosetto@commercelibrary.info; *Youth Serv Librn,* Amanda Vorce; Tel: 248-669-8101, Ext 112, E-mail: avorce@commercelibrary.info; *Adult Serv Mgr,* Marika Zemke; Tel: 248-669-8101, Ext 108, E-mail: mzemke@commercelibrary.info; *Youth & Teen Serv Mgr,* Trista Reno; Tel: 248-669-8101, Ext 106, E-mail: treno@commercelibrary.info; Staff 11 (MLS 11)
Pop 41,000
Wireless access
Function: 24/7 Electronic res, 24/7 Online cat, Activity rm, Adult bk club, Adult literacy prog, After school storytime, Art programs, Audiobks via web, AV serv, Bk club(s), Bks on CD, Children's prog, Computer training, Computers for patron use, Digital talking bks, Electronic databases & coll, Free DVD rentals, ILL available, Literacy & newcomer serv, Magazines, Mail & tel request accepted, Mango lang, Meeting rooms, Movies, Museum passes, Music CDs, Online cat, OverDrive digital audio bks, Photocopying/Printing, Preschool outreach, Preschool reading prog, Printer for laptops & handheld devices, Prog for adults, Prog for children & young adult, Ref & res, Ref serv available, Res assist avail, Scanner, Spoken cassettes & CDs, Spoken cassettes & DVDs, STEM programs, Story hour, Study rm, Summer & winter reading prog, Summer reading prog, Tax forms, Teen prog, Telephone ref, Wheelchair accessible, Winter reading prog, Workshops, Writing prog
Open Mon-Thurs 10-9, Fri & Sat 10-5, Sun 1-5
Friends of the Library Group

COMSTOCK

P COMSTOCK TOWNSHIP LIBRARY*, 6130 King Hwy, 49041. (Mail add: PO Box 25, 49041-0025), SAN 307-9619. Tel: 269-345-0136. FAX: 269-345-0138. E-mail: comstockreferencelibrarian@gmail.com. Web Site: www.comstocklibrary.org. *Dir,* Myla-Jean Stuart; *Ad,* Rachel Wiegmann; *Ref Librn,* Marian Veld; *Adult Serv,* Joey Ives; Staff 15 (MLS 7, Non-MLS 8)
Founded 1938. Pop 13,851; Circ 128,500
Library Holdings: Bk Titles 70,617; Bk Vols 78,643; Per Subs 125
Subject Interests: Local hist
Automation Activity & Vendor Info: (Cataloging) TLC (The Library Corporation); (Circulation) TLC (The Library Corporation); (ILL) Mel Cat; (OPAC) TLC (The Library Corporation); (Serials) TLC (The Library Corporation)
Wireless access
Function: Computers for patron use, Online cat, Photocopying/Printing, Preschool outreach, Prog for children & young adult, Ref serv available, Spoken cassettes & CDs, Spoken cassettes & DVDs, Story hour, Summer reading prog, Tax forms, Telephone ref, Wheelchair accessible
Partic in Southwest Michigan Library Cooperative
Open Mon-Thurs 9:30-8:30, Fri 10-6, Sat 10-4

COMSTOCK PARK

P KENT DISTRICT LIBRARY*, 814 West River Center Dr NE, 49321. SAN 346-5489. Tel: 616-784-2007. Administration Tel: 616-784-2016, Ext 2093. Automation Services Tel: 616-453-2575. Toll Free Tel: 877-243-2466. FAX: 616-647-3828. Web Site: www.kdl.org. *Dir,* Lance M Werner; E-mail: lwerner@kdl.org; Staff 192 (MLS 57, Non-MLS 135)
Founded 1927. Pop 395,660; Circ 5,586,894
Jan 2013-Dec 2013 Income (Main & Associated Libraries) $15,122,563. Mats Exp $2,237,436. Sal $7,848,869
Library Holdings: Braille Volumes 187; CDs 86,105; DVDs 63,022; e-books 10,853; Bk Vols 828,654; Per Subs 2,467
Subject Interests: Antiques, Careers, Collectibles, Health
Automation Activity & Vendor Info: (Acquisitions) Innovative Interfaces, Inc; (Cataloging) Innovative Interfaces, Inc; (Circulation) Innovative Interfaces, Inc; (OPAC) Innovative Interfaces, Inc
Wireless access
Publications: What's Next: Books in Series
Partic in Lakeland Library Cooperative
Special Services for the Blind - Audio mat; Bks & mags in Braille, on rec, tape & cassette; Braille equip; Descriptive video serv (DVS); Digital talking bk machines; Newsletter (in large print, Braille or on cassette)
Friends of the Library Group
Branches: 20
ALPINE TOWNSHIP BRANCH, 5255 Alpine Ave NW, 49321, SAN 346-5608. *Br Mgr,* Shaunna Martz; E-mail: smartz@kdl.org
Founded 1934. Pop 13,336; Circ 55,051
Open Mon & Wed 12-8, Tues & Thurs 9:30-5, Fri 12-5, Sat 9:30-1:30
Friends of the Library Group
ALTO BRANCH, 6071 Linfield Ave, Alto, 49302, SAN 346-5632. *Br Mgr,* Sandy Graham; E-mail: sgraham@kdl.org
Founded 1937. Pop 2,793; Circ 33,145
Open Mon & Sat 9:30-1:30, Tues & Wed 12-8, Thurs 1-6, Fri 9:30-6
Friends of the Library Group
BYRON TOWNSHIP BRANCH, 8191 Byron Center Ave SW, Byron Center, 49315, SAN 346-5667. *Br Mgr,* Eric DeHaan; E-mail: edehaan@kdl.org
Founded 1887. Pop 20,317; Circ 346,157
Open Mon-Wed 9:30-8, Thurs 12-8, Fri & Sat 9:30-5
CALEDONIA TOWNSHIP BRANCH, 6260 92nd St SE, Caledonia, 49316, SAN 346-5691. *Br Mgr,* Liz Guarino-Kozlowicz; E-mail: eguarino@kdl.org
Founded 1926. Pop 12,294; Circ 190,189
Subject Interests: Local hist
Open Mon 9:30-8, Tues & Thurs 12-8, Wed, Fri & Sat 9:30-5
Friends of the Library Group

CASCADE TOWNSHIP BRANCH, 2870 Jack Smith Ave SE, Grand Rapids, 49546, SAN 346-5721. *Br Mgr,* Vanesa Walstra; E-mail: vwalstra@kdl.org
Founded 1965. Pop 17,134; Circ 589,629
Open Mon-Thurs 9:30-8, Fri 9:30-6, Sat 9:30-5, Sun (Sept-May) 1-5
Friends of the Library Group
COMSTOCK PARK BRANCH, 3943 West River Dr NE, 49321, SAN 346-5756. *Br Mgr,* Nancy Mulder; E-mail: nmulder@kdl.org
Founded 1961. Pop 30,952; Circ 151,804
Open Mon 9:30-8, Tues & Thurs 12-8, Wed & Fri 9:30-5, Sat 1-5
EAST GRAND RAPIDS BRANCH, 746 Lakeside Dr SE, East Grand Rapids, 49506, SAN 346-5780. *Br Mgr,* Dawn Lewis; E-mail: dlewis@kdl.org
Founded 1959. Pop 10,694; Circ 451,306
Open Mon-Thurs 9:30-8, Fri 9:30-6, Sat 9:30-5, Sun (Sept-May) 1-5
Friends of the Library Group
ENGLEHARDT BRANCH, 200 N Monroe St, Lowell, 49331, SAN 346-5969. *Interim Mgr,* Sandra Graham; E-mail: sgraham@kdl.org
Founded 1878. Pop 3,783; Circ 182,055
Open Mon-Wed 12-8, Thurs-Sat 9:30-5
Friends of the Library Group
GAINES TOWNSHIP BRANCH, 421 68th St SE, Grand Rapids, 49548, SAN 346-5810. *Br Mgr,* Anjie Gleisner; E-mail: agleisner@kdl.org
Founded 1969. Pop 25,146; Circ 280,853
Open Mon, Tues & Thurs 9:30-8, Wed, Fri & Sat 9:30-5
Friends of the Library Group
GRANDVILLE BRANCH, 4055 Maple St SW, Grandville, 49418, SAN 346-5845. *Br Mgr,* Josh Bernstein; E-mail: jbernstein@kdl.org
Founded 1952. Pop 15,378; Circ 579,706
Open Mon-Thurs 9:30-8, Fri 9:30-6, Sat 9:30-5, Sun (Winter) 1-5
Friends of the Library Group
KELLOGGSVILLE BRANCH, Kelloggsville High School, 4787 Division Ave S, Grand Rapids, 49548. Web Site: www.kdl.org/locations/kelloggsville. *Br Mgr,* Lori Holland; E-mail: lholland@kdl.org
Open Tues-Thurs (Sept-May) 3-8, Sat 9:30-1:30; Mon, Wed, Fri & Sat (June-Aug) 9:30-1:30, Tues & Thurs Noon-8
KENTWOOD BRANCH, 4950 Breton SE, Kentwood, 49508, SAN 346-590X. *Br Mgr,* Cheryl Cammenga; E-mail: ccammenga@kdl.org
Founded 1955. Pop 48,707; Circ 547,211
Open Mon-Thurs 9:30-8, Fri 9:30-6, Sat 9:30-5, Sun (Sept-May) 1-5
Friends of the Library Group
KRAUSE MEMORIAL BRANCH, 140 E Bridge St, Rockford, 49341, SAN 346-5934. *Br Mgr,* Jennifer German; E-mail: jgerman@kdl.org
Founded 1937. Pop 5,719; Circ 395,196
Open Mon-Wed 9:30-8, Thurs 12-8, Fri & Sat 9:30-5
Friends of the Library Group
P LIBRARY FOR THE BLIND & PHYSICALLY HANDICAPPED, 3350 Michael Ave SW, Wyoming, 49509, SAN 346-5519. Tel: 616-647-3988. E-mail: lbphstaff@kdl.org. *Br Mgr,* Lori Holland; E-mail: lholland@kdl.org
Circ 47,315
Open Mon-Thurs 9:30-8, Fri 9:30-6, Sat 9:30-5, Sun (Sept-May) 1-5
NELSON TOWNSHIP/SAND LAKE BRANCH, 88 Eighth St, Sand Lake, 49343-9737, SAN 346-6027. *Br Mgr,* Paula Wright; E-mail: pwright@kdl.org
Founded 1920. Pop 4,764; Circ 96,605
Open Mon 9:30-8, Tues & Sat 9:30-5, Wed 12-8, Fri 9:30-6
Friends of the Library Group
PLAINFIELD TOWNSHIP BRANCH, 2650 Five Mile Rd NE, Grand Rapids, 49525, SAN 346-5993. *Br Mgr,* Kaitlin Tang; E-mail: ktang@kdl.org
Founded 1968. Pop 30,952; Circ 615,398
Open Mon-Thurs 9:30-8, Fri 9:30-6, Sat 9:30-5, Sun (Sept-May) 1-5
Friends of the Library Group
SPENCER TOWNSHIP BRANCH, 14960 Meddler Ave, Gowen, 49326, SAN 378-1615. *Br Mgr,* Kaitlin Tang
Founded 1998. Pop 3,960; Circ 44,888
Open Mon & Wed 9:30-5, Tues & Thurs 12-8, Fri 12-5, Sat 9:30-1:30
Friends of the Library Group
TYRONE TOWNSHIP BRANCH, 43 S Main St, Kent City, 49330, SAN 346-587X. *Br Mgr,* Liz Knapp; E-mail: lknapp@kdl.org
Founded 1935. Pop 4,731; Circ 46,295
Open Mon & Sat 9:30-1:30, Tues & Thurs 12-8, Wed 9:30-5, Fri 1-5
WALKER BRANCH, 4293 Remembrance Rd NW, Walker, 49534-7502, SAN 346-6051. *Br Mgr,* Craig Buno; E-mail: cbuno@kdl.org
Founded 1991. Pop 23,537; Circ 284,478
Open Mon-Thurs 9:30-8, Fri & Sat 9:30-5
Friends of the Library Group
WYOMING BRANCH, 3350 Michael Ave SW, Wyoming, 49509, SAN 346-6086. *Br Mgr,* Lori Holland
Founded 1940. Pop 72,125; Circ 597,746
Open Mon-Thurs 9:30-8, Fri 9:30-6, Sat 9:30-5, Sun (Sept-May) 1-5
Friends of the Library Group
Bookmobiles: 1

CONSTANTINE

P CONSTANTINE TOWNSHIP LIBRARY, 165 Canaris St, 49042-1015. SAN 307-9627. Tel: 269-435-7957. FAX: 269-435-5800. Web Site: www.constantine.michlibrary.org. *Dir,* Jane Moe; E-mail: jmoe@monroe.lib.mi.us; Staff 4 (Non-MLS 4)
Founded 1915. Pop 5,030; Circ 32,000
Library Holdings: AV Mats 700; Large Print Bks 150; Bk Vols 18,000; Per Subs 61; Talking Bks 350
Automation Activity & Vendor Info: (Circulation) AmLib Library Management System; (ILL) Auto-Graphics, Inc
Wireless access
Mem of Woodlands Library Cooperative
Open Mon & Wed-Fri 10-4, Tues & Thurs 10-6, Sat 10-3, Sun (Sept-May) 12-3

COOPERSVILLE

P COOPERSVILLE AREA DISTRICT LIBRARY, 333 Ottawa St, 49404-1243. SAN 307-9635. Tel: 616-837-6809. FAX: 616-837-7689. E-mail: coo@llcoop.org. Web Site: www.coopersvillelibrary.org. *Dir,* Elyshia Hoekstra; E-mail: cooeh@llcoop.org; Staff 3 (Non-MLS 3)
Founded 1915. Pop 11,862; Circ 91,528
Library Holdings: Bk Vols 36,537; Per Subs 72
Special Collections: Coopersville Observers 1880's-1970
Wireless access
Function: Adult bk club, Art exhibits, Audiobks via web, Bks on CD, CD-ROM, Children's prog, Computer training, Computers for patron use, Digital talking bks, Electronic databases & coll, Family literacy, Free DVD rentals, Holiday prog, ILL available, Magnifiers for reading, Mail & tel request accepted, Microfiche/film & reading machines, Music CDs, Online cat, OverDrive digital audio bks, Photocopying/Printing, Preschool outreach, Preschool reading prog, Prog for adults, Prog for children & young adult, Scanner, Senior computer classes, Spanish lang bks, Spoken cassettes & CDs, Spoken cassettes & DVDs, Story hour, Summer & winter reading prog, Summer reading prog, Tax forms, Teen prog, Visual arts prog, Wheelchair accessible, Winter reading prog
Partic in Lakeland Library Cooperative
Open Mon & Thurs 12-8, Tues, Wed & Fri 10-5:30, Sat 10-2
Friends of the Library Group

CORUNNA

P COMMUNITY DISTRICT LIBRARY*, Administration Office, 210 E Corunna Ave, 48817. SAN 346-1041. Tel: 989-743-3287. FAX: 989-743-5496. Web Site: www.mycdl.org. *Dir,* Jami Cromley; E-mail: director@mycdl.org; Staff 10 (MLS 1, Non-MLS 9)
Founded 2004. Pop 23,617; Circ 94,772
Library Holdings: Bk Vols 53,000
Special Collections: Corunna Journal 1887-1913
Automation Activity & Vendor Info: (Cataloging) Horizon; (Circulation) Horizon; (OPAC) Horizon
Wireless access
Partic in Midwest Collaborative for Library Services
Friends of the Library Group
Branches: 7
BANCROFT-SHIAWASSEE TOWNSHIP BRANCH, 625 Grand River Rd, Bancroft, 48414, SAN 346-1165. Tel: 989-634-5689. FAX: 989-634-5689. *Br Librn,* Kim Kennedy
Pop 18,298
Partic in Mideastern Michigan Library Cooperative
Open Mon & Wed 10-3, Tues & Thurs 10-7
Friends of the Library Group
BENTLEY MEMORIAL, 135 S Main St, Perry, 48872-0017, SAN 308-3373. Tel: 517-625-3166. FAX: 517-625-7214. E-mail: perry@mycdl.org. *Br Librn,* Carol Pavlica; *Libr Asst,* Tony Moore
Founded 1929. Pop 3,990; Circ 27,000
Library Holdings: AV Mats 847; Large Print Bks 469; Bk Vols 9,929; Per Subs 33; Talking Bks 300
Automation Activity & Vendor Info: (Cataloging) Follett Software; (Circulation) Follett Software; (OPAC) Follett Software
Partic in Mideastern Michigan Library Cooperative
Open Mon & Wed 12-8, Tues & Thurs 10-6, Fri 10-4, Sat 10-2
Friends of the Library Group
BYRON BRANCH, 312 W Maple St, Byron, 48418, SAN 377-6042. Tel: 810-266-4620, Ext 312. FAX: 810-266-5010. E-mail: byroncommlib@yahoo.com. *Br Librn,* Melissa Brown
Partic in Mideastern Mich Libr Coop
Open Mon-Wed 2-5
Friends of the Library Group
CORUNNA BRANCH, 210 E Corunna Ave, 48817, SAN 307-9643. Tel: 989-743-4800. FAX: 989-743-5502. E-mail: corunna@mycdl.org. *Br Librn,* Cathy Cramner; Staff 1 (MLS 1)
Founded 2004

Open Mon, Wed & Fri 10-5, Tues & Thurs 10-8, Sat 10-2
Friends of the Library Group
LENNON-VENICE TOWNSHIP, 11904 Lennon Rd, Lennon, 48449. (Mail add: PO Box 349, Lennon, 48449-0349), SAN 346-1106. Tel: 810-621-3202. FAX: 810-621-4896. *Br Libm,* Debbie Shaw
Open Mon & Wed 11-6, Tues & Thurs 11-5
MORRICE-PERRY TOWNSHIP, 300 Main St, Morrice, 48857, SAN 346-1130. Tel: 517-625-7911. FAX: 517-625-7911. *Br Librn,* Jeni Oliver
Open Mon & Tues 1-7, Wed & Fri 10-5
Friends of the Library Group
NEW LOTHROP-HAZELTON TOWNSHIP, 9387 Genesee St, New Lothrop, 48460. (Mail add: PO Box 279, New Lothrop, 48460-0279), SAN 346-1076. Tel: 810-638-7575. FAX: 810-638-2101. *Br Librn,* Elaine Prine
Open Mon & Wed (Winter) 1-7, Tues & Thurs 1-5; Tues (Summer) 2-7, Wed 10-6, Thurs 10-5

CROSWELL

P AITKIN MEMORIAL DISTRICT LIBRARY*, 111 N Howard Ave, 48422. SAN 307-9651. Tel: 810-679-3627. FAX: 810-679-3392. E-mail: aitkinlibrary@sbcglobal.net. Web Site: croswell-library.com. *Dir,* Marty Rheaume; Staff 4 (MLS 1, Non-MLS 3)
Founded 1911. Pop 7,333; Circ 39,000
Library Holdings: Bk Vols 39,396; Per Subs 77
Automation Activity & Vendor Info: (Circulation) Follett Software
Wireless access
Function: Bks on cassette, Bks on CD, Children's prog, Computer training, Computers for patron use, Homebound delivery serv, ILL available, Magnifiers for reading, Online cat, Photocopying/Printing, Prog for adults, Prog for children & young adult, Ref serv available, Story hour, Summer reading prog, Tax forms, Teen prog, VHS videos, Wheelchair accessible, Workshops
Partic in White Pine Library Cooperative
Open Mon-Thurs 10-7, Fri 10-5, Sat 10-2
Friends of the Library Group

CRYSTAL FALLS

P CRYSTAL FALLS DISTRICT COMMUNITY LIBRARY*, 237 Superior Ave, 49920-1331. SAN 307-966X. Tel: 906-875-3344. FAX: 906-874-0077. E-mail: cflib@uproc.lib.mi.us. Web Site: www.uproc.lib.mi.us/CrystalFalls. *Dir,* Mary J Thoreson
Founded 1955. Pop 3,453
Automation Activity & Vendor Info: (Cataloging) SirsiDynix; (Circulation) SirsiDynix
Wireless access
Partic in Superiorland Library Cooperative; Upper Peninsula Region of Library Cooperation, Inc
Open Mon-Thurs 9-7, Fri 9-4, Sat 9-1

DAVISBURG

P SPRINGFIELD TOWNSHIP LIBRARY*, 12000 Davisburg Rd, 48350. SAN 307-9678. Tel: 248-846-6550. FAX: 248-846-6555. Web Site: springfield.lib.mi.us. *Libr Dir,* Cathy Forst; E-mail: cforst@springfield.lib.mi.us; *Head, Circ,* Gretchen Mayville; E-mail: gmayville@springfield.lib.mi.us; *Head, Tech Serv,* Kathryn Kraepel; Tel: 248-846-6552, E-mail: kraepel@springfield.lib.mi.us; Staff 9 (MLS 4, Non-MLS 5)
Founded 1976. Pop 13,338
Library Holdings: Bk Vols 40,000; Per Subs 105
Automation Activity & Vendor Info: (Acquisitions) SirsiDynix; (Cataloging) SirsiDynix; (Circulation) SirsiDynix; (OPAC) SirsiDynix; (Serials) SirsiDynix
Wireless access
Function: 24/7 Electronic res, 24/7 Online cat, Activity rm, Adult bk club
Partic in The Library Network
Open Mon, Tues & Thurs 10-8, Wed 12-8, Fri 10-6, Sat 10-4
Friends of the Library Group

DEARBORN

M BEAUMONT HOSPITAL-DEARBORN MEDICAL LIBRARY*, 18101 Oakwood Blvd, 48124-2500. SAN 307-9732. Tel: 313-593-7685, E-mail: medlibrary@beaumont.org. Web Site: beaumont.libguides.com/dearborn. *Mgr,* Valerie L Reid; Tel: 313-593-7692, E-mail: valerie.reid@beaumont.org; *Librn,* Courtney Mandarino; Tel: 313-593-8652, E-mail: courtney.mandarino@beaumont.org; *ILL,* Sally J Castillo; Tel: 313-593-7687, E-mail: sally.castillo@beaumont.org; *Libr Tech,* Barbara Maynarich; E-mail: barbara.maynarich@beaumont.org; Staff 4 (MLS 2, Non-MLS 2)
Founded 1953
Library Holdings: AV Mats 500; CDs 200; DVDs 100; Bk Titles 5,500; Bk Vols 12,000; Per Subs 400
Special Collections: Consumer Health Coll, AV mats, bks, online info; Management Coll, AV, bks; Transcultural Resources Coll, AV mat, bks, govt doc, journals, teaching tools
Subject Interests: Clinical med, Health sci, Hospital admin, Nursing
Automation Activity & Vendor Info: (Cataloging) Sydney Enterprise; (Circulation) Sydney Enterprise; (ILL) OCLC WorldShare Interlibrary Loan; (OPAC) Sydney Enterprise
Wireless access
Partic in Michigan Health Sciences Libraries Association; Midwest Collaborative for Library Services
Open Mon-Fri 7:30-5
Restriction: Badge access after hrs

S DEARBORN HISTORICAL MUSEUM LIBRARY*, Dearborn Historical Museum, 915 Brady St, 48126. SAN 307-9708. Tel: 313-565-3000. FAX: 313-565-4848. Web Site: thedhm.com. *Curator,* Jack Tate; E-mail: jtate@ci.dearborn.mi.us; *Asst Curator, Chief,* Paul Talpos; E-mail: ptalpos@ci.dearborn.mi.us; *Archivist,* Mason Christensen; E-mail: mchristensen@ci.dearborn.mi.us; *Archivist,* Amanda Ford; E-mail: aford@ci.dearborn.mi.us; Staff 5 (Non-MLS 5)
Founded 1950
Library Holdings: Bk Titles 1,172; Bk Vols 2,556; Per Subs 10
Special Collections: Local Historical Records & Manuscripts
Publications: Dearborn Historian
Restriction: Non-circulating

P DEARBORN PUBLIC LIBRARY*, Henry Ford Centennial Library, 16301 Michigan Ave, 48126. SAN 346-1289. Tel: 313-943-2330. Administration Tel: 313-943-2037. FAX: 313-943-2853. Administration FAX: 313-943-3063. E-mail: library@ci.dearborn.mi.us. Web Site: www.dearbornlibrary.org. *Libr Dir,* Maryanne Bartles; Tel: 313-943-2049; *Dep Dir,* Julie Schaefer; Tel: 313-943-2338; *Admin Librn,* Steve Smith; Tel: 313-943-2812; *Br Serv Supvr,* James Knapp; Staff 29 (MLS 15, Non-MLS 14)
Founded 1919. Pop 98,153; Circ 874,771
Library Holdings: CDs 15,773; DVDs 25,949; Large Print Bks 2,731; Bk Vols 94,690; Talking Bks 6,141; Videos 6,060
Special Collections: City of Dearborn Coll; Ford Coll
Automation Activity & Vendor Info: (Acquisitions) SirsiDynix; (Cataloging) SirsiDynix; (Circulation) SirsiDynix; (OPAC) SirsiDynix
Wireless access
Open Mon-Thurs 9:30-8:30, Fri & Sat 9:30-5:30, Sun (Sept-May) 1-5
Friends of the Library Group
Branches: 2
BRYANT BRANCH LIBRARY, 22100 Michigan Ave, 48124, SAN 346-1319. Tel: 313-943-4091. FAX: 313-943-3099.
Library Holdings: Bk Vols 29,430
Open Mon & Tues 11-7, Wed, Thurs & Sat 11-5:30
Friends of the Library Group
ESPER BRANCH LIBRARY, 12929 W Warren, 48126, SAN 346-1343. Tel: 313-943-4096. FAX: 313-943-4097.
Library Holdings: Bk Vols 26,486
Open Mon & Tues 11-7, Wed, Thurs & Sat 11-5:30
Friends of the Library Group

S THE HENRY FORD, Benson Ford Research Center, 20900 Oakwood Blvd, 48124. (Mail add: PO Box 1970, 48121-1970), SAN 307-9716. Tel: 313-982-6020. FAX: 313-982-6244. E-mail: research.center@thehenryford.org. Web Site: www.thehenryford.org/collections-and-research/about. *Sr Mgr, Archives & Library,* Brian Wilson; Tel: 313-982-6100, Ext 2293, E-mail: brianw@thehenryford.org; Staff 15 (MLS 12, Non-MLS 3)
Founded 1929
Library Holdings: Bk Vols 45,000; Per Subs 200; Videos 380
Special Collections: Dave Friedman Racing Photogs; Detroit Publishing Company, archives, photogs; Edison Recording Artists; Ephemera Coll, trade lit; Fire Insurance Maps; Ford Motor Company Records; Gebelein Silversmiths; Henry & Clara Ford Papers; Henry Austin Clark Coll; HJ Heinz Co Records; Images Ford Motor Company; Industrial Design Coll; John Burroughs Papers; Stickley Furniture Co Records
Subject Interests: Hist, Mat culture
Automation Activity & Vendor Info: (Acquisitions) Ex Libris Group; (Cataloging) Ex Libris Group; (Circulation) Ex Libris Group; (Discovery) Ex Libris Group; (ILL) OCLC WorldShare Interlibrary Loan; (OPAC) Ex Libris Group; (Serials) Ex Libris Group
Wireless access
Function: 24/7 Online cat, Audio & video playback equip for onsite use, Bus archives, Computers for patron use, Electronic databases & coll, For res purposes, ILL available, Internet access, Magazines, Mail & tel request accepted, Microfiche/film & reading machines, Online cat, Online ref, Outside serv via phone, mail, e-mail & web, Photocopying/Printing, Ref & res, Res libr, Res performed for a fee
Partic in Detroit Area Library Network; Midwest Collaborative for Library Services; OCLC Online Computer Library Center, Inc; The Library Network

Open Mon-Fri 9-5
Restriction: Circulates for staff only, Closed stack, In-house use for visitors, Non-circulating to the pub

J HENRY FORD COLLEGE*, Eshleman Library, 5101 Evergreen Rd, 48128-1495. SAN 307-9724. Tel: 313-845-6375. Reference Tel: 313-845-6377. Information Services Tel: 313-845-9606. FAX: 313-845-9795. Web Site: library.hfcc.edu. *Dir, Academic Support, Libr Dir,* Kate Harger; Tel: 313-845-9760, E-mail: kharger@hfcc.edu; *Acq,* Pat Doline; Tel: 313-845-9762, E-mail: pdoline@hfcc.edu; *Cataloger, Govt Doc,* Vicki Morris; Tel: 313-845-9761, E-mail: vmorris@hfcc.edu; *Ref Serv,* Theresa Betts; Tel: 313-845-9763, E-mail: tbetts2@hfcc.edu; *Ser,* Clark Heath; Tel: 313-845-6518, E-mail: ceheath@hfcc.edu; *Syst Adminr,* Daniel Harrison; Tel: 313-845-6376, E-mail: dharrisn@hfcc.edu; Staff 6 (MLS 6)
Founded 1938. Enrl 12,525; Fac 216; Highest Degree: Bachelor
Library Holdings: Bk Titles 67,510; Bk Vols 130,000; Per Subs 590
Subject Interests: Law, Nursing, Performing arts
Automation Activity & Vendor Info: (Acquisitions) Innovative Interfaces, Inc - Sierra; (Cataloging) Innovative Interfaces, Inc - Sierra; (Circulation) Innovative Interfaces, Inc - Sierra; (Course Reserve) Innovative Interfaces, Inc - Sierra; (Discovery) Ex Libris Group
Wireless access
Open Mon-Thurs (Fall & Winter) 7:30-8:30, Fri 7:30-4, Sat 10-3; Mon-Thurs (Spring & Summer) 7:30-7

C UNIVERSITY OF MICHIGAN-DEARBORN*, Mardigian Library, 4901 Evergreen Rd, 48128-2406. SAN 307-9759. Tel: 313-593-5400. Circulation Tel: 313-593-5598. FAX: 313-593-5478. Reference FAX: 313-593-5561. E-mail: ask-the-mardigian@umich.edu. Web Site: library.umd.umich.edu. *Dir,* Maureen Linker; Tel: 313-593-5545, E-mail: mlinker@umich.edu; *Assoc Dir, Head, User Serv,* Holly Sorscher; Tel: 313-593-5695, E-mail: hrs@umich.edu; *Digital Initiatives Coordr, Head Archivist,* Julia Daniel Walkuski; Tel: 313-593-5615, E-mail: jcdaniel@umich.edu; *Head, Tech Serv,* Beth Taylor; Tel: 313-593-5402, E-mail: bjtaylor@umich.edu; *Asst Librn,* Nadine Anderson; Tel: 313-583-6324, E-mail: nfanders@umich.edu; *Librn,* Carla Brooks; Tel: 313-593-5616, E-mail: ctbrooks@umich.edu; *Cat Librn,* Barbara Bolek; Tel: 313-593-5401, E-mail: bbolek@umich.edu; *Cat Librn,* Lavada Smith; Tel: 313-593-3284, E-mail: lavadas@umich.edu; *Sci, Tech, Eng & Math Librn,* Joel Seewald; Tel: 313-583-6326, E-mail: seewaldj@umich.edu. Subject Specialists: *Behav sci, Psychol, Women's studies,* Nadine Anderson; *Educ, Health, Lit,* Carla Brooks; Staff 25 (MLS 12, Non-MLS 13)
Founded 1959
Jul 2012-Jun 2013 Income $2,498,755. Mats Exp $307,566, Books $154,126, Per/Ser (Incl. Access Fees) $121,000, AV Mat $4,914, Electronic Ref Mat (Incl. Access Fees) $25,023, Presv $2,503. Sal $1,358,555 (Prof $753,679)
Library Holdings: AV Mats 4,148; e-books 460,187; e-journals 70,458; Microforms 47,983; Bk Titles 265,531; Bk Vols 300,501; Per Subs 131; Videos 3,397
Special Collections: Juvenile Historic Coll; Voice/Vision Holocaust Survivor Oral History Archive
Automation Activity & Vendor Info: (Acquisitions) Innovative Interfaces, Inc; (Cataloging) Innovative Interfaces, Inc; (Circulation) Innovative Interfaces, Inc; (Course Reserve) Innovative Interfaces, Inc; (ILL) OCLC ILLiad; (Media Booking) Innovative Interfaces, Inc; (OPAC) Innovative Interfaces, Inc; (Serials) Innovative Interfaces, Inc
Wireless access
Publications: Occasional Bibliographic Series
Partic in OCLC Online Computer Library Center, Inc
Open Mon-Thurs 8am-11:45pm, Fri 8-8, Sat 10-6, Sun Noon-11:45 (Fall & Winter); Mon-Thurs 8am-9pm, Fri 8-6, Sat & Sun 12-6 (Summer)

DEARBORN HEIGHTS

DEARBORN HEIGHTS CITY LIBRARIES
CAROLINE KENNEDY LIBRARY*, 24590 George St, 48127, SAN 307-9767. Tel: 313-791-3800. Administration Tel: 313-791-3804. FAX: 313-791-3801. *Dir, Libr Serv,* Michael McCaffery; E-mail: mmccaffery@ci.dearborn-heights.mi.us; *Supv Librn,* Mary Howard; Tel: 313-791-3824, E-mail: mhoward@ci.dearborn-heights.mi.us; *Head, Circ,* Emily Kleszcz; Tel: 313-791-3805, E-mail: ekleszcz@ci.dearborn-heights.mi.us; Staff 5 (MLS 5)
Founded 1961. Pop 59,600; Circ 83,092
Library Holdings: Bk Vols 59,000; Per Subs 120
Automation Activity & Vendor Info: (Cataloging) SirsiDynix; (Circulation) SirsiDynix; (OPAC) SirsiDynix
Partic in The Library Network
Open Mon-Thurs 10-9, Fri & Sat 10-5, Sun 12-5
Friends of the Library Group
JOHN F KENNEDY JR LIBRARY*, 24602 Van Born Rd, 48125, SAN 307-9775. Tel: 313-791-6050. FAX: 313-791-6051. *Supv Librn,* Michael Wrona; Tel: 313-791-6053, E-mail: mwrona@ci.dearborn-heights.mi.us; *Head, Circ,* Janelle Martin; Tel: 313-791-6055, E-mail: jmartin@ci.dearborn-heights.mi.us; Staff 6.5 (MLS 1.5, Non-MLS 5)
Pop 59,600
Library Holdings: Bk Vols 55,000; Per Subs 120
Automation Activity & Vendor Info: (Cataloging) SirsiDynix; (Circulation) SirsiDynix; (OPAC) SirsiDynix
Open Mon-Thurs 12-8, Sat & Sun 12-5
Friends of the Library Group

DECATUR

P VAN BUREN DISTRICT LIBRARY*, Webster Memorial Library, 200 N Phelps St, 49045. SAN 346-1491. Tel: 269-423-4771. FAX: 269-423-8373. E-mail: info@bdl.org. Web Site: vbdl.org. *Dir,* Dan Hutchins; E-mail: dhutchins@vbdl.org; *Assoc Dir,* Molly Wunderlich; E-mail: mwundelich@vbdl.org; *Ch,* Emily Leestma; E-mail: eleestma@vbdl.org; *Local Hist Librn,* Amy Druskovich; E-mail: adruskovich@vbdl.org; *ILL,* Amber Blauer; E-mail: ablauer@vbdl.org; Staff 41 (MLS 3, Non-MLS 38)
Founded 1941. Pop 44,711; Circ 266,136
Library Holdings: AV Mats 7,290; e-books 11,000; Large Print Bks 4,404; Bk Vols 154,169; Per Subs 303; Talking Bks 4,719
Subject Interests: Civil War, Genealogy, Mich
Automation Activity & Vendor Info: (Cataloging) TLC (The Library Corporation); (Circulation) TLC (The Library Corporation)
Wireless access
Function: Wheelchair accessible
Open Mon-Thurs 9-8, Fri 9-5, Sat 9-3
Friends of the Library Group
Branches: 6
ANTWERP SUNSHINE BRANCH, 24823 Front Ave, Mattawan, 49071, SAN 346-167X. Tel: 269-668-2534. FAX: 269-668-5332. *Br Mgr,* Kayla Jellies; E-mail: kjellies@vbdl.org
Open Mon-Wed 10-7, Thurs & Fri 10-5, Sat 10-4
Friends of the Library Group
BANGOR BRANCH, 420 Division St, Bangor, 49013, SAN 346-1521. Tel: 269-427-8810. FAX: 269-427-0588. *Br Mgr,* Yvette Salomon; E-mail: ysalomon@vbdl.org
Open Mon-Wed 9-7, Thurs & Fri 9-5, Sat 9-2
Friends of the Library Group
BLOOMINGDALE BRANCH, 109 E Kalamazoo St, Bloomingdale, 49026. (Mail add: PO Box 218, Bloomingdale, 49026-0218), SAN 346-1556. Tel: 269-521-7601. FAX: 269-521-7614. *Br Mgr,* Cheryl Bull; E-mail: cbull@vbdl.org
Open Mon-Wed 10-7, Thurs & Fri 10-5, Sat 10-3
COVERT BRANCH, 33680 M-140 Hwy, Covert, 49043. (Mail add: PO Box 7, Covert, 49043-0007), SAN 346-1580. Tel: 269-764-1298. FAX: 269-764-0433. *Br Mgr,* Lois Brigham; E-mail: lbrigham@vbdl.org
Open Mon-Wed 10-7, Thurs 10-6, Fri 10-5, Sat 10-3
GOBLES BRANCH, 105 E Main St, Gobles, 49055. (Mail add: PO Box 247, Gobles, 49055-0247), SAN 346-1610. Tel: 269-628-4537. FAX: 269-628-0362. *Br Mgr,* Barb Insidioso; E-mail: binsidioso@vbdl.org
Open Mon-Wed 10-7, Thurs & Fri 10-5, Sat 10-3
Friends of the Library Group
LAWRENCE COMMUNITY, 212 N Paw Paw St, Lawrence, 49064. (Mail add: PO Box 186, Lawrence, 49064-0186), SAN 346-1645. Tel: 269-674-3200. FAX: 269-674-3704. *Br Mgr,* Anne Cox; E-mail: acox@vbdl.org
Open Mon-Wed 10-7, Thurs & Fri 10-5, Sat 10-3
Friends of the Library Group

DECKERVILLE

P DECKERVILLE PUBLIC LIBRARY*, 3542 N Main St, 48427. (Mail add: PO Box 8, 48427), SAN 307-9783. Tel: 810-376-8015. FAX: 810-376-8593. E-mail: deckervillelibrary@gmail.com. Web Site: deckerville.lib.mi.us. *Interim Dir,* Beth Schumacher
Founded 1924. Pop 4,908; Circ 106,279
Library Holdings: Bk Titles 18,793; Per Subs 80
Special Collections: Census of Sanilac County Cemeteries - Evergreen, Marion Twp, Mt Zion, Rosbury & Tucker; History of Sanilac County 1834-1984; Michigan Census Bk, 1904; Michigan Pioneer & Historical Coll (1881-1912); Sanilac County Atlas, 1906; Sanilac County Portrait & Biographical Album, 1884 & 1984
Automation Activity & Vendor Info: (Cataloging) Follett Software; (Circulation) Follett Software
Wireless access
Partic in White Pine Library Cooperative
Open Tues, Wed & Fri 10-7, Sat 10-1

DELTON

P DELTON DISTRICT LIBRARY*, 330 N Grove St, 49046. (Mail add: PO Box 155, 49046-0155), SAN 307-9791. Tel: 269-623-8040. FAX: 269-623-6740. E-mail: deltonlib@mei.net. Web Site: deltonlib.org. *Dir,* Cheryl Bower; Staff 7 (MLS 1, Non-MLS 6)
Founded 1974. Pop 13,000; Circ 70,000

Library Holdings: High Interest/Low Vocabulary Bk Vols 100; Large Print Bks 655; Bk Titles 30,000; Per Subs 30; Talking Bks 1,536; Videos 2,112
Special Collections: Tractor Manuals
Automation Activity & Vendor Info: (Cataloging) AmLib Library Management System; (Circulation) AmLib Library Management System; (ILL) Auto-Graphics, Inc
Wireless access
Function: Adult bk club, Art exhibits, CD-ROM, Computer training, Digital talking bks, Genealogy discussion group, ILL available, Internet access, Mail & tel request accepted, Outside serv via phone, mail, e-mail & web, Photocopying/Printing, Preschool outreach, Prog for adults, Prog for children & young adult, Spoken cassettes & CDs, Spoken cassettes & DVDs, Summer reading prog, Tax forms, Telephone ref, VHS videos, Wheelchair accessible
Mem of Woodlands Library Cooperative
Open Mon, Wed & Fri 9-5, Tues & Thurs 9-6, Sat 9-1
Friends of the Library Group

DETROIT

M ASCENSION SAINT JOHN HOSPITAL & MEDICAL CENTER LIBRARY*, 22101 Moross Rd, 48236. SAN 308-0358. Tel: 313-343-3733. FAX: 313-417-0538. E-mail: sjhmedicallibrary@ascension.org. Web Site: healthcare.ascension.org. *Med Librn,* Deborah Cicchini; E-mail: deborah.cicchini@ascension.org; Staff 3 (MLS 1, Non-MLS 2)
Founded 1952
Library Holdings: Bk Titles 2,500; Per Subs 320
Subject Interests: Hospital admin, Med, Nursing

L BODMAN PLC LAW LIBRARY*, Ford Field, 6th Flr, 1901 Saint Antoine St, 48226. SAN 372-2902. Tel: 313-259-7777. FAX: 313-393-7579. Web Site: www.bodmanlaw.com.
Founded 1927
Library Holdings: Bk Vols 10,000; Per Subs 15
Function: ILL available
Restriction: Staff use only

CHILDREN'S HOSPITAL OF MICHIGAN

M PHYLLIS ANN COLBURN MEMORIAL FAMILY LIBRARY*, 3901 Beaubien Blvd, 5th Flr, 48201. Tel: 313-745-5653. FAX: 313-993-0148. E-mail: cmedical@dmc.org. *Librn,* Patricia Supnick; Tel: 313-745-5437, E-mail: psupnick@dmc.org
Library Holdings: AV Mats 100; Bk Titles 1,000
Open Mon-Fri 9:30-4

M MEDICAL LIBRARY*, 3901 Beaubien Blvd, 1st Flr, 48201. SAN 307-9899. Tel: 313-745-0252, 313-745-5322. Toll Free Tel: 888-362-2500. E-mail: cmedical@dmc.org. Web Site: www.childrensdmc.org. *Head Librn,* Cathy Eames; *Librn,* Misa Mi; E-mail: mmi@dmc.org
Library Holdings: Bk Vols 3,300; Per Subs 200
Subject Interests: Pediatrics
Automation Activity & Vendor Info: (Cataloging) SirsiDynix; (Circulation) SirsiDynix; (OPAC) SirsiDynix
Open Mon-Thurs 8-7, Fri 8-6, Sat 9-1

L CLARK HILL PLC*, Law Library, 500 Woodward Ave, Ste 3500, 48226-3435. SAN 326-3851. Tel: 313-965-8277. FAX: 313-309-6977. *Librn,* Kathleen A Gamache; E-mail: kgamache@clarkhill.com; Staff 2 (MLS 2)
Wireless access

C COLLEGE FOR CREATIVE STUDIES LIBRARY, Manoogian Visual Resource Ctr, 301 Frederick Douglass Dr, 48202-4034. SAN 307-9880. Tel: 313-664-7642. FAX: 313-664-7880. Web Site: libguides.collegeforcreativestudies.edu/home, www.collegeforcreativestudies.edu/life-at-ccs/resources/library. *Dir,* Pad Becca; Tel: 313-664-7641, E-mail: rpad@collegeforcreativestudies.edu; Staff 6 (MLS 4, Non-MLS 2)
Founded 1966. Enrl 1,406; Highest Degree: Master
Library Holdings: e-books 150,000; Bk Titles 60,000; Bk Vols 63,000; Per Subs 303; Videos 3,200
Subject Interests: Animation, Applied arts, Fine arts, Graphic design, Photog
Automation Activity & Vendor Info: (Cataloging) Koha; (OPAC) Koha
Partic in Association of Independent Colleges of Art & Design; Midwest Collaborative for Library Services
Open Mon-Thurs 8am-10pm, Fri 8-6, Sat 10-5, Sun 1-8
Restriction: Open to pub for ref & circ; with some limitations

GM DEPARTMENT OF VETERANS AFFAIRS LIBRARY SERVICE*, John D Dingell VA Medical Center, 4646 John R St, 48201. SAN 307-8566. Tel: 313-576-1000, Ext 63380. FAX: 313-576-1048. *Med Librn,* Position Currently Open
Library Holdings: Bk Titles 5,000; Per Subs 250
Automation Activity & Vendor Info: (Cataloging) Horizon; (Circulation) Horizon; (OPAC) Horizon; (Serials) Horizon
Partic in Detroit Area Library Network
Open Mon-Fri 7:30-4

S DETROIT GARDEN CENTER, INC LIBRARY*, 1900 E Jefferson Ave, Ste 227, 48207. SAN 324-1017. Tel: 313-259-6363. E-mail: detroitgardenctr@yahoo.com. *Pres,* Ronald J Smith
Library Holdings: Bk Titles 4,000
Subject Interests: Hort
Wireless access
Function: Photocopying/Printing, Telephone ref
Publications: Detroit Garden Center Bulletin
Restriction: Circ to mem only, Non-circulating to the pub, Open by appt only, Open to pub for ref only

S DETROIT INSTITUTE OF ARTS*, Research Library & Archives, 5200 Woodward Ave, 48202. SAN 308-0005. Tel: 313-833-3460. Administration Tel: 313-833-7929. FAX: 313-833-6405. E-mail: libraryadmin@dia.org. Web Site: www.dia.org/art/research-library. *Dept Head,* Maria Ketcham; E-mail: mketcham@dia.org; Staff 5 (MLS 1, Non-MLS 4)
Founded 1905
Library Holdings: Bk Vols 180,000; Per Subs 200
Special Collections: Albert Kahn Architecture Library; Grace Whitney Hoff Coll, fine bindings; Puppetry (Paul McPharlin Coll)
Subject Interests: Art, Art hist, Conserv, Decorative art, Films & filmmaking, Furniture, Paintings, Sculpture
Automation Activity & Vendor Info: (Cataloging) OCLC Connexion; (OPAC) Horizon
Partic in Detroit Area Library Network; Midwest Collaborative for Library Services; OCLC Online Computer Library Center, Inc
Restriction: Open by appt only

P DETROIT PUBLIC LIBRARY*, 5201 Woodward Ave, 48202. SAN 346-1769. Tel: 313-481-1300. Circulation Tel: 313-481-1376. Interlibrary Loan Service Tel: 313-481-1378. Circulation FAX: 313-833-5333. E-mail: main@detroitpubliclibrary.org. Web Site: www.detroitpubliclibrary.org. *Exec Dir,* Jo Anne G Mondowney; E-mail: dir@detroitpubliclibrary.org; Staff 298 (MLS 88, Non-MLS 210)
Founded 1865. Pop 713,777; Circ 1,102,902
Jul 2016-Jun 2017 Income (Main & Associated Libraries) $33,238,585. Mats Exp $1,543,946. Sal $11,654,699
Special Collections: Burton Historical Coll (Genealogy); E Azalia Hackley Coll (African Americans & Africans in the performing arts); Ernie Harwell Sports Coll; National Automotive History Coll (History of automobile). Municipal Document Depository
Subject Interests: Archit, Art, Bus & mgt, Econ, Ethnic studies, Hist, Maps, Music, Natural sci, Soc sci, Tech
Automation Activity & Vendor Info: (Cataloging) SirsiDynix; (Circulation) SirsiDynix; (OPAC) SirsiDynix
Wireless access
Function: 24/7 Electronic res, 24/7 Online cat, 3D Printer, Activity rm, Adult bk club, Adult literacy prog, After school storytime, Archival coll, Art exhibits, BA reader (adult literacy), Bk club(s), Bks on cassette, Bks on CD, Bus archives, CD-ROM, Children's prog, Computer training, Computers for patron use, Digital talking bks, Electronic databases & coll, Family literacy, For res purposes, Games & aids for people with disabilities, Genealogy discussion group, Govt ref serv, Health sci info serv, Holiday prog, Home delivery & serv to seniorr ctr & nursing homes, Homebound delivery serv, Homework prog, ILL available, Instruction & testing, Internet access, Jazz prog, Life-long learning prog for all ages, Literacy & newcomer serv, Magazines, Magnifiers for reading, Makerspace, Meeting rooms, Microfiche/film & reading machines, Movies, Museum passes, Music CDs, Online cat, Online ref, Outreach serv, Outside serv via phone, mail, e-mail & web, OverDrive digital audio bks, Photocopying/Printing, Preschool outreach, Preschool reading prog, Printer for laptops & handheld devices, Prog for adults, Prog for children & young adult, Ref & res, Ref serv available, Res assist avail, Res libr, Senior computer classes, Spanish lang bks, Spoken cassettes & CDs, Spoken cassettes & DVDs, STEM programs, Story hour, Study rm, Summer & winter reading prog, Summer reading prog, Tax forms, Teen prog, Telephone ref, Visual arts prog, Wheelchair accessible, Winter reading prog, Workshops, Writing prog
Special Services for the Deaf - Staff with knowledge of sign lang; TTY equip
Special Services for the Blind - Assistive/Adapted tech devices, equip & products
Open Tues & Wed Noon-8, Thurs-Sat 10-6, Sun (Oct-May) 1-5
Friends of the Library Group
Branches: 22
BOWEN, 3648 Vernor Hwy, 48216-1441, SAN 346-1823. Tel: 313-481-1540. E-mail: bowen@detroitpubliclibrary.org. Web Site: detroitpubliclibrary.org/locations/bowen.
Subject Interests: Spanish lang mat

Open Mon, Wed & Sat 10-6, Tues & Thurs 12-8
Friends of the Library Group
CAMPBELL BRANCH, 8733 W Vernor Hwy, 48209-1434. Tel: 313-481-1550. E-mail: campbell@detroitpubliclibrary.org. Web Site: detroitpubliclibrary.org/locations/campbell.
Open Mon & Wed 12-8, Tues, Thurs & Sat 10-6
CHANDLER PARK, 12800 Harper Ave, 48213-1823, SAN 346-1912. Tel: 313-481-1560. E-mail: chandlerpark@detroitpubliclibrary.org. Web Site: detroitpubliclibrary.org/locations/chandler.
Open Wed & Sat 10-6, Thurs 12-8
Friends of the Library Group
CHANEY, 16101 Grand River, 48227-1821, SAN 346-1947. Tel: 313-481-1570. E-mail: chaney@detroitpubliclibrary.org. Web Site: detroitpubliclibrary.org/locations/chaney.
Open Mon, Wed & Sat 10-6, Tues & Thurs 12-8
Friends of the Library Group
CHASE, 17731 W Seven Mile Rd, 48235-3050, SAN 346-1971. Tel: 313-481-1580. E-mail: chase@detroitpubliclibrary.org. Web Site: detroitpubliclibrary.org/locations/chase.
Open Mon, Wed & Sat 10-6, Tues & Thurs 12-8
Friends of the Library Group
CONELY, 4600 Martin St, 48210-2343, SAN 346-2005. Tel: 313-481-1590. E-mail: conely@detroitpubliclibrary.org. Web Site: detroitpubliclibrary.org/locations/conely.
Open Mon, Wed & Sat 10-6, Tues & Thurs 12-8
Friends of the Library Group

P DETROIT SUBREGIONAL LIBRARY FOR THE BLIND & PHYSICALLY HANDICAPPED, 3666 Grand River Ave, 48208-2880, SAN 346-1777. Tel: 313-481-1701. FAX: 313-833-4941. TDD: 313-831-3779. Web Site: detroitpubliclibrary.org/services/lbph.
Founded 1980
Subject Interests: Braille
Publications: In-Focus (Newsletter)
Special Services for the Deaf - TTY equip
Special Services for the Blind - Assistive/Adapted tech devices, equip & products; Audio mat; Bks & mags in Braille, on rec, tape & cassette; Bks on cassette; Bks on CD; Braille servs; Extensive large print coll; Large print bks; Ref serv
Open Mon-Fri 8-4
Friends of the Library Group
FREDERICK DOUGLASS BRANCH FOR SPECIALIZED SERVICES, 3666 Grand River, 48208-2880, SAN 346-203X. Tel: 313-481-1707. E-mail: douglas@detroitpubliclibrary.org. Web Site: detroitpubliclibrary.org/locations/douglass.
Subject Interests: Children's bks
Open Mon-Fri 10-6
Friends of the Library Group
DUFFIELD, 2507 W Grand Blvd, 48208-1236, SAN 346-2099. Tel: 313-481-1710. E-mail: duffield@detroitpublibrary.org. Web Site: detroitpubliclibrary.org/locations/duffield.
Open Mon, Wed & Sat 10-6, Tues & Thurs 12-8
Friends of the Library Group
EDISON, 18400 Joy Rd, 48228-3131, SAN 346-2129. Tel: 313-481-1720. E-mail: edison@detroitpubliclibrary.org. Web Site: detroitpubliclibrary.org/locations/edison.
Open Mon & Wed 12-8, Tues, Thurs & Sat 10-6
Friends of the Library Group
ELMWOOD PARK, 550 Chene St, 48207, SAN 346-2153. Tel: 313-481-1730. E-mail: elmwood@detroitpubliclibrary.org. Web Site: detroitpubliclibrary.org/locations/elmwood.
Open Mon, Wed & Sat 10-6, Tues & Thurs 12-8
Friends of the Library Group
FRANKLIN, 13651 E McNichols Rd, 48205-3457, SAN 346-2188. Tel: 313-481-1740. E-mail: franklin@detroitpubliclibrary.org. Web Site: detroitpubliclibrary.org/locations/franklin.
Open Mon, Wed & Sat 10-6, Tues & Thurs 12-8
Friends of the Library Group
HUBBARD, 12929 W McNichols Rd, 48235-4106, SAN 346-2242. Tel: 313-481-1750. E-mail: hubbard@detroitpubliclibrary.org. Web Site: detroitpubliclibrary.org/locations/hubbard.
Open Mon & Wed 12-8, Tues, Thurs & Sat 10-6
Friends of the Library Group
JEFFERSON, 12350 E Outer Dr, 48224, SAN 346-2277. Tel: 313-481-1760. E-mail: jefferson@detroitpubliclibrary.org. Web Site: detroitpubliclibrary.org/locations/jefferson.
Closed for renovation 2020-
Friends of the Library Group
KNAPP, 13330 Conant St, 48212, SAN 346-2307. Tel: 313-481-1770. E-mail: knapp@detroitpubliclibrary.org. Web Site: detroitpubliclibrary.org/locations/knapp.
Open Mon & Wed 12-8, Tues, Thurs & Sat 10-6
Friends of the Library Group
LINCOLN, 1221 E Seven Mile Rd, 48203-2103, SAN 346-2331. Tel: 313-481-1780. E-mail: lincoln@detroitpubliclibrary.org. Web Site: detroitpubliclibrary.org/locations/lincoln.
Open Mon 12-8, Tues & Sat 10-6
Friends of the Library Group
MONTEITH, 14100 Kercheval St, 48215-2810, SAN 346-2420. Tel: 313-481-1800. E-mail: monteith@detroitpubliclibrary.org. Web Site: detroitpubliclibrary.org/locations/monteith.
Open Mon 12-8, Tues 10-6
Friends of the Library Group
PARKMAN, 1766 Oakman Blvd, 48238-2735, SAN 346-2455. Tel: 313-481-1810. E-mail: parkman@detroitpubliclibrary.org. Web Site: detroitpubliclibrary.org/locations/parkman.
Open Mon & Wed Noon-8, Tues, Thurs & Sat 10-6
Friends of the Library Group
REDFORD, 21200 Grand River/W McNichols, 48219-3851, SAN 346-248X. Tel: 313-481-1820. E-mail: redford@detroitpubliclibrary.org. Web Site: detroitpubliclibrary.org/locations/redford.
Open Mon & Wed 12-8, Tues, Thurs & Sat 10-6, Sun (Oct-May) 1-5
Friends of the Library Group
SHERWOOD FOREST, 7117 W Seven Mile Rd, 48221-2240, SAN 346-2544. Tel: 313-481-1840. E-mail: sherwoodforest@detroitpubliclibrary.org. Web Site: detroitpubliclibrary.org/locations/sherwood.
Open Mon, Wed & Sat 10-6, Tues & Thurs 12-8
Friends of the Library Group
SKILLMAN, 121 Gratiot Ave, 48226-2203, SAN 346-2064. Tel: 313-481-1850. E-mail: skillman@detroitpubliclibrary.org. Web Site: detroitpubliclibrary.org/locations/skillman.
Special Collections: National Automotive History Coll
Open Mon-Thurs & Sat 10-6
Friends of the Library Group
WILDER, 7140 E Seven Mile Rd, 48234-3065, SAN 346-2579. Tel: 313-481-1870. E-mail: wilder@detroitpubliclibrary.org. Web Site: detroitpubliclibrary.org/locations/wilder.
Open Mon & Wed 12-8, Tues, Thurs, Fri & Sat 10-6, Sun (Oct-May) 1-5
Friends of the Library Group
Bookmobiles: 1

S DETROIT SYMPHONY ORCHESTRA LIBRARY*, 3711 Woodward Ave, 48201. SAN 329-8876. Tel: 313-576-5171. FAX: 313-576-5101. Web Site: www.dso.org. *Principal Librn,* Robert Stiles; Tel: 313-576-5172, E-mail: rstiles@dso.org; *Librn,* Ethan Allen; E-mail: eallen@dso.org
Library Holdings: Music Scores 5,000; Bk Vols 200
Special Collections: Rare Scores
Restriction: Not a lending libr, Not open to pub

L DICKINSON WRIGHT PLLC LIBRARY*, 500 Woodward Ave, Ste 4000, 48226-3425. SAN 308-0048. Tel: 313-223-3500. FAX: 313-223-3598. Web Site: www.dickinson-wright.com. *Head Librn,* Mark A Heinrich; E-mail: mheinrich@dickinson-wright.com; *Tech Serv,* Carol M Darga; Staff 2 (MLS 2)
Founded 1878
Library Holdings: Bk Vols 25,000; Per Subs 4,000
Subject Interests: Law
Automation Activity & Vendor Info: (Cataloging) EOS International; (OPAC) EOS International; (Serials) EOS International
Wireless access
Publications: Current Awareness Bulletin; Library Guide; Research Guides (Biannually)
Partic in Dun & Bradstreet Info Servs; OCLC Online Computer Library Center, Inc
Restriction: Staff use only

S DOSSIN GREAT LAKES MUSEUM, 100 Strand Dr on Belle Isle, 48207. SAN 327-0289. Tel: 313-821-2661, 313-833-1805. FAX: 313-833-5342. Web Site: www.detroithistorical.org. *Dir, Exhibitions & Coll,* Tracy Irwin; E-mail: tracyi@detroithistorical.org
Founded 1960
Library Holdings: Bk Vols 1,000
Special Collections: Great Lakes Coll
Restriction: Open to staff only

M HENRY FORD HOSPITAL*, Sladen Library, 2799 W Grand Blvd, 48202. SAN 308-0080. Tel: 313-916-2550. FAX: 313-874-4730. E-mail: sladen@hfhs.org. Web Site: henryford.libguides.com/sladen. *Archives Dir, Syst Dir of Libr,* Gayle Williams; E-mail: gwillia3@hfhs.org; Staff 8.4 (MLS 6.4, Non-MLS 2)
Founded 1915
Library Holdings: e-journals 1,773; Bk Vols 7,726; Per Subs 1,060
Special Collections: Archives of Henry Ford Health System; Medical History Coll
Subject Interests: Hospital admin, Med, Nursing

Automation Activity & Vendor Info: (Acquisitions) SirsiDynix; (Cataloging) SirsiDynix; (Circulation) SirsiDynix; (ILL) OCLC ILLiad; (OPAC) SirsiDynix; (Serials) SirsiDynix
Wireless access
Partic in Midwest Collaborative for Library Services; OCLC Online Computer Library Center, Inc
Open Mon-Thurs 8:30-7:30, Fri 8-5

GL RALPH M FREEMAN MEMORIAL LIBRARY FOR THE US COURTS, 436 US Courthouse, 231 W Lafayette Blvd, 48226-2719. SAN 308-0420. Tel: 313-234-5255. FAX: 313-234-5383. *Satellite Librn,* Elise Keller; E-mail: elise_keller@ca6.uscourts.gov; Staff 2 (MLS 1, Non-MLS 1)
Founded 1975
Subject Interests: Law
Partic in OCLC Online Computer Library Center, Inc

L HONIGMAN MILLER SCHWARTZ & COHN LLP*, Law Library, 2290 First National Bldg, 660 Woodward Ave, 48226-3583. SAN 321-8090. Tel: 313-465-7169. FAX: 313-465-8000. *Mgr,* Leanna R Simon; E-mail: lsimon@honigman.com
Library Holdings: Bk Titles 8,000; Bk Vols 15,000; Per Subs 350
Wireless access
Restriction: Staff use only

C MARYGROVE COLLEGE*, Nancy A McDonough Geschke Library, 8425 W McNichols Rd, 48221-2599. SAN 308-0188. Tel: 313-927-1355. Reference Tel: 313-927-1346. Web Site: www.marygrove.edu/library. *Dir, Libr Serv,* Mary Kickhan-Samy; Tel: 313-927-1344, E-mail: mkickham@marygrove.edu; *Head, Tech Serv,* Crystal Agnew; Tel: 313-927-1340, E-mail: cagnew@marygrove.edu; *Tech Asst,* Esther Jefferson; Tel: 313-927-1377, E-mail: ejeffers@marygrove.edu; Staff 12 (MLS 7, Non-MLS 5)
Founded 1927. Enrl 5,600; Highest Degree: Master
Library Holdings: Bk Titles 82,350; Bk Vols 99,000; Per Subs 450
Wireless access
Partic in Detroit Area Library Network; Midwest Collaborative for Library Services; Southeastern Michigan League of Libraries

L MILLER CANFIELD PADDOCK & STONE LIBRARY, PLC*, 150 W Jefferson, Ste 2500, 48226. SAN 327-0424. Tel: 313-963-6420. FAX: 313-496-8452. Web Site: millercanfield.com. *Dir, Libr Serv,* Catherine Mulla; E-mail: mulla@millercanfield.com; Staff 3 (MLS 2, Non-MLS 1)
Library Holdings: Per Subs 100
Subject Interests: Educ, Labor, Real estate, Securities
Wireless access

S PRICE WATERHOUSE COOPERS LLP*, Information Center, 500 Woodward Ave, 48226. SAN 308-0293. Tel: 313-394-6000. FAX: 313-394-6010. Web Site: www.pwc.com. *Info Spec,* John Monoco
Founded 1975
Library Holdings: Bk Titles 500; Per Subs 50
Subject Interests: Acctg, Taxes
Publications: Booklets on Tax, Accounting & Auditing
Partic in Proquest Dialog

R SACRED HEART MAJOR SEMINARY*, Cardinal Edmund Szoka Library, 2701 Chicago Blvd, 48206. SAN 323-5793. Tel: 313-883-8650. Interlibrary Loan Service Tel: 313-883-8654. Web Site: www.shms.edu/content/cardinal-szoka-library. *Dir,* Chris Spilker; Tel: 313-883-8651, E-mail: spilker.chris@shms.edu. Subject Specialists: *Theol,* Chris Spilker; Staff 6 (MLS 1, Non-MLS 5)
Founded 1921. Enrl 590; Fac 65; Highest Degree: Master
Library Holdings: Bk Titles 120,000; Bk Vols 122,800; Per Subs 500
Special Collections: Church History; Early Michigan (Gabriel Richard Coll), bks, ms
Subject Interests: Philos, Theol
Automation Activity & Vendor Info: (Cataloging) SirsiDynix; (Circulation) SirsiDynix; (OPAC) SirsiDynix; (Serials) SirsiDynix
Wireless access
Publications: Accessions Lists; Brochure; Straight From the Heart (Newsletter)
Open Mon-Fri 8:30-4:30
Restriction: Circ limited

L THIRD JUDICIAL CIRCUIT COURT, WAYNE COUNTY, OFFICE OF THE GENERAL COUNSEL*, Law Library, Coleman A Young Municipal Ctr, Two Woodward Ave, Ste 780, 48226-3461. SAN 308-0455. Tel: 313-224-5265. FAX: 313-967-3562. *Dep Law Librn,* Lynn Reeves; E-mail: Lynn.Reeves@3rdcc.org
Library Holdings: Bk Vols 20,000
Wireless access
Partic in Mich Asn of Law Librs; Ohio Regional Asn of Law Librs

CR UNIVERSITY OF DETROIT MERCY LIBRARIES, McNichols Campus, 4001 W McNichols Rd, 48221-3038. SAN 346-3087. Tel: 313-993-1071. Circulation Tel: 313-993-1795. Administration Tel: 313-993-1090. E-mail: refdesk@udmercy.edu. Web Site: libraries.udmercy.edu. *Dean, Univ Librs & Instrul Tech,* Jennifer Dean; E-mail: deanjl@udmercy.edu; *Assoc Dean, Instrul Tech,* Russell Davidson, III; Tel: 313-993-1129, E-mail: davidsor@udmercy.edu; *Assoc Dean, Pub Serv,* George H Libbey; Tel: 313-993-1078, E-mail: libbeygh@udmercy.edu; *Assoc Dean, Tech Serv & Libr Syst,* Sara Armstrong; Tel: 313-993-1074, E-mail: armstrsj1@udmercy.edu; *Head, Circulation & User Servs,* Megan E Novell; Tel: 313-993-1070, E-mail: novellme@udmercy.edu; *Archive Collection Mgmt, Assoc Librn,* Patricia Higo; Tel: 313-578-0435, E-mail: higopa@udmercy.edu; *Assoc Librn, Cataloging & Database Mgmt,* Kris McLonis; Tel: 313-578-0457, E-mail: mclonika@udmercy.edu; *Assoc Librn, Reference Services,* Sandra Wilson; Tel: 313-578-0577, E-mail: wilsonsh@udmercy.edu; *ILL Tech,* Katherine Miller; Tel: 313-993-1072, E-mail: millerk1@udmercy.edu; *Libr Tech,* Joshua D Duffy; Tel: 313-993-1073, 313-993-7148, E-mail: duffyjo@udmercy.edu; *Libr Tech,* Laureen Ilasenko; Tel: 313-993-1130, E-mail: ilasenla@udmercy.edu; Staff 28 (MLS 14, Non-MLS 14)
Founded 1877. Enrl 5,231; Fac 654; Highest Degree: Doctorate
Jul 2012-Jun 2013 Income (Main Library Only) $3,448,200, Locally Generated Income $16,837, Parent Institution $3,409,178, Other $22,185. Mats Exp $968,319, Books $145,724, Per/Ser (Incl. Access Fees) $798,526, AV Mat $8,797, Electronic Ref Mat (Incl. Access Fees) $11,329, Presv $3,943. Sal $1,630,477 (Prof $1,140,259)
Library Holdings: Audiobooks 441; AV Mats 2,940; CDs 2,734; DVDs 4,328; e-books 114,417; e-journals 41,952; Microforms 10,833; Bk Titles 378,666; Per Subs 200
Special Collections: Black Abolitionist Archives, digital; Carney Latin American Solidarity Archive, print; Celebrating Scholarly Achievement Coll, digital; Dichotomy: School of Architecture Student Journal, digital; Dudley Randall Broadside Press Coll, print; Father Charles E Coughlin Coll, digital; Father Edward J Dowling Marine Historical Coll, digital, print; Lawrence DeVine Playbill Coll, print; Marie Corelli Coll, print; Maurice Greenia Jr Coll, digital; Sisters of Mercy Coll, digital; Society of Jesus Publs, print; Student Arts Journal, digital; Theses, digital, print; University Archives, AV mats, publs, rec; University Commencement Coll; University Honors Coll, digital; University of Detroit Football Coll, digital; University of Detroit Yearbook Coll, digital; William Kienzle Manuscripts, print. US Document Depository
Subject Interests: Archit, Philos, Theol
Automation Activity & Vendor Info: (Cataloging) Ex Libris Group; (ILL) OCLC; (OPAC) Ex Libris Group
Wireless access
Function: Archival coll, Art exhibits, Bks on CD, Computers for patron use, Distance learning, Doc delivery serv, Electronic databases & coll, Free DVD rentals, ILL available, Online cat, Online info literacy tutorials on the web & in blackboard, Online ref, Orientations, Photocopying/Printing, Ref & res, Ref serv available, Scanner, Telephone ref, Wheelchair accessible
Publications: User Guide
Partic in Association of Jesuit Colleges & Universities; Detroit Area Consortium of Catholic Colleges; Detroit Area Library Network; Michigan Health Sciences Libraries Association; Midwest Collaborative for Library Services
Open Mon-Thurs 8-8, Fri 8-5
Restriction: Access for corporate affiliates

Departmental Libraries:

SCHOOL OF DENTISTRY, CORKTOWN CAMPUS, 2700 Martin Luther King Jr Blvd, 48208-2576. Tel: 313-494-6900. Administration Tel: 313-494-6905. FAX: 313-494-6838. Web Site: libraries.udmercy.edu/dental. *Dir,* Marilyn Dow; E-mail: dowmk@udmercy.edu; *Libr Tech,* Jessica Grimes; Tel: 313-494-6901, E-mail: szubecjs@udmercy.edu; *Libr Asst,* Vivian Palmer; Tel: 313-494-6902, E-mail: palmervl1@udmercy.edu; Staff 5 (MLS 3, Non-MLS 2)
Founded 1877. Enrl 5,231; Fac 654; Highest Degree: Doctorate
Jul 2012-Jun 2013 Income $433,870, Locally Generated Income $213, Parent Institution $433,657. Mats Exp $108,350, Books $10,433, Per/Ser (Incl. Access Fees) $63,485, Electronic Ref Mat (Incl. Access Fees) $33,730, Presv $702. Sal $186,741 (Prof $133,289)
Library Holdings: AV Mats 1,175; CDs 193; DVDs 78; e-books 100,162; e-journals 41,449; Bk Titles 14,813; Per Subs 103
Special Collections: Antique Dental Instruments & Equipment Coll
Subject Interests: Dentistry
Automation Activity & Vendor Info: (OPAC) Horizon
Partic in Metrop Detroit Med Libr Group
Restriction: Authorized patrons, Borrowing privileges limited to fac & registered students, Not open to pub

CL UNIVERSITY OF DETROIT MERCY SCHOOL OF LAW, Kresge Law Library, 651 E Jefferson, 48226. SAN 346-3206. Tel: 313-596-0239. Circulation Tel: 313-596-0241. Reference Tel: 313-596-0244. FAX: 313-596-0245. E-mail: lawlibrary@udmercy.edu. Web Site: lawschool.udmercy.edu/library. *Libr Dir,* Patrick Meyer; Tel: 313-596-0240,

E-mail: meyerpj@udmercy.edu; *Head, Tech Serv,* Latha Rangarajan; Tel: 313-596-9824, E-mail: rangarl@udmercy.edu; *Ref & Ser Librn,* Benjamin Houston; Tel: 313-596-9414, E-mail: houstoboc@udmercy.edu; *Govt Doc, Ref Librn,* Jennifer Hostetler; Tel: 313-596-9415, E-mail: holzwojm@udmercy.edu; *Night Supvr, Res Spec,* Stephanie McCoy; Tel: 313-596-0241, E-mail: mccoysn@udmercy.edu; *Electronic Services Specialist,* Zachary Turk; E-mail: turkzp@udmercy.edu; *Cat Asst,* Elaine Manning; Tel: 313-596-0246, E-mail: manninec@udmercy.edu; *Circ Asst,* Haley Behr; E-mail: behrhp@udmercy.edu; Staff 8 (MLS 6, Non-MLS 2)
Founded 1912. Enrl 610; Fac 25; Highest Degree: Doctorate
Library Holdings: Bk Titles 47,170; Bk Vols 300,000; Per Subs 1,500; Videos 300
Special Collections: US Document Depository
Automation Activity & Vendor Info: (Acquisitions) Innovative Interfaces, Inc; (Circulation) Innovative Interfaces, Inc; (Course Reserve) Innovative Interfaces, Inc; (OPAC) Innovative Interfaces, Inc; (Serials) Innovative Interfaces, Inc
Function: Govt ref serv, Res libr
Partic in Midwest Collaborative for Library Services; OCLC Online Computer Library Center, Inc
Open Mon-Thurs 8am-10:50pm, Fri 8-5:50, Sat & Sun 10-5:50 (Winter); Mon-Fri 8-5:50 (Summer)
Restriction: Open to fac, students & qualified researchers

J WAYNE COUNTY COMMUNITY COLLEGE DISTRICT*, Learning Resource Center, 801 W Fort St, 48226-3010. SAN 308-0463. Tel: 313-496-2358. Web Site: www.wcccd.edu/dept/learning_resource_center.htm. *District Dean, LRC Serv,* Stephanie A Coffer; *Learning Res Ctr Coordr,* Traci Etheridge; E-mail: tetheri1@wcccd.edu
Founded 1974
Library Holdings: Bk Titles 70,000; Per Subs 559
Automation Activity & Vendor Info: (Acquisitions) SirsiDynix; (Cataloging) SirsiDynix; (Circulation) SirsiDynix; (Course Reserve) SirsiDynix; (ILL) SirsiDynix; (Media Booking) SirsiDynix; (OPAC) SirsiDynix; (Serials) SirsiDynix
Wireless access
Partic in Detroit Area Library Network
Open Mon-Thurs 8:30am-9pm, Fri 8:30-4:30, Sat 8:30-4

Departmental Libraries:

ARTHUR CARTWRIGHT LRC LIBRARY, 1001 W Fort St, 48226-3096. Tel: 313-496-2358, Ext 2063. FAX: 313-962-4506. E-mail: downtownlrc@wcccd.edu. *District Dean, LRC Serv,* Stephanie A Coffer; E-mail: scoffer1@wcccd.edu
Library Holdings: Bk Vols 29,000; Per Subs 100
Automation Activity & Vendor Info: (Cataloging) SirsiDynix; (Circulation) SirsiDynix; (OPAC) SirsiDynix
Open Mon-Thurs 7:30am-10pm, Fri 8-4:30, Sat & Sun 8-4

C WAYNE STATE UNIVERSITY LIBRARIES*, 5150 Gullen Mall, Ste 3100, 48202. SAN 346-3230. Tel: 313-577-4023. FAX: 313-577-5525. Web Site: library.wayne.edu. *Dean,* Jon E Cawthorne; Tel: 313-577-4020, E-mail: jon.cawthorne@wayne.edu; *Assoc Dean,* Alexis Macklin; Tel: 313-577-4176, E-mail: alexis.macklin@wayne.edu; Staff 132 (MLS 49, Non-MLS 83)
Enrl 26,894; Fac 2,790; Highest Degree: Doctorate
Library Holdings: e-books 819,540; Bk Vols 2,491,403; Per Subs 68,952
Special Collections: Arthur L Johnson African-American History Coll, bks, non-print mats, v-tapes; Curriculum Guide Coll; Florence Nightingale Coll (Purdy/Kresge Coll, items once owned by Florence Nightingale); Jeheskel (Hezy) Shoshani Library Endowed Coll; Judaic-Christian Heritage, Judaica, Hebraica & Yiddish Literature (Kasle Coll); Juvenile Coll; Leonard Simons Coll of Rare Michigan History Texts, mats; Literature for Young People 18th Century to Present (Ramsey Coll), rare bks, periodicals; Merril-Palmer Institute Coll early 1900s, bks, journals, monographs; Mildred Jeffrey Coll of Peace & Conflict Resolution; Urban Ethnic Materials (Millicent A Wills Coll); William Alfred Boyce Storytelling Coll. US Document Depository
Automation Activity & Vendor Info: (Acquisitions) Innovative Interfaces, Inc - Millennium; (Cataloging) Innovative Interfaces, Inc - Millennium; (Circulation) Innovative Interfaces, Inc - Millennium; (Course Reserve) Innovative Interfaces, Inc - Millennium; (ILL) OCLC ILLiad; (OPAC) Innovative Interfaces, Inc - Millennium; (Serials) Innovative Interfaces, Inc - Millennium
Wireless access
Publications: Annual report; Newsletters (Online only)
Partic in Association of Research Libraries; Greater Western Library Alliance; Midwest Collaborative for Library Services; OCLC Online Computer Library Center, Inc
Special Services for the Deaf - ADA equip

Departmental Libraries:

DAVID ADAMANY UNDERGRADUATE LIBRARY, 5150 Anthony Wayne, 48202. Tel: 313-577-5121. Circulation Tel: 313-577-8854. Interlibrary Loan Service Tel: 313-577-4011. Reference Tel: 313-577-8852. FAX: 313-577-5265. *Library Contact,* Megan Hakala; E-mail: ey7847@wayne.edu
Founded 1997

CL ARTHUR NEEF LAW LIBRARY, 474 Gilmour Mall, 48202, SAN 346-332X. Tel: 313-577-3925. Circulation Tel: 313-577-6181. Interlibrary Loan Service Tel: 313-577-6429. Reference Tel: 313-577-6180. FAX: 313-577-5498. Web Site: library.wayne.edu/neef. *Dir,* Virginia C Thomas; E-mail: ed5497@wayne.edu; Staff 8 (MLS 4, Non-MLS 4)
Special Collections: Law Libr Microform Consortium Publications; Social Studies; Women & the Law, flm. US Document Depository
Subject Interests: Bus & mgt, Hist
Publications: US Documents Information Guide

PURDY-KRESGE LIBRARY, 5265 Cass Ave, 48202, SAN 346-3389. Tel: 313-577-4042. Circulation Tel: 313-577-4043. Reference Tel: 313-577-6423. FAX: 313-577-3436. *Mgr,* Daniel Gamlin; E-mail: ad2887@wayne.edu
Special Collections: Children & Young People (Eloise Ramsey Coll); Peace & Conflict (Mildred Jeffrey Coll). State Document Depository; US Document Depository
Subject Interests: Bus, Educ, Humanities, Soc sci & issues

WALTER P REUTHER LIBRARY OF LABOR & URBAN AFFAIRS, 5401 Cass Ave, 48202, SAN 346-329X. Tel: 313-577-4024. *Interim Dir,* Mary Wallace; Tel: 313-577-4864, E-mail: ac7689@wayne.edu; Staff 18 (MLS 17, Non-MLS 1)
Founded 1960
Library Holdings: Bk Vols 9,000; Per Subs 650
Special Collections: Manuscript Coll; Metropolitan Detroit & University Archives; Photograph Coll. Oral History
Subject Interests: Archives, Labor
Publications: Reuther Library Newsletter
Open Mon-Fri 10-2

CM VERA P SHIFFMAN MEDICAL LIBRARY & LEARNING RESOURCES CENTERS, 320 E Canfield St, 48201, SAN 346-3354. Tel: 313-577-1088. Interlibrary Loan Service Tel: 313-577-1100. Information Services Tel: 313-577-1094. FAX: 313-577-6668. *Interim Dir,* LaVentra Ellis-Darquah; Tel: 313-577-9083, E-mail: laventra@wayne.edu; Staff 12 (MLS 2, Non-MLS 10)
Special Collections: Community Health Information Services; Detroit Community AIDS Library; Pharmacy & Allied Health Learning Resources Center Coll
Subject Interests: Allied health, Clinical med, Consumer health, Health sci, Med, Statistics
Automation Activity & Vendor Info: (Acquisitions) Innovative Interfaces, Inc; (Cataloging) Innovative Interfaces, Inc; (Circulation) Innovative Interfaces, Inc; (Course Reserve) Docutek; (ILL) OCLC ILLiad; (OPAC) Innovative Interfaces, Inc; (Serials) Innovative Interfaces, Inc
Function: Computer training, Computers for patron use, Doc delivery serv, E-Reserves, Electronic databases & coll, Health sci info serv, ILL available, Internet access, Magnifiers for reading, Online info literacy tutorials on the web & in blackboard, Online ref, Orientations, Outside serv via phone, mail, e-mail & web, Photocopying/Printing, Ref & res, Ref serv available, Res libr, Scanner, Senior computer classes, Telephone ref, VHS videos, Wheelchair accessible, Workshops
Special Services for the Blind - Aids for in-house use; Assistive/Adapted tech devices, equip & products; Cassette playback machines; Copier with enlargement capabilities; ZoomText magnification & reading software
Restriction: Non-circulating of rare bks, Off-site coll in storage - retrieval as requested

DEWITT

P DEWITT DISTRICT LIBRARY*, 13101 Schavey Rd, 48820-9008. Tel: 517-669-3156. FAX: 517-669-6408. E-mail: director@dewittlibrary.org. Web Site: www.dewittlibrary.org. *Dir,* Jennifer Balcom; E-mail: jbalcom@dewittlibrary.org; *Asst Dir, Youth Serv Coordr,* Mindy Schafer; E-mail: mschafer@dewittlibrary.org; Staff 19 (MLS 4, Non-MLS 15)
Founded 1934
Library Holdings: e-books 2,000; Bk Vols 58,000; Per Subs 124
Automation Activity & Vendor Info: (Acquisitions) SirsiDynix; (Cataloging) SirsiDynix; (Circulation) SirsiDynix; (OPAC) SirsiDynix
Wireless access
Function: 24/7 Electronic res, Butterfly Garden, Children's prog, Computer training, Internet access, Laminating, Online cat, OverDrive digital audio bks, STEM programs, Wheelchair accessible
Mem of Woodlands Library Cooperative
Open Mon-Thurs 10-8, Fri 1-6, Sat 10-4, Sun 1-5
Friends of the Library Group

DEXTER

P DEXTER DISTRICT LIBRARY*, 3255 Alpine St, 48130. SAN 308-048X. Tel: 734-426-4477. Administration Tel: 734-426-7731. FAX: 734-426-1217. Web Site: www.dexter.lib.mi.us. *Libr Dir,* Paul McCann; E-mail: pmccann@dexter.lib.mi.us; *Head, Adult Serv,* Lisa Ryan; E-mail:

lryan@dexter.lib.mi.us; *Head, Youth Serv,* Cathy Jurich; E-mail: cjurich@dexter.lib.mi.us; *Tech Librn,* Scott Wright; E-mail: swright@dexter.lib.mi.us; *Admin Serv Mgr,* Summer Powers; E-mail: spowers@dexter.lib.mi.us; *Circ Supvr,* Mary Graulich; E-mail: mgraulich@dexter.lib.mi.us; Staff 36 (MLS 13, Non-MLS 23)
Founded 1927. Pop 19,591; Circ 502,395
Oct 2015-Sept 2016 Income $1,505,521, State $12,811, Federal $5,703, County $35,512, Locally Generated Income $1,326,178, Other $69,064. Mats Exp $188,612, Books $116,285, Per/Ser (Incl. Access Fees) $15,228, AV Mat $35,622, Electronic Ref Mat (Incl. Access Fees) $21,477. Sal $754,903 (Prof $582,737)
Library Holdings: Audiobooks 3,274; CDs 8,978; DVDs 11,118; e-books 4,917; e-journals 296; Large Print Bks 812; Bk Titles 76,362; Bk Vols 84,212; Per Subs 190
Automation Activity & Vendor Info: (Cataloging) SirsiDynix; (Circulation) SirsiDynix; (OPAC) SirsiDynix; (Serials) SirsiDynix
Wireless access
Function: 24/7 Electronic res, 24/7 Online cat, Adult bk club, Art exhibits, AV serv, Bk club(s), Bks on CD, Children's prog, Computer training, Computers for patron use, Digital talking bks, Electronic databases & coll, Free DVD rentals, Holiday prog, ILL available, Internet access, Large print keyboards, Life-long learning prog for all ages, Magazines, Magnifiers for reading, Mail & tel request accepted, Mango lang, Meeting rooms, Movies, Museum passes, Music CDs, Online cat, Outside serv via phone, mail, e-mail & web, OverDrive digital audio bks, Photocopying/Printing, Preschool reading prog, Printer for laptops & handheld devices, Prog for adults, Prog for children & young adult, Ref serv available, Scanner, Senior computer classes, Spoken cassettes & CDs, Spoken cassettes & DVDs, Story hour, Study rm, Summer reading prog, Tax forms, Teen prog, Telephone ref, Wheelchair accessible, Workshops
Publications: Ex Libris (Newsletter)
Partic in MeLCat; The Library Network
Special Services for the Deaf - Video relay services
Open Mon-Fri 9-9, Sat 9-5, Sun 1-5
Friends of the Library Group

DIMONDALE

P DOROTHY HULL LIBRARY - WINDSOR CHARTER TOWNSHIP, 405 W Jefferson St, 48821. SAN 308-0498. Tel: 517-646-0633. FAX: 517-646-7061. E-mail: dimondalelibrary@gmail.com. Web Site: windsor-township.ploud.net. *Dir,* Ann Marie Sanders; *Asst Dir,* Rebecca Wagemaker; Staff 3 (MLS 2, Non-MLS 1)
Founded 1951. Pop 7,000; Circ 21,000
Library Holdings: Bk Vols 14,000; Per Subs 50
Wireless access
Function: 24/7 Online cat, Adult bk club, Audiobks via web, Bks on CD, Chess club, Children's prog, Computers for patron use, Electronic databases & coll, Family literacy, Free DVD rentals, Homebound delivery serv, ILL available, Internet access, Laminating, Magazines, Mango lang, Museum passes, Notary serv, Online cat, Photocopying/Printing, Preschool reading prog, Prog for adults, Prog for children & young adult, Res assist avail, Scanner, Story hour, Summer & winter reading prog, Tax forms, Teen prog, Telephone ref
Mem of Woodlands Library Cooperative
Open Mon-Fri 10-6, Sat 10-2

DOLLAR BAY

P OSCEOLA TOWNSHIP PUBLIC & SCHOOL LIBRARY, 48475 Maple Dr, 49922. (Mail add: PO Box 371, 49922-0371), SAN 308-0501. Tel: 906-482-5800. FAX: 989-455-4237. E-mail: info@dollarbay.k12.mi.us. Web Site: www.dollarbay.k12.mi.us/article/osceola-db-tc-school-library. *Librn,* Jennifer Strand; E-mail: strandj@dollarbay.k12.mi.us
Founded 1924. Circ 5,000
Library Holdings: AV Mats 60; Bk Vols 5,800
Partic in Upper Peninsula Region of Library Cooperation, Inc
Open Mon, Tues, Thurs & Fri 7:45-4:30, Wed 7:45-4:30 & 5:30-7:30

DORR

P DORR TOWNSHIP LIBRARY, 1804 Sunset Dr, 49323. SAN 346-3478. Tel: 616-681-9678. FAX: 616-681-5650. E-mail: dor@llcoop.org. Web Site: www.dorrlibrary.michlibrary.org. *Interim Dir,* Reilly Brower; E-mail: dorrb@llcoop.org; Staff 3.3 (Non-MLS 3.3)
Founded 1940. Pop 7,439; Circ 45,052. Sal $69,142
Library Holdings: Audiobooks 1,142; AV Mats 1,744; Bk Vols 25,037; Per Subs 61
Automation Activity & Vendor Info: (Acquisitions) OCLC; (Cataloging) Innovative Interfaces, Inc; (Circulation) Innovative Interfaces, Inc; (ILL) Innovative Interfaces, Inc; (OPAC) Innovative Interfaces, Inc
Wireless access
Function: Adult bk club, Bks on CD, Children's prog, Computers for patron use, Free DVD rentals, ILL available, Music CDs, Online cat, Photocopying/Printing, Preschool outreach, Prog for children & young adult, Story hour, Summer reading prog, Tax forms, Telephone ref, Wheelchair accessible
Partic in Lakeland Library Cooperative
Open Mon & Thurs 12-8, Tues & Sat 10-2, Wed & Fri 10-5
Friends of the Library Group

DOUGLAS

P SAUGATUCK-DOUGLAS DISTRICT LIBRARY*, 137 Center St, 49406. (Mail add: PO Box 789, 49406-0789), SAN 308-4027. Tel: 269-857-8241. FAX: 269-857-3005. E-mail: std@llcoop.org. Web Site: www.sdlibrary.org. *Dir,* Ingrid Steen Boyer; E-mail: stdib@llcoop.org
Founded 1965. Pop 7,202; Circ 28,223
Library Holdings: Bk Vols 20,000; Per Subs 62
Automation Activity & Vendor Info: (Cataloging) Innovative Interfaces, Inc; (Circulation) Innovative Interfaces, Inc
Wireless access
Partic in Lakeland Library Cooperative
Open Mon-Fri 10-6, Sat 10-2, Sun 1-4
Friends of the Library Group

DOWAGIAC

P DOWAGIAC DISTRICT LIBRARY, 211 Commercial St, 49047-1728. SAN 346-3567. Tel: 269-782-3826. FAX: 269-782-9798. Web Site: dowagiacdl.squarespace.com. *Dir,* Matthew Weston; E-mail: mweston@dowagiacdl.org; Staff 6 (MLS 1, Non-MLS 5)
Founded 1872. Pop 14,256; Circ 51,339
Library Holdings: Bk Titles 38,000; Per Subs 38
Subject Interests: Local hist
Automation Activity & Vendor Info: (Cataloging) Auto-Graphics, Inc; (Circulation) Auto-Graphics, Inc
Wireless access
Partic in Southwest Michigan Library Cooperative
Open Mon-Thurs 10-6, Fri 10-4, Sat 10-3
Friends of the Library Group

J SOUTHWESTERN MICHIGAN COLLEGE, Fred L Mathews Library, 58900 Cherry Grove Rd, 49047. SAN 308-051X. Tel: 269-782-1339. Interlibrary Loan Service Tel: 269-782-1339. Toll Free Tel: 800-456-8675. FAX: 269-783-2751. Web Site: www.swmich.edu/community/community-services/fred-l-mathews-library/. *Dir, Libr Serv,* Colleen Welsch; Tel: 269-782-1204, E-mail: cwelsch@swmich.edu; Staff 4 (MLS 2, Non-MLS 2)
Founded 1964. Enrl 1,900; Fac 138; Highest Degree: Associate
Library Holdings: Audiobooks 363; CDs 1,176; DVDs 2,317; e-books 1,137; e-journals 37,873; Bk Vols 19,753; Per Subs 6
Automation Activity & Vendor Info: (Cataloging) Auto-Graphics, Inc; (Circulation) Auto-Graphics, Inc; (ILL) OCLC Worldshare Management Services; (OPAC) Auto-Graphics, Inc
Wireless access
Partic in Midwest Collaborative for Library Services

DRYDEN

P DRYDEN TOWNSHIP LIBRARY*, 5480 Main St, 48428-9968. (Mail add: PO Box 280, 48428-0280), SAN 308-0528. Tel: 810-796-3586. FAX: 810-796-2634. E-mail: drydentownshiplibrary@hotmail.com. Web Site: www.drydentownshiplibrary.org. *Dir,* Diane Moyer
Founded 1975. Pop 3,399
Library Holdings: Large Print Bks 453; Bk Vols 19,495; Per Subs 105
Automation Activity & Vendor Info: (Cataloging) SirsiDynix; (Circulation) SirsiDynix; (OPAC) SirsiDynix
Wireless access
Partic in Mideastern Michigan Library Cooperative
Open Mon & Wed 10-7, Tues & Thurs 10-5, Sat 10-2

EAST JORDAN

P JORDAN VALLEY DISTRICT LIBRARY*, One Library Lane, 49727. (Mail add: PO Box 877, 49727-0877), SAN 308-0552. Tel: 231-536-7131. FAX: 231-536-3646. E-mail: dir@jvdl.info. Web Site: jvdl.info. *Libr Dir,* Dawn LaVanway; Staff 6 (MLS 1, Non-MLS 5)
Pop 6,997; Circ 45,233
Jul 2020-Jun 2021. Mats Exp $19,000, Per/Ser (Incl. Access Fees) $4,000, Electronic Ref Mat (Incl. Access Fees) $15,000. Sal $167,000
Library Holdings: Audiobooks 100; AV Mats 350; CDs 2,139; DVDs 3,600; e-books 20,138; Large Print Bks 150; Bk Titles 53,000; Per Subs 110
Automation Activity & Vendor Info: (Cataloging) Horizon; (Circulation) Horizon; (OPAC) Horizon
Wireless access
Function: 24/7 Electronic res, 24/7 Online cat, Art exhibits, Audiobks via web, Bks on CD, Computers for patron use, Digital talking bks, Electronic databases & coll, Free DVD rentals, ILL available, Internet access, Magazines, Mail & tel request accepted, Meeting rooms, Music CDs,

Notary serv, Online cat, OverDrive digital audio bks, Photocopying/Printing, Printer for laptops & handheld devices, Prog for adults, Prog for children & young adult, Ref & res, Res assist avail, Scanner, Story hour, Study rm, Summer reading prog, Tax forms, Teen prog, Telephone ref, VHS videos, Visual arts prog
Publications: Jordan Valley Library News (Newsletter)
Partic in Northland Library Cooperative
Open Mon-Fri 9-5
Restriction: Circ limited

EAST LANSING

P EAST LANSING PUBLIC LIBRARY*, 950 Abbot Rd, 48823-3105. SAN 308-0560. Tel: 517-351-2420. Administration Tel: 517-319-6863. FAX: 517-351-9536. Circulation E-mail: elplcirc@cityofeastlansing.com. Web Site: www.elpl.org. *Dir,* Kristin Shelley; Tel: 517-319-6913, E-mail: kshelley@cityofeastlansing.com; *Asst Dir, Head, Customer Experience,* Brice Bush; Tel: 517-319-6939, E-mail: bbush@cityofeastlansing.com; *Head, Tech,* Lauren Douglass; Tel: 517-319-6882, E-mail: ldougla@cityofeastlansing.com
Founded 1923. Pop 48,579; Circ 319,370. Sal $1,062,745
Library Holdings: Bk Vols 130,000
Special Collections: Local History
Automation Activity & Vendor Info: (Cataloging) Innovative Interfaces, Inc; (Circulation) Innovative Interfaces, Inc; (OPAC) Innovative Interfaces, Inc
Wireless access
Mem of Woodlands Library Cooperative
Open Mon-Thurs 10-9, Fri & Sat 10-6, Sun (Sept-May) 1-5
Friends of the Library Group

CL MICHIGAN STATE UNIVERSITY COLLEGE OF LAW LIBRARY*, John F Schaefer Law Library, Law College Bldg, Rm 115, 648 N Shaw Lane, 48824-1300. SAN 307-9953. Tel: 517-432-6860. Reference Tel: 517-432-6870. FAX: 517-432-6861. Reference E-mail: reference@law.msu.edu. Web Site: www.law.msu.edu/library/index.html. *Assoc Dean of Libr, Tech Serv,* Charles Ten Brink; Tel: 517-432-6862, E-mail: cjtb@law.msu.edu; *Assoc Dir,* Hildur Hanna; Tel: 517-432-6863, E-mail: hannahi@law.msu.edu; *Asst Dir, Coll Mgt,* Brooke Moynihan; Tel: 517-432-6864, E-mail: moynihbr@law.msu.edu; *Asst Dir, Pub Serv,* Jane Meland; Tel: 517-432-6867, E-mail: jane.meland@law.msu.edu; *Acq Librn,* Allison Eicher; E-mail: eicheral@law.msu.edu; *Ref Librn,* Barbara Bean; Tel: 517-432-6878, E-mail: beanbarb@law.msu.edu; *Ref Librn,* Brent Domann; Tel: 517-432-6851, E-mail: domannbr@law.msu.edu; *Ref Librn,* Daryl Thompson; Tel: 517-432-6957, E-mail: thomps43@law.msu.edu; *Circ Mgr,* Robin Doutre; Tel: 517-432-6869, E-mail: doutre@law.msu.edu; Staff 7 (MLS 7)
Founded 1891. Enrl 1,000; Fac 38; Highest Degree: Doctorate
Library Holdings: Bk Titles 147,748; Bk Vols 284,804
Special Collections: US Document Depository
Automation Activity & Vendor Info: (Acquisitions) Innovative Interfaces, Inc; (Cataloging) Innovative Interfaces, Inc; (Circulation) Innovative Interfaces, Inc; (OPAC) Innovative Interfaces, Inc; (Serials) Innovative Interfaces, Inc
Wireless access
Publications: Acquisitions List
Partic in Lexis, OCLC Online Computer Libr Ctr, Inc; Midwest Collaborative for Library Services
Open Mon-Thurs 8am-1am, Fri 8am-11pm, Sat 10am-11pm, Sun 10am-1am
Restriction: Pub use on premises

C MICHIGAN STATE UNIVERSITY LIBRARIES*, Main Library, 366 W Circle Dr, 48824-1048. SAN 346-3621. Tel: 517-432-6123. Interlibrary Loan Service Tel: 517-884-6399. Toll Free Tel: 800-500-1554. FAX: 517-432-3532. TDD: 517-353-9034. Web Site: www.lib.msu.edu. *Univ Librn,* Joe Salem; E-mail: jsalem@lib.msu.edu; *ILL Serv, Sr Assoc Univ Librn,* Arlene Weismantel; Tel: 517-884-6447, E-mail: weisman1@mail.lib.msu.edu; *Assoc Univ Librn, Coll,* Steven Sowards; Tel: 517-884-6391, E-mail: sowards@msu.edu; *Assoc Univ Librn, Syst, Tech Serv,* Kay Granskog; Tel: 517-884-0814, E-mail: granskog@msu.edu; *Asst Univ Librn, Digital Serv,* Shawn Nicholson; Tel: 517-884-6448, E-mail: nicho147@msu.edu; *Asst Univ Librn, Pub Serv,* Terri Miller; Tel: 517-884-0841, E-mail: ticklet@mail.lib.msu.edu. Subject Specialists: *Human resources,* Arlene Weismantel; Staff 210 (MLS 90, Non-MLS 120)
Founded 1855. Enrl 50,019; Fac 5,666; Highest Degree: Doctorate
Library Holdings: e-books 1,500,000; Bk Titles 7,606,499; Bk Vols 6,295,758
Special Collections: American Popular Culture; American Radical History; Apiculture Coll; Changing Men Coll; Comic Art; Cookery Coll; Early Works in Criminology; Eighteenth Century English Studies; English & American Authors; Fencing Coll; History of the French Monarchy; Illuminated Manuscripts in Facsimile; Italian Risorgimento History; Natural Science, especially Botany & Entomology; Veterinary History
Automation Activity & Vendor Info: (Acquisitions) Innovative Interfaces, Inc; (Circulation) Innovative Interfaces, Inc; (Serials) Innovative Interfaces, Inc
Wireless access
Partic in Association of Research Libraries; Big Ten Academic Alliance; Center for Research Libraries; Midwest Collaborative for Library Services; National Network of Libraries of Medicine Region 6
Departmental Libraries:
AREA STUDIES, Main Library, 366 W Circle Dr, 48824, SAN 346-4075. Tel: 517-884-6392. FAX: 517-432-3532. *Librn,* Jessica Achberger; E-mail: achberg2@mail.lib.msu.edu; *Librn,* Deborah Margolis; E-mail: deborahm@msu.edu; *Librn,* Erik Ponder; E-mail: ponderer@lib.msu.edu; *Librn,* Xian Wu; E-mail: wuxian@msu.edu; *Coordr, Area Studies, Librn,* Mary Jo Zeter; E-mail: zeter@msu.edu. Subject Specialists: *Africana,* Jessica Achberger; *Near Eastern studies,* Deborah Margolis; *Africana,* Erik Ponder; *Asian studies,* Xian Wu; *Latin Am studies,* Mary Jo Zeter
FINE ARTS-ART, W403 Main Library, 366 W Circle Dr, 48824, SAN 346-3745. Tel: 517-884-6469. FAX: 517-432-3532. Web Site: www.lib.msu.edu/coll/main/finearts. *Librn,* Terrie Wilson; E-mail: wilso398@msu.edu
FINE ARTS-MUSIC, W403 Main Library, 366 W Circle Dr, 48824, SAN 346-4164. Tel: 517-884-6469. FAX: 517-432-3532. Web Site: www.lib.msu.edu/coll/main/finearts. *Music Librn,* Grace Haynes; E-mail: haynesg3@mail.lib.msu.edu
WILLIAM C GAST BUSINESS LIBRARY, 50 Law College Bldg, 648 N Shaw Lane, 48824, SAN 346-380X. Tel: 517-355-3380. FAX: 517-353-6648. *Head Librn,* Laura Walesby; E-mail: leavitt9@mail.lib.msu.edu
GERALD M KLINE DIGITAL & MULTIMEDIA CENTER, W432 Main Library, 366 W Circle Dr, 48824, SAN 346-377X. Tel: 517-884-6470. FAX: 517-432-4795. Web Site: www.digital.lib.msu.edu. *Asst Dir, Digital Serv,* Shawn Nicholson; Tel: 517-884-6448, E-mail: nicho147@msu.edu
MAP LIBRARY, W308 Main Library, 366 W Circle Dr, 48824, SAN 329-6423. Tel: 517-884-6467. FAX: 517-432-3532. *Librn,* Kathleen Weessies
VOICE LIBRARY, W422 Library, 366 W Circle Dr, 48824, SAN 346-4318. Tel: 517-884-6470. FAX: 517-432-4795. *Asst Dir, Digital Serv,* Shawn Nicholson; E-mail: nicho147@msu.edu

EAST TAWAS

P IOSCO-ARENAC DISTRICT LIBRARY*, 120 W Westover St, 48730. SAN 347-0822. Tel: 989-362-2651. FAX: 989-362-6056. Web Site: www.ioscoarenaclibrary.org. *Dir,* Stephanie Mallak Olson; E-mail: director@ioscoarenaclibrary.org; *Commun Liaison Librn,* Arleen Wood; *Tech Coordr,* John Cargo; *Ch Serv, Youth Serv,* Lynne Bigelow; *ILL,* Richard Marx; Staff 9 (MLS 3, Non-MLS 6)
Founded 1935. Pop 41,786; Circ 141,990
Library Holdings: Audiobooks 1,619; CDs 4,161; e-books 2,321; Electronic Media & Resources 4; Bk Vols 100,368; Per Subs 246
Special Collections: Business Resource Center
Subject Interests: Genealogy, Local hist, Mich
Automation Activity & Vendor Info: (Cataloging) SirsiDynix; (Circulation) SirsiDynix; (ILL) Mel Cat; (OPAC) SirsiDynix
Wireless access
Publications: Annual Report
Partic in Valley Libr Consortium; White Pine Library Cooperative
Open Mon-Fri 8-4:30
Friends of the Library Group
Branches: 8
AU GRES COMMUNITY, 230 N MacKinaw, Au Gres, 48703. (Mail add: PO Box 146, Au Gres, 48703), SAN 347-0857. Tel: 989-876-8818. FAX: 989-876-8818. *Librn,* Linda Kauffman; Staff 2 (Non-MLS 2)
Circ 12,154
Open Mon & Tues 11-6, Wed-Fri 9-5, Sat 9:30-12:30
Friends of the Library Group
EAST TAWAS BRANCH, 760 Newman St, 48730. (Mail add: PO BOX 672, 48730), SAN 347-0881. Tel: 989-362-6162. E-mail: libraryet@yahoo.com. *Librn,* Luann Elvey; Staff 1 (Non-MLS 1)
Circ 17,916
Open Mon, Thurs & Fri 8-6, Tues 10-8:30, Sat 8-12
Friends of the Library Group
MARY JOHNSTON MEMORIAL LIBRARY - STANDISH BRANCH, 114 N Court, Standish, 48658-9416. (Mail add: PO Box 698, Standish, 48658-0698), SAN 347-0970. Tel: 989-846-6611. FAX: 989-846-6611. *Librn,* Hilda Carruthers; Staff 2.4 (Non-MLS 2.4)
Circ 29,050
Open Mon & Tues 11-7, Wed & Thurs 1-7, Fri & Sat 10-3
Friends of the Library Group
OMER LITTLE EAGLES NEST LIBRARY, 205 E Center St, Omer, 48749. (Mail add: PO Box 186, Omer, 48749), SAN 325-4283. Tel: 989-653-2230. FAX: 989-653-2230. *Librn,* Charmaine Ploof; Staff 1 (Non-MLS 1)

Circ 4,862
Open Mon 10-12 & 1-6, Tues 10-6, Wed 10-12 & 1-7, Thurs 1-7, Fri 1-6, Sat 9-12
ROBERT J PARKS LIBRARY - OSCODA BRANCH, 6010 N Skeel Ave, Oscoda, 48750, SAN 347-0946. Tel: 989-739-9581. FAX: 989-739-9581. *Librn,* Diana London; Staff 2.1 (Non-MLS 2.1)
Circ 33,416
Open Mon & Tues 9-5, Wed & Thurs 9-7, Fri & Sat 9-2
Friends of the Library Group
PLAINFIELD TOWNSHIP, 220 N Washington, Hale, 48739-9578. (Mail add: PO Box 247, Hale, 48739-0247), SAN 347-0911. Tel: 989-728-4086. FAX: 989-728-6491. *Librn,* Cheryl Tyler; Staff 2 (Non-MLS 2)
Circ 13,149
Open Mon, Tues, Thurs & Fri 8-4, Wed 8-6:30, Sat 9-12
Friends of the Library Group
TAWAS CITY BRANCH, 208 North St, Tawas City, 48763, SAN 347-1004. Tel: 989-362-6557. FAX: 989-362-6557. *Librn,* Terri Stein; Staff 1 (Non-MLS 1)
Circ 18,013
Open Mon-Fri 9-1 & 2-5, Sat 9-1
Friends of the Library Group
WHITTEMORE BRANCH, 483 Bullock St, Whittemore, 48770-5134. (Mail add: PO Box 247, Whittemore, 48770-0247), SAN 347-1039. Tel: 989-756-3186. FAX: 989-756-3186. *Librn,* Kathy Gibson; Staff 2 (Non-MLS 2)
Circ 6,603
Open Mon, Wed & Fri 10-6, Tues, Thurs & Sat 10-4
Friends of the Library Group

EASTPOINTE

P EASTPOINTE MEMORIAL LIBRARY*, 15875 Oak St, 48021-2390. SAN 308-0544. Tel: 586-445-5096. FAX: 586-775-0150. E-mail: eplweb@libcoop.net. Web Site: www.cityofeastpointe.net/library_main. *Dir,* Carol Sterling; E-mail: sterlinc@libcoop.net; *Asst Dir,* Sue Todd; E-mail: todds@libcoop.net; *Youth Serv Librn,* Abby Bond; E-mail: bonda@libcoop.net; Staff 6 (MLS 6)
Founded 1939. Pop 32,442; Circ 106,406
Library Holdings: AV Mats 8,909; Bk Vols 62,326; Per Subs 95
Special Collections: Automobile Manuals Coll
Automation Activity & Vendor Info: (Acquisitions) SirsiDynix; (Cataloging) SirsiDynix; (Circulation) SirsiDynix; (ILL) SirsiDynix; (OPAC) SirsiDynix; (Serials) SirsiDynix
Wireless access
Function: Accelerated reader prog
Partic in Suburban Library Cooperative
Open Mon-Thurs 10-8, Fri & Sat 12-5
Friends of the Library Group

EATON RAPIDS

P EATON RAPIDS AREA DISTRICT LIBRARY, 220 S Main St, 48827-1256. SAN 308-0595. Tel: 517-663-0950. FAX: 517-663-1940. E-mail: info@eradl.org. Web Site: eradl.org. *Libr Dir,* Anna M Curtis; Tel: 517-663-0950, Ext 401, E-mail: acurtis@eradl.org; Staff 5 (MLS 2, Non-MLS 3)
Founded 1876. Pop 12,670
Automation Activity & Vendor Info: (Acquisitions) Auto-Graphics, Inc; (Circulation) Auto-Graphics, Inc; (ILL) Mel Cat; (OPAC) Auto-Graphics, Inc
Wireless access
Function: 24/7 Electronic res, 24/7 Online cat, Adult bk club, Audiobks via web, Bk club(s), Bks on CD, Children's prog, Computer training, Computers for patron use, Digital talking bks, Distance learning, E-Readers, E-Reserves, Electronic databases & coll, Family literacy, Free DVD rentals, Holiday prog, ILL available, Internet access, Magazines, Magnifiers for reading, Mail & tel request accepted, Mango lang, Meeting rooms, Microfiche/film & reading machines, Movies, Museum passes, Music CDs, Online cat, Online ref, Outreach serv, Outside serv via phone, mail, e-mail & web, OverDrive digital audio bks, Photocopying/Printing, Preschool outreach, Preschool reading prog, Prog for adults, Prog for children & young adult, Ref serv available, Res performed for a fee, Scanner, Senior computer classes, STEM programs, Story hour, Summer & winter reading prog, Summer reading prog, Tax forms, Teen prog, Telephone ref, Winter reading prog, Workshops
Mem of Woodlands Library Cooperative
Open Mon, Wed & Thurs 10-7, Tues & Fri 10-5, Sat (Winter) 10-3
Restriction: Circ limited, Internal use only, Non-circulating coll, Non-circulating of rare bks, Non-resident fee
Friends of the Library Group

EAU CLAIRE

P EAU CLAIRE DISTRICT LIBRARY*, 6528 E Main St, 49111. (Mail add: PO Box 328, 49111-0328), SAN 308-0609. Tel: 269-461-6241. FAX: 269-461-3721. E-mail: eauclairedistrictlibrary@gmail.com. Web Site: www.eauclaire.michlibrary.org. *Dir,* Ann Greene; Staff 6 (MLS 1, Non-MLS 5)
Founded 1938. Pop 7,392; Circ 25,492
Library Holdings: Bk Titles 30,391; Per Subs 63
Subject Interests: Local hist, Spanish (Lang)
Automation Activity & Vendor Info: (Cataloging) Biblionix; (Circulation) Biblionix; (OPAC) Biblionix
Wireless access
Function: 24/7 Online cat, Adult bk club
Partic in Southwest Michigan Library Cooperative
Open Mon & Wed 12-9, Tues, Thurs & Fri 10-6, Sat 10-4

ECORSE

P ECORSE PUBLIC LIBRARY*, 4184 W Jefferson Ave, 48229. SAN 308-0617. Tel: 313-389-2030. FAX: 313-389-2032. Web Site: ecorse.lib.mi.us. *Dir,* Reginald B Williams; E-mail: rbwilliams@tln.lib.mi.us; *Libr Asst,* Cassandra Pinkston
Founded 1948
Library Holdings: Bk Titles 25,000; Bk Vols 35,000; Per Subs 70
Automation Activity & Vendor Info: (Cataloging) SirsiDynix; (Circulation) SirsiDynix; (OPAC) SirsiDynix
Wireless access
Function: Homework prog, Notary serv, Photocopying/Printing, Summer reading prog
Partic in The Library Network
Open Mon, Tues & Thurs 10-6

EDMORE

P HOME TOWNSHIP LIBRARY, 329 E Main St, 48829. (Mail add: PO Box 589, 48829-0589), SAN 308-0625. Tel: 989-427-5241. FAX: 989-427-3233. E-mail: edm@llcoop.org. Web Site: www.edmore.llcoop.org. *Dir,* Jonelle Ball
Pop 4,568; Circ 19,490
Library Holdings: AV Mats 610; Large Print Bks 1,500; Bk Vols 17,600; Per Subs 38; Talking Bks 630
Automation Activity & Vendor Info: (Cataloging) Innovative Interfaces, Inc; (Circulation) Innovative Interfaces, Inc; (ILL) Innovative Interfaces, Inc
Wireless access
Partic in Lakeland Library Cooperative
Open Mon & Wed 9-8, Tues, Thurs & Fri 9-5, Sat 10-2

ELK RAPIDS

P ELK RAPIDS DISTRICT LIBRARY, 300 Isle of Pines, 49629. (Mail add: PO Box 337, 49629-0337), SAN 308-065X. Tel: 231-264-9979. FAX: 231-264-9975. Web Site: www.elkrapidslibrary.org. *Dir,* Nannette D Miller; E-mail: erlib.director@gmail.com; Staff 1 (Non-MLS 1)
Founded 1939. Pop 5,432; Circ 54,837
Library Holdings: Bk Vols 18,014; Per Subs 56
Subject Interests: Local hist, Mich
Wireless access
Function: 24/7 Electronic res, 24/7 Online cat, Adult bk club
Partic in Northland Library Cooperative
Open Mon-Thurs 10-6, Fri & Sat 10-5, Sun 1-5
Friends of the Library Group

ELSIE

P ELSIE PUBLIC LIBRARY*, 145 W Main St, 48831. (Mail add: PO Box 545, 48831-0545), SAN 308-0676. Tel: 989-862-4633. FAX: 989-862-4633. E-mail: elsiepubliclibrary@gmail.com. *Dir,* Ann Trierweiler
Founded 1943. Pop 3,500; Circ 21,953
Library Holdings: CDs 500; DVDs 2,600; Bk Titles 25,000; Per Subs 89; Talking Bks 100
Automation Activity & Vendor Info: (Cataloging) Auto-Graphics, Inc; (Circulation) Auto-Graphics, Inc; (ILL) Auto-Graphics, Inc
Wireless access
Open Mon 11-5, Wed & Thurs 1-7, Sat 10-2

EMPIRE

P GLEN LAKE COMMUNITY LIBRARY, 10115 W Front St, 49630-9418. Tel: 231-326-5361. FAX: 231-326-5360. E-mail: info@glenlakelibrary.net. Web Site: www.glenlakelibrary.net. *Dir,* David F Diller; *Asst Librn,* Janette Berkshire
Founded 1977
Library Holdings: Bks on Deafness & Sign Lang 15; Bk Vols 20,000; Per Subs 50; Talking Bks 1,000

Wireless access
Partic in Mid-Michigan Library League
Open Mon, Wed, Fri & Sat 10-5, Tues & Thurs 10-7
Friends of the Library Group

ESCANABA

J BAY DE NOC COMMUNITY COLLEGE*, Bay College Library, 2001 N Lincoln Rd, 49829-2511. SAN 308-0684. Tel: 906-217-4055, 906-217-4076. Reference Tel: 906-217-4079. FAX: 906-217-1657. E-mail: libraryhelp@baycollege.edu. Web Site: library.baycollege.edu. *Libr Dir,* Oscar T DeLong; E-mail: oscar.delong@baycollege.edu; *Bibliog Instr, Coll Develop, Ref (Info Servs),* Ann Bissell; Fax: 906-217-1682, E-mail: bissella@baycollege.edu; Staff 3 (MLS 1, Non-MLS 2)
Founded 1963. Enrl 984; Fac 140; Highest Degree: Associate
Library Holdings: Audiobooks 357; CDs 300; DVDs 1,745; e-books 26,000; Bk Titles 30,000; Bk Vols 40,000; Per Subs 92; Videos 2,310
Special Collections: Delta County Oral History. Oral History
Automation Activity & Vendor Info: (Acquisitions) OCLC; (Cataloging) OCLC; (Circulation) OCLC; (Course Reserve) OCLC; (ILL) OCLC; (OPAC) OCLC WorldShare Interlibrary Loan
Wireless access
Partic in Mich Libr Asn; OCLC Online Computer Library Center, Inc; Upper Peninsula Region of Library Cooperation, Inc
Open Mon-Thurs (Fall & Winter) 8-7, Fri 8-4; Mon-Thurs (Summer) 8-4:30, Fri 8-4

P ESCANABA PUBLIC LIBRARY*, 400 Ludington St, 49829. SAN 308-0692. Tel: 906-789-7323. E-mail: epl@escanabalibrary.org. Web Site: www.uproc.lib.mi.us/eplwp. *Dir,* Carolyn Stacey; Tel: 906-789-7332, E-mail: cstacey@uproc.lib.mi.us; *Ch Serv,* Patricia J Fittante; *ILL,* Jessica McLamb; Staff 4 (MLS 2, Non-MLS 2)
Founded 1903. Pop 13,140; Circ 104,802
Library Holdings: AV Mats 500; Bk Vols 72,692; Per Subs 136; Talking Bks 800; Videos 628
Subject Interests: Genealogy, Local hist
Automation Activity & Vendor Info: (Circulation) SirsiDynix; (OPAC) SirsiDynix
Wireless access
Partic in Superiorland Library Cooperative; Upper Peninsula Region of Library Cooperation, Inc
Special Services for the Blind - Reader equip
Open Mon-Thurs 10-8, Fri 10-5, Sat 10-3
Friends of the Library Group

EVART

P EVART PUBLIC LIBRARY*, 104 N Main St, 49631. (Mail add: PO Box 576, 49631-0576), SAN 308-0714. Tel: 231-734-5542. FAX: 231-734-5542. E-mail: evartlibrary@yahoo.com. *Librn,* Lilas VanScoyoc; *Asst Librn,* Elsie Connor
Pop 6,000; Circ 34,580
Library Holdings: Bk Titles 24,000; Per Subs 65
Automation Activity & Vendor Info: (Cataloging) Auto-Graphics, Inc; (Circulation) Auto-Graphics, Inc
Wireless access
Partic in Mid-Michigan Library League
Open Mon, Tues, Thurs & Fri 9-4:30, Wed 9-6, Sat 9-Noon

EWEN

P MCMILLAN TOWNSHIP LIBRARY*, 200 Cedar St, 49925. (Mail add: PO Box 49, 49925-0049), SAN 376-7078. Tel: 906-988-2515. FAX: 906-988-2255. E-mail: mcmillan@uproc.lib.mi.us. Web Site: joomla.uproc.lib.mi.us/mcmillan. *Dir,* Gig Avromov
Library Holdings: Bk Titles 10,000; Per Subs 28
Automation Activity & Vendor Info: (Cataloging) Follett Software; (Circulation) Follett Software
Partic in Superiorland Library Cooperative; Upper Peninsula Region of Library Cooperation, Inc
Open Tues & Thurs 9:30-5:45, Wed 11-4:45

FAIRGROVE

P FAIRGROVE DISTRICT LIBRARY, 1959 Main St, 48733. SAN 308-0722. Tel: 989-693-6050. FAX: 989-693-6446. E-mail: libraryinfo@fairgrove.lib.mi.us. Web Site: www.fairgrove.michlibrary.org. *Dir,* Marcy Thompkins; E-mail: marcy@fairgrove.lib.mi.us
Founded 1884. Pop 5,500; Circ 18,000
Library Holdings: Bk Titles 22,000; Per Subs 50
Automation Activity & Vendor Info: (Cataloging) Follett Software; (Circulation) Follett Software
Wireless access
Function: Computers for patron use, Photocopying/Printing
Partic in OCLC Online Computer Library Center, Inc; White Pine Library Cooperative
Open Mon, Wed & Fri 9-8, Tues & Sat 9-1
Friends of the Library Group

FALMOUTH

P FALMOUTH AREA LIBRARY*, 219 E Prosper Rd, 49632-0602. Tel: 231-826-3738. *Dir,* Margaret B Rosenbrook; E-mail: rosenbrookm@gmail.com
Library Holdings: Bk Vols 13,000
Open Tues-Thurs 1-6, Sat 9-1

FARMINGTON HILLS

SR BIRMINGHAM TEMPLE LIBRARY, 28611 W Twelve Mile Rd, 48334. SAN 308-0749. Tel: 248-477-1410. FAX: 248-477-9014. E-mail: info@birminghamtemple.org. Web Site: www.birminghamtemple.com. *Exec Dir,* Ann-Marie Fisher; E-mail: fisher@birminghamtemple.org
Founded 1963
Library Holdings: Bk Vols 3,000; Per Subs 20
Subject Interests: Jewish hist & lit, Judaism (religion), Philos

P FARMINGTON COMMUNITY LIBRARY*, 32737 W 12 Mile Rd, 48334. SAN 346-4342. Tel: 248-553-0300. Reference Tel: 248-553-6880. Administration Tel: 248-848-4303. Automation Services Tel: 248-553-8678. FAX: 248-553-3228. Administration FAX: 248-553-6892. Web Site: www.farmlib.org. *Libr Dir,* Riti Grover; E-mail: riti.grover@farmlib.org; Staff 33 (MLS 23, Non-MLS 10)
Founded 1955. Pop 90,112; Circ 1,153,987
Library Holdings: Bk Vols 253,518; Per Subs 496
Special Collections: Business, Law Grantsmanship, parent, teacher, professional; Entrepreneur Coll for Small Business
Automation Activity & Vendor Info: (Acquisitions) Baker & Taylor; (Cataloging) Innovative Interfaces, Inc; (Circulation) Innovative Interfaces, Inc; (ILL) Mel Cat; (OPAC) Innovative Interfaces, Inc
Wireless access
Partic in Metro Net Libr Consortium; The Library Network
Open Mon-Thurs 9-9, Fri & Sat 10-6, Sun 1-5
Friends of the Library Group
Branches: 1
FARMINGTON BRANCH, 23500 Liberty St, Farmington, 48335, SAN 346-4407. Tel: 248-553-0321. FAX: 248-474-6915.
Library Holdings: Bk Vols 70,000; Per Subs 200
Open Mon-Thurs 9-9, Fri & Sat 10-6, Sun 1-5
Friends of the Library Group

S MICHIGAN PSYCHOANALYTIC INSTITUTE & SOCIETY*, Kulish Psychoanalytic Library, 32841 Middlebelt Rd, Ste 411D, 48334. SAN 327-7615. Tel: 248-851-3380. FAX: 248-851-1806. Web Site: mipsychoanalysis.org. *Librn,* Gina Labban; Staff 1 (MLS 1)
Founded 1957
Library Holdings: e-books 3; Bk Titles 2,200; Per Subs 29
Subject Interests: Psychoanalysis, Psychol
Wireless access
Function: For res purposes
Restriction: Staff & mem only

J OAKLAND COMMUNITY COLLEGE*, King Library, Orchard Ridge Campus, Bldg K, 27055 Orchard Lake Rd, 48334-4579. SAN 346-4431. Tel: 248-522-3525, 248-522-3526. Reference Tel: 248-522-3612. FAX: 248-522-3530. Web Site: www.oaklandcc.edu/library. *Librn, Ref (Info Servs),* Nadja Springer-Ali; Tel: 248-522-3531, E-mail: nmspring@oaklandcc.edu; *Librn, Ref (Info Servs),* Ann Walaskay; Tel: 248-522-3528, E-mail: aawalask@oaklandcc.edu. Subject Specialists: *Govt doc,* Nadja Springer-Ali; Staff 5 (MLS 2, Non-MLS 3)
Founded 1967. Enrl 8,462; Fac 65; Highest Degree: Associate
Jul 2019-Jun 2020. Mats Exp $35,815, Books $18,741, Per/Ser (Incl. Access Fees) $17,074. Sal $309,496 (Prof $211,439)
Library Holdings: CDs 344; DVDs 1,129; e-books 239,460; Electronic Media & Resources 14,115; Microforms 6,810; Bk Titles 82,739; Per Subs 159; Videos 210
Special Collections: US Document Depository
Automation Activity & Vendor Info: (Cataloging) Ex Libris Group; (Circulation) Ex Libris Group; (Course Reserve) Ex Libris Group; (Discovery) Ex Libris Group; (ILL) OCLC; (OPAC) Ex Libris Group; (Serials) EBSCO Online
Wireless access
Function: Audio & video playback equip for onsite use, Computers for patron use, Distance learning, Electronic databases & coll, Free DVD rentals, Govt ref serv, ILL available, Internet access, Microfiche/film & reading machines, Online cat, Online ref, Orientations, Photocopying/Printing, Ref & res, Ref serv available, Res assist avail, Scanner, Wheelchair accessible, Workshops
Special Services for the Blind - Computer with voice synthesizer for visually impaired persons; Reader equip
Open Mon-Thurs 8am-9pm, Fri 8-5

FARWELL

P SURREY TOWNSHIP PUBLIC LIBRARY*, 105 E Michigan, 48622. (Mail add: PO Box 189, 48622-0189), SAN 308-0773. Tel: 989-588-9782. FAX: 989-588-4488. Web Site: www.youseemore.com/Surrey. *Dir,* Jean Gaskill; E-mail: director@stpl.org; *Programming Dir,* Gina Hamilton; E-mail: ghamilton@stpl.org; *Circ,* Mary Beth DeSmith; E-mail: mdesmith@stpl.org; Staff 6 (MLS 1, Non-MLS 5)
Circ 24,227
Library Holdings: Bk Vols 35,000; Per Subs 80
Automation Activity & Vendor Info: (Acquisitions) Follett Software; (Cataloging) Follett Software; (Circulation) Follett Software; (OPAC) Follett Software
Wireless access
Function: Adult literacy prog, Distance learning, ILL available, Internet access, Magnifiers for reading, Outside serv via phone, mail, e-mail & web, Photocopying/Printing, Prog for children & young adult, Summer reading prog, Telephone ref, Wheelchair accessible
Partic in Mid-Michigan Library League
Special Services for the Deaf - Bks on deafness & sign lang; High interest/low vocabulary bks; Videos & decoder
Special Services for the Blind - Aids for in-house use; Audio mat; Bks on cassette; Braille bks; Children's Braille; Copier with enlargement capabilities; Extensive large print coll
Open Mon, Tues, Thurs & Fri 9-6, Wed 9-7, Sat 10-2
Friends of the Library Group

FENNVILLE

P FENNVILLE DISTRICT LIBRARY*, 400 W Main St, 49408. (Mail add: PO Box 1130, 49408-1130), SAN 308-0781. Tel: 269-561-5050. FAX: 269-561-5251. E-mail: fen@llcoop.org. Web Site: www.fennvilledl.michlibrary.org. *Dir,* Teresa Kline; E-mail: fentk@llcoop.org; Staff 11 (MLS 2, Non-MLS 9)
Founded 1924. Pop 14,564; Circ 41,000
Library Holdings: Bk Vols 37,000; Per Subs 150
Subject Interests: Mich
Automation Activity & Vendor Info: (Cataloging) Innovative Interfaces, Inc; (Circulation) Innovative Interfaces, Inc; (OPAC) Innovative Interfaces, Inc
Wireless access
Partic in Lakeland Library Cooperative; OCLC Online Computer Library Center, Inc
Special Services for the Deaf - Bks on deafness & sign lang; High interest/low vocabulary bks
Open Mon-Thurs 10-8, Fri 10-5, Sat 10-2, Sun 2-4
Friends of the Library Group

FERNDALE

P FERNDALE AREA DISTRICT LIBRARY*, 222 E Nine Mile Rd, 48220. SAN 308-0811. Tel: 248-546-2504. FAX: 248-545-5840. E-mail: info@ferndalepubliclibrary.org. Web Site: www.ferndalepubliclibrary.org. *Libr Dir,* Jenny Marr; Tel: 248-547-6000, E-mail: jmarr@ferndalepubliclibrary.org; *Asst Dir,* Darlene Hellenberg; Tel: 248-546-2504, Ext 691, E-mail: darlene@ferndalepubliclibrary.org; *Head, Circ,* Kelly Bennett; Tel: 248-546-2504, Ext 697, E-mail: kelly@ferndalepubliclibrary.org; *Head, Ref & Adult Serv,* Ed Burns; Tel: 248-546-2504, Ext 695, E-mail: edburnsiii@ferndalepubliclibrary.org; *Head, Youth Serv,* Jordan Wright; Tel: 248-546-2504, Ext 699, E-mail: jordan@ferndalepubliclibrary.org; Staff 10 (MLS 4, Non-MLS 6)
Founded 1930. Pop 22,105; Circ 125,000
Library Holdings: CDs 1,200; DVDs 1,600; Bk Vols 90,000; Per Subs 125; Talking Bks 1,000; Videos 5,000
Special Collections: Cookbook Coll
Automation Activity & Vendor Info: (Acquisitions) SirsiDynix; (Cataloging) SirsiDynix; (Circulation) SirsiDynix; (ILL) SirsiDynix; (OPAC) SirsiDynix
Wireless access
Partic in The Library Network
Open Mon-Thurs 10-8, Fri 10-6, Sat 12-5
Friends of the Library Group

FIFE LAKE

P FIFE LAKE PUBLIC LIBRARY*, 77 Lakecrest Lane, 49633. SAN 308-082X. Tel: 231-879-4101. FAX: 231-879-3360. E-mail: flpl@tadl.org. Web Site: www.tadl.org/fifelake. *Dir,* Julie Kintner
Founded 1887. Pop 1,517; Circ 12,000
Library Holdings: Large Print Bks 10; Bk Titles 16,000; Per Subs 52
Wireless access
Partic in Northland Library Cooperative
Open Tues 3-8, Wed & Fri 12-5, Thurs 12-8, Sat 10-3
Friends of the Library Group

FLAT ROCK

P FLAT ROCK PUBLIC LIBRARY, 25200 Gibraltar Rd, 48134. SAN 308-0838. Tel: 734-782-2430. Circulation Tel: 734-782-2430, Ext 106. Reference Tel: 734-782-2430, Ext 107. Administration Tel: 734-782-3444. FAX: 734-789-8265. Administration FAX: 734-789-8266. Circulation E-mail: circulation@frlib.org. Web Site: www.frlib.org. *Dir,* Michael D Cummings; E-mail: director@frlib.org; *Youth Serv Librn,* Connie Biccum; E-mail: youthlibrarian@frlib.org; Staff 14 (MLS 3, Non-MLS 11)
Founded 1999. Pop 17,823; Circ 62,545
Library Holdings: AV Mats 8,366; Bks on Deafness & Sign Lang 20; Large Print Bks 652; Bk Vols 29,896; Per Subs 72; Talking Bks 2,900
Special Collections: Local History Coll
Automation Activity & Vendor Info: (Acquisitions) CARL.Solution (TLC); (Cataloging) CARL.Solution (TLC); (Circulation) CARL.Solution (TLC); (ILL) CARL.Solution (TLC); (OPAC) CARL.Solution (TLC); (Serials) CARL.Solution (TLC)
Wireless access
Function: Activity rm, Adult bk club, Adult literacy prog, Bks on CD, Children's prog, Computers for patron use, ILL available, Internet access, Magazines, Magnifiers for reading, Meeting rooms, Movies, Music CDs, Online cat, OverDrive digital audio bks, Photocopying/Printing, Preschool reading prog, Prog for adults, Prog for children & young adult, Ref & res, Ref serv available, Scanner, Story hour, Study rm, Summer reading prog, Teen prog, Wheelchair accessible
Partic in The Library Network
Open Mon-Wed & Fri 10-6, Thurs 10-7, Sat 10-2
Friends of the Library Group

FLINT

C BAKER COLLEGE OF FLINT LIBRARY*, 1050 W Bristol Rd, 48507-5508. SAN 308-0846. Tel: 810-766-4239. Toll Free Tel: 888-854-1058. FAX: 810-766-4239. E-mail: library-fl@baker.edu. Web Site: www.baker.edu. *Acad Res Coordr,* Dr Brenda Brown; Tel: 810-766-4282, E-mail: brenda.brown@baker.edu; *Coordr of Info & Tech Res,* Bruce Childs; Staff 7 (MLS 1, Non-MLS 6)
Founded 1912. Enrl 28,800
Library Holdings: Bk Vols 80,000; Per Subs 125
Subject Interests: Aviation, Bus & mgt, Computer sci, Electronics, Engr, Fashion, Interior design, Occupational safety, Phys therapy, Travel
Automation Activity & Vendor Info: (Acquisitions) SirsiDynix; (Cataloging) SirsiDynix; (Circulation) SirsiDynix; (OPAC) SirsiDynix
Wireless access
Partic in MeLCat; PALnet
Open Mon-Thurs 9-6, Fri 9-5

SR FIRST PRESBYTERIAN CHURCH OF FLINT*, Pierce Memorial Library, 746 S Saginaw St, 48502-1508. SAN 329-8833. Tel: 810-234-8673. FAX: 810-234-1643. E-mail: info@fpcf.org. Web Site: www.fpcf.org. *Librn,* Steve Hill
Founded 1841
Library Holdings: AV Mats 3,076; CDs 1,021; DVDs 226; Bk Titles 4,823; Bk Vols 5,208; Talking Bks 633; Videos 2,848
Automation Activity & Vendor Info: (Cataloging) LibraryWorld, Inc; (Circulation) LibraryWorld, Inc
Open Mon-Fri (Winter) 8:30-4:30, Sun 8:30-12; Mon-Fri (Summer) 8-4, Sun 9:30-11

S FLINT INSTITUTE OF ARTS*, Reference Library, 1120 E Kearsley St, 48503-1915. SAN 308-0927. Tel: 810-234-1695. FAX: 810-234-1692. E-mail: info@flintarts.org. Web Site: www.flintarts.org. *Exec Dir,* John B Henry, III; E-mail: jhenry@flintarts.org; *Library Contact,* Tracee Glab
Founded 1928
Library Holdings: Bk Titles 8,000
Subject Interests: Art & archit
Publications: Exhibition Catalogues
Open Mon-Sat 10-5, Sun 1-5
Restriction: Non-circulating to the pub

P FLINT PUBLIC LIBRARY*, 1026 E Kearsley St, 48503. SAN 346-4466. Tel: 810-232-7111. Reference Tel: 810-249-2569. FAX: 810-249-2633. Web Site: www.fpl.info. *Dir, Libr Serv,* Kathryn Schwartz; Tel: 810-249-3038, E-mail: kschwartz@fpl.info; *Dir of Libr Operations,* Leslie Acevedo; Tel: 810-249-2046, E-mail: lacevedo@fpl.info; Staff 15 (MLS 14, Non-MLS 1)
Founded 1851. Pop 102,434
Jul 2014-Jun 2015 Income $3,408,501. Mats Exp $339,744. Sal $1,451,102
Special Collections: US Document Depository
Subject Interests: Children's lit, Genealogy, Local hist
Automation Activity & Vendor Info: (Circulation) Innovative Interfaces, Inc
Wireless access
Function: Activity rm, Adult bk club, Art exhibits, Audiobks via web, BA reader (adult literacy), Children's prog, Computer training, Computers for

patron use, Digital talking bks, Electronic databases & coll, Free DVD rentals, Govt ref serv, Internet access, Life-long learning prog for all ages, Online cat, Photocopying/Printing, Prog for adults, Prog for children & young adult, Ref serv available, Summer reading prog, Tax forms, Wheelchair accessible
Publications: Ring A Ring O'Roses (Library handbook)
Partic in Mideastern Michigan Library Cooperative
Special Services for the Deaf - High interest/low vocabulary bks
Open Tues-Thurs 11-8, Fri & Sat 9-6
Friends of the Library Group

L GENESEE COUNTY CIRCUIT COURT*, Law Library, County Court House, Ste 204, 900 S Saginaw St, 48502. SAN 329-7691. Tel: 810-257-3253. FAX: 810-257-0512. Web Site: www.7thcircuitcourt.com/law-library. *Library Contact,* Janet Patsy
Library Holdings: Bk Vols 10,000; Per Subs 10
Wireless access
Open Mon-Fri 8-5
Restriction: Limited access for the pub, Ref only

P GENESEE DISTRICT LIBRARY*, 4195 W Pasadena Ave, 48504. SAN 346-4709. Tel: 810-732-0110. Administration Tel: 810-732-5570. FAX: 810-732-3146. Web Site: www.thegdl.org. *Dir,* David Conklin; E-mail: dconklin@thegdl.org; *Br Librn,* Liz Kish; *Br Operations Mgr,* Mary Higginbottom; E-mail: mhigginbottom@thegdl.org; *Finance Mgr,* Amy Goldyn; E-mail: agoldyn@thegdl.org; *Human Res Mgr,* Jerilyn Klich; E-mail: jklich@thegdl.org; *IT Mgr,* Chris Wells; E-mail: cwells@thegdl.org; *Tech Serv Mgr,* Darwin McGuire; E-mail: dmcguire@thegdl.org; *Commun Relations Mgr,* Kelly Flynn; E-mail: kflynn@thegdl.org; Staff 35 (MLS 33, Non-MLS 2)
Founded 1942. Pop 332,567; Circ 4,555,186
Library Holdings: Audiobooks 4,828; AV Mats 253,292; Bks-By-Mail 7,000; Bks on Deafness & Sign Lang 80; Braille Volumes 21; CDs 8,142; DVDs 182,443; e-books 7,888; Electronic Media & Resources 52; High Interest/Low Vocabulary Bk Vols 30; Large Print Bks 137,999; Bk Vols 880,999; Per Subs 1,285; Talking Bks 14,011; Videos 11,004
Special Collections: American Indians Coll, bks, recs; Civil War (Robert L Calkins Memorial Coll); Genesee County Coll
Subject Interests: Genealogy
Automation Activity & Vendor Info: (Acquisitions) Innovative Interfaces, Inc; (Cataloging) Innovative Interfaces, Inc; (Circulation) Innovative Interfaces, Inc; (OPAC) Innovative Interfaces, Inc; (Serials) Innovative Interfaces, Inc
Wireless access
Function: Words travel prog
Special Services for the Deaf - Videos & decoder
Special Services for the Blind - Accessible computers; Aids for in-house use; Assistive/Adapted tech devices, equip & products; Audio mat; BiFolkal kits; Bks & mags in Braille, on rec, tape & cassette; Bks available with recordings; Bks on cassette; Blind Club (monthly newsletter); Braille bks; Braille Webster's dictionary; Cassette playback machines; Cassettes; Club for the blind; Computer access aids; Computer with voice synthesizer for visually impaired persons; Copier with enlargement capabilities; Descriptive video serv (DVS); Digital talking bk; Disability awareness prog; Duplicating spec requests; Home delivery serv; Info on spec aids & appliances; Internet workstation with adaptive software; Large print & cassettes; Large print bks; Large print bks & talking machines; Large screen computer & software; Lending of low vision aids; Low vision equip; Machine repair; Magnifiers; Networked computers with assistive software; Newsline for the Blind; Newsp on cassette; PC for people with disabilities; Playaways (bks on MP3); Sound rec; Spec cats; Spec prog; Talking bks & player equip; Talking bks from Braille Inst; Text reader; Volunteer serv
Open Mon-Fri 9-5
Friends of the Library Group
Branches: 20
BAKER PARK LIBRARY, G3410 S Grand Traverse, Burton, 48529, SAN 346-5128. Tel: 810-742-7860. FAX: 810-742-2927. E-mail: bakerpark@thegdl.org. *Br Librn,* Robert Gorney; E-mail: rgorney@thegdl.org; Staff 1.6 (MLS 1, Non-MLS 0.6)
Open Mon, Tues & Thurs 12-8, Fri & Sat 9-5
Friends of the Library Group
BURTON MEMORIAL LIBRARY, 4012 E Atherton Rd, Burton, 48519, SAN 346-4733. Tel: 810-742-0674. FAX: 810-742-2928. E-mail: burtonmemorial@thegdl.org. *Br Librn,* Brian Cutter; E-mail: bcutter@thegdl.org; Staff 2 (MLS 1, Non-MLS 1)
Open Mon 9-9, Tues & Thurs 10-6, Wed 12-8, Sat 9-5
Friends of the Library Group
CLIO AREA LIBRARY, 2080 W Vienna Rd, Clio, 48420, SAN 346-4768. Tel: 810-686-7130. FAX: 810-686-0071. E-mail: clio@thegdl.org. *Br Librn,* Roy Soncrant; E-mail: rsoncrant@thegdl.org; Staff 1 (MLS 1)
Open Mon & Wed 12-8, Tues & Thurs 10-6, Sat 9-5
Friends of the Library Group
DAVISON AREA LIBRARY, 203 E Fourth St, Davison, 48423, SAN 346-4792. Tel: 810-653-2022. FAX: 810-653-7633. E-mail: davison@thegdl.org. *Br Librn,* Sue Misra; E-mail: smisra@thegdl.org; Staff 1 (MLS 1)
Special Collections: Calkins Civil War Coll
Open Mon-9-9, Tues-Thurs 12-8, Fri & Sat 9-5, Sun (Winter) 1-5
Friends of the Library Group
FENTON-WINEGARDEN LIBRARY, 200 E Caroline St, Fenton, 48430, SAN 346-4822. Tel: 810-629-7612. FAX: 810-629-0855. E-mail: fenton@thegdl.org. *Br Librn,* Christine Heron; E-mail: cheron@thegdl.org; Staff 1 (MLS 1)
Open Mon & Wed 10-6, Tues & Thurs 12-8, Fri & Sat 9-5
Friends of the Library Group
FLINT TOWNSHIP-MCCARTY PUBLIC LIBRARY, 2071 S Graham Rd, 48532, SAN 346-4857. Tel: 810-732-9150. FAX: 810-732-0878. E-mail: flinttownship@thegdl.org. *Br Librn,* Amy Houser; E-mail: ahouser@thegdl.org; Staff 1 (MLS 1)
Open Mon & Wed 10-6, Tues & Thurs 12-8, Sat 9-5
Friends of the Library Group
FLUSHING AREA LIBRARY, 120 N Maple St, Flushing, 48433, SAN 346-4881. Tel: 810-659-9755. FAX: 810-659-1781. E-mail: flushing@thegdl.org. *Br Librn,* Cristen Jackson; E-mail: cjackson@thegdl.org; Staff 2 (MLS 2)
Open Mon & Wed 10-6, Tues & Thurs 12-8, Sat 9-5
Friends of the Library Group
FOREST TOWNSHIP LIBRARY, 123 W Main St, Otisville, 48463, SAN 346-5098. Tel: 810-631-6330. FAX: 810-631-6076. E-mail: foresttownship@thegdl.org. *Br Librn,* Marya Gutek; E-mail: mgutek@thegdl.org; Staff 1 (MLS 1)
Open Mon 10-6, Tues, Wed & Thurs 12-8, Sat 9-5
Friends of the Library Group
GAINES STATION LIBRARY, 103 E Walker St, Gaines, 48436, SAN 378-133X. Tel: 989-271-8720. FAX: 989-271-8816. E-mail: gaines@thegdl.org. *Br Librn,* Position Currently Open
Open Wed 4-8, Sat 9-5
GENESEE-JOHNSON LIBRARY, 7397 N Genesee Rd, Genesee, 48437, SAN 346-4970. Tel: 810-640-1410. FAX: 810-640-2413. E-mail: GeneseeTownship@thegdl.org. *Br Librn,* Shari Suarez; E-mail: ssuarez@thegdl.org; Staff 1 (MLS 1)
Open Mon 10-6, Tues & Thurs 12-8, Fri & Sat 9-5
Friends of the Library Group
GENESEE VALLEY CENTER LIBRARY, 3293 S Linden Rd, 48507. Tel: 810-732-1822. FAX: 810-732-1726. E-mail: GeneseeValley@thegdl.org. *Br Librn,* Kevin Collins; E-mail: kcollins@thegdl.org; Staff 1 (MLS 1)
Open Mon & Tues 10-9, Wed & Thurs 11-7, Fri & Sat 10-6, Sun 1-5
Friends of the Library Group
GOODRICH LIBRARY, 10237 Hegel Rd, Goodrich, 48438, SAN 346-4911. Tel: 810-636-2489. FAX: 810-636-3304. E-mail: goodrich@thegdl.org. *Br Librn,* Nicholas Badgley; E-mail: nbadgley@thegdl.org; Staff 1 (MLS 1)
Open Mon-Wed 12-8, Thurs 10-6, Sat 9-5
Friends of the Library Group
GRAND BLANC-MCFARLEN LIBRARY, 515 Perry Rd, Grand Blanc, 48439, SAN 346-4946. Tel: 810-694-5310. FAX: 810-694-5313. E-mail: grandblanc@thegdl.org. *Br Librn,* Kara Kvasnicka; E-mail: kkvasnicka@thegdl.org; Staff 3 (MLS 3)
Open Mon & Tues 9-9, Wed & Thurs 12-8, Fri & Sat 9-5, Sun (Winter) 1-5
Friends of the Library Group
HEADQUARTERS, 4195 W Pasadena Ave, 48504, SAN 346-4989. Tel: 810-732-0110. FAX: 810-732-3146. E-mail: headquarters@thegdl.org. *Br Librn,* Elizabeth Kish; E-mail: lkish@thegdl.org; Staff 3 (MLS 3)
Special Services for the Blind - Descriptive video serv (DVS); Talking bks
Open Mon & Tues 9-9, Wed & Thurs 12-8, Fri & Sat 9-5
Friends of the Library Group
LINDEN LIBRARY, 201 N Main St, Linden, 48451, SAN 346-5004. Tel: 810-735-7700. FAX: 810-735-9163. E-mail: linden@thegdl.org. *Br Librn,* John Eckleberry; E-mail: jeckleberry@thegdl.org; Staff 1 (MLS 1)
Open Mon, Wed & Thurs 12-8, Tues & Sat 9-5
Friends of the Library Group
MONTROSE-JENNINGS LIBRARY, 241 Feher Dr, Montrose, 48457, SAN 346-5039. Tel: 810-639-6388. FAX: 810-639-3675. E-mail: montrose@thegdl.org. *Br Librn,* Nancy Abbey; E-mail: nabbey@thegdl.org; Staff 1 (MLS 1)
Open Mon & Wed 10-6, Tues & Thurs 12-8, Sat 9-5
Friends of the Library Group
MOUNT MORRIS LIBRARY, 685 Van Buren Ave, Mount Morris, 48458, SAN 346-5063. Tel: 810-686-6120. FAX: 810-686-0661. E-mail: mtmorris@thegdl.org. *Br Librn,* Heather Van Fleet; E-mail: hvanfleet@thegdl.org; Staff 1 (MLS 1)
Open Mon 10-6, Tues & Wed 12-8, Fri & Sat 9-5
Friends of the Library Group

VERA B RISON-BEECHER LIBRARY, 1386 W Coldwater Rd, 48505. Tel: 810-789-2800. FAX: 810-789-2882. E-mail: beecher@thegdl.org. *Br Librn,* Sally-Adrina Taylor; E-mail: staylor@thegdl.org; Staff 1 (MLS 1)
Open Mon, Wed & Sat 9-5, Tues & Thurs 12-8
Friends of the Library Group

SWARTZ CREEK-PERKINS LIBRARY, 8095 Civic Dr, Swartz Creek, 48473, SAN 346-5152. Tel: 810-635-3900. FAX: 810-635-4179. E-mail: swartzcreek@thegdl.org. *Br Librn,* Ivan Smith; E-mail: ismith@thegdl.org; Staff 1 (MLS 1)
Open Mon, Tues & Wed 12-8, Thurs & Sat 9-5
Friends of the Library Group

P TALKING BOOK CENTER, 4195 W Pasadena Ave, 48504. Tel: 810-732-1120. FAX: 810-732-1715. E-mail: tbc@thegdl.org. *Librn,* Jason Bias; E-mail: jbias@thegdl.org; Staff 1 (MLS 1)
Partic in Mideastern Michigan Library Cooperative; Midwest Collaborative for Library Services
Special Services for the Blind - Bks on cassette; Descriptive video serv (DVS)
Open Mon-Fri 9-5

M HURLEY MEDICAL CENTER*, Michael H & Robert M Hamady Health Sciences Library, One Hurley Plaza, 48503. SAN 308-0919. Tel: 810-262-9427. Administration Tel: 810-262-9442. FAX: 810-262-7107. E-mail: library1@hurleymc.com. Web Site: education.hurleymc.com/research/medical-library. *Libr Mgr,* Jennifer Godlesky; E-mail: jgodles1@hurleymc.com; *Librn I,* Lorita Simon; Tel: 810-262-9055, E-mail: lsimon1@hurleymc.com; Staff 3 (MLS 2, Non-MLS 1)
Founded 1928
Library Holdings: Bk Titles 4,000; Per Subs 300
Special Collections: Consumer Health Information
Subject Interests: Health sci, Hospital admin, Med, Nursing
Automation Activity & Vendor Info: (Cataloging) EOS International; (Circulation) EOS International; (Serials) EOS International
Wireless access
Partic in Michigan Health Sciences Libraries Association; National Network of Libraries of Medicine Region 6
Restriction: Not open to pub

C KETTERING UNIVERSITY LIBRARY*, 1700 W University Ave, 48504. SAN 308-0900. Tel: 810-762-7814. Reference Tel: 810-762-9598. Administration Tel: 810-762-7812. FAX: 810-762-9744. E-mail: library@kettering.edu. Web Site: my.kettering.edu/academics/academic-resources/library. *Univ Librn,* Dr Dina Mein; E-mail: dmein@kettering.edu; *Head, Circ, Libr Asst IV,* Mary McNally; E-mail: mmcnally@kettering.edu; *Digital Tech/Ref Librn,* Jamie Niehof; Tel: 810-762-7815, E-mail: jniehof@kettering.edu; *Pub Serv Librn,* Dawn Winans; Tel: 810-762-9842, E-mail: dwinans@kettering.edu; *Cat, Tech Serv Librn,* Dawn Swanson; Tel: 810-762-7817, E-mail: dswanson@kettering.edu; Staff 5 (MLS 5)
Founded 1928. Enrl 2,675; Fac 154; Highest Degree: Master
Library Holdings: e-books 28,500; e-journals 3,400; Bk Titles 131,700; Bk Vols 147,900; Per Subs 400
Special Collections: ASTM Standards; NASA Technical Reports; SAE & SME Technical Papers
Subject Interests: Bus & mgt, Engr
Automation Activity & Vendor Info: (Acquisitions) SirsiDynix; (Cataloging) SirsiDynix; (Cataloging) OCLC; (Circulation) SirsiDynix; (Course Reserve) Blackboard Inc; (ILL) Clio; (OPAC) SirsiDynix; (Serials) EBSCO Online
Wireless access
Function: Res libr
Open Mon-Thurs 7:45am-Midnight, Fri 7:45-5:30, Sat 9-5, Sun 2pm-Midnight
Restriction: Open to fac, students & qualified researchers
Friends of the Library Group

M MCLAREN FLINT*, Medical Library, 401 S Ballenger Hwy, 48532-3685. SAN 324-3907. Tel: 810-342-2141. FAX: 810-342-2269. E-mail: medlib@mclaren.org. Web Site: www.mclaren.org/flint/gme-library.aspx. *Libr Mgr, Tech Serv,* Diane Gardner; E-mail: dianeg@mclaren.org; *Asst Librn,* Mary Fitzpatrick; Staff 3 (MLS 1, Non-MLS 2)
Founded 1951
Library Holdings: e-books 60; e-journals 2,500; Bk Titles 1,500; Per Subs 300
Subject Interests: Clinical med, Family practice, Health, Hospital admin, Nursing, Orthopedics, Radiology, Surgery
Automation Activity & Vendor Info: (Cataloging) EOS International; (Circulation) EOS International; (OPAC) EOS International; (Serials) EOS International
Partic in National Network of Libraries of Medicine Region 6; OCLC Online Computer Library Center, Inc
Open Mon-Fri 8-4:30

J MOTT COMMUNITY COLLEGE*, Mott Library, 1401 E Court St, 48503. SAN 308-0935. Tel: 810-762-0400. Circulation Tel: 810-762-0403. Reference Tel: 810-762-0411. Administration Tel: 810-762-0408. E-mail: library@mcc.edu. Web Site: library.mcc.edu. *Dir, Libr Serv,* Jill Sodt; E-mail: jill.sodt@mcc.edu; *Coordr, Circ & Tech Serv,* Linda Rutherford; *Coordr, Pub Serv,* Michael Ugorowski; Tel: 810-762-5662; Staff 9.5 (MLS 6.5, Non-MLS 3)
Founded 1923. Fac 554; Highest Degree: Associate
Jul 2012-Jun 2013 Income $1,039,808. Mats Exp $137,000, Books $40,000, Per/Ser (Incl. Access Fees) $32,000, Electronic Ref Mat (Incl. Access Fees) $65,000. Sal $483,429 (Prof $348,429)
Library Holdings: e-books 25,000; Bk Vols 75,000; Per Subs 150
Special Collections: College History Archive
Automation Activity & Vendor Info: (Acquisitions) SirsiDynix; (Cataloging) SirsiDynix; (Circulation) SirsiDynix; (Course Reserve) SirsiDynix; (ILL) OCLC; (OPAC) SirsiDynix; (Serials) SirsiDynix
Wireless access
Function: Audio & video playback equip for onsite use, Computers for patron use, Electronic databases & coll, Online cat, Online ref, Orientations, Photocopying/Printing, Scanner
Partic in Mideastern Michigan Library Cooperative; PALnet
Open Mon-Thurs 8am-9pm, Fri 8-5, Sat & Sun 12-5
Restriction: ID required to use computers (Ltd hrs), Lending limited to county residents, Open to students, fac & staff
Friends of the Library Group

S SLOAN MUSEUM*, Perry Archives, 303 Walnut St, 48503. SAN 325-920X. Tel: 810-237-3440. FAX: 810-237-3433. E-mail: Collections@sloanlongway.org. Web Site: sloanmuseum.org. *Curator,* Heather Moore; Tel: 810-237-3435
Library Holdings: Bk Vols 4,000
Special Collections: Archives Holdings for Flint & Genesee County
Restriction: Open by appt only

C UNIVERSITY OF MICHIGAN-FLINT*, Frances Willson Thompson Library, 303 E Kearsley St, 48502. SAN 308-0951. Tel: 810-762-3400. Reference Tel: 810-762-3408. E-mail: library-reference@umflint.edu. Web Site: libguides.umflint.edu/library, umflint.edu/library. *Dir,* Robert L Houbeck, Jr; Tel: 810-762-3018, E-mail: rhoubeck@umflint.edu; *Asst Dir, Ref Librn,* Mickey Doyle; Tel: 810-762-3401, E-mail: doylemd@umflint.edu; *Coll Develop Librn,* Paul Streby; Tel: 810-762-3405, E-mail: pgstreby@umflint.edu; *Syst Librn,* Kui-Bin Im; Tel: 810-762-3199, E-mail: kuibinim@umflint.edu; *Archivist,* Paul Gifford; Tel: 810-762-3402, E-mail: pgifford@umflint.edu; *Ser,* Anh Thach; Tel: 810-762-3414, E-mail: athach@umflint.edu; Staff 15 (MLS 10, Non-MLS 5)
Founded 1956. Enrl 7,200; Fac 333; Highest Degree: Master
Library Holdings: Bk Vols 235,000; Per Subs 905
Special Collections: Genesee Historical Coll Center
Automation Activity & Vendor Info: (Acquisitions) Ex Libris Group; (Cataloging) Ex Libris Group; (Circulation) Ex Libris Group; (Course Reserve) Ex Libris Group; (OPAC) Ex Libris Group; (Serials) Ex Libris Group
Wireless access
Function: Computers for patron use
Partic in Midwest Collaborative for Library Services
Special Services for the Deaf - Closed caption videos
Open Mon-Thurs (Fall-Winter) 8am-Midnight, Fri 8-8, Sat 10-8, Sun Noon-10; Mon-Thurs (Spring-Summer) 8am-10pm, Fri 8-6, Sat Noon-6, Sun Noon-8

FOSTORIA

P WATERTOWN TOWNSHIP FOSTORIA LIBRARY*, 9405 Foster St, 48435. (Mail add: PO Box 39, 48435-0039), SAN 308-096X. Tel: 989-795-2794. FAX: 989-795-2892. E-mail: clerk@watertowntownship.org, watertowntwplibrary@gmail.com. Web Site: watertowntwplibrary.wixsite.com/watertownlibrary. *Librn,* Sherry Walker
Founded 1964. Pop 2,100; Circ 4,800
Library Holdings: Bk Vols 7,000; Per Subs 10
Wireless access
Partic in White Pine Library Cooperative
Open Mon-Thurs 12-5 & Sat 10-12

FOWLERVILLE

P FOWLERVILLE DISTRICT LIBRARY, 130 S Grand Ave, 48836. SAN 308-0978. Tel: 517-223-9089. E-mail: info@fowlervillelibrary.org. Web Site: www.fowlervillelibrary.net. *Dir,* Ellen Peters; Staff 6 (MLS 4, Non-MLS 2)
Circ 23,000
Library Holdings: AV Mats 3,913; High Interest/Low Vocabulary Bk Vols 774; Large Print Bks 421; Bk Titles 28,248; Bk Vols 29,368; Per Subs 65
Subject Interests: Holidays

Automation Activity & Vendor Info: (Cataloging) Biblionix/Apollo; (Circulation) Biblionix/Apollo; (ILL) Biblionix/Apollo
Wireless access
Partic in The Library Network
Open Mon-Wed 9:30-7, Thurs 9:30-9, Fri 8:30-5, Sat 10-4

FRANKENMUTH

S FRANKENMUTH HISTORICAL ASSOCIATION*, Frankenmuth Historical Museum Library, 613 S Main St, 48734. SAN 326-0690. Tel: 989-652-9701. FAX: 989-652-9390. Web Site: www.frankenmuthmuseum.org. *Dir,* Alyssa Black; Tel: 989-652-9701, Ext 102, E-mail: fhadirector1963@gmail.com; *Colls Mgr,* Mary Nuechterlein; Tel: 989-652-9701, Ext 103, E-mail: fharesearch@airadv.net; Staff 1 (MLS 1)
Founded 1972
Library Holdings: Bk Titles 2,000; Bk Vols 2,500
Special Collections: Wilhelm Loehe Memorial Library; Wm Loehe Mission Activities. Oral History
Publications: Annual Booklet on History of Local Business or Organization
Restriction: Open by appt only, Pub use on premises

P FRANKENMUTH JAMES E WICKSON DISTRICT LIBRARY*, 359 S Franklin St, 48734. SAN 308-0986. Tel: 989-652-8323. FAX: 989-652-3450. E-mail: wicksonlibrary@gmail.com. Web Site: www.wicksonlibrary.org. *Libr Dir,* Pam Williams; *Asst Libr Dir,* Kathy Wiese; *Youth Serv Librn,* Barb Barger; E-mail: wicksonyouth@gmail.com; *Early Literacy Specialist,* Cheri Stainforth; E-mail: wicksonkids@gmail.com; Staff 12 (MLS 1, Non-MLS 11)
Founded 1974. Pop 6,887; Circ 95,953
Library Holdings: AV Mats 3,749; CDs 351; DVDs 114; Large Print Bks 1,249; Bk Vols 46,863; Per Subs 92; Talking Bks 1,015; Videos 1,832
Subject Interests: Genealogy, German lang, Local hist, Women studies
Automation Activity & Vendor Info: (Cataloging) Auto-Graphics, Inc; (Circulation) Auto-Graphics, Inc; (OPAC) Auto-Graphics, Inc
Wireless access
Publications: Newsletter (Quarterly)
Partic in Association for Rural & Small Libraries; White Pine Library Cooperative
Open Mon-Thurs 9-9, Fri 9-5, Sat 10-5, Sun (Oct-April) 1-4
Friends of the Library Group

FRANKFORT

P BENZIE SHORES DISTRICT LIBRARY*, 630 Main St, 49635. (Mail add: PO Box 631, 49635-0631), SAN 308-0994. Tel: 231-352-4671. FAX: 231-352-4671. E-mail: info@benzieshoreslibrary.org. Web Site: www.benzieshoreslibrary.org. *Libr Dir,* Cathy Carter; *Asst Libr Dir,* Stacy Pasche; *Tech Serv Librn,* Julie Morris; Staff 3 (MLS 1.5, Non-MLS 1.5)
Pop 4,000; Circ 64,253
Jul 2012-Jun 2013 Income $269,544. Mats Exp $269,555. Sal $138,400 (Prof $71,000)
Library Holdings: Audiobooks 800; DVDs 800; e-books 4,000; e-journals 50; Large Print Bks 2,000; Bk Vols 25,000; Per Subs 75; Talking Bks 1,114
Automation Activity & Vendor Info: (ILL) Mel Cat
Wireless access
Function: Adult bk club, Home delivery & serv to seniorr ctr & nursing homes, Homebound delivery serv, ILL available, Internet access, Photocopying/Printing, Prog for children & young adult, Ref & res, Ref serv available, Spoken cassettes & CDs, Summer reading prog, Wheelchair accessible, Workshops
Partic in Mid-Michigan Library League
Open Mon & Wed 10-8, Tues, Thurs & Fri 10-5, Sat 10-3
Restriction: Circ to mem only
Friends of the Library Group

FRANKLIN

P FRANKLIN PUBLIC LIBRARY*, 32455 Franklin Rd, 48025. SAN 308-1001. Tel: 248-851-2254. FAX: 248-851-5846. Web Site: www.franklin.lib.mi.us. *Dir,* Teresa Natzke; E-mail: tnatzke@franklin.lib.mi.us; Staff 7 (MLS 1, Non-MLS 6)
Founded 1939. Pop 3,000; Circ 24,000
Library Holdings: Bk Titles 14,000; Per Subs 50
Automation Activity & Vendor Info: (Cataloging) SirsiDynix; (Circulation) SirsiDynix; (OPAC) SirsiDynix
Wireless access
Function: 24/7 Electronic res, 24/7 Online cat, Adult bk club, Bks on CD, Children's prog, Computers for patron use, Free DVD rentals, ILL available, Internet access, Large print keyboards, Museum passes, Online cat, Photocopying/Printing, Preschool outreach, Prog for adults, Prog for children & young adult, Ref serv available, Story hour, Summer reading prog, Tax forms, Wheelchair accessible
Partic in The Library Network
Open Mon, Wed & Fri 11-6, Tues & Thurs 11-8, Sat 11-4
Friends of the Library Group

FRASER

P E C WEBER FRASER PUBLIC LIBRARY, 16330 East 14 Mile Rd, 48026-2034. SAN 308-101X. Tel: 586-293-2055. FAX: 586-294-5777. Web Site: www.fraserpubliclibrary.org. *Dir,* Lorena McDowell; E-mail: mcdowell@libcoop.net; Staff 6 (MLS 2, Non-MLS 4)
Founded 1963. Pop 14,400; Circ 111,382. Sal $248,587
Library Holdings: Audiobooks 386; CDs 3,640; DVDs 6,158; e-books 1,286; Electronic Media & Resources 49; Large Print Bks 609; Bk Vols 60,807; Per Subs 100; Videos 90
Automation Activity & Vendor Info: (Acquisitions) SirsiDynix; (Cataloging) SirsiDynix; (Circulation) SirsiDynix
Wireless access
Function: 24/7 Electronic res, Activity rm, Adult bk club, Art exhibits, Audiobks via web, AV serv, Bk club(s), Bks on CD, Children's prog, Computers for patron use, Electronic databases & coll, Free DVD rentals, Holiday prog, ILL available, Internet access, Magazines, Meeting rooms, Movies, Museum passes, Music CDs, Online cat, OverDrive digital audio bks, Photocopying/Printing, Prog for adults, Prog for children & young adult, Ref & res, Ref serv available, Scanner, Story hour, Summer reading prog, Tax forms, Teen prog, Telephone ref, Wheelchair accessible
Partic in Suburban Library Cooperative
Open Mon-Thurs 10-8, Fri & Sat 10-5
Restriction: Authorized patrons
Friends of the Library Group

FREELAND

S MICHIGAN DEPARTMENT OF CORRECTIONS, Saginaw Correctional Facility Library, 9625 Pierce Rd, 48623. Tel: 989-695-9880, Ext 2731314. FAX: 989-695-6345. Web Site: www.michigan.gov/corrections. *Librn,* Ervin Bell; E-mail: belled@michigan.gov
Library Holdings: Bk Vols 24,000; Per Subs 20
Automation Activity & Vendor Info: (Cataloging) Winnebago Software Co; (Circulation) Winnebago Software Co
Restriction: Not open to pub

FREEPORT

P FREEPORT DISTRICT LIBRARY, 208 S State St, 49325-9759. (Mail add: PO Box 4, 49325-0005), SAN 308-1028. Tel: 616-765-5181. FAX: 616-765-5181. E-mail: fretlb@llcoop.org. Web Site: freeportdl.michlibrary.org. *Dir,* Tammy Borden; *Asst Dir,* Kim Buehler; E-mail: freksb@llcoop.org; Staff 2 (Non-MLS 2)
Founded 1942. Pop 5,641; Circ 20,911
Library Holdings: Audiobooks 1,031; DVDs 1,647; e-books 4,792; Bk Titles 17,571; Per Subs 12; Talking Bks 570
Automation Activity & Vendor Info: (Cataloging) Innovative Interfaces, Inc; (Circulation) Innovative Interfaces, Inc; (ILL) Innovative Interfaces, Inc; (OPAC) Innovative Interfaces, Inc
Wireless access
Partic in Lakeland Library Cooperative
Open Mon & Thurs 1-8, Wed & Fri 9-5, Sat (Sept-April) 9am-11am
Friends of the Library Group

FREMONT

P FREMONT AREA DISTRICT LIBRARY*, 104 E Main St, 49412. SAN 308-1036. Tel: 231-924-3480. Circulation Tel: 231-928-0244. Reference Tel: 231-928-0256. Administration Tel: 231-928-0243. FAX: 231-924-2355. E-mail: fmt@llcoop.org. Web Site: www.fremontlibrary.net. *Dir,* Jackilyn Roseberry; E-mail: jroseberry@fremontlibrary.net; *Ref Serv, YA Serv,* Jill Hansen-Aune; E-mail: jeha@fremontlibrary.net; *Circ,* Lois Beekman; E-mail: lbeekman@fremontlibrary.net; Staff 18 (MLS 3, Non-MLS 15)
Founded 1996. Pop 13,413; Circ 170,000
Library Holdings: Bk Vols 81,000; Per Subs 200
Special Collections: Local History (Harry L Spooner Coll)
Automation Activity & Vendor Info: (Acquisitions) Innovative Interfaces, Inc; (Cataloging) Innovative Interfaces, Inc; (Circulation) Innovative Interfaces, Inc; (ILL) Innovative Interfaces, Inc; (OPAC) Innovative Interfaces, Inc; (Serials) Innovative Interfaces, Inc
Wireless access
Publications: Friends of the Library Newsletter (Quarterly)
Partic in Lakeland Library Cooperative
Special Services for the Blind - Audio mat; Bks on cassette; Bks on CD; Extensive large print coll
Open Mon, Tues & Thurs 10-7, Wed & Fri 10-5, Sat 10-1
Friends of the Library Group

GALESBURG

P GALESBURG CHARLESTON MEMORIAL DISTRICT LIBRARY*, 188 E Michigan Ave, 49053. SAN 308-1052. Tel: 269-665-7839. FAX: 269-665-7788. Web Site: www.galesburgcharlestonlibrary.org. *Dir,* Helena Hayes; E-mail: director@gcmdl.org
Pop 8,100; Circ 18,500
Library Holdings: Audiobooks 683; Bk Vols 30,490; Per Subs 21; Videos 1,001
Special Collections: Michigan Coll; Michigan Nut Growers Association; Michigan Pioneer Coll
Subject Interests: Local hist
Automation Activity & Vendor Info: (Acquisitions) Biblionix/Apollo; (Cataloging) Biblionix/Apollo; (Circulation) Biblionix/Apollo; (ILL) Mel Cat
Wireless access
Partic in Southwest Michigan Library Cooperative
Open Tues & Wed 10:30-6:30, Thurs & Fri 10:30-4:30, Sat 10-2
Friends of the Library Group

GALIEN

P GALIEN TOWNSHIP PUBLIC LIBRARY*, 302 N Main St, 49113. (Mail add: PO Box 278, 49113-0278), SAN 308-1060. Tel: 269-545-8281. FAX: 269-545-8281. E-mail: galienpl@sbcglobal.net. Web Site: www.galienpl.org. *Dir,* Sue Robinson
Library Holdings: Bk Vols 30,000; Per Subs 40
Automation Activity & Vendor Info: (Cataloging) Follett Software; (Circulation) Follett Software
Wireless access
Partic in Southwest Michigan Library Cooperative
Open Mon & Wed 12-8, Tues & Thurs 10-5:30, Fri 12-5:30, Sat 9-1

GARDEN CITY

P GARDEN CITY PUBLIC LIBRARY*, 31735 Maplewood St, 48135. SAN 308-1087. Tel: 734-793-1830. FAX: 734-793-1831. Web Site: www.gardencitylib.org. *Dir,* James B Lenze; E-mail: lenze@gardencitylib.org; *Ad,* Lisa Kleinert; E-mail: kleinert@gardencitylib.org; *Youth Librn,* Erin Look; E-mail: look@gardencitylib.org; Staff 12 (MLS 4, Non-MLS 8)
Founded 1923. Pop 30,047; Circ 75,000
Library Holdings: Bk Vols 50,000; Per Subs 80
Automation Activity & Vendor Info: (Circulation) SirsiDynix; (ILL) SirsiDynix; (OPAC) SirsiDynix
Wireless access
Function: AV serv, ILL available, Internet access, Magnifiers for reading, Photocopying/Printing, Prog for children & young adult, Summer reading prog, Telephone ref, Wheelchair accessible
Special Services for the Blind - Bks on cassette; Bks on CD; Large print bks; Magnifiers; Screen enlargement software for people with visual disabilities
Open Mon-Thurs 10-8, Fri & Sat 12-5
Friends of the Library Group

GAYLORD

P OTSEGO COUNTY LIBRARY*, 700 S Otsego Ave, 49735-1723. SAN 308-1095. Tel: 989-732-5841. FAX: 989-732-9401. E-mail: ocl@otsego.org. Web Site: otsego.lib.mi.us. *Dir,* Maureen Derenzy; E-mail: mderenzy@otsego.org; *Asst Dir,* Jackie Skinner; *Ch Serv,* Cathy Campbell; Staff 4 (MLS 2, Non-MLS 2)
Pop 23,301; Circ 152,451
Library Holdings: Bk Vols 59,280; Per Subs 355
Special Collections: State Document Depository
Subject Interests: Local hist
Automation Activity & Vendor Info: (Cataloging) SirsiDynix; (Circulation) SirsiDynix; (OPAC) SirsiDynix
Wireless access
Partic in Northland Library Cooperative
Special Services for the Blind - Bks on cassette; Closed circuit TV; Reader equip
Open Mon-Wed 9-8, Thurs & Fri 9-5, Sat 9-1, Sun 1-5
Friends of the Library Group
Branches: 2
JOHANNESBURG BRANCH, 10900 East M-32, Johannesburg, 49751, SAN 329-3548. Tel: 989-732-3928. FAX: 989-731-3365. E-mail: ocl@otsego.org. *Br Mgr,* Vickie Hoecherl; E-mail: jbl@otsego.org; Staff 2 (Non-MLS 2)
Open Mon 2-6, Tues 9-1, Wed, Thurs & Fri 1-5
Friends of the Library Group
VANDERBILT BRANCH, 8170 Mill St, Vanderbilt, 49795, SAN 329-3564. Tel: 989-983-3600. FAX: 989-983-3105. *Br Mgr,* Tianne Jones; Staff 1 (Non-MLS 1)
Open Mon 3-7, Tues-Thurs 1-5, Fri 9-1

GLADSTONE

P GLADSTONE AREA SCHOOL & PUBLIC LIBRARY*, 300 S Tenth St, 49837-1518. SAN 308-1109. Tel: 906-428-4224. FAX: 906-789-8452. Web Site: www.gladstoneschools.com/school__public_library. *Dir,* Lori Wells; E-mail: lwells@gladstone.k12.mi.us; Staff 3.8 (MLS 1, Non-MLS 2.8)
Founded 1913. Pop 11,700; Circ 99,884
Library Holdings: Bk Vols 45,000; Per Subs 150
Automation Activity & Vendor Info: (Cataloging) SirsiDynix; (Circulation) SirsiDynix; (OPAC) SirsiDynix
Wireless access
Function: 24/7 Electronic res, Accelerated reader prog, Activity rm, Adult bk club, Online cat, Wheelchair accessible
Partic in Superiorland Library Cooperative; Upper Peninsula Region of Library Cooperation, Inc
Open Mon-Thurs (Sept-May) 8-6:30, Fri 8-3:30; Mon-Thurs (June-Aug) 10-6
Friends of the Library Group

GLADWIN

P GLADWIN COUNTY DISTRICT LIBRARY*, 402 James Robertson Dr, 48624. SAN 308-1117. Tel: 989-426-8221. FAX: 989-426-6958. E-mail: gladwinlibrary@vlc.lib.mi.us. Web Site: gcdl.org. *Dir,* John Clexton; E-mail: director@gladwinlibrary.org; *Head, Circ,* Laura Rickord; E-mail: l.rickord@vlc.lib.mi.us; Staff 9 (MLS 1, Non-MLS 8)
Founded 1934. Pop 26,023; Circ 139,000
Library Holdings: Bk Vols 42,500; Per Subs 120
Special Collections: Genealogy room; Local History, local newsp on micro
Automation Activity & Vendor Info: (Cataloging) SirsiDynix; (Circulation) SirsiDynix; (OPAC) SirsiDynix
Wireless access
Publications: Annotated Catalog of Large Print Books; Index to Obituaries in the Gladwin County Record; Page 1 (newsletter)
Partic in Valley Libr Consortium
Open Mon-Thurs 9-8, Fri & Sat 9-5
Friends of the Library Group
Branches: 1
BEAVERTON BRANCH, 106 Tonkin St, Beaverton, 48612. Tel: 989-435-3981. FAX: 989-435-2577. *Library Contact,* Stacie Ann Fassett
Library Holdings: Bk Vols 11,500; Per Subs 28
Open Mon 9-8, Tues-Thurs 10-6, Fri 9-5, Sat 10-2
Friends of the Library Group

GLENNIE

P CURTIS TOWNSHIP LIBRARY, 4884 Bamfield Rd, 48737. Tel: 989-735-2601. FAX: 989-735-2601. Web Site: www.curtistownship.org. *Libr Dir,* Denise Bearre; E-mail: librarydirector@centurytel.net
Library Holdings: Bk Vols 9,000
Automation Activity & Vendor Info: (Cataloging) SirsiDynix; (Circulation) SirsiDynix; (OPAC) SirsiDynix
Wireless access
Partic in Superiorland Library Cooperative; Upper Peninsula Region of Library Cooperation, Inc
Open Tues, Thurs & Sat 11-4
Friends of the Library Group

GRAND HAVEN

S COUNCIL OF MICHIGAN FOUNDATIONS*, Library & Information Services, One S Harbor Dr, Ste 3, 49417. SAN 377-1598. Tel: 616-842-7080. FAX: 616-842-1760. E-mail: info@michiganfoundations.org. *Dir, Knowledge Mgt & Communications,* Bridget McGuiggan
Founded 1972
Library Holdings: AV Mats 500; Bk Titles 2,500; Per Subs 20
Subject Interests: Foundations, Grants, Philanthropy
Automation Activity & Vendor Info: (OPAC) Inmagic, Inc.
Function: Mail loans to mem
Restriction: Circ limited, Pub use on premises

P LOUTIT DISTRICT LIBRARY, 407 Columbus Ave, 49417. SAN 308-1125. Tel: 616-850-6900. E-mail: loutit@loutitlibrary.org. Web Site: www.loutitlibrary.org. *Dir,* John Martin; Tel: 616-850-6912, E-mail: jmartin@loutitlibrary.org; *Asst Dir,* Michelle Moore; Tel: 616-842-6920, E-mail: mmoore@loutitlibrary.org; *Ref Librn,* Amy Bailey; Tel: 616-850-6924, E-mail: abailey@loutitlibrary.org; *Local Hist/Genealogy,* Jeanette Weiden; Tel: 616-850-6925, E-mail: jweiden@loutitlibrary.org; *Youth Serv,* Allison Boyer; Tel: 616-850-6912, E-mail: aboyer@loutitlibrary.org; Staff 26 (MLS 5, Non-MLS 21)
Founded 1910. Pop 35,540; Circ 345,187
Library Holdings: Bk Vols 101,082; Per Subs 115
Special Collections: Genealogy & Local History Coll. Municipal Document Depository; Oral History

Automation Activity & Vendor Info: (Acquisitions) Innovative Interfaces, Inc; (Circulation) Innovative Interfaces, Inc; (OPAC) Innovative Interfaces, Inc
Wireless access
Partic in Lakeland Library Cooperative; Midwest Collaborative for Library Services
Open Mon & Tues 10-8, Wed-Fri 10-6, Sat 10-2
Friends of the Library Group

S TRI-CITIES HISTORICAL MUSEUM*, 200 Washington Ave, 49417. SAN 373-2061. Tel: 616-842-0700. FAX: 616-842-3698. Web Site: www.tri-citiesmuseum.org. *Curator of Coll,* Jared Yax; E-mail: jyax@tchmuseum.org
Founded 1959
Library Holdings: Bk Vols 500
Subject Interests: Local hist
Publications: Riverwinds (Newsletter)
Open Mon-Fri 10-5, Sat & Sun 12-5
Restriction: Not a lending libr

GRAND LEDGE

P GRAND LEDGE AREA DISTRICT LIBRARY*, 131 E Jefferson St, 48837-1534. SAN 308-1133. Tel: 517-627-7014. FAX: 517-627-6276. Web Site: grandledge.lib.mi.us. *Dir,* Lise Mitchell; Tel: 517-622-3550, E-mail: gladldirector@gmail.com; Staff 16 (MLS 1, Non-MLS 15)
Founded 1911. Pop 15,959
Library Holdings: Bk Vols 50,000; Per Subs 76
Subject Interests: Local hist
Automation Activity & Vendor Info: (Cataloging) TLC (The Library Corporation); (Circulation) TLC (The Library Corporation)
Wireless access
Function: 24/7 Electronic res, 24/7 Online cat, Children's prog, Free DVD rentals, Homework prog, Mango lang, OverDrive digital audio bks, Scanner, Study rm, Summer reading prog
Mem of Woodlands Library Cooperative
Partic in Association for Rural & Small Libraries; Midwest Collaborative for Library Services
Open Mon-Thurs 10-9, Fri & Sat 10-5, Sun 1-5
Friends of the Library Group

GRAND RAPIDS

C AQUINAS COLLEGE*, Grace Hauenstein Library, 1700 Fulton St E, 49506. SAN 308-1141. Tel: 616-632-2137. Reference Tel: 616-632-2140. Administration Tel: 616-632-2130, 616-632-2131. FAX: 616-732-4534. E-mail: library@aquinas.edu. Web Site: aquinas.libguides.com/library/home. *Co-Dir, Pub Serv,* Francine Paolini; E-mail: paolifra@aquinas.edu; *Co-Dir, Tech Serv,* Shellie Jeffries; E-mail: jeffrmic@aquinas.edu; *Electronic Res Librn, Ser Librn,* John Kroondyk; Tel: 616-632-2133, E-mail: kroonjoh@aquinas.edu; *Instruction Librn, Outreach Librn,* Christina Radisauskas; Tel: 616-632-2124, E-mail: radischr@aquinas.edu; Staff 7.5 (MLS 4, Non-MLS 3.5)
Founded 1936. Enrl 1,776; Fac 93; Highest Degree: Master
Jul 2017-Jun 2018. Mats Exp $327,802, Books $42,704, Per/Ser (Incl. Access Fees) $63,207, AV Mat $15,138, Electronic Ref Mat (Incl. Access Fees) $206,753. Sal $551,113 (Prof $265,805)
Library Holdings: CDs 2,187; DVDs 2,586; e-books 196,003; Electronic Media & Resources 85; Microforms 36,672; Bk Vols 85,348; Per Subs 231
Automation Activity & Vendor Info: (Acquisitions) Innovative Interfaces, Inc; (Cataloging) Innovative Interfaces, Inc; (Circulation) Innovative Interfaces, Inc; (OPAC) Innovative Interfaces, Inc; (Serials) Innovative Interfaces, Inc
Wireless access
Partic in Lakenet, Mich Libr Consortium; OCLC Online Computer Library Center, Inc

C CALVIN UNIVERSITY & CALVIN THEOLOGICAL SEMINARY*, Hekman Library, 1855 Knollcrest Circle SE, 49546-4402. SAN 308-1168. Tel: 616-526-7197. Interlibrary Loan Service Tel: 616-526-8573. Web Site: library.calvin.edu. *Dean of Libr,* David Malone; Tel: 616-526-6072, E-mail: david.malone@calvin.edu; *Head, Access Serv,* Carla Moyer Hotz; Tel: 616-526-5256, E-mail: Carla.Hotz@calvin.edu; *Cat Librn, Head, Coll,* Francene Lewis; Tel: 616-526-6308, E-mail: flewis@calvin.edu; *Head, Ref & Instruction,* Sarah Kolk; Tel: 616-526-6014, E-mail: smk23@calvin.edu; *Head, Tech,* Dan Wells; Tel: 616-526-7133, E-mail: dbw2@calvin.edu; *Research Librn,* Kathy DeMey; Tel: 616-526-6310, E-mail: kdemey@calvin.edu; *Theological Librn,* Anne Harrison; Tel: 616-526-6121, E-mail: amh99@calvin.edu; *ILL Coordr,* Elizabeth Steele; Tel: 616-526-8573, E-mail: eas36@calvin.edu; *Coll Develop,* Katherine Swart; Tel: 616-526-6311, E-mail: kswart20@calvin.edu; *Curator of Archives,* Dr William Katerberg; Tel: 616-526-6916, E-mail: wkaterbe@calvin.edu; Staff 11 (MLS 8, Non-MLS 3)
Founded 1892. Enrl 3,600; Fac 274; Highest Degree: Master
Library Holdings: Bk Titles 465,000; Bk Vols 765,000; Per Subs 2,658
Special Collections: Archives of Christian Reformed Church (Heritage Hall Archives), bk & microfilm; H Henry Meeter Calvinism Research Coll, bk & microfilm. State Document Depository; US Document Depository
Subject Interests: Humanities, Soc sci & issues, Theol
Automation Activity & Vendor Info: (Acquisitions) Evergreen; (Cataloging) Evergreen; (Circulation) Evergreen; (Course Reserve) Evergreen; (ILL) OCLC Tipasa; (OPAC) Evergreen; (Serials) Evergreen
Wireless access
Publications: Heritage Hall Publications; Origins
Partic in OCLC Online Computer Library Center, Inc
Open Mon-Thurs 7:30-Midnight, Fri 7:30am-8pm, Sat 9-8
Restriction: Circ limited

CR CORNERSTONE UNIVERSITY, Miller Library, 1001 E Beltline Ave NE, 49525. SAN 308-1265. Tel: 616-222-1458. Reference Tel: 616-254-1650, Ext 1382. E-mail: library.reference@cornerstone.edu. Web Site: library.cornerstone.edu. *Libr Dir & Theol Librn,* Jeff Lash; Tel: 616-254-1650, Ext 1451, E-mail: jeff.lash@cornerstone.edu; *Head, Tech Serv,* Jamie Tiemeyer; Tel: 616-254-1650, Ext 1628, E-mail: jamie.tiemeyer@cornerstone.edu; *Electronic Res Librn,* Jessica Shuck; Tel: 616-254-1650, Ext 2002, E-mail: jessica.shuck@cornerstone.edu; *ILL, Ref Librn,* Gina Bolger; Tel: 616-254-1650, Ext 1245, E-mail: gina.bolger@cornerstone.edu; *Circ Supvr,* Leah Peirce; Tel: 616-254-1650, Ext 1976, E-mail: leah.peirce@cornerstone.edu; *Acq Assoc,* Madison Drew; Tel: 616-254-1650, Ext 1232, E-mail: madison.drew@cornerstone.edu; *Cataloging Assoc,* Cathy Haan; Tel: 616-254-1650, Ext 1065, E-mail: cathy.haan@cornerstone.edu; *Metadata Library Assoc,* Brook Johnson; Tel: 616-254-1650, Ext 1358, E-mail: brook.johnson@cornerstone.edu. Subject Specialists: *Kinesiology, Math, Sci,* Jamie Tiemeyer; *Bus, Computer sci, Healthcare mgt,* Jessica Shuck; *Children's lit, Hist, Teacher educ,* Gina Bolger; *Communication, Media, Music,* Cathy Haan; Staff 8.5 (MLS 5, Non-MLS 3.5)
Founded 1941. Enrl 2,382; Fac 83; Highest Degree: Master
Library Holdings: DVDs 1,564; e-books 199,042; e-journals 44,661; Bk Titles 89,486; Per Subs 313
Subject Interests: Theol
Automation Activity & Vendor Info: (Acquisitions) Innovative Interfaces, Inc; (Cataloging) Innovative Interfaces, Inc; (Circulation) Innovative Interfaces, Inc; (Course Reserve) Innovative Interfaces, Inc; (ILL) OCLC Online; (OPAC) Innovative Interfaces, Inc; (Serials) Innovative Interfaces, Inc
Wireless access
Function: Archival coll, Doc delivery serv, ILL available, Ref serv available, Telephone ref
Partic in Christian Library Consortium
Open Mon-Thurs 8am-10pm, Fri 8-8, Sat Noon-8, Sun 5pm-8pm
Friends of the Library Group

C DAVENPORT UNIVERSITY*, Margaret D Sneden Library, 6191 Kraft Ave SE, 49512. SAN 308-1192. Tel: 616-554-5664. Reference Toll Free Tel: 800-632-9569. Toll Free Tel: 866-925-3884. FAX: 616-554-5226. E-mail: main_library@davenport.edu. Web Site: www.davenport.edu. *Dir, Acad Serv,* Karen McLaughlin; E-mail: karen.mclaughlin@davenport.edu; *Assoc Dir, Digital Serv,* Julie Gotch; E-mail: julie.gotch@davenport.edu; *Global Campus Librn,* Emily Hayes; E-mail: emily.hayes@davenport.edu; *Digital Serv Librn,* Brian Holda; E-mail: brian.holda@davenport.edu; *Libr Serv Spec,* Rachel Brown; E-mail: rachel.brown@davenport.edu; *Libr Serv Spec,* Sarah Gray; E-mail: sarah.gray@davenport.edu; *Libr Serv Spec,* Urszula Kassel; E-mail: urszula.kassel@davenport.edu; Staff 12 (MLS 9, Non-MLS 3)
Founded 1866. Highest Degree: Master
Subject Interests: Acctg, Allied health, Bus mgt, Computing, Info tech, Nursing
Automation Activity & Vendor Info: (Cataloging) Koha; (Circulation) Koha; (ILL) OCLC; (OPAC) Koha; (Serials) Koha
Wireless access
Partic in Midwest Collaborative for Library Services; OCLC Online Computer Library Center, Inc; Southeastern Michigan League of Libraries

C FERRIS STATE UNIVERSITY, Kendall College of Art & Design Library, 17 Fountain St NW, 49503-3002. SAN 308-1311. Tel: 616-259-1121. Toll Free Tel: 800-676-2787. FAX: 616-831-9689. Web Site: ferris.libguides.com/kcad-library. *Libr Dir,* Elise J Bohn; Tel: 616-259-1123, E-mail: elisebohn@ferris.edu; *Content Mgr, Scholarly Communications,* Benjamin Boss; Tel: 616-259-1126, E-mail: benboss@ferris.edu; Staff 3 (MLS 3)
Founded 1928. Enrl 1,100; Fac 166; Highest Degree: Master
Library Holdings: Audiobooks 77; CDs 525; DVDs 1,117; Electronic Media & Resources 200; Bk Titles 2,550; Bk Vols 2,698; Per Subs 95
Special Collections: 19th & Early 20th Century History of Furniture Design, Interiors & Ornament, auction cats, bks, company cats, exhibition cats, portfolios, prints
Subject Interests: Archit, Art educ, Art hist, Digital media, Drawing, Fine arts, Functional art & sculpture, Graphic design, Illustration, Interior design, Jewelry design, Metals design, Painting, Photog

Automation Activity & Vendor Info: (Acquisitions) Innovative Interfaces, Inc - Sierra; (Cataloging) OCLC; (Circulation) Innovative Interfaces, Inc - Sierra; (Discovery) Ex Libris Group; (ILL) OCLC WorldShare Interlibrary Loan; (Media Booking) Innovative Interfaces, Inc - Sierra; (OPAC) Innovative Interfaces, Inc - Sierra; (Serials) Innovative Interfaces, Inc - Sierra
Wireless access
Function: 24/7 Online cat, Archival coll, Audio & video playback equip for onsite use, Bks on CD, Computers for patron use, Electronic databases & coll, Free DVD rentals, ILL available, Internet access, Orientations, Photocopying/Printing, Ref serv available
Partic in Midwest Collaborative for Library Services
Open Mon-Thurs 8-5, Fri 8-4:30 (Fall & Spring)
Restriction: In-house use for visitors, Open to students, fac & staff

S FISHBECK, THOMPSON, CARR & HUBER*, Information Management Center, 1515 Arboretum Dr SE, 49546. Tel: 616-575-3824. FAX: 616-464-3993. E-mail: info@ftch.com. Web Site: www.ftch.com. *Info Res Spec,* Sandie Ross; E-mail: slross@ftch.com; Staff 1 (Non-MLS 1)
Founded 1956
Library Holdings: Bk Titles 7,000; Per Subs 164
Subject Interests: Archit, Engr

CR GRACE CHRISTIAN UNIVERSITY*, Bultema Memorial Library, 1011 Aldon St SW, 49509. SAN 308-1249. Tel: 616-261-8575. FAX: 616-538-0599. E-mail: library@gracechristian.edu. Web Site: gracechristian.libguides.com/libraryhome. *Univ Librn,* Erinn Huebner; E-mail: ehuebner@gracechristian.edu; Staff 3.5 (MLS 2, Non-MLS 1.5)
Founded 1945. Enrl 300; Fac 34; Highest Degree: Master
Library Holdings: Bk Vols 40,000; Per Subs 150
Subject Interests: Bible, Educ, Music, Soc serv, Theol
Automation Activity & Vendor Info: (Acquisitions) Follett Software; (Cataloging) Follett Software; (Circulation) Follett Software; (OPAC) Follett Software
Wireless access
Function: 24/7 Online cat
Open Mon-Thurs 8am-Midnight, Fri 8-4, Sat 11-4, Sun 8pm-11pm
Restriction: Open to students, fac & staff

S GRAND RAPIDS ART MUSEUM*, Reference Library, 101 Monroe Center St NW, 49503. SAN 308-1257. Tel: 616-831-1000. FAX: 616-831-1001. E-mail: info@artmuseumgr.org. Web Site: www.artmuseumgr.org. *Chief Curator,* Ron Platt; E-mail: rplatt@artmuseumgr.org; *Asst Curator,* Jennifer Wcisel; E-mail: jwcisel@artmuseumgr.org
Founded 1910
Library Holdings: Bk Titles 9,800
Special Collections: Art History Coll; Museum Archival Material
Wireless access
Open Tues-Sat 1-4
Restriction: Non-circulating, Restricted access

J GRAND RAPIDS COMMUNITY COLLEGE*, Arthur Andrews Memorial Library, 140 Ransom NE Ave, 49503. (Mail add: 143 Bostwick Ave NE, 49503), SAN 308-1281. Tel: 616-234-3868. Circulation Tel: 616-234-3872. Interlibrary Loan Service Tel: 616-234-3749. FAX: 616-234-3889. Web Site: www.grcc.edu/library. *Dir,* Brian Beecher; *Coll Develop Librn,* Sophia Brewer; *Ref & Instruction Librn,* Nan Schichtel; *Tech Serv Librn,* Lori DeBie; *Archivist, Ref Librn,* Michael Klawitter; *Syst Librn, Web Librn,* Steven Putt; *Circ Coordr,* Kevin Lyons; Staff 10 (MLS 5, Non-MLS 5)
Founded 1914. Enrl 9,000; Fac 600; Highest Degree: Associate
Library Holdings: e-books 156,000; Bk Titles 81,000; Bk Vols 85,000
Automation Activity & Vendor Info: (Acquisitions) Innovative Interfaces, Inc; (Cataloging) Innovative Interfaces, Inc; (Circulation) Innovative Interfaces, Inc; (Course Reserve) Innovative Interfaces, Inc; (ILL) OCLC; (OPAC) Innovative Interfaces, Inc; (Serials) Innovative Interfaces, Inc
Wireless access
Partic in MeLCat
Open Mon-Thurs (Fall & Winter) 7:30am-9:45pm, Fri 7:30-5, Sat 10-2; Mon-Thurs (Summer) 8-8, Fri 8-5

P GRAND RAPIDS PUBLIC LIBRARY*, 111 Library St NE, 49503-3268. SAN 346-5306. Tel: 616-988-5400. FAX: 616-988-5419. Web Site: www.grpl.org. *Dir,* John A McNaughton; Tel: 616-988-5402, Ext 5431, E-mail: jmcnaughton@grpl.org; *Asst Libr Dir,* Briana Trudell; E-mail: btrudell@grpl.org; *Youth Serv Librn,* Jessica Anne Bratt; E-mail: jbratt@grpl.org; *Circ Supvr,* Jen Vander Heide; Tel: 616-988-5402, Ext 5452, E-mail: jvanderh@grpl.org; *Coordr, Ref Serv-Adult,* Amy Cochran; E-mail: acochran@grpl.org; Staff 35 (MLS 35)
Founded 1871. Pop 197,800; Circ 1,523,566
Library Holdings: AV Mats 76,199; Electronic Media & Resources 21; Bk Titles 388,006; Bk Vols 722,280; Per Subs 1,163
Special Collections: Foundation Center Regional Coll; Furniture Coll; Genealogy (Lawrence Fund); History of Old Northwest Territory (Campbell Fund); Landscape Architecture & Gardening (Richmond Fund); Michigan History (Stuart Fund); Picture Books (Butler Fund). Oral History; State Document Depository; US Document Depository
Subject Interests: Art & archit, Bus & mgt, Educ, Hist, Music, Soc sci & issues
Automation Activity & Vendor Info: (Circulation) Innovative Interfaces, Inc
Wireless access
Function: Adult bk club, After school storytime, Archival coll, Computer training, Electronic databases & coll, Govt ref serv, Home delivery & serv to seniorr ctr & nursing homes, ILL available, Internet access, Online ref, Photocopying/Printing, Prog for adults, Prog for children & young adult, Ref serv available, Senior computer classes, Spoken cassettes & CDs, Spoken cassettes & DVDs, Summer reading prog, Tax forms, Telephone ref, Wheelchair accessible
Publications: Tree That Never Dies
Partic in OCLC Online Computer Library Center, Inc
Open Mon-Thurs 9-9, Fri & Sat 9-5:30, Sun (Sept-May) 1-5
Friends of the Library Group
Branches: 7
MADISON SQUARE, 1201 Madison SE, 49507, SAN 373-5362. Tel: 616-988-5411. FAX: 616-245-1403. E-mail: gms@grpl.org. *Librn,* Position Currently Open
Open Tues, Wed, Fri & Sat 10-6, Thurs 12-8
OTTAWA HILLS, 1150 Giddings Ave SE, 49506, SAN 346-5365. Tel: 616-988-5412. FAX: 616-241-1460. E-mail: gro@grpl.org. *Librn,* Madison Perian; E-mail: mperian@grpl.org
Open Tues & Thurs-Sat 10-6, Wed 12-8
Friends of the Library Group
SEYMOUR, 2350 Eastern Ave SE, 49507, SAN 346-539X. Tel: 616-988-5413. FAX: 616-241-1445. E-mail: grs@grpl.org. *Librn,* Zandra Blake; E-mail: zblake@grpl.org
Open Mon & Tues 12-8, Wed, Thurs & Sat 10-6
Friends of the Library Group
VAN BELKUM BRANCH, 1563 Plainfield Ave NE, 49505, SAN 346-5330. Tel: 616-988-5410. FAX: 616-365-2615. E-mail: grc@grpl.org. *Librn,* Bridget Ward; E-mail: bward@grpl.org
Open Tues & Thurs-Sat 10-6, Wed 12-8
WEST LEONARD BRANCH, 1017 Leonard St NW, 49504. Tel: 616-988-5416. FAX: 616-301-9438. E-mail: gnw@grpl.org. *Librn,* Kelly Karr; E-mail: kkarr@grpl.org
Open Mon & Tues 12-8, Wed, Thurs & Sat 10-6
WEST SIDE, 713 Bridge St NW, 49504, SAN 346-542X. Tel: 616-988-5414. FAX: 616-458-0103. E-mail: grw@grpl.org. *Librn,* Liz Sterling; E-mail: esterling@grpl.org
Open Tues, Wed, Fri & Sat 10-6, Thurs 12-8
Friends of the Library Group
YANKEE CLIPPER, 2025 Leonard NE, 49505, SAN 346-5454. Tel: 616-988-5415. FAX: 616-235-8349. E-mail: gry@grpl.org. *Librn,* Andrea Cosier; E-mail: acosier@grpl.org
Open Mon & Tues 12-8, Wed, Thurs & Sat 10-6
Friends of the Library Group

CR KUYPER COLLEGE*, Zondervan Library, 3333 E Beltline Ave NE, 49525. SAN 308-1362. Tel: 616-222-3000. Information Services Tel: 616-988-3700. FAX: 616-988-3608. E-mail: library@kuyper.edu. Web Site: www.kuyper.edu/library. *Dir, Libr Serv,* Michelle Norquist; Tel: 616-988-3660, E-mail: mnorquist@kuyper.edu; *Libr Serv Spec,* Libby Huizenga; Tel: 616-988-3777, E-mail: lhuizenga@kuyper.edu; Staff 1.5 (MLS 1, Non-MLS 0.5)
Founded 1940. Enrl 144; Fac 14; Highest Degree: Bachelor
Library Holdings: AV Mats 1,325; e-books 14,195; Microforms 4,754; Bk Titles 65,653; Per Subs 63
Special Collections: Zondervan Publishing House Coll
Subject Interests: Biblical studies, Educ, Hist, Relig, Theol
Automation Activity & Vendor Info: (Cataloging) Innovative Interfaces, Inc - Sierra; (Circulation) Innovative Interfaces, Inc - Sierra; (Discovery) EBSCO Discovery Service; (ILL) OCLC WorldShare Interlibrary Loan; (OPAC) Innovative Interfaces, Inc - Sierra
Wireless access
Partic in Asn of Christian Librs; Midwest Collaborative for Library Services
Open Mon-Thurs 8am-10pm, Fri 8-4:30, Sat 10-5

M MERCY HEALTH*, Health Services Library, Wege Center for Health & Learning, 300 Lafayette Ave SE, 49503. Tel: 616-685-6243. *Librn,* Caralee Witteveen-Lane; E-mail: caralee.witteveen-lane@mercyhealth.com
Function: Res libr
Open Mon-Fri 7-3

S MICHIGAN MASONIC MUSEUM & LIBRARY, 233 E Fulton St, Ste 10, 49503. Tel: 616-459-9336. Toll Free Tel: 888-748-4540. E-mail: library@mi-gl.org. Web Site: masonichistory.org. *Dir,* Dirk W Hughes; E-mail: dhughes@mmcfonline.org

Library Holdings: Bk Vols 8,000; Per Subs 15; Videos 25
Special Collections: Oral History
Subject Interests: Fraternal movement, Masonic heritage, Mich hist, Philos, Symbolism
Wireless access
Publications: Masonic Resources (Quarterly)
Open Tues, Wed, Fri & Sat 10-6, Thurs Noon-8
Friends of the Library Group

S RIGHT TO LIFE OF MICHIGAN*, State Central Resource Center, 2340 Porter St SW, 49509. (Mail add: PO Box 901, 49509-0901), SAN 375-1902. Tel: 616-532-2300. FAX: 616-532-3461. E-mail: info@rtl.org. Web Site: www.rtl.org. *Pub Relations,* Chris Gast; E-mail: cgast@rtl.org
Library Holdings: Bk Vols 300
Subject Interests: Abortion, Euthanasia
Open Mon-Fri 8:30-5

R SECOND CONGREGATIONAL UNITED CHURCH OF CHRIST LIBRARY*, 525 Cheshire Dr NE, 49505. SAN 308-1389. Tel: 616-361-2629. FAX: 616-361-8181. *Librn,* Janet Rinvett
Library Holdings: Bk Vols 2,050
Wireless access

L SMITH, HAUGHEY, RICE & ROEGGE*, Law Library, 100 Monroe Center NW, 49503. SAN 372-0454. Tel: 616-774-8000. FAX: 616-774-2461. Web Site: www.shrr.com. *Dir, Info Serv,* Penelope A Turner; Tel: 614-458-5315, E-mail: pturner@shrr.com; Staff 2 (Non-MLS 2)
Library Holdings: Bk Vols 6,000; Per Subs 101
Automation Activity & Vendor Info: (Cataloging) EOS International; (Serials) EOS International
Restriction: Co libr

M RICHARD R SMITH MEDICAL LIBRARY*, Spectrum Health Campus, 1840 Wealthy St SE, 49506. SAN 308-115X. Tel: 616-774-7931. FAX: 616-774-5290. E-mail: medical.library@spectrumhealth.org. Web Site: www.spectrumhealth.org/locations/spectrum-health-hospitals-blodgett-hospital. *Librn,* Diane Hummel; Staff 4 (MLS 3, Non-MLS 1)
Founded 1934
Library Holdings: Bk Vols 1,800; Per Subs 350
Subject Interests: Med, Neurology, Nursing, Oncology, Orthopedics, Pediatrics, Plastic surgery, Surgery
Partic in Midwest Collaborative for Library Services

M SPECTRUM HEALTH*, Amberg Health Sciences Library, A Level West Bldg, 100 Michigan St NE, 49503-2560. SAN 346-5276. Tel: 616-391-1655. FAX: 616-391-3527. E-mail: medical.library@spectrumhealth.org. Web Site: www.spectrumhealth.org/locations/spectrum-health-hospitals-butterworth-hospital. *Mgr,* Diane Hummel
Founded 1918
Library Holdings: e-books 100; e-journals 275; Bk Titles 6,000; Per Subs 650
Special Collections: American Nurse's Association Publications; National League for Nursing Publications Coll
Subject Interests: Med, Nursing
Automation Activity & Vendor Info: (Acquisitions) EOS International; (Cataloging) EOS International; (Circulation) EOS International; (Course Reserve) EOS International; (OPAC) EOS International; (Serials) EOS International
Publications: Ex Libris
Partic in Midwest Collaborative for Library Services
Open Mon-Thurs (Winter) 8:30-8, Fri 8:30-5; Mon-Thurs (Summer) 8:30-6, Fri 8:30-5

L WARNER, NORCROSS & JUDD, LLP LIBRARY*, 1500 Warner Bldg, 150 Ottawa Ave NW, 49503. SAN 308-1397. Tel: 616-752-2000. FAX: 616-752-2500. E-mail: library@wnj.com. Web Site: www.wnj.com. *Librn,* Kim Koscielntar; Staff 4 (MLS 1, Non-MLS 3)
Founded 1931
Library Holdings: Bk Titles 12,000
Automation Activity & Vendor Info: (Cataloging) Inmagic, Inc.; (Circulation) Inmagic, Inc.
Function: ILL available
Partic in Midwest Collaborative for Library Services
Restriction: Employees & their associates

GRANT

P GRANT AREA DISTRICT LIBRARY*, 122 Elder St, 49327. SAN 308-1419. Tel: 231-834-5713. FAX: 231-834-9705. E-mail: info@grantlibrary.net. Web Site: www.grantlibrary.net. *Dir,* Jessica Hunt; Tel: 231-834-5713, Ext 103, E-mail: jhunt@grantlibrary.net; Staff 1 (MLS 1)
Founded 1920. Pop 9,000; Circ 35,814
Library Holdings: Bk Titles 40,000; Per Subs 40
Special Collections: Oral History
Subject Interests: Local hist
Automation Activity & Vendor Info: (Cataloging) Innovative Interfaces, Inc - Sierra; (Circulation) Innovative Interfaces, Inc - Sierra
Wireless access
Function: 24/7 Electronic res, 24/7 Online cat, Adult bk club, Bk club(s), Bks on CD, Children's prog, Computers for patron use, Digital talking bks, Electronic databases & coll, Holiday prog, Homebound delivery serv, ILL available, Internet access, Laminating, Magazines, Meeting rooms, Museum passes, Music CDs, Notary serv, Online cat, OverDrive digital audio bks, Photocopying/Printing, Prog for adults, Prog for children & young adult, Ref serv available, Scanner, Spanish lang bks, Study rm, Summer reading prog, Tax forms, Wheelchair accessible
Publications: Grant Area, Yesterday-Today (local history book)
Partic in Lakeland Library Cooperative
Open Mon, Wed & Fri 9-5, Tues & Thurs 9-8, Sat 9-1
Friends of the Library Group

GRAYLING

P CRAWFORD COUNTY LIBRARY*, Devereaux Memorial Library, 201 Plum St, 49738. SAN 308-1427. Tel: 989-348-9214. FAX: 989-348-9294. E-mail: ccls@crawfordco.lib.mi.us. Web Site: www.crawfordco.lib.mi.us. *Dir,* Connie Meyer; E-mail: cmeyer@uproc.lib.mi.us; Staff 10 (MLS 1, Non-MLS 9)
Founded 1927. Pop 14,273; Circ 67,690
Library Holdings: AV Mats 3,012; Bks on Deafness & Sign Lang 35; CDs 300; e-books 14,000; Large Print Bks 1,205; Bk Vols 54,332; Per Subs 72; Talking Bks 4,024
Special Collections: Fly Fishing (George Griffith & Marion Wright Memorial Coll), prints; Local Newspaper Coll, 1879-present, micro & print
Subject Interests: Local hist, Popular mat
Automation Activity & Vendor Info: (Cataloging) SirsiDynix; (Circulation) SirsiDynix; (ILL) SirsiDynix; (OPAC) SirsiDynix
Wireless access
Partic in Superiorland Library Cooperative; Upper Peninsula Region of Library Cooperation, Inc
Special Services for the Blind - Audio mat; Bks on cassette; Bks on CD; Home delivery serv; HP Scan Jet with photo-finish software; Large screen computer & software; Low vision equip; Magnifiers; PC for people with disabilities; Ref serv; Talking bks
Open Mon-Fri 9-6
Restriction: Access for corporate affiliates
Friends of the Library Group
Branches: 1
FREDERIC TOWNSHIP LIBRARY, 6470 Manistee St, Frederic, 49733, SAN 376-0286. Tel: 989-348-4067. FAX: 989-348-0224. E-mail: frederic@crawfordco.lib.mi.us.
Library Holdings: Bk Vols 4,800; Per Subs 11
Special Services for the Blind - Computer with voice synthesizer for visually impaired persons
Open Mon-Fri 9-5, Sat 9-2
Friends of the Library Group

GREENVILLE

P FLAT RIVER COMMUNITY LIBRARY*, 200 W Judd St, 48838. SAN 308-1435. Tel: 616-754-6359. FAX: 616-754-1398. E-mail: gre@llcoop.org. Web Site: flatriverlibrary.org. *Dir,* Stefanie Reed; E-mail: gresr@llcoop.org; *YA Serv,* Tiffany Olman; E-mail: greto@llcoop.org; *Ref/Tech Serv,* Timothy J West; E-mail: gretjw@llcoop.org; Staff 6 (MLS 2, Non-MLS 4)
Founded 1868. Pop 17,626
Special Collections: Hans Christian Andersen Coll
Subject Interests: Local hist
Automation Activity & Vendor Info: (Cataloging) Innovative Interfaces, Inc; (Circulation) Innovative Interfaces, Inc; (OPAC) Innovative Interfaces, Inc; (Serials) Innovative Interfaces, Inc
Wireless access
Function: Art exhibits, AV serv, BA reader (adult literacy), Home delivery & serv to seniorr ctr & nursing homes, Homebound delivery serv, ILL available, Internet access, Magnifiers for reading, Outside serv via phone, mail, e-mail & web, Photocopying/Printing, Prog for adults, Prog for children & young adult, Ref serv available, Serves people with intellectual disabilities, Spoken cassettes & CDs, Summer reading prog, Telephone ref, VHS videos, Wheelchair accessible
Partic in Lakeland Library Cooperative
Open Mon-Thurs 9-8, Fri & Sat 9-5
Friends of the Library Group

GROSSE ILE

R GROSSE ILE PRESBYTERIAN CHURCH LIBRARY*, 7925 Horsemill Rd, 48138. SAN 308-1443. Tel: 734-676-8811. FAX: 734-676-2718. E-mail: gipc@gipc.org. Web Site: www.gipc.org. *Library Contact,* Lea Kohler
Founded 1960
Library Holdings: AV Mats 100; Bk Vols 1,200

GROSSE POINTE FARMS

P GROSSE POINTE PUBLIC LIBRARY*, Ten Kercheval Ave, 48236-3602. SAN 346-6116. Tel: 313-343-2074. FAX: 313-343-2437. Web Site: www.grossepointelibrary.org. *Dir,* Jessica Keyser; E-mail: jkeyser@grossepointelibrary.org; *Asst Dir,* Peggy Kitchel; E-mail: pkitchel@grossepointelibrary.org; Staff 18 (MLS 18)
Founded 1929. Pop 54,600
Library Holdings: Bk Vols 173,076; Per Subs 276
Special Collections: Oral History
Subject Interests: Bus & mgt, Med, Music
Automation Activity & Vendor Info: (Acquisitions) Innovative Interfaces, Inc; (Cataloging) Innovative Interfaces, Inc; (Circulation) Innovative Interfaces, Inc; (OPAC) Innovative Interfaces, Inc
Wireless access
Publications: Library Pointes
Open Mon-Thurs 9-9, Fri 9-6, Sat 9-5, Sun (Winter) 1-5
Friends of the Library Group
Branches: 2
EWALD, 15175 E Jefferson, Grosse Pointe Park, 48236, SAN 346-6140. Tel: 313-821-8830. FAX: 313-821-8356. *Br Mgr,* Danis Houser; E-mail: dhouser@grossepointelibrary.org; Staff 3 (MLS 3)
Library Holdings: Bk Vols 30,544; Per Subs 129
Open Mon-Thurs 9-9, Fri 9-6, Sat 9-5
Friends of the Library Group
WOODS, 20680 Mack Ave, Grosse Pointe Woods, 48236, SAN 346-6175. Tel: 313-343-2072. FAX: 313-343-2486. *Br Mgr,* Pat Mclary; Staff 4 (MLS 4)
Library Holdings: Bk Vols 45,816; Per Subs 135
Open Mon-Thurs 9-9, Fri 9-6, Sat 9-5, Sun (Winter) 1-5
Friends of the Library Group

GWINN

P FORSYTH TOWNSHIP PUBLIC LIBRARY*, 184 W Flint St, 49841. (Mail add: PO Box 1328, 49841-1328), SAN 308-146X. Tel: 906-346-3433. FAX: 906-346-9728. E-mail: fyill@uproc.lib.mi.us. Web Site: forsythtwplibrary.org. *Dir,* Leslie Makela; E-mail: lmakela@uproc.lib.mi.us
Pop 6,164; Circ 12,500
Library Holdings: AV Mats 200; Bk Vols 13,061; Per Subs 52
Wireless access
Partic in Superiorland Library Cooperative; Upper Peninsula Region of Library Cooperation, Inc
Open Mon & Wed 10-7, Tues, Thurs & Fri 10-5, Sat 10-1

HAMBURG

P HAMBURG TOWNSHIP LIBRARY, 10411 Merrill Rd, 48139. (Mail add: PO Box 247, 48139-0247), SAN 308-1478. Tel: 810-231-1771. FAX: 810-231-1520. E-mail: hamb@tln.lib.mi.us. Web Site: www.hamburglibrary.org. *Dir,* Holly Hentz; E-mail: hhentz@hamburglibrary.org; *Circ Librn,* Kim Roberts; E-mail: kroberts@hamburglibrary.org; *Financial Mgr,* Christine Weber; E-mail: cweber@hamburglibrary.org; *Adult Serv,* Bree Stokanovich; *Youth Serv,* Laura Strandt; E-mail: lstrandt@hamburglibrary.org; Staff 12 (MLS 3, Non-MLS 9)
Founded 1966. Pop 21,165; Circ 140,070
Library Holdings: Bk Vols 55,399; Per Subs 88
Special Collections: Arts & Crafts Coll; EPA Coll; Local History Coll; Michigan Coll; Speigleburg Rasmussen Sites
Automation Activity & Vendor Info: (Cataloging) Auto-Graphics, Inc; (Circulation) Auto-Graphics, Inc; (OPAC) Auto-Graphics, Inc
Wireless access
Function: 24/7 Electronic res, Accelerated reader prog, Activity rm, Adult bk club, Art exhibits, Audio & video playback equip for onsite use, AV serv, Bk club(s), Bks on CD, Children's prog, Computer training, Computers for patron use, E-Reserves, Electronic databases & coll, Free DVD rentals, ILL available, Laminating, Life-long learning prog for all ages, Literacy & newcomer serv, Magazines, Mail & tel request accepted, Movies, Museum passes, Music CDs, Online cat, Online ref, Photocopying/Printing, Preschool reading prog, Prog for adults, Prog for children & young adult, Ref serv available, Scanner, Spoken cassettes & CDs, Story hour, Study rm, Summer reading prog, Tax forms, Teen prog, Telephone ref, Wheelchair accessible
Publications: Newsletter
Partic in Midwest Collaborative for Library Services; The Library Network
Open Mon-Thurs 9-8, Fri 12-6, Sat 9-5

HAMTRAMCK

P HAMTRAMCK PUBLIC LIBRARY*, Albert J Zak Memorial Library, 2360 Caniff St, 48212. SAN 308-1486. Tel: 313-733-6822. FAX: 313-733-4456. Web Site: hamtramck.lib.mi.us. *Dir,* E Tamara Sochacka; E-mail: tamarasochacka@comcast.net; *Head, Circ,* Latisha Hill; *Youth Librn,* Katarina Quain; Staff 3 (MLS 2, Non-MLS 1)
Founded 1918. Pop 18,000; Circ 60,000
Library Holdings: AV Mats 410; Bk Vols 60,000; Per Subs 200; Talking Bks 830
Special Collections: City of Hamtramck Historical File, bks, clippings, microfilm, newsp; Polish, Ukrainian, Russian (Foreign Language Coll); Svengali, Hindi, Urdu, Serbian, Croatian, Bosnian, Arabic & Albanian Colls
Automation Activity & Vendor Info: (Cataloging) SirsiDynix; (Circulation) SirsiDynix; (OPAC) SirsiDynix
Partic in The Library Network
Open Mon, Wed & Fri 9-5, Tues & Thurs 11-7
Friends of the Library Group

HANCOCK

C FINLANDIA UNIVERSITY*, Maki Library, 601 Quincy St, 49930. SAN 346-6205. Tel: 906-487-7252. Administration Tel: 906-487-7253. Toll Free Tel: 800-682-7604, Ext 252. FAX: 906-487-7297. E-mail: maki.library@finlandia.edu. Web Site: www.finlandia.edu/library. *Head Librn,* Rebecca Daly; E-mail: rebecca.daly@finlandia.edu; *Asst Librn,* Airen Campbell-Olszewski; Tel: 906-487-7502, E-mail: airen.campbellolszewski@finlandia.edu; Staff 3 (MLS 2, Non-MLS 1)
Founded 1896. Enrl 580; Fac 35; Highest Degree: Bachelor
Library Holdings: Electronic Media & Resources 58; Bk Titles 37,296; Bk Vols 45,033; Per Subs 217
Special Collections: Finnish-American Life & Culture; Upper Peninsula of Michigan
Subject Interests: Art, Bus, Design, Educ, Nursing
Automation Activity & Vendor Info: (Acquisitions) Ex Libris Group; (Cataloging) Ex Libris Group; (Circulation) Ex Libris Group; (Course Reserve) Ex Libris Group; (ILL) Ex Libris Group; (OPAC) Ex Libris Group; (Serials) Ex Libris Group
Wireless access
Partic in Midwest Collaborative for Library Services; Upper Peninsula Region of Library Cooperation, Inc
Open Mon-Thurs (Fall & Spring) 8am-11pm, Fri 8-4, Sat 1-5, Sun 3-11; Mon-Fri (Summer) 9-5

HARBOR BEACH

P HARBOR BEACH AREA DISTRICT LIBRARY*, 105 N Huron Ave, 48441. SAN 308-1516. Tel: 989-479-3417. FAX: 989-479-6818. E-mail: librarian@hbadl.org. Web Site: www.hbadl.org. *Dir,* Vicki Mazure
Founded 1917. Circ 24,262
Library Holdings: Bk Vols 20,000; Per Subs 45
Open Mon, Wed & Fri 11-7, Tues & Thurs 9-5, Sat 10-2
Friends of the Library Group

HARPER WOODS

P HARPER WOODS PUBLIC LIBRARY*, 19601 Harper, 48225. SAN 308-1524. Tel: 313-343-2575. E-mail: hwl@libcoop.net. Web Site: www.harperwoodslibrary.org. *Dir,* Kristen Valyi-Hax; *Adult Serv,* Suzanne D Kent
Pop 14,236; Circ 50,000
Library Holdings: Bk Vols 42,000; Per Subs 50
Wireless access
Partic in Suburban Library Cooperative
Open Mon-Wed 11-7, Thurs & Fri 11-5
Friends of the Library Group

HARRISON

P HARRISON COMMUNITY LIBRARY*, 105 E Main St, 48625. (Mail add: PO Box 380, 48625-0380), SAN 308-1532. Tel: 989-539-6711. FAX: 989-539-6301. Web Site: hdl.org. *Dir,* Shelia Bissonnette; Tel: 989-539-6711, Ext 6, E-mail: sbissonnette@hdl.org; *Asst Dir,* Nick Loomis; Tel: 989-539-6711, Ext 5, E-mail: nloomis@hdl.org; *Pub Serv Librn,* Mary-Jane Ogg; Tel: 989-539-6711, Ext 2, E-mail: mogg@hdl.org; *Coordr, Prog, Youth Serv,* Cheryl Wagner; Tel: 989-539-6711, Ext 3, E-mail: cwagner@hdl.org; *Cat, Support Serv,* Angela Kellogg; Tel: 989-539-6711, Ext 4, E-mail: akellogg@hdl.org; Staff 4 (MLS 1, Non-MLS 3)
Founded 1948. Pop 13,415; Circ 50,000
Library Holdings: Bk Vols 32,000; Per Subs 90

Automation Activity & Vendor Info: (Cataloging) SirsiDynix; (Circulation) SirsiDynix; (ILL) SirsiDynix; (OPAC) SirsiDynix; (Serials) SirsiDynix
Wireless access
Partic in Valley Libr Consortium; White Pine Library Cooperative
Special Services for the Deaf - TDD equip
Open Mon 10-7, Tues-Fri 10-6, Sat 10-2
Friends of the Library Group

J MID MICHIGAN COMMUNITY COLLEGE*, Charles A Amble Library & Community Learning Center, 1375 S Clare Ave, 48625. SAN 346-6264. Tel: 989-386-6617. FAX: 989-386-2411. Web Site: www.midmich.edu/student-resources/lls/library. *Dir, Libr Serv,* Corey Goethe; E-mail: cgoethe@midmich.edu; Staff 2 (MLS 1, Non-MLS 1)
Founded 1969. Enrl 2,200; Fac 59; Highest Degree: Associate
Library Holdings: Bk Titles 22,000; Per Subs 100
Special Collections: Mid-Michigan History (Meek Coll), still pictures
Automation Activity & Vendor Info: (Cataloging) Horizon; (Circulation) Horizon
Wireless access
Partic in Valley Library Consortium; White Pine Library Cooperative
Open Mon-Thurs 8-8, Fri 8-4:30

HARRISVILLE

P ALCONA COUNTY LIBRARY SYSTEM*, Harrisville Branch Library & Headquarters, 312 W Main, 48740. SAN 308-1540. Tel: 989-724-6796. FAX: 989-724-6173. Web Site: alcona.lib.mi.us/. *Libr Dir,* Denise Bearre; E-mail: director@alcona.lib.mi.us; Staff 5 (MLS 1, Non-MLS 4)
Founded 1940. Pop 11,719; Circ 30,545
Library Holdings: Bk Titles 38,000; Bk Vols 50,000; Per Subs 50
Subject Interests: Local hist, Mich
Automation Activity & Vendor Info: (Acquisitions) SirsiDynix; (Cataloging) SirsiDynix; (Circulation) SirsiDynix
Wireless access
Member Libraries: Alcona County Library System
Partic in Northland Library Cooperative
Open Mon-Thurs 9:30-7, Fri 9:30-5:30, Sat 10-3
Friends of the Library Group
Branches: 3
CALEDONIA TOWNSHIP, 1499 Hurbert Rd, Hubbard Lake, 49747-9611. (Mail add: PO Box 56, Hubbard Lake, 49747-0056), SAN 376-7949. Tel: 989-727-3105. *Br Supvry Clerk,* Mary Jane Barkley
Open Mon-Thurs 1-5:30, Fri 12-4
Friends of the Library Group
LINCOLN BRANCH, 330 Traverse Bay Rd, Lincoln, 48742-0115. (Mail add: PO Box 115, Lincoln, 48742-0115), SAN 376-8058. Tel: 989-736-3388. *Br Supvry Clerk,* Sue Malski; Staff 1 (Non-MLS 1)
Open Mon-Thurs 12-6, Fri 10-4
MIKADO TOWNSHIP, 2291 S F-41, Mikado, 48745. (Mail add: PO Box 110, Mikado, 48745-0110), SAN 376-8066. Tel: 989-736-8389. *Br Supvry Clerk,* Melissa Leeseberg
Mem of Alcona County Library System
Open Mon-Thurs 2-6
Friends of the Library Group

HART

P HART AREA PUBLIC LIBRARY*, 415 S State St, 49420-1228. SAN 308-1559. Tel: 231-873-4476. FAX: 231-873-4476. E-mail: hapl@hartpubliclibrary.org. Web Site: www.hartpubliclibrary.org. *Dir,* Kathleen Rash; E-mail: kathleenrash@hartpubliclibrary.org
Pop 8,465; Circ 90,000
Library Holdings: Bk Vols 35,000; Per Subs 120
Subject Interests: Hist
Automation Activity & Vendor Info: (Acquisitions) Auto-Graphics, Inc; (Cataloging) Auto-Graphics, Inc; (Circulation) Auto-Graphics, Inc
Wireless access
Function: Art exhibits, Bilingual assistance for Spanish patrons, Bk club(s), Bks on cassette, Bks on CD, Children's prog, Computers for patron use, Digital talking bks, E-Reserves, Electronic databases & coll, Free DVD rentals, Health sci info serv, Holiday prog, Home delivery & serv to seniorr ctr & nursing homes, Homebound delivery serv, ILL available, Mail & tel request accepted, Music CDs, Notary serv, Online cat, Online ref, Photocopying/Printing, Preschool outreach, Prog for adults, Prog for children & young adult, Ref serv available, Spoken cassettes & CDs, Spoken cassettes & DVDs, Summer reading prog, Tax forms, Teen prog, Telephone ref, VHS videos, Wheelchair accessible, Writing prog
Partic in Mid-Michigan Library League
Special Services for the Blind - Audio mat; Bks on cassette; Bks on CD; Digital talking bk; Large print bks
Open Mon & Thurs 9-8:30, Tues, Wed & Fri 9-5, Sat 9-2
Friends of the Library Group

HARTFORD

P HARTFORD PUBLIC LIBRARY*, 12 Church Street, 49057. (Mail add: PO Box 8, 49057), SAN 308-1567. Tel: 616-621-3408. FAX: 616-621-3073. E-mail: hartfordlib@yahoo.com. Web Site: www.hartfordpl.michlibrary.org. *Dir,* Stephanie Daniels
Pop 6,580; Circ 33,100
Library Holdings: Bk Vols 47,300; Per Subs 30; Talking Bks 575
Special Collections: Hartford Day Spring Newspaper 1881-1973, microflm
Wireless access
Function: 3D Printer, Accelerated reader prog, Adult bk club, Adult literacy prog, After school storytime, Art programs, Bk club(s), Bk reviews (Group), Bks on CD, CD-ROM, Children's prog, Computer training, Computers for patron use, Electronic databases & coll, Family literacy, Holiday prog, Homework prog, ILL available, Internet access, Learning ctr, Life-long learning prog for all ages, Magazines, Movies, Music CDs, Online cat, Online ref, OverDrive digital audio bks, Photocopying/Printing, Preschool outreach, Preschool reading prog, Prog for adults, Prog for children & young adult, Ref & res, Scanner, Senior computer classes, Spanish lang bks, Specialized serv in classical studies, STEM programs, Story hour, Summer & winter reading prog, Summer reading prog, Tax forms, Teen prog, Telephone ref, Winter reading prog, Workshops, Writing prog
Partic in OCLC Online Computer Library Center, Inc; Southwest Michigan Library Cooperative
Open Mon 10-6, Tues-Fri 10-5, Sat 10-2
Friends of the Library Group

HARTLAND

P CROMAINE DISTRICT LIBRARY*, 3688 N Hartland Rd, 48353. (Mail add: PO Box 308, 48353-0308), SAN 308-1575. Tel: 810-632-5200. E-mail: cromaine@cromaine.org. Web Site: www.cromaine.org. *Libr Dir,* Cecilia Ann Marlow; Tel: 810-632-5200, Ext 105, E-mail: cmarlow@cromaine.org; *Mgr, Ad Serv,* Joshu Schu; Tel: 810-632-5200, Ext 113, E-mail: jschu@cromaine.org; *Circ Mgr,* Donna Janke; Tel: 810-632-5200, Ext 101, E-mail: djanke@cromaine.org; *Commun Relations Mgr,* Beth Schrader; Tel: 810-632-5200, Ext 118, E-mail: bschrader@cromaine.org; *Tech Mgr,* Glenn Fischer; Tel: 810-632-5200, Ext 110, E-mail: gfischer@cromaine.org; *Mgr, Youth & Teen Serv,* Marta-Kate Jackson; Tel: 810-632-5200, Ext 114, E-mail: mjackson@cromaine.org.
Subject Specialists: *Mkt,* Beth Schrader; Staff 30 (MLS 11, Non-MLS 19)
Founded 1927. Pop 26,391; Circ 277,367
Special Collections: Historical Documents of Hartland & Livingston County (J R Crouse Coll), art works, autographed letters, bks, doc, photog
Automation Activity & Vendor Info: (Acquisitions) CARL.Solution (TLC); (Cataloging) CARL.Solution (TLC); (Circulation) CARL.Solution (TLC); (OPAC) CARL.Solution (TLC)
Wireless access
Function: 24/7 Electronic res, 24/7 Online cat, 3D Printer, Activity rm, Adult bk club, After school storytime, Archival coll, Art exhibits, Art programs, Audiobks via web, Bk club(s), Bks on CD, Children's prog, Computer training, Computers for patron use, E-Readers, E-Reserves, Electronic databases & coll, Free DVD rentals, Games & aids for people with disabilities, Health sci info serv, Holiday prog, Home delivery & serv to seniorr ctr & nursing homes, Homebound delivery serv, Instruction & testing, Internet access, Jazz prog, Life-long learning prog for all ages, Magazines, Mail & tel request accepted, Makerspace, Mango lang, Meeting rooms, Movies, Museum passes, Music CDs, Notary serv, Online cat, Online ref, Orientations, Outreach serv, Outside serv via phone, mail, e-mail & web, OverDrive digital audio bks, Photocopying/Printing, Preschool outreach, Preschool reading prog, Printer for laptops & handheld devices, Prog for adults, Prog for children & young adult, Scanner, Senior computer classes, Senior outreach, STEM programs, Story hour, Study rm, Summer & winter reading prog, Summer reading prog, Tax forms, Teen prog, Telephone ref, Wheelchair accessible, Workshops
Partic in The Library Network
Open Mon-Thurs 9-9, Fri & Sat 10-5, Sun Noon-5
Friends of the Library Group

HASTINGS

P DOWLING PUBLIC LIBRARY*, 1765 E Dowling Rd, 49058-9332. Tel: 269-721-3743. FAX: 269-721-3743. E-mail: dowlinglibrary@gmail.com. Web Site: www.dowlingpubliclibrary.com. *Dir,* Kris Miller
Circ 2,800
Library Holdings: AV Mats 132; CDs 35; DVDs 120; Bk Vols 12,000; Per Subs 20
Automation Activity & Vendor Info: (Cataloging) Auto-Graphics, Inc
Wireless access
Mem of Woodlands Library Cooperative
Open Mon-Wed & Fri 11-6, Sat 10-2
Friends of the Library Group

P HASTINGS PUBLIC LIBRARY, 227 E State St, 49058-1817. SAN 308-1583. Tel: 269-945-4263. FAX: 269-948-3874. E-mail: has@llcoop.org. Web Site: www.hastingspubliclibrary.org. *Libr Dir,* Peggy Hemerling; *Asst Dir,* Diane Hawkins; *Circ Supvr,* David Edelman; Staff 13 (MLS 3, Non-MLS 10)
Founded 1896. Pop 13,033; Circ 106,000
Library Holdings: Bk Vols 37,781; Per Subs 110
Subject Interests: Genealogy, Local hist
Automation Activity & Vendor Info: (Circulation) Innovative Interfaces, Inc; (ILL) Innovative Interfaces, Inc; (OPAC) Innovative Interfaces, Inc
Wireless access
Function: 24/7 Electronic res, 24/7 Online cat, Activity rm, Adult bk club
Partic in Lakeland Library Cooperative
Open Mon-Thurs 9-8, Fri 9-6, Sat 9-3
Friends of the Library Group

HAZEL PARK

P HAZEL PARK MEMORIAL DISTRICT LIBRARY, 123 E Nine Mile Rd, 48030. SAN 308-1591. Tel: 248-542-0940, 248-546-4095. FAX: 248-546-4083. E-mail: hpmlibrary@gmail.com. Web Site: www.hazel-park.lib.mi.us. *Dir,* Corrine Stocker; E-mail: cstocker@hazel-park.lib.mi.us; *Dir of Circ,* Mary Boertmann; E-mail: mbentley@hazel-park.lib.mi.us; *IT Dir,* Jeanne Markowski; E-mail: jmarkowski@hazel-park.lib.mi.us; Staff 8 (MLS 5, Non-MLS 3)
Founded 1936. Pop 16,500; Circ 64,000
Library Holdings: Bk Vols 85,000; Per Subs 70
Automation Activity & Vendor Info: (Cataloging) SirsiDynix; (Circulation) SirsiDynix; (ILL) SirsiDynix; (OPAC) SirsiDynix; (Serials) SirsiDynix
Wireless access
Function: 24/7 Electronic res, 24/7 Online cat, Adult bk club, Art exhibits, Audiobks via web, Bks on CD, Bus archives, CD-ROM, Chess club, Children's prog, Computer training, Computers for patron use, E-Readers, Electronic databases & coll, Family literacy, Free DVD rentals, Home delivery & serv to seniorr ctr & nursing homes, ILL available, Internet access, Jazz prog, Life-long learning prog for all ages, Magazines, Magnifiers for reading, Mail & tel request accepted, Meeting rooms, Movies, Museum passes, Music CDs, Online cat, Orientations, Outreach serv, Outside serv via phone, mail, e-mail & web, OverDrive digital audio bks, Photocopying/Printing, Preschool outreach, Preschool reading prog, Prof lending libr, Prog for adults, Prog for children & young adult, Ref & res, Ref serv available, Scanner, Senior computer classes, Senior outreach, Spoken cassettes & CDs, Story hour, Summer & winter reading prog, Summer reading prog, Tax forms, Teen prog, Telephone ref, Wheelchair accessible, Winter reading prog
Partic in Libr Network of Mich
Open Mon-Thurs 12-8, Fri 1-5, Sat 12-4
Friends of the Library Group

HEMLOCK

P RAUCHHOLZ MEMORIAL LIBRARY*, 1140 N Hemlock Rd, 48626. SAN 308-1605. Tel: 989-642-8621. FAX: 989-642-5559. E-mail: library@rauchholzlibrary.org. Web Site: www.rauchholzlibrary.org. *Dir,* Billiejo Bluemer; Staff 2 (Non-MLS 2)
Founded 1942. Pop 6,380; Circ 63,629
Library Holdings: CDs 450; DVDs 604; Bk Titles 28,062; Per Subs 38; Talking Bks 1,068; Videos 730
Special Collections: Audio History, cassettes; Local History, slides. Oral History
Automation Activity & Vendor Info: (Cataloging) Follett Software; (Circulation) Follett Software; (OPAC) Follett Software
Wireless access
Function: AV serv, Home delivery & serv to seniorr ctr & nursing homes, Homebound delivery serv, ILL available, Photocopying/Printing, Prog for children & young adult, Summer reading prog, Wheelchair accessible
Partic in White Pine Library Cooperative
Open Mon, Tues & Fri 9-5, Wed & Thurs 1-8, Sat (Sept-May) 9-1
Friends of the Library Group

HESPERIA

P HESPERIA COMMUNITY LIBRARY, 80 S Division St, 49421-9004. SAN 308-1613. Tel: 231-854-5125. FAX: 231-854-5125. E-mail: hes@hesperialibrary.org. Web Site: hesperialibrary.org. *Dir,* Samantha Reid-Goldberg
Circ 31,942
Library Holdings: Bk Vols 22,510; Per Subs 69
Wireless access
Partic in Lakeland Library Cooperative
Open Mon-Thurs 10-7, Fri 10-5, Sat 10-3
Friends of the Library Group

HIGHLAND

P HIGHLAND TOWNSHIP PUBLIC LIBRARY*, 444 Beach Farm Circle, 48357. (Mail add: PO Box 277, 48357-0277), SAN 308-163X. Tel: 248-887-2218. FAX: 248-887-5179. E-mail: htplreply@highland.lib.mi.us. Web Site: www.highlandlibrary.info. *Dir,* Jude Halloran; Tel: 248-887-2218, Ext 110, E-mail: jhalloran@highland.lib.mi.us; *Head, Adult Serv,* Cathy Buehner; *Head, Teen Serv,* Dawn Dittmar; E-mail: ddittmar@highland.lib.mi.us; *Youth Serv Dept Head,* Brenda Dunseth; Staff 5 (MLS 5)
Founded 1856. Pop 19,202; Circ 187,103
Library Holdings: Audiobooks 2,637; CDs 2,083; DVDs 3,935; Large Print Bks 1,150; Bk Vols 76,549; Per Subs 165; Videos 2,030
Automation Activity & Vendor Info: (Circulation) SirsiDynix; (OPAC) SirsiDynix
Wireless access
Partic in The Library Network
Open Mon-Thurs 10-8, Fri & Sat 10-5
Friends of the Library Group

HILLSDALE

C HILLSDALE COLLEGE, Michael Alex Mossey Library, 33 E College St, 49242. SAN 308-1672. Tel: 517-607-2701. Circulation Tel: 517-607-2404. Administration Tel: 517-607-2400. FAX: 517-607-2248. Web Site: lib.hillsdale.edu. *Libr Dir,* Maurine McCourry; Tel: 517-610-2401, E-mail: mmccourry@hillsdale.edu; *Pub Serv Librn,* George Allen; Tel: 517-607-4370, E-mail: gallen@hillsdale.edu; *Pub Serv Librn,* Brenna Wade; Tel: 517-607-2606, E-mail: bwade@hillsdale.edu; *Archivist, Spec Coll Librn,* Lori Curtis; Tel: 517-607-2403, E-mail: lcurtis@hillsdale.edu; *Tech Serv Librn,* Aaron Kilgore; Tel: 517-607-2402, E-mail: akilgore@hillsdale.edu; *Tech Serv Librn,* LeAnne Rumler; Tel: 517-607-2405, E-mail: lrumler@hillsdale.edu; Staff 11 (MLS 6, Non-MLS 5)
Founded 1971. Enrl 1,488; Fac 171; Highest Degree: Doctorate
Library Holdings: CDs 7,744; DVDs 8,161; e-books 1,969,334; e-journals 104,055; Electronic Media & Resources 134,161; Microforms 50,950; Bk Vols 171,374; Per Subs 570; Videos 5,270
Special Collections: Ancient, Modern & US Currency (Alwin C Carus Coin Coll); Freewill Baptist Coll; Ludwig von Mises Library; Money, Banking & US Monetary Policy (George Edward Durell Coll); Richard Weaver Coll; Russell Kirk Library; Thomas Kimball Civil War Diary; Works by Founders of Western Civilization (Heritage Coll)
Subject Interests: Econ, Relig
Automation Activity & Vendor Info: (Acquisitions) Ex Libris Group; (Cataloging) Ex Libris Group; (Circulation) Ex Libris Group; (Course Reserve) Ex Libris Group; (Discovery) Ex Libris Group; (ILL) OCLC; (OPAC) Ex Libris Group; (Serials) Ex Libris Group
Wireless access
Partic in Midwest Collaborative for Library Services
Open Mon-Thurs 7:30am-1am, Fri 7:30am-9pm, Sat 9-9, Sun 1pm-1am; Mon-Fri (Summer) 7:30-4

P HILLSDALE COMMUNITY LIBRARY*, 11 E Bacon St, 49242. SAN 308-1680. Tel: 517-437-6470. Administration Tel: 517-437-6472. FAX: 517-437-6477. E-mail: info@hillsdale-library.org. Web Site: hillsdale-library.org. *Dir,* Mary Hill; E-mail: director@hillsdale-library.org; Staff 2 (MLS 1, Non-MLS 1)
Founded 1879. Pop 15,571; Circ 56,355
Library Holdings: Audiobooks 1,250; Electronic Media & Resources 9,122; Large Print Bks 2,093; Bk Vols 45,587; Per Subs 55; Videos 542
Automation Activity & Vendor Info: (Acquisitions) Auto-Graphics, Inc; (Cataloging) Auto-Graphics, Inc; (Circulation) Auto-Graphics, Inc; (Course Reserve) Auto-Graphics, Inc; (ILL) Auto-Graphics, Inc; (OPAC) Auto-Graphics, Inc; (Serials) Auto-Graphics, Inc
Wireless access
Function: Audiobks via web, Bks on cassette, Bks on CD, Children's prog, Computers for patron use, Electronic databases & coll, ILL available, Online cat, OverDrive digital audio bks, Photocopying/Printing, Prog for children & young adult, Summer reading prog, Tax forms, Teen prog, VHS videos, Wheelchair accessible
Mem of Woodlands Library Cooperative
Open Mon, Wed, Fri 11-5, Tues & Thurs 12-6
Friends of the Library Group

HOLLAND

P HERRICK DISTRICT LIBRARY*, 300 S River Ave, 49423. SAN 346-6299. Tel: 616-355-3100. Reference Tel: 616-355-3101. Administration Tel: 616-355-3723. Web Site: herrickdl.org. *Libr Dir,* Diane Kooiker; E-mail: dkooiker@herrickdl.org; *Asst Dir,* Mary Cook; Tel: 616-355-3724; *Colls Mgr, Digital Resources Mgr,* Karen Ginman; Tel: 616-355-3718; *Commun Relations Mgr,* Sara DeVries; Tel: 616-355-3728; *IT Mgr,* Pete Sneathen; Tel: 616-355-4948; *Pub Serv Mgr,* Dwayne Betcher; Tel:

616-355-3712; *Youth Serv Mgr,* Molly Rios; Tel: 616-355-3731; Staff 17.2 (MLS 17.2)
Founded 1867. Pop 102,212; Circ 1,307,639
Library Holdings: AV Mats 38,303; CDs 18,334; DVDs 14,886; e-books 5,083; Electronic Media & Resources 7,166; Bk Vols 256,698; Per Subs 500
Special Collections: Dutch, Spanish Periodicals; Indo-Chinese Language Coll; Local Genealogy Coll; Spanish Language Coll
Automation Activity & Vendor Info: (Cataloging) Innovative Interfaces, Inc; (Circulation) Innovative Interfaces, Inc; (OPAC) Innovative Interfaces, Inc
Wireless access
Function: Adult bk club, Audiobks via web, Bi-weekly Writer's Group, Bilingual assistance for Spanish patrons, Bk club(s), Bks on CD, Children's prog, Computer training, Computers for patron use, E-Reserves, Electronic databases & coll, Free DVD rentals, ILL available, Internet access, Magnifiers for reading, Music CDs, OverDrive digital audio bks, Photocopying/Printing, Preschool outreach, Prog for adults, Prog for children & young adult, Senior computer classes, Story hour, Summer & winter reading prog, Tax forms, Teen prog, Telephone ref, Wheelchair accessible
Partic in Lakeland Library Cooperative
Special Services for the Deaf - TDD equip
Open Mon-Wed 9-9, Thurs & Fri 9-6, Sat 9-2
Restriction: Restricted borrowing privileges
Friends of the Library Group
Branches: 1
NORTH BRANCH, 155 Riley St, 49424. Tel: 616-738-4360. FAX: 616-738-4359. *Br Mgr,* Rob Carpenter; Tel: 616-738-4365, E-mail: rcarpenter@herrickdl.org
Founded 2000
Library Holdings: Bk Vols 20,000; Per Subs 60
Open Mon-Fri 9-6
Friends of the Library Group

M HOLLAND HOSPITAL*, Medical Library, 602 Michigan Ave, 3rd Flr, 49423. SAN 325-9145. Tel: 616-392-5141, 616-494-4145. FAX: 616-392-8448. E-mail: medlib@hollandhospital.org. Web Site: www.hollandhospital.org/about/library.aspx. *Library Contact,* Kris Kamper
Founded 1917
Library Holdings: Bk Vols 5,000; Per Subs 240
Subject Interests: Cultural diversity
Partic in Michigan Health Sciences Libraries Association
Open Mon-Fri 8-4:30
Restriction: Employees only, Staff use only

HOPE COLLEGE

C THE JOINT ARCHIVES OF HOLLAND*, Theil Research Ctr, Nine E Tenth St, 49423-3513, SAN 327-5701. Tel: 616-395-7798. FAX: 616-395-7197. E-mail: archives@hope.edu. Web Site: www.jointarchives.org. *Dir,* Geoffrey D Reynolds; E-mail: reynoldsg@hope.edu; Staff 1 (MLS 1)
Founded 1988. Enrl 3,000; Highest Degree: Bachelor
Special Collections: Archival Coll of the Holland Historical Trust (Holland Museum); Coll of City of Holland, City of Saugatuck & Village of Douglas; Hope College & Western Theological Seminary
Subject Interests: Immigration, Oral hist, Reform Church hist, Regional hist
Function: Archival coll
Publications: A C Van Raalte: Dutch Leader & American Patriot, 1997; Campus Alive: A Walking Tour of Hope College, 1999; Guide to Collections of The Joint Archives of Holland, 1989; Supplement to The Guide to the Collection, 1991; The Joint Archives Quarterly
Open Mon-Fri 8-12 & 1-5
Restriction: Non-circulating to the pub
Friends of the Library Group

C VAN WYLEN LIBRARY*, 53 Graves Pl, 49422, SAN 308-1710. Tel: 616-395-7790. FAX: 616-395-7965. Web Site: www.hope.edu/lib. *Dir,* Kelly Jacobsma; E-mail: jacobsma@hope.edu; *Head, Access Serv,* David O'Brien; Tel: 616-395-7791, E-mail: obriend@hope.edu; *Head, Ref & Instruction,* Todd Wiebe; Tel: 616-395-7286, E-mail: wiebe@hope.edu; *Head, Tech Serv & Syst,* Brian Yost; Tel: 616-395-7492, E-mail: yostb@hope.edu; *Electronic Res Librn,* Jennifer Holman; E-mail: holman@hope.edu; *Ref & Instrul Serv Librn,* Rachel Bishop; Tel: 616-395-7299, E-mail: bishop@hope.edu; *Ref & Instrul Serv Librn,* Jessica Hronchek; Tel: 616-395-7124, E-mail: hronchek@hope.edu; *Spec Coll & Digital Projects Metadata Librn,* Jeremy Barney; *Circ Supvr,* Carla Kaminski; Tel: 616-395-7889, E-mail: kaminski@hope.edu; *TechLab Coordr,* Daphne Fairbanks; Tel: 616-395-7283, E-mail: fairbanks@hope.edu; *ILL Assoc,* Michelle Yost; Tel: 616-395-7794; Staff 9 (MLS 9)
Founded 1866. Enrl 3,075; Fac 239; Highest Degree: Bachelor
Library Holdings: Bk Vols 366,783; Per Subs 1,548
Special Collections: Church History (Reformed Church in America); Dutch American History; Holland Joint Archives
Subject Interests: Art hist
Automation Activity & Vendor Info: (Acquisitions) Innovative Interfaces, Inc; (Cataloging) Innovative Interfaces, Inc; (Circulation) Innovative Interfaces, Inc; (Course Reserve) Docutek; (OPAC) Innovative Interfaces, Inc; (Serials) Innovative Interfaces, Inc
Partic in OCLC Online Computer Library Center, Inc
Publications: Annual Bibliography of Faculty Scholarship
Special Services for the Deaf - Assistive tech
Special Services for the Blind - Assistive/Adapted tech devices, equip & products
Open Mon-Thurs (Winter) 8am-Midnight, Fri 8-6, Sat 10-6, Sun 1-Midnight; Mon-Fri (Summer) 8-5

R WESTERN THEOLOGICAL SEMINARY*, Cook Library, 101 E 13th St, 49423. SAN 308-1729. Tel: 616-392-8555. Circulation Tel: 616-392-8555, Ext 139. Administration Tel: 616-392-8555, Ext 141. Toll Free Tel: 800-392-8554. Web Site: guides.westernsem.edu. *Dir,* Rev Daniel F Flores; E-mail: dan.flores@westernsem.edu; *Emerging Tech Librn,* Steve Michaels; Tel: 616-392-8555, Ext 187, E-mail: steve.michaels@westernsem.edu; *Res Mgt Librn,* Margaret Wade; Tel: 616-392-8555, Ext 112, E-mail: margaret.wade@westernsem.edu; *Tech Serv Librn,* Position Currently Open; *Circ Supvr,* Allison Van Liere; Tel: 616-392-8555, Ext 146, E-mail: allison.vanliere@westernsem.edu; Staff 4 (MLS 3, Non-MLS 1)
Founded 1866. Enrl 337; Fac 20; Highest Degree: Doctorate
Library Holdings: AV Mats 2,228; e-books 100,847; Microforms 2,588; Bk Vols 94,486; Per Subs 132
Special Collections: 15th-18th Century; History of Reformed Church in America (Kolkman Memorial Archives), ms, mat; Theology (Rare bks), bd vols
Subject Interests: Art & archit, Biblical studies, Church hist, Educ, Relig, Theol
Automation Activity & Vendor Info: (Acquisitions) Innovative Interfaces, Inc - Millennium; (Cataloging) Innovative Interfaces, Inc - Millennium; (Circulation) Innovative Interfaces, Inc - Millennium; (ILL) OCLC; (OPAC) Innovative Interfaces, Inc; (Serials) Innovative Interfaces, Inc - Millennium
Wireless access
Partic in American Theological Library Association; Mich Libr Asn; Midwest Collaborative for Library Services; OCLC Online Computer Library Center, Inc

HOLLY

P HOLLY TOWNSHIP LIBRARY*, 1116 N Saginaw St, 48442-1395. SAN 308-1737. Tel: 248-634-1754. FAX: 248-634-8088. E-mail: hollytl1116@gmail.com. Web Site: hollylibrary.org. *Dir,* Gregory Hayes; E-mail: ghayeshollytl@gmail.com; *Adult Serv Mgr,* Tina Russette; *Circ Mgr,* Ruth Archer; *Youth Serv Mgr,* Debbie Hernan; E-mail: youthhollylibrary@gmail.com; Staff 1 (Non-MLS 1)
Founded 1852. Pop 23,088; Circ 81,391. Sal $224,500
Library Holdings: Audiobooks 5,200; Bks on Deafness & Sign Lang 15; CDs 2,300; DVDs 1,500; High Interest/Low Vocabulary Bk Vols 65; Large Print Bks 3,200; Per Subs 52
Special Collections: Municipal Document Depository
Subject Interests: Mich
Automation Activity & Vendor Info: (Circulation) Follett Software; (ILL) Follett Software
Wireless access
Function: Bk club(s), Bks on CD, CD-ROM, Children's prog, Computer training, Computers for patron use, E-Reserves, Electronic databases & coll, Free DVD rentals, Holiday prog, Home delivery & serv to seniorr ctr & nursing homes, ILL available, Internet access, Large print keyboards, Magnifiers for reading, Mail & tel request accepted, Microfiche/film & reading machines, Music CDs, Online cat, Photocopying/Printing, Preschool outreach, Printer for laptops & handheld devices, Prog for adults, Prog for children & young adult, Ref serv available, Scanner, Senior computer classes, Spanish lang bks, Story hour, Summer & winter reading prog, Tax forms, Wheelchair accessible
Partic in Mideastern Michigan Library Cooperative
Special Services for the Deaf - Staff with knowledge of sign lang
Open Mon-Thurs 9:30-8, Fri 9:30-5, Sat 9:30-3
Friends of the Library Group

HOMER

P HOMER PUBLIC LIBRARY*, 141 W Main St, 49245. SAN 376-7043. Tel: 517-568-3450. FAX: 517-568-4021. E-mail: hpl@wowway.biz. Web Site: homerpl.michlibrary.org. *Dir,* Trixie L McMeeking; *Asst Dir,* Glenda Ballentine
Founded 2015. Pop 3,901
Library Holdings: DVDs 600; Bk Titles 29,000; Per Subs 20
Wireless access
Mem of Woodlands Library Cooperative
Open Mon 10-7, Tues 10-6, Wed 10-5, Thurs 10-8, Fri 10-4, Sat 9-Noon

HOPKINS

P HOPKINS PUBLIC LIBRARY*, 118 E Main St, 49328-0366. SAN 308-1745. Tel: 269-793-7516. FAX: 269-793-7047. E-mail: hopkinslibrary@hotmail.com. Web Site: www.hopkinspl.michlibrary.org. *Dir,* Elyshia Schafer
Circ 16,186
Library Holdings: Bk Vols 18,000; Per Subs 20
Partic in Lakeland Library Cooperative
Open Mon & Wed 10-8, Tues & Fri 10-5, Sat 10-1

HOUGHTON

C MICHIGAN TECHNOLOGICAL UNIVERSITY*, J Robert Van Pelt & John & Ruanne Opie Library, 1400 Townsend Dr, 49931-1295. SAN 308-1753. Tel: 906-487-2508. FAX: 906-487-2357. E-mail: library@mtu.edu. Interlibrary Loan Service E-mail: ill@mtu.edu. Reference E-mail: reflib@mtu.edu. Web Site: www.mtu.edu/library. *Chief Info Officer,* Josh Olson; Tel: 906-487-1217, E-mail: jolson@mtu.edu; *Assoc Dir,* Pattie Luokkanen; Tel: 906-487-2484, E-mail: paluokka@mtu.edu; *Asst Dir, Coll & Scholarly Communications,* Nora Allred; Tel: 906-487-3208, E-mail: nsallred@mtu.edu; *Instruction & Learning Librn,* Jenn Sams; Tel: 906-487-2698, E-mail: jsams@mtu.edu; *Ref & Instruction Librn,* Amanda Binoniemi; Tel: 906-487-1814, E-mail: abinonie@mtu.edu; *Innovations Mgr, Tech Mgr,* David Holden; Tel: 906-487-1482, E-mail: doholden@mtu.edu; *Univ Archivist,* Allison Neely; Tel: 906-487-2816, E-mail: alneely@mtu.edu; *Cat, Metadata Specialist,* Georgeann Larson; Tel: 906-487-1443, E-mail: grlarson@mtu.edu; Staff 14.8 (MLS 11.8, Non-MLS 3)
Founded 1887. Enrl 6,976; Fac 47; Highest Degree: Doctorate. Sal $1,058,205 (Prof $711,560)
Library Holdings: Microforms 559,776; Bk Vols 796,179; Per Subs 30,226
Special Collections: Copper Country Historical; Copper Mining Company Records; University Archives; USBM Mine Maps of Michigan
Subject Interests: Engr
Automation Activity & Vendor Info: (Acquisitions) Ex Libris Group; (Cataloging) Ex Libris Group; (Circulation) Ex Libris Group; (Course Reserve) Ex Libris Group; (ILL) OCLC ILLiad; (OPAC) Ex Libris Group; (Serials) Ex Libris Group
Wireless access
Function: Archival coll, Art exhibits, Audio & video playback equip for onsite use, Computers for patron use, Distance learning, Doc delivery serv, E-Reserves, Electronic databases & coll, Equip loans & repairs, ILL available, Instruction & testing, Internet access, Magnifiers for reading, Microfiche/film & reading machines, Online cat, Online info literacy tutorials on the web & in blackboard, Online ref, Orientations, Photocopying/Printing, Ref & res, Ref serv available, Scanner, Telephone ref, VHS videos, Wheelchair accessible, Workshops
Partic in Midwest Collaborative for Library Services; OCLC Online Computer Library Center, Inc; Upper Peninsula Region of Library Cooperation, Inc
Open Mon-Thurs 7:45am-Midnight, Fri 7:45-5, Sat Noon-5, Sun Noon-Midnight
Friends of the Library Group

P PORTAGE LAKE DISTRICT LIBRARY*, 58 Huron St, 49931-2194. SAN 308-1761. Tel: 906-482-4570. FAX: 906-482-2129. E-mail: info@pldl.org. Web Site: www.uproc.lib.mi.us/pldl. *Dir,* Dillon Geshel; E-mail: dgeshel@pldl.org; Staff 22 (MLS 1, Non-MLS 21)
Founded 1910. Pop 14,243; Circ 101,200
Library Holdings: AV Mats 750; Bk Titles 50,000; Per Subs 100; Talking Bks 500
Automation Activity & Vendor Info: (Cataloging) SirsiDynix; (Circulation) SirsiDynix
Wireless access
Function: For res purposes, ILL available, Mail loans to mem, Photocopying/Printing, Prog for children & young adult, Ref serv available, Summer reading prog, Telephone ref
Partic in Superiorland Library Cooperative; Upper Peninsula Region of Library Cooperation, Inc
Open Mon-Thurs 10-8, Fri 10-5, Sat 10-3
Friends of the Library Group

HOUGHTON LAKE

P HOUGHTON LAKE PUBLIC LIBRARY*, 4431 W Houghton Lake Dr, 48629-8713. SAN 308-177X. Tel: 989-366-9230. E-mail: staff@hlpl.org. Web Site: www.hlpl.org. *Libr Dir,* Kimberly J Young; E-mail: kyoung@hlpl.org; Staff 2 (MLS 2)
Founded 1964. Pop 15,325
Jul 2014-Jun 2015 Income $607,950, State $9,022, Locally Generated Income $598,928. Mats Exp $573,382, Books $34,605, Per/Ser (Incl. Access Fees) $5,499, Other Print Mats $4,000, AV Mat $17,889, Electronic Ref Mat (Incl. Access Fees) $2,593. Sal $308,352
Library Holdings: Audiobooks 1,573; CDs 1,993; DVDs 2,632; Large Print Bks 1,135; Bk Titles 39,330; Per Subs 95
Automation Activity & Vendor Info: (Cataloging) Innovative Interfaces, Inc; (Circulation) Innovative Interfaces, Inc; (ILL) Mel Cat; (OPAC) Innovative Interfaces, Inc
Wireless access
Function: 24/7 Electronic res, Adult bk club, Bk club(s), Bks on CD, Children's prog, Computer training, Computers for patron use, E-Reserves, Free DVD rentals, ILL available, Magazines, Magnifiers for reading, Microfiche/film & reading machines, Movies, Music CDs, Online cat, OverDrive digital audio bks, Photocopying/Printing, Preschool outreach, Preschool reading prog, Printer for laptops & handheld devices, Prog for adults, Prog for children & young adult, Ref serv available, Scanner, Story hour, Summer & winter reading prog, Summer reading prog, Tax forms, Teen prog, Telephone ref, Wheelchair accessible, Winter reading prog
Partic in Midwest Collaborative for Library Services
Open Mon-Thurs 10-7, Fri & Sat 10-5

HOWARD CITY

P TIMOTHY C HAUENSTEIN REYNOLDS TOWNSHIP LIBRARY*, 117 W Williams St, 49329. (Mail add: PO Box 220, 49329-0220), SAN 308-1788. Tel: 231-937-5575. Reference Tel: 231-937-6175. FAX: 231-937-9240. E-mail: how@llcoop.org. Web Site: www.tchrtl.michlibrary.org. *Dir,* Janice Williams; E-mail: howjw@llcoop.org; *Asst Dir, Youth Serv,* Cheryl Smit
Library Holdings: Bk Titles 22,393; Per Subs 65
Special Collections: Howard City Record, microfilm
Automation Activity & Vendor Info: (Cataloging) Innovative Interfaces, Inc; (Circulation) Innovative Interfaces, Inc; (OPAC) Innovative Interfaces, Inc
Wireless access
Partic in Lakeland Library Cooperative; Mich Libr Asn
Open Mon, Tues & Thurs 10-7, Wed & Fri 10-5, Sat 10-2
Friends of the Library Group

HOWELL

C CLEARY UNIVERSITY LIBRARY, 3750 Cleary Dr, 48843. SAN 308-4930. Toll Free Tel: 800-686-1883, Ext 1611. E-mail: librarian@cleary.edu. Web Site: library.cleary.edu/students, www.cleary.edu/library. *Instrul Librn,* Jane Scales; E-mail: jscales@cleary.edu; Staff 1 (MLS 1)
Founded 1883. Enrl 1,011; Fac 48; Highest Degree: Master
Library Holdings: AV Mats 600; e-books 5,000; e-journals 20,000; Bk Titles 800; Bk Vols 1,000; Per Subs 20; Talking Bks 10
Subject Interests: Acctg, Mgt, Mkt
Wireless access
Function: Instruction & testing, Internet access, Online ref, Orientations
Partic in Midwest Collaborative for Library Services

P HOWELL CARNEGIE DISTRICT LIBRARY, 314 W Grand River Ave, 48843. SAN 308-1796. Tel: 517-546-0720. FAX: 517-546-1494. Web Site: www.howelllibrary.org. *Dir,* Holly Ward Lamb; Tel: 517-546-0720, Ext 112, E-mail: ward@howelllibrary.org; *Head, Ref,* Jerilee Cook; Tel: 517-546-0720, Ext 104, E-mail: cook@howelllibrary.org; *Head, Youth Serv,* Janice Heilman; Tel: 517-546-0720, Ext 121, E-mail: heilman@howelllibrary.org; Staff 37 (MLS 8, Non-MLS 29)
Founded 1906. Pop 41,916; Circ 555,003
Library Holdings: Bk Vols 126,264; Per Subs 398
Special Collections: Livingston County Local History, photog
Automation Activity & Vendor Info: (Cataloging) Innovative Interfaces, Inc - Millennium; (Circulation) Innovative Interfaces, Inc - Millennium; (OPAC) Innovative Interfaces, Inc - Millennium
Wireless access
Function: Adult literacy prog, Archival coll, Art exhibits, Bk club(s), Bks on cassette, Bks on CD, Bus archives, CD-ROM, Children's prog, Computer training, Computers for patron use, E-Reserves, Electronic databases & coll, Free DVD rentals, ILL available, Internet access, Music CDs, Online cat, Online ref, OverDrive digital audio bks, Photocopying/Printing, Preschool outreach, Printer for laptops & handheld devices, Prog for adults, Prog for children & young adult, Ref serv available, Satellite serv, Scanner, Spoken cassettes & CDs, Spoken cassettes & DVDs, Story hour, Summer reading prog, Tax forms, Telephone ref, VHS videos, Wheelchair accessible
Partic in The Library Network
Open Mon-Thurs 10-6, Fri & Sat 10-2
Friends of the Library Group

HUDSON

P HUDSON CARNEGIE DISTRICT LIBRARY*, 205 S Market, 49247. SAN 308-1818. Tel: 517-448-3801. FAX: 517-448-5095. E-mail: info@hudsoncdl.org, staff@hudsoncdl.org. Web Site: www.hudsoncdl.org. *Dir,* Joann Crater; E-mail: director@hudsoncdl.org; Staff 1 (Non-MLS 1)
Founded 1904. Pop 4,604; Circ 69,000

Library Holdings: Bk Vols 39,000; Per Subs 30
Special Collections: Carnegie Library; Hudson Historical Coll; Will Carleton Coll
Automation Activity & Vendor Info: (Cataloging) Follett Software; (Circulation) Follett Software; (ILL) Auto-Graphics, Inc
Wireless access
Mem of Woodlands Library Cooperative
Partic in OCLC Online Computer Library Center, Inc
Open Mon 1-6:30, Tues-Thurs 10-6:30, Fri 10-4, Sat 10-1
Friends of the Library Group

HUDSONVILLE

P GARY BYKER MEMORIAL LIBRARY, 3338 Van Buren St, 49426. SAN 308-1826. Tel: 616-669-1255. FAX: 616-669-5150. Web Site: www.hudsonville.org/library. *Dir,* Melissa Ann Huisman; E-mail: mhuisman@hudsonville.org; *Ch Serv,* Katie Kirk; E-mail: kkirk@hudsonville.org; Staff 15 (MLS 2, Non-MLS 13)
Founded 1967. Pop 9,067; Circ 133,701
Library Holdings: CDs 1,212; DVDs 1,013; Large Print Bks 1,397; Bk Titles 46,852; Per Subs 95; Talking Bks 1,697; Videos 2,867
Subject Interests: Local hist
Automation Activity & Vendor Info: (Cataloging) Innovative Interfaces, Inc; (Circulation) Innovative Interfaces, Inc; (ILL) Innovative Interfaces, Inc; (OPAC) Innovative Interfaces, Inc; (Serials) Innovative Interfaces, Inc
Wireless access
Function: 24/7 Electronic res, 24/7 Online cat, Adult bk club, Bk club(s), Bks on CD, Butterfly Garden, Children's prog, Digital talking bks, Electronic databases & coll, Free DVD rentals, Games & aids for people with disabilities, ILL available, Internet access, Laminating, Life-long learning prog for all ages, Magazines, Magnifiers for reading, Music CDs, Notary serv, Online cat, OverDrive digital audio bks, Photocopying/Printing, Prog for adults, Prog for children & young adult, Spoken cassettes & CDs, Story hour, Summer & winter reading prog, Tax forms, Teen prog, Telephone ref, Wheelchair accessible
Partic in Lakeland Library Cooperative
Open Mon, Tues & Thurs 10-8, Wed & Fri 10-5, Sat 10-1
Restriction: Open to pub for ref & circ; with some limitations
Friends of the Library Group

P PATMOS LIBRARY, 2445 Riley St, 49426. (Mail add: PO Box 87, Jamestown, 49427), SAN 346-6388. Tel: 616-896-9798. Interlibrary Loan Service Tel: 616-453-2575. FAX: 616-896-7645. E-mail: jamam@llcoop.org. Web Site: www.patmoslibrary.org. *Dir,* Amber McLain; Staff 5 (MLS 1, Non-MLS 4)
Pop 7,034; Circ 57,947
Library Holdings: AV Mats 2,015; Large Print Bks 151; Bk Vols 46,318; Per Subs 90; Talking Bks 1,718
Special Collections: Local History Coll
Automation Activity & Vendor Info: (Cataloging) Innovative Interfaces, Inc; (Circulation) Innovative Interfaces, Inc; (ILL) Innovative Interfaces, Inc; (OPAC) Innovative Interfaces, Inc; (Serials) Innovative Interfaces, Inc
Wireless access
Function: Adult bk club, Audiobks via web, Bk club(s), Bks on cassette, Bks on CD, CD-ROM, Children's prog, Computers for patron use, Digital talking bks, E-Reserves, Holiday prog, ILL available, Music CDs, Online cat, OverDrive digital audio bks, Photocopying/Printing, Prog for adults, Prog for children & young adult, Ref & res, Scanner, Spoken cassettes & CDs, Spoken cassettes & DVDs, Story hour, Summer & winter reading prog, Summer reading prog, Tax forms, VHS videos, Wheelchair accessible, Winter reading prog
Partic in Lakeland Library Cooperative
Open Mon & Thurs 12-8, Tues, Wed & Fri 10-5, Sat 10-1
Restriction: ID required to use computers (Ltd hrs)
Friends of the Library Group

HUNTINGTON WOODS

P HUNTINGTON WOODS PUBLIC LIBRARY*, 26415 Scotia Rd, 48070. SAN 308-1834. Tel: 248-543-9720. FAX: 248-543-2559. E-mail: htwd@huntingtonwoodslib.org. Web Site: huntingtonwoodslib.org. *Adult Serv, Dir,* Anne Hage; E-mail: ahage@huntingtonwoodslib.org; *Head, Circ,* Sally Kohlenberg; *Librn,* Joanne Johnson; *Librn,* Karen Tower; *Youth Serv Librn,* Joyce Krom; *Tech Serv,* Jesse Mitchell
Founded 1942. Pop 6,514; Circ 55,000
Library Holdings: Bks on Deafness & Sign Lang 50; High Interest/Low Vocabulary Bk Vols 100; Bk Vols 40,000; Per Subs 125
Special Collections: Early American Newspapers (Columbian Centinel of Boston 1792-1794)
Wireless access
Open Mon-Thurs (Fall & Winter) 10-9, Sat 10-5, Sun 1-5; Mon-Thurs (Summer) 10-9, Fri 10-5
Friends of the Library Group

IMLAY CITY

P RUTH HUGHES MEMORIAL DISTRICT LIBRARY*, 211 N Almont Ave, 48444-1004. SAN 308-1850. Tel: 810-724-8043. FAX: 810-724-2602. E-mail: info@ruthhughes.org. Web Site: ruthhughes.org. *Dir,* Tracy Aldrich; E-mail: taldrich@ruthhughes.org; Staff 4 (MLS 2, Non-MLS 2)
Founded 1923. Pop 11,480; Circ 110,000
Library Holdings: Bk Vols 49,000; Per Subs 80
Automation Activity & Vendor Info: (Cataloging) Horizon; (Circulation) Horizon; (OPAC) Horizon
Wireless access
Partic in Mideastern Michigan Library Cooperative
Open Mon, Wed & Thurs 10-8, Tues & Fri 10-5, Sat 10-3
Branches: 1
ATTICA TOWNSHIP LIBRARY, 4302 Peppermill Rd, Attica, 48412-9624. Tel: 810-724-2007. FAX: 810-724-2007. *Dir,* Tracy Aldrich; E-mail: taldrich@ruthhughes.org
Library Holdings: Bk Vols 8,000
Open Mon & Thurs 2-7, Tues & Fri 10-3

INDIAN RIVER

P INDIAN RIVER AREA LIBRARY*, 3546 S Straits Hwy, 49749. (Mail add: PO Box 160, 49749-0160), SAN 321-0405. Tel: 231-238-8581. FAX: 231-238-9494. E-mail: indriv1@northland.lib.mi.us. Web Site: www.indianriverarealibrary.michlibrary.org. *Dir,* Karen Magee; *Asst Librn,* Karen Vance; Staff 2 (MLS 1, Non-MLS 1)
Founded 1977. Pop 5,584; Circ 26,013
Jul 2013-Jun 2014 Income $118,969, State $2,266, City $62,398, County $29,644, Other $24,661. Mats Exp $26,840, Books $18,448, Per/Ser (Incl. Access Fees) $2,003, Other Print Mats $60, AV Mat $6,329. Sal $31,217
Library Holdings: AV Mats 3,191; Bks on Deafness & Sign Lang 18; CDs 1,769; DVDs 1,250; Large Print Bks 2,718; Bk Vols 43,094; Per Subs 146; Videos 1,941
Subject Interests: Careers, Dance, Music
Automation Activity & Vendor Info: (Circulation) Nugen Systems Inc; (ILL) Mel Cat
Wireless access
Partic in Northland Library Cooperative
Open Tues & Fri 11-8, Wed & Thurs 11-5:30
Friends of the Library Group

INKSTER

P LEANNA HICKS PUBLIC LIBRARY*, 1086 Inkster Rd, 48141. SAN 308-1869. Tel: 313-563-2822. FAX: 313-274-5130. E-mail: reference@inksterlibrary.org. Web Site: www.inkster.lib.mi.us. *Dir,* Betty Adams; E-mail: badams@inksterlibrary.org
Founded 1960. Pop 35,190
Library Holdings: Bk Vols 38,000; Per Subs 75
Wireless access
Publications: The Roots of Inkster
Open Mon 11-5, Tues & Thurs 12-6, Wed 10-7, Fri 1-6
Friends of the Library Group

INTERLOCHEN

INTERLOCHEN CENTER FOR THE ARTS

S BONISTEEL LIBRARY - SEABURY ACADEMIC LIBRARY*, 4000 M-137, 49643. (Mail add: PO Box 199, 49643), SAN 308-1877. Tel: 231-276-7420. FAX: 231-276-5232. Web Site: www.interlochen.org. *Dir of Libr,* Elizabeth Gourley; E-mail: beth.gourley@interlochen.org; *Academy Librn,* Carol Niemi; *Archivist,* Byron Hanson; *Libr Asst,* Joe Doerfer; Staff 3 (MLS 1, Non-MLS 2)
Founded 1962
Library Holdings: Bk Vols 27,000; Per Subs 80
Special Collections: Music Library Coll
Subject Interests: Art & archit, Dance, Drama, Music
Automation Activity & Vendor Info: (Cataloging) SirsiDynix; (Circulation) SirsiDynix; (OPAC) SirsiDynix

S FREDERICK & ELIZABETH LUDWIG FENNELL MUSIC LIBRARY*, 4000 Hwy M-137, 49643. (Mail add: PO Box 199, 49643-0199). Tel: 231-276-7230. FAX: 231-276-7882. Web Site: library.interlochen.org. *Dir of Libr,* Elizabeth Gourley; E-mail: beth.gourley@interlochen.org; *Head Librn,* Eleanor Lange; E-mail: eleanor.lange@interlochen.org; *Access Serv Coordr, Asst Music Librn,* Jacey Kepich
Founded 1928
Special Collections: Performance Materials
Automation Activity & Vendor Info: (Cataloging) SirsiDynix; (Circulation) SirsiDynix; (OPAC) SirsiDynix

P INTERLOCHEN PUBLIC LIBRARY, 9411 Tenth St, 49643. Tel: 231-276-6767. FAX: 231-276-5172. E-mail: interlochenpubliclibrary@gmail.com. Web Site: interlochenpubliclibrary.org. *Dir,* Jennifer Thomet; E-mail: jthomet@tadl.org; Staff 8 (MLS 1, Non-MLS 7)

Founded 1976. Pop 3,500
Library Holdings: Bks on Deafness & Sign Lang 10; Bk Vols 22,000; Per Subs 75
Special Collections: Interlochen History Coll
Automation Activity & Vendor Info: (Cataloging) Evergreen; (Circulation) Evergreen
Wireless access
Partic in Northland Library Cooperative
Open Mon, Tues, Fri & Sat 9-5, Wed & Thurs 9-7
Friends of the Library Group

IONIA

P IONIA COMMUNITY LIBRARY, 126 E Main St, 48846. SAN 308-1885. Tel: 616-527-3680. FAX: 616-527-6210. Web Site: www.ioniacommunitylibrary.org. *Dir,* Dale Parus; Tel: 616-527-3680, Ext 104, E-mail: daleparus.icl@gmail.com; *Ch,* Mike Golczynski; *Teen Librn,* Shanni Kerr; Staff 8 (Non-MLS 8)
Founded 1903. Pop 21,871; Circ 86,902
Jul 2012-Jun 2013 Income $549,640. Mats Exp $46,900, Books $28,500, Per/Ser (Incl. Access Fees) $4,300, AV Mat $8,500, Electronic Ref Mat (Incl. Access Fees) $5,600. Sal $264,064
Library Holdings: AV Mats 1,747; Bk Vols 33,547; Per Subs 84
Special Collections: Civil War Coll
Automation Activity & Vendor Info: (Cataloging) Innovative Interfaces, Inc; (Circulation) Innovative Interfaces, Inc; (OPAC) Innovative Interfaces, Inc
Wireless access
Open Mon-Thurs 10-8, Fri 10-6, Sat 10-2
Friends of the Library Group

IRON MOUNTAIN

P DICKINSON COUNTY LIBRARY*, 401 Iron Mountain St, 49801-3435. SAN 346-6442. Tel: 906-774-1218. Administration Tel: 906-774-3862. FAX: 906-774-4079. E-mail: dcl@dcl-lib.org. Web Site: www.dcl-lib.org. *Dir,* Megan Buck; E-mail: meg@dcl-lib.org; *Ch Serv,* Ginnie Adams; Staff 17 (MLS 1, Non-MLS 16)
Founded 1902. Pop 26,168; Circ 172,380
Library Holdings: AV Mats 11,060; Bk Titles 94,267; Per Subs 319
Subject Interests: Genealogy, Local hist, Mich
Automation Activity & Vendor Info: (Cataloging) SirsiDynix; (Circulation) SirsiDynix; (OPAC) SirsiDynix
Wireless access
Function: 24/7 Electronic res, Activity rm, Adult bk club, Art exhibits, Audiobks via web, AV serv, Bk club(s), Bks on cassette, Bks on CD, Children's prog, Computers for patron use, Digital talking bks, Electronic databases & coll, Family literacy, Free DVD rentals, Genealogy discussion group, Holiday prog, Home delivery & serv to seniorr ctr & nursing homes, Homebound delivery serv, ILL available, Internet access, Magazines, Magnifiers for reading, Mail & tel request accepted, Mango lang, Meeting rooms, Microfiche/film & reading machines, Movies, Museum passes, Music CDs, Online cat, Online ref, OverDrive digital audio bks, Photocopying/Printing, Preschool outreach, Preschool reading prog, Printer for laptops & handheld devices, Prog for adults, Prog for children & young adult, Ref serv available, Scanner, Story hour, Summer & winter reading prog, Summer reading prog, Tax forms, Teen prog, Telephone ref, VHS videos, Wheelchair accessible, Winter reading prog, Workshops
Publications: Ford Comes to Kingsford; The Evolution of the Public Library in Michigan's Dickinson County
Partic in Superiorland Library Cooperative; Upper Peninsula Region of Library Cooperation, Inc
Open Mon-Thurs (Winter) 9-9, Fri 9-6, Sat 9-5, Sun 1-4; Mon-Thurs (Summer) 9-8, Fri 9-6, Sat 9-1
Friends of the Library Group
Branches: 2
NORTH DICKINSON, W6588 M-69, Felch, 49831. Tel: 906-542-7230.
Open Mon & Fri 11-4, Tues & Thurs (Winter) 2-6 ; Mon, Tues & Thurs (Summer) 10-3
Friends of the Library Group
SOLOMONSON BRANCH, 620 Section St, Norway, 49870, SAN 346-6477. Tel: 906-563-8617.
Open Mon-Wed 10-8, Thurs & Fri 10-6, Sat 10-1
Friends of the Library Group

IRON RIVER

P WEST IRON DISTRICT LIBRARY*, 116 W Genesee St, 49935-1437. (Mail add: PO Box 328, 49935-0328), SAN 308-1915. Tel: 906-265-2831. FAX: 906-265-2062. Web Site: joomla.uproc.lib.mi.us/WestIron. *Dir,* Barbara Bartel; E-mail: lbbartel@uproc.lib.mi.us
Founded 1967. Pop 8,341; Circ 38,000
Library Holdings: Bk Titles 38,000; Bk Vols 980,000; Per Subs 90
Special Collections: Large Print Books
Wireless access
Partic in Superiorland Library Cooperative; Upper Peninsula Region of Library Cooperation, Inc
Open Mon-Wed & Fri 8:30-5, Thurs 8:30-7, Sat 10-2
Friends of the Library Group

IRONWOOD

J GOGEBIC COMMUNITY COLLEGE*, Alex D Chisholm Library, E4946 Jackson Rd, 49938. SAN 308-1931. Tel: 906-932-4231, Ext 344. FAX: 906-932-0868. Web Site: www.gogebic.edu/library. *Library Contact,* Position Currently Open
Founded 1932. Enrl 1,050; Fac 67; Highest Degree: Associate
Jul 2012-Jun 2013 Income $244,470. Mats Exp $45,000, Books $15,000, Per/Ser (Incl. Access Fees) $15,000, Electronic Ref Mat (Incl. Access Fees) $15,000. Sal $114,000
Library Holdings: Audiobooks 24; DVDs 30; Bk Titles 21,000; Bk Vols 22,000; Per Subs 100; Videos 1,500
Special Collections: Mining Memorabilia
Subject Interests: Great Lakes, Hist, Local hist
Automation Activity & Vendor Info: (Acquisitions) Ex Libris Group; (Cataloging) Ex Libris Group; (Circulation) Ex Libris Group; (Course Reserve) Ex Libris Group; (ILL) Ex Libris Group; (OPAC) Ex Libris Group; (Serials) Ex Libris Group
Wireless access
Function: Adult bk club
Partic in Upper Peninsula Region of Library Cooperation, Inc
Open Mon-Thurs 8-4, Fri 8-Noon

P IRONWOOD CARNEGIE PUBLIC LIBRARY*, 235 E Aurora St, 49938-2178. SAN 308-1923. Tel: 906-932-0203. FAX: 906-932-2447. Web Site: joomla.uproc.lib.mi.us/ironwood. *Dir,* Lynne Wiercinski; E-mail: Libraryboss@ironwoodcarnegie.org; Staff 4 (MLS 1, Non-MLS 3)
Founded 1901. Pop 9,629; Circ 54,607
Library Holdings: Bk Vols 29,152; Per Subs 85
Special Collections: Local newspapers on microfilm dating back to 1890; State of Michigan. State Document Depository
Subject Interests: Arts & crafts, Hist
Automation Activity & Vendor Info: (Cataloging) SirsiDynix; (Circulation) SirsiDynix
Wireless access
Partic in Superiorland Library Cooperative; Upper Peninsula Region of Library Cooperation, Inc
Open Mon & Fri 9-5, Tues & Thurs 12-7, Wed & Sat 9-12
Friends of the Library Group

ISHPEMING

P ISHPEMING CARNEGIE PUBLIC LIBRARY, 317 N Main St, 49849-1994. SAN 308-194X. Tel: 906-486-4381. FAX: 906-486-6226. Web Site: ishpeminglibrary.info. *Dir,* Jessica Shirtz; E-mail: jshirtz@uproc.lib.mi.us; *Asst Librn,* Kelsey Boldt; E-mail: krboldt@uproc.lib.mi.us; Staff 5 (MLS 2, Non-MLS 3)
Founded 1904. Pop 13,888; Circ 54,176
Library Holdings: AV Mats 620; Large Print Bks 175; Bk Vols 72,000; Per Subs 78; Talking Bks 270
Automation Activity & Vendor Info: (Cataloging) SirsiDynix; (Circulation) SirsiDynix; (OPAC) SirsiDynix
Wireless access
Partic in Superiorland Library Cooperative; Upper Peninsula Region of Library Cooperation, Inc
Open Tues & Fri 9-5, Wed & Thurs 9-7, Sat 10-4
Friends of the Library Group

S US NATIONAL SKI HALL OF FAME*, Roland Palmedo National Ski Library, 610 Palms Ave, 49849. (Mail add: PO Box 191, 49849-0191), SAN 308-1958. Tel: 906-485-6323. FAX: 906-486-4570. Web Site: www.skihall.com. *Exec Dir,* Justin Koski
Founded 1956
Library Holdings: Bk Titles 1,500
Special Collections: Roland Palmedo Coll
Subject Interests: Hist
Publications: Midwest Skiing - A Glance Back; Nine Thousand Years of Skis: Norwegian Wood to French Plastic; Seventy-Five Years of Skiing, 1904-79; Skiing Then & Now; The Flying Norseman
Open Mon-Sat 10-5
Friends of the Library Group

ITHACA

P THOMPSON HOME PUBLIC LIBRARY*, 125 W Center St, 48847. SAN 308-1966. Tel: 989-875-4184. FAX: 989-875-3374. Web Site: www.ithacalibrary.michlibrary.org. *Dir, Libr Serv,* Abby Hill; E-mail: thlibdir@edzone.net
Founded 1926. Pop 10,179
Library Holdings: Bk Vols 25,500; Per Subs 68

Subject Interests: Local hist, Mich
Automation Activity & Vendor Info: (Cataloging) Follett Software; (Circulation) Follett Software
Wireless access
Partic in White Pine Library Cooperative
Open Mon & Wed 10-8, Tues, Thurs & Fri 10-5, Sat (Sept-May) 10-2

JACKSON

C BAKER COLLEGE OF JACKSON*, Academic Resource Center, 2800 Springport Rd, 49202-1255. Tel: 517-841-4500. FAX: 517-789-7331. E-mail: library@baker.edu. Web Site: my.baker.edu/ICS/My_Services/Department_Resources/Academic_Resource_Center/Library. *Coordr, Info Tech,* Diane Childress; Tel: 810-766-4235, E-mail: dchild02@baker.edu
Founded 1994. Highest Degree: Doctorate
Library Holdings: Bk Vols 13,500; Per Subs 50
Automation Activity & Vendor Info: (Cataloging) Koha; (Circulation) Koha; (OPAC) Koha
Wireless access
Partic in LYRASIS; PALnet

CONSUMERS ENERGY

S CORPORATE LIBRARY*, One Energy Plaza, EP1-244, 49201, SAN 321-8104. Tel: 517-788-0541. FAX: 517-768-3804. *Dir,* Michele Morante Puckett; E-mail: michele.puckett@cmsenergy.com; *Asst Librn,* Joseph B Anteau; Tel: 517-788-2520, E-mail: joseph.anteau@cmsenergy.com. Subject Specialists: *Bus, Engr, Utilities,* Michele Morante Puckett; Staff 2 (MLS 2)
Founded 1977
Library Holdings: Audiobooks 200; DVDs 50; Bk Titles 6,000; Per Subs 225
Special Collections: Company & Industry Historical Archival Coll; Electric & Gas Industry Reports; Industry Standards
Subject Interests: Diversity, Energy disciplines, Health & wellness, Leadership, Safety
Automation Activity & Vendor Info: (ILL) OCLC FirstSearch; (Serials) EBSCO Online
Function: Archival coll, Audio & video playback equip for onsite use, Audiobks via web, Bks on CD, Bus archives, CD-ROM, Computers for patron use, Doc delivery serv, Electronic databases & coll, ILL available, Instruction & testing, Internet access, Learning ctr, Microfiche/film & reading machines, Online cat, Online ref, Orientations, Outside serv via phone, mail, e-mail & web, Res libr, Scanner, Tax forms, Telephone ref, Wheelchair accessible
Restriction: Access at librarian's discretion, Access for corporate affiliates, Borrowing requests are handled by ILL, By permission only, Circulates for staff only, External users must contact libr, Lending to staff only, No access to competitors, Non-circulating of rare bks, Not open to pub, Secured area only open to authorized personnel, Use of others with permission of librn
Friends of the Library Group

S LEGAL LIBRARY*, One Energy Plaza, 49201, SAN 308-1974. Tel: 517-788-1088. FAX: 517-788-1682. *Librn,* Betsy S Domschot
Founded 1955
Library Holdings: Bk Vols 32,000; Per Subs 25
Restriction: Restricted pub use

S G ROBERT COTTON REGIONAL CORRECTIONAL FACILITY LIBRARY, 3500 N Elm Rd, 49201. SAN 371-7585. Tel: 517-780-5000, 517-780-5172. FAX: 517-780-5100. *Librn,* Hatatu Elum; E-mail: elumh@michigan.gov; Staff 3 (MLS 1, Non-MLS 2)
Library Holdings: Bk Titles 10,000; Per Subs 14

J JACKSON COMMUNITY COLLEGE*, Atkinson Library, 2111 Emmons Rd, 49201-8399. SAN 308-2016. Tel: 517-796-8622. FAX: 517-796-8623. E-mail: jcclibrary@jccmi.edu. Web Site: www.jccmi.edu/library. *Libr Dir,* Jennifer Adams; *Coordr,* Debora Moyer; Tel: 517-796-8621, E-mail: moyerdeboraj@jccmi.edu; Staff 5 (MLS 2, Non-MLS 3)
Founded 1928. Enrl 6,328; Fac 95; Highest Degree: Associate
Library Holdings: Bk Vols 38,000; Per Subs 325
Special Collections: Historical Coll
Automation Activity & Vendor Info: (Cataloging) SirsiDynix; (Circulation) SirsiDynix; (Course Reserve) SirsiDynix; (ILL) OCLC; (OPAC) SirsiDynix; (Serials) SirsiDynix
Wireless access
Partic in Midwest Collaborative for Library Services
Open Mon-Thurs 7:30am-9pm, Fri 7:30-5, Sat 9-5, Sun 1-6

P JACKSON DISTRICT LIBRARY*, 244 W Michigan Ave, 49201. SAN 346-6507. Tel: 517-788-4087. Interlibrary Loan Service Tel: 517-788-4087, Ext 1486. Reference Tel: 517-788-4087, Ext 1339. Administration Tel: 517-788-1309, 517-788-4099. FAX: 517-782-8635. Web Site: myjdl.com. *Dir,* Sara Tackett; E-mail: tackettse@myjdl.com; *Asst Dir,* Liz Breed; E-mail: lizbreed810@gmail.com; *Ref Serv Coordr,* Deborah Sears; E-mail: searsdd@myjdl.com; *Tech Serv Coordr,* Lorraine Butchart; E-mail: butchartlk@myjdl.com; Staff 23 (MLS 15, Non-MLS 8)
Founded 1978. Pop 158,422; Circ 806,445
Library Holdings: Audiobooks 11,981; Bks on Deafness & Sign Lang 68; Braille Volumes 12; CDs 9,304; DVDs 14,459; e-books 20,147; Electronic Media & Resources 8,689; High Interest/Low Vocabulary Bk Vols 79; Large Print Bks 8,547; Microforms 4,044; Bk Titles 247,161; Per Subs 756; Videos 6,465
Special Collections: African American Coll; Genealogy Coll; Jackson & Michigan History Coll; Large Print Coll; Literacy Coll; Spanish Coll. US Document Depository
Automation Activity & Vendor Info: (Acquisitions) SirsiDynix; (Cataloging) SirsiDynix; (Circulation) SirsiDynix; (ILL) OCLC ILLiad; (Media Booking) SirsiDynix; (OPAC) SirsiDynix; (Serials) SirsiDynix
Wireless access
Function: Adult bk club, Adult literacy prog, After school storytime, Art exhibits, Audio & video playback equip for onsite use, Audiobks via web, Bk club(s), Bks on cassette, Bks on CD, CD-ROM, Children's prog, Computer training, Computers for patron use, Distance learning, E-Reserves, Electronic databases & coll, Family literacy, Games & aids for people with disabilities, Govt ref serv, Health sci info serv, Home delivery & serv to seniorr ctr & nursing homes, Homebound delivery serv, ILL available, Internet access, Magnifiers for reading, Mail & tel request accepted, Music CDs, Notary serv, Online cat, Online ref, Orientations, Outside serv via phone, mail, e-mail & web, Photocopying/Printing, Preschool outreach, Prog for adults, Prog for children & young adult, Ref serv available, Senior computer classes, Senior outreach, Serves people with intellectual disabilities, Spoken cassettes & CDs, Spoken cassettes & DVDs, Summer reading prog, Tax forms, Teen prog, Telephone ref, VHS videos, Wheelchair accessible, Workshops
Mem of Woodlands Library Cooperative
Special Services for the Deaf - Bks on deafness & sign lang
Special Services for the Blind - Large print bks & talking machines
Open Mon-Thurs 9-9, Fri 9-6, Sat 10-5
Friends of the Library Group
Branches: 13
BROOKLYN BRANCH, 207 N Main St, Brooklyn, 49230. (Mail add: PO Box 490, Brooklyn, 49230), SAN 378-1577. Tel: 517-905-1369. FAX: 517-592-3054. E-mail: brooklyn@myjdl.com. *Br Mgr,* Erica Grimm
Founded 1918. Pop 10,156; Circ 53,535
Open Mon & Wed 10-7, Tues & Fri 10-6, Thurs 12-6, Sat 10-2
Friends of the Library Group
CARNEGIE LIBRARY, 244 W Michigan Ave, 49201, SAN 378-1593. Tel: 517-788-4087. Automation Services Tel: 517-784-2280. FAX: 517-782-8635. *Dir,* Sara Tackett
Founded 1863. Pop 36,316; Circ 212,055
Special Services for the Deaf - Bks on deafness & sign lang
Open Mon-Thurs 9-9, Fri 9-6, Sat 10-5
Friends of the Library Group
CONCORD BRANCH, 108 S Main St, Concord, 49237. (Mail add: PO Box 458, Concord, 49237-0458), SAN 346-6590. Tel: 517-905-1379. FAX: 517-524-6971. E-mail: concord@myjdl.com. *Br Mgr,* Tammy Dotson
Founded 1903. Pop 5,641; Circ 25,307
Open Mon & Fri 1-6, Wed 10-7, Sat 10-2
Friends of the Library Group
EASTERN BRANCH, 3125 E Michigan Ave, 49201, SAN 346-6620. Tel: 517-788-4074. FAX: 517-788-4645. E-mail: eastern@myjdl.com. *Br Mgr,* Steven George
Founded 1914. Pop 30,278; Circ 105,004
Open Mon, Wed & Thurs 10-8, Tues & Fri 12-5, Sat 10-5, Sun 1-5
Friends of the Library Group
GRASS LAKE BRANCH, 130 W Michigan Ave, Grass Lake, 49240. (Mail add: PO Box 335, Grass Lake, 49240-0335), SAN 346-6655. Tel: 517-522-8211. FAX: 517-522-8215. E-mail: grasslake@myjdl.com. *Br Mgr,* Sue Weible
Founded 1935. Pop 5,353; Circ 38,244
Open Mon & Wed 10-7, Thurs & Fri 10-6, Sat 10-2
Friends of the Library Group
HANOVER BRANCH, 118 W Main St, Hanover, 49241. (Mail add: PO Box 130, Hanover, 49241-0130), SAN 346-668X. Tel: 517-905-1399. FAX: 517-563-8346. E-mail: hanover@myjdl.com. *Br Mgr,* Tammy Dotson
Founded 1927. Pop 7,661; Circ 19,659
Open Mon & Fri 1-6, Wed 10-7, Sat 10-2
Friends of the Library Group
HENRIETTA BRANCH, 11744 Bunkerhill Rd, Pleasant Lake, 49272. (Mail add: PO Box 88, Pleasant Lake, 49272-0088), SAN 346-6698. Tel: 517-769-6537. FAX: 517-769-6537. E-mail: henrietta@myjdl.com. *Br Mgr,* Kaitlyn Filip
Founded 1982. Pop 12,277; Circ 20,849
Open Mon & Fri 1-6, Wed 10-7, Sat 10-2
Friends of the Library Group

MEIJER BRANCH, 2699 Airport Rd, 49202, SAN 346-6736. Tel: 517-788-4480. FAX: 517-788-4481. E-mail: meijer@myjdl.com. *Br Mgr,* Patricia Snoblen
Founded 1928. Pop 27,432; Circ 159,659
Open Mon-Thurs 9-8, Fri 9-6, Sat 9-5, Sun 1-5
Friends of the Library Group

NAPOLEON BRANCH, 6755 S Brooklyn Rd, Napoleon, 49261. (Mail add: PO Box 476, Napoleon, 49261), SAN 346-6779. Tel: 517-536-4266. FAX: 517-536-0531. E-mail: napoleon@myjdl.com. *Br Mgr,* Nicole Gilbert
Founded 1930. Pop 6,273; Circ 25,806
Open Mon, Tues & Thurs 1-6, Wed 10-6
Friends of the Library Group

PARMA BRANCH, 102 Church St, Parma, 49269. (Mail add: PO Box 227, Parma, 49269-0227), SAN 346-6809. Tel: 517-531-4908. FAX: 517-531-5085. E-mail: parma@myjdl.com. *Br Mgr,* Jackie Merritt
Founded 1922. Pop 8,114; Circ 19,001
Open Mon & Fri 1-6, Wed 10-7, Sat 10-2
Friends of the Library Group

SPRING ARBOR BRANCH, 113 E Main St, Spring Arbor, 49283. (Mail add: PO Box 264, Spring Arbor, 49283-0264), SAN 346-6833. Tel: 517-750-2030. FAX: 517-750-2030. E-mail: springarbor@myjdl.com. *Br Mgr,* Dawn Iocca
Founded 1965. Pop 9,198; Circ 39,040
Open Mon & Wed 10-7, Fri 10-6, Sat 10-2
Friends of the Library Group

SPRINGPORT BRANCH, 116 Mechanic St, Springport, 49284. (Mail add: PO Box 172, Springport, 49284-0172), SAN 346-6868. Tel: 517-905-1459. FAX: 517-857-3833. E-mail: springport@myjdl.com. *Br Mgr,* Jackie Merritt
Founded 1901. Pop 5,612; Circ 10,644
Open Mon & Fri 1-6, Wed 10-7, Sat 10-2
Friends of the Library Group

SUMMIT BRANCH, 104 W Bird Ave, 49203, SAN 346-6892. Tel: 517-783-4030. FAX: 517-783-1788. E-mail: summit@myjdl.com. *Br Mgr,* Sarah Hashimoto
Founded 1939. Pop 26,640; Circ 63,601
Function: CD-ROM, Music CDs, Prog for adults, Prog for children & young adult, Ref serv available, Summer reading prog, VHS videos
Special Services for the Blind - Reader equip
Open Mon 9-8, Tues, Thurs & Fri 10-6, Wed 10-8, Sat 10-2
Friends of the Library Group

S MICHIGAN DEPARTMENT OF CORRECTIONS, Parnall Correctional Facility Library, 1790 E Parnall Rd, 49201. Tel: 517-780-6004. Web Site: www.michigan.gov/corrections. *Librn,* Sarah Gebbert; E-mail: gebberts@michigan.gov; *Libr Tech,* Mary Kalat; E-mail: kalatm1@michigan.gov
Library Holdings: Bk Vols 10,500
Restriction: Not open to pub

JENISON

P GEORGETOWN TOWNSHIP PUBLIC LIBRARY*, 1525 Baldwin St, 49428. SAN 308-2032. Tel: 616-457-9620. FAX: 616-457-3666. E-mail: jen@llcoop.org. Web Site: www.gtwp.com/186/Library. *Dir,* Rob Bristow; E-mail: jenrb@llcoop.org; Staff 21 (MLS 4, Non-MLS 17)
Founded 1965. Pop 50,446; Circ 263,000
Library Holdings: AV Mats 8,345; Large Print Bks 1,100; Bk Titles 95,000; Bk Vols 98,366; Per Subs 313; Talking Bks 2,525
Automation Activity & Vendor Info: (Cataloging) Innovative Interfaces, Inc; (Circulation) Innovative Interfaces, Inc; (OPAC) Innovative Interfaces, Inc
Function: ILL available
Partic in Lakeland Library Cooperative
Open Mon-Thurs (Winter) 10-9, Fri & Sat 10-5; Mon-Thurs (Summer) 9-9, Fri 9-5, Sat 9-1
Friends of the Library Group

JONESVILLE

P JONESVILLE DISTRICT LIBRARY*, 310 Church St, 49250-1087. (Mail add: PO Box 184, 49250-0184), SAN 308-2040. Tel: 517-849-9701. FAX: 517-849-0009. E-mail: jonesville.districtlibrary@monroe.lib.mi.us. Web Site: www.jonesvilledistrictlibrary.michlibrary.org. *Dir,* Laura Orlowski
Pop 5,894; Circ 28,209
Library Holdings: Bk Vols 26,000; Per Subs 32
Wireless access
Mem of Woodlands Library Cooperative
Open Mon & Wed (Spring) 10-8, Tues, Thurs & Fri 10-6, Sat 10-2; Mon-Fri (Winter) 10-6, Sat 10-2

KALAMAZOO

M ASCENSION BORGESS HOSPITAL LIBRARY, Borgess Library, 1521 Gull Rd, 49048-1666. SAN 314-4658. Tel: 269-226-7360. FAX: 269-226-6881. E-mail: borgess.library@ascension.org. Web Site: healthcare.ascension.org. *Clinical Librn,* Jennifer Barlow; E-mail: jennifer.barlow@ascension.org; Staff 1 (MLS 1)
Jul 2014-Jun 2015. Mats Exp $131,650, Books $12,000, Per/Ser (Incl. Access Fees) $20,000, Electronic Ref Mat (Incl. Access Fees) $99,650
Library Holdings: Bk Vols 3,000; Per Subs 120
Subject Interests: Bereavement, Clinical med, Ethics, Healthcare delivery, Mgt, Nursing
Automation Activity & Vendor Info: (Cataloging) Softlink America; (Circulation) Softlink America; (OPAC) Softlink America; (Serials) Softlink America
Wireless access
Partic in Medical Library Association; Michigan Health Sciences Libraries Association; Midwest Collaborative for Library Services; National Network of Libraries of Medicine Region 6; Southwest Michigan Library Cooperative
Open Mon-Fri 8-4:30

M BRONSON METHODIST HOSPITAL, Health Sciences Library, 601 John St, Box B, 49007. SAN 308-2067. Tel: 269-341-6318. FAX: 269-341-7043. E-mail: bronsonlibrary@bronsonhg.org. *Libr Serv Supvr,* Liz Colson; Tel: 269-341-8627, E-mail: colsone@bronsonhg.org; Staff 1 (MLS 1)
Founded 1961
Library Holdings: e-books 2,000; e-journals 2,375; Bk Titles 400; Bk Vols 450; Per Subs 7
Subject Interests: Allied health, Consumer health, Health sci, Hospital admin, Med, Nursing
Automation Activity & Vendor Info: (Cataloging) EOS International; (Discovery) TDNet; (ILL) OCLC WorldShare Interlibrary Loan; (OPAC) EOS International
Wireless access
Function: Prof lending libr
Partic in Michigan Health Sciences Libraries Association; Midwest Collaborative for Library Services; National Network of Libraries of Medicine Region 6; Southwest Michigan Library Cooperative
Open Mon-Fri 8-5
Restriction: Hospital staff & commun

R HERITAGE CHRISTIAN REFORMED CHURCH LIBRARY*, 2857 S 11th St, 49009. SAN 308-2075. Tel: 269-372-3830. *Librn,* Carol Bickle
Founded 1869
Library Holdings: Bk Titles 800; Bk Vols 1,000
Open Mon-Thurs 9-2

C KALAMAZOO COLLEGE LIBRARY*, 1200 Academy St, 49006-3285. SAN 308-2091. Tel: 269-337-7153. Interlibrary Loan Service Tel: 269-337-7148. Reference Tel: 269-337-7152. Web Site: library.kzoo.edu/. *Libr Dir,* Dr Stacy Nowicki; Tel: 269-337-5750, E-mail: stacy.nowicki@kzoo.edu; *Coll Serv Librn,* Leslie Burke; Tel: 269-337-7144, E-mail: leslie.burke@kzoo.edu; *Digital Serv Librn,* Ethan Cutler; Tel: 269-337-7147, E-mail: ethan.cutler@kzoo.edu; *Ref & Instruction Librn,* Kelly Frost; E-mail: kelly.frost@kzoo.edu; *Ref & Instruction Librn,* Robin Rank; E-mail: robin.rank@kzoo.edu; *Circ Supvr,* Hillary Berry; Tel: 269-337-5731, E-mail: hillary.berry@kzoo.edu; *Doc Delivery Spec,* Joisan Decker DeHaan; E-mail: joisan.decker@kzoo.edu; *Archivist,* Lisa Murphy; Tel: 269-337-7151, E-mail: lisa.murphy@kzoo.edu; *Curator, Rare Bks,* Mallory Heslinger; Tel: 269-337-5762, E-mail: mallory.heslinger@kzoo.edu; Staff 13 (MLS 8, Non-MLS 5)
Founded 1833. Enrl 1,461; Fac 124; Highest Degree: Bachelor
Special Collections: Fine Birds Coll; History of Books & Printing; History of Science; Michigan Baptist Coll; Private Presses
Automation Activity & Vendor Info: (Acquisitions) Ex Libris Group; (Cataloging) Ex Libris Group; (Circulation) Ex Libris Group; (Course Reserve) Ex Libris Group; (Discovery) Ex Libris Group; (ILL) OCLC Tipasa; (Serials) Ex Libris Group
Wireless access
Function: 24/7 Online cat, Wheelchair accessible
Partic in Midwest Collaborative for Library Services; Oberlin Group; OCLC Online Computer Library Center, Inc
Restriction: Circ limited, In-house use for visitors, Non-circulating of rare bks, Open to fac, students & qualified researchers, Open to pub for ref & circ; with some limitations, Open to students, fac & staff

S KALAMAZOO INSTITUTE OF ARTS, Mary & Edwin Meader Fine Arts Library, 314 S Park St, 49007. SAN 308-2113. Tel: 269-349-7775, Ext 3166. FAX: 269-349-9313. E-mail: library@kiarts.org. Web Site: www.kiarts.org/page.php?menu_id=68. *Head Librn,* Lauren McMullan; Staff 1 (MLS 1)
Founded 1956
Library Holdings: AV Mats 250; Bk Vols 11,000

Special Collections: 19th & 20th Century American Art; Local and Regional Artist Files
Subject Interests: Am Art 19th-20th Centuries, Fine arts, Photog
Automation Activity & Vendor Info: (Cataloging) Auto-Graphics, Inc; (Circulation) Auto-Graphics, Inc; (OPAC) Auto-Graphics, Inc
Wireless access
Function: Adult bk club, Computers for patron use, E-Reserves, Electronic databases & coll, Family literacy, Free DVD rentals, Internet access, Magazines, Movies, Music CDs, Online cat, Prog for adults, Prog for children & young adult, Ref serv available, Scanner, Spoken cassettes & CDs, Story hour, VHS videos, Wheelchair accessible
Publications: Exhibition Catalogs
Partic in Southwest Michigan Library Cooperative
Open Wed, Fri, & Sat 11-3
Restriction: Circ to mem only

P KALAMAZOO PUBLIC LIBRARY*, 315 S Rose St, 49007-5264. SAN 346-6981. Tel: 269-342-9897. Circulation Tel: 269-553-7806. Interlibrary Loan Service Tel: 269-553-7892. Reference Tel: 269-553-7801. FAX: 269-553-7999. Web Site: www.kpl.gov. *Dir,* Ryan Wieber; E-mail: ryanw@kpl.gov; *Head, Adult Serv,* Michael Cockrell; Tel: 269-553-7841, E-mail: michaelc@kpl.gov; *Head Fac Mgt,* Tom Sowell; Tel: 269-553-7883, E-mail: TomS@kpl.gov; *Head, Youth Serv,* Susan Warner; Tel: 269-553-7876, Fax: 269-553-7940, E-mail: susan@kpl.gov; *Br Head, Circ Serv,* Kevin King; Tel: 269-553-7881, E-mail: kevink@kpl.gov; *Human Res Mgr,* Terry New; Tel: 269-553-7931, E-mail: TerryN@kpl.gov; *Mkt & Communications Mgr,* Farrell Howe; Tel: 269-553-7879, E-mail: FarrellH@kpl.gov; *Budget Officer, Financial Serv,* Nnamdi Dike; Tel: 269-553-7856, E-mail: NnamdiD@kpl.gov; Staff 21 (MLS 21)
Founded 1872. Pop 123,979; Circ 1,398,360
Special Collections: Michigan & Kalamazoo History. US Document Depository
Wireless access
Function: 24/7 Electronic res, 24/7 Online cat, 3D Printer, Activity rm, Adult bk club, After school storytime, Archival coll, Art exhibits, Art programs, Audiobks via web, AV serv, Bilingual assistance for Spanish patrons, Bk club(s), Bks on CD, Children's prog, Citizenship assistance, Computers for patron use, Digital talking bks, Doc delivery serv, E-Readers, E-Reserves, Electronic databases & coll, Free DVD rentals, Govt ref serv, Holiday prog, Home delivery & serv to seniorr ctr & nursing homes, Homebound delivery serv, ILL available, Internet access, Magnifiers for reading, Mail & tel request accepted, Mail loans to mem, Makerspace, Meeting rooms, Microfiche/film & reading machines, Music CDs, Notary serv, Online cat, Online ref, Outreach serv, OverDrive digital audio bks, Photocopying/Printing, Preschool outreach, Printer for laptops & handheld devices, Prog for adults, Prog for children & young adult, Ref serv available, Scanner, Senior outreach, Spanish lang bks, Spoken cassettes & CDs, Spoken cassettes & DVDs, STEM programs, Story hour, Summer reading prog, Tax forms, Teen prog, Telephone ref, VHS videos, Wheelchair accessible, Workshops
Publications: LINK (Newsletter)
Partic in Southwest Michigan Library Cooperative
Open Mon-Thurs (Winter) 9-9, Fri 9-6, Sat 9-5, Sun 1-5; Mon-Wed (Summer) 9-9,Thurs & Fri 9-6, Sat 9-5
Restriction: Non-resident fee
Friends of the Library Group
Branches: 4
EASTWOOD, 1112 Gayle St, 49048, SAN 346-7163. Tel: 269-553-7810. FAX: 269-345-6095. *Lead Librn,* Judi Rambow
Open Mon 12-6, Tues 1-8, Wed & Thurs 10-6, Fri 12-5, Sat 10-5
Friends of the Library Group
OSHTEMO, 7265 W Main St, 49009, SAN 346-7198. Tel: 269-553-7980. FAX: 269-375-6610. *Lead Librn,* Nancy Smith; Staff 2 (MLS 2)
Open Mon & Wed 10-9, Tues 12-9, Thurs 10-6, Fri & Sat 10-5
Friends of the Library Group
ALMA POWELL BRANCH, 1000 W Paterson St, 49007, SAN 346-7139. Tel: 269-553-7960. FAX: 269-344-0782. *Lead Librn,* Judi Rambow; Tel: 269-553-7961, E-mail: judir@kpl.gov
Open Mon & Wed 1-6, Tues 1-8, Thurs 10-6, Fri 10-5
Friends of the Library Group
WASHINGTON SQUARE, 1244 Portage Rd, 49001, SAN 346-7228. Tel: 269-553-7970. FAX: 269-342-9261. *Lead Librn,* Nancy Stern
Open Mon & Wed 1-6, Tues 1-8, Thurs 10-6, Fri 10-5, Sat 9-Noon
Friends of the Library Group

J KALAMAZOO VALLEY COMMUNITY COLLEGE LIBRARIES*, 6767 West O Ave, Rm 3210, 49003. (Mail add: PO Box 4070, 49003-4070), SAN 308-213X. Tel: 269-488-4328, 269-488-4380. Circulation Tel: 269-488-5673. Interlibrary Loan Service Tel: 269-488-4331. Reference Tel: 269-488-4380. Administration Tel: 269-488-4326. Reference E-mail: libref@kvcc.edu. Web Site: www.kvcc.edu/library. *Libr Dir,* Mark Walters; E-mail: mwalters@kvcc.edu; *Instruction Librn, Librn, Arcadia Commons Campus,* Jim Ratliff; E-mail: jratliff@kvcc.edu; Staff 15 (MLS 6, Non-MLS 9)
Founded 1968. Enrl 15,000; Fac 136; Highest Degree: Associate
Library Holdings: AV Mats 22,767; Bks on Deafness & Sign Lang 300; Bk Titles 149,000; Per Subs 245
Special Collections: Alva Dorn Photography Coll; Mary Mace Spradling African American Coll; Michigan History (Ned Rubenstein Memorial Coll)
Subject Interests: Career res, Sign lang
Wireless access
Open Mon-Thurs 7:45am-9pm, Fri 7:45-5, Sat 10-2, Sun Noon-5 (Fall & Winter); Mon-Thurs 8am-9pm, Fri 8-Noon (Summer)

R SAINT LUKE'S EPISCOPAL CHURCH LIBRARY*, 247 W Lovell St, 49007. SAN 308-2148. Tel: 269-345-8553. FAX: 269-345-5559.
Library Holdings: Bk Vols 1,600
Friends of the Library Group

S W E UPJOHN INSTITUTE FOR EMPLOYMENT RESEARCH, Information Center, 300 S Westnedge Ave, 49007-4686. SAN 371-8174. Tel: 269-343-5541, Ext 418. FAX: 269-343-3308. Web Site: www.upjohn.org. *Dir, Info Serv,* Lisa M Abbott; E-mail: abbott@upjohn.org; Staff 3.3 (MLS 1, Non-MLS 2.3)
Founded 1945
Library Holdings: CDs 96; e-books 830; e-journals 298; Electronic Media & Resources 2,743; Bk Titles 14,353; Bk Vols 25,791; Per Subs 363
Subject Interests: Educ, Employment, Labor econ, Poverty & income support, Unemployment
Automation Activity & Vendor Info: (Cataloging) EOS International; (ILL) OCLC; (OPAC) EOS International; (Serials) EOS International
Wireless access
Function: Res libr
Partic in Midwest Collaborative for Library Services
Restriction: Staff use only

C WESTERN MICHIGAN UNIVERSITY, Dwight B Waldo Library, 1903 W Michigan Ave, WMU Mail Stop 5353, 49008-5353. Tel: 269-387-5059. Circulation Tel: 269-387-5156. Interlibrary Loan Service Tel: 269-387-5172. Reference Tel: 269-387-5178. Administration Tel: 269-387-5202. Automation Services Tel: 269-387-5039. FAX: 269-387-5077. Circulation FAX: 269-387-4343. Interlibrary Loan Service FAX: 269-387-5124. Reference FAX: 269-387-5836. Web Site: www.wmich.edu/library/visit/waldo. *Dean, Univ Libr,* Julie Ann Garrison; *Assoc Dean for Education & User Services,* Mary O'Kelly; Tel: 269-387-5239; *Assoc Dean for Resources & Digital Strategies,* Paul Gallagher; Tel: 269-387-5205; *Bus Librn,* LuMarie Guth; Tel: 269-387-5153; *Cataloging & Metadata Librn,* Marianne Swierenga; Tel: 269-387-4112; *Collections Strategist Librn,* Geri Rinna; Tel: 269-387-5196; *Data Librn,* Daria Orlowska; Tel: 269-387-5149; *Digital Projects Librn,* Amy Bocko; Tel: 269-387-5150; *Education & Human Dev Librn,* Bradford Dennis; Tel: 269-387-1581; *Engagement Librn,* Kate Langan; Tel: 269-387-5823; *Engineering & Natural Sciences Librn,* Edward Eckel; Tel: 269-387-5140; *Fine Arts Librn,* Mike Duffy; Tel: 269-387-5236; *Health & Human Services Librn,* Dianna Sachs; Tel: 269-387-5182; *Humanities Librn,* Alexis Smith; Tel: 269-387-5158; *Monographic Acquisitions & Gifts Librn,* Randle Gedeon; Tel: 269-387-5227; *Scholarly Comms & Open Educ'l Resources Librn,* Michele Behr; Tel: 269-387-5611; *Soc Sci Librn,* Carrie Leatherman; Tel: 269-387-5142; *Spec Coll Librn,* Susan Steuer; Tel: 269-387-5250; *User Serv Librn,* Jonathan Scherger; Tel: 269-387-5881; Staff 82 (MLS 31, Non-MLS 51)
Founded 1903. Enrl 24,433; Fac 885; Highest Degree: Doctorate
Library Holdings: Bk Titles 970,038; Bk Vols 1,910,778; Per Subs 7,743
Special Collections: African Studies (Ann Kercher Memorial); Cistercian Manuscript & Rare Book Coll; D B Waldo Lincoln Coll; Haenicke American Women's Poetry Coll; Historical Children's Book Coll; LeFevre Miniature Book Coll; Medieval Studies (Institute of Cistercian Studies), bks, mss; Regional History Coll. State Document Depository; US Document Depository
Automation Activity & Vendor Info: (Acquisitions) Ex Libris Group; (Cataloging) Ex Libris Group; (Circulation) Ex Libris Group; (ILL) Ex Libris Group; (Media Booking) Ex Libris Group; (OPAC) Ex Libris Group; (Serials) Ex Libris Group
Wireless access
Function: Archival coll, Audio & video playback equip for onsite use, CD-ROM, Doc delivery serv, E-Reserves, Electronic databases & coll, Govt ref serv, ILL available, Music CDs, Online cat, Online info literacy tutorials on the web & in blackboard, Online ref, Orientations, Photocopying/Printing, Ref & res, Ref serv available, Scanner, Tax forms, Telephone ref, Wheelchair accessible
Publications: Gatherings (Newsletter)
Partic in Midwest Collaborative for Library Services
Special Services for the Blind - Computer with voice synthesizer for visually impaired persons; Large print bks
Restriction: Borrowing privileges limited to fac & registered students, Non-circulating coll, Non-circulating of rare bks, Off-site coll in storage - retrieval as requested
Friends of the Library Group

Departmental Libraries:
ZHANG LEGACY COLLECTIONS CENTER, 1650 Oakland Dr, 49008, SAN 376-8864. Tel: 269-387-8490, 269-387-8497. FAX: 269-387-8484. E-mail: arch-collect@wmich.edu. Web Site: wmich.edu/library/visit/zhang. *Mgr,* Scott Smith; Tel: 269-387-8496, E-mail: scott.c.smith@wmich.edu; *Spec Coll Librn,* Susan Steuer; Tel: 269-387-5250; *Spec Coll Coordr,* Lori Kison; Tel: 269-387-5240; *Archives Curator,* John Winchell; Tel: 269-387-8485; *Regional History Curator,* Lynn Houghton; Tel: 269-387-8491; Staff 5 (MLS 1, Non-MLS 4)
Founded 1958. Enrl 28,500; Highest Degree: Doctorate
Library Holdings: Bk Vols 66,000
Special Collections: American Women's Poetry (Carol Ann Haenicke Coll); Book Arts & Graphic Design Colls; David Small & Sarah Stewart Archive; Historical Children's Coll; Regional History Colls; Western Michigan University Archives; World War II Propaganda & Print Colls
Subject Interests: Artists bks, Bk arts, Census data, Children's lit, Comic bks, County govt rec, Fine arts, Govt doc, Institutional hist, Poetry, Regional hist
Function: Archival coll
Open Tues-Fri 8-5, Sat 9-4 (Sept-June); Mon-Fri 9-5 (July-Aug)
Restriction: Non-circulating, Not a lending libr

KALKASKA

P KALKASKA COUNTY LIBRARY*, 247 S Cedar St, 49646. SAN 308-2164. Tel: 231-258-9411. Web Site: www.kalkaskalibrary.org. *Dir,* John Roberts; E-mail: john@kalkaskalibrary.org; *Ref Librn,* Bonnie Reed; Staff 4.5 (MLS 1.5, Non-MLS 3)
Founded 1934. Pop 17,500; Circ 32,305
Library Holdings: Audiobooks 1,150; Bks-By-Mail 200; Bks on Deafness & Sign Lang 10; Braille Volumes 8; CDs 415; DVDs 425; Large Print Bks 900; Bk Vols 40,200; Per Subs 20; Videos 800
Special Collections: Genealogy Coll; Northern Michigan History Coll
Wireless access
Function: Accelerated reader prog, Adult bk club, Art exhibits, Audio & video playback equip for onsite use, Audiobks via web, BA reader (adult literacy), Bi-weekly Writer's Group, Bilingual assistance for Spanish patrons, Bk club(s), Bks on cassette, Bks on CD, Children's prog, Computer training, Computers for patron use, Digital talking bks, E-Reserves, Electronic databases & coll, Equip loans & repairs, Free DVD rentals, Games & aids for people with disabilities, Genealogy discussion group, Holiday prog, Home delivery & serv to seniorr ctr & nursing homes, Homebound delivery serv, ILL available, Instruction & testing, Internet access, Jail serv, Magnifiers for reading, Mail & tel request accepted, Mail loans to mem, Microfiche/film & reading machines, Music CDs, Online cat, Online info literacy tutorials on the web & in blackboard, Orientations, Outreach serv, Outside serv via phone, mail, e-mail & web, OverDrive digital audio bks, Photocopying/Printing, Preschool outreach, Preschool reading prog, Prof lending libr, Prog for adults, Prog for children & young adult, Ref & res, Ref serv available, Res libr, Scanner, Senior computer classes, Senior outreach, Story hour, Summer reading prog, Tax forms, Teen prog, Telephone ref, VHS videos, Wheelchair accessible, Workshops
Partic in Proquest Dialog; SDC Info Servs
Open Mon, Tues, Thurs & Fri 9-6, Wed 9-8, Sat 9-2
Friends of the Library Group

KINGSTON

P JACQUELIN E OPPERMAN MEMORIAL LIBRARY, Kingston Community Public Library, 5790 State St, 48741. SAN 308-2180. Tel: 989-683-2500. FAX: 989-683-2081. E-mail: library@kingstonk12.org. Web Site: www.oppermanmemoriallibrary.com. *Libr Dir,* Glenna Ford; E-mail: gford@kingstonk12.org; Staff 2 (MLS 1, Non-MLS 1)
Founded 1970. Pop 4,080; Circ 6,399
Library Holdings: Audiobooks 220; CDs 122; DVDs 1,006; Large Print Bks 45; Per Subs 6
Automation Activity & Vendor Info: (Cataloging) Follett Software; (Circulation) Follett Software; (ILL) Innovative Interfaces, Inc - Millennium; (Media Booking) Follett Software
Wireless access
Partic in White Pine Library Cooperative
Open Mon 4-6, Tues,Wed & Thurs 4-8, Sat 9-3

LAINGSBURG

P LAINGSBURG PUBLIC LIBRARY*, 255 E Grand River, 48848. (Mail add: PO Box 280, 48848-0280), SAN 308-2210. Tel: 517-651-6282. FAX: 517-651-6371. E-mail: Laingsburglibrary@gmail.com. Web Site: www.laingsburg.michlibrary.org. *Dir,* Sandra Chavez
Founded 1905. Pop 7,132; Circ 26,667
Library Holdings: Bk Vols 15,000; Per Subs 42
Subject Interests: Local hist
Wireless access
Partic in Mideastern Michigan Library Cooperative
Open Mon 3-8, Tues-Thurs 9-6, Fri 9-5
Friends of the Library Group

LAKE CITY

P MISSAUKEE DISTRICT LIBRARY, 210 S Canal St, 49651. (Mail add: PO Box 340, 49651-0340), SAN 308-2229. Tel: 231-839-2166. FAX: 231-839-2166. Web Site: www.missaukeelibrary.org. *Dir & Librn,* Laura Marion; E-mail: director@missaukeelibrary.org; Staff 7 (Non-MLS 7)
Founded 1907. Pop 14,600; Circ 42,000
Library Holdings: Audiobooks 600; AV Mats 1,500; Bks on Deafness & Sign Lang 41; CDs 300; DVDs 1,300; Large Print Bks 1,122; Bk Titles 31,537; Bk Vols 40,000; Per Subs 56; Talking Bks 1,350; Videos 1,081
Special Collections: Local History
Wireless access
Function: 24/7 Electronic res, 24/7 Online cat, Activity rm, Adult bk club, Archival coll, Art programs, Audiobks via web, AV serv, Bk club(s), Bks on CD, Children's prog, Computer training, Computers for patron use, Digital talking bks, Doc delivery serv, E-Readers, Electronic databases & coll, Equip loans & repairs, Free DVD rentals, Genealogy discussion group, Holiday prog, Homebound delivery serv, Instruction & testing, Internet access, Laminating, Life-long learning prog for all ages, Magazines, Meeting rooms, Movies, Online cat, Online ref, OverDrive digital audio bks, Photocopying/Printing, Preschool outreach, Preschool reading prog, Printer for laptops & handheld devices, Prog for adults, Prog for children & young adult, Ref & res, Ref serv available, Scanner, Serves people with intellectual disabilities, Spanish lang bks, Story hour, Study rm, Summer & winter reading prog, Summer reading prog, Tax forms, Teen prog, Telephone ref, Wheelchair accessible, Winter reading prog, Workshops
Partic in Mid-Michigan Library League
Special Services for the Deaf - Bks on deafness & sign lang
Special Services for the Blind - Assistive/Adapted tech devices, equip & products; Bks on CD; Extensive large print coll; Large print bks; Talking bk & rec for the blind cat; Talking bks & player equip
Open Mon 9-7, Tues-Fri 9-6, Sat 9-2
Friends of the Library Group

LAKE ODESSA

P LAKE ODESSA COMMUNITY LIBRARY*, 1007 Fourth Ave, 48849-1023. SAN 376-3714. Tel: 616-374-4591. FAX: 616-374-3054. E-mail: lko@llcoop.org. Web Site: www.lakeodessalibrary.org. *Dir,* Jennifer Salgat
Founded 1986. Pop 4,434; Circ 33,500
Library Holdings: AV Mats 240; Bk Vols 18,000; Per Subs 35; Talking Bks 300
Wireless access
Partic in Lakeland Library Cooperative
Special Services for the Blind - Braille bks; Talking bks
Open Tues & Thurs 9-7, Wed & Fri 9-5, Sat 9-12
Friends of the Library Group

LAKE ORION

P ORION TOWNSHIP PUBLIC LIBRARY*, 825 Joslyn Rd, 48362. SAN 346-752X. Tel: 248-693-3000. FAX: 248-693-3009. Web Site: orionlibrary.org. *Dir,* Karen Knox; Tel: 248-693-3000, Ext 305, E-mail: kknox@orionlibrary.org; *Head, Adult Serv,* Beth Sheridan; Tel: 248-693-3000, Ext 332, E-mail: esheridan@orionlibrary.org; *Head, Info Tech,* Steve Saunders; Tel: 248-693-3000, Ext 334, E-mail: ssaunders@orionlibrary.org; *Head, Support Serv,* Shannon Schmidt; Tel: 248-693-3000, Ext 301, E-mail: sschmidt@orionlibrary.org; *Head, Youth Serv,* Debra Refior; Tel: 248-693-3000, Ext 341, E-mail: drefior@orionlibrary.org; *ILS Coordr,* Barnard Anne; Tel: 248-693-3000, Ext 339, E-mail: abarnard@orionlibrary.org; Staff 12 (MLS 12)
Founded 1926. Pop 35,394; Circ 505,910. Sal $1,210,000
Library Holdings: Audiobooks 10,118; CDs 7,973; DVDs 9,069; e-books 4,732; Large Print Bks 5,540; Bk Titles 151,036; Per Subs 357; Videos 4,431
Subject Interests: Genealogy, Mich
Automation Activity & Vendor Info: (Acquisitions) Horizon; (Cataloging) Horizon; (Circulation) Horizon; (Serials) Horizon
Wireless access
Function: Adult bk club, Art exhibits, Audio & video playback equip for onsite use, Audiobks via web, Bk club(s), Bks on cassette, Bks on CD, Chess club, Children's prog, Computer training, Computers for patron use, Electronic databases & coll, Free DVD rentals, Home delivery & serv to seniorr ctr & nursing homes, Homebound delivery serv, Homework prog, ILL available, Magnifiers for reading, Microfiche/film & reading machines, Museum passes, Music CDs, Notary serv, Online cat, Online ref, Outreach serv, OverDrive digital audio bks, Photocopying/Printing, Preschool outreach, Preschool reading prog, Printer for laptops & handheld devices, Prog for adults, Prog for children & young adult, Ref serv available, Scanner, Senior computer classes, Senior outreach, Serves people with

intellectual disabilities, Story hour, Summer reading prog, Tax forms, Teen prog, Telephone ref, Wheelchair accessible
Publications: Newsletter (Quarterly)
Partic in TLN
Special Services for the Deaf - Accessible learning ctr; Assisted listening device; Bks on deafness & sign lang; High interest/low vocabulary bks
Special Services for the Blind - BiFolkal kits; Bks on cassette; Bks on CD; Closed circuit TV magnifier; Extensive large print coll; Home delivery serv; Magnifiers; Reader equip
Open Mon-Thurs 9:30-9, Fri & Sat 9:30-5
Friends of the Library Group

LAKEVIEW

P TAMARACK DISTRICT LIBRARY*, 832 S Lincoln Ave, 48850. (Mail add: PO Box 469, 48850-0469), SAN 308-2245. Tel: 989-352-6274. FAX: 989-352-7713. E-mail: lvw@llcoop.org. Web Site: tamaracklibrary.org. *Libr Dir,* Hope Nobel; Staff 5 (MLS 2, Non-MLS 3)
Founded 1965. Pop 10,485; Circ 59,239
Automation Activity & Vendor Info: (Cataloging) Innovative Interfaces, Inc; (Circulation) Innovative Interfaces, Inc; (ILL) Innovative Interfaces, Inc; (OPAC) Innovative Interfaces, Inc; (Serials) Innovative Interfaces, Inc
Wireless access
Function: Adult bk club, After school storytime, Audiobks via web, Bk club(s), Bks on cassette, Bks on CD, CD-ROM, Children's prog, Computer training, Computers for patron use, Electronic databases & coll, Holiday prog, ILL available, Magnifiers for reading, Museum passes, Music CDs, Notary serv, Online cat, Outreach serv, OverDrive digital audio bks, Photocopying/Printing, Preschool outreach, Prog for adults, Prog for children & young adult, Ref serv available, Senior outreach, Story hour, Summer & winter reading prog, Summer reading prog, Tax forms, Teen prog, Telephone ref, VHS videos, Wheelchair accessible
Partic in Lakeland Library Cooperative
Open Mon, Wed & Fri 10-5, Tues & Thurs 10-8, Sat 10-2
Friends of the Library Group

L'ANSE

§J KEWEENAW BAY OJIBWA COMMUNITY COLLEGE LIBRARY, Wabanung Campus, Rm 206N, 770 N Main St, 49946. Tel: 906-524-8206. E-mail: library@kbocc.edu. Web Site: kbocc.edu/students/library. *Librn,* Joe Bouchard; E-mail: jbouchard@kbocc.edu
Wireless access
Function: Computers for patron use, Study rm
Partic in Upper Peninsula Region of Library Cooperation, Inc
Open Mon 10-6, Tues-Thurs 10-5

P L'ANSE AREA SCHOOL-PUBLIC LIBRARY, 201 N Fourth St, 49946-1499. SAN 308-2199. Tel: 906-524-0334, 906-524-6213. FAX: 906-524-5331. Web Site: joomla.uproc.lib.mi.us/lanse. *Libr Dir,* Sonya Evans; E-mail: sevans@laschools.k12.mi.us
Pop 9,140
Library Holdings: Bk Vols 16,500; Per Subs 63
Special Collections: Finnish American Coll; Native American Coll
Automation Activity & Vendor Info: (Cataloging) SirsiDynix; (Circulation) SirsiDynix
Wireless access
Partic in Superiorland Library Cooperative; Upper Peninsula Region of Library Cooperation, Inc
Open Mon-Fri 12-6; Tue-Thurs 9-2 (Summer)
Friends of the Library Group

LANSING

P CAPITAL AREA DISTRICT LIBRARIES*, 401 S Capitol Ave, 48933. (Mail add: PO Box 40719, 48901-7919), SAN 346-8453. Tel: 517-367-6300. Circulation Tel: 517-367-6350. Administration Tel: 517-367-0813. Information Services Tel: 517-367-6363. FAX: 517-374-1068. Web Site: www.cadl.org. *Exec Dir,* Scott Duimstra; E-mail: duimstras@cadl.org; *Dir of Finance,* Patrick Taylor; Tel: 517-367-6337, E-mail: taylorp@cadl.org; *Human Res Dir,* Julie Laxton; Tel: 517-367-6349, E-mail: laxtonj@cadl.org; *Dir, Mkt,* Trenton Smiley; Tel: 517-367-6348, E-mail: smileyt@cadl.org; *Tech Dir,* Sheryl Cormicle Knox; Tel: 517-367-6347, E-mail: knoxs@cadl.org; *Assoc Dir, Pub Serv, Sr Assoc Dir,* Jolee Hamlin; Tel: 517-367-0810, E-mail: hamlinj@cadl.org; *Assoc Dir, Coll Serv,* Thais Rousseau; Tel: 517-367-6325, E-mail: rousseaut@cadl.org; *Head Librn,* Michele Brussow; E-mail: brussowm@cadl.org; Staff 51 (MLS 44, Non-MLS 7)
Founded 1998. Pop 240,165
Library Holdings: Per Subs 316
Automation Activity & Vendor Info: (Acquisitions) Innovative Interfaces, Inc; (Cataloging) Innovative Interfaces, Inc; (Circulation) Innovative Interfaces, Inc; (ILL) Innovative Interfaces, Inc; (OPAC) Innovative Interfaces, Inc
Wireless access
Function: Bks on CD, CD-ROM, Children's prog, Computer training, Computers for patron use, Digital talking bks, Free DVD rentals, Home delivery & serv to seniorr ctr & nursing homes, Homebound delivery serv, Music CDs, Online cat, Online ref, OverDrive digital audio bks, Photocopying/Printing, Prog for adults, Prog for children & young adult, Ref serv available, Teen prog, Telephone ref
Partic in Mideastern Michigan Library Cooperative; Midwest Collaborative for Library Services
Open Mon-Fri 9-5
Restriction: Non-resident fee
Friends of the Library Group
Branches: 13
AURELIUS LIBRARY, 1939 S Aurelius Rd, Mason, 48854-9763, SAN 346-8488. Tel: 517-628-3743. FAX: 517-628-2141. *Head Librn,* Jennifer DeGroat; E-mail: degroatj@cadl.org; Staff 1 (MLS 1)
Founded 1936
Special Services for the Blind - Audiovision-a radio reading serv
Open Mon & Wed 11-7, Tues, Thurs & Fri 3-6, Sat 10- 1
Friends of the Library Group
DANSVILLE LIBRARY, 1379 E Mason St, Dansville, 48819, SAN 346-8518. Tel: 517-623-6511. FAX: 517-623-0520. *Head Librn,* Lynn Harper; E-mail: harperl@cadl.org; Staff 2 (MLS 2)
Open Mon & Wed 3-7, Tues & Thurs 11-6, Fri 3-6, Sat 10-2
Friends of the Library Group
DOWNTOWN LANSING LIBRARY, 401 S Capitol Ave, 48933. (Mail add: PO Box 40719, 48909-7919), SAN 377-7588. Tel: 517-367-6363. Reference Tel: 517-367-6346. FAX: 517-374-1068. *Interim Head Librn,* Jim MacLean; Tel: 517-367-6322, E-mail: macleanj@cadl.org; Staff 13 (MLS 13)
Open Mon-Thurs 9-9, Fri & Sat 9-6, Sun 1-6
Friends of the Library Group
FOSTER LIBRARY, 200 N Foster Ave, 48912, SAN 378-2425. Tel: 517-485-5185. FAX: 517-485-5239. *Head Librn,* Jean S Bolley; E-mail: bollej@cadl.org; Staff 1 (MLS 1)
Open Mon-Wed 1-7, Thurs & Fri 12-5, Sat 11-3
Friends of the Library Group
HASLETT LIBRARY, 1590 Franklin St, Haslett, 48840, SAN 346-8534. Tel: 517-339-2324. FAX: 517-339-0349. *Head Librn,* Ann Chapman; E-mail: chapmana@cadl.org; Staff 2 (MLS 2)
Open Mon-Thurs 10-9, Fri & Sat 10-7, Sun (Sept-May) 1-5
Friends of the Library Group
HOLT-DELHI LIBRARY, 2078 Aurelius Rd, Holt, 48842, SAN 346-8542. Tel: 517-694-9351. FAX: 517-699-3865. *Head Librn,* Karon Walter; E-mail: walterk@cadl.org; Staff 2 (MLS 2)
Open Mon-Wed 10-9, Thurs-Sat 10-7, Sun 12-5
Friends of the Library Group
LESLIE LIBRARY, 201 Pennsylvania St, Leslie, 49251, SAN 346-8607. Tel: 517-589-9400. FAX: 517-589-0536. *Head Librn,* Jeff Antaya; E-mail: antayaj@cadl.org; Staff 2 (MLS 2)
Open Mon 1-7, Tues, Thurs & Fri 1-6, Wed 11-7, Sat 10-2
Friends of the Library Group
MASON LIBRARY, 145 W Ash St, Mason, 48854, SAN 346-8631. Tel: 517-676-9088. FAX: 517-676-3780. *Head Librn,* Cheryl Lindemann; E-mail: lindemannc@cadl.org; Staff 2 (MLS 2)
Open Mon-Thurs 11-8, Fri 10-6, Sat 10-5, Sun (Sept-May) 1-5
Friends of the Library Group
OKEMOS LIBRARY, 4321 Okemos Rd, Okemos, 48864, SAN 346-8666. Tel: 517-347-2021. FAX: 517-347-2034. *Head Librn,* Betsy Hull; E-mail: hullb@cadl.org; Staff 4 (MLS 4)
Function: Adult bk club, After school storytime, Art exhibits, AV serv, Bk club(s), Bks on cassette, Bks on CD, Children's prog, Computer training, Computers for patron use, Digital talking bks, E-Reserves, Electronic databases & coll, Free DVD rentals, Holiday prog, ILL available, Mail & tel request accepted, Music CDs, Online cat, Online ref, Photocopying/Printing, Prog for adults, Prog for children & young adult, Spoken cassettes & CDs, Spoken cassettes & DVDs, Summer reading prog, Tax forms, Teen prog, Telephone ref, VHS videos, Wheelchair accessible
Open Mon-Thurs 9-9, Fri & Sat 9-7, Sun 12-6
Friends of the Library Group
SOUTH LANSING LIBRARY, 3500 S Cedar St, Ste 108, 48910, SAN 378-2441. Tel: 517-272-9840. FAX: 517-272-9901. *Head Librn,* Melissa Cole; E-mail: colem@cadl.org; Staff 3 (MLS 3)
Open Mon-Thurs 10-8, Fri 10-7, Sat 10-6, Sun 12-5
Friends of the Library Group
STOCKBRIDGE LIBRARY, 200 Wood St, Stockbridge, 49285. (Mail add: PO Box 245, Stockbridge, 49285), SAN 346-8690. Tel: 517-851-7810. FAX: 517-851-8612. *Head Librn,* Sherri McConnell; E-mail: mcconnells@cadl.org; Staff 1 (MLS 1)
Open Mon-Fri 11-7, Sat 11-5, Sun (Sept-May) 1-5
Friends of the Library Group
WEBBERVILLE LIBRARY, 115 S Main St, Webberville, 48892. (Mail add: PO Box 689, Webberville, 48892-0689), SAN 346-8755. Tel: 517-521-3643. FAX: 517-521-1079. *Head Librn,* Peg Mawby; E-mail: mawbyp@cadl.org; Staff 1 (MLS 1)

Open Mon 1-6, Tues & Thurs 2-8, Wed 10-6, Fri 2-6, Sat 10-2
Friends of the Library Group
WILLIAMSTON LIBRARY, 3845 Vanneter Rd, Williamston, 48895, SAN 346-878X. Tel: 517-655-1191. FAX: 517-655-5243. *Head Librn,* Julie Chrisinske; E-mail: chrisinskej@cadl.org; Staff 1 (MLS 1)
Open Mon-Thurs 10-7, Fri 10-6, Sat 12-4, Sun (Sept-May) 12-4
Friends of the Library Group
Bookmobiles: 1

P DELTA TOWNSHIP DISTRICT LIBRARY*, 5130 Davenport Dr, 48917-2040. Tel: 517-321-4014. FAX: 517-323-3272. Web Site: www.dtdl.org. *Dir,* Mary Rzepczynski; E-mail: mrzepczynski@dtdl.org; *Ad,* Tom Moore; E-mail: tmoore@dtdl.org; *Circ Serv Librn,* Melissa Gaus; E-mail: mgaus@dtdl.org; *Youth Serv Librn,* Becky Leboeuf; E-mail: bleboeuf@dtdl.org; *Tech Serv Coordr,* Stephanie Conarton; E-mail: sconarton@dtdl.org; *IT Tech,* Erica Gupton; E-mail: egupton@dtdl.org; Staff 13 (MLS 2, Non-MLS 11)
Pop 30,056; Circ 162,802
Library Holdings: AV Mats 2,939; Bks on Deafness & Sign Lang 25; Large Print Bks 1,022; Bk Titles 24,471; Per Subs 110
Automation Activity & Vendor Info: (Cataloging) SirsiDynix; (Circulation) SirsiDynix; (ILL) Auto-Graphics, Inc; (OPAC) SirsiDynix; (Serials) SirsiDynix
Wireless access
Publications: @ Your Library (Newsletter)
Mem of Woodlands Library Cooperative
Partic in Capitol Area Librs Coop
Open Mon-Thurs 10-8, Fri 10-6, Sat 10-4
Friends of the Library Group

CR GREAT LAKES CHRISTIAN COLLEGE*, Louis M Detro Memorial Library, 6211 W Willow Hwy, 48917. SAN 308-227X. Tel: 517-321-0242, Ext 237. FAX: 517-321-5902. E-mail: library@glcc.edu. Web Site: www.glcc.edu/academic/library. *Dir, Libr Serv,* Heather Bunce; Tel: 517-321-0242, Ext 251, E-mail: hbunce@glcc.edu; Staff 3 (MLS 1, Non-MLS 2)
Founded 1949. Enrl 220; Fac 13; Highest Degree: Bachelor
Library Holdings: Bk Vols 47,000; Per Subs 239
Special Collections: Bibles; C S Lewis
Subject Interests: Hist, Lang arts, Music, Theol
Automation Activity & Vendor Info: (Cataloging) Winnebago Software Co; (Circulation) Winnebago Software Co; (Course Reserve) Winnebago Software Co; (ILL) Winnebago Software Co; (OPAC) Winnebago Software Co; (Serials) Winnebago Software Co
Wireless access
Partic in Asn of Christian Librs; Midwest Collaborative for Library Services; OCLC-LVIS
Open Mon (Winter) 9-9, Tues-Thurs 7:45-9, Fri 7:45-5, Sat 2-4; Mon-Fri (Summer) 9-12 & 1-4

S HISTORICAL SOCIETY OF MICHIGAN, 7435 Westshire Dr, 48917. SAN 371-8778. Tel: 517-324-1828. FAX: 517-324-4370. E-mail: hsm@hsmichigan.org. Web Site: www.hsmichigan.org. *Exec Dir,* Larry J Wagenaar
Founded 1828
Library Holdings: Bk Titles 1,700
Special Collections: Michigan History Books
Subject Interests: Local hist, Mich hist
Wireless access
Publications: Historic Michigan Travel Guide (Biannually); Michigan History for Kids (Bimonthly); Michigan History magazine (Bimonthly); The Chronicle (Quarterly); The Michigan Historical Review; The Michigan History Directory (Reference guide)
Restriction: Mem only, Not a lending libr, Open by appt only

J LANSING COMMUNITY COLLEGE LIBRARY*, Technology & Learning Ctr, 400 N Capitol Ave, 48933. SAN 346-7589. Tel: 517-483-1657. Circulation Tel: 517-483-1626. Interlibrary Loan Service Tel: 517-483-1665. Reference Tel: 517-483-1615. Administration Tel: 517-483-1647. Toll Free Tel: 800-644-4522. FAX: 517-483-5300. Web Site: www.lcc.edu/library. *Libr Dir,* Elenka Raschkow; Tel: 517-483-1639, E-mail: raschke@lcc.edu; *Electronic Res Librn,* Frances Krempasky; Tel: 517-483-1651, E-mail: krempf@lcc.edu; *Instrul Serv Librn,* Ami Ewald; Tel: 517-483-5241, E-mail: ewalda@lcc.edu; *Lead Ref Librn, Liaison Librn,* Suzanne Sawyer; Tel: 517-483-9717, E-mail: sawyers@lcc.edu; *Web Serv Librn,* Suzanne Bernsten; Tel: 517-483-1644, E-mail: bernss@lcc.edu; Staff 18 (MLS 11, Non-MLS 7)
Founded 1959. Enrl 14,851; Highest Degree: Associate
Library Holdings: AV Mats 205; e-books 228,539; e-journals 34,574; Electronic Media & Resources 123; Bk Titles 64,429; Per Subs 114
Special Collections: Career Coll; Easy Reading Browsing
Subject Interests: Criminal justice, Nursing, Travel info
Automation Activity & Vendor Info: (Acquisitions) Innovative Interfaces, Inc; (Cataloging) Innovative Interfaces, Inc; (Circulation) Innovative Interfaces, Inc; (ILL) Innovative Interfaces, Inc; (Media Booking) Innovative Interfaces, Inc; (OPAC) Innovative Interfaces, Inc; (Serials) Innovative Interfaces, Inc
Wireless access
Publications: Link (Newsletter)
Partic in Midwest Collaborative for Library Services
Special Services for the Deaf - TDD equip
Special Services for the Blind - Computer with voice synthesizer for visually impaired persons; Reader equip
Open Mon-Thurs 8-8, Fri 8-5, Sat 11-5, Sun 1-5
Friends of the Library Group

P LIBRARY OF MICHIGAN*, 702 W Kalamazoo St, 48915. (Mail add: PO Box 30007, 48909-0007), SAN 346-7708. Tel: 517-373-1580. Interlibrary Loan Service Tel: 517-373-8926. Reference Tel: 517-373-1300. Toll Free Tel: 877-479-0021. FAX: 517-373-5700. Reference FAX: 517-373-3381. Toll Free FAX: 800-292-2431 (MI only). E-mail: librarian@michigan.gov. Web Site: www.michigan.gov/libraryofmichigan. *State Librn,* Randy Riley; Tel: 517-373-5860, E-mail: rileyr@michigan.gov; *Dir, Instrul Design, Libr Consult,* Sonya Schryer Norris; E-mail: librarian@sonyanorris.com; *Manager, Access & Tech Serv,* Don Todaro; Tel: 517-373-2583, E-mail: todarod@michigan.gov; *Mgr, Libr Develop,* Shannon White; Tel: 517-373-9489, E-mail: whites29@michigan.gov; *Mgr, Spec Coll,* Tim Gleisner; Tel: 517-373-8389, E-mail: gleisnert@michigan.gov; *Law Librn,* Kim Koscielniak; Tel: 517-373-4697, E-mail: koscielniakk@michigan.gov; *Librn, Mich Doc,* Bernadette Bartlett; Tel: 517-373-2971, E-mail: bartlettb@michigan.gov; *ILL/Ref Librn,* Karen J White; Tel: 517-373-2985, E-mail: whitek@michigan.gov; *E-Library & Outreach Coordr,* Position Currently Open; *Youth Serv Coordr,* Cathy Lancaster; Tel: 517-373-8129, E-mail: lancasterc5@michigan.gov; Staff 33 (MLS 22, Non-MLS 11)
Founded 1828
Special Collections: Federal & Michigan Government Document Coll; Michigan Resources Coll; Rare Book Room. State Document Depository; US Document Depository
Subject Interests: Law, Mich, Pub policy
Automation Activity & Vendor Info: (Acquisitions) Innovative Interfaces, Inc; (Cataloging) Innovative Interfaces, Inc; (Circulation) Innovative Interfaces, Inc; (ILL) OCLC; (OPAC) Innovative Interfaces, Inc; (Serials) Innovative Interfaces, Inc
Wireless access
Publications: Certification Handbook; Library Laws Handbook (Online only); Library of Michigan/Library of Michigan Foundation Annual Report; LM4X (Online only); LSTA 5-Year Plan; LSTA Report; Michigan Interactive Library Directory (Online only); Michigan Public Libraries Data Digest
Partic in Association for Rural & Small Libraries
Open Mon-Fri 10-5, Sat 10-4

L LIBRARY OF MICHIGAN*, State Law Library, 702 W Kalamazoo St, 48909. (Mail add: PO Box 30007, 48909-7507), SAN 370-9353. Tel: 517-373-0630. FAX: 517-373-3915. E-mail: lmlawlib@michigan.gov. Web Site: www.michigan.gov/lawlibrary. *Law Librn,* Kimberly Koscielniak; E-mail: koscielniakk@michigan.gov; *Ref Librn,* Timothy Watters; E-mail: watterst@michigan.gov. Subject Specialists: *Law,* Kimberly Koscielniak; *Law,* Timothy Watters; Staff 2.5 (MLS 2.5)
Library Holdings: Bk Vols 200,000; Per Subs 200
Automation Activity & Vendor Info: (Cataloging) Innovative Interfaces, Inc; (Circulation) Innovative Interfaces, Inc; (OPAC) Innovative Interfaces, Inc
Wireless access
Open Mon-Fri 10-5

M MCLAREN GREATER LANSING*, John W Chi Memorial Medical Library, 401 W Greenlawn Ave, 48910. SAN 320-3840. Tel: 517-975-6075. Web Site: www.mclaren.org/lansing/GME-Library.aspx. *Med Librn,* Judy Barners; E-mail: judith.barnes@mclaren.org; Staff 5 (MLS 1, Non-MLS 4)
Founded 1976
Library Holdings: e-books 2,000; e-journals 1,000; Bk Titles 4,000
Subject Interests: Allied health, Consumer health, Med, Nursing, Osteopathy, Pharmacology
Automation Activity & Vendor Info: (ILL) OCLC
Wireless access
Publications: Acquisition List (Monthly)
Partic in Michigan Health Sciences Libraries Association; MLC; National Network of Libraries of Medicine Region 6; OCLC Online Computer Library Center, Inc
Open Mon-Fri 9-5

P MICHIGAN BUREAU OF SERVICES FOR BLIND PERSONS - BRAILLE & TALKING BOOK LIBRARY*, Michigan Library & Historical Ctr, 702 W Kalamazoo St, 48915-1703. (Mail add: PO Box 30007, 48909-7507), SAN 308-2334. Tel: 517-284-2880. Toll Free Tel: 800-992-9012. FAX: 517-284-2885. Toll Free FAX: 800-726-7323. E-mail:

btbl@michigan.gov. Web Site: www.michigan.gov/btbl. *Mgr,* Sue Chinault; Tel: 517-284-2870, E-mail: chinaults@michigan.gov; Staff 11 (MLS 7, Non-MLS 4)
Founded 1931
Special Collections: Finnish Language; Michigan History & Authors
Wireless access
Publications: InFocus (Newsletter)
Special Services for the Blind - Accessible computers; Aids for in-house use; Assistive/Adapted tech devices, equip & products; Audio mat; Volunteer serv
Open Mon-Fri 8-5
Restriction: Restricted access

G MICHIGAN DEPARTMENT OF TRANSPORTATION LIBRARY, 425 W Ottawa, 48909-7550. (Mail add: PO Box 30050, Library B155, 48909-7550), SAN 308-2318. Tel: 517-230-6103. *Librn,* Jennifer Herron; E-mail: HerronJ1@michigan.gov; Staff 1 (MLS 1)
Founded 1964
Library Holdings: Bk Titles 18,100
Special Collections: Transportation Research Board
Subject Interests: Transportation
Automation Activity & Vendor Info: (Acquisitions) Cuadra Associates, Inc; (Cataloging) OCLC Connexion; (Circulation) Cuadra Associates, Inc; (ILL) OCLC WorldShare Interlibrary Loan
Wireless access
Partic in Cap Area Libr Consortium; Midwest Collaborative for Library Services; Midwest Transportation Knowledge Network; OCLC Online Computer Library Center, Inc
Restriction: Govt use only, Staff use only

G MICHIGAN LEGISLATIVE SERVICE BUREAU LIBRARY, Boji Tower, 4th Flr, 48909. (Mail add: PO Box 30036, 48909-7773), SAN 326-4203. Tel: 517-373-5200. FAX: 517-373-0171. E-mail: Researchrqsts@Legislature.mi.gov. *Dir,* Shonda Greco; Staff 2 (Non-MLS 2)
Founded 1941
Library Holdings: Bk Titles 15,750; Bk Vols 17,350; Per Subs 115
Special Collections: Legislative Reports (docs); Michigan Law (bks)
Subject Interests: Govt, Law
Publications: Guide to Legal Research in the Legislative Service Bureau Library; Recent Acquisitions in the Legislative Service Bureau Library
Restriction: Not open to pub

S RIGHT TO LIFE OF MICHIGAN*, Mid-Michigan Resource Center, 233 N Walnut St, 48933-1121. SAN 373-210X. Tel: 517-487-3376. FAX: 517-487-6453. E-mail: info@rtl.org. Web Site: www.rtl.org. *Pub Relations,* Chris Gast
Library Holdings: Bk Vols 200
Subject Interests: Abortion, Euthanasia
Open Mon-Fri 8:30-4:30

M SPARROW HEALTH SYSTEM, Sparrow Health Sciences Library, Two South, Sparrow Hospital, 1215 E Michigan Ave, 48912. SAN 308-2342. Tel: 517-364-2200. Reference Tel: 517-364-5660, Ext 1. FAX: 517-364-2201. E-mail: medical.library@sparrow.org. Web Site: www.sparrow.org/sparrow-community-health/sparrow-health-sciences-library. *Libr Mgr, Med Librn,* Michael Simmons; E-mail: michael.simmons@sparrow.org; Staff 3 (MLS 1, Non-MLS 2)
Library Holdings: e-books 2,500; e-journals 25,000; Bk Titles 7,000; Per Subs 2,500
Subject Interests: Evidence-based med, Nursing, Point-of-care res
Automation Activity & Vendor Info: (Cataloging) EOS International; (Circulation) EOS International; (OPAC) EOS International; (Serials) EOS International
Wireless access
Function: For res purposes, Health sci info serv, Internet access, Ref serv available
Partic in Michigan Health Sciences Libraries Association; Midwest Collaborative for Library Services; National Network of Libraries of Medicine Region 6
Open Mon-Fri 7-5
Restriction: Open to fac, students & qualified researchers, Open to pub for ref & circ; with some limitations

CL WESTERN MICHIGAN UNIVERSITY-COOLEY LAW SCHOOL LIBRARIES*, Brennan Law Library, 300 S Capitol Ave, 48901. SAN 308-2261. Tel: 517-371-5140. Circulation Tel: 517-371-5140, Ext 3100. Reference Tel: 517-371-5140, Ext 3111. Toll Free Tel: 866-733-3375. FAX: 517-334-5715, 517-334-5717. Web Site: www.cooley.edu/library. *Assoc Dean,* Duane Strojny; Tel: 517-371-5140, Ext 3401, E-mail: strojnyd@cooley.edu; *Head, Pub Serv,* Rita Marsala; Tel: 517-371-5140, Ext 3301, E-mail: marsalar@cooley.edu; *Head, Tech Serv,* Ron Reynolds; Tel: 517-371-5140, Ext 3405, E-mail: reynolro@cooley.edu; *Ref Librn,* Eric Kennedy; Tel: 517-371-5140, Ext 3306, E-mail: kennedye@cooley.edu; *Ref Librn,* Alissa Raasch; Tel: 517-371-5140, Ext 3305, E-mail: raascha@cooley.edu; Staff 13 (MLS 13)
Founded 1972. Enrl 1,300; Fac 54; Highest Degree: Doctorate
Library Holdings: e-books 6,332; Bk Titles 175,000; Bk Vols 535,000; Per Subs 4,335
Special Collections: Michigan Supreme Court Records & Briefs (1907-present), bound volumes. US Document Depository
Automation Activity & Vendor Info: (Acquisitions) Innovative Interfaces, Inc; (Cataloging) Innovative Interfaces, Inc; (Circulation) Innovative Interfaces, Inc; (Course Reserve) Innovative Interfaces, Inc; (OPAC) Innovative Interfaces, Inc; (Serials) Innovative Interfaces, Inc
Wireless access
Function: 24/7 Online cat, Doc delivery serv, Online ref, Ref serv available
Publications: Library Research Guides (various subjects); User's Guide to the Thomas M Cooley Law School Library
Partic in Midwest Collaborative for Library Services; NELLCO Law Library Consortium, Inc.; OCLC Online Computer Library Center, Inc
Open Mon-Thurs 8am-Midnight, Fri-Sun 8am-10pm
Restriction: Circ limited, Pub access for legal res only

LAPEER

P LAPEER DISTRICT LIBRARY*, 201 Village West Dr S, 48446-1699. SAN 346-7791. Tel: 810-664-9521. FAX: 810-664-8527. E-mail: ldlsupport@lib.lapeer.org. Web Site: www.library.lapeer.org. *Dir,* Amy Churchill; E-mail: achurchill@lib.lapeer.org; *Asst Dir, Tech Serv,* Yvonne Brown; *Head, Children's Dept,* Mary Cowles; *Head, Fiction Serv,* Janelle Martin; *Head, Ref,* Laura Fromwiller; Staff 19 (MLS 7, Non-MLS 12)
Founded 1939. Pop 62,378; Circ 177,293
Library Holdings: Bk Vols 102,148; Per Subs 246
Special Collections: Local History Coll, bks, news clippings; Marguerite de Angeli Coll
Wireless access
Partic in Mideastern Michigan Library Cooperative; Valley Library Consortium
Special Services for the Blind - Aids for in-house use; Assistive/Adapted tech devices, equip & products
Open Mon-Fri 8-5
Restriction: Access for corporate affiliates
Friends of the Library Group
Branches: 7
CLIFFORD BRANCH, 9530 Main St, Clifford, 48727. (Mail add: PO Box 233, Clifford, 48727-0233), SAN 346-7821. Tel: 989-761-7393. FAX: 989-761-7541. *Librn,* Denise Edwards
Library Holdings: Bk Vols 4,966; Per Subs 10
Function: Audiobks on Playaways & MP3, Audiobks via web, Bks on CD, Children's prog, Computers for patron use, Electronic databases & coll, Family literacy, Free DVD rentals, ILL available, Internet access, Magazines, Movies, OverDrive digital audio bks, Photocopying/Printing, Prog for adults, Prog for children & young adult, Story hour, Summer reading prog
Open Mon & Thurs 11-4, Wed 2-7
COLUMBIAVILLE BRANCH, 4718 First St, Columbiaville, 48421-9143. (Mail add: PO Box 190, Columbiaville, 48421-0190), SAN 346-7856. Tel: 810-793-6100. FAX: 810-793-6243. *Librn,* Susan Francis
Founded 1876
Library Holdings: Bk Vols 7,385; Per Subs 15
Open Mon & Wed 1-7, Fri 11-5
Friends of the Library Group
MARGUERITE DEANGELI BRANCH, 921 W Nepessing St, 48446, SAN 346-797X. Tel: 810-664-6971. FAX: 810-664-5581. *Head, Fiction Serv,* Janelle Martin; *Head, Ref,* Laura Fromwiller
Library Holdings: Bk Vols 79,659; Per Subs 121
Special Collections: Career Resource Center; Coll & Exhibit on Marguerite deAngeli; Genealogy Coll
Function: Adult bk club, Archival coll, Audiobks on Playaways & MP3, Audiobks via web, Bi-weekly Writer's Group, Bk club(s), Bk reviews (Group), Bks on CD, Children's prog, Computer training, Computers for patron use, Electronic databases & coll, Family literacy, Free DVD rentals, Holiday prog, ILL available, Internet access, Life-long learning prog for all ages, Magazines, Magnifiers for reading, Meeting rooms, Microfiche/film & reading machines, Movies, Music CDs, Notary serv, Online cat, OverDrive digital audio bks, Photocopying/Printing, Prog for adults, Prog for children & young adult, Story hour, Summer & winter reading prog, Summer reading prog, Tax forms, Teen prog, Wheelchair accessible
Open Mon-Thurs 9-8, Fri & Sat 9-5, Sun (Sept-May) 1-5
Friends of the Library Group
ELBA BRANCH, 5508 Davison Rd, 48446, SAN 346-7880. Tel: 810-653-7200. FAX: 810-653-4267. *Librn,* Sarena Hanson
Library Holdings: Bk Vols 3,214; Per Subs 10
Open Mon 11-5, Thurs 1-7

HADLEY BRANCH, 3556 Hadley Rd, Hadley, 48440. (Mail add: PO Box 199, Hadley, 48440-0199), SAN 346-7945. Tel: 810-797-4101. FAX: 810-797-2912. *Librn*, Jacalyn Woolbright
Library Holdings: Bk Vols 9,716; Per Subs 33
Open Mon & Tues 11-8, Wed & Thurs 2-8, Sat 9-2
Friends of the Library Group

METAMORA BRANCH, 4018 Oak St, Metamora, 48455. (Mail add: PO Box 77, Metamora, 48455-0077), SAN 346-8003. Tel: 810-678-2991. FAX: 810-678-3253. *Librn*, Shelia Ruby; *Librn*, Lorry Traver
Library Holdings: Bk Vols 9,618; Per Subs 27
Special Collections: Michigan Coll
Open Mon 9-5, Wed & Thurs 11-8, Fri 9-2
Friends of the Library Group

OTTER LAKE BRANCH, 6361 Detroit St, Otter Lake, 48464-9104. (Mail add: PO Box 185, Otter Lake, 48464-0185), SAN 346-8038. Tel: 810-793-6300. FAX: 810-793-7040. *Librn*, Gena Bunch
Library Holdings: Bk Vols 4,157; Per Subs 16
Open Mon 10-3, Tues & Thurs 2-7
Friends of the Library Group

LAWTON

P LAWTON PUBLIC LIBRARY*, 125 S Main St, 49065. (Mail add: PO Box 520, 49065-0520), SAN 308-2369. Tel: 269-624-5481. FAX: 269-624-1909. Web Site: www.lawtonlibrary.com. *Dir*, Lyn Tone; E-mail: ltone@lawtonlibrary.org; Staff 3 (MLS 1, Non-MLS 2)
Pop 1,865; Circ 17,680
Library Holdings: Bks on Deafness & Sign Lang 15; Bk Titles 32,000; Per Subs 49
Automation Activity & Vendor Info: (Cataloging) Follett Software; (Circulation) Follett Software; (OPAC) Follett Software
Wireless access
Open Mon-Wed 10-7, Fri 10-5, Sat 10-2

LELAND

S LEELANAU HISTORICAL SOCIETY, Leelanau Historical Museum Archives, 203 E Cedar St, 49654. (Mail add: PO Box 246, 49654-0246), SAN 371-5698. Tel: 231-256-7475. E-mail: info@leelanauhistory.org. Web Site: www.leelanauhistory.org. *Exec Dir*, Kim Kelderhouse
Founded 1957
Library Holdings: Bk Vols 500
Special Collections: Oral History
Restriction: Open by appt only

P LELAND TOWNSHIP PUBLIC LIBRARY*, 203 E Cedar, 49654. (Mail add: PO Box 736, 49654-0736), SAN 308-2385. Tel: 231-256-9152. FAX: 231-256-8847. E-mail: lelandlibrary@lelandtownshiplibrary.org. Web Site: www.lelandlibrary.org. *Dir*, Mark Morton; *Prog Coordr*, Laura Touhey; E-mail: programs@lelandtownshiplibrary.org; Staff 3 (Non-MLS 3)
Founded 1942. Pop 5,800; Circ 35,000
Apr 2015-Mar 2016 Income $171,000, State $2,000, Locally Generated Income $93,500, Other $75,500. Mats Exp $27,000, Books $15,500, Per/Ser (Incl. Access Fees) $2,500, AV Mat $6,500, Electronic Ref Mat (Incl. Access Fees) $2,500
Library Holdings: AV Mats 10,100; CDs 2,500; DVDs 6,500; e-books 15,600; Large Print Bks 500; Bk Vols 44,700; Per Subs 60
Special Collections: Michigan History Coll
Wireless access
Function: Bks on cassette, Bks on CD
Partic in Mid-Michigan Library League
Open Mon, Tues, Thurs & Fri 10-5, Wed 10-6, Sat 10-2
Friends of the Library Group

LEONARD

P ADDISON TOWNSHIP PUBLIC LIBRARY*, 1440 Rochester Rd, 48367-3555. SAN 376-6152. Tel: 248-628-4228, 248-628-7180. FAX: 248-628-6109. Web Site: www.addisontwp.michlibrary.org. *Dir*, Jaema Berman; E-mail: jberman@tln.lib.mi.us
Pop 6,439
Library Holdings: AV Mats 1,306; Bk Titles 27,000; Per Subs 52
Automation Activity & Vendor Info: (Cataloging) SirsiDynix; (Circulation) SirsiDynix; (OPAC) SirsiDynix
Wireless access
Partic in Midwest Collaborative for Library Services
Open Mon-Thurs 10-8, Fri & Sat 10-4
Friends of the Library Group

LEROY

P LEROY COMMUNITY LIBRARY*, 104 W Gilbert St, 49655. (Mail add: PO Box 157, 49655-0157), SAN 308-2377. Tel: 231-768-4493. E-mail: leroylibrary@att.net. *Dir*, Sigrid A Robertson; *Asst Librn*, Tom Shook
Circ 11,584
Jul 2015-Jun 2016 Income $30,444, State $1,522, Locally Generated Income $23,627, Other $5,295. Mats Exp $5,188, Books $2,914, Per/Ser (Incl. Access Fees) $764, Other Print Mats $502, Electronic Ref Mat (Incl. Access Fees) $1,008. Sal $14,298 (Prof $14,298)
Library Holdings: Audiobooks 261; DVDs 240; e-books 25; Bk Vols 21,928; Per Subs 49; Talking Bks 270
Subject Interests: Mich
Automation Activity & Vendor Info: (Circulation) Auto-Graphics, Inc
Wireless access
Partic in Mich Libr Asn; Mid-Michigan Library League
Open Mon & Fri 10-2, Tues & Thurs 1-6, Wed 12-5, Sat 10-1

LEXINGTON

P MOORE PUBLIC LIBRARY*, 7239 Huron Ave, 48450. (Mail add: PO Box 189, 48450-0189), SAN 308-2393. Tel: 810-359-8267. FAX: 810-359-2986. E-mail: lexlibrary@yahoo.com. Web Site: www.lexingtonlibrary.net. *Dir*, Beth Schumacher
Founded 1903. Pop 5,125; Circ 25,000
Library Holdings: Audiobooks 607; Bks on Deafness & Sign Lang 2; CDs 75; DVDs 60; Large Print Bks 150; Bk Titles 16,703; Per Subs 50; Videos 500
Automation Activity & Vendor Info: (Circulation) Follett Software
Wireless access
Partic in White Pine Library Cooperative
Open Mon & Thurs 10-7, Tues, Wed & Fri 10-5, Sat 10-1
Friends of the Library Group

LINCOLN PARK

P LINCOLN PARK PUBLIC LIBRARY*, 1381 Southfield Rd, 48146. SAN 308-2415. Tel: 313-381-0374. Web Site: www.lincoln-park.lib.mi.us. *Dir*, Nicole Kessler; E-mail: nkessler@lincoln-park.lib.mi.us; Staff 5 (MLS 2, Non-MLS 3)
Founded 1925. Pop 40,008; Circ 89,500
Library Holdings: Bk Titles 56,000; Per Subs 120
Automation Activity & Vendor Info: (Cataloging) SirsiDynix; (Circulation) SirsiDynix
Wireless access
Function: 24/7 Electronic res, 24/7 Online cat, Activity rm, Adult bk club, After school storytime, Audiobks via web, AV serv, Bk club(s), Bks on CD, Children's prog, Computer training, Computers for patron use, Electronic databases & coll, For res purposes, Holiday prog, ILL available, Magazines, Movies, Music CDs, Online cat, OverDrive digital audio bks, Photocopying/Printing, Prog for adults, Prog for children & young adult, Ref & res, Ref serv available, Scanner, Spanish lang bks, Story hour, Summer & winter reading prog, Tax forms, Teen prog, Winter reading prog
Partic in Morris Automated Information Network; The Library Network
Open Mon-Thurs 11-8, Fri & Sat 10-5
Restriction: ID required to use computers (Ltd hrs)
Friends of the Library Group

LITCHFIELD

P LITCHFIELD DISTRICT LIBRARY*, 108 N Chicago St, 49252-9738. (Mail add: PO Box 357, 49252-0357), SAN 308-2423. Tel: 517-542-3887. FAX: 517-542-3887. E-mail: litchfielddistrictlibrary@yahoo.com. Web Site: www.litchfielddistrictlibrary.org. *Libr Dir*, Shelly Wykes
Library Holdings: Audiobooks 1,265; Bks-By-Mail 571; CDs 129; DVDs 2,993; Large Print Bks 635; Bk Titles 10,000; Bk Vols 16,912
Automation Activity & Vendor Info: (Acquisitions) Follett Software; (Cataloging) Follett Software; (Circulation) Follett Software; (Course Reserve) Follett Software
Wireless access
Mem of Woodlands Library Cooperative
Open Mon, Wed & Fri 10-6, Sat 9-1

LIVONIA

P LIVONIA PUBLIC LIBRARY*, 32777 Five Mile Rd, 48154-3045, SAN 346-8062. Tel: 734-466-2491. FAX: 734-458-6011. E-mail: lvcc@livonia.lib.mi.us. Web Site: livoniapubliclibrary.org. *Libr Dir*, Ms Toni LaPorte; E-mail: laporte@livoniapubliclibrary.org
Founded 1958. Pop 100,545; Circ 761,307
Library Holdings: Bk Vols 256,442; Per Subs 672
Special Collections: US Document Depository
Automation Activity & Vendor Info: (Cataloging) SirsiDynix; (Circulation) SirsiDynix; (ILL) SirsiDynix
Wireless access
Special Services for the Deaf - TTY equip
Special Services for the Blind - Braille bks; Magnifiers
Open Mon-Thurs 9-9, Fri & Sat 9-5, Sun (Winter) 1-5
Friends of the Library Group

Branches: 4
CIVIC CENTER, 32777 Five Mile Rd, 48154-3045, SAN 328-9796. Tel: 734-466-2450. Circulation Tel: 734-466-2491. Reference Tel: 734-466-2490. FAX: 734-458-6011. Web Site: livonia.lib.mi.us/civic.html. *Dir,* Toni LaPorte; Tel: 734-466-2451, E-mail: tlaporte@livoniapubliclibrary.org; *Asst Dir,* Margaret Hainsworth; Tel: 734-466-2452, E-mail: mhainsworth@livoniapubliclibrary.org; *Head, Adult Serv,* Carl Katafiasz; E-mail: ckatafiasz@livoniapubliclibrary.org; *Head, Youth Serv,* Karen Smith; E-mail: ksmith@livoniapubliclibrary.org; Staff 35 (MLS 15, Non-MLS 20)
Founded 1988. Circ 419,165
Library Holdings: Bk Vols 169,219; Per Subs 70
Special Services for the Blind - Braille bks; Magnifiers
Open Mon-Thurs 9-9, Fri & Sat 9-5, Sun (Winter) 1-5
Friends of the Library Group

ALFRED NOBLE BRANCH, 32901 Plymouth Rd, 48150-1793, SAN 346-8151. Tel: 734-421-6600. FAX: 734-421-6606. Web Site: livonia.lib.mi.us/noble.html. *Br Librn,* Toni LaPorte; E-mail: laporte@livonia.lib.mi.us; *Librn,* Patty Goonis; E-mail: pgoonis@livonia.lib.mi.us; *Ch Serv,* Michelle Stiennon; E-mail: msteinnon@livonia.lib.mi.us; *YA Serv,* Ken Bignotti; E-mail: bignotti@tln.lib.mi.us; Staff 7 (MLS 4, Non-MLS 3)
Founded 1958. Circ 115,909
Library Holdings: Bk Vols 51,450; Per Subs 162
Open Mon 12-8, Wed 10-6
Friends of the Library Group

CARL SANDBURG BRANCH, 30100 W Seven Mile Rd, 48152-1918, SAN 346-8127. Tel: 248-893-4010. FAX: 248-476-6230. Web Site: livonia.lib.mi.us/sandburg.html. *Br Librn,* Toni LaPorte; E-mail: laporte@tln.lib.mi.us; *Ch Serv,* Michelle Stiennon; E-mail: mstiennon@livonia.lib.mi.us; *YA Serv,* Patty Goonis; E-mail: pgoonis@livonia.lib.mi.us; Staff 6 (MLS 3, Non-MLS 3)
Founded 1961. Circ 158,941
Library Holdings: Bk Vols 42,171; Per Subs 125
Open Tues 12-8, Sat 9-5
Friends of the Library Group

VEST POCKET, 15128 Farmington Rd, 48154-5417. Tel: 734-466-2559. Web Site: livonia.lib.mi.us/vest.html. *Br Librn,* Toni LaPorte; E-mail: laporte@livonia.lib.mi.us; Staff 1 (MLS 1)
Founded 1972
Library Holdings: Bk Vols 6,475
Open Mon-Fri 9:30-3:30
Friends of the Library Group

C MADONNA UNIVERSITY LIBRARY*, 36600 Schoolcraft Rd, 48150-1173. SAN 346-8186. Tel: 734-432-5703. Interlibrary Loan Service Tel: 734-432-5692. Reference Tel: 734-432-5767. Toll Free Tel: 800-852-4951. FAX: 734-432-5687. Web Site: library.madonna.edu/. *Dir,* Position Currently Open; *Coll Mgt Librn,* Lijun Xue; Tel: 734-432-5683, E-mail: lxue@madonna.edu; Staff 6 (MLS 2, Non-MLS 4)
Founded 1947
Special Collections: Artifacts from Diverse Ethnic Cultures; Institutional Archives; Transcultural Nursing Materials (Madeline Leininger Coll)
Subject Interests: Bus, Educ, Lang arts, Lit, Nursing, Paralegal studies, Sign lang
Automation Activity & Vendor Info: (Acquisitions) SirsiDynix; (Cataloging) SirsiDynix; (Circulation) SirsiDynix; (Course Reserve) SirsiDynix; (OPAC) SirsiDynix; (Serials) SirsiDynix
Wireless access
Function: 24/7 Electronic res, 24/7 Online cat
Partic in OCLC Online Computer Library Center, Inc; Southeastern Michigan League of Libraries
Friends of the Library Group

J SCHOOLCRAFT COLLEGE*, Eric J Bradner Library, 18600 Haggerty Rd, 48152-2696. SAN 308-244X. Tel: 734-462-4440. FAX: 734-462-4495. E-mail: library@schoolcraft.edu. Web Site: www.schoolcraft.edu/library. *Librn,* Wayne Pricer; Tel: 734-462-5317, E-mail: wpricer@schoolcraft.edu; *Tech Serv Librn,* Ozlem Gumeci; Tel: 734-462-4437, E-mail: ogumeci@schoolcraft.edu; *Circ Supvr,* Lissa McCarthy; Tel: 734-462-5326
Founded 1964
Library Holdings: Bk Vols 70,000; Per Subs 300
Special Collections: US Document Depository
Automation Activity & Vendor Info: (Acquisitions) SirsiDynix; (Cataloging) SirsiDynix; (Circulation) SirsiDynix; (Course Reserve) SirsiDynix; (ILL) SirsiDynix; (Media Booking) SirsiDynix; (OPAC) SirsiDynix; (Serials) SirsiDynix
Wireless access

LUDINGTON

P MASON COUNTY DISTRICT LIBRARY, Ludington Branch, 217 E Ludington Ave, 49431. (Mail add: PO Box 549, 49431-0549), SAN 308-2458. Tel: 231-843-8465. FAX: 231-843-1491. Interlibrary Loan Service E-mail: librarian@masoncounty.lib.mi.us. Web Site: www.masoncounty.lib.mi.us. *Libr Dir,* Susan Carlson; E-mail: scarlson@MCDLibrary.org; *Libr Dir,* Eric Smith; E-mail: esmith@MCDLibrary.org; Staff 10 (MLS 1, Non-MLS 9)
Founded 1905. Pop 28,800; Circ 180,000
Library Holdings: Bk Vols 120,000; Per Subs 200
Special Collections: State Document Depository
Automation Activity & Vendor Info: (Acquisitions) Auto-Graphics, Inc; (Cataloging) Auto-Graphics, Inc; (Circulation) Auto-Graphics, Inc
Wireless access
Publications: Friends of LPL Potpourri (Newsletter); Subject bibliographies
Partic in Mid-Michigan Library League; OCLC Online Computer Library Center, Inc
Open Mon-Wed 9-8, Thurs & Fri 9-6, Sat 9-5, Sun (Sept-May) 12-4
Friends of the Library Group
Branches: 1
SCOTTVILLE BRANCH, 204 E State St, Scottville, 49454, SAN 308-406X. Tel: 231-757-2588. FAX: 231-757-3401. *Libr Dir,* Patti Skinner; E-mail: PSkinner@MCDLibrary.org
Founded 1941. Pop 28,000; Circ 75,000
Automation Activity & Vendor Info: (Cataloging) Auto-Graphics, Inc; (Circulation) Auto-Graphics, Inc
Open Mon-Wed 9-8, Thurs & Fri 9-6, Sat 9-5, Sun (Sept-May) 12-4
Friends of the Library Group

S MASON COUNTY HISTORICAL SOCIETY*, Historic White Pine Village Research Library, 1687 S Lakeshore Dr, 49431. SAN 321-4702. Tel: 231-843-4808. E-mail: info@historicwhitepinevillage.org. Web Site: www.historicwhitepinevillage.org. *Exec Dir,* Rick Plummer; *Managing Dir,* Rebecca Berringer
Founded 1937
Library Holdings: Bk Titles 700; Per Subs 10
Special Collections: Business-Lumbering (Charles Mears Coll), diaries; Civil War (B S Mills Coll); Civil War (Hazel Oldt Coll), letters; Documentary on Wintertime Car Ferry Service across Lake Michigan, video; Lumbering (Jake Lunde Coll), a-tapes, microfilm of Mason County Papers, slides; Maritime Coll. Oral History
Subject Interests: Agr, Civil War, Genealogy, Local hist, Lumbering, Maritime
Function: Res libr
Publications: Centennial Farms of Mason County; Historic Mason County - 1980; Mason County Pictorial History - 1987; Mason Memories; Nature Power Then & Now
Open Tues-Sat (May-Sept) 10-5; Tues & Thurs (Oct-April) 11-4
Restriction: Non-circulating

LUTHER

P LUTHER AREA PUBLIC LIBRARY*, 115 State St, 49656. (Mail add: PO Box 86, 49656-0086). Tel: 231-797-8006. FAX: 231-797-8010. E-mail: lutherlibrary@att.net. *Dir,* Amy J Shank; *Co-Dir,* Jody Lucas
Founded 1979. Pop 3,540
Library Holdings: Bk Vols 12,000
Wireless access
Partic in Mid-Michigan Library League
Open Mon, Wed & Fri 10:30-6, Tues & Thurs 2-6, Sat 10:30-1:30
Friends of the Library Group

LYONS

P LYONS TOWNSHIP DISTRICT LIBRARY*, 240 E Bridge St, 48851. (Mail add: PO Box 185, 48851-0185). Tel: 989-855-3414. FAX: 989-855-2069. E-mail: lyonslib@hotmail.com. Web Site: www.lyons.michlibrary.org. *Dir,* Jennifer Kreiner
Library Holdings: Bk Vols 20,000; Per Subs 36
Wireless access
Mem of Woodlands Library Cooperative

MACKINAC ISLAND

P MACKINAC ISLAND PUBLIC LIBRARY*, 903 Main St, 49757. (Mail add: PO Box 903, 49757-0903), SAN 308-2466. Tel: 906-847-3421. FAX: 906-847-3368. E-mail: mcislib@mackisland.com. Web Site: www.uproc.lib.mi.us/mackisle. *Librn,* Anne L St Onge
Founded 1936. Pop 469; Circ 6,500
Library Holdings: Bk Vols 12,000; Per Subs 28
Subject Interests: Hist
Partic in OCLC Online Computer Library Center, Inc; Upper Peninsula Region of Library Cooperation, Inc
Open Tues & Fri 11-5:30 & 6:30-8:30, Wed & Thurs 11-5:30
Friends of the Library Group

MACKINAW CITY

P MACKINAW AREA PUBLIC LIBRARY*, 528 W Central Ave, 49701-9681. (Mail add: PO Box 67, 49701-0067), SAN 346-8240. Tel: 231-436-5451. FAX: 231-436-7344. E-mail: mackinaw3@gmail.com. Web Site: www.mackinawareapl.michlibrary.org. *Dir,* Jolene E Michaels. Subject Specialists: *Local hist, Mich,* Jolene E Michaels; Staff 3 (Non-MLS 3)
Founded 1968. Pop 4,689; Circ 66,182
Library Holdings: Audiobooks 607; CDs 2,000; DVDs 1,643; Bk Titles 39,384; Per Subs 72; Videos 3,151
Special Collections: Durant Rolls; Extensive Michigan History Coll
Automation Activity & Vendor Info: (ILL) Mel Cat
Wireless access
Publications: Memories of Mackinaw by Judy Ranville & Nancy Campbell (Local historical information)
Partic in Northland Library Cooperative
Special Services for the Deaf - Bks on deafness & sign lang
Special Services for the Blind - Audio mat; Bks on cassette; Bks on CD; Cassettes; Large print bks; Talking bks
Open Mon, Tues, Thurs & Fri 11-5, Wed 12-8; Mon, Tues, Thurs & Fri 11-5, Wed 12-8, Sat 10-2 (April-Dec)
Branches: 2
BLISS BRANCH, 265 Sturgeon Bay Trail, Levering, 49755, SAN 346-8259. Tel: 231-537-2927. FAX: 231-537-2927. E-mail: BlissBranch@gmail.com. *Br Head,* Mary Hohlbein. Subject Specialists: *Local hist,* Mary Hohlbein; Staff 1 (Non-MLS 1)
Pop 572; Circ 6,106
Subject Interests: Local hist
Automation Activity & Vendor Info: (ILL) Mel Cat
Function: Prog for adults, Prog for children & young adult, Spoken cassettes & CDs, Summer reading prog, VHS videos
Special Services for the Blind - Audio mat; Bks on cassette; Bks on CD; Large print bks; Talking bks; Videos on blindness & physical disabilties
Open Wed 2-8, Fri 1-5
Restriction: Open to pub for ref & circ; with some limitations
PELLSTON BRANCH, 125 N Milton St, Pellston, 49769-9301, SAN 346-8275. Tel: 231-539-8858. FAX: 231-539-8858. E-mail: pellstonbranch@gmail.com. *Br Head,* Tammy Gregory; Staff 1 (Non-MLS 1)
Circ 18,705
Function: ILL available, Photocopying/Printing, Prog for children & young adult, Spoken cassettes & CDs, Summer reading prog, VHS videos
Special Services for the Blind - Audio mat; Bks on cassette; Bks on CD; Large print bks; Talking bks; Videos on blindness & physical disabilties
Open Mon 11-4, Tues & Thurs 2-7
Restriction: Open to pub for ref & circ; with some limitations

MADISON HEIGHTS

P MADISON HEIGHTS PUBLIC LIBRARY*, 240 W 13 Mile Rd, 48071-1894. SAN 308-2474. Tel: 248-588-7763. Information Services Tel: 248-837-2851. FAX: 248-588-2470. E-mail: library@madison-heights.org. Web Site: www.madison-heights.org/library. *Libr Dir,* Roslyn F Yerman; Tel: 248-837-2852, E-mail: roslynyerman@madison-heights.org; *Head Ref Librn,* Sally Arrivee; E-mail: arrivee@madison-hgts.lib.mi.us; *Adult Ref Librn,* Krista Ghazar; Tel: 248-837-2850, E-mail: kghazar@madison-hgts.lib.mi.us; *Commun Serv Librn,* Jane Haigh; Tel: 248-837-2856, E-mail: jhaigh@madison-hgts.lib.mi.us; *Youth Serv Librn,* Amanda Gehrke; E-mail: gehrke@madison-hgts.lib.mi.us; *Libr Tech,* Rebecca Willemsen; Tel: 248-837-2854, E-mail: rebeccaw@madison-hgts.lib.mi.us; Staff 6.2 (MLS 3.1, Non-MLS 3.1)
Founded 1954. Pop 29,694; Circ 100,392
Jul 2012-Jun 2013 Income $584,233. Mats Exp $56,207, Books $40,707, Per/Ser (Incl. Access Fees) $6,500, AV Mat $9,000. Sal $310,893 (Prof $197,530)
Library Holdings: Audiobooks 2,957; CDs 3,097; DVDs 4,362; e-books 8,138; Bk Vols 95,760; Per Subs 100; Videos 4,362
Special Collections: Historical. US Document Depository
Automation Activity & Vendor Info: (Acquisitions) SirsiDynix; (Cataloging) SirsiDynix; (Circulation) SirsiDynix; (ILL) SirsiDynix; (OPAC) SirsiDynix; (Serials) SirsiDynix
Wireless access
Function: Archival coll, Art exhibits, Audiobks via web, AV serv, Bk club(s), Bks on cassette, Bks on CD, Children's prog, Computers for patron use, Free DVD rentals, Govt ref serv, Holiday prog, Homebound delivery serv, ILL available, Large print keyboards, Magnifiers for reading, Mail & tel request accepted, Music CDs, Online cat, Outreach serv, OverDrive digital audio bks, Photocopying/Printing, Preschool reading prog, Prog for children & young adult, Ref & res, Ref serv available, Story hour, Summer reading prog, Tax forms, Telephone ref, VHS videos, Wheelchair accessible
Partic in The Library Network
Open Mon, Tues & Thurs 9-8, Wed & Fri 9-5, Sat 10-5
Friends of the Library Group

MANCELONA

P MANCELONA TOWNSHIP LIBRARY, 202 W State St, 49659. (Mail add: PO Box 499, 49659-0499), SAN 308-2490. Tel: 231-587-9451. E-mail: mancelona.twp.library@gmail.com. Web Site: www.mancelonatownship.com/library. *Librn,* Kathleen Pintcke
Circ 16,983
Library Holdings: Bk Vols 16,000; Per Subs 10
Wireless access
Partic in Mid-Michigan Library League
Open Mon-Fri 10-6, Sat 10-Noon
Friends of the Library Group

MANCHESTER

P MANCHESTER DISTRICT LIBRARY, 912 City Rd M-52, 48158-0540. (Mail add: PO Box 540, 48158-5140), SAN 308-2504. Tel: 734-428-8045. Web Site: www.manchesterlibrary.info. *Dir,* Kathleen Dimond; E-mail: kdimond@manchesterlibrary.info; Staff 4 (MLS 2, Non-MLS 2)
Founded 1838. Pop 7,300
Library Holdings: AV Mats 1,500; Large Print Bks 100; Bk Titles 28,000; Per Subs 83; Talking Bks 500
Special Collections: Manchester Michigan Area History
Automation Activity & Vendor Info: (OPAC) CARL.Solution (TLC)
Wireless access
Function: Archival coll, ILL available, Prog for children & young adult, Ref serv available, Summer reading prog, Telephone ref, Wheelchair accessible
Partic in Midwest Collaborative for Library Services; The Library Network
Special Services for the Blind - Bks on cassette; Bks on CD; Copier with enlargement capabilities; Large print bks; Ref serv; Videos on blindness & physical disabilties
Open Mon-Wed 10-8, Fri 10-6, Sat 10-2, Sun 1-5
Restriction: Open to pub for ref & circ; with some limitations
Friends of the Library Group

MANISTEE

S MANISTEE COUNTY HISTORICAL MUSEUM*, Fortier Memorial Library, 425 River St, 49660. SAN 323-5394. Tel: 231-723-5531. E-mail: manisteemuseum@yahoo.com. Web Site: www.manisteemuseum.org. *Dir,* Mark Fedder; Staff 1 (Non-MLS 1)
Library Holdings: Bk Titles 1,000
Subject Interests: Great Lakes maritime hist, Manistee County hist
Open Tues-Sat 10-5
Restriction: Ref only

P MANISTEE COUNTY LIBRARY SYSTEM*, 95 Maple St, 49660. SAN 346-8305. Tel: 231-723-2519. FAX: 231-723-8270. Web Site: www.manisteelibrary.org. *Libr Dir,* Debra Greenacre; E-mail: dgreenacre@manisteelibrary.org; *Asst Dir,* Julie Herringa; E-mail: jherringa@manisteelibrary.org; Staff 20 (MLS 2, Non-MLS 18)
Founded 1903
Oct 2014-Sept 2015 Income (Main & Associated Libraries) $1,413,771, State $16,396, County $153,500, Locally Generated Income $1,129,999, Other $113,876. Mats Exp $158,277, Per/Ser (Incl. Access Fees) $11,847, Micro $800, AV Mat $46,430, Electronic Ref Mat (Incl. Access Fees) $19,000. Sal $462,577 (Prof $126,832)
Library Holdings: Audiobooks 6,080; AV Mats 631; Bks on Deafness & Sign Lang 176; CDs 3,009; DVDs 11,651; Electronic Media & Resources 8; Large Print Bks 6,369; Microforms 527; Bk Vols 93,588; Per Subs 748; Videos 0
Subject Interests: Local hist
Automation Activity & Vendor Info: (Cataloging) TLC (The Library Corporation); (Circulation) TLC (The Library Corporation); (OPAC) TLC (The Library Corporation)
Wireless access
Function: 24/7 Electronic res, Activity rm, Adult literacy prog, Audiobks via web, Computer training, Computers for patron use, Electronic databases & coll, Home delivery & serv to seniorr ctr & nursing homes, ILL available, Magazines, Magnifiers for reading, Music CDs, Online cat, Online info literacy tutorials on the web & in blackboard, OverDrive digital audio bks, Photocopying/Printing, Preschool outreach, Prog for adults, Prog for children & young adult, Ref serv available, Spoken cassettes & CDs, Story hour, Summer reading prog, Tax forms, Teen prog, Telephone ref
Partic in Mid-Michigan Library League
Special Services for the Blind - Accessible computers; Large print bks; Magnifiers; Playaways (bks on MP3); Talking bk serv referral
Open Mon & Tues 9:30-8, Wed-Fri 9:30-5, Sat 10-3
Friends of the Library Group

Branches: 5
ARCADIA BRANCH, 3586 Glovers Lake Rd, Arcadia, 49613. (Mail add: PO Box 109, Arcadia, 49613-0109), SAN 374-4582. Tel: 231-889-4230. FAX: 231-889-4230. *Br Mgr,* Jessica Hopkins; E-mail: jhopkins@manisteelibrary.org; Staff 1 (Non-MLS 1)
Function: 24/7 Electronic res, 24/7 Online cat
Open Tues 10:30-4, Thurs 12:30-6, Fri 11-4
Friends of the Library Group
KALEVA BRANCH, 14618 Walta St, Kaleva, 49645. (Mail add: PO Box 125, Kaleva, 49645-0125), SAN 346-8364. Tel: 231-362-3178. FAX: 231-362-3180. *Br Mgr,* Debbie Bostwick; E-mail: dbostwick@manisteelibrary.org; Staff 1 (Non-MLS 1)
Function: 24/7 Electronic res, 24/7 Online cat, Adult bk club
Open Mon & Tue 10:30-5, Wed 12:30-7, Thu 2-5, Fri 10:30-5
Friends of the Library Group
KEDDIE NORCONK MEMORIAL LIBRARY, 12325 Virginia St, Bear Lake, 49614. (Mail add: PO Box 266, Bear Lake, 49614-0266), SAN 346-833X. Tel: 231-864-2700. FAX: 231-864-2500. *Br Mgr,* Amy Cross; E-mail: across@manisteelibrary.org; Staff 1 (Non-MLS 1)
Function: 24/7 Electronic res, 24/7 Online cat
Open Mon & Tues 10:30-5, Wed 2-5, Thurs 12:30-7, Fri 10:30-5
Friends of the Library Group
ONEKAMA BRANCH, 5283 Main St, Onekama, 49675-9701. (Mail add: PO Box 149, Onekama, 49675-0149), SAN 346-8399. Tel: 231-889-4041. FAX: 231-889-5420. *Br Mgr,* Laurel Sproul; E-mail: lsproul@manisteelibrary.org; Staff 1 (Non-MLS 1)
Function: 24/7 Electronic res, 24/7 Online cat
Open Mon 10:30-5, Tues 1-5, Wed 12:30-7, Thu & Fri 10:30-5
WELLSTON BRANCH, 1273 Seaman Rd, Wellston, 49689. (Mail add: PO Box 62, Wellston, 49689), SAN 346-8429. Tel: 231-848-4013. FAX: 231-848-7113. *Br Mgr,* Michaelyn Crawford; E-mail: mcrawford@manisteelibrary.org; Staff 1 (Non-MLS 1)
Function: 24/7 Electronic res, 24/7 Online cat
Open Mon 12:30-7, Tues 10:30-6, Thurs & Fri 10:30-5

S MICHIGAN DEPARTMENT OF CORRECTIONS*, Oaks Correctional Facility Library, 1500 Caberfae Hwy, 49660. Tel: 231-723-8272. Web Site: www.michigan.gov/corrections. *Librn,* Leah Berean; E-mail: bereanl@michigan.gov
Library Holdings: Bk Vols 2,000
Restriction: Not open to pub

M MUNSON HEALTHCARE*, Manistee Hospital Library, 1465 Parkdale Ave, 49660-9785. Tel: 231-398-1171. *Coordr,* Karen Miller; E-mail: kmiller@mhc.net
Library Holdings: Bk Vols 350
Restriction: Staff use only

MANISTIQUE

P MANISTIQUE SCHOOL & PUBLIC LIBRARY, 100 N Cedar St, 49854-1293. SAN 308-2512. Tel: 906-341-4316. FAX: 906-252-4604. E-mail: mspl@manistiqueschools.org. Web Site: www.manistiquelibrary.org. *Dir,* Mary Hook; E-mail: mhook@manistiqueschools.org
Pop 8,401; Circ 44,459
Library Holdings: Bk Titles 35,000; Per Subs 78
Automation Activity & Vendor Info: (Cataloging) SirsiDynix; (Circulation) SirsiDynix
Wireless access
Partic in Upper Peninsula Region of Library Cooperation, Inc
Open Mon, Wed & Thurs 8-6, Tues & Fri 8-4; Mon 11:30-6, Tues-Thurs 11:30-4 (Summer)
Friends of the Library Group

MAPLE RAPIDS

P MAPLE RAPIDS PUBLIC LIBRARY*, 130 S Maple Ave, 48853. (Mail add: PO Box 410, 48853-0410), SAN 321-4672. Tel: 989-682-4464. FAX: 989-682-4149. E-mail: mrplibrary@gmail.com. Web Site: www.wplc.org/mrpl. *Dir,* Kim Salisbury; *Asst Dir,* Marvia Nemetz
Founded 1935. Circ 3,935
Library Holdings: Audiobooks 54; DVDs 1,117; Large Print Bks 53; Bk Titles 13,463; Per Subs 40
Subject Interests: Local hist
Automation Activity & Vendor Info: (Cataloging) Follett Software; (Circulation) Follett Software; (ILL) Mel Cat
Wireless access
Open Mon & Wed 10-7, Fri 10-5

MARCELLUS

P MARCELLUS TOWNSHIP-WOOD MEMORIAL LIBRARY*, 205 E Main St, 49067. (Mail add: PO Box 49, 49067-0049), SAN 308-2520. Tel: 269-646-9654. FAX: 269-646-9603. E-mail: marcellusmichiganlibrary@gmail.com. Web Site: www.marcellus.michlibrary.org. *Librn,* Christine Nofsinger
Circ 15,860
Library Holdings: Bk Titles 30,000; Per Subs 108
Automation Activity & Vendor Info: (Cataloging) Follett Software; (Circulation) Follett Software
Wireless access
Partic in Southwest Michigan Library Cooperative
Open Mon-Thurs 10-7, Fri 10-5, Sat 10-2
Friends of the Library Group

MARION

P M ALICE CHAPIN MEMORIAL LIBRARY*, 120 E Main St, 49665. (Mail add: PO Box 549, 49665), SAN 308-2539. Tel: 231-743-2421. FAX: 231-743-2421. E-mail: marionlibrary@sbcglobal.net. *Dir,* Shelley Ann Scott; Staff 3 (Non-MLS 3)
Library Holdings: Bk Vols 22,500
Wireless access
Partic in Mid-Michigan Library League
Open Mon-Fri 10-5, Sat 10-Noon

MARLETTE

P MARLETTE DISTRICT LIBRARY*, 3116 Main St, 48453. SAN 308-2547. Tel: 989-635-2838. FAX: 989-635-8005. Web Site: www.marlettelibrary.org. *Dir,* Jessica Moore; E-mail: j.moore@vlc.lib.mi.us; Staff 3 (Non-MLS 3)
Founded 1921. Pop 5,815; Circ 48,608
Library Holdings: DVDs 200; Bk Titles 20,505; Per Subs 55; Talking Bks 650
Special Collections: Local Newspaper, microfilm; Michigan Coll
Automation Activity & Vendor Info: (Cataloging) SirsiDynix; (Circulation) SirsiDynix; (OPAC) SirsiDynix; (Serials) SirsiDynix
Wireless access
Partic in Valley Libr Consortium; White Pine Library Cooperative
Open Mon, Wed & Fri 9-5, Tues & Thurs 10-8, Sat 10-2

MARQUETTE

P GREAT LAKES TALKING BOOKS, Reader Advisory & Outreach Center, 1615 Presque Isle Ave, 49855. SAN 308-0706. Tel: 906-228-7697, Ext 0. Toll Free Tel: 800-562-8985, Ext 0. FAX: 906-228-5627. E-mail: tb@greatlakestalkingbooks.org. Web Site: greatlakestalkingbooks.org. *Readers' Advisory,* Tonia Bickford; Staff 1 (Non-MLS 1)
Founded 1980. Pop 594; Circ 53,000
Function: Audiobks via web, Digital talking bks, Mail & tel request accepted, Mail loans to mem, Outreach serv
Partic in Superiorland Library Cooperative
Special Services for the Blind - Bks on flash-memory cartridges; Braille bks; Descriptive video serv (DVS); Digital talking bk; Digital talking bk machines; Home delivery serv; Info on spec aids & appliances; Newsletter (in large print, Braille or on cassette); Newsp reading serv; Ref serv
Open Mon, Tues & Thurs 9-5

S MARQUETTE REGIONAL HISTORY CENTER*, John M Longyear Research Library, 145 W Spring St, 49855. SAN 308-2555. Tel: 906-226-3571. Web Site: www.marquettehistory.org. *Research Librn,* Elizabeth Gruber; E-mail: beth@marquettehistory.org; Staff 1 (MLS 1)
Founded 1925
Library Holdings: Microforms 200; Per Subs 45
Special Collections: Breitung-Kaufman Papers; Burt Papers; Business Records; Carroll Watson Rankin Papers; Closser Appraisel Records; Family Records; J M Longyear Coll; Local Newspapers on Microfilm from 1870s; Military (Local Service Men); Municipal Records; Regional Genealogy Coll. Oral History
Subject Interests: Ethnology, Genealogy, Geol, Great Lakes, Local hist, Mining, Native Am studies, Railroads
Function: Archival coll, Bus archives
Publications: Harlow's Wooden Man (Quarterly)
Partic in Upper Peninsula Region of Library Cooperation, Inc
Open Tues, Thurs & Fri 10-5, Wed 10-8, Sat 10-3
Restriction: Closed stack, Fee for pub use, Non-circulating, Private libr

C NORTHERN MICHIGAN UNIVERSITY*, Lydia M Olson Library, 1401 Presque Isle Ave, 49855-5376. SAN 308-258X. Tel: 906-227-2260. Interlibrary Loan Service Tel: 906-227-2065. Reference Tel: 906-227-2294. Information Services Tel: 906-227-2117. FAX: 906-227-1333. TDD: 906-227-1232. Reference E-mail: info@nmu.edu. Web Site: www.nmu.edu/library. *Dean, Acad Info Access,* Leslie A Warren; E-mail: lwarren@nmu.edu; *Head, Coll,* Krista Clumpner; Tel: 906-227-1205, E-mail: kclumpne@nmu.edu; *Head, Libr Syst,* Michael Burgmeier; Tel: 906-227-2187, E-mail: mburgmei@nmu.edu; *Head, Pub Serv,* Mollie Freier; Tel: 906-227-1061, E-mail: mfreier@nmu.edu; *Cat Librn,* Catherine Oliver; Tel: 906-227-2123, E-mail: coliver@nmu.edu; *Ref/Electronic Res*

Librn, Kevin McDonough; Tel: 906-227-2118, E-mail: kmcdonou@nmu.edu; *Coordr, Instruction,* Michael Strahan; Tel: 906-227-2463, E-mail: mstrahan@nmu.edu; *Libr Syst Spec,* John Hambleton; Tel: 906-227-2741, E-mail: jhamblet@nmu.edu; *Circ, Sr Libr Asst,* Molly Anderson; Tel: 906-227-2250, E-mail: moanders@nmu.edu; *Govt Doc,* Bruce Sarjeant; Tel: 906-227-1580, E-mail: bsarjean@nmu.edu; Staff 14 (MLS 10, Non-MLS 4)
Founded 1899. Enrl 9,347; Fac 326; Highest Degree: Master
Library Holdings: AV Mats 8,251; e-books 20,372; e-journals 77; Electronic Media & Resources 4,573; Bk Vols 615,406; Per Subs 1,722
Special Collections: Holocaust Coll; Moses Coit Tyler Coll. State Document Depository; US Document Depository
Automation Activity & Vendor Info: (Acquisitions) Ex Libris Group; (Cataloging) Ex Libris Group; (Circulation) Ex Libris Group; (ILL) OCLC ILLiad; (OPAC) Ex Libris Group
Wireless access
Partic in Midwest Collaborative for Library Services; OCLC Online Computer Library Center, Inc; Upper Peninsula Region of Library Cooperation, Inc

M UP HEALTH SYSTEM - MARQUETTE*, Library Services, 850 W Baraga Ave, 49855. SAN 308-2563. Tel: 906-449-3346. *Library Services,* Janis Lubenow; E-mail: janis.lubenow@mghs.org
Founded 1974
Library Holdings: e-books 40; e-journals 200; Bk Titles 1,200
Automation Activity & Vendor Info: (Cataloging) SirsiDynix-WorkFlows; (Discovery) OVID Technologies; (OPAC) SirsiDynix; (Serials) OVID Technologies
Wireless access
Function: 24/7 Electronic res
Partic in Greater Midwest Regional Medical Libr Network; Michigan Health Sciences Libraries Association; Upper Peninsula Region of Library Cooperation, Inc
Restriction: Authorized personnel only

P PETER WHITE PUBLIC LIBRARY*, 217 N Front St, 49855. SAN 308-2601. Tel: 906-228-9510. Interlibrary Loan Service Tel: 906-226-4315. Reference Tel: 906-226-4311. Administration Tel: 906-228-4300. FAX: 906-226-1783. E-mail: pwpl@uproc.lib.mi.us. Web Site: www.pwpl.info. *Dir,* Andrea Ingmire; Tel: 906-226-4303, E-mail: aingpwpl@gmail.com; *Acq & Ref,* Samantha Ashby; Tel: 906-226-4309, E-mail: sashby@uproc.lib.mi.us; *Ch Serv,* Sarah Rehborg; Tel: 906-226-4319, E-mail: srehborg@uproc.lib.mi.us; *Circ,* Amy Salminen; Tel: 906-226-4310; *Tech Serv,* Ellen Moore; Tel: 906-226-4316, E-mail: emoore@uproc.lib.mi.us; Staff 24 (MLS 4.5, Non-MLS 19.5)
Founded 1871. Pop 36,441; Circ 217,947
Oct 2018-Sept 2019 Income $1,965,990. Mats Exp $96,790. Sal $911,863
Library Holdings: Audiobooks 4,051; AV Mats 22,978; CDs 11,006; DVDs 7,728; e-books 5,866; Large Print Bks 1,195; Microforms 925; Bk Vols 162,158; Per Subs 299
Special Collections: Children's Historical Book Coll; Finnish Coll; Guns, Railroads, Ships (Miller Coll); Library of Things; Local History Coll; Merrit Coll; Nadeau Coll; Shiras Coll; Sister City Coll; Submarines (William Nelson Coll). Municipal Document Depository
Automation Activity & Vendor Info: (Cataloging) SirsiDynix-WorkFlows; (Circulation) SirsiDynix-WorkFlows; (Discovery) Mel Cat; (ILL) Mel Cat; (OPAC) SirsiDynix-Enterprise; (Serials) SirsiDynix-WorkFlows
Wireless access
Function: 24/7 Electronic res, 24/7 Online cat, Activity rm, Adult bk club, Adult literacy prog, After school storytime, Art exhibits, Art programs, Audio & video playback equip for onsite use, Audiobks via web, AV serv, Bk club(s), Bks on CD, Bus archives, Butterfly Garden, CD-ROM, Chess club, Children's prog, Computer training, Computers for patron use, Digital talking bks, Distance learning, Doc delivery serv, Electronic databases & coll, Equip loans & repairs, Family literacy, Games & aids for people with disabilities, Govt ref serv, Holiday prog, Homebound delivery serv, Homework prog, ILL available, Instruction & testing, Internet access, Jazz prog, Large print keyboards, Magazines, Magnifiers for reading, Mail & tel request accepted, Mango lang, Meeting rooms, Microfiche/film & reading machines, Movies, Museum passes, Music CDs, Online cat, Orientations, Outside serv via phone, mail, e-mail & web, OverDrive digital audio bks, Passport agency, Photocopying/Printing, Preschool reading prog, Printer for laptops & handheld devices, Prog for adults, Prog for children & young adult, Ref serv available, Res assist avail, Scanner, Senior computer classes, Serves people with intellectual disabilities, Spoken cassettes & CDs, Spoken cassettes & DVDs, STEM programs, Story hour, Summer reading prog, Tax forms, Teen prog, Telephone ref, Wheelchair accessible, Workshops, Writing prog
Partic in Superiorland Library Cooperative; Upper Peninsula Region of Library Cooperation, Inc
Special Services for the Blind - Web-Braille
Open Mon-Thurs 10-9, Fri 10-6, Sat 10-5
Restriction: Non-resident fee
Friends of the Library Group

MARSHALL

P MARSHALL DISTRICT LIBRARY, 124 W Green St, 49068. SAN 308-2628. Tel: 269-781-7821. FAX: 269-781-7090. Web Site: www.yourmdl.org. *Dir,* Angela Semifero; Tel: 269-781-7821, Ext 11, E-mail: semiferoa@yourmdl.org; *Asst Dir,* Nate Palmer; Tel: 269-781-7821, Ext 13, E-mail: palmern@yourmdl.org; *Head, Info Tech,* Matt Harmon; Tel: 269-781-7821, Ext 16, E-mail: harmonm@yourmdl.org; *Head, Pub Serv,* Shuana Swantek; Tel: 269-781-7821, Ext 18, E-mail: swanteks@yourmdl.org; Staff 22 (MLS 5, Non-MLS 17)
Founded 1912. Pop 14,911; Circ 166,845
Jul 2015-Jun 2016 Income $1,036,094, State $9,298, Locally Generated Income $927,334, Other $99,462. Mats Exp $65,000, Books $45,500, Per/Ser (Incl. Access Fees) $3,500, AV Mat $10,000, Electronic Ref Mat (Incl. Access Fees) $6,000. Sal $3,314,843 (Prof $195,399)
Library Holdings: Audiobooks 4,403; CDs 895; DVDs 6,538; Bk Titles 46,325; Per Subs 100
Automation Activity & Vendor Info: (Cataloging) Innovative Interfaces, Inc; (Circulation) Innovative Interfaces, Inc; (ILL) Innovative Interfaces, Inc; (OPAC) Innovative Interfaces, Inc
Wireless access
Function: 24/7 Electronic res, 24/7 Online cat, Activity rm, Adult bk club, Archival coll, Audiobks via web, AV serv, Bk club(s), Bks on CD, Children's prog, Computer training, Computers for patron use, Distance learning, E-Readers, Electronic databases & coll, Equip loans & repairs, Family literacy, Free DVD rentals, Govt ref serv, Health sci info serv, Holiday prog, Home delivery & serv to seniorr ctr & nursing homes, Homebound delivery serv, ILL available, Internet access, Large print keyboards, Learning ctr, Life-long learning prog for all ages, Literacy & newcomer serv, Magazines, Magnifiers for reading, Mail & tel request accepted, Meeting rooms, Microfiche/film & reading machines, Movies, Museum passes, Music CDs, Notary serv, Online cat, Online ref, Outreach serv, Outside serv via phone, mail, e-mail & web, OverDrive digital audio bks, Photocopying/Printing, Preschool outreach, Preschool reading prog, Prog for adults, Prog for children & young adult, Ref & res, Ref serv available, Scanner, Senior computer classes, Senior outreach, Spanish lang bks, Spoken cassettes & CDs, Story hour, Study rm, Summer & winter reading prog, Summer reading prog, Tax forms, Teen prog, Telephone ref, Visual arts prog, Wheelchair accessible, Winter reading prog, Workshops, Writing prog
Mem of Woodlands Library Cooperative
Partic in Midwest Collaborative for Library Services
Special Services for the Blind - Bks available with recordings; Bks on CD; Closed circuit TV; Extensive large print coll; Large print bks; Magnifiers
Open Mon 10-8:30, Tues-Fri 10-5:30, Sat 10-3
Restriction: Non-resident fee

MARTIN

P J C WHEELER PUBLIC LIBRARY, 1576 S Main St, 49070-9728. (Mail add: PO Box 226, 49070-0226), SAN 308-2636. Tel: 269-672-7875. E-mail: lovemylibrary@live.com. Web Site: www.wheelerpl.michlibrary.org. *Dir,* Alicia Kershaw
Founded 1922. Circ 15,000
Library Holdings: Bk Vols 11,290; Per Subs 23
Wireless access
Partic in Lakeland Library Cooperative
Open Mon 12-7, Tues, Wed & Fri 10-5, Sat 9-1
Friends of the Library Group

MAYVILLE

P MAYVILLE DISTRICT PUBLIC LIBRARY*, 6090 Fulton St, 48744. (Mail add: PO Box 440, 48744-0440), SAN 308-2652. Tel: 989-843-6522. FAX: 989-843-0078. Web Site: www.mayvillelibrary.org. *Dir,* Jill Fox; E-mail: jill@mayvillelibrary.org
Founded 1950. Pop 6,094; Circ 47,366
Library Holdings: AV Mats 1,247; Bks on Deafness & Sign Lang 22; Large Print Bks 50; Bk Vols 21,000; Per Subs 65; Talking Bks 717
Automation Activity & Vendor Info: (Cataloging) Auto-Graphics, Inc; (Circulation) Auto-Graphics, Inc
Wireless access
Partic in Mich Libr Asn; White Pine Library Cooperative
Open Mon, Wed, Thurs & Fri 10-6, Tues 10-8, Sat 10-2
Friends of the Library Group

MCBAIN

P MCBAIN COMMUNITY LIBRARY, 107 E Maple St, 49657-9672. Tel: 231-825-2197. FAX: 231-825-2477. E-mail: mcbainlibrary@gmail.com. Web Site: mcbain.michlibrary.org. *Dir,* Diane Eisenga; E-mail: diane.eisenga@mcbain.org
Library Holdings: Bks on Deafness & Sign Lang 15; Bk Vols 20,000; Per Subs 40
Automation Activity & Vendor Info: (Cataloging) Biblionix/Apollo; (Circulation) Biblionix/Apollo; (OPAC) Biblionix/Apollo

Wireless access
Partic in Mid-Michigan Library League
Open Mon-Thurs 10-5, Fri 10-4, Sat 9-1 (June-Aug); Mon-Thurs 8-6, Fri 8-4, Sat 9-1 (Sept-May)
Friends of the Library Group

MECOSTA

P MORTON TOWNSHIP LIBRARY*, 110 S James, 49332-9334. (Mail add: PO Box 246, 49332-0246), SAN 308-2660. Tel: 231-972-8315. FAX: 231-972-4332. E-mail: info@mtplibrary.org. Web Site: morton.michlibrary.org. *Libr Dir,* Mary Ann Lenon; Tel: 231-972-8315, Ext 203, E-mail: mlenon@mtplibrary.org; *Asst Libr Dir,* Holly Swincicki; Tel: 231-972-8315, Ext 204, E-mail: hswincicki@mtplibrary.org; *Ch,* Juliane Schafer; Tel: 231-972-8315, Ext 209, E-mail: jschafer@mtplibrary.org; *Circ,* Deb Maculey; E-mail: dmacauley@mtplibrary.org; *Tech Serv,* Jeff Spedowski; E-mail: jspedowski@mtplibrary.org; Staff 4 (MLS 1, Non-MLS 3)
Founded 1966. Pop 6,634; Circ 63,296
Library Holdings: Bks on Deafness & Sign Lang 30; Large Print Bks 225; Large Print Bks 225; Bk Vols 22,137; Bk Vols 22,137; Per Subs 80; Per Subs 80; Talking Bks 880; Talking Bks 880
Automation Activity & Vendor Info: (Acquisitions) Auto-Graphics, Inc; (Cataloging) Auto-Graphics, Inc; (Circulation) Auto-Graphics, Inc
Wireless access
Function: Homebound delivery serv, ILL available, Online cat, Preschool reading prog, Prog for adults, Prog for children & young adult, Scanner, Senior computer classes, Story hour, Summer reading prog, Tax forms, Teen prog, Wheelchair accessible
Partic in Mid-Michigan Library League
Special Services for the Deaf - Bks on deafness & sign lang
Open Tues, Thurs & Fri 10-5, Wed 10-7, Sat 10-1
Friends of the Library Group

MELVINDALE

P MELVINDALE PUBLIC LIBRARY*, 18650 Allen Rd, 48122. SAN 308-2679. Tel: 313-429-1090. FAX: 313-388-0432. Web Site: www.melvindale.lib.mi.us. *Dir,* Theresa Kieltyka; E-mail: kieltyka@melvindale.lib.mi.us
Founded 1928. Pop 11,216; Circ 42,668
Library Holdings: Bks on Deafness & Sign Lang 15; DVDs 200; Large Print Bks 300; Bk Vols 47,000; Per Subs 85; Talking Bks 680; Videos 600
Automation Activity & Vendor Info: (Cataloging) SirsiDynix; (Circulation) SirsiDynix; (OPAC) SirsiDynix
Wireless access
Special Services for the Deaf - TDD equip
Special Services for the Blind - Bks on cassette; Large print bks
Open Mon & Wed (Winter) 12-6, Tues & Thurs 12-8, Sat 12-5; Mon & Wed (Summer) 12-6, Tues & Thurs 12-8, Fri 12-5

MENDON

P MENDON TOWNSHIP LIBRARY*, 314 W Main St, 49072. (Mail add: PO Box 39, 49072-8753), SAN 308-2687. Tel: 269-496-4865. FAX: 269-496-4635. E-mail: mendon@monroe.lib.mi.us. Web Site: www.mendontownshiplibrary.michlibrary.org. *Dir,* Kimberly Foghino
Founded 1882. Pop 4,999; Circ 10,916
Library Holdings: Bk Vols 17,000
Special Collections: Local History, scrapbks, bks; Mich & Local History; Mich & Local History, albums
Subject Interests: Foreign lang, Genealogy
Wireless access
Mem of Woodlands Library Cooperative
Open Tues, Wed & Fri 10-5, Thurs 12-7, Sat 10-2
Friends of the Library Group

MENOMINEE

P SPIES PUBLIC LIBRARY*, 940 First St, 49858-3296. SAN 308-2695. Tel: 906-863-3911. FAX: 906-863-5000. TDD: 800-649-3777. E-mail: spies@uproc.lib.mi.us. Web Site: joomla.uproc.lib.mi.us/spies. *Dir,* Cheryl Hoffman; Tel: 906-863-2900, E-mail: cherylh@uproc.lib.mi.us; *Cataloger, Syst Adminr,* Amber Allard; Staff 10 (MLS 1, Non-MLS 9)
Founded 1903. Pop 10,313; Circ 66,682
Library Holdings: AV Mats 2,248; e-books 35; Bk Vols 56,907; Per Subs 126
Automation Activity & Vendor Info: (Acquisitions) SirsiDynix; (Cataloging) SirsiDynix; (Circulation) SirsiDynix; (ILL) SirsiDynix; (OPAC) SirsiDynix; (Serials) SirsiDynix
Wireless access
Partic in Superiorland Library Cooperative; Upper Peninsula Region of Library Cooperation, Inc
Open Mon & Fri 9-5, Tues-Thurs 9-8, Sat 9-1
Friends of the Library Group

MERRILL

P MERRILL DISTRICT LIBRARY*, 321 W Saginaw St, 48637. (Mail add: PO Box 97, 48637), SAN 308-2709. Tel: 989-643-7300. FAX: 989-643-7300. E-mail: mer_ill@yahoo.com. Web Site: merrilllibrary.org. *Dir,* Brenda Francetic
Circ 24,512
Library Holdings: Bk Vols 23,158; Per Subs 52
Subject Interests: Mich
Partic in White Pine Library Cooperative
Open Mon & Wed 11-6, Tues & Thurs 11-4:30, Sat (Oct-May) 11-1

MIDDLEVILLE

P THORNAPPLE KELLOGG SCHOOL & COMMUNITY LIBRARY, 3885 Bender Rd, 49333-9273. SAN 308-2717. Tel: 269-795-5434. FAX: 269-795-8997. E-mail: tklibrary@tkschools.org. Web Site: www.tkschools.org/community/library. *Dir,* Barb Hubers; E-mail: bhubers@tkschools.org
Circ 45,000
Library Holdings: Bk Titles 38,000; Per Subs 26
Automation Activity & Vendor Info: (Cataloging) Innovative Interfaces, Inc; (Circulation) Innovative Interfaces, Inc
Wireless access
Partic in Lakeland Library Cooperative
Open Mon & Wed 8-5, Tues & Thurs 8-7:30, Fri 8-3, Sat 9:30-12:30
Friends of the Library Group

MIDLAND

P GRACE A DOW MEMORIAL LIBRARY*, 1710 W St Andrews Ave, 48640-2698. SAN 308-2725. Tel: 989-837-3430. Reference Tel: 989-837-3449. FAX: 989-837-3468. Web Site: www.midland-mi.org/gracedowlibrary. *Dir,* Miriam Andrus; E-mail: mandrus@midland-mi.org; Staff 19 (MLS 14, Non-MLS 5)
Founded 1899. Pop 76,707; Circ 789,851
Jul 2012-Jun 2013 Income $3,735,060. Mats Exp $372,349, Books $186,947, Per/Ser (Incl. Access Fees) $15,188, AV Mat $50,031, Electronic Ref Mat (Incl. Access Fees) $120,183
Library Holdings: Audiobooks 9,610; CDs 8,975; DVDs 10,032; e-books 2,290; Large Print Bks 6,062; Bk Vols 214,983; Per Subs 291
Special Collections: Municipal Document Depository
Subject Interests: Local hist
Automation Activity & Vendor Info: (Acquisitions) Biblionix/Apollo; (Cataloging) Biblionix/Apollo; (Circulation) Biblionix/Apollo; (ILL) Mel Cat; (Media Booking) Biblionix/Apollo; (OPAC) Biblionix/Apollo
Wireless access
Function: 24/7 Electronic res, 24/7 Online cat, Activity rm, Adult literacy prog, Art programs, Audiobks on Playaways & MP3, Audiobks via web, AV serv, Bk club(s), Bks on CD, Bus archives, Children's prog, Computer training, Computers for patron use, Digital talking bks, Electronic databases & coll, Family literacy, For res purposes, Free DVD rentals, Holiday prog, ILL available, Instruction & testing, Internet access, Life-long learning prog for all ages, Magazines, Magnifiers for reading, Meeting rooms, Microfiche/film & reading machines, Movies, Music CDs, Online cat, Online info literacy tutorials on the web & in blackboard, Online ref, Outreach serv, OverDrive digital audio bks, Photocopying/Printing, Preschool outreach, Preschool reading prog, Printer for laptops & handheld devices, Prof lending libr, Prog for adults, Prog for children & young adult, Ref & res, Ref serv available, Res assist avail, Res performed for a fee, Scanner, Senior computer classes, Senior outreach, Story hour, Study rm, Summer reading prog, Tax forms, Teen prog, Telephone ref, Visual arts prog, Wheelchair accessible, Workshops, Writing prog
Partic in Mideastern Michigan Library Cooperative
Special Services for the Blind - Aids for in-house use
Open Mon-Fri 9:30-8:30, Sat 10-5, Sun (Sept-May) 1-5
Restriction: Non-resident fee
Friends of the Library Group

R MEMORIAL PRESBYTERIAN CHURCH, Greenhoe Library-Rainbow Children's Library, 1310 Ashman St, 48640. SAN 308-2733. Tel: 989-835-6759. FAX: 989-835-6770. E-mail: info@mempres.org. Web Site: www.mempres.org/new-page. *Library Contact,* Sheryl Hnizda; E-mail: sherylh@mempres.org; Staff 2 (MLS 1, Non-MLS 1)
Founded 1945
Library Holdings: AV Mats 1,600; CDs 321; DVDs 89; Large Print Bks 167; Bk Titles 8,018; Bk Vols 7,189; Per Subs 6; Talking Bks 10; Videos 624
Special Collections: Children's Library, bks, flm, tapes
Subject Interests: Biblical studies, Church hist, Fiction

S MIDLAND COUNTY HISTORICAL SOCIETY LIBRARY*, 3417 W Main St, 48640. (Mail add: 1801 West St, Andrews Rd, 48640-2695), SAN 327-4373. Tel: 989-631-5930, Ext 1300. Web Site:

www.midlandcenter.org/museums/midland-county-historical-society. *Dir,* Julie Johnson; E-mail: johnsonj@midlandcenter.org; Staff 4 (Non-MLS 4)
Founded 1952
Library Holdings: Bk Titles 1,500; Per Subs 10
Special Collections: Area Genealogy Coll; Dow Chemical Company Archival Material, photos; Midland County Circuit Court Records. Municipal Document Depository; Oral History
Restriction: Open by appt only

M MIDMICHIGAN MEDICAL CENTER*, Health Sciences Library, 4005 Orchard Dr, 48670. SAN 325-2248. Tel: 989-839-3262. FAX: 989-631-1401. Web Site: www.midmichigan.org. *Mgr,* Kristin LaLonde; E-mail: kristin.lalonde@midmichigan.org
Library Holdings: Bk Vols 3,000; Per Subs 400
Special Collections: Health Sciences Coll
Wireless access
Open Mon-Fri 9-4:30

C NORTHWOOD UNIVERSITY*, Strosacker Library, 4000 Whiting Dr, 48640-2398. SAN 346-8933. Tel: 989-837-4333. FAX: 989-832-5031. Web Site: www.northwood.edu/academics/undergraduate/academics/library-services. *Head Librn,* Eric Palmer; Tel: 989-837-4338, E-mail: palmerer@northwood.edu; *Head, Circ,* Rebecca Grai; E-mail: grai@northwood.edu; *Ref (Info Servs),* Rochelle Zimmerman; Tel: 989-837-4275, E-mail: zimmerma@northwood.edu; Staff 9 (MLS 3, Non-MLS 6)
Founded 1959. Enrl 1,936; Fac 45; Highest Degree: Master
Library Holdings: AV Mats 86; Bk Titles 33,892; Bk Vols 39,671; Per Subs 334
Automation Activity & Vendor Info: (Cataloging) SirsiDynix; (Circulation) SirsiDynix; (Course Reserve) Docutek; (ILL) SirsiDynix; (OPAC) SirsiDynix
Wireless access
Partic in OCLC Online Computer Library Center, Inc; Valley Libr Consortium
Open Mon-Thurs 7:30am-10:30pm, Fri 7:30-4, Sat 1-5, Sun 2-10

MILAN

S FEDERAL CORRECTIONAL INSTITUTION LIBRARY*, 4004 E Arkona Rd, 48160. (Mail add: PO Box 49999, 48160), SAN 308-2741. Tel: 734-439-1511, Ext 3241. FAX: 734-439-3608. *Library Contact,* Tasha Harkness
Library Holdings: Bk Vols 20,000; Per Subs 35
Special Collections: Bureau of Prison Program Statements & Institutions Supplements; Federal Law Books & Statutes; Reference Works
Partic in Washtenaw-Livingston Libr Network
Open Mon-Sun 7:30-4:30 & 5-8:30

P MILAN PUBLIC LIBRARY*, 151 Wabash St, 48160. SAN 308-275X. Tel: 734-439-1240. FAX: 734-439-5625. E-mail: info@milanlibrary.org. Web Site: milanlibrary.org. *Dir,* Susan Wess; E-mail: susan.wess@milanlibrary.org; *Asst Dir/Ref Librn,* Barbara Beaton; Staff 7 (MLS 2, Non-MLS 5)
Founded 1935. Pop 17,462; Circ 79,995
Library Holdings: Large Print Bks 400; Bk Titles 33,000; Bk Vols 33,324; Per Subs 90; Videos 1,606
Subject Interests: Genealogy, Local hist
Wireless access
Function: Homebound delivery serv, ILL available, Photocopying/Printing, Prog for adults, Prog for children & young adult, Ref serv available, Summer reading prog, Telephone ref
Mem of Woodlands Library Cooperative
Partic in OCLC Online Computer Library Center, Inc
Open Mon-Thurs 10-8, Fri 10-6, Sat 10-4
Friends of the Library Group

MILFORD

P MILFORD PUBLIC LIBRARY*, 330 Family Dr, 48381-2000. SAN 308-2768. Tel: 248-684-0845. FAX: 248-684-2923. Web Site: milfordlibrary.info. *Dir,* Tina Hatch; E-mail: thatch@milfordlibrary.info; *Head, Adult Serv,* Karin Boughey; E-mail: kboughey@milfordlibrary.info; *Head, Circ,* Dawn Chlebo; E-mail: dchlebo@milfordlibrary.info; *Head, Youth Serv,* Karen Dobson; E-mail: kdobson@milfordlibrary.info; Staff 20 (MLS 7, Non-MLS 13)
Founded 1929. Pop 19,512; Circ 124,457
Library Holdings: Bk Vols 45,000; Per Subs 120
Special Collections: Art Geyer Civil War Coll
Subject Interests: Local hist, Mich
Wireless access
Publications: Library Register (Newsletter)
Partic in Midwest Collaborative for Library Services
Open Mon-Thurs 9:30-8, Fri & Sat 9:30-5, Sun 1-5
Friends of the Library Group

MILLINGTON

P MILLINGTON ARBELA DISTRICT LIBRARY, 8530 Depot St, 48746. SAN 308-2776. Tel: 989-871-2003. FAX: 989-871-5594. Web Site: www.millingtonlibrary.info. *Dir,* Sarah Rick; E-mail: director@millingtonlibrary.info; *Asst Dir,* Amy Beckman
Founded 1937. Pop 7,678; Circ 40,000
Library Holdings: Bk Titles 27,351; Bk Vols 29,653; Per Subs 65
Automation Activity & Vendor Info: (Circulation) Auto-Graphics, Inc; (OPAC) Auto-Graphics, Inc
Wireless access
Open Mon & Thurs 9-8, Tues & Wed 9-2, Fri 9-6, Sat 9-1

MIO

P OSCODA COUNTY LIBRARY*, 430 W Eighth St, 48647. SAN 308-2784. Tel: 989-826-3613. FAX: 989-826-5461. E-mail: ocl@m33access.com. Web Site: www.oscoda.lib.mi.us. *Dir,* Amy R Knepp; Staff 2 (MLS 1, Non-MLS 1)
Founded 1948. Pop 9,000; Circ 41,249
Library Holdings: Audiobooks 50; Bks on Deafness & Sign Lang 10; High Interest/Low Vocabulary Bk Vols 100; Bk Titles 30,000; Videos 200
Special Collections: County Papers 1932-Present
Automation Activity & Vendor Info: (Cataloging) Evergreen; (Circulation) Evergreen; (ILL) Evergreen; (OPAC) Evergreen
Wireless access
Function: 24/7 Online cat, Adult bk club, Adult literacy prog, AV serv, Bks on CD, Children's prog, Computers for patron use, Holiday prog, ILL available, Internet access, Meeting rooms, Movies, Notary serv, OverDrive digital audio bks, Photocopying/Printing, Preschool outreach, Printer for laptops & handheld devices, Prog for adults, Prog for children & young adult, Story hour, Summer reading prog, Tax forms, Wheelchair accessible
Partic in Northland Library Cooperative
Open Mon-Fri 9-5:30, Sat 9-1

MONROE

SR IHM LIBRARY/RESOURCE CENTER, Congregational Library, 610 W Elm Ave, 48162-7909. SAN 308-2806. Tel: 734-240-9713. Circulation Tel: 734-240-9678. FAX: 734-240-8347. E-mail: library@ihmsisters.org. Web Site: www.ihmsisters.org. *Dir,* Sister Anne Marie Murphy; *Librn,* Carol Kelly; Staff 7 (MLS 3, Non-MLS 4)
Founded 1927
Library Holdings: Audiobooks 150; CDs 350; DVDs 450; Large Print Bks 450; Bk Vols 30,000; Per Subs 100; Spec Interest Per Sub 20; Videos 2,200
Subject Interests: Art, Ecology, Fiction, Relig, Theol
Function: AV serv, Bk club(s), Bks on cassette, Bks on CD, CD-ROM, Computers for patron use, Free DVD rentals, Home delivery & serv to seniorr ctr & nursing homes, Internet access, Learning ctr, Magnifiers for reading, Mail loans to mem, Music CDs, Photocopying/Printing, Ref serv available, Res libr, Spoken cassettes & CDs, VHS videos, Wheelchair accessible
Special Services for the Blind - Assistive/Adapted tech devices, equip & products
Open Mon-Fri 10:30-4:30, Sat 9:30-12, Sun 1-3
Restriction: Authorized patrons, Authorized scholars by appt, Circ to mem only, External users must contact libr, Open to pub for ref & circ; with some limitations, Open to researchers by request, Private libr, Restricted pub use, Sub libr
Friends of the Library Group

J MONROE COUNTY COMMUNITY COLLEGE*, Campbell Learning Resources Center, 1555 S Raisinville Rd, 48161-9047. SAN 308-2792. Tel: 734-384-4204. FAX: 734-384-4160. Web Site: www.monroeccc.edu/library. *Libr Dir,* Laura Manley, PhD; Tel: 734-384-4244, E-mail: lmanley@monroeccc.edu; *Head, Tech Serv, Ref (Info Servs),* Terri Kovach; Tel: 734-384-4161, E-mail: tkovach@monroeccc.edu; *Adjunct Librn,* Mary Bullard; E-mail: mbullard@monroeccc.edu; *Adjunct Librn,* David Peck; E-mail: dpeck@monroeccc.edu; *Adjunct Librn,* Corinne Thompson; E-mail: cthompson@monroeccc.edu; *Pub Serv Librn, Ref,* Cindy Yonovich; Tel: 734-384-4162, E-mail: cyonovich@monroeccc.edu; *Ref/Tech Serv Librn,* Thomas Adamich; E-mail: tadamich@monroeccc.edu; *Circ, Digital Serv,* Janice Hylinski; Tel: 734-384-4399, E-mail: jhylinski@monroeccc.edu; *Tech Serv Asst,* Stacy Lehr; Tel: 734-384-4401, E-mail: slehr@monroeccc.edu; Staff 6 (MLS 3, Non-MLS 3)
Founded 1966. Enrl 4,500; Fac 3; Highest Degree: Associate
Library Holdings: AV Mats 4,944; Bk Titles 50,333; Bk Vols 56,000; Per Subs 335
Special Collections: Professional Library
Automation Activity & Vendor Info: (Acquisitions) SirsiDynix; (Cataloging) SirsiDynix; (Circulation) SirsiDynix; (ILL) OCLC; (OPAC) SirsiDynix; (Serials) SirsiDynix

Wireless access
Open Mon-Thurs 8-8, Fri 8-4:30

S MONROE COUNTY HISTORICAL MUSEUM*, 126 S Monroe St, 48161. SAN 327-439X. Tel: 734-240-7787, 734-240-7794. FAX: 734-240-7788. Web Site: www.co.monroe.mi.us/officials_and_departments/departments/museum. *Curator of Coll,* Caitlyn Riehle; E-mail: caitlyn_riehle@monroemi.org; Staff 1 (Non-MLS 1)
Library Holdings: Bk Vols 600
Subject Interests: County hist, Mich hist
Function: Archival coll
Open Mon-Sat 10-5, Sun 12-5
Restriction: Access at librarian's discretion

P MONROE COUNTY LIBRARY SYSTEM*, Mary K Daume Library Service Center, Administrative Offices, 840 S Roessler St, 48161. Tel: 734-241-5770. FAX: 734-241-4722. Web Site: monroe.lib.mi.us. *Dir,* Nancy Bellaire; E-mail: nancy.bellaire@monroe.lib.mi.us; Staff 24 (MLS 23, Non-MLS 1)
Founded 1934
Jan 2016-Dec 2016. Mats Exp $772,823, Books $451,675, Per/Ser (Incl. Access Fees) $57,838, AV Mat $125,846, Electronic Ref Mat (Incl. Access Fees) $137,464
Library Holdings: e-books 10,447; Bk Vols 419,472; Videos 42,019
Special Collections: General George A Custer Coll, bks, media, microfilm
Automation Activity & Vendor Info: (Acquisitions) Baker & Taylor; (Cataloging) Baker & Taylor; (Circulation) Innovative Interfaces, Inc - Sierra; (ILL) Mel Cat; (OPAC) Innovative Interfaces, Inc; (Serials) Baker & Taylor
Wireless access
Function: 24/7 Electronic res, Adult bk club, After school storytime, Archival coll, Art exhibits, Audiobks via web, AV serv, Bk club(s), Bks on CD, Children's prog, Computer training, Computers for patron use, Digital talking bks, Electronic databases & coll, Free DVD rentals, Genealogy discussion group, Govt ref serv, Holiday prog, Home delivery & serv to seniorr ctr & nursing homes, Homebound delivery serv, Homework prog, ILL available, Internet access, Magazines, Magnifiers for reading, Meeting rooms, Microfiche/film & reading machines, Movies, Museum passes, Music CDs, Online cat, Online ref, Outreach serv, OverDrive digital audio bks, Photocopying/Printing, Preschool outreach, Preschool reading prog, Prog for adults, Prog for children & young adult, Ref & res, Ref serv available, Res libr, Scanner, Senior computer classes, Senior outreach, Spanish lang bks, Spoken cassettes & CDs, Spoken cassettes & DVDs, Story hour, Study rm, Summer reading prog, Tax forms, Teen prog, Telephone ref, Wheelchair accessible
Mem of Woodlands Library Cooperative
Special Services for the Deaf - TDD equip
Special Services for the Blind - Large print bks
Restriction: Not open to pub
Friends of the Library Group
Branches: 16
BEDFORD BRANCH LIBRARY, 8575 Jackman Rd, Temperance, 48182, SAN 346-9387. Tel: 734-847-6747. FAX: 734-847-6591. *Commun Librn,* Jodi Russ
Subject Interests: Genealogy, Local hist
Open Mon-Thurs 9-9, Fri & Sat 9-5, Sun 12-5
Friends of the Library Group
BLUE BUSH BRANCH LIBRARY, 2210 Blue Bush Rd, 48162-9643, SAN 328-7505. Tel: 734-242-4085. FAX: 734-242-4085. *Commun Librn,* Jane Steed; *Br Tech,* Elizabeth Pifer
Founded 1986
Open Mon, Tues & Thurs 1-5, Wed 1-8, Fri 10-5, Sat 10-2
Friends of the Library Group
CARLETON BRANCH LIBRARY, 1444 Kent St, Carleton, 48117. (Mail add: PO Box 267, Carleton, 48117-0267), SAN 346-8992. Tel: 734-654-2180. FAX: 734-654-8767. *Commun Librn,* David Ross
Open Mon & Thurs 12-8, Tues & Wed 9-8, Fri & Sat 9-5
Friends of the Library Group
DORSCH MEMORIAL BRANCH LIBRARY, 18 E First St, 48161-2227, SAN 346-9026. Tel: 734-241-7878. FAX: 734-241-7879. *Commun Librn,* Amber Reed
Open Mon, Tues & Thurs 9-8, Wed & Fri 9-5
Friends of the Library Group
DUNDEE BRANCH, 144 E Main St, Dundee, 48131-1202, SAN 346-9050. Tel: 734-529-3310. FAX: 734-529-7415. *Commun Librn,* Jennifer Grudnoski
Founded 1934
Special Services for the Deaf - TDD equip
Open Mon & Wed 9-6, Tues & Thurs 10-8, Fri 9-5, Sat 10-2
Friends of the Library Group
ELLIS LIBRARY & REFERENCE CENTER, 3700 S Custer Rd, 48161-9716, SAN 346-9085. Tel: 734-241-5277. Toll Free Tel: 800-462-2050. FAX: 734-242-9037. *Libr Mgr,* Bill Reiser; *Ref Ctr Mgr,* Louis Komorowski
Special Services for the Deaf - TDD equip
Open Mon-Thurs 9-9, Fri & Sat 9-5, Sun 12-5
Friends of the Library Group
ERIE BRANCH, 2065 Erie Rd, Erie, 48133-9757, SAN 346-9115. Tel: 734-848-4420. *Commun Librn,* Shannen McMahon
Founded 1935
Open Mon 1-8, Tues, Thurs & Fri 1-5, Wed 9-5
Friends of the Library Group
FRENCHTOWN-DIXIE, 2881 Nadeau Rd, 48162-9355, SAN 346-914X. Tel: 734-289-1035. FAX: 734-289-3867. *Commun Librn,* Jane Steed
Open Mon & Tues 9-8, Wed, Fri & Sat 9-5, Thurs 12-8
Friends of the Library Group
IDA BRANCH, 3016 Lewis Ave, Ida, 48140. (Mail add: PO Box 56, Ida, 48140-0056), SAN 346-9174. Tel: 734-269-2191. FAX: 734-269-3315. *Commun Librn,* Suzanne Krueger
Founded 1934
Special Services for the Deaf - TDD equip
Open Mon 10-8, Tues 10-6, Wed-Fri 10-5, Sat 10-1
Friends of the Library Group
MAYBEE BRANCH, 9060 Raisin St, Maybee, 48159. (Mail add: PO Box 165, Maybee, 48159-0165), SAN 346-9239. Tel: 734-587-3680. FAX: 734-587-3680. *Br Tech,* Catherine Masson
Open Mon 12-8, Tues 12-5, Thurs 9-1, Fri 9-5, Sat 9-2
Friends of the Library Group
L S NAVARRE BRANCH, 1135 E Second St, 48161-1920, SAN 346-9263. Tel: 734-241-5577. FAX: 734-241-5577. *Commun Librn,* Amber Reed
Open Mon, Wed & Thurs 1-6, Tues 10-8, Fri & Sat 1-5
NEWPORT BRANCH, 8120 N Dixie Hwy, Newport, 48166. Tel: 734-586-2117. FAX: 734-586-1116. *Commun Librn,* David E Ross; *Br Tech,* Sue Young
Open Mon 12-6, Tues 10-8, Wed 10-6, Thurs 12-8, Fri 10-5, Sat 10-2
Friends of the Library Group
RASEY MEMORIAL, 4349 Oak St, Luna Pier, 48157-4572. (Mail add: PO Box 416, Luna Pier, 48157-0416), SAN 346-9204. Tel: 734-848-4572. FAX: 734-848-4572. *Commun Librn,* Shannen McMahon
Founded 1934
Special Services for the Deaf - TDD equip
Open Mon, Thurs & Sat 9-1, Tues & Wed 2-8, Fri 1-5
SOUTH ROCKWOOD BRANCH, 5676 Carleton Rockwood Rd, Ste C, South Rockwood, 48179. (Mail add: PO Box 47, South Rockwood, 48179-0047), SAN 346-9352. Tel: 734-379-3333. FAX: 734-479-7485. *Commun Librn,* David Ross; *Br Tech,* Kelli Venier
Open Mon 10-5, Tues & Thurs 1-6, Wed 1-8, Fri 1-5, Sat 9-1
Friends of the Library Group
SUMMERFIELD-PETERSBURG BRANCH, 60 E Center St, Petersburg, 49270. (Mail add: PO Box 567, Petersburg, 49270-0567), SAN 346-9328. Tel: 734-279-1025. FAX: 734-279-2328. *Commun Librn,* Ashley Liford
Founded 1934
Open Mon & Tues 10-7, Wed & Thurs 12-8, Fri 10-5, Sat 10-1
Friends of the Library Group
ROBERT A VIVIAN BRANCH, 2664 Vivian Rd, 48162-9212, SAN 346-9417. Tel: 734-241-1430. FAX: 734-241-1430. *Commun Librn,* Jane Steed; *Br Tech,* Diane Martel
Founded 1934
Open Mon & Wed 12-8, Thurs 9-2, Fri 12-5
Friends of the Library Group
Bookmobiles: 1

MORENCI

P STAIR PUBLIC LIBRARY*, 228 W Main St, 49256-1421. SAN 308-2822. Tel: 517-458-6510. E-mail: stairlibrary@gmail.com. Web Site: www.stairlib.org. *Dir,* Colleen Leddy; *Asst Dir,* Sheri Frost
Founded 1930. Pop 3,134; Circ 17,402
Library Holdings: Bk Vols 19,000; Per Subs 85
Automation Activity & Vendor Info: (Cataloging) Auto-Graphics, Inc; (Circulation) Auto-Graphics, Inc
Wireless access
Mem of Woodlands Library Cooperative
Open Mon & Wed 10-7, Tues, Thurs & Fri 1-5, Sat 9-1; Mon (June-Aug) 10-7, Tues, Thurs & Fri 1-5, Wed 10-5, Sat 9-1
Friends of the Library Group

MORLEY

P WALTON ERICKSON PUBLIC LIBRARY*, 4808 Northland Dr, 49336-9522. SAN 308-2830. Tel: 231-856-4298. FAX: 231-856-0307. *Dir,* Cory Taylor
Founded 1965. Pop 8,840; Circ 23,112
Library Holdings: Bk Titles 28,000; Per Subs 40
Wireless access
Partic in Mid-Michigan Library League
Open Mon & Wed 9-4:30, Tues 12:30-8, Thurs 9-8, Fri 9-12

MOUNT CLEMENS

S MACOMB COUNTY HISTORICAL SOCIETY, The Crocker House Museum Library, 15 Union St, 48043. SAN 328-560X. Tel: 586-465-2488. E-mail: info@crockerhousemuseum.org. Web Site: www.crockerhousemuseum.org. *Dir,* Position Currently Open
Founded 1869
Library Holdings: Bk Titles 2,500
Subject Interests: County hist, Local hist
Function: Res performed for a fee
Restriction: Non-circulating, Open by appt only

M MCLAREN MACOMB MEDICAL CENTER*, Stuck Medical Library, 1000 Harrington Blvd, 48043. SAN 308-2865. Tel: 586-493-8047. FAX: 586-493-8739. *Mgr,* Mary Carr; E-mail: Mary.Carr@mclaren.org; Staff 1 (MLS 1)
Founded 1957
Library Holdings: CDs 100; e-books 400; e-journals 6,000; Bk Titles 3,000; Spec Interest Per Sub 30
Subject Interests: Allied health, Health bus, Med, Nursing, Orthopedics
Automation Activity & Vendor Info: (Acquisitions) Ex Libris Group; (Cataloging) Ex Libris Group; (Circulation) Ex Libris Group; (Course Reserve) Ex Libris Group; (Discovery) Ex Libris Group; (ILL) Ex Libris Group; (OPAC) Ex Libris Group; (Serials) Ex Libris Group
Wireless access
Function: 24/7 Electronic res, 24/7 Online cat, Doc delivery serv, Electronic databases & coll, For res purposes, Health sci info serv, ILL available, Internet access, Online cat, Online ref, Photocopying/Printing, Prof lending libr, Ref & res, Res assist avail, Scanner
Partic in Detroit Area Library Network; Michigan Health Sciences Libraries Association
Open Mon-Fri 8-4:30
Restriction: Badge access after hrs, Circ limited, Circulates for staff only, Hospital employees & physicians only, In-house use for visitors, Lending to staff only, Limited access for the pub, Med & nursing staff, patients & families, Med staff & students, Non-circulating coll, Open to pub upon request, Open to staff, patients & family mem, Prof mat only, Restricted borrowing privileges, Restricted pub use, Staff & prof res

P MOUNT CLEMENS PUBLIC LIBRARY, 300 N Groesbeck Ave, 48043. SAN 308-2873. Tel: 586-469-6200. FAX: 586-469-6668. E-mail: askmcpl@libcoop.net. Web Site: www.mtclib.org. *Dir,* Brandon Bowman, Jr; E-mail: brandon.b.bowman@gmail.com; Staff 17 (MLS 7, Non-MLS 10)
Founded 1865. Pop 23,937; Circ 161,000
Library Holdings: Bk Vols 124,000; Per Subs 212
Special Collections: Local History & Genealogy (Michigan Coll) bks, doc, flm, pamphlets, per. Oral History
Automation Activity & Vendor Info: (Acquisitions) SirsiDynix; (Cataloging) SirsiDynix; (Circulation) SirsiDynix; (OPAC) SirsiDynix; (Serials) SirsiDynix
Wireless access
Function: 24/7 Electronic res, 24/7 Online cat, Archival coll, Audiobks via web, Bks on CD, Children's prog, Computers for patron use, Electronic databases & coll, Free DVD rentals, Genealogy discussion group, ILL available, Internet access, Magazines, Meeting rooms, Microfiche/film & reading machines, Museum passes, Music CDs, Online cat, Outside serv via phone, mail, e-mail & web, OverDrive digital audio bks, Prog for adults, Prog for children & young adult, Scanner, Story hour, Summer reading prog, Tax forms, Telephone ref, Wheelchair accessible
Publications: Library Online (Newsletter)
Partic in Suburban Library Cooperative
Open Mon-Thurs 10-8, Fri & Sat 10-5

MOUNT PLEASANT

C CENTRAL MICHIGAN UNIVERSITY*, Charles V Park Library, Park 407, 48859. (Mail add: 300 E Preston, 48859), SAN 308-2881. Tel: 989-774-3500. Circulation Tel: 989-774-3114. Interlibrary Loan Service Tel: 989-774-3022. Reference Tel: 989-774-3470. Automation Services Tel: 989-774-2338. FAX: 989-774-2179. Interlibrary Loan Service FAX: 989-774-4459. Reference FAX: 989-774-1350. Automation Services FAX: 989-774-2656. Web Site: www.lib.cmich.edu. *Dean of Libr,* Thomas J Moore; E-mail: thomas.j.moore@cmich.edu; *Assoc Dean of Libr,* Katherine M Irwin; Tel: 989-774-6421, E-mail: irwin1km@cmich.edu; *Dir, Coll Develop,* Matthew I Ismail; Tel: 989-774-2143, E-mail: ismai1md@cmich.edu; *Dir, Info Serv,* Timothy Peters; Tel: 989-774-3720, E-mail: peter1t@cmich.edu; *Head, Syst,* Daniel Ferrer; E-mail: daniel.ferrer@cmich.edu; *Head, Tech Serv,* Pamela Grudzien; Tel: 989-774-6488, E-mail: pamela.grudzien@cmich.edu; *Bus Mgr,* Bradley Stambaugh; Tel: 989-774-6415, E-mail: stamb1bb@cmich.edu; *Access Serv,* Diane Thomas; Tel: 989-774-2286, E-mail: diane.k.thomas@cmich.edu; Staff 67 (MLS 33, Non-MLS 34)
Founded 1892. Enrl 29,315; Fac 1,233; Highest Degree: Doctorate. Sal $3,546,345 (Prof $2,215,314)
Library Holdings: CDs 18,318; DVDs 3,262; e-books 18,917; e-journals 8,443; Microforms 1,358,172; Music Scores 7,440; Bk Titles 1,512,490; Per Subs 2,973; Videos 5,156
Special Collections: State Document Depository; US Document Depository
Automation Activity & Vendor Info: (Acquisitions) Innovative Interfaces, Inc; (Cataloging) Innovative Interfaces, Inc; (Circulation) Innovative Interfaces, Inc; (Course Reserve) Innovative Interfaces, Inc; (OPAC) Innovative Interfaces, Inc; (Serials) Innovative Interfaces, Inc
Wireless access
Function: Art exhibits, Computers for patron use, Distance learning, Doc delivery serv, E-Reserves, Electronic databases & coll, ILL available, Internet access, Music CDs, Online cat, Online ref, Orientations, Photocopying/Printing, Ref serv available, Scanner, Telephone ref, Wheelchair accessible
Publications: The Off-Campus Library Services Conference Proceedings
Partic in Midwest Collaborative for Library Services; OCLC Online Computer Library Center, Inc
Special Services for the Deaf - Assistive tech
Special Services for the Blind - Assistive/Adapted tech devices, equip & products
Open Mon-Thurs 7:50am-Midnight, Fri 7:50am-8pm, Sat 9-6, Sun Noon-Midnight
Friends of the Library Group
Departmental Libraries:
CLARKE HISTORICAL LIBRARY, 250 E Preston, 48859, SAN 323-8741. Tel: 989-774-3352. Reference Tel: 989-774-3864. FAX: 989-774-2160. E-mail: clarke@cmich.edu. Web Site: www.clarke.cmich.edu. *Dir,* Frank Boles; Tel: 989-774-3965, E-mail: frank.j.boles@cmich.edu; *Archivist,* Marian Matyn; Tel: 989-774-3990, E-mail: matyn1mj@cmich.edu; *Ref Librn,* John Fierst; Tel: 989-774-2601, E-mail: fiers1j@cmich.edu; Staff 3 (MLS 2, Non-MLS 1)
Founded 1954
Library Holdings: Microforms 11,000; Bk Titles 80,000
Special Collections: Africana & Afro-American (Wilbert Wright Coll); Aladdin Manufacturing Company Records; Angling (Reed T Draper Coll); Class of 1968 Presidential Campaign Biography Coll; Former US Senator & Michigan State Supreme Court Justice Robert P Griffin Papers; Literacy (Lucile Clarke Memorial Children's Library), fiction, textbks; Maureen Hathawy Michigan Culinary Archive, cookbks (M); Michigan Hemingway Coll; Molson Children's Art Coll; Russell Kirk Papers. State Document Depository
Subject Interests: African-Am, Am hist, Children's lit, Mich, Presidents (US)
Function: Archival coll, Electronic databases & coll, Ref serv available
Publications: Michigan Historical Review
Open Mon-Fri 8-5
Restriction: Closed stack, Internal use only, Non-circulating
Friends of the Library Group
KROMER INSTRUCTIONAL MATERIALS CENTER, 134 EHS Bldg, 48859, SAN 320-0531. Tel: 989-774-3549. *Interim Dir,* Mary Jo Davis

P CHIPPEWA RIVER DISTRICT LIBRARY*, Veterans Memorial Library, 301 S University Ave, 48858-2597. SAN 346-9476. Tel: 989-773-3242. FAX: 989-772-3280. Web Site: www.crdl.org. *Libr Dir,* Corey Friedrich; Tel: 989-773-3242, Ext 210, E-mail: cfriedri@crdl.org; *Mkt, Pub Relations Coordr,* Lisa McCartney; Tel: 989-773-3242, Ext 212, E-mail: lmccartney@crdl.org; *Syst Librn,* Arielle Hemingway; Tel: 989-773-3242, Ext 220, E-mail: ahemingway@crdl.org; *Cat,* Katrina Gormley; Tel: 989-773-3242, Ext 221, E-mail: kgormley@crdl.org; *Dir of Finance,* Kristin Ellison; Tel: 989-773-3242, Ext 226, E-mail: kellison@crdl.org; Staff 13 (MLS 6, Non-MLS 7)
Founded 1909. Pop 51,884; Circ 250,000
Library Holdings: Bk Titles 109,032; Bk Vols 160,918; Per Subs 300
Automation Activity & Vendor Info: (Acquisitions) TLC (The Library Corporation); (Cataloging) TLC (The Library Corporation); (Circulation) TLC (The Library Corporation); (OPAC) TLC (The Library Corporation); (Serials) TLC (The Library Corporation)
Wireless access
Function: 24/7 Electronic res, 24/7 Online cat, Adult bk club, Art exhibits, Audiobks via web, Bks on CD, Children's prog, Computer training, Computers for patron use, Electronic databases & coll, Free DVD rentals, Genealogy discussion group, ILL available, Internet access, Jazz prog, Life-long learning prog for all ages, Magazines, Mail & tel request accepted, Meeting rooms, Movies, Museum passes, Music CDs, Notary serv, Online cat, Online ref, OverDrive digital audio bks, Photocopying/Printing, Preschool outreach, Prog for adults, Prog for children & young adult, Ref serv available, Scanner, Story hour, Study rm, Summer reading prog, Tax forms, Teen prog, Telephone ref, Wheelchair accessible
Partic in Mideastern Michigan Library Cooperative; Midwest Collaborative for Library Services; OCLC Online Computer Library Center, Inc
Open Mon-Thurs 9-8, Fri & Sat 10-6, Sun (Sept-May) 1-5
Friends of the Library Group

Branches: 4
SHEPHERD COMMUNITY LIBRARY, 257 W Wright Ave, Shepherd, 48883, SAN 346-9506. Tel: 989-828-6801. FAX: 989-828-6801. *Br Mgr,* Tim Castillo; Staff 1 (Non-MLS 1)
Library Holdings: Bk Titles 14,225
Open Mon, Wed & Fri 10-6, Tues & Thurs 12-8, Sat 10-2
Friends of the Library Group
FREMONT TOWNSHIP COMMUNITY LIBRARY, 7959 South Winn Rd, Winn, 48896. (Mail add: PO Box 368, Winn, 48896-0368), SAN 346-9573. Tel: 989-866-2550. FAX: 989-866-2550. *Br Mgr,* Wes Umstead; E-mail: wumstead@crdl.org; Staff 1 (Non-MLS 1)
Library Holdings: Bk Titles 8,923
Open Mon 10-6, Tues & Wed 3-8, Thurs 12-8, Sun 12-4
FAITH JOHNSTON MEMORIAL, 4035 N Mission, Rosebush, 48878. (Mail add: PO Box 151, Rosebush, 48878-0235), SAN 325-4178. Tel: 989-433-0006. FAX: 989-433-0006. *Br Mgr,* Rebecca Bundy; E-mail: rbundy@crdl.org; Staff 1 (Non-MLS 1)
Library Holdings: Bk Titles 9,384
Open Mon, Wed & Fri 10-6, Tues & Thurs 12-8, Sun 1-5
Friends of the Library Group
TATE MEMORIAL LIBRARY, 324 Main St, Blanchard, 49310. (Mail add: PO Box 39, Blanchard, 49310-0039), SAN 346-9565. Tel: 989-561-2480. FAX: 989-561-2480. *Br Mgr,* Ken Newman; E-mail: knewman@crdl.org; Staff 1 (Non-MLS 1)
Library Holdings: Bk Titles 11,156
Open Tues & Wed 10-6, Thurs 2-8, Fri 1-5, Sat 10-2

MULLIKEN

P MULLIKEN DISTRICT LIBRARY*, 135 Main St, 48861. (Mail add: PO Box 246, 48861-0246), SAN 308-292X. Tel: 517-649-8611. FAX: 517-649-2207. E-mail: mulldistlib@gmail.com. Web Site: www.mullikendistrictlibrary.org. *Dir,* Dawn Hufnagel; Staff 3 (Non-MLS 3)
Founded 1903. Pop 1,903; Circ 23,385
Library Holdings: Bk Titles 13,668; Bk Vols 15,638; Per Subs 30
Automation Activity & Vendor Info: (Cataloging) Follett Software; (Circulation) Follett Software
Mem of Woodlands Library Cooperative
Open Mon & Fri 1-6, Tues & Thurs 3-8

MUNISING

S MICHIGAN DEPARTMENT OF CORRECTIONS*, Alger Correctional Facility Library, N6141 Industrial Park Dr, 49862. SAN 371-6759. Tel: 906-387-5000. *Librn,* Patricia Supnick; Staff 1 (MLS 1)
Founded 1990
Library Holdings: Bk Vols 8,200
Special Collections: ABE, preGED & GED Prepatory Materials; Native American, African-American & Hispanic History
Subject Interests: Law
Restriction: Staff & inmates only

MUSKEGON

C BAKER COLLEGE OF MUSKEGON LIBRARY*, Academic Resource Center, 1903 Marquette Ave, 49442-3404. SAN 308-2970. Tel: 231-777-5330. Reference Tel: 231-777-5333, 231-777-5335. Toll Free Tel: 800-937-0337. FAX: 231-777-5334. E-mail: library-mu@baker.edu. Web Site: www.baker.edu. Staff 1 (Non-MLS 1)
Founded 1883. Enrl 4,000; Fac 270; Highest Degree: Doctorate
Library Holdings: Bk Vols 35,000; Per Subs 125
Automation Activity & Vendor Info: (Cataloging) Koha; (Circulation) Koha; (Course Reserve) Koha; (Discovery) EBSCO Discovery Service; (ILL) OCLC; (OPAC) Koha; (Serials) EBSCO Online
Wireless access
Partic in Midwest Collaborative for Library Services; PALnet
Special Services for the Deaf - Accessible learning ctr; ADA equip; Assisted listening device; Assistive tech; Bks on deafness & sign lang; Closed caption videos; Coll on deaf educ; Deaf publ
Special Services for the Blind - Accessible computers; Assistive/Adapted tech devices, equip & products; Audio mat; Bks on CD; Magnifiers

P HACKLEY PUBLIC LIBRARY*, 316 W Webster Ave, 49440. SAN 308-2962. Tel: 231-722-8000. Reference Tel: 231-722-8011. FAX: 231-726-5567. E-mail: askus@hackleylibrary.org. Web Site: www.hackleylibrary.org. *Dir,* Joe Zappacosta; Tel: 231-722-8003, E-mail: jzappacosta@hackleylibrary.org; *Asst Dir,* Mary Murphy; Tel: 231-722-8004, E-mail: mmurphy@hackleylibrary.org; *Youth Serv Librn,* Lydia Schmidt; Tel: 231-722-8013, E-mail: ldaniels@hackleylibrary.org; *Circ Mgr,* Dorothy Johnson; Tel: 231-722-8024, E-mail: djohnson@hackleylibrary.org; *Ref Serv, Ad, Website Mgr,* Jocelyn Shaw; Tel: 231-722-8005, E-mail: jshaw@hackleylibrary.org; *Technology Spec,* Adam Skodack; Tel: 231-722-8006, E-mail: askodack@hackleylibrary.org; Staff 5.5 (MLS 5.5)
Founded 1890. Pop 40,898; Circ 170,880
Jul 2012-Jun 2013 Income $1,784,569, State $18,281, Locally Generated Income $1,766,288. Mats Exp $123,423, Books $80,658, Per/Ser (Incl. Access Fees) $9,898, Micro $4,238, AV Mat $26,394, Electronic Ref Mat (Incl. Access Fees) $2,235. Sal $934,037 (Prof $205,506)
Library Holdings: CDs 5,898; DVDs 5,478; e-books 3,009; Bk Vols 128,514; Per Subs 169
Special Collections: US Document Depository
Subject Interests: Civil War, Genealogy, Lumbering, Regional hist
Automation Activity & Vendor Info: (Cataloging) OCLC; (Circulation) Innovative Interfaces, Inc; (ILL) Innovative Interfaces, Inc; (OPAC) Innovative Interfaces, Inc; (Serials) Innovative Interfaces, Inc
Wireless access
Publications: Community Ink (Quarterly)
Partic in Lakeland Library Cooperative; Midwest Collaborative for Library Services
Open Mon & Tues 12-8, Wed-Sat 10-5
Friends of the Library Group

S LAKESHORE MUSEUM CENTER ARCHIVES*, 430 W Clay Ave, 49440-1002. SAN 372-8013. Tel: 231-722-0278. FAX: 231-728-4119. E-mail: info@lakeshoremuseum.org. Web Site: www.lakeshoremuseum.org. *Archivist,* Jeff Bessinger; E-mail: jeff@lakeshoremuseum.org. Subject Specialists: *Muskegon County,* Jeff Bessinger
Founded 1937
Library Holdings: Bk Titles 1,728; Bk Vols 2,230; Per Subs 10; Spec Interest Per Sub 10
Special Collections: Lumbering (Charles Yates Coll), photogs; Muskegon County History, bks, ms, photogs. Oral History
Subject Interests: Local hist
Function: Archival coll
Restriction: Open by appt only

S MICHIGAN DEPARTMENT OF CORRECTIONS, Muskegon Correctional Facility Library, 2400 S Sheridan Dr, 49442. Tel: 231-773-3201, Ext 2271. FAX: 231-773-3657. *Librn,* Elisia Hardiman; E-mail: hardimane@michigan.gov
Library Holdings: Bk Vols 13,000; Per Subs 20
Open Mon, Fri & Sat 7:30-4, Tues-Thurs 7:30am-9pm, Sun 12-9

P MUSKEGON AREA DISTRICT LIBRARY*, 4845 Airline Rd, Unit 5, 49444-4503. SAN 346-959X. Tel: 231-737-6248. FAX: 231-737-6307. Web Site: www.madl.org. *Dir,* Kelly Richards; E-mail: krichards@madl.org; *Dir of Finance,* Brenda Hall; Staff 33 (MLS 9, Non-MLS 24)
Pop 119,450; Circ 600,908
Special Collections: Blind & Physically Handicapped Library
Automation Activity & Vendor Info: (Cataloging) Innovative Interfaces, Inc; (Circulation) Innovative Interfaces, Inc; (ILL) Innovative Interfaces, Inc; (OPAC) Innovative Interfaces, Inc
Wireless access
Function: 24/7 Electronic res, 24/7 Online cat, Activity rm, Adult bk club, Audiobks on Playaways & MP3, Audiobks via web
Partic in Lakeland Library Cooperative
Special Services for the Deaf - TDD equip
Special Services for the Blind - Aids for in-house use; Audio mat; Bks & mags in Braille, on rec, tape & cassette; Bks available with recordings; Bks on CD; Braille equip; Children's Braille; Closed circuit TV; Descriptive video serv (DVS); Reader equip
Open Mon-Fri 8-5
Friends of the Library Group
Branches: 10
P BLIND & PHYSICALLY HANDICAPPED LIBRARY, 4845 Airline Rd, Unit 5, 49444. Tel: 231-737-6310. Toll Free Tel: 877-569-4801. FAX: 231-737-6307. *Librn,* Sarah Mahoney; E-mail: smahoney@madl.org
Founded 1979
Special Services for the Deaf - TDD equip
Special Services for the Blind - Bks on cassette; Descriptive video serv (DVS)
Open Mon-Fri 9-5
DALTON BRANCH, 3175 Fifth St, Twin Lake, 49457-9501, SAN 346-9654. Tel: 231-828-4188. E-mail: dal@madl.org. *Team Leader,* Rachel Church
Circ 32,512
Library Holdings: Audiobooks 2,202; CDs 295; DVDs 625; e-books 5,612; Bk Vols 13,752; Per Subs 781
Open Mon & Wed 9-7, Tues, Thurs & Fri 9-5, Sat 9-12
EGELSTON BRANCH, 5428 E Apple Ave, 49442-3008, SAN 346-9689. Tel: 231-788-6477. E-mail: ege@madl.org. *Librn,* Andrew Hammond; Staff 1 (MLS 1)
Circ 75,849
Library Holdings: Audiobooks 2,422; CDs 790; DVDs 3,533; e-books 5,612; Bk Vols 22,163; Per Subs 1,018
Special Services for the Deaf - TDD equip
Open Mon-Wed 9:30-8, Thurs-Sat 9:30-5

HOLTON BRANCH, 8776 Holton Duck Lake Rd, Holton, 49425, SAN 346-9743. Tel: 231-821-0268. E-mail: hlt@madl.org. *Lead Librn,* Heidi Gatzke
Circ 15,161
Library Holdings: Audiobooks 2,197; CDs 306; DVDs 644; e-books 5,611; Bk Vols 9,758; Per Subs 899
Open Mon-Wed 10:30-7, Fri 10:30-5, Sat 9-12
Friends of the Library Group

MONTAGUE BRANCH, 8778 Ferry St, Montague, 49437-1233, SAN 346-9778. Tel: 231-893-2675. E-mail: mon@madl.org. *Lead Librn,* Heidi Gatzke
Circ 27,156
Library Holdings: Audiobooks 2,211; CDs 287; DVDs 647; e-books 5,611; Bk Vols 20,085; Per Subs 1,019
Special Services for the Deaf - TDD equip
Open Mon-Wed 9:30-7, Thurs 12-5, Fri 9:30-5, Sat 9-1
Friends of the Library Group

MUSKEGON HEIGHTS BRANCH, 2808 Sanford St, Muskegon Heights, 49444-2010, SAN 346-9808. Tel: 231-739-6075. E-mail: muh@madl.org. *Team Leader,* Jonathan Blocher
Circ 17,319
Library Holdings: Audiobooks 2,201; CDs 297; DVDs 651; e-books 5,611; Bk Vols 16,154; Per Subs 821
Special Services for the Deaf - TDD equip
Open Mon-Fri 10-6, Sat 10-3
Friends of the Library Group

MUSKEGON TOWNSHIP BRANCH, 1765 Ada Ave, 49442. Tel: 231-760-4329. E-mail: mcb@madl.org. *Lead Librn,* Kathryn Ames
Circ 19,568
Library Holdings: Audiobooks 2,199; CDs 291; DVDs 633; e-books 5,612; Bk Vols 11,669; Per Subs 1,115
Open Mon-Wed 10:30-7, Fri 10:30-5, Sat 9-Noon

NORTH MUSKEGON WALKER BRANCH, 1522 Ruddiman Dr, North Muskegon, 49445-3038, SAN 346-9891. Tel: 231-744-6080. E-mail: nmu@madl.org. *Librn,* Holly Pelkey; Staff 1 (MLS 1)
Circ 85,154
Library Holdings: Audiobooks 2,590; CDs 385; DVDs 1,796; e-books 5,611; Bk Vols 30,048; Per Subs 759
Special Services for the Deaf - TDD equip
Open Mon-Wed 9:30-8, Thurs-Sat 9:30-5
Friends of the Library Group

NORTON SHORES BRANCH, 705 Seminole Rd, 49441-4797, SAN 346-9832. Tel: 231-780-8844. FAX: 231-780-5436. E-mail: nor@madl.org. *Librn,* Alison Purgiel; *Youth Serv Librn,* Gillian Streeter; Staff 2 (MLS 2)
Founded 1974. Circ 211,801
Library Holdings: Audiobooks 3,843; CDs 723; DVDs 3,250; e-books 5,611; Bk Vols 50,837; Per Subs 1,595
Open Mon-Wed 9-8, Thurs-Sat 9-5
Friends of the Library Group

RAVENNA BRANCH, 12278 Stafford, Ravenna, 49451-9410, SAN 346-9867. Tel: 231-853-6975. E-mail: rav@madl.org. *Lead Librn,* Katie Ames
Circ 37,006
Library Holdings: Audiobooks 2,377; CDs 304; DVDs 628; e-books 5,611; Bk Vols 19,814; Per Subs 1,245
Special Services for the Deaf - TDD equip
Open Mon-Wed 9:30-7, Thurs 12-5, Fri 9:30-5, Sat 9-1
Friends of the Library Group

J MUSKEGON COMMUNITY COLLEGE*, Hendrik Meijer Library, 221 S Quarterline Rd, 49442. SAN 308-2989. Tel: 231-777-0269. Circulation Tel: 231-777-0270. Interlibrary Loan Service Tel: 231-777-0205. Reference Tel: 231-777-0326. Automation Services Tel: 231-777-0416. Toll Free Tel: 866-711-4622. FAX: 231-777-0279. TDD: 231-777-0410. Web Site: www.muskegoncc.edu/library. *Adjunct Librn,* Lisa Anderson; Tel: 231-777-0274, E-mail: lisa.anderson@muskegoncc.edu; *Adjunct Ref Librn,* Darlene DeHudy; E-mail: darlene.dehudy@muskegoncc.edu; *Coordr, Ref Librn,* Carol Briggs-Erickson; E-mail: carol.briggs-erickson@muskegoncc.edu; *Ref Librn,* Charlotte Griffith; Tel: 231-777-0260; *Cataloger, Ref Librn,* Robert J Vanderlaan; Tel: 231-777-0267; Staff 7 (MLS 7)
Founded 1926. Enrl 5,000; Fac 105; Highest Degree: Associate
Library Holdings: CDs 472; DVDs 817; e-books 170,000; e-journals 19,000; Bk Titles 55,000; Bk Vols 62,000; Per Subs 150; Videos 1,250
Subject Interests: Careers, Children's lit
Automation Activity & Vendor Info: (Cataloging) OCLC; (Circulation) SirsiDynix; (OPAC) SirsiDynix
Wireless access
Partic in Midwest Collaborative for Library Services; OCLC Online Computer Library Center, Inc
Special Services for the Blind - Computer with voice synthesizer for visually impaired persons
Open Mon-Thurs (Fall & Winter) 7:30am-9pm, Fri 7:30-4:30, Sun 1-6

NASHVILLE

P PUTNAM DISTRICT LIBRARY, 327 N Main St, 49073-9578. (Mail add: PO Box 920, 49073-0920), SAN 308-2997. Tel: 517-852-9723. FAX: 517-852-9723. Web Site: www.putnamlib.org. *Dir,* Savannah Shilton; E-mail: SShilton@putnamlib.org; Staff 2 (Non-MLS 2)
Founded 1923
Subject Interests: Local hist
Automation Activity & Vendor Info: (Acquisitions) Follett Software; (Cataloging) Follett Software; (Circulation) Follett Software; (ILL) Mel Cat; (OPAC) Mel Cat
Wireless access
Mem of Woodlands Library Cooperative
Open Mon, Wed & Fri 10-6, Tues & Thurs 3-8, Sat 10-1

NEGAUNEE

P NEGAUNEE PUBLIC LIBRARY, 319 W Case St, 49866. (Mail add: PO Box 548, 49866-0548), SAN 308-3012. Tel: 906-475-7700, Ext 18. FAX: 906-475-4880. Web Site: cityofnegaunee.com/government/city-directory/negaunee-public-library. *Dir,* Jessica Holman; E-mail: jdholman@uproc.lib.mi.us
Founded 1890. Pop 7,656; Circ 40,190
Library Holdings: Audiobooks 737; CDs 212; DVDs 258; e-books 3,783; Large Print Bks 154; Bk Vols 31,209; Per Subs 20
Wireless access
Function: 24/7 Electronic res, 24/7 Online cat, Bks on CD, Children's prog, Computers for patron use, E-Reserves, Electronic databases & coll, Family literacy, Free DVD rentals, ILL available, Instruction & testing, Internet access, Magazines, Meeting rooms, Microfiche/film & reading machines, Online cat, OverDrive digital audio bks, Preschool outreach, Ref serv available, Story hour, Summer reading prog, Telephone ref, Wheelchair accessible, Writing prog
Partic in Superiorland Library Cooperative; Upper Peninsula Region of Library Cooperation, Inc
Open Mon-Wed 10-7, Thurs 10-6, Fri 10-5, Sat 9-12
Friends of the Library Group

NEW BALTIMORE

P MACDONALD PUBLIC LIBRARY*, 36480 Main St, 48047-2509. SAN 308-3020. Tel: 586-725-0273. FAX: 586-725-8360. E-mail: goikea@libcoop.net. Web Site: www.macdonaldlibrary.org. *Dir,* Margaret A Thomas; E-mail: thomasm@libcoop.net; *Asst Dir,* Annette Goike; E-mail: goikea@libcoop.net; *Ad,* Mary Jo Beranek; E-mail: beranekm@libcoop.net; *Ch,* Kelly Marra; E-mail: marrak@libcoop.net; Staff 11 (MLS 4, Non-MLS 7)
Founded 1941
Library Holdings: CDs 450; DVDs 800; Bk Vols 42,000; Per Subs 130; Talking Bks 1,200; Videos 1,450
Automation Activity & Vendor Info: (Cataloging) SirsiDynix; (Circulation) SirsiDynix; (ILL) SirsiDynix; (OPAC) SirsiDynix; (Serials) SirsiDynix
Wireless access
Function: 24/7 Electronic res, 24/7 Online cat, Adult bk club, Bks on CD, Children's prog, Computers for patron use, Electronic databases & coll, Free DVD rentals, Home delivery & serv to seniorr ctr & nursing homes, ILL available, Internet access, Magazines, Magnifiers for reading, Meeting rooms, Museum passes, Music CDs, Online cat, OverDrive digital audio bks, Photocopying/Printing, Preschool reading prog, Prog for children & young adult, Ref serv available, Study rm, Summer & winter reading prog, Tax forms, Telephone ref, Wheelchair accessible
Partic in Suburban Library Cooperative
Open Mon-Thurs 10-8, Fri 10-5, Sat 10-4
Friends of the Library Group

NEW BUFFALO

P NEW BUFFALO TOWNSHIP PUBLIC LIBRARY*, 33 N Thompson St, 49117. SAN 308-3039. Tel: 269-469-2933. FAX: 269-469-3521. E-mail: nbtlstaff@gmail.com. Web Site: www.newbuffalotownshiplibrary.org. *Dir,* Julie Grynwich; E-mail: nblibrary@comcast.net; *Asst Dir,* Courtney Kliss; E-mail: nbtlcreate@gmail.com
Founded 1938
Library Holdings: Bk Vols 50,000; Per Subs 112
Subject Interests: Local hist, Mich
Automation Activity & Vendor Info: (Cataloging) Follett Software; (Circulation) Follett Software
Wireless access
Partic in Southwest Michigan Library Cooperative
Open Mon, Tues & Thurs 10-8, Wed & Fri 10-5:30, Sat 10-4
Friends of the Library Group

NEW HAVEN

P LENOX TOWNSHIP LIBRARY, 58976 Main St, 48048-2685. SAN 308-3047. Tel: 586-749-3430. FAX: 586-749-3245. E-mail: lenstaff@libcoop.net. Web Site: www.lenoxlibrary.org. *Dir,* Beth Bogaert; E-mail: bogaertb@libcoop.net; *Syst Mgr,* Lynn Couck; E-mail: coucklm@libcoop.net; Staff 2 (MLS 1, Non-MLS 1)
Founded 1948. Pop 8,433; Circ 19,450
Library Holdings: Bk Vols 20,000; Per Subs 51
Automation Activity & Vendor Info: (Acquisitions) SirsiDynix; (Cataloging) SirsiDynix; (Circulation) SirsiDynix; (OPAC) SirsiDynix; (Serials) SirsiDynix
Wireless access
Partic in Suburban Library Cooperative
Open Mon-Thurs 10-8, Fri 10-5, Sat (Sept-May) 10-4

NEWAYGO

P NEWAYGO AREA DISTRICT LIBRARY*, 44 N State Rd, 49337-8969. SAN 308-3063. Tel: 231-652-6723. FAX: 231-652-6616. E-mail: new@llcoop.org. Web Site: www.newaygolibrary.org. *Libr Dir,* Kelly Tinkham; E-mail: newkt@llcoop.org; *Youth Serv Librn,* Carly Abbott
Founded 1914. Pop 10,268
Wireless access
Partic in Lakeland Library Cooperative
Special Services for the Blind - Talking bks
Open Mon-Fri 10-6, Sat 10-1
Friends of the Library Group

NEWBERRY

S NEWBERRY CORRECTIONAL FACILITY LIBRARY*, 13747 E County Rd 428, 49868. SAN 377-161X. Tel: 906-293-6200. FAX: 906-293-6323. *Librn,* Pat Supnick; Staff 1 (MLS 1)
Founded 1995
Library Holdings: High Interest/Low Vocabulary Bk Vols 150; Bk Vols 7,200; Per Subs 31
Restriction: Residents only

§P TAHQUAMENON AREA LIBRARY, 700 Newberry Ave, 49868. Tel: 906-293-5214. E-mail: tahquamcirc@gmail.com. Web Site: facebook.com/tahquamenonlibrary. *Dir,* Brian Freitag; E-mail: tqdirector@tahquamlibrary.org
Library Holdings: Audiobooks 500; DVDs 800; Bk Vols 28,000
Wireless access
Function: Computers for patron use, Scanner
Partic in Upper Peninsula Region of Library Cooperation, Inc
Open Mon & Wed 8:30-6:30, Tues & Fri 8:30-5, Thurs 8:15-7
Friends of the Library Group

NILES

M LAKELAND HOSPITAL-NILES*, Health Sciences Library, 31 N St Joseph Ave, 49120. Tel: 269-683-5510. Web Site: www.lakelandhealth.org. *Librn,* Michael Dill
Library Holdings: Bk Vols 200; Per Subs 85
Restriction: Staff use only

P NILES DISTRICT LIBRARY*, 620 E Main St, 49120. SAN 308-308X. Tel: 269-683-8545. FAX: 269-683-0075. E-mail: info@nileslibrary.net. Web Site: www.nileslibrary.com. *Dir,* Nancy Studebaker-Barringer; Tel: 269-683-8545, Ext 122, E-mail: director@nileslibrary.net; *Asst Dir,* Stevyn Compoe; Tel: 269-683-8545, Ext 105, E-mail: adminassist@nileslibrary.net; *Head, Adult Serv,* Laura Hollister; Tel: 269-683-8545, Ext 117, E-mail: laura.hollister@nileslibrary.net; *Head, Cat & Circ,* Deb Solloway; Tel: 269-683-8545, Ext 101, E-mail: circulation@nileslibrary.net; *Head, Youth Serv,* Tara Hunsberger; Tel: 269-683-8545, Ext 109, E-mail: youthservices@nileslibrary.net; Staff 21 (MLS 3, Non-MLS 18)
Founded 1903. Pop 25,565; Circ 135,443
Library Holdings: Bk Vols 126,764; Per Subs 250
Special Collections: Niles Newspapers, 1834 to date, microflm; Ring Lardner (Complete Works). Oral History
Automation Activity & Vendor Info: (Cataloging) Evergreen; (Circulation) Evergreen; (OPAC) Evergreen; (Serials) EBSCO Online
Wireless access
Partic in Southwest Michigan Library Cooperative
Open Mon-Thurs 9-8, Fri & Sat 10-6
Friends of the Library Group

NORTH ADAMS

P NORTH ADAMS COMMUNITY MEMORIAL LIBRARY*, 110 E Main St, 49262. (Mail add: PO Box 248, 49262-0248). Tel: 517-287-4426. E-mail: northadamslibrarian@gmail.com. Web Site: www.northadamscml.michlibrary.org. *Dir,* Phyllis J Rickard; *Ch Serv, Libr Asst,* Kristen Finnegan; Staff 2 (Non-MLS 2)
Founded 1921. Pop 4,469
Library Holdings: DVDs 181; Large Print Bks 300; Bk Vols 17,000; Per Subs 30; Talking Bks 39
Special Collections: Local History (North Adams-Jerome High School yearbooks)
Automation Activity & Vendor Info: (Cataloging) Auto-Graphics, Inc; (Circulation) Auto-Graphics, Inc; (ILL) Mel Cat; (OPAC) Auto-Graphics, Inc
Wireless access
Function: Adult bk club, Archival coll, Audiobks via web, Children's prog, Computers for patron use, Free DVD rentals, Holiday prog, ILL available, Internet access, Magazines, Mango lang, Movies, Museum passes, Online cat, OverDrive digital audio bks, Photocopying/Printing, Preschool reading prog, Printer for laptops & handheld devices, Prog for children & young adult, Ref serv available, Scanner, Story hour, Summer reading prog, Tax forms, Telephone ref, Wheelchair accessible
Mem of Woodlands Library Cooperative
Open Tues 12-7, Wed 11-7, Thurs & Fri 11-5, Sat 9-12
Restriction: In-house use for visitors

NORTH BRANCH

P NORTH BRANCH TOWNSHIP LIBRARY, 3714 Huron St, 48461-8117. (Mail add: PO Box 705, 48461-0705), SAN 308-3101. Tel: 810-688-2282. FAX: 810-688-3165. E-mail: northbranchlibrary@northbranchlibrary.net. Web Site: northbranch.ploud.net. *Dir,* Kelli Lovasz
Pop 9,124; Circ 38,523
Library Holdings: AV Mats 2,547; Bk Titles 30,000; Per Subs 67; Videos 1,047
Partic in Mideastern Michigan Library Cooperative
Open Mon & Fri 9-5:30, Tues-Thurs 9-8, Sat 9-2

NORTHPORT

P LEELANAU TOWNSHIP PUBLIC LIBRARY, 119 E Nagonaba St, 49670. (Mail add: PO Box 235, 49670-0235), SAN 308-311X. Tel: 231-386-5131. Web Site: www.leelanautownshiplibrary.org.
Founded 1856. Pop 3,000; Circ 30,000
Library Holdings: AV Mats 2,000; CDs 1,800; Large Print Bks 700; Bk Titles 17,000; Bk Vols 20,000; Per Subs 46; Talking Bks 500
Special Collections: US Constitution Coll
Subject Interests: Local hist
Wireless access
Function: ILL available, Internet access, Photocopying/Printing, Prog for adults, Prog for children & young adult, Ref serv available, Summer reading prog, Telephone ref, Wheelchair accessible
Publications: Library Report (Newsletter)
Partic in Mid-Michigan Library League
Open Tues, Thurs & Fri 9:30-5, Wed 3-8, Sat 9:30-1
Friends of the Library Group

NORTHVILLE

P NORTHVILLE DISTRICT LIBRARY, 212 W Cady St, 48167. SAN 308-3136. Tel: 248-349-3020. FAX: 248-349-8250. Web Site: northvillelibrary.org. *Libr Dir,* Laura Mancini; Tel: 248-349-3020, Ext 206, E-mail: lmancini@northvillelibrary.org; Staff 13 (MLS 13)
Founded 1889. Pop 34,467; Circ 255,185
Library Holdings: Large Print Bks 800; Bk Titles 96,000; Per Subs 214
Subject Interests: Local hist
Automation Activity & Vendor Info: (Cataloging) TLC (The Library Corporation); (Circulation) TLC (The Library Corporation); (OPAC) TLC (The Library Corporation); (Serials) TLC (The Library Corporation)
Wireless access
Function: Home delivery & serv to seniorr ctr & nursing homes, Homebound delivery serv, ILL available, Internet access, Large print keyboards, Magnifiers for reading, Photocopying/Printing, Prog for adults, Prog for children & young adult, Ref serv available, Summer reading prog, Wheelchair accessible
Partic in The Library Network
Open Mon-Thurs 10-9, Fri & Sat 10-5, Sun (Sept-May) 1-5
Friends of the Library Group

NOVI

P NOVI PUBLIC LIBRARY*, 45255 W Ten Mile Rd, 48375. SAN 308-3152. Tel: 248-349-0720. Web Site: www.novilibrary.org. *Dir,* Julie Farkas; E-mail: jfarkas@novilibrary.org; *Head, Info Serv,* April Stevenson; E-mail: astevenson@novilibrary.org; *Head, Info Tech,* Barb Rutkowski; E-mail: brutkowski@novilibrary.org; *Head, Support Serv,* Maryann Zurmuehlen; E-mail: mzurmuehlen@novilibrary.org; Staff 59 (MLS 17, Non-MLS 42)
Founded 1960
Automation Activity & Vendor Info: (Acquisitions) CARL.Solution (TLC); (Cataloging) CARL.Solution (TLC); (Circulation) CARL.Solution (TLC); (ILL) CARL.Solution (TLC); (OPAC) CARL.Solution (TLC)

Wireless access
Function: 24/7 Electronic res, 24/7 Online cat, 3D Printer, Activity rm, Adult bk club, After school storytime, Archival coll, Art exhibits, Art programs, Audiobks via web, AV serv, Bk club(s), Bk reviews (Group), Bks on CD, Chess club, Children's prog, Computer training, Computers for patron use, Digital talking bks, Distance learning, Electronic databases & coll, Family literacy, Free DVD rentals, Home delivery & serv to seniorr ctr & nursing homes, Homework prog, ILL available, Internet access, Laminating, Large print keyboards, Life-long learning prog for all ages, Magazines, Magnifiers for reading, Mail & tel request accepted, Makerspace, Meeting rooms, Microfiche/film & reading machines, Movies, Museum passes, Music CDs, Online ref, Outreach serv, Photocopying/Printing, Preschool outreach, Prog for adults, Prog for children & young adult, Ref serv available, Res assist avail, Res performed for a fee, Scanner, Senior computer classes, Senior outreach, Serves people with intellectual disabilities, Spanish lang bks, Spoken cassettes & CDs, STEM programs, Story hour, Study rm, Summer & winter reading prog, Summer reading prog, Tax forms, Teen prog, Telephone ref, Wheelchair accessible, Winter reading prog, Writing prog
Partic in The Library Network
Special Services for the Deaf - Assistive tech; Bks on deafness & sign lang; Closed caption videos; High interest/low vocabulary bks; Sign lang interpreter upon request for prog; TDD equip
Special Services for the Blind - Accessible computers; Assistive/Adapted tech devices, equip & products; BiFolkal kits; Bks available with recordings; Bks on cassette; Bks on CD; Closed circuit TV magnifier; Computer with voice synthesizer for visually impaired persons; Copier with enlargement capabilities; Extensive large print coll; Home delivery serv; Low vision equip; Magnifiers
Open Mon-Thurs 10-9, Fri & Sat 10-6, Sun 12-6
Friends of the Library Group

OAK PARK

R CONGREGATION BETH SHALOM, Rabbi Mordecai S Halpern Memorial Library, 14601 W Lincoln Rd, 48237-1391. SAN 308-3160. Tel: 248-547-7970. FAX: 248-547-0421. E-mail: info@congbethshalom.org. Web Site: www.congbethshalom.org.
Founded 1953
Library Holdings: Bk Vols 8,000
Subject Interests: Judaica (lit or hist of Jews)
Wireless access

P OAK PARK PUBLIC LIBRARY*, 14200 Oak Park Blvd, 48237-2089. SAN 308-3209. Tel: 248-691-7480. FAX: 248-691-7155. E-mail: Library@OakParkMI.gov. Web Site: www.oakparkmi.gov/departments/library. *Dir,* Sarah Jones; E-mail: sjones@oakparkmi.gov; Staff 10.5 (MLS 5, Non-MLS 5.5)
Founded 1957. Pop 32,493; Circ 131,377
Library Holdings: High Interest/Low Vocabulary Bk Vols 300; Bk Vols 97,530; Per Subs 185; Spec Interest Per Sub 9
Subject Interests: Arabic lang, Judaica (lit or hist of Jews), Russian (Lang)
Automation Activity & Vendor Info: (Acquisitions) SirsiDynix; (Cataloging) SirsiDynix; (Circulation) SirsiDynix; (ILL) SirsiDynix; (OPAC) SirsiDynix; (Serials) SirsiDynix
Wireless access
Special Services for the Deaf - TDD equip
Open Mon-Thurs 10-8, Fri Noon-6
Friends of the Library Group

OLIVET

C OLIVET COLLEGE LIBRARY, Burrage Library, 320 S Main St, 49076-9730. SAN 346-9921. Tel: 269-749-7608. FAX: 269-749-7121. Web Site: www.olivetcollege.edu/campus/burrage-library. *Dir,* Judy M Fales; Tel: 269-749-7595, E-mail: jfales@olivetcollege.edu; Staff 1 (MLS 1)
Founded 1844. Enrl 850; Fac 48; Highest Degree: Master
Library Holdings: Bk Titles 60,918; Bk Vols 68,811; Per Subs 180
Automation Activity & Vendor Info: (Acquisitions) Civica; (Cataloging) Civica; (Circulation) Civica; (ILL) OCLC; (OPAC) Civica
Wireless access
Function: Computers for patron use, Doc delivery serv, Electronic databases & coll, Free DVD rentals, Magazines, Meeting rooms, Movies, Online cat, Online ref, Scanner, Spanish lang bks, Study rm, Wheelchair accessible
Partic in OCLC Online Computer Library Center, Inc
Open Mon-Thurs 7:30-11, Fri 7:30-5, Sun 2-11; Mon-Fri 8:30-4 (Summer)
Restriction: Authorized patrons, Borrowing requests are handled by ILL, ID required to use computers (Ltd hrs), Limited access for the pub, Open to students, fac & staff, Open to students, fac, staff & alumni

ONTONAGON

P ONTONAGON TOWNSHIP LIBRARY*, 311 N Steel St, 49953-1398. SAN 308-3233. Tel: 906-884-4411. FAX: 906-884-2829. E-mail: OntLibrary@OntonagonLibrary.org. Web Site: joomla.uproc.lib.mi.us/ontonagon2. *Libr Dir,* Leo Siren; E-mail: LSiren@OntonagonLibrary.org; Staff 1 (Non-MLS 1)
Founded 1904. Pop 4,225; Circ 32,146
Library Holdings: Electronic Media & Resources 297; Large Print Bks 795; Bk Vols 38,953; Per Subs 76; Talking Bks 1,254; Videos 299
Special Collections: Michigan Local History Coll
Automation Activity & Vendor Info: (Cataloging) Follett Software; (Circulation) Follett Software; (ILL) OCLC FirstSearch
Function: ILL available, Internet access, Photocopying/Printing, Summer reading prog, Wheelchair accessible
Partic in Upper Peninsula Region of Library Cooperation, Inc
Open Mon & Wed 11-8, Tues & Fri 11-5, Sat 10-2
Branches: 1
ROCKLAND TOWNSHIP, 40 National Ave, Rockland, 49960. (Mail add: PO Box 251, Rockland, 49960-0251). Tel: 906-886-2821. FAX: 906-886-2821. E-mail: rocklib@chartermi.net. *Dir,* Kathleen Preiss; E-mail: merwin24_42@hotmail.com; Staff 2 (Non-MLS 2)
Founded 1968
Library Holdings: Bk Vols 1,000
Open Mon-Wed & Fri 2-5, Sat 12:30-3:30

ORCHARD LAKE

R CARDINAL ADAM MAIDA ALUMNI LIBRARY*, SS Cyril & Methodius Seminary, 3535 Indian Trail, 48324. SAN 308-3241. Tel: 248-392-9965. Reference Tel: 248-683-0524. FAX: 248-683-0526. E-mail: library@orchardlakeschools.com, library@sscms.edu. Web Site: www.orchardlakelibrary.com. *Dir,* Beata Owczarski; Tel: 248-392-9963, E-mail: bowczarski@sscms.edu; Staff 2 (MLS 2)
Founded 1885. Enrl 74; Fac 18; Highest Degree: Master
Library Holdings: AV Mats 1,639; High Interest/Low Vocabulary Bk Vols 50; Bk Titles 86,214; Bk Vols 90,000; Per Subs 150
Special Collections: Polish Language Coll; Polish Language Rare Books
Subject Interests: Culture, Ethnic studies, Lang, Polish (Lang), Theol
Automation Activity & Vendor Info: (Cataloging) SirsiDynix; (Circulation) SirsiDynix; (ILL) OCLC Online; (OPAC) SirsiDynix
Wireless access
Function: ILL available
Partic in Detroit Area Consortium of Catholic Colleges; Midwest Collaborative for Library Services; OCLC Online Computer Library Center, Inc
Open Mon-Fri 9-5
Restriction: In-house use for visitors

ORTONVILLE

P BRANDON TOWNSHIP PUBLIC LIBRARY, 304 South St, 48462. SAN 308-325X. Tel: 248-627-1460. Administration Tel: 248-627-1464. FAX: 248-627-9880. Web Site: www.brandonlibrary.org. *Adult Serv Mgr, Dir,* Rebecca Higgerson; Tel: 248-627-1474, E-mail: rhiggerson@brandonlibrary.org; *Librn,* Shuana Quick; Tel: 248-627-1472, E-mail: squick@brandonlibrary.org; *Youth Serv Mgr,* Kate Scheid; Tel: 248-627-1473, E-mail: kscheid@brandonlibrary.org; Staff 19 (MLS 3, Non-MLS 16)
Founded 1924
Wireless access
Function: Activity rm, Adult bk club, Adult literacy prog, After school storytime, Archival coll, Art exhibits, Bk club(s), Bks on CD, Children's prog, Computer training, Computers for patron use, Digital talking bks, E-Readers, Electronic databases & coll, Free DVD rentals, Holiday prog, Homebound delivery serv, ILL available, Instruction & testing, Internet access, Laminating, Large print keyboards, Life-long learning prog for all ages, Magazines, Magnifiers for reading, Mail & tel request accepted, Meeting rooms, Movies, Museum passes, Music CDs, Online cat, OverDrive digital audio bks, Photocopying/Printing, Preschool outreach, Preschool reading prog, Printer for laptops & handheld devices, Prog for adults, Prog for children & young adult, Ref & res, Ref serv available, Scanner, Serves people with intellectual disabilities, Spoken cassettes & CDs, Spoken cassettes & DVDs, Story hour, Study rm, Summer reading prog, Tax forms, Teen prog, Telephone ref, VHS videos, Wheelchair accessible
Partic in Association for Rural & Small Libraries; TLN
Open Mon & Tues 9-7, Wed & Thurs 10-6, Fri 9-5, Sat 11-4
Friends of the Library Group

OTSEGO

P OTSEGO DISTRICT PUBLIC LIBRARY*, 401 Dix St, 49078. SAN 308-3268. Tel: 269-694-9690. FAX: 269-694-9129. Web Site: www.otsegolibrary.org. *Dir,* Andrea Estelle; E-mail:

aestelle@otsegolibrary.org; *Asst Dir,* Diane DeVries; E-mail: ddevries@otsegolibrary.org; Staff 15 (MLS 1, Non-MLS 14)
Founded 1844. Pop 14,952; Circ 152,812
Jan 2019-Dec 2019 Income $584,165, State $11,099, County $75,000, Locally Generated Income $420,966, Other $77,100. Mats Exp $65,670, Books $34,000, Per/Ser (Incl. Access Fees) $1,670, AV Mat $20,000, Electronic Ref Mat (Incl. Access Fees) $10,000. Sal $229,000 (Prof $67,000)
Library Holdings: AV Mats 435; CDs 2,892; DVDs 3,834; Bk Titles 40,224; Per Subs 100
Special Collections: History of Otsego, 12 volume Coll, bks & micro; Michigan Pioneer Coll
Automation Activity & Vendor Info: (Acquisitions) Auto-Graphics, Inc; (Cataloging) Auto-Graphics, Inc; (Circulation) Auto-Graphics, Inc; (OPAC) Auto-Graphics, Inc
Wireless access
Function: Adult bk club, Archival coll, Art exhibits, Audiobks on Playaways & MP3, Bk club(s), Bks on CD, Chess club, Children's prog, Computer training, Computers for patron use, Electronic databases & coll, Free DVD rentals, Homebound delivery serv, ILL available, Internet access, Laminating, Magazines, Meeting rooms, Movies, Music CDs, OverDrive digital audio bks, Photocopying/Printing, Preschool outreach, Preschool reading prog, Prog for adults, Prog for children & young adult, Spanish lang bks, Story hour, Study rm, Summer & winter reading prog, Summer reading prog, Tax forms, Teen prog, Wheelchair accessible
Partic in Midwest Collaborative for Library Services; Southwest Michigan Library Cooperative
Open Mon-Thurs 9-8, Fri 9-5:30, Sat 9-2:30
Restriction: Borrowing requests are handled by ILL, Non-resident fee
Friends of the Library Group

OVID

P OVID PUBLIC LIBRARY, 206 N Main St, 48866. (Mail add: PO Box 105, 48866-0105), SAN 320-4847. Tel: 989-834-5800. FAX: 989-834-5113. E-mail: ovidlibrary1949@gmail.com. Web Site: ovidpubliclibrary.weebly.com. *Dir,* Sharlyn S Huyck; Staff 2 (Non-MLS 2)
Founded 1949. Pop 5,569; Circ 42,152
Library Holdings: Bk Titles 20,000; Per Subs 72
Automation Activity & Vendor Info: (Cataloging) Auto-Graphics, Inc; (Circulation) Auto-Graphics, Inc; (ILL) Mel Cat
Wireless access
Partic in White Pine Library Cooperative
Open Mon-Wed 10-8, Fri 10-5, Sat 10-1

OWOSSO

C BAKER COLLEGE OF OWOSSO LIBRARY*, 1020 S Washington St, 48867-4400. SAN 370-0097. Toll Free Tel: 800-879-3797. FAX: 989-729-3429. E-mail: library@baker.edu. Web Site: my.baker.edu/ICS/My_Services/Department_Resources/Academic_Resource_Center/Library. *Coordr of Info & Tech Res,* Diane Childress; Tel: 810-766-4235, E-mail: dchild02@baker.edu
Founded 1984. Highest Degree: Doctorate
Library Holdings: Bk Titles 200
Automation Activity & Vendor Info: (Cataloging) Koha; (Circulation) Koha; (Discovery) EBSCO Discovery Service; (ILL) Koha; (OPAC) Koha
Wireless access
Partic in PALnet

P SHIAWASSEE DISTRICT LIBRARY*, Owosso Branch, 502 W Main St, 48867-2607. SAN 308-3306. Tel: 989-725-5134. FAX: 989-723-5444. E-mail: info@sdl.lib.mi.us. Web Site: www.sdl.lib.mi.us. *Dir,* Steven H Flayer; E-mail: steven.flayer@sdl.lib.mi.us; *Ad, Asst Dir,* Margaret Ann Bentley; E-mail: margaret.bentley@sdl.lib.mi.us; *Ch Serv Librn,* Natalie Young; E-mail: natalie.young@sdl.lib.mi.us; Staff 7 (MLS 2, Non-MLS 5)
Founded 1910. Pop 28,742; Circ 90,815
Library Holdings: AV Mats 5,600; Bk Vols 60,387; Per Subs 158; Videos 1,149
Special Collections: Genealogy, includes surname file; James Oliver Curwood Coll, bks, ms, pictures. Oral History
Subject Interests: Local hist
Automation Activity & Vendor Info: (Circulation) Biblionix/Apollo; (ILL) Mel Cat; (OPAC) Biblionix/Apollo
Wireless access
Function: ILL available, Magnifiers for reading, Prog for children & young adult, Ref serv available, Summer reading prog, Telephone ref
Open Mon-Thurs (Winter) 9-8:30, Fri 1-5, Sat 10-5; Mon-Thurs (Summer) 9-8:30, Fri 9-5, Sat 10-2
Restriction: Open to pub for ref & circ; with some limitations
Friends of the Library Group

Branches: 1
DURAND MEMORIAL BRANCH, 700 N Saginaw St, Durand, 48429-1245, SAN 308-0536. Tel: 989-288-3743. FAX: 989-288-3743. *Asst Dir,* Nancy Folaron; E-mail: nancy.folaron@sdl.lib.mi.us; Staff 4 (Non-MLS 4)
Founded 1954. Pop 3,446
Library Holdings: AV Mats 1,928; Bk Vols 21,000; Per Subs 69
Special Collections: City of Durand Coll
Subject Interests: Genealogy, Mich
Automation Activity & Vendor Info: (Cataloging) Biblionix/Apollo; (Circulation) Biblionix/Apollo; (ILL) Mel Cat
Open Mon-Thurs 9:30-8, Fri 9:30-6, Sat 9:30-3
Friends of the Library Group

OXFORD

P OXFORD PUBLIC LIBRARY, 530 Pontiac St, 48371-4844. (Mail add: PO Box 538, 48371), SAN 308-3314. Tel: 248-628-3034. Administration Tel: 248-628-3034, Ext 210. FAX: 248-969-9492. Web Site: www.miopl.org. *Dir,* Bryan Cloutier; E-mail: bcloutier@miopl.org; *Head, Adult Serv,* Laura Fromwiller; *Head, Support Serv,* Jacqueline Seimer; *Head, Youth Serv,* Kim Burean; Staff 25 (MLS 7, Non-MLS 18)
Founded 1916. Pop 16,025; Circ 95,000
Library Holdings: Bk Titles 47,000; Per Subs 120
Automation Activity & Vendor Info: (Cataloging) SirsiDynix; (Circulation) SirsiDynix; (OPAC) SirsiDynix
Wireless access
Open Mon-Thurs 10-9, Fri & Sat 10-5
Friends of the Library Group

PALMER

P RICHMOND TOWNSHIP LIBRARY*, 304 Snyder St, 49871. (Mail add: PO Box 339, 49871-0339), SAN 308-3322. Tel: 906-475-5241. FAX: 906-475-7516. E-mail: richtown@uproc.lib.mi.us. Web Site: www.uproc.lib.mi.us/rich. *Dir,* Jan St Germain; Staff 1 (MLS 1)
Founded 1975. Pop 1,095
Library Holdings: Bk Titles 5,600; Bk Vols 7,000; Per Subs 32
Special Collections: Finnish Coll
Partic in Superiorland Library Cooperative; Upper Peninsula Region of Library Cooperation, Inc
Open Mon 1-7, Tues 11-5 & 7-9, Wed & Thurs 11-5

PARADISE

P WHITEFISH TOWNSHIP COMMUNITY LIBRARY*, 7247 North M Hwy 123, 49768. (Mail add: PO Box 197, 49768-0197), SAN 376-7086. Tel: 906-492-3500. FAX: 906-492-3504. E-mail: staff@whitefishtownshiplibrary.org. Web Site: whitefishtownshiplibrary.org. *Libr Dir,* Christine Hickman
Founded 1975. Circ 1,470
Library Holdings: Bk Titles 8,700; Bk Vols 10,000; Per Subs 30
Automation Activity & Vendor Info: (Cataloging) SirsiDynix; (Circulation) SirsiDynix
Partic in Upper Peninsula Region of Library Cooperation, Inc
Open Tues, Thurs & Fri 10-4, Wed 12-8, Sat 10-2

PARCHMENT

P PARCHMENT COMMUNITY LIBRARY*, 401 S Riverview Dr, 49004. SAN 308-3330. Tel: 269-343-7747. FAX: 269-343-7749. E-mail: ref@parchmentlibrary.org. Web Site: www.parchmentlibrary.org. *Dir,* Teresa L Stannard; Tel: 269-343-7747, Ext 203, E-mail: tstannard@parchmentlibrary.org; Staff 12 (MLS 3, Non-MLS 9)
Founded 1963. Pop 9,969; Circ 109,180
Library Holdings: Audiobooks 1,741; DVDs 2,298; Large Print Bks 1,122; Bk Vols 34,124; Per Subs 50
Special Collections: Parchment History Coll, newsp, pictures. Oral History
Automation Activity & Vendor Info: (Cataloging) Biblionix/Apollo; (Circulation) Biblionix/Apollo; (ILL) Innovative Interfaces, Inc - Millennium; (OPAC) Biblionix/Apollo; (Serials) Biblionix/Apollo
Wireless access
Function: Adult bk club, Archival coll, Audio & video playback equip for onsite use, Audiobks via web, Bks on CD, Children's prog, Computers for patron use, Free DVD rentals, Notary serv, Online cat, Photocopying/Printing, Preschool reading prog, Printer for laptops & handheld devices, Prog for adults, Prog for children & young adult, Ref serv available, Scanner, Story hour, Summer reading prog, Tax forms, Teen prog, Telephone ref, Wheelchair accessible
Partic in Southwest Michigan Library Cooperative
Open Mon & Tues 9-7, Wed & Thurs 9-5, Fri & Sat 9-1
Friends of the Library Group

PAW PAW

P PAW PAW DISTRICT LIBRARY, 609 W Michigan Ave, 49079-1072. SAN 308-3349. Tel: 269-657-3800. FAX: 269-657-2603. E-mail: ppdl49079@yahoo.com. Web Site; www.pawpaw.lib.mi.us. *Dir,* Gretchen Evans; Staff 3 (MLS 3)
Founded 1920. Pop 13,579; Circ 64,950
Library Holdings: Bk Vols 66,636; Per Subs 142
Special Collections: Michigan Coll
Automation Activity & Vendor Info: (Cataloging) Auto-Graphics, Inc; (Circulation) Auto-Graphics, Inc; (ILL) Auto-Graphics, Inc; (OPAC) Auto-Graphics, Inc; (Serials) Auto-Graphics, Inc
Partic in Mich Libr Asn; Southwest Michigan Library Cooperative
Open Mon, Tues & Thurs 9-8, Wed 12-8, Fri & Sat 9-5
Friends of the Library Group

PECK

P ELK TOWNSHIP LIBRARY*, 29 E Lapeer St, 48466. (Mail add: PO Box 268, 48466-0268), SAN 308-3357. Tel: 810-378-5409. FAX: 810-378-5016. E-mail: library@airadv.net. Web Site: www.elktwplibrary.org. *Dir,* Janet Dyki
Founded 1938. Pop 4,088; Circ 10,000
Library Holdings: CDs 131; Large Print Bks 450; Bk Vols 10,000; Per Subs 30; Videos 100
Wireless access
Partic in White Pine Library Cooperative
Open Tues & Thurs 9-12 & 1-7, Wed & Fri 9-12 & 1-5, Sat 9-Noon

PENTWATER

P PENTWATER TOWNSHIP LIBRARY*, 402 E Park, 49449. (Mail add: PO Box 946, 49449), SAN 308-3365. Tel: 231-869-8581. FAX: 231-869-4000. E-mail: librarian@pentwaterlibrary.org. Web Site: www.pentwaterlibrary.org. *Dir,* Mary Barker; E-mail: mbarker@pentwaterlibrary.org
Circ 19,000
Library Holdings: Bk Vols 17,000; Per Subs 100
Special Collections: Michigan Coll
Automation Activity & Vendor Info: (Cataloging) Auto-Graphics, Inc; (Circulation) Auto-Graphics, Inc
Wireless access
Partic in Mid-Michigan Library League
Open Mon & Wed 9:30-7, Tues, Thurs & Fri 9:30-5:30, Sat 9:30-2
Friends of the Library Group

PETOSKEY

S LITTLE TRAVERSE HISTORY MUSEUM LIBRARY*, 100 Depot Ct, 49770. (Mail add: PO Box 2418, 49770), SAN 321-2335. Tel: 231-347-2620. E-mail: info@petoskeymuseum.org. Web Site: www.petoskeymuseum.org. *Dir,* Jane Garver; E-mail: jane@petoskeymuseum.org; *Dir,* Dylan Taylor; E-mail: dylan@petoskeymuseum.org; *Archivist,* Phil Deloria; Staff 1 (Non-MLS 1)
Founded 1905
Library Holdings: Bk Vols 4,400
Special Collections: Little Traverse Bay Area; Petoskey Newspapers 1875-1979
Subject Interests: Local hist
Open Mon-Sat (May-Oct) 10-4

M MCLAREN NORTHERN MICHIGAN*, Dean C Burns Health Sciences Library, 416 Connable Ave, 49770. SAN 308-339X. Tel: 231-487-4500. Toll Free Tel: 800-248-6777. FAX: 231-487-7892. E-mail: library@northernhealth.org. Web Site: www.mclaren.org. *Librn,* Anne Foster
Library Holdings: Per Subs 400
Subject Interests: Health sci
Open Mon-Fri 8:30-5

J NORTH CENTRAL MICHIGAN COLLEGE LIBRARY*, 1515 Howard St, 49770. SAN 308-3381. Tel: 231-348-6615. FAX: 231-348-6629. E-mail: library@ncmich.edu. Web Site: www.ncmich.edu/resources-support/library/. *Librn,* Beth K Lieberman; E-mail: blieberman1@ncmich.edu; Staff 2 (MLS 1, Non-MLS 1)
Founded 1958. Enrl 3,200; Fac 32; Highest Degree: Associate
Library Holdings: e-books 67,000; Bk Titles 36,000; Per Subs 300
Special Collections: Nuclear Documents. US Document Depository
Subject Interests: Hist, Soc sci & issues
Automation Activity & Vendor Info: (Circulation) Follett Software; (Course Reserve) Follett Software; (OPAC) Follett Software
Wireless access
Special Services for the Blind - Aids for in-house use

P PETOSKEY DISTRICT LIBRARY, 500 E Mitchell St, 49770. SAN 308-3403. Tel: 231-758-3100. Circulation Tel: 231-758-3111. Reference Tel: 231-758-3114. FAX: 231-758-3301. Web Site: www.petoskeylibrary.org. *Dir,* Valerie Meyerson; E-mail: vmeyerson@petoskeylibrary.org; *Ch Serv,* Megan Goedge; E-mail: mgoedge@petoskeylibrary.org; *Pub Serv Librn,* Jodi Haven; E-mail: jhaven@petoskeylibrary.org
Founded 1905. Pop 14,568; Circ 124,000
Library Holdings: Bk Vols 81,525; Per Subs 140
Special Collections: Great Lakes Americana (William H Ohle Coll)
Automation Activity & Vendor Info: (Cataloging) SirsiDynix; (Circulation) SirsiDynix; (ILL) Mel Cat; (OPAC) BiblioCommons
Wireless access
Function: 24/7 Online cat, Adult literacy prog, Archival coll, Art exhibits, Audiobks via web, Bi-weekly Writer's Group, Bks on CD, Chess club, Children's prog, Computer training, Computers for patron use, Digital talking bks, Doc delivery serv, E-Readers, E-Reserves, Electronic databases & coll, Family literacy, Free DVD rentals, Games & aids for people with disabilities, Genealogy discussion group, Health sci info serv, Holiday prog, Home delivery & serv to seniorr ctr & nursing homes, ILL available, Instruction & testing, Internet access, Magazines, Magnifiers for reading, Mail & tel request accepted, Mango lang, Meeting rooms, Microfiche/film & reading machines, Movies, Museum passes, Music CDs, Online cat, Online ref, Outreach serv, OverDrive digital audio bks, Photocopying/Printing, Preschool outreach, Preschool reading prog, Printer for laptops & handheld devices, Prog for adults, Prog for children & young adult, Ref & res, Ref serv available, Scanner, Senior outreach, Serves people with intellectual disabilities, Spoken cassettes & CDs, Spoken cassettes & DVDs, Story hour, Study rm, Summer reading prog, Tax forms, Teen prog, Telephone ref, Wheelchair accessible, Writing prog
Partic in Northland Library Cooperative
Open Mon-Fri 10-6, Sat 10-5, Sun 12-5
Restriction: Non-resident fee
Friends of the Library Group

PIGEON

P PIGEON DISTRICT LIBRARY*, 7236 Nitz St, 48755. (Mail add: PO Box 357, 48755-0357), SAN 308-3411. Tel: 989-453-2341. FAX: 989-453-2266. E-mail: pdl@pigeondistrictlibrary.com. Web Site: www.pigeondistrictlibrary.com. *Dir,* Jane Himmel; E-mail: jane@pigeondistrictlibrary.com; Staff 8 (Non-MLS 8)
Founded 1913. Pop 9,300; Circ 59,116
Library Holdings: Bks on Deafness & Sign Lang 36; CDs 308; DVDs 289; High Interest/Low Vocabulary Bk Vols 339; Large Print Bks 1,042; Bk Vols 44,000; Per Subs 98; Talking Bks 805; Videos 3,227
Special Collections: Joann Haist Coll, births, deaths, marriages & hist of businesses from 1987; Michigan Vertical File, Newsp clippings; Parent Resource Center
Subject Interests: Adult lit, Local hist
Automation Activity & Vendor Info: (Circulation) SirsiDynix; (ILL) SirsiDynix
Wireless access
Function: Home delivery & serv to seniorr ctr & nursing homes, ILL available, Magnifiers for reading, Photocopying/Printing, Prog for children & young adult, Summer reading prog, Wheelchair accessible
Partic in White Pine Library Cooperative
Special Services for the Deaf - Assistive tech; Bks on deafness & sign lang; High interest/low vocabulary bks
Special Services for the Blind - Aids for in-house use; Bks on CD; Copier with enlargement capabilities; Extensive large print coll; Large print bks; Lending of low vision aids; Low vision equip; Magnifiers; Talking bks
Open Mon, Wed & Fri 9-5, Tues & Thurs 9-7, Sat 9-2
Friends of the Library Group

PINCKNEY

P PINCKNEY COMMUNITY PUBLIC LIBRARY*, 125 Putnam St, 48169. SAN 308-342X. Tel: 734-878-3888. Administration Tel: 734-878-2952. FAX: 734-878-2907. Web Site: pinckneylibrary.org. *Dir,* Hope Siasoco; *Youth/Young Adult Librn,* Sara Castle; Staff 9 (MLS 2, Non-MLS 7)
Founded 1953. Pop 10,548; Circ 34,675
Library Holdings: AV Mats 1,363; High Interest/Low Vocabulary Bk Vols 150; Large Print Bks 277; Bk Vols 18,820; Per Subs 55
Special Collections: Graphic Novels; Michigan/Local History (Village of Pinckney), doc, microfilms, newsp, yearbks
Automation Activity & Vendor Info: (Acquisitions) Brodart; (Cataloging) Follett Software; (Circulation) Follett Software; (OPAC) Follett Software
Wireless access
Function: Home delivery & serv to seniorr ctr & nursing homes, Homebound delivery serv, ILL available, Photocopying/Printing, Prog for children & young adult, Summer reading prog
Partic in Mich Libr Asn; Midwest Collaborative for Library Services; The Library Network

Open Mon, Wed & Fri 10-6, Tues & Thurs 10-8, Sat 10-4
Friends of the Library Group

PITTSFORD

P PITTSFORD PUBLIC LIBRARY, 9268 E Hudson Rd, 49271. SAN 308-3438. Tel: 517-523-2565. FAX: 517-523-2565. *Dir,* Susan Ruder; E-mail: sruder@monroe.lib.mi.us
Founded 1962. Pop 4,291; Circ 11,281
Library Holdings: Large Print Bks 400; Bk Vols 14,000; Per Subs 40; Talking Bks 64; Videos 300
Automation Activity & Vendor Info: (Cataloging) Book Systems; (Circulation) Book Systems; (OPAC) Book Systems
Mem of Woodlands Library Cooperative
Open Tues-Fri 12-5, Sat 10-Noon

PLAINWELL

P CHARLES A RANSOM DISTRICT LIBRARY*, 180 S Sherwood Ave, 49080-1896. SAN 308-3446. Tel: 269-685-8024. FAX: 269-685-2266. Web Site: www.ransomlibrary.org. *Dir,* Joe Gross; E-mail: jgross@ransomlibrary.org; *Asst Dir, Youth Serv,* Erin Marsh; E-mail: emarsh@ransomlibrary.org; *Circ,* Karena Chapman; E-mail: kchapman@ransomlibrary.org; *Circ,* Julie Stout; E-mail: jstout@ransomlibrary.org; *ILL,* Dawn Holtman; E-mail: dholtman@ransomlibrary.org; Staff 2 (MLS 1, Non-MLS 1)
Founded 1868. Pop 13,593
Library Holdings: Bk Vols 55,000; Per Subs 79
Special Collections: Burchfield Room; Sandy Stamm Archives Room
Subject Interests: Adult educ
Automation Activity & Vendor Info: (Cataloging) Follett Software; (Circulation) Follett Software
Wireless access
Partic in Southwest Michigan Library Cooperative
Special Services for the Blind - Reader equip
Open Mon-Thurs 10-9, Fri & Sat 10-5, Sun (Sept-May) 1-5
Friends of the Library Group

PLYMOUTH

P PLYMOUTH DISTRICT LIBRARY*, 223 S Main St, 48170-1687. SAN 308-3454. Tel: 734-453-0750. Circulation Tel: 734-453-0750, Ext 3. Reference Tel: 734-453-0750, Ext 1. FAX: 734-453-0733. E-mail: info@plymouthlibrary.org. Web Site: plymouthlibrary.org. *Dir,* Carol Souchock; Tel: 734-453-0750, Ext 218, E-mail: csouchock@plymouthlibrary.org; *Head, Info & Tech,* Frank Ferguson; Tel: 734-453-0750, Ext 239; *Teen Serv Librn,* Barb Dinan; Tel: 734-453-0750, Ext 271, E-mail: bdinan@plymouthlibrary.org; *Bus Mgr, Human Res Adminr,* Robyn Lowenstein; Tel: 734-453-0750, Ext 215; *Adult Serv Coordr,* Holly Hibner; Tel: 734-453-0750, Ext 213; *Youth Serv Coordr,* Carol Champagne; Tel: 734-453-0750, Ext 237; Staff 42 (MLS 15, Non-MLS 27)
Founded 1923. Pop 57,031; Circ 882,147
Library Holdings: Bk Vols 220,000; Per Subs 200
Automation Activity & Vendor Info: (Acquisitions) SirsiDynix; (Cataloging) SirsiDynix; (Circulation) SirsiDynix; (OPAC) SirsiDynix; (Serials) SirsiDynix
Wireless access
Partic in TLN
Open Mon-Thurs 9:30-9, Fri 9:30-6, Sat 9:30-5, Sun 12-5
Friends of the Library Group

S PLYMOUTH HISTORICAL MUSEUM ARCHIVES*, 155 S Main St, 48170-1635. SAN 371-6546. Tel: 734-455-8940, Ext 3. FAX: 734-455-7797. E-mail: archivist@plymouthhistory.org. Web Site: www.plymouthhistory.org. *Exec Dir,* Elizabeth Kelley Kerstens; E-mail: director@plymouthhistory.org; *Archivist,* Pam Yockey; E-mail: archivist@plymouthhistory.org; Staff 1 (MLS 1)
Founded 1976
Library Holdings: Bk Titles 5,000; Per Subs 10
Special Collections: Civil War History (War of the Rebellion Coll), bks, rec; Local Newspapers & Census Records, microfilm; Michigan History; Petz Abraham Lincoln Coll, bks, papers, photos; Plymouth Birth/Death Records; Schrader Funeral Home Records
Wireless access
Publications: Plymouth's First Century - Innovators & Industry

PONTIAC

M MCLAREN OAKLAND*, Medical Library, 50 N Perry St, 48342-2217. SAN 308-3543. Tel: 248-338-5000, Ext 3155. FAX: 248-338-5025. *Med Librn,* Sheela John; E-mail: sheela.john@mclaren.org; Staff 1 (MLS 1)
Founded 1962
Library Holdings: e-books 1,000; e-journals 600; Bk Titles 250; Per Subs 15
Wireless access
Partic in Metrop Detroit Med Libr Group; Michigan Health Sciences Libraries Association; MLC
Open Mon-Sun 7-3:30

S OAKLAND COUNTY JAIL LIBRARY*, 1201 N Telegraph Rd, 48341-1044. Tel: 248-858-2925. Web Site: www.oakgov.com/sheriff/Corrections-Courts/jail/Pages/default.aspx. *Supvr,* Kurt Rachar; E-mail: rachark@oakgov.com

S OAKLAND COUNTY PIONEER & HISTORICAL SOCIETY, Library & Archives, 405 Cesar E Chavez Ave, 48342-1068. SAN 373-2169. Tel: 248-338-6732. FAX: 248-338-6731. E-mail: office@ocphs.org. Web Site: www.ocphs.org/research-library. *Exec Dir,* Mike McGinness
Founded 1874
Library Holdings: Bk Vols 3,800
Special Collections: Oral History
Subject Interests: Civil War, Local hist, Manuscripts, Oral hist
Wireless access
Function: Res performed for a fee
Publications: Oakland Gazette (Newsletter)
Open Tues & Thurs 11-4, Wed 11-8
Restriction: Non-circulating

P PONTIAC PUBLIC LIBRARY*, 60 E Pike St, 48342. SAN 346-9980. Tel: 248-758-3942. FAX: 248-430-8254. E-mail: pont@tln.lib.mi.us. Web Site: www.pontiac.lib.mi.us. *Dir,* Ms Devan Green; Tel: 248-758-3940, E-mail: dbgreen@tln.lib.mi.us
Library Holdings: Bk Titles 80,000; Bk Vols 90,000; Per Subs 150
Subject Interests: Hist
Wireless access
Open Mon-Thurs 10-8, Fri & Sat 10-5:30
Friends of the Library Group

PORT AUSTIN

P PORT AUSTIN TOWNSHIP LIBRARY*, 114 Railroad St, 48467. (Mail add: P.O. Box 325, 48467), SAN 308-3586. Tel: 989-738-7212. FAX: 989-738-7983. E-mail: patl114@yahoo.com. Web Site: www.portaustinlibrary.org. *Dir,* Mary Jaworski
Founded 1947. Pop 4,074; Circ 17,500
Library Holdings: Large Print Bks 300; Bk Titles 10,100; Bk Vols 10,890; Per Subs 50; Talking Bks 250; Videos 2,500
Subject Interests: Local hist
Wireless access
Partic in White Pine Library Cooperative
Open Mon-Thurs 10-7, Fri 10-5, Sat 10-2
Friends of the Library Group

PORT HURON

J SAINT CLAIR COUNTY COMMUNITY COLLEGE LIBRARY*, 323 Erie St, 48060. (Mail add: PO Box 5015, 48061-5015), SAN 308-3608. Tel: 810-984-3881, 810-989-5640. Reference Tel: 810-989-5640, Ext 2. Toll Free Tel: 800-553-2427, Ext 5640. FAX: 810-984-2852. E-mail: lrc@sc4.edu. Web Site: www.sc4.edu/lrc. *Dir, Libr Serv,* Kendra lake; *Pub Serv,* Jane Lewandoski; Staff 10 (MLS 4, Non-MLS 6)
Founded 1923. Enrl 3,033; Fac 80; Highest Degree: Associate
Library Holdings: Bk Titles 56,541; Bk Vols 61,960; Per Subs 575
Automation Activity & Vendor Info: (Cataloging) Horizon; (Circulation) Horizon; (Discovery) ProQuest; (ILL) OCLC WorldShare Interlibrary Loan; (OPAC) Horizon; (Serials) Horizon
Wireless access
Partic in Midwest Collaborative for Library Services; OCLC Online Computer Library Center, Inc
Special Services for the Deaf - ADA equip
Open Mon-Thurs (Fall & Winter) 7:30am-9pm, Fri 7:30-4, Sat 8-4

P SAINT CLAIR COUNTY LIBRARY SYSTEM*, 210 McMorran Blvd, 48060-4098. SAN 347-0199. Tel: 810-987-7323. Toll Free Tel: 877-987-7323. FAX: 810-987-7874. Web Site: www.sccl.lib.mi.us. *Libr Dir,* Allison Arnold; E-mail: aarnold@sccl.lib.mi.us; *Ch Serv Librn,* Tarri Ryan; E-mail: tryan@sccl.lib.mi.us; *Circ Serv Librn,* Anne Marie Bedard; E-mail: abedard@sccl.lib.mi.us; *Ref Serv Librn,* Barbara King; E-mail: bking@sccl.lib.mi.us; *Tech Serv Librn,* Angela Klocek; E-mail: aklocek@sccl.lib.mi.us; *Coll Coordr, Tech Innovation Librn,* Nicole Pinskey; E-mail: npinskey@sccl.lib.mi.us; *Commun Relations Coordr, Friends Coordr,* Mike Mercatante; E-mail: mmercatante@sccl.lib.mi.us; *Coordr, Pub Serv,* Melba Moss; E-mail: mmoss@sccl.lib.mi.us; *Admin Serv,* Position Currently Open; Staff 11 (MLS 11)
Founded 1917. Pop 163,040; Circ 793,748
Library Holdings: Bk Vols 389,519; Per Subs 1,161
Special Collections: Michigan & the Great Lakes (W L Jenks Historical Coll), bks, maps, microfilm, ms, per, photog. Canadian and Provincial; State Document Depository; US Document Depository
Subject Interests: Local hist

Automation Activity & Vendor Info: (Acquisitions) SirsiDynix; (Cataloging) SirsiDynix; (Circulation) SirsiDynix; (OPAC) SirsiDynix; (Serials) SirsiDynix
Wireless access
Publications: Annual Report; Library Links (Newsletter)
Member Libraries: St Clair County Literacy Project
Partic in Midwest Collaborative for Library Services; The Library Network
Special Services for the Deaf - TTY equip
Special Services for the Blind - Aids for in-house use; Bks on cassette; Bks on CD; Braille servs; Closed circuit TV; Computer with voice synthesizer for visually impaired persons; Descriptive video serv (DVS); Dragon Naturally Speaking software; Large print bks & talking machines; Low vision equip; Machine repair; Magnifiers; Reader equip; Talking bk & rec for the blind cat; Talking bks
Open Mon-Thurs 8:30am-9pm, Fri & Sat 8:30-5
Friends of the Library Group
Branches: 11
ALGONAC-CLAY BRANCH LIBRARY, 2011 St Clair River Dr, Algonac, 48001, SAN 347-0288. Tel: 810-794-4471. FAX: 810-794-2940. *Branch Lead,* Scott Nichols; E-mail: snichols@sccl.lib.mi.us
Library Holdings: Bk Vols 20,065
Open Mon-Thurs 9-8, Fri & Sat 9-5
Friends of the Library Group
P BLIND & PHYSICALLY HANDICAPPED LIBRARY, 210 McMorran Blvd, 48060, SAN 347-0164. Tel: 810-982-3600. Toll Free Tel: 800-272-8570. E-mail: lbph@sccl.lib.mi.us. *Coordr,* Mary Redigan; E-mail: mredigan@sccl.lib.mi.us
Special Services for the Deaf - TTY equip
BURTCHVILLE TOWNSHIP BRANCH LIBRARY, 7093 Second St, Lakeport, 48059. Tel: 810-385-8550. FAX: 810-385-2968. *Branch Lead,* Jane Fortushniak; E-mail: jfortushniak@sccl.lib.mi.us
Pop 3,500
Open Mon & Thurs 12-8, Tues, Wed, Fri & Sat 9-5
Friends of the Library Group
G LYNN CAMPBELL BRANCH LIBRARY, 1955 N Allen Rd, Kimball, 48074, SAN 347-0229. Tel: 810-982-9171. FAX: 810-987-9689. *Branch Lead,* Jenna Reed; E-mail: jreed@sccl.lib.mi.us
Founded 1962
Library Holdings: Bk Vols 12,939
Open Mon & Thurs 12-8, Tues, Wed, Fri & Sat 9-5
Friends of the Library Group
CAPAC BRANCH LIBRARY, 111 N Main St, Capac, 48014, SAN 347-0253. Tel: 810-395-7000. FAX: 810-395-2863. *Branch Lead,* Breezy Wallace; E-mail: bwallace@sccl.lib.mi.us
Founded 1919. Pop 2,000
Open Mon & Thurs 12-8, Tues, Wed, Fri & Sat 9-5
Friends of the Library Group
IRA TOWNSHIP BRANCH LIBRARY, 7013 Meldrum Rd, Fair Haven, 48023, SAN 347-0318. Tel: 586-725-9081. FAX: 586-725-1256. *Branch Lead,* Gary Kupper; E-mail: gkupper@sccl.lib.mi.us
Founded 1965. Pop 5,500
Open Mon & Thurs 12-8, Tues, Wed, Fri & Sat 9-5
Friends of the Library Group
MARINE CITY BRANCH LIBRARY, 300 S Parker Rd, Marine City, 48039, SAN 347-0342. Tel: 810-765-5233. FAX: 810-765-4376. *Branch Lead,* Andrew Webb; E-mail: awebb@sccl.lib.mi.us
Founded 1889. Pop 4,500
Library Holdings: Bk Vols 21,475
Open Mon-Thurs 9-8, Fri & Sat 9-5
Friends of the Library Group
MARYSVILLE BRANCH LIBRARY, 1175 Delaware, Marysville, 48040, SAN 347-0377. Tel: 810-364-9493. FAX: 810-364-7491. *Branch Lead,* Nancy Gearhart; E-mail: ngearhart@sccl.lib.mi.us
Pop 8,500
Open Mon-Thurs 9-8, Fri & Sat 9-5
Friends of the Library Group
MEMPHIS BRANCH LIBRARY, 34830 Potter St, Memphis, 48041, SAN 347-0407. Tel: 810-392-2980. FAX: 810-392-3206. *Branch Lead,* Karyl Birkett; E-mail: kbirkett@sccl.lib.mi.us
Founded 1973
Open Mon & Thurs 12-8, Tues, Wed, Fri & Sat 9-5
Friends of the Library Group
SAINT CLAIR BRANCH LIBRARY, 310 S Second St, Saint Clair, 48079, SAN 347-0466. Tel: 810-329-3951. FAX: 810-329-7142. *Branch Lead,* Julie Alef; E-mail: jalef@sccl.lib.mi.us
Founded 1869. Pop 5,000
Open Mon-Thurs 9-8, Fri & Sat 9-5
Friends of the Library Group
YALE BRANCH LIBRARY, Two Jones St, Yale, 48097, SAN 347-0490. Tel: 810-387-2940. FAX: 810-387-2051. *Branch Lead,* Lori Herrington; E-mail: lherrington@sccl.lib.mi.us
Open Mon-Thurs 9-8, Fri & Sat 9-5
Friends of the Library Group

S ST CLAIR COUNTY LITERACY PROJECT*, 210 McMorran Blvd, 48060. SAN 371-8808. Tel: 810-987-7323, Ext 156. FAX: 810-987-7327. E-mail: sccliteracyproject@gmail.com. Web Site: www.sccliteracyproject.org. *Pres, Literacy Project,* Suzanne Langlois
Wireless access
Mem of Saint Clair County Library System
Friends of the Library Group

PORT SANILAC

P SANILAC DISTRICT LIBRARY*, 7130 Main St, 48469. (Mail add: PO Box 525, 48469-0525), SAN 308-3616. Tel: 810-622-8623. E-mail: sanilacdistrictlibrary@yahoo.com. Circulation E-mail: sdlcircdesk@yahoo.com. Web Site: www.sanilacdistrictlibrary.lib.mi.us. *Dir,* Beverly Dear; Staff 4 (Non-MLS 4)
Founded 1936. Pop 4,545; Circ 40,430
Library Holdings: Bk Vols 39,018
Subject Interests: Aviation, Local hist
Automation Activity & Vendor Info: (Acquisitions) Follett Software; (Circulation) Follett Software
Wireless access
Publications: BookTalk (newsletter)
Partic in White Pine Library Cooperative
Open Mon & Wed 11-7, Tues, Thurs & Fri 11-5, Sat 11-2
Friends of the Library Group

PORTAGE

P PORTAGE DISTRICT LIBRARY*, 300 Library Lane, 49002. SAN 308-3624. Tel: 269-329-4544. FAX: 269-324-9222. E-mail: info@portagelibrary.info. Web Site: www.portagelibrary.info. *Dir,* Christy Klien; E-mail: cklien@portagelibrary.info; *Asst to the Dir,* Quyen Edwards; E-mail: gedwards@portagelibrary.info; *Libr Syst Adminr,* Rolfe Behrje; Tel: 269-329-4542, Ext 704, E-mail: rbehrje@portagelibrary.info; *Head, Adult Serv,* Lawrence Kapture; Tel: 269-329-4542, Ext 710, E-mail: lkapture@portagelibrary.info; *Head, Youth Serv,* Laura Wright; E-mail: lwright@portagelibrary.info; *Bus Mgr,* Robert Foti; Tel: 269-329-4542, Ext 702, E-mail: rfoti@portagelibrary.info; *Circ Supvr,* Jill Austin; Tel: 269-329-4542, Ext 706, E-mail: jaustin@portagelibrary.info; Staff 19 (MLS 16, Non-MLS 3)
Founded 1962. Pop 49,265; Circ 357,248
Library Holdings: Bk Titles 113,077; Bk Vols 136,034; Per Subs 211
Special Collections: John Todd Coll, aerial photos; Local History (Heritage Room Coll), letters, bks, archival mat. Oral History
Automation Activity & Vendor Info: (Acquisitions) Horizon; (Cataloging) Horizon; (OPAC) Horizon; (Serials) Horizon
Wireless access
Publications: Portage & Its Past; Women in Business & Management - A Bibliography
Partic in OCLC Online Computer Library Center, Inc; Southwest Michigan Library Cooperative
Special Services for the Deaf - Bks on deafness & sign lang; Spec interest per; Videos & decoder
Open Mon-Thurs 9-9, Fri 9-6, Sat 9-5, Sun (Sept-May) 1-5
Friends of the Library Group

PORTLAND

P PORTLAND DISTRICT LIBRARY*, 334 Kent St, 48875-1735. SAN 308-3632. Tel: 517-647-6981. FAX: 517-647-2738. Web Site: www.pdl.michlibrary.org. *Dir,* Cory E Grimminck; E-mail: cgrimminck@portlandmilibrary.com; *Youth Librn,* Kristie Reynolds; Staff 7 (Non-MLS 7)
Founded 1905. Pop 12,449; Circ 59,529
Library Holdings: AV Mats 3,138; Bks on Deafness & Sign Lang 10; Large Print Bks 353; Bk Vols 26,010; Per Subs 100; Talking Bks 818
Subject Interests: Genealogy, Local hist
Automation Activity & Vendor Info: (Cataloging) Follett Software; (Circulation) Follett Software; (ILL) Mel Cat
Wireless access
Function: AV serv, For res purposes, Health sci info serv, ILL available, Internet access, Photocopying/Printing, Prog for children & young adult, Ref serv available, Summer reading prog
Mem of Woodlands Library Cooperative
Open Mon-Thurs 9-8, Fri 9-5, Sat 9-2
Friends of the Library Group

POTTERVILLE

P POTTERVILLE BENTON TOWNSHIP DISTRICT LIBRARY*, 150 Library Lane, 48876. (Mail add: PO Box 158, 48876-0158), SAN 308-3640. Tel: 517-645-2989. FAX: 517-645-0268. Web Site: pottervillelibrary.org. *Dir,* Lu Ann Stachnik; E-mail: director@pottervillelibrary.org
Pop 4,880; Circ 19,000
Library Holdings: Bk Vols 16,000; Per Subs 30

Automation Activity & Vendor Info: (Acquisitions) Baker & Taylor; (Circulation) Auto-Graphics, Inc; (ILL) Auto-Graphics, Inc
Mem of Woodlands Library Cooperative
Open Mon, Thurs & Fri 12:30-5:30, Tues 10-6, Wed 12:30-7, Sat 10-1
Friends of the Library Group

RAY

P RAY TOWNSHIP PUBLIC LIBRARY, 64255 Wolcott Rd, 48096. Tel: 586-749-7130. FAX: 586-749-6190. E-mail: info@raylibrary.org. Web Site: www.raylibrary.org. *Dir,* Christy DeMeulenaere
Founded 1983
Library Holdings: Audiobooks 120; DVDs 300; Bk Vols 10,000
Automation Activity & Vendor Info: (Cataloging) SirsiDynix
Wireless access
Function: Photocopying/Printing
Partic in Suburban Library Cooperative
Open Mon-Thurs 11-7, Sat 10-2
Friends of the Library Group

READING

P READING COMMUNITY LIBRARY*, 104 N Main St, 49274. (Mail add: PO Box 184, 49274), SAN 308-3659. Tel: 517-283-3916. FAX: 517-283-2510. E-mail: reading@monroe.lib.mi.us. Web Site: www.rcl.michlibrary.org. *Librn,* Jeri Mosher; Staff 2 (Non-MLS 2)
Founded 1939. Pop 4,110; Circ 10,000
Jul 2012-Jun 2013. Mats Exp $5,500, Books $4,500, Per/Ser (Incl. Access Fees) $900, AV Mat $100
Library Holdings: Audiobooks 192; CDs 180; DVDs 309; Large Print Bks 216; Bk Vols 11,674; Per Subs 36
Automation Activity & Vendor Info: (Acquisitions) Auto-Graphics, Inc; (Cataloging) Auto-Graphics, Inc; (Circulation) Auto-Graphics, Inc; (ILL) Mel Cat
Wireless access
Function: ILL available
Mem of Woodlands Library Cooperative
Open Mon & Thurs 2-6, Tues, Wed & Fri 10-5, Sat 10-2

REDFORD

P REDFORD TOWNSHIP DISTRICT LIBRARY*, 25320 W Six Mile, 48240. SAN 308-0307. Tel: 313-531-5960. FAX: 313-531-1721. E-mail: rtdl@redfordlibrary.org. Web Site: rtdl.org. *Dir,* Garrett Hungerford; Tel: 313-531-5960, Ext 100, E-mail: ghungerford@rtdl.org; *Head, Adult Serv,* Carol Deckert; E-mail: cdeckert@rtdl.org; *Head, Automation,* Martin Smith; E-mail: msmith@rtdl.org; *Head, Children's Servx,* Suzanne Migrin; E-mail: smigrin@rtdl.org; *Adult Prog Coordr, Adult Ref Librn,* Linda Pride; E-mail: lpride@rtdl.org; *Teen Librn,* Kendra Wesner; E-mail: kwesner@rtdl.org; *Bus Mgr, Fac Mgr,* Michael Gazzarari; E-mail: mgazzarari@rtdl.org; *Circ Supvr,* Teneia Combs; E-mail: tcombs@rtdl.org; *Ad,* Brooke Galbreath; E-mail: bgalbreath@rtdl.org; *Mkt Coordr,* Megan Grant; E-mail: mgrant@rtdl.org; Staff 11 (MLS 7, Non-MLS 4)
Founded 1947. Pop 48,362; Circ 297,454
Automation Activity & Vendor Info: (Circulation) CARL.Solution (TLC); (ILL) Mel Cat; (OPAC) CARL.Solution (TLC)
Wireless access
Partic in Midwest Collaborative for Library Services; The Library Network
Special Services for the Deaf - ADA equip; Assistive tech; Closed caption videos
Special Services for the Blind - BiFolkal kits; Bks on CD; Braille bks; Internet workstation with adaptive software; Large print bks; Large screen computer & software; Low vision equip; Magnifiers; Optolec clearview video magnifier; Screen reader software
Open Mon-Thurs 10-8:30, Fri & Sat 10-5, Sun (Sept-May) Noon-5
Restriction: Restricted access
Friends of the Library Group

REED CITY

P REED CITY AREA DISTRICT LIBRARY*, 829 S Chestnut St, 49677-1152. SAN 308-3667. Tel: 231-832-2131. FAX: 231-832-2131. Web Site: www.reedcitylibrary.org. *Dir,* Thomas Burnosky; E-mail: tburnosky@reedcitylibrary.org; *Asst Dir,* Jennifer Thorson; Staff 5 (MLS 1, Non-MLS 4)
Pop 8,508; Circ 47,874
Library Holdings: AV Mats 486; Large Print Bks 450; Bk Titles 21,000; Per Subs 58; Talking Bks 385
Special Collections: Memorial Cookbook Coll
Wireless access
Function: ILL available, Photocopying/Printing, Prog for adults, Prog for children & young adult, Ref serv available, Spoken cassettes & CDs, Summer reading prog
Partic in Mid-Michigan Library League
Open Mon, Wed & Fri 11-5, Tues & Thurs 11-7, Sat (Sept-May) 11-2

REESE

P REESE UNITY DISTRICT LIBRARY, 2065 Gates St, 48757. (Mail add: PO Box 413, 48757), SAN 376-6322. Tel: 989-868-4120. FAX: 989-868-4123. Web Site: reeseunitylibrary.org. *Dir,* Danielle Reid; E-mail: dreid@reeseunitylibrary.org
Founded 1990. Pop 6,295; Circ 28,000
Library Holdings: Large Print Bks 400; Bk Titles 22,000; Bk Vols 23,500; Per Subs 41; Talking Bks 450
Wireless access
Partic in White Pine Library Cooperative
Open Mon-Thurs 9-7, Fri 9-6, Sat 9-2

REMUS

P WHEATLAND TOWNSHIP LIBRARY*, 207 Michigan Ave, 49340. (Mail add: PO Box 217, 49340-0217), SAN 308-3675. Tel: 989-967-8271. FAX: 989-967-8271. E-mail: vitrumpet@yahoo.com. Web Site: remus.org/library. *Dir,* Becky Kurtz
Pop 2,929
Library Holdings: Bk Vols 15,000; Per Subs 26; Talking Bks 342; Videos 335
Wireless access
Partic in Mid-Michigan Library League
Open Tues-Fri 10-5, Sat 9-12
Friends of the Library Group

REPUBLIC

P REPUBLIC-MICHIGAMME PUBLIC LIBRARY*, 227 Maple St, 49879-9998. SAN 308-3683. Tel: 906-376-2239, 906-376-2277. FAX: 906-376-8299. Web Site: sites.google.com/site/republicmichigammeschools/public-library. *Dir,* Larry Woukko; E-mail: lwuokko@r-mschool.org
Library Holdings: Audiobooks 112; DVDs 50; Bk Titles 12,028; Per Subs 25
Wireless access
Partic in Superiorland Library Cooperative; Upper Peninsula Region of Library Cooperation, Inc
Open Tues-Fri (Winter) 3:15-7; Tues & Thurs (Summer) 9-12, Wed 3-7

RICHMOND

P LOIS WAGNER MEMORIAL LIBRARY*, 35200 Division Rd, 48062. SAN 308-3691. Tel: 586-727-2665. FAX: 586-727-3774. E-mail: lwml@libcoop.net. Web Site: www.cityofrichmond.net/191/Lois-Wagner-Memorial-Library. *Dir,* Julianne Kammer; E-mail: kammerj@libcoop.net; *Syst Mgr,* Rebecca Brockett; E-mail: lwmsysman@gmail.com; *Libr Tech,* Colleen Kelley; E-mail: kelleyc@libcoop.net
Founded 1912. Circ 58,076
Library Holdings: Bk Vols 35,636; Per Subs 44
Special Collections: Pictorial History of Richmond, photos
Automation Activity & Vendor Info: (Cataloging) SirsiDynix; (Circulation) SirsiDynix
Wireless access
Publications: Library Information Hand-outs; Newsletter (Quarterly)
Partic in Suburban Library Cooperative
Open Mon-Wed 9-7, Thurs & Fri 9-5, Sat 10-2
Friends of the Library Group

RIVER ROUGE

P RIVER ROUGE PUBLIC LIBRARY, 221 Burke St, 48218. SAN 308-3705. Tel: 313-843-2040. FAX: 313-842-4716. Web Site: www.river-rouge.lib.mi.us. *Libr Dir,* Gurpreet Samra; E-mail: gsamra@tln.lib.mi.us; *Youth Serv Librn,* Lynn Shymwell
Founded 1958. Pop 10,060; Circ 14,984
Library Holdings: Bk Vols 26,179; Per Subs 75
Automation Activity & Vendor Info: (Cataloging) SirsiDynix; (Circulation) SirsiDynix; (OPAC) SirsiDynix
Wireless access
Open Mon-Wed 12-7, Thurs 12-6, Fri 12-5

RIVERDALE

P SEVILLE TOWNSHIP PUBLIC LIBRARY, 6734 N Lumberjack Rd, 48877. (Mail add: PO Box 160, 48877-0160), SAN 308-3713. Tel: 989-833-7776. FAX: 989-833-2588. E-mail: SevilleTownshipLibrary@gmail.com. Web Site: www.seville.michlibrary.org/. *Dir,* Justine Peterson
Founded 1941. Pop 2,948; Circ 13,222
Library Holdings: Bk Titles 11,217; Bk Vols 12,200; Per Subs 50
Wireless access
Partic in Mid-Michigan Library League
Open Mon, Tues & Fri 9-5, Wed 2-7, Sat 9-12

ROCHESTER

M CRITTENTON HOSPITAL MEDICAL CENTER*, Ullmann Medical Library, 1101 W University Dr, 48307. *Dir,* Paula Grube; E-mail: paula.grube@ascension.org
Founded 1967
Library Holdings: Bk Vols 541; Per Subs 50
Automation Activity & Vendor Info: (Cataloging) Inmagic, Inc.; (Circulation) Inmagic, Inc.
Restriction: Med staff only

C OAKLAND UNIVERSITY LIBRARY*, Kresge Library, 100 Library Dr, 48309-4479. SAN 308-3756. Tel: 248-370-4426. Interlibrary Loan Service Tel: 248-370-2132. FAX: 248-370-2474. Reference E-mail: ref@oakland.edu. Web Site: library.oakland.edu. *Assoc Prof, Dean, Libr Serv,* Stephen P Weiter; *Asst Dean,* Linda Kreger; Tel: 248-370-2488, E-mail: kreger@oakland.edu; *Dir, Med Libr,* Nancy Bulgarelli; Tel: 248-370-2481, E-mail: bulgarel@oakland.edu; *Digital Assets Librn,* Meghan Finch; Tel: 248-370-2457, E-mail: mmfinch@oakland.edu; *First Year Experience Librn,* Katie Greer; Tel: 248-370-2480, E-mail: greer@oakland.edu; *Health Sci, Nursing & Fac Res Support Librn,* Julia Rodriguez; Tel: 248-370-2490, E-mail: juliar@oakland.edu; *Humanities Librn, Hist & Modern Lang,* Dominique Daniel; Tel: 248-370-2478, E-mail: daniel@oakland.edu; *Outreach Librn,* Anne Switzer; Tel: 248-370-2475, E-mail: switzer2@oakland.edu; *Tech/eLearning,* Amanda Hess; Tel: 248-370-2487, E-mail: nichols@oakland.edu; *Coll Develop, Govt Doc,* Helen Levenson; Tel: 248-370-2497, E-mail: hlevenson@oakland.edu; *Bus Librn,* Shawn McCann; Tel: 248-370-2456, E-mail: mccann@oakland.edu; *Humanities Librn,* Emily Spunaugle; Tel: 248-370-2498, E-mail: spunaugle@oakland.edu; *Res Support & Data Serv Librn,* Joanna Thielen; Tel: 248-370-2477, E-mail: jthielen@oakland.edu.
Subject Specialists: *Health sci, Nursing,* Julia Rodriguez; *Linguistics, Modern lang,* Dominique Daniel; Staff 21 (MLS 16, Non-MLS 5)
Founded 1959. Enrl 18,920; Fac 992; Highest Degree: Doctorate
Jul 2016-Jun 2017. Mats Exp $1,868,000, Books $359,000, Per/Ser (Incl. Access Fees) $757,000, Electronic Ref Mat (Incl. Access Fees) $752,000. Sal $2,570,000 (Prof $759,000)
Library Holdings: e-books 50,000; Bk Vols 800,000; Per Subs 75,000
Special Collections: 17th-19th Century Books by Women (Hicks Coll); Bingham Historical Children's Literature Coll; China Coll; Folklore & Witchcraft (James Coll); Gaylor Coll of GLBT Literature; Lincolniana (Springer Coll); University Archives. US Document Depository
Automation Activity & Vendor Info: (Acquisitions) Ex Libris Group; (Cataloging) Ex Libris Group; (Circulation) Ex Libris Group; (Course Reserve) Ex Libris Group; (ILL) OCLC ILLiad; (OPAC) Ex Libris Group; (Serials) Ex Libris Group
Wireless access
Partic in Midwest Collaborative for Library Services; OCLC Online Computer Library Center, Inc

P ROCHESTER HILLS PUBLIC LIBRARY, 500 Olde Towne Rd, 48307-2043. SAN 308-373X. Tel: 248-656-2900. Circulation Tel: 248-650-7174. Reference Tel: 248-650-7130. Administration Tel: 248-650-7122. FAX: 248-650-7121. Web Site: www.rhpl.org. *Libr Dir,* Juliane Morian; E-mail: juliane.morian@rhpl.org; *Dir, Info Tech,* Derek Brown; Tel: 248-650-7123, E-mail: derek.brown@rhpl.org; *Head, Adult Serv,* Allison Sartwell; Tel: 248-650-7132; *Head, Youth Serv,* Betsy Raczkowski; Tel: 248-650-7142; *Bkmobile/Outreach Serv,* Mary Davis; Tel: 248-650-7152, E-mail: Mary.Davis@rhpl.org; *Circ, User Experience Mgr,* Meggie Brody; Tel: 248-650-7162, E-mail: meggie.brody@rhpl.org; Staff 60 (MLS 24, Non-MLS 36)
Founded 1924. Pop 100,485; Circ 2,000,000
Jan 2020-Dec 2020 Income $3,154,100, State $120,400, City $2,749,700, County $284,000. Mats Exp $4,824,700, Books $358,000, Per/Ser (Incl. Access Fees) $25,000, AV Mat $142,900, Electronic Ref Mat (Incl. Access Fees) $246,500. Sal $3,249,400
Library Holdings: AV Mats 18,059; e-books 12,219; Bk Vols 194,066; Per Subs 400; Videos 44,780
Special Collections: Photographic Archives. Oral History
Automation Activity & Vendor Info: (Acquisitions) Innovative Interfaces, Inc; (Cataloging) Innovative Interfaces, Inc; (Circulation) Innovative Interfaces, Inc; (OPAC) Innovative Interfaces, Inc; (Serials) Innovative Interfaces, Inc
Wireless access
Function: Home delivery & serv to seniorr ctr & nursing homes, Homebound delivery serv, ILL available, Internet access, Photocopying/Printing, Prog for adults, Prog for children & young adult, Ref serv available, Summer reading prog, Wheelchair accessible
Publications: News & Views (Newsletter)
Partic in Metro Net Libr Consortium; The Library Network
Special Services for the Blind - Accessible computers; Aids for in-house use; Assistive/Adapted tech devices, equip & products; BiFolkal kits; Bks & mags in Braille, on rec, tape & cassette; Bks on flash-memory cartridges; Braille & cassettes; Braille alphabet card; Braille bks; Braille equip; Children's Braille; Closed circuit TV magnifier; Compressed speech equip; Computer access aids; Computer with voice synthesizer for visually impaired persons; Copier with enlargement capabilities; Descriptive video serv (DVS); Digital talking bk; Digital talking bk machines; Disability awareness prog; Extensive large print coll; Home delivery serv; Large print bks; Large print bks & talking machines; Large screen computer & software; Large type calculator; Lending of low vision aids; PC for people with disabilities; Screen enlargement software for people with visual disabilities; Talking bk & rec for the blind cat; Talking bk serv referral
Open Mon-Thurs 9-9, Fri & Sat 9-6, Sun (Sept-May) 1-6
Friends of the Library Group
Bookmobiles: 2

ROCHESTER HILLS

C ROCHESTER COLLEGE*, Ennis & Nancy Ham Library, 800 W Avon Rd, 48307. SAN 308-3748. Tel: 248-218-2260. E-mail: librarystaff@rc.edu. Web Site: library.rochesteru.edu. *Dir, Libr Serv,* Allison Jimenez; Tel: 248-218-2268, E-mail: ajimenez@rc.edu; *Per Asst,* Karen Liston; Staff 5 (MLS 5)
Founded 1959. Enrl 1,160; Fac 41; Highest Degree: Master
May 2013-Apr 2014. Mats Exp $104,599, Books $18,596, Per/Ser (Incl. Access Fees) $12,726, AV Mat $2,958, Electronic Ref Mat (Incl. Access Fees) $69,519, Presv $800. Sal $142,226 (Prof $127,716)
Library Holdings: AV Mats 2,131; Bks on Deafness & Sign Lang 14; CDs 779; DVDs 1,131; e-books 11,646; Electronic Media & Resources 60; Microforms 44,987; Music Scores 80; Bk Titles 55,969; Bk Vols 55,471; Per Subs 99; Talking Bks 71; Videos 19
Subject Interests: Biblical studies, Bus, Communications, Early childhood educ, Hist, Lit, Music, Psychol, Relig
Automation Activity & Vendor Info: (Acquisitions) SirsiDynix; (Cataloging) SirsiDynix; (Circulation) SirsiDynix; (Course Reserve) SirsiDynix; (ILL) OCLC; (OPAC) SirsiDynix; (Serials) SirsiDynix
Wireless access
Partic in Detroit Area Library Network; Midwest Collaborative for Library Services
Special Services for the Blind - Bks on CD
Open Mon, Tues & Thurs (Winter) 9am-11pm, Wed 9-6 & 8:30-11, Fri 9-6, Sat 12-5, Sun 7am-11pm; Mon-Fri (Summer) 9-6, Sat 12-5

ROGERS CITY

P PRESQUE ISLE DISTRICT LIBRARY*, 181 E Erie St, 49779-1709. SAN 308-3764. Tel: 989-734-2477. Circulation Tel: 989-734-2477, Ext 224. Interlibrary Loan Service Tel: 989-734-2477, Ext 226. Reference Tel: 989-734-2477, Ext 225. FAX: 989-734-4899. E-mail: librarian@pidl.org. Web Site: www.pidl.org. *Libr Dir,* Amber L Alexander; Tel: 989-734-2477, Ext 222, E-mail: director@pidl.org; *Prog Dir,* Anne Belanger; E-mail: annebelanger@pidl.org; *Children & Youth Serv Librn,* Don Dimick; *Cat Supvr,* Kay Spomer; Staff 11 (MLS 1, Non-MLS 10)
Founded 1945. Pop 14,646; Circ 69,297
Library Holdings: Bk Vols 64,800; Per Subs 65
Special Collections: Great Lakes Nautical Coll; Michigan Coll
Automation Activity & Vendor Info: (Acquisitions) Baker & Taylor; (Cataloging) SirsiDynix-WorkFlows; (Circulation) SirsiDynix-WorkFlows; (ILL) SirsiDynix-WorkFlows; (OPAC) BiblioCommons; (Serials) EBSCO Online
Wireless access
Function: Adult bk club, Adult literacy prog, Art exhibits, Audiobks via web, AV serv, Bk club(s), Bks on cassette, Bks on CD, CD-ROM, Children's prog, Computer training, Computers for patron use, Distance learning, E-Reserves, Electronic databases & coll, Free DVD rentals, Games & aids for people with disabilities, Holiday prog, Home delivery & serv to seniorr ctr & nursing homes, Homebound delivery serv, ILL available, Jail serv, Magazines, Magnifiers for reading, Mail & tel request accepted, Meeting rooms, Online cat, Online ref, Outreach serv, Outside serv via phone, mail, e-mail & web, Photocopying/Printing, Preschool outreach, Prog for adults, Prog for children & young adult, Ref serv available, Senior computer classes, Senior outreach, Serves people with intellectual disabilities, Spoken cassettes & CDs, Spoken cassettes & DVDs, Story hour, Study rm, Summer reading prog, Tax forms, Teen prog, VHS videos, Wheelchair accessible, Workshops
Publications: November Requiem (Local historical information)
Partic in Michicard Borrowing Serv; Northland Library Cooperative
Special Services for the Deaf - ADA equip; Adult & family literacy prog; Bks on deafness & sign lang; Closed caption videos; Coll on deaf educ; High interest/low vocabulary bks; Sign lang interpreter upon request for prog
Special Services for the Blind - Accessible computers; Assistive/Adapted tech devices, equip & products; Audio mat; Bks & mags in Braille, on rec, tape & cassette; Bks available with recordings; Bks on cassette; Bks on CD; Cassettes; Computer with voice synthesizer for visually impaired persons; Copier with enlargement capabilities; Extensive large print coll; Home delivery serv; Large print & cassettes; Large print bks; Magnifiers; Recorded bks; Ref serv; Screen enlargement software for people with visual disabilities; Sound rec; Talking bks

Open Mon & Thurs 9:30-7:30, Tues, Wed & Fri 10-5:30, Sat 10-3
Friends of the Library Group
Branches: 4
GRAND LAKE BRANCH, 18132 Lake Esau Hwy, Presque Isle, 49777, SAN 321-4087. Tel: 989-595-5051. FAX: 989-595-3146. *Br Mgr,* Sandy Dion
Special Services for the Blind - Computer with voice synthesizer for visually impaired persons
Open Tues & Thurs 2-7, Wed, Fri & Sat 10-4
Friends of the Library Group
MILLERSBURG BRANCH, 5561 Main St, Millersburg, 49759. (Mail add: PO Box 160, Millersburg, 49759). Tel: 989-733-4411. E-mail: millersburg@pidl.org. *Br Mgr,* Lena Prichard; Tel: 989-733-4411
ONAWAY BRANCH, 20774 State St, Onaway, 49765, SAN 321-4079. Tel: 989-733-6621. FAX: 989-733-7842. E-mail: onaway@pidl.org. *Librn,* JoLynn Zalewski; E-mail: onawaybranch@pidl.org
Special Services for the Blind - Computer with voice synthesizer for visually impaired persons
Open Mon, Wed & Thurs 2-7, Tues & Fri 10-5, Sat 10-2:30
Friends of the Library Group
POSEN BRANCH, 6987 Turtle St, Posen, 49776, SAN 321-4095. Tel: 989-766-2233. FAX: 989-766-9977. E-mail: posen@pidl.org. *Br Mgr,* Nicole Grulke
Open Mon 1-7, Tues, Wed & Thurs 1-5, Fri 10-2
Friends of the Library Group

ROMULUS

P ROMULUS PUBLIC LIBRARY*, 11121 Wayne Rd, 48174. SAN 308-3780. Tel: 734-942-7589. FAX: 734-941-3575. E-mail: romuluspubliclibrary@gmail.com. Web Site: www.romuluslibrary.org. *Dir,* Patty Braden; Tel: 734-955-4516, E-mail: pbraden@romuluslibrary.org; *Asst Dir, Youth Serv,* Jessica Wilhoite; Tel: 734-955-4517, E-mail: jwilhoite@romuluslibrary.org; Staff 10 (MLS 3, Non-MLS 7)
Founded 1923. Pop 39,868
Library Holdings: Bk Vols 51,000; Per Subs 19
Special Collections: Michigan Coll
Wireless access
Function: 24/7 Electronic res, 24/7 Online cat, Activity rm, Adult bk club, Adult literacy prog, After school storytime, Art exhibits, Art programs, AV serv, Bk club(s), Bks on CD, Children's prog, Computer training, Computers for patron use, Electronic databases & coll, Family literacy, Free DVD rentals, Holiday prog, ILL available, Internet access, Laminating, Life-long learning prog for all ages, Literacy & newcomer serv, Magazines, Meeting rooms, Movies, Museum passes, Music CDs, Online cat, Online info literacy tutorials on the web & in blackboard, Outreach serv, Outside serv via phone, mail, e-mail & web, OverDrive digital audio bks, Photocopying/Printing, Preschool outreach, Preschool reading prog, Printer for laptops & handheld devices, Prof lending libr, Prog for adults, Prog for children & young adult, Ref & res, Scanner, Senior computer classes, Senior outreach, Serves people with intellectual disabilities, STEM programs, Story hour, Study rm, Summer & winter reading prog, Summer reading prog, Tax forms, Teen prog, Wheelchair accessible, Winter reading prog
Partic in The Library Network
Open Mon-Thurs 10-8, Fri 10-6, Sat 10-5
Friends of the Library Group

ROSCOMMON

J KIRTLAND COMMUNITY COLLEGE LIBRARY*, 10775 N St Helen Rd, 48653. SAN 308-3799. Tel: 989-275-5000, Ext 246. FAX: 989-275-8510. E-mail: library@kirtland.edu. Web Site: www.kirtland.edu/library. *Dir,* Deb Shumaker; Tel: 989-275-5000, Ext 235, E-mail: deb.shumaker@kirtland.edu; *Ref Librn,* Pat Ellisor; Tel: 989-275-5000, Ext 246, E-mail: pat.ellisor@kirtland.edu; Staff 2 (MLS 2)
Founded 1966. Enrl 1,800; Fac 75; Highest Degree: Associate
Library Holdings: AV Mats 1,000; Bks on Deafness & Sign Lang 12; e-books 19,000; Bk Titles 29,000; Bk Vols 31,000; Per Subs 205; Talking Bks 150
Automation Activity & Vendor Info: (Cataloging) SirsiDynix; (Circulation) SirsiDynix; (OPAC) SirsiDynix
Wireless access
Function: Archival coll, Distance learning, Health sci info serv, ILL available, Orientations, Photocopying/Printing, Ref serv available, Spoken cassettes & CDs, Telephone ref, Wheelchair accessible
Open Mon-Fri 8-4:30
Restriction: Open to pub for ref & circ; with some limitations

§P ROSCOMMON AREA DISTRICT LIBRARY, 106 Lake St, 48653. (Mail add: PO Box 888, 48653). Tel: 989-281-1305. E-mail: radlcirc@uproc.lib.mi.us. Web Site: roscommonlibrary.org. *Libr Dir,* Colleen Dyke
Founded 2010
Library Holdings: Bk Vols 30,000
Wireless access
Function: Computers for patron use, Meeting rooms, Photocopying/Printing, Scanner
Partic in Upper Peninsula Region of Library Cooperation, Inc
Open Tues-Thurs 10-7, Fri 10-5, Sat 10-3
Friends of the Library Group
Branches: 1
LYON BRANCH, 7851 W Higgins Lake Dr, Higgins Lake, 48627. (Mail add: PO Box 232, Higgins Lake, 48627). Tel: 989-281-9111. *Br Mgr,* Cindy Post-Petkus
Open Mon-Fri 10-3

ROSE CITY

P OGEMAW DISTRICT LIBRARY*, 107 W Main St, 48654. SAN 322-6484. Tel: 989-685-3300. FAX: 989-685-3647. E-mail: ogemawdistrictlibrary@hotmail.com. Web Site: www.ogemawlibrary.net. *Dir,* Jeanette Leathorn; E-mail: librarianzim@aol.com
Founded 1977. Pop 12,561; Circ 74,321
Library Holdings: Bk Titles 24,193; Bk Vols 37,817
Subject Interests: Genealogy, Local hist
Wireless access
Open Mon 10-7, Tues-Thurs 10-5, Fri & Sat 10-2
Friends of the Library Group
Branches: 2
OGEMAW EAST, 200 Washington, Prescott, 48756, SAN 325-3406. Tel: 989-873-5807. E-mail: prescottlibrary@hotmail.com. *Dir,* Jeanette Leathorn
Library Holdings: Bk Vols 15,000; Per Subs 20
Open Mon, Wed & Thurs 12-5
SKIDWAY LAKE, 2196 Greenwood Rd, Prescott, 48756. (Mail add: PO Box 4520, Prescott, 48756). Tel: 989-873-5086. FAX: 989-873-4646. *Librn,* Melissa Rousseau
Open Mon 10-7, Tues-Thurs 10-5, Fri 10-2

ROSEVILLE

P ROSEVILLE PUBLIC LIBRARY, 29777 Gratiot Ave, 48066. SAN 308-3802. Tel: 586-445-5407. Automation Services Tel: 586-203-8725. E-mail: rsvlibraryadmin@roseville-mi.gov. Web Site: rosevillelibrary.org. *Dir,* Jacalynn Harvey; *Adult Serv Coordr, Asst Dir,* Tracy Wilson; Staff 21 (MLS 8, Non-MLS 13)
Founded 1936. Pop 48,129; Circ 235,067
Library Holdings: Bk Titles 132,171; Per Subs 301
Automation Activity & Vendor Info: (Acquisitions) SirsiDynix; (Cataloging) SirsiDynix; (Circulation) SirsiDynix; (OPAC) SirsiDynix; (Serials) SirsiDynix
Wireless access
Function: 24/7 Electronic res, 24/7 Online cat, Adult bk club, Bks on CD, Children's prog, Computers for patron use, Electronic databases & coll, Free DVD rentals, Homebound delivery serv, ILL available, Internet access, Magazines, Online cat, OverDrive digital audio bks, Prog for adults, Prog for children & young adult, Ref serv available, Scanner, STEM programs, Story hour, Study rm, Summer reading prog, Tax forms, Teen prog, Telephone ref, Wheelchair accessible
Partic in Suburban Library Cooperative
Open Mon-Thurs 9-8, Fri 9-5, Sat (Sept-May) 10-4
Friends of the Library Group

ROYAL OAK

M BEAUMONT HOSPITAL*, Medical Library, 3601 W 13 Mile Rd, 48073-6769. SAN 308-3810. Tel: 248-898-1750. FAX: 248-898-1060. Web Site: www.beaumonthospitals.com. *Librn,* Andrea Rogers-Snyr; E-mail: andrea.rogerssnyr@beaumont.edu; Staff 8 (MLS 4, Non-MLS 4)
Founded 1956
Library Holdings: e-books 325; e-journals 15,550; Bk Titles 10,000; Per Subs 30
Wireless access
Restriction: Badge access after hrs, Hospital employees & physicians only

J OAKLAND COMMUNITY COLLEGE*, Royal Oak Campus Library, 739 S Washington Ave, Bldg C, 48067-3898. SAN 308-3829. Tel: 248-246-2525. Interlibrary Loan Service Tel: 248-246-2527. Reference Tel: 248-246-2519. FAX: 248-246-2520. Web Site: libguides.oaklandcc.edu/about/royal_oak, www.oaklandcc.edu/library. *Librn, Ref (Info Servs),* Carol Benson; Tel: 248-246-2528, E-mail: ctbenson@oaklandcc.edu; *Ref Librn,* Darlene Johnson-Bignotti; Tel: 248-246-2526, E-mail: dxjohnso@oaklandcc.edu; Staff 5 (MLS 2, Non-MLS 3)
Founded 1974. Enrl 4,812; Fac 63; Highest Degree: Associate
Library Holdings: CDs 29; DVDs 435; e-books 239,460; Electronic Media & Resources 108; Microforms 3,741; Bk Vols 40,114; Per Subs 160
Special Collections: Career Coll; Children's Literature Coll; Dante Alighieri Society Coll, bks in Italian & English; ESL Coll

Automation Activity & Vendor Info: (Acquisitions) Ex Libris Group; (Cataloging) Ex Libris Group; (Circulation) Ex Libris Group; (Course Reserve) Ex Libris Group; (Discovery) Ex Libris Group; (ILL) Ex Libris Group; (OPAC) Ex Libris Group; (Serials) Ex Libris Group
Wireless access
Partic in Midwest Collaborative for Library Services
Special Services for the Deaf - Accessible learning ctr; ADA equip
Special Services for the Blind - Accessible computers; Assistive/Adapted tech devices, equip & products
Open Mon-Thurs (Fall & Winter) 8am-9pm, Fri 8-7, Sat 10-2; Mon-Thurs (Summer) 8am-9pm, Fri 8-5

P ROYAL OAK PUBLIC LIBRARY*, 222 E Eleven Mile Rd, 48067-2633. (Mail add: PO Box 494, 48068-0494), SAN 308-3837. Tel: 248-246-3700. Interlibrary Loan Service Tel: 248-246-3720. Reference Tel: 248-246-3727. Administration Tel: 248-246-3711. FAX: 248-246-3701. Web Site: www.ropl.org. *Dir,* Mary Karshner; Tel: 248-246-3710, E-mail: mary@ropl.org; *Head, Adult Serv,* Mary Ann DeKane; Tel: 248-246-3714, E-mail: maryann@ropl.org; *Head, Support Serv,* Matthew Day; Tel: 248-246-3732, E-mail: matthew@ropl.org; *Head, Youth & Teen Serv,* Emily Dumas; Tel: 248-246-3716, E-mail: emily@ropl.org; *Tech Serv, Webmaster,* Ed Pank; Tel: 248-246-3751; Staff 13 (MLS 13)
Founded 1856. Pop 57,000
Library Holdings: AV Mats 22,882; Large Print Bks 960; Bk Vols 131,675
Special Collections: Auto Repair Manuals; Royal Oak History Coll
Automation Activity & Vendor Info: (Cataloging) SirsiDynix; (Circulation) SirsiDynix; (OPAC) SirsiDynix; (Serials) SirsiDynix
Wireless access
Function: 24/7 Electronic res, 24/7 Online cat, Activity rm, Adult bk club, After school storytime
Publications: Leaflet (Newsletter); Twigs (Newsletter)
Partic in The Library Network
Open Mon-Thurs 10-9, Fri & Sat 10-6
Friends of the Library Group

SAGINAW

M CMU HEALTH*, Knowledge Services, CMU College of Medicine, Educ Bldg, 1632 Stone St, 48602. SAN 320-8109. Tel: 989-746-7577. FAX: 989-746-7582. E-mail: cmedlibrary@cmich.edu. Web Site: med.cmich.edu/ks. *Libr Mgr,* Tamara Sawyer; E-mail: tamara.sawyer@cmich.edu; *Libr Asst, Ref,* Courtney Cooney; E-mail: courtney.cooney@cmich.edu; *Libr Asst,* Jane Murphy; E-mail: jane.murphy@cmich.edu; *Libr Asst,* Amy Smethwick; E-mail: amy.smethwick@cmich.edu; Staff 4 (MLS 1, Non-MLS 3)
Founded 1978
Library Holdings: Bk Titles 3,600; Bk Vols 4,500; Per Subs 150
Subject Interests: Allied health, Human med
Automation Activity & Vendor Info: (Cataloging) EOS International; (Circulation) EOS International; (Discovery) EBSCO Discovery Service; (ILL) OCLC WorldShare Interlibrary Loan; (OPAC) EOS International; (Serials) EOS International
Wireless access
Partic in Michigan Health Sciences Libraries Association
Open Mon-Fri 8-4:30
Branches:
ST MARY'S BRANCH, 800 S Washington, 2nd Flr, 48601-2551. Tel: 989-907-8204. FAX: 989-907-8616. *Knowledge Mgr,* Tamara Sawyer; Tel: 989-746-7577, E-mail: tamara.sawyer@cmich.edu; *Libr Asst, Ref,* Courtney Cooney; Tel: 989-746-7577, E-mail: courtney.cooney@cmich.edu; *Libr Asst,* Amy Smethwick; Tel: 989-746-7577, E-mail: amy.smethwich@cmich.edu; Staff 3.5 (MLS 1, Non-MLS 2.5)
Library Holdings: Bk Vols 1,000; Per Subs 36
Open Mon-Fri 8-4:30
Restriction: Open to pub for ref only

GM DEPARTMENT OF VETERANS AFFAIRS*, Aleta E Lutz VA Medical Center & Health Science Library, 1500 Weiss St, 48602. SAN 308-3896. Tel: 989-497-2500, Ext 11870. FAX: 989-321-4902. *Librn,* Susie Sheltraw; E-mail: susanna.sheltraw@va.gov
Library Holdings: Bk Vols 825; Per Subs 100
Special Collections: AV Coll
Wireless access
Function: AV serv, Bks on CD, Electronic databases & coll, ILL available, Internet access, Magnifiers for reading, Microfiche/film & reading machines, VHS videos
Open Mon-Fri 7:30-4
Restriction: Access at librarian's discretion, Authorized patrons, Authorized personnel only, Badge access after hrs, Employee & client use only, Govt use only, Open to authorized patrons, Staff & patient use

P PUBLIC LIBRARIES OF SAGINAW*, Hoyt Main Library, 505 Janes Ave, 48607. SAN 347-058X. Tel: 989-755-0904. FAX: 989-755-9829. TDD: 989-755-9831. Web Site: www.saginawlibrary.org. *Dir,* Maria McCarville; E-mail: mmccarville@saginawlibrary.org; Staff 70 (MLS 16, Non-MLS 54)
Founded 1890. Pop 135,000
Library Holdings: AV Mats 23,635; Electronic Media & Resources 60; Bk Vols 411,598; Per Subs 762
Special Collections: African Heritage Coll; Genealogy, Saginaw Valley History & Michigan History (Eddy Historical & Genealogy Coll). US Document Depository
Subject Interests: Art, Genealogy, Local hist, Multicultural, Parenting, Sci tech
Automation Activity & Vendor Info: (Acquisitions) SirsiDynix; (Circulation) SirsiDynix; (OPAC) SirsiDynix
Wireless access
Partic in Mideastern Michigan Library Cooperative
Open Mon-Thurs 9-8, Fri & Sat 9-5
Friends of the Library Group
Branches: 3
BUTMAN-FISH, 1716 Hancock St, 48602, SAN 347-061X. Tel: 989-799-9160. FAX: 989-799-8149. *Head of Libr,* Lynn Heitkamp
Library Holdings: Bk Vols 92,754
Special Collections: African Heritage Coll; Hispanic Heritage Coll; Large Print Books
Open Mon-Thurs 11-7, Fri & Sat 9-5
Friends of the Library Group
RUTH BRADY WICKES LIBRARY, 1713 Hess St, 48601, SAN 347-0679. Tel: 989-752-3821. FAX: 989-752-8685. *Head of Libr,* Roy Bishop
Library Holdings: Bk Vols 43,492
Special Collections: African Heritage Coll; Hispanic Heritage Coll; Spanish Language Materials
Open Mon-Thurs 12-6, Sat 12-5
Friends of the Library Group
ZAUEL MEMORIAL LIBRARY, 3100 N Center Rd, 48603, SAN 347-0709. Tel: 989-799-2771. FAX: 989-799-1771. *Head of Libr,* Bill O'Brien; Staff 5 (MLS 3, Non-MLS 2)
Library Holdings: Bk Vols 117,102
Special Collections: African Heritage Coll; Hispanic Heritage Coll; Parenting Coll
Open Mon, Tues & Thurs 9-9, Wed Noon-9, Fri & Sat 9-5
Friends of the Library Group

S SAGINAW ART MUSEUM*, The John & Michele Bueker Research Library, 1126 N Michigan Ave, 48602. SAN 308-3861. Tel: 989-754-2491. FAX: 989-754-9387. E-mail: registrar@saginawartmuseum.org. Web Site: www.saginawartmuseum.org. *Exec Dir,* Mike Kolleth; *Curatorial Asst, Educ Coordr,* Tim Faris; E-mail: registrar@saginawartmuseum.org
Founded 1948
Library Holdings: Bk Titles 1,100
Special Collections: Eanger Irving Couse Coll (bks, per, doc, correspondences, photog, etc)
Subject Interests: Archit, Fine arts, Graphic design, Photog
Wireless access
Open Tues-Sat Noon-5
Restriction: Not a lending libr

P THOMAS TOWNSHIP LIBRARY*, 8207 Shields Dr, 48609-4814. SAN 376-7884. Tel: 989-781-3770. FAX: 989-781-3881. E-mail: info@thomastownshiplibrary.org. Web Site: thomastownshiplibrary.org. *Dir,* Tari L Dusek
Library Holdings: Bk Titles 68,000; Bk Vols 71,100; Per Subs 160
Automation Activity & Vendor Info: (Cataloging) Follett Software; (Circulation) Follett Software; (OPAC) Follett Software
Partic in White Pine Library Cooperative
Open Mon-Thurs 10-8, Fri & Sat 10-5, Sun (Oct-April) 1-5

SAINT CHARLES

P SAINT CHARLES DISTRICT LIBRARY*, 104 W Spruce St, 48655. SAN 308-3918. Tel: 989-865-9451. FAX: 989-865-6666. E-mail: info@stcharlesdistrictlibrary.org. Web Site: www.stcharlesdistrictlibrary.org. *Dir,* Nannette Pretzer; E-mail: n.pretzer@stcharlesdistrictlibrary.org; Staff 7 (Non-MLS 7)
Founded 1907. Pop 7,798; Circ 30,135
Library Holdings: Bk Vols 24,202; Per Subs 99
Special Collections: Michigan Coll
Automation Activity & Vendor Info: (Acquisitions) Horizon; (Cataloging) Horizon; (Circulation) Horizon; (Course Reserve) Horizon; (ILL) Horizon; (Media Booking) Horizon; (OPAC) Horizon; (Serials) Horizon
Wireless access
Function: Accelerated reader prog, Adult bk club, After school storytime, Bks on cassette, Bks on CD, CD-ROM, Children's prog, Computers for

patron use, Electronic databases & coll, Free DVD rentals, Holiday prog, ILL available, Music CDs, Online cat, Photocopying/Printing, Preschool reading prog, Prog for adults, Prog for children & young adult, Scanner, Story hour, Summer & winter reading prog, Tax forms, VHS videos
Partic in White Pine Library Cooperative
Open Mon-Thurs 10-7, Fri 10-5
Restriction: Badge access after hrs
Friends of the Library Group

SAINT CLAIR SHORES

S RIGHT TO LIFE OF MICHIGAN*, Macomb County Educational Resource Center, 27417 Harper, 48081. Tel: 586-774-6050. FAX: 586-774-5192. E-mail: info@rtl.org. Web Site: www.rtl.org.
Founded 1987
Library Holdings: AV Mats 339; Bk Titles 251; Videos 112
Subject Interests: Abortion, Euthanasia
Open Mon & Fri 9-4, Tues & Thurs 10-5, Wed 9-5

P SAINT CLAIR SHORES PUBLIC LIBRARY*, 22500 11 Mile Rd, 48081-1399. SAN 308-3926. Tel: 586-771-9020. FAX: 586-771-8935. TDD: 586-771-7384. Web Site: www.scslibrary.org. *Libr Dir,* Rosemary Orlando; E-mail: orlandor@libcoop.net; *Ad, Archivist,* Heidi Christein; *Ad,* Kathleen Harville; *Ad,* Alexandra Reading; *Youth Serv Librn,* Elizabeth Drewek; Staff 21 (MLS 7, Non-MLS 14)
Founded 1935
Library Holdings: Bk Vols 114,259; Per Subs 385
Special Collections: Great Lakes History; Local History, bks, photogs. Oral History
Subject Interests: Careers, Great Lakes, Mich
Automation Activity & Vendor Info: (Acquisitions) SirsiDynix; (Cataloging) SirsiDynix; (Circulation) SirsiDynix; (ILL) SirsiDynix; (OPAC) SirsiDynix; (Serials) SirsiDynix
Wireless access
Function: 24/7 Electronic res, 24/7 Online cat, Accelerated reader prog, Adult bk club, Adult literacy prog, Archival coll, Art exhibits, Audiobks on Playaways & MP3, Audiobks via web, AV serv, Bk club(s), Bks on CD, Children's prog, Computers for patron use, Digital talking bks, E-Reserves, Electronic databases & coll, Free DVD rentals, Genealogy discussion group, Holiday prog, ILL available, Instruction & testing, Internet access, Life-long learning prog for all ages, Magazines, Magnifiers for reading, Mail & tel request accepted, Mango lang, Meeting rooms, Microfiche/film & reading machines, Movies, Museum passes, Music CDs, Online cat, Online info literacy tutorials on the web & in blackboard, Online ref, Outside serv via phone, mail, e-mail & web, OverDrive digital audio bks, Photocopying/Printing, Preschool outreach, Preschool reading prog, Printer for laptops & handheld devices, Prog for adults, Prog for children & young adult, Ref & res, Ref serv available, Res assist avail, Spanish lang bks, Spoken cassettes & CDs, Spoken cassettes & DVDs, STEM programs, Story hour, Study rm, Summer reading prog, Tax forms, Teen prog, Telephone ref, VHS videos, Wheelchair accessible
Publications: Inside the Library (Newsletter); Muskrat Tales (Local history magazine)
Partic in Suburban Library Cooperative
Special Services for the Deaf - TDD equip
Open Mon-Thurs 9-9, Fri 9-5, Sat (Sept-May) 9-5
Friends of the Library Group

SAINT HELEN

P RICHFIELD TOWNSHIP PUBLIC LIBRARY*, 1410 Saint Helen Rd, 48656. (Mail add: PO Box 402, 48656-0402), SAN 308-3934. Tel: 989-389-7630. FAX: 989-389-4956. E-mail: library@richfieldtownship.com. Web Site: www.richfieldtpl.michlibrary.org. *Dir,* Lynn Taylor; Staff 2 (MLS 1, Non-MLS 1)
Founded 1965. Pop 4,500; Circ 16,000
Library Holdings: CDs 250; DVDs 600; Bk Vols 16,000; Per Subs 52
Wireless access
Partic in Mid-Michigan Library League
Open Mon 9:30-7:30, Tues 9:30-4:30, Sat 10-1

SAINT IGNACE

P SAINT IGNACE PUBLIC LIBRARY*, 110 W Spruce St, 49781-1649. SAN 308-3942. Tel: 906-643-8318. FAX: 906-643-9809. Web Site: www.uproc.lib.mi.us/Stignace. *Dir,* Alycia McKowen; E-mail: alyciamc@uproc.lib.mi.us
Pop 4,284; Circ 26,000
Library Holdings: Bk Vols 23,000; Per Subs 70
Automation Activity & Vendor Info: (Acquisitions) SirsiDynix; (Cataloging) SirsiDynix; (Circulation) SirsiDynix; (ILL) SirsiDynix
Wireless access
Partic in Upper Peninsula Region of Library Cooperation, Inc
Open Mon & Fri 9-5, Tues-Thurs 9-7, Sat 9-3
Friends of the Library Group

SAINT JOHNS

P BRIGGS DISTRICT LIBRARY*, 108 E Railroad St, 48879-1526. SAN 308-3950. Tel: 989-224-4702. FAX: 989-224-1205. Web Site: www.briggsdistrictlibrary.org. *Dir,* Sara B Morrison; E-mail: director@briggsdistrictlibrary.org; *Asst Dir,* Brett Harger; Staff 4 (MLS 1, Non-MLS 3)
Founded 1939. Pop 18,189; Circ 129,984
Library Holdings: Audiobooks 2,039; DVDs 1,205; Large Print Bks 691; Bk Vols 34,621; Per Subs 79; Videos 1,518
Special Collections: Local Genealogy Coll; Local History Coll
Automation Activity & Vendor Info: (Cataloging) Follett Software; (Circulation) Follett Software; (OPAC) Follett Software
Wireless access
Open Mon-Thurs 10-8, Fri 10-6, Sat 10-3
Friends of the Library Group

SAINT JOSEPH

R FIRST CONGREGATIONAL UNITED CHURCH OF CHRIST LIBRARY*, 2001 Niles Ave, 49085-1614. SAN 308-3969. Tel: 269-983-5519. FAX: 269-983-5988. E-mail: office@fccstjoseph.org.
Founded 1854
Library Holdings: Bk Vols 3,692
Special Collections: Video Tapes for Children & Adults
Subject Interests: Biblical studies, Educ, Psychol
Restriction: Congregants only

S THE HERITAGE MUSEUM & CULTURAL CENTER, Research Library & Archives, 601 Main St, 49085. Tel: 269-983-1191. FAX: 269-983-1274. E-mail: info@theheritagemcc.org. Web Site: www.theheritagemcc.org. *Pres,* Laurie Marshall; *Curator,* Tracy Gierada Payovich
Library Holdings: Bk Vols 1,000; Per Subs 12
Special Collections: Oral History
Subject Interests: Local hist
Wireless access
Partic in Southwest Michigan Library Cooperative
Restriction: Open by appt only

M LAKELAND HEALTH CARE*, Physician's Health Sciences Library, 1234 Napier Ave, 49085-2158. Tel: 269-983-8300. Web Site: www.lakelandhealth.org. *Med Librn,* Mike Dill; E-mail: mdill@lakelandregional.org
Library Holdings: Bk Vols 200; Per Subs 240
Wireless access
Restriction: Staff use only

P MAUD PRESTON PALENSKE MEMORIAL LIBRARY*, 500 Market St, 49085. SAN 308-3977. Tel: 269-983-7167. Reference Tel: 269-983-7167, Ext 10. Automation Services Tel: 269-983-7167, Ext 15. FAX: 269-983-5804. E-mail: publiclibrary@sjcity.com. Web Site: www.youseemore.com/maudpreston. *Libr Dir,* Stephanie Masin; Tel: 269-983-7167, Ext 12; Staff 7 (MLS 2, Non-MLS 5)
Founded 1903. Pop 18,831; Circ 250,000
Library Holdings: Bk Titles 94,366; Bk Vols 113,093; Per Subs 180
Subject Interests: Local hist
Automation Activity & Vendor Info: (Cataloging) TLC (The Library Corporation); (Circulation) TLC (The Library Corporation); (ILL) Mel Cat; (OPAC) TLC (The Library Corporation)
Wireless access
Function: Art exhibits, Bks on cassette, Bks on CD, Chess club, Children's prog, Computers for patron use, Electronic databases & coll, Homebound delivery serv, ILL available, Magnifiers for reading, Mail & tel request accepted, Music CDs, Online cat, Photocopying/Printing, Preschool outreach, Prog for adults, Prog for children & young adult, Scanner, Story hour, Summer reading prog, Tax forms, Teen prog, Wheelchair accessible
Partic in Southwest Michigan Library Cooperative
Open Mon-Thurs 10-8, Fri 10-6, Sat 10-5
Friends of the Library Group

SAINT LOUIS

P SAINT LOUIS PUBLIC LIBRARY, T A Cutler Memorial Library, 312 Michigan Ave, 48880. SAN 308-3985. Tel: 989-681-5141. FAX: 989-681-2077. E-mail: cutlerlibrary@live.com. Web Site: tacml.agverso.com. *Libr Dir,* Jessica Little; Staff 2 (MLS 1, Non-MLS 1)
Founded 1936. Pop 10,662
Jul 2019-Jun 2020 Income $314,415, State $8,546, City $64,774, County $223,535, Locally Generated Income $17,560. Mats Exp $14,226, Books $6,976, Per/Ser (Incl. Access Fees) $2,186, AV Mat $2,289, Electronic Ref Mat (Incl. Access Fees) $2,775. Sal $109,314 (Prof $79,644)
Library Holdings: Audiobooks 830; CDs 248; e-books 20,896; e-journals 3,500; Electronic Media & Resources 1; Large Print Bks 737; Microforms 97; Bk Vols 25,754; Per Subs 47; Videos 1,722

Special Collections: Local History Coll (St Louis, Alma, Breckenridge & Gratiot County), bks, newsp clippings, pamplets, yearbks; Pine River Superfund Documents
Automation Activity & Vendor Info: (Cataloging) Auto-Graphics, Inc; (Circulation) Auto-Graphics, Inc; (ILL) Mel Cat; (OPAC) Auto-Graphics, Inc
Wireless access
Function: 24/7 Electronic res, 24/7 Online cat, Audiobks on Playaways & MP3, Audiobks via web, Bk club(s), Bks on CD, Computers for patron use, Free DVD rentals, ILL available, Internet access, Laminating, Magazines, Movies, Music CDs, Online cat, OverDrive digital audio bks, Photocopying/Printing, Preschool reading prog, Printer for laptops & handheld devices, Prog for children & young adult, Ref serv available, Scanner, Story hour, Summer reading prog, Tax forms, Teen prog, Telephone ref
Partic in White Pine Library Cooperative
Special Services for the Deaf - Closed caption videos
Special Services for the Blind - Bks on CD; Large print bks
Open Mon-Fri 10-6, Sat 10-2
Friends of the Library Group

SALINE

G MICHIGAN DEPARTMENT OF HEALTH AND HUMAN SERVICES, Center for Forensic Psychiatry Library, 8303 Platt Rd, 48176. (Mail add: PO Box 2060, Ann Arbor, 48106-2060), SAN 371-5671. Tel: 734-429-2531, Ext 4296. Administration Tel: 734-295-4296. FAX: 734-429-7951. TDD: 734-994-7012. *Dir,* Patricia Supnick; E-mail: supnickp@michigan.gov; Staff 1 (MLS 1)
Founded 1974
Library Holdings: Bk Titles 5,724; Bk Vols 7,104; Per Subs 75
Subject Interests: Forensic psychiat, Forensic psychol
Automation Activity & Vendor Info: (Acquisitions) Inmagic, Inc.; (Cataloging) Inmagic, Inc.; (Circulation) Inmagic, Inc.; (Serials) EBSCO Online
Wireless access
Partic in Metrop Detroit Med Libr Group
Special Services for the Deaf - TDD equip
Restriction: Not open to pub

P SALINE DISTRICT LIBRARY, 555 N Maple Rd, 48176. SAN 308-3993. Tel: 734-429-5450. FAX: 734-944-0600. Web Site: www.salinelibrary.org. *Dir,* Mary Ellen Mulcrone; E-mail: maryellen@saline.lib.mi.us; *Asst Dir,* Karrie Waarala; E-mail: karrie@saline.lib.mi.us; Staff 42 (MLS 10, Non-MLS 32)
Founded 1900
Subject Interests: Local hist
Automation Activity & Vendor Info: (Cataloging) Innovative Interfaces, Inc; (Circulation) Innovative Interfaces, Inc; (OPAC) Innovative Interfaces, Inc; (Serials) Innovative Interfaces, Inc
Wireless access
Function: 24/7 Electronic res, 24/7 Online cat, Activity rm, Adult bk club, Art exhibits, Audiobks via web, Bk club(s), Bks on CD, Butterfly Garden, Children's prog, Computer training, Computers for patron use, Electronic databases & coll, Free DVD rentals, Home delivery & serv to seniorr ctr & nursing homes, Homebound delivery serv, ILL available, Internet access, Life-long learning prog for all ages, Magazines, Mail & tel request accepted, Mango lang, Meeting rooms, Movies, Museum passes, Music CDs, Online cat, Outreach serv, OverDrive digital audio bks, Photocopying/Printing, Prog for adults, Prog for children & young adult, Ref serv available, Serves people with intellectual disabilities, Story hour, Study rm, Summer reading prog, Tax forms, Teen prog, Telephone ref, Wheelchair accessible, Workshops
Partic in The Library Network
Open Mon-Thurs 9-9, Fri & Sat 10-5, Sun 1-5
Restriction: Non-circulating coll, Non-resident fee
Friends of the Library Group

SANDUSKY

P SANDUSKY DISTRICT LIBRARY*, 55 E Sanilac Ave, 48471-1146. SAN 308-4000. Tel: 810-648-2644. FAX: 810-648-1904. Web Site: www.sandusky.lib.mi.us. *Dir,* Gail Ann Nartker; E-mail: gnartker@sandusky.lib.mi.us; *Asst Librn,* Jackie Graves; Staff 6 (Non-MLS 6)
Founded 1937. Pop 7,333; Circ 80,000
Library Holdings: Large Print Bks 667; Bk Titles 25,000; Bk Vols 35,000; Per Subs 100; Talking Bks 1,000
Subject Interests: Genealogy, Local hist
Automation Activity & Vendor Info: (Cataloging) Follett Software; (Circulation) Follett Software; (OPAC) Follett Software
Wireless access
Partic in White Pine Library Cooperative
Open Mon-Fri 9-6, Sat 9-1
Friends of the Library Group

SARANAC

P SARANAC PUBLIC LIBRARY*, 61 Bridge St, 48881. (Mail add: PO Box 27, 48881-0027), SAN 308-4019. Tel: 616-642-9146. FAX: 616-642-6430. E-mail: sar@llcoop.org. Web Site: www.saranac.michlibrary.org. *Dir,* Kerry Fountain; E-mail: sarkf@llcoop.org
Circ 18,726
Library Holdings: Bk Vols 35,000; Per Subs 100
Automation Activity & Vendor Info: (Cataloging) Innovative Interfaces, Inc; (Circulation) Innovative Interfaces, Inc; (OPAC) Innovative Interfaces, Inc
Wireless access
Partic in Lakeland Library Cooperative; Mich Libr Asn
Open Mon 12-7, Tues & Wed 9-5, Thurs 9-7, Fri & Sat 9-1
Branches: 1
CLARKSVILLE BRANCH, 130 S Main St, Clarksville, 48815. (Mail add: PO Box 200, Clarksville, 48815-0200). Tel: 616-693-1001. FAX: 616-693-2365. E-mail: cla@llcoop.org. Web Site: www.clarksville.llcoop.org. *Librn,* Noreen Steward
Library Holdings: Bk Vols 9,652
Open Wed 12-7, Thurs & Fri 9-5, Sat 9-1

SAULT SAINTE MARIE

C LAKE SUPERIOR STATE UNIVERSITY, Kenneth J Shouldice Library, 906 Ryan Ave, 49783. SAN 308-4051. Tel: 906-635-2815. FAX: 906-635-2193. Web Site: www.lssu.edu/library. *Libr Dir,* Marc Boucher; E-mail: marc.boucher@lssu.edu; *Acad Librn,* Karen Harag; Tel: 906-635-2862, E-mail: kharag@lssu.edu; *Acad Librn,* Ali Van Doren; Tel: 906-635-2124, E-mail: avandoren@lssu.edu; *Acq Librn, Ser Librn,* Bonnie Speas; Tel: 906-635-2861, E-mail: bspeas@lssu.edu; *Circ Supvr,* Teresa Yelverton-Johnson; E-mail: tyelvertonjohnso@lssu.edu; *Cataloger,* Position Currently Open. Subject Specialists: *Archives, Spec coll,* Karen Harag; Staff 6 (MLS 3, Non-MLS 3)
Founded 1946. Enrl 1,960; Fac 100; Highest Degree: Bachelor
Library Holdings: Bk Vols 111,429; Per Subs 811
Special Collections: Great Lakes (Marine-Laker); Michigan History (Michigan Room). US Document Depository
Automation Activity & Vendor Info: (Acquisitions) Ex Libris Group; (Cataloging) Ex Libris Group; (Circulation) Ex Libris Group; (Course Reserve) Ex Libris Group; (ILL) Ex Libris Group; (Media Booking) Ex Libris Group; (OPAC) Ex Libris Group; (Serials) Ex Libris Group
Wireless access
Function: Electronic databases & coll, ILL available, Laminating, Microfiche/film & reading machines, Music CDs, Online cat, Photocopying/Printing, Scanner
Partic in Midwest Collaborative for Library Services; Upper Peninsula Region of Library Cooperation, Inc
Open Mon-Wed 7:30am-Midnight, Thurs 7:30am-11pm, Fri 7:30-6, Sat 11-6, Sun 1pm-Midnight (Winter); Mon, Thurs & Fri 8-5, Tues & Wed 8am-9pm, Sat 10-2 (Summer)

P SUPERIOR DISTRICT LIBRARY*, Bayliss Public Library & Administrative Offices, 541 Library Dr, 49783. SAN 308-4035. Tel: 906-632-9331. FAX: 906-635-0210. Web Site: www.sdl.michlibrary.org. *Dir,* Lisa Waskin; E-mail: lisaw@uproc.lib.mi.us; *Financial Mgr, Human Res Mgr,* Angela Lane; E-mail: alane@uproc.lib.mi.us; *Br Mgr,* Pam Flood; E-mail: pamf@uproc.lib.mi.us; *Head, Circ,* Victor Beeker; E-mail: vbeeker@uproc.lib.mi.us; *Head, Ref,* Meredith Sommers; E-mail: msommers@uproc.libmi.us; *Ch,* Sabrina Neveu; E-mail: sneveu@uproc.lib.mi.us; Staff 3 (MLS 1, Non-MLS 2)
Special Collections: State Document Depository
Automation Activity & Vendor Info: (Cataloging) SirsiDynix; (Circulation) SirsiDynix; (OPAC) SirsiDynix
Wireless access
Partic in Superiorland Library Cooperative; Upper Peninsula Region of Library Cooperation, Inc
Open Tues & Thurs 9-9, Wed & Fri 9-5:30, Sat 9-4
Friends of the Library Group
Branches: 8
BREVORT TOWNSHIP COMMUNITY LIBRARY, 1941 W Church St, Moran, 49760. (Mail add: PO Box 92, Moran, 49760). FAX: 906-643-8098. E-mail: brevort@sault.com. *Mgr,* Lori Brownson; E-mail: lbrownson@uproc.lib.mi.us
Open Tues 3-8, Wed, Fri & Sat 12-5
Friends of the Library Group
CURTIS LIBRARY, N 9220 Portage Ave, Curtis, 49820. Tel: 906-586-9411. FAX: 906-586-6166. E-mail: curtislib@uproc.lib.mi.us. *Mgr,* Linda Blanchard
Open Mon 9-7, Tues, Thurs & Fri 9-4:30

P DETOUR PUBLIC LIBRARY, 202 S Division St, DeTour Village, 49725. (Mail add: PO Box 429, DeTour Village, 49725-0429), SAN 307-9686. Tel: 906-297-2011. FAX: 906-297-3403. Web Site: detour.eupschools.org/domain/44. *Libr Mgr,* Megan Stanfanski; E-mail: megans@uproc.lib.mi.us

Pop 1,829; Circ 11,449
Library Holdings: Bk Vols 21,000; Per Subs 55
Automation Activity & Vendor Info: (Cataloging) Follett Software; (Circulation) Follett Software
Open Mon, Tues, Thurs & Fri (Winter) 10-5, Wed 1-8, Sat 10-2; Tues & Thurs (Summer) 10-4, Wed 4-8, Sat 10-2
Friends of the Library Group

DRUMMOND ISLAND LIBRARY, 29934 E Court St, Drummond Island, 49726. Tel: 906-493-5243. FAX: 906-493-5924. *Mgr,* Laura Hintz; E-mail: laurah@uproc.lib.mi.us
Open Mon, Tues & Fri 10:30-3:30, Wed 9:30-5, Thurs 2-7
Friends of the Library Group

ENGADINE LIBRARY, W13920 Melville St, Engadine, 49827. Tel: 906-477-6313, Ext 140. *Mgr,* Melanie Chaffin; E-mail: mchaffin@eupschools.org
Open Mon & Thurs 10-4 & 7-10, Tues, Wed & Fri 10-4, Sat 9-Noon; Mon 12-4:30 & 7-10, Wed & Fri 12-4:30, Thurs 7pm-10pm, Sat 9-Noon (Summer)
Friends of the Library Group

LES CHENEAUX COMMUNITY LIBRARY, 75 E Hodeck St, Cedarville, 49719. Tel: 906-484-3547. FAX: 906-484-3547. E-mail: lcclib@uproc.lib.mi.us. *Mgr,* Jane French
Open Tues, Wed & Fri 10-5:30, Thurs 10-8, Sat 10-3
Friends of the Library Group

PICKFORD COMMUNITY LIBRARY, 230 E Main St, Pickford, 49774. (Mail add: PO Box 277, Pickford, 49774). Tel: 906-647-1288. FAX: 906-647-1288. Web Site: www.pickfordlibrary.org. *Mgr,* Emily Hyde; E-mail: ehyde@uproc.lib.mi.us
Friends of the Library Group

SCHOOLCRAFT

P SCHOOLCRAFT COMMUNITY LIBRARY, 330 N Centre St, 49087. SAN 371-5701. Tel: 269-679-5959. FAX: 269-679-5599. Web Site: schoolcraftlibrary.org. *Dir,* Pamela Ballett; E-mail: director@schoolcraftlibrary.org; Staff 6 (MLS 1, Non-MLS 5)
Founded 1988. Pop 3,686
Mar 2019-Feb 2020 Income $192,430, State $7,940, Locally Generated Income $145,286, Other $39,204. Mats Exp $12,877, Books $10,150, Per/Ser (Incl. Access Fees) $900, AV Equip $450, AV Mat $1,000, Electronic Ref Mat (Incl. Access Fees) $377. Sal $116,038
Library Holdings: Audiobooks 686; DVDs 842; e-books 8,341; Electronic Media & Resources 1; Large Print Bks 556; Bk Titles 26,819; Per Subs 25
Automation Activity & Vendor Info: (Acquisitions) Biblionix/Apollo; (Cataloging) Biblionix/Apollo; (Circulation) Biblionix/Apollo; (ILL) Mel Cat
Wireless access
Function: 24/7 Electronic res, 24/7 Online cat, 3D Printer, Activity rm, Adult bk club, Art exhibits, Audiobks via web, Bk club(s), Bks on cassette, Bks on CD, Butterfly Garden, CD-ROM, Children's prog, Computers for patron use, Electronic databases & coll, Family literacy, For res purposes, Holiday prog, Home delivery & serv to seniorr ctr & nursing homes, Homebound delivery serv, Homework prog, ILL available, Internet access, Laminating, Life-long learning prog for all ages, Magazines, Mango lang, Meeting rooms, Movies, Online cat, Outreach serv, Outside serv via phone, mail, e-mail & web, OverDrive digital audio bks, Photocopying/Printing, Preschool outreach, Preschool reading prog, Prog for adults, Prog for children & young adult, Ref & res, Ref serv available, Scanner, Spoken cassettes & CDs, STEM programs, Story hour, Study rm, Summer & winter reading prog, Summer reading prog, Tax forms, Teen prog, Telephone ref, VHS videos, Wheelchair accessible
Mem of Woodlands Library Cooperative
Open Mon, Tues & Thurs 10-5, Wed 10-7:30, Fri & Sat 10-1
Friends of the Library Group

SCOTTVILLE

J WEST SHORE COMMUNITY COLLEGE*, William M Anderson Library, 3000 N Stiles Rd, 49454. SAN 308-4078. Tel: 231-843-5529, 231-845-6211. Toll Free Tel: 800-848-9722. Web Site: www.westshore.edu/community/library. *Dir,* Renee Snodgrass; E-mail: rsnodgrass@westshore.edu
Founded 1967. Enrl 1,400
Library Holdings: CDs 2,000; e-books 50; Bk Titles 10,000; Bk Vols 23,000; Per Subs 150
Automation Activity & Vendor Info: (Cataloging) Book Systems; (Circulation) Book Systems
Wireless access
Partic in Mid-Michigan Library League
Open Mon-Thurs 8am-8:30pm, Fri 8-4:30

SEBEWAING

P SEBEWAING TOWNSHIP LIBRARY*, 41 N Center St, 48759-1406. SAN 308-4086. Tel: 989-883-3520. FAX: 989-883-3520. E-mail: sebewainglibrary@att.net. Web Site: www.sebewainglibrary.org. *Dir,* Angela Pike
Pop 4,509; Circ 26,000
Library Holdings: Bk Vols 20,000; Per Subs 50
Special Collections: Local Newspapers on Microfilm
Wireless access
Partic in White Pine Library Cooperative
Open Mon & Wed 10-6, Tues & Fri 10-5, Sat 10-1

SHELBY

P SHELBY AREA DISTRICT LIBRARY*, 189 Maple St, 49455-1134. SAN 308-4094. Tel: 231-861-4565. FAX: 231-861-6868. E-mail: shelbyadl@gmail.com. Web Site: www.shelbylibrary.org. *Libr Dir,* Tiffany Haight; E-mail: tifhaight@shelbylibrary.org; *Asst Dir,* Quinn Maynard; Staff 9 (Non-MLS 9)
Founded 1907. Pop 11,377
Library Holdings: Audiobooks 1,187; CDs 150; DVDs 1,211; Bk Titles 40,139; Per Subs 73
Automation Activity & Vendor Info: (Cataloging) Auto-Graphics, Inc; (Circulation) Auto-Graphics, Inc; (OPAC) Auto-Graphics, Inc
Wireless access
Function: 24/7 Online cat, Activity rm, Adult bk club, Archival coll, Art exhibits, Audiobks via web, Bk club(s), Bks on cassette, Bks on CD, Children's prog, Computer training, Computers for patron use, E-Readers, Electronic databases & coll, Free DVD rentals, Holiday prog, ILL available, Internet access, Laminating, Magazines, Mail & tel request accepted, Meeting rooms, Microfiche/film & reading machines, Movies, Music CDs, Online cat, OverDrive digital audio bks, Photocopying/Printing, Printer for laptops & handheld devices, Prog for adults, Prog for children & young adult, Ref & res, Scanner, Spanish lang bks, Story hour, Summer & winter reading prog, Summer reading prog, Tax forms, Teen prog, Telephone ref, Wheelchair accessible, Winter reading prog, Workshops
Partic in Mich Libr Asn; Mid-Michigan Library League
Open Mon-Thurs 9-7, Fri 9-5, Sat 9-1
Friends of the Library Group

SHELBY TOWNSHIP

P SHELBY TOWNSHIP LIBRARY*, 51680 Van Dyke, 48316-4448. SAN 308-4604. Tel: 586-739-7414. FAX: 586-726-0535. Web Site: www.shelbytwplib.org. *Dir,* Katie Ester; Tel: 586-726-2344, E-mail: esterk@libcoop.net; *Asst Dir,* Catherine Schmidt; *Adult Serv,* Elizabeth Campion; E-mail: campione@libcoop.net; *Ch Serv,* Jennifer Sunderhaus; E-mail: sunderhausj@libcoop.net; Staff 17 (MLS 5, Non-MLS 12)
Founded 1972. Pop 65,159; Circ 261,689
Library Holdings: AV Mats 14,056; Electronic Media & Resources 543; Large Print Bks 2,592; Bk Vols 116,327; Per Subs 262; Talking Bks 3,755
Automation Activity & Vendor Info: (Cataloging) SirsiDynix; (Circulation) SirsiDynix; (ILL) OCLC; (OPAC) SirsiDynix; (Serials) EBSCO Online
Wireless access
Function: Homebound delivery serv, ILL available, Internet access, Prog for children & young adult, Serves people with intellectual disabilities, Summer reading prog, Telephone ref, Wheelchair accessible
Publications: Friends of the Shelby Township Library (Newsletter); Shelby News Worth Knowing (Newsletter)
Partic in Suburban Library Cooperative
Open Mon-Thurs 9-8, Fri & Sat 9-5
Friends of the Library Group

SIDNEY

J MONTCALM COMMUNITY COLLEGE LIBRARY*, 2800 College Dr, 48885. SAN 308-4108. Tel: 989-328-2111, Ext 261, 989-328-2111, Ext 291. Web Site: www.montcalm.edu/library. *Libr Dir,* Katie Arwood; E-mail: katiea@montcalm.edu
Founded 1965. Enrl 2,000; Fac 24; Highest Degree: Associate
Library Holdings: Bk Titles 30,000; Per Subs 220
Wireless access
Function: ILL available
Open Mon-Thurs 8:30am-9pm, Fri 8:30-1

SODUS

P SODUS TOWNSHIP LIBRARY*, 3776 Naomi Rd, 49126-9783. SAN 308-4116. Tel: 269-925-0903. FAX: 269-925-1823. E-mail: sodustwplib@comcast.net. Web Site: sodustwp.ploud.net. *Dir,* Danette Albrecht; Staff 1 (Non-MLS 1)
Founded 1939. Pop 1,932; Circ 7,200
Library Holdings: Bk Titles 15,000; Per Subs 53

Wireless access
Partic in Southwest Michigan Library Cooperative
Open Mon 2-7, Tues 10-6, Wed & Thurs 2-6, Fri 2-5, Sat 10-1

SOUTH HAVEN

S MICHIGAN MARITIME MUSEUM, Marialyce Canonie Great Lakes Research Library, 91 Michigan Ave, 49090. Tel: 269-637-9156. Administration Tel: 269-637-8078. E-mail: library@mimaritime.org. Web Site: www.michiganmaritimemuseum.org/. *Exec Dir,* Patti Montgomery Reinert; *Dir of Educ,* Ashley Deming; E-mail: ashley@mimaritime.org; *Archive & Coll Mgr,* Emily E Stap; Staff 1 (Non-MLS 1)
Founded 1985
Library Holdings: Bk Vols 4,000; Per Subs 45
Special Collections: Oral History
Subject Interests: Great Lakes maritime hist
Wireless access
Function: Archival coll, Internet access, Ref & res, Res libr, Res performed for a fee
Partic in Southwest Michigan Library Cooperative
Restriction: Access at librarian's discretion, Authorized scholars by appt, Open by appt only

P SOUTH HAVEN MEMORIAL LIBRARY*, 314 Broadway St, 49090. SAN 308-4124. Tel: 269-637-2403. FAX: 269-639-1685. E-mail: shml@shmlibrary.org. Web Site: www.shmlibrary.org. *Dir,* Jim France; E-mail: jimfrance@shmlibrary.org; *Children & Teen Librn,* Gail Patterson; E-mail: gailpatterson@shmlibrary.org; Staff 5 (MLS 2, Non-MLS 3)
Founded 1910. Pop 9,059; Circ 51,814
Jul 2014-Jun 2015 Income $345,860. Mats Exp $371,973. Sal $191,528
Library Holdings: Bks on Deafness & Sign Lang 10; High Interest/Low Vocabulary Bk Vols 120; Bk Titles 57,000; Per Subs 120
Subject Interests: Great Lakes, Local hist
Automation Activity & Vendor Info: (Cataloging) Follett Software; (Circulation) Follett Software; (ILL) Auto-Graphics, Inc; (OPAC) Follett Software
Wireless access
Partic in Southwest Michigan Library Cooperative
Special Services for the Deaf - Bks on deafness & sign lang; High interest/low vocabulary bks
Special Services for the Blind - Aids for in-house use
Open Mon-Thurs 10-8, Fri 10-6, Sat 10-4
Restriction: Open to pub for ref & circ; with some limitations
Friends of the Library Group

SOUTH LYON

P LYON TOWNSHIP PUBLIC LIBRARY*, 27005 S Milford Rd, 48178. SAN 308-3055. Tel: 248-437-8800. FAX: 248-437-4621. Web Site; www.lyon.lib.mi.us. *Dir,* Holly Teasdle; E-mail: hteasdle@lyon.lib.mi.us; *Computer Tech,* Marjorie O'Donnel; E-mail: modonnel@lyon.lib.mi.us; *Genealogist,* Cathy Cottone; E-mail: ccottone@lyon.lib.mi.us; *Tech Serv,* Pam Quackenbush; E-mail: pquackenbush@lyon.lib.mi.us; *Youth Serv,* Jocelyn Levin; E-mail: jlevin@lyon.lib.mi.us; Staff 2.5 (MLS 1.5, Non-MLS 1)
Founded 1956. Pop 11,041; Circ 81,634
Library Holdings: Bk Vols 50,000; Per Subs 120
Subject Interests: Genealogy
Automation Activity & Vendor Info: (Cataloging) SirsiDynix; (Circulation) SirsiDynix; (OPAC) SirsiDynix
Wireless access
Function: Adult bk club, Archival coll, Bks on CD, Children's prog, Computer training, Computers for patron use, Free DVD rentals, Genealogy discussion group, ILL available, Internet access, Museum passes, Music CDs, Online cat, Photocopying/Printing, Preschool outreach, Prog for adults, Prog for children & young adult, Scanner, Senior computer classes, Story hour, Summer reading prog, Tax forms, Teen prog, VHS videos, Wheelchair accessible
Partic in Upper Peninsula Region of Library Cooperation, Inc
Open Mon-Thurs 10-8, Fri & Sat 12-5
Friends of the Library Group

P SALEM-SOUTH LYON DISTRICT LIBRARY, 9800 Pontiac Trail, 48178-7021. SAN 308-4132. Tel: 248-437-6431. FAX: 248-437-6593. Web Site: www.ssldl.info. *Interim Dir,* Kathy Merucci; E-mail: kmerucci@ssldl.info; *Asst Dir,* Kathy Hutchinson; Tel: 248-437-6431, Ext 207; *Head, Adult Serv,* Amelia Yunker; E-mail: ayunker@ssldl.info; *Head, Youth Serv,* Kathy Merucci; Tel: 248-437-6431, Ext 205; *Pub Relations Coordr,* Tracy Robinson; E-mail: trobinson@ssldl.info. Subject Specialists: *Acctg,* Kathy Hutchinson; *Mkt,* Tracy Robinson; Staff 43 (MLS 9, Non-MLS 34)
Founded 1939. Pop 16,954; Circ 318,433
Jul 2021-Jun 2022. Mats Exp $165,374. Sal $639,959
Library Holdings: CDs 2,999; DVDs 1,515; Large Print Bks 1,402; Bk Vols 58,034; Per Subs 103; Talking Bks 2,342; Videos 3,662
Special Collections: South Lyon Herald from 1929, CD-ROM
Automation Activity & Vendor Info: (Acquisitions) CARL.Solution (TLC); (Cataloging) CARL.Solution (TLC); (Circulation) CARL.Solution (TLC); (ILL) CARL.Solution (TLC); (OPAC) CARL.Solution (TLC); (Serials) CARL.Solution (TLC)
Wireless access
Function: 24/7 Electronic res, 24/7 Online cat, 3D Printer, Activity rm, Adult bk club, After school storytime, Art exhibits, Art programs, Audio & video playback equip for onsite use, Audiobks on Playaways & MP3, Audiobks via web, AV serv, Bk club(s), Bks on CD, Butterfly Garden, CD-ROM, Children's prog, Computer training, Computers for patron use, Digital talking bks, Electronic databases & coll, Equip loans & repairs, Family literacy, Free DVD rentals, Games & aids for people with disabilities, Genealogy discussion group, Holiday prog, Home delivery & serv to seniorr ctr & nursing homes, Homebound delivery serv, Homework prog, ILL available, Internet access, Jazz prog, Life-long learning prog for all ages, Magazines, Magnifiers for reading, Mail & tel request accepted, Mango lang, Meeting rooms, Museum passes, Music CDs, Notary serv, Online cat, Online ref, Orientations, Outreach serv, Outside serv via phone, mail, e-mail & web, OverDrive digital audio bks, Photocopying/Printing, Preschool outreach, Prog for adults, Prog for children & young adult, Ref & res, Ref serv available, Res assist avail, Scanner, Senior computer classes, Senior outreach, STEM programs, Story hour, Study rm, Summer & winter reading prog, Summer reading prog, Tax forms, Teen prog, Telephone ref, VHS videos, Wheelchair accessible, Winter reading prog, Workshops
Partic in The Library Network
Special Services for the Blind - Closed circuit TV magnifier; Magnifiers; ZoomText magnification & reading software
Open Mon-Thurs 10-7, Fri & Sat 10-5, Sun 1-5
Friends of the Library Group

SOUTHFIELD

R CONGREGATION SHAAREY ZEDEK LIBRARY & AUDIO VISUAL CENTER*, 27375 Bell Rd, 48034. SAN 308-4191. Tel: 248-357-5544. FAX: 248-357-0227. E-mail: csz.info@shaareyzedek.org. Web Site: www.shaareyzedek.org. *Exec Dir,* Sheila Shapiro; *Dir of Youth & Family Learning,* Ari Reis; E-mail: areis@shaareyzedek.org
Founded 1861
Library Holdings: Bk Titles 35,250; Bk Vols 40,250; Per Subs 12
Special Collections: Modern Hebrew lit, Holtzman Coll
Subject Interests: Holocaust, Judaica (lit or hist of Jews), Juv delinquency, Lit
Automation Activity & Vendor Info: (Cataloging) Follett Software

M HELEN L DEROY MEDICAL LIBRARY*, 16001 W Nine Mile Rd, 48075. SAN 308-4272. Tel: 248-849-3294. FAX: 248-849-3201. E-mail: deroy.library@providencehospital.org. *Librn,* Alexia Estabrook; E-mail: alexia.estabrook@ascension.org; Staff 2 (MLS 1, Non-MLS 1)
Founded 1950
Library Holdings: e-books 5,000; e-journals 10,000; Bk Vols 200; Per Subs 5
Subject Interests: Med
Automation Activity & Vendor Info: (Cataloging) OCLC Connexion; (Circulation) CyberTools for Libraries; (OPAC) CyberTools for Libraries; (Serials) CyberTools for Libraries
Wireless access
Open Mon-Fri 8-4:30

L JAFFE RAITT HEUER & WEISS*, Law Library, 27777 Franklin Rd, Ste 2500, 48034-8214. SAN 372-0403. Tel: 248-351-3000. FAX: 248-351-3082. E-mail: libreq@jaffelaw.com. Web Site: www.jaffelaw.com. *Head Librn,* Maria Kuechler; Staff 1.3 (MLS 1, Non-MLS 0.3)
Founded 1968
Restriction: Access at librarian's discretion

C LAWRENCE TECHNOLOGICAL UNIVERSITY LIBRARY*, 21000 W Ten Mile Rd, 48075-1058. SAN 308-4256. Tel: 248-204-3000. FAX: 248-204-3005. E-mail: refdesk@ltu.edu. Web Site: library.ltu.edu. *Libr Dir,* Gary R Cocozzoli; E-mail: gcocozzol@ltu.edu; *Head of Ref & Instrul Serv,* Gretchen Young Weiner; E-mail: gweiner@ltu.edu; *Head, Tech Serv,* Cathy Phillips; E-mail: cphillips@ltu.edu; *Digital Projects Librn,* Adrienne Aluzzo; Tel: 248-204-2821, E-mail: aaluzzo@ltu.edu; *Ref & ILL Librn,* Natalie Zebula; E-mail: nzebula@ltu.edu; *Ref & Ser Librn,* Suzanne Schimanski-Gross; E-mail: sschimans@ltu.edu; *Ref Librn,* Sheila Gaddie; E-mail: sgaddie@ltu.edu; *Ref Librn,* Steven Kish; E-mail: skish@ltu.edu; *Ref Librn,* Mary Alice Power; E-mail: mpower@ltu.edu; *Coordr, Access Serv,* Cynthia Simpson; E-mail: csimpson@ltu.edu; *Digital Projects, Libr Asst,* Sherry Tuffin; Tel: 248-204-2800, E-mail: stuffin@ltu.edu. Subject Specialists: *Archives, Oral hist,* Sherry Tuffin; Staff 12 (MLS 9, Non-MLS 3)
Founded 1932. Enrl 2,593; Fac 725; Highest Degree: Doctorate
Jul 2018-Jun 2019 Income $12,000,000

Library Holdings: Audiobooks 144,187; CDs 100; DVDs 3,160; e-books 457,714; e-journals 65,445; Microforms 2,020; Bk Titles 62,388; Bk Vols 113,550; Per Subs 100
Special Collections: Architectural Materials (Albert F Kahn Coll)
Subject Interests: Archit, Engr, Mgt
Automation Activity & Vendor Info: (Acquisitions) OCLC Worldshare Management Services; (Cataloging) OCLC Worldshare Management Services; (Circulation) OCLC Worldshare Management Services; (Course Reserve) OCLC Worldshare Management Services; (Discovery) OCLC Worldshare Management Services; (ILL) OCLC WorldShare Interlibrary Loan; (OPAC) OCLC Worldshare Management Services; (Serials) OCLC Worldshare Management Services
Wireless access
Function: Bk reviews (Group), Computers for patron use, Distance learning, Doc delivery serv, Electronic databases & coll, Free DVD rentals, ILL available, Mail & tel request accepted, Microfiche/film & reading machines, Online cat, Outside serv via phone, mail, e-mail & web, Photocopying/Printing, Ref serv available, Spoken cassettes & CDs, Telephone ref
Partic in Midwest Collaborative for Library Services; OCLC Online Computer Library Center, Inc; Southeastern Michigan League of Libraries
Open Mon-Thurs 8:30am-9:30pm, Fri 8:30-7:30, Sat 11-4, Sun 1-6

J OAKLAND COMMUNITY COLLEGE*, Southfield Campus Library-Information Commons, 22322 Rutland Dr, Rm A212, 48075-4793. SAN 376-9801. Tel: 248-233-2830. Circulation Tel: 248-233-2825. Reference Tel: 248-233-2826. FAX: 248-233-2828. Web Site: www.oaklandcc.edu/library. *Fac Librn, Ref (Info Servs),* Stacy Charlesbois-Nordan; E-mail: sbcharle@oaklandcc.edu; Staff 3 (MLS 1, Non-MLS 2)
Founded 1998. Enrl 4,200; Fac 8; Highest Degree: Associate
Jul 2016-Jun 2017. Mats Exp $16,000, Books $12,000, Per/Ser (Incl. Access Fees) $4,000. Sal $131,595
Library Holdings: DVDs 100; Bk Vols 3,000; Per Subs 20; Talking Bks 55
Special Collections: Browsing (Urban Fiction Specialty)
Subject Interests: African-Am studies, Allied health, Nursing
Automation Activity & Vendor Info: (Cataloging) SirsiDynix; (Circulation) SirsiDynix; (Course Reserve) SirsiDynix; (Discovery) EBSCO Discovery Service; (ILL) Mel Cat; (OPAC) SirsiDynix; (Serials) SirsiDynix
Wireless access
Function: Audio & video playback equip for onsite use, Bks on CD, Computers for patron use, Doc delivery serv, Electronic databases & coll, Health sci info serv, ILL available, Magnifiers for reading, Online info literacy tutorials on the web & in blackboard, Online ref, Orientations, Photocopying/Printing, Ref & res, Ref serv available, Tax forms, Wheelchair accessible
Partic in Midwest Collaborative for Library Services
Special Services for the Blind - Assistive/Adapted tech devices, equip & products; Computer with voice synthesizer for visually impaired persons; Low vision equip; Magnifiers
Open Mon-Thurs 8:30am-9:45pm, Fri & Sat 8:30-4:45

L PEPPER, HAMILTON LLP*, Law Library, 4000 Town Ctr, Ste 1800, 48075. SAN 372-042X. Tel: 248-359-7300. FAX: 248-359-7700. Web Site: www.pepperlaw.com. *Dir, Libr Serv,* Maureen Rossi; E-mail: maureen.rossi@troutman.com; Staff 1 (MLS 1)
Library Holdings: Bk Vols 12,000; Per Subs 20

P SOUTHFIELD PUBLIC LIBRARY*, David Stewart Memorial Library, 26300 Evergreen Rd, 48076. SAN 308-4299. Tel: 248-796-4200. Circulation Tel: 248-796-4208. Reference Tel: 248-796-4280. FAX: 248-796-4305. Web Site: www.southfieldlibrary.org. *Dir,* Dave Ewick; Tel: 248-796-4300, E-mail: dewick@sfldlib.org; *Dep Librn,* Mary Beall; Tel: 248-796-4302, E-mail: mbeall@sfldlib.org; *Coordr, Tech Serv,* Robin Gardella; Tel: 248-796-4340, E-mail: rgardella@sfldlib.org; Staff 37 (MLS 23, Non-MLS 14)
Founded 1960. Pop 71,000; Circ 714,326
Library Holdings: Bk Vols 254,926; Per Subs 445
Special Collections: United States Census Affiliate Center
Automation Activity & Vendor Info: (Acquisitions) Innovative Interfaces, Inc; (Cataloging) Innovative Interfaces, Inc; (Circulation) Innovative Interfaces, Inc; (OPAC) Innovative Interfaces, Inc; (Serials) Innovative Interfaces, Inc
Wireless access
Publications: Newsletter (Bimonthly)
Partic in Metronet; Midwest Collaborative for Library Services; The Library Network
Open Mon 1-9, Tues 10-9, Fri 1-5, Sat 10-5
Friends of the Library Group

SOUTHGATE

P SOUTHGATE VETERANS MEMORIAL LIBRARY*, 14680 Dix-Toledo Rd, 48195. SAN 308-4310. Tel: 734-258-3002. FAX: 734-284-9477. Web Site: www.southgate.lib.mi.us. *Dir,* Don Priest; Tel: 734-258-3003, E-mail: dpriest@southgate.lib.mi.us; *Ad,* Barbara Keresztury; E-mail: bkeresztury@southgate.lib.mi.us; *Youth Serv Librn,* Michael DiMuzio; E-mail: mdimuzio@southgate.lib.mi.us
Pop 30,771; Circ 92,159
Library Holdings: Bk Vols 77,000; Per Subs 122
Function: Prog for children & young adult, Summer reading prog
Partic in The Library Network
Open Mon-Thurs 10-9, Fri & Sat 10-5

SPARTA

P SPARTA TOWNSHIP LIBRARY*, 80 N Union St, 49345. SAN 308-4329. Tel: 616-887-9937. FAX: 616-887-0179. E-mail: spa@llcoop.org. Web Site: www.sparta.llcoop.org. *Libr Dir,* Merri-Jo Tuinstra; E-mail: spamt@llcoop.org
Founded 1917. Pop 8,938; Circ 42,915
Library Holdings: Bk Vols 59,965; Per Subs 48
Subject Interests: Genealogy, Local hist
Automation Activity & Vendor Info: (Cataloging) Innovative Interfaces, Inc - Sierra; (Circulation) Innovative Interfaces, Inc - Sierra
Wireless access
Partic in Lakeland Library Cooperative
Open Mon-Wed 9-8, Fri 9-5, Sat 9-1

SPRING ARBOR

C SPRING ARBOR UNIVERSITY, Hugh A & Edna C White Library, 106 E Main St, 49283. SAN 308-4337. Tel: 517-750-6742. Circulation Tel: 517-750-6742. Interlibrary Loan Service Tel: 517-750-6439. Toll Free Tel: 800-968-9103, Ext 1742. FAX: 517-750-2108. E-mail: saulibrary@gmail.com. Web Site: library.arbor.edu. *Dir,* Robbie Bolton; Tel: 517-750-6435, E-mail: robbie@arbor.edu; *Online & Distance Learning Librn,* Elizabeth Walker-Papke; Tel: 517-750-6443, E-mail: elizabeth.walker2@arbor.edu; *Ref Librn,* Karen Parsons; Tel: 517-750-6436, E-mail: kparsons@arbor.edu; *Coordr, User Serv,* Katherine Moyer; Tel: 517-750-6439, E-mail: kmoyer@arbor.edu; *Acq, University Archives,* Susan Panak; Tel: 517-750-6434, E-mail: spanak@arbor.edu; *Cataloger,* Wendy Clark; Tel: 517-750-6437, E-mail: wclark@arbor.edu; *Circ,* Kelly Baker; Tel: 517-750-6442, E-mail: kelly.baker@arbor.edu; Staff 7 (MLS 3, Non-MLS 4)
Founded 1873. Enrl 2,478; Fac 77; Highest Degree: Doctorate
Library Holdings: Bk Vols 95,137; Per Subs 93
Wireless access
Mem of Woodlands Library Cooperative
Partic in Midwest Collaborative for Library Services; OCLC Online Computer Library Center, Inc
Open Mon-Thurs 7:30am-10pm, Fri 7:30-5, Sun 6pm-10pm

SPRING LAKE

P SPRING LAKE DISTRICT LIBRARY, 123 E Exchange St, 49456. SAN 308-4353. Tel: 616-846-5770. FAX: 616-844-2129. E-mail: contactus@sllib.org. Web Site: www.sllib.org. *Dir,* Maggie McKeithan; E-mail: mmckeithan@sllib.org; Staff 3 (MLS 2, Non-MLS 1)
Pop 13,140
Library Holdings: AV Mats 3,210; Bk Titles 69,000; Per Subs 175
Automation Activity & Vendor Info: (Cataloging) Innovative Interfaces, Inc; (Circulation) Innovative Interfaces, Inc; (ILL) Innovative Interfaces, Inc; (OPAC) Innovative Interfaces, Inc; (Serials) Innovative Interfaces, Inc
Wireless access
Partic in Lakeland Library Cooperative
Open Mon-Fri 10-6, Sat 10-2
Friends of the Library Group

STANTON

P WHITE PINE LIBRARY*, 106 E Walnut, 48888-9294. SAN 308-4361. Tel: 989-831-4327. FAX: 989-831-4976. E-mail: whitepinelibrary1@hotmail.com. Web Site: whitepinelibrary.org. *Dir,* Patty Rockafellow; *Asst Librn,* Gail Rinard
Founded 1935. Pop 10,320; Circ 44,000
Library Holdings: Bk Vols 22,000; Per Subs 50
Subject Interests: Genealogy, Local hist
Automation Activity & Vendor Info: (Cataloging) Follett Software; (Circulation) Follett Software; (OPAC) Follett Software
Wireless access
Partic in Mid-Michigan Library League
Open Mon, Thurs & Fri 9-5:30, Tues 12:30-5:30, Wed 12-7, Sat 10-12
Friends of the Library Group

STEPHENSON

P MENOMINEE COUNTY LIBRARY, S319 Railroad St, 49887. (Mail add: PO Box 128, 49887-0128), SAN 347-0768. Tel: 906-753-6923. Toll Free Tel: 800-559-8194. FAX: 906-753-4678. E-mail: mcl@uproc.lib.mi.us. Web Site: www.menomineecountylibrary.org. *Dir,* Amanda Winnicki; E-mail: winnickia@uproc.lib.mi.us; *Outreach Coordr,* Ann Best; E-mail: besta@uproc.lib.mi.us; Staff 4.5 (MLS 1, Non-MLS 3.5)
Founded 1944. Pop 15,013
Library Holdings: Audiobooks 800; CDs 300; DVDs 1,100; Large Print Bks 4,000; Bk Vols 48,000; Per Subs 60; Videos 5
Automation Activity & Vendor Info: (Cataloging) SirsiDynix-WorkFlows; (Circulation) SirsiDynix-WorkFlows; (OPAC) SirsiDynix-iBistro
Wireless access
Function: ILL available
Partic in Superiorland Library Cooperative; Upper Peninsula Region of Library Cooperation, Inc
Open Mon 9-1, Tues-Fri 9-6, Sat 9-3
Friends of the Library Group
Branches: 1
HERMANSVILLE BRANCH, W5480 First St, Hermansville, 49847, SAN 347-0792. Tel: 906-498-2253. *Br Librn,* Ann Murray; E-mail: murraya@uproc.lib.mi.us
Open Tues & Wed 9-2:30, Thurs 9-2
Friends of the Library Group
Bookmobiles: 1

STERLING HEIGHTS

P STERLING HEIGHTS PUBLIC LIBRARY*, 40255 Dodge Park Rd, 48313-4140. SAN 308-4388. Tel: 586-446-2665. Reference Tel: 586-446-2642. Administration Tel: 586-446-2640. FAX: 586-276-4067. E-mail: shpl@libcoop.net. Web Site: www.shpl.net. *Dir,* Tammy Turgeon; Tel: 586-446-2641, E-mail: turgeont@libcoop.net; *Supvr, Circ,* Loa Stanislawski; E-mail: stanisll@libcoop.net; *Supvr, Pub Serv,* Karen Stine; E-mail: stinek@libcoop.net; *Supvr, Tech Serv,* Catherine Les; Tel: 586-446-2649, E-mail: lesc@libcoop.net; Staff 16 (MLS 16)
Founded 1971. Pop 129,699; Circ 568,736
Library Holdings: AV Mats 28,254; Bk Vols 196,019; Per Subs 295
Special Collections: International Language Coll. Oral History
Subject Interests: Careers, Children's lit
Automation Activity & Vendor Info: (Acquisitions) SirsiDynix; (Cataloging) SirsiDynix; (Circulation) SirsiDynix; (ILL) SirsiDynix; (OPAC) SirsiDynix; (Serials) SirsiDynix
Wireless access
Function: 24/7 Electronic res, 24/7 Online cat, Audiobks via web, Bi-weekly Writer's Group, Bk club(s), Bks on CD, Children's prog, Computer training, Computers for patron use, Electronic databases & coll, Free DVD rentals, Holiday prog, Home delivery & serv to seniorr ctr & nursing homes, Homebound delivery serv, Internet access, Life-long learning prog for all ages, Magazines, Mango lang, Meeting rooms, Microfiche/film & reading machines, Movies, Museum passes, Music CDs, Online cat, Outreach serv, OverDrive digital audio bks, Photocopying/Printing, Printer for laptops & handheld devices, Prog for adults, Prog for children & young adult, Ref serv available, Scanner, Senior computer classes, Senior outreach, Spanish lang bks, Story hour, Study rm, Summer & winter reading prog, Summer reading prog, Tax forms, Teen prog, Telephone ref, Wheelchair accessible, Winter reading prog, Workshops, Writing prog
Partic in Suburban Library Cooperative
Open Mon-Thurs 9:30-9, Fri 1-5, Sat 9:30-5, Sun (Sept-May) 1-5
Friends of the Library Group

STEVENSVILLE

P LINCOLN TOWNSHIP PUBLIC LIBRARY, 2099 W John Beers Rd, 49127. SAN 308-4396. Tel: 269-429-9575. FAX: 269-429-3500. Web Site: www.lincolntownshiplibrary.org. *Dir,* Jessica Ishmael; E-mail: jishmael@lincolnlib.org; Staff 6 (MLS 3, Non-MLS 3)
Founded 1959. Pop 22,258; Circ 231,285
Library Holdings: Electronic Media & Resources 57; High Interest/Low Vocabulary Bk Vols 265; Bk Titles 81,242; Per Subs 214
Special Collections: Bartz Poetry Coll; Michigan Governors (Towne Square Coll)
Subject Interests: Gardening
Automation Activity & Vendor Info: (Cataloging) TLC (The Library Corporation); (Circulation) TLC (The Library Corporation); (ILL) Auto-Graphics, Inc; (OPAC) TLC (The Library Corporation)
Wireless access
Function: 24/7 Electronic res, 24/7 Online cat, Activity rm, Adult bk club, Adult literacy prog, After school storytime, Audiobks via web, AV serv, Bk club(s), Bks on CD, Children's prog, Computer training, Computers for patron use, Digital talking bks, E-Readers, Electronic databases & coll, Free DVD rentals, Holiday prog, Home delivery & serv to seniorr ctr & nursing homes, Homebound delivery serv, ILL available, Internet access, Jazz prog, Life-long learning prog for all ages, Magazines, Magnifiers for reading, Meeting rooms, Movies, Museum passes, Music CDs, Online cat, Outreach serv, OverDrive digital audio bks, Photocopying/Printing, Prog for adults, Prog for children & young adult, Ref & res, Ref serv available, Res assist avail, Scanner, Senior outreach, Serves people with intellectual disabilities, Spanish lang bks, Spoken cassettes & CDs, Spoken cassettes & DVDs, STEM programs, Story hour, Study rm, Summer & winter reading prog, Summer reading prog, Tax forms, Teen prog, Wheelchair accessible, Winter reading prog, Workshops, Writing prog
Partic in Southwest Michigan Library Cooperative
Special Services for the Deaf - TDD equip
Open Mon-Thurs 10-9, Fri & Sat 10-5
Restriction: Lending limited to county residents
Friends of the Library Group

STURGIS

P STURGIS DISTRICT LIBRARY*, 255 North St, 49091. SAN 308-440X. Tel: 269-659-7224. FAX: 269-651-4534. E-mail: Research@sturgis-library.org. Web Site: www.sturgis-library.org. *Dir,* Todd Reed; Tel: 269-659-7225, E-mail: treed@sturgis-library.org; *Circ Supvr,* Cyndi Holther; E-mail: circulation@sturgis-library.org; *Youth Serv - Prog,* Michele Frost; E-mail: mfrost@sturgis-library.org; Staff 11 (MLS 1, Non-MLS 10)
Founded 2006. Pop 18,500; Circ 175,000
Library Holdings: Bk Vols 57,275; Per Subs 160
Special Collections: Genealogy, bks, microfilm; Local History, maps, bks, pictures; Michigan History
Subject Interests: Bus & mgt
Wireless access
Open Mon, Tues & Thurs 9:30-8, Wed & Fri 9:30-5:30, Sat 9:30-2
Friends of the Library Group

SUNFIELD

P SUNFIELD DISTRICT LIBRARY*, 112 Main St, 48890. (Mail add: PO Box 97, 48890-0097), SAN 308-4418. Tel: 517-566-8065. FAX: 517-566-8065. Web Site: www.sunfieldlibrary.michlibrary.org.
Pop 2,578; Circ 23,237
Library Holdings: Bk Vols 18,000; Per Subs 40
Special Collections: Local History (Loretta L Peabody Memorial Coll)
Mem of Woodlands Library Cooperative
Open Tues-Fri 2-8, Sat 9-1
Friends of the Library Group

SUTTONS BAY

P SUTTONS BAY BINGHAM DISTRICT LIBRARY*, 416 Front St, 49682. (Mail add: PO Box 340, 49682-0340), SAN 308-4426. Tel: 231-271-3512. E-mail: info@sbbdl.org. Web Site: www.sbbdl.org. *Dir,* Bradley Chaplin; E-mail: librarian@sbbdl.org; *Asst Librn,* Jane Suppes; E-mail: jane@sbbdl.org; Staff 3 (MLS 1, Non-MLS 2)
Pop 5,400; Circ 46,042
Library Holdings: Audiobooks 982; Bks-By-Mail 207; Bks on Deafness & Sign Lang 5; Braille Volumes 1; CDs 1,601; DVDs 934; High Interest/Low Vocabulary Bk Vols 1,861; Large Print Bks 804; Bk Vols 26,289; Per Subs 70; Videos 594
Special Collections: Adult & Children Graphic Novels Coll; Michigan Local History Coll
Wireless access
Publications: Annual Report; Newsletter
Special Services for the Deaf - Accessible learning ctr; Assistive tech; Bks on deafness & sign lang; Closed caption videos; High interest/low vocabulary bks
Special Services for the Blind - Accessible computers; Audio mat; Bks available with recordings; Bks on cassette; Bks on CD; Internet workstation with adaptive software
Open Mon-Wed 10-6, Thurs 10-7:30, Fri 10-4, Sat 10-2
Friends of the Library Group

TAYLOR

P TAYLOR COMMUNITY LIBRARY*, 12303 Pardee Rd, 48180-4219. SAN 308-4434. Tel: 734-287-4840. FAX: 734-287-4141. Web Site: www.taylor.lib.mi.us. *Dir,* Vanessa Verdun-Morris; E-mail: vmorris@ci.taylor.mi.us
Pop 70,800
Library Holdings: Bk Titles 132,000; Per Subs 210
Automation Activity & Vendor Info: (Circulation) SirsiDynix
Wireless access
Open Mon-Thurs 10-8, Fri & Sat 10-5, Sun 1-5
Friends of the Library Group

J WAYNE COUNTY COMMUNITY COLLEGE*, John Dingell LRC Library, 21000 North Line Rd, 48180-4798. Tel: 734-374-3228. Administration Tel: 734-374-3524. FAX: 734-374-0240. Web Site:

www.wcccd.edu/dept/learning_resource_center_downriver.htm. *Learning Res Coordr,* Ronghua Luo; E-mail: rluo1@wcccd.edu
Library Holdings: Bk Vols 19,500; Per Subs 85
Automation Activity & Vendor Info: (Cataloging) Ex Libris Group; (Circulation) Ex Libris Group; (OPAC) Ex Libris Group
Open Mon & Tues 11-7, Wed-Fri 8:30-4:30

TECUMSEH

P TECUMSEH DISTRICT LIBRARY*, 215 N Ottawa St, 49286-1564. SAN 308-4450. Tel: 517-423-2238. FAX: 517-423-5519. Web Site: www.tecumsehlibrary.org. *Dir,* Susan Bach; E-mail: sbach@tecumsehlibrary.org; *Ch Serv Librn,* Mary Beth Reasoner; E-mail: mbreasoner@tecumsehlibrary.org; *Hist Coll Librn, Ref Librn,* Chuck Harpst; E-mail: charpst@tecumsehlibrary.org; *Teen Serv Librn,* Anne Keller; E-mail: akeller@tecumsehlibrary.org; *Circ Serv Supvr,* Sonja Downey; E-mail: sdowney@tecumsehlibrary.org; *Supvr, Tech Serv,* Gina Walmsley; E-mail: gwalmsley@tecumsehlibrary.org; Staff 6 (MLS 3, Non-MLS 3)
Founded 2003. Pop 18,100; Circ 139,000
Library Holdings: Bk Vols 53,087; Per Subs 157
Special Collections: Tecumseh Herald Newspaper, 1850-present, micro. Oral History
Subject Interests: Civil War, Indians, Local hist
Automation Activity & Vendor Info: (Acquisitions) Auto-Graphics, Inc; (Cataloging) Auto-Graphics, Inc; (Circulation) Auto-Graphics, Inc
Wireless access
Function: Archival coll, ILL available, Photocopying/Printing, Prog for children & young adult, Ref serv available, Summer reading prog, Telephone ref, Wheelchair accessible
Mem of Woodlands Library Cooperative
Partic in Midwest Collaborative for Library Services
Open Mon-Thurs 10-8, Fri & Sat 10-5, Sun (Oct-April) 1-5
Friends of the Library Group

TEKONSHA

P TEKONSHA PUBLIC LIBRARY, 230 S Church St, 49092. SAN 308-4469. Tel: 517-767-4769. FAX: 517-767-4769. E-mail: tekonlib@tekonshalibrary.org. Web Site: www.tekonlib.michlibrary.org. *Dir,* Sharla A Vincent
Pop 1,873; Circ 8,500
Library Holdings: Bk Vols 17,000
Wireless access
Mem of Woodlands Library Cooperative
Open Mon & Fri 10-5, Tues, Wed & Thurs 3-7, Sat 10-2
Friends of the Library Group

THOMPSONVILLE

P BETSIE VALLEY DISTRICT LIBRARY, 14744 Thompson Ave, 49683. (Mail add: PO Box 185, 49683-0185). Tel: 231-378-2716. FAX: 231-378-2716. E-mail: bvdlibrary@acegroup.cc. Web Site: www.betsievalleydistrictlibrary.org. *Librn,* Michelle Guerra
Library Holdings: Bk Vols 9,500; Per Subs 10
Wireless access
Partic in Mid-Michigan Library League
Open Mon, Tues & Thurs 11-5, Wed 11-7, Fri 11-6, Sat 10-2
Friends of the Library Group

THREE OAKS

P THREE OAKS TOWNSHIP PUBLIC LIBRARY*, Three N Elm St, 49128-1303. SAN 308-4477. Tel: 269-756-5621. FAX: 269-756-3004. E-mail: threeoakspubliclibrary@yahoo.com. Web Site: www.threeoaks.michlibrary.org. *Dir,* Cheryl Kersey; Staff 5 (Non-MLS 5)
Founded 1859
Library Holdings: Bk Titles 27,500; Per Subs 80
Automation Activity & Vendor Info: (Cataloging) Biblionix/Apollo; (Circulation) Biblionix/Apollo
Wireless access
Function: 24/7 Electronic res, 24/7 Online cat, Accelerated reader prog, Activity rm, Archival coll, Audiobks via web, AV serv, Bks on CD, Children's prog, Computers for patron use, Electronic databases & coll, For res purposes, Free DVD rentals, ILL available, Internet access, Laminating, Magazines, Meeting rooms, Microfiche/film & reading machines, Movies, Museum passes, Online cat, OverDrive digital audio bks, Photocopying/Printing, Preschool reading prog, Prog for adults, Prog for children & young adult, Ref & res, Ref serv available, Res assist avail, Scanner, Story hour, Summer & winter reading prog, Summer reading prog, Wheelchair accessible
Partic in Southwest Michigan Library Cooperative
Open Mon, Wed & Fri 10-5, Tues & Thurs 10-7, Sat 10-2
Friends of the Library Group

THREE RIVERS

P THREE RIVERS PUBLIC LIBRARY, 88 N Main St, 49093-2137. SAN 308-4485. Tel: 269-273-8666. FAX: 833-966-2330. E-mail: info@threeriverslibrary.org. Web Site: www.threeriverslibrary.org. *Libr Dir,* Bobbi Schoon; E-mail: bschoon@threeriverslibrary.org; *Asst Dir,* Erin Zabonick; E-mail: ezabonick@threeriverslibrary.org; *Ch,* Peter Butts; E-mail: pbutts@threeriverslibrary.org; Staff 3 (MLS 2, Non-MLS 1)
Founded 1889. Pop 14,253; Circ 84,885
Jul 2021-Jun 2022. Mats Exp $526,512, Books $30,000, Other Print Mats $2,450, Electronic Ref Mat (Incl. Access Fees) $4,000. Sal $226,770 (Prof $110,000)
Library Holdings: Audiobooks 1,558; Bks on Deafness & Sign Lang 353; CDs 35; DVDs 2,882; e-books 6,344; Electronic Media & Resources 300; High Interest/Low Vocabulary Bk Vols 100; Large Print Bks 1,422; Music Scores 15; Bk Titles 42,625; Talking Bks 12
Subject Interests: Local hist
Automation Activity & Vendor Info: (Acquisitions) Biblionix/Apollo; (Cataloging) Biblionix/Apollo; (Circulation) Biblionix/Apollo; (ILL) Biblionix/Apollo; (OPAC) Biblionix/Apollo
Wireless access
Partic in Southwest Michigan Library Cooperative
Open Mon-Fri 10-5:30, Sat 10-4
Friends of the Library Group

TOPINABEE

P TOPINABEE PUBLIC LIBRARY*, 1576 N Straits Hwy, 49791. (Mail add: PO Box 266, 49791-0266), SAN 308-4493. Tel: 231-238-7514. FAX: 231-238-2112. Web Site: www.topinabeepl.michlibrary.org. *Dir,* Patricia King
Pop 1,197; Circ 13,021
Library Holdings: Bk Vols 7,126; Per Subs 40
Wireless access
Partic in Northland Library Cooperative
Open Tues, Wed & Fri 10-5, Thurs 10-6, Sat 10-2
Friends of the Library Group

TRAVERSE CITY

MUNSON HEALTHCARE
M COMMUNITY HEALTH LIBRARY*, 550 Munson Ave, Ste 100, 49686. Tel: 231-935-9265. Toll Free Tel: 800-468-6766. FAX: 231-935-9267. Web Site: www.munsonhealthcare.org. *Coordr,* Roberta Craig. Subject Specialists: *Consumer health,* Roberta Craig; Staff 3 (MLS 2, Non-MLS 1)
Founded 2000
Library Holdings: AV Mats 500; Bk Vols 2,700; Per Subs 20
Subject Interests: Consumer health
Automation Activity & Vendor Info: (Cataloging) Follett Software; (Circulation) Follett Software; (OPAC) Follett Software; (Serials) Follett Software
Function: For res purposes, Games & aids for people with disabilities, Health sci info serv, Homebound delivery serv, ILL available, Internet access, Magnifiers for reading, Mail loans to mem, Outside serv via phone, mail, e-mail & web, Photocopying/Printing, Prog for adults, Prog for children & young adult, Ref serv available, Telephone ref, Wheelchair accessible, Workshops
Partic in Midwest Collaborative for Library Services; National Network of Libraries of Medicine Region 6
Open Mon-Thurs 8:30-12 & 12:30-5:30, Fri 8:30-12:30

M DEPARTMENT OF LIBRARY SERVICES*, 1105 Sixth St, 49684. Tel: 231-935-6170. FAX: 231-935-7124. *Mgr, Libr Serv,* Barbara Platts; Tel: 231-935-6544; Staff 7 (MLS 4, Non-MLS 3)
Library Holdings: e-books 225; e-journals 250; Bk Vols 3,500; Per Subs 200
Subject Interests: Allied health, Leadership develop, Med, Nursing
Automation Activity & Vendor Info: (Cataloging) Follett Software; (Circulation) Gateway; (OPAC) Follett Software; (Serials) Follett Software
Function: Archival coll, Audio & video playback equip for onsite use, Bks on CD, CD-ROM, Computer training, Computers for patron use, Doc delivery serv, Electronic databases & coll, For res purposes, Health sci info serv, ILL available, Instruction & testing, Internet access, Mail loans to mem, Online cat, Orientations, Outreach serv, Outside serv via phone, mail, e-mail & web, Photocopying/Printing, Prof lending libr, Ref serv available, Res libr, Scanner, Telephone ref, VHS videos
Restriction: Authorized personnel only, Badge access after hrs, Circulates for staff only, Med & health res only, Med staff & students, Not open to pub, Open to researchers by request, Prof mat only, Restricted access

J NORTHWESTERN MICHIGAN COLLEGE*, Mark & Helen Osterlin Library, 1701 E Front St, 49686-3061. SAN 347-1063. Tel: 231-995-1060. Reference Tel: 231-995-1540. FAX: 231-995-1056. E-mail: library@nmc.edu. Web Site: www.nmc.edu/library. *Dir, Libr Serv,* Kerrey

Woughter; E-mail: kwoughter@nmc.edu; *Librn,* Mary Beeker; E-mail: mbeeker@nmc.edu; Staff 6 (MLS 3, Non-MLS 3)
Founded 1951. Enrl 4,000; Fac 125; Highest Degree: Associate
Library Holdings: e-books 15; Electronic Media & Resources 2,000; Bk Titles 4,950; Bk Vols 50,480; Per Subs 258
Special Collections: New York Times Index. State Document Depository; US Document Depository
Automation Activity & Vendor Info: (Cataloging) SirsiDynix; (Circulation) SirsiDynix; (Course Reserve) SirsiDynix; (OPAC) SirsiDynix; (Serials) SirsiDynix
Wireless access
Function: Archival coll, Distance learning, Govt ref serv, ILL available, Internet access, Learning ctr, Photocopying/Printing, Ref serv available, Telephone ref

P PENINSULA COMMUNITY LIBRARY*, 2699 Island View Rd, 49686. SAN 308-4515. Tel: 231-223-7700. FAX: 231-223-7708. E-mail: pcl@tadl.org. Web Site: www.peninsulacommunitylibrary.org. *Dir,* Victoria Shurly
Founded 1957. Pop 5,265; Circ 39,107
Library Holdings: Bk Vols 28,000; Per Subs 110
Wireless access
Open Mon & Thurs 9-8, Tues, Wed & Fri 9-5:30, Sat (Sept-May) 9-1
Friends of the Library Group

P TRAVERSE AREA DISTRICT LIBRARY*, 610 Woodmere Ave, 49686. SAN 347-1128. Tel: 231-932-8500. Circulation Tel: 231-932-8504. Reference Tel: 231-932-8502. FAX: 231-932-8578. TDD: 231-932-8507. E-mail: libadmin@tadl.tcnet.org. Web Site: www.tadl.org. *Dir,* Gail Parsons; Tel: 231-932-8527, E-mail: gparsons@tadl.org; *Asst Dir,* Barbara Nowinski; Staff 53 (MLS 9, Non-MLS 44)
Founded 1897. Pop 70,279; Circ 789,081
Library Holdings: Audiobooks 29,834; CDs 137,532; DVDs 102,846; Bk Vols 410,323; Per Subs 808; Videos 12,343
Subject Interests: Deaf, Genealogy, Hearing impaired, Local hist, Sheet music
Automation Activity & Vendor Info: (Acquisitions) Baker & Taylor; (Cataloging) Evergreen; (Circulation) Evergreen; (ILL) Evergreen; (OPAC) Evergreen
Wireless access
Function: Adult bk club, Art exhibits, Audio & video playback equip for onsite use, Bks on cassette, Bks on CD, Children's prog, Computer training, Computers for patron use, E-Reserves, Free DVD rentals, ILL available, Internet access, Jazz prog, Magnifiers for reading, Mail & tel request accepted, Music CDs, Notary serv, Online cat, Online ref, Photocopying/Printing, Prog for adults, Prog for children & young adult, Ref & res, Scanner, Story hour, Summer reading prog, Tax forms, Teen prog, VHS videos, Wheelchair accessible
Publications: TADL-Tales (Monthly newsletter)
Open Mon-Thurs 9-9, Fri & Sat 9-6, Sun 12-5
Friends of the Library Group
Branches: 3
EAST BAY BRANCH, 1989 Three Mile Rd N, 49686, SAN 347-1152. Tel: 231-922-2085. FAX: 231-922-2087. E-mail: ebb@tadl.tcnet.org. *Library Contact,* Barbara Nowinski
Founded 1972
Library Holdings: Bk Vols 18,000
Special Services for the Blind - Rec of textbk mat
Open Tues & Thurs 10-8, Wed & Fri 10-6, Sat 10-3
Friends of the Library Group
KINGSLEY BRANCH, 104 S Brownson Ave, Kingsley, 49649. (Mail add: PO Box 427, Kingsley, 49649-0427), SAN 308-2172. Tel: 231-263-5484. FAX: 231-263-5526. E-mail: kpl@tadl.tcnet.org. Web Site: www.tadl.org/branchmemberlibs/kingsleylib.htm. *Librn,* Mary Fraquelli
Founded 1910. Pop 3,475; Circ 13,423
Library Holdings: Bk Vols 18,000
Partic in OCLC Online Computer Library Center, Inc
Open Tues, Wed & Fri 9-5, Thurs 10-6, Sat 10-3
Friends of the Library Group
P SUBREGIONAL LIBRARY FOR THE BLIND & PHYSICALLY HANDICAPPED, 610 Woodmere, 49686, SAN 377-7782. Tel: 231-932-8558. Toll Free Tel: 877-931-8558. FAX: 231-932-8578. E-mail: lbph@tadl.tcnet.org. *Librn,* Kathy Kelto
Founded 1972
Special Services for the Blind - Audio mat; Bks & mags in Braille, on rec, tape & cassette; Digital talking bk; Talking bks
Open Mon-Fri 9-5
Friends of the Library Group

TRENTON

P TRENTON VETERANS MEMORIAL LIBRARY*, 2790 Westfield Rd, 48183-2482. SAN 308-4523. Tel: 734-676-9777. FAX: 734-676-9895. E-mail: tpubliclibrary@trenton-mi.com. Web Site: www.trenton.lib.mi.us. *Dir,* Erin Chapman; E-mail: EChapman@trenton-mi.com; Staff 6 (MLS 4, Non-MLS 2)
Founded 1928. Pop 72,726; Circ 177,954
Library Holdings: Audiobooks 2,941; CDs 2,729; DVDs 3,563; Electronic Media & Resources 3; Bk Vols 99,611; Per Subs 162; Talking Bks 1,610
Automation Activity & Vendor Info: (Cataloging) SirsiDynix; (Circulation) SirsiDynix; (OPAC) SirsiDynix
Wireless access
Function: 24/7 Electronic res, 24/7 Online cat, Adult bk club, Audiobks via web, Bks on CD, Children's prog, Computer training, Computers for patron use, Electronic databases & coll, Homebound delivery serv, ILL available, Internet access, Magazines, Magnifiers for reading, Microfiche/film & reading machines, Movies, Museum passes, Music CDs, Online cat, Online info literacy tutorials on the web & in blackboard, Outreach serv, Outside serv via phone, mail, e-mail & web, OverDrive digital audio bks, Photocopying/Printing, Preschool reading prog, Prog for adults, Prog for children & young adult, Ref serv available, Scanner, Senior computer classes, Story hour, Study rm, Summer reading prog, Tax forms, Teen prog, Telephone ref, Wheelchair accessible
Partic in The Library Network
Special Services for the Deaf - Bks on deafness & sign lang
Special Services for the Blind - Closed circuit TV magnifier; Home delivery serv; Magnifiers
Open Mon-Thurs 10-9, Fri & Sat 10-6, Sun 1-5
Friends of the Library Group

TROY

L HARNESS, DICKEY & PIERCE, PLC*, Law Library, 5445 Corporate Dr, Ste 200, 48098. SAN 372-0489. Tel: 248-641-1600, Ext 1250. FAX: 248-641-0270. Web Site: www.hdp.com. *Librn,* Kristine Potter
Founded 1921
Library Holdings: Bk Vols 10,000; Per Subs 37
Restriction: Staff use only

P TROY PUBLIC LIBRARY*, 510 W Big Beaver Rd, 48084-5289. SAN 347-1187. Tel: 248-524-3538. FAX: 248-524-0112. E-mail: info@troypl.org. Web Site: troypl.org. *Libr Dir,* Cathy Russ; E-mail: c.russ@troymi.gov; *Asst Dir,* Phillip Kwik; E-mail: KwikPJ@troymi.gov; Staff 35 (MLS 35)
Founded 1962. Pop 80,959; Circ 1,418,442
Library Holdings: DVDs 21,657; e-books 3,719; Electronic Media & Resources 85; Bk Vols 206,198; Per Subs 656; Talking Bks 26,890
Special Collections: Frances Teasdale (Civil War Coll); International Language; Morgan - West White House Memorabilia
Automation Activity & Vendor Info: (Acquisitions) SirsiDynix; (Cataloging) SirsiDynix; (Circulation) SirsiDynix; (OPAC) SirsiDynix; (Serials) SirsiDynix
Wireless access
Partic in Suburban Library Cooperative
Special Services for the Deaf - TDD equip
Open Mon-Thurs 10-9, Sat 10-5, Sun 1-5
Friends of the Library Group

C WALSH COLLEGE, Troy Campus Library, 3838 Livernois Rd, 48083-5066. SAN 308-454X. Tel: 248-823-1640. E-mail: librarian@walshcollege.edu. Web Site: www.walshcollege.edu/library. *Libr Dir,* Caryn Noel; Tel: 248-823-1254, E-mail: cnoel@walshcollege.edu; *Ref Librn,* Dianne White; Tel: 248-823-1338, E-mail: dwhite@walshcollege.edu; Staff 2.5 (MLS 2.5)
Founded 1922. Enrl 1,750; Fac 130; Highest Degree: Doctorate
Sept 2020-Aug 2021. Mats Exp $307,854, Books $385, Per/Ser (Incl. Access Fees) $24,328, Electronic Ref Mat (Incl. Access Fees) $283,141. Sal $244,435 (Prof $196,494)
Library Holdings: CDs 105; DVDs 40; e-books 646,537; e-journals 201,826; Bk Titles 25,981; Per Subs 80
Subject Interests: Acctg, Bus & mgt, Bus law, Econ, Finance, Info tech, Mkt, Tax
Automation Activity & Vendor Info: (Acquisitions) Ex Libris Group; (Cataloging) Ex Libris Group; (Circulation) Ex Libris Group; (Course Reserve) Ex Libris Group; (Discovery) Ex Libris Group; (ILL) Mel Cat; (OPAC) Ex Libris Group; (Serials) Ex Libris Group
Wireless access
Function: Doc delivery serv
Partic in Detroit Area Library Network; Midwest Collaborative for Library Services
Special Services for the Blind - Bks on CD; Screen reader software
Open Mon-Thurs 12-6, Fri & Sat (by appt) 9-5
Restriction: Pub use on premises

UBLY

P SLEEPER PUBLIC LIBRARY, 2236 E Main St, 48475-9726. SAN 308-4558. Tel: 989-658-8901. FAX: 989-658-8788. Web Site: www.sleeper.michlibrary.org. *Dir,* Barbara Butch; E-mail: ublylibrary1908@gmail.com
Circ 8,117
Library Holdings: Bk Vols 16,495; Per Subs 95
Wireless access
Open Mon-Fri 10-5

UNIONVILLE

P COLUMBIA TOWNSHIP LIBRARY*, 6456 Center St, 48767. SAN 308-4574. Tel: 989-674-2651. FAX: 989-674-2138. E-mail: columbiatwplibrary@gmail.com. Web Site: www.columbiatwplibrary.org. *Dir,* Briynne McCrea; *Librn,* Sandra Gnagey; Staff 1.1 (MLS 0.6, Non-MLS 0.5)
Founded 1952. Pop 2,193; Circ 15,000
Library Holdings: Audiobooks 10; AV Mats 2,705; CDs 111; DVDs 1,251; Large Print Bks 280; Bk Vols 17,417; Per Subs 20
Automation Activity & Vendor Info: (Cataloging) Biblionix; (Circulation) Biblionix; (ILL) Mel Cat
Wireless access
Function: Accelerated reader prog, After school storytime, Bks on CD, Computer training, Computers for patron use, E-Reserves, Electronic databases & coll, Homework prog, ILL available, Music CDs, Online cat, OverDrive digital audio bks, Photocopying/Printing, Preschool reading prog, Scanner, Senior computer classes, Spoken cassettes & DVDs, Story hour, Summer reading prog, Tax forms, VHS videos, Wheelchair accessible
Open Mon-Thurs 10-7, Sat 9-1

UNIVERSITY CENTER

J DELTA COLLEGE LIBRARY*, 1961 Delta Rd, 48710. SAN 308-4582. Tel: 989-686-9006. Circulation Tel: 989-686-9310. E-mail: library@delta.edu. Web Site: www.delta.edu/community/services-for-our-community/library.html. *Dir,* Michele Pratt; E-mail: michelepratt@delta.edu; *Ref Librn,* Krysta Vincent; E-mail: krystavincent@delta.edu; *Ref Librn, Govt Doc,* Anne Elias; E-mail: anneelias@delta.edu; Staff 10 (MLS 4, Non-MLS 6)
Founded 1961. Enrl 11,300; Highest Degree: Associate
Library Holdings: Bk Titles 59,663; Per Subs 296
Special Collections: Delta College Archives. US Document Depository
Automation Activity & Vendor Info: (Acquisitions) Horizon; (Cataloging) Horizon; (Circulation) Horizon; (Course Reserve) Horizon; (ILL) Horizon; (OPAC) SirsiDynix; (Serials) SirsiDynix
Wireless access
Function: Art exhibits
Partic in Midwest Collaborative for Library Services; Valley Libr Consortium
Open Mon-Thurs 7:30am-9pm, Fri 7:30-3, Sat 10-2, Sun 1-4

C SAGINAW VALLEY STATE UNIVERSITY*, Melvin J Zahnow Library, 7400 Bay Rd, 48710. SAN 308-4590. Tel: 989-964-4240. Reference Tel: 989-964-4242. Administration Tel: 989-964-4237. Toll Free Tel: 866-381-7878. FAX: 989-964-4383. E-mail: library@svsu.edu. Web Site: www.svsu.edu/library. *Dir,* Anita Dey; Tel: 989-964-4236, E-mail: adey@svsu.edu; *Head, Access Serv,* Thomas Zantow; Tel: 989-964-4238, E-mail: tzantow@svsu.edu; *Coll Develop & Res Librn,* Matt Buckley; Tel: 989-964-2844, E-mail: mjbuck1@svsu.edu; Staff 20 (MLS 10, Non-MLS 10)
Founded 1963. Enrl 10,250; Fac 295; Highest Degree: Master. Sal $1,109,115 (Prof $692,000)
Library Holdings: AV Mats 27,023; e-books 102,228; e-journals 41,794; Microforms 370,628; Bk Vols 200,451; Per Subs 105
Special Collections: Cramton Jazz Coll; Flying Melzoras Circus Coll; Ken Follett Coll; Local History Coll; University Archives
Automation Activity & Vendor Info: (Cataloging) Innovative Interfaces, Inc; (Circulation) Innovative Interfaces, Inc; (Course Reserve) Innovative Interfaces, Inc; (ILL) OCLC ILLiad; (OPAC) Innovative Interfaces, Inc; (Serials) Innovative Interfaces, Inc
Wireless access
Partic in Midwest Collaborative for Library Services; OCLC Online Computer Library Center, Inc
Open Mon-Thurs 8am-Midnight, Fri 8am-11pm, Sat 10-6, Sun Noon-Midnight

UTICA

P UTICA PUBLIC LIBRARY*, 7530 Auburn Rd, 48317-5216. SAN 308-4612. Tel: 586-731-4141. FAX: 586-731-0769. E-mail: upl-info@libcoop.net. Web Site: www.uticalibrary.com. *Dir,* Marsha C Doege; E-mail: doegem@libcoop.net; Staff 3 (Non-MLS 3)
Founded 1933. Pop 4,750; Circ 37,000
Library Holdings: Bk Vols 20,000; Per Subs 40
Special Collections: Utica Sentinel Newspaper Coll (1876-1971), micro (1986 to present)
Automation Activity & Vendor Info: (Acquisitions) SirsiDynix; (Cataloging) SirsiDynix; (Circulation) SirsiDynix; (Serials) SirsiDynix
Wireless access
Function: Homebound delivery serv, ILL available, Photocopying/Printing, Prog for adults, Prog for children & young adult, Ref serv available, Summer reading prog, Wheelchair accessible
Partic in Suburban Library Cooperative
Open Mon, Tues & Thurs 11-7, Wed 11-8, Fri 11-4, Sat 11-2:30

VASSAR

P BULLARD SANFORD MEMORIAL LIBRARY, 520 W Huron Ave, 48768. SAN 308-4620. Tel: 989-823-2171. FAX: 989-823-8573. E-mail: info@vassarlibrary.org. Web Site: www.vassarlibrary.org. *Libr Dir,* Christian D Dunham; E-mail: christian@vassarlibrary.org; *Dep Dir,* Jennifer Santoviz; E-mail: jsantoviz@vassarlib.org; *Libr Asst,* Patricia Kreiner; Staff 6 (MLS 1, Non-MLS 5)
Founded 1906. Pop 10,000; Circ 52,000
Library Holdings: Bk Vols 45,000; Per Subs 100
Special Collections: Large Print Coll
Automation Activity & Vendor Info: (Cataloging) Auto-Graphics, Inc; (Circulation) Auto-Graphics, Inc; (OPAC) Auto-Graphics, Inc
Wireless access
Partic in White Pine Library Cooperative
Special Services for the Deaf - TDD equip
Special Services for the Blind - Talking bks
Open Tues-Fri 10-6, Sat 10-4
Friends of the Library Group
Bookmobiles: 1. Bk vols 1,500

VERMONTVILLE

P VERMONTVILLE TOWNSHIP LIBRARY*, 120 E First St, 49096. (Mail add: PO Box G, 49096-0910), SAN 308-4639. Tel: 517-726-1362. FAX: 517-726-1362. E-mail: vermontvillelibrary@yahoo.com. Web Site: www.vmtlib.michlibrary.org. *Dir,* Carla Rumsey; *Asst Dir,* Rita Miller; *Librn,* Kim Eldred; *Librn,* Diana Reid
Founded 1949. Pop 3,842; Circ 10,309
Library Holdings: Bk Vols 21,933
Automation Activity & Vendor Info: (Acquisitions) Follett Software; (Cataloging) Follett Software; (Circulation) Follett Software; (ILL) Follett Software; (OPAC) Follett Software; (Serials) Follett Software
Wireless access
Mem of Woodlands Library Cooperative
Open Tues 1-8, Wed-Fri 11-6, Sat 9-1

VERNON

P VERNON DISTRICT PUBLIC LIBRARY*, 115 E Main St, 48476. (Mail add: PO Box 416, 48476-0416), SAN 308-4647. Tel: 989-288-6486. FAX: 989-288-2422. E-mail: vernonlibrary@hotmail.com. Web Site: vernon.michlibrary.org. *Dir,* Cheryl Davenport
Founded 1969. Pop 4,989; Circ 12,044
Library Holdings: Audiobooks 296; Bks on Deafness & Sign Lang 20; DVDs 384; e-books 1,982; Large Print Bks 200; Bk Vols 15,895; Per Subs 12
Automation Activity & Vendor Info: (Cataloging) OCLC; (Circulation) Follett Software; (OPAC) Follett Software
Wireless access
Partic in Mideastern Michigan Library Cooperative
Open Mon, Tues & Thurs 10-7, Wed & Fri 10-5, Sat 10-2

VESTABURG

P RICHLAND TOWNSHIP LIBRARY*, 8821 Third St, 48891. (Mail add: PO Box 220, 48891-0220), SAN 308-4655. Tel: 989-268-5044. FAX: 989-268-5629. TDD: 989-268-5044. E-mail: rtl@richlandtownshiplibrary.com. Web Site: richlandtownshiplibrary.com. *Dir,* Sherma M Horrocks
Founded 1912. Pop 3,674
Library Holdings: Audiobooks 326; DVDs 2,310
Automation Activity & Vendor Info: (Cataloging) Auto-Graphics, Inc; (Circulation) Auto-Graphics, Inc
Wireless access
Function: Accelerated reader prog, Adult bk club, Audiobks on Playaways & MP3, Audiobks via web, Bk club(s), Bks on CD, Children's prog, Computers for patron use, ILL available, Magazines, Online cat, Prog for adults, Scanner, Teen prog
Partic in Mid-Michigan Library League
Open Mon 2-6, Tues 10-5, Wed-Fri 11-5
Friends of the Library Group

VICKSBURG

P VICKSBURG DISTRICT LIBRARY, 215 S Michigan Ave, 49097. SAN 308-4663. Tel: 269-649-1648. FAX: 269-649-3666. E-mail: info@vicksburglibrary.org. Web Site: www.vicksburglibrary.org. *Dir,* Eric Richard Hansen; E-mail: ehansen@vicksburglibrary.org; *Head, Circ & Ref,* Adrianne Schinkai; *Youth Serv Librn,* Stephanie Willoughby. Subject Specialists: *English lit, Writing,* Eric Richard Hansen; Staff 3 (MLS 2, Non-MLS 1)
Founded 1902. Pop 12,238; Circ 65,734
Library Holdings: CDs 500; DVDs 2,100; Bk Vols 41,525; Per Subs 71; Talking Bks 720
Subject Interests: Local hist
Automation Activity & Vendor Info: (Circulation) Auto-Graphics, Inc; (ILL) Auto-Graphics, Inc; (OPAC) Auto-Graphics, Inc
Wireless access
Function: 24/7 Online cat, Activity rm, Adult bk club, Audiobks via web, Bk club(s), Bks on CD, Children's prog, Computers for patron use, Electronic databases & coll, For res purposes, Free DVD rentals, Holiday prog, ILL available, Internet access, Laminating, Magazines, Magnifiers for reading, Meeting rooms, Microfiche/film & reading machines, Movies, Music CDs, Online cat, Outreach serv, OverDrive digital audio bks, Photocopying/Printing, Prog for adults, Prog for children & young adult, Ref & res, Ref serv available, Res assist avail, Res performed for a fee, Scanner, Story hour, Summer & winter reading prog, Summer reading prog, Tax forms, Teen prog, Winter reading prog, Writing prog
Partic in Southwest Michigan Library Cooperative
Open Mon-Thurs 10-8:30, Fri & Sat 10-5, Sun 1-5

WAKEFIELD

P WAKEFIELD PUBLIC LIBRARY*, 401 Hancock St, 49968. SAN 308-4671. Tel: 906-229-5236. FAX: 906-229-5974. Web Site: www.uproc.lib.mi.us/wakefield. *Dir,* Joell Laessig; E-mail: jlaessig@uproc.lib.mi.us
Founded 1934. Circ 23,584
Library Holdings: Bk Vols 20,000; Per Subs 30
Special Collections: Foreign Language (Italian, Polish & Finnish)
Automation Activity & Vendor Info: (Cataloging) Follett Software; (Circulation) Follett Software
Wireless access
Partic in Superiorland Library Cooperative; Upper Peninsula Region of Library Cooperation, Inc
Open Mon 10-6, Tues & Thurs 12-4:30, Wed 12-6, Fri 10:30-4:30, Sat (Sept-May) 10-12
Friends of the Library Group

WALDRON

P WALDRON DISTRICT LIBRARY*, 107 N Main St, 49288. (Mail add: PO Box 136, 49288-0136), SAN 376-7051. Tel: 517-286-6511. FAX: 517-286-6511. E-mail: books@wcomco.net. Web Site: waldrondistlib.michlibrary.org. *Dir,* Joyce Gendron
Pop 2,475. Sal $42,337
Library Holdings: Audiobooks 183; CDs 56; DVDs 192; Bk Vols 16,656; Per Subs 4; Talking Bks 229; Videos 764
Automation Activity & Vendor Info: (Cataloging) Follett Software; (Circulation) Follett Software
Wireless access
Mem of Woodlands Library Cooperative
Open Tues-Thurs 11-7, Fri 11-4:30, Sat 9-12
Friends of the Library Group

WALLED LAKE

P WALLED LAKE CITY LIBRARY*, 1499 E West Maple Rd, 48390. SAN 308-4698. Tel: 248-624-3772. FAX: 248-624-0041. Web Site: walledlake.ploud.net. *Dir,* Alyson Lobert; E-mail: alyson@walledlakelibrary.org; *Asst Dir,* Carrie Ralston; E-mail: carrie@walledlakelibrary.org; Staff 6 (MLS 2, Non-MLS 4)
Founded 1963. Pop 6,900; Circ 50,000
Library Holdings: Bk Vols 50,500; Per Subs 70
Automation Activity & Vendor Info: (Cataloging) SirsiDynix; (Circulation) SirsiDynix; (ILL) SirsiDynix; (OPAC) SirsiDynix-iBistro
Wireless access
Function: Adult literacy prog, Audiobks via web, Bks on CD, Computer training, Computers for patron use, Digital talking bks, Electronic databases & coll, Home delivery & serv to seniorr ctr & nursing homes, Homebound delivery serv, ILL available, Mail & tel request accepted, Museum passes, Music CDs, Online cat, Photocopying/Printing, Prog for adults, Prog for children & young adult, Senior computer classes, Story hour, Summer reading prog, Tax forms, Telephone ref, Wheelchair accessible
Partic in The Library Network
Open Mon-Thurs 10-8, Fri 10-6, Sat 10-5
Friends of the Library Group

WALLOON LAKE

P CROOKED TREE DISTRICT LIBRARY, Walloon Lake Library, 2203 Walloon St, 49796. (Mail add: PO Box 518, 49796-0518), SAN 376-6470. Tel: 231-535-2111. FAX: 231-535-2790. E-mail: walloon@crookedtreelibrary.com. Web Site: www.crookedtreelibrary.org. *Dir,* Karen Felde; E-mail: karen@crookedtreelibrary.com; Staff 1 (MLS 1)
Founded 1977. Pop 3,953
Automation Activity & Vendor Info: (Cataloging) SirsiDynix; (Circulation) SirsiDynix; (OPAC) SirsiDynix
Wireless access
Partic in Northland Library Cooperative
Open Mon-Wed 12-4
Friends of the Library Group
Branches: 1
BOYNE FALLS BRANCH, 3008 Railroad St, Boyne Falls, 49713. (Mail add: PO Box 17, Boyne Falls, 49713-0017), SAN 376-8201. Tel: 231-549-2277. E-mail: bflibrary@centurytel.net. *Dir,* Karen Felde
Founded 1977
Open Thurs 12-4, Sat 10-1

WARREN

J MACOMB COMMUNITY COLLEGE LIBRARIES*, South Campus, 14500 E 12 Mile Rd, J-Bldg, 48088-3896. SAN 308-4728. Tel: 586-445-7401, Ext 2. Reference Tel: 586-445-7779. FAX: 586-445-7157. Web Site: www.macomb.edu. *Dean, Libr & Learning Res,* Michael Balsamo; Tel: 586-445-7141, E-mail: balsamom@macomb.edu; *Electronic Serv Librn,* Mary Kickham-Samy; Tel: 586-445-7419, E-mail: kickham-samym@macomb.edu; *Syst Librn,* Bruce Bett; Tel: 586-445-7880, E-mail: bettb@macomb.edu; Staff 10 (MLS 5, Non-MLS 5)
Founded 1954. Enrl 5,500; Fac 900; Highest Degree: Associate
Library Holdings: AV Mats 5,281; CDs 242; DVDs 840; e-books 10,000; Bk Titles 83,734; Bk Vols 102,500; Per Subs 160
Subject Interests: Law
Automation Activity & Vendor Info: (Acquisitions) SirsiDynix; (Cataloging) SirsiDynix; (Circulation) SirsiDynix; (OPAC) SirsiDynix; (Serials) SirsiDynix
Wireless access
Function: Online ref
Partic in Detroit Area Library Network; OCLC Online Computer Library Center, Inc
Open Mon-Thurs 8am-9:45pm, Fri 8-2:15, Sat 9-4:15, Sun 12-5:45
Departmental Libraries:
CENTER CAMPUS, 44575 Garfield Rd, C-Bldg, Clinton Township, 48038-1139, SAN 346-9441. Tel: 586-286-2104, Ext 2. Reference Tel: 586-286-2056. Web Site: www.macomb.edu/future-students/student-resources/library/index.html. *Coll & Res Librn,* Cassandra Spieles; Tel: 586-445-7778, E-mail: spielesc@macomb.edu; *Electronic Info Librn,* Teresa Biegun; Tel: 586-286-2233, E-mail: biegunt@macomb.edu; *Pub Serv Librn,* Steve Rybicki; Tel: 586-286-2026, E-mail: rybickis@macomb.edu; Staff 7 (MLS 4, Non-MLS 3)
Founded 1963. Enrl 15,000; Highest Degree: Associate
Library Holdings: AV Mats 4,935; CDs 187; DVDs 125; e-books 10,000; Bk Titles 60,541; Bk Vols 86,000; Per Subs 100
Automation Activity & Vendor Info: (Cataloging) Horizon; (Circulation) Horizon; (Discovery) EBSCO Discovery Service; (OPAC) Horizon
Partic in Midwest Collaborative for Library Services
Open Mon-Thurs 8am-9:45pm, Fri 8-2:15, Sat 9-4:15, Sun 12-5:45

M ST JOHN MACOMB HOSPITAL CENTER LIBRARY*, 11800 E 12 Mile Rd, 48093. SAN 320-3859. Tel: 586-573-5117. FAX: 586-573-5042. Web Site: www.stjohnprovidence.org/macomb-oakland. *Library Contact,* Jennifer Randazzo; E-mail: jennifer.randazzo@stjohn.org; Staff 1 (MLS 1)
Library Holdings: Bk Titles 2,200; Bk Vols 2,500; Per Subs 180
Subject Interests: Allied health, Med, Nursing
Wireless access
Open Mon-Thurs 8-4

P WARREN PUBLIC LIBRARY*, Civic Center Library, One City Sq, Ste 100, 48093-2396. SAN 347-1454. Tel: 586-751-0770. Web Site: www.warrenlibrary.net. *Libr Dir,* Oksana Urban; E-mail: ourban@cityofwarren.org; *Br Supvr,* Lynn Bieszka; Staff 7 (MLS 5, Non-MLS 2)
Founded 1958. Pop 138,247; Circ 603,725
Library Holdings: Bk Vols 258,623; Per Subs 525
Automation Activity & Vendor Info: (Acquisitions) SirsiDynix; (Cataloging) SirsiDynix; (Circulation) SirsiDynix; (ILL) SirsiDynix; (OPAC) SirsiDynix; (Serials) SirsiDynix
Wireless access

Open Mon & Wed 12-8, Tues & Thurs 9-8, Fri & Sat 9-5 Sun(Summer) 12-5
Friends of the Library Group
Branches: 3
MAYBELLE BURNETTE BRANCH, 23345 Van Dyke Ave, 48089, SAN 347-1489. Tel: 586-353-0579. *Br Supvr,* Sharon Linsday; Staff 4 (MLS 2, Non-MLS 2)
Founded 1965
Library Holdings: Per Subs 90
Subject Interests: Irish
Function: 24/7 Electronic res, 24/7 Online cat, After school storytime
Special Services for the Blind - Closed circuit TV magnifier; Magnifiers; Reader equip
Open Mon, Wed, Fri, Sat, 9-5; Tues & Thurs 12-8
Friends of the Library Group
DOROTHY M BUSCH BRANCH, 23333 Ryan Rd, 48091, SAN 347-1519. Tel: 586-353-0580. *Br Supvr,* Jamie Babcock; Staff 2 (MLS 1, Non-MLS 1)
Library Holdings: Per Subs 98
Friends of the Library Group
ARTHUR J MILLER BRANCH, 5460 Arden St, Ste 303, 48092, SAN 347-1578. Tel: 586-751-5377. *Br Supvr,* John Robertson; Staff 4 (MLS 3, Non-MLS 1)
Library Holdings: Per Subs 221
Special Collections: State Document Depository; US Document Depository
Subject Interests: Bus, Sheet music
Function: 24/7 Electronic res, 24/7 Online cat, Adult bk club, After school storytime
Special Services for the Deaf - TDD equip
Open Mon, Fri, Sat, 9-5; Wed, 9-8; Tues, Thurs, 12-8
Friends of the Library Group

WASHINGTON

P ROMEO DISTRICT LIBRARY, Graubner Library, 65821 Van Dyke, 48095. SAN 370-758X. Tel: 586-752-0603. Circulation Tel: 586-752-0603, Ext 1000. Reference Tel: 586-752-0603, Ext 1021. FAX: 586-752-8416. Web Site: romeodistrictlibrary.org. *Dir,* Claire Lopiccolo; E-mail: claire@romeodistrictlibary.org; *Ad,* Glen Sowles; E-mail: glen@romeodistrictlibary.org; *Operations Mgr,* William Blevins; E-mail: william@romeodistrictlibrary.org; Staff 32 (MLS 10, Non-MLS 22)
Founded 1909. Pop 17,294; Circ 329,952
Library Holdings: AV Mats 9,475; Electronic Media & Resources 420; Bk Titles 79,500; Bk Vols 83,516; Per Subs 311; Talking Bks 4,679
Automation Activity & Vendor Info: (Acquisitions) SirsiDynix; (Cataloging) SirsiDynix; (Circulation) SirsiDynix; (OPAC) SirsiDynix; (Serials) SirsiDynix
Wireless access
Partic in Suburban Library Cooperative
Open Mon-Thurs 11-7, Fri & Sat 11-3
Friends of the Library Group
Branches: 1
KEZAR BRANCH, 107 Church St, Romeo, 48065, SAN 308-3772. Tel: 586-752-2583. FAX: 586-336-7300. *Br Libm,* Stacie Guzzo; E-mail: stacie@romeodistrictlibrary.org; Staff 2 (MLS 1, Non-MLS 1)
Founded 1909
Open Mon-Thurs 11-7, Fri & Sat 11-3
Friends of the Library Group

WATERFORD

J OAKLAND COMMUNITY COLLEGE, Highland Lakes Campus Library, Woodland Hall, 7350 Cooley Lake Rd, 48327-4187. SAN 308-4566. Tel: 248-942-3125. Reference Tel: 248-942-3126. FAX: 248-942-3132. Web Site: www.oaklandcc.edu/library. *Librn,* Beth Garnsey; Tel: 248-942-3128, E-mail: bagarnse@oaklandcc.edu; *Librn,* Allison McFadden-Keesling; Tel: 248-942-3127, E-mail: acmcfadd@oaklandcc.edu; Staff 4.5 (MLS 2, Non-MLS 2.5)
Founded 1965. Enrl 6,161; Fac 54; Highest Degree: Associate
Jul 2018-Jun 2019. Mats Exp $62,816, Books $30,563, Per/Ser (Incl. Access Fees) $32,253. Sal $306,326 (Prof $219,267)
Library Holdings: Bks on Deafness & Sign Lang 114; DVDs 736; e-books 239,460; Bk Titles 35,717; Videos 210
Subject Interests: Allied health, Dental hygiene, Nursing
Automation Activity & Vendor Info: (Cataloging) Ex Libris Group; (Circulation) Ex Libris Group; (Course Reserve) Ex Libris Group; (Discovery) EBSCO Discovery Service; (ILL) OCLC; (OPAC) Ex Libris Group; (Serials) EBSCO Online
Wireless access
Function: Audio & video playback equip for onsite use, CD-ROM, Doc delivery serv, Electronic databases & coll, Health sci info serv, ILL available, Internet access, Music CDs, Online ref, Orientations, Photocopying/Printing, Ref & res, Ref serv available, Res assist avail, VHS videos, Wheelchair accessible
Special Services for the Blind - Computer with voice synthesizer for visually impaired persons
Open Mon-Thurs (Sept-June) 8am-9pm, Fri 8-5; Mon-Thurs (July-Aug) 8-8, Fri 8-5

P WATERFORD TOWNSHIP PUBLIC LIBRARY, 5168 Civic Center Dr, 48329. SAN 347-0075. Tel: 248-674-4831. FAX: 248-674-1910. Web Site: www.waterfordmi.gov/Library. *Libr Dir,* Joan M Rogers; Tel: 248-618-7691, E-mail: jrogers@waterfordmi.gov; *Head, Adult & Outreach Serv,* Jean Hansen; Tel: 248-618-7682, E-mail: jhansen@waterfordmi.gov; *Head, Children's Servx,* Cynthia Walker; Tel: 248-618-7684, E-mail: cwalker@waterfordmi.gov; *Coordr, Circ,* Jonathan Deahl; Tel: 248-618-7678, E-mail: jdeahl@waterfordmi.gov; Staff 24 (MLS 10, Non-MLS 14)
Founded 1964. Pop 73,767; Circ 223,743
Jan 2020-Dec 2020 Income $2,187,590, State $57,640, County $123,994, Locally Generated Income $1,974,102, Other $31,854
Library Holdings: AV Mats 21,221; e-books 31,366; Bk Titles 120,190; Per Subs 198
Subject Interests: Careers, Mich
Automation Activity & Vendor Info: (Acquisitions) TLC (The Library Corporation); (Circulation) CARL.Solution (TLC); (ILL) TLC (The Library Corporation); (OPAC) TLC (The Library Corporation)
Wireless access
Function: 24/7 Electronic res, 24/7 Online cat, Adult bk club, Adult literacy prog, Audiobks via web, BA reader (adult literacy), Bi-weekly Writer's Group, Bk club(s), Bk reviews (Group), Bks on CD, Children's prog, Computer training, Computers for patron use, Digital talking bks, Electronic databases & coll, Free DVD rentals, Genealogy discussion group, Home delivery & serv to seniorr ctr & nursing homes, Homebound delivery serv, ILL available, Instruction & testing, Internet access, Life-long learning prog for all ages, Literacy & newcomer serv, Magazines, Magnifiers for reading, Mail & tel request accepted, Meeting rooms, Microfiche/film & reading machines, Movies, Museum passes, Music CDs, Online cat, Online ref, Orientations, Outreach serv, OverDrive digital audio bks, Photocopying/Printing, Preschool outreach, Preschool reading prog, Printer for laptops & handheld devices, Prog for adults, Prog for children & young adult, Ref & res, Ref serv available, Scanner, Senior outreach, Serves people with intellectual disabilities, Spanish lang bks, Spoken cassettes & CDs, Story hour, Study rm, Summer & winter reading prog, Summer reading prog, Tax forms, Teen prog, Telephone ref, Wheelchair accessible, Winter reading prog, Writing prog
Partic in The Library Network
Special Services for the Blind - BiFolkal kits; Bks on cassette; Bks on CD; Home delivery serv; Large print bks; Large screen computer & software; Low vision equip; Magnifiers; Scanner for conversion & translation of mats; Screen enlargement software for people with visual disabilities; ZoomText magnification & reading software
Open Mon-Thurs 10-9, Sat 10-5, Sun 1-5
Restriction: Access for corporate affiliates, Circ limited, In-house use for visitors, Non-circulating coll
Friends of the Library Group

WATERVLIET

P WATERVLIET DISTRICT LIBRARY, 333 N Main St, 49098-9793. SAN 308-4760. Tel: 269-463-6382. FAX: 269-463-3117. E-mail: info@wdlib.org. Web Site: www.watervlietlibrary.org. *Dir,* Sharon L Crotser-Toy; Staff 5 (MLS 1, Non-MLS 4)
Founded 1923. Pop 5,235; Circ 34,439
Library Holdings: Bks on Deafness & Sign Lang 30; High Interest/Low Vocabulary Bk Vols 25; Bk Titles 23,000; Bk Vols 26,500; Per Subs 53
Special Collections: Civil War Coll; Local History
Automation Activity & Vendor Info: (Cataloging) Biblionix/Apollo; (Circulation) Biblionix/Apollo; (OPAC) Biblionix/Apollo
Wireless access
Function: 24/7 Electronic res, 24/7 Online cat, Activity rm, Adult bk club, Adult literacy prog, Archival coll, Art programs, Audiobks on Playaways & MP3, Audiobks via web, Bk club(s), Bks on CD, Bus archives, Butterfly Garden, CD-ROM, Children's prog, Computer training, Computers for patron use, Doc delivery serv, E-Reserves, Electronic databases & coll, For res purposes, Free DVD rentals, Holiday prog, Homebound delivery serv, ILL available, Internet access, Laminating, Life-long learning prog for all ages, Magazines, Mail & tel request accepted, Mail loans to mem, Meeting rooms, Movies, Museum passes, Online cat, Online ref, Outreach serv, Outside serv via phone, mail, e-mail & web, OverDrive digital audio bks, Photocopying/Printing, Preschool outreach, Preschool reading prog, Prog for adults, Prog for children & young adult, Ref & res, Ref serv available, Res assist avail, Scanner, Spanish lang bks, STEM programs, Story hour, Summer & winter reading prog, Summer reading prog, Tax forms, Teen prog, Telephone ref, Wheelchair accessible, Winter reading prog, Workshops
Partic in Midwest Collaborative for Library Services; Southwest Michigan Library Cooperative

Open Mon & Wed 10-7, Tues & Thurs 10-6, Fri 10-5, Sat 9-3
Restriction: Non-circulating of rare bks, Non-resident fee

WAYLAND

P HENIKA DISTRICT LIBRARY, 149 S Main St, 49348-1208. SAN 308-4779. Tel: 269-792-2891. FAX: 269-792-0399. Web Site: www.henikalibrary.com. *Dir,* Cierra Bakovka; E-mail: waycb@llcoop.org
Founded 1899. Pop 6,921; Circ 39,363
Library Holdings: Bk Vols 37,000; Per Subs 56
Wireless access
Partic in Lakeland Library Cooperative; Mich Libr Asn
Open Mon & Wed 9-8, Tues, Thurs & Fri 9-6, Sat 9-3
Friends of the Library Group

P LEIGHTON TOWNSHIP PUBLIC LIBRARY*, 4451 12th St, 49348. (Mail add: PO Drawer H, Moline, 49335-0250), SAN 346-3508. Tel: 616-877-4143. FAX: 616-877-4484. E-mail: molkmk@llcoop.org. Web Site: www.leightonlibrary.org. *Libr Dir,* Karen McKinnon
Founded 1999. Pop 4,934
Library Holdings: Bk Vols 18,290; Per Subs 60
Wireless access
Function: 24/7 Online cat, Activity rm, Audiobks via web, Bks on CD, Children's prog, Computers for patron use, Free DVD rentals, ILL available, Internet access, Laminating, Magazines, Music CDs, Online cat, OverDrive digital audio bks, Prog for adults, Prog for children & young adult, Ref & res, Story hour, Summer reading prog, Teen prog, Wheelchair accessible, Winter reading prog
Partic in Lakeland Library Cooperative
Open Mon, Wed & Thurs 10-8, Fri 10-4, Sat 9-1

WAYNE

P WAYNE PUBLIC LIBRARY*, 3737 S Wayne Rd, 48184. SAN 308-4809. Tel: 734-721-7832. FAX: 734-721-0341. Web Site: wayne.lib.mi.us. *Dir,* Steven McGladdery; E-mail: smcgladdery@wayne.lib.mi.us; *Librn,* Carola Fisher; E-mail: cfisher@wayne.lib.mi.us; *Librn,* Sean Glasgow; *Ad,* Kathleen Kozakowski; E-mail: kkozakowski@wayne.lib.mi.us; *Youth Serv Librn,* Nancy Voigt; E-mail: nvoigt@wayne.lib.mi.us; Staff 9 (MLS 6, Non-MLS 3)
Founded 1927. Pop 17,593; Circ 49,194
Library Holdings: AV Mats 12,371; High Interest/Low Vocabulary Bk Vols 75; Large Print Bks 1,841; Bk Vols 95,034; Per Subs 138
Automation Activity & Vendor Info: (Acquisitions) SirsiDynix; (Cataloging) SirsiDynix; (Circulation) SirsiDynix; (OPAC) SirsiDynix; (Serials) SirsiDynix
Wireless access
Publications: Communique (Newsletter)
Partic in Libr Network of Mich
Special Services for the Deaf - TDD equip
Special Services for the Blind - Closed circuit TV magnifier
Open Mon-Thurs 10-9, Fri & Sat 12-5, Sun (Sept-May) 1-5
Friends of the Library Group

WEST BLOOMFIELD

R JEWISH COMMUNITY CENTER OF METROPOLITAN DETROIT*, Henry & Delia Meyers Library, 6600 W Maple Rd, 48322-3022. SAN 308-4825. Tel: 248-432-5547. FAX: 248-432-5552. Web Site: www.jccdet.org. *Libr Dir,* Francine Menken; Tel: 248-432-5546, E-mail: fmenken@jccdet.org; Staff 1 (Non-MLS 1)
Founded 1959
Library Holdings: DVDs 100; Large Print Bks 100; Bk Vols 12,000; Per Subs 35; Talking Bks 15; Videos 50
Special Collections: American-Jewish Coll, per & newsp
Subject Interests: Judaica (lit or hist of Jews)
Automation Activity & Vendor Info: (Cataloging) Follett Software; (Circulation) Follett Software
Function: Bk club(s), Prog for adults, Prog for children & young adult
Special Services for the Blind - Magnifiers; Telesensory screen enlarger & speech synthesis interface to the OPAC
Open Mon-Thurs 10-5, Fri 10-Noon, Sun 11-2
Friends of the Library Group

R TEMPLE ISRAEL LIBRARIES & MEDIA CENTER*, 5725 Walnut Lake Rd, 48323. SAN 308-0390. Tel: 248-661-5700. FAX: 248-661-1302. E-mail: info@temple-israel.org. Web Site: www.temple-israel.org/CheckItOut. *Dir,* Lauren Johnson; *Archivist, Asst Librn,* Kylie Gignac; E-mail: kgignac@temple-israel.org; Staff 2 (MLS 2)
Founded 1941
Library Holdings: Bk Titles 13,560; Bk Vols 16,010; Per Subs 20
Special Collections: Jewish Children's Literature Coll; Jewish Heritage Coll, video; Reform Judaism Coll
Subject Interests: Holocaust, Israel, Jewish hist, Judaism
Automation Activity & Vendor Info: (Cataloging) Follett Software; (Circulation) Follett Software

P WEST BLOOMFIELD TOWNSHIP PUBLIC LIBRARY*, 4600 Walnut Lake Rd, 48323. SAN 347-1756. Tel: 248-682-2120. Circulation Tel: 248-232-2201. FAX: 248-232-2291. TDD: 248-232-2292. Web Site: www.wblib.org. *Dir,* Clara Nalli Bohrer; E-mail: director@wblib.org; *IT Coordr,* Robert Pesale; Tel: 248-232-2315, E-mail: pesalero@wblib.org; Staff 95 (MLS 27, Non-MLS 68)
Founded 1934. Pop 64,860; Circ 1,885,986
Library Holdings: AV Mats 39,376; Bk Vols 225,617; Per Subs 525
Automation Activity & Vendor Info: (Acquisitions) Innovative Interfaces, Inc; (Cataloging) Innovative Interfaces, Inc; (Circulation) Innovative Interfaces, Inc; (ILL) Innovative Interfaces, Inc; (OPAC) Innovative Interfaces, Inc; (Serials) Innovative Interfaces, Inc
Wireless access
Partic in Metro Net Libr Consortium; The Library Network
Special Services for the Deaf - Assistive tech; Bks on deafness & sign lang; Closed caption videos; TTY equip
Special Services for the Blind - Audio mat; Bks on cassette; Bks on CD; Computer with voice synthesizer for visually impaired persons; Large print bks; Magnifiers; Reader equip
Open Mon-Thurs 9-9, Fri & Sat 9-6, Sun 12-8
Friends of the Library Group
Branches: 1
WESTACRES, 7321 Commerce Rd, 48324, SAN 347-1780. Tel: 248-363-4022. Circulation Tel: 248-232-2410. Reference Tel: 248-232-2420. FAX: 248-363-7243. *Br Mgr,* Steve Ketchan; Tel: 248-232-2401
Founded 1938
Library Holdings: Bk Titles 43,651; Per Subs 150
Open Mon-Thurs 9-9, Fri & Sat 9-6, Sun 12-8 (12-5 Summer)
Friends of the Library Group

WEST BRANCH

P WEST BRANCH DISTRICT LIBRARY*, 119 N Fourth St, 48661. SAN 308-4833. Tel: 989-345-2235. FAX: 989-345-8735. Web Site: westbranchlibrary.org. *Dir,* John Sheridan; E-mail: jsheridanwbdlibrary@gmail.com; Staff 8 (MLS 1, Non-MLS 7)
Founded 1905. Pop 9,922; Circ 50,466
Automation Activity & Vendor Info: (Acquisitions) SirsiDynix; (Cataloging) SirsiDynix; (Circulation) SirsiDynix; (Course Reserve) SirsiDynix; (ILL) SirsiDynix; (Media Booking) SirsiDynix; (OPAC) SirsiDynix; (Serials) SirsiDynix
Wireless access
Partic in Valley Library Consortium; White Pine Library Cooperative
Open Mon & Wed 10-7, Tues, Thurs & Fri 10-5, Sat 10-2
Friends of the Library Group

WESTLAND

P WESTLAND PUBLIC LIBRARY*, William P Faust Library, 6123 Central City Pkwy, 48185. Tel: 734-326-6123. FAX: 734-595-4612. Administration E-mail: questions@westlandlibrary.org. Web Site: www.westland.lib.mi.us. *Libr Dir,* Jennifer Roth; E-mail: jennifer.roth@westlandlibrary.org; *Head, Tech Serv,* Susan Hanson; E-mail: susan.hanson@westlandlibrary.org; *Head, Tech, Librn,* Daniel Wetterstrom; E-mail: dan.wetterstrom@westlandlibrary.org; *Head, Youth Serv,* Cari Fry; E-mail: cari.fry@westlandlibrary.org; *Homebound Delivery Coordr,* Yvonne Lopetrone; E-mail: yvonne.lopetrone@westlandlibrary.org
Wireless access
Open Mon-Thurs 9-9, Fri & Sat 9-5, Sun Noon-5
Friends of the Library Group

WHITE CLOUD

P WHITE CLOUD COMMUNITY LIBRARY*, 1038 Wilcox Ave, 49349. (Mail add: PO Box 995, 49349-0995), SAN 308-485X. Tel: 231-689-6631. FAX: 231-689-6699. Circulation E-mail: circ1@whitecloudlibrary.net. Web Site: www.whitecloudlibrary.net. *Dir,* Nancy L Harper; E-mail: director@whitecloudlibrary.net; *Asst Dir, Head, Circ,* Jessie Long; E-mail: circ1@whitecloudlibrary.net; *Circ Librn,* Angie Ditlow; E-mail: circ2@whitecloudlibrary.net; *Genealogy & Hist Librn,* Pamela Miller; E-mail: localhistory@whitecloudlibrary.net; *Cat,* Amy Maike; E-mail: processing@whitecloudlibrary.net; *Ch Serv,* Katie Hoffman; E-mail: childrens@whitecloudlibrary.net; Staff 8 (Non-MLS 8)
Founded 1955. Pop 8,536; Circ 70,000
Jul 2019-Jun 2020 Income $317,205, State $5,581, Locally Generated Income $301,500, Other $10,124. Mats Exp $308,000. Sal $189,000
Library Holdings: AV Mats 6,300; CDs 1,300; DVDs 1,910; e-books 3,853; Electronic Media & Resources 232; Large Print Bks 1,099; Bk Titles 51,082; Per Subs 120; Videos 6,720

Special Collections: Civil War-Lincoln Coll (Louis Fry); Local History (Douglass Coll), bks & photos; Local History (Martha Evans Coll); Newaygo County Genealogy & History Coll
Automation Activity & Vendor Info: (Acquisitions) Innovative Interfaces, Inc; (Cataloging) Innovative Interfaces, Inc; (Circulation) Innovative Interfaces, Inc; (ILL) Innovative Interfaces, Inc; (OPAC) Innovative Interfaces, Inc
Wireless access
Function: 24/7 Electronic res, 24/7 Online cat, Activity rm, Adult bk club, After school storytime, Archival coll, Art exhibits, Audiobks on Playaways & MP3, Bk club(s), Bks on cassette, Bks on CD, CD-ROM, Children's prog, Computer training, Computers for patron use, Electronic databases & coll, Free DVD rentals, Holiday prog, ILL available, Instruction & testing, Internet access, Laminating, Magazines, Magnifiers for reading, Mail & tel request accepted, Meeting rooms, Microfiche/film & reading machines, Movies, Music CDs, Notary serv, Online cat, Online ref, OverDrive digital audio bks, Photocopying/Printing, Prog for adults, Prog for children & young adult, Ref serv available, Scanner, Spoken cassettes & CDs, Spoken cassettes & DVDs, Story hour, Summer & winter reading prog, Summer reading prog, Tax forms, Teen prog, Telephone ref, Wheelchair accessible, Winter reading prog, Workshops
Publications: Library News (Newsletter)
Partic in Lakeland Library Cooperative; Midwest Collaborative for Library Services
Open Mon & Wed 9:30-7, Tues, Thurs & Fri 9:30-5:30, Sat 9:30-1
Friends of the Library Group

WHITE LAKE

P WHITE LAKE TOWNSHIP LIBRARY*, 7527 E Highland Rd, 48383-2938. SAN 375-376X. Tel: 248-698-4942. FAX: 248-698-2550. Web Site: www.whitelakelibrary.org. *Dir,* Denise Stefanick; Tel: 248-698-4942, Ext 5, E-mail: dstefanick@whitelakelibrary.org; Staff 16 (MLS 6, Non-MLS 10)
Founded 1975. Pop 29,000; Circ 153,000
Library Holdings: Bk Vols 50,000; Per Subs 85
Automation Activity & Vendor Info: (Cataloging) SirsiDynix; (Circulation) SirsiDynix
Wireless access
Function: Wheelchair accessible
Publications: News & Reviews from White Lake Township Library (Newsletter)
Partic in The Library Network
Open Mon-Thurs 10-8, Fri & Sat 10-5
Friends of the Library Group

WHITE PIGEON

P WHITE PIGEON TOWNSHIP LIBRARY, 102 N Kalamazoo St, 49099-9726. (Mail add: PO Box 399, 49099-0399), SAN 308-4868. Tel: 269-483-7409. FAX: 269-483-9923. Web Site: www.whitepigeonlibrary.org. *Dir,* Perri Saunders; E-mail: p.saunders@woodlands.lib.mi.us
Founded 1881. Pop 5,239; Circ 35,408
Jul 2020-Jun 2021 Income $215,000
Automation Activity & Vendor Info: (Acquisitions) Evolve; (Cataloging) Evolve; (Circulation) Evolve
Wireless access
Function: 24/7 Electronic res, 24/7 Online cat, Adult bk club, Archival coll, Art programs, Bk club(s), Bk reviews (Group), Bks on CD, Children's prog, Computer training, Computers for patron use, Electronic databases & coll, Free DVD rentals, Holiday prog, Home delivery & serv to seniorr ctr & nursing homes, Homebound delivery serv, ILL available, Internet access, Laminating, Magazines, Mail & tel request accepted, Mango lang, Meeting rooms, Microfiche/film & reading machines, Movies, Music CDs, Notary serv, Online cat, OverDrive digital audio bks, Photocopying/Printing, Preschool outreach, Preschool reading prog, Printer for laptops & handheld devices, Prog for adults, Prog for children & young adult, Ref serv available, Scanner, Spanish lang bks, Spoken cassettes & CDs, Story hour, Summer & winter reading prog, Summer reading prog, Tax forms, Teen prog, Telephone ref, VHS videos, Wheelchair accessible, Winter reading prog
Mem of Woodlands Library Cooperative
Open Mon-Fri 9-6, Sat 9-1
Friends of the Library Group

WHITE PINE

P CARP LAKE TOWNSHIP LIBRARY*, 36349 Mall Circle Dr, 49971. (Mail add: PO Box 157, 49971-0157), SAN 308-4876. Tel: 906-885-5888. FAX: 906-885-5888. E-mail: cltlibrary@uproc.lib.mi.us. Web Site: www.uproc.lib.mi.us/CarpLake. *Dir,* Wanda Tessmer
Founded 1954. Circ 5,702
Library Holdings: Bk Vols 10,000; Per Subs 42
Automation Activity & Vendor Info: (Cataloging) Brodart; (Circulation) Brodart; (OPAC) Brodart
Partic in Superiorland Library Cooperative; Upper Peninsula Region of Library Cooperation, Inc
Open Tues 2-6, Wed & Thurs 10-3, Sat 11-2

WHITEHALL

P WHITE LAKE COMMUNITY LIBRARY, 3900 White Lake Dr, 49461-9257. SAN 308-4884. Tel: 231-894-9531. FAX: 231-893-8821. E-mail: info@wlclib.org. Web Site: wlclib.org. *Dir,* Virginia DeMumbrum; E-mail: vdemumbrum@wlclib.org; *Asst Dir,* Pam Osborn; E-mail: posborn@wlclib.org; Staff 6 (Non-MLS 6)
Founded 1880. Pop 11,811; Circ 152,513
Library Holdings: Bk Titles 35,952; Per Subs 95; Videos 2,568
Subject Interests: Local hist, Mich
Wireless access
Function: 24/7 Electronic res, 24/7 Online cat, Activity rm, Adult bk club
Partic in Lakeland Library Cooperative
Open Mon-Thurs 10-8, Fri & Sat 10-5
Friends of the Library Group

WIXOM

P WIXOM PUBLIC LIBRARY*, 49015 Pontiac Trail, 48393-2567. SAN 308-4892. Tel: 248-624-2512. FAX: 248-624-0862. E-mail: wixom@wixomlibrary.org. Web Site: www.wixomlibrary.org. *Dir,* Andrea Dickson; *Support Serv Librn,* Hannah Lesniak; *Ch Serv,* Sara Fifield; *Ref (Info Servs),* Karla Gibson; Staff 6 (MLS 5.5, Non-MLS 0.5)
Founded 1973. Pop 13,498; Circ 158,860
Jul 2018-Jun 2019. Mats Exp $89,900
Special Collections: ESL Coll; Large Print Coll
Automation Activity & Vendor Info: (Circulation) CARL.Solution (TLC); (OPAC) CARL.Solution (TLC); (Serials) CARL.Solution (TLC)
Wireless access
Function: 24/7 Electronic res, 24/7 Online cat, 3D Printer, Adult bk club, Bk club(s), Bks on CD, Children's prog, Computer training, Computers for patron use, Electronic databases & coll, Free DVD rentals, ILL available, Internet access, Large print keyboards, Life-long learning prog for all ages, Magazines, Magnifiers for reading, Museum passes, Music CDs, Online cat, OverDrive digital audio bks, Photocopying/Printing, Printer for laptops & handheld devices, Prog for adults, Prog for children & young adult, Ref serv available, Scanner, Summer reading prog, Tax forms, Teen prog, Telephone ref, Wheelchair accessible
Partic in TLN
Special Services for the Deaf - Bks on deafness & sign lang; TTY equip
Special Services for the Blind - Bks on CD; Copier with enlargement capabilities; Large print bks; Magnifiers; Sound rec; ZoomText magnification & reading software
Open Mon-Thurs 10-8, Fri 10-6, Sat 10-5
Friends of the Library Group

WOLVERINE

P WOLVERINE COMMUNITY LIBRARY*, 5716 W Main St, 49799-9403. (Mail add: PO Box 310, 49799-9403), SAN 308-4906. Tel: 231-525-8800. FAX: 231-525-8713. E-mail: wolveri1@northland.lib.mi.us. *Dir,* Susan Warner
Founded 1950. Circ 6,620
Library Holdings: Bk Vols 16,000; Per Subs 42
Partic in Northland Library Cooperative
Open Mon-Fri 10-5

WOODLAND

P GEORGE W SPINDLER MEMORIAL LIBRARY*, 186 N Main St, 48897-0068. Tel: 269-367-4694. E-mail: gwspindlerlibrary@gmail.com. Web Site: spindler.michlibrary.org. *Dir,* Kay Bursley
Library Holdings: Bk Vols 8,300
Mem of Woodlands Library Cooperative
Open Mon 3-7, Wed 12-6, Thurs 9-4, Sat 10-1

WYANDOTTE

P BACON MEMORIAL DISTRICT LIBRARY*, 45 Vinewood, 48192-5221. SAN 308-4914. Tel: 734-246-8357. FAX: 734-282-1540. Web Site: www.baconlibrary.org. *Dir,* Laura Gramlich; E-mail: lgramlich@baconlibrary.org; *Head, Circ,* Jayne Johnson; *Hist Librn,* Jakki Malnar; *Ref Librn,* Wally Hayden; *Ref Librn,* Kelly Ray; *Youth Librn,* Lynne Bustin; Staff 19 (MLS 5, Non-MLS 14)
Founded 1869. Pop 25,883
Library Holdings: Audiobooks 1,731; CDs 2,451; DVDs 6,916; Large Print Bks 1,409; Bk Vols 53,969; Per Subs 112
Subject Interests: Local hist, Mil hist
Automation Activity & Vendor Info: (Acquisitions) SirsiDynix; (Cataloging) SirsiDynix; (Circulation) SirsiDynix; (ILL) SirsiDynix; (OPAC) SirsiDynix; (Serials) SirsiDynix
Wireless access

Function: Adult bk club, Archival coll, Children's prog, Computer training, Computers for patron use, Homebound delivery serv, ILL available, Notary serv, OverDrive digital audio bks, Photocopying/Printing, Prog for children & young adult, Ref serv available, Summer reading prog, Wheelchair accessible
Partic in The Library Network
Open Mon-Thurs 10-9, Fri & Sat 10-5
Friends of the Library Group

M HENRY FORD WYANDOTTE HOSPITAL*, Medical Library, Rehabilitation Bldg, 4th Flr, 2333 Biddle Ave, 48192-4668. Tel: 734-246-7361. FAX: 734-246-6069. E-mail: wylibrary@hfhs.org. Web Site: henryford.libguides.com/hfwhlibrary. *Librn,* Laurie Arrick; E-mail: larrick1@hfhs.org; Staff 1 (MLS 1)
Library Holdings: AV Mats 600; Bk Vols 2,000; Per Subs 85
Wireless access
Open Mon-Fri 8-4:30
Restriction: Non-circulating to the pub

S FORD-MACNICHOL HOME, WYANDOTTE MUSEUM, ARCHIVES*, 2610 Biddle Ave, 48192. SAN 321-0413. Tel: 734-324-7297. FAX: 734-324-7283. E-mail: museum@wyan.org. Web Site: www.wyandottemuseums.org. *Dir,* Jody Egen
Founded 1958
Library Holdings: Bk Titles 2,000; Per Subs 10
Special Collections: Oral History
Subject Interests: Detroit hist, Local hist, Mich hist, Wayne County hist
Open Mon-Fri 9-5

WYOMING

M METRO HEALTH HOSPITAL*, Skytron Medical Library, 5900 Byron Ctr Ave SW, 49519. (Mail add: PO Box 916, 49509). Tel: 616-252-7200. Toll Free Tel: 800-968-0051. FAX: 616-252-7265. Web Site: www.metrohealth.net. *Librn,* Mary B Loftis; E-mail: mary.loftis@metrogr.org
Founded 1942
Library Holdings: Bk Vols 2,500; Per Subs 100
Open Mon-Fri 8-4:30

R THEOLOGICAL SCHOOL OF PROTESTANT REFORMED CHURCHES LIBRARY*, 4949 Ivanrest Ave SW, 49418-9709. Tel: 616-531-1490. FAX: 616-531-3033. E-mail: prcseminary1925@gmail.com. Web Site: www.prca.org/Seminary/SeminaryMainPg.htm. *Archivist, Librn,* Charles Terpstra
Library Holdings: Bk Vols 8,000

YPSILANTI

C EASTERN MICHIGAN UNIVERSITY*, Bruce T Halle Library, Administrative Office, Rm 200, 955 W Circle Dr, 48197. SAN 308-4949. Circulation Tel: 734-487-2562. Interlibrary Loan Service Tel: 734-487-2596. Reference Tel: 734-487-2445. Administration Tel: 734-487-2633. Interlibrary Loan Service FAX: 734-487-5399. Administration FAX: 734-484-1151. Web Site: www.emich.edu/halle. *Interim Dept Head,* Rhonda Fowler; E-mail: rhonda.fowler@emich.edu; *Acq Librn,* Joe Badics; Tel: 734-487-2402, E-mail: joseph.badics@emich.edu; *Info Literacy Librn, Women's & Gender Studies Librn,* Suzanne Gray; Tel: 734-487-2517, E-mail: suzanne.gray@emich.edu; *Maps Librn,* Rhonda Fowler; Tel: 734-487-2587, E-mail: rhonda.fowler@emich.edu; *Pub Serv Librn,* Keith Stanger; Tel: 734-487-2509, E-mail: keith@stanger.com; *Tech Serv Coordr,* Position Currently Open; *Archivist,* Alexis Braun Marks; Tel: 734-487-2594, E-mail: abraunma@emich.edu; Staff 32 (MLS 26, Non-MLS 6)
Founded 1849. Enrl 23,341; Fac 688; Highest Degree: Doctorate
Jul 2012-Jun 2013. Mats Exp $3,134,156. Sal $4,593,991
Library Holdings: AV Mats 15,759; e-books 90,000; Bk Titles 695,000; Bk Vols 785,000; Per Subs 44,145
Special Collections: State Document Depository; US Document Depository
Subject Interests: Educ
Automation Activity & Vendor Info: (Acquisitions) Ex Libris Group; (Cataloging) Ex Libris Group; (Circulation) Ex Libris Group; (Course Reserve) Docutek; (ILL) OCLC ILLiad; (OPAC) Ex Libris Group; (Serials) Ex Libris Group
Wireless access
Publications: Numbered Bibliography Series; Study Guides
Partic in Midwest Collaborative for Library Services; OCLC Online Computer Library Center, Inc
Open Mon-Thurs 7:30am-Midnight, Fri 7:30am-8pm, Sat 9-6, Sun Noon-Midnight
Friends of the Library Group

P YPSILANTI DISTRICT LIBRARY*, Whittaker Road Library, 5577 Whittaker Rd, 48197. Tel: 734-482-4110. FAX: 734-482-0047. Web Site: www.ypsilibrary.org. *Dir,* Lisa Hoenig; Tel: 734-879-1300, E-mail: lisa@ypsilibrary.org; *Asst Dir,* Julianne Smith; Tel: 734-879-1301, E-mail: smith@ypsilibrary.org; Staff 45 (MLS 18, Non-MLS 27)
Founded 1863. Pop 82,974; Circ 685,621
Dec 2016-Nov 2017 Income (Main & Associated Libraries) $3,722,198. Mats Exp $350,000. Sal $1,953,290
Library Holdings: Bk Vols 343,688
Special Collections: AP Marshall African-American Oral History Archive; Library of Congress Veterans' History Project; Ypsilanti & Michigan History Coll
Automation Activity & Vendor Info: (Acquisitions) SirsiDynix; (Cataloging) SirsiDynix; (Circulation) SirsiDynix; (OPAC) SirsiDynix
Wireless access
Function: 24/7 Electronic res, 24/7 Online cat, Activity rm, Adult bk club, Adult literacy prog, Art exhibits, Audiobks on Playaways & MP3, Audiobks via web, AV serv, Bk club(s), Bks on CD, Children's prog, Computer training, Computers for patron use, Digital talking bks, E-Reserves, Electronic databases & coll, Family literacy, For res purposes, Free DVD rentals, Holiday prog, Home delivery & serv to seniorr ctr & nursing homes, Homebound delivery serv, Homework prog, ILL available, Instruction & testing, Internet access, Large print keyboards, Life-long learning prog for all ages, Literacy & newcomer serv, Magazines, Magnifiers for reading, Mail & tel request accepted, Mango lang, Meeting rooms, Microfiche/film & reading machines, Movies, Museum passes, Music CDs, Online cat, Online ref, Orientations, Outreach serv, Outside serv via phone, mail, e-mail & web, OverDrive digital audio bks, Photocopying/Printing, Preschool outreach, Preschool reading prog, Printer for laptops & handheld devices, Prog for adults, Prog for children & young adult, Ref & res, Ref serv available, Scanner, Senior computer classes, Senior outreach, Spanish lang bks, Spoken cassettes & CDs, Spoken cassettes & DVDs, STEM programs, Story hour, Study rm, Summer reading prog, Tax forms, Teen prog, Telephone ref, Visual arts prog, Wheelchair accessible, Workshops, Writing prog
Publications: The Loop (Newsletter)
Partic in The Library Network
Special Services for the Deaf - Adult & family literacy prog; Bks on deafness & sign lang; Closed caption videos; High interest/low vocabulary bks
Special Services for the Blind - Accessible computers; Audio mat; Bks available with recordings; Bks on CD; Computer with voice synthesizer for visually impaired persons; Copier with enlargement capabilities; Digital talking bk; Extensive large print coll; Home delivery serv; Large print bks; Large screen computer & software; Lending of low vision aids; Low vision equip; Magnifiers; Optolec clearview video magnifier; Playaways (bks on MP3); Recorded bks; Ref serv; Screen enlargement software for people with visual disabilities; Screen reader software; Talking bks; Talking bks & player equip; ZoomText magnification & reading software
Open Mon-Thurs 9-9, Fri & Sat 10-6, Sun 1-5
Restriction: In-house use for visitors
Friends of the Library Group
Branches: 2
SUPERIOR TOWNSHIP, 8975 MacArthur Blvd, 48198. Tel: 734-482-3747. Automation Services Tel: 734-482-4110. FAX: 734-482-3757. Automation Services FAX: 734-482-0047. *Head, Outreach Serv,* Mary Garboden; E-mail: garboden@ypsilibrary.org
Open Mon 12-8, Tues & Sat 10-6, Wed & Thurs 4-8
Friends of the Library Group
WEST MICHIGAN AVENUE, 229 W Michigan Ave, 48197-5485, SAN 308-4957. Tel: 734-482-4110. FAX: 734-482-0047. *Br Mgr,* Joy Cichewicz
Open Mon-Thurs 10-9, Fri & Sat 10-6
Friends of the Library Group
Bookmobiles: 1. Head, Outreach Servs, Mary Garboden. Bk titles 3,600

ZEELAND

R FIRST CRC ZEELAND LIBRARY*, 15 S Church St, 49464. SAN 308-4965. Tel: 616-772-2866. FAX: 616-772-2620. E-mail: office@firstzeeland.org. Web Site: firstzeeland.org.
Founded 1930
Library Holdings: Bk Titles 4,500; Per Subs 15
Special Collections: Church History (Acts of Synod, 1857-present), bound
Subject Interests: Biographies, Fiction, Inspirational
Restriction: Mem only

P HOWARD MILLER PUBLIC LIBRARY*, 14 S Church St, 49464-1728. SAN 308-499X. Tel: 616-772-0874. FAX: 616-772-3253. E-mail: zee@llcoop.org. Web Site: www.cityofzeeland.com/168/Library. *Dir,* Heather Wood-Gramza; E-mail: hwood-gramza@cityofzeeland.com; Staff 15 (MLS 2, Non-MLS 13)
Founded 1969. Pop 23,096; Circ 272,064
Library Holdings: Bks on Deafness & Sign Lang 40; High Interest/Low Vocabulary Bk Vols 60; Bk Vols 71,000; Per Subs 90

Automation Activity & Vendor Info: (Cataloging) Innovative Interfaces, Inc; (Circulation) Innovative Interfaces, Inc; (ILL) Innovative Interfaces, Inc; (OPAC) Innovative Interfaces, Inc
Wireless access
Publications: Children's Services (Quarterly newsletter)
Open Mon-Thurs 9-8, Fri 9-5, Sat 9-3

MINNESOTA

Date of Statistics: FY 2019
Population, 2020 U.S. Census: 5,657,342
Number of Public Libraries: 140 administrative units comprising 355 buildings and eight bookmobiles
Total Materials in Public Libraries: 16,629,333
Items Per Capita: 2.74
Total Public Library Circulation: 51,235,969
Circulation Per Capita: 9.08
Income and Expenditures:
Source of Income: Local: 84.9%, State: 7.02%, Federal: 0.1%, Other: 8.01%
Local Tax Support: 90% of the 2011 state-certified level of library support
Income and Expenditures:
Total Public Library Operating Expenditures (includes grants): $246,463,754
Operating Expenditures Per Capita: $43.70
Number of Regional Public Library Systems: 12
Number of Bookmobiles: 8
Number of Multi-type Library Systems: 7
State Aid: (12 regional public library systems) $13,570,000
Regional Library Telecommunication Aid: $2,300,000
Multi-type Library Systems: (Seven multi-county, multi-type library systems) $1,300,000
Information provided courtesy of: Verena Getahun, Library Data Coordinator; Minnesota Department of Education

ALBERT LEA

P ALBERT LEA PUBLIC LIBRARY, 211 E Clark St, 56007. SAN 308-5015. Tel: 507-377-4350. FAX: 507-377-4339. E-mail: alpl.library@gmail.com. Web Site: alplonline.org. *Dir,* Peggy Havener; Tel: 507-377-4355, E-mail: phavener@selco.info; *Asst Dir,* Annice Sevett; E-mail: asevett@selco.info; *Ch Serv Librn,* Patty Greibrok; Staff 10 (MLS 2, Non-MLS 8)
Founded 1897. Pop 32,238; Circ 417,035
Library Holdings: Bk Vols 71,000; Per Subs 300
Special Collections: Obituary Index to Local Newspaper
Wireless access
Partic in Southeastern Libraries Cooperating
Open Mon-Thurs 9-6
Friends of the Library Group

S FREEBORN COUNTY HISTORICAL MUSEUM LIBRARY*, 1031 N Bridge Ave, 56007. SAN 308-5023. Tel: 507-373-8003. FAX: 507-552-1269. Web Site: www.freeborncountyhistory.org. *Librn,* Linda Evenson
Founded 1968
Library Holdings: Bk Titles 600
Special Collections: Lea College 1966-72; Local Newspapers, 1860-present, microfilm; Lt Col Albert Miller Lea Coll; Morin Coll; Obituaries; Photo Coll of County; Sorenson Cartoon Coll; Spicer Coll
Subject Interests: Genealogy, Local hist
Function: For res purposes
Open Wed-Sat 10-4
Restriction: Not a lending libr

ALEXANDRIA

J ALEXANDRIA TECHNICAL COLLEGE LIBRARY*, 1601 Jefferson St, Rm 302, 56308. SAN 378-3863. Tel: 320-762-4465. Toll Free Tel: 888-234-1222, Ext 4465. E-mail: library@alextech.edu. Web Site: www.alextech.edu/college-services/library. *Librn,* Nina Battistini; E-mail: ti5676kp@alextech.edu
Library Holdings: Bk Titles 11,000; Per Subs 125
Subject Interests: Communication arts, Interior design
Automation Activity & Vendor Info: (Cataloging) PALS; (Circulation) PALS; (Course Reserve) PALS; (ILL) PALS
Wireless access
Partic in MnPALS
Open Mon-Thurs 7:30-6, Fri 7:30-4, Sat 8-12

P DOUGLAS COUNTY LIBRARY, 720 Fillmore St, 56308. SAN 308-504X. Tel: 320-762-3014. FAX: 320-762-3036. E-mail: library@douglascountylibrary.org. Web Site: douglascountylibrary.org. *Dir,* Dawn Dailey; E-mail: ddailey@douglascountylibrary.org; *Youth Librn,* Sarah Wethem; Staff 2 (MLS 2)
Founded 1878. Pop 30,000; Circ 311,000
Library Holdings: Bk Vols 60,150; Per Subs 176
Special Collections: Kensington Runestone
Wireless access
Mem of Viking Library System
Open Mon-Thurs 10-8, Fri 10-5, Sat 10-3
Friends of the Library Group
Bookmobiles: 1

ANOKA

S ANOKA COUNTY HISTORICAL SOCIETY, History Center & Library, 2135 Third Ave N, 55303. SAN 308-5066. Tel: 763-421-0600. Web Site: anokacountyhistory.org. *Exec Dir,* Rebecca Ebnet-Desens; E-mail: rebecca@anokacountyhistory.org
Founded 1934
Library Holdings: Bk Titles 1,020; Per Subs 20
Special Collections: Genealogical Books for Research throughout US & Foreign Countries
Subject Interests: Census records, Family hist, Local hist, Maps
Wireless access
Function: Archival coll, Art exhibits, Bus archives, For res purposes, Internet access, Magazines, Meeting rooms, Microfiche/film & reading machines, Online cat, Online ref, Outside serv via phone, mail, e-mail & web, Prog for adults, Prog for children & young adult, Ref & res, Res assist avail, Res libr, Res performed for a fee, Teen prog, Wheelchair accessible, Workshops
Open Tues-Fri 10-4

L ANOKA COUNTY LAW LIBRARY*, 325 E Main St, 55303. SAN 323-8563. Tel: 763-422-7487. FAX: 763-422-7453. E-mail: LawLibrarian@co.anoka.mn.us. Web Site: www.anokacounty.us/346/Law-Library. *Law Libr Dir/Law Librn,* John Murphy; E-mail: john.murphy@co.anoka.mn.us; *Assoc Librn,* Merry Conway; Staff 2 (Non-MLS 2)
Library Holdings: Bk Titles 1,750; Bk Vols 42,000
Special Collections: Local Municipal Ordinances. US Document Depository
Wireless access
Open Mon-Fri 8-4:30

J ANOKA TECHNICAL COLLEGE LIBRARY*, 1355 W Hwy 10, 55303. SAN 308-5058. Tel: 763-576-7850. FAX: 763-576-4821. E-mail: librarian@anokatech.edu. Web Site: anokatech.edu/StudentServices/Library.aspx.
Highest Degree: Associate
Subject Interests: Allied health, Nursing
Wireless access
Partic in Metronet; MnPALS
Open Mon-Thurs 7:30am-8pm, Fri 7:30-4

APPLETON

P APPLETON PUBLIC LIBRARY*, 322 W Schlieman Ave, 56208. SAN 347-6855. Tel: 320-289-1681. FAX: 320-289-1681. Web Site: appletonpubliclibrarymn.webs.com. *Librn,* Cindy Hendrickx; E-mail: cindy.hendrickx@pioneerland.lib.mn.us
Pop 3,482; Circ 23,801
Library Holdings: Bk Vols 18,000; Per Subs 25
Automation Activity & Vendor Info: (Cataloging) Innovative Interfaces, Inc; (Circulation) Innovative Interfaces, Inc; (OPAC) Innovative Interfaces, Inc
Mem of Pioneerland Library System
Open Mon & Fri 10:30-5:30, Tues-Thurs 10:30-7:30, Sat 10:30-2:30

ARLINGTON

P ARLINGTON PUBLIC LIBRARY*, 321 W Main St, 55307. (Mail add: PO Box 391, 55307-0391), SAN 347-4216. Tel: 507-964-2490. FAX: 507-964-2490. E-mail: libtsa@tds.lib.mn.us. *Dir,* Kathy Homme
Library Holdings: Bk Vols 10,530
Wireless access
Function: Home delivery & serv to seniorr ctr & nursing homes, Photocopying/Printing
Mem of Traverse Des Sioux Library Cooperative
Open Mon 9-12 & 12:30-7:30, Tues & Fri 9-12 & 12:30-5:30, Wed 9-12 & 12:30-6:30, Sat 9-12
Friends of the Library Group

ATWATER

P ATWATER PUBLIC LIBRARY*, 322 Atlantic Ave W, 56209. SAN 348-0992. Tel: 320-974-3363. E-mail: atwater.staff@pioneerland.lib.mn.us. Web Site: www.atwater.lib.mn.us. *Head Librn,* Ria Newhouse; E-mail: ria.newhouse@pioneerland.lib.mn.us
Founded 1956. Pop 2,358; Circ 11,188
Library Holdings: AV Mats 716; Bk Titles 14,700; Per Subs 18; Talking Bks 171
Subject Interests: Animals, Farming
Wireless access
Mem of Pioneerland Library System
Open Mon 11-6, Tues-Thurs 2-6, Fri 12-3

AURORA

P AURORA PUBLIC LIBRARY*, 14 W Second Ave N, 55705-1314. SAN 308-5120. Tel: 218-229-2021. *Librn,* Paula J Chapman; *Asst Librn,* Kathy Schultz
Founded 1914. Pop 1,650; Circ 20,868
Library Holdings: AV Mats 2,758; Bk Vols 20,301; Per Subs 43
Wireless access
Function: 24/7 Electronic res, Audiobks via web, Bks on cassette, Bks on CD, Children's prog, Computers for patron use, E-Readers, E-Reserves, Free DVD rentals, Holiday prog, ILL available, Instruction & testing, Internet access, Magazines, Movies, Music CDs, Online cat, Outreach serv, OverDrive digital audio bks, Photocopying/Printing, Preschool outreach, Prog for adults, Prog for children & young adult, Senior outreach, Spoken cassettes & CDs, Summer & winter reading prog, Summer reading prog, Tax forms, VHS videos, Wheelchair accessible, Workshops
Mem of Arrowhead Library System
Open Mon 10-7:30, Tues-Thurs 1-7:30, Fri 10-5
Friends of the Library Group

AUSTIN

P AUSTIN PUBLIC LIBRARY*, 323 Fourth Ave NE, 55912-3370. SAN 347-190X. Tel: 507-433-2391. Reference E-mail: aplref@selco.info. Web Site: www.austinpubliclibrary.org. *Dir,* Julie Clinefelter; Staff 5 (MLS 5)
Founded 1904. Pop 38,890; Circ 280,069
Library Holdings: Bk Titles 89,051; Per Subs 352
Subject Interests: Local hist
Automation Activity & Vendor Info: (Cataloging) Horizon; (Circulation) Horizon; (OPAC) Horizon
Wireless access
Function: 24/7 Electronic res, 24/7 Online cat, Activity rm, Adult bk club, Audiobks on Playaways & MP3, Audiobks via web, Bks on CD, Children's prog, Computer training, Computers for patron use, Electronic databases & coll, Homebound delivery serv, ILL available, Internet access, Magazines, Mango lang, Meeting rooms, Microfiche/film & reading machines, Movies, Music CDs, Online cat, OverDrive digital audio bks, Printer for laptops & handheld devices, Ref serv available, Scanner, Story hour, Study rm, Summer reading prog, Wheelchair accessible
Partic in Southeastern Libraries Cooperating
Open Mon-Thurs 10-8, Fri & Sat 10-6, Sun 1-5
Friends of the Library Group

J RIVERLAND COMMUNITY COLLEGE*, Austin Campus Library, 1600 Eighth Ave NW, 55912. SAN 308-5139. Tel: 507-433-0533. FAX: 507-433-0515. E-mail: library@riverland.edu. Web Site: www.riverland.edu/library. *Librn,* Jeannie Kearney; Staff 2 (MLS 1, Non-MLS 1)
Founded 1940. Enrl 2,500
Library Holdings: Bk Vols 26,147; Per Subs 100
Automation Activity & Vendor Info: (Cataloging) OCLC; (Circulation) Ex Libris Group; (Course Reserve) Ex Libris Group; (ILL) PALS; (OPAC) Ex Libris Group
Wireless access
Partic in Minitex; MnPALS; OCLC Online Computer Library Center, Inc
Open Mon-Fri 9-6:30

BABBITT

P BABBITT PUBLIC LIBRARY, 71 South Dr, 55706. SAN 308-5155. Tel: 218-827-3345. FAX: 218-827-3345. Web Site: babbitt-mn.com/library/library.html, babbittlibrary.blogspot.com. *Dir,* Lisa Pennala; E-mail: Lisa.Pennala@alslib.info
Founded 1959. Pop 1,562; Circ 37,043
Library Holdings: Bk Vols 33,429; Per Subs 16
Special Collections: Babbitt History Coll, bulletins, clippings, pictures
Automation Activity & Vendor Info: (Cataloging) SirsiDynix; (Circulation) SirsiDynix; (OPAC) SirsiDynix
Wireless access
Mem of Arrowhead Library System
Open Mon-Thurs 12-6, Fri 12-5
Friends of the Library Group

BAUDETTE

P BAUDETTE PUBLIC LIBRARY*, 110 First Ave SW, 56623. (Mail add: PO Box 739, 56623-0739), SAN 308-5163. Tel: 218-634-2329. FAX: 218-634-2329. Web Site: www.alslib.info. *Dir,* Kelli Pelland; E-mail: kellip@ci.baudette.mn.us
Founded 1912. Pop 1,170; Circ 25,281
Library Holdings: Bk Vols 10,413; Per Subs 38
Automation Activity & Vendor Info: (Cataloging) SirsiDynix; (Circulation) SirsiDynix; (OPAC) SirsiDynix
Wireless access
Mem of Arrowhead Library System
Open Mon-Fri 10-5, Sat 10-2

BAYPORT

P BAYPORT PUBLIC LIBRARY*, 582 N Fourth St, 55003-1111. SAN 308-5171. Tel: 651-275-4416. FAX: 651-275-4417. E-mail: books@bayportlibrary.org. Web Site: www.bayportlibrary.org. *Dir,* Jill Smith; E-mail: jsmith@ci.bayport.mn.us
Founded 1960. Pop 3,471; Circ 69,000
Library Holdings: Bk Vols 30,244; Per Subs 96
Special Collections: Large Print Coll; Local History Coll
Automation Activity & Vendor Info: (Cataloging) SirsiDynix; (Circulation) SirsiDynix; (OPAC) SirsiDynix
Wireless access
Open Mon 10-8, Tues 10-6, Wed & Thurs 12-8, Fri 10-5, Sat (Sept-May) 10-3
Friends of the Library Group

S MINNESOTA CORRECTIONAL FACILITY*, Education Library, 970 Pickett St N, Education/Library, 55003-1490. SAN 308-8103. Tel: 651-779-2700, Ext 2575. *Librn,* David Coward; Staff 1 (MLS 1)
Founded 1979
Library Holdings: Bk Titles 11,600; Per Subs 20
Subject Interests: Law
Automation Activity & Vendor Info: (Cataloging) Follett Software; (Circulation) Follett Software; (OPAC) Follett Software; (Serials) Follett Software
Open Mon-Thurs 1-8:45, Fri 8-3

BEMIDJI

P BEMIDJI PUBLIC LIBRARY*, 509 America Ave NW, 56601. SAN 320-4529. Tel: 218-751-3963. FAX: 218-333-0523. E-mail: bemidji@krls.org. Web Site: www.krls.org/index.php/bemidji-home-page. *Br Mgr,* Sherilyn Brumback; Staff 8 (MLS 1, Non-MLS 7)
Founded 1907. Pop 45,264; Circ 219,959
Library Holdings: Bk Titles 62,932
Subject Interests: Native Am studies
Automation Activity & Vendor Info: (Acquisitions) Innovative Interfaces, Inc; (Circulation) Innovative Interfaces, Inc; (OPAC) Innovative Interfaces, Inc
Wireless access
Publications: Friends (Newsletter)
Mem of Kitchigami Regional Library

Special Services for the Deaf - Assisted listening device; Bks on deafness & sign lang
Special Services for the Blind - Accessible computers; Assistive/Adapted tech devices, equip & products; Extensive large print coll; Low vision equip
Open Mon-Thurs 9-7, Fri & Sat 9-5
Friends of the Library Group

C BEMIDJI STATE UNIVERSITY*, A C Clark Library, 1500 Birchmont Dr NE, No 28, 56601-2699. SAN 308-518X. Tel: 218-755-3342. Circulation Tel: 218-755-3345. Interlibrary Loan Service Tel: 218-755-2968. Toll Free Tel: 800-860-0234. FAX: 218-755-2051. Web Site: www.bemidjistate.edu/library. *Associ Vice Pres, Academic Affairs,* Randall Westhoff; Tel: 218-755-2016, E-mail: rwesthoff@bemidjistate.edu; *Acq/Ser Librn,* Tammy Bobrowsky; Tel: 218-755-4110; *Cat Librn,* Dianne Narum; Tel: 218-755-3340; *Coll Mgt Librn, ILL Librn,* Colleen Deel; Tel: 218-755-3339; *Res & Instruction Librn,* Patrick Lee; Tel: 218-755-3349; *Circ, Syst & Distance Learning Librn,* Peter McDonnell; Tel: 218-755-2967; *Circ, Libr Tech,* Mary K Leuthard; Tel: 218-755-2956; Staff 10 (MLS 5, Non-MLS 5)
Founded 1919. Enrl 4,955; Fac 311; Highest Degree: Master
Library Holdings: Bk Titles 361,317; Bk Vols 459,421
Special Collections: US Document Depository
Subject Interests: Native American hist, Northern Minn hist
Wireless access
Partic in MnPALS; OCLC Online Computer Library Center, Inc
Open Mon-Thurs 7am-11:45pm, Fri 7-4:45, Sat 11-4:45, Sun 1-11:45
Friends of the Library Group

§C NORTHWEST TECHNICAL COLLEGE LIBRARY, 905 Grant Ave SE, 56601-4907. Tel: 218-333-6633. Web Site: www.ntcmn.edu/academics/library. *Library Contact,* Paula DeMars; E-mail: paula.demars.@ntcmn.edu
Wireless access
Function: ILL available, Study rm
Partic in MnPALS
Open Mon-Thurs 7:30-4, Fri 7:30-2

JR OAK HILLS CHRISTIAN COLLEGE*, Cummings Library, 1600 Oak Hills Rd SW, 56601-8832. SAN 308-5198. Tel: 218-333-9961. E-mail: it@oakhills.edu. Web Site: www.oakhills.edu/academics/cummings-library. *Dir,* Keith Bush; Staff 2 (Non-MLS 2)
Founded 1946. Enrl 155; Fac 13
Library Holdings: Bk Vols 25,000; Per Subs 160
Subject Interests: Philos, Relig studies

BENSON

P BENSON PUBLIC LIBRARY*, 200 13th St N, 56215-1223. SAN 308-5201. Tel: 320-842-7981. FAX: 320-843-4948. E-mail: benson.staff@pioneerland.lib.mn.us. Web Site: www.benson.lib.mn.us. *Head Librn,* Dawn Dailey; E-mail: dawn.dailey@pioneerland.lib.mn.us
Founded 1913. Circ 53,129
Library Holdings: Bk Vols 19,000; Per Subs 50
Wireless access
Mem of Pioneerland Library System
Open Mon, Tues & Thurs 10-7, Wed & Fri 10-6, Sat 10-4
Friends of the Library Group

SR OUR REDEEMERS LUTHERAN CHURCH LIBRARY*, 800 Tenth St S, 56215. SAN 308-521X. Tel: 320-843-3151. FAX: 320-843-3469. Web Site: www.our-redeemers.com. *Library Contact,* Ms Hege Herfindahl
Founded 1956
Library Holdings: Bk Vols 1,900; Videos 30
Open Mon-Fri 8-4:30

BIRD ISLAND

P BIRD ISLAND PUBLIC LIBRARY*, 260 S Main St, 55310-1226. (Mail add: PO Box 217, 55310-0217), SAN 348-1026. Tel: 320-365-4640. FAX: 320-365-4640. E-mail: birdisland.staff@pionerland.lib.mn.us. Web Site: www.birdisland.lib.mn.us. *Head Librn,* Jake Fejedelem; E-mail: jake.fejedelem@pioneerland.lib.mn.us
Pop 1,320; Circ 16,414
Library Holdings: Large Print Bks 120; Bk Vols 11,400; Per Subs 23; Talking Bks 275
Automation Activity & Vendor Info: (Cataloging) Innovative Interfaces, Inc; (Circulation) Innovative Interfaces, Inc; (OPAC) Innovative Interfaces, Inc
Wireless access
Function: Homebound delivery serv, ILL available, Internet access, Photocopying/Printing, Prog for adults, Prog for children & young adult, Summer reading prog, Wheelchair accessible
Mem of Pioneerland Library System
Open Mon 6-8, Tues & Wed 10-5, Thurs 10-4 & 6-8, Fri 9-2

BLACKDUCK

P BLACKDUCK COMMUNITY LIBRARY*, 72 First St SE, 56630. (Mail add: PO Box 326, 56630-0326), SAN 347-772X. Tel: 218-835-6600. FAX: 218-835-6600. E-mail: blackduck@krls.org. Web Site: www.krls.org/index.php/blackduck-home-page. *Head Librn,* Alayna Nestberg; *Asst Librn,* Danielle Theisen; Staff 2 (Non-MLS 2)
Founded 1909. Pop 5,000; Circ 20,000
Library Holdings: Bks on Deafness & Sign Lang 4; Braille Volumes 1; CDs 100; DVDs 60; High Interest/Low Vocabulary Bk Vols 10; Large Print Bks 600; Bk Vols 16,500; Per Subs 35; Talking Bks 200; Videos 500
Special Collections: Hispanic Materials Coll
Automation Activity & Vendor Info: (Acquisitions) Innovative Interfaces, Inc
Wireless access
Function: ILL available
Mem of Kitchigami Regional Library
Open Tues & Fri 1-6, Wed & Sat 9-1, Thurs 1-7

BLAINE

P ANOKA COUNTY LIBRARY*, Administrative Office, 707 County Hwy 10 Frontage Rd, 55434-2398. SAN 347-2027. Tel: 763-324-1500. FAX: 763-717-3262. E-mail: aclref@co.anoka.mn.us, register@co.anoka.mn.us. Web Site: anokacountylibrary.org. *Libr Dir,* Colleen Haubner; E-mail: colleen.haubner@co.anoka.mn.us; Staff 33 (MLS 21, Non-MLS 12)
Founded 1958. Pop 313,033; Circ 2,920,574
Library Holdings: Bk Vols 614,106; Per Subs 1,377
Automation Activity & Vendor Info: (Acquisitions) SirsiDynix; (Cataloging) SirsiDynix; (Circulation) SirsiDynix; (OPAC) SirsiDynix; (Serials) SirsiDynix
Wireless access
Partic in Metropolitan Library Service Agency; Minitex
Open Mon-Fri 8-4:30
Friends of the Library Group
Branches: 8
CENTENNIAL, 100 Civic Heights Circle, Circle Pines, 55014. (Mail add: 707 County Rd Ten NE, 55434-2398), SAN 347-2051. Tel: 763-324-1540. *Br Mgr,* Mary Healy; Staff 3 (MLS 1, Non-MLS 2)
Library Holdings: Bk Vols 44,083; Per Subs 100
Open Tues & Thurs-Sat 10-4, Wed 1-7
Friends of the Library Group
CROOKED LAKE, 11440 Crooked Lake Blvd NW, Coon Rapids, 55433, SAN 347-2116. Tel: 763-324-1530. *Br Mgr,* Becky Walpole; Staff 5 (MLS 1, Non-MLS 4)
Library Holdings: Bk Vols 63,226; Per Subs 137
Open Mon & Wed 1-7, Tues, Thurs & Sat 10-4
Friends of the Library Group
JOHNSVILLE, 12461 Oak Park Blvd, 55434. (Mail add: 707 County Rd 10 NE, 55434-2398), SAN 326-8039. Tel: 763-324-1550. *Br Mgr,* Position Currently Open
Open Tues & Thurs-Sat 10-4, Wed 1-7
Friends of the Library Group
MISSISSIPPI, 410 Mississippi St NE, Fridley, 55432. (Mail add: 707 County Rd 10 NE, 55434-2398), SAN 347-2140. Tel: 763-324-1560. *Br Mgr,* Shannon Melham; Staff 3 (MLS 3)
Library Holdings: Bk Vols 52,880; Per Subs 155
Open Tues & Thurs-Sat 10-4, Wed 1-7
Friends of the Library Group
NORTH CENTRAL, 17565 Central Ave NE, Ham Lake, 55304, SAN 347-2175. Tel: 763-324-1570. *Br Mgr,* Mary Oliver; Staff 1 (Non-MLS 1)
Library Holdings: Bk Vols 29,549; Per Subs 70
Open Mon & Wed 1-7, Tues, Thurs & Sat 10-4
Friends of the Library Group
NORTHTOWN, 711 County Hwy 10 Frontage Rd, 55434. (Mail add: 707 County Rd 10 NE, 55434-2398), SAN 347-2035. Tel: 763-324-1510. *Br Mgr,* Stacey Hendren
Open Mon & Wed 1-7, Tues, Thurs & Sat 10-4
Friends of the Library Group
RUM RIVER, 4201 Sixth Ave, Anoka, 55303. (Mail add: 707 County Rd 10 NE, 55434-2398), SAN 329-5842. Tel: 763-324-1520. *Br Mgr,* Janet Kleckner
Open Tues & Thurs-Sat 10-4, Wed 1-7
Friends of the Library Group
ST FRANCIS BRANCH, 3519 Bridge St NW, Saint Francis, 55070. (Mail add: 707 County Rd 10 NE, 55434), SAN 347-2191. Tel: 763-324-1580. *Br Mgr,* Olivia Hedlund
Open Tues & Thurs-Sat 10-4, Wed 1-7
Friends of the Library Group

BLOOMINGTON

J NORMANDALE COMMUNITY COLLEGE LIBRARY*, 9700 France Ave S, 55431. SAN 308-5252. Tel: 952-487-8290. Reference Tel: 952-487-8295. FAX: 952-487-8101. Web Site: www.normandale.edu/library. *Cat, Chair,* Adam Kauwenberg-Marsnik; Tel: 952-487-8297, E-mail: Adam.Kauwenberg-Marsnik@normandale.edu; *Acq,* Rosalie Bunge; Tel: 952-487-8296, E-mail: Rosalie.Bunge@normandale.edu; *Acq,* Lorna I Redding; Tel: 952-487-8292, E-mail: Lorna.Redding@normandale.edu; *Cat, Libr Tech,* Jacqueline Burns; Tel: 952-487-8293, E-mail: Jacqueline.Burns@normandale.edu; *Libr Tech, Per,* Kimberly Christianson; Tel: 952-487-8291, E-mail: Kimberly.Christianson@normandale.edu; Staff 14 (MLS 5, Non-MLS 9)
Founded 1968. Enrl 14,129; Fac 349; Highest Degree: Associate
Library Holdings: AV Mats 12,671; Bks on Deafness & Sign Lang 27; Electronic Media & Resources 1,211; High Interest/Low Vocabulary Bk Vols 15; Large Print Bks 133; Bk Titles 89,733; Bk Vols 95,477; Per Subs 650; Talking Bks 118
Special Collections: Career & Academic Planning Center; College Success Center; Minnesota Authors Coll; Picture Books Coll; Writing Center
Subject Interests: Juv lit, Minn hist
Automation Activity & Vendor Info: (Acquisitions) Ex Libris Group; (Cataloging) Ex Libris Group; (Circulation) Ex Libris Group; (Course Reserve) Ex Libris Group; (ILL) Ex Libris Group; (OPAC) Ex Libris Group; (Serials) Ex Libris Group
Wireless access
Function: AV serv, Distance learning, Doc delivery serv, ILL available, Photocopying/Printing, Ref serv available, Wheelchair accessible
Publications: New Materials Added to the Normandale Library (Acquisition list)
Partic in Minitex; MnPALS; OCLC Online Computer Library Center, Inc
Open Mon-Thurs 7:45am-9:50pm, Fri 7:45-5:50, Sat 9-3:50

C NORTHWESTERN HEALTH SCIENCES UNIVERSITY, Greenawalt Library, 2501 W 84th St, 55431-1599. SAN 308-7816. Tel: 952-885-5419. Interlibrary Loan Service Tel: 952-885-5463. FAX: 952-884-3318. Web Site: www.nwhealth.edu. *Dir, Libr Serv,* Emily Waitz; Tel: 952-300-3567, E-mail: ewaitz@nwhealth.edu; *Ser Librn,* Monica Howell; Tel: 952-204-5325, E-mail: mhowell@nwhealth.edu; *Pub Serv,* Krista Jacobson; Tel: 952-885-5463, E-mail: kjacobson@nwhealth.edu; *Tech Serv,* Susan Vossberg; Tel: 952-204-5361, E-mail: svossberg@nwhealth.edu; Staff 3.8 (MLS 3.8)
Founded 1966. Enrl 1,136; Fac 51; Highest Degree: Doctorate
Library Holdings: Bk Titles 18,015; Per Subs 146
Special Collections: Acupuncture & Oriental Medicine Journals & Other Materials; Chiropractic Journals & Other Materials; Complementary & Alternative Medicine Journals & Other Materials; Therapeutic Massage Coll
Automation Activity & Vendor Info: (Cataloging) TLC (The Library Corporation); (Circulation) TLC (The Library Corporation); (OPAC) TLC (The Library Corporation); (Serials) TLC (The Library Corporation)
Wireless access
Publications: Library newsletter; New Materials List (Acquisition list)
Partic in Chiropractic Libr Consortium; Health Scis Librs of Minn; Twin Cities Biomedical Consortium

BLUE EARTH

P BLUE EARTH COMMUNITY LIBRARY*, 124 W Seventh St, 56013-1308. SAN 372-5790. Tel: 507-526-5012. FAX: 507-526-4683. E-mail: libtfb@tds.lib.mn.us. Web Site: becity.org/library. *Dir,* Eva Gaydon; E-mail: egaydo@tds.lib.mn.us; Staff 7 (MLS 1, Non-MLS 6)
Founded 1902. Pop 4,000
Library Holdings: Bk Titles 35,212; Bk Vols 38,322; Per Subs 70
Special Collections: DVD videos; Local newspapers from 1861
Subject Interests: Local hist
Automation Activity & Vendor Info: (Cataloging) PALS; (Circulation) PALS; (ILL) PALS; (OPAC) PALS
Mem of Traverse Des Sioux Library Cooperative
Special Services for the Deaf - TDD equip
Open Mon-Thurs 10-8, Fri 10-5, Sat 10-1

BOVEY

P BOVEY PUBLIC LIBRARY*, 402 Second St, 55709. (Mail add: PO Box 130, 55709-0130), SAN 308-5279. Tel: 218-245-3691. FAX: 218-245-3691. Web Site: cityofbovey.org/library.html. *Dir,* Tara DeGuiseppi; E-mail: tdeguiseppi@arrowhead.lib.mn.us
Founded 1930. Pop 858; Circ 12,574
Library Holdings: Bk Vols 20,000; Per Subs 50
Special Collections: Genealogy Coll
Automation Activity & Vendor Info: (Cataloging) SirsiDynix; (Circulation) SirsiDynix; (OPAC) SirsiDynix
Wireless access
Mem of Arrowhead Library System
Open Mon 9-5, Tues & Fri 11-5, Wed 12-6, Thurs 10-5

BRAINERD

P BRAINERD PUBLIC LIBRARY, 416 S Fifth St, 56401. SAN 320-4537. Tel: 218-829-5574. FAX: 218-829-0055. E-mail: brainerd@krls.org. Web Site: www.brainerd.com/library. *Br Mgr,* Jenny Hill
Founded 1882. Pop 40,000; Circ 322,555
Library Holdings: Bk Vols 80,000
Special Collections: Foundation Center Cooperating Coll
Automation Activity & Vendor Info: (Acquisitions) Innovative Interfaces, Inc; (Cataloging) Innovative Interfaces, Inc; (Circulation) Innovative Interfaces, Inc; (Course Reserve) Innovative Interfaces, Inc; (ILL) Innovative Interfaces, Inc; (Media Booking) Innovative Interfaces, Inc; (OPAC) Innovative Interfaces, Inc; (Serials) Innovative Interfaces, Inc
Wireless access
Function: ILL available, Photocopying/Printing, Prog for children & young adult, Summer reading prog, Telephone ref, Wheelchair accessible, Workshops
Mem of Kitchigami Regional Library
Open Mon-Thurs 9-7:30, Fri 9-6, Sat 9-4
Friends of the Library Group
Bookmobiles: 1

J CENTRAL LAKES COLLEGE LIBRARY*, 501 W College Dr, 56401. SAN 308-5287. Tel: 218-855-8180. Toll Free Tel: 800-933-0346. FAX: 218-855-8179. Web Site: www.clcmn.edu/library. *Librn,* David Bissonette; Tel: 218-855-8178
Founded 1938. Enrl 3,600; Fac 130; Highest Degree: Associate
Library Holdings: AV Mats 3,100; Bk Titles 41,000; Bk Vols 45,600; Per Subs 65
Special Collections: American Indian Coll
Subject Interests: Hist, Law enforcement, Local govt, Nursing
Automation Activity & Vendor Info: (Cataloging) Ex Libris Group; (Circulation) Ex Libris Group; (Course Reserve) Ex Libris Group; (ILL) Ex Libris Group; (OPAC) Ex Libris Group
Wireless access
Publications: Library Handbook
Partic in MnPALS; OCLC Online Computer Library Center, Inc
Open Mon-Thurs 8-8, Fri 8-4

S CROW WING COUNTY HISTORICAL SOCIETY ARCHIVES LIBRARY*, 320 Laurel St, 56401-3523. (Mail add: PO Box 722, 56401-0722), SAN 326-0291. Tel: 218-829-3268. FAX: 218-828-4434. E-mail: history@crowwing.us. Web Site: www.crowwinghistory.org/research_library.html. *Adminr, Exec Dir,* Hillary Swanson
Founded 1983
Library Holdings: Bk Vols 300
Special Collections: Brainerd Address Directories 1901-present; Forsythe-Hoffman Diaries
Subject Interests: Local hist
Partic in Northern Lights Library Network
Open Tues-Sat 10-3
Restriction: Non-circulating to the pub

BRECKENRIDGE

S WILKIN COUNTY MUSEUM LIBRARY*, 704 Nebraska Ave, 56520. SAN 373-224X. Tel: 218-643-1303. Web Site: www.co.wilkin.mn.us/historicalsociety. *Library Contact,* Sylvia Peterson; E-mail: sylviawchs@hotmail.com
Library Holdings: Bk Vols 1,000
Subject Interests: Genealogy, Local hist
Open Tues-Thurs (May-Oct) 1:30-4

BROOKLYN PARK

§J HENNEPIN TECHNICAL COLLEGE LIBRARY, Brooklyn Park Campus, 9000 Brooklyn Blvd, 55445. Tel: 763-488-2929. Web Site: hennepintech.edu/current-students/library. *Fac Librn,* Adam Bezdicek; Tel: 763-488-2634, E-mail: adam.bezdicek@hennepintech.edu; *Libr Tech,* Judi Harju; Tel: 763-488-2437, E-mail: judi.harju@hennepintech.edu; *Libr Tech,* Monica Wigdahl; Tel: 952-995-1300, E-mail: monica.wigdahl@hennepintech.edu
Function: ILL available, Meeting rooms, Online Chat, Res assist avail, Study rm
Partic in Minitex; MnPALS
Open Mon-Thurs 9-5:30, Fri 8-4:30
Departmental Libraries:
EDEN PRAIRIE CAMPUS, 13100 College View Dr, Eden Prairie, 55347. Tel: 952-995-1650. *Libr Tech,* Laurie Brown; Tel: 952-995-1535, E-mail: laurie.brown@hennepintech.edu; *Libr Tech,* Denise Weir; Tel: 952-995-1534, E-mail: denise.weir@hennepintech.edu
Open Mon-Thurs 9-5:30, Fri 8-4:30

J NORTH HENNEPIN COMMUNITY COLLEGE LIBRARY*, 7411 85th Ave N, 55445-2298. SAN 308-5295. Tel: 763-424-0732. Circulation Tel: 763-424-0739. Interlibrary Loan Service Tel: 763-424-0935. Reference Tel: 763-424-0734. Administration Tel: 763-424-0738. FAX: 763-493-3569. E-mail: librarian@nhcc.edu. Web Site: www.nhcc.edu/library. *Librn,* Lisa Forslund; E-mail: lforslun@nhcc.edu; *Librn,* Craig Larson; Tel: 763-424-0733, E-mail: clarson@nhcc.edu; Staff 5 (MLS 2, Non-MLS 3)
Founded 1966. Enrl 8,100; Fac 200; Highest Degree: Associate
Library Holdings: AV Mats 3,162; Bk Titles 37,178; Bk Vols 42,000
Automation Activity & Vendor Info: (Acquisitions) Ex Libris Group; (Cataloging) Ex Libris Group; (Circulation) Ex Libris Group; (Course Reserve) Ex Libris Group; (ILL) Ex Libris Group; (OPAC) Ex Libris Group
Wireless access
Partic in Minitex; MnPALS; OCLC Online Computer Library Center, Inc
Open Mon-Thurs 8am-9:45pm, Fri 8-3:45, Sat 8:30-3:45

BROWNS VALLEY

P BROWNS VALLEY PUBLIC LIBRARY, 15 S Third St, 56219. (Mail add: PO Box 307, 56219-0307), SAN 320-894X. Tel: 320-695-2318. FAX: 320-695-2125. Web Site: brownsvalleymnpubliclibrary.org. *Libr Dir,* Bernice Piechowski; E-mail: bpiechowski@bvpubliclibrary.org
Founded 1908. Pop 957
Library Holdings: Audiobooks 148; AV Mats 1,275; Bks on Deafness & Sign Lang 10; CDs 175; DVDs 2,350; Large Print Bks 350; Bk Vols 16,630; Per Subs 43
Special Collections: Native American Coll
Automation Activity & Vendor Info: (Cataloging) Horizon; (Circulation) Horizon; (OPAC) Horizon
Wireless access
Mem of Viking Library System
Open Mon, Tues & Thurs 1-6, Wed & Fri 10-6, Sat 9-12

BROWNSDALE

P BROWNSDALE GRACE GILLETTE PUBLIC LIBRARY*, 103 E Main St, 55918-8817. (Mail add: PO Box 302, 55918-0302), SAN 347-1934. Tel: 507-567-9951. FAX: 507-567-2250. Web Site: brownsdale.lib.mn.us. *Libr Dir,* Debara Smith; E-mail: dsmith@selco.info
Library Holdings: Bk Vols 9,574; Per Subs 10
Partic in Southeastern Libraries Cooperating
Open Mon, Wed & Fri 12:30-5:30, Tues 9-2, Thurs 3-8

BROWNTON

P BROWNTON PUBLIC LIBRARY*, Brownton Civic Ctr, 335 Third St S, 55312. (Mail add: PO Box 97, 55312-0097), SAN 348-1050. Tel: 320-328-5900. E-mail: brownton.staff@pioneerland.lib.mn.us. Web Site: www.brownton.lib.mn.us. *Head Librn,* Jackee Fountain; E-mail: jackee.fountain@pioneerland.lib.mn.us
Founded 1978. Pop 801; Circ 10,176
Library Holdings: AV Mats 45; DVDs 35; Large Print Bks 200; Bk Vols 6,295; Per Subs 21; Videos 70
Wireless access
Mem of Pioneerland Library System
Open Mon 3-7, Tues & Thurs 2-6, Wed 9-11:30 & 3-6, Fri 2-4; Mon (Fall) 3-7, Tues 3-6, Wed 9-11:30 & 3-6, Thurs 12-5, Sat 9-11:30

BUHL

P BUHL PUBLIC LIBRARY, 400 Jones Ave, 55713. (Mail add: PO Box 664, 55713-0664), SAN 308-5309. Tel: 218-258-3391. FAX: 218-489-1052. Web Site: cityofbuhlmn.com/community/library. *Lead Libr Tech,* Cari Oberstar
Founded 1918. Circ 14,000
Automation Activity & Vendor Info: (Cataloging) Horizon; (Circulation) Horizon; (OPAC) Horizon
Wireless access
Mem of Arrowhead Library System
Open Mon-Thurs 10-6, Fri 1-5

BURNSVILLE

M FAIRVIEW-RIDGES HOSPITAL*, Medical Staff Library, 201 E Nicollet Blvd, 55337. SAN 370-8519. Tel: 952-892-2414. FAX: 952-892-2277. Web Site: www.fairview.org. *Librn,* Janet Erdman; E-mail: jerdman2@fairview.org
Library Holdings: Bk Titles 1,200; Per Subs 75
Wireless access

CALEDONIA

P CALEDONIA PUBLIC LIBRARY*, 231 E Main St, 55921-1321. SAN 308-5317. Tel: 507-725-2671. Web Site: caledonia.lib.mn.us. *Dir,* Stephanie Eggert; E-mail: seggert@selco.info; *Asst Librn,* Karen Gran; E-mail: kgran@selco.info; Staff 2 (Non-MLS 2)
Founded 1895. Pop 6,319; Circ 20,961
Library Holdings: DVDs 888; Bk Titles 13,507; Per Subs 49; Talking Bks 314
Special Collections: Caledonia Argus (newspaper) 1900 - present; Caledonia Journal, 1868-1956
Wireless access
Function: 24/7 Electronic res, 24/7 Online cat, Adult bk club, Audiobks via web, Bks on CD, Children's prog, Computer training, Computers for patron use, Electronic databases & coll, Free DVD rentals, ILL available, Instruction & testing, Internet access, Laminating, Magazines, Meeting rooms, Microfiche/film & reading machines, Online cat, Online ref, OverDrive digital audio bks, Photocopying/Printing, Preschool reading prog, Prog for adults, Prog for children & young adult, Scanner, Senior computer classes, Story hour, Study rm, Summer reading prog, Tax forms, Telephone ref, Wheelchair accessible
Partic in Southeastern Libraries Cooperating
Open Tues-Fri 10-8, Sat 10-2
Restriction: Non-resident fee
Friends of the Library Group

CALUMET

P CALUMET PUBLIC LIBRARY*, City Hall, 932 Gary St, 55716. (Mail add: PO Box 356, 55716), SAN 308-5325. Tel: 218-247-3108. FAX: 218-247-3108. Web Site: www.alslib.info/services/find-my-public-library/calumet-public-library. *Dir,* Melanie Lefebvre; E-mail: melanie.lefebvre@alslib.info
Pop 460; Circ 2,446
Library Holdings: Bk Vols 7,000; Per Subs 15
Wireless access
Mem of Arrowhead Library System
Open Mon 11-7, Tues & Thurs 12-5, Wed 9-5 (Winter); Mon 11-7, Tues & Thurs 9-3 (Summer)

CAMBRIDGE

J ANOKA-RAMSEY COMMUNITY COLLEGE, Cambridge Campus Library, 300 Spirit River Dr S, 55008. SAN 377-838X. Tel: 763-433-1950. E-mail: ARCC.Library@anokaramsey.edu. Web Site: www.anokaramsey.edu/resources/library/. *Librn,* Juliana Boner; Tel: 763-433-1358, E-mail: Juliana.Boner@anokaramsey.edu; Staff 1.5 (MLS 1, Non-MLS 0.5)
Founded 1987. Enrl 1,000; Highest Degree: Associate
Library Holdings: AV Mats 1,200; CDs 285; e-books 8,000; Bk Titles 12,200; Bk Vols 14,600; Per Subs 129; Talking Bks 35
Special Collections: State Document Depository
Subject Interests: Art, Minn hist
Wireless access

P EAST CENTRAL REGIONAL LIBRARY*, Cambridge Public Library (Headquarters), 111 Dellwood St, 55008-1588. SAN 347-2353. Tel: 763-689-7390. Toll Free Tel: 888-234-1293. FAX: 763-689-7436. E-mail: ecregion@ecrlib.org. Web Site: www.ecrlib.org. *Exec Dir,* Carla Lydon; E-mail: clydon@ecrlib.org; *Asst Dir,* Rachel Howell; *Br Librn,* Kirsten Vaughan; E-mail: kvaughan@ecrlib.org; *Program Librn,* Erica Myhre; E-mail: emyhre@ecrlib.org; *Resource Librn,* Mindy Hicks; E-mail: mhicks@ecrlib.org; *Syst Adminr,* Andy Nordin; E-mail: anordin@ecrlib.org; *Tech Serv Mgr,* Marcia Ledin; E-mail: mledin@ecrlib.org; Staff 8 (MLS 6, Non-MLS 2)
Founded 1959. Pop 175,494; Circ 1,271,237
Library Holdings: Bk Titles 217,676; Bk Vols 388,155; Per Subs 635
Automation Activity & Vendor Info: (Cataloging) Evergreen; (Circulation) Evergreen; (ILL) OCLC CatExpress; (OPAC) Evergreen
Wireless access
Partic in Central Minnesota Libraries Exchange; Minitex
Friends of the Library Group
Branches: 13
AITKIN PUBLIC LIBRARY, 110 First Ave NE, Aitkin, 56431-1319, SAN 347-2388. Tel: 218-927-2339. FAX: 218-927-1432. Web Site: ecrlib.org/locations/aitkin-public-library. *Librn II,* Mandie Kruger
Pop 7,450; Circ 58,110
Library Holdings: Bk Vols 10,000; Per Subs 60
Automation Activity & Vendor Info: (Cataloging) SirsiDynix; (Circulation) SirsiDynix; (OPAC) SirsiDynix
Open Mon & Wed-Fri 10-5:30, Tues 10-7, Sat 9-1
Friends of the Library Group
CHISAGO LAKES AREA PUBLIC LIBRARY, 11754 302nd St, Chisago City, 55013, SAN 347-2442. Tel: 651-257-2817. FAX: 651-257-3576. Web Site: ecrlib.org/locations/chisago-lakes-area-library. *Br Librn,*

Kerstin Finsness; E-mail: kfinsness@ecrlib.org; Staff 4 (MLS 1, Non-MLS 3)
Pop 10,500; Circ 27,310
Library Holdings: Bk Vols 18,000; Per Subs 50
Open Mon, Wed & Fri 10-6, Tues & Thurs 10-8, Sat 10-4
Friends of the Library Group

WYOMING AREA GIESE MEMORIAL LIBRARY, 26855 Forest Blvd, Wyoming, 55092. (Mail add: PO Box 39, Wyoming, 55092-0039). Tel: 651-462-9001. FAX: 651-462-6634. Web Site: ecrlib.org/locations/195-2. *Br Librn,* Steve Karlson; E-mail: skarlson@ecrlib.org
Open Mon 12-6, Tues 10-8, Wed & Thurs 10-6, Sat 10-2

HINCKLEY PUBLIC LIBRARY, 106 First St SE, Hinckley, 55037. (Mail add: PO Box 336, Hinckley, 55037-0336), SAN 347-2418. Tel: 320-384-6351. FAX: 320-384-9931. Web Site: ecrlib.org/locations/chisago-lakes-area-library. *Br Librn,* Joshua Menter; E-mail: jmenter@ecrlib.org; Staff 1 (Non-MLS 1)
Pop 2,602; Circ 26,413
Library Holdings: Bk Vols 10,000; Per Subs 80
Automation Activity & Vendor Info: (Cataloging) SirsiDynix; (Circulation) SirsiDynix; (OPAC) SirsiDynix
Open Tues 10-7, Wed-Fri 10-5, Sat 10-1

MCGREGOR PUBLIC LIBRARY, 111 E Center Ave, McGregor, 55760. (Mail add: PO Box 56, McGregor, 55760), SAN 347-2477. Tel: 218-768-3305. FAX: 218-768-4652. Web Site: ecrlib.org/locations/mcgregor-public-library. *Br Librn,* Mandie Krueger; E-mail: mkrueger@ecrlib.org
Pop 3,250; Circ 30,153
Library Holdings: AV Mats 1,805; Bk Titles 8,511; Per Subs 20
Automation Activity & Vendor Info: (Acquisitions) SirsiDynix; (Cataloging) SirsiDynix; (Circulation) SirsiDynix; (ILL) PALS; (OPAC) SirsiDynix
Open Tues & Fri 10-4, Thurs 10-7, Sat 10-1
Friends of the Library Group

MILACA COMMUNITY LIBRARY, 235 First St E, Milaca, 56353-1122, SAN 347-2507. Tel: 320-983-3677. FAX: 320-983-5784. Web Site: ecrlib.org/locations/milaca-community-library. *Br Librn,* Lisa Vievering; E-mail: lvievering@ecrlib.org
Pop 7,587; Circ 30,568
Library Holdings: AV Mats 760; Bk Titles 9,847; Per Subs 40
Automation Activity & Vendor Info: (Cataloging) SirsiDynix; (Circulation) SirsiDynix; (OPAC) SirsiDynix
Open Tues 10-7, Wed & Thurs 10-5, Fri 10-2, Sat 10-1
Friends of the Library Group

MILLE LACS LAKE COMMUNITY LIBRARY, 285 Second Ave S, Isle, 56342-0147. (Mail add: PO Box 147, Isle, 56342), SAN 329-1510. Tel: 320-676-3929. FAX: 320-676-8478. Web Site: ecrlib.org/locations/mille-lacs-lake-community-library. *Br Librn,* Carolyn Avaire; E-mail: cavaire@ecrlib.org
Founded 1985. Pop 3,915; Circ 20,230
Library Holdings: Large Print Bks 400; Bk Vols 10,000; Per Subs 48
Automation Activity & Vendor Info: (Cataloging) SirsiDynix; (Circulation) SirsiDynix; (OPAC) SirsiDynix
Open Mon 10-3, Wed 10-5, Thurs 2-7, Sat 9-Noon
Friends of the Library Group

MORA PUBLIC LIBRARY, 200 W Maple Ave, Mora, 55051, SAN 347-2531. Tel: 320-679-2642. Web Site: ecrlib.org/locations/mora-public-library. *Br Librn,* Katherine Jordan; E-mail: kjordan@ecrlib.org
Pop 11,266; Circ 71,622
Library Holdings: Bk Vols 15,000; Per Subs 40
Automation Activity & Vendor Info: (Circulation) SirsiDynix; (OPAC) SirsiDynix
Open Mon, Wed & Fri 10-5:30, Tues & Thurs 12-8, Sat 10-2
Friends of the Library Group

NORTH BRANCH AREA LIBRARY, 6355 379th St, North Branch, 55056, SAN 321-9240. Tel: 651-674-8443. FAX: 651-674-4870. Web Site: ecrlib.org/locations/north-branch-area-library. *Br Librn,* Amelia Birkholz; E-mail: abirkholz@ecrlib.org; Staff 3 (Non-MLS 3)
Pop 10,427; Circ 58,030
Library Holdings: Bk Vols 20,000; Per Subs 45
Open Mon-Thurs 10-8, Fri 10-6, Sat 10-4
Friends of the Library Group

PINE CITY PUBLIC LIBRARY, 300 Fifth St SE, Pine City, 55063, SAN 347-2566. Tel: 320-629-6403. FAX: 320-629-4642. Web Site: ecrlib.org/locations/pine-city-public-library. *Br Librn,* Heidi Anderson-Ferdinand; E-mail: handersonferdinand@ecrlib.org
Founded 1921. Pop 8,858; Circ 51,225
Library Holdings: Bk Vols 11,000; Per Subs 50
Open Mon & Wed 10-7, Tues, Thurs & Fri 10-5, Sat 9-1
Friends of the Library Group

PRINCETON AREA LIBRARY, 100 Fourth Ave S, Princeton, 55371, SAN 347-2590. Tel: 763-389-3753. FAX: 763-631-0514. Web Site: ecrlib.org/locations/princeton-area-library. *Br Librn,* Steve Karlson; E-mail: skarlson@ecrlib.org
Founded 1959. Pop 17,000; Circ 90,000
Library Holdings: Bk Vols 30,000; Per Subs 85
Automation Activity & Vendor Info: (Cataloging) Horizon; (Circulation) Horizon; (OPAC) Horizon
Open Mon, Wed & Fri 10-5, Tues & Thurs Noon-7, Sat 9-1
Friends of the Library Group

RUSH CITY PUBLIC LIBRARY, 240 W Fourth St, Rush City, 55069. (Mail add: PO Box 556, Rush City, 55069-0556), SAN 347-2612. Tel: 320-358-3948. FAX: 320-358-9905. Web Site: ecrlib.org/locations/rush-city-public-library. *Br Librn,* Donna Larson; E-mail: dlarson1@ecrlib.org
Pop 4,832; Circ 30,939
Library Holdings: Bk Vols 18,000; Per Subs 42
Automation Activity & Vendor Info: (Cataloging) SirsiDynix; (Circulation) SirsiDynix; (OPAC) SirsiDynix
Open Tues 10-7, Wed 10-5, Thurs & Fri 12-5, Sat 10-1
Friends of the Library Group

SANDSTONE PUBLIC LIBRARY, 119 N Fourth St, Sandstone, 55072. (Mail add: PO Box 599, Sandstone, 55072-0599), SAN 347-2620. Tel: 320-245-2270. Web Site: ecrlib.org/locations/sandstone-public-library. *Br Librn,* Joshua Menter; E-mail: jmenter@ecrlib.org
Pop 6,582; Circ 45,250
Library Holdings: Bk Vols 14,500; Per Subs 40
Open Tues 10-5, Wed & Fri 12-5, Thurs 10-7, Sat 9-12
Friends of the Library Group

S ISANTI COUNTY HISTORICAL SOCIETY*, Reference Research Library, 33525 Flanders St NE, 55008. SAN 323-7257. Tel: 763-689-4229. Web Site: www.isanticountyhistory.org. *Exec Dir,* Sam Klocksien; E-mail: director@isanticountyhistory.org; Staff 3 (Non-MLS 3)
Founded 1965
Library Holdings: Bk Vols 400; Per Subs 10; Spec Interest Per Sub 10
Special Collections: Swedish Immigration from Dalarna Sweden to Isanti County, bks, photogs, tapes. Oral History
Subject Interests: Swedish immigrants hist
Function: Archival coll, Bus archives, Photocopying/Printing, Ref serv available, Res libr
Publications: Art & History Passport; Braham Minnesota, 100 Years 1899-1999; Home Folks II; Isanti County College; Isonti, Minnesota Centennial; Local Cemetery Records; Preserving a Sense of Heritage
Restriction: In-house use for visitors, Not a lending libr, Open to students, Pub by appt only, Pub use on premises

CANBY

P CANBY PUBLIC LIBRARY*, 110 Oscar Ave N, 56220-1332. SAN 308-5341. Tel: 507-223-5738. FAX: 507-223-5738. E-mail: canby.staff@pioneerland.lib.mn.us. Web Site: www.canby.lib.mn.us. *Head Librn,* Deb Lanthier; E-mail: deb.lanthier@pioneerland.lib.mn.us; Staff 4 (Non-MLS 4)
Founded 1928. Pop 2,081; Circ 51,399
Library Holdings: Bk Vols 20,000; Per Subs 81
Automation Activity & Vendor Info: (Cataloging) Innovative Interfaces, Inc; (Circulation) Innovative Interfaces, Inc; (OPAC) Innovative Interfaces, Inc
Wireless access
Function: ILL available, Instruction & testing, Internet access, Life-long learning prog for all ages, Magazines, Microfiche/film & reading machines, Music CDs, Online cat, OverDrive digital audio bks, Photocopying/Printing, Preschool reading prog, Printer for laptops & handheld devices, Prog for adults, Prog for children & young adult, Scanner, Senior computer classes, Spoken cassettes & CDs, Story hour, Summer & winter reading prog, Teen prog, Winter reading prog
Mem of Pioneerland Library System
Partic in Library Information Network of Clackamas County
Open Mon, Tues, Thurs & Fri 10:30-1 & 1:30-6, Wed 12-6 & 6:30-7:30, Sat 10-3
Restriction: Non-resident fee

CANNON FALLS

P CANNON FALLS LIBRARY*, 306 W Mill St, 55009-2045. SAN 308-535X. Tel: 507-263-2804. E-mail: cfl_ill@selco.info. *Dir,* Nicole Miller; Staff 1 (MLS 1)
Founded 1951
Special Collections: Cannon Falls Beacon, microfilm, bd per; Family Search Geneological; Local Cemetery Indexes; Minnesota Census, microfilm (Goodhue County & Dakota County)
Subject Interests: Regional hist especially city, Regional hist especially county
Automation Activity & Vendor Info: (Acquisitions) SirsiDynix; (Cataloging) SirsiDynix; (Circulation) SirsiDynix; (OPAC) SirsiDynix; (Serials) SirsiDynix
Mem of Southeast Library System (SELS)
Partic in Southeastern Libraries Cooperating
Special Services for the Deaf - TTY equip

Special Services for the Blind - Reader equip
Open Mon & Fri 10-5, Tues-Thurs 12-8, Sat 9-2
Friends of the Library Group

CARLTON

P CARLTON AREA PUBLIC LIBRARY*, 310 Chestnut Ave, 55718. (Mail add: PO Box 309, 55718-0309), SAN 308-5368. Tel: 218-384-3322. FAX: 218-384-4229. Web Site: www.cityofcarlton.com/public-library. *Dir,* Bethany Leseman; E-mail: bethany.leseman@alslib.info
Pop 884; Circ 5,661
Library Holdings: Large Print Bks 60; Bk Vols 7,500; Per Subs 21; Talking Bks 100; Videos 150
Mem of Arrowhead Library System
Open Mon 1-6, Tues-Thurs 1-5, Sat 11-2
Friends of the Library Group

CASS LAKE

P CASS LAKE COMMUNITY LIBRARY*, 223 Cedar, 56633. (Mail add: PO Box 836, 56633-0836), SAN 347-7789. Tel: 218-335-8865. FAX: 218-335-8865. E-mail: casslake@krls.org. Web Site: www.krls.org/index.php/cass-lake-home-page. *Br Mgr,* Bethany Norenberg
Pop 3,500; Circ 22,091
Library Holdings: Bk Vols 10,420; Per Subs 12
Automation Activity & Vendor Info: (Cataloging) Innovative Interfaces, Inc; (Circulation) Innovative Interfaces, Inc; (OPAC) Innovative Interfaces, Inc
Wireless access
Mem of Kitchigami Regional Library
Open Tues 4-8, Wed & Sat 10-2, Thurs & Fri 1-5

J LEECH LAKE TRIBAL COLLEGE*, Bezhigoogahbow Library, 6945 Little Wolf Rd NW, 56633. Tel: 218-335-4240. FAX: 218-335-4282. Web Site: www.lltc.edu/resources/library. *Dir, Libr Serv,* Paula DeMars; E-mail: paula.demars@lltc.edu; Staff 1 (MLS 1)
Enrl 200; Fac 30; Highest Degree: Associate
Library Holdings: AV Mats 206; Bk Vols 5,805; Per Subs 11
Wireless access
Partic in MnPALS
Open Mon-Fri 8-4:30
Restriction: Non-circulating to the pub

CENTER CITY

S HAZELDEN BETTY FORD FOUNDATION LIBRARY*, 15251 Pleasant Valley Rd, CO-4, 55012. SAN 371-7372. Tel: 651-213-4093. E-mail: librarian@hazeldenbettyford.org. Web Site: www.hazeldenbettyford.org. *Libr Dir,* Ann Geht. Subject Specialists: *Addictions,* Ann Geht; Staff 1 (MLS 1)
Founded 1966
Library Holdings: AV Mats 2,500; Bk Titles 17,500; Per Subs 50
Special Collections: History of Alcoholism; Spirituality & Temperance (Hazelden Pittman Archives) manuscripts
Subject Interests: Addictions, Alcohol & drug counseling, Alcohol & drug treatment, Alcohol abuse, Alcohol addiction, Alcohol, drug & tobacco prevention, Drug abuse, Drug addiction, Drug rehab, Recovery, Self help, Spirituality, Substance abuse
Automation Activity & Vendor Info: (OPAC) Inmagic, Inc.
Wireless access
Partic in Central Minnesota Libraries Exchange; Health Scis Librs of Minn; Minitex
Restriction: Not open to pub

CHASKA

P CARVER COUNTY LIBRARY*, Four City Hall Plaza, 55318. SAN 347-2655. Tel: 952-448-9395. Administration Tel: 952-448-9395, Ext 1. FAX: 952-448-9392. Web Site: www.carverlib.org. *Libr Dir,* Heidi Hoks; E-mail: hhoks@co.carver.mn.us; Staff 5 (MLS 5)
Founded 1975
Library Holdings: Bk Vols 193,129; Per Subs 680
Automation Activity & Vendor Info: (Acquisitions) Innovative Interfaces, Inc; (Cataloging) Innovative Interfaces, Inc; (Circulation) Innovative Interfaces, Inc; (OPAC) Innovative Interfaces, Inc; (Serials) Innovative Interfaces, Inc
Wireless access
Partic in Metropolitan Library Service Agency; Minitex
Open Mon-Fri 10-5
Friends of the Library Group
Branches: 7
CHANHASSEN BRANCH, 7711 Kerber Blvd, Chanhassen, 55317, SAN 347-2671. Tel: 952-227-1500. FAX: 952-227-1510. *Br Mgr,* Kathy Bognanni; E-mail: kbognanni@co.carver.mn.us
Open Mon-Thurs 10-8, Fri & Sat 10-5, Sun 1-5
Friends of the Library Group
CHASKA BRANCH, Three City Hall Plaza, 55318, SAN 347-268X. Tel: 952-448-3886. FAX: 952-279-5216. *Br Mgr,* Jodi Edstrom; E-mail: jedstrom@co.carver.mn.us
Open Mon-Thurs 10-8, Fri 10-5, Sat 10-3
Friends of the Library Group
LAW LIBRARY, Carver County Government Ctr, 604 E Fourth St, 55318. Tel: 952-361-1564. *Law Librn,* Elissa Blees; E-mail: eblees@co.carver.mn.us
Open Mon-Fri 8-4:30
NORWOOD YOUNG AMERICA BRANCH, 314 Elm St W, Norwood Young America, 55397, SAN 347-2779. Tel: 952-467-2665. FAX: 952-467-4219. *Br Mgr,* Paul Ericsson; E-mail: pericsson@co.carver.mn.us
Open Mon & Thurs 1-7, Tues & Fri 10-5, Wed 1-5, Sat 1-4
Friends of the Library Group
VICTORIA BRANCH, 1670 Stieger Lake Lane, Victoria, 55386. Tel: 952-442-3050. FAX: 952-442-3059. *Br Mgr,* Kathy Bognanni
Open Mon & Wed 10-6, Tues & Thurs 1-8, Fri 12-5, Sat 10-3
Friends of the Library Group
WACONIA BRANCH, 217 S Vine St, Waconia, 55387, SAN 347-271X. Tel: 952-442-4714. FAX: 952-856-4242. *Br Mgr,* Paul Ericsson
Open Mon & Tues 10-8, Wed & Thurs 10-6, Fri 10-5, Sat 10-3
Friends of the Library Group
WATERTOWN BRANCH, 309 Lewis Ave SW, Watertown, 55388, SAN 347-2744. Tel: 952-955-2939. FAX: 952-388-1350. *Br Mgr,* Paul Ericsson
Open Mon & Wed 1-8, Tues & Fri 1-5, Thurs 10-5, Sat 9-Noon
Friends of the Library Group

CHATFIELD

S CHATFIELD MUSIC LENDING LIBRARY*, 81 Library Lane SW, 55923. (Mail add: PO Box 578, 55923-0578), SAN 326-0658. Tel: 507-867-3275. E-mail: chatband@selco.info. Web Site: www.chatfieldband.lib.mn.us. *Libr Mgr,* Jerel Nielsen; E-mail; JNielsen@selco.info; Staff 6 (Non-MLS 6)
Founded 1971
Library Holdings: Music Scores 75,000
Special Collections: Jan Bily Small Orchestra Coll
Wireless access
Publications: Newsletter
Mem of Southeast Library System (SELS)
Open Mon & Tues 9-3, Wed 9-Noon

P CHATFIELD PUBLIC LIBRARY, 314 S Main St, 55923. SAN 308-5384. Tel: 507-867-3480. FAX: 507-867-3480. E-mail: chat_dir@selco.info. Web Site: www.chatfieldpubliclibrary.org. *Dir,* Monica Erickson; E-mail: monica@selco.info; *Libr Assoc,* Christy Hyke; Staff 4 (Non-MLS 4)
Founded 1911. Pop 5,436; Circ 37,934
Library Holdings: Bk Vols 19,000; Per Subs 42
Special Collections: Local History Coll
Automation Activity & Vendor Info: (Cataloging) SirsiDynix; (Circulation) SirsiDynix; (OPAC) SirsiDynix
Wireless access
Partic in Southeastern Libraries Cooperating
Open Tues & Wed 10-6:30, Thurs 10-8:30, Fri 9-5, Sat 9-2
Friends of the Library Group

CHISHOLM

P CHISHOLM PUBLIC LIBRARY*, 300 W Lake St, 55719-1718. SAN 308-5392. Tel: 218-254-7913. Web Site: www.ci.chisholm.mn.us/library. *Dir,* Katie Christenson; E-mail: kchristenson@ci.chisholm.mn.us
Pop 5,000; Circ 45,000
Library Holdings: Bk Vols 17,000; Per Subs 25
Automation Activity & Vendor Info: (Cataloging) SirsiDynix; (Circulation) SirsiDynix; (OPAC) SirsiDynix
Wireless access
Mem of Arrowhead Library System
Open Mon-Fri 9-6
Friends of the Library Group

S MINNESOTA DISCOVERY CENTER*, Iron Range Research Center Library, 1005 Discovery Dr, 55719. SAN 324-7716. Tel: 218-254-1229. Toll Free Tel: 800-372-6437. FAX: 218-254-7971. E-mail: archivist@mndiscoverycenter.com. Web Site: mndiscoverycenter.com. *Archivist,* Christopher Welter; *Res Spec,* Sue Godfrey; E-mail: sue.godfrey@mndiscoverycenter.com. Subject Specialists: *Hist rec,* Christopher Welter; *Genealogy,* Sue Godfrey; Staff 5 (MLS 1, Non-MLS 4)
Founded 1979
Library Holdings: AV Mats 12,400; Bk Titles 7,000; Bk Vols 8,000; Spec Interest Per Sub 50
Special Collections: Federal & Local Government Coll (Chippewa & Superior National Forest, Itasca & St Louis Counties) maps, papers, rec. Municipal Document Depository; Oral History; State Document Depository

Subject Interests: Genealogy, Geol, Immigration, Labor, Local hist, Logging, Mining, Oral hist
Automation Activity & Vendor Info: (OPAC) SirsiDynix
Wireless access
Function: 24/7 Electronic res, 24/7 Online cat, Archival coll, Computers for patron use, Doc delivery serv, Electronic databases & coll, Genealogy discussion group, Internet access, Magazines, Mail & tel request accepted, Microfiche/film & reading machines, Online cat, Orientations, Outreach serv, Photocopying/Printing, Ref & res, Ref serv available, Res assist avail, Res libr, Res performed for a fee, Telephone ref, Wheelchair accessible
Mem of Arrowhead Library System
Partic in Minitex
Open Tues-Sat 10-5

CLARA CITY

P CLARA CITY PUBLIC LIBRARY, 126 N Main St, 56222. SAN 347-688X. Tel: 320-847-3535. FAX: 320-847-3535. Web Site: www.claracity.lib.mn.us. *Head Librn,* Larissa Schwenk; E-mail: larissa.schwenk@pioneerland.lib.mn.us
Library Holdings: Bk Vols 14,577; Per Subs 60
Wireless access
Mem of Pioneerland Library System
Open Mon, Tues, Thurs & Fri 10-6, Sat 10-2

CLOQUET

S CARLTON COUNTY HISTORICAL SOCIETY*, 406 Cloquet Ave, 55720. SAN 328-1639. Tel: 218-879-1938. FAX: 218-879-1938. E-mail: director@carltoncountyhistory.org. Web Site: www.carltoncountyhistory.org. *Dir,* Mark King; E-mail: mjking@carltoncountyhistory.org
Founded 1949
Library Holdings: Bk Titles 450; Videos 50
Special Collections: Carlton County History Coll; The Fires of 1918 Coll, photog. Oral History
Subject Interests: Local hist
Wireless access
Open Tues-Sat 9-4
Restriction: Non-circulating to the pub

P CLOQUET PUBLIC LIBRARY, 320 14th St, 55720. SAN 308-5406. Tel: 218-879-1531. FAX: 218-879-6531. E-mail: cloquet.library@gmail.com. Web Site: www.cloquetlibrary.org. *Libr Dir,* Beth Sorenson; E-mail: beth.sorenson@alslib.info; Staff 8 (MLS 1, Non-MLS 7)
Founded 1895. Pop 11,463; Circ 144,528
Library Holdings: Bk Vols 54,197; Per Subs 155
Automation Activity & Vendor Info: (Acquisitions) Horizon; (Cataloging) Horizon; (Circulation) Horizon; (OPAC) Horizon
Wireless access
Function: Prog for children & young adult, Wheelchair accessible
Mem of Arrowhead Library System
Open Mon-Wed & Fri 9:30-5:30, Thurs 9:30-7
Friends of the Library Group

§J FOND DU LAC TRIBAL & COMMUNITY COLLEGE, Ruth A Myers Library, 2101 14th St, 55720. Tel: 218-879-0838. E-mail: library@fdltcc.edu. Web Site: fdltcc.edu/academics/library-services/library-information. *Librn,* Keith Cich; Tel: 218-879-0837, E-mail: keith.cich@fdltcc.edu
Special Collections: American Indian Mats (Juvenile/Young Adult Coll); Anishinaabe Regional Coll; Minnesota Regional Coll. State Document Depository; US Document Depository
Subject Interests: Native Am lit, Native American issues, Regional hist
Wireless access
Function: ILL available, Res assist avail
Partic in MnPALS

COLERAINE

P COLERAINE PUBLIC LIBRARY*, 203 Cole Ave, 55722. (Mail add: PO Box 225, 55722-0225), SAN 308-5422. Tel: 218-245-2315. FAX: 218-245-2315. Web Site: www.alslib.info/services/find-my-public-library/coleraine-public-library. *Dir,* Liv Mostad-Jensen; E-mail: liv.mostad-jensen@alslib.info
Founded 1911. Pop 2,921; Circ 23,283
Library Holdings: Bk Titles 17,000; Per Subs 60
Special Collections: Historic Photographs of Local Area; Local History Items; Promotional Items of Local Businesses of the Past
Wireless access
Mem of Arrowhead Library System
Open Mon-Thurs 9-6, Fri 9-4; Mon, Tues & Thurs (Summer) 9-5, Wed 9-6, Fri 9-4

COLLEGEVILLE

C SAINT JOHN'S UNIVERSITY, Alcuin Library, 2835 Abbey Plaza, 56321. (Mail add: PO Box 2500, 56321), SAN 308-5430. Tel: 320-363-2122. Administration Tel: 320-363-2119. E-mail: askalibrarian@csbsju.edu. Web Site: www.csbsju.edu/library. *Dir of Libraries & Archives,* Kathleen Parker; Tel: 320-363-2121, E-mail: kparker@csbsju.edu; *Bus Librn,* Kelly Kraemer; Tel: 320-363-2601, E-mail: kelly.k.kreamer@csbsju.edu; *Coll Develop Librn,* David Wuolu; Tel: 320-363-2128, E-mail: dwuolu@csbsju.edu; *Sci Librn,* Jonathan Carlson; Tel: 320-363-2579, E-mail: jcarlson@csbsju.edu; *Archivist,* Peggy Roske; Tel: 320-363-2129, E-mail: proske@csbsju.edu; Staff 14 (MLS 11, Non-MLS 3)
Founded 1856. Enrl 2,048; Fac 159; Highest Degree: Master
Subject Interests: Benedictina, Bks, Liturgical design, Liturgy, Printing, Theol
Automation Activity & Vendor Info: (Acquisitions) OCLC Worldshare Management Services; (Cataloging) OCLC Worldshare Management Services; (Circulation) OCLC Worldshare Management Services; (Course Reserve) OCLC Worldshare Management Services; (Discovery) OCLC Worldshare Management Services; (ILL) OCLC Tipasa; (OPAC) OCLC Worldshare Management Services; (Serials) OCLC Worldshare Management Services
Wireless access
Partic in Central Minnesota Libraries Exchange; Minnesota Theological Library Association; OCLC Online Computer Library Center, Inc
Open Mon-Thurs 8am-Midnight, Fri 8-5, Sat 10-10, Sun 1-Midnight
Restriction: Limited access for the pub

COLUMBIA HEIGHTS

P COLUMBIA HEIGHTS PUBLIC LIBRARY, 3939 Central Ave NE, 55421. SAN 308-5449. Tel: 763-706-3690. FAX: 763-706-3691. Web Site: columbiaheightsmn.gov/departments/library. *Dir,* Renee Dougherty; E-mail: rdougherty@columbiaheightsmn.gov; *Ad,* Cortni O'Brien; E-mail: cobrien@columbiaheightsmn.gov; *Youth Librn,* Bri Belanger; E-mail: bbelanger@columbiaheightsmn.gov; Staff 3 (MLS 1, Non-MLS 2)
Founded 1928. Pop 23,977; Circ 120,000
Library Holdings: Bk Titles 71,000; Per Subs 110
Automation Activity & Vendor Info: (Cataloging) SirsiDynix; (Circulation) SirsiDynix; (OPAC) SirsiDynix
Wireless access
Special Services for the Deaf - TTY equip
Open Mon-Wed 11-7, Thurs & Fri 10-4, Sat 11-3
Friends of the Library Group

COMFREY

P COMFREY AREA LIBRARY, 306 Brown St W, 56019-1167. SAN 308-5457. Tel: 507-877-6600. E-mail: libtbc1@tds.lib.mn.us. *Dir,* Sharon Lang
Pop 1,051; Circ 14,620
Library Holdings: Bk Titles 11,000; Bk Vols 12,000; Per Subs 10
Wireless access
Mem of Traverse Des Sioux Library Cooperative
Open Mon & Fri (Winter) 8:30-11:30 &12:30-5,Tues,Wed & Thurs 8:30-11:30 & 12:30-6; Mon-Fri(Summer)1-6
Friends of the Library Group

COOK

P COOK PUBLIC LIBRARY*, 103 S River St, 55723. (Mail add: PO Box 126, 55723-0126), SAN 320-8958. Tel: 218-666-2210. Web Site: www.cookmn.us/pages/library.html, www.cookpubliclibrary.org. *Librn,* Crystal Phillips; E-mail: crystal.phillips@alslib.info
Pop 800; Circ 4,885
Library Holdings: Bk Vols 13,000
Special Collections: Fishing Coll; Hunting Coll; Outdoors Coll
Wireless access
Mem of Arrowhead Library System
Open Tues 1-5, Wed & Thurs 10-6, Fri 10-5
Friends of the Library Group

COON RAPIDS

J ANOKA-RAMSEY COMMUNITY COLLEGE*, Coon Rapids Campus Library, 11200 Mississippi Blvd NW, 55433-3470. SAN 308-5465. Tel: 763-433-1150. Web Site: www.anokaramsey.edu/resources/library. *Librn,* Al Mamaril; Tel: 763-433-1552, E-mail: al.mamaril@anokaramsey.edu; *Librn,* Gina Pancerella-Willis; Tel: 763-433-1197, E-mail: gina.pancerella-willis@anokaramsey.edu; *Librn,* Barbara Sandarin; Tel: 763-433-1466, E-mail: barbara.sandarin@anokaramsey.edu; Staff 4 (MLS 3, Non-MLS 1)
Founded 1965
Library Holdings: Bks on Deafness & Sign Lang 26; Electronic Media & Resources 38,000; Bk Titles 41,000; Per Subs 260

Automation Activity & Vendor Info: (Acquisitions) Baker & Taylor; (Cataloging) PALS; (Circulation) PALS; (Course Reserve) PALS; (ILL) PALS; (OPAC) PALS
Wireless access
Partic in Minitex; MnPALS
Open Mon-Thurs (Winter) 7:30am-8pm, Fri 7:30-4, Sat 9-1; Mon & Thurs (Summer) 7:30-4, Tues & Wed 11-7

COSMOS

P COSMOS PUBLIC LIBRARY*, 230 Milky Way S, 56228. (Mail add: PO Box 595, 56228). Tel: 320-440-1012. E-mail: cosmos.staff@pioneerland.lib.mn.us. Web Site: www.cosmos.lib.mn.us. *Head Librn,* Beth Cronk; E-mail: elizabeth.cronk@pioneerland.lib.mn.us
Wireless access
Mem of Pioneerland Library System; Pioneerland Library System
Open Mon 10-5, Tues & Fri 2-5, Thurs 2-6, Sat 10-1

CROOKSTON

C UNIVERSITY OF MINNESOTA CROOKSTON, UMC Library, 2900 University Ave, 56716-0801. SAN 308-5481. Tel: 218-281-8399. Interlibrary Loan Service Tel: 218-281-8398. FAX: 218-281-8080. E-mail: umclib@umn.edu. Web Site: www.crk.umn.edu/units/library. *Dir,* Keri Youngstrand; Tel: 218-281-8395, E-mail: kyoungst@crk.umn.edu; *Asst Librn,* Betsy Ferwerda; Tel: 218-281-8404, E-mail: bferwer@crk.umn.edu; *ILL, Ser,* Krista Proulx
Founded 1966. Enrl 1,650; Fac 75
Library Holdings: AV Mats 1,544; e-books 300,000; e-journals 150,000; Microforms 26,170; Bk Titles 27,600; Per Subs 110
Special Collections: Agriculture, Business, Foods, Equine Research Center, Hospitality, Minnesota Census Data, UMC Archives
Automation Activity & Vendor Info: (Cataloging) Ex Libris Group; (Circulation) Ex Libris Group; (Course Reserve) Ex Libris Group; (ILL) Ex Libris Group
Wireless access
Partic in Minitex; OCLC Online Computer Library Center, Inc
Open Mon-Thurs 8am-9pm, Fri 8-4:30, Sun 5-9

CROSBY

P JESSIE F HALLETT MEMORIAL LIBRARY*, 101 First St SE, 56441. SAN 308-549X. Tel: 218-546-8005. FAX: 218-546-7287. E-mail: hallett@hallettlibrary.com. Web Site: www.hallettlibrary.org. *Head Librn,* Peggi Beseres; E-mail: librarian@hallettlibrary.org; *Ch,* Deb Weide
Founded 1978. Pop 11,400; Circ 36,000
Library Holdings: e-books 2,750; Bk Vols 43,000; Per Subs 108
Automation Activity & Vendor Info: (ILL) Biblionix
Wireless access
Open Mon & Wed 10-6, Tues & Thurs 10-8, Fri & Sat 10-2
Friends of the Library Group

DASSEL

P DASSEL PUBLIC LIBRARY, 460 Third St N, 55325. (Mail add: PO Box 385, 55325-0385), SAN 348-1115. Tel: 320-275-3756. Web Site: www.dassel.lib.mn.us. *Head Librn,* Elizabeth Cronk; E-mail: elizabeth.cronk@pioneerland.lib.mn.us
Founded 1972
Library Holdings: Bk Titles 6,837; Per Subs 25
Automation Activity & Vendor Info: (Cataloging) PALS; (Circulation) PALS; (OPAC) PALS
Mem of Pioneerland Library System
Open Mon, Tues & Thurs 2-6, Wed & Sat 10-1, Fri 2-5

DAWSON

P DAWSON PUBLIC LIBRARY*, 676 Pine St, 56232. SAN 347-691X. Tel: 320-769-2069. FAX: 320-769-2069. E-mail: dawson.staff@pioneerland.lib.mn.us. Web Site: www.dawson.lib.mn.us. *Head Librn,* Deb Lanthier; E-mail: deb.lanthier@pioneerland.lib.mn.us
Pop 2,100; Circ 28,434
Library Holdings: Bk Vols 25,000; Per Subs 55
Wireless access
Publications: Article Dawson Sentinel
Mem of Pioneerland Library System
Special Services for the Blind - Reader equip
Open Mon & Thurs 10-1 & 1:30-6, Tues, Wed & Fri 10-1 & 1:30-5:30, Sat 10-2

DETROIT LAKES

S BECKER COUNTY HISTORICAL SOCIETY*, Walter D Bird Memorial Library & Archives, 714 Summit Ave, 56501. (Mail add: PO Box 622, 56502-0622), SAN 327-831X. Tel: 218-847-2938. E-mail: research@beckercountyhistory.org. Web Site: www.beckercountyhistory.org. *Librn & Archivist,* Position Currently Open
Library Holdings: Microforms 500; Bk Vols 4,000; Spec Interest Per Sub 5
Special Collections: Minnesota Historical Photos (Becker County Coll)
Open Tues-Sat 10-4

DODGE CENTER

P DODGE CENTER PUBLIC LIBRARY*, 13 First Ave NW, 55927. (Mail add: PO Box 430, 55927-0430), SAN 308-5503. Tel: 507-374-2275. FAX: 507-374-2275. Web Site: dodgecenter.lib.mn.us. *Libr Dir,* Ingvild Herfindahl; E-mail: DC_Dir@selco.info; *Libr Asst,* Wendy Kenworthy; Staff 1.8 (MLS 1, Non-MLS 0.8)
Founded 1909. Pop 6,000; Circ 29,000
Library Holdings: Audiobooks 664; CDs 251; DVDs 1,110; Large Print Bks 729; Bk Vols 20,148; Per Subs 15; Videos 514
Automation Activity & Vendor Info: (Cataloging) SirsiDynix; (Circulation) SirsiDynix; (OPAC) SirsiDynix
Wireless access
Function: 24/7 Electronic res, Adult bk club, Audio & video playback equip for onsite use, AV serv, Bks on cassette, Bks on CD, Children's prog, Computer training, Computers for patron use, Digital talking bks, Family literacy, Free DVD rentals, Home delivery & serv to seniorr ctr & nursing homes, Homebound delivery serv, ILL available, Instruction & testing, Internet access, Life-long learning prog for all ages, Literacy & newcomer serv, Magazines, Microfiche/film & reading machines, Movies, Music CDs, Online cat, Outreach serv, OverDrive digital audio bks, Photocopying/Printing, Preschool outreach, Preschool reading prog, Printer for laptops & handheld devices, Prog for adults, Prog for children & young adult, Ref serv available, Scanner, Senior outreach, Spoken cassettes & CDs, Story hour, Summer & winter reading prog, Summer reading prog, Tax forms, VHS videos, Visual arts prog, Winter reading prog
Partic in Southeastern Libraries Cooperating
Open Mon, Wed & Fri 10-5, Tues & Thurs 10-7, Sat 9-Noon
Friends of the Library Group

DULUTH

C THE COLLEGE OF SAINT SCHOLASTICA LIBRARY*, 1200 Kenwood Ave, 55811-4199. SAN 347-2809. Tel: 218-723-6140. Interlibrary Loan Service Tel: 218-723-6178. Reference Tel: 218-723-6473. FAX: 218-723-5948. TDD: 218-422-6942. E-mail: library@css.edu. Interlibrary Loan Service E-mail: cssill@css.edu. Web Site: libguides.css.edu/csslibrary. *Asst Prof, Libr Dir,* Kevin McGrew; Tel: 218-723-6198, E-mail: kmcgrew@css.edu; *Access Serv Librn, Asst Prof,* Jennifer Lund; E-mail: jlund1@css.edu; *Asst Prof, Cat & Syst Librn,* Laura Hoelter; Tel: 218-723-6141, E-mail: lhoelter@css.edu; *Asst Prof, Distance Educ Librn,* Julie Rustad; Tel: 218-723-6535, E-mail: jrustad@css.edu; *Asst Prof, Electronic Res, Head Ref Librn,* Todd White; E-mail: twhite@css.edu; *Asst Prof, Info Literacy, Instruction Librn,* Heidi Johnson; Tel: 218-723-6488, E-mail: hjohnso2@css.edu; *Asst Prof, Coll Develop, Per Librn,* Brad Snelling; Tel: 218-723-6644, E-mail: bsnellin@css.edu; *Acq, Libr Asst,* Julie Walkowiak; Tel: 218-723-6649, E-mail: jwalkowi@css.edu; *Libr Asst, ILL,* Angie Mason; E-mail: amason2@css.edu; Staff 9 (MLS 7, Non-MLS 2)
Founded 1912. Enrl 3,334; Fac 265; Highest Degree: Doctorate
Jul 2018-Jun 2019. Mats Exp $584,814, Books $53,341, Per/Ser (Incl. Access Fees) $196,571, Manu Arch $7,920, AV Mat $13,608, Electronic Ref Mat (Incl. Access Fees) $305,454, Presv $910. Sal $566,451 (Prof $387,035)
Special Collections: Children's Literature; James Franklin Louis Archives; North American Indian Studies Coll
Subject Interests: Health sci, Indians of NAm, Relig, Theol
Automation Activity & Vendor Info: (Acquisitions) Ex Libris Group; (Cataloging) Ex Libris Group; (Circulation) Ex Libris Group; (Course Reserve) Ex Libris Group; (Discovery) EBSCO Discovery Service; (ILL) Ex Libris Group; (Media Booking) Ex Libris Group; (OPAC) Ex Libris Group; (Serials) Ex Libris Group
Wireless access
Function: Archival coll, Art exhibits, Computers for patron use, Electronic databases & coll, Games & aids for people with disabilities, ILL available, Online cat, Online info literacy tutorials on the web & in blackboard, Photocopying/Printing, Ref serv available, Tax forms, Wheelchair accessible
Publications: The Browser (Bibliographies)
Partic in Minitex; MnPALS; OCLC Online Computer Library Center, Inc
Open Mon-Thurs 7:45am-11pm, Fri 7:45-5, Sat 9-7, Sun Noon-11
Restriction: Borrowing requests are handled by ILL, In-house use for visitors, Open to researchers by request, Open to students, fac, staff & alumni
Friends of the Library Group

P DULUTH PUBLIC LIBRARY*, 520 W Superior St, 55802. SAN 347-2922. Tel: 218-730-4200. Interlibrary Loan Service Tel: 218-730-4228. Administration Tel: 218-730-4221. Automation Services Tel: 218-730-4246. FAX: 218-730-5926. TDD: 218-730-4201. E-mail: webmail@duluthmn.gov. Web Site: www.duluthlibrary.org. *Libr Mgr,* Carla Powers; Tel: 218-730-4225, E-mail: cpowers@duluthmn.gov; *ILL Librn,* Stacy LaVres; E-mail: slavres@duluthmn.gov; *Librn II, Tech Serv & Automation,* Jessica Bellini; Tel: 218-730-4251, E-mail: jbellini@duluthmn.gov; *Bus Coordr,* Marie Weber; Tel: 218-730-4223, E-mail: mweber@duluthmn.gov; *Adult Serv Supvr, Tech Serv,* Steph Myers; Tel: 218-730-4246, E-mail: smyers@duluthmn.gov; *Commun Serv, Libr Supvr, Youth Serv,* Susan Schumacher; Tel: 218-730-4219, E-mail: sschumacher@duluthmn.gov; *Circ,* Byron Johnson; Tel: 218-730-4242, E-mail: bjohnson@duluthmn.gov; *Circ Serv, Libr Supvr,* Renee Zurn; Tel: 218-730-4240, E-mail: rzurn@duluthmn.gov; *Govt Doc,* Andrea Pearson; Tel: 218-730-4243, E-mail: apearson@duluthmn.gov; *Non-Fiction & Ref Coordr,* Julie Levang; Tel: 218-730-4247, E-mail: jlevang@duluthmn.gov; *Pub Relations, Webmaster,* Laura Selden; Tel: 218-730-4236, E-mail: lselden@duluthmn.gov; Staff 48.7 (MLS 20, Non-MLS 28.7)
Founded 1890. Pop 86,859; Circ 848,293
Jan 2018-Dec 2018 Income (Main & Associated Libraries) $4,732,713, State $5,054, City $4,599,600, Other $128,059. Mats Exp $393,776, Books $272,112, Other Print Mats $64,813, Micro $3,898, AV Mat $60,195, Electronic Ref Mat (Incl. Access Fees) $74,252. Sal $2,787,172
Library Holdings: Audiobooks 4,731; CDs 4,888; DVDs 8,017; Microforms 8,017; Bk Vols 192,036; Per Subs 330
Special Collections: Local History (Duluth Coll); Regional History (Great Lakes Region); Regional History (Minnesota Coll). US Document Depository
Subject Interests: Great Lakes
Automation Activity & Vendor Info: (Acquisitions) Innovative Interfaces, Inc; (Cataloging) Innovative Interfaces, Inc; (Circulation) Innovative Interfaces, Inc; (ILL) Innovative Interfaces, Inc; (OPAC) Innovative Interfaces, Inc; (Serials) Innovative Interfaces, Inc
Wireless access
Function: 24/7 Electronic res, 24/7 Online cat, Adult bk club, Archival coll, Audiobks on Playaways & MP3, Audiobks via web, Bks on CD, Children's prog, Computer training, Computers for patron use, E-Readers, Electronic databases & coll, Free DVD rentals, Genealogy discussion group, Govt ref serv, Homebound delivery serv, ILL available, Internet access, Jail serv, Life-long learning prog for all ages, Magazines, Magnifiers for reading, Mail & tel request accepted, Meeting rooms, Microfiche/film & reading machines, Movies, Music CDs, Online cat, Online ref, Outreach serv, Outside serv via phone, mail, e-mail & web, OverDrive digital audio bks, Photocopying/Printing, Prog for adults, Prog for children & young adult, Ref serv available, Scanner, Senior computer classes, STEM programs, Story hour, Summer & winter reading prog, Summer reading prog, Tax forms, Teen prog, Telephone ref, Wheelchair accessible, Winter reading prog
Publications: How Do I Contact? (Reference guide)
Mem of Arrowhead Library System
Partic in Minitex
Special Services for the Deaf - Sign lang interpreter upon request for prog; Sorenson video relay syst; TDD equip
Special Services for the Blind - Accessible computers; Audio mat; Bks on CD; Extensive large print coll; Internet workstation with adaptive software; Large print bks; Magnifiers; Playaways (bks on MP3); Reader equip; Recorded bks; Sound rec; ZoomText magnification & reading software
Friends of the Library Group
Branches: 2
MOUNT ROYAL, 105 Mount Royal Shopping Circle, 55803, SAN 378-1976. Tel: 218-730-4290. *Sr Libr Tech,* Paul Griffin; E-mail: pgriffin@duluthmn.gov
Founded 1998
Library Holdings: Audiobooks 2,804; CDs 2,049; DVDs 5,772; Bk Vols 49,893; Per Subs 77
Friends of the Library Group
WEST DULUTH, 5830 Grand Ave, 55807, SAN 372-4905. Tel: 218-730-4280. *Sr Libr Tech,* Jodi Johnson; E-mail: jjohnson@duluthmn.gov
Founded 1991
Library Holdings: Audiobooks 1,639; CDs 915; DVDs 3,769; Bk Vols 30,192; Per Subs 54

M ESSENTIA INSTITUTE OF RURAL HEALTH*, Health Sciences Library, Essentia Health St Mary's Medical Center, 407 E Third St, 55805-1984. SAN 308-5635. Tel: 218-786-4396. E-mail: library@essentiahealth.org. *Libr Supvr,* Elizabeth Sobczak; Tel: 218-786-4145; *Electronic Serv Librn,* Anna Robbins; Tel: 218-786-5488, E-mail: Anna.Robbins@EssentiaHealth.org; *Med Librn, Ref,* Diane Wennberg; Tel: 218-786-4009, E-mail: Diane.Wennberg@EssentiaHealth.org; *Doc Delivery, ILL,* Kaylinn Stormo; E-mail: Kaylinn.Stormo@EssentiaHealth.org; *ILL/Doc Delivery Serv,* Renee Lamoureux; E-mail: Renee.Lamoureux@EssentiaHealth.org; Staff 4 (Non-MLS 4)
Library Holdings: e-journals 10,000; Bk Vols 2,000
Subject Interests: Allied health, Leadership, Med, Nursing, Wellness
Wireless access
Open Mon-Fri 8-4:30

§J LAKE SUPERIOR COLLEGE, Erickson Library, 2101 Trinity Rd, East Bldg, 55811. Tel: 218-733-5912. E-mail: lsclibrary@lsc.edu. Web Site: www.lsc.edu/current-students/library. *Dept Chair, Librn,* Bridget Reistad; Tel: 218-733-5913, E-mail: bridget.reistad@lsc.edu; *Librn,* Kate Rolfe; Tel: 218-733-5980, E-mail: katharyn.rolfe@lsc.edu
Wireless access
Function: Computers for patron use, ILL available, Res assist avail, Study rm
Partic in MnPALS
Open Mon-Thurs 8-4:30, Fri 8-4

R PILGRIM CONGREGATIONAL CHURCH LIBRARY, 2310 E Fourth St, 55812. SAN 328-1159. Tel: 218-724-8503. FAX: 218-724-0848. E-mail: office@pilgrimduluth.org. Web Site: www.pilgrimduluth.org. *Library Contact,* Patrick Colvin
Founded 1918
Library Holdings: Bk Titles 1,850; Bk Vols 1,900
Special Collections: Bible (Liberal Theology Coll), bks; UCC & Congregational History Coll
Wireless access
Open Mon-Thurs 9:30-4

L SAINT LOUIS COUNTY LAW LIBRARY*, Alan Mitchell Law Library, 100 N Fifth Ave W, Rm 15, 55802. SAN 308-5538. Tel: 218-726-2611. E-mail: lawlibrary@stlouiscountymn.gov.
Library Holdings: Bk Vols 20,000; Per Subs 15
Wireless access
Open Mon-Fri 8-4:30

M ST LUKE'S HOSPITAL*, Hilding Medical & Health Sciences Library, 915 E First St, 55805. SAN 308-5627. Tel: 218-249-5320. FAX: 218-249-5926. Web Site: www.slhduluth.com/Healthcare-Professionals/Hilding-Medical-Library.aspx. *Med Librn,* Doreen Roberts; E-mail: droberts@slhduluth.com; Staff 1 (MLS 1)
Founded 1941
Library Holdings: Per Subs 80
Subject Interests: Clinical med, Nursing
Wireless access
Open Mon-Fri 8-4:30

G UNITED STATES ENVIRONMENTAL PROTECTION, Mid Continent Ecology Division, 6201 Congdon Blvd, 55804-2595. SAN 308-5554. Tel: 218-529-5000, 218-529-5085. Web Site: www.epa.gov/med. *Librn,* John Bankson; E-mail: bankson.john@epa.gov; Staff 1 (MLS 1)
Founded 1967
Library Holdings: e-books 1,200; e-journals 350; Bk Titles 5,000; Bk Vols 12,000; Per Subs 25
Subject Interests: Effluent testing, Freshwater toxicology, Predictive toxicity model, Wetland ecology
Wireless access
Partic in Federal Library & Information Network; OCLC-LVIS
Open Mon-Fri 8-4:30
Restriction: Authorized personnel only, Authorized scholars by appt, Borrowing requests are handled by ILL

C UNIVERSITY OF MINNESOTA DULUTH*, Kathryn A Martin Library, 416 Library Dr, 55812. SAN 347-3104. Tel: 218-726-8120. Circulation Tel: 218-726-6120. Interlibrary Loan Service Tel: 218-726-6628. Reference Tel: 218-726-8100. Administration Tel: 218-726-8130. FAX: 218-726-8019. E-mail: lib@d.umn.edu. Web Site: lib.d.umn.edu. *Libr Dir,* Matt Rosendahl; Tel: 218-726-6562, E-mail: mrosenda@d.umn.edu; *Head, Access & Coll Serv,* Elizabeth Benson Johnson; Tel: 218-726-6561, E-mail: ejohnso1@d.umn.edu; *Head, Res Serv,* Tom Ambrosi; Tel: 218-726-7681, E-mail: tambrosi@d.umn.edu; *Access Serv, Coll Serv,* Anne Hovde; Tel: 218-726-7887, E-mail: ahovde@d.umn.edu; Staff 33 (MLS 14, Non-MLS 19)
Founded 1947. Enrl 11,184; Fac 523; Highest Degree: Doctorate
Library Holdings: AV Mats 18,196; e-books 30,886; e-journals 26,272; Bk Vols 368,904; Per Subs 1,411
Special Collections: Northeast Minnesota Historical Center; Ramseyer Bible; UMD Archives; Voyager Coll. Oral History; US Document Depository
Automation Activity & Vendor Info: (Acquisitions) Ex Libris Group; (Cataloging) Ex Libris Group; (Circulation) Ex Libris Group; (Course Reserve) Ex Libris Group; (ILL) OCLC; (OPAC) Ex Libris Group; (Serials) Ex Libris Group
Wireless access
Publications: Newsletter
Partic in Minitex; OCLC Online Computer Library Center, Inc

Special Services for the Deaf - Assistive tech; Closed caption videos; High interest/low vocabulary bks; Sorenson video relay syst
Special Services for the Blind - Accessible computers; Assistive/Adapted tech devices, equip & products; Audio mat; Bks on cassette; Bks on CD; Braille equip; Cassette playback machines; Cassettes; Closed caption display syst; Computer with voice synthesizer for visually impaired persons; Copier with enlargement capabilities; Dragon Naturally Speaking software; Inspiration software; Integrated libr/media serv; Internet workstation with adaptive software; Low vision equip; Networked computers with assistive software; PC for people with disabilities; Reader equip; Scanner for conversion & translation of mats; Screen enlargement software for people with visual disabilities; Screen reader software; Sound rec; Text reader

EAGAN

P DAKOTA COUNTY LIBRARY SYSTEM*, 1340 Wescott Rd, 55123-1099. SAN 347-2205. Tel: 651-450-2900. Administration Tel: 651-450-2925. FAX: 651-450-2915. Administration FAX: 651-450-2934. E-mail: askalibrarian@co.dakota.mn.us. Web Site: www.co.dakota.mn.us/libraries. *Dir,* Margaret Stone; E-mail: margaret.stone@co.dakota.mn.us; *Dep Dir,* Jennifer Reichert-Simpson; E-mail: jennifer.reichert.simpson@co.dakota.mn.us; Staff 61.2 (MLS 61.2)
Founded 1959. Pop 384,233; Circ 4,456,891
Jan 2017-Dec 2017 Income $12,344,606, State $63,471, County $10,086,507, Other $2,194,628. Mats Exp $1,831,186, Books $1,260,991, AV Mat $232,764, Electronic Ref Mat (Incl. Access Fees) $337,431. Sal $9,831,094
Library Holdings: AV Mats 125,834; e-books 131,565; Bk Vols 639,496; Per Subs 1,297
Special Collections: US Document Depository
Automation Activity & Vendor Info: (Acquisitions) SirsiDynix; (Cataloging) SirsiDynix; (Circulation) SirsiDynix; (OPAC) SirsiDynix; (Serials) EBSCO Online
Function: Homebound delivery serv, ILL available, Photocopying/Printing, Prog for adults, Prog for children & young adult, Ref serv available, Summer reading prog, VHS videos
Member Libraries: South Saint Paul Public Library
Partic in Metropolitan Library Service Agency; Minitex
Open Mon-Thurs 10-8:30, Fri & Sat 10-5:30, Sun 1-5
Friends of the Library Group
Branches: 9
BURNHAVEN LIBRARY, 1101 W County Rd 42, Burnsville, 55306, SAN 347-223X. Tel: 952-891-0300. FAX: 952-435-3476. *Br Mgr,* Chad Lubbers; E-mail: chad.lubbers@co.dakota.mn.us
Open Mon-Thurs 9-8, Fri & Sat 9-5, Sun 1-5
FARMINGTON LIBRARY, 508 Third St, Farmington, 55024-1357, SAN 347-2264. Tel: 651-438-0250. FAX: 651-463-7979.
Open Mon-Wed Noon-8, Thurs-Sat 9-5
Friends of the Library Group
GALAXIE LIBRARY, 14955 Galaxie Ave, Apple Valley, 55124, SAN 370-9272. Tel: 952-891-7045. FAX: 952-891-7048.
Open Mon-Thurs 9-8, Fri & Sat 9-5, Sun 1-5
HERITAGE LIBRARY, 20085 Heritage Dr, Lakeville, 55044. Tel: 952-891-0360.
Circ 558,088
Open Mon-Thurs 9-8, Fri & Sat 9-5, Sun (Winter) 1-5
Friends of the Library Group
INVER GLEN LIBRARY, 8098 Blaine Ave, Inver Grove Heights, 55076. Tel: 651-554-6840. FAX: 651-552-7522.
Open Mon-Wed 12-8, Thurs-Sat 9-5
Friends of the Library Group
PLEASANT HILL LIBRARY, 1490 S Frontage Rd, Hastings, 55033, SAN 347-2299. Tel: 651-437-0200. FAX: 651-480-4944.
Open Mon-Thurs 9-8, Fri & Sat 9-5, Sun (Winter) 1-5
ROBERT TRAIL LIBRARY, 14395 S Robert Trail, Rosemount, 55068. Tel: 651-480-1200. FAX: 651-480-1212.
Open Mon-Thurs 9-8, Fri & Sat 9-5, Sun 1-5
WENTWORTH LIBRARY, 199 E Wentworth Ave, West Saint Paul, 55118, SAN 347-2329. Tel: 651-554-6800. FAX: 651-451-1914.
Open Mon-Thurs 9-8, Fri & Sat 9-5, Sun 1-5
WESCOTT LIBRARY, 1340 Wescott Rd, 55123, SAN 347-2256. Tel: 651-450-2900. Administration Tel: 651-450-2925. FAX: 651-450-2955. Administration FAX: 651-450-2934. TDD: 651-450-2921.
Open Mon-Thurs 9-8, Fri & Sat 9-5, Sun 1-5
Friends of the Library Group
Bookmobiles: 1

L THOMSON REUTERS WESTLAW*, Library Services, 610 Opperman Dr, MS DLL N750, 55123. SAN 371-7143. Tel: 651-848-2760. FAX: 651-848-2627. E-mail: eagan.libraryservices@thomsonreuters.com. *Librn,* Cynthia Schriber; E-mail: cindy.schriber@thomsonreuters.com; Staff 5 (MLS 1, Non-MLS 4)
Library Holdings: Bk Titles 6,000; Bk Vols 300,000; Per Subs 500

EAST GRAND FORKS

P EAST GRAND FORKS CAMPBELL LIBRARY, 422 Fourth St NW, 56721. SAN 308-5651. Tel: 218-773-9121. FAX: 218-773-2645. Web Site: www.egf.mn/185/Library. *Dir,* Charlotte Helgeson; E-mail: chelgeson@egflibrary.org
Founded 1963. Pop 8,950; Circ 41,321
Library Holdings: Bk Vols 50,050; Per Subs 35
Wireless access
Function: 24/7 Electronic res, 24/7 Online cat, Activity rm, Adult bk club, After school storytime, Art exhibits, Art programs, Audiobks via web, Bk club(s), Bks on CD, Children's prog, Computers for patron use, Electronic databases & coll, ILL available, Internet access, Life-long learning prog for all ages, Magazines, Mail & tel request accepted, Meeting rooms, Movies, Online cat, OverDrive digital audio bks, Photocopying/Printing, Preschool reading prog, Prog for adults, Prog for children & young adult, Scanner, Serves people with intellectual disabilities, STEM programs, Story hour, Study rm, Summer reading prog, Teen prog, Visual arts prog, Wheelchair accessible
Restriction: Non-resident fee
Friends of the Library Group

J NORTHLAND COMMUNITY & TECHNICAL COLLEGE LIBRARY*, East Grand Forks Campus, 2022 Central Ave NE, 56721. Tel: 218-793-2435. Web Site: www.northlandcollege.edu/library. *Libr Tech,* Amanda Johnson; E-mail: amanda.johnson@northlandcollege.edu
Enrl 1,749; Fac 123
Library Holdings: Bk Titles 6,049; Bk Vols 8,040; Per Subs 123
Automation Activity & Vendor Info: (Cataloging) Ex Libris Group; (Circulation) Ex Libris Group; (OPAC) Ex Libris Group
Wireless access
Partic in OCLC Online Computer Library Center, Inc
Open Mon-Thurs 8-4:30, Fri 8:30-4
Friends of the Library Group

EDGERTON

P EDGERTON PUBLIC LIBRARY*, 811 First Ave W, 56128. (Mail add: PO Box 25, 56128-0025), SAN 324-1416. Tel: 507-442-7071. FAX: 507-442-7071. Web Site: edgertonmn.com/community/library.php, www.plumcreeklibrary.org/edgerton. *Dir,* Elberta DeJager; E-mail: edejager@plumcreeklibrary.net
Founded 1950. Pop 1,189; Circ 77,539
Library Holdings: Audiobooks 1,065; CDs 600; DVDs 2,235; e-books 2,000; Electronic Media & Resources 76; Bk Vols 20,883; Videos 1,000
Wireless access
Function: ILL available, Photocopying/Printing, Prog for children & young adult, Summer reading prog
Mem of Plum Creek Library System
Open Mon, Tues & Thurs-Sat 9:30-5, Wed 9-8

EDINA

M FAIRVIEW-SOUTHDALE HOSPITAL*, Mary Ann King Health Sciences Library, 6401 France Ave S, 55435. SAN 308-5678. Tel: 952-924-5005. FAX: 952-924-5933. Web Site: www.fairview.org/hospitals/southdale. *Librn,* Brett Demars; E-mail: bdemars1@fairview.org; *Librn,* Janet Erdman; E-mail: jerdman2@fairview.org
Founded 1975
Library Holdings: Bk Vols 1,000; Per Subs 100
Subject Interests: Bus, Cardiology, Nursing, Obstetrics, Orthopedics
Wireless access
Partic in Metronet; Midwest Health Sci Libr Network; Twin Cities Biomedical Consortium
Open Mon-Fri 7-3:30

ELBOW LAKE

P THORSON MEMORIAL PUBLIC LIBRARY*, 117 Central Ave, 56531. (Mail add: PO Box 1040, 56531-1040), SAN 308-5686. Tel: 218-685-6850. FAX: 218-685-6852. E-mail: library@elbowlakelibrary.org. Web Site: elbowlakepubliclibrary.org. *Libr Dir,* Gail Hedstrom; Tel: 320-808-6394, E-mail: ghedstrom@elbowlakelibrary.org; *Libr Asst,* Pat Anderson; *Ch Prog,* Susan Frykman
Founded 1903. Pop 2,220; Circ 44,527
Automation Activity & Vendor Info: (Cataloging) SirsiDynix; (Circulation) SirsiDynix; (ILL) SirsiDynix; (OPAC) SirsiDynix
Function: 24/7 Electronic res, 24/7 Online cat, 3D Printer, Adult bk club, Adult literacy prog, Archival coll, Art exhibits, Audio & video playback equip for onsite use, Bk club(s), Bks on CD, Children's prog, Computer training, Computers for patron use, Digital talking bks, Distance learning, E-Reserves, Electronic databases & coll, Equip loans & repairs, Free DVD rentals, ILL available, Internet access, Life-long learning prog for all ages, Magazines, Magnifiers for reading, Mail & tel request accepted, Meeting rooms, Movies, Music CDs, Online cat, Outside serv via phone, mail, e-mail & web, Photocopying/Printing, Preschool outreach, Preschool

reading prog, Prog for adults, Prog for children & young adult, Ref & res, Ref serv available, Serves people with intellectual disabilities, Spanish lang bks, Spoken cassettes & CDs, Spoken cassettes & DVDs, Story hour, Summer reading prog, Tax forms, Telephone ref, VHS videos, Wheelchair accessible, Winter reading prog, Workshops, Writing prog
Mem of Viking Library System
Open Mon, Wed & Fri 9-5, Tues & Thurs 12-8, Sat 9-2
Friends of the Library Group

ELMORE

P ELMORE PUBLIC LIBRARY*, 107 E Willis St, 56027. (Mail add: PO Box 56, 56027-0056), SAN 376-7159. Tel: 507-943-7159. Tel: 507-943-3150. FAX: 507-943-3434. E-mail: libtfe@tds.lib.mn.us. Web Site: www.elmoremn.com. *Librn,* Pamela Engelking
Library Holdings: Bk Titles 1,000
Wireless access
Mem of Traverse Des Sioux Library Cooperative
Open Mon, Tues, Thurs & Fri 3-6, Wed 1-7, Sat 9-11

ELY

P ELY PUBLIC LIBRARY*, 224 E Chapman St, 55731. SAN 308-5708. Tel: 218-365-5140. FAX: 218-365-6107. Web Site: www.elylibrary.org. *Dir,* Rachel Heinrich; E-mail: rachel.heinrich@alslib.info; Staff 3 (MLS 1, Non-MLS 2)
Founded 1922. Pop 3,883; Circ 54,791
Library Holdings: Bk Vols 35,000; Per Subs 80
Function: ILL available, Photocopying/Printing, Prog for children & young adult, Summer reading prog
Mem of Arrowhead Library System
Open Mon-Fri 10-6, Sat 8-Noon
Friends of the Library Group

J VERMILION COMMUNITY COLLEGE LIBRARY*, 1900 E Camp St, 55731. SAN 308-5716. Tel: 218-235-2158. E-mail: library@vcc.edu. Web Site: www.vcc.mnscu.edu/info_sru/library/libmain.htm. *Librn,* Sharon Evensen; E-mail: s.evensen@vcc.edu
Founded 1922. Enrl 670; Highest Degree: Associate
Library Holdings: Bk Vols 36,000; Per Subs 200
Special Collections: Ojibway Native American Coll
Subject Interests: Natural res
Automation Activity & Vendor Info: (Cataloging) PALS; (Circulation) PALS; (ILL) PALS; (OPAC) PALS; (Serials) PALS
Partic in MnPALS; OCLC Online Computer Library Center, Inc
Open Mon-Thurs 8am-9pm, Fri 9-3, Sun 4-8

EVELETH

P EVELETH PUBLIC LIBRARY, 614 Pierce St, 55734. SAN 308-5724. Tel: 218-744-7499. E-mail: evepublib@gmail.com. Web Site: evelethpubliclibrary.com. *Libr Dir,* Mary Ellen Higgins; E-mail: maryellen.higgins@alslib.info; Staff 1 (Non-MLS 1)
Founded 1914. Pop 7,384; Circ 36,015
Library Holdings: Bk Vols 27,000; Per Subs 83
Special Collections: Multi-Sensory Materials Coll
Automation Activity & Vendor Info: (Cataloging) SirsiDynix; (Circulation) SirsiDynix; (OPAC) SirsiDynix
Wireless access
Function: 24/7 Electronic res, 24/7 Online cat, Bks on CD, Children's prog, Computers for patron use, Electronic databases & coll, Free DVD rentals, Genealogy discussion group, ILL available, Internet access, Magazines, Magnifiers for reading, Mail & tel request accepted, Music CDs, OverDrive digital audio bks, Photocopying/Printing, Summer reading prog, Tax forms, Wheelchair accessible
Mem of Arrowhead Library System
Open Mon-Wed 12-7, Thurs & Fri 9-5, Sat 10-2 (Winter); Mon, Tues & Thurs-Sat 9-5 (Summer)
Friends of the Library Group

FAIRFAX

P FAIRFAX PUBLIC LIBRARY*, 101 First St SE, 55332. SAN 376-7728. Tel: 507-426-7269. FAX: 507-426-7269. E-mail: fairfax.staff@pioneerland.lib.mn.us. Web Site: www.fairfax.lib.mn.us. *Head Librn,* Jake Fejedelem; E-mail: jake.fejedelem@pioneerland.lib.mn.us
Library Holdings: Bk Vols 6,000; Per Subs 18
Wireless access
Mem of Pioneerland Library System
Open Tues & Thurs 9-12 & 12:30-5, Wed 12-5 & 5:30-8, Fri 9-12 & 12:30-3, Sat 9-1

FAIRMONT

S MARTIN COUNTY HISTORICAL SOCIETY, INC, Pioneer Museum Research Library, 304 E Blue Earth Ave, 56031. SAN 370-1557. Tel: 507-235-5178. FAX: 507-235-5179. E-mail: mchsfairmont@gmail.com. Web Site: www.fairmont.org/mchs. *Exec Dir,* Lenny Tvedten; *Asst Admin,* Dona Paris; *Curator,* James Marushin; Staff 6 (MLS 3, Non-MLS 3)
Founded 1929. Pop 21,000
Special Collections: Fairmont Railway Motors, Inc. build records of motor cars; Martin County - City Directories, Family Histories, History Files, Microfilm, Obituaries, Picture Files, Plat Books, Telephone Directories, Video Library; Martin County Local Newspapers, 1874-. Oral History
Subject Interests: Civil War, County hist, Minn
Wireless access
Function: Archival coll, For res purposes, Photocopying/Printing, Res libr
Open Mon-Fri 8:30-12 & 1-4:30
Restriction: Open to pub for ref & circ; with some limitations, Open to researchers by request, Open to students, fac & staff, Pub use on premises

P MARTIN COUNTY LIBRARY*, 110 N Park St, 56031-2822. SAN 308-5767. Tel: 507-238-4207. FAX: 507-238-4208. Web Site: www.martincountylibrary.org. *Dir,* Jenny Trushenski; E-mail: jjepse@tds.lib.mn.us; *Ch,* Mackenzie Geiger; Staff 1 (MLS 1)
Founded 1943. Pop 22,000; Circ 200,000
Library Holdings: Bk Titles 100,000; Per Subs 225
Wireless access
Mem of Traverse Des Sioux Library Cooperative
Partic in OCLC Online Computer Library Center, Inc
Open Mon, Wed & Thurs 9-9, Tues 9-6, Fri & Sat 9-5
Branches: 3
SHERBURN BRANCH, 21 N Main St, Sherburn, 56171-1052, SAN 376-9917. Tel: 507-764-7611. E-mail: libtms@tds.lib.mn.us.
Library Holdings: Bk Vols 8,560; Per Subs 17
Open Mon-Fri 1:30-5:30
Friends of the Library Group
TRIMONT BRANCH, 190 W Main St, Trimont, 56176, SAN 378-2018. Tel: 507-639-2571. E-mail: libtmt@tds.lib.mn.us.
Library Holdings: Bk Vols 5,000; Per Subs 13
Open Mon & Tues 1:30-5, Wed 2:30-6, Thurs 9-12 & 1:30-5, Sat 9-12
Friends of the Library Group
TRUMAN BRANCH, 101 E Ciro St, Truman, 56088-2017, SAN 376-9925. Tel: 507-776-2717.
Library Holdings: Bk Titles 5,000; Per Subs 12
Open Mon-Thurs 1:30-5, Fri 12-6
Friends of the Library Group

FARIBAULT

S ANTIQUE STOVE ASSOCIATION LIBRARY*, 823 Lincoln Ave SW, 55021-6636. SAN 328-090X. Tel: 507-210-4304. *Librn,* David Petricka
Founded 1985
Library Holdings: Bk Vols 2,500
Special Collections: Stove Manufacturers Catalogs 1860-1935
Restriction: Open by appt only

P BUCKHAM MEMORIAL LIBRARY*, 11 Division St E, 55021-6000. SAN 308-5775. Tel: 507-334-2089. FAX: 507-384-0503. Web Site: www.faribault.org/library. *Dir,* Delane James; E-mail: djames@ci.faribault.mn.us; *Ch,* Deni Buendorf; E-mail: dbuendorf@ci.faribault.mn.us; *Pub Serv Librn,* Allyn McColley; E-mail: amccolley@ci.faribault.mn.us; Staff 3 (MLS 3)
Founded 1897. Pop 32,000; Circ 270,000
Library Holdings: AV Mats 1,400; CDs 3,400; DVDs 1,500; Electronic Media & Resources 1,200; Large Print Bks 500; Bk Vols 85,000; Per Subs 225; Videos 3,000
Wireless access
Function: Adult bk club, Bk club(s), Computer training, Digital talking bks, E-Reserves, Home delivery & serv to seniorr ctr & nursing homes, Homebound delivery serv, ILL available, Photocopying/Printing, Prog for adults, Prog for children & young adult, Ref serv available, Summer reading prog, Tax forms, Wheelchair accessible
Partic in Southeastern Libraries Cooperating
Open Mon & Wed 9-6, Tues 9-8, Thurs 9-8 (9-6 Summer), Fri & Sat 9-5
Friends of the Library Group

P MINNESOTA BRAILLE & TALKING BOOK LIBRARY*, 388 SE Sixth Ave, 55021-6340. SAN 308-5791. Tel: 507-333-4828. Toll Free Tel: 800-722-0550. FAX: 507-333-4832. E-mail: mn.btbl@state.mn.us. Web Site: education.mn.gov/btbl. *Dir,* Catherine A Durivage; Tel: 507-384-6860, E-mail: catherine.durivage@state.mn.us; *Studio Dir,* David J Statz; Tel: 507-384-6865, E-mail: david.statz@state.mn.us; *Librn,* Rene Perrance; Tel: 507-384-6870, E-mail: rene.perrance@state.mn.us; *Syst & Digital Serv Librn,* Dan Malosh; Tel: 507-384-6869, E-mail: dan.malosh@state.mn.us; Staff 8 (MLS 4, Non-MLS 4)
Founded 1933

Library Holdings: Braille Volumes 36,321; DVDs 62; Large Print Bks 8,395; Talking Bks 217,152; Videos 357
Automation Activity & Vendor Info: (Cataloging) Keystone Systems, Inc (KLAS); (Circulation) Keystone Systems, Inc (KLAS); (OPAC) Keystone Systems, Inc (KLAS); (Serials) Keystone Systems, Inc (KLAS)
Function: 24/7 Online cat, Audiobks via web, Digital talking bks, Magazines, Mail & tel request accepted, Mail loans to mem, Online cat, Ref serv available, Spanish lang bks, Wheelchair accessible
Special Services for the Blind - Assistive/Adapted tech devices, equip & products; Audio mat; Bks & mags in Braille, on rec, tape & cassette; Bks on flash-memory cartridges; Braille bks; Braille servs; Children's Braille; Digital talking bk; Digital talking bk machines; Home delivery serv; Info on spec aids & appliances; Internet workstation with adaptive software; Large print bks; Local mags & bks recorded; Mags & bk reproduction/duplication; Newsletter (in large print, Braille or on cassette); Newsline for the Blind; Newsp reading serv; Production of talking bks; Radio reading serv; Recorded bks; Ref serv; Soundproof reading booth; Spanish Braille mags & bks; Talking bk & rec for the blind cat; Talking bks; Transcribing serv; Volunteer serv
Open Mon-Fri 8-4:30
Restriction: Authorized patrons, Registered patrons only

S MINNESOTA DEPARTMENT OF CORRECTIONS, Minnesota Correctional Facility - Faribault-Rogers Library, 1101 Linden Lane, 55021-0730. Tel: 507-334-0700. FAX: 507-334-0880. Web Site: mn.gov/doc/facilities/faribault. *Educ Dir,* Nancy Rosman; E-mail: nancy.rosman@state.mn.us
Library Holdings: Bk Vols 15,400; Per Subs 33
Special Collections: Law Coll
Automation Activity & Vendor Info: (Cataloging) EOS International; (Circulation) EOS International
Restriction: Staff & inmates only

S RICE COUNTY HISTORICAL SOCIETY*, Rice County Museum of History Archives Library, 1814 Second Ave NW, 55021. SAN 327-8336. Tel: 507-332-2121. FAX: 507-332-2121. E-mail: rchs@rchistory.org. Web Site: www.rchistory.org. *Exec Dir,* Susan Garwood; E-mail: sgarwood@rchistory.org. Subject Specialists: *Genealogy, Hist,* Susan Garwood; Staff 3 (MLS 1, Non-MLS 2)
Founded 1926
Library Holdings: Bk Vols 1,400
Function: Online cat, Ref & res, Ref serv available, Res performed for a fee, Wheelchair accessible, Workshops
Publications: 2000 Rice County Pictorial History; Portraits & Memories of Rice County; Reprinted Rice County 1882; Rice County Families
Open Mon-Fri 9-4
Restriction: Fee for pub use, Non-circulating, Not a lending libr, Open to pub for ref only

C SOUTH CENTRAL COLLEGE LIBRARY*, Faribault Campus, 1225 SW Third St, 55021. SAN 375-4286. Tel: 507-332-5883. FAX: 507-332-5888. Web Site: www.southcentral.edu/Library/scc-library-home.html. *Librn,* Ala Garlinska; E-mail: ala.garlinska@southcentral.edu
Library Holdings: Bk Vols 4,000; Per Subs 19
Subject Interests: Carpentry
Wireless access
Open Mon-Thurs 7:30am-8pm, Fri 7:30-4

FERGUS FALLS

P FERGUS FALLS PUBLIC LIBRARY*, 205 E Hampden, 56537. SAN 308-5813. Tel: 218-739-9387. FAX: 218-736-5131. E-mail: library@ffpubliclibrary.org. Web Site: www.ffpubliclibrary.org. *Libr Dir,* Gail Hedstrom; E-mail: ghedstrom@ffpubliclibrary.org; *Ref (Info Servs),* Candace Herbert; Staff 7 (MLS 3, Non-MLS 4)
Founded 1891. Pop 19,242; Circ 218,298
Library Holdings: Bk Vols 93,924; Per Subs 195
Automation Activity & Vendor Info: (Acquisitions) SirsiDynix; (Cataloging) TLC (The Library Corporation); (Circulation) SirsiDynix; (OPAC) SirsiDynix
Wireless access
Mem of Viking Library System
Partic in Northern Lights Library Network
Open Mon-Thurs 9-8, Fri 9-6, Sat 9-1
Friends of the Library Group

R LUTHERAN BRETHREN SEMINARY*, Christiansen Memorial Library, 1036 W Alcott Ave, 56537. SAN 327-7747. Tel: 218-739-1211. Administration Tel: 218-739-3375. Administration FAX: 218-739-1259. E-mail: library@lbs.edu. Web Site: www.lbs.edu/library. *Librn,* Brent Andrews; E-mail: bandrews@lbs.edu. Subject Specialists: *Res,* Brent Andrews; Staff 3 (MLS 1, Non-MLS 2)
Founded 1902. Enrl 35; Highest Degree: Master. Sal $16,000
Library Holdings: CDs 100; DVDs 20; Bk Titles 20,000; Bk Vols 22,000; Per Subs 70; Videos 100
Subject Interests: Church hist, Missions, New Testament, Old Testament, Relig, Theol
Automation Activity & Vendor Info: (Acquisitions) Surpass; (Cataloging) Surpass; (Circulation) Surpass; (Serials) EBSCO Online
Wireless access
Function: Photocopying/Printing, Wheelchair accessible
Partic in Northern Lights Library Network
Open Mon-Fri 7:30-4
Restriction: Not a lending libr

J MINNESOTA STATE COMMUNITY & TECHNICAL COLLEGE*, Fergus Falls Campus Library, 1414 College Way, 56537-1000. SAN 308-5805. Tel: 218-736-1650. FAX: 218-736-1510. Web Site: www.minnesota.edu/library. *Libr Tech,* Marci King; E-mail: marci.king@minnesota.edu
Founded 1960. Enrl 1,208; Fac 77
Library Holdings: Bk Titles 33,000; Per Subs 102
Subject Interests: Environ
Automation Activity & Vendor Info: (Cataloging) PALS; (Circulation) PALS; (Course Reserve) PALS
Wireless access
Partic in MnPALS; Northern Lights Library Network; OCLC Online Computer Library Center, Inc
Open Mon-Thurs 7:45am-9pm, Fri 7:45-5

S OTTER TAIL COUNTY HISTORICAL SOCIETY, E T Barnard Library, 1110 Lincoln Ave W, 56537. SAN 329-2789. Tel: 218-736-6038. FAX: 218-739-3075. E-mail: otchs@prtel.com. Web Site: www.otchs.org/LibraryResearch/libraryHome.html. *Curator of Coll,* Kathy Evavold; E-mail: kevavold@otchs.org; *Res Asst,* Vicky Anderson; E-mail: vanderson@otchs.org
Founded 1927
Library Holdings: Bk Titles 2,906; Per Subs 25
Special Collections: Otter Tail County Newspapers (1871-present). Oral History
Subject Interests: Bus, Church, Educ, Genealogy, Local hist, Rural educ, Township History
Wireless access
Publications: Otter Tail Record (Quarterly)
Open Mon-Fri 9-5
Restriction: Non-circulating to the pub

P VIKING LIBRARY SYSTEM*, 1915 Fir Ave W, 56537. SAN 308-583X. Tel: 218-739-5286. FAX: 218-739-5287. Web Site: www.viking.lib.mn.us. *Dir,* Position Currently Open; *Pub Libr Consult,* Gail Nordstrom; E-mail: gnordstrom@vikinglibrarysystem.org; Staff 11 (MLS 2, Non-MLS 9)
Founded 1975. Pop 124,698
Library Holdings: CDs 2,247; Bk Vols 13,789; Per Subs 58; Videos 4,135
Automation Activity & Vendor Info: (Acquisitions) Horizon; (Cataloging) Horizon; (Circulation) Horizon; (ILL) Horizon; (OPAC) Horizon
Wireless access
Function: Internet access, Online cat, Outreach serv
Member Libraries: Browns Valley Public Library; Douglas County Library; Fergus Falls Public Library; Glenwood Public Library; Hancock Community Library; Morris Public Library; New York Mills Public Library; Pelican Rapids Public Library; Perham Area Public Library; Thorson Memorial Public Library; Wheaton Community Library
Partic in Northern Lights Library Network
Restriction: Not open to pub
Bookmobiles: 2

FOUNTAIN

S FILLMORE COUNTY HISTORY CENTER*, The Emery & Almeda Eickhoff Genealogy Library, 202 County Rd 8, 55935. SAN 373-3696. Tel: 507-268-4449. E-mail: fchc@frontier.com. Web Site: fillmorecountyhistory.wordpress.com. *Exec Dir,* Debra J Richardson
Library Holdings: Bk Vols 2,500
Subject Interests: Local hist
Open Tues-Sat 9-4

FULDA

P FULDA MEMORIAL LIBRARY*, 101 Third St NE, 56131-1106. (Mail add: PO Box 346, 56131-0346), SAN 308-5872. Tel: 507-425-3277. E-mail: fuldalibrary@gmail.com. Web Site: fuldamn.com/fulda-memorial-library. *Dir,* Beth Cuperus; E-mail: bcuperus@plumcreeklibrary.net
Pop 1,330
Library Holdings: Bk Vols 14,890; Per Subs 60
Automation Activity & Vendor Info: (Cataloging) Koha; (Circulation) Koha; (OPAC) Koha

Wireless access
Function: 24/7 Electronic res, 24/7 Online cat, Bks on CD, Children's prog, Computers for patron use, Electronic databases & coll, Free DVD rentals, ILL available, Internet access, Magazines, Music CDs, Online cat, OverDrive digital audio bks, Photocopying/Printing, Prog for adults, Prog for children & young adult, Scanner, Story hour, Summer & winter reading prog, Teen prog, Wheelchair accessible, Winter reading prog
Mem of Plum Creek Library System
Open Mon-Thurs 10-5:30, Fri 12-5:30, Sat 9-1

GAYLORD

P GAYLORD PUBLIC LIBRARY*, 428 Main Ave, 55334. (Mail add: PO Box 797, 55334-0797), SAN 347-4240. Tel: 507-237-2280. FAX: 507-237-4177. E-mail: libtsg@tds.lib.mn.us. Web Site: gaylordlibrary.tdslib.org. *Dir,* Barbara Kranz; *Asst Dir,* Cindy DeVries
Library Holdings: Bk Vols 14,000; Per Subs 56
Automation Activity & Vendor Info: (Cataloging) SirsiDynix; (Circulation) SirsiDynix; (OPAC) SirsiDynix
Wireless access
Mem of Traverse Des Sioux Library Cooperative
Open Mon, Tues & Thurs 12-7, Wed & Fri 9-6, Sat 9-1
Friends of the Library Group

GIBBON

P GIBBON PUBLIC LIBRARY*, 1050 Adams Ave, 55335. (Mail add: PO Box 138, 55335-0138), SAN 347-4275. Tel: 507-834-6640. FAX: 507-834-6640. E-mail: libtsb@tds.lib.mn.us. Web Site: www.cityofgibbon.com. *Dir,* Kimberly J Holmquist; Staff 1.5 (Non-MLS 1.5)
Founded 1975
Library Holdings: Bk Vols 9,824; Per Subs 50
Automation Activity & Vendor Info: (Cataloging) Innovative Interfaces, Inc - Sierra; (Circulation) Innovative Interfaces, Inc - Sierra; (OPAC) Innovative Interfaces, Inc - Sierra
Wireless access
Mem of Traverse Des Sioux Library Cooperative
Open Mon & Thurs 10-7, Tues, Wed & Fri 10-6, Sat (Summer) 9-12
Friends of the Library Group

GILBERT

P GILBERT PUBLIC LIBRARY*, 17 N Broadway, 55741. (Mail add: PO Box 758, 55741-0758), SAN 308-5880. Tel: 218-748-2230. FAX: 218-600-0506. Web Site: www.gilbert.lib.mn.us. *Dir,* Su Dabbas; E-mail: su.dabbas@alslib.info; *Circ,* Taryn Greiner; E-mail: taryn.greiner@alslib.info; *Circ,* Sue Samargia; E-mail: sue.samargia@alslib.info; Staff 3 (Non-MLS 3)
Founded 1924. Pop 1,799; Circ 17,726
Jan 2015-Dec 2015 Income $125,190, City $110,548, Other $11,332. Mats Exp $12,500, Books $10,000, Per/Ser (Incl. Access Fees) $1,000, AV Mat $1,500. Sal $83,111
Library Holdings: Audiobooks 263; DVDs 1,276; Bk Titles 9,931; Per Subs 22
Special Collections: Careers; NE Minnesota
Automation Activity & Vendor Info: (Cataloging) Horizon; (Circulation) Horizon; (OPAC) Horizon
Wireless access
Function: 24/7 Electronic res, 24/7 Online cat, Audiobks on Playaways & MP3, Audiobks via web, Bks on cassette, Bks on CD, Children's prog, Computer training, Computers for patron use, Digital talking bks, E-Readers, E-Reserves, Electronic databases & coll, Equip loans & repairs, Family literacy, For res purposes, Free DVD rentals, Holiday prog, ILL available, Instruction & testing, Internet access, Life-long learning prog for all ages, Magazines, Meeting rooms, Movies, Music CDs, Online cat, Online info literacy tutorials on the web & in blackboard, Outreach serv, OverDrive digital audio bks, Photocopying/Printing, Preschool outreach, Prof lending libr, Prog for adults, Prog for children & young adult, Ref & res, Ref serv available, Res performed for a fee, Scanner, Senior computer classes, Story hour, Summer & winter reading prog, Summer reading prog, Tax forms, Teen prog, Telephone ref, Wheelchair accessible, Winter reading prog, Workshops
Mem of Arrowhead Library System
Partic in Minitex
Open Mon-Fri 10-6

GLENCOE

P GLENCOE PUBLIC LIBRARY*, 1107 11th St E, Ste 207, 55336. SAN 348-114X. Tel: 320-864-3919. FAX: 320-864-1919. E-mail: glencoe.staff@pioneerland.lib.mn.us. Web Site: www.glencoe.lib.mn.us. *Head Librn,* Jackee Fountain; E-mail: jackee.fountain@pioneerland.lib.mn.us
Pop 5,247; Circ 39,686
Library Holdings: Bk Vols 26,000; Per Subs 102
Automation Activity & Vendor Info: (Cataloging) Innovative Interfaces, Inc; (Circulation) Innovative Interfaces, Inc; (OPAC) Innovative Interfaces, Inc
Wireless access
Mem of Pioneerland Library System
Open Mon, Tues & Thurs 10-8, Wed 1-8, Fri 10-5, Sat 10-2
Friends of the Library Group

GLENWOOD

P GLENWOOD PUBLIC LIBRARY*, 108 SE First Ave, 56334-1622. SAN 308-5899. Tel: 320-634-3375. FAX: 320-634-5099. Web Site: viking.lib.mn.us/glenwood-public-library. *Dir,* Leslie Randall; E-mail: lrandall@glenwoodpubliclibrary.org
Founded 1907. Pop 5,002; Circ 67,943
Library Holdings: AV Mats 440; Bks on Deafness & Sign Lang 5; CDs 1,094; DVDs 1,652; Large Print Bks 376; Music Scores 45; Bk Vols 23,777; Per Subs 61; Videos 361
Wireless access
Mem of Viking Library System
Open Mon & Wed 1-8, Tues & Thurs 10-5:30, Fri 1-5:30, Sat 10-2
Friends of the Library Group

S POPE COUNTY HISTORICAL SOCIETY*, 809 S Lakeshore Dr, 56334. SAN 326-0631. Tel: 320-634-3293. E-mail: popecountymuseum@gmail.com. Web Site: popecountymuseum.wordpress.com. *Dir,* Merlin Peterson; *Coll Mgr,* Ann Grandy; *Archivist,* Brent Gulsvig
Founded 1932
Jan 2019-Dec 2019 Income $127,000. Sal $80,000
Library Holdings: Bk Vols 1,000
Special Collections: History of Pope County, bks, bibles, ed, fiction; Newspapers (1891-present); Pope County Platt Book (from 1874); Population Census 1880-1920 (not 1890), microfilm
Subject Interests: Genealogy
Wireless access
Open Tues-Sat 10-5
Restriction: Open to pub for ref only

GOLDEN VALLEY

§S PERPICH CENTER FOR ARTS EDUCATION, Perpich Arts Library, 6125 Olson Memorial Hwy, 55422. Tel: 763-279-4170. E-mail: library@pcae.k12.mn.us. Web Site: perpich.mn.gov/arts-library. *Librn,* Anne Dennison; E-mail: anne.dennison@pcae.k12.mn.us
Subject Interests: Dance, Diversity, Literary arts, Media arts, Music, Native Am studies, Theatre, Visual arts
Wireless access
Function: ILL available
Partic in MnPALS
Open Mon-Fri 8-4

GRACEVILLE

P GRACEVILLE PUBLIC LIBRARY, 415 Studdart Ave, 56240. (Mail add: PO Box 457, 56240-0457), SAN 347-6944. Tel: 320-748-7332. E-mail: graceville.staff@pioneerland.lib.mn.us. Web Site: www.graceville.lib.mn.us. *Head Librn,* Vicki Bartz; E-mail: vicki.bartz@pioneerland.lib.mn.us
Pop 659; Circ 16,794
Library Holdings: Bk Vols 17,371; Per Subs 15
Automation Activity & Vendor Info: (Circulation) Innovative Interfaces, Inc; (OPAC) Innovative Interfaces, Inc
Wireless access
Mem of Pioneerland Library System
Open Tues 11-6, Wed & Thurs 1-6, Fri 1-5, Sat 10-1
Friends of the Library Group

GRAND MARAIS

P GRAND MARAIS PUBLIC LIBRARY*, 104 Second Ave W, 55604. (Mail add: PO Box 280, 55604-0280), SAN 308-5929. Tel: 218-387-1140. E-mail: gmlib@alslib.info. Web Site: www.grandmaraislibrary.org. *Dir,* Steve Harsin; E-mail: steve.harsin@alslib.info; *Asst Dir,* Amanda St John; E-mail: amanda.stjohn@alslib.info; *Cataloger,* Melissa Wickwire; E-mail: melissa.wickwire@alslib.info; *Ch Serv,* Erika Ternes; E-mail: erika.ternes@aslib.info; Staff 5 (MLS 2, Non-MLS 3)
Founded 1904. Pop 5,286; Circ 69,461
Library Holdings: Bk Vols 22,936; Per Subs 155
Subject Interests: Cook County, Local hist, North Eastern Minn
Automation Activity & Vendor Info: (Cataloging) SirsiDynix; (Circulation) SirsiDynix; (ILL) SirsiDynix; (OPAC) SirsiDynix
Wireless access
Function: 24/7 Electronic res, 24/7 Online cat, Audio & video playback equip for onsite use, Audiobks on Playaways & MP3, Audiobks via web, AV serv, Bks on CD, CD-ROM, Children's prog, Computers for patron use, Digital talking bks, E-Readers, Electronic databases & coll, Equip

loans & repairs, Family literacy, For res purposes, Free DVD rentals, Home delivery & serv to seniorr ctr & nursing homes, Homebound delivery serv, ILL available, Internet access, Life-long learning prog for all ages, Magazines, Magnifiers for reading, Mail & tel request accepted, Mail loans to mem, Meeting rooms, Microfiche/film & reading machines, Movies, Online cat, Online info literacy tutorials on the web & in blackboard, Outreach serv, OverDrive digital audio bks, Photocopying/Printing, Preschool outreach, Preschool reading prog, Printer for laptops & handheld devices, Prof lending libr, Prog for adults, Prog for children & young adult, Ref & res, Ref serv available, Scanner, Spoken cassettes & CDs, Spoken cassettes & DVDs, Story hour, Study rm, Summer & winter reading prog, Summer reading prog, Tax forms, Teen prog, Wheelchair accessible, Winter reading prog, Workshops, Writing prog
Mem of Arrowhead Library System
Partic in Minnesota Library Information Network
Open Mon, Tues, Thurs & Fri 10-5, Wed 10-8, Sat 10-2
Friends of the Library Group

GRAND MEADOW

P GRAND MEADOW PUBLIC LIBRARY*, 125 Grand Ave E, 55936. SAN 347-1969. Tel: 507-754-5859. FAX: 507-754-5859. Web Site: www.grandmeadow.lib.mn.us. *Head Librn,* Alicia Fernsemer; E-mail: afernsemer@selco.info
Library Holdings: Bk Vols 14,000; Per Subs 20
Wireless access
Partic in Southeastern Libraries Cooperating
Open Tues & Thurs 9-6, Wed 9-5, Fri & Sat 9-1

GRAND PORTAGE

S US NATIONAL PARK SERVICE, Grand Portage National Monument Library, 170 Mile Creek Rd, 55605. (Mail add: PO Box 426, 55605-0426), SAN 370-3134. Tel: 218-475-0123. FAX: 218-475-0174. Web Site: www.nps.gov/grpo. *Pub Info Officer,* Anna Deschampe; E-mail: anna_deschampe@nps.gov
Library Holdings: Bk Vols 1,211; Per Subs 50
Subject Interests: Fur trade, Ojibwe culture
Restriction: Open by appt only, Open to pub for ref only

GRAND RAPIDS

P GRAND RAPIDS AREA LIBRARY*, 140 NE Second St, 55744. SAN 308-5937. Tel: 218-326-7640. E-mail: library@cityofgrandrapidsmn.com. Web Site: www.cityofgrandrapidsmn.com/library. *Dir,* Marcia Anderson; Tel: 218-326-7643; *Asst Dir,* Amy Dettmer Dettmer; Staff 7.8 (MLS 3, Non-MLS 4.8)
Founded 1900. Pop 19,138; Circ 195,000
Library Holdings: AV Mats 500; CDs 2,000; DVDs 1,215; Large Print Bks 3,650; Bk Titles 68,000; Per Subs 200; Talking Bks 1,714; Videos 1,118
Subject Interests: Judy Garland, Local authors, World War I
Automation Activity & Vendor Info: (Acquisitions) SirsiDynix; (Cataloging) OCLC CatExpress; (Circulation) SirsiDynix; (Course Reserve) SirsiDynix; (OPAC) SirsiDynix; (Serials) SirsiDynix
Wireless access
Function: Adult bk club, Adult literacy prog, Art exhibits, AV serv, Bk club(s), Digital talking bks, Distance learning, E-Reserves, Electronic databases & coll, Equip loans & repairs, Family literacy, Homework prog, ILL available, Internet access, Mail & tel request accepted, Photocopying/Printing, Prog for adults, Prog for children & young adult, Ref & res, Spoken cassettes & CDs, Summer reading prog, Tax forms, Telephone ref, VHS videos, Wheelchair accessible
Mem of Arrowhead Library System
Special Services for the Deaf - TDD equip
Open Mon-Thurs 9-7, Fri 9-5, Sat 10-2
Friends of the Library Group

C ITASCA COMMUNITY COLLEGE LIBRARY, 1851 E Hwy 169, 55744. SAN 308-5945. Tel: 218-322-2351. Web Site: www.itascacc.edu/campus-services/library. *Fac Librn,* Steven Bean; E-mail: steve.bean@itascacc.edu
Founded 1922. Enrl 920; Fac 40
Library Holdings: Bk Titles 30,000; Per Subs 150
Automation Activity & Vendor Info: (Cataloging) Ex Libris Group; (Circulation) Ex Libris Group; (Course Reserve) Ex Libris Group; (ILL) Ex Libris Group; (OPAC) Ex Libris Group; (Serials) Ex Libris Group
Wireless access
Partic in MnPALS; OCLC Online Computer Library Center, Inc; Project for Automated Systs
Open Mon-Thurs 8-8, Fri 8-4:30, Sun 2-8

S ITASCA COUNTY HISTORICAL SOCIETY, Karjala Genealogy & History Research Center/Itasca Veterans, 201 Pokegama Ave N, 55744. SAN 373-2258. Tel: 218-326-6431. E-mail: ichs@paulbunyan.net. Web Site: www.itascahistorical.org/research-center. *Exec Dir,* Lilah J Crowe
Library Holdings: Bk Vols 750
Special Collections: Itasca Veterans
Subject Interests: Local hist
Wireless access
Open Mon-Fri 9-5, Sat 10-4

GRANITE FALLS

P GRANITE FALLS PUBLIC LIBRARY, 155 Seventh Ave, 56241. SAN 308-5953. Tel: 320-564-3738. E-mail: granitefalls.staff@pioneerland.lib.mn.us. Web Site: www.granitefalls.lib.mn.us. *Head Librn,* Larissa Schwenk; E-mail: larissa.schwenk@pioneerland.lib.mn.us; Staff 2 (Non-MLS 2)
Founded 1877. Pop 5,000; Circ 26,421
Library Holdings: Large Print Bks 1,200; Bk Vols 20,500; Per Subs 87; Talking Bks 540; Videos 725
Special Collections: Large Print Coll; Local History Coll; Native American Coll; Norway (Sons of Norway Coll)
Wireless access
Mem of Pioneerland Library System
Open Mon-Thurs 9-6:30, Fri 9-3, Sat 9-2

GROVE CITY

P GROVE CITY PUBLIC LIBRARY*, 210 Atlantic Ave W, 56243. (Mail add: PO Box 248, 56243-0248), SAN 348-1174. Tel: 320-857-2550. FAX: 320-857-2322. E-mail: grovecity.staff@pioneerland.lib.mn.us. Web Site: www.grovecity.lib.mn.us. *Head Librn,* Elizabeth Cronk; E-mail: elizabeth.cronk@pioneerland.lib.mn.us; Staff 1 (Non-MLS 1)
Pop 597; Circ 6,330
Library Holdings: Bk Vols 5,618; Per Subs 39
Automation Activity & Vendor Info: (Circulation) Innovative Interfaces, Inc; (OPAC) Innovative Interfaces, Inc
Wireless access
Mem of Pioneerland Library System
Open Mon 10-5, Tues 2-6, Wed & Thurs 3-6, Fri 2-5

HANCOCK

P HANCOCK COMMUNITY LIBRARY*, 662 Sixth St, 56244-9998. SAN 308-5961. Tel: 320-392-5666. FAX: 320-392-5666. Web Site: www.hancockcommunitylibrary.org/client/en_US/ha. *Dir,* Michelle Hanson; E-mail: mhanson@hancockcommunitylibrary.org
Founded 1920. Pop 750; Circ 10,083
Library Holdings: Bk Titles 7,890; Per Subs 36
Special Collections: Large Print Coll
Automation Activity & Vendor Info: (Cataloging) Horizon; (Circulation) Horizon; (OPAC) Horizon
Wireless access
Mem of Viking Library System
Partic in Northern Lights Library Network
Open Mon, Tues & Thurs 11-6
Friends of the Library Group

HANSKA

P HANSKA COMMUNITY LIBRARY*, 201 W Broadway St, 56041. (Mail add: PO Box 91, 56041-0091), SAN 376-7167. Tel: 507-439-7323. Web Site: cityofhanska.com/community-library. *Dir,* Tricia Conner; *Libr Asst,* Rhonda Froehling; Staff 2 (Non-MLS 2)
Pop 380
Library Holdings: Bk Titles 6,300
Special Collections: Hanska History Coll
Automation Activity & Vendor Info: (Cataloging) SirsiDynix; (Circulation) SirsiDynix; (OPAC) SirsiDynix
Wireless access
Function: Archival coll
Mem of Traverse Des Sioux Library Cooperative
Open Mon 9-5, Tues & Wed 12-5, Thurs 2-6

HARMONY

P HARMONY PUBLIC LIBRARY*, 225 Third Ave SW, 55939-6635. (Mail add: PO Box 488, 55939-0488), SAN 308-597X. Tel: 507-886-8133. FAX: 507-886-1433. E-mail: har_dir@selco.info. Web Site: harmony.lib.mn.us. *Libr Dir,* Stephanie Silvers; E-mail: ssilvers@selco.info; Staff 2 (MLS 1, Non-MLS 1)
Founded 1916. Pop 2,500; Circ 24,125
Library Holdings: Bk Vols 17,000; Per Subs 60
Special Collections: Beginning Genealogy; Local Old Photographs & History
Function: 24/7 Electronic res, 24/7 Online cat, Activity rm, Adult bk club, Adult literacy prog, Bk club(s), Bks on CD, Children's prog, Computer training, Computers for patron use, Electronic databases & coll, Family literacy, Free DVD rentals, Holiday prog, ILL available, Internet access, Magazines, Movies, Online cat, Outreach serv, Outside serv via phone,

mail, e-mail & web, OverDrive digital audio bks, Photocopying/Printing, Preschool reading prog, Prog for adults, Prog for children & young adult, Ref & res, Ref serv available, Scanner, Senior computer classes, Story hour, Summer & winter reading prog, Summer reading prog, Winter reading prog, Workshops
Partic in Southeastern Libraries Cooperating
Open Mon, Wed & Fri 10-6, Tues & Thurs 2-8, Sat 10-1

HECTOR

P HECTOR PUBLIC LIBRARY*, 126 S Main St, 55342. (Mail add: PO Box 625, 55342), SAN 376-7191. Tel: 320-848-2841. FAX: 320-848-2841. E-mail: hector.staff@pioneerland.lib.mn.us. Web Site: www.hector.lib.mn.us. *Head Librn,* Jake Fejedelen; E-mail: jake.fejedelen@pioneerland.lib.mn.us; *Librn,* Jill Budach; E-mail: jill.budach@pioneerland.lib.mn.us; Staff 1 (Non-MLS 1)
Founded 1985. Pop 1,146; Circ 20,152
Jan 2016-Dec 2016 Income $45,381. Mats Exp $4,500. Sal $27,500
Library Holdings: AV Mats 625; Large Print Bks 277; Bk Vols 12,250; Per Subs 20
Automation Activity & Vendor Info: (Acquisitions) Baker & Taylor
Wireless access
Mem of Pioneerland Library System
Open Mon, Tues & Fri 11:30-4:30, Wed 10-12 & 1-4:30, Thurs 11:30-4:30 & 6:30-8, Sat 10-12
Friends of the Library Group

HENDERSON

P HENDERSON PUBLIC LIBRARY*, 110 S Sixth St, 56044-7734. (Mail add: PO Box 404, 56044), SAN 347-4305. Tel: 507-248-3880. E-mail: libtsh@tds.lib.mn.us. Web Site: www.hendersonmnlibrary.org. *Dir,* Kathy Engel
Library Holdings: Bk Vols 9,376
Automation Activity & Vendor Info: (Acquisitions) SirsiDynix; (Cataloging) SirsiDynix; (Circulation) SirsiDynix; (Course Reserve) SirsiDynix; (Media Booking) SirsiDynix; (Serials) SirsiDynix
Wireless access
Mem of Traverse Des Sioux Library Cooperative
Friends of the Library Group

HIBBING

§J HIBBING COMMUNITY COLLEGE, Marinelli Library, Bldg M, Rm 160, 1515 E 25th St, 55746. Tel: 218-262-6746. Web Site: hibbing.edu/campus-services/library. *Libr Tech,* Rachel Milani; Tel: 218-262-7258, E-mail: rachelmilani@hibbing.edu
Wireless access
Function: Computers for patron use, ILL available
Mem of Arrowhead Library System
Partic in MnPALS
Open Mon & Wed 8-8, Tues & Thurs 8-6, Fri 8-4

P HIBBING PUBLIC LIBRARY*, 2020 E Fifth Ave, 55746. SAN 308-5996. Tel: 218-362-5959. FAX: 218-312-9779. E-mail: hibbingpl@arrowhead.lib.mn.us. Web Site: www.hibbing.lib.mn.us. *Dir,* Tyler Pulkkinen; E-mail: tyler.pulkkinen@alslib.info; Staff 3 (MLS 1, Non-MLS 2)
Founded 1908. Pop 17,017; Circ 138,822
Library Holdings: Bk Vols 80,000; Per Subs 125
Special Collections: Bob Dylan Coll
Automation Activity & Vendor Info: (Acquisitions) SirsiDynix; (Cataloging) OCLC CatExpress; (Circulation) SirsiDynix; (OPAC) SirsiDynix; (Serials) SirsiDynix
Wireless access
Function: Art exhibits, Bks on cassette, Bks on CD, Children's prog, Computers for patron use, Electronic databases & coll, Homebound delivery serv, ILL available, Music CDs, Photocopying/Printing, Story hour, Summer reading prog, Tax forms
Mem of Arrowhead Library System
Special Services for the Deaf - TDD equip
Open Mon-Thurs 10-7, Fri 10-5
Friends of the Library Group

HOKAH

P HOKAH PUBLIC LIBRARY*, 57 Main, 55941. (Mail add: PO Box 503, 55941-0503), SAN 376-7833. Tel: 507-894-2665. Web Site: www.cityofhokah-mn.gov/library.html. *Librn,* Kirsten Plummer; E-mail: kplummer@selco.info
Library Holdings: CDs 600; DVDs 500; Bk Vols 20,600; Per Subs 34; Talking Bks 55; Videos 1,500
Automation Activity & Vendor Info: (Cataloging) Horizon; (Circulation) Horizon; (OPAC) Horizon
Wireless access
Partic in Southeastern Libraries Cooperating
Open Mon & Wed 8-1, Tues & Thurs 3-8, Fri 1-6
Friends of the Library Group

HOYT LAKES

P HOYT LAKES PUBLIC LIBRARY, 206 Kennedy Memorial Dr, 55750. SAN 308-6011. Tel: 218-225-2412. FAX: 218-225-2399. Web Site: hoytlakeslibrary.org. *Libr Dir,* Susan Sowers; E-mail: sue.sowers@alslib.info
Founded 1959. Circ 36,000
Library Holdings: Bk Vols 23,000; Per Subs 62
Automation Activity & Vendor Info: (Cataloging) SirsiDynix; (Circulation) SirsiDynix; (OPAC) SirsiDynix; (Serials) SirsiDynix
Wireless access
Mem of Arrowhead Library System
Open Mon-Fri 11-5
Friends of the Library Group

HUTCHINSON

P HUTCHINSON PUBLIC LIBRARY*, 50 Hassan St SE, 55350-1881. SAN 348-1204. Tel: 320-587-2368. FAX: 320-587-4286. Web Site: www.hutchinson.lib.mn.us. *Head Librn,* Katy Hiltner; E-mail: katy.hiltner@pioneerland.lib.mn.us; *Ch,* Sherry Lund; E-mail: sherry.lund@pioneerland.lib.mn.us; Staff 4 (Non-MLS 4)
Pop 12,989; Circ 90,355
Library Holdings: Bk Vols 40,865; Per Subs 129
Automation Activity & Vendor Info: (Circulation) PALS; (OPAC) PALS
Wireless access
Mem of Pioneerland Library System
Open Mon-Thurs 10-9, Fri & Sat 10-5
Friends of the Library Group

J RIDGEWATER COLLEGE LIBRARY*, Hutchinson Campus, Two Century Ave SE, 55350. SAN 378-3715. Tel: 320-234-8567. Interlibrary Loan Service Tel: 320-234-8566. Web Site: www.ridgewater.edu/library. *Librn,* Terrence Edwards; Tel: 320-222-7537, E-mail: terrence.edwards@ridgewater.edu; *Libr Tech,* Karen Kaczmarek; Tel: 320-234-8566, E-mail: karen.kaczmarek@ridgewater.edu; Staff 2 (MLS 1, Non-MLS 1)
Founded 1997. Enrl 1,200; Fac 56; Highest Degree: Associate
Library Holdings: Bk Vols 11,000; Per Subs 120
Automation Activity & Vendor Info: (Cataloging) Ex Libris Group; (Circulation) Ex Libris Group; (OPAC) Ex Libris Group
Wireless access
Open Mon-Thurs 7:30-7; Fri 7:30-6

INTERNATIONAL FALLS

P INTERNATIONAL FALLS PUBLIC LIBRARY, 750 Fourth St, 56649. SAN 308-602X. Tel: 218-283-8051. Web Site: www.internationalfallslibrary.us. *Libr Dir,* Diane Adams; E-mail: diane.adams@alslib.info; Staff 3 (MLS 1, Non-MLS 2)
Founded 1911. Pop 5,906; Circ 89,858
Library Holdings: AV Mats 1,966; Bk Titles 48,687; Per Subs 85
Subject Interests: Minn hist
Automation Activity & Vendor Info: (Acquisitions) SirsiDynix; (Cataloging) SirsiDynix; (Circulation) SirsiDynix; (ILL) SirsiDynix; (OPAC) SirsiDynix; (Serials) SirsiDynix
Wireless access
Mem of Arrowhead Library System
Open Mon-Wed 10-8, Thurs & Fri 10-6, Sat (Winter) 10-3
Friends of the Library Group

S KOOCHICHING COUNTY HISTORICAL MUSEUM LIBRARY, 214 Sixth Ave, 56649. SAN 326-2456. Tel: 218-283-4316. FAX: 218-283-8243. E-mail: koochmuseums@gmail.com. Web Site: www.koochichingmuseums.org. *Exec Dir,* Ashley LaVigna
Library Holdings: Bk Vols 1,950; Per Subs 12
Special Collections: International Lumber Co Coll, photogs & records; Mando/Boise Cascade Coll, photogs & records; Sawmill, Logging, Papermill Coll. Oral History
Open Mon-Fri 9-5

J RAINY RIVER COMMUNITY COLLEGE LIBRARY, 1501 Hwy 71, 56649. SAN 308-6038. Tel: 218-285-7722, Ext 220. FAX: 218-285-2239. Web Site: www.rainyriver.edu/college-services/library. *Librn,* Diane Raboin; Tel: 218-285-2250, E-mail: diane.raboin@rainyriver.edu; Staff 1 (MLS 1)
Founded 1967. Enrl 399
Library Holdings: Bk Titles 16,500; Bk Vols 19,000; Per Subs 32; Videos 740
Publications: LRC Handbook
Partic in MnPALS; Proquest Dialog
Open Mon 7:30am-8pm, Tues-Thurs 7:30am-9pm, Fri 7:30-4

INVER GROVE HEIGHTS

J INVER HILLS COMMUNITY COLLEGE LIBRARY*, 2500 80th St E, 55076-3209. SAN 308-6046. Tel: 651-450-3625. Interlibrary Loan Service Tel: 651-450-3624. E-mail: library@inverhills.edu. Web Site: www.inverhills.edu/library. *Instr, Librn,* Brenda Besser; Tel: 651-450-3798, E-mail: bbesser@inverhills.edu; *Acq, Instruction Librn,* Julie Benolken; Tel: 651-450-8622, E-mail: jbenolken@inverhills.edu; *Tech Serv,* David Colwell; E-mail: dcolwell@inverhills.edu; Staff 4 (MLS 3, Non-MLS 1)
Founded 1970. Enrl 6,100; Fac 180; Highest Degree: Associate
Library Holdings: Bk Titles 64,000; Per Subs 200
Automation Activity & Vendor Info: (Acquisitions) Ex Libris Group; (Cataloging) Ex Libris Group; (Circulation) Ex Libris Group; (Course Reserve) Ex Libris Group; (ILL) Ex Libris Group; (OPAC) Ex Libris Group; (Serials) Ex Libris Group
Wireless access
Partic in Minitex; MnPALS; OCLC Online Computer Library Center, Inc
Open Mon-Thurs 8am-9pm, Fri 8-4, Sat 9-3

IVANHOE

P IVANHOE PUBLIC LIBRARY*, 401 N Harold, 56142. (Mail add: PO Box 25, 56142-0025), SAN 376-7574. Tel: 507-694-1555. FAX: 507-694-1278. E-mail: Ivanhoemnlibrary@gmail.com. Web Site: www.plumcreeklibrary.org/Ivanhoe. *Dir,* Susan Vizecky; E-mail: Svizecky@plumcreeklibrary.net
Library Holdings: Bk Titles 10,000; Bk Vols 15,000; Per Subs 20
Wireless access
Mem of Plum Creek Library System
Open Mon, Wed & Fri 9-1 & 2-4, Thurs 12-3 & 4-7
Friends of the Library Group

JACKSON

P JACKSON COUNTY LIBRARY*, 311 Third St, 56143-1600. SAN 308-6054. Tel: 507-847-4748. FAX: 507-847-5470. E-mail: jacksoncolibrary@plumcreeklibrary.net. Web Site: www.co.jackson.mn.us/library. *Dir,* Tamera Marie Erickson; E-mail: tamera.erickson@co.jackson.mn.us; *Asst Librn,* Pam Grussing; E-mail: pgrussing@plumcreeklibrary.net; *Asst Librn,* Dawn Skow; E-mail: dskow@plumcreeklibrary.net; *Ch Serv,* Carrie Dose; E-mail: cdose@plumcreeklibrary.net; Staff 7 (Non-MLS 7)
Pop 11,636; Circ 109,825
Library Holdings: CDs 200; Bk Vols 22,829; Per Subs 100; Talking Bks 1,684; Videos 1,358
Automation Activity & Vendor Info: (Cataloging) TLC (The Library Corporation); (Circulation) TLC (The Library Corporation); (OPAC) TLC (The Library Corporation)
Wireless access
Mem of Plum Creek Library System
Open Mon, Tues & Thurs (Winter) 10-7, Wed & Fri 10-5, Sat 10-3; Mon, Tues & Thurs (Summer) 10-7, Wed & Fri 10-5
Friends of the Library Group
Branches: 2
HERON LAKE BRANCH, 401 Ninth St, Heron Lake, 56137-1440. (Mail add: PO Box 348, Heron Lake, 56137-0348), SAN 322-6719. Tel: 507-793-2641. FAX: 507-793-2641. *Br Mgr,* Sunny Osland
Pop 1,000; Circ 9,723
Library Holdings: Bk Vols 7,521; Per Subs 22
Open Tues & Thurs 1-5:30, Wed 3-8 (1-8 Summer), Fri 1-5, Sat 10-12
LAKEFIELD BRANCH, 410 Main St, Lakefield, 56150-1201. (Mail add: PO Box 723, Lakefield, 56150-0723). Tel: 507-662-5782. FAX: 507-662-5782. *Br Mgr,* Kathy Weeks-Wegner
Library Holdings: Bk Vols 10,608; Per Subs 34
Open Mon-Wed 11-5:30, Thurs 11-7, Fri 11-5, Sat 10-1

KASSON

P KASSON PUBLIC LIBRARY, 607 First St NW, 55944. SAN 308-6062. Tel: 507-634-7615. E-mail: kassonlibrary@gmail.com. Web Site: www.kasson.lib.mn.us. *Dir,* Patricia Shaffer-Gottschalk; E-mail: ka_dir@selco.info; Staff 5 (MLS 2, Non-MLS 3)
Founded 1899. Pop 9,761; Circ 60,547
Library Holdings: AV Mats 5,000; Bk Titles 22,272
Wireless access
Function: 24/7 Electronic res, 24/7 Online cat, 3D Printer, Activity rm, Adult bk club, After school storytime
Partic in Southeastern Libraries Cooperating
Open Mon & Tues 10-6, Wed, Thurs & Fri 10-5, Sat 9-12
Friends of the Library Group

KEEWATIN

P KEEWATIN PUBLIC LIBRARY, 125 W Third Ave, 55753. SAN 308-6070. Tel: 218-778-6377. FAX: 218-778-6193. Web Site: www.keewatin.govoffice.com. *Libr Dir,* Paula Fowler; E-mail: paula.fowler@alslib.info; *Libr Assoc,* Janice Kunze
Pop 1,300; Circ 11,614
Library Holdings: Bk Vols 7,390; Per Subs 20
Wireless access
Mem of Arrowhead Library System
Open Mon-Thurs 10-7, Fri 10-4

KENYON

P KENYON PUBLIC LIBRARY, 709 Second St, 55946-1339. SAN 308-6089. Tel: 507-789-6821. FAX: 507-789-5604. Web Site: www.kenyon.lib.mn.us. *Dir,* Michelle Otte; E-mail: motte@selco.info; Staff 3 (MLS 1, Non-MLS 2)
Founded 1907. Pop 4,500; Circ 28,000
Library Holdings: Audiobooks 200; CDs 125; DVDs 800; Large Print Bks 900; Bk Vols 14,000
Wireless access
Partic in Southeastern Libraries Cooperating
Open Mon, Wed & Fri 10-4:30, Tues & Thurs 10-6:30

KERKHOVEN

P KERKHOVEN PUBLIC LIBRARY*, 208 N Tenth St, 56252. (Mail add: PO Box 508, 56252-0508), SAN 347-6952. Tel: 320-264-2141. FAX: 320-264-2141. E-mail: kerkhoven.staff@pioneerland.lib.mn.us. Web Site: www.kerkhoven.lib.mn.us. *Head Librn,* Andrew Kelton; E-mail: andrew.kelton@pioneerland.lib.mn.us; Staff 1 (MLS 1)
Pop 740; Circ 7,787
Library Holdings: Bk Vols 4,323; Per Subs 16
Automation Activity & Vendor Info: (Circulation) PALS; (OPAC) PALS
Wireless access
Mem of Pioneerland Library System
Open Mon & Tues 2-5, Wed 2-7, Thurs 11-5, Fri 1-5

KINNEY

P KINNEY PUBLIC LIBRARY*, 400 Main St, 55758. (Mail add: PO Box D7, 55758), SAN 308-6097. Tel: 218-258-2232. *Dir,* Judy Holcomb
Pop 447; Circ 4,270
Library Holdings: Bk Vols 8,500; Per Subs 30
Open Mon-Thurs 4-7

LA CRESCENT

P LA CRESCENT PUBLIC LIBRARY*, 321 Main St, 55947. SAN 375-6157. Tel: 507-895-4047. FAX: 507-895-7153. Web Site: lacrescent.lib.mn.us. *Libr Dir,* Kayce Gentry; E-mail: lcr_dir@selco.info; *Libr Asst,* Kristen Boeshans; E-mail: kboeshans@selco.info; Staff 4 (MLS 1, Non-MLS 3)
Founded 1985. Pop 7,925; Circ 53,227
Library Holdings: Audiobooks 1,208; AV Mats 18; CDs 310; DVDs 2,267; e-books 2,100; Large Print Bks 1,543; Microforms 32; Bk Vols 34,800; Per Subs 60
Special Collections: State Document Depository
Automation Activity & Vendor Info: (Cataloging) Horizon; (Circulation) Horizon; (OPAC) Horizon
Wireless access
Function: 24/7 Electronic res, 24/7 Online cat, Adult bk club, After school storytime, Audiobks on Playaways & MP3, Audiobks via web, Bk club(s), Bks on CD, Children's prog, Computers for patron use, Digital talking bks, E-Reserves, Electronic databases & coll, Free DVD rentals, Holiday prog, ILL available, Internet access, Magazines, Magnifiers for reading, Mail & tel request accepted, Masonic res mat, Meeting rooms, Microfiche/film & reading machines, Movies, Music CDs, Online cat, OverDrive digital audio bks, Photocopying/Printing, Preschool reading prog, Prog for adults, Prog for children & young adult, Scanner, Story hour, Summer reading prog, Wheelchair accessible
Partic in Southeastern Libraries Cooperating
Special Services for the Deaf - Bks on deafness & sign lang
Special Services for the Blind - Bks on CD
Open Mon, Tues & Fri 10-6, Wed & Thurs 10-7, Sat 10-2
Friends of the Library Group

LAKE BENTON

P LAKE BENTON PUBLIC LIBRARY*, 110 E Benton, 56149. (Mail add: PO Box 377, 56149), SAN 376-690X. Tel: 507-368-4641. E-mail: lbpubliclibrary@gmail.com. *Dir,* Shelly Finzen; *Librn,* Faith McCullough
Library Holdings: Bk Titles 8,100; Per Subs 40
Wireless access
Function: Adult bk club, Chess club, Outreach serv, Workshops

Mem of Plum Creek Library System
Open Mon & Wed 11-5:30, Tues & Thurs 12-6:30, Fri 10-5:30, Sat 9-Noon
Friends of the Library Group

LAKE CITY

P LAKE CITY PUBLIC LIBRARY*, 201 S High St, 55041. SAN 308-6100. Tel: 651-345-4013. FAX: 651-345-5923. Web Site: lakecity.lib.mn.us. *Dir,* Patti Bross; E-mail: pbross@selco.info
Founded 1904. Pop 4,505; Circ 40,174
Library Holdings: Bk Titles 42,000; Per Subs 125
Open Mon-Thurs 10-8, Fri 10-5, Sat 9-Noon
Friends of the Library Group

LAKE LILLIAN

P LAKE LILLIAN PUBLIC LIBRARY*, 431 Lakeview St, 56253. (Mail add: PO Box 38, 56253-0038), SAN 348-1239. Tel: 320-664-4514. FAX: 320-664-4514. Web Site: www.lakelillian.lib.mn.us. *Head Librn,* Ria Newhouse; E-mail: ria.newhouse@pioneerland.lib.mn.us; Staff 1 (Non-MLS 1)
Pop 228; Circ 22,282
Library Holdings: Bk Vols 6,393; Per Subs 43
Wireless access
Mem of Pioneerland Library System
Open Mon & Tues 11-5, Thurs 11-7

LAKEFIELD

S JACKSON COUNTY HISTORICAL SOCIETY LIBRARY*, 307 N Hwy 86, 56150. SAN 328-820X. Tel: 507-662-5505. E-mail: jchslakefield@gmail.com. *Exec Dir,* Michael Kirchmeier
Library Holdings: Bk Titles 200
Special Collections: Cemetery & Census Records; Genealogical Publications
Subject Interests: County hist
Wireless access
Open Mon-Fri 9:30-4:30, Sat 8-12

LAMBERTON

P LAMBERTON PUBLIC LIBRARY*, 101 E Second Ave, 56152. (Mail add: PO Box 505, 56152-0505), SAN 308-6127. Tel: 507-752-7220. FAX: 507-752-7220. E-mail: lambertonlib@plumcreeklibrary.net. Web Site: www.plumcreeklibrary.org/lamberton. *Dir,* Alicia Vogel
Founded 1933. Pop 1,010; Circ 8,000
Library Holdings: Audiobooks 211; AV Mats 1,415; CDs 50; DVDs 360; Large Print Bks 218; Bk Titles 9,350; Bk Vols 9,356; Per Subs 12; Videos 1,235
Automation Activity & Vendor Info: (Acquisitions) SirsiDynix; (Cataloging) SirsiDynix; (Circulation) SirsiDynix; (ILL) SirsiDynix; (OPAC) SirsiDynix; (Serials) SirsiDynix
Wireless access
Mem of Plum Creek Library System
Open Mon-Fri 9:30-1 & 1:30-6
Friends of the Library Group

LANESBORO

P LANESBORO PUBLIC LIBRARY, 202 Parkway Ave S, 55949. (Mail add: PO Box 330, 55949-0330), SAN 376-7892. Tel: 507-467-2649. FAX: 507-467-2346. Web Site: www.lanesboro.lib.mn.us. *Dir,* Tara Johnson; E-mail: tjohnson@selco.info
Founded 1927
Library Holdings: Bk Vols 15,000; Per Subs 25
Wireless access
Partic in Southeastern Libraries Cooperating
Open Mon, Wed & Fri 1-6, Tues & Thurs 2-7, Sat 9-2
Friends of the Library Group

LEROY

P LE ROY PUBLIC LIBRARY*, 605 N Broadway, 55951. (Mail add: PO Box 357, 55951-0357), SAN 347-1993. Tel: 507-324-5641. FAX: 507-324-5641. Web Site: leroy.lib.mn.us. *Dir,* Rhonda Lee Barnes; E-mail: rbarnes@selco.info
Founded 1915. Pop 1,000
Library Holdings: Bk Vols 15,000; Per Subs 29
Wireless access
Partic in Southeastern Libraries Cooperating
Open Mon-Thurs 1-8, Sat 9-1

LINO LAKES

S MINNESOTA DEPARTMENT OF CORRECTIONS*, Minnesota Correctional Facility - Lino Lakes, 7525 Fourth Ave, 55014. Tel: 651-717-6100. FAX: 651-717-6598. Web Site: mn.gov/doc/facilities/lino-lakes. *Librn,* Michael Schneider; Tel: 651-717-6100, Ext 684
Library Holdings: Bk Vols 9,700
Special Collections: Law Coll
Automation Activity & Vendor Info: (Cataloging) Follett Software; (Circulation) Follett Software

LITCHFIELD

P LITCHFIELD PUBLIC LIBRARY, 216 N Marshall Ave, 55355. SAN 320-5274. Tel: 320-693-2483. E-mail: litchfield.staff@pioneerland.lib.mn.us. Web Site: www.ci.litchfield.mn.us/1079/Library, www.litchfield.lib.mn.us. *Head Librn,* Beth Cronk; E-mail: elizabeth.cronk@pioneerland.lib.mn.us; Staff 3 (MLS 1, Non-MLS 2)
Founded 1904. Pop 12,000; Circ 110,000
Library Holdings: AV Mats 1,754; DVDs 274; Large Print Bks 1,057; Per Subs 65; Talking Bks 692; Videos 788
Subject Interests: County hist
Automation Activity & Vendor Info: (Acquisitions) Innovative Interfaces, Inc; (Cataloging) Innovative Interfaces, Inc; (Circulation) Innovative Interfaces, Inc; (ILL) Fretwell-Downing; (OPAC) Innovative Interfaces, Inc; (Serials) Innovative Interfaces, Inc
Wireless access
Mem of Pioneerland Library System
Open Mon-Thurs 10-8, Fri & Sat 10-5
Friends of the Library Group

LITTLE FALLS

S CHARLES A WEYERHAEUSER MEMORIAL MUSEUM*, R D Musser Library, 2151 Lindbergh Dr S, 56345. (Mail add: PO Box 239, 56345-0239), SAN 326-470X. Tel: 320-632-4007. E-mail: contactstaff@morrisoncountyhistory.org. Web Site: www.morrisoncountyhistory.org. *Exec Dir,* Mary Warner; *Presv,* Anne Marie Johnson; Staff 2 (Non-MLS 2)
Founded 1975
Library Holdings: Bk Vols 2,000; Per Subs 8
Special Collections: County Newspapers & Census Materials, micro; Little Falls Transcript 1892-1982, bd vols; Morrison County Record 1969-present
Subject Interests: Genealogy, Local hist
Function: Ref serv available
Open Tues, Wed, Fri & Sat 10-5
Restriction: Non-circulating to the pub

LONG LAKE

S WEST HENNEPIN COUNTY PIONEERS ASSOCIATION LIBRARY*, 1953 W Wayzata Blvd, 55356. (Mail add: PO Box 332, 55356-0332), SAN 326-4416. Tel: 952-473-6557. E-mail: museum@whcpa-museum.org. Web Site: www.whcpa-museum.org. *Interim Pres,* Gary White; Tel: 612-227-6560
Founded 1907
Library Holdings: Bk Titles 600; Per Subs 25
Special Collections: Oral History
Subject Interests: Local hist
Publications: Newsletter (Quarterly)
Open Sat 10-1

LONGVILLE

P MARGARET WELCH MEMORIAL LIBRARY, Longville Library, 5051 State Hwy 84, 56655. (Mail add: PO Box 106, 56655-0106), SAN 347-7878. Tel: 218-363-2710. FAX: 218-363-2710. E-mail: longville@krls.org. Web Site: krls.org/index.php/longville-home-page, longville.com/local/library. *Br Mgr,* Cheryl Martin
Founded 1954. Pop 2,500; Circ 28,000
Library Holdings: AV Mats 500; Bk Titles 15,700; Bk Vols 16,000; Per Subs 30; Talking Bks 504
Subject Interests: Mysteries, World War II
Wireless access
Mem of Kitchigami Regional Library
Open Tues, Thurs & Sat 10-2, Wed & Fri 1-5
Friends of the Library Group

LUVERNE

P ROCK COUNTY COMMUNITY LIBRARY*, 201 W Main, 56156. SAN 308-6151. Tel: 507-449-5040. FAX: 507-449-5034. E-mail: rocklibrarystaff@gmail.com. Web Site: rockcountycommunitylibrary.org.

Dir, Calla Jarvie; E-mail: cjarvie@plumcreeklibrary.net; *Asst Librn,* Barb Verhey; *Ch Serv,* Bronwyn Wenzel; Staff 3 (Non-MLS 3)
Founded 1907. Pop 9,966; Circ 94,001
Library Holdings: Bk Vols 38,000; Per Subs 75
Automation Activity & Vendor Info: (Cataloging) SirsiDynix-WorkFlows; (Circulation) SirsiDynix-WorkFlows; (OPAC) SirsiDynix-iLink
Wireless access
Mem of Plum Creek Library System
Open Mon-Thurs 10-8, Fri 10-5, Sat 10-2
Friends of the Library Group

MABEL

P MABEL PUBLIC LIBRARY*, 110 E Newburg Ave, 55954. (Mail add: PO Box 118, 55954-0118), SAN 308-616X. Tel: 507-493-5336. FAX: 507-493-3336. E-mail: mab_dir@selco.info. Web Site: mabel.lib.mn.us. *Dir,* Donna Johnson; E-mail: donnaj@selco.info
Founded 1920. Pop 900; Circ 5,791
Library Holdings: Bk Titles 8,000
Wireless access
Partic in Southeastern Libraries Cooperating
Open Mon & Wed 2-7, Tues, Thurs & Fri 9-2, Sat 9-12
Friends of the Library Group

MADISON

S LAC QUI PARLE COUNTY HISTORICAL SOCIETY*, Museum Library, 250 Eighth Ave S, 56256. SAN 328-3771. Tel: 320-598-7678. E-mail: lqphistorycenter@lqphc.org. Web Site: lqphc.org. *Curator,* Barb Redepenning
Founded 1948
Library Holdings: Bk Vols 1,500
Function: Res libr
Open Mon-Fri (May-Oct) 10-4, Sat 10-3; Tues-Fri (Nov-April) 10-4

P MADISON PUBLIC LIBRARY*, 401 Sixth Ave, 56256-1236. SAN 347-6979. Tel: 320-598-7938. E-mail: madison.staff@pioneerland.lib.mn.us. Web Site: www.madison.lib.mn.us. *Head Librn,* Deb Lanthier; E-mail: deb.lanthier@pioneerland.lib.mn.us
Founded 1904. Pop 1,930; Circ 37,578
Library Holdings: AV Mats 2,167; CDs 345; DVDs 867; Large Print Bks 475; Bk Vols 23,894; Per Subs 61; Talking Bks 753; Videos 1,236
Wireless access
Mem of Pioneerland Library System
Open Mon & Wed 10-1 & 1:30-5:30, Tues & Thurs 10-1 & 1:30-7:30, Fri & Sat 1:30-5:30

MANKATO

CR BETHANY LUTHERAN COLLEGE MEMORIAL LIBRARY*, 700 Luther Dr, 56001-4490. SAN 308-6194. Tel: 507-344-7000. Interlibrary Loan Service Tel: 507-344-7437. Reference Tel: 507-344-7349. Administration Tel: 507-344-7874. FAX: 507-344-7376. E-mail: library@blc.edu. Web Site: www.blc.edu/library. *Dir, Libr Serv,* Alyssa Inniger; E-mail: alyssa.inniger@blc.edu; *Cat Librn, Tech Serv Librn,* Mae Gagnon; Tel: 507-344-7850; *Library Services, Ref & Instruction Librn,* Jessica Zimmerman; *Circ & ILL Coordr,* Annie Williams; Staff 7 (MLS 2, Non-MLS 5)
Founded 1927. Enrl 592; Fac 48; Highest Degree: Bachelor
Jul 2012-Jun 2013 Income $124,400. Mats Exp $99,400, Books $12,000, Per/Ser (Incl. Access Fees) $18,000, Other Print Mats $10,000, AV Equip $3,000, AV Mat $7,000, Electronic Ref Mat (Incl. Access Fees) $48,900, Presv $500. Sal $185,000 (Prof $55,000)
Library Holdings: Audiobooks 68; AV Mats 5,190; CDs 2,657; DVDs 1,590; e-books 2,725; Electronic Media & Resources 25,000; Music Scores 648; Bk Titles 67,465; Bk Vols 70,469; Per Subs 174; Videos 875
Automation Activity & Vendor Info: (Acquisitions) Ex Libris Group; (Cataloging) Ex Libris Group; (Circulation) Ex Libris Group; (Course Reserve) Ex Libris Group; (ILL) Ex Libris Group; (Media Booking) Ex Libris Group; (OPAC) Ex Libris Group; (Serials) Ex Libris Group
Wireless access
Function: Archival coll, Audio & video playback equip for onsite use, Bks on CD, CD-ROM, Computer training, Computers for patron use, Electronic databases & coll, Free DVD rentals, ILL available, Instruction & testing, Internet access, Learning ctr, Music CDs, Online cat, Online info literacy tutorials on the web & in blackboard, Online ref, Orientations, Photocopying/Printing, Ref serv available, Scanner, Tax forms, VHS videos, Wheelchair accessible
Partic in Minitex; MnPALS
Open Mon-Thurs 8am-11pm, Fri 8-4:30, Sat 1-5, Sun 1-11
Restriction: Borrowing requests are handled by ILL, Non-circulating coll, Non-circulating of rare bks, Open to students, fac, staff & alumni, Photo ID required for access

P BLUE EARTH COUNTY LIBRARY SYSTEM*, 100 E Main St, 56001. SAN 347-4186. Tel: 507-304-4001. Circulation Tel: 507-304-4010. Reference Tel: 507-304-4022. Administration Tel: 507-304-4007. FAX: 507-304-4013. E-mail: library@blueearthcountylibrary.gov. Web Site: www.beclibrary.org. *Dir,* Kelly McBride; E-mail: kelly.mcbride@blueearthcountymn.gov; Staff 2 (MLS 2)
Founded 1902. Pop 55,810; Circ 400,613
Library Holdings: Bk Titles 250,000; Bk Vols 300,000; Per Subs 520
Special Collections: Maud Hart Lovelace Coll; Minnesota Print Material
Automation Activity & Vendor Info: (Cataloging) SirsiDynix; (Circulation) SirsiDynix; (OPAC) SirsiDynix; (Serials) SirsiDynix
Wireless access
Function: AV serv, ILL available, Magnifiers for reading, Orientations, Photocopying/Printing, Prog for adults, Prog for children & young adult, Ref serv available, Spoken cassettes & CDs, VHS videos, Wheelchair accessible
Mem of Traverse Des Sioux Library Cooperative
Open Mon-Fri 10-6, Sat 11-3
Friends of the Library Group
Branches: 2
LAKE CRYSTAL PUBLIC LIBRARY, 100 Robinson St, Lake Crystal, 56055, SAN 347-433X. Tel: 507-726-2726. FAX: 507-726-2265. *Dir,* Kelly McBride; Staff 1 (Non-MLS 1)
Founded 1919. Pop 2,085; Circ 16,465
Open Mon, Tues & Thurs 12-5, Wed & Fri 9-5, Sat 9-Noon
Friends of the Library Group
MAPLETON BRANCH, 104 First Ave, Mapleton, 56065. (Mail add: PO Box 405, Mapleton, 56065). Tel: 507-524-3513. FAX: 507-524-4536. *Dir,* Kelly McBride; Staff 1 (Non-MLS 1)
Founded 1910. Pop 1,515; Circ 5,460
Open Tues & Thurs 1-5, Wed & Fri 1-5 & 6-8, Sat 10-12
Friends of the Library Group
Bookmobiles: 1

C MINNESOTA STATE UNIVERSITY, MANKATO*, Library Services, 601 Maywood Ave, 56001. (Mail add: PO Box 8419 - ML3097, 56002-8419), SAN 308-6216. Tel: 507-389-5952. Circulation Tel: 507-389-5759. Interlibrary Loan Service Tel: 507-389-5959. Reference Tel: 507-389-5958. FAX: 507-389-5155. Web Site: www.lib.mnsu.edu. *Dean, Libr Serv,* Joan Roca; Tel: 507-389-5953, E-mail: joan.roca@mnsu.edu; *Asst Dean,* Leslie M Peterson; Tel: 507-389-2290, E-mail: leslie.peterson-1@mnsu.edu; *Librn, Ref Coordr,* Casey Duevel; *Cat Librn,* Jessica Schomberg; *Faculty Res Librn,* Mark McCullough; *Instrul Serv Librn, Ref Librn,* Kellian Clink; *Media Librn,* Barbara Bergman; *Music Librn,* Lynne Weber; *Ref Librn,* Lisa Baures; *Archivist, Spec Coll Librn,* Daardi Sizemore; *Circ Mgr,* Joni Myers; *Govt Doc,* Evan Rusch; *Info Tech,* Dawn Clyne; Staff 40 (MLS 19, Non-MLS 21)
Founded 1868. Enrl 13,000; Fac 650
Library Holdings: Bk Titles 450,498; Bk Vols 827,341; Per Subs 2,195
Special Collections: Curriculum Materials Coll; Minnesota History (Center for Minnesota Studies Coll); University Archives. Oral History; State Document Depository; US Document Depository
Automation Activity & Vendor Info: (Acquisitions) Ex Libris Group; (Cataloging) Ex Libris Group; (Circulation) Ex Libris Group; (Course Reserve) Ex Libris Group; (ILL) Ex Libris Group; (Media Booking) Ex Libris Group; (OPAC) Ex Libris Group; (Serials) Ex Libris Group
Wireless access
Function: ILL available, Ref serv available
Publications: Quarterly Newsletter
Partic in Minitex; MnPALS; OCLC Online Computer Library Center, Inc; South Central Minnesota Interlibrary Exchange
Special Services for the Blind - Reader equip
Open Mon-Thurs 7:30am-2am, Fri 7:30-7, Sat 10-6, Sun 11am-2am

P TRAVERSE DES SIOUX LIBRARY COOPERATIVE*, 1400 Madison Ave, Ste 622, 56001-5488. SAN 308-6224. Tel: 833-837-5422. E-mail: tds@tds.lib.mn.us. Web Site: tdslib.org. *Exec Dir,* Ann Hokanson; E-mail: ahokanson@tds.lib.mn.us; *Head, Cat, Tech Serv Librn,* Casie Reiner; E-mail: creiner@tds.lib.mn.us; *Syst Librn, Tech Serv & Automation,* Seth Erickson; E-mail: serickson@tds.lib.mn.us; *Tech Librn,* John Miller; E-mail: jmille@tds.lib.mn.us; *Libr Spec,* Connie Haugen; E-mail: chaugen@tds.lib.mn.us; *Outreach Coordr,* Jessica Roschen; E-mail: jroschen@tds.lib.mn.us; *ILL Assoc,* Sara White; E-mail: swhite@tds.lib.mn.us; Staff 11 (MLS 7, Non-MLS 4)
Founded 1975. Pop 220,000
Automation Activity & Vendor Info: (Acquisitions) Innovative Interfaces, Inc - Sierra; (Cataloging) Innovative Interfaces, Inc - Sierra; (Circulation) Innovative Interfaces, Inc - Sierra; (OPAC) Innovative Interfaces, Inc - Sierra; (Serials) Innovative Interfaces, Inc - Sierra
Wireless access
Member Libraries: Arlington Public Library; Blue Earth Community Library; Blue Earth County Library System; Comfrey Area Library; Dyckman Free Library; Elmore Public Library; Gaylord Public Library; Gibbon Public Library; Hanska Community Library; Henderson Public Library; Martin County Library; Martin Luther College Library; Muir

Library; New Ulm Public Library; North Mankato Taylor Library; Saint Peter Public Library; Springfield Public Library; Waseca-Le Sueur Regional Library; Watonwan County Library; Wells Public Library
Open Mon-Fri 8-5

MANTORVILLE

S DODGE COUNTY HISTORICAL SOCIETY LIBRARY*, 615 N Main St, 55955. SAN 373-370X. Tel: 507-635-5508. E-mail: dodgecountyhistoricalsociety@gmail.com.
Library Holdings: Bk Vols 1,000
Subject Interests: Genealogy, Local hist
Wireless access

MARBLE

P MARBLE PUBLIC LIBRARY*, 302 Alice Ave, 55764. (Mail add: PO Box 409, 55764-0409), SAN 308-6232. Tel: 218-247-7676. FAX: 218-247-7676. *Dir,* Tanja Smith; E-mail: Tanja.Smith@alslib.info; *Asst Dir,* Alicia Wikstrom; E-mail: Alicia.Wikstrom@alslib.info
Pop 699
Library Holdings: Bk Vols 17,000
Special Collections: Christian Romances & Inspirational Series; Stephen King, Dean Koontz & Danielle Steel Colls
Wireless access
Mem of Arrowhead Library System
Open Mon & Fri 1-5, Tues & Thurs 1-6, Wed 12-7 (Sept-May); Mon, Tues & Thurs 1-5, Wed 2-7, Fri 10-1 (June-Aug)

MARSHALL

P MARSHALL-LYON COUNTY LIBRARY*, 201 C St, 56258. SAN 347-4488. Tel: 507-537-7003. E-mail: library@marshalllyonlibrary.org. Web Site: www.marshalllyonlibrary.org. *Libr Dir,* Michele Leininger; Tel: 507-337-6183, E-mail: michele.leininger@marshalllyonlibrary.org; *Ch,* Mary Beth Sinclair; Tel: 507-337-6184, E-mail: marybeth.sinclair@marshalllyonlibrary.org; *Pub Serv Mgr,* Paula Nemes; Tel: 507-337-6186, E-mail: paula.nemes@marshalllyonlibrary.org; Staff 6 (MLS 2, Non-MLS 4)
Founded 1886. Pop 21,605; Circ 205,403
Library Holdings: AV Mats 6,218; Bk Vols 81,795; Per Subs 188
Special Collections: Cake Pans
Automation Activity & Vendor Info: (Cataloging) TLC (The Library Corporation); (Circulation) TLC (The Library Corporation); (OPAC) TLC (The Library Corporation)
Wireless access
Mem of Plum Creek Library System
Partic in Association for Rural & Small Libraries
Open Mon-Fri 10-5:30
Friends of the Library Group
Branches: 2
BALATON COMMUNITY, 134 Third St, Balaton, 56115-9451. (Mail add: PO Box 326, Balaton, 56115-0326), SAN 347-4518. Tel: 507-734-2034. FAX: 507-734-2316. *Librn,* Thomas Flynn
Open Mon & Wed 2-7, Fri 12:30-6, Sat 9:30-2
Friends of the Library Group
COTTONWOOD COMMUNITY, 86 W Main St, Cottonwood, 56229. (Mail add: PO Box 106, Cottonwood, 56229-0106), SAN 347-4542. Tel: 507-423-6488. FAX: 507-423-5368. *Librn,* Mary Roseland
Library Holdings: AV Mats 589; Bk Vols 7,092
Open Mon 9-12 & 1-7, Wed & Fri 12-5:30

C SOUTHWEST MINNESOTA STATE UNIVERSITY LIBRARY*, McFarland Library, 1501 State St, 56258. SAN 347-4577. Tel: 507-537-7278. Interlibrary Loan Service Tel: 507-537-6127. Reference Tel: 507-537-6176. FAX: 507-537-6200. Web Site: www.smsu.edu/library. *Dept Chair, Librn,* Pam Gladis; Tel: 507-537-6813, E-mail: pam.gladis@smsu.edu; *Adjunct Fac Librn,* Joann Robasse; Tel: 507-537-6231, E-mail: joann.robasse@smsu.edu; *Coll Mgt Librn, Electronic Res Librn,* Maria Wiggins; Tel: 507-537-6134, E-mail: maria.wiggins@smsu.edu; *Ref Librn,* Chelsea Wyman; Tel: 507-537-6453, E-mail: chelsea.wyman@smsu.edu; *Libr Tech,* Peggy Anderson; Tel: 507-537-6148, E-mail: peggy.anderson@smsu.edu; *Libr Tech,* Elizabeth Fladhamer; Tel: 507-537-6158, E-mail: liz.fladhammer@smsu.edu; *Libr Tech,* Kristi Petersen; Tel: 507-537-6162, E-mail: Kristi.Petersen@smsu.edu; *Libr Tech,* Conni Stensrud; Tel: 507-537-6127, E-mail: conni.stensrud@smsu.edu; Staff 9 (MLS 5, Non-MLS 4)
Founded 1967. Enrl 3,800; Fac 5; Highest Degree: Master
Library Holdings: AV Mats 5,296; e-books 8,166; Bk Vols 197,057; Per Subs 804
Special Collections: Autographs (Z L Begin Coll); Grants-Scholarship Coll; Rare Books Coll. Oral History; US Document Depository
Automation Activity & Vendor Info: (Acquisitions) PALS; (Cataloging) PALS; (Circulation) PALS; (Course Reserve) PALS; (ILL) PALS; (Media Booking) PALS; (OPAC) PALS; (Serials) PALS
Wireless access
Function: Archival coll, Wheelchair accessible
Partic in Minitex; MnPALS; OCLC Online Computer Library Center, Inc

MAYNARD

P MAYNARD PUBLIC LIBRARY*, 331 Mason Ave, 56260. SAN 347-7002. Tel: 320-367-2143. FAX: 320-367-2143. Web Site: www.maynard.lib.mn.us. *Head Librn,* Gloria Sims; E-mail: gloria.sims@pioneerland.lib.mn.us; Staff 1 (Non-MLS 1)
Pop 388; Circ 9,611
Library Holdings: Bk Vols 10,000; Per Subs 19
Automation Activity & Vendor Info: (Cataloging) Innovative Interfaces, Inc; (Circulation) Innovative Interfaces, Inc; (OPAC) Innovative Interfaces, Inc
Wireless access
Mem of Pioneerland Library System
Open Mon, Tues & Thurs 1-5:30, Wed 1-7:30

MILAN

P MILAN PUBLIC LIBRARY*, 235 Main St, 56262. (Mail add: PO Box 187, 56262-0187), SAN 347-7037. Tel: 320-734-4792. FAX: 320-734-4792. E-mail: milan.staff@pioneerland.lib.mn.us. Web Site: www.milan.lib.mn.us. *Head Librn,* Larissa Schwenk
Pop 341; Circ 9,167
Library Holdings: Bk Vols 9,335; Per Subs 16
Automation Activity & Vendor Info: (Cataloging) Innovative Interfaces, Inc; (Circulation) Innovative Interfaces, Inc; (OPAC) Innovative Interfaces, Inc
Wireless access
Mem of Pioneerland Library System
Open Tues-Fri 2-6, Sat 9-1
Friends of the Library Group

MINNEAPOLIS

M ALLINA HEALTH LIBRARY SERVICES*, Abbott Northwestern Hospital, 800 E 28th St, Mail Stop 11008, 55407. SAN 308-6917. Tel: 612-863-4312. FAX: 612-863-5695. E-mail: library.services@allina.com. *Mgr,* Jim Bulger
Founded 1943
Subject Interests: Cardiology, Neurology, Nursing, Pediatrics, Perinatology, Rehabilitation med, Spinal cord injury
Wireless access
Open Mon-Fri 8-4:30
Restriction: Open to pub for ref only

S AMERICAN CRAFT COUNCIL LIBRARY, 1224 Marshall St NE, Ste 200, 55413. SAN 311-5755. Tel: 612-206-3118. FAX: 612-355-2330. E-mail: library@craftcouncil.org. Web Site: craftcouncil.org/library. *Librn & Archivist,* Beth Goodrich; E-mail: bgoodrich@craftcouncil.org. Subject Specialists: *Digital media, Info mgt,* Beth Goodrich; Staff 1 (MLS 1)
Founded 1956
Library Holdings: AV Mats 230; DVDs 75; Bk Titles 17,000; Bk Vols 20,000; Per Subs 99; Videos 225
Special Collections: American Craft Council Archives (1940-Present); Craft Artist Files; Craft Students League of New York Archives (1920s-2005); Museum of Contemporary Craft/American Craft Museum Archives (1956-1990); World Craft Council Archives (1964-2006)
Subject Interests: Am, Contemporary, Craft
Automation Activity & Vendor Info: (Cataloging) OCLC Connexion; (Discovery) OCLC FirstSearch; (OPAC) Koha; (Serials) EBSCO Discovery Service
Wireless access
Function: Archival coll, Art exhibits, Online cat, Ref & res, Ref serv available
Publications: Crafty Librarian (Newsletter)
Open Mon-Fri 10-4 by appointment
Restriction: Open to pub for ref only
Friends of the Library Group

S AMERICAN SWEDISH INSTITUTE*, Wallenberg Library & Archives, 2600 Park Ave, 55407. SAN 308-6291. Tel: 612-871-4907. FAX: 612-871-8682. E-mail: info@asimn.org. Web Site: www.asimn.org/exhibitions-collections/library-and-archives. *Chief Exec Officer, Pres,* Bruce N Karstadt; *Colls Mgr,* Inga Theissen; E-mail: ingat@asimn.org; Staff 1 (MLS 1)
Founded 1929
Library Holdings: Bk Vols 17,000; Per Subs 2
Special Collections: Swedish History & Literature (Swan J Turnblad Library); Swedish Immigration History Coll (Victor Lawson Coll); Turnblad Lending Library
Subject Interests: Swedish hist
Open Wed 4-8, Fri 12-4, Sat 10-2
Restriction: Closed stack, Non-circulating

C AUGSBURG UNIVERSITY*, Lindell Library, 2211 Riverside Ave, 55454. SAN 308-6305. Tel: 612-330-1604. Circulation Tel: 612-330-1017. Web Site: library.augsburg.edu. *Dir, Libr Serv,* Mary Hollerich; E-mail: holleric@augsburg.edu; *Ref & 1st Year Learning Experience Librn,* Stacy Cutinella; *Ref & Pub Serv Librn,* William Wittenbreer; *Circ, Syst Librn,* Mike Bloomberg; *Coll Mgt,* Ron Kurpiers; Staff 8 (MLS 8)
Founded 1869. Enrl 3,317; Fac 211; Highest Degree: Master
Library Holdings: Bk Vols 185,000; Per Subs 620
Special Collections: Meridel LeSueur Papers; Modern Scandinavian Music, rec, tapes & scores
Automation Activity & Vendor Info: (Circulation) Innovative Interfaces, Inc
Wireless access
Partic in Minitex; MnPALS; OCLC Online Computer Library Center, Inc
Open Mon-Thurs 7:45am-Midnight, Fri 7:45-6:30, Sat 10-6, Sun 2pm-Midnight

S THE BAKKEN MUSEUM, The Bakken Library of Electricity in Life, 3537 Zenith Ave S, 55416. SAN 326-4459. Tel: 612-926-3878. Reference Tel: 612-926-3878, Ext 201. FAX: 612-927-7265. Web Site: thebakken.org. *Pres & Chief Exec Officer,* Michael Sanders; *Exhibits Curator, Spec Coll,* Adrian Fischer; E-mail: fischer@thebakken.org; *Asst Curator,* Nicholas Williams; E-mail: williams@thebakken.org; Staff 2 (Non-MLS 2)
Founded 1975
Library Holdings: Bk Vols 12,000; Per Subs 3
Special Collections: Instrument Coll
Subject Interests: Hist of electricity, Hist of magnetism, Hist of med, Hist of sci
Wireless access
Function: Ref serv available, Res libr
Partic in OCLC Online Computer Library Center, Inc
Open Mon-Fri 10-4
Restriction: Not a lending libr

§CR BETHLEHEM COLLEGE & SEMINARY LIBRARY, 720 13th Ave S, 55415. Tel: 612-455-3420. E-mail: library.requests@bcsmn.edu. Web Site: bcsmn.edu/academics, bcsmn.libguides.com. *Head Librn,* Barbara Winters; E-mail: barbara.winters@bcsmn.edu
Library Holdings: Bk Vols 10,000
Wireless access
Partic in Minnesota Theological Library Association
Open Mon-Thurs 7am-9pm, Fri 7-5, Sat 9-5
Restriction: Not a lending libr

L BOWMAN & BROOKE*, Law Library, 150 S Fifth St, Ste 3000, 55402. SAN 372-0500. Tel: 612-339-8682. FAX: 612-672-3200. Web Site: www.bowmanandbrooke.com. *Librn,* Donna Trimble; E-mail: donna.trimble@bowmanandbrooke.com
Wireless access
Restriction: Staff use only

M A CHANCE TO GROW*, Kretsch Brain Resource Library, 1800 Second St NE, 55418. SAN 370-3282. Tel: 612-789-1236. FAX: 612-706-5555. E-mail: actg@actg.org. Web Site: actg.org. *Dir,* Position Currently Open
Library Holdings: Bk Vols 2,000
Open Mon-Fri 9-4

GM DEPARTMENT OF VETERANS AFFAIRS*, Medical Center Library, One Veterans Dr, Mail Stop 142 D, 55417. SAN 308-6976. Tel: 612-467-4200. *Lead Librn, Tech Serv, Ref & Instruction,* Brian Conn; E-mail: brian.conn@va.gov; *Patient Educ Librn,* Thomas Keeler; E-mail: Thomas.Keeler@va.gov; *Libr Tech,* Michele Mackey; E-mail: michele.mackey@va.gov. Subject Specialists: *Consumer health info,* Thomas Keeler; Staff 3 (MLS 2, Non-MLS 1)
Special Collections: Medical AV Coll; Patient Education
Subject Interests: Allied health, Hospital admin, Med, Nursing
Automation Activity & Vendor Info: (Circulation) EOS International; (Discovery) EOS International; (OPAC) EOS International
Wireless access
Open Mon-Fri 7:30-4:30
Branches:
PATIENT EDUCATION LIBRARY, One Veterans Dr,Mail Stop 142D1, 55417. Tel: 612-467-4212. *Patient Educ Librn,* Thomas Keeler; E-mail: Thomas.Keeler@va.gov. Subject Specialists: *Consumer health,* Thomas Keeler; Staff 1 (MLS 1)
Founded 1978
Subject Interests: Patient health educ

L DORSEY & WHITNEY*, Information Resource Center, 50 S Sixth St, 55402. SAN 308-6402. Tel: 612-340-2600. FAX: 612-492-2868. Web Site: www.dorsey.com. *Dir,* Jan Rivers; E-mail: rivers.jan@dorsey.com; Staff 33 (MLS 10, Non-MLS 23)
Library Holdings: Bk Vols 60,000; Per Subs 400
Restriction: Not open to pub

J DUNWOODY COLLEGE OF TECHNOLOGY*, John A Butler Learning Resource Center, 818 Dunwoody Blvd, 55403. SAN 308-6410. Tel: 612-374-5800. Web Site: www.dunwoody.edu/library. *Head Librn,* Marcus Seraphine; Tel: 612-381-3306, E-mail: mseraphine@dunwoody.edu; *Librn,* Kristina Oberstar; Tel: 612-381-3345, E-mail: koberstar@dunwoody.edu
Library Holdings: Bk Vols 10,000; Per Subs 150
Wireless access
Partic in MnPALS
Open Mon-Fri 6:30am-9pm

L FAEGRE BAKER DANIELS*, Information Resources, 2200 Wells Fargo Ctr, 90 South Seventh St, 55402-3901. SAN 308-6437. Tel: 612-766-7000. Toll Free Tel: 800-328-4393. FAX: 612-766-1600. *Law Librn,* Constance Matts
Automation Activity & Vendor Info: (Acquisitions) SydneyPlus
Restriction: Staff use only

S FEDERAL RESERVE BANK OF MINNEAPOLIS*, Research Information Services, 90 Hennepin Ave, 55401. (Mail add: PO Box 291, 55480-0291), SAN 308-6461. Tel: 612-204-5000. E-mail: mpls.research.info.svcs@mpls.frb.org. *Dir,* Brooke Tosi
Founded 1940
Library Holdings: Bk Vols 15,000; Per Subs 2,000
Special Collections: Federal Reserve System Publications Coll
Subject Interests: Econ, Finance, Monetary policy
Automation Activity & Vendor Info: (ILL) OCLC
Wireless access
Restriction: Open by appt only, Staff use only

L FELHABER, LARSON, FENLON & VOGT*, Law Library, 220 S Sixth St, Ste 2200, 55402-4302. SAN 372-2864. Tel: 612-339-6321. FAX: 612-338-0535. Web Site: www.felhaber.com. *Librn,* Annette C Borer; Tel: 612-373-8441
Library Holdings: Bk Vols 10,500; Per Subs 107

R FIRST BAPTIST CHURCH LIBRARY*, 1021 Hennepin Ave, 55403. SAN 308-647X. Tel: 612-332-3651. FAX: 612-332-3661. Web Site: fbcminneapolis.org. *Library Contact,* Mary Krizon
Library Holdings: Bk Vols 3,000
Special Collections: Commentaries & Sermons (Dr W B Riley, founder of Northwestern Bible College)
Open Sun 9am-11am

L FREDRIKSON & BRYON*, Law Library, 200 S Sixth St, Ste 4000, 55402. SAN 372-0519. Tel: 612-492-7000. FAX: 612-492-7077. Web Site: www.fredlaw.com. *Dir, Libr & Res Serv,* Jeanette Woessner; E-mail: jwoessner@fredlaw.com; Staff 7 (MLS 6, Non-MLS 1)
Library Holdings: Bk Vols 20,000; Per Subs 300
Wireless access

GENERAL MILLS, INC

S JAMES FORD BELL LIBRARY & INFORMATION SERVICES*, 9000 Plymouth Ave N, 55427, SAN 347-4666. Tel: 763-764-6460. Interlibrary Loan Service Tel: 763-764-2761. FAX: 763-764-3166. *Dir, Knowledge Discovery Serv,* Fred Hulting
Founded 1961
Library Holdings: Bk Titles 18,000; Bk Vols 20,000; Per Subs 750
Subject Interests: Food sci
Automation Activity & Vendor Info: (Acquisitions) Sydney; (Cataloging) Sydney; (Circulation) Sydney; (OPAC) Sydney; (Serials) Sydney
Partic in Dow Jones News Retrieval; OCLC Online Computer Library Center, Inc; Proquest Dialog
Publications: Foods Adlibra; Internal newsletters; Periodical Holdings List (Annual)
Restriction: Not open to pub

S BUSINESS INFORMATION CENTER*, One General Mills Blvd, 55426-1347, SAN 347-4631. Tel: 763-764-5461. Web Site: www.generalmills.com. *Sr Assoc,* Gail Wolfson; Staff 2 (MLS 1, Non-MLS 1)
Founded 1965
Library Holdings: Bk Vols 1,500; Per Subs 200
Subject Interests: Consumerism, Food indust
Automation Activity & Vendor Info: (Acquisitions) SydneyPlus; (Cataloging) SydneyPlus; (Circulation) SydneyPlus; (OPAC) SydneyPlus; (Serials) SydneyPlus
Restriction: Not open to pub

L GRAY, PLANT, MOOTY*, Law Library, 500 IDS Ctr, 80 S Eighth St, 55402. SAN 329-9678. Tel: 612-632-3000. Web Site: www.gpmlaw.com. *Res Spec,* Teresa Myers; Staff 3 (MLS 2, Non-MLS 1)
Library Holdings: Bk Titles 2,000; Per Subs 150

Subject Interests: Law
Wireless access
Restriction: Staff use only

GL HENNEPIN COUNTY LAW LIBRARY, Anne W Grande Law Library, C-2451 Government Ctr, 300 S Sixth St, 55487. SAN 308-6526. Tel: 612-348-3022. Circulation Tel: 612-348-3024. Reference Tel: 612-348-2903. FAX: 612-632-8773. Reference E-mail: law.library@hennepin.us. Web Site: hclawlib.org. *Dir,* Karen Westwood; Tel: 612-348-7977, E-mail: karen.westwood@hennepin.us; *Law Librn,* Richard Harrington; Tel: 612-348-2952, E-mail: richard.harrington@hennepin.us; *Ref Librn,* Edward W Carroll; Tel: 612-348-8860, E-mail: edward.carroll@hennepin.us; Staff 4 (MLS 3, Non-MLS 1)
Founded 1883
Automation Activity & Vendor Info: (OPAC) Koha
Wireless access
Function: 24/7 Electronic res, 24/7 Online cat, Computers for patron use, Electronic databases & coll, Internet access, Mail & tel request accepted, Microfiche/film & reading machines, Notary serv, Online cat, Photocopying/Printing, Ref serv available, Wheelchair accessible
Open Mon-Fri 8-5
Restriction: Circ limited

M HENNEPIN COUNTY MEDICAL CENTER*, Medical Library Services, Mail Code R2, 701 Park Ave, 55415. SAN 308-6585. Tel: 612-873-2710. Reference Tel: 612-873-2714. FAX: 612-904-4248. *Med Librn,* Danielle Becker; E-mail: danielle.becker@hcmed.org; *Circ, ILL,* Paul Reid; E-mail: paul.reid@hcmed.org; *Ser,* Bonnie Moore; Tel: 612-873-2711, E-mail: bonnie.moore@hcmed.org; Staff 3 (MLS 1, Non-MLS 2)
Founded 1976
Jul 2014-Jun 2015. Mats Exp $645,000
Library Holdings: e-books 165; e-journals 2,000; Bk Titles 7,700; Bk Vols 8,000; Per Subs 530; Videos 144
Subject Interests: Clinical med
Automation Activity & Vendor Info: (Cataloging) CyberTools for Libraries; (Circulation) CyberTools for Libraries; (OPAC) CyberTools for Libraries; (Serials) CyberTools for Libraries
Wireless access
Function: Computers for patron use, Doc delivery serv, Electronic databases & coll, Health sci info serv, Internet access, Learning ctr, Online cat, Orientations
Partic in Health Scis Librs of Minn; Minitex; OCLC Online Computer Library Center, Inc
Open Mon-Fri 8-5
Restriction: Med staff only, Open to staff, patients & family mem, Open to students, fac & staff, Residents only

S HENNEPIN HISTORY MUSEUM LIBRARY, 2303 Third Ave S, 55404-3599. SAN 326-5773. Tel: 612-870-1329. FAX: 612-870-1320. E-mail: history@hennepinhistory.org. Web Site: hennepinhistory.org. *Archivist,* Michele Pollard
Library Holdings: Bk Vols 1,300
Special Collections: Historic Photographs; Manuscripts
Subject Interests: Civil War hist
Publications: Hennepin History Magazine (Periodical)
Open Tues 10-2, Wed, Fri & Sat 1-5, Thurs 1-8

R HOLY TRINITY LUTHERAN CHURCH LIBRARY, 2730 E 31st St, 55406. SAN 308-6542. Tel: 612-729-8358. E-mail: office@htlcmpls.org. Web Site: www.htlcmpls.org. *Library Contact,* Roberta Shaw
Founded 1963
Library Holdings: Bk Vols 5,000
Subject Interests: Soc justice, Spiritual life, Theol
Wireless access

S JEWISH COMMUNITY RELATIONS COUNCIL*, 12 N 12th St, Ste 480, 55403. SAN 327-8212. Tel: 612-338-7816. FAX: 612-349-6569. E-mail: info@minndakjcrc.org. Web Site: www.minndakjcrc.org. *Exec Dir,* Steve Hunegs
Library Holdings: Bk Vols 100
Open Mon-Fri 9-5

L LARKIN, HOFFMAN, DALY & LINDGREN*, Law Library, 8300 Norman Center Dr, Ste 1000, 55437-1060. SAN 372-283X. Tel: 952-835-3800. FAX: 952-896-3333. Web Site: larkinhoffman.com. *Dir, Res Serv,* Patrick Butler; E-mail: pbutler@larkinhoffman.com
Library Holdings: Bk Vols 15,000; Per Subs 125
Wireless access
Open Mon-Fri 8:30-5

C MINNEAPOLIS COLLEGE OF ART & DESIGN LIBRARY*, 2501 Stevens Ave, 55404-3593. SAN 308-6674. Tel: 612-874-3791. FAX: 612-874-3704. E-mail: library@mcad.edu. Web Site: mcad.edu/facilities-and-services/library. *Libr Dir,* Amy Naughton; Tel: 612-874-3752, E-mail: amy_naughton@mcad.edu; *Tech Serv Librn,* Kay Kroeff-Streng; Tel: 612-874-3734, E-mail: kay_streng@mcad.edu; *Circ Coordr,* Dan Leanio; E-mail: dan_leanio@mcad.edu; *Visual Res,* Allan Kohl; Tel: 612-874-3781, E-mail: allan_kohl@mcad.edu; Staff 5.8 (MLS 3.1, Non-MLS 2.7)
Founded 1886. Enrl 772; Fac 125; Highest Degree: Master
Library Holdings: CDs 221; DVDs 331; Bk Titles 45,760; Bk Vols 54,700; Per Subs 115; Videos 1,000
Special Collections: Artists Books; College Archives
Subject Interests: Contemporary art
Automation Activity & Vendor Info: (Cataloging) Ex Libris Group; (Circulation) Ex Libris Group; (Course Reserve) Ex Libris Group; (ILL) Ex Libris Group; (OPAC) Ex Libris Group
Wireless access
Publications: Accessions List
Partic in Minitex; MnPALS
Open Mon-Thurs 9am-10pm, Fri 9-5, Sat 12-5, Sun 12-7
Restriction: Circ limited

J MINNEAPOLIS COMMUNITY & TECHNICAL COLLEGE LIBRARY*, Wheelock Whitney Hall, 1501 Hennepin Ave, 55403. SAN 308-664X. Tel: 612-659-6290. E-mail: circdesk@minneapolis.edu. Web Site: library.minneapolis.edu. *Libr Tech,* Cory Cain; Tel: 612-659-6297, E-mail: cory.cain@minneapolis.edu; *Libr Tech,* John Daniels; E-mail: john.daniels@minneapolis.edu; *Ref Serv,* Kathleen Daniels; Tel: 612-659-6285; *Ref Serv,* Jane Jurgens; Tel: 612-659-6287; Staff 10 (MLS 6, Non-MLS 4)
Founded 1965. Enrl 10,000; Highest Degree: Associate
Library Holdings: Bk Titles 65,000; Per Subs 600
Special Collections: Alternative & Small Press Coll, bks, cd's, dvd's, periodicals, zines
Wireless access
Partic in Minitex; Minn Interlibr; MnPALS

S MINNEAPOLIS INSTITUTE OF ART*, Art Research & Reference Library, 2400 Third Ave S, 55404. SAN 308-6682. Tel: 612-870-3117. Toll Free Tel: 888-642-2787. FAX: 612-870-3004. Web Site: new.artsmia.org/visit/museum-library. *Head Librn,* Janice Lurie; E-mail: jlurie@artsmia.org; Staff 2 (MLS 2)
Founded 1915
Library Holdings: Bk Titles 65,000; Per Subs 120
Special Collections: Botany & Fashion (Minnich Coll); Five Hundred Years of Sporting Books (John Daniels Coll), drawings; History of Printing (Leslie Coll)
Subject Interests: Art hist, Chinese bronzes, Drawing, English silver, Furniture, Jades, Painting, Prints, Sculpture, Textiles
Automation Activity & Vendor Info: (Cataloging) OCLC Worldshare Management Services; (Circulation) OCLC Worldshare Management Services
Wireless access
Publications: Arts; Surrealism: Beyond the Printed Word; The Minneapolis Institute of Art Research & Reference Library: History & Guide; Villa I Tatti
Open Tues-Fri 11:30-4:30
Restriction: Non-circulating to the pub, Pub use on premises
Friends of the Library Group

C NORTH CENTRAL UNIVERSITY LIBRARY*, T J Jones Library, 915 E 14th St, 55404. (Mail add: 910 Elliot Ave, 55404-1391), SAN 308-6798. Tel: 612-343-4490. FAX: 612-343-8069. E-mail: library@northcentral.edu. Web Site: www.northcentral.edu/library. *Dir, Libr Serv,* Judy Pruitt; Tel: 612-343-4491, E-mail: japruitt@northcentral.edu; Staff 3 (MLS 2, Non-MLS 1)
Founded 1930. Enrl 1,135; Fac 41; Highest Degree: Master
Library Holdings: Bks on Deafness & Sign Lang 117; DVDs 891; e-books 16,167; Bk Vols 78,717
Special Collections: Pentecostal Studies
Automation Activity & Vendor Info: (Acquisitions) OCLC Worldshare Management Services; (Cataloging) OCLC Worldshare Management Services; (Circulation) OCLC Worldshare Management Services; (Course Reserve) OCLC Worldshare Management Services; (Discovery) OCLC Worldshare Management Services; (ILL) OCLC WorldShare Interlibrary Loan; (OPAC) OCLC Worldshare Management Services; (Serials) OCLC Worldshare Management Services
Wireless access
Partic in Christian Library Consortium; Minitex; OCLC Online Computer Library Center, Inc
Open Mon-Thurs 7am-11pm, Fri 7-5, Sat 1-5, Sun 7pm-11pm

S QUATREFOIL LIBRARY, 1220 E Lake St, 55407. SAN 329-1588. Tel: 612-729-2543. E-mail: info@qlibrary.org. Web Site: www.qlibrary.org. *Librn,* Kathy Robbins
Founded 1986

Library Holdings: CDs 100; DVDs 4,000; Bk Vols 20,000; Per Subs 40; Videos 20
Subject Interests: Bisexual, Gay & lesbian, Queer, Transgender
Automation Activity & Vendor Info: (Cataloging) LibraryWorld, Inc; (Circulation) LibraryWorld, Inc; (OPAC) LibraryWorld, Inc
Wireless access
Publications: Quatrefolio (Newsletter)
Open Mon, Tues, Thurs & Fri 7pm-9pm, Wed 1-5 & 7-9, Sat & Sun 10-5

R SAINT OLAF LUTHERAN CHURCH, Carlsen Memorial Library, 2901 Emerson Ave N, 55411. SAN 308-6909. Tel: 612-529-7726. FAX: 612-529-4385. Web Site: stolaflutheran.wordpress.com. *Library Contact,* Rev Dale Hulme; E-mail: pastor@stolaflutheran.org
Founded 1963
Library Holdings: Bk Titles 1,750

S SONS OF NORWAY, Heritage Library, 1455 W Lake St, 55408. SAN 308-6925. Tel: 612-827-3611. Toll Free Tel: 800-945-8851. FAX: 612-827-0658. E-mail: culture@sofn.com. Web Site: www.sofn.com. *Librn,* Jana Velo; E-mail: jvelo@sofn.com
Founded 1962
Library Holdings: Bk Titles 1,000; Bk Vols 2,500
Special Collections: Norwegian-American Culture & Immigration Coll
Wireless access
Open Mon-Thurs 7:30-5, Fri 8-Noon
Friends of the Library Group

S STAR TRIBUNE*, News Research Library, 650 Thurd Ave S, Ste 1300, 55488. SAN 308-6690. Tel: 612-673-4375, 612-673-7759. FAX: 612-673-4359. Web Site: www.startribune.com. *Library Contact, Researcher,* John Wareham; E-mail: john.wareham@startribune.com
Founded 1946
Library Holdings: Bk Vols 1,000
Wireless access
Restriction: Not open to pub, Staff use only

L STINSON LLP*, Law Library, 50 S Sixth St, 55402. SAN 372-0527. Tel: 612-335-1500. E-mail: research.services@stinson.com. Web Site: www.stinson.com. *Dir, Res Serv,* Stephanie DeClue; Staff 10 (MLS 5, Non-MLS 5)
Library Holdings: Bk Vols 15,000; Per Subs 150
Open Mon-Fri 8-5

L TAFT, STETTINIUS & HOLLISTER LLP*, Law Library, 2200 IDS Ctr, 80 S Eighth St, 55402. SAN 372-2856. Tel: 612-977-8400. FAX: 612-977-8650. E-mail: briggs@briggs.com. Web Site: www.taftlaw.com. *Ref Serv Mgr, Research Librn,* Chris Sexton; Staff 3 (MLS 2, Non-MLS 1)
Automation Activity & Vendor Info: (Cataloging) Inmagic, Inc.
Open Mon-Fri 8-5

R TEMPLE ISRAEL LIBRARY*, 2324 Emerson Ave S, 55405. SAN 308-6933. Tel: 612-377-8680. FAX: 612-377-6630. E-mail: info@templeisrael.com. Web Site: templeisrael.com. *Librn,* Georgia Kalman; Tel: 612-374-0355, E-mail: gkalman@templeisrael.com; Staff 2 (MLS 1, Non-MLS 1)
Founded 1929
Library Holdings: Bk Titles 15,000; Per Subs 20
Subject Interests: Art, Childrens' bks, Fiction, Hist, Holocaust
Open Mon-Thurs 2-5, Sat & Sun 9-12

G UNITED STATES COURT OF APPEALS*, Branch Library, 1102 US Courthouse, 300 S Fourth St, Rm 1102, 55415. SAN 325-4348. Tel: 612-664-5830. E-mail: library8th@ca8.uscourts.gov. Web Site: lb8.uscourts.gov:444/aboutus/minneapolis.htm. *Br Librn,* Andrea Wambach; E-mail: Andrea_Wambach@ca8.uscourts.gov; Staff 1.5 (MLS 1, Non-MLS 0.5)
Library Holdings: Bk Vols 28,000; Per Subs 25
Open Mon-Fri 8:30-5
Restriction: Limited access for the pub, Ref only to non-staff, Restricted borrowing privileges

C UNIVERSITY OF MINNESOTA LIBRARIES-TWIN CITIES*, 499 Wilson Library, 309 19th Ave S, 55455. SAN 347-5298. Tel: 612-624-3321. FAX: 612-626-9353. Web Site: www.lib.umn.edu. *Univ Librn & Dean of Libr,* Lisa Pradt German; E-mail: lgerman@umn.edu; *Assoc Univ Librn, Info Tech,* John Butler; E-mail: j-butl@umn.edu
Founded 1851. Enrl 47,568; Fac 3,911; Highest Degree: Doctorate
Library Holdings: Bk Vols 6,587,430; Per Subs 43,303
Special Collections: African-American Literature & Life (Givens Coll); Berman Upper Midwest Jewish Archives; British-Indian Interaction (Ames Library of South Asia); Children's Literature Research Coll; Gay, Lesbian, Bisexual & Transgender (Jean-Nickolaus Tretter Coll); History of European Expansion Prior to 1800 (James Ford Bell Library); History of Immigration from Eastern & Southeastern Europe (Immigration History Research Center); History of Information Processing (Charles Babbage Institute); History of Photomechanics (Mertle Coll); Kautz Family YMCA Archives; Literary Manuscripts Coll; Northwest Architectural Archives; Performing Arts Archives; Plants, Plant Cultivation, Landscape Architecture (Andersen Horticultural Library); Sherlock Holmes Coll; Social Welfare History Archives; Swedish Americana (Dahllof Coll); University of Minnesota Archives; Wangensteen Historical Library of Biology & Medicine. State Document Depository; UN Document Depository; US Document Depository
Automation Activity & Vendor Info: (Acquisitions) Ex Libris Group; (Cataloging) Ex Libris Group; (Circulation) Ex Libris Group; (Course Reserve) Ex Libris Group; (ILL) OCLC; (OPAC) Ex Libris Group; (Serials) Ex Libris Group
Wireless access
Publications: Continuum (Periodical)
Partic in Association of Research Libraries; Big Ten Academic Alliance; Council of Independent Colleges; Digital Libr Fedn; Minitex; OCLC Online Computer Library Center, Inc; OCLC Research Library Partnership
Friends of the Library Group

Departmental Libraries:

AMES LIBRARY OF SOUTH ASIA, S-10 Wilson Library, 309 19th Ave S, 55455, SAN 347-5719. Tel: 612-624-4857. FAX: 612-626-9353. Web Site: lib.umn.edu/ames. *Librn,* Dr David Faust; Tel: 612-624-5801, E-mail: faust011@umn.edu; Staff 1 (MLS 1)

ANDERSEN HORTICULTURAL LIBRARY, 3675 Arboretum Dr, Chaska, 55318, SAN 378-0759. Tel: 612-301-1239. E-mail: HortLib@umn.edu. Web Site: www.lib.umn.edu/ahl. *Librn,* Katherine Allen; E-mail: kallen@umn.edu
Open Tues-Fri 8:30-4:30, Sat 10:30-4:30
Friends of the Library Group

ARCHITECTURE & LANDSCAPE ARCHITECTURE LIBRARY, 210 Rapson Hall, 89 Church St SE, 55455, SAN 329-756X. Tel: 612-624-6383. FAX: 612-625-5597. E-mail: arlalib@umn.edu. Web Site: lib.umn.edu/architecture. *Librn,* Deborah K Ultan; E-mail: ultan004@umn.edu. Subject Specialists: *Archit, Art, Performing arts,* Deborah K Ultan
Open Mon-Thurs 9-9, Fri 9-6, Sat & Sun 1-5

ARCHIVES & SPECIAL COLLECTIONS, Elmer L Andersen Library, 222 21st Ave S, Ste 111, 55455, SAN 347-6731. Tel: 612-624-7469. E-mail: ascref@umn.edu. Web Site: lib.umn.edu/special. *Assoc Librn, Curator,* Timothy Johnson; E-mail: johns976@umn.edu

CHARLES BABBAGE INSTITUTE, 211 Elmer L Andersen Library, 222 21st Ave S, 55455, SAN 371-3083. Tel: 612-624-5050. FAX: 612-625-8054. E-mail: cbi@umn.edu. Web Site: www.cbi.umn.edu. *Archivist,* Amanda Wick; E-mail: abwick@umn.edu

JAMES FORD BELL LIBRARY, Elmer L Andersen Library, 222 21st Ave S, Ste 15, 55455, SAN 347-5328. Tel: 612-624-1528. FAX: 612-626-9353. E-mail: jfbell@umn.edu. Web Site: lib.umn.edu/bell. *Curator,* Dr Marguerite Ragnow; E-mail: ragn0001@umn.edu
Friends of the Library Group

CM BIO-MEDICAL LIBRARY, Diehl Hall, 505 Essex St SE, 55455, SAN 347-5352. Tel: 612-626-4045. FAX: 612-626-5822. E-mail: medref@umn.edu. Web Site: hsl.lib.umn.edu/biomed. *Assoc Univ Librn, Dir,* Janice Jaguszewski; Tel: 612-626-7039, E-mail: j-jagu@umn.edu; Staff 42 (MLS 13, Non-MLS 29)

JOHN R BORCHERT MAP LIBRARY, S-76 Wilson Library, 309 19th Ave S, 55455, SAN 347-6642. Tel: 612-624-4549. FAX: 612-626-9353. E-mail: mapref@umn.edu. Web Site: lib.umn.edu/borchert. *Head of Libr, Maps Librn,* Ryan Mattke; E-mail: matt0089@umn.edu

CHILDREN'S LITERATURE RESEARCH COLLECTIONS, Elmer L Andersen Library, 222 21st Ave S, Ste 113, 55455, SAN 347-6103. Tel: 612-624-4576. FAX: 612-626-0377. E-mail: asc-clrc@umn.edu. Web Site: lib.umn.edu/clrc. *Curator,* Lisa Von Drasek; E-mail: lvondras@umn.edu
Open Mon, Tues & Fri 8:30-4:30, Wed & Thurs 8:30-7

EAST ASIAN LIBRARY, S-75 Wilson Library, 309 19th Ave S, 55455, SAN 347-657X. Tel: 612-624-5863. Web Site: lib.umn.edu/eastasian. *Librn,* Yao Chen; E-mail: chen3200@umn.edu

IMMIGRATION HISTORY RESEARCH CENTER ARCHIVES, Elmer L Andersen Library, 222 21st Ave S, Ste 311, 55455, SAN 378-0996. Tel: 612-625-4800. FAX: 612-626-0018. E-mail: ihrc@umn.edu. Web Site: cla.umn.edu/ihrc. *Actg Dir,* Yuichiro Onishi; E-mail: ohni0001@umn.edu
Open Mon-Fri 8:30-11:30 & 12:30-4:30
Friends of the Library Group

CL LAW LIBRARY, 120 Mondale Hall, 229 19th Ave S, 55455, SAN 378-1046. Tel: 612-625-4300. Interlibrary Loan Service Tel: 612-625-9534. Reference Tel: 612-625-4309. FAX: 612-625-3478. E-mail: law-ref@umn.edu. Web Site: www.law.umn.edu/library. *Assoc Dean, Info Tech,* Joan Howland; E-mail: howla001@umn.edu
Special Collections: The Papers of Clarence Darrow

MAGRATH LIBRARY, 1984 Buford Ave, Saint Paul, 55108. Tel: 612-624-2233. Web Site: www.lib.umn.edu/magrath. *Dir,* Philip Herold; Tel: 612-624-2779, E-mail: herol008@umn.edu

MATHEMATICS LIBRARY, 310 Vincent Hall, 206 Church St SE, 55455, SAN 347-5891. Tel: 612-624-6075. FAX: 612-624-4302. E-mail: library@math.umn.edu. Web Site: lib.umn.edu/math. *Librn,* Kristine Fowler; E-mail: fowle013@umn.edu; Staff 4 (MLS 1, Non-MLS 3)

MUSIC LIBRARY, 70 Ferguson Hall, 2106 S Fourth St, 55455, SAN 347-6251. Tel: 612-624-5890. FAX: 612-625-6994. E-mail: musiclib@umn.edu. Web Site: lib.umn.edu/music. *Music Librn,* Jessica Abbazio; E-mail: jabbazio@umn.edu

NATURAL RESOURCES LIBRARY, 375 Hodson Hall, 1980 Folwell Ave, Saint Paul, 55108. Tel: 612-624-9288. FAX: 612-624-0719. E-mail: nrl@umn.edu. Web Site: www.lib.umn.edu/naturalresources. *Ref Librn,* Shannon Farrell; Tel: 612-624-4799, E-mail: sfarrell@umn.edu

CM VETERINARY MEDICAL LIBRARY, 450 Veterinary Science Bldg, 1971 Commonwealth Ave, Saint Paul, 55108, SAN 378-1224. Tel: 612-624-4281. FAX: 612-624-9782. E-mail: vetlib@umn.edu. Web Site: hsl.lib.umn.edu/vetmed. *Head Librn,* Andre J Nault; Tel: 612-624-5376, E-mail: naulta@umn.edu. Subject Specialists: *Veterinary med,* Andre J Nault

WALTER LIBRARY, 117 Pleasant St SE, 55455. Tel: 612-624-3366. Web Site: www.lib.umn.edu/walter.

CM WANGENSTEEN HISTORICAL LIBRARY OF BIOLOGY & MEDICINE, 568 Diehl Hall, 505 Essex St SE, 55455, SAN 347-5506. Tel: 612-626-6881. FAX: 612-626-6500. E-mail: wanghist@umn.edu. Web Site: hsl.lib.umn.edu/wangensteen. *Curator,* Lois Hendrickson; E-mail: l-hend@umn.edu

CM UNIVERSITY OF MINNESOTA MEDICAL CENTER - FAIRVIEW, LIBRARY*, 2450 Riverside Ave, 55454. SAN 308-6615. Tel: 612-273-6546. FAX: 612-273-2675. E-mail: library10@fairview.org. Web Site: www.mhealth.org/locations/buildings/east-building. *Mgr, Libr Serv,* Brett Demars; Tel: 612-273-6595, E-mail: bdemars1@fairview.org; *ILL, Per,* Renee Jacobson; E-mail: rjacobs2@fairview.org; Staff 3 (MLS 2, Non-MLS 1)

Library Holdings: e-journals 15,000; Bk Vols 2,500; Per Subs 350
Subject Interests: Nursing
Automation Activity & Vendor Info: (Acquisitions) EOS International; (Cataloging) EOS International; (Circulation) EOS International; (OPAC) EOS International; (Serials) EOS International
Wireless access
Function: Doc delivery serv, For res purposes, Health sci info serv, ILL available, Internet access, Orientations, Photocopying/Printing, Prof lending libr, Ref serv available, Res libr, Telephone ref
Partic in Minitex; Twin Cities Biomedical Consortium
Open Mon-Fri 8-4
Restriction: In-house use for visitors, Open to pub for ref only, Prof mat only

C WALDEN UNIVERSITY LIBRARY*, 100 Washington Ave S, Ste 900, 55401. SAN 303-0857. Toll Free Tel: 855-764-4433. E-mail: library@waldenu.edu. Web Site: academicguides.waldenu.edu/library. *Dir, Libr Serv,* Michelle Hajder; Tel: 612-312-2379, Fax: 612-338-5092, E-mail: michelle.hajder@waldenu.edu; *Assoc Dir, Info Tech,* Heather Westerlund; E-mail: heather.westerlund@waldenu.edu; *Assoc Dir, Ref, Outreach & Instruction Librn,* Kerry Sullivan; E-mail: kerry.sullivan@waldenu.edu; *Mgr, Information Literacy & Instruction,* Susan Stekel; *Mgr, Liaisons & Outreach,* Nykol Eystad; *Coll Mgr,* Miki Scholl; E-mail: miki.scholl@waldenu.edu; *Ref Serv Mgr,* Kristina Green; Staff 17 (MLS 17)

Founded 1992. Enrl 45,619; Fac 1,000; Highest Degree: Doctorate
Library Holdings: e-books 164,703; e-journals 64,136
Automation Activity & Vendor Info: (Acquisitions) SerialsSolutions; (Cataloging) SerialsSolutions; (OPAC) LibLime; (Serials) EBSCO Online
Function: Distance learning, Doc delivery serv, Electronic databases & coll, Online info literacy tutorials on the web & in blackboard, Online ref, Ref serv available, Telephone ref
Open Mon-Fri 8am-1am, Sat & Sun Noon-1am
Restriction: Not a lending libr

L WINTHROP & WEINSTINE*, Law Library, Capella Tower, Ste 3500, 225 S Sixth St, 55402. SAN 372-2872. Tel: 612-604-6450. FAX: 612-604-6850. E-mail: wwlibrary@winthrop.com. Web Site: www.winthrop.com. *Res Serv Spec,* Position Currently Open
Wireless access
Restriction: Private libr

L ZELLE, HOFMANN, VOELBEL, MASON & GETTE*, Law Library, 500 Washington Ave S, Ste 4000, 55415. SAN 372-2813. Tel: 612-339-2020. FAX: 612-336-9100. Web Site: www.zelle.com. *Librn,* Elaine Ray; E-mail: eray@zelle.com
Library Holdings: Bk Vols 10,000; Per Subs 200
Wireless access
Open Mon-Fri 8-5

MINNEOTA

P MINNEOTA PUBLIC LIBRARY*, 200 N Jefferson St, 56264. SAN 308-6992. Tel: 507-872-5473. FAX: 507-872-6144. Web Site: www.plumcreeklibrary.org/Minneota. *Librn,* Mary Buysse; E-mail: mbuysse@plumcreeklibrary.net; *Asst Librn,* Elana Nomeland; Staff 2 (Non-MLS 2)

Founded 1902. Pop 1,500; Circ 7,310
Library Holdings: Bk Titles 6,369; Per Subs 14
Wireless access
Function: Home delivery & serv to seniorr ctr & nursing homes
Mem of Plum Creek Library System
Open Tues & Thurs 9-5, Wed 10:30-6:30, Fri 10-5, Sat 9-Noon
Friends of the Library Group

MINNETONKA

P HENNEPIN COUNTY LIBRARY*, 12601 Ridgedale Dr, 55305-1909. SAN 347-3163. Tel: 612-543-8593. Interlibrary Loan Service Tel: 612-543-8318. Reference Tel: 612-543-5669. Administration Tel: 612-543-8518. FAX: 612-543-8600. Interlibrary Loan Service FAX: 612-543-8148. Web Site: www.hclib.org. *Libr Dir,* Chad Helton; Tel: 612-543-8505, E-mail: chelton@hclib.org; *Dep Dir,* Janet Mills; Tel: 612-543-8535, E-mail: jmills@hclib.org; *Div Mgr, Res Serv,* Johannah Genett; Tel: 612-543-8639, E-mail: jrgenett@hclib.org; *Div Mgr, Syst Serv,* Ali Turner; Tel: 612-543-8516, E-mail: aturner@hclib.org; *Head, Patron Serv,* Samantha Jekot-Graham; Tel: 612-543-5919, E-mail: sjekot-graham@hclib.org; *Libr Serv Mgr,* Michael Boe; Tel: 612-543-5627, E-mail: mkboe@hclib.org; *Libr Serv Mgr,* Tonya DePriest; Tel: 612-543-8126, E-mail: tdepriest@hclib.org; *Libr Serv Mgr,* Kevin Lian-Anderson; Tel: 612-543-8515, E-mail: klian-anderson@hclib.org; *Libr Serv Mgr,* Amy McNally; Tel: 612-543-8513, E-mail: amcnally@hclib.org; *Libr Serv Mgr,* Kelly Stade; Tel: 612-543-8749, E-mail: kcstade@hclib.org; *Libr Serv Mgr,* Tammy Wallin; Tel: 612-543-8519, E-mail: twallin@hclib.org; Staff 600 (MLS 172, Non-MLS 428)

Founded 1885. Pop 1,210,720; Circ 16,185,356
Jan 2015-Dec 2015 Income (Main & Associated Libraries) $73,418,169. Mats Exp $73,418,169
Library Holdings: AV Mats 28,156; e-books 227,318; e-journals 112; Electronic Media & Resources 45,462; Music Scores 52,497; Bk Vols 4,240,897; Per Subs 5,413
Special Collections: 19th Century American Studies Coll; Heffelfinger Aesop's & Others' Fables Coll; History of Books & Printing Coll; Hoag Mark Twain Coll; Huttner Abolition & Anti-Slavery Coll; Kittleson World War II Coll; Louis Dodge Autograph Coll; Minneapolis Athenaeum (includes Early American Exploration & Travel Coll); Minneapolis Coll including Oral History; North American Indians Coll; Picture Coll; Spencer Natural History Coll. Oral History; US Document Depository
Wireless access
Partic in Metropolitan Library Service Agency; Minitex; OCLC Online Computer Library Center, Inc
Special Services for the Deaf - Accessible learning ctr; ADA equip; Assisted listening device; Assistive tech; Closed caption videos; Sign lang interpreter upon request for prog; Videos & decoder
Special Services for the Blind - Assistive/Adapted tech devices, equip & products; Audio mat; Bks on cassette; Bks on CD; Internet workstation with adaptive software; Large print & cassettes; Magnifiers; Micro-computer access & training; Reader equip
Friends of the Library Group
Branches: 41

AUGSBURG PARK, 7100 Nicollet Ave S, Richfield, 55423-3117, SAN 347-3198. Tel: 612-543-6200. FAX: 612-543-6202.
Open Mon, Tues & Thurs 9-5, Wed 12-8, Sun 12-5
Friends of the Library Group

PIERRE BOTTINEAU, 55 Broadway St NE, Minneapolis, 55413-1811, SAN 347-4992. Tel: 612-543-6850. FAX: 612-543-6852.
Open Mon & Thurs 12-8, Tues, Wed, Fri & Sat 9-5
Friends of the Library Group

BROOKDALE, 6125 Shingle Creek Pkwy, Brooklyn Center, 55430-2110, SAN 347-3228. Tel: 612-543-5600. FAX: 612-543-5602.
Open Tues 12-8, Wed-Sat 9-5
Friends of the Library Group

BROOKLYN PARK, 8500 W Broadway Ave, Brooklyn Park, 55445, SAN 347-3252. Tel: 612-543-6225. FAX: 612-543-6227. *Patron Experience Supvr,* Michelle Lewis; Tel: 612-543-6229, E-mail: mylewis@hclib.org; *Patron Experience Supvr,* Kathryn Zimmerman; Tel: 612-543-6228, E-mail: kzimmerman@hclib.org
Friends of the Library Group

CHAMPLIN, 12154 Ensign Ave N, Champlin, 55316-9998, SAN 347-3287. Tel: 612-543-6250. FAX: 612-543-6252.
Open Tues 12-8, Wed-Sat 9-5
Friends of the Library Group

EAST LAKE, 2727 E Lake St, Minneapolis, 55406, SAN 347-481X. Tel: 612-543-8425. FAX: 612-543-8427.
Open Mon, Tues & Thurs 9-8, Wed, Fri & Sat 9-5, Sun 12-5
Friends of the Library Group
EDEN PRAIRIE, 565 Prairie Center Dr, Eden Prairie, 55344-5319, SAN 347-3317. Tel: 612-543-6275. FAX: 612-543-6277.
Open Mon-Wed 9-5, Thurs 12-8, Sun 12-5
Friends of the Library Group
EDINA, 5280 Grandview Sq, Edina, 55436, SAN 347-3341. Tel: 612-543-6325. FAX: 612-543-6327.
Open Mon 12-8, Tues-Thurs 9-5, Sun 12-5
Friends of the Library Group
EXCELSIOR, 337 Water St, Excelsior, 55331-1878, SAN 347-3376. Tel: 612-543-6350. FAX: 612-543-6352.
Open Tues, Wed, Fri & Sat 9-5, Thurs 12-8
Friends of the Library Group
FRANKLIN, 1314 E Franklin Ave, Minneapolis, 55404-2924, SAN 347-4844. Tel: 612-543-6925. FAX: 612-543-6927.
Open Tues, Wed, Fri & Sat 9-5, Thurs 12-8
Friends of the Library Group
ARVONNE FRASER, 1222 Fourth St SE, Minneapolis, 55414, SAN 347-5050. Tel: 612-543-6725. FAX: 612-543-6727.
Open Tues & Sat 9-5, Thurs 12-8
Friends of the Library Group
GOLDEN VALLEY, 830 Winnetka Ave N, Golden Valley, 55427-4532, SAN 347-3406. Tel: 612-543-6375. FAX: 612-543-6377.
Open Mon-Wed 9-8, Thurs-Sat 9-5, Sun 12-5
Friends of the Library Group
HOPKINS, 22 11th Ave N, Hopkins, 55343-7575, SAN 347-3430. Tel: 612-543-6400. FAX: 612-543-6402.
Open Tues & Thurs-Sat 9-5, Wed 12-8
Friends of the Library Group
HOSMER, 347 E 36th St, Minneapolis, 55408-4567, SAN 347-4879. Tel: 612-543-6900. FAX: 612-543-6902.
Open Mon 12-8, Tues-Thurs 9-5, Sun 12-5
Friends of the Library Group
LINDEN HILLS, 2900 W 43rd St, Minneapolis, 55410-1515, SAN 347-4909. Tel: 612-543-6825. FAX: 612-543-6827.
Open Mon, Wed, Fri & Sat 9-5, Tues & Thurs 12-8
Friends of the Library Group
LONG LAKE, 1865 Wayzata Blvd W, Long Lake, 55356-9587, SAN 328-7335. Tel: 612-543-6425. FAX: 612-543-6427.
Open Mon 12-8, Wed & Fri 9-5
Friends of the Library Group
MAPLE GROVE, 8001 Main St N, Maple Grove, 55369-4617, SAN 328-9184. Tel: 612-543-6450. FAX: 612-543-6452.
Open Tues, Wed, Fri & Sat 9-5, Thurs 12-8
Friends of the Library Group
MAPLE PLAIN, 5184 Main St E, Maple Plain, 55359-9648, SAN 347-349X. Tel: 612-543-5700. FAX: 612-543-6452.
Open Tues 12-8, Wed-Sat 9-5
Friends of the Library Group
MINNEAPOLIS CENTRAL, 300 Nicollet Mall, Minneapolis, 55401, SAN 347-4755. Tel: 612-543-8000. FAX: 612-543-8173.
Special Collections: 19th Century American Studies Coll; History of Books & Printing Coll; Hoag Mark Twain Coll; Huttner Abolition & Anti-Slavery Coll; Kittleson World War II Coll; Louis Dodge Autograph Coll; Minneapolis Athenaeum (includes Early American Exploration & Travel Coll, Heffelfinger Aesop's & Others' Fables Coll, North American Indians Coll, Spencer Natural History Coll); Minneapolis Coll including Oral History; Picture Coll. Oral History; US Document Depository
Special Services for the Deaf - Accessible learning ctr
Special Services for the Blind - Assistive/Adapted tech devices, equip & products; Networked computers with assistive software
Open Mon, Tues & Thurs 9-5, Wed 12-8, Sun 12-5
Friends of the Library Group
MINNETONKA, 17524 Excelsior Blvd, 55345-1099, SAN 347-3554. Tel: 612-543-5725. FAX: 612-543-5727.
Open Mon & Tues 12-8, Wed-Sat 9-5
Friends of the Library Group
NOKOMIS, 5100 34th Ave S, Minneapolis, 55417-1545, SAN 347-4933. Tel: 612-543-6800. FAX: 612-543-6802.
Open Tues, Wed, Fri & Sat 9-5, Thurs 12-8
Friends of the Library Group
NORTH REGIONAL, 1315 Lowry Ave N, Minneapolis, 55411, SAN 347-478X. Tel: 612-543-8450. FAX: 612-543-8452.
Open Mon, Wed & Thurs 9-5, Tues 12-8
Friends of the Library Group
NORTHEAST, 2200 Central Ave NE, Minneapolis, 55418-3708, SAN 347-4968. Tel: 612-543-6775. FAX: 612-543-6777.
Open Tues, Thurs, Fri & Sat 9-5, Wed 12-8
Friends of the Library Group
OSSEO, 415 Central Ave, Osseo, 55369-1194, SAN 347-3589. Tel: 612-543-5750. FAX: 612-543-5752.
Open Mon 12-8, Tues & Thurs 9-5
Friends of the Library Group
OXBORO, 8801 Portland Ave S, Bloomington, 55420-2997, SAN 347-3619. Tel: 612-543-5775. FAX: 612-543-5777.
Open Tues 12-8, Wed-Sat 9-5
Friends of the Library Group
PENN LAKE, 8800 Penn Ave S, Bloomington, 55431-2022, SAN 347-3643. Tel: 612-543-5800. FAX: 612-543-5802.
Open Mon, Tues & Thurs 9-5, Wed 12-8, Sun 12-5
Friends of the Library Group
PLYMOUTH, 15700 36th Ave N, Plymouth, 55446, SAN 375-6130. Tel: 612-543-5825. FAX: 612-543-5827.
Open Mon 12-8, Tues-Thurs 9-5, Sun 12-5
Friends of the Library Group
RIDGEDALE, 12601 Ridgedale Dr, 55305-1909. Tel: 612-543-8800. FAX: 612-543-8819.
Open Tues 12-8, Wed-Sat 9-5
Friends of the Library Group
ROCKFORD ROAD, 6401 42nd Ave N, Crystal, 55427-1499, SAN 347-3678. Tel: 612-543-5875. FAX: 612-543-5877.
Open Mon, Tues & Thurs 9-5, Wed 12-8, Sun 12-5
Friends of the Library Group
ROGERS, 21300 John Milless Dr, Rogers, 55374-9998, SAN 347-3686. Tel: 612-543-6050. FAX: 612-543-6052.
Open Tues, Wed, Fri & Sat 9-5, Thurs 12-8
Friends of the Library Group
ROOSEVELT, 4026 28th Ave S, Minneapolis, 55406, SAN 347-5026. Tel: 612-543-6700. FAX: 612-543-6702.
Open Tues & Thurs 12-8, Sat 9-5
Friends of the Library Group
SAINT ANTHONY, 2941 Pentagon Dr NE, Saint Anthony, 55418-3209, SAN 347-3708. Tel: 612-543-6075. FAX: 612-543-6077.
Open Tues 12-8, Wed-Sat 9-5
Friends of the Library Group
SAINT BONIFACIUS, 8624 Kennedy Memorial Dr, Saint Bonifacius, 55375-9998, SAN 347-3732. Tel: 612-543-6100. FAX: 612-543-6102.
Open Mon & Wed 12-8, Sat 9-5
Friends of the Library Group
SAINT LOUIS PARK, 3240 Library Lane, Saint Louis Park, 55426-4101, SAN 347-3767. Tel: 612-543-6125. FAX: 612-543-6127.
Open Mon-Wed 9-5, Thurs 12-8, Sun 12-5
Friends of the Library Group
SOUTHDALE, 7001 York Ave S, Edina, 55435-4287, SAN 347-3791. Tel: 612-543-5900. FAX: 612-543-5976.
Open Tues 12-8, Wed-Sat 9-5
Friends of the Library Group
SUMNER, 611 Van White Memorial Blvd, Minneapolis, 55411-4196, SAN 347-5085. Tel: 612-543-6875. FAX: 612-543-6877.
Special Collections: African American History (Gary N Sudduth Coll)
Open Mon 12-8, Tues-Thurs 9-5, Sun 12-5
Friends of the Library Group
WALKER, 2880 Hennepin Ave, Minneapolis, 55408-1957, SAN 347-5115. Tel: 612-543-8400. FAX: 612-543-8402.
Open Tues & Thurs-Sat 9-5, Wed 12-8
Friends of the Library Group
WASHBURN, 5244 Lyndale Ave S, Minneapolis, 55419-1222, SAN 347-514X. Tel: 612-543-8375. FAX: 612-543-8377.
Open Tues 12-8, Wed-Sat 9-5
Friends of the Library Group
WAYZATA, 620 Rice St, Wayzata, 55391-1734, SAN 347-3821. Tel: 612-543-6150. FAX: 612-543-6152.
Open Tues & Thurs-Sat 9-5, Wed 12-8
Friends of the Library Group
WEBBER PARK, 4440 Humboldt Ave N, Minneapolis, 55412, SAN 347-5174. Tel: 612-543-6750. FAX: 612-543-6752.
Open Tues, Wed, Fri & Sat 9-5, Thurs 12-8
Friends of the Library Group
WESTONKA, 2079 Commerce Blvd, Mound, 55364-1594, SAN 347-3856. Tel: 612-543-6175. FAX: 612-543-6184.
Open Tues & Thurs-Sat 9-5, Wed 12-8
Friends of the Library Group

MONTEVIDEO

P MONTEVIDEO PUBLIC LIBRARY*, 224 S First St, 56265. SAN 347-6820. Tel: 320-269-6501. FAX: 320-269-8696. Web Site: www.montevideolibrary.org. *Head Librn*, Larissa Schwenk; E-mail: larissa.schwenk@pioneerland.lib.mn.us; Staff 1 (Non-MLS 1)
Founded 1879. Pop 8,000; Circ 80,000
Jan 2014-Dec 2014 Income $217,530, City $94,730, County $117,800, Locally Generated Income $5,000. Mats Exp $31,600, Books $25,000, Per/Ser (Incl. Access Fees) $3,600, AV Mat $3,000. Sal $105,600 (Prof $48,600)

Library Holdings: Audiobooks 823; AV Mats 54; Bks on Deafness & Sign Lang 10; CDs 112; DVDs 1,292; High Interest/Low Vocabulary Bk Vols 426; Large Print Bks 2,046; Microforms 325; Bk Titles 56,000; Bk Vols 57,800; Per Subs 170; Spec Interest Per Sub 20; Talking Bks 84; Videos 1,169
Special Collections: 16mm Film Coll; Spanish Language (Uruguayan Materials Coll)
Subject Interests: Film
Automation Activity & Vendor Info: (Acquisitions) Innovative Interfaces, Inc; (Cataloging) Innovative Interfaces, Inc; (Circulation) Innovative Interfaces, Inc; (ILL) Innovative Interfaces, Inc; (Media Booking) Innovative Interfaces, Inc; (OPAC) Innovative Interfaces, Inc
Wireless access
Mem of Pioneerland Library System
Special Services for the Blind - Closed circuit TV magnifier
Open Mon-Thurs 9-7:30, Fri 9-5, Sat 9-2

GL C A ROLLOFF TRI-COUNTY LAW LIBRARY*, Chippewa County Courthouse, 629 N 11th St, Ste 9, 56265. SAN 321-8317. Tel: 320-269-8550. FAX: 320-269-7733. *Librn,* Michelle Day
Founded 1951
Library Holdings: Bk Titles 3,000
Wireless access
Open Mon-Fri 8-4:30

MOORHEAD

C CONCORDIA COLLEGE*, Carl B Ylvisaker Library, 901 S Eighth St, 56562. SAN 308-700X. Tel: 218-299-4640. Circulation Tel: 218-299-4641. Reference Tel: 218-299-4656. FAX: 218-299-4253. Web Site: www.concordiacollege.edu/library. *Dir,* Laura Probst; Tel: 218-299-4642, E-mail: lprobst@cord.edu; *Assoc Librn,* Virginia Connell; Tel: 218-299-3237, E-mail: vconnell@cord.edu; *Asst Librn,* Theresa Borchert; Tel: 218-299-3235, E-mail: borchert@cord.edu; *Col Archivist/Librn,* Lisa Sjoberg; Tel: 218-299-3180, E-mail: sjoberg@cord.edu; *Syst & Web Mgt Librn,* Allie Thome; Tel: 218-299-3904, E-mail: athome@cord.edu; *Cat Mgr,* Suzanne M Anderson; Tel: 218-299-4402, E-mail: sanderso@cord.edu; *Circ & ILL Mgr,* Leah Anderson; E-mail: landerso@cord.edu; Staff 20 (MLS 10, Non-MLS 10)
Founded 1891. Enrl 2,823; Fac 218; Highest Degree: Master
Library Holdings: AV Mats 25,015; e-books 12,741; Microforms 44,055; Bk Vols 333,367; Per Subs 3,425
Subject Interests: Lutheran hist, Philos, Relig studies, Scandinavian studies
Automation Activity & Vendor Info: (Acquisitions) Ex Libris Group; (Cataloging) Ex Libris Group; (Circulation) Ex Libris Group; (Course Reserve) Ex Libris Group; (ILL) Ex Libris Group; (Media Booking) Ex Libris Group; (OPAC) Ex Libris Group; (Serials) Ex Libris Group
Wireless access
Function: Archival coll, Art exhibits, Audio & video playback equip for onsite use, Bks on CD, Computers for patron use, Doc delivery serv, E-Reserves, Electronic databases & coll, ILL available, Instruction & testing, Internet access, Online cat, Online ref, Orientations, Outside serv via phone, mail, e-mail & web, Photocopying/Printing, Prof lending libr, Ref & res, Ref serv available, Scanner, Spoken cassettes & CDs, Spoken cassettes & DVDs, Telephone ref, VHS videos, Wheelchair accessible
Partic in Minitex
Special Services for the Deaf - ADA equip; Assistive tech; High interest/low vocabulary bks
Special Services for the Blind - Accessible computers; Bks on CD; Computer with voice synthesizer for visually impaired persons; Copier with enlargement capabilities; Large screen computer & software
Open Mon-Thurs 7:45am-Midnight, Fri 7:45-5, Sat 10-5, Sun Noon-Midnight
Restriction: Borrowing requests are handled by ILL, In-house use for visitors, Non-circulating coll, Non-circulating of rare bks, Open to pub for ref & circ; with some limitations, Restricted access

P LAKE AGASSIZ REGIONAL LIBRARY*, 118 S Fifth St, 56560-2756. (Mail add: PO Box 900, 56561-0900), SAN 347-7096. Tel: 218-233-3757. Toll Free Tel: 800-247-0449. FAX: 218-233-7556. Web Site: larl.org. *Regional Libr Dir,* Liz Lynch; Tel: 218-233-3757, Ext 127, E-mail: lynchl@larl.org; *Coll Develop Librn,* Jeanne Anderson; Tel: 218-233-3757, Ext 122, E-mail: andersonj@larl.org; *Automation Coordr,* Sharon Douglas; Tel: 218-233-3757, Ext 138, E-mail: douglass@larl.org; Staff 9 (MLS 9)
Founded 1961. Pop 130,981; Circ 815,385
Library Holdings: Bk Vols 332,247
Automation Activity & Vendor Info: (Acquisitions) Innovative Interfaces, Inc; (Cataloging) Innovative Interfaces, Inc; (Circulation) Innovative Interfaces, Inc; (OPAC) Innovative Interfaces, Inc
Wireless access
Open Mon-Fri 7:30-4:30

Branches: 13
ADA PUBLIC LIBRARY, 107 E Fourth Ave, Ada, 56510, SAN 347-7126. Tel: 218-784-4480. FAX: 218-784-2594. E-mail: ada@larl.org. Web Site: larl.org/locations/ada.
Founded 1945. Pop 3,964
Library Holdings: Bk Vols 14,000; Per Subs 52
Open Tues & Thurs 12-8, Wed & Fri 10-6
Friends of the Library Group
BAGLEY PUBLIC LIBRARY, 79 Spencer Ave SW, Bagley, 56621. (Mail add: PO Box G, Bagley, 56621-1008), SAN 328-6975. Tel: 218-694-6201. FAX: 218-694-6201. E-mail: bagley@larl.org. Web Site: larl.org/locations/bagley.
Founded 1910. Pop 9,500; Circ 19,247
Library Holdings: Bk Vols 5,400; Per Subs 30
Open Tues & Thurs 2-8, Wed & Fri 10-6, Sat 10-2
Friends of the Library Group
BARNESVILLE PUBLIC LIBRARY, 104 N Front St, Barnesville, 56514. (Mail add: PO Box 549, Barnesville, 56514-0549), SAN 347-7150. Tel: 218-354-2301. FAX: 218-354-2301. E-mail: barnesville@larl.org. Web Site: larl.org/locations/barnesville.
Founded 1949. Pop 3,452
Library Holdings: Bk Vols 12,064; Per Subs 80
Open Tues & Wed 11-7, Thurs & Fri 10-6, Sat 10-2
Friends of the Library Group
BRECKENRIDGE PUBLIC LIBRARY, 205 N Seventh St, Breckenridge, 56520, SAN 347-7185. Tel: 218-643-2113. FAX: 218-643-2113. E-mail: breckenridge@larl.org. Web Site: larl.org/locations/breckenridge.
Founded 1912. Pop 6,554
Library Holdings: Bk Vols 16,653; Per Subs 61
Automation Activity & Vendor Info: (Cataloging) SirsiDynix; (Circulation) SirsiDynix; (Course Reserve) SirsiDynix; (ILL) SirsiDynix; (Media Booking) SirsiDynix; (OPAC) SirsiDynix
Open Mon & Tues 11-7, Wed & Thurs 10-6, Fri 9-5, Sat 9-1
Friends of the Library Group
CLIMAX PUBLIC LIBRARY, 104 W Broadway, Climax, 56523, SAN 347-7215. Tel: 218-857-2455. FAX: 218-857-2455. E-mail: climax@larl.org. Web Site: larl.org/locations/climax.
Founded 1960. Pop 787
Library Holdings: Bk Vols 5,410; Per Subs 18
Open Mon 4-8, Tues 1-6, Thurs 1-8, Fri 10-2
Friends of the Library Group
CROOKSTON PUBLIC LIBRARY, 110 N Ash St, Crookston, 56716, SAN 347-724X. Tel: 218-281-4522. FAX: 218-281-4523. E-mail: crookston@larl.org. Web Site: larl.org/locations/crookston.
Founded 1903. Pop 11,000
Library Holdings: Bk Vols 56,590; Per Subs 85
Open Mon-Wed 10-8, Thurs & Fri 10-6, Sat 10-5, Sun (Winter) 1-5
Friends of the Library Group
DETROIT LAKES PUBLIC LIBRARY, 1000 Washington Ave, Detroit Lakes, 56501, SAN 347-7274. Tel: 218-847-2168. FAX: 218-847-2160. E-mail: detroit@larl.org. Web Site: larl.org/locations/detroitlakes.
Founded 1908. Pop 30,000
Library Holdings: Bk Vols 32,669; Per Subs 134
Open Mon-Thurs 9-7, Fri 9-6, Sat 10-4
Friends of the Library Group
FERTILE PUBLIC LIBRARY, 101 S Mill St, Fertile, 56540. (Mail add: PO Box 418, Fertile, 56540-0418). Tel: 218-945-6137. FAX: 218-945-6137. E-mail: fertile@larl.org. Web Site: larl.org/locations/fertile.
Founded 1967. Pop 803
Library Holdings: Bk Vols 6,700; Per Subs 31
Open Tues, Thurs & Fri 10-6, Wed 12-8
Friends of the Library Group
FOSSTON PUBLIC LIBRARY, 403 Foss Ave N, Fosston, 56542, SAN 347-7339. Tel: 218-435-1320. FAX: 218-435-1320. E-mail: fosston@larl.org. Web Site: larl.org/locations/fosston.
Founded 1918. Pop 4,530
Library Holdings: Bk Vols 13,150; Per Subs 34
Open Mon, Wed & Fri 10-6, Tues & Thurs 12-8, Sat 11-2
Friends of the Library Group
HAWLEY PUBLIC LIBRARY, 422 Hartford St, Hawley, 56549. (Mail add: PO Box 519, Hawley, 56549-0519), SAN 347-7363. Tel: 218-483-4549. FAX: 218-483-4549. E-mail: hawley@larl.org. Web Site: larl.org/locations/hawley.
Founded 1950. Pop 3,580
Library Holdings: Bk Vols 11,508; Per Subs 45
Open Tues & Wed 2-8, Thurs & Fri 10-6, Sat 10-2
MAHNOMEN PUBLIC LIBRARY, 203 S Main St, Mahnomen, 56557. (Mail add: PO Box 476, Mahnomen, 56557-0476), SAN 308-6186. Tel: 218-935-2843. FAX: 218-935-2574. E-mail: mahnomen@larl.org. Web Site: larl.org/locations/mahnomen.
Pop 5,000; Circ 10,000
Library Holdings: Bk Vols 13,000; Per Subs 24
Open Tues 1-7, Wed & Fri 10-6, Thurs 12-6, Sat 10-2
Friends of the Library Group

MCINTOSH PUBLIC LIBRARY, 115 Broadway NW, McIntosh, 56556. (Mail add: PO Box 39, McIntosh, 56556-0039), SAN 347-7398. Tel: 218-563-4555. FAX: 218-563-3042. E-mail: mcintosh@larl.org. Web Site: larl.org/locations/mcintosh.
Founded 1941. Pop 977
Library Holdings: Bk Vols 7,000; Per Subs 15
Open Mon 10-3, Tues & Thurs 4-7, Wed & Fri 12-5

MOORHEAD PUBLIC LIBRARY, 118 Fifth St S, 56560. (Mail add: PO Box 900, 56561-0900), SAN 347-7428. Tel: 218-233-7594. FAX: 218-236-7405. E-mail: moorhead@larl.org. Web Site: larl.org/locations/moorhead.
Founded 1906. Pop 41,245
Library Holdings: Bk Vols 123,228; Per Subs 299
Open Mon-Thurs 9-9, Fri & Sat 10-6
Friends of the Library Group

C MINNESOTA STATE UNIVERSITY MOORHEAD*, Livingston Lord Library, 1104 Seventh Ave S, 56563. (Mail add: PO Box 101, 56563), SAN 308-7018. Tel: 218-477-2922. Circulation Tel: 218-477-2355. Interlibrary Loan Service Tel: 218-477-2924. Reference Tel: 218-477-2345. FAX: 218-477-5924. Web Site: www.mnstate.edu/library. *Exec Dir, Libr Serv,* Martina Haines; Tel: 218-477-4728, E-mail: martina.haines@mnstate.edu; *Distance Learning & Web Librn,* Travis Dolence; E-mail: dolence@mnstate.edu; *Electronic Res Librn,* Mary Muehlberg; E-mail: mary.muehlberg@mnstate.edu; *Info Serv Librn,* Larry Schwartz; E-mail: schwartz@mnstate.edu; *Librn, Info Literacy Initiatives,* Brittney Goodman; E-mail: brittney.goodman@mnstate.edu; *Pub Serv Librn,* Stacy Voeller; E-mail: voeller@mnstate.edu; *Archivist,* Trista Raezer-Stursa; E-mail: trista.raezerstursa@mnstate.edu; *ILL,* Wendy Gibson; E-mail: gibson@mnstate.edu; *Pub Serv,* Pam Werre; E-mail: werrepa@mnstate.edu; *Tech Serv,* Jean Kramer; E-mail: kramer@mnstate.edu; Staff 17 (MLS 10, Non-MLS 7)
Founded 1887. Enrl 7,600; Fac 349; Highest Degree: Master
Library Holdings: Bk Vols 570,000; Per Subs 4,000
Special Collections: State Document Depository; US Document Depository
Subject Interests: Juv, Media, Res
Automation Activity & Vendor Info: (Acquisitions) PALS; (Cataloging) PALS; (Circulation) PALS; (Course Reserve) PALS; (ILL) PALS; (Media Booking) PALS; (OPAC) PALS; (Serials) PALS
Wireless access
Function: ILL available, Internet access, Photocopying/Printing, Ref serv available, Wheelchair accessible
Partic in Minn Interlibr Teletype Exchange; MnPALS; OCLC Online Computer Library Center, Inc
Open Mon-Thurs 8am-11pm, Fri 8-5, Sat 11-5, Sun 1-11

R TRINITY LUTHERAN CHURCH LIBRARY*, 210 S Seventh St, 56560-2794. (Mail add: PO Box 188, 56561-0188), SAN 308-7026. Tel: 218-236-1333. FAX: 218-236-8918. *Librn,* Lou Trowbridge; Staff 4 (MLS 1, Non-MLS 3)
Founded 1959
Library Holdings: DVDs 110; Large Print Bks 60; Bk Titles 4,200; Spec Interest Per Sub 2; Videos 230
Subject Interests: Bible study resources, Biblical ref, Personal faith

MOOSE LAKE

S MINNESOTA DEPARTMENT OF CORRECTIONS*, Minnesota Correctional Facility - Willow River/Moose Lake, 1000 Lakeshore Dr, 55767. Tel: 218-485-5000, Ext 5202. Web Site: mn.gov/doc/facilities/willow-river-moose-lake/moose-lake.jsp. *Librn,* Becky Pemberton; E-mail: becky.pemberton@state.mn.us
Library Holdings: DVDs 645; Bk Vols 14,000; Per Subs 48
Automation Activity & Vendor Info: (Cataloging) Follett Software; (Circulation) Follett Software

P MOOSE LAKE PUBLIC LIBRARY, 313 Elm Ave, 55767. (Mail add: PO Box 277, 55767-0277), SAN 308-7034. Tel: 218-485-4424. Administration Tel: 218-485-0394. Web Site: www.cityofmooselake.net/284/Public-Library. *Libr Dir,* Laura Helwig; E-mail: laura.helwig@alslib.info; Staff 2.3 (Non-MLS 2.3)
Founded 1938. Pop 2,751; Circ 48,434
Library Holdings: Audiobooks 788; DVDs 1,597; Bk Titles 14,800; Per Subs 101
Automation Activity & Vendor Info: (Cataloging) Horizon; (Circulation) Horizon; (OPAC) Horizon
Wireless access
Mem of Arrowhead Library System
Open Mon-Wed & Fri 10-5, Thurs 10-7

MORA

S KANABEC COUNTY HISTORICAL SOCIETY, Kanabec History Center, 805 W Forest Ave, 55051-1466. (Mail add: PO Box 113, 55051-0113), SAN 373-2274. Tel: 320-679-1665. FAX: 320-679-1673. E-mail: center@kanabechistory.org. Web Site: www.kanabechistory.org. *Exec Dir,* Barb Burnes
Founded 1978
Library Holdings: Bk Vols 2,800
Subject Interests: Genealogy

MORGAN

P MORGAN PUBLIC LIBRARY*, 210 Vernon Ave, 56266. (Mail add: PO Box 128, 56266-0128), SAN 308-7050. Tel: 507-249-3153. FAX: 507-249-3839. E-mail: morganlibrary@redred.com. Web Site: www.plumcreeklibrary.org/morgan. *Dir,* Mandi Kuehn; Staff 3 (Non-MLS 3)
Founded 1939. Pop 76,053; Circ 320,061
Library Holdings: Bk Titles 13,000; Per Subs 25
Wireless access
Mem of Plum Creek Library System
Open Mon, Wed & Fri 9-5, Tues & Thurs 1-7

MORRIS

P MORRIS PUBLIC LIBRARY*, 102 E Sixth St, 56267-1211. SAN 308-7069. Tel: 320-589-1634. FAX: 320-589-8892. Web Site: viking.lib.mn.us/morris-public-library, www.morris.lib.mn.us. *Dir,* Anne Barber; E-mail: abarber@morrispublib.org; Staff 4 (MLS 1, Non-MLS 3)
Pop 5,366; Circ 128,000
Library Holdings: Bk Vols 50,000; Per Subs 100
Special Collections: Local History Coll
Automation Activity & Vendor Info: (Cataloging) SirsiDynix; (Circulation) SirsiDynix; (OPAC) SirsiDynix
Wireless access
Mem of Viking Library System
Open Mon-Thurs 10-8, Fri & Sat 10-5
Friends of the Library Group

C UNIVERSITY OF MINNESOTA-MORRIS*, Rodney A Briggs Library, 600 E Fourth St, 56267. SAN 308-7077. Tel: 320-589-6175. Reference Tel: 320-589-6176. FAX: 320-589-6168. Web Site: library.morris.umn.edu. *Dir,* LeAnn Lindquist Dean; Tel: 320-589-6226, E-mail: deanl@morris.umn.edu; *Digital Serv Coordr,* Angela Stangl; Tel: 320-589-6164, E-mail: amstangl@morris.umn.edu; *Instruction Coordr,* Kellie Meehlhause; Tel: 320-589-6227, E-mail: kmeehlha@morris.umn.edu; *Metadata Coordr, Tech Serv Coordr,* Naomi Skulan; Tel: 320-589-6174, E-mail: skulann@morris.umn.edu; *Ref Coordr,* Peter Bremer; Tel: 320-589-6173, E-mail: pbremer@morris.umn.edu; Staff 9 (MLS 5, Non-MLS 4)
Founded 1960. Enrl 1,872; Fac 121; Highest Degree: Bachelor
Jul 2016-Jun 2017. Mats Exp $399,433, Books $48,002, Per/Ser (Incl. Access Fees) $30,000, Manu Arch $280, AV Mat $900, Electronic Ref Mat (Incl. Access Fees) $420,251. Sal $593,660
Library Holdings: e-books 99,810; Bk Vols 265,000; Per Subs 64,000
Special Collections: Archives; Career Center Resources; Children's Literature; Faculty Teaching & Learning Coll; Little Magazines Coll; Native American Boarding School Coll; Poetry Coll; UMM Scholarship Coll; West Central Minnesota Historical Research Coll. US Document Depository
Automation Activity & Vendor Info: (Acquisitions) Ex Libris Group; (Cataloging) Ex Libris Group; (Circulation) Ex Libris Group; (Course Reserve) Ex Libris Group; (ILL) Ex Libris Group; (OPAC) Ex Libris Group; (Serials) Ex Libris Group
Wireless access
Partic in Minitex; Northern Lights Library Network; OCLC Online Computer Library Center, Inc
Open Mon-Thurs 8am-1am, Fri 8-6, Sat 11-7, Sun Noon-1am
Friends of the Library Group

S WEST CENTRAL MINNESOTA HISTORICAL RESEARCH CENTER*, University of Minnesota, 600 E Fourth St, 56267. SAN 371-6236. Tel: 320-589-6172. Web Site: library.morris.umn.edu/collections/west-central-minnesota-historical-research-center. *Dir,* Stephen Gross; E-mail: grosssj@morris.umn.edu
Founded 1960
Library Holdings: Bk Vols 457
Special Collections: Campus Archives, Local Records & Manuscripts; Univ. Oral History; State Document Depository
Subject Interests: Local hist
Wireless access

MOUNTAIN IRON

P ARROWHEAD LIBRARY SYSTEM*, 5528 Emerald Ave, 55768-2069. SAN 308-8189. Tel: 218-741-3840. Toll Free Tel: 800-257-1442. FAX: 218-748-2171. E-mail: als@alslib.info. Web Site: www.alslib.info. *Exec Dir,* Jim Weikum; E-mail: jim.weikum@alslib.info; *Asst Dir,* Shari Fisher; E-mail: shari.fisher@alslib.info; Staff 21.3 (MLS 6, Non-MLS 15.3)
Founded 1966. Pop 313,284; Circ 178,382
Jan 2018-Dec 2018 Income (Main Library Only) $3,161,769, State $1,623,709, County $1,217,437, Other $320,623. Mats Exp $270,456. Sal $1,092,131
Library Holdings: Audiobooks 1,240; AV Mats 7,598; Bks-By-Mail 27,997; Bks on Deafness & Sign Lang 30; CDs 244; DVDs 5,758; e-books 42,290; Large Print Bks 3,785; Bk Vols 32,775; Per Subs 19; Talking Bks 1,732; Videos 5,758
Special Collections: Bifolkal Kits; STEAM Kits; Storytime Kits; Video Games; Video Gaming Equipment
Automation Activity & Vendor Info: (Acquisitions) SirsiDynix; (Cataloging) SirsiDynix; (Circulation) SirsiDynix; (Discovery) SirsiDynix; (OPAC) SirsiDynix; (Serials) SirsiDynix
Wireless access
Function: 24/7 Electronic res, 24/7 Online cat, Art programs, Audiobks on Playaways & MP3, Audiobks via web, Bks on CD, Children's prog, Electronic databases & coll, Free DVD rentals, Home delivery & serv to seniorr ctr & nursing homes, Homebound delivery serv, Homework prog, ILL available, Life-long learning prog for all ages, Mail loans to mem, Music CDs, Online cat, Online info literacy tutorials on the web & in blackboard, Outreach serv, OverDrive digital audio bks, Preschool reading prog, Prog for adults, Prog for children & young adult, Res assist avail, Senior outreach, Summer & winter reading prog, Summer reading prog, Teen prog, Visual arts prog, Wheelchair accessible, Winter reading prog, Workshops, Writing prog
Member Libraries: Aurora Public Library; Babbitt Public Library; Baudette Public Library; Bovey Public Library; Buhl Public Library; Calumet Public Library; Carlton Area Public Library; Chisholm Public Library; Cloquet Public Library; Coleraine Public Library; Cook Public Library; Duluth Public Library; Ely Public Library; Eveleth Public Library; Gilbert Public Library; Grand Marais Public Library; Grand Rapids Area Library; Hibbing Community College; Hibbing Public Library; Hoyt Lakes Public Library; International Falls Public Library; Keewatin Public Library; Marble Public Library; Minnesota Discovery Center; Moose Lake Public Library; Mountain Iron Public Library; Silver Bay Public Library; Two Harbors Public Library; Virginia Public Library
Partic in Minitex; Minnesota Library Information Network
Open Mon-Fri 7:30-4:30
Bookmobiles: 1. Bkmobile Coord, Sophia Anderson. Bk vols 8,674

P MOUNTAIN IRON PUBLIC LIBRARY*, 5742 Mountain Ave, 55768-9636. (Mail add: PO Box 477, 55768-0477), SAN 308-7085. Tel: 218-735-8625. FAX: 218-748-7573. Web Site: mountainironlibrary.com. *Dir,* Anna Amundson; E-mail: anna.amundson@alslib.info; *Asst Librn,* Julie Hansen
Pop 4,134; Circ 29,300
Library Holdings: Bk Vols 30,000; Per Subs 90
Special Collections: Local History Coll
Automation Activity & Vendor Info: (Cataloging) Horizon; (Circulation) Horizon; (OPAC) Horizon
Wireless access
Mem of Arrowhead Library System
Open Mon-Thurs 10-6, Fri 10-2

MOUNTAIN LAKE

P MOUNTAIN LAKE PUBLIC LIBRARY*, 1054 Fourth Ave, 56159-1455. (Mail add: PO Box 477, 56159-0477), SAN 308-7093. Tel: 507-427-2506. FAX: 507-427-2506. Web Site: www.mountainlakepubliclibrary.org. *Librn,* Carol Lehman; E-mail: clehman@plumcreeklibrary.net
Pop 2,000; Circ 35,408
Library Holdings: Bk Vols 25,000; Per Subs 95
Special Collections: Mennonite Heritage Coll
Automation Activity & Vendor Info: (Cataloging) TLC (The Library Corporation); (Circulation) TLC (The Library Corporation); (ILL) TLC (The Library Corporation); (OPAC) TLC (The Library Corporation)
Mem of Plum Creek Library System
Open Mon & Wed-Fri 10-5:30, Tues 10-8, Sat 10-1
Friends of the Library Group

NEW BRIGHTON

R UNITED THEOLOGICAL SEMINARY OF THE TWIN CITIES*, The Spencer Library, 3000 Fifth St NW, 55112-2598. SAN 308-7115. Tel: 651-255-6142. Web Site: unitedseminary.libguides.com, www.unitedseminary.edu/culture/united-life/campus/library. *Dir,* Dale Dobias; E-mail: ddobias@unitedseminary.edu; Staff 3 (MLS 2, Non-MLS 1)
Founded 1962. Enrl 191; Fac 13; Highest Degree: Doctorate
Library Holdings: Bk Titles 85,106; Per Subs 189
Subject Interests: Liberation theol, Native Am, Reformed tradition, Sexuality, Theol, Women's studies in relig
Automation Activity & Vendor Info: (Acquisitions) OCLC; (Cataloging) OCLC; (Circulation) OCLC; (Course Reserve) OCLC; (ILL) OCLC WorldShare Interlibrary Loan; (OPAC) OCLC; (Serials) OCLC
Wireless access
Partic in Minnesota Theological Library Association
Open Mon, Wed & Fri 8-5, Tues & Thurs 8am-9pm, Sat 10-2

NEW LONDON

P NEW LONDON PUBLIC LIBRARY*, 15 Ash St S, 56273-9567. (Mail add: PO Box 156, 56273-0156), SAN 348-1298. Tel: 320-354-2943. E-mail: newlondon.staff@pioneerland.lib.mn.us. Web Site: www.newlondon.lib.mn.us. *Head Librn,* Ria Newhouse; E-mail: ria.newhouse@pioneerland.lib.mn.us
Pop 1,000; Circ 12,253
Library Holdings: Bk Vols 10,500; Per Subs 20
Automation Activity & Vendor Info: (Cataloging) Innovative Interfaces, Inc; (Circulation) Innovative Interfaces, Inc; (OPAC) Innovative Interfaces, Inc
Wireless access
Mem of Pioneerland Library System
Open Mon 12-5, Tues & Fri 1-5, Wed 10-2, Sat 9-12

NEW ULM

S BROWN COUNTY HISTORICAL SOCIETY*, Research Library, Two N Broadway, 56073. SAN 370-5250. Tel: 507-233-2616, 507-233-2619. E-mail: research@browncountyhistorymn.org. Web Site: www.browncountyhistorymn.org/research-library.html. *Research Librn,* Darla Gebhard; Staff 1 (MLS 1)
Founded 1930
Library Holdings: Bk Titles 1,000
Special Collections: Dakota War Coll; New Ulm POW Camp Coll; New Ulm Turnverein Coll; Wanda Gag Coll; World War I & World War II Coll
Wireless access
Publications: Brown County Mile Posts (Quarterly)
Open Tues-Fri 10-12 & 1-4, Sat 10-3
Restriction: Non-circulating to the pub

C MARTIN LUTHER COLLEGE LIBRARY*, 1995 Luther Ct, 56073-3965. SAN 308-7123. Tel: 507-233-9131. Web Site: mlc-wels.edu/library. *Libr Dir,* Linda M Kramer; Tel: 507-354-8221, Ext 296, E-mail: kramerlm@mlc-wels.edu; *Mgr, Ser,* Janice Nass; Tel: 507-354-8221, Ext 327, E-mail: nassja@mlc-wels.edu; *Tech Serv Mgr,* Grace Bases; Tel: 507-354-8221, Ext 364, E-mail: basesgm@mlc-wels.edu; *Acq, Circ,* Elizabeth Wessel; Staff 3.8 (MLS 1, Non-MLS 2.8)
Founded 1995. Enrl 707; Fac 64; Highest Degree: Master
Automation Activity & Vendor Info: (Cataloging) OCLC Connexion; (Circulation) Innovative Interfaces, Inc - Sierra; (Discovery) EBSCO Discovery Service; (OPAC) Innovative Interfaces, Inc - Sierra
Wireless access
Mem of Traverse Des Sioux Library Cooperative
Partic in OCLC Online Computer Library Center, Inc
Open Mon-Thurs 7:15am-Midnight, Fri 7:15-5, Sat 11-5, Sun 1-Midnight

P NEW ULM PUBLIC LIBRARY, 17 N Broadway, 56073-1786. SAN 308-7131. Tel: 507-359-8331. FAX: 507-354-3255. Web Site: www.newulmlibrary.org. *Libr Dir,* Paulina Poplawska; E-mail: ppoplawska@tds.lib.mn.us; *Asst Dir,* April Ide; E-mail: aide@tds.lib.mn.us; *Ref Librn,* Leasa Sieve; E-mail: lsieve@tds.lib.mn.us; *Programming, Tech Serv Librn,* LeRoy Nosker Tanner; E-mail: ltanner@tds.lib.mn.us; *Youth Serv Librn,* Kathryn Tatnall; E-mail: ktatnall@tds.lib.mn.us; Staff 12 (MLS 3, Non-MLS 9)
Founded 1937. Pop 13,610; Circ 182,272
Library Holdings: Audiobooks 4,095; Bk Vols 80,750; Per Subs 173; Videos 3,090
Special Collections: German-American Heritage Coll; New Ulm Journal Coll, 1940-present
Automation Activity & Vendor Info: (Cataloging) SirsiDynix; (Circulation) SirsiDynix; (OPAC) SirsiDynix
Wireless access
Function: Adult bk club, Bks on cassette, Bks on CD, Children's prog, Computers for patron use, Electronic databases & coll, Free DVD rentals, ILL available, Online cat, Photocopying/Printing, Prog for adults, Prog for children & young adult, Ref & res, Ref serv available, Spoken cassettes & CDs, Spoken cassettes & DVDs, Story hour, Summer reading prog, Tax forms, Teen prog, Telephone ref, VHS videos, Wheelchair accessible, Workshops
Mem of Traverse Des Sioux Library Cooperative
Open Mon-Thurs 9:30-8, Fri & Sat 9:30-5
Friends of the Library Group

NEW YORK MILLS

P NEW YORK MILLS PUBLIC LIBRARY*, 30 Main Ave N, 56567-4318. (Mail add: PO Box 279, 56567-0279), SAN 376-7175. Tel: 218-385-2436. FAX: 218-385-2508. Web Site: www.viking.lib.mn.us/new-york-mills-public-library. *Dir,* Julie Adams; E-mail: jadams@nympubliclibrary.org
Library Holdings: Bk Vols 15,000; Per Subs 75
Automation Activity & Vendor Info: (Cataloging) SirsiDynix; (Circulation) SirsiDynix; (OPAC) SirsiDynix
Wireless access
Mem of Viking Library System
Open Mon & Tues 10-6, Wed & Thurs 10-7, Fri 10-5, Sat 10-2
Friends of the Library Group

NORTH MANKATO

P NORTH MANKATO TAYLOR LIBRARY*, 1001 Belgrade Ave, 56003. SAN 347-4399. Tel: 507-345-5120. FAX: 507-345-1861. Web Site: www.northmankato.com/taylorlibrary. *Libr Dir,* Katie Heintz; E-mail: kheintz@nmlibrary.org; *Asst Dir,* Angela Kelly; E-mail: akelly@nmlibrary.org; *Ch,* Michelle Zimmermann; E-mail: mzimmermann@nmlibrary.org; Staff 4 (MLS 1, Non-MLS 3)
Founded 1907
Library Holdings: Bk Vols 25,965; Per Subs 128
Wireless access
Mem of Traverse Des Sioux Library Cooperative
Open Mon-Thurs 10-8, Fri 10-6, Sat 10-4
Friends of the Library Group
Bookmobiles: 1. Librn, Amy Hunt

J SOUTH CENTRAL COLLEGE*, North Mankato Campus Library, 1920 Lee Blvd, 56003-2504. SAN 374-7263. Tel: 507-389-7223. Interlibrary Loan Service Tel: 507-389-7251. E-mail: library@southcentral.edu. Web Site: southcentral.edu/library. *Dir, Libr Serv,* Johnna Horton; E-mail: johnna.horton@southcentral.edu; *Libr Mgr,* Kim DeMarce; E-mail: kim.demarce@southcentral.edu; Staff 2 (MLS 1, Non-MLS 1)
Founded 1946. Highest Degree: Associate
Library Holdings: CDs 200; DVDs 100; e-books 9,000; Large Print Bks 15; Bk Vols 32,000; Per Subs 165
Automation Activity & Vendor Info: (Cataloging) Ex Libris Group; (Circulation) Ex Libris Group; (Course Reserve) Ex Libris Group; (ILL) Ex Libris Group; (Media Booking) Ex Libris Group; (OPAC) Ex Libris Group
Wireless access
Partic in Minitex; MnPALS
Open Mon-Thurs 7:30am-8pm, Fri 7:30-4

NORTH SAINT PAUL

S NORTH SAINT PAUL HISTORICAL SOCIETY*, Museum Library, 2666 E Seventh Ave, 55109. SAN 373-2282. Tel: 651-747-2432. E-mail: nsphistorical@gmail.com. Web Site: www.northstpaul.org/306/Historical-Society-Museum. *Curator,* Paul J Anderson; Tel: 651-777-8965
Founded 1976
Library Holdings: Bk Vols 1,000; Videos 20
Special Collections: Henry A Castle Coll; Local Authors, bks, vf. Oral History
Subject Interests: Hist of North St Paul
Open Fri 1-4, Sat 10-1 & by appointment
Friends of the Library Group

NORTHFIELD

C CARLETON COLLEGE*, Laurence McKinley Gould Library, One N College St, 55057-4097. SAN 347-7452. Tel: 507-222-4260. Interlibrary Loan Service Tel: 507-222-4257. Reference Tel: 507-222-4264. Administration Tel: 507-222-4261. Web Site: www.carleton.edu/library/. *Librn,* Brad Schaffner; Tel: 507-222-4267, E-mail: bschaffner@carleton.edu; *Head, Loan Services,* Lisa Pillow; Tel: 507-222-5447, E-mail: lpillow@carleton.edu; *Head, Ref & Instruction,* Emily Scharf; Tel: 507-222-5304, E-mail: escharf@carleton.edu; *Head, Spec Coll & Archives,* Tom Lamb; Tel: 507-222-7015, E-mail: tlamb@carleton.edu; *Librn Emeritus,* Samuel Demas; E-mail: sdemas@carleton.edu; Staff 31 (MLS 18, Non-MLS 13)
Founded 1867. Enrl 2,000; Fac 195; Highest Degree: Bachelor
Library Holdings: AV Mats 10,422; Bks on Deafness & Sign Lang 428; CDs 2,087; DVDs 4,646; e-books 338,679; e-journals 33,214; Electronic Media & Resources 49,949; Microforms 220,278; Bk Titles 641,350; Bk Vols 841,418; Per Subs 1,049; Videos 4,874
Special Collections: Lucas Jazz Records; Photos of Famous Authors by Famous Photographers; Thorsten Veblen's Library; Warming Orchid Books; Western Americana (Donald Beaty Bloch Coll). US Document Depository
Subject Interests: Geol, Liberal arts
Automation Activity & Vendor Info: (Acquisitions) Ex Libris Group; (Cataloging) Ex Libris Group; (Circulation) Ex Libris Group; (ILL) OCLC ILLiad; (OPAC) Ex Libris Group; (Serials) Ex Libris Group
Wireless access
Function: Doc delivery serv, E-Reserves, Electronic databases & coll, ILL available, Internet access, Online ref, Photocopying/Printing, VHS videos
Partic in Minitex; OCLC Online Computer Library Center, Inc
Open Mon-Fri 8am-1am, Sat 9am-Midnight, Sun 9am-1am
Friends of the Library Group

P NORTHFIELD PUBLIC LIBRARY*, 210 Washington St, 55057. SAN 308-7158. Tel: 507-645-6606. Web Site: www.ci.northfield.mn.us/library. *Dir, Libr & Info Tech,* Teresa Jensen; Tel: 507-645-1801, E-mail: Teresa.Jensen@ci.northfield.mn.us; *Children's Prog Librn,* Emily Lloyd; E-mail: emily.lloyd@ci.northfield.mn.us; *Ref Librn,* Joan Ennis; Tel: 507-645-1802, E-mail: joan.ennis@ci.northfield.mn.us; *Libr Asst, Ref,* Tyler Gardner; E-mail: tyler.gardner@ci.northfield.mn.us; *Ref Librn,* Jamie Stanley; E-mail: jamie.stanley@ci.northfield.mn.us; *Mgr, Ref Serv,* Katlin Heidgerken Greene; Tel: 507-645-1804, E-mail: katlin.greene@ci.northfield.mn.us; *Circ, Tech Serv Mgr,* Katherine Rush; Tel: 507-645-1800, E-mail: kathy.rush@ci.northfield.mn.us; Staff 6 (MLS 4, Non-MLS 2)
Founded 1857. Pop 26,851; Circ 385,737
Jan 2018-Dec 2018 Income $1,263,830, County $188,470. Mats Exp $102,000
Library Holdings: Audiobooks 8,256; AV Mats 5,274; DVDs 9,077; e-books 32,893; e-journals 145; Electronic Media & Resources 63; Bk Titles 55,794; Per Subs 156
Special Collections: Local History Coll
Automation Activity & Vendor Info: (Acquisitions) SirsiDynix; (Cataloging) SirsiDynix; (Circulation) SirsiDynix; (OPAC) SirsiDynix; (Serials) SirsiDynix
Wireless access
Function: 24/7 Electronic res, 24/7 Online cat, Adult bk club, Audiobks on Playaways & MP3, Audiobks via web, Bk club(s), Bks on CD, Butterfly Garden, CD-ROM, Children's prog, Computers for patron use, Digital talking bks, Doc delivery serv, E-Readers, Electronic databases & coll, Family literacy, Free DVD rentals, Holiday prog, Home delivery & serv to seniorr ctr & nursing homes, Homebound delivery serv, ILL available, Internet access, Magazines, Magnifiers for reading, Mail & tel request accepted, Meeting rooms, Microfiche/film & reading machines, Music CDs, Notary serv, Online cat, Outreach serv, Outside serv via phone, mail, e-mail & web, OverDrive digital audio bks, Photocopying/Printing, Prog for adults, Prog for children & young adult, Ref serv available, Scanner, Spanish lang bks, Story hour, Summer reading prog, Tax forms, Teen prog, Telephone ref, Wheelchair accessible, Winter reading prog
Partic in Southeastern Libraries Cooperating
Special Services for the Deaf - Closed caption videos
Special Services for the Blind - Bks on CD; Home delivery serv; Large print bks; Magnifiers; Playaways (bks on MP3); Recorded bks; Talking bks
Open Mon-Thurs 9-8, Fri 9-6, Sat 9-5, Sun (Sept-May) 1-5
Friends of the Library Group
Bookmobiles: 1

S NORWEGIAN-AMERICAN HISTORICAL ASSOCIATION ARCHIVES, 1510 St Olaf Ave, 55057. SAN 327-1692. Tel: 507-786-3221. FAX: 507-786-3734. E-mail: naha-archivist@stolaf.edu, naha@stolaf.edu. Web Site: www.naha.stolaf.edu. *Exec Dir,* Amy Boxrud; *Archivist,* Kristina Warner; Tel: 507-786-3450, E-mail: warner3@stolaf.edu
Founded 1925
Library Holdings: Bk Vols 8,000
Function: Res libr
Restriction: Open by appt only

SAINT OLAF COLLEGE

C HOWARD V & EDNA H HONG KIERKEGAARD LIBRARY*, 1510 Saint Olaf Ave, 55057-1097, SAN 374-7077. Tel: 507-646-3846. FAX: 507-646-3858. Web Site: www.stolaf.edu/collections/kierkegaard. *Spec Coll Librn,* Cynthia Wales Lund; *Curator,* Gordon Marino; Tel: 507-646-3609, E-mail: marino@stolaf.edu; Staff 2 (MLS 1, Non-MLS 1)
Founded 1976
Library Holdings: Bk Vols 11,000
Automation Activity & Vendor Info: (Cataloging) Innovative Interfaces, Inc; (OPAC) Innovative Interfaces, Inc; (Serials) Innovative Interfaces, Inc
Partic in OCLC Online Computer Library Center, Inc
Publications: Soren Kierkegaard Society Newsletter
Open Mon-Fri 9-5
Restriction: Not a lending libr
Friends of the Library Group

C ROLVAAG MEMORIAL LIBRARY, HUSTAD SCIENCE LIBRARY, HALVORSON MUSIC LIBRARY*, 1510 Saint Olaf Ave, 55057-1097, SAN 347-7517. Tel: 507-786-3634. Circulation Tel: 507-786-3224. Interlibrary Loan Service Tel: 507-786-3223. Reference Tel:

507-786-3452. FAX: 507-786-3734. Web Site: www.stolaf.edu/library. *Dir, Libr & Info Serv,* Roberta Lembke; Tel: 507-786-3097, E-mail: lembke@stolaf.edu; *Head, Coll Develop,* Mary Barbosa-Jerez; *Head, Res & Instruction,* Kasia Gonnerman; Tel: 507-786-3501, E-mail: gonnermk@stolaf.edu; *Cat Librn, Music,* Kathy Blough; Tel: 507-786-3794; *Music Librn,* Beth Christensen; Tel: 507-786-3362, E-mail: christeb@stolaf.edu; *Ref & Instrul Serv Librn,* Ken Johnson; Tel: 507-786-3793, E-mail: johnsonk@stolaf.edu; *Sci Librn,* Charles Priore; Tel: 507-786-3099, E-mail: priore@stolaf.edu; *Syst & Web Develop Librn,* Sarah Johnston; Tel: 507-786-3771, E-mail: johnsts@stolaf.edu; Staff 22.5 (MLS 13.5, Non-MLS 9)
Founded 1874. Enrl 3,096; Fac 278; Highest Degree: Bachelor
Special Collections: Norwegian-American Historical Association Coll, bks & per; Pre-1801 Imprints (Vault Coll), bks & per. US Document Depository
Subject Interests: Relig studies, Scandinavian hist, Scandinavian lit
Automation Activity & Vendor Info: (Acquisitions) Innovative Interfaces, Inc; (Cataloging) Innovative Interfaces, Inc; (Circulation) Innovative Interfaces, Inc; (Course Reserve) Innovative Interfaces, Inc; (ILL) OCLC ILLiad; (OPAC) Innovative Interfaces, Inc; (Serials) Innovative Interfaces, Inc
Partic in Minitex
Open Mon-Thurs 8am-2am, Fri 8am-9pm, Sat 9-9, Sun Noon-2am

OLIVIA

P OLIVIA PUBLIC LIBRARY*, 405 S Tenth St, 56277-1287. SAN 308-7166. Tel: 320-523-1738. E-mail: olivia.staff@pioneerland.lib.mn.us. Web Site: www.olivia.lib.mn.us. *Head Librn,* Jake Fejedelem; E-mail: jake.fejedelem@pioneerland.lib.mn.us; Staff 5 (MLS 1, Non-MLS 4)
Founded 1916
Library Holdings: Bk Vols 27,198; Per Subs 25
Special Collections: Local Newspaper Depository
Automation Activity & Vendor Info: (Acquisitions) Innovative Interfaces, Inc - Millennium; (Circulation) Innovative Interfaces, Inc - Millennium; (OPAC) Innovative Interfaces, Inc - Millennium
Wireless access
Mem of Pioneerland Library System
Open Mon, Wed & Thurs 12-8, Tues 10-6, Fri 10-5, Sat 9-Noon

ORTONVILLE

P ORTONVILLE PUBLIC LIBRARY*, 412 NW Second St, 56278-1415. SAN 308-7182. Tel: 320-839-2494. FAX: 320-839-3784. E-mail: ortonville.staff@pioneerland.lib.mn.us. Web Site: www.ortonville.lib.mn.us. *Head Librn,* Vicki Bartz; E-mail: vicki.bartz@pioneerland.lib.mn.us; Staff 2 (Non-MLS 2)
Founded 1915. Pop 4,126; Circ 41,336
Library Holdings: Audiobooks 422; DVDs 1,856; Bk Titles 20,011; Per Subs 65; Videos 175
Automation Activity & Vendor Info: (Acquisitions) Innovative Interfaces, Inc; (Cataloging) Innovative Interfaces, Inc; (Circulation) Innovative Interfaces, Inc; (ILL) Innovative Interfaces, Inc; (OPAC) Innovative Interfaces, Inc
Wireless access
Function: Computers for patron use, Orientations, Photocopying/Printing, Prog for adults, Prog for children & young adult, Scanner, Senior computer classes, Spoken cassettes & CDs, Story hour, Summer & winter reading prog, Summer reading prog, Tax forms, Teen prog, VHS videos, Wheelchair accessible
Mem of Pioneerland Library System
Open Mon-Thurs 11-7, Fri 12-5, Sat 10-3
Friends of the Library Group

OWATONNA

P OWATONNA PUBLIC LIBRARY, 105 N Elm Ave, 55060. SAN 347-7606. Tel: 507-444-2460. FAX: 507-444-2465. Web Site: owatonna.info/190/Library. *Libr Dir,* Mark L Blando; E-mail: mark.blando@ci.owatonna.mn.us; *Asst Dir,* Renee Lowery; E-mail: renee@owatonna.info; *Cat Librn, Sr Ref Librn,* Bonnie Krueger; E-mail: bonnie@owatonna.info; *Ch,* Darla Lager; E-mail: darla@owatonna.info; Staff 5 (MLS 4, Non-MLS 1)
Founded 1900. Pop 25,373; Circ 340,000
Library Holdings: Bk Vols 169,000
Special Collections: Genealogy Coll
Automation Activity & Vendor Info: (Cataloging) SirsiDynix; (Circulation) SirsiDynix; (ILL) SirsiDynix; (OPAC) SirsiDynix; (Serials) SirsiDynix
Wireless access
Partic in Southeastern Libraries Cooperating
Open Mon-Thurs 9-9, Fri & Sat 9-5, Sun (Oct-April) 1-5

Branches: 1
BLOOMING PRAIRIE BRANCH, 138 Highway Ave S, Blooming Prairie, 55917, SAN 347-7630. Tel: 507-583-7750. FAX: 507-583-4520. E-mail: bpbl@selco.info. *Br Mgr,* Nancy Vaillancourt; Staff 3 (Non-MLS 3)
Founded 1976. Pop 2,043; Circ 30,459
Library Holdings: Bk Vols 24,411
Open Mon-Wed 10-6, Thurs 10-8, Fri 10-5, Sat 10-1
Friends of the Library Group

PARK RAPIDS

P PARK RAPIDS AREA LIBRARY*, 210 W First St, 56470-8925. SAN 308-7190. Tel: 218-732-4966. FAX: 218-732-4966. E-mail: parkrapids@krls.org. Web Site: www.krls.org/index.php/park-rapids-home-page. *Br Mgr,* Jodi Schultz
Founded 1903. Circ 105,815
Library Holdings: Bk Vols 25,000; Per Subs 90
Automation Activity & Vendor Info: (Cataloging) Innovative Interfaces, Inc; (Circulation) Innovative Interfaces, Inc; (OPAC) Innovative Interfaces, Inc
Wireless access
Mem of Kitchigami Regional Library
Open Mon 9:30-6:30, Tues-Thurs 9:30-5:30, Fri 9:30-4:30, Sat 9:30-1:30
Friends of the Library Group
Bookmobiles: 1

PELICAN RAPIDS

P PELICAN RAPIDS PUBLIC LIBRARY, Multicultural Learning Center, 25 W Mill Ave, 56572. (Mail add: PO Box 371, 56572-0371), SAN 376-7183. Tel: 218-863-7055. FAX: 218-863-7056. E-mail: prpl@prpubliclibrary.org. Web Site: viking.lib.mn.us/pelican-rapids-public-library. *Dir,* Annie M Wrigg; E-mail: awrigg@prpubliclibrary.org; Staff 1 (MLS 1)
Library Holdings: Bk Vols 30,000; Per Subs 115
Automation Activity & Vendor Info: (Cataloging) Horizon; (Circulation) Horizon; (ILL) Horizon; (OPAC) Horizon
Wireless access
Mem of Viking Library System
Open Mon & Tues 10-7, Wed-Fri 10-6, Sat 10-2
Friends of the Library Group

PERHAM

P PERHAM AREA PUBLIC LIBRARY*, 225 Second Ave NE, 56573-1819. SAN 308-7212. Tel: 218-346-4892. FAX: 218-346-4906. Web Site: www.perhamlibrary.org. *Librn,* Susan Heusser-Ladwig; E-mail: susanhl@perhamlibrary.org; Staff 2.9 (MLS 1, Non-MLS 1.9)
Founded 1922. Pop 5,879; Circ 64,409
Automation Activity & Vendor Info: (Acquisitions) Horizon; (Cataloging) Horizon; (Circulation) Horizon; (Discovery) Horizon; (OPAC) Horizon
Wireless access
Function: 24/7 Electronic res, 24/7 Online cat, Adult bk club, Art exhibits, Audiobks via web, Bks on CD, Children's prog, Computers for patron use, ILL available, Internet access, Magazines, Meeting rooms, Online cat, OverDrive digital audio bks, Photocopying/Printing, Preschool reading prog, Prog for adults, Prog for children & young adult, Ref serv available, Scanner, Story hour, Summer & winter reading prog, Tax forms, Wheelchair accessible
Mem of Viking Library System
Open Mon & Wed 10-8, Tues, Thurs & Fri 10-5, Sat 10-3
Friends of the Library Group

PINE CITY

§J PINE TECHNICAL & COMMUNITY COLLEGE LIBRARY, 900 Fourth St SE, 55063. Tel: 320-629-5100. Web Site: www.pine.edu/academics/college-library. *Librn,* Sara Carman; Tel: 320-629-5169, E-mail: sara.carman@pine.edu; *Library & Information Technologist,* Laurie Jorgensen; Tel: 320-629-5145, E-mail: laurie.jorgensen@pine.edu
Library Holdings: Per Subs 44
Wireless access
Function: Computers for patron use, ILL available, Meeting rooms, Photocopying/Printing, Res assist avail, Scanner, Study rm
Partic in MnPALS
Open Mon-Thurs 7:30am-8pm, Fri 7:30-4; Mon-Fri 7:30-4 (Summer)

PINE ISLAND

P VAN HORN PUBLIC LIBRARY, Pine Island Public Library, 115 SE Third St, 55963. (Mail add: PO Box 38, 55963-0038), SAN 308-7239. Tel: 507-356-8558. FAX: 507-356-8599. E-mail: pipl@selco.info. Web Site: pineisland.lib.mn.us. *Dir,* Rachel Gray; E-mail: rgray@selco.info; Staff 1.6 (MLS 1, Non-MLS 0.6)
Founded 1918. Pop 9,403; Circ 63,652

Jan 2015-Dec 2015 Income $177,923, City $108,875, County $69,048. Mats Exp $24,083, Books $15,325, Per/Ser (Incl. Access Fees) $2,150, AV Mat $6,608. Sal $90,825 (Prof $44,725)
Library Holdings: CDs 1,393; DVDs 2,212; Bk Vols 18,151; Per Subs 25
Special Collections: Oral History
Automation Activity & Vendor Info: (Cataloging) Horizon; (Circulation) Horizon; (OPAC) Horizon; (Serials) Horizon
Wireless access
Partic in Southeastern Libraries Cooperating
Open Mon, Wed & Thurs 10-6, Tues 12-7, Fri 10-5, Sat 10-2

PINE RIVER

P KITCHIGAMI REGIONAL LIBRARY*, 310 Second St N, 56474. (Mail add: PO Box 84, 56474-0084), SAN 347-7665. Tel: 218-587-2171. FAX: 218-587-4855. Web Site: www.krls.org. *Dir,* Stephanie Johnson; E-mail: johnsons@krls.org
Founded 1969. Pop 150,000; Circ 825,000
Library Holdings: AV Mats 12,730; Large Print Bks 10,699; Bk Titles 146,949; Bk Vols 300,364; Per Subs 525; Talking Bks 7,307
Subject Interests: Native Americans-Chippewa (Ojibway)
Wireless access
Member Libraries: Bemidji Public Library; Blackduck Community Library; Brainerd Public Library; Cass Lake Community Library; Margaret Welch Memorial Library; Park Rapids Area Library; Pine River Public Library; Wadena City Library; Walker Public Library
Partic in Association for Rural & Small Libraries; Northern Lights Library Network; OCLC Online Computer Library Center, Inc
Special Services for the Deaf - Bks on deafness & sign lang; High interest/low vocabulary bks
Open Mon-Fri 9-4

P PINE RIVER PUBLIC LIBRARY*, 212 Park Ave, 56474. (Mail add: PO Box 14, 56474-0014), SAN 347-7800. Tel: 218-587-4639. FAX: 218-587-3107. E-mail: pineriver@krls.org. Web Site: krls.org/index.php/pine-river-home-page. *Br Mgr,* Tami Beto
Founded 1965
Library Holdings: Audiobooks 948; CDs 216; DVDs 559; Large Print Bks 1,453; Bk Vols 15,233; Per Subs 35; Videos 348
Automation Activity & Vendor Info: (Acquisitions) Innovative Interfaces, Inc; (Cataloging) Innovative Interfaces, Inc; (Circulation) Innovative Interfaces, Inc; (Course Reserve) Innovative Interfaces, Inc; (OPAC) Innovative Interfaces, Inc; (Serials) Innovative Interfaces, Inc
Wireless access
Mem of Kitchigami Regional Library
Open Mon 1-5, Tues & Thurs 10-5, Wed 12-7, Fri 10-3, Sat 10-1
Friends of the Library Group

PIPESTONE

P MEINDERS COMMUNITY LIBRARY, 1401 Seventh St SW, 56164. SAN 376-7132. Tel: 507-825-6714. FAX: 507-562-7374. E-mail: meinders@pas.k12.mn.us. Web Site: plumcreeklibrary.org/places/meinders-community-library. *Libr Dir,* Jody Wacker; E-mail: jody.wacker@pas.k12.mn.us; Staff 4 (MLS 1, Non-MLS 3)
Founded 1904. Pop 8,400; Circ 46,720
Library Holdings: Bk Titles 27,000; Bk Vols 32,000; Per Subs 42
Automation Activity & Vendor Info: (Cataloging) Koha; (Circulation) Koha; (OPAC) Koha
Wireless access
Function: Adult bk club, Audio & video playback equip for onsite use, Audiobks on Playaways & MP3, Audiobks via web, Bks on CD, Children's prog, Computer training, Computers for patron use, Electronic databases & coll, Family literacy, Free DVD rentals, Home delivery & serv to seniorr ctr & nursing homes, ILL available, Internet access, Life-long learning prog for all ages, Magazines, Magnifiers for reading, Movies, Music CDs, Online cat, Orientations, Outreach serv, OverDrive digital audio bks, Photocopying/Printing, Preschool outreach, Prog for adults, Prog for children & young adult, Scanner, Spanish lang bks, Story hour, Study rm, Summer & winter reading prog, Summer reading prog, Tax forms, Teen prog, Telephone ref, Wheelchair accessible, Winter reading prog, Workshops, Writing prog
Mem of Plum Creek Library System
Open Mon-Thurs 10-6, Fri 10-5, Sat 10-2
Friends of the Library Group

S PIPESTONE COUNTY HISTORICAL SOCIETY*, Pipestone County Museum Research Library, 113 S Hiawatha, 56164. SAN 328-1175. Tel: 507-825-2563. Toll Free Tel: 866-747-3687. FAX: 507-825-2563. Toll Free FAX: 866-747-3687. E-mail: pipctymu@iw.net. Web Site: www.pipestoneminnesota.com/museum. *Exec Dir,* Susan Hoskins
Library Holdings: Bk Titles 500
Special Collections: County Newspapers Coll (1879-present); Doctors' Records Coll; Indian School Coll; Photo Coll. Oral History
Subject Interests: Genealogy, Local hist
Open Mon-Sat 10-5
Restriction: Non-circulating, Ref only

PLAINVIEW

P PLAINVIEW PUBLIC LIBRARY, 345 First Ave NW, 55964. SAN 308-7247. Tel: 507-534-3425. E-mail: pla_dir@selco.info. Web Site: plainview.lib.mn.us. *Dir,* Alice Henderson; E-mail: ahenderson@selco.info
Founded 1865. Pop 7,438; Circ 73,139
Library Holdings: DVDs 600; Bk Titles 28,000; Per Subs 15
Automation Activity & Vendor Info: (Cataloging) Horizon; (Circulation) Horizon; (OPAC) Horizon
Wireless access
Partic in Southeastern Libraries Cooperating
Open Mon-Fri 10-7

PLATO

S FAR EASTERN RESEARCH LIBRARY*, Nine First Ave NE, 55370. (Mail add: PO Box 181, 55370-0181), SAN 324-0304. Tel: 612-926-6887. E-mail: emenglang@163.com. *Dir,* Dr Jerome Cavanaugh; E-mail: emenglang@163.com; *Acq of Monographs, Acq of New Ser/Per, Cat,* Jiaqing Liao; *Acq of Monographs & Journals, Acq of New Ser/Per,* Mingzhi Lin. Subject Specialists: *Chinese lang mat, Japanese lang mat, SE Asian lang mat,* Dr Jerome Cavanaugh; *Chinese art, Chinese modern hist,* Jiaqing Liao; *Japanese lang mat, Korean (Lang),* Mingzhi Lin; Staff 4 (MLS 3, Non-MLS 1)
Founded 1969
Library Holdings: AV Mats 135; CDs 170; DVDs 200; Bk Titles 56,220; Bk Vols 58,321; Per Subs 222; Videos 80
Special Collections: Chinese & Tibetan Linguistics (Feng Coll); Chinese Cultural Revolution Coll, doc, monographs, newsp; Chinese Dialect Materials Coll, bks, journals, ms; Chinese Internal Distribution Publications 8000+ titles; Chinese language serials 6000+ titles; Chinese Local History Studies, monographs, ser; Chinese Proverbs, Slang & Colloquialisms Coll; Song Yuan & Ming Drama (Chinese Pre-Modern Drama Coll); Studies on the City of Tianjin Coll
Subject Interests: China, E Asia, Japan, SE Asia
Function: Ref serv available, Res libr
Publications: Far Eastern Research Library Bibliographical Aids Series (Bibliographies)

PLYMOUTH

§CR FREE LUTHERAN BIBLE COLLEGE & SEMINARY, Francis W Monseth Library, Heritage Hall, 2nd Flr, 3134 E Medicine Lake Blvd, 55441-3008. Tel: 763-412-2035. FAX: 763-412-2047. E-mail: library@flbc.edu. Web Site: flbc.edu/library. *Dir, Learning Res,* Dr Jerry Moan; E-mail: jmoan@aflc.org; *Librn,* Rachel Molstre; E-mail: rachel.molstre@flbc.edu
Library Holdings: Bk Vols 25,000
Subject Interests: Relig
Wireless access
Function: Computers for patron use, Photocopying/Printing, Scanner, Study rm
Partic in Minnesota Theological Library Association
Open Mon, Tues, Thurs & Fri 8am-10pm, Wed 8-5, Sat 1-5 (Winter); Mon-Fri 8-4:30 (Summer)

PRESTON

P PRESTON PUBLIC LIBRARY*, 101 St Paul St NW, 55965. (Mail add: PO Box 439, 55965-0439), SAN 308-7271. Tel: 507-765-4511. Web Site: preston.lib.mn.us. *Libr Dir,* Elizabeth Anderson; E-mail: bethand@selco.info
Founded 1908. Pop 3,322; Circ 27,000
Library Holdings: Audiobooks 1,600; DVDs 5,000; Bk Vols 32,000; Per Subs 46; Videos 1,000
Automation Activity & Vendor Info: (Cataloging) SirsiDynix; (Circulation) SirsiDynix; (OPAC) SirsiDynix
Wireless access
Function: 24/7 Online cat, Art exhibits, Audiobks on Playaways & MP3, Audiobks via web, Bks on cassette, Bks on CD, Children's prog, Computers for patron use, Digital talking bks, Electronic databases & coll, Free DVD rentals, ILL available, Internet access, Magazines, Music CDs, Online cat, Online ref, OverDrive digital audio bks, Photocopying/Printing, Prog for adults, Prog for children & young adult, Scanner, Spoken cassettes & CDs, Story hour, Summer & winter reading prog, Summer reading prog, Tax forms, Teen prog, VHS videos, Wheelchair accessible, Winter reading prog
Partic in Southeastern Libraries Cooperating
Open Mon & Fri 10-5, Tues & Thurs 2-8, Wed 10-8, Sat 10-3
Friends of the Library Group

RAYMOND

P RAYMOND PUBLIC LIBRARY, 208 Cofield St N, 56282. (Mail add: PO Box 203, 56282-0203), SAN 348-1328. Tel: 320-967-4411. Web Site: www.raymond.lib.mn.us. *Head Librn,* Ria Newhouse; E-mail: ria.newhouse@pioneerland.lib.mn.us
Pop 1,553; Circ 14,732
Library Holdings: Bk Vols 6,200; Per Subs 19
Automation Activity & Vendor Info: (Cataloging) Innovative Interfaces, Inc; (Circulation) Innovative Interfaces, Inc; (OPAC) Innovative Interfaces, Inc
Wireless access
Mem of Pioneerland Library System
Open Mon, Wed & Fri 1-6, Tues 10-3

RED WING

R FIRST LUTHERAN CHURCH, Schendel Memorial Library, 615 W Fifth St, 55066. SAN 308-728X. Tel: 651-388-9311. FAX: 651-388-1714. E-mail: office@firstlutheranrw.com. Web Site: www.firstlutheranrw.com. *Vols Librn,* Nancy Thorson
Founded 1951
Library Holdings: Bk Titles 3,000
Subject Interests: Attitudes, Beliefs, Bible study, Children's lit, Christian life, Christianity, Devotional studies, Inspirational reading, Interpersonal relations, Recreational reading
Wireless access

S GOODHUE COUNTY HISTORICAL SOCIETY LIBRARY*, 1166 Oak St, 55066. SAN 327-1714. Tel: 651-388-6024. FAX: 651-388-3577. E-mail: library@goodhistory.org. Web Site: goodhuehistory.org/research-library. *Exec Dir,* Robin Whipperling; E-mail: director@goodhistory.org; *Libr & Archives Mgr,* Mr Afton Esson
Library Holdings: Bk Vols 2,050
Publications: Goodhue County Historical News
Open Tues-Fri 9-5, Sat 9-3 & by appointment

S MINNESOTA DEPARTMENT OF CORRECTIONS*, Minnesota Correctional Facility - Red Wing, 1079 Hwy 292, 55066. Tel: 651-267-3644. FAX: 651-385-6425. Web Site: mn.gov/doc. *Libr Tech,* Brad Wronski; E-mail: brad.wronski@state.mn.us
Library Holdings: AV Mats 350; Bk Vols 5,500; Per Subs 27
Special Collections: Law Coll
Automation Activity & Vendor Info: (Cataloging) EOS International; (Circulation) EOS International; (OPAC) EOS International

P RED WING PUBLIC LIBRARY*, 225 East Ave, 55066-2298. SAN 308-7298. Tel: 651-385-3673. Reference Tel: 651-385-3645. FAX: 651-385-3644. E-mail: rwpl@selco.info. Web Site: www.redwing.lib.mn.us. *Libr Dir,* Jessica McGee; Tel: 651-385-5105, E-mail: jmcgee@selco.info; *Children's & Teen Serv,* Megan Seeland; Tel: 651-385-5108, E-mail: mseeland@selco.info; *Circ Serv, Ref Serv,* Randy Decker; E-mail: rdecker@selco.info; *Tech Serv,* Janet Elizabeth Brandt; Tel: 651-385-5100, E-mail: janetb@selco.info; Staff 13 (MLS 5, Non-MLS 8)
Founded 1894. Pop 18,900; Circ 183,000
Library Holdings: Audiobooks 2,061; CDs 1,494; DVDs 3,961; Large Print Bks 1,870; Bk Titles 64,068; Per Subs 225; Videos 110
Special Collections: Red Wing Area Genealogy Index; Red Wing History
Automation Activity & Vendor Info: (Acquisitions) SirsiDynix; (Cataloging) SirsiDynix; (Circulation) SirsiDynix; (ILL) SirsiDynix; (Media Booking) SirsiDynix; (OPAC) SirsiDynix; (Serials) SirsiDynix
Wireless access
Function: 24/7 Electronic res, 24/7 Online cat, Adult bk club, Audiobks on Playaways & MP3, Audiobks via web, Bk club(s), Bks on CD, Children's prog, Computer training, Computers for patron use, Electronic databases & coll, Free DVD rentals, Holiday prog, ILL available, Instruction & testing, Internet access, Magazines, Mango lang, Movies, Music CDs, Notary serv, Online cat, OverDrive digital audio bks, Photocopying/Printing, Prog for adults, Prog for children & young adult, Ref & res, Ref serv available, Spanish lang bks, Story hour, Study rm, Wheelchair accessible
Partic in Southeastern Libraries Cooperating
Special Services for the Deaf - Assistive tech; Closed caption videos; Spec interest per
Special Services for the Blind - Assistive/Adapted tech devices, equip & products; Home delivery serv; Large print bks; Large screen computer & software; Low vision equip; Magnifiers
Open Mon-Wed 10-7, Thurs & Fri 10-6, Sat 9-3
Friends of the Library Group

REDWOOD FALLS

P REDWOOD FALLS PUBLIC LIBRARY*, 509 S Lincoln St, 56283. SAN 308-7301. Tel: 507-616-7420. FAX: 507-627-5004. E-mail: rwf@ci.redwood-falls.mn.us. Web Site: www.redwoodfallslibrary.org. *Dir, Libr Serv,* Teri Smith; E-mail: tsmith@ci.redwood-falls.mn.us; *Ch,* Jill Deinken; E-mail: jdeinken@ci.redwood-falls.mn.us; Staff 4 (MLS 1, Non-MLS 3)
Founded 1904. Pop 7,070; Circ 109,883
Library Holdings: Bk Titles 54,000; Per Subs 70
Wireless access
Publications: American Libraries; Library Journal
Mem of Plum Creek Library System
Open Mon-Thurs 10-8, Fri 10-5, Sat 10-2 (Sept-May)
Friends of the Library Group

RENVILLE

P RENVILLE CITY LIBRARY*, 221 N Main St, 56284. (Mail add: PO Box 609, 56284-0609), SAN 348-1336. Tel: 320-329-8193. E-mail: renville.staff@pioneerland.lib.mn.us. Web Site: www.renville.lib.mn.us. *Head Librn,* Jake Fejedelem; E-mail: jake.fejedelem@pioneerland.lib.mn.us
Pop 1,375; Circ 27,220
Library Holdings: Bk Vols 23,000; Per Subs 62
Automation Activity & Vendor Info: (Acquisitions) Innovative Interfaces, Inc - Millennium; (Cataloging) Innovative Interfaces, Inc - Millennium; (Circulation) Innovative Interfaces, Inc - Millennium; (OPAC) Innovative Interfaces, Inc - Millennium
Wireless access
Mem of Pioneerland Library System
Open Mon, Wed & Fri 12:30-5:30, Tues 10-4, Thurs 12:30-5:30

RICHFIELD

R OAK GROVE LUTHERAN CHURCH, Juanita Carpenter Library, 7045 Lyndale Ave S, 55423-3099. SAN 308-731X. Tel: 612-869-4917. Web Site: www.oakgrovelutheran.org. *Librn,* Richard Jefferson
Founded 1959
Library Holdings: Bk Titles 5,800
Subject Interests: Admin, Adult, Aging, Biblical studies, Educ of ch, Ethics, Family life, Fiction, Marriage, Psychol, Relig
Special Services for the Blind - Large print bks
Open Mon-Fri 9-4 (Winter); Mon-Fri 9-3 (Summer)

ROBBINSDALE

M NORTH MEMORIAL HEALTH CARE*, Medical Library, 3300 Oakdale Ave N, 55422. SAN 308-681X. Tel: 763-581-4740. FAX: 763-581-4750. E-mail: library@northmemorial.com. Web Site: www.northmemorial.com. *Librn,* Janet Crow; *Librn,* Dawn Krist; Staff 1 (MLS 0.5, Non-MLS 0.5)
Founded 1968
Library Holdings: AV Mats 825; Bk Titles 4,800; Per Subs 30
Subject Interests: Hospitals, Med, Nursing, Paramedical training
Automation Activity & Vendor Info: (Cataloging) EOS International; (OPAC) EOS International; (Serials) EOS International
Wireless access
Partic in Minitex; National Network of Libraries of Medicine Region 6
Restriction: Med & nursing staff, patients & families

ROCHESTER

S MAYO CLINIC LIBRARIES, (Formerly Mayo Foundation), 200 First St SW, 55905. SAN 377-869X. Tel: 507-284-2061. FAX: 507-266-4910. E-mail: library@mayo.edu. Web Site: college.mayo.edu/academics/libraries. *Exec Dir,* Anna Beth Morgan
Founded 1972
Library Holdings: e-journals 4,900; Bk Vols 100,000
Automation Activity & Vendor Info: (Cataloging) Innovative Interfaces, Inc
Wireless access
Open Mon-Thurs 7:30am-11pm, Fri 7:30-5, Sat 10-6, Sun 12-8
Restriction: Open to students, fac & staff

S MAYO CLINIC LIBRARIES*, Saint Marys Patients' Library, 1216 Second St SW, 55902. SAN 347-7967. Tel: 507-255-5434. FAX: 507-255-5254. E-mail: patientlib@mayo.edu. Web Site: libraryguides.mayo.edu/hospitalpatients. *Librn,* Stephanie Wentz; E-mail: wentz.stephanie@mayo.edu; Staff 3 (MLS 1, Non-MLS 2)
Founded 1921
Library Holdings: CDs 2,000; DVDs 300; Large Print Bks 200; Bk Vols 7,000; Per Subs 110; Videos 2,000
Subject Interests: Consumer health info
Automation Activity & Vendor Info: (Acquisitions) Innovative Interfaces, Inc; (Cataloging) Innovative Interfaces, Inc; (Circulation) Innovative Interfaces, Inc; (ILL) Innovative Interfaces, Inc; (Media Booking) Innovative Interfaces, Inc; (OPAC) Innovative Interfaces, Inc; (Serials) Innovative Interfaces, Inc
Wireless access
Special Services for the Blind - Talking bks; Talking bks & player equip
Open Mon-Fri 9:30-4:30, Sat & Sun 1-4:30
Restriction: Non-circulating to the pub

S OLMSTED COUNTY HISTORICAL SOCIETY, Willson Wicklund Research Center, 1195 W Circle Dr SW, 55902. SAN 326-114X. Tel: 507-282-9447. E-mail: services@olmstedhistory.com. Web Site: www.olmstedhistory.com/resources-wicklund. *Exec Dir,* Wayne Gannaway; E-mail: execdirector@olmstedhistory.com; *Archivist,* Krista Lewis; E-mail: archivist@olmstedhistory.com
Founded 1926
Special Collections: Funeral Home, Cemetery Records; Minnesota Census 1857-1930; Olmsted County & Rochester Coll; Olmsted County Probate & Guardianship Records; Rochester Newspapers 1859-present; Vital Records, Olmsted County & other Southeastern Minnesota Counties; World War I Draft Registrations
Subject Interests: Genealogy, Hist
Wireless access
Open Tues-Sat 9-5
Restriction: Non-circulating to the pub

J ROCHESTER COMMUNITY & TECHNICAL COLLEGE*, Goddard Library, 851 30 Ave SE, 55904. SAN 308-7360. Tel: 507-285-7233. FAX: 507-281-7772. Web Site: rctc.libguides.com/library. *Libr Coord,* Diane Pollock; Tel: 507-285-7229, E-mail: diane.pollock@rctc.edu; *Librn,* Jen Bruce; *Librn,* Mary Dennison; *Librn,* May Jesseph; *Librn,* Michele McCaughtry; Staff 7.6 (MLS 3.6, Non-MLS 4)
Founded 1915. Enrl 9,000; Fac 4
Wireless access
Partic in Minitex; MnPALS; OCLC Online Computer Library Center, Inc
Open Mon-Thurs 8am-9pm, Fri 8-4:30, Sat 9-5, Sun 1-5

P ROCHESTER PUBLIC LIBRARY*, 101 Second St SE, 55904-3776. SAN 308-7387. Tel: 507-328-2300. Circulation Tel: 507-328-2304. Interlibrary Loan Service Tel: 507-328-2366. Reference Tel: 507-328-2309. Administration Tel: 507-328-2320. Automation Services Tel: 507-328-2363. FAX: 507-328-2384. Web Site: www.rplm.org. *Libr Dir,* Audrey Betcher; Tel: 507-328-2344, E-mail: audrey@rplmn.org; *Head of Mkt,* Karen Lemke; Tel: 507-328-2343, E-mail: klemke@rplmn.org; *Head, Reader Serv,* Kimberly Edson; Tel: 507-328-2325, E-mail: kedson@rplmn.org; *Head, Ref Serv,* Sara Patalita; Tel: 507-328-2369, E-mail: spatalita@rplmn.org; *Head, Tech Serv,* Keri Ostby; Tel: 507-328-2355, E-mail: kostby@rplmn.org; *Head, Youth Serv,* Heather Acerro; Tel: 507-328-2339, E-mail: hacerro@rplmn.org; *Admin Serv Mgr,* Purna Gurung; E-mail: pgurung@rplmn.org; *Automation Syst Mgr,* Steve Mosing; Tel: 507-328-2361, E-mail: stevem@rplmn.org; *Circ Serv Mgr,* Andy Stehr; Tel: 507-328-2322, E-mail: astehr@rplmn.org; Staff 72 (MLS 20, Non-MLS 52)
Founded 1895. Pop 144,743; Circ 1,897,802
Jan 2017-Dec 2017 Income $7,644,994, State $58,370, City $6,191,826, Federal $25,704, County $949,394, Other $419,700. Mats Exp $822,738. Sal $4,118,996
Automation Activity & Vendor Info: (Acquisitions) SirsiDynix; (Cataloging) SirsiDynix; (Circulation) SirsiDynix; (ILL) OCLC; (OPAC) SirsiDynix; (Serials) SirsiDynix
Wireless access
Function: 24/7 Electronic res, 24/7 Online cat, 3D Printer, Activity rm, Adult bk club, Adult literacy prog, After school storytime, Archival coll, Art exhibits, Art programs, Audio & video playback equip for onsite use, Audiobks via web, AV serv, Bi-weekly Writer's Group, Bk club(s), Bks on CD, CD-ROM, Chess club, Children's prog, Computer training, Computers for patron use, Doc delivery serv, E-Reserves, Electronic databases & coll, Equip loans & repairs, Family literacy, For res purposes, Free DVD rentals, Govt ref serv, Health sci info serv, Home delivery & serv to seniorr ctr & nursing homes, Homebound delivery serv, Homework prog, ILL available, Instruction & testing, Internet access, Jail serv, Large print keyboards, Life-long learning prog for all ages, Literacy & newcomer serv, Magazines, Magnifiers for reading, Mail & tel request accepted, Makerspace, Mango lang, Meeting rooms, Microfiche/film & reading machines, Movies, Music CDs, Online cat, Online ref, Outreach serv, Outside serv via phone, mail, e-mail & web, OverDrive digital audio bks, Photocopying/Printing, Preschool outreach, Preschool reading prog, Printer for laptops & handheld devices, Prog for adults, Prog for children & young adult, Ref & res, Ref serv available, Scanner, Senior computer classes, Senior outreach, Serves people with intellectual disabilities, Spanish lang bks, Spoken cassettes & CDs, Spoken cassettes & DVDs, Story hour, Study rm, Summer & winter reading prog, Summer reading prog, Tax forms, Teen prog, Telephone ref, VHS videos, Visual arts prog, Wheelchair accessible, Workshops, Writing prog
Partic in OCLC Online Computer Library Center, Inc; Rochester Regional Library Council; Southeastern Libraries Cooperating
Special Services for the Deaf - ADA equip; Bks on deafness & sign lang; Closed caption videos; High interest/low vocabulary bks
Special Services for the Blind - Accessible computers; Assistive/Adapted tech devices, equip & products; Audio mat; Bks on cassette; Bks on CD; Braille equip; Cassette playback machines; Computer with voice synthesizer for visually impaired persons; Descriptive video serv (DVS); Digital talking bk; Home delivery serv; Large print & cassettes; Large print bks; Magnifiers; Videos on blindness & physical disabilties; ZoomText magnification & reading software
Open Mon-Thurs 9:30-9, Sat 9:30-5:30, Sun 1:30-5:30
Friends of the Library Group
Bookmobiles: 1. Head, Reader Servs, Kimberly Edson. Bk vols 20,028

P SOUTHEAST LIBRARY SYSTEM (SELS)*, 2600 19th St, 55901. Tel: 507-288-5513. Toll Free Tel: 800-992-5061. FAX: 507-288-8697. Web Site: www.selco.info. *Exec Dir,* Krista Ross; E-mail: kross@selco.info
Member Libraries: Cannon Falls Library; Chatfield Music Lending Library; Winona County Historical Society

ROSEMOUNT

J DAKOTA COUNTY TECHNICAL COLLEGE LIBRARY, 1300 145th St E, 55068. SAN 320-6831. Tel: 651-423-8366. Circulation Tel: 651-423-8345. Interlibrary Loan Service Tel: 651-423-8654. Administration Tel: 651-423-8406. FAX: 651-423-8043. E-mail: library@dctc.edu. Web Site: dctc.edu/support-services/library. *Head Librn,* Michael Kirby; E-mail: Michael.Kirby@dctc.edu; *Circ Mgr,* Melanie Ellston; E-mail: Melanie.Ellston@dctc.edu; *Cat, ILL Mgr,* Danielle Hoveland; E-mail: Danielle.Hoveland@dctc.edu; Staff 2.6 (MLS 1, Non-MLS 1.6)
Founded 1973
Library Holdings: AV Mats 1,165; e-books 216,570; Bk Titles 15,963; Per Subs 38
Automation Activity & Vendor Info: (Cataloging) PALS; (Circulation) PALS; (Course Reserve) PALS; (ILL) PALS; (OPAC) PALS
Wireless access
Partic in MnPALS
Open Mon-Thurs 7:30-5, Fri 7:30-3:30 (Fall & Spring); Mon-Thurs (Summer) 8-1

ROSEVILLE

S MINNESOTA STATE HORTICULTURAL SOCIETY LIBRARY*, 2705 Lincoln Dr, 55113. SAN 328-4034. Tel: 651-643-3601. Toll Free Tel: 800-676-6747. FAX: 651-643-3638. E-mail: info@northerngardener.org. Web Site: northerngardener.org/library. *Chief Exec Officer,* Rose Eggert; E-mail: reggert@northerngardener.org
Founded 1866
Library Holdings: CDs 20; DVDs 130; Bk Titles 2,000
Special Collections: Historical Volumes relating to horticulture; Minnesota Horticulturist bound volumes from 1870s to present; Video tapes-topics relating to Northern horticultural
Subject Interests: Hort
Open Mon, Wed & Thurs 8-4:30, Tues 8-7, Fri 8-Noon
Restriction: Circ limited, In-house use for visitors
Friends of the Library Group

RUSH CITY

S MINNESOTA DEPARTMENT OF CORRECTIONS*, Minnesota Correctional Facility - Rush City, 7600 - 525th St, 55069. Tel: 320-358-0400, Ext 373. FAX: 763-689-7555. Web Site: www.doc.state.mn.us. *Librn,* Jonathan P Chapman; E-mail: jonathan.chapman@state.mn.us; *Libr Tech,* Lisa Beynon; Staff 1 (MLS 1)
Founded 2000
Library Holdings: Bk Titles 15,054; Bk Vols 16,793; Per Subs 60; Videos 400
Special Collections: Minnesota Law Library
Automation Activity & Vendor Info: (Cataloging) Follett Software; (Circulation) Follett Software
Restriction: Staff & inmates only

RUSHFORD

P RUSHFORD PUBLIC LIBRARY*, 101 N Mill St, 55971. (Mail add: PO Box 250, 55971-0250), SAN 308-7433. Tel: 507-864-7600. FAX: 507-864-7003. Web Site: www.rushford.lib.mn.us. *Dir,* Susan Hart; E-mail: rush_dir@selco.info; Staff 2 (Non-MLS 2)
Founded 1922. Pop 4,340; Circ 28,173
Jan 2015-Dec 2015 Income $149,357, State $2,736, City $107,920, County $33,022, Locally Generated Income $5,679. Mats Exp $17,015, Books $9,540, AV Equip $83, AV Mat $4,382, Electronic Ref Mat (Incl. Access Fees) $3,010. Sal $102,082
Library Holdings: Audiobooks 812; CDs 694; DVDs 1,642; e-books 10,000; e-journals 22; Large Print Bks 1,601; Bk Vols 19,241; Per Subs 19; Videos 887
Subject Interests: Local hist
Automation Activity & Vendor Info: (Cataloging) SirsiDynix; (Circulation) SirsiDynix; (ILL) SirsiDynix; (Media Booking) SirsiDynix; (OPAC) SirsiDynix; (Serials) SirsiDynix
Wireless access
Function: Audiobks on Playaways & MP3, Audiobks via web, Bks on CD, Children's prog, Computers for patron use, Free DVD rentals, Home delivery & serv to seniorr ctr & nursing homes, Homebound delivery serv,

ILL available, Internet access, Magazines, Online cat, Outreach serv, Photocopying/Printing, Preschool reading prog, Prog for adults, Prog for children & young adult, Scanner, Story hour, Summer & winter reading prog, VHS videos, Winter reading prog
Partic in Southeastern Libraries Cooperating
Special Services for the Blind - Large print bks; Talking bks
Open Mon 12-7, Tues & Thurs 10-7, Wed & Fri 10-6, Sat 10-2

SAINT BONIFACIUS

CR CROWN COLLEGE*, Watne Memorial Library, 8700 College View Dr, 55375-9002. SAN 308-5228. Tel: 952-446-4241. Interlibrary Loan Service Tel: 952-446-4414. FAX: 952-446-4149. Web Site: www.crownlibrary.com. *Interim Libr Dir,* Mary Meehan; E-mail: meehanm@crown.edu; *Tech Serv & Syst Librn,* Position Currently Open; *ILL Mgr, Ref Librn,* Mary Meehan; E-mail: interlibraryloan@crown.edu; *Pub Serv Mgr,* Kathleen McBride; E-mail: McBridek@crown.edu; Staff 2 (MLS 1, Non-MLS 1)
Founded 1916. Enrl 1,050; Fac 42; Highest Degree: Master
Library Holdings: AV Mats 1,376; CDs 160; DVDs 855; e-books 179,431; e-journals 39,088; Bk Titles 259,553; Bk Vols 266,702; Per Subs 70
Automation Activity & Vendor Info: (Acquisitions) OCLC; (Cataloging) OCLC; (Circulation) OCLC; (Course Reserve) OCLC; (ILL) OCLC WorldShare Interlibrary Loan; (OPAC) OCLC
Wireless access
Function: 24/7 Online cat, Archival coll, Internet access, Mango lang, Online cat, Ref & res, Ref serv available, Study rm
Partic in Christian Library Consortium; Minitex; OCLC Online Computer Library Center, Inc
Open Mon-Thurs 7:30am-Midnight, Fri 7:30-5, Sat 1-5, Sun 6pm-11pm; Mon-Fri (Summer) 8-4
Restriction: Authorized patrons, Badge access after hrs, Open to authorized patrons, Open to students, fac & staff

SAINT CHARLES

P SAINT CHARLES PUBLIC LIBRARY*, 125 W 11th St, 55972-1141. SAN 308-7441. Tel: 507-932-3227. E-mail: scill@selco.info. Web Site: stcharles.lib.mn.us. *Dir,* Sharon Grossardt; E-mail: sherryg@selco.info; Staff 1 (MLS 1)
Founded 1913. Pop 7,811; Circ 36,227
Jan 2014-Dec 2014 Income $149,537, City $97,786, County $28,069, Locally Generated Income $22,073, Other $1,609. Mats Exp $16,142, Books $12,133, AV Mat $4,009. Sal $67,507
Library Holdings: AV Mats 2,658; e-books 25,827; Bk Vols 23,484; Per Subs 50
Special Collections: Photographs of Early St Charles
Automation Activity & Vendor Info: (Cataloging) Horizon; (Circulation) Horizon; (ILL) Horizon; (OPAC) Horizon; (Serials) Horizon
Wireless access
Function: Children's prog, Computers for patron use, Free DVD rentals, ILL available, Mail & tel request accepted, Music CDs, Online cat, OverDrive digital audio bks, Photocopying/Printing, Preschool outreach, Prog for children & young adult, Spoken cassettes & CDs, Summer & winter reading prog, Tax forms, VHS videos, Wheelchair accessible
Partic in Southeastern Libraries Cooperating
Open Mon & Wed 10-6, Tues, Thurs & Fri 1-6
Friends of the Library Group

SAINT CLOUD

M CENTRACARE - SAINT CLOUD HOSPITAL*, Health Sciences Library, 1406 Sixth Ave N, 56303. SAN 327-8271. Tel: 320-251-2700, Ext 54686. FAX: 320-656-7039. E-mail: library@centracare.com. *Librn,* Susan Schleper; *Libr Asst,* Stephanie Ronning
Library Holdings: Bk Vols 1,000; Per Subs 160
Wireless access
Open Mon-Fri 8-4:30
Restriction: Open to pub for ref only

GM DEPARTMENT OF VETERANS AFFAIRS MEDICAL CENTER*, Medical Library, 4801 Veterans Dr, 56303. SAN 308-745X. Tel: 320-255-6342. FAX: 320-255-6493. Web Site: www.stcloud.va.gov/. *Librn,* Patricia Grelson; E-mail: patricia.grelson@va.gov; Staff 1 (Non-MLS 1)
Founded 1925
Library Holdings: Bk Vols 1,500; Per Subs 205
Subject Interests: Geriatrics, Nursing, Psychiat, Psychol
Open Mon-Fri 7-4

P GREAT RIVER REGIONAL LIBRARY*, 1300 W St Germain St, 56301. SAN 347-8173. Tel: 320-650-2500. Circulation Tel: 320-650-2522. Web Site: www.griver.org. *Exec Dir,* Karen Pundsack; Tel: 320-650-2512, E-mail: karenp@grrl.lib.mn.us; *Assoc Dir, Coll Develop,* Jami Trenam; Tel: 320-650-2531, E-mail: jamit@grrl.lib.mn.us; *Assoc Dir, Human Res,* Julie Schmitz; Tel: 320-650-2511, E-mail: julies@grrl.lib.mn.us; *Assoc Dir, Info Tech,* Jay Roos; Tel: 320-650-2534, E-mail: jayr@grrl.lib.mn.us; *Patron Serv Supvr,* Brandi Canter; Tel: 320-650-2530, E-mail: brandic@grrl.lib.mn.us; *Patron Serv Supvr,* Ryan McCormick; Tel: 320-650-2527, E-mail: ryanm@grrl.lib.mn.us; *Patron Serv Supvr,* Rachel Thomas; Tel: 320-650-2525, E-mail: rachelt@grrl.lib.mn.us; Staff 19 (MLS 19)
Founded 1969. Pop 467,188; Circ 3,820,661
Jan 2013-Dec 2013 Income $9,507,437. Mats Exp $947,100. Sal $6,915,000
Library Holdings: Audiobooks 29,523; CDs 39,595; DVDs 64,202; Bk Vols 797,293
Automation Activity & Vendor Info: (Cataloging) Horizon; (Circulation) Horizon; (OPAC) Horizon
Wireless access
Function: Adult bk club, Art exhibits, Audiobks via web, Bk club(s), Bks on cassette, Bks on CD, Children's prog, Computer training, Computers for patron use, Digital talking bks, Electronic databases & coll, Free DVD rentals, Home delivery & serv to seniorr ctr & nursing homes, ILL available, Large print keyboards, Magnifiers for reading, Music CDs, Online cat, OverDrive digital audio bks, Photocopying/Printing, Prog for adults, Prog for children & young adult, Ref serv available, Senior computer classes, Spoken cassettes & CDs, Spoken cassettes & DVDs, Story hour, Summer reading prog, Tax forms, Teen prog, Telephone ref, VHS videos, Wheelchair accessible
Publications: Index of St Cloud Daily Times
Partic in Minitex
Open Mon-Thurs 10-9, Fri 10-6, Sat 10-5
Friends of the Library Group
Branches: 32
ALBANY PUBLIC LIBRARY, 400 Railroad Ave, Albany, 56307. (Mail add: PO Box 519, Albany, 56307), SAN 347-8203. Tel: 320-845-4843. Web Site: griver.org/locations/albany. *Libr Serv Coordr,* John Hannon; E-mail: johnha@grrl.lib.mn.us
Founded 1960. Pop 12,488; Circ 82,071
Library Holdings: Audiobooks 520; AV Mats 520; CDs 619; DVDs 1,119; Bk Vols 16,043; Videos 1,119
Open Mon 12-7, Tues 12-8, Wed 10-6, Thurs 12-6, Fri 12-5, Sat 10-1
Friends of the Library Group
ANNANDALE PUBLIC LIBRARY, 30 Cedar St E, Annandale, 55302-1113. (Mail add: PO Box 207, Annandale, 55302-0207), SAN 347-8238. Tel: 320-274-8448. Web Site: griver.org/locations/annandale. *Br Mgr,* Carla Asfeld; E-mail: carlaa@grrl.lib.mn.us
Pop 8,139; Circ 58,558
Library Holdings: Audiobooks 738; AV Mats 99; CDs 591; DVDs 1,373; Bk Vols 13,702; Per Subs 30
Open Mon 2-5, Tues 9-1 & 2-5, Wed 2-8, Fri 9-12 & 2-5, Sat 9-12
Friends of the Library Group
BECKER LIBRARY, 11500 Sherburne Ave, Becker, 55308. (Mail add: PO Box 414, Becker, 55308-0414), SAN 322-564X. Tel: 763-261-4454. Web Site: griver.org/locations/becker. *Libr Serv Coordr,* Jeannette Burkhardt; E-mail: jeannetteb@grrl.lib.mn.us
Founded 1984. Pop 10,504; Circ 83,009
Library Holdings: Audiobooks 501; AV Mats 586; CDs 384; DVDs 516; Bk Vols 16,851; Per Subs 28; Videos 516
Open Mon & Thurs 2-8, Tues 10-6, Wed & Fri 2-6, Sat 10-1
Friends of the Library Group
BIG LAKE LIBRARY, 790 Minnesota Ave, Ste 500, Big Lake, 55309, SAN 322-6336. Tel: 763-263-6445. Web Site: griver.org/locations/big-lake. *Libr Serv Coordr,* Jeannette Burkhardt
Founded 1984. Pop 15,115; Circ 75,355
Library Holdings: Audiobooks 967; AV Mats 960; CDs 547; DVDs 683; Bk Vols 20,230; Per Subs 41; Videos 684
Open Mon & Wed 1-7, Tues 10-7, Thurs 2-6, Fri 10-5, Sat 10-1
Friends of the Library Group
BRYANT LIBRARY, 430 Main St, Unit 1, Sauk Centre, 56378, SAN 308-8006. Tel: 320-352-3016. Web Site: griver.org/locations/sauk-centre. *Libr Serv Coordr,* Marisa George; E-mail: marisag@grrl.lib.mn.us
Founded 1878. Pop 7,973; Circ 96,111
Library Holdings: Audiobooks 701; AV Mats 181; CDs 1,357; DVDs 1,865; Bk Vols 20,739; Per Subs 56
Special Collections: James Hendryx Coll; Sinclair Lewis Coll
Open Mon & Fri 12-5, Tues & Thurs 2-8, Wed 10-5, Sat 10-1
Friends of the Library Group
BUFFALO LIBRARY, 18 NW Lake Blvd, Buffalo, 55313, SAN 347-8262. Tel: 763-682-2753. Web Site: griver.org/locations/buffalo. *Libr Serv Coordr,* Position Currently Open
Founded 1907. Pop 25,000; Circ 256,357
Library Holdings: Audiobooks 1,538; AV Mats 245; CDs 1,791; Bk Vols 38,333; Per Subs 96; Videos 3,604
Special Services for the Deaf - TDD equip
Open Mon-Wed 10-8, Thurs 12-8, Fri 11-5, Sat 10-2
Friends of the Library Group

COKATO LIBRARY, 175 Fourth St W, Cokato, 55321. (Mail add: PO Box 686, Cokato, 55321-0686), SAN 347-8297. Tel: 320-286-5760. Web Site: griver.org/locations/cokato. *Libr Serv Coordr,* Sara Koivisto; E-mail: sarak@grrl.lib.mn.us
Pop 6,010; Circ 72,224
Library Holdings: Audiobooks 583; AV Mats 112; CDs 292; Bk Vols 12,386; Per Subs 45; Videos 1,082
Open Mon 2-6, Tues & Thurs 2-8, Wed 10-2, Fri 11-5, Sat 10-12
Friends of the Library Group

COLD SPRING LIBRARY, 27 Red River Rd S, Cold Spring, 56320, SAN 347-8327. Tel: 320-685-8281. Web Site: griver.org/locations/cold-spring. *Libr Serv Coordr,* Jason Kirchoff; E-mail: jasonk@grrl.lib.mn.us
Pop 9,544; Circ 116,595
Library Holdings: Audiobooks 549; AV Mats 624; CDs 563; DVDs 625; Bk Vols 12,794; Per Subs 30; Videos 626
Open Mon 12-6, Tues & Thurs 2-8, Wed 10-5, Fri 11-5, Sat 10-1
Friends of the Library Group

DELANO LIBRARY, 160 Railroad Ave E, Delano, 55328. (Mail add: PO Box 677, Delano, 55328-0677), SAN 347-8351. Tel: 763-972-3467. Web Site: griver.org/locations/delano. *Libr Serv Coordr,* Theresa Jacobs; E-mail: theresaj@grrl.lib.mn.us
Pop 7,390; Circ 145,640
Library Holdings: Audiobooks 1,039; AV Mats 254; CDs 1,247; DVDs 2,731; Bk Vols 25,018; Per Subs 70; Videos 992
Open Mon & Thurs 10-6, Tues 10-8, Wed 1-8, Fri 1-6, Sat 10-1
Friends of the Library Group

EAGLE BEND LIBRARY, 127 E Main, Eagle Bend, 56446. (Mail add: PO Box 238, Eagle Bend, 56446-0238), SAN 321-9267. Tel: 218-738-4590. Web Site: griver.org/locations/eagle-bend. *Libr Serv Coordr,* Cathy Perish; E-mail: cathyp@grrl.lib.mn.us
Pop 4,221; Circ 24,036
Library Holdings: Audiobooks 244; AV Mats 119; CDs 315; DVDs 1,183; Bk Vols 9,450; Per Subs 40
Open Mon & Tues 10-5, Thurs 4-7, Sat 9-12
Friends of the Library Group

ELK RIVER LIBRARY, 13020 Orono Pkwy, Elk River, 55330, SAN 347-8386. Tel: 763-441-1641. Web Site: griver.org/locations/elk-river. *Libr Serv Coordr,* Robbie Schake; E-mail: robbies@grrl.lib.mn.us
Pop 41,927; Circ 313,199
Library Holdings: Audiobooks 1,911; AV Mats 1,590; CDs 1,336; DVDs 1,266; Bk Vols 41,407; Per Subs 69; Videos 1,267
Open Mon-Thurs 12-8, Fri 10-5, Sat 10-2
Friends of the Library Group

FOLEY LIBRARY, 251 N Fourth Ave, Foley, 56329. (Mail add: PO Box 340, Foley, 56329), SAN 347-8416. Tel: 320-968-6612. Web Site: griver.org/locations/foley. *Libr Serv Coordr,* Position Currently Open
Pop 9,135; Circ 68,914
Library Holdings: Audiobooks 467; AV Mats 100; CDs 590; DVDs 1,573; Bk Vols 13,757; Per Subs 41; Videos 611
Open Mon & Wed 2-8, Tues & Fri 9-12 & 1-6, Thurs 2-6, Sat 10-1
Friends of the Library Group

GREY EAGLE COMMUNITY LIBRARY, 118 State St E, Grey Eagle, 56336. (Mail add: PO Box 157, Grey Eagle, 56336-0157), SAN 375-6114. Tel: 320-285-2505. Web Site: griver.org/locations/grey-eagle. *Libr Serv Coordr,* Jennifer Shattuck; E-mail: jennifers@grrl.lib.mn.us
Pop 2,290; Circ 26,025
Library Holdings: Audiobooks 2,204; AV Mats 68; CDs 178; DVDs 462; Bk Vols 9,355; Per Subs 36
Open Mon 10-4, Wed 2-8, Fri 1-6, Sat 10-1
Friends of the Library Group

HOWARD LAKE LIBRARY, 617 Sixth Ave, Howard Lake, 55349-5644, SAN 347-8440. Tel: 320-543-2020. Web Site: griver.org/locations/howard-lake. *Libr Serv Coordr,* Sara Koivisto
Pop 6,255; Circ 49,844
Library Holdings: Audiobooks 477; AV Mats 139; CDs 493; DVDs 1,230; Bk Vols 9,911; Per Subs 40; Videos 1,230
Open Mon & Wed 2-8, Tues 2-6, Thurs 3-6, Fri 10-1 & 3-6, Sat 10-1
Friends of the Library Group

KIMBALL LIBRARY, Five Main St N, Kimball, 55353. (Mail add: PO Box 540, Kimball, 55353-0540), SAN 347-8475. Tel: 320-398-3915. Web Site: griver.org/locations/kimball. *Libr Serv Coordr,* Carla Asfeld; E-mail: carlaa@grrl.lib.mn.us
Pop 4,104; Circ 30,986
Library Holdings: Audiobooks 444; AV Mats 50; CDs 345; DVDs 1,058; Bk Vols 7,886; Per Subs 27
Open Mon 10-1 & 2-7, Wed 10-1 & 3-6, Fri 3-6, Sat 9-12
Friends of the Library Group

LITTLE FALLS PUBLIC LIBRARY, 108 NE Third St, Little Falls, 56345-2708, SAN 308-6143. Tel: 320-632-9676. Web Site: griver.org/locations/little-falls. *Libr Serv Coordr,* Cindy Bruggenthies; E-mail: cindyb@grrl.lib.mn.us
Founded 1904. Pop 16,326; Circ 122,168
Library Holdings: Audiobooks 1,335; AV Mats 1,773; CDs 809; DVDs 867; Bk Vols 31,297; Per Subs 116; Videos 868
Open Mon & Wed 12-7, Tues & Thurs 10-7, Fri 12-6, Sat 10-3
Friends of the Library Group

LONG PRAIRIE LIBRARY, 42 Third St N, Ste 1, Long Prairie, 56347, SAN 347-8505. Tel: 320-732-2332. Web Site: griver.org/locations/long-prairie. *Libr Serv Coordr,* Nancy Potter; E-mail: nancyp@grrl.lib.mn.us
Pop 10,293; Circ 59,800
Library Holdings: Audiobooks 410; AV Mats 124; CDs 577; DVDs 1,537; Bk Vols 10,308; Per Subs 60
Open Mon & Thurs 1-7, Tues 10-6, Wed & Fri 12-6, Sat 9-12

MYRTLE MABEE LIBRARY, 324 Washburn Ave, Belgrade, 56312. (Mail add: PO Box 388, Belgrade, 56312-0388), SAN 347-853X. Tel: 320-254-8842. Web Site: griver.org/locations/belgrade. *Libr Serv Coordr,* Gretchen Vork; E-mail: gretchenv@grrl.lib.mn.us
Pop 2,289; Circ 18,475
Library Holdings: Audiobooks 268; AV Mats 104; CDs 421; DVDs 738; Bk Vols 6,898; Per Subs 36
Open Mon & Wed 2-5, Thurs 10-1 & 2-5, Fri 2-5 & 6-8, Sat 9-12

MELROSE LIBRARY, 225 E First St N, Melrose, 56352-1153. (Mail add: PO Box 027, Melrose, 56352-0027), SAN 347-8564. Tel: 320-256-3885. Web Site: griver.org/locations/melrose. *Libr Serv Coordr,* Janet Atkinson; E-mail: janeta@grrl.lib.mn.us
Pop 6,624; Circ 93,446
Library Holdings: Audiobooks 604; AV Mats 105; CDs 1,240; DVDs 1,678; Bk Vols 11,435; Per Subs 40
Open Mon 2-8, Tues & Fri 2-5, Wed 2-7, Thurs 10-12 & 2-5, Sat 9-12
Friends of the Library Group

MONTICELLO LIBRARY, 200 W Sixth St, Monticello, 55362-8832, SAN 347-8599. Tel: 763-295-2322. Web Site: griver.org/locations/monticello. *Libr Serv Coordr,* Marla Scherber; E-mail: marlas@grrl.lib.mn.us
Pop 13,388; Circ 236,220
Library Holdings: Audiobooks 1,221; AV Mats 335; CDs 1,957; DVDs 3,399; Bk Vols 39,594; Per Subs 69
Open Mon 10-8, Tues & Thurs 1-8, Wed 10-6, Fri 10-5, Sat 10-2
Friends of the Library Group

PAYNESVILLE LIBRARY, 119 Washburne Ave, Paynesville, 56362, SAN 308-7204. Tel: 320-243-7343. Web Site: griver.org/locations/paynesville. *Libr Serv Coordr,* Gretchen Vork
Founded 1908. Pop 5,989; Circ 52,670
Library Holdings: Audiobooks 569; AV Mats 114; CDs 580; DVDs 1,385; Bk Vols 12,887; Per Subs 32
Open Mon & Fri 2-8, Tues & Thurs 2-6, Wed 10-6, Sat 10-1
Friends of the Library Group

PIERZ LIBRARY, 117 S Main St, Pierz, 56364, SAN 347-8629. Tel: 320-468-6486. Web Site: griver.org/locations/pierz. *Libr Serv Coordr,* Grace Heschke; E-mail: graceh@grrl.lib.mn.us
Pop 7,404; Circ 20,820
Library Holdings: Audiobooks 234; AV Mats 536; CDs 112; DVDs 186; Bk Vols 7,852; Per Subs 30; Videos 187
Open Mon 1-5:30, Wed 2-7, Thurs 10-5, Fri 2-5:30, Sat 10-1
Friends of the Library Group

RICHMOND LIBRARY, 63 Hall Ave SW, Richmond, 56368-8108. (Mail add: PO Box 130, Richmond, 56368-0130), SAN 347-8653. Tel: 320-597-3739. Web Site: griver.org/locations/richmond. *Libr Serv Coordr,* Jason Kirchoff
Pop 3,009; Circ 29,374
Library Holdings: Audiobooks 254; AV Mats 179; CDs 218; DVDs 253; Bk Vols 6,258; Per Subs 32; Videos 253
Open Mon 2-8, Tues & Sat 10-1, Wed 11-1 & 3-6, Fri 3-6
Friends of the Library Group

AL RINGSMUTH LIBRARY, 253 N Fifth Ave, Waite Park, 56387-0395. (Mail add: PO Box 307, Waite Park, 56387-0307), SAN 347-8777. Tel: 320-253-9359. Web Site: griver.org/locations/waite-park. *Libr Serv Coordr,* Michelle Goebel; E-mail: michelleg@grrl.lib.mn.us
Pop 15,818; Circ 138,573
Library Holdings: Audiobooks 823; AV Mats 149; CDs 794; DVDs 2,155; Bk Vols 15,640; Per Subs 38
Open Mon 12-8, Tues 10-2, Wed & Fri 2-6, Thurs 1-8, Sat 10-1
Friends of the Library Group

ROCKFORD PUBLIC LIBRARY, 8220 Cedar St, Rockford, 55373, SAN 373-904X. Tel: 763-477-4216. Web Site: griver.org/locations/rockford. *Libr Serv Coordr,* Julie Eskritt; E-mail: juliee@grrl.lib.mn.us
Pop 6,932; Circ 82,877
Library Holdings: Audiobooks 859; AV Mats 920; CDs 542; DVDs 746; Bk Vols 18,657; Per Subs 56; Videos 746
Open Mon & Tues 2-8, Wed 10-6, Thurs 3-8, Fri 3-6, Sat 10-1
Friends of the Library Group

ROYALTON LIBRARY, 12 N Birch St, Royalton, 56373. (Mail add: PO Box 285, Royalton, 56373-0285), SAN 347-8688. Tel: 320-584-8151. Web Site: griver.org/locations/royalton. *Libr Serv Coordr,* Terri Deal-Hansen; E-mail: terrid@grrl.lib.mn.us
Pop 8,153; Circ 25,487
Library Holdings: Audiobooks 351; AV Mats 106; CDs 713; DVDs 1,154; Bk Vols 9,168; Per Subs 12

Open Mon 2-6, Wed 2-8, Thurs 10-1 & 2-6, Sat 10-1
Friends of the Library Group
SAINT CLOUD PUBLIC LIBRARY, 1300 W Saint Germain St, 56301, SAN 347-8718. Tel: 320-650-2500. Web Site: griver.org/locations/st-cloud. *Patron Serv Supvr,* Ryan McCormick; E-mail: ryanm@grrl.lib.mn.us
Pop 101,506; Circ 1,075,161
Library Holdings: Audiobooks 5,626; AV Mats 1,602; CDs 14,086; DVDs 10,416; Bk Vols 271,308; Per Subs 421
Open Mon-Thurs 10-9, Fri 10-6, Sat 10-5
Friends of the Library Group
ST MICHAEL PUBLIC LIBRARY, 11800 Town Center Dr NE, Ste 100, Saint Michael, 55376, SAN 373-9058. Tel: 763-497-1998. Web Site: griver.org/locations/st-michael. *Libr Serv Coordr,* Nancy Bunting; E-mail: nancyb@grrl.lib.mn.us
Pop 23,689; Circ 210,000
Open Mon & Wed 10-8, Tues 10-6, Thurs 1-8, Fri 12-5, Sat 10-1
Friends of the Library Group
STAPLES PUBLIC LIBRARY, 122 Sixth St NE, Staples, 56479, SAN 308-8081. Tel: 218-894-1401. Web Site: griver.org/locations/staples. *Libr Serv Coordr,* Cathy Perish
Founded 1909. Pop 7,560; Circ 88,123
Library Holdings: Audiobooks 666; AV Mats 161; CDs 606; DVDs 2,322; Bk Vols 15,640; Per Subs 73
Open Mon & Wed 10-6, Tues & Thurs 2-8, Fri 1-5, Sat 10-1
Friends of the Library Group
STICKNEY CROSSING LIBRARY, 740 Clearwater Ctr, Clearwater, 55320. (Mail add: PO Box 335, Clearwater, 55320). Tel: 320-558-6001. Web Site: griver.org/locations/clearwater. *Libr Serv Coordr,* Position Currently Open
Open Mon 1-4, Tues 10-1 & 3-6, Wed & Fri 3-6, Thurs 10-1
Friends of the Library Group
SWANVILLE LIBRARY, 213 DeGraff Ave, Swanville, 56382. (Mail add: PO Box 295, Swanville, 56382-0295), SAN 347-8742. Tel: 320-547-2346. Web Site: griver.org/locations/swanville. *Libr Serv Coordr,* Cindy Bruggenthies
Pop 2,791; Circ 20,295
Library Holdings: Audiobooks 415; AV Mats 175; CDs 136; DVDs 249; Bk Vols 6,349; Per Subs 26; Videos 250
Open Mon 10-1 & 3-6, Tues & Thurs 3-6, Wed 1-7:30, Sat 10-2
UPSALA LIBRARY, 117 Main St, Upsala, 56384. (Mail add: PO Box 248, Upsala, 56384), SAN 328-8870. Tel: 320-573-4282. Web Site: griver.org/locations/upsala. *Libr Serv Coordr,* Wanda Erickson; E-mail: wandae@grrl.lib.mn.us
Pop 1,928; Circ 42,561
Library Holdings: Audiobooks 324; AV Mats 96; CDs 357; DVDs 1,093; Bk Vols 5,861; Per Subs 37
Open Mon 10-3, Tues 3-6, Wed & Fri 2-8, Sat 10-1
Friends of the Library Group

S MINNESOTA DEPARTMENT OF CORRECTIONS*, Minnesota Correctional Facility - St Cloud, 2305 Minnesota Blvd SE, 56304. Tel: 320-240-3071. Web Site: mn.gov/doc/facilities/st-cloud. *Librn,* Teri Hams; E-mail: teri.hams@state.mn.us
Library Holdings: Bk Vols 12,600; Per Subs 25
Special Collections: Law Coll
Automation Activity & Vendor Info: (Cataloging) EOS International; (Circulation) EOS International
Restriction: Staff & inmates only

C ST CLOUD STATE UNIVERSITY LIBRARY*, James W Miller Learning Resource Center, 400 Sixth St S, 56301. (Mail add: Saint Cloud State University, 720 Fourth Ave S, 56301-4498), SAN 347-8807. Tel: 320-308-3083. Interlibrary Loan Service Tel: 320-308-2085. Administration Tel: 320-308-2022. E-mail: library@stcloudstate.edu. Web Site: stcloudstate.edu/library. *Dean of Libr,* Rhonda Huisman; Tel: 320-308-2022, E-mail: rkhuisman@stcloudstate.edu; *Govt Pub Librn,* Michael Gorman; Tel: 320-308-2028, E-mail: msgorman@stcloudstate.edu; *Libr Serv Mgr,* Joe Franklin; Tel: 320-308-4675, E-mail: jpfranklin@stcloudstate.edu; *ILL,* Hannah Topp-Schefers; Tel: 320-308-2085, E-mail: hschefers@stcloudstate.edu
Founded 1869. Enrl 15,000; Fac 570; Highest Degree: Doctorate
Special Collections: Archives, Government Documents & Maps; ERIC Documents of Education, micro; Library of American Civilization; Minnesota Coll; Rare Book Coll; State Author Manuscript Coll. State Document Depository; US Document Depository
Automation Activity & Vendor Info: (Acquisitions) Ex Libris Group; (Cataloging) Ex Libris Group; (Circulation) Ex Libris Group; (Course Reserve) Ex Libris Group; (ILL) Ex Libris Group; (Media Booking) Ex Libris Group; (OPAC) Ex Libris Group; (Serials) Ex Libris Group
Partic in Minitex; OCLC Online Computer Library Center, Inc

J SAINT CLOUD TECHNICAL & COMMUNITY COLLEGE LIBRARY*, 1520 Whitney Ct, 56303-1240. (Mail add: 1540 Northway Dr, 56303), SAN 320-6858. Tel: 320-308-5141. Reference Tel: 320-308-5966. Administration Tel: 320-308-5177. Toll Free Tel: 800-222-1009. FAX: 320-308-5027. E-mail: library@sctcc.edu. Web Site: www.sctcc.edu/library. *Chief Info Officer, Libr Dir,* Vi Bergquist; E-mail: vbergquist@sctcc.edu; *Librn,* Patricia Akerman; E-mail: pakerman@sctcc.edu; Staff 3 (MLS 2, Non-MLS 1)
Founded 1975. Enrl 3,400; Fac 375; Highest Degree: Associate
Subject Interests: Genocide, Holocaust
Automation Activity & Vendor Info: (Cataloging) Ex Libris Group; (Circulation) Ex Libris Group; (Course Reserve) Ex Libris Group; (ILL) Ex Libris Group; (OPAC) Ex Libris Group
Wireless access
Function: 24/7 Online cat, Bks on CD, CD-ROM, Computers for patron use, Electronic databases & coll, Free DVD rentals, ILL available, Internet access, Learning ctr, Magazines, Magnifiers for reading, Music CDs, Online cat, Online info literacy tutorials on the web & in blackboard, Online ref, Orientations, Photocopying/Printing, Printer for laptops & handheld devices, Prof lending libr, Ref & res, Ref serv available, Scanner, Spanish lang bks, Spoken cassettes & CDs, Spoken cassettes & DVDs, Study rm, Telephone ref, Wheelchair accessible
Partic in Central Minnesota Libraries Exchange; Minitex; MnPALS
Special Services for the Deaf - Accessible learning ctr; ADA equip; Assistive tech; Bks on deafness & sign lang; Closed caption videos; Interpreter on staff; Sign lang interpreter upon request for prog
Special Services for the Blind - Accessible computers; Aids for in-house use; Assistive/Adapted tech devices, equip & products; Bks on CD; Closed caption display syst; Computer with voice synthesizer for visually impaired persons; Copier with enlargement capabilities; Dragon Naturally Speaking software; Duplicating spec requests; Info on spec aids & appliances; Internet workstation with adaptive software; Large screen computer & software; Low vision equip; PC for people with disabilities; Sound rec; Text reader
Open Mon-Thurs 8-6, Fri (Summer) 8-4

S STEARNS HISTORY MUSEUM*, Research Center Library & Archives, 235 33rd Ave S, 56301-3752. SAN 325-4712. Tel: 320-253-8424. Toll Free Tel: 866-253-8424. FAX: 320-253-2172. E-mail: info@stearns-museum.org. Web Site: www.stearnshistorymuseum.org/research. *Head Archivist, Ref (Info Servs),* Steve Penick; E-mail: spenick@sterns-museum.org; *Archivist, Ref (Info Servs),* Jessica Storlien; E-mail: jstorlien@sterns-museum.org; *Archivist,* John W Decker; E-mail: jdecker@stearns-museum.org; Staff 4 (MLS 2, Non-MLS 2)
Founded 1936
Library Holdings: CDs 50; Microforms 1,665; Bk Titles 2,290; Bk Vols 2,810; Per Subs 20; Videos 190
Special Collections: Myron Hall Photo Coll. Oral History
Subject Interests: Dairying, Genealogy, German, Granite indust, Immigration, Luxembourg settlement, Stearns County hist
Wireless access
Partic in Central Minnesota Libraries Exchange
Open Mon-Sat 10-5, Sun 12-5

SAINT JAMES

P WATONWAN COUNTY LIBRARY, 125 Fifth St S, 56081. SAN 308-7468. Tel: 507-375-1278. FAX: 507-375-5415. E-mail: libtwa@tds.lib.mn.us. Web Site: www.co.watonwan.mn.us/index.aspx?nid=175. *Dir,* Matt Pannkuk; E-mail: mpannkuk@tds.lib.mn.us; *Asst Dir,* Shirley Coleman; E-mail: scolem@tds.lib.mn.us; Staff 9.5 (MLS 2, Non-MLS 7.5)
Founded 1943. Pop 11,876; Circ 128,015. Sal $298,567 (Prof $99,039)
Library Holdings: AV Mats 4,451; Bk Titles 47,685; Per Subs 79
Subject Interests: Agr, Antique tractor repair, Tractors
Automation Activity & Vendor Info: (Cataloging) Innovative Interfaces, Inc; (Circulation) Innovative Interfaces, Inc; (ILL) Innovative Interfaces, Inc
Wireless access
Function: Bks on CD, Children's prog, Computer training, Computers for patron use, Digital talking bks, Free DVD rentals, ILL available, Instruction & testing, Magnifiers for reading, Mail & tel request accepted, Music CDs, Online cat, OverDrive digital audio bks, Photocopying/Printing, Preschool outreach, Prog for adults, Prog for children & young adult, Ref serv available, Spanish lang bks, Spoken cassettes & CDs, Spoken cassettes & DVDs, Story hour, Summer & winter reading prog, Summer reading prog, Tax forms, Teen prog, Telephone ref, VHS videos, Wheelchair accessible, Winter reading prog, Writing prog
Mem of Traverse Des Sioux Library Cooperative
Partic in OCLC Online Computer Library Center, Inc
Open Mon, Wed & Thurs 10-8, Tues & Fri 10-5:30, Sat 10-2
Friends of the Library Group
Branches: 4
BUTTERFIELD BRANCH, 111 Second St N, Butterfield, 56120. (Mail add: PO Box L, Butterfield, 56120-0237), SAN 328-6819. Tel: 507-956-2361. FAX: 507-956-2361. E-mail: libtwb@tds.lib.mn.us. *Br Mgr,* Rose Carston; *Circ,* Angela Lenz; Staff 1 (Non-MLS 1)

Founded 1970. Pop 573; Circ 12,702
Library Holdings: AV Mats 1,012; Bk Vols 9,249; Per Subs 16
Automation Activity & Vendor Info: (OPAC) SirsiDynix
Function: Computers for patron use, Health sci info serv, Holiday prog, Home delivery & serv to seniorr ctr & nursing homes, Homebound delivery serv, Homework prog, ILL available, Instruction & testing, Internet access, Jail serv, Jazz prog, Large print keyboards, Learning ctr, Legal assistance to inmates, Literacy & newcomer serv, Magnifiers for reading, Mail & tel request accepted, Mail loans to mem, Masonic res mat, Microfiche/film & reading machines, Museum passes, Music CDs, Notary serv, Online cat, Online info literacy tutorials on the web & in blackboard, Online ref, Orientations, Outreach serv, Outside serv via phone, mail, e-mail & web, OverDrive digital audio bks, Passport agency, Photocopying/Printing, Preschool outreach, Preschool reading prog, Printer for laptops & handheld devices, Prof lending libr, Prog for adults, Prog for children & young adult, Serves people with intellectual disabilities, Story hour, Summer & winter reading prog, Tax forms, Wheelchair accessible
Open Mon 1:30-7, Tues-Fri 1:30-5, Sat 9:30-11:30

DARFUR BRANCH, 200 Adrian St, Darfur, 56022, SAN 328-6835. Tel: 507-877-5010. FAX: 507-877-5522. E-mail: libtwd@tds.lib.mn.us. *Branch Services,* Dawn Junker
Founded 1941. Pop 138; Circ 2,999
Library Holdings: AV Mats 597; Bk Vols 2,114
Function: Bks on cassette, Bks on CD, Children's prog, Computers for patron use, ILL available, Music CDs, Photocopying/Printing, Prog for children & young adult, Spoken cassettes & CDs, Spoken cassettes & DVDs, Tax forms, Telephone ref
Open Tues & Thurs 2-5:30, Sat Noon-2

LEWISVILLE BRANCH, 129 Lewis St W, Lewisville, 56060. (Mail add: PO Box 314, Lewisville, 56060-0314), SAN 325-1748. Tel: 507-435-2781. FAX: 507-435-2781. E-mail: libtwl@tds.lib.mn.us. *Br Mgr,* John Hocker; *Branch Services,* Heidi Cooling; Staff 1 (Non-MLS 1)
Founded 1941. Pop 249; Circ 4,430
Library Holdings: AV Mats 1,159; Bk Vols 4,664
Automation Activity & Vendor Info: (Cataloging) OCLC; (OPAC) SirsiDynix
Function: Bks on cassette, Bks on CD, Children's prog, ILL available, Internet access, Music CDs, Photocopying/Printing, Prog for children & young adult, Tax forms, VHS videos
Open Mon & Fri 3-6, Wed 3-7, Sat 9-12
Friends of the Library Group

MADELIA BRANCH, 23 First St NW, Madelia, 56062, SAN 328-6797. Tel: 507-642-3511. FAX: 507-642-8144. E-mail: libtwm@tds.lib.mn.us. *Br Mgr,* Cheryl Lindell; *Branch Services,* John Hocker; Staff 3 (Non-MLS 3)
Founded 1941. Pop 2,234; Circ 30,761
Library Holdings: AV Mats 2,206; Bk Vols 20,083; Per Subs 40
Function: Wheelchair accessible
Open Mon-Wed 10:30-7:30, Thurs & Fri 10:30-5, Sat 10:30-1:30
Friends of the Library Group

SAINT JOSEPH

C COLLEGE OF SAINT BENEDICT, Clemens Library, 37 S College Ave, 56374. Tel: 320-363-5611. Interlibrary Loan Service Tel: 320-363-5604. Administration Tel: 320-363-2119. E-mail: askalibrarian@csbsju.edu. Web Site: www.csbsju.edu/libraries. *Dir of Libraries & Archives,* Kathleen Parker; Tel: 320-363-5195, E-mail: kparker@csbsju.edu; *Assoc Dir, Learning & Research,* Diana Symons; Tel: 320-363-5296, E-mail: dsymons@csbsju.edu; *Fine Arts Librn,* Bonnie Finn; Tel: 320-363-5513, E-mail: bfinn001@csbsju.edu; *Humanities Librn,* Annie Larson; Tel: 320-363-2127, E-mail: alarson002@csbsju.edu; *Sci Librn,* Jonathan Carlson; Tel: 320-363-2579, E-mail: jcarlson@csbsju.edu; *Soc Sci Librn,* Sarah Gewirtz; Tel: 320-363-5802, E-mail: sgewirtz@csbsju.edu; *Access Serv Mgr,* Nicole Reuter; Tel: 320-363-5159, E-mail: nreuter@csbsju.edu; *Archivist,* Peggy Roske; Tel: 320-363-5019, E-mail: proske@csbsju.edu; Staff 14 (MLS 11, Non-MLS 3)
Founded 1913. Enrl 2,057; Fac 173; Highest Degree: Bachelor
Subject Interests: Nursing, Women studies
Automation Activity & Vendor Info: (Acquisitions) OCLC Worldshare Management Services; (Cataloging) OCLC Worldshare Management Services; (Circulation) OCLC Worldshare Management Services; (Course Reserve) OCLC Worldshare Management Services; (Discovery) OCLC Worldshare Management Services; (ILL) OCLC Tipasa; (OPAC) OCLC Worldshare Management Services; (Serials) OCLC Worldshare Management Services
Wireless access
Partic in Central Minnesota Libraries Exchange; OCLC Online Computer Library Center, Inc
Open Mon-Thurs 8am-Midnight, Fri 8am-10pm, Sat 10-10, Sun 10am-Midnight
Restriction: Open to students, fac & staff

SAINT LOUIS PARK

R BETH-EL SYNAGOGUE*, Max Shapiro Memorial Library, 5225 Barry St W, 55416. SAN 308-7484. Tel: 952-873-7300, Ext 7329. FAX: 952-873-7301. Web Site: www.bethelsynagogue.org. *Librn,* Marcia Oleisky; E-mail: moleisky@bethelsynagogue.org
Founded 1929
Library Holdings: Bk Titles 6,000; Per Subs 26
Special Collections: Music Coll

S PARK NICOLLET METHODIST HOSPITAL, Arneson Methodist Library, 6600 Excelsior Blvd, Ste 101, 55426. SAN 308-6879. Tel: 952-993-5451. E-mail: library@parknicollet.com. *Dir,* Penny Marsala; *Librn,* Mark Mershon; Staff 3 (MLS 3)
Founded 1952
Library Holdings: e-journals 2,500; Bk Vols 6,500; Per Subs 291
Automation Activity & Vendor Info: (Cataloging) Inmagic, Inc.; (Circulation) Inmagic, Inc.
Wireless access
Function: Computers for patron use, Meeting rooms, Photocopying/Printing, Study rm
Open Mon-Fri 8-5

SAINT PAUL

S AERO SYSTEMS ENGINEERING INC LIBRARY*, 358 E Fillmore Ave, 55107. SAN 308-6488. Tel: 651-220-1209. FAX: 651-227-0519. *Librn,* Glenn Payton; Staff 1 (MLS 1)
Founded 1967
Library Holdings: Bk Titles 2,800; Per Subs 150
Subject Interests: Aerospace res, Aircraft engine, Develop, Hush houses, Test cells, Testing, Wind tunnel design
Partic in Metronet; Proquest Dialog
Open Mon-Fri 9-5

CR BETHEL UNIVERSITY LIBRARY, (Formerly Bethel Seminary Library), 3900 Bethel Dr, 55112. SAN 308-7530. Tel: 651-638-6540. Interlibrary Loan Service Tel: 651-635-8797. Administration Tel: 651-635-8717. E-mail: srefdesk@bethel.edu. Web Site: libguides.bethel.edu, www.bethel.edu/library. *Dir,* David Stewart; E-mail: d-stewart@bethel.edu
Founded 1871. Highest Degree: Doctorate
Library Holdings: e-books 200,000; Bk Vols 260,000; Per Subs 293
Special Collections: 19th Century Pietism (Skarstedt Coll); Baptist General Conference History Center; Bethel University Archives; Devotional Literature (Nelson-Lundquist Coll); Klingberg Puritan Coll
Wireless access
Partic in Minitex; Minnesota Theological Library Association; MnPALS
Open Mon-Thurs 7:30am-11pm, Fri 7:30-6, Sat 9-6, Sun 2-11
Friends of the Library Group

C CONCORDIA UNIVERSITY*, Library Technology Center, 1282 Concordia Ave, 55104. (Mail add: 275 N Syndicate St, 55104), SAN 308-759X. Tel: 651-641-8237. Reference Tel: 651-641-8812. Administration Tel: 651-641-8241. FAX: 651-641-8782. Reference E-mail: library@csp.edu. Web Site: library.csp.edu. *Dir, Libr Serv,* Jonathan Burnell Neilson; E-mail: neilson@csp.edu; *Assoc Dir, Instruction & Outreach,* Rachel Wightman; E-mail: rwightman@csp.edu; *Head, Metadata Serv, Head, Tech Serv,* Jeanine Gatzke; Tel: 651-641-8242, E-mail: gatzke@csp.edu; *Digital Scholarship Librn, Univ Archivist,* Megan Johnson-Saylor; Tel: 651-641-8244, E-mail: johnsonsaylor@csp.edu; *Instruction & Outreach Librn,* Jennifer Carlson; Tel: 651-641-8770, E-mail: jcarlson@csp.edu; *Access Serv Coordr,* Netanya Roden; Tel: 651-641-8240, E-mail: roden@csp.edu
Founded 1893. Enrl 1,866; Fac 85; Highest Degree: Master
Library Holdings: AV Mats 3,321; Bk Vols 127,000; Per Subs 450
Special Collections: 16th-19th Century Coll (mainly German & Theological); Education (Children's Coll); Historical Textbooks; Hymnbook Coll. Oral History
Subject Interests: Educ, Hist, Music, Organizational mgt
Automation Activity & Vendor Info: (Cataloging) Innovative Interfaces, Inc; (Circulation) Innovative Interfaces, Inc; (Course Reserve) Innovative Interfaces, Inc; (ILL) Innovative Interfaces, Inc; (Media Booking) Innovative Interfaces, Inc; (OPAC) Innovative Interfaces, Inc; (Serials) EBSCO Online
Wireless access
Publications: The Reformation as Media Event: A Bibliography of 16th Century Materials
Partic in MnPALS; OCLC Online Computer Library Center, Inc
Open Mon-Thurs (Winter) 7:45am-11pm, Fri 7:45-5, Sat 8-5, Sun 1-11; Mon-Thurs (Summer) 9-8, Fri 9-4, Sat 12-4

S DEBRA S FISH EARLY CHILDHOOD RESOURCE LIBRARY, Ten Yorkton Ct, 55117. SAN 327-2184. Tel: 651-641-3544. TDD: 651-641-0332. E-mail: librarian@thinksmall.org. Web Site: www.thinksmall.org/for-early-childhood-professionals/debra_s_fish_library.

Chief Exec Officer, Pres, Barbara Yates; Tel: 651-641-6645, E-mail: byates@thinksmall.org; *Librn,* Jennie Walker Knoot; E-mail: jwalkerknoot@thinksmall.org; Staff 1 (MLS 1)
Founded 1997
Library Holdings: CDs 65; DVDs 275; Bk Titles 5,300
Subject Interests: Child develop, Early childhood, Early childhood educ
Wireless access
Function: 24/7 Online cat, CD-ROM, Computers for patron use, For res purposes, Free DVD rentals, ILL available, Internet access, Mail & tel request accepted, Meeting rooms, Music CDs, Online cat, Outside serv via phone, mail, e-mail & web, Photocopying/Printing, Preschool outreach, Prof lending libr, Ref & res, Ref serv available, Res assist avail, Scanner, Spanish lang bks, Study rm, Telephone ref
Special Services for the Deaf - TDD equip
Open Mon-Fri 8:30-5
Friends of the Library Group

HAMLINE UNIVERSITY
C BUSH MEMORIAL LIBRARY*, 1536 Hewitt, 55104, SAN 347-8920. Tel: 651-523-2375. FAX: 651-523-2199. E-mail: bush_reference_email@gw.hamline.edu. Web Site: www.hamline.edu/bushlibrary/index.html. *Dir,* Diane Clayton; E-mail: dclayton@gw.hamline.edu; *Dir,* Julie Rochat; *Cat,* Deb Kerkvliet; *Circ,* Barbara Brokopp; *Ref (Info Servs),* Kate Borowske; *Ref (Info Servs),* Kimberly Feilmeyer; *Ref (Info Servs),* Kristofer Scheid; *Ref (Info Servs),* Amy Sheehan; *Ser,* Jan Griffith
Founded 1854. Enrl 2,000
Library Holdings: Bk Vols 154,000; Per Subs 1,148
Special Collections: Brass Rubbing Coll
Automation Activity & Vendor Info: (Acquisitions) Innovative Interfaces, Inc; (Cataloging) Innovative Interfaces, Inc; (Circulation) Innovative Interfaces, Inc; (Course Reserve) Innovative Interfaces, Inc; (ILL) Innovative Interfaces, Inc; (OPAC) Innovative Interfaces, Inc; (Serials) Innovative Interfaces, Inc
Partic in Metronet; Minitex; MnPALS; OCLC Online Computer Library Center, Inc
Open Mon-Thurs 7:30am-11:45pm, Fri 7:30am-8:45pm, Sat 7:30-6:45, Sun 12-11:45

CL SCHOOL OF LAW LIBRARY*, 1536 Hewitt Ave, 55104, SAN 347-8955. Tel: 651-523-2379. Interlibrary Loan Service Tel: 651-523-2737. FAX: 651-523-2863. Web Site: lawlibrary.hamline.edu. *Head, Pub Serv, Interim Co-Dir,* Barb Kallusky; Tel: 651-523-2131; *Head, Tech Serv, Interim Co-Dir,* Emily Waitz; *Access & Circ Serv Librn,* Selva Palani; *Cat Librn,* Susan J Vossberg; *Pub Serv Librn,* Megan Koltes; Staff 4 (MLS 4)
Founded 1972. Enrl 587; Fac 30; Highest Degree: Doctorate
Library Holdings: Bk Vols 274,195
Automation Activity & Vendor Info: (Acquisitions) Innovative Interfaces, Inc; (Cataloging) Innovative Interfaces, Inc; (Circulation) Innovative Interfaces, Inc; (Course Reserve) Innovative Interfaces, Inc; (ILL) Innovative Interfaces, Inc; (Media Booking) Innovative Interfaces, Inc; (OPAC) Innovative Interfaces, Inc; (Serials) Innovative Interfaces, Inc
Partic in OCLC Online Computer Library Center, Inc
Publications: Library Guide; Pathfinders
Open Mon-Thurs, Sat & Sun (Fall & Spring) 7:30am-11pm, Fri 7:30am-10pm; Mon-Fri (Summer) 8am-10pm, Sat & Sun 9-6

S LEAGUE OF MINNESOTA CITIES LIBRARY*, 145 University Ave W, 55103-2044. SAN 327-1943. Tel: 651-281-1200. Toll Free Tel: 800-925-1122. FAX: 651-281-1299. Web Site: www.lmc.org. *Mgr, Res,* Amber Eisenschenk; E-mail: aeisenschenk@lmc.org; Staff 4 (Non-MLS 4)
Founded 1913
Library Holdings: Bk Titles 100; Spec Interest Per Sub 60
Special Collections: Minnesota City Charters
Subject Interests: City hist, Govt
Function: Govt ref serv
Publications: Cities Bulletin; Handbook for Minnesota Cities; Human Resources Reference Manual; Information Memos on Municipal Topics; Minnesota Cities; Minnesota Mayors Handbook
Open Mon-Fri 8:30-4:30
Restriction: Authorized patrons

R LUTHER SEMINARY LIBRARY*, 2375 Como Ave, 55108. (Mail add: 2481 Como Ave, 55108), SAN 308-7689. Tel: 651-641-3447. Reference Tel: 651-641-3226. E-mail: reference@luthersem.edu. Web Site: www.luthersem.edu/library. *Assoc Dir,* Peter Susag; E-mail: psusag001@luthersem.edu; *Cat Librn,* Mary Ann Teske; Tel: 651-641-3446, E-mail: mteske@luthersem.edu; *Coordr, Circ, Coordr, ILL,* Peter Watters; E-mail: pwatters002@luthersem.edu; Staff 6 (MLS 6)
Founded 1869. Enrl 764; Fac 28; Highest Degree: Doctorate
Library Holdings: Microforms 46,820; Bk Vols 230,000; Per Subs 292
Special Collections: Doving Hymnal Coll; Pre-1800 Book Coll; Tanner Catechism Coll; Thrivent Reformation Research Coll
Subject Interests: Reformation
Automation Activity & Vendor Info: (OPAC) OCLC
Wireless access
Partic in Minnesota Theological Library Association
Special Services for the Blind - Assistive/Adapted tech devices, equip & products
Open Mon-Thurs 7:45am-10pm, Fri 7:45-5, Sat 1-5, Sun 6pm-10pm

C MACALESTER COLLEGE*, DeWitt Wallace Library, 1600 Grand Ave, 55105-1899. SAN 347-9013. Tel: 651-696-6346. Circulation Tel: 651-696-6610. Interlibrary Loan Service Tel: 651-696-6545. Reference Tel: 651-696-6618. FAX: 651-696-6617. Administration FAX: 651-696-6782. Web Site: www.macalester.edu/library. *Libr Dir,* Angi Faiks; Tel: 651-696-6208, E-mail: faiks@macalester.edu; *Asst Libr Dir, Coll & Discovery,* Katy Gabrio; Tel: 651-696-6703, E-mail: gabrio@macalester.edu; Staff 21 (MLS 12, Non-MLS 9)
Founded 1874. Enrl 2,000; Fac 147; Highest Degree: Bachelor
Library Holdings: AV Mats 11,000; e-books 5,196; Bk Titles 327,156; Bk Vols 439,568; Per Subs 2,038
Special Collections: Early Minnesota; Sinclair Lewis, bks, per, letters & ephemera
Automation Activity & Vendor Info: (Acquisitions) OCLC; (Cataloging) OCLC; (Circulation) OCLC; (Course Reserve) OCLC; (ILL) OCLC; (Media Booking) OCLC; (OPAC) OCLC; (Serials) OCLC
Wireless access
Partic in Minitex; OCLC Online Computer Library Center, Inc

S METROPOLITAN COUNCIL LIBRARY*, 390 Robert St N, 55101. SAN 308-7697. Tel: 651-602-1412. Web Site: www.metrocouncil.org. *Libr & Info Res Coordr,* Jan Price; E-mail: jan.price@metc.state.mn.us; Staff 1 (MLS 1)
Founded 1967
Library Holdings: AV Mats 350; Bk Titles 10,000; Per Subs 150
Special Collections: Local Government Comprehensive Plans; Metropolitan Council, doc
Subject Interests: Housing, Regional planning, Transportation, Urban planning
Automation Activity & Vendor Info: (Cataloging) LibraryWorld, Inc; (OPAC) LibraryWorld, Inc
Wireless access
Publications: New Books in the Library (Online only)
Partic in Capital Area Library Consortium; Minitex
Open Mon-Fri 8:15-4:30
Restriction: Non-circulating to the pub

C METROPOLITAN STATE UNIVERSITY*, Library & Learning Center, 645 E Seventh St, 55106. (Mail add: 700 E Seventh St, 55106), SAN 378-3766. Tel: 651-793-1616. Reference Tel: 651-793-1614. Administration Tel: 651-793-1622. FAX: 651-793-1615. E-mail: library.services@metrostate.edu. Web Site: www.metrostate.edu/library. *Dean, Libr Serv,* Beth Claussen; Tel: 651-793-1618, E-mail: beth.clausen@metrostate.edu; *Pub Serv Mgr,* Eric Nelsen; Tel: 651-793-1627, E-mail: eric.nelsen@metrostate.edu; *Head, Ref & Res Serv,* Michelle Filkins; Tel: 651-793-1621, E-mail: michelle.filkins@metrostate.edu; Staff 21 (MLS 10, Non-MLS 11)
Founded 1992. Enrl 11,277; Fac 10; Highest Degree: Doctorate
Special Collections: Minnesota Cookbook Coll; Musical Theatre Coll, CDs
Automation Activity & Vendor Info: (Acquisitions) Ex Libris Group; (Cataloging) Ex Libris Group; (Circulation) Ex Libris Group; (Course Reserve) Docutek; (ILL) PALS; (Media Booking) PALS; (OPAC) Ex Libris Group; (Serials) Ex Libris Group
Wireless access
Partic in Metronet; Minitex; Minnesota Library Information Network; MnPALS
Open Mon-Thurs 8am-11pm, Fri 8-6, Sat 8-6, Sun 12-11

GL MINNESOTA ATTORNEY GENERAL LIBRARY*, Bremer Tower, Ste 1050, 445 Minnesota St, 55101-2109. SAN 321-8325. Tel: 651-757-1055. FAX: 651-296-7000. TDD: 651-296-1410. E-mail: library.ag@ag.state.mn.us. Web Site: www.ag.state.mn.us. *Law Libm,* Sadie Snyder; E-mail: sadie.snyder@ag.state.mn.us; Staff 1 (MLS 1)
Library Holdings: Bk Titles 3,014; Bk Vols 20,607; Per Subs 600
Special Collections: Minnesota Attorney General Opinions Coll, micro, VF
Automation Activity & Vendor Info: (Cataloging) PALS; (ILL) PALS; (OPAC) PALS
Partic in MnPALS; OCLC Online Computer Library Center, Inc
Restriction: Staff use only

G MINNESOTA DEPARTMENT OF EMPLOYMENT & ECONOMIC DEVELOPMENT LIBRARY*, 1st National Bank Bldg, 332 Minnesota St, Ste E200, 55101-1351. SAN 308-7743. Tel: 651-259-7188. Toll Free Tel: 800-657-3858. FAX: 651-215-3841. E-mail: DEED.Library@state.mn.us.

Web Site: mn.gov/library/deed.html. *Librn,* Dru Frykberg; E-mail: dru.frykberg@state.mn.us; Staff 2 (MLS 1.5, Non-MLS 0.5)
Founded 1976
Library Holdings: Bk Titles 7,700; Per Subs 100
Subject Interests: Econ develop, Intl trade, Workforce develop
Automation Activity & Vendor Info: (Acquisitions) Ex Libris Group; (Cataloging) Ex Libris Group; (Circulation) Ex Libris Group; (ILL) Ex Libris Group; (OPAC) Ex Libris Group; (Serials) Ex Libris Group
Function: ILL available
Partic in Capital Area Library Consortium; Minitex; OCLC Online Computer Library Center, Inc
Restriction: Open by appt only

G MINNESOTA DEPARTMENT OF HEALTH*, R N Barr Library, 2079 Ellis Ave, 55114. SAN 308-6704. Tel: 651-201-5093. E-mail: health.library@state.mn.us. Web Site: www.health.state.mn.us/library. *Librn,* Mark Smith; E-mail: mark.a.smith@state.mn.us. Subject Specialists: *Health,* Mark Smith
Founded 1872
Library Holdings: AV Mats 547; DVDs 253; e-journals 75; Bk Titles 300; Per Subs 73
Subject Interests: Environ health, Health planning, Health promotion, Pub health, Socio-econ aspects of health care
Automation Activity & Vendor Info: (Acquisitions) Ex Libris Group; (Cataloging) Ex Libris Group; (Circulation) Ex Libris Group; (ILL) Ex Libris Group; (Media Booking) Ex Libris Group; (OPAC) PALS; (Serials) Ex Libris Group
Partic in Capitol Area Library Consortium; Minitex; OCLC Online Computer Library Center, Inc
Open Mon-Fri 8-4:30

§G MINNESOTA DEPARTMENT OF NATURAL RESOURCES LIBRARY, 500 Lafayette Rd, 55155. Tel: 651-259-5506. Toll Free Tel: 800-766-6000. FAX: 651-296-8029. E-mail: info.dnr@state.mn.us. Web Site: www.dnr.state.mn.us/library. *Librn,* Tracy Waterman; E-mail: tracy.waterman@state.mn.us
Special Collections: Natural Resource Management (DNR Archives), bks, journals, rpts
Subject Interests: Ecology, Fish, Forestry, Geol, Parks, Recreation, Water, Wildlife
Partic in MnPALS
Restriction: Open by appt only

S MINNESOTA DEPARTMENT OF REVENUE LIBRARY*, 600 N Robert St, 55101. SAN 327-1846. Tel: 651-556-6134. FAX: 651-556-3103. E-mail: dor.library@state.mn.us. *Librn,* Chris Anning; E-mail: chris.anning@state.mn.us; Staff 1 (Non-MLS 1)
Founded 1986
Jul 2012-Jun 2013. Mats Exp $50,000, Books $20,000, Per/Ser (Incl. Access Fees) $9,000, Other Print Mats $5,000, Electronic Ref Mat (Incl. Access Fees) $16,000. Sal $50,000
Library Holdings: Bk Titles 5,000; Bk Vols 10,000; Per Subs 100
Subject Interests: Taxation
Automation Activity & Vendor Info: (Cataloging) OCLC Connexion; (Circulation) PALS; (ILL) PALS; (OPAC) PALS
Partic in Capital Area Library Consortium; Metronet; Minitex; MnPALS; OCLC Online Computer Library Center, Inc
Open Mon-Fri 8-4:30 by appointment

G MINNESOTA DEPARTMENT OF TRANSPORTATION LIBRARY, 395 John Ireland Blvd, MS 155, 55155. SAN 308-7735. Tel: 651-366-3791. Toll Free Tel: 800-657-3774. FAX: 651-366-3789. TDD: 800-627-3529. E-mail: library.dot@state.mn.us. Web Site: www.mndot.gov/library. *Libr Dir,* Sheila Hatchell; Tel: 651-366-3733, E-mail: sheila.hatchell@state.mn.us; *Contract Librn,* Marilee Tuite; Tel: 651-366-3797, E-mail: Marilee.tuite@state.mn.us; *Electronic Res Librn,* Jim Byerly; Tel: 651-366-3739, E-mail: jim.byerly@state.mn.us; *Ref/Outreach Librn,* Karen Neinstadt; Tel: 651-366-3796, E-mail: karen.neinstadt@state.mn.us; *Tech Serv Librn,* Qin Tang; Tel: 651-366-3784, E-mail: qin.tang@state.mn.us; *Libr Tech,* Madeline Kuncio; Tel: 651-366-3749, E-mail: Madeline.Kuncio@state.mn.us. Subject Specialists: *Transportation,* Sheila Hatchell; *Transportation,* Marilee Tuite; *Transportation,* Jim Byerly; *Transportation,* Karen Neinstadt; *Transportation,* Qin Tang; *Transportation,* Madeline Kuncio; Staff 6 (MLS 6)
Founded 1957
Library Holdings: Audiobooks 12; CDs 100; DVDs 81; e-journals 46; Electronic Media & Resources 718; Bk Titles 17,000; Bk Vols 20,000; Per Subs 200; Videos 150
Subject Interests: Civil engr, Diversity, Mgt, Transportation
Automation Activity & Vendor Info: (Acquisitions) Ex Libris Group; (Cataloging) OCLC; (Circulation) Ex Libris Group; (Course Reserve) Ex Libris Group; (Discovery) Ex Libris Group; (ILL) OCLC; (OPAC) Ex Libris Group; (Serials) Ex Libris Group
Wireless access
Publications: Minnesota Transportation Libraries New Library Materials
Partic in Capitol Area Library Consortium; Metronet; Midwest Transportation Knowledge Network; Minitex; MnPALS; OCLC Online Computer Library Center, Inc
Open Mon-Fri 8-4:30

G MINNESOTA GEOLOGICAL SURVEY LIBRARY*, 2609 W Territorial Rd, 55114-1009. SAN 324-766X. Tel: 612-626-2969. E-mail: mgs@umn.edu. Web Site: www.mngs.umn.edu. *Dir,* Harvey Thorleifson; E-mail: thorleif@umn.edu
Founded 1974
Library Holdings: Bk Vols 2,000
Subject Interests: Minn geology, Seasonal thermal energy storage, Underground construction, Underground space
Restriction: Non-circulating to the pub

S MINNESOTA HISTORICAL SOCIETY*, Gale Family Library, 345 Kellogg Blvd W, 55102-1906. SAN 347-9137. Tel: 651-259-3300. Interlibrary Loan Service Tel: 651-259-3308. FAX: 651-297-7436. E-mail: collections@mnhs.org. Web Site: www.mnhs.org/library. *Dir,* Jennifer Jones; E-mail: jennifer.jones@mnhs.org; Staff 41 (MLS 10, Non-MLS 31)
Founded 1849
Library Holdings: Bk Titles 411,884; Per Subs 1,300
Special Collections: Art; Great Northern & Northern Pacific Railroad Papers; History of Native Peoples of Minnesota; Hubert H Humphrey Papers; Minnesota Newspapers, 1849-2008; Photographs; Posters; State & Local Government (Minnesota State Archives), rec; Walter Mondale Papers. Oral History; State Document Depository
Subject Interests: Genealogy, Minn hist
Automation Activity & Vendor Info: (Cataloging) PALS; (OPAC) PALS
Wireless access
Function: Archival coll, Art exhibits, Audio & video playback equip for onsite use, Computers for patron use, Electronic databases & coll, ILL available, Online cat, Orientations, Photocopying/Printing, Ref & res, Res performed for a fee, Telephone ref
Partic in Capitol Area Librs Coop; MnPALS; OCLC Online Computer Library Center, Inc; OCLC Research Library Partnership
Open Tues 9-8, Wed-Sat 9-4
Restriction: Non-circulating, Photo ID required for access, Registered patrons only

G MINNESOTA LEGISLATIVE REFERENCE LIBRARY, 645 State Office Bldg, 100 Rev Dr Martin Luther King Jr Blvd, 55155-1050. SAN 308-7751. Tel: 651-296-3398. Reference Tel: 651-296-8338. FAX: 651-296-9731. E-mail: refdesk@lrl.mn.gov. Web Site: www.lrl.mn.gov/lrl. *Dir,* Elizabeth Lincoln; Tel: 651-296-0594, E-mail: elincoln@lrl.mn.gov; *Dep Dir,* David Schmidtke; Tel: 651-215-9058, E-mail: davids@lrl.mn.gov; Staff 13 (MLS 6, Non-MLS 7)
Founded 1969
Jul 2021-Jun 2022 Income State $1,793,000. Mats Exp $74,500, Books $10,000, Per/Ser (Incl. Access Fees) $45,500, Electronic Ref Mat (Incl. Access Fees) $19,000. Sal $1,050,000
Library Holdings: Bk Titles 45,000; Per Subs 400
Special Collections: Bills Introduced for Ten Years; Interim Committee Reports; Minnesota Documents Coll; Minnesota Government Manual, 1887-present; Minnesota Government Publications; Senate & House Journals, tapes, committee minutes. State Document Depository
Subject Interests: Govt
Automation Activity & Vendor Info: (Cataloging) Ex Libris Group; (Circulation) Ex Libris Group; (OPAC) Ex Libris Group
Wireless access
Function: Govt ref serv, ILL available, Movies, Res libr
Publications: Just In (Monthly bulletin)
Partic in Capital Area Library Consortium; Minitex; MnPALS; OCLC Online Computer Library Center, Inc
Open Mon-Fri 8-4:30
Restriction: In-house use for visitors, Non-circulating to the pub, Open to pub for ref only, Pub use on premises, Restricted borrowing privileges

G MINNESOTA POLLUTION CONTROL AGENCY LIBRARY*, 520 Lafayette Rd, 55155-4194. SAN 320-684X. Tel: 651-757-2547. Web Site: www.pca.state.mn.us. *Librn,* Leslie Hunter-Larson; Tel: 651-757-2314, E-mail: Leslie.Hunter-Larson@state.mn.us; Staff 1 (MLS 1)
Library Holdings: Bk Vols 12,000; Per Subs 125
Special Collections: EPA Coll; MPCA Coll
Subject Interests: Air pollution, Pollution control, Solid wastes, Sustainable develop, Water pollution
Partic in OCLC Online Computer Library Center, Inc
Open Mon-Fri 8-4

GL MINNESOTA STATE LAW LIBRARY*, Minnesota Judicial Ctr, Rm G25, 25 Rev Dr Martin Luther King Jr Blvd, 55155. SAN 308-7794. Tel: 651-297-7651. FAX: 651-296-6740. Web Site: mn.gov/law-library. *State*

Law Librn, Liz Reppe; E-mail: liz.reppe@courts.state.mn.us; *Head, Pub Serv,* Elvira Embser-Herbert; Tel: 651-297-7657, E-mail: Elvira.Embser-Herbert@courts.state.mn.us; *Head, Tech Serv,* Erica Nutzman; Tel: 651-297-2090, E-mail: erica.nutzman@courts.state.mn.us; Staff 14 (MLS 9.5, Non-MLS 4.5)
Founded 1849
Library Holdings: Bk Vols 260,000; Per Subs 600
Special Collections: Minnesota Legal Periodical Index; Minnesota Trial Coll; Program to Collect Prof Papers of Retired Justices of Minnesota Supreme Court
Subject Interests: Am law, Minn law
Automation Activity & Vendor Info: (Cataloging) Ex Libris Group; (Circulation) Ex Libris Group; (ILL) OCLC; (OPAC) Ex Libris Group; (Serials) Ex Libris Group
Wireless access
Partic in Capitol Area Library Consortium; Metronet; Minitex; MnPALS; OCLC Online Computer Library Center, Inc
Open Mon-Fri 8:30-5

CL MITCHELL HAMLINE SCHOOL OF LAW, Warren E Burger Library, 875 Summit Ave, 55105. SAN 308-7980. Tel: 651-290-6333. Reference Tel: 651-290-6424. FAX: 651-290-6318. Reference E-mail: reference@mitchellhamline.edu. Web Site: mitchellhamline.edu/library. *Interim Libr Dir,* Lisa Heidenreich; E-mail: lisa.heidenreich@mitchellhamline.edu; Staff 7.8 (MLS 7.8)
Founded 1958. Highest Degree: Doctorate
Library Holdings: AV Mats 809; e-books 700,000; Electronic Media & Resources 28,851; Microforms 156,248; Bk Titles 74,599; Bk Vols 334,739
Subject Interests: Law, Taxation
Automation Activity & Vendor Info: (Acquisitions) Innovative Interfaces, Inc; (Cataloging) Innovative Interfaces, Inc; (Circulation) Innovative Interfaces, Inc; (Course Reserve) Innovative Interfaces, Inc; (OPAC) Innovative Interfaces, Inc; (Serials) Innovative Interfaces, Inc
Wireless access
Partic in Minitex
Open Mon-Fri 7:30am-10pm, Sat & Sun 9am-10pm

R MOUNT ZION TEMPLE*, Bloom Library, 1300 Summit Ave, 55105. SAN 308-7808. Tel: 651-698-3881. FAX: 651-698-1263. E-mail: librarian@mzion.org. Web Site: www.mzion.org. *Librn,* Robert A Epstein; Staff 1 (MLS 1)
Founded 1929
Library Holdings: Bks on Deafness & Sign Lang 2; CDs 288; DVDs 696; Large Print Bks 2; Bk Titles 10,138; Per Subs 4
Special Collections: Children's Coll; Jewish Feminism (Margolis Coll)
Subject Interests: Judaica
Automation Activity & Vendor Info: (Cataloging) ComPanion Corp; (Circulation) ComPanion Corp
Wireless access

GL RAMSEY COUNTY LAW LIBRARY, 1815 Court House, 55102. SAN 308-7832. Tel: 651-266-8391. FAX: 651-266-8399. *Dir,* Sara Galligan; E-mail: sara.galligan@co.ramsey.mn.us; Staff 3 (MLS 2, Non-MLS 1)
Founded 1936
Special Collections: Self-Represented Litigants; Westlaw
Subject Interests: Minn law
Automation Activity & Vendor Info: (Serials) Inmagic, Inc.
Wireless access
Partic in Metronet
Open Mon-Fri 8-4:30

M REGIONS HOSPITAL*, Medical Library, 640 Jackson St, 55101. SAN 308-7883. Tel: 651-254-3607. FAX: 651-254-3427. *Head Librn,* Mary Wittenbreer
Founded 1940
Library Holdings: Bk Vols 800; Per Subs 270
Automation Activity & Vendor Info: (Cataloging) EOS International
Wireless access
Partic in Twin Cities Biomedical Consortium
Open Mon-Fri 7:30-5

C SAINT CATHERINE UNIVERSITY*, Libraries, Media Services & Archives, 2004 Randolph Ave, Mail F-10, 55105-1794. SAN 347-8866. Tel: 651-690-6650. Circulation Tel: 651-690-8737. Interlibrary Loan Service Tel: 651-690-6655. Reference Tel: 651-690-6652. E-mail: library@stkate.edu. Web Site: library.stkate.edu. *Dir, Libr Serv,* Emily Asch; E-mail: ejasch@stkate.edu; *Head Archivist, Head, Spec Coll,* Deborah Kloiber; Tel: 651-690-6599, E-mail: d.kloiber@stkate.edu; *Head, Media Serv,* Rodney Fillmore; Tel: 651-690-6658, E-mail: rwfillmore@stkate.edu; *Librn,* Cynthia Graham; Tel: 651-690-7780, E-mail: ckgraham@stkate.edu; *Syst Librn,* Amy Shaw; Tel: 651-690-6423, E-mail: amshaw@stkate.edu; *Access Serv, ILL Assoc,* Jade Erickson; Tel: 651-690-6655, E-mail: jnerickson@stkate.edu. Subject Specialists: *Music,* Amy Shaw; Staff 14.5 (MLS 10.9, Non-MLS 3.6)
Founded 1905. Enrl 5,328; Fac 261; Highest Degree: Doctorate. Sal $962,361 (Prof $781,674)
Library Holdings: AV Mats 7,218; Bks on Deafness & Sign Lang 699; CDs 2,278; DVDs 4,648; e-books 17,437; e-journals 60,316; Electronic Media & Resources 8,000; Microforms 180,946; Music Scores 6,079; Bk Titles 155,094; Bk Vols 185,537; Per Subs 312; Videos 4,648
Special Collections: Autographs & Manuscripts (Mother Antonia McHugh Coll), bks, letters; Children's Literature (Ruth Sawyer Coll), multi media; Liturgical Art (Ade Bethune Coll); Muellerleile Coll of Printing; Rare Bks (Charlotte Hill Slade Coll & Mitsch Coll), first editions & fine bindings. Oral History
Automation Activity & Vendor Info: (Acquisitions) Innovative Interfaces, Inc; (Cataloging) Innovative Interfaces, Inc; (Circulation) Innovative Interfaces, Inc; (Course Reserve) Innovative Interfaces, Inc; (ILL) OCLC ILLiad; (Media Booking) Innovative Interfaces, Inc; (OPAC) Innovative Interfaces, Inc; (Serials) Innovative Interfaces, Inc
Wireless access
Partic in Metronet; Minitex; MnPALS; OCLC Online Computer Library Center, Inc
Special Services for the Deaf - ADA equip; Am sign lang & deaf culture; Bks on deafness & sign lang; Closed caption videos; Coll on deaf educ; Deaf publ; Sorenson video relay syst
Special Services for the Blind - Computer with voice synthesizer for visually impaired persons
Open Mon-Thurs 8am-11:30pm, Fri 8am-9:30pm, Sat 8-8, Sun 10am-11pm
Friends of the Library Group

Departmental Libraries:

MINNEAPOLIS CAMPUS, 601 25th Ave S, Minneapolis, 55454, SAN 308-6895. Tel: 651-690-7784. Web Site: www.stkate.edu. *Librn,* Cynthia Graham; Tel: 651-690-7780, E-mail: ckgraham@stkate.edu; *Media Serv Supvr,* Ronnie Carlson; Tel: 651-690-7792, E-mail: rcarlson@stkate.edu; *Circ,* Sue Gray; Tel: 651-690-7898; *ILL,* Monica Olmschenk; Tel: 651-690-7782. Subject Specialists: *Health sci,* Cynthia Graham; Staff 3 (MLS 2, Non-MLS 1)
Founded 1964. Highest Degree: Doctorate
Subject Interests: Allied health, Nursing, Phys therapy
Special Services for the Deaf - Captioned film dep; Spec interest per
Special Services for the Blind - Braille bks; Computer with voice synthesizer for visually impaired persons
Restriction: Open to students, fac & staff
Friends of the Library Group

J SAINT PAUL COLLEGE LIBRARY*, 235 Marshall Ave, 55102. SAN 308-7905. Tel: 651-846-1646. FAX: 651-221-1416. E-mail: librarywebemail@saintpaul.edu. Web Site: www.saintpaul.edu/library. *Librn,* Ben Tri; Tel: 651-846-1489, E-mail: ben.tri@saintpaul.edu; Staff 1 (MLS 1)
Founded 1966. Enrl 3,000; Fac 170
Library Holdings: Bk Vols 32,000; Per Subs 200
Wireless access
Partic in Minitex; MnPALS
Open Mon-Thurs 7:15am-8pm, Fri 7:15-4, Sat 8-Noon

P SAINT PAUL PUBLIC LIBRARY, George Latimer Central, 90 W Fourth St, 55102-1668. SAN 347-9226. Tel: 651-266-7000. Interlibrary Loan Service Tel: 651-501-6306. Administration Tel: 651-266-7073. FAX: 651-266-7060. E-mail: centrallibrary@ci.stpaul.mn.us, spplweb@ci.stpaul.mn.us. Web Site: www.sppl.org. *Dir,* Catherine Penkert; E-mail: catherine.penkert@ci.stpaul.mn.us; Staff 3 (MLS 3)
Special Collections: US Document Depository
Automation Activity & Vendor Info: (Acquisitions) Innovative Interfaces, Inc; (Cataloging) Innovative Interfaces, Inc; (Circulation) Innovative Interfaces, Inc; (ILL) Innovative Interfaces, Inc; (OPAC) Innovative Interfaces, Inc; (Serials) Innovative Interfaces, Inc
Wireless access
Function: Archival coll, AV serv, Govt ref serv, Homebound delivery serv, ILL available, Internet access, Magnifiers for reading, Outside serv via phone, mail, e-mail & web, Photocopying/Printing, Prog for adults, Prog for children & young adult, Ref serv available, Summer reading prog, Wheelchair accessible, Workshops
Publications: Communique (Newsletter)
Partic in Metropolitan Library Service Agency; Minitex
Special Services for the Deaf - Accessible learning ctr
Restriction: 24-hr pass syst for students only
Friends of the Library Group

Branches: 12

ARLINGTON HILLS, 1200 Payne Ave, 55130, SAN 347-9250. Tel: 651-632-3870. E-mail: arlingtonhills@ci.stpaul.mn.us.
DAYTON'S BLUFF, 645 E Seventh St, 55106, SAN 328-8005. Tel: 651-793-1699. FAX: 651-793-1697. E-mail: daytonsbluff@ci.stpaul.mn.us.
HAMLINE - MIDWAY, 1558 W Minnehaha Ave, 55104-1264, SAN 347-9285. Tel: 651-642-0293. FAX: 651-642-0323. E-mail: hamlinemidway@ci.stpaul.mn.us.

HAYDEN HEIGHTS, 1456 White Bear Ave, 55106-2405, SAN 347-9315. Tel: 651-793-3934. FAX: 651-793-3936. E-mail: haydenheights@ci.stpaul.mn.us.
HIGHLAND PARK, 1974 Ford Pkwy, 55116-1922, SAN 347-934X. Tel: 651-695-3700. FAX: 651-695-3701. E-mail: highlandpark@ci.stpaul.mn.us.
MERRIAM PARK, 1831 Marshall Ave, 55104-6010, SAN 347-9404. Tel: 651-642-0385. FAX: 651-642-0391. E-mail: merriampark@ci.stpaul.mn.us.
RICE STREET, 1011 Rice St, 55117, SAN 347-9439. Tel: 651-558-2223. FAX: 651-558-2225. E-mail: ricestreet@ci.stpaul.mn.us.
RIVERVIEW, One E George St, 55107-2906, SAN 347-9463. Tel: 651-292-6626. FAX: 651-292-6575. E-mail: riverview@ci.stpaul.mn.us.
RONDO COMMUNITY OUTREACH LIBRARY, 461 N Dale St, 55103. FAX: 651-266-7410. E-mail: rondolibrary@ci.stpaul.mn.us.
Library Holdings: CDs 5,835; DVDs 8,569; Bk Vols 77,382; Per Subs 85
Special Collections: ESL Coll; IBWT Coll; Small Business Partnership Coll
Subject Interests: African-Am culture, Hist
Open Mon-Thurs 10-9, Fri & Sat 10-5:30, Sun 1-5
Friends of the Library Group
SAINT ANTHONY PARK, 2245 Como Ave, 55108-1719, SAN 347-9498. Tel: 651-642-0411. FAX: 651-642-0358. E-mail: saintanthonypark@ci.stpaul.mn.us.
SUN RAY, 2105 Wilson Ave, 55119-4033, SAN 347-9528. Tel: 651-501-6300. E-mail: sunray@ci.stpaul.mn.us.
WEST SEVENTH, 265 Oneida St, 55102. Tel: 651-298-5516. E-mail: west7th@ci.stpaul.mn.us.
Library Holdings: CDs 819; DVDs 1,380; Bk Titles 7,823; Per Subs 14; Talking Bks 304
Open Mon & Thurs 12:30-8, Tues 11:30-5:30, Wed & Fri 10-5:30
Friends of the Library Group
Bookmobiles: 1

S 3M INFORMATION RESEARCH & SOLUTIONS*, 3M Corporate Headquarters, 2701 Hudson Rd, 55144. SAN 347-9560. Tel: 651-575-1300, 651-733-1110. FAX: 651-736-6495. *Library Contact,* Tom Koehler
Library Holdings: Bk Titles 67,000; Bk Vols 100,000; Per Subs 1,550
Automation Activity & Vendor Info: (OPAC) Ex Libris Group; (Serials) Ex Libris Group
Publications: 3M Union List of Serials
Partic in OCLC Online Computer Library Center, Inc; Proquest Dialog; Questal Orbit
Open Mon-Fri 8-5

A UNITED STATES ARMY*, Corps of Engineers Saint Paul District Technical Library, 180 Fifth St E, Ste 700, 55101-1678. SAN 347-9854. Tel: 651-290-5807. FAX: 651-290-5256. E-mail: library@usace.army.mil. Web Site: www.mvp.usace.army.mil/Library. *Librn,* Position Currently Open
Founded 1972
Library Holdings: Bk Vols 4,884; Per Subs 350
Special Collections: Annual Reports of the Chief of Engineers, US Army
Subject Interests: DM construction, Engr, Environ studies, Hydrol, Water res
Wireless access
Partic in OCLC Online Computer Library Center, Inc
Open Mon-Fri 7:30-4:30

GL US COURTS LIBRARY*, Eighth Circuit Library, 512 Federal Court Bldg, 316 N Robert St, 55101. SAN 308-7964. Tel: 651-848-1320. FAX: 651-848-1325. E-mail: library8th@ca8.uscourts.gov. Web Site: www.ca8.uscourts.gov. *Librn,* Andrea Wambach; E-mail: andrea_wambach@ca8.uscourts.gov; Staff 2 (MLS 1, Non-MLS 1)
Library Holdings: Bk Vols 20,000; Per Subs 30
Automation Activity & Vendor Info: (Cataloging) SirsiDynix; (OPAC) SirsiDynix
Restriction: Staff use only

C UNIVERSITY OF NORTHWESTERN-ST PAUL*, Berntsen Library, 3003 Snelling Ave N, 55113. SAN 320-9326. Tel: 651-631-5241. Reference Tel: 651-286-7708. E-mail: unwlibrary@unwsp.edu. Web Site: guide.unwsp.edu. *Dir,* Ruth McGuire; E-mail: ramcguire@unwsp.edu; *Electronic Res Librn,* Linda Rust; E-mail: lorust@unwsp.edu; *Ref & Instruction Librn,* Jessica Moore; E-mail: jmmoore@unwsp.edu; *Syst Librn,* Nathan Farley; E-mail: nrfarley@unwsp.edu; *Access Serv Supvr,* Becky Schleicher; E-mail: bjschleicher@unwsp.edu; *Coordr, Acq, Coord, Weekend & Periodicals,* Lindsey Brooks; E-mail: lsbrooks@unwsp.edu; *Coordr, Cat,* Katie Hagen; E-mail: kahagen@unwsp.edu; *Web Coordr,* Kong Yang; E-mail: kmyang@unwsp.edu; *Archivist,* Greg Rosauer; E-mail: gjrosauer@unwsp.edu; Staff 9 (MLS 5, Non-MLS 4)
Founded 1902. Enrl 2,640; Fac 99; Highest Degree: Master
Library Holdings: e-books 457,912; e-journals 76,260; Bk Titles 88,459
Special Collections: W B Riley Coll, bks, ms, scrapbks
Automation Activity & Vendor Info: (Acquisitions) Ex Libris Group; (Cataloging) Ex Libris Group; (Circulation) Ex Libris Group; (Course Reserve) Ex Libris Group; (Discovery) Ex Libris Group; (ILL) OCLC ILLiad; (Serials) Ex Libris Group
Wireless access
Partic in Christian Library Consortium; Minitex; MnPALS; OCLC Online Computer Library Center, Inc
Open Mon-Thurs 7:30am-11:30pm, Fri 7:30-7, Sat 10-6, Sun 1-10

CR UNIVERSITY OF SAINT THOMAS*, O'Shaughnessy-Frey Library, 2115 Summit Ave, Mail Box 5004, 55105. SAN 308-7581. Tel: 651-962-5001. Circulation Tel: 651-962-5494. Administration Tel: 651-962-5014. FAX: 651-962-5406. Web Site: www.stthomas.edu/libraries/. *Assoc Vice-Provost, Univ Librn,* Dan Gjelten; Tel: 651-962-5005, E-mail: drgjelten@stthomas.edu; *Assoc Dir, Coll Mgt,* Meg Manahan; Tel: 651-962-5016, E-mail: mkmanahan@stthomas.edu; *Assoc Dir, Digital Serv,* Greg Argo; Tel: 651-962-5498, E-mail: gargo@stthomas.edu; *Assoc Dir, Res & Info Serv,* Ann Zawistoski; Tel: 651-962-5412, E-mail: ann.zawistoski@stthomas.edu; *Coordr, Libr Serv,* Julie Kimlinger; E-mail: jakimlinger@stthomas.edu; *ILL,* Faith E Bonitz; E-mail: febonitz@stthomas.edu; *Univ Archivist,* Ann M Kenne; Tel: 651-962-5461. Subject Specialists: *English, Polit sci,* Dan Gjelten; *Hist,* Ann M Kenne; Staff 32 (MLS 21, Non-MLS 11)
Founded 1885. Enrl 10,245; Fac 461; Highest Degree: Doctorate
Special Collections: Belloc-Chesterton Coll; Celtic Coll; Luxembourg Coll; University Archives; UST Research Online
Automation Activity & Vendor Info: (Acquisitions) Ex Libris Group; (Cataloging) Ex Libris Group; (Circulation) Ex Libris Group; (Course Reserve) Ex Libris Group; (Discovery) Ex Libris Group; (ILL) OCLC ILLiad; (OPAC) Ex Libris Group; (Serials) Ex Libris Group
Wireless access
Function: Archival coll, Audio & video playback equip for onsite use, Computers for patron use, Doc delivery serv, E-Reserves, Electronic databases & coll, ILL available, Internet access, Music CDs, Online cat, Online ref, Orientations, Outside serv via phone, mail, e-mail & web, Photocopying/Printing, Printer for laptops & handheld devices, Ref & res, Ref serv available, Res libr, Scanner, Spoken cassettes & DVDs, Telephone ref, VHS videos, Wheelchair accessible
Partic in Minitex; MnPALS; OCLC Online Computer Library Center, Inc; TexSHARE - Texas State Library & Archives Commission
Special Services for the Deaf - Assistive tech; Bks on deafness & sign lang
Special Services for the Blind - Assistive/Adapted tech devices, equip & products; Computer with voice synthesizer for visually impaired persons
Open Mon-Thurs 7:30am-2am, Fri 7:30am-8pm, Sat 10-6, Sun Noon-2am

Departmental Libraries:

ARCHBISHOP IRELAND MEMORIAL LIBRARY, 2260 Summit Ave, Mail No IRL, 55105, SAN 377-0214. Tel: 651-962-5453. Administration Tel: 651-962-5451. FAX: 651-962-5460. Web Site: www.stthomas.edu/libraries/ireland. *Dir,* N Curtis Lemay; E-mail: nclemay@stthomas.edu; *Circ Mgr,* Conie Borchardt; E-mail: clborchardt@stthomas.edu; *Tech Serv,* Betsy J Polakowski; Tel: 651-962-5452, E-mail: ejpolakowski@stthomas.edu; Staff 3 (MLS 2, Non-MLS 1)
Founded 1894. Enrl 110; Fac 24; Highest Degree: Doctorate
Library Holdings: AV Mats 51; e-books 108,861; e-journals 44,256; Microforms 1,249; Bk Vols 109,149; Per Subs 160
Subject Interests: Theol
Partic in Minnesota Theological Library Association
Open Mon-Thurs 8am-10pm, Fri 8-6, Sat 10-5, Sun 1-10
Friends of the Library Group
CHARLES J KEFFER LIBRARY, 1000 LaSalle Ave, MOH 206, Minneapolis, 55403, SAN 377-0230. Tel: 651-962-4642. FAX: 651-962-4648. Web Site: www.stthomas.edu/libraries/keffer. *Libr Dir,* Janice Kragness; Tel: 651-962-4645, E-mail: jlkragness@stthomas.edu; *Ref Librn,* Merrie Davidson; Tel: 651-962-4661, E-mail: merrie.davidson@stthomas.edu; *Ref Librn,* Laura Hansen; Tel: 651-962-4646, E-mail: laura.hansen@stthomas.edu; *Ref Librn,* Andrea Koeppe; Tel: 651-962-4647, E-mail: arhudson@stthomas.edu; *Ref Librn,* Donna Nix; Tel: 651-962-4662, E-mail: denix@stthomas.edu; *Circ,* Linnae Weinrich; Tel: 651-962-4644, E-mail: ljweinrich@stthomas.edu; *Circ,* William Zych; Tel: 651-962-4667, E-mail: wrzych@stthomas.edu. Subject Specialists: *Bus,* Janice Kragness; *Educ,* Merrie Davidson; *Bus,* Laura Hansen; *Bus,* Andrea Koeppe; *Educ,* Donna Nix; Staff 6 (MLS 4, Non-MLS 2)
Founded 1992. Highest Degree: Doctorate
Library Holdings: AV Mats 135; e-books 108,861; e-journals 44,256; Microforms 835,727; Bk Vols 32,000; Per Subs 261
Subject Interests: Bus, Educ, Psychol
Function: Computers for patron use, E-Reserves, Electronic databases & coll, ILL available, Internet access, Online cat, Online info literacy tutorials on the web & in blackboard, Online ref, Photocopying/Printing, Ref & res, Ref serv available, Res libr, Scanner, Wheelchair accessible
Open Mon-Thurs 8am-10pm, Fri 8-6, Sat 10-5, Sun 1-10

SAINT PETER

C GUSTAVUS ADOLPHUS COLLEGE*, Folke Bernadotte Memorial Library, 800 W College Ave, 56082. SAN 348-0097. Tel: 507-933-7556. Circulation Tel: 507-933-7558. Interlibrary Loan Service Tel: 507-933-7564. Reference Tel: 507-933-7567. FAX: 507-933-6292. E-mail: folke@gustavus.edu. Web Site: www.gustavus.edu/library. *Chair/Ref Librn,* Daniel Mollner; Tel: 507-933-7569, E-mail: dmollner@gustavus.edu; *Coll Access & Ref Librn,* Julie Gilbert; Tel: 507-933-7552, E-mail: jgilber2@gustavus.edu; *Electronic Res & Ref Librn,* Anna Hulseberg; Tel: 507-933-7566, E-mail: ahulsebe@gustavus.edu; *Ref & Instruction Librn,* Barbara Fister; Tel: 507-933-7553, E-mail: fister@gustavus.edu; *Ref Librn,* Michelle Twait; Tel: 507-933-7563, E-mail: mtwait@gustavus.edu; *ILL Mgr,* Sonja Timmerman; E-mail: stimmer2@gustavus.edu; *Col Archivist,* Jeff Jenson; Tel: 507-933-7572, E-mail: jjenson@gustavus.edu; Staff 15 (MLS 6, Non-MLS 9)
Founded 1862. Enrl 2,443; Fac 214; Highest Degree: Bachelor
Jun 2013-May 2014 Income $1,871,211. Mats Exp $624,742. Sal $856,364 (Prof $760,456)
Library Holdings: AV Mats 19,509; CDs 5,284; DVDs 3,207; e-journals 149; Electronic Media & Resources 64; Microforms 43,075; Music Scores 5,356; Bk Vols 280,616; Per Subs 424; Videos 2,124
Special Collections: College Archives; Gene Basset Political Cartoons; Hasselquist International Studies Coll; Heitzig Coll; John Updike Coll; Lutheran Church Archives; Mettetal Record Coll; Rezmerski Science Fiction Coll; Scandinavian American Coll; Scullin Jazz Coll; Selma Lagerloff (Nils Sahlin Coll), bks, pamphlets. US Document Depository
Automation Activity & Vendor Info: (Acquisitions) Ex Libris Group; (Cataloging) OCLC; (Circulation) Ex Libris Group; (Course Reserve) Ex Libris Group; (ILL) Ex Libris Group; (OPAC) Ex Libris Group; (Serials) EBSCO Online
Wireless access
Function: 24/7 Electronic res, Archival coll, Audio & video playback equip for onsite use, AV serv, Computers for patron use, Doc delivery serv, E-Reserves, Electronic databases & coll, Free DVD rentals, ILL available, Internet access, Magnifiers for reading, Microfiche/film & reading machines, Music CDs, Online cat, Online ref, Printer for laptops & handheld devices, Ref serv available, Scanner, Telephone ref, VHS videos, Wheelchair accessible
Partic in Minitex; OCLC Online Computer Library Center, Inc
Special Services for the Blind - Magnifiers; Reader equip; Screen enlargement software for people with visual disabilities
Open Mon-Thurs 8am-1am, Fri 8-6, Sat 10-6, Sun 11am-1am
Restriction: Authorized patrons
Friends of the Library Group

S NICOLLET COUNTY HISTORICAL SOCIETY*, Treaty Site History Center, 1851 N Minnesota Ave, 56082. SAN 325-500X. Tel: 507-934-2160. FAX: 507-934-0172. E-mail: museum@nchsmn.org. Web Site: www.nchsmn.org/sites/treaty-site-history-center. *Research Coordr,* Ruth Einstein; E-mail: researchcoordinator@nchsmn.org
Library Holdings: Bk Titles 2,000
Subject Interests: County hist, Genealogy, Hist, Southern Minn
Open Tues-Fri 10-4, Sun 1-4

P SAINT PETER PUBLIC LIBRARY*, 601 S Washington Ave, 56082. SAN 347-4429. Tel: 507-934-7420. FAX: 507-934-1204. E-mail: lib@saintpetermn.gov. Web Site: www.saintpetermn.gov/library. *Head Librn,* Doug Wolfe; *Asst Head Librn, Ch,* Brenda McHugh; *Libr Assoc,* Tosha Anderson; Staff 4 (MLS 1, Non-MLS 3)
Library Holdings: Bk Vols 45,000; Per Subs 183
Automation Activity & Vendor Info: (Acquisitions) SirsiDynix; (Cataloging) SirsiDynix; (Circulation) SirsiDynix; (Course Reserve) SirsiDynix; (ILL) SirsiDynix; (Media Booking) SirsiDynix; (OPAC) SirsiDynix; (Serials) SirsiDynix
Wireless access
Mem of Traverse Des Sioux Library Cooperative
Open Mon-Thurs 10-8, Fri 10-5, Sat 9-4
Friends of the Library Group

M SAINT PETER REGIONAL TREATMENT CENTER LIBRARIES*, MSH Education Dept Library, 2100 Sheppard Dr, 56082. SAN 348-0151. Tel: 507-985-2121. *Library Contact,* Thomas Rosburg; Tel: 507-985-2320, E-mail: tom.rosburg@state.mn.us; Staff 5 (MLS 1, Non-MLS 4)
Founded 1878
Library Holdings: CDs 500; DVDs 550; Bk Titles 12,000; Bk Vols 12,600; Per Subs 12
Subject Interests: Alcoholic dependents, Bks in gen for retarded readers, Drug dependence, Media in gen for retarded readers, Mentally ill patients
Wireless access
Partic in South Central Minnesota Interlibrary Exchange
Open Mon-Fri 8-4

R TRINITY LUTHERAN PARISH LIBRARY*, 511 S Fifth St, 56082. SAN 308-7999. Tel: 507-934-4786. FAX: 507-934-4562. E-mail: office@trinitystpeter.org. Web Site: www.trinitystpeter.org. *Librn,* Position Currently Open
Founded 1959
Library Holdings: Bk Vols 4,500
Subject Interests: Bible, Christian life, Martin Luther, Psychol, Relig studies
Friends of the Library Group

SHAKOPEE

S MINNESOTA DEPARTMENT OF CORRECTIONS, Minnesota Correctional Facility - Shakopee, 1010 6th Ave W, 55379-2213. Tel: 952-496-4440. FAX: 952-496-4460. Web Site: mn.gov/doc/facilities/shakopee. *Librn,* Andrea Smith; E-mail: andrea.a.smith@state.mn.us; Staff 1 (MLS 1)
Library Holdings: Audiobooks 250; DVDs 100; Bk Vols 9,500; Talking Bks 2
Special Collections: Law Coll
Automation Activity & Vendor Info: (Cataloging) EOS International; (Circulation) EOS International

P SCOTT COUNTY LIBRARY SYSTEM*, Library Administration, 1615 Weston Ct, 55379. SAN 348-0305. Tel: 952-496-8010. FAX: 952-707-1775. Web Site: www.scottlib.org. *Dir,* Jake J Grussing; E-mail: jgrussing@scottlib.org; *Assoc Dir,* Cynthia Purser; E-mail: cpurser@co.scott.mn.us; *Librn,* Mary Kay Baden; *Youth Serv Coordr,* Lisa Pollard; *Libr Assoc,* Julie Svenningsen; Staff 36.9 (MLS 7.9, Non-MLS 29)
Founded 1969. Pop 119,646; Circ 908,693
Library Holdings: AV Mats 23,832; Bk Vols 266,195; Per Subs 366; Talking Bks 5,361
Automation Activity & Vendor Info: (Cataloging) SirsiDynix-Unicorn; (Circulation) SirsiDynix-Unicorn; (OPAC) SirsiDynix-iBistro; (Serials) SirsiDynix-Unicorn
Wireless access
Function: Art exhibits, Audio & video playback equip for onsite use, Bk club(s), Bks on cassette, Bks on CD, Children's prog, Computers for patron use, Electronic databases & coll, Free DVD rentals, Home delivery & serv to seniorr ctr & nursing homes, Homework prog, ILL available, Internet access, Jail serv, Magnifiers for reading, Museum passes, Music CDs, Notary serv, Online cat, Online ref, Outreach serv, Outside serv via phone, mail, e-mail & web, Photocopying/Printing, Preschool outreach, Prog for adults, Prog for children & young adult, Ref & res, Ref serv available, Spoken cassettes & CDs, Spoken cassettes & DVDs, Story hour, Summer reading prog, Tax forms, Teen prog, Telephone ref, VHS videos, Wheelchair accessible
Partic in Metropolitan Library Service Agency; Minitex
Open Mon-Fri 8-4:30
Friends of the Library Group
Branches: 7
BELLE PLAINE PUBLIC LIBRARY, 125 W Main St, Belle Plaine, 56011-1245, SAN 348-033X. Tel: 952-873-6767. FAX: 952-873-6767. E-mail: bplibrary@scottlib.org.
Library Holdings: Bk Vols 13,409
Open Tues 10-6, Wed 2-8:30, Thurs 2-8, Fri 10-5, Sat (Sept-May) 10-2
ELKO NEW MARKET PUBLIC LIBRARY, 110 J Roberts Way, Elko New Market, 55054, SAN 348-0399. Tel: 952-496-8030. FAX: 952-496-8030. E-mail: nmlibrary@scottlib.org.
Library Holdings: Bk Vols 6,156
Open Mon & Wed 1-8, Fri 10-5
JORDAN PUBLIC LIBRARY, 275 Creek Lane S, Jordan, 55352, SAN 348-0364. Tel: 952-492-8050. FAX: 952-492-2500. E-mail: jolibrary@scottlib.org.
Library Holdings: Bk Vols 15,677
Open Mon & Wed 2-8, Tues & Thurs 10-5:30, Sat (Winter) 10-2
NEW PRAGUE PUBLIC LIBRARY, 400 E Main St, New Prague, 56071-2429, SAN 348-0429. Tel: 952-496-8026. FAX: 952-758-2391. E-mail: nplibrary@scottlib.org.
Library Holdings: Bk Vols 21,980
Open Mon-Thurs 10-8, Sat 10-4, Sun (Winter) 1-5
PRIOR LAKE PUBLIC LIBRARY, 16210 Eagle Creek Ave SE, Prior Lake, 55372-9202, SAN 348-0453. Tel: 952-447-3375. FAX: 952-447-3375. E-mail: pllibrary@scottlib.org.
Library Holdings: Bk Vols 26,595
Open Mon-Wed 10-8, Thurs 10-5, Fri 1-5, Sat 10-4, Sun (Winter) 1-5
SAVAGE PUBLIC LIBRARY, 13090 Alabama Ave S, Savage, 55378, SAN 348-0488. Tel: 952-707-1770. FAX: 952-707-1775. E-mail: salibrary@scottlib.org.
Library Holdings: Bk Vols 17,964
Open Mon-Thurs 10-8, Fri 10-5, Sat 10-4, Sun 1-5

SHAKOPEE PUBLIC LIBRARY, 235 Lewis St S, 55379, SAN 348-0518. Tel: 952-233-9590. FAX: 952-233-3851. E-mail: shlibrary@scottlib.org.
Library Holdings: Bk Vols 35,925
Open Mon, Tues & Thurs 10-8, Wed 10-5, Fri 1-5, Sat 10-4, Sun (Jan-May) 1-5

SHOREVIEW

P RAMSEY COUNTY LIBRARY*, Administration, 4570 N Victoria St, 55126. SAN 347-8025. Tel: 651-486-2200. FAX: 651-486-2220. Web Site: rclreads.org. *Libr Dir,* Jill Boldenow; Tel: 651-486-2201, E-mail: jill.boldenow@co.ramsey.mn.us; *Dep Dir,* Lynn Wyman; Tel: 651-724-6010, E-mail: lynn.wyman@co.ramsey.mn.us; Staff 160 (MLS 50, Non-MLS 110)
Founded 1951
Special Collections: Minnesota Coll
Subject Interests: State geog, State hist
Automation Activity & Vendor Info: (Acquisitions) SirsiDynix; (Cataloging) SirsiDynix; (Circulation) SirsiDynix
Wireless access
Partic in Metronet; Metropolitan Library Service Agency
Friends of the Library Group
Branches: 7
MAPLEWOOD BRANCH, 3025 Southlawn Dr, Maplewood, 55109, SAN 347-8084. Tel: 651-724-6003. FAX: 651-704-2038. *Br Mgr,* Monica Stratton; Tel: 651-724-6063, E-mail: monica.stratton@co.ramsey.mn.us
Open Mon-Thurs 10-9, Fri & Sat 10-5, Sun 12-5
Friends of the Library Group
MOUNDS VIEW BRANCH, 2576 Mounds View Blvd, Mounds View, 55112-4032, SAN 370-1298. Tel: 651-724-6004. FAX: 763-717-3275. *Br Mgr,* Marcus Lowry; Tel: 651-724-6097, E-mail: marcus.lowry@co.ramsey.mn.us
Open Mon & Thurs 1-8, Wed, Fri & Sat 10-5
Friends of the Library Group
NEW BRIGHTON BRANCH, 400 Tenth St NW, New Brighton, 55112-6806, SAN 347-805X. Tel: 651-724-6002. *Br Mgr,* Meg Robertson; Tel: 651-724-6050, E-mail: margaret.l.robertson@co.ramsey.mn.us; Staff 8 (MLS 2, Non-MLS 6)
Open Mon, Tues, Thurs & Fri 10-5, Wed 10-7
Friends of the Library Group
NORTH SAINT PAUL BRANCH, 2300 N St Paul Dr, North Saint Paul, 55109, SAN 347-8114. Tel: 651-724-6005. FAX: 651-747-2705. *Br Mgr,* Ann Wahlstrom; Tel: 651-747-2701, E-mail: ann.wahlstrom@co.ramsey.mn.us
Open Mon, Wed, Thurs & Sat 10-5, Tues 1-8
Friends of the Library Group
ROSEVILLE BRANCH, 2180 N Hamline Ave, Roseville, 55113-4241, SAN 347-8122. Tel: 651-724-6001. FAX: 651-628-6818. *Br Mgr,* Jeff Eide; Tel: 651-724-6061, E-mail: jeffrey@eide@co.ramsey.mn.us
Open Mon-Thurs 10-9, Fri & Sat 10-5, Sun 12-5
Friends of the Library Group
SHOREVIEW BRANCH, 4560 N Victoria St, 55126, SAN 373-5184. Tel: 651-724-6006. FAX: 651-486-2313. *Br Mgr,* Carol Jackson; Tel: 651-724-6090, E-mail: carol.l.jackson@co.ramsey.mn.us
Open Mon-Thurs 10-9, Fri & Sat 10-5, Sun 12-5
Friends of the Library Group
WHITE BEAR LAKE BRANCH, 2150 Second St, White Bear Lake, 55110, SAN 347-8149. Tel: 651-724-6007. FAX: 651-407-5305. *Br Mgr,* Therese Sonnek; Tel: 651-724-6130, E-mail: therese.m.sonnek@co.ramsey.mn.us
Open Mon 10-8, Tues & Wed 1-8, Thurs, Fri & Sat 10-5
Friends of the Library Group

SILVER BAY

P SILVER BAY PUBLIC LIBRARY*, Nine Davis Dr, 55614-1318. SAN 308-8014. Tel: 218-226-4331. E-mail: silverbaypubliclibrary@gmail.com. Web Site: www.silverbay.com. *Dir,* J Billings
Founded 1955. Pop 1,800
Automation Activity & Vendor Info: (Acquisitions) SirsiDynix; (Cataloging) SirsiDynix; (Serials) SirsiDynix
Wireless access
Mem of Arrowhead Library System
Open Mon-Thurs 10-6:30, Fri 10-6
Friends of the Library Group

SLAYTON

P SLAYTON PUBLIC LIBRARY*, 2451 Broadway Ave, 56172. SAN 308-8022. Tel: 507-836-8778. FAX: 507-393-0029. Web Site: slayton.govoffice.com. *Dir,* Lori Stainer; E-mail: lstainer@plumcreeklibrary.net; *Asst Librn,* Trish Grieme; E-mail: pgrieme@plumcreeklibrary.net
Founded 1946. Pop 2,451; Circ 30,573
Library Holdings: Bk Vols 32,000; Per Subs 50
Special Collections: Song Books
Automation Activity & Vendor Info: (Cataloging) Koha; (Circulation) Koha; (OPAC) Koha
Wireless access
Mem of Plum Creek Library System
Open Mon & Thurs 10-4, Tues, Wed & Fri 9-4
Friends of the Library Group

SLEEPY EYE

P DYCKMAN FREE LIBRARY*, 345 W Main St, 56085-1331. SAN 308-8030. Tel: 507-794-7655. Web Site: www.dyckmanlibrarymn.org. *Libr Dir,* Andrew Kelton; Tel: 507-794-7655, E-mail: akelton@tds.lib.mn.us; Staff 1 (MLS 1)
Founded 1900. Pop 5,200; Circ 20,000
Jan 2014-Dec 2014 Income $135,450, Provincial $200, City $116,000, County $14,000, Locally Generated Income $5,250. Mats Exp $9,538, Books $7,500, AV Mat $1,500, Electronic Ref Mat (Incl. Access Fees) $538. Sal $93,500 (Prof $44,600)
Library Holdings: Audiobooks 962; AV Mats 659; e-books 3,070; e-journals 40; Bk Vols 21,495; Per Subs 22
Special Collections: Local History Artifacts
Automation Activity & Vendor Info: (Acquisitions) Innovative Interfaces, Inc; (Cataloging) Innovative Interfaces, Inc; (Circulation) Innovative Interfaces, Inc; (Course Reserve) Innovative Interfaces, Inc; (ILL) Innovative Interfaces, Inc; (OPAC) Innovative Interfaces, Inc
Wireless access
Mem of Traverse Des Sioux Library Cooperative
Open Mon & Wed 9:30-8, Tues, Thurs & Fri 9:30-5, Sat 9:30-Noon

SOUTH SAINT PAUL

S DAKOTA COUNTY HISTORICAL SOCIETY, Research Library, 130 Third Ave N, 55075. SAN 329-7268. Tel: 651-552-7548. FAX: 651-552-7265. E-mail: dakotahistory@co.dakota.mn.us. Web Site: www.dakotahistory.org. *Dir, Res,* Rebecca Snyder; E-mail: rebecca.snyder@co.dakota.mn.us; Staff 3 (Non-MLS 3)
Founded 1935
Library Holdings: Bk Titles 600; Per Subs 20
Special Collections: Oral History
Subject Interests: Dakota County, Hist
Publications: Census Transcription; Over the Years; Society Happenings (Newsletter)
Open Wed & Fri 9-5, Thurs 9-8, Sat 10-3

P SOUTH SAINT PAUL PUBLIC LIBRARY, 106 Third Ave N, 55075. SAN 308-8057. Tel: 651-554-3240. FAX: 651-554-3241. Web Site: www.southstpaul.org/library. *Libr Dir,* Kathy Halgren; Tel: 651-554-3242, E-mail: khalgren@sspmn.org; *Ad,* Honora Greenwood Rodriguez; Tel: 651-554-3243, E-mail: Hrodriguez@sspmn.org; *Youth Serv Librn,* Sarah Connolly; Tel: 651-554-3244, E-mail: sconnolly@southstpaul.org; Staff 7.1 (MLS 3, Non-MLS 4.1)
Founded 1922. Pop 20,800; Circ 110,000
Library Holdings: AV Mats 6,800; Bk Vols 64,000; Per Subs 129
Automation Activity & Vendor Info: (Cataloging) SirsiDynix; (Circulation) SirsiDynix; (OPAC) SirsiDynix
Wireless access
Function: 24/7 Electronic res, 24/7 Online cat, Adult bk club, Art programs, Audiobks on Playaways & MP3, Audiobks via web, Bks on CD, Children's prog, Computer training, Computers for patron use, Doc delivery serv, Electronic databases & coll, Family literacy, Free DVD rentals, Homebound delivery serv, ILL available, Internet access, Life-long learning prog for all ages, Magazines, Mango lang, Meeting rooms, Music CDs, Online ref, Outreach serv, Outside serv via phone, mail, e-mail & web, Photocopying/Printing, Preschool outreach, Preschool reading prog, Prog for adults, Prog for children & young adult, Ref serv available, Senior outreach, Spanish lang bks, STEM programs, Story hour, Summer & winter reading prog, Tax forms, Teen prog, Telephone ref, Wheelchair accessible
Mem of Dakota County Library System
Special Services for the Deaf - Bks on deafness & sign lang; Closed caption videos; Sign lang interpreter upon request for prog
Special Services for the Blind - Audio mat; Bks available with recordings; Bks on CD; Copier with enlargement capabilities; Descriptive video serv (DVS); Home delivery serv; Large print bks; Merlin electronic magnifier reader; Playaways (bks on MP3)
Open Mon & Thurs 9-8, Tues, Wed & Fri 9-6, Sat (Sept-May) 10-4

SPICER

P SPICER LIBRARY*, 198 Manitoba St, 56288-9629. (Mail add: PO Box 160, 56288-0160), SAN 348-1352. Tel: 320-796-5560. FAX: 320-796-3013. E-mail: spicer.staff@pioneerland.lib.mn.us. Web Site: www.spicer.lib.mn.us. *Head Librn,* Ria Newhouse; E-mail: ria.newhouse@pioneerland.lib.mn.us
Pop 1,164; Circ 19,660
Library Holdings: Bk Vols 32,000; Per Subs 37

Automation Activity & Vendor Info: (Cataloging) Innovative Interfaces, Inc; (Circulation) Innovative Interfaces, Inc; (OPAC) Innovative Interfaces, Inc
Wireless access
Mem of Pioneerland Library System
Open Tues 10-5, Wed 12-7, Thurs & Fri 11-5, Sat 9-1
Friends of the Library Group

SPRING VALLEY

P SPRING VALLEY PUBLIC LIBRARY, 121 W Jefferson St, 55975. SAN 308-8065. Tel: 507-346-2100. E-mail: sv_dir@selco.info. Web Site: springvalley.lib.mn.us. *Dir,* Jenny Simon; E-mail: jsimon@selco.info
Founded 1901. Circ 46,000
Library Holdings: Bk Titles 22,000; Per Subs 35
Automation Activity & Vendor Info: (Cataloging) SirsiDynix; (Circulation) SirsiDynix; (OPAC) SirsiDynix
Wireless access
Partic in Southeastern Libraries Cooperating
Open Mon & Fri 10-6, Tues-Thurs 12-7

SPRINGFIELD

P SPRINGFIELD PUBLIC LIBRARY*, 120 N Cass Ave, 56087-1506. SAN 308-8073. Tel: 507-723-3510. FAX: 507-723-6422. E-mail: libtbs@tds.lib.mn.us. Web Site: www.springfieldpubliclibrarymn.org. *Dir,* Linda Roiger; E-mail: lroige@tds.lib.mn.us
Founded 1932. Pop 2,211; Circ 38,280
Library Holdings: Bks on Deafness & Sign Lang 15; Large Print Bks 900; Bk Titles 25,000; Bk Vols 30,000; Per Subs 100; Talking Bks 625
Subject Interests: Local hist
Wireless access
Function: AV serv, Home delivery & serv to seniorr ctr & nursing homes, ILL available, Internet access, Prog for adults, Prog for children & young adult, Summer reading prog, Wheelchair accessible
Mem of Traverse Des Sioux Library Cooperative
Partic in OCLC Online Computer Library Center, Inc
Special Services for the Deaf - Bks on deafness & sign lang
Special Services for the Blind - Audio mat; Bks on cassette; Bks on CD; Braille bks; Children's Braille; Large print bks; Talking bks
Open Mon-Thurs 9-7, Fri 9-5, Sat (Sept-May) 9-Noon

STEWARTVILLE

P STEWARTVILLE PUBLIC LIBRARY*, 110 Second St SE, 55976-1306. SAN 308-809X. Tel: 507-533-4902. FAX: 507-533-4746. E-mail: stew_notices@selco.info. Web Site: www.stewartvillelibrary.org. *Libr Dir,* Nate Deprey; E-mail: ndeprey@selco.info; *Assoc Librn,* Debora Lofgren; E-mail: debora@selco.info; Staff 3 (Non-MLS 3)
Founded 1938. Pop 6,519
Library Holdings: Bk Titles 33,000; Per Subs 30
Special Collections: Holocaust Coll
Automation Activity & Vendor Info: (Cataloging) SirsiDynix; (Circulation) SirsiDynix; (ILL) SirsiDynix; (OPAC) SirsiDynix; (Serials) SirsiDynix
Partic in Southeastern Libraries Cooperating
Open Mon 12-8, Tues 10-6, Wed 12-6, Thurs 10-8, Fri 12-5, Sat 10-1
Friends of the Library Group

STILLWATER

S MINNESOTA DEPARTMENT OF CORRECTIONS*, Minnesota Correctional Facility - Oak Park Heights, 5329 Osgood Ave N, 55082. Tel: 651-779-1410. FAX: 651-779-1323. Web Site: mn.gov/doc/facilities/oak-park-heights. *Librn,* Sue Farmer; Tel: 651-779-1409
Library Holdings: AV Mats 1,475; Bk Vols 4,000; Per Subs 24
Special Collections: Law Coll
Automation Activity & Vendor Info: (Cataloging) Follett Software; (Circulation) Follett Software
Restriction: Not open to pub

P STILLWATER PUBLIC LIBRARY*, 224 N Third St, 55082. SAN 308-8111. Tel: 651-275-4338. Circulation Tel: 651-275-4338, Ext 4873. Reference Tel: 651-275-4338, Ext 4876. Administration Tel: 651-430-8755. FAX: 651-275-4342. E-mail: splinfo@ci.stillwater.mn.us. Web Site: www.stillwaterlibrary.org. *Dir,* Mark Troendle; E-mail: mtroendle@ci.stillwater.mn.us; *Youth Serv,* Angela Petrie; Staff 5 (MLS 5)
Founded 1897. Pop 18,000; Circ 335,000
Library Holdings: AV Mats 9,600; Bk Titles 89,491; Per Subs 224
Special Collections: St Croix Coll
Subject Interests: Local hist
Automation Activity & Vendor Info: (Acquisitions) Horizon; (Cataloging) Horizon; (Circulation) Horizon; (ILL) OCLC Online; (OPAC) Horizon
Wireless access
Open Mon-Thurs 10-8, Fri & Sat 10-5, Sun (Sept-May) 1-5
Friends of the Library Group

TAYLORS FALLS

P TAYLORS FALLS PUBLIC LIBRARY*, 473 Bench St, 55084. (Mail add: PO Box 195, 55084-0195), SAN 325-1608. Tel: 651-465-6905. Web Site: www.ci.taylors-falls.mn.us. *Librn,* Diane Dedon; E-mail: dianed46@frontier.com
Founded 1871. Pop 1,010; Circ 2,499
Library Holdings: Bk Titles 11,680
Special Collections: History of Taylors Falls Coll; The St Croix River Valley Coll
Wireless access
Open Wed 2-5 & 6:30-8, Sat 9:30-12:30

THIEF RIVER FALLS

J NORTHLAND COMMUNITY & TECHNICAL COLLEGE LIBRARY, 1101 Hwy One E, 56701. SAN 308-812X. Tel: 218-683-8757. Web Site: www.northlandcollege.edu/library. *Librn,* Cynthia Jorstad; E-mail: cynthia.jorstad@northlandcollege.edu
Founded 1965. Enrl 2,131; Fac 90; Highest Degree: Associate
Library Holdings: Bk Titles 27,000; Bk Vols 30,000; Per Subs 100
Special Collections: Oral History
Automation Activity & Vendor Info: (Cataloging) Ex Libris Group; (Circulation) Ex Libris Group; (OPAC) Ex Libris Group
Wireless access
Partic in Minitex; MnPALS; Northern Lights Library Network
Open Mon-Thurs 8:30-5, Fri 8:30-4

P NORTHWEST REGIONAL LIBRARY*, 210 LaBree Ave N, 56701. (Mail add: PO Box 593, 56701), SAN 348-0542. Tel: 218-681-1066. FAX: 218-681-1095. E-mail: info@nwrlib.org. Web Site: www.nwrlib.org. *Regional Dir,* James Trojanowski; E-mail: trojanowskij@gsuite.nwrlib.org; *Tech Serv,* Tammee Bacon; E-mail: nwrltech@gsuite.nwrlib.org
Pop 49,617; Circ 304,318
Library Holdings: Bk Vols 142,668; Per Subs 400; Talking Bks 843
Special Collections: Large Print; Literacy; Toddler's
Automation Activity & Vendor Info: (Acquisitions) Innovative Interfaces, Inc; (Cataloging) Innovative Interfaces, Inc; (Circulation) Innovative Interfaces, Inc; (ILL) Innovative Interfaces, Inc; (OPAC) Innovative Interfaces, Inc
Wireless access
Open Mon-Fri 8-5
Friends of the Library Group
Branches: 8
GODEL MEMORIAL LIBRARY, 314 E Johnson Ave, Warren, 56762, SAN 348-0577. Tel: 218-745-5465. FAX: 218-745-8807. E-mail: warren@gsuite.nwrlib.org. *Librn,* Jodi Gulden
Pop 2,105; Circ 19,561
Library Holdings: Bk Vols 10,000; Per Subs 27; Talking Bks 1,086; Videos 1,283
Open Mon & Thurs 12-8, Tues, Wed & Fri 10-5
GREENBUSH PUBLIC LIBRARY, 234 Main St N, Greenbush, 56726, SAN 348-0607. Tel: 218-782-2218. FAX: 218-782-2218. E-mail: greenbush@nwrlib.org. *Librn,* Linda Andersen; *Librn,* Katie Andersen
Founded 1970. Pop 817; Circ 14,082
Library Holdings: Bk Vols 5,500; Per Subs 19
Open Tues, Wed & Fri 10-5, Thurs 10-6, Sat 9-Noon
Friends of the Library Group
HALLOCK PUBLIC LIBRARY, 163 Third St S, Hallock, 56728, SAN 348-0631. Tel: 218-843-2401. FAX: 218-843-2401. E-mail: hallock@gsuite.nwrlib.org. *Librn,* Peggy Pearson
Pop 2,000; Circ 19,895
Library Holdings: Bk Vols 14,236; Per Subs 21; Talking Bks 892; Videos 2,003
Open Tues, Wed & Fri 10-5, Thurs 10-8, Sat 10-1
KARLSTAD PUBLIC LIBRARY, 104 First St S, Karlstad, 56732. Tel: 218-436-7323. FAX: 218-843-2401. E-mail: karlstad@nwrlib.org. *Librn,* Peggy Pearson
Open Wed 2:30-6:30
RED LAKE FALLS PUBLIC LIBRARY, 105 Champagne Ave SW, Red Lake Falls, 56750, SAN 348-0666. Tel: 218-253-2992. E-mail: redlake@nwrlib.org. *Librn,* Mary Casavan; *Librn,* Laura Schafer
Pop 2,100; Circ 20,729
Library Holdings: Bk Vols 8,600; Per Subs 25
Open Tues-Fri 12-6, Sat 10-2
Friends of the Library Group
ROSEAU PUBLIC LIBRARY, 121 Center St E, Ste 100, Roseau, 56751, SAN 348-0690. Tel: 218-463-2825. FAX: 218-463-2825. E-mail: roseau@gsuite.nwrlib.org. *Librn,* Stacey Rusek; *Librn,* Melissa Wilson
Pop 2,272; Circ 25,258
Library Holdings: Bk Vols 6,000; Per Subs 20

Open Mon-Wed & Fri 9-5, Thurs 9-8, Sat 11-4 (Oct-April)
Friends of the Library Group

THIEF RIVER FALLS PUBLIC LIBRARY, 102 First St E, 56701. (Mail add: PO Box 674, 56701). Tel: 218-681-4325. FAX: 218-681-4355. Circulation E-mail: trfcirc@gsuite.nwrlib.org. *Librn,* Sarah Villanueva
Open Mon-Thurs 9-8:30, Fri 9-5, Sat 10-5

WARROAD PUBLIC LIBRARY, 202 Main Ave NE, Warroad, 56763, SAN 348-0720. Tel: 218-386-1283. FAX: 218-386-1283. E-mail: warroad@gsuite.nwrlib.org. *Librn,* Kelly Benjamin
Pop 2,187; Circ 9,189
Library Holdings: Bk Vols 15,000; Per Subs 97; Talking Bks 999; Videos 1,522
Open Mon-Wed & Fri 10-5, Thurs 10-8
Friends of the Library Group

TRACY

P TRACY PUBLIC LIBRARY*, 189 Third St, 56175. SAN 308-8138. Tel: 507-629-5548. FAX: 507-629-5549. Web Site: www.tracypubliclibrary.org. *Librn,* Valerie Quist; E-mail: vquist@plumcreeklibrary.net
Founded 1936. Pop 2,516; Circ 18,000
Library Holdings: Bk Vols 30,000; Per Subs 46
Wireless access
Function: 24/7 Electronic res, 24/7 Online cat, Adult bk club, Audiobks via web, Bks on CD, Children's prog, Computer training, Computers for patron use, E-Readers, Free DVD rentals, Home delivery & serv to seniorr ctr & nursing homes, Homebound delivery serv, ILL available, Internet access, Magazines, Meeting rooms, Movies, Music CDs, Online cat, OverDrive digital audio bks, Photocopying/Printing, Preschool outreach, Printer for laptops & handheld devices, Prog for adults, Prog for children & young adult, Scanner, Senior computer classes, Serves people with intellectual disabilities, Spanish lang bks, Story hour, Summer & winter reading prog, Summer reading prog, Wheelchair accessible, Winter reading prog
Mem of Plum Creek Library System
Open Mon-Thurs 10-6, Fri & Sat 10-12

TWO HARBORS

P TWO HARBORS PUBLIC LIBRARY*, 320 Waterfront Dr, 55616. SAN 308-8162. Tel: 218-834-3148. E-mail: thplinfo@gmail.com. Web Site: www.twoharborspubliclibrary.com. *Dir,* Katie Sundstrom; E-mail: katie.sundstrom@alslib.info
Founded 1896. Pop 6,500; Circ 67,800
Library Holdings: Bk Vols 28,000; Per Subs 80
Wireless access
Mem of Arrowhead Library System
Open Mon-Thurs 11-8, Fri 11-5, Sat 11-4
Friends of the Library Group

TYLER

P TYLER PUBLIC LIBRARY*, 230 Tyler St N, 56178-1161. (Mail add: PO Box L, 56178-0461), SAN 308-8170. Tel: 507-247-5556. FAX: 507-247-5557. Web Site: www.plumcreeklibrary.org/tyler. *Dir,* Shelly L Finzen; E-mail: tylerlib@plumcreeklibrary.net
Library Holdings: Bk Titles 11,000; Per Subs 15
Automation Activity & Vendor Info: (Cataloging) TLC (The Library Corporation); (Circulation) TLC (The Library Corporation); (OPAC) TLC (The Library Corporation)
Wireless access
Function: 24/7 Online cat, Audiobks via web, Bks on CD, Children's prog, Computers for patron use, Free DVD rentals, ILL available, Internet access, Magazines, Mail & tel request accepted, Online cat, Photocopying/Printing, Prog for adults, Prog for children & young adult, Summer & winter reading prog, Summer reading prog
Mem of Plum Creek Library System
Open Mon & Tues 10-5, Wed 12-6, Thurs & Fri 1-5, Sat 10-Noon

VICTORIA

S LOWRY NATURE CENTER LIBRARY*, Carver Park Reserve, Three Rivers Park District, 7025 Victoria Dr, 55386. SAN 308-5759. Tel: 763-694-7650. FAX: 952-472-5420. Web Site: www.threeriversparks.org. *Supvr,* Allison Neaton; E-mail: allison.neaton@threeriversparks.org
Founded 1969
Library Holdings: Bk Vols 800
Subject Interests: Birding, Conserv, General reading, Natural hist, Outdoor educ
Function: Ref serv available
Open Mon-Sat 9-5, Sun 12-5
Restriction: Non-circulating to the pub

VIRGINIA

J MESABI RANGE COMMUNITY & TECHNICAL COLLEGE LIBRARY*, 1001 Chestnut St W, 55792. SAN 308-8197. Tel: 218-749-7740. Web Site: www.mesabirange.edu/college-services/mrc-library. *Libr Tech,* Kim Johnson; E-mail: v.johnson@mesabirange.edu
Founded 1922. Enrl 1,000
Library Holdings: AV Mats 2,400; CDs 380; DVDs 1,300; e-books 10,000; Large Print Bks 40; Bk Titles 24,200; Per Subs 40; Videos 480
Wireless access
Partic in MnPALS
Open Mon-Thurs (Fall & Spring) 8-6, Fri 8-4; Mon-Thurs (Summer) 10-3

P VIRGINIA PUBLIC LIBRARY*, 215 Fifth Ave S, 55792-2642. SAN 308-8200. Tel: 218-748-7525. FAX: 218-748-7527. Web Site: www.virginiapubliclibrary.info. *Libr Dir,* Jodi Grebinoski; E-mail: jodi.grebinoski@alslib.info; *Ch Serv,* Stephanie Wichlacz; E-mail: stephanie.wichlacz@alslib.info; *Tech Serv,* Susan Hoppe; E-mail: susan.hoppe@alslib.info; Staff 8 (MLS 3, Non-MLS 5)
Founded 1905. Pop 9,157; Circ 224,148
Library Holdings: AV Mats 4,000; Bk Vols 60,000; Per Subs 170
Automation Activity & Vendor Info: (Acquisitions) SirsiDynix; (Cataloging) SirsiDynix; (Circulation) SirsiDynix; (OPAC) SirsiDynix; (Serials) SirsiDynix
Wireless access
Function: 24/7 Electronic res, 24/7 Online cat, Accelerated reader prog, Activity rm, After school storytime, Art exhibits, Audio & video playback equip for onsite use, Audiobks on Playaways & MP3, Audiobks via web, Bks on cassette, Bks on CD, CD-ROM, Children's prog, Computer training, Computers for patron use, Digital talking bks, E-Readers, E-Reserves, Electronic databases & coll, Equip loans & repairs, Free DVD rentals, Holiday prog, Homework prog, ILL available, Internet access, Laminating, Large print keyboards, Life-long learning prog for all ages, Magazines, Magnifiers for reading, Mail & tel request accepted, Mango lang, Meeting rooms, Microfiche/film & reading machines, Movies, Music CDs, Online cat, Online info literacy tutorials on the web & in blackboard, Online ref, Orientations, Outreach serv, OverDrive digital audio bks, Photocopying/Printing, Preschool outreach, Preschool reading prog, Prog for adults, Prog for children & young adult, Ref & res, Ref serv available, Res libr, Scanner, Senior computer classes, Senior outreach, Serves people with intellectual disabilities, Spoken cassettes & CDs, Spoken cassettes & DVDs, Story hour, Study rm, Summer & winter reading prog, Summer reading prog, Tax forms, Teen prog, Telephone ref, Visual arts prog, Wheelchair accessible, Winter reading prog, Workshops
Mem of Arrowhead Library System
Special Services for the Deaf - TDD equip
Open Mon & Thurs 9-7, Tues, Wed & Fri 9-5
Friends of the Library Group

WABASHA

P WABASHA PUBLIC LIBRARY*, 168 Alleghany Ave, 55981-1286. SAN 308-8219. Tel: 651-565-3927. FAX: 651-565-3927. E-mail: wablib@yahoo.com. Web Site: wabasha.lib.mn.us. *Dir,* Beverly Hall; E-mail: bhall@selco.info
Founded 1868. Pop 2,812
Library Holdings: Bk Vols 20,000; Per Subs 70
Special Collections: Local History (Wabasha-A Sense of Place); Local Paper, Wabasha County Herald 1863-present, micro
Automation Activity & Vendor Info: (Cataloging) SirsiDynix; (Circulation) SirsiDynix; (OPAC) SirsiDynix
Wireless access
Function: 24/7 Electronic res, 24/7 Online cat, Adult bk club, Audiobks on Playaways & MP3, Audiobks via web, Bk club(s), Bks on CD, Children's prog, Computers for patron use, Electronic databases & coll, Free DVD rentals, Holiday prog, Homebound delivery serv, ILL available, Internet access, Laminating, Life-long learning prog for all ages, Magazines, Microfiche/film & reading machines, Movies, Music CDs, Online cat, Online ref, Outreach serv, Photocopying/Printing, Preschool outreach, Preschool reading prog, Printer for laptops & handheld devices, Prog for children & young adult, Scanner, Senior computer classes, Story hour, Summer & winter reading prog, Summer reading prog, Tax forms, Wheelchair accessible, Workshops
Partic in Southeastern Libraries Cooperating
Open Mon-Thurs 10-7, Fri 10-5, Sat 9-noon
Friends of the Library Group

WABASSO

P WABASSO PUBLIC LIBRARY, 1248 Oak St, 56293. (Mail add: PO Box 190, 56293-0190), SAN 320-8966. Tel: 507-342-5279. FAX: 507-342-2329. Web Site: www.plumcreeklibrary.org/Wabasso. *Dir,* Scott Sobocinski; E-mail: ssobocinski@plumcreeklibrary.net; *Libr Asst,* Joanne Krause

Pop 1,090; Circ 24,950
Library Holdings: DVDs 500; Bk Vols 11,000; Per Subs 24; Talking Bks 600; Videos 1,400
Automation Activity & Vendor Info: (Cataloging) TLC (The Library Corporation); (Circulation) TLC (The Library Corporation); (OPAC) TLC (The Library Corporation)
Wireless access
Mem of Plum Creek Library System
Open Mon-Fri 10-12 & 1-6; Mon-Fri 9-12:30 & 1:30-6 (Summer)
Friends of the Library Group

WACONIA

S CARVER COUNTY HISTORICAL SOCIETY LIBRARY*, 555 W First St, 55387. SAN 325-5182. Tel: 952-442-4234. FAX: 952-442-3025. E-mail: historical@co.carver.mn.us. Web Site: www.carvercountyhistoricalsociety.org/library_resources.php. *Dir,* Wendy Biorn; *Researcher,* Marilyn Braun; E-mail: mbraun@co.carver.mn.us; Staff 1 (Non-MLS 1)
Founded 1940
Library Holdings: Bk Titles 1,000
Special Collections: German & Swedish Language Reading Society Coll c 1860
Open Mon-Fri 9-4:30, Sat 10-3
Restriction: Non-circulating to the pub

WADENA

P WADENA CITY LIBRARY*, 304 First St SW, 56482-1460. SAN 347-7819. Tel: 218-631-2476. FAX: 218-632-5029. E-mail: wadena@krls.org. Web Site: www.krls.org/index.php/wadena-home-page. *Br Mgr,* Renee Frethem
Pop 4,699; Circ 27,238
Library Holdings: Bk Vols 17,000; Per Subs 40
Wireless access
Mem of Kitchigami Regional Library
Open Mon 10-3, Tues 10-6, Wed & Fri 10-5, Thurs 10-7, Sat 10-2
Friends of the Library Group

WALKER

P WALKER PUBLIC LIBRARY*, 207 Fourth St, 56484. (Mail add: PO Box 550, 56484-0550), SAN 347-7843. Tel: 218-547-1019. FAX: 218-547-1019. E-mail: walker@krls.org. Web Site: krls.org/index.php/walker-home-page. *Br Mgr,* Carrie Huston; Staff 2 (Non-MLS 2)
Founded 1909. Circ 46,084
Library Holdings: Bk Titles 19,746; Per Subs 33
Automation Activity & Vendor Info: (Cataloging) Innovative Interfaces, Inc; (Circulation) Innovative Interfaces, Inc; (Course Reserve) Innovative Interfaces, Inc; (OPAC) Innovative Interfaces, Inc
Wireless access
Mem of Kitchigami Regional Library
Open Tues & Wed 10-6, Thurs 10-7, Fri 10-4, Sat 10-2
Friends of the Library Group

WASECA

G WASECA COUNTY HISTORICAL SOCIETY LIBRARY*, Research Center, 315 Second Ave NE, 56093. SAN 326-5102. Tel: 507-835-7700. Web Site: www.historical.waseca.mn.us. *Exec Dir,* Joan Mooney; E-mail: director@historical.waseca.mn.us; *Curator,* Pauline Fenelon; *Curator,* Vanessa Zimprich; *Res,* Linda Taylor; E-mail: research@historical.waseca.mn.us. Subject Specialists: *Genealogy,* Linda Taylor
Founded 1938
Library Holdings: Bk Titles 350; Per Subs 10
Special Collections: Business & Organization Records; Diaries; Waseca County Genealogy
Subject Interests: Archives, Family hist, Manuscripts
Wireless access
Function: Microfiche/film & reading machines, Online ref, Outreach serv, Ref & res, Ref serv available, Res libr, Res performed for a fee, Scanner
Partic in S Minnesota Interlibr Res Exchange
Open Tues-Fri 8-12 & 1-5
Restriction: Fee for pub use, Free to mem, In-house use for visitors, Not a lending libr, Open to pub for ref only, Open to researchers by request, Secured area only open to authorized personnel, Visitors must make appt to use bks in the libr
Friends of the Library Group

P WASECA-LE SUEUR REGIONAL LIBRARY*, 408 N State St, 56093. SAN 348-0755. Tel: 507-835-2910. FAX: 507-835-3700. E-mail: libtlr@tds.lib.mn.us. Web Site: www.wasecalesueurlibraries.com. *Dir,* Stacy Lienemann; E-mail: lienemann@tds.lib.mn.us; Staff 4 (MLS 4)
Founded 1965. Pop 41,882; Circ 241,437
Library Holdings: Electronic Media & Resources 11,000; Bk Vols 150,000; Per Subs 460
Automation Activity & Vendor Info: (Cataloging) SirsiDynix; (Circulation) SirsiDynix; (OPAC) SirsiDynix; (Serials) SirsiDynix
Wireless access
Mem of Traverse Des Sioux Library Cooperative
Partic in OCLC Online Computer Library Center, Inc
Open Mon-Wed 9-8:30, Thurs & Fri 9-5, Sat 9-1
Branches: 8
ELYSIAN BRANCH, 196 W Main St, Elysian, 56028. (Mail add: PO Box 10, Elysian, 56028), SAN 376-2106. Tel: 507-267-4411. *Librn,* Anne Davies
Library Holdings: Bk Vols 3,000
Open Mon & Fri 1-5, Tues 9-12, Wed 12:30-5:30, Sat 10-12
JANESVILLE PUBLIC, 102 W Second, Janesville, 56048-3009. (Mail add: PO Box H, Janesville, 56048-0608), SAN 348-078X. Tel: 507-234-6605. E-mail: libtlj@tds.lib.mn.us. *Br Supvr,* Nicole Krienke
Library Holdings: Bk Vols 10,480
Open Mon 12-6, Tues 9-12 & 1-6, Thurs 2-8
Friends of the Library Group
LE CENTER PUBLIC, Ten W Tyrone St, Le Center, 56057, SAN 348-081X. Tel: 507-357-6792. E-mail: libtlc@tds.lib.mn.us. *Br Mgr,* Diane Wild
Library Holdings: Bk Vols 10,000
Open Mon & Tues 1-7, Thurs & Fri 1-5
Friends of the Library Group
LE SUEUR PUBLIC, 118 E Ferry St, Le Sueur, 56058, SAN 348-0844. Tel: 507-665-2662. *Librn,* Dianne Pinney
Library Holdings: Bk Vols 35,000
Open Mon 10-8, Tues & Thurs 1-8, Wed & Fri 10-5, Sat 10-2
MONTGOMERY PUBLIC, 104 Oak Ave SE, Montgomery, 56069, SAN 348-0879. Tel: 507-364-7615. E-mail: libtlm@tds.lib.mn.us. *Librn,* Nancy Noffke
Library Holdings: Bk Vols 15,000
Open Mon & Wed 10-5, Tues & Thurs 10-8, Sat 9-12, Sun (Sept-May) 1-4
Friends of the Library Group
NEW RICHLAND PUBLIC, 129 S Broadway Ave, New Richland, 56072. (Mail add: PO Box 385, New Richland, 56072-0385), SAN 348-0909. Tel: 507-465-3708. *Librn,* Linda Lynne
Library Holdings: Bk Vols 10,000
Open Mon, Wed & Thurs 12:30-6, Sat 9-12:30
WALDORF BRANCH, 109 Main St N, Waldorf, 56091. (Mail add: PO Box 166, Waldorf, 56091-0166), SAN 376-2130. Tel: 507-239-2248. *Librn,* Cheryl Marquardt
Library Holdings: Bk Vols 3,000
Open Tues 1-4:30, Wed 9-11:30 & 1-5, Thurs 12:30-5:30
WATERVILLE PUBLIC, 210 E Paquin St, Waterville, 56096, SAN 348-0933. Tel: 507-362-8462. *Librn,* Lynne Coleman
Library Holdings: Bk Vols 8,000
Open Mon 12:30-4:30, Tues & Thurs 3-7:30, Wed 9-11 & 12:30-5

WELLS

P WELLS PUBLIC LIBRARY*, 54 First St SW, 56097-1913. SAN 308-8251. Tel: 507-553-3702. FAX: 800-878-9678. E-mail: libtfl@tds.lib.mn.us. Web Site: www.cityofwells.net/index.php/library. *Libr Dir,* Tami Beto; Staff 3 (Non-MLS 3)
Founded 1976. Pop 5,451; Circ 39,000
Library Holdings: Audiobooks 542; CDs 339; DVDs 1,935; Large Print Bks 1,001; Bk Titles 20,000; Bk Vols 21,875; Per Subs 26
Special Collections: Faribault County Genealogy Files, cemetery listings, newsp clippings; USC Community Yearbooks, 1934-1959 & 1961 to present
Automation Activity & Vendor Info: (Cataloging) Innovative Interfaces, Inc - Sierra; (Circulation) Innovative Interfaces, Inc - Sierra; (OPAC) Innovative Interfaces, Inc - Sierra
Wireless access
Function: Art exhibits, Bks on cassette, Bks on CD, Computers for patron use, Free DVD rentals, ILL available, Internet access, Music CDs, Online cat, Outreach serv, Photocopying/Printing, Prog for adults, Prog for children & young adult, Scanner, Summer reading prog, Tax forms, VHS videos, Wheelchair accessible
Mem of Traverse Des Sioux Library Cooperative
Open Mon & Wed 10-7, Tues, Thurs & Fri 10-5, Sat (Sept-May) 10-1

WEST CONCORD

P WEST CONCORD PUBLIC LIBRARY*, 180 E Main St, 55985. (Mail add: PO Box 468, 55985-0468), SAN 376-7140. Tel: 507-527-2031. FAX: 507-527-2031. Web Site: westconcord.lib.mn.us. *Librn,* Nancy Schollmeier; E-mail: nschollmeier@selco.info
Library Holdings: Bk Titles 15,000; Per Subs 10
Automation Activity & Vendor Info: (Cataloging) Horizon; (Circulation) Horizon; (OPAC) Horizon

Wireless access
Function: ILL available
Partic in Southeastern Libraries Cooperating
Open Mon & Thurs 1-7, Tues, Wed & Fri 10-5, Sat 10-Noon
Friends of the Library Group

WESTBROOK

P WESTBROOK PUBLIC LIBRARY, 556 First Ave, 56183. (Mail add: PO Box 26, 56183-0026), SAN 376-6527. Tel: 507-274-6174. FAX: 507-274-6174. E-mail: westbrook@plumcreeklibrary.net. Web Site: www.plumcreeklibrary.org/westbrook-public-library. *Dir,* Kari Ourada; E-mail: kourada@woodstocktel.net
Library Holdings: Bk Vols 11,362; Per Subs 35; Talking Bks 593; Videos 299
Automation Activity & Vendor Info: (Cataloging) Koha; (Circulation) Koha; (OPAC) Koha
Wireless access
Open Mon & Tues 10-6, Wed 1-6, Thurs & Fri 10-5, Sat 10-2

WHEATON

P WHEATON COMMUNITY LIBRARY, 901 First Ave N, 56296. SAN 320-8974. Tel: 320-563-8487. FAX: 320-563-8815. Web Site: www.viking.lib.mn.us/wheaton-community-library, www.wheatoncommunitylibrary.org. *Dir,* Jacquie Peeples; E-mail: jpeeples@wheatoncommunitylibrary.org; *Ch,* Terry Anderson; *Libr Asst,* Gayle Ballhagen; Staff 3 (Non-MLS 3)
Founded 1972. Pop 2,288; Circ 50,000
Library Holdings: Audiobooks 515; CDs 501; DVDs 2,515; e-books 8,845; Electronic Media & Resources 1,379; Large Print Bks 2,021; Bk Titles 22,071; Per Subs 82
Automation Activity & Vendor Info: (Cataloging) Horizon; (Circulation) Horizon; (OPAC) Horizon
Wireless access
Function: 24/7 Electronic res, 24/7 Online cat, Adult literacy prog, Audiobks via web, Bks on CD, Children's prog, Computers for patron use, Electronic databases & coll, Free DVD rentals, Home delivery & serv to seniorr ctr & nursing homes, ILL available, Internet access, Magazines, Magnifiers for reading, Mail & tel request accepted, Meeting rooms, Movies, Music CDs, Online cat, Outreach serv, Outside serv via phone, mail, e-mail & web, OverDrive digital audio bks, Photocopying/Printing, Preschool outreach, Printer for laptops & handheld devices, Prog for children & young adult, Ref & res, Res assist avail, Story hour, Summer & winter reading prog, Summer reading prog, Tax forms, Telephone ref, Wheelchair accessible, Winter reading prog
Mem of Viking Library System
Partic in Minitex
Open Mon & Fri 10-5, Tues & Thurs 10-6, Sat 9-Noon
Friends of the Library Group

WHITE BEAR LAKE

J CENTURY COLLEGE LIBRARY*, 3300 N Century Ave, 55110. SAN 308-826X. Tel: 651-779-3968. Interlibrary Loan Service Tel: 651-779-3260. Reference Tel: 651-747-4004. FAX: 651-779-3963. Web Site: www.century.edu/library. *Acq Librn,* James Nalen; Tel: 651-779-3969, E-mail: james.nalen@century.edu; *Electronic Res Librn,* Randi Madisen; Tel: 651-779-3292, E-mail: randi.madisen@century.edu; *Libr Instruction, Ref Librn,* Maura Smyth; Tel: 651-773-1762, E-mail: maura.smyth@century.edu; *Circ, Tech Serv,* Jane Young; Tel: 651-779-3264, E-mail: jane.young@century.edu; *ILL,* Cathy Adams; E-mail: cathy.adams@century.edu; Staff 10.5 (MLS 3.5, Non-MLS 7)
Founded 1967. Enrl 5,900; Fac 300; Highest Degree: Associate
Library Holdings: Audiobooks 600; AV Mats 23,000; e-books 174,000; Bk Titles 59,000; Per Subs 154
Special Collections: Fire/EMS/Safety Coll; Orthotics & Prosthetics (A Bennett Wilson Coll); Partial College Archives
Automation Activity & Vendor Info: (Acquisitions) Ex Libris Group; (Cataloging) Ex Libris Group; (Circulation) Ex Libris Group; (Course Reserve) Ex Libris Group; (Discovery) PALS; (ILL) Ex Libris Group; (OPAC) Ex Libris Group; (Serials) Ex Libris Group
Wireless access
Function: For res purposes
Partic in Minitex; MnPALS; OCLC Online Computer Library Center, Inc
Special Services for the Deaf - Assistive tech
Special Services for the Blind - Assistive/Adapted tech devices, equip & products
Open Mon-Thurs 7:30am-8pm, Fri 7:30-4, Sat 9-3

WILLMAR

S KANDIYOHI COUNTY HISTORICAL SOCIETY*, Lawson Research Library, 610 NE Hwy 71, 56201. SAN 326-3045. Tel: 320-235-1881. FAX: 320-235-1881. E-mail: kandhist@msn.com. Web Site: www.kandiyohicountyhistory.com/research%20library.html. *Exec Dir,* Jill Wohnoutka; *Dep Dir,* Bob Larson; E-mail: research@kandiyohicountyhistory.com; Staff 2 (MLS 1, Non-MLS 1)
Founded 1969
Library Holdings: Bk Titles 1,500; Bk Vols 1,700; Per Subs 100
Special Collections: Local Newspapers Coll, microfilm
Subject Interests: Archives, Local hist
Publications: Kandi Express (Quarterly)
Open Mon-Fri 9-4
Restriction: Non-circulating to the pub

P PIONEERLAND LIBRARY SYSTEM, Wilmar Public Library, 410 Fifth St SW, 2nd Flr, 56201. (Mail add: PO Box 327, 56201-0327), SAN 348-0968. Tel: 320-235-6106. FAX: 320-214-0187. Web Site: www.pioneerland.lib.mn.us. *Exec Dir,* Laurie Ortega; Tel: 320-235-6106, Ext 28, E-mail: laurie.ortega@pioneerland.lib.mn.us; *Automation Coordr,* Beth Lunn; Tel: 320-235-6106, Ext 29, E-mail: beth.lunn@pioneerland.lib.mn.us; Staff 56 (MLS 6, Non-MLS 50)
Founded 1983. Pop 166,431; Circ 896,418
Library Holdings: Bk Titles 270,000; Bk Vols 675,000; Per Subs 415
Automation Activity & Vendor Info: (Cataloging) Innovative Interfaces, Inc; (Circulation) Innovative Interfaces, Inc; (ILL) Innovative Interfaces, Inc; (OPAC) Innovative Interfaces, Inc
Wireless access
Member Libraries: Appleton Public Library; Atwater Public Library; Benson Public Library; Bird Island Public Library; Brownton Public Library; Canby Public Library; Clara City Public Library; Cosmos Public Library; Dassel Public Library; Dawson Public Library; Fairfax Public Library; Glencoe Public Library; Graceville Public Library; Granite Falls Public Library; Grove City Public Library; Hector Public Library; Hutchinson Public Library; Kerkhoven Public Library; Lake Lillian Public Library; Litchfield Public Library; Madison Public Library; Maynard Public Library; Milan Public Library; Montevideo Public Library; New London Public Library; Olivia Public Library; Ortonville Public Library; Raymond Public Library; Renville City Library; Spicer Library; Willmar Public Library; Winsted Public Library
Partic in OCLC Online Computer Library Center, Inc
Open Mon-Fri 8-4:30
Friends of the Library Group

C RIDGEWATER COLLEGE LIBRARY*, 2101 15th Ave NW, 56201. SAN 308-8278. Tel: 320-222-7536. Toll Free Tel: 800-722-1151. Web Site: www.ridgewater.edu/library. *Librn,* Terrence B Edwards; E-mail: terrence.edwards@ridgewater.edu; *Libr Tech,* Karen Kaczmarek; E-mail: karen.kaczmarek@ridgewater.edu; *Cat, Libr Tech,* Jolene Spanier; E-mail: jolene.spanier@ridgewater.edu; Staff 2 (MLS 1, Non-MLS 1)
Founded 1962. Enrl 3,000; Fac 80; Highest Degree: Bachelor
Jul 2013-Jun 2014. Mats Exp $73,500, Books $10,000, Per/Ser (Incl. Access Fees) $15,000, AV Equip $5,000, Electronic Ref Mat (Incl. Access Fees) $40,500, Presv $3,000. Sal $105,000 (Prof $75,000)
Library Holdings: AV Mats 798; DVDs 112; e-books 143,328; e-journals 10; Microforms 45,629; Bk Vols 32,128; Per Subs 99; Talking Bks 206; Videos 918
Special Collections: Private Library of Local Publisher (Lawson Library)
Automation Activity & Vendor Info: (Cataloging) Ex Libris Group; (Circulation) Ex Libris Group; (ILL) Ex Libris Group; (OPAC) Ex Libris Group
Wireless access
Partic in Minitex; MnPALS; Prairielands Library Exchange
Open Mon-Thurs 7:30-7, Fri 7:30-4

P WILLMAR PUBLIC LIBRARY*, 410 Fifth St SW, 56201-3298. SAN 372-8536. Tel: 320-235-3162. FAX: 320-235-3169. E-mail: willmar.staff@pioneerland.lib.mn.us. Web Site: www.willmarpubliclibrary.org. *Head Librn,* Position Currently Open; *Ad,* Syrena Maranell; Tel: 320-235-3162, Ext 16, E-mail: syrena.maranell@pioneerland.lib.mn.us; *YA Librn,* Sam Plessel; E-mail: samantha.plessel@pioneerland.lib.mn.us; *Ch Serv,* Kathy Torkelson; Tel: 320-235-3162, Ext 14, E-mail: kathy.torkelson@pioneerland.lib.mn.us; Staff 8 (MLS 2, Non-MLS 6)
Founded 1904. Pop 19,886; Circ 130,848
Library Holdings: e-books 3,000; Bk Vols 78,954; Per Subs 213
Automation Activity & Vendor Info: (Circulation) Innovative Interfaces, Inc; (OPAC) Innovative Interfaces, Inc
Wireless access
Function: Computers for patron use, Electronic databases & coll, ILL available, Online cat, OverDrive digital audio bks, Photocopying/Printing, Printer for laptops & handheld devices, Prog for adults, Prog for children & young adult, Ref serv available, Story hour, Summer & winter reading prog
Mem of Pioneerland Library System
Partic in Minitex
Open Mon-Thurs 9-8, Fri 9-5:30, Sat 9-4
Friends of the Library Group

WINDOM

S COTTONWOOD COUNTY HISTORICAL SOCIETY LIBRARY*, 812 Fourth Ave, 56101. SAN 326-3975. Tel: 507-831-1134. FAX: 507-831-2665. E-mail: cchs@windomnet.com. Web Site: www.cchsmn1901.org. *Dir,* Linda Fransen; Staff 2 (Non-MLS 2)
Founded 1901
Library Holdings: Bk Vols 720; Videos 12
Special Collections: Local Newspapers, 1871-present, micro. Oral History
Wireless access
Function: Photocopying/Printing, Wheelchair accessible
Publications: Cottonwood County Courthouse, 1904-2004 (Reference guide); Give It Your Best Shot: Focus on Cottonwood County's Doors & Windows; Newsletter; Robert Remick: His Life, His Art and His Legacy
Open Mon-Fri 8-4, Sat 10-4
Restriction: In-house use for visitors, Non-circulating, Pub use on premises

P WINDOM PUBLIC LIBRARY, 904 Fourth Ave, 56101. SAN 308-8294. Tel: 507-831-6131. Web Site: www.windom-mn.com/city-facilities/windom-public-library. *Libr Dir,* Dawn Aamot; E-mail: daamot@plumcreeklibrary.net
Founded 1883. Pop 5,306; Circ 53,326
Library Holdings: Audiobooks 1,275; DVDs 1,020; Large Print Bks 400; Bk Vols 28,582; Per Subs 98; Talking Bks 1,680; Videos 100
Automation Activity & Vendor Info: (Cataloging) ByWater Solutions; (Circulation) ByWater Solutions; (OPAC) ByWater Solutions
Wireless access
Mem of Plum Creek Library System
Open Mon 9-7, Tues-Fri 9-5:30, Sat 9-1
Friends of the Library Group

WINNEBAGO

P MUIR LIBRARY, 36 Main St N, 56098. SAN 308-8308. Tel: 507-893-3196. FAX: 507-893-4766. E-mail: tfwstaff@tds.lib.mn.us. Web Site: cityofwinnebago.com/index.php/library, winnebago.tdslib.org. *Libr Dir,* Nicole Krienke
Pop 1,562; Circ 29,761
Library Holdings: Bk Titles 21,000; Per Subs 30
Automation Activity & Vendor Info: (Cataloging) SirsiDynix; (Circulation) SirsiDynix; (OPAC) SirsiDynix
Wireless access
Mem of Traverse Des Sioux Library Cooperative
Open Mon 9-12, 2-5 & 7-9, Tues-Thurs 2-5 & 7-9, Fri 10-12 & 2-5, Sat 10-12
Friends of the Library Group

WINONA

S WILLET HAUSER ARCHITECTURAL GLASS LIBRARY*, 1685 Wilke Dr, 55987. SAN 315-0275. Toll Free Tel: 800-533-3960, Ext 738. Toll Free FAX: 877-495-9486. E-mail: info@Willethauser.com. *Adminr, Library Contact,* Kimberly Jass-Mahoney; Staff 1 (Non-MLS 1)
Library Holdings: Bk Titles 1,000
Special Collections: Out-of-Print Research Books on Costumes, Animals & Art; Willet Studio Archives
Subject Interests: Bible commentaries, Christian symbolism, Church archit, Lives of saints, Stained glass
Function: Ref serv available
Restriction: Not open to pub

CR SAINT MARY'S UNIVERSITY OF MINNESOTA*, Fitzgerald Library, 700 Terrace Heights, No 26, 55987-1399. SAN 308-8324. Tel: 507-457-1561. Interlibrary Loan Service Tel: 507-457-1564. Reference Tel: 507-457-1562. Administration Tel: 507-457-6909. E-mail: wlibrary@smumn.edu. Web Site: fitzlibrary.smumn.edu. *Libr Dir,* Laura Oanes; Tel: 507-457-6909, E-mail: loanes@smumn.edu; *Cat Librn,* Lori Pesik; Tel: 507-457-6665, E-mail: lpesik@smumn.edu; *Digital Serv Librn, Instruction Librn,* Megan Peterson; Tel: 507-457-1511, E-mail: mepeters@smumn.edu; *ILL Librn, Per Librn,* Lauren Leighton; Tel: 507-457-1564, E-mail: lleighto@smumn.edu; *Ref Librn,* Ruth Ann Torstenson; Tel: 507-457-6664, E-mail: rtorstern@smumn.edu; Staff 8 (MLS 5, Non-MLS 3)
Founded 1925. Enrl 5,931; Fac 428; Highest Degree: Doctorate
Library Holdings: CDs 2,212; DVDs 3,761; e-books 5,408; Bk Titles 170,270; Bk Vols 183,412; Per Subs 4,965
Automation Activity & Vendor Info: (Acquisitions) Ex Libris Group; (Cataloging) Ex Libris Group; (Circulation) Ex Libris Group; (Discovery) EBSCO Discovery Service; (ILL) Ex Libris Group; (OPAC) Ex Libris Group; (Serials) Ex Libris Group
Wireless access
Partic in Minitex; MnPALS; OCLC Online Computer Library Center, Inc
Open Mon-Thurs 7:30am-Midnight, Fri 7:30-6, Sat 10-6, Sun Noon-Midnight

Departmental Libraries:
TWIN CITIES CAMPUS LIBRARY, LaSalle Hall, Rm 108, 2500 Park Ave, Minneapolis, 55404. Tel: 612-728-5108. Web Site: lib.smumn.edu. *Assoc Dir, Univ Libr,* Rachel McGee; Tel: 612-728-5172, E-mail: rmcgee@smumn.edu
Function: Computers for patron use, ILL available, Photocopying/Printing, Res assist avail, Scanner, Study rm
Open Mon-Fri 9-5, Sat 9-3

S WINONA COUNTY HISTORICAL SOCIETY*, Laird Lucas Memorial Library & Archives, 160 Johnson St, 55987. SAN 308-8332. Tel: 507-454-2723. FAX: 507-454-0006. E-mail: archives@winonahistory.org. Information Services E-mail: info@winonahistory.org. Web Site: www.winonahistory.org. *Exec Dir,* Mark Peterson; Tel: 507-454-2723, Ext 1, E-mail: director@winonahistory.org; *Archivist,* Walter Bennick; Tel: 507-454-2723, Ext 2; *Archivist, Curator of Coll,* Andy Bloedorn; Tel: 507-454-2723, Ext 4, E-mail: curator@winonahistory.org; Staff 3 (MLS 2, Non-MLS 1)
Founded 1935
Library Holdings: Bk Vols 4,000
Subject Interests: Genealogy, Local hist, Lumbering, Railroading, Steamboating
Automation Activity & Vendor Info: (Cataloging) Horizon; (OPAC) Horizon
Function: Archival coll
Publications: Argus: A Winona County Historical Society Newsletter (Bimonthly)
Mem of Southeast Library System (SELS)
Open Mon-Fri 10-12 & 1-5
Restriction: Non-circulating to the pub

P WINONA PUBLIC LIBRARY*, 151 W Fifth St, 55987. (Mail add: PO Box 1247, 55987-7247), SAN 308-8340. Tel: 507-452-4582. Reference Tel: 507-452-4860. E-mail: winonapl@selco.info. Web Site: www.winona.lib.mn.us. *Libr Dir,* Lezlea Dahlke; E-mail: ldahlke@selco.info; *Ad,* Samantha Berhow; *Tech Serv Librn,* Linda Weinmann; *Youth Serv Librn,* Tricia Wehrenberg; Staff 5 (MLS 2, Non-MLS 3)
Founded 1899. Pop 51,386; Circ 306,122
Library Holdings: Audiobooks 739; CDs 6,670; DVDs 5,085; Large Print Bks 2,604; Bk Vols 107,353; Per Subs 120
Subject Interests: Minn mat, Winona city, Winona County
Automation Activity & Vendor Info: (Acquisitions) SirsiDynix; (Cataloging) SirsiDynix; (Circulation) SirsiDynix; (OPAC) SirsiDynix
Wireless access
Partic in Minn Interlibr Teletype Exchange; OCLC Online Computer Library Center, Inc; Southeastern Libraries Cooperating
Open Mon, Wed & Fri 9-2, Tues & Thurs 12-6, Sat 9-Noon
Friends of the Library Group

C WINONA STATE UNIVERSITY*, Darrell W Krueger Library, 175 W Mark St, 55987. (Mail add: PO Box 5838, 55987-5838). Tel: 507-457-5140. Circulation Tel: 507-457-5149. Interlibrary Loan Service Tel: 507-457-5139. Reference Tel: 507-457-5146. Administration Tel: 507-457-5151. FAX: 507-457-5594. E-mail: library@winona.edu. Web Site: www.winona.edu/library. *Dean of Libr,* Kenneth Janz; E-mail: kjanz@winona.edu; *Chair, Archives,* Russ Dennison; Tel: 507-457-5143, E-mail: rdennison@winona.edu; *Cat Librn,* Joe Jackson; Tel: 507-457-5152, E-mail: jjackson@winona.edu; *Access Serv,* Carol Daul-Elhindi; Tel: 507-457-5147, E-mail: cdaulelhindi@winona.edu; *Ref Serv, Spec Coll,* Allison Quam; Tel: 507-457-2644, E-mail: aquam@winona.edu; *Acq, Coll Develop,* Vernon Leighton; Tel: 507-457-5148, E-mail: vleighton@winona.edu; *Coll Mgt & Digital Initiatives,* Kendall Larson; Tel: 507-457-5367, E-mail: klarson@winona.edu; Staff 17 (MLS 9, Non-MLS 8)
Founded 1860. Enrl 8,100; Fac 858; Highest Degree: Doctorate
Jul 2014-Jun 2015 Income $1,968,570. Mats Exp $904,092, Books $175,000, Per/Ser (Incl. Access Fees) $729,092. Sal $918,238 (Prof $650,190)
Library Holdings: AV Mats 4,399; CDs 1,593; DVDs 2,151; e-books 55,808; e-journals 34,393; Electronic Media & Resources 1,126; Microforms 120,000; Music Scores 1,600; Bk Titles 344,659; Bk Vols 479,521; Per Subs 700; Videos 4,399
Special Collections: Winona State University Archives. State Document Depository; US Document Depository
Automation Activity & Vendor Info: (Acquisitions) PALS; (Cataloging) PALS; (Circulation) PALS; (Course Reserve) PALS; (ILL) PALS; (OPAC) PALS; (Serials) PALS
Wireless access
Partic in Minitex; MnPALS; OCLC Online Computer Library Center, Inc
Open Mon-Thurs 7:30am-9pm, Fri 7:30-5, Sun 1-9

WINSTED

P WINSTED PUBLIC LIBRARY*, 180 Main Ave W, 55395. (Mail add: PO Box 175, 55395-0175), SAN 348-1387. Tel: 320-485-3909. FAX: 320-485-3909. E-mail: winsted.staff@pioneerland.lib.mn.us. Web Site: www.winsted.lib.mn.us. *Head Librn,* Katy Hiltner; E-mail: katy.hiltner@pioneerland.lib.mn.us; Staff 2 (MLS 2)
Founded 1976. Pop 2,698; Circ 8,049
Library Holdings: Bk Vols 7,200; Per Subs 15
Wireless access
Function: 24/7 Electronic res, 24/7 Online cat, Audiobks via web, Bks on CD, Computers for patron use, Free DVD rentals, ILL available, Internet access, Magazines, Online cat, OverDrive digital audio bks, Photocopying/Printing, Prog for adults, Prog for children & young adult, Summer & winter reading prog, Summer reading prog, Tax forms, Winter reading prog
Mem of Pioneerland Library System
Partic in Minitex
Open Mon & Wed 2-7, Tues & Thurs 10-1, Fri 2-5, Sat 10-12

WINTHROP

P WINTHROP PUBLIC LIBRARY, 305 N Main St, 55396. (Mail add: PO Box Y, 55396), SAN 347-4453. Tel: 507-647-5308. FAX: 507-647-3200. E-mail: libtsw@tds.lib.mn.us. Web Site: winthropmnlibrary.org. *Libr Dir,* Elizabeth M Niebuhr
Library Holdings: Bk Vols 7,869
Wireless access
Open Mon 12-7, Tues-Fri 10-12 & 12:30-5:30, Sat 9-12
Friends of the Library Group

WOODBURY

P WASHINGTON COUNTY LIBRARY*, 8595 Central Park Pl, 55125-9453. SAN 347-3880. Tel: 651-275-8500. FAX: 651-275-8509. Web Site: www.washcolib.org. *Dir,* Keith Ryskoski; Tel: 651-275-8501, E-mail: keith.ryskoski@co.washington.mn.us; *Tech Serv Mgr,* Brian Kraft; E-mail: Brian.Kraft@co.washington.mn.us; *Youth Serv Librn,* Dawn LaBrosse; E-mail: Dawn.LaBrosse@co.washington.mn.us
Founded 1966. Pop 213,085; Circ 2,201,828
Library Holdings: Bk Vols 392,613; Per Subs 1,186
Automation Activity & Vendor Info: (Acquisitions) SirsiDynix; (Cataloging) SirsiDynix; (Circulation) SirsiDynix; (OPAC) SirsiDynix; (Serials) SirsiDynix
Wireless access
Partic in Metropolitan Library Service Agency; Minitex
Branches: 9
HARDWOOD CREEK BRANCH, 19955 Forest Rd N, Forest Lake, 55025, SAN 376-2149. Tel: 651-275-7300. Administration Tel: 651-275-8500. Administration FAX: 651-275-8509. *Mgr,* Amy Worwa; E-mail: amy.worwa@co.washington.mn.us
Pop 31,000; Circ 490,000
Library Holdings: Bk Vols 91,300
Open Mon-Thurs 9:30-8, Fri & Sat 9:30-5, Sun 1-5
NEWPORT BRANCH, 405 Seventh Ave, Newport, 55055-1410, SAN 347-3953. Tel: 651-459-9631. FAX: 651-459-9631. *Mgr,* Chad Lubbers; E-mail: chad.lubbers@co.washington.mn.us
Library Holdings: Bk Vols 3,187
Open Mon & Fri 10-2, Tues-Thurs 2-6
OAKDALE BRANCH, 1010 Heron Ave N, Oakdale, 55128, SAN 373-9104. Tel: 651-730-0504. FAX: 651-275-8591. *Assoc Mgr,* Lynne Michaels; E-mail: lynne.michaels@co.washington.mn.us
Library Holdings: Bk Vols 42,526
Open Mon 9:30-8, Tues-Thurs 12:30-8, Fri 12:30-5, Sat 9:30-5, Sun 1-5
PARK GROVE BRANCH, 7900 Hemingway Ave S, Cottage Grove, 55016-1833, SAN 347-397X. Tel: 651-459-2040. FAX: 651-275-8581. *Mgr,* Megan Sockness; E-mail: megan.sockness@co.washington.mn.us
Library Holdings: Bk Vols 76,623
Open Mon-Thurs 9:30-8, Fri & Sat 9:30-5, Sun 1-5
R H STAFFORD BRANCH, 8595 Central Park Pl, 55125-9613, SAN 347-4062. Tel: 651-731-1320. FAX: 651-275-8562. *Mgr,* Chad Lubbers; E-mail: chad.lubbers@co.washington.mn.us
Library Holdings: Bk Vols 119,612
Open Mon-Thurs 9:30-8, Fri & Sat 9:30-5, Sun 1-5
VALLEY BRANCH, 380 St Croix Trail S, Lakeland, 55043, SAN 347-4003. Tel: 651-436-5882. FAX: 651-436-5882. *Mgr,* Chad Lubbers; E-mail: chad.lubbers@co.washington.mn.us
Library Holdings: Bk Vols 13,609
Open Mon & Fri 10-2, Tues-Thurs 2-6
ROSALIE E WAHL BRANCH, 3479 Lake Elmo Ave N, Lake Elmo, 55042. Tel: 651-777-7415. FAX: 651-777-7416. *Assoc Mgr,* Lynne Michaels; E-mail: lynne.michaels@co.washington.mn.us
Library Holdings: Bk Vols 8,380
Open Mon & Fri 10-2, Tues-Thurs 2-6

L WASHINGTON COUNTY LAW LIBRARY, Washington County Courthouse, 14949 62nd St N, Rm 1005, Stillwater, 55082. (Mail add: PO Box 6, Stillwater, 55082-0006). Tel: 651-430-6330. FAX: 651-430-6331. E-mail: lawlibrary@co.washington.mn.us. *County Law Librn,* Pauline Afuso; Tel: 651-430-6954; *Librn,* Pat Dolan; *Asst Librn,* Phyllis Kittle; Staff 2 (MLS 1.5, Non-MLS 0.5)
Founded 1956
Library Holdings: Bk Vols 8,000
Open Mon-Fri 8-4:30
Restriction: Open to pub for ref & circ; with some limitations
WILDWOOD BRANCH, 763 Stillwater Rd, Mahtomedi, 55115-2008, SAN 347-4038. Tel: 651-426-2042. FAX: 651-275-8541. *Mgr,* Margaret Stone; E-mail: margaret.stone@co.washington.mn.us
Library Holdings: Bk Vols 37,395
Open Mon 9:30-8, Tues-Thurs 12:30-8, Fri 12:30-5, Sat 9:30-5, Sun 1-5

WORTHINGTON

J MINNESOTA WEST COMMUNITY & TECHNICAL COLLEGE LIBRARIES*, Worthington Campus, 1450 College Way, 56187. SAN 308-8383. Tel: 507-372-3462. FAX: 507-372-5803. *Dir,* Kip Thorson; E-mail: kip.thorson@mnwest.edu; *Librn,* Sandi Mead; Tel: 507-372-3481, E-mail: sandi.mead@mnwest.edu; Staff 5 (MLS 4, Non-MLS 1)
Founded 1936. Enrl 1,900
Library Holdings: Bk Titles 37,000; Per Subs 200
Automation Activity & Vendor Info: (Acquisitions) Ex Libris Group; (Cataloging) Ex Libris Group; (Circulation) Ex Libris Group; (Course Reserve) Ex Libris Group; (ILL) PALS; (OPAC) Ex Libris Group
Wireless access
Partic in MnPALS
Open Mon-Thurs 8-8, Fri 8-4; Mon-Thurs (Summer) 9-2
Departmental Libraries:
CANBY CAMPUS, 1011 First St W, Canby, 56220. Tel: 507-223-7252. FAX: 507-223-5291. Web Site: www.mnwest.edu/larc. *Info Res Spec,* Deb Full; E-mail: deb.full@mnwest.edu
Open Mon-Thurs 8-4, Fri (Fall-Spring) 8-Noon
GRANITE FALLS CAMPUS, 1593 11th Ave, Granite Falls, 56241. Tel: 320-564-5056. FAX: 320-564-2318. *Coordr,* Julie Williams; E-mail: julie.williams@mnwest.edu
Open Mon-Thurs 8-4:30; Tues-Thurs (Summer) 8-4
JACKSON CAMPUS, 401 West St, Jackson, 56143. Tel: 507-847-7920.
Open Mon-Thurs 7am-9pm, Fri 8-5; Mon-Thurs (Summer) 8-4
PIPESTONE CAMPUS, 1314 N Hiawatha Ave, Pipestone, 56164. (Mail add: PO Box 250, Pipestone, 56164-0250). Tel: 507-825-6832. FAX: 507-825-4656. *Library Contact,* Terry Peterson; E-mail: terry.peterson@mnwest.edu
Open Mon-Thurs 8:30-4; Wed (Summer) 9-2

P NOBLES COUNTY LIBRARY, 407 12th St, 56187. (Mail add: PO Box 1049, 56187-5049), SAN 308-8367. Tel: 507-295-5340. FAX: 507-372-2982. E-mail: nobleslib@co.nobles.mn.us. Web Site: www.nclibrary.org. *Libr Dir,* David Bradford; *Ch Serv,* Jackie Van Horsen; *Ref (Info Servs),* Laurie Ebbers; Staff 6 (MLS 1, Non-MLS 5)
Founded 1947. Pop 19,920; Circ 179,663. Sal $254,000
Library Holdings: Bk Vols 72,124; Per Subs 100; Talking Bks 2,054; Videos 4,000
Special Collections: ESL for Spanish-Speaking Adults
Automation Activity & Vendor Info: (Cataloging) LibLime; (Circulation) LibLime; (OPAC) LibLime
Wireless access
Mem of Plum Creek Library System
Open Mon-Thurs 9-8, Fri 9-5, Sat 9-1
Friends of the Library Group
Branches: 1
ADRIAN BRANCH, 214 Maine Ave, Adrian, 56110. (Mail add: PO Box 39, Adrian, 56110-0039), SAN 325-1713. Tel: 507-483-2541. FAX: 507-483-2541. E-mail: adrianlib@co.nobles.mn.us. Web Site: www.plumcreeklibrary.org/adrian. *Librn,* Christine Hornstein
Pop 1,500; Circ 14,301
Library Holdings: Audiobooks 50; CDs 10; DVDs 200; Large Print Bks 50; Bk Titles 14,000; Per Subs 8; Videos 30
Open Mon-Thurs 12-6, Fri 12-5, Sat 10-1

P PLUM CREEK LIBRARY SYSTEM*, 290 S Lake St, 56187. (Mail add: PO Box 697, 56187-0697), SAN 308-8375. Tel: 507-376-5803. Toll Free Tel: 800-439-3492. FAX: 507-376-9244. Web Site: www.plumcreeklibrary.org. *Dir,* Jim Trojanowski; E-mail: jtrojanowski@plumcreeklibrary.net; Staff 2 (MLS 2)
Founded 1974. Pop 119,523
Library Holdings: Bk Vols 655,319
Special Collections: Framed Art Prints; Large Print Coll; Puppet Resources; Song Book Coll
Automation Activity & Vendor Info: (Cataloging) TLC (The Library Corporation); (Circulation) TLC (The Library Corporation); (OPAC) TLC (The Library Corporation)

Member Libraries: Edgerton Public Library; Fulda Memorial Library; Ivanhoe Public Library; Jackson County Library; Lake Benton Public Library; Lamberton Public Library; Marshall-Lyon County Library; Meinders Community Library; Minneota Public Library; Morgan Public Library; Mountain Lake Public Library; Nobles County Library; Redwood Falls Public Library; Rock County Community Library; Slayton Public Library; Tracy Public Library; Tyler Public Library; Wabasso Public Library; Windom Public Library
Partic in Prairielands Library Exchange
Open Mon-Fri 8-5
Bookmobiles: 1

ZUMBROTA

P ZUMBROTA PUBLIC LIBRARY*, 100 West Ave, 55992. SAN 308-8391. Tel: 507-732-5211. FAX: 507-732-5212. E-mail: zpl@selco.info. Web Site: www.zumbrota.info. *Dir*, James Hill; E-mail: jhill@selco.info; *Asst Dir*, Angela Gustafson; E-mail: agustafson@selco.info
Pop 6,901
Library Holdings: Bk Vols 31,348; Per Subs 98
Automation Activity & Vendor Info: (Acquisitions) Horizon; (Cataloging) Horizon; (Circulation) Horizon; (OPAC) Horizon; (Serials) Horizon
Wireless access
Partic in Southeastern Libraries Cooperating
Open Mon, Wed & Thurs 12-8, Tues 10-6, Fri 10-5, Sat 9-3

MISSISSIPPI

Date of Statistics: FY 2020
Population, 2020 U.S. Census: 2,956,871
Population Served by Public Libraries: 2,986,490
Total Volumes in Public Libraries: 5,328,723
Volumes Per Capita: 1.8
Total Public Library Circulation: 7,012,060
Digital Resources:
Total e-books: 867,166
Total audio items (physical & downloadable units): 377,441
Total video items (physical & downloadable units): 438,730
Total computers for use by the public: 2,738
Total annual wireless sessions: 2,013,789

Income and Expenditures:
Total Public Library Income (includes Grants-in-Aid): $51,220,504
Source of Income: Mainly public funds
Expenditures Per Capita: $15.99
Number of County or Multi-County (Regional) Libraries: 51
Counties Served: 82
Number of Bookmobiles in State: 3
Grants-in-Aid to Public Libraries: $6,925,002
Federal & State: $7,500,944
Information provided courtesy of: Lacy Ellinwood, Library Consultant; Mississippi Library Commission

ACKERMAN

P CHOCTAW COUNTY LIBRARY*, 511 S Louisville St, 39735. (Mail add: PO Box 755, 39735-0755), SAN 348-9213. Tel: 662-285-6348. FAX: 662-285-3042. E-mail: choctawcountylibrary@gmail.com. *Dir,* Cristen Chandler; Staff 2 (Non-MLS 2)
Circ 7,070
Library Holdings: AV Mats 850; Bk Vols 14,000
Special Collections: Genealogy & Local History (J P Coleman Coll)
Automation Activity & Vendor Info: (Cataloging) Biblionix; (ILL) SirsiDynix
Wireless access
Function: 24/7 Electronic res, Accelerated reader prog, Bks on CD, Children's prog, Computers for patron use, E-Reserves, Electronic databases & coll, Free DVD rentals, ILL available, Internet access, Meeting rooms, Movies, Music CDs, Online cat, Preschool reading prog, Prog for adults, Prog for children & young adult, Ref & res, Scanner, STEM programs, Story hour, Summer reading prog, Teen prog, Wheelchair accessible
Open Mon, Tues, Thurs & Fri 9-6, Wed 9-1
Friends of the Library Group

ALCORN STATE

C ALCORN STATE UNIVERSITY*, J D Boyd Library, 1000 ASU Dr, 39096-7500. SAN 308-8901. Tel: 601-877-6350. FAX: 601-877-2459. Web Site: www.alcorn.edu/academics/library. *Dean, Univ Libr,* Dr Blanche Sanders; E-mail: blanche@alcorn.edu; *Acq Librn,* Brenda Jackson; Tel: 601-877-6354, E-mail: brendajackson@alcorn.edu; *Govt Doc Librn,* Danielle Terrell; Tel: 601-877-6358, E-mail: danielle@alcorn.edu; *Ref Librn,* Joanna Williams; Tel: 601-877-2392, E-mail: jwwilliams@alcorn.edu; *Ser Librn,* Floyce Thomas; Tel: 601-877-6362, E-mail: floyce@alcorn.edu; *Instrul Media,* Patrice Savoy; Tel: 601-877-6359, E-mail: patrice@alcorn.edu; Staff 26 (MLS 9, Non-MLS 17)
Founded 1871. Enrl 3,400; Fac 193
Library Holdings: e-books 18,836; Bk Vols 287,133; Per Subs 1,046
Special Collections: Alcorn Archives. State Document Depository; US Document Depository
Subject Interests: Agr, Educ
Automation Activity & Vendor Info: (Acquisitions) Ex Libris Group; (Cataloging) Ex Libris Group; (Circulation) Ex Libris Group; (Course Reserve) Ex Libris Group; (Media Booking) Ex Libris Group; (OPAC) Ex Libris Group; (Serials) Ex Libris Group
Wireless access
Partic in LYRASIS
Open Mon-Thurs 8am-11pm, Fri 8-7, Sat 9-5, Sun 2-11

ASHLAND

P BENTON COUNTY LIBRARY SYSTEM*, Bond Memorial Library, 247 Court St, 38603. (Mail add: PO Box 308, 38603), SAN 376-6357. Tel: 662-224-6400. FAX: 662-224-6304. Web Site: www.benton.lib.ms.us. *Dir,* Jeannie Burton; E-mail: jburton@benton.lib.ms.us; Staff 4 (MLS 1, Non-MLS 3)
Founded 1959. Pop 8,000
Automation Activity & Vendor Info: (Cataloging) Book Systems; (Circulation) Book Systems
Wireless access
Open Mon-Fri 8-5
Friends of the Library Group
Branches: 1
HICKORY FLAT PUBLIC LIBRARY, 1067 Spruce St, Hickory Flat, 38633. (Mail add: PO Box 309, Hickory Flat, 38633-0309), SAN 376-6268. Tel: 662-333-7663. FAX: 662-333-7663. E-mail: hickory@benton.lib.ms.us. *Librn,* Tina Burks; Staff 1 (Non-MLS 1)
Founded 1959
Open Mon-Fri 9-12 & 1-5

BAY SAINT LOUIS

P HANCOCK COUNTY LIBRARY SYSTEM*, 312 Hwy 90, 39520-3595. SAN 348-1417. Tel: 228-467-5282. Administration Tel: 228-467-6836. FAX: 228-467-5503. E-mail: hcls@hancock.lib.ms.us. Web Site: www.hancocklibraries.info. *Interim Dir,* Amber Stephenson; E-mail: astephson@hancock.lib.ms.us; *Info & Tech Serv,* Matthew Armstrong; Staff 34 (MLS 2, Non-MLS 32)
Founded 1934. Pop 45,556; Circ 156,000
Oct 2015-Sept 2016 Income (Main & Associated Libraries) $2,088,315, State $186,952, City $387,187, Federal $23,504, County $1,399,098, Other $91,574. Mats Exp $145,248, Books $97,156, AV Mat $21,544, Electronic Ref Mat (Incl. Access Fees) $26,548. Sal $864,200
Library Holdings: Audiobooks 4,751; DVDs 11,577; e-books 1,200; Electronic Media & Resources 8; High Interest/Low Vocabulary Bk Vols 200; Large Print Bks 3,976; Microforms 133; Bk Vols 96,470; Per Subs 75
Special Collections: Mississippi-Louisiana (Mississippiana Coll)
Automation Activity & Vendor Info: (Acquisitions) SirsiDynix-WorkFlows; (Cataloging) SirsiDynix-WorkFlows; (Circulation) SirsiDynix-WorkFlows; (OPAC) SirsiDynix; (Serials) SirsiDynix-WorkFlows
Wireless access
Function: 24/7 Electronic res, 24/7 Online cat, Accelerated reader prog, Activity rm, Adult bk club, Audiobks via web, Bk club(s), Bks on CD, Children's prog, Computer training, Computers for patron use, Digital talking bks, Electronic databases & coll, Free DVD rentals, Holiday prog, ILL available, Internet access, Learning ctr, Life-long learning prog for all ages, Magazines, Magnifiers for reading, Mail & tel request accepted, Mango lang, Meeting rooms, Microfiche/film & reading machines, Movies, Online cat, Online info literacy tutorials on the web & in blackboard, Outreach serv, Outside serv via phone, mail, e-mail & web, Photocopying/Printing, Prog for adults, Prog for children & young adult, Ref serv available, Scanner, Senior computer classes, Senior outreach, Story hour, Summer reading prog, Tax forms, Telephone ref, Wheelchair accessible

Special Services for the Deaf - Bks on deafness & sign lang; Closed caption videos; High interest/low vocabulary bks
Special Services for the Blind - Copier with enlargement capabilities; Digital talking bk; Free checkout of audio mat; Large print bks; Playaways (bks on MP3); Talking bks
Open Mon, Tues & Thurs 9-7, Wed & Fri 9-5, Sat 9-4
Friends of the Library Group
Branches: 4
EAST HANCOCK PUBLIC LIBRARY, 4545 Shepherd Sq, Diamondhead, 39525. Tel: 228-255-6337. FAX: 228-255-6450. *Br Mgr,* Gerri McClesky; E-mail: gmcclesky@hancock.lib.ms.us; Staff 3 (Non-MLS 3)
Founded 2012. Pop 8,425; Circ 26,000
Library Holdings: CDs 426; DVDs 1,074; Large Print Bks 243; Bk Vols 9,029; Per Subs 14
Function: Art exhibits, Bks on CD, Children's prog, Computer training, Computers for patron use, Electronic databases & coll, Free DVD rentals, ILL available, Online cat, Photocopying/Printing, Prog for adults, Ref serv available, Story hour, Summer reading prog, Wheelchair accessible
Open Mon, Tues & Thurs 10-6, Wed & Sat 10-2, Fri 10-5
KILN PUBLIC LIBRARY, 17065 Hwy 603, Kiln, 39556, SAN 348-1433. Tel: 228-255-1724. FAX: 228-255-0644. *Br Mgr,* Laura Mills; E-mail: lmills@hancock.lib.ms.us; Staff 4 (Non-MLS 4)
Founded 2000. Circ 36,928
Library Holdings: CDs 952; DVDs 2,505; Large Print Bks 1,051; Bk Vols 20,198; Per Subs 18
Function: 24/7 Electronic res, 24/7 Online cat, Accelerated reader prog, Adult bk club, Audiobks via web, Bk club(s), Bks on CD, Children's prog, Computer training, Computers for patron use, Digital talking bks, Electronic databases & coll, Free DVD rentals, Holiday prog, ILL available, Internet access, Life-long learning prog for all ages, Magazines, Magnifiers for reading, Mango lang, Meeting rooms, Online cat, Photocopying/Printing, Prog for adults, Prog for children & young adult, Ref serv available, Story hour, Summer reading prog, Tax forms, Wheelchair accessible
Open Mon, Tues & Thurs 9-6, Wed & Fri 9-5, Sat 9-4
PEARLINGTON PUBLIC LIBRARY, 6096 First St, Pearlington, 39572, SAN 378-1585. Tel: 228-533-0755. FAX: 228-533-0125. *Br Mgr,* Andrea Coote Pack; E-mail: apack@hancock.lib.ms.us; Staff 2 (Non-MLS 2)
Founded 1999. Circ 5,013
Library Holdings: CDs 382; DVDs 1,319; Large Print Bks 306; Bk Vols 7,265; Per Subs 6
Function: 24/7 Electronic res, 24/7 Online cat, Accelerated reader prog, Audiobks via web, Bks on CD, Children's prog, Computers for patron use, Electronic databases & coll, Free DVD rentals, Holiday prog, ILL available, Internet access, Magazines, Mango lang, Meeting rooms, Online cat, Photocopying/Printing, Prog for adults, Prog for children & young adult, Ref serv available, Scanner, Story hour, Summer reading prog, Tax forms, Wheelchair accessible
Open Tues & Thurs 10-6, Wed 11-5, Fri 10-2, Sat 9-1
WAVELAND PUBLIC LIBRARY, 345 Coleman Ave, Waveland, 39576, SAN 348-1441. Tel: 228-467-9240. FAX: 228-467-1336. *Br Mgr,* Angela Christoffer; E-mail: achristoffer@hancock.lib.ms.us; Staff 3 (Non-MLS 3)
Circ 24,294
Library Holdings: CDs 511; DVDs 1,963; Large Print Bks 367; Bk Vols 11,045; Per Subs 11
Function: 24/7 Electronic res, 24/7 Online cat, Accelerated reader prog, Audiobks via web, Bks on CD, Computers for patron use, Electronic databases & coll, Free DVD rentals, Holiday prog, ILL available, Internet access, Magazines, Mail & tel request accepted, Mango lang, Meeting rooms, Online cat, Photocopying/Printing, Prog for adults, Prog for children & young adult, Ref serv available, Story hour, Summer reading prog, Tax forms, Wheelchair accessible
Open Tues & Thurs 10-6, Wed & Sat 10-2, Fri 10-5

BELZONI

P HUMPHREYS COUNTY LIBRARY SYSTEM*, 105 S Hayden, 39038. SAN 348-1476. Tel: 662-247-3606. FAX: 662-247-3443. Web Site: www.humphreys.lib.ms.us. *Dir,* Thomas Cobbs
Founded 1958. Pop 18,706; Circ 44,493
Library Holdings: Audiobooks 2,086; Bk Vols 40,433; Per Subs 84; Videos 2,399
Special Collections: Oral History
Automation Activity & Vendor Info: (Acquisitions) A-G Canada Ltd; (Cataloging) A-G Canada Ltd; (Circulation) A-G Canada Ltd
Wireless access
Partic in Dancing Rabbit Library Consortium; MAGNOLIA
Open Mon-Thurs 9:30-5, Fri 9:30-2

BLUE MOUNTAIN

C BLUE MOUNTAIN COLLEGE, Guyton Library, 201 W Main St, 38610. (Mail add: PO Box 160, 38610-0160), SAN 308-8448. Tel: 662-685-4771, Ext 147. E-mail: library@bmc.edu. Web Site: www.librarybmc.com. *Dir, Libr Serv,* Hannah Johnson; E-mail: hjohnson@bmc.edu; *Coll Develop Librn,* Shelby Carmichael; E-mail: scarmichael@bmc.edu; Staff 2 (Non-MLS 2)
Founded 1873. Enrl 641; Fac 37; Highest Degree: Master
Library Holdings: DVDs 145; e-books 35,991; Music Scores 840; Bk Titles 41,411; Per Subs 63
Special Collections: Blue Mountain College Archives (archives, artifacts, furniture & pictures); Blue Mountain College Hist (May Gardner Black Alumnae Coll); China (Mary Raleigh Anderson); Mary Dean Hollis Historical Doll Coll
Subject Interests: Liberal arts
Automation Activity & Vendor Info: (Cataloging) Book Systems; (Circulation) Book Systems; (OPAC) Book Systems; (Serials) Book Systems
Wireless access
Open Mon-Thurs 8am-10pm, Fri 8-4:30

BOONEVILLE

J NORTHEAST MISSISSIPPI COMMUNITY COLLEGE*, Eula Dees Memorial Library, 101 Cunningham Blvd, 38829. SAN 308-8464. Tel: 662-720-7237, 662-728-7751. Interlibrary Loan Service Tel: 662-720-7408. Toll Free Tel: 800-555-2154. FAX: 662-720-7171. Web Site: www.nemcc.edu/library. *Dir,* Glenice Stone; E-mail: gwstone@nemcc.edu; *Librn,* Sherita Taylor; Tel: 662-720-7583, E-mail: shtaylor@nemcc.edu; *Librn,* Ellice Yager; Tel: 662-720-7584, E-mail: leyager@nemcc.edu; *Evening Librn,* Kalah Rogers; E-mail: klrogers@nemcc.edu; *Libr Asst,* Susan Brackeen; Tel: 662-720-7407, E-mail: sibrackeen@nemcc.edu; Staff 6 (MLS 4, Non-MLS 2)
Founded 1948
Library Holdings: AV Mats 2,839; e-books 27,186; Microforms 63,092; Bk Vols 47,900; Per Subs 89
Subject Interests: Miss
Wireless access
Open Mon-Thurs (Sept-May) 7:30am-9pm, Fri 8-Noon, Sun 6:30pm-9pm; Mon-Thurs (June-Aug) 8-4, Fri 8-Noon

BRANDON

P BRANDON PUBLIC LIBRARY*, 1475 W Government St, 39042. SAN 329-2835. Tel: 601-825-2672. FAX: 601-825-4156. E-mail: brandon@cmrls.lib.ms.us. Web Site: www.cmrls.lib.ms.us/cmrlsbrances/brandon. *Br Mgr,* Linda Wolfe; E-mail: brbm@cmrls.lib.ms.us; *Circ Supvr,* Nora Anderson; *Ref Supvr,* Kayla Martin-Gant; E-mail: brref@cmrls.lib.ms.us. Subject Specialists: *Circ & libr serv,* Nora Anderson; Staff 10 (Non-MLS 10)
Founded 1958. Pop 16,000; Circ 100,000
Library Holdings: Bk Vols 24,500; Per Subs 60
Subject Interests: Genealogy
Wireless access
Mem of Central Mississippi Regional Library System
Partic in National Network of Libraries of Medicine Region 2
Open Mon-Thurs 10-8, Fri 10-5, Sat 10-4
Friends of the Library Group

P CENTRAL MISSISSIPPI REGIONAL LIBRARY SYSTEM*, 100 Tamberline St, 39042. (Mail add: PO Box 1749, 39043-1749), SAN 329-5109. Tel: 601-825-0100. FAX: 601-825-0199. E-mail: custsvc@cmrls.lib.ms.us. Web Site: www.cmrls.lib.ms.us. *Dir,* Mara Polk; E-mail: mara@cmrls.lib.ms.us; *Br Serv Coordr,* Kimberly Cook; *Children's & Youth Serv, Coordr,* Kathy Roberts; *Pub Relations Coordr,* Dorothy Vance; *Coordr, Tech Serv & Automation,* Tammy Jones; Staff 102 (MLS 4, Non-MLS 98)
Founded 1986. Pop 200,000; Circ 745,122
Library Holdings: CDs 6,778; DVDs 6,793; e-books 10; Large Print Bks 11,781; Bk Vols 294,806; Per Subs 530; Talking Bks 9,571; Videos 15,446
Automation Activity & Vendor Info: (Acquisitions) SirsiDynix; (Cataloging) SirsiDynix; (Circulation) SirsiDynix; (OPAC) SirsiDynix; (Serials) SirsiDynix
Wireless access
Member Libraries: Brandon Public Library; Evon A Ford Public Library; Forest Public Library; Lake Public Library; Magee Public Library; Mendenhall Public Library; Mize Public Library; Morton Public Library; Northwest Point Reservoir Library; Pearl Public Library; Pelahatchie Public Library; Polkville Public Library; Puckett Public Library; Raleigh Public Library; Sandhill Pisgah Library & Community Center; Sebastopol Public Library
Open Mon-Thurs 9-8, Fri 9-5, Sat 11-4
Friends of the Library Group

P NORTHWEST POINT RESERVOIR LIBRARY*, 2230 Spillway Rd, 39047. SAN 377-5755. Tel: 601-992-2539. FAX: 601-992-7870. E-mail: reservoi@cmrls.lib.ms.us. Web Site: cmrls.lib.ms.us/cmrlsbranches/reservoir. *Br Mgr,* Charlie Simpkins
Library Holdings: Bk Vols 15,000; Per Subs 35

Mem of Central Mississippi Regional Library System
Open Mon 11:30-5, Tues 10-8, Wed & Thurs 10-6, Fri 10-5, Sat 10-Noon
Friends of the Library Group

P SANDHILL PISGAH LIBRARY & COMMUNITY CENTER*, 727 Sandhill Rd, 39047. SAN 376-6381. Tel: 601-829-1653. FAX: 601-829-1653. E-mail: sandhill@cmrls.lib.ms.us. Web Site: cmrls.lib.ms.us/cmrlsbranches/sandhill-pisgah. *Br Mgr,* Jessica Ward
Library Holdings: Bk Vols 15,903; Per Subs 10
Wireless access
Mem of Central Mississippi Regional Library System
Open Mon-Thurs 8:30-12 & 12:30-4

BROOKHAVEN

P LINCOLN-LAWRENCE-FRANKLIN REGIONAL LIBRARY*, 100 S Jackson St, 39601. SAN 348-1654. Tel: 601-833-3369, 601-833-5038. FAX: 601-833-3381. Web Site: www.llf.lib.ms.us. *Dir,* Katrina Castilaw; E-mail: kcastilaw@llf.lib.ms.us; Staff 19 (MLS 3, Non-MLS 16)
Founded 1956. Pop 50,861
Library Holdings: AV Mats 2,659; CDs 1,149; Large Print Bks 3,581; Bk Titles 105,415; Per Subs 159; Talking Bks 1,278; Videos 2,985
Special Collections: John H Williams Photo Coll; Lincoln County History Coll; Whitworth College Digital Coll. Oral History
Automation Activity & Vendor Info: (Circulation) Follett Software; (OPAC) Follett Software
Wireless access
Partic in Longleaf Library Consortium
Open Mon & Wed 9-6, Tues & Thurs 9-8, Fri & Sat 9-5
Branches: 3
FRANKLIN COUNTY PUBLIC LIBRARY, 38 First St, Meadville, 39653. (Mail add: PO Box 336, Meadville, 39653-0336), SAN 348-1719. Tel: 601-384-2997. FAX: 601-384-3003. *Librn,* Susan Adams; Staff 2 (MLS 1, Non-MLS 1)
Library Holdings: Bk Vols 22,000
Open Mon & Wed 9-5, Tues & Thurs 9-6, Fri & Sat 9-Noon
LAWRENCE COUNTY PUBLIC LIBRARY, 142 Courthouse Sq, Monticello, 39654, SAN 348-1743. Tel: 601-587-2471. FAX: 601-587-7582. *Librn,* Kendra Smith; Staff 3 (MLS 1, Non-MLS 2)
Library Holdings: Bk Vols 15,067
Open Mon-Thurs 10-6, Fri & Sat 10-5
NEW HEBRON PUBLIC LIBRARY, 209 Jones St, New Hebron, 39140, SAN 348-176X. Tel: 601-694-2623. FAX: 601-694-2155. *Br Mgr,* Karen Turnage; Staff 1 (Non-MLS 1)
Open Mon & Tues 9:30-5:30, Wed 9:30-5, Thurs 9-4

CANTON

P MADISON COUNTY LIBRARY SYSTEM*, 102 Priestley St, 39046. SAN 348-1808. Administration Tel: 601-859-7733. Administration FAX: 601-859-0014. E-mail: feedback@mcls.ms. Web Site: www.mcls.ms. *Dir,* Tonja Johnson; E-mail: tjohnson@mcls.ms; *Asst Dir,* Ray Myers; Staff 13 (MLS 8, Non-MLS 5)
Pop 79,758; Circ 360,060
Library Holdings: Bk Vols 176,926; Per Subs 224; Talking Bks 5,038; Videos 7,604
Special Collections: Local Picture Coll; Madison County Historical Materials. Oral History
Subject Interests: African-Am hist, Local hist, Miss writers
Automation Activity & Vendor Info: (Acquisitions) SirsiDynix; (Cataloging) SirsiDynix; (Circulation) SirsiDynix
Wireless access
Publications: Newsletter (Quarterly)
Partic in Association for Rural & Small Libraries; OCLC Online Computer Library Center, Inc
Open Mon-Fri 8-4:30
Friends of the Library Group
Branches: 5
REBECCA BAINE RIGBY LIBRARY, 994 Madison Ave, Madison, 39110. (Mail add: PO Box 1153, Madison, 39139), SAN 348-1867. Tel: 601-856-2749. FAX: 601-856-2681. *Br Mgr,* Tammie Terry; Staff 5 (MLS 1, Non-MLS 4)
Pop 14,692; Circ 119,887
Library Holdings: Bk Vols 42,187; Per Subs 43
Open Mon-Thurs 9-7, Fri & Sat 9-5
Friends of the Library Group
CANTON PUBLIC LIBRARY, 102 Priestley St, 39046. Tel: 601-859-3202. FAX: 601-859-2728. *Br Mgr,* Christine Greenwood; Staff 4 (MLS 1, Non-MLS 3)
Pop 12,911; Circ 54,333
Library Holdings: Bk Vols 61,000; Per Subs 50
Open Mon & Wed 9-6, Tues & Thurs 9-7, Fri & Sat 9-5
Friends of the Library Group
FLORA PUBLIC LIBRARY, 144 Clark St, Flora, 39071. (Mail add: PO Box 356, Flora, 39071-0356), SAN 348-1832. Tel: 601-879-8835. FAX: 601-879-3934. *Br Supvr,* Presley Posey; Staff 2 (Non-MLS 2)
Pop 1,546; Circ 11,969
Library Holdings: Bk Vols 20,596; Per Subs 14
Special Collections: Local History Coll
Open Mon-Thurs 9-6, Fri 9-5, Sat 9-1
Friends of the Library Group
PAUL E GRIFFIN LIBRARY, 116 Parkside Ave, Camden, 39045. Tel: 662-468-0309. FAX: 662-468-0309. *Br Mgr,* Lennie Beamon
Founded 2004. Pop 1,379
Library Holdings: Bk Vols 12,000
Open Mon & Wed 10-7, Tues & Thurs 9-6, Fri 12-5, Sat 9-Noon
Friends of the Library Group
ELSIE E JURGENS LIBRARY, 397 Hwy 51 N, Ridgeland, 39157, SAN 348-1891. Tel: 601-856-4536. FAX: 601-856-3748. *Br Mgr,* Antoinette Giamalva; Staff 7 (MLS 4, Non-MLS 3)
Pop 20,173; Circ 85,542
Library Holdings: Bk Vols 55,000; Per Subs 50
Open Mon-Thurs 9-7, Fri & Sat 9-5
Friends of the Library Group

CARROLLTON

P CARROLLTON NORTH-CARROLLTON PUBLIC LIBRARY*, 1102 Lexington St, 38917. (Mail add: PO Box 329, 38917-0329), SAN 376-6411. Tel: 662-237-6268. FAX: 662-237-6268. Web Site: cpls-verso.auto-graphics.com. *Dir,* Sharon Tollison; E-mail: stollison@carroll.lib.ms.us; Staff 3 (MLS 1, Non-MLS 2)
Pop 10,517; Circ 13,491
Library Holdings: Bk Titles 18,000; Per Subs 20; Talking Bks 300
Function: Photocopying/Printing, Summer reading prog, VHS videos, Wheelchair accessible
Open Mon-Fri 8-12 & 1-5
Friends of the Library Group

CHARLESTON

P TALLAHATCHIE COUNTY LIBRARY SYSTEM*, 102 N Walnut, 38921. (Mail add: PO Box 219, 38921-0219), SAN 348-1921. Tel: 662-647-2638. FAX: 662-647-0975. Web Site: tallahatchie.lib.ms.us. *Dir,* Roshella Cole
Founded 1939. Pop 17,800; Circ 104,000
Library Holdings: Bk Vols 42,000
Partic in Dancing Rabbit Library Consortium
Open Mon, Tues & Fri 12-5, Wed 10-3
Branches: 1
TUTWILER BRANCH, 303 Second Ave, Tutwiler, 38963, SAN 348-1956. Tel: 662-345-8475. FAX: 662-345-6315.
Library Holdings: Bk Titles 10,000
Open Mon-Fri 3-7

CLARKSDALE

P CARNEGIE PUBLIC LIBRARY*, 114 Delta Ave, 38614-4212. (Mail add: PO Box 280, 38614-0280), SAN 348-2014. Tel: 662-624-4461. FAX: 662-627-4344. Web Site: www.cplclarksdale.lib.ms.us. *Dir,* JoAnn Blue; E-mail: jblue@cplclarksdale.lib.ms.us; *Ch,* Mary Jenkins; Staff 11 (MLS 1, Non-MLS 10)
Founded 1914. Pop 27,272; Circ 75,000
Special Collections: State Document Depository
Automation Activity & Vendor Info: (Acquisitions) TLC (The Library Corporation); (Cataloging) TLC (The Library Corporation); (Circulation) TLC (The Library Corporation); (OPAC) TLC (The Library Corporation)
Wireless access
Partic in Miss Libr Comn Interlibr Loan Network
Open Mon-Thurs 9-5:30, Fri 9-5, Sat 9-1
Friends of the Library Group

J COAHOMA COMMUNITY COLLEGE*, Dickerson-Johnson Library & Learning Resource Center, 3240 Friars Point Rd, 38614. SAN 308-8480. Tel: 662-621-4287. FAX: 662-627-9530. Web Site: coahomacc.edu/library. *Dir, Libr Serv,* Rose Lockett; E-mail: rlockett@coahomacc.edu; *Librn,* Mary L Caradine; Tel: 662-621-4289, E-mail: mcaradine@coahomacc.edu
Founded 1949. Enrl 1,362
Library Holdings: Bk Vols 36,000; Per Subs 400
Special Collections: Special Black Studies Coll
Subject Interests: Child growth, Educ
Wireless access
Partic in Dancing Rabbit Library Consortium
Open Mon-Thurs (Winter) 8am-9pm, Fri 8-4; Mon-Fri (Summer) 8-4

CLEVELAND

P BOLIVAR COUNTY LIBRARY SYSTEM*, Robinson-Carpenter Memorial Library, 104 S Leflore Ave, 38732. SAN 348-2073. Tel: 662-843-2774. FAX: 662-843-4701. Web Site: bolivar.lib.ms.us. *Dir,* Emily

Bell; E-mail: ebell@bolivar.lib.ms.us; *Asst Dir,* Sharon Williamson; E-mail: swilliamson@bolivar.lib.ms.us; *Circ Mgr,* Megan Fleming; E-mail: mfleming@bolivar.lib.ms.us; *Adult/Ref Serv,* Tamara Blackwell; E-mail: tdblackwell@bolivar.lib.ms.us; *Youth Serv,* Bobbie Matheney; E-mail: bmatheney@bolivar.lib.ms.us; Staff 15 (MLS 2, Non-MLS 13)
Founded 1958. Pop 34,145; Circ 41,044
Library Holdings: Audiobooks 819; DVDs 237; Bk Vols 56,088; Per Subs 103
Subject Interests: Genealogy, Local hist
Automation Activity & Vendor Info: (Acquisitions) Innovative Interfaces, Inc; (Cataloging) Innovative Interfaces, Inc; (Circulation) Innovative Interfaces, Inc; (ILL) Innovative Interfaces, Inc; (OPAC) Innovative Interfaces, Inc; (Serials) EBSCO Online
Wireless access
Function: Accelerated reader prog, Archival coll, Art exhibits, AV serv, Bk reviews (Group), Bks on CD, CD-ROM, Children's prog, Computers for patron use, E-Reserves, Electronic databases & coll, Equip loans & repairs, Free DVD rentals, Games & aids for people with disabilities, Holiday prog, ILL available, Jail serv, Mail & tel request accepted, Music CDs, Online cat, Outreach serv, Photocopying/Printing, Preschool outreach, Preschool reading prog, Prog for adults, Prog for children & young adult, Ref & res, Ref serv available, Scanner, Senior outreach, Story hour, Summer reading prog, Tax forms, Teen prog, Telephone ref, Wheelchair accessible
Partic in Dancing Rabbit Library Consortium
Open Mon-Thurs 9-6, Fri 9-5, Sat 9-1
Friends of the Library Group
Branches: 6
BENOIT PUBLIC LIBRARY, 109 W Preston St, Benoit, 38725. (Mail add: 104 S Leflore Ave, 38732), SAN 372-7912. Tel: 662-742-3112. FAX: 662-742-3112. Web Site: bolivar.lib.ms.us/about-us/branches/benoit-public-library. *Librn,* Tina McGee; E-mail: emcgee@bolivar.lib.ms.us
Open Mon & Thurs 1-5
Friends of the Library Group
FIELD MEMORIAL LIBRARY, 132 N Peeler Ave, Shaw, 38773. (Mail add: 104 S Leflore Ave, 38732), SAN 348-2103. Tel: 662-754-4597. FAX: 662-754-4597. E-mail: shaw@bolivar.lib.ms.us.
Closed until further notice 2021-
Friends of the Library Group
DR ROBERT T HOLLINGSWORTH PUBLIC LIBRARY, Old Hwy 61 N, Shelby, 38774. (Mail add: 104 S Leflore Ave, 38732), SAN 348-2197. Tel: 662-398-7748. FAX: 662-398-7748. Web Site: bolivar.lib.ms.us/about-us/branches/hollingsworth. *Librn,* Marie Shorter; E-mail: shelby@bolivar.lib.ms.us
Open Mon & Wed 10-5, Fri 12-5
Friends of the Library Group
MOUND BAYOU PUBLIC, 301 E Martin Luther King St, Mound Bayou, 38762. (Mail add: 104 S Leflore Ave, 38732). E-mail: moundbayou@bolivar.lib.ms.us.
Founded 2002
closed until further notice due to funding 2021-
Friends of the Library Group
THELMA RAYNER MEMORIAL LIBRARY, 201 Front St, Merigold, 38759. (Mail add: 104 S Leflore Ave, 38732), SAN 348-2227. Tel: 662-748-2105. FAX: 662-748-2596. E-mail: merigold@bolivar.lib.ms.us. Web Site: bolivar.lib.ms.us/about-us/branches/rayner. *Librn,* Evelyn Brown
Open Mon-Thurs 1-5
ROSEDALE PUBLIC LIBRARY, 702 Front St, Rosedale, 38769, SAN 348-2162. Tel: 662-759-6332. FAX: 662-759-6332. Web Site: bolivar.lib.ms.us/about-us/branches/rosedale. *Librn,* Martha Lawson; E-mail: mlawson@bolivar.lib.ms.us
Open Mon & Wed 10-5, Fri 12-5

C DELTA STATE UNIVERSITY*, Roberts-LaForge Library, Laflore Circle at Fifth Ave, 38733-2599. SAN 308-8499. Tel: 662-846-4430. Interlibrary Loan Service Tel: 662-846-4448. Reference Tel: 662-846-4431. FAX: 662-846-4443. E-mail: refdesk@deltastate.edu. Web Site: www.deltastate.edu/library. *Dean of Libr,* Jeff M Slagell; E-mail: jslagell@deltastate.edu; *Asst Dir,* Joi Phillips; E-mail: jjphilip@deltastate.edu; *Access Serv Librn,* Jerome Billingsley; E-mail: jbilling@deltastate.edu; *Electronic Res Librn,* Lynne Lambdin; Tel: 662-846-4456, E-mail: llambdin@deltastate.edu; *Archivist,* Emily Jones; Tel: 662-846-4781, E-mail: ejones@deltastate.edu; *Doc, Ref (Info Servs),* David Salinero; E-mail: dsaliner@deltastate.edu; *Ref (Info Servs),* Ann Ashmore; E-mail: aashmore@deltastate.edu; *Ref (Info Servs),* Michael Mounce; E-mail: mmounce@deltastate.edu; *Tech Serv,* Rick Torgerson; Tel: 662-846-4438, E-mail: rick@deltastate.edu; Staff 25 (MLS 12, Non-MLS 13)
Founded 1925. Enrl 4,200; Fac 250; Highest Degree: Doctorate
Library Holdings: AV Mats 19,302; e-books 50,786; Bk Vols 360,286; Per Subs 17,368
Special Collections: Archives (Walter Sillers Coll); Art Coll; Mississippi Delta History; Mississippiana, mss. Oral History; State Document Depository; US Document Depository
Automation Activity & Vendor Info: (Acquisitions) SirsiDynix; (Cataloging) SirsiDynix; (Circulation) SirsiDynix; (Course Reserve) SirsiDynix; (ILL) SirsiDynix; (OPAC) SirsiDynix; (Serials) SirsiDynix
Wireless access
Partic in Dancing Rabbit Library Consortium; LYRASIS; MAGNOLIA
Open Mon-Thurs 7:30am-10pm, Fri 7:30-4, Sun 2-10
Friends of the Library Group

CLINTON

C MISSISSIPPI COLLEGE*, Leland Speed Library, 130 W College St, 39058. (Mail add: PO Box 4047, 39058-4047), SAN 348-2251. Tel: 601-925-3232. Reference Tel: 601-925-3916. FAX: 601-925-3435. Web Site: library.mc.edu. *Libr Dir,* Kathleen Hutchison; Tel: 601-925-3870, E-mail: khutchis@mc.edu; *Head, Pub Serv,* Claudia Conklin; Tel: 601-925-3943, E-mail: cconklin@mc.edu; *Head, Spec Coll,* Heather Moore; Tel: 601-925-3434, E-mail: hsmoore@mc.edu; *Head, Tech Serv,* Julie Thornton; Tel: 601-925-3436, E-mail: jthornto@mc.edu; *Ref & Instruction Librn,* Ben Van Horn; Tel: 601-925-7390, E-mail: vanhor00@mc.edu; Staff 7 (Non-MLS 7)
Founded 1826. Fac 160; Highest Degree: Doctorate
Library Holdings: Bk Vols 241,620; Per Subs 770
Special Collections: Mississippi Baptist Historical Coll
Automation Activity & Vendor Info: (Acquisitions) Innovative Interfaces, Inc; (Cataloging) Innovative Interfaces, Inc; (Circulation) Innovative Interfaces, Inc; (Course Reserve) Innovative Interfaces, Inc; (ILL) Innovative Interfaces, Inc; (Media Booking) Innovative Interfaces, Inc; (OPAC) Innovative Interfaces, Inc; (Serials) Innovative Interfaces, Inc
Wireless access
Function: ILL available
Partic in LYRASIS
Open Mon-Thurs 7:30am-1am, Fri 7:30am-Midnight, Sat Noon-Midnight, Sun 2pm-1am
Restriction: Pub use on premises
Departmental Libraries:
LAW LIBRARY
See Separate Entry Under Mississippi College in Jackson

COFFEEVILLE

P YALOBUSHA COUNTY PUBLIC LIBRARY SYSTEM*, Coffeeville Public Library, 14432 Main St, 38922-2590. (Mail add: PO Box 359, 38922-0359), SAN 324-3737. Tel: 662-675-8822. FAX: 662-675-2001. E-mail: info@yalobusha.lib.ms.us. Web Site: yalobusha.lib.ms.us/branches/coffeeville-public-library. *Dir,* Patty M Bailey; E-mail: patty@yalobusha.lib.ms.us; *Asst Librn,* Dianne Brewer; *Asst Librn, Cataloger,* Sandy Vaughn; E-mail: svaughn@yalobusha.lib.ms.us
Founded 1960. Pop 1,100; Circ 10,337
Library Holdings: Bk Vols 9,040; Per Subs 45
Automation Activity & Vendor Info: (Cataloging) Book Systems; (Circulation) Book Systems
Wireless access
Function: Adult bk club, Bks on CD, Children's prog, Computers for patron use, Free DVD rentals, ILL available, Internet access, Magazines, Online cat, Prog for adults, Prog for children & young adult, Tax forms
Open Mon & Fri 9-12 & 1-5, Tues & Wed 1-5, Thurs 1-8
Restriction: Authorized patrons, ID required to use computers (Ltd hrs)
Friends of the Library Group
Branches: 1
OAKLAND PUBLIC LIBRARY, 324 Holly St, Oakland, 38948. (Mail add: PO Box 69, Oakland, 38948-0069), SAN 308-9029. Tel: 662-623-8651. FAX: 662-623-0089. Web Site: yalobusha.lib.ms.us/branches/oakland-public-library. *Br Librn, Cataloger,* Gretchen T McCain; E-mail: gtumelson@yalobusha.lib.ms.us
Pop 2,000; Circ 2,300
Library Holdings: Bk Vols 10,000; Per Subs 18
Subject Interests: Local hist
Function: 24/7 Online cat, Bks on CD, Free DVD rentals, ILL available, Internet access, Magazines, Online cat, Prog for adults, Prog for children & young adult, Tax forms
Partic in Miss Libr Comn Interlibr Loan Network
Open Mon & Fri 9-12 & 1-5, Wed 10-12 & 1-6
Restriction: Authorized patrons
Friends of the Library Group

COLLINS

P COVINGTON COUNTY LIBRARY SYSTEM*, R E Blackwell Memorial Library, 403 S Fir Ave, 39428. (Mail add: PO Box 1539, 39428-1539), SAN 348-8195. Tel: 601-765-4612. FAX: 601-765-3317. E-mail: collins@ccls.lib.ms.us. Web Site: www.ccls.lib.ms.us/collins-ms. *Dir,* James Pinkard; E-mail: jpinkard@ccls.lib.ms.us; *Mgr,* David Hollingsworth
Wireless access

Open Mon-Fri 8:30-5:30, Sat 9:30-1:30
Friends of the Library Group
Branches: 2
JANE BLAIN BREWER MEMORIAL, 102 S Fifth St, Mount Olive, 39119. (Mail add: PO Box 936, Mount Olive, 39119-0936), SAN 348-8373. Tel: 601-797-4955. FAX: 601-797-4955. E-mail: mtolive@ccls.lib.ms.us. Web Site: www.ccls.lib.ms/mount-olive-ms. *Mgr,* Martha Diehl
Open Mon-Fri 9:30-5:30
Friends of the Library Group
CONNER-GRAHAM MEMORIAL, 101 Willow St, Seminary, 39479. (Mail add: PO Box 95, Seminary, 39479-0095), SAN 348-8497. Tel: 601-722-9041. FAX: 601-722-9041. E-mail: seminary@ccls.lib.ms.us. Web Site: www.ccls.lib.ms.us/seminary-ms. *Mgr,* Alison Stringer
Open Mon-Fri 8:30-5:30
Friends of the Library Group

COLUMBIA

P SOUTH MISSISSIPPI REGIONAL LIBRARY*, Columbia Marion County Library, 900 Broad St, 39429. SAN 348-2316. Tel: 601-736-5516. FAX: 601-736-1379. Web Site: smrl.lib.ms.us. *Dir,* Ryda Worthy; E-mail: rworthy@smrl.lib.ms.us; *Tech Serv,* Kendra Smith; E-mail: ksmith@smrl.lib.ms.us; Staff 4 (MLS 2, Non-MLS 2)
Founded 1972. Pop 41,508
Library Holdings: Audiobooks 1,200; DVDs 4,800; e-books 600; e-journals 2; Bk Titles 31,602; Bk Vols 574,990; Per Subs 228
Automation Activity & Vendor Info: (Cataloging) Innovative Interfaces, Inc; (Circulation) Innovative Interfaces, Inc; (OPAC) Innovative Interfaces, Inc
Wireless access
Partic in Longleaf Library Consortium
Open Mon-Thurs 8:30-6, Fri 8:30-5, Sat 8:30-3
Friends of the Library Group
Branches: 2
FRANK L LEGGETT PUBLIC LIBRARY, 161 General Robert E Blount Blvd, Bassfield, 39421. (Mail add: PO Box 310, Bassfield, 39421-0310), SAN 348-2340. Tel: 601-943-5420. FAX: 601-943-5142. *Br Mgr,* Jackie Miller
Open Mon-Fri 8:30-12 & 1-5
Friends of the Library Group
PRENTISS PUBLIC, 2229 Pearl St, Prentiss, 39474. (Mail add: PO Box 1315, Prentiss, 39474-1315), SAN 348-2375. Tel: 601-792-5845. FAX: 601-792-8159. E-mail: smrlprentiss@gmail.com. *Libr Supvr,* Jackie Miller
Open Mon-Thurs 8:30-5:30, Fri 8:30-5
Friends of the Library Group

COLUMBUS

P COLUMBUS-LOWNDES PUBLIC LIBRARY*, 314 Seventh St N, 39701. SAN 348-2405. Tel: 662-329-5300. FAX: 662-329-5156. Web Site: www.lowndeslibrary.com. *Dir,* Erin Busbea; E-mail: ebusbea@lowndes.lib.ms.us; *Bus Mgr,* Pam Rhea; E-mail: prhea@lowndes.lib.ms.us; *Cat Asst, Circ Coordr,* Wil'Lani Turner; E-mail: wturner@lowndes.lib.ms.us; *Archivist,* Mona Vance; E-mail: mvance@lowndes.lib.ms.us. Subject Specialists: *Local hist,* Mona Vance; Staff 22 (MLS 3, Non-MLS 19)
Founded 1940. Pop 60,933; Circ 108,868
Library Holdings: Bk Vols 94,995; Per Subs 151
Special Collections: Billups-Garth Archives; Eudora Welty Special Coll; Genealogy & Local History (Margaret Latimer Buckley Room), bks, pers & micro
Automation Activity & Vendor Info: (Acquisitions) SirsiDynix; (Cataloging) SirsiDynix; (Circulation) SirsiDynix; (ILL) SirsiDynix; (OPAC) SirsiDynix; (Serials) EBSCO Online
Wireless access
Partic in Mississippi Library Partnership
Special Services for the Blind - Bks on CD; Large print bks; Playaways (bks on MP3); Talking bk encyclopedia
Open Mon-Thurs 9-7, Fri & Sat 9-2
Friends of the Library Group
Branches: 3
ARTESIA PUBLIC, 323 Front St, Artesia, 39736, SAN 348-243X. Tel: 662-272-5255. FAX: 662-370-1054. *Br Mgr,* Bernice Wilson; E-mail: bwilson@lowndes.lib.ms.us; Staff 5 (MLS 3, Non-MLS 2)
Automation Activity & Vendor Info: (Course Reserve) SirsiDynix
Function: Art exhibits, Bks on CD, Children's prog, Computer training, Computers for patron use, Free DVD rentals, Holiday prog, ILL available, Online cat, Online ref, Photocopying/Printing, Prog for adults, Prog for children & young adult, Ref & res, Story hour, Summer reading prog, Tax forms, Teen prog, Telephone ref, Wheelchair accessible, Workshops
Partic in MAGNOLIA
Open Tues & Thurs 10-1 & 2-5:30
Friends of the Library Group
CALEDONIA PUBLIC, 754 Main St, Caledonia, 39740, SAN 348-2464. Tel: 662-356-6384. FAX: 662-370-1603. *Br Mgr,* Tori Sansing; E-mail: thawkins@lowndes.lib.ms.us
Open Mon, Wed & Thurs 8:30-12 & 1-5:30
Friends of the Library Group
CRAWFORD PUBLIC, 320 Main St, Crawford, 39743, SAN 348-2472. Tel: 662-272-5144. FAX: 662-370-1238. *Br Mgr,* Bernice Wilson
Open Mon & Wed 10-1 & 2-5:30
Friends of the Library Group

C MISSISSIPPI UNIVERSITY FOR WOMEN*, John Clayton Fant Memorial Library, PO Box W1625, 39701. SAN 348-2499. Circulation Tel: 662-329-7332. Interlibrary Loan Service Tel: 662-329-7333. Reference Tel: 662-329-7336. FAX: 662-329-7348. E-mail: library@muw.edu. Web Site: www.muw.edu/library. *Dean, Libr Serv,* Amanda Clay Powers; E-mail: acpowers@muw.edu; *Spec Projects Librn,* Nancy J Wheeley; E-mail: njwheeley@muw.edu; *Syst Librn, Webmaster,* Bobby Fugitt; E-mail: bfugitt@muw.edu; Staff 14 (MLS 6, Non-MLS 8)
Founded 1884
Library Holdings: Bk Vols 255,487; Per Subs 1,619
Special Collections: George Eliot (Blanche Colton Williams' Biography of George Eliot), original mss; George Eliot First Editions & Criticisms; Mississippiana; Southern Women's History, Specializing in Mississippi; State & Local Histroy (General E T Sykes Scrapbook Coll), clippings; University history, bks, micro. State Document Depository; US Document Depository
Subject Interests: Art & archit, Behav sci, Creative writing, Educ, Feminism, Music, Nursing, Soc sci, Women's hist
Wireless access
Partic in LYRASIS; MAGNOLIA
Open Mon-Thurs 7:30am-10pm, Fri 7:30-5, Sat 9-5, Sun 2-10pm
Friends of the Library Group

COLUMBUS AFB

A UNITED STATES AIR FORCE, Columbus Air Force Base Library, 37 Harris St, 39710-5102. SAN 348-2553. Tel: 662-434-2934. Web Site: www.columbusafbliving.com. *Dir,* Europonda Stone; E-mail: europonda.stone@us.af.mil; Staff 3 (Non-MLS 3)
Library Holdings: Audiobooks 100; DVDs 700; Bk Vols 5,500; Per Subs 20
Subject Interests: Aviation, Mil strategy
Wireless access
Open Mon, Wed & Fri 10:30-2:30, Sun 1-5

CORINTH

P NORTHEAST REGIONAL LIBRARY*, 1023 Fillmore St, 38834-4199. SAN 348-2588. Tel: 662-287-7311. FAX: 662-286-8010. Web Site: nereg.lib.ms.us. *Syst Dir,* Dee Hare; E-mail: dee@nereg.lib.ms.us; *Coll Develop Librn,* Hope Morton; E-mail: hope@nereg.lib.ms.us; Staff 24 (MLS 4, Non-MLS 20)
Founded 1951. Pop 101,564; Circ 346,035
Library Holdings: AV Mats 18,231; Electronic Media & Resources 49; Bk Vols 200,146; Per Subs 211
Special Collections: Oral History
Subject Interests: Genealogy
Automation Activity & Vendor Info: (Cataloging) OCLC CatExpress; (Circulation) SirsiDynix; (ILL) OCLC FirstSearch; (OPAC) Horizon
Wireless access
Function: Adult bk club, Adult literacy prog, Art exhibits, Bks on cassette, Bks on CD, Computer training, Computers for patron use, Electronic databases & coll, ILL available, Mail & tel request accepted, Music CDs, Online cat, Photocopying/Printing, Prog for children & young adult, Ref serv available, Spoken cassettes & CDs, Spoken cassettes & DVDs, Summer reading prog, Tax forms, Telephone ref, VHS videos, Wheelchair accessible
Partic in Collaborative Libraries of Vermont
Open Mon-Fri 8-5
Friends of the Library Group
Branches: 13
GEORGE E ALLEN LIBRARY, 500 W Church St, Booneville, 38829-3353, SAN 348-2820. Tel: 662-728-6553. FAX: 662-728-4127. E-mail: boon@nereg.lib.ms.us. *Librn,* Leigh Hood; E-mail: klhood@nereg.lib.ms.us
Library Holdings: Bk Vols 29,927
Special Collections: George E Allen Coll, (papers & memorabilia belonging to George E Allen)
Open Mon-Thurs 9-6, Fri 9-5, Sat 9-4
Friends of the Library Group

BELMONT PUBLIC LIBRARY, 102 S Third St, Belmont, 38827. (Mail add: PO Box 629, Belmont, 38827-0629), SAN 348-2677. Tel: 662-454-7841. FAX: 662-454-7841. E-mail: be@nereg.lib.ms.us. *Librn,* Andrea Green; E-mail: agreen@nereg.lib.ms.us
Library Holdings: Bk Vols 13,689
Open Mon-Wed & Fri 9:30-5
Friends of the Library Group

BLUE MOUNTAIN PUBLIC LIBRARY, 125 S Railroad Ave, Blue Mountain, 38610, SAN 348-2707. Tel: 662-685-4559. FAX: 662-685-4559. E-mail: bl@nereg.lib.ms.us. *Librn,* Stacy Hull
Library Holdings: Bk Vols 5,473
Open Tues & Thurs 12-5

BURNSVILLE PUBLIC LIBRARY, Norman Ave, Burnsville, 38833. (Mail add: PO Box 188, Burnsville, 38833-0188), SAN 348-2731. Tel: 662-427-9258. FAX: 662-427-9258. E-mail: bu@nereg.lib.ms.us. *Librn,* Charlotte Morris; E-mail: charlotte@nereg.lib.ms.us
Library Holdings: Bk Vols 10,006
Open Mon-Fri 10-4
Friends of the Library Group

CHALYBEATE PUBLIC LIBRARY, 2501-A Hwy 354, Walnut, 38683-9762, SAN 348-2766. Tel: 662-223-6768. FAX: 662-223-6768. *Librn,* Genette McKinney
Library Holdings: Bk Vols 4,248
Open Mon & Wed 1-4, Fri 12-4

CORINTH PUBLIC LIBRARY, 1023 Fillmore St, 38834. Tel: 662-287-2441. FAX: 662-286-8010. E-mail: co@nereg.lib.ms.us. *Librn,* Cody Daniel; E-mail: cdaniel@nereg.lib.ms.us
Founded 1951. Pop 35,000; Circ 123,856
Library Holdings: Bk Vols 68,173
Open Mon-Thurs 9-8, Fri & Sat 9-5
Friends of the Library Group

ANNE SPENCER COX LIBRARY, 303 N Third St, Baldwyn, 38824-1517, SAN 348-2642. Tel: 662-365-3305. FAX: 662-365-3305. E-mail: ba@nereg.lib.ms.us. *Librn,* Simone Chandler; E-mail: simone@nereg.lib.ms.us
Library Holdings: Bk Vols 14,926
Open Mon-Thurs 10-6, Fri & Sat 9-1
Friends of the Library Group

IUKA PUBLIC LIBRARY, 204 N Main St, Iuka, 38852, SAN 348-288X. Tel: 662-423-6300. FAX: 662-423-6300. E-mail: iu@nereg.lib.ms.us. *Librn,* Gwen Spain; E-mail: gwen@nereg.lib.ms.us
Library Holdings: Bk Vols 29,478
Open Mon-Thurs 9-6, Fri 9-5, Sat 9-4
Friends of the Library Group

MARGARET RAE MEMORIAL, Margaret Rae Memorial Bldg, Hwy 25 & Main St, Tishomingo, 38873. (Mail add: PO Box 128, Tishomingo, 38873-0128), SAN 348-3002. Tel: 662-438-7640. FAX: 662-438-7640. E-mail: ti@nereg.lib.ms.us. *Librn,* Beverly Parker
Library Holdings: Bk Vols 8,332
Open Mon, Wed & Fri 10-5, Sat 10-3
Friends of the Library Group

MARIETTA PUBLIC LIBRARY, Park Rd, Marietta, 38856. (Mail add: PO Box 88, Marietta, 38856-0088), SAN 348-291X. Tel: 662-728-9320. FAX: 662-728-9320. E-mail: ma@nereg.lib.ms.us. *Librn,* Cindy Ramey
Library Holdings: Bk Vols 3,348
Open Mon, Tues & Fri 9-5, Wed 9-Noon

RIENZI PUBLIC LIBRARY, School St, Rienzi, 38865. (Mail add: PO Box 69, Rienzi, 38865-0069), SAN 348-2944. Tel: 662-462-5015. FAX: 662-462-5015. *Librn,* Erica Will; E-mail: ewill@nereg.lib.ms.us
Library Holdings: Bk Vols 6,303
Open Mon, Wed & Fri 11:30-4:30

RIPLEY PUBLIC LIBRARY, 308 N Commerce St, Ripley, 38663-1721, SAN 348-2979. Tel: 662-837-7773. FAX: 662-993-9117. E-mail: rp@nereg.lib.ms.us. *Librn,* Eric Melton; E-mail: eric@nereg.lib.ms.us
Library Holdings: Bk Vols 21,955
Open Mon, Wed, Fri & Sat 9-5, Tues & Thurs 9-8
Friends of the Library Group

WALNUT PUBLIC LIBRARY, 650 N Main St, Walnut, 38683, SAN 348-3037. Tel: 662-223-6768. FAX: 662-223-6768. E-mail: wa@nereg.lib.ms.us. *Librn,* Gayle Newby; E-mail: gayle@nereg.lib.ms.us
Library Holdings: Bk Vols 7,538
Open Mon-Wed & Fri 11-5

DECATUR

J EAST CENTRAL COMMUNITY COLLEGE*, Mamie Ethel Burton Memorial Library, 275 E Broad St, 39327. (Mail add: PO Box 129, 39327-0129), SAN 308-8510. Tel: 601-635-2111, Ext 219, 601-635-6219. Toll Free Tel: 877-462-3222. FAX: 601-635-2150. Web Site: www.eccc.edu/library. *Dean, Learning Res,* Leslie Hughes; E-mail: lhughes@eccc.edu; *Librn,* Elizabeth Minter; E-mail: eminter@eccc.edu
Founded 1977. Enrl 2,400
Library Holdings: Bk Vols 41,000; Per Subs 210
Wireless access
Open Mon-Thurs (Winter) 7:30am-9pm, Fri 7:30-3, Sun 6pm-8:30pm; Mon-Thurs (Summer) 7:30-3:30, Fri 7:30-3

ELLISVILLE

J JONES COUNTY JUNIOR COLLEGE*, T Terrell Tisdale Library, 900 S Court St, 39437. SAN 308-8529. Tel: 601-477-4055. FAX: 601-477-2600. E-mail: library@jcjc.edu. Web Site: jcjc.edu/library. *Dir,* Andrew Sharp; *Acq,* Julie Atwood; E-mail: julie.atwood@jcjc.edu; *Cat,* Gary Herring; Staff 4 (MLS 4)
Founded 1924. Enrl 5,186; Fac 275
Library Holdings: AV Mats 44,426; Bk Vols 65,000; Per Subs 160
Special Collections: Literary Criticism on William Faulkner & Eudora Welty, bks & flm; Mississippi Coll
Subject Interests: Genealogy
Automation Activity & Vendor Info: (Acquisitions) SirsiDynix; (Cataloging) SirsiDynix; (Circulation) SirsiDynix; (Course Reserve) SirsiDynix; (ILL) OCLC; (OPAC) SirsiDynix; (Serials) SirsiDynix
Wireless access
Publications: Library Handbook
Open Mon-Thurs 7am-9pm, Fri 7-3:30

FLORENCE

P FLORENCE PUBLIC LIBRARY*, 115 W Main St, 39073. (Mail add: PO Box 95, 39073-0095), SAN 376-6276. Tel: 601-845-6032. FAX: 601-845-4625. E-mail: florence@cmrls.lib.ms.us. Web Site: cmrls.lib.ms.us/cmrlsbranches/florence. *Br Mgr,* Jill Hodges
Library Holdings: Bk Titles 15,000; Bk Vols 16,000; Per Subs 12
Automation Activity & Vendor Info: (Circulation) SirsiDynix; (ILL) SirsiDynix; (Media Booking) SirsiDynix; (Serials) SirsiDynix
Wireless access
Open Mon & Thurs 9:30-7, Tues & Wed 9:30-5, Fri 1-5, Sat 9-12:30
Friends of the Library Group

FOREST

P FOREST PUBLIC LIBRARY*, 210 S Raleigh St, 39074. (Mail add: PO Box 737, 39074-0737), SAN 376-6233. Tel: 601-469-1481. FAX: 601-469-5903. E-mail: forest@cmrls.lib.ms.us. Web Site: cityofforest.com/home/community/library, cmrls.lib.ms.us/cmrlsbranches/forest. *Br Mgr,* Dianne McLaurin
Library Holdings: Bk Titles 38,000; Per Subs 25
Wireless access
Function: Photocopying/Printing
Mem of Central Mississippi Regional Library System
Open Mon, Wed & Thurs 9-5:30, Tues 10-7, Fri 9-5, Sat 9-12
Friends of the Library Group

FULTON

J ITAWAMBA COMMUNITY COLLEGE*, Learning Resource Center, 602 W Hill St, 38843. SAN 348-324X. Tel: 662-862-8384. FAX: 662-862-8410. Web Site: iccms.libguides.com/c.php?g=941087. *Dir, Learning Res,* Janet Armour; E-mail: jyarmour@iccms.edu; *Librn,* Holly Gray; E-mail: ehgray@iccms.edu; *Librn,* Holly Karr; Tel: 662-862-8378, E-mail: kmkarr@iccms.edu; Staff 2 (MLS 2)
Library Holdings: Bk Titles 50,000; Per Subs 254
Wireless access
Partic in Loanet; LYRASIS; Miss Interlibr Loan Syst
Open Mon-Thurs (Winter) 7:30am-9pm, Fri 7:30-4:30, Sun 4-8; Mon-Fri (Summer) 7:30-4:30

GAUTIER

J MISSISSIPPI GULF COAST COMMUNITY COLLEGE*, Jackson County Campus Library, 2300 Hwy 90, 39553. (Mail add: PO Box 100, 39553-0100), SAN 308-8545. Tel: 228-497-7715. Administration Tel: 228-497-7825. E-mail: jc.library@mgccc.edu. Web Site: www.mgccc.edu/library. *Asst Dean of Libr,* Melissa Davis; Tel: 228-497-7642, E-mail: melissa.davis@mgccc.edu; *Librn,* Dr Gwendolyn Carter; E-mail: gwendolyn.carter@mgccc.edu; *Librn,* Tim Koehn; Tel: 228-497-7716, E-mail: tim.koehn@mgccc.edu; Staff 4 (MLS 2, Non-MLS 2)
Founded 1965. Enrl 3,189; Fac 185; Highest Degree: Associate
Automation Activity & Vendor Info: (Acquisitions) SirsiDynix
Wireless access
Partic in LYRASIS
Open Mon-Thurs (Fall-Spring) 7:30am-8pm, Fri 7:30-4:30; Mon-Thurs (Summer) 7:30-7, Fri 7:30-4:30

GOODMAN

J HOLMES COMMUNITY COLLEGE*, McMorrough Library, Goodman Campus, One Hill St, 39079. (Mail add: PO Box 439, 39079), SAN 308-8553. Tel: 662-472-9021. FAX: 662-472-9155. Web Site: www.holmescc.edu/library. *Dir, Libr Serv,* James Thompson; E-mail: jathompson@holmescc.edu; *Librn,* Sarah Clay; E-mail: sclay@holmescc.edu; Staff 4 (MLS 2, Non-MLS 2)
Founded 1928. Enrl 3,805; Fac 132; Highest Degree: Associate
Library Holdings: e-books 40,000; Bk Vols 57,875; Per Subs 64
Subject Interests: Juv, Miss, Shakespeare
Automation Activity & Vendor Info: (Acquisitions) SirsiDynix-WorkFlows; (Cataloging) SirsiDynix-WorkFlows; (OPAC) SirsiDynix-iBistro
Wireless access
Partic in MAGNOLIA
Open Mon-Wed (Fall & Spring) 7:30am-9pm, Thurs 7:30-5, Fri 8-3:30, Sun 9-5; Mon-Fri (Summer) 8-3:30
Restriction: In-house use for visitors

GREENVILLE

P WASHINGTON COUNTY LIBRARY SYSTEM*, William Alexander Percy Memorial Library, 341 Main St, 38701. SAN 348-3274. Tel: 662-335-2331. FAX: 662-390-4758. Web Site: www.washington.lib.ms.us. *Dir,* Kay Clanton; E-mail: kclanton@washington.lib.ms.us; Staff 6 (MLS 1, Non-MLS 5)
Founded 1964
Library Holdings: Bk Vols 281,325; Per Subs 394
Special Collections: Greenville Writers Exhibit. Oral History
Subject Interests: Genealogy, Local hist, Miss hist
Automation Activity & Vendor Info: (Cataloging) Auto-Graphics, Inc
Partic in Dancing Rabbit Library Consortium; National Network of Libraries of Medicine Region 2
Open Mon & Tues 9-7, Wed-Fri 10-5, Sat 10-1
Friends of the Library Group
Branches: 5
ARCOLA LIBRARY, 106 Martin Luther King Dr, Arcola, 38722, SAN 348-3304. Tel: 662-827-5262. *Br Mgr,* Joan Milton
Open Mon (Winter) 2-6, Tues-Fri 3-6; Mon (Summer) 1-5, Tues-Fri 2-5
AVON LIBRARY, 874 Riverside Rd, Avon, 38723, SAN 348-3339, Tel: 662-332-9346. *Br Mgr,* Joan Davis
Open Mon-Thurs 2-5
GLEN ALLAN LIBRARY, 970 E Lake Washington Rd, Glen Allan, 38744, SAN 348-3428. Tel: 662-839-4066. *Br Mgr,* Winnie Darnell
Open Mon 1-5, Tues-Fri 2-5
LELAND LIBRARY, 107 N Broad St, Leland, 38756, SAN 348-3363. Tel: 601-686-7353. E-mail: leland@washington.lib.ms.us. *Br Mgr,* Audrey Lee
Open Mon & Tues 9-6, Wed-Fri 10-5
Friends of the Library Group
TORREY WOOD MEMORIAL, 302 East Ave N, Hollandale, 38748-3714, SAN 348-3398. Tel: 662-827-2335. *Br Mgr,* Andrea Ross
Open Mon 2-6, Tues-Fri 3-6
Bookmobiles: 1

GREENWOOD

P GREENWOOD-LEFLORE PUBLIC LIBRARY SYSTEM, 405 W Washington St, 38930-4297. SAN 348-3452. Tel: 662-453-3634. Interlibrary Loan Service Tel: 662-453-3635. FAX: 662-453-0683. E-mail: info@glpls.com. Web Site: www.glpls.com. *Dir,* Naomi Jones; *Circ Supvr, Mgr, ILL,* Candace Hony; E-mail: candyhony@greenwood.lib.ms.us; *Acq,* Sue Lott; *Circ, Libr Asst,* Tad Russell. Subject Specialists: *Hist,* Tad Russell; Staff 9.5 (MLS 3, Non-MLS 6.5)
Founded 1914. Pop 31,861; Circ 42,171
Library Holdings: AV Mats 727; Bk Vols 87,947; Per Subs 176
Special Collections: Genealogy (Mae Wilson McBee Coll), bk, microfilm
Subject Interests: Genealogy
Automation Activity & Vendor Info: (Cataloging) Auto-Graphics, Inc; (Circulation) Auto-Graphics, Inc; (ILL) Auto-Graphics, Inc; (OPAC) Auto-Graphics, Inc
Wireless access
Function: Bk club(s), Bks on cassette, Bks on CD, Children's prog, Computer training, Computers for patron use, Distance learning, Electronic databases & coll, Holiday prog, ILL available, Mail & tel request accepted, Microfiche/film & reading machines, Online cat, Outreach serv, Outside serv via phone, mail, e-mail & web, Photocopying/Printing, Preschool outreach, Prog for children & young adult, Ref & res, Ref serv available, Res performed for a fee, Spoken cassettes & CDs, Story hour, Summer reading prog, Tax forms, Teen prog, Telephone ref, Wheelchair accessible
Special Services for the Blind - Bks on cassette; Bks on CD; Large print bks
Open Mon-Fri 8:30-5:30, Sat 8:30-Noon
Restriction: ID required to use computers (Ltd hrs), Open to pub for ref & circ; with some limitations
Branches: 1
JODIE WILSON BRANCH, 209 ½ E Martin Luther King Jr Dr, 38930, SAN 348-3606. Tel: 662-453-1761. *Br Mgr,* Zhycurie Dobbins; E-mail: z.dobbins98@gmail.com
Circ 815
Library Holdings: Bk Vols 8,377; Per Subs 14
Open Mon-Fri 9-12 & 2-5

S MUSEUM OF THE MISSISSIPPI DELTA*, R A Billups Memorial Library, 1608 Hwy 82 W, 38930. SAN 370-7555. Tel: 662-453-0925. FAX: 662-455-7556. E-mail: info@museumofthemississippidelta.com. Web Site: www.museumofthemississippidelta.com. *Exec Dir,* Cheryl Thornhill; E-mail: director@museumofthemississippidelta.com
Founded 1969
Library Holdings: Bk Titles 400; Per Subs 5
Special Collections: Mississippi Archeology & History, bks, papers
Wireless access
Open Mon-Sat 9-5
Restriction: Non-circulating

GRENADA

J HOLMES COMMUNITY COLLEGE*, Grenada Center Library, 1180 W Monroe St, 38901. Tel: 662-227-2363. FAX: 662-227-2290. Web Site: www.holmescc.edu/library. *Dir, Libr Serv,* James Thompson; E-mail: jathompson@holmescc.edu; *Librn,* Carla Ross; E-mail: cross@holmescc.edu
Library Holdings: Bk Titles 6,000; Per Subs 125
Automation Activity & Vendor Info: (Acquisitions) SirsiDynix; (Cataloging) SirsiDynix; (Circulation) SirsiDynix; (Course Reserve) SirsiDynix; (ILL) SirsiDynix; (OPAC) SirsiDynix
Wireless access
Open Mon-Thurs (Fall & Spring) 7:30-7:30, Fri 8-3:30; Mon-Fri (Summer) 8-3:30

P ELIZABETH JONES LIBRARY, 1050 Fairfield Ave, 38901. SAN 308-8561. Tel: 662-226-2072. FAX: 662-226-8747. Web Site: www.elizabeth.lib.ms.us. *Dir,* Crystal M Osborne; E-mail: crystalosborne@elizabeth.lib.ms.us; *Cataloger, ILL,* Sarah Mims; *Circ, Ref,* Sandra McCaulla; Staff 4 (MLS 1, Non-MLS 3)
Founded 1933. Pop 23,000; Circ 87,563
Library Holdings: Bk Vols 50,000; Per Subs 80
Automation Activity & Vendor Info: (Acquisitions) Innovative Interfaces, Inc
Wireless access
Partic in Miss Libr Asn; Miss Libr Comn Interlibr Loan Network
Open Mon, Wed & Fri 8:30-5, Tues & Thurs 8:30-5:30

GULFPORT

GL HARRISON COUNTY LAW LIBRARY*, 1801 23rd Ave, 39501. SAN 308-8588. Tel: 228-865-4004, 228-865-4068. FAX: 228-865-4067. Web Site: co.harrison.ms.us/departments/law%20library. *Dir,* Ali Kokce; E-mail: akokce@co.harrison.ms.us
Founded 1967
Library Holdings: Bk Titles 1,500; Bk Vols 24,000
Subject Interests: Miss
Wireless access
Open Mon-Fri 8-5

P HARRISON COUNTY LIBRARY SYSTEM*, 12135 Old Hwy 49, 39501. SAN 308-8596. Tel: 228-539-0110. FAX: 228-539-0111. E-mail: reflib@harrison.lib.ms.us. Web Site: www.harrison.lib.ms.us. *Libr Dir,* Sarah Crisler-Ruskey; E-mail: s.ruskey@harrison.lib.ms.us; *Outreach Serv Librn,* Gen Thompson; E-mail: g.thompson@harrison.lib.ms.us; *Acq,* Carrie Turner; E-mail: c.turner@harrison.lib.ms.us; *Cataloger,* Jan Delaune; E-mail: j.delaune@harrison.lib.ms.us; *Info Tech,* Mick McCormick; E-mail: m.mccormick@harrison.lib.ms.us; *ILL,* Diane P McGee; E-mail: d.mcgee@harrison.lib.ms.us; Staff 74 (MLS 7, Non-MLS 67)
Founded 1898. Pop 195,000; Circ 768,332
Library Holdings: Bk Vols 275,560; Per Subs 608
Special Collections: Oral History
Subject Interests: Art, Careers, Genealogy, Local hist, Maps
Automation Activity & Vendor Info: (Acquisitions) Brodart; (Cataloging) SirsiDynix; (Circulation) SirsiDynix
Wireless access
Function: Ref serv available
Publications: Directory of Academic, High School, Public & Special Libraries in Harrison County
Friends of the Library Group
Branches: 9
BILOXI CENTRAL LIBRARY, 580 Howard Ave, Biloxi, 39530, SAN 348-159X. Tel: 228-436-3095. FAX: 228-436-3097. *Head Librn,* Sharon Davis; E-mail: s.davis@harrison.lib.ms.us; Staff 1 (Non-MLS 1)
Founded 2007

Library Holdings: CDs 70; DVDs 200; Bk Vols 6,000
Automation Activity & Vendor Info: (Circulation) Horizon; (OPAC) Horizon
Function: Bks on CD, Children's prog, Computers for patron use, Electronic databases & coll, Holiday prog, Online cat, Photocopying/Printing, Story hour, Summer reading prog, Tax forms
Open Mon-Thurs 9-6, Fri & Sat 10-4
Friends of the Library Group

GULFPORT LIBRARY, 1708 25th Ave, 39501. Tel: 228-871-7171. FAX: 228-871-7067. *Br Mgr,* Jamie Ellston; E-mail: j.ellston@harrison.lib.ms.us; Staff 17 (MLS 2, Non-MLS 15)
Founded 1916. Circ 211,535
Library Holdings: Bk Vols 85,000; Per Subs 150
Open Mon-Thurs 9-6, Fri & Sat 10-4

JERRY LAWRENCE MEMORIAL LIBRARY, 10391 AutoMall Pkwy, D'Iberville, 39540, SAN 376-625X. Tel: 228-392-2279. FAX: 228-396-9573. *Head Librn,* Lucienne Gautier; E-mail: l.gautier@harrison.lib.ms.us; *Ch,* Missy Lucas; E-mail: mlucas@harrison.lib.ms.us; Staff 6 (Non-MLS 6)
Founded 1978. Circ 112,096
Library Holdings: Bk Vols 25,000; Per Subs 30
Open Mon-Thurs 9-5:30, Fri & Sat 9-3
Friends of the Library Group

ORANGE GROVE PUBLIC, 12135 Old Hwy 49, 39503, SAN 377-0001. Tel: 228-832-6924. FAX: 228-832-6926. *Br Mgr,* Mike Alexander; E-mail: m.alexander@harrison.lib.ms.us; Staff 6 (MLS 1, Non-MLS 5)
Founded 1975
Library Holdings: Bk Titles 22,000; Per Subs 15
Open Mon, Wed & Thurs 9-6, Tues 9-7, Fri & Sat 10-4
Friends of the Library Group

PASS CHRISTIAN PUBLIC, 111 Hiern Ave, Pass Christian, 39571, SAN 308-9053. Tel: 228-452-4596. FAX: 228-452-1111. *Br Mgr,* Wendy Allard; E-mail: w.allard@harrison.lib.ms.us; Staff 7 (MLS 1, Non-MLS 6)
Founded 1970
Library Holdings: Bk Titles 34,250; Per Subs 57
Special Collections: Postage Stamps
Open Mon-Thurs 8-6, Fri 9-5, Sat 9-2
Friends of the Library Group

SAUCIER CHILDREN'S LIBRARY, 24014 Church Ave, Saucier, 39574. Tel: 228-539-4419. *Br Mgr,* Rita Aalbertsburg; E-mail: r.aalbertsberg@harrison.lib.ms.us
Automation Activity & Vendor Info: (Circulation) Horizon
Open Mon 12-6, Tues & Thurs 11-5

MARGARET SHERRY BRANCH LIBRARY, 2141 Popps Ferry Rd, Biloxi, 39532-4251, SAN 348-1611. Tel: 228-388-1633. FAX: 228-388-0920. *Br Mgr,* Tara Morgan; E-mail: t.morgan@harrison.lib.ms.us; Staff 3 (MLS 1, Non-MLS 2)
Founded 1983
Library Holdings: Bk Vols 23,157; Per Subs 42
Automation Activity & Vendor Info: (Circulation) Horizon; (OPAC) Horizon
Function: After school storytime, Art exhibits, Bks on cassette, Bks on CD, Children's prog, Computers for patron use, Electronic databases & coll, Holiday prog, ILL available, Mail & tel request accepted, Music CDs, Photocopying/Printing, Prog for adults, Prog for children & young adult, Ref & res, Story hour, Summer reading prog, Tax forms, Teen prog, Wheelchair accessible
Open Mon-Sat 9-5
Friends of the Library Group

WEST BILOXI LIBRARY, 2047 Pass Rd, Biloxi, 39531-3125, SAN 348-162X. Tel: 228-388-5696. FAX: 228-388-5652. *Br Mgr,* Deborah Lundy; E-mail: d.lundy@harrison.lib.ms.us; Staff 2 (MLS 2)
Founded 1968. Circ 90,593
Library Holdings: Bk Vols 35,195; Per Subs 60
Automation Activity & Vendor Info: (Circulation) Horizon; (OPAC) Horizon
Function: After school storytime, Art exhibits, Bks on cassette, Bks on CD, Children's prog, Computers for patron use, Doc delivery serv, Electronic databases & coll, Holiday prog, ILL available, Mail & tel request accepted, Music CDs, Online cat, Photocopying/Printing, Prog for adults, Prog for children & young adult, Ref serv available, Story hour, Summer reading prog, Tax forms, VHS videos
Open Mon-Thurs 9-6, Fri & Sat 10-4
Friends of the Library Group

WOOLMARKET LIBRARY, 13034 Kayleigh Cove, Biloxi, 39532. Tel: 228-354-9464. FAX: 228-354-9466. *Br Mgr,* Donna Posey; E-mail: d.posey@harrison.lib.ms.us; Staff 1 (Non-MLS 1)
Founded 2007. Pop 15,000
Library Holdings: CDs 75; DVDs 250; Bk Titles 4,000
Automation Activity & Vendor Info: (Circulation) Horizon; (OPAC) Horizon
Function: After school storytime, Bks on CD, Children's prog, Computers for patron use, Holiday prog, ILL available, Mail & tel request accepted, Online cat, Photocopying/Printing, Prog for children & young adult, Story hour, Summer reading prog, Tax forms, Teen prog
Open Mon-Thurs 9-6, Fri & Sat 10-4
Restriction: Lending limited to county residents, Non-resident fee
Friends of the Library Group

M MEMORIAL HOSPITAL AT GULFPORT*, Roberta L Burman Medical Library, 4500 13th St, 39501. (Mail add: PO Box 1810, 39502-1810). Tel: 228-865-3157. FAX: 228-867-5141. Web Site: www.gulfportmemorial.com. *Dir,* Connie Keel
Library Holdings: Bk Titles 250
Restriction: Employees & their associates, Staff use only

J MISSISSIPPI GULF COAST COMMUNITY COLLEGE*, Jefferson Davis Campus Learning Resource Center, 2226 Switzer Rd, 39507, SAN 308-860X. Tel: 228-896-2536. Web Site: mgccc.edu/about-the-library/harrison-county-library. *Asst Dean,* Adrienne McPhaul; Tel: 228-895-2514, E-mail: adrienne.mcphaul@mgccc.edu; *Librn,* Kristen Barnett; E-mail: kristen.barnett@mgccc.edu; Staff 5 (MLS 4, Non-MLS 1)
Founded 1966. Enrl 3,862; Fac 125; Highest Degree: Associate
Library Holdings: AV Mats 2,364; Bk Titles 44,208; Per Subs 225
Special Collections: McNaughton Coll
Automation Activity & Vendor Info: (Acquisitions) SirsiDynix; (Circulation) SirsiDynix; (OPAC) SirsiDynix
Wireless access
Function: ILL available, Ref serv available
Publications: Bibliographie Materials; Orientation & Reference Guides
Partic in LYRASIS
Special Services for the Blind - Reader equip
Open Mon-Thurs 7:30am-8:30pm, Fri 7:30-4

HARRISVILLE

P HARRISVILLE PUBLIC LIBRARY*, 1767 Simpson Hwy 469, 39082-4005. (Mail add: PO Box 307, 39082-0307), SAN 376-6373. Tel: 601-847-1268. FAX: 601-847-1268. E-mail: harrisvi@cmrls.lib.ms.us. Web Site: cmrls.lib.ms.us/cmrlsbranches/harrisville. *Br Mgr,* Kathie Ward
Library Holdings: Bk Titles 4,000
Function: Photocopying/Printing
Open Mon & Thurs 2-6, Tues 3-6, Sat 9-Noon
Friends of the Library Group

HATTIESBURG

M FORREST COUNTY GENERAL HOSPITAL*, Library Services, 6051 Hwy 49 S, 39402. (Mail add: PO Box 16389, 39404-6389), SAN 325-478X. Tel: 601-288-4214. FAX: 601-288-4209. E-mail: medicallibrary@forrestgeneral.com. Web Site: www.forresthealth.org. *Dir,* Vicky Buxton; Fax: 601-288-4209, E-mail: vbuxton@forrestgeneral.com; Staff 1 (Non-MLS 1)
Founded 1973
Library Holdings: Bk Vols 1,500; Per Subs 42
Subject Interests: Med
Wireless access
Partic in National Network of Libraries of Medicine Region 2; SEND
Restriction: Staff use only

P THE LIBRARY OF HATTIESBURG, PETAL, FORREST COUNTY*, 329 Hardy St, 39401-3496. SAN 348-3754. Tel: 601-582-4461. FAX: 601-582-5338. Web Site: hattlibrary.org. *Dir,* Sean Farrell; E-mail: sean@hpfc.lib.ms.us; *Assoc Dir,* Christina Keiper; E-mail: chris@hpfc.lib.ms.us; *Assoc Dir,* Adam Singletary; E-mail: adam@hpfc.lib.ms.us; *Youth Serv Librn,* Deb White; E-mail: dw@hpfc.lib.ms.us; Staff 37 (MLS 5, Non-MLS 32)
Founded 1916. Pop 74,927; Circ 184,569
Library Holdings: Bk Vols 150,000; Per Subs 222
Special Collections: Adult New Reader's Coll. State Document Depository
Subject Interests: Genealogy, Miss
Automation Activity & Vendor Info: (Cataloging) Innovative Interfaces, Inc
Wireless access
Publications: The Library (Newsletter)
Partic in National Network of Libraries of Medicine Region 2
Open Mon-Thurs 8-8, Fri & Sat 10-4
Friends of the Library Group
Branches: 1

PETAL BRANCH, 714 S Main St, Petal, 39465, SAN 348-3789. Tel: 601-584-7610. *Dir,* Pamela J Pridgen; E-mail: pamela@hpfc.lib.ms.us
Library Holdings: Bk Vols 12,748
Open Mon-Fri 9-6, Sat 9-1
Friends of the Library Group

C UNIVERSITY OF SOUTHERN MISSISSIPPI LIBRARY*, Joseph Anderson Cook Library, 124 Golden Eagle Dr, 39406. (Mail add: 118 College Dr, No 5053, 39406), SAN 348-3843. Tel: 601-266-4241. Circulation Tel: 601-266-4250. Interlibrary Loan Service Tel: 601-266-4256. Reference Tel: 601-266-4249. FAX: 601-266-6033. Web Site: www.lib.usm.edu. *Dean of Libr,* John Eye; Tel: 601-266-4362, E-mail: john.eye@usm.edu; *Head, Libr Tech,* Lisa R Jones; Tel: 601-266-4244, E-mail: Lisa.R.Jones@usm.edu; *Head, Pub Serv,* Tisha Zelner; Tel: 601-266-6167, E-mail: Tisha.Zelner@usm.edu; *Head, Tech Serv,* Position Currently Open; Staff 31 (MLS 12, Non-MLS 19)
Founded 1912. Enrl 14,478; Fac 896; Highest Degree: Doctorate
Library Holdings: AV Mats 26,502; e-books 160,853; Bk Titles 1,389,511; Bk Vols 1,658,991; Per Subs 25,748
Subject Interests: Biology, Chem, Computers, Criminal justice, Educ, Letters, Libr sci, Music, Nursing, Polymer sci, Psychol
Automation Activity & Vendor Info: (Acquisitions) SirsiDynix; (Cataloging) SirsiDynix; (Circulation) SirsiDynix; (Course Reserve) SirsiDynix; (ILL) OCLC ILLiad; (Media Booking) SirsiDynix; (OPAC) SirsiDynix; (Serials) SirsiDynix
Wireless access
Publications: Juvenile Miscellany; Library Focus (Newsletter)
Partic in LYRASIS
Open Mon-Thurs 7am- 2am, Fri 7-6, Sat 9-6, Sun Noon-2am
Friends of the Library Group
Departmental Libraries:
GULF COAST LIBRARY
See Separate Entry in Long Beach
WILLIAM DAVID MCCAIN LIBRARY & ARCHIVES, 118 College Dr, No 5148, 39406, SAN 369-772X. Tel: 601-266-4345. FAX: 601-226-6269. *Spec Coll Librn,* Jennifer Brannock; Tel: 601-266-4347, E-mail: jennifer.brannock@usm.edu
Founded 1976
Library Holdings: Bk Vols 151,877
Special Collections: Association of American Editorial Cartoonists Coll; Association of American Railroads Coll; Children's Literature (Lena Y de Grummond Coll); Cleanth Brooks Literature Coll; Confederate Literature (Ernest A Walen Coll); Gulf, Mobile & Ohio Railroad Records Coll; Mississippiana Coll; Papers of Mississippi Governor & United States Senator Theodore C Bilbo, 1915-1947; Papers of Mississippi Governors Paul Johnson Sr & Paul Johnson Jr, 1917-1970; Papers of United States Representative William M Colmer, 1933-1973; Paul Yoder Marching Band Music Coll; Rare Book Coll; University Archives
Subject Interests: 19th-20th Century Am Lit, 19th-20th Century British, Art for children, Civil War, Drawings, Editorial cartoons, Genealogy, Hist of South, Lit for children, Literary criticism, Miss docs, Miss fiction, Miss publs
Partic in LYRASIS; OCLC Online Computer Library Center, Inc
Open Mon-Fri 8-5

C WILLIAM CAREY UNIVERSITY LIBRARIES*, Dumas L Smith/ I E Rouse Library, 710 William Carey Pkwy, 39401. SAN 348-3878. Tel: 601-318-6169. FAX: 601-318-6171. Web Site: libguides.wmcarey.edu. *Dir of Libr,* Reese Powell; E-mail: rpowell@wmcarey.edu; *Archival Librn,* Christy Calhoun; E-mail: ccalhoun@wmcarey.edu; *Cat Librn,* Erin Small; E-mail: esmall@wmcarey.edu; *Pub Serv Librn,* Nicole Aranda; E-mail: naranda@wmcarey.edu; *Syst/Ref Librn,* Dee Lumpkin; E-mail: dlumpkin@wmcarey.edu
Founded 1906. Enrl 2,400; Fac 96; Highest Degree: Master
Library Holdings: AV Mats 1,220; Bk Titles 75,000; Bk Vols 94,995; Per Subs 773
Special Collections: Church Music (Clarence Dickinson Coll)
Subject Interests: Art, Bus, Educ, Music, Nursing, Relig studies
Automation Activity & Vendor Info: (Acquisitions) OCLC ILLiad; (Cataloging) OCLC ILLiad; (Circulation) OCLC ILLiad; (Course Reserve) OCLC ILLiad; (OPAC) OCLC ILLiad; (Serials) OCLC ILLiad
Wireless access
Function: Electronic databases & coll, ILL available, Photocopying/Printing, Ref serv available, VHS videos, Wheelchair accessible
Partic in LYRASIS
Restriction: Open to researchers by request, Open to students, fac & staff, Res pass required for non-affiliated visitors, Use of others with permission of librn
Friends of the Library Group
Departmental Libraries:
TRADITION LIBRARY, 19640 Hwy 67, Biloxi, 39532-8666, SAN 348-3932. Tel: 228-702-1890. *Regional Librn,* Peggy H Gossage; E-mail: pgossage@wmcarey.edu
Library Holdings: Bk Vols 18,000; Per Subs 100
Open Mon-Thurs 8am-10pm, Fri 8-4, Sat 10-2

HAZLEHURST

P COPIAH-JEFFERSON REGIONAL LIBRARY SYSTEM*, George W Covington Memorial Library, 223 S Extension St, 39083-3339. SAN 348-3967. Tel: 601-894-1681. FAX: 601-894-1672. Web Site: www.copjeflibrary.blogspot.com. *Dir,* Roxanne Mack; E-mail: director@copjef.lib.ms.us; Staff 16 (Non-MLS 16)
Founded 1950. Pop 36,500; Circ 70,760
Library Holdings: Bk Vols 45,000
Special Collections: Mississippi Coll (Archives Room)
Subject Interests: African-Am hist
Automation Activity & Vendor Info: (Cataloging) Innovative Interfaces, Inc; (Circulation) Innovative Interfaces, Inc
Wireless access
Partic in Longleaf Library Consortium
Open Mon-Fri 9-6, Sat 9-12
Friends of the Library Group
Branches: 4
J T BIGGS JR MEMORIAL LIBRARY, 200 S Jackson St, Crystal Springs, 39059, SAN 348-4025. Tel: 601-892-3205. FAX: 601-892-2138. E-mail: cslibmgr@gmail.com.
Partic in National Network of Libraries of Medicine Region 2
Open Mon-Fri 9-5, Sat 9-11:30
Friends of the Library Group
GEORGETOWN LIBRARY, 1164 Railroad Ave, Georgetown, 39078, SAN 377-9955. Tel: 601-858-2202. FAX: 601-858-2202. E-mail: georgetownlib@gmail.com.
Open Mon-Fri 9-11:30 & 12:30-5
LONGIE DALE HAMILTON MEMORIAL LIBRARY, 1012 Spring St, Wesson, 39191. (Mail add: PO Box 299, Wesson, 39191-0299), SAN 348-4084. Tel: 601-643-5725. FAX: 601-643-5725. E-mail: welibmgr@gmail.com.
Special Collections: Wesson Historical Artifacts & Information
Open Mon-Fri 10-12 & 1-5
Friends of the Library Group
JEFFERSON COUNTY LIBRARY, 1269 S Main St, Fayette, 39069, SAN 348-405X. Tel: 601-786-3982. FAX: 601-786-9646. E-mail: falibmgr@gmail.com.
Open Mon-Thurs 9-6, Fri 9-5

HERNANDO

P FIRST REGIONAL LIBRARY*, Headquarters Library, 370 W Commerce St, 38632. SAN 348-4114. Tel: 662-429-4439. FAX: 662-429-8853. Web Site: www.firstregional.org. *Dir,* Meredith Wickham; E-mail: mwickham@firstregional.org; *Asst Dir, Pub Serv,* Barbara Evans; E-mail: bevans@firstregional.org; *Youth Serv Coordr,* Hanna Lee; E-mail: hlee@firstregional.org; Staff 149 (MLS 19, Non-MLS 130)
Founded 1950. Pop 289,167; Circ 1,306,906. Sal $3,490,313
Library Holdings: AV Mats 49,891; e-books 8,235; Electronic Media & Resources 44; Large Print Bks 15,561; Bk Titles 561,380; Per Subs 1,013; Talking Bks 31,967; Videos 31,206
Special Collections: Mississippi History & Literature. State Document Depository
Automation Activity & Vendor Info: (Acquisitions) SirsiDynix; (Cataloging) SirsiDynix; (Circulation) SirsiDynix; (Discovery) EBSCO Discovery Service; (OPAC) SirsiDynix
Wireless access
Function: Adult bk club, After school storytime, Art exhibits, Audiobks via web, Bilingual assistance for Spanish patrons, Bk club(s), Bks on CD, Children's prog, Computers for patron use, Distance learning, Electronic databases & coll, Free DVD rentals, Genealogy discussion group, Holiday prog, Home delivery & serv to seniorr ctr & nursing homes, Homework prog, ILL available, Learning ctr, Legal assistance to inmates, Mail & tel request accepted, Microfiche/film & reading machines, Music CDs, Online cat, Outreach serv, Outside serv via phone, mail, e-mail & web, OverDrive digital audio bks, Photocopying/Printing, Preschool outreach, Preschool reading prog, Printer for laptops & handheld devices, Prog for adults, Prog for children & young adult, Ref serv available, Scanner, Senior computer classes, Senior outreach, Spoken cassettes & CDs, Story hour, Summer & winter reading prog, Summer reading prog, Tax forms, Teen prog, Telephone ref, Wheelchair accessible, Workshops, Writing prog
Publications: What's Happening (Newsletter)
Partic in Dancing Rabbit Library Consortium; Mississippi Library Partnership
Special Services for the Blind - Assistive/Adapted tech devices, equip & products; BiFolkal kits; Bks on CD; Closed circuit TV magnifier; Computer access aids; Large print bks; Playaways (bks on MP3); Recorded bks; ZoomText magnification & reading software
Open Mon-Thurs 10-7, Fri 10-5:30, Sat 10-5
Friends of the Library Group

Branches: 13

BATESVILLE PUBLIC LIBRARY, 206 Hwy 51 N, Batesville, 38606, SAN 348-4149. Tel: 662-563-1038. FAX: 662-563-6640. *Head Libra,* Emily Burton; E-mail: eburton@firstregional.org; Staff 7 (MLS 1, Non-MLS 6)
Founded 1932
Open Mon 10-8, Tues-Thurs 10-6, Fri 10-5:30, Sat 10-4:30
Friends of the Library Group

B J CHAIN PUBLIC LIBRARY, 6619 Hwy 305 N, Olive Branch, 38654, SAN 348-4173. Tel: 662-895-5900. FAX: 662-895-9171. *Head Librn,* Suzanne Argo; E-mail: suzannea@firstregional.org; *Asst Mgr, Ref Spec,* Sherry Mosley; E-mail: sherryj@firstregional.org; *Youth Serv Spec,* Teresa Spiers; E-mail: tspiers@firstregional.org
Founded 1951
Open Mon-Thurs 10-8, Fri 10-6, Sat 10-5, Sun 2-5
Friends of the Library Group

M R DAVIS PUBLIC LIBRARY, 8554 Northwest Dr, Southaven, 38671, SAN 348-4440. Tel: 662-342-0102. FAX: 662-342-0556. *Head Librn,* Caroline Barnett; E-mail: cbarnett@firstregional.org; *Asst Br Mgr,* Linda Willis; E-mail: lwillis@firstregional.org; Staff 11 (MLS 1, Non-MLS 10)
Founded 1962
Open Mon-Thurs 10-8, Fri 10-6, Sat 10-5, Sun 2-5
Friends of the Library Group

M R DYE PUBLIC LIBRARY, 2885 Goodman Rd, Horn Lake, 38637, SAN 348-4297. Tel: 662-393-5654. FAX: 662-342-9468. *Head Librn,* Debra Gilbert; E-mail: dgilbert@firstregional.org; Staff 1 (MLS 1)
Founded 1979
Open Mon & Tues 10-7, Wed & Thurs 10-6, Fri & Sat 10-5:30
Friends of the Library Group

JESSIE J EDWARDS PUBLIC LIBRARY, 610 E Central Ave, Coldwater, 38618. (Mail add: PO Box 591, Coldwater, 38618-0591), SAN 348-4203. Tel: 662-622-5573. FAX: 662-622-5846. *Head Librn,* Kristin Causey; E-mail: kcausey@firstregional.org; *Asst Br Mgr,* Kiras Daniel
Founded 1951
Open Mon 10-6, Tues-Thurs 12-6, Sat 10-Noon
Friends of the Library Group

HERNANDO PUBLIC LIBRARY, 370 W Commerce St, 38632. Tel: 662-429-4439. FAX: 662-429-8625. *Head Librn,* Jesse Pool; E-mail: jpool@firstregional.org; *Youth Spec,* Denise McOwen; E-mail: dmcowen@firstregional.org
Founded 1950
Open Mon-Thurs 10-7, Fri 10-5:30, Sat 10-5

ROBERT C IRWIN PUBLIC LIBRARY, 1285 Kenny Hill Ave, Tunica, 38676, SAN 348-4327. Tel: 662-363-2162. FAX: 662-357-5929. *Br Mgr,* Tasha Jackson-Sow; E-mail: tjackson-sow@firstregional.org; *Youth Spec,* Brenda Garrett; E-mail: brendag@firstregional.org
Founded 1969
Open Mon-Thurs 9-6, Fri 9:30-5:30, Sat 10-2
Friends of the Library Group

LAFAYETTE COUNTY-OXFORD PUBLIC LIBRARY, 401 Bramlett Blvd, Oxford, 38655, SAN 348-4351. Tel: 662-234-5751. FAX: 662-234-3155. *Head Librn,* Laura Beth Walker; E-mail: lbwalker@firstregional.org; *Ref Librn,* Corey Vinson; E-mail: cvinson@firstregional.org; *Youth Librn,* Ally Watkins; E-mail: awatkins@firstregional.org; *Youth Spec,* Meredith Wulff; E-mail: mwulff@firstregional.org; Staff 6 (MLS 3, Non-MLS 3)
Founded 1930. Pop 40,000; Circ 250,000
Open Mon-Thurs 10-8, Fri & Sat 10-5:30, Sun 2-5
Friends of the Library Group

SAM LAPIDUS MEMORIAL PUBLIC LIBRARY, 108 Missouri Ave, Crenshaw, 38621, SAN 348-4238. Tel: 662-382-7479. FAX: 662-382-7479. *Br Mgr,* Charlene Bradford; E-mail: cbradford@firstregional.org
Founded 1951
Open Mon & Wed 10-5:30, Fri 10-5, Sat 10-Noon
Friends of the Library Group

EMILY JONES POINTER PUBLIC LIBRARY, 104 Main St, Como, 38619. (Mail add: PO Box 128, Como, 38632), SAN 348-4262. Tel: 662-526-5283. FAX: 662-526-5200. *Br Mgr,* Amy Henderson; E-mail: ahenderson@firstregional.org; *Youth Spec,* Veneda Ruby; E-mail: vruby@firstregional.org
Founded 1951
Open Mon & Wed-Fri 10-6, Sat 10-Noon
Friends of the Library Group

SARDIS PUBLIC LIBRARY, 101 McLaurin St, Sardis, 38666, SAN 348-4386. Tel: 662-487-2126. FAX: 662-487-2126. *Br Mgr,* Charlene Bradford; E-mail: charleneb@firstregional.org; *Youth Spec,* Ciardi Love; E-mail: clove@firstregional.org
Founded 1947
Open Tues 10-6, Wed & Thurs 12-6, Fri 12-5, Sat 12-3
Friends of the Library Group

SENATOBIA PUBLIC LIBRARY, 222 Ward St, Senatobia, 38668, SAN 348-4416. Tel: 662-562-6791. FAX: 662-562-0414. *Head Librn,* Kristin Causey; E-mail: kcausey@firstregional.org; *Youth Spec,* Laura Sellers; E-mail: lauras@firstregional.org
Open Mon-Thurs 10-6, Fri 10-5:30, Sat 10-1
Friends of the Library Group

WALLS PUBLIC LIBRARY, 7181 Delta Bluff Pkwy, Walls, 38680, SAN 378-0287. Tel: 662-781-3664. FAX: 662-781-3427. *Head Librn,* Jesse Pool; E-mail: jpool@firstregional.org; *Asst Br Mgr,* Yolanda Priddy; E-mail: ypriddy@firstregional.org
Founded 1998
Open Mon-Thurs 10-6, Fri 10-5:30, Sat 10-4
Friends of the Library Group

Bookmobiles: 1. Early Childhood Servs Coordr, Victoria Penny

HOLLY SPRINGS

P MARSHALL COUNTY LIBRARY SYSTEM*, 109 E Gholson Ave, 38635. SAN 348-4475. Tel: 662-252-3823. FAX: 662-252-3066. E-mail: holly@marshall.lib.ms.us. Web Site: marshall.lib.ms.us. *Dir,* Amanda McDonald; E-mail: amcdonald@marshall.lib.ms.us; Staff 10.5 (MLS 1.5, Non-MLS 9)
Founded 1955. Pop 38,000; Circ 20,000
Library Holdings: Audiobooks 799; Bks on Deafness & Sign Lang 6; Braille Volumes 1; DVDs 234; Electronic Media & Resources 93; Large Print Bks 286; Microforms 60; Bk Titles 30,000; Bk Vols 38,000; Per Subs 75
Special Collections: Marshall County Historical & Genealogical Coll
Automation Activity & Vendor Info: (Cataloging) Book Systems; (Circulation) Book Systems; (OPAC) Book Systems; (Serials) EBSCO Online
Wireless access
Function: 24/7 Online cat, Activity rm, Archival coll, Audiobks on Playaways & MP3, Bks on CD, Children's prog, Computers for patron use, For res purposes, Free DVD rentals, Genealogy discussion group, Govt ref serv, ILL available, Internet access, Laminating, Large print keyboards, Magazines, Meeting rooms, Microfiche/film & reading machines, Notary serv, Online cat, Outreach serv, Photocopying/Printing, Printer for laptops & handheld devices, Scanner, Spanish lang bks, Summer reading prog, Tax forms, Telephone ref, Wheelchair accessible
Partic in MAGNOLIA
Open Mon & Wed 9-6, Tues & Thurs 9-8, Fri 9-5, Sat 8-2
Friends of the Library Group

Branches: 2

RUTH B FRENCH LIBRARY, 161 S Hwy 309, Byhalia, 38611. (Mail add: PO Box 412, Byhalia, 38611), SAN 348-4505. Tel: 662-838-4024. FAX: 662-838-6900. *Br Mgr,* Position Currently Open; *Br Mgr,* Adrian Florence; E-mail: aflorence@marshall.lib.ms.us
Open Mon 12-7, Tues & Fri 1-5, Wed 10-6, Thurs 2-7

POTTS CAMP PUBLIC, 20 S Center St, Potts Camp, 38659. Tel: 601-333-7068. FAX: 601-333-7096. *Br Mgr,* Liz Boyett; E-mail: lboyett@marshall.lib.ms.us
Open Mon-Fri 1-5

C RUST COLLEGE*, Leontyne Price Library, 150 E Rust Ave, 38635. SAN 308-8669. Tel: 662-252-8000, Ext 4100. FAX: 662-252-8873. Web Site: www.rustcollege.edu/leontyneprice_about_the_library.html. *Head Librn,* Anita W Moore; E-mail: amoore@rustcollege.edu; *Pub Serv Librn,* Marjorie Sise; E-mail: msise@rustcollege.edu; *Reader Serv Librn,* Mattie Walker; E-mail: mwalker@rustcollege.edu; *Ref Serv, Ser, Spec Coll Librn,* Cynthia Cole; E-mail: ccole@rustcollege.edu; *AV, Ref Serv,* Freddie Jeffries; E-mail: fjeffries@rustcollege.edu; *Tech Serv,* Gwendolyn Jones; E-mail: gjones@rustcollege.edu; Staff 7 (MLS 2, Non-MLS 5)
Founded 1866. Enrl 1,100; Fac 56; Highest Degree: Bachelor
Library Holdings: Bk Titles 122,033; Per Subs 366
Special Collections: International Coll; Roy Wilkins Coll; United Methodist Religious Coll
Wireless access
Publications: Acquisition List (Quarterly); Circulation Handbook; Collection Development Handbook; Library Manual; Roy Wilkins Special Collections Book
Partic in Coop Col Libr Ctr, Inc; LYRASIS
Open Mon-Thurs 7:45am-Midnight, Fri 7:45-6, Sat 10-2, Sun 4-10

HORN LAKE

S AMERICAN CONTRACT BRIDGE LEAGUE*, Albert H Morehead Memorial Library, 6575 Windchase Blvd, 38637. SAN 371-9464. Tel: 662-253-3100. FAX: 662-253-3187. E-mail: service@acbl.org. Web Site: www.acbl.org. *Librn,* Tracey Yarbro; Tel: 662-253-3106, E-mail: tracey.yarbro@acbl.org
Founded 1969
Library Holdings: Bk Titles 3,200; Per Subs 500
Wireless access
Open Mon-Fri 8-4:30

INDIANOLA

P SUNFLOWER COUNTY LIBRARY SYSTEM*, Administrative Offices, 201 Cypress Dr, 38751. SAN 348-4599. Tel: 622-887-2153. FAX: 662-887-1618. Web Site: www.sunflower.lib.ms.us. *Dir,* Mary Ann Griffin; E-mail: magriffin@sunflower.lib.ms.us; *Asst Dir,* Kay Slater; E-mail: kslater@sunflower.lib.ms.us; *Coordr, Br Serv,* Nita Dill; E-mail: ndill@sunflower.lib.ms.us
Founded 1938. Pop 35,129; Circ 63,129
Library Holdings: Bk Titles 58,259; Bk Vols 93,788; Per Subs 147
Partic in Dancing Rabbit Library Consortium; OCLC Online Computer Library Center, Inc
Open Mon-Fri 8:30-5
Friends of the Library Group
Branches: 5
DREW PUBLIC, 290 W Park Ave, Drew, 38737, SAN 348-4629. Tel: 662-745-2237. FAX: 662-745-3778. E-mail: drew@sunflower.lib.ms.us.
Library Holdings: Bk Vols 17,000
Open Mon & Wed 12-6, Fri 10-5
INVERNESS PUBLIC, 802 E Grand Ave, Inverness, 38753, SAN 348-4688. Tel: 662-265-5179. FAX: 662-265-5502. E-mail: inverness@sunflower.lib.ms.us.
Library Holdings: Bk Vols 10,000
Open Tues & Thurs 11-5, Wed 1-5
HENRY M SEYMOUR LIBRARY, 201 Cypress Dr, 38751, SAN 348-4718. Tel: 662-887-1672. FAX: 662-887-1618. E-mail: seymour@sunflower.lib.ms.us.
Library Holdings: Bk Vols 45,588
Open Mon, Tues & Thurs 9-6, Wed & Fri 9-5, Sat 10-3
Friends of the Library Group
KATHY JUNE SHERIFF LIBRARY, 802 Johnny Russell Dr, Moorhead, 38761, SAN 348-4742. Tel: 662-246-8070. E-mail: moorhead@sunflower.lib.ms.us.
Library Holdings: Bk Vols 10,000
Open Mon & Wed 12-6
HORACE STANSEL MEMORIAL, 128 S Ruby St, Ruleville, 38771, SAN 348-4653. Tel: 662-756-2226. FAX: 662-756-2809. E-mail: ruleville@sunflower.lib.ms.us.
Pop 3,000
Library Holdings: Bk Vols 12,200
Function: After school storytime, Art exhibits, Bks on cassette, Bks on CD, Children's prog, Computers for patron use, Holiday prog, Internet access, Online cat, Online ref, Photocopying/Printing, Prog for adults, Prog for children & young adult, Ref serv available, Story hour, Summer reading prog, Tax forms, Teen prog, Wheelchair accessible
Open Tues & Thurs 1-6
Friends of the Library Group

ITTA BENA

C MISSISSIPPI VALLEY STATE UNIVERSITY*, James Herbert White Library, 14000 Hwy 82 W, 38941. SAN 308-8685. Tel: 662-254-3494. Circulation Tel: 662-254-3500. Reference Tel: 662-254-3497. FAX: 662-254-3499. E-mail: jhwhitelibrary@mvsu.edu. Web Site: www.mvsu.edu/library. *Dir,* Mantra Henderson; E-mail: mlhenderson@mvsu.edu; Staff 10 (MLS 5, Non-MLS 5)
Founded 1950. Enrl 2,138; Highest Degree: Master
Library Holdings: e-books 40,000; e-journals 3,217; Bk Titles 127,541; Per Subs 402
Special Collections: Martin Luther King Shelf; Mississippi Coll. State Document Depository
Subject Interests: Educ, Miss, Negroes
Automation Activity & Vendor Info: (Acquisitions) Ex Libris Group; (Cataloging) Ex Libris Group; (Circulation) Ex Libris Group; (Course Reserve) Docutek; (ILL) OCLC; (Media Booking) Ex Libris Group; (OPAC) Ex Libris Group; (Serials) Ex Libris Group
Wireless access
Function: Ref serv available
Publications: James Herbert White Library (Newsletter)
Partic in Dancing Rabbit Library Consortium; LYRASIS; National Network of Libraries of Medicine Region 2
Open Mon-Thurs 7:30am-10pm, Fri 7:30-7, Sat 10-4, Sun 2-10

JACKSON

CR BELHAVEN UNIVERSITY*, Warren A Hood Library, 1500 Peachtree St, 39202. SAN 308-8693. Tel: 601-968-5948. FAX: 601-968-5968. E-mail: libcomments@belhaven.edu. Web Site: www.belhaven.edu/library. *Dir of Libr,* Chris Cullnane; Tel: 601-968-5947, E-mail: ccullnane@belhaven.edu; *Cat Librn,* Position Currently Open; *Circ Librn,* Daylan Stephens; E-mail: dstephens@belhaven.edu; *Database Librn,* Tracy Harrington; E-mail: tharrington@belhaven.edu; *Mat Mgr,* Position Currently Open; *Per,* Charles Gaudin; Tel: 601-968-5951, E-mail: cgaudin@belhaven.edu; Staff 5 (MLS 5)
Founded 1910. Enrl 3,152; Fac 111; Highest Degree: Master
Library Holdings: CDs 623; DVDs 582; e-books 41,200; e-journals 10,000; Music Scores 327; Bk Titles 167,000; Per Subs 223
Subject Interests: Art, Music, Presbyterian records, Relig studies
Automation Activity & Vendor Info: (Cataloging) Innovative Interfaces, Inc; (Circulation) Innovative Interfaces, Inc; (ILL) OCLC; (OPAC) Innovative Interfaces, Inc
Wireless access
Partic in LYRASIS
Restriction: Private libr

P JACKSON/HINDS LIBRARY SYSTEM*, Administrative Office, 300 N State St, 39201-1705. SAN 348-4807. Tel: 601-968-5825. Toll Free Tel: 800-968-5803. FAX: 601-968-5817. E-mail: info@jhlibrary.org. Web Site: www.jhlibrary.com. *Exec Dir,* Patty Furr; E-mail: pfurr@jhlibrary.org; *Dep Dir,* Kim Corbett; E-mail: kcorbett@jhlibrary.org; *Dir, Human Res,* Brenette Nichols; E-mail: bnichols@jhlibrary.org
Wireless access
Open Mon-Fri 8-5
Friends of the Library Group
Branches: 14
ELLA BESS AUSTIN LIBRARY, 420 W Cunningham Ave, Terry, 39170. (Mail add: PO Box 155, Terry, 39170-0155), SAN 348-5765. Tel: 601-878-5336. FAX: 601-878-0609. E-mail: terry@jhlibrary.org. *Br Mgr,* Cassandra Cooper; Staff 4 (Non-MLS 4)
Automation Activity & Vendor Info: (Acquisitions) SirsiDynix-WorkFlows; (Cataloging) SirsiDynix-WorkFlows; (Circulation) SirsiDynix-WorkFlows
Function: 24/7 Online cat, Bks on CD, Children's prog, Computers for patron use, Electronic databases & coll, Free DVD rentals, ILL available, Magazines, Movies, Online cat, Online ref, Photocopying/Printing, Prog for adults, Prog for children & young adult, Story hour, Summer reading prog, Tax forms, Wheelchair accessible
Open Mon-Fri 9-6, Sat 9-1
Friends of the Library Group
R G BOLDEN/ANNA BELL-MOORE LIBRARY, 1444 Wiggins Rd, 39209-4430, SAN 348-5889. Tel: 601-922-6076. FAX: 601-923-8144. E-mail: boldenmoore@jhlibrary.org. *Br Mgr,* Patrick McCarty; Staff 1 (Non-MLS 1)
Open Mon, Wed & Thurs 9-6, Tues 9-7, Fri & Sat 10-2
Friends of the Library Group
BEVERLEY J BROWN LIBRARY, 7395 South Siwell Rd, Byram, 39272-8741, SAN 374-4159. Tel: 601-372-0954. FAX: 601-373-7164. E-mail: byram@jhlibrary.org. *Br Mgr,* Debra Perkins; Staff 3 (Non-MLS 3)
Open Mon, Wed & Thurs 9-6, Tues 9-7, Fri 9-4, Sat 10-2
Friends of the Library Group
MEDGAR EVERS LIBRARY, 4215 Medgar Evers Blvd, 39213-5210, SAN 348-5048. Tel: 601-982-2867. FAX: 601-982-2598. E-mail: evers@jhlibrary.org. *Br Librn,* Anne Sanders; Staff 3 (Non-MLS 3)
Open Mon, Wed & Thurs 9-6, Tues 9-7, Fri 9-5, Sat 10-4
Friends of the Library Group
LOIS A FLAGG LIBRARY, 105 Williamson Ave, Edwards, 39066. (Mail add: PO Box 140, Edwards, 39066-0140), SAN 328-8196. Tel: 601-852-2230. FAX: 601-852-4539. E-mail: edwards@jhlibrary.org. *Br Mgr,* Jessica Johnson-Williams; Staff 1 (Non-MLS 1)
Open Mon-Thurs 9-6, Sat 9-1
Friends of the Library Group
FANNIE LOU HAMER LIBRARY, 3450 Albermarle Rd, 39213-6507, SAN 348-4831. Tel: 601-362-3012. FAX: 601-362-1505. E-mail: hamer@jhlibrary.org. *Interim Br Mgr,* Rosemary Luckett; Staff 1 (Non-MLS 1)
Open Mon-Fri 9-5
Friends of the Library Group
ANNIE THOMPSON JEFFERS LIBRARY, 111 Madison St, Bolton, 39041. (Mail add: PO Box 358, Bolton, 39041-0358), SAN 370-7911. Tel: 601-866-4247. FAX: 601-866-4653. E-mail: bolton@jhlibrary.org. *Br Mgr,* Alfenette Robinson; Staff 1 (Non-MLS 1)
Open Mon-Thurs 9-6, Fri & Sat 9-1
Friends of the Library Group
EVELYN TAYLOR MAJURE LIBRARY, 217 W Main St, Utica, 39175-0340, SAN 348-582X. Tel: 601-885-8381. FAX: 601-885-2612. E-mail: utica@jhlibrary.org. *Br Librn,* Kristin Finch; Staff 1 (Non-MLS 1)
Open Mon-Thurs 9-6, Sat 9-1
Friends of the Library Group
MARGARET WALKER ALEXANDER LIBRARY, 2525 Robinson Rd, 39209-6256, SAN 348-5226. Tel: 601-354-8911. FAX: 601-354-8912. E-mail: alexander@jhlibrary.org. *Br Mgr,* Karen Wilson; Staff 4 (Non-MLS 4)
Automation Activity & Vendor Info: (Acquisitions) SirsiDynix-WorkFlows; (Cataloging) SirsiDynix-WorkFlows; (Circulation) SirsiDynix-WorkFlows; (OPAC) SirsiDynix
Function: 24/7 Online cat, Bks on CD, Computers for patron use, Free DVD rentals, ILL available, Internet access, Meeting rooms, Movies, Online cat, Online ref, Outside serv via phone, mail, e-mail & web,

Photocopying/Printing, Prog for adults, Prog for children & young adult, Story hour, Summer reading prog, Tax forms, Wheelchair accessible
Open Mon, Wed & Thurs 9-6, Tues 9-7, Fri 9-5, Sat 10-4
Friends of the Library Group
WILLIE MORRIS BRANCH, 4912 Old Canton Rd, 39211-5404, SAN 370-7903. Tel: 601-987-8181. FAX: 601-987-8212. E-mail: morris@jhlibrary.org. *Br Mgr,* Carolyn Carter; Staff 4 (Non-MLS 4)
Open Mon, Wed & Thurs 9-6, Tues 9-7, Fri 9-5, Sat 10-4
Friends of the Library Group
QUISENBERRY LIBRARY, 605 E Northside Dr, Clinton, 39056-5121, SAN 348-498X. Tel: 601-924-5684. FAX: 601-924-1953. E-mail: quisenberry@jhlibrary.org. *Br Libr*n, Susan Delmas; Staff 6 (Non-MLS 6)
Open Mon & Wed 9-7, Tues & Thurs 9-8, Fri & Sat 10-4
Friends of the Library Group
RAYMOND PUBLIC LIBRARY, 126 W Court St, Raymond, 39154. (Mail add: PO Box 14, Raymond, 39154-0014), SAN 348-5587. Tel: 601-857-8721. FAX: 601-857-4281. E-mail: raymond@jhlibrary.org. *Br Mgr,* Austin Farmer; Staff 2 (Non-MLS 2)
Open Mon, Tues & Thurs 9-6, Wed 9-1, Fri 9-5
Friends of the Library Group
EUDORA WELTY LIBRARY (MAIN LIBRARY), 300 North State St, 39201-1705. Tel: 601-968-5811. Toll Free Tel: 800-968-5803. FAX: 601-968-5806. E-mail: welty@jhlibrary.org. *Ref Mgr,* Sue Prendergust; Staff 15 (MLS 1, Non-MLS 14)
Open Mon-Thurs 9-8, Fri & Sat 9-9
Friends of the Library Group
RICHARD WRIGHT LIBRARY, 515 W McDowell Rd, 39204-5547, SAN 348-5706. Tel: 601-372-1621. FAX: 601-372-7083. E-mail: wright@jhlibrary.org. *Br Mgr,* Tammy Smith; Staff 4 (Non-MLS 4)
Open Mon, Wed & Thurs 9-6, Tues 9-7, Fri 9-5, Sat 10-4
Friends of the Library Group

C JACKSON STATE UNIVERSITY, Henry Thomas Sampson Library, 1325 J R Lynch St, 39217. SAN 308-8723. Tel: 601-979-2123, 601-979-4270. FAX: 601-979-2239. E-mail: library@jsums.edu. Web Site: sampson.jsums.edu. *Interim Dean, Library & Info Services,* Dr Locord Wilson; E-mail: locord.d.wilson@jsums.edu; *Electronic Res Librn,* Bernice Shelwood; E-mail: bernice.shelwood@jsums.edu; *Metadata Librn,* Crystal Brown; E-mail: crystal.n.brown@jsums.edu; *Digital Archivist,* Darlita Ballard; E-mail: darlita.r.ballard@jsums.edu; *Libr Asst I,* Denise Brown; E-mail: denise.brown@jsums.edu; Staff 35 (MLS 10, Non-MLS 25)
Founded 1877. Enrl 6,700; Fac 330; Highest Degree: Doctorate
Library Holdings: Bk Titles 625,000; Bk Vols 1,000,000; Per Subs 1,600
Special Collections: Ayers Decision Coll; Black Studies (Afro-American), bks, discs, pamphlets; Census & Demographic Information; Gibbs-Green Coll; Select Government Repository Library. Oral History; State Document Depository; US Document Depository
Subject Interests: African-Am studies, Engr, Ethnic studies, Soc issues, Urban planning
Automation Activity & Vendor Info: (Acquisitions) Innovative Interfaces, Inc; (Cataloging) Innovative Interfaces, Inc; (Circulation) Innovative Interfaces, Inc; (Course Reserve) Innovative Interfaces, Inc; (Media Booking) Innovative Interfaces, Inc; (OPAC) Innovative Interfaces, Inc; (Serials) Innovative Interfaces, Inc
Wireless access
Function: Telephone ref
Publications: Annual Report; H T Sampson Communicator; Media Highlights
Partic in LYRASIS; MAGNOLIA
Open Mon-Thurs 8-8, Fri 8-5
Restriction: Circ limited

L JONES WALKER*, Law Library, 190 E Capital St, Ste 800, 39201. (Mail add: PO Box 427, 39205-0427), SAN 372-2899. Tel: 601-949-4792. FAX: 601-949-4804. Web Site: www.joneswalker.com. *Librn,* Joe Xu; E-mail: jxu@joneswalker.com
Library Holdings: Bk Titles 3,000; Bk Vols 14,000; Per Subs 52

C MILLSAPS COLLEGE*, Millsaps-Wilson Library, 1701 N State St, 39210. (Mail add: PO Box 151066, 39210), SAN 308-8731. Tel: 601-974-1073. Interlibrary Loan Service Tel: 601-974-1083. FAX: 601-974-1082. E-mail: librarian@millsaps.edu. Web Site: www.millsaps.edu/library. *Col Librn,* Jamie Bounds Wilson; Tel: 601-974-1086, E-mail: jamie.wilson@millsaps.edu; *Cat & Syst Librn,* Elizabeth Beck; Tel: 601-974-1076, E-mail: beckea@millsaps.edu; *Col Archivist,* Debra McIntosh; Tel: 601-974-1077, E-mail: mcintdw@millsaps.edu; Staff 6.5 (MLS 5, Non-MLS 1.5)
Founded 1890. Enrl 900; Fac 90; Highest Degree: Master
Library Holdings: Bk Titles 144,206; Bk Vols 205,427; Per Subs 300
Special Collections: Anthropology (Munro Edmonson Coll); Ethics (Paul Ramsey Coll); Eudora Welty Coll; Medical Ethics (Harmon Smith Coll); Military History (Johnson Coll); Millsaps College Archives; Mississippi Methodist Archives; Rare Books; Theater & Performing Arts (Lehman Engel Coll)
Subject Interests: Applied ethics, Art, Lit, Relig studies
Automation Activity & Vendor Info: (Acquisitions) SirsiDynix; (Cataloging) SirsiDynix; (Circulation) SirsiDynix; (Course Reserve) SirsiDynix; (OPAC) SirsiDynix; (Serials) SirsiDynix
Wireless access
Partic in Associated Colleges of the South; Central Mississippi Library Council; LYRASIS; Private Academic Libraries of Mississippi
Restriction: Limited access for the pub

CL MISSISSIPPI COLLEGE*, Law Library, 151 E Griffith St, 39201-1391. SAN 348-2286. Tel: 601-925-7120. FAX: 601-925-7112. Web Site: law.mc.edu/library. *Libr Dir,* Mary Miller; E-mail: mmiller@mc.edu; *Acq & Cat Librn,* Daniel Shemwell; E-mail: dshemwell@mc.edu; *Circ Librn, Research & Instruction Services,* Cymber Hubbard; E-mail: cdhubbard@mc.edu; *Computer Librn, Ref Librn,* Thomas B Walter; E-mail: walter@mc.edu; Staff 4 (MLS 2, Non-MLS 2)
Founded 1975. Enrl 350; Fac 19; Highest Degree: Doctorate
Library Holdings: Bk Vols 314,000; Per Subs 3,500
Automation Activity & Vendor Info: (Acquisitions) Innovative Interfaces, Inc; (Cataloging) Innovative Interfaces, Inc; (Circulation) Innovative Interfaces, Inc; (Course Reserve) Innovative Interfaces, Inc; (Media Booking) Innovative Interfaces, Inc; (OPAC) Innovative Interfaces, Inc; (Serials) Innovative Interfaces, Inc
Wireless access
Partic in LYRASIS; OCLC Online Computer Library Center, Inc
Open Mon-Thurs (Winter) 7am-Midnight, Fri 7-7, Sat 9-7, Sun Noon-Midnight; Mon-Fri (Summer) 7-5

G MISSISSIPPI DEPARTMENT OF ARCHIVES & HISTORY, Archives & Records Services Division, 200 North St, 39201. (Mail add: PO Box 571, 39205), SAN 308-8790. Tel: 601-576-6876. FAX: 601-576-6964. E-mail: refdesk@mdah.state.ms.us. Web Site: www.mdah.state.ms.us. *Dir,* David Pilcher; E-mail: dpilcher@mdah.ms.gov; Staff 36 (MLS 10, Non-MLS 26)
Founded 1902
Library Holdings: Bk Vols 70,233; Per Subs 300
Special Collections: County Records, micro; Federal Government Records Pertaining to Mississippi; Map Coll; Mississippi Businesses & Organizations, private papers, mss; Mississippi Coll, newspapers; Mississippi Confederate Records; newsfilm; Photograph Coll; State, Territorial & Provincial Government, archives. Oral History; State Document Depository
Subject Interests: Civil rights, Civil War, Mississippiana
Automation Activity & Vendor Info: (Cataloging) ByWater Solutions; (Circulation) ByWater Solutions; (OPAC) ByWater Solutions; (Serials) ByWater Solutions
Wireless access
Function: Archival coll
Publications: Guide to Official Records in the Department of Archives & History; Research in the Department of Archives & History
Open Mon 9-5, Tues-Fri 8-5, Sat 8-1
Restriction: Non-circulating to the pub

G MISSISSIPPI DEPARTMENT OF ENVIRONMENTAL QUALITY LIBRARY*, 700 N State St, 39202. (Mail add: PO Box 2279, 39225), SAN 308-8758. Tel: 601-961-5501. Administration Tel: 601-961-5528. Administration FAX: 601-961-5521. Web Site: www.deq.state.ms.us/MDEQ.nsf/page/HR_Library?OpenDocument. *Dir,* Dr David Dockery, III; Tel: 601-961-5544, E-mail: ddockery@mdeq.ms.gov
Founded 1850
Library Holdings: Bk Vols 48,000; Per Subs 100
Special Collections: National, State & International Government Publications; Topographic Maps; United States & State Geological Survey Publications
Subject Interests: Environ engr, Environ geol, Geohydrology, Geol, Hazardous waste mgt, Paleontology, Petroleum geol
Function: Res libr
Open Mon-Fri 1-4:30
Restriction: Access at librarian's discretion, Authorized patrons, Authorized scholars by appt, By permission only, Circulates for staff only, Employees only, External users must contact libr, In-house use for visitors, Non-circulating to the pub, Not a lending libr, Staff use only

P MISSISSIPPI LIBRARY COMMISSION, 3881 Eastwood Dr, 39211. SAN 348-5919. Tel: 601-432-4111. Circulation Tel: 601-432-4153. Reference Tel: 601-432-4127. Information Services Tel: 601-432-4492. Toll Free Tel: 800-647-7542, 877-594-5733. FAX: 601-432-4476, 601-432-4480. Information Services FAX: 601-432-4478. E-mail: mslib@mlc.lib.ms.us. Reference E-mail: mlcref@mlc.lib.ms.us. Web Site: mlc.lib.ms.us. *Exec Dir,* Dr Hulen E Bivins; Tel: 601-432-4038, E-mail: hbivins@mlc.lib.ms.us; *Dir, Admin Serv Bur,* Jennifer Peacock; Tel: 601-432-4042, E-mail: jpeacock@mlc.lib.ms.us; *Dir, Libr Serv Bur,* Tracy Carr; Tel: 601-432-4450, E-mail: tcarr@mlc.lib.ms.us; *Dir of Develop,* Lacy Ellinwood; Tel: 601-432-4154, E-mail: lellinwood@mlc.lib.ms.us; *Coll Mgt Serv Dir,* Lawrence Smith; Tel: 601-432-4120, E-mail:

lsmith@mlc.lib.ms.us; *Dir, Info Serv,* Ally Mellon; Tel: 601-432-4117, E-mail: amellon@mlc.lib.ms.us; *Dir, Talking Bks,* Mary Rogers Beal; Tel: 601-432-4116, E-mail: mrogers@mlc.lib.ms.us; Staff 49 (MLS 11, Non-MLS 38)
Founded 1926
Special Collections: Blind & Physically Handicapped Coll; Large Print Coll; US Patent & Trademark Depository. State Document Depository; US Document Depository
Subject Interests: Libr sci, Mississippiana, Patents
Automation Activity & Vendor Info: (Acquisitions) Auto-Graphics, Inc; (Cataloging) OCLC; (Circulation) Auto-Graphics, Inc; (ILL) Auto-Graphics, Inc; (OPAC) Auto-Graphics, Inc; (Serials) Auto-Graphics, Inc
Wireless access
Publications: Large Print New Books Catalog (Bibliographies); Mississippi State Government Publications Index (Quarterly); Public Library Statistics (Online only); Reading Light (Newsletter); The Packet (Newsletter)
Partic in MAGNOLIA
Special Services for the Deaf - Bks on deafness & sign lang
Special Services for the Blind - Accessible computers; Assistive/Adapted tech devices, equip & products; Bks & mags in Braille, on rec, tape & cassette; Braille equip; Braille servs; Cassette playback machines; Closed circuit TV; Club for the blind; Computer with voice synthesizer for visually impaired persons; Copier with enlargement capabilities; Descriptive video serv (DVS); Digital talking bk; Disability awareness prog; Duplicating spec requests; Extensive large print coll; Home delivery serv; Info on spec aids & appliances; Low vision equip; Machine repair; Magnifiers; Newsletter (in large print, Braille or on cassette); Production of talking bks; Reader equip; Soundproof reading booth; Spanish Braille mags & bks; Spec cats; Spec prog; Talking bk & rec for the blind cat; Talking bks; Tel Pioneers equip repair group; Volunteer serv; ZoomText magnification & reading software
Open Mon-Fri 8-5
Friends of the Library Group

P MISSISSIPPI LIBRARY COMMISSION*, Talking Book Library Services, 3881 Eastwood Dr, 39211-6473. SAN 308-8766. Tel: 601-432-4151. Toll Free Tel: 800-446-0892. FAX: 601-432-4476. E-mail: talkingbooks@mlc.lib.ms.us. Web Site: www.mlc.lib.ms.us/tbs. *Dir,* Mary Rogers Beal; Tel: 601-432-4116, E-mail: mrbeal@mlc.lib.ms.us; Staff 8 (MLS 2, Non-MLS 6)
Founded 1970
Library Holdings: Audiobooks 296; Braille Volumes 1,688; CDs 179; DVDs 114; Electronic Media & Resources 420; Per Subs 85; Talking Bks 60,035; Videos 819
Special Collections: Lobe Library Consortium Member, digital bks; Mississippiana Coll, descriptive videos; Playaway, digital bks; Print Reference Coll
Automation Activity & Vendor Info: (Acquisitions) Keystone Systems, Inc (KLAS); (Cataloging) Keystone Systems, Inc (KLAS); (Circulation) Keystone Systems, Inc (KLAS); (ILL) Keystone Systems, Inc (KLAS); (OPAC) Keystone Systems, Inc (KLAS); (Serials) Keystone Systems, Inc (KLAS)
Wireless access
Publications: Bibliography of Locally Recorded Materials; Instruction Manual for Institutions & Libraries; Patron Handbook; Reader Newsletter (Quarterly); The Reading Light (Newsletter); User Manual
Special Services for the Blind - Accessible computers; Aids for in-house use; Assistive/Adapted tech devices, equip & products; Audio mat; Bks & mags in Braille, on rec, tape & cassette; Bks available with recordings; Bks on cassette; Bks on CD; Blind Club (monthly newsletter); Braille & cassettes; Braille alphabet card; Braille bks; Braille equip; Braille servs; Cassette playback machines; Cassettes; Children's Braille; Closed circuit TV; Closed circuit TV magnifier; Computer access aids; Computer with voice synthesizer for visually impaired persons; Copier with enlargement capabilities; Daisy reader; Descriptive video serv (DVS); Digital talking bk; Disability awareness prog; Duplicating spec requests; Extensive large print coll; Info on spec aids & appliances; Internet workstation with adaptive software; Large print & cassettes; Large print bks; Large screen computer & software; Local mags & bks recorded; Machine repair; Magnifiers; Mags & bk reproduction/duplication; Musical scores in Braille & large print; Newsletter (in large print, Braille or on cassette); PC for people with disabilities; Photo duplicator for making large print; Playaways (bks on MP3); Production of talking bks; Reader equip; Recorded bks; Ref in Braille; Ref serv; Screen enlargement software for people with visual disabilities; Screen reader software; Sound rec; Soundproof reading booth; Spanish Braille mags & bks; Spec cats; Spec prog; Talking bk & rec for the blind cat; Talking bk serv referral; Talking bks; Talking bks & player equip; Talking bks plus; Tel Pioneers equip repair group; Variable speed audiotape players; Videos on blindness & physical disabilties; Volunteer serv; Web-Braille; ZoomText magnification & reading software
Open Mon-Fri 8-5
Friends of the Library Group

S MISSISSIPPI MUSEUM OF ART*, Howorth Library, 380 S Lamar St, 39201. SAN 327-2141. Tel: 601-960-1515. FAX: 601-960-1505. Web Site: www.msmuseumart.org. *Chief Curator, Dir,* Ryan Dennis; E-mail: mmacuratorial@msmuseumart.org; *Curator, Dep Dir,* Holly Harrison; E-mail: hharrison@msmuseumart.org
Library Holdings: Bk Vols 45,000
Open Tues-Thurs 11-7, Fri-Sat 11-5

GM G V MONTGOMERY VA MEDICAL CENTER LIBRARY*, 1500 E Woodrow Wilson Dr, 39216. SAN 308-8855. Tel: 601-364-1273. FAX: 601-364-1316. Web Site: www.jackson.va.gov. *Librn,* Betty Townsend; Staff 1 (MLS 1)
Founded 1946
Library Holdings: Bk Titles 3,100; Per Subs 300
Automation Activity & Vendor Info: (Acquisitions) CyberTools for Libraries; (Cataloging) EOS International; (Circulation) CyberTools for Libraries; (OPAC) CyberTools for Libraries; (Serials) CyberTools for Libraries
Function: Computer training, Computers for patron use, Doc delivery serv, Electronic databases & coll, ILL available, Internet access, Online cat, Photocopying/Printing, Ref serv available, Wheelchair accessible
Open Mon-Fri 8-4:30
Restriction: Authorized patrons, Badge access after hrs, Circ limited, Circulates for staff only, Hospital employees & physicians only, Med & nursing staff, patients & families

L PHELPS DUNBAR, LLP*, Law Library, 4270 Interstate 55 N, 39211-6391. (Mail add: PO Box 16114, 39236-6114), SAN 372-4662. Tel: 601-352-2300. FAX: 601-360-9777. Web Site: www.phelpsdunbar.com. *Libr Mgr,* Jennifer Dabbs; E-mail: dabbsj@phelps.com; Staff 2 (MLS 2)
Library Holdings: Bk Vols 5,000; Per Subs 20
Subject Interests: Labor
Restriction: Staff use only

R REFORMED THEOLOGICAL SEMINARY LIBRARY, 5422 Clinton Blvd, 39209. SAN 308-8812. Tel: 601-923-1623. FAX: 601-923-1621. E-mail: library.jackson@rts.edu. Web Site: library.rts.edu, www.rts.edu/site/resources. *Libr Dir,* John Crabb; *Asst Librn,* David Jackson; Tel: 601-923-1622, E-mail: djackson@rts.edu; Staff 2 (MLS 2)
Founded 1965. Enrl 285; Fac 18; Highest Degree: Doctorate
Library Holdings: Bk Vols 150,000; Per Subs 320
Special Collections: Southern Presbyterianism (Blackburn Coll)
Wireless access
Partic in LYRASIS
Open Mon-Thurs 8am-9pm, Fri 8-4, Sat 9-4

M ST DOMINIC HOSPITAL, Luther Manship Medical Library, 969 Lakeland Dr, 39216. SAN 308-8820. Tel: 601-200-6944. FAX: 601-200-8075. E-mail: library@stdom.com. Web Site: www.stdom.com. *Libr Engagement Facilitator,* Michelle Vincent
Founded 1974
Special Services for the Blind - Cassettes
Open Mon-Thurs 8-4:30, Fri 8-Noon

GL STATE OF MISSISSIPPI JUDICIARY, State Law Library of Mississippi, Carroll Gartin Justice Bldg, 450 High St, 39201. (Mail add: PO Box 1040, 39215-1040), SAN 308-8804. Tel: 601-359-3672. FAX: 601-359-2912. Web Site: courts.ms.gov/newsite2/research/statelibrary/library.php. *State Librn,* Stephen Parks; *Circ Librn,* Casandra Noel; E-mail: cnoel@courts.ms.gov; *Info Processing Librn,* Judy Nettles; E-mail: jnettles@courts.ms.gov; *Ref Librn,* LaTavius Jackson; E-mail: ljackson@courts.ms.gov; Staff 4 (MLS 3, Non-MLS 1)
Founded 1838
Library Holdings: Bk Vols 225,000; Per Subs 267
Special Collections: Mississippiana. US Document Depository
Subject Interests: Fed law, State law
Automation Activity & Vendor Info: (Cataloging) Book Systems; (OPAC) Book Systems
Function: ILL available
Open Mon-Fri 8-5
Restriction: Circ limited

CM UNIVERSITY OF MISSISSIPPI MEDICAL CENTER*, Rowland Medical Library, 2500 N State St, 39216-4505. SAN 308-8847. Tel: 601-984-1290. Circulation Tel: 601-984-1230. Interlibrary Loan Service Tel: 601-984-1247. Reference Tel: 601-984-1231. FAX: 601-984-1251. Interlibrary Loan Service FAX: 601-984-1262. E-mail: lib-library@rowland.umsmed.edu. Web Site: www.umc.edu/library/. *Dir,* Susan Clark; E-mail: sbclark2@umc.edu; *Assoc Dir,* Connie K Machado; Tel: 601-984-1273, E-mail: cmachado@umc.edu; *Div Mgr, Operations,* Linda Bouchillon; E-mail: lbouchillon@umc.edu; *Libr Tech II,* Antronette Bell; Tel: 601-984-1230, E-mail: lbell@umc.edu; *Ser,* Dean James; Tel: 601-984-1277, E-mail: ddjames@umc.edu; Staff 27 (MLS 11, Non-MLS 16)

Founded 1955. Enrl 2,200; Fac 713; Highest Degree: Doctorate
Library Holdings: AV Mats 888; Bk Titles 66,803; Bk Vols 72,679; Per Subs 2,202
Special Collections: History of Medicine; UMC Theses & Dissertations
Subject Interests: Allied health, Dentistry, Health educ, Med, Nursing, Prof mat
Automation Activity & Vendor Info: (Acquisitions) SirsiDynix; (Cataloging) SirsiDynix; (Circulation) SirsiDynix; (Course Reserve) SirsiDynix; (OPAC) SirsiDynix; (Serials) SirsiDynix
Wireless access
Publications: Handbook; Reference Guide; Rowland Medical Library Source; Topic Tracks
Partic in Consortium of Southern Biomedical Libraries; National Network of Libraries of Medicine Region 2
Open Mon-Thurs 7am-Midnight, Fri 7am-9pm, Sat 8-7, Sun Noon-Midnight
Friends of the Library Group

KEESLER AFB

UNITED STATES AIR FORCE
A MCBRIDE LIBRARY*, 81 FSS/FSDL McBride Library, 512 Larcher Blvd Bldg 2222, 39534-2345, SAN 348-6036. Tel: 228-377-2181. Administration Tel: 228-377-2604. FAX: 228-435-0203. Web Site: www.keesler.af.mil. *Dir,* Rebecca Chapman; Staff 5 (MLS 1, Non-MLS 4)
Founded 1942
Library Holdings: Bk Vols 4,000; Per Subs 150
Special Collections: Air War College; Chief of Staff Professional Reading Test; McNaughton Lease Books; Professional Military Education; Transition Assistance Program; US Air Force Periodicals
Subject Interests: Bus admin, Computer engr, Computer sci, Data communications, Electronics, Hist, Math, Mil sci, Television, Weather
Automation Activity & Vendor Info: (Cataloging) Softlink America; (Circulation) Softlink America; (ILL) OCLC; (OPAC) Softlink America
Partic in OCLC Online Computer Library Center, Inc
Special Services for the Blind - Closed circuit TV magnifier
Open Mon-Thurs 10-8, Fri-Sun 12-7
AM MEDICAL CENTER LIBRARY*, 81st Medical Group/SGGMEL, 301 Fisher St, Rm 1A132, 39534-2519, SAN 348-6044. Tel: 228-376-4949. FAX: 228-377-6127. *Librn,* Mary Altman; Staff 2 (MLS 1, Non-MLS 1)
Founded 1942
Library Holdings: Bk Titles 6,200; Per Subs 350
Subject Interests: Allied health, Clinical med, Dentistry, Nursing
Automation Activity & Vendor Info: (Cataloging) EOS International; (Circulation) EOS International; (Serials) EOS International
Partic in Gulf Coast Biomedical Libr Consortium; SE-Atlantic Regional Med Libr Servs

KOSCIUSKO

P MID-MISSISSIPPI REGIONAL LIBRARY SYSTEM*, 201 S Huntington St, 39090-9002. SAN 348-6095. Tel: 662-289-5151. FAX: 662-289-5106. Web Site: mmrls.lib.ms.us. *Exec Dir,* Josh Haidet; E-mail: director@mmrls.lib.ms.us; *Asst Dir,* Position Currently Open; *Tech Coordr,* Michael Davide; *Cat,* Jannine Hutchison; *Ch Serv,* Lindsay Fitts; Staff 7 (MLS 2, Non-MLS 5)
Founded 1957. Pop 93,429; Circ 299,534
Library Holdings: Bk Titles 160,000; Per Subs 531
Special Collections: Barrett Civil War Coll (Lexington); Hendrix Genealogy Coll (Louisville); Sanders Genealogy Coll (Attala)
Subject Interests: Educ, Genealogy
Automation Activity & Vendor Info: (Acquisitions) EOS International; (Cataloging) EOS International; (Circulation) EOS International; (OPAC) EOS International
Wireless access
Function: ILL available
Open Mon-Thurs & Sat 9-6, Fri 9-5
Friends of the Library Group
Branches: 13
ATTALA COUNTY, 201 S Huntington St, 39090-9002, SAN 348-6125. Tel: 662-289-5141. FAX: 662-289-9983. E-mail: attala@mmrls.lib.ms.us. *Librn,* Charla Grace; Staff 7 (Non-MLS 7)
Special Collections: Blaylock-Sanders Coll; Education (Reavis Coll); Miss History & Genealogy
Open Mon-Thurs 9-6, Fri 9-5, Sat 9-12:30
Friends of the Library Group
CARTHAGE-LEAKE COUNTY, 114 E Franklin St, Carthage, 39051-3716, SAN 348-615X. Tel: 601-267-7821. FAX: 601-267-5530. E-mail: carthage@mmrls.lib.ms.us. *Librn,* Nancy Cain; Staff 4 (Non-MLS 4)
Open Mon, Tues, Thurs & Fri 8-5:30, Wed & Sat 8-12
Friends of the Library Group
DUCK HILL PUBLIC, 127 N State St, Duck Hill, 38925-9287. (Mail add: PO Box 279, Duck Hill, 38925-0279), SAN 348-6184. Tel: 662-565-2391. FAX: 662-565-2392. E-mail: duckhill@mmrls.lib.ms.us. *Librn,* Jessie Mann; Staff 1 (Non-MLS 1)
Open Mon, Tues, Thurs & Fri 1-5, Sat 8-12
Friends of the Library Group
DURANT PUBLIC, 15338 N Jackson St, Durant, 39063-3708, SAN 348-6214. Tel: 662-653-3451. FAX: 662-653-3108. E-mail: durant@mmrls.lib.ms.us. *Librn,* Martha Ellington; Staff 2 (Non-MLS 2)
Open Mon-Fri 8-5
Friends of the Library Group
GOODMAN PUBLIC, 9792 Main St, Goodman, 39079. (Mail add: PO Box 374, Goodman, 39079-0374), SAN 348-6249. Tel: 662-472-0550. FAX: 662-472-0599. E-mail: goodman@mmrls.lib.ms.us. *Librn,* Jennette Moore; Staff 1 (Non-MLS 1)
Open Tues & Thurs 9-12 & 1-5
Friends of the Library Group
KILMICHAEL PUBLIC, 102 First St, Kilmichael, 39747. (Mail add: PO Box 316, Kilmichael, 39747-0316), SAN 348-6273. Tel: 662-262-7615. FAX: 662-262-7615. E-mail: kilmichael@mmrls.lib.ms.us. *Librn,* Kerri Varnes
Open Mon, Tues & Fri 1-5, Thurs 8-12 & 1-5
Friends of the Library Group
LEXINGTON PUBLIC, 208 Tchula St, Lexington, 39095-3134, SAN 348-6303. Tel: 662-834-2571. FAX: 662-834-4578. E-mail: lexington@mmrls.lib.ms.us. *Librn,* Laura Lawson; Staff 2 (Non-MLS 2)
Open Mon, Wed & Thurs 9-12 & 1-5, Tues & Fri 9-5
Friends of the Library Group
PICKENS PUBLIC, 309 Hwy 51, Pickens, 39146. (Mail add: PO Box 188, Pickens, 39146-0188), SAN 348-6338. Tel: 662-468-2391. FAX: 662-468-2392. E-mail: pickens@mmrls.lib.ms.us. *Librn,* Dedra Edwards; Staff 1 (Non-MLS 1)
Open Mon, Wed & Fri 9-12 & 1-5, Tues 9-5
Friends of the Library Group
TCHULA PUBLIC, 105 Mercer St, Tchula, 39169-5235. (Mail add: PO Box 248, Tchula, 39169-0248), SAN 348-6362. Tel: 662-235-5235. FAX: 662-235-4925. E-mail: tchula@mmrls.lib.ms.us. *Librn,* Yvonne Clark; Staff 1 (Non-MLS 1)
Open Tues & Wed 10-5, Thurs 10-4
Friends of the Library Group
WALNUT GROVE PUBLIC, 146 Main St, Walnut Grove, 39189. (Mail add: PO Box 206, Walnut Grove, 39189-0206), SAN 348-6397. Tel: 601-253-2483. FAX: 601-253-9374. E-mail: walnutgrove@mmrls.lib.ms.us. *Librn,* Katie Mills; Staff 1 (Non-MLS 1)
Open Mon-Sat 1-5
Friends of the Library Group
WEST PUBLIC, 24843 Hwy 51, West, 39192. (Mail add: PO Box 9, West, 39192-0009), SAN 348-6427. Tel: 662-967-2510. FAX: 662-967-2511. E-mail: west@mmrls.lib.ms.us. *Interim Librn,* Ann Polk; Staff 1 (Non-MLS 1)
Open Mon & Fri 8-12 & 1-5, Wed 12-4
Friends of the Library Group
WINONA-MONTGOMERY COUNTY, 115 N Quitman St, Winona, 38967-2228, SAN 348-6451. Tel: 662-283-3443. FAX: 662-283-2642. E-mail: winona@mmrls.lib.ms.us. *Librn,* Virginia Weed; Staff 2 (Non-MLS 2)
Open Mon-Fri 8-5
Friends of the Library Group
WINSTON COUNTY, 100 W Park St, Louisville, 39339-3018, SAN 348-6486. Tel: 662-773-3212. FAX: 662-773-8434. E-mail: winston@mmrls.lib.ms.us. *Librn,* Beth Edwards; Staff 4 (Non-MLS 4)
Special Collections: Miss Genealogy Coll
Open Mon & Tues 8:30-6, Wed 8:30-5:30, Thurs & Sat 8:30-12, Fri 8:30-5
Friends of the Library Group

LAKE

P LAKE PUBLIC LIBRARY*, City Hall, 100 Front St, 39092. (Mail add: PO Box 160, 39092-0160), SAN 376-6179. Tel: 601-775-3560. E-mail: lake@cmrls.lib.ms.us. Web Site: cmrls.lib.ms.us/cmrlsbranches/lake. *Br Mgr,* Selena Swink; E-mail: sswink@cmrls.lib.ms.us
Library Holdings: Bk Titles 4,500
Subject Interests: Local hist
Wireless access
Mem of Central Mississippi Regional Library System
Special Services for the Deaf - Bks on deafness & sign lang; Closed caption videos
Special Services for the Blind - Audio mat; Bks on CD; Large print bks
Open Mon 1-6, Wed & Thurs 9-12 & 12:30-5
Friends of the Library Group

LAUREL

P LAUREL-JONES COUNTY LIBRARY SYSTEM, INC*, Laurel-Jones County Library, 530 Commerce St, 39440. SAN 348-6516. Tel: 601-428-4313, Ext 104. FAX: 601-428-0597. Web Site: www.laurel.lib.ms.us. *Dir,* Mary-Louise Breland; Tel: 601-428-4313, Ext 101, E-mail: marylouise.breland@laurel.lib.ms.us; *Asst Dir,* Carolyn Russell; Tel: 601-428-4313, Ext 103, E-mail: crussell@laurel.lib.ms.us; Staff 4 (MLS 2, Non-MLS 2)
Founded 1919. Pop 62,500; Circ 184,393
Library Holdings: Bk Vols 82,050; Per Subs 85
Special Collections: Genealogy Library; Laurel Newspaper Coll, 1892-present, micro & print; Local Family Records
Subject Interests: Genealogy, Local hist
Automation Activity & Vendor Info: (Acquisitions) Baker & Taylor; (Cataloging) Biblionix/Apollo; (Circulation) Biblionix/Apollo; (Course Reserve) Biblionix/Apollo; (ILL) Auto-Graphics, Inc; (OPAC) Biblionix/Apollo; (Serials) EBSCO Online
Wireless access
Open Mon, Tues, Thurs & Fri 8-6, Sat 10-2
Friends of the Library Group
Branches: 1
ELLISVILLE PUBLIC, 201 Poplar St, Ellisville, 39437, SAN 348-6540. Tel: 601-477-9271. FAX: 601-477-3004. *Br Mgr,* Joanna Ashley; Staff 2.5 (Non-MLS 2.5)
Pop 3,500
Function: Children's prog, Computers for patron use, Free DVD rentals, Online cat, Online info literacy tutorials on the web & in blackboard, Photocopying/Printing
Open Mon & Wed-Fri 10-6, Sat 10-2
Friends of the Library Group

S LAUREN ROGERS MUSEUM OF ART LIBRARY*, 565 N Fifth Ave, 39440. (Mail add: PO Box 1108, 39441-1108), SAN 308-8863. Tel: 601-649-6374. FAX: 601-649-6379. E-mail: LRMAlibrary@LRMA.org. Web Site: lrma.org/collections/library. *Curator,* Kristen Zohn; E-mail: kzohn@LRMA.org; Staff 2 (MLS 1, Non-MLS 1)
Founded 1923
Library Holdings: Bk Vols 10,000; Per Subs 75
Special Collections: Artists' Clipping Files; Bookplates; Local History, photog, ms; Museum Archives; Postcard Coll; Rare Books
Subject Interests: Am art, Georgian silver, Local hist, Mississippiana, Native Am basket
Function: Ref serv available
Publications: Jean Leon Gerome Ferris (1863-1930), American Painter Historian; Lauren Rogers Museum of Art Handbook of Collections; Lauren Rogers Museum of Art Handbook of the Collections, Revised Ed (Collection catalog); Lauren Rogers Museum of Art Newsletter (Quarterly); Mississippi Art Colony; Mississippi Portraiture; Recent Acquisitions, Lauren Rogers Museum of Art; Sam Gilliam: Folded & Hinged; The French Legacy; The Gibbons Silver Collection (Collection catalog)
Open Tues, Fri & Sat 10-4:45, Sun 1-4
Restriction: Non-circulating

CR SOUTHEASTERN BAPTIST COLLEGE*, A R Reddin Memorial Library, 4229 Hwy 15 N, 39440. SAN 308-8871. Tel: 601-426-6346. FAX: 601-426-6347. Web Site: southeasternbaptist.edu. *Librn,* Amy Hinton; E-mail: ahinton@southeasternbaptist.edu; Staff 1 (MLS 1)
Founded 1955. Enrl 111; Fac 12; Highest Degree: Doctorate
Library Holdings: Bk Titles 30,000; Per Subs 45
Special Collections: Baptist Missionary Association of America Coll, doc
Open Mon & Tues 8-6, Wed & Thurs 8-2:30

LEAKESVILLE

S MISSISSIPPI DEPARTMENT OF CORRECTIONS*, South Mississippi Correctional Institution Library, 22689 Hwy 63 N, 39451. Tel: 601-394-5600, Ext 1079. FAX: 601-394-5600, Ext 1182. Web Site: www.mdoc.state.ms.us. *Librn,* Position Currently Open
Library Holdings: Bk Vols 9,000

LONG BEACH

P LONG BEACH PUBLIC LIBRARY*, 209 Jeff Davis Ave, 39560. SAN 308-8898. Tel: 228-863-0711. FAX: 228-863-8511. Web Site: longbeach.lib.ms.us. *Dir,* Denise Saucier; E-mail: dsaucier@longbeach.lib.ms.us; Staff 4 (Non-MLS 4)
Founded 1895. Pop 17,320; Circ 115,495
Library Holdings: Bks on Deafness & Sign Lang 30; Bk Titles 20,000
Special Collections: Cook Books & Craft Coll
Automation Activity & Vendor Info: (Cataloging) Follett Software; (Circulation) Follett Software; (OPAC) Follett Software
Wireless access
Open Mon-Fri 9-5, Sat 9-1
Friends of the Library Group

C UNIVERSITY OF SOUTHERN MISSISSIPPI*, Gulf Coast Library, 730 E Beach Blvd, 39560-2698. SAN 325-3422. Tel: 228-214-3450. Web Site: www.lib.usm.edu. *Dean, Univ Libr,* John Eye; E-mail: John.Eye@usm.edu; *Assoc Dean,* Edward McCormack; Tel: 228-214-3466, E-mail: Edward.McCormack@usm.edu; *Circ Spec,* Mr Cameron Faulk; Tel: 228-214-3414, E-mail: cameron.faulk@usm.edu; *Coll Mgt Librn,* Allisa Beck; Tel: 228-214-3468, E-mail: allisa.beck@usm.edu; Staff 13 (MLS 5, Non-MLS 8)
Founded 1972. Enrl 2,300; Fac 111
Library Holdings: Bk Vols 60,000; Per Subs 630
Special Collections: Curriculum Materials Center; Gulf of Mexico Program; PDK Fastbacks
Subject Interests: Bus admin, Educ, Hospitality mgt, Humanities, Nursing, Psychol
Automation Activity & Vendor Info: (Circulation) SirsiDynix; (ILL) OCLC ILLiad; (Media Booking) SirsiDynix; (OPAC) SirsiDynix
Wireless access
Publications: USMGC Library Link
Partic in LYRASIS; MAGNOLIA
Open Mon-Thurs 7:30am-11pm, Fri 7:30-5, Sat & Sun 12-9

MACON

P NOXUBEE COUNTY LIBRARY SYSTEM*, Ada S Fant Memorial Library, 145 Dr Martin Luther King Jr Dr, 39341. SAN 308-891X. Tel: 662-726-5461. FAX: 662-726-4694. Web Site: www.noxubee.lib.ms.us. *Dir,* Shemeka Conner; *Librn,* Loraine Walker; *Librn,* Sharon Young
Founded 1933. Pop 12,604; Circ 21,762
Library Holdings: Bk Vols 26,925
Special Collections: Reference Classics (Harold Gibson Brown Memorial Coll)
Subject Interests: Mississippiana
Automation Activity & Vendor Info: (Acquisitions) Auto-Graphics, Inc; (Cataloging) Auto-Graphics, Inc; (Circulation) Auto-Graphics, Inc; (ILL) Auto-Graphics, Inc
Wireless access
Open Mon, Tues, Thurs & Fri 8-6
Friends of the Library Group
Branches: 2
BROOKSVILLE BRANCH, 13758 W Main St, Brooksville, 39739, SAN 321-9429. Tel: 662-738-4559. *Librn,* Barbara Mickens
Open Mon & Thurs 2-5
Friends of the Library Group
VISTA J DANIEL MEMORIAL, 402 Residence St, Shuqualak, 39361-9740. (Mail add: PO Box 248, Shuqualak, 39361-0248), SAN 321-9437. Tel: 662-793-9576. *Br Librn,* Eddie P Fox
Library Holdings: Bk Vols 12,000
Automation Activity & Vendor Info: (Serials) Auto-Graphics, Inc
Open Mon & Thurs 2-5
Friends of the Library Group

MAGEE

P MAGEE PUBLIC LIBRARY, Mims Williams Memorial Library, 120 First St NW, 39111. SAN 376-6195. Tel: 601-849-3747. FAX: 601-849-6609. E-mail: magee@cmrls.lib.ms.us. Web Site: cmrls.lib.ms.us. *Br Mgr,* Frances T Meadows; E-mail: mabm@cmrls.lib.ms.us; *Ch Serv,* Matt Pudas; *Ch Serv,* Kathie Jo Ward; *Circ,* Barbara Gauthier; Staff 1 (Non-MLS 1)
Founded 1935. Pop 4,298; Circ 46,400
Library Holdings: Audiobooks 200; CDs 150; DVDs 2,500; e-books 1,500; e-journals 20; Large Print Bks 1,000; Bk Titles 30,000; Per Subs 6
Automation Activity & Vendor Info: (Circulation) Horizon
Wireless access
Function: 24/7 Electronic res, 24/7 Online cat, Adult bk club, Audiobks on Playaways & MP3, Audiobks via web, Bk club(s), Bks on CD, Children's prog, Computer training, Computers for patron use, Electronic databases & coll, Free DVD rentals, ILL available, Internet access, Laminating, Magazines, Meeting rooms, Movies, Music CDs, Notary serv, Online cat, Online info literacy tutorials on the web & in blackboard, Online ref, Outreach serv, Photocopying/Printing, Printer for laptops & handheld devices, Prog for adults, Prog for children & young adult, Scanner, Spanish lang bks, Story hour, Summer & winter reading prog, Summer reading prog, Tax forms, Teen prog, Telephone ref, Wheelchair accessible
Mem of Central Mississippi Regional Library System
Open Mon, Wed & Fri 8:30-5:30, Tues & Thurs 10-7, Sat 9-1
Friends of the Library Group

MARKS

P MARKS-QUITMAN COUNTY LIBRARY*, 315 E Main St, 38646. SAN 308-8928. Tel: 662-326-7141. FAX: 662-326-7369. E-mail: mqcl@marks.lib.ms.us. Web Site: www.marksquitmancountylibrary.org. *Dir,* William Bahr; E-mail: wlbahr@marks.lib.ms.us
Pop 10,500; Circ 23,202

Library Holdings: Bk Titles 13,000; Per Subs 29
Subject Interests: Agr, Genealogy, Hist, Miss
Wireless access
Partic in Dancing Rabbit Library Consortium
Open Mon, Tues, Thurs & Fri 8-4, Wed 8-5

MCCOMB

P PIKE-AMITE-WALTHALL LIBRARY SYSTEM*, McComb Public Library (Headquarters), 1022 Virginia Ave, 39648. SAN 348-663X. Tel: 601-684-2661. Administration Tel: 601-684-7034, Ext 10. FAX: 601-250-1213. Web Site: www.pawls.org. *Dir,* Darlene Morgan; Tel: 601-684-7034, Ext 11, E-mail: dmorgan@pawls.lib.ms.us; *Asst Dir,* Kelli Miller; Tel: 601-684-7034, Ext 15, E-mail: kelli@pawls.lib.ms.us; *Children's Activities Dir,* Laura Stokes; Tel: 601-684-2661, Ext 12, E-mail: lstokes@pawls.lib.ms.us; *Cat Librn,* Patrick Sanders; Tel: 601-684-2661, Ext 14, E-mail: psanders@pawls.lib.ms.us; *Ref Librn,* Monica Wilkinson; Tel: 601-684-2661, Ext 18, E-mail: monica@pawls.lib.ms.us; *Circ Mgr,* Aaron Wilkinson; Tel: 601-684-2661, Ext 17, E-mail: awilkinson@pawls.lib.ms.us. Subject Specialists: *Genealogy,* Monica Wilkinson; Staff 14 (MLS 2, Non-MLS 12)
Founded 1964. Pop 68,796; Circ 136,780
Library Holdings: Audiobooks 2,016; AV Mats 11,298; CDs 334; DVDs 2,519; e-books 100; Electronic Media & Resources 55; Large Print Bks 3,555; Microforms 140; Bk Titles 88,234; Bk Vols 145,085; Per Subs 225; Videos 4,098
Subject Interests: Genealogy
Automation Activity & Vendor Info: (Acquisitions) SirsiDynix-WorkFlows; (Cataloging) SirsiDynix-WorkFlows; (Circulation) SirsiDynix-WorkFlows; (ILL) OCLC WorldShare Interlibrary Loan; (OPAC) SirsiDynix-WorkFlows; (Serials) SirsiDynix-WorkFlows
Wireless access
Function: Art exhibits, Bks on cassette, Bks on CD, Children's prog, Computers for patron use, Electronic databases & coll, Free DVD rentals, ILL available, Internet access, Microfiche/film & reading machines, Online cat, Online ref, Photocopying/Printing, Preschool reading prog, Prog for children & young adult, Story hour, Summer reading prog, Tax forms, Wheelchair accessible
Partic in Longleaf Library Consortium; National Network of Libraries of Medicine Region 2
Restriction: 24-hr pass syst for students only
Branches: 8
ALPHA CENTER, 414 McComb Ave, 39648, SAN 348-6664. Tel: 601-684-8312. E-mail: alphacen@pawls.lib.ms.us. *Librn,* Michele Brister; Staff 1 (Non-MLS 1)
Founded 1964
Library Holdings: Bk Vols 1,933
Function: 24/7 Electronic res, 24/7 Online cat, After school storytime, Archival coll, Art exhibits, Audiobks via web, Bk club(s), Bks on CD, Children's prog, Computers for patron use, Electronic databases & coll, For res purposes, Free DVD rentals, Holiday prog, ILL available, Internet access, Laminating, Magazines, Mail & tel request accepted, Meeting rooms, Microfiche/film & reading machines, Online cat, Online ref, Photocopying/Printing, Preschool outreach, Preschool reading prog, Prog for adults, Prog for children & young adult, Ref & res, Ref serv available, Res assist avail, Scanner, Story hour, Study rm, Summer & winter reading prog, Summer reading prog
Open Mon-Thurs 2-5, Fri 3-5
CROSBY BRANCH, 106 W Pine St, Crosby, 39633. (Mail add: PO Box 427, Crosby, 39633-0427), SAN 348-6699. Tel: 601-639-4633. E-mail: crosby@pawls.lib.ms.us. *Librn,* Kathy Cassels; Staff 1 (Non-MLS 1)
Founded 1959
Library Holdings: Bk Vols 3,260
Open Mon-Thurs 1:30-5:30
GLOSTER BRANCH, 229 E Main St, Gloster, 39638. (Mail add: PO Drawer 460, Gloster, 39638-0460), SAN 348-6729. Tel: 601-225-4341. E-mail: gloster@pawls.lib.ms.us. *Librn,* Joyce H Waugh; Staff 1 (Non-MLS 1)
Founded 1959
Library Holdings: Bk Vols 10,992
Open Mon-Wed & Fri 10:30-4:30, Sat 8am-10am
LIBERTY BRANCH, 196 Clinic Dr, Liberty, 39654. (Mail add: PO Box 187, Liberty, 39654-0187), SAN 348-6753. Tel: 601-657-8781. E-mail: liberty@pawls.lib.ms.us. *Br Mgr,* Michael Maltese; Staff 1 (Non-MLS 1)
Library Holdings: Bk Vols 11,550
Open Mon-Wed & Fri 11-5, Sat 10-12
MAGNOLIA BRANCH, 230 S Cherry St, Magnolia, 39652, SAN 348-6788. Tel: 601-783-6565. FAX: 601-783-6565. E-mail: magnolia@pawls.lib.ms.us. *Librn,* Edythe Lensing; Staff 1 (Non-MLS 1)
Founded 1933
Library Holdings: Bk Vols 10,610
Open Mon-Wed & Fri 11-5, Thurs 1-7
OSYKA BRANCH, 112 W Railroad Ave, Osyka, 39657. (Mail add: P.O. Box 129, Osyka, 39657), SAN 348-6842. Tel: 601-542-5147. E-mail: osyka@pawls.lib.ms.us. *Librn,* Nancy Sitton; Staff 1 (Non-MLS 1)
Library Holdings: Bk Vols 6,164
Open Mon, Tues, Thurs & Fri 11-5
PROGRESS, 5071 Mt Herman Rd, 39648-9767. Tel: 601-542-5501. E-mail: progress@pawls.lib.ms.us. *Librn,* Andrea Traylor; Staff 1 (Non-MLS 1)
Library Holdings: Bk Vols 4,873
Open Mon-Thurs 1-5
Friends of the Library Group
WALTHALL, 707 Union Rd, Tylertown, 39667, SAN 348-6931. Tel: 601-876-4348. FAX: 601-876-4677. E-mail: walthall@pawls.lib.ms.us. *Br Librn,* Anita Beard; Staff 3 (MLS 1, Non-MLS 2)
Founded 1933
Library Holdings: Bk Vols 18,203
Open Mon, Tues & Thurs 9-6, Wed 9-3, Fri 9:30-4:30, Sat 9:30-11:30
Friends of the Library Group

MENDENHALL

J COPIAH-LINCOLN COMMUNITY COLLEGE*, Fred & Jewett Taylor Library, Simpson County Ctr, 151 Co-Lin Dr, 39114. Tel: 601-849-0116. FAX: 601-849-0160. Web Site: www.colin.edu/library-tips/simpson-county-center-library. *Dir,* Bryon Conville; E-mail: bryon.conville@colin.edu; *Evening Librn,* Jennifer Parker; Tel: 601-849-0118; *Evening Librn,* Marcia Winningham
Library Holdings: Bk Vols 7,000; Per Subs 23
Open Mon & Wed (Fall-Spring) 7:30-4:30, Tues & Thurs 7:30am-8pm, Fri 7:30-3; Mon-Thurs (Summer) 7:30-4:30, Fri 7:30am-12:30pm

P MENDENHALL PUBLIC LIBRARY*, 1630 Simpson Hwy 149, 39114. SAN 376-6187. Tel: 601-847-2181. FAX: 601-847-2188. E-mail: menden@cmrls.lib.ms.us. Web Site: cmrls.lib.ms.us/cmrlsbranches/mendenhall. *Br Mgr,* Rhoda Benton; *Ch,* Sylvia Kennedy
Library Holdings: Bk Titles 25,000; Bk Vols 30,000; Per Subs 30
Automation Activity & Vendor Info: (Cataloging) SirsiDynix; (Circulation) SirsiDynix
Wireless access
Mem of Central Mississippi Regional Library System
Open Mon 10-7, Tues & Thurs 9:30-5:30, Fri 9-5, Sat 9-Noon
Friends of the Library Group

MERIDIAN

J MERIDIAN COMMUNITY COLLEGE*, L O Todd Library Resource Center, 910 Hwy 19 N, 39307. SAN 308-8944. Tel: 601-484-8760. FAX: 601-482-3936. Web Site: www.mcc.cc.ms.us/library. *Libr Dir,* Doug Jernigan; Tel: 601-484-8762, E-mail: djerniga@meridiancc.edu; *Asst Dir,* Rita McClure; Tel: 601-484-8761, E-mail: rmcclure@meridiancc.edu; *Tech Serv Librn,* Suzanne Grafton; Tel: 601-484-8766, E-mail: sgrafton@meridiancc.edu; Staff 10 (MLS 3, Non-MLS 7)
Founded 1937. Enrl 3,800
Library Holdings: Bk Vols 12,000; Per Subs 180
Special Collections: Ulysses S Grant Presidential Coll
Subject Interests: Allied health
Wireless access
Partic in National Network of Libraries of Medicine Region 2
Open Mon-Thurs 7:30am-9pm, Fri 7:30-3:30

P MERIDIAN-LAUDERDALE COUNTY PUBLIC LIBRARY*, 2517 Seventh St, 39301. SAN 308-8952. Tel: 601-693-6771. FAX: 601-486-2270. E-mail: library@meridian.lib.ms.us. Web Site: meridianlauderdalecolibrary.com. *Dir,* Alice Markey; Tel: 601-486-2261, E-mail: director@meridian.lib.ms.us; *Asst Dir,* Walt Barrett; Tel: 601-693-6771, Ext 230, E-mail: wbarrett@meridian.lib.ms.us; Staff 16 (MLS 2, Non-MLS 14)
Founded 1913. Pop 79,000; Circ 135,000
Oct 2020-Sept 2021 Income $1,046,500, State $102,000, County $917,000, Locally Generated Income $13,000, Other $14,500. Mats Exp $128,147, Books $92,177, Per/Ser (Incl. Access Fees) $130, Micro $26,000, AV Mat $5,178, Electronic Ref Mat (Incl. Access Fees) $2,500, Presv $2,162. Sal $631,286
Library Holdings: AV Mats 36,710; Bk Titles 137,915; Bk Vols 176,452; Per Subs 124; Talking Bks 1,767
Special Collections: State Document Depository
Subject Interests: Genealogy, Local hist, Meridian star, Miss
Automation Activity & Vendor Info: (Cataloging) Biblionix/Apollo; (Circulation) Biblionix/Apollo; (ILL) Biblionix/Apollo; (OPAC) Biblionix/Apollo
Wireless access
Function: Bks on cassette, Bks on CD, Children's prog, Computers for patron use, Electronic databases & coll, Free DVD rentals, Homebound delivery serv, Notary serv, Outreach serv, Preschool outreach, Prog for

children & young adult, Ref & res, Ref serv available, Spoken cassettes & CDs, Story hour, Summer reading prog, Telephone ref
Publications: Mailibrary Catalog (Monthly)
Partic in Association for Rural & Small Libraries
Open Mon-Fri 9-5
Restriction: Non-resident fee
Friends of the Library Group

A NAS MERIDIAN*, Andrew Triplett Library, 220 Fuller Rd, 39309. SAN 348-6966. Tel: 601-679-2326. FAX: 601-679-5106. Web Site: www.navymwrmeridian.com. *Supvry Librn,* Lacey Mills; Staff 1 (Non-MLS 1)
Founded 1960
Library Holdings: Bk Titles 9,893; Per Subs 54
Automation Activity & Vendor Info: (Cataloging) EOS International; (Circulation) EOS International
Wireless access
Function: Photocopying/Printing, Prog for children & young adult, Ref serv available, Summer reading prog, Wheelchair accessible
Open Mon & Thurs 10-8, Tues, Wed & Fri 10-6, Sat 10-4
Restriction: Circ to mil employees only, Open to govt employees only

MISSISSIPPI STATE

S COBB INSTITUTE OF ARCHAELOGY LIBRARY, Mississippi State University, Rm 206, 340 Lee Blvd, 39762. (Mail add: PO Box AR, 39762), SAN 348-7024. Tel: 662-325-3826. FAX: 662-325-8690. Web Site: www.cobb.msstate.edu. *Library Contact,* Kathleen Elliott; E-mail: kathleen.elliott@msstate.edu
Founded 1975
Library Holdings: Bk Titles 1,604
Special Collections: Indians of the Southeastern United States; Middle Eastern & Biblical Archaeology; North American Archaeology; Numismatic literature
Wireless access
Restriction: Non-circulating, Open by appt only

C MISSISSIPPI STATE UNIVERSITY*, Mitchell Memorial Library, 395 Hardy Rd, 39762. (Mail add: PO Box 5408, 39762-5408), SAN 348-6990. Tel: 662-325-7668. FAX: 662-325-0011. Web Site: lib.msstate.edu. *Dean of Libr,* Frances N Coleman; E-mail: fcoleman@library.msstate.edu; *Assoc Dean, Univ Libr,* Stephen Cunetto; E-mail: scunetto@library.msstate.edu; *Univ Archivist,* Jessica Parker Smith; E-mail: jsmith@library.msstate.edu; Staff 26 (MLS 26)
Founded 1881. Highest Degree: Doctorate
Library Holdings: Bk Vols 2,051,615; Per Subs 18,103
Special Collections: David Bowen Coll; Delta & Pineland Company Papers; Eugene Butler; Gil Carmichael; GV (Sonny) Montgomery Coll; Hodding Carter Papers; John C Stennis Coll, correspondence, genealogy, mss, notes, papers, photogs; John Grisham; Mike Esty Coll; Mississippi Journalists; Mississippiana, bks, mss, newsp; Republican Party of Mississippi Papers; Sid Salter; Southern History & Politics, micro; State & Local History; Turner Catledge Papers. Oral History; State Document Depository; US Document Depository
Subject Interests: Agr, Energy, Engr, Forestry
Automation Activity & Vendor Info: (Circulation) SirsiDynix
Wireless access
Publications: Guide to Resources in Mammology; Guide to Resources in Ornithology; Guide to Resources of MSU Library in Education; Science Resources
Partic in LYRASIS
Open Mon-Thurs 7am-9:45pm, Fri 7-5:45, Sat 10-5:45
Friends of the Library Group
Departmental Libraries:
ARCHITECTURE, 121 Giles Hall, 889 Collegeview St, 39762. (Mail add: PO Box AQ, 39762), SAN 348-7059. Tel: 662-325-2204. FAX: 662-325-8872. E-mail: jhammett@library.msstate.edu. *Assoc Prof, Librn,* Susan Hall; E-mail: shall@library.msstate.edu; *Info Spec,* Kathrin Dodds; E-mail: kdodds@library.msstate.edu
Open Mon-Thurs 8am-10pm, Fri 8-5, Sat 1-5, Sun 2-10
Friends of the Library Group
JACKSON ARCHITECTURE, 509 E Capitol St, Jackson, 39201. Tel: 622-325-0679. FAX: 601-354-6481. *Libr Assoc,* Pamela Berberette; Tel: 601-354-6184, E-mail: pberberette@library.msstate.edu
Open Mon, Wed & Thurs 9:30-3, Tues 10-3:30
Friends of the Library Group
MERIDIAN CAMPUS, 1000 Hwy 19 N, Meridian, 39307. Tel: 601-484-0236. Reference Tel: 662-325-7667. FAX: 601-484-0139. Web Site: library.msstate.edu/content/templates/?a=142&z=49. *Librn,* Melanie Thomas; E-mail: mthomas@library.msstate.edu
Open Mon, Wed & Thurs 9-6, Tues 12-9, Fri 8-5
Friends of the Library Group
VETERINARY MEDICINE, 240 Wise Center Dr, 39762. (Mail add: PO Box 9825, 39762), SAN 348-7083. Tel: 662-325-1256. FAX: 662-325-1144. Web Site: library.msstate.edu/cvm. *Coordr,* Derek Marshall; Tel: 662-325-1114, E-mail: dmarshall@library.msstate.edu
Open Mon-Thurs 7am-11pm, Fri 7-5, Sat 10-6, Sun 2-10
Friends of the Library Group

MIZE

P MIZE PUBLIC LIBRARY, R T Prince Memorial, 302 Hwy 28 E, 39116. (Mail add: PO Box 247, 39116-0247), SAN 376-639X. Tel: 601-733-2272. E-mail: mize@cmrls.lib.ms.us. Web Site: cmrls.lib.ms.us/cmrlsbranches/mize. *Br Mgr,* Frances Meadows
Library Holdings: Bk Vols 1,800
Automation Activity & Vendor Info: (Circulation) SirsiDynix
Wireless access
Mem of Central Mississippi Regional Library System
Open Mon & Wed 1-5:30
Friends of the Library Group

MOORHEAD

J MISSISSIPPI DELTA COMMUNITY COLLEGE*, Stanny Sanders Library, 414 Hwy 3 South, 38761. (Mail add: PO Box 668, 38761-0668), SAN 308-8960. Tel: 662-246-6376. Circulation Tel: 662-246-6380. Reference Tel: 662-246-6235. Administration Tel: 662-246-6301. FAX: 662-246-8627. Administration FAX: 662-246-6321. E-mail: mdcc_library@msdelta.edu. Web Site: www.msdelta.edu. *Dir, Libr Serv,* Kristy Aust Bariola; Tel: 662-246-6378, E-mail: kbariola@msdelta.edu; *Resource Librn,* Audrey H Beach; E-mail: abeach@msdelta.edu; *Media Ctr Coordr,* Johnnie Davis; Tel: 662-246-6384, E-mail: jdavis@msdelta.edu; *Cataloger,* Position Currently Open; Staff 7 (MLS 2, Non-MLS 5)
Founded 1929. Enrl 2,900; Highest Degree: Associate
Library Holdings: DVDs 700; Bk Titles 55,000; Per Subs 207
Automation Activity & Vendor Info: (Cataloging) SirsiDynix-WorkFlows; (Circulation) SirsiDynix; (ILL) OCLC FirstSearch
Wireless access
Publications: Library Handbook
Partic in Dancing Rabbit Library Consortium
Open Mon-Wed 7:30am-9pm, Thurs 7:30-5
Departmental Libraries:
DREW LIBRARY, 153 N Main St, Drew, 38737. Tel: 662-745-6322. FAX: 662-745-0194. *Librn,* Audrey H Beach; E-mail: abeach@msdelta.edu; *Librn,* Merrie Knight; E-mail: mknight@msdelta.edu; Staff 2 (MLS 2)
Highest Degree: Associate
GHEC LIBRARY, 2900A Hwy 1 S, Greenville, 38701. Tel: 662-332-8467. FAX: 662-332-8931. *Librn,* Alice Permenter; E-mail: apermenter@msdelta.edu; *Librn,* Melody Sample Stapleton; E-mail: mstapleton@msdelta.edu; Staff 2 (MLS 1, Non-MLS 1)
Highest Degree: Associate
Automation Activity & Vendor Info: (Acquisitions) SirsiDynix-WorkFlows; (Circulation) SirsiDynix-WorkFlows; (Course Reserve) SirsiDynix-WorkFlows; (ILL) SirsiDynix-WorkFlows; (Media Booking) SirsiDynix-WorkFlows; (OPAC) SirsiDynix-WorkFlows; (Serials) SirsiDynix-WorkFlows
Open Mon-Thurs 7:30am-9pm
GREENWOOD LIBRARY, 207 W Park Ave, Greenwood, 38930. Tel: 662-453-7377. FAX: 662-453-2043. *Librn,* Audrey Horn Beach; E-mail: abeach@msdelta.edu; *Librn,* Merrie Knight; E-mail: mknight@msdelta.edu; Staff 2 (MLS 2)
Highest Degree: Associate
Open Mon-Thurs 8-4

MORTON

P MORTON PUBLIC LIBRARY*, 16 E Fourth Ave, 39117. SAN 376-6160. Tel: 601-732-6288. FAX: 601-732-6282. E-mail: morton@cmrls.lib.ms.us. Web Site: cmrls.lib.ms.us/cmrlsbranches/morton. *Br Mgr,* Carrie Harrison; E-mail: mobm@cmrls.lib.ms.us
Library Holdings: Bk Titles 10,000; Per Subs 25
Automation Activity & Vendor Info: (Cataloging) SirsiDynix; (Circulation) SirsiDynix
Wireless access
Mem of Central Mississippi Regional Library System
Open Mon-Wed 9:30-5, Thurs 11:30-7, Fri 9-5
Friends of the Library Group

P POLKVILLE PUBLIC LIBRARY*, 6334 Hwy 13, 39117. SAN 376-6012. Tel: 601-537-3116. E-mail: polkvill@cmrls.lib.ms.us. Web Site: www.cmrls.lib.ms.us/cmrlsbranches/polkville. *Br Mgr,* Joyce Bradshaw
Library Holdings: Bk Vols 600
Mem of Central Mississippi Regional Library System
Open Mon 3-7, Wed & Thurs 1:30-5:30
Friends of the Library Group

NATCHEZ

J COPIAH-LINCOLN COMMUNITY COLLEGE*, Willie Mae Dunn Library, 11 Co-Lin Circle, 39120. SAN 308-8987. Tel: 601-446-1101. Administration Tel: 601-446-1107. FAX: 601-446-1297. Web Site: www.colin.edu/students/student-services/libraries. *Libr Dir,* Beth Richard; E-mail: beth.richard@colin.edu; Staff 1 (MLS 1)
Founded 1972. Enrl 959; Fac 25; Highest Degree: Associate
Library Holdings: AV Mats 780; e-books 11,000; Bk Vols 23,275; Per Subs 135
Automation Activity & Vendor Info: (OPAC) SirsiDynix
Wireless access
Open Mon & Wed 7:30-4:30, Tues & Thurs 7:30-6, Fri 7:30-2

P JUDGE GEORGE W ARMSTRONG LIBRARY*, 220 S Commerce St, 39120. SAN 308-8979. Tel: 601-445-8862. FAX: 601-446-7795. E-mail: judge@armstronglibrary.org. Web Site: armstronglibrary.org. *Dir,* Pamela Plummer; E-mail: pam@armstronglibrary.org; *Ch,* Stephanie Johnson; E-mail: stephanie@armstronglibrary.org; *Circ Mgr,* Marianne Raley; E-mail: marianne@armstronglibrary.org; *Cataloger,* Chris Shirey; E-mail: chris@armstronglibrary.org; Staff 11 (MLS 2, Non-MLS 9)
Founded 1883. Pop 42,000
Library Holdings: Bk Titles 92,000; Per Subs 230
Special Collections: Natchez Mississippi Coll
Subject Interests: Local hist
Automation Activity & Vendor Info: (Cataloging) Innovative Interfaces, Inc; (Circulation) Innovative Interfaces, Inc; (ILL) Auto-Graphics, Inc; (OPAC) Innovative Interfaces, Inc
Wireless access
Function: Bks on cassette, Bks on CD, Children's prog, Computers for patron use, ILL available, Online cat, Photocopying/Printing, Preschool outreach, Prog for children & young adult, Spoken cassettes & CDs, Story hour, Summer reading prog, Teen prog, Telephone ref, VHS videos, Wheelchair accessible
Open Mon-Wed & Fri 9-5, Thurs 9-7, Sat 9-1
Friends of the Library Group
Branches: 2
KEVIN POOLE VAN CLEAVE MEMORIAL LIBRARY, 141 W Park St, Centreville, 39631. Tel: 601-645-5771. FAX: 601-645-5771. E-mail: vancleave@naw.lib.ms.us.
Library Holdings: Bk Vols 6,890
Open Mon-Thurs 9-5, Sat 9-1
WOODVILLE PUBLIC LIBRARY, 489 Main St, Woodville, 39669. Tel: 601-888-6712. FAX: 601-888-6885.
Library Holdings: Bk Vols 6,805
Open Tues-Fri 10-5, Sat 10-2
Friends of the Library Group

NEW ALBANY

P UNION COUNTY LIBRARY*, Jennie Stephens Smith Library, 219 King St, 38652. (Mail add: PO Box 846, 38652-0846), SAN 348-7113. Tel: 662-534-1991. FAX: 662-534-1937. Web Site: unioncountylibrary.org/unioncounty. *Dir,* Kay Sappington; E-mail: ksappington@union.lib.ms.us; Staff 9 (MLS 1, Non-MLS 8)
Founded 1933. Pop 26,000; Circ 43,500
Library Holdings: Bk Vols 70,000; Per Subs 75
Special Collections: Genealogy Coll
Subject Interests: Miss hist
Automation Activity & Vendor Info: (Cataloging) Follett Software; (Circulation) Follett Software; (ILL) Follett Software; (OPAC) Follett Software
Wireless access
Open Tues & Thurs 9-8, Wed & Fri 9-6, Sat 11-4
Friends of the Library Group
Branches: 1
NANCE MCNEELY PUBLIC, 1177 B Springdale Ave, Myrtle, 38650. (Mail add: PO Box 225, Myrtle, 38650-0225), SAN 374-731X. Tel: 662-988-2895. FAX: 662-988-2895. *Librn,* Betty McNeely
Open Mon, Tues, Thurs & Fri 1:30-5:30, Sat 9-1
Friends of the Library Group

NEW AUGUSTA

P NEW AUGUSTA PUBLIC*, PO Box 401, 39462. SAN 348-8403. Tel: 601-964-3710. E-mail: nacityhall@ftcweb.net. *Library Contact,* Sarah Magee

OCEAN SPRINGS

C UNIVERSITY OF SOUTHERN MISSISSIPPI-GULF COAST RESEARCH LABORATORY, Gunter Library, 703 E Beach Dr, 39564. SAN 308-9037. Tel: 228-872-4213, 228-872-4253. FAX: 228-872-4264. Web Site: gcrl.usm.edu/library.gcrl. *Head Librn, Prof,* Joyce M Shaw; E-mail: joyce.shaw@usm.edu; *Libr Coord,* MaryAnne Anthony; E-mail: maryanne.anthony@usm.edu; *Libr Asst,* Martha Brown; E-mail: martha.brown@usm.edu; *Tech Asst,* Marjorie Williams; E-mail: marjorie.williams@usm.edu; Staff 2.5 (MLS 1, Non-MLS 1.5)
Founded 1955. Enrl 54; Fac 1; Highest Degree: Doctorate
Library Holdings: Bk Titles 7,148; Per Subs 120
Special Collections: GCRL History; GCRL Publications; Marine Biology (Expedition Reports); Marine Invertebrate Zoology Coll
Subject Interests: Botany, Ecology, Geol, Ichthyology, Marine biol, Microbiology, Toxicology
Wireless access
Function: Archival coll, Bks on CD, Computers for patron use, Doc delivery serv, ILL available, Photocopying/Printing, Scanner
Publications: Gulf & Caribbean Research (Periodical); Master Serial List (Serials catalog)
Partic in MAGNOLIA; National Network of Libraries of Medicine Region 2
Open Mon-Thurs 8-12 & 1-6:30, Fri 8-12 & 1-5
Restriction: Borrowing privileges limited to fac & registered students, Circulates for staff only, In-house use for visitors, Non-circulating to the pub, Open to fac, students & qualified researchers, Open to pub for ref only

OXFORD

J NORTHWEST MISSISSIPPI COMMUNITY COLLEGE, Lafayette-Yalobusha Learning Resource Center Library, 1310 Belk Dr, 38655. SAN 370-4939. Tel: 662-238-7953. Web Site: www.northwestms.edu/index.php/?page_id=2095. *Head Librn,* Laura McCain; E-mail: lmccain@northwestms.edu
Founded 1988
Library Holdings: Bk Vols 16,000; Per Subs 60
Wireless access
Open Mon-Thurs 8-7, Fri 8-3

GL USDA-ARS, National Sedimentation Laboratory Library, 598 McElroy Dr, 38655-2117. SAN 373-0778. Tel: 662-232-2996. FAX: 662-281-5706. *Dir,* Martin Locke; E-mail: martin.locke@ars.usda.gov
Library Holdings: Bk Vols 20,000; Per Subs 15
Open Mon-Fri 8-5

PARCHMAN

S MISSISSIPPI DEPARTMENT OF CORRECTIONS*, Mississippi State Penitentiary Library, PO Box 1057, 38738. Tel: 662-745-6611, Ext 3101. Web Site: www.mdoc.ms.gov. *Librn,* Melinda Buckner; E-mail: mbuckner@mdoc.state.ms.us
Library Holdings: Bk Vols 3,000; Per Subs 100
Automation Activity & Vendor Info: (Cataloging) Follett Software; (Circulation) Follett Software
Open Mon-Sun 6:30-2:30 & 4:30-8

PASCAGOULA

P JACKSON-GEORGE REGIONAL LIBRARY SYSTEM*, 3214 Pascagoula St, 39567. SAN 348-7202. Tel: 228-769-3227. FAX: 228-769-3146. Web Site: www.jgrls.org. *Libr Dir,* Lori Barnes; E-mail: lbarnes@jgrls.org; *Asst Dir of Br,* Pamela Armstrong; E-mail: parmstrong@jgrls.org; *Asst Dir, Coll Mgt,* Alisa St Amant; E-mail: astamant@jgrls.org; *Bus Mgr,* Janet Beatty; Tel: 228-769-3092, E-mail: jbeatty@jgrls.org; Staff 89 (MLS 14, Non-MLS 75)
Founded 1940. Pop 155,000; Circ 950,000
Library Holdings: DVDs 13,293; Large Print Bks 12,176; Bk Vols 308,500; Per Subs 936; Talking Bks 19,137
Special Collections: Genealogy & Local History Coll
Automation Activity & Vendor Info: (Acquisitions) SirsiDynix-WorkFlows; (Cataloging) SirsiDynix-WorkFlows; (Circulation) SirsiDynix-WorkFlows; (OPAC) SirsiDynix-Enterprise
Wireless access
Function: 24/7 Electronic res, 24/7 Online cat, 3D Printer, Accelerated reader prog, Adult bk club, After school storytime, ILL available, Photocopying/Printing, Prog for children & young adult, Ref serv available, Summer reading prog, Wheelchair accessible
Open Mon-Thurs 9-8, Fri & Sat 9-4
Friends of the Library Group
Branches: 8
EAST CENTRAL PUBLIC LIBRARY, 21801 Slider Rd, Moss Point, 39562, SAN 348-7237. Tel: 228-588-6263. *Br Mgr,* Ann Rushing; E-mail: mrushing@jgrls.org; Staff 5 (MLS 1, Non-MLS 4)
Open Mon-Thurs 8-6, Fri & Sat 8-4
Friends of the Library Group
LUCEDALE-GEORGE COUNTY PUBLIC LIBRARY, 507 Oak St, Lucedale, 39452, SAN 348-7261. Tel: 601-947-2123. FAX: 601-766-3360. *Br Mgr,* Cynthia Morgan; E-mail: cmorgan@jgrls.org; Staff 5 (MLS 1, Non-MLS 4)
Open Mon-Thurs 9-7, Fri & Sat 9-5
Friends of the Library Group

KATHLEEN MCILWAIN-GAUTIER PUBLIC LIBRARY, 2100 Library Lane, Gautier, 39553, SAN 348-7326. Tel: 228-497-4531. FAX: 228-497-4560. *Br Mgr,* Angela Thompson; E-mail: athompson@jgrls.org
Open Mon-Thurs 9-8, Fri & Sat 9-5
Friends of the Library Group
OCEAN SPRINGS MUNICIPAL LIBRARY, 525 Dewey Ave, Ocean Springs, 39564, SAN 348-7350. Tel: 228-875-1193. FAX: 228-875-1535. *Br Mgr,* Yvonne Parton; E-mail: yparton@jgrls.org
Open Mon-Thurs 9-8, Fri & Sat 9-5
Friends of the Library Group
PASCAGOULA PUBLIC LIBRARY, 3214 Pascagoula St, 39567, SAN 348-7385. FAX: 228-769-3060. *Br Mgr,* Leanna Hamburg; E-mail: jlhamburg@jgrls.org
Open Mon-Thurs 9-8, Fri & Sat 9-5
Friends of the Library Group
ST MARTIN PUBLIC LIBRARY, 15004 LeMoyne Blvd, Biloxi, 39532, SAN 348-7415. Tel: 228-392-3250. FAX: 228-392-0522. *Br Mgr,* Janis Zuleeg; E-mail: jzuleeg@jgrls.org
Open Mon-Thurs 9-7, Fri & Sat 9-5
Friends of the Library Group
INA THOMPSON MOSS POINT LIBRARY, 4119 Bellview St, Moss Point, 39563, SAN 348-7296. Tel: 228-475-7462. FAX: 228-475-7484. *Br Mgr,* Jamie Elston; E-mail: jelston@jgrls.org; Staff 5 (MLS 1, Non-MLS 4)
Founded 1900
Library Holdings: Per Subs 102
Open Mon-Thurs 9-8, Fri & Sat 9-5
Friends of the Library Group
VANCLEAVE PUBLIC LIBRARY, 12604 Hwy 57, Vancleave, 39565, SAN 348-744X. Tel: 228-826-5857. FAX: 228-826-5893. *Br Mgr,* Jeanne Damiano; E-mail: jdamiano@jgrls.org
Open Mon-Thurs 9-7, Fri & Sat 9-5
Friends of the Library Group

G NATIONAL MARINE FISHERIES SERVICE*, Pascagoula Laboratory Library, NMFS/SE Fisheries Science Ctr, 3209 Frederick St, 39568. (Mail add: PO Mailing Drawer 1207, 39568-1207), SAN 308-9045. Tel: 228-549-1617, 228-762-4591. FAX: 228-769-9200. Web Site: www.aoml.noaa.gov/general/lib/pasca2.html, www.lib.noaa.gov. *Librn,* Lagena Fantroy; E-mail: lagena.fantroy@noaa.gov; Staff 1 (MLS 1)
Founded 1950
Library Holdings: Bk Vols 5,000; Per Subs 88
Subject Interests: Marine biol, Oceanography, Seafood analysis, Seafood tech
Automation Activity & Vendor Info: (ILL) OCLC
Partic in NOAA Libraries Network; Proquest Dialog
Open Mon-Fri 8-4:30

PEARL

P PEARL PUBLIC LIBRARY*, 2416 Old Brandon Rd, 39208-4601. SAN 377-5739. Tel: 601-932-2562. FAX: 601-932-3535. E-mail: pearl@cmrls.lib.ms.us. Web Site: cmrls.lib.ms.us/cmrlsbranches/pearl. *Br Mgr,* Position Currently Open; E-mail: rcbm@cmrls.lib.ms.us; *Circ Supvr,* Carolyn Anderson; E-mail: rccirc@cmrls.lib.ms.us; *Ref Supvr,* Amy Lee; E-mail: rcref@cmrls.lib.ms.us; *Youth Serv,* Adrianne Manning; E-mail: rcchild@cmrls.lib.ms.us; Staff 4 (MLS 1, Non-MLS 3)
Pop 25,000
Library Holdings: Bk Vols 53,000; Per Subs 120
Automation Activity & Vendor Info: (Circulation) Horizon; (OPAC) Horizon
Wireless access
Function: Accelerated reader prog, Adult bk club, After school storytime, Art exhibits, Audiobks via web, Bk club(s), Bks on cassette, Bks on CD, Children's prog, Computer training, Computers for patron use, Electronic databases & coll, Free DVD rentals, Holiday prog, ILL available, Internet access, Music CDs, Online cat, Online ref, Outreach serv, Photocopying/Printing, Preschool outreach, Prog for adults, Prog for children & young adult, Ref serv available, Senior computer classes, Spoken cassettes & CDs, Spoken cassettes & DVDs, Story hour, Summer reading prog, Tax forms, Teen prog, Telephone ref, VHS videos, Wheelchair accessible
Mem of Central Mississippi Regional Library System
Open Mon-Thurs 9-8, Fri 9-5, Sat 10-4
Friends of the Library Group

PELAHATCHIE

P PELAHATCHIE PUBLIC LIBRARY*, 718 Second St, 39145. (Mail add: PO Box 959, 39145), SAN 376-6225. Tel: 601-854-8764. FAX: 601-854-8764. E-mail: pelahat@cmrls.lib.ms.us. Web Site: cmrls.lib.ms.us/cmrlsbranches/pelahatchie. *Br Mgr,* Tina Mauney
Library Holdings: Bk Titles 13,347
Wireless access
Mem of Central Mississippi Regional Library System
Open Mon-Wed 10:30-5, Thurs 12-7

PERKINSTON

J MISSISSIPPI GULF COAST COMMUNITY COLLEGE*, Perkinston Campus Learning Resources Center, Hwy 49 S, 39573. SAN 348-7474. Tel: 601-928-5211. FAX: 601-928-6345. Web Site: www.mgccc.edu/library/perkinston-library. *Asst Dean,* Vanessa Ritchie; Tel: 601-928-6242, E-mail: vanessa.ritchie@mgccc.edu; *Librn,* Laura Savage; Tel: 601-928-6380, E-mail: laura.savage@mgccc.edu; *Librn,* Shugana Williams; Tel: 601-928-6259, E-mail: shugana.williams@mgccc.edu; Staff 5 (MLS 3, Non-MLS 2)
Founded 1925. Enrl 1,200; Fac 45
Library Holdings: Bk Vols 31,000; Per Subs 212
Subject Interests: Career, Faculty
Wireless access
Open Mon-Thurs (Winter) 7:30am-9pm, Fri 7:30-2:30, Sun 6-9; Mon-Thurs (Summer) 7:30-5, Fri 7:30-2:30

PHILADELPHIA

P NESHOBA COUNTY PUBLIC LIBRARY, 230 Beacon St, 39350. SAN 308-907X. Tel: 601-656-4911. FAX: 601-656-6894. E-mail: neshobalibrary@gmail.com. Web Site: neshobalibrary.net. *Libr Dir,* Position Currently Open; *Youth Librn,* Leaha Winstead; *Tech Serv,* Jason Msyo; Staff 5 (MLS 1, Non-MLS 4)
Founded 1929. Pop 29,905; Circ 40,000
Library Holdings: Audiobooks 400; DVDs 1,500; e-books 3,000; Bk Titles 36,000; Per Subs 30
Subject Interests: Choctaw Indians, Genealogy, Local hist
Automation Activity & Vendor Info: (Acquisitions) Biblionix/Apollo; (Cataloging) Biblionix/Apollo; (Circulation) Biblionix/Apollo; (Course Reserve) Biblionix/Apollo; (OPAC) Biblionix/Apollo; (Serials) Biblionix/Apollo
Wireless access
Publications: Cemetery Records of Neshoba County; Our Links to the Past; The Red Clay Hills of Neshoba
Open Mon-Fri 10-4
Friends of the Library Group
Bookmobiles: 1. Libr Dir, Jacob Starks. Bk titles 1,500

PICAYUNE

P PEARL RIVER COUNTY LIBRARY SYSTEM*, Margaret Reed Crosby Memorial Library, 900 Goodyear Blvd, 39466. SAN 348-7504. Tel: 601-798-5081. FAX: 601-798-5082. Web Site: www.pearlriver.lib.ms.us. *Syst Dir,* Carol Phares; E-mail: cphares@pearlriver.lib.ms.us; *Head, Tech Proc,* Phyllis Gage; E-mail: pgage@pearlriver.lib.ms.us; *Head, Circ,* Renee Buford; Staff 1 (MLS 1)
Founded 1926. Pop 39,700; Circ 150,000
Library Holdings: Bk Vols 90,000; Per Subs 70
Special Collections: Genealogy Family Files; Miss Municipal Assn Digitizing Project; W A Zeltner Mississippi Coll. Oral History; State Document Depository
Subject Interests: Drug abuse, Genealogy, Local hist
Automation Activity & Vendor Info: (Cataloging) Book Systems; (Circulation) Book Systems
Wireless access
Function: 24/7 Online cat, Adult bk club, Bk club(s), Bks on CD, CD-ROM, Children's prog, Computers for patron use, Free DVD rentals, ILL available, Internet access, Magazines, Magnifiers for reading, Meeting rooms, Microfiche/film & reading machines, Online cat, Photocopying/Printing, Printer for laptops & handheld devices, Prog for adults, Prog for children & young adult, Ref serv available, Scanner, Serves people with intellectual disabilities, Spanish lang bks, Story hour, Summer reading prog, Wheelchair accessible
Special Services for the Deaf - Bks on deafness & sign lang; High interest/low vocabulary bks
Special Services for the Blind - Extensive large print coll; Low vision equip; Magnifiers
Open Mon & Thurs 9-6, Tues 9-7, Fri 9-5, Sat 9-1
Friends of the Library Group
Branches: 1
POPLARVILLE PUBLIC LIBRARY, 202 W Beers St, Poplarville, 39470, SAN 348-7539. Tel: 601-795-8411. FAX: 601-795-8411. *Br Mgr,* Denise Davis; E-mail: ddavis@pearlriver.lib.ms.us; *Head, Circ,* Ronnie Rawls; E-mail: prclssocial@gmail.com; Staff 3 (Non-MLS 3)
Library Holdings: Bk Vols 30,000; Per Subs 20
Automation Activity & Vendor Info: (Circulation) Book Systems
Function: Activity rm, Bks on CD, CD-ROM, Children's prog, Computers for patron use, Free DVD rentals, ILL available, Internet access, Magazines, Magnifiers for reading, Movies, Online cat, Photocopying/Printing, Preschool reading prog, Prog for children & young adult, Ref serv available, Scanner, Serves people with intellectual

disabilities, Spanish lang bks, Story hour, Summer reading prog, Wheelchair accessible
Open Mon, Thurs & Fri 9-5, Tues 10-6
Friends of the Library Group

PONTOTOC

P DIXIE REGIONAL LIBRARY SYSTEM*, 111 N Main St, 38863. SAN 348-7598. Tel: 662-489-3961. FAX: 662-489-3929. E-mail: pclib@dixie.lib.ms.us. Web Site: www.dixie.lib.ms.us. *Dir,* Regina Graham; E-mail: rgraham@dixie.lib.ms.us; *Tech Serv,* Pam Morton; E-mail: pmorton@dixie.lib.ms.us; Staff 3 (MLS 3)
Founded 1961. Pop 62,427; Circ 174,876
Library Holdings: Bk Vols 133,248; Per Subs 143
Subject Interests: Genealogy, Local hist
Automation Activity & Vendor Info: (Cataloging) Book Systems; (Circulation) Book Systems; (ILL) Auto-Graphics, Inc; (OPAC) Book Systems
Wireless access
Function: Accelerated reader prog, Art exhibits, Children's prog, Computers for patron use, Electronic databases & coll, Holiday prog, ILL available, Internet access, Music CDs, Online cat, Online ref, Outside serv via phone, mail, e-mail & web, Photocopying/Printing, Preschool outreach, Prog for adults, Prog for children & young adult, Spoken cassettes & CDs, Spoken cassettes & DVDs, Story hour, Summer reading prog, Tax forms, Telephone ref, VHS videos, Wheelchair accessible
Publications: Dixie News (Quarterly)
Partic in MAGNOLIA
Special Services for the Blind - Large print & cassettes
Open Mon-Thurs 9-6, Fri 9-5, Sat 9-1
Friends of the Library Group
Branches: 8
CALHOUN CITY BRANCH, 113 E Burkitt St, Calhoun City, 38916, SAN 348-7652. Tel: 662-628-6331. FAX: 662-628-6331. E-mail: cclib@dixie.lib.ms.us. *Br Mgr,* Debbie Hunter
Library Holdings: Bk Vols 10,645
Function: Bks on cassette, Bks on CD, Children's prog, Computers for patron use, ILL available, Online cat, Photocopying/Printing, Spoken cassettes & CDs, Story hour, Summer reading prog, Tax forms, VHS videos
Open Mon & Fri 10-5, Tues 12-6, Thurs 10-6, Sat 10-Noon
EDMONDSON MEMORIAL, 109 Stovall St, Vardaman, 38878, SAN 348-7776. Tel: 662-682-7333. FAX: 662-682-7333. E-mail: valib@dixie.lib.ms.us. *Br Mgr,* Janet Swindle
Library Holdings: Bk Vols 4,024
Open Mon, Tues & Thurs 10-5, Fri 10-4, Sat 10-Noon
HOULKA PUBLIC, 113 Hwy 32 E, Houlka, 38850, SAN 348-7687. Tel: 662-568-2747. FAX: 662-568-2747. E-mail: hllib@dixie.lib.ms.us. *Br Mgr,* Martha Hinton
Pop 1,657; Circ 4,316
Library Holdings: Bk Vols 4,923
Open Mon-Fri 1-5
HOUSTON CARNEGIE BRANCH, 105 W Madison St, Houston, 38851, SAN 348-7717. Tel: 662-456-3381. FAX: 662-456-3381. E-mail: holib@dixie.lib.ms.us. *Br Mgr,* Lisa M Mims; Staff 1.8 (Non-MLS 1.8)
Founded 1909
Library Holdings: Bk Vols 10,000
Open Tues-Fri 9-5, Sat 9-Noon
Friends of the Library Group
OKOLONA CARNEGIE BRANCH, 321 Main St, Okolona, 38860. (Mail add: PO Box 126, Okolona, 38860-0126), SAN 348-7741. Tel: 662-447-2401. FAX: 662-447-2401. E-mail: oklib@dixie.lib.ms.us. *Br Mgr,* Estelle Ivy
Library Holdings: Bk Vols 15,000
Open Mon, Tues, Thurs & Fri 9-1, Sat 9-Noon
Friends of the Library Group
PONTOTOC COUNTY LIBRARY, 111 N Main St, 38863, SAN 348-7628. FAX: 662-489-7777. *Br Mgr,* Annette McGregor; E-mail: amcgregor@dixie.lib.ms.us
Founded 1934. Pop 20,918
Library Holdings: Bk Vols 25,148
Special Collections: James Garrison Civil War Exhibit
Subject Interests: Local hist
Open Mon-Thurs 9-6, Fri 9-5, Sat 9-1
Friends of the Library Group
SHERMAN PUBLIC, 20 W Lamar St, Sherman, 38869. (Mail add: PO Box 181, Sherman, 38869-0181), SAN 373-1766. Tel: 662-840-2513. FAX: 662-840-2513. E-mail: shlib@dixie.lib.ms.us. *Br Mgr,* Celisa Russell
Library Holdings: Bk Vols 3,265
Open Mon-Fri 12-5
Friends of the Library Group
JESSE YANCY MEMORIAL LIBRARY, 314 N Newberger Ave, Bruce, 38915. (Mail add: PO Box 517, Bruce, 38915-0096), SAN 348-7806. Tel: 662-983-2220. FAX: 662-983-2934. E-mail: brlib@dixie.lib.ms.us. *Br Mgr,* Janaice Vaughn; Staff 1 (Non-MLS 1)
Founded 1959
Library Holdings: Bk Vols 20,000
Function: ILL available, Photocopying/Printing, Prog for adults, Prog for children & young adult, Spoken cassettes & CDs, Summer reading prog, VHS videos
Open Mon, Wed & Fri 9-5, Tues 10-6, Sat 10-2
Friends of the Library Group

POPLARVILLE

J PEARL RIVER COMMUNITY COLLEGE*, Garvin H Johnston Library, 101 Hwy 11 N, 39470. (Mail add: PO Box 5660, 39470-5660), SAN 308-9088. Reference Tel: 601-403-1332. Automation Services Tel: 601-403-1337. E-mail: ghjlibrary@prcc.edu. Web Site: www.prcc.edu/libraries. *Dir of Libr,* Tracy H Smith; E-mail: tsmith@prcc.edu; *Pub Serv Librn,* Amanda Myers; E-mail: acmyers@price.edu; Staff 3 (MLS 3)
Founded 1926. Enrl 3,500; Fac 175; Highest Degree: Associate
Library Holdings: DVDs 12; e-books 17,706; Bk Vols 57,407; Per Subs 326; Videos 4,174
Special Collections: Mississippi Coll
Subject Interests: Behav sci, Hist, Lit, Soc sci
Automation Activity & Vendor Info: (Cataloging) SirsiDynix; (Circulation) SirsiDynix; (Course Reserve) SirsiDynix; (OPAC) SirsiDynix; (Serials) SirsiDynix
Wireless access
Partic in LYRASIS
Open Mon-Thurs 7am-9pm, Fri 7-4:30 (Fall-Spring); Mon-Wed 7:30-6:30, Thurs 7:30-5 (Summer)
Departmental Libraries:
FORREST COUNTY CENTER LIBRARY, 5448 US Hwy 49 S, Hattiesburg, 39401, SAN 377-7758. Tel: 601-554-5522. *Librn,* Sarah Welch; E-mail: swelch@prcc.edu
Founded 1995
Library Holdings: Bk Vols 4,000; Per Subs 46
Subject Interests: Allied health
Open Mon-Thurs 7am-9pm, Fri 7-3 (Fall-Spring); Mon-Wed 7-6:30, Thurs 7:30-5 (Summer)
HANCOCK CENTER LIBRARY, 454 Hwy 90, Ste D, Waveland, 39756. Tel: 228-252-7000. *Librn,* Caroline Clark
Founded 2005
Library Holdings: Bk Vols 2,000
Open Tues & Fri 8-4, Thurs 11-7 (Fall-Spring); Mon-Wed 10-6:30, Thurs 10-5 (Summer)

PORT GIBSON

P HARRIETTE PERSON MEMORIAL LIBRARY*, 606 Market St, 39150. SAN 308-910X. Tel: 601-437-5202. FAX: 601-437-5787. E-mail: harrietteperson.library@gmail.com. Web Site: hpml.lib.ms.us. *Dir,* Helen McComb
Founded 1914. Pop 11,831; Circ 28,350
Library Holdings: DVDs 196; Bk Titles 21,151; Per Subs 57; Talking Bks 689; Videos 1,981
Special Collections: Miss Coll
Automation Activity & Vendor Info: (Cataloging) Book Systems; (Circulation) Book Systems; (ILL) Auto-Graphics, Inc; (OPAC) Book Systems; (Serials) EBSCO Online
Wireless access
Open Mon-Wed & Fri 8:30-5, Thurs & Sat 9-12
Friends of the Library Group

PUCKETT

P PUCKETT PUBLIC LIBRARY*, 118 Cemetery Rd, 39151. (Mail add: PO Box 550, 39151-0550), SAN 376-6217. Tel: 601-824-0180. E-mail: puckett@cmrls.lib.ms.us. Web Site: www.cmrls.lib.ms.us/cmrlsbranches/puckett. *Br Mgr,* Regina Hutson
Library Holdings: Bk Titles 13,294; Per Subs 14
Wireless access
Mem of Central Mississippi Regional Library System
Open Mon 2-6, Tues & Thurs 11-5
Friends of the Library Group

PURVIS

P LAMAR COUNTY LIBRARY SYSTEM*, Library Administration, 144 Shelby Speights Dr, 39475. (Mail add: PO Box 289, 39475). Web Site: lclsms.org. *Dir,* Phillip Carter; Tel: 601-794-3220, E-mail: director@lamarcountylibraries.org; *Asst Dir,* Mr Terry Lajaunie; Tel: 601-794-3222, E-mail: tlajaunie@lamarcountylibraries.org; Staff 4 (MLS 2, Non-MLS 2)

Founded 1997. Pop 40,000
Subject Interests: Genealogy, Local hist, Miss authors
Automation Activity & Vendor Info: (Cataloging) SirsiDynix; (Circulation) SirsiDynix; (ILL) OCLC; (OPAC) SirsiDynix
Wireless access
Open Mon-Fri 9-5
Friends of the Library Group
Branches: 4
L R BOYER MEMORIAL LIBRARY - SUMRALL, 121 Poplar St, Sumrall, 39482. (Mail add: PO Box 327, Sumrall, 39482-0327), SAN 329-3335. Tel: 601-758-4711. FAX: 601-758-4711. Web Site: lclsms.org/sumrall. *Br Mgr,* Misty Davis; Staff 2 (Non-MLS 2)
Founded 1933
Library Holdings: AV Mats 379; Large Print Bks 500; Bk Vols 13,000; Per Subs 12; Talking Bks 250
Partic in MAGNOLIA
Open Mon-Fri 8-5, Sat 10-2
Friends of the Library Group
LUMBERTON PUBLIC, 106 W Main Ave, Lumberton, 39455, SAN 348-8284. Tel: 601-796-2505. FAX: 601-794-4584. Web Site: lclsms.org/lumberton. *Mgr,* Sherri McSorley; Staff 2 (Non-MLS 2)
Founded 1922
Library Holdings: AV Mats 296; Large Print Bks 425; Bk Vols 10,711; Per Subs 18; Talking Bks 117
Subject Interests: Local hist
Partic in MAGNOLIA
Open Mon-Fri 9-6, Sat 10-2
Friends of the Library Group
OAK GROVE PUBLIC, 4958 Old Hwy 11, Hattiesburg, 39402. Tel: 601-296-1620. Reference Tel: 601-296-1704. FAX: 601-296-1620. Web Site: lclsms.org/oakgrove. *Br Mgr,* Alice Markey; Staff 7 (MLS 2, Non-MLS 5)
Founded 2003
Library Holdings: AV Mats 133; Large Print Bks 127; Bk Vols 8,826; Per Subs 62; Talking Bks 51
Subject Interests: Genealogy, Local hist, Miss authors
Partic in MAGNOLIA
Open Mon-Fri 9-6, Sat 10-2
Friends of the Library Group
PURVIS PUBLIC, 122 Shelby Speights Dr, 39475, SAN 348-8438. Tel: 601-794-6291. FAX: 601-794-6291. Web Site: lclsms.org/purvis. *Br Mgr,* Christina Broome; Staff 3 (MLS 1, Non-MLS 2)
Founded 1934
Library Holdings: AV Mats 441; Large Print Bks 519; Bk Vols 13,023; Per Subs 27; Talking Bks 185
Partic in MAGNOLIA
Open Mon-Fri 9-6, Sat 10-2
Friends of the Library Group

QUITMAN

P EAST MISSISSIPPI REGIONAL LIBRARY SYSTEM*, 116 Water St, 39355-2336. SAN 348-7830. Tel: 601-776-3881. FAX: 601-776-6599. E-mail: info@emrl.lib.ms.us. Web Site: emrl.lib.ms.us. *Dir,* Joshua Haidet; E-mail: jhaidet@emrl.lib.ms.us; Staff 10 (MLS 2, Non-MLS 8)
Founded 1966. Pop 36,555; Circ 83,350
Library Holdings: AV Mats 6,035; CDs 769; DVDs 483; Large Print Bks 4,628; Bk Vols 62,930; Per Subs 56; Talking Bks 2,423; Videos 2,151
Automation Activity & Vendor Info: (Cataloging) Innovative Interfaces, Inc; (Circulation) Innovative Interfaces, Inc; (ILL) Auto-Graphics, Inc; (OPAC) Innovative Interfaces, Inc
Wireless access
Function: Bks on cassette, Bks on CD, CD-ROM, Children's prog, Computers for patron use, Free DVD rentals, ILL available, Music CDs, Online cat, Photocopying/Printing, Ref serv available, Spoken cassettes & CDs, Summer reading prog, Tax forms, VHS videos, Wheelchair accessible
Open Mon-Thurs 8-6
Branches: 6
BAY SPRINGS MUNICIPAL, 2747 Hwy 15, Bay Springs, 39422. (Mail add: PO Drawer N, Bay Springs, 39422-1914), SAN 348-7865. Tel: 601-764-2291. FAX: 601-764-2290. Web Site: emrl.lib.ms.us/branches/bay-springs-municipal-library. *Librn,* Libby Thornton; E-mail: ethornton@emrl.lib.ms.us; *Librn,* Melissa Anne Blocker; E-mail: mblocker@emrl.lib.ms.us
Library Holdings: Bk Vols 10,000
Open Mon, Tues & Thurs 8-6:30, Wed 7:30-6
CLARKE COUNTY-QUITMAN PUBLIC, 116 Water St, 39355. Tel: 601-776-3881. FAX: 601-776-6599. Web Site: emrl.lib.ms.us/branches/ccquitman-public-library. *Librn,* Barbara O'Neil; E-mail: boneil@emrl.lib.ms.us; *Librn,* Alicia Underwood; E-mail: aunderwood@erml.lib.ms.us; Staff 2 (Non-MLS 2)
Founded 1966. Pop 16,743; Circ 11,351
Library Holdings: DVDs 757; Bk Titles 16,089; Per Subs 40
Function: Computers for patron use, Free DVD rentals, ILL available, Microfiche/film & reading machines, Online cat, Online ref, Photocopying/Printing, Spoken cassettes & CDs, Summer reading prog, VHS videos
Open Mon, Tues & Thurs 8-6:30, Wed 7:30-6
ENTERPRISE PUBLIC, 500 River Rd, Enterprise, 39330, SAN 348-789X. Tel: 601-659-3564. Web Site: emrl.lib.ms.us/branches/enterprise-public-library. *Librn,* Jane Evans; E-mail: jevans@emrl.lib.ms.us
Library Holdings: Bk Vols 8,250
Open Mon-Fri 12-5
PACHUTA PUBLIC, Hwy 11N, Pachuta, 39347. (Mail add: PO Box 189, Pachuta, 39347-0189). Tel: 601-776-7209. Web Site: emrl.lib.ms.us/branches/pachuta-public-library. *Librn,* Wilma Johnson; E-mail: wjohnson@emrl.lib.ms.us
Library Holdings: Bk Vols 5,000
Open Mon-Thurs 1-6
MARY WEEMS PARKER MEMORIAL, 1016 N Pine Ave, Heidelberg, 39439, SAN 348-792X. Tel: 601-787-3857. FAX: 601-787-3857. E-mail: hlib@emrl.lib.ms.us. Web Site: emrl.lib.ms.us/branches/mary-weems-parker-memorial-library. *Librn,* Margie McClellan
Library Holdings: Bk Vols 12,000
Open Mon-Thurs 1-6, Sat 9-1
STONEWALL PUBLIC, 801 Erwin Rd, Stonewall, 39363-9610. (Mail add: PO Box 700, Stonewall, 39363-0700), SAN 348-8047. Tel: 601-659-3080. FAX: 601-659-3080. Web Site: emrl.lib.ms.us/branches/stonewall-public-library. *Librn,* Michelle Kulick; E-mail: mkulick@emrl.lib.ms.us
Library Holdings: Bk Vols 12,000
Open Mon-Thurs 1-6

RALEIGH

P RALEIGH PUBLIC LIBRARY*, Floyd J Robinson Memorial Library, 150 Main St, 39153. (Mail add: PO Box 266, 39153-0266), SAN 376-6349. Tel: 601-782-4277. FAX: 601-782-4400. E-mail: raleigh@cmrls.lib.ms.us. Web Site: cmrls.lib.ms.us/cmrlsbranches/raleigh. *Br Mgr,* Betty Medlock
Library Holdings: Bk Titles 13,500; Per Subs 18
Function: Photocopying/Printing
Mem of Central Mississippi Regional Library System
Open Mon-Fri 9-5:30
Friends of the Library Group

RAYMOND

J HINDS COMMUNITY COLLEGE*, Raymond Campus Learning Resources/Library, 505 E Main St, 39154. (Mail add: PO Box 1100, 39154-1100), SAN 348-8101. Tel: 601-857-3255. Administration Tel: 601-857-3380. E-mail: lrcraymondcirculation@hindscc.edu. Web Site: lrc.hindscc.edu. *Dean, Learning Res,* Dr Mary Beth Applin; E-mail: mary.applin@hindscc.edu; *Librn,* Judy Hilkert; Tel: 601-857-3355, E-mail: jrhilkert@hindscc.edu; Staff 10 (MLS 9, Non-MLS 1)
Founded 1922. Enrl 12,164; Fac 488; Highest Degree: Associate
Library Holdings: Bk Titles 103,793; Bk Vols 173,675; Per Subs 1,180
Special Collections: Black Heritage Coll; Government (John Bell Williams Coll)
Automation Activity & Vendor Info: (Acquisitions) SirsiDynix
Publications: HLR Spotlight (Newsletter)
Partic in LYRASIS
Open Mon-Thurs (Winter) 7:45am-9pm, Fri 7:45-4; Mon-Thurs (Summer) 7:15am-8pm, Fri 7:15-3
Departmental Libraries:
JACKSON ACADEMIC & TECHNICAL CENTER LEARNING RESOURCES/LIBRARY, 3925 Sunset Dr, Jackson, 39213-5899, SAN 308-8715. Tel: 601-987-8123. FAX: 601-982-5804. E-mail: lrcsunsetcirculation@hindscc.edu. *Head Librn,* Jackie Quinn; E-mail: JYQuinn@hindscc.edu; Staff 2 (MLS 1, Non-MLS 1)
Highest Degree: Associate
Function: Res libr
Open Mon-Thurs 7:30-7:30, Fri 7:30-3
NURSING/ALLIED HEALTH CENTER LIBRARY, 1750 Chadwick Dr, Jackson, 39204-3490, SAN 324-427X. Tel: 601-376-4816. FAX: 601-376-4966. Circulation E-mail: lrcnursingcirculation@hindscc.edu. *Librn,* Sybyl A Stringer; E-mail: sybyl.stringer@hindscc.edu
Open Mon, Tues & Thurs 7:30-7:30, Wed 7:30-4, Fri 7:30-3
RANKIN CAMPUS LEARNING RESOURCES/LIBRARY, 3805 Hwy 80 E, Pearl, 39208-4295, SAN 324-4288. Tel: 601-936-5538. FAX: 601-936-5542. E-mail: lrcrankincirculation@hindscc.edu. *Admin Librn,* Renita Lane; E-mail: rlane@hindscc.edu
Open Mon-Thurs (Winter) 7:30-7:30, Fri 7:30-3; Mon-Thurs (Summer) 7am-7:30pm, Fri 7-3
VICKSBURG LEARNING RESOURCES/LIBRARY, 755 Hwy 27, Vicksburg, 39180-8699, SAN 324-4261. Tel: 601-629-6846. FAX: 601-629-6862. E-mail: lrcvicksburgcirculation@hindscc.edu. *Admin Librn,* George Sellers; E-mail: george.sellers@hindscc.edu; Staff 2 (MLS 1, Non-MLS 1)

Highest Degree: Associate
Automation Activity & Vendor Info: (OPAC) SirsiDynix
Open Mon-Thurs (Winter) 8-6:45, Fri 8-3; Mon-Thurs (Summer) 7:30-6, Fri 7:30-2
WILLIAM H HOLTZDAW LIBRARY UTICA CAMPUS, 3417 MS-18 West, Utica, 39175-9599, SAN 308-9207. Tel: 601-885-7035. E-mail: lrcuticacirculation@hindscc.edu. *Admin Librn,* Jean Greene; E-mail: jbgreene@hindscc.edu; *Tech Serv,* Diana Brown; E-mail: dcbrown@hindscc.edu; Staff 3 (MLS 3)
Founded 1903. Enrl 751
Special Collections: Black Heritage Coll
Subject Interests: Behav sci, Educ, English lit, Soc sci
Open Mon-Thurs (Winter) 8-7:30, Fri 8-4; Mon-Fri (Summer) 8-4:30
Friends of the Library Group

RICHLAND

P RICHLAND PUBLIC LIBRARY*, 370 Scarbrough St, 39218. (Mail add: PO Box 180098, 39218), SAN 376-6284. Tel: 601-932-1846. FAX: 601-932-1688. E-mail: richland@cmrls.lib.ms.us. Web Site: cmrls.lib.ms.us/cmrlsbranches/richland. *Br Mgr,* Dewayne Hellums
Founded 1986. Pop 8,000
Library Holdings: Bk Titles 20,000; Bk Vols 25,000; Per Subs 65
Wireless access
Open Mon & Thurs 10-8, Tues & Wed 10-6, Fri & Sat 10-5
Friends of the Library Group

RICHTON

P PINE FOREST REGIONAL LIBRARY*, Headquarters, 210 Front St, 39476-1510. (Mail add: PO Box 1208, 39746-1208), SAN 348-8136. Tel: 601-788-6539. Toll Free Tel: 800-437-2941. FAX: 601-788-9743. Web Site: www.pineforest.lib.ms.us. *Dir,* Cheri Godwin; E-mail: cgodwin@pineforest.lib.ms.us; Staff 29 (MLS 3, Non-MLS 26)
Founded 1958. Pop 70,638; Circ 184,283
Library Holdings: Bk Titles 150,000; Per Subs 2,400
Subject Interests: Local hist
Wireless access
Open Tues-Thurs 9-5:30
Branches: 6
LEAKESVILLE PUBLIC LIBRARY, 301 Lafayette Ave, Leakesville, 39451, SAN 348-825X. Tel: 601-394-2897. FAX: 601-394-2897. E-mail: lea@pineforest.lib.ms.us. *Br Mgr,* Sara Smith
Open Mon, Wed & Thurs 9-5:30
WILLIAM & DOLORES MAULDIN LIBRARY, 25 McHenry School Dr, McHenry, 39561, SAN 348-8314. Tel: 601-528-9465. FAX: 601-528-9465. E-mail: mch@pineforest.lib.ms.us. *Br Mgr,* Rhonda Darby; *Asst Br Mgr,* Heather Donohoe
Special Services for the Deaf - Bks on deafness & sign lang; Closed caption videos
Special Services for the Blind - Bks on cassette; Bks on CD; Copier with enlargement capabilities; Large print bks
Open Tues-Thurs 9-5
Friends of the Library Group
MCLAIN PUBLIC, 117 Church Ave, McLain, 39456. (Mail add: PO Box 65, McLain, 39456-0065), SAN 348-8349. Tel: 601-753-9207. FAX: 601-753-9207. E-mail: mcl@pineforest.lib.ms.us. *Br Mgr,* Martha Byrd
Open Mon 9-1, Tues & Thurs 9-3
RICHTON PUBLIC, 210 Front St, 39476. (Mail add: PO Box 1208, 39476-1208). Tel: 601-788-6539. FAX: 601-788-9743. E-mail: ric@pineforest.lib.ms.us. *Br Mgr,* Donna Shipley
Open Tues 9-5, Thurs & Fri 1-5
STATE LINE PUBLIC, Eight Farrier St, State Line, 39362. (Mail add: PO Box 279, State Line, 39362-0279), SAN 348-8527. Tel: 601-848-7011. FAX: 601-848-7011. E-mail: stl@pineforest.lib.ms.us. *Br Mgr,* Pam Brown
Open Mon & Fri 9-5:30, Tues, Wed & Thurs 12-5
STONE COUNTY PUBLIC, 242 Second St SE, Wiggins, 39577, SAN 348-8551. Tel: 601-928-4993. FAX: 601-928-4993. E-mail: wig@pineforest.lib.ms.us. *Asst Mgr,* Karma Howze
Open Mon-Fri 9-5:30
Friends of the Library Group

RIDGELAND

J HOLMES COMMUNITY COLLEGE, Ernest J Adcock Library, Ridgeland Campus, 412 W Ridgeland Ave, 39158-1410. Tel: 601-605-3303. FAX: 601-605-3410. Web Site: www.holmescc.edu/library. *Libr Dir,* James Thompson; E-mail: jathompson@holmescc.edu; *Librn,* Nacole Adams; E-mail: nadams@holmescc.edu
Library Holdings: Bk Vols 11,000; Per Subs 175
Automation Activity & Vendor Info: (Acquisitions) SirsiDynix; (Cataloging) SirsiDynix; (Circulation) SirsiDynix; (Course Reserve) SirsiDynix; (ILL) SirsiDynix; (Serials) SirsiDynix
Wireless access
Open Mon-Thurs (Winter) 7:30-7:30, Fri 7:30-3:30; Mon, Thurs & Fri (Summer) 7:30-3:30, Tues & Wed 7:30-6:30

R WESLEY BIBLICAL SEMINARY LIBRARY, 1880 E County Line rd, 39157. SAN 375-2143. Tel: 601-366-8880. FAX: 601-366-8832. Web Site: www.wbs.edu/academics/library. *Dir, Libr Serv,* Grace Andrews; E-mail: gandrews@wbs.edu
Library Holdings: e-books 2,600; e-journals 500; Bk Vols 17,000; Per Subs 270
Subject Interests: Relig
Automation Activity & Vendor Info: (Cataloging) ProQuest; (Circulation) EBSCO Discovery Service; (OPAC) EBSCO Discovery Service; (Serials) EBSCO Discovery Service
Wireless access
Open Mon, Tues & Thurs 8am-9pm, Wed & Fri 8-5, Sat 9-2
Restriction: Circ privileges for students & alumni only

ROLLING FORK

P SHARKEY-ISSAQUENA COUNTY LIBRARY*, 116 E China St, 39159. SAN 323-794X. Tel: 662-873-4076. FAX: 662-873-0614. E-mail: sicl@sicl.lib.ms.us. Web Site: www.sicl.lib.ms.us. *Librn,* Elissa Tucker
Library Holdings: Bk Vols 20,000; Per Subs 45
Automation Activity & Vendor Info: (Cataloging) TLC (The Library Corporation); (Circulation) TLC (The Library Corporation)
Wireless access
Open Mon-Thurs 8:30-5:30, Fri 8:30-4:30
Friends of the Library Group

SCOOBA

J EAST MISSISSIPPI COMMUNITY COLLEGE*, Tubb-May Memorial Library, 1512 Kemper St, 39358, (Mail add: PO Box 158, 39358-0158), SAN 348-8586. Tel: 662-476-5054. FAX: 662-476-5053. Web Site: www.eastms.edu. *Dir, Libr Serv,* Donna Ballard; E-mail: dballard@eastms.edu; *Librn,* Christina Jurusik; E-mail: cjurusik@eastms.edu; Staff 3 (MLS 1, Non-MLS 2)
Founded 1927. Enrl 4,000
Library Holdings: Bk Vols 46,000; Per Subs 200; Videos 26,000
Special Collections: Mississippi Coll
Subject Interests: Miss hist
Automation Activity & Vendor Info: (Cataloging) SirsiDynix; (Circulation) SirsiDynix; (Course Reserve) SirsiDynix; (OPAC) SirsiDynix; (Serials) SirsiDynix
Wireless access
Open Mon-Thurs 8am-9pm, Fri 8-4:30, Sun 3-9
Departmental Libraries:
GOLDEN TRIANGLE CAMPUS LIBRARY, 8731 S Frontage Rd, Mayhew, 39753. (Mail add: PO Box 100, Mayhew, 39753). Tel: 662-243-1914. FAX: 662-243-1952. *District Librn,* Donna S Ballard; E-mail: dballard@eastms.edu; *Asst Librn,* Edwina Hogue; E-mail: whogue@eastms.edu; *Libr Asst,* Rosemary Rice; E-mail: rrice@eastms.edu; Staff 2 (MLS 1, Non-MLS 1)
Enrl 5,000; Highest Degree: Associate
Function: Computers for patron use, Distance learning, Electronic databases & coll, ILL available, Instruction & testing, Outside serv via phone, mail, e-mail & web, Photocopying/Printing, Scanner, Wheelchair accessible
Partic in Mississippi Library Partnership
Open Mon-Thurs 7:30am-9pm, Fri 7:30-4:30

SEBASTOPOL

P SEBASTOPOL PUBLIC LIBRARY*, 17403 Hwy 21 N, 39359. Tel: 601-625-8826. FAX: 601-625-8826. E-mail: sebastop@cmrls.lib.ms.us. Web Site: www.cmrls.lib.ms.us/cmrlsbranches/sebastopol. *Br Mgr,* Megan Perkins
Library Holdings: Bk Titles 6,334; Bk Vols 7,500
Automation Activity & Vendor Info: (Cataloging) SirsiDynix; (Circulation) SirsiDynix
Wireless access
Mem of Central Mississippi Regional Library System
Open Tues 11-2 & 2:30-7, Wed 9-12 & 12:30-5

SENATOBIA

J NORTHWEST MISSISSIPPI COMMUNITY COLLEGE*, R C Pugh Library, Senatobia Learning Resource Ctr, 4975 Hwy 51 N, 38668-1701. SAN 348-8640. Tel: 662-562-3278. FAX: 662-562-3280. Web Site: www.northwestms.edu/index.php/?page_id=962. *Dir, Learning Res,* Melissa Wright; Tel: 662-562-3268, E-mail: mwright@northwestms.edu; *Digital Serv Librn,* Maya Berry; E-mail: mberry@northwestms.edu; *Instrul Librn,* Victoria Penny; E-mail: vpenny@northwestms.edu; *Tech Serv Librn,* Crystal Giles; E-mail: cgiles@northwestms.edu; Staff 8.5 (MLS 4, Non-MLS 4.5)

Founded 1926. Enrl 7,172; Fac 122; Highest Degree: Associate
Library Holdings: AV Mats 9,711; CDs 1,733; DVDs 928; Bk Vols 85,863; Per Subs 286; Videos 4,288
Automation Activity & Vendor Info: (Cataloging) SirsiDynix; (Circulation) SirsiDynix; (OPAC) SirsiDynix; (Serials) SirsiDynix
Wireless access
Partic in LYRASIS
Open Mon-Thurs (Winter) 8am-9pm, Fri 8-3:30, Sun 2-7; Mon-Fri (Summer) 8-3:30

SOUTHAVEN

J NORTHWEST MISSISSIPPI COMMUNITY COLLEGE*, DeSoto Center Library, 5197 WE Ross Pkwy, 38671. SAN 308-9142. Tel: 662-280-6164. E-mail: librarydesoto@gmail.com. Web Site: www.northwestms.edu/l/current-students/library/desoto-learning-resource-center. *Head Librn,* Tenise Faulkner; E-mail: tfaulkner@northwestms.edu; *Instrul Librn,* Courtney Hicks; E-mail: chicks@northwestms.edu
Founded 1979. Enrl 600; Fac 41
Library Holdings: Bk Vols 18,000; Per Subs 250
Wireless access
Open Mon-Thurs 7:30am-9pm, Fri 7:30-4

STARKVILLE

P STARKVILLE-OKTIBBEHA COUNTY PUBLIC LIBRARY SYSTEM*, 326 University Dr, 39759. SAN 348-8675. Tel: 662-323-2766. FAX: 662-323-9140. E-mail: starkvillelibrary@gmail.com. Web Site: www.starkville.lib.ms.us. *Dir,* Virginia Holtcamp; Staff 3 (MLS 3)
Pop 36,600; Circ 113,000
Library Holdings: Bk Vols 59,000; Per Subs 115
Special Collections: Genealogy (Katie-Prince Eskar Coll)
Automation Activity & Vendor Info: (Acquisitions) SirsiDynix; (Cataloging) SirsiDynix; (Circulation) SirsiDynix; (ILL) Auto-Graphics, Inc; (OPAC) SirsiDynix
Wireless access
Function: Archival coll, Audiobks via web, AV serv, Bk club(s), Bks on cassette, Bks on CD, Children's prog, Computers for patron use, Electronic databases & coll, ILL available, Large print keyboards, Music CDs, Online cat, OverDrive digital audio bks, Photocopying/Printing, Prog for adults, Prog for children & young adult, Story hour, Summer reading prog, Tax forms, Teen prog, VHS videos, Wheelchair accessible
Partic in Mississippi Library Partnership
Open Mon-Thurs 9-6, Fri & Sat 9-4
Friends of the Library Group
Branches: 2
MABEN BRANCH, 3982 Second Ave, Maben, 39750. (Mail add: PO Box 507, Maben, 39750-0507), SAN 348-8705. Tel: 662-263-5619. FAX: 662-263-5619. *Librn,* Mary Boutwell
Open Mon, Tues, Thurs & Fri 8:30-11:30 & 12-4:30
Friends of the Library Group
STURGIS PUBLIC LIBRARY, 2732 Hwy 12 W, Sturgis, 39769. (Mail add: PO Box 8, Sturgis, 39769), SAN 348-8764. Tel: 662-465-7493. FAX: 662-465-7493. E-mail: sturgispubliclib@yahoo.com. *Br Mgr, Librn,* Perian P Kerr; *Asst Librn,* Shelby Jean Griffin; Staff 32 (MLS 16, Non-MLS 16)
Founded 1967. Pop 300
Function: Bks on cassette, Bks on CD, Children's prog, Computers for patron use, Digital talking bks, Free DVD rentals, ILL available, Music CDs, Online cat, Photocopying/Printing, Story hour, Summer reading prog, Tax forms, VHS videos
Partic in Mississippi Library Partnership
Special Services for the Deaf - Bks on deafness & sign lang
Special Services for the Blind - Bks on cassette; Bks on CD; Large print bks
Open Mon, Tues, Thurs & Fri 9-5

STENNIS SPACE CENTER

A UNITED STATES NAVY*, Matthew Fontaine Maury Oceanographic Library, 1002 Balch Blvd, 39522-5001. Tel: 228-688-4597. FAX: 228-688-4191. E-mail: NAVO_STNS_Maury_Library@navy.mil. Web Site: www.public.navy.mil/fltfor/cnmoc/Pages/m2.aspx. *Dir,* Beth Morgan; Tel: 228-688-4398, E-mail: mary.b.morgan@navy.mil; Staff 6 (MLS 4, Non-MLS 2)
Founded 1871
Library Holdings: e-journals 60; Bk Vols 400,000; Per Subs 250
Special Collections: Hydrographic Office Publications Coll; Oceanographic Expeditions Coll
Subject Interests: Biological, Cartography, Chem, Engr, Geol oceanog, Meteorology, Ocean engr, Photogrammetry, Phys oceanog
Function: Archival coll, Bks on CD, CD-ROM, Computers for patron use, Electronic databases & coll, ILL available, Internet access, Online cat, Online ref, Photocopying/Printing, Ref & res, Ref serv available, Res libr, Spoken cassettes & CDs
Publications: Accessions List
Partic in OCLC Online Computer Library Center, Inc
Open Mon-Fri 7:30-3:30
Restriction: Circ limited

STONEVILLE

C MISSISSIPPI STATE UNIVERSITY*, Delta Research & Extension Center Library, Bldg 1532, 82 Stoneville Rd, 38776. (Mail add: PO Box 197, 38776-0197), SAN 308-9150. Tel: 662-686-3260. FAX: 662-686-3342. Web Site: drec.msstate.edu. *Librn,* Bess Moss; E-mail: bbm68@msstate.edu; Staff 1 (MLS 1)
Founded 1966
Library Holdings: Bk Vols 25,000
Subject Interests: Agr, Botany, Chem, Econ, Entomology, Math, Mechanical engr, Meteorology, Publ of all state experiment stations, Zoology
Wireless access
Function: Res libr
Publications: Serials Catalog
Open Mon-Fri 8-4:30

SUMMIT

J SOUTHWEST MISSISSIPPI COMMUNITY COLLEGE*, Ford Library-Learning Resources Center, 1156 College Dr, 39666. (Mail add: 1036 College Dr, 39666), SAN 308-9169. Tel: 601-276-2004. FAX: 601-276-3748. Web Site: www.smcc.edu/library/library.php. *Dir,* Natalie McMahon; E-mail: nmcmahon@smcc.edu; *Librn,* Laura Riddle; E-mail: lporta@smcc.edu; Staff 2 (MLS 2)
Founded 1977. Enrl 1,816
Library Holdings: e-books 11,173; Bk Vols 38,808; Per Subs 123
Special Collections: Mississippi Coll
Wireless access
Open Mon-Thurs 8-6, Fri 8-3:30

TAYLORSVILLE

P EVON A FORD PUBLIC LIBRARY*, 208 Spring St, 39168. (Mail add: PO Box 430, 39168-0430), SAN 376-6241. Tel: 601-785-4361. FAX: 601-785-6611. E-mail: taylorsv@cmrls.lib.ms.us. Web Site: cmrls.lib.ms.us/cmrlsbranches/taylorsville. *Br Mgr,* Joyce McKinley
Library Holdings: Bk Titles 13,000; Per Subs 12
Wireless access
Mem of Central Mississippi Regional Library System
Open Mon-Wed 9-5:30, Fri 8:30-5:30, Sat 9-Noon

TOUGALOO

C TOUGALOO COLLEGE, L Zenobia Coleman Library, 500 W County Line Rd, 39174-9799. SAN 308-9177. Tel: 601-977-7706. FAX: 601-977-7714. E-mail: libraryservices@tougaloo.edu. Web Site: www.tougaloo.edu/library. *Interim Dir,* Stephanie Taylor; Tel: 601-977-7703, E-mail: sltaylor@tougaloo.edu; Staff 4 (MLS 1, Non-MLS 3)
Founded 1869. Enrl 600; Fac 89; Highest Degree: Master
Library Holdings: Bk Titles 143,579; Per Subs 389
Special Collections: African Materials (Ross Coll); Baily-Ward African American Coll (archives); Civil Rights & Liberties (Charles Horowitz Papers); Civil Rights Movement (Tracy Sugarman Print Coll of 1964), prints; Mississippi Civil Rights Lawsuits of the 1960's, bks, papers; Music (B B King Coll), awards, pamphlets, papers, per; Radical Papers (Kudzu File). Oral History
Automation Activity & Vendor Info: (Acquisitions) OCLC; (Cataloging) OCLC; (Circulation) OCLC; (Course Reserve) OCLC; (ILL) OCLC; (Media Booking) OCLC; (OPAC) OCLC; (Serials) OCLC
Wireless access
Function: Archival coll, ILL available, Ref serv available
Publications: A Classified Bibliography of the Special Collections in the L Zenobia Coleman Library
Partic in Central Mississippi Library Council; OCLC Online Computer Library Center, Inc; Private Academic Libraries of Mississippi
Open Mon-Thurs 7:45am-11pm, Fri 7:45-5, Sat 11-4, Sun 2-9

TUPELO

J ITAWAMBA COMMUNITY COLLEGE*, Learning Resource Center, 2176 S Eason Blvd, 38804. SAN 308-9185. Tel: 662-620-5091. FAX: 662-620-5095. Web Site: www.iccms.edu/LRCResources. *Dir,* Janet Armour; Tel: 662-620-5092, E-mail: jyarmour@iccms.edu; *Librn,* Casandra L Ifie; Tel: 662-620-5090, E-mail: clifie@iccms.edu
Founded 1975. Enrl 1,400; Fac 125
Library Holdings: Bk Titles 20,000; Per Subs 225
Open Mon & Tues 7:45am-8:45pm, Wed & Thurs 7:30-6, Fri 7:30-4; Mon-Thurs (Summer) 7:30am-8:45pm, Fri 7:30-4:30

P LEE-ITAWAMBA LIBRARY SYSTEM*, Lee County Library, 219 N Madison St, 38804-3899. SAN 348-8799. Tel: 662-841-9027. Reference Tel: 662-841-9013. Administration Tel: 662-841-9029. FAX: 662-840-7615. Web Site: www.li.lib.ms.us. *Dir,* Jeff Tomlinson; E-mail: jtomlinson@li.lib.ms.us; *Circ Librn,* Juanita Easley; E-mail: jeasley@li.lib.ms.us; *Genealogy Librn,* Brian Hargett; E-mail: bhargett@li.lib.ms.us; *Ref Librn,* David Prather; E-mail: dprather@li.lib.ms.us; *Youth Librn,* Grace Hall; E-mail: ghall@li.lib.ms.us; Staff 14 (MLS 2, Non-MLS 12)
Founded 1942. Pop 100,195
Library Holdings: Bk Vols 142,369; Per Subs 279; Talking Bks 2,794
Subject Interests: Genealogy
Automation Activity & Vendor Info: (Acquisitions) TLC (The Library Corporation); (Cataloging) TLC (The Library Corporation); (Circulation) TLC (The Library Corporation); (OPAC) TLC (The Library Corporation); (Serials) TLC (The Library Corporation)
Wireless access
Special Services for the Deaf - Bks on deafness & sign lang; Closed caption videos
Special Services for the Blind - Assistive/Adapted tech devices, equip & products; Computer with voice synthesizer for visually impaired persons
Open Mon-Thurs 9-8, Fri & Sat 9-5
Friends of the Library Group
Branches: 1
PRATT MEMORIAL LIBRARY, 210 Cedar St, Fulton, 38843, SAN 348-8829. Tel: 662-862-4926. FAX: 662-862-2477. *Librn,* Jeffrey Martin; E-mail: icpl1@li.lib.ms.us; Staff 4 (MLS 4)
Founded 1966
Function: Bk reviews (Group), Bks on cassette, Bks on CD, Computer training, Computers for patron use, Free DVD rentals, Holiday prog, ILL available, Internet access, Online cat, Online ref, Outreach serv, Photocopying/Printing, Preschool outreach, Prog for adults, Prog for children & young adult, Senior computer classes, Spoken cassettes & CDs, Story hour, Summer reading prog, Tax forms, VHS videos, Wheelchair accessible
Open Mon, Tues, Thurs & Fri 9-6, Sat 10-2
Friends of the Library Group
Bookmobiles: 1. Librn, Barbara Carouthers

M NORTH MISSISSIPPI HEALTH SERVICES*, Medical Library, 830 S Gloster St, 38801. SAN 371-0947. Tel: 662-377-4399. FAX: 662-377-7239. Web Site: www.nmhs.net. *Med Librn,* Loralei T McGee; E-mail: lmcgee@nmhs.net; Staff 1 (Non-MLS 1)
Founded 1975
Library Holdings: Audiobooks 10; DVDs 5; e-journals 10; Bk Titles 300; Bk Vols 340; Per Subs 60; Videos 100
Wireless access
Partic in SEND
Open Mon-Fri 8-4:30

UNION

P KEMPER-NEWTON REGIONAL LIBRARY SYSTEM*, 101 Peachtree St, 39365-2617. SAN 348-8888. Tel: 601-774-9297. FAX: 601-774-9297. Web Site: knrls.lib.ms.us. *Dir,* Hannah Berryhill; E-mail: hannah@kemper.lib.ms.us; *Asst Dir, Bus Mgr,* Brenda Williams; E-mail: brenwill@kemper.lib.ms.us; Staff 11 (MLS 1, Non-MLS 10)
Founded 1969. Pop 31,685; Circ 50,312
Library Holdings: CDs 198; DVDs 30; Bk Titles 48,094; Per Subs 65
Subject Interests: Genealogy, Miss authors, Miss hist
Wireless access
Function: ILL available
Open Mon-Thurs 8:30-5, Fri 8:30-3:30
Friends of the Library Group
Branches: 5
DEKALB BRANCH, 141 Bell St, DeKalb, 39328, SAN 348-8977. Tel: 601-743-5981. *Br Head,* Lawson Smith; E-mail: lawsonknrls@gmail.com
Library Holdings: Bk Titles 9,500
Special Collections: Kemper County History Coll
Open Mon-Thurs 9-5, Fri 9-4
Friends of the Library Group
JESSIE MAE EVERETT PUBLIC LIBRARY, 306 W Broad St, Decatur, 39365, SAN 348-8942. Tel: 601-635-2777. *Br Mgr,* Barbara Divine; E-mail: barbaraknrls@gmail.com
Library Holdings: Bk Titles 7,492
Open Mon-Thurs 10-5
J ELLIOTT MCMULLAN LIBRARY, 300 W Church St, Newton, 39345-2208, SAN 348-9000. Tel: 601-683-3367. FAX: 601-683-3367. *Br Librn,* Maxine Dawkins; E-mail: Maxineknrls@gmail.com
Library Holdings: Bk Titles 14,500
Special Collections: Mississippi Authors & History Coll
Open Mon-Thurs 9-5, Fri 9-4
Friends of the Library Group
SCOOBA BRANCH, 801-1099 Kemper St, Scooba, 39358, SAN 348-9035. Tel: 662-476-8454. *Br Librn,* Judith Howard; E-mail: judithknrls@gmail.com
Library Holdings: Bk Titles 4,897
Open Tues & Thurs 1-5
Friends of the Library Group
UNION PUBLIC, 101 Peachtree, 39365-2617. Tel: 601-774-5096. FAX: 601-774-5096. *Br Librn,* Donna Neils; E-mail: donnaknrls@gmail.com
Library Holdings: Bk Titles 14,082
Special Collections: Newton County History Coll
Open Mon-Thurs 9-5, Fri 9-4

UNIVERSITY

CL UNIVERSITY OF MISSISSIPPI*, Grisham Law Library, 481 Chuckie Mullins Dr, 38677. (Mail add: PO Box 1848, 38677-1848), SAN 308-9193. Tel: 662-915-6824. Reference Tel: 662-915-6812. FAX: 662-915-7731. E-mail: lawref@olemiss.edu. Web Site: library.law.olemiss.edu. *Dir,* Kris Gilliland; E-mail: gillilan@olemiss.edu; *Asst Dir, Head, Pub Serv,* Christopher Noe; Tel: 662-915-6850, E-mail: noe@olemiss.edu; *Pub Serv Librn,* Scott DeLeve; Tel: 662-915-6834, E-mail: sdeleve@olemiss.edu; *Pub Serv Librn,* Justin Huckaby; E-mail: jrhuckab@olemiss.edu; *Pub Serv Librn,* Susan Winters; E-mail: swinters@olemiss.edu; *Tech Serv Librn,* Julianna S Davis; Tel: 662-915-6832, E-mail: uldavis@olemiss.edu; Staff 8 (MLS 8)
Founded 1854. Enrl 540; Fac 26; Highest Degree: Doctorate
Library Holdings: e-books 24,013; Bk Vols 336,487
Special Collections: State Document Depository; US Document Depository
Subject Interests: Law, Space law
Publications: Law Library (Online only)
Partic in Association of Southeastern Research Libraries; LYRASIS
Open Mon-Thurs 7:30am-Midnight, Fri 7:30am-10pm, Sat 10-10, Sun 10am-Midnight

C UNIVERSITY OF MISSISSIPPI*, John Davis Williams Library, One Library Loop, 38677. (Mail add: PO Box 1848, 38677-1848), SAN 348-906X. Tel: 662-915-5858. Interlibrary Loan Service Tel: 662-915-7936. FAX: 662-915-5734. Interlibrary Loan Service FAX: 662-915-5453. Web Site: libraries.olemiss.edu. *Dean of Libr,* Cecilia Botero; Tel: 662-915-7091, E-mail: cbotero@olemiss.edu; *Asst Dean, Tech Serv,* Gail Herrera; Tel: 662-915-5674, E-mail: gherrera@olemiss.edu; *Head, Library Facilities,* Stanley Whitehorn; Tel: 662-915-7935, E-mail: swhithrn@olemiss.edu; *Res & Instruction Librn,* Savannah Kelly; Tel: 662-915-5877, E-mail: slkelly@olemiss.edu; Staff 55 (MLS 27, Non-MLS 28)
Founded 1848. Enrl 18,000; Fac 830; Highest Degree: Doctorate
Library Holdings: Bk Vols 1,268,318; Per Subs 8,500
Special Collections: Mississippi Writers; Mississippiana; William Faulkner Coll. State Document Depository; US Document Depository
Subject Interests: Blues music, Culture, Lit, Southern culture, Southern hist
Automation Activity & Vendor Info: (Acquisitions) Innovative Interfaces, Inc; (Cataloging) Innovative Interfaces, Inc; (Circulation) Innovative Interfaces, Inc
Wireless access
Special Services for the Deaf - Staff with knowledge of sign lang; TDD equip
Friends of the Library Group
Departmental Libraries:
SCIENCE, 1031 Natural Products Ctr, 38677, SAN 369-7800. Tel: 662-915-7381. Interlibrary Loan Service Tel: 662-915-5668. FAX: 662-915-7549. Web Site: www.libraries.olemiss.edu/science-library. *Lead Librn,* Jason Burton; Tel: 662-915-7910, E-mail: jtburto1@olemiss.edu; *Librn, Res Assoc,* Deborah V McCain; E-mail: dmccain@olemiss.edu; Staff 5 (MLS 4, Non-MLS 1)
Founded 1997. Highest Degree: Doctorate
Library Holdings: Bk Vols 70,000; Per Subs 450
Subject Interests: Analytical chem, Biochem, Inorganic chem, Organic chem, Pharmaceutics, Pharmacognosy-natural products, Pharmacology, Phys chem
Function: Doc delivery serv, Homebound delivery serv, ILL available, Photocopying/Printing, Ref serv available, Res libr, Telephone ref

VAIDEN

P VAIDEN PUBLIC LIBRARY*, 507 Lee St, 39176-0108. SAN 376-6365. Tel: 662-464-7736. FAX: 662-464-7736. *Dir,* Sharon Tollison; E-mail: stollison@carroll.lib.ms.us
Library Holdings: Bk Titles 1,200; Bk Vols 1,500; Per Subs 13
Wireless access
Open Mon-Fri 8-12 & 1-5
Friends of the Library Group

VICKSBURG

A UNITED STATES ARMY*, Engineer Research & Development Center Library, 3909 Halls Ferry Rd, 39180-6199. SAN 308-9223. Tel: 601-634-2355. FAX: 601-634-2306. Web Site: acwc.sdp.sirsi.net/client/default. *Br Chief,* Molly McManus; Staff 7 (MLS 7)
Founded 1930
Library Holdings: e-books 39,000; e-journals 30,000; Bk Titles 225,000; Bk Vols 250,000; Per Subs 1,500
Subject Interests: Aquatic plant control, Coastal engr, Computer sci, Concrete, Dredged mat res, Environ effects, Explosive excavation, Hydraulics, Info tech, Pavements, Soil mechanics, Trafficability, Vehicle mobility, Weapons effects
Wireless access
Partic in OCLC Online Computer Library Center, Inc

S VICKSBURG & WARREN COUNTY HISTORICAL SOCIETY*, McCardle Library, Old Court House Museum, 1008 Cherry St, 39183. SAN 370-3045. Tel: 601-636-0741. E-mail: societyhistorica@bellsouth.net. Web Site: www.oldcourthouse.org. *Dir,* George C Bolm
Library Holdings: Bk Vols 1,400
Special Collections: J Mack Moore Photo Coll
Subject Interests: Genealogy, Hist
Open Mon-Fri 8:30-4:30

G VICKSBURG NATIONAL MILITARY PARK LIBRARY, 3201 Clay St, 39183-3495. SAN 308-9231. Tel: 601-636-0583. FAX: 601-636-9497. Web Site: www.nps.gov/vick. *Library Contact,* Jenny Lesor; Tel: 601-630-6313, E-mail: jenny_lesor@nps.gov
Library Holdings: Bk Vols 2,500
Special Collections: American Civil War Coll
Restriction: Open by appt only

P WARREN COUNTY-VICKSBURG PUBLIC LIBRARY*, 700 Veto St, 39180-3595. SAN 308-9266. Tel: 601-636-6411. FAX: 601-634-4809. Web Site: www.warren.lib.ms.us. *Dir,* Katrina Stokes; E-mail: kstokes@warren.lib.ms.us; *Asst Dir,* Paula Benard; E-mail: benard@warren.lib.ms.us; *Head, Circ,* Sandra Mayfield; E-mail: mayfield@warren.lib.ms.us; *Circ Librn,* Marie Cunningham; E-mail: mcunningham@warren.lib.ms.us; *ILL Librn,* Lesa Foster; E-mail: lfoster@warren.lib.ms.us; *AV,* Zandra Demby-Miller; E-mail: zdemby@warren.lib.ms.us; *Cataloger,* Denise Hogan; E-mail: whit10@warren.lib.ms.us; Staff 15 (MLS 4, Non-MLS 11)
Founded 1915. Pop 49,800; Circ 227,925
Library Holdings: Audiobooks 7,696; Electronic Media & Resources 41; Bk Vols 131,748; Per Subs 169; Videos 13,490
Subject Interests: Civil War, Miss, Miss river, Mystery novels
Automation Activity & Vendor Info: (Acquisitions) Innovative Interfaces, Inc; (Cataloging) Innovative Interfaces, Inc; (Circulation) Innovative Interfaces, Inc; (OPAC) Innovative Interfaces, Inc; (Serials) Innovative Interfaces, Inc
Wireless access
Function: Adult bk club, Art exhibits, AV serv, Bk club(s), Bks on cassette, Bks on CD, Children's prog, Computers for patron use, Electronic databases & coll, Free DVD rentals, ILL available, Mail & tel request accepted, Music CDs, Online cat, Photocopying/Printing, Preschool outreach, Prog for adults, Prog for children & young adult, Ref & res, Ref serv available, Spoken cassettes & CDs, Spoken cassettes & DVDs, Story hour, Summer reading prog, Tax forms, Telephone ref, VHS videos, Wheelchair accessible
Publications: Newsletter
Open Mon-Thurs 9-7, Fri & Sat 9-5
Friends of the Library Group

WATER VALLEY

P BLACKMUR MEMORIAL LIBRARY*, 608 Blackmur Dr, 38965-6070. SAN 308-9274. Tel: 662-473-2444. FAX: 662-473-2444. E-mail: blackmurlibrary@gmail.com. Web Site: www.blackmur.lib.ms.us. *Dir,* Joseph Gurner; E-mail: jgurner@blackmur.lib.ms.us; Staff 2 (Non-MLS 2)
Founded 1959. Pop 8,000; Circ 16,610
Library Holdings: High Interest/Low Vocabulary Bk Vols 200; Large Print Bks 150; Bk Titles 10,000; Bk Vols 16,351; Per Subs 39
Special Collections: Black History Coll; Mississippi History
Subject Interests: Genealogy, Local hist
Automation Activity & Vendor Info: (Cataloging) Book Systems; (Circulation) Book Systems; (OPAC) Book Systems
Partic in Dancing Rabbit Library Consortium
Open Mon-Fri 8-5
Friends of the Library Group

WAYNESBORO

P WAYNESBORO-WAYNE COUNTY LIBRARY SYSTEM, 1103A Mississippi Dr, 39367. SAN 348-8071. Tel: 601-735-2268. FAX: 601-735-6407. E-mail: librarywayne39367@gmail.com. Web Site: www.wwcls.lib.ms.us. *Libr Dir,* Patsy Brewer; Staff 11 (MLS 1, Non-MLS 10)
Founded 1934
Library Holdings: Bk Vols 46,000; Per Subs 40
Subject Interests: Genealogy
Automation Activity & Vendor Info: (Cataloging) Biblionix/Apollo; (Circulation) Biblionix/Apollo; (ILL) Auto-Graphics, Inc; (OPAC) Biblionix/Apollo
Wireless access
Function: 24/7 Electronic res, 24/7 Online cat, 3D Printer, Adult bk club, Archival coll, Art exhibits, Bk club(s), Bks on cassette, Bks on CD, CD-ROM, Children's prog, Computer training, Computers for patron use, Electronic databases & coll, Equip loans & repairs, For res purposes, Free DVD rentals, Games & aids for people with disabilities, Genealogy discussion group, Holiday prog, ILL available, Internet access, Laminating, Large print keyboards, Literacy & newcomer serv, Magazines, Mail & tel request accepted, Makerspace, Meeting rooms, Microfiche/film & reading machines, Movies, Music CDs, Notary serv, Online cat, Outreach serv, Photocopying/Printing, Preschool outreach, Preschool reading prog, Printer for laptops & handheld devices, Prog for adults, Prog for children & young adult, Ref & res, Ref serv available, Res assist avail, Scanner, Senior computer classes, Spanish lang bks, STEM programs, Story hour, Study rm, Summer reading prog, Tax forms, Telephone ref, VHS videos, Wheelchair accessible
Open Mon-Fri 9-6, Sat 9-1
Restriction: Non-circulating of rare bks
Friends of the Library Group

WESSON

J COPIAH-LINCOLN COMMUNITY COLLEGE*, Evelyn W Oswalt Library, 1028 J C Redd Dr, 39191. (Mail add: PO Box 649, 39191-0649), SAN 308-9282. Tel: 601-643-8363. Web Site: www.colin.edu/students/student-services/libraries. *Dir of Libr,* Dr Jacqueline Quinn; Tel: 601-643-8364, E-mail: jacqueline.quinn@colin.edu; Staff 5 (MLS 1, Non-MLS 4)
Founded 1928. Enrl 2,033; Fac 135; Highest Degree: Associate
Jul 2013-Jun 2014 Income $256,301. Mats Exp $96,040, Books $10,000, Per/Ser (Incl. Access Fees) $2,700, Electronic Ref Mat (Incl. Access Fees) $83,340. Sal $160,261 (Prof $71,585)
Library Holdings: Bk Vols 33,819; Per Subs 26; Videos 1,293
Automation Activity & Vendor Info: (Cataloging) SirsiDynix; (Circulation) SirsiDynix; (Discovery) EBSCO Discovery Service; (OPAC) SirsiDynix
Wireless access
Partic in MAGNOLIA; Mississippi Electronic Libraries Online
Open Mon-Thurs (Fall & Spring) 7:30am-9:30pm, Fri 7:30am-2pm; Mon-Thurs (Summer) 7:30pm-8pm, Fri 7:30am-12:30pm

WEST POINT

P TOMBIGBEE REGIONAL LIBRARY SYSTEM*, Bryan Public Library, Headquarters, 436 Commerce St, 39773-2923. SAN 348-9159. Tel: 662-494-4872. FAX: 662-494-0300. Web Site: tombigbee.lib.ms.us. *Dir,* Tanna Taylor; E-mail: ttaylor@trlsms.com; *Cat Librn,* Debbie Brownlee; E-mail: dbrownlee@trlsms.com; *Circ Librn,* Valerie Hargrove; E-mail: vhargrove@trlsms.com; *Ref Librn,* Priscilla Ivy; E-mail: pivy@trlsms.com; *Bus Mgr,* Brenda McVay; E-mail: bmcvay@trlsms.com; Staff 19 (MLS 1, Non-MLS 18)
Founded 1916. Pop 79,800; Circ 133,892. Sal $475,043
Library Holdings: AV Mats 11,505; Bk Vols 129,556; Per Subs 157
Subject Interests: Genealogy, Local hist
Automation Activity & Vendor Info: (Cataloging) SirsiDynix; (Circulation) SirsiDynix; (ILL) OCLC; (OPAC) SirsiDynix
Wireless access
Function: Accelerated reader prog, Archival coll, Art exhibits, Bk reviews (Group), Bks on cassette, Bks on CD, Children's prog, Computer training, Computers for patron use, Electronic databases & coll, Free DVD rentals, Genealogy discussion group, Holiday prog, ILL available, Music CDs, Notary serv, Online cat, Orientations, OverDrive digital audio bks, Photocopying/Printing, Preschool outreach, Preschool reading prog, Prog for adults, Prog for children & young adult, Spoken cassettes & CDs, Spoken cassettes & DVDs, Story hour, Summer reading prog, Tax forms, Teen prog, Wheelchair accessible
Publications: BPL-News from Friends (Newsletter)
Partic in Mississippi Library Partnership
Open Mon-Thurs 10-6, Fri 10-5
Friends of the Library Group

Branches: 7

AMORY MUNICIPAL LIBRARY, 401 Second Ave N, Amory, 38821-3514, SAN 348-9183. Tel: 662-256-5261. FAX: 662-256-6321. Web Site: tombigbee.lib.ms.us/amory. *Br Librn,* Ruby Holman; E-mail: rholman@tombigbee.lib.ms.us; *Asst Librn, Ch,* Michelle Bond; E-mail: mbond@tombigbee.lib.ms.us; Staff 2 (Non-MLS 2)
Circ 44,333
Library Holdings: AV Mats 4,662; Bk Vols 19,894
Subject Interests: Genealogy, Local hist
Automation Activity & Vendor Info: (ILL) SirsiDynix
Function: Art exhibits, Bks on cassette, Bks on CD, Children's prog, Computers for patron use, Free DVD rentals, ILL available, Music CDs, Online cat, Photocopying/Printing, Prog for adults, Prog for children & young adult, Ref & res, Spoken cassettes & CDs, Spoken cassettes & DVDs, Story hour, Summer reading prog, Tax forms, VHS videos, Wheelchair accessible
Open Mon-Thurs 10-6, Fri & Sat 9-5
Friends of the Library Group

EVANS MEMORIAL LIBRARY, 105 N Long St, Aberdeen, 39730, SAN 348-9248. Tel: 662-369-4601. FAX: 662-369-2971. Web Site: tombigbee.lib.ms.us/evans. *Br Librn,* Barbara Blair; E-mail: bblair@trlsms.com; *Ch,* Patricia Waldrop; *Circ Librn,* Laverne Luker; Staff 2 (Non-MLS 2)
Circ 26,787
Library Holdings: AV Mats 1,238; Bk Vols 28,705
Special Collections: Photographs (McKnight Coll)
Subject Interests: Genealogy, Local hist
Automation Activity & Vendor Info: (ILL) SirsiDynix
Open Mon-Thurs 10-6, Fri & Sat 10-4
Friends of the Library Group

HAMILTON PUBLIC LIBRARY, Hwy 45 S, Hamilton, 39746, SAN 348-9272. Tel: 601-343-8962. FAX: 601-343-8962. Web Site: tombigbee.lib.ms.us/hamilton. *Librn,* Charlotte Wathen; E-mail: cwathen@trlsms.com
Circ 2,014
Library Holdings: AV Mats 149; Bk Vols 4,256
Automation Activity & Vendor Info: (ILL) SirsiDynix
Open Tues & Thurs 12-5
Friends of the Library Group

DOROTHY J LOWE MEMORIAL PUBLIC LIBRARY, 165 Young Ave, Nettleton, 38858, SAN 348-9337. Tel: 662-963-2011. FAX: 662-963-2014. Web Site: tombigbee.lib.ms.us/nettleton. *Librn,* Maridelle Dickerson; E-mail: mdickerson@trlsms.com
Circ 2,311
Library Holdings: AV Mats 144; Bk Vols 3,117
Automation Activity & Vendor Info: (ILL) SirsiDynix
Open Mon-Thurs 12-5
Friends of the Library Group

MATHISTON PUBLIC LIBRARY, 298 Scott Ave, Mathiston, 39752, SAN 348-9302. Tel: 662-263-4772. FAX: 662-263-4488. Web Site: tombigbee.lib.ms.us/mathiston. *Librn,* Susan Curry; E-mail: scurry@trlsms.com
Circ 2,462
Library Holdings: AV Mats 102; Bk Vols 4,115
Automation Activity & Vendor Info: (ILL) SirsiDynix
Open Tues, Wed & Fri 1:30-5, Thurs 9-12:30
Friends of the Library Group

WEBSTER COUNTY PUBLIC LIBRARY, 445 W Fox Ave, Eupora, 39744, SAN 348-9396. Tel: 662-258-7515. FAX: 662-258-7519. Web Site: tombigbee.lib.ms.us/webster. *Br Librn,* Fran Smith; E-mail: fsmith@trlsms.com
Circ 10,026
Library Holdings: AV Mats 1,084; Bk Vols 8,227
Subject Interests: Genealogy, Local hist
Automation Activity & Vendor Info: (ILL) SirsiDynix
Open Mon & Wed 10-5, Tues 10-4
Friends of the Library Group

WREN PUBLIC LIBRARY, 32655 Hwy 45 N, Aberdeen, 39730-9796, SAN 348-9450. Tel: 662-256-4957. FAX: 662-256-4957. Web Site: tombigbee.lib.ms.us/wren. *Librn,* Charlotte Wathen
Circ 2,685
Library Holdings: AV Mats 151; Bk Vols 4,693
Automation Activity & Vendor Info: (ILL) SirsiDynix
Open Mon & Wed 12-5
Friends of the Library Group

WHITFIELD

MISSISSIPPI STATE HOSPITAL

M MEDICAL LIBRARY*, Whitfield Rd, 39193, SAN 308-9304. Tel: 601-351-8000, Ext 4278. *Librn,* Jane Hull
Library Holdings: Bk Vols 1,000; Per Subs 25
Subject Interests: Alcoholism, Drug addiction, Psychiat
Open Mon & Wed 8-4, Fri 8-3

M PATIENT LIBRARY*, Whitfield Rd, 39193, SAN 376-0324. Tel: 601-351-8000, Ext 4278. *Librn,* Jane Hull
Library Holdings: Bk Vols 14,000
Open Mon & Wed 8-4, Fri 8-3

YAZOO CITY

P B S RICKS MEMORIAL LIBRARY*, 310 N Main St, 39194, SAN 348-9574. Tel: 662-746-5557. Administration Tel: 662-746-5586. FAX: 662-746-7309. E-mail: yazoolibraryassociation@gmail.com. Web Site: yazoolibraryassociation.org. *Dir, Syst Adminr,* Craig Wooten; E-mail: cwooten@yazoo.lib.ms.us; *Librn,* Karen Dunaway; E-mail: karen@yazoo.lib.ms.us; Staff 4 (MLS 4)
Founded 1838. Pop 27,886; Circ 46,500
Library Holdings: Bk Vols 42,000; Per Subs 110
Special Collections: Local History Coll. Oral History; State Document Depository
Automation Activity & Vendor Info: (Circulation) Auto-Graphics, Inc
Wireless access
Partic in Dancing Rabbit Library Consortium; LYRASIS
Open Mon, Wed & Fri 8-5, Tues & Thus 8-7, Sat 8:30-Noon
Friends of the Library Group

Date of Statistics: FY 2020
Population, 2020 U.S. Census: 6,151,548
Population Served by Public Libraries: 5,483,526
  Unserved: 505,401
Total Volumes in Public Libraries: 15,341,903
  Volumes Per Capita: 2.56
Total Public Library Circulation: 49,445,167
  Circulation Per Capita: 8.26
Digital Resources:
  Total e-books: 7,511,565 (includes duplicated consortia materials)
  Total audio items (physical and downloadable units): 4,014,066
  Total video items (physical and downloadable units): 1,866,657
  Total computers for use by the public: 4,675
  Total computer uses: 3,200,993
  Total annual wireless sessions: 3,547,819
Income and Expenditures:
Total Public Library Income: $310,247,899
  Source of Income: Local 92.82%, State 1.50%, Federal 0.77%, Other 4.90%
  Expenditure Per Capita: $46.07
Number of County & Multi-county: 67
Counties Served: 86
Number of Bookmobiles: 23
Grants-in-Aid:
  State Aid: $4,284,371
  Federal $2,401,249
Information provided courtesy of: Cory Mihalik, Statistical Research Consultant; Missouri State Library

ALBANY

P CARNEGIE PUBLIC LIBRARY, 101 W Clay, 64402. SAN 308-9320. Tel: 660-726-5615. FAX: 660-726-4213. Web Site: carnegie.lib.mo.us. *Dir,* Traci Clair; E-mail: librarian@carnegie.lib.mo.us; Staff 1 (MLS 1)
Founded 1906. Pop 1,937; Circ 15,117
Library Holdings: Audiobooks 349; DVDs 1,580; e-books 9,600; Electronic Media & Resources 3; Large Print Bks 230; Bk Titles 15,900; Per Subs 14
Special Collections: Gentry County Geneaology
Automation Activity & Vendor Info: (Cataloging) Evergreen
Wireless access
Partic in Grand Rivers Libr Conference
Open Mon & Thurs 9-7, Tues, Wed, Fri & Sat 9-5
Friends of the Library Group

ALTON

P OREGON COUNTY LIBRARY DISTRICT*, Alton Public Library, 20 Court Sq, 65606. (Mail add: PO Box 158, 65606-0158), SAN 377-1016. Tel: 417-778-6414. FAX: 417-778-6414. E-mail: altonpubliclibrary@hotmail.com. *Br Mgr,* Janice Richardson; Staff 1 (MLS 1)
Pop 710
Library Holdings: Bk Titles 11,775; Bk Vols 12,000; Per Subs 13
Open Mon-Fri 8:30-5
Branches: 4
KOSHKONONG PUBLIC, 302 Diggins St, Koshkonong, 65692, SAN 377-5542. Tel: 417-867-5472. FAX: 417-867-5472. E-mail: koshlibrary@gmail.com. *Head Librn,* Paula Miller; Staff 1 (MLS 1)
Pop 610
Library Holdings: Bk Titles 4,980; Bk Vols 5,126; Per Subs 11; Videos 100
Open Mon 10:30-4:30, Tues & Wed 10:30-5:30
MYRTLE PUBLIC, General Delivery, State Hwy V, Myrtle, 65778. Tel: 417-938-4350. FAX: 417-938-4350. *Head Librn,* Janis Campbell
Open Tues & Wed 9-5, Sat 9-1
THAYER PUBLIC, 121 N Second St, Thayer, 65791, SAN 377-2160. Tel: 417-264-3091. FAX: 417-264-3091. *Head Librn,* Grace Mainprize; Staff 1 (MLS 1)
Library Holdings: Bk Titles 20,000; Bk Vols 25,000; Per Subs 24; Talking Bks 56; Videos 78
Open Mon-Sat 8:30-4:30
THOMASVILLE PUBLIC LIBRARY, Rte HC3, Box 62, Birch Tree, 65438. Tel: 417-764-3603. FAX: 417-764-3603. E-mail: librarytville@yahoo.com. *Head Librn,* Joyce Cates
Open Tues & Wed 9-4, Thurs 10-4

APPLETON CITY

P APPLETON CITY PUBLIC LIBRARY, 105 W Fourth St, 64724. SAN 308-9339. Tel: 660-476-5513. E-mail: acpubliclibrary@yahoo.com. Web Site: acmogov.com/library. *Dir,* Sandra Bain; Staff 1 (Non-MLS 1)
Founded 1870. Pop 1,120
Library Holdings: DVDs 460; Large Print Bks 900; Bk Titles 24,000; Per Subs 8; Talking Bks 356; Videos 612
Open Tues & Thurs 8:30-5, Sat 8-12

AVA

P DOUGLAS COUNTY PUBLIC LIBRARY, 301 W Webster Ave, 65608. (Mail add: PO Box 277, 65608-0277), SAN 308-9355. Tel: 417-683-5633. FAX: 417-683-5633. Web Site: douglascountylibrary.lib.mo.us. *Access Serv, Librn,* Anita Dodd; E-mail: doddanita@gmail.com; Staff 2 (Non-MLS 2)
Founded 1979. Pop 13,084; Circ 39,316
Library Holdings: Bks-By-Mail 518; DVDs 212; Large Print Bks 873; Bk Vols 38,908; Per Subs 34; Talking Bks 1,141; Videos 840
Automation Activity & Vendor Info: (Cataloging) TLC (The Library Corporation); (Circulation) TLC (The Library Corporation); (OPAC) TLC (The Library Corporation)
Partic in Mo State Database
Open Mon-Fri 9-5, Sat 9-12
Friends of the Library Group

BLOOMFIELD

P BLOOMFIELD PUBLIC LIBRARY*, 200 Seneca St, 63825. (Mail add: PO Box 294, 63825-0294), SAN 308-9363. Tel: 573-568-3626. FAX: 573-568-3626. *Dir,* Linda Myers; Staff 1 (MLS 1)
Founded 1967. Pop 1,924; Circ 8,167
Library Holdings: Bk Titles 14,182; Bk Vols 14,391; Per Subs 12; Talking Bks 15; Videos 31
Special Collections: 1850 Newspaper Coll, microfilm; Stoddard County Records, bks, microfilm; War of the Rebellion
Automation Activity & Vendor Info: (Circulation) TLC (The Library Corporation)
Wireless access
Open Mon-Wed 10-5, Thurs 10-6, Fri 9-5, Sat 9-12

BLUE SPRINGS

S BLUE SPRINGS HISTORICAL SOCIETY*, Archives & Research Library, 101 SW 15th St, 64015. (Mail add: PO Box 762, 64013), SAN 373-2347. Tel: 816-224-8979, 816-304-1740. Web Site: www.bluespringshistory.org. *Archivist,* Kaye Burrus; E-mail: k.f.burrus@att.net
Founded 1976
Special Collections: Oral History
Subject Interests: Local hist
Function: Archival coll
Restriction: Not open to pub

BOLIVAR

P POLK COUNTY LIBRARY*, 1690 W Broadway St, 65613. SAN 348-9639. Tel: 417-326-4531. FAX: 417-326-4366. Web Site: polkcolibrary.org. *Dir,* Cindy Youngblood; E-mail: director@polkcolibrary.org; *Asst Dir,* Jeannie Saltkill; Staff 2 (MLS 1, Non-MLS 1)
Founded 1947. Pop 26,992
Library Holdings: CDs 873; DVDs 416; Large Print Bks 2,563; Bk Vols 50,000; Per Subs 57; Videos 2,089
Automation Activity & Vendor Info: (Cataloging) Book Systems; (Circulation) Book Systems; (ILL) OCLC; (OPAC) Book Systems
Wireless access
Open Mon, Tues & Thurs 9-8, Wed, Fri & Sat 9-5
Friends of the Library Group
Branches: 1
HUMANSVILLE BRANCH, 101 S Ohio St, Humansville, 65674. (Mail add: PO Box 201, Humansville, 65674-0201), SAN 348-9752. Tel: 417-754-2455. FAX: 417-754-2455. *Br Mgr,* Sharon Anderson
Library Holdings: CDs 42; DVDs 120; Large Print Bks 508; Bk Vols 11,600; Videos 629
Open Tues, Thurs & Fri 8:30-12:30 & 1-5, Sat 8:30-12:30
Friends of the Library Group

CR SOUTHWEST BAPTIST UNIVERSITY LIBRARIES*, Harriet K Hutchens Library, 1600 University Ave, 65613. SAN 308-9371. Tel: 417-328-1604, 417-328-1621. Toll Free Tel: 800-743-5774. FAX: 417-328-1652. Web Site: www.sbuniv.edu/library. *Dean, Univ Libr,* Dr Edward W Walton; Tel: 417-328-1619, E-mail: ewalton@sbuniv.edu; *Acq & Coll Develop Librn,* Susan Kromrie; Tel: 417-328-1629, E-mail: skromrie@sbuniv.edu; *Cat Librn,* Coleen Rose; Tel: 417-328-1631, E-mail: crose@sbuniv.edu; *Info Literacy Librn,* Bethany Messersmith; Tel: 417-328-1626, E-mail: bmessersmith@sbuniv.edu; *Digital Serv Librn,* Doyin Adenuga; Tel: 417-328-1624, E-mail: aadenuga@sbuniv.edu. Subject Specialists: *Admin, Electronic res,* Dr Edward W Walton; Staff 6 (MLS 6)
Founded 1878. Enrl 3,099; Fac 130; Highest Degree: Doctorate
Library Holdings: AV Mats 11,202; CDs 892; e-books 16,325; e-journals 9,823; Electronic Media & Resources 397; Music Scores 3,090; Bk Titles 121,204; Bk Vols 177,526; Per Subs 407; Videos 2,520
Special Collections: Butler Baptist Heritage Coll; Christian Education Resource Lab; Library of American Civilization - Microbook Coll; Southern Baptist Convention Resource Lab. State Document Depository
Automation Activity & Vendor Info: (Acquisitions) Innovative Interfaces, Inc; (Cataloging) Innovative Interfaces, Inc; (Circulation) Innovative Interfaces, Inc; (Course Reserve) Innovative Interfaces, Inc; (ILL) OCLC; (Media Booking) Innovative Interfaces, Inc; (OPAC) Innovative Interfaces, Inc; (Serials) Innovative Interfaces, Inc
Function: Archival coll, Audio & video playback equip for onsite use, Doc delivery serv, ILL available, Internet access, Mail loans to mem, Music CDs, Photocopying/Printing, Ref serv available, VHS videos
Publications: Southern Baptist Periodical Index (Index to science materials)
Partic in Amigos Library Services, Inc; MOBIUS
Restriction: Open to pub for ref & circ; with some limitations, Open to students, fac & staff
Departmental Libraries:
MERCY COLLEGE OF NURSING & HEALTH SCIENCES LIBRARY, 4431 S Fremont, Springfield, 65804-7307, SAN 309-2372. Tel: 417-820-2103. FAX: 417-820-4847. *Libr Dir,* Position Currently Open; Staff 3 (MLS 1, Non-MLS 2)
Founded 1909
Library Holdings: Bk Titles 3,059; Bk Vols 4,347; Per Subs 88
Special Collections: Archive Coll
Subject Interests: Nursing
Open Mon-Thurs 8am-9pm, Fri 8-12
MOUNTAIN VIEW CAMPUS LIBRARY, 209 W First St, Mountain View, 65548. (Mail add: PO Box 489, Mountain View, 65548). Tel: 417-934-5057. FAX: 417-934-5056.
Library Holdings: Bk Titles 10,972; Bk Vols 13,257
Automation Activity & Vendor Info: (Cataloging) Innovative Interfaces, Inc; (Circulation) Innovative Interfaces, Inc; (OPAC) Innovative Interfaces, Inc
Open Mon-Tues & Thurs 8-12 & 1-9, Wed & Fri 8-12 & 1-5
WISDOM LIBRARY, SBU Salem Ctr, 501 S Grand St, Salem, 65560. Tel: 573-729-7071. FAX: 573-729-6949. *Libr Supvr,* Nancy Eudy; E-mail: neudy@sbuniv.edu
Library Holdings: Bk Titles 4,256; Bk Vols 4,962
Automation Activity & Vendor Info: (Cataloging) Innovative Interfaces, Inc; (Circulation) Innovative Interfaces, Inc; (OPAC) Innovative Interfaces, Inc
Open Mon-Thurs 10-7, Fri 10-4

BONNE TERRE

P BONNE TERRE MEMORIAL LIBRARY, Five SW Main St, 63628. SAN 308-938X. Tel: 573-358-2260. FAX: 573-358-5941. E-mail: btml@bonneterre.net. Web Site: www.bonneterrelibrary.org. *Libr Dir,* Amanda Miller; *Ch, Circ Serv,* Rachel Howard; *Tech Serv Librn,* Peggy Haring; *Librn/Teen & Tween Serv,* Tina Johnston; *Spec Serv,* Beverly King
Founded 1867. Pop 5,000; Circ 36,909
Library Holdings: Audiobooks 595; CDs 117; DVDs 175; Large Print Bks 1,292; Bk Vols 23,050; Per Subs 29; Videos 1,102
Subject Interests: Local hist
Automation Activity & Vendor Info: (Cataloging) Follett Software; (Circulation) Follett Software
Wireless access
Function: After school storytime, Bk club(s), Bks on cassette, Bks on CD, Children's prog
Open Mon-Wed & Fri 10-6, Thurs 10-7, Sat 10-2
Friends of the Library Group

BOONVILLE

S FRIENDS OF HISTORIC BOONVILLE*, Archival Collection, 614 E Morgan, 65233. (Mail add: PO Box 1776, 65233), SAN 373-2312. Tel: 660-882-7977. Toll Free Tel: 888-588-1477. FAX: 660-882-9194. E-mail: fohboonville@gmail.com. Web Site: www.friendsofhistoricboonvillemo.org. *Dir,* Laura Wax; *Archivist,* Kathleen Conway; Staff 1 (MLS 1)
Founded 1971
Library Holdings: Bk Titles 460; Bk Vols 530
Subject Interests: Local hist
Restriction: Open by appt only

BRANSON

P TANEYHILLS COMMUNITY LIBRARY*, 200 S Fourth St, 65616-2738. SAN 308-9401. Tel: 417-334-1418. FAX: 417-334-1629. E-mail: tanlib100@gmail.com. Web Site: bransoncommunitylibrary.org. *Dir,* Marsha Schemper-Carlock; Staff 1 (MLS 1)
Founded 1933
Library Holdings: Bk Titles 44,552; Bk Vols 46,732; Per Subs 50
Special Collections: DAR Genealogy Coll; Missouri Coll; Taney County & Ozark Region Coll
Automation Activity & Vendor Info: (Cataloging) Follett Software; (Circulation) Follett Software
Publications: Newsletter, semi-annual
Open Mon, Tues, Thurs & Fri 10-5, Wed 10-7, Sat 10-1
Friends of the Library Group

BRENTWOOD

P BRENTWOOD PUBLIC LIBRARY*, 8765 Eulalie Ave, 63144. SAN 308-941X. Tel: 314-963-8630. Circulation Tel: 314-963-8631. FAX: 314-962-8675. E-mail: circulation@bplmo.org. Web Site: www.brentwoodlibrarymo.org. *Dir,* Gina Gibbons; Tel: 314-963-8636, E-mail: ggibbons@bplmo.org; *Youth Librn,* Lindsay Beckman; Tel: 314-963-8649, E-mail: lbeckman@bplmo.org; *Tech Serv Supvr,* Susan Holt; Tel: 314-963-8632; Staff 9 (MLS 3, Non-MLS 6)
Founded 1939. Pop 7,800; Circ 100,000
Library Holdings: Large Print Bks 31; Bk Titles 53,702; Bk Vols 54,238; Per Subs 81; Talking Bks 90; Videos 210
Automation Activity & Vendor Info: (Cataloging) SirsiDynix; (Circulation) SirsiDynix
Wireless access
Partic in Municipal Library Consortium; Saint Louis Regional Library Network
Open Mon-Thurs 9-8, Fri 9-6, Sat 9-5, Sun 1-5
Friends of the Library Group

BROOKFIELD

P BROOKFIELD PUBLIC LIBRARY*, 102 E Boston St, 64628. SAN 308-9428. Tel: 660-258-7439. FAX: 660-258-5626. E-mail: director@brookfieldpubliclibrary.org. Web Site: www.brookfieldpubliclibrary.org. *Dir,* Gina Smith; E-mail: director@brookfieldpubliclibrary.org; Staff 4 (Non-MLS 4)
Founded 1918. Pop 4,888; Circ 31,434
Library Holdings: Bk Vols 33,000; Per Subs 78
Subject Interests: Genealogy, Linn Co hist
Automation Activity & Vendor Info: (Cataloging) Mandarin Library Automation; (Circulation) Mandarin Library Automation
Wireless access
Function: 24/7 Electronic res, 24/7 Online cat, Bks on CD, Children's prog, Computers for patron use, Electronic databases & coll, For res purposes, ILL available, Internet access, Magazines, Meeting rooms, Microfiche/film & reading machines, Movies, Online cat, OverDrive digital audio bks, Photocopying/Printing, Preschool reading prog, Prog for adults,

Prog for children & young adult, Ref & res, Ref serv available, Res assist avail, Story hour, Summer reading prog, Wheelchair accessible
Partic in Grand Rivers Libr Conference
Open Mon-Fri 10-6, Sat 10-4

BRUNSWICK

P BRUNSWICK PUBLIC LIBRARY*, 115 W Broadway, 65236-1214. (Mail add: 310 W Broadway, 65236), SAN 375-0299. Tel: 660-548-1026. FAX: 660-548-1026. E-mail: brunswickarealibrary@gmail.com. *Library Contact,* Mary Jane Meyer; Staff 1 (MLS 1)
Founded 1973. Pop 1,000
Library Holdings: Large Print Bks 34; Bk Titles 14,500; Bk Vols 15,000; Talking Bks 20; Videos 95
Function: Res libr
Partic in OCLC Online Computer Library Center, Inc
Open Mon 10-12 & 2-4, Tues 3pm-4pm, Wed 10-12 & 2- , Thurs 2-4, Fri 10-Noon

BUFFALO

S DALLAS COUNTY HISTORICAL SOCIETY*, Historical & Genealogical Library, 1107 S Ash, 65622-8649. (Mail add: PO Box 594, 65622), SAN 373-2320. Tel: 417-267-2433. E-mail: dchsmo@gmail.com.
Library Holdings: Bk Vols 705
Restriction: Open by appt only

P DALLAS COUNTY LIBRARY, 219 W Main, 65622. (Mail add: PO Box 1008, 65622-1008), SAN 308-9436. Tel: 417-345-2647. FAX: 417-345-2647. E-mail: dallascountylibrary@gmail.com. Web Site: dallascountylibrary.missouri.org. *Dir,* Debra Woodyard; Staff 4 (Non-MLS 4)
Pop 16,107; Circ 99,556
Library Holdings: Audiobooks 1,225; Microforms 164; Bk Titles 26,970; Per Subs 25; Videos 2,361
Automation Activity & Vendor Info: (Cataloging) OCLC CatExpress; (Circulation) Book Systems; (ILL) OCLC FirstSearch; (OPAC) Book Systems
Wireless access
Partic in Amigos Library Services, Inc
Open Mon-Fri 8-5:30, Sat 8-12
Friends of the Library Group

BUTLER

P BUTLER PUBLIC LIBRARY, 100 W Atkison Ave, 64730. SAN 308-9444. Tel: 660-679-4321. FAX: 660-679-4321. Web Site: www.butlerpubliclibrary.org. *Libr Dir,* Tifany Fugate; E-mail: tifanyfugate@butlerpubliclibrary.org
Founded 1926. Pop 15,000
Library Holdings: Bk Titles 33,000; Per Subs 17
Automation Activity & Vendor Info: (Cataloging) Follett Software; (Circulation) Follett Software
Open Mon-Wed & Fri 9:30-5:30, Thurs 9:30-7, Sat 9:30-1:30
Friends of the Library Group

CALIFORNIA

P MONITEAU COUNTY LIBRARY @ WOOD PLACE, 501 S Oak St, 65018. SAN 308-9452. Tel: 573-796-2642. E-mail: librarian@moniteaucountylibrary.org. Web Site: www.moniteaucountylibrary.org. *Libr Dir,* Connie Walker
Founded 1956. Pop 10,472
Library Holdings: Bk Titles 19,360; Bk Vols 17,209; Per Subs 22; Talking Bks 760; Videos 1,125
Automation Activity & Vendor Info: (Acquisitions) Follett Software; (Cataloging) Follett Software; (Circulation) Follett Software; (Media Booking) Follett Software; (OPAC) Follett Software
Wireless access
Open Mon, Wed & Fri 9-5, Tues & Thurs 9-6, Sat 9-12
Friends of the Library Group

CAMDENTON

P CAMDEN COUNTY LIBRARY DISTRICT*, Camdenton Library, 89 Rodeo Rd, 65020. (Mail add: PO Box 1320, 65020-1320), SAN 377-1032. Tel: 573-346-5954. FAX: 573-346-1263. Web Site: www.ccld.us. *Dir,* Michael Davis; *Br Mgr,* Karen Colgan; E-mail: karenc@ccld.us; Staff 15 (MLS 1, Non-MLS 14)
Founded 1934. Pop 38,702; Circ 188,017
Library Holdings: Audiobooks 2,019; CDs 214; DVDs 3,536; Bk Vols 97,109; Per Subs 243; Videos 192
Automation Activity & Vendor Info: (Cataloging) Innovative Interfaces, Inc; (Circulation) Innovative Interfaces, Inc; (ILL) OCLC; (OPAC) Innovative Interfaces, Inc
Wireless access
Function: Bks on cassette, Bks on CD, Children's prog, Computer training, Computers for patron use, Doc delivery serv, Electronic databases & coll, Free DVD rentals, Genealogy discussion group, ILL available, Magnifiers for reading, Photocopying/Printing, Prog for children & young adult, Summer reading prog, Tax forms, VHS videos, Wheelchair accessible
Partic in Mo Libr Asn
Open Mon 9-8, Tues-Fri 9-6, Sat 9-5
Restriction: Open to pub for ref & circ; with some limitations
Branches: 5
CLIMAX SPRINGS BRANCH, 14157 N State Hwy 7, Climax Springs, 65324, SAN 377-4147. Tel: 573-347-2722. FAX: 573-347-2722. *Br Mgr,* Carolee Apperson; Staff 1 (MLS 1)
Library Holdings: Bk Titles 7,280; Bk Vols 7,410; Per Subs 24; Talking Bks 50; Videos 50
Partic in Mo Libr Asn
Open Tues-Thurs 9-5, Sat 9-1
MACKS CREEK BRANCH, 90 State Rd N, Macks Creek, 65786. Tel: 573-363-5530. FAX: 573-363-5530. *Br Mgr,* Jennie Smith; Staff 1 (Non-MLS 1)
Function: Children's prog, Computers for patron use, Electronic databases & coll, Free DVD rentals, ILL available, Online cat, OverDrive digital audio bks, Photocopying/Printing, Preschool reading prog, Prog for children & young adult, Story hour, Summer reading prog, Tax forms
Open Tues-Thurs 9-5, Sat 9-1
OSAGE BEACH BRANCH, 1064 Gutridge Lane, Osage Beach, 65065. Tel: 573-348-3282. FAX: 573-348-2883. *Br Mgr,* Vicky Moore; Staff 1 (Non-MLS 1)
Open Mon-Thurs 9-8, Fri 9-6, Sat 9-5
STOUTLAND BRANCH, 132 Starling Ave, Stoutland, 65567. Tel: 417-286-3611. FAX: 417-286-3611. *Br Mgr,* Marie Brown; Staff 1 (Non-MLS 1)
Open Tues-Thurs 9-5, Sat 9-1
SUNRISE BEACH BRANCH, 14156 N State Hwy 5, Sunrise Beach, 65079. (Mail add: PO Box 1206, Sunrise Beach, 65079), SAN 377-2764. Tel: 573-374-6982. FAX: 573-374-6982. *Br Mgr,* Claire Hammerschmidt; Staff 1 (MLS 1)
Library Holdings: Large Print Bks 10; Bk Titles 9,680; Bk Vols 9,830; Per Subs 38; Talking Bks 51; Videos 76
Open Mon, Wed & Fri 9-5, Tues & Thurs 9-6, Sat 9-1

CANTON

P CANTON PUBLIC LIBRARY*, 403 Lewis St, 63435. SAN 308-9460. Tel: 573-288-5279. FAX: 573-288-5279. E-mail: cantonmopubliclibrary@gmail.com. Web Site: www.cantonmopubliclibrary.org. *Libr Dir,* Trina Karl; Staff 3 (Non-MLS 3)
Founded 1929. Pop 2,377; Circ 18,618
Library Holdings: Bk Titles 18,115; Bk Vols 18,448; Per Subs 13
Special Collections: Meridian Library; War of the Rebellion
Subject Interests: Adult fiction, Adult non-fiction, Juv fiction, Juv non-fiction
Wireless access
Function: 24/7 Electronic res, 24/7 Online cat, Activity rm, Adult literacy prog, After school storytime
Partic in Grand Rivers Libr Conference
Open Mon-Fri 9-5, Sat 10-2

CR CULVER-STOCKTON COLLEGE*, Carl Johann Memorial Library, One College Hill, 63435. SAN 308-9479. Tel: 573-288-6321. FAX: 573-288-6615. Web Site: www.culver.edu/library. *Libr Dir,* Katie Marney; Tel: 573-288-6478, E-mail: kmarney@culver.edu; *Circ & Tech Serv Coordr,* Julie Wright; Tel: 573-288-6640, E-mail: jwright@culver.edu; *Cat Tech, Ref Tech,* Amber Strub-Lay; Tel: 573-288-6369, E-mail: astrublay@culver.edu; Staff 4 (MLS 1, Non-MLS 3)
Founded 1853. Enrl 855; Fac 50; Highest Degree: Bachelor
Library Holdings: e-books 6,000; Bk Vols 164,611; Per Subs 196
Special Collections: American Freedom Studies; History & Literature of Missouri & Midwest; History of Christian Church (Disciples of Christ Coll); Mark Twain Coll; Midwest Americana. Oral History
Subject Interests: Hist, Relig studies
Automation Activity & Vendor Info: (Acquisitions) Innovative Interfaces, Inc; (Cataloging) Innovative Interfaces, Inc; (Circulation) Innovative Interfaces, Inc; (Course Reserve) Innovative Interfaces, Inc; (ILL) Innovative Interfaces, Inc; (OPAC) Innovative Interfaces, Inc; (Serials) Innovative Interfaces, Inc
Wireless access
Function: Art exhibits, AV serv, Homework prog, ILL available, Internet access, VHS videos
Publications: ExLibris (Newsletter)
Partic in Amigos Library Services, Inc; Missouri Research & Education Network; MOBIUS; OCLC Online Computer Library Center, Inc
Open Mon-Thurs 8am-11:30pm, Fri 8-5, Sat 1-5, Sun 1-11:30
Friends of the Library Group

CAPE GIRARDEAU

P CAPE GIRARDEAU PUBLIC LIBRARY, 711 N Clark St, 63701. SAN 308-9487. Tel: 573-334-5279. FAX: 573-334-8334. Web Site: www.capelibrary.org. *Libr Dir,* Katie Earnhart; E-mail: katie@capelibrary.org; Staff 6 (MLS 3, Non-MLS 3)
Founded 1922. Pop 35,590; Circ 243,507
Jul 2017-Jun 2018 Income $1,843,668, Federal $29,980, Locally Generated Income $1,763,688, Other $50,000. Mats Exp $147,367, Books $96,072, Per/Ser (Incl. Access Fees) $6,141, Micro $1,133, AV Mat $11,000, Electronic Ref Mat (Incl. Access Fees) $33,021. Sal $547,193 (Prof $159,930)
Library Holdings: Audiobooks 6,949; CDs 2,084; DVDs 6,305; e-books 18,029; Large Print Bks 2,565; Microforms 731; Bk Titles 99,165; Bk Vols 102,156; Per Subs 135; Videos 400
Special Collections: DAC & DAR Coll; Groves Genealogy Coll; Hirsch Foreign Language for Children; Mississippi River Valley Coll
Automation Activity & Vendor Info: (Acquisitions) SirsiDynix; (Cataloging) SirsiDynix; (Circulation) SirsiDynix; (ILL) OCLC FirstSearch; (OPAC) SirsiDynix
Wireless access
Function: 24/7 Electronic res, 24/7 Online cat, Activity rm, Adult bk club, Adult literacy prog, Art exhibits, Art programs, Audiobks on Playaways & MP3, Audiobks via web, Bk club(s), Bk reviews (Group), Bks on cassette, Bks on CD, Children's prog, Computer training, Computers for patron use, Doc delivery serv, Electronic databases & coll, Free DVD rentals, Holiday prog, Home delivery & serv to seniorr ctr & nursing homes, Homebound delivery serv, ILL available, Internet access, Magazines, Magnifiers for reading, Meeting rooms, Microfiche/film & reading machines, Movies, Music CDs, Notary serv, Online cat, OverDrive digital audio bks, Passport agency, Photocopying/Printing, Preschool outreach, Preschool reading prog, Printer for laptops & handheld devices, Prog for adults, Prog for children & young adult, Ref serv available, Scanner, Senior computer classes, Serves people with intellectual disabilities, Spanish lang bks, Spoken cassettes & CDs, STEM programs, Story hour, Study rm, Summer & winter reading prog, Summer reading prog, Tax forms, Teen prog, Telephone ref, VHS videos, Wheelchair accessible, Winter reading prog
Partic in Amigos Library Services, Inc
Special Services for the Blind - Volunteer serv
Open Mon-Thurs 9-9, Fri & Sat 9-5, Sun 1-5
Restriction: Non-resident fee
Friends of the Library Group

C SOUTHEAST MISSOURI STATE UNIVERSITY*, Kent Library, 929 Normal Ave, 63701. (Mail add: One University Plaza, MS 4600, 63701), SAN 308-9495. Tel: 573-651-2235. Circulation Tel: 573-651-2232. Interlibrary Loan Service Tel: 573-651-2152. Information Services Tel: 573-651-2230. Circulation E-mail: circulationdesk@semo.edu. Web Site: library.semo.edu. *Dean,* Barbara Glackin; E-mail: bglackin@semo.edu; *Access Serv Mgr,* Leah McAlister; Tel: 573-986-7308, E-mail: lrmcalister@semo.edu; *Libr Syst Mgr,* Jason Bruenderman; Tel: 573-986-6833, E-mail: jbruenderman@semo.edu; Staff 18 (MLS 9, Non-MLS 9)
Founded 1873. Enrl 11,069; Fac 415; Highest Degree: Master
Library Holdings: Audiobooks 190; CDs 1,627; DVDs 6,312; e-books 393,420; e-journals 90,590; Electronic Media & Resources 199,543; Large Print Bks 18; Microforms 1,231,155; Music Scores 794; Bk Titles 360,172; Bk Vols 411,173; Per Subs 194
Special Collections: Brodsky Coll of William Faulkner Materials; Charles Harrison Rare Books Coll; Little River Drainage District Coll; Regional History Coll of Southeast Missouri. State Document Depository; US Document Depository
Automation Activity & Vendor Info: (Acquisitions) Innovative Interfaces, Inc; (Cataloging) Innovative Interfaces, Inc; (Circulation) Innovative Interfaces, Inc; (Course Reserve) Innovative Interfaces, Inc; (ILL) OCLC ILLiad; (OPAC) Innovative Interfaces, Inc; (Serials) Ex Libris Group
Wireless access
Partic in Amigos Library Services, Inc; MOBIUS; OCLC Online Computer Library Center, Inc
Open Mon-Thurs 7:30am-11pm, Fri 7:30-6, Sat 11-5, Sun 1-11

S SOUTHEAST MISSOURIAN NEWSPAPER LIBRARY*, 301 Broadway, 63701. (Mail add: PO Box 699, 63702-0699), SAN 329-7128. Tel: 573-388-3653. Toll Free Tel: 800-879-1210. Web Site: www.semissourian.com. *Librn,* Sharon K Sanders; E-mail: ssanders@semissourian.com; Staff 1 (MLS 1)
Founded 1965
Library Holdings: AV Mats 750; Bk Titles 700; Per Subs 10
Special Collections: Historical Research Notes; Newspaper Clippings (1965-present); Southeast Missourian & Bulletin-Journal Newspapers, microfilm
Restriction: Not open to pub

CARROLLTON

P CARROLLTON PUBLIC LIBRARY, One N Folger St, 64633. SAN 308-9509. Tel: 660-542-0183. FAX: 660-542-0654. Web Site: www.carrolltonlibrary.com. *Dir,* Susan Lightfoot; E-mail: director@carrolltonlibrary.com; Staff 4 (MLS 1, Non-MLS 3)
Founded 1938. Pop 3,784; Circ 65,000
Library Holdings: Audiobooks 450; AV Mats 450; Bks on Deafness & Sign Lang 25; Braille Volumes 1; DVDs 1,000; e-books 175; Large Print Bks 1,500; Microforms 150; Bk Titles 35,000; Per Subs 75; Talking Bks 2; Videos 500
Special Collections: DAR History Books of Carroll County, MO
Automation Activity & Vendor Info: (Acquisitions) Baker & Taylor; (Cataloging) Evergreen; (Circulation) Evergreen; (Course Reserve) Evergreen; (Discovery) Evergreen; (ILL) Evergreen; (Media Booking) Evergreen; (OPAC) Evergreen; (Serials) Evergreen
Wireless access
Function: 24/7 Electronic res, 24/7 Online cat, Accelerated reader prog, Activity rm, Adult bk club, Adult literacy prog, After school storytime, Archival coll, Art exhibits, Audio & video playback equip for onsite use, Audiobks on Playaways & MP3, Audiobks via web, AV serv, BA reader (adult literacy), Bilingual assistance for Spanish patrons, Bk club(s), Bk reviews (Group), Bks on CD, Bus archives, CD-ROM, Chess club, Children's prog, Citizenship assistance, Computer training, Computers for patron use, Digital talking bks, Distance learning, Doc delivery serv, Electronic databases & coll, Equip loans & repairs, Family literacy, For res purposes, Free DVD rentals, Games & aids for people with disabilities, Genealogy discussion group, Govt ref serv, Health sci info serv, Holiday prog, Home delivery & serv to seniorr ctr & nursing homes, Homebound delivery serv, Homework prog, ILL available, Instruction & testing, Internet access, Jazz prog, Laminating, Large print keyboards, Learning ctr, Legal assistance to inmates, Life-long learning prog for all ages, Literacy & newcomer serv, Magazines, Magnifiers for reading, Mail & tel request accepted, Mail loans to mem, Masonic res mat, Meeting rooms, Microfiche/film & reading machines, Movies, Museum passes, Music CDs, Online cat, Online info literacy tutorials on the web & in blackboard, Online ref, Orientations, Outreach serv, Outside serv via phone, mail, e-mail & web, OverDrive digital audio bks, Photocopying/Printing, Preschool outreach, Preschool reading prog, Printer for laptops & handheld devices, Prof lending libr, Prog for adults, Prog for children & young adult, Ref & res, Ref serv available, Res libr, Res performed for a fee, Scanner, Senior computer classes, Senior outreach, Serves people with intellectual disabilities, Spanish lang bks, Specialized serv in classical studies, Story hour, Study rm, Summer & winter reading prog, Summer reading prog, Tax forms, Teen prog, Telephone ref, VHS videos, Visual arts prog, Wheelchair accessible, Winter reading prog, Words travel prog, Workshops, Writing prog
Partic in Grand Rivers Libr Conference; Missouri Evergreen; Missouri Research & Education Network
Special Services for the Deaf - Adult & family literacy prog
Special Services for the Blind - Bks on CD; Large print bks; Magnifiers; Photo duplicator for making large print; Playaways (bks on MP3); Web-Braille
Open Mon, Tues, Thurs & Fri 9-5:30, Wed 9-8, Sat 9-1, Sun 1-5
Friends of the Library Group

CARTHAGE

P CARTHAGE PUBLIC LIBRARY*, 612 S Garrison Ave, 64836. SAN 308-9517. Tel: 417-237-7040. FAX: 417-237-7041. E-mail: carthage@carthagelibrary.net. Web Site: carthage.lib.mo.us. *Dir,* Julie Yockey; E-mail: jyockey@carthagelibrary.net; Staff 11 (Non-MLS 11)
Founded 1902. Pop 12,668; Circ 88,738
Library Holdings: AV Mats 1,114; Bks on Deafness & Sign Lang 25; e-books 6,700; Large Print Bks 2,481; Bk Titles 48,879; Bk Vols 52,984; Per Subs 139; Talking Bks 1,135
Automation Activity & Vendor Info: (Cataloging) Follett Software; (Circulation) Follett Software; (ILL) OCLC Online; (OPAC) Follett Software
Wireless access
Function: AV serv, ILL available, Internet access, Magnifiers for reading, Photocopying/Printing, Prog for children & young adult, Ref serv available, Summer reading prog, Telephone ref, Wheelchair accessible
Partic in Amigos Library Services, Inc
Special Services for the Deaf - TTY equip
Open Mon & Tues 9-8, Wed-Fri 9-6, Sat 9-4
Friends of the Library Group

CARUTHERSVILLE

P CARUTHERSVILLE PUBLIC LIBRARY*, 707 W 13th St, 63830. SAN 308-9525. Tel: 573-333-2480. FAX: 573-333-0552. Web Site: cville.lib.mo.us. *Dir,* Teresa Tidwell; E-mail: ttidwell@cville.lib.mo.us; Staff 8 (Non-MLS 8)
Founded 1923. Pop 5,068; Circ 44,000

Jul 2016-Jun 2017 Income $164,858, State $8,000, City $42,000, Locally Generated Income $5,000, Other $95,000. Mats Exp $20,093
Library Holdings: Bk Titles 24,117; Bk Vols 25,684; Per Subs 32; Talking Bks 371; Videos 718
Subject Interests: Behav sci, Educ, Genealogy, Law, Relig studies, Soc sci
Automation Activity & Vendor Info: (Acquisitions) Evergreen; (Cataloging) Evergreen; (Circulation) Evergreen; (ILL) Evergreen; (OPAC) Evergreen
Wireless access
Function: 24/7 Electronic res, 24/7 Online cat, Accelerated reader prog, Activity rm, Adult bk club, Adult literacy prog, After school storytime
Partic in Association for Rural & Small Libraries
Special Services for the Deaf - High interest/low vocabulary bks
Special Services for the Blind - Talking bk serv referral
Open Mon, Wed, Thurs & Fri 9:30-5:30, Tues 9:30-7:30, Sat 9:30-1:30, Sun 1-4
Restriction: Circ to mem only, Free to mem, Lending limited to county residents, Residents only
Friends of the Library Group

CENTER

P RALLS COUNTY LIBRARY*, 102 N Public St, 63436-1000. (Mail add: PO Box 259, 63436-0259), SAN 377-2721. Tel: 573-267-3200. FAX: 573-267-3200. E-mail: rallscountylibrary@gmail.com. Web Site: rallscountylibrary.com. *Dir,* Brian Cleveland; Staff 2 (MLS 1, Non-MLS 1)
Founded 1992. Pop 9,626; Circ 17,231
Library Holdings: DVDs 30; Bk Titles 16,000; Bk Vols 16,400; Per Subs 61; Talking Bks 250; Videos 652
Wireless access
Open Mon-Fri 8:30-5:30, Sat 8:30-Noon
Friends of the Library Group

CENTERVILLE

P REYNOLDS COUNTY LIBRARY DISTRICT*, Centerville Branch, 2306 Pine St, 63633. (Mail add: PO Box 175, 63633-0175), SAN 349-8727. Tel: 573-648-2471. FAX: 573-648-2471. E-mail: reynoldscountylibrary@yahoo.com. Web Site: reynoldscountylibrary.missouri.org. *Dir,* Pat Rainwater; Staff 2 (Non-MLS 2)
Pop 6,689; Circ 35,952
Library Holdings: Audiobooks 344; DVDs 41; Bk Titles 8,421; Per Subs 4
Wireless access
Open Mon, Wed & Fri 8-4:30
Branches: 4
BUNKER BRANCH, 203 N Main St, Bunker, 63629, SAN 349-8697. Tel: 573-689-2718. FAX: 573-689-2718. E-mail: bunkerbranchlibrary@yahoo.com. *Br Librn,* Lesa Bishop; Staff 1 (Non-MLS 1)
Library Holdings: Audiobooks 245; Bk Titles 9,363; Per Subs 4; Videos 170
Open Mon-Fri 8:30-4:30
ELLINGTON BRANCH, 130 S Main, Ellington, 63638. (Mail add: PO Box 485, Ellington, 63638), SAN 349-8751. Tel: 573-663-7289. FAX: 573-663-7289. E-mail: ellingtonbranchlibrary@yahoo.com. *Br Librn,* Stephanie Lambert; Staff 1 (Non-MLS 1)
Library Holdings: Audiobooks 302; Bk Titles 10,782; Per Subs 5; Videos 194
Open Mon-Fri 8:30-5
LESTERVILLE BRANCH, 33285 Hwy 21, Lesterville, 63654. (Mail add: PO Box 222, Lesterville, 63654), SAN 349-8875. Tel: 573-637-2532. Administration Tel: 573-648-2471. FAX: 573-637-2532. E-mail: lestervillebranchlibrary@yahoo.com. *Br Librn,* Mary Dement; Staff 1 (Non-MLS 1)
Library Holdings: Audiobooks 257; Bk Titles 7,466; Per Subs 3
Open Tues & Thurs 8-4:30, Wed 8-12
OATES BRANCH, 8483 Hwy J, Black, 63625, SAN 349-8964. Tel: 573-269-1117. *Br Librn,* Phoebe White; Staff 1 (Non-MLS 1)
Library Holdings: Audiobooks 44; Bk Titles 3,079; Per Subs 2
Open Mon & Wed 9-5

CENTRALIA

P CENTRALIA PUBLIC LIBRARY*, 210 S Jefferson St, 65240. SAN 308-9533. Tel: 573-682-2036. FAX: 573-682-5556. E-mail: centraliapl@gmail.com. Web Site: www.centraliapubliclibrary.com. *Dir,* Becky Wilson; Staff 4 (MLS 1, Non-MLS 3)
Founded 1903. Pop 4,300; Circ 50,000
Library Holdings: e-books 19,446; e-journals 25; Bk Titles 28,545; Per Subs 15
Special Collections: Missouri Bks
Automation Activity & Vendor Info: (Cataloging) OCLC CatExpress; (Circulation) Follett Software; (ILL) OCLC WorldShare Interlibrary Loan
Wireless access
Function: 24/7 Electronic res, Adult bk club, Online cat
Open Mon, Wed, Fri & Sat 9-5, Tues & Thurs 9-8, Sun 1-4
Friends of the Library Group

CHAFFEE

P CHAFFEE PUBLIC LIBRARY*, 202 Wright Ave, 63740. SAN 308-9541. Tel: 573-887-3298. FAX: 573-887-3298. Web Site: cityofchaffee.com/chflibrary. *Librn,* Tina Horton; *Librn,* Jennifer Nolen; Staff 1 (MLS 1)
Founded 1929. Pop 3,041; Circ 11,306
Library Holdings: Audiobooks 22; Bks-By-Mail 150; Bks on Deafness & Sign Lang 4; Braille Volumes 2; CDs 43; DVDs 434; Large Print Bks 17; Bk Titles 13,113; Bk Vols 16,614; Per Subs 12; Talking Bks 91; Videos 79
Automation Activity & Vendor Info: (Cataloging) Follett Software
Open Mon-Fri 10-12:30 & 1:30-6, Sat 10-1

CHARLESTON

P MISSISSIPPI COUNTY LIBRARY DISTRICT*, Clara Drinkwater Newnam Library, 105 E Marshall St, 63834. (Mail add: PO Box 160, 63834-0160), SAN 348-9817. Tel: 573-683-6748. FAX: 573-683-2761. E-mail: mx92000@yahoo.com. Web Site: www.youseemore.com/mcld. *Dir,* Stephanie R Bledsoe
Founded 1945. Pop 14,442; Circ 59,579
Library Holdings: Bks on Deafness & Sign Lang 15; Bk Vols 41,983; Per Subs 196
Special Collections: State & Local History Coll, micro, print, VF
Automation Activity & Vendor Info: (Acquisitions) TLC (The Library Corporation); (Cataloging) TLC (The Library Corporation); (Circulation) TLC (The Library Corporation)
Wireless access
Partic in Amigos Library Services, Inc
Open Mon-Fri 8-5:30, Sat 9-4
Branches: 1
MITCHELL MEMORIAL, 204 E Washington St, East Prairie, 63845, SAN 348-9841. Tel: 573-649-2131. FAX: 573-649-9100. *Dir,* Stephanie Bledsoe
Open Mon-Fri 10-5:30, Sat 10-2

CHESTERFIELD

CM LOGAN UNIVERSITY/COLLEGE OF CHIROPRACTIC LIBRARY*, Learning Resources Center, 1851 Schoettler Rd, 63006. (Mail add: PO Box 1065, 63006-1065), SAN 308-955X. Tel: 636-230-1781. Reference Tel: 636-227-1788. Toll Free Tel: 800-782-3344. FAX: 636-207-2448. E-mail: library@logan.edu. Web Site: www.logan.edu/campus-resources/lrc. *Dir,* Ellen Dickman; Tel: 636-230-1878, E-mail: ellen.dickman@logan.edu; *Cataloger, Librn,* Tori Lyons; Tel: 636-230-1783, E-mail: victoria.lyons@logan.edu; *Ref Librn,* Sheryl Walters; E-mail: sheryl.walters@logan.edu; Staff 2 (MLS 2)
Founded 1960. Enrl 1,100; Fac 94; Highest Degree: Doctorate
Library Holdings: AV Mats 1,500; CDs 250; DVDs 500; Bk Titles 11,000; Bk Vols 13,000; Per Subs 240; Videos 750
Special Collections: Osseous, Human & Synthetic; State Chiropractic Association Newsletters
Subject Interests: Chiropractic, Neurology, Nutrition, Orthopedics, Radiology
Automation Activity & Vendor Info: (Acquisitions) Innovative Interfaces, Inc; (Cataloging) Innovative Interfaces, Inc; (Circulation) Innovative Interfaces, Inc; (OPAC) Innovative Interfaces, Inc; (Serials) Innovative Interfaces, Inc
Wireless access
Function: Ref serv available
Publications: In Touch (Bibliographies)
Partic in Chiropractic Libr Consortium; MOBIUS; Saint Louis Regional Library Network
Open Mon-Fri 7-6

CHILLICOTHE

P LIVINGSTON COUNTY LIBRARY*, 450 Locust St, 64601-2597. SAN 308-9568. Tel: 660-646-0547. FAX: 660-646-5504. E-mail: librarian@livingstoncountylibrary.org. Web Site: www.livingstoncountylibrary.org. *Dir,* Cindy Warren; Staff 11 (MLS 2, Non-MLS 9)
Founded 1921. Pop 14,558; Circ 145,483
Library Holdings: AV Mats 2,084; e-books 6,000; Bk Titles 44,000; Bk Vols 54,000; Per Subs 100; Videos 1,000
Special Collections: Missouri History (George Somerville Coll)
Wireless access
Open Mon-Thurs 9-7, Fri 9-5, Sat 9-4
Friends of the Library Group

CLAYTON

GL SAINT LOUIS COUNTY LAW LIBRARY*, Courts Bldg, 105 S Central Ave, 6th Flr, 63105. SAN 308-9584. Tel: 314-615-4726. E-mail: stlouiscountylawlibrary@gmail.com. Web Site: www.stlouisco.com/lawandpublicsafety/lawlibrary. *Dir,* Lacy Rakestraw; Staff 2 (MLS 2)
Library Holdings: Bk Titles 30,000; Bk Vols 31,000; Per Subs 20
Wireless access
Open Mon-Fri 8-4:50
Restriction: Circ to mil employees only, Limited access for the pub, Non-circulating, Not a lending libr, Open to pub for ref only

CLEVER

P CLEVER PUBLIC LIBRARY*, 7450 W Veterans Blvd, 65631. (Mail add: PO Box 44, 65631). Tel: 417-743-2277. FAX: 417-743-2277. E-mail: clever@christiancountylibrary.org. *Dir,* Ms Geri Godber; Tel: 417-209-7126, E-mail: ggodber@christiancountylibrary.org; *Libr Asst,* Ms Dale Maisel; E-mail: dmaisel@christiancountylibrary.org
Founded 1949
Library Holdings: Bk Vols 9,000
Automation Activity & Vendor Info: (Cataloging) Innovative Interfaces, Inc; (Circulation) Innovative Interfaces, Inc; (ILL) OCLC; (OPAC) Innovative Interfaces, Inc
Wireless access
Open Mon-Thurs 10-7, Fri 2-6, Sat 9-2
Friends of the Library Group

CLINTON

P HENRY COUNTY LIBRARY, 123 E Green St, 64735. SAN 308-9592. Tel: 660-885-2612. FAX: 660-885-8953. Web Site: www.henrycolib.org. *Libr Dir,* Stephanie Rogers; E-mail: stephanie.rogers@henrycolib.org; *Asst Dir,* Debbie Jones; Staff 14 (MLS 3, Non-MLS 11)
Founded 1946. Pop 19,215; Circ 147,319
Library Holdings: Large Print Bks 115; Bk Titles 80,000; Per Subs 96; Talking Bks 2,115; Videos 1,284
Subject Interests: Local hist
Automation Activity & Vendor Info: (Cataloging) Book Systems; (Circulation) Book Systems
Wireless access
Open Mon-Sat 8-5
Friends of the Library Group
Branches: 1
LENORA BLACKMORE BRANCH, 105 W Benton St, Windsor, 65360, SAN 309-2623. Tel: 660-647-2298. FAX: 660-647-2275. *Libr Dir,* Stephanie Rogers; Staff 3 (MLS 2, Non-MLS 1)
Founded 1937. Pop 3,053; Circ 19,307
Library Holdings: AV Mats 183; Bk Titles 18,000; Per Subs 15
Open Mon-Fri 8-5, Sat 8-Noon

COLUMBIA

P DANIEL BOONE REGIONAL LIBRARY*, Columbia Public Library-Headquarters, 100 W Broadway, 65203. (Mail add: PO Box 1267, 65205-1267), SAN 348-9876. Tel: 573-443-3161. Toll Free Tel: 800-324-4806. FAX: 573-443-3281. TDD: 573-642-0662. Web Site: www.dbrl.org. *Dir,* Margaret Conroy; E-mail: mconroy@dbrl.org; *Chief Financial Officer,* Jim Smith; *Assoc Dir,* Elinor Barrett; *Tech Serv Mgr,* Nathan Pauley; Staff 122 (MLS 25, Non-MLS 97)
Founded 1959
Library Holdings: Per Subs 925
Automation Activity & Vendor Info: (Acquisitions) SirsiDynix; (Cataloging) SirsiDynix; (Circulation) SirsiDynix; (OPAC) SirsiDynix
Wireless access
Function: Adult literacy prog, Archival coll, Art exhibits, Audiobks on Playaways & MP3, Audiobks via web, Bk club(s), Bks on CD, Children's prog, Computer training, Computers for patron use, Electronic databases & coll, Free DVD rentals, Genealogy discussion group, Home delivery & serv to seniorr ctr & nursing homes, Homebound delivery serv, ILL available, Internet access, Life-long learning prog for all ages, Magazines, Mail & tel request accepted, Meeting rooms, Microfiche/film & reading machines, Movies, Music CDs, Notary serv, Online cat, Online info literacy tutorials on the web & in blackboard, Online ref, Outreach serv, Outside serv via phone, mail, e-mail & web, OverDrive digital audio bks, Photocopying/Printing, Printer for laptops & handheld devices, Prog for adults, Prog for children & young adult, Ref & res, Ref serv available, Scanner, Senior computer classes, Spanish lang bks, Spoken cassettes & CDs, Spoken cassettes & DVDs, Story hour, Study rm, Summer reading prog, Teen prog, Telephone ref, Wheelchair accessible
Special Services for the Deaf - TDD equip
Open Mon-Thurs 9-9, Fri 9-6, Sat 9-5, Sun 1-5
Restriction: ID required to use computers (Ltd hrs)
Friends of the Library Group
Branches: 3
CALLAWAY COUNTY PUBLIC LIBRARY, 710 Court St, Fulton, 65251, SAN 348-9906. Tel: 573-642-7261. FAX: 573-642-4439. *Libr Mgr,* Greg Reeves
Special Services for the Deaf - TDD equip
Open Mon-Thurs 9-7, Fri & Sat 9-5
Friends of the Library Group
HOLTS SUMMIT PUBLIC LIBRARY, 188 W Simon Blvd, Holts Summit, 65043. Tel: 573-606-8770. *Libr Serv Mgr,* Sara Henry; E-mail: shenry@dbrl.org; Staff 4 (Non-MLS 4)
Founded 2019
Open Mon-Fri 9-6, Sat 9-3
SOUTHERN BOONE COUNTY PUBLIC LIBRARY, 109 N Main St, Ashland, 65010. Tel: 573-657-7378. FAX: 573-657-0448. *Libr Mgr,* Ronda Mitchell
Founded 1999
Open Mon-Thurs 9-7, Fri 9-6, Sat 9-3
Friends of the Library Group
Bookmobiles: 2

SR CALVARY EPISCOPAL CHURCH LIBRARY*, 123 S Ninth St, 65201. SAN 326-0771. Tel: 573-449-3194. FAX: 573-442-9392. Web Site: www.calvaryonninth.org.
Founded 1975
Library Holdings: Bk Titles 1,500; Bk Vols 1,750; Videos 15
Subject Interests: Biblical studies, Church hist

C COLUMBIA COLLEGE*, J W & Lois Stafford Library, 1001 Rogers St, 65216. SAN 308-9606. Tel: 573-875-7381. Toll Free Tel: 800-231-2391, Ext 7381. Reference E-mail: library@ccis.edu. Web Site: library.ccis.edu. *Interim Libr Dir,* Susan Townsend; E-mail: stownsend@ccis.edu; *Asst Dir,* M Jordan Rustemeyer; Tel: 573-875-4591, E-mail: mjrustemeyer1@ccis.edu; *Access Serv Librn,* Mary Batterson; Tel: 573-875-7373, E-mail: mebatterson@ccis.edu; *Tech Serv Librn,* Vandy Evermon; Tel: 573-875-7370, E-mail: vlevermon@ccis.edu; *ILL, Libr Asst,* Peter Neely; Tel: 573-875-7372, E-mail: pdneely@ccis.edu; Staff 4 (MLS 4)
Founded 1851. Highest Degree: Master
Jul 2017-Jun 2018. Mats Exp $291,000, Books $15,000, Per/Ser (Incl. Access Fees) $29,000, Electronic Ref Mat (Incl. Access Fees) $246,000, Presv $1,000
Library Holdings: CDs 490; DVDs 515; e-books 208,000; Bk Vols 61,000; Per Subs 110; Videos 870
Automation Activity & Vendor Info: (Acquisitions) Innovative Interfaces, Inc - Sierra; (Cataloging) Innovative Interfaces, Inc - Sierra; (Circulation) Innovative Interfaces, Inc - Sierra; (Course Reserve) Innovative Interfaces, Inc - Sierra; (Discovery) EBSCO Discovery Service; (ILL) Clio; (Media Booking) Innovative Interfaces, Inc - Sierra; (OPAC) Innovative Interfaces, Inc - Sierra; (Serials) Innovative Interfaces, Inc - Sierra
Wireless access
Partic in Amigos Library Services, Inc; MOBIUS; OCLC Online Computer Library Center, Inc
Open Mon-Thurs 8am-Midnight, Fri 8-8, Sat 9-5, Sun 2-Midnight

G COLUMBIA ENVIRONMENTAL RESEARCH CENTER LIBRARY*, US Geological Survey, 4200 New Haven Rd, 65201-8709. SAN 308-9657. Tel: 573-876-1853. FAX: 573-876-1833. Web Site: www.cerc.usgs.gov/default.aspx. *Librn,* Julia Towns-Campbell; E-mail: jtowns@usgs.gov
Founded 1968
Library Holdings: Bk Titles 7,308; Bk Vols 9,000; Per Subs 80
Special Collections: Pesticides (Reprint Coll)
Subject Interests: Biol toxicity, Chem pesticides, Environ contaminants, Mo river, Water quality
Partic in OCLC Online Computer Library Center, Inc
Restriction: Open by appt only

S STATE HISTORICAL SOCIETY OF MISSOURI LIBRARY*, 605 Elm St, 65201. SAN 308-9649. Tel: 573-882-1187. Interlibrary Loan Service Tel: 573-882-6029. Administration Tel: 573-882-7083. Toll Free Tel: 800-747-6366. FAX: 573-884-4950. E-mail: columbia@shsmo.org. Web Site: shsmo.org. *Exec Dir,* Dr Gary R Kremer; E-mail: kremerg@shsmo.org; *Sr Assoc Dir,* Gerald Hirsch; Tel: 573-884-7906, E-mail: hirschg@shsmo.org; *Asst Dir, Ref Serv,* Tatyana N Shinn; Tel: 573-882-1187, E-mail: shinntn@shsmo.org; *Librn,* Kevin George; E-mail: georgeke@shsmo.org; Staff 21 (MLS 8, Non-MLS 13)
Founded 1898
Special Collections: Church History (Bishop William F McMurry Coll); Literature (Mahan Memorial Mark Twain Coll & Eugene Field Coll); Manuscript Coll; Map Coll; Mid-Western History (J Christian Bay Coll); Missouri Newspapers (1808-present); Missouri's Literary Heritage for Children & Youth (Alice Irene Fitzgerald Coll); Photograph Coll; United States Census Coll, micro. Oral History
Subject Interests: Genealogy, Mo hist, Western hist
Wireless access

Function: Archival coll, Art exhibits, Audio & video playback equip for onsite use, ILL available, Mail & tel request accepted, Online cat, Photocopying/Printing, Prog for adults, Ref serv available, Res performed for a fee
Publications: Missouri Historical Review (Quarterly); Missouri Times (Newsletter)
Open Tues-Fri 8:30-4:30, Sat 8:30-3
Restriction: Non-circulating
Friends of the Library Group

C STEPHENS COLLEGE*, Hugh Stephens Library, 1200 E Broadway, 65215. SAN 348-9930. Tel: 573-876-7182. Reference Tel: 573-876-7181. Circulation E-mail: library@stephens.edu. Web Site: stephens.libguides.com/library. *Dir,* Dan Kammer; Tel: 573-876-7273, E-mail: dkammer@stephens.edu; *Coll Develop & Res Librn,* James Walter; E-mail: jwalter@stephens.edu; *Access Serv,* Nina Stawski; E-mail: nstawski@stephens.edu; Staff 6 (MLS 3, Non-MLS 3)
Founded 1833. Enrl 740; Fac 76; Highest Degree: Master
Library Holdings: Bk Titles 115,000; Bk Vols 130,000
Special Collections: Educational Resources & Childrens Literature; Women's Studies Coll (Monographic)
Subject Interests: Women's studies
Automation Activity & Vendor Info: (Acquisitions) Innovative Interfaces, Inc; (Cataloging) Innovative Interfaces, Inc; (Circulation) Innovative Interfaces, Inc; (Course Reserve) Innovative Interfaces, Inc; (ILL) Innovative Interfaces, Inc; (Media Booking) Innovative Interfaces, Inc; (OPAC) Innovative Interfaces, Inc; (Serials) Innovative Interfaces, Inc
Wireless access
Publications: Annual report; Bibliographies
Partic in MOBIUS; OCLC Online Computer Library Center, Inc
Open Mon-Thurs 8-5, Fri 8-1

UNIVERSITY OF MISSOURI-COLUMBIA

C ACADEMIC SUPPORT CENTER MEDIA RENTAL LIBRARY*, 505 E Stewart Rd, 65211-2040, SAN 308-9665. Tel: 573-882-3601. FAX: 573-882-6110. E-mail: asc-media-lib@missouri.edu. Web Site: asc.missouri.edu/medialib.html. *Assoc Dir,* John S Fick; Staff 3 (Non-MLS 3)
Library Holdings: AV Mats 13,500; DVDs 1,400; Videos 8,000
Partic in MOBIUS
Open Mon-Fri 8-5
Restriction: Closed stack, Fee for pub use

C COLUMBIA MISSOURIAN NEWSPAPER LIBRARY*, School of Journalism, 315 Lee Hills Hall, 65205, SAN 329-8124. Tel: 573-882-4876. FAX: 573-882-5702. Web Site: www.missouri.edu/~jlibrwww. *Librn,* Dorothy Carner; Tel: 573-882-6591, E-mail: carnerd@missouri.edu; Staff 2 (MLS 1, Non-MLS 1)
Founded 1974. Enrl 23,000; Fac 106; Highest Degree: Doctorate
Library Holdings: Bk Vols 400
Special Collections: Newspaper Bound Volumes
Open Mon-Fri 8-5

C ELMER ELLIS LIBRARY*, 104 Ellis Library, 65201-5149, SAN 348-999X. Tel: 573-882-4701. Circulation Tel: 573-882-3362. Interlibrary Loan Service Tel: 573-882-1101. Reference Tel: 573-882-4581. FAX: 573-882-8044. Reference E-mail: ellisref@missouri.edu. Web Site: library.missouri.edu. *Dir of Libr,* James A Cogswell; E-mail: cogswellja@missouri.edu; *Assoc Dir, Res & Info Serv,* Jeannette Pierce; E-mail: pierceja@missouri.edu; *Asst Dir, Tech Serv,* Ann Riley; Tel: 573-882-1685, E-mail: rileyac@missouri.edu; *Head, Access Serv,* June L DeWeese; Tel: 573-882-7315, E-mail: deweesej@missouri.edu; *Humanities Librn,* Anne Barker; Tel: 573-882-6324, E-mail: barkera@missouri.edu; *Humanities Librn,* Rachel Brekhus; Tel: 573-882-7563, E-mail: brekhusr@missouri.edu; *Humanities Librn,* Michael Muchow; Tel: 573-882-6824; *Sci Librn,* Janice Dysart; Tel: 573-882-1828, E-mail: dysartj@missouri.edu; *Soc Sci Librn,* Wayne Barnes; Tel: 573-882-3310, E-mail: barnese@missouri.edu; *Soc Sci Librn,* Gwen Gray; Tel: 573-882-9162, E-mail: grayg@missouri.edu; *Soc Sci Librn,* Paula Roper; Tel: 573-882-3326, E-mail: roperp@missouri.edu; *Coordr, Libr Instruction,* Goodie Bhullar; Tel: 573-882-9163, E-mail: bhullarp@missouri.edu; *Electronic Res,* Rhonda Whithaus; Tel: 573-882-9164, E-mail: whithausr@missouri.edu; *ILL,* Delores Fisher; Tel: 573-882-1101, E-mail: fisherd@missouri.edu; *ILL,* Tammy Green; Tel: 573-882-3224, E-mail: greenta@missouri.edu; *Ref Serv,* Cindy Cotner; Tel: 573-882-4693, E-mail: cotnerc@missouri.edu; *Univ Archivist,* Michael Holland; Tel: 573-882-4602, E-mail: hollandm@missouri.edu. Subject Specialists: *Lang arts, Lit, Sound rec,* Anne Barker; *Anthrop, Hist,* Rachel Brekhus; *Communications, Fine arts, Linguistics,* Michael Muchow; *Atmospheric sci, Biochem,* Janice Dysart; *Children's lit, Educ, Psychol,* Wayne Barnes; *Bus & mgt, Econ,* Gwen Gray; *African-Am studies, Educ,* Paula Roper; *Geog, S Asia,* Goodie Bhullar; Staff 211 (MLS 62, Non-MLS 149)
Founded 1839. Enrl 25,000; Fac 1,669; Highest Degree: Doctorate
Library Holdings: Bk Titles 667,119; Bk Vols 691,714; Per Subs 26,886; Talking Bks 2,451; Videos 3,119
Special Collections: American Best Sellers (Frank Luther Mott Coll); Cartoons (John Tinney McCutcheon Coll); Fourth of July Oration Coll; Philosophy (Thomas Moore Johnson Coll); Rare Book Coll; World War I & II Poster Coll. State Document Depository; UN Document Depository; US Document Depository
Automation Activity & Vendor Info: (Acquisitions) Innovative Interfaces, Inc; (Cataloging) Innovative Interfaces, Inc; (Circulation) Innovative Interfaces, Inc; (Course Reserve) Innovative Interfaces, Inc; (OPAC) Innovative Interfaces, Inc; (Serials) Innovative Interfaces, Inc
Partic in Merlin
Publications: UMC Libraries (Newsletter); University of Missouri Library Series
Open Mon-Thurs 7:30am-2am, Fri 7:30am-8pm, Sat 9-8, Sun Noon-2am
Friends of the Library Group

C ENGINEERING LIBRARY & TECHNOLOGY COMMONS*, W2001 Lafferre Hall, 65211, SAN 349-0025. Tel: 573-882-2379. FAX: 573-884-4499. Web Site: library.missouri.edu/engineering. *Librn,* Judy Siebert Maseles; Tel: 573-882-2715, E-mail: maselesj@missouri.edu; Staff 3 (MLS 1, Non-MLS 2)
Founded 1906. Highest Degree: Doctorate
Library Holdings: CDs 612; e-books 71,656; e-journals 500; Bk Vols 34,138; Per Subs 736
Subject Interests: Computer sci, Engr
Automation Activity & Vendor Info: (Circulation) Innovative Interfaces, Inc; (Course Reserve) Innovative Interfaces, Inc; (ILL) OCLC ILLiad; (OPAC) Innovative Interfaces, Inc
Partic in Merlin
Open Mon-Thurs (Winter) 8am-Midnight, Fri 8-5, Sat 1-5, Sun 1-Midnight; Mon-Thurs (Summer) 8am-9pm, Fri 8-5, Sat 1-5, Sun 1-9

C GEOLOGICAL SCIENCES LIBRARY*, 201 Geological Sciences, 65211, SAN 349-005X. Tel: 573-882-4860. Interlibrary Loan Service Tel: 573-882-3224. FAX: 573-882-5458. Web Site: mulibraries.missouri.edu/geology. *Librn,* Stephen Stanton; E-mail: stantons@missouri.edu; Staff 3 (MLS 1, Non-MLS 2)
Library Holdings: Bk Titles 67,091; Bk Vols 68,774; Per Subs 663
Special Collections: 19th Century Federal Survey Publications; 19th Century State Geological Survey Publications
Subject Interests: Econ geol, Exploration, Geochemistry, Geophysics, Hydrol, Paleontology, Petrology, Siesmology, Solid earth geophysics, Stratigraphy, Structural geol
Automation Activity & Vendor Info: (Cataloging) Innovative Interfaces, Inc; (Circulation) Innovative Interfaces, Inc
Partic in Merlin
Open Mon-Thurs 8-12 & 1-9, Fri 8-12 & 1-5, Sun 2-5

CL LAW LIBRARY*, 203 Hulston Hall, 65211-4190, SAN 349-0114. Tel: 573-882-4597. Reference Tel: 573-884-6362. FAX: 573-882-9676. Web Site: www.law.missouri.edu/library. *Dir,* Randy Diamond; Tel: 573-882-2935, E-mail: diamondrj@missouri.edu; *Assoc Law Librn,* Resa Kerns; Tel: 573-882-5108, E-mail: kernsr@missouri.edu; *Assoc Law Librn,* Cindy Shearrer; Tel: 573-882-1125, E-mail: shearrerc@missouri.edu; *Sr Res Librn,* Steven Lambson; Tel: 573-882-6464, E-mail: lambsons@missouri.edu; *Access Serv,* John Dethman; Tel: 573-884-1760, E-mail: dethmanj@missouri.edu; *Tech Serv,* Needra Jackson; Tel: 573-882-9675, E-mail: jacksonn@missouri.edu; Staff 7 (MLS 7)
Founded 1872. Enrl 500; Fac 40; Highest Degree: Doctorate
Library Holdings: Bk Titles 180,000; Bk Vols 343,000; Per Subs 1,700
Special Collections: 19th Century Trials (John D Lawson Coll). US Document Depository
Automation Activity & Vendor Info: (Acquisitions) Innovative Interfaces, Inc; (Cataloging) Innovative Interfaces, Inc; (Circulation) Innovative Interfaces, Inc; (OPAC) Innovative Interfaces, Inc; (Serials) Innovative Interfaces, Inc
Partic in Merlin; Mid-America Law Library Consortium
Publications: Law Library Guide (Library handbook)
Open Mon-Thurs 8-7:45, Fri 8-4:45, Sat 10-5:45, Sun 12-7:45
Restriction: Open to pub for ref & circ; with some limitations

CM LIBRARY FOR FAMILY & COMMUNITY MEDICINE*, M246 Medical Sciences Bldg, 65212, SAN 349-0130. Tel: 573-882-6183. FAX: 573-882-9096. *Librn,* Susan Meadows; Staff 1 (MLS 1)
Founded 1966. Highest Degree: Master
Library Holdings: Bk Vols 200; Per Subs 40
Subject Interests: Gerontology, Healthcare syst, Med ethics, Primary health care, Rural health, Soc aspects of med care
Open Mon-Fri 8-5

CM J OTTO LOTTES HEALTH SCIENCES LIBRARY*, One Hospital Dr, 65212. Tel: 573-882-0471. Circulation Tel: 573-882-4153. Administration Tel: 573-882-7033. FAX: 573-882-5574. E-mail: referencequestions@missouri.edu. Web Site: www.muhealth.org/~library. *Dir,* Deborah Ward; E-mail: warddh@missouri.edu
Partic in Greater Western Library Alliance

C FRANK LEE MARTIN MEMORIAL JOURNALISM LIBRARY*, 449 S Ninth St, 102 Reynolds Journalism Institute, 65211, SAN 349-0084. Tel: 573-882-7502. Administration Tel: 573-882-6591. FAX: 573-884-4963. E-mail: jlib@missouri.edu. Web Site:

mulibraries.missouri.edu/journalism. *Head, Journalism Libr,* Dorothy J Carner; E-mail: carnerd@missouri.edu. Subject Specialists: *Advertising, Journalism, Pub relations,* Dorothy J Carner; Staff 4 (MLS 1, Non-MLS 3)
Founded 1908. Enrl 4,000; Fac 104; Highest Degree: Doctorate
Special Collections: Fields Photojournalism Coll; McDougall Photojournalism Coll; Pictures of the Year Photojournalism Coll; Weinberg Journalism Fiction Coll
Partic in Amigos Library Services, Inc
Restriction: Borrowing privileges limited to fac & registered students

C MATH SCIENCES LIBRARY*, 206 Math Sciences Bldg, 65211, SAN 349-0173. Tel: 573-882-7286. Interlibrary Loan Service Tel: 573-882-3224. FAX: 573-884-0058. Web Site: mulibraries.missouri.edu/math. *Libr Spec II,* John Meyer; E-mail: meyerjl@missouri.edu. Subject Specialists: *Math,* John Meyer; Staff 1 (Non-MLS 1)
Founded 1969
Library Holdings: Bk Vols 26,000; Per Subs 258
Subject Interests: Math
Partic in Merlin
Restriction: Badge access after hrs

CM ZALK VETERINARY MEDICAL LIBRARY*, W-218 Veterinary-Medicine Bldg, 65211, SAN 349-0262. Tel: 573-882-2461. FAX: 573-882-2950. E-mail: vetlib@missouri.edu. Web Site: vetmedlibrary.missouri.edu. *Head Librn,* Trenton Boyd; E-mail: boydt@missouri.edu; *Info Spec I,* Laura Buck; E-mail: buckl@missouri.edu; Staff 1 (MLS 1)
Founded 1951. Enrl 252; Fac 100; Highest Degree: Doctorate
Library Holdings: Per Subs 290
Subject Interests: Clydesdales, Mules, Veterinary hist
Partic in Merlin
Open Mon-Thurs 7:30am-9pm, Fri 7:30-5, Sat 10-2, Sun 1-8

CONCEPTION

CR CONCEPTION ABBEY & SEMINARY LIBRARY*, 37174 State Hwy VV, 64433. (Mail add: PO Box 501, 64433-0501), SAN 308-9681. Tel: 660-944-2803. FAX: 660-944-2833. E-mail: library@conception.edu. Web Site: www.conceptionabbey.org/library. *Libr Dir,* Brother Thomas Sullivan; Tel: 660-944-2860, E-mail: thomas@conception.edu; *Asst Librn,* Christopher Brite; Tel: 660-944-2863, E-mail: cbrite@conception.edu; *Asst Librn,* Patricia Danner; Tel: 660-944-2882, E-mail: pdanner@conception.edu; *Libr Office Mgr,* Barbara Cowan; E-mail: bcowan@conception.edu; *Archives,* Brother Bernard Montgomery; Tel: 660-944-2828, E-mail: bernard@conception.edu; *Spec Coll,* Fr Aidan McSorley; E-mail: aidan@conception.edu; Staff 6 (MLS 3, Non-MLS 3)
Founded 1873. Enrl 93; Fac 15; Highest Degree: Bachelor
Library Holdings: Bk Titles 115,000; Bk Vols 121,000; Per Subs 364; Videos 110
Special Collections: 17th-19th Century Catholic Theology Coll; American Catholic Church History Coll; Incunabula & Manuscripts
Subject Interests: Art, Medieval European hist, Philos, Relig studies, Roman Catholic relig
Partic in OCLC Online Computer Library Center, Inc
Open Mon-Sat 8am-10pm, Sun 1-10

COTTLEVILLE

J ST CHARLES COMMUNITY COLLEGE*, Paul & Helen Schnare Library, 4601 Mid Rivers Mall Dr, 63376. SAN 309-1090. Tel: 636-922-8620. Circulation Tel: 636-922-8434. Interlibrary Loan Service Tel: 636-922-8340. Administration Tel: 636-922-8512. FAX: 636-922-8433. E-mail: refdrop@stchas.edu. Web Site: www.stchas.edu/library. *Dean, Learning Res,* Dr Stephanie Tolson; *Libr Dir,* Theresa Flett; Tel: 636-922-8587, E-mail: tflett@stchas.edu; *Ref Librn,* Kelly Mitchell; Tel: 636-922-8798, E-mail: kmitchell@stchas.edu; *Ref Librn,* Julia Wilbers; Tel: 636-922-8450, E-mail: jwilbers@stchas.edu; *Pub Serv Mgr,* Ying Li; Tel: 636-922-8438, E-mail: yli@stchas.edu; *Tech Serv Mgr,* Jean Rose; Tel: 636-922-8439, E-mail: jrose@stchas.edu; *Cataloger,* Rebecca Klemme Eliceiri; E-mail: rkeliceiri@stchas.edu; Staff 11.5 (MLS 7, Non-MLS 4.5)
Founded 1987. Enrl 4,620; Fac 300; Highest Degree: Associate
Jul 2016-Jun 2017 Income $940,192. Mats Exp $207,682, Books $49,221, Per/Ser (Incl. Access Fees) $51,043, AV Mat $12,283, Electronic Ref Mat (Incl. Access Fees) $95,135. Sal $533,075 (Prof $385,362)
Library Holdings: AV Mats 939; e-books 30,170; Electronic Media & Resources 27; Bk Titles 68,244; Per Subs 348; Videos 6,611
Automation Activity & Vendor Info: (Acquisitions) Innovative Interfaces, Inc; (Cataloging) Innovative Interfaces, Inc; (Circulation) Innovative Interfaces, Inc; (Course Reserve) Innovative Interfaces, Inc; (Discovery) EBSCO Discovery Service; (ILL) OCLC; (Media Booking) Innovative Interfaces, Inc; (OPAC) Innovative Interfaces, Inc; (Serials) Innovative Interfaces, Inc
Wireless access
Function: Adult bk club, Audio & video playback equip for onsite use, Bk club(s), Bk reviews (Group), Computers for patron use, E-Readers, Electronic databases & coll, Games & aids for people with disabilities, ILL available, Internet access, Magazines, Magnifiers for reading, Microfiche/film & reading machines, Music CDs, Online cat, Online info literacy tutorials on the web & in blackboard, Online ref, Orientations, Photocopying/Printing, Ref serv available, Scanner, Study rm, Wheelchair accessible
Publications: Library Editions (Newsletter)
Partic in MOBIUS; Network of Illinois Learning Resources in Community Colleges; Northern Illinois Learning Resources Cooperative; Saint Louis Regional Library Network
Special Services for the Deaf - Assistive tech
Special Services for the Blind - Text reader; ZoomText magnification & reading software
Open Mon-Thurs 7:30am-10pm, Fri 7:30-4:30, Sat (Fall & Spring) 9-2
Restriction: Borrowing privileges limited to fac & registered students, Borrowing requests are handled by ILL, Restricted borrowing privileges

CRYSTAL CITY

P CRYSTAL CITY PUBLIC LIBRARY*, 736 Mississippi Ave, 63019-1646. SAN 308-9711. Tel: 636-937-7166. FAX: 636-937-3193. E-mail: cclib63019@yahoo.com. Web Site: www.crystalcitymo.org/departments/public-library.html. *Dir,* Tania Laughlin; *Asst Librn,* Kirsten Goings; *Asst Librn,* Marilyn Parr
Founded 1916. Pop 4,300; Circ 30,497
Library Holdings: AV Mats 2,000; Large Print Bks 697; Bk Titles 20,496; Bk Vols 21,447; Per Subs 48; Talking Bks 1,000
Special Collections: Genealogy Coll. Oral History
Automation Activity & Vendor Info: (Cataloging) Follett Software; (Circulation) Follett Software; (ILL) OCLC; (OPAC) Follett Software
Wireless access
Function: ILL available, Photocopying/Printing, Prog for children & young adult, Summer reading prog, Wheelchair accessible
Open Mon-Thurs 10-7, Fri 12-5, Sat 10-1

DE SOTO

P DE SOTO PUBLIC LIBRARY*, 712 S Main St, 63020. SAN 308-972X. Tel: 636-586-3858. FAX: 636-586-1707. E-mail: dspl1935@gmail.com. Web Site: desotopubliclibrary.lib.mo.us. *Dir,* Tony Benningfield; Staff 5 (MLS 1, Non-MLS 4)
Founded 1935. Pop 6,400; Circ 35,000
Library Holdings: Bks on Deafness & Sign Lang 5; CDs 1,021; DVDs 950; Large Print Bks 1,215; Microforms 132; Bk Titles 31,360; Per Subs 50; Videos 538
Special Collections: Local History (Felix Milfeld), negatives, photog. Oral History
Subject Interests: Jefferson County hist
Automation Activity & Vendor Info: (Acquisitions) Evergreen; (Cataloging) Evergreen; (Circulation) Evergreen; (ILL) Evergreen; (OPAC) Evergreen
Wireless access
Function: 24/7 Electronic res, 24/7 Online cat, Activity rm, Adult bk club, Archival coll, Art exhibits, Audiobks via web, Bi-weekly Writer's Group, Bks on CD, Chess club, Children's prog, Citizenship assistance, Computer training, Computers for patron use, Digital talking bks, E-Reserves, Electronic databases & coll, Family literacy, For res purposes, Holiday prog, ILL available, Internet access, Laminating, Life-long learning prog for all ages, Literacy & newcomer serv, Magazines, Magnifiers for reading, Mail & tel request accepted, Meeting rooms, Microfiche/film & reading machines, Movies, Notary serv, Online cat, Outreach serv, OverDrive digital audio bks, Photocopying/Printing, Preschool outreach, Preschool reading prog, Printer for laptops & handheld devices, Prog for adults, Prog for children & young adult, Ref & res, Ref serv available, Scanner, Senior computer classes, Serves people with intellectual disabilities, Spanish lang bks, Story hour, Study rm, Summer reading prog, Tax forms, Teen prog, Telephone ref, Wheelchair accessible
Publications: Quarterly newsletter
Partic in Missouri Evergreen
Open Mon, Wed, Thurs & Fri 9-5, Tues 9-7, Sat 9-2
Restriction: Borrowing requests are handled by ILL, ID required to use computers (Ltd hrs), In-house use for visitors, Non-resident fee
Friends of the Library Group

DEXTER

P KELLER PUBLIC LIBRARY*, 402 W Grant St, 63841. SAN 308-9738. Tel: 573-624-3764. FAX: 573-614-1051. E-mail: info@kellerpl.org. Web Site: www.kellerpl.org. *Dir,* Pamela Trammell; Staff 6 (MLS 1, Non-MLS 5)
Founded 1934. Pop 7,035
Library Holdings: AV Mats 1,175; Large Print Bks 250; Bk Titles 38,950; Bk Vols 39,016; Per Subs 62; Talking Bks 525; Videos 119
Subject Interests: Genealogy
Automation Activity & Vendor Info: (Acquisitions) SirsiDynix; (Cataloging) SirsiDynix; (Circulation) SirsiDynix

Open Mon-Wed & Fri 10-5, Thurs 10-6, Sat 10-2
Friends of the Library Group

DIAMOND

G US NATIONAL PARK SERVICE*, George Washington Carver National Monument Library, 5646 Carver Rd, 64840-8314. SAN 370-3142. Tel: 417-325-4151. FAX: 417-325-4231. E-mail: GWCA_interpretation@nps.gov. Web Site: www.nps.gov/gwca. *Library Contact,* Curtis Gregory; E-mail: curtis_gregory@nps.gov; Staff 2 (Non-MLS 2)
Library Holdings: Bk Titles 4,000; Per Subs 3
Special Collections: Carver Coll, archives & artifacts; Original Carver Letters
Open Mon-Sun 9-5

EDINA

S KNOX COUNTY HISTORICAL SOCIETY LIBRARY*, 408 E Lafayette St, 63537. (Mail add: PO Box 75, 63537-0075), SAN 373-3718. Tel: 660-397-2349. FAX: 660-397-3331. *Pres,* Brent Karhoff; Staff 1 (Non-MLS 1)
Library Holdings: Bk Titles 1,907; Bk Vols 2,041

FARMINGTON

P FARMINGTON PUBLIC LIBRARY, 101 North A St, 63640. SAN 308-9762. Tel: 573-756-5779. E-mail: library@farmington-mo.gov. Web Site: farmington-mo.gov/library. *Dir,* Travis Trokey; E-mail: ttrokey@farmington-mo.gov; *Librn,* Bonnie Coleman; E-mail: bcoleman@farmington-mo.gov; *Librn,* Rachel Mullins; E-mail: rmullins@farmington-mo.gov; Staff 13 (MLS 1, Non-MLS 12)
Founded 1916. Pop 19,000; Circ 114,000
Special Collections: Local History & Genealogy Coll
Automation Activity & Vendor Info: (Cataloging) OCLC CatExpress; (Circulation) Book Systems; (ILL) OCLC FirstSearch; (OPAC) Book Systems
Wireless access
Function: 24/7 Electronic res, 24/7 Online cat, Adult bk club, Archival coll, Audiobks on Playaways & MP3, Audiobks via web, Bi-weekly Writer's Group, Bk club(s), Bks on CD, Chess club, Children's prog, Computer training, Computers for patron use, Doc delivery serv, E-Readers, E-Reserves, Electronic databases & coll, For res purposes, Free DVD rentals, Holiday prog, Home delivery & serv to seniorr ctr & nursing homes, Homebound delivery serv, ILL available, Instruction & testing, Internet access, Laminating, Magazines, Magnifiers for reading, Mail & tel request accepted, Meeting rooms, Microfiche/film & reading machines, Movies, Music CDs, Online cat, Online ref, Outside serv via phone, mail, e-mail & web, OverDrive digital audio bks, Photocopying/Printing, Prog for adults, Prog for children & young adult, Ref & res, Ref serv available, Res performed for a fee, Senior computer classes, Serves people with intellectual disabilities, Story hour, Study rm, Summer reading prog, Tax forms, Teen prog, Telephone ref, Workshops, Writing prog
Publications: Farmington, Missouri (Local historical information)
Open Mon-Thurs 10-9, Fri 10-6, Sat 10-4
Restriction: Non-resident fee

FAYETTE

CR CENTRAL METHODIST UNIVERSITY*, Smiley Memorial Library, 411 Central Methodist Sq, 65248. SAN 308-9770. Tel: 660-248-6271. Toll Free Tel: 877-268-1854. FAX: 660-248-6226. E-mail: library@centralmethodist.edu. Web Site: www.centralmethodist.edu/academics/library. *Dir, Info Res,* Cynthia Dudenhoffer; E-mail: cmdudenh@centralmethodist.edu; *Archivist,* John Finley; E-mail: jfinley@centralmethodist.edu; *Tech Serv,* Leasa Strodtman; E-mail: lstrodtm@centralmethodist.edu; Staff 7 (MLS 3, Non-MLS 4)
Founded 1857. Enrl 1,200; Highest Degree: Master
Library Holdings: Large Print Bks 109; Bk Titles 80,000; Bk Vols 99,142; Per Subs 200; Talking Bks 281; Videos 310
Special Collections: Religion (Missouri United Methodist Archives). State Document Depository
Subject Interests: Methodism
Automation Activity & Vendor Info: (Acquisitions) Innovative Interfaces, Inc; (Cataloging) Innovative Interfaces, Inc; (Circulation) Innovative Interfaces, Inc; (Course Reserve) Innovative Interfaces, Inc; (OPAC) Innovative Interfaces, Inc; (Serials) Innovative Interfaces, Inc
Wireless access
Partic in Amigos Library Services, Inc; MOBIUS
Open Mon-Thurs 7:30am-11pm, Fri 7:30-5, Sat 10-1, Sun 4-11

FERGUSON

P FERGUSON MUNICIPAL PUBLIC LIBRARY, 35 N Florissant Rd, 63135. SAN 308-9800. Tel: 314-521-4820. FAX: 314-521-1275. Web Site: www.ferguson.lib.mo.us. *Dir,* Scott Bonner; E-mail: sbonner@fergusonlibrary.net; Staff 9 (MLS 2, Non-MLS 7)
Founded 1933. Pop 22,984; Circ 173,103
Library Holdings: Bk Titles 78,931; Bk Vols 79,804; Per Subs 126; Talking Bks 1,579; Videos 2,236
Subject Interests: City hist
Automation Activity & Vendor Info: (Cataloging) SirsiDynix; (Circulation) SirsiDynix; (OPAC) SirsiDynix
Wireless access
Function: ILL available
Partic in Municipal Library Consortium; Saint Louis Regional Library Network
Special Services for the Deaf - TDD equip
Open Mon-Thurs 9-8, Fri 9-6, Sat 9-4
Friends of the Library Group

FESTUS

P FESTUS PUBLIC LIBRARY, 400 W Main, 63028. SAN 308-9819. Tel: 636-937-2017. FAX: 636-937-3439. E-mail: library@cityoffestus.org. Web Site: www.cityoffestus.org/221/Fsetus-Public-Library. *Dir,* Elizabeth Steffen; E-mail: esteffen@cityoffestus.org
Founded 1934. Pop 11,000; Circ 40,025
Library Holdings: Bk Titles 35,000; Per Subs 52
Automation Activity & Vendor Info: (Cataloging) Follett Software; (Circulation) Follett Software; (OPAC) Follett Software
Partic in Saint Louis Regional Library Network
Open Mon-Thurs 9-7 Fri 9-5, Sat 9-2
Friends of the Library Group

FLORISSANT

CR SAINT LOUIS CHRISTIAN COLLEGE LIBRARY*, 1360 Grandview Dr, 63033. SAN 308-9843. Tel: 314-837-6777, Ext 1512. FAX: 314-837-8291. E-mail: librarian@stlchristian.edu. Web Site: stlchristian.edu/library. *Libr Dir,* Pamela Withrow; Staff 1 (MLS 1)
Founded 1956
Library Holdings: Bk Vols 30,000; Per Subs 91
Special Collections: Stone Campbell Movement Coll
Subject Interests: Bible, Biblical theol, Church hist, Linguistics, Restoration movement hist (19th century Am relig movement)
Partic in Christian Library Consortium
Open Mon-Thurs 8am-10pm, Fri 8-4, Sat 9-3

FORT LEONARD WOOD

UNITED STATES ARMY

A BRUCE C CLARKE LIBRARY ACADEMIC SERVICES DIVISION*, Bldg 3202, 14020 MSCOE Loop, Ste 200, 65473-8928, SAN 362-8957. Tel: 573-563-4109. FAX: 573-563-4156. Web Site: www.wood.army.mil/library. *Libr Dir,* Claretta Crawford; Tel: 573-563-5608, E-mail: claretta.t.crawford.civ@mail.mil; *Supvry Librn,* Travis Ferrell; Tel: 573-563-6111, E-mail: travis.a.ferrell.civ@mail.mil; *Librn,* Kenneth Howard; Tel: 573-563-5318, E-mail: kenneth.r.howard.civ@mail.mil. Subject Specialists: *Chem, Law enforcement, Mil hist,* Claretta Crawford; Staff 8 (MLS 2, Non-MLS 6)
Founded 1935
Library Holdings: Audiobooks 539; CDs 314; DVDs 1,222; Bk Vols 53,100; Per Subs 45; Videos 949
Special Collections: Chemical Corps; Military Police; Military Unit Histories; Rare Book Room
Subject Interests: Chem, Law enforcement, Mil engr, Mil hist
Automation Activity & Vendor Info: (Acquisitions) SirsiDynix; (Cataloging) SirsiDynix; (Circulation) SirsiDynix; (Course Reserve) SirsiDynix; (ILL) SirsiDynix; (Media Booking) SirsiDynix; (OPAC) SirsiDynix; (Serials) SirsiDynix
Function: Bks on CD, CD-ROM, Computers for patron use, Electronic databases & coll, Free DVD rentals, ILL available, Online cat, Orientations, OverDrive digital audio bks, Photocopying/Printing, Ref serv available, Scanner
Partic in OCLC Online Computer Library Center, Inc
Open Mon-Thurs 7:15-7, Fri 7:15-5
Restriction: Mil, family mem, retirees, Civil Serv personnel NAF only, Non-circulating of rare bks

A BRUCE C CLARKE LIBRARY COMMUNITY SERVICES DIVISION*, Bldg 3202, 597 Manscen Loop, Ste 100, 65473-8928, SAN 349-0297. Tel: 573-563-4113. FAX: 573-563-4118. Web Site: www.library.wood.army.mil. *Librn,* Joyce Waybright; Staff 1 (MLS 1)
Founded 1941
Library Holdings: Bk Titles 66,012; Bk Vols 68,000; Per Subs 120
Special Collections: Children's Library
Subject Interests: Foreign lang, Mil art, Sci

Automation Activity & Vendor Info: (Acquisitions) SirsiDynix; (Cataloging) SirsiDynix; (Circulation) SirsiDynix; (ILL) SirsiDynix; (Media Booking) SirsiDynix; (OPAC) SirsiDynix; (Serials) SirsiDynix
Partic in OCLC Online Computer Library Center, Inc
Open Mon-Wed 7:30-7:30, Sat & Sun 10-5

AM GENERAL LEONARD WOOD ARMY COMMUNITY HOSPITAL MEDICAL LIBRARY*, 4430 Missouri Ave, 65473, SAN 349-0378. Tel: 573-596-0131, Ext 69110. FAX: 573-596-5359.
Founded 1945
Library Holdings: Bk Titles 2,792; Bk Vols 2,816; Per Subs 69
Automation Activity & Vendor Info: (Acquisitions) Ex Libris Group; (Cataloging) Ex Libris Group; (Circulation) Ex Libris Group; (Serials) Ex Libris Group
Restriction: Staff use only

FULTON

FULTON STATE HOSPITAL

M PATIENT'S LIBRARY*, 600 E Fifth St, 65251, SAN 349-0440. Tel: 573-592-2261. FAX: 573-592-3011. *Librn,* Tonya Hayes-Martin; Staff 2 (MLS 1, Non-MLS 1)
Founded 1949
Library Holdings: Bk Titles 7,120; Bk Vols 7,280; Per Subs 100
Restriction: Open by appt only

M PROFESSIONAL LIBRARY*, 600 E Fifth St, 65251, SAN 349-0416. Tel: 573-592-2261. FAX: 573-592-3011. *Librn,* Tonya Hayes-Martin; Staff 2 (MLS 1, Non-MLS 1)
Founded 1949
Library Holdings: Bk Titles 1,590; Bk Vols 1,900; Per Subs 101
Subject Interests: Med, Nursing, Psychiat, Psychol, Soc work
Open Mon-Fri 8-Noon

WESTMINSTER COLLEGE

C NATIONAL CHURCHILL MUSEUM*, 501 Westminster Ave, 65251-1299, SAN 308-9878. Tel: 573-592-5626. FAX: 573-592-5222. Web Site: www.nationalchurchillmuseum.org. *Exec Dir,* Dr Rob Havers; Tel: 573-592-5233; *Develop Dir,* Kit Freudenberg; Tel: 573-592-5022; *Asst Dir,* Sara Winingear; Tel: 573-592-5234; *Archivist, Curator,* Liz Murphy; E-mail: liz.murphy@churchillmemorial.org; *Educ & Pub Prog Coordr,* Amanda Plybon; Tel: 573-592-6242, E-mail: mandy.plybon@churchillmemorial.org; Staff 6 (Non-MLS 6)
Founded 1962
Library Holdings: Bk Titles 1,196; Bk Vols 1,300
Special Collections: British-American Relations; Christopher Wren Coll; Sir Winston Churchill Coll
Partic in OCLC Online Computer Library Center, Inc
Publications: The Churchillian (Quarterly)
Restriction: Non-circulating of rare bks, Non-circulating to the pub, Not a lending libr, Open to pub by appt only, Open to pub for ref only, Open to qualified scholars, Open to researchers by request
Friends of the Library Group

C REEVES MEMORIAL LIBRARY*, 501 Westminster Ave, 65251-1299, SAN 308-9886. Tel: 573-592-5245. Circulation Tel: 573-592-5247. Reference Tel: 573-592-5246. Automation Services Tel: 573-592-5209. FAX: 573-642-6356. E-mail: Reeves.Library@westminster-mo.edu. Web Site: www.westminster-mo.edu/academics/resources/library/pages/default.aspx. *Dir, Libr Serv,* Angela Grogan; E-mail: angela.grogan@westminster-mo.edu; *Head, Pub Serv,* Kathryn Barden; *Head, Tech Serv,* Corinne Caputo; *Res Sharing Librn,* Cindy Schoolcraft; *Coordr, Ser & Electronic Res,* Kathy Renner; Tel: 573-592-5248, E-mail: kathy.renner@westminster-mo.edu; Staff 8 (MLS 4, Non-MLS 4)
Founded 1851. Enrl 1,141; Fac 90; Highest Degree: Bachelor
Library Holdings: AV Mats 7,311; CDs 285; DVDs 331; e-books 9,367; e-journals 27,437; Microforms 7,068; Bk Titles 83,888; Bk Vols 123,994; Per Subs 207; Videos 1,585
Automation Activity & Vendor Info: (Acquisitions) Innovative Interfaces, Inc; (Cataloging) Innovative Interfaces, Inc; (Circulation) Innovative Interfaces, Inc; (Course Reserve) Innovative Interfaces, Inc; (ILL) OCLC; (OPAC) Innovative Interfaces, Inc; (Serials) Innovative Interfaces, Inc
Partic in MOBIUS; Utah Academic Library Consortium
Open Mon-Thurs 7:30am-12:30am, Fri 7:30-4:30, Sat Noon-6, Sun 1:30pm-12:30am

C WILLIAM WOODS UNIVERSITY*, Dulany Memorial Library, One University Ave, 65251. SAN 308-9894. Tel: 573-592-4291. Circulation Tel: 573-592-4289. Interlibrary Loan Service Tel: 573-592-1160. Toll Free Tel: 800-995-3159. FAX: 573-592-1159. Web Site: www.williamwoods.edu/current_students/library. *Dir of the Univ Libr,* Erlene A Dudley; E-mail: erlene.dudley@williamwoods.edu; *Tech Serv Librn,* Rachel Utrecht; E-mail: rachel.utrecht@williamwoods.edu; *Access Serv Coordr,* Melissa Martin; E-mail: melissa.martin@williamwoods.edu; Staff 4 (MLS 4)
Founded 1870. Enrl 1,150; Fac 59; Highest Degree: Master
Library Holdings: Bk Vols 130,427; Per Subs 419
Special Collections: Education Coll; Equestrian Science Coll
Subject Interests: Equestrian studies, Interpreter training
Automation Activity & Vendor Info: (Acquisitions) Innovative Interfaces, Inc; (Cataloging) Innovative Interfaces, Inc; (Circulation) Innovative Interfaces, Inc; (Course Reserve) Innovative Interfaces, Inc; (ILL) Innovative Interfaces, Inc; (Media Booking) Innovative Interfaces, Inc; (OPAC) Innovative Interfaces, Inc; (Serials) Innovative Interfaces, Inc
Wireless access
Publications: Dulany Library Handbook
Partic in Amigos Library Services, Inc; MOBIUS
Special Services for the Deaf - Bks on deafness & sign lang

GAINESVILLE

P OZARK COUNTY LIBRARY*, 200 Elm St, 65655. (Mail add: PO Box 518, 65655), SAN 377-2233. Tel: 417-679-4442. *Libr Board of Trustees Pres,* Kathryn Atkinson; *Ch Serv,* Alitta Moore
Founded 1947. Pop 2,000
Mar 2014-Feb 2015 Income $7,500. Mats Exp $1,000
Library Holdings: Audiobooks 343; Bks on Deafness & Sign Lang 3; DVDs 1,000; Electronic Media & Resources 9; Large Print Bks 200; Bk Titles 19,260; Bk Vols 20,000; Videos 50
Automation Activity & Vendor Info: (Cataloging) JayWil Software Development, Inc; (Circulation) JayWil Software Development, Inc
Wireless access
Open Mon-Fri 9-3:30, Sat 9-12

GALENA

P STONE COUNTY LIBRARY*, 322 West State Hwy 248, 65656. (Mail add: PO Box 225, 65656-0225), SAN 308-9908. Tel: 417-357-6410. FAX: 417-357-6695. Web Site: www.stonecountylibrary.org. *Dir,* Rebecca Payne; E-mail: rpayne@scl.lib.mo.us; *Cat Mgr,* Debbie Bridges; E-mail: dbridges@scl.lib.mo.us; Staff 6 (MLS 1, Non-MLS 5)
Founded 1948. Pop 28,658; Circ 29,769
Jan 2018-Dec 2018 Income (Main & Associated Libraries) $556,243, State $15,762, County $507,113, Locally Generated Income $27,517. Mats Exp $58,390. Sal $141,474
Library Holdings: AV Mats 8,235; Bk Titles 47,180; Bk Vols 55,415; Per Subs 60
Subject Interests: Genealogy, Local hist
Automation Activity & Vendor Info: (Cataloging) Innovative Interfaces, Inc; (Circulation) Innovative Interfaces, Inc; (OPAC) Innovative Interfaces, Inc
Wireless access
Partic in Consortium of Ozarks Libraries
Open Mon 8-8, Tues-Fri 8-4:30, Sat 8-12
Friends of the Library Group
Branches: 2
BLUE EYE BRANCH, 138 State Hwy EE, Blue Eye, 65611. (Mail add: PO Box 54, Blue Eye, 65611). Tel: 417-779-3500. FAX: 417-779-3535. *Br Mgr,* Beth McConnell; Tel: 417-357-6510, E-mail: bmcconnell@scl.lib.mo.us; Staff 1 (Non-MLS 1)
Open Mon, Wed & Fri 9-5, Tues & Thurs 9-8, Sat 9-1
CRANE AREA BRANCH, 201 Main St, Crane, 65633. (Mail add: PO Box 25, Crane, 65633-0025), SAN 308-9703. Tel: 417-723-8261. FAX: 417-723-8851. *Br Mgr,* Alice Cumming; Staff 2 (Non-MLS 2)
Founded 1938
Automation Activity & Vendor Info: (Circulation) Innovative Interfaces, Inc; (OPAC) Innovative Interfaces, Inc
Open Mon-Fri 9-5, Sat 9-1
Bookmobiles: 1. Librn, Fred Daugherty

GALLATIN

P DAVIESS COUNTY LIBRARY*, 306 W Grand, 64640-1132. SAN 349-0475. Tel: 660-663-3222. FAX: 660-663-3250. Web Site: www.daviesscountylibrary.org. *Libr Dir,* Elizabeth Plotner; E-mail: davieslibrarydirector@gmail.com; Staff 2 (Non-MLS 2)
Founded 1947. Pop 8,433; Circ 40,053
Jan 2020-Dec 2020 Income (Main & Associated Libraries) $234,000
Library Holdings: AV Mats 2,240; Large Print Bks 300; Bk Titles 38,561; Per Subs 142; Talking Bks 1,220
Automation Activity & Vendor Info: (Cataloging) Mandarin Library Automation; (Circulation) Mandarin Library Automation; (ILL) OCLC; (OPAC) Mandarin Library Automation
Wireless access
Function: 24/7 Electronic res, 24/7 Online cat, Activity rm, Adult literacy prog, After school storytime, Audio & video playback equip for onsite use, Audiobks on Playaways & MP3, Audiobks via web, Bks on cassette, Bks on CD, Children's prog, Computer training, Computers for patron use, Digital talking bks, Electronic databases & coll, Family literacy, Free DVD rentals, Home delivery & serv to seniorr ctr & nursing homes, Homebound delivery serv, ILL available, Internet access, Laminating, Life-long learning prog for all ages, Magazines, Meeting rooms, Microfiche/film & reading

machines, Movies, Online cat, Online info literacy tutorials on the web & in blackboard, Online ref, Outreach serv, OverDrive digital audio bks, Photocopying/Printing, Printer for laptops & handheld devices, Prog for adults, Prog for children & young adult, Satellite serv, Scanner, Senior computer classes, Senior outreach, Spoken cassettes & CDs, Spoken cassettes & DVDs, STEM programs, Story hour, Study rm, Summer & winter reading prog, Summer reading prog, Tax forms, Wheelchair accessible
Special Services for the Deaf - Bks on deafness & sign lang
Special Services for the Blind - Accessible computers; Assistive/Adapted tech devices, equip & products; Bks on CD; Large print bks; Playaways (bks on MP3); ZoomText magnification & reading software
Open Tues-Thurs 9-6, Fri 9-5, Sat 9-12
Restriction: Authorized patrons, ID required to use computers (Ltd hrs), In-house use for visitors
Friends of the Library Group
Branches: 1
JAMESPORT BRANCH, 101 E Main, Jamesport, 64648. (Mail add: PO Box 197, Jamesport, 64648-0197), SAN 349-0505. Tel: 660-684-6120. *Br Librn,* Pam Parton; E-mail: pparton@daviesscountylibrary.org
Open Thurs & Fri 12-5, Sat 8-1

GERALD

P GERALD AREA LIBRARY*, 357 S Main St, 63037. (Mail add: PO Box 212, 63037-0212), SAN 377-2217. Tel: 573-764-7323. Web Site: geraldmo.com/library. *Libr Dir,* Beatrice Sheer; Staff 1 (MLS 1)
Founded 1994
Library Holdings: Audiobooks 150; CDs 11; DVDs 35; Large Print Bks 300; Bk Titles 12,688; Bk Vols 13,192; Per Subs 42; Talking Bks 100; Videos 300
Automation Activity & Vendor Info: (Cataloging) TLC (The Library Corporation); (Circulation) TLC (The Library Corporation)
Wireless access
Open Tues, Wed & Fri 9-5, Sat 9-12

GLASGOW

P LEWIS LIBRARY OF GLASGOW*, 315 Market St, 65254. SAN 308-9924. Tel: 660-338-2395. E-mail: librarian@lewislibrary.org. Web Site: www.lewislibrary.org. *Dir,* Rosetta Fuemmeler; Staff 4 (MLS 2, Non-MLS 2)
Founded 1866. Pop 1,408; Circ 21,112
Library Holdings: AV Mats 410; Large Print Bks 42; Bk Titles 18,091; Bk Vols 19,712; Per Subs 62; Videos 308
Special Collections: Local Papers (dated back to 1840)
Open Mon & Wed 2-7, Tues, Thurs & Fri 3-7, Sat 1-5
Friends of the Library Group

HAMILTON

P HAMILTON PUBLIC LIBRARY, 312 N Davis St, 64644. SAN 308-9932. Tel: 816-583-4832. FAX: 816-583-7501. E-mail: hamiltonpubliclibrary@gmail.com. Web Site: hamiltonpubliclibrary.com. *Dir,* Kate Adams; *Libr Asst,* Annette Hignight; Staff 2 (MLS 1, Non-MLS 1)
Founded 1919. Pop 1,657; Circ 13,890
Library Holdings: e-books 3,485; Large Print Bks 734; Bk Vols 11,620; Per Subs 10; Talking Bks 98; Videos 263
Automation Activity & Vendor Info: (Acquisitions) Mandarin Library Automation; (Cataloging) Mandarin Library Automation; (Circulation) Mandarin Library Automation
Wireless access
Open Tues, Wed & Fri 9-5, Thurs 9-7, Sat 9-Noon

HANNIBAL

P HANNIBAL FREE PUBLIC LIBRARY*, 200 S Fifth St, 63401. SAN 308-9940. Tel: 573-221-0222. FAX: 573-221-0369. E-mail: ref@hannibal.lib.mo.us. Web Site: hannibal.lib.mo.us. *Dir,* Hallie Yundt Silver; E-mail: hallieys@hannibal.lib.mo.us; Staff 9 (MLS 2, Non-MLS 7)
Founded 1845. Pop 17,757; Circ 132,380
Library Holdings: e-books 9,842; Microforms 797; Bk Vols 92,333; Per Subs 121
Subject Interests: Hannibal hist, Mark Twain
Automation Activity & Vendor Info: (Cataloging) SirsiDynix; (Circulation) SirsiDynix; (OPAC) SirsiDynix; (Serials) SirsiDynix
Wireless access
Publications: Story of Hannibal by the Hagoods (Local historical information)
Open Mon & Tues 10-8, Wed-Sat 10-6
Restriction: Non-resident fee, Open to pub for ref & circ; with some limitations
Friends of the Library Group

C HANNIBAL-LAGRANGE UNIVERSITY*, Roland Library, 2800 Palmyra Rd, 63401-1999. SAN 308-9959. Tel: 573-629-3132. Interlibrary Loan Service Tel: 573-629-3137. Administration Tel: 573-629-3130. E-mail: library@hlg.edu. Web Site: hlg.edu/student-life/library/. *Dir,* Julie Andresen; Tel: 573-629-3130, E-mail: jandresen@hlg.edu; Staff 5.5 (MLS 1, Non-MLS 4.5)
Founded 1858. Enrl 930; Fac 78; Highest Degree: Master
Jul 2015-Jun 2016 Income $382,517. Mats Exp $382,517, Books $11,477, Per/Ser (Incl. Access Fees) $85,325, AV Mat $628, Presv $1,448. Sal $190,055
Library Holdings: AV Mats 7,003; e-books 11,020; Bk Vols 115,394; Per Subs 205
Subject Interests: Archives, Baptist mat, Rare bks
Automation Activity & Vendor Info: (Cataloging) Innovative Interfaces, Inc; (Circulation) Innovative Interfaces, Inc; (Course Reserve) Innovative Interfaces, Inc; (ILL) OCLC; (Media Booking) Innovative Interfaces, Inc; (OPAC) Innovative Interfaces, Inc; (Serials) Innovative Interfaces, Inc
Wireless access
Function: 24/7 Electronic res, Archival coll, Art exhibits, Audio & video playback equip for onsite use, Computers for patron use, E-Readers, Electronic databases & coll, Equip loans & repairs, ILL available, Internet access, Laminating, Magazines, Microfiche/film & reading machines, Online cat, Orientations, Photocopying/Printing, Ref serv available, Scanner, Study rm, Tax forms, VHS videos, Wheelchair accessible, Workshops
Partic in Amigos Library Services, Inc; Missouri Research & Education Network; MOBIUS; OCLC Online Computer Library Center, Inc
Special Services for the Blind - Daisy reader; ZoomText magnification & reading software
Open Mon-Fri (Sept-April) 7:30am-Midnight, Sat Noon-5; Mon, Tues & Thurs (May-Aug) 8-6, Wed & Fri 8-4
Restriction: Fee for pub use, Open to students, fac & staff

S MARK TWAIN HOME FOUNDATION*, Mark Twain Museum Library, 120 N Main St, 63401-3537. SAN 326-0542. Tel: 573-221-9010. FAX: 573-221-7975. Web Site: www.marktwainmuseum.org. *Exec Dir,* Henry Sweets; Tel: 573-221-9010, Ext 405, E-mail: henry.sweets@marktwainmuseum.org
Founded 1937
Library Holdings: DVDs 15; Bk Titles 3,900; Per Subs 5; Videos 50
Special Collections: Mark Twain Coll (First Editions & Works about Him)
Wireless access
Publications: The Fence Painter (Bimonthly)
Restriction: Open by appt only

HARRISONVILLE

P CASS COUNTY PUBLIC LIBRARY*, Administration Office, 400 E Mechanic St, 64701. SAN 349-0564. Tel: 816-380-4600. FAX: 816-884-2301. Web Site: www.casscolibrary.org. *Dir,* Christie Kessler; E-mail: ckessler@casscolibrary.org; *Asst Dir, Head, Pub Serv,* Dan Brower; Staff 1 (MLS 1)
Founded 1947. Pop 94,232; Circ 545,400
Library Holdings: Bk Vols 214,000; Per Subs 586
Special Collections: Cass County & Missouri, hist doc
Subject Interests: Genealogy
Automation Activity & Vendor Info: (Acquisitions) SirsiDynix; (Cataloging) SirsiDynix; (Circulation) SirsiDynix; (ILL) SirsiDynix; (OPAC) SirsiDynix; (Serials) SirsiDynix
Wireless access
Function: Adult bk club, Archival coll, Bilingual assistance for Spanish patrons, Bks on cassette, Bks on CD, Children's prog, Citizenship assistance, Computer training, Computers for patron use, Doc delivery serv, Electronic databases & coll, Genealogy discussion group, Holiday prog, Music CDs, Photocopying/Printing, Preschool outreach, Prog for children & young adult, Senior computer classes
Publications: Annual Report; Summer Reading Kit
Partic in Kansas City Library Service Program; Mid-America Library Alliance; Missouri Research & Education Network
Special Services for the Deaf - TDD equip
Open Mon-Fri 8-5
Friends of the Library Group
Branches: 7
ARCHIE BRANCH, 315 S Main, Archie, 64725, SAN 349-0599. Tel: 816-293-5579.
Open Mon 2-6, Tues & Wed 9-6, Thurs 2-7, Sat 9-1
Friends of the Library Group
MARY B B CROUCH GENEOLOGY LIBRARY, 400 E Mechanic, 64701. Tel: 816-884-6285.
Open Mon, Fri & Sat 10-12 & 1-5, Tues & Thurs 12-6, Wed 12-5 & 6-8
Friends of the Library Group
DREXEL BRANCH, 211 E Main St, Drexel, 64742, SAN 349-0688. Tel: 816-928-1010.
Open Mon 9-1 & 2-7, Wed & Thurs 9-1 & 2-6, Fri 2-5, Sat 9-12
Friends of the Library Group

GARDEN CITY BRANCH, 201 C Date St, Garden City, 64747-9211, SAN 349-0718. Tel: 816-755-3030.
Open Mon & Wed 9-7, Thurs 9-6, Sat 9-3
Friends of the Library Group
HARRISONVILLE BRANCH, 400 E Mechanic St, 64701, SAN 349-0742. Tel: 816-884-3483.
Open Mon-Thurs 9-8, Fri 9-6, Sat 9-5
Friends of the Library Group
NORTHERN RESOURCE CENTER, 1741 E North Ave, Belton, 64012, SAN 349-0629. Tel: 816-331-0049.
Open Mon-Thurs 9-8, Fri 9-6, Sat 9-5
Friends of the Library Group
PLEASANT HILL BRANCH, 1108 N Hwy No 7, Pleasant Hill, 64080, SAN 349-0807. Tel: 816-987-2231.
Open Mon & Wed 9-6, Tues 9-7, Thurs 12-6, Fri 12-5, Sat 9-3
Friends of the Library Group
Bookmobiles: 1

HARTVILLE

P WRIGHT COUNTY LIBRARY*, Administrative Headquarters, 160 E Marshfield St, 65667-9998. (Mail add: PO Box 70, 65667-0070). Tel: 417-741-7595. FAX: 417-741-7927. E-mail: htvlib@wrightcounty.lib.mo.us. Web Site: www.wrightcounty.lib.mo.us. *Dir,* Karen Moore; E-mail: kmoore@wrightcounty.lib.mo.us; Staff 3 (MLS 1, Non-MLS 2)
Founded 1947
Library Holdings: Bk Titles 72,129; Bk Vols 73,048; Per Subs 71
Automation Activity & Vendor Info: (ILL) OCLC
Wireless access
Open Mon, Tues, Thurs & Fri 9-12:30 & 1-4:30, Sat 9-Noon
Friends of the Library Group
Branches: 2
MOUNTAIN GROVE BRANCH, 206 Green Ave, Mountain Grove, 65711, SAN 349-098X. Tel: 417-926-4453. FAX: 417-926-6240. E-mail: mglib@wrightcounty.lib.mo.us. *Br Mgr,* Barbara Flageolle; Staff 3 (MLS 3)
Library Holdings: Bk Titles 7,012; Bk Vols 7,690; Per Subs 11
Open Mon-Fri 9-4:30, Sat 9-12
Friends of the Library Group
LAURA INGALLS WILDER LIBRARY, 120 Business 60, Hwy 5, Mansfield, 65804, SAN 349-0955. Tel: 417-924-8068. FAX: 417-924-3045. E-mail: manlib@wrightcounty.lib.mo.us. *Br Mgr,* Marissa Crewse; Staff 3 (MLS 2, Non-MLS 1)
Library Holdings: Bk Titles 9,500; Bk Vols 10,000; Per Subs 16
Open Mon, Tues, Thurs & Fri 9-12:30 & 1-4:30, Sat 9-Noon
Friends of the Library Group
Bookmobiles: 1

HAYTI

P CONRAN MEMORIAL LIBRARY*, 302 E Main St, 63851. (Mail add: PO Box 552, 63851), SAN 308-9967. Tel: 573-359-0599. FAX: 573-359-0599. E-mail: conranlibrary@hotmail.com. Web Site: haytimo.org/2156/library. *Librn,* Amy Boone
Founded 1934. Pop 3,841
Library Holdings: AV Mats 150; Large Print Bks 300; Bk Vols 19,000; Per Subs 20; Talking Bks 100; Videos 100
Subject Interests: Town hist
Wireless access
Open Mon-Fri 11-5

HERMANN

S DEUTSCHHEIM STATE HISTORIC SITE LIBRARY*, 107 W Second St, 65041-1045. SAN 372-7459. Tel: 573-486-2200. FAX: 573-486-2249. Web Site: mostateparks.com/park/deutschheim-state-historic-site. *Adminr,* Katy Holmer; E-mail: katy.holmer@dnr.mo.gov
Founded 1978
Library Holdings: Bk Vols 300
Special Collections: German Immigrants & German Americans in Missouri 1785-1900
Open Mon-Sun 10-4; Thurs-Sun (Nov-March) 10-4

HIGGINSVILLE

P ROBERTSON MEMORIAL LIBRARY*, 19 W 20th St, 64037. SAN 308-9975. Tel: 660-584-2880. FAX: 660-584-8181. Web Site: higginsvillelibrary.org. *Dir,* Tina Myrick; Staff 2 (MLS 1, Non-MLS 1)
Founded 1928. Pop 4,723
Automation Activity & Vendor Info: (Acquisitions) Book Systems; (Cataloging) Book Systems; (Circulation) Book Systems; (OPAC) Book Systems
Wireless access
Open Tues, Thurs & Fri 10-5, Wed 10-7, Sat 10-2
Friends of the Library Group

HIGH RIDGE

P JEFFERSON COUNTY LIBRARY*, 5678 State Rd PP, 63049-2216. SAN 372-7505. Tel: 636-677-8689. FAX: 636-677-1769. E-mail: info@jeffersoncountylibrary.org. Web Site: www.jeffcolib.org. *Dir,* Pamela R Klipsch; *Asst Dir, Bus Operations,* Debby Byron; E-mail: dbyron@jeffcolib.org; *Asst Dir, Libr Operations,* Pamela Withrow; E-mail: pwithrow@jeffcolib.org; *Tech Serv Mgr,* Kate Coleman; E-mail: kcoleman@jeffcolib.org; *Tech Mgr,* Jay Manning; E-mail: jmanning@jeffcolib.org; Staff 16 (MLS 13, Non-MLS 3)
Founded 1989. Pop 131,842; Circ 568,191
Jan 2018-Dec 2018. Mats Exp $2,601,279
Special Collections: State Document Depository
Subject Interests: Genealogy, Local hist, Parenting
Automation Activity & Vendor Info: (Acquisitions) Evergreen; (Cataloging) Evergreen; (Circulation) Evergreen; (OPAC) Evergreen
Wireless access
Special Services for the Deaf - Adult & family literacy prog; Bks on deafness & sign lang; Coll on deaf educ
Special Services for the Blind - Assistive/Adapted tech devices, equip & products; Audio mat; Bks on cassette; Bks on CD; Cassettes; Closed circuit TV; Computer with voice synthesizer for visually impaired persons; Home delivery serv; Large print bks; Large screen computer & software; Talking bks
Open Mon-Thurs 9-9, Fri 9-6, Sat 9-5
Friends of the Library Group
Branches: 3
ARNOLD BRANCH, 1701 Missouri State Rd, Arnold, 63010, SAN 372-7513. Tel: 636-296-2204. FAX: 636-296-5975. *Br Mgr,* Meredith McCarthy; E-mail: mmccarthy@jeffcolib.org; *Ch,* Amy Held; E-mail: aheld@jeffcolib.org; *Ref Librn,* Joshua Henry; E-mail: jhenry@jeffcolib.org; *Ref Librn,* Myra Hill; E-mail: mhill@jeffcolib.org; *Circ,* Marcia Shrader; E-mail: mshrader@jeffcolib.org; Staff 5.7 (MLS 4, Non-MLS 1.7)
Founded 1989. Pop 67,955; Circ 231,896
Special Collections: State Document Depository
Subject Interests: Bus
Open Mon-Thurs 9-9, Fri 9-6, Sat 9-5
Friends of the Library Group
NORTHWEST, 5680 State Rd PP, 63049, SAN 372-8064. Tel: 636-677-8186. FAX: 636-677-8243. E-mail: northwest@jeffcolib.org. *Br Mgr,* Cindy Hayes; E-mail: chayes@jeffcolib.org; *Ref Librn,* Brenda Rahmoeller; E-mail: brahmoeller@jeffcolib.org; *Ch Assoc,* Julia Click; E-mail: jclick@jeffcolib.org; *Circ,* Karen Jones; E-mail: kjones@jeffcolib.org; *Genealogy Serv,* Mindy Hudson; E-mail: mhudson@jeffcolib.org; Staff 6.1 (MLS 2.8, Non-MLS 3.3)
Founded 1989. Pop 45,694; Circ 246,588
Library Holdings: Audiobooks 3,160; CDs 2,658; DVDs 2,486; High Interest/Low Vocabulary Bk Vols 658; Large Print Bks 2,174; Microforms 2,300; Bk Vols 70,991; Videos 2,501
Subject Interests: Genealogy, Local hist
Open Mon-Thurs 9-9, Fri 9-6, Sat 9-5
Friends of the Library Group
WINDSOR, 7479 Metropolitian Blvd, Barnhart, 63012, SAN 378-2182. Tel: 636-461-1914. FAX: 636-461-1915. *Br Mgr,* Adam Tucker; E-mail: atucker@jeffcolib.org; *Ref Librn,* Jason Phinney; E-mail: jphinney@jeffcolib.org; *Ch Serv,* Patty Lagermann; E-mail: plagermann@jeffcolib.org; *Circ Supvr,* Dawn Zubic; E-mail: dzubic@jeffcolib.org; *Ref Serv,* Elizabeth Cobb; E-mail: bcobb@jeffcolib.org; *Ref Serv,* Karen Graham; E-mail: kgraham@jeffcolib.org; Staff 7.4 (MLS 2, Non-MLS 5.4)
Founded 1989. Pop 18,193; Circ 145,624
Subject Interests: Parenting
Open Mon-Thurs 9-9, Fri 9-6, Sat 9-5
Friends of the Library Group

HILLSBORO

C JEFFERSON COLLEGE LIBRARY*, 1000 Viking Dr, 63050. SAN 308-9983. Tel: 636-481-3000, 636-797-3000. Circulation Tel: 636-789-3167. FAX: 636-789-3954. E-mail: refdesk@jeffco.edu. Web Site: www.jeffco.edu/library. *Dir, Libr Serv,* Lisa Pritchard; Tel: 636-481-3160, E-mail: lpritcha@jeffco.edu; *Access Serv Librn,* Elizabeth Steffen; Tel: 636-481-3174, E-mail: esteffe2@jeffco.edu; Staff 9 (MLS 3, Non-MLS 6)
Founded 1964. Enrl 2,930; Fac 88; Highest Degree: Associate
Library Holdings: Bk Titles 70,831; Bk Vols 72,415; Per Subs 130; Videos 1,000
Special Collections: Jefferson County History Center. State Document Depository; US Document Depository
Automation Activity & Vendor Info: (Circulation) Innovative Interfaces, Inc; (Course Reserve) Innovative Interfaces, Inc; (OPAC) Innovative Interfaces, Inc; (Serials) Innovative Interfaces, Inc
Wireless access

Partic in Amigos Library Services, Inc; MOBIUS; Network of Illinois Learning Resources in Community Colleges; Saint Louis Regional Library Network
Open Mon-Thurs 7:30am-9pm, Fri 7:30-4, Sat 10-2
Departmental Libraries:
ARNOLD CAMPUS LIBRARY, 1687 Missouri State Rd, Arnold, 63010. Tel: 636-481-3597.
Open Mon-Thurs 8-2:30

HOUSTON

P TEXAS COUNTY LIBRARY*, 117 W Walnut St, 65483. SAN 349-1048. Tel: 417-967-2258. Toll Free Tel: 888-609-4469. FAX: 417-967-2262. E-mail: httexascountylibrary@gmail.com. Web Site: texascountylibrary.lib.mo.us. *Dir,* Loretta Smith; Staff 7 (MLS 1, Non-MLS 6)
Founded 1946. Pop 22,000; Circ 140,330
Library Holdings: Bk Titles 58,720; Bk Vols 60,000; Per Subs 60; Talking Bks 729; Videos 836
Wireless access
Partic in SW Mo Libr Network
Open Mon, Wed & Fri 9-5, Tues & Thurs 9-7 (9-5 Winter), Sat 9-1
Friends of the Library Group
Branches: 3
CABOOL BRANCH, 418 Walnut Ave, Cabool, 65689, SAN 349-1072. Tel: 417-962-3722. Toll Free Tel: 888-609-4474. FAX: 417-962-3723. E-mail: cblib@texascountylibrary.lib.mo.us. Web Site: texascountylibrary.lib.mo.us/content/cabool-branch. *Librn,* Eliza Cannon; *Librn,* Lanie Jeep; Staff 3 (MLS 1, Non-MLS 2)
Open Mon-Fri 11-5, Sat 9-1
Friends of the Library Group
LICKING BRANCH, 126 S Main St, Licking, 65542, SAN 349-1102. Tel: 573-674-2038. Toll Free Tel: 888-609-4479. FAX: 573-674-2148. E-mail: lklib@texascountylibrary.lib.mo.us. Web Site: texascountylibrary.lib.mo.us/content/licking-branch. *Librn,* Cynthia Floyd; *Librn,* Brandie Smith; Staff 2 (Non-MLS 2)
Open Mon & Fri 11-5, Tues-Thurs 11-6, Sat 9-1
Friends of the Library Group
SUMMERSVILLE BRANCH, 480 First St, Summersville, 65571, SAN 349-1137. Tel: 417-932-5261. FAX: 417-932-5262. E-mail: svlibrary@texascountylibrary.lib.mo.us. Web Site: texascountylibrary.lib.mo.us/content/summersville-branch. *Librn,* Kathie Cox; *Librn,* Diana Richardson; Staff 1 (Non-MLS 1)
Open Mon-Fri 11-5, Sat 9-1
Friends of the Library Group

IBERIA

P HEARTLAND REGIONAL LIBRARY SYSTEM*, Iberia Library, 304 N St Louis St, 65486. (Mail add: PO Box 386, 65486-0386), SAN 377-1113. Tel: 573-793-6746. FAX: 573-793-6037. Web Site: heartland.lib.mo.us/iberia-branch. *Br Mgr,* Carrie Fritchey; Staff 3 (MLS 1, Non-MLS 2)
Library Holdings: Bk Titles 17,398; Bk Vols 17,991; Per Subs 20
Wireless access
Open Tues, Wed & Fri 1-5, Thurs 1-7, Sat 9-1
Branches: 3
BELLE BRANCH, 206 B S Alvarado, Belle, 65013. (Mail add: PO Box 663, Belle, 65013-0663). Tel: 573-859-6285. FAX: 573-859-6961. Web Site: heartland.lib.mo.us/belle-branch. *Br Mgr,* Tammy Baxter
Open Tues, Wed & Fri 1-5, Thurs 1-7, Sat 9-1
ELDON PUBLIC LIBRARY, 308 E First St, Eldon, 65026-1802, SAN 377-1075. Tel: 573-392-6657. FAX: 573-392-4071. Web Site: heartland.lib.mo.us/eldon-branch. *Br Mgr,* Ruby Bunch; Staff 1 (MLS 1)
Library Holdings: Bk Titles 21,119; Bk Vols 23,240; Per Subs 32; Talking Bks 64; Videos 57
Automation Activity & Vendor Info: (Cataloging) SirsiDynix; (Circulation) SirsiDynix
Open Mon-Wed & Fri 9-5, Thurs 9-7, Sat 9-1
VIENNA BRANCH, 315 Third St, Vienna, 65582. (Mail add: PO Box 231, Vienna, 65582-0231). Tel: 573-422-9866. FAX: 573-422-3771. Web Site: heartland.lib.mo.us/viennabranch. *Dir,* Lisa Garro; E-mail: lisa.garro@heartland.lib.mo.us; *Br Mgr,* Amanda Kremer
Open Tues, Wed & Fri 1-5, Thurs 1-7, Sat 9-1

INDEPENDENCE

R COMMUNITY OF CHRIST LIBRARY*, The Temple, 201 S River, 64050. SAN 349-1919. Tel: 816-833-1000, Ext 2400. E-mail: rkillebrew@cofchrist.org. Web Site: www.cofchrist.org/library/default.asp. *Libr Dir,* Rachel Killebrew; Tel: 816-833-1000, Ext 2399, E-mail: rkillebrew@CofChrist.org; Staff 1 (MLS 1)
Founded 1865
Library Holdings: Audiobooks 2,000; Bk Titles 30,000; Per Subs 150; Videos 400
Special Collections: Book of Mormon, ms; Early Origins of the Mormon Church; Herald Publishing House Publications; Histories of States Related to Latter Day Saints Movement; Inspired Version of the Bible; Latter Day Saints History & Theology, archives, foreign language scriptures, Herald House Preservation, pamphlets,vault, unpublished, audios & videos; Latter Day Saints Pamphlets; Reorganized Church of Jesus Christ of Latter Day Saints, journals, papers, photog & rec
Subject Interests: Christianity, Mormon (Latter Day Saints) hist, Mormon (Latter Day Saints) theol, Peace studies
Automation Activity & Vendor Info: (Cataloging) SirsiDynix; (Circulation) SirsiDynix
Restriction: Non-circulating, Open to pub by appt only

S JACKSON COUNTY HISTORICAL SOCIETY, Archives & Research Library, 112 W Lexington Ave, 64050-3700. (Mail add: PO Box 4241, 64051), SAN 320-197X. Tel: 816-252-7454. FAX: 816-461-1510. E-mail: info@jchs.org. Web Site: jchs.org. *Archivist,* Danielle Hall; Staff 3 (MLS 1, Non-MLS 2)
Founded 1940
Library Holdings: Bk Titles 1,500; Per Subs 10
Subject Interests: Jackson County, Mo hist, Mo hist
Wireless access
Function: Archival coll, Photocopying/Printing, Ref & res, Ref serv available, Res assist avail
Publications: The Jackson County Historical Society e-Journal (Monthly)
Restriction: Not a lending libr, Open by appt only, Pub use on premises

P MID-CONTINENT PUBLIC LIBRARY*, 15616 E US Hwy 24, 64050. SAN 349-1161. Tel: 816-836-5200. E-mail: info@mymcpl.org. Web Site: www.mymcpl.org. *Dir of Libr,* Steven V Potter; Fax: spotter@mymcpl.org; *Asst Dir,* Susan Wray; Tel: 816-521-7220, E-mail: swray@mymcpl.org; *Dir, Human Res,* Jennifer Ridley; Staff 34 (MLS 34)
Founded 1965. Pop 688,000; Circ 9,060,960
Library Holdings: AV Mats 330,341; CDs 93,441; DVDs 36,329; High Interest/Low Vocabulary Bk Vols 6,965; Bk Titles 681,528; Bk Vols 3,106,319; Per Subs 8,283; Talking Bks 73,848
Special Collections: Handicapped Coll, AV, bks, puzzles, toys; Missouriana & Genealogy Coll; United States Census Coll, micro
Automation Activity & Vendor Info: (Acquisitions) SirsiDynix; (Cataloging) SirsiDynix; (Circulation) SirsiDynix; (ILL) SirsiDynix; (Media Booking) SirsiDynix; (OPAC) SirsiDynix; (Serials) SirsiDynix
Wireless access
Function: Adult bk club, Adult literacy prog, Audiobks via web, AV serv, Bk club(s), Bks on cassette, Bks on CD, Children's prog, Computers for patron use, Digital talking bks, Electronic databases & coll, Family literacy, Free DVD rentals, Genealogy discussion group, Homebound delivery serv, Homework prog, ILL available, Internet access, Magnifiers for reading, Mail & tel request accepted, Music CDs, Online cat, Online ref, Outside serv via phone, mail, e-mail & web, OverDrive digital audio bks, Photocopying/Printing, Prog for adults, Prog for children & young adult, Ref serv available, Spoken cassettes & CDs, Spoken cassettes & DVDs, Story hour, Summer reading prog, Tax forms, Teen prog, Telephone ref, VHS videos, Wheelchair accessible
Partic in Amigos Library Services, Inc; Mid-America Library Alliance; OCLC Online Computer Library Center, Inc
Special Services for the Deaf - Bks on deafness & sign lang; High interest/low vocabulary bks; Spec interest per
Open Mon-Fri 8-5
Friends of the Library Group
Branches: 30
ANTIOCH BRANCH, 6060 N Chestnut Ave, Gladstone, 64119, SAN 349-1196. Tel: 816-454-1306. Web Site: www.mymcpl.org/locations/antioch. *Br Mgr,* Rosalyn Spring; E-mail: RSpring@mymcpl.org; Staff 2 (MLS 1, Non-MLS 1)
Library Holdings: Bk Titles 21,221; Bk Vols 22,390; Per Subs 54; Talking Bks 81; Videos 178
Open Mon-Thurs 9-9, Fri 9-6, Sat 10-6, Sun 1-5
Friends of the Library Group
BLUE RIDGE BRANCH, 9253 Blue Ridge Blvd, Kansas City, 64138, SAN 349-1765. Tel: 816-761-3382. Web Site: www.mymcpl.org/locations/blue-ridge. *Br Mgr,* Geri Haile; E-mail: GHaile@mymcpl.org; Staff 2 (MLS 1, Non-MLS 1)
Founded 1956
Library Holdings: Bk Titles 20,195; Bk Vols 21,071; Per Subs 34; Videos 389
Open Mon-Thurs 9-9, Fri 9-6, Sat 10-6, Sun 1-5
Friends of the Library Group
BLUE SPRINGS NORTH BRANCH, 850 NW Hunter Dr, Blue Springs, 64015, SAN 373-7195. Tel: 816-224-8772. Web Site: www.mymcpl.org/locations/blue-springs-north. *Br Mgr,* Ms Robin Hudson; E-mail: RHudson@mymcpl.org; Staff 3 (MLS 1, Non-MLS 2)
Library Holdings: Bk Titles 20,075; Bk Vols 21,192; Per Subs 36; Videos 370
Open Mon-Thurs 9-9, Fri 9-6, Sat 10-6, Sun 1-5
Friends of the Library Group

BLUE SPRINGS SOUTH BRANCH, 2220 South Hwy 7, Blue Springs, 64014, SAN 349-1226. Tel: 816-229-3571. Web Site: www.mymcpl.org/locations/blue-springs-south. *Br Mgr,* Sarah Stansberry; E-mail: SStansberry@mymcpl.org; Staff 2 (MLS 1, Non-MLS 1)
Library Holdings: Bk Titles 22,717; Bk Vols 23,081; Per Subs 40; Videos 315
Open Mon-Thurs 9-9, Fri 9-6, Sat 10-6, Sun 1-5
Friends of the Library Group

BOARDWALK BRANCH, 8656 N Ambassador Dr, Kansas City, 64154, SAN 375-5681. Tel: 816-741-9011. Web Site: www.mymcpl.org/locations/boardwalk. *Br Mgr,* Rebecca Richardson; E-mail: rrichardson@mymcpl.org; Staff 3 (MLS 1, Non-MLS 2)
Library Holdings: Bk Titles 23,133; Bk Vols 23,609; Per Subs 36; Videos 387
Open Mon-Thurs 9-9, Fri 9-6, Sat 10-6, Sun 1-5
Friends of the Library Group

BUCKNER BRANCH, 19 E Jefferson St, Buckner, 64016, SAN 349-1250. Tel: 816-650-3212. Web Site: www.mymcpl.org/locations/buckner. *Br Mgr,* LynnDee Wathen; E-mail: LWathen@mymcpl.org; Staff 3 (MLS 1, Non-MLS 2)
Library Holdings: Bk Titles 21,779; Bk Vols 22,011; Per Subs 33; Videos 341
Open Mon-Thurs 9-8, Tues, Fri 9-6, Sat 10-6
Friends of the Library Group

CAMDEN POINT BRANCH, 401 Hardesty St, Camden Point, 64018, SAN 349-1285. Tel: 816-280-3384. Web Site: www.mymcpl.org/locations/camden-point. *Br Mgr,* Tiara Dixon; E-mail: tdixon@mymcpl.org; Staff 2 (MLS 1, Non-MLS 1)
Library Holdings: Bk Titles 19,881; Bk Vols 20,177; Per Subs 29; Videos 305
Open Mon 9-8, Tues-Fri 9-6, Sat 10-6
Friends of the Library Group

CLAYCOMO BRANCH, 309 NE US Hwy 69, Claycomo, 64119, SAN 373-7209. Tel: 816-455-5030. Web Site: www.mymcpl.org/locations/claycomo. *Br Mgr,* Stephanie Shade; E-mail: SShade@mymcpl.org; Staff 3 (MLS 1, Non-MLS 2)
Library Holdings: Bk Titles 20,079; Bk Vols 20,181; Per Subs 31; Videos 379
Open Mon-Thurs 9-8, Fri 9-6, Sat 10-6
Friends of the Library Group

COLBERN ROAD BRANCH, 1000 NE Colbern Rd, Lee's Summit, 64086, SAN 373-7217. Tel: 816-525-9924. Web Site: www.mymcpl.org/locations/colbern-road. *Br Mgr,* Seth Moses; E-mail: smoses@mymcpl.org; Staff 2 (MLS 1, Non-MLS 1)
Library Holdings: Bk Titles 20,199; Bk Vols 20,409; Per Subs 31; Videos 336
Open Mon-Thurs 9-9, Fri 9-6, Sat 10-6, Sun 1-5
Friends of the Library Group

DEARBORN BRANCH, 206 Maple Leaf Ave, Dearborn, 64439, SAN 349-1315. Tel: 816-450-3502. Web Site: www.mymcpl.org/locations/dearborn. *Br Mgr,* Tiara Dixon; E-mail: tdixon@mymcpl.org
Open Mon & Wed-Fri 9-6, Tues 9-8, Sat 10-6

EDGERTON BRANCH, 404 Frank St, Edgerton, 64444, SAN 349-134X. Tel: 816-790-3569. Web Site: www.mymcpl.org/locations/edgerton. *Br Mgr,* Tiara Dixon; E-mail: tdixon@mymcpl.org; Staff 2 (MLS 1, Non-MLS 1)
Library Holdings: Bk Titles 21,113; Bk Vols 21,449; Per Subs 31; Videos 309
Open Mon-Wed & Fri 9-6, Thurs 9-8, Sat 10-6
Friends of the Library Group

EXCELSIOR SPRINGS BRANCH, 1460 Kearney Rd, Excelsior Springs, 64024, SAN 349-1374. Tel: 816-630-6721. Web Site: www.mymcpl.org/locations/excelsior-springs. *Br Mgr,* Stephen Chalmers; E-mail: schalmers@mymcpl.org; Staff 2 (MLS 1, Non-MLS 1)
Library Holdings: Bk Titles 21,143; Bk Vols 22,059; Per Subs 32; Videos 312
Open Mon-Thurs 9-9, Fri 9-6, Sat 10-6, Sun 1-5
Friends of the Library Group

GRAIN VALLEY BRANCH, 101 SW Eagles Pkwy, Grain Valley, 64029, SAN 349-1439. Tel: 816-228-4020. Web Site: www.mymcpl.org/locations/grain-valley. *Br Mgr,* Peyton Jenkins; E-mail: PJenkins@mymcpl.org; Staff 2 (MLS 1, Non-MLS 1)
Library Holdings: Bk Titles 21,481; Bk Vols 22,112; Per Subs 37
Open Mon-Thurs 9-8, Fri 9-6, Sat 10-6
Friends of the Library Group

GRANDVIEW BRANCH, 12930 Booth Lane, Grandview, 64030, SAN 349-1463. Tel: 816-763-0550. Web Site: www.mymcpl.org/locations/grandview. *Br Mgr,* Ashley Durkee; E-mail: ADurkee@mymcpl.org; Staff 3 (MLS 1, Non-MLS 2)
Library Holdings: Bk Titles 22,391; Bk Vols 22,911; Per Subs 27; Videos 281
Open Mon-Thurs 9-9, Fri 9-6, Sat 10-6, Sun 1-5
Friends of the Library Group

KEARNEY BRANCH, 100 S Platte-Clay Way, Kearney, 64060, SAN 349-1498. Tel: 816-628-5055. Web Site: www.mymcpl.org/locations/kearney. *Br Mgr,* Angela Gillette; E-mail: AGillette@mymcpl.org; Staff 2 (MLS 1, Non-MLS 1)
Library Holdings: Bk Titles 19,761; Bk Vols 20,359; Per Subs 31
Open Mon-Thurs 9-9, Fri 9-6, Sat 10-6, Sun 1-5
Friends of the Library Group

LEE'S SUMMIT BRANCH, 150 NW Oldham Pkwy, Lee's Summit, 64081, SAN 349-1528. Tel: 816-524-0567. Web Site: www.mymcpl.org/locations/lees-summit. *Br Mgr,* Megan Garrett; E-mail: mgarrett@mymcpl.org
Open Mon-Thurs 9-9, Fri 9-6, Sat 10-6, Sun 1-5

LIBERTY BRANCH, 1000 Kent St, Liberty, 64068, SAN 349-1536. Tel: 816-781-9240. Web Site: www.mymcpl.org/locations/liberty. *Br Mgr,* Kara Drury; E-mail: KDrury@mymcpl.org; Staff 2 (MLS 1, Non-MLS 1)
Library Holdings: Bk Titles 21,760; Bk Vols 22,549; Per Subs 39; Videos 301
Open Mon-Thurs 9-9, Fri 9-6, Sat 10-6, Sun 1-5
Friends of the Library Group

LONE JACK BRANCH, 211 N Bynum Rd, Lone Jack, 64070, SAN 326-8365. Tel: 816-697-2528. Web Site: www.mymcpl.org/locations/lone-jack. *Br Mgr,* Naphtali Faris; E-mail: NFaris@mymcpl.org; Staff 3 (MLS 1, Non-MLS 2)
Library Holdings: Bk Titles 21,507; Bk Vols 22,410; Per Subs 30; Videos 310
Open Mon-Thurs 9-8, Fri 9-6, Sat 10-6
Friends of the Library Group

MIDWEST GENEALOGY CENTER, 3440 S Lee's Summit Rd, 64055. Tel: 816-252-7228. E-mail: mgc@mymcpl.org. Web Site: www.mymcpl.org/locations/midwest-genealogy-center. *Br Mgr,* Cheryl Lang; E-mail: clang@mymcpl.org; *Asst Br Mgr,* Nicole Schlagel; E-mail: nschlagel@mymcpl.org; Staff 19 (MLS 3, Non-MLS 16)
Library Holdings: CDs 392; DVDs 32; Microforms 607,297; Bk Vols 174,000; Per Subs 500; Videos 99
Subject Interests: Genealogy, Local hist
Open Mon-Sat 10-8, Sun 1-8
Friends of the Library Group

NORTH INDEPENDENCE BRANCH, 317 W US Hwy 24, 64050, SAN 349-1552. Tel: 816-252-0950. Web Site: www.mymcpl.org/locations/north-independence. *Br Mgr,* Andrew Phillips; E-mail: aphillips@mymcpl.org; Staff 3 (MLS 1, Non-MLS 2)
Library Holdings: Bk Titles 19,808; Bk Vols 21,112; Per Subs 26; Videos 261
Open Mon-Thurs 9-9, Fri 9-6, Sat 10-6, Sun 1-5
Friends of the Library Group

NORTH OAK BRANCH, 8700 N Oak Trafficway, Kansas City, 64155, SAN 349-1404. Tel: 816-436-4385. Web Site: www.mymcpl.org/locations/north-oak. *Br Mgr,* Leigh Hallenberg; E-mail: LHallenberg@mymcpl.org; Staff 3 (MLS 1, Non-MLS 2)
Library Holdings: Bk Titles 21,136; Bk Vols 22,311; Per Subs 33
Open Mon-Thurs 9-9, Fri 9-6, Sat 10-6, Sun 1-5
Friends of the Library Group

OAK GROVE BRANCH, 2320 S Broadway St, Oak Grove, 64075, SAN 349-1587. Tel: 816-690-3213. Web Site: www.mymcpl.org/locations/oak-grove. *Br Mgr,* Amy Vajnar; E-mail: AVajnar@mymcpl.org; Staff 2 (MLS 1, Non-MLS 1)
Library Holdings: Bk Titles 21,088; Bk Vols 22,961; Per Subs 30; Videos 151
Open Mon-Thurs 9-8, Fri 9-6, Sat 10-6
Friends of the Library Group

PARKVILLE BRANCH, 8815 Tom Watson Pkwy, Parkville, 64152, SAN 373-7225. Tel: 816-741-4721. Web Site: www.mymcpl.org/locations/parkville. *Br Mgr,* Eric Bullock; E-mail: EBullock@mymcpl.org; Staff 2 (MLS 1, Non-MLS 1)
Library Holdings: Bk Titles 19,988; Bk Vols 21,042; Per Subs 29
Open Mon-Thurs 9-9, Fri 9-6, Sat 10-6, Sun 1-5
Friends of the Library Group

PLATTE CITY BRANCH, 2702 NW Prairie View Rd, Platte City, 64079, SAN 349-1617. Tel: 816-858-2322. Web Site: www.mymcpl.org/locations/platte-city. *Br Mgr,* Rachael Rafuse; E-mail: RRafuse@mymcpl.org
Open Mon-Thurs 9-8, Fri 9-6, Sat 10-6

RAYTOWN BRANCH, 6131 Raytown Rd, Raytown, 64133, SAN 349-1676. Tel: 816-353-2052. Web Site: www.mymcpl.org/locations/raytown. *Br Mgr,* Jane Mulvihill-Jones; E-mail: JMulvihill-Jones@mymcpl.org; Staff 2 (MLS 1, Non-MLS 1)
Library Holdings: Bk Titles 20,712; Bk Vols 21,516; Per Subs 23
Open Mon-Thurs 9-9, Fri 9-6, Sat 10-6, Sun 1-5
Friends of the Library Group

RED BRIDGE BRANCH, 11140 Locust St, Kansas City, 64131, SAN 349-1706. Tel: 816-942-1780. Web Site: www.mymcpl.org/locations/red-bridge. *Br Mgr,* Sherry Bridges; E-mail: SBridges@mymcpl.org; Staff 2 (MLS 1, Non-MLS 1)
Library Holdings: Bk Titles 18,889; Bk Vols 20,118; Per Subs 22

Open Mon-Thurs 9-9, Fri 9-6, Sat 10-6, Sun 1-5
Friends of the Library Group
RIVERSIDE BRANCH, 2700 NW Vivion Rd, Riverside, 64150, SAN 349-1730. Tel: 816-741-6288. Web Site: www.mymcpl.org/locations/riverside. *Br Mgr,* Patrice Nollette; E-mail: PNollette@mymcpl.org; Staff 2 (MLS 1, Non-MLS 1)
Library Holdings: Bk Titles 20,514; Bk Vols 21,769; Per Subs 27
Open Mon-Thurs 9-8, Fri 9-6, Sat 10-6
Friends of the Library Group
SMITHVILLE BRANCH, 120 Richardson St, Smithville, 64089, SAN 349-179X. Tel: 816-532-0116. Web Site: www.mymcpl.org/locations/smithville. *Br Mgr,* Sheryl Williams; E-mail: SWilliams@mymcpl.org; Staff 2 (MLS 1, Non-MLS 1)
Library Holdings: Audiobooks 2,767; CDs 1,869; DVDs 3,169; Bk Vols 53,682; Per Subs 28; Videos 798
Open Mon-Thurs 9-9, Fri 9-6, Sat 10-6, Sun 1-5
SOUTH INDEPENDENCE BRANCH, 13700 E 35th St S, 64055, SAN 349-182X. Tel: 816-461-2050. Web Site: www.mymcpl.org/locations/south-independence. *Br Mgr,* Tiffany Mautino; E-mail: tmautino@mymcpl.org; Staff 2 (MLS 1, Non-MLS 1)
Library Holdings: Bk Titles 20,818; Bk Vols 21,216; Per Subs 27
Open Mon-Thurs 9-9, Fri 9-6, Sat 10-6, Sun 1-5
Friends of the Library Group
WESTON BRANCH, 18204 Library Dr, Weston, 64098, SAN 349-1889. Tel: 816-640-2874. Web Site: www.mymcpl.org/locations/weston. *Br Mgr,* Rachel Rafuse; E-mail: rrafuse@mymcpl.org; Staff 2 (MLS 1, Non-MLS 1)
Library Holdings: Bk Titles 21,654; Bk Vols 21,938; Per Subs 36
Open Mon-Thurs 9-7, Fri 9-6, Sat 10-6
Friends of the Library Group

S NATIONAL ARCHIVES & RECORDS ADMINISTRATION, Harry S Truman Presidential Library & Museum, 500 W US Hwy 24, 64050-1798. SAN 309-0035. Tel: 816-268-8200. Reference Tel: 816-268-8272. Toll Free Tel: 800-833-1225. FAX: 816-268-8295. E-mail: truman.library@nara.gov. Reference E-mail: truman.reference@nara.gov. Web Site: www.trumanlibrary.gov. *Dir,* Dr Kurt Graham; E-mail: kurt.graham@nara.gov; *Dep Dir,* Kelly Anders; E-mail: kelly.anders@nara.gov; *Supvry Archivist,* Samuel W Rushay; E-mail: samuel.rushay@nara.gov; Staff 28 (MLS 2, Non-MLS 26)
Founded 1957
Library Holdings: Bk Titles 25,000
Special Collections: Papers of Harry S. Truman & Other Individuals
Automation Activity & Vendor Info: (Cataloging) OCLC
Wireless access
Function: Archival coll, For res purposes, Ref serv available
Open Wed-Sat 9-3, Sun 12-5
Restriction: Closed stack, Non-circulating, Photo ID required for access
Friends of the Library Group

IRONTON

P OZARK REGIONAL LIBRARY*, 402 N Main St, 63650. SAN 349-1978. Tel: 573-546-2615. FAX: 573-546-7225. Web Site: ozarkregional.org. *Dir,* Holly Martin Huffman; E-mail: hmh@ozarkregional.org; *Ch,* Kelsy Fitzgerald; Staff 18.6 (MLS 4, Non-MLS 14.6)
Founded 1947. Pop 61,819; Circ 128,792
Library Holdings: Audiobooks 2,205; AV Mats 3,513; DVDs 245; Microforms 1,001; Bk Titles 91,333; Bk Vols 146,960; Per Subs 250; Videos 1,444
Special Collections: Eastern US Genealogy (Floyd Coll)
Wireless access
Open Mon & Wed-Fri 8-5, Tues 8-8, Sat 8-Noon
Branches: 7
ANNAPOLIS BRANCH, 204 N Allen St, Annapolis, 63620. (Mail add: PO Box 274, Annapolis, 63620-0274), SAN 349-2001. Tel: 573-598-3706. *Librn,* Charlotte Brown
Circ 4,941
Library Holdings: Bk Vols 4,409
Open Tues-Fri 2-6, Sat 10-2
BOURBON BRANCH, 575 Elm, Bourbon, 65441. (Mail add: PO Box 475, Bourbon, 65441-0475), SAN 349-2036. Tel: 573-732-5313. *Librn,* Sharon Fann
Circ 8,328
Library Holdings: Bk Vols 10,287
Open Tues, Wed & Fri 1-5:30, Sat 10-2
FREDERICKTOWN BRANCH, 115 S Main St, Fredericktown, 63645, SAN 349-2060. Tel: 573-783-2120. *Librn,* Deborah Anderson
Circ 21,635
Library Holdings: Bk Vols 17,635
Open Mon, Wed-Fri 10-5:30, Tues 10-8, Sat 10-3
IRONTON BRANCH, 402 N Main St, 63650, SAN 349-2095. Tel: 573-546-2615. *Librn,* John F Mertens
Circ 24,466
Library Holdings: Bk Vols 41,149
Open Mon & Wed-Fri 8-5, Tues 8-8, Sat 9-4
RECKLEIN MEMORIAL, 305 N Smith St, Cuba, 65453, SAN 349-2125. Tel: 573-885-3431. *Librn,* Cheryl Bach
Circ 14,292
Library Holdings: Bk Vols 11,757
Open Tues 10:30-7, Wed-Fri 10:30-5, Sat 10:30-2
STEELVILLE BRANCH, 210 S Fourth St, Steelville, 65565. (Mail add: PO Box 266, Steelville, 65565-0266), SAN 349-2184. Tel: 573-775-2338. *Librn,* Rosemary Kehr
Circ 18,613
Library Holdings: Bk Vols 20,574
Open Tues 10-8, Wed-Fri 12-5:30, Sat 10-4
VIBURNUM BRANCH, City Hall Missouri Ave, Viburnum, 65566. (Mail add: PO Box 33, Viburnum, 65566-0033), SAN 349-2214. Tel: 573-244-5986. *Librn,* Kathryn Snyder
Circ 1,174
Library Holdings: Bk Vols 4,409
Open Mon & Wed 2:30-4:30, Thurs 7-9, Sat 10-12
Bookmobiles: 1. Bk vols 2,700

JACKSON

P RIVERSIDE REGIONAL LIBRARY*, 1997 E Jackson Blvd, 63755-1949. (Mail add: PO Box 389, 63755-0389), SAN 349-2249. Tel: 573-243-8141. FAX: 573-243-8142. E-mail: riversideregionallibrary@gmail.com. Web Site: www.riversideregionallibrary.org. *Dir,* Jeff Trinkle; Staff 23 (MLS 1, Non-MLS 22)
Founded 1955. Pop 66,199; Circ 272,808
Library Holdings: Bk Titles 147,028; Bk Vols 148,020; Per Subs 135; Talking Bks 2,080; Videos 11,446
Special Collections: Large Print
Subject Interests: Genealogy for local families
Automation Activity & Vendor Info: (Cataloging) TLC (The Library Corporation); (Circulation) TLC (The Library Corporation); (OPAC) TLC (The Library Corporation)
Wireless access
Function: ILL available
Partic in Amigos Library Services, Inc; Missouri Research & Education Network
Special Services for the Blind - Closed circuit TV; Talking bks
Open Mon-Fri 9-7, Sat 9-4
Friends of the Library Group
Branches: 5
ALTENBURG BRANCH, 66 Poplar St, Altenburg, 63732. (Mail add: PO Box 32, Altenburg, 63732-0032), SAN 349-2362. Tel: 573-824-5267. FAX: 573-824-5357. *Br Librn,* Eunice Schlichting; Staff 1 (Non-MLS 1)
Library Holdings: Bk Titles 13,214; Bk Vols 14,110; Per Subs 10; Talking Bks 101; Videos 75
Open Tues & Thurs 1-6, Wed 12-6, Sat 8-12
Friends of the Library Group
BENTON BRANCH, 54 N Winchester, Hwy 61, Benton, 63736. (Mail add: PO Box 108, Benton, 63736-0108), SAN 349-2303. Tel: 573-545-3581. FAX: 573-545-3656. *Br Librn,* Tina Powers; Staff 1 (Non-MLS 1)
Library Holdings: Audiobooks 252; CDs 80; DVDs 350; Large Print Bks 100; Bk Titles 11,213; Bk Vols 12,191; Per Subs 10; Videos 50
Open Mon, Tues & Fri 1-6, Wed 9-6, Sat 8-12
Friends of the Library Group
ORAN BRANCH, 120 Mountain St, Oran, 63771. (Mail add: PO Box 298, Oran, 63771-0298), SAN 328-8447. Tel: 573-262-3745. FAX: 573-262-3776. *Br Mgr,* Tiffany Whitmore; Staff 1 (Non-MLS 1)
Library Holdings: Bk Titles 9,757; Bk Vols 10,130; Per Subs 15; Talking Bks 101; Videos 119
Open Mon, Wed & Thurs 9-12 & 1-6, Sat 9-12
Friends of the Library Group
PERRYVILLE BRANCH, 800 City Park Dr, Ste A, Perryville, 63775, SAN 349-2338. Tel: 573-547-6508. FAX: 573-547-3715. *Br Librn,* Melissa Haymaker; Staff 4 (Non-MLS 4)
Library Holdings: Bk Titles 61,238; Bk Vols 62,010; Per Subs 15; Talking Bks 103; Videos 148
Open Mon-Fri 9-6, Sat 9-1
Friends of the Library Group
SCOTT CITY BRANCH, 2016 Main St, Scott City, 63780, SAN 349-2273. Tel: 573-264-2413. FAX: 573-264-2299. *Br Librn,* Joyce Luten; Staff 1 (Non-MLS 1)
Library Holdings: Bk Titles 22,197; Bk Vols 23,198; Per Subs 15; Talking Bks 116; Videos 152
Open Mon, Thurs & Fri 1-6, Tues & Wed 11-6, Sat 9-1
Friends of the Library Group

JEFFERSON CITY

GL COMMITTEE ON LEGISLATIVE RESEARCH*, Legislative Library, State Capitol Bldg, 117A, 65101. SAN 309-0086. Tel: 573-751-4633. FAX: 573-751-0130. E-mail: leg.library@lr.mo.gov. Web Site: www.senate.mo.gov/jcfo. *Librn,* Barb G Wilde; E-mail: barb.wilde@senate.mo.gov; Staff 3 (MLS 1, Non-MLS 2)
Founded 1943
Library Holdings: Bk Titles 5,560; Bk Vols 5,780; Per Subs 125
Special Collections: Missouri Bills, 1909 to date; Missouri House & Senate Journals, 1837 to date; Missouri Laws from Territorial days to date
Open Mon-Fri 8-5

C LINCOLN UNIVERSITY OF MISSOURI*, Inman E Page Library, 712 Lee Dr, 65101. SAN 309-006X. Tel: 573-681-5504. Administration Tel: 573-681-5518. Information Services Tel: 573-681-5512. FAX: 573-681-5511. E-mail: teampage@lincolnu.edu. Web Site: www.lincolnu.edu/web/library. *Dir, Libr Serv,* Waheedah Bilal; E-mail: bilald@lincolnu.edu; Staff 9 (MLS 6, Non-MLS 3)
Founded 1866. Enrl 3,600; Fac 154; Highest Degree: Master
Library Holdings: AV Mats 5,488; CDs 687; Bk Titles 162,169; Bk Vols 208,229; Per Subs 240
Special Collections: Ethnic Studies Center Coll. Oral History
Automation Activity & Vendor Info: (Acquisitions) Innovative Interfaces, Inc; (Cataloging) Innovative Interfaces, Inc; (Circulation) Innovative Interfaces, Inc; (Course Reserve) Innovative Interfaces, Inc; (ILL) Innovative Interfaces, Inc; (OPAC) Innovative Interfaces, Inc; (Serials) Innovative Interfaces, Inc
Wireless access
Publications: Bibliography of Books by & About Blacks
Partic in Amigos Library Services, Inc; MOBIUS; OCLC Online Computer Library Center, Inc
Open Mon-Thurs (Fall & Spring) 7:30am-Midnight, Fri 8-5, Sat 11-8, Sun 3-Midnight; Mon-Thurs (Summer) 7:30am-11pm
Friends of the Library Group

S MISSOURI DEPARTMENT OF CORRECTIONS*, Offender Libraries, 2729 Plaza Dr, 65109-1146. (Mail add: PO Box 236, 65102-0236), SAN 349-2540. Tel: 573-522-1928. FAX: 573-751-4099. Web Site: doc.mo.gov. *Coordr, Libr Serv,* Kimberly Bresnahan; Tel: 573-526-6540, E-mail: kimberly.bresnahan@doc.mo.gov
Subject Interests: Civil rights, Law
Function: Photocopying/Printing, Ref serv available
Restriction: Internal circ only
Branches:
ALGOA CORRECTIONAL CENTER, 8501 No More Victims Rd, 65101-4567. Tel: 573-751-3911, Ext 640. FAX: 573-751-7375. *Librn,* Julie Koenigsfeld; Staff 1 (Non-MLS 1)
BOONVILLE CORRECTIONAL CENTER, 1216 E Morgan St, Boonville, 65233-1300, SAN 349-2575. Tel: 660-882-6521. FAX: 660-882-3427. *Librn,* Position Currently Open
FARMINGTON CORRECTIONAL CENTER, 1012 W Columbia St, Farmington, 63640-2902, SAN 377-1091. Tel: 573-218-7100. FAX: 573-218-7106. *Librn,* Wanda Kreitler
Library Holdings: Bk Vols 17,014; Per Subs 96
FULTON RECEPTION & DIAGNOSTIC CENTER, PO Box 190, Fulton, 65251-0190. Tel: 573-592-4040. FAX: 573-592-4020. *Librn,* Jane Swartz
JEFFERSON CITY CORRECTIONAL CENTER, 8200 No More Victims Rd, 65101-4539, SAN 349-263X. Tel: 573-751-3224. FAX: 573-751-0355. *Librn,* Robyn Combs
MARYVILLE TREATMENT CENTER, 30227 US Hwy 136, Maryville, 64468-8353. Tel: 660-582-6542. FAX: 660-582-8071. *Librn,* Brenda Jennings
MISSOURI EASTERN CORRECTIONAL CENTER, 18701 US Hwy 66, Pacific, 63069-3525, SAN 329-9171. Tel: 636-257-3322. FAX: 636-257-5296. *Librn,* Mary Merseal
Founded 1981
Library Holdings: Bk Titles 17,800; Bk Vols 21,000; Per Subs 60
MOBERLY CORRECTIONAL CENTER, 5201 S Morley, Moberly, 65270. (Mail add: PO Box 7, Moberly, 65270-0007). Tel: 660-263-3778. FAX: 660-263-1730. *Librn,* Ms Terri Lucas
Founded 1963
Library Holdings: AV Mats 300; High Interest/Low Vocabulary Bk Vols 50; Large Print Bks 250; Bk Titles 8,190; Bk Vols 8,318; Per Subs 64; Spec Interest Per Sub 12
Subject Interests: Law
NORTHEAST CORRECTIONAL CENTER, 13698 Airport Rd, Bowling Green, 63334. Tel: 573-324-9975. FAX: 573-324-5028. *Librn,* Sherry Courtney; Staff 2 (Non-MLS 2)
OZARK CORRECTIONAL CENTER, 929 Honor Camp Lane, Fordland, 65652-9700. Tel: 417-767-4491. FAX: 417-738-2400. *Librn,* Aleta Juergens; Staff 1 (MLS 1)
POTOSI CORRECTIONAL CENTER, 11593 State Hwy O, Mineral Point, 63660. Tel: 573-438-6000. FAX: 573-438-6006. *Librn,* Doris Brooks; Staff 1 (Non-MLS 1)
SOUTH CENTRAL CORRECTIONAL CENTER, 255 W Hwy 32, Licking, 65542-9069. Tel: 573-674-4470. FAX: 573-674-4428. *Librn,* Melba Miller; Staff 2 (Non-MLS 2)
SOUTHEAST CORRECTIONAL CENTER, 300 E Pedro Simmons Dr, Charleston, 63834. Tel: 573-683-4409. FAX: 573-683-7022. *Librn,* Sandria Hutcheson; Staff 2 (Non-MLS 2)
TIPTON CORRECTIONAL CENTER, 619 N Osage Ave, Tipton, 65081-8038. Tel: 660-433-2031. FAX: 660-433-2804. *Librn,* Position Currently Open
WESTERN MISSOURI CORRECTIONAL CENTER, 609 E Pence Rd, Cameron, 64429-8823, SAN 372-5758. Tel: 816-632-1390. FAX: 816-632-7882. *Librn,* Rita Taylor; Staff 1 (Non-MLS 1)
WESTERN RECEPTION & DIAGNOSTIC CORRECTIONAL CENTER, 3401 Faraon St, Saint Joseph, 64506-5101. Tel: 816-387-2158. FAX: 816-387-2217. *Librn,* Joyce Russell; Staff 1 (MLS 1)
WOMEN'S EASTERN RECEPTION & DIAGNOSTIC CORRECTIONAL CENTER, 1101 E Hwy 54, Vandalia, 63382-2905. (Mail add: PO Box 300, Vandalia, 63382-0300). Tel: 573-594-6686. FAX: 573-594-6789. *Librn,* Janet Armstrong; *Librn,* Janet Shaw; Staff 2 (MLS 1, Non-MLS 1)

P MISSOURI RIVER REGIONAL LIBRARY, 214 Adams St, 65101. (Mail add: PO Box 89, 65102-0089), SAN 349-2427. Tel: 573-634-2464. Administration Tel: 573-634-6064. FAX: 573-634-7028. Web Site: www.mrrl.org. *Dir,* Claudia Cook; E-mail: cookc@mrrl.org; *Asst Dir,* Betty Hagenhoff; E-mail: hagenhoffb@mrrl.org; *Br Mgr,* Position Currently Open; *Teen Librn,* Courtney Waters; *Mgr, Children's Dept,* Angie Bayne; E-mail: baynea@mrrl.org; *Circ Mgr,* Jessica Wieberg; E-mail: wiebergj@mrrl.org; *IT Mgr,* Jason Shelvy; *Tech Serv Mgr,* Bryan Dunlap; E-mail: dunlapb@mrrl.org; *Adult Prog Coordr,* Madeline Matson; E-mail: matsonm@mrrl.org; *Human Res Officer,* Diane Clingman; *Lead Children's Programmer,* Eric Lyons; *Pub Info,* Natalie Newville; Staff 56 (MLS 8, Non-MLS 48)
Founded 1994. Pop 89,832; Circ 734,181. Sal $2,137,686
Library Holdings: AV Mats 26,570; Bk Vols 190,719; Per Subs 500
Subject Interests: Local hist
Automation Activity & Vendor Info: (Acquisitions) Innovative Interfaces, Inc; (Cataloging) Innovative Interfaces, Inc; (Circulation) Innovative Interfaces, Inc; (OPAC) Innovative Interfaces, Inc; (Serials) Innovative Interfaces, Inc
Wireless access
Function: Audio & video playback equip for onsite use
Publications: MRRL News (Monthly newsletter)
Partic in MOBIUS
Special Services for the Deaf - Bks on deafness & sign lang; Closed caption videos
Special Services for the Blind - Assistive/Adapted tech devices, equip & products; Braille equip; Computer with voice synthesizer for visually impaired persons; Home delivery serv; Large print bks; Talking bks
Open Mon-Thurs 9-7, Fri 9-6, Sat 9-5, Sun 1-5
Branches: 1
OSAGE COUNTY, 22 Library Lane, Linn, 65051, SAN 378-2468. Tel: 573-897-2951. *Br Mgr,* Position Currently Open; Staff 3 (Non-MLS 3)
Founded 1994
Open Mon-Fri 9-6, Sat 9-1
Friends of the Library Group
Bookmobiles: 1

P MISSOURI STATE LIBRARY, James C Kirkpatrick State Information Ctr, 600 W Main St, 65101. (Mail add: PO Box 387, 65102-0387), SAN 309-0094. Tel: 573-751-0586. Reference Tel: 573-751-3615. Administration Tel: 573-522-4036. Toll Free Tel: 800-325-0131 (MO only). FAX: 573-751-3612. E-mail: mostlib@sos.mo.gov. Web Site: www.sos.mo.gov/library. *State Librn,* Ms Robin Westphal; E-mail: robin.westphal@sos.mo.gov; *Dir, Ref,* Laura Kromer; Tel: 573-751-2862, E-mail: laura.kromer@sos.mo.gov; Staff 20 (MLS 16, Non-MLS 4)
Founded 1907
Library Holdings: Audiobooks 4; Braille Volumes 23,417; CDs 521; DVDs 449; Electronic Media & Resources 20; Large Print Bks 2,974; Microforms 715; Bk Titles 131,886; Bk Vols 143,056; Per Subs 30; Talking Bks 83,799; Videos 55
Special Collections: Missouri Authors Coll; Missouriana. State Document Depository; US Document Depository
Subject Interests: State govt
Automation Activity & Vendor Info: (Cataloging) OCLC; (Circulation) Innovative Interfaces, Inc; (ILL) OCLC; (OPAC) Innovative Interfaces, Inc
Wireless access
Function: Digital talking bks, Govt ref serv, ILL available, Prof lending libr
Publications: Keeping Up (Online only); Show Me Express (Newsletter)
Partic in Association for Rural & Small Libraries; MOBIUS
Open Mon-Fri 8-5
Restriction: Open to pub for ref & circ; with some limitations, Pub use on premises

P MISSOURI STATE LIBRARY*, Wolfner Talking Book & Braille Library, 600 W Main St, 65101. (Mail add: PO Box 387, 65102-0387). SAN 309-2216. Tel: 573-751-8720. Administration Tel: 573-522-2767. Toll Free Tel: 800-392-2614. FAX: 573-751-3612. TDD: 800-347-1379. E-mail: wolfner@sos.mo.gov. Web Site: www.sos.mo.gov/wolfner. *Dir,* Leslie Bowman; E-mail: leslie.bowman@sos.mo.gov; *Dep Dir, Pub Serv,* Abbey Rimel; E-mail: abbey.rimel@sos.mo.gov; Staff 5 (MLS 4, Non-MLS 1)
Founded 1924
Library Holdings: Braille Volumes 52,755; DVDs 106; Large Print Bks 4,711; Bk Titles 84,000; Bk Vols 405,477; Per Subs 70; Talking Bks 70,065; Videos 580
Automation Activity & Vendor Info: (Cataloging) Keystone Systems, Inc (KLAS); (Circulation) Keystone Systems, Inc (KLAS); (OPAC) Keystone Systems, Inc (KLAS); (Serials) Keystone Systems, Inc (KLAS)
Wireless access
Function: Audiobks via web, Digital talking bks, Online cat, Summer reading prog, Winter reading prog
Publications: Wolfner Library News (Quarterly)
Special Services for the Deaf - TDD equip
Special Services for the Blind - Braille bks; Descriptive video serv (DVS); Digital talking bk; Digital talking bk machines; Web-Braille
Open Mon-Fri 8-5
Friends of the Library Group

GL MISSOURI SUPREME COURT LIBRARY*, Supreme Court Bldg, 207 W High St, 2nd Flr, 65101. SAN 309-0108. Tel: 573-751-2636. FAX: 573-751-2573. Web Site: www.courts.mo.gov/page.jsp?id=218. *Dir, Libr Serv, Pub Serv Dir,* Gail Cross Miller; E-mail: gail.miller@courts.mo.gov; Staff 5 (MLS 1, Non-MLS 4)
Founded 1820
Library Holdings: Bk Vols 120,000; Per Subs 180
Automation Activity & Vendor Info: (Cataloging) LibraryWorld, Inc
Wireless access
Open Mon-Fri 8-5

JOPLIN

P JOPLIN PUBLIC LIBRARY, 1901 E 20th St, 64804. SAN 309-0116. Tel: 417-623-7953. Reference Tel: 417-624-5465. E-mail: jpl@joplinpubliclibrary.org. Web Site: www.joplinpubliclibrary.org. *Dir,* Jeana Gockley; *Ch,* Christina Matekel-Gibson; *Coll Develop Librn,* Linda Cannon; *Ref Librn,* Patty Crane; *Tech Serv Librn,* Alyssa Berry; *Teen Serv Librn,* Beth Snow; *Circ Supvr,* Eden Elliott; *Info Tech,* Lee Cushing; Staff 29 (MLS 6, Non-MLS 23)
Founded 1902. Pop 48,109; Circ 299,956
Nov 2020-Oct 2021. Mats Exp $312,500, Books $122,738, Per/Ser (Incl. Access Fees) $26,226, Other Print Mats $78,329, AV Mat $38,550, Electronic Ref Mat (Incl. Access Fees) $46,657
Library Holdings: Audiobooks 8,758; Bks on Deafness & Sign Lang 27; Braille Volumes 4; CDs 3,573; DVDs 11,455; e-books 84,806; Large Print Bks 7,113; Microforms 1,337; Bk Titles 90,723; Bk Vols 171,720; Per Subs 253
Special Collections: Fine & Decorative Arts (Winfred L & Elizabeth C Post Memorial Art Reference Library); Genealogy Coll
Automation Activity & Vendor Info: (Acquisitions) Innovative Interfaces, Inc; (Cataloging) Innovative Interfaces, Inc; (Circulation) Innovative Interfaces, Inc; (Discovery) EBSCO Discovery Service; (ILL) Innovative Interfaces, Inc; (OPAC) Innovative Interfaces, Inc; (Serials) Innovative Interfaces, Inc
Wireless access
Function: 24/7 Electronic res, 24/7 Online cat, 3D Printer, Art exhibits, Audiobks on Playaways & MP3, Audiobks via web, Bks on CD, Chess club, Children's prog, Computers for patron use, Electronic databases & coll, Free DVD rentals, ILL available, Instruction & testing, Internet access, Magazines, Magnifiers for reading, Makerspace, Mango lang, Meeting rooms, Microfiche/film & reading machines, Music CDs, Notary serv, Online cat, OverDrive digital audio bks, Passport agency, Photocopying/Printing, Preschool outreach, Preschool reading prog, Prog for adults, Prog for children & young adult, Ref & res, Ref serv available, Scanner, Serves people with intellectual disabilities, Spanish lang bks, STEM programs, Story hour, Study rm, Summer reading prog, Teen prog, Telephone ref, Wheelchair accessible
Special Services for the Deaf - Bks on deafness & sign lang; Closed caption videos
Special Services for the Blind - Audio mat; Bks on CD; Large print bks; Magnifiers
Open Mon-Wed & Fri 9-6, Thurs 9-8, Sat 9-5, Sun 1-5
Restriction: Circ limited, ID required to use computers (Ltd hrs), Non-resident fee

C MISSOURI SOUTHERN STATE UNIVERSITY, George A Spiva Library, 3950 E Newman Rd, 64801-1595. SAN 309-0132. Tel: 417-625-9342. Circulation Tel: 417-625-9362. FAX: 417-625-9734. Reference E-mail: librref@mssu.edu. Web Site: www.mssu.edu/library. *Libr Dir,* James Capeci; Tel: 417-625-9806, E-mail: capeci-j@mssu.edu; *Asst Libr Dir,* Amber Carr; Tel: 417-625-3124, E-mail: Carr-A@mssu.edu; *Spec Coll Librn, Univ Archivist,* Whitney Hamm; *Cat Spec,* DeAnn Isenhower; *Library Content & Colls Specialist,* Melissa Forsythe; *Libr Operations Spec,* McKayla Clark; Staff 13 (MLS 3, Non-MLS 10)
Founded 1937. Enrl 4,861; Fac 353; Highest Degree: Master
Library Holdings: Bk Vols 228,945; Per Subs 499
Special Collections: Arrell Morgan Gibson Coll; Gene Taylor Congressional papers; Tri-State Mining Maps. State Document Depository; US Document Depository
Subject Interests: Educ, Nursing
Automation Activity & Vendor Info: (Acquisitions) Innovative Interfaces, Inc; (Cataloging) Innovative Interfaces, Inc; (Circulation) Innovative Interfaces, Inc; (Course Reserve) Innovative Interfaces, Inc; (Media Booking) Innovative Interfaces, Inc; (OPAC) Innovative Interfaces, Inc; (Serials) Innovative Interfaces, Inc
Wireless access
Function: Archival coll, Bk club(s), Computers for patron use, Doc delivery serv, Electronic databases & coll, ILL available, Internet access, Meeting rooms, Microfiche/film & reading machines, Movies, Music CDs, Online cat, OverDrive digital audio bks, Photocopying/Printing, Ref & res, Ref serv available, Res assist avail, Spoken cassettes & CDs, Spoken cassettes & DVDs, Study rm, Telephone ref
Partic in MOBIUS
Open Mon-Thurs 7:30am-9pm, Fri 7:30-5, Sun 1-9 (Fall & Spring); Mon-Thurs 7am-9pm, Sun 1-9 (Summer)
Friends of the Library Group

C OZARK CHRISTIAN COLLEGE, Seth Wilson Library, 1111 N Main St, 64801-4804. SAN 309-0140. Tel: 417-626-1234, Ext 1209. E-mail: library@occ.edu. Web Site: occ.edu/academics/library. *Interim Libr Dir,* Jacque Gage; E-mail: gage.jacque@occ.edu; Staff 2 (MLS 1, Non-MLS 1)
Founded 1942. Enrl 620; Highest Degree: Master
Library Holdings: Bks on Deafness & Sign Lang 50; Bk Titles 62,491; Bk Vols 71,104; Per Subs 300; Talking Bks 439; Videos 756
Special Collections: Restoration Movement (Christianity)
Subject Interests: Archaeology, Biblical studies
Automation Activity & Vendor Info: (Cataloging) Innovative Interfaces, Inc - Sierra; (Circulation) Innovative Interfaces, Inc - Sierra; (Course Reserve) Innovative Interfaces, Inc - Sierra; (ILL) Innovative Interfaces, Inc - Sierra; (OPAC) Innovative Interfaces, Inc - Sierra; (Serials) EBSCO Online
Wireless access
Function: ILL available, Photocopying/Printing, Ref serv available
Partic in Asn of Christian Librs; MOBIUS
Open Mon-Wed 7:30am-Midnight, Thurs 7:30am-9:30pm, Fri 7:30am-9pm, Sat 9-9, Sun 1:30-9

S WINFRED L & ELIZABETH C POST FOUNDATION*, Post Art Library, 1901 E 20th St, 64804. SAN 325-1756. Tel: 417-623-7953, Ext 1041. E-mail: pal@postartlibrary.org. Web Site: postartlibrary.org. *Exec Dir,* Jill Sullivan; E-mail: jhsullivan@postartlibrary.org; Staff 1 (MLS 1)
Founded 1981
Library Holdings: Per Subs 30
Special Collections: Joplin Local History Archives; Yi Dynasty Reproductions
Subject Interests: Archit, Art, Hist, Historic presv
Wireless access
Function: Ref serv available
Open Mon-Thurs 9-8, Fri & Sat 9-6, Sun 1-5
Restriction: Non-circulating

KAHOKA

P NORTHEAST MISSOURI LIBRARY SERVICE*, 207 W Chestnut, 63445-1489. SAN 349-2729. Tel: 660-727-2327. FAX: 660-727-2327. TDD: 660-727-3262. *Dir,* Cathy James; E-mail: viojam@hotmail.com; Staff 13 (MLS 1, Non-MLS 12)
Founded 1961. Pop 27,991; Circ 137,000
Library Holdings: Bk Titles 117,000; Bk Vols 118,000; Per Subs 49
Special Collections: Large Print Material
Subject Interests: Genealogy
Wireless access
Special Services for the Deaf - TDD equip
Open Mon-Fri 8-5, Sat 9-1
Friends of the Library Group
Branches: 4
KNOX COUNTY PUBLIC, 120 S Main St, Edina, 63537-1427, SAN 349-2753. Tel: 660-397-2460. FAX: 660-397-2460. *Dir,* Cathy James; E-mail: viojam@hotmail.com; Staff 1 (Non-MLS 1)
Pop 5,615
Library Holdings: DVDs 621; Bk Titles 21,017; Bk Vols 22,136; Per Subs 33
Special Services for the Blind - Large print bks; Talking bks
Open Mon-Fri 8-12 & 12:30-5, Sat 8-12 & 12:30-4

LEWIS COUNTY BRANCH-LABELLE, 425 State St, La Belle, 63447. (Mail add: PO Box 34, La Belle, 63447), SAN 349-2788. Tel: 660-213-3600. FAX: 660-462-3600. *Br Mgr,* Roxanne Lewis; Staff 1 (Non-MLS 1)
Library Holdings: Bk Titles 7,892; Bk Vols 10,632; Per Subs 18
Open Mon, Wed & Fri 8-12 & 1-5, Sat 8-12
Friends of the Library Group

LEWIS COUNTY BRANCH-LAGRANGE, 114 S Main, LaGrange, 63448. (Mail add: PO Box 8, LaGrange, 63448-0008), SAN 349-2818. Tel: 573-655-2288. FAX: 573-655-2288. *Br Mgr,* Michele Adair; Staff 1 (Non-MLS 1)
Library Holdings: Bk Titles 11,191; Bk Vols 12,309; Per Subs 23
Open Mon 12-6, Tues-Fri 12-5:30, Sat 9-12
Friends of the Library Group

H E SEVER MEMORIAL, 207 W Chestnut, 63445, SAN 349-2877. Tel: 660-727-3262. FAX: 660-727-1055. E-mail: severmemoriallibrary@hotmail.com. *Br Mgr,* Brenda Brown; Staff 3 (MLS 1, Non-MLS 2)
Library Holdings: Bk Titles 53,765; Bk Vols 58,922; Per Subs 31
Special Collections: Large Print Materials; Three County (Knox, Lewis, Clark) Histories & Genealogy Coll, micro
Subject Interests: Med
Special Services for the Deaf - TDD equip
Open Mon 9-6, Tues-Fri 8-5, Sat 9-1
Friends of the Library Group

KANSAS CITY

S AMERICAN TRUCK HISTORICAL SOCIETY*, Zoe James Memorial Library, 10380 N Ambassador Dr, Ste 101, 64153-1378. SAN 370-9698. Tel: 816-891-9900. FAX: 816-891-9903. E-mail: library@aths.org. Web Site: www.aths.org. *Libr Dir,* Courtney Cesar; Tel: 816-777-0924; Staff 8 (MLS 1, Non-MLS 7)
Founded 1971
Special Collections: Ernie Sternberg - Sterling Truck; PIE; White Motor Company Archives
Wireless access
Function: Archival coll, Art exhibits, Bus archives, For res purposes, Internet access, Magazines, Meeting rooms, Microfiche/film & reading machines, Online cat, Online ref, Photocopying/Printing, Ref & res, Ref serv available, Res libr, Res performed for a fee, Telephone ref, Wheelchair accessible
Publications: Show Time (Annual); Wheels of Time (Bimonthly)
Open Mon-Fri 8-4:30
Restriction: Non-circulating, Not a lending libr

C AVILA UNIVERSITY*, Hooley-Bundschu Library/Learning Commons, 11901 Wornall Rd, 64145. SAN 309-0183. Tel: 816-501-3621. Web Site: www.avila.edu/academics/learning-commons. *Interim Libr Dir,* Rebecca Nichols; Tel: 816-501-2428, E-mail: Rebecca.Nichols@avila.edu; *ILL Librn,* Larry Kramer; Tel: 816-501-3712, E-mail: Larry.Kramer@avila.edu; *Archivist,* Amy Moorman; Tel: 816-501-3620, E-mail: Amy.Moorman@avila.edu. Subject Specialists: *Women relig,* Amy Moorman; Staff 3 (MLS 1, Non-MLS 2)
Founded 1916. Enrl 1,500; Fac 70; Highest Degree: Master
Library Holdings: Bk Vols 35,000; Per Subs 284
Special Collections: Women Religious
Wireless access
Partic in MOBIUS
Open Mon-Thurs 7:30am-11pm, Fri 7:30-6, Sun Noon-11; Mon-Thurs (Summer) 8am-9pm, Fri 8-6, Sat 10-5

CR CALVARY UNIVERSITY*, Hilda Kroeker Library, 15800 Calvary Rd, 67417. SAN 309-0264. Tel: 816-322-5152, Ext 1205. FAX: 816-331-4474. Web Site: www.calvary.edu/library. *Librn,* Tiffany Smith; E-mail: tiffany.smith@calvary.edu; Staff 1 (MLS 1)
Founded 1932. Enrl 309; Fac 40; Highest Degree: Master
Library Holdings: AV Mats 1,338; CDs 985; DVDs 15; e-books 397; Bk Titles 49,000; Bk Vols 59,000; Per Subs 70; Videos 338
Subject Interests: Bible, Educ, Missions, Music
Automation Activity & Vendor Info: (Cataloging) SirsiDynix; (Circulation) SirsiDynix; (Course Reserve) SirsiDynix; (OPAC) SirsiDynix
Wireless access
Publications: Calvary Today
Partic in Kansas City Library Service Program
Open Mon-Fri 7:45am-10pm, Sat 1-5
Restriction: Fee for pub use, Open to students, fac, staff & alumni
Friends of the Library Group

M CENTER FOR BEHAVIORAL MEDICINE*, Charles B Wilkinson MD Memorial Library, 1000 E 24th St, 64108. SAN 309-071X. Tel: 816-512-7302. FAX: 816-512-7308. Web Site: dmh.mo.gov/cbm. *Librn,* Lewis Arnold; Staff 1 (Non-MLS 1)
Founded 1968
Library Holdings: AV Mats 1,225; Bk Vols 2,600; Per Subs 19; Spec Interest Per Sub 30; Talking Bks 325; Videos 900
Special Collections: Charles B Wilkinson's Professional Coll
Subject Interests: Behav sci, Psychiat, Psychol, Soc sci
Automation Activity & Vendor Info: (Cataloging) Marcive, Inc; (ILL) OCLC; (Serials) EBSCO Online
Partic in Health Sciences Library Network of Kansas City, Inc; OCLC Online Computer Library Center, Inc
Open Mon-Fri 9-4

M CHILDREN'S MERCY HOSPITAL*, Library Services, 2401 Gillham Rd, 64108. SAN 309-0272. Tel: 816-234-3800, 816-234-3900. E-mail: library@cmh.edu. Web Site: libguides.childrensmercy.org. *Mgr, Libr Serv,* Katie Dayani; E-mail: kddayani@cmh.edu; *Clinical Serv Librn,* Keri Swaggart; E-mail: kswaggart@cmh.edu; *Med Librn,* Jennifer Lyon; Tel: 816-302-8255, E-mail: jalyon@cmh.edu. Subject Specialists: *Bioinformatics, Clinical med, Educ, Med res, Molecular biol,* Jennifer Lyon; Staff 5 (MLS 4, Non-MLS 1)
Founded 1914
Library Holdings: e-books 1,000; e-journals 950; Bk Titles 6,000; Bk Vols 7,200; Per Subs 4
Special Collections: Library of History of Pediatrics (William L Bradford, MD)
Subject Interests: Pediatrics
Automation Activity & Vendor Info: (Cataloging) EOS International; (Circulation) EOS International; (Discovery) SerialsSolutions; (ILL) OCLC ILLiad; (OPAC) EOS International; (Serials) EOS International
Wireless access
Partic in Health Sciences Library Network of Kansas City, Inc; National Network of Libraries of Medicine Region 3; OCLC Online Computer Library Center, Inc
Restriction: Authorized patrons, Employee & client use only, Open to others by appt, Secured area only open to authorized personnel

GM DEPARTMENT OF VETERANS AFFAIRS MEDICAL LIBRARY*, 4801 E Linwood Blvd, 64128-2295. SAN 309-068X. Tel: 816-922-2315. FAX: 816-922-3340. *Dir,* Elizabeth Burns
Founded 1932
Library Holdings: Bk Vols 2,500; Per Subs 198
Subject Interests: Allied health, Med
Publications: Current New Acquistion Lists
Partic in Health Sciences Library Network of Kansas City, Inc; Midcontinental Regional Med Libr Program
Open Mon-Fri 8-4:30
Restriction: Med staff only

S FEDERAL RESERVE BANK OF KANSAS CITY*, Research Library, One Memorial Dr, 64198. SAN 309-0345. Tel: 816-881-2970. Toll Free Tel: 800-333-1010. E-mail: research.library@kc.frb.org. *Librn,* Lu Dayrit; E-mail: lu.o.dayrit@kc.frb.org; Staff 5 (MLS 2, Non-MLS 3)
Library Holdings: Bk Titles 14,000; Bk Vols 15,500; Per Subs 20
Subject Interests: Agr, Econ, Finance, Statistics
Partic in OCLC Online Computer Library Center, Inc
Restriction: Open by appt only

S LINDA HALL LIBRARY OF SCIENCE, ENGINEERING & TECHNOLOGY, 5109 Cherry St, 64110. SAN 309-0353. Tel: 816-363-4600. Toll Free Tel: 800-662-1545. E-mail: communications@lindahall.org, library@lindahall.org. Web Site: www.lindahall.org. *Pres,* Lisa Browar; Tel: 816-926-8745, E-mail: president@lindahall.org; *Dir, Communications,* Sara Kincaid Makara; Tel: 816-926-8765, E-mail: kincaids@lindahall.org; Staff 57 (MLS 17, Non-MLS 40)
Founded 1946
Library Holdings: Bk Titles 799,998; Per Subs 2,316
Special Collections: History of Science; NASA & DOE Reports; Sci-Tech Conference Proceedings; Soviet & European Sci-Tech Publications; Standards & Specifications; US Patent & Trademark Specifications
Subject Interests: Aeronaut, Astronomy, Chemistry, Earth sci, Engr, Environ sci, Life sci, Maps, Natural hist, Physics
Automation Activity & Vendor Info: (Acquisitions) Ex Libris Group; (Cataloging) Ex Libris Group; (Circulation) Ex Libris Group; (Discovery) Ex Libris Group; (OPAC) Ex Libris Group; (Serials) Ex Libris Group
Partic in Center for Research Libraries; OCLC Online Computer Library Center, Inc; OCLC Research Library Partnership
Open Mon-Wed & Fri 10-4, Thurs 10-7
Friends of the Library Group

S HALLMARK CARDS, INC*, Creative Research Library, 2501 McGee Trafficway, MD 912, 64108. SAN 349-2907. Tel: 816-274-5525. Web Site: www.hallmark.com. *Res Mgr,* Sally Anderson; Staff 4 (MLS 2, Non-MLS 2)
Founded 1930
Library Holdings: Bk Titles 2,000; Bk Vols 25,000; Per Subs 150
Subject Interests: Design, Fine arts

Publications: Monthly Newsletter
Restriction: Employees only
Branches:
BUSINESS RESEARCH LIBRARY, 2501 McGee, No 203, 64108, SAN 349-2931. Tel: 816-274-4648. FAX: 816-274-7394. *Librn,* Isidro de la Herran; Staff 1 (MLS 1)
Founded 1980
Library Holdings: Bk Vols 2,000; Per Subs 55
Subject Interests: Retailing
Open Mon-Fri 9-5

S IRISH GENEALOGICAL FOUNDATION LIBRARY*, PO Box 7575, 64116. SAN 378-0015. Tel: 816-399-0905. FAX: 816-454-2410. Web Site: www.irishroots.com. *Library Contact,* Mike O'Laughlin; E-mail: Mike@irishroots.com; Staff 1 (Non-MLS 1)
Library Holdings: Bk Titles 3,890; Bk Vols 4,261
Special Collections: Journal of the American Irish Historical Society 1898-various by county in Ireland
Subject Interests: Genealogy, Heraldry, Irish hist
Restriction: Open by appt only
Friends of the Library Group

GL JACKSON COUNTY LAW LIBRARY, INC, 1301 Oak St, Ste 310, 64106. SAN 321-8333. Tel: 816-221-2221. FAX: 816-221-6607. E-mail: info@jcll.org. Web Site: www.jcll.org. *Dir,* Kelly Lynn Anders; *Law Librn,* Dale Magariel; Staff 4 (MLS 2, Non-MLS 2)
Founded 1871
Library Holdings: Bk Titles 27,800; Bk Vols 46,914; Per Subs 31
Subject Interests: Fed law, Jury instructions, Legal res, Regulations, State law, Statute law
Automation Activity & Vendor Info: (Acquisitions) LibraryWorld, Inc; (Cataloging) LibraryWorld, Inc; (OPAC) LibraryWorld, Inc; (Serials) LibraryWorld, Inc
Function: Res libr
Publications: Brochure; Pathfinder
Open Mon-Fri 8:30-5
Restriction: Not a lending libr, Staff & mem only, Sub libr

C KANSAS CITY ART INSTITUTE LIBRARY*, Jannes Library, 4538 Warwick Blvd, 64111. (Mail add: 4415 Warwick Blvd, 64111-1874), SAN 309-037X. Tel: 816-802-3390. FAX: 816-802-3338. E-mail: library@kcai.edu. Web Site: kcai.edu/campus-life/jannes-library. *Dir,* M J Poehler; E-mail: mpoehler@kcai.edu; *Cat, Digital Serv Librn,* Lora Farrell; Tel: 816-802-3394, E-mail: lfarrell@kcai.edu; Staff 4 (MLS 2, Non-MLS 2)
Founded 1885. Enrl 660; Fac 115; Highest Degree: Bachelor
Library Holdings: e-books 231,365; Electronic Media & Resources 9,082; Bk Titles 28,918; Bk Vols 35,503; Per Subs 70; Videos 427
Special Collections: Artists books
Subject Interests: Fine arts
Automation Activity & Vendor Info: (Cataloging) Innovative Interfaces, Inc; (Circulation) Innovative Interfaces, Inc; (Course Reserve) Innovative Interfaces, Inc; (ILL) OCLC WorldShare Interlibrary Loan; (OPAC) Innovative Interfaces, Inc; (Serials) Innovative Interfaces, Inc
Wireless access
Partic in MOBIUS
Open Mon-Thurs 8am-11pm, Fri 8-5, Sat 1-4, Sun 1-11
Restriction: Badge access after hrs, Open to pub for ref only, Open to students, fac & staff

P THE KANSAS CITY PUBLIC LIBRARY, Central Library, 14 W Tenth St, 64105. SAN 349-2990. Tel: 816-701-3400. Circulation Tel: 816-701-3449. Interlibrary Loan Service Tel: 816-701-3463. Reference Tel: 816-701-3433. FAX: 816-701-3401. TDD: 816-701-3403. Web Site: www.kclibrary.org/library-locations/central-library. *Dir, Human Res,* Karen Weitzel; Tel: 816-701-3517, E-mail: karenweitzel@kclibrary.org; *Dir, Operations,* Teresa Bolton; Tel: 816-701-3747, E-mail: teresabolton@kclibrary.org; *Dir, Teen Serv,* Crystal Faris; Tel: 816-701-3513, E-mail: crystalfaris@kclibrary.org; *Dep Dir, Libr Serv,* Joel Jones; Tel: 816-701-3504, E-mail: joeljones@kclibrary.org; *Dep Dir, Pub Affairs,* Carrie Coogan; Tel: 816-701-3514, E-mail: carriecoogan@kclibrary.org; *Asst Dir,* Debbie Siragusa; Tel: 816-701-3515, E-mail: debbiesiragusa@kclibrary.org; Staff 249 (MLS 41, Non-MLS 208)
Founded 1873. Pop 194,122; Circ 2,348,408
Library Holdings: Audiobooks 11,559; CDs 12,702; DVDs 22,972; Bk Vols 390,997; Videos 7,633
Special Collections: African American History Coll (John F Ramos); Civil War Coll; Kansas City Latino Heritage Coll; Missouri Valley History & Genealogy; Western Migration & Trails Coll. Oral History; State Document Depository; US Document Depository
Automation Activity & Vendor Info: (Circulation) SirsiDynix
Wireless access
Publications: Annual Report; Comprehensive Annual Financial Report
Partic in Kansas City Library Service Program; Mid-America Library Alliance; OCLC Online Computer Library Center, Inc
Open Mon & Thurs-Sat 10-5, Tues & Wed 10-9
Friends of the Library Group
Branches: 9
LUCILE H BLUFORD BRANCH, 3050 Prospect Ave, 64128, SAN 349-3202. Tel: 816-701-3482. FAX: 816-701-3492. *Dir, Br Operations,* Cindy Hohl; Tel: 816-701-3482, E-mail: cindyhohl@kclibrary.org
Library Holdings: Audiobooks 959; CDs 1,237; DVDs 1,431; Bk Vols 25,685; Videos 210
Open Mon-Fri 10-7, Sat 10-5
NORTH-EAST, 6000 Wilson Rd, 64123, SAN 349-3148. Tel: 816-701-3485. FAX: 816-701-3495. *Br Mgr,* Amanda Barnhart; Tel: 816-701-3589, E-mail: amandabarnhart@kclibrary.org
Library Holdings: Audiobooks 1,818; CDs 2,343; DVDs 2,938; Bk Vols 48,107; Videos 749
Open Mon-Fri 10-6, Sat 10-5
PLAZA, 4801 Main St, 64112, SAN 349-3172. Tel: 816-701-3481. FAX: 816-701-3491. *Br Dir,* April Roy; Tel: 816-701-3690, E-mail: aprilroy@kclibrary.org; Staff 6.5 (MLS 6.5)
Library Holdings: Audiobooks 4,906; CDs 8,110; DVDs 8,826; Bk Vols 122,474; Videos 62
Open Mon-Wed 10-9, Thurs-Sat 10-6
IRENE H RUIZ BIBLIOTECA DE LAS AMERICAS, 2017 W Pennway St, 64108, SAN 349-3350. Tel: 816-701-3487. FAX: 816-701-3497. *Br Mgr,* Amy Morris; Tel: 816-701-3565, E-mail: amymorris@kclibrary.org
Library Holdings: Audiobooks 561; CDs 1,504; DVDs 2,922; Bk Vols 10,451; Videos 474
SOUTHEAST, 6242 Swope Pkwy, 64130, SAN 349-3261. Tel: 816-701-3484. FAX: 816-701-3494. *Br Mgr,* Monica Jedine; Tel: 816-701-3582, E-mail: monicajedine@kclibrary.org
Library Holdings: Audiobooks 1,254; CDs 1,857; DVDs 1,990; Bk Vols 43,590; Videos 243
Open Mon-Sat 10-5
SUGAR CREEK BRANCH, 102 S Sterling Ave, Sugar Creek, 64054. Tel: 816-701-3489. FAX: 816-701-3499. *Br Mgr,* Ruth Stephens; Tel: 816-701-3583, E-mail: ruthstephens@kclibrary.org
Library Holdings: Audiobooks 577; CDs 1,229; DVDs 1,644; Bk Vols 10,356; Videos 187
TRAILS WEST, 11401 E 23rd St, Independence, 64052, SAN 349-3326. Tel: 816-701-3483. FAX: 816-701-3493. *Mgr,* Ruth Stephens
Library Holdings: Audiobooks 3,042; CDs 4,264; DVDs 5,350; Bk Vols 56,296; Videos 1,641
Open Mon-Fri 10-7, Sat 10-5
WALDO COMMUNITY, 201 E 75th St, 64114, SAN 349-3296. Tel: 816-701-3486. FAX: 816-701-3496. *Br Mgr,* Jim Poplau; Tel: 816-701-3586, E-mail: jimpoplau@kclibrary.org
Library Holdings: Audiobooks 2,034; CDs 4,919; DVDs 3,638; Bk Vols 44,868; Videos 634
Open Mon-Fri 10-7, Sat 10-5
WESTPORT, 118 Westport Rd, 64111, SAN 349-3385. Tel: 816-701-3488. FAX: 816-701-3498. *Br Mgr,* MaShonda Harris; Tel: 816-701-3588, E-mail: mashondaharris@kclibrary.org
Library Holdings: Audiobooks 2,677; CDs 4,341; DVDs 4,660; Bk Vols 36,197; Videos 2,293
Open Mon-Fri 10-5

CM KANSAS CITY UNIVERSITY OF MEDICINE & BIOSCIENCES D'ANGELO*, 1750 Independence Ave, 64106-1453. SAN 309-0388. Tel: 816-654-7260. Interlibrary Loan Service Tel: 816-654-7266. Reference Tel: 816-654-7264. Automation Services Tel: 816-654-7262. Toll Free Tel: 800-234-4847. FAX: 816-654-7261. E-mail: library@kcumb.edu. Web Site: www.kcumb.edu/library. *Dir,* Marilyn J DeGeus; E-mail: mdegeus@kcumb.edu; *Ref Librn,* Lori A Fitterling; E-mail: lfitterling@kcumb.edu; *Tech Serv Librn,* Jessica R Berry; Tel: 816-654-7265, E-mail: jberry@kcumb.edu; *ILL Coordr,* Laurie A Sims; E-mail: lsims@kcumb.edu; *Access Serv, Spec Coll Coordr,* Robyn R Oro; Tel: 816-654-7267, E-mail: roro@kcumb.edu; Staff 6 (MLS 4, Non-MLS 2)
Founded 1916. Enrl 985; Fac 176; Highest Degree: Doctorate
Jul 2015-Jun 2016. Mats Exp $800,881, Books $9,000, Per/Ser (Incl. Access Fees) $477,594, AV Equip $120, AV Mat $700, Electronic Ref Mat (Incl. Access Fees) $312,967, Presv $500
Library Holdings: Audiobooks 50; AV Mats 18; CDs 2,208; DVDs 120; e-books 1,443; e-journals 1,674; Electronic Media & Resources 33; Bk Titles 7,588; Bk Vols 8,280; Per Subs 511; Videos 10
Special Collections: Osteopathic History & Medicine (Osteopathic Coll), bk, flm, slides, tapes
Subject Interests: Med
Automation Activity & Vendor Info: (Cataloging) Innovative Interfaces, Inc - Sierra; (Circulation) Innovative Interfaces, Inc - Sierra; (Course Reserve) Innovative Interfaces, Inc - Sierra; (ILL) Innovative Interfaces, Inc - Sierra; (OPAC) Innovative Interfaces, Inc - Sierra; (Serials) Innovative Interfaces, Inc - Sierra
Wireless access

Partic in Health Sciences Library Network of Kansas City, Inc; Mid-America Library Alliance; MOBIUS; National Network of Libraries of Medicine Region 3
Open Mon-Fri 7am-11:30pm, Sat & Sun 9am-11:30pm
Restriction: Borrowing privileges limited to fac & registered students, Borrowing requests are handled by ILL

METROPOLITAN COMMUNITY COLLEGE

J BLUE RIVER LIBRARY*, 20301 E 78 Hwy, Independence, 64057, SAN 377-8258. Tel: 816-604-6642. Interlibrary Loan Service Tel: 816-604-6650. FAX: 816-220-6751. Web Site: brlibrary.mcckc.edu. *Libr Dir,* Jared Rinck; Tel: 816-604-6740, E-mail: jared.rinck@mcckc.edu; *Libr Spec,* Amy Campbell; E-mail: amy.campbell@mcckc.edu; Staff 2 (MLS 1, Non-MLS 1)
Founded 1990. Enrl 2,691; Fac 29; Highest Degree: Associate
Library Holdings: Bk Vols 16,191; Per Subs 85
Automation Activity & Vendor Info: (Circulation) Innovative Interfaces, Inc; (OPAC) Innovative Interfaces, Inc
Special Services for the Deaf - Assistive tech
Special Services for the Blind - Assistive/Adapted tech devices, equip & products
Open Mon-Thurs (Fall-Spring) 8am-9pm, Fri 8-4:30, Sat 9-1

J LONGVIEW CAMPUS LIBRARY*, 500 SW Longview Rd, Lee's Summit, 64081-2105, SAN 309-0787. Tel: 816-604-2080. Interlibrary Loan Service Tel: 816-604-2243. Reference Tel: 816-604-2268. Administration Tel: 816-604-2266. FAX: 816-604-2087. Web Site: www.mcckc.edu. *Libr Mgr,* Judy Rice; Tel: 816-604-2278, E-mail: judy.rice@mcckc.edu; *Librn,* Candice Baldwin; E-mail: candice.baldwin@mcckc.edu; *Ref Librn,* Marty Miller; Tel: 816-604-2654, E-mail: marty.miller@mcckc.edu; *ILL,* Sandy Findley; E-mail: sandy.findley@mcckc.edu; Staff 9.5 (MLS 4, Non-MLS 5.5)
Founded 1969. Enrl 8,000; Fac 86; Highest Degree: Associate
Library Holdings: Audiobooks 10; AV Mats 840; e-books 10,098; Microforms 4,200; Bk Titles 37,781; Bk Vols 44,411; Per Subs 158
Automation Activity & Vendor Info: (Acquisitions) Innovative Interfaces, Inc - Millennium; (Cataloging) Innovative Interfaces, Inc - Millennium; (Circulation) Innovative Interfaces, Inc - Millennium; (Course Reserve) Innovative Interfaces, Inc - Millennium; (ILL) Innovative Interfaces, Inc - Millennium; (Media Booking) Innovative Interfaces, Inc - Millennium; (OPAC) Innovative Interfaces, Inc - Millennium; (Serials) Innovative Interfaces, Inc - Millennium
Open Mon-Thurs (Fall-Spring) 8-8, Fri 8-4, Sat 10-2; Mon-Thurs (Summer) 8-7, Fri 8-4

J MAPLE WOODS LIBRARY, 2601 NE Barry Rd, 64156, SAN 309-0434. Tel: 816-604-3080. Interlibrary Loan Service Tel: 816-604-3083. Reference Tel: 816-604-3042. FAX: 816-437-3082. Web Site: mcckc.edu/library/maple-woods. *Dir,* Linda Carter; *Ref Librn,* Erin Niederberger; Staff 7.9 (MLS 4.4, Non-MLS 3.5)
Founded 1969. Enrl 4,191; Fac 49; Highest Degree: Associate
Jul 2019-Jun 2020. Mats Exp $125,393. Sal $356,853 (Prof $262,914)
Library Holdings: e-books 267,707; Bk Titles 26,120; Bk Vols 302,256; Per Subs 68; Videos 375
Special Collections: Veterinary Medicine Coll, bks & per
Automation Activity & Vendor Info: (Acquisitions) Innovative Interfaces, Inc; (Circulation) Innovative Interfaces, Inc; (Course Reserve) Innovative Interfaces, Inc; (ILL) Innovative Interfaces, Inc; (OPAC) Innovative Interfaces, Inc; (Serials) Innovative Interfaces, Inc
Partic in Mid-America Library Alliance; MOBIUS
Open Mon-Thurs 8-7, Fri 8-3:30

PENN VALLEY LIBRARY*, 3201 SW Trafficway, 64111-2764, SAN 309-0574. Tel: 816-604-4080. Web Site: mcckc.edu. *Libr Mgr,* Jackie Roberts; E-mail: jackie.roberts@mcckc.edu; *Librn,* Michael Korklan; Tel: 816-759-4090, E-mail: michael.korklan@mcckc.edu; *Tech Serv Coordr,* Ted Ostaszewski; Tel: 816-759-4095, E-mail: ted.ostaszewski@mcckc.edu; Staff 7 (MLS 7)
Founded 1969. Enrl 4,500; Fac 110
Library Holdings: e-books 6,296; Bk Vols 84,252; Per Subs 184
Automation Activity & Vendor Info: (Acquisitions) Innovative Interfaces, Inc; (Cataloging) Innovative Interfaces, Inc; (Circulation) Innovative Interfaces, Inc; (Course Reserve) Innovative Interfaces, Inc; (ILL) Innovative Interfaces, Inc; (Media Booking) Innovative Interfaces, Inc; (OPAC) Innovative Interfaces, Inc; (Serials) Innovative Interfaces, Inc
Partic in Amigos Library Services, Inc; Missouri Research & Education Network
Publications: Bookmarks; New Books List; Student Guides
Open Mon-Thurs 8-8, Fri 8-3:30

R MIDWESTERN BAPTIST THEOLOGICAL SEMINARY LIBRARY*, 5001 N Oak Trafficway, 64118-4620. SAN 309-0477. Tel: 816-414-3729. Reference Tel: 816-414-3728. Administration Tel: 816-414-3730. E-mail: circ@mbts.edu. Web Site: libguides.mbts.edu, www.mbts.edu/current-students/#library. *Dir,* Kenette Harder; E-mail: kharder@mbts.edu; *Asst Dir,* Matt Millsap; E-mail: mmillsap@mbt.edu; *Cat, Head, Ref,* Judy Howie; E-mail: jhowie@mbts.edu; *Electronic Res Librn,* Chris Vaughn; E-mail: cvaughn@mbts.edu; Staff 4 (MLS 3, Non-MLS 1)
Founded 1951. Highest Degree: Doctorate
Library Holdings: AV Mats 4,196; CDs 623; DVDs 419; e-books 114,684; e-journals 223; Microforms 3,100; Music Scores 1,118; Bk Vols 102,493; Per Subs 371; Videos 865
Special Collections: Baptist Denominational Coll; Charles Haddon Spurgeon Personal Library; Rawlings Interfaith Evangelism Coll
Subject Interests: Biblical studies
Automation Activity & Vendor Info: (Acquisitions) Innovative Interfaces, Inc; (Cataloging) Innovative Interfaces, Inc; (Circulation) Innovative Interfaces, Inc; (ILL) Innovative Interfaces, Inc; (OPAC) Innovative Interfaces, Inc; (Serials) Innovative Interfaces, Inc
Wireless access
Function: ILL available
Partic in MOBIUS
Open Mon-Fri 7:30-6, Sat 9:30-3
Restriction: Staff use only, Students only

GL MISSOURI COURT OF APPEALS LIBRARY*, Western District, 1300 Oak St, 64106-2970. SAN 309-0485. Tel: 816-889-3600. FAX: 816-889-3668. Web Site: www.courts.mo.gov. *Librn,* Janine Estrada-Lopez
Founded 1885
Library Holdings: Bk Titles 31,190; Bk Vols 32,500; Per Subs 150
Restriction: Staff use only

G NATIONAL ARCHIVES & RECORDS ADMINISTRATION*, National Archives at Kansas City, 400 W Pershing Rd, 64108. SAN 309-0515. Tel: 816-268-8000. FAX: 816-268-8038. E-mail: kansascity.archives@nara.gov. Web Site: www.archives.gov/kansas-city. *Archival Operations, Dir,* Lori Cox-Paul; Tel: 816-268-8017, E-mail: lori.cox-paul@nara.gov
Founded 1969
Library Holdings: Bk Titles 35,112; Bk Vols 37,696; Per Subs 41
Special Collections: Archival records of Federal agencies & courts in Iowa, Kansas, Missouri & Nebraska; Federal Government Field Office Records of Federal Agencies within the states of Iowa, Kansas, Minnesota, Missouri, Nebraska, North Dakota, & South Dakota, 1850-1950; Federal Population Censuses, 1790-1930, microfilm; Records of Indian Territory, Kansas, Nebraska & Dakota Territories, 1854-89
Subject Interests: Econ, Ethnology, Frontier, Genealogy, Hist, Law, Natural res, Polit sci, Pub admin
Function: Photocopying/Printing
Open Mon-Fri 8-4
Restriction: Ref only to non-staff

S NATIONAL ASSOCIATION OF INSURANCE COMMISSIONERS, Research Library, 1100 Walnut St, Ste 1500, 64106. SAN 329-8345. Tel: 816-783-8250. E-mail: reslib@naic.org. Web Site: naic.soutronglobal.net/portal/public/en-gb/search/simplesearch. *Libr Mgr,* Eryn Campbell; Tel: 816-783-8253, E-mail: eecampbell@naic.org; Staff 2 (MLS 1, Non-MLS 1)
Subject Interests: Ins regulation
Automation Activity & Vendor Info: (Acquisitions) Softlink America; (Cataloging) Softlink America; (Circulation) Softlink America; (OPAC) Softlink America; (Serials) Softlink America
Function: Archival coll, For res purposes, Res libr

R NAZARENE THEOLOGICAL SEMINARY*, William Broadhurst Library, 1700 E Meyer Blvd, 64131. SAN 309-0531. Tel: 816-268-5471. Toll Free Tel: 800-831-3011. FAX: 816-268-5475. E-mail: library@nts.edu. Web Site: www.nts.edu/library. *Dir, Libr Serv,* Debra Bradshaw; Tel: 816-268-5472, E-mail: dlbradshaw@nts.edu; *Asst Librn, ILL, Asst Librn, Tech Support,* Alexandra Duenow; Tel: 816-268-5474, E-mail: aduenow@nts.edu; *Asst Librn, Electronic Serv, Ser,* Sarah Jones; Tel: 816-268-5473, E-mail: sjones@nts.edu; Staff 10 (MLS 2, Non-MLS 8)
Founded 1945. Enrl 396; Fac 18; Highest Degree: Doctorate
Library Holdings: Bk Vols 140,588; Per Subs 526
Special Collections: Carl Bangs Arminianism Coll; History of the Holiness Movement; Methodistica-Wesleyana Coll
Wireless access
Partic in Amigos Library Services, Inc; Kansas City Library Service Program; Mid-America Library Alliance; OCLC Online Computer Library Center, Inc; Proquest Dialog
Open Mon & Tues 8am-8:30pm, Wed-Fri 8-5, Sat 12-4; Mon-Thurs (Summer) 8-6

S NELSON-ATKINS MUSEUM OF ART*, Spencer Art Reference Library, Bloch Bldg, 2nd Flr, 4525 Oak St, 64111-1873. SAN 309-054X. Tel: 816-751-1216. FAX: 816-751-0498. Web Site: www.nelson-atkins.org/library. *Pub Serv Librn, Sr Librn,* Amelia Nelson; Tel: 816-751-1215, E-mail: anelson@nelson-atkins.org; *Archivist,* Tara Laver; Tel: 816-751-1354; Staff 14 (MLS 5, Non-MLS 9)
Founded 1933

Library Holdings: AV Mats 300; Microforms 100; Bk Titles 140,000; Bk Vols 200,000; Per Subs 500; Spec Interest Per Sub 45,800
Special Collections: Auction Catalogs; Decorative Arts, per; Oriental Art; Prints & Drawings (The John H Bender Library)
Subject Interests: Art hist, Asian art, Decorative art, European art
Automation Activity & Vendor Info: (Acquisitions) Ex Libris Group; (Cataloging) Ex Libris Group; (Circulation) Ex Libris Group; (Course Reserve) Ex Libris Group; (ILL) OCLC; (OPAC) Ex Libris Group; (Serials) Ex Libris Group
Wireless access
Function: Archival coll, Ref & res
Partic in Amigos Library Services, Inc; OCLC Research Library Partnership
Open Wed 10-5, Thurs & Fri 10-6, Sat & Sun 10-4
Restriction: Non-circulating

L POLSINELLI*, Law Library, 900 W 48th St Pl, 64112. SAN 323-8911. Tel: 816-753-1000. FAX: 816-753-1536. Web Site: www.polsinelli.com. *Mgr, Libr Serv,* Betty Sola; E-mail: bsola@polsinelli.com; Staff 6 (MLS 3, Non-MLS 3)
Library Holdings: Bk Titles 4,000; Bk Vols 15,000; Per Subs 150
Automation Activity & Vendor Info: (Acquisitions) Inmagic, Inc.; (Serials) Inmagic, Inc.
Wireless access
Restriction: Staff use only

M RESEARCH MEDICAL CENTER*, Carl R Ferris Medical Library, 2316 E Meyer Blvd, 64132-1199. SAN 309-0582. Tel: 816-276-4309. FAX: 816-276-3106. Web Site: hcamidwest.com. *Med Librn,* Kitty Serling; E-mail: kitty.serling@hcamidwest.com. Subject Specialists: *Consumer health, Nursing,* Kitty Serling; Staff 1 (MLS 1)
Founded 1963
Library Holdings: e-journals 2,000; Bk Titles 2,000; Per Subs 730
Subject Interests: Nursing
Wireless access
Function: Archival coll, Doc delivery serv, For res purposes, Health sci info serv, ILL available, Internet access, Orientations, Photocopying/Printing, Prof lending libr, Ref serv available, Res libr, Wheelchair accessible
Partic in Health Sciences Library Network of Kansas City, Inc; National Network of Libraries of Medicine Region 3
Open Mon-Fri 8-4:30
Restriction: Access for corporate affiliates, Authorized patrons, Circulates for staff only, Co libr, In-house use for visitors, Pub use on premises, Restricted borrowing privileges, Use of others with permission of librn

C ROCKHURST UNIVERSITY, Greenlease Library, 1100 Rockhurst Rd, 64110-2561. SAN 309-0590. Tel: 816-501-4142. Reference Tel: 816-501-4749. FAX: 816-501-4666. E-mail: library@rockhurst.edu. Web Site: www.rockhurst.edu/library. *Libr Dir,* Laura Horne-Popp; Tel: 816-501-4655, E-mail: laura.hornepopp@rockhurst.edu; *Access & Learning Serv Librn,* Robert Powers; Tel: 816-501-4121, E-mail: robert.powers@rockhurst.edu; *Content Serv Librn,* Catherine Price; Tel: 816-501-4143, E-mail: catherine.price@rockhurst.edu; *E-Resources Librn,* Kassie McLaughlin; Tel: 816-501-4161, E-mail: kassie.mclaughlin@rockhurst.edu; *Liaison Librn,* Position Currently Open; *Metadata Librn,* Julianne Newberry; Tel: 816-501-4131, E-mail: julianne.newberry@rockhurst.edu; *Research, Learning & Assessment Librn,* Tyler Johnson; E-mail: tyler.johnson@rockhurst.edu; *Access Serv Asst,* David Reeves; E-mail: david.reeves@rockhurst.edu; *Research Services Asst,* Jamie Banister; E-mail: jamie.banister@rockhurst.edu; *Research Services Asst,* Ben Stevenson; E-mail: benjamin.stevenson@rockhurst.edu; Staff 9.5 (MLS 7, Non-MLS 2.5)
Founded 1917. Enrl 2,435; Fac 238; Highest Degree: Doctorate
Special Collections: US Document Depository
Automation Activity & Vendor Info: (Acquisitions) Innovative Interfaces, Inc - Sierra; (Cataloging) Innovative Interfaces, Inc - Sierra; (Circulation) Innovative Interfaces, Inc - Sierra; (Course Reserve) Innovative Interfaces, Inc - Sierra; (ILL) OCLC; (OPAC) Innovative Interfaces, Inc - Sierra; (Serials) Innovative Interfaces, Inc - Sierra
Wireless access
Function: 24/7 Electronic res, 24/7 Online cat, Archival coll, Computers for patron use, Electronic databases & coll, Equip loans & repairs, Govt ref serv, ILL available, Internet access, Online cat, Online info literacy tutorials on the web & in blackboard, Online ref, Photocopying/Printing, Ref & res, Ref serv available, Study rm, VHS videos, Wheelchair accessible
Partic in Association of Jesuit Colleges & Universities; Missouri Research & Education Network; MOBIUS
Special Services for the Deaf - TDD equip
Open Mon-Thurs 8am-10pm, Fri 8-4:30, Sat Noon-4:30, Sun Noon-10
Restriction: Circ limited, In-house use for visitors, Limited access for the pub, Open to students, fac, staff & alumni, Private libr, Pub use on premises, Restricted borrowing privileges, Restricted loan policy, Restricted pub use
Friends of the Library Group

M SAINT LUKE'S HOSPITAL*, Health Sciences Library, 4401 Wornall Rd, 64111. SAN 309-0612. Tel: 816-502-8710. E-mail: library@saint-lukes.org. Web Site: www.saintlukeskc.org/locations/saint-lukes-hospital-kansas-city. *Dir, Libr Serv,* Beth Edson; Tel: 816-502-8704
Founded 1948
Library Holdings: e-journals 4,746; Bk Titles 2,416; Bk Vols 2,611; Per Subs 21
Wireless access
Function: ILL available
Publications: Newsletter
Open Mon-Fri 8:30-5
Restriction: Circulates for staff only

L SHOOK, HARDY & BACON*, Law Library, 2555 Grand Blvd, 3rd Flr, 64108-2613. SAN 309-0647. Tel: 816-474-6550. FAX: 816-421-5547. *Dir,* Jeff Sewell; E-mail: jsewell@shb.com; *Cat,* Brian Adkins; *Electronic Res,* Janet McKinney; *Info/Res Spec,* Leslie Gasper; *Ref (Info Servs),* Valerie Vogt
Library Holdings: Bk Vols 40,000; Per Subs 900
Wireless access
Partic in Health Sciences Library Network of Kansas City, Inc

S STATE HISTORICAL SOCIETY OF MISSOURI*, Research Center-Kansas City, 302 Newcomb Hall, 5123 Holmes St, 64110-2499. SAN 329-2754. Tel: 816-235-1543. E-mail: kansascity@shsmo.org. Web Site: shsmo.org/about/kansascity/. *Assoc Dir,* Lucinda Adams; Tel: 816-235-1544, E-mail: adamslu@shsmo.org; Staff 4.5 (MLS 4, Non-MLS 0.5)
Library Holdings: Bk Titles 1,500; Bk Vols 1,684
Special Collections: Oral History
Subject Interests: Kansas City area hist, Mo hist
Function: 24/7 Electronic res, 24/7 Online cat, Archival coll, Electronic databases & coll, For res purposes
Restriction: Non-circulating coll

GL US COURT LIBRARY - EIGHTH CIRCUIT, Kansas City Branch, 9440 Charles Evans Whittaker US Courthouse, 400 E Ninth St, 64106. SAN 309-0663. Tel: 816-512-5790. FAX: 816-512-5799. E-mail: library8th@ca8.uscourts.gov. Web Site: www.lb8.uscourts.gov. *Circuit Librn,* Eric W Brust; Staff 2 (MLS 1, Non-MLS 1)
Library Holdings: Bk Titles 40,355
Special Collections: Historic Missouri Legal Materials
Open Mon-Fri 9-5:30

C UNIVERSITY OF MISSOURI-KANSAS CITY LIBRARIES*, University Libraries, 800 E 51st St, 64110. (Mail add: 5100 Rockhill Rd, 64110-2446), SAN 349-3687. Tel: 816-235-1531. Interlibrary Loan Service Tel: 816-235-1586. FAX: 816-333-5584. Interlibrary Loan Service FAX: 816-235-5531. Web Site: library.umkc.edu. *Dean, Univ Libr,* Bonnie Postlethwaite; *Assoc Dean, Coll,* Stuart Hinds; Tel: 816-235-1532, E-mail: hindss@umkc.edu; *Assoc Dean, Pub Serv,* Cynthia Thompson; Tel: 816-235-1511, E-mail: thompsoncym@umkc.edu; *Dir of Advan,* Nicole Leone; Tel: 816-235-5828; *Dir, Coll & Access Mgt,* Brenda Dingley; Tel: 816-235-2226, E-mail: dingleyb@umkc.edu; *Asst Dir, Admin Serv,* Jennifer Eigsti; Tel: 816-235-1533, E-mail: eigstij@umkc.edu; *Head, Circ Serv,* Mary Anderson; Tel: 816-235-1678, E-mail: andersonme@umkc.edu; *Head, Coll Develop,* Steve Alleman; Tel: 816-235-1580, E-mail: allemans@umkc.edu; *Acq, Head, Electronic Res,* Mariah Harvey; Tel: 816-235-6461, E-mail: harveym@umkc.edu; *Head, Metadata Serv, Presv,* Wendy Sistrunk; Tel: 816-235-5291, E-mail: sistrunkw@umkc.edu; *Head, Resource Sharing,* Jen Salvo-Eaton; Tel: 816-235-2225, E-mail: salvoeatonj@umkc.edu; *Head Music Libr, Media Serv,* Nara Newcomer; Tel: 816-235-1679, E-mail: newcomern@umkc.edu; *Head, Teaching & Learning Serv,* Mardi Mahaffy; Tel: 816-235-1537, E-mail: mahaffym@umkc.edu
Founded 1933. Highest Degree: Doctorate
Special Collections: American Sheet Music Coll; Americana (Snyder Coll) bks, ms; English & American; English & American Literature (Baker Coll); Holocaust Studies; Midwest Center for American Music (Amy Beach & Paul Creston Coll); Sound Archives. State Document Depository; US Document Depository
Automation Activity & Vendor Info: (Acquisitions) Innovative Interfaces, Inc; (Cataloging) Innovative Interfaces, Inc; (Circulation) Innovative Interfaces, Inc; (Course Reserve) Innovative Interfaces, Inc; (ILL) Innovative Interfaces, Inc; (Media Booking) Innovative Interfaces, Inc; (OPAC) Innovative Interfaces, Inc; (Serials) Innovative Interfaces, Inc
Wireless access
Function: 24/7 Electronic res, 24/7 Online cat, E-Reserves, Electronic databases & coll, ILL available, Online cat
Partic in Center for Research Libraries; Merlin; Mo Res Consortium of Libraries; MOBIUS; OCLC Online Computer Library Center, Inc

Open Mon-Thurs 7:30am-11pm, Fri 7:30-6, Sat 11-6, Sun 1-11
Restriction: Borrowing privileges limited to fac & registered students, Borrowing requests are handled by ILL, Circ limited
Friends of the Library Group
Departmental Libraries:
DENTAL LIBRARY, 650 E 25th St, 64108, SAN 349-3806. Tel: 816-235-2030. FAX: 816-235-6540. *Dental Librn,* Marie Thompson; Tel: 816-235-2063, E-mail: thompsonmarie@umkc.edu
Founded 1916. Highest Degree: Doctorate
Special Collections: History of Dentistry Coll
Partic in Health Sciences Library Network of Kansas City, Inc
Open Mon-Thurs 7:30am-9pm, Fri 7:30-6, Sat & Sun 12-5
Restriction: Authorized patrons, Borrowing privileges limited to fac & registered students, Borrowing requests are handled by ILL, Circ limited, External users must contact libr, ID required to use computers (Ltd hrs)
HEALTH SCIENCES LIBRARY, 2411 Holmes St, 64108, SAN 349-3717. Tel: 816-235-1880. FAX: 816-235-6570. *Head, Libr Operations,* Brent Sweany; Tel: 816-235-2062, E-mail: sweanyb@umkc.edu; *Sr Med Librn,* Kristy Steigerwalt; Tel: 816-235-1876, E-mail: steigerwaltk@umkc.edu; *Clinical Med Librn,* Nora Franco; Tel: 816-235-1884, E-mail: franconl@umkc.edu
Founded 1965. Highest Degree: Doctorate
Subject Interests: Clinical med, Nursing
Partic in Midcontinental Regional Med Libr Program; National Network of Libraries of Medicine Region 3; Proquest Dialog; SDC Search Serv
Open Mon-Thurs 8am-10pm, Fri 8-5:30, Sat 9-5, Sun 2-10

CL UNIVERSITY OF MISSOURI-KANSAS CITY LIBRARIES*, Leon E Bloch Law Library, 500 E 52nd St, 64110. SAN 349-3741. Tel: 816-235-1650. FAX: 816-235-5274. E-mail: umkclawlibrary@umkc.edu. Web Site: law.umkc.edu/library. *Libr Dir,* Paul D Callister; E-mail: callisterp@umkc.edu; *Assoc Dir,* Ayyoub Ajmi; E-mail: ajmia@umkc.edu; Staff 7 (MLS 6, Non-MLS 1)
Founded 1895. Highest Degree: Doctorate
Library Holdings: Bk Vols 202,809; Per Subs 1,820
Special Collections: Urban Law Coll. US Document Depository
Subject Interests: Law
Automation Activity & Vendor Info: (Acquisitions) Innovative Interfaces, Inc - Millennium; (Cataloging) Innovative Interfaces, Inc - Millennium; (Circulation) Innovative Interfaces, Inc - Millennium; (ILL) OCLC; (OPAC) Innovative Interfaces, Inc
Wireless access
Publications: Acquisitions List
Partic in Merlin; Mid-America Law Library Consortium; MOBIUS

CR WESTERN BAPTIST BIBLE COLLEGE MEMORIAL LIBRARY*, 2119 Tracy Ave, 64108. SAN 309-0701. Tel: 816-842-4195. FAX: 816-842-3050. E-mail: wbbible@sbcglobal.net. Web Site: www.wbbckc.org. *Dean,* Dr Sandra Jones; Staff 1 (MLS 1)
Library Holdings: Bk Titles 14,601; Bk Vols 15,089; Per Subs 39; Talking Bks 67; Videos 52
Subject Interests: African-Am hist, Archaeology, Bible hist, Drama, English lit, European hist, Music, Philos, Psychol, Relig, Relig hist educ, Sociol, Theol, World hist
Open Mon-Fri 10-3

KENNETT

P DUNKLIN COUNTY LIBRARY*, 209 N Main, 63857. SAN 349-3865. Tel: 573-888-2261, 573-888-3561. FAX: 573-888-6393. Web Site: dunklin-co.lib.mo.us. *Dir,* JoNell Minton; E-mail: jonell@dunklin-co.lib.mo.us; Staff 1 (MLS 1)
Founded 1947. Pop 32,000; Circ 316,825
Library Holdings: Bk Vols 180,000; Per Subs 150; Talking Bks 1,000; Videos 1,000
Special Collections: Charles H Baker Military Coll. Oral History
Subject Interests: Genealogy
Automation Activity & Vendor Info: (Acquisitions) Innovative Interfaces, Inc; (Cataloging) TLC (The Library Corporation); (Circulation) Innovative Interfaces, Inc; (ILL) OCLC
Open Mon-Sat 8:30-5:30
Friends of the Library Group
Branches: 7
CAMPBELL BRANCH, 404 W Grand, Campbell, 63933, SAN 349-392X. Tel: 573-246-2112. *Librn,* Sara Shepherd
Library Holdings: Bk Titles 19,000
Open Mon-Fri 1-5
CARDWELL BRANCH, Main St, Cardwell, 63829, SAN 349-3954. Tel: 573-654-3366. *Librn,* Janice Cureton
Open Mon, Wed & Thurs 12-5, Tues 9-2, Fri 1-5
CLARKTON BRANCH, 113 S Main St, Clarkton, 63837, SAN 349-3989. Tel: 573-448-3803. *Librn,* Margaret Pilsing
Library Holdings: Bk Titles 15,000
Open Mon-Fri 1-5
HOLCOMB BRANCH, W Main St, Holcomb, 63852, SAN 349-4012. Tel: 573-792-3268. *Librn,* Nancy Hardin
Library Holdings: Bk Titles 7,000
Open Mon, Wed & Fri 1-5
HORNERSVILLE BRANCH, 502 School St, Hornersville, 63855, SAN 349-4047. Tel: 573-737-2728. *Librn,* Glenda Scott
Library Holdings: Bk Titles 10,000
Open Mon, Wed & Fri 1-5
MALDEN BRANCH, 1203 Stokelan, Malden, 63863, SAN 349-4071. Tel: 573-276-3674. *Librn,* Sarah Snider
Library Holdings: Bk Titles 32,000
Open Mon-Sat 8:30-5:30
SENATH BRANCH, 108 N Main St, Senath, 63876, SAN 349-4101. Tel: 573-738-2363. *Librn,* Terri Long
Library Holdings: Bk Titles 20,000
Open Mon-Fri 1-5

R FIRST BAPTIST CHURCH LIBRARY*, 300 Saint Francis St, 63857. SAN 309-0728. Tel: 573-888-4689. FAX: 573-888-4680. E-mail: fbc@fbckennett.com. Web Site: www.fbckennett.com/ministries/library. *Librn,* Sara LaGore; Staff 2 (Non-MLS 2)
Founded 1948
Library Holdings: Bk Vols 3,450; Per Subs 27; Videos 10
Subject Interests: Bible characters, Child missionaries, Devotions, Holidays
Open Wed 5:45pm-6:15pm, Sun 9-9:30 & 5-6

KIRKSVILLE

CM A T STILL UNIVERSITY*, Missouri Campus Library, Kirksville Campus, 800 W Jefferson St, 63501. SAN 309-0736. Tel: 660-626-2345. Interlibrary Loan Service Tel: 660-626-2030. Reference Tel: 660-626-2336. FAX: 660-626-2333. E-mail: libmo@atsu.edu. Web Site: www.atsu.edu/library. *Campus Libr Dir, Distance Support Librn, Liaison Librn,* Susan E Swogger; Tel: 660-626-2340, E-mail: susanswogger@atsu.edu; *Liaison Librn,* Laura Lipke; E-mail: lauralipke@atsu.edu; *Tech Serv Librn,* Mary Sims; Tel: 660-626-2635, E-mail: msims@atsu.edu; *Pub Serv Mgr,* Debra Loguda-Summers; Tel: 660-626-2645, E-mail: dsummers@atsu.edu; *Circ,* Carlo Caroli; E-mail: ccaroli@atsu.edu; *ILL Serv,* Leisa Walter; Tel: 660-626-2030, E-mail: lwalter@atsu.edu. Subject Specialists: *Dentistry, Health sci, Pub health,* Susan E Swogger; *Med,* Laura Lipke; *3D printing, Hist of med,* Debra Loguda-Summers; Staff 6 (MLS 3, Non-MLS 3)
Founded 1897. Enrl 3,293; Fac 165; Highest Degree: Doctorate
Library Holdings: DVDs 192; e-books 32,000; e-journals 12,000; Bk Titles 25,250; Bk Vols 74,098; Per Subs 627
Special Collections: Osteopathic Medical Literature
Subject Interests: Dentistry, Educ, Health bus, Osteopathic med, Pub health
Automation Activity & Vendor Info: (Acquisitions) Innovative Interfaces, Inc; (Cataloging) Innovative Interfaces, Inc; (Circulation) Innovative Interfaces, Inc; (Discovery) EBSCO Discovery Service; (ILL) OCLC; (OPAC) Innovative Interfaces, Inc
Wireless access
Function: Computers for patron use
Partic in MOBIUS; OCLC Online Computer Library Center, Inc
Open Mon-Fri 7am-Midnight, Sat & Sun 9am-Midnight
Restriction: Borrowing requests are handled by ILL, Open to students, fac, staff & alumni

P ADAIR COUNTY PUBLIC LIBRARY*, One Library Lane, 63501. SAN 309-0752. Tel: 660-665-6038. FAX: 660-627-0028. E-mail: acpl@adairco.org. Web Site: youseemore.com/adaircpl. *Libr Dir,* Jami Livingston; *Ch,* Mr Cory Landon; Staff 4 (MLS 1, Non-MLS 3)
Founded 1986. Pop 25,572; Circ 207,407
Jan 2013-Dec 2013 Income $422,285, State $12,804, County $347,931, Locally Generated Income $44,507, Other $17,043. Mats Exp $73,205, Books $56,140, AV Mat $17,065. Sal $205,689
Library Holdings: Audiobooks 1,805; CDs 1,192; DVDs 2,565; e-books 21,095; Large Print Bks 1,453; Microforms 400; Bk Titles 58,014; Bk Vols 60,108; Per Subs 70
Special Collections: Adair County
Subject Interests: Mo hist
Automation Activity & Vendor Info: (Cataloging) TLC (The Library Corporation); (Circulation) TLC (The Library Corporation); (OPAC) TLC (The Library Corporation)
Wireless access
Partic in Grand Rivers Libr Conference
Open Tues & Wed 9-8, Thurs & Fri 9-6, Sat 10-4
Friends of the Library Group

C TRUMAN STATE UNIVERSITY*, Pickler Memorial Library, 100 E Normal, 63501-4211. SAN 309-0744. Tel: 660-785-4038. Circulation Tel: 660-785-4533. Interlibrary Loan Service Tel: 660-785-4534. Reference Tel: 660-785-4051. FAX: 660-785-4538. Web Site: library.truman.edu. *Assoc*

Dean, Res & Instruction, Janet Romine; Tel: 660-785-4051, E-mail: jiromine@truman.edu; *Assoc Dean, Tech Serv & Libr Syst,* Stephen Wynn; Tel: 660-785-4535, E-mail: swynn@truman.edu; *Assoc Dean, Spec Coll,* Amanda Langendoerfer; Tel: 660-785-7546, E-mail: alang@truman.edu; *Head, Access Serv, Head, Circ Serv,* Gayla McHenry; Tel: 660-785-4037, E-mail: gmchenry@truman.edu; *Head, Curric Mat(s) Ctr, Head, Media Libr,* Sharon Hackney; Tel: 660-785-7366, E-mail: shackney@truman.edu; *Res & Instruction Librn,* Daisy Rearick; Tel: 660-785-4048, E-mail: drearick@truman.edu; Staff 13 (MLS 12, Non-MLS 1)
Founded 1867. Enrl 5,615; Fac 357; Highest Degree: Master. Sal $1,008,564 (Prof $544,606)
Library Holdings: Audiobooks 1,618; AV Mats 52,534; CDs 6,360; DVDs 11,904; e-books 83,887; Music Scores 7,585; Bk Vols 505,210; Videos 12,864
Special Collections: Eugenics Coll (Harry Laughlin), ms; Glenn Frank Coll, ms; Lincoln (Fred & Ethel Schwengel Coll), artifacts & bks; Missouriana (Violette McClure Coll); Rare Books Coll. US Document Depository
Subject Interests: Bus, Health, Liberal arts, Sciences
Wireless access
Partic in Amigos Library Services, Inc; MOBIUS
Special Services for the Blind - Scanner for conversion & translation of mats
Open Mon-Thurs 7:30am-1am, Fri 7:30am-9pm, Sat 11-6, Sun 1-1

KIRKWOOD

P KIRKWOOD PUBLIC LIBRARY*, 140 E Jefferson Ave, 63122. SAN 309-0760. Tel: 314-821-5770. FAX: 314-822-3755. E-mail: circulation@kirkwoodpubliclibrary.org. Web Site: kirkwoodpubliclibrary.org. *Dir,* Sarah Erwin; Tel: 314-821-5770, Ext 1016, E-mail: serwin@kirkwoodpubliclibrary.org; *Dir, Adult Serv, Dir, Commun Serv,* Emma DeLooze-Klein; Tel: 314-821-5770, Ext 1025; *Dir of Libr Operations,* Lisa Henry; Tel: 314-821-5770, Ext 1013, E-mail: lhenry@kirkwoodpubliclibrary.org; *Dir, Prog & Youth Serv,* Rachel Johannigmeier; Tel: 314-821-5770, Ext 1011; *Dir, Tech Serv,* Nick O'Neal; Tel: 314-821-5770, Ext 1027, E-mail: noneal@kirkwoodpubliclibrary.org; Staff 14 (MLS 5, Non-MLS 9)
Founded 1924. Pop 27,156; Circ 316,526
Library Holdings: AV Mats 18,062; Bk Vols 81,000; Per Subs 342
Special Collections: Kirkwood History Coll; Nonprofit Resources Special Coll
Automation Activity & Vendor Info: (Acquisitions) Innovative Interfaces, Inc; (Cataloging) Innovative Interfaces, Inc; (Circulation) Innovative Interfaces, Inc; (ILL) OCLC FirstSearch; (OPAC) Innovative Interfaces, Inc; (Serials) Innovative Interfaces, Inc
Wireless access
Function: Adult bk club, Audiobks via web, Bk club(s), Bks on CD, Chess club, Children's prog, Computer training, Computers for patron use, Electronic databases & coll, Free DVD rentals, Home delivery & serv to seniorr ctr & nursing homes, Homebound delivery serv, ILL available, Internet access, Magnifiers for reading, Music CDs, Online cat, Outreach serv, OverDrive digital audio bks, Passport agency, Photocopying/Printing, Preschool outreach, Preschool reading prog, Prog for adults, Prog for children & young adult, Ref serv available, Scanner, Senior outreach, Story hour, Summer reading prog, Tax forms, Teen prog, Telephone ref, Wheelchair accessible, Writing prog
Partic in Municipal Library Consortium; Saint Louis Regional Library Network
Open Mon-Thurs 9-9, Fri & Sat 9-5, Sun 1-5
Friends of the Library Group

LA PLATA

P LA PLATA PUBLIC LIBRARY, 103 E Moore St, 63549. SAN 309-0779. Tel: 660-332-4945. FAX: 660-332-4945. E-mail: laplatamolibrary@gmail.com. Web Site: laplatalibrary.wixsite.com/mysite. *Librn,* Breann Turner
Founded 1939. Pop 1,486
Library Holdings: Per Subs 3
Special Collections: Doc Savage Coll
Subject Interests: Genealogy, Local hist
Wireless access
Function: Adult bk club, Bks on CD, Children's prog, Computers for patron use, Free DVD rentals, Genealogy discussion group, Govt ref serv, Home delivery & serv to seniorr ctr & nursing homes, Homebound delivery serv, ILL available, Magazines, Meeting rooms, Microfiche/film & reading machines, Movies, Prog for children & young adult, Res performed for a fee, Scanner, Senior outreach, Wheelchair accessible
Open Tues & Thurs 9-1, Wed & Fri 2-6

LAMAR

P BARTON COUNTY LIBRARY*, Mary K Finley Library & Administrative Offices, 300 W Tenth St, 64759. Tel: 417-682-5355. FAX: 417-682-3206. Web Site: www.bclib.info. *Dir,* Carol Darrow; E-mail: cdarrow@bclib.info
Founded 1932. Pop 12,541
Automation Activity & Vendor Info: (Cataloging) TLC (The Library Corporation); (Circulation) TLC (The Library Corporation); (ILL) OCLC; (OPAC) TLC (The Library Corporation)
Wireless access
Function: Accelerated reader prog, After school storytime, AV serv, Bks on cassette, Bks on CD, Children's prog, Computer training, Computers for patron use, Electronic databases & coll, Free DVD rentals, ILL available, Magnifiers for reading, Mail & tel request accepted, Photocopying/Printing, Prog for children & young adult, Ref serv available, Scanner, Senior computer classes, Story hour, Summer reading prog, Teen prog, VHS videos, Wheelchair accessible
Open Mon, Tues, Thurs & Fri 10-5:30, Wed 10-7, Sat 10-2
Branches: 2
HAPPY & MARY CURLESS LIBRARY - LIBERAL BRANCH, 201 S Main St, Liberal, 64762-9315. Tel: 417-843-5791. FAX: 417-843-5910. *Br Mgr,* Connie King
Open Mon-Wed & Fri 11-5, Thurs 1-6, Sat 10-Noon
HYLTON LIBRARY - GOLDEN CITY BRANCH, 607 Main St, Golden City, 64748-8211. Tel: 417-537-4991. FAX: 417-537-4249. *Br Mgr,* Carol Pyle
Open Tues, Wed & Fri 11-5, Thurs 1-5:30, Sat 10-1

LAWSON

G MISSOURI DEPARTMENT OF NATURAL RESOURCES*, Watkins Woolen Mill State Historic Site Archives, 26600 Park Rd N, 64062. SAN 327-8808. Tel: 816-580-3387. FAX: 816-580-3782. Web Site: mostateparks.com/park/watkins-woolen-mill-state-historic-site. *Adminr,* Michael Beckett; E-mail: michael.beckett@dnr.mo.gov; Staff 1 (Non-MLS 1)
Founded 1964
Library Holdings: Bk Titles 690; Bk Vols 750; Per Subs 1,000
Special Collections: 19th Century Agriculture, 19th Century Woolen Textile Manufacturing; 19th Century Gristmilling; Watkins Family Letters 1820's-1940's; Watkins Mill Association Records 1959-1990
Function: Archival coll
Restriction: Open by appt only
Friends of the Library Group

LEBANON

P LEBANON-LACLEDE COUNTY LIBRARY*, 915 S Jefferson Ave, 65536. SAN 349-4136. Tel: 417-532-2148. Administration Tel: 417-532-4212. FAX: 417-532-7424. Reference E-mail: askref@lebanon-laclede.lib.mo.us. Web Site: www.lebanon-laclede.lib.mo.us. *Dir,* Cathy Dame; E-mail: cdame@lebanon-laclede.lib.mo.us; *Circ Mgr,* Sonja Brown; E-mail: sbrown@lebanon-laclede.lib.mo.us; Staff 9 (MLS 3, Non-MLS 6)
Pop 89,281; Circ 357,389
Library Holdings: Large Print Bks 215; Bk Titles 91,864; Bk Vols 93,410; Per Subs 119; Talking Bks 338; Videos 490
Subject Interests: Genealogy, Local hist
Automation Activity & Vendor Info: (Cataloging) Innovative Interfaces, Inc; (Circulation) Innovative Interfaces, Inc
Partic in Mo Libr Film Coop; SW Mo Libr Network
Open Mon-Thurs 8-8, Fri & Sat 8-5
Friends of the Library Group
Bookmobiles: 2

LIBERTY

S CLAY COUNTY ARCHIVES & HISTORICAL LIBRARY*, 210 E Franklin St, 64068. (Mail add: PO Box 99, 64069-0099), SAN 323-5238. Tel: 816-781-3611. E-mail: info@claycountyarchives.org. Web Site: www.claycountyarchives.org/. *Pres,* Stuart Elliott; Staff 1 (MLS 1)
Library Holdings: Bk Titles 1,200; Bk Vols 1,340; Per Subs 15
Subject Interests: Family hist, Genealogy
Wireless access
Open Mon-Wed 9-4
Restriction: Not a lending libr
Friends of the Library Group

C WILLIAM JEWELL COLLEGE*, Charles F Curry Library, 500 College Hill, 64068. SAN 309-0825. Tel: 816-415-7620. Information Services Tel: 816-415-7610. FAX: 816-415-5021. Web Site: www.jewell.edu/curry-library. *Dir, Libr Serv,* Rebecca Hamlett; Tel: 816-415-7613, E-mail: hamlettr@william.jewell.edu; *Archives, Tech Serv Librn,* Abigal Broadbent; E-mail: broadbenta@william.jewell.edu; *Libr Support Spec,* Chris Vaughn; Tel: 816-415-5062, E-mail: vaughnc@william.jewell.edu; Staff 5 (MLS 4, Non-MLS 1)

Founded 1849. Enrl 1,170; Fac 95; Highest Degree: Bachelor
Library Holdings: Bk Vols 258,352; Per Subs 613
Special Collections: Baptist History (Partee Center for Baptist Historical Studies); Children"s Literature (Lois Lenski Coll), bk, drawing; Missouri History (Missouri Coll); Puritan Literature (Charles Haddon Spurgeon Coll); Western Americana (Settle Coll), bk, photo, slides. US Document Depository
Automation Activity & Vendor Info: (Acquisitions) Innovative Interfaces, Inc; (Cataloging) Innovative Interfaces, Inc; (Circulation) Innovative Interfaces, Inc; (Course Reserve) Docutek; (ILL) Innovative Interfaces, Inc; (OPAC) Innovative Interfaces, Inc; (Serials) Innovative Interfaces, Inc
Wireless access
Partic in Amigos Library Services, Inc; Mid-America Library Alliance; MOBIUS; OCLC Online Computer Library Center, Inc
Open Mon-Fri 8-4; Mon-Fri (Summer) 8-6:30

LILBOURN

P LILBOURN MEMORIAL LIBRARY, 210 E Lewis Ave, 63862. (Mail add: PO Box 282, 63862), SAN 309-0833. Tel: 573-688-2622. E-mail: lilbournlibrary@outlook.com. *Librn,* Betty Allred; Staff 1 (MLS 1)
Founded 1936. Pop 1,297; Circ 7,854
Library Holdings: Large Print Bks 44; Bk Titles 11,542; Bk Vols 11,900; Per Subs 30; Talking Bks 200; Videos 390
Open Tues-Fri 1-5

LOCKWOOD

P LOCKWOOD PUBLIC LIBRARY*, 721 Main St, 65682. (Mail add: PO Box 286, 65682-0286), SAN 309-0841. Tel: 417-232-4204. E-mail: librarian@lockwoodmo.com. *Head Librn,* Phyllis Hagerman; Staff 2 (MLS 1, Non-MLS 1)
Pop 1,050; Circ 14,500
Library Holdings: Audiobooks 175; AV Mats 12; DVDs 285; Bk Titles 11,866; Bk Vols 11,890; Videos 280
Special Collections: Dade County History; Lockwood Newspapers from 1890-1980
Automation Activity & Vendor Info: (Acquisitions) Book Systems; (Cataloging) Book Systems; (Circulation) Book Systems; (OPAC) Book Systems
Wireless access
Open Mon & Thurs 9-5, Tues 9-6, Wed & Sat 9-Noon

LOUISIANA

P LOUISIANA PUBLIC LIBRARY*, 121 N Third St, 63353. SAN 309-085X. Tel: 573-754-4491. FAX: 573-754-4208. *Librn,* Holly Mabry; E-mail: hollymabry4@aol.com; Staff 1 (MLS 1)
Founded 1904. Pop 3,954; Circ 17,323
Library Holdings: Bk Vols 29,000; Per Subs 30; Talking Bks 328; Videos 281
Automation Activity & Vendor Info: (Cataloging) Book Systems; (Circulation) Book Systems
Open Mon & Wed-Fri 10:30-5:30, Tues 12-8, Sat 9:30-1:30
Friends of the Library Group

MACON

P MACON PUBLIC LIBRARY*, 210 N Rutherford St, 63552. SAN 309-0868. Tel: 660-385-3314. FAX: 660-385-6610. E-mail: maconlibrary@yahoo.com. Web Site: www.cityofmacon-mo.com/living-in-macon/library, www.maconlibrary.org. *Libr Dir,* Sharon Brown; E-mail: director@maconlibrary.org
Founded 1912. Pop 5,680; Circ 34,538
Library Holdings: Bk Vols 34,000; Per Subs 75
Subject Interests: Genealogy, Macon County
Automation Activity & Vendor Info: (Cataloging) SirsiDynix; (Circulation) SirsiDynix
Wireless access
Partic in NE Mo Libr Network
Open Mon, Tues, Thurs & Fri 10-8, Wed 10-5, Sat 10-3
Friends of the Library Group

MAPLEWOOD

P MAPLEWOOD PUBLIC LIBRARY*, 7550 Lohmeyer Ave, 63143. SAN 309-0876. Tel: 314-781-7323. FAX: 314-781-2191. E-mail: info@maplewoodpubliclibrary.com. Web Site: www.maplewood.lib.mo.us. *Dir,* Terrence Donnelly; Staff 7 (MLS 1, Non-MLS 6)
Founded 1935. Pop 9,228; Circ 124,602
Library Holdings: AV Mats 1,509; Bk Titles 31,907; Bk Vols 47,521; Per Subs 118
Subject Interests: Local hist
Automation Activity & Vendor Info: (Cataloging) SirsiDynix; (Circulation) SirsiDynix; (ILL) SirsiDynix; (OPAC) SirsiDynix; (Serials) SirsiDynix
Function: Homebound delivery serv, ILL available, Photocopying/Printing, Prog for children & young adult, Ref serv available, Summer reading prog, Telephone ref, Wheelchair accessible
Publications: Booked Up (Newsletter)
Partic in Municipal Library Consortium; Saint Louis Regional Library Network
Open Mon-Thurs 9-9, Fri 9-7, Sat 9-5

MARBLE HILL

P BOLLINGER COUNTY LIBRARY*, 207 Mayfield Dr, 63764. SAN 309-0884. Tel: 573-238-2713. FAX: 573-238-2879. E-mail: bollynger@yahoo.com. Web Site: www.bocolib.com. *Dir,* Eva Dunn; *Asst Dir,* Joyce James
Founded 1947. Pop 12,024
Library Holdings: Bk Vols 90,000; Per Subs 50
Subject Interests: Agr, Feminism, Genealogy, Handicraft, Hist, Natural sci
Automation Activity & Vendor Info: (Cataloging) Mandarin Library Automation; (Circulation) Mandarin Library Automation
Wireless access
Open Tues-Fri 10-6
Friends of the Library Group

MARCELINE

P MARCELINE CARNEGIE LIBRARY*, 119 E California Ave, 64658. SAN 309-0892. Tel: 660-376-3223. FAX: 660-376-3577. E-mail: marcelinelibrary@hotmail.com. Web Site: marcelinelibrary.org. *Libr Dir,* Joyce Clapp; Staff 2 (MLS 1, Non-MLS 1)
Founded 1920. Pop 2,781; Circ 7,096
Library Holdings: Bk Titles 15,000; Bk Vols 15,181; Per Subs 32; Talking Bks 50; Videos 110
Special Collections: Walt Disney Coll
Open Mon-Fri 9-5, Sat 9-12
Friends of the Library Group

MARSHALL

P MARSHALL PUBLIC LIBRARY*, 214 N Lafayette, 65340. SAN 370-6680. Tel: 660-886-3391. FAX: 660-886-2492. Web Site: marshallmolibrary.org. *Libr Dir,* Annmarie Gibson; Tel: 660-886-3391, Ext 3, E-mail: agibson@marshallmolibrary.org; *Asst Dir,* Mary Bays; Tel: 660-886-3391, Ext 4, E-mail: mary@marshallmolibrary.org; Staff 10 (MLS 1, Non-MLS 9)
Founded 1990. Pop 12,711; Circ 83,941
Library Holdings: Bks on Deafness & Sign Lang 35; Bk Titles 37,500; Per Subs 98
Special Collections: Saline County Genealogy & Local History Coll
Automation Activity & Vendor Info: (Cataloging) Evergreen; (Circulation) Evergreen
Wireless access
Open Mon-Thurs 9-7, Fri 9-5, Sat 10-5, Sun 1-5
Friends of the Library Group

C MURRELL LIBRARY & COMMONS*, Missouri Valley College, 500 E College St, 65340. SAN 309-0906. Tel: 660-831-4180, 660-831-4181. Reference Tel: 660-831-4187. Administration Tel: 660-831-4123. Information Services Tel: 660-831-4005. FAX: 660-831-4068. E-mail: library@moval.edu. Web Site: www.moval.edu/library. *Libr Dir, Prof,* Dr Bryan M Carson; Tel: 660-831-4123, E-mail: carsonb@moval.edu; *Asst Prof, Librn,* Mary C Slater; Tel: 660-831-4187, E-mail: slaterm@moval.edu; *Cataloger, Learning Commons Coord,* Sarah Haug; Tel: 660-831-4005, E-mail: haugs@moval.edu; *Circ Serv Coordr,* Bathsheba Love; Tel: 660-831-4180, E-mail: loveb@moval.edu; *Coordr, Pub Relations & Outreach, Mkt,* Margot Mirabal; Tel: 660-831-4181, E-mail: mirabalm@moval.edu; *Evening Libr Asst,* Susan Hughes; Tel: 660-831-4180, E-mail: hughess@moval.edu; *Evening Libr Asst,* Cheyanna Weaver; Tel: 660-831-4013, E-mail: weaverc2@moval.edu; *Libr Asst,* Jenny Hare; Tel: 660-831-4013, E-mail: harej@moval.edu; *Per Asst,* Abigail Edwards; Tel: 660-831-4180 (evenings), E-mail: edwardsa@moval.edu. Subject Specialists: *Graphic design, Mkt,* Cheyanna Weaver; *Hist, Libr sci,* Abigail Edwards; Staff 7 (MLS 2, Non-MLS 5)
Founded 1889. Enrl 1,437; Fac 59; Highest Degree: Master
Jul 2019-Jun 2020 Income $188,350, Parent Institution $188,350. Mats Exp $149,637, Books $17,464, Per/Ser (Incl. Access Fees) $30,000, AV Mat $2,000, Electronic Ref Mat (Incl. Access Fees) $100,173. Sal $228,049 (Prof $89,000)
Library Holdings: Audiobooks 145; AV Mats 3,528; CDs 235; DVDs 3,293; e-books 54,559; e-journals 225; Electronic Media & Resources 14,251; Microforms 29,423; Bk Titles 57,817; Bk Vols 67; Per Subs 410; Videos 2
Special Collections: Cumberland Presbyterian Church Archives; Missouri History (John Ashford Coll
Subject Interests: Bus, Educ, Hist, Missouriana, Psychol, US
Automation Activity & Vendor Info: (Acquisitions) Innovative Interfaces, Inc; (Cataloging) Innovative Interfaces, Inc; (Circulation) Innovative

Interfaces, Inc; (Course Reserve) Innovative Interfaces, Inc; (ILL) OCLC; (Media Booking) Innovative Interfaces, Inc; (OPAC) Innovative Interfaces, Inc; (Serials) Innovative Interfaces, Inc
Wireless access
Function: 24/7 Electronic res, 24/7 Online cat, Adult bk club, Archival coll, Art exhibits, Audio & video playback equip for onsite use, Audiobks via web, AV serv, Bk club(s), Bks on CD, Children's prog, Computer training, Computers for patron use, E-Readers, Electronic databases & coll, Equip loans & repairs, For res purposes, Free DVD rentals, Health sci info serv, Holiday prog, Homework prog, ILL available, Instruction & testing, Internet access, Life-long learning prog for all ages, Magazines, Mango lang, Microfiche/film & reading machines, Movies, Music CDs, Online cat, Online info literacy tutorials on the web & in blackboard, Orientations, Outreach serv, OverDrive digital audio bks, Photocopying/Printing, Preschool reading prog, Printer for laptops & handheld devices, Prog for adults, Ref & res, Ref serv available, Res assist avail, Scanner, Spoken cassettes & CDs, Wheelchair accessible
Publications: Acquisition List; Annual Report; Library Guide
Partic in Amigos Library Services, Inc; MOBIUS
Open Mon-Thurs 7:30am-Midnight, Fri 7:30-4, Sun 1-Midnight
Restriction: Borrowing privileges limited to fac & registered students, Circ privileges for students & alumni only, Circulates for staff only, Fee for pub use, In-house use for visitors, Non-circulating of rare bks, Non-circulating to the pub, Open to students, fac & staff

MARYVILLE

P MARYVILLE PUBLIC LIBRARY*, 509 N Main St, 64468. SAN 309-0914. Tel: 660-582-5281. FAX: 660-582-2411. Administration E-mail: admin@maryvillepubliclibrary.org. Web Site: www.maryvillepubliclibrary.lib.mo.us. *Dir,* Stephanie Patterson; *Asst Dir,* Wilma Henggeler; *YA Librn,* Kelsey Noble; Staff 4 (MLS 1, Non-MLS 3)
Founded 1904. Pop 10,557; Circ 77,587
Library Holdings: Bk Vols 55,000; Per Subs 45; Talking Bks 1,114; Videos 375
Automation Activity & Vendor Info: (Cataloging) Mandarin Library Automation; (Circulation) Mandarin Library Automation
Wireless access
Open Mon-Fri 9-6, Sat 9-3
Friends of the Library Group

S NODAWAY COUNTY HISTORICAL SOCIETY, Mary H Jackson Research Center, 110 N Walnut St, 64468. (Mail add: PO Box 324, 64468-0324), SAN 373-2363. Tel: 660-582-8176. FAX: 660-562-3377. E-mail: nodawaycountyhistoricalsociety@embarqmail.com, nodawaymuseumresearch@embarqmail.com. Web Site: nodawaymuseumresea.wixsite.com/nchs. *Coll Coordr,* Margaret Kelley; *Curator,* Tom Carneal
Founded 1944
Library Holdings: Bk Titles 8,900; Bk Vols 12,000
Special Collections: Oral History
Subject Interests: Genealogy, Local hist
Open Tues-Fri (March-Dec) 1-4

C NORTHWEST MISSOURI STATE UNIVERSITY*, B D Owens Library, 800 University Dr, 64468-6001. SAN 349-4284. Tel: 660-562-1192. Interlibrary Loan Service Tel: 660-562-1193. Reference Tel: 660-562-1629. FAX: 660-562-1049. E-mail: library@nwmissouri.edu. Web Site: www.nwmissouri.edu/library/index.html. *Access Serv, Asst Dir,* Terra Feick; E-mail: terraf@nwmissouri.edu; *Asst Libr Dir, Res Serv,* Frank Baudino; E-mail: baudino@nwmissouri.edu; *Asst Libr Dir, Coll Develop,* Brandy Brady; E-mail: bbrady@nwmissouri.edu; *Research Librn,* Carolyn Johnson; E-mail: carolyn@nwmissouri.edu; *Research Librn,* Lori Mardis; E-mail: lmardis@nwmissouri.edu; Staff 10 (MLS 6, Non-MLS 4)
Founded 1905. Enrl 7,076; Fac 275; Highest Degree: Master
Jul 2018-Jun 2019 Income (Main Library Only) $2,179,219. Mats Exp $736,055. Sal $913,443 (Prof $532,099)
Library Holdings: AV Mats 7,517; e-books 48,895; e-journals 25,375; Bk Titles 215,890; Bk Vols 259,651; Per Subs 459
Special Collections: Missouri History & Government (Missouriana), multi-media. State Document Depository; US Document Depository
Automation Activity & Vendor Info: (Acquisitions) Innovative Interfaces, Inc; (Cataloging) Innovative Interfaces, Inc; (Circulation) Innovative Interfaces, Inc; (Course Reserve) Innovative Interfaces, Inc; (ILL) Innovative Interfaces, Inc; (Media Booking) Innovative Interfaces, Inc; (OPAC) Innovative Interfaces, Inc; (Serials) Innovative Interfaces, Inc
Wireless access
Partic in Amigos Library Services, Inc; MOBIUS; OCLC Online Computer Library Center, Inc
Open Mon-Thurs 7:30am-11:45pm, Fri 7:30-4:45, Sat 9-4:45, Sun 1-11:45
Restriction: In-house use for visitors, Restricted pub use

Departmental Libraries:
HORACE MANN LIBRARY, Brown Hall 121, 800 University Dr, 64468, SAN 349-4314. Tel: 660-562-1271. FAX: 660-562-1992. *Librn,* Mary Shields; E-mail: mshield@nwmissouri.edu; Staff 3 (MLS 1, Non-MLS 2)
Special Collections: Elementary Curricula
Subject Interests: Children's lit
Automation Activity & Vendor Info: (Cataloging) Innovative Interfaces, Inc - Millennium; (Circulation) Innovative Interfaces, Inc - Millennium
Open Mon-Fri (Aug-May) 7:45-4

MEMPHIS

P SCOTLAND COUNTY MEMORIAL LIBRARY*, 306 W Madison, 63555. SAN 309-0922. Tel: 660-465-7042. FAX: 660-465-7334. E-mail: scmlib@gmail.com. Web Site: scotland.lib.mo.us. *Dir,* Melissa Schuster; Staff 3.2 (Non-MLS 3.2)
Founded 1958. Pop 4,843; Circ 38,081
Jan 2018-Dec 2018 Income $155,849, State $4,963, County $133,283, Other $17,603. Mats Exp $158,297, Books $17,053, Per/Ser (Incl. Access Fees) $764, AV Mat $7,012. Sal $75,534
Library Holdings: Audiobooks 990; CDs 241; DVDs 1,608; Large Print Bks 2,160; Microforms 364; Bk Vols 25,445; Per Subs 35; Talking Bks 1,152
Subject Interests: Consumer health, Genealogy, Local hist
Automation Activity & Vendor Info: (Cataloging) Book Systems; (Circulation) Book Systems; (ILL) OCLC; (OPAC) Book Systems
Wireless access
Function: 24/7 Electronic res, 24/7 Online cat, Bks on CD, Computers for patron use, Free DVD rentals, ILL available, Internet access, Magazines, Microfiche/film & reading machines, Online cat, OverDrive digital audio bks, Summer reading prog
Publications: Ella Ewing, Missouri Giantess
Partic in OCLC Online Computer Library Center, Inc
Special Services for the Deaf - Closed caption videos
Special Services for the Blind - Bks on CD
Open Mon, Wed & Fri 9-5:30, Tues & Thurs 9-7, Sat 9-1

MEXICO

P MEXICO-AUDRAIN COUNTY LIBRARY DISTRICT*, 305 W Jackson St, 65265. SAN 349-4349. Tel: 573-581-4939. FAX: 573-581-7510. E-mail: mexicoaudrain@netscape.net. Web Site: mexico-audrain.lib.mo.us. *Libr Dir,* Christal Bruner; *Asst Dir,* Mare Prosso; Staff 22 (MLS 3, Non-MLS 19)
Founded 1912
Library Holdings: Bk Titles 86,000; Bk Vols 150,000; Per Subs 154
Special Collections: Audrain County Genealogy
Automation Activity & Vendor Info: (Cataloging) TLC (The Library Corporation); (Circulation) TLC (The Library Corporation)
Wireless access
Function: 24/7 Electronic res, 24/7 Online cat, Art exhibits, Audiobks via web, Bks on CD, Children's prog, Computer training, Free DVD rentals, ILL available, Internet access, Magazines, Magnifiers for reading, Mail & tel request accepted, Meeting rooms, Microfiche/film & reading machines, Movies, Online cat, OverDrive digital audio bks, Photocopying/Printing, Preschool outreach, Prog for adults, Prog for children & young adult, Story hour, Study rm, Summer reading prog, Tax forms, Telephone ref, Wheelchair accessible
Partic in Amigos Library Services, Inc; Missouri Research & Education Network
Open Mon & Wed 9-8, Tues, Thurs & Fri 9-5:30, Sat 9-1
Friends of the Library Group
Branches: 4
FARBER BRANCH, 113 W Front St, Farber, 63345, SAN 349-4373. Tel: 573-249-2012. FAX: 573-249-2012. E-mail: frbrlibrary0@gmail.com. *Br Mgr,* Vernelle Hull; Staff 1 (Non-MLS 1)
Library Holdings: CDs 20; DVDs 35; Large Print Bks 200; Bk Titles 8,919; Bk Vols 9,636; Per Subs 21; Talking Bks 25; Videos 30
Open Mon & Tues 1:30-5, Wed 9-12 & 1:30-5, Sat 9-12
Friends of the Library Group
ED FRENCH MEMORIAL, 204 E Second St, Laddonia, 63352, SAN 349-4403. Tel: 573-373-2393. FAX: 573-373-2393. E-mail: 2laddonialibrary@gmail.com. *Br Mgr,* Pam Mozee; Staff 1 (Non-MLS 1)
Open Mon & Thurs 9-1, Tues & Wed 1-5, Sat 9-Noon
Friends of the Library Group
MARTINSBURG BRANCH, 201 E Washington St, Martinsburg, 65264, SAN 370-002X. Tel: 573-492-6254. FAX: 573-492-6254. *Br Mgr,* Kim Boyle
Open Tues-Thurs 1-5, Fri & Sat 9-Noon
Friends of the Library Group
VANDALIA BRANCH, 312 S Main St, Vandalia, 63382, SAN 349-4438. Tel: 573-594-6600. FAX: 573-594-3590. *Br Mgr,* Crystal McCurdy; Staff 3 (Non-MLS 3)
Special Collections: Vandalia History Coll

Open Mon-Fri 9-5:30, Sat 9-1
Friends of the Library Group

MILAN

P SULLIVAN COUNTY PUBLIC LIBRARY, 109 E Second St, 63556. SAN 309-0930. Tel: 660-265-3911. FAX: 660-265-3911. E-mail: sullivanco63556@gmail.com. Web Site: sullivan.mogenweb.org/sclibrary.html. *Dir,* Pamela Branson; Staff 5 (MLS 1, Non-MLS 4)
Founded 1972
Library Holdings: Bk Titles 21,113; Bk Vols 23,165; Per Subs 18; Talking Bks 200; Videos 150
Automation Activity & Vendor Info: (Cataloging) Book Systems; (Circulation) Book Systems; (Course Reserve) Book Systems; (ILL) Book Systems; (OPAC) Book Systems
Open Tues, Wed & Fri 9-5, Thurs 9-8, Sat 9-3

MOBERLY

CR CENTRAL CHRISTIAN COLLEGE OF THE BIBLE LIBRARY, Reese Resource Center Library, 911 E Urbandale Dr, 65270. SAN 321-1819. Tel: 660-263-3933. Administration Tel: 660-263-3900. Toll Free Tel: 888-263-3900. FAX: 660-263-3533. Administration FAX: 660-263-3936. E-mail: library@cccb.edu. Web Site: cccb.edu/media-resources/library. *Dir,* Patricia A Agee; E-mail: pattyagee@cccb.edu; *Asst Librn,* Crystal Applegarth; E-mail: crystalapplegarth@cccb.edu; *Cataloger, Libr Asst,* Teresa Ammon; Tel: 660-263-2933, E-mail: teresaammon@cccb.edu; Staff 2.7 (MLS 1.7, Non-MLS 1)
Founded 1957. Enrl 200; Fac 19; Highest Degree: Master
Library Holdings: Audiobooks 50; AV Mats 9,866; Bks on Deafness & Sign Lang 24; DVDs 300; e-books 260,774; e-journals 120; Electronic Media & Resources 3; Large Print Bks 10; Bk Titles 77,700; Bk Vols 92,362; Per Subs 190; Spec Interest Per Sub 180; Talking Bks 100; Videos 250
Special Collections: Preaching Charts of John Hall & Edsil Dale; Rosetta Stone Language Program; Walter S Coble Mission File Coll
Subject Interests: Bible, Communication, Counseling, Missions, Theol
Automation Activity & Vendor Info: (Cataloging) Follett Software; (Circulation) Follett Software; (Course Reserve) Follett Software; (ILL) OCLC WorldShare Interlibrary Loan; (OPAC) Follett Software
Wireless access
Function: Computers for patron use, ILL available, Photocopying/Printing, Ref & res, Scanner, VHS videos, Wheelchair accessible
Partic in Amigos Library Services, Inc; Christian Library Consortium
Open Mon-Thurs 7:30am-11:30pm, Fri 7:30-5, Sat 1-7 (Winter); Mon-Fri 7:30-4:30 (Summer)
Restriction: Open to pub for ref & circ; with some limitations, Open to students, fac, staff & alumni, Photo ID required for access

P LITTLE DIXIE REGIONAL LIBRARIES*, 111 N Fourth St, 65270-1577. SAN 349-4462. Tel: 660-263-4426. FAX: 660-263-4024. Web Site: www.little-dixie.lib.mo.us. *Dir, Librn,* Rachael Grime; E-mail: director@little-dixie.lib.mo.us; Staff 3 (MLS 1, Non-MLS 2)
Founded 1966. Pop 34,451; Circ 20,500
Library Holdings: Audiobooks 3,772; DVDs 4,800; Large Print Bks 12,000; Microforms 1,000; Bk Titles 122,059; Bk Vols 181,343; Per Subs 214; Videos 5,480
Special Collections: Missouri Civil War Coll; Randolph County Genealogy
Automation Activity & Vendor Info: (Cataloging) Book Systems; (Circulation) Book Systems; (Media Booking) Book Systems; (OPAC) Book Systems; (Serials) Book Systems
Wireless access
Function: AV serv, Games & aids for people with disabilities, Home delivery & serv to seniorr ctr & nursing homes, Homebound delivery serv, ILL available, Large print keyboards, Magnifiers for reading, Outside serv via phone, mail, e-mail & web, Photocopying/Printing, Prog for adults, Prog for children & young adult, Ref serv available, Spoken cassettes & CDs, Summer reading prog, Telephone ref, VHS videos, Wheelchair accessible, Workshops
Special Services for the Deaf - Assistive tech; TTY equip
Special Services for the Blind - Assistive/Adapted tech devices, equip & products; Computer with voice synthesizer for visually impaired persons
Open Mon, Tues & Thurs 9-8, Wed & Fri 9-6, Sat 9-4
Friends of the Library Group
Branches: 3
DULANY MEMORIAL, 101 N Main, Paris, 65275-1398, SAN 349-4551. Tel: 660-327-4707. FAX: 660-327-4094. *Librn,* Sue Mattingly; E-mail: smattingly@little-dixie.lib.mo.us
Special Collections: Monroe County Genealogy
Special Services for the Deaf - Assistive tech
Special Services for the Blind - Aids for in-house use; Assistive/Adapted tech devices, equip & products; Computer with voice synthesizer for visually impaired persons
Open Mon, Tues & Fri 12-5, Wed 9:30-5, Thurs 12-7, Sat 9-12
Friends of the Library Group
HUNTSVILLE BRANCH, 102 E Library St, Huntsville, 65259-1125, SAN 349-4497. Tel: 660-277-4518. FAX: 660-277-4333. *Librn,* Lora Colley; E-mail: lcolley@little-dixie.lib.mo.us
Special Services for the Deaf - Assistive tech
Special Services for the Blind - Aids for in-house use; Assistive/Adapted tech devices, equip & products; Computer with voice synthesizer for visually impaired persons
Open Mon 12-7, Tues, Thurs & Fri 12-5, Wed 9:30-5, Sat 9-12
Friends of the Library Group
MADISON BRANCH, 113 E Broadway, Madison, 65263, SAN 349-4527. Tel: 660-291-3695. FAX: 660-291-8695. *Librn,* Carol Kroeckel; E-mail: ckroekel@little-dixie.lib.mo.us
Special Services for the Deaf - Assistive tech
Special Services for the Blind - Aids for in-house use; Assistive/Adapted tech devices, equip & products; Computer with voice synthesizer for visually impaired persons
Open Mon, Thurs & Fri 12-5, Tues 12-7, Wed 9:30-5, Sat 9-12
Friends of the Library Group

J MOBERLY AREA COMMUNITY COLLEGE*, Kate Stamper Wilhite Library, Main Bldg, 2nd Flr, 101 College Ave, 65270-1304. SAN 309-0957. Tel: 660-263-4110, Ext 11210. Toll Free Tel: 800-622-2070. FAX: 660-263-6448. E-mail: info@macc.edu. Web Site: www.macc.edu/library-resources. *Dir, Libr Serv,* Valerie J Darst; Tel: 660-263-4110, Ext 11244, E-mail: ValerieDarst@macc.edu; Staff 3 (MLS 1, Non-MLS 2)
Founded 1927. Enrl 2,500; Highest Degree: Associate
Library Holdings: Bk Titles 21,899; Bk Vols 22,170; Per Subs 50; Talking Bks 48; Videos 118
Special Collections: Jack Conroy American Studies Coll; Stamper Science & Technology Coll
Subject Interests: Behav sci, Hist, Natural sci, Soc sci
Automation Activity & Vendor Info: (Cataloging) Innovative Interfaces, Inc; (Circulation) Innovative Interfaces, Inc
Wireless access
Partic in MOBIUS
Open Mon-Thurs (Fall & Spring) 7am-8:30pm, Fri 7-4; Mon & Tues (Summer) 7-4 & 5:30-7:30, Wed-Fri 7-4

MONETT

P BARRY-LAWRENCE REGIONAL LIBRARY*, 213 Sixth St, 65708-2147. SAN 349-4586. Tel: 417-235-6646. FAX: 417-235-6799. E-mail: libinfo@blrlibrary.org. Web Site: www.blrlibrary.com. *Dir,* Gina Gail Milburn; E-mail: execdir@blrlibrary.org; *Cataloger, Coll Develop,* Rhonda Duff; E-mail: rhonda@blrlibrary.org; *Cataloger,* Joyce Frazier; E-mail: joycefrazier@blrlibrary.org; *Computer Tech,* Lee Ann Rosewicz; E-mail: leeann@blrlibrary.org; Staff 27 (MLS 1, Non-MLS 26)
Founded 1954. Pop 74,231; Circ 467,974
Jul 2013-Jun 2014 Income (Main & Associated Libraries) $1,732,663, State $81,933, County $1,366,700, Locally Generated Income $232,160, Other $51,870. Mats Exp $152,315, Books $126,673, Per/Ser (Incl. Access Fees) $6,708, Micro $523, AV Mat $18,411. Sal $796,129 (Prof $756,925)
Library Holdings: Audiobooks 180; CDs 4,479; DVDs 18,409; Large Print Bks 10,280; Microforms 605; Bk Titles 174,076; Bk Vols 178,805; Per Subs 115; Videos 1,729
Special Collections: Local History (Missouri Coll)
Automation Activity & Vendor Info: (Cataloging) TLC (The Library Corporation); (Circulation) TLC (The Library Corporation); (OPAC) TLC (The Library Corporation)
Wireless access
Function: Adult bk club, After school storytime, Bk club(s), Bks on CD, Children's prog, Computer training, Computers for patron use, Electronic databases & coll, Free DVD rentals, Home delivery & serv to seniorr ctr & nursing homes, Homebound delivery serv, ILL available, Internet access, Life-long learning prog for all ages, Magazines, Meeting rooms, Notary serv, Photocopying/Printing, Preschool reading prog, Prog for adults, Prog for children & young adult, Story hour, Summer reading prog, Tax forms, Teen prog, Wheelchair accessible
Special Services for the Deaf - ADA equip; Bks on deafness & sign lang
Special Services for the Blind - Bks on cassette; Bks on CD; Free checkout of audio mat; Large print bks
Open Mon & Tues 8:30-7, Wed-Sat 8:30-5:30
Friends of the Library Group
Branches: 9
AURORA BRANCH, 202 Jefferson, Aurora, 65605, SAN 349-4594. Tel: 417-678-2036. FAX: 417-678-2041. E-mail: aurora@blrlibrary.org. *Br Supvr,* Martha Pettegrew; *Adult Serv,* Vickey Maples; *Youth Serv,* Maria Cross
Circ 64,106
Library Holdings: Audiobooks 31; CDs 746; DVDs 2,076; Large Print Bks 1,867; Microforms 42; Bk Titles 29,353; Bk Vols 30,164; Per Subs 14; Videos 323

Open Mon-Sat 8:30-5:30
Friends of the Library Group
CASSVILLE BRANCH, 301 W 17th St, Cassville, 65625-1044. (Mail add: PO Box D, Cassville, 65625), SAN 349-4616. Tel: 417-847-2121. FAX: 417-847-4679. E-mail: cassville@blrlibrary.org. *Br Supvr,* Cheryl Williams; *Adult Serv,* Donna Lawson; *Youth Serv,* Verna Fry
Circ 87,629
Library Holdings: Audiobooks 48; CDs 799; DVDs 2,672; Large Print Bks 1,390; Microforms 73; Bk Titles 24,755; Bk Vols 25,690; Per Subs 13; Videos 384
Special Collections: Barry County Genealogy
Open Mon, Wed, Fri & Sat 8:30-5:30, Tues & Thurs 8:30-6:30
Friends of the Library Group
EAGLE ROCK BRANCH, 27824 State Hwy 86, Eagle Rock, 65641. (Mail add: PO Box 147, Eagle Rock, 65641-0147), SAN 375-8745. Tel: 417-271-3186. FAX: 417-271-3186. E-mail: eaglerock@blrlibrary.org. *Br Supvr,* Jennifer Cochran; *Youth Serv,* Tracey Crook
Circ 20,498
Library Holdings: Audiobooks 8; CDs 134; DVDs 1,144; Large Print Bks 339; Bk Titles 4,999; Bk Vols 5,084; Per Subs 6; Videos 32
Open Mon, Wed & Fri 8:30-5:30
Friends of the Library Group
MARIONVILLE BRANCH, 303 W Washington St, Marionville, 65705, SAN 349-4640. Tel: 417-463-2675. FAX: 417-463-2116. E-mail: marionville@blrlibrary.org. *Br Supvr, Youth Serv Coordr,* Janea Kay Coker; *Adult Serv,* Delora Manning; *Youth Serv,* Cindy Magallanes
Circ 30,323
Library Holdings: Audiobooks 6; CDs 337; DVDs 1,564; Large Print Bks 974; Bk Titles 16,368; Bk Vols 16,630; Per Subs 11; Videos 112
Open Mon-Fri 8:30-5:30
Friends of the Library Group
MILLER BRANCH, 112 E Main St, Miller, 65707. (Mail add: PO Box 84, Miller, 65707-0084), SAN 349-4675. Tel: 417-452-3466. FAX: 417-452-3466. E-mail: miller@blrlibrary.org. *Br Supvr,* Cindy Rinker; *Libr Asst,* Kathy Wells
Circ 13,353
Library Holdings: Audiobooks 1; CDs 151; DVDs 1,093; Large Print Bks 374; Bk Titles 8,476; Bk Vols 8,685; Per Subs 7; Videos 81
Open Mon, Wed & Fri 9-6
Friends of the Library Group
MONETT BRANCH, 213 Sixth St, 65708, SAN 349-4705. Tel: 417-235-6646. FAX: 417-235-6799. E-mail: monett@blrlibrary.org. *Br Supvr,* Cindy Frazier; *Adult Serv,* Betty Kay Alyea; *Youth Serv,* Korrlyn Cantwell
Circ 88,968
Library Holdings: Audiobooks 28; CDs 874; DVDs 2,570; Large Print Bks 1,833; Microforms 357; Bk Titles 29,186; Bk Vols 30,379; Per Subs 24; Videos 381
Open Mon 8:30-7, Tues-Fri 8:30-5:30, Sat 9-1
Friends of the Library Group
MOUNT VERNON BRANCH, 206 W Water St, Mount Vernon, 65712, SAN 349-4764. Tel: 417-466-2921. FAX: 417-466-2936. E-mail: mtvernon@blrlibrary.org. *Br Supvr,* Cindy Rinker; *Adult Serv,* Edwana Kennedy; *Youth Serv,* Julie McCollum
Circ 91,316
Library Holdings: Audiobooks 34; CDs 828; DVDs 2,663; Large Print Bks 1,575; Microforms 357; Bk Titles 29,862; Bk Vols 30,615; Per Subs 13; Videos 254
Special Collections: Lawrence County Genealogy & Historical Coll
Open Mon 8:30-7, Tues-Sat 8:30-5:30
Friends of the Library Group
PIERCE CITY BRANCH, 101 N Walnut St, Pierce City, 65723. Tel: 417-476-5110. FAX: 417-476-5110. E-mail: piercecity@blrlibrary.org. *Br Supvr,* Cindy Frazier; *Adult Serv,* Rebecca Mayberry; *Youth Serv,* Carolyn Dean
Circ 18,931
Library Holdings: Audiobooks 8; CDs 219; DVDs 1,472; Large Print Bks 814; Microforms 42; Bk Titles 15,678; Bk Vols 15,924; Per Subs 11; Videos 14
Open Mon, Wed, Thurs & Fri 8:30-5:30
Friends of the Library Group
SHELL KNOB BRANCH, 24931 State Hwy 39, Shell Knob, 65747. (Mail add: PO Box 349, Shell Knob, 65747-0349), SAN 349-4756. Tel: 417-858-3618. FAX: 417-858-3618. E-mail: shellknob@blrlibrary.org. *Br Supvr,* Jennifer Cochran; *Youth Serv,* Tracey Crook
Circ 23,589
Library Holdings: Audiobooks 10; CDs 286; DVDs 1,721; Large Print Bks 735; Bk Titles 8,267; Bk Vols 8,374; Per Subs 8; Videos 50
Open Mon, Wed, Thurs & Fri 8:30-5:30
Friends of the Library Group

MONROE CITY

P MONROE CITY PUBLIC LIBRARY, 109A Second St, 63456. SAN 309-0965. Tel: 573-735-2665. E-mail: mopublib@gmail.com. Web Site: www.monroecitymo.org/monroe-city-library. *Libr Dir,* Karen Seward; Staff 1 (Non-MLS 1)
Founded 1918. Pop 2,557; Circ 10,110
Library Holdings: Bk Titles 11,050; Bk Vols 11,561; Per Subs 35; Talking Bks 33
Subject Interests: Recreation
Automation Activity & Vendor Info: (Cataloging) Mandarin Library Automation; (Circulation) Mandarin Library Automation
Wireless access
Open Mon-Fri 11-6, Sat 9-12

MONTGOMERY CITY

P MONTGOMERY CITY PUBLIC LIBRARY, 224 N Allen St, 63361. SAN 309-0973. Tel: 573-564-8022. Web Site: www.mcplmo.com. *Interim Dir,* Gaylee Harris; E-mail: mcplmo@gmail.com; Staff 5 (Non-MLS 5)
Founded 1927. Pop 2,800; Circ 39,486
Jul 2016-Jun 2017 Income $158,985
Library Holdings: Audiobooks 899; DVDs 1,044; e-books 26,066; Bk Vols 23,053; Per Subs 62
Automation Activity & Vendor Info: (Acquisitions) Evergreen; (Cataloging) Evergreen; (Circulation) Evergreen; (ILL) Evergreen; (OPAC) Evergreen
Wireless access
Function: Adult bk club, After school storytime, Audiobks via web, Bk club(s), Bks on CD, Children's prog, Computer training, Computers for patron use, Digital talking bks, Distance learning, Free DVD rentals, ILL available, Internet access, Magazines, Meeting rooms, Movies, Online cat, OverDrive digital audio bks, Photocopying/Printing, Preschool outreach, Preschool reading prog, Prog for adults, Ref & res, Scanner, Story hour, Summer reading prog
Partic in Amigos Library Services, Inc; Missouri Evergreen; Missouri Research & Education Network
Open Mon-Thurs 8:30-6, Fri 8:30-5, Sat 9-1

MOUND CITY

P MOUND CITY PUBLIC LIBRARY*, 207 E Sixth St, 64470. SAN 309-0981. Tel: 660-442-5700. FAX: 660-442-3149. Web Site: www.moundcitypubliclibrary.org. *Libr Dir,* Susan Nauman; E-mail: mclibdirector@outlook.com; *Asst Dir,* Jane Gegen
Founded 1908. Pop 1,358; Circ 8,400
Library Holdings: DVDs 225; Bk Titles 18,500; Bk Vols 19,450; Per Subs 31; Talking Bks 60; Videos 100
Subject Interests: Fiction
Wireless access
Open Mon & Wed-Fri 12-5, Tues 10-5, Sat 9-12
Friends of the Library Group

MOUNT VERNON

S MISSOURI VETERANS' HOME LIBRARY, 1600 S Hickory, 65712. SAN 377-1148. Tel: 417-466-7103. FAX: 417-466-4040. Web Site: mvc.dps.mo.gov/homes/mtvernon.php. *Librn, Vols Coordr,* David Kloppenborg; E-mail: david.kloppenborg@mvc.dps.mo.gov
Library Holdings: Bk Vols 600; Per Subs 10
Restriction: Not open to pub

MOUNTAIN VIEW

P MOUNTAIN VIEW PUBLIC LIBRARY*, 125 S Oak St, 65548. (Mail add: PO Box 1389, 65548-1389), SAN 309-1007. Tel: 417-934-6154. FAX: 417-934-5100. Web Site: mvpubliclibrary.webs.com. *Dir,* Beth Smith; E-mail: bethsmithlib@gmail.com; *Asst Dir,* Katrina Tripp; E-mail: katrina_janae@hotmail.com; Staff 2 (MLS 1, Non-MLS 1)
Founded 1950. Pop 2,719
Jul 2017-Jun 2018 Income $118,583
Library Holdings: Large Print Bks 1,000; Bk Titles 50,000; Per Subs 30; Videos 12,000
Subject Interests: Hist of Ozarks scenic river
Automation Activity & Vendor Info: (Cataloging) TLC (The Library Corporation); (Circulation) TLC (The Library Corporation); (ILL) OCLC; (OPAC) TLC (The Library Corporation)
Wireless access
Function: 24/7 Electronic res, 24/7 Online cat, Adult bk club, Bk club(s), Bks on CD, Children's prog, Computers for patron use, E-Readers, Electronic databases & coll, Family literacy, Free DVD rentals, Holiday prog, ILL available, Instruction & testing, Internet access, Magazines, Magnifiers for reading, Mail & tel request accepted, Meeting rooms, Movies, Music CDs, Online cat, Preschool outreach, Preschool reading prog, Prog for children & young adult, Scanner, Spoken cassettes & CDs,

Spoken cassettes & DVDs, Story hour, Summer reading prog, Tax forms, VHS videos, Wheelchair accessible
Open Mon-Wed & Fri 8:30-5, Thurs 8:30-7, Sat 8-Noon
Restriction: Borrowing requests are handled by ILL, Fee for pub use, ID required to use computers (Ltd hrs), In-house use for visitors, Non-circulating, Non-circulating coll, Non-circulating to the pub, Photo ID required for access
Friends of the Library Group

NEOSHO

J CROWDER COLLEGE*, Bill & Margot Lee Library, 601 Laclede Ave, 64850. SAN 309-1015. Tel: 417-455-5606. Reference Tel: 417-455-5689. Administration Tel: 417-455-5610. FAX: 417-455-5702. E-mail: circ@crowder.edu. Web Site: www.crowder.edu/academics/lee-library. *Dir,* Eric Deatherage; E-mail: ericdeatherage@crowder.edu; *Access Serv Librn,* Robin Wolven; E-mail: robinwolven@crowder.edu; *Pub Serv Librn,* Jason Smith; E-mail: jasonsmith@crowder.edu; Staff 1 (MLS 1)
Founded 1964. Enrl 2,102; Fac 75; Highest Degree: Associate
Library Holdings: AV Mats 4,200; DVDs 200; e-books 21,500; Bk Titles 39,500; Per Subs 170; Videos 316
Automation Activity & Vendor Info: (Acquisitions) Innovative Interfaces, Inc - Millennium; (Cataloging) Innovative Interfaces, Inc; (Circulation) Innovative Interfaces, Inc; (ILL) OCLC FirstSearch; (OPAC) Innovative Interfaces, Inc; (Serials) Innovative Interfaces, Inc
Wireless access
Function: Audio & video playback equip for onsite use, Bks on cassette, Bks on CD, CD-ROM, Distance learning, Doc delivery serv, Electronic databases & coll, ILL available, Instruction & testing, Internet access, Orientations, Outside serv via phone, mail, e-mail & web, Photocopying/Printing, Ref & res, Ref serv available, Scanner, Spoken cassettes & CDs, Spoken cassettes & DVDs, Telephone ref, VHS videos, Wheelchair accessible
Partic in Amigos Library Services, Inc; Missouri Research & Education Network; MOBIUS
Open Mon-Thurs (Fall-Spring) 8:30-8:30, Fri 8:30-4:30, Sun 1:30-4:30; Mon-Thurs (Summer) 8:30-6:30, Fri 8:30-4:30
Restriction: Non-circulating coll, Open to students, fac & staff, Restricted pub use
Friends of the Library Group

P NEOSHO/NEWTON COUNTY LIBRARY*, 201 W Spring St, 64850. SAN 349-4799. Tel: 417-451-4231. FAX: 417-451-6438. E-mail: info@neosho.lib.mo.us. Web Site: www.newtoncolib.org. *Dir,* Carrie Cline; E-mail: carrie@neosho.lib.mo.us; Staff 8 (MLS 1, Non-MLS 7)
Founded 1966. Pop 55,000; Circ 180,000
Library Holdings: Bk Titles 50,000; Bk Vols 51,118; Per Subs 132; Talking Bks 618; Videos 2,891
Automation Activity & Vendor Info: (Acquisitions) SirsiDynix; (Cataloging) SirsiDynix; (Circulation) SirsiDynix; (OPAC) SirsiDynix
Wireless access
Partic in OCLC Online Computer Library Center, Inc
Open Mon-Thurs 9-7, Fri & Sat 9-5
Friends of the Library Group
Branches: 1
SENECA BRANCH, 1216 Cherokee, Seneca, 64865. Tel: 417-776-2705. FAX: 417-776-8003. *Br Mgr,* Georgia Wilkes; E-mail: georgia@neosho.lib.mo.us
Library Holdings: DVDs 250; Bk Vols 11,000; Per Subs 19; Videos 100
Open Mon-Thurs 11-6, Sat 11-2
Friends of the Library Group

NEVADA

J COTTEY COLLEGE*, Blanche Skiff Ross Memorial Library, 1000 W Austin, 64772-2763. Tel: 417-667-8181, Ext 2153. FAX: 417-448-1040. E-mail: library@cottey.edu. Web Site: cottey.edu/campus-community/library. *Libr Dir,* Courtney Trautweiler; E-mail: ctrautweiler@cottey.edu; Staff 4 (MLS 1, Non-MLS 3)
Founded 1884. Enrl 324; Fac 35; Highest Degree: Bachelor
Library Holdings: CDs 641; Bk Titles 56,000; Per Subs 205
Special Collections: College Archives; Henry Moore Coll; bks, cats
Subject Interests: Gen liberal arts, Women's leadership
Automation Activity & Vendor Info: (Acquisitions) OCLC CatExpress; (Cataloging) Innovative Interfaces, Inc - Sierra; (Circulation) Innovative Interfaces, Inc - Sierra; (Course Reserve) Innovative Interfaces, Inc - Sierra; (ILL) OCLC WorldShare Interlibrary Loan; (Media Booking) Innovative Interfaces, Inc - Sierra; (OPAC) Innovative Interfaces, Inc - Sierra; (Serials) Innovative Interfaces, Inc - Sierra
Wireless access
Function: 24/7 Electronic res, Archival coll, Art exhibits, Audio & video playback equip for onsite use, Bks on CD, Computers for patron use, Doc delivery serv, Electronic databases & coll, ILL available, Internet access, Learning ctr, Magazines, Microfiche/film & reading machines, Music CDs, Online cat, Orientations, Photocopying/Printing, Scanner, VHS videos, Wheelchair accessible
Open Mon-Thurs 7:30am-11pm, Fri 7:30-6, Sat 12-6, Sun 2-11

P NEVADA PUBLIC LIBRARY*, 212 W Walnut, 64772-0931. SAN 309-1031. Tel: 417-448-2770. FAX: 417-448-2771. E-mail: nevadapubliclibrary@gmail.com. Web Site: www.nevadapubliclibrary.com. *Exec Dir,* Jodi L Polk; E-mail: jodipolk@gmail.com; Staff 5 (MLS 2, Non-MLS 3)
Founded 1898. Pop 8,691; Circ 80,000
Library Holdings: Bks on Deafness & Sign Lang 18; High Interest/Low Vocabulary Bk Vols 25; Large Print Bks 36; Bk Titles 40,600; Bk Vols 40,710; Per Subs 72; Spec Interest Per Sub 12; Talking Bks 698; Videos 1,115
Special Collections: State Document Depository
Wireless access
Special Services for the Deaf - TDD equip
Special Services for the Blind - Computer with voice synthesizer for visually impaired persons
Open Mon, Wed & Fri 9-5, Tues & Thurs 9-8, Sat 9-1
Friends of the Library Group

NORBORNE

P NORBORNE PUBLIC LIBRARY*, 109 E Second St, 64668. SAN 309-1066. Tel: 660-593-3514. FAX: 660-593-3737. Web Site: cityofnorborne.org/city-hall. *Librn,* Pamela Penrod; E-mail: PPenrod@cityofnorborne.org
Founded 1930. Pop 931; Circ 7,844
Library Holdings: High Interest/Low Vocabulary Bk Vols 10; Large Print Bks 75; Bk Titles 1,200; Bk Vols 10,000; Per Subs 18; Talking Bks 125; Videos 103
Subject Interests: Town hist
Open Mon-Fri 8-12 & 1-5, Sat 8-12

NORTH KANSAS CITY

P NORTH KANSAS CITY PUBLIC LIBRARY, 2251 Howell St, 64116. SAN 309-1082. Tel: 816-221-3360. FAX: 816-221-8298. Web Site: www.nkcpl.org. *Libr Dir,* Lori Mangan; E-mail: lmangan@nkcpl.org; *Asst Dir,* Doris Rogers; E-mail: drogers@nkcpl.org; Staff 10 (MLS 2, Non-MLS 8)
Founded 1939. Pop 5,750; Circ 77,400
Library Holdings: e-books 73,000; Large Print Bks 98; Bk Titles 58,552; Bk Vols 70,000; Per Subs 200; Talking Bks 1,144; Videos 2,816
Automation Activity & Vendor Info: (Acquisitions) SirsiDynix; (Cataloging) SirsiDynix; (Circulation) SirsiDynix; (ILL) SirsiDynix; (OPAC) SirsiDynix; (Serials) SirsiDynix
Wireless access
Partic in Kansas City Library Service Program
Open Mon & Thurs 9-9, Tues 3-9, Wed 9-4:30, Fri 9-6, Sat 1-5
Friends of the Library Group

OREGON

P OREGON PUBLIC LIBRARY*, 103 S Washington St, 64473. (Mail add: PO Box 288, 64473-0288), SAN 309-1112. Tel: 660-446-3586. FAX: 660-446-3586. E-mail: oregonlibrary@hotmail.com. *Librn,* Allison Russell; Staff 2 (MLS 1, Non-MLS 1)
Founded 1938. Pop 1,500; Circ 6,741
Library Holdings: Large Print Bks 75; Bk Titles 15,161; Bk Vols 15,878; Per Subs 32; Talking Bks 138; Videos 147
Open Mon & Thurs-Sat 2-5, Tues 10-5, Wed 1-7

OSCEOLA

P SAINT CLAIR COUNTY LIBRARY*, 115 Chestnut St, 64776. SAN 309-1120. Tel: 417-646-2214. FAX: 417-646-8643. E-mail: stclaircountylibrary@gmail.com. Web Site: mostclair.lib.mo.us. *Dir,* Angie Jones
Founded 1948. Pop 9,862; Circ 60,885
Library Holdings: Bk Titles 34,697; Per Subs 32
Special Collections: County Historical Society
Automation Activity & Vendor Info: (Acquisitions) Book Systems; (Cataloging) Book Systems; (Circulation) Book Systems; (ILL) OCLC FirstSearch; (Media Booking) Book Systems; (OPAC) Book Systems; (Serials) Book Systems
Wireless access
Open Mon-Thurs 8am-9pm, Fri 8-5, Sat 9-2
Friends of the Library Group
Branches: 1
LOWRY CITY BRANCH, 406 Fourth St, Lowry City, 64763. Tel: 417-644-2255. FAX: 417-644-2257. *Dir,* Angie Jones
Open Tues-Thurs 1-7, Fri 9-5, Sat 9-2
Bookmobiles: 1

OZARK

P CHRISTIAN COUNTY LIBRARY*, 1005 N Fourth Ave, 65721. SAN 309-1139. Tel: 417-581-2432. FAX: 417-581-8855. E-mail: info@christiancountylibrary.org. Web Site: christiancountylibrary.org. *Dir,* Geri Godber; E-mail: ggodber@christiancountylibrary.org; *Asst Dir,* Katy Pattison; E-mail: kpattison@christiancountylibrary.org; Staff 24 (MLS 3, Non-MLS 21)
Founded 1956. Pop 77,422; Circ 216,538
Library Holdings: AV Mats 2,658; e-books 7,575; Electronic Media & Resources 82; Large Print Bks 8,200; Bk Titles 69,701; Bk Vols 75,858; Per Subs 203; Talking Bks 1,613
Special Collections: Southwest Missouri & the Ozarks. Oral History
Subject Interests: Antiques
Automation Activity & Vendor Info: (Acquisitions) Innovative Interfaces, Inc - Sierra; (Cataloging) Innovative Interfaces, Inc; (Circulation) Innovative Interfaces, Inc; (ILL) OCLC FirstSearch; (OPAC) Innovative Interfaces, Inc
Wireless access
Function: 24/7 Electronic res, 24/7 Online cat, Activity rm, Adult bk club, Archival coll, Art exhibits, Audiobks on Playaways & MP3, Audiobks via web, Bks on CD, Children's prog, Computer training, Computers for patron use, Digital talking bks, Electronic databases & coll, Free DVD rentals, Holiday prog, Home delivery & serv to seniorr ctr & nursing homes, ILL available, Instruction & testing, Internet access, Laminating, Large print keyboards, Life-long learning prog for all ages, Magazines, Mail & tel request accepted, Mango lang, Meeting rooms, Microfiche/film & reading machines, Movies, Notary serv, Online cat, Outreach serv, OverDrive digital audio bks, Photocopying/Printing, Preschool outreach, Prog for adults, Prog for children & young adult, Ref & res, Res performed for a fee, Scanner, Senior computer classes, Story hour, Study rm, Summer & winter reading prog, Tax forms, Teen prog, Wheelchair accessible, Workshops, Writing prog
Partic in Consortium of Ozarks Libraries; Missouri Research & Education Network; MOBIUS
Open Mon-Thurs 8:30-8, Fri & Sat 8:30-5
Restriction: Authorized patrons, In-house use for visitors
Friends of the Library Group

PALMYRA

P MARION COUNTY SUB-DISTRICT LIBRARY*, 212 S Main St, 63461. SAN 309-1147. Tel: 573-769-2830. FAX: 573-769-0405. E-mail: palmyralibrary@gmail.com. Web Site: marioncounty1.lib.mo.us. *Dir,* Peggy Northcraft; *Circ Mgr,* Kris Abbott; *Ch Serv,* Mary Lynne Jones; Staff 2 (MLS 1, Non-MLS 1)
Founded 1913. Pop 6,000
Library Holdings: Bk Titles 21,040; Bk Vols 22,000; Per Subs 17; Talking Bks 413; Videos 546
Special Collections: Civil War; History Local Battles; Mark Twain Coll
Subject Interests: Local hist
Automation Activity & Vendor Info: (Cataloging) ComPanion Corp; (Circulation) ComPanion Corp; (ILL) OCLC FirstSearch; (OPAC) ComPanion Corp
Wireless access
Publications: Local Paper Column (Weekly)
Open Mon, Wed & Fri 10-5:30, Tues & Thurs 10-6, Sat 10-2

PARK HILLS

J MINERAL AREA COLLEGE*, C H Cozean Library, 5270 Flat River Rd, 63601. (Mail add: PO Box 1000, 63601-1000), SAN 308-9835. Tel: 573-518-2141. FAX: 573-518-2162. Web Site: www.mineralarea.edu/library. *Libr Dir,* Ryan Harrington; Tel: 573-518-2236, E-mail: rkharrin@mineralarea.edu
Founded 1969. Enrl 3,000; Fac 81; Highest Degree: Associate
Library Holdings: AV Mats 5,046; Bk Titles 29,389; Bk Vols 33,999; Per Subs 166; Videos 868
Automation Activity & Vendor Info: (Acquisitions) Innovative Interfaces, Inc; (Cataloging) Innovative Interfaces, Inc; (Circulation) Innovative Interfaces, Inc; (Course Reserve) Innovative Interfaces, Inc; (ILL) Innovative Interfaces, Inc; (Media Booking) Innovative Interfaces, Inc; (OPAC) Innovative Interfaces, Inc; (Serials) Innovative Interfaces, Inc
Wireless access
Partic in Amigos Library Services, Inc; MOBIUS
Open Mon-Thurs 7:30am-8pm, Fri 7:30-4

P PARK HILLS PUBLIC LIBRARY*, 16 S Coffman St, 63601. SAN 308-9827. Tel: 573-431-4842. FAX: 573-431-2110. E-mail: parkhillspubliclibrary@parkhillsmo.net. Web Site: parkhillsmo.net/services/library. *Dir,* Lisa Sisk; Staff 3 (MLS 1, Non-MLS 2)
Founded 1934. Pop 12,000; Circ 32,000
Library Holdings: Bk Titles 45,000; Bk Vols 46,000; Per Subs 43; Talking Bks 838; Videos 392
Subject Interests: Local hist
Automation Activity & Vendor Info: (Acquisitions) Follett Software; (Cataloging) Follett Software; (Circulation) Follett Software
Open Mon & Tues 10-7, Wed-Fri 11-5, Sat (Sept-May) 9-12
Friends of the Library Group

PARKVILLE

C PARK UNIVERSITY LIBRARY*, McAfee Memorial Library, Park University - Norrington Ctr, 8700 NW River Park Dr, 64152. (Mail add: 8700 NW River Park Dr, CMB #61, 64152), SAN 309-1155. Tel: 816-584-6285. Administration Tel: 816-584-6707. Toll Free Tel: 800-270-4347. Web Site: library.park.edu. *Libr Dir,* Brent Short; E-mail: brent.short@park.edu; *Ref & Instruction Librn,* Katelyn Handler; Tel: 816-584-6282, E-mail: katelyn.handler@park.edu; *Coll Mgt/Res Sharing,* Karen Bleier; Tel: 816-584-6704, E-mail: karen.bleier@park.edu; *Archivist,* Carolyn Elwess; Tel: 816-584-6891, E-mail: carolyn.elwess@park.edu; *Acq,* Veronica Spottswood; Tel: 816-741-6284, E-mail: veronica.spottswood@park.edu; *Cat,* Betty Dusing; Tel: 816-584-6281, E-mail: betty.dusing@park.edu; Staff 6 (MLS 3, Non-MLS 3)
Founded 1875. Fac 106; Highest Degree: Master
Library Holdings: DVDs 150; e-books 204,630; e-journals 43,939; Electronic Media & Resources 73; Bk Titles 90,933; Bk Vols 108,074
Special Collections: History (Platte County Historical Society Archives); Park College & Park University History Coll. Oral History
Automation Activity & Vendor Info: (Cataloging) Innovative Interfaces, Inc - Sierra; (Circulation) Innovative Interfaces, Inc - Sierra; (Course Reserve) Innovative Interfaces, Inc - Sierra; (Discovery) EBSCO Discovery Service; (OPAC) Innovative Interfaces, Inc - Sierra; (Serials) Innovative Interfaces, Inc - Sierra
Wireless access
Partic in MOBIUS
Open Mon-Thurs (Fall/Spring) 7:30am-9:30pm, Fri 7:30-4:30, Sat 10-4, Sun 4-9:30

PINEVILLE

P MCDONALD COUNTY LIBRARY*, Pineville Library, 808 Bailey Rd, 64856. SAN 309-118X. Tel: 417-223-4489. FAX: 417-223-4011. Web Site: librarymail.org. *Dir,* Amy Wallain; E-mail: amywallain@gmail.com; Staff 9 (MLS 1, Non-MLS 8)
Founded 1949. Pop 21,681; Circ 68,539
Library Holdings: Bks on Deafness & Sign Lang 14; Bk Titles 33,000; Bk Vols 36,000; Per Subs 50; Talking Bks 1,023; Videos 3,633
Special Collections: Jesse James Coll
Automation Activity & Vendor Info: (Cataloging) Book Systems; (Circulation) Book Systems; (OPAC) Book Systems
Wireless access
Open Mon-Thurs 9-6, Fri 1-6, Sat 9-3
Branches: 2
ANNE CROXDALE MEMORIAL LIBRARY, 102 N Main St, Southwest City, 64863. Tel: 417-762-7323. FAX: 417-762-7322. *Br Mgr,* Retha Mitchell
Open Tues-Thurs 10-6, Fri 1-6, Sat 10-3
NOEL LIBRARY, 626 Johnson Dr, Noel, 64854. Tel: 417-475-3223. FAX: 417-475-3223. *Br Mgr,* Wes Ferguson
Library Holdings: DVDs 550; Bk Vols 4,000; Talking Bks 50; Videos 600
Open Tues-Thurs 11-6, Fri 1-6, Sat 9-3

POINT LOOKOUT

COLLEGE OF THE OZARKS
C BROWNELL RESEARCH CENTER LIBRARY*, Ralph Foster Museum, One Cultural Ct, 65726. (Mail add: PO Box 17, 65726-0017). Tel: 417-690-3407. FAX: 417-690-2606. *Dir,* Annette Sain; E-mail: sain@cofo.edu
Founded 1975
Library Holdings: Bk Titles 4,000; Per Subs 4
Special Collections: Artifacts & Antiques Coll
Subject Interests: Hist
Function: For res purposes
Restriction: Not a lending libr, Staff & prof res

C LYONS MEMORIAL LIBRARY*, One Opportunity Ave, 65726. (Mail add: PO Box 17, 65726-0017). Tel: 417-690-3411. FAX: 417-334-3085. Web Site: www.cofo.edu/library/default.asp. *Libr Supvr-Popular Libr,* Karla Jenkins; E-mail: kjenkins@cofo.edu; *ILL, Pub Serv, Ref Serv,* Linda Schmidt; *Media Spec, Spec Coll,* Gwen Simmons; E-mail: simmons@cofo.edu; *Tech Serv,* Ronald D Wyly; E-mail: wyly@cofo.edu; Staff 4 (MLS 4)
Founded 1906. Enrl 1,440; Fac 83; Highest Degree: Bachelor
Library Holdings: AV Mats 3,306; Bk Vols 120,782; Per Subs 715
Special Collections: Ozarks (Ozarkiana Coll), bks, photogs, tapes, mss, letters
Automation Activity & Vendor Info: (Circulation) Innovative Interfaces, Inc; (OPAC) Innovative Interfaces, Inc

Partic in Amigos Library Services, Inc; Missouri Research & Education Network; OCLC Online Computer Library Center, Inc
Open Mon-Thurs 8am-10pm, Fri 8-5, Sat 1-5, Sun 2-5

POPLAR BLUFF

P POPLAR BLUFF MUNICIPAL LIBRARY*, 318 N Main St, 63901. SAN 349-4918. Tel: 573-686-8639. FAX: 573-785-6876. E-mail: library@poplarbluff.org. Web Site: poplarbluff.org. *Dir,* Sue Crites Szostak; Tel: 573-686-8639, Ext 25, E-mail: director@poplarbluff.org; *Asst Dir,* Shannon Midyett; Tel: 573-686-8639, Ext 21, E-mail: assistantdirector@poplarbluff.org; *Children & Youth Serv Librn,* Belinda Birrer; Tel: 573-686-8639, Ext 28, E-mail: childrens@poplarbluff.org; *Adult Serv Mgr,* Cole Bearden; Tel: 573-686-8639, Ext 22, E-mail: adultservices@poplarbluff.org; *Tech Serv Mgr,* Shon Griffin; Tel: 573-686-8639, Ext 24, E-mail: techservices@poplarbluff.org; Staff 8 (MLS 3, Non-MLS 5)
Founded 1916. Pop 17,000; Circ 200,000
Jan 2019-Dec 2019 Income $1,372,000, State $10,980, Locally Generated Income $1,361,020
Library Holdings: Bk Vols 70,000; Per Subs 105
Automation Activity & Vendor Info: (Acquisitions) Evergreen; (Cataloging) Evergreen; (Circulation) Evergreen; (ILL) OCLC FirstSearch; (OPAC) Evergreen
Wireless access
Function: 24/7 Electronic res, 24/7 Online cat, Activity rm, Adult bk club, Archival coll, Art exhibits, Audio & video playback equip for onsite use, Audiobks via web, Bk club(s), Bks on CD, Children's prog, Computer training, Computers for patron use, Distance learning, Electronic databases & coll, Free DVD rentals, Holiday prog, ILL available, Internet access, Makerspace, Meeting rooms, Microfiche/film & reading machines, Movies, Online cat, Outreach serv, Outside serv via phone, mail, e-mail & web, OverDrive digital audio bks, Passport agency, Photocopying/Printing, Preschool outreach, Preschool reading prog, Printer for laptops & handheld devices, Prog for adults, Prog for children & young adult, Ref serv available, Scanner, STEM programs, Story hour, Study rm, Summer & winter reading prog, Tax forms, Teen prog, Telephone ref, Wheelchair accessible, Winter reading prog, Workshops
Partic in Mid-America Library Alliance; Missouri Evergreen
Friends of the Library Group

J THREE RIVERS COMMUNITY COLLEGE LIBRARY*, Rutland Library, 2080 Three Rivers Blvd, 63901. SAN 309-1201. Tel: 573-840-9654. FAX: 573-840-9659. E-mail: library@trcc.edu. Web Site: trcc.edu/arc. *Actg Libr Dir,* Kathy Sanders; E-mail: ksanders@trcc.edu; *Outreach Coordr,* Sheila Ursery; E-mail: sursery@trcc.edu; Staff 1 (MLS 1)
Founded 1966. Enrl 3,400; Highest Degree: Associate
Library Holdings: Bk Vols 35,000; Per Subs 175; Videos 500
Special Collections: McManus Civil War Coll; Ozarks & Southeast Missouri History. State Document Depository
Automation Activity & Vendor Info: (Cataloging) OCLC Online; (Circulation) Innovative Interfaces, Inc; (ILL) OCLC Online; (OPAC) Innovative Interfaces, Inc
Wireless access
Partic in Amigos Library Services, Inc; MOBIUS; OCLC Online Computer Library Center, Inc
Open Mon-Fri 8-5
Restriction: Open to pub for ref & circ; with some limitations

PORTAGEVILLE

P NEW MADRID COUNTY LIBRARY*, 309 E Main St, 63873. SAN 309-1228. Tel: 573-379-3583. FAX: 573-379-9220. E-mail: nmcl1@newmadridcountylibrary.com. Web Site: www.newmadridcountylibrary.com. *Dir,* Susan Newman
Founded 1948. Pop 18,954; Circ 69,243
Library Holdings: Bk Vols 85,857; Per Subs 52
Subject Interests: Genealogy, Local hist
Automation Activity & Vendor Info: (Acquisitions) Follett Software; (Cataloging) TLC (The Library Corporation); (Circulation) Follett Software; (ILL) Follett Software; (OPAC) Follett Software
Open Mon-Sat 8-5
Branches: 6
MATTHEWS SERVICE CENTER, 105 Main St, Matthews, 63867.
Open Tues & Fri Noon-4
MOREHOUSE SERVICE CENTER, 113 E Beech St, Morehouse, 63868. (Mail add: 309 E Main St, 63873), SAN 377-3744. Tel: 573-379-3583. *Libr Dir,* Judith Hankins
Library Holdings: Bk Vols 4,500
NEW MADRID MEMORIAL, 431 Mill St, New Madrid, 63869. (Mail add: 309 E Main St, 63873), SAN 321-9453. Tel: 573-748-2378. FAX: 573-748-7637. *Librn,* Rhonda Bickerstaff; *Librn,* Sheila Halford
Library Holdings: Bk Titles 25,669; Per Subs 10
Automation Activity & Vendor Info: (Circulation) Follett Software
Open Mon-Fri 9-5, Sat 9-12
PARMA SERVICE CENTER, 209 Broad, Parma, 63870. (Mail add: 309 East Main, 63873). *Br Librn,* Barbie Brannon
Open Tues & Fri 1-5
, 303 S Main St, Gideon, 63848. (Mail add: 309 E Main St, 63873), SAN 308-9916. Tel: 573-379-3583. *Br Librn,* Gina McGinley
Library Holdings: Bk Titles 12,290
Automation Activity & Vendor Info: (Circulation) Follett Software; (OPAC) Follett Software
Open Mon, Wed & Fri 1-5, Tues & Thurs 8-5
RISCO SERVICE CENTER, 210 Missouri St, Risco, 63874. *Br Librn,* Tiffany McGinley
Open Tues & Thurs Noon-4

POTOSI

P WASHINGTON COUNTY LIBRARY*, 235 E High St, 63664. SAN 309-1236. Tel: 573-438-4691. FAX: 573-438-6423. E-mail: washingtoncolibrary@hotmail.com. Web Site: thewashingtoncountylibrary.com. *Librn,* Melissa G Mercer
Founded 1948. Pop 23,344; Circ 65,197
Library Holdings: Bk Titles 58,366; Bk Vols 66,561; Per Subs 138
Special Collections: Historical Coll, bks & micro
Automation Activity & Vendor Info: (Cataloging) Follett Software; (Circulation) Follett Software
Wireless access
Open Mon 9-8, Tues-Fri 9-5, Sat 9-1
Bookmobiles: 1

PRINCETON

P MERCER COUNTY LIBRARY*, 601 W Grant St, 64673. SAN 309-1244. Tel: 660-748-3725. FAX: 660-748-3723. TDD: 660-748-4514. E-mail: mercoulib@gmail.com. Web Site: www.mcl.lib.mo.us. *Dir,* Paula Fagan; *Ch & Youth Librn,* Marilyn Hardy; *Circ Librn,* Billie Day; *Tech Librn,* Aimee Kenagy; Staff 6 (Non-MLS 6)
Founded 1926. Pop 4,610; Circ 35,475
Library Holdings: Bk Titles 19,435; Bk Vols 20,000; Per Subs 36; Talking Bks 117; Videos 538
Subject Interests: Genealogy
Automation Activity & Vendor Info: (Cataloging) Book Systems; (Circulation) Book Systems
Wireless access
Partic in LYRASIS; OCLC Online Computer Library Center, Inc
Open Mon-Wed & Fri 9-5, Thurs 9-8, Sat 9-12

REPUBLIC

S NATIONAL PARK SERVICE*, Mr & Mrs John K Hulston Civil War Library, Wilson's Creek National Battlefield, 6424 W Farm Rd 182, 65738-9514. SAN 321-0006. Tel: 417-732-2662. FAX: 417-732-1167. Web Site: www.nps.gov/wicr. *Mgr,* Jeffrey Patrick; E-mail: jeffrey_patrick@nps.gov; Staff 1 (Non-MLS 1)
Founded 1985
Library Holdings: Bk Vols 14,000
Subject Interests: Civil War, Mo
Function: Res libr
Restriction: Not a lending libr
Friends of the Library Group

RICHLAND

P PULASKI COUNTY LIBRARY DISTRICT*, Richland Library (Headquarters), 111 Camden St, 65556. (Mail add: PO Box 340, 65556-0340), SAN 349-4225. Tel: 573-765-3642. FAX: 573-765-5395. Web Site: pulaskicounty.lib.mo.us. *Dir,* Emily Slama; Tel: 573-774-5026, E-mail: emily@pulaskilibraries.org; *Br Mgr,* Liz Hable; Staff 10 (Non-MLS 10)
Founded 1965
Library Holdings: Bk Vols 50,000; Per Subs 27
Automation Activity & Vendor Info: (Acquisitions) Innovative Interfaces, Inc; (Cataloging) Innovative Interfaces, Inc; (Circulation) Innovative Interfaces, Inc; (Course Reserve) Innovative Interfaces, Inc; (ILL) Innovative Interfaces, Inc; (Media Booking) Innovative Interfaces, Inc; (OPAC) Innovative Interfaces, Inc; (Serials) Innovative Interfaces, Inc
Wireless access
Partic in National Network of Libraries of Medicine Region 3
Open Tues 9-7, Wed & Thurs 9-6, Fri 9-5, Sat 9-1
Friends of the Library Group
Branches: 2
CROCKER LIBRARY, 602 N Commercial St, Crocker, 65452. Tel: 573-736-5592. FAX: 573-736-5427. *Br Mgr,* Donna Morgan
Founded 1999
Open Tues 9-7, Wed & Thurs 9-6, Fri 9-5, Sat 9-1
Friends of the Library Group

WAYNESVILLE LIBRARY, 306 Historic 66 W, Waynesville, 65583, SAN 349-425X. Tel: 573-774-2965. FAX: 573-774-6429. *Br Mgr,* B J Pierce
Open Mon, Wed & Fri 9-6, Tues & Thurs 9-5, Sat 9-1
Friends of the Library Group

RICHMOND

S RAY COUNTY HISTORICAL SOCIETY & MUSEUM LIBRARY, 901 W Royle St, 64085. SAN 372-6568. Tel: 816-776-2305. E-mail: raycohistory@aol.com. Web Site: raycountyhistory.webs.com. *Mus Spec,* Cathy Gottsch; *Curator,* Linda Emley; Staff 1 (MLS 1)
Founded 1973
Library Holdings: Bk Titles 1,376; Bk Vols 3,000
Special Collections: Jesse James Coll; Russell Ogg Coll; William Burke Coll
Wireless access
Publications: The Looking Glass (Newsletter)
Open Wed-Sat 10-4

P RAY COUNTY LIBRARY*, 215 E Lexington St, 64085-1834. SAN 309-1252. Tel: 816-776-5102, 816-776-5104. FAX: 816-776-5103. E-mail: rclibraryservices@gmail.com. Web Site: www.raycountylibrary.com. *Libr Dir,* Stacy Hisle-Chaudri; E-mail: library.director.rcl@gmail.com; Staff 1 (MLS 1)
Founded 1947. Pop 23,494; Circ 76,143
Jan 2013-Dec 2013 Income $377,974, State $12,564, Federal $24,742, County $310,137, Locally Generated Income $30,531. Mats Exp $85,779, Books $61,074, Per/Ser (Incl. Access Fees) $1,250, AV Mat $3,661, Electronic Ref Mat (Incl. Access Fees) $19,794. Sal $166,320 (Prof $52,500)
Library Holdings: Audiobooks 1,285; Large Print Bks 1,350; Microforms 161; Bk Titles 60,000; Bk Vols 62,500; Per Subs 89; Videos 2,860
Automation Activity & Vendor Info: (Cataloging) Book Systems; (Circulation) Book Systems; (ILL) OCLC WorldShare Interlibrary Loan
Wireless access
Open Mon-Fri 9-7, Sat 9-5
Friends of the Library Group

RICHMOND HEIGHTS

P RICHMOND HEIGHTS MEMORIAL LIBRARY*, 8001 Dale Ave, 63117. SAN 309-1260. Tel: 314-645-6202. FAX: 314-781-3434. E-mail: staff@rhmlibrary.org. Web Site: www.richmondheightslibrary.org. *Libr Dir,* Jeanette Piquet; E-mail: jpiquet@rhmlibrary.org; Staff 9 (MLS 4, Non-MLS 5)
Founded 1935. Pop 9,600; Circ 195,738
Library Holdings: Bk Titles 59,432; Bk Vols 61,402; Per Subs 117; Talking Bks 448; Videos 349
Automation Activity & Vendor Info: (Acquisitions) Innovative Interfaces, Inc; (Cataloging) Innovative Interfaces, Inc; (Circulation) Innovative Interfaces, Inc; (ILL) OCLC WorldShare Interlibrary Loan; (OPAC) Innovative Interfaces, Inc; (Serials) Innovative Interfaces, Inc
Wireless access
Function: Adult bk club, After school storytime, Art exhibits, Audiobks via web, Bk club(s), Bks on CD, Children's prog, Computer training, Computers for patron use, Digital talking bks, Electronic databases & coll, Free DVD rentals, Holiday prog, ILL available, Magnifiers for reading, Mail & tel request accepted, Music CDs, Online cat, OverDrive digital audio bks, Photocopying/Printing, Preschool outreach, Preschool reading prog, Prog for adults, Prog for children & young adult, Ref serv available, Scanner, Senior outreach, Story hour, Summer & winter reading prog, Tax forms, Teen prog, Telephone ref, VHS videos, Wheelchair accessible
Partic in MLC; Saint Louis Regional Library Network
Special Services for the Blind - Aids for in-house use; Audio mat; Bks on CD; Copier with enlargement capabilities; Extensive large print coll; Large print bks; Low vision equip; Magnifiers; Playaways (bks on MP3); Ref serv; Sound rec
Open Mon-Thurs 9-9, Fri 9-8, Sat 9-5, Sun 1-5
Friends of the Library Group

ROCK HILL

P ROCK HILL PUBLIC LIBRARY, 9811 Manchester Rd, 63119. SAN 309-1279. Tel: 314-962-4723. FAX: 314-962-3932. Web Site: www.rockhillpubliclibrary.org. *Dir,* Position Currently Open; *Asst Dir, Tech Serv,* Susan Hoch; E-mail: shoch@rhplmo.org; Staff 7 (Non-MLS 7)
Founded 1943. Pop 4,765; Circ 50,418
Library Holdings: Audiobooks 400; CDs 1,020; DVDs 2,099; Bk Titles 26,898; Per Subs 70; Videos 495
Automation Activity & Vendor Info: (Cataloging) SirsiDynix; (Circulation) SirsiDynix; (ILL) OCLC Online; (OPAC) SirsiDynix; (Serials) SirsiDynix
Wireless access
Function: ILL available, Prog for children & young adult, Ref serv available, Summer reading prog, Wheelchair accessible
Partic in Municipal Library Consortium; Saint Louis Regional Library Network
Open Mon-Fri 2-6, Sat 10-2
Restriction: Open to pub for ref & circ; with some limitations

ROCK PORT

P ATCHISON COUNTY LIBRARY*, 200 S Main St, 64482. SAN 349-5000. Tel: 660-744-5404. FAX: 660-744-2861. E-mail: rockport@aclibrary.net. Web Site: acl.tlcdelivers.com. *Dir,* Robert Simpson; *Libn,* Rebecca Adams; Staff 5 (MLS 1, Non-MLS 4)
Founded 1946. Pop 6,430; Circ 42,535
Library Holdings: Large Print Bks 350; Bk Vols 60,836; Per Subs 95; Talking Bks 1,555; Videos 5,067
Subject Interests: Genealogy, Local hist
Automation Activity & Vendor Info: (Cataloging) OCLC CatExpress; (Circulation) TLC (The Library Corporation); (ILL) OCLC; (OPAC) TLC (The Library Corporation)
Wireless access
Partic in Amigos Library Services, Inc; Grand Rivers Libr Conference; Missouri Research & Education Network; Mo Libr Asn
Open Mon, Wed & Fri 9-5, Tues & Thurs 9-8, Sat 9-Noon
Branches: 2
FAIRFAX BRANCH, 118 Main St, Fairfax, 64446, SAN 349-5035. Tel: 660-686-2204. *Librn,* Amanda Agnew; Staff 1 (MLS 1)
Open Mon 9-11:30 & 12-5, Wed & Fri 12-5, Thurs 12-7
TARKIO BRANCH, 405 S 11th St, Tarkio, 64491, SAN 349-506X. Tel: 660-736-5832. *Librn,* Cheryl Freeman; Staff 1 (Non-MLS 1)
Open Mon & Fri 9-12 & 1-5, Tues 12-5, Thurs 12-5 & 6-8

ROLLA

S MISSOURI DEPARTMENT OF NATURAL RESOURCES - MISSOURI GEOLOGICAL SURVEY, Frank C Greene Memorial Library, 111 Fairgrounds Rd, 65401-2909. (Mail add: PO Box 250, 65402-0250), SAN 309-1287. Tel: 573-368-2100. FAX: 573-368-2111. E-mail: geology@dnr.mo.gov. Web Site: dnr.mo.gov. *Library Contact,* Patrick Mulvany; Tel: 573-368-2139, E-mail: patrick.mulvany@dnr.mo.gov; Staff 1 (MLS 1)
Founded 1853
Library Holdings: Bk Titles 57,400; Bk Vols 58,112; Per Subs 37
Special Collections: Ed Clark Museum of Missouri Geology; Missouri Geoscience Information Repository; Missouri Mine Map Repository
Subject Interests: Econ geol, Engr geol, Geoscience, Paleontology
Wireless access
Open Mon-Fri 8-5

P ROLLA FREE PUBLIC LIBRARY*, 900 Pine St, 65401. SAN 309-1295. Tel: 573-364-2604. FAX: 573-341-5768. E-mail: director@rollapubliclibrary.org. Web Site: rollapubliclibrary.org. *Dir,* Rebecca Buckley; E-mail: director@rollapubliclibrary.org; Staff 1 (MLS 1)
Founded 1938. Pop 16,000; Circ 104,000
Library Holdings: AV Mats 8,000; Bk Vols 53,000; Per Subs 121
Special Collections: Local Paper, 1860-present, micro
Subject Interests: Missouriana
Automation Activity & Vendor Info: (Cataloging) TLC (The Library Corporation); (Circulation) TLC (The Library Corporation); (ILL) OCLC; (OPAC) TLC (The Library Corporation)
Wireless access
Function: 24/7 Electronic res, 24/7 Online cat, Activity rm, Adult bk club, After school storytime, Audiobks via web, Bk club(s), Bks on CD, Chess club, Children's prog, Computers for patron use, E-Readers, Electronic databases & coll, Free DVD rentals, Holiday prog, ILL available, Internet access, Magazines, Magnifiers for reading, Mail & tel request accepted, Meeting rooms, Movies, Music CDs, Online cat, Online ref, OverDrive digital audio bks, Photocopying/Printing, Preschool outreach, Prog for adults, Prog for children & young adult, Ref serv available, Scanner, Senior outreach, Serves people with intellectual disabilities, Story hour, Summer reading prog, Tax forms, Teen prog, Telephone ref, Wheelchair accessible, Writing prog
Special Services for the Deaf - TDD equip
Special Services for the Blind - Bks on CD; Braille bks; Large print bks; Magnifiers
Open Mon-Fri 9-8, Sat 9-5, Sun 1:30-5
Friends of the Library Group

C STATE HISTORICAL SOCIETY OF MISSOURI - ROLLA*, Western Historical Manuscript Collection - Rolla, University of Missouri, G-3 Curtis Laws Wilson Library, 400 W 14th St, 65409-0060. SAN 326-4548. Tel: 573-341-4874. E-mail: rolla@shsmo.org. Web Site: shsmo.org/about/rolla. *Sr Archivist,* Kathleen Seale; Tel: 573-341-4440, E-mail: SealeK@shsmo.org; *Info Serv,* Carole Goggin; E-mail: GogginCJ@shsmo.org; Staff 2 (Non-MLS 2)
Special Collections: State Historical Society of Missouri; Western Historical Manuscript Coll

Subject Interests: Hist, Mineral, Mining, Mo hist
Function: Archival coll
Partic in Association of Research Libraries
Open Tues-Fri 8-4:45

C CURTIS LAWS WILSON LIBRARY, 400 W 14th St, 65409-0060. SAN 309-1317. Tel: 573-341-4008. FAX: 573-341-4233. E-mail: library@mst.edu. Web Site: library.mst.edu. *Dean of Libr,* Hsin-liang Cheng; Tel: 573-341-4011, E-mail: chenhs@mst.edu; *Dir,* Roger Weaver; Tel: 573-341-4221, E-mail: weaverjr@mst.edu; *Ref Librn,* Ellen Cline; Tel: 573-341-7839, E-mail: ecline@mst.edu; *Ref Librn,* Sherry Mahnken; Tel: 573-341-7843, E-mail: mahnkens@mst.edu; *Acq,* Becky Merrell; Tel: 573-341-4013, E-mail: rmerrell@mst.edu; Staff 14 (MLS 6, Non-MLS 8)
Founded 1871. Enrl 8,823; Fac 359; Highest Degree: Doctorate
Library Holdings: AV Mats 1,556; CDs 662; e-books 583,803; e-journals 79,731; Electronic Media & Resources 8,726; Microforms 67,337; Music Scores 677; Bk Vols 295,644; Per Subs 45
Special Collections: John H Dougherty Coll. US Document Depository
Subject Interests: Chem, Engr, Geol, Mat sci, Metallurgy, Mgt, Mining
Automation Activity & Vendor Info: (Acquisitions) Innovative Interfaces, Inc; (Cataloging) Innovative Interfaces, Inc; (Circulation) Innovative Interfaces, Inc; (Course Reserve) Innovative Interfaces, Inc; (OPAC) Innovative Interfaces, Inc; (Serials) Innovative Interfaces, Inc
Wireless access
Function: 24/7 Electronic res, 24/7 Online cat, Computers for patron use, Distance learning, Doc delivery serv, E-Reserves, Electronic databases & coll, Govt ref serv, ILL available, Internet access, Online cat, Photocopying/Printing, Ref serv available
Partic in Amigos Library Services, Inc; Merlin; MOBIUS; OCLC Online Computer Library Center, Inc
Special Services for the Blind - Magnifiers; Reader equip; Ref serv
Open Mon-Fri 7:30am-Midnight, Sat & Sun 8am-Midnight

SAINT ANN

§CR BROOKES BIBLE COLLEGE LIBRARY, 10257 St Charles Rock Rd, 63074. (Mail add: PO Box 404, 63074). Tel: 314-773-0083. Web Site: brookes.libguides.com/library, www.brookes.edu/library. *Librn,* Amy Pearce; E-mail: apearce@brookes.edu
Wireless access
Function: Computers for patron use, ILL available, Photocopying/Printing, Scanner
Partic in Saint Louis Regional Library Network
Open Mon-Fri 9-5

SAINT CHARLES

C LINDENWOOD UNIVERSITY LIBRARY, 209 S Kingshighway, 63301. SAN 309-1333. Tel: 636-949-4820. Reference Tel: 636-949-4144. E-mail: librarystc@lindenwood.edu. Web Site: www.lindenwood.edu/library. *Dir, Libr Serv,* MacDonald Elizabeth; Tel: 636-949-4396, E-mail: emacdonald@lindenwood.edu; *Digital Librn,* Michael Anthony Fetters; Tel: 636-949-4574, E-mail: mfetters@lindenwood.edu; *Ref/Outreach Librn,* Leah Rosenmiller; E-mail: lrosenmiller@lindenwood.edu; *Tech Serv Librn,* Suzanne Gleason; Tel: 636-949-4881, E-mail: sgleason@lindenwood.edu; *Mgr, Access Serv,* Lisa Young; Tel: 636-949-4670, E-mail: lyoung@lindenwood.edu; *Mgr, Ref Serv,* Nancy Messina; Tel: 636-949-4842, E-mail: nmessina@lindenwood.edu; *Circ Supvr,* Chris Smentkowski; Tel: 636-949-2529, E-mail: csmentkowski@lindenwood.edu; *Coordr, Acq,* Joanna DeYoung; Tel: 636-949-2250, E-mail: jdeyoung@lindenwood.edu; *ILL Coordr,* Jake Morrissey; Tel: 636-949-4758, E-mail: jmorrissey@lindenwood.edu; *Archivist,* Paul Huffman; Tel: 636-949-4823, E-mail: phuffman@lindenwood.edu; Staff 10 (MLS 7, Non-MLS 3)
Founded 1827. Enrl 10,000; Fac 200; Highest Degree: Doctorate
Library Holdings: Bk Vols 70,038; Per Subs 151
Special Collections: Mary E Ambler Archival Coll; The Sporting News Archives Research Coll. US Document Depository
Automation Activity & Vendor Info: (Acquisitions) Innovative Interfaces, Inc; (Cataloging) Innovative Interfaces, Inc; (Circulation) Innovative Interfaces, Inc; (Course Reserve) Innovative Interfaces, Inc; (OPAC) Innovative Interfaces, Inc; (Serials) Innovative Interfaces, Inc
Wireless access
Function: Archival coll, ILL available, Photocopying/Printing, Telephone ref
Publications: Bibliographies; Newsletter; Research Guide
Partic in Amigos Library Services, Inc; MOBIUS; OCLC Online Computer Library Center, Inc; Statewide California Electronic Library Consortium
Open Mon-Thurs 8am-10pm, Fri 8-5, Sat 10-5, Sun 2-10
Restriction: Open to pub for ref & circ; with some limitations

S SAINT CHARLES COUNTY HISTORICAL SOCIETY ARCHIVES*, Old Market House, 101 S Main St, 63301-2802. SAN 329-9295. Tel: 636-946-9828. E-mail: archives@scchs.org. Web Site: www.scchs.org. *Archivist,* Amy Haake
Founded 1956
Library Holdings: Bk Titles 500
Special Collections: Circuit & Probate Court Records-St Charles County, indexes, photographs
Open Mon, Wed & Fri 10-3
Restriction: Non-circulating

SAINT JAMES

P JAMES MEMORIAL LIBRARY*, 300 W Scioto St, 65559. SAN 309-135X. Tel: 573-265-7211. FAX: 573-265-8771. E-mail: library@stjames-mo.org. Web Site: jmpl.weebly.com. *Libr Dir,* Linda Ray; E-mail: lray@stjamesmo.org; *Ch Serv,* Niki Moen; E-mail: nmoen@stjamesmo.org; Staff 4 (MLS 1, Non-MLS 3)
Founded 1951. Pop 6,500; Circ 54,829
Library Holdings: CDs 240; Large Print Bks 500; Bk Titles 30,100; Bk Vols 30,640; Per Subs 58; Talking Bks 586; Videos 722
Special Collections: History of Ozarks, photog
Automation Activity & Vendor Info: (Cataloging) Follett Software; (Circulation) Follett Software
Wireless access
Open Mon & Tues 10-5, Wed & Sat 10-2, Thurs & Fri 10-6
Friends of the Library Group

SAINT JOSEPH

R HUFFMAN MEMORIAL UNITED METHODIST CHURCH LIBRARY, 2802 Renick St, 64507-1897. SAN 309-1406. Tel: 816-233-0239. FAX: 816-233-5427. E-mail: office@huffman-umc.org. Web Site: www.huffman-umc.org. *Librn,* Kathy George; Tel: 816-232-7809; Staff 1 (Non-MLS 1)
Founded 1958
Library Holdings: Bk Titles 4,391; Bk Vols 4,562; Per Subs 10
Subject Interests: Christian living, Devotions, Missions, Relig, Sermons
Wireless access
Open Mon-Fri 9-1

C MISSOURI WESTERN STATE UNIVERSITY, Hearnes Center, 4525 Downs Dr, 64507-2294. SAN 309-1414. Tel: 816-271-4368. Circulation Tel: 816-271-4360. Interlibrary Loan Service Tel: 816-271-4572. Reference Tel: 816-271-4573. Administration Tel: 816-271-4369. E-mail: refdesk@missouriwestern.edu. *Libr Dir,* Sally Gibson; E-mail: sgibson14@missouriwestern.edu; *Asst Dir, Tech Serv,* Stephanie Spratt; E-mail: sspratt@missouriwestern.edu; *Cat Librn,* Jennifer Callow; E-mail: jcallow@missouriwestern.edu; *Distance Educ, ILL,* Jackie Burns; E-mail: jburns@missouriwestern.edu; *Info Serv Librn,* Jim Mulder; E-mail: mulder@missouriwestern.edu; *Info Serv Librn/Spec Coll,* Rachel Lundy; E-mail: rlundy3@missouriwestern.edu; *Sr Libr Tech, Tech Serv,* Position Currently Open; *Circ,* Lisa Hensley; E-mail: lhensley1@missouriwestern.edu; *Coll Develop,* Michelle Diaz; E-mail: diaz@missouriwestern.edu; *ILL,* Jennifer Galloway; E-mail: jgalloway3@missouriwestern.edu; Staff 10 (MLS 7, Non-MLS 3)
Founded 1915. Enrl 4,800; Fac 250; Highest Degree: Master
Jul 2021-Jun 2022. Mats Exp $7,000. Sal $603,582
Library Holdings: Bk Titles 166,649; Bk Vols 229,693; Per Subs 1,585
Special Collections: Women Writers Along the Rivers. State Document Depository
Automation Activity & Vendor Info: (Acquisitions) Innovative Interfaces, Inc; (Cataloging) Innovative Interfaces, Inc; (Circulation) Innovative Interfaces, Inc; (Course Reserve) Innovative Interfaces, Inc; (ILL) Innovative Interfaces, Inc; (OPAC) Innovative Interfaces, Inc; (Serials) Innovative Interfaces, Inc
Wireless access
Publications: Library Link
Partic in MOBIUS
Special Services for the Blind - Braille equip; Reader equip; ZoomText magnification & reading software

M MOSAIC LIFE CARE*, Library Services, 5325 Faraon St, 64506. SAN 326-4831. Tel: 816-271-6075. FAX: 816-271-6074. *Librn,* Cindi Kerns; E-mail: cindi.kerns@mymlc.com
Library Holdings: Bk Titles 1,200; Per Subs 456
Subject Interests: Med, Nursing
Wireless access
Publications: Newsletter
Partic in Health Sci Libr Network
Open Mon-Fri 8-4:30

P ROLLING HILLS CONSOLIDATED LIBRARY*, 1912 N Belt Hwy, 64506. Tel: 816-232-5479. Administration Tel: 816-236-2106. FAX: 816-236-2133. E-mail: admin@rhcl.org. Web Site: rhcl.org. *Libr Dir,* Michelle Mears; E-mail: mmears@rhcl.org; Staff 37 (MLS 6, Non-MLS 31)
Founded 1961. Pop 41,428; Circ 341,420

Automation Activity & Vendor Info: (Acquisitions) Biblionix/Apollo; (Cataloging) Biblionix/Apollo; (Circulation) Biblionix/Apollo; (OPAC) Biblionix/Apollo
Wireless access
Function: 24/7 Electronic res, 24/7 Online cat, Activity rm, Adult bk club, Audiobks via web, Bk club(s), Bks on CD, Chess club, Children's prog, Computer training, Computers for patron use, Digital talking bks, Electronic databases & coll, Free DVD rentals, Holiday prog, Home delivery & serv to seniorr ctr & nursing homes, Homebound delivery serv, ILL available, Internet access, Life-long learning prog for all ages, Magazines, Mail & tel request accepted, Mail loans to mem, Mango lang, Meeting rooms, Movies, Music CDs, Online cat, Outreach serv, OverDrive digital audio bks, Passport agency, Photocopying/Printing, Preschool outreach, Preschool reading prog, Prog for adults, Prog for children & young adult, Ref serv available, Scanner, Senior computer classes, Senior outreach, Spanish lang bks, Story hour, Study rm, Summer reading prog, Tax forms, Teen prog, Wheelchair accessible, Winter reading prog, Writing prog
Open Mon-Fri 9-5
Friends of the Library Group
Branches: 2
BELT, 1904 N Belt Hwy, 64506-2201. ; Staff 16 (MLS 5, Non-MLS 11)
Founded 1961
Open Mon-Sat 9-8, Sun Noon-6
Friends of the Library Group
SAVANNAH, 514 W Main St, Savannah, 64485-1670, SAN 349-5426. Tel: 816-324-4569. Administration Tel: 816-232-5479, Ext 2401. Administration FAX: 816-236-2133. *Dir,* Michelle Mears; Staff 2 (Non-MLS 2)
Founded 1963
Open Mon-Fri 9-7, Sat 9-5, Sun Noon-5
Friends of the Library Group

S ST JOSEPH MUSEUMS INC*, Nancy Hillyard Hampton Library and Archives, 3406 Frederick Ave, 64506. (Mail add: PO Box 8096, 64508-8096), SAN 309-1430. Tel: 816-232-8471. FAX: 816-232-8482. E-mail: sjm@stjosephmuseum.org. Web Site: www.stjosephmuseum.org. *Colls Mgr,* Emily Zeman; E-mail: emily@stjosephmuseum.org; Staff 10 (Non-MLS 10)
Founded 1927
Library Holdings: Bk Titles 5,000; Bk Vols 5,280; Per Subs 15
Special Collections: History of St Joseph State Hospital (number two); Missouri History; Natural History; Oregon-California Trail; Pony Express; St Joseph During the Civil War; St Joseph History; Western Expansion
Function: Ref serv available
Publications: Museum Graphic (Newsletter)
Open Mon-Fri 9-12 & 1-4
Restriction: In-house use for visitors, Non-circulating

P ST JOSEPH PUBLIC LIBRARY*, Downtown Library, 927 Felix St, 64501-2799. SAN 349-5450. Tel: 816-232-7729. Reference Tel: 816-232-8151. Administration Tel: 816-232-4038. FAX: 816-279-3372. TDD: 816-236-2160. Web Site: sjpl.lib.mo.us. *Dir,* Mary Beth Revels; E-mail: mrevels@sjpl.lib.mo.us; *Br Mgr,* Jen Wildhagen; Staff 31 (MLS 6, Non-MLS 25)
Founded 1890. Pop 65,064; Circ 389,864
Jul 2018-Jun 2019 Income (Main & Associated Libraries) $3,394,045. Mats Exp $202,919, Books $145,985, Per/Ser (Incl. Access Fees) $15,782, Micro $2,281, AV Mat $20,567, Electronic Ref Mat (Incl. Access Fees) $18,304. Sal $1,161,609
Library Holdings: AV Mats 48,184; Bks-By-Mail 3,148; e-books 5,948; Large Print Bks 8,542; Bk Vols 242,308; Per Subs 192
Special Collections: Literature (Eugene Field Coll); Local History Coll; Medicine (Dr Wayne Toothaker Medical Library). State Document Depository; US Document Depository
Automation Activity & Vendor Info: (Acquisitions) SirsiDynix; (Cataloging) SirsiDynix; (Circulation) SirsiDynix; (ILL) OCLC WorldShare Interlibrary Loan; (OPAC) SirsiDynix
Wireless access
Function: 24/7 Online cat, 3D Printer, Activity rm, Adult bk club, Art programs, Audiobks on Playaways & MP3, Audiobks via web, Bk club(s), Bks on CD, Children's prog, Computer training, Computers for patron use, Electronic databases & coll, Family literacy, For res purposes, Free DVD rentals, Govt ref serv, Homebound delivery serv, ILL available, Internet access, Laminating, Life-long learning prog for all ages, Magazines, Magnifiers for reading, Mail & tel request accepted, Makerspace, Meeting rooms, Microfiche/film & reading machines, Movies, Music CDs, Notary serv, Online cat, Online ref, Outreach serv, OverDrive digital audio bks, Preschool outreach, Prog for adults, Prog for children & young adult, Ref & res, Ref serv available, Res performed for a fee, Scanner, Senior computer classes, Serves people with intellectual disabilities, STEM programs, Story hour, Summer & winter reading prog, Summer reading prog, Tax forms, Teen prog, Telephone ref, Wheelchair accessible
Publications: Library Matters (Monthly newsletter)
Special Services for the Deaf - TTY equip
Open Mon-Thurs 9-8, Fri & Sat 9-5, Sun 11-3
Friends of the Library Group
Branches: 3
CARNEGIE PUBLIC, 316 Massachusetts St, 64504-1449, SAN 349-5485. Tel: 816-238-0526. FAX: 816-238-9438. *Br Mgr,* Audrey Sheets
Founded 1902
Library Holdings: AV Mats 4,828; Bk Vols 29,295
Open Mon, Wed, Fri & Sat 10-6, Tues & Thurs 11-7
Friends of the Library Group
EAST HILLS LIBRARY, 502 N Woodbine Rd, 64506. Tel: 816-236-2136. FAX: 816-236-1429. *Br Mgr,* Shirley Blakeney
Founded 2004
Library Holdings: AV Mats 22,156; Bks-By-Mail 3,148; Bk Vols 93,035
Open Mon-Thurs 9-9, Fri & Sat 9-5, Sun 11-3
Friends of the Library Group
WASHINGTON PARK, 1821 N Third St, 64505-2533, SAN 349-5515. Tel: 816-232-2052. FAX: 816-236-2151. *Br Mgr,* Karen Schultz
Founded 1910
Library Holdings: AV Mats 5,312; Bk Vols 30,879
Open Mon, Wed, Fri & Sat 9-5, Tues & Thurs 12-8
Friends of the Library Group

SAINT LOUIS

M AMERICAN ASSOCIATION OF ORTHODONTISTS, Charles R Baker Memorial Library, 401 N Lindbergh Blvd, 63141. SAN 372-6207. Tel: 314-292-6542. FAX: 314-997-1745. E-mail: library@aaortho.org. *Libr Serv Mgr,* Jackie Hittner; Staff 1 (MLS 1)
Library Holdings: Bk Titles 2,000; Per Subs 80
Subject Interests: Dentistry, Orthodontics
Automation Activity & Vendor Info: (Cataloging) CyberTools for Libraries; (Circulation) CyberTools for Libraries; (OPAC) CyberTools for Libraries; (Serials) CyberTools for Libraries
Wireless access
Function: Archival coll
Restriction: Mem only

R SAUL BRODSKY JEWISH COMMUNITY LIBRARY, 12 Millstone Campus Dr, 63146. SAN 309-1732. Tel: 314-442-3720. FAX: 314-432-1277. E-mail: brodsky-library@jfedstl.org. Web Site: www.jfedstl.org. *Asst Librn,* Lorraine Landy; E-mail: LLandy@JFedSTL.org; *Archivist,* Diane M Everman; E-mail: DEverman@JFedSTL.org; Staff 4 (MLS 2, Non-MLS 2)
Founded 1983
Special Collections: Hebrew Literature; Holocaust
Subject Interests: Hist, Holocaust, Israel, Jewish art, Lit, Philos
Automation Activity & Vendor Info: (Cataloging) Follett Software; (Circulation) Follett Software
Wireless access
Open Mon & Tues 9-3, Wed-Fri 9-1
Friends of the Library Group

L BRYAN CAVE LLP*, Law Library, One Metropolitan Sq, 211 N Broadway, Ste 3600, 63102-2750. SAN 328-3054. Tel: 314-259-2298. Web Site: www.bryancave.com. *Chief Libr Officer, Res Serv,* Judy Harris; E-mail: jlharris@bryancave.com; Staff 1 (MLS 1)
Library Holdings: Bk Titles 21,815; Bk Vols 22,000; Per Subs 100
Special Collections: Annual Reports
Wireless access
Publications: Annual Report; Library Bulletin; Library Guide
Partic in OCLC Online Computer Library Center, Inc
Open Mon-Fri 8:30-5

SR CATHOLIC CENTRAL VEREIN OF AMERICA*, Central Bureau Library, 3835 Westminster Pl, 63108. SAN 328-5618. Tel: 314-371-1653. FAX: 314-371-0889. E-mail: centbur@sbcglobal.net. Web Site: www.socialjusticereview.org. *Dir,* Fr Edward Krause; Staff 2 (MLS 1, Non-MLS 1)
Founded 1908
Library Holdings: Bk Vols 250,000; Per Subs 20
Special Collections: German Americana Coll
Subject Interests: Hist, Philos, Theol
Publications: Social Justice Review (Bimonthly)
Restriction: Non-circulating to the pub, Open to students

R CONCORDIA HISTORICAL INSTITUTE*, 804 Seminary Pl, 63105-3014. SAN 309-1783. Tel: 314-505-7900. Reference Tel: 314-505-7935. Administration Tel: 314-505-7911. FAX: 314-505-7901. E-mail: chi@lutheranhistory.org. Reference E-mail: reference@lutheranhistory.org. Web Site: www.concordiahistoricalinstitute.org. *Exec Dir,* Daniel Harmelink; E-mail: dharmelink@lutheranhistory.org; *Archivist,* Todd Zittlow; E-mail: tzittlow@lutheranhistory.org; Staff 7 (MLS 1, Non-MLS 6)

Founded 1927
Library Holdings: AV Mats 800; Braille Volumes 100; CDs 200; DVDs 50; Microforms 200; Music Scores 400; Bk Vols 59,000; Per Subs 180
Special Collections: Archives of the Lutheran Church-Missouri Synod, 1839-present, ms; Carl Ferdinand Wilhelm Walther Coll; Creation Research Society; History of Lutheranism, bks, ms; Jacob Aall Otteson Preus; Lutheran Foreign Missions (Walter A Maier, Buenger, Graebner, Behnken & Rehwinkel Manuscript Coll); Lutheran Hour, broadcast discs; Lutheranism in America, History & Theology; Martin Scharlemann
Subject Interests: Lutheran churches, Lutheranism, Lutheranism in Am, Lutheranism in hist, Lutheranism in theol
Automation Activity & Vendor Info: (Cataloging) OCLC
Wireless access
Function: Archival coll
Publications: Concordia Historical Institute Quarterly (Journal); Historical Footnotes (Newsletter)
Open Mon-Fri 8:30-4
Restriction: Non-circulating
Friends of the Library Group

R CONCORDIA SEMINARY LIBRARY*, Kristine Kay Hasse Memorial Library, 801 Seminary Pl, 63105-3199. SAN 991-7276. Tel: 314-505-7038. Circulation E-mail: librarycirc@csl.edu. Web Site: www.csl.edu/resources/library. *Dir, Libr Serv,* Rev Benjamin Haupt; E-mail: hauptb@csl.edu; *Asst Dir, Libr Serv,* Eric Stancliff; E-mail: stancliffe@csl.edu; *Pub Serv Librn,* Donna Church; E-mail: churchd@csl.edu; *Tech Serv Librn,* Joel Shedlofsky; E-mail: shedlofskyj@csl.edu; Staff 5 (MLS 3, Non-MLS 2)
Founded 1839. Enrl 448; Fac 49; Highest Degree: Doctorate
Library Holdings: AV Mats 25,500; Bks on Deafness & Sign Lang 200; Braille Volumes 10; CDs 3,020; DVDs 417; e-journals 75; Music Scores 1,200; Bk Titles 195,450; Bk Vols 229,950; Per Subs 983; Videos 2,417
Special Collections: Hymnology & Liturgics; Lutherana Coll; Peasant's War
Subject Interests: Biblical studies, Lutheranism, Reformation
Automation Activity & Vendor Info: (Course Reserve) Blackboard Inc; (ILL) OCLC
Wireless access
Function: Art exhibits, Distance learning, Doc delivery serv, E-Reserves, Electronic databases & coll, ILL available, Magnifiers for reading, Online cat, Photocopying/Printing, Ref serv available, Res libr, Wheelchair accessible
Partic in Amigos Library Services, Inc; Saint Louis Regional Library Network
Open Mon-Thurs 7am-10pm, Fri 7-5, Sat 1-5, Sun 6pm-10pm
Restriction: Open to students, fac, staff & alumni, Pub use on premises

R CONGREGATION SHAARE EMETH, Hyman A Rubin Library, 11645 Ladue Rd, 63141. SAN 321-5822. Tel: 314-569-0010. FAX: 314-569-0271. Web Site: www.sestl.org/learn/hyman-a-rubin-library. *Libr Dir,* Debbie Bram; Tel: 314-692-5308, E-mail: dbram@sestl.org
Founded 1960
Library Holdings: DVDs 15; Bk Vols 15,000
Special Collections: St. Louis Authors
Wireless access
Friends of the Library Group

R COVENANT THEOLOGICAL SEMINARY, J Oliver Buswell Jr Library, 478 Covenant Ln, 63141. (Mail add: 12330 Conway Rd, 63141), SAN 309-1589. Tel: 314-392-4100, 314-434-4044. FAX: 314-392-4116, 314-434-4819. E-mail: library@covenantseminary.edu. Web Site: www.covenantseminary.edu/library. *Libr Dir,* Steve Jamieson; E-mail: steve.jamieson@covenantseminary.edu; *Coll Develop Librn,* Andy Thomas; E-mail: andy.thomas@covenantseminary.edu; *Tech Serv Librn,* Rebecca Givens; E-mail: becky.givens@covenantseminary.edu; *Assoc Librn, Pub Serv,* Andrew Stout; E-mail: andrew.stout@covenantseminary.edu; *Libr Office Mgr,* Karen Heirendt; E-mail: karen.heirendt@covenantseminary.edu; *Circ Coordr,* Alex Cain; E-mail: alex.cain@covenantseminary.edu; *Writing Center Coord,* Katie Kinney; E-mail: katie.kinney@covenantseminary.edu; Staff 5.5 (MLS 4, Non-MLS 1.5)
Founded 1956. Enrl 599; Fac 26; Highest Degree: Doctorate
Jul 2019-Jun 2020 Income $438,506. Mats Exp $387,210, Books $20,531, Per/Ser (Incl. Access Fees) $9,209, Electronic Ref Mat (Incl. Access Fees) $28,355, Presv $1,140. Sal $294,568 (Prof $180,849)
Library Holdings: AV Mats 2,725; e-books 11,281; e-journals 9,946; Electronic Media & Resources 20; Microforms 1,333; Bk Titles 68,754; Bk Vols 81,170; Per Subs 131
Special Collections: Curriculum Resource Center; Presbyterian Church in America Archives; Tait Rare Book Coll; W Harold Mare Institute for Biblical & Archaeological Studies
Subject Interests: Biblical studies, Church hist, Counseling, Puritans, Relig, Theol
Automation Activity & Vendor Info: (Acquisitions) Innovative Interfaces, Inc; (Cataloging) Innovative Interfaces, Inc; (Circulation) Innovative Interfaces, Inc; (ILL) OCLC WorldShare Interlibrary Loan; (OPAC) Innovative Interfaces, Inc; (Serials) Innovative Interfaces, Inc
Wireless access
Partic in American Theological Library Association; Association of Christian Librarians; MOBIUS; Saint Louis Regional Library Network; Saint Louis Theological Consortium; Statewide California Electronic Library Consortium

GM DEPARTMENT OF VETERANS AFFAIRS*, Medical Library, 142D/JC, 915 N Grand Blvd, 63106. SAN 309-2186. Tel: 314-289-6421. FAX: 314-289-6321. *Libr Tech,* Kevin McLaughlin; E-mail: kevin.mclaughlin3@va.gov; Staff 2 (MLS 1, Non-MLS 1)
Founded 1954
Library Holdings: e-books 78; e-journals 98; Electronic Media & Resources 10; Bk Titles 985; Per Subs 110; Videos 82
Automation Activity & Vendor Info: (Cataloging) EOS International; (Circulation) EOS International; (OPAC) EOS International
Open Mon-Fri 7:30-4

G EAST WEST GATEWAY COUNCIL OF GOVERNMENTS LIBRARY, One Memorial Dr, Ste 1600, 63102. SAN 327-1676. Tel: 314-421-4220, Ext 201. FAX: 314-231-6120. Web Site: www.ewgateway.org/library. *Library Contact,* Mary Rocchio; E-mail: mary.rocchio@ewgateway.org; Staff 1 (MLS 1)
Library Holdings: Bk Titles 5,280; Bk Vols 5,590; Per Subs 16; Talking Bks 50; Videos 50
Open Mon-Fri 8-5

SR THE EPISCOPAL DIOCESE OF MISSOURI ARCHIVES, 1210 Locust St, 63103-2322. SAN 325-2280. Tel: 314-231-1220, Ext 1375. Web Site: www.diocesemo.org. *Archivist, Registrar,* Sue Rehkopf; E-mail: srehkopf@diocesemo.org; Staff 1 (Non-MLS 1)
Founded 1840
Library Holdings: Bk Vols 1,600
Special Collections: Diocesan Archives & Historical Coll
Subject Interests: Anglican Church, Church hist, Episcopal Church
Wireless access
Restriction: Open by appt only

S FEDERAL RESERVE BANK OF SAINT LOUIS*, Research Library, One Federal Reserve Bank Plaza, 63102-2005. (Mail add: PO Box 442, 63166-0442), SAN 309-1643. Tel: 314-444-8552. Toll Free Tel: 800-333-0810. FAX: 314-444-8694. Web Site: research.stlouisfed.org. *Libr Dir, Res Serv,* Katrina L Stierholz; E-mail: katrina.l.stierholz@stls.frb.org; *Digital Projects Librn,* Pamela Campbell; Tel: 314-444-8907, E-mail: pamela.d.campbell@stls.frb.org; *Res Info Spec,* Adrienne Brennecke; Tel: 314-444-7479, E-mail: adrienne.j.brennecke@stls.frb.org; Staff 7 (MLS 6, Non-MLS 1)
Founded 1923
Library Holdings: Bk Vols 20,000; Per Subs 350
Special Collections: Federal Reserve System Publications
Subject Interests: Banking, Econ
Automation Activity & Vendor Info: (Acquisitions) SirsiDynix; (Cataloging) SirsiDynix; (Circulation) SirsiDynix; (OPAC) SirsiDynix; (Serials) SirsiDynix
Function: Res libr
Partic in Amigos Library Services, Inc; OCLC Online Computer Library Center, Inc

CR FONTBONNE UNIVERSITY*, Jack C Taylor Library, 6800 Wydown Blvd, 63105. SAN 309-1651. Tel: 314-889-1417. FAX: 314-719-8040. E-mail: libraryhelp@fontbonne.edu. Web Site: library.fontbonne.edu, www.fontbonne.edu/library. *Univ Librn,* Sharon McCaslin; Tel: 314-889-4567, E-mail: smccaslin@fontbonne.edu; *Metadata Librn, Tech Serv Librn,* Julie Portman; Tel: 314-889-4569, E-mail: jportman@fontbonne.edu; *Ref & Digital Librn,* Megahan Justin; Tel: 314-719-4566, E-mail: jmegahan@fontbonne.edu; *Ref & Instrul Serv Librn,* Peggy Ridlen; Tel: 314-889-1443, E-mail: pridlen@fontbonne.edu; *Scholarly Resources Librn,* Brady Shuman; Tel: 314-719-4666, E-mail: bshuman@fontbonne.edu; Staff 10.5 (MLS 6, Non-MLS 4.5)
Founded 1923. Enrl 2,298; Fac 118; Highest Degree: Master. Sal $435,643
Library Holdings: AV Mats 5,000; CDs 828; e-books 8,691; e-journals 73,234; Bk Titles 66,739; Bk Vols 75,235; Per Subs 251; Videos 4,076
Subject Interests: Educ
Automation Activity & Vendor Info: (Acquisitions) Innovative Interfaces, Inc; (Cataloging) Innovative Interfaces, Inc; (Circulation) Innovative Interfaces, Inc; (Course Reserve) Innovative Interfaces, Inc; (ILL) Innovative Interfaces, Inc; (Media Booking) Innovative Interfaces, Inc; (OPAC) Innovative Interfaces, Inc; (Serials) Innovative Interfaces, Inc
Wireless access
Partic in Amigos Library Services, Inc; Missouri Research & Education Network; MOBIUS; OCLC Online Computer Library Center, Inc; Saint Louis Regional Library Network
Open Mon-Thurs 7:30am-10pm, Fri 7:30-3, Sat 9:30-5, Sun 1:30-9

CM GOLDFARB SCHOOL OF NURSING AT BARNES-JEWISH COLLEGE LIBRARY, 4483 Duncan Ave, Mail Stop 90-30-697, 63110. SAN 349-5639. Tel: 314-362-1699, 314-454-7055. Toll Free Tel: 800-832-9009. Web Site: www.barnesjewishcollege.edu. *Dir, Libr & Info Serv,* Renee Gorrell; Tel: 314-454-8171, E-mail: renee.gorrell@barnesjewishcollege.edu; *Libr Asst,* Anise Gilliam; E-mail: anise.gilliam@barnesjewishcollege.edu; Staff 3.5 (MLS 1.5, Non-MLS 2)
Founded 1984. Enrl 800; Highest Degree: Doctorate
Library Holdings: AV Mats 50; e-books 20,000; e-journals 4,000; Bk Titles 1,000
Special Collections: American Nurses Association (ANA) Publications
Subject Interests: Clinical labs, Health serv admin, Holistic health, Nursing, Pain mgt, Palliative care
Automation Activity & Vendor Info: (Cataloging) Innovative Interfaces, Inc - Sierra; (Circulation) Innovative Interfaces, Inc - Sierra
Wireless access
Partic in Amigos Library Services, Inc; Mid Continental Med Libr Asn; MOBIUS; OCLC-LVIS; Saint Louis Regional Library Network
Open Mon-Thurs 7:30-8, Fri 7:30-5
Restriction: In-house use for visitors, Open to students, fac & staff

C HARRIS-STOWE STATE UNIVERSITY LIBRARY, AT&T Library & Technology Resource Center, 3026 Laclede Ave, 63103. SAN 309-1708. Tel: 314-340-3624. FAX: 314-340-3630. E-mail: library@hssu.edu. Web Site: www.hssu.edu/rsp_index.cfm?wid=20. *Coordr, Spec Serv, Interim Dir,* Linda Orzel; E-mail: orzell@hssu.edu; Staff 3 (MLS 2, Non-MLS 1)
Founded 1857. Highest Degree: Bachelor
Library Holdings: CDs 105; Bk Titles 79,500; Bk Vols 79,600; Per Subs 100; Videos 227
Special Collections: St Louis Public School Archives
Subject Interests: Educ, Ethnic studies, Urban studies
Automation Activity & Vendor Info: (Acquisitions) Innovative Interfaces, Inc - Sierra; (Cataloging) Innovative Interfaces, Inc - Sierra; (Circulation) Innovative Interfaces, Inc - Sierra; (OPAC) Innovative Interfaces, Inc - Sierra; (Serials) Innovative Interfaces, Inc - Sierra
Wireless access
Partic in MOBIUS; Saint Louis Regional Library Network
Restriction: Authorized patrons

S HEALTH CAPITAL CONSULTANTS, LLC LIBRARY, 2127 Innerbelt Business Center Dr, Ste 107, 63114-5700. SAN 377-824X. Tel: 314-994-7641. Toll Free Tel: 800-394-8258. FAX: 314-991-3435. E-mail: books@healthcapital.com. Web Site: www.healthcapital.com. *Pres,* Todd Zigrang; Staff 3 (MLS 1, Non-MLS 2)
Founded 1993
Library Holdings: Bk Titles 3,500; Bk Vols 3,800; Per Subs 80
Special Collections: Business Valuation; Healthcare Industry (Financial, Economic & Policy Areas of Healthcare Services)
Automation Activity & Vendor Info: (Cataloging) Inmagic, Inc.; (Circulation) Inmagic, Inc.
Wireless access

L HUSCH BLACKWELL LLP*, Law Library, 190 Carondelet Plaza, Ste 600, 63105. SAN 372-4751. Tel: 314-480-1500. FAX: 314-480-1505. Web Site: www.huschblackwell.com. *Mgr, Res,* Karla A Morris-Holmes; E-mail: karla.morris-holmes@huschblackwell.com; Staff 1 (Non-MLS 1)
Library Holdings: Bk Titles 9,500; Bk Vols 10,000; Per Subs 95
Restriction: Staff use only

S JEFFERSON NATIONAL EXPANSION MEMORIAL LIBRARY*, 11 N Fourth St, 63102. SAN 309-1724. Tel: 314-655-1600. FAX: 314-655-1652. Web Site: www.nps.gov/jeff. *Librn,* Tom Dewey; Tel: 314-655-1632, E-mail: tom_dewey@partner.nps.gov
Founded 1935
Library Holdings: Bk Vols 6,150; Per Subs 60
Special Collections: Jefferson National Expansion Memorial Archives
Subject Interests: St Louis hist, Westward expansion
Function: Res libr
Open Mon-Fri 8-4:30
Restriction: Non-circulating to the pub

R KENRICK-GLENNON SEMINARY*, Charles L Souvay Memorial Library, 5200 Glennon Dr, 63119. SAN 309-1740. Tel: 314-792-6100. FAX: 314-792-6503. E-mail: souvaylibrary@kenrick.edu. Web Site: souvaylibrarykgs.org, www.kenrick.edu. *Libr Dir,* Mary Ann Aubin; Tel: 314-792-6302, E-mail: aubin@kenrick.edu; *Electronic Res Librn,* Frances Behrman; Tel: 314-792-6144, E-mail: francesbehrman@kenrick.edu; *Acq & Ser,* Rose Lawson; Tel: 314-792-6131, E-mail: lawson@kenrick.edu; *Tech Asst,* Mary Grosch; Tel: 314-792-6126, E-mail: grosch@kenrick.edu; Staff 4 (MLS 3, Non-MLS 1)
Founded 1893. Enrl 1,141; Fac 26; Highest Degree: Master
Library Holdings: Bk Vols 80,000
Special Collections: Official Catholic Directory; Pre-Vatican II Catechism Coll; Rare Book Coll; Thomas Merton Coll
Subject Interests: Archives, Canon law, Liturgics, Patristics, Roman Catholic theol, Scripture
Wireless access
Partic in MOBIUS; OCLC Online Computer Library Center, Inc

S LAUMEIER SCULPTURE PARK LIBRARY & ARCHIVE*, 12580 Rott Rd, 63127. SAN 374-5708. Tel: 314-615-5280. E-mail: info@laumeier.org. Web Site: www.laumeiersculpturepark.org. *Curator,* Dana Turkovic; E-mail: dturkovic@laumeier.org; Staff 1 (MLS 1)
Founded 1986
Library Holdings: Bk Titles 3,200; Per Subs 18
Special Collections: Contemporary Sculpture Coll
Function: Ref serv available
Restriction: Open by appt only

L LAW LIBRARY ASSOCIATION OF SAINT LOUIS, 1300 Civil Courts Bldg, Ten N Tucker Blvd, 63101. SAN 309-1775. Tel: 314-622-4470. FAX: 314-241-0911. Web Site: llastl.org. *Libr Dir,* Gail Wechsler; E-mail: gwechsler@llastl.org; Staff 3 (MLS 1, Non-MLS 2)
Founded 1838
Library Holdings: Bk Vols 70,000; Per Subs 120
Wireless access
Open Mon-Fri 8:30-6

S LEWIS RICE LLC LAW LIBRARY, 600 Washington Ave, Ste 2500, 63101. SAN 327-7437. Tel: 314-444-7600. FAX: 314-241-6056. Web Site: www.lewisrice.com. *Librn,* Leslie Carnemolla; Staff 1 (MLS 1)
Publications: Monthly accessions list
Restriction: Staff use only

M LUTHERAN SCHOOL OF NURSING*, Louise Kraus-Ament Memorial Library, St Alexas Hospital, Education Bldg, 3547 S Jefferson Ave, 63118. SAN 309-1791. Tel: 314-577-5864. FAX: 314-268-6160. Web Site: www.nursingschoollmc.com/liabrary.php. *Med Librn,* Brian McFerron; E-mail: brian.mcferron@southcityhospitalstl.com; Staff 2 (MLS 1, Non-MLS 1)
Library Holdings: Bk Titles 4,675; Bk Vols 5,000; Per Subs 73
Subject Interests: Nursing educ, Primary educ

S MALLINCKRODT*, Pharma Info Center, 3600 N Second St, 63147-3457. SAN 309-1813. Administration Tel: 314-654-1511. FAX: 314-654-1513. Web Site: www.mallinckrodt.com. *Sr Info Spec,* Dennis Eliceiri; Staff 7 (MLS 5, Non-MLS 2)
Founded 1867
Library Holdings: Bk Titles 10,740; Bk Vols 11,500; Per Subs 150
Special Collections: Pre-1900 German Chemistry & Pharmaceutical Monographs; Pre-1900 Pharmacopeias
Subject Interests: Chem, Pharmaceutical chem
Automation Activity & Vendor Info: (Cataloging) EOS International; (ILL) OCLC; (Serials) EOS International
Wireless access
Partic in OCLC Online Computer Library Center, Inc
Restriction: Staff use only

C MARYVILLE UNIVERSITY LIBRARY*, 650 Maryville University Dr, 63141. SAN 309-1821. Tel: 314-529-9595. Interlibrary Loan Service Tel: 314-529-9591. FAX: 314-529-9941. E-mail: reference@maryville.edu. Web Site: www.maryville.edu/library. *Libr Operations Mgr,* Theresa Olson; E-mail: tolson@maryville.edu; *Med Librn,* Jacob Beard; Tel: 314-529-6528, E-mail: jbeard1@maryville.edu; *Libr Operations Mgr,* Thomas Olson; Tel: 314-529-9493, E-mail: tolson@maryville.edu; *Univ Archivist,* Emma Prince; Tel: 314-529-9491, E-mail: eprince1@maryville.edu; *Access Serv, Ref Serv,* Stacey Bradley; Tel: 314-529-9595, E-mail: sbradley@maryville.edu; Staff 11 (MLS 5, Non-MLS 6)
Founded 1872. Enrl 3,564; Fac 502; Highest Degree: Doctorate
Jun 2013-May 2014. Mats Exp $403,385. Sal $593,952 (Prof $304,806)
Library Holdings: AV Mats 148,111; e-books 187,193; e-journals 84,496; Microforms 29,773; Bk Vols 64,248; Per Subs 262
Special Collections: Maryville Archives; Papers of Edward S Dowling. US Document Depository
Subject Interests: Actuarial sci, Educ, Music therapy, Nursing
Automation Activity & Vendor Info: (Acquisitions) Innovative Interfaces, Inc; (Cataloging) Innovative Interfaces, Inc; (Circulation) Innovative Interfaces, Inc; (Course Reserve) Innovative Interfaces, Inc; (Discovery) EBSCO Discovery Service; (ILL) OCLC ILLiad; (OPAC) Innovative Interfaces, Inc; (Serials) Innovative Interfaces, Inc
Wireless access
Partic in Amigos Library Services, Inc; MOBIUS; OCLC Online Computer Library Center, Inc; Saint Louis Regional Library Network
Open Mon-Thurs 8am-10pm, Fri 8-6, Sat 9-6, Sun 11-6
Friends of the Library Group

M MERCY HOSPITAL*, Thomas F Frawley Medical Library, Tower B, Ste 1000, 621 S New Ballas Rd, 63141. SAN 309-1988. Tel: 314-251-6340. FAX: 314-251-4299. E-mail: medlib@mercy.net. Web Site: mercy.net/practice/mercy-hospital-st-louis/thomas-f-frawley-medical-library. *Dir,* Jennifer P Plaat; E-mail: jennifer.plaat@mercy.net; *Asst Dir,* Kathleen Alsup; E-mail: alsuks@stlo.mercy.net
Library Holdings: e-books 700; e-journals 2,000; Bk Vols 1,000; Per Subs 350
Subject Interests: Clinical med, Dentistry, Nursing
Partic in National Network of Libraries of Medicine Region 3; OCLC Online Computer Library Center, Inc
Open Mon-Fri 7-5

M MISSOURI BAPTIST MEDICAL CENTER*, Medical Library, 3015 N Ballas Rd, 63131. SAN 321-6209. Tel: 314-996-5000. FAX: 314-996-5031. E-mail: library@bjc.org. Web Site: www.missouribaptist.org. *Librn,* David Owens; Tel: 314-996-5531, E-mail: david.owens@bjc.org
Founded 1965
Library Holdings: Bk Titles 100; Per Subs 125
Open Mon-Fri 7-5

C MISSOURI BAPTIST UNIVERSITY*, Jung-Kellogg Library, One College Park Dr, 63141-8698. SAN 309-1864. Tel: 314-434-1115. Circulation Tel: 314-392-2320. FAX: 314-392-2343. Circulation E-mail: library@mobap.edu. Web Site: www.mobap.edu/library. *Dir, Libr Serv,* Zana Sueme; E-mail: zana.sueme@mobap.edu; *Ref Librn,* Ling Thumin; E-mail: ling.thumin@mobap.edu; *Circ Mgr,* Linda Webb; E-mail: linda.webb@mobap.edu; Staff 11 (MLS 4, Non-MLS 7)
Founded 1968. Enrl 5,276; Fac 69; Highest Degree: Doctorate
Library Holdings: AV Mats 4,598; Bk Titles 65,612; Bk Vols 70,210; Per Subs 165
Automation Activity & Vendor Info: (Acquisitions) Innovative Interfaces, Inc; (Cataloging) OCLC; (Circulation) Innovative Interfaces, Inc; (Course Reserve) Innovative Interfaces, Inc; (ILL) OCLC; (OPAC) Innovative Interfaces, Inc; (Serials) Innovative Interfaces, Inc
Wireless access
Partic in Amigos Library Services, Inc; Missouri Research & Education Network; MOBIUS; Saint Louis Regional Library Network
Open Mon, Tues & Thurs (Winter) 7:30-9:30, Wed & Fri 7:30-5, Sat 10-2; Mon, Tues & Thurs (Summer) 8-7, Wed 8-4:30, Fri 8-12

S MISSOURI BOTANICAL GARDEN*, Peter H Raven Library, 4500 Shaw Blvd, 4th Flr, 63110. (Mail add: 4344 Shaw Blvd, 63110), SAN 309-1872. Tel: 314-577-5155. Reference Tel: 314-577-5159. FAX: 314-577-0840. E-mail: library@mobot.org. Web Site: www.missouribotanicalgarden.org/plant-science/plant-science/resources/raven-library. *Dir,* Douglas L Holland; Tel: 314-577-0842, E-mail: doug.holland@mobot.org; Staff 12 (MLS 7, Non-MLS 5)
Founded 1859
Library Holdings: Bk Vols 200,000; Per Subs 800
Special Collections: Archives; Bryology (Steere Coll); Ewan Coll; Folio Coll; Post-Linnaean Rare Book Coll; Pre-Linnaean Coll; Pre-Linnean Botany (Sturtevant Coll); Rare Book Coll. Oral History
Subject Interests: Bot exploration, Botanical hist, Botany, Hort
Automation Activity & Vendor Info: (Acquisitions) Innovative Interfaces, Inc; (Cataloging) Innovative Interfaces, Inc; (Circulation) Innovative Interfaces, Inc; (OPAC) Innovative Interfaces, Inc; (Serials) Innovative Interfaces, Inc
Publications: Accessions List (Monthly)
Partic in OCLC Online Computer Library Center, Inc
Open Mon-Fri 8:30-5

L MISSOURI COURT OF APPEALS*, Eastern District Library, One Old Post Office Sq, Rm 304, 815 Olive St, 63101. SAN 372-4131. Tel: 314-539-4300. FAX: 314-539-4324. Web Site: www.courts.mo.gov/page.jsp?id=99. *Librn,* Maureen Jacquot; Staff 1 (MLS 1)
Library Holdings: Bk Titles 28,618; Bk Vols 30,000; Per Subs 12
Restriction: Staff use only

GM MISSOURI DEPARTMENT OF MENTAL HEALTH*, 5400 Arsenal St, 63139-1403. SAN 309-1899. Tel: 314-877-5967. *Dir,* Amanda Hunyar. Subject Specialists: *Educ, Mental health, Psychiat,* Amanda Hunyar; Staff 2 (MLS 1, Non-MLS 1)
Founded 1962
Special Collections: Saint Louis State Hospital Archives
Subject Interests: Psychiat, Psychiat nursing, Psychol, Substance abuse
Automation Activity & Vendor Info: (Circulation) Follett Software; (OPAC) TLC (The Library Corporation)

S MISSOURI HISTORICAL SOCIETY*, Library & Research Center, 225 S Skinker Blvd, 63105. (Mail add: PO Box 775460, 63177), SAN 309-1880. Tel: 314-746-4500. FAX: 314-746-4548. E-mail: library@mohistory.org. Web Site: www.mohistory.org. *Librn,* Emily Jaycox; *Cat Librn,* Debbie Schraut; *Ref & Info Serv, Web Coordr,* Jason D Stratman; *Acq, ILL,* Kelly Brown; Tel: 314-746-4506, E-mail: kbrown@mohistory.org; *Presv Spec,* Randall Blomquist. Subject Specialists: *Maps,* Emily Jaycox; Staff 6.2 (MLS 3, Non-MLS 3.2)
Founded 1866
Library Holdings: Bk Titles 77,623; Bk Vols 81,496; Per Subs 250
Special Collections: Charles Lindbergh; Lewis & Clark Expedition; Trade Catalogs
Subject Interests: Genealogy, Hist, Music
Automation Activity & Vendor Info: (Acquisitions) Innovative Interfaces, Inc - Sierra; (Cataloging) OCLC Connexion; (Circulation) Innovative Interfaces, Inc - Sierra; (OPAC) Innovative Interfaces, Inc - Sierra; (Serials) Innovative Interfaces, Inc - Sierra
Wireless access
Function: 24/7 Online cat, Archival coll, Electronic databases & coll, Internet access, Microfiche/film & reading machines, Online cat, Orientations, Outside serv via phone, mail, e-mail & web, Ref serv available, Res assist avail, Res libr, Wheelchair accessible
Publications: In Her Own Write
Partic in Amigos Library Services, Inc; MOBIUS; Saint Louis Regional Library Network; Saint Louis Research Libraries Consortium
Open Tues-Fri 12-5, Sat 10-5
Restriction: Closed stack, Non-circulating, Not a lending libr

S MISSOURI SCHOOL FOR THE BLIND LIBRARY*, 3815 Magnolia Ave, 63110. SAN 372-6703. Tel: 314-633-1566. FAX: 314-773-3762. Web Site: msb.dese.mo.gov/library-media-center. *Librn,* Steven Daley; E-mail: Steven.Daley@msb.dese.mo.gov; *Asst Librn,* Chris Davidson; E-mail: Christine.Davidson@msb.dese.mo.gov; Staff 2 (MLS 1, Non-MLS 1)
Library Holdings: Braille Volumes 10,500; DVDs 304; Large Print Bks 3,800; Bk Titles 21,400; Bk Vols 26,000; Per Subs 52; Talking Bks 10,000; Videos 350
Special Collections: Blind Education Coll
Automation Activity & Vendor Info: (Cataloging) Follett Software; (Circulation) Follett Software; (OPAC) Follett Software
Special Services for the Blind - Accessible computers; Assistive/Adapted tech devices, equip & products; Bks on cassette; Bks on CD; Bks on flash-memory cartridges; Braille bks; Braille Webster's dictionary; Cassette playback machines; Closed circuit TV magnifier; Digital talking bk; Digital talking bk machines; Extensive large print coll; Internet workstation with adaptive software; Large print bks; Magnifiers; Ref in Braille; Screen enlargement software for people with visual disabilities; Screen reader software; Talking bks & player equip; ZoomText magnification & reading software
Open Mon-Fri 8:15-4
Restriction: Open to students, fac & staff, Pub use on premises

S MUSEUM OF TRANSPORTATION*, Reference Library, 2933 Barrett Station Rd, 63122. SAN 309-1910. Tel: 314-615-8668, 314-965-6885. FAX: 314-965-0242. Web Site: transportmuseumassociation.org, www.museumoftransport.org. *Archivist,* Teresa Militello
Founded 1944
Library Holdings: Bk Vols 8,000; Per Subs 10
Special Collections: Transportation Coll
Subject Interests: Air, Automobiles, Marine, Rail
Restriction: Open by appt only
Friends of the Library Group

S NESTLE PURINA PET CARE CO*, Library & Information Services, Checkerboard Sq 2S, 63164. SAN 309-1961. Tel: 314-982-5913. Interlibrary Loan Service Tel: 314-982-2150. Web Site: www.purina.com. *Mgr,* Justin Smith; *Coordr, Search Serv,* Geri Heberlie; Staff 5 (MLS 3, Non-MLS 2)
Founded 1929
Library Holdings: e-journals 100; Bk Titles 8,000; Per Subs 150
Subject Interests: Animal, Food proc, Human nutrition, Sanitation, Veterinary med
Automation Activity & Vendor Info: (Cataloging) EOS International; (Circulation) EOS International; (ILL) OCLC; (OPAC) EOS International; (Serials) EOS International
Wireless access
Partic in Amigos Library Services, Inc; OCLC Online Computer Library Center, Inc; Proquest Dialog
Open Mon-Fri 8-4:30

L POLSINELLI PC*, Law Library, 100 S Fourth St, Ste 1000, 63102. SAN 372-4727. Tel: 314-889-8000. Web Site: www.polsinelli.com. *Librn,* Mary K Macaulay; E-mail: mmacaulay@polsinelli.com; Staff 1 (MLS 1)
Library Holdings: Bk Vols 500
Wireless access
Open Mon-Fri 8:30-5

S PULITZER, INC, Saint Louis Post-Dispatch News Research Department, 900 N Tucker Blvd, 63101. SAN 309-1953. Tel: 314-340-8270. Toll Free Tel: 800-365-0820, Ext 8728. Web Site: www.stltoday.com. *Dir,* Mike Meiners; Staff 15 (MLS 3, Non-MLS 12)
Founded 1922
Library Holdings: Bk Titles 4,100
Special Collections: Housing (Pruitt-Igoe Housing Development Coll), flm; Post-Dispatch Authors Coll; Saint Louis Sun Times, microfilm; St. Louis Post-Dispatch Archives; Theater (St Louis Municipal Opera Coll), clippings
Subject Interests: Intl news, Newsp clipping files, Newsp photogs, Newsp subjects related to nat
Function: Archival coll, Res libr
Restriction: Not open to pub

S SAINT LOUIS ART MUSEUM*, Richardson Memorial Library, One Fine Arts Dr, Forest Park, 63110. SAN 309-1996. Tel: 314-655-5252. FAX: 314-721-6172. E-mail: library@slam.org. Web Site: www.slam.org/research/library-archives. *Archivist,* Jenna Stout; Tel: 314-655-5452, E-mail: jenna.stout@slam.org; Staff 4 (MLS 3, Non-MLS 1)
Founded 1915
Library Holdings: AV Mats 6,000; Bk Titles 83,000; Bk Vols 112,000; Per Subs 200
Special Collections: Contemporary Art Ephemera; Louisiana Purchase Exposition 1904 Records; Museum History Coll; Rare Art Books Coll
Subject Interests: Art hist
Automation Activity & Vendor Info: (Acquisitions) Innovative Interfaces, Inc; (Cataloging) Innovative Interfaces, Inc; (Circulation) Innovative Interfaces, Inc; (OPAC) Innovative Interfaces, Inc; (Serials) Innovative Interfaces, Inc
Partic in OCLC Online Computer Library Center, Inc; OCLC Research Library Partnership; Saint Louis Research Libraries Consortium
Open Tues-Fri 10-5
Restriction: Non-circulating to the pub

M SAINT LOUIS CHILDREN'S HOSPITAL*, Medical Library, One Children's Pl, 3rd Flr, Ste 3N-34, 63110. SAN 329-3823. Tel: 314-454-2768. FAX: 314-454-2340. Web Site: www.stlouischildrens.org/health-care-professionals/education/medical-staff-library. Staff 1 (Non-MLS 1)
Library Holdings: Bk Titles 1,226; Per Subs 28
Subject Interests: Med, Nursing, Pediatrics
Wireless access
Restriction: Staff use only

SAINT LOUIS COMMUNITY COLLEGE

J FLORISSANT VALLEY CAMPUS LIBRARY*, 3400 Pershall Rd, Ferguson, 63135-1408, SAN 349-5965. Tel: 314-513-4511. Circulation Tel: 314-513-4514. Reference Tel: 314-513-4420, 314-513-4517. FAX: 314-513-4053. Web Site: www.stlcc.edu. *Libr Serv Supvr,* Roger Thomas; Tel: 314-513-4529, E-mail: rthomas1@stlcc.edu; *Coordr, Libr Serv,* Christopher C White; Tel: 314-513-4484, E-mail: cwhite@stlcc.cc.mo.us; Staff 24 (MLS 7, Non-MLS 17)
Founded 1963. Enrl 3,639; Fac 244; Highest Degree: Associate
Library Holdings: Bk Titles 91,853; Bk Vols 102,439; Per Subs 584; Talking Bks 589; Videos 1,260
Automation Activity & Vendor Info: (Acquisitions) Innovative Interfaces, Inc; (Cataloging) Innovative Interfaces, Inc; (Circulation) Innovative Interfaces, Inc; (Course Reserve) Innovative Interfaces, Inc; (OPAC) Innovative Interfaces, Inc; (Serials) Innovative Interfaces, Inc
Function: Ref serv available
Partic in Amigos Library Services, Inc
Special Services for the Deaf - TDD equip

J FOREST PARK CAMPUS LIBRARY*, 5600 Oakland Ave, 63110-1316, SAN 349-599X. Tel: 314-644-9209. Circulation Tel: 314-644-9210. Reference Tel: 314-644-9214. FAX: 314-644-9240. TDD: 314-644-9969. Web Site: www.stlcc.edu. *Libr Mgr,* June S Williams; E-mail: jswilliams@stlcc.edu; *Coordr, Libr Serv,* Jean Thomas; Tel: 314-644-9206, E-mail: jthomas@stlcc.edu; *Libr Spec,* Renee Potts; Tel: 314-644-9681, E-mail: rpotts@stlcc.edu; Staff 11 (MLS 4, Non-MLS 7)
Founded 1965. Enrl 4,095; Fac 127; Highest Degree: Associate
Library Holdings: AV Mats 5,481; Bk Vols 82,766; Per Subs 624
Special Collections: Black Studies (Afro-American) bks, per
Subject Interests: Allied health, Food indust, Med, Nursing, Restaurant mgt, Tourism
Automation Activity & Vendor Info: (Circulation) Innovative Interfaces, Inc; (Course Reserve) Innovative Interfaces, Inc; (OPAC) Innovative Interfaces, Inc; (Serials) Innovative Interfaces, Inc
Partic in Missouri Research & Education Network
Publications: Collection Development Statement; Library Guide; Library Services for the Faculty
Special Services for the Deaf - TDD equip

J INSTRUCTIONAL RESOURCES*, 5460 Highland Park Dr, 63110, SAN 349-5930. Tel: 314-644-9555. Interlibrary Loan Service Tel: 314-644-9560. Web Site: www.stlcc.edu. *Dir,* Sheila Ouellette; Tel: 314-644-9557, E-mail: souellette@stlcc.edu; *Acq, Coordr, Libr Serv,* Kimberly Linkous; Tel: 314-644-9559, E-mail: klinkous@stlcc.edu; *Libr Spec, ILL,* Bridgette Lee; E-mail: blee@stlcc.edu; Staff 12 (MLS 6, Non-MLS 6)
Founded 1962. Highest Degree: Associate
Library Holdings: AV Mats 94; DVDs 35; e-books 10,000; Bk Vols 393; Per Subs 21; Videos 1,731
Special Collections: College Archives; Video Library
Automation Activity & Vendor Info: (Acquisitions) Innovative Interfaces, Inc; (Cataloging) Innovative Interfaces, Inc; (Circulation) Innovative Interfaces, Inc; (ILL) OCLC; (Media Booking) Dymaxion; (OPAC) Innovative Interfaces, Inc; (Serials) Innovative Interfaces, Inc
Partic in Higher Educ Coun of St Louis; Missouri Research & Education Network; MOBIUS; Saint Louis Regional Library Network

J MERAMEC CAMPUS LIBRARY*, 11333 Big Bend Rd, 63122-5720, SAN 349-6023. Tel: 314-984-7616. Circulation Tel: 314-984-7797. Reference Tel: 314-984-7613. FAX: 314-984-7225. Web Site: www.stlcc.edu/libraries. *Sr Mgr, Campus Libr & Instrul Res,* Bonnie Sanguinet; Tel: 314-984-7624, E-mail: bsanguinet@stlcc.edu; *Supvr, Libr Serv,* Patrick Mallory; Tel: 314-984-7615, E-mail: pmallory1@stlcc.edu; Staff 8.5 (MLS 6.5, Non-MLS 2)
Founded 1963. Enrl 11,500; Fac 8; Highest Degree: Associate
Library Holdings: AV Mats 12,945; e-books 17,218; Bk Titles 113,306; Bk Vols 120,906; Per Subs 553
Automation Activity & Vendor Info: (Cataloging) Innovative Interfaces, Inc - Millennium; (Circulation) Innovative Interfaces, Inc - Millennium; (Course Reserve) Innovative Interfaces, Inc - Millennium; (OPAC) Innovative Interfaces, Inc; (Serials) Innovative Interfaces, Inc - Millennium
Function: Audio & video playback equip for onsite use, Bks on cassette, Bks on CD, Computers for patron use, Doc delivery serv, Electronic databases & coll, Free DVD rentals, Games & aids for people with disabilities, ILL available, Internet access, Magnifiers for reading, Music CDs, Notary serv, Online cat, Online info literacy tutorials on the web & in blackboard, Online ref, Orientations, Outside serv via phone, mail, e-mail & web, Photocopying/Printing, Prof lending libr, Ref & res, Ref serv available, Serves people with intellectual disabilities, Spoken cassettes & CDs, Spoken cassettes & DVDs, Telephone ref, VHS videos, Wheelchair accessible
Partic in Higher Educ Coun of Metrop St Louis; Missouri Research & Education Network
Publications: A Guide to Meramec Library; Services & Products Booklets
Special Services for the Deaf - Accessible learning ctr; ADA equip; Assisted listening device; Assistive tech; Bks on deafness & sign lang; Closed caption videos; High interest/low vocabulary bks
Special Services for the Blind - Accessible computers; Aids for in-house use; Assistive/Adapted tech devices, equip & products; Bks on cassette; Bks on CD; Braille equip; Computer with voice synthesizer for visually impaired persons; Copier with enlargement capabilities; Daisy reader; Dragon Naturally Speaking software; Integrated libr/media serv; Internet workstation with adaptive software; Networked computers with assistive software; Rec of textbk mat; Recorded bks; Scanner for conversion & translation of mats; Screen enlargement software for people with visual disabilities; Screen reader software; Soundproof reading booth; Talking bks; Talking bks & player equip
Open Mon-Thurs 7:30am-10pm, Fri 7:30-5, Sat 8-5, Sun 1-5

P SAINT LOUIS COUNTY LIBRARY*, Headquarters, 1640 S Lindbergh Blvd, 63131-3598. SAN 349-6058. Tel: 314-994-3300. FAX: 314-997-7602. Web Site: www.slcl.org. *Libr Dir,* Kristen L Sorth; E-mail: ksorth@slcl.org; *Dep Dir,* Eric Button; Tel: 314-994-3300, Ext 3253, E-mail: ebutton@slcl.org; *Asst Dir, Admin,* Mr Kris Mooney; E-mail: kmooney@slcl.org; *Asst Dir, Advan,* Barbara Turkington; Tel: 314-994-3300, Ext 2152, E-mail: bturkington@slcl.org; *Asst Dir, Fac,* Steve Hunter; E-mail: shunter@slcl.org; *Adminr, Support Serv,* Stephanie Nordmann; Tel: 314-994-3300, Ext 2220, E-mail: snordmann@slcl.org; *Develop Mgr,* Jim Bogart; Tel: 314-994-3300, Ext 2156; *Mgr, Youth Serv,* Nicole Clawson; Tel: 314-994-3300, Ext 2230; *Libr Planner,* Marie Conlin; E-mail: mconlin@slcl.org. Subject Specialists: *Develop, Foundations,* Barbara Turkington; Staff 645 (MLS 85, Non-MLS 560)
Founded 1946. Pop 860,000; Circ 10,876,070
Jan 2020-Dec 2020 Income $64,269,446, State $762,593, Federal $64,943, County $62,005,281, Other $1,436,629. Mats Exp $7,986,315, Books $2,990,000, Per/Ser (Incl. Access Fees) $200,000, Other Print Mats $105,000, Micro $23,000, AV Mat $1,847,000, Electronic Ref Mat (Incl. Access Fees) $2,635,000. Sal $20,274,055 (Prof $5,476,600)
Library Holdings: Audiobooks 47,039; AV Mats 315,421; CDs 9,353; DVDs 228,398; e-books 131,127; e-journals 9,313; Electronic Media & Resources 181,296; High Interest/Low Vocabulary Bk Vols 1,650,568; Large Print Bks 53,520; Microforms 221,787; Bk Vols 1,204,714; Per Subs 3,516; Videos 228,398
Special Collections: State Document Depository; US Document Depository

Subject Interests: Asian mat, Bus, Fiction, Finance, Genealogy, Local hist, Mgt
Automation Activity & Vendor Info: (Acquisitions) Innovative Interfaces, Inc; (Cataloging) Innovative Interfaces, Inc; (Circulation) Innovative Interfaces, Inc; (Course Reserve) Innovative Interfaces, Inc; (ILL) Innovative Interfaces, Inc; (Media Booking) Innovative Interfaces, Inc; (OPAC) Innovative Interfaces, Inc; (Serials) Innovative Interfaces, Inc
Wireless access
Function: Adult bk club, Adult literacy prog, Archival coll, Audiobks on Playaways & MP3, Audiobks via web, Bk club(s), Bks on CD, Children's prog, Computer training, Computers for patron use, Electronic databases & coll, Free DVD rentals, Govt ref serv, Holiday prog, Home delivery & serv to seniorr ctr & nursing homes, Homebound delivery serv, ILL available, Instruction & testing, Internet access, Jail serv, Life-long learning prog for all ages, Magazines, Magnifiers for reading, Mango lang, Meeting rooms, Microfiche/film & reading machines, Movies, Music CDs, Online cat, Online ref, Outreach serv, OverDrive digital audio bks, Photocopying/Printing, Preschool outreach, Preschool reading prog, Printer for laptops & handheld devices, Prog for adults, Prog for children & young adult, Ref & res, Ref serv available, Res assist avail, Scanner, Senior outreach, Story hour, Study rm, Summer & winter reading prog, Summer reading prog, Tax forms, Teen prog, Wheelchair accessible, Winter reading prog, Workshops, Writing prog
Publications: Co-Lib Chronicle (Newsletter); Friends (Quarterly); Guide to St Louis Catholic Archdiocesan Parish Records (Research guide)
Partic in Amigos Library Services, Inc; Saint Louis Regional Library Network
Special Services for the Deaf - Bks on deafness & sign lang; Closed caption videos; Spec interest per; Staff with knowledge of sign lang; TDD equip; TTY equip
Special Services for the Blind - BiFolkal kits; Bks on CD; Playaways (bks on MP3); Recorded bks; Videos on blindness & physical disabilties
Open Mon-Thurs 9-9, Fri & Sat 9-5, Sun (Sept-May) 1-5
Restriction: Open to pub for ref & circ; with some limitations
Friends of the Library Group
Branches: 20
DANIEL BOONE BRANCH, 300 Clarkson Rd, Ellisville, 63011-2222, SAN 349-6112. Tel: 314-994-3300, Ext 3100. *Br Mgr,* Laura Kasak; *Asst Mgr,* Anne Bradley
Open Mon-Thurs 9-9, Fri & Sat 9-5, Sun 1-5
Friends of the Library Group
BRIDGETON TRAILS BRANCH, 3455 McKelvey Rd, Bridgeton, 63044-2500, SAN 349-6082. Tel: 314-994-3300, Ext 3000. *Br Mgr,* Donna Spaulding; *Asst Mgr,* Danielle Nenninger
Founded 1978
Library Holdings: Bk Vols 80,000
Open Mon-Thurs 9-9, Fri & Sat 9-5
Friends of the Library Group
CLIFF CAVE BRANCH, 5430 Telegraph Rd, 63129, SAN 374-4590. Tel: 314-994-3300, Ext 3050. *Br Mgr,* Katie Keeven; *Asst Mgr,* Nora Marino
Open Mon-Thurs 9-9, Fri & Sat 9-5, Sun 1-5
EUREKA HILLS BRANCH, 156 Eureka Towne Center Dr, Eureka, 63025-1032, SAN 323-8113. Tel: 314-994-3300, Ext 3200. *Br Mgr,* Anna Schurk; *Asst Mgr,* Nicole Walsh
Open Mon-Thurs 9-9, Fri & Sat 9-5
FLORISSANT VALLEY BRANCH, 195 New Florissant Rd S, Florissant, 63031-6796, SAN 349-6147. Tel: 314-994-3300, Ext 3250. *Br Mgr,* Rachel Nowell; *Asst Mgr,* Will LaChance
Open Mon-Thurs 9-9, Fri & Sat 9-5, Sun 1-5
GRAND GLAIZE BRANCH, 1010 Meramec Station Rd, Manchester, 63021-6943, SAN 349-6171. Tel: 314-994-3300, Ext 3300. *Br Mgr,* Paul Bayless; *Asst Mgr,* Conrad Rader
Open Mon-Thurs 9-9, Fri & Sat 9-5
GRANT'S VIEW BRANCH, 9700 Musick Rd, 63123-3935, SAN 349-6384. Tel: 314-994-3300, Ext 3850. *Br Mgr,* Lori Boschert; *Asst Mgr,* Emma Figueroa
Open Mon-Thurs 9-9, Fri & Sat 9-5, Sun 1-5
HISTORY & GENEALOGY DEPARTMENT, 1640 S Lindbergh Blvd, 63131-3598, SAN 328-476X. Tel: 314-994-3300. *Genealogy Dept Mgr, History Dept Mgr,* Scott Holl
Special Collections: African-American Research (Julius K Hunter & Friends Coll); Jewish Genealogical Society of St Louis Coll; National Genealogical Society Library Coll; St Louis Genealogical Society Library Coll
Subject Interests: Genealogy, Local hist
Open Mon-Thurs 9-9, Fri & Sat 9-5, Sun 1-5
INDIAN TRAILS BRANCH, 8400 Delport Dr, 63114-5904, SAN 349-6201. Tel: 314-994-3300, Ext 3350. *Br Mgr,* Stacy Berger; *Asst Mgr,* Carla Maxwell
Open Mon-Thurs 9-9, Fri & Sat 9-5
JAMESTOWN BLUFFS BRANCH, 4153 N Hwy 67, Florissant, 63034-2825, SAN 377-6085. Tel: 314-994-3300, Ext 3400. *Br Mgr,* Andrea Johnson; *Asst Mgr,* Aaron Seidel
Open Mon-Thurs 9-9, Fri & Sat 9-5
LEWIS & CLARK BRANCH, 9909 Lewis-Clark Blvd, 63136-5322, SAN 349-6260. Tel: 314-994-3300, Ext 3450. *Br Mgr,* Gina Sheridan; *Asst Mgr,* Chasidy Allen
Open Mon-Thurs 9-9, Fri & Sat 9-5
Friends of the Library Group
MERAMEC VALLEY BRANCH, 1501 San Simeon Way, Fenton, 63026-3479, SAN 328-6878. Tel: 314-994-3300, Ext 3550. *Br Mgr,* Anne Arthur; *Asst Mgr,* Terra Baca
Open Mon-Thurs 9-9, Fri & Sat 9-5, Sun 1-5
Friends of the Library Group
MID-COUNTY BRANCH, 7821 Maryland Ave, 63105-3875, SAN 349-6295. Tel: 314-994-3300, Ext 3500. *Br Mgr,* Annie Fuller; *Asst Mgr,* Andrea Carter
Friends of the Library Group
NATURAL BRIDGE BRANCH, 7606 Natural Bridge Rd, 63121-4905, SAN 349-6325. Tel: 314-994-3300, Ext 3600. *Br Mgr,* Anna Maria Gonzalez
Open Mon-Thurs 9-9, Fri & Sat 9-5, Sun 1-5
Friends of the Library Group
OAK BEND BRANCH, 842 S Holmes Ave, 63122-6507, SAN 328-6894. Tel: 314-994-3300, Ext 3650. *Br Mgr,* Allison Wisniewski; *Asst Mgr,* Devon Harris
Open Mon-Thurs 9-9, Fri & Sat 9-5
Friends of the Library Group
PRAIRIE COMMONS BRANCH, 915 Utz Lane, Hazelwood, 63042-2739, SAN 328-6851. Tel: 314-994-3300, Ext 3700. *Br Mgr,* Keir Haug; *Asst Mgr,* Ross Brand
Open Mon-Thurs 9-9, Fri & Sat 9-5
Friends of the Library Group
ROCK ROAD BRANCH, 10267 St Charles Rock Rd, Saint Ann, 63074-1812, SAN 349-635X. Tel: 314-994-3300, Ext 3750. *Br Mgr,* Connie Dee; *Asst Mgr,* Michelle Hawkins
Open Mon-Thurs 9-9, Fri & Sat 9-5
Friends of the Library Group
SAMUEL C SACHS BRANCH, 16400 Burkhardt Pl, Chesterfield, 63017-4660. Tel: 314-994-3300, Ext 3800. *Br Mgr,* Cheri Remington; *Asst Mgr,* Miriam Whatley
Open Mon-Thurs 9-9, Fri & Sat 9-5
Friends of the Library Group
THORNHILL BRANCH, 12863 Willowyck Dr, 63146-3771, SAN 349-6414. Tel: 314-994-3300, Ext 3900. *Br Mgr,* Kathy Muller; *Asst Mgr,* Andrew Freshwater
Open Mon-Thurs 9-9, Fri & Sat 9-5, Sun 1-5
WEBER ROAD BRANCH, 4444 Weber Rd, 63123-6744, SAN 349-6449. Tel: 314-994-3300, Ext 3950. *Br Mgr,* Lisa Haddox; *Asst Mgr,* Heather Neill
Open Mon-Thurs 9-9, Fri & Sat 9-5
Friends of the Library Group
Bookmobiles: 5. Outreach Mgr, Crystal Harris

S SAINT LOUIS MERCANTILE LIBRARY AT THE UNIVERSITY OF MISSOURI-ST LOUIS, Thomas Jefferson Library Bldg, One University Blvd, 63121-4400. SAN 309-2054. Tel: 314-516-7240. FAX: 314-516-7241. E-mail: mercantilelibrary@umsl.com. Web Site: www.umsl.edu/mercantile. *Head, Ref,* Charles E Brown; Tel: 314-516-7243, E-mail: cbrown@umsl.edu; *Curator,* Julie Dunn-Morton; Tel: 314-516-6740, E-mail: dunnmortonj@umsl.edu; *Curator,* Nick Fry; Tel: 314-516-7253, E-mail: fryn@umsl.edu; Staff 5 (MLS 3, Non-MLS 2)
Founded 1846
Library Holdings: Bk Vols 250,000
Special Collections: Alchemy Coll; American Railroads 1840's - Present (John W Barriger III Coll), bks, comn rpts, monographs, ms, pamphlets, papers, photogs, speeches; Art Coll; Early Western Americana; Herman T Pott Coll; National Inland Waterways Coll, bks, ms, maps, photogs, rpts & pamphlets; St Louis History Coll, atlases, maps, newsp, photogs from the early 19th century
Wireless access
Publications: Annual Report
Partic in Amigos Library Services, Inc; OCLC Online Computer Library Center, Inc
Open Mon-Thurs 8am-9pm
Friends of the Library Group

S SAINT LOUIS METROPOLITAN POLICE DEPARTMENT*, Saint Louis Police Library, 315 S Tucker Blvd, 63102. SAN 325-447X. Tel: 314-444-5581. FAX: 314-444-5689. Web Site: www.slmpd.org/library.shtml. *Librn,* Barbara Miksicek; E-mail: blmiksicek@slmpd.org; Staff 1 (Non-MLS 1)
Founded 1947
Library Holdings: Audiobooks 50; CDs 50; DVDs 50; Bk Vols 20,000; Per Subs 120
Special Collections: Police Department Annual Reports, 1861-present
Subject Interests: Law enforcement
Automation Activity & Vendor Info: (Cataloging) TLC (The Library Corporation); (Circulation) TLC (The Library Corporation); (ILL) TLC

(The Library Corporation); (OPAC) TLC (The Library Corporation); (Serials) TLC (The Library Corporation)
Publications: Directory of Law Enforcement Agencies in Metropolitan St Louis; In the Line of Duty
Restriction: Open by appt only

S SAINT LOUIS PSYCHIATRIC REHABILITATION CENTER*, Clients Library, 5300 Arsenal St, 63139. SAN 372-6363. Tel: 314-877-6500. *Librn,* Amanda Hunyar
Library Holdings: Bk Titles 6,000; Bk Vols 6,202; Per Subs 30
Special Services for the Deaf - Bks on deafness & sign lang; High interest/low vocabulary bks
Open Mon-Fri 8:30-4

S SAINT LOUIS PSYCHOANALYTIC INSTITUTE*, Betty Golde Smith Library, 8820 Ladue Rd, 3rd Flr, 63124-2079. SAN 309-2062. Tel: 314-361-7075. FAX: 314-361-6269. E-mail: library@stlpi.org. Web Site: www.stlpi.org/betty-golde-smith-library. *Librn,* David Bachman; Tel: 314-361-7075, Ext 324; Staff 1 (MLS 1)
Founded 1957
Library Holdings: CDs 20; Bk Titles 4,500; Per Subs 35
Subject Interests: Psychiat, Psychoanalysis, Psychol
Function: AV serv
Open Mon-Fri 8:30-3:30

P SAINT LOUIS PUBLIC LIBRARY*, Administrative Offices, 1301 Olive St, 63103. SAN 349-6597. Tel: 314-539-0300. TDD: 314-539-0364. Web Site: www.slpl.org. *Exec Dir,* Waller McGuire; E-mail: wmcguire@slpl.org; *Dir, Br Serv,* Tiffany Davis; E-mail: tdavis@slpl.org; *Dir, Technology,* John Brakesmith; E-mail: jbrakesmith@slpl.org; *Assoc Dep Dir,* Kathy Leitle; E-mail: kleitle@slpl.org; *Head, Coll Mgt,* Anna Strackeljahn; E-mail: jstrackeljahn@slpl.org; *Chief Public Services Officer,* Daisy Porter-Reynolds; E-mail: dporter-reynolds@slpl.org; *Youth Serv,* Carrie Betz; E-mail: cbetz@slpl.org; Staff 300 (MLS 52, Non-MLS 248)
Founded 1865. Pop 348,189; Circ 2,500,000
Library Holdings: Audiobooks 2,200; AV Mats 132,400; e-books 1,850; Electronic Media & Resources 70; Microforms 727,600; Bk Vols 3,843,627; Per Subs 6,618
Special Collections: Architecture (Steedman Coll); Black History (Julia Davis Coll); Foundation Center/Grants Coll; Genealogy Coll; NJ Werner Coll of Typography; St Louis Media Archives. State Document Depository; US Document Depository
Subject Interests: Civil War, Genealogy, Heraldry, St Louis hist
Automation Activity & Vendor Info: (Acquisitions) SirsiDynix; (Cataloging) SirsiDynix; (Circulation) SirsiDynix; (ILL) SirsiDynix; (OPAC) SirsiDynix; (Serials) SirsiDynix
Wireless access
Publications: African-American Heritage of St Louis; German-American Heritage of St Louis; St Louis by the Numbers
Partic in OCLC Online Computer Library Center, Inc
Special Services for the Deaf - Bks on deafness & sign lang; Spec interest per; TDD equip
Special Services for the Blind - Assistive/Adapted tech devices, equip & products; Audio mat; BiFolkal kits; Bks on CD; Braille equip; Braille servs; Copier with enlargement capabilities; Large print bks; Magnifiers; Playaways (bks on MP3); Screen enlargement software for people with visual disabilities
Open Mon-Fri 8-5
Friends of the Library Group
Branches: 16
BADEN, 8448 Church Rd, 63147-1898, SAN 349-6627. Tel: 314-388-2400. FAX: 314-388-0529. *Br Mgr,* Jan Daley; Staff 4 (MLS 1, Non-MLS 3)
Library Holdings: Bk Vols 27,270
Open Mon & Sat 9-6, Tues-Thurs 12-7, Fri 11-6
BARR, 1701 S Jefferson Ave, 63104, SAN 349-6651. Tel: 314-771-7040. FAX: 314-771-9054. *Br Mgr,* Erin Guss; Staff 4 (MLS 2, Non-MLS 2)
Library Holdings: Bk Vols 28,085
Open Mon & Sat 9-6, Tues-Thurs 12-7, Fri 11-6
BUDER, 4401 Hampton Ave, 63109-2237, SAN 349-6716. Tel: 314-352-2900. FAX: 314-352-5387. *Br Mgr,* James Moses; Staff 20 (MLS 5, Non-MLS 15)
Library Holdings: Bk Vols 86,783
Open Mon-Thurs 9-9, Fri & Sat 9-6, Sun 1-5
CABANNE, 1106 Union Blvd, 63113, SAN 349-6740. Tel: 314-367-0717. FAX: 314-367-7802. *Br Mgr,* Barbara Henderson; Staff 4 (MLS 1, Non-MLS 3)
Library Holdings: Bk Vols 35,956
Open Mon & Sat 9-6, Tues-Thurs 12-7, Fri 11-6
Friends of the Library Group
CARONDELET, 6800 Michigan Ave, 63111, SAN 349-6775. Tel: 314-752-9224. FAX: 314-752-7794. *Br Mgr,* Jennifer Halla-Sindelar; Staff 4 (MLS 1, Non-MLS 3)
Library Holdings: Bk Vols 53,840
Open Mon & Sat 9-6, Tues-Thurs 12-7, Fri 11-6
CARPENTER, 3309 S Grand Blvd, 63118, SAN 349-6805. Tel: 314-772-6586. FAX: 314-772-1871. *Regional Br Mgr,* Cynthia E Jones; Staff 13 (MLS 3, Non-MLS 10)
Library Holdings: Bk Vols 65,726
Open Mon-Thurs 9-9, Fri & Sat 9-6, Sun 1-5
CENTRAL EXPRESS, 815 Olive St, Ste 160, 63101. Tel: 314-206-6755. *Br Mgr,* Ed Witowski; Staff 2 (MLS 1, Non-MLS 1)
Open Mon-Fri 9-6
CENTRAL LIBRARY, 1301 Olive St, 63103. Tel: 314-241-2288. FAX: 314-539-0393. *Dir, Cent Serv,* Brenda McDonald
Special Collections: Architecture (Steedman Coll); Foundation Center/Grants Coll; Genealogy Coll; NJ Werner Coll of Typography; Saint Louis Media Archives. Municipal Document Depository; State Document Depository; UN Document Depository
Subject Interests: Civil War, Genealogy, Heraldry' Saint Louis hist
Special Services for the Deaf - Bks on deafness & sign lang; Spec interest per; TDD equip
Special Services for the Blind - Assistive/Adapted tech devices, equip & products; Audio mat; BiFolkal kits; Bks on CD; Braille equip; Braille servs; Copier with enlargement capabilities; Large print bks; Magnifiers; Playaways (bks on MP3); Screen enlargement software for people with visual disabilities
Open Mon-Thurs 10-9, Fri & Sat 10-6, Sun 1-5
CHARING CROSS, 356 N Skinker Blvd, 63130, SAN 322-5917. Tel: 314-726-2653. FAX: 314-726-6541. *Br Mgr,* Charles Lamkin; Staff 1 (Non-MLS 1)
Library Holdings: Bk Vols 3,863
Open Tues-Fri 1-6, Sat 9-12 & 1-6
JULIA DAVIS BRANCH, 4415 Natural Bridge Rd, 63115, SAN 349-6864. Tel: 314-383-3021. FAX: 314-383-0251. *Regional Mgr,* Floyd Council; Staff 9 (MLS 2, Non-MLS 7)
Library Holdings: Bk Vols 71,850
Open Mon-Thurs 9-9, Fri & Sat 9-6, Sun 1-5
Friends of the Library Group
DIVOLL, 4234 N Grand Blvd, 63107, SAN 349-6929. Tel: 314-534-0313. FAX: 314-534-3353. *Br Mgr,* Scott Morris; Staff 4 (MLS 1, Non-MLS 3)
Library Holdings: Bk Vols 28,051
Open Mon & Sat 9-6, Tues-Thurs 12-7, Fri 11-6
KINGSHIGHWAY, 2260 S Vandeventer Ave, 63110, SAN 349-6988. Tel: 314-771-5450. FAX: 314-771-9877. *Br Mgr,* Joe Sedey; Staff 4 (MLS 1, Non-MLS 3)
Library Holdings: Bk Vols 41,578
Function: Adult bk club, Art exhibits, Audio & video playback equip for onsite use, Children's prog, Computers for patron use, Electronic databases & coll, Homework prog, ILL available, Music CDs, Online cat, Photocopying/Printing, Prog for adults, Prog for children & young adult, Spoken cassettes & CDs, Summer reading prog, Tax forms, Teen prog, VHS videos, Wheelchair accessible
Open Mon & Sat 9-6, Tues-Thurs 12-7, Fri 11-6
Friends of the Library Group
MACHACEK, 6424 Scanlan Ave, 63139, SAN 349-7046. Tel: 314-781-2948. FAX: 314-781-8441. *Br Mgr,* Nancy Doerhoff; Staff 4 (MLS 2, Non-MLS 2)
Library Holdings: Bk Vols 58,240
Open Mon & Sat 9-6, Tues-Thurs 12-7, Fri 11-6
MARKETPLACE LIBRARY, 6548 Manchester Ave, 63139, SAN 376-9526. Tel: 314-647-0939. FAX: 314-647-1062. *Br Mgr,* Homer Hudson; Staff 2 (Non-MLS 2)
Open Tues-Thurs 11-7, Fri 11-6, Sat 9-6
SCHLAFLY, 225 N Euclid Ave, 63108, SAN 349-7011. Tel: 314-367-4120. FAX: 314-367-4814. *Regional Br Mgr,* Leandrea Lucas; Staff 13 (MLS 3, Non-MLS 10)
Library Holdings: Bk Vols 50,160
Open Mon-Thurs 9-9, Fri & Sat 9-6, Sun 1-5
WALNUT PARK, 5760 W Florissant Ave, 63120, SAN 349-7135. Tel: 314-383-1210. FAX: 314-383-2079. *Br Mgr,* Rodney Freeman; Staff 4 (MLS 1, Non-MLS 3)
Library Holdings: Bk Vols 36,888
Open Mon & Sat 9-6, Tues-Thurs 12-7, Fri 11-6
Bookmobiles: 3

C SAINT LOUIS UNIVERSITY*, Pius XII Memorial Library, 3650 Lindell Blvd, 63108-3302. SAN 349-7194. Tel: 314-977-3087. Interlibrary Loan Service Tel: 314-977-3104. Reference Tel: 314-977-3103. Administration Tel: 314-977-3100. Automation Services Tel: 314-977-3112. Information Services Tel: 314-977-3580. FAX: 314-977-3108. E-mail: piusweb@slu.edu. Web Site: lib.slu.edu. *Dean of Libr,* David Cassens; Tel: 314-977-3095, E-mail: david.cassens@slu.edu; *Asst Dean for Coll Mgt, Head, Coll Mgt,* Jean Parker; Tel: 314-977-3093, E-mail: jean.parker@slu.edu; *Asst Dean, Research Librn,* Patricia Gregory, PhD; Tel: 314-977-3107, E-mail: patricia.gregory@slu.edu; *Asst Dean, Spec Coll,* Gregory Pass, PhD; Tel: 314-977-3096, E-mail: gregory.pass@slu.edu; *Chair, Res & Instrul Serv,* Martha Allen; Tel: 314-977-3596, E-mail:

martha.allen@slu.edu; *Research Librn,* Rebecca Hyde; Tel: 314-977-3106, E-mail: rebecca.hyde@slu.edu; *ILL Coordr,* Shawnee Magparangalan; E-mail: shawnee.magparangalan@slu.edu; *Outreach Coordr,* John Waide; Tel: 314-977-9359, E-mail: john.waide@slu.edu; Staff 58 (MLS 26, Non-MLS 32)
Founded 1818. Enrl 12,225; Fac 26; Highest Degree: Doctorate
Jul 2012-Jun 2013. Mats Exp $2,954,597. Sal $2,732,017 (Prof $2,099,732)
Library Holdings: AV Mats 70,839; DVDs 2,549; e-books 12,398; e-journals 7,043; Microforms 1,265,054; Bk Vols 1,338,279; Per Subs 7,735
Special Collections: 16th-19th Century Theology, Church History, Patristics & Jesuitica (Rare Books Coll); Medieval & Renaissance Manuscript Studies (Knights of Columbus Vatican Film Library), microfilm; University Archives & Manuscripts (Walter J Ong & Tristan da Cunha Colls). US Document Depository
Subject Interests: Medieval & Renaissance studies, Philos, Theol
Automation Activity & Vendor Info: (Acquisitions) Innovative Interfaces, Inc; (Cataloging) Innovative Interfaces, Inc; (Circulation) Innovative Interfaces, Inc; (Course Reserve) Docutek; (Discovery) EBSCO Discovery Service; (ILL) OCLC ILLiad; (OPAC) Innovative Interfaces, Inc; (Serials) SerialsSolutions
Wireless access
Function: Archival coll, Art exhibits, Audio & video playback equip for onsite use, Bks on cassette, Bks on CD, CD-ROM, Computers for patron use, Doc delivery serv, E-Reserves, Electronic databases & coll, Govt ref serv, Health sci info serv, ILL available, Internet access, Music CDs, Online cat, Online info literacy tutorials on the web & in blackboard, Online ref, Orientations, Outreach serv, Outside serv via phone, mail, e-mail & web, Photocopying/Printing, Ref & res, Ref serv available, Scanner, Spoken cassettes & CDs, Spoken cassettes & DVDs, Telephone ref, VHS videos, Wheelchair accessible
Publications: Library Guides/research aids; Manuscripta: A Journal for Manuscript Research; University Libraries (Monthly newsletter)
Partic in Amigos Library Services, Inc; Mid-America Law Library Consortium; MOBIUS; OCLC Online Computer Library Center, Inc; Saint Louis Regional Library Network
Restriction: Off-site coll in storage - retrieval as requested, Photo ID required for access
Friends of the Library Group

Departmental Libraries:

CL VINCENT C IMMEL LAW LIBRARY, 100 N Tucker Blvd, Flrs 5 & 6, 63101, SAN 349-7283. Tel: 314-977-3081. Interlibrary Loan Service Tel: 314-977-3314. Reference Tel: 314-977-1447. Administration Tel: 314-977-2759. FAX: 314-977-3966. Web Site: www.slu.edu/law/library/index.php. *Adminr,* Erika Cohn; Tel: 314-977-2759, E-mail: erika.cohn@slu.edu; *Govt Doc,* Kathleen Casey; Tel: 314-977-2742, E-mail: kathleen.casey@slu.edu; Staff 10 (MLS 10)
Founded 1842. Highest Degree: Doctorate
Library Holdings: AV Mats 677; Microforms 1,392,051; Bk Titles 664,083; Per Subs 3,565
Special Collections: Early State Records, microfilm; Father Brown Labor Arbitration Coll; Missouri & Illinois Briefs; Smurfit Irish Law Coll; Sullivan Manuscript Coll; US Briefs, microcard & fiche. State Document Depository; US Document Depository
Subject Interests: Constitutional law, Illinois law, Irish law, Labor law, Legal hist, Med legal, Mo law, Polish law, Urban problems
Automation Activity & Vendor Info: (Acquisitions) Innovative Interfaces, Inc; (Cataloging) OCLC Online; (Circulation) Innovative Interfaces, Inc; (Course Reserve) Innovative Interfaces, Inc; (ILL) OCLC Online; (OPAC) Innovative Interfaces, Inc; (Serials) Innovative Interfaces, Inc
Partic in Council of Law Librs of AJCU
Open Mon-Thurs 7:30am-Midnight, Fri 7:30-7, Sat 9-7, Sun 9am-Midnight
Restriction: Access for corporate affiliates
Friends of the Library Group

CM MEDICAL CENTER LIBRARY, 1402 S Grand Blvd, 63104, SAN 349-7259. Tel: 314-977-8800. Interlibrary Loan Service Tel: 314-977-8805. Reference Tel: 314-977-8801. Administration Tel: 314-977-8803. FAX: 314-977-3587. Web Site: lib.slu.edu/mcl. *Dir,* Patrick McCarthy; E-mail: patrick.mccarthy@slu.edu; *ILL,* PJ Koch; Tel: 314-977-8806, E-mail: pj.koch@slu.edu; Staff 6 (MLS 5, Non-MLS 1)
Founded 1890. Enrl 11,977; Highest Degree: Doctorate
Jul 2012-Jun 2013. Mats Exp $1,434,763. Sal $654,538 (Prof $393,537)
Library Holdings: DVDs 241; e-books 355; Microforms 23,472; Bk Vols 152,241; Per Subs 205
Special Collections: US Document Depository
Subject Interests: Allied health, Med, Nursing, Pub health
Automation Activity & Vendor Info: (OPAC) Innovative Interfaces, Inc
Function: Computers for patron use, Doc delivery serv, E-Reserves, Electronic databases & coll, Health sci info serv, ILL available, Online cat, Online info literacy tutorials on the web & in blackboard, Photocopying/Printing, Ref serv available, Wheelchair accessible
Partic in National Network of Libraries of Medicine Region 3; OCLC Online Computer Library Center, Inc
Friends of the Library Group

S SAINT LOUIS ZOO LIBRARY, One Government Dr, 63110. SAN 328-4018. Tel: 314-646-4555. FAX: 314-646-5535. Web Site: www.stlzoo.org. *Librn,* Jill Gordon; Tel: 314-781-0900, Ext 4554, E-mail: gordon@stlzoo.org; Staff 1 (MLS 1)
Library Holdings: Bk Vols 6,000; Per Subs 40
Special Collections: St Louis Zoo History Coll
Subject Interests: Conserv, Natural hist, Zoology
Automation Activity & Vendor Info: (Cataloging) SirsiDynix; (OPAC) SirsiDynix
Partic in Saint Louis Regional Library Network
Open Mon-Fri 9-5

L THOMPSON COBURN LLP*, Law Library, One US Bank Plaza, 63101-1693. SAN 372-4468. Tel: 314-552-6000. Circulation Tel: 314-552-6323. Interlibrary Loan Service Tel: 314-552-6052. Reference Tel: 314-552-6000, Ext 1483. Administration Tel: 314-552-6275. Automation Services Tel: 314-552-6382. FAX: 314-552-7000. Circulation FAX: 314-552-7323. Web Site: www.thompsoncoburn.com. *Dir,* Kathleen Dunagin; E-mail: kdunagin@thompsoncoburn.com; *Head, Pub Serv,* Brenda Foote; Tel: 314-552-6260, E-mail: bfoote@thompsoncoburn.com; *Head, Tech Serv,* Donna Barratt; Tel: 314-552-6347, E-mail: dbarratt@thompsoncoburn.com; *Bus & Intelligence Librn,* Susan Daubard; Tel: 314-552-6424, E-mail: sdaubard@thompsoncoburn.com; *Computer Serv,* Jennifer Spector; E-mail: jspector@thompsoncoburn.com; Staff 7 (MLS 4, Non-MLS 3)
Library Holdings: Bk Titles 4,800; Bk Vols 26,000; Per Subs 3,600
Automation Activity & Vendor Info: (Cataloging) EOS International; (Circulation) EOS International; (ILL) OCLC; (OPAC) EOS International; (Serials) EOS International
Wireless access
Partic in Amigos Library Services, Inc
Restriction: Not open to pub

R UNITED HEBREW CONGREGATION, Millstone Library, 13788 Conway Rd, 63141. SAN 309-2151. Tel: 314-469-0700. FAX: 314-434-7821. E-mail: temple@unitedhebrew.org. Web Site: unitedhebrew.org/learning/millstone-library. *Library Contact,* Jessica Nelson; E-mail: jnelson@unitedhebrew.org
Library Holdings: Bk Titles 3,814
Subject Interests: Hist, Jewish holidays
Wireless access

A UNITED STATES ARMY CORPS OF ENGINEERS, Saint Louis District Library, Ray Bldg, Rm No 4202, 1222 Spruce St, 63033. SAN 349-7437. Tel: 314-331-8883. FAX: 314-331-8005. E-mail: TeamsSTL-PAO@usace.army.mil. Web Site: www.mvs.usace.army.mil/library. *Librn,* Phyllis Thomas; Staff 1 (Non-MLS 1)
Founded 1968
Library Holdings: Bk Titles 8,500; Bk Vols 8,510; Per Subs 688
Special Collections: River & Harbor acts, Congressional Documents, 1899-date; River Basin Studies
Subject Interests: Civil engr, Environ, Outdoor recreation, Water res
Wireless access
Publications: Holdings List (biannual); Library Users Guide; New Books List (quarterly)
Partic in OCLC Online Computer Library Center, Inc; Proquest Dialog
Restriction: Pub by appt only, Staff use only

GL UNITED STATES COURT OF APPEALS LIBRARY*, US Courts Library Eighth Circuit (Headquarters), Thomas F Eagleton US Courthouse, 111 S Tenth St, Rm 22-300, 63102. SAN 309-216X. Tel: 314-244-2665. Administration Tel: 314-244-2660. FAX: 314-244-2675. Administration FAX: 314-244-2676. E-mail: library8th@ca8.uscourts.gov. Web Site: www.lb8.uscourts.gov. *Circuit Librn,* Eric Brust; Staff 10.7 (MLS 4.6, Non-MLS 6.1)
Library Holdings: Bk Vols 63,776
Subject Interests: Fed law
Automation Activity & Vendor Info: (Acquisitions) SirsiDynix; (Cataloging) SirsiDynix; (OPAC) SirsiDynix; (Serials) SirsiDynix
Partic in Federal Library & Information Network
Open Mon-Fri 8-5
Restriction: Non-circulating to the pub

CM UNIVERSITY OF HEALTH SCIENCES & PHARMACY IN SAINT LOUIS LIBRARY, 4588 Parkview Pl, 63110. SAN 309-2003. Tel: 314-446-8361. FAX: 314-446-8360. E-mail: library@uhsp.edu. Web Site: www.uhsp.edu/library. *Dir,* Jill Nissen; Tel: 314-446-8362, E-mail: Jill.Nissen@uhsp.edu; *Cat Librn,* Shirley Moreno; Tel: 314-446-8364, E-mail: Shirley.Moreno@uhsp.edu; *Electronic Res Librn,* Kristina Coley; Tel: 314-446-8558, E-mail: Kristina.Coley@uhsp.edu; *Ref & Instruction*

Librn, Susan Fuchs; Tel: 314-446-8365, E-mail: Susan.Fuchs@uhsp.edu; Staff 4 (MLS 4)
Founded 1948. Enrl 978; Fac 100; Highest Degree: Doctorate
Library Holdings: Bk Titles 29,204; Bk Vols 54,221; Per Subs 400
Special Collections: Archives
Automation Activity & Vendor Info: (Cataloging) Innovative Interfaces, Inc - Sierra; (Circulation) Innovative Interfaces, Inc - Sierra; (Course Reserve) Innovative Interfaces, Inc - Sierra; (Discovery) EBSCO Discovery Service; (ILL) OCLC; (OPAC) Innovative Interfaces, Inc - Sierra; (Serials) Innovative Interfaces, Inc - Sierra
Wireless access
Partic in Amigos Library Services, Inc; Missouri Research & Education Network; MOBIUS; OCLC Online Computer Library Center, Inc; Saint Louis Regional Library Network
Open Mon-Thurs 8am-Midnight, Fri 8-8, Sat 10-8, Sun Noon-Midnight
Restriction: Badge access after hrs, Circ privileges for students & alumni only

C UNIVERSITY OF MISSOURI-SAINT LOUIS LIBRARIES*, Thomas Jefferson Library, One University Blvd, 63121-4400. SAN 349-7496. Tel: 314-516-5060. Interlibrary Loan Service Tel: 314-516-5066. Administration Tel: 314-516-5050. FAX: 314-516-5853. Web Site: www.umsl.edu. *Dean of Libr,* Christopher Dames; E-mail: cdames@umsl.edu; *Assoc Dean of Libr,* Jaleh Fazelian; E-mail: jfazelian@umsl.edu; *Head, Tech Serv,* David Owens; *ILL Supvr,* Mary Zettwoch; *Libr Operations,* Linda Hearst; E-mail: lmhearst@umsl.edu; Staff 47 (MLS 27, Non-MLS 20)
Founded 1963. Enrl 16,802; Fac 539; Highest Degree: Doctorate
Library Holdings: e-books 1,190; Microforms 1,335,705; Bk Vols 1,228,382; Per Subs 3,000
Special Collections: Colonial Latin American History; Historic Rail & River Travel; Mercantile; Utopian Literature & Science Fiction; Western Americana. US Document Depository
Automation Activity & Vendor Info: (Acquisitions) Innovative Interfaces, Inc; (Cataloging) Innovative Interfaces, Inc; (Circulation) Innovative Interfaces, Inc; (Course Reserve) Innovative Interfaces, Inc; (OPAC) Innovative Interfaces, Inc; (Serials) Innovative Interfaces, Inc
Wireless access
Publications: Libraries' (Newsletter)
Partic in Merlin; Midwest Region Libr Network; MOBIUS; OCLC Online Computer Library Center, Inc
Open Mon-Thurs 7:30am-10:30pm, Fri 7:30-5, Sat 9-5, Sun 1-9
Friends of the Library Group

C WASHINGTON UNIVERSITY LIBRARIES*, John M Olin Library, One Brookings Dr, Campus Box 1061, 63130-4862. SAN 349-7550. Tel: 314-935-5400. Circulation Tel: 314-935-5420. Interlibrary Loan Service Tel: 314-935-5442. FAX: 314-935-4045. Web Site: library.wustl.edu/units/olinlibrary. *Univ Librn,* Denise Stephens; E-mail: dstephens@wustl.edu; *Assoc Univ Librn,* Jackie Lorraine; E-mail: jlorraine@wustl.edu; Staff 108 (MLS 104, Non-MLS 4)
Founded 1853. Enrl 13,210; Fac 757; Highest Degree: Doctorate
Library Holdings: AV Mats 74,196; CDs 6,146; DVDs 1,973; e-books 198,091; Bk Titles 1,723,043; Bk Vols 3,745,746; Per Subs 44,806; Videos 23,189
Special Collections: 19th Century & Modern Literature, bks, ms; American & New; Classical Archaeology & Numismatics (John M Wolfing Coll); Early History of Communications-Semantics (Philip M Arnold Coll); Ernst Krohn Musicological Coll; George N Meissner Rare Book Department; German Language & Literature (Praetorius Memorial Coll); Henry Hampton Archives; History of Architecture (Bruce Coll); History of Printing (Isador Mendle Coll); History of Russian Revolutionary Movement & the Soviet Union (Edna Gellhorn Coll); Literature Coll (Conrad Aiken, Samuel Beckett, Robert Creely, James Dickey & Ford Maddox Ford); Romance Languages & Literature (Max W Bryant Coll); York Stock Exchange Reports. US Document Depository
Subject Interests: Behav sci, Soc sci
Automation Activity & Vendor Info: (Acquisitions) Innovative Interfaces, Inc; (Cataloging) Innovative Interfaces, Inc; (Circulation) Innovative Interfaces, Inc; (Course Reserve) Innovative Interfaces, Inc; (ILL) Innovative Interfaces, Inc; (OPAC) Innovative Interfaces, Inc; (Serials) Innovative Interfaces, Inc
Wireless access
Partic in Amigos Library Services, Inc; Greater Western Library Alliance; Higher Educ Coun of Metrop St Louis; Mid-America Law Library Consortium; MOBIUS; OCLC Online Computer Library Center, Inc; OCLC Research Library Partnership; Saint Louis Regional Library Network
Open Mon-Thurs 7:30am-2am, Fri 7:30am-8pm, Sat 9am-10pm, Sun 10am-2am

Departmental Libraries:

CM BERNARD BECKER MEDICAL LIBRARY, 660 S Euclid Ave, Campus Box 8132, 63110, SAN 349-7828. Tel: 314-362-7080. FAX: 314-454-6606. Web Site: becker.wustl.edu. *Assoc Dean & Dir,* Paul Schoening; Tel: 314-362-3119, E-mail: paschoening@wustl.edu; *Assoc Dir, Coll Mgt,* Marysue Schaffer; Tel: 314-362-0997, E-mail: schaffem@wustl.edu; *Assoc Dir, Health Info Res,* Deborah Thomas; Tel: 314-362-9729, E-mail: dathomas@wustl.edu; *Assoc Dir, Translational Res Support,* Robert Engeszer; Tel: 314-362-4735, E-mail: engeszer@wustl.edu; *Head Archivist,* Stephen Logsdon; Tel: 314-362-4239, E-mail: logsdons@wustl.edu; *Cat Librn,* Anna Vani; Tel: 314-362-3481, E-mail: vanianna@wustl.edu; *Rare Bk Librn,* Elisabeth Brander; Tel: 314-362-4235, E-mail: ebrander@wustl.edu; *Educ Coordr,* Kim Lipsey; Tel: 314-362-4733, E-mail: lipseyk@wustl.edu; Staff 48 (MLS 15, Non-MLS 33)
Founded 1837. Enrl 1,062; Fac 831
Library Holdings: CDs 582; e-books 176; e-journals 1,612; Bk Vols 295,748; Per Subs 2,595
Special Collections: Dental Medicine (Henry J McKellops Coll); Opthalmology (Bernard Becker Coll); Otology & Deaf Education (Max A Goldstein - CID Coll); Robert E Schlueter Paracelsus Coll. Oral History
Subject Interests: Health admin, Med, Occupational therapy, Phys therapy
Partic in Saint Louis Regional Library Network
Publications: Library Guide; Special Collections Guide
Open Mon-Thurs 7:30am-Midnight, Fri 7:30am-10pm, Sat 9-6, Sun 11-11

GEORGE WARREN BROWN SCHOOL OF SOCIAL WORK, One Brookings Dr, Campus Box 1196, 63130-4899, SAN 349-7917. Tel: 314-935-6633. FAX: 314-935-8511. Web Site: brownschool.wustl.edu/Life-at-Brown/Pages/Library.aspx. *Dir,* Susan Fowler; Tel: 314-935-8644, E-mail: fowler@wustl.edu; *Ref Librn,* Lori Siegel; Tel: 314-935-4064, E-mail: lsiegel@wustl.edu; Staff 3 (MLS 2, Non-MLS 1)
Enrl 500; Fac 72; Highest Degree: Doctorate
Library Holdings: DVDs 226; Bk Vols 56,966; Per Subs 494; Videos 562
Subject Interests: Alcoholism, Econ develop, Epidemiology, Family therapy, Gerontology, Mental health, Pub health, Soc develop, Soc work, Women's issues, Youth
Open Mon-Fri 8:30-6

CHEMISTRY, 549 Louderman Hall, Rm 549, Campus Box 1061, 63130. Tel: 314-935-4818. FAX: 314-935-4778. E-mail: chem@wumail.wustl.edu. Web Site: library.wustl.edu/units/chemistry. *Interim Librn,* Rina Vecchiola; E-mail: rvecchio@wustl.edu; Staff 1 (MLS 1)
Library Holdings: Bk Vols 45,979; Per Subs 321
Subject Interests: Inorganic, Organic, Phys chem, Spectroscopy
Partic in CDP
Open Mon-Fri 8:30-5

EAST ASIAN, January Hall, 2nd Flr, One Brookings Dr, Campus Box 1061, 63130-4862. Tel: 314-935-5525. E-mail: ea@wumail.wustl.edu. Web Site: library.wustl.edu/units/ea. *Librn,* Joan Wang; Tel: 314-935-4816, E-mail: joan.wang@wustl.edu; Staff 2 (MLS 2)
Library Holdings: Bk Vols 141,191; Per Subs 272
Special Collections: Cultural Revolution of China, 1966-69 (Robert Elegant Coll)
Subject Interests: Art hist, Hist, Lang, Lit, Philos, Relig, Soc sci
Publications: A Guide to Library Resources for Japanese Studies
Open Mon-Fri 8:30-5

GAYLORD MUSIC LIBRARY, 6500 Forsyth Blvd, Campus Box 1061, 63130. Tel: 314-935-5563. E-mail: music@wumail.wustl.edu. Web Site: library.wustl.edu/units/music. *Librn,* Bradley Short; Tel: 314-935-5529, E-mail: short@wustl.edu; Staff 4 (MLS 2, Non-MLS 2)
Founded 1948. Enrl 10,889; Fac 3,098; Highest Degree: Doctorate
Library Holdings: AV Mats 27,683; CDs 20,661; DVDs 528; e-journals 379; Electronic Media & Resources 10; Microforms 3,719; Music Scores 51,177; Bk Vols 62,603; Per Subs 592; Videos 613
Special Collections: American Hymnals & Tune Books; Early Music Editions (Beethoven, Mozart, 19th Century French Opera); Local Music Manuscripts; Sheet Music
Automation Activity & Vendor Info: (Course Reserve) Atlas Systems; (ILL) OCLC ILLiad
Open Mon-Fri 8:30-5

KOPOLOW BUSINESS LIBRARY, One Brookings Dr, Campus Box 1061, 63130, SAN 349-764X. Tel: 314-935-6963. FAX: 314-935-4970. Web Site: library.wustl.edu/units/business. *Interim Librn,* Jennifer Moore; Tel: 314-935-6739, E-mail: j.moore@wustl.edu; *Libr Assoc,* Ellen Riney; E-mail: eriney@wustl.edu; *Data Res Assoc,* Madjid Zeggane; E-mail: zeggane@wustl.edu; Staff 4.6 (MLS 1, Non-MLS 3.6)
Enrl 1,974; Highest Degree: Doctorate
Library Holdings: Bk Vols 15,000
Function: Art exhibits, E-Reserves, Electronic databases & coll, ILL available, Internet access, Mail & tel request accepted, Online cat, Online info literacy tutorials on the web & in blackboard, Online ref, Orientations, Outreach serv, Photocopying/Printing, Ref & res, Ref serv available, Res libr, Scanner, Wheelchair accessible
Publications: Recent Acquisitions
Open Mon-Fri 8-5

Restriction: Access at librarian's discretion, Access for corporate affiliates, Borrowing requests are handled by ILL, In-house use for visitors
Friends of the Library Group
KRANZBERG ART & ARCHITECTURE LIBRARY, One Brookings Dr, Campus Box 1061, 63130-4862. Tel: 314-935-5268. E-mail: artarch@wumail.wustl.edu. Web Site: library.wustl.edu/units/artarch. *Librn,* Rina Vecchiola; Tel: 314-935-7658; Staff 2 (MLS 2)
Library Holdings: Bk Vols 105,882; Per Subs 310
Special Collections: Bryce Coll; Eames & Young Coll; East Asian Coll (oriental art); Sorger Coll
Subject Interests: Archit, Art, Art hist, Classical archeol, Communication arts, E Asian art, Fashion design, Landscape archit, Planning design
Open Mon-Thurs 8:30am-9pm, Fri 8:30-5, Sat Noon-5, Sun 1-9

CL LAW LIBRARY, Washington Univ Sch Law, Anheuser-Busch Hall, One Brookings Dr, Campus Box 1171, 63130, SAN 349-7798. Tel: 314-935-6450. FAX: 314-935-7125. Web Site: law.wustl.edu/library. *Assoc Dean,* Joyce A McCray Pearson; Tel: 314-935-2929, E-mail: jmccraypearson@wulaw.wustl.edu; *Dir, Pub Serv,* Dorie Bertram; Tel: 314-935-6484, E-mail: bertram@wulaw.wustl.edu; *Dir, Tech Serv,* Wei Luo; Tel: 314-935-8045, E-mail: luo@wulaw.wustl.edu; *Sr Cat Librn,* Frederick Chan; Tel: 314-935-6415, E-mail: fchan@wulaw.wustl.edu; *Electronic Res Librn,* Hyla Bondareff; Tel: 314-935-6434, E-mail: bondareh@wulaw.wustl.edu; *Ref (Info Servs),* Anne Cleester Taylor; Tel: 314-935-4829, E-mail: actaylor@wulaw.wustl.edu; Staff 9 (MLS 9)
Founded 1867. Enrl 800; Fac 44; Highest Degree: Doctorate
Library Holdings: Bk Titles 148,270; Bk Vols 675,776; Per Subs 6,109
Special Collections: Ashman British Coll; Neuhoff Rare Book Coll. State Document Depository; US Document Depository
Subject Interests: Chinese law, Corporate law, European Union law, Intellectual property law, Intl trade law, Tax law
Publications: Faculty Services Guide; Law Library Guide; New Student Orientation Guide; Research Guides; Select Acquisitions List
Open Mon-Thurs 7am-11pm, Fri 7-7, Sat 10-6, Sun Noon-6
Friends of the Library Group
PFEIFFER PHYSICS LIBRARY, One Brookings Dr, Physics Library Box 1105, 63130, SAN 349-7887. Tel: 314-935-6215. FAX: 314-935-6219. Web Site: library.wustl.edu/units/physics. *Librn,* Alison Verbeck; E-mail: alison@wustl.edu; Staff 1 (MLS 1)
Library Holdings: Bk Vols 49,106; Per Subs 233
Subject Interests: Astronomy, Astrophysics, Atomic, High energy particles, Math, Nuclear physics, Physics, Quantum mechanics, Solid state physics
Open Mon-Fri 7:15-4:30
RONALD RETTNER EARTH & PLANETARY SCIENCE LIBRARY, One Brookings Dr, Campus Box 1061, 63130. Tel: 314-935-5406. E-mail: eps@wumail.wustl.edu. Web Site: library.wustl.edu/units/epsc. *Librn,* Clara McLeod; Tel: 314-935-4817, E-mail: cpmcleod@wustl.edu; Staff 1 (MLS 1)
Highest Degree: Doctorate
Library Holdings: Bk Vols 39,968; Per Subs 215
Special Collections: Missouri State Geological Survey; USGS Maps. US Document Depository
Subject Interests: Geochemistry, Geol, Geomorphology, Geophysics, Petrology, Planetary sci, Sedimentation, Structural geol
Open Mon-Fri 8:30-5, Sun 12-3

C WEBSTER UNIVERSITY*, Emerson Library, 101 Edgar Rd, 63119. (Mail add: 470 E Lockwood Ave, 63119-3194), SAN 309-2208. Tel: 314-968-6952. Reference Tel: 314-968-6950. Toll Free Tel: 800-985-4279. FAX: 314-968-7113. Web Site: library.webster.edu. *Dean, Univ Libr,* Eileen Condon; Tel: 314-968-7154, E-mail: econdon@webster.edu; *Head, Instruction, Liaison & Ref Serv,* Holly Hubenschmidt; Tel: 314-968-8673, E-mail: hollyh@webster.edu; *Head, Access Serv,* Matt Wier; Tel: 314-246-7806, E-mail: mwier@webster.edu; *ILL Coordr,* Rick Kaeser; Tel: 314-968-5994, E-mail: rick@webster.edu; Staff 29 (MLS 13, Non-MLS 16)
Founded 1969. Enrl 21,500; Highest Degree: Doctorate
Library Holdings: Bk Vols 242,425; Per Subs 1,500
Special Collections: Children's Literature (Hochschild Coll); Harry James Cargas Coll; Reformed Church History (James I Good Coll)
Automation Activity & Vendor Info: (Acquisitions) Innovative Interfaces, Inc; (Cataloging) Innovative Interfaces, Inc; (Circulation) Innovative Interfaces, Inc; (Course Reserve) Docutek; (OPAC) Innovative Interfaces, Inc; (Serials) Innovative Interfaces, Inc
Wireless access
Partic in Amigos Library Services, Inc; Higher Educ Coun of St Louis; MOBIUS; OCLC Online Computer Library Center, Inc; Saint Louis Regional Library Network
Open Mon-Thurs 8am-Midnight, Fri & Sat 8-8, Sun Noon-Midnight

SAINT PETERS

P SAINT CHARLES CITY-COUNTY LIBRARY DISTRICT*, 77 Boone Hills Dr, 63376. (Mail add: PO Box 529, 63376-0529), SAN 349-5094. Tel: 636-441-2300. FAX: 636-441-3132. Web Site: www.mylibrary.org. *Dir,* Jason Kuhl; E-mail: jkuhl@stchlibrary.org; *Dep Dir,* Laurie St Laurent; E-mail: lstlaurent@stchlibrary.org; *Chief Financial Officer,* Julie Wolfe; *Adult Serv Mgr,* Sara Nielsen; *Coll Serv Mgr,* Carol Schrey; *Develop Mgr,* Erica Land; *Human Res Mgr,* Patricia Batzel; *IT Mgr,* Gary Brinker; *Mkt Mgr,* Jan Bardon; E-mail: jbardon@stchlibrary.org; *Youth Serv Mgr,* Maggie Melson; Staff 35 (MLS 35)
Founded 1973. Pop 353,000; Circ 6,367,709
Library Holdings: Audiobooks 36,336; CDs 27,751; DVDs 64,070; e-books 9,356; Electronic Media & Resources 186; Large Print Bks 18,001; Bk Titles 376,688; Bk Vols 839,034; Per Subs 8,507; Videos 8,828
Special Collections: Bizelli-Fleming Local History Coll; Business Coll; Non-Profit Coll; Your Healthy Answer Place
Subject Interests: Bus info, Consumer health info, Genealogy, Local hist
Wireless access
Function: Bks on CD, Children's prog, Computers for patron use, E-Reserves, Electronic databases & coll, Family literacy, Govt ref serv, Health sci info serv, Holiday prog, Home delivery & serv to seniorr ctr & nursing homes, ILL available, Internet access, Life-long learning prog for all ages, Magazines, Mail & tel request accepted, Mango lang, Meeting rooms, Music CDs, Online cat, Online ref, Outreach serv, OverDrive digital audio bks, Photocopying/Printing, Preschool outreach, Printer for laptops & handheld devices, Prog for adults, Prog for children & young adult, Ref serv available, Senior computer classes, Senior outreach, Spanish lang bks, Story hour, Study rm, Summer reading prog, Tax forms, Teen prog, Telephone ref, Wheelchair accessible
Partic in MOBIUS; Saint Louis Regional Library Network
Open Mon-Fri 8:30-5
Friends of the Library Group
Branches: 12
AUGUSTA BRANCH, 198 Jackson St, Augusta, 63332-1772. (Mail add: PO Box 128, Augusta, 63332-0128), SAN 349-5272. Tel: 636-228-4855. FAX: 636-228-4855. *Br Mgr,* Jennifer Jung; E-mail: jjung@stchlibrary.org
Circ 35,793
Library Holdings: Bk Vols 11,581
Open Mon, Tues & Thurs 9-8, Sat 9-Noon
Friends of the Library Group
BOONE'S TRAIL BRANCH, Ten Fiddlecreek Ridge Rd, New Melle, 63365. (Mail add: PO Box 277, New Melle, 63365-0277), SAN 377-676X. Tel: 636-398-6200. FAX: 636-398-6200. *Br Mgr,* Jennifer Jung; E-mail: jjung@stchlibrary.org
Circ 58,293
Library Holdings: Bk Vols 13,000
Open Mon, Tues & Thurs 9-8, Sat 9-Noon
Friends of the Library Group
CORPORATE PARKWAY BRANCH, 1200 Corporate Pkwy, Wentzville, 63385-4828, SAN 349-5302. Tel: 636-327-4010, 636-332-8280. Administration Tel: 636-441-2300. FAX: 636-327-0548. Administration FAX: 636-441-3132. *Br Mgr,* Madison Morris; E-mail: mmorris@stchlibrary.org; *Ch,* Shelly Bretsnyder; E-mail: mbretsnyder@stchlibrary.org; Staff 2 (MLS 2)
Circ 491,298
Library Holdings: Bk Vols 162,341
Special Services for the Deaf - TDD equip
Open Mon-Thurs 9-9, Fri & Sat 9-6, Sat 1-5
Friends of the Library Group
DEER RUN BRANCH, 1300 N Main, O'Fallon, 63366-2013, SAN 375-6270. Tel: 636-978-3251, 636-980-1332. FAX: 636-978-3209. *Br Mgr,* Cindy Miller; E-mail: cmiller@stchlibrary.org; *Youth Serv,* Jessie Park; E-mail: jpark@stchlibrary.org
Founded 1995. Circ 469,817
Library Holdings: Bk Vols 85,694
Special Services for the Deaf - TDD equip
Open Mon-Thurs 9-9, Fri & Sat 9-6, Sun 1-5
Friends of the Library Group
KISKER ROAD BRANCH, 1000 Kisker Rd, Saint Charles, 63304-8726, SAN 370-1115. Tel: 636-447-7323, 636-926-7323. FAX: 636-926-0869. *Br Mgr,* Diana Tucker; E-mail: dtucker@stchlibrary.org; *Ch Serv,* Ashley Runyon; E-mail: arunyon@stchlibrary.org
Circ 504,038
Library Holdings: Bk Vols 100,272
Open Mon-Thurs 9-9, Fri & Sat 9-6, Sun 1-5
Friends of the Library Group
LIBRARY EXPRESS @ DISCOVERY VILLAGE, 378 Shadow Pines Dr, Wentzville, 63385-3745. Tel: 636-332-6476. FAX: 636-332-4165. *Br Mgr,* Asia Gross; E-mail: agross@stchlibrary.org
Circ 186,410
Library Holdings: Bk Vols 15,000
Open Mon-Thurs 9-9, Fri & Sat 9-6, Sun 1-5
Friends of the Library Group

LIBRARY EXPRESS @ WINGHAVEN, 7435 Village Center Dr, O'Fallon, 63368-4768. Tel: 636-561-3385. FAX: 636-561-3819. *Br Mgr,* Aaron Eller; E-mail: aeller@stchlibrary.org
Circ 219,920
Library Holdings: Bk Vols 15,000
Open Mon-Thurs 9-9, Fri & Sat 9-6, Sun 1-5
Friends of the Library Group

KATHRYN LINNEMANN BRANCH, 2323 Elm St, Saint Charles, 63301, SAN 349-5159. Tel: 636-723-0232, 636-946-6294. FAX: 636-947-0692. *Br Mgr,* Asia Gross; E-mail: agross@stchlibrary.org; *Supvr, Youth Serv,* Julie Jackson; E-mail: jjackson@stchlibrary.org; Staff 7 (MLS 7)
Circ 840,000
Library Holdings: Bk Vols 193,030
Subject Interests: Local hist
Open Mon-Thurs 9-9, Fri & Sat 9-6, Sun 1-5
Friends of the Library Group

MCCLAY, 2760 McClay Rd, Saint Charles, 63303-5427, SAN 377-6786. Tel: 636-441-7577. FAX: 636-441-5898. *Br Mgr,* Alison Griffith; E-mail: agriffith@stchlibrary.org; *Ch Serv,* Ann Randolph; E-mail: arandolph@stchlibrary.org
Circ 662,524
Library Holdings: Bk Vols 94,592
Open Mon-Thurs 9-9, Fri & Sat 9-6, Sun 1-5
Friends of the Library Group

MIDDENDORF-KREDELL BRANCH, 2750 Hwy K, O'Fallon, 63368-7859, SAN 375-6289. Tel: 636-272-4999, 636-978-7926. FAX: 636-978-7998. *Br Mgr,* Aaron Eller; E-mail: aeller@stchlibrary.org; *Asst Mgr,* Melissa Whatley; E-mail: mwhatley@stchlibrary.org
Circ 1,155,443
Library Holdings: Bk Vols 179,097
Special Collections: US Document Depository
Special Services for the Deaf - TDD equip
Open Mon-Thurs 9-9, Fri & Sat 9-6, Sun 1-5
Friends of the Library Group

PORTAGE DES SIOUX BRANCH, 1825 Commonfield Rd, Portage des Sioux, 63373. (Mail add: PO Box 190, Portage des Sioux, 63373-0190), SAN 349-5183. Tel: 636-753-3070. FAX: 636-753-3070. *Br Mgr,* Jennifer Jung; E-mail: jjung@stchlibrary.org; Staff 2 (Non-MLS 2)
Circ 19,994
Library Holdings: Bk Vols 9,410
Open Mon & Tues 12-8, Thurs 9-8, Sat 9-12
Friends of the Library Group

SPENCER ROAD BRANCH, 427 Spencer Rd, 63376. (Mail add: PO Box 529, 63376-0529), SAN 349-5248. Tel: 636-441-0522, 636-447-2320. FAX: 636-926-3948. *Br Mgr,* Jennifer Jung
Circ 743,682
Library Holdings: Bk Vols 185,200
Special Collections: Business Services
Special Services for the Deaf - TDD equip
Open Mon-Thurs 9-9, Fri & Sat 9-6, Sun 1-5
Friends of the Library Group

SAINTE GENEVIEVE

P SAINTE GENEVIEVE COUNTY LIBRARY*, 21388 Hwy 32, 63670. SAN 349-215X. Tel: 573-883-3358. E-mail: contact@sgcl.org. Web Site: sgclib.org. *Dir,* Jodi Ralston; E-mail: ralstonj@sgclib.org; Staff 1 (Non-MLS 1)
Founded 2016. Pop 18,145
Automation Activity & Vendor Info: (ILL) Evergreen; (OPAC) Evergreen
Wireless access
Function: 24/7 Online cat, Adult bk club, Computers for patron use, Free DVD rentals, ILL available, Meeting rooms, Microfiche/film & reading machines, Online cat, OverDrive digital audio bks, Photocopying/Printing, Prog for adults, Prog for children & young adult, Scanner, Story hour, Summer reading prog
Partic in Missouri Evergreen
Open Mon-Fri 9-7, Sat 10-4
Friends of the Library Group

SALEM

P SALEM PUBLIC LIBRARY*, 403 N Jackson St, 65560. SAN 309-2224. Tel: 573-729-4331. FAX: 573-729-2123. Web Site: salempubliclibrary.net. *Dir,* Glenda Wofford; E-mail: glendabrown1@gmail.com; Staff 3 (MLS 1, Non-MLS 2)
Founded 1930. Pop 4,854; Circ 40,436
Library Holdings: Bk Titles 30,763; Bk Vols 32,123; Per Subs 75; Talking Bks 742; Videos 848
Subject Interests: Genealogy
Automation Activity & Vendor Info: (Cataloging) TLC (The Library Corporation); (Circulation) TLC (The Library Corporation)
Wireless access
Open Mon-Wed & Fri 10-5, Thurs 10-7, Sat 10-1
Friends of the Library Group

SALISBURY

P DULANY MEMORIAL LIBRARY*, 501 S Broadway, 65281. SAN 309-2232. Tel: 660-388-5712. FAX: 660-388-5712. E-mail: contact@dulanylibrary.org. Web Site: dulanylibrary.org. *Dir,* Cheryl Springer; *Asst Dir,* Carolyn McNeall; Staff 2 (MLS 1, Non-MLS 1)
Founded 1928. Pop 1,960; Circ 19,600
Library Holdings: Large Print Bks 30; Bk Titles 14,890; Bk Vols 15,795; Per Subs 37; Talking Bks 78; Videos 230
Automation Activity & Vendor Info: (Cataloging) Mandarin Library Automation; (Circulation) Mandarin Library Automation; (OPAC) Mandarin Library Automation
Open Mon-Fri Noon-5, Sat 10-Noon

SARCOXIE

P SARCOXIE PUBLIC LIBRARY*, 508 Center St, 64862. (Mail add: PO Box 130, 64862-0130), SAN 329-2533. Tel: 417-548-2736. FAX: 417-548-3104. Web Site: www.sarcoxiemo.com/library. *Dir,* Carolina Chapman; E-mail: librarydirector@sarcoxiemo.com; Staff 3 (MLS 1, Non-MLS 2)
Founded 1960. Pop 1,470; Circ 13,591
Library Holdings: AV Mats 110; Bk Titles 13,551; Bk Vols 13,872; Per Subs 16; Talking Bks 151; Videos 389
Wireless access
Open Mon-Fri 9-6, Sat 9-1
Friends of the Library Group

SEDALIA

P BOONSLICK REGIONAL LIBRARY*, Administrative Office, 219 W Third St, 65301. SAN 349-7941. Tel: 660-827-7111. FAX: 660-827-4668. Web Site: www.boonslickregionallibrary.com. *Dir, Ref (Info Servs),* Linda Allcorn; E-mail: allcornl@brl.lib.mo.us; Staff 12 (MLS 1, Non-MLS 11)
Founded 1953. Pop 53,068; Circ 402,333
Library Holdings: Bk Vols 200,000; Per Subs 175
Automation Activity & Vendor Info: (Acquisitions) TLC (The Library Corporation); (Cataloging) TLC (The Library Corporation); (Circulation) TLC (The Library Corporation)
Wireless access
Publications: Adult Book List; Annual Report; BRL2GO Schedule; Childrens Newsletter; Informational Brochures; Seasonal Ideas
Partic in Mid-Mo Libr Network; Mo Libr Asn
Open Mon-Fri 8-5
Friends of the Library Group
Branches: 4

BOONVILLE BRANCH, 618 Main St, Boonville, 65233, SAN 349-7976. Tel: 660-882-5864. FAX: 660-882-7953. Web Site: www.boonslickregionallibrary.com/Boonville. *Br Supvr,* Cathy Birk; E-mail: birkc@boonslicklibrary.com; Staff 2 (MLS 1, Non-MLS 1)
Open Mon & Wed-Fri 9-6, Tues 9-7, Sat 9-5
Friends of the Library Group

COLE CAMP BRANCH, 701 W Main St, Cole Camp, 65325, SAN 349-800X. Tel: 660-668-3887. FAX: 660-668-3852. Web Site: www.boonslickregionallibrary.com/Cole-Camp. *Br Supvr,* Greg Burel; E-mail: burelg@brl.lib.mo.us; Staff 1 (MLS 1)
Open Tues & Thurs 10-6, Wed 1-6, Sat 9-2
Friends of the Library Group

SEDALIA BRANCH, 219 W Third St, 65301, SAN 329-5834. Tel: 660-827-7323. Administration Tel: 660-827-7111. FAX: 660-827-4668. Web Site: www.boonslickregionallibrary.com/Sedalia. *Br Supvr,* Jo Boger; E-mail: bogerj@brl.lib.mo.us; Staff 2 (MLS 1, Non-MLS 1)
Open Mon-Wed & Fri 9-6, Thurs 9-7, Sat 9-5
Friends of the Library Group

WARSAW BRANCH, 102 E Jackson, Warsaw, 65355, SAN 349-8034. Tel: 660-438-5211. FAX: 660-438-9567. Web Site: www.boonslickregionallibrary.com/Warsaw. *Br Supvr,* Joanne Glowczewski; E-mail: glowczewskim@brl.lib.mo.us; Staff 2 (MLS 1, Non-MLS 1)
Open Mon-Sat 9-5:30
Friends of the Library Group

P SEDALIA PUBLIC LIBRARY*, 311 W Third St, 65301-4399. SAN 309-2240. Tel: 660-826-1314. FAX: 660-826-0396. Web Site: www.sedalialibrary.com. *Dir,* Pam Hunter; E-mail: phunter@sedalialibrary.com; Staff 12 (MLS 1, Non-MLS 11)
Founded 1895. Pop 20,185; Circ 120,708
Library Holdings: Audiobooks 680; Bks on Deafness & Sign Lang 47; Braille Volumes 10; CDs 50; DVDs 1,500; Electronic Media & Resources 213; Large Print Bks 3,113; Microforms 110; Bk Titles 85,000; Per Subs 155; Videos 100
Subject Interests: Local hist
Automation Activity & Vendor Info: (Cataloging) OCLC CatExpress; (Circulation) SirsiDynix; (OPAC) SirsiDynix
Wireless access

Special Services for the Deaf - Assistive tech; Bks on deafness & sign lang; Closed caption videos; Coll on deaf educ; Staff with knowledge of sign lang; TDD equip
Special Services for the Blind - Assistive/Adapted tech devices, equip & products; Audio mat; Bks on cassette; Bks on CD; Large print & cassettes; Large print bks; Low vision equip; Magnifiers; Talking bks; Videos on blindness & physical disabilties
Open Mon 9-7, Tues-Fri 9-6, Sat 9-5, Sun 1-5

J STATE FAIR COMMUNITY COLLEGE*, Donald C Proctor Library, 3201 W 16th St, 65301. SAN 309-2259. Tel: 660-530-5842. FAX: 660-596-7468. E-mail: library@sfccmo.edu. Web Site: www.sfccmo.edu/library. *Dir,* Michelle Franklin; E-mail: mfranklin2@sfccmo.edu; *Libr Coord,* Malinda McBride; E-mail: mmcbride1@sfccmo.edu; Staff 4 (MLS 1, Non-MLS 3)
Founded 1969
Library Holdings: AV Mats 2,300; Bk Titles 36,000; Per Subs 65
Special Collections: Audio Visual (videotapes & cassette tape kits); Juvenile Coll; Missouri Coll
Subject Interests: Agr, Art, Automotive, Bus educ, Nursing
Automation Activity & Vendor Info: (Cataloging) Innovative Interfaces, Inc; (Circulation) Innovative Interfaces, Inc; (ILL) OCLC; (OPAC) Innovative Interfaces, Inc; (Serials) Innovative Interfaces, Inc
Wireless access
Publications: Library Handbook; Recent Acquisitions Bulletin
Partic in Amigos Library Services, Inc; MOBIUS
Open Mon, Wed & Fri 8-5, Tues & Thurs 8-7

SHELBINA

P SHELBINA CARNEGIE PUBLIC LIBRARY*, 102 N Center St, 63468. SAN 309-2267. Tel: 573-588-2271. FAX: 573-588-2271. E-mail: shelbinalibrary@gmail.com. Web Site: shelbinacarnegie.lib.mo.us. *Libr Dir,* Linda K Kropf; *Ch,* Janie Wood; *Cat/Circ,* Cheryl Kendrick; Staff 1 (MLS 1)
Founded 1917. Pop 2,175; Circ 36,000
Library Holdings: AV Mats 827; Bk Titles 30,362; Per Subs 73; Videos 305
Special Collections: Centennial Farms Records of Shelby County; Early Census Records of Shelby County; Genealogy (Burial Records of Shelby County, History of Schools, Churches & Families in Area); Shelby County Newspapers
Wireless access
Open Mon, Wed-Fri 11-5:30, Tues 11-8, Sat 9-Noon

SHELDON

P SHELDON LIBRARY*, 216 W Main St, 64784. SAN 377-2179. Tel: 417-884-2909. *Chmn of Libr Board,* Marlene Moran; *Librn,* Sharon Butcher
Pop 700
Library Holdings: Bk Titles 5,816; Bk Vols 6,000; Per Subs 17; Talking Bks 128; Videos 290
Wireless access
Function: Activity rm, After school storytime, Computers for patron use, Free DVD rentals, Internet access, Magazines, Movies, Story hour, Tax forms
Open Tues, Thurs & Fri 1-5
Friends of the Library Group

SIKESTON

P SIKESTON PUBLIC LIBRARY*, 121 E North St, 63801. (Mail add: PO Box 1279, 63801-1279), SAN 309-2275. Tel: 573-471-4140. FAX: 573-471-6048. E-mail: info@sikeston.lib.mo.us. Web Site: sikeston.lib.mo.us. *Dir,* Ron Eifert; E-mail: reifert@sikeston.lib.mo.us; Staff 6 (Non-MLS 6)
Founded 1938. Pop 17,100; Circ 52,000
Library Holdings: Audiobooks 735; AV Mats 1,852; Bks on Deafness & Sign Lang 13; CDs 84; DVDs 135; Large Print Bks 1,134; Microforms 363; Bk Titles 42,500; Per Subs 109; Videos 932
Automation Activity & Vendor Info: (Cataloging) Evergreen; (Circulation) Evergreen; (ILL) OCLC FirstSearch; (OPAC) Evergreen; (Serials) EBSCO Online
Wireless access
Function: Adult bk club, Art exhibits, Audiobks via web, Bk club(s), Bks on CD, Children's prog, Computers for patron use, Electronic databases & coll, Free DVD rentals, Holiday prog, ILL available, Instruction & testing, Internet access, Magazines, Microfiche/film & reading machines, Online cat, OverDrive digital audio bks, Photocopying/Printing, Preschool outreach, Preschool reading prog, Prog for adults, Prog for children & young adult, Story hour, Summer reading prog, Tax forms, Wheelchair accessible
Partic in Missouri Evergreen; Missouri Research & Education Network
Open Mon-Thurs 10-8, Fri 10-6, Sat 10-4, Sun 1-5
Friends of the Library Group

SLATER

P SLATER PUBLIC LIBRARY, 201 N Main, 65349. SAN 309-2291. Tel: 660-529-3100. E-mail: library2@ctcis.net. Web Site: cityofslater.com/library. *Librn,* Donna Haynie
Founded 1927. Pop 2,610; Circ 22,752
Library Holdings: Bk Vols 40,438
Special Collections: Dickens & Mark Twain Coll
Open Mon-Thurs 9-7, Fri 9-5

SPRINGFIELD

CR ASSEMBLIES OF GOD THEOLOGICAL SEMINARY*, Cordas C Burnett Library, 1435 N Glenstone Ave, 65802-2131. SAN 309-2305. Tel: 417-268-1000. Toll Free Tel: 800-467-2487. FAX: 417-268-1001. E-mail: library@agseminary.edu. Web Site: www.agts.edu/lib. *Libr Adminr,* Rick Oliver; Tel: 417-268-1059, E-mail: oliverr@evangel.edu; *Cat,* Nancy Donnelly; Tel: 417-268-1061, E-mail: donnellyn@evangel.edu; *Evening Circ Supvr,* Jacqueline Smith; Tel: 417-268-1063, E-mail: smithj@evangel.edu; Staff 2 (MLS 1, Non-MLS 1)
Founded 1973. Highest Degree: Doctorate
Library Holdings: AV Mats 5,557; Microforms 79,929; Bk Vols 121,279; Per Subs 250
Subject Interests: Anthrop, Biblical studies, Communication, Missions, Pentecostalism, Psychol, Theol
Automation Activity & Vendor Info: (Acquisitions) Innovative Interfaces, Inc; (Cataloging) Innovative Interfaces, Inc; (Circulation) Innovative Interfaces, Inc; (Course Reserve) Innovative Interfaces, Inc; (ILL) OCLC; (OPAC) Innovative Interfaces, Inc; (Serials) Innovative Interfaces, Inc
Wireless access
Partic in Amigos Library Services, Inc; Missouri Research & Education Network; MOBIUS; OCLC Online Computer Library Center, Inc
Open Mon-Fri 9am-9:30pm, Sat 10-6

CR BAPTIST BIBLE COLLEGE & THEOLOGICAL SEMINARY*, G B Vick Memorial Library, 730 E Kearney St, 65803. (Mail add: 628 E Kearney St, 65803), SAN 349-8069. Tel: 417-268-6048. Administration Tel: 417-268-6049. FAX: 417-268-6690. E-mail: library@gobbc.edu. Web Site: library.gobbc.edu. *Dir, Libr Serv,* Jon Jones; E-mail: jjones@gobbc.edu; Staff 2.1 (MLS 1.3, Non-MLS 0.8)
Founded 1950. Enrl 256; Fac 14; Highest Degree: Master
Library Holdings: Bk Vols 55,923; Per Subs 332
Special Collections: Baptist History; Fellowship Authors
Subject Interests: Educ, Music, Relig studies
Automation Activity & Vendor Info: (Acquisitions) Innovative Interfaces, Inc - Sierra; (Cataloging) Innovative Interfaces, Inc - Sierra; (Circulation) Innovative Interfaces, Inc - Sierra; (Course Reserve) Innovative Interfaces, Inc - Sierra; (ILL) OCLC Online; (OPAC) Innovative Interfaces, Inc - Sierra; (Serials) Innovative Interfaces, Inc - Sierra
Function: For res purposes, ILL available, Internet access, Ref serv available, Telephone ref
Partic in Christian Library Consortium; MOBIUS
Open Mon, Tues & Thurs 7:30am-11:30pm, Wed & Fri 7:30-5, Sat 12-7, Sun 8pm-11:30pm

M COXHEALTH LIBRARIES*, North Library, Cox Medical Ctr N, 1423 N Jefferson Ave, J-209-210, 65802. SAN 323-5580. Tel: 417-269-3460. FAX: 417-269-3492. E-mail: library@coxhealth.com. Web Site: www.coxhealth.com/our-hospitals-and-clinics/our-locations/cox-north. *Librn,* Mary Melvin; E-mail: mary.melvin@coxhealth.com; *Librn,* Nicole Montgomery; Tel: 417-269-8018, E-mail: nicole.montgomery@coxhealth.com; Staff 7 (MLS 4, Non-MLS 3)
Library Holdings: Bk Titles 7,891; Bk Vols 8,744; Per Subs 514
Subject Interests: Health sci, Med, Nursing
Automation Activity & Vendor Info: (Acquisitions) Marcive, Inc; (Cataloging) EOS International; (OPAC) EOS International; (Serials) EOS International
Wireless access
Function: CD-ROM, Computers for patron use, Electronic databases & coll, Online cat, Orientations, Photocopying/Printing
Partic in Health Sciences Library Network of Kansas City, Inc; MCMLA; Medical Library Association; OCLC Online Computer Library Center, Inc
Open Mon-Fri 8-4:30
Restriction: Circ limited, Med & nursing staff, patients & families, Open to students, fac & staff

CR DRURY UNIVERSITY*, F W Olin Library, 900 N Benton Ave, 65802. SAN 309-2321. Tel: 417-873-7282. Circulation Tel: 417-873-7338. Interlibrary Loan Service Tel: 417-873-7277. Reference Tel: 417-873-7337. FAX: 417-873-7432. E-mail: refdesk@drury.edu. Circulation E-mail: circdesk@drury.edu. Web Site: library.drury.edu. *Dir,* William Garvin; Tel: 417-873-7282, E-mail: wgarvin@drury.edu; *Assoc Librn,* Katherine

Bohnenkamper; Tel: 417-873-7485, E-mail: kbohnenk@drury.edu; *Assoc Librn, Cat/ILL Librn,* Phyllis Holzenberg; Tel: 417-873-7487, E-mail: pholzenb@drury.edu; *Assoc Librn, Curator, Art & Spec Coll,* Jacqueline Tygart; Tel: 417-873-7496, E-mail: jtygart@drury.edu; *Sr Asst Librn, Tech Serv Coordr,* Holli Henslee; Tel: 417-873-7483, E-mail: hhenslee@drury.edu; *Circ Serv Mgr,* Barbi Dickensheet; Tel: 417-873-7486, E-mail: bdickensheet@drury.edu; Staff 12 (MLS 7, Non-MLS 5)
Founded 1873. Enrl 4,635; Fac 440; Highest Degree: Master
Library Holdings: AV Mats 3,706; CDs 330; DVDs 341; e-books 16,325; e-journals 590; Music Scores 527; Bk Titles 121,896; Bk Vols 176,304; Per Subs 993; Videos 3,459
Special Collections: Claude Thornhill Music Coll; John F Kennedy Memorabilia. US Document Depository
Subject Interests: Archit
Automation Activity & Vendor Info: (Acquisitions) Innovative Interfaces, Inc; (Cataloging) Innovative Interfaces, Inc; (Circulation) Innovative Interfaces, Inc; (Course Reserve) Docutek; (ILL) OCLC; (Media Booking) Innovative Interfaces, Inc; (OPAC) Innovative Interfaces, Inc; (Serials) Innovative Interfaces, Inc
Partic in Amigos Library Services, Inc; Missouri Research & Education Network; MOBIUS
Open Mon-Thurs (Winter) 7:45am-Midnight, Fri 7:45-6, Sat 10-5, Sun 1-Midnight; Mon-Fri (Summer) 8-5

C EVANGEL UNIVERSITY*, Klaude Kendrick Library, 1111 N Glenstone Ave, 65802. SAN 309-233X. Tel: 417-865-2815, Ext 7268. Web Site: www.evangel.edu/library/index.asp. *Dir of Libr/Media Serv,* Dale R Jensen; E-mail: jensend@evangel.edu; *Cat Librn,* Rumyana Hristova; *Instruction & Outreach Librn,* Keri Kirby; *Circ Supvr,* Melanie Box; *Archivist,* Shirley Shedd; Staff 9 (MLS 3, Non-MLS 6)
Founded 1955. Enrl 2,100; Fac 100; Highest Degree: Doctorate
May 2016-Apr 2017 Income $582,805. Mats Exp $230,200, Books $50,000, Per/Ser (Incl. Access Fees) $75,000, Micro $40,000, AV Equip $4,000, AV Mat $9,000, Electronic Ref Mat (Incl. Access Fees) $50,000, Presv $2,200. Sal $297,855 (Prof $148,748)
Library Holdings: CDs 1,250; DVDs 400; e-books 138,000; e-journals 12,000; Bk Titles 120,000; Bk Vols 130,000; Per Subs 700; Videos 500
Special Collections: Library of American Civilization, micro; O'Reilly Hospital, photog & doc; University Archives
Automation Activity & Vendor Info: (Acquisitions) Innovative Interfaces, Inc - Sierra; (Cataloging) Innovative Interfaces, Inc - Sierra; (Circulation) Innovative Interfaces, Inc - Sierra; (Course Reserve) Innovative Interfaces, Inc - Sierra; (ILL) Innovative Interfaces, Inc - Sierra; (Media Booking) Innovative Interfaces, Inc - Sierra; (OPAC) Innovative Interfaces, Inc - Sierra; (Serials) Innovative Interfaces, Inc - Sierra
Wireless access
Function: Archival coll, Computers for patron use, Electronic databases & coll, Free DVD rentals, ILL available, Learning ctr, Music CDs, Online cat, Online ref, Photocopying/Printing, Ref & res, Ref serv available, Wheelchair accessible
Partic in Amigos Library Services, Inc; MOBIUS; OCLC Online Computer Library Center, Inc
Open Mon-Thurs 7:30am-11:45pm, Fri 7:30-4, Sun 4-Midnight
Restriction: Borrowing privileges limited to fac & registered students, In-house use for visitors, Mem organizations only, Non-circulating coll, Non-circulating of rare bks, Non-circulating to the pub, Pub use on premises

M MERCY HEALTH*, Springfield Medical Library, 1235 E Cherokee St, 65804-2263. SAN 326-4823. Tel: 417-820-2795. Administration Tel: 417-820-3253. FAX: 417-820-5399. E-mail: libstaff@mercy.net. Web Site: www.mercy.net/417library. *Mgr, Libr Serv,* Holly Henderson; *Librn,* Jean M Lewis; Staff 2 (MLS 1, Non-MLS 1)
Founded 1940
Subject Interests: Allied health, Healthcare mgt, Med, Nursing
Automation Activity & Vendor Info: (Circulation) Innovative Interfaces, Inc; (ILL) OCLC; (OPAC) Innovative Interfaces, Inc
Wireless access
Function: Health sci info serv
Partic in Health Sciences Library Network of Kansas City, Inc; National Network of Libraries of Medicine Region 3
Restriction: Hospital employees & physicians only, Med & health res only
Branches:
VAN K SMITH CONSUMER HEALTH INFORMATION SERVICE, 1235 E Cherokee St, 65804. Tel: 417-820-2539. E-mail: libstaff@mercy.net. *Libr Mgr,* Holly Henderson; Staff 2 (MLS 1, Non-MLS 1)
Founded 1990
Subject Interests: Consumer health
Function: Doc delivery serv, Mail & tel request accepted, Ref serv available, Res assist avail, Telephone ref
Open Mon-Fri 8-4:30
Restriction: Not a lending libr

GL MISSOURI STATE COURT OF APPEALS*, Southern District Law Library, University Plaza, 300 Hammons Pkwy, 65806. (Mail add: 300 S Hammons Pkwy, Ste 300, 65806), SAN 309-2364. Tel: 417-895-1398. FAX: 417-895-6817. *Librn,* Amy Bailey; E-mail: amy.bailey@courts.mo.gov; Staff 1 (Non-MLS 1)
Library Holdings: Bk Titles 17,500; Bk Vols 19,500; Per Subs 30
Restriction: Not open to pub

C MISSOURI STATE UNIVERSITY*, Duane G Meyer Library, 850 S John Q Hammons Pkwy, 65807. (Mail add: 901 S National, 65897-0001), SAN 349-8158. Tel: 417-836-4535. Circulation Tel: 417-836-4700. Interlibrary Loan Service Tel: 417-836-4540. Administration Tel: 417-836-4525. Web Site: www.library.missouristate.edu/Meyer. *Dean, Libr Serv,* Thomas Peters; E-mail: TPeters@missouristate.edu; *Head, Access Serv,* Joshua Lambert; Tel: 417-836-3183, E-mail: JLambert@missouristate.edu; *Head, Cat,* Marilyn A McCroskey; Tel: 417-836-4541, E-mail: marilynmccroskey@missouristate.edu; *Head Music Libr,* Jir Shin Boey; Tel: 417-836-5428, E-mail: JSBoey@missouristate.edu; *Archivist,* Anne Baker; Tel: 417-836-4298, E-mail: AnneBaker@missouristate.edu; Staff 65 (MLS 29, Non-MLS 36)
Founded 1907. Enrl 18,700; Fac 673; Highest Degree: Doctorate
Library Holdings: AV Mats 34,097; Bk Vols 1,738,708; Per Subs 4,200
Special Collections: African-American History of the Ozarks (Katherine Lederer Coll); Jean Arthur Rimbaud (William Jack Jones Coll); Michel Butor Coll; Ozarks Labor Union Archives; Ozarks Lesbian and Gay Archives; Robert Wallace Coll; University Archives. Oral History; State Document Depository; UN Document Depository; US Document Depository
Automation Activity & Vendor Info: (Acquisitions) Innovative Interfaces, Inc; (Cataloging) Innovative Interfaces, Inc; (Circulation) Innovative Interfaces, Inc; (Course Reserve) Innovative Interfaces, Inc; (ILL) Innovative Interfaces, Inc; (Media Booking) Innovative Interfaces, Inc; (OPAC) Innovative Interfaces, Inc; (Serials) Innovative Interfaces, Inc
Wireless access
Publications: "Check It Out" (Newsletter)
Partic in Amigos Library Services, Inc; Missouri Research & Education Network; MOBIUS
Special Services for the Deaf - TDD equip
Open Mon-Thurs 7am-2am, Fri 7-6, Sat 9-6, Sun Noon-2am
Friends of the Library Group
Departmental Libraries:
HASELTINE LIBRARY, Greenwood Laboratory School, 901 S National, Rm 3, 65897, SAN 349-8182. Tel: 417-836-8563. *Libr Assoc,* Rhonda O'Connor; E-mail: rhondaoconnor@missouristate.edu; *Media Spec,* Dea Borneman; E-mail: deaborneman@missouristate.edu; Staff 1 (MLS 1)
Library Holdings: Bk Titles 1,986; Bk Vols 2,100; Per Subs 43
Open Mon-Fri 8-5
Friends of the Library Group
MUSIC LIBRARY, Ellis Hall, Rm 209, 901 S National, 65804-0095, SAN 328-6916. Tel: 417-836-5434. *Head of Libr,* Drew Beisswenger; Tel: 417-836-5499, E-mail: drewbeisswenger@missouristate.edu; *Supvr,* Sue Reichling; E-mail: suereichling@missouristate.edu; Staff 1 (MLS 1)
Library Holdings: Bk Titles 4,886; Bk Vols 5,000; Per Subs 100
Special Collections: Missouri Music Educators Association Archives
Open Mon-Thurs 8am-10pm, Fri 8-5, Sat 12-4, Sun 1-10
Friends of the Library Group

P SPRINGFIELD-GREENE COUNTY LIBRARY DISTRICT*, 4653 S Campbell Ave, 65810-1723. SAN 349-8212. Tel: 417-882-0714. Reference Tel: 417-883-5341. Administration Tel: 417-883-5366. FAX: 417-883-9348. Administration FAX: 417-889-2547. Web Site: thelibrary.org. *Exec Dir,* Regina Cooper; E-mail: reginac@thelibrary.org; *Assoc Dir,* Jim Schmidt; E-mail: jims@thelibrary.org; *Libr Found Dir,* Adler Melissa; E-mail: foundation@thelibrary.org; *Electronic Res Librn,* Renee Brumett; E-mail: reneeb@thelibrary.org; *Planning & Develop Librn,* Gay Wilson; E-mail: gayw@thelibrary.org; *Commun Relations Mgr,* Kathleen O'Dell; E-mail: kathleeno@thelibrary.org; *Human Res Mgr,* Lori Ruzicka; E-mail: humanresources@thelibrary.org; *Youth Serv Coordr,* Nancee Dahms-Stinson; E-mail: nanceed@thelibrary.org; *Coll Serv,* Lisa Sampley; E-mail: lisas@thelibrary.org; *Info Tech,* David Patillo; E-mail: davidp@thelibrary.org; Staff 250 (MLS 28, Non-MLS 222)
Founded 1903. Pop 283,870; Circ 3,627,707
Jul 2014-Jun 2015 Income (Main & Associated Libraries) $12,859,207. Mats Exp $2,026,672. Sal $5,934,133
Library Holdings: Audiobooks 29,594; CDs 29,571; DVDs 54,534; e-books 10,614; Electronic Media & Resources 46; Bk Vols 413,900; Per Subs 1,184
Special Collections: Burt Buhrman Music Coll; Genealogy & Missouri History; Max Hunter Folk Songs Coll; Turnbo Papers
Automation Activity & Vendor Info: (Acquisitions) Innovative Interfaces, Inc; (Cataloging) Innovative Interfaces, Inc; (Circulation) Innovative Interfaces, Inc; (ILL) Innovative Interfaces, Inc; (OPAC) Innovative Interfaces, Inc; (Serials) Innovative Interfaces, Inc
Wireless access

Function: Homebound delivery serv, ILL available, Internet access, Photocopying/Printing, Prog for adults, Prog for children & young adult, Ref serv available, Summer reading prog, Wheelchair accessible
Partic in MOBIUS; OCLC Online Computer Library Center, Inc
Special Services for the Deaf - Closed caption videos; TDD equip; Videos & decoder
Special Services for the Blind - Assistive/Adapted tech devices, equip & products; Newsline for the Blind; Talking bks
Open Mon-Fri 8:30-5
Friends of the Library Group
Branches: 11
ASH GROVE BRANCH, 101 E Main St, Ash Grove, 65604-0248, SAN 349-8247. Tel: 417-751-2933. Web Site: thelibrary.org/branches/agr.cfm. *Br Mgr,* Sarah Francka-Jones; E-mail: sarahf@thelibrary.org; Staff 3.7 (MLS 1, Non-MLS 2.7)
Circ 38,377
Function: Internet access, Photocopying/Printing, Prog for adults, Prog for children & young adult, Ref serv available, Summer reading prog
Open Mon-Fri 8:30-6
Friends of the Library Group
FAIR GROVE BRANCH, 81 S Orchard Blvd, Fair Grove, 65648-8421. Tel: 417-759-2637. Web Site: thelibrary.org/branches/fgr.cfm. *Br Mgr,* Whitney Austin; E-mail: whitneya@thelibrary.org; Staff 4 (MLS 1, Non-MLS 3)
Circ 72,353
Function: Internet access, Photocopying/Printing, Prog for adults, Prog for children & young adult, Ref serv available, Summer reading prog
Open Mon-Thurs 9:30-7, Fri & Sat 9:30-6
Friends of the Library Group
THE LIBRARY CENTER, 4653 S Campbell Ave, 65810-1723, SAN 349-8328. Tel: 417-882-0714. Web Site: thelibrary.org/branches/tlc.cfm. *Br Mgr,* Jessie Alexander-East; E-mail: jessieae@thelibrary.org; Staff 48 (MLS 6.5, Non-MLS 41.5)
Circ 1,043,343
Special Collections: Ozarks history, Civil War history in Trans-Mississippi Theater; historic Ozarks photograph digital coll
Subject Interests: Genealogy, Local hist
Function: ILL available, Internet access, Photocopying/Printing, Prog for adults, Prog for children & young adult, Ref serv available, Summer reading prog, Wheelchair accessible
Open Mon-Sat 8:30am-9pm, Sun 1-5
Friends of the Library Group
LIBRARY STATION, 2535 N Kansas Expressway, 65803-1114, SAN 349-8301. Tel: 417-865-1340. Web Site: thelibrary.org/branches/lst.cfm. *Br Mgr,* Kim Flores; E-mail: kimf@thelibrary.org; Staff 25 (MLS 5, Non-MLS 20)
Circ 565,501
Special Collections: Historical Ozarks photograph digital coll; Ozarks history, Civil War history in Trans-Mississippi Theater
Subject Interests: Genealogy, Local hist
Function: Internet access, Photocopying/Printing, Prog for adults, Prog for children & young adult, Ref serv available, Summer reading prog
Open Mon-Sat 8:30am-9pm, Sun 1-5
Friends of the Library Group
MIDTOWN CARNEGIE BRANCH, 397 E Central St, 65802-3834. Tel: 417-862-0135. Web Site: thelibrary.org/branches/mid.cfm. *Br Mgr,* Eva Pelkey; E-mail: evap@thelibrary.org; Staff 14 (MLS 3, Non-MLS 11)
Circ 222,532
Open Mon-Thurs 8:30-7:30, Fri 8:30-6, Sat 8:30-5
Friends of the Library Group
OUTREACH SERVICES, 4653 S Campbell, 65810-8113, SAN 376-2386. Tel: 417-883-6112. Web Site: thelibrary.org/services/bkm.cfm. *Mgr, Outreach Serv,* Allison Eckhardt; E-mail: allisone@thelibrary.org; Staff 8 (Non-MLS 8)
Circ 186,195
Function: Home delivery & serv to seniorr ctr & nursing homes, Homebound delivery serv, Summer reading prog
Friends of the Library Group
PARK CENTRAL BRANCH, 128 Park Central Sq, 65806-1311. Tel: 417-831-1342. Web Site: thelibrary.org/branches/prk.cfm. *Br Mgr,* Ingrid Bohnenkamp; E-mail: ingridb@thelibrary.org
Circ 63,597
Open Mon-Sat 8:30-7
Friends of the Library Group
REPUBLIC BRANCH, 921 N Lindsey Ave, Republic, 65738-1248, SAN 349-8360. Tel: 417-732-7284. Web Site: thelibrary.org/branches/rep.cfm. *Br Mgr,* Erin Gray; E-mail: ering@thelibrary.org; Staff 7 (MLS 1, Non-MLS 6)
Circ 194,142
Function: Internet access, Photocopying/Printing, Prog for adults, Prog for children & young adult, Ref serv available, Summer reading prog
Open Mon-Thurs 8:30-9, Fri & Sat 8:30-6
Friends of the Library Group
SCHWEITZER BRENTWOOD BRANCH, 2214 Brentwood Blvd, 65804. (Mail add: PO Box 248, 65804), SAN 349-8271. Tel: 417-883-1974. Web Site: thelibrary.org/branches/bwd.cfm. *Br Mgr,* Jeana Gockley; E-mail: jeanag@thelibrary.org; Staff 17 (MLS 3, Non-MLS 14)
Founded 1970. Circ 495,651
Function: Internet access, Photocopying/Printing, Prog for adults, Prog for children & young adult, Ref serv available, Summer reading prog
Open Mon-Thurs 8:30am-9pm, Fri & Sat 8:30-6, Sun 1-5
Friends of the Library Group
STRAFFORD BRANCH, 101 S State Hwy 125, Strafford, 65757-8998. (Mail add: PO Box 248, Strafford, 65757). Tel: 417-736-9233. Web Site: thelibrary.org/branches/str.cfm. *Br Mgr,* Whitney Austin; E-mail: whitneya@thelibrary.org
Circ 68,985
Open Mon-Thurs 9:30-7, Fri & Sat 9:30-6
Friends of the Library Group
WILLARD BRANCH, East Shopping Ctr, 304 E Jackson St, Willard, 65781-0517. (Mail add: PO Box 248, Willard, 65781), SAN 376-2378. Tel: 417-742-4258. Web Site: thelibrary.org/branches/wld.cfm. *Br Mgr,* Sarah Francka-Jones; E-mail: sarahf@thelibrary.org; Staff 4 (MLS 1, Non-MLS 3)
Circ 102,350
Function: Internet access, Photocopying/Printing, Prog for adults, Prog for children & young adult, Ref serv available, Summer reading prog
Open Mon-Thurs 9:30-7, Fri & Sat 9:30-6
Friends of the Library Group
Bookmobiles: 1. Outreach Servs Mgr, Allison Eckhardt. Bk vols 3,800

STANBERRY

P GENTRY COUNTY LIBRARY, 304 N Park St, 64489. SAN 309-2402. Tel: 660-783-2335. FAX: 660-783-2335. Web Site: www.gentrycountylibrary.org. *Dir,* Judy Garrett; E-mail: jgarrett@gentrycountylibrary.org; *Asst Dir,* Sharon Luke; Staff 5 (MLS 2, Non-MLS 3)
Founded 1955. Pop 6,488; Circ 74,290
Library Holdings: CDs 19; Large Print Bks 37; Bk Titles 53,731; Bk Vols 54,121; Per Subs 70; Talking Bks 431; Videos 1,581
Subject Interests: Genealogy, Mo
Open Tues, Thurs & Fri 8-5, Wed 8-7, Sat 8-Noon
Friends of the Library Group
Bookmobiles: 1

STEELE

P STEELE PUBLIC LIBRARY*, 108 E Main St, 63877-1528. SAN 309-2410. Tel: 573-695-3561. FAX: 573-695-3021. E-mail: steelepubliclibrary19@gmail.com. *Dir,* Myrna McKay; Staff 3 (MLS 1, Non-MLS 2)
Founded 1937. Pop 2,419; Circ 10,426
Library Holdings: Bk Titles 15,678; Bk Vols 16,323; Per Subs 22; Talking Bks 237; Videos 562
Wireless access
Partic in Missouri Research & Education Network
Open Tues-Fri 12:30-4:30
Friends of the Library Group

SWEET SPRINGS

P SWEET SPRINGS PUBLIC LIBRARY*, 217 Turner St, 65351. SAN 309-2429. Tel: 660-335-4314. E-mail: sweetspringslibrary@hotmail.com. *Librn,* Janet L Scott; *Asst Librn,* Jennie Aiken; Staff 2 (Non-MLS 2)
Founded 1939. Pop 1,596
Library Holdings: Audiobooks 25; AV Mats 100; Bks on Deafness & Sign Lang 2; DVDs 100; Bk Titles 13,465; Bk Vols 13,475; Per Subs 12
Special Collections: Books on Missouri Coll
Wireless access
Function: ILL available, Photocopying/Printing
Open Tues & Fri 12-5, Thurs 12-7, Sat 9-12
Friends of the Library Group

TIPTON

P PRICE JAMES MEMORIAL LIBRARY*, 104 E Morgan, 65081. (Mail add: PO Box 187, 65081-0187), SAN 309-2445. Tel: 660-433-5622. *Dir,* Marsha Nelson; E-mail: mnelson@pricejameslibrary.com; Staff 1 (MLS 1)
Pop 6,623; Circ 20,000
Library Holdings: Large Print Bks 3,000; Bk Titles 15,000; Talking Bks 203; Videos 125
Subject Interests: Classics, Fiction, Humanities, Juv, Relig studies, Sci
Automation Activity & Vendor Info: (Cataloging) Biblionix; (Circulation) Biblionix
Open Mon 10-5, Tues & Wed 10-7, Fr 10-4

TRENTON

P GRUNDY COUNTY-JEWETT NORRIS LIBRARY*, 1331 Main St, 64683. SAN 309-2453. Tel: 660-359-3577. FAX: 660-359-6220. Web Site: grundycountylibrary.org. *Dir,* Theresa Hunsaker; E-mail: theresa@grundycountylibrary.org; *Asst Dir,* Doris Baker; E-mail: doris@grundycountylibrary.org; *Librn,* Carolyn Dickerson; E-mail: carolyn@grundycountylibrary.org; *Ch,* Charity Halstead; E-mail: charity@grundycountylibrary.org
Founded 1890. Pop 10,500; Circ 36,000
Library Holdings: Bk Titles 31,252; Per Subs 53
Subject Interests: Genealogy
Automation Activity & Vendor Info: (Acquisitions) Follett Software; (Cataloging) Follett Software; (Circulation) Follett Software
Wireless access
Function: Bks on cassette, Bks on CD, CD-ROM, Children's prog, Computer training, Computers for patron use, Free DVD rentals, Genealogy discussion group, ILL available, Instruction & testing, Internet access, Magnifiers for reading, Outreach serv, Photocopying/Printing, Preschool outreach, Printer for laptops & handheld devices, Prog for children & young adult, Scanner, Senior computer classes, Serves people with intellectual disabilities, Story hour, Summer reading prog, Tax forms, Teen prog, Wheelchair accessible
Open Mon 8:30-7, Tues-Fri 8:30-5, Sat 8:30-12
Friends of the Library Group

J NORTH CENTRAL MISSOURI COLLEGE LIBRARY*, Geyer Hall, 1st & 2nd Flr, 1301 Main St, 64683. SAN 309-2461. Tel: 660-359-3948, Ext 1322, 660-359-3948, Ext 1325, 660-359-3948, Ext 1335. Web Site: www.ncmissouri.edu/library. *Libr Dir,* Dr Beth Ann Caldarello; E-mail: bcaldarello@mail.ncmissouri.edu; *ILL, Mkt Librn,* Ronna Owens; E-mail: rowens@mail.ncmissouri.edu; *Testing Ctr Coord,* Shellee Castanada; E-mail: scastanada@mail.ncmissouri.edu; Staff 4 (MLS 2, Non-MLS 2)
Founded 1967
Library Holdings: Bk Vols 30,000
Automation Activity & Vendor Info: (Acquisitions) Innovative Interfaces, Inc; (Cataloging) Innovative Interfaces, Inc; (Circulation) Innovative Interfaces, Inc; (OPAC) Innovative Interfaces, Inc
Wireless access
Partic in MOBIUS
Open Mon-Wed 7:30am-9pm, Thurs 7:30-6, Fri 7:30-4:30, Sun 4-8
Restriction: Badge access after hrs, Borrowing privileges limited to anthropology fac & libr staff, Borrowing privileges limited to fac & registered students, Borrowing requests are handled by ILL, By permission only, Circ limited, Circ privileges for students & alumni only, Circ to mem only

TROY

P POWELL MEMORIAL LIBRARY, 951 W College St, 63379. SAN 309-247X. Tel: 636-462-4874. FAX: 636-462-4875. Web Site: www.troy.k12.mo.us/domain/48. *Dir,* Sharon Hasekamp; E-mail: hasekamp@troy.k12.mo.us; *Librn,* Kathy Rowe; E-mail: rowek@troy.k12.mo.us
Founded 1949. Pop 12,000; Circ 45,000
Library Holdings: AV Mats 50; Large Print Bks 100; Bk Titles 30,000; Per Subs 10; Talking Bks 250
Special Collections: Missouri Genealogical Coll. Oral History
Subject Interests: Local hist
Automation Activity & Vendor Info: (Cataloging) Follett Software; (Circulation) Follett Software; (OPAC) Follett Software
Wireless access
Open Mon & Tues 8:30-7, Wed 10-6, Thurs & Fri 8:30-4:30, Sat 8:30-12:30 (Summer); Mon 8:30-4:30, Tues & Wed 10-6, Thurs & Fri 8:30-4:30 (Winter)
Restriction: Residents only

UNION

J EAST CENTRAL COLLEGE LIBRARY*, 1964 Prairie Dell Rd, 63084. SAN 309-2488. Tel: 636-584-6560. FAX: 636-583-1897. E-mail: library@eastcentral.edu. Web Site: www.eastcentral.edu/library. *Dir, Libr Serv,* Lisa Farrell; E-mail: lisa.farrell@eastcentral.edu; Staff 2 (MLS 2)
Founded 1969. Enrl 2,700; Fac 190; Highest Degree: Associate
Library Holdings: AV Mats 2,100; Bks on Deafness & Sign Lang 14; CDs 421; DVDs 1,500; e-books 10,232; Bk Vols 20,000; Per Subs 175; Talking Bks 316
Special Collections: Abraham Lincoln (John E Baker, Jr Memorial Coll); Harrison Eaton Children's Coll
Automation Activity & Vendor Info: (Cataloging) Innovative Interfaces, Inc; (Circulation) Innovative Interfaces, Inc; (Course Reserve) Innovative Interfaces, Inc; (ILL) OCLC; (OPAC) Innovative Interfaces, Inc; (Serials) Innovative Interfaces, Inc
Wireless access
Partic in Amigos Library Services, Inc; Missouri Research & Education Network; MOBIUS; Network of Illinois Learning Resources in Community Colleges
Open Mon-Thurs 7:30am-7:30pm, Fri 7:30-2
Friends of the Library Group

P SCENIC REGIONAL LIBRARY*, Administrative Offices, 304 Hawthorne Dr, 63084. SAN 349-8395. Tel: 636-583-0652. Web Site: scenicregional.org. *Libr Dir,* Steve Campbell; Tel: 636-583-0652, Ext 101, E-mail: swcampbell@scenicregional.org; *Asst Dir,* Megan Maurer; Tel: 636-583-0652, Ext 102, E-mail: mmaurer@scenicregional.org; *Youth Serv Librn,* Christy Schink; Tel: 636-583-0652, Ext 105, E-mail: cschink@scenicregional.org; Staff 28.7 (MLS 5, Non-MLS 23.7)
Founded 1959. Pop 116,117; Circ 536,742
Library Holdings: Audiobooks 5,746; CDs 7,476; DVDs 2,675; Large Print Bks 6,595; Bk Vols 245,509; Per Subs 464; Videos 3,583
Wireless access
Function: Adult bk club, Art exhibits, Audio & video playback equip for onsite use, AV serv, Electronic databases & coll, Health sci info serv, Home delivery & serv to seniorr ctr & nursing homes, ILL available, Internet access, Magnifiers for reading, Mail & tel request accepted, Mail loans to mem, Music CDs, Online ref, Photocopying/Printing, Preschool outreach, Prog for adults, Prog for children & young adult, Ref & res, Ref serv available, Spoken cassettes & CDs, Spoken cassettes & DVDs, Summer reading prog, Tax forms, Telephone ref, VHS videos, Wheelchair accessible
Partic in Saint Louis Regional Library Network
Open Mon-Fri 8-4:30
Branches: 8
HERMANN BRANCH, 601 Market St, Hermann, 65041, SAN 349-8425. Tel: 573-486-2024. *Br Supvr,* Sheri Hausman
Circ 36,130
Library Holdings: Audiobooks 904; CDs 883; DVDs 258; Large Print Bks 888; Bk Vols 28,347; Per Subs 41; Videos 414
Special Collections: City Newspapers, micro; City Records, micro; County Census Records, micro
Open Tues, Thurs & Fri 9-6, Wed 11-8, Sat 9-3
NEW HAVEN BRANCH, 901 Maupin, New Haven, 63068, SAN 349-845X. Tel: 573-237-2189. *Br Supvr,* Judy Brock
Circ 16,023
Library Holdings: Audiobooks 385; CDs 634; DVDs 180; Large Print Bks 446; Bk Vols 15,410; Per Subs 42; Videos 380
Function: ILL available, Internet access, Mail & tel request accepted, Online ref, Photocopying/Printing, Ref serv available, Spoken cassettes & CDs, Spoken cassettes & DVDs, Summer reading prog, Tax forms, Telephone ref, VHS videos, Wheelchair accessible
Open Tues, Thurs & Fri 8:30-12:30 & 1-5:30, Wed 8:30-12:30 & 1-7, Sat 8:30-1
OWENSVILLE BRANCH, 107 N First St, Owensville, 65066, SAN 349-8484. Tel: 573-437-2188. *Br Supvr,* Linda G Little
Circ 27,567
Library Holdings: Audiobooks 631; CDs 867; DVDs 211; Large Print Bks 684; Bk Vols 21,278; Per Subs 40; Videos 393
Function: AV serv, Digital talking bks, Electronic databases & coll, ILL available, Internet access, Music CDs, Online ref, Photocopying/Printing, Ref & res, Ref serv available, Spoken cassettes & CDs, Spoken cassettes & DVDs, Summer reading prog, Tax forms, Telephone ref, VHS videos, Wheelchair accessible
Open Tues, Thurs & Fri 8:30-12:30 & 1-5:30, Wed 8:30-12:30 & 1-7, Sat 8:30-1
Friends of the Library Group
PACIFIC BRANCH, 119 W Saint Louis St, Pacific, 63069, SAN 349-8514. Tel: 636-257-2712. *Br Supvr,* Georgia Mofield
Circ 54,454
Library Holdings: Audiobooks 505; CDs 999; DVDs 318; Large Print Bks 811; Bk Vols 22,665; Per Subs 40; Videos 421
Function: AV serv, Digital talking bks, Electronic databases & coll, ILL available, Internet access, Music CDs, Online ref, Photocopying/Printing, Prog for children & young adult, Ref & res, Ref serv available, Spoken cassettes & CDs, Spoken cassettes & DVDs, Summer reading prog, Tax forms, Telephone ref, VHS videos, Wheelchair accessible
Open Tues, Thurs & Fri 9-6, Wed 9-8, Sat 9-3
SAINT CLAIR BRANCH, 570 S Main St, Saint Clair, 63077, SAN 349-8549. Tel: 636-629-2546. *Br Supvr,* Karen Fogelbach
Circ 37,477
Library Holdings: Audiobooks 619; CDs 741; DVDs 204; Large Print Bks 756; Bk Vols 23,153; Per Subs 32; Videos 503
Function: Digital talking bks, E-Reserves, Electronic databases & coll, ILL available, Internet access, Music CDs, Online ref, Photocopying/Printing, Prog for children & young adult, Ref & res, Ref serv available, Spoken cassettes & CDs, Spoken cassettes & DVDs, Summer reading prog, Tax forms, Telephone ref, VHS videos, Wheelchair accessible
Open Tues, Thurs & Fri 8:30-12:30 & 1-5:30, Wed 8:30-12:30 & 1-7, Sat 9-1:30

SULLIVAN PUBLIC LIBRARY, 104 W Vine St, Sullivan, 63080, SAN 329-1057. Tel: 573-468-4372. FAX: 573-860-4648. *Mgr,* Lori Jane Perdew; Staff 2 (MLS 1, Non-MLS 1)
Founded 1948. Pop 6,351
Library Holdings: Large Print Bks 500; Bk Titles 12,900; Bk Vols 13,000; Per Subs 50; Talking Bks 673
Open Mon & Fri 9-5, Tues & Thurs 9-6, Wed 9-7, Sat 9-1

UNION BRANCH, 308 Hawthorne Dr, 63084, SAN 349-8573. Tel: 636-583-3224. FAX: 636-583-6519. *Dir,* Sallie Hancox; *Asst Dir,* Kenneth Rohrbach; E-mail: scenic2@real.more.net; *Access Serv/Reserves/Ref Librn, ILL,* Carolyn Scheer; E-mail: scenic3@real.more.net; *Ch Serv,* Christy Schink; E-mail: scenic4@real.more.net; Staff 4 (MLS 4)
Library Holdings: CDs 422; DVDs 383; Large Print Bks 1,126; Bk Vols 87,773; Per Subs 60; Talking Bks 2,412; Videos 1,103
Special Collections: Area Newspapers, micro; County Census Records; Selected County Records, micro
Function: Audio & video playback equip for onsite use, AV serv, Digital talking bks, Electronic databases & coll, Home delivery & serv to seniorr ctr & nursing homes, ILL available, Internet access, Magnifiers for reading, Mail & tel request accepted, Music CDs, Online ref, Photocopying/Printing, Preschool outreach, Prog for children & young adult, Ref & res, Ref serv available, Spoken cassettes & CDs, Spoken cassettes & DVDs, Summer reading prog, Tax forms, Telephone ref, VHS videos, Wheelchair accessible
Open Mon, Tues, Thurs & Fri 8-6, Wed 8-8, Sat 9-3

WARREN COUNTY, 912 S Hwy 47, Warrenton, 63383-2600, SAN 349-8603. Tel: 636-456-3321. *Br Supvr,* Marlys Mertens
Circ 116,705
Library Holdings: Audiobooks 1,007; CDs 1,325; DVDs 529; Large Print Bks 1,140; Bk Vols 41,413; Per Subs 43; Videos 684
Special Collections: Census records & area newspapers, micro
Function: Audio & video playback equip for onsite use, AV serv, Digital talking bks, Electronic databases & coll, Home delivery & serv to seniorr ctr & nursing homes, ILL available, Internet access, Music CDs, Online ref, Photocopying/Printing, Prog for children & young adult, Ref & res, Ref serv available, Spoken cassettes & CDs, Spoken cassettes & DVDs, Summer reading prog, Tax forms, Telephone ref, VHS videos, Wheelchair accessible
Open Mon, Thurs & Fri 9-6, Tues & Wed 9-8, Sat 9-3

Bookmobiles: 1. Mgr, Connie Vest. Bk vols 11,236

UNIONVILLE

P PUTNAM COUNTY PUBLIC LIBRARY*, 115 S 16th St, 63565-1624. SAN 309-250X. Tel: 660-947-3192. FAX: 660-947-7039. E-mail: pclib@yahoo.com. Web Site: putnamcl.lib.mo.us. *Dir,* Leatha Walsh; Staff 4 (Non-MLS 4)
Founded 1946. Pop 5,223; Circ 50,375
Jan 2016-Dec 2016. Mats Exp $32,385, Books $18,040, Per/Ser (Incl. Access Fees) $1,500, AV Equip $10,045, AV Mat $2,000, Electronic Ref Mat (Incl. Access Fees) $800. Sal $54,761 (Prof $28,571)
Library Holdings: Audiobooks 5,388; AV Mats 8; CDs 82; DVDs 2,092; Electronic Media & Resources 17,226; Large Print Bks 777; Microforms 140; Bk Titles 33,998; Bk Vols 34,125; Per Subs 86
Subject Interests: Genealogy of Putnam County, Local hist
Automation Activity & Vendor Info: (Cataloging) Evergreen; (Circulation) Evergreen; (OPAC) EOS International
Wireless access
Function: 24/7 Electronic res, 24/7 Online cat, Audiobks via web, Bks on CD, Children's prog, Computer training, Computers for patron use, Electronic databases & coll, Free DVD rentals, ILL available, Internet access, Jail serv, Magazines, Magnifiers for reading, Mail & tel request accepted, Meeting rooms, Microfiche/film & reading machines, Movies, Online cat, Outside serv via phone, mail, e-mail & web, OverDrive digital audio bks, Photocopying/Printing, Preschool outreach, Preschool reading prog, Printer for laptops & handheld devices, Prog for adults, Prog for children & young adult, Ref serv available, Res assist avail, Senior computer classes, Story hour, Summer reading prog, Telephone ref, Workshops
Publications: Atlas of Putnam County, 1877 & 1897
Partic in Grand Rivers Libr Conference; Midwest Collaborative for Library Services; Missouri Research & Education Network
Special Services for the Blind - Aids for in-house use; Assistive/Adapted tech devices, equip & products; Audio mat; Bks on cassette; Bks on CD; Copier with enlargement capabilities; Extensive large print coll; Large print bks; Lending of low vision aids; Low vision equip; Magnifiers; Playaways (bks on MP3)
Open Mon 9-7, Tues-Fri 9-5, Sat 9-12
Friends of the Library Group

UNITY VILLAGE

R UNITY ARCHIVES, 1901 NW Blue Pkwy, 64065-0001. SAN 309-2518. Tel: 816-347-5539, 816-524-3550, Ext 2020. E-mail: archivescontact@unityonline.org. Web Site: www.unity.org/archives. *Dir, Archives,* Jolene Clark; *Asst Archivist,* Karren Scapple; Staff 2 (MLS 1, Non-MLS 1)
Founded 1942
Special Collections: Unity Archives from 1889, AV, bks, per
Subject Interests: Relig studies
Automation Activity & Vendor Info: (Cataloging) SirsiDynix; (Circulation) SirsiDynix; (Course Reserve) SirsiDynix; (ILL) SirsiDynix; (OPAC) SirsiDynix; (Serials) SirsiDynix
Wireless access
Function: Archival coll, For res purposes, Online cat, Photocopying/Printing, Ref serv available, Telephone ref, VHS videos
Restriction: Open by appt only, Pub ref by request

UNIVERSITY CITY

P UNIVERSITY CITY PUBLIC LIBRARY*, 6701 Delmar Blvd, 63130. SAN 309-2534. Tel: 314-727-3150. FAX: 314-727-6005. Web Site: www.ucpl.lib.mo.us. *Dir,* Patrick Wall; E-mail: pjwall@ucitylibrary.org; *Dir, Tech Serv,* Sally Master; E-mail: smaster@ucpl.lib.mo.us; Staff 11 (MLS 8, Non-MLS 3)
Founded 1939. Pop 37,428; Circ 491,420
Library Holdings: Audiobooks 3,826; CDs 6,803; DVDs 5,718; e-books 6,850; Electronic Media & Resources 10; High Interest/Low Vocabulary Bk Vols 628; Large Print Bks 3,091; Music Scores 745; Bk Titles 186,441; Per Subs 250; Videos 3,375
Special Collections: Archive of Local History; Locally Produced Art Pottery & Artifacts, circa 1910
Automation Activity & Vendor Info: (Acquisitions) SirsiDynix; (Cataloging) SirsiDynix; (Circulation) SirsiDynix; (OPAC) SirsiDynix; (Serials) SirsiDynix
Wireless access
Publications: Checkout (Newsletter)
Partic in Municipal Library Consortium; Saint Louis Regional Library Network
Open Mon-Fri 9-9, Sat 9-5, Sun 1-5
Friends of the Library Group

VALLEY PARK

P VALLEY PARK LIBRARY, 320 Benton St, 63088. SAN 309-2542. Tel: 636-225-5608. FAX: 636-825-0079. Web Site: www.valleyparklibrary.org. *Dir,* Pamela Kettler; E-mail: pkettler@valleyparklibrary.org; Staff 2 (MLS 2)
Founded 1943. Pop 3,859; Circ 9,041
Library Holdings: Bk Vols 14,000
Subject Interests: Local hist
Wireless access
Partic in Municipal Library Consortium; Saint Louis Regional Library Network
Open Mon-Wed 10-6, Thurs 10-7, Fri 10-5, Sat 10-2

VAN BUREN

P CARTER COUNTY LIBRARY DISTRICT*, Van Buren Library, 403 Ash St, 63965. (Mail add: PO Box 309, 63965-0309), SAN 349-8638. Tel: 573-323-4315. FAX: 573-323-0188. E-mail: library_vb@yahoo.com. Web Site: cartercountylibrary.org. *Dir,* Donna Sutton
Founded 1947. Pop 6,265; Circ 50,381
Library Holdings: Audiobooks 560; DVDs 354; Large Print Bks 600; Bk Titles 20,403
Special Collections: State Document Depository
Subject Interests: Children's folklore, Genealogy, Local hist
Automation Activity & Vendor Info: (Acquisitions) Book Systems; (Cataloging) Book Systems; (Circulation) Book Systems
Wireless access
Partic in Missouri Research & Education Network; SE Mo Libr Network
Open Mon, Wed-Fri 8-5, Tues 8-6
Branches: 2

ELLSINORE BRANCH, PO Box 312, Ellsinore, 63937. Tel: 573-322-0015. *Librn,* Gloria Copeland; Staff 1 (Non-MLS 1)
Circ 500
Library Holdings: Bk Titles 1,200
Open Tues & Fri 9-5, Sat 9-12

GRANDIN BRANCH, PO Box 274, Grandin, 63943-0274, SAN 349-8816. Tel: 573-593-4084. *Librn,* John Grow; Staff 1 (Non-MLS 1)
Library Holdings: Bk Titles 1,000
Open Tues & Thurs 1-6

S NATIONAL PARK SERVICE*, Ozark National Scenic Riverways Reference Library, 404 Watercress Dr, 63965. (Mail add: PO Box 490, 63965-0490), SAN 309-2550. Tel: 573-323-4236. FAX: 573-323-4140. Web Site: www.nps.gov/ozar. *Library Contact,* Position Currently Open
Founded 1974
Library Holdings: Bk Vols 2,000; Per Subs 14
Special Collections: Oral History
Subject Interests: Background studies associated with Riverways area, General natural, Hist data relative to Ozark area
Wireless access
Function: Res libr
Open Mon-Fri 8-4:30

VERSAILLES

P MORGAN COUNTY LIBRARY*, 600 N Hunter, 65084-1830. SAN 309-2569. Tel: 573-378-5319. FAX: 573-378-6166. E-mail: mocolibrary@hotmail.com. Web Site: morgancountylibrary.org. *Dir,* Stacey Embry; *Ch,* Berenice Clark; Staff 4 (Non-MLS 4)
Founded 1946. Pop 22,000; Circ 87,808
Library Holdings: Bks on Deafness & Sign Lang 15; CDs 1,878; DVDs 7,147; Electronic Media & Resources 226; Bk Vols 36,500; Per Subs 89; Talking Bks 2,890; Videos 7,147
Subject Interests: Genealogy, Local hist
Automation Activity & Vendor Info: (Cataloging) Follett Software; (Circulation) Follett Software
Wireless access
Partic in Missouri Research & Education Network
Open Mon-Fri 9-5:30, Sat 9-1
Friends of the Library Group

WARRENSBURG

S JOHNSON COUNTY HISTORICAL SOCIETY*, Mary Miller Smiser Heritage Library, 302 N Main St, 64093. SAN 328-0195. Tel: 660-747-6480. E-mail: curator@jocomohistory.org. Web Site: jocomohistory.org/mary-miller-smiser-heritage-library. *Curator,* Mike Shaw
Founded 1969
Library Holdings: Bk Titles 2,110; Bk Vols 2,340; Per Subs 11
Special Collections: Johnson County; Local History, Newsp. Oral History
Open Tues-Sat 1-4

P TRAILS REGIONAL LIBRARY*, 432 N Holden St, 64093. SAN 349-9170. Tel: 660-747-1699. Circulation Tel: 660-747-9177. Web Site: www.trailslibrary.org. *Dir,* Rochelle McCaulley; E-mail: mccaulleyr@trailslibrary.org; *Asst Dir,* Anita Love; E-mail: lovea@trailslibrary.org; *Head, Tech Serv,* Kathy Cox; E-mail: coxk@trailslibrary.org; *Br Mgr,* Carol Nolte; E-mail: noltec@trailslibrary.org; Staff 52 (MLS 5, Non-MLS 47)
Founded 1957. Pop 81,482; Circ 316,257
Jul 2016-Jun 2017 Income (Main & Associated Libraries) $2,837,018. Mats Exp $3,031,037, Books $243,485, Per/Ser (Incl. Access Fees) $14,009, AV Mat $75,246, Electronic Ref Mat (Incl. Access Fees) $24,941. Sal $1,583,284
Library Holdings: CDs 4,757; DVDs 12,425; e-books 22,730; Bk Vols 126,000
Automation Activity & Vendor Info: (Acquisitions) Evergreen; (Cataloging) Evergreen; (Circulation) Evergreen; (ILL) OCLC; (OPAC) Evergreen
Wireless access
Partic in Mid-America Library Alliance; Missouri Evergreen
Friends of the Library Group
Branches: 9
CONCORDIA BRANCH, 813 S Main, Concordia, 64020, SAN 349-9200. Tel: 660-463-2277. *Br Mgr,* Debra Kirchhoff; E-mail: kirchhoffd@trailslibrary.org
Open Mon-Fri 9:30-5:30, Sat 9:30-4:30
Friends of the Library Group
CORDER BRANCH, 221 N Lafayette, Corder, 64021, SAN 349-9235. Tel: 660-394-2565. *Br Mgr,* Linda Markworth; E-mail: markworthl@trailslibrary.org
Open Mon, Wed & Fri 9-5, Sat 9-3
HOLDEN BRANCH, 207 S Main St, Holden, 64040, SAN 308-9991. Tel: 816-732-4545. *Br Mgr,* Jeannae Dickerson; E-mail: dickersonj@trailslibrary.org; Staff 1 (MLS 1)
Founded 1941. Pop 2,389; Circ 10,901
Library Holdings: CDs 51; Large Print Bks 88; Bk Titles 18,941; Bk Vols 19,802; Per Subs 35; Talking Bks 80; Videos 112
Open Mon, Wed & Fri 9-5, Tues & Thurs 9-7, Sat 9-4
Friends of the Library Group
KNOB NOSTER BRANCH, 202 N Adams, Knob Noster, 65336, SAN 349-926X. Tel: 660-563-2997. FAX: 660-563-2997. *Br Mgr,* Julie Dolph; E-mail: dolphj@trailslibrary.org
Open Mon-Fri 9:30-5:30, Sat 9:30-4:30
LEETON EXPRESS BRANCH, 500 N Main St, Leeton, 64761. Tel: 660-653-2301, Ext 125, 660-653-4731. *Br Mgr,* Cherie Tibbetts; E-mail: tibbetts@leeton.k12.mo.us
Library Holdings: AV Mats 500; Bk Vols 14,000; Per Subs 35
Automation Activity & Vendor Info: (Cataloging) Follett Software; (Circulation) Follett Software; (OPAC) Follett Software
Open Tues-Thurs 3:30-7, Sat 9-Noon
LEXINGTON BRANCH, 1008 Main St, Lexington, 64067, SAN 349-9294. Tel: 660-259-3071. FAX: 660-259-3071. *Br Mgr,* Carol Nolte; E-mail: noltec@trailslibrary.org
Open Mon-Thurs 8:30-7, Fri & Sat 8:30-5
Friends of the Library Group
ODESSA BRANCH, 204 S First, Odessa, 64076, SAN 349-9324. Tel: 816-633-4089. *Br Mgr,* Linda Washam; E-mail: washaml@trailslibrary.org
Open Mon-Thurs 9-7, Fri & Sat 9-5
Friends of the Library Group
WARRENSBURG BRANCH, 432 N Holden, 64093, SAN 349-9359. Tel: 660-747-9177. FAX: 660-747-7928. *Br Mgr,* Mary Barnhart; E-mail: barnhartm@trailslibrary.org
Open Mon-Thurs 8-7, Fri 8-5:30, Sat 8-5
Friends of the Library Group
WAVERLY BRANCH, 203 E Kelling, Waverly, 64096, SAN 349-9383. Tel: 660-493-2987. *Br Mgr,* Amy Boland; E-mail: bolanda@trailslibrary.org
Open Mon, Wed & Fri 9-5, Sat 9-3

C UNIVERSITY OF CENTRAL MISSOURI*, James C Kirkpatrick Library, 601 S Missouri, 64093-5020. SAN 349-9111. Tel: 660-543-4140. Circulation Tel: 660-543-4154. Interlibrary Loan Service Tel: 660-543-4508. FAX: 660-543-4144. Web Site: library.ucmo.edu. *Univ Librn,* Dr Gail Staines; E-mail: staines@ucmo.edu; *Asst Univ Librn,* Laura Horne-Popp; Tel: 660-543-8639, E-mail: horne-popp@ucmo.edu; Staff 26 (MLS 10, Non-MLS 16)
Founded 1871. Enrl 11,487; Fac 463; Highest Degree: Master
Library Holdings: e-books 275,666; e-journals 106,657; Bk Titles 397,215; Per Subs 4,741
Special Collections: Faculty Publications; Geography (Missouri & International Speleology); Literature (Izaac Walton's Compleat Angler); Missouri Coll; Research Coll in Children's Literature. US Document Depository
Automation Activity & Vendor Info: (Acquisitions) Ex Libris Group; (Cataloging) Ex Libris Group; (Circulation) Ex Libris Group; (Course Reserve) Ex Libris Group; (Discovery) Ex Libris Group; (ILL) OCLC Tipasa; (Media Booking) Ex Libris Group; (OPAC) Ex Libris Group; (Serials) Ex Libris Group
Wireless access
Partic in Amigos Library Services, Inc; Mid-America Library Alliance; OCLC Online Computer Library Center, Inc
Open Mon-Thurs 7:30am-Midnight, Fri 7:30am-8pm, Sat 10-6, Sun 1-Midnight

WARRENTON

S WARREN COUNTY HISTORICAL SOCIETY, Museum & Historical Library, 102 W Walton St, 63383. SAN 373-4668. Tel: 636-456-3820. E-mail: museum@warrencountymohistory.com. Web Site: warrencountymohistory.com. *Mgr,* Janet Sutherland; *Curator,* Susie Busekrus
Founded 1982
Library Holdings: Bk Vols 500
Special Collections: Central Wesleyen College
Subject Interests: Local hist
Wireless access
Open Thurs & Fri 10-4, Sun 1-4

WASHINGTON

P WASHINGTON PUBLIC LIBRARY*, 410 Lafayette St, 63090. SAN 309-2577. Tel: 636-390-1070. FAX: 636-390-0171. E-mail: library@ci.washintgon.mo.us. Web Site: scenicregional.org/about-us/locations-and-hours, www.washmolib.org. *Libr Dir,* Claire Miller; E-mail: cmiller@ci.washington.mo.us; Staff 3 (MLS 1, Non-MLS 2)
Founded 1924. Pop 8,713; Circ 154,000
Library Holdings: Audiobooks 800; CDs 276; DVDs 1,000; Electronic Media & Resources 13; Large Print Bks 8,082; Bk Vols 47,000; Per Subs 125
Automation Activity & Vendor Info: (Cataloging) OCLC CatExpress; (ILL) OCLC Connexion
Wireless access
Function: Adult bk club, Art exhibits, Bk club(s), Bks on CD, Chess club, Children's prog, Computer training, Computers for patron use, Electronic databases & coll, Free DVD rentals, ILL available, Internet access, Magnifiers for reading, Music CDs, Notary serv, Online cat, Passport

agency, Photocopying/Printing, Preschool reading prog, Printer for laptops & handheld devices, Prog for adults, Prog for children & young adult, Ref serv available, Senior computer classes, Spanish lang bks, Story hour, Summer reading prog, Tax forms, Teen prog, Wheelchair accessible
Partic in Amigos Library Services, Inc; Missouri Evergreen
Open Mon-Thurs 8-8, Fri 8-6, Sat 9-5, Sun Noon-4
Restriction: ID required to use computers (Ltd hrs), Non-resident fee, Residents only
Friends of the Library Group

WEBB CITY

P WEBB CITY PUBLIC LIBRARY, 101 S Liberty St, 64870. SAN 309-2585. Tel: 417-673-4326. FAX: 417-673-5703. E-mail: info@webbcitylibrary.org. Web Site: www.webbcitylibrary.org. *Dir,* Jacob Johnson; E-mail: jjohnson@webbcitylibrary.org; Staff 3 (MLS 1, Non-MLS 2)
Founded 1913. Pop 10,705; Circ 100,340
Library Holdings: Bk Titles 28,490; Bk Vols 30,000; Per Subs 70; Talking Bks 491; Videos 452
Subject Interests: Genealogy, Local hist
Automation Activity & Vendor Info: (Cataloging) Inlex; (Circulation) Inlex
Wireless access
Publications: The Miner (Quarterly)
Open Mon, Wed, Fri & Sat 9-5, Tues & Thurs 8-8
Friends of the Library Group

WEBSTER GROVES

P WEBSTER GROVES PUBLIC LIBRARY, 301 E Lockwood Ave, 63119-3102. SAN 309-2593. Tel: 314-961-3784. Reference Tel: 314-961-7277. FAX: 314-961-4233. E-mail: reference@wgpl.org. Web Site: www.wgpl.org. *Dir,* Tom Cooper; E-mail: tcooper@wgpl.org; *Ad,* Deborah Ladd; E-mail: dladd@wgpl.org; *Ref Librn,* Jeraca Fite; E-mail: jfite@wgpl.org; *Ch Serv,* Michelle Haffer; Tel: 314-961-7262, E-mail: mhaffer@wgpl.org; Staff 11 (MLS 3, Non-MLS 8)
Founded 1928. Pop 23,230; Circ 335,776
Library Holdings: Bk Titles 68,363; Bk Vols 69,406; Per Subs 152; Talking Bks 6,529; Videos 2,900
Subject Interests: Local hist
Automation Activity & Vendor Info: (Cataloging) Innovative Interfaces, Inc; (Circulation) Innovative Interfaces, Inc; (OPAC) Innovative Interfaces, Inc
Wireless access
Function: 24/7 Electronic res, 24/7 Online cat, Activity rm, Adult bk club
Publications: Page 61 (Newsletter)
Partic in Municipal Library Consortium; Saint Louis Regional Library Network
Open Mon-Thurs 9-9, Fri & Sat 9-4:30, Sun 2-5
Friends of the Library Group

WELLSVILLE

P WELLSVILLE PUBLIC LIBRARY*, 108 W Hudson St, 63384. SAN 309-2607. Tel: 573-684-6151. FAX: 573-684-6151. E-mail: wellsvillelibrary@gmail.com. Web Site: wellsvillelibrary.lib.mo.us. *Libr Dir,* Jeana Houf; Staff 1 (MLS 1)
Founded 1944. Pop 1,216; Circ 4,434
Apr 2018-Mar 2019 Income $24,758. Mats Exp $2,344. Sal $14,112
Library Holdings: Audiobooks 45; DVDs 250; Bk Titles 12,716; Per Subs 4; Videos 48
Wireless access
Function: Adult bk club, Bks on CD, Computers for patron use, Free DVD rentals, ILL available, Photocopying/Printing, Ref serv available, Summer reading prog, Tax forms, Telephone ref, VHS videos
Open Mon, Tues & Wed 12-5:30, Fri 10-5
Friends of the Library Group

WENTZVILLE

§CR URSHAN COLLEGE LIBRARY, 1151 Century Tel Dr, 63385. Tel: 314-838-8858. FAX: 636-538-5317. Web Site: urshancollege.org/academics/library. *Dir, Libr Serv, Theological Librn,* Gary D Erickson; E-mail: gerickson@ugst.edu; *Asst Dir, Libr Serv,* Russ Faubert; E-mail: faubert@ugst.edu
Automation Activity & Vendor Info: (Cataloging) Follett Software; (OPAC) Follett Software
Wireless access
Partic in Saint Louis Regional Library Network
Open Mon, Tues & Thurs 8am-11:30pm, Wed 8-6 & 9-11:30, Fri 8am-9pm, Sat 9-9, Sun 5pm-11:30pm

WEST PLAINS

C MISSOURI STATE UNIVERSITY-WEST PLAINS*, Garnett Library, 304 W Trish Knight St, 65775. SAN 376-2300. Tel: 417-255-7945. Administration Tel: 417-255-7949. FAX: 417-255-7944. Web Site: libraries.missouristate.edu/Garnett. *Dir, Libr Serv,* Rebekah J McKinney; E-mail: RebekahMcKinney@MissouriState.edu; *Ref/Cat Librn,* Rose Scarlet; E-mail: RoseScarlet@missouristate.edu; *Asst Librn,* Neva Parrott; Tel: 417-255-7947, E-mail: NevaParrott@missouristate.edu; *Circ/Shelving Supvr,* Sophia Skinner; E-mail: SophiaSkinner@missouristate.edu; Staff 4 (MLS 3, Non-MLS 1)
Founded 1963. Enrl 1,995; Fac 155; Highest Degree: Associate
Library Holdings: Bk Vols 42,701; Per Subs 127
Special Collections: Civil War Letters; Local History Audiocassette Coll
Subject Interests: Gen, Nursing, Rare bks
Automation Activity & Vendor Info: (Acquisitions) Baker & Taylor; (Cataloging) OCLC Connexion; (Circulation) Innovative Interfaces, Inc - Sierra; (Course Reserve) Innovative Interfaces, Inc - Sierra; (ILL) Innovative Interfaces, Inc - Sierra; (Media Booking) Innovative Interfaces, Inc - Sierra; (OPAC) Innovative Interfaces, Inc - Sierra; (Serials) EBSCO Online
Wireless access
Publications: Footnotes (Newsletter)
Open Mon-Thurs 8am-10pm, Fri 8-6, Sat 1-5, Sun 1-9
Friends of the Library Group

P WEST PLAINS PUBLIC LIBRARY*, 750 W Broadway, 65775. SAN 309-2615. Tel: 417-256-4775. FAX: 417-256-8316. Web Site: www.westplainslibrary.org. *Libr Dir,* Sherry Russell; *Ch,* Kelli Cook; *Tech Serv Coordr,* Marietta Caldwell; Staff 9 (Non-MLS 9)
Founded 1948. Pop 10,065; Circ 135,776
Library Holdings: Audiobooks 2,574; Large Print Bks 3,141; Bk Titles 77,908; Per Subs 117; Videos 2,568
Automation Activity & Vendor Info: (Cataloging) SirsiDynix; (Circulation) SirsiDynix; (ILL) OCLC; (OPAC) SirsiDynix
Wireless access
Special Services for the Blind - Aids for in-house use; Audio mat; Bks on cassette; Bks on CD; Cassettes; Computer access aids; Large print & cassettes; Large print bks; Large screen computer & software; Magnifiers; Reading & writing aids; Recorded bks
Open Mon-Fri 9-6, Sat 9-5
Friends of the Library Group

WHITEMAN AFB

A UNITED STATES AIR FORCE*, Whiteman Air Force Base Library FL4625, 509 FSS/FSDL, 511 Spirit Blvd, 65305-5019. SAN 349-9413. Tel: 660-687-5614. FAX: 660-687-6228. Web Site: www.whitemanfss.com/library. *Dir,* Dennis Wilson; Staff 2 (MLS 1, Non-MLS 1)
Subject Interests: Mil, Polit sci
Automation Activity & Vendor Info: (Cataloging) SirsiDynix-WorkFlows; (Circulation) SirsiDynix-WorkFlows; (ILL) OCLC WorldShare Interlibrary Loan; (OPAC) SirsiDynix-WorkFlows
Wireless access
Open Mon-Fri 8:30-6, Sat 8:30-4

MONTANA

Date of Statistics: FY 2020
Population, 2020 U.S. Census: 1,084,225
Population Served by Public Libraries: 988,533
Counties Served: 56
Number of Public Libraries: 82
Number of Public Library Branches: 34
Number of Academic Libraries: 27
Number of Institutional Libraries: 3
Number of Special Libraries: 57
Number of School Libraries: 562
Total Volumes in Public Libraries: 2,736,135
Volumes Per Capita: 2.8
Total Public Library Circulation: 4,961,567

Income and Expenditures:
Total Public Library Income: $33,207,459
Income per Capita: $33.59
Source of Income: Mainly public funds
State Tax Rate: 5-mill county tax (permissive); 7-mill for cities & towns (permissive)
Total Public Library Expenditures: $29,216,416
Expenditures Per Capita: $29.55
Number of Bookmobiles in State: 9
Federal Grants-in-Aid to Public Libraries-Library Services and Technology Act: $1,088,834
Grants-in-State Aid to Public Libraries: $433,960
Information provided courtesy of: Tracy Cook, Lead Consulting and Learning Librarian; Montana State Library

ANACONDA

P HEARST FREE LIBRARY*, 401 Main St, 59711. SAN 309-2631. Tel: 406-563-6932. FAX: 406-563-5393. Web Site: www.hearstfreelibrary.org. *Dir,* Sam Walters; E-mail: swalters@mtlib.org; *Asst Dir,* Colleen Fergusen; E-mail: cferg@mtlib.org; Staff 4.3 (MLS 1, Non-MLS 3.3)
Founded 1895. Pop 8,000; Circ 41,000
Library Holdings: Bk Titles 31,000; Per Subs 86
Automation Activity & Vendor Info: (Cataloging) SirsiDynix; (Circulation) SirsiDynix; (ILL) OCLC FirstSearch; (OPAC) SirsiDynix-iBistro
Wireless access
Publications: Anaconda's Treasure: Hearst Free Library (Local historical information)
Mem of Broad Valleys Federation of Libraries
Open Mon, Fri & Sat 9-5, Tues-Thurs 9-8
Friends of the Library Group

ARLEE

P JOCKO VALLEY LIBRARY*, 212 Culloyah St, 59821. (Mail add: PO Box 158, 59821-0158). Tel: 406-726-3572. E-mail: jockovalleylibraryarlee@hotmail.com. *Dir,* Suzy Black
Library Holdings: Bk Titles 8,000
Subject Interests: Montana, Native Am
Automation Activity & Vendor Info: (Acquisitions) LibraryWorld, Inc; (Cataloging) LibraryWorld, Inc; (Circulation) LibraryWorld, Inc; (ILL) LibraryWorld, Inc
Wireless access
Open Mon & Thurs 1-5, Fri 12-4
Bookmobiles: 1

BAKER

P FALLON COUNTY LIBRARY, Six W Fallon Ave, 59313. (Mail add: PO Box 1037, 59313-1037), SAN 309-2666. Tel: 406-778-7160. FAX: 406-778-7116. E-mail: falloncountylibrary@gmail.com. Web Site: www.falloncountylibrary.net. *Dir, Libr Serv,* Stacey Moore; E-mail: moores@falloncounty.net; Staff 3 (Non-MLS 3)
Founded 1922. Pop 2,837
Library Holdings: Audiobooks 24,692; CDs 1,138; DVDs 1,708; e-books 33,252; Large Print Bks 2,881; Bk Titles 18,739; Per Subs 12
Automation Activity & Vendor Info: (Cataloging) SirsiDynix; (Circulation) SirsiDynix; (ILL) OCLC; (OPAC) SirsiDynix
Wireless access
Function: 24/7 Electronic res, 24/7 Online cat, Accelerated reader prog, Activity rm, Adult bk club, Archival coll, Audio & video playback equip for onsite use, Audiobks via web, Bks on CD, Children's prog, Citizenship assistance, Computers for patron use, Digital talking bks, Distance learning, E-Readers, Electronic databases & coll, Free DVD rentals, Home delivery & serv to seniorr ctr & nursing homes, Homebound delivery serv, ILL available, Internet access, Laminating, Magazines, Mail & tel request accepted, Meeting rooms, Microfiche/film & reading machines, Online cat, Online ref, Outreach serv, OverDrive digital audio bks, Photocopying/Printing, Preschool reading prog, Prog for children & young adult, Scanner, Story hour, Summer reading prog, Tax forms, Wheelchair accessible
Mem of Sagebrush Federation
Open Mon-Fri 8-5
Friends of the Library Group

BELGRADE

P BELGRADE COMMUNITY LIBRARY*, 106 N Broadway, 59714. SAN 309-2674. Tel: 406-388-4346. FAX: 406-388-6586. E-mail: bcl@belgradelibrary.org. Web Site: www.belgradelibrary.org. *Dir,* Gale Bacon; *Youth Serv Librn,* Meghan Salisbury; *Tech Adminr,* Aaron Canen; *Adult Serv Coordr,* Sarah Creech; *Circ Spec,* Kathleen Godfrey; Staff 7 (MLS 2, Non-MLS 5)
Founded 1932. Pop 12,960; Circ 84,053
Jul 2016-Jun 2017. Mats Exp $38,900, Books $35,000, Per/Ser (Incl. Access Fees) $2,000, Electronic Ref Mat (Incl. Access Fees) $1,900. Sal $192,744 (Prof $150,960)
Library Holdings: Audiobooks 1,226; Bks on Deafness & Sign Lang 25; DVDs 2,011; e-books 15,682; Large Print Bks 930; Bk Titles 39,021; Per Subs 58
Automation Activity & Vendor Info: (Cataloging) SirsiDynix; (Circulation) SirsiDynix; (ILL) OCLC
Wireless access
Function: Adult bk club, After school storytime, Art exhibits, Audiobks via web, Bk club(s), Bks on CD, Children's prog, Computer training, Computers for patron use, Electronic databases & coll, Family literacy, Free DVD rentals, Holiday prog, ILL available, Internet access, Life-long learning prog for all ages, Magazines, Movies, Online cat, Photocopying/Printing, Preschool outreach, Preschool reading prog, Prog for adults, Prog for children & young adult, Scanner, Story hour, Summer reading prog, Tax forms, Teen prog, Telephone ref, Wheelchair accessible, Winter reading prog
Mem of Broad Valleys Federation of Libraries
Open Mon-Thurs 11-7, Fri & Sat 11-5
Friends of the Library Group

BELT

P BELT PUBLIC LIBRARY*, 404 Millard St, 59412. (Mail add: PO Box 467, 59412-0467), SAN 309-2682. Tel: 406-277-3136. FAX: 406-277-3136. E-mail: beltlib@3rivers.net. Web Site: www.beltlibrary.org. *Libr Dir,* Gladys Rayhill; Staff 1 (Non-MLS 1)
Founded 1898. Pop 1,100; Circ 61,524
Jul 2014-Jun 2015 Income $15,325, State $525, County $13,000, Other $1,800. Mats Exp $5,000. Sal $16,000
Library Holdings: Audiobooks 80; DVDs 461; Large Print Bks 350; Bk Titles 6,351; Bk Vols 6,391; Per Subs 15
Automation Activity & Vendor Info: (Cataloging) Follett Software; (Circulation) Follett Software; (ILL) OCLC FirstSearch

Wireless access
Special Services for the Blind - Accessible computers; Aids for in-house use; Bks on cassette; Bks on CD; Large print bks; Low vision equip; Magnifiers; ZoomText magnification & reading software
Open Mon-Fri 11-5

BIG TIMBER

P CARNEGIE PUBLIC LIBRARY*, 314 McLeod St, 59011. (Mail add: PO Box 846, 59011-0846), SAN 309-2690. Tel: 406-932-5608. E-mail: bigtlib@itstriangle.com. Web Site: www.bigtimberlibrary.org. *Dir,* Jacque Scott
Pop 3,500; Circ 29,953
Library Holdings: Bk Titles 16,000; Per Subs 60
Special Collections: County Newspapers
Automation Activity & Vendor Info: (Cataloging) SirsiDynix; (Circulation) SirsiDynix
Wireless access
Partic in S Cent Fedn of Libr
Open Tues-Sat 10-6
Friends of the Library Group

BILLINGS

P BILLINGS PUBLIC LIBRARY*, 510 N Broadway, 59101. SAN 309-2747. Tel: 406-657-8258. Administration Tel: 406-657-8391. FAX: 406-657-8293. E-mail: refdesk@ci.billings.mt.us. Web Site: billingslibrary.org. *Libr Dir,* Gavin Woltjer; Tel: 406-657-8292, E-mail: woltjerg@ci.billings.mt.us; *Asst Dir,* Tori Koch; Tel: 406-657-8295, E-mail: kocht@ci.billings.mt.us; *Senior Admin Coord,* Mary Murphrey; E-mail: murphreym@ci.billings.mt.us; *Syst Adminr,* Kathy Robins; E-mail: robinsk@ci.billings.mt.us; Staff 29 (MLS 9, Non-MLS 20)
Founded 1901. Pop 147,126; Circ 858,087
Jul 2012-Jun 2013 Income $3,068,898, State $14,585, City $2,084,607, County $730,975, Other $238,731. Mats Exp $375,334, Books $144,750, Per/Ser (Incl. Access Fees) $35,000, Other Print Mats $72,040, AV Mat $60,600, Electronic Ref Mat (Incl. Access Fees) $62,944. Sal $1,827,495
Library Holdings: Audiobooks 12,170; DVDs 23,242; e-books 10,669; Electronic Media & Resources 44; Bk Vols 220,359; Per Subs 144
Special Collections: Montana Room
Subject Interests: Genealogy
Automation Activity & Vendor Info: (Acquisitions) SirsiDynix-WorkFlows; (Cataloging) SirsiDynix-WorkFlows; (Circulation) SirsiDynix-WorkFlows; (Discovery) EBSCO Discovery Service; (OPAC) SirsiDynix-iBistro
Wireless access
Function: Archival coll, Home delivery & serv to seniorr ctr & nursing homes, Large print keyboards, Notary serv
Publications: The Turning Page (Newsletter)
Special Services for the Deaf - Assisted listening device; Closed caption videos
Special Services for the Blind - Accessible computers; Assistive/Adapted tech devices, equip & products; Audio mat; Bks on CD; Home delivery serv; Large print bks; Large screen computer & software; Low vision equip
Open Mon-Fri (Winter) 10-9, Sat 9-5; Mon-Thurs (Summer) 10-9, Fri 10-6, Sat 9-5
Friends of the Library Group
Bookmobiles: 2. Sr Outreach, Kelsie Raddas

L CROWLEY FLECK PLLP LIBRARY, 490 N 31st St, Ste 500, 59101-1267. (Mail add: PO Box 2529, 59103-2529), SAN 329-1669. Tel: 406-252-3441. FAX: 406-259-4159. E-mail: library@crowleyfleck.com. *Mgr, Libr Serv,* Diane Paszkowski; E-mail: dpaszkowski@crowleyfleck.com; Staff 1 (Non-MLS 1)
Founded 1895
Library Holdings: Bk Vols 32,000
Subject Interests: Law
Wireless access
Function: ILL available
Partic in OCLC Online Computer Library Center, Inc
Restriction: Not open to pub

S DOWL LIBRARY*, 222 N 32nd, Ste 700, 59101-1976. SAN 327-1471. Tel: 406-656-6399. FAX: 406-656-6398. *Librn,* Kimberly Ann Guy; Tel: 406-869-6357, E-mail: kguy@dowl.com; Staff 1 (Non-MLS 1)
Library Holdings: Bk Vols 13,000
Subject Interests: Civil engr, Structural engr, Water res

C MONTANA STATE UNIVERSITY-BILLINGS LIBRARY, 1500 University Dr, 59101. SAN 309-2720. Tel: 406-657-2262. Interlibrary Loan Service Tel: 406-657-1666. Reference Tel: 406-657-1662. Web Site: www.msubillings.edu/Library. *Dir,* Darlene Hert; Tel: 406-657-1655, E-mail: dhert@msubillings.edu; *Assessment Librn,* Megan Thomas; Tel: 406-657-1663, E-mail: megan.thomas@msubillings.edu; *Distance Learning Librn,* Victoria Conteraz; Tel: 406-657-1691, E-mail: victoria.contreraz@msubillings.edu; *Instruction Coordr, Ref Librn,* Jenks TyRee; Tel: 406-657-1654, E-mail: tjenks@msubillings.edu; *Ref Librn,* Eileen Wright; Tel: 406-657-1656, E-mail: ewright@msubillings.edu; *Cat/Acq Tech,* Jessica Torgerson Lundin; Tel: 406-657-1664, E-mail: jessica.torgerson@msubillings.edu; *Circ Tech,* Chandra Shaw; Tel: 406-657-1671, E-mail: chandra.shaw@msubillings.edu; *Govt Doc & Ser Tech,* Position Currently Open; *Admin Assoc,* Shelby Alcorn; E-mail: shelby.alcorn@msubillings.edu; Staff 11 (MLS 6, Non-MLS 5)
Founded 1927. Enrl 4,000; Fac 172; Highest Degree: Master
Library Holdings: Bk Vols 338,933; Per Subs 1,713
Special Collections: Billings, Yellowstone County & Eastern Montana, ms; Montana & Western History (Dora C White Memorial Coll); Terry C Johnston Research Coll. State Document Depository; US Document Depository
Subject Interests: Bus, Educ, Health, Native Am studies, Spec educ
Automation Activity & Vendor Info: (Cataloging) Ex Libris Group; (Circulation) Ex Libris Group; (ILL) OCLC Tipasa; (OPAC) Ex Libris Group
Wireless access
Partic in OCLC Online Computer Library Center, Inc; Treasure State Academic Information & Library Services
Special Services for the Blind - Assistive/Adapted tech devices, equip & products; Closed circuit TV; Computer with voice synthesizer for visually impaired persons; Reader equip
Open Mon-Thurs 8-8, Fri 8-5, Sun 4-8

S RIMROCK FOUNDATION LIBRARY*, 1231 N 29th St, 59101. SAN 324-0711. Tel: 406-248-3175. Toll Free Tel: 800-227-3953, Ext 404. FAX: 406-248-3821. E-mail: comm@rimrock.org. Web Site: www.rimrock.org. *Dir,* Hugh Kilbourne
Founded 1985
Library Holdings: CDs 150; DVDs 200; Bk Titles 2,000; Videos 75
Subject Interests: Adult children of alcoholics, Co-dependency, Compulsive behaviors, Eating disorders, Mental health, Substance abuse
Partic in Billings Area Health Sciences Information Consortium

C ROCKY MOUNTAIN COLLEGE*, Paul M Adams Memorial Library, 1511 Poly Dr, 59102-1796. SAN 309-2755. Tel: 406-657-1087. FAX: 406-259-9751. Interlibrary Loan Service E-mail: ill@rocky.edu. Web Site: rocky.edu/academics/library. *Libr Dir,* Bobbi Otte; Tel: 406-657-1086, E-mail: otteb@rocky.edu; *Asst Libr Dir,* Alana Mueller-Brunckhorst; Tel: 406-657-1140; *Libr Assoc,* Bethany Schatzke; E-mail: bethany.schatzke@rocky.edu; Staff 3 (MLS 2, Non-MLS 1)
Founded 1878. Enrl 1,000; Fac 63; Highest Degree: Master
Library Holdings: Audiobooks 25; AV Mats 45; CDs 381; DVDs 1,515; e-books 150,000; e-journals 60; Music Scores 1,088; Bk Titles 45,000; Bk Vols 67,701; Per Subs 375; Spec Interest Per Sub 12; Videos 250
Special Collections: College Archives; Geology Coll; Rare Books Coll
Subject Interests: Aviation, Equestrian
Automation Activity & Vendor Info: (Cataloging) OCLC Connexion; (Circulation) Ex Libris Group; (Course Reserve) Ex Libris Group; (ILL) OCLC; (OPAC) Ex Libris Group
Wireless access
Function: 24/7 Electronic res, 24/7 Online cat, Archival coll, Audio & video playback equip for onsite use, AV serv, Computers for patron use, E-Readers, Electronic databases & coll, ILL available, Internet access, Magazines, Mail & tel request accepted, Mango lang, Microfiche/film & reading machines, Movies, Music CDs, Online cat, Orientations, Ref & res, Ref serv available, Res assist avail, Study rm, Telephone ref, Wheelchair accessible
Partic in Billings Area Health Sciences Information Consortium; LYRASIS; OCLC Online Computer Library Center, Inc; Treasure State Academic Information & Library Services; Westchester Academic Library Directors Organization
Open Mon-Thurs (Winter) 7:30am-11pm, Fri 7:30-4:30, Sat 1-5, Sun 1-11; Mon-Fri (Summer) 8:30-4:30

S WESTERN ORGANIZATION OF RESOURCE COUNCILS LIBRARY*, 220 S 27th St, Ste B, 59101. SAN 371-4535. Tel: 406-252-9672. FAX: 406-252-1092. Web Site: www.worc.org. *Exec Dir,* John Smillie; E-mail: jssmillie@worc.org
Library Holdings: Bk Titles 200; Per Subs 31
Wireless access

CR YELLOWSTONE CHRISTIAN COLLEGE, Ida Dockery Owen Library, 1515 S Shiloh Rd, 59106. SAN 377-242X. Tel: 406-606-9950. E-mail: library@yellowstonechristian.edu. Web Site: www.yellowstonechristian.edu/library. *Libr Dir,* Vanessa Lund; E-mail: vlund@yellowstonechristian.edu; Staff 1 (MLS 1)
Founded 1974. Enrl 57; Fac 23; Highest Degree: Bachelor
Library Holdings: DVDs 459; Bk Titles 27,479; Bk Vols 29,987; Per Subs 60
Special Collections: Native American Resource Center
Wireless access

Function: Activity rm, Audio & video playback equip for onsite use, Bks on CD, Computers for patron use, Internet access, Mail & tel request accepted, Mail loans to mem, Meeting rooms, Movies, Study rm
Partic in Treasure State Academic Information & Library Services
Open Mon & Tues 9-9, Wed & Thurs 9-3
Restriction: Fee for pub use, Non-circulating of rare bks

BOULDER

P JEFFERSON COUNTY LIBRARY SYSTEM*, Boulder Community Library, 202 S Main St, 59632. (Mail add: PO Box 589, 59632-0589), SAN 376-6888. Tel: 406-225-3241. FAX: 406-225-3241. E-mail: bldrlib@mtlib.org. Web Site: sites.google.com/site/bouldercommunitylibrary. *Head Librn,* Jodi K Smiley; E-mail: jsmiley@mtlib.org; Staff 3 (Non-MLS 3)
Founded 1974. Pop 10,049; Circ 51,514
Jul 2017-Jun 2018 Income (Main & Associated Libraries) $319,414, State $3,724, City $8,144, County $301,325, Other $6,221. Mats Exp $86,550, Books $30,785, Per/Ser (Incl. Access Fees) $2,202, Other Print Mats $26,432, AV Equip $4,373, AV Mat $7,801, Electronic Ref Mat (Incl. Access Fees) $8,655, Presv $6,302. Sal $145,063
Library Holdings: Audiobooks 968; AV Mats 1,500; Bks-By-Mail 5,002; CDs 881; DVDs 6,763; e-books 21,348; Electronic Media & Resources 4; Large Print Bks 315; Bk Vols 30,441; Per Subs 62; Talking Bks 39
Special Collections: Montana Coll
Automation Activity & Vendor Info: (Cataloging) SirsiDynix; (Circulation) SirsiDynix; (ILL) OCLC; (OPAC) SirsiDynix
Wireless access
Function: 24/7 Electronic res, 24/7 Online cat, Adult bk club, Audiobks via web, AV serv, Bk club(s), Bks on CD, Children's prog, Computer training, Computers for patron use, E-Readers, Electronic databases & coll, Free DVD rentals, Games & aids for people with disabilities, ILL available, Internet access, Jail serv, Life-long learning prog for all ages, Magazines, Magnifiers for reading, Mail & tel request accepted, Meeting rooms, Movies, Museum passes, Online cat, Online ref, OverDrive digital audio bks, Photocopying/Printing, Preschool reading prog, Prog for adults, Prog for children & young adult, Res assist avail, Scanner, Senior computer classes, Serves people with intellectual disabilities, Story hour, Summer reading prog, Tax forms, Teen prog, VHS videos, Wheelchair accessible
Mem of Broad Valleys Federation of Libraries
Partic in Four Rivers Area Libr Serv Authority
Open Mon 6:30pm-8:30pm, Tues & Thurs 10-7:30, Wed 10-8:30, Fri & Sun 1-5
Friends of the Library Group
Branches: 1
WHITEHALL COMMUNITY LIBRARY, 110 First St W, Whitehall, 59759. (Mail add: PO Box 659, Whitehall, 59759-0659), SAN 376-6462. Tel: 406-287-3763. FAX: 406-287-3763. *Librn,* Jeannie Ferriss; E-mail: jfluvbks@gmail.com; Staff 2 (MLS 1, Non-MLS 1)
Founded 1974
Open Mon & Wed 9-7, Tues & Thurs 1-7, Fri 9-5, Sat 9-1
Friends of the Library Group

BOX ELDER

J STONE CHILD COLLEGE*, Rocky Boy Community Library, 8294 Upper Box Elder Rd, 59521. SAN 375-6262. Tel: 406-395-4875, Ext 3213/3214. Web Site: stonechild.edu/2015-02-03-23-38-56/scc-library. *Libr Dir,* Joy Bridwell; Tel: 406-395-4875, Ext 3213, E-mail: jbridwell@stonechild.edu; *Libr Asst,* Samantha Courchane; Tel: 406-395-4875, Ext 3214, E-mail: scourchane@stonechild.edu; Staff 2 (MLS 1, Non-MLS 1)
Founded 1984. Enrl 200
Library Holdings: Bk Titles 11,000; Bk Vols 12,000; Per Subs 136
Automation Activity & Vendor Info: (Acquisitions) Follett Software; (Cataloging) Follett Software; (Circulation) Follett Software; (Course Reserve) Follett Software; (ILL) Follett Software; (Media Booking) Follett Software; (OPAC) Follett Software; (Serials) Follett Software
Wireless access
Partic in Treasure State Academic Information & Library Services
Open Mon-Thurs 8-4:30, Fri 8-3

BOZEMAN

P BOZEMAN PUBLIC LIBRARY*, 626 E Main St, 59715. SAN 309-2798. Tel: 406-582-2400. Circulation Tel: 406-582-2408. Reference Tel: 406-582-2410. Information Services Tel: 406-582-2427. FAX: 406-582-2424. Web Site: www.bozemanlibrary.org. *Dir,* Susan Gregory; E-mail: sgregory@bozeman.net; *Asst Dir,* Kit Stephenson; E-mail: kstephenson@bozeman.net; *Head, Circ,* Brittany Dolezal; E-mail: bdolezal@bozeman.net; *Head, Coll Develop, Head, Tech Serv,* Lois Dissly; E-mail: ldissly@bozeman.net; Staff 23 (MLS 8.5, Non-MLS 14.5)
Founded 1891. Pop 47,805; Circ 671,501
Library Holdings: Audiobooks 4,134; AV Mats 15,690; Bks on Deafness & Sign Lang 68; Braille Volumes 21; CDs 6,312; DVDs 4,317; e-books 12,707; Electronic Media & Resources 22; Large Print Bks 3,248; Bk Vols 117,365; Per Subs 246; Videos 6,396
Special Collections: Foundation Center. US Document Depository
Subject Interests: Montana hist
Automation Activity & Vendor Info: (Cataloging) SirsiDynix; (Circulation) SirsiDynix; (OPAC) SirsiDynix; (Serials) EBSCO Online
Wireless access
Function: Adult bk club, Archival coll, Art exhibits, Bi-weekly Writer's Group, Bks on cassette, Bks on CD, CD-ROM, Chess club, Children's prog, Computer training, Computers for patron use, E-Reserves, Electronic databases & coll, Free DVD rentals, Holiday prog, Homebound delivery serv, ILL available, Internet access, Jazz prog, Magnifiers for reading, Mail & tel request accepted, Museum passes, Music CDs, Notary serv, Online cat, OverDrive digital audio bks, Photocopying/Printing, Preschool outreach, Prof lending libr, Prog for adults, Prog for children & young adult, Ref & res, Scanner, Senior computer classes, Senior outreach, Spoken cassettes & CDs, Spoken cassettes & DVDs, Story hour, Summer reading prog, Teen prog, Telephone ref, VHS videos, Wheelchair accessible
Publications: Check It Out (Newsletter)
Mem of Broad Valleys Federation of Libraries
Open Mon-Thurs 10-8, Fri & Sat 10-5, Sun 1-5
Restriction: Non-circulating of rare bks, Non-resident fee
Friends of the Library Group
Bookmobiles: 1. Librn, Jessica Carlson

CR MONTANA BIBLE COLLEGE*, Gail Horton Library, 100 Discovery Dr, 59718. SAN 377-5577. Tel: 406-586-3585, Ext 25. E-mail: library@montanabiblecollege.edu. Web Site: www.montanabiblecollege.edu/library. *Libr Dir,* Jessica Carlson; E-mail: jessica.carlson@montanabiblecollege.edu; Staff 2 (Non-MLS 2)
Founded 1987. Enrl 99; Fac 14; Highest Degree: Bachelor
Library Holdings: e-books 6,500; Bk Titles 10,000; Per Subs 15
Wireless access
Open Mon & Wed 7:30am-9pm, Tues 7-11 & 1-9, Thurs 7-11 & 12-6, Fri 9:30-3, Sat 9-12, Sun 5-9

C MONTANA STATE UNIVERSITY LIBRARY, One Centennial Mall, 59717. (Mail add: PO Box 173320, 59717-3320), SAN 349-9448. Tel: 406-994-3119. Circulation Tel: 406-994-3139. Interlibrary Loan Service Tel: 406-994-3161. Reference Tel: 406-994-3171. FAX: 406-994-2851. Web Site: ask.lib.montana.edu, www.lib.montana.edu. *Dean of Libr,* Kenning Arlitsch; Tel: 406-994-6978, E-mail: kenning.arlitsch@montana.edu; *Assoc Dean of Libr,* Brian Rossmann; Tel: 406-994-5298, E-mail: brossmann@montana.edu; *Head, Archives & Spec Coll, Univ Archivist,* Jodi Allison-Bunnell; Tel: 406-994-5297, E-mail: jodi.allisonbunnell@montana.edu; *Access & Tech Serv Librn, Head, Coll,* Amy Foster; Tel: 406-994-5301, E-mail: amy.foster3@montana.edu; *Head, Digital Libr Initiatives,* Doralyn Rossman; Tel: 406-994-3153, E-mail: doralyn@montana.edu; *Head, Learning & Research Servs,* Kris Johnson; Tel: 406-994-7708, E-mail: krisjohnson@montana.edu; Staff 22 (MLS 19, Non-MLS 3)
Founded 1893. Enrl 16,841; Fac 978; Highest Degree: Doctorate
Library Holdings: CDs 2,446; DVDs 5,540; e-journals 6,000; Music Scores 4,117; Bk Vols 883,844; Per Subs 15,805
Special Collections: Acoustic Atlas Natural Sound Archive; Architecture & Engineering Coll; Montana History Coll; Montana Native American Coll; Montana State University History Coll; Regional Writers Coll; Trout & Angling History Coll; Yellowstone National Park & the Greater Yellowstone Ecosystem Coll. State Document Depository; US Document Depository
Subject Interests: Agr, Engr, Health sci, Natural sci, Sci tech
Automation Activity & Vendor Info: (Cataloging) OCLC; (Circulation) Ex Libris Group; (Course Reserve) Ex Libris Group; (ILL) OCLC ILLiad; (OPAC) Ex Libris Group; (Serials) Ex Libris Group
Wireless access
Function: 24/7 Online cat
Partic in OCLC Research Library Partnership; Treasure State Academic Information & Library Services
Open Mon-Thurs 7am-Midnight, Fri 7-6, Sat 10-5, Sun 10am-Midnight
Friends of the Library Group

BRIDGER

P BRIDGER PUBLIC LIBRARY*, 119 W Broadway Ave, 59014. (Mail add: PO Box 428, 59014-0428), SAN 309-281X. Tel: 406-662-3598. FAX: 406-662-9975. E-mail: info@bridgerpubliclibrary.org. Web Site: bridgerpubliclibrary.org. *Libr Dir,* Krystal Zentner
Founded 1906. Pop 2,778; Circ 12,000
Library Holdings: Bk Vols 12,000
Special Collections: Bridger Times, 1909-1958
Automation Activity & Vendor Info: (Acquisitions) Follett Software
Wireless access
Function: Adult bk club, Bks on cassette, Bks on CD, Computers for patron use, Free DVD rentals, ILL available, Photocopying/Printing, Summer reading prog

Mem of South Central Federation
Partic in Association for Rural & Small Libraries
Open Mon-Thurs 10-6
Friends of the Library Group

BROADUS

P HENRY A MALLEY MEMORIAL LIBRARY*, 101 S Lincoln, 59317. (Mail add: PO Box 345, 59317-0345), SAN 309-2828. Tel: 406-436-2812. E-mail: broaduslibrary@rangeweb.net. Web Site: prco.mt.gov/Library. *Dir,* June Ray; *Librn,* Barb Mitchell
Pop 1,900; Circ 17,000
Library Holdings: Bk Vols 20,000; Per Subs 35
Wireless access
Mem of Sagebrush Federation
Open Mon & Thurs 11-6, Tues, Wed, Fri & Sat 12-5

BROWNING

J BLACKFEET COMMUNITY COLLEGE, Medicine Spring Library, 504 SE Boundary St, 59417. (Mail add: PO Box 819, 59417-0819), SAN 321-107X. Tel: 406-338-5441. Toll Free Tel: 800-549-7457. FAX: 406-338-5454. Web Site: bfcc.edu/medicine-spring-library. *Dir, Libr Serv,* Aaron LaFromboise; E-mail: alafromboise@bfcc.edu; *Libr Tech,* Michael Fast Buffalo Horse; *Libr Tech,* Kimberly Old Chief; *Network Tech,* Joseph D Rutherford. Subject Specialists: *Communications, Grant writing, Staff training,* Aaron LaFromboise; *Cultural prog, Libr instruction,* Michael Fast Buffalo Horse; *Gen ref,* Kimberly Old Chief; *Digital asset mgt, Digitization,* Joseph D Rutherford; Staff 4 (MLS 1, Non-MLS 3)
Founded 1981. Enrl 350; Fac 52; Highest Degree: Associate
Library Holdings: AV Mats 100; Bks on Deafness & Sign Lang 20; Large Print Bks 50; Bk Titles 14,500; Bk Vols 15,000; Per Subs 250; Talking Bks 50
Special Collections: Blackfeet Tribal Coll
Subject Interests: Blackfeet hist, Culture, Native Am studies
Automation Activity & Vendor Info: (Cataloging) SirsiDynix-WorkFlows; (Circulation) SirsiDynix; (ILL) OCLC Connexion
Wireless access
Function: 24/7 Electronic res, 24/7 Online cat, Activity rm, Adult bk club, Archival coll, Art exhibits, Art programs, Audio & video playback equip for onsite use, AV serv, Children's prog, Computer training, Computers for patron use, Distance learning, Electronic databases & coll, For res purposes, ILL available, Instruction & testing, Internet access, Life-long learning prog for all ages, Magazines, Magnifiers for reading, Mail & tel request accepted, Meeting rooms, Microfiche/film & reading machines, Movies, Online cat, Orientations, Outreach serv, Photocopying/Printing, Printer for laptops & handheld devices, Prog for adults, Prog for children & young adult, Ref & res, Ref serv available, Scanner, Senior computer classes, Telephone ref, Wheelchair accessible, Workshops
Partic in Treasure State Academic Information & Library Services
Open Mon-Fri 8-6

BUTTE

P BUTTE-SILVER BOW PUBLIC LIBRARY*, 226 W Broadway, 59701. SAN 309-2836. Tel: 406-723-3361. Automation Services Tel: 406-723-2138. FAX: 406-782-1825. E-mail: info@buttepubliclibrary.info. Web Site: www.buttepubliclibrary.info. *Dir,* Stef Johnson; E-mail: stjohnson@buttepubliclibrary.info; *Head, Tech Serv,* Vickie Peck; E-mail: vpeck@buttepubliclibrary.info; *Ch,* Cathy Friel; Staff 18 (MLS 3, Non-MLS 15)
Founded 1890. Pop 34,606; Circ 92,875
Library Holdings: AV Mats 4,955; Bk Vols 96,655; Per Subs 226; Talking Bks 2,578; Videos 2,374
Subject Interests: Fishing, Local hist, Montana hist
Automation Activity & Vendor Info: (Circulation) Follett Software; (OPAC) LibLime
Wireless access
Function: AV serv, Doc delivery serv, Govt ref serv, Homebound delivery serv, ILL available, Internet access, Magnifiers for reading, Outside serv via phone, mail, e-mail & web, Photocopying/Printing, Prog for adults, Prog for children & young adult, Ref serv available, Summer reading prog, Telephone ref, Wheelchair accessible
Mem of Broad Valleys Federation of Libraries
Open Mon, Fri & Sat 10-5, Tues-Thurs 10-8
Friends of the Library Group
Branches: 1
SOUTH BRANCH, Butte Plaza Mall, 3100 Harrison Ave, 59701. Tel: 406-723-3361, Ext 6400. *Br Mgr,* Linda Zeller
Library Holdings: CDs 40; DVDs 100; Bk Vols 300; Per Subs 8

C MONTANA TECH LIBRARY*, 1300 W Park St, 59701. SAN 309-2844. Tel: 406-496-4281. Reference Tel: 406-496-4282. FAX: 406-496-4133. E-mail: librequests@mtech.edu. Web Site: www.mtech.edu/library. *Dir,* Scott Juskiewicz; Tel: 406-496-4284, E-mail: sjuskiewicz@mtech.edu; *Head, Pub Serv,* Frances Holmes; Tel: 406-496-4222, E-mail: fholmes@mtech.edu; *Head, Tech Serv,* Kristi Carroll; Tel: 406-496-4668, E-mail: kcarroll@mtech.edu; *Ref Librn,* Adrian Kien; Tel: 406-496-4839, E-mail: akien@mtech.edu; *Computer Support Spec,* Marcia Lubick; Tel: 406-496-4287, E-mail: mlubick@mtech.edu; Staff 9 (MLS 4, Non-MLS 5)
Founded 1900. Enrl 2,363; Fac 122; Highest Degree: Master
Library Holdings: AV Mats 148; CDs 4,316; e-books 109,025; e-journals 50,690; Electronic Media & Resources 3,962; Microforms 5,302; Bk Titles 51,865; Bk Vols 75,584; Per Subs 400; Videos 148
Special Collections: US Patent & Trademark Coll. US Document Depository
Subject Interests: Environ engr, Geochemistry, Geol, Geophysics, Metallurgy, Mining, Petroleum engr
Automation Activity & Vendor Info: (Acquisitions) Ex Libris Group; (Cataloging) Ex Libris Group; (Circulation) Ex Libris Group; (Course Reserve) Ex Libris Group; (ILL) OCLC ILLiad; (OPAC) Ex Libris Group; (Serials) Ex Libris Group
Wireless access
Partic in Treasure State Academic Information & Library Services
Open Mon-Thurs 7:30am-10pm, Fri 7:30-5, Sat Noon-4, Sun 1-9
Friends of the Library Group

S NATIONAL CENTER FOR APPROPRIATE TECHNOLOGY*, Research Library, 3040 Continental Dr, 59701. (Mail add: PO Box 3838, 59702-3838), SAN 320-3921. Tel: 406-494-8643. FAX: 406-494-2905. Web Site: www.ncat.org. *Dir,* Rose Sullivan; E-mail: roses@ncat.org
Founded 1978
Library Holdings: Bk Titles 7,000; Per Subs 300
Subject Interests: Biofuels, Commun develop, Greenhouses, Internet, Low cost tech, Low income housing, Micro-hydro power, Mkt, Small scale, Solar energy, Superinsulation
Restriction: Staff use only

M ST JAMES HEALTHCARE*, Medical Library, 400 S Clark St, 59701. SAN 323-6323. Tel: 406-723-2523. FAX: 406-723-2813. *Librn,* Laurel Egan
Founded 1981
Library Holdings: Bk Titles 125; Per Subs 83
Wireless access

CASCADE

P WEDSWORTH MEMORIAL LIBRARY, 13 Front St N, 59421. (Mail add: PO Box 526, 59421-0526), SAN 309-2852. Tel: 406-468-2848. FAX: 406-468-2848. E-mail: wedsworth.library@gmail.com. Web Site: www.cascademtwedsworthlibrary.wordpress.com. *Dir,* Nancy Royan; Staff 1 (Non-MLS 1)
Founded 1936. Pop 900; Circ 26,535
Jul 2020-Jun 2021 Income $36,194, State $2,990, County $19,000, Locally Generated Income $3,088, Other $11,000. Mats Exp $33,344, Books $11,453, Per/Ser (Incl. Access Fees) $243, AV Mat $3,440, Electronic Ref Mat (Incl. Access Fees) $2,132. Sal $11,960
Library Holdings: Audiobooks 256; Bks on Deafness & Sign Lang 1; CDs 130; DVDs 1,600; e-books 9,932; Bk Titles 8,281; Per Subs 6; Talking Bks 520; Videos 30
Special Collections: Cascade Historical Coll, photog; Digitized Cascade High School Annuals; Local Newspaper, microfilm; Town Little League Baseball Trophies & Pictures
Automation Activity & Vendor Info: (Cataloging) Follett Software; (Circulation) Follett Software; (ILL) OCLC
Wireless access
Function: 24/7 Online cat, Activity rm, Adult bk club, Archival coll, Art exhibits, Bk club(s), Bks on CD, CD-ROM, Children's prog, Computer training, Computers for patron use, Free DVD rentals, Holiday prog, Homebound delivery serv, ILL available, Internet access, Laminating, Magazines, Mail & tel request accepted, Meeting rooms, Microfiche/film & reading machines, Movies, Music CDs, Online cat, OverDrive digital audio bks, Photocopying/Printing, Printer for laptops & handheld devices, Prog for children & young adult, Ref serv available, Scanner, Senior computer classes, Story hour, Study rm, Summer reading prog, Tax forms, VHS videos, Wheelchair accessible
Open Mon 9-1 & 2-6, Tues 9-1 & 3-5, Wed-Fri 2-5 (Winter); Mon 9-1 & 2-6, Tues-Fri 9-1 (Summer)
Restriction: Borrowing requests are handled by ILL, Non-circulating of rare bks
Friends of the Library Group

CHESTER

P LIBERTY COUNTY LIBRARY*, 100 E First St, 59522. (Mail add: PO Box 458, 59522-0458), SAN 309-2860. Tel: 406-759-5445. FAX: 406-759-5445. E-mail: library@libertycountymt.gov. Web Site: co.liberty.mt.us/liberty-county-library. *Dir,* Julie Erickson; E-mail: library@libertycountymt.gov
Founded 1945. Pop 2,500; Circ 16,000

Library Holdings: Bk Vols 25,000; Per Subs 51
Special Collections: Broken Mountains Genealogical Library Coll
Automation Activity & Vendor Info: (Acquisitions) Follett Software; (Cataloging) Follett Software; (Circulation) Follett Software; (Course Reserve) Follett Software; (ILL) Follett Software; (Media Booking) Follett Software; (OPAC) Follett Software
Wireless access
Open Mon 11-6, Tues-Thurs 9-4:30, Fri 9-3
Friends of the Library Group

CHINOOK

P BLAINE COUNTY LIBRARY*, 112 Fourth St W, 59523. (Mail add: PO Box 610, 59523-0610), SAN 349-9502. Tel: 406-357-2932. FAX: 406-357-2552. E-mail: blcolib@itstriangle.com. Web Site: www.blainecountylibrary.org. *Dir,* Valerie Frank
Founded 1920. Pop 6,800; Circ 25,000
Library Holdings: Bk Vols 18,000; Per Subs 39
Automation Activity & Vendor Info: (Acquisitions) SirsiDynix; (Cataloging) SirsiDynix; (Circulation) SirsiDynix; (Course Reserve) SirsiDynix; (ILL) SirsiDynix; (Media Booking) SirsiDynix; (OPAC) SirsiDynix; (Serials) SirsiDynix
Wireless access
Open Mon & Wed 12-7, Tues & Thurs 10-6 Fri 12-5

CHOTEAU

P CHOTEAU/TETON PUBLIC LIBRARY*, 17 N Main Ave, 59422. (Mail add: PO Box 876, 59422-0876), SAN 309-2879. Tel: 406-466-2052. FAX: 406-466-2052. E-mail: cpl@3rivers.net. Web Site: www.choteau-tetonpubliclibrary.com. *Libr Dir,* Della Yeager; *Asst Librn,* Sally Heuscher
Pop 5,000; Circ 35,000
Library Holdings: Bk Titles 20,100; Per Subs 13
Subject Interests: Authors, Montana hist
Automation Activity & Vendor Info: (Cataloging) Follett Software; (Circulation) Follett Software
Wireless access
Special Services for the Blind - Bks on cassette; Talking bks
Open Mon-Wed 12-8, Thurs 10-8, Fri 12-6
Friends of the Library Group

CIRCLE

P GEORGE MCCONE MEMORIAL COUNTY LIBRARY*, 1101 C Ave, 59215. (Mail add: PO Box 49, 59215-0049), SAN 309-2887. Tel: 406-485-2350. E-mail: mcl@midrivers.com. *Libr Dir,* Emmie Loberg
Founded 1930. Pop 1,900
Library Holdings: Bk Vols 19,314; Per Subs 42
Subject Interests: Montana, Western states
Wireless access
Mem of Sagebrush Federation
Open Mon-Fri 12-6

COLUMBUS

P STILLWATER COUNTY LIBRARY, 27 N Fourth St, 59019. (Mail add: PO Box 266, 59019-0266), SAN 349-9561. Tel: 406-322-5009. FAX: 406-322-8071. E-mail: slibrary@mtlib.org. *Dir,* Jennifer Reed; *Asst Librn,* Andrew Boll; Staff 3.5 (MLS 1, Non-MLS 2.5)
Founded 1928. Pop 9,117
Library Holdings: Audiobooks 2,151; CDs 200; DVDs 2,607; e-books 5,230; Electronic Media & Resources 5,237; Bk Titles 20,554; Per Subs 38; Videos 367
Special Collections: Montana; Stillwater County
Automation Activity & Vendor Info: (Acquisitions) SirsiDynix-WorkFlows; (Cataloging) SirsiDynix-WorkFlows; (Circulation) SirsiDynix-WorkFlows; (ILL) OCLC
Wireless access
Function: 24/7 Electronic res, 24/7 Online cat, 3D Printer, Activity rm, Adult bk club, Adult literacy prog, After school storytime, Art exhibits, Art programs, Audiobks via web, Bk club(s), Bks on CD, Children's prog, Computer training, Computers for patron use, Digital talking bks, Distance learning, E-Readers, Electronic databases & coll, Equip loans & repairs, Family literacy, For res purposes, Free DVD rentals, Holiday prog, ILL available, Instruction & testing, Internet access, Life-long learning prog for all ages, Literacy & newcomer serv, Magazines, Mail & tel request accepted, Makerspace, Meeting rooms, Movies, Online cat, Online info literacy tutorials on the web & in blackboard, Online ref, Outreach serv, OverDrive digital audio bks, Photocopying/Printing, Preschool outreach, Preschool reading prog, Printer for laptops & handheld devices, Prog for adults, Prog for children & young adult, Scanner, Senior outreach, Serves people with intellectual disabilities, STEM programs, Story hour, Summer & winter reading prog, Summer reading prog, Tax forms, Teen prog, Telephone ref, Visual arts prog, Wheelchair accessible, Winter reading prog, Workshops
Special Services for the Blind - Bks on cassette; Bks on CD
Open Mon-Fri 9:30-5:30, Sat 9-4
Friends of the Library Group

CONRAD

P CONRAD PUBLIC LIBRARY, 15 Fourth Ave SW, 59425. SAN 309-2909. Tel: 406-271-5751. FAX: 406-271-5051. E-mail: conrdlib@3rivers.net. Web Site: www.conradlibrary.com. *Dir,* Carolyn Donath; Staff 3 (Non-MLS 3)
Founded 1925. Pop 4,270; Circ 28,500
Library Holdings: Bks on Deafness & Sign Lang 45; Bk Titles 20,891; Per Subs 6
Special Collections: Montana Coll
Automation Activity & Vendor Info: (Acquisitions) Follett Software; (Cataloging) Follett Software; (Circulation) Follett Software; (Course Reserve) Follett Software; (ILL) Follett Software; (Media Booking) Follett Software; (OPAC) Follett Software; (Serials) Follett Software
Wireless access
Special Services for the Blind - Talking bks
Open Mon, Wed & Fri 9-5, Tues & Thurs 9-7
Friends of the Library Group

CROW AGENCY

J LITTLE BIG HORN COLLEGE LIBRARY*, 8645 S Weaver Dr, 59022. (Mail add: PO Box 370, 59022-0370). Tel: 406-638-3123. Interlibrary Loan Service Tel: 406-638-3174. FAX: 406-638-3170. Web Site: lib.lbhc.edu. *Libr Dir,* Tim Bernardis; Tel: 406-638-3113, E-mail: tim@lbhc.edu; *Asst Librn,* Edwin Springfield; Tel: 406-638-3160, E-mail: springfielde@lbhc.edu; *Archivist,* Jon Ille; Tel: 406-638-3182, E-mail: ille@lbhc.edu
Library Holdings: Bk Vols 22,000; Per Subs 30
Wireless access
Partic in Treasure State Academic Information & Library Services
Open Mon-Thurs (Fall-Spring) 8-5:30, Fri 8-12; Mon-Thurs (Summer) 8-5

CUT BANK

P GLACIER COUNTY LIBRARY*, 21 First Ave SE, 59427. SAN 349-9715. Tel: 406-873-4572. FAX: 406-873-4845. E-mail: gclibrary@bresnan.net. *Dir,* Jamie Greco; Staff 5 (MLS 1, Non-MLS 4)
Founded 1944. Pop 13,578; Circ 38,121
Library Holdings: Audiobooks 879; AV Mats 899; CDs 20; DVDs 192; Large Print Bks 267; Bk Vols 38,290; Per Subs 57; Videos 707
Special Collections: Lewis & Clark Coll; Montana Authors & History
Automation Activity & Vendor Info: (Cataloging) OCLC Connexion; (Circulation) SirsiDynix-WorkFlows; (ILL) OCLC FirstSearch
Wireless access
Function: 24/7 Online cat, Adult bk club, Adult literacy prog, Archival coll, Audiobks via web, Bks on CD, Children's prog, Computers for patron use, Digital talking bks, Electronic databases & coll, Family literacy, Free DVD rentals, ILL available, Internet access, Magazines, Online cat, Prog for children & young adult, Story hour, Summer reading prog, Tax forms, Wheelchair accessible
Open Mon, Tues & Thurs 10-7, Wed & Fri 10-5, Sat 10-2
Friends of the Library Group
Branches: 2
BROWNING BRANCH, 214 First St NW, Browning, 59417, SAN 349-974X. Tel: 406-338-7105. FAX: 406-338-5436. E-mail: gcl.browning@gmail.com. *Librn,* Vananda Yazzie; Staff 1 (Non-MLS 1)
Open Mon 2-8, Tues-Fri 11:30-5:30, Sat 10-2
EAST GLACIER PARK BRANCH, Hwy Two, East Glacier Park, 59434, SAN 349-9774. *Dir,* Jamie Greco
Open Wed 4-6

DARBY

P DARBY COMMUNITY PUBLIC LIBRARY*, 101 1/2 Marshall St, 59829. (Mail add: PO Box 909, 59829-0909), SAN 309-2917. Tel: 406-821-4771. FAX: 406-821-3964. E-mail: staff@darbylibrary.net. Web Site: www.darbylibrary.net. *Libr Dir,* Wendy Campbell; E-mail: librarian@darbylibrary.net; Staff 1 (Non-MLS 1)
Founded 1921. Circ 4,300
Library Holdings: Bk Titles 7,500
Wireless access
Mem of Tamarack Federation of Libraries
Open Tues 10-7, Wed, Thurs & Fri 11-6, Sat 11-2
Friends of the Library Group

DEER LODGE

P WILLIAM K KOHRS MEMORIAL LIBRARY*, 501 Missouri Ave, 59722-1152. SAN 309-2933. Tel: 406-846-2622. FAX: 406-846-2622. E-mail: wkkohrs@yahoo.com. Web Site: www.kohrslibrarymt.org. *Dir,* Cindy Griefhaber; Staff 3 (Non-MLS 3)
Founded 1902. Pop 7,000; Circ 25,500

Library Holdings: AV Mats 4,200; Bk Titles 30,000; Per Subs 41
Special Collections: Newspapers (The New Northwest 1869-1885 & Silver State Post 1893-Present), bd
Automation Activity & Vendor Info: (OPAC) Follett Software
Wireless access
Open Mon-Thurs 11-7, Fri & Sat 11-5
Friends of the Library Group

S MONTANA STATE PRISON*, Cottonwood Union Library, 600 Conley Lake Rd, 59722. SAN 309-2941. Tel: 406-415-6410. FAX: 406-846-2950. Web Site: cor.mt.gov/adult/msp. *Librn,* Wendy Zuber; Tel: 406 415 6410, E-mail: wzuber@mt.gov; Staff 4 (Non-MLS 4)
Pop 1,600
Subject Interests: Law
Automation Activity & Vendor Info: (ILL) OCLC WorldShare Interlibrary Loan
Function: 24/7 Electronic res, Bk club(s), Computer training, Computers for patron use, Distance learning, Equip loans & repairs, ILL available, Legal assistance to inmates, Magazines, Notary serv, Photocopying/Printing, Ref & res, Satellite serv, Serves people with intellectual disabilities, Spanish lang bks, Tax forms, Wheelchair accessible
Special Services for the Blind - Bks & mags in Braille, on rec, tape & cassette; Talking bks; Talking bks & player equip; Talking bks from Braille Inst
Open Mon-Fri 7-3
Restriction: Inmate patrons, facility staff & vols direct access. All others through ILL only, Photo ID required for access

S NATIONAL PARK SERVICE*, Grant-Kohrs Ranch National Historic Site Library, 266 Warren Lane, 59722. SAN 323-8504. Tel: 406-846-2070, Ext 224, 406-846-2070, Ext 250. FAX: 406-846-3962. Web Site: www.nps.gov/grko. *Librn,* Christine Ford; Tel: 406-846-2070, Ext 242
Founded 1972
Library Holdings: Bk Titles 2,000; Per Subs 20
Special Collections: Oral History
Open Mon-Fri 8-4:30
Restriction: Limited access for the pub, Open to pub for ref & circ; with some limitations

DENTON

P DENTON PUBLIC LIBRARY*, 515 Broadway, 59430. (Mail add: PO Box 986, 59430-0986), SAN 376-7841. Tel: 406-567-2571. E-mail: dentonpl@itstriangle.com. Web Site: dentonpubliclibrary.wordpress.com. *Libr Dir,* Kellie Davis; Staff 1 (Non-MLS 1)
Pop 300
Library Holdings: Bk Titles 6,000
Mem of South Central Federation
Partic in Amigos Library Services, Inc
Open Mon, Wed & Fri 9-4, Tues & Thurs Noon-6:30

DILLON

S BEAVERHEAD COUNTY MUSEUM RESEARCH LIBRARY, 15 S Montana St, 59725. SAN 321-8481. Tel: 406-683-5027. E-mail: bvhdmuseum@hotmail.com. Web Site: beaverheadcounty.org/departments/beaverhead-county-museum. *Exec Dir,* Candi Whitworth
Founded 1947
Library Holdings: Bk Titles 250
Special Collections: Oral History
Subject Interests: SW Montana
Publications: Newsletter (Quarterly)
Open Mon-Fri 10-5 (May-Oct) or by appointment
Restriction: Non-circulating to the pub

P DILLON CITY LIBRARY, 121 S Idaho St, 59725-2500. SAN 309-2976. Toll Free Tel: 877-683-4544. Web Site: dillonpubliclibrary.org. *Libr Dir,* Lori Roberts; E-mail: dpldirector@dillonmt.org; Staff 2 (Non-MLS 2)
Founded 1890. Pop 9,246; Circ 26,741
Library Holdings: Bk Titles 17,996; Per Subs 31
Automation Activity & Vendor Info: (Circulation) SirsiDynix
Wireless access
Mem of Broad Valleys Federation of Libraries
Open Mon, Wed & Thurs 9-6, Tues 9-8, Fri 9-5, Sat 11-3
Friends of the Library Group

C UNIVERSITY OF MONTANA WESTERN, Lucy Carson Memorial Library, 710 S Atlantic St, 59725. SAN 309-2984. Tel: 406-683-7541. FAX: 406-683-7493. Web Site: www.umwestern.edu/library. *Dir,* Anne Kish; Tel: 406-683-7494, E-mail: anne.kish@umwestern.edu; *Acq,* Kayla Schmeisser; Tel: 406-683-7542, E-mail: kayla.schmeisser@umwestern.edu; Staff 2 (MLS 1, Non-MLS 1)
Founded 1893. Enrl 1,100; Fac 55; Highest Degree: Bachelor
Jul 2020-Jun 2021. Mats Exp $83,000, Books $30,000, Per/Ser (Incl. Access Fees) $53,000. Sal $109,707
Library Holdings: DVDs 600; e-books 30,000; Bk Titles 54,870; Per Subs 82
Subject Interests: Educ
Automation Activity & Vendor Info: (Acquisitions) Ex Libris Group; (Cataloging) Ex Libris Group; (Circulation) Ex Libris Group; (Course Reserve) Ex Libris Group; (Discovery) Ex Libris Group; (ILL) Ex Libris Group; (Media Booking) Ex Libris Group; (OPAC) Ex Libris Group; (Serials) Ex Libris Group
Wireless access
Publications: Unravelling the Patchwork: A Handbook for Rural School Librarians
Partic in OCLC Online Computer Library Center, Inc; Treasure State Academic Information & Library Services
Open Mon-Thurs 8-8, Fri 8-5

DRUMMOND

P DRUMMOND SCHOOL & COMMUNITY LIBRARY*, 124 First St, 59832. (Mail add: PO Box 266, 59832-0349), SAN 325-2590. Tel: 406-288-3700. E-mail: librarydhs@blackfoot.net. Web Site: drummondlibrary.org. *Dir,* Jodi Oberweiser
Pop 1,117; Circ 13,000
Library Holdings: Audiobooks 125; CDs 28; DVDs 214; e-books 9,111; Large Print Bks 250; Bk Titles 14,499; Per Subs 4; Videos 416
Special Collections: Fiction & Non-fiction; Montana Coll
Automation Activity & Vendor Info: (Cataloging) SirsiDynix; (Circulation) SirsiDynix; (OPAC) SirsiDynix
Wireless access
Function: 24/7 Online cat, Accelerated reader prog, Adult bk club, After school storytime, Bk club(s), Bks on cassette, Bks on CD, Chess club, Children's prog, Electronic databases & coll, Free DVD rentals, ILL available, Internet access, Life-long learning prog for all ages, Magazines, Mail & tel request accepted, Meeting rooms, Online cat, Photocopying/Printing, Prog for adults, Prog for children & young adult, Scanner, Story hour, Summer & winter reading prog, Summer reading prog, Teen prog, VHS videos
Mem of Broad Valleys Federation of Libraries
Open Mon & Thurs 1-7, Tues & Wed 1-5, Sat 10-4
Friends of the Library Group

DUTTON

P DUTTON/TETON PUBLIC LIBRARY*, 22 Main St W, 59433. SAN 309-295X. Tel: 406-476-3382. FAX: 406-476-3382. E-mail: duttonpubliclibrary@gmail.com. Web Site: duttonlibrary.com. *Libr Dir,* Cheri Fuhringer
Pop 1,389; Circ 4,035
Library Holdings: AV Mats 89; Bk Titles 5,000; Bk Vols 7,000
Automation Activity & Vendor Info: (Cataloging) Follett Software
Wireless access
Open Mon, Tues, Thurs & Fri 10-1:30, Wed 10-6

EKALAKA

P EKALAKA PUBLIC LIBRARY, 105 Main St, 59324. (Mail add: PO Box 482, 59324-0482), SAN 325-0199. Tel: 406-775-6336. FAX: 406-775-6336. E-mail: ekalakalibrary@gmail.com, epl@midrivers.com. Web Site: sites.google.com/site/ekalakapubliclibrary. *Dir,* Pat Kalstrom
Founded 1976. Pop 1,000; Circ 33,000
Library Holdings: AV Mats 827; Large Print Bks 220; Bk Titles 6,900
Special Collections: Carter County History Books Coll; Local History Coll; Local Literature Coll; Montana History Coll
Automation Activity & Vendor Info: (Cataloging) SirsiDynix; (Circulation) SirsiDynix
Wireless access
Function: Computers for patron use
Open Tues-Fri 11-5

ENNIS

P MADISON VALLEY PUBLIC LIBRARY*, 210 Main St, 59729. SAN 309-300X. Tel: 406-682-7244. FAX: 406-682-7669. E-mail: ennislib@3rivers.net. Web Site: www.ennislib.org. *Dir,* Karen Ketchu; Staff 1 (MLS 1)
Founded 1974. Pop 1,700; Circ 16,407
Library Holdings: Bk Vols 16,000; Per Subs 40
Special Collections: Western Coll
Wireless access
Mem of Broad Valleys Federation of Libraries
Open Mon-Fri 9-6, Sat 10-2
Friends of the Library Group

FAIRFIELD

P FAIRFIELD/TETON PUBLIC LIBRARY*, 14 N Fourth St, 59436. (Mail add: PO Box 324, 59436-0324), SAN 309-3018. Tel: 406-467-2477. FAX: 406-467-2477. E-mail: ffpubliclibrary@3rivers.net. *Libr Dir,* Brett Allen; *Asst Librn,* Tracie Roeder
Pop 1,350; Circ 14,441
Library Holdings: Bk Vols 9,000; Per Subs 12
Automation Activity & Vendor Info: (Acquisitions) Follett Software; (Cataloging) Follett Software; (Circulation) Follett Software; (ILL) Follett Software; (Media Booking) Follett Software; (OPAC) Follett Software; (Serials) Follett Software
Wireless access
Open Tues-Thurs 11-6
Friends of the Library Group

FORSYTH

P ROSEBUD COUNTY LIBRARY*, 201 N Ninth Ave, 59327. (Mail add: PO Box 7, 59327-0007), SAN 309-3026. Tel: 406-346-7561. FAX: 406-346-7685. Web Site: rosebudcountymt.gov/department/library-rosebud-county-library-forsyth. *Dir,* Heather A Johnstone; E-mail: rosebuddirector@gmail.com; *Asst Librn,* Susan Martin; E-mail: smartin@rosebudcountymt.gov; *Tech Librn, Teen Librn,* Yvonne Redding; E-mail: yredding@rosebudcountymt.gov; Staff 5 (Non-MLS 5)
Founded 1919. Pop 9,951; Circ 40,514
Library Holdings: High Interest/Low Vocabulary Bk Vols 25; Bk Vols 31,350; Per Subs 50; Spec Interest Per Sub 10
Special Collections: Local newspapers from 1894-present
Subject Interests: Western hist
Automation Activity & Vendor Info: (Acquisitions) SirsiDynix; (Cataloging) SirsiDynix; (Circulation) SirsiDynix; (ILL) SirsiDynix; (OPAC) SirsiDynix; (Serials) SirsiDynix
Wireless access
Function: 24/7 Online cat, Activity rm, Adult bk club, Archival coll, Art exhibits, Audio & video playback equip for onsite use, Audiobks via web, AV serv, Bk club(s), Bk reviews (Group), Bks on cassette, Bks on CD, CD-ROM, Children's prog, Citizenship assistance, Computer training, Computers for patron use, Digital talking bks, E-Readers, Electronic databases & coll, Family literacy, For res purposes, Free DVD rentals, Genealogy discussion group, Govt ref serv, Holiday prog, Home delivery & serv to seniorr ctr & nursing homes, Homebound delivery serv, Homework prog, ILL available, Instruction & testing, Internet access, Large print keyboards, Life-long learning prog for all ages, Magazines, Magnifiers for reading, Mail & tel request accepted, Mail loans to mem, Meeting rooms, Movies, Music CDs, Online cat, Online ref, Orientations, Outreach serv, Outside serv via phone, mail, e-mail & web, OverDrive digital audio bks, Photocopying/Printing, Preschool outreach, Preschool reading prog, Printer for laptops & handheld devices, Prog for adults, Prog for children & young adult, Ref & res, Ref serv available, Scanner, Senior computer classes, Senior outreach, Serves people with intellectual disabilities, Spanish lang bks, Spoken cassettes & CDs, Spoken cassettes & DVDs, Story hour, Study rm, Summer reading prog, Teen prog, Telephone ref, Wheelchair accessible, Workshops
Mem of South Central Federation
Partic in Partners Library Network
Special Services for the Deaf - Adult & family literacy prog; Bks on deafness & sign lang; Closed caption videos; High interest/low vocabulary bks; Spec interest per
Special Services for the Blind - Audio mat; Bks on cassette; Bks on CD; Cassette playback machines; Cassettes; Computer with voice synthesizer for visually impaired persons; Copier with enlargement capabilities; Extensive large print coll; HP Scan Jet with photo-finish software; Large print & cassettes; Large print bks; Reader equip; Videos on blindness & physical disabilties
Open Mon-Thurs 11-7, Fri 11-5, Sat 10-1
Friends of the Library Group
Branches: 1
BICENTENNIAL LIBRARY OF COLSTRIP, 419 Willow Ave, Colstrip, 59323. (Mail add: PO Box 1947, Colstrip, 59323-1947), SAN 373-9120. Tel: 406-748-3040. FAX: 406-748-2133. Web Site: rosebudcountymt.gov/departments/library-bicentennial-library-colstrip. *Dir,* Mary Kay Bullard; E-mail: colstriplibrarymk@gmail.com; *Asst Librn,* Rachel Grafton; E-mail: geekgamergirlrach@gmail.com; *Ch,* Stephanie Gregg; E-mail: steph.colstriplibrary@gmail.com; *Ref Librn,* Jill Hanson; E-mail: jill.colstriplibrary@gmail.com; Staff 4 (Non-MLS 4)
Founded 1976. Pop 5,689; Circ 30,158
Library Holdings: Bk Titles 21,860; Per Subs 45
Automation Activity & Vendor Info: (Circulation) SirsiDynix-WorkFlows; (ILL) OCLC; (OPAC) OCLC WorldShare Interlibrary Loan
Special Services for the Deaf - Bks on deafness & sign lang
Open Mon-Thurs 11-7, Fri 12-5, Sat 10-1
Friends of the Library Group

FORT BENTON

P CHOUTEAU COUNTY LIBRARY*, 1518 Main St, 59442. (Mail add: PO Box 639, 59442-0639), SAN 349-9804. Tel: 406-622-5222. FAX: 406-622-5294. E-mail: choctylibrary@gmail.com. Web Site: www.chouteaucountylibrary.net. *Dir,* Sandra Larson; *Asst Librn,* Maren Engen
Founded 1915. Pop 5,900; Circ 57,000
Library Holdings: Bk Vols 47,000; Per Subs 80
Subject Interests: Chouteau County, Fort Benton, Lewis & Clark expedition, Mo river, Montana
Automation Activity & Vendor Info: (Acquisitions) Follett Software; (Cataloging) OCLC CatExpress; (Circulation) Follett Software; (Course Reserve) Follett Software; (ILL) OCLC FirstSearch; (Media Booking) Follett Software; (OPAC) Follett Software; (Serials) Follett Software
Wireless access
Open Mon-Wed (Summer) 9-8, Thurs & Fri 9-5; Mon (Winter) 9-8, Tues-Fri 9-5
Friends of the Library Group
Branches: 2
BIG SANDY BRANCH, 60 Johannes Ave, Big Sandy, 59520. (Mail add: PO Box 1247, Big Sandy, 59520-0007), SAN 349-9839. Tel: 406-378-2161. *Br Librn,* Darlene Cline
Circ 800
Special Collections: Big Sandy Mountaineer
Automation Activity & Vendor Info: (Acquisitions) Horizon; (Circulation) Horizon; (ILL) Horizon
Function: After school storytime, Home delivery & serv to seniorr ctr & nursing homes, Homebound delivery serv, ILL available, Photocopying/Printing, Preschool outreach, Prog for children & young adult, Spoken cassettes & CDs, Spoken cassettes & DVDs, Summer reading prog, Tax forms, VHS videos, Wheelchair accessible
Open Tues & Thurs 12-6, Wed 10-4, Fri 10-2
Friends of the Library Group
GERALDINE BRANCH, 254 Main St, Geraldine, 59446. (Mail add: PO Box 316, Geraldine, 59446-0326), SAN 349-9863. Tel: 406-737-4331. *Br Librn,* Joan Trindle
Special Collections: Geraldine Review, newsp
Open Tues & Thurs 12:30-5:30, Wed & Fri 10-3

FORT HARRISON

GM VETERANS ADMINISTRATION CENTER*, Fort Harrison, 3687 Veterans Dr, 59636. (Mail add: PO Box 1500, 59636-0196), SAN 309-3034. Tel: 406-447-7347. FAX: 406-447-7992. *Dir,* Gail Wilkerson; *Librn,* Kathryn Poelman; E-mail: kathryn.poelman@va.gov; Staff 1 (MLS 1)
Founded 1930
Library Holdings: Bk Titles 200
Subject Interests: Health, Veterans
Open Mon-Fri 8-4:30

GARDINER

S YELLOWSTONE NATIONAL PARK*, Research Library & Archives, 20 Old Yellowstone Trail, 59030. (Mail add: PO Box 168, Yellowstone National Park, 82190), SAN 318-515X. Tel: 307-344-2264. FAX: 406-848-9958. E-mail: yell_research_library@nps.gov. Web Site: www.nps.gov/yell/learn/historyculture/library.htm, wyld.ent.sirsi.net/client/en_US/yrl. *Librn,* Melanie Cutietta; *Librn,* Sarah Marino; Staff 2 (MLS 1, Non-MLS 1)
Founded 1933
Library Holdings: Bk Titles 12,000; Per Subs 10
Special Collections: Montana Historical Society Coll (1876-present); Yellowstone Area (Rare Bks Coll). US Document Depository
Subject Interests: Yellowstone National Park
Function: Archival coll, For res purposes
Partic in WYLD Network
Open Mon-Thurs 9-4

GLASGOW

P GLASGOW CITY-COUNTY LIBRARY*, 408 Third Ave S, 59230. SAN 309-3050. Tel: 406-228-2731. FAX: 406-228-8193. E-mail: glasgowcitycountylibrary@gmail.com. Web Site: www.glasgowlibrary.org. *Dir,* Megan Haddix
Founded 1904. Pop 7,675; Circ 41,733. Sal $95,502 (Prof $36,480)
Library Holdings: Audiobooks 1,139; AV Mats 2,203; CDs 333; e-books 7,684; Bk Titles 43,641; Per Subs 65
Special Collections: Glasgow Courier 1895-1988
Subject Interests: Culinary, Montana genealogy
Automation Activity & Vendor Info: (Acquisitions) Follett Software; (Cataloging) OCLC CatExpress; (Circulation) Follett Software; (ILL) OCLC; (OPAC) Follett Software
Wireless access
Mem of Golden Plains Library Federation

Open Mon-Thurs 10-7, Fri 10-5, Sat 10-3
Friends of the Library Group

GLENDIVE

J DAWSON COMMUNITY COLLEGE LIBRARY*, Jane Carey Memorial Library, 300 College Dr, 59330. (Mail add: PO Box 421, 59330-0421), SAN 309-3077. Tel: 406-377-9413. Reference Tel: 406-377-9414. FAX: 406-377-8132. E-mail: info@dawson.edu. Web Site: dawson.edu/academics/library. *Dir,* Jerushe Shipstead; *Asst Dir,* Tami Johnson; Staff 2 (MLS 1, Non-MLS 1)
Founded 1940. Enrl 350; Fac 26; Highest Degree: Associate
Library Holdings: AV Mats 1,150; Bk Vols 20,468; Per Subs 160
Special Collections: State Document Depository
Subject Interests: Art, Law enforcement
Automation Activity & Vendor Info: (Acquisitions) SirsiDynix; (Cataloging) SirsiDynix; (Circulation) SirsiDynix; (Course Reserve) SirsiDynix; (ILL) OCLC; (OPAC) SirsiDynix; (Serials) SirsiDynix
Wireless access
Partic in OCLC Online Computer Library Center, Inc; Treasure State Academic Information & Library Services
Open Mon & Fri 8-4, Tues-Thurs 8-4 & 6:30-9

P GLENDIVE PUBLIC LIBRARY*, 200 S Kendrick Ave, 59330. SAN 349-9928. Tel: 406-377-3633. FAX: 406-377-4568. E-mail: booksrus@midrivers.com. Web Site: www.glendivelibrary.com. *Dir,* Dawn Kingstad
Founded 1915. Pop 9,000; Circ 45,000
Library Holdings: Bk Titles 20,000; Bk Vols 23,000; Per Subs 85
Special Collections: German-Russian Immigrations; Montana History
Automation Activity & Vendor Info: (Cataloging) SirsiDynix
Wireless access
Function: ILL available
Mem of Sagebrush Federation
Open Mon-Wed 9-7, Thurs & Fri 10-5, Sat 9-1
Friends of the Library Group
Branches: 1
RICHEY PUBLIC LIBRARY, 223 S Main St, Richey, 59259. (Mail add: PO Box 149, Richey, 59259-0149), SAN 349-9952. Tel: 406-773-5585. *Librn,* Betty Keysor
Library Holdings: Bk Vols 10,000; Per Subs 12
Function: ILL available
Open Mon, Wed & Fri 12:30-4:30

GREAT FALLS

J GREAT FALLS COLLEGE MONTANA STATE UNIVERSITY, Weaver Library, 2100 16th Ave S, 59405. SAN 373-6784. Tel: 406-771-4398. Administration Tel: 406-268-3713. E-mail: library@gfcmsu.edu. Web Site: library.gfcmsu.edu, research.gfcmsu.edu. *Dir, Libr Serv,* Mandy Wright; E-mail: mandy.wright@gfcmsu.edu; Staff 2 (MLS 1, Non-MLS 1)
Founded 1976. Enrl 900; Fac 50; Highest Degree: Associate
Library Holdings: AV Mats 972; e-books 22,465; e-journals 43,130; Bk Vols 8,813; Per Subs 72
Automation Activity & Vendor Info: (Acquisitions) SirsiDynix; (Cataloging) SirsiDynix; (Circulation) SirsiDynix; (Course Reserve) SirsiDynix; (ILL) OCLC ILLiad; (OPAC) SirsiDynix; (Serials) SerialsSolutions
Wireless access
Function: Audio & video playback equip for onsite use, Audiobks via web, Bk club(s), Bks on cassette, Bks on CD, Computers for patron use, Distance learning, E-Readers, E-Reserves, Electronic databases & coll, Free DVD rentals, ILL available, Instruction & testing, Internet access, Laminating, Magazines, Magnifiers for reading, Online cat, Online ref, Orientations, Outside serv via phone, mail, e-mail & web, Photocopying/Printing, Printer for laptops & handheld devices, Ref & res, Ref serv available, Scanner, Study rm, Telephone ref, VHS videos, Wheelchair accessible
Partic in Treasure State Academic Information & Library Services
Open Mon-Thurs 8am-9pm, Fri 8-5, Sun 12:30-9
Restriction: Borrowing requests are handled by ILL

S GREAT FALLS GENEALOGY SOCIETY LIBRARY, 301 Second Ave N, 3rd Flr, 59404. SAN 326-4025. Tel: 406-727-3922. E-mail: gfgenealogy@genlibrary.org. Web Site: gfgenealogy.org/library. *Pres,* Larry Spicer
Founded 1975
Library Holdings: Bk Vols 8,000; Per Subs 105
Special Collections: Cascade County High School Annuals; Local Cemetery Listings & Records; Marriage Records; Vital Records, Inquests
Subject Interests: Genealogy
Wireless access
Publications: Treasure State Lines (Quarterly)
Open Mon-Sat 1-4

P GREAT FALLS PUBLIC LIBRARY*, 301 Second Ave N, 59401-2593. SAN 309-3115. Tel: 406-453-0349. FAX: 406-453-0181. E-mail: questions@greatfallslibrary.org. Web Site: www.greatfallslibrary.org. *Libr Dir,* Susie McIntyre; Tel: 406-453-0181, Ext 216, E-mail: smcintyre@greatfallslibrary.org; *IT Coordr,* Sara Kegel; Tel: 406-453-0181, Ext 230; *Pub Relations,* Jude Smith; Tel: 406-453-0181, Ext 220; *Pub Serv,* Kat Wilson; Tel: 406-453-0181, Ext 213; *Youth Serv,* Rae McFadden; Tel: 406-453-0349, Ext 215; Staff 26 (MLS 4, Non-MLS 22)
Founded 1890. Pop 77,128; Circ 370,291
Library Holdings: Bk Titles 124,071; Bk Vols 159,769; Per Subs 354
Special Collections: City; Montana History Coll
Automation Activity & Vendor Info: (Acquisitions) SirsiDynix; (Cataloging) SirsiDynix; (Circulation) SirsiDynix; (ILL) OCLC Connexion; (OPAC) SirsiDynix
Wireless access
Function: ILL available
Open tues-thurs 10-8, Fri & Sat 10-6, Sun (Oct-May) 1-5
Friends of the Library Group
Bookmobiles: 1

S LEWIS & CLARK TRAIL HERITAGE FOUNDATION, INC, William P Sherman Library & Archives, 4201 Giant Spring Rd, Ste 2, 59405. Tel: 406-454-1234. Toll Free Tel: 888-701-3434. E-mail: library@lewisandclark.org. Web Site: www.lewisandclark.org. *Exec Dir,* Sarah Cawley; E-mail: director@lewisandclark.org; *Libr Tech,* Della Van Setten; E-mail: della@lewisandclark.org
Founded 1968
Library Holdings: Bk Vols 3,000
Open Mon-Fri 9-4

S MONTANA SCHOOL FOR THE DEAF & BLIND LIBRARY*, 3911 Central Ave, 59405. SAN 320-6904. Tel: 406-771-6051. Toll Free Tel: 800-882-6732. FAX: 406-771-6164. TDD: 406-771-6063. E-mail: info@msdb.mt.gov. Web Site: msdb.mt.gov/campus/library.html. *Librn,* Staci Bechard; E-mail: sbechard@msdb.mt.gov; Staff 1 (Non-MLS 1)
Library Holdings: Bks on Deafness & Sign Lang 300; Braille Volumes 1,000; Large Print Bks 500; Bk Vols 9,500
Automation Activity & Vendor Info: (Cataloging) SirsiDynix; (Circulation) SirsiDynix
Wireless access
Special Services for the Deaf - Accessible learning ctr; Captioned film dep; Described encaptioned media prog
Special Services for the Blind - Braille bks; Large print bks
Restriction: Not open to pub

S C M RUSSELL MUSEUM LIBRARY, Frederic G & Ginger K Renner Research Center, 400 13th St N, 59401. SAN 327-1552. Tel: 406-727-8787. FAX: 406-727-2402. Web Site: cmrussell.org/experience/research-center. *Mgr,* Kathryn Marie Kramer; Tel: 406-727-8787, Ext 336, E-mail: kkramer@cmrussell.org; Staff 1 (MLS 1)
Founded 1980
Library Holdings: Bk Titles 3,700; Bk Vols 4,000; Per Subs 15; Spec Interest Per Sub 9
Special Collections: Frederic G & Ginger K Renner Coll; J H Sharp Coll, photog; John Taliaferro Papers; Karl Yost papers; Richard Flood Coll
Subject Interests: Art, Artists, Western Am art, Western US hist
Restriction: Non-circulating, Open by appt only

CR UNIVERSITY OF PROVIDENCE LIBRARY, 1301 20th St S, 59405-4948. SAN 309-3085. Tel: 406-791-5315. Administration Tel: 406-791-5318. E-mail: library@uprovidence.edu. Web Site: www.uprovidence.edu/academics/library-services. *E-Resources Librn, Sr Librn, Ref,* Susan M Lee; E-mail: susan.lee@uprovidence.edu; *Evening/Weekend Supvr, Libr Asst,* Jean Kronebusch; Tel: 406-791-5316, E-mail: jean.kronebusch@uprovidence.edu; Staff 2 (MLS 1, Non-MLS 1)
Founded 1932. Enrl 940; Highest Degree: Master
Library Holdings: e-books 10,903; e-journals 191,000; Bk Titles 47,436; Per Subs 74
Subject Interests: Criminal justice, Educ, Law, Relig
Automation Activity & Vendor Info: (Acquisitions) Ex Libris Group; (Cataloging) Ex Libris Group; (Circulation) Ex Libris Group; (Course Reserve) Ex Libris Group; (Discovery) Ex Libris Group; (ILL) OCLC WorldShare Interlibrary Loan; (Media Booking) Ex Libris Group; (OPAC) Ex Libris Group; (Serials) EBSCO Online
Wireless access
Function: 24/7 Electronic res, 24/7 Online cat, Audiobks via web, Computers for patron use, Distance learning, Electronic databases & coll, ILL available, Internet access, Mail & tel request accepted, Online cat, Online ref, Orientations, Photocopying/Printing, Ref & res, Ref serv available, Scanner, Study rm, Wheelchair accessible
Partic in Treasure State Academic Information & Library Services
Open Mon-Thurs 7:30am-10pm, Fri 7:30-5, Sun 2-10 (Winter); Mon-Fri 8-5 (Summer)
Restriction: 24-hr pass syst for students only, Non-circulating of rare bks

HAMILTON

P BITTERROOT PUBLIC LIBRARY, 306 State St, 59840. SAN 309-3123. Tel: 406-363-1670. FAX: 406-363-1678. E-mail: info@bitterrootpubliclibrary.org. Web Site: www.bitterrootpubliclibrary.org. *Libr Dir,* Mark Wetherington; E-mail: mark@bitterrootpubliclibrary.org; *Asst Dir, Youth Serv Librn,* Wendy Campbell; E-mail: wendy@bitterrootpubliclibrary.org; *Commun Librn,* Daniel Ray; E-mail: daniel@bitterrootpubliclibrary.org; Staff 6 (Non-MLS 6)
Founded 1903. Pop 24,945; Circ 120,716
Library Holdings: AV Mats 2,592; e-books 9,058; Electronic Media & Resources 28; Large Print Bks 1,423; Bk Titles 43,345; Bk Vols 46,907; Per Subs 74
Special Collections: Bitterroot Valley, Montana; Lewis & Clark Expedition; Ravalli County, Montana
Automation Activity & Vendor Info: (Circulation) SirsiDynix; (ILL) OCLC Online
Wireless access
Mem of Tamarack Federation of Libraries
Special Services for the Deaf - Closed caption videos
Open Mon-Thurs 9:30-7, Fri & Sat 9:30-5
Friends of the Library Group

G NIH, NATIONAL INSTITUTE OF ALLERGY & INFECTIOUS DISEASES*, Rocky Mountain Laboratories Library, 903 S Fourth St, 59840-2932. SAN 309-3131. Tel: 406-363-9212. Administration Tel: 406-363-9211. *Librn,* Taylor Robinson; E-mail: taylor.robinson@nih.gov; Staff 1 (MLS 1)
Founded 1927
Library Holdings: Bk Titles 3,250; Bk Vols 3,500; Per Subs 11
Subject Interests: Allergy, Bacteriology, Biochem, Immunology, Med entomology, Microbiology, Parasitology, Venereal disease, Veterinary sci, Virology, Wildlife, Zoology
Automation Activity & Vendor Info: (Cataloging) OCLC; (Circulation) Innovative Interfaces, Inc; (OPAC) Innovative Interfaces, Inc; (Serials) Innovative Interfaces, Inc
Wireless access
Partic in Nat Libr of Med Regional Med Libr Prog
Open Mon-Fri 8-4:30
Restriction: Badge access after hrs, External users must contact libr

S RAVALLI COUNTY MUSEUM*, Miles Romney Memorial Library, 205 Bedford, 59840. SAN 324-3605. Tel: 406-363-3338. FAX: 406-363-6588. E-mail: rcmuseum@gmail.com. Web Site: ravallimuseum.org. *Exec Dir,* Tamar Stanley; E-mail: director@ravallimuseum.org; *Prog Coordr,* Sarah Monson; E-mail: marketing@ravallimuseum.org
Founded 1979
Library Holdings: Bk Titles 500; Per Subs 15
Special Collections: Bitter Root Valley Historical Society Coll; Bitter Root Valley Newspapers. Oral History
Function: Res libr
Open Mon, Thurs & Fri 10-4, Sat 10-2, Sun 1-4
Restriction: Not a lending libr

HARDIN

P BIG HORN COUNTY PUBLIC LIBRARY, 419 N Custer Ave, 59034. SAN 309-314X. Tel: 406-665-1808. FAX: 406-665-1804. Web Site: bighorncountymt.gov/departments/library/. *Dir,* Ray Dale; E-mail: rdale@bighorncountymt.gov; *Instr,* Anita Shoppe; Tel: 406-665-9747, E-mail: anitaschoppe@hotmail.com; *Librn,* Donna Howe; Tel: 406-665-9742, E-mail: dhowe@bighorncountymt.gov; *Ch,* Angie LittleLight; E-mail: alittlelight@bighorncountymt.gov. Subject Specialists: *Adult educ,* Anita Shoppe; Staff 4 (Non-MLS 4)
Founded 1909. Pop 12,290; Circ 51,865
Jul 2015-Jun 2016 Income $299,000. Mats Exp $12,500, Books $10,000, Per/Ser (Incl. Access Fees) $2,500. Sal $90,000
Library Holdings: AV Mats 2,500; Bks on Deafness & Sign Lang 10; CDs 450; Large Print Bks 2,500; Bk Titles 29,500; Per Subs 30; Videos 1,500
Special Collections: Battle of Little Big Horn; Cheyenne Indian Culture & History; Crow Indian Culture & History
Automation Activity & Vendor Info: (Cataloging) SirsiDynix; (Circulation) SirsiDynix; (ILL) OCLC; (OPAC) SirsiDynix
Wireless access
Open Mon-Thurs 10-7, Fri 10-6
Restriction: Residents only
Friends of the Library Group

HARLEM

J AANIIIH NAKODA COLLEGE LIBRARY*, Fort Belknap Agency, 330 Assiniboine Ave, 59526. (Mail add: PO Box 159, 59526-0159), SAN 375-3522. Tel: 406-353-2607, Ext 311. FAX: 406-353-2898. E-mail: fortbelknaplibrary@yahoo.com. Web Site: www.ancollege.edu/Library. *Libr Dir,* Eva English; E-mail: eenglish@ancollege.edu; Staff 1 (MLS 1)
Founded 1984. Enrl 176; Fac 10
Library Holdings: Bk Titles 8,000; Bk Vols 10,000; Per Subs 25
Special Collections: Oral History
Automation Activity & Vendor Info: (Acquisitions) SirsiDynix; (Cataloging) SirsiDynix; (Circulation) SirsiDynix; (Course Reserve) SirsiDynix; (ILL) SirsiDynix; (Media Booking) SirsiDynix; (OPAC) SirsiDynix; (Serials) SirsiDynix
Wireless access
Partic in Treasure State Academic Information & Library Services
Open Mon-Thurs 8-5, Fri 10-5

P HARLEM PUBLIC LIBRARY*, 37 First Ave SE, 59526. (Mail add: PO Box 519, 59526-0519), SAN 349-9537. Tel: 406-353-2712. FAX: 406-353-2224. E-mail: harlemlib@live.com. Web Site: www.harlempubliclibrary.org. *Libr Dir,* Colleen Brommer; *Asst Librn,* Carly Vauthier
Pop 2,555; Circ 16,271
Library Holdings: Audiobooks 157; DVDs 536; Large Print Bks 60; Bk Titles 13,416; Per Subs 54
Automation Activity & Vendor Info: (Acquisitions) SirsiDynix; (Cataloging) SirsiDynix; (Circulation) SirsiDynix; (Course Reserve) SirsiDynix; (ILL) SirsiDynix; (Media Booking) SirsiDynix; (OPAC) SirsiDynix; (Serials) SirsiDynix
Wireless access
Open Mon 11-7, Tues & Fri 9-2, Wed & Thurs 12-6
Friends of the Library Group

HARLOWTON

P HARLOWTON PUBLIC LIBRARY, 13 S Central Ave, 59036. (Mail add: PO Box 663, 59036-0663), SAN 309-3158. Tel: 406-632-5584. FAX: 406-632-5583. E-mail: harlolib@mtintouch.net. Web Site: www.harlowtonlibrary.com. *Libr Dir,* Kathleen Schreiber
Founded 1932. Pop 2,246; Circ 10,168
Library Holdings: Bk Titles 10,000; Bk Vols 11,500; Per Subs 38
Open Mon-Wed 9:30-12 & 1-8, Thurs 1-8, Fri 9:30-12 & 1-5

HAVRE

P HAVRE HILL COUNTY LIBRARY, 402 Third St, 59501. SAN 309-3174. Tel: 406-265-2123. FAX: 406-262-2418. E-mail: library@havrehill.org. Web Site: havrehilllibrary.org. *Dir,* Rachel Rawn; *Youth Serv Librn,* Ashley Martin; *Cat,* Shelma Seidel; Staff 5 (Non-MLS 5)
Founded 1983. Pop 16,663; Circ 93,215
Library Holdings: Bks on Deafness & Sign Lang 180; Braille Volumes 15; CDs 150; DVDs 25; Large Print Bks 4,500; Bk Titles 63,937; Per Subs 137; Talking Bks 1,122; Videos 1,382
Subject Interests: Genealogy, Montana
Automation Activity & Vendor Info: (Cataloging) SirsiDynix; (Circulation) SirsiDynix
Wireless access
Open Mon & Tues 9-9, Wed & Thurs 9-6, Fri 9-5, Sat 12-5
Friends of the Library Group

C MONTANA STATE UNIVERSITY-NORTHERN*, Vande Bogart Library, 300 13th St W, 59501. (Mail add: PO Box 7751, 59501-7751), SAN 309-3182. Tel: 406-265-3706. FAX: 406-265-3799. Web Site: www.msun.edu/library. *Electronic Access Librn, Libr Dir,* Vicki Gist; Tel: 406-265-4140, E-mail: gist@msun.edu; *Govt Doc, ILL & Ser, Info & Instruction Librn,* Belinda Potter; Tel: 406-265-3544, E-mail: bpotter@msun.edu; *Archivist, Pub Serv, Tech Serv,* Valerie Hickman; Tel: 406-265-3506, E-mail: hickman@msun.edu; Staff 4 (MLS 1, Non-MLS 3)
Founded 1929. Enrl 1,058; Fac 98; Highest Degree: Master
Library Holdings: CDs 671; DVDs 132; e-books 216,409; e-journals 41,507; Bk Vols 133,910; Per Subs 98; Videos 11
Special Collections: Education (Educational Resources Information Center Coll), micro. State Document Depository; US Document Depository
Subject Interests: Applied tech, Educ, Nursing, Western hist
Automation Activity & Vendor Info: (Cataloging) SirsiDynix; (Circulation) SirsiDynix; (Course Reserve) SirsiDynix; (ILL) OCLC ILLiad; (OPAC) SirsiDynix; (Serials) SirsiDynix
Wireless access
Partic in Treasure State Academic Information & Library Services
Open Mon-Thurs 8am-10pm, Fri 8-5, Sun 1-10

HELENA

P BROAD VALLEYS FEDERATION OF LIBRARIES*, 120 S Last Chance Gulch, 59601-4133. Tel: 406-447-1690. FAX: 406-447-1687. *Coordr,* John Finn; E-mail: jfinn@lclibrary.org
Wireless access
Member Libraries: Belgrade Community Library; Bozeman Public Library; Broadwater School & Community Library; Butte-Silver Bow

Public Library; Dillon City Library; Drummond School & Community Library; Hearst Free Library; Jefferson County Library System; Lewis & Clark Library; Madison Valley Public Library; Manhattan Community Library; Meagher County City Library; Philipsburg Public Library; Sheridan Public Library; Thompson-Hickman Free County Library; Three Forks Community Library; West Yellowstone Public Library

C CARROLL COLLEGE, Jack & Sallie Corette Library, 1601 N Benton Ave, 59625. SAN 309-3204. Tel: 406-447-4340. Administration Tel: 406-447-4344. FAX: 406-447-4525. E-mail: libstaff@carroll.edu. Web Site: www.carroll.edu/academics/library. *Dir,* Dr Jennifer Oates; *Cat/Ref Librn,* Heather Navratil; E-mail: hnavratil@carroll.edu; *Electronic Res Librn,* Stephen Haddad; E-mail: shaddad@carroll.edu; *Web Serv Librn,* Terence Kratz; Tel: 406-447-5450, E-mail: tkratz@carroll.edu; *Circ Supvr,* Cindy Bennett; E-mail: cbennett@carroll.edu; Staff 5 (MLS 4, Non-MLS 1)
Founded 1909. Enrl 1,400; Fac 100; Highest Degree: Master
Library Holdings: Bk Titles 83,425; Bk Vols 98,257; Videos 1,000
Subject Interests: Allied health, Natural sci, State hist, Theol
Automation Activity & Vendor Info: (Acquisitions) SirsiDynix; (Cataloging) OCLC; (Circulation) Ex Libris Group; (ILL) OCLC; (OPAC) Ex Libris Group; (Serials) Ex Libris Group
Wireless access
Partic in National Network of Libraries of Medicine Region 4; OCLC Online Computer Library Center, Inc; OMNI; Treasure State Academic Information & Library Services

P LEWIS & CLARK LIBRARY*, 120 S Last Chance Gulch, 59601. SAN 349-9987. Tel: 406-447-1690. Circulation Tel: 406-447-1690, Ext 123. FAX: 406-447-1687. E-mail: lclreference@lclibrary.org. Web Site: www.lewisandclarklibrary.org. *Dir,* John Finn; E-mail: jfinn@lclibrary.org; *Pub Info Officer,* Patricia Spencer; E-mail: pspencer@mtlib.org; *Coll Develop Librn,* James Parrott; E-mail: jparrott@lclibrary.org; *Youth Serv Librn,* Molly Hudson; E-mail: mhudson@lclibrary.org; *Bus Mgr,* Patricia Stemberg; E-mail: tsberg@lclibrary.org; *Syst Mgr,* Matthew A Beckstrom; E-mail: mbeckstrom@lclibrary.org; *Adult Serv,* Suzanne Schwichtenberg; E-mail: sschwich@lclibrary.org; Staff 27.1 (MLS 6.5, Non-MLS 20.6)
Founded 1868. Pop 56,335; Circ 647,806
Library Holdings: Bk Titles 129,420; Per Subs 203
Special Collections: Local Energy Resource Center; Local Government Info Center; Local Montana History Coll. Oral History
Subject Interests: Energy resources, Govt info
Automation Activity & Vendor Info: (Acquisitions) Infor Library & Information Solutions; (Cataloging) Infor Library & Information Solutions; (Circulation) Infor Library & Information Solutions; (ILL) Infor Library & Information Solutions; (OPAC) Infor Library & Information Solutions
Wireless access
Function: Adult bk club, Adult literacy prog, Art exhibits, CD-ROM, Computer training, Doc delivery serv, Electronic databases & coll, Genealogy discussion group, Homebound delivery serv, ILL available, Internet access, Online ref, Photocopying/Printing, Preschool outreach, Prog for adults, Prog for children & young adult, Ref serv available, Senior computer classes, Serves people with intellectual disabilities, Spoken cassettes & CDs, Spoken cassettes & DVDs, Summer reading prog, Tax forms, Telephone ref, VHS videos, Wheelchair accessible, Workshops
Publications: Annual Report
Mem of Broad Valleys Federation of Libraries
Partic in OCLC Online Computer Library Center, Inc
Open Mon-Fri 11-6, Sat 11-5, Sun 1-5
Restriction: Lending limited to county residents, Non-resident fee
Friends of the Library Group
Branches: 3
AUGUSTA BRANCH, 205 Main St, Augusta, 59410. (Mail add: PO Box 387, Augusta, 59410-0387). Tel: 406-562-3348. FAX: 406-562-3358. *Br Librn,* Holly Herring; E-mail: hherring@lclibrary.org
Open Mon 3-7, Tues-Thurs 10-5, Sun 1-5
EAST HELENA BRANCH, 16 E Main St, East Helena, 59635. (Mail add: PO Box 1398, East Helena, 59635). Tel: 406-227-5750. FAX: 406-227-5751. *Br Mgr,* Andrea Eckerson; E-mail: aeckerson@lclibrary.org
Open Mon-Thurs 11-6, Fri 11-5
LINCOLN BRANCH, 102 Ninth Ave S, Lincoln, 59639. (Mail add: PO Box 309, Lincoln, 59639-0309). Tel: 406-362-4300. FAX: 406-362-4039. *Br Librn,* Kate Radford; E-mail: kradford@lclibrary.org
Automation Activity & Vendor Info: (Course Reserve) Infor Library & Information Solutions
Open Mon-Fri 10-2
Bookmobiles: 1. Librn, Bretagne Byrd

G MONTANA DEPARTMENT OF COMMERCE*, Census & Economic Information Center, 301 S Park Ave, 59620. (Mail add: PO Box 200505, 59620-0505), SAN 320-1996. Tel: 406-841-2870. FAX: 406-841-2871. E-mail: ceic@mt.gov. Web Site: ceic.mt.gov. *Actg Chief,* Tom Kaiserski; *Sr Res Economist,* Joe Ramler; Tel: 406-841-2719, E-mail: jramler@mt.gov; Staff 5 (Non-MLS 5)
Founded 1970
Library Holdings: CDs 150; DVDs 50; Bk Titles 100; Bk Vols 250
Subject Interests: Demographics, Econ
Open Mon-Fri 7:30-4:30

S MONTANA HISTORICAL SOCIETY, Research Center, 225 N Roberts St, 59601-4514. (Mail add: PO Box 201201, 59620-1201), SAN 309-3220. Tel: 406-444-2681. Administration Tel: 406-444-4787. Toll Free Tel: 800-243-9900. FAX: 406-444-2696. *Dir,* Roberta Gebhardt; Tel: 406-444-4702, E-mail: rgebhardt@mt.gov; *Digital Projects Librn,* Position Currently Open; *Librn,* Maggie Meredith; Tel: 406-444-9526, E-mail: maggie.meredith@mt.gov; *Tech Serv Librn,* Laurie Chipps; Tel: 406-444-4787, E-mail: laurie.chipps@mt.gov; *Libr Mgr,* Laura Tretter; Tel: 406-444-7415, E-mail: ltretter@mt.gov; *Photog Archives Mgr,* Jeff Malcomsom; Tel: 406-444-0261; *Sr Archivist,* Heather Hultman; Tel: 406-444-3668, E-mail: heather.hultman@mt.gov; *Sr Archivist,* Kellyn Younggren; Tel: 406-444-3317, E-mail: kellyn.younggren@mt.gov; *State Archivist,* Rich Aarstad; Tel: 406-444-6779, E-mail: raarstad@mt.gov; *Archivist, Oral Historian,* Anneliese Warhank; Tel: 406-444-4774, E-mail: awarhank@mt.gov; *Digital Projects Tech,* Position Currently Open; *Archivist, Govt Doc,* Hannah Soukup; Tel: 406-444-7427, E-mail: hannah.soukup@mt.gov; *Film Archivist,* Position Currently Open; *Archives, Tech,* Pam Smith; Tel: 406-444-4739, E-mail: psmith2@mt.gov; *Photo Archivist,* Tom Ferris; E-mail: tferris@mt.gov; *Ref Historian,* Zoe Ann Stoltz; Tel: 406-444-1988, E-mail: zstoltz@mt.gov. Subject Specialists: *Photog,* Heather Hultman; *Manuscripts,* Anneliese Warhank; Staff 13 (MLS 8, Non-MLS 5)
Founded 1865
Library Holdings: Bk Vols 56,000; Per Subs 385
Special Collections: 20th Century Homesteading Photos (Cameron Coll); Cattle Industry (Huffmann Coll), photog; Genealogy (Daughters of American Revolution Coll); George Armstrong Custer (Edgar I Stewart Coll); Montana Newspapers; Montana State Archives; Range Cattle Industry 1860-1945 (Teakle Coll); Yellowstone Park, Pacific Northwest & North Plains Photos (Haynes Coll). Oral History; State Document Depository
Subject Interests: Montana, Western Americana
Automation Activity & Vendor Info: (Cataloging) SirsiDynix; (Circulation) SirsiDynix; (OPAC) SirsiDynix; (Serials) SirsiDynix
Wireless access
Function: 24/7 Online cat, Govt ref serv, ILL available, Ref serv available, Telephone ref
Publications: Montana: The Magazine of Western History (Quarterly)
Partic in OCLC Online Computer Library Center, Inc
Open Tues-Fri 9-5
Restriction: Circulates for staff only, Closed stack, In-house use for visitors, Non-circulating coll

G MONTANA LEGISLATIVE REFERENCE CENTER, State Capitol, Rm 10, 59620. (Mail add: PO Box 201706, 59620-1706), SAN 320-2003. Tel: 406-444-4043. E-mail: leglib@mt.gov. Web Site: leg.mt.gov. *Libr Dir,* Sonia Gavin; *Libr Tech,* Pam Weitz; E-mail: pweitz@mt.gov; Staff 2 (MLS 1, Non-MLS 1)
Founded 1975
Library Holdings: Bk Titles 7,581; Bk Vols 10,456; Per Subs 489
Special Collections: Montana Legislature Interim Study Archives
Subject Interests: Law, Legis hist, Montana constitutional, Pub admin, Pub affairs
Automation Activity & Vendor Info: (Acquisitions) Inmagic, Inc.; (Cataloging) Inmagic, Inc.; (Circulation) Inmagic, Inc.; (ILL) Inmagic, Inc.; (OPAC) Inmagic, Inc.; (Serials) Inmagic, Inc.
Function: ILL available, Photocopying/Printing, Telephone ref
Publications: Catalog of Publications & Interim Study Final Reports (1957-1999); Sources of Information & Publications (8th ed 2000)
Open Mon-Fri 8-5

S MONTANA MASONIC LIBRARY*, 425 N Park Ave, 59624. (Mail add: PO Box 1158, 59624-1158), SAN 309-3212. Tel: 406-442-7774. E-mail: brodan@grandlodgemontana.org. Web Site: www.grandlodgemontana.org. *Librn,* Daniel Gardiner
Founded 1866
Library Holdings: Bk Titles 3,000
Special Collections: Early Montana & Masonic History, first issue copies & original handwritten ms
Subject Interests: Freemasonry, Masonry
Wireless access
Function: ILL available
Open Mon-Fri 8:30-4:30
Friends of the Library Group

G MONTANA STATE DEPARTMENT OF NATURAL RESOURCES & CONSERVATION, Research & Information Center, PO Box 201601, 59620-1601. SAN 320-6912. Tel: 406-444-6603. FAX: 406-444-0533. Web Site: www.dnrc.mt.gov. *Admin Mgr,* Cindy Forgey; E-mail: cforgey@mt.gov

Library Holdings: Bk Titles 9,000; Per Subs 91
Special Collections: (includes Columbia, Missouri & Yellowstone River basin studies & general natural resource planning); Energy Planning & Development; Environmental Impact Statements; Montana Department of Natural Resources Publications & Water Planning
Publications: DNRC Publications List & Addendum
Restriction: Staff use only

P MONTANA STATE LIBRARY, 1515 E Sixth Ave, 59620. (Mail add: PO Box 201800, 59620-1800), SAN 350-0136. Tel: 406-444-3115. Information Services Tel: 406-444-3016. Toll Free Tel: 800-338-5087. FAX: 406-444-0266. Information Services FAX: 406-444-0204. Reference E-mail: MSLReference@mt.gov. Web Site: home.msl.mt.gov. *State Librn,* Jennie Stapp; *Dir, Statewide Libr Res,* Tracy Cook; E-mail: tcook2@mt.gov; *Digital Library Admin,* Evan Hammer; *Electronic Res Librn, Outreach Librn,* Marilyn Bennett; E-mail: MBennett@mt.gov; *State Publ Librn,* James Kammerer; Tel: 406-444-5432, E-mail: jkammerer@mt.gov; *Central Servs Mgr,* Kris Schmitz; Tel: 406-444-3117, E-mail: kschmitz@mt.gov; *Circ Mgr,* Bert Rinderle; E-mail: brinderle@mt.gov; Staff 35 (MLS 9, Non-MLS 26)
Founded 1929
Library Holdings: Braille Volumes 129,000; CDs 339; e-books 500; e-journals 6; Electronic Media & Resources 3,067; Bk Titles 30,000; Bk Vols 38,000; Talking Bks 151,576
Special Collections: Braille Twin Vision, combined textile & vision bks; Descriptive Videos (DV's); Geographic Information System; Library & Information Science; MT Natural Resource Index; Natural Resource Information System; Talking Book Library; Water Information System. State Document Depository
Subject Interests: Librarianship, Natural res, State govt, Water
Automation Activity & Vendor Info: (Cataloging) SirsiDynix; (Circulation) SirsiDynix; (ILL) OCLC FirstSearch; (OPAC) Keystone Systems, Inc (KLAS); (Serials) EBSCO Online
Wireless access
Function: Govt ref serv, Homebound delivery serv, ILL available, Ref serv available, Wheelchair accessible, Workshops
Publications: Big Sky (Newsletter); Bits of Gold (Newsletter); Montana Certification Program Manual; Montana Library Directory (Online only); Montana Public Library Annual Statistics
Partic in Association for Rural & Small Libraries; Mountain Plains Libr Asn; Nat Libr Serv READS Prog; OCLC Online Computer Library Center, Inc; Pac NW Libr Asn
Special Services for the Deaf - Assisted listening device; Assistive tech; Staff with knowledge of sign lang; TTY equip
Special Services for the Blind - Accessible computers; Assistive/Adapted tech devices, equip & products; Audio mat; Braille alphabet card; Braille servs; Cassette playback machines; Children's Braille; Closed circuit TV; Computer with voice synthesizer for visually impaired persons; Digital talking bk; Digital talking bk machines; Duplicating spec requests; Info on spec aids & appliances; Internet workstation with adaptive software; Local mags & bks recorded; Low vision equip; Machine repair; Magnifiers; Mags & bk reproduction/duplication; Networked computers with assistive software; Newsline for the Blind; Production of talking bks; Ref serv; Screen enlargement software for people with visual disabilities; Soundproof reading booth; Spec cats; Talking bk & rec for the blind cat; Tel Pioneers equip repair group; Volunteer serv; Web-Braille
Open Mon-Fri 8-5

M ST PETER'S HOSPITAL*, Medical Library, 2475 Broadway, 59601. SAN 320-8656. Tel: 406-444-2312. FAX: 406-447-2609. E-mail: medlibrary@sphealth.org. Web Site: www.sphealth.org/employee-resources/provider-resources. *Library Contact,* Sevda Raghib; E-mail: SRaghib@sphealth.org
Founded 1973
Library Holdings: Bk Titles 250; Per Subs 40
Subject Interests: Med
Wireless access
Function: Doc delivery serv, Electronic databases & coll, ILL available, Internet access, Mail & tel request accepted, Photocopying/Printing, Ref serv available
Open Mon-Fri 8-3

M SHODAIR CHILDREN'S HOSPITAL*, Medical Library, 2755 Colonial Dr, 59601. (Mail add: PO Box 5539, 59604-5539), SAN 320-6920. Tel: 406-444-7500. Toll Free Tel: 800-447-6614. Web Site: shodair.org. *Dir of Educ,* Mandy Countryman; Tel: 406-444-7564, E-mail: mcountryman@shodair.org; Staff 1 (Non-MLS 1)
Founded 1979
Library Holdings: AV Mats 100; Bk Titles 1,800; Per Subs 100
Special Collections: Lay Information on Genetic Disorders
Subject Interests: Birth defects, Child psychology, Clinical genetics, Cytogenetics, Genetic counseling, Genetic disorders, Med genetics, Prenatal diagnosis
Partic in National Network of Libraries of Medicine Region 4; OCLC Online Computer Library Center, Inc
Open Mon-Fri 8- 5

GL STATE LAW LIBRARY OF MONTANA*, 215 N Sanders, 59601-4522. (Mail add: PO Box 203004, 59620-3004). Tel: 406-444-3660. Toll Free Tel: 800-710-9827 (MT only). FAX: 406-444-3603. E-mail: lawlibcirc@mt.gov. Web Site: courts.mt.gov/library. *Dir,* Sarah McClain; E-mail: SMcClain@mt.gov; *Ref Librn,* Christine Mandiloff; *Tech Serv Librn,* Stephan Licitra; *Access Serv Coordr,* Rita Gibson; *Electronic Res,* Kevin Cook. Subject Specialists: *Legal ref,* Christine Mandiloff; Staff 8 (MLS 3, Non-MLS 5)
Founded 1866
Library Holdings: Bk Titles 19,000; Bk Vols 190,000; Per Subs 550
Special Collections: State Justice Institute Depository. US Document Depository
Subject Interests: Legal hist, Legis hist
Automation Activity & Vendor Info: (Acquisitions) SirsiDynix; (Cataloging) SirsiDynix; (Circulation) SirsiDynix; (Course Reserve) SirsiDynix; (ILL) SirsiDynix; (Media Booking) SirsiDynix; (OPAC) SirsiDynix; (Serials) SirsiDynix
Wireless access
Publications: A Guide to Montana Legal Research; Audio/Visual Catalogs; Historic Sketch of the State Law Library of Montana; Legal Materials for Non-lawyers; Periodicals Catalog; State Law Library Users Guide
Partic in OCLC Online Computer Library Center, Inc
Open Mon-Fri 8-5

C UNIVERSITY OF MONTANA HELENA*, Donaldson Campus Library, 1115 N Roberts St, 59601. SAN 373-6865. Tel: 406-444-2743. FAX: 406-444-6892. E-mail: library@helenacollege.edu. Web Site: www.helenacollege.edu/library. *Dir, Libr Serv,* Della Dubbe; E-mail: della.dubbe@HelenaCollege.edu; *Librn,* Jessie Pate; E-mail: jessie.pate@HelenaCollege.edu; *Libr Tech,* Mary Ann George; E-mail: maryann.george@HelenaCollege.edu; Staff 2 (MLS 2)
Founded 1992. Enrl 1,300; Highest Degree: Associate
Library Holdings: Audiobooks 2,400; AV Mats 200; DVDs 300; e-books 92,000; e-journals 41,600; Bk Vols 10,000; Per Subs 90; Videos 200
Subject Interests: Aviation, Computer tech, Construction, Diesel, Electronic, Fire protection, Nursing, Teaching, Technologies, Trades
Automation Activity & Vendor Info: (Cataloging) Ex Libris Group; (Circulation) Ex Libris Group; (OPAC) Ex Libris Group
Wireless access
Function: Audio & video playback equip for onsite use, Computers for patron use, Electronic databases & coll, Free DVD rentals, ILL available, Internet access, Online cat, Online info literacy tutorials on the web & in blackboard, Online ref, Orientations, OverDrive digital audio bks, Photocopying/Printing, Printer for laptops & handheld devices, Ref serv available, VHS videos, Wheelchair accessible
Partic in LYRASIS; OCLC Online Computer Library Center, Inc; Treasure State Academic Information & Library Services
Open Mon-Thurs 8-6, Fri 8-5
Restriction: Open to pub for ref & circ; with some limitations, Open to students, fac & staff

HERON

P LAURIE HILL LIBRARY*, PO Box 128, 59844-0128. SAN 376-7701. Tel: 406-847-2520.
Library Holdings: Bk Titles 8,000; Bk Vols 9,000
Wireless access
Open Wed 3-5:30, Thurs 11-1, Sat 11-3

HOT SPRINGS

P PRESTON TOWN-COUNTY LIBRARY OF HOT SPRINGS*, 203 E Main St, 59845. (Mail add: PO Box 850, 59845-0850), SAN 309-328X. Tel: 406-741-3491. E-mail: prestonhotspringslibrary@yahoo.com. Web Site: prestonhotspringslibrary.wordpress.com/. *Libr Dir,* Starla Rice
Founded 1963
Library Holdings: Bk Titles 12,313
Special Collections: Chinese-Herbal Therapy Coll; Montana & Western Coll. Oral History
Wireless access
Function: Wheelchair accessible
Open Tues & Wed 12-5, Thurs & Fri 12-4
Friends of the Library Group

JOLIET

P JOLIET PUBLIC LIBRARY*, 211 E Front Ave, 59041. (Mail add: PO Box 213, 59041-0213), SAN 376-785X. Tel: 406-962-3013. E-mail: jolietlib@yahoo.com. Web Site: mtsc.ent.sirsi.net/client/en_US/JOLIET. *Dir,* Alyson Green
Founded 2004
Wireless access

Open Tues-Fri 10-6, Sat 9-1
Friends of the Library Group

JORDAN

P GARFIELD COUNTY FREE LIBRARY, 208 Main St, 59337. (Mail add: PO Box 81, 59337), SAN 309-3298. Tel: 406-557-2297. E-mail: garfieldcountylibrary@gmail.com. Web Site: garflibr.wixsite.com/books. *Libr Dir,* Carrie Murnion
Founded 1948. Pop 1,589; Circ 7,000
Library Holdings: Bk Titles 10,261
Automation Activity & Vendor Info: (Acquisitions) Follett Software; (Cataloging) Follett Software; (Circulation) Follett Software; (Course Reserve) Follett Software; (ILL) Follett Software; (Media Booking) Follett Software; (OPAC) Follett Software; (Serials) Follett Software
Mem of Sagebrush Federation
Open Mon 10-4, Tues & Thurs 1-6, Wed 10-5, Fri 10-3

KALISPELL

J FLATHEAD VALLEY COMMUNITY COLLEGE LIBRARY*, 777 Grandview Dr, 59901. SAN 309-331X. Tel: 406-756-3856. Administration Tel: 406-756-3853. FAX: 406-756-3854. Web Site: www.fvcc.edu/p/library. *Dir, Libr Serv,* Susan H Matter; E-mail: smatter@fvcc.edu; *Acq, Tech Serv,* Carrie Nelson; Tel: 406-756-3855, E-mail: cnelson@fvcc.edu; *Circ, ILL,* Darrah Rogers; E-mail: drogers@fvcc.edu; Staff 3 (MLS 1, Non-MLS 2)
Founded 1967. Enrl 1,988; Fac 48; Highest Degree: Associate
Library Holdings: DVDs 1,109; e-books 2,700; Bk Titles 34,050; Bk Vols 39,990; Per Subs 138; Videos 1,721
Subject Interests: Allied health, Forestry, Indians of NAm, Montana hist, Tourism
Automation Activity & Vendor Info: (Acquisitions) Ex Libris Group; (Cataloging) Ex Libris Group; (Circulation) Ex Libris Group; (Course Reserve) Ex Libris Group; (Discovery) Ex Libris Group; (ILL) OCLC; (Media Booking) Ex Libris Group; (OPAC) Ex Libris Group; (Serials) Ex Libris Group
Wireless access
Function: 24/7 Electronic res, 24/7 Online cat, 3D Printer, Art exhibits, Audiobks via web, Bilingual assistance for Spanish patrons, Computer training, Computers for patron use, Electronic databases & coll, Free DVD rentals, ILL available, Instruction & testing, Internet access, Large print keyboards, Magazines, Magnifiers for reading, Mail & tel request accepted, Makerspace, Online cat, Online ref, Orientations, Outside serv via phone, mail, e-mail & web, Photocopying/Printing, Ref & res, Ref serv available, Study rm, Telephone ref, VHS videos, Wheelchair accessible
Partic in OCLC Online Computer Library Center, Inc; Treasure State Academic Information & Library Services
Special Services for the Blind - Braille equip; Scanner for conversion & translation of mats
Open Mon-Thurs 8-8, Fri 8-5, Sat & Sun 12-4:30

P IMAGINEIF LIBRARIES*, 247 First Ave E, 59901. SAN 350-0195. Tel: 406-758-5820. Circulation Tel: 406-758-5819. Interlibrary Loan Service Tel: 406-758-2446. Reference Tel: 406-758-5815. FAX: 406-758-5868. Web Site: imagineiflibraries.org. *Dir,* Connie Behe; Tel: 406-758-5826, E-mail: cbehe@imagineiflibraries.org; *Tech Coordr,* Sam Crompton; Staff 26 (MLS 4, Non-MLS 22)
Founded 1943. Pop 96,400; Circ 625,117
Library Holdings: AV Mats 6,750; e-books 4,521; Bk Vols 125,000; Per Subs 117
Automation Activity & Vendor Info: (Acquisitions) SirsiDynix; (Cataloging) SirsiDynix; (Circulation) SirsiDynix; (Media Booking) SirsiDynix; (OPAC) SirsiDynix; (Serials) SirsiDynix
Wireless access
Function: ILL available, Photocopying/Printing, Prog for children & young adult, Ref serv available, Summer reading prog, Telephone ref
Mem of Tamarack Federation of Libraries
Partic in OCLC Online Computer Library Center, Inc
Open Mon-Wed 10-8, Thurs & Fri 10-6, Sat 10-5
Friends of the Library Group
Branches: 3
BIGFORK BRANCH, 525 Electric Ave, Bigfork, 59911. Tel: 406-837-6976. *Br Mgr,* Deidre McMullin
Open Tues, Thurs & Sat 11-5, Wed 10-6, Fri 11-6
Friends of the Library Group
COLUMBIA FALLS BRANCH, 130 Sixth St W, # C, Columbia Falls, 59912, SAN 350-025X. Tel: 406-892-5919. FAX: 406-892-5919. *Br Mgr,* Tony Edmundson; Staff 4 (Non-MLS 4)
Open Mon & Thurs 10-6, Tues & Wed 10-7, Fri 12-6, Sat 12-4
Friends of the Library Group
MARION BRANCH, 205 Gopher Lane, Marion, 59925, SAN 323-8105. Tel: 406-854-2333. *Br Mgr,* Position Currently Open
Open Wed 3:30-5

M LOGAN HEALTH MEDICAL LIBRARY, (Formerly Kalispell Regional Medical Center), 310 Sunnyview Lane, 59901. SAN 309-3328. Tel: 406-752-1739. E-mail: medicallibrarian@logan.org. Web Site: www.logan.org. *Lead Med Librn,* Heidi Sue Adams; E-mail: hadams@logan.org; *PRN Med Librn,* Laurel Egan; E-mail: legan@logan.org; Staff 2 (MLS 2)
Founded 1976
Library Holdings: e-books 175; e-journals 4,000; Bk Titles 400; Per Subs 10
Subject Interests: Allied health, Med, Nursing
Automation Activity & Vendor Info: (Cataloging) SirsiDynix-WorkFlows; (Circulation) SirsiDynix-WorkFlows; (ILL) OCLC WorldShare Interlibrary Loan; (OPAC) SirsiDynix-Enterprise
Function: Online cat
Partic in National Network of Libraries of Medicine Region 4; OCLC Online Computer Library Center, Inc
Restriction: Authorized personnel only, Badge access after hrs, Closed stack, Med & health res only, Non-circulating, Not open to pub, Prof mat only, Secured area only open to authorized personnel

LAME DEER

J CHIEF DULL KNIFE COLLEGE*, Dr John Woodenlegs Memorial Library, One College Dr, 59043. (Mail add: PO Box 98, 59043-0098), SAN 321-8120. Tel: 406-477-8293. FAX: 406-477-6575. E-mail: library@cdkc.edu. Web Site: woodenlegslibrary.us. *Dir,* Jerusha Shipstead; E-mail: jshipstead@cdkc.edu; *Asst Librn, ILL,* Audrey Arpen; Staff 2 (MLS 1, Non-MLS 1)
Founded 1979. Enrl 405; Fac 18
Library Holdings: High Interest/Low Vocabulary Bk Vols 4,000; Bk Titles 22,000; Bk Vols 24,000; Per Subs 119; Spec Interest Per Sub 10
Special Collections: Local History; Native American Studies
Automation Activity & Vendor Info: (Acquisitions) SirsiDynix; (Cataloging) SirsiDynix; (Circulation) SirsiDynix; (Course Reserve) SirsiDynix; (ILL) SirsiDynix; (Media Booking) SirsiDynix; (OPAC) SirsiDynix; (Serials) SirsiDynix
Wireless access
Partic in Treasure State Academic Information & Library Services
Open Mon-Thurs 8-6, Fri (Winter) 8-4:30

LAUREL

P LAUREL PUBLIC LIBRARY*, 720 W Third St, 59044. SAN 309-3336. Tel: 406-628-4961. FAX: 406-628-9323. E-mail: laurelpl@mtlib.org, library@laurelpubliclibrary.org. Web Site: www.laurelpubliclibrary.org. *Libr Dir,* Nancy L Schmidt; E-mail: nschmidt@mtlib.org; Staff 3.4 (Non-MLS 3.4)
Founded 1916. Pop 6,718; Circ 38,910
Jul 2018-Jun 2019 Income $225,219, Locally Generated Income $216,232, Other $8,987. Mats Exp $39,890, Books $27,928, AV Mat $4,065, Electronic Ref Mat (Incl. Access Fees) $7,897. Sal $112,078
Library Holdings: Large Print Bks 620; Bk Vols 19,700; Per Subs 25; Talking Bks 300; Videos 770
Special Collections: Laurel High School yearbooks, digital content; Local History Coll (Laurel Outlook 1919-2000), microfilm
Automation Activity & Vendor Info: (Acquisitions) SirsiDynix; (Cataloging) SirsiDynix; (Circulation) SirsiDynix-WorkFlows; (OPAC) SirsiDynix-iBistro
Wireless access
Function: 24/7 Electronic res, Activity rm, Adult bk club, Archival coll, Art exhibits, Bk club(s), Bks on CD, Computer training, Computers for patron use, Free DVD rentals, ILL available, Internet access, Large print keyboards, Magazines, Mail & tel request accepted, Microfiche/film & reading machines, Movies, Music CDs, Online cat, OverDrive digital audio bks, Photocopying/Printing, Prog for children & young adult, Ref & res, Scanner, Story hour, Tax forms, Wheelchair accessible
Mem of South Central Federation
Special Services for the Deaf - ADA equip; Bks on deafness & sign lang
Special Services for the Blind - Accessible computers; Bks on cassette; Bks on CD; Braille alphabet card; Large print bks; Low vision equip; Screen reader software; ZoomText magnification & reading software
Open Mon-Thurs 9-7:30, Sat 9-3

P SOUTH CENTRAL FEDERATION, 720 W Third St, 59044. Tel: 406-628-4961. FAX: 406-628-9323. *Coordr,* Nancy Schmidt; Staff 4 (Non-MLS 4)
Founded 1916. Pop 6,715
Wireless access
Function: 24/7 Electronic res, 24/7 Online cat, 3D Printer, Activity rm, Adult bk club, Archival coll, Art exhibits, Audiobks via web, Bk club(s), Bks on CD, CD-ROM, Children's prog, Computer training, Computers for patron use, Digital talking bks, E-Readers, Electronic databases & coll, For res purposes, Free DVD rentals, Holiday prog, ILL available, Instruction & testing, Internet access, Large print keyboards, Magazines, Magnifiers for reading, Mail & tel request accepted, Meeting rooms, Microfiche/film &

reading machines, Movies, Music CDs, Online cat, OverDrive digital audio bks, Photocopying/Printing, Printer for laptops & handheld devices, Prog for adults, Prog for children & young adult, Ref & res, Res assist avail, Scanner, Story hour, Summer & winter reading prog, Summer reading prog, Tax forms, Telephone ref, Wheelchair accessible
Member Libraries: Bridger Public Library; Denton Public Library; Laurel Public Library; Lewistown Public Library; Moore Public Library; Rosebud County Library; Roundup Community Library
Open Mon-Thurs 9-7, Sat 9-3

LEWISTOWN

P LEWISTOWN PUBLIC LIBRARY*, 701 W Main St, 59457. SAN 309-3344. Tel: 406-538-5212. FAX: 406-538-3920. E-mail: library@lewistownlibrary.org, lpldirector@lewistownlibrary.org. Web Site: lewistownlibrary.org. *Dir,* Dani Buehler; E-mail: danib@lewistownlibrary.org; *Circ Librn, Pub Serv Librn,* Kari Albertson-Denison; E-mail: kari@lewistownlibrary.org; *Local Hist Librn,* Nancy Watts; E-mail: nancyw@lewistownlibrary.org; *Outreach Serv Librn,* Nancy Sackett; E-mail: bkloner@lewistownlibrary.org; Staff 5 (MLS 1, Non-MLS 4)
Founded 1905. Pop 11,080; Circ 88,925
Library Holdings: Bks on Deafness & Sign Lang 10; CDs 150; DVDs 30; Electronic Media & Resources 20; Large Print Bks 1,500; Bk Titles 36,000; Bk Vols 38,500; Per Subs 54; Talking Bks 1,500; Videos 250
Special Collections: Local Historic Photographs. Oral History
Subject Interests: Local hist, Montana
Automation Activity & Vendor Info: (Acquisitions) SirsiDynix-WorkFlows; (Cataloging) SirsiDynix; (Circulation) SirsiDynix; (ILL) OCLC; (Media Booking) SirsiDynix-WorkFlows; (OPAC) SirsiDynix-iBistro
Wireless access
Function: After school storytime, Archival coll, Audio & video playback equip for onsite use, Audiobks via web, AV serv, Bks on cassette, Bks on CD, CD-ROM, Children's prog, Computer training, Computers for patron use, Digital talking bks, E-Reserves, Electronic databases & coll, Free DVD rentals, Genealogy discussion group, Govt ref serv, Home delivery & serv to seniorr ctr & nursing homes, ILL available, Internet access, Learning ctr, Magnifiers for reading, Mail & tel request accepted, Mail loans to mem, Music CDs, Online cat, Online ref, Outside serv via phone, mail, e-mail & web, OverDrive digital audio bks, Photocopying/Printing, Preschool outreach, Prog for adults, Prog for children & young adult, Ref & res, Ref serv available, Senior computer classes, Senior outreach, Serves people with intellectual disabilities, Spoken cassettes & CDs, Spoken cassettes & DVDs, Story hour, Summer reading prog, Tax forms, Teen prog, Telephone ref, VHS videos, Wheelchair accessible
Mem of South Central Federation
Special Services for the Blind - Talking bks & player equip
Open Tues-Fri 9-6, Sat 10-2
Friends of the Library Group

LIBBY

P LINCOLN COUNTY PUBLIC LIBRARIES*, 220 W Sixth St, 59923-1898. SAN 350-0403. Tel: 406-293-2778. FAX: 406-293-4235. E-mail: library@lincolncountylibraries.com. Web Site: www.lincolncountylibraries.com. *Dir,* Alyssa Ramirez; E-mail: aramirez@lincolncountylibraries.com; *Circ, Youth Serv,* Dustina Deans; E-mail: ddeans@lincolncountylibraries.com
Founded 1920. Pop 19,000; Circ 79,401
Library Holdings: Bk Titles 45,000; Per Subs 125
Automation Activity & Vendor Info: (Acquisitions) AmLib Library Management System; (Cataloging) AmLib Library Management System; (Circulation) AmLib Library Management System; (Course Reserve) AmLib Library Management System; (ILL) AmLib Library Management System; (OPAC) AmLib Library Management System; (Serials) AmLib Library Management System
Wireless access
Publications: Library Journal
Mem of Tamarack Federation of Libraries
Open Mon-Fri 9-5, Sat 10-2
Friends of the Library Group
Branches: 2
EUREKA BRANCH, 318 Dewey Ave, Eureka, 59917. (Mail add: PO Box 401, Eureka, 59917-0401), SAN 350-0438. Tel: 406-296-2613. FAX: 406-296-2613. *Librn,* Esther Brandt; E-mail: ebrandt@lincolncountylibraries.com; Staff 2 (Non-MLS 2)
Library Holdings: Bk Vols 7,000; Per Subs 35
Open Tues-Fri 11-5, Sat 11-2
Friends of the Library Group
TROY BRANCH, Third & Kalispell Ave, Troy, 59935. (Mail add: PO Box 430, Troy, 59935-0430), SAN 350-0462. Tel: 406-295-4040. FAX: 406-295-4040. *Librn,* Stacy Walenter
Open Tues-Fri (Winter) 11-6, Sat 11-1; Tues & Thurs (Summer) 11-6, Wed 1-6, Sat 11-1
Friends of the Library Group

LIVINGSTON

S FLY FISHERS INTERNATIONAL, Learning Center, (Formerly International Federation of Flyfishers), 5237 US Hwy 89 S, Ste 11, 59047. SAN 374-8227. Tel: 406-222-9369. FAX: 406-222-5823. E-mail: museum@flyfishersinternational.org. Web Site: flyfishersinternational.org. *Operations Mgr, VPres,* Rhonda Sellers; Tel: 406-222-9369, Ext 4, E-mail: operations@flyfishersinternational.org
Founded 1983
Library Holdings: AV Mats 200; Bk Titles 1,500; Bk Vols 2,500; Per Subs 15; Spec Interest Per Sub 15
Subject Interests: Fly fishing
Function: Ref & res, Res libr
Open Mon-Fri 9-5

P LIVINGSTON-PARK COUNTY PUBLIC LIBRARY*, 228 W Callender St, 59047. SAN 309-3379. Tel: 406-222-0862. FAX: 406-222-6522. E-mail: info.lpcpl@mtlib.org. Web Site: livingstonparkcountylibrary.blogspot.com. *Libr Dir,* Mitch Grady; Staff 6.4 (MLS 2, Non-MLS 4.4)
Founded 1901. Circ 93,600
Library Holdings: AV Mats 3,309; Bk Titles 49,771; Bk Vols 53,000; Per Subs 239
Special Collections: Fly Fishing Coll; Montana Coll
Automation Activity & Vendor Info: (Cataloging) OCLC Connexion; (Circulation) Follett Software; (ILL) OCLC WorldShare Interlibrary Loan; (OPAC) Follett Software
Wireless access
Function: After school storytime, Audio & video playback equip for onsite use, CD-ROM, Computer training, ILL available, Mail & tel request accepted, Music CDs, Online ref, Photocopying/Printing, Preschool outreach, Prog for adults, Prog for children & young adult, Ref serv available, Summer reading prog, Tax forms, Telephone ref, VHS videos, Wheelchair accessible
Open Mon & Tues 12-8, Wed & Thurs 10-8, Fri 10-6, Sat 10-5
Friends of the Library Group

MALMSTROM AFB

A UNITED STATES AIR FORCE*, Arden G Hill Memorial Library Malmstrom Air Force Base FL4626, Bldg 1152, 7356 Fourth Ave N, 59402-7506. SAN 350-0497. Tel: 406-731-4638. Administration Tel: 406-731-2748. FAX: 406-731-3667. Web Site: www.341fss.com/library-military-resources. *Librn,* Linda Paronto; E-mail: linda.paronto.1@us.af.mil; Staff 4 (MLS 1, Non-MLS 3)
Founded 1953
Library Holdings: Bk Vols 31,000; Per Subs 125
Automation Activity & Vendor Info: (Acquisitions) Softlink America; (Cataloging) Softlink America; (Circulation) Softlink America; (Course Reserve) Softlink America; (ILL) Softlink America; (Media Booking) Softlink America; (Serials) Softlink America
Wireless access
Publications: Bulletin (Monthly)
Partic in OCLC Online Computer Library Center, Inc; Proquest Dialog
Open Mon-Thurs 9-5:30, Fri 9-5, Sat 12-4

MALTA

P PHILLIPS COUNTY LIBRARY*, 10 S Fourth St E, 59538. (Mail add: PO Box 840, 59538-0840), SAN 350-0527. Tel: 406-654-2407. FAX: 406-654-2407. E-mail: philibr@itstriangle.com. *Dir,* Janeen Brookie; *Libr Asst,* Michelle Mitchell; *Libr Asst,* Sarah Osmundson; *Libr Asst,* Halle Williamson; Staff 3 (Non-MLS 3)
Founded 1917. Pop 4,100
Library Holdings: Bk Titles 23,000
Wireless access
Mem of Golden Plains Library Federation
Open Mon-Thurs 10-12 & 1-6, Fri 10-12 & 1-5, Sat 10-2 (Sept-May)
Branches: 2
DODSON BRANCH, 121 Second St E, Dodson, 59524, SAN 350-0551. *Librn,* Halle Williamson
Open Tues 1-6
SACO BRANCH, 201 B Taylor St, Saco, 59261. (Mail add: PO Box 74, Saco, 59261), SAN 350-0586. *Librn,* Esther Brosseau
Open Tues & Sat 2-4:30

MANHATTAN

P MANHATTAN COMMUNITY LIBRARY*, 200 W Fulton Ave, 59741. (Mail add: PO Box 9, 59741), SAN 309-3395. Tel: 406-284-3341, Ext 222. Web Site: www.manhattancommunitylibrary.com. *Dir,* Kari Eliason; E-mail: keliason@mhstigers.org
Pop 2,500; Circ 10,400
Library Holdings: Large Print Bks 324; Bk Titles 10,800; Bk Vols 11,200; Per Subs 36; Talking Bks 212
Automation Activity & Vendor Info: (Cataloging) Follett Software; (Circulation) Follett Software; (OPAC) Follett Software
Wireless access
Mem of Broad Valleys Federation of Libraries
Open Mon-Thurs 1-7, Fri 1-6, Sat 10-3

MILES CITY

P MILES CITY PUBLIC LIBRARY*, One S Tenth St, 59301. SAN 309-3409. Tel: 406-234-1496. FAX: 406-234-2095. E-mail: mcpl@midrivers.com. Web Site: milescitypubliclibrary.org. *Dir,* Sonja A Woods; *Cataloger,* Michelle Cunningham; *Ch Serv,* Hannah Nash; *Hist Archivist,* Jean Nielsen; *ILL,* Gloria Archdale; Staff 5 (MLS 1, Non-MLS 4)
Founded 1902. Pop 12,000
Library Holdings: Bk Titles 47,000; Bk Vols 60,000; Per Subs 25
Subject Interests: Montana, State hist
Automation Activity & Vendor Info: (Circulation) SirsiDynix; (ILL) OCLC; (OPAC) SirsiDynix
Wireless access
Function: Doc delivery serv, ILL available, Internet access, Photocopying/Printing, Prog for children & young adult, Summer reading prog, Telephone ref, Wheelchair accessible
Open Tues-Fri 10-6, Sat 9-5
Friends of the Library Group

J MILES COMMUNITY COLLEGE*, Judson H Flower Jr Library, 2715 Dickinson, 59301. SAN 309-3417. Tel: 406-874-6105. Toll Free Tel: 800-541-9281. FAX: 406-874-6282. E-mail: library@milescc.edu. Web Site: www.milescc.edu/campusservices/library. *Libr Dir,* Jerusha Shipstead; E-mail: shipsteadJ@milescc.edu
Library Holdings: Bk Vols 15,000; Per Subs 275
Partic in Treasure State Academic Information & Library Services
Open Mon-Thurs 8:15-7, Fri 8:15-5

S MONTANA DEPARTMENT OF CORRECTIONS*, Pine Hills Youth Correctional Facility, Four N Haynes Ave, 59301. SAN 375-314X. Tel: 406-232-1377, 406-233-2230. FAX: 406-233-2204. Web Site: cor.mt.gov/Youth/pinehills. *Librn,* Lana Seagren; E-mail: lseagren@mt.gov
Library Holdings: Bk Titles 7,500
Special Collections: Native American Coll, bks & videos
Restriction: Not open to pub

P SAGEBRUSH FEDERATION*, One S Tenth St, 59301-3398. Tel: 406-234-1496. E-mail: mcpl@midrivers.com. *Coordr,* Sonja Woods
Wireless access
Member Libraries: Fallon County Library; Garfield County Free Library; George McCone Memorial County Library; Glendive Public Library; Henry A Malley Memorial Library; Prairie County Library; Sidney Public Library; Wibaux Public Library
Open Tues-Fri 10-6, Sat 9-5

MISSOULA

M THE LEARNING CENTER*, Medical Library, 500 W Broadway, 59802. SAN 309-3441. Tel: 406-329-5710. FAX: 406-329-5688. E-mail: library@saintpatrick.org. Web Site: montana.providence.org/health-resources/the-learning-center. *Med Librn,* Dana Kopp; Tel: 406-329-5711, E-mail: Dana.Kopp@providence.org; *Libr Tech,* Amanda Steinvall; Tel: 406-329-5712, E-mail: Amanda.Steinvall@providence.org; Staff 2 (MLS 1, Non-MLS 1)
Founded 1946
Library Holdings: Audiobooks 30; AV Mats 50; CDs 50; DVDs 25; e-books 1,200; e-journals 3,500; Electronic Media & Resources 200; Bk Titles 2,500
Special Collections: Consumer Health & Nursing Coll; Death, Dying & Grieving Coll; General Hospital Leadership (LEAD Coll); Medical Humanities & Ethics (Ridge Coll)
Subject Interests: Admin, Consumer health, Nursing
Automation Activity & Vendor Info: (Acquisitions) Ex Libris Group; (Cataloging) Ex Libris Group; (Circulation) Ex Libris Group; (Course Reserve) Ex Libris Group; (Media Booking) Ex Libris Group; (OPAC) Ex Libris Group; (Serials) EBSCO Online
Wireless access
Partic in Consortium of Acad & Spec Libr in Mont
Open Mon-Fri 8-4:30

P MISSOULA PUBLIC LIBRARY*, 301 E Main, 59802-4799. SAN 350-0616. Tel: 406-721-2665. FAX: 406-728-5900. E-mail: mslaplib@missoula.lib.mt.us. Web Site: www.missoulapubliclibrary.org. *Dir,* Honore Bray; E-mail: hbray@missoula.lib.mt.us; *Asst Dir,* Elizabeth Jonkel; E-mail: ejonkel@missoula.lib.mt.us; *Cat Librn,* Paulette Parpart; E-mail: parpart@missoula.lib.mt.us; *Ch,* Pam Carlton; *ILL/Ref Librn,* Annie Alger; *Ser Librn,* Lyndy Parke; *YA Librn,* Linette Greene; Staff 32 (MLS 3, Non-MLS 29)
Founded 1894. Pop 99,000; Circ 802,216
Library Holdings: Audiobooks 2,215; AV Mats 133; CDs 11,215; DVDs 7,224; e-books 2,524; Large Print Bks 3,206; Bk Titles 210,234; Bk Vols 236,714; Per Subs 571; Videos 3,242
Special Collections: Montana Hist Coll; Northwest Hist Coll, bks, docs. State Document Depository
Automation Activity & Vendor Info: (Acquisitions) SirsiDynix; (Cataloging) SirsiDynix; (Circulation) SirsiDynix
Wireless access
Function: Home delivery & serv to seniorr ctr & nursing homes, Homebound delivery serv, ILL available, Internet access, Photocopying/Printing, Prog for adults, Prog for children & young adult, Ref serv available, Summer reading prog, Telephone ref, Wheelchair accessible
Special Services for the Deaf - Assistive tech
Open Mon-Wed 10-9, Thurs-Sat 10-6, Sun 1-5
Friends of the Library Group
Branches: 6
BIG SKY BRANCH, Big Sky High School, 3100 South Ave W, 59804. Tel: 406-728-2400, Ext 8605. *Library Contact,* Joleen Jin; E-mail: joleenj@missoula.lib.mt.us
Open Mon-Wed 3:30-7:30, Thurs 2:30-6:30
FRENCHTOWN BRANCH, Frenchtown High School - School/Community Library, 17620 Frontage Rd, Frenchtown, 59834. (Mail add: Frenchtown High School, PO Box 117, Frenchtown, 59834). Tel: 406-626-2730. *Library Contact,* Jane Guest; E-mail: jlguest@missoula.lib.mt.us
Open Mon-Thurs 4:30-8
LOLO BRANCH, Lolo School/Community Library, 11395 Hwy 93 S, Lolo, 59847. Tel: 406-273-0451, Ext 211. *Library Contact,* Erin Casey; E-mail: ecasey@missoula.lib.mt.us
Open Mon-Thurs 4-8:15
POTOMAC BRANCH, Potomac School District II, 29750 Potomac Rd, Potomac, 59823. Tel: 406-244-5581, Ext 227. *Library Contact,* Kirk Vriesman; E-mail: kirkv@missoula.lib.mt.us
Open Wed 1-4
SEELEY LAKE COMMUNITY, 456 Airport Rd, Seeley Lake, 59868. (Mail add: PO Box 416, Seeley Lake, 59868-0416), SAN 329-5575. Tel: 406-677-8995. FAX: 406-677-2949. *Librn,* Sue Stone; E-mail: sstone@missoula.lib.mt.us
Open Tues & Thurs 10:30-4, Wed 10:30-6
Friends of the Library Group
SWAN VALLEY COMMUNITY, 6811 Hwy 83, Condon, 59826. (Mail add: PO Box 1165, Condon, 59826), SAN 350-0691. Tel: 406-754-2521. *Librn,* Colleen Kesterson; E-mail: Colleenk@missoula.lib.mt.us; Staff 1 (Non-MLS 1)
Founded 1988
Library Holdings: Audiobooks 30; CDs 20; DVDs 50; Large Print Bks 30; Bk Titles 5,000; Videos 300
Open Mon & Fri 10-4, Wed 11-4:30
Bookmobiles: 1. Contact, Kirk Vriesman

P TAMARACK FEDERATION OF LIBRARIES*, 455 E Main, 59802. Tel: 406-721-2665. FAX: 406-258-0500. *Coordr,* Honore Bray; E-mail: hbray@missoula.lib.mt.us
Wireless access
Member Libraries: Bitterroot Public Library; Darby Community Public Library; ImagineIF Libraries; Lincoln County Public Libraries; Mineral County Public Library; Plains Public Library District; Polson City Library; Ronan Library District; Swan Lake Public Library

CL UNIVERSITY OF MONTANA*, William J Jameson Law Library, 32 Campus Dr, 59812. SAN 350-073X. Tel: 406-243-2699. Web Site: www.umt.edu/law/library. *Dir,* Stacey Gordon; Tel: 406-243-6808, E-mail: stacey.gordon@umontana.edu; Staff 5 (MLS 3, Non-MLS 2)
Founded 1911. Enrl 226; Fac 17; Highest Degree: Doctorate
Library Holdings: Bk Titles 20,000; Per Subs 1,795
Special Collections: Indian Law, bks & micro
Automation Activity & Vendor Info: (Acquisitions) Ex Libris Group; (Cataloging) Ex Libris Group; (Circulation) Ex Libris Group; (Course Reserve) Ex Libris Group; (ILL) Ex Libris Group; (Media Booking) Ex Libris Group; (OPAC) Ex Libris Group; (Serials) Ex Libris Group
Partic in Treasure State Academic Information & Library Services
Open Mon-Thurs 7:30am-9pm, Fri 7:30-5, Sat 8:30-5, Sun 12-5

C UNIVERSITY OF MONTANA MISSOULA, Maureen & Mike Mansfield Library, 32 Campus Dr, 59812-4968. Tel: 406-243-4072, 406-243-6866. FAX: 406-243-6864. Web Site: www.lib.umt.edu. *Dean of Libr,* Barry Brown
Library Holdings: Bk Titles 1,000,000; Bk Vols 1,500,000
Automation Activity & Vendor Info: (Acquisitions) Ex Libris Group; (Cataloging) Ex Libris Group; (Circulation) Ex Libris Group; (Course Reserve) Ex Libris Group; (ILL) Ex Libris Group; (Media Booking) Ex Libris Group; (OPAC) Ex Libris Group; (Serials) Ex Libris Group
Partic in Treasure State Academic Information & Library Services

MOORE

P MOORE PUBLIC LIBRARY*, 403 Fergus Ave, 59464. (Mail add: PO Box 125, 59464-0125), SAN 309-3476. Tel: 406-374-2364. FAX: 406-374-2364. E-mail: moorelib2002@gmail.com. *Dir,* Sunny De Long; Staff 1 (MLS 1)
Founded 1918. Pop 212; Circ 2,739
Library Holdings: AV Mats 211; Large Print Bks 140; Bk Titles 7,621; Talking Bks 40
Wireless access
Function: Home delivery & serv to seniorr ctr & nursing homes, Homebound delivery serv, ILL available, Magnifiers for reading, Photocopying/Printing, Prog for children & young adult, Summer reading prog, Wheelchair accessible
Mem of South Central Federation
Open Tues-Thurs 12-5

OPHEIM

P OPHEIM COMMUNITY LIBRARY*, 100 Rock St, 59250. (Mail add: PO Box 108, 59250-0108), SAN 376-7876. Tel: 406-762-3213. FAX: 406-762-3348. Web Site: sites.google.com/site/opheimschool/library. *Librn,* Nikki Taylor; E-mail: ntaylor@ohsvikings.org
Library Holdings: Bk Titles 9,000; Bk Vols 10,000; Per Subs 35
Automation Activity & Vendor Info: (Acquisitions) Follett Software; (Cataloging) Follett Software; (Circulation) Follett Software; (Course Reserve) Follett Software; (ILL) Follett Software; (Media Booking) Follett Software; (OPAC) Follett Software; (Serials) Follett Software
Mem of Golden Plains Library Federation
Open Mon & Fri 9-Noon, Tues & Thurs 10-Noon
Friends of the Library Group

PABLO

C SALISH KOOTENAI COLLEGE*, D'Arcy McNickle Library, PO Box 70, 59855. SAN 373-6326. Tel: 406-275-4875. FAX: 406-275-4812. Web Site: library.skc.edu. *Libr Dir,* Fred Noel; Tel: 406-275-4873, E-mail: fred_noel@skc.edu; *Instruction & Outreach Librn,* Jani Costilla; Tel: 406-275-4874, E-mail: jani_costilla@skc.edu; *ILL,* Jamie Shepard; Tel: 406-275-4876, E-mail: jamie_shepard@skc.edu; Staff 5 (MLS 3, Non-MLS 2)
Founded 1979. Enrl 954; Fac 56; Highest Degree: Bachelor
Library Holdings: Bk Vols 47,000; Per Subs 200
Special Collections: Confederated Salish & Kootenai Tribal History
Subject Interests: Environ studies, Native Am studies, Nursing
Automation Activity & Vendor Info: (Acquisitions) Ex Libris Group; (Cataloging) Ex Libris Group; (Circulation) Ex Libris Group; (Course Reserve) Docutek; (ILL) OCLC; (OPAC) Ex Libris Group; (Serials) Ex Libris Group
Wireless access
Partic in Treasure State Academic Information & Library Services
Open Mon-Thurs 7:30am-8pm, Fri 7:30-4:30, Sat 10-4:30

PHILIPSBURG

P PHILIPSBURG PUBLIC LIBRARY, 106 W Broadway St, 59858. (Mail add: PO Box 797, 59858-0797), SAN 321-7817. Tel: 406-859-5030. E-mail: phl5030@blackfoot.net. Web Site: pburglibrary.org. *Dir,* Gina Vale
Pop 1,680; Circ 3,485
Library Holdings: Bk Vols 4,500
Wireless access
Mem of Broad Valleys Federation of Libraries
Open Mon, Thurs & Fri 12-5, Tues 9-5, Wed 12-7, Sat 12-4
Friends of the Library Group

PLAINS

P PLAINS PUBLIC LIBRARY DISTRICT*, 108 W Railroad, 59859. (Mail add: PO Box 399, 59859-0399), SAN 309-3484. Tel: 406-826-3101. FAX: 406-826-3101. Web Site: www.plainslibrary.org. *Dir,* Carrie M Terrell; E-mail: cterrell@mtlib.org; Staff 3 (Non-MLS 3)
Founded 1918. Pop 3,801; Circ 30,000
Library Holdings: Bk Titles 14,000; Bk Vols 15,000; Per Subs 42
Special Collections: Montana Coll
Automation Activity & Vendor Info: (Acquisitions) SirsiDynix; (Cataloging) SirsiDynix; (Circulation) SirsiDynix; (ILL) SirsiDynix; (OPAC) SirsiDynix
Wireless access
Mem of Tamarack Federation of Libraries
Open Mon & Tues 11-6, Wed & Thurs 12-7, Sat 10-12; Mon & Tues (Summer) 11-7, Wed & Thurs 12-7
Friends of the Library Group

PLENTYWOOD

P GOLDEN PLAINS LIBRARY FEDERATION, 100 W Laurel Ave, 59254. SAN 309-3069. Tel: 406-765-3510. FAX: 406-765-3586. *Coordr,* Jonna Underwood; Tel: 406-765-3463, E-mail: junderwood@co.sheridan.mt.us
Automation Activity & Vendor Info: (Cataloging) OCLC; (Circulation) SirsiDynix-Enterprise
Wireless access
Member Libraries: Daniels County Free Library; Fort Peck Community College Library; Glasgow City-County Library; Opheim Community Library; Phillips County Library; Roosevelt County Library; Sheridan County Library

P SHERIDAN COUNTY LIBRARY*, 100 W Laurel Ave, 59254. SAN 309-3492. Tel: 406-765-3510. FAX: 406-765-3586. E-mail: library@co.sheridan.mt.us. Web Site: www.shercolibrary.org. *Dir,* Jonna Underwood; E-mail: junderwood@co.sheridan.mt.us; Staff 2 (Non-MLS 2)
Founded 1914. Pop 3,524; Circ 23,066
Library Holdings: AV Mats 1,728; Large Print Bks 816; Bk Titles 34,802; Bk Vols 36,485; Per Subs 63
Special Collections: Local Newspapers on Microfilm; Sheet Music Coll
Wireless access
Mem of Golden Plains Library Federation
Open Mon-Fri 9-5

POLSON

P POLSON CITY LIBRARY*, Two First Ave E, 59860. (Mail add: PO Box 820, 59860-0820), SAN 309-3506. Tel: 406-883-8225. FAX: 406-883-8239. E-mail: polsoncl@polson.lib.mt.us. Web Site: northlakecountylibrary.org. *Dir,* Abbi Dooley; E-mail: abbid@polson.lib.mt.us
Founded 1910. Pop 15,000; Circ 62,619
Library Holdings: Bk Vols 45,000; Per Subs 35
Automation Activity & Vendor Info: (Cataloging) SirsiDynix; (Circulation) SirsiDynix
Wireless access
Mem of Tamarack Federation of Libraries
Open Mon-Thurs 10-7, Fri 10-6, Sat 10-4; Mon-Fri 10-1 & 3-5, Wed & Fri 9am-10pm (Summer)
Friends of the Library Group

POPLAR

J FORT PECK COMMUNITY COLLEGE LIBRARY*, James E Shanley Tribal Library, 604 Assiniboine Ave, 59255. (Mail add: PO Box 398, 59255-0398), SAN 326-7032. Tel: 406-768-6340. Toll Free Tel: 866-650-5148. FAX: 406-768-6303. Web Site: fpcc.edu/library. *Dir,* Anita A Scheetz; E-mail: Ascheetz@fpcc.edu; Staff 2 (MLS 1, Non-MLS 1)
Founded 1981. Enrl 350; Fac 20; Highest Degree: Associate
Library Holdings: DVDs 1,200; Bk Titles 11,000; Per Subs 100; Spec Interest Per Sub 25
Special Collections: Fort Peck Assiniboine
Subject Interests: Native Am, Western Americana
Automation Activity & Vendor Info: (Acquisitions) Follett Software; (Cataloging) SirsiDynix-WorkFlows; (Circulation) SirsiDynix-WorkFlows; (Course Reserve) SirsiDynix-WorkFlows; (ILL) OCLC FirstSearch; (Media Booking) SirsiDynix-WorkFlows; (OPAC) SirsiDynix-WorkFlows; (Serials) SirsiDynix-WorkFlows
Wireless access
Function: 24/7 Electronic res, 24/7 Online cat, Adult bk club, ILL available
Mem of Golden Plains Library Federation
Partic in Treasure State Academic Information & Library Services
Open Mon-Thurs 8-5, Fri 8-3

RED LODGE

P RED LODGE CARNEGIE LIBRARY*, Three W Eighth St, 59068. (Mail add: PO Box 1068, 59068-1068), SAN 309-3514. Tel: 406-446-1905. E-mail: rlibrary@bresnan.net. Web Site: cityofredlodge.net/library. *Libr Dir,* Jodie Moore; Staff 1.5 (MLS 1, Non-MLS 0.5)
Founded 1915. Pop 5,000; Circ 21,910
Jul 2016-Jun 2017 Income $155,381, State $3,654, City $44,795, County $105,832, Other $1,100. Mats Exp $49,680, Books $34,670, Per/Ser (Incl. Access Fees) $22, AV Mat $14,988. Sal $90,723

Library Holdings: Audiobooks 823; Bks on Deafness & Sign Lang 12; DVDs 423; High Interest/Low Vocabulary Bk Vols 450; Large Print Bks 162; Bk Titles 14,252; Bk Vols 14,539; Per Subs 26; Videos 865
Automation Activity & Vendor Info: (Acquisitions) SirsiDynix; (Cataloging) SirsiDynix; (Circulation) SirsiDynix; (ILL) OCLC WorldShare Interlibrary Loan; (OPAC) SirsiDynix
Wireless access
Function: Audiobks via web, Bks on cassette, Bks on CD, Children's prog, Computers for patron use, Electronic databases & coll, Free DVD rentals, ILL available, Internet access, Life-long learning prog for all ages, Magazines, Movies, Online cat, Outreach serv, Outside serv via phone, mail, e-mail & web, OverDrive digital audio bks, Photocopying/Printing, Preschool outreach, Preschool reading prog, Printer for laptops & handheld devices, Prog for adults, Prog for children & young adult, Ref & res, Ref serv available, Scanner, Summer reading prog, Spoken cassettes & CDs, Story hour, Summer & winter reading prog, Tax forms, Telephone ref, VHS videos, Wheelchair accessible, Winter reading prog
Open Tues-Fri 10-6, Sat 12-6
Friends of the Library Group

RONAN

P RONAN LIBRARY DISTRICT*, 203 Main St SW, 59864. SAN 309-3522. Tel: 406-676-3682. FAX: 406-676-3683. E-mail: ronanlibrarydistrict@gmail.com. Web Site: ronanlibrary.org. *Dir,* Michelle Fenger; *Technology Spec,* Dylan Carey; E-mail: ronanlibrarytech@gmail.com; Staff 2 (MLS 1, Non-MLS 1)
Founded 1923. Pop 8,645; Circ 31,379
Library Holdings: Audiobooks 855; DVDs 481; Large Print Bks 664; Per Subs 7; Videos 691
Special Collections: Montana Coll
Automation Activity & Vendor Info: (Acquisitions) Follett Software; (Cataloging) Follett Software; (Circulation) Follett Software; (Course Reserve) Follett Software; (ILL) Follett Software; (OPAC) Follett Software; (Serials) Follett Software
Wireless access
Function: Bks on cassette, Bks on CD, Children's prog, Computers for patron use, Family literacy, Free DVD rentals, ILL available, Photocopying/Printing, Prog for adults, Prog for children & young adult, Scanner, Story hour, Summer & winter reading prog, Summer reading prog, Tax forms, Telephone ref
Mem of Tamarack Federation of Libraries
Partic in Mont Libr Asn
Open Mon-Fri 10-7, Sat 10-5
Friends of the Library Group

ROUNDUP

P ROUNDUP COMMUNITY LIBRARY, 526 Sixth Ave W, 59072. SAN 309-3530. Tel: 406-323-1802. FAX: 406-323-1346. E-mail: rounduplibrary@roundup.k12.mt.us. *Dir,* Sandy Larson; Staff 1 (MLS 1)
Founded 1931. Pop 4,106; Circ 15,000
Library Holdings: Bk Vols 22,000; Per Subs 30
Automation Activity & Vendor Info: (Cataloging) SirsiDynix; (Circulation) SirsiDynix; (ILL) OCLC FirstSearch; (OPAC) SirsiDynix-iBistro
Wireless access
Mem of South Central Federation
Open Mon & Fri (Winter) 8-4, Tues & Thurs 8-8, Wed 8-5, Sat 10-2; Tues & Thurs (Summer) 4-8, Wed, Fri & Sat 10-2
Friends of the Library Group

SCOBEY

P DANIELS COUNTY FREE LIBRARY*, 203 Timmons St, 59263. (Mail add: PO Box 190, 59263-0190), SAN 309-3557. Tel: 406-487-5502. FAX: 406-487-5502. *Librn,* Valerie Landeraaer
Founded 1946. Pop 2,000; Circ 23,286
Library Holdings: Bk Vols 20,000; Per Subs 35
Automation Activity & Vendor Info: (Acquisitions) Follett Software; (Cataloging) Follett Software; (Circulation) Follett Software; (Course Reserve) Follett Software; (ILL) Follett Software; (Media Booking) Follett Software; (OPAC) Follett Software; (Serials) Follett Software
Wireless access
Mem of Golden Plains Library Federation
Open Mon-Fri 8-6, Sat 8-2
Friends of the Library Group

SHELBY

P TOOLE COUNTY LIBRARY*, 229 Second Ave S, 59474. SAN 350-0764. Tel: 406-424-8345. FAX: 406-424-8346. E-mail: toolelib@yahoo.com. Web Site: toolecountylibrary.com. *Dir,* Heidi Alford
Founded 1948. Pop 5,046; Circ 19,000
Library Holdings: Bk Titles 20,000; Per Subs 30
Special Collections: Montana Indian Coll
Automation Activity & Vendor Info: (Cataloging) Follett Software; (Circulation) Follett Software
Wireless access
Open Mon, Wed & Thurs 1-5 & 7-9, Tues 10-5 & 7-9, Fri 10-12 & 1-5, Sat 1-4
Friends of the Library Group
Branches: 1
SUNBURST BRANCH, 105 First St N, Sunburst, 59482. (Mail add: PO Box 158, Sunburst, 59482), SAN 350-0799. Tel: 406-937-6980. FAX: 406-937-6980. *Librn,* Mary Jo Aschim; E-mail: aschim@northerntel.net
Library Holdings: Bk Titles 8,000
Open Mon 12-7:30, Wed 10-5:30, Fri 10-3

SHERIDAN

P SHERIDAN PUBLIC LIBRARY*, 109 E Hamilton St, 59749. (Mail add: PO Box 107, 59749-0107), SAN 309-3565. Tel: 406-842-5770. FAX: 406-842-5770. E-mail: sheridanlibrary@gmail.com. Web Site: sites.google.com/site/sheridanlibrary. *Libr Dir,* William Talbott
Founded 1902. Pop 1,005; Circ 11,491
Library Holdings: AV Mats 24; Bk Vols 12,300; Per Subs 3
Special Collections: Montana Authors Coll
Wireless access
Mem of Broad Valleys Federation of Libraries
Open Tues 9-5, Wed 10-7, Thurs-Sat 10-5
Friends of the Library Group

SIDNEY

S MONDAK HERITAGE CENTER*, Lillian Anderson Jensen Memorial Library, 120 Third Ave SE, 59270. SAN 309-3573. Tel: 406-433-3500. E-mail: mdhc@richland.org. Web Site: mondakheritagecenter.org. *Exec Dir,* Cheri Friedman; E-mail: cfriedman@richland.org
Founded 1967
Library Holdings: Microforms 100; Bk Titles 2,000; Spec Interest Per Sub 5
Subject Interests: Genealogy, Montana, NDak
Wireless access
Function: Archival coll, Electronic databases & coll, Meeting rooms, Microfiche/film & reading machines, Photocopying/Printing, Printer for laptops & handheld devices, Scanner
Open Tues-Fri 10-4, Sat 1-4
Restriction: In-house use for visitors

P SIDNEY PUBLIC LIBRARY*, 121 Third Ave NW, 59270-4025. SAN 309-3581. Tel: 406-433-1917. FAX: 406-433-4642. E-mail: sidneypublic@richland.org. Web Site: www.richland.org/index.aspx?nid=362. *Dir,* Kelly Reisig; E-mail: kreisig@richland.org; Staff 1 (MLS 1)
Founded 1914. Pop 9,800; Circ 163,604
Library Holdings: Bk Titles 25,518; Bk Vols 25,718; Per Subs 60
Automation Activity & Vendor Info: (Cataloging) Follett Software; (Circulation) Follett Software; (OPAC) Follett Software
Wireless access
Mem of Sagebrush Federation
Open Mon, Fri & Sat 10-5, Tues-Thurs 11:30-7:30

STANFORD

P JUDITH BASIN COUNTY FREE LIBRARY*, 93 Third St N, 59479. (Mail add: PO Box 486, 59479-0486), SAN 350-0829. Tel: 406-566-2277, Ext 123. FAX: 406-566-2211. E-mail: jbclibrary@mtintouch.net. Web Site: judithbasinlibrary.com. *Dir,* Jeanne M Lillegard; *Asst Librn,* Norma Zimmer; Staff 2 (Non-MLS 2)
Founded 1946. Pop 2,329; Circ 14,125
Library Holdings: CDs 250; Large Print Bks 50; Bk Vols 21,322; Per Subs 30; Talking Bks 152
Automation Activity & Vendor Info: (Cataloging) Follett Software; (Circulation) Follett Software
Wireless access
Function: AV serv, Homebound delivery serv, ILL available, Prog for adults, Prog for children & young adult, Wheelchair accessible
Special Services for the Blind - Audio mat; Bks on cassette; Bks on CD; Large print bks; Talking bks
Open Mon, Tues, Thurs & Fri 9:30-5:30, Wed 9:30-9
Branches: 1
HOBSON COMMUNITY LIBRARY, 210 Central Ave, Hobson, 59452, SAN 350-0861. Tel: 406-423-5453. Web Site: www.hobsonlibrary.org. *Librn,* Jennifer Hammontree
Library Holdings: Bk Vols 7,000
Automation Activity & Vendor Info: (Cataloging) LiBRARYSOFT; (Circulation) LiBRARYSOFT; (OPAC) LiBRARYSOFT
Open Mon & Wed 2-6, Tues & Thurs 10-6
Friends of the Library Group

STEVENSVILLE

P NORTH VALLEY PUBLIC LIBRARY*, Stevensville Library, 208 Main St, 59870. SAN 309-359X. Tel: 406-777-5061. E-mail: circ@northvalleylibrary.org. Web Site: www.northvalleylibrary.org. *Dir,* Denise Ard; E-mail: DeniseA@northvalleylibrary.org; *Libr Spec,* Daniel Ray; E-mail: danielr@northvalleylibrary.org; *Youth Serv,* Annika Riley; E-mail: annikar@northvalleylibrary.org; Staff 9 (MLS 2, Non-MLS 7)
Founded 1909. Pop 10,283; Circ 75,073
Jul 2017-Jun 2018 Income $348,275, State $27,443, Federal $3,678, Locally Generated Income $304,792, Other $12,362. Mats Exp $30,367, Books $18,639, AV Mat $11,728
Special Collections: Montana Coll
Automation Activity & Vendor Info: (Cataloging) SirsiDynix-WorkFlows; (Circulation) SirsiDynix-WorkFlows; (ILL) OCLC FirstSearch; (OPAC) SirsiDynix-Enterprise
Wireless access
Function: 24/7 Electronic res, 24/7 Online cat, Adult bk club, After school storytime, Art exhibits, Art programs, Audiobks on Playaways & MP3, Audiobks via web, AV serv, Bks on CD, Children's prog, Computer training, Computers for patron use, Digital talking bks, Free DVD rentals, Homework prog, ILL available, Internet access, Large print keyboards, Life-long learning prog for all ages, Magazines, Meeting rooms, Music CDs, Online cat, Orientations, OverDrive digital audio bks, Photocopying/Printing, Preschool reading prog, Prog for adults, Prog for children & young adult, Ref serv available, Scanner, Spoken cassettes & CDs, Story hour, Summer & winter reading prog, Summer reading prog, Telephone ref, Wheelchair accessible, Workshops
Special Services for the Blind - Large print bks
Open Mon-Fri 10-7, Sat 10-5
Friends of the Library Group

SUPERIOR

P MINERAL COUNTY PUBLIC LIBRARY*, 301 Second Ave E, 59872. (Mail add: PO Box 430, 59872-0430), SAN 350-0977. Tel: 406-822-3563. FAX: 406-822-3569. E-mail: mcpl@blackfoot.net. Web Site: www.mineralcountylibrary.org. *Dir,* Guna K Chaberek; E-mail: gchaberek@co.mineral.mt.us; Staff 5 (Non-MLS 5)
Founded 1936. Pop 3,633; Circ 28,835
Library Holdings: Bks on Deafness & Sign Lang 20; CDs 324; DVDs 70; High Interest/Low Vocabulary Bk Vols 150; Large Print Bks 186; Bk Titles 25,434; Per Subs 17; Talking Bks 560; Videos 1,064
Subject Interests: Montana hist
Automation Activity & Vendor Info: (Acquisitions) SirsiDynix-Unicorn; (Cataloging) OCLC; (Circulation) SirsiDynix-WorkFlows; (ILL) OCLC FirstSearch; (OPAC) SirsiDynix-iBistro
Wireless access
Function: Bks on cassette, Bks on CD, CD-ROM, Children's prog, Computers for patron use, Electronic databases & coll, Free DVD rentals, Holiday prog, ILL available, Music CDs, Online cat, Online ref, Photocopying/Printing, Scanner, Summer reading prog, VHS videos, Wheelchair accessible
Mem of Tamarack Federation of Libraries
Special Services for the Blind - Talking bks
Open Mon-Thurs 10:30-5, Sat 10:30-2:30
Friends of the Library Group

SWAN LAKE

P SWAN LAKE PUBLIC LIBRARY*, 22782 Hwy 83 S, 59911. SAN 376-5067. Tel: 406-886-2086. FAX: 406-886-2086. *Librn,* Anne Morley
Library Holdings: Bk Titles 9,000; Bk Vols 10,000
Mem of Tamarack Federation of Libraries
Open Wed (May-Oct) 10-4

TERRY

P PRAIRIE COUNTY LIBRARY*, 309 Garfield Ave, 59349. (Mail add: PO Box 275, 59349-0275), SAN 309-3603. Tel: 406-635-5546. FAX: 406-635-5546. E-mail: prairielib@midrivers.com. *Dir,* Rolane Christofferson; Staff 1 (Non-MLS 1)
Pop 1,179
Jul 2017-Jun 2018 Income $45,071, State $1,206, County $42,400, Other $1,465. Mats Exp $4,603, Books $4,353, AV Mat $250. Sal $28,515
Library Holdings: Audiobooks 450; DVDs 680; Large Print Bks 550; Bk Titles 12,118
Automation Activity & Vendor Info: (Cataloging) SirsiDynix; (Circulation) SirsiDynix
Wireless access
Function: 24/7 Online cat, Audiobks via web, Bk club(s), Bks on CD, Children's prog, Computers for patron use, Free DVD rentals, Homebound delivery serv, ILL available, Internet access, Mail & tel request accepted, Online cat, OverDrive digital audio bks, Photocopying/Printing, Prog for children & young adult, Story hour, Wheelchair accessible
Mem of Sagebrush Federation
Open Tues 2-5 & 7-8:30, Wed-Fri 2-5

THOMPSON FALLS

P THOMPSON FALLS PUBLIC LIBRARY*, 911 Main St, 59873. (Mail add: PO Box 337, 59873-0337), SAN 309-3611. Tel: 406-827-3547. E-mail: tflibrary@blackfoot.net. Web Site: thompsonfallspubliclibrary.org. *Libr Dir,* Position Currently Open
Pop 4,500; Circ 19,000
Library Holdings: Bk Titles 18,000; Per Subs 40
Automation Activity & Vendor Info: (Cataloging) SirsiDynix; (Circulation) SirsiDynix
Wireless access
Open Tues-Thurs 10-6, Fri 10-5, Sat 10-2
Friends of the Library Group

THREE FORKS

P THREE FORKS COMMUNITY LIBRARY*, 607 Main St, 59752. (Mail add: PO Box 1350, 59752-1350), SAN 309-362X. Tel: 406-285-3747. E-mail: tflibrary@hotmail.com. Web Site: threeforkslibrary.weebly.com, www.threeforksmontana.us/library. *Libr Dir,* Melissa Christoffersen; Staff 3 (Non-MLS 3)
Founded 1934. Pop 4,500
Library Holdings: AV Mats 98; Bk Titles 16,800; Per Subs 25
Automation Activity & Vendor Info: (Acquisitions) SirsiDynix-WorkFlows; (Cataloging) SirsiDynix-WorkFlows; (Circulation) SirsiDynix-WorkFlows; (Course Reserve) SirsiDynix-WorkFlows; (ILL) OCLC FirstSearch; (OPAC) SirsiDynix-WorkFlows
Wireless access
Mem of Broad Valleys Federation of Libraries
Special Services for the Blind - Audio mat; Large print & cassettes
Open Mon & Wed-Fri 10-5, Tues 1-8, Sat 12-4
Friends of the Library Group

TOWNSEND

P BROADWATER SCHOOL & COMMUNITY LIBRARY, 201 N Spruce St, 59644. SAN 309-3638. Tel: 406-441-3430. FAX: 406-441-3457. Web Site: www.townsend.k12.mt.us/o/tsdmt/page/broadwater-school-and-community-library. *Head Librn,* Angela Giono; Tel: 406-266-5060, E-mail: agiono@townsend.k12.mt.us; Staff 4 (Non-MLS 4)
Founded 1995. Pop 5,600; Circ 24,053
Library Holdings: Bks on Deafness & Sign Lang 25; Bk Vols 40,000; Per Subs 59
Automation Activity & Vendor Info: (Cataloging) Follett Software; (Circulation) Follett Software
Mem of Broad Valleys Federation of Libraries
Open Mon-Fri 2-7, Sat 9-3
Friends of the Library Group

TWIN BRIDGES

P TWIN BRIDGES PUBLIC LIBRARY*, 206 S Main St, 59754. (Mail add: PO Box 246, 59754-0246), SAN 373-790X. Tel: 406-684-5416. FAX: 406-684-5260. E-mail: twin@3rivers.net. Web Site: twinbridges.weebly.com. *Libr Dir,* Brenda Pollorena; Staff 3 (MLS 1, Non-MLS 2)
Founded 1897. Pop 700; Circ 5,805. Sal $17,091
Library Holdings: Audiobooks 200; DVDs 350; Large Print Bks 30; Bk Vols 9,000; Per Subs 16; Videos 1,458
Subject Interests: Archives, Local hist
Automation Activity & Vendor Info: (Acquisitions) OCLC FirstSearch; (Cataloging) SirsiDynix; (Circulation) SirsiDynix; (ILL) OCLC FirstSearch
Wireless access
Special Services for the Blind - BiFolkal kits
Open Mon-Fri 10-6, Sat 10-3
Restriction: Authorized patrons
Friends of the Library Group

VALIER

P VALIER PUBLIC LIBRARY, 400 Teton Ave, 59486. (Mail add: PO Box 247, 59486-0247), SAN 309-3646. Tel: 406-279-3366. FAX: 406-279-3368. E-mail: valierlibrary@gmail.com. Web Site: www.townofvalier.com/public-library. *Dir & Librn,* Cathy S Brandvold
Pop 1,986; Circ 12,687
Library Holdings: Bk Vols 12,000; Per Subs 10
Automation Activity & Vendor Info: (Acquisitions) SirsiDynix; (Cataloging) SirsiDynix; (Circulation) SirsiDynix; (Course Reserve) SirsiDynix; (ILL) SirsiDynix; (Media Booking) SirsiDynix; (OPAC) SirsiDynix
Wireless access
Open Mon, Tues, Thurs & Fri 9-5, Wed 9:30-5:30
Friends of the Library Group

VIRGINIA CITY

P THOMPSON-HICKMAN FREE COUNTY LIBRARY, Madison County Library, 217 Idaho St, 59755. (Mail add: PO Box 128, 59755-0128), SAN 309-3654. Tel: 406-843-5346. FAX: 406-843-5347. E-mail: thlibrary@madisoncountymt.gov. Web Site: madisoncountymt.gov/295/Thompson-Hickman-County-Library. *Dir,* Jack Albrecht; E-mail: jalbrecht@madisoncountymt.gov; *Asst Librn,* Christina Koch; E-mail: ckoch@madisoncountymt.gov
Founded 1923. Pop 4,875; Circ 17,810
Library Holdings: Bk Titles 10,208; Per Subs 18
Special Collections: Dick Pace Archives
Automation Activity & Vendor Info: (Cataloging) SirsiDynix; (Circulation) SirsiDynix
Wireless access
Function: Audiobks via web, Children's prog, Computers for patron use, E-Readers, E-Reserves, Free DVD rentals, ILL available, Internet access, Magazines, Meeting rooms, Movies, Photocopying/Printing, Preschool outreach, Ref serv available, Wheelchair accessible
Mem of Broad Valleys Federation of Libraries
Open Mon 10-7, Tues-Fri 10-5:30, Sat 10-2
Friends of the Library Group

WARM SPRINGS

S MONTANA STATE HOSPITAL LIBRARY, 151 Blizzard Way, 59756. (Mail add: PO Box 300, 59756-0300), SAN 309-2925. Tel: 406-693-7133. FAX: 406-693-7127. Web Site: dphhs.mt.gov/amdd/msh. *Libr Dir,* Terry Ferguson; Staff 2 (Non-MLS 2)
Founded 1968
Library Holdings: CDs 54; DVDs 21; e-journals 2; Large Print Bks 76; Bk Titles 6,000; Per Subs 35; Videos 106
Subject Interests: Music, Psychol
Automation Activity & Vendor Info: (OPAC) Follett Software
Wireless access
Partic in Docline; OCLC Online Computer Library Center, Inc
Open Mon-Fri 8-4

WEST YELLOWSTONE

P WEST YELLOWSTONE PUBLIC LIBRARY, 23 N Dunraven St, 59758. (Mail add: PO Box 370, 59758-0370), SAN 321-7825. Tel: 406-646-9017. E-mail: library@townofwestyellowstone.com. Web Site: westyellowstonepubliclibrary.org. *Dir,* Bruce McPherson
Founded 1981. Pop 1,200; Circ 6,000
Library Holdings: Bk Titles 12,500; Bk Vols 15,000; Per Subs 5
Automation Activity & Vendor Info: (Cataloging) SirsiDynix; (Circulation) SirsiDynix
Wireless access
Mem of Broad Valleys Federation of Libraries
Open Tues-Fri 10-6, Sat 10-2 (Summer); Tues-Fri 10-5, Sat 10-2 (Winter)

WHITE SULPHUR SPRINGS

P MEAGHER COUNTY CITY LIBRARY, 205 SW Garfield, 59645. (Mail add: PO Box S, 59645), SAN 309-3689. Tel: 406-547-2250. FAX: 406-547-3691. E-mail: mccl@itstriangle.com. Web Site: www.meaghercountycitylibrary.org. *Dir,* Jessica Ketola; *Asst Librn,* Shannon Washburn; *Asst Librn,* Rachel Wahlstrom; Staff 1 (Non-MLS 1)
Founded 1940. Pop 2,500; Circ 9,730
Library Holdings: Audiobooks 250; AV Mats 75; CDs 50; DVDs 300; e-books 300; High Interest/Low Vocabulary Bk Vols 100; Large Print Bks 300; Bk Titles 15,000; Bk Vols 15,500; Per Subs 15; Talking Bks 275; Videos 350
Special Collections: Meagher County History; Montana History (Historical Society); Rare Books
Automation Activity & Vendor Info: (Cataloging) SirsiDynix; (Circulation) SirsiDynix
Wireless access
Function: 24/7 Online cat, Activity rm, After school storytime, Audiobks on Playaways & MP3, Audiobks via web, AV serv, Bk club(s), Bk reviews (Group), Bks on cassette, Bks on CD, Children's prog, Citizenship assistance, Computer training, Computers for patron use, Digital talking bks, Distance learning, E-Readers, Electronic databases & coll, Equip loans & repairs, Family literacy, For res purposes, Free DVD rentals, Govt ref serv, Health sci info serv, Holiday prog, Home delivery & serv to seniorr ctr & nursing homes, Homebound delivery serv, Homework prog, ILL available, Instruction & testing, Internet access, Laminating, Life-long learning prog for all ages, Literacy & newcomer serv, Magazines, Magnifiers for reading, Mail & tel request accepted, Meeting rooms, Movies, Music CDs, Online cat, Online info literacy tutorials on the web & in blackboard, Online ref, Outreach serv, OverDrive digital audio bks, Photocopying/Printing, Preschool outreach, Preschool reading prog, Printer for laptops & handheld devices, Prof lending libr, Prog for adults, Prog for children & young adult, Ref serv available, Scanner, Senior computer classes, Serves people with intellectual disabilities, Spoken cassettes & CDs, Story hour, Study rm, Summer & winter reading prog, Summer reading prog, Tax forms, Teen prog, Telephone ref, VHS videos, Visual arts prog, Wheelchair accessible, Winter reading prog, Workshops, Writing prog
Mem of Broad Valleys Federation of Libraries
Special Services for the Deaf - Bks on deafness & sign lang; High interest/low vocabulary bks
Special Services for the Blind - Audio mat; Audiovision-a radio reading serv; Bks on cassette; Bks on CD; Blind Club (monthly newsletter); Copier with enlargement capabilities; Home delivery serv; HP Scan Jet with photo-finish software; Large print bks; Magnifiers; Mags & bk reproduction/duplication; Talking bks
Open Tues, Thurs & Fri 10-5, Wed 1-7, Sat 10-3
Friends of the Library Group

WHITEFISH

P WHITEFISH COMMUNITY LIBRARY*, Nine Spokane Ave, 59937. SAN 350-0373. Tel: 406-862-9914. FAX: 406-862-1407. Web Site: whitefishlibrary.org. *Dir,* Joey Kositzky; E-mail: joeyk@whitefishlibrary.org
Library Holdings: Bk Vols 47,000
Automation Activity & Vendor Info: (ILL) OCLC WorldShare Interlibrary Loan
Wireless access
Open Mon 10-7, Tues-Thurs 10-6, Fri & Sat 12-5
Friends of the Library Group

WIBAUX

P WIBAUX PUBLIC LIBRARY*, 115 S Wibaux, 59353. (Mail add: PO Box 332, 59353-0332), SAN 309-3697. Tel: 406-796-2452. FAX: 406-795-5779. E-mail: wibauxpubliclibrarymt@gmail.com. *Libr Dir,* Mindy Van Vleet
Pop 1,068; Circ 7,434
Library Holdings: Bk Vols 14,595
Automation Activity & Vendor Info: (Cataloging) Follett Software; (Circulation) Follett Software
Mem of Sagebrush Federation
Open Mon, Tues, Thurs & Fri 9-5, Wed 9-8
Friends of the Library Group

WINNETT

P PETROLEUM COUNTY COMMUNITY LIBRARY*, Winnett School Library, 305 S Broadway, 59087. (Mail add: PO Box 188, 59087), SAN 309-3700. Tel: 406-429-2451. FAX: 406-429-7631. E-mail: pcclibrary55@gmail.com. Web Site: petroleumcolibrary.wixsite.com/petroleum-county. *County Librn,* Lori Olsen; *Sch Librn,* Kim Jensen; Staff 4 (Non-MLS 4)
Founded 1974. Pop 565; Circ 10,214
Library Holdings: Audiobooks 636; AV Mats 500; Bks on Deafness & Sign Lang 28; CDs 200; DVDs 50; Electronic Media & Resources 26; Large Print Bks 68; Bk Titles 14,833; Bk Vols 15,470; Per Subs 51; Videos 1,500
Special Collections: Local History; Montana. Oral History
Automation Activity & Vendor Info: (Cataloging) Follett Software; (Circulation) Follett Software; (ILL) OCLC
Wireless access
Function: Adult bk club, Audio & video playback equip for onsite use, AV serv, CD-ROM, Computer training, Electronic databases & coll, Free DVD rentals, Homebound delivery serv, ILL available, Internet access, Magnifiers for reading, Mail & tel request accepted, Mail loans to mem, Music CDs, Online ref, Photocopying/Printing, Prof lending libr, Prog for children & young adult, Ref & res, Ref serv available, Satellite serv, Spoken cassettes & CDs, Spoken cassettes & DVDs, Story hour, Telephone ref, VHS videos, Wheelchair accessible
Open Mon-Thurs 9-4, Fri 9-Noon

WOLF POINT

P ROOSEVELT COUNTY LIBRARY*, 220 Second Ave S, 59201-1599. SAN 350-106X. Tel: 406-653-2411. FAX: 406-653-1365. E-mail: read@nemont.net. Web Site: rooseveltcountylibrary.org. *Dir,* Andrea Hayes
Pop 10,999
Library Holdings: Bk Titles 53,394; Per Subs 96
Automation Activity & Vendor Info: (Cataloging) SirsiDynix; (Circulation) SirsiDynix
Wireless access
Mem of Golden Plains Library Federation
Open Mon, Wed & Fri 9-5, Tues & Thurs 9-7, Sat 9-3
Friends of the Library Group
Branches: 2
CULBERTSON PUBLIC, 307 Broadway Ave, Culbertson, 59218. (Mail add: PO Box 415, Culbertson, 59218-0415), SAN 350-1124. Tel: 406-787-5275. E-mail: culbertsonpubliclibrary@yahoo.com. *Br Librn,* Leona Colvin

Library Holdings: Bk Titles 7,000
Open Mon, Tues & Thurs 11-5
FROID PUBLIC, 101 Second St N, Froid, 59226, SAN 350-1159. Tel: 406-766-2492. E-mail: froidlibrary@yahoo.com. *Br Librn,* Sheri Harvey
Library Holdings: Bk Titles 7,000
Open Mon, Tues & Thurs 11-5
Friends of the Library Group

NEBRASKA

Date of Statistics: FY 2020
Population, 2020 U.S. Census: 1,961,504
Population Served by Public Libraries: 1,595,049
Total Book Volumes in Public Libraries: 5,418,610
Total Items in Public Libraries: 6,656,143 (excludes shared consortia held titles)
Total Public Library Circulation: 9,470,979
Income and Expenditures:
Total Public Library Income: $66,664,606
Source of Income: Property Tax 93%
Grants-in-Aid to Public Libraries: $704,319
Number of County or Multi-County (Regional) Libraries: 10
Number of Bookmobiles in State: 7
Information provided courtesy of: Sam Shaw, Planning & Data Services Coordinator; Nebraska Library Commission

AINSWORTH

P AINSWORTH PUBLIC LIBRARY*, 445 N Main St, 69210. (Mail add: PO Box 207, 69210-0207), SAN 309-3727. Tel: 402-387-2032. FAX: 402-387-0209. E-mail: aplibrary@threeriver.net. Web Site: libraries.ne.gov/ainsworth. *Libr Dir,* Gail J Irwin
Founded 1911. Pop 4,031; Circ 35,000
Library Holdings: Bk Vols 25,300; Per Subs 88
Special Collections: Oral History
Automation Activity & Vendor Info: (Cataloging) Follett Software; (Circulation) Follett Software
Mem of Central Plains Library System
Partic in Ill Networking
Open Mon & Fri 11-6, Tues & Thurs 11-8, Wed & Sat 1-5

ALBION

P ALBION PUBLIC LIBRARY*, 437 S Third St, 68620. SAN 309-3735. Tel: 402-395-2021. E-mail: albionpubliclibrary@gmail.com. Web Site: libraries.ne.gov/albion. *Libr Dir,* Staci Wright; E-mail: albionlibrarydirector@gmail.com; *Asst Librn,* Joye Anderson
Founded 1900. Pop 2,500; Circ 23,394
Library Holdings: Bk Titles 18,773; Per Subs 37
Automation Activity & Vendor Info: (Cataloging) Follett Software; (Circulation) Follett Software; (OPAC) Follett Software
Wireless access
Mem of Three Rivers Library System
Open Mon & Wed 10-8, Tues, Thurs & Fri 10-6, Sat 10-2
Friends of the Library Group

ALLEN

P SPRINGBANK TOWNSHIP LIBRARY*, 100 E Second St, 68710. (Mail add: PO Box 158, 68710-0158), SAN 309-3751. Tel: 402-635-2444. *Dir,* Brian Fuoss
Pop 411; Circ 2,007
Library Holdings: Bk Vols 7,627; Per Subs 30
Wireless access
Mem of Three Rivers Library System
Open Mon 9am-11am, Wed 3-5, Fri 9-Noon

ALLIANCE

P ALLIANCE PUBLIC LIBRARY*, 1750 Sweetwater Ave, Ste 101, 69301-4438. SAN 309-376X. Tel: 308-762-1387. Web Site: libraries.ne.gov/alliance. *Dir,* Stephanie O'Connor; E-mail: soconnor@cityofalliance.net
Pop 8,491; Circ 69,906
Library Holdings: Bk Vols 43,392; Per Subs 127
Automation Activity & Vendor Info: (Cataloging) Biblionix/Apollo; (Circulation) Biblionix/Apollo
Wireless access
Open Mon-Thurs 8-6, Fri 8-5, Sat 10-2
Friends of the Library Group

ALMA

P HOESCH MEMORIAL PUBLIC LIBRARY*, City Park W Second St, 68920. (Mail add: PO Box 438, 68920-0438), SAN 309-3778. Tel: 308-928-2600. FAX: 308-928-2662. E-mail: libry@megavision.com. *Dir,* Keri Anderson
Founded 1910. Pop 1,674; Circ 18,748
Library Holdings: Bk Vols 17,048; Per Subs 16
Subject Interests: Hist
Automation Activity & Vendor Info: (Cataloging) LibLime Koha; (Circulation) LibLime Koha; (OPAC) LibLime Koha
Wireless access
Mem of Central Plains Library System
Open Tues-Thurs 10-8, Fri & Sat 10-5
Friends of the Library Group

ARAPAHOE

P ARAPAHOE PUBLIC LIBRARY, 306 Nebraska Ave, 68922. (Mail add: PO Box 598, 68922-0598), SAN 309-3794. Tel: 308-962-7806. FAX: 308-962-7321. E-mail: arapahoereads@gmail.com. Web Site: libraries.ne.gov/arapahoe. *Dir,* Jennifer Einspahr; *Asst Librn,* Jill Snyder
Founded 1985. Pop 1,050; Circ 33,000
Library Holdings: Bk Titles 19,000; Per Subs 33
Automation Activity & Vendor Info: (Cataloging) LibLime Koha; (Circulation) LibLime Koha
Wireless access
Mem of Central Plains Library System
Partic in Pioneer
Open Mon & Fri 1-5, Tues 10-5:30, Wed 9-3, Thurs 1-7, Sat 9-Noon
Friends of the Library Group

ARCADIA

P ARCADIA TOWNSHIP LIBRARY*, 100 S Reynolds, 68815. (Mail add: PO Box 355, 68815-0355), SAN 309-3808. Tel: 308-789-6346. FAX: 308-789-6346. E-mail: arcadialibrary@nctc.net. *Librn,* Terri Pierson
Pop 530; Circ 6,337
Library Holdings: Bk Vols 7,500; Per Subs 27
Wireless access
Mem of Central Plains Library System

ARLINGTON

P ARLINGTON PUBLIC LIBRARY*, 410 W Elm St, 68002. (Mail add: PO Box 39, 68002-0039), SAN 309-3816. Tel: 402-478-4545. E-mail: arlopublib@gmail.com. Web Site: www.arlingtonne.org/government/public-facilities/arlington-public-library. *Librn,* Debra Wesch
Pop 1,117; Circ 6,809

Library Holdings: Bk Titles 7,251; Per Subs 21
Wireless access
Mem of Three Rivers Library System
Open Mon 2-6, Tues-Fri 3-6, Sat 10-1

ARNOLD

P FINCH MEMORIAL PUBLIC LIBRARY, 205 N Walnut St, 69120. (Mail add: PO Box 247, 69120-0247), SAN 309-3824. Tel: 308-848-2219. FAX: 308-848-4729. E-mail: finlib@yahoo.com. Web Site: finchmemoriallibrary.weebly.com. *Dir,* Marcy Lucas
Pop 1,400; Circ 5,600
Library Holdings: Bk Vols 11,000; Per Subs 28
Mem of Central Plains Library System
Open Mon-Fri 1-5:30, Sat 10-Noon
Friends of the Library Group

ARTHUR

P ARTHUR COUNTY PUBLIC LIBRARY*, 205 Fir St, 69121. (Mail add: PO Box 146, 69121-0146), SAN 309-3832. Tel: 308-764-2219. FAX: 308-764-2216. E-mail: arthurcountylibrary@gmail.com. Web Site: libraries.ne.gov/arthur. *Libr Dir,* Evanna Hardin
Founded 1939. Pop 450
Library Holdings: Bk Titles 6,939
Wireless access
Mem of Western Library System
Open Mon-Fri 1-4

ASHLAND

P ASHLAND PUBLIC LIBRARY*, 1324 Silver St, 68003-1816. SAN 309-3840. Tel: 402-521-2012. FAX: 402-521-2012. Web Site: libraries.ne.gov/ashland. *Dir,* Amanda Pena; E-mail: librarydir@ashland-ne.com
Founded 1904. Pop 2,514; Circ 25,000
Library Holdings: Bk Titles 13,332; Per Subs 5
Automation Activity & Vendor Info: (Cataloging) Biblionix/Apollo; (Circulation) Biblionix/Apollo
Wireless access
Open Mon-Wed 9:30-6, Thurs 9:30-8, Fri & Sat 12-5

ATKINSON

P ATKINSON PUBLIC LIBRARY, 210 W State St, 68713. (Mail add: PO Box 938, 68713-0938), SAN 309-3859. Tel: 402-925-2855. FAX: 402-925-2855. E-mail: atkplib@gpcom.net. Web Site: libraries.ne.gov/atkinson. *Dir,* Judy Hagan
Founded 1927. Pop 1,300; Circ 28,592
Library Holdings: Bk Vols 21,000; Per Subs 54
Automation Activity & Vendor Info: (Cataloging) LibLime Koha; (Circulation) LibLime Koha; (OPAC) LibLime Koha
Wireless access
Mem of Central Plains Library System
Open Mon & Thurs 9-5, Tues 9-6, Wed 12-6, Fri & Sat 9-3
Friends of the Library Group

AUBURN

P AUBURN MEMORIAL LIBRARY*, 1810 Courthouse Ave, 68305-2323. SAN 309-3867. Tel: 402-274-4023. FAX: 402-274-4433. E-mail: auburnlibraryne@yahoo.com. Web Site: www.auburnmemoriallibrary.com. *Dir,* Heather Koeneke; Staff 6 (Non-MLS 6)
Founded 1914. Pop 8,367; Circ 65,393
Library Holdings: Bk Titles 29,985; Per Subs 80
Automation Activity & Vendor Info: (Cataloging) Follett Software; (Circulation) Follett Software
Wireless access
Mem of Southeast Library System
Open Mon, Wed & Fri 10-5, Tues & Thurs 10-8, Sat 9-2
Friends of the Library Group

AURORA

P ALICE M FARR LIBRARY, 1603 L St, 68818-2132. SAN 309-3875. Tel: 402-694-2272. FAX: 402-694-2273. E-mail: afl@hamilton.net, amfplibrary@gmail.com. Web Site: auroranelibrary.org. *Dir,* Janette Thomsen; *Asst Dir, Ch,* Jackie Bowman
Pop 8,600; Circ 53,500
Library Holdings: Bk Vols 49,000; Per Subs 124
Special Collections: Hamilton County History
Automation Activity & Vendor Info: (Cataloging) OCLC CatExpress; (Circulation) Follett Software
Mem of Southeast Library System
Special Services for the Deaf - Bks on deafness & sign lang; Captioned film dep; High interest/low vocabulary bks; Spec interest per; Videos & decoder
Open Mon-Thurs 10-8, Fri 10-5, Sat 10-2
Friends of the Library Group

AXTELL

P AXTELL PUBLIC LIBRARY*, 305 N Main St, 68924. (Mail add: PO Box 65, 68924-0065). Tel: 308-743-2592. E-mail: axtellpubliclib@gmail.com. Web Site: libraries.ne.gov/axtell. *Dir,* Darcie Senff
Pop 696; Circ 2,500
Library Holdings: CDs 40; DVDs 50; Bk Vols 8,000; Per Subs 20; Talking Bks 75
Automation Activity & Vendor Info: (Cataloging) Follett Software; (Circulation) Follett Software
Wireless access
Mem of Central Plains Library System
Open Mon, Wed & Fri (Sept-May) 8-12 & 3:30-6, Tues & Thurs 3:30-6; Mon, Tues & Thurs (June-May) 9-2, Wed 9-2 & 4-8
Friends of the Library Group

BANCROFT

P BANCROFT PUBLIC LIBRARY*, 103 E Poplar St, 68004. (Mail add: PO Box 67, 68004-0067), SAN 309-3891. Tel: 402-648-3350. E-mail: library@gpcom.net. Web Site: libraries.ne.gov/bancroft. *Dir,* Lesa Bargmann; *Asst Librn,* JoDee Flock; Staff 5.3 (MLS 5.3)
Founded 1974. Pop 750; Circ 5,831
Oct 2012-Sept 2013 Income $18,895, State $695, City $15,950, County $2,250. Mats Exp $3,725, Books $3,500, Per/Ser (Incl. Access Fees) $225. Sal $8,100
Library Holdings: DVDs 121; Large Print Bks 75; Bk Vols 8,400; Per Subs 20; Talking Bks 140; Videos 208
Special Collections: Cakepans; Games
Automation Activity & Vendor Info: (Cataloging) Follett Software; (Circulation) Follett Software; (OPAC) Follett Software
Wireless access
Function: Adult bk club
Mem of Three Rivers Library System
Open Tues 9-12 & 1-5, Wed 1-6, Thurs 4:30-7:30, Fri & Sat 9-Noon
Friends of the Library Group

S NEBRASKA STATE HISTORICAL SOCIETY*, John G Neihardt State Historic Site, 306 W Elm, 68004. (Mail add: PO Box 344, 68004-0344), SAN 309-3905. Tel: 402-648-3388. Toll Free Tel: 888-777-HOOP. E-mail: neihardt@gpcom.net. Web Site: www.neihardtcenter.org. *Exec Dir,* Marianne Reynolds; E-mail: neihardt@gpcom.net; Staff 2 (MLS 1, Non-MLS 1)
Founded 1976
Library Holdings: Bk Titles 200; Bk Vols 300
Special Collections: Bound Nebraska History Coll; Dr John G Neihardt Coll, bks, critiques, ms
Subject Interests: Hist, Native American
Wireless access
Function: Archival coll, Art exhibits, Audio & video playback equip for onsite use, Bk club(s), Butterfly Garden, For res purposes, Internet access, Mail & tel request accepted, Meeting rooms, Outreach serv, Prog for adults, Res libr, Study rm, Wheelchair accessible
Open Tues-Sat 10-4
Restriction: Authorized scholars by appt, By permission only, Non-circulating

BARTLEY

P BARTLEY PUBLIC LIBRARY, 411 Commercial St, 69020. (Mail add: PO Box 194, 69020-0194), SAN 309-3913. Tel: 308-692-3313. E-mail: bartleylibrary@outlook.com. Web Site: libraries.ne.gov/bartley. *Dir,* Sam Badilla; *Asst Dir,* Ronni Renee Harding
Pop 339; Circ 1,811
Library Holdings: Bk Vols 5,725; Per Subs 18
Special Collections: Oral History
Mem of Central Plains Library System
Open Tues 10-5, Wed & Thurs 12-5

BASSETT

P ROCK COUNTY PUBLIC LIBRARY, 201 E Bertha St, 68714. (Mail add: PO Box 465, 68714-0465), SAN 309-3921. Tel: 402-684-3800. FAX: 402-684-3930. E-mail: rockcolib@abbnebraska.com. Web Site: libraries.ne.gov/rockcounty. *Dir,* Macey Lackaff; *Asst Dir,* Kim Ost
Founded 1929. Pop 2,019; Circ 22,181
Library Holdings: Audiobooks 771; Electronic Media & Resources 28,744; Bk Vols 17,000; Per Subs 31; Videos 494
Mem of Central Plains Library System

Open Mon, Tues, Thurs & Fri 10-5:30, Wed 10-6:30, Sat 9-Noon
Friends of the Library Group
Bookmobiles: 1

BATTLE CREEK

P LIED BATTLE CREEK PUBLIC LIBRARY*, 100 S Fourth St, 68715. (Mail add: PO Box D, 68715-0106), SAN 309-393X. Tel: 402-675-6934. FAX: 402-675-3911. Web Site: libraries.ne.gov/battlecreek. *Dir,* Jessica Fouts; E-mail: bclibrarydirector@cableone.net; *Asst Dir,* Mae Toelle; E-mail: mtoelle@cableone.net; Staff 1 (Non-MLS 1)
Pop 1,158; Circ 35,000
Library Holdings: CDs 170; DVDs 196; e-books 10,540; Large Print Bks 325; Bk Titles 34,810; Per Subs 48; Talking Bks 972; Videos 2,232
Special Collections: Nebraska Authors or Subjects
Automation Activity & Vendor Info: (Cataloging) Follett Software; (Circulation) Follett Software; (OPAC) Follett Software
Wireless access
Mem of Three Rivers Library System
Open Mon-Fri 10-6, Sat 10-2
Friends of the Library Group

BAYARD

P BAYARD PUBLIC LIBRARY, 509 Ave A, 69334. (Mail add: PO Box B, 69334-0676), SAN 309-3948. Tel: 308-586-1144. FAX: 308-545-1042. E-mail: bayardpubliclibrary@cityofbayard.net. Web Site: libraries.ne.gov/bayard. *Dir,* Becky Henkel
Founded 1921. Pop 1,435
Library Holdings: Bk Vols 14,365; Per Subs 50
Automation Activity & Vendor Info: (Cataloging) Follett Software; (Circulation) Follett Software
Wireless access
Function: 24/7 Online cat, Accelerated reader prog, Adult bk club, Adult literacy prog, Audiobks via web, Bk club(s), Bks on CD, Children's prog, Computers for patron use, E-Readers, Free DVD rentals, Home delivery & serv to seniorr ctr & nursing homes, Homebound delivery serv, ILL available, Internet access, Magazines, Magnifiers for reading, Makerspace, Microfiche/film & reading machines, Online cat, Outreach serv, Prog for adults, Prog for children & young adult, Ref & res, STEM programs, Summer reading prog
Open Tues-Fri 9-5, Sat 9-Noon

BEATRICE

P BEATRICE PUBLIC LIBRARY*, 100 N 16th St, 68310-4100. SAN 309-3956. Tel: 402-223-3584. FAX: 402-223-3913. Web Site: www.beatrice.ne.gov/library. *Libr Dir,* Joanne Neemann; E-mail: jneemann@beatrice.ne.gov; Staff 3 (MLS 3)
Founded 1893. Pop 12,388; Circ 105,035
Library Holdings: Audiobooks 2,588; e-books 41,451; Bk Vols 98,045; Per Subs 70; Videos 5,543
Special Collections: Nebraska State Genealogical Society Coll
Automation Activity & Vendor Info: (Cataloging) LibLime Koha; (Circulation) LibLime Koha; (ILL) OCLC WorldShare Interlibrary Loan; (OPAC) LibLime Koha; (Serials) LibLime Koha
Wireless access
Function: 24/7 Electronic res, 24/7 Online cat, 3D Printer, Audiobks via web, Bks on cassette, Bks on CD, Children's prog, Computers for patron use, Electronic databases & coll, Free DVD rentals, Home delivery & serv to seniorr ctr & nursing homes, Homebound delivery serv, ILL available, Internet access, Magazines, Meeting rooms, Microfiche/film & reading machines, Movies, Music CDs, Online cat, Online ref, OverDrive digital audio bks, Photocopying/Printing, Ref & res, Ref serv available, Scanner, Story hour, Study rm, Summer reading prog, Telephone ref, VHS videos, Wheelchair accessible
Mem of Southeast Library System
Open Mon-Thurs 10-7:30, Fri & Sat 10-5:30, Sun 2-5
Friends of the Library Group

J SOUTHEAST COMMUNITY COLLEGE LIBRARY*, 4771 W Scott Rd, 68310-7042. Tel: 402-228-8224. Toll Free Tel: 800-233-5027. FAX: 402-228-2218. Web Site: www.southeast.edu/libraryresourcecenters. *Dir,* Lyndsi Rasmussen; E-mail: lrasmussen@southeast.edu; Staff 2 (MLS 1, Non-MLS 1)
Founded 1986. Enrl 1,000
Library Holdings: Bk Titles 15,000; Per Subs 100
Automation Activity & Vendor Info: (Cataloging) Mandarin Library Automation; (Circulation) Mandarin Library Automation; (ILL) OCLC; (OPAC) Mandarin Library Automation
Wireless access
Partic in OCLC Online Computer Library Center, Inc
Open Mon-Fri 7:30-5

S US NATIONAL PARK SERVICE*, Homestead National Monument of America Research Library, 8523 W State Hwy 4, 68310. SAN 370-2944. Tel: 402-223-3514. FAX: 402-228-4231. Web Site: www.nps.gov/home. *Historian,* Jonathan Fairchild; E-mail: jonathan_fairchild@nps.gov
Library Holdings: Bk Vols 1,700; Per Subs 15
Restriction: Open to pub for ref only

BEAVER CITY

P BEAVER CITY PUBLIC LIBRARY, 408 Tenth St, 68926. (Mail add: PO Box 431, 68926-0431), SAN 309-3964. Tel: 308-268-4115. E-mail: bclibrary@atcjet.net. Web Site: libraries.ne.gov/beavercity. *Dir,* Dawn C Brown; *Asst Dir,* Karen MacDonald; *Libr Asst,* Holly Hunt; *Libr Asst,* Shelby Rickert; *Libr Asst,* Janet McClain
Founded 1922. Circ 7,000
Library Holdings: Bk Titles 10,000; Per Subs 41
Automation Activity & Vendor Info: (Cataloging) Follett Software; (Circulation) Follett Software
Mem of Central Plains Library System
Open Tues & Thurs 1-7, Wed 9-12 & 1-5, Fri 1-5, Sat 9-Noon

GL FURNAS COUNTY LAW LIBRARY*, Courthouse, 912 R St, 68926. (Mail add: PO Box 373, 68926-0373), SAN 374-8294. Tel: 308-268-4025. *Library Contact,* Victoria Barnett
Library Holdings: Bk Vols 1,000
Wireless access
Open Mon-Fri 10-12 & 1-3

BEEMER

P KARLEN MEMORIAL LIBRARY*, 215 Blaine St, 68716. (Mail add: PO Box 248, 68716-0248), SAN 309-3972. Tel: 402-528-3476. FAX: 402-528-3476. Web Site: libraries.ne.gov/beemer. *Dir,* Stephanie Payton; E-mail: sheinema1980@gmail.com; Staff 2 (Non-MLS 2)
Founded 1924. Pop 665; Circ 1,990
Library Holdings: Audiobooks 17; DVDs 626; Large Print Bks 175; Bk Vols 7,768; Per Subs 15
Special Collections: Accu-Cut Dies (For use with the Accu-Cut Machine); Cricut Cartridges (For use with the Cricut Machine)
Automation Activity & Vendor Info: (Acquisitions) Follett Software; (Cataloging) Follett Software; (Circulation) Follett Software; (OPAC) Follett Software; (Serials) Follett Software
Wireless access
Function: Children's prog, Computers for patron use, Homebound delivery serv, ILL available, Internet access, Laminating, Online cat, OverDrive digital audio bks, Photocopying/Printing, Scanner, Summer reading prog
Mem of Three Rivers Library System
Open Mon, Wed & Fri 9-12 & 1-5, Tues 2-6, Sat 9-12
Friends of the Library Group

BELLEVUE

P BELLEVUE PUBLIC LIBRARY, 1003 Lincoln Dr, 68005. SAN 309-3999. Tel: 402-293-3157. FAX: 402-293-3163. Web Site: www.bellevuelibrary.org. *Dir,* Julie Dinville; E-mail: julie.dinville@bellevue.net; *Asst Dir, Head, Tech Serv,* Sandra Astleford; E-mail: sandra.astleford@bellevue.net; Staff 22 (MLS 4, Non-MLS 18)
Founded 1929. Pop 53,900; Circ 285,000
Library Holdings: Bk Titles 127,900; Per Subs 204
Special Collections: Local History Coll
Subject Interests: Local hist
Automation Activity & Vendor Info: (Acquisitions) SirsiDynix; (Cataloging) SirsiDynix; (Circulation) SirsiDynix; (ILL) SirsiDynix; (OPAC) SirsiDynix; (Serials) SirsiDynix
Wireless access
Function: ILL available
Publications: Bellevue Library Times (Bimonthly)
Mem of Three Rivers Library System
Open Mon-Thurs 9-8, Fri 9-6, Sat 9-5, Sun 12-5
Friends of the Library Group

C BELLEVUE UNIVERSITY, Freeman-Lozier Library, 1000 Galvin Rd S, 68005. SAN 309-3980. Tel: 402-557-7314. Interlibrary Loan Service Tel: 402-557-7311. Reference Tel: 402-557-7313. Toll Free Tel: 800-756-7920. FAX: 402-557-5427. E-mail: library@bellevue.edu. Web Site: library.bellevue.edu. *Sr Dir for Libr Serv,* Robin R Bernstein; Tel: 402-557-7300, E-mail: robin.bernstein@bellevue.edu; *Asst Dir, Syst,* Joel Hartung; Tel: 402-557-7317, E-mail: joel.hartung@bellevue.edu; *Pub Serv Librn,* Christine Armstrong; Tel: 402-557-7301, E-mail: christine.armstrong@bellevue.edu; *Ref & Instruction Librn,* Matthew Colbert; Tel: 402-557-7303, E-mail: matthew.colbert@bellevue.edu; *Ref & Instruction Librn,* Lorraine Patrick; Tel: 402-557-7316, E-mail: lorraine.patrick@bellevue.edu; *Tech Serv Librn,* Megan McIntosh; Tel: 402-557-7305, E-mail: mmcintosh@bellevue.edu; *Access Serv Spec, Outreach Serv Spec,* Alicia James; Tel: 402-557-7309, E-mail:

aljames@bellevue.edu; *Electronic Services Specialist,* Brandi Bengtson; Tel: 402-557-7307, E-mail: brandi.bengtson@bellevue.edu; *Reference Support Specialist,* Mary Barrett; Tel: 402-557-7315, E-mail: mary.barrett@bellevue.edu; *Reference Support Specialist,* Margie McCandless; Tel: 402-557-7302, E-mail: margie.mccandless@bellevue.edu; *Resource Sharing Circulation Specialist,* Allison Schafer; E-mail: allison.schafer@bellevue.edu; *Tech Serv Spec,* Diane Osborne; Tel: 402-557-7312, E-mail: diane.osborne@bellevue.edu; *Archives Admin, Scholarly Communications,* Sierra Whitfield; Tel: 402-557-7299, E-mail: swhitfield@bellevue.edu; *Senior Circulation Asst,* Jessica Omer; Tel: 402-557-7308, E-mail: jessica.omer@bellevue.edu; *Circ Asst,* Haley Wert; E-mail: haley.wert@bellevue.edu; *Tech Serv Asst,* Sarah Araujo; E-mail: sarah.araujo@bellevue.edu; Staff 15.5 (MLS 9.5, Non-MLS 6)
Founded 1966. Enrl 9,215; Fac 300; Highest Degree: Doctorate
Jul 2020-Jun 2021. Mats Exp $785,310, Books $27,876, Per/Ser (Incl. Access Fees) $79,306, Electronic Ref Mat (Incl. Access Fees) $673,976, Presv $4,152. Sal $650,653
Library Holdings: AV Mats 136,713; e-books 528,084; e-journals 57,790; Bk Vols 61,172; Per Subs 58
Special Collections: Thomas Dolly Coll, writings
Automation Activity & Vendor Info: (Acquisitions) SirsiDynix; (Cataloging) SirsiDynix; (Circulation) SirsiDynix; (Discovery) EBSCO Discovery Service; (ILL) OCLC; (Media Booking) SirsiDynix; (OPAC) SirsiDynix; (Serials) SirsiDynix
Wireless access
Function: 24/7 Electronic res, 24/7 Online cat
Publications: More Than Books (Newsletter)
Mem of Three Rivers Library System
Partic in ICON Library Consortium; OCLC Online Computer Library Center, Inc
Open Mon-Fri 7:30am-10:30pm, Sat 8-5, Sun 10-7
Restriction: Authorized patrons

BELVIDERE

S THAYER COUNTY MUSEUM*, Historical & Genealogical Library, 110 Ninth St, 68315. SAN 373-3726. Tel: 402-768-2147. E-mail: thayercountymuseum@gmail.com. Web Site: www.thayercountymuseum.com. *Curator,* Ms Jackie Williamson; Tel: 402-768-6845, E-mail: kjwmson@windstream.net
Subject Interests: Genealogy, Local hist
Wireless access
Open Sun & Wed 2-4

BENKELMAN

P DUNDY COUNTY LIBRARY*, 102 Sixth Ave E, 69021. (Mail add: PO Box 53, 69021-0053). Tel: 308-423-2333. E-mail: ducolibrary@bwtelcom.net. Web Site: libraries.ne.gov/dundycounty. *Dir,* Christine Egger; Staff 2 (MLS 1, Non-MLS 1)
Founded 1932. Pop 1,006; Circ 6,289
Library Holdings: Audiobooks 35; AV Mats 46; Bks on Deafness & Sign Lang 2; CDs 50; DVDs 1,595; Large Print Bks 1,249; Bk Vols 10,443; Per Subs 2; Talking Bks 35
Automation Activity & Vendor Info: (Cataloging) Koha; (Circulation) Koha
Wireless access
Function: 24/7 Online cat, Activity rm, Adult bk club, ILL available
Mem of Western Library System
Open Mon, Wed & Fri 2-7, Tues & Thurs 10-1 & 2-7, Sat 10-3
Restriction: Access at librarian's discretion

BENNINGTON

P BENNINGTON PUBLIC LIBRARY*, 11401 N 156th St, 68007. (Mail add: PO Box 32, 68007-0032), SAN 309-4006. Tel: 402-238-2201. FAX: 402-238-2218. E-mail: info@benningtonlibrary.org. Web Site: benningtonlibrary.org. *Dir,* Lisa M Flaxbeard; *Asst Dir,* Dalene Clark; *Libr Spec, Youth Serv,* Joanne Mancuso; *Libr Asst,* Chase Martin; *Libr Asst,* Cassandra Ozbirn; Staff 4 (Non-MLS 4)
Founded 1948. Pop 4,692; Circ 31,652
Library Holdings: Bk Vols 24,155; Per Subs 28
Special Collections: Cake Pans
Wireless access
Function: 24/7 Electronic res, 24/7 Online cat, Adult bk club, Audiobks on Playaways & MP3, Audiobks via web, AV serv, Bk club(s), Bks on CD, Children's prog, Computers for patron use, E-Readers, Free DVD rentals, ILL available, Internet access, Life-long learning prog for all ages, Magazines, Meeting rooms, Movies, Online cat, Outreach serv, OverDrive digital audio bks, Photocopying/Printing, Preschool outreach, Prog for adults, Ref serv available, Scanner, STEM programs, Story hour, Study rm, Summer reading prog, Teen prog, Telephone ref
Mem of Three Rivers Library System
Open Mon 10-7:30, Tues-Thurs 10-6, Sat 9-Noon
Friends of the Library Group

BIG SPRINGS

P BIG SPRINGS PUBLIC LIBRARY, 400 Pine St, 69122. (Mail add: PO Box 192, 69122-0192), SAN 309-4022. Tel: 308-889-3482. E-mail: mjlibrarians@atcjet.net. *Librn,* Janie Jimenez
Founded 1927. Pop 700; Circ 2,000
Library Holdings: Bk Vols 12,000; Per Subs 16
Wireless access
Mem of Western Library System
Open Mon 1:30-4:30, Thurs 1:30-6:30, Sat 9-11

BLAIR

P BLAIR PUBLIC LIBRARY, 2233 Civic Dr, 68008. SAN 309-4030. Tel: 402-426-3617. FAX: 402-426-3633. Web Site: libraries.ne.gov/blair. *Dir,* Brooke Zarco; E-mail: bzarco@blairnebraska.org; *Pub Serv Librn,* Wendy Lukert; E-mail: wlukert@blairnebraska.org; *Tech Serv Librn,* Connie Hagedorn; E-mail: chagedorn@blairnebraska.org; Staff 5 (Non-MLS 5)
Founded 1915. Pop 7,500; Circ 75,730
Library Holdings: AV Mats 1,023; CDs 50; DVDs 324; Large Print Bks 1,769; Bk Titles 35,029; Per Subs 96; Talking Bks 1,104; Videos 1,100
Automation Activity & Vendor Info: (Cataloging) Follett Software; (Circulation) Follett Software; (ILL) OCLC; (OPAC) Follett Software
Wireless access
Mem of Three Rivers Library System
Open Mon-Thurs 10-7, Fri 10-5, Sat 10-4
Friends of the Library Group

BLOOMFIELD

P BLOOMFIELD PUBLIC LIBRARY*, 121 S Broadway, 68718. (Mail add: PO Box 548, 68718-0548), SAN 309-4057. Tel: 402-373-4588. FAX: 402-373-2601. E-mail: plibrary548@gmail.com. *Dir,* Jennifer Lauck; Staff 1 (Non-MLS 1)
Founded 1915. Pop 1,393; Circ 8,821
Library Holdings: Audiobooks 30; Bks on Deafness & Sign Lang 5; Braille Volumes 1; DVDs 50; Bk Titles 500; Per Subs 35
Automation Activity & Vendor Info: (Cataloging) Follett Software; (Circulation) Follett Software; (OPAC) Follett Software
Wireless access
Mem of Three Rivers Library System
Open Mon & Wed 12:30-7, Tues, Thurs & Fri 12:30-5:30, Sat 9-12:30
Friends of the Library Group

BLUE HILL

P BLUE HILL PUBLIC LIBRARY, 317 W Gage St, 68930. (Mail add: PO Box 278, 68930-0278), SAN 309-4065. Tel: 402-756-2701. E-mail: bhpublibr@gtmc.net. Web Site: libraries.ne.gov/bluehill. *Dir,* Tammy Lowery; Staff 1 (Non-MLS 1)
Founded 1929. Pop 883; Circ 4,200
Library Holdings: Bk Vols 7,000; Per Subs 35
Automation Activity & Vendor Info: (Cataloging) Follett Software; (Circulation) Follett Software; (OPAC) Follett Software
Wireless access
Mem of Central Plains Library System
Open Mon & Thurs 9-3:30, Wed 9-7, Sat 9-12
Friends of the Library Group

BOYS TOWN

S FATHER FLANAGAN'S BOYS HOME*, Boys Town Library Services, 13727 Flanagan Blvd, 68010. SAN 309-4073. Tel: 531-355-8340. *Media Spec,* Shanna Crosby-Wilson; Staff 1 (MLS 1)
Founded 1975
Library Holdings: Bk Titles 3,500; Per Subs 25
Wireless access
Partic in OCLC Online Computer Library Center, Inc; Proquest Dialog

BRIDGEPORT

P BRIDGEPORT PUBLIC LIBRARY*, 722 Main St, 69336. (Mail add: PO Box 940, 69336-0940), SAN 309-4081. Tel: 308-262-0326. FAX: 308-262-1412. Web Site: www.cityofbport.com/city-library. *Dir,* Tammy Howitt-Covalt; E-mail: tammycovalt@gmail.com; *Libr Asst,* Lori Leonard
Founded 1905. Pop 1,650; Circ 15,507
Library Holdings: Bk Titles 15,000; Per Subs 41
Automation Activity & Vendor Info: (Cataloging) Follett Software; (Circulation) Follett Software
Wireless access
Partic in LYRASIS; Valley Library Consortium
Open Tues & Thurs 9-7, Wed & Fri 9-5, Sat 9-2
Friends of the Library Group

BROADWATER

P BROADWATER PUBLIC LIBRARY, 251 N Starr St, 69125. (Mail add: PO Box 91, 69125-0091). Tel: 308-489-0199. E-mail: broadwaterpl@gmail.com. Web Site: libraries.ne.gov/broadwater. *Dir,* Position Currently Open
Library Holdings: Bk Vols 9,500
Wireless access
Mem of Western Library System
Open Wed & Fri 3-7, Sat 10-1

BROKEN BOW

P BROKEN BOW PUBLIC LIBRARY*, 626 South D St, 68822. SAN 309-4103. Tel: 308-872-2927. FAX: 308-872-2927. E-mail: bbpl@kdsi.net. Web Site: www.brokenbowlibrary.net. *Dir,* K Joan Birnie; Staff 3 (Non-MLS 3)
Founded 1885. Pop 3,491; Circ 44,718
Library Holdings: Audiobooks 350; CDs 157; DVDs 25; Electronic Media & Resources 21; Large Print Bks 350; Bk Vols 25,438; Per Subs 117; Talking Bks 507; Videos 375
Special Collections: DAR Holdings; Genealogy Coll; Local History Coll; Local Newspapers from 1882, bound; Nebraska History & Authors. Municipal Document Depository
Automation Activity & Vendor Info: (Cataloging) Follett Software; (Circulation) Follett Software; (ILL) OCLC FirstSearch; (OPAC) Follett Software
Wireless access
Function: Adult bk club, Adult literacy prog, After school storytime, Audiobks via web, BA reader (adult literacy), Bk club(s), Bks on cassette, Bks on CD, CD-ROM, Children's prog, Computers for patron use, Distance learning, Electronic databases & coll, Family literacy, Free DVD rentals, Home delivery & serv to seniorr ctr & nursing homes, Homebound delivery serv, ILL available, Large print keyboards, Online cat, OverDrive digital audio bks, Photocopying/Printing, Prog for adults, Prog for children & young adult, Satellite serv, Story hour, Summer reading prog, Tax forms, Teen prog, VHS videos, Wheelchair accessible
Mem of Central Plains Library System
Open Mon-Thurs 10-8, Fri 10-6, Sat 10-2
Friends of the Library Group

L CUSTER COUNTY LAW LIBRARY*, 604 Heritage Dr, 68822. SAN 375-1287. Tel: 308-872-2121. FAX: 308-872-5826. *Library Contact,* Amy Oxford
Founded 1910
Library Holdings: Bk Titles 1,000
Wireless access
Open Mon-Fri 8-12 & 1-5

BRUNING

P BRUNING PUBLIC LIBRARY, 117 E Main St, 68322. (Mail add: PO Box 250, 68322-0250), SAN 328-0233. Tel: 402-353-4610. E-mail: bruning.library@windstream.net. Web Site: www.bruninglibrary.com. *Librn,* Sarah Krehnke
Founded 1922. Pop 332; Circ 3,000
Library Holdings: Large Print Bks 50; Bk Titles 7,000
Subject Interests: Quilting
Wireless access
Mem of Southeast Library System
Open Tues & Thurs 4:5:30, Wed 9-12 & 2:30-5:30, Sat 9-Noon
Friends of the Library Group

BURWELL

P GARFIELD COUNTY LIBRARY, 217 G St, 68823. (Mail add: PO Box 307, 68823-0307), SAN 309-412X. Tel: 308-346-4711. FAX: 308-346-4711. E-mail: gcl@nctc.net. Web Site: garfieldcountylibrary.org. *Dir,* Shelley Ruterbories
Pop 2,363; Circ 14,154
Library Holdings: Bk Vols 15,399; Per Subs 37
Wireless access
Mem of Central Plains Library System
Open Mon & Wed 2-7, Fri 2-5, Sat 9-12
Friends of the Library Group

BUTTE

P DAVIES MEMORIAL LIBRARY*, 612 Thayer St, 68722. (Mail add: PO Box 276, 68722-0276). Tel: 402-775-2325. FAX: 402-775-2426. *Librn,* Norma Vanderbeck
Open Mon-Thurs 9-4

BYRON

P BYRON PUBLIC LIBRARY, 119 Kansas Ave, 68325. (Mail add: PO Box 91, 68325-0091), SAN 309-4146. Tel: 402-236-8752. Web Site: byroncommunitycenter.org/library.html. *Librn,* Lynda Ivers
Founded 1964. Pop 300; Circ 3,000. Sal $2,452
Library Holdings: Audiobooks 1; Bks-By-Mail 120; CDs 42; DVDs 33; Large Print Bks 55; Bk Vols 13,456; Videos 295
Mem of Southeast Library System
Open Wed 5:30-9, Sat 9-12

CALLAWAY

P NIGEL SPROUSE MEMORIAL LIBRARY*, 102 E Kimball, 68825. (Mail add: PO Box 277, 68825-0277), SAN 309-4154. Tel: 308-836-2610. E-mail: sprouseml@yahoo.com. *Dir,* Laura Seng
Pop 1,052; Circ 4,508
Library Holdings: Bk Vols 12,500
Wireless access
Mem of Central Plains Library System
Open Mon, Wed & Fri 1-6:30, Sat 9-1

CAMBRIDGE

P BUTLER MEMORIAL LIBRARY, 621 Penn St, 69022. (Mail add: PO Box 448, 69022-0448), SAN 309-4162. Tel: 308-697-3836. FAX: 308-697-3173. E-mail: bumemlib@gmail.com. Web Site: libraries.ne.gov/cambridge. *Dir,* Maria Downer
Founded 1951. Pop 1,000; Circ 15,500
Library Holdings: Bk Vols 16,000; Per Subs 21
Automation Activity & Vendor Info: (Cataloging) Follett Software; (Circulation) Follett Software; (OPAC) Follett Software
Wireless access
Mem of Central Plains Library System
Open Mon, Wed & Fri 2-5, Tues & Thurs 9-7 Sat 9-Noon

CAMPBELL

P CAMPBELL PUBLIC LIBRARY*, 721 Broad St, 68932. (Mail add: PO Box 101, 68932-0101), SAN 377-1814. Tel: 402-756-8121. E-mail: cvclerk@gtmc.net. Web Site: campbellne.com/campbell-library. *Dir & Librn,* Jeanne Penney
Library Holdings: Bk Vols 15,000
Mem of Central Plains Library System
Open Tues & Sat 9-Noon

CARROLL

P LIED CARROLL PUBLIC LIBRARY*, 506 Main St, 68723. (Mail add: PO Box 215, 68723-0215), SAN 309-4197. Tel: 402-585-4586. *Dir,* Norene Klinger; Tel: 402-585-4768, E-mail: noreneklinger@gmail.com
Library Holdings: Bk Vols 850
Wireless access
Mem of Three Rivers Library System
Open Thurs 6-8, Sat 9:30-11:30

CEDAR RAPIDS

P CEDAR RAPIDS PUBLIC LIBRARY*, 423 W Main St, 68627. (Mail add: PO Box 344, 68627-0344), SAN 309-4200. Tel: 308-358-0603. FAX: 308-358-0117. E-mail: licedrap@gpcom.net. Web Site: www.megavision.net/crpl. *Dir,* Marilyn Jo Schuele; *Asst Librn,* Veronica Ann Pfeifer
Founded 1914. Pop 407; Circ 5,000
Library Holdings: AV Mats 650; CDs 120; Large Print Bks 100; Bk Vols 10,821; Per Subs 10; Talking Bks 395; Videos 725
Special Collections: Cedar Rapids Nebraska Newspaper Items 1901-1935
Wireless access
Mem of Three Rivers Library System
Open Wed & Fri 9-11 & 2:30-5:30, Sat 2-5 & 7-9

CENTRAL CITY

P CENTRAL CITY PUBLIC LIBRARY*, 1604 15th Ave, 68826. SAN 309-4219. Tel: 308-946-2512. FAX: 308-946-3290. E-mail: cc.library.ne@gmail.com. Web Site: libraries.ne.gov/centralcity. *Libr Dir,* Sara Lee; *Asst Librn,* Adele Maynard; *Asst Librn,* Jamie Wright; *Youth Librn,* Judy Marco
Founded 1895. Pop 2,868; Circ 68,004
Library Holdings: Bks on Deafness & Sign Lang 17; e-books 4,079; Bk Vols 34,274; Per Subs 75
Subject Interests: Genealogy, Music
Automation Activity & Vendor Info: (Cataloging) LibLime; (Circulation) LibLime; (ILL) OCLC; (OPAC) LibLime
Wireless access
Open Mon-Thurs 10-8, Fri 10-6, Sat 10-2

CERESCO

P CERESCO COMMUNITY LIBRARY*, 425 S Second St, 68017. (Mail add: PO Box 158, 68017-0158), SAN 309-4227. Tel: 402-665-2112. E-mail: ceresco@microlnk.com.
Founded 1976. Pop 1,001
Library Holdings: Bks-By-Mail 25; CDs 45; Bk Titles 8,480; Per Subs 12; Talking Bks 55; Videos 220
Automation Activity & Vendor Info: (Cataloging) Biblionix; (Circulation) Biblionix; (OPAC) Biblionix
Wireless access
Open Tues-Thurs 10-12 & 2:30-7, Sat 10-3
Friends of the Library Group

CHADRON

P CHADRON PUBLIC LIBRARY*, 507 Bordeaux, 69337. SAN 309-4235. Tel: 308-432-0531. FAX: 308-432-0534. Web Site: www.chadron-nebraska.com/274/Public-Library. *Dir,* Rosella Tesch; E-mail: rtesch@chadronpubliclibrary.com; *Asst Dir,* Susan Rolfsmeier; E-mail: srolfsmeier@chadronpubliclibrary.com; Staff 4 (MLS 3, Non-MLS 1)
Founded 1911. Pop 5,933; Circ 73,000
Library Holdings: Bk Vols 30,000; Per Subs 82
Automation Activity & Vendor Info: (Cataloging) Follett Software; (Circulation) Follett Software; (OPAC) Follett Software
Wireless access
Publications: Annual Special Library Edition: 1989, A 100-year History
Mem of Western Library System
Open Mon-Thurs 10-8, Fri & Sat 12-5
Friends of the Library Group

C CHADRON STATE COLLEGE, Reta E King Library, 300 E 12th St, 69337. SAN 309-4243. Tel: 308-432-7062. E-mail: library@csc.edu. Web Site: www.csc.edu/library. *Librn, Pub Serv,* Christine Fullerton; E-mail: cfullerton@csc.edu; *Librn, Outreach Serv,* Shawn Hartman; E-mail: shartman@csc.edu; Staff 3 (MLS 3)
Founded 1911. Fac 110; Highest Degree: Master
Library Holdings: Bk Vols 215,000; Per Subs 140
Wireless access
Mem of Western Library System
Partic in OCLC Online Computer Library Center, Inc
Special Services for the Blind - Reader equip
Open Mon-Thurs 7am-10pm, Fri 7-4:30, Sun 1-9
Restriction: Access at librarian's discretion

S MUSEUM OF THE FUR TRADE LIBRARY, 6321 Hwy 20, 69337. Tel: 308-432-3843. FAX: 308-432-5963. E-mail: museum@furtrade.org. Web Site: www.furtrade.org. *Dir,* NaKaya Fester
Library Holdings: Bk Vols 10,000
Function: Res libr
Restriction: Not open to pub

CHAPPELL

P CHAPPELL MEMORIAL LIBRARY & ART GALLERY, 289 Babcock Ave, 69129. (Mail add: PO Box 248, 69129-0248), SAN 309-4251. Tel: 308-874-2626. FAX: 308-874-2626. E-mail: chappelllibrary35@outlook.com. Web Site: www.chappellne.org/library. *Dir,* Cheri Leach; *Asst Librn,* Peggy Hayden
Pop 1,095; Circ 7,823
Library Holdings: Bk Vols 11,170; Per Subs 15
Automation Activity & Vendor Info: (Circulation) Follett Software
Wireless access
Mem of Western Library System
Open Tues & Thurs 12-6, Sat 9-Noon
Friends of the Library Group

CLARKS

P CLARKS PUBLIC LIBRARY*, 101 W Amity, 68628. (Mail add: PO Box 223, 68628-0223), SAN 377-1830. Tel: 308-548-2864. E-mail: clarkspubliclibrary@yahoo.com. Web Site: www.nlc.state.ne.us/scripts/libraries/basiclibrarydata.asp?libcode=NE0053. *Dir,* Barbee Sweet
Founded 1917
Library Holdings: Bk Vols 6,500; Per Subs 23
Wireless access
Partic in NE Nebr Libr Asn
Open Mon 1-7, Tues-Fri 1-5
Friends of the Library Group

CLARKSON

P CLARKSON PUBLIC LIBRARY*, 318 Pine St, 68629. SAN 309-4278. Tel: 402-892-3235. E-mail: clarksonpubliclibrary@gmail.com. Web Site: libraries.ne.gov/clarkson. *Libr Dir,* Debra Nadrchal; Staff 3 (MLS 1, Non-MLS 2)
Founded 1921. Pop 699; Circ 3,620
Library Holdings: Bk Vols 12,000; Per Subs 24
Special Collections: Czechoslavakian Coll
Automation Activity & Vendor Info: (Cataloging) Follett Software; (Circulation) Follett Software
Wireless access
Function: Art exhibits, Bks on CD, Children's prog, Computer training, Computers for patron use, Home delivery & serv to seniorr ctr & nursing homes, ILL available, Internet access, Laminating, Large print keyboards, Magazines, Mail & tel request accepted, Microfiche/film & reading machines, Movies, Notary serv, Photocopying/Printing, Printer for laptops & handheld devices, Prog for adults, Prog for children & young adult, Scanner, Story hour, Wheelchair accessible
Mem of Three Rivers Library System
Open Mon, Tues, Thurs & Fri 2-6, Wed 10-1 & 4-7, Sat 10-1

CLAY CENTER

P CLAY CENTER PUBLIC LIBRARY*, 117 W Edgar St, 68933. SAN 309-4286. Tel: 402-762-3861. FAX: 402-762-3861. E-mail: claycenterlibrary@gmail.com. Web Site: libraries.ne.gov/claycenter. *Dir,* Cheryl Green
Founded 1912. Pop 1,000; Circ 10,931
Library Holdings: Bk Titles 15,267; Per Subs 50
Automation Activity & Vendor Info: (Cataloging) Follett Software; (Circulation) Follett Software
Wireless access
Open Mon-Thurs 1-6:30, Sat 10-3
Friends of the Library Group

CLEARWATER

P CLEARWATER PUBLIC LIBRARY*, 626 Main St, 68726. (Mail add: PO Box 24, 68726), SAN 309-4294. Tel: 402-485-2034. FAX: 402-485-2034. Web Site: libraries.ne.gov/clearwater. *Dir,* Kathy Feusse; E-mail: kfeusse@aol.com
Pop 409; Circ 3,077
Library Holdings: Bk Vols 5,271
Wireless access
Mem of Three Rivers Library System
Open Mon, Wed & Fri 1-5, Sat 10-2

COLUMBUS

J CENTRAL COMMUNITY COLLEGE, Columbus Resource Center, 4500 63rd St, 68602. (Mail add: PO Box 1027, 68602-1027), SAN 309-4316. Tel: 402-562-1202. Administration Tel: 402-562-1418. Toll Free Tel: 877-222-0780 (in-state). Web Site: libguides.cccneb.edu/libraries, www.cccneb.edu. *Dir,* Dee Johnson, II; E-mail: djohnson@cccneb.edu; *Assoc Dir,* Denette Drum; Tel: 402-562-1445, E-mail: ddrum@cccneb.edu
Founded 1969. Enrl 2,000; Fac 100; Highest Degree: Associate
Library Holdings: Bk Vols 24,000; Per Subs 150
Automation Activity & Vendor Info: (Cataloging) SirsiDynix; (Circulation) SirsiDynix; (OPAC) SirsiDynix; (Serials) OCLC
Wireless access
Mem of Three Rivers Library System
Open Mon-Thurs (Winter) 7:30am-9pm, Fri 7:30-4; Mon-Thurs (Summer) 7-5

P COLUMBUS PUBLIC LIBRARY*, 2504 14th St, 68601-4988. SAN 309-4308. Tel: 402-564-7116. FAX: 402-563-3378. Web Site: www.columbusne.us/library. *Dir,* Laura Whitehead; *Ch Serv,* Brad Hruska; Staff 15 (MLS 1, Non-MLS 14)
Founded 1900. Pop 33,000; Circ 197,700
Library Holdings: AV Mats 6,500; CDs 2,000; DVDs 1,200; Large Print Bks 2,200; Bk Titles 81,500; Bk Vols 88,880; Per Subs 170; Talking Bks 3,400; Videos 3,200
Special Collections: Play & Theatre Coll. State Document Depository
Automation Activity & Vendor Info: (Acquisitions) SirsiDynix; (Cataloging) SirsiDynix; (Circulation) SirsiDynix; (Media Booking) SirsiDynix; (OPAC) SirsiDynix; (Serials) SirsiDynix
Wireless access
Mem of Three Rivers Library System
Partic in ONELibrary Consortium
Open Mon-Thurs 9:30-9, Fri 9:30-5, Sat 10-5, Sun 1:30-5
Friends of the Library Group
Bookmobiles: 1. Librn, Stephanie Meyers

COMSTOCK

P COMSTOCK TOWNSHIP LIBRARY*, 119 W Main St, 68828. (Mail add: PO Box 15, 68828-0015). Tel: 308-750-7457. *Library Contact*, Pam Roth
Open Tues & Thurs 1-3

COZAD

P WILSON PUBLIC LIBRARY*, 910 Meridian, 69130-1755. SAN 309-4340. Tel: 308-784-2019. E-mail: wpublib@cozadtel.net. Web Site: www.wilsonpubliclibrary.org. *Dir*, Laurie Yocom
Pop 3,828; Circ 51,286
Library Holdings: Bk Vols 27,444; Per Subs 48
Subject Interests: Local hist
Wireless access
Mem of Central Plains Library System
Open Mon-Thurs 10-7, Fri 10-5, Sat 10-1
Friends of the Library Group

CRAWFORD

P CRAWFORD PUBLIC LIBRARY*, 601 Second St, 69339. SAN 309-4367. Tel: 308-665-1780. FAX: 308-665-3932. E-mail: crawlib@yahoo.com. Web Site: www.crawfordpubliclibrary.com. *Head Librn*, Marcella Thompson; *Ch, Libr Asst*, Cleone Hoyda
Founded 1916. Circ 26,889
Library Holdings: Bk Vols 14,000; Per Subs 22
Automation Activity & Vendor Info: (Cataloging) Follett Software; (Circulation) Follett Software; (OPAC) Follett Software
Mem of Western Library System
Open Mon-Fri 1-6, Sat 10-2
Friends of the Library Group

CREIGHTON

P CREIGHTON PUBLIC LIBRARY, 701 State St, 68729-4000. (Mail add: PO Box 158, 68729-0158), SAN 309-4375. Tel: 402-358-5115. FAX: 402-358-3767. E-mail: crpulib@gpcom.net. Web Site: creighton.org/public-library.html. *Dir*, Lisa Macke; Staff 3 (Non-MLS 3)
Founded 1914. Pop 1,223; Circ 15,000
Library Holdings: Bk Titles 13,108; Per Subs 54
Special Collections: Old West Coll; Second World War Coll
Automation Activity & Vendor Info: (Cataloging) Follett Software; (Circulation) Follett Software
Wireless access
Mem of Three Rivers Library System
Special Services for the Deaf - High interest/low vocabulary bks; Spec interest per
Open Mon & Wed 12-7, Tues & Thurs 10-5, Fri 12-5, Sat 9-1

CRETE

P CRETE PUBLIC LIBRARY, 1515 Forest Ave, 68333. SAN 309-4383. Tel: 402-826-3809. E-mail: crete.library@crete.ne.gov. Web Site: www.crete.ne.gov/vnews/display.v/SEC/Library. *Libr Dir*, Joy Stevenson; E-mail: joy.stevenson@crete.ne.gov; *Asst Dir, Youth Librn*, Laura Renker; E-mail: laura.renker@crete.ne.gov; *Outreach Serv*, Susan Church; E-mail: susan.church@crete.ne.gov; Staff 9 (MLS 2, Non-MLS 7)
Founded 1878. Pop 10,000; Circ 72,601
Library Holdings: Audiobooks 1,258; CDs 7; DVDs 3,207; Large Print Bks 2,171; Bk Vols 27,548; Per Subs 45
Special Collections: Czechoslovakian Coll; Nebraska Coll
Automation Activity & Vendor Info: (Cataloging) Biblionix/Apollo; (Circulation) Biblionix/Apollo
Wireless access
Function: 24/7 Electronic res, 24/7 Online cat, 3D Printer, Activity rm, Adult bk club, Art exhibits, Audiobks via web, Bilingual assistance for Spanish patrons, Bk club(s), Bks on CD, Children's prog, Computer training, Computers for patron use, Electronic databases & coll, Family literacy, Free DVD rentals, Home delivery & serv to seniorr ctr & nursing homes, Homebound delivery serv, ILL available, Instruction & testing, Internet access, Laminating, Magazines, Mail & tel request accepted, Makerspace, Meeting rooms, Movies, Music CDs, Online cat, Outreach serv, Outside serv via phone, mail, e-mail & web, OverDrive digital audio bks, Photocopying/Printing, Preschool reading prog, Printer for laptops & handheld devices, Prog for adults, Prog for children & young adult, Ref & res, Ref serv available, Scanner, Senior outreach, Serves people with intellectual disabilities, Spanish lang bks, STEM programs, Story hour, Study rm, Summer reading prog, Tax forms, Teen prog, Telephone ref, Wheelchair accessible
Mem of Southeast Library System
Open Mon, Wed & Fri 10-5, Tues & Thurs 10-7, Sat 10-4
Restriction: Circ limited
Friends of the Library Group

C DOANE COLLEGE*, Perkins Library, 1014 Boswell Ave, 68333-2421. SAN 309-4391. Tel: 402-826-8287. FAX: 402-826-8303. E-mail: library@doane.edu. Web Site: www.doane.edu/library. *Interim Libr Dir*, Cali Biaggi; E-mail: cali.biaggi@doane.edu; *E-Resources Librn, Learning Librn*, Jayne Germer; Tel: 402-826-8567, E-mail: jayne.germer@doane.edu; *Cataloger*, Holly Baber; Tel: 402-826-8569, E-mail: holly.baber@doane.edu; Staff 3 (MLS 3)
Founded 1872. Enrl 1,794; Fac 104; Highest Degree: Master
Library Holdings: AV Mats 3,418; e-books 6,000; Bk Vols 96,000; Per Subs 515
Special Collections: Doane College Archives Coll; Rall Art Gallery; Rossman Historiography; United Church of Christ Coll. State Document Depository; US Document Depository
Subject Interests: Liberal arts
Automation Activity & Vendor Info: (Acquisitions) SirsiDynix; (Cataloging) OCLC; (Circulation) SirsiDynix; (Course Reserve) SirsiDynix; (ILL) OCLC; (OPAC) SirsiDynix; (Serials) EBSCO Online
Publications: Accessions List
Partic in LYRASIS; NICLC; OCLC Online Computer Library Center, Inc
Open Mon-Thurs 8am-11pm, Fri 8-5, Sun 2-11

CROFTON

P EASTERN TOWNSHIP PUBLIC LIBRARY*, 206 W Main St, 68730. (Mail add: PO Box 455, 68730-0455), SAN 377-5380. Tel: 402-388-4915. FAX: 402-388-4915. E-mail: easterntownshiplib@gpcom.net. *Dir*, Diane Limoges; Staff 1 (Non-MLS 1)
Pop 853
Library Holdings: Bk Titles 6,500; Per Subs 15; Videos 75
Mem of Three Rivers Library System
Open Mon, Tues & Thurs 1-5, Wed 9-8:30, Sat 9-11

CULBERTSON

P CULBERTSON PUBLIC LIBRARY*, 507 New York St, 69024. (Mail add: PO Box 327, 69024-0327), SAN 309-4405. Tel: 308-278-2135. E-mail: culbertsonpubliclibrary@gmail.com. Web Site: libraries.ne.gov/culbertson. *Librn*, Connie McCoy; *Asst Librn*, Dana Wade; E-mail: danawade2003@yahoo.com
Founded 1908. Pop 795; Circ 2,898
Library Holdings: Bk Vols 10,430; Per Subs 22
Special Collections: Art Prints; Old Books; Old History of Hitchcock County (Otis Rogers Coll), clippings & pictures
Mem of Western Library System
Open Tues & Wed 2-7, Fri 9-1, Sat 12-5

CURTIS

P KLYTE BURT MEMORIAL PUBLIC LIBRARY*, 316 Center Ave, 69025. (Mail add: PO Box 29, 69025-0029), SAN 309-4413. Tel: 308-367-4148. E-mail: kbmlib@curtis-ne.com. Web Site: libraries.ne.gov/curtis. *Libr Dir*, Waneta Storm; Staff 1 (Non-MLS 1)
Founded 1940. Pop 3,416; Circ 10,800
Library Holdings: Audiobooks 278; DVDs 614; Large Print Bks 327; Bk Titles 9,781; Per Subs 5; Videos 26
Wireless access
Function: Adult bk club, After school storytime, Bks on CD, Children's prog, Computers for patron use, Electronic databases & coll, Free DVD rentals, ILL available, Internet access, Laminating, Magazines, Movies, OverDrive digital audio bks, Photocopying/Printing, Preschool reading prog, Prog for children & young adult, Scanner, Story hour, Summer & winter reading prog, Summer reading prog, Telephone ref
Mem of Central Plains Library System
Open Mon & Wed-Fri 1:30-5:30, Tues 2-7, Sat 2-5

C NEBRASKA COLLEGE OF TECHNICAL AGRICULTURE LIBRARY*, 404 E Seventh St, 69025. (Mail add: RR 3 Box 23A, 69025-0069), SAN 371-702X. Tel: 308-367-5213. FAX: 308-367-5209. Web Site: ncta.unl.edu. *Libr Serv Spec*, Mo Khamouna; E-mail: mkhamouna1@unl.edu; Staff 1 (Non-MLS 1)
Enrl 234; Fac 22
Library Holdings: Bk Titles 6,410; Per Subs 320
Automation Activity & Vendor Info: (Acquisitions) Follett Software; (Cataloging) Follett Software; (Circulation) Follett Software; (ILL) Follett Software; (OPAC) Follett Software; (Serials) Follett Software
Wireless access
Mem of Central Plains Library System
Open Mon-Fri 8am-10pm, Sun 6pm-10pm

DAKOTA CITY

P DAKOTA CITY PUBLIC LIBRARY*, 1710 Broadway, 68731. (Mail add: PO Box 482, 68731-0189), SAN 309-4421. Tel: 402-987-3778. FAX: 402-987-3778. E-mail: library@dakotacity.net. Web Site: www.dakota-city.net/city/library. *Dir*, Kathy Schable; Staff 2 (MLS 1, Non-MLS 1)

Pop 1,900; Circ 6,444
Library Holdings: Audiobooks 167; DVDs 765; Bk Vols 5,257; Per Subs 20
Special Collections: Library of America Classics; War of the Rebellion Coll
Automation Activity & Vendor Info: (Cataloging) Follett Software; (Circulation) Follett Software
Wireless access
Function: 24/7 Online cat, Activity rm, Adult bk club, After school storytime, Bks on CD, Children's prog, Computers for patron use, Free DVD rentals, Internet access, Magazines, Meeting rooms, Online cat, Photocopying/Printing, Prog for children & young adult, Spanish lang bks, Story hour, Summer & winter reading prog, Summer reading prog, Wheelchair accessible
Mem of Three Rivers Library System
Open Mon & Thurs 1-8, Tues, Wed & Fri 1-5, Sat 9-Noon
Friends of the Library Group

DALTON

P DALTON PUBLIC LIBRARY*, 306 Main St, 69131. (Mail add: PO Box 353, 69131-0353), SAN 309-443X. Tel: 308-377-2413. E-mail: daltonlibrary@daltontel.net. *Dir,* Charles Powell
Pop 568; Circ 2,247
Library Holdings: Audiobooks 18; Large Print Bks 90; Bk Vols 3,000; Videos 23
Mem of Western Library System
Open Mon & Tues 10-1 & 3-5
Friends of the Library Group

DAVENPORT

P DAVENPORT PUBLIC LIBRARY*, 109 N Maple Ave, 68335. (Mail add: PO Box 236, 68335-0236), SAN 309-4448. Tel: 402-364-2147. E-mail: davenportlib@superiorinet.net. *Librn,* Sharon Littrel
Pop 339; Circ 19,624
Library Holdings: Bk Vols 12,000; Per Subs 17
Wireless access
Mem of Southeast Library System
Open Mon-Thurs 2:30-5

DAVID CITY

P ROMAN L & VICTORIA E HRUSKA MEMORIAL PUBLIC LIBRARY*, 399 N Fifth St, 68632. SAN 309-4456. Tel: 402-367-3100. FAX: 402-367-3105. E-mail: hruskalibrary@gmail.com. Web Site: www.davidcitylibrary.com. *Libr Dir,* Kay Schmid
Founded 1891
Subject Interests: County hist
Automation Activity & Vendor Info: (Acquisitions) Koha; (Cataloging) Koha; (Circulation) Koha; (ILL) Koha
Wireless access
Function: Adult bk club, After school storytime, Archival coll, Art exhibits, Audiobks via web, Bks on CD, Children's prog, Computer training, Computers for patron use, Electronic databases & coll, Free DVD rentals, Home delivery & serv to seniorr ctr & nursing homes, ILL available, Instruction & testing, Mail & tel request accepted, Microfiche/film & reading machines, Music CDs, Online cat, OverDrive digital audio bks, Photocopying/Printing, Preschool reading prog, Prog for adults, Prog for children & young adult, Scanner, Senior computer classes, Senior outreach, Serves people with intellectual disabilities, Story hour, Summer & winter reading prog, Tax forms, Wheelchair accessible
Open Mon-Thurs 10-7, Sat 9-1
Friends of the Library Group

DAYKIN

P DAYKIN PUBLIC LIBRARY, 201 Mary Ave, 68338. (Mail add: PO Box 215, 68338-0215), *Dir,* Clarice Meyer; E-mail: dcmeyer@diodecom.net
Library Holdings: Bk Vols 6,000
Wireless access
Mem of Southeast Library System
Open Wed 4-6

DENTON

R OUR LADY OF GUADALUPE SEMINARY LIBRARY*, 7880 W Denton Rd, 68339. (Mail add: PO Box 147, 68339-0147). Tel: 402-797-7700. FAX: 402-797-7705. Web Site: www.fsspolgs.org. *Librn,* Sister Stephen Larson; E-mail: srstephenl@yahoo.com
Library Holdings: Bk Vols 28,000

DESHLER

P JENNIFER REINKE PUBLIC LIBRARY, Deshler Public Library, (Formerly Deshler Public Library), 311 E Pearl St, 68340. (Mail add: PO Box 520, 68340-0520), SAN 309-4472. Tel: 402-365-4107. FAX: 402-365-4107. E-mail: ansdad@yahoo.com. *Librn,* Brant Fegter; *Asst Librn,* Lisa Monk
Founded 1937. Pop 810; Circ 4,050
Library Holdings: AV Mats 20; Bk Vols 13,900; Per Subs 15
Wireless access
Function: ILL available
Mem of Southeast Library System
Open Mon-Wed 3-6, Fri 10-12:30, Sat 9-Noon

DEWITT

P BURKLEY LIBRARY & RESOURCE CENTER*, 208 E Fillmore Ave, 68341. (Mail add: PO Box 375, 68341-0375). Tel: 402-683-2145. FAX: 402-683-2145. E-mail: brc@galaxycable.net. Web Site: dewitt.ne.gov/our-community/library. *Dir,* Geraldine Powers
Pop 577; Circ 2,363
Library Holdings: AV Mats 210; DVDs 200; Bk Vols 10,000; Per Subs 20; Talking Bks 237
Automation Activity & Vendor Info: (Cataloging) Biblionix; (Circulation) Biblionix; (OPAC) Biblionix
Mem of Southeast Library System
Open Mon & Thurs 2-5, Tues & Wed 2-6, Sat 9-12

DODGE

P JOHN ROGERS MEMORIAL PUBLIC LIBRARY*, 703 Second St, 68633. SAN 309-4502. Tel: 402-693-2512. E-mail: johnrogerslibrary@yahoo.com. Web Site: libraries.ne.gov/dodge. *Libr Dir,* Jenny Praest; *Asst Librn,* Mary Mandel
Pop 700; Circ 1,000
Library Holdings: Bk Vols 6,500; Per Subs 22
Automation Activity & Vendor Info: (Cataloging) OCLC WorldShare Interlibrary Loan; (Circulation) OCLC WorldShare Interlibrary Loan; (OPAC) OCLC WorldShare Interlibrary Loan
Wireless access
Mem of Three Rivers Library System
Open Tues & Wed 11:30-5, Thurs 11:30-8, Sat 9-Noon

DORCHESTER

P DORCHESTER PUBLIC LIBRARY*, Sixth & Washington, 68343. (Mail add: PO Box 268, 68343-0268), SAN 377-2489. Tel: 402-802-7250. *Dir,* Vanessa Willison; E-mail: whiteskies312@gmail.com
Pop 614; Circ 732
Library Holdings: Bk Vols 5,875
Mem of Southeast Library System
Open Wed 4-6, Sat 9:30-11:30
Friends of the Library Group

ELGIN

P ELGIN PUBLIC LIBRARY, 503 S Second St, 68636-3222. (Mail add: PO Box 240, 68636-0240), SAN 309-4529. Tel: 402-843-2460. FAX: 402-843-2460. E-mail: elgpblib@gpcom.net. *Co-Dir,* Barb Bode; *Co-Dir,* Dianne Gunderson
Pop 661; Circ 5,300
Library Holdings: CDs 75; DVDs 60; Large Print Bks 680; Bk Titles 11,900; Per Subs 17; Talking Bks 101; Videos 184
Automation Activity & Vendor Info: (Cataloging) Biblionix; (Circulation) Biblionix; (Course Reserve) Biblionix
Wireless access
Function: Adult bk club, Bks on cassette, Bks on CD, Children's prog, Computers for patron use, Free DVD rentals, Home delivery & serv to seniorr ctr & nursing homes, Homebound delivery serv, ILL available, Photocopying/Printing, Spoken cassettes & CDs, Spoken cassettes & DVDs, Story hour, Summer reading prog, VHS videos, Wheelchair accessible
Mem of Three Rivers Library System
Open Mon 4-7, Tues & Thurs 1-5, Wed 1-7, Fri 9-Noon

ELM CREEK

P ELM CREEK PUBLIC LIBRARY*, 241 N Tyler St, 68836. (Mail add: PO Box 489, 68836-0489), SAN 377-189X. Tel: 308-856-4394. E-mail: library@elmcreekne.com. Web Site: elmcreekne.com/library. *Librn,* Jane Walker
Library Holdings: Bk Vols 9,000; Per Subs 16
Wireless access
Mem of Central Plains Library System
Open Mon 3:30-5:30, Tues 9-12 & 3:30-5:30, Wed 2-7, Thurs 9-12, Sat 9-5

ELMWOOD

P ELMWOOD PUBLIC LIBRARY*, 124 West D St, 68349. (Mail add: PO Box 283, 68349-0283), SAN 309-4545. Tel: 402-994-4125. FAX: 402-994-4125. E-mail: elmwoodlibrary@outlook.com. Web Site: libraries.ne.gov/elmwood, www.elmwoodnebraska.com/nl/index.php/community/library. *Libr Dir,* Janet Sorensen
Founded 1917. Pop 600; Circ 4,636
Library Holdings: Bk Vols 11,089; Per Subs 23
Special Collections: Autographed Books (Bess Streeter Aldrich Coll)
Automation Activity & Vendor Info: (Cataloging) Follett Software; (Circulation) Follett Software
Wireless access
Mem of Southeast Library System; Three Rivers Library System
Open Mon 3-8, Tues & Wed 2-6, Thurs & Sat 10-2
Friends of the Library Group

ELWOOD

P ELWOOD PUBLIC LIBRARY*, 306 Calvert St, 68937. (Mail add: PO Box 327, 68937-0327), SAN 309-4553. Tel: 308-785-8155. FAX: 308-785-2035. E-mail: elwood.public@outlook.com. Web Site: libraries.ne.gov/elwood. *Dir,* Jane Hilton
Pop 2,140; Circ 18,492
Library Holdings: Bk Vols 18,226; Per Subs 18
Mem of Central Plains Library System
Open Mon 4pm-8pm, Tues & Thurs 1-5:30, Wed & Sat 9-2, Fri 1:30-4:30

EMERSON

P EMERSON PUBLIC LIBRARY*, 110 Main St, 68733. (Mail add: PO Box 160, 68733-0160), SAN 309-4561. Tel: 402-695-2449. FAX: 402-695-2449. E-mail: libraryemersonpublic@gmail.com. Web Site: libraries.ne.gov/emersonpubliclibrary. *Library Contact,* LaVaille Reifenrath
Founded 1930. Pop 874; Circ 7,001
Library Holdings: Bk Titles 10,000; Per Subs 20
Subject Interests: Alaskana
Automation Activity & Vendor Info: (Acquisitions) OCLC Online; (Cataloging) Follett Software; (Circulation) Follett Software; (OPAC) Follett Software
Wireless access
Function: Accelerated reader prog, Adult bk club, Adult literacy prog, After school storytime, Archival coll, Art exhibits, Audio & video playback equip for onsite use, Audiobks via web, AV serv, BA reader (adult literacy), Bi-weekly Writer's Group, Bilingual assistance for Spanish patrons, Bk club(s), Bk reviews (Group), Bks on cassette, Bks on CD, Bus archives, CD-ROM, Chess club, Citizenship assistance, Computer training, Computers for patron use, Digital talking bks, Distance learning, Doc delivery serv, E-Reserves, Electronic databases & coll, Equip loans & repairs, Family literacy, For res purposes, Free DVD rentals, Games & aids for people with disabilities, Genealogy discussion group, Govt ref serv, Health sci info serv, Holiday prog, Home delivery & serv to seniorr ctr & nursing homes, Homebound delivery serv, Homework prog, ILL available, Instruction & testing, Internet access, Jail serv, Jazz prog, Large print keyboards, Learning ctr, Legal assistance to inmates, Literacy & newcomer serv, Magnifiers for reading, Mail & tel request accepted, Mail loans to mem, Masonic res mat, Microfiche/film & reading machines, Museum passes, Music CDs, Notary serv, Online cat, Online info literacy tutorials on the web & in blackboard, Online ref, Orientations, Outreach serv, Outside serv via phone, mail, e-mail & web, OverDrive digital audio bks, Passport agency, Photocopying/Printing, Preschool outreach, Preschool reading prog, Printer for laptops & handheld devices, Prof lending libr, Prog for adults, Prog for children & young adult, Ref & res, Ref serv available, Res libr, Res performed for a fee, Satellite serv, Scanner, Senior computer classes, Senior outreach, Serves people with intellectual disabilities, Spanish lang bks, Specialized serv in classical studies, Spoken cassettes & CDs, Spoken cassettes & DVDs, Story hour, Summer & winter reading prog, Tax forms, Teen prog, Telephone ref, VHS videos, Visual arts prog, Wheelchair accessible, Words travel prog, Workshops
Mem of Three Rivers Library System
Special Services for the Blind - Web-Braille
Open Mon & Fri 9-12 & 1-5, Wed 2-7, Sat 9-11
Friends of the Library Group

EUSTIS

P EUSTIS PUBLIC LIBRARY, 108 N Morton St, 69028. (Mail add: PO Box 68, 69028-0068), SAN 309-457X. Tel: 308-486-2651. E-mail: eustislibrary@gmail.com. *Librn,* Ramona Koch
Founded 1935. Pop 401; Circ 3,765
Library Holdings: Bk Vols 6,485
Wireless access
Mem of Central Plains Library System
Open Wed 3-6, Sat 9:30-11

EWING

P EWING TOWNSHIP LIBRARY*, 202 E Nebraska, 68735. (Mail add: PO Box 55, 68735-0055), SAN 309-4588. E-mail: ewinglibrary@yahoo.com. *Librn,* Idella Tuttle
Founded 1927. Pop 387
Library Holdings: Audiobooks 9; DVDs 77; Large Print Bks 324; Bk Titles 5,296; Videos 131
Wireless access
Mem of Central Plains Library System
Partic in Nebr Network
Open Tues 9-12 & 3-5, Thurs 2-5, Sat 9-12

EXETER

P EXETER PUBLIC LIBRARY*, 202 S Exeter Ave, 68351. (Mail add: PO Box 96, 68351-0096), SAN 309-4596. Tel: 402-266-3031. FAX: 402-266-3061. E-mail: epublib@hotmail.com. *Dir,* Jessica Votipka; Staff 2 (Non-MLS 2)
Pop 712; Circ 5,194
Library Holdings: AV Mats 348; Bk Titles 12,160; Per Subs 14; Talking Bks 81
Automation Activity & Vendor Info: (Circulation) ComPanion Corp
Mem of Southeast Library System
Open Mon, Wed & Fri 8-12 & 1-5, Sat 9-12

FAIRBURY

P FAIRBURY PUBLIC LIBRARY*, 601 Seventh St, 68352. SAN 309-460X. Tel: 402-729-2843. FAX: 402-729-2880. E-mail: fairburypubliclibrary@yahoo.com. Web Site: www.fairburylibrary.org. *Libr Dir,* Debbie Aden; *Ch,* Linda Dux; Staff 6 (MLS 1, Non-MLS 5)
Founded 1909. Pop 3,803; Circ 23,295
Oct 2015-Sept 2016 Income $202,645, State $883, City $192,611, Federal $2,353, Locally Generated Income $3,260, Parent Institution $3,250, Other $288. Mats Exp $18,631, Books $11,728, Per/Ser (Incl. Access Fees) $3,001, Micro $440, AV Mat $1,000, Electronic Ref Mat (Incl. Access Fees) $2,462. Sal Prof $99,420
Library Holdings: Audiobooks 1,289; Braille Volumes 1; CDs 229; DVDs 814; Electronic Media & Resources 2; Large Print Bks 2,810; Microforms 249; Bk Titles 27,521; Per Subs 61; Videos 160
Automation Activity & Vendor Info: (Cataloging) Biblionix/Apollo; (Circulation) Biblionix/Apollo; (OPAC) Biblionix/Apollo
Wireless access
Function: 24/7 Electronic res, 24/7 Online cat, 3D Printer, Accelerated reader prog, Adult bk club, Audiobks on Playaways & MP3, Audiobks via web, Bilingual assistance for Spanish patrons, Bks on CD, Children's prog, Computers for patron use, E-Reserves, Electronic databases & coll, Free DVD rentals, Home delivery & serv to seniorr ctr & nursing homes, ILL available, Internet access, Large print keyboards, Magazines, Mango lang, Microfiche/film & reading machines, Movies, Music CDs, Online cat, OverDrive digital audio bks, Photocopying/Printing, Prog for adults, Prog for children & young adult, Scanner, Spanish lang bks, STEM programs, Story hour, Summer reading prog, Tax forms, Wheelchair accessible
Mem of Southeast Library System
Open Mon-Thurs 10-7, Fri 10-6, Sat 9-1
Restriction: Non-resident fee

FAIRFIELD

P FAIRFIELD PUBLIC LIBRARY*, 412 North D St, 68938. (Mail add: PO Box 278, 68938-0278), SAN 309-4626. Tel: 402-726-2104. FAX: 402-726-2388. E-mail: fplibrary@hotmail.com. Web Site: libraries.ne.gov/fairfield. *Libr Dir,* Stephanie Haack
Founded 1914. Pop 367; Circ 2,699
Oct 2014-Sept 2015 Income $16,000. Sal $8,060
Library Holdings: Bk Vols 5,000; Per Subs 13
Automation Activity & Vendor Info: (Acquisitions) Book Systems; (Cataloging) Book Systems; (Circulation) Book Systems
Wireless access
Function: Accelerated reader prog, Bks on CD, Computers for patron use, Electronic databases & coll, Free DVD rentals, Homebound delivery serv, ILL available, Internet access, Laminating, Magazines, Movies, Online cat, Outside serv via phone, mail, e-mail & web, OverDrive digital audio bks, Photocopying/Printing, Printer for laptops & handheld devices, Scanner, VHS videos
Open Mon & Wed 1:30-5:30, Sat 8-Noon
Friends of the Library Group

FAIRMONT

P FAIRMONT PUBLIC LIBRARY, 600 F St, 68354. (Mail add: PO Box 428, 68354-0428), SAN 309-4634. Tel: 402-268-6081. FAX: 402-268-6081. E-mail: fairmontpubliclibrary@gmail.com. Web Site: www.fairmont-nebraska.org/vnews/display.v/SEC/Public%20Library. *Dir,* Wanda Marget; E-mail: wmarget@windstream.net; Staff 1 (Non-MLS 1)

Founded 1916. Pop 709
Library Holdings: Bk Vols 10,966; Per Subs 57
Automation Activity & Vendor Info: (Cataloging) Follett Software; (Circulation) Follett Software; (OPAC) Follett Software
Wireless access
Mem of Southeast Library System
Open Mon 8-12, 1-5:30 & 6:30-9, Wed 6:30pm-9pm, Fri 1-5:30, Sat 8-12

FALLS CITY

P THE FALLS CITY LIBRARY & ARTS CENTER*, 1400 Stone St, 68355. SAN 309-4642. Tel: 402-245-2913. FAX: 402-245-3031. E-mail: info@fallscitylibrary.org. Web Site: www.fallscitylibrary.org. *Dir,* Hope Schawang
Pop 4,671
Library Holdings: Bk Vols 50,000; Per Subs 100
Special Collections: Local Artists Coll, paintings
Wireless access
Open Mon-Thurs 10-8, Fri 10-5:30, Sat 9-Noon
Friends of the Library Group

FARNAM

P FARNAM PUBLIC LIBRARY*, 313 Main St, 69029. (Mail add: PO Box 8, 69029-0008), SAN 309-4650. Tel: 308-569-2318. E-mail: farnamlibrary@gmail.com. Web Site: farnampubliclibrary.com. *Dir,* Kaylin Craig
Pop 220; Circ 3,663
Library Holdings: Bk Vols 9,000
Mem of Central Plains Library System
Open Wed 10-12 & 4-5, Thurs 3-6, Sat 1-5

FORT CALHOUN

S WASHINGTON COUNTY HISTORICAL ASSOCIATION*, Museum Library, 102 N 14th St, 68023. (Mail add: PO Box 25, 68023-0025), SAN 326-5811. Tel: 402-468-5740. Web Site: www.wchamuseum.com/. *Curator,* Faith Norwood; E-mail: Curator@wchamuseum.com
Founded 1938
Special Collections: Books with Copyright Date from 1850's to 1950's & Histories Principly Midwest/Nebraska
Wireless access
Publications: 1876 History of Washington, with index
Open Tues-Fri 9-5, Sat 9-1
Restriction: Non-circulating to the pub

FRANKLIN

P FRANKLIN PUBLIC LIBRARY*, 1502 P St, 68939. SAN 309-4669. Tel: 308-425-3162. E-mail: fpl@cityoffranklin.net. Web Site: libraries.ne.gov/franklin. *Librn,* Elizabeth Williams; *Asst Librn,* Cindy Seifert
Pop 1,000; Circ 11,500
Library Holdings: Bk Titles 12,000; Per Subs 21
Automation Activity & Vendor Info: (Cataloging) Follett Software; (Circulation) Follett Software; (OPAC) Follett Software
Wireless access
Mem of Central Plains Library System
Open Mon 1-8, Wed & Fri 10-5, Thurs 10-6, Sat 9-Noon
Friends of the Library Group

FREMONT

S DODGE COUNTY HISTORICAL SOCIETY*, Louis E May Museum Library, 1643 N Nye Ave, 68025. SAN 327-2265. Tel: 402-721-4515. E-mail: louisemaymuseum@gmail.com. Web Site: maymuseum.com. *Dir,* Jeff Kappeler
Library Holdings: Bk Titles 1,000
Wireless access

S EASTERN NEBRASKA GENEALOGICAL SOCIETY LIBRARY*, 1643 N Nye Ave, 68025. (Mail add: PO Box 541, 68026-0541), SAN 370-8551. Tel: 402-721-4515. Web Site: www.usgennet.org/usa/ne/county/dodge/ENGSociety.HTM. *Library Contact,* Renee Bunck; E-mail: reneebunck@gmail.com
Founded 1972
Library Holdings: Bk Vols 800; Per Subs 200
Publications: Newsletter (Quarterly); Roots & Leaves (Quarterly)
Open Wed-Sat 1:30-3:30 or by appointment

P KEENE MEMORIAL LIBRARY*, 1030 N Broad St, 68025-4199. SAN 309-4677. Tel: 402-727-2694. FAX: 402-727-2693. Web Site: www.fremontne.gov/library. *Interim Dir, Youth Serv Librn,* Laura England-Biggs; E-mail: laura.biggs@fremontne.gov; *Adult Serv/Circ Librn,* Elisa Cruz; E-mail: elisa.cruz@fremontne.gov. Subject Specialists: *Educ,* Elisa Cruz; Staff 3 (MLS 3)
Founded 1901. Pop 26,500; Circ 194,654
Library Holdings: Bk Titles 90,000; Per Subs 235
Special Collections: Classics (Taylor)
Automation Activity & Vendor Info: (Acquisitions) SirsiDynix; (Cataloging) SirsiDynix; (Circulation) SirsiDynix; (OPAC) SirsiDynix; (Serials) SirsiDynix
Wireless access
Function: 24/7 Electronic res, 24/7 Online cat, Activity rm, Adult bk club, After school storytime, Archival coll, Audiobks on Playaways & MP3, Audiobks via web, Bilingual assistance for Spanish patrons, Bk club(s), Bks on CD, Children's prog, Computer training, Computers for patron use, Distance learning, Doc delivery serv, E-Readers, E-Reserves, Electronic databases & coll, Equip loans & repairs, Family literacy, Free DVD rentals, Games & aids for people with disabilities, Holiday prog, Home delivery & serv to seniorr ctr & nursing homes, Homebound delivery serv, Homework prog, ILL available, Instruction & testing, Internet access, Magazines, Mango lang, Meeting rooms, Microfiche/film & reading machines, Movies, Music CDs, Online cat, Online ref, Outreach serv, OverDrive digital audio bks, Photocopying/Printing, Preschool outreach, Preschool reading prog, Printer for laptops & handheld devices, Prog for adults, Prog for children & young adult, Ref & res, Ref serv available, Res performed for a fee, Scanner, Senior outreach, Serves people with intellectual disabilities, Spanish lang bks, Story hour, Study rm, Summer & winter reading prog, Summer reading prog, Tax forms, Teen prog, Telephone ref, Workshops
Mem of Three Rivers Library System
Partic in OCLC Online Computer Library Center, Inc
Open Mon-Thurs 9:30-8:30, Fri & Sat 9:30-5:30, Sun 12:30-4:30
Restriction: Circ limited, In-house use for visitors, Non-resident fee
Friends of the Library Group

CR MIDLAND UNIVERSITY, Luther Library, 900 N Clarkson, 68025. SAN 309-4685. Tel: 402-941-6250. FAX: 402-727-6223. E-mail: library@midlandu.edu. Web Site: www.midlandu.edu/academics/luther-library. *Chief Info Officer,* Shane Perrien; E-mail: perrien@midlandu.edu; *Head Librn,* Laura Hinman; E-mail: hinmanl@midlandu.edu; Staff 4 (MLS 2, Non-MLS 2)
Founded 1883. Enrl 720; Fac 53; Highest Degree: Bachelor
Library Holdings: AV Mats 500; CDs 1,400; DVDs 500; e-books 172,000; e-journals 12,000; Bk Titles 51,000; Bk Vols 88,600; Per Subs 125; Videos 1,000
Special Collections: Biblical Literature. US Document Depository
Automation Activity & Vendor Info: (Acquisitions) OCLC WorldShare Interlibrary Loan; (Cataloging) OCLC WorldShare Interlibrary Loan; (Circulation) OCLC WorldShare Interlibrary Loan; (Course Reserve) OCLC WorldShare Interlibrary Loan; (ILL) OCLC WorldShare Interlibrary Loan; (Media Booking) OCLC WorldShare Interlibrary Loan; (OPAC) OCLC WorldShare Interlibrary Loan; (Serials) OCLC WorldShare Interlibrary Loan
Wireless access
Mem of Three Rivers Library System
Partic in Nebr Independent Col Libr Consortium; OCLC Online Computer Library Center, Inc
Open Mon-Thurs 7:45am-11pm, Fri 7:45-4:30, Sat 1-4, Sun 3-11

FRIEND

P GILBERT PUBLIC LIBRARY*, 628 Second St, 68359. SAN 309-4693. Tel: 402-947-5081. E-mail: gilbertlibrary@diodecom.net. Web Site: www.ci.friend.ne.us/library.htm. *Dir,* Diane Odoski
Founded 1916. Circ 3,046
Library Holdings: Bk Vols 11,391; Per Subs 35
Wireless access
Mem of Southeast Library System
Open Mon & Wed 1:30-7:30, Tues & Thurs 9-1, Sat 9-Noon

FULLERTON

P FULLERTON PUBLIC LIBRARY*, 903 Broadway, 68638. (Mail add: PO Box 578, 68638-0578), SAN 309-4707. Tel: 308-536-2382. FAX: 308-536-2382. E-mail: fullertonpubliclibrary13@gmail.com. Web Site: www.libraries.ne.gov/fullerton. *Dir,* Lacey Bittner
Founded 1913. Pop 1,452; Circ 12,008
Library Holdings: Bk Vols 13,000; Per Subs 40
Automation Activity & Vendor Info: (Cataloging) Follett Software; (Circulation) Follett Software
Wireless access
Mem of Three Rivers Library System
Open Mon 12-5 & 7-9, Tues 10-5, Wed 2-6 & 7-9, Thurs & Fri 1-5, Sat 10-Noon
Friends of the Library Group

GENEVA

P GENEVA PUBLIC LIBRARY, 1043 G St, 68361. SAN 309-4715. Tel: 402-759-3416. FAX: 402-759-3416. Web Site: GenevaLibrary.com. *Libr Dir,* Sarah Johnson; E-mail: sjohnson@cityofgeneva.org; Staff 5 (MLS 1, Non-MLS 4)
Founded 1906. Pop 3,032; Circ 40,536
Library Holdings: Audiobooks 633; AV Mats 2,890; CDs 322; DVDs 3,303; e-books 24,802; Electronic Media & Resources 22; Large Print Bks 442; Bk Vols 17,790; Per Subs 25; Talking Bks 12,100; Videos 622
Automation Activity & Vendor Info: (Cataloging) Biblionix/Apollo; (Circulation) Biblionix/Apollo; (OPAC) Biblionix/Apollo; (Serials) Biblionix/Apollo
Function: 24/7 Electronic res, 24/7 Online cat, 3D Printer, Audiobks via web, Bks on CD, Children's prog, Computers for patron use, Electronic databases & coll, Free DVD rentals, Genealogy discussion group, Home delivery & serv to seniorr ctr & nursing homes, Homebound delivery serv, ILL available, Instruction & testing, Internet access, Laminating, Magazines, Mail & tel request accepted, Makerspace, Meeting rooms, Online cat, Outreach serv, OverDrive digital audio bks, Photocopying/Printing, Prog for adults, Prog for children & young adult, Ref serv available, Res assist avail, Scanner, Senior computer classes, Senior outreach, STEM programs, Story hour, Study rm, Summer reading prog, Teen prog, Wheelchair accessible
Mem of Southeast Library System
Open Mon, Wed & Fri 10-6, Tues & Thurs 12-8, Sat 10-4

GENOA

P GENOA PUBLIC LIBRARY*, 421 Willard Ave, 68640. (Mail add: PO Box 279, 68640-0279), SAN 309-4723. Tel: 402-993-2943. E-mail: genoanebraskapubliclibrary@gmail.com. Web Site: libraries.ne.gov/genoa. *Libr Dir,* Tammi Thiem; *Children's Activities Dir,* Kimberly Thiem
Pop 1,090; Circ 12,079
Library Holdings: Bk Vols 8,597; Per Subs 29
Automation Activity & Vendor Info: (Cataloging) Follett Software; (Circulation) Follett Software
Function: Computer training, Electronic databases & coll, Homebound delivery serv, ILL available, Magnifiers for reading, Music CDs, Photocopying/Printing, Prog for children & young adult, Summer reading prog, Tax forms, VHS videos, Wheelchair accessible
Mem of Three Rivers Library System
Open Mon & Fri 10-12 & 2-5, Tues & Thurs 10-12, 2-5 & 6-8, Wed 3-6, Sat 10-2
Friends of the Library Group

GERING

P GERING PUBLIC LIBRARY*, 1055 P St, 69341. SAN 309-4731. Tel: 308-436-7433. FAX: 308-436-6869. E-mail: gpl@geringlibrary.org. Web Site: www.gering.org/departments-services/gering-public-library. *Dir,* Diane Downer; E-mail: ddowner@geringlibrary.org; *Pub Serv Librn,* Sherry Preston; *Tech Serv Librn,* Tammie Gitschel; *Youth Serv Librn,* Christie Clarke; Staff 5.5 (MLS 2, Non-MLS 3.5)
Founded 1895. Pop 7,886; Circ 35,000
Library Holdings: Audiobooks 1,200; DVDs 1,800; Bk Titles 30,000; Per Subs 50
Automation Activity & Vendor Info: (Cataloging) Biblionix/Apollo; (Circulation) Biblionix/Apollo; (OPAC) Biblionix/Apollo
Wireless access
Function: 24/7 Online cat, Adult bk club, Bks on CD, Children's prog, Computers for patron use, Electronic databases & coll, Free DVD rentals, Home delivery & serv to seniorr ctr & nursing homes, Homebound delivery serv, ILL available, Internet access, Magazines, Meeting rooms, Microfiche/film & reading machines, Notary serv, Online cat, OverDrive digital audio bks, Photocopying/Printing, Prog for adults, Prog for children & young adult, Ref serv available, Story hour, Summer reading prog, Tax forms, Teen prog, Wheelchair accessible
Mem of Western Library System
Open Mon-Thurs 9-7, Fri & Sat 10-5
Friends of the Library Group

CR SUMMIT CHRISTIAN COLLEGE LIBRARY*, 2025 21st St, 69341. SAN 309-6246. Tel: 308-632-6933, Ext 208. FAX: 308-632-8599. Web Site: www.summitcc.edu. *Libr Coord,* LaVern Allbaugh; E-mail: Lallbaugh@summitcc.edu; Staff 1 (Non-MLS 1)
Founded 1952. Enrl 50; Fac 10; Highest Degree: Bachelor
Library Holdings: Bk Vols 15,000; Per Subs 25
Wireless access
Function: CD-ROM, Computers for patron use, Distance learning, Electronic databases & coll, ILL available, Internet access, VHS videos
Mem of Western Library System
Restriction: Fee for pub use, Open to fac, students & qualified researchers, Photo ID required for access

GIBBON

P GIBBON PUBLIC LIBRARY*, 116 LaBarre, 68840. (Mail add: PO Box 309, 68840-0309), SAN 309-4758. Tel: 308-468-5889. FAX: 308-468-5501. E-mail: gpl@nctc.net. Web Site: libraries.ne.gov/gibbon. *Dir,* Missy Onate; *Libr Asst,* Susan Webster
Founded 1909. Pop 1,792
Library Holdings: Bk Vols 10,223; Per Subs 72
Automation Activity & Vendor Info: (Cataloging) Book Systems; (Circulation) Book Systems
Wireless access
Function: Adult bk club, After school storytime, Bks on cassette, Bks on CD, Children's prog, Computers for patron use, Electronic databases & coll, Free DVD rentals, ILL available, Mail & tel request accepted, Photocopying/Printing, Preschool outreach, Prog for adults, Prog for children & young adult, Story hour, Summer reading prog, Tax forms, Teen prog, VHS videos, Wheelchair accessible
Mem of Central Plains Library System
Open Mon-Fri 11-6, Sat 11-2
Friends of the Library Group

GILTNER

P GILTNER PUBLIC LIBRARY, 4020 N Commercial Ave, 68841. (Mail add: PO Box 67, 68841-0067), SAN 377-1903. Tel: 402-849-2290.
Library Holdings: Large Print Bks 150; Bk Vols 2,500
Wireless access
Mem of Southeast Library System
Open Tues 3:30-5

GORDON

P GORDON CITY LIBRARY, 101 W Fifth St, 69343. SAN 309-4766. Tel: 308-282-1198. FAX: 308-282-0417. E-mail: gordoncitylibrary@gmail.com. Web Site: www.gordoncitylibrary.org. *Libr Dir,* Rachael Price; *Asst Librn,* Amy Lefler
Founded 1922. Pop 1,924
Library Holdings: Bk Titles 12,067; Per Subs 82
Special Collections: Gordon Journal Coll from 1894, micro; Interpreter's Bible; Large Print Coll; Nebraska History Coll
Subject Interests: Hist, Literary criticism
Automation Activity & Vendor Info: (Cataloging) Biblionix; (Circulation) Biblionix; (OPAC) Biblionix
Wireless access
Mem of Western Library System
Open Mon-Thurs 11-5:30, Sat 10-3
Friends of the Library Group

GOTHENBURG

P GOTHENBURG PUBLIC LIBRARY, 1104 Lake Ave, 69138-1903. SAN 309-4774. Tel: 308-537-2591. FAX: 308-537-3667. E-mail: gothlibrary@yahoo.com. Web Site: www.ci.gothenburg.ne.us/library.asp. *Dir,* Mary Koch; E-mail: mkoch@cityofgothenburg.org; *Librn,* Thaine Freeze
Founded 1915. Pop 3,480; Circ 50,000
Library Holdings: Bk Vols 30,000; Per Subs 50
Automation Activity & Vendor Info: (Cataloging) Biblionix/Apollo; (Circulation) Biblionix/Apollo; (OPAC) Biblionix/Apollo
Wireless access
Mem of Central Plains Library System
Open Mon-Thurs 9-8, Fri 9-5

GRAND ISLAND

J CENTRAL COMMUNITY COLLEGE*, Grand Island Campus Library, 3134 W Hwy 34, 68802. (Mail add: PO Box 4903, 68802-4903), SAN 377-1741. Tel: 308-398-7395, 308-398-7396. Web Site: libguides.cccneb.edu. *Supvr,* Dixie Codner; E-mail: dcodner@cccneb.edu; Staff 2 (MLS 1, Non-MLS 1)
Highest Degree: Associate
Library Holdings: DVDs 100; Bk Vols 3,000; Per Subs 20
Automation Activity & Vendor Info: (Circulation) SirsiDynix-WorkFlows; (ILL) OCLC WorldShare Interlibrary Loan; (OPAC) SirsiDynix-Enterprise
Wireless access
Mem of Central Plains Library System
Partic in OCLC Online Computer Library Center, Inc
Open Mon-Thurs 8-7, Fri 8-4; Mon-Thurs 8-4:30 (Summer)

P GRAND ISLAND PUBLIC LIBRARY, Edith Abbott Memorial Library, 1124 W Second St, 68801. SAN 309-4782. Tel: 308-385-5333. Administration Tel: 308-385-5333, Ext 101. FAX: 308-385-5339. E-mail: LibrarySupervisors@gilibrary.org, refdesk@gilibrary.org. Web Site: www.gilibrary.org. *Libr Dir,* Celine Swan; E-mail: celines@gilibrary.org; *Ad, Tech Serv Librn,* Shaun Klee; Staff 4 (MLS 1, Non-MLS 3)

Founded 1884. Pop 50,550
Library Holdings: AV Mats 10,713; Bk Vols 123,032; Per Subs 300
Special Collections: Abbott Sisters Research Center; Genealogy (Lue R Spencer State DAR Coll & Ella Sprague Coll)
Automation Activity & Vendor Info: (Cataloging) OCLC; (Circulation) TLC (The Library Corporation); (ILL) OCLC; (OPAC) TLC (The Library Corporation); (Serials) TLC (The Library Corporation)
Wireless access
Function: 24/7 Electronic res, 24/7 Online cat, Activity rm, Adult bk club, After school storytime, Art exhibits, Audiobks via web, AV serv, Bilingual assistance for Spanish patrons, Bk club(s), Bks on CD, CD-ROM, Children's prog, Citizenship assistance, Computer training, Computers for patron use, Electronic databases & coll, Family literacy, Free DVD rentals, Holiday prog, Home delivery & serv to seniorr ctr & nursing homes, Homebound delivery serv, ILL available, Internet access, Life-long learning prog for all ages, Magazines, Magnifiers for reading, Mail & tel request accepted, Mango lang, Meeting rooms, Microfiche/film & reading machines, Music CDs, Online cat, OverDrive digital audio bks, Photocopying/Printing, Preschool outreach, Preschool reading prog, Printer for laptops & handheld devices, Prog for adults, Prog for children & young adult, Ref serv available, Scanner, Senior computer classes, Serves people with intellectual disabilities, Spanish lang bks, Spoken cassettes & CDs, Spoken cassettes & DVDs, Story hour, Study rm, Summer reading prog, Tax forms, Teen prog, Telephone ref, Wheelchair accessible
Mem of Central Plains Library System
Partic in Pioneer
Open Mon-Fri 9:30-6, Sat 9:30-1
Restriction: Non-resident fee
Friends of the Library Group

S STUHR MUSEUM OF THE PRAIRIE PIONEER*, Research Library, 3133 W Hwy 34, 68801-7280. SAN 309-4790. Tel: 308-385-5316, Ext 241. FAX: 308-385-5028. E-mail: research@stuhrmuseum.org. Web Site: stuhrmuseum.org/research/. *Curator,* Kari Stofer; E-mail: kstofer@stuhrmuseum.org; Staff 1 (Non-MLS 1)
Founded 1967
Library Holdings: Bk Titles 10,000; Per Subs 10
Special Collections: Arthur F Bentley Coll; Judge Bayard H Paine Coll
Publications: Bartenbach Opera House; Prairie Pioneer Press; Schimmer's Sand Krog-Resort on the Platte; Sheep King; Townbuilders

GRANT

P HASTINGS MEMORIAL LIBRARY*, Grant Public Library, 505 Central Ave, 69140-3017. SAN 309-4812. Tel: 308-352-4894. FAX: 308-352-2358. E-mail: hml@gpcom.net. Web Site: libraries.ne.gov/grant. *Dir,* Robin Quinn
Pop 1,270; Circ 13,299
Library Holdings: Bk Vols 15,000; Per Subs 10
Wireless access
Mem of Western Library System
Open Mon-Fri 10-1 & 1:30-5:30, Sat 9-Noon
Friends of the Library Group

GREELEY

P GREELEY VILLAGE PUBLIC LIBRARY*, 102 S Kildare St, 68842. (Mail add: PO Box 330, 68842-0330), SAN 309-4820. Tel: 308-428-4010. E-mail: vog@centercable.tv. *Librn,* Carla Costello
Pop 562; Circ 2,392
Library Holdings: Large Print Bks 200; Bk Vols 3,000
Wireless access
Mem of Central Plains Library System
Open Mon-Fri 8-12 & 1-3

GREENWOOD

P GREENWOOD PUBLIC LIBRARY*, 619 Main St, 68366. (Mail add: PO Box 29, 68366-0029), SAN 309-4839. Tel: 402-789-2301. FAX: 402-789-2323. *Dir,* Karen Frank; E-mail: kfranklibrary@hotmail.com
Pop 587; Circ 2,663
Library Holdings: Bk Titles 13,500; Per Subs 12; Talking Bks 91
Wireless access
Mem of Southeast Library System; Three Rivers Library System
Open Wed 9-12 & 1-5, Thurs & Fri 1-6, Sat 10-2
Friends of the Library Group

GRETNA

P GRETNA PUBLIC LIBRARY*, 736 South St, 68028. SAN 309-4855. Tel: 402-332-4480. FAX: 402-332-2506. E-mail: Gretna.Library@gmail.com. Web Site: www.gretnapubliclibrary.org. *Dir,* Krissy Reed; E-mail: gretna.librarydirector@gmail.com; *Asst Dir,* Rebecca McCorkindale; Staff 8 (MLS 2, Non-MLS 6)
Founded 1929. Pop 23,000; Circ 117,308
Library Holdings: Bk Titles 21,398; Bk Vols 23,677; Per Subs 99
Wireless access
Function: 24/7 Electronic res, 24/7 Online cat, Accelerated reader prog, Activity rm, Adult bk club, Adult literacy prog, After school storytime, Archival coll, Art programs, Audiobks via web, Bk club(s), Bks on CD, Butterfly Garden, Children's prog, Computer training, Computers for patron use, Digital talking bks, Doc delivery serv, E-Reserves, Electronic databases & coll, Family literacy, For res purposes, Free DVD rentals, Games & aids for people with disabilities, Govt ref serv, Health sci info serv, Holiday prog, Homework prog, ILL available, Instruction & testing, Internet access, Life-long learning prog for all ages, Literacy & newcomer serv, Magazines, Mail & tel request accepted, Makerspace, Mango lang, Meeting rooms, Microfiche/film & reading machines, Movies, Music CDs, Online cat, Online info literacy tutorials on the web & in blackboard, Online ref, Outreach serv, Outside serv via phone, mail, e-mail & web, OverDrive digital audio bks, Photocopying/Printing, Preschool outreach, Preschool reading prog, Prof lending libr, Prog for adults, Prog for children & young adult, Ref & res, Ref serv available, Res assist avail, Scanner, Senior outreach, Serves people with intellectual disabilities, Spoken cassettes & CDs, STEM programs, Story hour, Study rm, Summer & winter reading prog, Summer reading prog, Tax forms, Teen prog, Visual arts prog, Wheelchair accessible, Winter reading prog, Workshops, Writing prog
Mem of Three Rivers Library System
Open Mon, Thurs & Fri 3-8, Tues & Wed 10-2, Sat 1-3
Restriction: Borrowing requests are handled by ILL
Friends of the Library Group
Branches: 1
CHILDREN'S LIBRARY, 119 N McKenna St, 68028. Tel: 402-502-9088.
Founded 2012
Open Mon-Fri 10-2, Sat 10-Noon

GUIDE ROCK

P AULD-DOUDNA PUBLIC LIBRARY*, 155 W Grant St, 68942. (Mail add: PO Box 126, 68942-0126), SAN 309-4863. Tel: 402-257-4015. E-mail: aulddoudnapubliclibrary@gmail.com. *Dir,* Carol Morris
Founded 1918. Pop 245; Circ 1,559
Library Holdings: AV Mats 50; Bk Titles 10,892; Per Subs 11
Wireless access
Mem of Central Plains Library System
Open Tues & Fri 12:30-5

HARRISON

P SIOUX COUNTY PUBLIC LIBRARY*, 182 W Third St, 69346. (Mail add: PO Box 31, 69346). Tel: 308-668-9431. E-mail: sioux_county_public_library@hotmail.com. *Dir,* Sarah Sanderson
Pop 2,000; Circ 2,149
Library Holdings: DVDs 50; Bk Vols 11,000; Talking Bks 152; Videos 400
Automation Activity & Vendor Info: (Cataloging) Book Systems
Wireless access
Mem of Western Library System
Open Mon 9-12 & 1-5, Tues & Wed 1-5, Thurs 3:30-6:30, Fri 9-1, Sat 9-Noon
Friends of the Library Group

HARTINGTON

P HARTINGTON PUBLIC LIBRARY, 106 S Broadway, 68739. (Mail add: PO Box 458, 68739-0458), SAN 309-4871. Tel: 402-254-6245. FAX: 402-254-6245. E-mail: citylibrary@hartel.net. Web Site: libraries.ne.gov/hartington. *Libr Dir,* Tami L Anderson; *Ch,* Kim Emanuel; Staff 5 (Non-MLS 5)
Founded 1914. Pop 2,000; Circ 3,600
Library Holdings: Bk Vols 20,000; Per Subs 50
Automation Activity & Vendor Info: (Cataloging) Follett Software; (Circulation) Follett Software; (OPAC) Follett Software
Wireless access
Mem of Three Rivers Library System
Open Mon-Thurs 9-6, Fri 9-5, Sat 9-1
Friends of the Library Group

HARVARD

P HARVARD PUBLIC LIBRARY*, 309 N Clay Ave, 68944. (Mail add: PO Box 130, 68944-0130), SAN 309-488X. Tel: 402-772-7201. Reference E-mail: harpublib@gmail.com. *Librn,* Sharon Steenbarger
Founded 1915. Pop 998; Circ 4,416
Library Holdings: Bk Vols 6,560; Per Subs 30
Wireless access
Open Mon 4-8, Tues 3-8, Wed & Thurs 12-5, Fri 9-2

HASTINGS

S ADAMS COUNTY HISTORICAL SOCIETY ARCHIVES*, Hastings Museum of Natural & Cultural History, 1330 N Burlington Ave, 68902. (Mail add: PO Box 102, 68902-0102), SAN 309-4898. Tel: 402-463-5838. E-mail: achs@inebraska.com. Web Site: www.adamshistory.org. *Library Contact,* Elizabeth Spilinek. Subject Specialists: *Adams County hist,* Elizabeth Spilinek
Founded 1965
Library Holdings: Bk Vols 1,500
Special Collections: Adams County Archives; Adams County Newspapers, micro; Church Records Coll; Dust Bowl Years, oral hist; Friborg Architectural Coll, drawings; Probate Records; School Records Coll
Subject Interests: Genealogy, Local hist
Publications: Historical News (Bimonthly)
Open Tues-Thurs 10-4, Fri 10-1, Sat 10-3
Restriction: Non-circulating to the pub

J CENTRAL COMMUNITY COLLEGE, HASTINGS CAMPUS*, Nuckolls Library, 550 S Technical Blvd, 68902. (Mail add: PO Box 1024, 68902-1024), SAN 309-4901. Tel: 402-461-2538. Web Site: libguides.cccneb.edu/libraries, www.cccneb.edu. *Supvr,* Sherrie Dux-Ideus; E-mail: sideus@cccneb.edu; Staff 3 (MLS 1, Non-MLS 2)
Founded 1970. Enrl 1,420; Fac 135
Library Holdings: Bk Titles 3,939; Bk Vols 4,112; Per Subs 70
Wireless access
Mem of Central Plains Library System
Open Mon-Thurs (Fall & Spring) 7:30am-9pm, Fri 7:30-4; Mon-Thurs (Summer) 7:30-4

P CENTRAL PLAINS LIBRARY SYSTEM*, 2727 W Second St, Ste 233, 68901. Tel: 402-462-1975. Toll Free Tel: 800-569-4961. FAX: 402-462-1974. Web Site: libraries.ne.gov/cpls. *Co-Dir,* Denise Harders; E-mail: denise.cpls@gmail.com; *Co-Dir,* Autumn Carlson; E-mail: autumn.cpls@gmail.com
Publications: Plain Speaking (Newsletter)
Member Libraries: Ainsworth Public Library; Arapahoe Public Library; Arcadia Township Library; Atkinson Public Library; Auld Public Library; Auld-Doudna Public Library; Axtell Public Library; Bartley Public Library; Beaver City Public Library; Blue Hill Public Library; Brenizer Public Library; Broken Bow Public Library; Butler Memorial Library; Campbell Public Library; Central Community College; Central Community College, Hastings Campus; Elm Creek Public Library; Elwood Public Library; Eustis Public Library; Ewing Township Library; Farnam Public Library; Finch Memorial Public Library; Franklin Public Library; Garfield County Library; Gibbon Public Library; Good Samaritan Society - Hastings Village; Gothenburg Public Library; Grand Island Public Library; Greeley Village Public Library; Hastings College; Hastings Public Library; Hastings Regional Center; Hildreth Public Library; Hoesch Memorial Public Library; Holdrege Area Public Library; Indianola Public Library; Jensen Memorial Library; Kearney Public Library; Keya Paha County Library; Klyte Burt Memorial Public Library; Lexington Public Library; Litchfield Public Library; Logan County Public Library; Loup City Public Library; Lynch Public Library; Maltman Memorial Public Library; McCook Public Library; Mid Plains Community College; Mid-Plains Community College; Nebraska College of Technical Agriculture Library; Nigel Sprouse Memorial Library; North Loup Township Library; North Platte Public Library; O'Neill Public Library; Ord Township Library; Overton Community Library; Oxford Public Library; Ravenna Public Library; Rock County Public Library; Saint Paul Library; Sargent Township Library; Scotia Public Library; Shelton Public Library; Spalding Public Library; Spencer Township Library; Stuart Township Library; Sunshine Township Library; Sutherland Public Library; Taylor Public Library; The Willa Cather Foundation; Thomas County Library; University of Nebraska at Kearney; Valentine Public Library; Wilcox Public Library; Wilson Public Library; Wilsonville Public Library

R FIRST PRESBYTERIAN CHURCH LIBRARY, 621 N Lincoln, 68901. SAN 309-491X. Tel: 402-462-5147. E-mail: fpc@fpchastings.org. Web Site: www.fpchastings.org/our-library. *Librn,* Susan Medsker-Nedderman; Tel: 402-984-3545; Staff 1 (MLS 1)
Founded 1950
Library Holdings: Audiobooks 5; CDs 20; DVDs 75; Large Print Bks 125; Bk Titles 5,000; Per Subs 6
Subject Interests: Philos, Relig
Wireless access
Open Mon-Fri 8:30-4:30
Friends of the Library Group

C HASTINGS COLLEGE*, Perkins Library, 705 E Seventh St, 68901. SAN 309-4928. Tel: 402-461-7454. Interlibrary Loan Service Tel: 402-461-7701. E-mail: HCLibrary@hastings.edu. Web Site: www.hastings.edu/perkins-library. *Dir,* Susan Franklin; Tel: 402-461-7411, E-mail: sfranklin@hastings.edu; *Pub Serv Librn,* Pam Bohmfalk; E-mail: pbohmfalk@hastings.edu; Staff 5 (MLS 3, Non-MLS 2)
Founded 1882. Enrl 1,400; Fac 80; Highest Degree: Master
Library Holdings: AV Mats 4,500; e-books 95,000; Bk Titles 105,000; Bk Vols 140,000; Per Subs 450
Special Collections: Holcomb Lewis & Clark Coll; Plains & Western History (Brown Coll)
Automation Activity & Vendor Info: (Acquisitions) OCLC; (Cataloging) OCLC; (Circulation) OCLC; (Course Reserve) OCLC; (ILL) OCLC; (Media Booking) OCLC; (OPAC) OCLC; (Serials) OCLC
Wireless access
Mem of Central Plains Library System
Partic in Nebr Independent Col Libr Consortium; OCLC Online Computer Library Center, Inc
Open Mon-Thurs 7:30am-11pm, Fri 7:30-5, Sun 4-11; Mon-Fri (Summer) 8:30-4:30

S HASTINGS MUSEUM OF NATURAL & CULTURAL HISTORY LIBRARY*, 1330 N Burlington Ave, 68901. (Mail add: PO Box 1286, 68902-1286), SAN 309-4936. Tel: 402-461-2399, 402-461-4629. E-mail: collections@hastingsmuseum.org. Web Site: hastingsmuseum.org. *Dir,* Rebecca Matticks; E-mail: rmatticks@hastingsmuseum.org; *Curator,* Teresa Kreutzer-Hodson
Library Holdings: Bk Vols 1,000; Per Subs 15
Special Collections: Bureau of American Ethnology Reports: Smithsonian Institution, (1880 to 1930)
Wireless access
Open Tues-Fri 9-5
Restriction: Non-circulating to the pub

P HASTINGS PUBLIC LIBRARY*, 314 N Denver Ave, 68901. (Mail add: PO Box 849, 68902-0849), SAN 309-4944. Tel: 402-461-2346. FAX: 402-461-2359. E-mail: staff@hastings.lib.ne.us. Web Site: hastingslibrary.us. *Dir,* Amy Hafer; E-mail: amy@hastingslibrary.us; *Librn,* Kristy Hruska; Tel: 402-461-2354, E-mail: Khruska@hastingslibrary.us; *Librn,* Tim Lentz; Tel: 402-461-2373, E-mail: Tlentz@hastingslibrary.us; Staff 22 (MLS 3, Non-MLS 19)
Founded 1903. Pop 32,769; Circ 259,846
Library Holdings: Audiobooks 4,025; AV Mats 1,104; CDs 2,463; DVDs 1,087; Large Print Bks 7,242; Microforms 798; Bk Vols 142,632; Per Subs 157; Videos 2,115
Automation Activity & Vendor Info: (Acquisitions) SirsiDynix; (Cataloging) SirsiDynix; (Circulation) SirsiDynix; (ILL) OCLC; (OPAC) SirsiDynix; (Serials) SirsiDynix
Wireless access
Function: 24/7 Electronic res, 24/7 Online cat, 3D Printer, Adult bk club, Audiobks via web, Bilingual assistance for Spanish patrons, Bk club(s), Bks on CD, Children's prog, Computer training, Computers for patron use, E-Readers, Electronic databases & coll, Free DVD rentals, Home delivery & serv to seniorr ctr & nursing homes, Homebound delivery serv, ILL available, Internet access, Laminating, Life-long learning prog for all ages, Magazines, Mail & tel request accepted, Makerspace, Mango lang, Meeting rooms, Microfiche/film & reading machines, Movies, Museum passes, Online cat, OverDrive digital audio bks, Photocopying/Printing, Preschool reading prog, Printer for laptops & handheld devices, Prog for adults, Prog for children & young adult, Ref & res, Ref serv available, Res assist avail, Scanner, Serves people with intellectual disabilities, Spanish lang bks, Spoken cassettes & CDs, STEM programs, Story hour, Study rm, Summer & winter reading prog, Summer reading prog, Tax forms, Teen prog, Telephone ref, Wheelchair accessible, Winter reading prog
Publications: Friends News (Newsletter)
Mem of Central Plains Library System
Special Services for the Deaf - Closed caption videos; Staff with knowledge of sign lang; TDD equip
Special Services for the Blind - Magnifiers
Open Mon-Thurs 9-8, Fri & Sat 9-6, Sun 12-6
Friends of the Library Group
Bookmobiles: 1

HAY SPRINGS

P CRAVATH MEMORIAL LIBRARY*, 243 N Main, 69347. (Mail add: PO Box 309, 69347-0309). Tel: 308-638-4541. E-mail: cravath@gpcom.net. *Dir,* Marlene Benson
Pop 652; Circ 2,500
Library Holdings: Bk Vols 11,747; Videos 190
Mem of Western Library System
Open Tues & Wed 9-4, Fri 9-3

HAYES CENTER

P HAYES CENTER PUBLIC LIBRARY*, 407 Troth St, 69032. (Mail add: PO Box 174, 69032-0174), SAN 309-4960. Tel: 308-286-3411. E-mail: hayescenterlibrary@yahoo.com. *Libr Dir,* Deb Lawson
Pop 231; Circ 2,010

Library Holdings: Bk Vols 6,000; Per Subs 12
Wireless access
Mem of Western Library System
Open Mon & Thurs 1-5

HEBRON

P HEBRON SECREST LIBRARY, 146 N Fourth St, 68370. (Mail add: PO Box 125, 68370-0125), SAN 309-4979. Tel: 402-768-6701. FAX: 402-768-6701. E-mail: hslibrary@diodecom.net. Web Site: libraries.ne.gov/hebron. *Libr Dir,* Chuck Reichwein; E-mail: mrcreic4343@yahoo.com; *Asst Librn,* Judy Kassebaum
Founded 1921. Pop 1,565; Circ 11,309
Library Holdings: Bk Vols 11,052; Per Subs 27
Special Collections: Local Memorabilia
Subject Interests: Church hist
Automation Activity & Vendor Info: (Cataloging) Follett Software; (Circulation) Follett Software; (OPAC) Follett Software
Wireless access
Publications: Library Folder for 60th Anniversary, 1921-81
Mem of Southeast Library System
Open Mon, Wed & Fri 10-5, Tues & Thurs 12-7, Sat 10-1

HEMINGFORD

P HEMINGFORD PUBLIC LIBRARY, 812 Box Butte Ave, 69348. (Mail add: PO Box 6, 69348-0006), SAN 309-4987. Tel: 308-487-3454. FAX: 308-487-3835. E-mail: hpl@bbc.net. Web Site: hemingfordsite.wordpress.com. *Dir & Librn,* Colleen Garner
Pop 1,023; Circ 2,058
Library Holdings: Bk Vols 10,000; Per Subs 17
Wireless access
Mem of Western Library System
Open Tues & Wed 12-6, Thurs & Sat 9-12, Fri 12-5

HENDERSON

SR BETHESDA MENNONITE CHURCH LIBRARY, 930 16th St, 68371. (Mail add: PO Box 130, 68371-0130). Tel: 402-723-4562. FAX: 402-723-4567. E-mail: bethesda@mainstaycomm.net. Web Site: bethesdamc.org. *Library Contact,* Brent Swartzendruber
Library Holdings: Bk Vols 4,500
Special Collections: Children's & Christian Literature Coll
Wireless access

HILDRETH

P HILDRETH PUBLIC LIBRARY, 248 Commercial Ave, 68947. (Mail add: PO Box 112, 68947-0112), SAN 309-5002. Tel: 308-938-3008. FAX: 308-938-2545. E-mail: hildrethlibrary@gmail.com. Web Site: libraries.ne.gov/hildreth. *Dir,* Vicki Casper
Pop 370; Circ 8,000
Library Holdings: Bk Vols 8,000; Per Subs 12
Automation Activity & Vendor Info: (Cataloging) Follett Software; (Circulation) Follett Software; (OPAC) Follett Software
Wireless access
Mem of Central Plains Library System
Open Mon-Thurs 10-12 & 1-6, Fri 10-12 & 1-5
Friends of the Library Group

HOLDREGE

P HOLDREGE AREA PUBLIC LIBRARY*, 604 East Ave, 68949. SAN 309-5029. Tel: 308-995-6556. FAX: 308-995-5732. E-mail: info@holdregelibrary.org. Web Site: www.holdregelibrary.org. *Dir,* Mike Burris; E-mail: director@holdregelibrary.org; *Cat,* Cynthia Blum; *Ch Serv,* Cynthia Gitt; *Circ, Ref (Info Servs),* Linda Davey; Staff 10 (MLS 1, Non-MLS 9)
Founded 1895. Pop 9,175; Circ 131,983
Library Holdings: Audiobooks 2,135; DVDs 1,612; Large Print Bks 2,928; Bk Titles 58,773; Per Subs 90; Videos 1,096
Special Collections: State Document Depository
Automation Activity & Vendor Info: (Cataloging) Follett Software; (Circulation) Follett Software
Wireless access
Function: Audiobks via web, Bks on cassette, Bks on CD, Children's prog, Computers for patron use, Electronic databases & coll, Free DVD rentals, Home delivery & serv to seniorr ctr & nursing homes, ILL available, Magnifiers for reading, Online cat, Outreach serv, OverDrive digital audio bks, Photocopying/Printing, Prog for adults, Prog for children & young adult, Scanner, Story hour, Summer reading prog, Tax forms, Teen prog, Wheelchair accessible
Mem of Central Plains Library System
Open Mon-Thurs 9-8, Fri & Sat 9-5
Friends of the Library Group

S NEBRASKA PRAIRIE MUSEUM*, Don O Lindgren Library, 2701 Burlington St., 68949. (Mail add: PO Box 164, 68949-0164), SAN 325-2256. Tel: 308-995-5015. FAX: 308-995-2241. E-mail: prairie@gmail.com. Web Site: nebraskaprairiemuseum.com. *Exec Dir,* Dan Christensen; *Head, Genealogy Libr,* Sandy Slater; Staff 1 (Non-MLS 1)
Founded 1972
Library Holdings: Bk Vols 4,200
Special Collections: POW Archives. Oral History
Subject Interests: Genealogy, Local hist, Phelps County
Wireless access
Open Mon-Fri 9-5

HOOPER

P HOOPER PUBLIC LIBRARY*, 128 N Main St, 68031. (Mail add: PO Box 45, 68031-0045), SAN 309-5037. Tel: 402-654-3833. E-mail: hooperlib@hotmail.com. Web Site: libraries.ne.gov/hooper. *Dir,* Milissa Wimer
Pop 1,000
Library Holdings: DVDs 30; Large Print Bks 200; Bk Vols 10,169; Per Subs 35; Talking Bks 50; Videos 200
Automation Activity & Vendor Info: (Acquisitions) Follett Software; (Cataloging) Follett Software
Wireless access
Function: Adult bk club, After school storytime, Audio & video playback equip for onsite use, ILL available, Internet access, Photocopying/Printing, Prog for children & young adult, Summer reading prog, Workshops
Mem of Three Rivers Library System
Partic in Eastern Nebr Libr Asn
Open Tues, Wed & Thurs 2-7, Fri & Sat 9-1
Friends of the Library Group

HOWELLS

P HOWELLS PUBLIC LIBRARY*, 128 N Third St, 68641. (Mail add: PO Box 337, 68641-0337), SAN 309-5045. Tel: 402-986-1210. FAX: 402-986-1210. E-mail: howellspubliclibrary@yahoo.com. Web Site: howellsnebraska.com/resources/library. *Dir,* Victoria Vacha
Pop 632; Circ 927
Library Holdings: Bk Vols 9,600; Per Subs 71
Automation Activity & Vendor Info: (Cataloging) Chancery SMS; (Circulation) Chancery SMS
Wireless access
Publications: Booklist
Mem of Three Rivers Library System
Open Mon 2-6:30, Wed 9-2 & 4-9, Fri 2-5:30, Sat 9-Noon
Friends of the Library Group

HUMBOLDT

P BRUUN MEMORIAL PUBLIC LIBRARY*, 730 Third St, 68376. (Mail add: PO Box 368, 68376-0368), SAN 309-5053. Tel: 402-862-2914. E-mail: bmemorial@neb.rr.com. *Libr Dir,* Jorene Herr
Founded 1884. Pop 877; Circ 23,524
Library Holdings: Audiobooks 629; CDs 146; DVDs 426; Large Print Bks 335; Bk Titles 17,584; Per Subs 15; Videos 572
Special Collections: State Document Depository; UN Document Depository; US Document Depository
Automation Activity & Vendor Info: (Cataloging) Biblionix; (Circulation) Biblionix; (OPAC) Biblionix
Wireless access
Mem of Southeast Library System
Open Mon 2-8:30, Tues & Thurs 10-12 & 2-5:30, Wed & Fri 2-5:30, Sat 9-12
Friends of the Library Group

HUMPHREY

P HUMPHREY PUBLIC LIBRARY, 307 Main St, 68642. (Mail add: PO Box 266, 68642-0266), SAN 309-5061. Tel: 402-923-0957. FAX: 402-923-0957. E-mail: humphreypl@hotmail.com. Web Site: www.cityofhumphrey.com/library. *Dir,* Michele Hastreiter; *Asst Librn,* Becky Bender
Founded 1938
Library Holdings: Audiobooks 326; Per Subs 26
Automation Activity & Vendor Info: (Circulation) Follett Software
Wireless access
Function: 24/7 Electronic res, 24/7 Online cat, Bks on CD, Children's prog, Computers for patron use, Free DVD rentals, Homebound delivery serv, ILL available, Internet access, Magazines, Mail & tel request accepted, Meeting rooms, Online cat, OverDrive digital audio bks, Photocopying/Printing, Preschool outreach, Prog for adults, Scanner, Story hour, Tax forms, Telephone ref
Mem of Three Rivers Library System
Open Mon & Wed 1-8, Tues & Fri 9-12, Thurs 9-12 & 2-6, Sat 8-12

HYANNIS

P GRANT COUNTY LIBRARY*, 105 E Harrison St, 69350. (Mail add: PO Box 328, 69350-0328), SAN 309-507X. Tel: 308-458-2218. FAX: 308-458-2485. Web Site: grantco.panhandlelibraries.org. *Libr Dir,* Vickie Retzlaff
Founded 1929. Pop 747; Circ 3,030
Library Holdings: Bk Vols 8,000; Per Subs 42
Automation Activity & Vendor Info: (Cataloging) Follett Software; (Circulation) Follett Software; (OPAC) Follett Software
Wireless access
Open Mon & Fri 9-12 & 1-5, Wed 9-12 & 1-6

IMPERIAL

P LIED IMPERIAL PUBLIC LIBRARY*, 703 Broadway, 69033. (Mail add: PO Box 728, 69033-0728), SAN 309-5088. Tel: 308-882-4754. FAX: 308-882-2914. E-mail: imperiallibrary1@gpcom.net. Web Site: libraries.ne.gov/imperial. *Dir,* Beth Falla; E-mail: read@imperiallibrary.org
Pop 4,000; Circ 59,026
Automation Activity & Vendor Info: (Cataloging) Follett Software; (Circulation) Follett Software; (ILL) OCLC
Wireless access
Mem of Western Library System
Open Mon 9-5, Tues-Thurs 9-6, Fri 10-5, Sat 9-Noon
Friends of the Library Group

INDIANOLA

P INDIANOLA PUBLIC LIBRARY*, 122 N Fourth St, 69034. (Mail add: PO Box 300, 69034-0300). Tel: 308-364-9259. E-mail: inpuli01@gpcom.net. Web Site: libraries.ne.gov/indianola. *Librn,* Judith Hollers
Pop 642; Circ 700
Library Holdings: AV Mats 170; Bk Vols 6,370; Per Subs 12; Talking Bks 24
Wireless access
Mem of Central Plains Library System
Open Tues & Thurs 1-5, Wed 4-8, Sat 9-12

KEARNEY

P KEARNEY PUBLIC LIBRARY*, 2020 First Ave, 68847. SAN 309-510X. Tel: 308-233-3282. Reference Tel: 308-233-3256. FAX: 308-233-3291. Web Site: cityofkearney.org/1475/Library. *Dir,* Matthew R Williams; Tel: 308-233-3280, E-mail: mwilliams@kearneygov.org; *Asst Libr Dir,* Christine Walsh; Tel: 308-233-3283, E-mail: cwalsh@kearneygov.org; *Ref Serv Librn,* Sarah Haack; E-mail: shaack@kearneygov.org; *Tech Serv Librn,* Mike Marchand; Tel: 308-233-3285, E-mail: mmarchand@kearneygov.org; *Youth Serv Librn,* Shawna Lindner; Tel: 308-233-3284, E-mail: slindner@kearneygov.org; Staff 26 (MLS 3, Non-MLS 23)
Founded 1890. Pop 27,431; Circ 489,078
Library Holdings: Bk Vols 109,985; Per Subs 169
Special Collections: Kearney Coll, VF
Subject Interests: Genealogy
Automation Activity & Vendor Info: (Acquisitions) SirsiDynix; (Cataloging) OCLC; (Circulation) SirsiDynix; (ILL) OCLC; (OPAC) SirsiDynix; (Serials) SirsiDynix
Wireless access
Mem of Central Plains Library System
Open Mon-Thurs 9-9, Fri & Sat 9-5, Sun 1-5
Friends of the Library Group
Bookmobiles: 1

C UNIVERSITY OF NEBRASKA AT KEARNEY*, Calvin T Ryan Library, 2508 11th Ave, 68849-2240. Tel: 308-865-8535. Circulation Tel: 308-865-8599. Interlibrary Loan Service Tel: 308-865-8594. Reference Tel: 308-865-8586. FAX: 308-865-8722. Web Site: library.unk.edu. *Dean,* Janet Stoeger Wilke; Tel: 308-865-8546, E-mail: wilkej@unk.edu; *Coll Serv Librn,* David Arredondo; Tel: 308-865-8992, E-mail: arredondodr@unk.edu; *Curric Librn,* Rochelle Reeves; Tel: 308-865-8276, E-mail: reevesr@unk.edu; *Ref & Instruction Librn,* Lindsay Brownfield; Tel: 308-865-8853, E-mail: brownfieldj@unk.edu; *Spec Projects Librn,* Susan Mueller; Tel: 308-865-8143, E-mail: muellersm@unk.edu; *Circ Mgr,* Lisa Mount; Tel: 308-865-8850, E-mail: mountll@unk.edu; *Doc Delivery Mgr, ILL Mgr,* Alta Kramer; Tel: 308-865-8594, E-mail: kramera@unk.edu; *Univ Archivist,* Laurinda Weisse; Tel: 308-865-8593, E-mail: weissell@unk.edu; *Access Services Assoc,* Marshall Dorr; Tel: 308-865-8598, E-mail: dorrmb3@unk.edu; *Tech Serv Assoc,* Autumn Bartek-Jensen; Tel: 308-865-8846, E-mail: bartakae@unk.edu; Staff 13 (MLS 10, Non-MLS 3)
Founded 1906. Enrl 6,902; Fac 330; Highest Degree: Master
Jul 2014-Jun 2015 Income $3,813,199, State $3,135,968, Locally Generated Income $671,858, Parent Institution $5,373. Mats Exp $1,175,710, Books $123,406, Per/Ser (Incl. Access Fees) $491,799, Micro $34,226, AV Mat $18,468, Electronic Ref Mat (Incl. Access Fees) $507,651, Presv $160. Sal $1,377,586 (Prof $825,135)
Library Holdings: AV Mats 93,431; Bks on Deafness & Sign Lang 244; Braille Volumes 154; CDs 1,766; DVDs 1,978; e-books 176,556; e-journals 83,506; Electronic Media & Resources 97,832; High Interest/Low Vocabulary Bk Vols 26; Microforms 46,046; Music Scores 4,000; Bk Titles 242,263; Bk Vols 410,948; Per Subs 442; Videos 185
Special Collections: State Document Depository; US Document Depository
Subject Interests: Great Plains, Nebr
Automation Activity & Vendor Info: (Acquisitions) Innovative Interfaces, Inc; (Cataloging) Innovative Interfaces, Inc; (Circulation) Innovative Interfaces, Inc; (Course Reserve) Innovative Interfaces, Inc; (ILL) OCLC ILLiad; (OPAC) Innovative Interfaces, Inc; (Serials) Innovative Interfaces, Inc
Wireless access
Publications: In Brief (Newsletter)
Mem of Central Plains Library System
Partic in LYRASIS; OCLC Online Computer Library Center, Inc
Open Mon-Thurs 7:30am-Midnight, Fri 7:30-5, Sat 10-5, Sun 2-Midnight

S YOUTH REHABILITATION & TREATMENT CENTER LIBRARY, 2802 30th Ave, 68845. SAN 377-1806. Tel: 308-865-5313, Ext 287. FAX: 308-865-5323. *Librn,* Lisa Irwin; E-mail: lisa.irwin@nebraska.gov
Founded 1879
Library Holdings: Bk Titles 7,000; Bk Vols 7,300; Per Subs 25
Automation Activity & Vendor Info: (Cataloging) Follett Software; (Circulation) Follett Software; (OPAC) Follett Software
Wireless access
Open Mon-Fri 8-4

KIMBALL

P KIMBALL PUBLIC LIBRARY*, 208 S Walnut St, 69145. SAN 309-5126. Tel: 308-235-4523. FAX: 308-235-2165. E-mail: kimballpubliclibrary@gmail.com. Web Site: www.kimballpubliclibrary.org. *Dir,* Jan Sears; Staff 3 (Non-MLS 3)
Founded 1888. Pop 2,200; Circ 11,590
Library Holdings: Bk Vols 26,500; Per Subs 40
Special Collections: Kimball County History Coll, newsp clippings, photog. Municipal Document Depository; Oral History
Automation Activity & Vendor Info: (Cataloging) Biblionix/Apollo; (Circulation) Biblionix/Apollo
Wireless access
Function: 24/7 Online cat, 3D Printer, Accelerated reader prog, Adult bk club, After school storytime, Archival coll, Art exhibits, Audiobks via web, AV serv, Bk club(s), Bks on CD, Chess club, Children's prog, Computer training, Computers for patron use, Digital talking bks, Distance learning, Doc delivery serv, Electronic databases & coll, Free DVD rentals, Genealogy discussion group, Home delivery & serv to seniorr ctr & nursing homes, Homebound delivery serv, Homework prog, ILL available, Internet access, Laminating, Magazines, Magnifiers for reading, Mail & tel request accepted, Makerspace, Meeting rooms, Microfiche/film & reading machines, Movies, Music CDs, Notary serv, Online cat, Online ref, OverDrive digital audio bks, Photocopying/Printing, Printer for laptops & handheld devices, Prog for adults, Prog for children & young adult, Scanner, Senior computer classes, STEM programs, Story hour, Summer & winter reading prog, Summer reading prog, Wheelchair accessible
Mem of Western Library System
Special Services for the Blind - Accessible computers; Audio mat; Bks on CD; Copier with enlargement capabilities; Digital talking bk; Home delivery serv; Large print bks; Magnifiers
Open Mon, Wed & Fri 10-5:30, Tues & Thurs 1-7, Sat 10-1
Restriction: Borrowing requests are handled by ILL
Friends of the Library Group

LA VISTA

P LA VISTA PUBLIC LIBRARY, 9110 Giles Rd, 68128. SAN 309-5134. Tel: 402-537-3900. FAX: 402-932-6352. E-mail: lvlibrary@cityoflavista.org. Web Site: www.cityoflavista.org/library. *Libr Dir,* Rose Barcal; E-mail: rbarcal@cityoflavista.org; *Asst Dir,* Jodi Norton; E-mail: jnorton@cityoflavista.org; Staff 6 (MLS 3, Non-MLS 3)
Founded 1972. Pop 17,344; Circ 117,517
Library Holdings: Audiobooks 3,121; CDs 354; DVDs 3,287; e-books 51,223; e-journals 230; Large Print Bks 3,067; Bk Vols 51,028; Per Subs 128
Special Collections: Harold "Andy" Anderson Civic Leadership Coll; Howard Hamilton Coll; Joseph J Barmettler Law Coll
Automation Activity & Vendor Info: (Cataloging) Biblionix/Apollo; (Circulation) Biblionix/Apollo; (OPAC) Biblionix/Apollo
Wireless access
Function: 24/7 Electronic res, 24/7 Online cat, Adult bk club, Adult literacy prog, Audiobks via web, Bk club(s), Bks on CD, CD-ROM, Children's prog, Computer training, Computers for patron use, Electronic

databases & coll, Free DVD rentals, Holiday prog, ILL available, Internet access, Laminating, Large print keyboards, Magazines, Mango lang, Movies, Music CDs, Notary serv, Online cat, Online ref, Outreach serv, OverDrive digital audio bks, Photocopying/Printing, Preschool outreach, Printer for laptops & handheld devices, Prog for adults, Prog for children & young adult, Ref serv available, Scanner, Study rm, Summer & winter reading prog, Summer reading prog, Tax forms, Teen prog, Telephone ref, Wheelchair accessible, Winter reading prog
Mem of Three Rivers Library System
Open Mon-Thurs 8am-9pm, Fri & Sat 8-5, Sun 1-5
Restriction: Circ to mem only, Non-resident fee

LAUREL

P LAUREL COMMUNITY LEARNING CENTER & PUBLIC LIBRARY*, 502 Wakefield St, 68745-0248. (Mail add: PO Box 8, 68745). Tel: 402-256-3133, Ext 4144. E-mail: lcclibrary@lccschool.org. Web Site: lclearningcenter.org. *Dir,* Robert Parsons; E-mail: robert.parsons@lccschool.org; Staff 1.5 (Non-MLS 1.5)
Pop 870; Circ 21,000
Oct 2020-Sept 2021 Income $34,263, State $852, City $27,411, County $6,000. Mats Exp $6,000. Sal $19,200
Library Holdings: Bk Vols 18,763; Per Subs 15; Talking Bks 346
Automation Activity & Vendor Info: (Acquisitions) Baker & Taylor; (Cataloging) ComPanion Corp; (Circulation) ComPanion Corp; (OPAC) ComPanion Corp
Wireless access
Function: Activity rm, Adult bk club, Computers for patron use, Digital talking bks, Electronic databases & coll, Free DVD rentals, ILL available, Internet access, Laminating, Life-long learning prog for all ages, Magazines, Mail loans to mem, Meeting rooms, Microfiche/film & reading machines, Movies, Online cat, OverDrive digital audio bks, Photocopying/Printing, Preschool outreach, Printer for laptops & handheld devices, Prog for adults, Prog for children & young adult, Res assist avail, Scanner, Summer reading prog, Wheelchair accessible
Mem of Three Rivers Library System
Open Mon-Thurs 8-8, Fri 8-4, Sat 9-2
Friends of the Library Group

LEIGH

P LEIGH PUBLIC LIBRARY, 153 N Main St, 68643. (Mail add: PO Box 158, 06843-0158), SAN 309-5142. Tel: 402-487-2507. FAX: 402-487-8507. E-mail: leighpubliclibrary@gmail.com. *Dir,* Kathy Stender; E-mail: leighpubliclibrary@gmail.com
Pop 509; Circ 4,703
Library Holdings: DVDs 259
Special Collections: Nebraska History/Authors Coll
Wireless access
Mem of Three Rivers Library System
Open Tues 12-4:30, Thurs 12- 6, Wed 3-7, Sat 9-12

LEWELLEN

P LEWELLEN PUBLIC LIBRARY*, 208 Main St, 69147. (Mail add: PO Box 104, 69147-0104), SAN 309-5150. Tel: 308-778-5421. E-mail: clerklew@gmail.com. *Dir,* Ruth Radke
Founded 1920. Pop 280
Library Holdings: Bk Vols 4,500
Wireless access
Mem of Western Library System
Open Tues & Fri 9-4

LEXINGTON

P LEXINGTON PUBLIC LIBRARY*, 907 N Washington St, 68850. (Mail add: PO Box 778, 68850-0778), SAN 309-5169. Tel: 308-324-2151. FAX: 308-324-2140. Web Site: lexingtonlibrary.org. *Libr Dir,* Kathleen Thomsen; E-mail: kthomsen@cityoflex.com; *Asst Libr Dir,* JoAnn Grove; E-mail: jfrove@cityoflex.com; *Youth Serv Librn,* Brenda Schwarz; E-mail: bschwarz@cityoflex.com
Pop 10,011; Circ 73,019
Library Holdings: Bk Titles 30,179; Per Subs 109
Automation Activity & Vendor Info: (Cataloging) Follett Software; (Circulation) Follett Software; (Course Reserve) Follett Software; (ILL) Follett Software; (OPAC) Follett Software
Wireless access
Mem of Central Plains Library System
Open Mon-Thurs 9-9, Fri & Sat 9-5, Sun 1-5
Friends of the Library Group

LINCOLN

S AMERICAN HISTORICAL SOCIETY OF GERMANS FROM RUSSIA, Library & Archives, 631 D St, 68502. SAN 328-0454. Tel: 402-474-3363. FAX: 402-474-7229. E-mail: ahsgr_librarian@ahsgr.org. Web Site: www.ahsgr.org/page/library. *Librn,* Ellen Vorderstrasse; E-mail: evorderstrasse@ahsgr.org; Staff 1 (MLS 1)
Founded 1968
Library Holdings: Bk Titles 8,116
Special Collections: Ancestor database; Censuses; Family histories; Surname charts
Subject Interests: Germans from Russia
Automation Activity & Vendor Info: (ILL) OCLC
Wireless access
Function: Archival coll, ILL available, Ref & res, Res performed for a fee
Publications: AHSGR Journal (Quarterly); AHSGR Newsletter (Quarterly)
Mem of Southeast Library System
Open Mon-Fri 9-4
Restriction: Restricted loan policy

JM BRYAN COLLEGE OF THE HEALTH SCIENCES*, Bryan Medical Center Library, 5035 Everett St, 68506. SAN 327-2281. Tel: 402-481-3908. FAX: 402-481-3138. Web Site: library.bryanhealthcollege.edu. *Dir, Libr Serv,* Heather St Clair; E-mail: Heather.stclair@bryanhealth.org; Staff 3 (MLS 2, Non-MLS 1)
Library Holdings: Bk Titles 2,500; Per Subs 150
Subject Interests: Nursing
Automation Activity & Vendor Info: (Acquisitions) Follett Software; (Cataloging) Follett Software; (Circulation) Follett Software; (Course Reserve) Follett Software
Restriction: Open to pub for ref only, Open to students, fac & staff

M CATHOLIC HEALTH INITIATIVES, CHI Health Medical Library, CHI Health St Elizabeth, 555 S 70th St, 68510. SAN 309-5290. Tel: 402-219-7306. FAX: 402-219-7335. Web Site: culibraries.creighton.edu/CHIlibrary. *Division Librn,* Maria Ford; E-mail: maria.ford@chihealth.com; Staff 1 (MLS 1)
Founded 1928
Library Holdings: Bk Vols 2,579; Per Subs 97
Special Collections: Allied Health Coll; Cultural Diversity Coll; Leadership Coll; Medical Coll; Nursing Coll
Subject Interests: Burn therapy, Family practice, Neonatal med, Obgyn, Pediatrics
Automation Activity & Vendor Info: (Cataloging) LibraryWorld, Inc; (Circulation) LibraryWorld, Inc; (OPAC) LibraryWorld, Inc; (Serials) LibraryWorld, Inc
Wireless access
Publications: AV Catalog
Partic in ICON Library Consortium; National Network of Libraries of Medicine Region 4
Open Mon-Thurs 8-4:30, Fri 8am-12:30pm

R CHRIST UNITED METHODIST CHURCH LIBRARY*, 4530 A St, 68510. SAN 309-5185. Tel: 402-489-9618. FAX: 402-489-9675. Web Site: www.christumclinc.org. *Prog Dir,* Kim Garrison; E-mail: kim.garrison1970@gmail.com; *Librn,* Sandra Herzinger
Library Holdings: Bk Vols 4,550
Automation Activity & Vendor Info: (Cataloging) Church Related Online Software Systems (CROSS)
Wireless access
Open Mon-Fri 8-4, Sun 8-Noon

S CHRISTIAN RECORD SERVICES FOR THE BLIND*, Lending Library, 5900 S 58th St, Ste M, 68516. (Mail add: PO Box 6097, 68506-0097), SAN 327-6058. Tel: 402-488-0981. FAX: 402-488-7582. Administration FAX: 402-488-1902. E-mail: info@ChristianRecord.org. Web Site: Lib.Guide. *Library Contact,* Kalvin Follett
Founded 1899
Library Holdings: Bk Titles 1,200
Wireless access
Special Services for the Blind - Braille bks; Talking bks
Open Mon-Thurs 9-12 & 1-5

S CHURCH OF JESUS CHRIST OF LATTER-DAY SAINTS*, Family History Center, 3000 Old Cheney Rd, 68516-2775. (Mail add: PO Box 22512, 68542-2512), SAN 377-3825. Tel: 402-423-4561. *Dir,* Tina Wells; E-mail: tmwells@radiks.net
Library Holdings: Bk Vols 350
Open Tues 10-4 & 6-9, Wed 10-2 & 6-9, Thurs 6-9, Fri 1-4, Sat 10-2

S DIAGNOSTIC & EVALUATION CENTER LIBRARY*, 3220 W Van Dorn St, 68522-9278. (Mail add: PO Box 22800, 68542-2800). Tel: 402-471-3330. FAX: 402-479-6368. Web Site: corrections.nebraska.gov/facilities/diagnostic-evaluation-center. *Librn,* Position Currently Open
Library Holdings: Bk Vols 4,750; Per Subs 20
Open Mon-Fri 7-3:30

P LINCOLN CITY LIBRARIES*, Bennett Martin Public Library, 136 S 14th St, 68508-1899. SAN 350-1272. Tel: 402-441-8500. Interlibrary Loan Service Tel: 402-441-8537. Reference Tel: 402-441-8530. Administration Tel: 402-441-8512. FAX: 402-441-8586. TDD: 402-441-8589. E-mail: library@lincolnlibraries.org. Web Site: www.lincolnlibraries.org. *Libr Dir,* Pat Leach; Tel: 402-441-8510, E-mail: p.leach@lincolnlibraries.org; *Asst Dir,* Julee Hammer; Tel: 402-441-8511, E-mail: jhammer@lincoln.ne.gov; *Automation Syst Coordr,* Rod Cummings; Tel: 402-441-8522, E-mail: r.cummings@lincolnlibraries.org; *Coordr, Youth Serv,* Vicki Wood; Tel: 402-441-8565, E-mail: v.wood@lincolnlibraries.org; *Libr Res Coordr,* Tammy Teasley; Tel: 402-441-8575, E-mail: t.teasley@lincolnlibraries.org; *Pub Serv Coordr,* Julie Beno; Tel: 402-441-8535, E-mail: j.beno@lincolnlibraries.org; Staff 126 (MLS 21, Non-MLS 105)
Founded 1877
Sept 2017-Aug 2018 Income (Main & Associated Libraries) $10,640,667, State $99,484, City $8,236,094, Federal $6,721, County $776,770, Locally Generated Income $678,400, Other $843,198. Mats Exp $10,327,122, Other Print Mats $119,000, Electronic Ref Mat (Incl. Access Fees) $725,957. Sal $4,910,162
Library Holdings: CDs 43,053; DVDs 57,912; e-books 25,995; Electronic Media & Resources 836; Microforms 5,829; Bk Vols 646,261; Per Subs 350; Videos 16
Special Collections: Nebraska Authors; Polley Music Library (sheet music). State Document Depository
Automation Activity & Vendor Info: (Acquisitions) Baker & Taylor; (Cataloging) SirsiDynix; (Circulation) SirsiDynix; (ILL) OCLC ILLiad; (OPAC) SirsiDynix; (Serials) EBSCO Online
Wireless access
Function: 24/7 Electronic res, 24/7 Online cat, 3D Printer, Activity rm, Adult bk club, After school storytime, Art exhibits, Audiobks on Playaways & MP3, Audiobks via web, BA reader (adult literacy), Bk club(s), Bks on CD, CD-ROM, Children's prog, Computer training, Computers for patron use, Digital talking bks, E-Reserves, Electronic databases & coll, Family literacy, Free DVD rentals, Homebound delivery serv, ILL available, Internet access, Magazines, Magnifiers for reading, Mail & tel request accepted, Meeting rooms, Microfiche/film & reading machines, Movies, Music CDs, Online cat, Online ref, Outreach serv, Outside serv via phone, mail, e-mail & web, OverDrive digital audio bks, Photocopying/Printing, Preschool outreach, Printer for laptops & handheld devices, Prog for adults, Prog for children & young adult, Ref & res, Ref serv available, Res assist avail, Res performed for a fee, Scanner, Spanish lang bks, Spoken cassettes & CDs, Story hour, Study rm, Summer & winter reading prog, Summer reading prog, Tax forms, Teen prog, Telephone ref, Wheelchair accessible, Winter reading prog
Partic in OCLC Online Computer Library Center, Inc
Special Services for the Blind - Assistive/Adapted tech devices, equip & products; Audio mat; Bks on CD; Closed circuit TV; Computer with voice synthesizer for visually impaired persons; Large print bks; Reader equip
Restriction: Non-resident fee
Friends of the Library Group
Branches: 7
VICTOR E ANDERSON BRANCH, 3635 Touzalin Ave, 68507-1698, SAN 350-1302. Tel: 402-441-8540. FAX: 402-441-8543. *Br Supvr,* Kim Shelley; Tel: 402-441-8542, E-mail: k.shelley@lincolnlibraries.org
Open Mon-Thurs 10-8, Fri & Sat 10-6, Sun 12-8
BETHANY BRANCH, 1810 N Cotner Blvd, 68505, SAN 350-1396. Tel: 402-441-8550. FAX: 402-441-8552. *Br Supvr,* Kim Shelley
Open Mon-Sat 12-8
Friends of the Library Group
LOREN COREY EISELEY BRANCH, 1530 Superior St, 68521. Tel: 402-441-4250. FAX: 402-441-4253. *Br Mgr,* Ms Lisa Olivigni; Tel: 402-441-4252, E-mail: l.olivigni@lincolnlibraries.org
Open Mon-Thurs 10-8, Fri & Sat 10-6, Sun 12-8
CHARLES H GERE BRANCH, 2400 S 56th St, 68506-3599, SAN 350-1426. Tel: 402-441-8560. FAX: 402-441-8563. *Br Supvr,* Brenda Ealey; Tel: 402-441-8562, E-mail: b.ealey@lincolnlibraries.org
Open Mon-Thurs 10-8, Fri & Sat 10-6, Sun 12-8
SOUTH BRANCH, 2675 South St, 68502-3099, SAN 350-1485. Tel: 402-441-8570. FAX: 402-441-8572. *Br Supvr,* Julie Beno; Tel: 402-441-8535, E-mail: j.beno@lincolnlibraries.org
Open Mon-Thurs 10-8, Fri & Sat 10-6, Sun 12-8
BESS DODSON WALT BRANCH, 6701 S 14th St, 68512. Tel: 402-441-4460. FAX: 402-441-4463. *Br Supvr,* Jodene Glaesemann
Open Mon-Thurs 10-8, Fri & Sat 10-6, Sun 12-8
DAN A WILLIAMS BRANCH, 5000 Mike Scholl St, 68524. Tel: 402-441-8580. *Br Mgr,* Ms Lisa Olivigni; Tel: 402-441-4252, E-mail: l.olivigni@lincolnlibraries.org
Open Mon-Thurs 4-8, Fri 4-6, Sat & Sun 1-6
Bookmobiles: 1. Librn, Rebecca Hueske. Bk vols 4,500

S LINCOLN CORRECTIONAL CENTER LIBRARY*, 3216 W Van Dorn St, 68522. (Mail add: PO Box 22800, 68542-2800), SAN 377-1601. Tel: 402-471-2861. FAX: 402-479-6100. Web Site: corrections.nebraska.gov/facilities/lincoln-correctional-center. *Librn,* Position Currently Open
Library Holdings: Bk Vols 10,000; Per Subs 44

S LINCOLN FAMILY MEDICINE PROGRAM LIBRARY*, 4600 Valley Rd, Ste 210, 68510-4892. SAN 377-1563. Tel: 402-483-4591. FAX: 402-483-5079. Web Site: www.lmep.com. *Library Contact,* Carole Ortmeier; E-mail: cortmeier@lmep.com
Library Holdings: Bk Vols 300; Per Subs 16
Wireless access
Partic in Lincoln Libr Group

M MADONNA REHABILITATION HOSPITAL*, Medical Library, 5401 South St, 68506-2134. SAN 327-6074. Tel: 402-489-7102. FAX: 402-486-8381. *Library Contact,* Marcie Stoner
Library Holdings: Bk Titles 300
Wireless access
Restriction: Not open to pub

S NATIONAL PARK SERVICE*, Midwest Archeological Center Library, Federal Bldg, Rm 474, 100 Centennial Mall North, 68508. SAN 309-5231. Tel: 402-437-5392, Ext 110. FAX: 402-437-5098. E-mail: MWAC_Library@nps.gov. Web Site: www.nps.gov/mwac.
Founded 1969
Library Holdings: Bk Titles 34,369; Per Subs 46
Special Collections: Archeology Coll, ms
Subject Interests: Archaeology, Hist
Function: For res purposes, Res libr
Restriction: Authorized scholars by appt, Circulates for staff only, Internal circ only, Lending to staff only, Not a lending libr, Prof mat only

G NDOR TRANSPORTATION LIBRARY*, Nebraska Department of Roads, 1500 Hwy 2, 68502. (Mail add: PO Box 94759, 68509-4759), SAN 377-1628. Tel: 402-479-4316. FAX: 402-479-3989. E-mail: ndot.library@nebraska.gov. *Librn,* Denise Matulka; Staff 1 (MLS 1)
Founded 1968
Subject Interests: Hwys, Rail, Roads, Transportation
Automation Activity & Vendor Info: (Cataloging) OCLC CatExpress; (OPAC) Mandarin Library Automation
Restriction: Open by appt only

S NEBRASKA DEPARTMENT OF CORRECTIONS, Nebraska State Penitentiary Library, PO Box 2500, Sta B, 68502. SAN 377-3922. Tel: 402-471-3161, Ext 3267. FAX: 402-479-5819. *Libr Coord,* Position Currently Open
Library Holdings: Bk Titles 15,000; Per Subs 79
Subject Interests: Classics
Automation Activity & Vendor Info: (ILL) OCLC
Partic in SE Nebr Libr Asn
Restriction: Not open to pub

G NEBRASKA DEPARTMENT OF ECONOMIC DEVELOPMENT LIBRARY, 301 Centennial Mall S, 68509. (Mail add: PO Box 94666, 68509-4666), SAN 370-6443. Tel: 402-471-3111. Toll Free Tel: 800-426-6505. FAX: 402-471-3778. Web Site: www.neded.org. *Dir, Res,* Dave Dearmont; Tel: 402-471-3777, E-mail: dave.dearmont@nebraska.gov
Library Holdings: Bk Vols 2,000
Wireless access
Mem of Southeast Library System
Open Mon-Fri 8-5

G NEBRASKA DEPARTMENT OF NATURAL RESOURCES LIBRARY*, State Office Bldg, 4th Flr, 301 Centennial Mall S, 68509-4676. (Mail add: PO Box 94676, 68509-4676), SAN 377-371X. Tel: 402-471-1684. Administration Tel: 402-471-2363. FAX: 402-471-2900. Web Site: www.dnr.nebraska.gov. *Mgr, Spec Proj,* Susan France; E-mail: susan.france@nebraska.gov
Library Holdings: Bk Vols 2,000; Per Subs 30
Wireless access

M NEBRASKA HEALTH CARE ASSOCIATION LIBRARY*, 1200 Libra Dr, Ste 100, 68512. SAN 375-6750. Tel: 402-435-3551. FAX: 402-475-6289. Web Site: www.nehca.org. *Dir of Develop,* Pam Truscott; E-mail: pamt@nehca.org
Library Holdings: Bk Titles 900; Bk Vols 920; Per Subs 25
Open Mon-Fri 8-5

S NEBRASKA HISTORY LIBRARY*, History Nebraska-Nebraska State Historical Society, 1500 R St, 68508. SAN 309-5266. Tel: 402-471-4751. Toll Free Tel: 800-833-6747. FAX: 402-471-3100. Reference E-mail: hn.reference@nebraska.gov. Web Site: nebraskahistory.org. *Curator, Head, Ref,* Andrea Faling; Tel: 402-471-4785; *Curator, Head, Tech Serv, Librn,* Cindy S Drake; Tel: 402-471-4786, E-mail: cindy.drake@nebraska.gov; *Curator, State Archivist,* Gayla Koerting; Tel: 402-471-4783, E-mail: gayla.koerting@nebraska.gov; *Curator for Photog,* Karen Keehr; Tel:

402-471-4750, E-mail: karen.keehr@nebraska.gov; *Curator of Ms,* Tom Mooney; Tel: 402-471-6396, E-mail: tom.mooney@nebraska.gov; *Visual Image Curator,* Paul J Eisloeffel; Tel: 402-471-7837, E-mail: paul.eisloeffel@nebraska.gov. Subject Specialists: *Archives, Nebr,* Andrea Faling; *Genealogy, Local hist, Nebr,* Cindy S Drake; *Govt rec,* Gayla Koerting
Founded 1893
Library Holdings: Bk Vols 80,000; Per Subs 50
Special Collections: Nebraska Historical Society Photo Coll; Nebraska Public Records (State & County). State Document Depository
Subject Interests: Genealogy, Native American, Western hist
Automation Activity & Vendor Info: (Cataloging) Mandarin Library Automation; (OPAC) Mandarin Library Automation
Wireless access
Function: 24/7 Online cat, Magazines, Microfiche/film & reading machines, Online cat, Outside serv via phone, mail, e-mail & web, Photocopying/Printing, Ref & res, Ref serv available, Res libr
Open Tues-Sat 10-4
Restriction: Non-circulating, Pub use on premises

G NEBRASKA LEGISLATIVE COUNCIL*, Legislative Research Library, 1201 State Capitol Bldg, 1445 K St, 68508. SAN 328-1760. Tel: 402-471-2222. FAX: 402-471-2126. Web Site: news.legislature.ne.gov/lrd/legislative-research-library. *Librn,* Elice Hubbert; E-mail: ehubbert@leg.ne.gov; Staff 2 (Non-MLS 2)
Founded 1980
Library Holdings: Bk Titles 6,000; Per Subs 124
Subject Interests: Legis mat
Automation Activity & Vendor Info: (Acquisitions) EOS International; (Cataloging) EOS International; (Circulation) EOS International; (OPAC) EOS International; (Serials) EOS International
Wireless access
Publications: Acquisitions List (Monthly); Annotated Periodicals List
Restriction: Not open to pub

P NEBRASKA LIBRARY COMMISSION*, The Atrium, 1200 N St, Ste 120, 68508-2023. SAN 350-1604. Tel: 402-471-2045. Reference Tel: 402-471-4016. Toll Free Tel: 800-307-2665 (NE only). FAX: 402-471-2083. Web Site: www.nlc.nebraska.gov. *Dir,* Rod Wagner; Tel: 402-471-4001, E-mail: rod.wagner@nebraska.gov; *Dir, Info Serv,* Lisa Kelly; Tel: 402-471-4015, E-mail: lisa.kelly@nebraska.gov; *Dir, Libr Develop,* Christa Porter; *Talking Bk/Braille Serv Dir,* Gabe Kramer; Tel: 402-471-6242, E-mail: gabe.kramer@nebraska.gov; *Tech & Access Serv Dir,* Devra Dragos; *Acq Librn,* Cathy Hatterman; Tel: 402-471-4034, E-mail: cathy.hatterman@nebraska.gov; *Govt Info Librn,* Mary Sauers; Tel: 402-471-4017, E-mail: mary.sauers@nebraska.gov; *Online Serv Librn,* Susan Knisely; Tel: 402-471-3849; *Tech & Access Serv Librn,* Allana Novotny; Tel: 402-471-6681; *Tech Innovation Librn,* Amanda Sweet; Tel: 402-471-3106; *Bus Mgr,* Jerry Breazile; E-mail: jerry.breazile@nebraska.gov; *Children's Coordr, Young Adult Serv Coordr,* Sally Snyder; Tel: 402-471-4003, E-mail: sally.snyder@nebraska.gov; *Communications Coordr,* Tessa Terry; Tel: 402-471-3434, E-mail: tessa.terry@nebraska.gov; *Continuing Educ Coordr,* Holli Duggan; Tel: 402-471-2694, E-mail: holli.duggan@nebraska.gov; *Planning & Data Serv Coordr,* Sam Shaw; Tel: 402-471-3216, E-mail: sam.shaw@nebraska.gov; Staff 29 (MLS 17, Non-MLS 12)
Founded 1901
Jul 2019-Jun 2020 Income $5,348,685, State $3,989,781, Federal $1,358,904. Mats Exp $659,979. Sal $2,189,192
Special Collections: State Document Depository; US Document Depository
Automation Activity & Vendor Info: (Cataloging) OCLC; (Circulation) Mandarin Library Automation; (ILL) OCLC; (Media Booking) Mandarin Library Automation; (OPAC) Mandarin Library Automation; (Serials) Mandarin Library Automation
Wireless access
Function: Online cat
Publications: Interchange (Quarterly); Magazine in Special Format; NCompass (Annual report); What's Up Doc (Bimonthly)
Partic in Association for Rural & Small Libraries; OCLC Online Computer Library Center, Inc
Special Services for the Blind - Braille bks; Talking bks
Open Mon-Fri 8-5
Branches: 1
TALKING BOOK & BRAILLE SERVICE
See Separate Entry

P NEBRASKA LIBRARY COMMISSION*, Talking Book & Braille Service, The Atrium, 1200 N St, Ste 120, 68508-2023. SAN 309-5258. Tel: 402-471-4038. Toll Free Tel: 800-742-7691. FAX: 402-471-2083. Web Site: www.nlc.nebraska.gov/tbbs. *Dir,* Gabe Kramer; E-mail: gabe.kramer@nebraska.gov
Founded 1952
Library Holdings: Braille Volumes 2,855; CDs 690; DVDs 154; Bk Titles 62,153; Bk Vols 106,958; Talking Bks 59,496; Videos 607
Special Collections: Children's Braille; Nebraska Coll (cassette bks, digital bks)
Wireless access
Publications: Interchange (Newsletter)
Special Services for the Blind - Aids for in-house use; Assistive/Adapted tech devices, equip & products; Audio mat; Bks & mags in Braille, on rec, tape & cassette; Bks on cassette; Bks on flash-memory cartridges; Braille servs

GL NEBRASKA STATE LIBRARY*, 325 State Capitol, 1445 K St, 68509. (Mail add: PO Box 98931, 65809-8931), SAN 309-5274. Tel: 402-471-3189. FAX: 402-471-1011. E-mail: nsc.lawlibrary@nebraska.gov. Web Site: supremecourt.nebraska.gov/administration/state-library. *Actg Dep Dir,* Maureen Eck; E-mail: maureen.eck@nebraska.gov
Founded 1871
Library Holdings: Bk Titles 140,000
Special Collections: US Document Depository
Subject Interests: Law
Wireless access
Mem of Southeast Library System
Open Mon-Fri 8-4:30

R NEBRASKA UNITED METHODIST HISTORICAL CENTER ARCHIVES, Nebraska Wesleyan University, Cochrane-Woods Library, Lower Level, 5000 Saint Paul Ave, 68504. SAN 309-5215. Tel: 402-465-2175. E-mail: gpcarchives@greatplainsumc.org. Web Site: greatplainsumc.org/archivesandhistory. *Dir/Curator,* Karrie L Dvorak. Subject Specialists: *Evangelism,* Karrie L Dvorak; Staff 1 (Non-MLS 1)
Founded 1942
Jan 2020-Dec 2021 Income $250. Mats Exp $4,000, Books $1,500. Sal $28,000
Library Holdings: Microforms 19; Bk Titles 1,500
Special Collections: Nebraska Annual Conference Minutes Coll, 1856-2019
Wireless access
Function: Archival coll
Restriction: Closed stack, Open by appt only

C NEBRASKA WESLEYAN UNIVERSITY*, Cochrane-Woods Library, 5000 St Paul Ave, 68504. SAN 309-5282. Tel: 402-465-2400. Circulation Tel: 402-465-2402. Reference Tel: 402-465-2406. Administration Tel: 402-465-2401. FAX: 402-465-2189. E-mail: library@nebrwesleyan.edu. Web Site: www.nebrwesleyan.edu/inside-nwu/cochrane-woods-library. *Univ Librn,* Julie Pinnell; Tel: 402-465-2405, E-mail: jpinnell@nebrwesleyan.edu; *Head, Access Serv, Head, Electronic Res,* Annie Erdmann; Tel: 402-465-2404, E-mail: aerdmann@nebrwesleyan.edu; *Head, Archives, Head, Res Serv,* Dr Martha Tanner; Tel: 402-465-2407, E-mail: mtanner@nebrwesleyan.edu; Staff 7 (MLS 4, Non-MLS 3)
Founded 1888. Enrl 1,809; Fac 130; Highest Degree: Master
Library Holdings: Bk Vols 203,000; Per Subs 641
Special Collections: Mignon G Eberhart Coll; Publications of Faculty, bks, ms; Rare Books/College Archives
Wireless access
Publications: Newsletter
Partic in Nebr Independent Col Libr Consortium; OCLC Online Computer Library Center, Inc
Open Mon-Thurs 7:45am-Midnight, Fri 7:45-6, Sat 12-6, Sun Noon-Midnight

J SOUTHEAST COMMUNITY COLLEGE-LINCOLN CAMPUS*, LRC Library, 8800 O St, 68520. SAN 350-1663. Tel: 402-437-2585. Toll Free Tel: 800-642-4075. FAX: 402-437-2404. Web Site: www.southeast.edu/libraryresourcecenters. *Admin Dir,* Lyndsi Elias; Tel: 402-437-2586, E-mail: lelias@southeast.edu; *Libr Spec,* Michael Elsener; Tel: 402-437-2589, E-mail: melsener@southeast.edu; Staff 4 (MLS 2, Non-MLS 2)
Founded 1973. Highest Degree: Associate
Library Holdings: Bk Titles 13,000; Per Subs 300
Automation Activity & Vendor Info: (Cataloging) Mandarin Library Automation; (Circulation) Mandarin Library Automation; (OPAC) Mandarin Library Automation
Wireless access
Open Mon-Thurs 7:30am-9pm, Fri 7:30-5

P SOUTHEAST LIBRARY SYSTEM*, 5730 R St, Ste C1, 68505. Tel: 402-467-6188. Toll Free Tel: 800-288-6063. FAX: 402-467-6196. *Dir,* Scott Childers; E-mail: scott.childers.sels@gmail.com
Publications: Southeast Signal (Newsletter)
Member Libraries: Alice M Farr Library; American Historical Society of Germans from Russia; Auburn Memorial Library; Beatrice Public Library; Bruning Public Library; Bruun Memorial Public Library; Burkley Library & Resource Center; Byron Public Library; Crete Public Library; Davenport Public Library; Daykin Public Library; Dorchester Public Library; Douglas

Public Library; Dvoracek Memorial Library; Elmwood Public Library; Exeter Public Library; Fairbury Public Library; Fairmont Public Library; Geneva Public Library; Gilbert Public Library; Giltner Public Library; Greenwood Public Library; Hebron Secrest Library; Jennifer Reinke Public Library; John G Smith Memorial Public Library; Kilgore Memorial Library; Lincoln Journal Star Library; Lincoln Regional Center; Nebraska Center for the Education of Children Who Are Blind or Visually Impaired; Nebraska Department of Economic Development Library; Nebraska State Library; Osceola Public Library; Pawnee City Public Library; Plymouth Public Library; Seward Memorial Library; Shubert Public Library & Museum; Stella Community Library; Sterling Public Library; Struckman-Baatz Public Library; Syracuse Public Library; Table Rock Public Library; Tecumseh Public Library; Tobias Public Library; Tucker Memorial Public Library; Virgil Biegert Public Library; Webermeier Memorial Library; Weeping Water Public Library; Wymore Public Library

C UNION COLLEGE LIBRARY, 3800 S 48th St, 68506-4386. SAN 350-1728. Tel: 402-486-2514. FAX: 402-486-2678. Web Site: www.ucollege.edu/library. *Instrul Libr, Libr Dir, Res,* Bliss Kuntz; Tel: 402-486-2600, Ext 150, E-mail: bliss.kuntz@ucollege.edu; *Outreach Libr, Pub Serv,* Jill Kline; Tel: 402-486-2600, Ext 2149, E-mail: jill.kline@ucollege.edu; *Circ & Ref Asst,* Marcia Nordmeyer; Tel: 402-486-2600, Ext 2151, E-mail: marcia.nordmeyer@ucollege.edu; Staff 3 (MLS 2, Non-MLS 1)
Founded 1891. Enrl 800; Fac 3; Highest Degree: Master
Library Holdings: DVDs 243; e-books 36,474; Bk Vols 161,546; Per Subs 594; Videos 715
Special Collections: College Archives; E N Dick Coll; Heritage Room
Subject Interests: Seventh Day Adventists
Automation Activity & Vendor Info: (Acquisitions) OCLC; (Cataloging) OCLC; (Circulation) OCLC; (Course Reserve) OCLC; (ILL) OCLC WorldShare Interlibrary Loan; (OPAC) OCLC; (Serials) OCLC
Wireless access
Function: Archival coll, Art exhibits, Computers for patron use, Electronic databases & coll, ILL available, Laminating, Magazines, Mango lang, Microfiche/film & reading machines, Movies, Online cat, Photocopying/Printing, Prog for adults, Ref serv available, Study rm, Telephone ref, Wheelchair accessible
Partic in Adventist Librs Info Coop; OCLC Online Computer Library Center, Inc
Open Mon-Thurs 8:30am-11pm, Fri 8:30-4, Sun 5-11
Restriction: Open to pub for ref & circ; with some limitations, Open to students, fac, staff & alumni

C UNIVERSITY OF NEBRASKA-LINCOLN*, University Libraries, 318 Love Library, 13th & R Strs, 68588. (Mail add: PO Box 884100, 68588-4100). Tel: 402-472-2526. Interlibrary Loan Service Tel: 402-472-2522. Reference Tel: 402-472-9568. Administration FAX: 402-472-5181. Web Site: libraries.unl.edu. *Dean of Libr,* Dr Nancy Busch; E-mail: nbusch2@unl.edu; *Chair, Access Serv, Chair, Discovery & Res Mgt,* Judith Wolfe; E-mail: jwolfe4@unl.edu; *Chair, Digital Initiatives & Spec Coll,* Katherine Walter; E-mail: kwalter1@unl.edu; *Chair, Res & Instrul Serv,* Charlene Maxey-Harris; E-mail: cmaxeyharris2@unl.edu; *Dir, Computing Operations & Research Serv,* DeeAnn Allison; E-mail: dallison1@unl.edu; *Head, User Experience,* Jeanetta Drueke; E-mail: mdrueke1@unl.edu; *Bus Officer,* Kay Richter; E-mail: krichter4@unl.edu; *Fac Mgr,* Debra Pearson; E-mail: dpearson1@unl.edu; *Spec Coll & Archives Libr,* Mary Ellen Ducey; E-mail: mducey2@unl.edu; Staff 140 (MLS 46, Non-MLS 94)
Founded 1869. Enrl 25,260; Fac 1,643; Highest Degree: Doctorate
Jul 2015-Jun 2016. Mats Exp $8,907,856. Sal $7,614,241 (Prof $3,600,582)
Library Holdings: Bk Vols 3,801,630
Special Collections: French & Russian Revolutions; Literary Papers & Manuscripts; Ted Kooser, Wright Morris, Hilda Raz & others); Natural History & Science; Political papers including congressional papers; Quilt Archives & Manuscripts; Ruth Etting and Kees-Helm Music; U.S. Secretary of Agriculture and Trade Ambassador Papers; US Military & Wartime History; Walt Whitman and Willa Cather Archive. State Document Depository; UN Document Depository; US Document Depository
Automation Activity & Vendor Info: (Acquisitions) Innovative Interfaces, Inc; (Cataloging) Innovative Interfaces, Inc; (Circulation) Innovative Interfaces, Inc; (Course Reserve) Innovative Interfaces, Inc; (ILL) OCLC ILLiad; (OPAC) Innovative Interfaces, Inc; (Serials) Innovative Interfaces, Inc
Wireless access
Partic in Big Ten Academic Alliance; OCLC Online Computer Library Center, Inc; University of Nebraska Consortium of Libraries
Departmental Libraries:
ARCHITECTURE LIBRARY, Architecture Hall, Rm 308, City Campus 0108, 68588-0108. Tel: 402-472-1208. *Library Contact,* Kay Logan-Peters; E-mail: klogan-peters1@unl.edu
ENGINEERING LIBRARY, Nebraska Hall, Rm W204, City Campus 0516, 68588-0516. Tel: 402-472-3411. *Library Contact,* Ted Naylor; E-mail: tnaylor2@unl.edu
EXTENSION CENTER, 4502 Ave I, Scottsbluff, 69361. Tel: 308-632-1230. FAX: 308-632-1365. *Librn,* Joan Giesecke; E-mail: jgiesecke@unl.edu
Library Holdings: Bk Vols 3,000
Restriction: Not open to pub
GEOLOGY LIBRARY, Bessey Hall, Rm 10, City Campus 0344, 68588-0344. Tel: 402-472-2653. *Library Contact,* Adonna Fleming; E-mail: dfleming2@unl.edu
MATHEMATICS LIBRARY, 14 Avery Hall, 68588-0129. Tel: 402-472-6900. *Library Contact,* Adonna Fleming; E-mail: dfleming2@unl.edu
MUSIC LIBRARY, Westbrook Music Bldg, Rm 30, 68588-0101. Tel: 402-472-6300. *Library Contact,* Anita Breckbill; E-mail: abreckbill1@unl.edu
Founded 1980

CL MARVIN & VIRGINIA SCHMID LAW LIBRARY, 1875 N 42nd St, 68583. (Mail add: PO Box 830902, 68583-0902). Tel: 402-472-3547. Reference Tel: 402-472-3548. FAX: 402-472-8260. Web Site: www.law.unl.edu. *Dir,* Richard Leiter; Tel: 402-472-5737; *Assoc Dir,* Sandy Placzek; *Ref (Info Servs),* Stefanie Pearlman; *Ref (Info Servs),* Matt Novak; *Tech Serv,* Emily Nimsakont
Founded 1891
Special Collections: Anglo-American Law Coll; Space Telecommunications Law Coll; Tax Law Coll
Partic in Mid-America Law Library Consortium
C Y THOMPSON LIBRARY, East Campus, 1625 N 38th St, 68583-0717, SAN 350-1841. Circulation Tel: 402-472-4401. Reference Tel: 402-472-4407. FAX: 402-472-7005. *Library Contact,* Judith Wolfe; E-mail: jwolfe4@unl.edu

LITCHFIELD

P LITCHFIELD PUBLIC LIBRARY*, 102 W Buford St, 68852. (Mail add: PO Box 79, 68852-0079), SAN 309-5355. Tel: 308-446-2285. E-mail: litchfieldnelibrary@gmail.com. *Dir,* Position Currently Open
Library Holdings: Bk Vols 5,000
Wireless access
Mem of Central Plains Library System
Open Wed 3-5

LODGEPOLE

P NANCY FAWCETT MEMORIAL LIBRARY, 724 Oberfelder St, 69149-0318. (Mail add: PO Box 318, 69149-0318), SAN 309-5363. Tel: 308-483-5714. E-mail: nafameli@daltontel.net. *Pres,* Diana Bruns; *Dir, Librn,* Norma Michelman
Founded 1930. Pop 368; Circ 2,330
Library Holdings: Bk Vols 6,200; Per Subs 10
Wireless access
Mem of Western Library System
Open Mon-Thurs 2:30-6:30

LOUISVILLE

P LOUISVILLE PUBLIC LIBRARY*, 217 Main St, 68037. (Mail add: PO Box 39, 68037-0039), SAN 309-5371. Tel: 402-234-6265. E-mail: louisvillelibrary@gmail.com. Web Site: www.louisvillenelibrary.org. *Libr Dir,* Michelle Daniels
Pop 1,048; Circ 9,299
Library Holdings: Bk Titles 12,000
Automation Activity & Vendor Info: (Cataloging) Biblionix; (Circulation) Biblionix; (OPAC) Biblionix
Wireless access
Function: 24/7 Electronic res, 24/7 Online cat, After school storytime, Bks on cassette, Bks on CD, CD-ROM, Children's prog, Computers for patron use, Free DVD rentals, ILL available, Internet access, Magazines, Movies, Online cat, OverDrive digital audio bks, Photocopying/Printing, Preschool reading prog, Prog for children & young adult, Ref & res, Ref serv available, Res assist avail, Spoken cassettes & CDs, Story hour, Summer & winter reading prog, Summer reading prog, Teen prog, Telephone ref, VHS videos, Wheelchair accessible
Mem of Three Rivers Library System
Open Mon & Wed 10-6, Fri 10-5, Sat 9-Noon

LOUP CITY

P LOUP CITY PUBLIC LIBRARY*, 800 N Eighth St, 68853. SAN 309-538X. Tel: 308-745-1589. E-mail: loupcity@hotmail.com, loupcitylibrary@yahoo.com. *Libr Dir,* Audrey L Heil
Founded 1917. Pop 3,999; Circ 16,000
Library Holdings: High Interest/Low Vocabulary Bk Vols 500; Large Print Bks 200; Bk Vols 27,000; Per Subs 60; Talking Bks 100; Videos 350
Special Collections: Nebraska History Coll

Automation Activity & Vendor Info: (Cataloging) OPALS (Open-source Automated Library System); (Circulation) OPALS (Open-source Automated Library System); (OPAC) OPALS (Open-source Automated Library System)
Wireless access
Mem of Central Plains Library System
Open Tues & Thurs 9-1 & 2-6, Wed 2-8, Fri 2-6, Sat 2-5

LYMAN

P LYMAN PUBLIC LIBRARY*, 313 Jeffers St, 69352. (Mail add: PO Box 384, 69352-0384), SAN 309-5398. Tel: 308-787-1366. FAX: 308-787-1366. Web Site: lyman.panhandlelibraries.org. *Dir,* Keitha Green; *Asst Librn,* Mary Haagensen
Pop 551; Circ 3,552
Library Holdings: Bk Titles 8,000; Per Subs 20
Wireless access
Mem of Western Library System
Open Mon 2-5, Tues, Thurs & Sat 9-12, Wed 9-12 & 2-5

LYNCH

P LYNCH PUBLIC LIBRARY*, 423 W Hoffman, 68746. (Mail add: PO Box 385, 68746-0385), SAN 377-208X. Tel: 402-569-3491. *Library Contact,* Janice Hull
Library Holdings: Bk Vols 13,000
Mem of Central Plains Library System
Open Mon & Wed 2-5, Fri 9-12

LYONS

P LYONS PUBLIC LIBRARY*, 305 Main, 68038. (Mail add: PO Box 198, 68038-0198), SAN 309-5401. Tel: 402-687-2895. FAX: 402-687-4112. E-mail: lyonslibrary@abbnebraska.com. Web Site: lyonscity.nebraska.gov/library. *Libr Dir,* Michael Heavrin
Pop 851
Library Holdings: CDs 38; Large Print Bks 800; Bk Titles 10,400; Per Subs 20; Talking Bks 205; Videos 483
Automation Activity & Vendor Info: (Cataloging) Biblionix; (Circulation) Biblionix; (ILL) OCLC; (OPAC) Biblionix
Mem of Three Rivers Library System
Special Services for the Blind - Audio mat; Bks available with recordings; Bks on cassette; Bks on CD; Extensive large print coll; Home delivery serv
Open Mon & Wed 12-8, Tues & Thurs 9-12 & 5-8, Fri 4-8, Sat 9-1
Friends of the Library Group

MACY

J NEBRASKA INDIAN COMMUNITY COLLEGE*, Macy Campus Library, 1111 Hwy 75, 68039. (Mail add: PO Box 428, 68039-0428), SAN 377-1733. Tel: 402-837-4183. *Librn,* Susan Tyndall; E-mail: styndall@thenicc.edu
Library Holdings: Bk Vols 3,000; Per Subs 10
Open Mon-Fri 9-5

MADISON

P MADISON PUBLIC LIBRARY*, 208 W Third St, 68748. (Mail add: PO Box 387, 68748-0387), SAN 309-5444. Tel: 402-454-3500. FAX: 402-454-3376. E-mail: madlibr@cableone.net. Web Site: www.madisonlibrary.net. *Dir,* Lori Porter
Pop 2,425; Circ 12,000
Library Holdings: Bk Titles 19,000; Per Subs 41
Mem of Three Rivers Library System
Open Mon-Thurs 11:30-7, Fri 11:30-5

MASON CITY

P SUNSHINE TOWNSHIP LIBRARY, 417 Main St, 68855. (Mail add: PO Box 12, 68855-0012), SAN 309-5452. E-mail: masonnews@nctc.net.
Founded 1926. Pop 305; Circ 619
Library Holdings: Bk Titles 4,487
Special Collections: Central Nebraska Authors; History Books of Area Towns
Mem of Central Plains Library System
Open Wed & Sat 2-5

MCCOOK

S HIGH PLAINS MUSEUM LIBRARY*, 413 Norris Ave, 69001. SAN 309-541X. Tel: 308-345-3661. *Curator,* Marilyn Hawkins
Founded 1961
Library Holdings: Bk Vols 1,000
Special Collections: Frank Lloyd Wright Coll; German Bibles & School Books; Men & Women Fashion Catalogues; Old Medical Books & Equipment. Oral History
Subject Interests: Cooking
Wireless access
Open Tues-Sat 1-5

P MCCOOK PUBLIC LIBRARY, 802 Norris Ave, 69001-3143. SAN 309-5436. Tel: 308-345-1906. FAX: 308-345-1461. E-mail: mlibrary@cityofmccook.com. Web Site: libraries.ne.gov/mccook, www.cityofmccook.com/124/Library. *Dir,* Jody Crocker; *Ch,* Diane Lyons; E-mail: pdlyons@gpcom.net
Pop 8,500
Library Holdings: Large Print Bks 4,000; Bk Titles 30,000; Per Subs 90
Subject Interests: Braille
Wireless access
Mem of Central Plains Library System
Open Mon-Fri 9-8, Sat 9-5

J MID-PLAINS COMMUNITY COLLEGE*, McCook Community College Von Riesen Library, 1205 E Third St, 69001. SAN 309-5428. Tel: 308-345-8117. Toll Free Tel: 800-658-4348. FAX: 308-345-8193. E-mail: library@mpcc.edu. Web Site: mpcc-verso.auto-graphics.com/mvc. *Area Asst Dir,* Sky Seery; E-mail: seerys@mpcc.edu; Staff 2 (MLS 2)
Founded 1926. Enrl 801; Fac 44
Library Holdings: Bk Titles 25,000; Per Subs 240
Wireless access
Mem of Central Plains Library System
Partic in OCLC Online Computer Library Center, Inc
Open Mon-Thurs 7:30am-9:30pm, Fri 8-4:30, Sun 5pm-9:30pm

S NEBRASKA DEPARTMENT OF CORRECTIONAL SERVICES*, Work Ethic Camp Library, 2309 N Hwy 83, 69001. Tel: 308-345-8405. FAX: 308-345-8407. Web Site: corrections.nebraska.gov/facilities/work-ethic-camp. *Library Contact,* Jane Keith
Library Holdings: Bk Vols 700
Restriction: Not open to pub

MEAD

P MEAD PUBLIC LIBRARY*, 316 S Vine, 68041. (Mail add: PO Box 203, 68041-0203), SAN 309-5460. Tel: 402-624-6605. FAX: 402-624-6605. Web Site: www.meadnebraska.net/library. *Dir,* Laurie Van Ackeren; *Asst Dir,* Lori Moseman; E-mail: meadlibrary@outlook.com; *Libr Asst,* Mary Mayfield
Pop 595; Circ 2,800
Library Holdings: Audiobooks 80; CDs 30; DVDs 180; Large Print Bks 40; Bk Titles 11,000; Per Subs 20; Videos 545
Special Collections: Mead Ordnance Plant Administrative Records
Automation Activity & Vendor Info: (Cataloging) Follett Software; (Circulation) Follett Software; (OPAC) Follett Software
Wireless access
Open Tues 10-1 & 4-7, Wed 4-7, Thurs 9-6, Fri 9-1, Sat 9-noon
Friends of the Library Group

MEADOW GROVE

P MEADOW GROVE PUBLIC LIBRARY*, 205 Main St, 68752. (Mail add: PO Box 198, 68752-0198). Tel: 402-634-2266. FAX: 402-634-2266. E-mail: mglibrary@telebeep.com. Web Site: libraries.ne.gov/meadowgrove. *Dir,* Mardell Kohl; Staff 2 (MLS 2)
Founded 1926. Pop 332; Circ 11,614
Library Holdings: Large Print Bks 60; Bk Vols 6,877; Per Subs 27; Talking Bks 92
Automation Activity & Vendor Info: (Cataloging) Follett Software
Wireless access
Mem of Three Rivers Library System
Open Mon & Sat 9-12, Tues & Thurs 1-5:30, Wed & Fri 3-7
Friends of the Library Group

MERNA

P BRENIZER PUBLIC LIBRARY*, 430 W Center Ave, 68856. (Mail add: PO Box 8, 68856-0008), SAN 309-5487. Tel: 308-643-2268. FAX: 308-643-2268. *Dir,* Vickie Burnett; *Asst Librn,* Carol Squier
Founded 1916. Pop 1,000; Circ 9,200. Sal $6,000
Library Holdings: Audiobooks 25; CDs 100; DVDs 20; Bk Titles 17,500; Per Subs 36; Videos 300
Wireless access
Mem of Central Plains Library System
Open Tues, Thurs & Sat 12:30-5

MILFORD

J SOUTHEAST COMMUNITY COLLEGE*, Stanley A Matzke Learning Resource Center, 600 State St, 68405. SAN 309-5495. Tel: 402-761-2131, Ext 8245. FAX: 402-761-2324. Web Site: www.southeast.edu/libraryresourcecenters. *Dir,* Janalee Petsch; E-mail: jpetsch@southeast.edu

Founded 1975. Enrl 1,000; Fac 82
Library Holdings: Bk Titles 23,000; Per Subs 350
Special Collections: Vocational/Technical
Automation Activity & Vendor Info: (Acquisitions) Mandarin Library Automation; (Cataloging) Mandarin Library Automation; (Circulation) Mandarin Library Automation; (Course Reserve) Mandarin Library Automation; (ILL) Mandarin Library Automation; (Media Booking) Mandarin Library Automation; (OPAC) Mandarin Library Automation; (Serials) Mandarin Library Automation
Wireless access
Open Mon-Thurs 7:30-6, Fri 7:30-4:30

P WEBERMEIER MEMORIAL LIBRARY*, 617 Second St, 68405. (Mail add: PO Box 705, 68405-0705), SAN 309-5509. Tel: 402-761-2937. FAX: 402-761-2937. E-mail: milfordlibrary@gmail.com. Web Site: libraries.ne.gov/milford. *Dir,* George Matzen
Founded 1930. Pop 2,110; Circ 15,513
Library Holdings: Bk Vols 17,940; Per Subs 51
Wireless access
Mem of Southeast Library System
Open Mon-Thurs 10-7, Fri 10-5, Sat 10-3
Friends of the Library Group

MILLIGAN

P MILLIGAN PUBLIC LIBRARY*, 507 Main St, 68406. SAN 309-5517. Tel: 402-629-4302. E-mail: milliganlibrary@windstream.net. *Dir,* Shirley Brunkow; *Librn,* Betty Zelenka
Pop 350
Library Holdings: Audiobooks 25; AV Mats 150; Large Print Bks 20; Bk Vols 3,377; Per Subs 3; Spec Interest Per Sub 1; Videos 635
Wireless access
Function: After school storytime
Open Mon & Wed 3-5, Sat 9-11

MINATARE

P MINATARE PUBLIC LIBRARY*, 309 Main St, 69356. (Mail add: PO Box 483, 69356-0483), SAN 309-5525. Tel: 308-783-1414. FAX: 308-783-1414. E-mail: minatarelibrary@gmail.com. *Librn,* Caryle Covalt
Pop 1,100; Circ 5,761
Library Holdings: Large Print Bks 30; Bk Vols 7,550; Talking Bks 30
Mem of Western Library System
Open Mon-Fri 1-4:30

MINDEN

P JENSEN MEMORIAL LIBRARY, 443 N Kearney, 68959. (Mail add: PO Box 264, 68959-0264), SAN 309-5533. Tel: 308-832-2648. FAX: 308-832-1642. E-mail: library@mindennebraska.org. Web Site: libraries.ne.gov/jensen. *Dir,* Janene Hill
Founded 1906. Pop 2,939; Circ 29,814
Library Holdings: Bk Vols 18,000; Per Subs 69; Videos 2,066
Special Collections: Genealogy Reference Coll. Oral History
Automation Activity & Vendor Info: (Cataloging) Follett Software; (Circulation) Follett Software; (OPAC) Follett Software
Wireless access
Mem of Central Plains Library System
Partic in Association for Rural & Small Libraries
Open Mon, Tues & Thurs 9-7, Wed & Fri 9-5:30, Sat 9-1

MITCHELL

P MITCHELL PUBLIC LIBRARY, 1449 Center Ave, 69357. SAN 309-5541. Tel: 308-623-2222. FAX: 308-623-2222. E-mail: mipl@actcom.net. Web Site: www.mitchellcity.net/library. *Libr Dir,* Maryruth Reed; Staff 1 (MLS 1)
Founded 1920. Pop 1,666; Circ 11,287
Oct 2015-Sept 2016 Income $95,092, State $701, Other $28,156. Mats Exp $10,800. Sal $38,396
Library Holdings: AV Mats 30; DVDs 10; Microforms 1; Bk Titles 12,819; Per Subs 6
Subject Interests: Nebr hist
Automation Activity & Vendor Info: (Cataloging) Follett Software; (Circulation) Follett Software; (ILL) OCLC; (OPAC) Follett Software
Wireless access
Function: 24/7 Electronic res, 24/7 Online cat, Adult bk club
Mem of Western Library System
Open Mon-Thurs 11-6, Fri & Sat 11-5
Friends of the Library Group

MORRILL

P MORRILL PUBLIC LIBRARY, 119 E Webster, 69358. (Mail add: PO Box 402, 69358-0402), SAN 309-555X. Tel: 308-247-2611. FAX: 308-247-2309. E-mail: morrillpl@charter.net. Web Site: libraries.ne.gov/morrill. *Dir,* Sarah Alfred; *Libr Asst,* John Hudson; Staff 3 (Non-MLS 3)
Founded 1916. Pop 940; Circ 5,410
Library Holdings: AV Mats 87; Large Print Bks 196; Bk Vols 10,825; Per Subs 28; Talking Bks 135
Automation Activity & Vendor Info: (Cataloging) ComPanion Corp; (OPAC) ComPanion Corp
Wireless access
Function: Audiobks on Playaways & MP3, Bks on CD, Children's prog, Computers for patron use, Free DVD rentals, ILL available, Internet access, Laminating, Large print keyboards, Movies, Online cat, Photocopying/Printing, Preschool outreach, Preschool reading prog, Prog for adults, Prog for children & young adult, Ref serv available, Scanner, STEM programs, Story hour, Summer reading prog, Teen prog, Wheelchair accessible
Mem of Western Library System
Special Services for the Deaf - Bks on deafness & sign lang
Special Services for the Blind - Bks on cassette; Bks on CD; Large print bks
Open Mon & Thurs 1-7, Tues & Wed 1-5:30, Fri 9-5:30
Friends of the Library Group

MULLEN

P HOOKER COUNTY LIBRARY*, 102 N Cleveland Ave, 69152. (Mail add: PO Box 479, 69152-0479), SAN 309-5568. Tel: 308-546-2240. FAX: 308-546-2240. *Librn,* Julie Pfeiffer; E-mail: jpfeiffer41@hotmail.com
Pop 977; Circ 16,630
Library Holdings: Bk Vols 12,000; Per Subs 22
Wireless access
Mem of Western Library System
Open Mon, Wed & Fri 2-5, Tues & Thurs 11-5

NEBRASKA CITY

P MORTON-JAMES PUBLIC LIBRARY*, 923 First Corso, 68410. SAN 309-5576. Tel: 402-873-5609. E-mail: mortonjameslibrary@gmail.com. Web Site: www.morton-jamespubliclibrary.com. *Dir,* Donna S Kruse; E-mail: dkruse@nebraskacity.com; *Asst Dir,* Louan Beard; E-mail: louanbeard@gmail.com; Staff 6 (MLS 2, Non-MLS 4)
Founded 1896. Pop 7,228; Circ 88,889
Oct 2017-Sept 2018 Income $1,300. Mats Exp $37,000, Books $24,950, Per/Ser (Incl. Access Fees) $2,000, AV Mat $10,050
Library Holdings: CDs 2,236; DVDs 4,514; Large Print Bks 2,356; Microforms 589; Bk Vols 29,336; Per Subs 50
Special Collections: Nebraska City & Otoe County Genealogy & History Coll
Automation Activity & Vendor Info: (Acquisitions) Biblionix; (Cataloging) OCLC CatExpress; (Circulation) Biblionix; (ILL) OCLC; (OPAC) Biblionix; (Serials) Biblionix
Wireless access
Function: 24/7 Electronic res, 24/7 Online cat, Adult bk club, Archival coll, Art exhibits, Audiobks via web, Bk club(s), Bks on CD, Children's prog, Computers for patron use, Electronic databases & coll, Free DVD rentals, Holiday prog, Home delivery & serv to seniorr ctr & nursing homes, Homebound delivery serv, ILL available, Internet access, Magazines, Mail & tel request accepted, Mango lang, Meeting rooms, Microfiche/film & reading machines, Music CDs, Online cat, Online ref, Outside serv via phone, mail, e-mail & web, OverDrive digital audio bks, Photocopying/Printing, Preschool outreach, Prog for adults, Prog for children & young adult, Scanner, Spanish lang bks, Summer reading prog, Tax forms, Telephone ref, Wheelchair accessible
Open Mon-Thurs 9-6, Fri & Sat 9-5
Restriction: Borrowing requests are handled by ILL, Non-circulating coll, Non-circulating of rare bks, Non-resident fee

S NEBRASKA CENTER FOR THE EDUCATION OF CHILDREN WHO ARE BLIND OR VISUALLY IMPAIRED, 824 Tenth Ave, 68410. (Mail add: PO Box 129, 68410-0129), SAN 377-0982. Tel: 402-873-5513. Toll Free Tel: 800-826-4355. FAX: 402-873-3463. Web Site: www.ncecbvi.org. *Adminr,* Sally Schreiner; E-mail: sschreiner@esu4.net; *Prog Dir,* Dr Tanya Armstrong; E-mail: tarmstrong@esu4.net
Library Holdings: Bk Vols 15,000; Per Subs 25
Mem of Southeast Library System
Open Mon-Fri 7:30-4

NELIGH

P NELIGH PUBLIC LIBRARY*, 710 Main St, 68756-1246. SAN 309-5584. Tel: 402-887-5140. FAX: 402-887-4530. Web Site: www.libraries.ne.gov/neligh. *Dir,* Jennifer Norton; E-mail: jn@nelighlibrary.com; *Youth Serv Dir,* Anne Dexter; *Ref Librn,* Danielle Reynolds; *Asst Librn,* Mary Klinetobe; Staff 4 (Non-MLS 4)
Founded 1905. Pop 1,599; Circ 67,149
Library Holdings: Audiobooks 683; AV Mats 635; e-books 3,000; Electronic Media & Resources 21; Bk Titles 28,000; Per Subs 73

Special Collections: Art Prints/Posters; Nebraska Coll; Wood Carving Patterns
Automation Activity & Vendor Info: (Cataloging) Follett Software; (Circulation) Follett Software; (ILL) OCLC; (OPAC) Follett Software
Wireless access
Mem of Three Rivers Library System
Open Mon-Thurs 10-8, Fri & Sat 10-2
Friends of the Library Group

NELSON

P NELSON PUBLIC LIBRARY*, Ten W Third St, 68961. (Mail add: PO Box 322, 68961-0322), SAN 309-5592. Tel: 402-225-7111. FAX: 402-225-7111. E-mail: nelsonlibrary@superiorinet.net. Web Site: libraries.ne.gov/nelson. *Dir,* Mary Statz; *Ch,* Tina Albrecht; *Asst Librn,* Dawn Shaw
Founded 1907. Circ 2,854
Library Holdings: Large Print Bks 275; Bk Vols 9,100; Per Subs 12; Talking Bks 54; Videos 300
Automation Activity & Vendor Info: (Acquisitions) Follett Software; (Cataloging) Follett Software; (Circulation) Follett Software; (ILL) OCLC WorldShare Interlibrary Loan
Wireless access
Open Tues & Thurs 3:30-8, Wed 2-8, Sat 9-12
Friends of the Library Group

NEWMAN GROVE

P NEWMAN GROVE PUBLIC LIBRARY, 615 Hale Ave, 68758. (Mail add: PO Box 430, 68758-0430), SAN 309-5606. Tel: 402-447-2331. FAX: 402-447-2331. E-mail: ngplread64@gmail.com. Web Site: libraries.ne.gov/newmangrove. *Dir,* Kathy Strong; E-mail: kmstrong84@gmail.com; Staff 1 (Non-MLS 1)
Founded 1923. Pop 730; Circ 9,341
Library Holdings: AV Mats 337; Large Print Bks 150; Bk Titles 13,795; Bk Vols 14,494; Per Subs 12; Talking Bks 125; Videos 283
Special Collections: Local Newspaper, micro
Automation Activity & Vendor Info: (Cataloging) Follett Software; (Circulation) Follett Software; (OPAC) Follett Software
Wireless access
Mem of Three Rivers Library System
Open Tues & Wed 9-12 & 1-7, Thurs 9-12 & 1-6, Fri & Sat 9-12

NIOBRARA

J NEBRASKA INDIAN COMMUNITY COLLEGE*, Santee Campus Library, 415 N River Rd, 68760. SAN 377-3590. Tel: 402-241-5945. Web Site: www.thenicc.edu/index.php/en/library. *Librn,* Cheryl Maloney; E-mail: CMaloney@thenicc.edu
Library Holdings: Bk Vols 5,500
Open Mon-Fri 9-5

P NIOBRARA PUBLIC LIBRARY*, 25414 Park Ave, Ste 3, 68760. (Mail add: PO Box 15, 68760-0015), SAN 309-5614. Tel: 402-857-3565. FAX: 402-857-3824. E-mail: niolib2@gpcom.net. Web Site: www.niobrarane.com/library. *Librn,* Judy L Kopp
Pop 419
Library Holdings: CDs 15; DVDs 120; Large Print Bks 300; Bk Vols 8,500; Per Subs 25; Talking Bks 200; Videos 300
Special Collections: Niobrara Nebraska Centennial History Coll
Subject Interests: Local hist
Automation Activity & Vendor Info: (Cataloging) Follett Software; (OPAC) Follett Software
Wireless access
Mem of Three Rivers Library System
Special Services for the Blind - Audio mat; Bks on cassette; Bks on CD
Open Tues 9-2, Wed 12-7, Thurs 1-6, Sat 9-12

NORFOLK

P NORFOLK PUBLIC LIBRARY*, 308 W Prospect Ave, 68701-4138. SAN 309-5630. Tel: 402-844-2100. Web Site: norfolkne.gov/government/departments/library. *Dir,* Jessica Chamberlain; E-mail: jchamberlain@norfolkne.gov; *Librn I, Youth Serv Supvr,* Karen Drevo; Tel: 402-844-2108, E-mail: kdrevo@norfolkne.gov; *Circ Supvr,* Doug Collier; Tel: 402-844-2105, E-mail: dcollier@norfolkne.gov; *Tech Serv Supvr,* Sally Stahlecker; Tel: 402-844-2107, E-mail: sstahlec@norfolkne.gov; Staff 16 (MLS 2, Non-MLS 14)
Founded 1906. Pop 24,210
Subject Interests: Genealogy, Nebr hist, Poetry
Automation Activity & Vendor Info: (Acquisitions) SirsiDynix; (Cataloging) SirsiDynix; (Circulation) SirsiDynix; (Course Reserve) SirsiDynix; (ILL) SirsiDynix; (Media Booking) SirsiDynix; (OPAC) SirsiDynix; (Serials) SirsiDynix
Wireless access
Function: 24/7 Electronic res, 24/7 Online cat, Adult bk club, Audiobks via web, AV serv, Bk club(s), Bks on CD, Children's prog, Computer training, Computers for patron use, Electronic databases & coll, Free DVD rentals, Homebound delivery serv, ILL available, Internet access, Laminating, Life-long learning prog for all ages, Magazines, Makerspace, Mango lang, Meeting rooms, Movies, Museum passes, Notary serv, Online cat, OverDrive digital audio bks, Photocopying/Printing, Preschool reading prog, Printer for laptops & handheld devices, Prog for adults, Prog for children & young adult, Ref & res, Scanner, Spanish lang bks, STEM programs, Story hour, Study rm, Summer reading prog, Teen prog, Wheelchair accessible, Writing prog
Mem of Three Rivers Library System
Partic in ONELibrary Consortium
Special Services for the Blind - Audio mat; Bks on CD; Computer access aids; Computer with voice synthesizer for visually impaired persons; Copier with enlargement capabilities; Large print bks; Low vision equip
Open Mon-Thurs 9-8, Fri & Sat 9-5, Sun 1:30-4:30

M NORFOLK REGIONAL CENTER, Resident Library, 1700 N Victory Rd, 68701. (Mail add: PO Box 1209, 68701-1209), SAN 350-1930. Tel: 402-370-3290. FAX: 402-370-3194. *Activity Spec, Librn,* Lisa Weible; E-mail: lisa.weible@nebraska.gov
Library Holdings: Bk Titles 3,000; Per Subs 20
Subject Interests: Educ, Recreation
Automation Activity & Vendor Info: (Cataloging) Follett Software; (Circulation) Follett Software; (ILL) Follett Software; (OPAC) Follett Software
Mem of Three Rivers Library System
Open Mon-Fri 8-5

J NORTHEAST COMMUNITY COLLEGE*, Library Resource Center, 801 E Benjamin Ave, 68702. (Mail add: PO Box 469, 68702-0469), SAN 309-5649. Tel: 402-844-7130. FAX: 402-844-7293. Web Site: northeast.edu/Library-Resources/. *Dir, Libr Serv,* Mary Louise Irene Foster; Tel: 402-844-7131, E-mail: marylouise@northeast.edu; Staff 2 (MLS 1, Non-MLS 1)
Founded 1928. Enrl 3,200; Fac 120; Highest Degree: Associate
Library Holdings: Audiobooks 238; Per Subs 143
Automation Activity & Vendor Info: (Acquisitions) SirsiDynix; (Cataloging) SirsiDynix; (Circulation) SirsiDynix; (Discovery) EBSCO Discovery Service; (OPAC) SirsiDynix; (Serials) SirsiDynix
Wireless access
Partic in OCLC Online Computer Library Center, Inc
Open Mon-Thurs (Fall & Spring) 7am-10pm, Fri 7-5, Sun 1-9

NORTH BEND

P NORTH BEND PUBLIC LIBRARY*, 110 E 13th St, 68649. (Mail add: PO Box 279, 68649-0279), SAN 309-5657. Tel: 402-652-8356. FAX: 402-652-8356. E-mail: northbendlibrary@gpcom.net. Web Site: libraries.ne.gov/northbend. *Dir,* Amy Reznicek; *Librn,* Lisa Dvorak; *Librn,* Joyce Ruzicka
Pop 1,368; Circ 14,970
Library Holdings: Audiobooks 436; DVDs 735; Electronic Media & Resources 19; Large Print Bks 125; Bk Titles 10,467; Per Subs 18
Special Collections: Cake Pans
Automation Activity & Vendor Info: (Cataloging) Follett Software; (Circulation) Follett Software; (OPAC) Follett Software
Wireless access
Mem of Three Rivers Library System
Partic in Eastern Nebr Libr Asn
Open Mon-Thurs 1-6:30, Fri 10-5, Sat 10-2
Friends of the Library Group

NORTH LOUP

P NORTH LOUP TOWNSHIP LIBRARY, 112 South B St, 68859. (Mail add: PO Box 157, 68859-0157), SAN 309-5665. Tel: 308-496-4230. E-mail: nlpl@nctc.net. *Librn,* Linda Markvicka
Founded 1925. Pop 563; Circ 1,433
Library Holdings: Bk Vols 6,044; Per Subs 12
Special Collections: North Loup Newspapers, 1887-1942, microfilm & reader printer
Mem of Central Plains Library System
Special Services for the Blind - Bks on cassette; Large print bks
Open Mon, Wed & Fri 2:30-4:30

NORTH PLATTE

J MID PLAINS COMMUNITY COLLEGE*, North Platte Learning Resource Center, 601 W State Farm Rd, 69101. SAN 309-5673. Tel: 308-535-3600, 308-535-3726. FAX: 308-535-3794. E-mail: library@mpcc.edu. Web Site: mpcc-verso.auto-graphics.com/mvc. *Asst Dir, Learning Res,* Sky Seery; Tel: 308-535-3727, E-mail: seerys@mpcc.edu; Staff 7 (MLS 2, Non-MLS 5)
Founded 1965. Enrl 1,500; Fac 65; Highest Degree: Associate

Library Holdings: Audiobooks 274; CDs 847; DVDs 1,353; e-books 150,000; Music Scores 45,272; Bk Titles 16,243; Per Subs 55
Automation Activity & Vendor Info: (Cataloging) Auto-Graphics, Inc; (Circulation) Auto-Graphics, Inc; (Course Reserve) Auto-Graphics, Inc; (ILL) OCLC; (OPAC) Auto-Graphics, Inc
Wireless access
Function: 24/7 Electronic res, 24/7 Online cat, Bks on CD, Computers for patron use, Electronic databases & coll, Free DVD rentals, ILL available, Instruction & testing, Internet access, Magazines, Movies, Music CDs, Online cat, Online info literacy tutorials on the web & in blackboard, Online ref, Outside serv via phone, mail, e-mail & web, Photocopying/Printing, Ref serv available, Scanner, Telephone ref, Wheelchair accessible
Mem of Central Plains Library System
Open Mon-Thurs 7:30am-9:30pm, Fri 7:30-4:30, Sun 3:30-8

P NORTH PLATTE PUBLIC LIBRARY*, 120 W Fourth St, 69101-3993. SAN 309-5681. Tel: 308-535-8036. FAX: 308-535-8296. E-mail: library@ci.north-platte.ne.us. Web Site: www.ci.north-platte.ne.us/library. *Dir,* Cecelia C Lawrence; E-mail: lawrencecc@ci.north-platte.ne.us; *Info Syst Mgr,* Sara Aden; E-mail: adensj@ci.north-platte.ne.us; *Acq, Tech Serv,* Brenda Anderson; E-mail: andersonbl@ci.north-platte.ne.us; *Ch Serv,* Mitzi Mueller; E-mail: muellermm@ci.north-platte.ne.us; *Circ,* Kaycee Anderson; E-mail: Andersonkm@ci.north-platte.ne.us; *ILL, Ref (Info Servs),* Sharon Lohoefener; E-mail: lohoefenersm@ci.north-platte.ne.us; Staff 17 (MLS 2, Non-MLS 15)
Founded 1912. Pop 34,632; Circ 225,403
Oct 2013-Sept 2014 Income $1,118,084, State $5,300, City $1,072,574, County $40,210. Mats Exp $113,725, Books $79,000, Per/Ser (Incl. Access Fees) $5,160, AV Mat $14,000, Electronic Ref Mat (Incl. Access Fees) $15,565. Sal $640,101 (Prof $142,267)
Library Holdings: Audiobooks 4,412; CDs 2,025; DVDs 5,047; e-books 10,816; Large Print Bks 9,205; Bk Titles 102,338; Bk Vols 118,497; Per Subs 94
Special Collections: Travel Packets. Oral History
Subject Interests: Genealogy, Local hist, Nebr hist
Automation Activity & Vendor Info: (Cataloging) SirsiDynix; (Circulation) SirsiDynix; (OPAC) SirsiDynix; (Serials) SirsiDynix
Wireless access
Function: 24/7 Electronic res, Accelerated reader prog, Adult literacy prog, Archival coll, Audio & video playback equip for onsite use, Audiobks via web, Bks on CD, Children's prog, Computer training, Computers for patron use, Electronic databases & coll, Free DVD rentals, Genealogy discussion group, Health sci info serv, ILL available, Instruction & testing, Large print keyboards, Life-long learning prog for all ages, Magazines, Magnifiers for reading, Mail & tel request accepted, Microfiche/film & reading machines, Music CDs, Online cat, Online ref, Outreach serv, OverDrive digital audio bks, Photocopying/Printing, Preschool reading prog, Prog for adults, Prog for children & young adult, Ref & res, Ref serv available, Res performed for a fee, Scanner, Senior computer classes, Serves people with intellectual disabilities, Story hour, Summer reading prog, Tax forms, Teen prog, Wheelchair accessible
Publications: Friends of the Library (Newsletter)
Mem of Central Plains Library System
Partic in OCLC Online Computer Library Center, Inc
Open Mon-Thurs 9-9, Fri & Sat 9-6
Friends of the Library Group

OAKDALE

P LOIS JOHNSON MEMORIAL LIBRARY*, 406 Fifth St, 68761. (Mail add: PO Box 187, 68761-0187), SAN 309-569X. Tel: 402-776-2602. FAX: 402-776-2602. E-mail: libra68761@gmail.com. *Dir,* Charlotte Tracy; Staff 2 (Non-MLS 2)
Pop 350; Circ 7,273
Library Holdings: Bk Titles 4,800; Per Subs 54
Special Collections: Large Print Book Coll; Oakdale Sentinel Newspaper Back Issues, 1887-1960, microfilm
Wireless access
Mem of Three Rivers Library System
Open Mon & Fri 1-6, Wed 1-7, Sat 10-Noon

OAKLAND

P OAKLAND PUBLIC LIBRARY, 110 E Third St, 68045-1356. SAN 309-5703. Tel: 402-685-5113. FAX: 402-685-4140. E-mail: oaklandlibrary68045@gmail.com. *Dir,* Rosa Schmidt
Pop 1,393; Circ 158,001
Library Holdings: Bk Vols 20,365; Per Subs 42
Wireless access
Mem of Three Rivers Library System
Open Mon & Wed 1:30-8:30, Tues & Thurs 8:30-12 & 1:30-6, Sat 8:30-Noon
Friends of the Library Group

OCONTO

P OCONTO PUBLIC LIBRARY*, 43352 Rd 780, 68860. (Mail add: PO Box 25, 68722-0025). Tel: 308-858-4920. *Dir,* Penny Jeffrey; E-mail: pennyjeffrey@gmail.com
Open Wed 10-5

OGALLALA

P GOODALL CITY LIBRARY*, 203 West A St, 69153. SAN 309-5711. Tel: 308-284-4354. Administration Tel: 308-284-8467. FAX: 308-284-6390. E-mail: goodall@megavision.com. Web Site: www.ogallalapubliclibrary.com. *Dir,* Kendra Caskey; E-mail: kcaskeygcl@gmail.com; *Ad,* Kasia Helmuth; *Youth Serv Librn,* Chelsea Foust; Staff 1 (MLS 1)
Founded 1913. Pop 8,800; Circ 85,713
Library Holdings: CDs 69; Large Print Bks 863; Bk Titles 35,968; Per Subs 87; Talking Bks 1,527; Videos 1,033
Special Collections: Nebraska History & Western Culture
Automation Activity & Vendor Info: (Cataloging) Follett Software; (Circulation) Follett Software; (ILL) OCLC; (OPAC) Follett Software
Wireless access
Mem of Western Library System
Open Mon-Thurs 9-8, Fri 9-5, Sat 10-1
Friends of the Library Group

OMAHA

M BOY'S TOWN NATIONAL RESEARCH HOSPITAL*, Information Resources Center, 555 N 30th St, 68131. SAN 377-435X. Tel: 402-498-6511. FAX: 402-498-6351.
Library Holdings: Bk Vols 200
Partic in Info Consortium; Mid-Continental Regional Med Librs Asn

M CHI HEALTH CREIGHTON UNIVERSITY MEDICAL CENTER-BERGAN MERCY*, John D Hartigan Medical Library, 7500 Mercy Rd, 68124-9832. SAN 325-3228. Tel: 402-398-6092. FAX: 402-398-6923. Web Site: www.chihealth.com/en/location-search/creighton-bergan.html. *Librn,* Cindy Perkins; E-mail: CindyPerkins@creighton.edu; Staff 1 (MLS 1)
Founded 1975
Library Holdings: e-books 3; High Interest/Low Vocabulary Bk Vols 80; Bk Titles 800; Bk Vols 824; Per Subs 187
Partic in ICON Library Consortium; Info Consortium; Medical Library Association
Open Mon-Fri 8-4

C CLARKSON COLLEGE LIBRARY*, 101 S 42nd St, 68131-2739, SAN 327-4764. Tel: 402-552-3387. FAX: 402-552-2899. E-mail: library@clarksoncollege.edu. Web Site: library.clarksoncollege.edu. *Dir,* Anne Heimann; E-mail: heimannanne@clarksoncollege.edu; *Access Serv Librn,* Amy Masek; E-mail: masekamy@clarksoncollege.edu; *Resources Librn,* Nicole Caskey; E-mail: caskeynicole@clarksoncollege.edu; Staff 4 (MLS 4)
Highest Degree: Doctorate
Library Holdings: DVDs 50; Bk Titles 8,000; Bk Vols 12,000; Per Subs 264
Automation Activity & Vendor Info: (Cataloging) Sydney; (Circulation) EOS International; (OPAC) EOS International
Wireless access
Mem of Three Rivers Library System
Partic in ICON Library Consortium; OCLC-LVIS
Open Mon-Thurs 8-8, Fri 8-5, Sat 9-5, Sun 1-8; Mon-Thurs (Spring) 7:30am-8pm, Fri 7:30-5, Sat 9-5, Sun 1-8

CR COLLEGE OF SAINT MARY LIBRARY*, 7000 Mercy Rd, 68106-2606. SAN 309-572X. Tel: 402-399-2471. Interlibrary Loan Service Tel: 402-399-2631. Reference Tel: 402-399-2468. FAX: 402-399-2686. E-mail: csmlibrary@csm.edu. Web Site: www.csm.edu/student-life/library. *Libr Dir,* Sara Williams; Tel: 402-399-2467, E-mail: swilliams@csm.edu; *Electronic Access Librn, Res,* Melissa Tiemann; E-mail: mtiemann@csm.edu; *ILL Librn,* Sister Judy Pat Healy; E-mail: jhealy@csm.edu; *Archivist, Cataloger,* Danielle Kessler; Tel: 402-399-2464, E-mail: dkessler@csm.edu; Staff 4 (MLS 3, Non-MLS 1)
Founded 1923. Enrl 1,000; Fac 125; Highest Degree: Doctorate
Subject Interests: Educ, Leadership, Nursing, Occupational therapy
Automation Activity & Vendor Info: (Acquisitions) OCLC; (Cataloging) OCLC Connexion; (Circulation) OCLC; (Course Reserve) OCLC; (ILL) OCLC; (OPAC) OCLC; (Serials) OCLC
Wireless access
Function: Archival coll, Electronic databases & coll, ILL available, Online cat, Orientations, Photocopying/Printing, Printer for laptops & handheld devices, Ref serv available
Mem of Three Rivers Library System
Partic in OCLC Online Computer Library Center, Inc

Open Mon-Thurs 8am-10pm, Fri 8-5, Sat 10-4, Sun 1-10
Restriction: Open to students, fac, staff & alumni, Pub use on premises

C CREIGHTON UNIVERSITY*, Reinert-Alumni Memorial Library, 2500 California Plaza, 68178-0209. SAN 350-2023. Tel: 402-280-2260. Interlibrary Loan Service Tel: 402-280-2219. Reference Tel: 402-280-2227. Administration Tel: 402-280-2706. Automation Services Tel: 402-280-3065. FAX: 402-280-2435. E-mail: askus@creighton.edu. Web Site: www.creighton.edu/libraries/. *Dir,* Michael J LaCroix; Tel: 402-280-2217, E-mail: michaellacroix@creighton.edu; *Univ Librn,* Jim Bothmer; E-mail: jbothmer@creighton.edu; *Head, Access Serv,* Debra Sturges; Tel: 402-280-4756, E-mail: dsturges@creighton.edu; *Head, Ref (Info Serv),* Mary Nash; Tel: 402-280-2226, E-mail: mdnash@creighton.edu; *Head, Tech Serv & Electronic Res,* Rick Kerns; Tel: 402-280-2228, E-mail: rickkerns@creighton.edu; *Ref Librn/Instrul Serv,* Maoria Kirker; Tel: 402-280-2927, E-mail: mjkirker@creighton.edu; *Syst Librn,* Becky Wymer; Tel: 402-280-2220, E-mail: beckywymer@creighton.edu; *Archivist,* David Crawford; Tel: 402-280-2746, E-mail: davidecrawford@creighton.edu; *Cat,* Arnette Payne; Tel: 402-280-1806, E-mail: apayne@creighton.edu; *ILL,* Lynn Schneidermann; E-mail: lynns@creighton.edu; *Ref (Info Servs), Webmaster,* Christine Carmichael; Tel: 402-280-1757, E-mail: christinecarmichael@creighton.edu; *Ref Serv,* Mike Poma; Tel: 402-280-2298, E-mail: mapoma@creighton.edu. Subject Specialists: *Soc sci,* Maoria Kirker; Staff 20 (MLS 9, Non-MLS 11)
Founded 1878. Enrl 4,949; Fac 291; Highest Degree: Doctorate
Jul 2012-Jun 2013 Income (Main Library Only) $3,080,099. Mats Exp $3,130,447, Books $221,076, Per/Ser (Incl. Access Fees) $504,270, Manu Arch $15,000, Other Print Mats $86,211, Micro $32,439, AV Mat $20,443, Electronic Ref Mat (Incl. Access Fees) $382,509, Presv $4,500. Sal $1,083,372 (Prof $703,718)
Library Holdings: AV Mats 11,362; CDs 3,462; DVDs 3,037; e-books 114,380; e-journals 56,798; Electronic Media & Resources 328; Bk Titles 369,000; Bk Vols 383,000; Per Subs 420; Videos 3,865
Special Collections: Early Christian Writings, bks, micro; Fables of Aesop & La Fontaine. US Document Depository
Subject Interests: Physics, Theol
Automation Activity & Vendor Info: (Acquisitions) SirsiDynix; (Cataloging) SirsiDynix; (Circulation) SirsiDynix; (Course Reserve) Docutek; (ILL) OCLC; (OPAC) SirsiDynix; (Serials) SirsiDynix
Wireless access
Publications: Creighton Cornerstone (Newsletter)
Mem of Three Rivers Library System
Partic in Mid-America Law Library Consortium; OCLC Online Computer Library Center, Inc; OCLC-LVIS
Open Mon-Thurs 6:30am-2am, Fri 6:30am-11pm, Sat 9am-10pm, Sun 10am-2am
Restriction: Access for corporate affiliates, Borrowing privileges limited to anthropology fac & libr staff, Borrowing privileges limited to fac & registered students, By permission only, Circ to mem only, Circ to mil employees only, Circulates for staff only, Clients only, Closed stack, Co libr

Departmental Libraries:

CM HEALTH SCIENCES LIBRARY-LEARNING RESOURCE CENTER, 2770 Webster St, 68178-0210. (Mail add: 2500 California Plaza, 68178), SAN 350-2058. Tel: 402-280-5108. Circulation Tel: 402-280-5109. Interlibrary Loan Service Tel: 402-280-5144. Reference Tel: 402-280-5138. Administration Tel: 402-280-5135. FAX: 402-280-5134. E-mail: refdesk@creighton.edu. Web Site: hsl.creighton.edu. *Dir,* James Bothmer; Tel: 402-280-5120, E-mail: jbothmer@creighton.edu; *Dept Head,* Diana Boone; Tel: 402-280-5175, E-mail: dboone@creighton.edu; *Head, Info Serv,* Richard Jizba; Tel: 402-280-5142, E-mail: rjizba@creighton.edu; *Head, User Serv,* John Mitchell; Tel: 402-280-4127, E-mail: jmitchell@creighton.edu; *Outreach Serv Librn,* Judi Bergjord; Tel: 402-280-5199; *Educ Coordr,* Jeanne Burke; *Ser,* Bryan Stack; Tel: 402-280-5137. Subject Specialists: *Educ,* Jeanne Burke; Staff 22 (MLS 10, Non-MLS 12)
Founded 1977. Enrl 2,200; Fac 641; Highest Degree: Doctorate
Jul 2012-Jun 2013 Income $355,211. Mats Exp $1,342,988, Books $14,576, Per/Ser (Incl. Access Fees) $1,046,000, AV Mat $23,110, Electronic Ref Mat (Incl. Access Fees) $251,302, Presv $8,000. Sal $1,005,820 (Prof $715,865)
Library Holdings: AV Mats 4,598; e-books 12,635; e-journals 4,056; Bk Titles 32,610; Per Subs 249
Special Collections: Mulitcultural Health. State Document Depository; US Document Depository
Subject Interests: Dentistry, Med, Nursing, Occupational therapy, Pharm, Phys therapy
Automation Activity & Vendor Info: (Acquisitions) SirsiDynix-iLink; (Cataloging) OCLC; (Circulation) SirsiDynix-iLink; (OPAC) SirsiDynix-iLink; (Serials) SerialsSolutions
Function: Art exhibits, Audio & video playback equip for onsite use, CD-ROM, Computer training, Computers for patron use, Distance learning, Doc delivery serv, E-Reserves, Electronic databases & coll, Health sci info serv, ILL available, Internet access, Learning ctr, Online cat, Orientations, Outreach serv, Outside serv via phone, mail, e-mail & web, Photocopying/Printing, Ref & res, Ref serv available, Res libr, Res performed for a fee, Telephone ref, VHS videos, Wheelchair accessible
Partic in ICON Library Consortium; MCMLA
Publications: BicInformer (Newsletter)
Mem of Three Rivers Library System
Special Services for the Deaf - Accessible learning ctr
Open Mon-Thurs 7am-Midnight, Fri 7am-10pm, Sat 10-6, Sun 10am-Midnight

CL KLUTZNICK LAW LIBRARY - MCGRATH NORTH MULLIN & KRATZ LEGAL RESEARCH CENTER, School of Law, 2500 California Plaza, 68178-0340, SAN 350-2082. Tel: 402-280-2251, 402-280-2875. FAX: 402-280-2244. Reference E-mail: lawref@lists.creighton.edu. Web Site: law.creighton.edu/current-students/law-library. *Dir,* Kay L Andrus; *Ref/Electronic Serv Librn,* Troy Johnson; *Acq, Ser,* Heather Buckwalter; *Cat, Ref (Info Servs),* Corinne Jacox; *Ref (Info Servs),* George Butterfield; Staff 12 (MLS 5, Non-MLS 7)
Founded 1904. Enrl 435; Fac 26
Library Holdings: CDs 263; DVDs 237; e-books 42,290; e-journals 2,574; Microforms 96,883; Bk Titles 48,050; Bk Vols 205,389; Videos 138
Special Collections: History of Anglo-American Law (Te Poel Coll); US Supreme Court Coll, briefs & rec. US Document Depository
Subject Interests: Jury instructions
Automation Activity & Vendor Info: (OPAC) SirsiDynix
Partic in OCLC Online Computer Library Center, Inc
Publications: Acquisitions List (Monthly)
Mem of Three Rivers Library System
Open Mon-Thurs 7am-Midnight, Fri 7am-8pm, Sat 9-8, Sun 10am-Midnight

GL DOUGLAS COUNTY DISTRICT COURT*, Honorable Michael W Amdor Memorial Law Library, Rm H07 Civic Ctr, Harney Street Level, 1819 Farnam St, 68183. SAN 309-5738. Tel: 402-444-7174. FAX: 402-444-3927. Web Site: www.dc4dc.com/law-library. *Librn,* Ann Borer; E-mail: aborer@dc4dc.com; Staff 2 (Non-MLS 2)
Founded 1905
Wireless access
Function: Computers for patron use, Doc delivery serv, Electronic databases & coll, Res assist avail, Res libr
Open Mon-Fri 8:30-4:30
Friends of the Library Group

S DOUGLAS COUNTY HISTORICAL SOCIETY*, Library Archives Center, 5730 N 30th St, No 11A, 68111. SAN 328-3178. Tel: 402-455-9990. E-mail: research@douglascohistory.org. Web Site: www.douglascohistory.org. *Exec Dir,* Kathy Aultz; E-mail: director@douglascohistory.org; *Res Spec,* Ana Somers
Library Holdings: Bk Titles 3,000; Per Subs 30
Special Collections: Company & Individual Official Archives of Douglas County: Documents to early 1800; Omaha World-Herald Newspaper Clipping Coll
Subject Interests: Local hist
Function: Photocopying/Printing, Ref serv available
Publications: History Lectures; Local Historical Works; Newsletter
Open Mon-Fri 10-4, Sat by appointment
Restriction: Non-circulating, Not a lending libr, Open to pub with supv only

S DOUGLAS COUNTY YOUTH CENTER LIBRARY*, 1301 S 41st St, 68105. SAN 377-5658. Tel: 402-444-7492. FAX: 402-444-4188. *Library Contact,* Sue Helming; E-mail: susan.helming@douglascounty-ne.gov
Library Holdings: Bks on Deafness & Sign Lang 1; e-books 5; High Interest/Low Vocabulary Bk Vols 1,000; Large Print Bks 100; Bk Vols 5,000
Restriction: Not open to pub
Friends of the Library Group

SR FIRST CHRISTIAN CHURCH (DISCIPLES OF CHRIST) LIBRARY, 6630 Dodge St, 68132. SAN 328-5626. Tel: 402-558-1939. FAX: 402-558-1941. E-mail: fccomaha@firstchristian-omaha.org. Web Site: www.firstchristian-omaha.org.
Library Holdings: Bk Titles 1,500; Per Subs 10
Wireless access
Open Mon-Fri 9-3, Sun 8-12

M IMMANUEL MEDICAL CENTER*, Professional Library, 6901 N 72nd St, 68122. SAN 325-3767. Tel: 402-572-2345. FAX: 402-572-2797. Web Site: www.chihealth.com. *Librn,* Joy A Winkler
Library Holdings: Bk Titles 750; Per Subs 225
Wireless access
Restriction: Staff use only

S JOSLYN ART MUSEUM*, Milton R & Pauline S Abrahams Library, 2200 Dodge St, 68102-1292. SAN 309-5770. Tel: 402-661-3300. FAX: 402-342-2376. Web Site: www.joslyn.org. *Dir Educ & Outreach,* Nancy Round; Tel: 402-661-3859, E-mail: nround@joslyn.org
Founded 1931
Library Holdings: Bk Vols 30,000; Per Subs 50; Spec Interest Per Sub 45
Special Collections: Artists' Clipping Files; Publications of the Metropolitan Museum of Art, microfiche set; Western Americana: Frontier History of the Trans-Mississippi West, microfilm set
Subject Interests: Art, Native Am art, Western Am art
Automation Activity & Vendor Info: (Cataloging) TLC (The Library Corporation); (Circulation) TLC (The Library Corporation); (OPAC) TLC (The Library Corporation)
Partic in OCLC Online Computer Library Center, Inc; OCLC-LVIS
Open Tues, Wed & Fri-Sun 10-4, Thurs 10-8
Restriction: Not a lending libr

R KRIPKE JEWISH FEDERATION LIBRARY*, 333 S 132nd St, 68154. SAN 309-5762. Tel: 402-334-6462. FAX: 402-334-1330. E-mail: sbanner@jewishomaha.org. Web Site: www.jewishomaha.org/education/kripke-jewish-federation-library. *Libr Spec,* Shirly Banner; E-mail: sbanner@jewishomaha.org; Staff 3 (MLS 1, Non-MLS 2)
Founded 1945
Library Holdings: Audiobooks 60; CDs 500; DVDs 600; e-books 50; Electronic Media & Resources 3; Large Print Bks 300; Bk Titles 34,000; Bk Vols 36,500; Per Subs 15
Subject Interests: Archaeology, Bible, Comparative relig, Holocaust, Israel, Judaica, Middle East
Automation Activity & Vendor Info: (Cataloging) Follett Software; (Circulation) Follett Software
Wireless access
Publications: Index to the Omaha Jewish Press
Open Mon-Thurs 9-6, Fri 9-4

L KUTAK ROCK LLP*, Law Library, 1650 Farnam St, 68102-2186. SAN 327-490X. Tel: 402-346-6000. FAX: 402-346-1148. Web Site: www.kutakrock.com. *Librn,* Lynn Koperski; E-mail: lynn.koperski@kutakrock.com
Library Holdings: Bk Vols 10,000; Per Subs 100
Wireless access
Restriction: Open by appt only

J METROPOLITAN COMMUNITY COLLEGE LIBRARY*, 30th & Fort Sts, Bldg 8, 68103. (Mail add: PO Box 3777, 68103-0777), SAN 350-2112. Tel: 402-457-2705. Toll Free Tel: 800-228-9553. FAX: 402-457-2655. Web Site: www.mccneb.edu/current-students/student-tools/Library.aspx. *Dean,* Susan R Raftery; E-mail: sraftery@mccneb.edu; *Libr Supvr,* Ann Wills; Tel: 402-457-2630, E-mail: awills@mccneb.edu; *Cat,* Diane Schram; Tel: 402-457-2761, E-mail: dschram@mccneb.edu; *ILL,* Pam Neseth; Tel: 402-289-1320, E-mail: pneseth@mccneb.edu; Staff 20 (MLS 1, Non-MLS 19)
Founded 1974. Enrl 12,000; Fac 186; Highest Degree: Associate
Library Holdings: AV Mats 7,995; Bks on Deafness & Sign Lang 649; e-books 40,000; e-journals 9,000; High Interest/Low Vocabulary Bk Vols 246; Large Print Bks 18; Bk Titles 34,899; Bk Vols 44,851; Per Subs 575
Automation Activity & Vendor Info: (Acquisitions) Infor Library & Information Solutions; (Cataloging) Infor Library & Information Solutions; (Circulation) Infor Library & Information Solutions; (OPAC) Infor Library & Information Solutions; (Serials) Infor Library & Information Solutions
Wireless access
Function: ILL available, Photocopying/Printing, Ref serv available, Telephone ref, Wheelchair accessible
Special Services for the Deaf - Bks on deafness & sign lang; TDD equip
Open Mon-Fri 7:30am-10pm, Sat 7:30-4:30, Sun 1-5
Departmental Libraries:
ELKHORN VALLEY CAMPUS, 204th & W Dodge Rd, 68022. (Mail add: PO Box 3777, 68103-0777), SAN 350-2201. Tel: 402-289-1206. FAX: 402-289-1286. *Libr Supvr,* Scott Mahoney; E-mail: smahoney@mccneb.edu
FORT OMAHA CAMPUS, 30th & Fort St, 68111. (Mail add: PO Box 3777, 68103-0777), SAN 350-2147. Tel: 402-457-2306. FAX: 402-457-2859. *Libr Supvr,* Ann Wills; Tel: 402-457-2630, E-mail: awills@mccneb.edu
SOUTH OMAHA CAMPUS, Mahoney Bldg, 2909 Edward "Babe" Gomez Ave, 68107. (Mail add: PO Box 3777, 68103-0777), SAN 350-2171. Tel: 402-738-4506. FAX: 402-738-4738. *Br Mgr,* Scott Mahoney; E-mail: smahoney@mccneb.edu

S NATIONAL PARK SERVICE*, Midwest Regional Library, 601 Riverfront Dr, 68102-4226. SAN 309-5797. Tel: 402-661-3006. *Dir,* Position Currently Open
Founded 1938
Library Holdings: Bk Titles 9,000
Special Collections: Early Western Travels; Pacific Railroad Surveys; Westerners Brand Book
Subject Interests: Archaeology, Botany, Ethnology, Geol, Western Americana, Zoology
Publications: National Park Service Reports on the Midwest Region
Restriction: Employees only

CM NEBRASKA METHODIST COLLEGE*, John Moritz Library, 720 N 87th St, 68114. SAN 327-4888. Tel: 402-354-7251. FAX: 402-354-7250. E-mail: library@methodistcollege.edu. Web Site: libguides.methodistcollege.edu/libraryFAQ, www.methodistcollege.edu/library. *Libr Dir,* Emily McIllece; Tel: 402-354-7246, E-mail: Emily.McIllece@methodistcollege.edu; *Electronic Res Librn,* Sonja Maddox; Tel: 402-354-7252, E-mail: Sonja.Maddox@methodistcollege.edu; *ILL, Ref,* Deborah Divis; Tel: 402-354-7248, E-mail: Deborah.Divis@methodistcollege.edu; Staff 4 (MLS 2, Non-MLS 2)
Enrl 950; Fac 100; Highest Degree: Master
Library Holdings: DVDs 100; e-books 50; e-journals 2,000; Bk Titles 2,000; Per Subs 120
Subject Interests: Nursing, Nursing educ
Automation Activity & Vendor Info: (Acquisitions) SirsiDynix; (Cataloging) SirsiDynix; (Circulation) SirsiDynix; (Course Reserve) SirsiDynix; (Media Booking) SirsiDynix; (OPAC) SirsiDynix; (Serials) SirsiDynix
Wireless access
Mem of Three Rivers Library System
Partic in National Network of Libraries of Medicine Region 3; OCLC-LVIS
Open Mon-Fri 8-4:30

S OMAHA CORRECTIONAL CENTER LIBRARY*, 2323 E Ave J, 68110-0099. (Mail add: PO Box 11099, 68110-2766), SAN 377-4511. Tel: 402-595-3964. FAX: 402-595-2227. Web Site: corrections.nebraska.gov/facilities/omaha-correctional-center. *Dir,* Denise Morton
Library Holdings: Bk Vols 10,600; Per Subs 32
Automation Activity & Vendor Info: (Cataloging) LiBRARYSOFT; (Circulation) LiBRARYSOFT; (ILL) OCLC; (OPAC) LiBRARYSOFT
Partic in Nebr Inst Librs
Restriction: Staff & inmates only

P OMAHA PUBLIC LIBRARY*, W Dale Clark Library, 215 S 15th St, 68102-1629. SAN 350-2295. Tel: 402-444-4800. Circulation Tel: 402-444-4809. Administration Tel: 402-444-4844. FAX: 402-444-4504. Web Site: omahalibrary.org. *Exec Dir,* Laura Marlane; E-mail: lmarlane@omahalibrary.org; *Asst Dir,* Rachel Steiner; E-mail: rsteiner@omahalibrary.org; *Mgr,* Matt Couch; E-mail: mcouch@omahalibrary.org; *Mgr, Br,* Sarah VanRaden; E-mail: svanraden@omahalibrary.org; *Adult Serv Mgr,* Amy Mather; E-mail: amather@omahalibrary.org; *Operations Mgr,* Elizabeth Johnson; E-mail: eajohnson@omahalibrary.org; *Youth Serv Mgr,* Julie Humphrey; E-mail: jhumphrey@omahalibrary.org; Staff 47 (MLS 41, Non-MLS 6)
Founded 1872. Pop 552,806; Circ 299,219
Library Holdings: AV Mats 86,329; CDs 17,571; Large Print Bks 16,955; Bk Titles 255,160; Bk Vols 898,395; Per Subs 2,282; Talking Bks 29,918; Videos 19,671
Special Collections: African-American History (Black Culture Coll); Local History Coll; TransMississippi Exposition Photo Coll. State Document Depository; US Document Depository
Subject Interests: Foreign lang, Genealogy, Local hist
Automation Activity & Vendor Info: (Acquisitions) SirsiDynix; (Cataloging) SirsiDynix; (Circulation) SirsiDynix; (ILL) OCLC; (OPAC) SirsiDynix; (Serials) SirsiDynix
Wireless access
Function: Archival coll, AV serv, Home delivery & serv to seniorr ctr & nursing homes, Homebound delivery serv, ILL available, Internet access, Prog for adults, Prog for children & young adult, Ref serv available, Summer reading prog, Telephone ref, Wheelchair accessible
Publications: BST Bulletin (Monthly); Omaha Public Library Connection (Quarterly)
Mem of Three Rivers Library System
Special Services for the Deaf - TTY equip
Special Services for the Blind - Bks on cassette; Bks on CD; Braille equip; Home delivery serv; Large print & cassettes; Large print bks
Open Mon-Sat 9-5
Friends of the Library Group
Branches: 11
MILTON R ABRAHAMS BRANCH, 5111 N 90th St, 68134-2829, SAN 329-6032. Tel: 402-444-6284. FAX: 402-444-6590. *Mgr,* Jennifer Jazynka; E-mail: jjazynka@omahalibrary.org
Founded 1988. Circ 344,719
Library Holdings: AV Mats 11,987; Bk Vols 94,628

Open Mon-Thurs 9-9, Fri & Sat 9-6, Sun 1-6
Friends of the Library Group
BENSON BRANCH, 6015 Binney St, 68104-3498, SAN 350-2325. Tel: 402-444-4846. FAX: 402-444-6595. *Mgr,* Karen Pietsch; E-mail: kpietsch@omahalibrary.org
Founded 1923. Circ 149,261
Library Holdings: AV Mats 6,913; Bk Vols 57,528
Open Tues-Thurs 9-8, Fri & Sat 9-6
Friends of the Library Group
WILLA CATHER BRANCH, 1905 S 44th St, 68105-2807, SAN 350-235X. Tel: 402-444-4851. FAX: 402-444-6662. *Mgr,* Lori Nelson; E-mail: lnelson@omahalibrary.org
Founded 1956. Circ 150,364
Library Holdings: AV Mats 6,133; Bk Vols 49,471
Open Tues & Thurs 10-8, Wed, Fri & Sat 10-6
Friends of the Library Group
BESS JOHNSON ELKHORN LIBRARY, 2100 Reading Plaza, Elkhorn, 68022, SAN 309-4537. Tel: 402-289-4367. FAX: 402-289-0420. *Br Mgr,* Joanne Ferguson Cavanaugh; E-mail: jferguson@omahalibrary.org
Pop 7,635; Circ 41,485
Library Holdings: Bk Vols 37,264; Per Subs 60
Open Mon-Thurs 9-8, Fri & Sat 9-6
Friends of the Library Group
FLORENCE BRANCH, 2920 Bondesson St, 68112-1822, SAN 350-2384. Tel: 402-444-5299. FAX: 402-444-6607. *Mgr,* Lois Imig; E-mail: lcimig@omahalibrary.org
Founded 1923. Circ 73,585
Library Holdings: AV Mats 4,213; Bk Vols 34,517
Open Tues & Wed 10-8, Thurs-Sat 10-6
Friends of the Library Group
MILLARD BRANCH, 13214 Westwood Lane, 68144-3556, SAN 350-2449. Tel: 402-444-4848. FAX: 402-444-6623. *Mgr,* Evonne Edgington; E-mail: eedgington@omahalibrary.org
Founded 1952. Circ 827,517
Library Holdings: AV Mats 12,206; Bk Vols 129,033
Open Mon-Thurs 9-9, Fri-Sun 9-6
Friends of the Library Group
SADDLEBROOK BRANCH, 14850 Laurel Ave, 68116. Tel: 402-444-5780. Web Site: omahalibrary.org/locations/OK. *Mgr,* Amy Wenzl; E-mail: ajwenzl@omahalibrary.org
Open Tues-Thurs 8-8, Fri 8-5, Sat 9-4
Friends of the Library Group
A V SORENSEN BRANCH, 4808 Cass St, 68132-3031, SAN 350-2503. Tel: 402-444-5274. FAX: 402-444-6592. *Mgr,* Autumn Hill; E-mail: ahill@omahalibrary.org
Founded 1976. Circ 119,065
Library Holdings: AV Mats 5,864; Bk Vols 41,200
Open Tues & Thurs 10-8, Wed, Fri & Sat 10-6
Friends of the Library Group
SOUTH OMAHA LIBRARY, 2808 Q St, 68107-2828, SAN 350-2538. Tel: 402-444-4850. FAX: 402-444-6644. *Mgr,* Marvel Maring; E-mail: mamaring@omahalibrary.org
Founded 1904. Circ 82,860
Library Holdings: AV Mats 5,034; Bk Vols 41,865
Special Collections: ESL Materials
Open Mon-Thurs 7:30am-9pm, Fri & Sat 9-6
Friends of the Library Group
W CLARKE SWANSON BRANCH, 9101 W Dodge Rd, 68114-3305, SAN 350-2562. Tel: 402-444-4852. FAX: 402-444-6651. *Mgr,* Ms Casey Kralik; E-mail: ckralik@omahalibrary.org
Founded 1966. Circ 235,860
Library Holdings: AV Mats 9,084; Bk Vols 103,355
Special Collections: Children's Historic Literature Coll
Open Tues-Thurs 8-8, Fri 8-6, Sat 9-6
Friends of the Library Group
CHARLES B WASHINGTON BRANCH, 2868 Ames Ave, 68111-2426, SAN 350-2473. Tel: 402-444-4849. FAX: 402-444-6658. *Mgr,* Micki Dietrich; E-mail: mdietrich@omahalibrary.org
Founded 1921. Circ 34,354
Library Holdings: AV Mats 4,222; Bk Vols 36,239
Special Collections: African-American History (Black Culture Coll)
Open Mon-Wed 9–8, Thurs-Sat 9–6
Friends of the Library Group

S OMAHA WORLD-HERALD LIBRARY*, 1314 Douglas St, Ste 700, 68102. SAN 325-0938. Tel: 402-444-1000. FAX: 402-345-0183. Web Site: www.omaha.com. *Chief Librn,* Sheritha Jones; E-mail: sheritha.jones@owh.com; Staff 5 (Non-MLS 5)
Founded 1900
Library Holdings: Bk Titles 150; Bk Vols 400
Restriction: Not open to pub

P THREE RIVERS LIBRARY SYSTEM*, 11929 Elm St, Ste 18, 68144. Tel: 402-330-7884. Toll Free Tel: 800-627-7884. FAX: 402-330-1859. E-mail: trls.director@gmail.com. Web Site: libraries.ne.gov/trls. *Dir,* Tammi Thiem; E-mail: tammi.thiem.trls@gmail.com; *Libr Asst, Library Services,* Chelsea Morlan; E-mail: trls.assistant@gmail.com
Founded 2015
Publications: TRaiLS (Newsletter)
Member Libraries: Agnes Robinson Waterloo Public Library; Albion Public Library; Arlington Public Library; Bancroft Public Library; Bellevue Public Library; Bellevue University; Bennington Public Library; Blair Public Library; Bloomfield Public Library; Brunswick Public Library; Cedar Rapids Public Library; Central Community College; Clarkson College Library; Clarkson Public Library; Clearwater Public Library; College of Saint Mary Library; Columbus Public Library; Creighton Public Library; Creighton University; Dakota City Public Library; Eastern Township Public Library; Elgin Public Library; Elmwood Public Library; Emerson Public Library; Fullerton Public Library; Gardner Public Library; Genoa Public Library; Grace University; Greenwood Public Library; Gretna Public Library; Hartington Public Library; Hooper Public Library; House Memorial Public Library; Howells Public Library; Humphrey Public Library; John A Stahl Library; John Rogers Memorial Public Library; Karlen Memorial Library; Keene Memorial Library; La Vista Public Library; Laurel Community Learning Center & Public Library; Leigh Public Library; Lied Battle Creek Public Library; Lied Carroll Public Library; Lied Lincoln Township Library; Lied Pierce Public Library; Lied Winside Public Library; Lois Johnson Memorial Library; Louisville Public Library; Lyons Public Library; Madison Public Library; Meadow Grove Public Library; Midland University; Nebraska Christian College; Nebraska Methodist College; Neligh Public Library; Newman Grove Public Library; Niobrara Public Library; Norfolk Public Library; Norfolk Regional Center; North Bend Public Library; Oakland Public Library; Omaha Public Library; Orchard Public Library; Osmond Public Library; Petersburg Public Library; Pilger Public Library; Plainview Public Library; Plattsmouth Public Library; Ponca Carnegie Library; Raymond A Whitwer Tilden Public Library; Saint Edward Public Library; Schuyler Public Library; Scribner Public Library; Snyder Public Library; South Sioux City Public Library; Springbank Township Library; Springfield Memorial Library; Stanton Public Library; Sump Memorial Library; Tekamah Public Library; University of Nebraska at Omaha; University of Nebraska Medical Center; Valley Public Library; Verdigre Public Library; Veterans Affairs Medical Library; Walthill Public Library; Wayne Public Library; Wayne State College; Weeping Water Public Library; Wisner Public Library
Open Mon-Fri 10:30-5

A UNITED STATES ARMY*, Corps of Engineers Omaha District Library, 1616 Capitol Ave, Rm 764, 68102-4909. SAN 309-5827. Tel: 402-995-2534. FAX: 402-995-2623. E-mail: cenwo.library@usace.army.mil. Web Site: www.nwo.usace.army.mil/Library. *Librn,* Barbara L Slater; Tel: 402-995-2535, E-mail: barbara.l.slater@usace.army.mil; Staff 1 (MLS 1)
Library Holdings: Bk Titles 8,862; Bk Vols 13,665; Per Subs 100
Special Collections: Engineering Design Memo Coll; Sediment Series Coll
Subject Interests: Engr, Law
Automation Activity & Vendor Info: (Cataloging) EOS International; (Circulation) EOS International; (ILL) OCLC; (OPAC) EOS International; (Serials) EOS International
Function: Internet access, Mail & tel request accepted, Online cat, Online ref, Scanner, Telephone ref
Partic in OCLC Online Computer Library Center, Inc
Restriction: Authorized personnel only, Circ limited, Co libr, Employees only, Not open to pub, Photo ID required for access

C UNIVERSITY OF NEBRASKA AT OMAHA*, Dr C C & Mabel L Criss Library, 6001 Dodge St, 68182-0237. SAN 309-5835. Circulation Tel: 402-554-3206. Toll Free Tel: 800-858-8648, Ext 43206. FAX: 402-554-3215. Web Site: library.unomaha.edu. *Dean,* David Richards; Tel: 402-554-3208, E-mail: drichards@unomaha.edu; *Dir, Archives & Spec Coll,* Amy Schindler; Tel: 402-554-6046, E-mail: aschindler@unomaha.edu; *Dir, Patron Serv,* Joyce Neujahr; Tel: 402-554-3607, E-mail: jneujahr@unomaha.edu; *Dir, Res & Instruction Serv,* Katie Bishop; Tel: 402-554-2992, E-mail: kbishop@unomaha.edu; *Coll Coordr, Govt Doc Librn,* James Shaw; Tel: 402-554-2225, E-mail: jshaw@unomaha.edu; *Rare Bk Librn, Spec Coll,* Robert Nash; Tel: 402-554-2884, E-mail: rnash@unomaha.edu; *Bus Mgr,* Beau Malnack; Tel: 402-554-2916, E-mail: bmalnack@unomaha.edu; *Electronic Res Mgr,* Jeff Kuskie; Tel: 402-554-2363, E-mail: jkuskie@unomaha.edu; Staff 20 (MLS 13, Non-MLS 7)
Founded 1908. Enrl 15,300; Fac 723; Highest Degree: Doctorate
Library Holdings: Bk Vols 750,000
Special Collections: Arthur Paul Afghanistan Coll; Icarian Community Coll; Mary L Richmond - Cummings Press Coll; Nebraska Authors & History; Omaha Federal Writers Project Papers (WPA). State Document Depository; US Document Depository
Automation Activity & Vendor Info: (Acquisitions) Innovative Interfaces, Inc; (Cataloging) Innovative Interfaces, Inc; (Circulation) Innovative Interfaces, Inc; (Course Reserve) Docutek; (ILL) OCLC; (OPAC) Innovative Interfaces, Inc; (Serials) Innovative Interfaces, Inc
Wireless access

Function: Archival coll, Art exhibits, Audio & video playback equip for onsite use, CD-ROM, Computers for patron use, Distance learning, E-Reserves, Electronic databases & coll, Equip loans & repairs, Govt ref serv, ILL available, Instruction & testing, Internet access, Large print keyboards, Magnifiers for reading, Music CDs, Online cat, Online info literacy tutorials on the web & in blackboard, Online ref, Photocopying/Printing, Ref & res, Ref serv available, Res libr, Scanner, Tax forms, VHS videos, Wheelchair accessible
Mem of Three Rivers Library System
Partic in OCLC Online Computer Library Center, Inc; Proquest Dialog
Open Mon-Thurs 7am-Midnight, Fri 7-5, Sat 9-5, Sun Noon-Midnight; Mon-Thurs (Summer) 7am-9pm, Fri 7-5, Sat Noon-5, Sun Noon-9
Friends of the Library Group

CM UNIVERSITY OF NEBRASKA MEDICAL CENTER, McGoogan Library of Medicine, 600 S 42nd St, 68198. (Mail add: 986705 Nebraska Medical Ctr, 68198-6705), SAN 350-2597. Tel: 402-559-7079. Interlibrary Loan Service Tel: 402-559-7085. Reference Tel: 402-559-6221. FAX: 402-559-5498. E-mail: askus@unmc.edu. Web Site: www.unmc.edu/library. *Dean,* Emily McElroy; Tel: 402-559-7078; *Assoc Dean,* Heather Brown; Tel: 402-559-7097, E-mail: hlbrown@unmc.edu; *Adminr,* Laura Bashus; Tel: 462-559-7080, E-mail: lbashus@unmc.edu; *ILL,* Mr Dana Boden; Tel: 402-559-3732, E-mail: dhboden@unmc.edu; *Media Spec,* Stuart K Dayton; Tel: 402-559-6334, E-mail: sdayton@unmc.edu; Staff 37 (MLS 13, Non-MLS 24)
Founded 1902. Enrl 2,044; Fac 926; Highest Degree: Doctorate
Library Holdings: Bk Titles 65,294; Bk Vols 234,011; Per Subs 1,427
Special Collections: Consumer Health Information Resource Services Coll, bks, journals; History of Medicine, bks, memorabilia; Obstetrics & Gynecology (Moon Coll); Surgery & Related Subjects (H Winnett Orr Coll & American College of Surgeons Coll), bks, memorabilia
Subject Interests: Allied health, Med
Automation Activity & Vendor Info: (Cataloging) Innovative Interfaces, Inc; (Circulation) Innovative Interfaces, Inc; (ILL) OCLC; (Media Booking) Innovative Interfaces, Inc; (OPAC) Innovative Interfaces, Inc; (Serials) Innovative Interfaces, Inc
Wireless access
Publications: Focus on Friends (Semi-annual); Point of Access (Quarterly)
Mem of Three Rivers Library System
Partic in National Network of Libraries of Medicine Region 3
Open Mon-Thurs 7:30am-12am, Fri 7:30am-9pm, Sat 9-5, Sun 1-Midnight
Friends of the Library Group

GM VETERANS AFFAIRS MEDICAL LIBRARY*, 4101 Woolworth Ave, 68105. SAN 309-5843. Tel: 402-995-3530. Web Site: www.nebraska.va.gov. *Librn,* Darrel Willoughby; E-mail: darrel.willoughby@va.gov; Staff 1 (MLS 1)
Founded 1950
Library Holdings: Bk Titles 650; Per Subs 5
Subject Interests: Allied health, Med
Wireless access
Mem of Three Rivers Library System
Open Mon-Fri 8-4:30

O'NEILL

P O'NEILL PUBLIC LIBRARY*, 601 E Douglas, 68763. SAN 309-586X. Tel: 402-336-3110. FAX: 402-336-3268. E-mail: oneilllibrary@hotmail.com. Web Site: libraries.ne.gov/oneill. *Dir,* Jeannie Mejstrik; Tel: 402-336-3110; *Ch,* M Menish; *Asst Librn,* Sue Tooker
Founded 1913. Pop 3,700; Circ 84,000
Library Holdings: Bk Titles 27,000; Per Subs 138
Automation Activity & Vendor Info: (Acquisitions) Biblionix/Apollo; (Cataloging) Biblionix/Apollo; (Circulation) Biblionix/Apollo; (ILL) OCLC ILLiad; (OPAC) Biblionix
Wireless access
Mem of Central Plains Library System
Partic in OCLC Online Computer Library Center, Inc
Open Mon, Tues, Fri & Sat 10:30-5:30, Wed & Thurs 10:30-9
Friends of the Library Group

ORCHARD

P ORCHARD PUBLIC LIBRARY*, 232 Windom, 68764. (Mail add: PO Box 317, 68764-0317), SAN 309-5878. Tel: 402-893-4606. FAX: 402-893-4606. E-mail: orchpl@gmail.com. Web Site: orchardpubliclibrary.org. *Dir,* Donna Hamilton; Staff 3 (Non-MLS 3)
Founded 1902. Pop 650; Circ 6,218
Library Holdings: AV Mats 363; DVDs 430; Bk Titles 14,103; Per Subs 30; Talking Bks 215
Special Collections: Orchard News, 1902-to-date, 1903-2003 on micro-film
Function: Accelerated reader prog, Adult bk club, Audio & video playback equip for onsite use, Bks on cassette, Bks on CD, Children's prog, Computers for patron use, Electronic databases & coll, Free DVD rentals, Homebound delivery serv, ILL available, Online cat, Photocopying/Printing, Ref serv available, Scanner, Story hour, Summer reading prog, Tax forms, VHS videos, Wheelchair accessible
Mem of Three Rivers Library System
Open Mon & Thurs 1-8, Wed 7-9, Sat 10-3
Friends of the Library Group

ORD

P ORD TOWNSHIP LIBRARY*, 1718 M St, 68862. (Mail add: PO Box 206, 68862-0206), SAN 309-5886. Tel: 308-728-3012. FAX: 308-728-3126. Web Site: www.ordlibrary.org. *Dir,* Kristi Hagstrom; E-mail: director@ordlibrary.org; *Librn,* Diane Breitkreutz; E-mail: librarian1@ordlibrary.org; *Prog Coordr,* Corky Michalski; E-mail: librarian2@ordlibrary.org
Founded 1993. Pop 3,000; Circ 18,000
Library Holdings: Bk Vols 23,000; Per Subs 65
Automation Activity & Vendor Info: (Cataloging) Biblionix; (Circulation) Biblionix; (ILL) OCLC WorldShare Interlibrary Loan; (OPAC) Biblionix
Wireless access
Function: Summer reading prog
Mem of Central Plains Library System
Partic in OCLC Online Computer Library Center, Inc
Open Mon, Wed & Fri 12-5:30, Tues & Thurs 12-8, Sat 12:30-3, Sun 12-3

ORLEANS

P CORDELIA B PRESTON MEMORIAL LIBRARY*, 510 Orleans Ave, 68966. (Mail add: PO Box 430, 68966-0430), SAN 309-5894. Tel: 308-473-3425. FAX: 308-473-3425. E-mail: olibry@frontiernet.net. Web Site: libraries.ne.gov/orleans. *Librn,* Stephanie Branham; *Asst Librn,* Raylene Stephens
Founded 1917. Pop 523; Circ 5,592
Library Holdings: Bk Vols 10,000; Per Subs 10
Special Collections: Civil War (War of Rebellion)
Automation Activity & Vendor Info: (Cataloging) Follett Software; (Circulation) Follett Software
Wireless access
Open Mon 3-8, Tues & Sat 9-Noon, Wed & Thurs 3-6
Friends of the Library Group

OSCEOLA

P OSCEOLA PUBLIC LIBRARY*, 131 N Main, 68651. (Mail add: PO Box 448, 68651-0448), SAN 309-5908. Tel: 402-747-4301. FAX: 402-747-4991. E-mail: osceolalibraryne@gmail.com. Web Site: libraries.ne.gov/osceola. *Dir,* April Stevens; E-mail: osceolalibrary@windstream.net; *Asst Ch,* Allie Ray; E-mail: osceolalibrary@windstream.net
Founded 1895. Pop 1,400; Circ 10,000
Library Holdings: Audiobooks 183; CDs 70; DVDs 500; Large Print Bks 1,100; Bk Titles 14,800; Per Subs 27; Videos 338
Special Collections: Cake Pans
Automation Activity & Vendor Info: (Cataloging) Book Systems; (Circulation) Book Systems; (OPAC) Book Systems
Wireless access
Function: 24/7 Online cat, Bks on CD, Computers for patron use, Electronic databases & coll, ILL available, Internet access, Magazines, Movies, Online cat, OverDrive digital audio bks, Photocopying/Printing, Prog for adults, Prog for children & young adult, Scanner, Story hour, Summer reading prog, VHS videos
Mem of Southeast Library System
Open Mon 12:30-7:30, Tues 9-12, Wed 12:30-8, Fri 12:30-5:30
Friends of the Library Group

OSHKOSH

P OSHKOSH PUBLIC LIBRARY, 307 W First St, 69154. (Mail add: PO Box 140, 69154-0140), SAN 309-5916. Tel: 308-772-4554. FAX: 308-772-4554. E-mail: oshkoshlib@gmail.com. Web Site: oshkosh.panhandlelibraries.org. *Dir,* Elaine Lake; Staff 2 (Non-MLS 2)
Founded 1943. Pop 887; Circ 7,535
Library Holdings: DVDs 1,000; e-books 29,000; Large Print Bks 500; Bk Titles 8,500; Per Subs 17; Talking Bks 279; Videos 100
Special Collections: Cake Pan Coll
Automation Activity & Vendor Info: (Cataloging) Biblionix/Apollo; (Circulation) Biblionix/Apollo; (ILL) OCLC
Wireless access
Mem of Western Library System
Partic in OCLC Online Computer Library Center, Inc; WiLS
Open Mon 10-6, Tues-Fri 1-5:30
Friends of the Library Group

OSMOND

P OSMOND PUBLIC LIBRARY*, 412 N State St, 68765. (Mail add: PO Box 478, 68765-0478), SAN 309-5924. Tel: 402-748-3382. FAX: 402-748-3382. E-mail: ospuli@abbnebraska.com. *Dir,* Donna Kahny; *Automation Librn,* Helen Steckelberg; Staff 1 (Non-MLS 1)
Founded 1937. Pop 1,419; Circ 14,500
Library Holdings: AV Mats 807; Bks on Deafness & Sign Lang 10; Large Print Bks 185; Bk Vols 14,000; Per Subs 40; Talking Bks 212
Automation Activity & Vendor Info: (Cataloging) Follett Software
Wireless access
Mem of Three Rivers Library System
Open Mon, Tues, Thurs & Fri 12-6, Wed 12-7, Sat 9-Noon
Friends of the Library Group

OVERTON

P OVERTON COMMUNITY LIBRARY*, 407 Hwy 30, 68863. (Mail add: PO Box 117, 68863-0117), SAN 309-5932. Tel: 308-987-2543. *Dir,* Deb Weiland
Pop 660; Circ 3,238
Library Holdings: Bk Vols 6,500
Mem of Central Plains Library System
Open Tues 10-Noon, Thurs 3-5

OXFORD

P OXFORD PUBLIC LIBRARY*, 411 Ogden St, 68967. (Mail add: PO Box 156, 68967-0156), SAN 309-5940. Tel: 308-824-3381. FAX: 308-824-3381. E-mail: oxfordlibrary13@gmail.com. Web Site: villageofoxfordne.com/oxford-public-library. *Dir,* Danielle Burns; E-mail: danielleburns5@gmail.com
Founded 1941. Pop 1,109
Library Holdings: Bk Vols 14,000; Per Subs 36
Special Collections: American Heritage, History of the United States; Bess Streeter Aldrich; Civil War; Encyclopedia of Collectibles; Lexicon Universal - World Book; Louisa May Alcott; Mari Sandoz; Mark Twain; Nebraska Authors; The Old West; Time-Life, History of World War II; Vietnam, encyclopedia; Willa Cather; Winston Churchill; World War II; Zane Gray
Mem of Central Plains Library System
Open Mon-Thurs 2-7, Fri 9-12 & 1-5, Sat 12-4

PALISADE

P PALISADE PUBLIC LIBRARY*, 124 N Main St, 69040. (Mail add: PO Box 308, 69040-0308), SAN 309-5959. Tel: 308-285-3525. FAX: 308-285-3525. E-mail: palisade.library@gmail.com. Web Site: libraries.ne.gov/palisade. *Dir,* Cindee Wagner
Founded 1917. Pop 351; Circ 1,040; Fac 1
Library Holdings: Audiobooks 15; CDs 10; DVDs 285; Large Print Bks 45; Bk Vols 5,000; Per Subs 6
Wireless access
Function: Adult bk club, After school storytime, Bks on CD, Children's prog, Computers for patron use, Electronic databases & coll, Free DVD rentals, Homebound delivery serv, ILL available, Internet access, Magazines, Movies, Online cat, OverDrive digital audio bks, Photocopying/Printing, Printer for laptops & handheld devices, Prog for adults, Prog for children & young adult, Scanner, Senior computer classes, Story hour, Summer reading prog, Wheelchair accessible
Mem of Western Library System
Open Mon & Wed 9-5

PALMYRA

P PALMYRA MEMORIAL LIBRARY, 525 Illinois Pl, 68418. SAN 322-6816. Tel: 402-780-5344. FAX: 402-780-5344. E-mail: palmyramemoriallibrary@gmail.com. Web Site: libraries.ne.gov/palmyra. *Libr Dir,* Carey Shapiro
Pop 510; Circ 1,725
Wireless access
Open Mon, Tues & Sun 2-8

PAPILLION

CR NEBRASKA CHRISTIAN COLLEGE*, Loren T & Melva M Swedburg Library, 12550 S 114th St, 68046. SAN 309-5622. Tel: 402-935-9400. FAX: 402-935-9500. E-mail: library@nechristian.edu. Web Site: www.nechristian.edu/library. *Dir, Libr Serv,* Becky Wymer; E-mail: becky.wymer@nechristian.edu; Staff 1 (MLS 1)
Founded 1945
Library Holdings: Bk Vols 27,000; Per Subs 173
Special Collections: Rare Bibles
Subject Interests: Christian Church, Relig studies, Restoration hist
Automation Activity & Vendor Info: (Cataloging) Mandarin Library Automation; (Circulation) Mandarin Library Automation; (OPAC) Mandarin Library Automation
Wireless access
Mem of Three Rivers Library System
Open Mon-Thurs 8:30am-11pm, Fri 8:30-5, Sun 7pm-11pm

P SUMP MEMORIAL LIBRARY*, 222 N Jefferson St, 68046. SAN 309-5975. Tel: 402-597-2040. FAX: 531-329-3349. E-mail: sumplibrary@gmail.com. Web Site: www.sumplibrary.org. *Dir,* Rebecca Sims; Tel: 402-597-2042, E-mail: rsims@papillion.org; *Asst Dir,* Matt Kovar; E-mail: mkovar@papillion.org; *Youth Serv,* Cathy McMahon; Staff 5 (Non-MLS 5)
Founded 1921. Pop 15,700
Library Holdings: DVDs 540; Bk Vols 54,619; Per Subs 169; Talking Bks 2,337; Videos 1,104
Automation Activity & Vendor Info: (Cataloging) Follett Software; (Circulation) Follett Software; (OPAC) Follett Software
Wireless access
Mem of Three Rivers Library System
Special Services for the Deaf - Closed caption videos
Special Services for the Blind - Audio mat; BiFolkal kits; Bks on cassette; Bks on CD; Copier with enlargement capabilities; Descriptive video serv (DVS); Large print bks; Reader equip; Talking bks
Open Mon-Thurs 9-9, Fri & Sat 9-5, Sun 1-5
Friends of the Library Group

PAWNEE CITY

P PAWNEE CITY PUBLIC LIBRARY*, 735 Eighth St, 68420. (Mail add: PO Box 311, 68420-0311), SAN 309-5983. Tel: 402-852-2118. FAX: 402-852-3134. E-mail: plibrary2@gmail.com. Web Site: pawneecitylibrary.com. *Dir,* Lola Seitz; Staff 2 (Non-MLS 2)
Founded 2011. Pop 932; Circ 12,151
Library Holdings: Bks on Deafness & Sign Lang 5; DVDs 668; Large Print Bks 1,041; Bk Titles 12,733; Talking Bks 271; Videos 608
Special Collections: Adult Fiction Coll; Children's Fiction Coll; Harold Lloyd Coll
Automation Activity & Vendor Info: (Cataloging) Biblionix; (Circulation) Biblionix; (OPAC) Biblionix
Wireless access
Mem of Southeast Library System
Open Mon, Tues, Thurs & Fri 9:30-12:30 & 1:30-6, Wed 12-8, Sat 9:30-1:30
Friends of the Library Group

PAXTON

P PAXTON PUBLIC LIBRARY*, 110 N Oak St, 69155. (Mail add: PO Box 278, 69155-0278), SAN 309-5991. Tel: 308-239-4763. E-mail: paxtonlibrary@nebnet.net. Web Site: libraries.ne.gov/paxton. *Librn,* Dianne Jay; Staff 1 (MLS 1)
Founded 1932. Pop 1,175; Circ 3,878
Library Holdings: Large Print Bks 30; Bk Vols 8,590; Per Subs 28; Talking Bks 114; Videos 82
Special Collections: Local History Coll; Nebraska Coll
Wireless access
Mem of Western Library System
Open Mon 2-6:30, Tues 9-1, Thurs 3-6:30, Sat 9-2
Friends of the Library Group

PENDER

P HOUSE MEMORIAL PUBLIC LIBRARY, 220 Thurston Ave, 68047. (Mail add: PO Box 509, 68047-0509), SAN 309-6009. Tel: 402-385-2521. FAX: 402-385-2521. E-mail: hmlibrary@abbnebraska.com. Web Site: www.penderlibrary.org. *Dir,* Ann Bachman; *Asst Dir,* Carol Springer
Pop 1,148; Circ 18,298
Library Holdings: Bk Titles 14,000; Per Subs 70
Automation Activity & Vendor Info: (Cataloging) Follett Software; (Circulation) Follett Software; (OPAC) Follett Software
Wireless access
Mem of Three Rivers Library System
Open Mon & Thurs 2-8, Tues, Wed & Fri 2-5, Sat 10-4

PERU

C PERU STATE COLLEGE LIBRARY, 600 Hoyt St, 68421. SAN 309-6017. Tel: 402-872-2311. E-mail: library@campus.peru.edu. Web Site: www.peru.edu/library. *Libr Dir,* Veronica Meier; E-mail: vmeier@peru.edu; Staff 3 (MLS 1, Non-MLS 2)
Founded 1867. Enrl 1,316; Fac 47; Highest Degree: Master
Library Holdings: Audiobooks 119; AV Mats 2,583; CDs 294; DVDs 2,982; e-books 455,979; e-journals 12; Microforms 1,771; Bk Titles 77,433; Videos 145

Automation Activity & Vendor Info: (Cataloging) Innovative Interfaces, Inc - Millennium; (Circulation) Innovative Interfaces, Inc - Millennium; (Course Reserve) Innovative Interfaces, Inc - Millennium; (Discovery) EBSCO Discovery Service; (ILL) OCLC WorldShare Interlibrary Loan; (OPAC) Innovative Interfaces, Inc - Millennium
Wireless access
Partic in OCLC Online Computer Library Center, Inc
Open Mon-Wed 7:30am-11:00pm, Thurs 7:30am-10:00pm, Fri 7:30-5, Sat 1-5, Sun 3-11

PETERSBURG

P PETERSBURG PUBLIC LIBRARY*, 103 S Second St, 68652. (Mail add: PO Box 60, 68652-0060), SAN 325-2582. Tel: 402-386-5755. Web Site: www.ci.petersburg.ne.us/library.asp. *Vols Librn,* Jennifer Leifeld; E-mail: leifelds@frontiernet.net
Founded 1984. Pop 380; Circ 917
Library Holdings: Bk Titles 5,000; Per Subs 40
Wireless access
Mem of Three Rivers Library System
Open Mon, Wed & Thurs 2-5

PIERCE

P LIED PIERCE PUBLIC LIBRARY*, 207 W Court St, 68767. (Mail add: PO Box 39, 68767-0039), SAN 309-6025. Tel: 402-329-6324. FAX: 402-329-6442. E-mail: pplib@ptcnet.net. Web Site: piercepubliclibrary.org. *Dir,* Dawnn Tucker; E-mail: director@ptcnet.net; Staff 4 (Non-MLS 4)
Founded 1911. Pop 1,779; Circ 24,000
Library Holdings: Bk Vols 23,150; Per Subs 45
Automation Activity & Vendor Info: (Circulation) Follett Software
Wireless access
Mem of Three Rivers Library System
Open Mon-Wed 1-8, Thurs 10-6, Fri 1-6, Sat 10-4
Friends of the Library Group

PILGER

P PILGER PUBLIC LIBRARY*, 120 Main St, 68768. (Mail add: PO Box 54, 68768-0054), SAN 309-6033. Tel: 402-396-3550. FAX: 402-396-3550. E-mail: pilgerlibrary@gmail.com. Web Site: libraries.ne.gov/pilgerlibrary. *Librn,* Lori Ruskamp
Founded 1934. Pop 378; Circ 2,500
Library Holdings: DVDs 350; Bk Vols 7,200; Per Subs 30; Talking Bks 38; Videos 127
Automation Activity & Vendor Info: (Acquisitions) LibraryWorld, Inc
Wireless access
Mem of Three Rivers Library System
Open Mon & Thurs 2-6, Wed 2-7, Sat 10-12

PLAINVIEW

P PLAINVIEW PUBLIC LIBRARY, 209 N Pine St, 68769. (Mail add: PO Box 728, 68769-0728), SAN 309-6041. Tel: 402-582-4507. FAX: 402-582-4813. E-mail: plibrary@plvwtelco.net. Web Site: www.libraries.ne.gov/plainview. *Dir,* Donna Christiansen; *Ch,* Eileen Bramer; *Asst Librn,* Kristine Hingst-Sims
Founded 1917
Oct 2019-Sept 2020 Income $91,380, State $2,390, City $79,990, County $5,500, Locally Generated Income $3,500. Mats Exp $8,195, Books $7,695, Electronic Ref Mat (Incl. Access Fees) $500. Sal $65,526
Library Holdings: Audiobooks 881; DVDs 569; Bk Vols 15,453; Per Subs 25
Wireless access
Function: 24/7 Online cat, 3D Printer, Adult bk club, After school storytime, Bks on CD, Children's prog, Computer training, Computers for patron use, Distance learning, E-Readers, Electronic databases & coll, Free DVD rentals, Home delivery & serv to seniorr ctr & nursing homes, Homebound delivery serv, ILL available, Internet access, Laminating, Large print keyboards, Life-long learning prog for all ages, Magazines, Magnifiers for reading, Makerspace, Meeting rooms, Movies, Online cat, Online ref, Outreach serv, OverDrive digital audio bks, Photocopying/Printing, Preschool outreach, Preschool reading prog, Printer for laptops & handheld devices, Prog for adults, Prog for children & young adult, Ref & res, Res assist avail, Scanner, Senior computer classes, Senior outreach, STEM programs, Story hour, Study rm, Summer & winter reading prog, Summer reading prog, Tax forms, Teen prog, Wheelchair accessible, Winter reading prog
Mem of Three Rivers Library System
Open Mon-Thurs 10-8, Fri 10-5, Sat 10-2
Friends of the Library Group

PLATTSMOUTH

P PLATTSMOUTH PUBLIC LIBRARY*, 401 Ave A, 68048. SAN 309-605X. Tel: 402-296-4154. FAX: 402-296-4712. E-mail: plattsmouthpubliclibrary@hotmail.com. *Dir,* Karen Mier; *Asst Dir,* Barb Miller; *Youth Serv Librn,* Kirsten Wood; *Libr Supvr,* Stacey Ewing; Staff 9 (MLS 1, Non-MLS 8)
Founded 1885. Pop 6,451; Circ 68,000
Oct 2017-Sept 2018 Income City $347,640. Mats Exp $42,000. Sal $197,000
Library Holdings: Audiobooks 1,968; CDs 817; DVDs 7,389; Large Print Bks 2,053; Microforms 144; Bk Vols 32,753; Per Subs 49
Special Collections: Local & Nebraska History, Local newspapers and yearbooks digitized
Subject Interests: Local genealogy
Automation Activity & Vendor Info: (Cataloging) Innovative Interfaces, Inc; (Circulation) Innovative Interfaces, Inc; (OPAC) Innovative Interfaces, Inc
Wireless access
Function: 24/7 Electronic res, 24/7 Online cat, Activity rm, Adult literacy prog, Archival coll, Audio & video playback equip for onsite use, Audiobks on Playaways & MP3, Audiobks via web, Bks on CD, Children's prog, Computer training, Computers for patron use, Digital talking bks, Electronic databases & coll, Equip loans & repairs, Free DVD rentals, Holiday prog, Home delivery & serv to seniorr ctr & nursing homes, Homebound delivery serv, ILL available, Internet access, Laminating, Life-long learning prog for all ages, Magazines, Magnifiers for reading, Mail & tel request accepted, Makerspace, Meeting rooms, Microfiche/film & reading machines, Movies, Music CDs, Online cat, OverDrive digital audio bks, Photocopying/Printing, Preschool reading prog, Prog for adults, Prog for children & young adult, Ref & res, Ref serv available, Res assist avail, Scanner, Senior computer classes, Spanish lang bks, Spoken cassettes & CDs, STEM programs, Story hour, Summer reading prog, Tax forms, Teen prog, Telephone ref, Wheelchair accessible
Mem of Three Rivers Library System
Special Services for the Blind - Bks on CD; Copier with enlargement capabilities; Free checkout of audio mat; Home delivery serv; Large print bks; Magnifiers
Open Mon-Thurs 9-8, Fr 9-5, Sat 9-4, Sun 12-4:30
Friends of the Library Group

PLYMOUTH

P PLYMOUTH PUBLIC LIBRARY*, 103 N Jefferson Ave, 68424. (Mail add: PO Box 378, 68424-0378). Tel: 402-656-4335. E-mail: plymouthlibrary@diodecom.net. *Dir,* Niki Bare
Pop 3,681
Library Holdings: AV Mats 50; Bk Vols 6,500
Wireless access
Mem of Southeast Library System
Open Mon & Thurs 9-3, Tues 4:30-6:30, Wed & Fri 9-2
Friends of the Library Group

POLK

P POLK PUBLIC LIBRARY, 180 N Main St, 68654. (Mail add: PO Box 49, 68654-0049), SAN 309-6068. Tel: 402-765-7266. FAX: 402-765-7266. E-mail: polknelibrary@gmail.com. *Dir,* Ann Garey; Staff 1 (Non-MLS 1)
Founded 1913. Pop 322; Circ 7,838
Library Holdings: Audiobooks 78; DVDs 120; Large Print Bks 527; Bk Titles 7,901; Per Subs 21
Subject Interests: Nebr
Wireless access
Function: Adult bk club, Children's prog, Computers for patron use, Holiday prog, Homebound delivery serv, ILL available, Photocopying/Printing, Prog for adults, Prog for children & young adult, Story hour, Summer reading prog, VHS videos, Wheelchair accessible
Open Mon 1:30-4:30, Wed 1:30-5, Thurs 4:30-8, Sat 9-2

PONCA

P PONCA CARNEGIE LIBRARY*, 203 W Second St, 68770. (Mail add: PO Box 368, 68770-0368), SAN 309-6084. Tel: 402-755-2739. E-mail: poncalib@gpcom.net. Web Site: libraries.ne.gov/ponca/. *Dir,* Mary Climer; E-mail: director4pcl@gmail.com; *Librn,* Patti Goodier; E-mail: librarian@cityofponca.org; Staff 2 (Non-MLS 2)
Founded 1913. Pop 982; Circ 1,562
Library Holdings: Bk Titles 11,235; Per Subs 30
Special Collections: Dixon County Census, 1860-1930, microfilm; Lewis & Clark Materials; Newspapers, 1884-1996, microfilm
Subject Interests: Genealogy
Automation Activity & Vendor Info: (Cataloging) Follett Software; (Circulation) Follett Software
Wireless access
Mem of Three Rivers Library System

Open Mon & Thurs 3:30-6, Tues 3:30-8, Wed & Fri 1-6, Sat 10-4
Friends of the Library Group

POTTER

P POTTER PUBLIC LIBRARY*, 333 Chestnut, 69156. (Mail add: PO Box 317, 69156-0317), SAN 377-192X. Tel: 308-879-4345. FAX: 308-879-4456. E-mail: potterslibrary@gmail.com. *Dir,* Kathleen Gorman; Staff 1 (Non-MLS 1)
Pop 750; Circ 1,520
Library Holdings: Bk Vols 7,000; Per Subs 10
Automation Activity & Vendor Info: (Circulation) JayWil Software Development, Inc
Wireless access
Mem of Western Library System
Special Services for the Blind - Talking bks
Open Wed 10-6, Sat 1:30-5

RALSTON

P HOLLIS & HELEN BARIGHT PUBLIC LIBRARY*, 5555 S 77th St, 68127-2899. SAN 309-6092. Tel: 402-331-7636. FAX: 402-331-1168. Web Site: ralstonlibrary.org. *Dir,* Bailey Halbur; E-mail: baileyhalbur@ralstonlibrary.org; *Asst Dir, Youth Serv Librn,* Justine Ridder; E-mail: justineridder@ralstonlibrary.org; Staff 5.5 (MLS 3.5, Non-MLS 2)
Founded 1922. Pop 6,214
Oct 2015-Sept 2016 Income $508,000. Mats Exp $69,000, Books $43,000, Per/Ser (Incl. Access Fees) $4,000, AV Mat $10,000, Electronic Ref Mat (Incl. Access Fees) $12,000. Sal $270,000
Library Holdings: Bk Titles 27,650; Bk Vols 31,000; Per Subs 87
Automation Activity & Vendor Info: (OPAC) Innovative Interfaces, Inc
Wireless access
Function: 24/7 Electronic res, 24/7 Online cat, Adult bk club, Adult literacy prog, Audiobks via web, Bks on CD, Children's prog, Computer training, Computers for patron use, Electronic databases & coll, Free DVD rentals, ILL available, Internet access, Laminating, Magazines, Meeting rooms, Online cat, Photocopying/Printing, Preschool reading prog, Prog for adults, Prog for children & young adult, Scanner, Summer & winter reading prog, Wheelchair accessible
Open Mon-Thurs 10-9, Fri & Sat 10-5, Sun 1-5
Friends of the Library Group

RANDOLPH

P LIED RANDOLPH PUBLIC LIBRARY*, 111 N Douglas St, 68771-5510. (Mail add: PO Box 307, 68771-0307), SAN 309-6106. Tel: 402-337-0046. FAX: 402-337-0046. E-mail: librarian@rlibrary.org. Web Site: www.rlibrary.org. *Dir,* Peggy Leiting; *Libr Asst,* Julie Pfanstiel
Founded 1918. Pop 930
Library Holdings: CDs 43; DVDs 65; Large Print Bks 40; Bk Vols 16,000; Per Subs 35; Talking Bks 52; Videos 360
Special Collections: Agriculture Coll; History Coll
Automation Activity & Vendor Info: (Cataloging) Follett Software; (Circulation) Follett Software
Wireless access
Open Mon, Tues & Thurs 10-12 & 1-6, Wed 10-12 & 1-7, Sat 10-12 & 1-4
Friends of the Library Group

RAVENNA

P RAVENNA PUBLIC LIBRARY, 324 Milan Ave, 68869. SAN 309-6114. Tel: 308-452-4213. FAX: 308-452-4210. E-mail: library@myravenna.com. Web Site: myravenna.com/public-library/. *Libr Dir,* Joy Kyhn; Staff 1 (Non-MLS 1)
Founded 1918. Pop 1,360; Circ 10,672
Library Holdings: Audiobooks 560; DVDs 85; Large Print Bks 480; Bk Titles 8,400; Per Subs 38; Videos 440
Automation Activity & Vendor Info: (Cataloging) Book Systems; (Circulation) Book Systems; (OPAC) Book Systems
Wireless access
Function: After school storytime, Bks on CD, Children's prog, Computers for patron use, Free DVD rentals, Holiday prog, Homebound delivery serv, ILL available, Internet access, Microfiche/film & reading machines, Movies, Online cat, OverDrive digital audio bks, Photocopying/Printing, Printer for laptops & handheld devices, Prog for children & young adult, Scanner, Spoken cassettes & CDs, Story hour, Summer reading prog, Tax forms, Teen prog, VHS videos
Mem of Central Plains Library System
Open Mon 1-8, Tues-Fri, 9-5, Sat 9-12
Friends of the Library Group

RED CLOUD

P AULD PUBLIC LIBRARY*, 537 N Webster St, 68970. (Mail add: PO Box 287, 68970), SAN 309-6122. Tel: 402-746-3352. E-mail: rclibr@hotmail.com. Web Site: libraries.ne.gov/redcloud. *Dir,* Terri Eberly
Founded 1917. Pop 960; Circ 9,491
Library Holdings: Audiobooks 50; Bks on Deafness & Sign Lang 2; DVDs 260; Large Print Bks 100; Bk Titles 9,000; Per Subs 31; Videos 234
Automation Activity & Vendor Info: (Cataloging) Follett Software
Wireless access
Function: Bks on CD, Free DVD rentals, Homebound delivery serv, Photocopying/Printing, VHS videos
Mem of Central Plains Library System
Open Mon-Wed & Fri 1-6, Thurs 1-7, Sat 9-Noon

S THE WILLA CATHER FOUNDATION*, 413 N Webster St, 68970-2466. SAN 309-6130. Tel: 402-746-2653. Toll Free Tel: 866-731-7304. FAX: 402-746-2652. E-mail: info@willacather.org. Web Site: www.willacather.org. *Exec Dir,* Ashley Olson; E-mail: aolson@willacather.org; *Archivist, Educ Dir,* Tracy Tucker; E-mail: ttucker@willcather.org
Founded 1955
Library Holdings: Bk Titles 300; Bk Vols 400
Special Collections: Willa Cather Pioneer Memorial & Educational Foundation Coll
Subject Interests: Webster County, Willa Cather
Mem of Central Plains Library System

S WEBSTER COUNTY HISTORICAL MUSEUM LIBRARY*, 721 W Fourth Ave, 68970. (Mail add: PO Box 464, 68970-0464), SAN 377-1474. Tel: 402-746-2444. E-mail: wchmdirector@gpcom.net. *Dir,* Teresa Young
Library Holdings: Bk Vols 300
Wireless access

RISING CITY

P RISING CITY COMMUNITY LIBRARY, 675 Main St, 68658. (Mail add: PO Box 190, 68658-0190), SAN 309-6149. Tel: 402-954-0270. E-mail: risingcitylibrary@gmail.com. *Dir,* Melissa Praught; E-mail: mel.praught@gmail.com
Founded 1963. Pop 419; Circ 2,000
Library Holdings: Audiobooks 50; DVDs 100; Large Print Bks 150; Bk Titles 6,600; Per Subs 15
Special Collections: Large Print Coll; Zane Grey Series
Open Tues 3-7, Thurs 9-1, Sat 9-2

RUSHVILLE

P RUSHVILLE PUBLIC LIBRARY*, 207 Sprague St, 69360. (Mail add: PO Box 389, 69360-0389), SAN 309-6157. Tel: 308-327-2740. FAX: 308-327-2740. E-mail: rpublib@gpcom.net. *Libr Dir,* Dela DeSersa; Staff 1 (Non-MLS 1)
Pop 999; Circ 8,300
Library Holdings: Bk Vols 10,000; Per Subs 17
Special Collections: Native American History & Literature Coll; Nebraska & South Dakota Authors (Local Author Coll)
Automation Activity & Vendor Info: (Acquisitions) Winnebago Software Co; (Cataloging) Winnebago Software Co; (Circulation) Winnebago Software Co; (Serials) Winnebago Software Co
Wireless access
Function: Bks on cassette, Bks on CD, Computers for patron use, ILL available, Photocopying/Printing, Story hour, Summer reading prog, VHS videos
Mem of Western Library System
Special Services for the Blind - Audio mat; Bks on cassette; Bks on CD; Large print bks
Open Mon-Fri 10-6
Friends of the Library Group

S SHERIDAN COUNTY HISTORICAL SOCIETY, INC*, Benschoter Memorial Library, Hwy 20 & Nelson Ave, 69360. (Mail add: PO Box 274, 69360-0274), SAN 371-6627. Tel: 308-327-2985, 308-360-0299. Web Site: sheridancountyhistoricalsociety.com. *Curator,* Jerry Willnitz; E-mail: nitz@gpcom.net; Staff 1 (Non-MLS 1)
Founded 1960
Library Holdings: Bk Titles 700
Special Collections: Camp Sheridan Nebraska 1874-1881, bks, micro, monographs
Open Mon-Fri 9-4
Restriction: Non-circulating to the pub

SAINT EDWARD

P SAINT EDWARD PUBLIC LIBRARY, 302 Beaver St, 68660. (Mail add: PO Box 249, 68660-0249), SAN 309-6173. Tel: 402-678-2204. FAX: 402-678-2204. E-mail: sepl@gpcom.net. Web Site: www.megavision.net/sepl. *Dir,* Vickie Fritzges; *Librn,* Deanna Reardon
Founded 1925. Pop 800; Circ 5,948
Library Holdings: Bk Vols 11,850; Per Subs 20
Wireless access
Mem of Three Rivers Library System
Open Tues 12-6, Wed 10-8, Thurs 9-12 & 1-6, Sat 9-12
Friends of the Library Group

SAINT PAUL

P SAINT PAUL LIBRARY, 1301 Howard Ave, 68873-2021. SAN 309-6181. Tel: 308-754-5223. Web Site: www.stpaulwildcatslibrary.org. *Dir,* Aubrie Brown; E-mail: aubrie.brown@spwildcat.org
Pop 2,094; Circ 21,011
Library Holdings: Bk Vols 40,000; Per Subs 67
Wireless access
Mem of Central Plains Library System
Open Mon-Fri 10-8, Sat 10-4, Sun 12-4

SARGENT

P SARGENT TOWNSHIP LIBRARY*, 506 Main St, 68874. (Mail add: PO Box 476, 68874-0476), SAN 309-6203. Tel: 308-527-4241. E-mail: sargentlibrary@gmail.com. Web Site: libraries.ne.gov/sargent. *Librn,* Gayle Mattox
Founded 1928. Pop 800; Circ 2,741
Library Holdings: Bk Vols 9,000
Wireless access
Mem of Central Plains Library System
Open Mon 9-3, Wed 1-7, Sat 9-Noon

SCHUYLER

P SCHUYLER PUBLIC LIBRARY*, 108 E 18th St, 68661-1929. SAN 309-6211. Tel: 402-352-2221. FAX: 402-352-5377. E-mail: schuylerpublib@yahoo.com. Web Site: schuylernebraska.net/library. *Dir,* Jenny White; *Asst Dir,* Michael Rea
Founded 1909. Pop 6,370
Library Holdings: Bk Titles 27,000; Per Subs 75
Mem of Three Rivers Library System
Open Mon-Thurs 10-8, Fri 10-5, Sat 10-1

SCOTIA

P SCOTIA PUBLIC LIBRARY, 110 S Main St, 68875. (Mail add: PO Box 188, 68875-0188), SAN 309-622X. Tel: 308-245-3191. FAX: 308-245-3191. E-mail: scotialibrary@nctc.net. Web Site: libraries.ne.gov/scotia. *Dir,* Julie Middendorf; E-mail: mjmiddendorf94@gmail.com
Pop 349; Circ 5,094
Library Holdings: Audiobooks 13; DVDs 12; Large Print Bks 68; Bk Vols 6,046
Special Collections: Pioneer
Wireless access
Mem of Central Plains Library System
Open Mon-Sat 10:30-12:30

SCOTTSBLUFF

P LIED SCOTTSBLUFF PUBLIC LIBRARY*, 1809 Third Ave, 69361-2493. SAN 309-6254. Tel: 308-630-6250. Interlibrary Loan Service Tel: 308-630-6252. FAX: 308-630-6293. E-mail: librarydirector@scottsbluff.org. Web Site: www.scottsbluff.org/government/library. *Dir,* Erin Aschenbrenner; Tel: 308-630-6251, E-mail: easchenbrenner@scottsbluff.org; *Adult Serv,* Jana Kehn; E-mail: jkehn@scottsbluff.org; *Ch Serv,* Debra Carlson; Tel: 308-630-6284, E-mail: dcarlson@scottsbluff.org; *ILL,* Roberta Boyd; E-mail: rboyd@scottsbluff.org; *Tech Serv,* Judith Oltmanns; Tel: 308-630-6207, E-mail: judyo@scottsbluff.org; Staff 11 (MLS 2, Non-MLS 9)
Founded 1917. Pop 14,737; Circ 146,968
Library Holdings: Bk Titles 65,666; Per Subs 105
Special Collections: DAR Coll; Rebecca Winter Genealogical Coll; Western Americana (Western History Coll). State Document Depository; US Document Depository
Automation Activity & Vendor Info: (Acquisitions) SirsiDynix; (Cataloging) SirsiDynix; (Circulation) SirsiDynix; (OPAC) SirsiDynix; (Serials) SirsiDynix
Wireless access
Function: 24/7 Electronic res, Adult bk club, After school storytime, Audiobks via web, Bk club(s), Children's prog, Computer training, Computers for patron use, Electronic databases & coll, Free DVD rentals, ILL available, Magazines, Mango lang, Movies, Music CDs, Notary serv, Online cat, OverDrive digital audio bks, Photocopying/Printing, Prog for adults, Prog for children & young adult, Scanner, Senior computer classes, Story hour, Summer & winter reading prog, Summer reading prog, Tax forms, Teen prog
Mem of Western Library System
Special Services for the Deaf - Pocket talkers
Special Services for the Blind - Bks on cassette; Bks on CD; Talking bk serv referral
Open Mon-Thurs 9-7, Fri & Sat 9-5
Friends of the Library Group

M REGIONAL WEST MEDICAL CENTER LIBRARY*, St Mary Plaza, 3700 Avenue B, 69361. SAN 377-1458. Tel: 308-635-3711. FAX: 308-630-1721. Web Site: www.rwhs.org/patients/patient-education-other-resources/hospital-library. *Dir of Educ,* Jason Stratman; E-mail: jason.stratman@rwhs.org
Library Holdings: Bk Vols 3,300; Per Subs 250
Partic in Mid-Continental Regional Med Librs Asn
Open Mon-Fri 8-4:30

P WESTERN LIBRARY SYSTEM*, 615 S Beltline Hwy W, 69361. Tel: 308-632-1350. Toll Free Tel: 888-879-5303. FAX: 308-632-3978. Web Site: libraries.ne.gov/wls. *Dir,* Cindy Osborne; E-mail: cindy.osborne@nebraska.gov
Publications: Western Sun (Newsletter)
Member Libraries: Arthur County Public Library; Big Springs Public Library; Broadwater Public Library; Chadron Public Library; Chadron State College; Chappell Memorial Library & Art Gallery; Cravath Memorial Library; Crawford Public Library; Culbertson Public Library; Dalton Public Library; Dundy County Library; Gering Public Library; Goodall City Library; Gordon City Library; Hastings Memorial Library; Hayes Center Public Library; Hemingford Public Library; Hooker County Library; Kimball Public Library; Lewellen Public Library; Lied Imperial Public Library; Lied Scottsbluff Public Library; Lyman Public Library; Minatare Public Library; Mitchell Public Library; Morrill Public Library; Nancy Fawcett Memorial Library; Oshkosh Public Library; Palisade Public Library; Paxton Public Library; Potter Public Library; Rushville Public Library; Sidney Public Library; Sioux County Public Library; Stratton Public Library; Summit Christian College Library; Trenton Public Library; Wauneta Public Library; Western Nebraska Veterans Home Library

J WESTERN NEBRASKA COMMUNITY COLLEGE LIBRARY*, 1601 E 27th NE, 69361-1899. SAN 309-6238. Tel: 308-635-6040. Circulation Tel: 308-635-6068. Reference Tel: 308-635-6041. FAX: 308-635-6086. E-mail: library@wncc.net. Web Site: www.wncc.net/library. *Gen Serv Librn,* Deb Kildow; E-mail: kildowd@wncc.edu; *Pub Serv,* Andrea Gonzales; *Libr Tech II,* Allison Reisig; E-mail: reisigj2@wncc.edu
Founded 1926. Enrl 1,398; Fac 43
Automation Activity & Vendor Info: (Cataloging) Follett Software; (Circulation) OCLC Online; (OPAC) Follett Software
Wireless access
Partic in OCLC Online Computer Library Center, Inc
Special Services for the Deaf - Pocket talkers
Special Services for the Blind - Braille bks; Braille equip
Open Mon-Thurs 7:30am-9pm, Fri 7:30-4, Sat 10-2

Departmental Libraries:

SIDNEY LEARNING RESOURCE CENTER, Sidney Campus, 371 College Dr, Sidney, 69162. (Mail add: 1601 E 27th St, 69361), SAN 374-5287. Tel: 308-254-7452. *Library Contact,* Donna Maddox; E-mail: maddoxd@wncc.edu
Open Mon-Thurs 8am-9pm, Fri 8-4

S WESTERN NEBRASKA VETERANS HOME LIBRARY, 1102 W 42nd St, 69361-4713. SAN 377-3779. Tel: 308-632-0300. FAX: 308-632-1384. Web Site: veterans.nebraska.gov/cnvh. *Library Contact,* Kilee Oliverius; E-mail: kilee.oliverius@nebraska.gov
Founded 1975
Library Holdings: DVDs 29; Bk Titles 1,500; Per Subs 15; Talking Bks 10
Wireless access
Mem of Western Library System

SCRIBNER

P SCRIBNER PUBLIC LIBRARY*, 530 Main St, 68057. (Mail add: PO Box M, 68057), SAN 309-6262. Tel: 402-664-3540. FAX: 402-664-3540. E-mail: scribnerlibrary@yahoo.com. *Dir,* Angela Brainard; *Librn,* Arlene Alsmeyer
Founded 1902. Pop 950; Circ 10,000
Library Holdings: Bk Titles 10,000; Per Subs 30
Automation Activity & Vendor Info: (Cataloging) Follett Software; (Circulation) Follett Software; (Course Reserve) Follett Software; (ILL) OCLC WorldShare Interlibrary Loan; (OPAC) Follett Software

Wireless access
Mem of Three Rivers Library System
Open Mon 10-7, Tues 1-5, Wed 2-6 Thurs 1-7, Fri 10-5, Sat 10-1
Friends of the Library Group

SEWARD

C CONCORDIA UNIVERSITY*, Link Library, 800 N Columbia Ave, 68434. SAN 309-6270. Tel: 402-643-7254. Interlibrary Loan Service Tel: 402-643-7255. Reference Tel: 402-643-7256. Administration Tel: 402-643-7358. Toll Free Tel: 800-535-5494. FAX: 402-643-4218. E-mail: library@cune.edu. Web Site: www.cune.edu/library. *Dir, Libr Serv,* Philip Hendrickson; E-mail: philip.hendrickson@cune.edu; *Cat Librn,* Holly Helmer; E-mail: holly.helmer@cune.edu; *Ref & Instruction Librn,* Billy Moore; E-mail: billy.moore@cune.edu; *Circ Supvr,* Kathy Rippstein; E-mail: kathy.rippstein@cune.edu; *ILL, Ser,* Sarah Jurchen; E-mail: sarah.jurchen@cune.edu; Staff 4.3 (MLS 3, Non-MLS 1.3)
Founded 1912. Enrl 2,200; Fac 85; Highest Degree: Master
Special Collections: Board Games; Children's Literature; Curriculum
Subject Interests: Educ, Music, Relig
Automation Activity & Vendor Info: (Cataloging) OCLC; (Circulation) OCLC; (Course Reserve) OCLC; (ILL) OCLC; (Media Booking) OCLC; (OPAC) OCLC; (Serials) OCLC
Wireless access
Partic in OCLC Online Computer Library Center, Inc
Special Services for the Blind - Magnifiers
Open Mon-Thurs 8am-Midnight, Fri 8-5, Sat 1-5, Sun 1pm-Midnight

R SAINT GREGORY THE GREAT SEMINARY*, Our Lady Seat of Wisdom Library, 800 Fletcher Rd, 68434. Tel: 402-643-4052. FAX: 402-643-6964. E-mail: sggs@sggs.edu. Web Site: sggs.edu. *Librn,* Dr Terrence D Nollen
Founded 1998
Library Holdings: Bk Vols 41,000
Subject Interests: Hist, Liberal arts, Lit, Philos, Sacred scripture, Spirituality, Theol

P SEWARD MEMORIAL LIBRARY, 233 S Fifth St, 68434. SAN 309-6289. Tel: 402-643-3318. E-mail: info@sewardlibrary.org. Web Site: www.sewardlibrary.org. *Libr Dir,* Becky Baker; Staff 8 (Non-MLS 8)
Founded 1888. Pop 5,700; Circ 97,002
Library Holdings: Bk Titles 33,000; Per Subs 99
Special Collections: Large Print Coll; Nebraska Coll
Wireless access
Mem of Southeast Library System
Open Mon-Wed 9-6, Thurs 9-8, Fri 9-5, Sat 9-1
Friends of the Library Group

SHELBY

P SHELBY COMMUNITY LIBRARY*, 648 N Walnut, 68662. (Mail add: PO Box 146, 68662-0146), SAN 377-1989. Tel: 402-527-5181. FAX: 402-527-5181. Web Site: libraries.ne.gov/shelby. *Dir,* Laura Alt; Tel: 402-527-5256; *Media Spec,* Sherri Nielsen; Tel: 402-669-9726
Library Holdings: Bk Vols 6,000
Wireless access
Open Mon-Fri 8-3:30; Mon, Tues & Thurs (Summer) 9:30-12 & 12:30-4:30, Wed 12:30-4:30 & 5-7:30, Fri & Sat 9:30-1:30
Friends of the Library Group

SHELTON

P SHELTON PUBLIC LIBRARY, 313 C St, 68876. (Mail add: PO Box 10, 68876-0010), SAN 309-6297. Tel: 308-647-5182. FAX: 308-647-9132. E-mail: sheltonlibrary@nctc.net. *Dir,* Tony Crouse
Pop 1,497
Library Holdings: Bk Vols 8,500; Per Subs 33
Mem of Central Plains Library System
Open Mon 11-5, Tues & Thurs 1-7, Wed Noon-6, Fri 10-4
Friends of the Library Group

SHICKLEY

P VIRGIL BIEGERT PUBLIC LIBRARY*, 214 N Market, 68436. (Mail add: PO Box 412, 68436-0412), SAN 309-6300. Tel: 402-627-3365. FAX: 402-627-3365. E-mail: shickleylibrary@windstream.net. Web Site: www.biglittletown.us/library. *Librn,* Carolyn Schlegel
Pop 376; Circ 5,202
Library Holdings: Large Print Bks 154; Bk Vols 15,051; Per Subs 65; Talking Bks 130; Videos 551
Automation Activity & Vendor Info: (Cataloging) Follett Software
Mem of Southeast Library System
Open Mon & Fri 9-11:30 & 1:30-5:30, Wed 2:30-6:30, Sat 9:30am-11:30am

SHUBERT

P SHUBERT PUBLIC LIBRARY & MUSEUM*, 313 Main St, 68437. (Mail add: PO Box 148, 68437-0148), SAN 377-2004. Tel: 402-883-2059. *Library Contact,* Peggy Oliver
Pop 147
Library Holdings: Bk Vols 3,500; Per Subs 20
Mem of Southeast Library System
Open Sat (Winter) 9am-11:30am

SIDNEY

P SIDNEY PUBLIC LIBRARY, 1112 12th Ave, 69162. (Mail add: PO Box 119, 69162), SAN 309-6319. Tel: 308-254-3110. FAX: 308-254-3710. E-mail: spl@sidneypubliclibrary.org. Web Site: sidneypubliclibrary.org. *Ch,* Eileen Nightingale; E-mail: eileen@sidneypubliclibrary.org; *Circ Librn,* Larami Bruner; E-mail: larami@sidneypubliclibrary.org; *ILL, Libr Office Mgr,* Stephanie Mika; E-mail: stephanie@sidneypubliclibrary.org; *Adult Serv,* Jenny Gilbert; E-mail: jenny@sidneypubliclibrary.org; *Cat, Tech Serv,* Sandy Nelson; E-mail: sandy@sidneypubliclibrary.org; Staff 5 (Non-MLS 5)
Founded 1914. Pop 9,830; Circ 40,000
Library Holdings: CDs 3,659; DVDs 1,235; Large Print Bks 1,596; Bk Titles 28,510; Per Subs 45; Talking Bks 3,659
Special Collections: The Sidney Telegraph, 1875-, microfilm
Subject Interests: Local hist, Nebr authors
Automation Activity & Vendor Info: (Cataloging) OCLC CatExpress; (ILL) OCLC
Wireless access
Function: 24/7 Electronic res, 24/7 Online cat, 3D Printer, AV serv, Bks on CD, Children's prog, Computers for patron use, Electronic databases & coll, Free DVD rentals, Homebound delivery serv, ILL available, Internet access, Magazines, Mail & tel request accepted, Makerspace, Meeting rooms, Microfiche/film & reading machines, Movies, Online cat, Outreach serv, OverDrive digital audio bks, Photocopying/Printing, Preschool outreach, Printer for laptops & handheld devices, Prog for adults, Prog for children & young adult, Ref & res, Ref serv available, Scanner, Spoken cassettes & CDs, Story hour, Summer reading prog, Tax forms, Telephone ref, Wheelchair accessible
Mem of Western Library System
Open Mon-Fri 9-6, Sat 9-5
Friends of the Library Group
Bookmobiles: 1. Librn, Jenny Gilbert

SILVER CREEK

P TOWNSHIP LIBRARY OF SILVER CREEK*, 309 Vine St, 68663. (Mail add: PO Box 249, 68663-0249), SAN 309-6327. Tel: 308-773-2594. E-mail: sclibraryts@gmail.com. *Librn,* Cheryl Kershaw; *Librn,* Linda Reed; *Librn,* Rick Tank
Founded 1934. Pop 437; Circ 1,975
Library Holdings: Bk Vols 6,400
Wireless access
Open Mon-Fri 3-6

SNYDER

P SNYDER PUBLIC LIBRARY*, 203 Ash St, 68664. (Mail add: PO Box 26, 68664-0026), SAN 309-6335. Tel: 402-568-2570. E-mail: snyderlibrary@yahoo.com. Web Site: libraries.ne.gov/snyder. *Dir,* Elizabeth Hittle
Pop 300; Fac 1
Library Holdings: DVDs 500; Large Print Bks 85; Bk Vols 3,082; Per Subs 15
Wireless access
Function: Adult bk club, Children's prog, Computers for patron use, For res purposes, Free DVD rentals, Holiday prog, ILL available, Internet access, Literacy & newcomer serv, Movies, Photocopying/Printing, Printer for laptops & handheld devices, Prog for adults, Prog for children & young adult, Ref & res, Story hour, Summer reading prog, Teen prog, Wheelchair accessible
Mem of Three Rivers Library System
Open Tues 3pm-6:30pm, Wed 5:30-7:30, Sun 1-4:30

SOUTH SIOUX CITY

P SOUTH SIOUX CITY PUBLIC LIBRARY*, 2121 Dakota Ave, 68776. SAN 309-6343. Tel: 402-494-7545. FAX: 402-494-7546. E-mail: publiclibrary@southsiouxcity.org. Web Site: www.southsiouxcity.org/department/?structureid=10. *Libr Dir,* David Mixdorf; E-mail: dwmixdorf@southsiouxcity.org; *Asst Dir,* Dan Nieman; E-mail: dnieman@southsiouxcity.org; *Ch,* Odessa Meyer; E-mail: omeyer@southsiouxcity.org; Staff 6 (MLS 1, Non-MLS 5)
Founded 1920. Pop 12,000; Circ 35,000
Library Holdings: AV Mats 112; Bks-By-Mail 578; Bks on Deafness & Sign Lang 13; CDs 200; DVDs 200; e-books 15,179; Electronic Media &

Resources 7; High Interest/Low Vocabulary Bk Vols 944; Large Print Bks 2,000; Bk Titles 36,222; Per Subs 100; Talking Bks 658; Videos 1,000
Special Collections: Nebraska
Automation Activity & Vendor Info: (Acquisitions) LibLime; (Cataloging) LibLime; (Circulation) LibLime; (OPAC) LibLime; (Serials) LibLime
Wireless access
Mem of Three Rivers Library System
Open Mon-Thurs 9-8, Fri & Sat 9-5

SPALDING

P SPALDING PUBLIC LIBRARY*, 159 W St Joseph St, 68665. (Mail add: PO Box 74, 68665-0074), SAN 309-6351. Tel: 308-497-2705. Web Site: libraries.ne.gov/spalding. *Dir,* Debra Pritchard; E-mail: debpritchard2013@gmail.com
Library Holdings: Bk Vols 7,000
Wireless access
Mem of Central Plains Library System
Open Mon & Thurs 10-12 & 3:30-6:30

SPENCER

P SPENCER TOWNSHIP LIBRARY*, 110 Main St, 68777. (Mail add: PO Box 189, 68777-0189), SAN 309-636X. Tel: 402-589-1131. E-mail: spnlib@nntc.net. *Librn,* Steven Marcum
Pop 596; Circ 1,200
Library Holdings: Bk Vols 6,355; Per Subs 15
Mem of Central Plains Library System
Open Mon, Wed & Fri 1:30-5

SPRINGFIELD

P SPRINGFIELD MEMORIAL LIBRARY*, 665 Main St, 68059. (Mail add: PO Box 40, 68059-0040), SAN 309-6378. Tel: 402-253-2797. FAX: 402-253-2797. E-mail: smlibrary665@gmail.com. Web Site: libraries.ne.gov/springfield. *Dir,* Constance Manzer; *Asst Dir,* Kellie Seiber
Pop 1,526; Circ 13,694
Library Holdings: Bk Vols 17,000; Per Subs 70
Automation Activity & Vendor Info: (Acquisitions) Biblionix; (Cataloging) Biblionix; (Circulation) Biblionix; (OPAC) Biblionix
Wireless access
Mem of Three Rivers Library System
Open Mon & Wed 10-5, Tues & Thurs 1-7, Sat 9-1
Friends of the Library Group

SPRINGVIEW

P KEYA PAHA COUNTY LIBRARY*, 118 Main St, 68778. (Mail add: PO Box 134, 68778-0134). Tel: 402-497-2626. E-mail: keyapahalibrary@gmail.com. *Dir,* Marge Hespe
Pop 1,000; Circ 2,800
Library Holdings: CDs 15; DVDs 30; Bk Vols 13,000; Talking Bks 30; Videos 270
Wireless access
Mem of Central Plains Library System
Open Tues & Fri 1-5, Wed 10-2, Thurs 4-7

STANTON

P STANTON PUBLIC LIBRARY*, 1009 Jackpine St, 68779. (Mail add: PO Box 497, 68779-0497), SAN 309-6386. Tel: 402-439-2230. FAX: 402-439-2248. E-mail: spl68779@stanton.net. Web Site: www.stanton.net/library.html. *Dir,* Laura Hess; E-mail: laura55_68779@yahoo.com; *Asst Librn,* Tami Barth
Founded 1886. Pop 1,627; Circ 16,609
Library Holdings: DVDs 1,428; Large Print Bks 247; Bk Titles 16,000; Per Subs 24
Automation Activity & Vendor Info: (Acquisitions) Follett Software; (Cataloging) Follett Software; (Circulation) Follett Software; (OPAC) Follett Software
Wireless access
Mem of Three Rivers Library System
Open Mon 2-8, Tues-Thurs 12-6, Fri 10-4
Friends of the Library Group

STAPLETON

P LOGAN COUNTY PUBLIC LIBRARY*, 317 Main St, 69163. (Mail add: PO Box 8, 69163-0008), SAN 309-6394. Tel: 308-636-2343. *Libr Dir,* Kathryn Trimble; E-mail: ktlibr@hotmail.com
Founded 1939. Pop 340; Circ 3,400
Library Holdings: Bk Titles 6,688
Wireless access
Mem of Central Plains Library System
Open Tues & Thurs 8:30-5:30
Friends of the Library Group

STELLA

P STELLA COMMUNITY LIBRARY*, 224 N Main St, 68442. (Mail add: PO Box 5, 68442-0005), SAN 321-2408. Tel: 402-883-2232. FAX: 402-883-2232. E-mail: stellalibrary@sentco.net. *Librn,* Shadow J Loveless; Tel: 402-245-8190
Founded 1908. Pop 280
Library Holdings: Bk Vols 2,344
Wireless access
Mem of Southeast Library System
Open Wed & Sat 9-11:30

STERLING

P STERLING PUBLIC LIBRARY*, 150 Broadway St, 68443. (Mail add: PO Box 57, 68443-0057), SAN 309-6408. Tel: 402-866-2056. E-mail: skw8754@live.com. *Dir,* Susan Wilken
Pop 510; Circ 5,759
Library Holdings: Bk Titles 9,955; Per Subs 35
Wireless access
Mem of Southeast Library System
Open Tues & Thurs 2-5, Sat 8-Noon

STRATTON

P STRATTON PUBLIC LIBRARY*, 502 Bailey St, 69043. (Mail add: PO Box 182, 69043-0182), SAN 309-6416. Tel: 308-276-2463. E-mail: straplib@gpcom.net. *Dir,* Beverly Henderson
Library Holdings: Bk Vols 5,000
Mem of Western Library System
Open Mon 1-5, Thurs 12-5, Sat 1-4

STROMSBURG

P STROMSBURG PUBLIC LIBRARY*, 320 Central St, 68666. (Mail add: PO Box 366, 68666-0366), SAN 309-6424. Tel: 402-764-7681. FAX: 402-764-7681. E-mail: stromsburgpl@windstream.net. Web Site: libraries.ne.gov/Stromsburg. *Dir,* Monica Tidyman; *Asst Librn,* Dorinda Brown
Founded 1918. Pop 1,241; Circ 14,084
Library Holdings: DVDs 300; Bk Vols 15,000; Per Subs 53
Automation Activity & Vendor Info: (Cataloging) Follett Software; (Circulation) Follett Software
Wireless access
Open Mon, Wed & Fri 12-5:30, Tues 12-8, Thurs 10-Noon
Friends of the Library Group

STUART

P STUART TOWNSHIP LIBRARY*, Second & Main St, 68780. (Mail add: PO Box 207, 68780-0207), SAN 309-6432. Tel: 402-924-3242. *Dir,* Angie Olberding; E-mail: aolberding6@hotmail.com
Pop 1,102; Circ 2,123
Library Holdings: Bk Vols 4,897; Per Subs 23
Wireless access
Mem of Central Plains Library System
Open Mon & Wed 2-5:30, Fri 11-5:30
Friends of the Library Group

SUPERIOR

P SUPERIOR PUBLIC LIBRARY*, 449 N Kansas, 68978-1852. SAN 309-6440. Tel: 402-879-4200. FAX: 402-879-4202. E-mail: superiorlibrary@hotmail.com. Web Site: libraries.ne.gov/superior. *Dir,* Vicki Perrie; *Librn,* Peggy Lipker
Founded 1901. Pop 2,010; Circ 23,200
Library Holdings: Bk Vols 24,000
Wireless access
Open Mon-Fri 1:30-8, Sat 10-12 & 1:30-5:30

SUTHERLAND

P SUTHERLAND PUBLIC LIBRARY, Maxine White Public Library, 900 Second St, 69165. (Mail add: PO Box 275, 69165-0275), SAN 309-6459. Tel: 308-386-2228. E-mail: sutherlandpubliclib@gmail.com. Web Site: libraries.ne.gov/sutherland. *Libr Dir,* Amy Coffman
Pop 1,200
Oct 2021-Sept 2022. Mats Exp $7,500
Library Holdings: DVDs 655; Large Print Bks 771; Bk Vols 11,771
Wireless access
Mem of Central Plains Library System
Open Tues & Thurs 10-12 & 1-7, Sat 9-1

SUTTON

P SUTTON MEMORIAL LIBRARY, 201 S Saunders, 68979. (Mail add: PO Box 433, 68979-0433), SAN 309-6467. Tel: 402-773-5259. FAX: 402-773-5259. E-mail: memlibrary@suttonne.com. Web Site: libraries.ne.gov/sutton/about-2. *Head Librn,* Amanda Eastin; *Asst Librn,* Shelly A Reed
Founded 1908. Pop 1,447; Circ 15,213
Library Holdings: AV Mats 671; Large Print Bks 127; Bk Vols 17,136; Per Subs 40; Talking Bks 193; Videos 636
Automation Activity & Vendor Info: (Circulation) Follett Software
Wireless access
Open Mon, Tues & Thurs 12-7, Wed 12-5, Fri 10-5, Sat 10-12
Friends of the Library Group

SYRACUSE

P SYRACUSE PUBLIC LIBRARY*, 480 Fifth St, 68446. (Mail add: PO Box 8, 68446-0008), SAN 309-6475. Tel: 402-269-2336. Web Site: syracusene.com/library. *Librn,* Susan Antes
Pop 2,000; Circ 17,917
Library Holdings: Bk Titles 24,000; Per Subs 27
Automation Activity & Vendor Info: (Acquisitions) Biblionix; (Cataloging) Biblionix; (Circulation) Biblionix; (Course Reserve) Biblionix; (Serials) Biblionix
Wireless access
Mem of Southeast Library System
Partic in LYRASIS
Open Mon & Fri 9-5, Wed 9-8, Thurs 4-8, Sat 9-12
Friends of the Library Group

TABLE ROCK

P TABLE ROCK PUBLIC LIBRARY*, 511 Luzerne St, 68447. (Mail add: PO Box 86, 68447-0143), SAN 309-6483, *Co-Dir,* Lindsay Kostecka; E-mail: jlkostecka@hotmail.com; *Co-Dir,* Frances Workman
Pop 308
Library Holdings: Bk Vols 5,700
Wireless access
Mem of Southeast Library System
Open Tues & Thurs 1-5, Sat 9-Noon

TALMAGE

P TALMAGE PUBLIC LIBRARY*, 405 Main, 68448. (Mail add: PO Box 7, 68448-0007), SAN 309-6491. Tel: 402-264-3875. E-mail: talmagepl@jagwireless.net. Web Site: talmagepubliclibrary.weebly.com. *Librn,* Carol Fisher
Founded 1904. Pop 268; Circ 1,564
Library Holdings: Bk Vols 6,000
Wireless access
Special Services for the Deaf - Captioned film dep
Open Mon & Wed 4-7, Sat 8-11
Friends of the Library Group

TAYLOR

P TAYLOR PUBLIC LIBRARY*, PO Box 207, 68879-0207. SAN 309-6505. Tel: 308-942-6125. *Dir,* Cheryl Sue Roblyer; Tel: 308-346-4395, E-mail: croblyer2009@hotmail.com
Pop 683; Circ 2,714
Library Holdings: Large Print Bks 70; Bk Vols 5,300
Wireless access
Function: ILL available
Mem of Central Plains Library System
Special Services for the Blind - Large print bks
Open Tues 11-3, Thurs 1-5

TECUMSEH

S NEBRASKA DEPARTMENT OF CORRECTIONS*, Tecumseh State Correctional Institution Library, 2725 N Hwy 50, 68450. Tel: 402-335-5998. FAX: 402-335-5115. *Librn,* Position Currently Open
Library Holdings: Bk Vols 9,000; Per Subs 59; Talking Bks 10
Restriction: Not open to pub

P TECUMSEH PUBLIC LIBRARY*, 170 Branch St, 68450. SAN 309-6513. Tel: 402-335-2060. FAX: 402-335-2069. E-mail: tlibrary@neb.rr.com. Web Site: www.tecumsehne.com/library. *Librn,* Susie Kerner
Founded 1907. Pop 1,702; Circ 16,014
Library Holdings: Bk Titles 11,680; Per Subs 28
Automation Activity & Vendor Info: (Cataloging) Follett Software; (Circulation) Follett Software; (OPAC) Follett Software
Mem of Southeast Library System
Open Mon, Wed & Fri 9-5:30, Sat 8:30-1

TEKAMAH

S BURT COUNTY MUSEUM, INC LIBRARY*, 319 N 13th St, 68061. (Mail add: PO Box 125, 68061-0125), SAN 372-6088. Tel: 402-374-1505. E-mail: burtcomuseum@abbnebraska.com. Web Site: sites.google.com/site/officialburtcountymuseum. *Curator,* Bonnie Newell
Founded 1967
Library Holdings: Bk Titles 625; Bk Vols 950
Special Collections: History of Burt County 1929; Story of an Old Town 1902; Tekamah Book 1904; Tekamah Cemetery Book 1984; Tekamah Centennial Book 1854-1954; The Life & Times
Subject Interests: Genealogy
Wireless access
Friends of the Library Group

P TEKAMAH PUBLIC LIBRARY*, 204 S 13th St, 68061. SAN 309-6521. Tel: 402-374-2453. FAX: 402-374-2553. E-mail: teklibrary@abbnebraska.com. *Dir,* Megan Tomasiewicz; E-mail: teklibdirector@gmail.com; *Ch,* Theresa Lawton; Staff 1 (Non-MLS 1)
Founded 1916. Pop 3,409; Circ 27,000
Library Holdings: CDs 75; DVDs 500; Large Print Bks 150; Bk Titles 15,510; Per Subs 50; Talking Bks 219
Automation Activity & Vendor Info: (Cataloging) Follett Software; (Circulation) Follett Software; (OPAC) Follett Software
Wireless access
Function: Art exhibits, Bks on cassette, Bks on CD, Children's prog, Computers for patron use, Home delivery & serv to seniorr ctr & nursing homes, Homebound delivery serv, ILL available, Music CDs, Photocopying/Printing, Prog for children & young adult, Scanner, Story hour, Summer reading prog, Teen prog, Telephone ref, VHS videos
Mem of Three Rivers Library System
Special Services for the Blind - Bks on cassette; Bks on CD; Large print bks
Open Mon & Wed 10-7, Tues & Thurs 10-5, Sat 10-2

THEDFORD

P THOMAS COUNTY LIBRARY*, 503 Main St, 69166. (Mail add: PO Box 228, 69166-0228), SAN 350-2686. Tel: 308-645-2237. E-mail: thomascolibrary@neb-sandhills.net. *Libr Dir,* Kim Mills; *Asst Librn,* Dawn Bryant
Founded 1958. Pop 3,079; Circ 38,006
Library Holdings: Bks on Deafness & Sign Lang 10; High Interest/Low Vocabulary Bk Vols 200; Large Print Bks 30; Bk Vols 21,107; Per Subs 37; Talking Bks 25
Special Collections: Indians of North America; Library of American Literature Coll; Western History (especially Nebraska)
Subject Interests: Archit, Art, Educ, Natural sci
Wireless access
Mem of Central Plains Library System
Open Mon 4pm-7pm, Tues-Thurs 1-6, Fri 1-4
Bookmobiles: 1. Librn, Josephine Morris. Bk titles 1,000

TILDEN

P RAYMOND A WHITWER TILDEN PUBLIC LIBRARY*, 202 S Center St, 68781. (Mail add: PO Box 457, 68781-0457), SAN 309-653X. Tel: 402-368-5306. FAX: 402-368-5515. Web Site: libraries.ne.gov/tilden. *Libr Dir,* Cindy Lee Simeon; E-mail: csimeon@tildenlibrary.org; *Head Librn,* Hella Bauer; E-mail: hbauer@tildenlibrary.org; *Asst Librn, Ch,* Jeanmarie Shermer; E-mail: jmshermer@tildenlibrary.org; *Asst Librn, Genealogy Librn,* Jeanne Dahl; E-mail: jdahl@tildenlibrary.org
Founded 1922. Pop 953; Circ 22,321
Library Holdings: Audiobooks 370; CDs 25; Large Print Bks 450; Bk Vols 20,354; Per Subs 51; Videos 1,233
Automation Activity & Vendor Info: (Cataloging) Follett Software; (Circulation) Follett Software; (OPAC) Follett Software
Wireless access
Function: Adult bk club, Archival coll, Art exhibits, Audio & video playback equip for onsite use, Bks on CD, Children's prog, Computers for patron use, Electronic databases & coll, Free DVD rentals, Holiday prog, Home delivery & serv to seniorr ctr & nursing homes, ILL available, Jazz prog, Large print keyboards, Magnifiers for reading, Microfiche/film & reading machines, Music CDs, Online cat, OverDrive digital audio bks, Photocopying/Printing, Scanner, Summer reading prog, Tax forms, VHS videos, Wheelchair accessible
Mem of Three Rivers Library System
Special Services for the Deaf - ADA equip
Special Services for the Blind - Bks on CD; Dragon Naturally Speaking software; ZoomText magnification & reading software
Open Mon & Thurs 10-7, Tues, Wed & Fri 10-6, Sat 10-2
Friends of the Library Group

TRENTON

P TRENTON PUBLIC LIBRARY*, 406 Main St, 69044. (Mail add: PO Box 307, 69044-0307), SAN 309-6556. Tel: 308-334-5413. E-mail: read2trenton@gpcom.net. Web Site: www.villageoftrenton.net/library/library.php. *Dir,* Larry Evans; *Librn,* Nadine Dewey; Staff 2 (Non-MLS 2)
Pop 560; Circ 2,600
Oct 2018-Sept 2019 Income $19,126, City $18,500, Federal $526, County $100. Mats Exp $3,600, Books $3,000, Per/Ser (Incl. Access Fees) $100, AV Mat $500. Sal $6,600
Library Holdings: Audiobooks 11,290; DVDs 238; e-books 22,659; Large Print Bks 210; Bk Vols 10,500; Per Subs 15
Automation Activity & Vendor Info: (OPAC) OpenBiblio
Wireless access
Mem of Western Library System
Open Wed 1-5, Thurs 2-7, Sat 9-2
Friends of the Library Group

ULYSSES

P ULYSSES TOWNSHIP LIBRARY, 410 C St, 68669. (Mail add: PO Box 217, 68669-0217), SAN 309-6564. Tel: 402-549-2451. FAX: 402-549-2450. E-mail: ulysses.library@gmail.com. Web Site: libraries.ne.gov/ulysses. *Librn,* Diane Schroeder; Tel: 402-641-3652
Founded 1914. Pop 504; Circ 3,540
Library Holdings: Bk Vols 8,000; Per Subs 22; Videos 690
Open Tues & Thurs 2-6, Wed 3-7, Sat 9-12
Friends of the Library Group

VALENTINE

S CHERRY COUNTY HISTORICAL SOCIETY ARCHIVES*, PO Box 284, 69201-0284. SAN 377-4295. Tel: 402-376-2015. *Pres,* Joyce Muirhead
Library Holdings: Bk Vols 1,500
Open Thurs-Sat (May-Sept) 1-4:30

SR SAINT JOHN'S EPISCOPAL CHURCH LIBRARY*, 372 N Main St, 69201. (Mail add: PO Box 261, 69201-0261), SAN 373-8205. Tel: 402-376-1723. E-mail: churchsolveig@live.com. Web Site: www.episcopalassetmap.org/dioceses/diocese-nebraska/list/st-johns-episcopal-church-0.
Founded 1993
Library Holdings: Bk Titles 575; Bk Vols 668
Special Collections: Episcopal Church Holdings Coll

P VALENTINE PUBLIC LIBRARY*, 324 N Main St, 69201. SAN 309-6572. Tel: 402-376-3160. FAX: 402-376-3160. E-mail: vallibrary@shwisp.net. Web Site: valentinelibrary.org. *Dir,* Anne Quigley; Staff 3 (Non-MLS 3)
Founded 1921. Pop 5,713; Circ 35,138
Library Holdings: DVDs 1,228; Bk Vols 28,383; Per Subs 30
Special Collections: Mari Sandoz American Indian Coll
Automation Activity & Vendor Info: (Acquisitions) OCLC; (Cataloging) Biblionix; (Circulation) Biblionix; (ILL) OCLC FirstSearch; (OPAC) Biblionix
Wireless access
Function: Adult bk club, Art exhibits, Audiobks via web, Bk club(s), Bks on CD, Computer training, Computers for patron use, E-Reserves, Electronic databases & coll, Free DVD rentals, Health sci info serv, Holiday prog, Home delivery & serv to seniorr ctr & nursing homes, Homebound delivery serv, ILL available, Internet access, Microfiche/film & reading machines, Online cat, Online ref, Outside serv via phone, mail, e-mail & web, OverDrive digital audio bks, Photocopying/Printing, Printer for laptops & handheld devices, Prog for adults, Prog for children & young adult, Ref & res, Scanner, Senior outreach, Serves people with intellectual disabilities, Spoken cassettes & CDs, Spoken cassettes & DVDs, Story hour, Summer reading prog, Wheelchair accessible, Workshops
Mem of Central Plains Library System
Special Services for the Blind - Audio mat; Bks on cassette; Bks on CD
Open Mon-Fri 9-6, Sat 10-3
Restriction: Non-resident fee, Open to pub for ref & circ; with some limitations
Friends of the Library Group
Bookmobiles: 1

VALLEY

P VALLEY PUBLIC LIBRARY*, 232 N Spruce St, 68064. (Mail add: PO Box 353, 68064-0353), SAN 309-6580. Tel: 402-359-9924. FAX: 402-932-6258. E-mail: valleypubliclibrary@gmail.com. Web Site: libraries.ne.gov/valley. *Dir,* Sami Voshell; E-mail: svoshell@valley.omhcoxmail.com; *Asst Librn,* Gail White; E-mail: gwhite@valley.omhcoxmail.com
Founded 1902. Pop 1,788; Circ 14,000
Library Holdings: Bk Vols 12,000; Per Subs 25
Special Collections: Nebraska Authors Coll
Wireless access
Mem of Three Rivers Library System
Open Mon, Wed & Fri 10-5, Tues & Thurs 3-8, Sat 10-2
Friends of the Library Group

VALPARAISO

P VALPARAISO PUBLIC LIBRARY*, 300 W Second St, 68065. (Mail add: PO Box 440, 68065-0440), SAN 309-6599. Tel: 402-784-6141. FAX: 402-784-6141. E-mail: VPLibraryweb@gmail.com. Web Site: libraries.ne.gov/valparaiso. *Dir,* Lori Springer; *Asst Librn,* Sue Blackman; Staff 2 (MLS 1, Non-MLS 1)
Pop 600
Library Holdings: Bk Vols 6,652
Automation Activity & Vendor Info: (Circulation) Follett Software
Wireless access
Partic in Saunders County Libr Coop
Open Tues 3-8, Wed 3-8 (Summer 1-8), Thurs 1-8, Sat 9-Noon
Friends of the Library Group

VERDIGRE

P VERDIGRE PUBLIC LIBRARY, 101 E Third St, 68783. (Mail add: PO Box 40, 68783-0040), SAN 309-6602. Tel: 402-668-2677. FAX: 402-668-2677. E-mail: verdigrelibrary@gmail.com. Web Site: libraries.ne.gov/verdigre. *Libr Dir,* Katrina Hollmann; Staff 1 (Non-MLS 1)
Founded 1952. Pop 519; Circ 5,223
Oct 2019-Sept 2020 Income $39,384, State $864, City $27,362, County $4,500, Locally Generated Income $6,658. Mats Exp $21,492. Sal $19,502
Library Holdings: Audiobooks 482; DVDs 848; e-books 29,666; Bk Vols 10,132; Per Subs 7
Automation Activity & Vendor Info: (Acquisitions) Biblionix/Apollo; (Cataloging) Biblionix/Apollo; (Circulation) Biblionix/Apollo
Wireless access
Function: 24/7 Electronic res, 24/7 Online cat, Archival coll, Art exhibits, Art programs, Audio & video playback equip for onsite use, Audiobks via web, AV serv, Bks on CD, CD-ROM, Children's prog, Computer training, Computers for patron use, Digital talking bks, Doc delivery serv, Electronic databases & coll, Equip loans & repairs, Family literacy, Free DVD rentals, Govt ref serv, Health sci info serv, Holiday prog, Home delivery & serv to seniorr ctr & nursing homes, Homebound delivery serv, ILL available, Internet access, Laminating, Large print keyboards, Learning ctr, Life-long learning prog for all ages, Magazines, Mail & tel request accepted, Makerspace, Microfiche/film & reading machines, Movies, Music CDs, Online cat, Online ref, Outreach serv, Outside serv via phone, mail, e-mail & web, OverDrive digital audio bks, Photocopying/Printing, Preschool outreach, Printer for laptops & handheld devices, Prog for adults, Prog for children & young adult, Ref serv available, Res performed for a fee, Scanner, Spoken cassettes & CDs, Spoken cassettes & DVDs, Story hour, Summer reading prog, Tax forms, Teen prog, Telephone ref, Visual arts prog, Wheelchair accessible, Workshops
Mem of Three Rivers Library System
Open Tues & Fri 12-5, Wed 12-6, Thurs 12-7, Sat 10-1
Restriction: Non-circulating coll
Friends of the Library Group

VERDON

P VILLAGE OF VERDON LIBRARY*, 312 1/2 Main St, 68457. (Mail add: PO Box 62, 68457-0062). Tel: 402-883-2044. *Library Contact,* Leota Specht; E-mail: leotaspecht@yahoo.com
Library Holdings: Bk Vols 7,500
Open Mon & Thurs 6pm-8pm, Sat 1-3

WAHOO

P WAHOO PUBLIC LIBRARY*, 637 N Maple St, 68066-1673. SAN 309-6610. Tel: 402-443-3871. FAX: 402-443-3877. Web Site: www.wahoo.ne.us. *Libr Dir,* Denise Lawver; E-mail: denise@wahoo.ne.us; *Children's Serv Coordr,* Carrie Trutna; E-mail: carrie@wahoo.ne.us
Founded 1923. Pop 4,100; Circ 93,000
Oct 2018-Sept 2019. Mats Exp $26,800, Books $18,000, Per/Ser (Incl. Access Fees) $1,800, AV Mat $7,000. Sal $136,000
Library Holdings: Bk Vols 33,000; Per Subs 70
Automation Activity & Vendor Info: (Cataloging) Biblionix; (Circulation) Biblionix; (Course Reserve) Biblionix; (Serials) EBSCO Online
Wireless access
Partic in Association for Rural & Small Libraries; Saunders County Libr Coop
Open Mon-Thurs 9-8, Fri 9:30-5, Sat 9:30-1
Friends of the Library Group

WAKEFIELD

P GARDNER PUBLIC LIBRARY*, 114 W Third St, 68784. (Mail add: PO Box 150, 68784-0150), SAN 309-6629. Tel: 402-287-2334. FAX: 402-287-2334. E-mail: gplibrarian@gmail.com. Web Site: gardnerpubliclibrary.com. *Librn,* Elizabeth Carlson; *Youth Librn,* Blake Craig
Founded 1915. Pop 1,451; Circ 7,001
Wireless access
Mem of Three Rivers Library System
Special Services for the Blind - Computer with voice synthesizer for visually impaired persons; Copier with enlargement capabilities; Large print bks
Open Mon, Tues, Thurs & Fri 9-6, Wed 9-5, Sat 9-11
Friends of the Library Group

WALLACE

P FAITH MEMORIAL LIBRARY*, 122 N Garrison Ave, 69169. (Mail add: PO Box 40, 69169). Tel: 308-387-4537. *Dir,* Donna Hahn; E-mail: donnah@elsiecomm.net
Pop 320; Circ 952
Library Holdings: DVDs 25; Bk Vols 9,959; Talking Bks 180; Videos 955
Wireless access
Open Tues-Thurs 1-5
Friends of the Library Group

WALTHILL

P WALTHILL PUBLIC LIBRARY*, 323 Main St, 68067. (Mail add: PO Box 466, 68067), SAN 309-6637. Tel: 402-846-5051. E-mail: walthillplibrary@gmail.com. *Librn,* Nola Briggs
Pop 847
Library Holdings: Bk Vols 6,500
Wireless access
Mem of Three Rivers Library System
Open Mon, Wed & Thurs 10-6
Friends of the Library Group

WATERLOO

P AGNES ROBINSON WATERLOO PUBLIC LIBRARY*, 23704 Cedar Dr, 68069. SAN 309-6645. Tel: 402-779-4171. FAX: 402-779-4369. E-mail: Waterloolibrary@me.com. Web Site: www.waterloonepubliclibrary.com. *Dir,* Julie Jorgensen
Pop 450; Circ 2,478
Library Holdings: Bk Vols 10,000; Per Subs 12
Wireless access
Mem of Three Rivers Library System
Open Mon 9:30-12 & 1-6, Tues & Thurs 9:30-12 & 1:30-7:30, Sat 9:30-12:30
Friends of the Library Group

WAUNETA

P WAUNETA PUBLIC LIBRARY, 319 N Tecumseh Ave, 69045. SAN 309-6653. Tel: 308-394-5243. FAX: 308-394-5243. E-mail: wvlibrary@bwtelcom.net. Web Site: libraries.ne.gov/wauneta. *Librn,* Marsha Cameron
Pop 675; Circ 5,690
Library Holdings: Bk Vols 5,700
Wireless access
Mem of Western Library System
Open Mon & Thurs 12:30-5:30, Sat 9-11

WAUSA

P LIED LINCOLN TOWNSHIP LIBRARY*, 603 E Norris St, 68786. (Mail add: PO Box H, 68786-0319), SAN 309-6661. Tel: 402-586-2454. FAX: 402-586-2454. E-mail: linctnlb@gpcom.net. Web Site: libraries.ne.gov/wausalibrary. *Dir,* Virginia Lindquist; *Asst Librn,* Wendy Ketelsen
Pop 900; Circ 3,921
Library Holdings: Bk Vols 20,000; Per Subs 70
Automation Activity & Vendor Info: (Cataloging) Follett Software; (Circulation) Follett Software; (OPAC) Follett Software
Mem of Three Rivers Library System
Open Mon, Tues & Thurs 1:30-5:30, Wed 3-8, Fri 9-1

WAYNE

P WAYNE PUBLIC LIBRARY, Robert B & Mary Y Benthack Library-Senior Ctr, 410 Pearl St, 68787. SAN 309-667X. Tel: 402-375-3135. FAX: 402-375-5772. Web Site: www.cityofwayne.org/82/library. *Libr Dir,* Heather Headley; E-mail: hheadley@cityofwayne.org; *Ad,* Sharon Carr; E-mail: scarr@cityofwayne.org; *Youth Serv Librn,* Kim Warner; E-mail: kwarner@cityofwayne.org; Staff 1 (MLS 1)
Founded 1902. Pop 5,583; Circ 38,000
Library Holdings: AV Mats 1,665; Bk Vols 30,000; Per Subs 40
Special Collections: Nebraska Coll, video, book on tape, art reproduction
Subject Interests: Nebr
Automation Activity & Vendor Info: (Cataloging) SirsiDynix; (Circulation) SirsiDynix; (OPAC) SirsiDynix; (Serials) SirsiDynix
Wireless access
Mem of Three Rivers Library System
Open Mon-Thurs 10-8, Fri 10-6, Sat 10-4, Sun (Sept-May) 2-5
Friends of the Library Group

C WAYNE STATE COLLEGE*, Conn Library, 1111 Main St, 68787. SAN 309-6688. Tel: 402-375-7258. Administration Tel: 402-375-7257. E-mail: asklibrary@wsc.edu. Web Site: www.wsc.edu/library. *Dir,* David Graber; Tel: 402-375-7272, E-mail: dagrabe1@wsc.edu; *Acq Librn, Archivist,* Marcus Schlichter; Tel: 402-375-7266, E-mail: maschli1@wsc.edu; *Distance Learning Librn,* Valerie Knight; Tel: 402-375-7443, E-mail: vaknigh1@wsc.edu; *Coll Develop, Ref Librn,* Charissa Loftis; Tel: 402-375-7729, E-mail: chlofti1@wsc.edu; *Circ, Syst Librn,* Evan Swan; Tel: 402-375-7161, E-mail: evswan1@wsc.edu; *Tech Serv Librn,* Marilyn Quance; Tel: 402-375-7474, E-mail: maquanc1@wsc.edu; *Instrul Res Coordr,* Jenny Putnam; Tel: 402-375-7732, E-mail: jeputna1@wsc.edu. Subject Specialists: *Bus, Hist,* David Graber; *Journalism, Philos, Relig,* Marcus Schlichter; *Educ,* Valerie Knight; *Art, Med,* Charissa Loftis; *Anthrop, Biology, Geog,* Evan Swan; *Physics, Psychol,* Marilyn Quance; *Curric, Educ,* Jenny Putnam; Staff 13 (MLS 6, Non-MLS 7)
Founded 1892. Enrl 2,849; Fac 187; Highest Degree: Master
Library Holdings: AV Mats 13,310; CDs 1,853; e-journals 15,295; Electronic Media & Resources 372; High Interest/Low Vocabulary Bk Vols 5,110; Large Print Bks 10; Music Scores 4,485; Bk Titles 185,067; Bk Vols 886,079; Per Subs 2,180; Videos 6,502
Special Collections: Instructional Resources; Juvenile & Young Adults; Kessler Art Coll; Musical Score Coll; Val Peterson Archives. State Document Depository; US Document Depository
Automation Activity & Vendor Info: (Acquisitions) Innovative Interfaces, Inc; (Cataloging) Innovative Interfaces, Inc; (Circulation) Innovative Interfaces, Inc; (OPAC) Innovative Interfaces, Inc; (Serials) Innovative Interfaces, Inc
Wireless access
Function: Audio & video playback equip for onsite use, AV serv, BA reader (adult literacy), Digital talking bks, Distance learning, Doc delivery serv, Govt ref serv, Homebound delivery serv, ILL available, Internet access, Magnifiers for reading, Mail loans to mem, Outside serv via phone, mail, e-mail & web, Photocopying/Printing, Prog for adults, Ref serv available, Satellite serv, Wheelchair accessible, Workshops
Publications: Children/Young Adults Materials Review; Nebraska Young Adult Authors Anthology; Northeast Nebraska Young Authors Anthology
Mem of Three Rivers Library System
Partic in Nebr State Col Syst; OCLC Online Computer Library Center, Inc
Open Mon-Thurs 7:30am-Midnight, Fri 7:30-5, Sat 1-6, Sun 3-Midnight

WEEPING WATER

P WEEPING WATER PUBLIC LIBRARY*, 101 W Eldora Ave, Ste 2, 68463. (Mail add: PO Box 425, 68463-0425), SAN 309-6696. Tel: 402-267-3050. E-mail: weepingwaterlibrary@gmail.com. Web Site: www.weepingwaterlibrary.org. *Dir,* Aimee Morlan
Founded 1914. Pop 1,100; Circ 9,741
Library Holdings: Bk Titles 15,000; Per Subs 10
Wireless access
Mem of Southeast Library System; Three Rivers Library System
Open Mon, Wed & Fri 10-5, Tues & Thurs 1-8, Sat 9-1
Friends of the Library Group

WEST POINT

P JOHN A STAHL LIBRARY*, 330 N Colfax St, 68788. SAN 309-670X. Tel: 402-372-3831. FAX: 402-372-5931. E-mail: info@wplibrary.com. *Dir,* Mary Jo Mack; E-mail: maryjo@wplibrary.com
Circ 37,717
Library Holdings: Bk Vols 28,000; Per Subs 86
Special Collections: Leila Stahl Buffett Genealogy Center
Mem of Three Rivers Library System
Open Mon, Wed & Thurs 10-9, Tues, Fri & Sat 10-5:30

WESTERN

P STRUCKMAN-BAATZ PUBLIC LIBRARY, 104 S West St, 68464. (Mail add: PO Box 338, 68464-0338), SAN 309-6718. Tel: 402-433-2177. FAX: 402-433-2177. E-mail: struckbaatz@gmail.com. *Dir,* Patsy Meyer
Pop 287; Circ 1,682
Library Holdings: Bk Titles 14,000; Per Subs 4
Wireless access

Mem of Southeast Library System
Open Tues-Fri 2-6, Sat 9:30-Noon

WILBER

P DVORACEK MEMORIAL LIBRARY*, 419 W Third St, 68465. (Mail add: PO Box 803, 68465-0803), SAN 309-6726. Tel: 402-821-2832. E-mail: dmlibrary@windstream.net. Web Site: www.czechlibrary.org. *Dir,* Susie Homolka; *Dir,* Nancy Vacek; Staff 2 (MLS 2)
Founded 1968. Pop 1,760; Circ 15,952
Library Holdings: Bk Titles 16,000; Per Subs 15
Special Collections: Czech Materials, bks
Automation Activity & Vendor Info: (Cataloging) Follett Software; (Circulation) Follett Software
Wireless access
Mem of Southeast Library System
Open Tues, Thurs & Fri 9:30-5, Wed 9:30-7, Sat 9-Noon
Friends of the Library Group

WILCOX

P WILCOX PUBLIC LIBRARY*, 107 W Sapp St, 68982. (Mail add: PO Box 88, 68982-0088), SAN 377-4627. Tel: 308-478-5510. E-mail: wilcox@gpcom.net. *Librn,* Melinda Ferree
Library Holdings: Bk Vols 3,000
Wireless access
Mem of Central Plains Library System
Open Mon-Fri 8-12

WILSONVILLE

P WILSONVILLE PUBLIC LIBRARY*, 203 Iva St, 69046. (Mail add: PO Box 100, 69046-0100), SAN 309-6734, *Librn,* Connie Holliday
Pop 100; Circ 3,729
Library Holdings: Bk Vols 6,128
Special Collections: Memorials
Mem of Central Plains Library System
Open Mon 9-2:30

WINNEBAGO

J LITTLE PRIEST TRIBAL COLLEGE LIBRARY*, 601 E College Dr, 68071. (Mail add: PO Box 270, 68071). Tel: 402-878-2380. Web Site: littlepriest.edu/lptc-winnebago-public-library. *Librn,* Yatty Mohammed; Tel: 402-878-2380, Ext 131, E-mail: yattym@littlepriest.edu; Staff 1 (MLS 1)
Enrl 165; Highest Degree: Associate
Library Holdings: Audiobooks 861; AV Mats 768; CDs 88; DVDs 1,788; e-journals 1,700; Large Print Bks 831; Bk Vols 23,465; Per Subs 83
Special Collections: Native American Coll, adult & children's bks, Indian Law mats, journals, newsp, ref works, DVDs
Automation Activity & Vendor Info: (Cataloging) TLC (The Library Corporation); (Circulation) TLC (The Library Corporation); (OPAC) TLC (The Library Corporation)
Wireless access
Function: ILL available, Photocopying/Printing
Partic in National Network of Libraries of Medicine Region 3
Open Mon-Fri 9-5

WINSIDE

P LIED WINSIDE PUBLIC LIBRARY*, 417 Main St, 68790. (Mail add: PO Box 217, 68790-0217), SAN 309-6750. Tel: 402-286-1122. E-mail: liedwinpublib@yahoo.com. *Librn,* JoAnn V Field; *Librn,* Lara Lanphear; Staff 1 (Non-MLS 1)
Founded 1911. Pop 434; Circ 4,966
Library Holdings: Audiobooks 20; Bk Titles 9,543; Per Subs 35
Wireless access
Mem of Three Rivers Library System
Open Mon & Wed (Winter) 1-6, Tues 3-7, Sat 9-12 & 1-4; Mon (Summer) 1-5 & 7-9, Tues 4-7, Wed 1-6, Sat 9-12 & 1-4
Friends of the Library Group

WISNER

P WISNER PUBLIC LIBRARY*, 1015 Ave E, 68791. SAN 309-6769. Tel: 402-529-6018. FAX: 402-529-6018. *Dir,* Carol Duncan; E-mail: director324@hotmail.com
Pop 1,270; Circ 13,999
Library Holdings: Bk Vols 8,700; Per Subs 16
Automation Activity & Vendor Info: (Cataloging) Follett Software; (Circulation) Follett Software
Mem of Three Rivers Library System
Open Mon & Fri 9-5, Wed 9:30-7:30, Sat 10-Noon

WOOD RIVER

P MALTMAN MEMORIAL PUBLIC LIBRARY*, 910 Main St, 68883. (Mail add: PO Box 10, 68883), SAN 309-6785. Tel: 308-583-2349. Web Site: woodriverne.com/library. *Librn,* Deb Fairbanks
Founded 1905. Pop 1,250; Circ 8,826
Library Holdings: Bk Titles 17,500; Per Subs 34
Wireless access
Mem of Central Plains Library System
Open Mon & Wed 8-11:30 & 3-7, Tues & Thurs 8-11:30 & 1-5

WYMORE

P WYMORE PUBLIC LIBRARY*, 116 W F St, 68466. SAN 309-6793. Tel: 402-645-3787. E-mail: wymorelibrary@hotmail.com. Web Site: wymorelibrary.org. *Dir,* Janet Roberts
Founded 1917. Pop 1,841; Circ 16,494
Library Holdings: Bk Vols 15,000; Per Subs 55
Wireless access
Mem of Southeast Library System
Open Mon, Tues & Thurs 11:30-6, Wed 11:30-7, Fri 11:30-5:30
Friends of the Library Group

YORK

P KILGORE MEMORIAL LIBRARY, 520 N Nebraska Ave, 68467-3035. SAN 309-6815. Tel: 402-363-2620. FAX: 402-363-2601. E-mail: kilgore@cityofyork.net. Web Site: libraries.ne.gov/york. *Dir,* Deb Robertson; E-mail: drobertson@cityofyork.net; Staff 5 (MLS 1, Non-MLS 4)
Founded 1885. Pop 7,862; Circ 76,000
Automation Activity & Vendor Info: (Acquisitions) Biblionix/Apollo; (Cataloging) Biblionix/Apollo; (Circulation) Biblionix/Apollo; (ILL) OCLC WorldShare Interlibrary Loan; (OPAC) Biblionix/Apollo
Wireless access
Function: 24/7 Electronic res, 24/7 Online cat
Mem of Southeast Library System
Open Mon-Thurs 10-7, Fri & Sat 10-5
Friends of the Library Group

S NEBRASKA DEPARTMENT OF CORRECTIONS*, Nebraska Correctional Center for Women Library, 1107 Recharge Rd, 68467-8003. SAN 377-1334. Tel: 402-362-3317. FAX: 402-362-3892. *Librn,* Robin Lewis; Staff 6 (Non-MLS 6)
Library Holdings: CDs 43; High Interest/Low Vocabulary Bk Vols 75; Large Print Bks 150; Bk Titles 4,000; Per Subs 25; Spec Interest Per Sub 10
Subject Interests: African-Am culture, Law, Spanish lang mat
Partic in Nebr Institutional Asn for Librs
Restriction: Not open to pub

C YORK COLLEGE*, Levitt Library Learning Center, 1125 E Eighth St, 68467-2699. SAN 309-6807. Tel: 402-363-5703. Circulation Tel: 402-363-5708. Interlibrary Loan Service Tel: 402-363-5706. FAX: 402-363-5685. Web Site: www.york.edu/levitt/index.asp. *Libr Dir,* Ruth Carlock; E-mail: rmcarlock@york.edu; *Asst Dir,* Ramona Ratliff; E-mail: rjratliff@york.edu; *ILL,* Leo Miller; E-mail: leo.miller@york.edu; Staff 3 (MLS 2, Non-MLS 1)
Founded 1956. Enrl 394; Fac 35; Highest Degree: Master
Jul 2016-Jun 2017. Mats Exp $61,642, Books $103, Per/Ser (Incl. Access Fees) $14,397, Other Print Mats $3,620, Electronic Ref Mat (Incl. Access Fees) $29,180. Sal $75,671 (Prof $56,307)
Library Holdings: AV Mats 142; Bks on Deafness & Sign Lang 64; CDs 188; DVDs 102; e-books 211,658; Electronic Media & Resources 113,399; Microforms 19,757; Bk Titles 47,347; Bk Vols 60,013; Per Subs 83; Videos 36
Special Collections: Church History (Restoration Movement); Missions; Yorkana. Oral History
Automation Activity & Vendor Info: (Acquisitions) Koha; (Cataloging) OCLC Connexion; (Circulation) Koha; (ILL) OCLC WorldShare Interlibrary Loan; (OPAC) Koha; (Serials) Koha
Wireless access
Partic in OCLC Online Computer Library Center, Inc
Open Mon, Tues, Thurs (Fall & Spring) 7:45am-9:55am & 10:30-10; Wed 7:45am-9:55am, 10:30-5:30 & 7:30-10; Fri 8-9:55 & 10:30-5; Sat 1-5, Sun 2-5:30 & 7:30-10; Mon-Fri (Summer) 8-5
Friends of the Library Group

YUTAN

P YUTAN PUBLIC LIBRARY, 410 First St, 68073. (Mail add: PO Box 241, 68073-0241), SAN 309-6823. Tel: 402-625-2111. FAX: 402-625-2111. E-mail: yutanlibrary22@gmail.com. Web Site: libraries.ne.gov/yutan. *Dir,* Laurie Van Ackeren; E-mail: lvanackeren@gmail.com; *Asst Dir,* Viki Miller

Founded 1966. Pop 1,350; Circ 5,179
Library Holdings: Bk Vols 6,700
Wireless access
Open Mon 9-1, Tues & Fri 9-3, Wed 3-7, Thurs 9-8, Sat 9-12

NEVADA

Date of Statistics: FY 2019
Population, 2020 U.S. Census: 3,138,259
Population Served by Public Libraries: 3,056,542
Total Holdings in Public Libraries: 5,738,955
Holdings Per Capita: 1.88
Total Public Library Circulation (excluding bookmobiles): 17,396,697
Circulation Per Capita: 5.69
Digital Resources:
Total e-books: 834,038
Total audio items (physical and downloadable units): 558,117
Total video items (physical and downloadable units): 658,464
Total computers for use by the public: 1,465
Total number of public computer sessions: 2,526,052
Total annual wireless sessions: 1,437,836
Income and Expenditures:
Total Public Library Operating Expenditures (including Grants-in-Aid): $100,677,446
Expenditure Per Capita: $32.93
Source of Income: Local Funds, State Grants, Federal LSTA
Number of County & Regional Libraries: County 12, District 9
Number of Bookmobiles in State: 3
State Grants-in-Aid to Public Libraries (FY 2019): $325,226
Information provided courtesy of: Norma Fowler, Library Planning and Development Consultant; Nevada State Library, Archives and Public Records

AMARGOSA VALLEY

P THE AMARGOSA VALLEY LIBRARY*, 829 E Farm Rd, 89020. SAN 320-488X. Tel: 775-372-5340. FAX: 775-372-1188. E-mail: amargosalibrary@gmail.com. Web Site: www.amargosalibrary.com. *Libr Dir,* Leslie Scott; *ILL,* Osvaldo Granados; Staff 3 (Non-MLS 3)
Founded 1977. Pop 1,400
Special Collections: US Document Depository
Subject Interests: Local hist
Automation Activity & Vendor Info: (Cataloging) Follett Software; (Circulation) Follett Software
Wireless access
Open Mon & Fri 10-6, Tues-Thurs 9-5

BEATTY

P BEATTY LIBRARY DISTRICT*, 400 N Fourth St, 89003. (Mail add: PO Box 129, 89003-0129), SAN 309-684X. Tel: 775-553-2257. FAX: 775-553-2257. E-mail: beattylibrary@att.net. Web Site: www.beattylibrarydistrict.org, www.clan.lib.nv.us/polpac/library/clan/beatty.htm. *Dir,* Sharon Jennings; E-mail: spjennin@clan.lib.nv.us; *Libr Asst,* Dianna Smith; Staff 3 (MLS 1, Non-MLS 2)
Founded 1966. Pop 1,060; Circ 6,591
Library Holdings: AV Mats 480; DVDs 795; Large Print Bks 200; Bk Vols 17,129; Per Subs 39; Videos 828
Special Collections: Nevada Coll
Subject Interests: Local hist, Nev
Automation Activity & Vendor Info: (Serials) Innovative Interfaces, Inc
Wireless access
Function: E-Reserves, Electronic databases & coll, ILL available, Internet access, Magnifiers for reading, Mail & tel request accepted, Music CDs, Photocopying/Printing, Prog for adults, Prog for children & young adult, Ref serv available, Spoken cassettes & CDs, Summer reading prog, Tax forms, Telephone ref, VHS videos, Wheelchair accessible
Partic in Information Nevada
Open Mon & Wed 10-4, Tues 12-7, Sat 10-Noon

BOULDER CITY

P BOULDER CITY LIBRARY*, 701 Adams Blvd, 89005-2207. SAN 309-6858. Tel: 702-293-1281. Web Site: bclibrary.org. *Dir,* Kimberly Diehm; E-mail: bcdirector@bclibrary.org; *Asst Dir,* Anne Karr; E-mail: catwoman@bclibrary.org; *Youth Serv Librn,* Jessica Jones; E-mail: jessica@bclibrary.org; *Info Serv, Tech,* Samantha Evangelho; E-mail: tech@bclibrary.org; *Acq & Cat Mgr,* Jill Donahue; E-mail: jill@bclibrary.org; Staff 26 (MLS 5, Non-MLS 21)
Founded 1943. Pop 16,000; Circ 103,787
Library Holdings: AV Mats 4,000; Large Print Bks 6,000; Bk Titles 95,000; Bk Vols 100,000; Per Subs 250; Talking Bks 4,000
Special Collections: Local History Coll
Automation Activity & Vendor Info: (Cataloging) Innovative Interfaces, Inc; (Circulation) Innovative Interfaces, Inc; (ILL) OCLC; (OPAC) Innovative Interfaces, Inc
Wireless access
Function: 24/7 Electronic res, 24/7 Online cat, Adult bk club, Archival coll, Art exhibits, Art programs, Audiobks via web, Bk club(s), Bks on CD, Chess club, Children's prog, Computer training, Computers for patron use, Electronic databases & coll, Family literacy, Free DVD rentals, Holiday prog, Homebound delivery serv, ILL available, Instruction & testing, Internet access, Life-long learning prog for all ages, Magazines, Meeting rooms, Microfiche/film & reading machines, Movies, Music CDs, Online cat, Online ref, Outreach serv, OverDrive digital audio bks, Photocopying/Printing, Preschool outreach, Preschool reading prog, Printer for laptops & handheld devices, Prog for adults, Prog for children & young adult, Ref serv available, Res libr, Scanner, Senior outreach, Spanish lang bks, STEM programs, Story hour, Summer & winter reading prog, Summer reading prog, Tax forms, Teen prog, Telephone ref, Wheelchair accessible, Winter reading prog
Open Mon-Thurs 9-8:30, Fri 9-5, Sat 11-4, Sun (Winter) 1-4

S LAKE MEAD NATIONAL RECREATION AREA LIBRARY*, Alan Bible Visitor Ctr, Intersection of Hwys 93 & 166, 89005. (Mail add: 601 Nevada Hwy, 89005), SAN 309-6874. Tel: 702-293-8990. E-mail: lake_interpretation@nps.gov. Web Site: nps.gov/lake. *Library Contact,* Thomas Valencia; Staff 1 (MLS 1)
Founded 1962
Library Holdings: Bk Titles 1,650
Subject Interests: Amphibians, Archaeology, Botany, Geol, Hist, Indians, Interpretation, Nat Park Serv, Natural hist, Reptiles, Water res
Restriction: Staff use only

CARSON CITY

P CARSON CITY LIBRARY*, 900 N Roop St, 89701. SAN 309-6963. Tel: 775-887-2244. FAX: 775-887-2273. Web Site: www.carsoncitylibrary.org. *Libr Dir,* Tod Colegrove; Tel: 775-283-7591, E-mail: tcolegrove@carson.org; *Access Serv Mgr,* Ermal Reinhart; Tel: 775-283-7595; *Bus Mgr, Project Mgr,* Diane Baker; Tel: 775-887-2244, Ext 7554, E-mail: dbaker@carson.org; *Coll Develop Mgr,* Amy Lauder; Tel: 775-283-7599, E-mail: alauder@carson.org; *Creative Learning Mgr,* Maria Klesta; Tel: 775-283-7593, E-mail: mklesta@carson.org; Staff 20 (MLS 7, Non-MLS 13)
Founded 1966. Pop 75,000; Circ 365,900
Library Holdings: AV Mats 10,000; Bk Vols 125,000; Per Subs 327
Special Collections: Large Print Coll; Nevada Coll
Automation Activity & Vendor Info: (Cataloging) Innovative Interfaces, Inc; (Circulation) Innovative Interfaces, Inc; (ILL) OCLC; (OPAC) Innovative Interfaces, Inc; (Serials) Innovative Interfaces, Inc
Wireless access
Function: 24/7 Electronic res, 24/7 Online cat, Homebound delivery serv
Partic in Information Nevada

Open Mon & Fri 10-6, Tues-Thurs 10-8, Sat 10-4, Sun Noon-4
Friends of the Library Group

S NEVADA DEPARTMENT OF CORRECTIONS*, Warm Springs Correctional Center Library, 3301 E Fifth St, 89701. (Mail add: PO Box 7007, 89702). Tel: 775-684-3000. FAX: 775-684-3051. Web Site: doc.nv.gov/Facilities/WSCC_Facility. *Library Contact,* Christina Evans
Library Holdings: Bk Vols 1,500
Restriction: Staff & inmates only

S NEVADA LEGISLATIVE COUNSEL BUREAU*, Research Library, 401 S Carson St, 89701-4747. Tel: 775-684-6827. Toll Free Tel: 800-992-0973. FAX: 775-684-6400. E-mail: library@lcb.state.nv.us. Web Site: www.leg.state.nv.us/Division/Research/Library. *Legislative Librn,* Teresa Wilt; *Sr Asst Librn,* Stephanie Hegroth Wilcox; Staff 3 (MLS 2, Non-MLS 1)
Founded 1971
Library Holdings: Bk Titles 12,000; Bk Vols 14,500; Per Subs 250
Special Collections: Nevada Legislative History Coll. State Document Depository
Automation Activity & Vendor Info: (Acquisitions) Inmagic, Inc.; (Cataloging) Inmagic, Inc.; (OPAC) Inmagic, Inc.
Open Mon-Fri 8-5
Restriction: Non-circulating

P NEVADA STATE LIBRARY, ARCHIVES & PUBLIC RECORDS, 100 N Stewart St, 89701-4285. SAN 350-2740. Tel: 775-684-3310, 775-684-3360. Circulation Tel: 775-684-3365. FAX: 775-684-3330, 775-684-3371. Web Site: nsla.nv.gov. *State Archivist,* Cynthia Laframboise; E-mail: claframboise@admin.nv.gov; Staff 39 (MLS 9, Non-MLS 30)
Founded 1859
Library Holdings: Bk Vols 67,350; Per Subs 150
Special Collections: Nevada Newspaper Coll (microform, retrospective); US Bureau of the Census Data Center. Oral History; State Document Depository; US Document Depository
Subject Interests: Govt affairs, Nev, Statistics
Automation Activity & Vendor Info: (Acquisitions) Innovative Interfaces, Inc; (Cataloging) Innovative Interfaces, Inc; (Circulation) Innovative Interfaces, Inc; (ILL) Innovative Interfaces, Inc; (Media Booking) Innovative Interfaces, Inc; (OPAC) Innovative Interfaces, Inc; (Serials) Innovative Interfaces, Inc
Wireless access
Publications: Nevada Library Directory & Statistics; Nevada Official Publications; Nevada Records; Silver Lining (Talking Books); State Data Center Report
Partic in Association for Rural & Small Libraries; Information Nevada; OCLC Online Computer Library Center, Inc; Research Libraries Information Network
Branches: 1

P REGIONAL LIBRARY FOR THE BLIND & PHYSICALLY HANDICAPPED, 100 N Stewart St, 89701-4285, SAN 309-6939. Tel: 775-684-3354. Toll Free Tel: 800-922-9334. FAX: 775-684-3355. TDD: 775-687-8338. *Librn,* Hope Williams; Staff 5 (MLS 1, Non-MLS 4)
Founded 1968. Pop 1,907,815
Library Holdings: Bk Titles 45,680; Bk Vols 77,455
Special Collections: Nevada Authors; Nevada Titles
Subject Interests: Gen fiction
Publications: Silver Lining (Newsletter)
Special Services for the Blind - Bks & mags in Braille, on rec, tape & cassette; Braille music coll; Closed circuit TV; Digital talking bk
Open Mon-Fri 8-5

GL NEVADA SUPREME COURT LAW LIBRARY*, Supreme Court Bldg, 201 S Carson St, Ste 100, 89701-4702. SAN 309-6955. Tel: 775-684-1640. FAX: 775-684-1662. Reference E-mail: Reference@nvcourts.nv.gov. Web Site: nvcourts.gov/lawlibrary. *Librn,* Jason Sowards; Tel: 775-684-1671, E-mail: jsowards@nvcourts.nv.gov; Staff 4 (MLS 3, Non-MLS 1)
Founded 1973
Library Holdings: Bk Titles 11,625; Bk Vols 135,896; Per Subs 330
Special Collections: American & English Law. US Document Depository
Automation Activity & Vendor Info: (Cataloging) Innovative Interfaces, Inc; (OPAC) Innovative Interfaces, Inc
Wireless access
Publications: New Titles List
Open Mon-Fri 8-5

J WESTERN NEVADA COMMUNITY COLLEGE*, Library & Media Services, 2201 W College Pkwy, 89703. SAN 350-2805. Tel: 775-445-3229. E-mail: refdesk@wnc.edu. Web Site: library.wnc.edu/home. *Dir,* Ken Sullivan; Tel: 775-445-4246, E-mail: ken.sullivan@wnc.edu; *Librn,* Larry Calkins; *Libr Serv Supvr,* Kristie Gangestad; E-mail: kgangest@wnc.edu; *Circ Spec,* Erich Holcombe; *Media Serv,* Ralph Schilling; Staff 11 (MLS 4, Non-MLS 7)
Founded 1972. Enrl 5,688; Fac 90
Library Holdings: Bk Vols 40,000; Per Subs 180
Automation Activity & Vendor Info: (Acquisitions) Innovative Interfaces, Inc; (Cataloging) Innovative Interfaces, Inc; (Circulation) Innovative Interfaces, Inc; (Course Reserve) Innovative Interfaces, Inc; (ILL) Innovative Interfaces, Inc; (Media Booking) Innovative Interfaces, Inc; (OPAC) Innovative Interfaces, Inc; (Serials) Innovative Interfaces, Inc
Wireless access
Open Mon-Thurs 8-8, Fri 8-5, Sat 11-3
Departmental Libraries:
BECK LIBRARY & MEDIA SERVICES, 160 Campus Way, Fallon, 89406, SAN 372-8420. Tel: 775-423-5330. *Libr Support Spec,* Ron Belbin; E-mail: ron.belbin@wnc.edu
Library Holdings: Bk Vols 7,222; Per Subs 52
Open Mon-Thurs 8:30-8, Fri 8:30-5, Sat 9-1

ELKO

P ELKO-LANDER-EUREKA COUNTY LIBRARY SYSTEM*, Elko County Library, 720 Court St, 89801. SAN 350-283X. Tel: 775-738-3066. FAX: 775-738-8262. Web Site: www.elkocountylibrary.org. *Libr Dir,* Kassie M Antonucci; E-mail: krkincai@elkocountynv.net; *Asst Dir,* Melissa Spence; E-mail: mspence@elkocountynv.net; *Youth Librn,* Holly Whittle; *Ref Librn,* Patrick Dunn; E-mail: pfdunn@elkocountynv.net; *Supvr, Circ,* Annette Robinson; *Cataloger,* Athena Laprade; Staff 37 (MLS 2, Non-MLS 35)
Founded 1922. Pop 59,000; Circ 250,000
Library Holdings: AV Mats 4,000; CDs 500; DVDs 2,000; Bk Titles 180,000; Per Subs 151; Videos 6,000
Special Collections: State Document Depository; US Document Depository
Subject Interests: Mining, Nev
Automation Activity & Vendor Info: (Cataloging) Innovative Interfaces, Inc; (Circulation) Innovative Interfaces, Inc; (ILL) Innovative Interfaces, Inc; (OPAC) Innovative Interfaces, Inc
Wireless access
Function: ILL available
Partic in Information Nevada
Open Mon & Tues 9-8, Wed & Thurs 9-6, Fri & Sat 9-5
Friends of the Library Group
Branches: 9
AUSTIN BRANCH LIBRARY, 88 Main St, Austin, 89310. (Mail add: PO Box 121, Austin, 89310), SAN 350-2864. Tel: 775-964-2428. FAX: 775-964-2426. *Br Asst,* Connie Vaughn; E-mail: cvaughn@elkocountynv.net
Library Holdings: Bk Vols 2,500
Special Collections: Mining; Nevada
Open Mon 1-5, Wed 1-6, Fri 9-Noon
Friends of the Library Group
BATTLE MOUNTAIN BRANCH LIBRARY, 625 S Broad St, Battle Mountain, 89820. (Mail add: PO Box 141, Battle Mountain, 89820-0141), SAN 350-2899. Tel: 775-635-2534. *Br Asst,* Clara Hamilton; E-mail: chamilton@elkocountynv.net
Library Holdings: Bk Vols 5,000
Special Collections: Mining; Nevada
Open Tues & Fri 12-5, Wed 1-6, Thurs 3-8, Sat 10-4
Friends of the Library Group
CARLIN BRANCH LIBRARY, 330 Memory Lane, Carlin, 89822. (Mail add: PO Box 1120, Carlin, 89822-1120), SAN 373-8558. Tel: 775-754-6766. FAX: 775-754-6621. *Br Asst,* Tammy Gregory; E-mail: tgregory@elkocountynv.net
Library Holdings: Bk Vols 2,500
Open Mon & Tues 11-5, Wed 2-8, Thurs & Fri 9-3
Friends of the Library Group
CRESCENT VALLEY BRANCH LIBRARY, Cresent Valley Town Ctr, 5045 Tenabo Ave, Ste 103, Crescent Valley, 89821, SAN 377-757X. Tel: 775-468-0249. *Br Asst,* Sharon Riddle; E-mail: sriddle@elkocountynv.net
Library Holdings: Bk Vols 1,000
Open Mon 10-2:30, Tues & Wed 12:30-5
Friends of the Library Group
EUREKA BRANCH LIBRARY, 80 S Monroe St, Eureka, 89316. (Mail add: PO Box 293, Eureka, 89316-0293), SAN 350-2953. Tel: 775-237-5307. *Br Asst,* Robin Evans; E-mail: revans@elkocountynv.net
Library Holdings: Bk Vols 4,000
Open Tues 10-4, Wed, Fri & Sat 12-6, Thurs 2-8
Friends of the Library Group
JACKPOT BRANCH LIBRARY, 2301 Progressive Rd, Jackpot, 89825. (Mail add: PO Box 530, Jackpot, 89825-0530). Tel: 775-755-2356. *Br Asst,* Leslie Martinez; E-mail: lmartinez@elkocountynv.net
Library Holdings: Bk Vols 20,000
Open Tues-Thurs 2-8, Fri 2-7, Sat 10-5
Friends of the Library Group
TUSCARORA BRANCH LIBRARY, 55 Weed St, Tuscarora, 89834, SAN 350-2988. Tel: 775-756-6597. *Br Asst,* George Aful
Library Holdings: Bk Vols 500
Open Mon-Fri 8-11 & 11:30-2:30, Sat 9am-10am

WELLS BRANCH LIBRARY, 208 Baker St, Wells, 89835. (Mail add: PO Box 691, Wells, 89835-0691), SAN 350-3011. Tel: 775-752-3856. *Br Asst,* Jessica Boyer; E-mail: jboyer@elkocountynv.net
Library Holdings: Bk Vols 6,000
Open Mon-Wed & Fri 11-5, Thurs 1-7
Friends of the Library Group

WEST WENDOVER BRANCH LIBRARY, 590 Camper Dr, West Wendover, 89883. (Mail add: PO Box 5040, West Wendover, 89883-5040), SAN 329-059X. Tel: 775-664-2510. FAX: 775-664-2226. *Br Asst,* Kelly Eveleth; E-mail: keveleth@elkocountynv.net
Library Holdings: Bk Vols 5,000
Open Mon & Wed 12-6, Tues 1-7, Thurs & Fri 11-5
Friends of the Library Group

Bookmobiles: 1. Contact, Kelvin Sanders. Bk vols 5,000

C GREAT BASIN COLLEGE LIBRARY, 1500 College Pkwy, 89801. SAN 309-7005. Tel: 775-327-2122. Interlibrary Loan Service Tel: 775-327-2124. E-mail: gbc-library@gbcnv.edu. Web Site: www.gbcnv.edu/library. *Libr Mgr,* Position Currently Open; *Ref Librn,* Eric Walsh; Tel: 775-327-2125, E-mail: eric.walsh@gbcnv.edu; *Libr Tech II,* David Stirm; E-mail: david.stirm@gbcnv.edu. Subject Specialists: *Career res, Educ res,* Eric Walsh; *Govt publ,* David Stirm; Staff 2 (MLS 1, Non-MLS 1)
Founded 1967. Fac 85; Highest Degree: Bachelor
Library Holdings: DVDs 200; e-books 300,000; Bk Vols 65,892; Per Subs 36
Special Collections: American Indian; Basque; Nevada. US Document Depository
Subject Interests: Juv lit
Automation Activity & Vendor Info: (Acquisitions) Ex Libris Group; (Circulation) Ex Libris Group; (OPAC) Ex Libris Group
Wireless access
Open Mon-Fri 9-5

S NEVADA YOUTH TRAINING CENTER LIBRARY*, 100 Youth Center Rd, 89801. (Mail add: PO Box 459, 89803). Tel: 775-738-7182. Web Site: dcfs.nv.gov/Programs/JJS/Nevada_Youth_Training_Center. *Library Contact,* Nocona Hassett
Library Holdings: Bk Titles 11,070; Per Subs 37
Automation Activity & Vendor Info: (Acquisitions) Follett Software; (Cataloging) Follett Software; (Circulation) Follett Software; (OPAC) Follett Software
Wireless access
Function: Prog for children & young adult
Restriction: Open to students, fac & staff

S NORTHEASTERN NEVADA MUSEUM LIBRARY*, 1515 Idaho St, 89801. SAN 309-6998. Tel: 775-738-3418. E-mail: archives@museumelko.org. Web Site: www.museumelko.org. *Archivist,* Toni Mendive
Founded 1968
Library Holdings: Bk Titles 2,500; Bk Vols 4,000
Special Collections: Area Newspaper Coll (1869-present), bd, micro; Elko Coll; Jarbidge, Lamoille, Wells, Metropolis & Area Railroads Coll, Pioneer vehicles; Tuscarora Coll
Subject Interests: Anthrop, Hist, Natural hist, NE Nev hist
Publications: Northeastern Nevada Historical Society Quarterly
Open Tues-Fri 9-5

ELY

NEVADA DEPARTMENT OF CORRECTIONS

S ELY STATE PRISON - LAW LIBRARY*, 4569 N State Rte 490, 89301. (Mail add: PO Box 1989, 89301). Tel: 775-289-8800, Ext 2264. FAX: 775-289-1263. E-mail: pio@doc.nv.gov.
Library Holdings: Bk Vols 3,000
Open Mon-Fri 8-4:30

S ELY STATE PRISON LIBRARY*, 4569 N State Rte 490, 89301. (Mail add: Mountain High School, Ave C, 89301). Tel: 775-289-8800, Ext 2244. FAX: 775-289-1273. Web Site: www.doc.nv.gov. *Library Contact,* Ron Schafer
Library Holdings: Bk Vols 14,000; Per Subs 10

P WHITE PINE COUNTY LIBRARY*, 950 Campton, 89301-1965. SAN 350-3046. Tel: 775-293-6900. Web Site: whitepinecounty.net/index.aspx?NID=284. *Dir,* Lori Romero; E-mail: lromero@clan.lib.nv.us; *Ch,* Hilary Peck
Founded 1961. Pop 10,600; Circ 51,680
Library Holdings: Bk Vols 42,000; Per Subs 72
Special Collections: Local History (White Pine County Historical Society), photog; Nevada Materials. Oral History
Automation Activity & Vendor Info: (Cataloging) Innovative Interfaces, Inc; (Circulation) Innovative Interfaces, Inc; (OPAC) Innovative Interfaces, Inc
Wireless access
Open Mon-Thurs 9-6, Fri 9-1, Sat 10-2
Friends of the Library Group

FALLON

P CHURCHILL COUNTY LIBRARY*, 553 S Maine St, 89406-3387. SAN 309-7021. Tel: 775-423-7581. FAX: 775-423-7766. E-mail: info@churchillcountylibrary.org. Web Site: www.churchillcountylibrary.org. *Libr Dir,* Carol Lloyd; E-mail: celloyd@churchillcountylibrary.org; *Ad,* Diane F Wargo; *Ch,* Jeslyn MacDiarmid; *Tech Serv Librn,* Joseph Salsman
Founded 1932. Pop 22,580; Circ 152,046
Library Holdings: e-journals 50; Bk Vols 90,843; Per Subs 45
Special Collections: Nevada History
Automation Activity & Vendor Info: (Cataloging) Innovative Interfaces, Inc; (Circulation) Innovative Interfaces, Inc; (OPAC) Innovative Interfaces, Inc
Wireless access
Function: 24/7 Electronic res, 24/7 Online cat
Publications: Footnotes (Newsletter)
Partic in Information Nevada
Open Mon, Thurs & Fri 9-6, Tues & Wed 9-8, Sat 9-5
Friends of the Library Group

GABBS

P GABBS COMMUNITY LIBRARY*, 602 Third St, 89409. (Mail add: PO Box 206, 89409), SAN 377-3434. Tel: 775-285-2686. *Dir,* Jan Basinger
Founded 1944. Pop 300
Library Holdings: Bks on Deafness & Sign Lang 5; High Interest/Low Vocabulary Bk Vols 75; Large Print Bks 400; Bk Titles 20,000; Bk Vols 25,000; Per Subs 15; Talking Bks 200; Videos 800
Special Collections: Nevada Coll. Oral History
Wireless access
Open Tues, Wed & Thurs Noon-3
Friends of the Library Group

HAWTHORNE

P MINERAL COUNTY LIBRARY*, 110 First St, 89415. (Mail add: PO Box 1390, 89415-1390), SAN 350-3135. Tel: 775-945-2778. Web Site: www.mineralcountynv.us/departments/library.php. *Dir,* Courtney Oberhansli; E-mail: coberhansli@mineralcountynv.org; *Asst Dir,* Kathy Kachelries; E-mail: kkachelries@mineralcountynv.org; *Circ Librn,* Katharine Pyatt; E-mail: kpyatt@mineralcountynv.org
Founded 1955. Pop 4,000; Circ 36,000
Library Holdings: Audiobooks 920; Large Print Bks 1,260; Bk Vols 30,600; Per Subs 20; Videos 1,720
Special Collections: State of Nevada History Coll
Automation Activity & Vendor Info: (Cataloging) Innovative Interfaces, Inc; (Circulation) Innovative Interfaces, Inc; (OPAC) Innovative Interfaces, Inc
Wireless access
Partic in Information Nevada
Open Mon-Fri 10-6, Sat 11-4
Friends of the Library Group

Branches: 1

MINA-LUNING LIBRARY, 908 B St, Mina, 89422. (Mail add: PO Box 143, Mina, 89422-0143), SAN 350-316X. Tel: 775-573-2505. FAX: 775-573-2505. *Br Mgr,* Carol Jean Souza
Library Holdings: Large Print Bks 340; Bk Vols 7,000; Videos 410
Special Collections: State of Nevada History Coll
Open Mon, Wed & Fri 1-5
Friends of the Library Group

HENDERSON

P HENDERSON DISTRICT PUBLIC LIBRARIES*, Henderson Library, 280 S Green Valley Pkwy, 89012. Tel: 702-492-7252. FAX: 702-492-1711. Web Site: hendersonlibraries.com. *Exec Dir,* Marcie Smedley; E-mail: mlsmedley@hendersonlibraries.com; *Asst Dir,* Gayle Hornaday; Tel: 702-492-6582, E-mail: gmhornaday@hendersonlibraries.com
Founded 1944. Pop 213,670; Circ 772,527
Library Holdings: Audiobooks 18,948; e-books 18,568; Electronic Media & Resources 44,453; Per Subs 163; Videos 29,460
Automation Activity & Vendor Info: (Cataloging) Innovative Interfaces, Inc; (Circulation) Innovative Interfaces, Inc; (OPAC) Innovative Interfaces, Inc
Wireless access
Friends of the Library Group

Branches: 2

JAMES I GIBSON LIBRARY, 100 W Lake Mead Pkwy, 89015, SAN 309-7056. Tel: 702-565-8402. Reference Tel: 702-564-9261. FAX: 702-565-8832. *Br Mgr,* Candace Kingsley; E-mail: clkingsley@hdpl.org
Library Holdings: Bk Vols 138,500
Open Mon-Thurs 9:30-8, Fri & Sat 9:30-5
Friends of the Library Group

GREEN VALLEY LIBRARY, 2797 N Green Valley Pkwy, 89014. Tel: 702-207-4260. *Br Mgr,* Stephen Platt; E-mail: smplatt@hdpl.org
Open Tues-Thurs 9:30-8, Fri & Sat 9:30-6

C NEVADA STATE COLLEGE*, Marydean Martin Library, 1125 Nevada State Dr, 89002. Tel: 702-992-2800. E-mail: library@nsc.edu. Web Site: nsc.edu/library. *Dir, Libr Serv,* Nathaniel King; Tel: 702-992-2806, E-mail: nathaniel.king@nsc.edu; Staff 1 (MLS 1)
Founded 2003. Enrl 2,000; Highest Degree: Bachelor
Library Holdings: Bk Vols 20,000; Per Subs 83; Videos 120
Automation Activity & Vendor Info: (Cataloging) Innovative Interfaces, Inc; (Circulation) Innovative Interfaces, Inc; (Course Reserve) Innovative Interfaces, Inc; (OPAC) Innovative Interfaces, Inc
Wireless access
Open Mon-Thurs 7:30am-9pm, Fri 7:30-5, Sat 9-5

S SPERLING-KRONBERG-MACK HOLOCAUST RESOURCE CENTER LIBRARY*, Midbar Kodesh Temple, 1940 Pasco Verde, 89012. SAN 375-7757. Tel: 702-433-0005. Web Site: www.lvhresourcecenter.com. *Libr Consult,* Susan H Dubin; E-mail: sdubin@offtheshelflibraryservices.net; Staff 1 (Non-MLS 1)
Founded 1980
Library Holdings: DVDs 120; Bk Titles 5,000; Videos 300
Special Collections: Leopold Page Coll
Subject Interests: Holocaust
Automation Activity & Vendor Info: (Acquisitions) OPALS (Open-source Automated Library System); (Cataloging) OPALS (Open-source Automated Library System); (Circulation) OPALS (Open-source Automated Library System); (Course Reserve) OPALS (Open-source Automated Library System); (ILL) OPALS (Open-source Automated Library System); (Media Booking) OPALS (Open-source Automated Library System); (OPAC) OPALS (Open-source Automated Library System); (Serials) OPALS (Open-source Automated Library System)
Wireless access
Restriction: Open by appt only

S TITANIUM METALS CORPORATION OF AMERICA*, Henderson Technical Library, PO Box 2128, 89009. SAN 323-4371. Tel: 702-564-2544, Ext 396. FAX: 702-564-9038. *Library Contact,* Courtney Sumpter
Library Holdings: Bk Titles 20,000; Per Subs 75
Restriction: Not open to pub

INCLINE VILLAGE

C SIERRA NEVADA COLLEGE*, Prim Library, 999 Tahoe Blvd, 89450-9500. SAN 309-7064. Tel: 775-881-7501, 775-881-7511. FAX: 775-832-6134. E-mail: library@sierranevada.edu. Web Site: www.sierranevada.edu. *Librn,* Dani Porter-Lansky; E-mail: dporterlansky@sierranevada.edu; *Libr Tech,* Marsha Tejeda; Tel: 775-881-7412, E-mail: mtejeda@sierranevada.edu; Staff 2 (MLS 1, Non-MLS 1)
Founded 1969. Enrl 500; Fac 30; Highest Degree: Bachelor
Library Holdings: Bk Titles 20,000; Bk Vols 23,000; Per Subs 100
Subject Interests: Calif, Environ, Nev, Sierra maps, Teacher, Visual arts
Automation Activity & Vendor Info: (Cataloging) Innovative Interfaces, Inc; (Circulation) Innovative Interfaces, Inc; (OPAC) Innovative Interfaces, Inc
Wireless access
Function: ILL available
Partic in Information Nevada
Open Mon-Thurs 8am-9pm, Fri 8-4, Sat 11-4, Sun Noon-9

LAS VEGAS

GL CLARK COUNTY LAW LIBRARY, 309 S Third St, Ste 400, 89101. (Mail add: PO Box 557340, 89155-7340), SAN 309-7099. Tel: 702-455-4696. E-mail: AskInfo@ClarkCountyNV.Gov. Web Site: www.clarkcountynv.gov/government/departments/law_library. *Dir,* Chanteyl Hasse; *Law Librn,* Tanner Henley; *Law Librn,* Justin Iverson; *Law Librn,* Summer Youngquest; Staff 9 (Non-MLS 9)
Founded 1923
Library Holdings: Bk Vols 84,000; Per Subs 420
Special Collections: Nevada Coll
Subject Interests: Treatises
Wireless access
Open Mon-Fri 8-5

C COLLEGE OF SOUTHERN NEVADA*, Charleston Campus, 6375 W Charleston Blvd, W10I, 89146. SAN 309-7188. Tel: 702-651-5716. Circulation Tel: 702-651-5723. Interlibrary Loan Service Tel: 702-651-5007. Reference Tel: 702-651-5729. FAX: 702-651-5718. Interlibrary Loan Service FAX: 702-651-5725. Reference FAX: 702-651-5003. Web Site: sites.csn.edu/library. *Interim Dir,* Caprice Roberson; Tel: 702-651-5863, E-mail: caprice.roberson@csn.edu; *Digital Serv Librn,* Emily King; Tel: 702-651-7511, E-mail: emily.king@csn.edu; *Instruction & Ref Librn,* Ted Chodock; Tel: 702-651-5509, E-mail: ted.chodock@csn.edu; *Instruction & Ref Librn,* Christine Shore; Tel: 702-651-5069, E-mail: christine.shore@csn.edu; *Tech Serv Librn,* Lynn Best; Tel: 702-651-5527, E-mail: lynn.best@csn.edu; *Libr Tech,* Corey Cohen; Tel: 702-651-5781; *Libr Tech,* Maggie Slomka; Tel: 702-651-5882, E-mail: maggie.slomka@csn.edu; Staff 27 (MLS 12, Non-MLS 15)
Founded 1972. Enrl 22,000; Highest Degree: Bachelor
Library Holdings: Bk Titles 96,704; Bk Vols 98,481; Per Subs 399
Subject Interests: Computer sci, Criminal justice, Culinary arts, Dental hygiene, Electronics, Fire sci, Gaming, Hort, Nursing, Resorts
Automation Activity & Vendor Info: (Acquisitions) Innovative Interfaces, Inc; (Circulation) Innovative Interfaces, Inc; (ILL) Innovative Interfaces, Inc; (Serials) Innovative Interfaces, Inc
Wireless access
Function: Ref serv available
Open Mon-Thurs 7:30am-10:30pm, Fri 7:30-5, Sat 9-5
Departmental Libraries:
CHEYENNE CAMPUS, 3200 E Cheyenne Ave, C2A, North Las Vegas, 89030, SAN 376-8805. Tel: 702-651-4419. FAX: 702-643-4812. *Ref Librn,* Susan Gregg; Tel: 702-651-4622, E-mail: susan.gregg@csn.edu; *Ref Librn,* Jack Sawyer; Tel: 702-651-4444, E-mail: jack.sawyer@csn.edu; *Circ,* Lazara Gonzalez; Tel: 702-651-4014, E-mail: lazara.gonzalez@csn.edu
HENDERSON CAMPUS, 700 S College Dr, H1A, Henderson, 89002, SAN 321-6071. Tel: 702-651-3066. Reference Tel: 702-651-3039. FAX: 702-651-3513. *Ref Librn,* Paula Grenell; E-mail: paula.grenell@csn.edu; *Ref Librn,* Jeanette Jones; *Circ,* Cleo Wilson; E-mail: cleo.wilson@csn.edu

S DESERT RESEARCH INSTITUTE*, Sulo & Aileen Maki Research Library, 755 E Flamingo Rd, 89119-7363. Tel: 702-862-5405. FAX: 702-862-5542. Web Site: www.dri.edu/library. *Research Librn,* Karen Stewart; E-mail: karen.j.stewart@dri.edu
Library Holdings: Bk Vols 3,000
Wireless access

P LAS VEGAS-CLARK COUNTY LIBRARY DISTRICT, Windmill Library & District Headquarters, 7060 W Windmill Lane, 89113. Tel: 702-507-6030, 702-734-7323. FAX: 702-507-6064. Administration E-mail: administration@lvccld.org. Web Site: www.lvccld.org. *Exec Dir,* Kelvin Watson; *Br Mgr,* Theron Nissen
Circ 909,791
Wireless access
Open Mon-Thurs 10-8, Fri-Sun 10-6
Branches: 26
BLUE DIAMOND LIBRARY, 14 Cottonwood Dr, Blue Diamond, 89004. (Mail add: PO Box 40, Blue Diamond, 89004-0040), SAN 350-3259. Tel: 702-875-4295. FAX: 702-875-4095. *Br Assoc,* Nina Mata; Staff 2 (Non-MLS 2)
Founded 1970. Circ 9,017
BUNKERVILLE LIBRARY, Ten W Virgin St, Bunkerville, 89007. (Mail add: PO Box 7208, Bunkerville, 89007-7208), SAN 350-3283. Tel: 702-346-5238. FAX: 702-346-5784. *Br Assoc,* Carolynn Leavitt; Staff 2 (Non-MLS 2)
Founded 1973. Circ 19,032
CENTENNIAL HILLS LIBRARY, 6711 N Buffalo Dr, 89131, SAN 325-4224. Tel: 702-507-6100. FAX: 702-507-6147. *Br Mgr,* Tammy Giesking
Founded 2009. Circ 935,867
CITY OF LAS VEGAS DETENTION FACILITY, 3100 E Stewart Ave, 89101. Tel: 702-384-4887. FAX: 702-671-3971. *Adminr,* Tom Olsen; Staff 1 (Non-MLS 1)
CLARK COUNTY DETENTION FACILITY, 330 S Casino Center Blvd, 89101, SAN 350-3453. Tel: 702-384-4887. FAX: 702-671-3971. *Librn,* Tom Olsen
Subject Interests: Circulating paperbacks, Fed law bk vols, Nev
CLARK COUNTY LIBRARY, 1401 E Flamingo Rd, 89119, SAN 350-3348. Tel: 702-507-3400. FAX: 702-507-3482. *Br Mgr,* Marie Nicholl-Lynam
Founded 1966. Circ 988,212
Special Collections: Government Documents; Southern Nevada Nonprofit Information Center
Open Mon-Thurs 10-8, Fri-Sun 10-6
EAST LAS VEGAS LIBRARY, 2851 E Bonanza Rd, 89101, SAN 350-3437. Tel: 702-507-3500. FAX: 702-507-3540. *Br Mgr,* Thomas Olson
Founded 1973. Circ 541,046
Special Collections: Nevada Data Center; State Publication Distribution Center. State Document Depository; US Document Depository
Subject Interests: Gaming, Local hist
Open Mon-Thurs 10-8, Fri-Sun 10-6

ENTERPRISE LIBRARY, 25 E Shelbourne Ave, 89123, SAN 377-6565. Tel: 702-507-3760. FAX: 702-507-3779. *Br Mgr,* Salvador Avila
Founded 1996. Circ 696,976
Open Mon-Thurs 10-8, Fri-Sun 10-6
GOODSPRINGS LIBRARY, 365 W San Pedro Ave, Goodsprings, 89019. (Mail add: PO Box 667, Goodsprings, 89019), SAN 350-3372. Tel: 702-874-1366. FAX: 702-874-1335. *Br Assoc,* Jacques Alimusa
Founded 1968. Circ 14,597
INDIAN SPRINGS LIBRARY, 715 Gretta Lane, Indian Springs, 89018. (Mail add: PO Box 628, Indian Springs, 89018-0628), SAN 350-3402. Tel: 702-879-3845. FAX: 702-879-5227. *Br Assoc,* Marie Reed
Founded 1969. Circ 31,237
LAUGHLIN LIBRARY, 2840S Needles Hwy, Laughlin, 89029. (Mail add: PO Box 32225, Laughlin, 89028-2225). Tel: 702-507-4070. FAX: 702-507-4067. *Br Mgr,* Karen Lassen
Founded 1987. Circ 199,493
Friends of the Library Group
MEADOWS LIBRARY, 251 W Boston Ave, 89102, SAN 378-1755. Tel: 702-474-0023. *Regional Br Serv Dir,* Mario Aguilar
Founded 1994. Circ 47,455
Subject Interests: Spanish lang
MESQUITE LIBRARY, 121 W First North St, Mesquite, 89027-4759, SAN 350-3550. Tel: 702-507-4312. Administration Tel: 702-507-4080. FAX: 702-346-5224, 702-346-5788. *Br Assoc,* Judith Sargent
Founded 1973. Circ 194,666
Library Holdings: High Interest/Low Vocabulary Bk Vols 28,000
MOAPA TOWN LIBRARY, 1340 E Hwy 168, Moapa, 89025. (Mail add: PO Box 250, Moapa, 89025-0250), SAN 374-4132. Tel: 702-864-2438. FAX: 702-864-2467. *Br Assoc,* Jan Johnson
Founded 1988. Circ 26,844
MOAPA VALLEY LIBRARY, 36 N Moapa Valley Blvd, Overton, 89040-0397. (Mail add: PO Box 397, Overton, 89040-0397), SAN 350-3461. Tel: 702-397-2690. FAX: 702-397-2698. *Br Assoc,* April Heath
Founded 1967. Circ 146,769
MOUNT CHARLESTON LIBRARY, 75 Ski Chalet Pl, HCR 38, Box 269, 89124, SAN 350-347X. Tel: 702-872-5585. FAX: 702-872-5631. *Br Assoc,* Raychel Lendis
Founded 1980. Circ 5,784
RAINBOW LIBRARY, 3150 N Buffalo Dr, 89128, SAN 325-4240. Tel: 702-507-3710. FAX: 702-507-3730. *Br Mgr,* Sufa Anderson
Founded 1985. Circ 1,024,639
Open Mon-Thurs 10-7, Fri-Sun 10-6
SAHARA WEST LIBRARY, 9600 W Sahara Ave, 89117. Tel: 702-507-3630. FAX: 702-507-3673. *Br Mgr,* Kim Clanton-Green
Founded 1992. Circ 1,025,356
Open Mon-Thurs 10-8, Fri-Sun 10-6
SANDY VALLEY LIBRARY, 650 W Quartz Ave, HCR 31 Box 377, Sandy Valley, 89019, SAN 322-5828. Tel: 702-723-5333. FAX: 702-723-1010. *Br Mgr,* Deborah Wadley
Founded 1984. Circ 39,997
SEARCHLIGHT LIBRARY, 200 Michael Wendell Way, Searchlight, 89046. (Mail add: PO Box 98, Searchlight, 89046-0098), SAN 350-3496. Tel: 702-297-1442. FAX: 702-297-1782. *Br Assoc,* Rebecca Wallace
Founded 1969. Circ 25,666
SPRING VALLEY LIBRARY, 4280 S Jones Blvd, 89103, SAN 325-4208. Tel: 702-507-3820. FAX: 702-507-3838. *Br Mgr,* Nikki Winslow
Founded 1985. Circ 961,092
Open Mon-Thurs 10-8, Fri-Sun 10-6
SUMMERLIN LIBRARY & PERFORMING ARTS CENTER, 1771 Inner Circle Dr, 89134, SAN 374-4140. Tel: 702-507-3860. FAX: 702-507-3880. *Br Mgr,* Gregory C Carr
Founded 1993. Circ 565,353
Open Mon-Thurs 10-8, Fri-Sun 10-6
SUNRISE LIBRARY, 5400 Harris Ave, 89110, SAN 350-3526. Tel: 702-507-3900. FAX: 702-507-3914. *Br Mgr,* Timothy McDonald
Founded 1987. Circ 887,167
Open Mon-Thurs 10-8, Fri-Sun 10-6
WEST CHARLESTON LIBRARY, 6301 W Charleston Blvd, 89146-1124, SAN 350-3313. Tel: 702-507-3940. FAX: 702-507-3950. *Br Mgr,* Florence Jakus
Founded 1973. Circ 739,428
Subject Interests: Health sci, Med
Open Mon-Thurs 10-8, Fri-Sun 10-6
WEST LAS VEGAS LIBRARY, 951 W Lake Mead Blvd, 89106, SAN 350-3585. Tel: 702-507-3980. FAX: 702-507-3996. *Br Mgr,* Leo Seguro
Founded 1973. Circ 349,983
Special Collections: African American Experience
Subject Interests: Local hist
Open Mon-Thurs 10-8, Fri-Sun 10-6
WHITNEY LIBRARY, 5175 E Tropicana Ave, 89122, SAN 370-9280. Tel: 702-507-4010. FAX: 702-507-4026. *Br Mgr,* Ann Lagumina
Founded 1994. Circ 866,652
Open Mon-Thurs 10-8, Fri-Sun 10-6

S LAS VEGAS FAMILYSEARCH GENEALOGY LIBRARY*, Family History Library, 509 S Ninth St, 89101. SAN 309-7080. Tel: 702-382-9695. E-mail: nv_lasvegas@ldsmail.net. Web Site: www.lvfamilysearchlibrary.org. *Co-Dir,* Sister Charlotte Openshaw; *Co-Dir,* Ken Openshaw; *Asst Dir,* Sister Sandy Jackson; Staff 85 (Non-MLS 85)
Founded 1965
Library Holdings: Bk Vols 10,000
Special Collections: Local Histories (Nevada); State & County History (US & Canada)
Subject Interests: Family hist
Open Mon & Fri 9-5, Tues-Thurs 9-8, Sat 9-3

S NATIONAL SECURITY TECHNOLOGIES*, Nuclear Testing Archive, 755 E Flamingo Rd, 89119. (Mail add: PO Box 98521, M/S 400, 89193-8521), SAN 373-4684. Tel: 702-794-5106. FAX: 702-794-5107. E-mail: cic@nv.doe.gov. Web Site: www.nnss.gov/pages/resources/NuclearTestingArchive.html. *Mgr,* Martha DeMarre
Founded 1981
Library Holdings: Bk Vols 420,000; Videos 102
Special Collections: Human Radiation Experiments Coll; Nuclear Testing Archive
Subject Interests: Nuclear weapons testing
Open Mon-Fri 9-4:30

S NEVADA STATE MUSEUM, Cahlan Research Library, 309 S Valley View Blvd, 89107. Tel: 702-486-5205, 702-822-8751. FAX: 702-486-5172. E-mail: infonsmlv@nevadaculture.org. Web Site: www.lasvegasnvmuseum.org/research/cahlan-research-library/. *Dir,* Hollis J Gillespie; E-mail: hgillespie@nevadaculture.org; Staff 1 (MLS 1)
Founded 1982
Library Holdings: Bk Titles 2,200
Special Collections: Clark County Civil Defense Coll, pamphlets, bus recs 1930s-1950s; Helen J Stewart Coll, papers; John Cahlan & Florence Lee Jones-Cahlan, papers
Wireless access
Function: For res purposes, Ref & res, Res libr
Partic in Information Nevada
Restriction: Authorized patrons, Circulates for staff only, Researchers by appt only

M SUNRISE HEALTH SYSTEM LIBRARY*, 3186 S Maryland Pkwy, 89109. SAN 309-7153. Tel: 702-731-8777. Toll Free FAX: 877-567-1075. Web Site: www.sunrisecme.com. *Med Librn,* Amber Carter; E-mail: amber@sunrisecme.com; Staff 3 (Non-MLS 3)
Founded 1975
Library Holdings: Bk Titles 1,000; Per Subs 1,500
Special Collections: Ciba slides
Subject Interests: Clinical med
Wireless access
Partic in National Network of Libraries of Medicine Region 5
Open Mon-Fri 8-4:30

M UNIVERSITY MEDICAL CENTER OF SOUTHERN NEVADA*, Medical Library, 2040 W Charleston Blvd, Ste 500, 89102. SAN 309-7145. Tel: 702-383-2368. FAX: 702-383-2369. Web Site: www.umcsn.com.
Founded 1960
Library Holdings: Bk Titles 2,000; Bk Vols 18,000; Per Subs 1,000
Subject Interests: Health sci, Med
Automation Activity & Vendor Info: (Cataloging) LibraryWorld, Inc; (Circulation) LibraryWorld, Inc; (Serials) LibraryWorld, Inc
Function: For res purposes
Partic in Nev Libr Asn
Open Mon-Fri 7:30-4

C UNIVERSITY OF NEVADA, LAS VEGAS LIBRARIES*, Lied Library, 4505 Maryland Pkwy, Box 457001, 89154-7001. SAN 350-3615. Tel: 702-895-2111. Interlibrary Loan Service Tel: 702-895-2152. Reference Tel: 702-895-2100. Administration Tel: 702-895-2286. FAX: 702-895-2287. Circulation FAX: 702-895-2281. Web Site: www.library.unlv.edu. *Dean, Univ Libr,* Maggie Farrell; *Assoc Dean,* Scott Smith; *Dir, Spec Coll,* Peter Michel; Tel: 702-895-2243, E-mail: peter.michel@unlv.edu; *Dir, Technology,* Jason Vaughan; Tel: 702-895-2179, E-mail: jason.vaughan@unlv.edu; *Head, Coll Mgt,* Cory Tucker; Staff 38 (MLS 34, Non-MLS 4)
Founded 1957. Enrl 24,000; Fac 1,405; Highest Degree: Doctorate
Library Holdings: AV Mats 800; CDs 900; Bk Vols 30,800; Per Subs 1,500; Talking Bks 560; Videos 300
Special Collections: Architectural Drawings (Martin Stern Coll); Gaming; Union Pacific Railroad Coll; Urban & Regional Historical Coll. State Document Depository; US Document Depository
Automation Activity & Vendor Info: (Cataloging) Innovative Interfaces, Inc; (Circulation) Innovative Interfaces, Inc; (Course Reserve) Innovative

Interfaces, Inc; (ILL) Innovative Interfaces, Inc; (OPAC) Innovative Interfaces, Inc; (Serials) Innovative Interfaces, Inc
Wireless access
Function: Res libr
Publications: Communications; Ex Libris (Newsletter); TechNotes
Partic in Greater Western Library Alliance; OCLC Research Library Partnership
Open Mon-Thurs 7:30am-Midnight, Fri 7:30-7, Sat 9-6, Sun 11am-Midnight
Departmental Libraries:
ARCHITECTURE STUDIES LIBRARY, Paul B Sogg Architecture Bldg, 4505 S Maryland Pkwy, Box 454049, 89154-4049. Tel: 702-895-1959. FAX: 702-895-1975. Web Site: www.library.unlv.edu/arch. *Libr Tech II,* Steven Baskin; E-mail: steven.baskin@unlv.edu; Staff 10 (MLS 2, Non-MLS 8)
Open Mon-Thurs 8-8, Fri 8-6, Sun 1-6
MUSIC LIBRARY, 4505 S Maryland Pkwy, Box 457002, 89154-7002. Tel: 702-895-2541. Web Site: library.unlv.edu/music. *Fine Arts Librn,* Kate Lambaria; E-mail: kate.lambaria@unlv.edu; Staff 1 (MLS 1)
Library Holdings: AV Mats 3,000; CDs 6,000; Music Scores 26,000; Videos 1,000
Open Mon-Thurs 9-7, Fri 9-5:30, Sun 1-5
TEACHER DEVELOPMENT & RESOURCES LIBRARY, 4505 S Maryland Pkwy, Box 453009, 89154-3009. Tel: 702-895-3593. FAX: 702-895-3528. Web Site: www.library.unlv.edu/tdrl. *Head of Libr,* Amanda Melilli; Tel: 702-895-1963, E-mail: amanda.melilli@unlv.edu; Staff 4 (MLS 1, Non-MLS 3)
Subject Interests: Children's lit
Open Mon-Thurs 8-8. Fri 8-5, Sat 9-5

CL WIENER-ROGERS LAW LIBRARY, William S Boyd School of Law, 4505 Maryland Pkwy, 89154. (Mail add: PO Box 451080, 89154-1080). Tel: 702-895-2400. Reference Tel: 702-895-2420. Administration Tel: 702-895-2327. FAX: 702-895-2410. Administration FAX: 702-895-2416. Web Site: law.unlv.edu/law-library. *Dir,* Jeanne Frazier Price; Tel: 702-895-2404, E-mail: jeanne.price@unlv.edu; *Assoc Dir,* David McClure; *Law Libr Operations Mgr,* Cindy Claus; *Head, Coll,* Jennifer L Gross; *Tech Serv Librn,* Jim Fitch; *Circ Supvr,* Beverly Galloway.
Subject Specialists: *Law,* Jeanne Frazier Price
Founded 1997
Library Holdings: Bk Titles 200,000; Bk Vols 350,000
Open Mon-Thurs 7:30am-11pm, Fri 7:30am-9pm, Sat 9-9, Sun 10am-11pm
Restriction: Circ limited

LOVELOCK

S NEVADA DEPARTMENT OF CORRECTIONS*, Lovelock Correctional Center Library, 1200 Prison Rd, 89419. Tel: 775-273-1300. FAX: 775-273-4277. Web Site: www.doc.nv.gov. *Library Contact,* Position Currently Open
Library Holdings: Bk Vols 1,000
Open Mon-Fri 7:30-4

P PERSHING COUNTY LIBRARY*, 1125 Central Ave, 89419. (Mail add: PO Box 781, 89419-0781), SAN 350-3674. Tel: 775-273-2216. FAX: 775-273-0421. Web Site: www.pershingcountynv.gov/community/county_library. *Libr Dir,* Kathie Brinkerhoff; E-mail: kbrinkerhoff@pershingcountynv.gov; Staff 3 (MLS 1, Non-MLS 2)
Founded 1930. Pop 6,753; Circ 25,048
Jul 2020-Jun 2021 Income $325,208, State $1,516, Federal $4,065, County $316,612, Locally Generated Income $3,015. Mats Exp $26,906, Books $22,003, Per/Ser (Incl. Access Fees) $621, AV Mat $3,388, Presv $894. Sal $149,870
Library Holdings: Audiobooks 2,188; DVDs 1,476; Large Print Bks 1,616; Microforms 101; Bk Vols 36,713; Per Subs 21
Special Collections: Nevada Coll
Automation Activity & Vendor Info: (Acquisitions) Innovative Interfaces, Inc; (Cataloging) Innovative Interfaces, Inc; (Circulation) Innovative Interfaces, Inc; (OPAC) Innovative Interfaces, Inc
Wireless access
Function: 24/7 Electronic res, 24/7 Online cat, Activity rm, Art exhibits, Audiobks on Playaways & MP3, Audiobks via web, Bks on CD, Children's prog, Computer training, Computers for patron use, Digital talking bks, Electronic databases & coll, Free DVD rentals, ILL available, Internet access, Magazines, Meeting rooms, Microfiche/film & reading machines, Online cat, OverDrive digital audio bks, Photocopying/Printing, Preschool reading prog, Prog for adults, Prog for children & young adult, Scanner, Spanish lang bks, Story hour, Summer reading prog, Tax forms, Wheelchair accessible, Workshops
Partic in Information Nevada; Nev Libr Asn
Open Mon, Tues & Fri 10-5, Wed & Thurs 10-6
Friends of the Library Group

MINDEN

P DOUGLAS COUNTY PUBLIC LIBRARY, Minden Library, 1625 Library Lane, 89423. (Mail add: PO Box 337, 89423), SAN 350-3739. Tel: 775-782-9841. FAX: 775-782-5754. Administration FAX: 775-782-6766. E-mail: info@douglas.lib.nv.us. Web Site: library.douglascountynv.gov. *Libr Dir,* Amy Dodson; E-mail: adodson@douglas.lib.nv.us; *Coll Develop Librn,* Luise Davis; E-mail: ldavis@douglas.lib.nv.us; *Tech Serv Coordr,* Karen Fitzgerald; E-mail: kfitzgerald@douglas.lib.nv.us; Staff 14.3 (MLS 5, Non-MLS 9.3)
Founded 1967. Pop 49,500; Circ 185,000
Jul 2014-Jun 2015 Income (Main & Associated Libraries) $1,515,000, County $1,500,000, Locally Generated Income $15,000. Mats Exp $164,000, Books $105,000, Per/Ser (Incl. Access Fees) $9,000, AV Mat $30,000, Electronic Ref Mat (Incl. Access Fees) $20,000. Sal $650,000 (Prof $350,000)
Library Holdings: Bk Titles 81,000; Bk Vols 114,030; Per Subs 140; Talking Bks 835
Special Collections: Carson Valley History (Van Sickle Coll), ms, micro; Nevada Historical Society. Municipal Document Depository; Oral History
Automation Activity & Vendor Info: (Acquisitions) Innovative Interfaces, Inc; (Cataloging) Innovative Interfaces, Inc; (Circulation) Innovative Interfaces, Inc; (ILL) Innovative Interfaces, Inc; (OPAC) Innovative Interfaces, Inc; (Serials) Innovative Interfaces, Inc
Wireless access
Function: After school storytime, Art exhibits, Audio & video playback equip for onsite use, Audiobks via web, Bks on cassette, Bks on CD, CD-ROM, Children's prog, Computer training, Computers for patron use, Digital talking bks, Electronic databases & coll, Equip loans & repairs, Free DVD rentals, Genealogy discussion group, Home delivery & serv to seniorr ctr & nursing homes, Homebound delivery serv, ILL available, Large print keyboards, Magnifiers for reading, Mail & tel request accepted, Music CDs, Online cat, Orientations, Outreach serv, Photocopying/Printing, Preschool outreach, Prog for adults, Prog for children & young adult, Ref serv available, Senior computer classes, Senior outreach, Spoken cassettes & CDs, Spoken cassettes & DVDs, Story hour, Summer reading prog, Tax forms, Teen prog, Telephone ref, VHS videos, Wheelchair accessible, Workshops
Publications: Douglas County's Architectural Heritage (Local historical information)
Special Services for the Deaf - Assistive tech; Bks on deafness & sign lang; High interest/low vocabulary bks; Videos & decoder
Special Services for the Blind - Assistive/Adapted tech devices, equip & products; Computer with voice synthesizer for visually impaired persons; Home delivery serv
Open Mon-Wed 10-7, Thurs & Fri 10-6, Sat 10-5
Friends of the Library Group
Branches: 1
LAKE TAHOE, 233 Warrior Way, Zephyr Cove, 89448. (Mail add: PO Box 4770, Stateline, 89449-4770), SAN 350-3763. Tel: 775-588-6411. Administration Tel: 775-782-9841. FAX: 775-588-6464. *Br Head,* Position Currently Open
Pop 50,000; Circ 185,000
Library Holdings: Bk Vols 32,696
Special Collections: Lake Tahoe Heritage Coll
Function: ILL available, Photocopying/Printing, Prog for children & young adult, Summer reading prog, Telephone ref
Open Wed 11-7, Thurs-Sat 9-5

NORTH LAS VEGAS

P NORTH LAS VEGAS LIBRARY DISTRICT*, 2250 Las Vegas Blvd, Ste 133, 89030. SAN 309-7196. Tel: 702-633-1070. FAX: 702-649-2576. Web Site: www.nlvld.org. *Dir,* Forrest Lewis; E-mail: lewisf@cityofnorthlasvegas.com; *Assoc Librn,* Liz Lucchesi
Founded 1962
Library Holdings: Bk Vols 80,000; Per Subs 40
Automation Activity & Vendor Info: (Cataloging) Innovative Interfaces, Inc - Sierra; (Circulation) Innovative Interfaces, Inc - Sierra; (OPAC) Innovative Interfaces, Inc - Sierra
Wireless access
Function: 24/7 Electronic res, 24/7 Online cat, Bilingual assistance for Spanish patrons, Children's prog, Computers for patron use, Electronic databases & coll, Free DVD rentals, Homework prog, ILL available, Internet access, Magazines, Online cat, Outreach serv, Photocopying/Printing, Preschool reading prog, Prog for children & young adult, Summer reading prog
Open Mon-Thurs 10:30-8
Friends of the Library Group
Branches: 2
ALEXANDER LIBRARY, 1755 W Alexander Rd, 89032. Tel: 702-633-2880. FAX: 702-399-9813. *Br Mgr,* Garett Dacay; E-mail: dacayg@cityofnorthlasvegas.com; *Pub Serv Librn,* Andrea Schreiber; E-mail: schreibera@cityofnorthlasvegas.com

Library Holdings: CDs 420; DVDs 2,500; Bk Vols 56,000; Per Subs 30; Talking Bks 300
Open Wed & Thurs 10:30-8, Fri & Sat 9-6
Friends of the Library Group
ALIANTE LIBRARY, 2400 Deer Springs Way, 89084. Tel: 702-839-2980. FAX: 702-839-5707. *Br Mgr,* Shelly Alexander; E-mail: alexanders@cityofnorthlasvegas.com; *Family Serv Librn,* Patrick Hinrichs; E-mail: hinrichsp@cityofnorthlasvegas.com
Open Mon-Thurs 10:30-8, Fri & Sat 9-6
Friends of the Library Group

PAHRUMP

P PAHRUMP COMMUNITY LIBRARY*, 701 E St, 89048. SAN 309-720X. Tel: 775-727-5930. FAX: 775-727-6209. Web Site: www.pahrumplibrary.org. *Dir,* Susan Wonderly; E-mail: director@pahrumplibrary.org; *Asst Dir,* Mandy Caffeo; E-mail: assistdir@pahrumplibrary.org; *Head, Youth Serv,* Alysha Wogee; E-mail: children@pahrumplibrary.org; *Ref Librn,* Amy Bruno; E-mail: reference@pahrumplibrary.org
Pop 30,000; Circ 90,000
Library Holdings: Bk Titles 50,000; Per Subs 54
Special Collections: Nevada Coll
Automation Activity & Vendor Info: (Cataloging) Follett Software; (Circulation) Follett Software; (OPAC) Follett Software
Wireless access
Open Mon-Thurs 9-6, Fri & Sat 10-5
Friends of the Library Group

PIOCHE

P LINCOLN COUNTY LIBRARY*, 63 Main St, 89043. (Mail add: PO Box 330, 89043-0330), SAN 309-7218. Tel: 775-962-5244. FAX: 775-962-5243. E-mail: piochelibrary@yahoo.com. *Dir,* Sharon Faehling; E-mail: sfaehling@lcturbonet.com
Pop 4,130; Circ 20,000
Library Holdings: Bk Vols 47,829
Automation Activity & Vendor Info: (Cataloging) Winnebago Software Co; (Circulation) Winnebago Software Co
Wireless access
Partic in Information Nevada; Nev Libr Asn
Open Mon, Wed & Thurs 11-4, Tues Noon-6
Branches: 2
ALAMO BRANCH, 100 S First Ave, Alamo, 89001. (Mail add: PO Box 239, Alamo, 89001-0239). Tel: 775-725-3343. FAX: 775-725-3344. E-mail: alamolibrary2017@yahoo.com. *Library Contact,* Laci Fiatoa
Library Holdings: Bk Vols 13,000
Open Mon 1-5:30, Tues-Thurs 11-4
CALIENTE BRANCH, 100 Depot Ave, Caliente, 89008. (Mail add: PO Box 306, Caliente, 89008-0306), SAN 324-1084. Tel: 775-726-3104. E-mail: calientelibrary@yahoo.com. *Library Contact,* Cheryl Lewis
Library Holdings: Bk Vols 12,000
Open Mon, Tues & Thurs 11-4, Wed 1-5:30
Bookmobiles: 1

RENO

S CHURCH OF JESUS CHRIST OF LATTER-DAY SAINTS*, Reno Family History Center, 4751 Neil Rd, 89502. SAN 370-6656. Tel: 775-240-5588. E-mail: NV_Reno@ldsmail.net. Web Site: www.familysearch.org/wiki/en/Reno_Nevada_Family_History_Center. *Dir,* Kathy Dougherty
Library Holdings: CDs 250; Microforms 8,000; Bk Titles 5,000; Per Subs 2
Special Collections: Genealogy Coll
Wireless access
Open Tues & Wed 10-5, Thurs 10-2 or by appointment

S DESERT RESEARCH INSTITUTE, Patrick Squires Library, 2215 Raggio Pkwy, 89512-1095. SAN 309-7323. Tel: 775-674-7042. FAX: 775-674-7183. Web Site: www.dri.edu/education/libraries. *Libr Mgr,* John Ford, Jr; E-mail: john.ford@dri.edu; Staff 2 (MLS 1, Non-MLS 1)
Founded 1977
Library Holdings: Bk Vols 13,350
Subject Interests: Atmospheric sci, Environ sci
Wireless access
Function: For res purposes
Publications: New Books; Newsletter
Open Mon-Fri 8-5

S NEVADA HISTORICAL SOCIETY*, Research Library, 1650 N Virginia St, 89503. SAN 309-7250. Tel: 775-688-1190, Ext 227. FAX: 775-688-2917. Web Site: www.nvhistoricalsociety.org/research-library. *Curator of Ms,* Sheryln L Hayes-Zorn; E-mail: shayeszorn@nevadaculture.org; *Libr Tech,* Karalea Clough; E-mail: Kclough@nevadaculture.org
Founded 1904
Library Holdings: Bk Titles 30,000; Per Subs 260
Special Collections: Nevada & the Great Basin Coll, ms, photogs; Nevada History Coll, ephemera, ms, maps, photogs. Oral History; US Document Depository
Subject Interests: Communication in Nev, Gambling, Genealogy, Lumber, Mining, Transportation, Water, Western US
Publications: Nevada Historical Society Quarterly
Open Tues-Sat 12-4

J TRUCKEE MEADOWS COMMUNITY COLLEGE*, Elizabeth Sturm Library, 7000 Dandini Blvd, 89512-3999. SAN 320-6947. Tel: 775-674-7600. Reference Tel: 775-674-7602. FAX: 775-673-8231. Web Site: www.tmcc.edu/library. *Dir, Libr Serv,* Position Currently Open; *Ref Librn,* John Fitzsimmons; Tel: 775-674-7609, E-mail: jfitzsimmons@tmcc.edu; *Ref Librn,* Neil Siegel; Tel: 775-674-7608, E-mail: nsiegel@tmcc.edu; Charlotte Lee; E-mail: clee@tmcc.edu; Staff 13 (MLS 5, Non-MLS 8)
Founded 1973. Enrl 6,210; Fac 175; Highest Degree: Associate
Library Holdings: AV Mats 8,097; Bks on Deafness & Sign Lang 61; Braille Volumes 6; CDs 700; DVDs 1,000; e-journals 35; Music Scores 6; Bk Titles 47,560; Per Subs 105; Videos 1,000
Subject Interests: Career educ, Folklore, Health educ, Indust, Tech fields
Automation Activity & Vendor Info: (Acquisitions) Ex Libris Group; (Cataloging) Ex Libris Group; (Circulation) Ex Libris Group; (Course Reserve) Ex Libris Group; (ILL) Ex Libris Group; (OPAC) Ex Libris Group; (Serials) Ex Libris Group
Wireless access
Special Services for the Deaf - Bks on deafness & sign lang
Special Services for the Blind - Accessible computers; Braille bks; Computer with voice synthesizer for visually impaired persons; Copier with enlargement capabilities; Networked computers with assistive software; Screen reader software; Ultimate talking dictionary
Open Mon-Tues (Summer) 7:30-7, Wed & Fri 7:30-5; Mon-Fri (Winter) 8-5
Departmental Libraries:
NELL J REDFIELD LEARNING RESOURCE CENTER, Technical Institute, 475 Edison Way, 89502-4103. Tel: 775-857-4990. FAX: 775-857-4976. *Libr Tech,* Avis Andrulli; E-mail: aandrulli@tmcc.edu
Library Holdings: Bks on Deafness & Sign Lang 25; e-journals 4,000; Bk Vols 300; Per Subs 20

L UNITED STATES COURTS FOR THE NINTH CIRCUIT LIBRARY*, Bruce R Thompson US Courthouse & Fed Bldg, 400 S Virginia St, Rm 705, 89501. SAN 372-3410. Tel: 775-686-5776. Web Site: www.ca9.uscourts.gov/library. *Librn,* Shannon Lynch; E-mail: shannon_lynch@lb9.uscourts.gov; Staff 1 (MLS 1)
Library Holdings: Bk Titles 1,102; Bk Vols 22,000
Restriction: Authorized patrons, Internal circ only, Not open to pub

C UNIVERSITY OF NEVADA-RENO*, Mathewson-IGT Knowledge Center, 1664 N Virginia St, Mailstop 0322, 89557-0322. SAN 350-3828. Tel: 775-682-5684. Circulation Tel: 775-682-5625. Interlibrary Loan Service Tel: 775-682-5636. Information Services Tel: 775-682-5657. FAX: 775-784-4529. Circulation FAX: 775-327-2181. Interlibrary Loan Service FAX: 775-784-1751. Web Site: library.unr.edu. *Dean, Libr & Teaching & Learning Tech,* Kathlin L Ray; E-mail: kray@unr.edu; *Asst Dean, Admin Serv,* Janita Jobe; Tel: 775-682-5688, E-mail: jobe@unr.edu; *Asst Dean, Coll & Knowledge Access Serv,* Steven R Harris; Tel: 775-682-5671, E-mail: stevenharris@unr.edu; *Access Serv, Outreach Serv, Spec Coll & Basque Libr,* Maggie Ressel; Tel: 775-682-5653, E-mail: ressel@unr.edu; *Acq, Electronic Res,* Paoshan Yue; Tel: 775-682-5599; *Cat & Metadata,* Emily Boss; Tel: 775-682-5614, E-mail: emilyboss@unr.edu; *Develop,* Robin Monteith; Tel: 775-682-5656, E-mail: robinmonteith@unr.edu; *Digital Media Tech,* Mark Gandolfo; Tel: 775-682-9299, E-mail: gandolfo@unr.edu; *Discovery Serv,* Molly Beisler; Tel: 775-682-5602, E-mail: abeisler@unr.edu; *Res Serv,* Ann Medaille; Tel: 775-682-5600, E-mail: amedaille@unr.edu; Staff 46 (MLS 25, Non-MLS 21)
Founded 1886. Enrl 22,209; Fac 792; Highest Degree: Doctorate
Special Collections: Basque Studies; Nevada & the Great Basin; Women in the West
Automation Activity & Vendor Info: (Acquisitions) Innovative Interfaces, Inc - Sierra; (Cataloging) Innovative Interfaces, Inc - Sierra; (Circulation) Innovative Interfaces, Inc - Sierra; (Course Reserve) Innovative Interfaces, Inc - Sierra; (Discovery) ProQuest; (ILL) Innovative Interfaces, Inc - Sierra; (Media Booking) Innovative Interfaces, Inc - Sierra; (OPAC) Innovative Interfaces, Inc - Sierra; (Serials) Innovative Interfaces, Inc - Sierra
Wireless access
Publications: Friends of the University Library Newsletter (Biannually); Knowledge Matters (Quarterly); Recently in the KC

Partic in National Network of Libraries of Medicine Region 5; OCLC Online Computer Library Center, Inc; OCLC Research Library Partnership
Friends of the Library Group
Departmental Libraries:
DELAMARE LIBRARY, 1664 N Virginia St, MS 262, 89557-0262. Tel: 775-784-6945. FAX: 775-784-6949. *Head Librn,* Tod Colegrove; Tel: 775-682-5644, E-mail: pcolegrove@unr.edu. Subject Specialists: *Physics,* Tod Colegrove; Staff 3 (MLS 3)
Founded 1997. Highest Degree: Doctorate
Special Collections: US Geological Survey. US Document Depository
Subject Interests: Computer sci, Earth sci, Engr, Geog, Maps
Friends of the Library Group

CM UNIVERSITY OF NEVADA-RENO*, Savitt Medical Library, Pennington Medical Education Bldg, 1664 N Virginia St, 89557. SAN 350-3976. Tel: 775-784-4625. FAX: 775-784-4489. E-mail: savitt@medicine.nevada.edu. Web Site: library.unr.edu/savitt. *Dir,* Mary Shultz; E-mail: mshultz@med.unr.edu; *Head, Outreach Serv,* Terry Henner; E-mail: thenner@med.unr.edu; *Clinical Librn,* Alexander Lyubechansky; E-mail: alexl@med.unr.edu; *Ref Librn, Web Librn,* Michelle Rachal; E-mail: mrachal@med.unr.edu; *Libr Office Mgr,* Melanie England; E-mail: mengland@med.unr.edu; *Libr Tech,* Jenny Costa; E-mail: costaj@unr.edu; *Bibliog Serv,* Bonnie Ragains; E-mail: bhragains@med.unr.edu; *ILL/Doc Delivery Serv,* Norman Huckle; E-mail: mhuckle@med.unr.edu; Staff 9 (MLS 2, Non-MLS 7)
Founded 1978. Highest Degree: Doctorate
Library Holdings: e-books 41; e-journals 3,417; Bk Titles 13,631; Bk Vols 72,180; Per Subs 3,443
Special Collections: Nevada Medical Archives; Sons of Italy Birth Defects & Genetics Coll
Subject Interests: Audiology, Consumer health, Med, Pub health, Speech pathology
Wireless access
Function: Doc delivery serv, Health sci info serv, Homebound delivery serv, ILL available, Internet access, Outside serv via phone, mail, e-mail & web, Ref serv available, Telephone ref, Wheelchair accessible
Open Mon-Thurs (Winter) 7:30am-10pm, Fri 8-6, Sat 9-5, Sun 1-10; Mon-Thurs (Summer) 8-8, Fri 8-5, Sat & Sun 1-5

GL WASHOE COUNTY LAW LIBRARY, 75 Courth St, Rm 101, 89501. (Mail add: PO Box 30083, Courthouse, 89520-3083), SAN 309-7293. Tel: 775-328-3250. FAX: 775-328-3441. E-mail: lawlib@washoecounty.us. Web Site: www.washoecourts.com/LawLibrary. *Law Librn,* Sara Bates; *Ref Librn,* Myndi Clive; *Tech Serv Librn,* Judy Chalmers; Staff 6 (MLS 3, Non-MLS 3)
Founded 1915
Library Holdings: Bk Titles 5,099; Bk Vols 52,755; Per Subs 315
Special Collections: General Law Library (Nevada Law, California Law Coll). US Document Depository
Automation Activity & Vendor Info: (Cataloging) SirsiDynix
Publications: Library Acquisitions Lists
Partic in Nev Educ Online Network; Research Libraries Information Network
Open Mon & Fri 8-5, Tues, Wed & Thurs 8-7, Sat 10-5
Friends of the Library Group

P WASHOE COUNTY LIBRARY SYSTEM*, 301 S Center St, 89501-2102. SAN 350-4069. Interlibrary Loan Service Tel: 775-327-8333. Administration Tel: 775-327-8341. Administration FAX: 775-327-8392. E-mail: library@washoecounty.us. Web Site: www.washoecountylibrary.us. *Dir,* Jeff Scott; E-mail: jscott@washoecounty.us; *Asst Libr Dir,* Joan Dalusung; E-mail: jdalusung@washoecounty.us; Staff 26 (MLS 13, Non-MLS 13)
Founded 1904. Pop 427,704
Special Collections: State Document Depository; US Document Depository
Subject Interests: Gambling, Literacy, Nev hist
Automation Activity & Vendor Info: (Acquisitions) ByWater Solutions; (Cataloging) ByWater Solutions; (Circulation) ByWater Solutions; (OPAC) ByWater Solutions; (Serials) ByWater Solutions
Wireless access
Function: Adult bk club, Art exhibits, Audiobks via web, Bk club(s), Bks on CD, CD-ROM, Children's prog, Computer training, Computers for patron use, Electronic databases & coll, Free DVD rentals, Govt ref serv, Holiday prog, ILL available, Microfiche/film & reading machines, Music CDs, Online cat, Online ref, OverDrive digital audio bks, Photocopying/Printing, Preschool outreach, Prog for adults, Prog for children & young adult, Ref serv available, Serves people with intellectual disabilities, Spoken cassettes & CDs, Story hour, Summer & winter reading prog, Summer reading prog, Tax forms, Teen prog, Telephone ref, Wheelchair accessible
Publications: Annual Report; Branch Monthly Calendars; Library Newsletter (Monthly); Listing of Branches (Reference guide)
Partic in Coop Libr Agency for Syst & Servs
Special Services for the Deaf - High interest/low vocabulary bks; Staff with knowledge of sign lang
Special Services for the Blind - Large print bks
Friends of the Library Group
Branches: 12
DOWNTOWN RENO LIBRARY, 301 S Center St, 89501. Tel: 775-327-8300. Circulation Tel: 775-327-8301. Reference Tel: 775-327-8312. FAX: 775-327-8390. *Mgr,* Scottie Wallace; Staff 16 (MLS 4, Non-MLS 12)
Special Collections: State Document Depository; US Document Depository
Function: 24/7 Electronic res, Activity rm, Archival coll, Art exhibits, Audiobks via web, Bilingual assistance for Spanish patrons, Bk club(s), Bks on CD, Children's prog, Computer training, Computers for patron use, E-Readers, Electronic databases & coll, Free DVD rentals, Govt ref serv, ILL available, Internet access, Life-long learning prog for all ages, Magazines, Magnifiers for reading, Mail & tel request accepted, Mango lang, Meeting rooms, Microfiche/film & reading machines, Movies, Music CDs, Online cat, Online ref, Outside serv via phone, mail, e-mail & web, OverDrive digital audio bks, Photocopying/Printing, Prog for adults, Prog for children & young adult, Ref & res, Ref serv available, Scanner, Spanish lang bks, Spoken cassettes & CDs, Spoken cassettes & DVDs, Story hour, Summer reading prog, Telephone ref, Wheelchair accessible
Open Mon-Fri 10-6, Sat & Sun 10-2
Friends of the Library Group
DUNCAN-TRANER COMMUNITY LIBRARY, 1650 Carville Dr, 89512, SAN 374-7131. Tel: 775-333-5134. FAX: 775-333-5076. *Actg Mgr,* Sarah Jaeck
Open Mon, Tues & Thurs 3-6, Wed 2:30-6, Sun 1-5
Friends of the Library Group
GERLACH COMMUNITY LIBRARY, 555 E Sunset Blvd, Gerlach, 89412, SAN 371-9782. Tel: 775-557-2326. FAX: 775-557-2450. *Mgr,* Position Currently Open
Library Holdings: Bk Vols 6,607
Friends of the Library Group
INCLINE VILLAGE LIBRARY, 845 Alder Ave, Incline Village, 89451, SAN 350-4093. Tel: 775-832-4130. FAX: 775-832-4180. *Mgr,* Pam Rasmussen; Staff 8 (MLS 2, Non-MLS 6)
Library Holdings: Bk Vols 37,023
Special Collections: Lake Tahoe Coll
Function: Activity rm, Art exhibits, Audiobks via web, Bi-weekly Writer's Group, Bks on CD, Children's prog, Computer training, Computers for patron use, Electronic databases & coll, Family literacy, Free DVD rentals, Games & aids for people with disabilities, Holiday prog, ILL available, Large print keyboards, Life-long learning prog for all ages, Magazines, Magnifiers for reading, Mango lang, Meeting rooms, Microfiche/film & reading machines, Movies, Music CDs, Online cat, Online info literacy tutorials on the web & in blackboard, Online ref, Outreach serv, Outside serv via phone, mail, e-mail & web, OverDrive digital audio bks, Photocopying/Printing, Preschool outreach, Preschool reading prog, Printer for laptops & handheld devices, Prog for adults, Prog for children & young adult, Ref serv available, Scanner, Senior computer classes, Senior outreach, Spanish lang bks, Spoken cassettes & CDs, Story hour, Study rm, Summer reading prog, Teen prog, Telephone ref, Visual arts prog, Wheelchair accessible, Workshops, Writing prog
Open Mon, Wed & Fri 11-6, Tues 11-7
Restriction: In-house use for visitors, Non-resident fee
Friends of the Library Group
NORTH VALLEYS LIBRARY, 1075 N Hills Blvd, No 340, 89506, SAN 350-4158. Tel: 775-972-0281. FAX: 775-971-3046. *Managing Librn,* Jonnica Bowen
Open Tues, Thurs & Fri 10-6, Wed 10-7, Sat 1-4
Friends of the Library Group
NORTHWEST RENO LIBRARY, 2325 Robb Dr, 89523, SAN 374-7123. Tel: 775-787-4100. FAX: 775-747-7845. *Managing Librn,* Kristin Reinke
Library Holdings: Bk Vols 94,487
Special Collections: Holocaust Education. State Document Depository; US Document Depository
Subject Interests: Nev
Open Mon, Tues, Thurs & Fri 10-6, Wed 10-7, Sat 10-5
Friends of the Library Group
SENIOR CENTER LIBRARY, 1155 E Ninth St, 89512, SAN 350-4115. Tel: 775-328-2586. FAX: 775-785-4610. *Managing Librn,* Scottie Wallace
Open Mon-Fri 9-1
Friends of the Library Group
SIERRA VIEW LIBRARY, 4001 S Virginia St, 89502, SAN 329-6385. Tel: 775-827-3232. FAX: 775-827-8792. *Managing Librn,* John Crockett
Founded 1987
Open Mon-Fri 10-6, Sat 10-5
Friends of the Library Group

SOUTH VALLEYS LIBRARY, 15650A Wedge Pkwy, 89511, SAN 373-5001. Tel: 775-851-5190. FAX: 775-851-5188. *Mgr,* Julie Ullman; Staff 16 (MLS 2, Non-MLS 14)
Library Holdings: Bk Vols 60,072
Function: 24/7 Electronic res, 24/7 Online cat, Adult bk club, Art exhibits, Bks on CD, Children's prog, Computers for patron use, Electronic databases & coll, Family literacy, Free DVD rentals, ILL available, Internet access, Large print keyboards, Life-long learning prog for all ages, Magazines, Mango lang, Meeting rooms, Movies, Music CDs, Online cat, Outreach serv, OverDrive digital audio bks, Photocopying/Printing, Preschool outreach, Printer for laptops & handheld devices, Prog for adults, Prog for children & young adult, Ref serv available, Scanner, Spanish lang bks, Story hour, Study rm, Summer reading prog, Wheelchair accessible
Open Mon, Tues, Thurs & Fri 10-6, Wed 10-7, Sat 10-5
Friends of the Library Group

SPANISH SPRINGS LIBRARY, 7100A Pyramid Lake Hwy, Sparks, 89436-6669. Tel: 775-424-1800. FAX: 775-424-1840. *Libr Mgr,* Julie Machado; Staff 12 (MLS 2, Non-MLS 10)
Library Holdings: Bk Vols 69,199
Function: 24/7 Online cat, Accelerated reader prog, Activity rm, Adult bk club, Art exhibits, Audio & video playback equip for onsite use, Audiobks via web, Bk club(s), Bks on CD, Children's prog, Computers for patron use, E-Readers, Electronic databases & coll, Family literacy, Free DVD rentals, Games & aids for people with disabilities, Holiday prog, ILL available, Internet access, Large print keyboards, Magazines, Magnifiers for reading, Mail & tel request accepted, Mango lang, Meeting rooms, Movies, Music CDs, Online cat, Outreach serv, OverDrive digital audio bks, Photocopying/Printing, Preschool outreach, Preschool reading prog, Prog for adults, Prog for children & young adult, Ref serv available, Scanner, Senior outreach, Serves people with intellectual disabilities, Spanish lang bks, Spoken cassettes & CDs, Spoken cassettes & DVDs, Story hour, Study rm, Summer reading prog, Tax forms, Teen prog, Telephone ref, Wheelchair accessible, Writing prog
Open Mon, Wed & Thurs 10-6, Tues 10-7, Sun 10-5
Friends of the Library Group

SPARKS LIBRARY, 1125 12th St, Sparks, 89431, SAN 350-4123. Tel: 775-352-3200. FAX: 775-352-3207. *Managing Librn,* Corinne Dickman; Staff 18 (MLS 2, Non-MLS 16)
Founded 1932
Special Collections: Auto Repair Manual Coll, classic-current; Rail City Coll, railroads & rails
Function: 24/7 Online cat, Adult bk club, Art exhibits, Audiobks via web, Bi-weekly Writer's Group, Bks on CD, Children's prog, Computer training, Computers for patron use, E-Readers, Electronic databases & coll, Free DVD rentals, Holiday prog, ILL available, Internet access, Life-long learning prog for all ages, Magazines, Magnifiers for reading, Mango lang, Meeting rooms, Microfiche/film & reading machines, Movies, Music CDs, Online cat, Outreach serv, OverDrive digital audio bks, Photocopying/Printing, Preschool reading prog, Prog for adults, Prog for children & young adult, Ref serv available, Scanner, Spanish lang bks, Story hour, Summer reading prog, Tax forms, Telephone ref, Wheelchair accessible
Special Services for the Blind - Talking bks
Open Mon-Wed & Fri 10-6, Thurs 10-7, Sat 10-5
Restriction: Circulates for staff only
Friends of the Library Group

VERDI COMMUNITY LIBRARY, 270 Bridge St, Verdi, 89439, SAN 371-9790. Tel: 775-345-8104. FAX: 775-345-8106. *Managing Librn,* Kristin Reinke; Staff 2 (Non-MLS 2)
Open Tues & Fri 3-6, Wed 2:30-6
Friends of the Library Group

ROUND MOUNTAIN

P SMOKY VALLEY LIBRARY DISTRICT*, Round Mountain Public Library, 73 Hadley Circle, 89045. (Mail add: PO Box 1428, 89045-1428). Tel: 775-377-2215. FAX: 775-377-2699. Web Site: www.svld.net. *Co-Dir,* Jeanne Bleecker; E-mail: jeanneb@svld.net; *Co-Dir,* Andrea Madziarek; E-mail: andream@svld.net; Staff 6 (Non-MLS 6)
Pop 1,841; Circ 60,608
Jul 2019-Jun 2020 Income (Main & Associated Libraries) $994,759, State $47,955, County $918,337, Locally Generated Income $19,509. Mats Exp $183,838. Sal $536,898 (Prof $420,000)
Library Holdings: Audiobooks 2,000; Braille Volumes 22; CDs 2,651; e-books 784; Large Print Bks 200; Bk Titles 30,000; Per Subs 3
Automation Activity & Vendor Info: (Cataloging) Follett Software; (Circulation) Follett Software; (Media Booking) Innovative Interfaces, Inc
Wireless access
Function: 24/7 Online cat, Accelerated reader prog, Art exhibits, Audiobks via web, Bilingual assistance for Spanish patrons, Bks on CD, Children's prog, Computers for patron use, Digital talking bks, Distance learning, Electronic databases & coll, Free DVD rentals, Holiday prog, Homework prog, ILL available, Internet access, Laminating, Mango lang, Meeting rooms, Music CDs, Notary serv, Online cat, Online ref, Photocopying/Printing, Printer for laptops & handheld devices, Prog for children & young adult, Scanner, Story hour, Summer reading prog, Tax forms, Wheelchair accessible
Open Mon-Fri 8-6
Friends of the Library Group
Branches: 1

MANHATTAN BRANCH, 555 W Mineral St, Manhattan, 89022. (Mail add: PO Box 95, Manhattan, 89022-0095). Tel: 775-487-2326. FAX: 775-487-2433. *Libr Asst,* Phyllis Cook; Tel: 775-487-2326, E-mail: phyllisc@svld.net
Pop 120; Circ 1,500
Library Holdings: Audiobooks 200; DVDs 2,000; Bk Vols 4,000; Per Subs 3
Function: Music CDs, Online ref, Photocopying/Printing, Tax forms, VHS videos, Wheelchair accessible
Open Wed, Fri & Sat 10-3, Thurs 2-7

SILVERPEAK

P ESMERALDA COUNTY PUBLIC LIBRARIES, Silverpeak Library, Ten Montezuma St, 89047. (Mail add: PO Box 128, 89047-0128). Tel: 775-937-2215. FAX: 775-937-2215. Web Site: www.accessesmeralda.com/county_offices/library.php, www.esmeraldacountylibraries.org. *Dir,* Nicole White; E-mail: nwhite@esmeraldacountynv.org
Library Holdings: Bk Vols 6,000
Automation Activity & Vendor Info: (Cataloging) Innovative Interfaces, Inc; (Circulation) Innovative Interfaces, Inc; (OPAC) Innovative Interfaces, Inc
Wireless access
Open Tues-Thurs 11-6
Branches: 2

FISH LAKE LIBRARY, Hwy 264 Bluebird Lane, Dyer, 89010. (Mail add: PO Box 105, Dyer, 89010-0105), SAN 309-703X. Tel: 775-572-3311. FAX: 775-572-3311. Web Site: www.accessesmeralda.com/fish_lake_valley.php. *Librn,* Sheila Stover; E-mail: sstover@esmeraldacountynv.org
Circ 8,900
Library Holdings: Bk Vols 6,000
Special Collections: Bilingual Coll; Nevada Local History; Spanish Coll
Partic in Information Nevada
Open Thurs-Sat 9-4

GOLDFIELD PUBLIC LIBRARY, Corner of Crook & Fourth St, Goldfield, 89013. (Mail add: PO Box 430, Goldfield, 89013-0430), SAN 309-7048. Tel: 775-485-3236. FAX: 775-485-3236. *Librn,* Amanda Elsea; E-mail: aelsea@esmeraldacountynv.org
Founded 1976. Pop 558
Library Holdings: Bk Vols 8,000
Open Tues 2-8, Wed-Fri 3-8

TONOPAH

S CENTRAL NEVADA MUSEUM & HISTORICAL SOCIETY*, 1900 Logan Field Rd, 89049. (Mail add: PO Box 326, 89049-0326), SAN 373-241X. Tel: 775-482-9676. FAX: 775-482-5423. E-mail: cnmuseum@citlink.net. Web Site: www.tonopahnevada.com/CentralNevadaMuseum.html. *Pres,* Allen Metscher; E-mail: metscher@citlink.net; Staff 2 (Non-MLS 2)
Founded 1981
Library Holdings: Bk Titles 2,000; Videos 200
Special Collections: Central Nevada History Coll. Oral History
Function: Audio & video playback equip for onsite use, Bus archives, CD-ROM, Photocopying/Printing, VHS videos, Wheelchair accessible
Open Tues-Sat 9-5
Restriction: Restricted access

P TONOPAH LIBRARY DISTRICT*, 167 S Central St, 89049. (Mail add: PO Box 449, 89049-0449). Tel: 775-482-3374. FAX: 775-482-5143. E-mail: tonopahlibrary@hotmail.com. Web Site: www.tonopahnevada.com/tonopahdistrictlibrary.html. *Librn,* Dianne Ryals
Circ 14,823
Library Holdings: DVDs 300; Bk Vols 9,679; Talking Bks 2,387
Special Collections: Topographic Maps
Subject Interests: Geol, Mining
Automation Activity & Vendor Info: (Acquisitions) Innovative Interfaces, Inc; (Cataloging) Innovative Interfaces, Inc; (Circulation) Innovative Interfaces, Inc; (OPAC) Innovative Interfaces, Inc
Wireless access
Partic in Information Nevada
Open Tues-Fri 1-6, Sat 11-2
Friends of the Library Group

WINNEMUCCA

P HUMBOLDT COUNTY LIBRARY*, 85 E Fifth St, 89445. SAN 350-4182. Tel: 775-623-6388. FAX: 775-623-6438. E-mail: library@hcnv.us. Web Site: hcnv.us/351/library. *Sr Libr Tech,* Jessica Anderson; E-mail: jessica.anderson@hcnv.us
Founded 1923. Pop 16,500; Circ 160,000
Library Holdings: Bk Vols 55,000; Per Subs 171
Special Collections: Local History Coll; Nevada Coll
Partic in Information Nevada
Open Mon & Thurs 9-6, Tues & Wed 9-8, Fri 9-5, Sat 10-4
Branches: 2
DENIO BRANCH, 190 Pueblo Dr, Denio, 89404. (Mail add: 85 E Fifth St, 89445). Tel: 775-941-0330. FAX: 775-941-0330. E-mail: deniolibrary@hotmail.com. *Libr Spec,* Sherry Ranf; E-mail: sherry.ranf@hcnv.us
Library Holdings: Bk Vols 2,000
Open Mon & Tues 12-5, Wed 3-8, Thurs 8-1
MCDERMITT BRANCH, 135 Oregon Rd, McDermitt, 89421. (Mail add: PO Box 444, McDermitt, 89421-0444). Tel: 775-532-8014. FAX: 775-532-8018. E-mail: mcdlibrary89421@yahoo.com. *Libr Spec,* Martica Crutcher; E-mail: martica.crutcher@hcnv.us
Library Holdings: Bk Titles 6,000
Open Mon, Tues & Thurs 8-5, Wed 10-7
Bookmobiles: 1. Librn, Ginny Dufurrena

S NORTH CENTRAL NEVADA HISTORICAL SOCIETY, Humboldt Museum Research Department, 175 Museum Ln, 89446. (Mail add: PO Box 819, 89446-0819), SAN 373-2428. Tel: 775-623-2912. FAX: 775-623-5640. Web Site: www.humboldtmuseum.org. *Exec Dir,* Dana Toth; E-mail: dana@humboldtmuseum.org
Library Holdings: Bk Vols 2,000
Wireless access
Open Wed-Fri 9-4, Sat 10-4

YERINGTON

P LYON COUNTY LIBRARY SYSTEM*, 20 Nevin Way, 89447. SAN 350-4271. Tel: 775-463-6645. FAX: 775-463-6646. Web Site: www.lyon-county.org/238/Library. *Libr Dir,* Amy Geddes; E-mail: ageddes@lyon-county.org; Staff 8.3 (MLS 1, Non-MLS 7.3)
Pop 57,510; Circ 86,354
Automation Activity & Vendor Info: (Acquisitions) Baker & Taylor; (Cataloging) Innovative Interfaces, Inc; (Circulation) Innovative Interfaces, Inc; (ILL) Innovative Interfaces, Inc - Millennium; (OPAC) Innovative Interfaces, Inc
Wireless access
Function: 24/7 Electronic res, 24/7 Online cat, 3D Printer, Art exhibits, Audiobks via web, Bilingual assistance for Spanish patrons, Bk club(s), Bks on CD, Children's prog, Computer training, Computers for patron use, Digital talking bks, Electronic databases & coll, Free DVD rentals, Holiday prog, ILL available, Internet access, Large print keyboards, Magazines, Magnifiers for reading, Mail & tel request accepted, Mail loans to mem, Makerspace, Meeting rooms, Microfiche/film & reading machines, Movies, Music CDs, Online cat, Online ref, Outside serv via phone, mail, e-mail & web, OverDrive digital audio bks, Photocopying/Printing, Preschool reading prog, Printer for laptops & handheld devices, Prog for adults, Prog for children & young adult, Ref serv available, Res assist avail, Scanner, Serves people with intellectual disabilities, Spanish lang bks, Story hour, Study rm, Summer reading prog, Tax forms, Teen prog, Telephone ref, Wheelchair accessible, Writing prog
Open Tues & Wed 9-5, Thurs 11-6, Fri & Sat 11-4
Friends of the Library Group
Branches: 4
DAYTON VALLEY BRANCH, 321 Old Dayton Valley Rd, Dayton, 89403-8902, SAN 377-0257. Tel: 775-246-6212. FAX: 775-246-6213. *Br Mgr,* Summer Bell; E-mail: sbell@lyon-county.org; Staff 2 (Non-MLS 2)
Open Tues, Thurs & Fri 9-5, Wed 11-6, Sat 11-4
Friends of the Library Group
FERNLEY BRANCH, 575 Silver Lace Blvd, Fernley, 89408, SAN 350-4301. Tel: 775-575-3366. FAX: 775-575-3368. *Br Mgr,* Lynn Evans; E-mail: levans@lyon-county.org; Staff 2 (Non-MLS 2)
Open Tues & Wed 9-6, Thurs 11-4, Sat 10-5
Friends of the Library Group
SILVER-STAGE BRANCH, 3905 Hwy 50 W, Silver Springs, 89429. (Mail add: PO Box 310, Silver Springs, 89429), SAN 350-428X. Tel: 775-577-5015. FAX: 775-577-5013. *Br Mgr,* Wynne Prindle; E-mail: wprindle@lyon-county.org; Staff 1 (Non-MLS 1)
Open Wed-Sat 11-5
Friends of the Library Group
SMITH VALLEY BRANCH, 22 Day Lane, Smith, 89430-9707, SAN 377-0273. Tel: 775-465-2369. FAX: 775-465-2309.
Open Tues & Thurs 3-6, Fri 9-5, Sat 11-5
Friends of the Library Group

NEW HAMPSHIRE

Date of Statistics: FY 2016
Population, U.S. Census 2020: 1,366,275
Population Served by Public Libraries: 1,448,496
Total Volumes in Public Libraries: 5,644,856
Volumes Per Capita: 3.90
Total Public Library Circulation: 10,372,411
Circulation Per Capita: 7.16
Income and Expenditures:
Total Public Library Income (not including Grants-in-Aid): $60,740,405
Income Per Capita: $41.93
Source of Income: Mainly public funds (2/3 public, 1/3 endowment)
Total Public Library Expenditures: $60,218,731
Expenditures Per Capita: $41.57

ACWORTH

P ACWORTH SILSBY LIBRARY*, Five Lynn Hill Rd, 03601. (Mail add: PO Box 179, 03601-0179), SAN 324-3729. Tel: 603-835-2150. E-mail: acworthlibrary@myfairpoint.net. Web Site: www.acworthlibrary.org. *Admnr,* Susan Metsack; *Admnr,* Linda Thomson-Mohr
Founded 1891. Pop 1,511; Circ 3,883
Library Holdings: AV Mats 361; Bk Titles 8,000; Per Subs 13; Talking Bks 210
Subject Interests: NH hist
Publications: Library & Town (Newsletter)
Open Tues & Thurs 11:30-5:30, Sat & Sun 11:30-4:30
Friends of the Library Group

ALEXANDRIA

P HAYNES LIBRARY*, 33 Washburn Rd, 03222. (Mail add: 567 Washburn Rd, 03222-6532), SAN 320-4898. Tel: 603-744-6529. E-mail: rinba@metrocast.net. *Dir,* Position Currently Open
Founded 1885. Circ 1,218
Library Holdings: Bk Vols 7,000
Special Collections: Local History Coll
Open Mon 1:30-4:30 & 7-8

ALLENSTOWN

P ALLENSTOWN PUBLIC LIBRARY, 59 Main St, 03275-1716. SAN 309-7358. Tel: 603-485-7651. E-mail: allenstownlib@comcast.net. Web Site: allenstownlibrary.org. *Dir,* Betsy Randlett
Pop 5,000; Circ 5,784
Library Holdings: Bk Vols 12,500; Per Subs 28
Subject Interests: Historic maps, Town hist
Wireless access
Partic in Suncook Interlibrary Cooperative
Open Tues 10-6, Thurs & Fri 10-5
Restriction: Residents only

ALSTEAD

P SHEDD-PORTER MEMORIAL LIBRARY*, Three Main St, 03602. SAN 309-7366. Tel: 603-835-6661. Web Site: www.sheddporter.org. *Dir,* Alyson Montgomery; E-mail: alyson.montgomery@sheddporter.org; *Asst Librn,* Gaale Klein; Staff 1 (Non-MLS 1)
Founded 1910. Pop 1,463; Circ 20,000
Library Holdings: Bk Vols 33,500; Per Subs 20
Wireless access
Open Wed & Fri 11-5, Thurs 11-7, Sat 9-Noon

ALTON

P GILMAN LIBRARY*, 100 Main St, 03809. (Mail add: PO Box 960, 03809-0960), SAN 309-7374. Tel: 603-875-2550. E-mail: info@gilmanlibrary.org. Web Site: gilmanlibrary.org. *Libr Dir,* Holly Brown; E-mail: hollybrown@gilmanlibrary.org; *Asst Dir,* Rozalind Benoit; E-mail: rozabenoit@gilmanlibrary.org
Founded 1951. Pop 3,800; Circ 23,426
Jan 2013-Dec 2013 Income $139,127. Mats Exp $14,530, Books $7,871, AV Mat $5,384, Electronic Ref Mat (Incl. Access Fees) $1,275. Sal $89,960
Library Holdings: CDs 1,134; DVDs 2,647; e-books 7,219; Bk Titles 18,265; Per Subs 51
Automation Activity & Vendor Info: (Acquisitions) Biblionix/Apollo; (Cataloging) Biblionix/Apollo; (Circulation) Biblionix/Apollo; (Course Reserve) Biblionix/Apollo
Wireless access
Partic in Rochester Area Librarians
Open Tues & Thurs 11-7, Wed & Fri 9-5, Sat 9-1
Friends of the Library Group

AMHERST

P AMHERST TOWN LIBRARY, 14 Main St, 03031. SAN 309-7382. Tel: 603-673-2288. E-mail: library@amherstlibrary.org. Web Site: www.amherstlibrary.org. *Dir,* Amy LaPointe; E-mail: alapointe@amherstlibrary.org; *Asst Dir,* Sarah Leonardi; E-mail: sleonardi@amherstlibrary.org; *Head, Children's Servx,* Sarah Hydorn; E-mail: shydorn@amherstlibrary.org; *Circ Librn, Reader Serv Librn,* Alexa Moore; E-mail: amoore@amherstlibrary.org; *Tech Serv Librn,* Angela Brown; E-mail: abrown@amherstlibrary.org; Staff 21 (MLS 4, Non-MLS 17)
Founded 1891. Pop 10,000; Circ 138,107
Library Holdings: Bk Titles 55,783; Bk Vols 60,000; Per Subs 136
Automation Activity & Vendor Info: (Cataloging) Innovative Interfaces, Inc; (Circulation) Innovative Interfaces, Inc; (OPAC) Innovative Interfaces, Inc; (Serials) Innovative Interfaces, Inc
Wireless access
Partic in GMILCS, Inc
Special Services for the Blind - Magnifiers; Screen enlargement software for people with visual disabilities; Talking bks
Open Mon, Tues, Thurs & Fri 9:30-5, Wed 9:30-7, Sat 9:30-12:30
Friends of the Library Group

ANDOVER

P ANDOVER PUBLIC LIBRARY*, 11 School St, 03216. SAN 309-7390. Tel: 603-735-5333. E-mail: andoverpl@comcast.net. Web Site: andovernhlibrary.weebly.com. *Librn,* Priscilla Poulin
Pop 1,584; Circ 10,328
Library Holdings: Bk Vols 11,000; Per Subs 20
Wireless access
Open Mon 6pm-8pm, Wed 9-12 & 6-8, Thurs 1-5, Sat 9-Noon
Friends of the Library Group

ANTRIM

P JAMES A TUTTLE LIBRARY*, 45 Main St, 03440-3906. (Mail add: PO Box 235, 03440-0235), SAN 309-7412. Tel: 603-588-6786. E-mail: tuttlelibrary@gmail.com. Web Site: www.antrimnh.org/james-tuttle-library. *Libr Dir,* Cynthia Jewett; Staff 5 (MLS 1, Non-MLS 4)
Founded 1908. Pop 2,600; Circ 14,000
Library Holdings: CDs 500; DVDs 2,500; e-books 21,000; Bk Titles 30,000; Per Subs 60
Subject Interests: Genealogy, NH hist
Automation Activity & Vendor Info: (Acquisitions) Biblionix/Apollo; (Cataloging) Biblionix/Apollo; (Circulation) Biblionix/Apollo; (ILL) SirsiDynix; (OPAC) Biblionix/Apollo
Wireless access
Function: 24/7 Electronic res, 24/7 Online cat, 3D Printer, Activity rm, Adult literacy prog, Archival coll, Art exhibits, Audiobks via web, Bk club(s), Bks on CD, Children's prog, Citizenship assistance, Computer training, Computers for patron use, Electronic databases & coll, Free DVD rentals, Games & aids for people with disabilities, Genealogy discussion group, Govt ref serv, Health sci info serv, Holiday prog, ILL available, Internet access, Magazines, Magnifiers for reading, Mail & tel request accepted, Makerspace, Museum passes, Music CDs, Notary serv, Online cat, Outside serv via phone, mail, e-mail & web, OverDrive digital audio bks, Prog for adults, Prog for children & young adult, Ref & res, Ref serv available, Res assist avail, Tax forms, Telephone ref, Wheelchair accessible
Partic in New Hampshire Automated Information Systems
Open Mon & Wed 2-6, Tues & Thurs 2-8, Fri 9-12, Sat 10-4
Restriction: Authorized patrons
Friends of the Library Group

ASHLAND

P ASHLAND TOWN LIBRARY*, 42 Main St, 03217. (Mail add: PO Box 660, 03217-0660), SAN 309-7420. Tel: 603-968-7928. FAX: 603-968-7928. E-mail: ashlandtownlibrary@gmail.com. Web Site: www.ashlandtownlibrary.org. *Dir,* Sara Weinberg; *Asst Dir,* Terry Fouts
Pop 1,915; Circ 4,777
Library Holdings: Bk Titles 18,000; Per Subs 28
Automation Activity & Vendor Info: (Circulation) Follett Software
Wireless access
Open Mon, Tues & Thurs 1-7, Fri & Sat 10-2

ASHUELOT

P THAYER PUBLIC LIBRARY*, Three Main St, 03441-2616. (Mail add: PO Box 67, 03441-0067). Tel: 603-329-0175. E-mail: thayer@thayerlibrary.net. *Dir,* Jennifer Bellan
Pop 4,200
Library Holdings: Bk Vols 5,600; Talking Bks 50
Wireless access
Open Tues & Thurs 3-7, Sat 9-1

ATKINSON

P KIMBALL LIBRARY*, Five Academy Ave, 03811-2202. SAN 309-7439. Tel: 603-362-5234. FAX: 603-362-6095. E-mail: staff@kimballlibrary.com. Web Site: www.kimballlibrary.com. *Dir,* Diane Heer; E-mail: director@kimballlibrary.com; *Asst Dir, Dir, Youth Serv,* Kathy Watson; E-mail: kwatson@kimballlibrary.com; Staff 11 (MLS 1, Non-MLS 10)
Founded 1894. Pop 7,000; Circ 93,880
Library Holdings: Audiobooks 1,925; CDs 816; DVDs 2,241; Large Print Bks 322; Bk Vols 31,605; Per Subs 98
Special Collections: New England, audio, bks, large-print bks
Subject Interests: Local hist
Automation Activity & Vendor Info: (Circulation) Follett Software; (OPAC) Follett Software; (Serials) Follett Software
Wireless access
Partic in WinnShare Libr Coop
Open Mon-Fri 10-8, Sat 10-3
Friends of the Library Group

AUBURN

P GRIFFIN FREE PUBLIC LIBRARY, 22 Hooksett Rd, 03032. (Mail add: PO Box 308, 03032-0308), SAN 309-7447. Tel: 603-483-5374. Web Site: griffinfree.org. *Dir,* Kathy Growney; E-mail: director@griffinfree.org; *Tech Serv Asst,* Chris Chickering
Pop 5,600
Library Holdings: Bk Vols 16,500; Per Subs 20
Automation Activity & Vendor Info: (Circulation) Koha
Wireless access
Open Tues & Thurs 10-6, Wed 1-8, Fri 10-5, Sat 10-2
Friends of the Library Group

BARRINGTON

P BARRINGTON PUBLIC LIBRARY*, 105 Ramsdell Lane, 03825-7469. SAN 309-7463. Tel: 603-664-9715. Administration Tel: 603 664-0193. FAX: 603-664-5219. E-mail: circulation@barringtonlibrary.com. Web Site: www.barringtonlibrary.com. *Dir,* Melissa Huette; E-mail: director@barringtonlibrary.com; *Ch,* Wendy Rowe; E-mail: children@barringtonlibrary.com; *ILL,* Amy Inglis; E-mail: interlibraryloan@barringtonlibrary.com; Staff 5 (MLS 1, Non-MLS 4)
Founded 1795. Pop 8,576; Circ 90,000
Jan 2014-Dec 2014 Income $305,724, City $284,594, Locally Generated Income $21,130. Mats Exp $27,888. Sal $180,954 (Prof $93,811)
Library Holdings: Audiobooks 9,487; Bks on Deafness & Sign Lang 40; CDs 725; DVDs 3,899; e-books 10,265; High Interest/Low Vocabulary Bk Vols 50; Large Print Bks 500; Bk Vols 42,984; Per Subs 46
Special Collections: Oral History
Automation Activity & Vendor Info: (Cataloging) Book Systems; (Circulation) Book Systems; (ILL) SirsiDynix; (OPAC) Book Systems
Wireless access
Function: Adult bk club, Art exhibits, Audiobks via web, Bks on CD, Children's prog, Computer training, Computers for patron use, E-Readers, E-Reserves, Electronic databases & coll, Equip loans & repairs, Free DVD rentals, Genealogy discussion group, Homebound delivery serv, ILL available, Internet access, Life-long learning prog for all ages, Magazines, Movies, Museum passes, Music CDs, Notary serv, Online cat, Outreach serv, OverDrive digital audio bks, Photocopying/Printing, Preschool outreach, Preschool reading prog, Prog for adults, Prog for children & young adult, Scanner, Story hour, Summer reading prog, Tax forms, Teen prog, Telephone ref, Visual arts prog, Workshops
Partic in New Hampshire Automated Information Systems; Suncook Interlibrary Cooperative
Special Services for the Blind - Bks on CD
Open Mon & Fri 10-6, Tues & Thurs 10-7, Wed 10-8, Sat 10-3
Friends of the Library Group

BARTLETT

P BARTLETT PUBLIC LIBRARY, 1313 US Rte 302, 03812. (Mail add: PO Box 399, 03812-0399), SAN 309-7471. Tel: 603-374-2755. FAX: 603-374-2755. E-mail: librarian@bartlettpubliclibrary.org. Web Site: bartlettpubliclibrary.org. *Libr Dir,* Kathy Van Deursen; *Asst Librn,* Elizabeth Kelsea
Library Holdings: Bk Titles 19,000; Per Subs 60
Automation Activity & Vendor Info: (Circulation) Follett Software
Wireless access
Open Mon & Wed 2-8, Tues & Thurs 2-5, Sat 11:30-3
Friends of the Library Group

BATH

P BATH PUBLIC LIBRARY*, Four W Bath Rd, 03740. SAN 309-748X. Tel: 603-747-3372. FAX: 603-747-3372. Web Site: www.bathlibrarynh.org. *Libr Dir,* Bernie Prochnik; E-mail: bathlibrarybbp@gmail.com; *Asst Librn,* Kathie Bonor; E-mail: bathlibrarykjb@gmail.com
Pop 893; Circ 2,900
Library Holdings: AV Mats 259; Bk Vols 13,748
Wireless access
Open Tues-Thurs 9-12 & 1-6, Sat 9-Noon
Friends of the Library Group

BEDFORD

P BEDFORD PUBLIC LIBRARY, Three Meetinghouse Rd, 03110. SAN 309-7498. Tel: 603-472-2300. FAX: 603-472-2978. E-mail: reference@bedfordnh.org. Web Site: bedfordnhlibrary.org. *Libr Dir,* Miriam Johnson; E-mail: mjohnson@bedfordnh.org; *Asst Dir,* Caitlin Loving; *Head, Children's Servx,* Emily Sennott; *Head, Ref & ILL Serv,* Emily Weiss; *Head, Tech Serv,* Anne Murphy; Staff 8 (MLS 7, Non-MLS 1)
Founded 1789. Pop 22,592; Circ 210,198
Library Holdings: Bk Vols 69,365; Per Subs 124
Special Collections: Sheet Music Coll. State Document Depository
Automation Activity & Vendor Info: (Acquisitions) Innovative Interfaces, Inc; (Cataloging) Innovative Interfaces, Inc; (Circulation) Innovative Interfaces, Inc; (OPAC) Innovative Interfaces, Inc; (Serials) Innovative Interfaces, Inc
Wireless access
Publications: Town Directory & Friends Newsletter
Partic in GMILCS, Inc
Open Mon-Thurs 9-8:30, Fri 9-5, Sat 10-3 (10-1 Summer), Sun (Winter) 1-5
Friends of the Library Group

BELMONT

P BELMONT PUBLIC LIBRARY*, 146 Main St, 03220. (Mail add: PO Box 308, 03220-0308), SAN 309-751X. Tel: 603-267-8331. FAX: 603-267-5924. E-mail: bpl@belmontnh.org. Web Site: belmontpubliclibrary.org. *Libr Dir,* Eileen Gilbert; *Libr Asst,* Katherine Bollenbach; Staff 1 (Non-MLS 1)
Founded 1928. Pop 7,100; Circ 14,932
Library Holdings: CDs 155; DVDs 165; Electronic Media & Resources 370; High Interest/Low Vocabulary Bk Vols 335; Large Print Bks 285; Bk Titles 13,677; Bk Vols 15,178; Per Subs 53; Videos 496
Automation Activity & Vendor Info: (Cataloging) Follett Software; (Circulation) Follett Software; (OPAC) Follett Software
Wireless access
Function: Accelerated reader prog, Adult bk club, Adult literacy prog, After school storytime
Open Mon & Wed 10-7, Tues & Thurs 10-5, Fri 10-4, Sat 9-1
Friends of the Library Group

BENNINGTON

P GEP DODGE LIBRARY, Two Main St, 03442. (Mail add: Seven School St, Unit 204, 03442), SAN 309-7528. Tel: 603-588-6585. FAX: 603-588-6585. E-mail: dodgelibrary1@comcast.net, dodgelibrary2@comcast.net. Web Site: www.dodgelibrary.com. *Dir,* Leslie MacGregor; *Asst Dir,* Melissa Searles
Founded 1906. Pop 1,183; Circ 13,618
Library Holdings: Audiobooks 973; AV Mats 1,245; CDs 453; Bk Vols 30,000; Per Subs 45; Talking Bks 839
Automation Activity & Vendor Info: (Cataloging) Follett Software; (Circulation) Follett Software
Wireless access
Open Mon & Fri 8-4, Tues 9-5, Thurs 12-7
Friends of the Library Group

BERLIN

M ANDROSCOGGIN VALLEY HOSPITAL*, Medical Library, 59 Page Hill Rd, 03570. SAN 327-747X. Tel: 603-326-5825, 603-752-2200. FAX: 603-326-5832. Web Site: www.avhnh.org.
Library Holdings: Bk Titles 200; Per Subs 85
Wireless access
Restriction: Open to staff only

P BERLIN PUBLIC LIBRARY*, 270 Main St, 03570. SAN 309-7536. Tel: 603-752-5210. FAX: 603-752-8568. E-mail: librarian@berlinnh.gov. Web Site: www.berlinnh.gov/library. *Head Librn,* Denise Jensen; *Ch,* Kathy Godin; Staff 4 (Non-MLS 4)
Founded 1893. Pop 9,743; Circ 31,327
Jul 2013-Jun 2014 Income $195,450. Mats Exp $19,000. Sal $54,946
Library Holdings: Audiobooks 3,868; CDs 8; DVDs 5,987; Large Print Bks 175; Bk Titles 14,733; Per Subs 462; Videos 1,119
Special Collections: French Fiction Coll
Wireless access
Partic in New Hampshire Automated Information Systems
Open Mon, Tues, Thurs & Fri 10-6, Wed 12-7

S NEW HAMPSHIRE DEPARTMENT OF CORRECTIONS, Northern New Hampshire Correctional Facility Library, 138 E Milan Rd, 03570. Tel: 603-752-0460. FAX: 603-752-0405. Web Site: www.nh.gov/nhdoc/facilities/berlin.html. *Librn,* Samantha Smalley-King; E-mail: samantha.smalley@doc.nh.gov
Founded 2000
Library Holdings: Bk Vols 8,250
Open Mon-Fri 8-2:30

J WHITE MOUNTAINS COMMUNITY COLLEGE*, Fortier Library, 2020 Riverside Dr, 03570-3799. SAN 309-7552. Tel: 603-342-3087. Toll Free Tel: 800-445-4525. E-mail: wmcclibrary@ccsnh.edu. Web Site: www.wmcc.edu/student-services/fortier-library. *Dir, Libr Serv,* Melissa Laplante; Tel: 603-342-3086, E-mail: mlaplante@ccsnh.edu; *Libr Tech II,* Denise Bergeron; E-mail: dbergeron@ccsnh.edu; Staff 2 (MLS 1, Non-MLS 1)
Founded 1970. Enrl 1,000; Fac 50
Library Holdings: Bk Vols 17,000; Per Subs 125
Special Collections: State Document Depository
Automation Activity & Vendor Info: (Cataloging) TLC (The Library Corporation); (OPAC) TLC (The Library Corporation)
Wireless access
Partic in OCLC Online Computer Library Center, Inc
Open Mon-Thurs 7:30-7, Fri 8-4

BETHLEHEM

P BETHLEHEM PUBLIC LIBRARY*, 2245 Main St, 03574. (Mail add: PO Box 250, 03574-0250), SAN 309-7560. Tel: 603-869-2409. FAX: 603-869-2410. Web Site: www.bethlehemlibrary.org. *Dir,* Laura Clerkin; E-mail: lclerkin@bethlehemlibrary.org; *Asst Dir,* Kathy Treamer; E-mail: ktreamer@bethlehemlibrary.org; Staff 4 (MLS 2, Non-MLS 2)
Founded 1913. Pop 2,526; Circ 27,603
Library Holdings: Audiobooks 432; DVDs 1,177; e-books 29; Bk Vols 13,554; Per Subs 40
Automation Activity & Vendor Info: (Cataloging) Book Systems; (Circulation) Book Systems; (OPAC) Book Systems
Wireless access
Function: 24/7 Online cat, Adult bk club, After school storytime, Audiobks via web, Bk club(s), Bks on CD, Children's prog, Computer training, Computers for patron use, E-Readers, E-Reserves, Electronic databases & coll, Free DVD rentals, Holiday prog, Homebound delivery serv, ILL available, Internet access, Magazines, Meeting rooms, Movies, Online cat, OverDrive digital audio bks, Photocopying/Printing, Printer for laptops & handheld devices, Prog for adults, Prog for children & young adult, Ref serv available, Scanner, Senior computer classes, Story hour, Summer & winter reading prog, Summer reading prog, Tax forms, Teen prog, Telephone ref, Wheelchair accessible
Open Mon, Wed & Thurs 1-7, Tues & Fri 10-4, Sat 9-1
Restriction: Circ to mem only, Free to mem, Non-resident fee
Friends of the Library Group

BOSCAWEN

P BOSCAWEN PUBLIC LIBRARY, 116 N Main St, 03303-1123. SAN 350-4336. Tel: 603-753-8576. E-mail: boscawenpl@gmail.com. Web Site: www.boscawenpubliclibrary.org. *Dir,* Bonny John; *Libr Asst,* Donna Raymond; Staff 1 (Non-MLS 1)
Founded 1897. Pop 4,696; Circ 20,000
Library Holdings: Audiobooks 200; CDs 60; DVDs 500; e-books 3,000; Large Print Bks 600; Bk Titles 16,000; Bk Vols 18,000; Per Subs 30; Videos 1,500
Special Collections: Local History Coll; Town Records Coll
Wireless access
Function: Adult bk club, After school storytime, Children's prog, Computer training, Computers for patron use, Electronic databases & coll, ILL available, Online cat, Outside serv via phone, mail, e-mail & web, OverDrive digital audio bks, Photocopying/Printing, Preschool reading prog, Prog for adults, Prog for children & young adult, Spoken cassettes & CDs, Spoken cassettes & DVDs, Story hour, Summer & winter reading prog
Partic in Suncook Interlibrary Cooperative
Open Mon 12-7, Tues-Thurs 10-6, Sat 9-1
Friends of the Library Group

BOW

P BAKER FREE LIBRARY*, 509 South St, 03304. SAN 309-7579. Tel: 603-224-7113. FAX: 603-224-2063. E-mail: info@bakerfreelib.org. Web Site: www.bowbakerfreelibrary.org. *Dir,* Lori A Fisher; E-mail: lori@bakerfreelib.org; *Youth Serv Librn,* Juliana Gallo; E-mail: juliana@bakerfreelib.org; Staff 2 (MLS 1, Non-MLS 1)
Founded 1914. Pop 7,900; Circ 75,456
Library Holdings: AV Mats 2,471; Bk Vols 34,786; Per Subs 138
Automation Activity & Vendor Info: (Cataloging) Follett Software; (Circulation) Follett Software; (OPAC) Follett Software
Wireless access
Function: Adult bk club, Art exhibits, Bks on CD, Children's prog, Computers for patron use, Electronic databases & coll, Homebound delivery serv, ILL available, Magnifiers for reading, Museum passes, Music CDs, Online cat, OverDrive digital audio bks, Photocopying/Printing, Prog for adults, Prog for children & young adult, Summer reading prog, Teen prog
Open Mon-Thurs 10-8, Fri 10-7, Sat 10-4
Friends of the Library Group

BRADFORD

P BROWN MEMORIAL LIBRARY*, 78 W Main St, 03221-3308. SAN 309-7587. Tel: 603-938-5562. E-mail: bmlbradford@gmail.com. Web Site: www.brownmemoriallibrary.org. *Librn,* Ellen Barselle; Staff 3 (Non-MLS 3)
Founded 1893. Pop 1,500; Circ 11,445
Library Holdings: Bk Vols 11,000; Per Subs 15
Wireless access
Open Mon & Fri 10-6, Wed 11-7, Sat 9-1
Friends of the Library Group

P SUTTON FREE LIBRARY*, Five Corporation Hill Rd, 03221. (Mail add: PO Box 202, North Sutton, 03260), SAN 309-9652. Tel: 603-927-4927. E-mail: suttonlibrarian@gmail.com.
Pop 1,850; Circ 13,369
Wireless access
Function: Activity rm, Adult bk club, Bks on CD, Children's prog, Computers for patron use, Free DVD rentals, ILL available, Internet access, Mail & tel request accepted, Meeting rooms, Museum passes, OverDrive digital audio bks, Photocopying/Printing, Printer for laptops & handheld devices, Prog for adults, Prog for children & young adult, Scanner, Story hour, Summer reading prog
Open Mon 10-12 & 3-7, Wed 8-12 & 3-7, Sat 10-2
Friends of the Library Group

BRENTWOOD

P MARY E BARTLETT MEMORIAL LIBRARY*, 22 Dalton Rd, 03833. SAN 309-7595. Tel: 603-642-3355. FAX: 603-642-3383. E-mail: bartlettlibrary@comcast.net. Web Site: www.brentwoodlibrary.org. *Libr Dir,* Kathy Sperounis; E-mail: director.meblib@gmail.com; *Ch,* Joyce Miller; Staff 2 (MLS 1, Non-MLS 1)
Founded 1893. Pop 4,486; Circ 55,000
Library Holdings: Audiobooks 1,200; Bks on Deafness & Sign Lang 15; CDs 1,200; DVDs 2,400; e-books 65; Electronic Media & Resources 5; Large Print Bks 40; Bk Vols 45,000; Per Subs 90
Automation Activity & Vendor Info: (Cataloging) Book Systems; (Circulation) Book Systems; (OPAC) Book Systems
Wireless access
Function: 24/7 Electronic res, Adult bk club, Bks on CD, Children's prog, Computer training, Computers for patron use, E-Readers, Electronic databases & coll, Equip loans & repairs, Free DVD rentals, ILL available, Instruction & testing, Internet access, Magazines, Mail & tel request accepted, Movies, Museum passes, Online cat, Online ref, Photocopying/Printing, Preschool reading prog, Prog for adults, Story hour, Study rm, Summer reading prog, Teen prog, Wheelchair accessible, Workshops
Partic in New Hampshire Automated Information Systems
Open Mon 2-7, Tues-Wed 9-5, Thurs 9-7, Fri & Sat 9-1
Friends of the Library Group

BRETTON WOODS

S APPALACHIAN MOUNTAIN CLUB*, Library & Archives, AMC Highland Center at Crawford Notch, US Route 302, 03575. SAN 307-1243. Tel: 603-374-8515. E-mail: bfullerton@outdoors.org. *Archivist,* Rebecca M Fullerton; Staff 1 (Non-MLS 1)
Founded 1876
Library Holdings: DVDs 50; Bk Titles 3,000; Bk Vols 3,500; Per Subs 20
Special Collections: Appalachian Mountain Club Map Coll; Appalachian Mountain Club Records, 1876-present; Outdoor Recreation in Northeast US (Appalachian Mountain Club Photographic Colls); White Mountains Coll, bks, images
Subject Interests: Environ conserv, Mountaineering, Outdoor educ, Outdoor recreation
Automation Activity & Vendor Info: (Acquisitions) LibraryWorld, Inc; (Cataloging) LibraryWorld, Inc; (OPAC) LibraryWorld, Inc; (Serials) LibraryWorld, Inc
Function: Archival coll
Restriction: Open to pub by appt only

BRISTOL

P MINOT-SLEEPER LIBRARY*, 35 Pleasant St, 03222-1407. SAN 309-7609. Tel: 603-744-3352. E-mail: minotsleeperlibrary@gmail.com. Web Site: www.minotsleeperlibrary.org. *Librn,* Brittany Overton
Pop 3,054; Circ 40,000
Library Holdings: AV Mats 888; Bk Vols 14,902; Per Subs 53
Special Collections: Stuffed Bird Coll
Wireless access
Open Mon, Wed & Fri 10-6, Tues & Thurs 1-8, Sat 10-2
Friends of the Library Group

BROOKLINE

P BROOKLINE PUBLIC LIBRARY*, 16 Main St, 03033. (Mail add: PO Box 157, 03033-0157), SAN 309-7617. Tel: 603-673-3330. FAX: 603-673-0735. Web Site: bplnh.weebly.com. *Dir,* Patricia Leonard; E-mail: patl@brookline.nh.us; *Ch,* Aimee Gaudette
Pop 4,800; Circ 41,000
Library Holdings: Bk Vols 29,000; Per Subs 200
Automation Activity & Vendor Info: (Cataloging) Follett Software; (Circulation) Follett Software
Wireless access
Open Mon-Thurs 10-8, Fri & Sat (Sept-June) 10-2
Friends of the Library Group

CAMPTON

P CAMPTON PUBLIC LIBRARY*, 1110 New Hampshire Rte 175, Ste B, 03223. SAN 376-5113. Tel: 603-726-4877. FAX: 603-726-4877. E-mail: camptonpubliclibrary@gmail.com. Web Site: www.camptonlibrary.com. *Dir,* Tara McKenzie
Library Holdings: DVDs 100; Bk Titles 13,000; Per Subs 16; Talking Bks 250; Videos 500
Automation Activity & Vendor Info: (Circulation) Follett Software
Wireless access
Open Mon & Wed-Fri 3:30-8:30, Sat 9-4

CANAAN

P CANAAN TOWN LIBRARY*, 1173 US Rte 4, 03741. (Mail add: PO Box 368, 03741-0368), SAN 309-7633. Tel: 603-523-9650. Circulation E-mail: circulationdesk@canaanlibrary.org. Interlibrary Loan Service E-mail: ill@canaanlibrary.org. Web Site: www.canaanlibrary.org. *Libr Dir,* Amy Thurber; E-mail: athurber@canaanlibrary.org; *ILL Librn,* Jenna McAlister; *Asst Librn,* Lori Dacier; *Asst Librn,* Nancy Pike; *Asst Librn,* Pam Wotton; Staff 5 (Non-MLS 5)
Founded 1804. Pop 2,464; Circ 20,211
Library Holdings: Bk Vols 27,000; Per Subs 65
Automation Activity & Vendor Info: (Cataloging) Follett Software; (Circulation) Follett Software; (OPAC) Follett Software
Wireless access
Open Mon 3-8, Tues & Wed 1-8, Thurs 1-5, Fri 9-Noon, Sat 9-3
Friends of the Library Group

CANDIA

P SMYTH PUBLIC LIBRARY, 55 High St, 03034. SAN 309-880X. Tel: 603-483-8245. E-mail: librarian@smythpl.org. Web Site: www.smythpl.org. *Dir,* Heidi Deacon; Staff 3 (Non-MLS 3)
Founded 1888. Pop 4,000; Circ 23,000
Library Holdings: Bk Vols 23,000; Per Subs 50
Special Collections: Local History Coll
Automation Activity & Vendor Info: (Cataloging) Follett Software; (Circulation) Follett Software; (OPAC) Follett Software
Wireless access
Open Mon, Wed, Thurs & Sat 10-2, Sun 10-1
Friends of the Library Group

CANTERBURY

P ELKINS PUBLIC LIBRARY, Nine Center Rd, 03224. (Mail add: PO Box 300, 03224-0300), SAN 309-7641. Tel: 603-783-4386. FAX: 603-783-4817. Web Site: www.elkinspubliclibrary.org. *Dir,* Susan LeClair; E-mail: sleclair@elkinspubliclibrary.org; *Youth Serv Librn,* Rachel Baker; E-mail: mrsbaker@elkinspubliclibrary.org; *Circ,* Roseann Howe; Staff 5 (MLS 5)
Founded 1927. Pop 2,040; Circ 22,330
Jan 2020-Dec 2020. Mats Exp $3,140, Per/Ser (Incl. Access Fees) $140, AV Mat $3,000
Library Holdings: AV Mats 1,932; Large Print Bks 53; Bk Titles 16,347; Per Subs 28; Talking Bks 783; Videos 1,171
Special Collections: Shaker Coll
Automation Activity & Vendor Info: (Acquisitions) Baker & Taylor; (Cataloging) Baker & Taylor; (Circulation) Follett Software; (OPAC) Follett Software
Wireless access
Function: 24/7 Electronic res, 24/7 Online cat, Adult bk club
Partic in New Hampshire Automated Information Systems; Suncook Interlibrary Cooperative
Open Mon & Tues 9-5, Wed & Thurs 9-7, Sat 9-12

CARROL

P TWIN MOUNTAIN PUBLIC LIBRARY*, 92 School St, 03595. (Mail add: PO Box 149, Twin Mountain, 03595-0149), SAN 309-765X. Tel: 603-846-5818. FAX: 603-846-5712. E-mail: twinmountainpl@roadrunner.com. *Dir,* Tom McCorkhill
Pop 722; Circ 900
Library Holdings: Bk Titles 6,000
Special Collections: White Mountain & Surrounding Region Material Coll (1800's), bks, pictures
Wireless access
Partic in New Hampshire Automated Information Systems
Open Mon 3-7, Tues 9-1, Wed 1-5, Sat 10-1
Friends of the Library Group

CENTER BARNSTEAD

P OSCAR FOSS MEMORIAL LIBRARY*, 111 S Barnstead Rd, 03225. (Mail add: Rte 126, PO Box 219, 03225-0219), SAN 309-7455. Tel: 603-269-3900. Web Site: www.oscarfoss.org. *Dir,* Danielle Hinton; E-mail:

danielle@oscarfoss.org; *Circ,* Jerissa Brown; E-mail: jerissa@oscarfoss.org; *ILL, Teen Prog,* Lindsey Smith; E-mail: lindsey@oscarfoss.org; *Youth Serv,* Christy Verville; E-mail: christy.ofml@oscarfoss.org
Pop 3,000; Circ 8,655
Library Holdings: Audiobooks 762; CDs 488; DVDs 606; e-books 5; Bk Vols 15,231; Per Subs 35
Automation Activity & Vendor Info: (Acquisitions) Book Systems; (Cataloging) Book Systems; (Circulation) Book Systems; (OPAC) Book Systems
Wireless access
Partic in Suncook Interlibrary Cooperative
Open Tues & Wed 2-6, Thurs & Fri 12-8, Sat 10-1
Friends of the Library Group

CENTER HARBOR

P THE JAMES E NICHOLS MEMORIAL LIBRARY*, 35 Plymouth St, 03226-3341. (Mail add: PO Box 1339, 03226-1339), SAN 309-7668. Tel: 603-253-6950. FAX: 603-253-7219. E-mail: ch_library@metrocast.net. Web Site: centerharborlibrary.org, jnml.wordpress.com. *Dir,* Allen Jon Kinnaman; Staff 1.5 (MLS 1, Non-MLS 0.5)
Founded 1910. Pop 1,018; Circ 13,405
Library Holdings: Audiobooks 1,023; DVDs 1,733; Large Print Bks 281; Bk Vols 12,834; Per Subs 26
Automation Activity & Vendor Info: (OPAC) Book Systems
Wireless access
Function: 24/7 Electronic res, 24/7 Online cat, Adult bk club, Audiobks via web, Children's prog, Digital talking bks, Doc delivery serv, E-Readers, Home delivery & serv to seniorr ctr & nursing homes, Homebound delivery serv, Magazines, Online cat, Ref serv available, Scanner, Spoken cassettes & CDs, Story hour
Special Services for the Deaf - Closed caption videos
Special Services for the Blind - Bks available with recordings
Open Mon, Wed & Fri 10-6, Tues, Thurs & Sat 10-1

CENTER OSSIPEE

P OSSIPEE PUBLIC LIBRARY*, 74 Main St, 03814. (Mail add: PO Box 638, 03814), SAN 309-9210. Tel: 603-539-6390. FAX: 603-539-5758. E-mail: opl@worldpath.net. Web Site: ossipee.lib.nh.us. *Dir,* Maria Moulton; *Librn,* Polly Sheffer; *Asst Librn,* Jen Allen
Pop 4,678; Circ 31,106
Library Holdings: Audiobooks 20,078; CDs 267; DVDs 1,482; e-books 29,514; Electronic Media & Resources 21; Large Print Bks 581; Bk Titles 21,837; Per Subs 36
Special Collections: Local Genealogy Coll; New England Coll; New Hampshire Coll
Automation Activity & Vendor Info: (Acquisitions) Baker & Taylor; (Cataloging) Book Systems; (Circulation) Book Systems; (OPAC) Book Systems
Wireless access
Partic in Rochester Area Librarians
Open Mon & Thurs 12-8, Tues & Fri 10-5, Sat 9-1
Friends of the Library Group

CENTER SANDWICH

P SAMUEL H WENTWORTH LIBRARY*, 35 Main St, 03227. SAN 309-9482. Tel: 603-284-6665. FAX: 603-284-9226. E-mail: sandwichlibrary@gmail.com. Web Site: sandwichnh.org/departments/library.php. *Dir,* Glynis Miner
Pop 1,300; Circ 24,000
Library Holdings: Bk Vols 21,000; Per Subs 50
Automation Activity & Vendor Info: (Circulation) Book Systems
Wireless access
Publications: Library History
Open Mon-Thurs 12-6, Fri 10-6, Sat 10-1
Friends of the Library Group

CENTER TUFTONBORO

P TUFTONBORO FREE LIBRARY*, 221 Middle Rd, Rte 109A, 03816. (Mail add: PO Box 73, 03816-0073), SAN 309-9733. Tel: 603-569-4256. FAX: 603-569-5885. E-mail: info@tuftonborolibrary.org. Web Site: www.tuftonborolibrary.org. *Dir & Librn,* Christie V Sarles; Staff 2 (MLS 1, Non-MLS 1)
Founded 1839. Pop 2,500; Circ 40,000
Library Holdings: AV Mats 917; High Interest/Low Vocabulary Bk Vols 237; Large Print Bks 324; Bk Titles 20,923; Per Subs 28; Talking Bks 544
Subject Interests: Country living, Local hist, Nature
Automation Activity & Vendor Info: (Circulation) Follett Software
Wireless access
Function: Adult bk club, Art exhibits, Audiobks via web, AV serv, Bk club(s), Bks on cassette, Bks on CD, Children's prog, Computers for patron use, Doc delivery serv, E-Reserves, Electronic databases & coll, Free DVD rentals, Holiday prog, Homebound delivery serv, ILL available, Internet access, Museum passes, Music CDs, Online cat, Orientations, Outreach serv, Outside serv via phone, mail, e-mail & web, OverDrive digital audio bks, Photocopying/Printing, Preschool outreach, Prog for adults, Prog for children & young adult, Ref serv available, Spoken cassettes & CDs, Spoken cassettes & DVDs, Story hour, Summer reading prog, Tax forms, Telephone ref, VHS videos, Wheelchair accessible, Workshops
Partic in New Hampshire Automated Information Systems; Rochester Area Librarians
Open Tues-Thurs 9-5:30, Fri 9-6:30, Sat 9-2
Restriction: Non-circulating coll, Non-resident fee, Open to pub for ref & circ; with some limitations
Friends of the Library Group

CHARLESTOWN

P SILSBY FREE PUBLIC LIBRARY, 226 Main St, 03603. (Mail add: PO Box 307, 03603-0307), SAN 309-7676. Tel: 603-826-7793. FAX: 603-826-7793. E-mail: silsby@charlestown-nh.gov. Web Site: www.charlestown-nh.gov/silsby-public-library, www.silsbyfree.org. *Ch, Dir,* Jennifer Haynes; *Asst Dir,* Sandra Perron; *ILL Librn,* Jennifer Clark; Staff 2 (MLS 1, Non-MLS 1)
Founded 1896. Pop 4,950; Circ 26,000
Library Holdings: AV Mats 360; CDs 180; DVDs 399; Large Print Bks 1,078; Bk Vols 21,332; Per Subs 71; Talking Bks 263; Videos 285
Subject Interests: Local genealogical mat, Local hist
Automation Activity & Vendor Info: (Cataloging) Follett Software; (Circulation) Follett Software; (OPAC) Follett Software
Wireless access
Partic in Librarians of the Upper Valley Coop
Special Services for the Blind - Large print bks
Open Tues & Fri 10-5, Wed 1-7, Thurs 1-5, Sat 10-1

CHESTER

P CHESTER PUBLIC LIBRARY, Three Chester St, Jct 121 & 102, 03036. (Mail add: PO Box 277, 03036-0277), SAN 309-7684. Tel: 603-887-3404. FAX: 603-887-2701. E-mail: chesterpubliclibrary@gmail.com. Web Site: www.chesternh.org/chester-public-library. *Libr Dir,* Kandace Knowlton; *Asst Dir,* Maryjo Siergiej
Pop 4,621; Circ 23,000
Library Holdings: Bk Vols 45,000; Per Subs 40
Subject Interests: New England
Automation Activity & Vendor Info: (Circulation) Follett Software
Wireless access
Partic in Merry-Hill Rock Libr Coop
Open Mon & Wed 3-7, Tues & Thurs 10-7, Fri 1-4, Sat 10-1
Friends of the Library Group

CHESTERFIELD

P CHESTERFIELD PUBLIC LIBRARY*, 524 Rte 63, 03443-0158. SAN 309-7706. Tel: 603-363-4621. FAX: 603-363-4958. E-mail: information@chesterfieldlibrary.org. Web Site: www.chesterfieldlibrary.org. *Interim Dir,* Claudette Russell; E-mail: crussell@chesterfieldlibrary.org; *Children & Youth Serv Librn,* Karen La Rue; *Asst Librn,* Melissa Baptiste
Founded 1939. Pop 3,600; Circ 16,446
Library Holdings: CDs 1,677; DVDs 1,161; Large Print Bks 1,200; Bk Titles 31,655; Per Subs 35
Special Collections: Large Print
Subject Interests: Biographies, Cooking, Health, Hist, Mysteries, Natural sci, New England hist, Relig studies
Automation Activity & Vendor Info: (Cataloging) OpenAccess Software, Inc; (Circulation) OpenAccess Software, Inc; (OPAC) OpenAccess Software, Inc
Wireless access
Function: Adult bk club, Art exhibits, Bk club(s), Bks on cassette, Bks on CD, Children's prog, Computers for patron use, Homebound delivery serv, ILL available, OverDrive digital audio bks, Photocopying/Printing, Preschool reading prog, Prog for adults, Prog for children & young adult, Ref serv available, Spoken cassettes & CDs, Spoken cassettes & DVDs, Story hour, Summer reading prog, Teen prog, Telephone ref, VHS videos, Wheelchair accessible
Partic in New Hampshire Automated Information Systems; Nubanusit Library Cooperative
Special Services for the Deaf - Assistive tech
Special Services for the Blind - Audio mat; Bks on CD; Large print bks; Low vision equip; Magnifiers; Talking bks; Volunteer serv
Open Mon-Thurs 11-7, Sat 9-Noon
Friends of the Library Group

CHICHESTER

P CHICHESTER TOWN LIBRARY, 161 Main St, 03258. SAN 309-7714. Tel: 603-798-5613. FAX: 603-798-5439. E-mail: clibrary@comcast.net. Web Site: www.chichesternh.org/town-library. *Libr Dir,* Caroline Pynes; Staff 5 (MLS 1, Non-MLS 4)
Founded 1899. Pop 2,500; Circ 15,000
Library Holdings: Audiobooks 418; AV Mats 1,200; DVDs 1,598; Large Print Bks 85; Bk Titles 14,199; Per Subs 28
Function: 24/7 Electronic res, 24/7 Online cat, Activity rm, Adult bk club, After school storytime, Archival coll, Art exhibits, Art programs, Audiobks on Playaways & MP3, Audiobks via web, Bi-weekly Writer's Group, Bk club(s), Bks on CD, Children's prog, Computer training, Computers for patron use, Digital talking bks, Electronic databases & coll, Family literacy, Free DVD rentals, Holiday prog, ILL available, Internet access, Magazines, Magnifiers for reading, Mail & tel request accepted, Mail loans to mem, Meeting rooms, Movies, Museum passes, Online cat, Online ref, Outside serv via phone, mail, e-mail & web, OverDrive digital audio bks, Photocopying/Printing, Preschool outreach, Preschool reading prog, Prof lending libr, Prog for adults, Prog for children & young adult, Ref serv available, Res assist avail, Scanner, Spoken cassettes & CDs, Spoken cassettes & DVDs, STEM programs, Story hour, Study rm, Summer & winter reading prog, Summer reading prog, Teen prog, Telephone ref, Wheelchair accessible, Winter reading prog, Writing prog
Partic in Suncook Interlibrary Cooperative
Special Services for the Deaf - Bks on deafness & sign lang
Open Mon & Wed 2:30-8:30, Tues & Thurs 10-1:30, Fri 1:30-4:30, Sat 9-12
Restriction: Non-resident fee, Registered patrons only, Residents only, Restricted access, Restricted borrowing privileges, Restricted loan policy, Restricted pub use, Staff & customers only
Friends of the Library Group

CHOCORUA

P CHOCORUA PUBLIC LIBRARY*, 25 Deer Hill Rd, 03817. (Mail add: PO Box 128, 03817), SAN 309-7722. Tel: 603-323-8610. E-mail: librarian@chocorualibrary.org. Web Site: www.chocorualibrary.org. *Libr Dir,* Cathy Daney
Founded 1888. Pop 2,200; Circ 4,000
Library Holdings: Bk Vols 12,500; Per Subs 30
Wireless access
Function: Adult bk club, After school storytime, Archival coll, Art exhibits, Audio & video playback equip for onsite use, Bk reviews (Group), Bks on cassette, Bks on CD, Chess club, Children's prog, Computer training, Computers for patron use, Digital talking bks, E-Reserves, Free DVD rentals, Health sci info serv, Holiday prog, Home delivery & serv to seniorr ctr & nursing homes, Homework prog, ILL available, Instruction & testing, Jail serv, Learning ctr, Magnifiers for reading, Mail & tel request accepted, Mail loans to mem, Music CDs, Photocopying/Printing, Prog for adults, Prog for children & young adult, Ref & res, Ref serv available, Satellite serv, Serves people with intellectual disabilities, Spoken cassettes & CDs, Spoken cassettes & DVDs, Story hour, Summer reading prog, Tax forms, Telephone ref, VHS videos, Wheelchair accessible
Open Mon & Thurs 1-7, Sun 1-5

CLAREMONT

P FISKE FREE LIBRARY, 108 Broad St, 03743-2673. SAN 309-7730. Tel: 603-542-7017. FAX: 603-542-7029. Web Site: www.claremontnh.com/library. *Dir,* Michael Grace; E-mail: mgrace@claremontnh.com; *Asst Dir,* Marta Smith; E-mail: msmith@claremontnh.com; *Circ Librn,* Colin Sanborn; E-mail: csanborn@claremontnh.com
Founded 1873. Pop 13,902; Circ 121,852
Library Holdings: Bk Vols 48,000; Per Subs 150
Special Collections: Local Genealogy Coll; Local History Coll
Automation Activity & Vendor Info: (Circulation) Follett Software; (OPAC) Follett Software
Wireless access
Open Mon, Tues & Thurs 9-7, Wed & Fri 11-5, Sat 9-1
Friends of the Library Group

J RIVER VALLEY COMMUNITY COLLEGE*, Charles P Puksta Library, One College Pl, 03743. SAN 309-7749. Tel: 603-542-7744, Ext 5465. FAX: 603-543-1844. E-mail: rivervalley@ccsnh.edu. Web Site: www.rivervalley.edu/student-resources/charles-p-puksta-library. *Libr Assoc,* Gloria Oakes; E-mail: goakes@ccsnh.edu
Founded 1969
Library Holdings: Bk Titles 13,505; Per Subs 90
Special Collections: Deaf Education; New Hampshire Local History
Subject Interests: Allied health educ, Nursing
Automation Activity & Vendor Info: (Acquisitions) TLC (The Library Corporation); (Cataloging) TLC (The Library Corporation); (Circulation) TLC (The Library Corporation); (Course Reserve) TLC (The Library Corporation); (ILL) TLC (The Library Corporation); (OPAC) TLC (The Library Corporation); (Serials) TLC (The Library Corporation)
Wireless access
Special Services for the Deaf - Bks on deafness & sign lang; Spec interest per; Staff with knowledge of sign lang
Open Mon-Thurs 7:30am-8pm, Fri 8-4

COLEBROOK

P COLEBROOK PUBLIC LIBRARY, 126 Main St, 03576. (Mail add: PO Box 58, 03576-0058), SAN 309-7757. Tel: 603-237-4808. FAX: 603-237-4386. E-mail: colebrookpublib@gmail.com. Web Site: colebrookpubliclibrary.weebly.com. *Dir,* Julie Colby; *Youth Serv,* Melissa Hall; Staff 2 (Non-MLS 2)
Founded 1928. Pop 2,744; Circ 26,350
Jan 2021-Dec 2021 Income $227,085, City $206,360, Locally Generated Income $20,725. Mats Exp $17,025, Books $14,750, Per/Ser (Incl. Access Fees) $875, AV Mat $1,400. Sal $86,400 (Prof $58,261)
Library Holdings: Audiobooks 1,350; DVDs 1,661; e-journals 25; Large Print Bks 2,098; Bk Titles 36,668; Per Subs 13
Special Collections: Canadian Church Records; Nancy Dodge Genealogical Coll
Automation Activity & Vendor Info: (Acquisitions) Koha; (Cataloging) Koha; (Circulation) Koha; (ILL) Auto-Graphics, Inc; (OPAC) Koha; (Serials) EBSCO Discovery Service
Wireless access
Open Mon, Wed & Fri 10-5, Tues 10-1, Thurs 1-5, Sat 9-Noon

CONCORD

P CONCORD PUBLIC LIBRARY, 45 Green St, 03301. SAN 350-4395. Tel: 603-225-8670. FAX: 603-230-3693. E-mail: library@concordnh.gov. Web Site: concordnh.gov/588/Library. *Libr Dir,* Todd Fabian; E-mail: tfabian@concordnh.gov; *Asst Dir, Head, Tech Serv,* Matthew Bose; Tel: 603-230-3686, E-mail: mbose@concordnh.gov; *Head, Youth Serv,* Rebecca Kasten; Tel: 603-230-3688, E-mail: rkasten@concordnh.gov; Staff 6 (MLS 6)
Founded 1855. Pop 42,970; Circ 310,618
Library Holdings: AV Mats 12,032; Bk Vols 123,744; Per Subs 302
Special Collections: Concord Historical Coll. State Document Depository
Automation Activity & Vendor Info: (Acquisitions) Innovative Interfaces, Inc - Millennium; (Cataloging) Innovative Interfaces, Inc - Millennium; (Circulation) Innovative Interfaces, Inc - Millennium; (OPAC) Innovative Interfaces, Inc - Millennium; (Serials) Innovative Interfaces, Inc - Millennium
Wireless access
Open Mon, Wed & Fri 9-11, 12-2 & 3-5, Tues & Thurs 11-1, 2-4 & 5-7, Sat 9-11 & 12-2
Branches: 1
PENACOOK BRANCH, Three Merrimack St, Penacook, 03303, SAN 350-4425. Tel: 603-753-4441. *Library Contact,* Rebecca Kasten
Library Holdings: Bk Vols 10,000
Open Mon 2:30-8:30, Wed 2:30-5:30, Sat 9-12
Friends of the Library Group

L THE JOHN W KING NEW HAMPSHIRE LAW LIBRARY*, Supreme Court Bldg, One Charles Doe Dr, 03301-6160. SAN 350-4514. Tel: 603-271-3777. FAX: 603-513-5450. E-mail: lawlibrary@courts.state.nh.us. Web Site: www.courts.state.nh.us/lawlibrary. *Dir,* Mary S Searles; E-mail: msearles@courts.state.nh.us; *Acq,* Erin Hubbard; E-mail: ehubbard@courts.state.nh.us; *Libr Asst,* Rachel Catano; E-mail: rcatano@courts.state.nh.us; Staff 3 (MLS 1, Non-MLS 2)
Founded 1819
Library Holdings: Bk Vols 100,100; Per Subs 110
Special Collections: Laws & Court Reports; New Hampshire Material. State Document Depository; US Document Depository
Automation Activity & Vendor Info: (Acquisitions) SirsiDynix; (Cataloging) SirsiDynix; (Circulation) SirsiDynix; (OPAC) SirsiDynix; (Serials) SirsiDynix
Wireless access
Function: 24/7 Online cat, Archival coll, CD-ROM, Computers for patron use, Doc delivery serv, Electronic databases & coll, Govt ref serv, ILL available, Internet access, Jail serv, Mail & tel request accepted, Mail loans to mem, Microfiche/film & reading machines, Online cat, Photocopying/Printing, Ref serv available, Res libr, Telephone ref
Open Mon-Fri 8:30-4:30
Restriction: Borrowing requests are handled by ILL, Circ limited

S NEW HAMPSHIRE AUDUBON*, Francis Beach White Library, McLane Center, 84 Silk Farm Rd, 03301-8311. SAN 323-8296. Tel: 603-224-9909. FAX: 603-226-0902. E-mail: nha@nhaudubon.org. Web Site: www.nhaudubon.org. *Libr Mgr,* Jane Kolias; Tel: 603-224-9909, Ext 310
Founded 1972

Library Holdings: Bk Titles 3,000; Per Subs 61
Subject Interests: Ecology, Natural hist, Ornithology

S NEW HAMPSHIRE CORRECTIONS FACILITY FOR WOMEN LIBRARY, 42 Perimeter Rd, 03301. Tel: 603-271-0892. Web Site: www.nh.gov/nhdoc/facilities/goffstown.html. *Media Generalist II,* Jeff Lyons
Library Holdings: Bk Vols 3,000

GL NEW HAMPSHIRE DEPARTMENT OF JUSTICE*, Office of the Attorney General Library, 33 Capitol St, 03301-6397. SAN 377-2713. Tel: 603-271-3658. FAX: 603-271-2110. Web Site: www.doj.nh.gov.
Library Holdings: Bk Vols 10,000
Restriction: Staff use only

G NEW HAMPSHIRE DIVISION OF PUBLIC HEALTH SERVICES*, Public Health Services Library, 29 Hazen Dr, 03301. Tel: 603-271-5557. Web Site: www.dhhs.nh.gov/dphs. *Library Contact,* Martha Wells; E-mail: martha.wells@dhhs.nh.gov
Library Holdings: AV Mats 50; Bk Vols 150
Subject Interests: Diabetes, Disaster preparedness, Fitness, Nutrition, Older adults, Pub health training, Sch health, Tobacco prevention
Open Mon-Fri 8-12:30

M NEW HAMPSHIRE FAMILY VOICES LIBRARY*, Dept Health & Human Servs, Spec Med Servs, Thayer Bldg, 129 Pleasant St, 03301. Tel: 603-271-4525. Toll Free Tel: 800-852-3345, Ext 4525 (NH only). FAX: 603-271-4902. E-mail: nhfamilyvoices@nhfv.org. Web Site: nhfv.org/how-we-can-help/lending-library. *Co-Dir,* Martha-Jean Madison; *Co-Dir,* Terry Ohlson-Martin; E-mail: tom@nhfv.org
Library Holdings: AV Mats 100; Bk Vols 1,700
Open Mon-Fri 9-5

S NEW HAMPSHIRE HISTORICAL SOCIETY LIBRARY*, 30 Park St, 03301-6384. SAN 309-7781. Tel: 603-228-6688. Reference Tel: 603-856-0641. Administration Tel: 603-856-0643. FAX: 603-224-0463. Web Site: www.nhhistory.org/Research. *Libr Dir,* Sarah E Galligan; E-mail: sgalligan@nhhistory.org; *Ref Librn,* Paul Friday; E-mail: pfridayl@nhhistory.org; Staff 3 (MLS 2, Non-MLS 1)
Founded 1823
Library Holdings: AV Mats 200,000; Microforms 400; Music Scores 300; Bk Titles 40,000; Bk Vols 50,000; Per Subs 130; Videos 200
Special Collections: New Hampshire Church Records, 1700-1900, ms vols; New Hampshire Manuscripts, 1700-1990; New Hampshire Maps, 1700-1960; New Hampshire Newspapers, 1790-1900, microfilm; New Hampshire Photographs, 1850-1990; New Hampshire Provincial Deeds, 1640-1770, micro
Subject Interests: Archit, Decorative art, Genealogy, Hist of NH, Local hist
Automation Activity & Vendor Info: (Cataloging) MINISIS Inc; (OPAC) MINISIS Inc
Wireless access
Function: Archival coll, Ref serv available
Special Services for the Deaf - Accessible learning ctr; ADA equip; Adult & family literacy prog; Am sign lang & deaf culture; Assisted listening device
Special Services for the Blind - Assistive/Adapted tech devices, equip & products
Open Tues-Sat 9:30-5
Restriction: Free to mem, Non-circulating

M NEW HAMPSHIRE HOSPITAL*, Dorothy M Breene Memorial Library, 36 Clinton St, 03301-3861. SAN 309-779X. Tel: 603-271-5420. FAX: 603-271-5425. E-mail: breenelibrary@dhhs.nh.gov. Web Site: www.dhhs.nh.gov/dcbcs/nhh/libraries.htm. *Med Librn,* Karen Goodman. Subject Specialists: *Med, Psychiat, Psychol,* Karen Goodman; Staff 1 (MLS 1)
Founded 1880
Jul 2013-Jun 2014. Mats Exp $64,353, Books $3,000, Per/Ser (Incl. Access Fees) $48,353
Library Holdings: AV Mats 700; Bk Titles 2,000; Per Subs 75
Subject Interests: Commun mental health, Geriatrics, Neurology, Nursing, Occupational therapy, Psychiat, Psychol, Recreational therapy, Soc sci, Soc work
Automation Activity & Vendor Info: (Acquisitions) EOS International; (Cataloging) EOS International; (Circulation) EOS International; (Course Reserve) EOS International; (ILL) EOS International; (Media Booking) EOS International; (OPAC) EOS International; (Serials) EOS International
Partic in National Network of Libraries of Medicine Region 7
Open Mon-Thurs 8-3:30

P NEW HAMPSHIRE STATE LIBRARY*, 20 Park St, 03301. SAN 350-445X. Tel: 603-271-2144. Circulation Tel: 603-271-2616. Administration Tel: 603-271-2392. FAX: 603-271-2205. Administration FAX: 603-271-6826. TDD: 800-735-2964. Web Site: www.nh.gov/nhsl. *State Librn,* Michael York; Tel: 603-271-2397, E-mail: michael.york@dncr.nh.gov; *Adminr, Libr Operations,* Lori Fisher; Tel: 603-271-2393, E-mail: lori.fisher@dncr.nh.gov; *Tech Res Librn,* Bobbi Lee Slossar; Tel: 603-271-2143, E-mail: bobbilee.slossar@dncr.nh.gov; *Youth & Adult Serv Librn,* Deborah Dutcher; Tel: 603-271-2865, E-mail: deborah.dutcher@dncr.nh.gov; *Ref/Info Serv Supvr,* Charles Shipman; Tel: 603-271-3302, E-mail: charles.shipman@dncr.nh.gov; *Tech Serv Supvr,* Mary Russell; Tel: 603-271-2866, E-mail: mary.russell@dncr.nh.gov; Staff 42 (MLS 13, Non-MLS 29)
Founded 1716
Library Holdings: Braille Volumes 570; Bk Vols 567,699; Per Subs 73; Talking Bks 72,683; Videos 3,888
Special Collections: Historical Children's Books; New Hampshire Authors; New Hampshire Government & History; New Hampshire Imprints; New Hampshire Maps. Oral History; State Document Depository; US Document Depository
Subject Interests: Biog, Genealogy, Info sci, Law, Libr sci, Pub admin, Soc sci
Automation Activity & Vendor Info: (Cataloging) SirsiDynix; (ILL) SirsiDynix; (OPAC) SirsiDynix
Publications: Checklist of New Hampshire State Departments' Publications (Biennial); Granite Bits (Irregularly); Granite State Libraries (Bi-monthly newsletter); New Hampshire Libraries (Annual directory); New Hampshire Library Statistics (Annual)
Partic in LYRASIS; New Hampshire Automated Information Systems
Open Mon-Fri 8-4:30

P NEW HAMPSHIRE STATE LIBRARY, Talking Book Services, Gallen State Office Park, Dolloff Bldg, 117 Pleasant St, 03301-3852. SAN 309-7803. Tel: 603-271-2417, 603-271-3429. Administration Tel: 603-271-1498. Toll Free Tel: 800-491-4200 (NH only). FAX: 603-271-8370. E-mail: talking@dncr.nh.gov. Web Site: www.nh.gov/nhsl/talking_books. *Librn III, Supvr,* Marilyn Stevenson; E-mail: marilyn.s.stevenson@dncr.nh.gov; *Libr Assoc I,* Brenda Corey; *Libr Assoc I,* Joan Nelson; E-mail: joan.k.nelson@dncr.nh.gov; *Libr Tech 1,* Jody Matisko; Staff 1 (MLS 1)
Founded 1970
Wireless access
Function: Digital talking bks, Equip loans & repairs, Mail & tel request accepted, Mail loans to mem, Online cat, Outreach serv, OverDrive digital audio bks, VHS videos
Special Services for the Blind - BiFolkal kits; Braille servs; Children's Braille; Digital talking bk; Newsline for the Blind; Ref serv; Talking bks & player equip; Tel Pioneers equip repair group; Web-Braille
Open Mon-Fri 8-4:30
Restriction: Registered patrons only

S NEW HAMPSHIRE STATE PRISON FOR MEN LIBRARY*, 281 N State St, 03301. (Mail add: PO Box 14, 03302-0014), SAN 309-7811. Tel: 603-271-1929. FAX: 603-271-0401. Web Site: www.nh.gov/nhdoc/facilities/concord.html. *Media Generalist II,* Dana Benner
Founded 1918. Sal $45,000
Library Holdings: Bks on Deafness & Sign Lang 50; Electronic Media & Resources 1; High Interest/Low Vocabulary Bk Vols 300; Large Print Bks 800; Music Scores 300; Bk Vols 3,000; Per Subs 8; Videos 325
Special Collections: Law Coll; Lois Law Coll
Subject Interests: Educ, Hobby craft, Law, Penology, Recreational
Special Services for the Deaf - Assisted listening device
Special Services for the Blind - Talking bks & player equip
Restriction: Staff & inmates only

J NHTI, CONCORD'S COMMUNITY COLLEGE*, 31 College Dr, 03301-7425. SAN 309-782X. Tel: 603-230-4028. FAX: 603-230-9310. E-mail: nhtilibrary@ccsnh.edu. Web Site: www.nhti.edu/support-success/library-research-resources. *Learning Commons Coord,* Sarah Hebert; Tel: 603-271-6484, Ext 4201, E-mail: shebert@ccsnh.edu; *Circ Supvr,* Tim Fisher; Tel: 603-271-6484, Ext 4338, E-mail: tfisher@ccsnh.edu; *Circ,* John Dennett; E-mail: jdennett@ccsnh.edu; *Ser,* Joyce Verdone; E-mail: jverdone@ccsnh.edu; Staff 6.5 (MLS 3.5, Non-MLS 3)
Founded 1965. Enrl 3,850; Fac 150; Highest Degree: Associate
Library Holdings: e-books 35,000; Bk Titles 80,000; Per Subs 200
Special Collections: College Archives; NEARA Coll; NH Chapter AIA
Subject Interests: Archit, Architectural engr tech, Autism, Dental hygiene, Diagnostic ultrasound, Early childhood educ, Electronic, Emergency med care, Landscape archit, Mental health, Nursing, Radiologic tech
Automation Activity & Vendor Info: (Cataloging) TLC (The Library Corporation); (Circulation) TLC (The Library Corporation); (OPAC) TLC (The Library Corporation)
Wireless access
Publications: Acquisitions List; Bibliographies; Page Notes
Friends of the Library Group

L ORR & RENO LAW LIBRARY*, 45 S Main St, 03302. (Mail add: PO Box 3550, 03302-3550), SAN 323-7419. Tel: 603-223-9105. FAX: 603-223-9005. E-mail: library@orr-reno.com. Web Site: orr-reno.com. Staff 1 (MLS 1)
Library Holdings: Bk Titles 500; Per Subs 35
Subject Interests: Bus law, Immigration, Tax law
Function: ILL available
Restriction: Staff use only

CL UNIVERSITY OF NEW HAMPSHIRE SCHOOL OF LAW*, Two White St, 03301. SAN 309-7838. Circulation Tel: 603-513-5130. Administration Tel: 603-513-5131. Web Site: www.library.law.unh.edu. *Dir, Law Libr,* Sue Zago; E-mail: sue.zago@law.unh.edu; *Cat Librn,* Matt Jenks; *Electronic Res Librn,* Tom Hemstock; *IP Librn,* Jon R Cavicchi; *Ref Librn, Pub Serv,* Kathy Fletcher; *Syst Librn,* Melanie Cornell; *Acq, Supvr,* Kathie Goodwin; *Supvr, Ser,* Ellen Phillips; Staff 8 (MLS 4, Non-MLS 4)
Founded 1973. Enrl 450; Fac 25; Highest Degree: Doctorate
Special Collections: US Document Depository
Subject Interests: Electronic commerce, Intellectual property
Automation Activity & Vendor Info: (Acquisitions) Innovative Interfaces, Inc; (Cataloging) Innovative Interfaces, Inc; (Circulation) Innovative Interfaces, Inc; (Course Reserve) Innovative Interfaces, Inc; (ILL) OCLC; (OPAC) Innovative Interfaces, Inc; (Serials) Innovative Interfaces, Inc
Wireless access
Function: ILL available
Partic in NELLCO Law Library Consortium, Inc.; NHCUC
Special Services for the Blind - Closed circuit TV magnifier
Restriction: Access at librarian's discretion, Closed stack, Open to students, fac & staff

CONTOOCOOK

P HOPKINTON TOWN LIBRARY*, 61 Houston Dr, 03229. (Mail add: PO Box 217, 03229-0217), SAN 309-8494. Tel: 603-746-3663. FAX: 603-746-6799. E-mail: info@hopkintontownlibrary.org. Web Site: www.hopkintontownlibrary.org. *Dir,* Donna Dunlop; E-mail: ddunlop@hopkintontownlibrary.org; *Ch,* Leigh Maynard; E-mail: lmaynard@hopkintontownlibrary.org; *Ref Librn,* Karen Dixon; E-mail: kdixon@hopkintontownlibrary.org; Staff 2 (MLS 2)
Founded 1870. Pop 5,617; Circ 70,195
Wireless access
Function: Adult bk club, Art exhibits, Audiobks via web, Bks on cassette, Bks on CD, Children's prog, Citizenship assistance, Computer training, Computers for patron use, E-Reserves, Electronic databases & coll, Homebound delivery serv, ILL available, Internet access, Mail & tel request accepted, Museum passes, Music CDs, Online cat, Outreach serv, OverDrive digital audio bks, Photocopying/Printing, Preschool outreach, Prog for adults, Prog for children & young adult, Ref serv available, Senior computer classes, Story hour, Summer reading prog, Tax forms, Teen prog, Telephone ref, VHS videos, Wheelchair accessible, Writing prog
Open Tues & Wed 10-8, Thurs 10-6, Fri 10-5, Sat 10-3; Sun (Winter) 1-5
Friends of the Library Group

CONWAY

P CONWAY PUBLIC LIBRARY*, 15 Main Ave, 03818. (Mail add: PO Box 2100, 03818-2100), SAN 350-4662. Tel: 603-447-5552. FAX: 603-447-6921. E-mail: info@conwaypubliclibrary.org. Web Site: conwaypubliclibrary.org. *Dir,* David Smolen; E-mail: dsmolen@conwaypubliclibrary.org; *Head, Youth Serv,* Tara McKenzie; E-mail: tmckenzie@conwaypubliclibrary.org; *Ad,* Betty Parker; E-mail: bparker@conwaypubliclibrary.org; *ILL Librn,* Cheryl O'Neil; *Circ Serv,* Glynis Knox; *Tech Serv,* Katie Cunningham; E-mail: kcunningham@conwaypubliclibrary.org; Staff 4 (MLS 1, Non-MLS 3)
Founded 1900. Pop 10,000; Circ 83,500
Library Holdings: Bk Vols 37,000; Per Subs 95
Subject Interests: Local hist
Automation Activity & Vendor Info: (Cataloging) TLC (The Library Corporation); (Circulation) TLC (The Library Corporation); (OPAC) TLC (The Library Corporation)
Wireless access
Open Mon-Thurs 10-8, Fri & Sat 10-5
Friends of the Library Group

CORNISH

S SAINT-GAUDENS NATIONAL HISTORIC SITE LIBRARY*, National Park Service, 139 Saint-Gaudens Rd, 03745-4232. SAN 309-7846. Tel: 603-675-2175, Ext 112. FAX: 603-675-2701. Web Site: www.nps.gov/saga/learn/photosmultimedia/collections.htm. *Curator,* Dr Henry Duffy; E-mail: henry_duffy@nps.gov
Founded 1919
Library Holdings: Bk Vols 2,000
Special Collections: Cornish Art Colony Coll 1885-1935
Subject Interests: Art, Sculpture
Open Mon-Fri 9-4:30

CORNISH FLAT

P GEORGE H STOWELL FREE LIBRARY*, 24 School St, 03746. (Mail add: PO Box 360, 03746-0360), SAN 309-7854. Tel: 603-543-3644. E-mail: stowelllibrary@comcast.net. Web Site: www.cornishnh.net/?page_id=129. *Dir,* Brenda Freeland
Pop 1,500; Circ 3,800
Library Holdings: Bks on Deafness & Sign Lang 10; High Interest/Low Vocabulary Bk Vols 50; Bk Titles 9,750; Bk Vols 10,620; Per Subs 30
Subject Interests: Cornish hist
Wireless access
Open Mon & Fri 4-6, Wed 3-6, Sat 9-Noon

DALTON

P DALTON PUBLIC LIBRARY, Town of Dalton Municipal Bldg, 756 Dalton Rd, 03598. SAN 309-7870. Tel: 603-837-2751. FAX: 603-837-2273. E-mail: library@townofdalton.com. Web Site: townofdalton.com/municipal-departments/dalton-public-library. *Librn,* Doris Mitton
Founded 1892. Pop 1,000; Circ 1,775. Sal $8,788
Library Holdings: AV Mats 414; Bk Vols 7,000; Per Subs 17
Open Mon & Wed 2-5

DANBURY

P GEORGE GAMBLE LIBRARY*, 29 Rte 104, 03230. (Mail add: PO Box 209, 03230-0209), SAN 309-7889. Tel: 603-768-3765. E-mail: georgegamblelibrary@comcast.net. *Dir,* Linda Olmsted
Founded 1911. Pop 1,200; Circ 1,050
Library Holdings: Audiobooks 21; CDs 3; DVDs 123; Large Print Bks 24; Bk Vols 6,238
Function: Adult bk club
Special Services for the Blind - Audio mat
Open Wed 1-6, Sat 10-3

DANVILLE

P COLBY MEMORIAL LIBRARY*, Seven Colby Rd, 03819-5104. (Mail add: PO Box 10, 03819-0010), SAN 309-7897. Tel: 603-382-6733. FAX: 603-382-0487. Web Site: www.colbymemoriallibrary.org. *Dir,* Ann Massoth; E-mail: Director@colbymemoriallibrary.org
Founded 1892. Pop 4,300; Circ 70,000
Library Holdings: Bk Titles 33,000; Per Subs 25
Automation Activity & Vendor Info: (Cataloging) Koha; (Circulation) Koha; (OPAC) Koha
Wireless access
Partic in Merri-Hill-Rock Library Cooperative
Open Mon & Tues 12-8, Wed & Thurs 10-6, Sat 10-1
Friends of the Library Group

DEERFIELD

P PHILBRICK-JAMES LIBRARY, Four Church St, 03037-1426. SAN 309-7919. Tel: 603-463-7187. E-mail: pjlibrary@townofdeerfieldnh.com. Web Site: philbrickjameslibrary.org. *Libr Dir,* Candace Yost; *Ch,* Sarah Gontarski; E-mail: pjlchildrens@townofdeerfieldnh.com; *Libr Asst,* Suzanne Krohn; E-mail: pjlill@townofdeerfieldnh.com; Staff 1.8 (Non-MLS 1.8)
Founded 1880. Pop 4,280; Circ 16,623
Jan 2016-Dec 2016 Income $91,229. Mats Exp $13,500, Books $10,000, Per/Ser (Incl. Access Fees) $500, AV Mat $2,500, Electronic Ref Mat (Incl. Access Fees) $180. Sal $43,264
Library Holdings: Audiobooks 358; DVDs 125; Large Print Bks 225; Bk Titles 24,092; Per Subs 19
Wireless access
Function: Adult bk club, Art exhibits, Audiobks via web, Bks on cassette, Bks on CD, Children's prog, Computer training, Computers for patron use, Electronic databases & coll, Free DVD rentals, ILL available, Museum passes, Music CDs, Online cat, OverDrive digital audio bks, Photocopying/Printing, Prog for adults, Prog for children & young adult, Spoken cassettes & CDs, Story hour, Summer reading prog, Teen prog, VHS videos, Wheelchair accessible
Partic in Suncook Interlibrary Cooperative
Special Services for the Deaf - Bks on deafness & sign lang
Special Services for the Blind - Audio mat; Bks on cassette; Bks on CD; Large print bks; Reader equip; Talking bk serv referral
Open Mon & Wed 10-7, Tues & Thurs 10-5, Fri 10-2, Sat 9-Noon
Friends of the Library Group

DEERING

P DEERING PUBLIC LIBRARY, 762 Deering Center Rd, 03244. SAN 309-7927. Tel: 603-464-3248. FAX: 603-464-3804. E-mail: library@deering.nh.us. Web Site: www.deeringpubliclibrary.blogspot.com.
Founded 1926. Pop 1,800
Library Holdings: Bk Titles 5,500; Per Subs 10
Open Mon-Thurs 9-5
Friends of the Library Group

DERRY

P DERRY PUBLIC LIBRARY, 64 E Broadway, 03038-2412. SAN 309-7935. Tel: 603-432-6140. E-mail: derrylib@derrypl.org. Web Site: www.derrypl.org. *Libr Dir,* Eric Stern; E-mail: erics@derrypl.org; *Asst Dir, Head, Adult Serv,* Susan Brown; E-mail: susanb@derrypl.org; *Head, Children's Servx,* Ray Fontaine; E-mail: rayf@derrypl.org; *Head, Tech Serv,* Jessica DeLangie; E-mail: jessicad@derrypl.org; *Circ, ILL Librn,* Julie Gilchrist; E-mail: julieg@derrypl.org; *YA Librn,* Yahira Vallario; E-mail: yahirav@derrypl.org; *Communications Coordr,* Jennifer Khoury; E-mail: jenniferk@derrypl.org; Staff 10 (MLS 5, Non-MLS 5)
Founded 1905. Pop 33,037; Circ 184,516
Jul 2020-Jun 2021 Income $1,491,421, City $1,393,738, Locally Generated Income $97,683. Mats Exp $95,498, Books $54,054, Per/Ser (Incl. Access Fees) $4,470, Micro $2,380, AV Mat $12,492, Electronic Ref Mat (Incl. Access Fees) $7,373. Sal $777,535
Library Holdings: Audiobooks 3,207; CDs 5,091; DVDs 6,991; e-books 20,687; Large Print Bks 1,971; Bk Titles 75,653; Bk Vols 79,546; Per Subs 101
Special Collections: Houses of Derry (Harriet Newell Books); Robert Frost Material; Tasha Tudor Drawings
Automation Activity & Vendor Info: (Acquisitions) Innovative Interfaces, Inc; (Cataloging) Innovative Interfaces, Inc; (Circulation) Innovative Interfaces, Inc; (ILL) Innovative Interfaces, Inc; (OPAC) Innovative Interfaces, Inc; (Serials) Innovative Interfaces, Inc
Wireless access
Function: 24/7 Online cat, Activity rm, Adult bk club, After school storytime, Archival coll, Art exhibits, Art programs, Audiobks on Playaways & MP3, Audiobks via web, BA reader (adult literacy), Bk club(s), Bks on CD, Children's prog, Computer training, Computers for patron use, Electronic databases & coll, Free DVD rentals, Genealogy discussion group, Holiday prog, ILL available, Internet access, Life-long learning prog for all ages, Literacy & newcomer serv, Magazines, Magnifiers for reading, Mail & tel request accepted, Meeting rooms, Microfiche/film & reading machines, Movies, Museum passes, Music CDs, Notary serv, Online cat, Outreach serv, OverDrive digital audio bks, Photocopying/Printing, Preschool outreach, Preschool reading prog, Printer for laptops & handheld devices, Prof lending libr, Prog for adults, Prog for children & young adult, Ref & res, Ref serv available, Res assist avail, Scanner, Senior computer classes, Senior outreach, Serves people with intellectual disabilities, Spoken cassettes & CDs, Spoken cassettes & DVDs, STEM programs, Story hour, Study rm, Summer & winter reading prog, Summer reading prog, Tax forms, Teen prog, Telephone ref, Wheelchair accessible, Winter reading prog, Writing prog
Partic in GMILCS, Inc
Open Mon-Wed 9:30-8, Fri & Sat 9:30-5
Restriction: Non-circulating of rare bks, Non-resident fee
Friends of the Library Group

M PARKLAND MEDICAL CENTER*, Health Sciences Library, One Parkland Dr, 03038. SAN 323-6889. Tel: 603-421-2318. FAX: 603-421-2060. Web Site: parklandmedicalcenter.com/hl. *Med Librn,* Elanor Pickens
Library Holdings: Bk Titles 260; Per Subs 77
Wireless access
Function: Electronic databases & coll, Health sci info serv, ILL available
Restriction: Hospital employees & physicians only

DOVER

P DOVER PUBLIC LIBRARY*, 73 Locust St, 03820-3785. SAN 309-796X. Tel: 603-516-6050. Reference Tel: 603-516-6082. FAX: 603-516-6053. Web Site: library.dover.nh.gov. *Libr Dir,* Cathleen C Beaudoin; E-mail: c.beaudoin@dover.nh.gov; *Ad,* Susan Dunker; E-mail: s.dunker@dover.nh.gov; *Ch,* Patty Falconer; E-mail: p.falconer@dover.nh.gov; *ILL Librn,* Sue Vincent; E-mail: s.vincent@dover.nh.gov; *Ref Librn,* Denise LaFrance; E-mail: d.lafrance@dover.nh.gov; *Ref Librn,* Carrie Tremblay; E-mail: c.tremblay@dover.nh.gov; *Tech & Syst Librn,* Peggy Thrasher; E-mail: p.thrasher@dover.nh.gov; *Cataloger,* Phuong Openo; E-mail: p.openo@dover.nh.gov; Staff 9 (MLS 9)
Founded 1883. Pop 31,000; Circ 294,000
Jul 2017-Jun 2018 Income $1,433,747, City $1,379,247, Locally Generated Income $47,000, Other $7,500. Mats Exp $161,548, Books $125,400, Per/Ser (Incl. Access Fees) $6,000, Micro $600, AV Mat $25,548, Electronic Ref Mat (Incl. Access Fees) $4,000. Sal $633,593 (Prof $360,325)
Library Holdings: AV Mats 5,266; CDs 2,057; DVDs 1,000; Large Print Bks 1,400; Music Scores 1,557; Bk Titles 94,323; Bk Vols 104,441; Per Subs 294; Talking Bks 1,637; Videos 2,565
Special Collections: New Hampshire & New England Historical & Genealogical Materials
Subject Interests: Local hist
Automation Activity & Vendor Info: (Acquisitions) ByWater Solutions; (Cataloging) ByWater Solutions; (Circulation) ByWater Solutions; (OPAC) ByWater Solutions; (Serials) ByWater Solutions
Wireless access
Function: 24/7 Electronic res, 24/7 Online cat, 3D Printer, Adult bk club, Archival coll, Art exhibits, Audio & video playback equip for onsite use, Audiobks via web, AV serv, Bk club(s), Bks on CD, Children's prog, Citizenship assistance, Computer training, Computers for patron use, E-Readers, Electronic databases & coll, Equip loans & repairs, Free DVD rentals, ILL available, Instruction & testing, Internet access, Life-long learning prog for all ages, Magnifiers for reading, Mail & tel request accepted, Mango lang, Meeting rooms, Microfiche/film & reading machines, Movies, Museum passes, Music CDs, Online cat, Online ref, OverDrive digital audio bks, Passport agency, Photocopying/Printing, Preschool outreach, Preschool reading prog, Printer for laptops & handheld devices, Prog for adults, Prog for children & young adult, Ref & res, Ref serv available, Res performed for a fee, Scanner, Senior computer classes, Spoken cassettes & CDs, Spoken cassettes & DVDs, Story hour, Study rm, Summer reading prog, Tax forms, Teen prog, Telephone ref, VHS videos, Wheelchair accessible, Workshops
Publications: DPL (Newsletter)
Open Mon-Thurs 9-8:30, Fri 9-5:30, Sat 9-5 (9-1 Summer), Sun (Sept-May) 1-5
Restriction: Circ to mem only, Non-resident fee
Friends of the Library Group

DUBLIN

P DUBLIN PUBLIC LIBRARY, 1114 Main St, 03444. (Mail add: PO Box 442, 03444-0442), SAN 309-7986. Tel: 603-563-8658. FAX: 603-563-8751. E-mail: librarypublicdublin@myfairpoint.net. Web Site: dublinnhpubliclibrary.org. *Dir,* Rachael Lovett
Pop 1,556; Circ 7,500
Library Holdings: Bk Vols 20,000; Per Subs 40
Automation Activity & Vendor Info: (Cataloging) Biblionix/Apollo; (Circulation) Biblionix/Apollo; (OPAC) Biblionix/Apollo
Wireless access
Open Mon, Tues & Thurs 4-8, Wed 9-12 & 4-8, Sat 9-1
Friends of the Library Group

DUNBARTON

P DUNBARTON PUBLIC LIBRARY*, 1004 School St, 03046-4816. SAN 309-8001. Tel: 603-774-3546. FAX: 603-774-5563. E-mail: dunlib@gsinet.net. Web Site: www.dunbartonlibrary.org. *Dir,* Mary Girard; Staff 1.5 (MLS 1, Non-MLS 0.5)
Founded 1893. Pop 2,600; Circ 11,000
Library Holdings: Bk Vols 14,000; Per Subs 40
Special Collections: Dunbarton History Coll
Automation Activity & Vendor Info: (Cataloging) Follett Software; (Circulation) Follett Software; (OPAC) Follett Software
Wireless access
Open Tues & Thurs 1-8, Wed & Fri 10-4, Sat 10-2

DURHAM

P DURHAM PUBLIC LIBRARY*, 49 Madbury Rd, 03824. SAN 377-5372. Tel: 603-868-6699. FAX: 603-868-9944. E-mail: durhampl@gmail.com. Web Site: www.durhampubliclibrary.org. *Dir,* Rose Bebris; E-mail: rbebris@ci.durham.nh.us; *Dir, Adult Serv,* Jessica Ross; E-mail: jross@ci.durham.nh.us; *Dir, Ch Serv, Youth Serv Dir,* Lisa Kleinmann; E-mail: ekleinmann@ci.durham.nh.us; Staff 3 (MLS 1, Non-MLS 2)
Founded 1997. Pop 15,182; Circ 62,432
Jan 2014-Dec 2014 Income $402,515, City $389,575, Locally Generated Income $12,940. Mats Exp $23,618, Books $15,768, Per/Ser (Incl. Access Fees) $2,800, AV Mat $5,050. Sal $186,623
Library Holdings: Bk Vols 31,176; Per Subs 35
Automation Activity & Vendor Info: (Cataloging) Innovative Interfaces, Inc; (Circulation) Innovative Interfaces, Inc; (OPAC) Innovative Interfaces, Inc
Wireless access
Partic in Rochester Area Librarians
Open Mon 12-8, Tues-Thurs 10-8, Fri 10-5, Sat 10-2
Friends of the Library Group

C UNIVERSITY OF NEW HAMPSHIRE LIBRARY*, 18 Library Way, 03824. SAN 350-4727. Tel: 603-862-1540. Circulation Tel: 603-862-1535. Reference Tel: 603-862-1544. FAX: 603-862-0247. Web Site:

www.library.unh.edu. *Dean, Univ Libr,* Tara Lynn Fulton, PhD; Tel: 603-862-1506; *Assoc Dean of Libr,* Kimberly Sweetman; Tel: 603-862-1974, E-mail: kimberly.sweetman@unh.edu; *Asst Dean, Libr Admin,* Tracey Lauder; Tel: 603-862-3041, E-mail: tracey.lauder@unh.edu; *Coll Develop Librn,* Jennifer Carroll; Tel: 603-862-4049, Fax: 603-862-0294, E-mail: jennifer.carroll@unh.edu; *Spec Coll Librn,* Dr William E Ross; Tel: 603-862-0346, E-mail: bill.ross@unh.edu; *Cat & Metadata,* Sarah Theimer; Tel: 603-862-5603, E-mail: sarah.theimer@unh.edu; *ILL,* Nancy Plimpton; Tel: 603-862-1173, E-mail: nancy.plimpon@unh.edu; *Ref (Info Servs),* Kathrine Aydelott; Tel: 603-862-0657, E-mail: kathrine.aydelott@unh.edu; Staff 83 (MLS 23, Non-MLS 60)
Founded 1868. Enrl 14,766; Fac 678; Highest Degree: Doctorate
Library Holdings: AV Mats 44,887; Bk Vols 1,804,960; Per Subs 54,691
Special Collections: Amy Beach Papers; Angling (Milne Coll); Contra Dance & Folk Music (Ralph Page Coll); Donald Hall Coll; Frost Archives; Galway Kinnell Coll; Senator McIntyre Papers; Senator Norris Cotton Papers; US Patent Document Depository. State Document Depository; UN Document Depository; US Document Depository
Automation Activity & Vendor Info: (Acquisitions) Innovative Interfaces, Inc; (Cataloging) Innovative Interfaces, Inc; (Circulation) Innovative Interfaces, Inc; (OPAC) Innovative Interfaces, Inc; (Serials) Innovative Interfaces, Inc
Wireless access
Function: Doc delivery serv
Partic in Boston Library Consortium, Inc; New Hampshire College & University Council; OCLC Online Computer Library Center, Inc
Friends of the Library Group

Departmental Libraries:

CHEMISTRY, Parsons Hall, 23 College Rd, 03824-3598, SAN 350-4816. Tel: 603-862-1083. FAX: 603-862-4278. Web Site: www.library.unh.edu/branches/chemgide.html. *Librn,* Emily LeViness Poworoznek; Tel: 603-862-4168, E-mail: el@cisunix.unh.edu; *Libr Assoc,* Robert Constantine; E-mail: rjc3@cisunix.unh.edu; Staff 2 (MLS 1, Non-MLS 1)
Library Holdings: Bk Vols 32,472; Per Subs 129
Subject Interests: Chem, Mat sci
Open Mon-Thurs 8am-10pm, Fri 8-5, Sat 1-5, Sun 2-10
Friends of the Library Group

DAVID G CLARK MEMORIAL PHYSICS LIBRARY, DeMeritt Hall, Nine Library Way, 03824-3568, SAN 350-4875. Tel: 603-862-2348. FAX: 603-862-2998. Web Site: www.library.unh.edu/branches/physlib.html. *Librn,* Emily LeViness Poworoznek; E-mail: el@cisunix.unh.edu; *Libr Assoc,* Heather Gagnon; Staff 2 (MLS 1, Non-MLS 1)
Founded 1976
Library Holdings: Bk Vols 29,654; Per Subs 161
Subject Interests: Astronomy, Physics
Partic in Northeast Research Libraries Consortium
Open Mon-Thurs 8am-10pm, Fri 8-4:30, Sat 1-5, Sun 2-10
Friends of the Library Group

ENGINEERING, MATHEMATICS & COMPUTER SCIENCE, Kingsbury Hall, 33 Academic Way, 03824, SAN 350-4840. Tel: 603-862-1196. FAX: 603-862-4112. Web Site: www.library.unh.edu/branches/engmathcs.html. *Librn,* Emily L Poworoznek; Tel: 603-862-4168, E-mail: el@cisunix.unh.edu; *Libr Assoc,* Alan L Bryce; Tel: 603-862-1740, E-mail: abryce@cisunix.unh.edu; Staff 2 (MLS 1, Non-MLS 1)
Founded 1949
Library Holdings: Bk Vols 49,642; Per Subs 720
Subject Interests: Computer sci, Engr, Mat sci, Math, Statistics
Open Mon-Thurs 8am-11pm, Fri 8-5, Sat 1-5, Sun 2-11
Friends of the Library Group

EAST ANDOVER

P WILLIAM ADAMS BACHELDER LIBRARY*, 12 Chase Hill Rd, 03231. SAN 309-801X. Tel: 603-735-5333. E-mail: wablibrary@comcast.net. Web Site: andovernhlibrary.weebly.com. *Libr Dir,* Lee Wells
Circ 1,960
Library Holdings: Bk Vols 6,000; Per Subs 21
Automation Activity & Vendor Info: (Cataloging) Readerware; (Circulation) Readerware
Wireless access
Open Tues 9-12:30 & 6:30-8:30, Thurs 6:30-8:30, Fri 1:30-5

EAST DERRY

P TAYLOR LIBRARY*, 49 E Derry Rd, 03041. (Mail add: PO Box 110, 03041-0110), SAN 309-7943. Tel: 603-432-7186. FAX: 603-432-0985. E-mail: taylorlibrary@comcast.net. Web Site: www.taylorlibrary.org. *Libr Dir,* Linda Merrill; *Asst Dir,* Frances Mears
Founded 1878. Pop 35,000
Library Holdings: Bk Vols 20,010; Per Subs 30
Wireless access
Open Mon & Wed 10-5, Tues & Thurs 12-8, Fri & Sun 10-3
Friends of the Library Group

EAST KINGSTON

P EAST KINGSTON PUBLIC LIBRARY*, 47 Maplevale Rd, 03827. (Mail add: PO Box 9, 03827-0009), SAN 320-8443. Tel: 603-642-8333. E-mail: ekpublib@comcast.net. Web Site: www.eastkingstonlibrary.org. *Dir,* Tracy Waldron; E-mail: directoreastkingston@gmail.com; *Asst Librn,* Diane Sheckells
Pop 1,775; Circ 14,500
Library Holdings: Bk Vols 18,000; Per Subs 30
Automation Activity & Vendor Info: (Circulation) Book Systems
Wireless access
Open Mon & Wed 9-7, Tues & Thurs 3-7, Fri 9-1, Sat 9-3
Friends of the Library Group

EAST LEMPSTER

P MINER MEMORIAL LIBRARY*, Three 2nd NH Tpk, 03605. (Mail add: PO Box 131, 03605-0131), SAN 321-0448. Tel: 603-863-0051. FAX: 603-863-8105. E-mail: MinerLibrary@gmail.com. Web Site: minermemoriallibrary.placeweb.site. *Dir & Librn,* Bonnie Cilley
Founded 1893. Pop 1,099; Circ 2,000
Library Holdings: AV Mats 560; Bk Vols 6,000
Automation Activity & Vendor Info: (Cataloging) LibraryWorld, Inc; (OPAC) LibraryWorld, Inc
Wireless access
Function: Adult bk club, Art exhibits, Bks on CD, Children's prog, Computers for patron use, Holiday prog, Photocopying/Printing, Summer reading prog
Partic in Librarians of the Upper Valley Coop
Open Mon 10-12 & 2-7, Wed 1:30-6, Sun 2-5, Sat (Summer) 10-12
Friends of the Library Group

EAST ROCHESTER

P EAST ROCHESTER PUBLIC LIBRARY*, 935 Portland St, 03868. SAN 309-9393. Tel: 603-923-0126. E-mail: erpl@metrocast.net. *Dir,* Carol Shannon
Pop 2,500
Library Holdings: Bk Vols 6,000
Wireless access
Open Mon & Thurs 12-5
Friends of the Library Group

EFFINGHAM

P EFFINGHAM PUBLIC LIBRARY*, 30 Town House Rd, 03882. SAN 309-8036. Tel: 603-539-1537. E-mail: effinghamlibrary@gmail.com. Web Site: effingham.lib.nh.us. Staff 1 (Non-MLS 1)
Founded 1893. Pop 1,273; Circ 1,500
Jan 2018-Dec 2018 Income $55,026. Mats Exp $14,495. Sal $46,940
Library Holdings: Audiobooks 475; AV Mats 895; Braille Volumes 2; CDs 100; DVDs 1,300; Large Print Bks 195; Bk Titles 8,278; Bk Vols 8,735; Per Subs 8
Special Collections: Local Authors Coll
Subject Interests: Classics, Local hist, New England, Northern Indians (New England), State hist
Automation Activity & Vendor Info: (Cataloging) Follett Software; (Circulation) Follett Software; (ILL) SirsiDynix; (OPAC) Follett Software
Wireless access
Function: ILL available, Internet access, Photocopying/Printing, Prog for adults, Prog for children & young adult, Summer reading prog, Telephone ref, Wheelchair accessible, Workshops
Special Services for the Deaf - Closed caption videos
Special Services for the Blind - Large print bks; Sound rec
Open Tues & Wed 1-7, Fri & Sat 9-3
Friends of the Library Group

ENFIELD

P ENFIELD FREE PUBLIC LIBRARY, 23 Main St, 03748. (Mail add: PO Box 1030, 03748-1030), SAN 309-8044. Tel: 603-632-7145. FAX: 603-632-4055. E-mail: library@enfield.nh.us. Web Site: www.enfield.nh.us/enfield-public-library. *Librn,* Melissa Hutson; E-mail: mhutson@enfield.nh.us; *Asst Librn,* Kate Minshall
Founded 1893. Pop 4,202; Circ 37,776
Library Holdings: Bk Vols 30,884; Per Subs 45
Special Collections: Shaker Coll; Town of Enfield Historical Records
Wireless access
Open Tues & Wed 10-12 & 2-4, Thurs 5-7 by appointment

EPPING

P HARVEY MITCHELL MEMORIAL LIBRARY*, 151 Main St, 03042. SAN 309-8052. Tel: 603-679-5944, 603-734-4587. FAX: 603-679-5884. E-mail: harvmitch@gmail.com. Web Site: www.eppinglibrary.com. *Dir,* Ben Brown; Staff 1 (MLS 1)
Pop 7,000; Circ 32,000
Jan 2015-Dec 2015 Income $168,800
Library Holdings: Bk Vols 24,000; Videos 2,100
Special Collections: New Hampshire Coll
Automation Activity & Vendor Info: (Cataloging) Follett Software; (Circulation) Follett Software
Wireless access
Open Mon & Fri 10-5, Tues-Thurs 10-8, Sat 10-2, Sun 12-4
Friends of the Library Group

EPSOM

P EPSOM PUBLIC LIBRARY*, 1606 Dover Rd, 03234. SAN 309-8060. Tel: 603-736-9920. FAX: 603-736-9920. E-mail: epl@metrocast.net. Web Site: www.epsomlibrary.com. *Dir,* Nancy Claris; *Youth Serv,* Vickie Benner
Pop 4,600
Library Holdings: Bk Vols 27,000; Per Subs 40
Automation Activity & Vendor Info: (Circulation) Book Systems
Wireless access
Partic in Suncook Interlibrary Cooperative
Open Mon-Thurs 10-7, Sat 9-1
Friends of the Library Group

ERROL

P ERROL PUBLIC LIBRARY*, 67 Main St, 03579. (Mail add: PO Box 130, 03579-0007), SAN 309-8079. Tel: 603-482-7720. E-mail: errolbks@gmail.com. *Co-Dir,* Pat Calder; *Co-Dir,* Carol Hall
Pop 292; Circ 1,549
Library Holdings: Audiobooks 88; CDs 10; DVDs 612; Large Print Bks 247; Bk Vols 6,288; Per Subs 12
Subject Interests: Christian living, Fiction, Handicrafts, Local hist
Wireless access
Function: 24/7 Electronic res
Open Mon 6pm-8pm, Wed, Fri & Sat 9-1, Thurs 1-5

ETNA

P HANOVER TOWN LIBRARY, 130 Etna Rd, 03750. (Mail add: PO Box 207, 03750-0207), SAN 309-8346. Tel: 603-643-3116. FAX: 603-643-3116. E-mail: etna.library@hanovernh.org. Web Site: www.hanovernh.org/etna-library. *Librn,* Barbara Prince; Staff 2 (Non-MLS 2)
Founded 1898. Pop 9,212
Library Holdings: Bk Titles 8,000; Per Subs 18; Talking Bks 441
Subject Interests: Local hist
Automation Activity & Vendor Info: (Circulation) Innovative Interfaces, Inc
Wireless access
Open Mon, Wed & Thurs 2:30-6:30, Tues & Fri 9:30-2:30, Sat 12:30-2:30

EXETER

S AMERICAN INDEPENDENCE MUSEUM LIBRARY*, One Governors Lane, 03833. SAN 373-2843. Tel: 603-772-2622. E-mail: info@independencemuseum.org. Web Site: www.independencemuseum.org. *Colls Mgr,* Rachel Passannant
Founded 1902
Library Holdings: Bk Vols 680
Special Collections: 18th Century NH & US History, bks, doc, pamphlets; Original 18th & 19th Century Documents, Maps & Letters
Subject Interests: Am Revolution
Wireless access
Restriction: Open by appt only

M EXETER HOSPITAL INC*, Health Sciences Library, Five Alumni Dr, 03833-2160. SAN 377-9556. Tel: 603-580-6226. E-mail: library@ehr.org. *Librn,* Gayle Tudisco; E-mail: gtudisco@ehr.org; Staff 1 (MLS 1)
Library Holdings: Bk Titles 500; Per Subs 100
Subject Interests: Med, Nursing
Function: ILL available
Partic in National Network of Libraries of Medicine Region 7; North Atlantic Health Sciences Libraries, Inc
Restriction: Open to others by appt, Staff use only

P EXETER PUBLIC LIBRARY*, Four Chestnut St, 03833. SAN 309-8087. Tel: 603-772-3101, 603-772-6036. FAX: 603-772-7548. E-mail: deweyexeter1@comcast.net. Web Site: www.exeternh.gov/library. *Dir,* Hope Godino; *Asst Dir,* Julia Lanter; *Asst Ch,* Denise De Les Dernier
Founded 1853. Pop 14,000; Circ 219,950
Library Holdings: Bk Vols 80,000; Per Subs 120
Special Collections: New Hampshire Coll
Automation Activity & Vendor Info: (Circulation) Follett Software
Wireless access
Open Mon-Thurs 8:30-8, Fri 8:30-5, Sat 9-5 (10-1 Summer)
Friends of the Library Group

FARMINGTON

P GOODWIN LIBRARY*, 422 Main St, 03835-1519. SAN 309-8095. Tel: 603-755-2944. Administration Tel: 603-755-2944, Ext 102. Administration FAX: 603-755-3681. Reference E-mail: reference@goodwinlibrary.org. Web Site: www.goodwinlibrary.org. *Dir,* Tami LaRock; E-mail: director@goodwinlibrary.org; Staff 9 (MLS 1, Non-MLS 8)
Founded 1928. Pop 6,800; Circ 42,000
Jan 2018-Dec 2018 Income $291,450, City $271,450, Locally Generated Income $20,000. Mats Exp $22,495, Books $16,000, Per/Ser (Incl. Access Fees) $1,000, Other Print Mats $900, AV Mat $4,500, Electronic Ref Mat (Incl. Access Fees) $1,795, Presv $100. Sal $174,870 (Prof $38,000)
Library Holdings: Audiobooks 771; DVDs 1,793; Electronic Media & Resources 6; Large Print Bks 120; Bk Vols 15,445; Per Subs 2,059
Special Collections: Farmington News, mid 1800-1970's, digitized online database, Family Burial index; New Hampshire History, Authors & Books; Town & Family Histories of Farmington (Museum Artifacts)
Automation Activity & Vendor Info: (Acquisitions) Biblionix/Apollo; (Cataloging) Biblionix/Apollo; (Circulation) Biblionix/Apollo; (ILL) Biblionix/Apollo; (OPAC) Biblionix
Wireless access
Function: 24/7 Electronic res, 24/7 Online cat, Adult bk club, Adult literacy prog, Audiobks via web, Bi-weekly Writer's Group, Bk club(s), Bks on CD, Children's prog, Computer training, Computers for patron use, Doc delivery serv, E-Readers, Electronic databases & coll, Family literacy, For res purposes, Free DVD rentals, Holiday prog, Homebound delivery serv, Homework prog, ILL available, Internet access, Laminating, Large print keyboards, Learning ctr, Literacy & newcomer serv, Magazines, Mail & tel request accepted, Meeting rooms, Movies, Museum passes, Notary serv, Online cat, Online ref, Outreach serv, OverDrive digital audio bks, Photocopying/Printing, Preschool outreach, Prog for adults, Prog for children & young adult, Ref & res, Ref serv available, Scanner, Spoken cassettes & CDs, Story hour, Summer reading prog, Tax forms, Teen prog, Telephone ref, Wheelchair accessible, Workshops, Writing prog
Partic in Rochester Area Librarians
Special Services for the Blind - Bks on CD; Large print bks
Open Mon & Fri 10-5, Tues & Thurs 2-8, Sat 10-2
Restriction: Non-circulating coll, Non-resident fee, Pub ref by request, Researchers by appt only
Friends of the Library Group

FITZWILLIAM

P FITZWILLIAM TOWN LIBRARY, 11 Templeton Tpk, 03447. SAN 309-8109. Tel: 603-585-6503. FAX: 603-585-6738. E-mail: info@fitzlib.org. Web Site: www.fitzlib.org. *Libr Dir,* Kate Thomas; *Asst Librn,* Winta Hay; Staff 3 (MLS 1, Non-MLS 2)
Founded 1913. Pop 2,300; Circ 20,000
Library Holdings: Audiobooks 1,100; DVDs 1,584; Large Print Bks 200; Bk Vols 17,321; Per Subs 43
Automation Activity & Vendor Info: (Cataloging) ByWater Solutions; (Circulation) ByWater Solutions; (OPAC) ByWater Solutions
Wireless access
Function: 24/7 Electronic res, Activity rm, Adult bk club, Art exhibits, Audiobks via web, Bk club(s), Children's prog, Computer training, Computers for patron use, E-Readers, E-Reserves, Electronic databases & coll, Equip loans & repairs, Free DVD rentals, Holiday prog, ILL available, Magazines, Magnifiers for reading, Mango lang, Movies, Online cat, Online ref, OverDrive digital audio bks, Photocopying/Printing, Preschool reading prog, Prog for adults, Prog for children & young adult, Summer reading prog, Tax forms, Teen prog, Telephone ref, Wheelchair accessible
Open Mon 2-8, Tues & Thurs 2-6, Wed 9-12 & 2-8, Sat 9-Noon
Friends of the Library Group

FRANCESTOWN

P GEORGE HOLMES BIXBY MEMORIAL LIBRARY*, 52 Main St, 03043-3025. (Mail add: PO Box 69, 03043-0069), SAN 309-8117. Tel: 603-547-2730. FAX: 603-547-2730. E-mail: francestownlibrary@gmail.com. *Dir,* Carol Brock; *Ch,* Mark Marony
Founded 1827. Pop 1,500; Circ 10,099
Library Holdings: Bk Titles 15,000; Per Subs 40; Talking Bks 150
Special Collections: Oral History
Wireless access
Publications: Conservation Letter; Monthly Calendar
Open Tues 2-7:30, Wed 10-5, Thurs 2-7, Fri 12-5, Sat 9-12:30
Friends of the Library Group

FRANCONIA

P ABBIE GREENLEAF LIBRARY*, 439 Main St, 03580. (Mail add: PO Box 787, 03580-0787), SAN 309-8125. Tel: 603-823-8424. E-mail: info@abbielibrary.org. Web Site: www.abbielibrary.org. *Dir,* Ann Steuernagel
Founded 1892. Pop 1,203; Circ 22,044
Library Holdings: Bk Vols 22,000; Per Subs 45
Special Collections: Franconia Coll; New Hampshire Coll
Subject Interests: NH Franconia Region
Wireless access
Open Mon & Tues 2-6, Wed 10-12 & 2-6, Thurs & Fri 2-5, Sat 10-2
Friends of the Library Group

FRANKLIN

P FRANKLIN PUBLIC LIBRARY*, 310 Central St, 03235. SAN 309-8133. Tel: 603-934-2911. FAX: 603-934-7413. Web Site: www.franklinnh.org/Pages/FranklinNH_Library/index. *Dir,* Robert Sargent; E-mail: rob.sargent@franklin.lib.nh.us; *Ch,* Rachel Stolworthy; E-mail: rachel.stolworthy@franklin.lib.nh.us; Staff 5 (MLS 1, Non-MLS 4)
Founded 1907. Pop 8,300; Circ 57,000
Library Holdings: AV Mats 3,000; Bk Titles 24,000; Bk Vols 27,000; Per Subs 100
Special Collections: Franklin History; New Hampshire History
Automation Activity & Vendor Info: (Cataloging) Follett Software; (Circulation) Follett Software; (OPAC) Follett Software
Open Tues 11-8, Wed-Sat 8-5

FREEDOM

P FREEDOM PUBLIC LIBRARY*, 38 Old Portland Rd, 03836. (Mail add: PO Box 159, 03836-0159), SAN 309-8141. Tel: 603-539-5176. E-mail: freedomlibrary@roadrunner.com. Web Site: www.freedompubliclibrary.org. *Dir,* Elizabeth Rhymer; E-mail: director@freedompubliclibrary.org; *Asst Librn,* Amanda Feuerborn; E-mail: circ@freedompubliclibrary.org; Staff 2 (MLS 1, Non-MLS 1)
Pop 1,440
Library Holdings: Bk Vols 14,000; Per Subs 13
Special Collections: Oral History
Subject Interests: NH
Wireless access
Open Tues & Thurs 2-7, Wed 10-2, Fri 12-5, Sat 10-1
Friends of the Library Group

FREMONT

P FREMONT PUBLIC LIBRARY*, Seven Jackie Bernier Dr, 03044. SAN 309-815X. Tel: 603-895-9543. FAX: 603-244-1724. E-mail: frelib@comcast.net. Web Site: fremont.nh.gov/Pages/FremontNH_Library. *Dir,* Eric Abney; *Asst Librn,* Catherine Murdock; *Ch,* Nancy Mason
Founded 1894. Pop 4,000; Circ 23,000
Automation Activity & Vendor Info: (Cataloging) Follett Software; (Circulation) Follett Software; (OPAC) Follett Software
Wireless access
Open Mon 12-6, Tues & Thurs 1-7, Wed & Fri 9-5, Sat 9-2
Friends of the Library Group

GILFORD

P GILFORD PUBLIC LIBRARY*, 31 Potter Hill Rd, 03249-6803. SAN 309-8168. Tel: 603-524-6042. FAX: 603-524-1218. E-mail: library@gilfordlibrary.org. Web Site: www.gilfordlibrary.org. *Dir,* Katherine Dormody; E-mail: katherine@gilfordlibrary.org; *Asst Dir,* Kayleigh Thomas; *Teen Librn,* Mark Thomas; Staff 8 (MLS 2, Non-MLS 6)
Founded 1894. Pop 6,800
Library Holdings: Bk Vols 49,000; Per Subs 100
Subject Interests: NH
Automation Activity & Vendor Info: (Circulation) SirsiDynix; (OPAC) SirsiDynix
Wireless access
Open Mon, Wed & Fri 9-6, Tues & Thurs 10-8, Sat 10-2
Friends of the Library Group

GILMANTON

P GILMANTON CORNER PUBLIC LIBRARY*, 509 Province Rd, 03237-9205. (Mail add: PO Box 504, 03237-0504), SAN 309-8176. Tel: 603-267-6200. E-mail: gilmantoncornerlibrary@metrocast.net. Web Site: www.gilmantonnh.org/corners-library-municipal-library.
Founded 1912. Pop 3,060
Mar 2014-Feb 2015 Income $4,700, City $3,700, Locally Generated Income $1,000. Mats Exp $2,700
Library Holdings: Audiobooks 170; Braille Volumes 2; CDs 150; DVDs 125; Large Print Bks 50; Music Scores 50; Bk Vols 8,010; Per Subs 3; Videos 15
Special Collections: State Document Depository
Open Mon, Wed & Fri 3-5

GILMANTON IRON WORKS

P GILMANTON YEAR-ROUND LIBRARY*, 1358 NH Rte 140, 03837. Tel: 603-364-2400. E-mail: gyrla@metrocast.org. Web Site: www.gyrla.org. *Librn,* Tasha LeRoux Stetson; *Youth Serv Librn,* Jennifer Landry MacLeod; Staff 1 (Non-MLS 1)
Founded 1916. Pop 1,500
Library Holdings: Bk Titles 5,000
Open Tues & Thurs 1-7, Wed & Fri 10-4, Sat 10-3
Friends of the Library Group

GILSUM

P GILSUM PUBLIC LIBRARY*, 650 Rte 10, 03448-7502. SAN 309-8206. Tel: 603-357-0320. FAX: 603-352-0845. E-mail: gilsumlibrary@comcast.net. Web Site: gilsum.org/community/gilsum-public-library. *Librn,* Gail Bardwell
Founded 1892. Pop 800; Circ 4,555
Library Holdings: Bk Vols 10,800; Per Subs 23
Wireless access
Open Mon 12-4 & 6-8, Tues 6-8, Wed 10-2, Sat 10-Noon

GOFFSTOWN

P GOFFSTOWN PUBLIC LIBRARY, Two High St, 03045-1910. SAN 309-8214. Tel: 603-497-2102. E-mail: goflib@goffstownlibrary.com. Web Site: www.goffstownlibrary.com. *Libr Dir,* Dianne Hathaway; E-mail: dianneh@goffstownlibrary.com; *Head, Youth Serv,* Patti Penick; E-mail: pattip@goffstownlibrary.com; Staff 12 (MLS 4, Non-MLS 8)
Founded 1888. Pop 18,000; Circ 103,150
Jan 2021-Dec 2021 Income $752,596. Mats Exp $63,126, Books $46,926, Electronic Ref Mat (Incl. Access Fees) $16,200
Automation Activity & Vendor Info: (Acquisitions) Innovative Interfaces, Inc; (Cataloging) Innovative Interfaces, Inc; (Circulation) Innovative Interfaces, Inc; (OPAC) Innovative Interfaces, Inc; (Serials) Innovative Interfaces, Inc
Wireless access
Function: 24/7 Electronic res, 24/7 Online cat, Adult bk club, Art programs, Audiobks on Playaways & MP3, Audiobks via web, Bk club(s), Bks on CD, Children's prog, Computer training, Computers for patron use, Digital talking bks, Electronic databases & coll, For res purposes, Free DVD rentals, Holiday prog, Home delivery & serv to seniorr ctr & nursing homes, Homebound delivery serv, ILL available, Instruction & testing, Internet access, Life-long learning prog for all ages, Magazines, Mail & tel request accepted, Mango lang, Museum passes, Music CDs, Online cat, Online ref, Outreach serv, OverDrive digital audio bks, Photocopying/Printing, Preschool outreach, Preschool reading prog, Prof lending libr, Prog for adults, Prog for children & young adult, Ref & res, Ref serv available, Res assist avail, Scanner, Senior outreach, Serves people with intellectual disabilities, STEM programs, Story hour, Summer & winter reading prog, Summer reading prog, Tax forms, Teen prog, Visual arts prog, Wheelchair accessible, Winter reading prog
Partic in GMILCS, Inc
Open Mon, Thurs & Fri 9-5, Tues & Wed 9-8, Sat (Sept-June) 9-2
Friends of the Library Group

GORHAM

P GORHAM PUBLIC LIBRARY*, 35 Railroad St, 03581. SAN 309-8222. Tel: 603-466-2525. FAX: 603-466-1146. E-mail: gorhampubliclibrary@ne.rr.com. Web Site: gorhamnh.org/Pages/GorhamNH_Library/index. *Dir,* Shannon Buteau
Founded 1895. Pop 3,600; Circ 24,856
Library Holdings: Bk Vols 30,000; Per Subs 28
Special Collections: New Hampshire Books Coll
Automation Activity & Vendor Info: (Acquisitions) Biblionix
Wireless access
Open Mon-Fri 10-6, Sat 10-Noon

GOSHEN

P OLIVE G PETTIS MEMORIAL LIBRARY, Goshen Library, 36 Mill Village Rd N, 03752. (Mail add: PO Box 57, 03752-0057), SAN 309-8230. Tel: 603-863-6921. E-mail: info@goshenlibrary.org. Web Site: www.goshenlibrary.org. *Libr Mgr,* Shelby Wood; E-mail: ogplibrarian@goshenlibrary.org; Staff 2 (Non-MLS 2)
Founded 1908. Pop 742; Circ 2,020
Apr 2013-Mar 2014 Income $24,628, City $24,128, Locally Generated Income $500. Mats Exp $2,100, Books $1,200, Per/Ser (Incl. Access Fees) $260, AV Mat $240, Electronic Ref Mat (Incl. Access Fees) $400. Sal $15,840
Library Holdings: Audiobooks 8,000; DVDs 200; e-books 10,000; Large Print Bks 20; Bk Vols 7,400; Per Subs 12; Spec Interest Per Sub 4

Special Collections: John Gunnison
Subject Interests: Local hist
Automation Activity & Vendor Info: (Cataloging) LibraryWorld, Inc; (Circulation) LibraryWorld, Inc
Wireless access
Function: Adult bk club, Audiobks via web, Bks on CD, Children's prog, Computer training, Computers for patron use, Electronic databases & coll, Free DVD rentals, Homebound delivery serv, Homework prog, ILL available, Internet access, Museum passes, Music CDs, Online cat, OverDrive digital audio bks, Photocopying/Printing, Preschool outreach, Preschool reading prog, Printer for laptops & handheld devices, Prog for adults, Prog for children & young adult, Satellite serv, Scanner, Senior computer classes, Senior outreach, Story hour, Summer reading prog, Teen prog, Wheelchair accessible
Open Tues 8-5, Wed 8-1, Thurs & Fri 3-8
Restriction: Authorized patrons, Circ to mem only, External users must contact libr, ID required to use computers (Ltd hrs), In-house use for visitors, Non-circulating of rare bks, Non-resident fee
Friends of the Library Group

GRAFTON

P GRAFTON PUBLIC LIBRARY, 47 Library Rd, 03240. (Mail add: PO Box 313, 03240-0310), SAN 309-8249. Tel: 603-523-7865. E-mail: library@townofgraftonnh.com. Web Site: graftonpubliclibrary.wixsite.com/graftonnh. *Libr Dir,* Stacey Glazier; *Librn,* Debra Clough
Pop 998; Circ 2,355
Library Holdings: Bk Vols 6,000; Per Subs 10
Open Mon 5-8, Wed 9-12 & 5-8, Sat 9-12

GRANTHAM

P DUNBAR FREE LIBRARY*, 401 Rte 10 S, 03753. (Mail add: PO Box 1580, 03753-1580), SAN 309-8257. Tel: 603-863-2172. FAX: 603-863-2172. E-mail: info@dunbarlibrary.org. Web Site: www.dunbarlibrary.org. *Dir,* Dawn Huston; *Asst Librn, ILL Librn,* Joey B Holmes; *Ch, Programming Librn,* Karen Goldstein; E-mail: dflprogramming@comcast.net; Staff 3 (MLS 1, Non-MLS 2)
Founded 1901. Pop 2,985; Circ 56,000
Jul 2017-Jun 2018 Income $226,764, City $226,164, Locally Generated Income $600. Mats Exp $24,227, Books $15,095, Per/Ser (Incl. Access Fees) $1,000, AV Mat $6,152, Electronic Ref Mat (Incl. Access Fees) $1,980. Sal $94,472 (Prof $44,772)
Library Holdings: Audiobooks 9,892; AV Mats 2,346; Bks on Deafness & Sign Lang 38; Braille Volumes 2; Large Print Bks 175; Bk Titles 18,076; Per Subs 69; Talking Bks 953; Videos 1,169
Automation Activity & Vendor Info: (Cataloging) Follett Software; (Circulation) Follett Software; (ILL) SirsiDynix; (OPAC) Follett Software
Wireless access
Function: 24/7 Electronic res, 24/7 Online cat, Adult bk club, Art exhibits, Audio & video playback equip for onsite use, Audiobks via web, Bk club(s), Bks on cassette, Bks on CD, Butterfly Garden, Children's prog, Citizenship assistance, Computer training, Computers for patron use, E-Readers, Electronic databases & coll, Free DVD rentals, Games & aids for people with disabilities, Holiday prog, Homebound delivery serv, ILL available, Instruction & testing, Internet access, Laminating, Life-long learning prog for all ages, Magazines, Mail & tel request accepted, Mango lang, Movies, Museum passes, Music CDs, Online cat, Outside serv via phone, mail, e-mail & web, OverDrive digital audio bks, Photocopying/Printing, Preschool reading prog, Printer for laptops & handheld devices, Prog for adults, Prog for children & young adult, Ref serv available, Scanner, Senior computer classes, Spanish lang bks, Spoken cassettes & CDs, Spoken cassettes & DVDs, Story hour, Summer reading prog, Tax forms, Teen prog, Telephone ref, VHS videos, Wheelchair accessible
Partic in Librarians of the Upper Valley Coop; New Hampshire Downloadable Books Consortium
Special Services for the Deaf - Bks on deafness & sign lang; Closed caption videos; High interest/low vocabulary bks
Special Services for the Blind - Bks & mags in Braille, on rec, tape & cassette; Bks available with recordings; Bks on CD; Home delivery serv; Large print bks; Recorded bks
Open Mon & Wed 9-7:30, Thurs 9-5, Fri 9-12, Sat 9-2
Restriction: Non-circulating of rare bks
Friends of the Library Group

GREENFIELD

P STEPHENSON MEMORIAL LIBRARY, Greenfield Library, 761 Forest Rd, 03047. (Mail add: PO Box 127, 03047-0127), SAN 309-8265. Tel: 603-547-2790. Web Site: www.greenfield-nh.gov/stephenson-memorial-library. *Dir,* David Bridgewater; E-mail: director@stephensonlibrary.org; Staff 1 (Non-MLS 1)
Founded 1903. Pop 1,749
Library Holdings: Bk Vols 15,000; Per Subs 25
Special Collections: American Anthology of Music, recs; Greenfield (Town & Local Events), photos
Automation Activity & Vendor Info: (Cataloging) Biblionix/Apollo
Function: 24/7 Electronic res, 24/7 Online cat, 3D Printer, Activity rm, Adult bk club, After school storytime, Art exhibits, Audiobks via web, Bk club(s), Bks on CD, Children's prog, Computer training, Computers for patron use, Digital talking bks, E-Readers, Electronic databases & coll, Family literacy, Free DVD rentals, Homebound delivery serv, Homework prog, ILL available, Internet access, Life-long learning prog for all ages, Magazines, Mail & tel request accepted, Meeting rooms, Online cat, Online info literacy tutorials on the web & in blackboard, Online ref, Outreach serv, OverDrive digital audio bks, Photocopying/Printing, Prog for adults, Prog for children & young adult, Ref & res, Ref serv available, Scanner, Senior outreach, STEM programs, Story hour, Study rm, Summer & winter reading prog, Wheelchair accessible, Writing prog
Publications: New Town History
Friends of the Library Group

GREENLAND

P WEEKS PUBLIC LIBRARY*, 36 Post Rd, 03840-2312. (Mail add: PO Box 430, 03840-0430), SAN 309-8273. Tel: 603-436-8548. FAX: 603-427-0913. E-mail: weekspl@comcast.net. Web Site: www.weekslibrary.org. *Dir,* Denise Grimse; E-mail: dgrimsewpl@comcast.net; *Asst Dir, Children's Librn,* Susan MacDonald; *Circ Librn,* Elaine Molleur; *ILL Librn,* Lee Atkinson; *Librn,* Position Currently Open; *Cataloger, Circ,* Carol Chamberlain; *Circ,* Margaret Mooers; Staff 3 (MLS 2, Non-MLS 1)
Founded 1897. Pop 3,724; Circ 37,154
Jan 2017-Dec 2017 Income $290,566, City $284,962, Locally Generated Income $5,604. Mats Exp $36,891, Books $19,325, Per/Ser (Incl. Access Fees) $1,973, AV Mat $10,895, Electronic Ref Mat (Incl. Access Fees) $4,698. Sal $176,452 (Prof $104,164)
Library Holdings: Audiobooks 1,239; CDs 794; DVDs 3,305; e-books 21,943; Large Print Bks 467; Bk Vols 22,302; Per Subs 36
Special Collections: Greenland; New Hampshire
Automation Activity & Vendor Info: (Cataloging) Book Systems; (Circulation) Book Systems; (OPAC) Book Systems
Wireless access
Function: 3D Printer, Adult bk club, Audiobks via web, Bk club(s), Bks on CD, Children's prog, Computers for patron use, Digital talking bks, Distance learning, E-Readers, Electronic databases & coll, Free DVD rentals, Holiday prog, ILL available, Internet access, Laminating, Magazines, Mail & tel request accepted, Mango lang, Movies, Museum passes, Music CDs, Online cat, Photocopying/Printing, Prog for adults, Prog for children & young adult, Scanner, Story hour, Summer reading prog, Tax forms, Teen prog, Workshops
Publications: Book Bytes (Bimonthly); Weeks Public Library (Monthly newsletter)
Open Mon-Thurs 10-8, Fri 10-5, Sat 9-1
Friends of the Library Group

GREENVILLE

P CHAMBERLIN FREE PUBLIC LIBRARY*, 46 Main St, 03048. (Mail add: PO Box 404, 03048-0499), SAN 309-8281. Tel: 603-878-1105. FAX: 603-878-4092. E-mail: cfpl_green@hotmail.com. Web Site: www.chamberlinlibrary.org. *Dir,* Charles Brault; *Asst Dir,* Diane Steele
Founded 1876. Pop 2,200; Circ 13,255
Library Holdings: Bk Vols 20,000; Per Subs 80
Special Collections: Cook Book Coll; Gardening Coll; Occult Coll
Automation Activity & Vendor Info: (Acquisitions) Koha; (Cataloging) Koha; (Circulation) Koha; (Course Reserve) Koha; (OPAC) Koha; (Serials) Koha
Wireless access
Open Mon & Wed 3-8, Tues & Thurs 9-8, Fri 9-5, Sat 9-1

GROVETON

P NORTHUMBERLAND PUBLIC LIBRARY*, 31 State St, 03582. Tel: 603-636-2066. FAX: 603-636-2066. E-mail: grovetonlibrary@gmail.com. *Librn,* Gail Rossetto
Pop 2,478; Circ 28,056
Library Holdings: Bk Vols 25,000; Per Subs 18
Open Tues-Fri 10-5, Sat 10-2

HAMPSTEAD

P HAMPSTEAD PUBLIC LIBRARY, Nine Mary E Clark Dr, 03841. SAN 309-829X. Tel: 603-329-6411. FAX: 603-329-6036. E-mail: circulation@hampsteadlibrary.org. Web Site: www.hampsteadlibrary.org. *Libr Dir,* Rosemary Krol; E-mail: rkrol@hampstead.lib.nh.us; *Asst Dir/Ref Librn,* Merrily Samuels; E-mail: msamuels@hampstead.lib.nh.us; *Youth Serv Librn,* Jenn MacLeod; E-mail: jmacleod@hampstead.lib.nh.us; *Adult Programmer, Coordr,* Janet Arden; E-mail: jarden@hampstead.lib.nh.us; Staff 9 (MLS 2, Non-MLS 7)

Founded 1888. Pop 8,600; Circ 70,660
Library Holdings: Audiobooks 1,903; AV Mats 3,328; Bks on Deafness & Sign Lang 7; CDs 549; DVDs 3,009; e-journals 25; Large Print Bks 859; Bk Titles 34,147; Per Subs 44
Special Collections: Civil War Coll
Automation Activity & Vendor Info: (Cataloging) Follett Software; (Circulation) Follett Software; (OPAC) Follett Software
Wireless access
Partic in Merri-Hill-Rock Library Cooperative
Open Mon, Tues & Thurs 9-8, Wed 1-8, Fri 9-5, Sat 9-3
Friends of the Library Group

HAMPTON

S HAMPTON HISTORICAL SOCIETY*, Tuck Museum Library, 40 Park Ave, 03842. (Mail add: PO Box 1601, 03843), SAN 373-2444. Tel: 603-929-0781. E-mail: info@hamptonhistoricalsociety.org. Web Site: www.hamptonhistoricalsociety.org. *Coll Mgr,* Betty Moore
Founded 1925
Library Holdings: Bk Vols 700
Special Collections: Local History, Genealogy & NH Town Histories, postcards, photos of Hampton area
Subject Interests: Educ, Genealogy
Wireless access
Restriction: Non-circulating, Open by appt only

P LANE MEMORIAL LIBRARY*, Two Academy Ave, 03842. SAN 309-8303. Tel: 603-926-3368. FAX: 603-926-1348. E-mail: library@hampton.lib.nh.us. Web Site: www.hampton.lib.nh.us. *Dir,* Amanda Reynolds Cooper; E-mail: acooper@hampton.lib.nh.us; *Head, Children's Servx,* Paulina Shadowens; E-mail: pshadowens@hampton.lib.nh.us; *Head, Pub Serv,* Darrell Eifert; E-mail: deifert@hampton.lib.nh.us; *Tech Serv,* Jenn Beigel; Staff 14 (MLS 4, Non-MLS 10)
Founded 1881. Pop 15,000; Circ 165,749
Library Holdings: Bk Vols 55,555; Per Subs 279; Talking Bks 4,556; Videos 3,585
Special Collections: Genealogy Coll; Local History Coll; New Hampshire Coll
Automation Activity & Vendor Info: (Cataloging) TLC (The Library Corporation); (Circulation) TLC (The Library Corporation); (OPAC) TLC (The Library Corporation)
Wireless access
Function: Adult literacy prog, Home delivery & serv to seniorr ctr & nursing homes, ILL available, Photocopying/Printing, Prog for children & young adult, Ref serv available, Summer reading prog, Telephone ref, Wheelchair accessible
Open Mon-Thurs 9-8, Fri & Sat 9-5
Friends of the Library Group

HAMPTON FALLS

P HAMPTON FALLS FREE PUBLIC LIBRARY*, Seven Drinkwater Rd, 03844. SAN 309-8311. Tel: 603-926-3682. FAX: 603-926-0170. E-mail: hamptonfalls.library@comcast.net. Web Site: www.hamptonfallslibrary.org. *Dir,* Barbara Tosiano; *Youth Serv Librn,* Leah Knowlton; *Libr Asst,* Francesca Schleppy; Staff 2 (MLS 1, Non-MLS 1)
Pop 2,100; Circ 21,400
Library Holdings: Bk Vols 15,000; Per Subs 45
Automation Activity & Vendor Info: (Acquisitions) Biblionix/Apollo; (Circulation) Biblionix/Apollo
Wireless access
Function: Adult bk club, After school storytime, Art exhibits, Audiobks via web, Bks on CD, Children's prog, Computers for patron use, Free DVD rentals, Homebound delivery serv, ILL available, Magnifiers for reading, Online cat, OverDrive digital audio bks, Photocopying/Printing, Prog for adults, Prog for children & young adult, Summer reading prog, Wheelchair accessible
Open Tues & Fri 10-5, Wed 1-8, Thurs 10-8, Sat 10-1
Friends of the Library Group

HANCOCK

P HANCOCK TOWN LIBRARY*, 25 Main St, 03449. (Mail add: PO Box 130, 03449-0130), SAN 309-832X. Tel: 603-525-4411. E-mail: hancocklibrary@comcast.net. Web Site: hancocktownlibrarynh.wordpress.com. *Dir,* Amy Markus; *Ch,* Jennifer Wood
Founded 1860. Pop 1,800; Circ 23,603
Library Holdings: Bk Titles 18,000; Per Subs 55
Subject Interests: Town hist
Automation Activity & Vendor Info: (Acquisitions) Follett Software
Wireless access
Open Mon & Wed 2-6, Tues & Thurs 10-7, Sat 10-4
Friends of the Library Group

HANOVER

C DARTMOUTH COLLEGE LIBRARY*, 6025 Baker Berry Library, Rm 115, 03755-3527. (Mail add: 25 N Main St, 03755), SAN 350-493X. Tel: 603-646-2236. FAX: 603-646-3702. Web Site: www.library.dartmouth.edu. *Dean of Libr,* Susanne Mehrer; E-mail: Susanne.Mehrer@Dartmouth.edu; *Dir, Mgt Serv,* Lora Coble; E-mail: Lora.L.Coble@Dartmouth.edu; *Assoc Librn, Access Serv,* Kenneth Peterson; E-mail: Kenneth.J.Peterson@Dartmouth.edu; Staff 184 (MLS 54, Non-MLS 130)
Founded 1769. Enrl 5,328; Fac 951; Highest Degree: Doctorate
Library Holdings: e-journals 40,731; Bk Vols 2,511,667; Per Subs 17,533
Wireless access
Partic in Association of Research Libraries; Coun of Libr Info Resources; Digital Libr Fedn; LYRASIS; New Eng Res Libs; OCLC Online Computer Library Center, Inc
Friends of the Library Group
Departmental Libraries:
BAKER-BERRY LIBRARY, 6025 Baker-Berry Library, 03755-3527. (Mail add: 25 N Main St, 03755). Tel: 603-646-2704. Interlibrary Loan Service Tel: 603-646-2596. FAX: 603-646-3702. E-mail: ris@dartmouth.edu. Web Site: www.dartmouth.edu/~library/bakerberry. *Head, Cat & Metadata Serv,* Cecilia Tittemore; Tel: 603-646-3236, E-mail: Cecilia.P.Tittemore@Dartmouth.edu; *Head, Digital Libr Tech,* Anthony Helm; Tel: 603-646-3830, E-mail: Anthony.Helm@Dartmouth.edu; Staff 42 (MLS 12, Non-MLS 30)
Founded 1928
Library Holdings: Bk Vols 1,695,575; Per Subs 11,366
Open Mon-Fri 8am-2am, Sat & Sun 10am-2am
Friends of the Library Group

CM DANA BIOMEDICAL LIBRARY, HB 6168, 37 Dewey Field Rd, 3rd Flr, 03755-1417, SAN 350-4964. Tel: 603-650-1658. Interlibrary Loan Service Tel: 603-646-8629. Reference Tel: 603-650-7660. Web Site: www.dartmouth.edu/~library/biomed. *Dir,* Stephanie Kerns; Tel: 603-650-1668, E-mail: Stephanie.C.Kerns@dartmouth.edu; *Research Coordr,* Pamela Bagley; Tel: 603-650-1749, E-mail: Pamela.Bagley@dartmouth.edu; Staff 8 (MLS 7, Non-MLS 1)
Subject Interests: Biology, Med, Nursing

FELDBERG BUSINESS & ENGINEERING LIBRARY, 6193 Murdough Ctr, 03755-3560, SAN 350-4999. Tel: 603-646-2191. FAX: 603-646-2384. Reference E-mail: feldberg.reference@dartmouth.edu. Web Site: www.dartmouth.edu/~library/feldberg. *Head, Res Serv,* Jane Quigley; E-mail: Jane.Quigley@dartmouth.edu; *Bus & Econ Librn, Eng Librn,* Janifer Holt; E-mail: Janifer.T.Holt@Dartmouth.edu; *Bus & Econ Librn, Eng Librn,* Mark Mounts; E-mail: Mark.Mounts@Dartmouth.edu; *Bus & Econ Librn, Eng Librn,* Karen Sluzenski; E-mail: Karen.L.Sluzenski@Dartmouth.edu; Staff 10 (MLS 5, Non-MLS 5)
Founded 1973. Highest Degree: Doctorate
Library Holdings: Bk Vols 115,988; Per Subs 2,673

KRESGE PHYSICAL SCIENCES LIBRARY, 6115 Fairchild Hall, 42 College St, 03755-3571, SAN 350-5022. Tel: 603-646-3563. E-mail: kresge.library@dartmouth.edu. Web Site: www.dartmouth.edu/~library/kresge. *Head, Data Serv, Head, Res Serv,* Jane Quigley; E-mail: Jane.Quigley@Dartmouth.EDU; *Phys Sci Librn,* Lora Leligdon; E-mail: Lora.C.Leligdon@Dartmouth.edu; *Libr Supvr,* Karen MacPhee; E-mail: Karen.A.MacPhee@Dartmouth.edu; *Coll Spec,* Lisa Ladd; E-mail: Lisa.A.Ladd@Darmouth.edu; Staff 6 (MLS 3, Non-MLS 3)
Library Holdings: Bk Vols 129,634; Per Subs 1,533

MATTHEWS-FULLER HEALTH SCIENCES LIBRARY, One Medical Center Dr, HB 7300, Lebanon, 03756-0001. Tel: 603-650-7658. Web Site: www.dartmouth.edu/~library/biomed. *Libr Supvr,* Jeremy Klockars; Tel: 603-650-5273, E-mail: Jeremy.P.Klockars@Dartmouth.edu

PADDOCK MUSIC LIBRARY, Hopkins Ctr for the Arts, Hinman Box 6245, Four E Wheelock St, 03755. Tel: 603-646-3234. Reference Tel: 603-646-3120. E-mail: Paddock.Music.Library@Dartmouth.edu. Web Site: www.dartmouth.edu/~library/paddock. *Music & Performing Arts Librn,* Memory Apata; E-mail: Memory.R.Apata@dartmouth.edu; *Coll Spec,* Craig Pallett; E-mail: Craig.S.Pallett@Dartmouth.edu; *Libr Spec,* David Bowden; E-mail: David.C.Bowden@Dartmouth.edu; Staff 4 (MLS 1, Non-MLS 3)
Library Holdings: CDs 29,200; DVDs 1,670; Bk Vols 75,600; Per Subs 378
Subject Interests: Dance, Music
Automation Activity & Vendor Info: (Acquisitions) Innovative Interfaces, Inc; (Cataloging) Innovative Interfaces, Inc; (Circulation) Innovative Interfaces, Inc - Millennium

RAUNER SPECIAL COLLECTIONS LIBRARY, 6065 Webster Hall, 03755-3519, SAN 378-0546. Tel: 603-646-0538. FAX: 603-646-0447. E-mail: rauner.reference@dartmouth.edu. Web Site: www.dartmouth.edu/~library/rauner. *Head, Spec Coll,* Jay Satterfield; E-mail: Jay.Satterfield@Dartmouth.edu; *Outreach & Spec Coll Librn,* Morgan Swan; E-mail: Morgan.R.Swan@Dartmouth.edu; *Col Archivist,* Peter Carini; E-mail: Peter.Carini@Dartmouth.edu; Staff 13 (MLS 3, Non-MLS 10)
Library Holdings: Bk Vols 126,797; Per Subs 489

Special Collections: American Calligraphy Coll; Bookplates; Dartmouth Archives; Don Quixote Coll; George Ticknor Library; German & English Plays (Barrett Clark Coll); Horace (Barlow Coll); New England Early Illustrated Books (1926 Memorial); New Hampshire History & Imprints Coll; Polar Regions (Stefansson Coll); Private Presses; Railroads (Chase Streeter Coll); Robert Frost Coll; Shakespeare (Hickmott Coll); Spanish Civilization (Bryant Coll); Spanish Plays; White Mountains
Open Mon-Fri 8-6
Friends of the Library Group

SHERMAN ART LIBRARY, Carpenter Hall, Hinman Box 6025, 03755-3570, SAN 350-5081. Tel: 603-646-2305. Reference E-mail: Sherman.library.reference@dartmouth.edu. Web Site: www.dartmouth.edu/~library/sherman. *Visual Arts Librn,* Laura Graveline; Tel: 603-646-3831, E-mail: Laura.K.Graveline@dartmouth.edu
Founded 1929
Library Holdings: Bk Vols 129,298; Per Subs 642
Special Collections: Artists Books
Subject Interests: Archit, Photog

P HOWE LIBRARY*, 13 South St, 03755. SAN 309-8354. Tel: 603-643-4120. Administration Tel: 603-640-3251. FAX: 603-643-0725. Reference E-mail: reference@thehowe.org. Web Site: thehowe.org. *Libr Dir,* Rubi Simon; E-mail: rubi.simon@thehowe.org; *Asst Dir,* Pam Smith; Tel: 603-640-3257, E-mail: pamela.smith@thehowe.org; *Circ Mgr,* Sondra VanderPloeg; Tel: 603-640-3262, E-mail: Sondra.Vanderploeg@thehowe.org; *Youth Serv Mgr,* Denise Reitsma; Tel: 603-640-3254, E-mail: denise.reitsma@thehowe.org; Staff 24 (MLS 10, Non-MLS 14)
Founded 1900. Pop 11,260; Circ 238,939
Library Holdings: Audiobooks 19,546; DVDs 11,300; e-books 14,000; Bk Vols 117,846; Per Subs 376
Automation Activity & Vendor Info: (Acquisitions) Evergreen; (Cataloging) Evergreen; (Circulation) Evergreen; (OPAC) Evergreen
Wireless access
Function: 24/7 Electronic res, 24/7 Online cat, 3D Printer, Activity rm, Adult bk club, After school storytime, Art exhibits, Art programs, Audio & video playback equip for onsite use, Audiobks via web, Bk club(s), Bks on CD, Chess club, Children's prog, Computer training, Computers for patron use, Digital talking bks, Electronic databases & coll, Free DVD rentals, Home delivery & serv to seniorr ctr & nursing homes, Homebound delivery serv, ILL available, Instruction & testing, Internet access, Large print keyboards, Magazines, Magnifiers for reading, Mail & tel request accepted, Makerspace, Meeting rooms, Microfiche/film & reading machines, Movies, Museum passes, Music CDs, Online cat, Online ref, Outreach serv, Outside serv via phone, mail, e-mail & web, OverDrive digital audio bks, Photocopying/Printing, Preschool outreach, Preschool reading prog, Prog for adults, Prog for children & young adult, Ref serv available, Senior outreach, Serves people with intellectual disabilities, Spanish lang bks, Spoken cassettes & CDs, Spoken cassettes & DVDs, STEM programs, Story hour, Study rm, Summer reading prog, Tax forms, Teen prog, Telephone ref, Visual arts prog, Wheelchair accessible, Workshops, Writing prog
Special Services for the Blind - Assistive/Adapted tech devices, equip & products; Computer with voice synthesizer for visually impaired persons; Home delivery serv
Open Mon-Thurs 10-8, Fri 10-6, Sat 10-5, Sun 1-5

A UNITED STATES ARMY*, Engineer Research & Development Center Library, 72 Lyme Rd, 03755-1290. SAN 350-5111. Tel: 603-646-4779. *Librn,* Kirsten Lahlum; Staff 3 (MLS 2, Non-MLS 1)
Founded 1952
Library Holdings: e-journals 1,500; Bk Titles 20,000; Per Subs 150
Special Collections: Cold Regions Science & Technology Bibliography
Subject Interests: Engr, Geol, Math, Meteorology, Physics
Automation Activity & Vendor Info: (Cataloging) SirsiDynix; (Circulation) SirsiDynix; (OPAC) SirsiDynix; (Serials) SirsiDynix
Wireless access
Function: Res libr
Publications: Bibliography of Cold Regions Science & Technology
Partic in OCLC Online Computer Library Center, Inc
Restriction: Internal use only, Open by appt only

HARRISVILLE

P HARRISVILLE PUBLIC LIBRARY*, Seven Canal St, 03450. (Mail add: PO Box 387, 03450-0387), SAN 309-8362. Tel: 603-827-2918. FAX: 603-827-2919. Web Site: www.harrisvillenh.org/library. *Dir,* Susan Weaver; E-mail: sweaver@harrisville.lib.nh.us; *Ch,* Kris Finnegan; E-mail: kofinnegan@harrisville.lib.nh.us
Pop 1,075; Circ 7,332
Library Holdings: AV Mats 400; DVDs 40; Bk Vols 5,500; Per Subs 18
Wireless access
Open Mon, Tues & Thurs 3-7, Wed 10-1 & 3-7, Sat 10-1
Friends of the Library Group

HAVERHILL

P HAVERHILL LIBRARY ASSOCIATION, 67 Court St, 03765. (Mail add: PO Box 117, 03765-0117), SAN 309-8370. Tel: 603-989-5578. E-mail: mail@haverhilllibrary.org. Web Site: hliba.blogspot.com. *Librn,* Nanci Myers; *Ch,* Anne Marie Ballam; Staff 3 (Non-MLS 3)
Founded 1880. Pop 350; Circ 7,850
Library Holdings: AV Mats 266; Bk Vols 15,235; Per Subs 27; Talking Bks 92; Videos 174
Special Collections: Oral History; State Document Depository
Wireless access
Special Services for the Blind - Large print bks
Open Tues 10-2, Thurs 3-7

HEBRON

P HEBRON LIBRARY*, Eight Church Lane, 03241. (Mail add: PO Box 90, 03241-0090), SAN 309-8419. Tel: 603-744-7998. E-mail: hebronlibrary@metrocast.net. *Dir,* Robin Orr
Pop 342; Circ 3,533
Library Holdings: AV Mats 152; Bk Vols 8,000; Per Subs 14
Wireless access
Open Mon 5-7, Wed 1-5, Sat 9-Noon
Friends of the Library Group

HENNIKER

C NEW ENGLAND COLLEGE*, H Raymond Danforth Library, 196 Bridge St, 03242-3298. (Mail add: 98 Bridge St, 03242-3298), SAN 350-5146. Tel: 603-428-2344. FAX: 603-428-4273. Web Site: www.nec.edu/library. *Dir,* Chelsea Hanrahan; *Assoc Dir,* Russ Rattray; *Distance Serv Librn, Instruction Librn,* Mark Rowland; *Ref & ILL Librn,* Catherine Ryan; *Circ, Pub Serv Coordr,* Shana Elburn; Staff 5 (MLS 4, Non-MLS 1)
Founded 1946. Enrl 3,000; Fac 42; Highest Degree: Doctorate
Library Holdings: Bk Vols 102,000; Per Subs 150
Special Collections: College Archives & Art Coll; New Hampshiriana; Shakespeare Coll (Adams Col)
Automation Activity & Vendor Info: (Acquisitions) Innovative Interfaces, Inc; (Cataloging) Innovative Interfaces, Inc; (Circulation) Innovative Interfaces, Inc; (Course Reserve) Innovative Interfaces, Inc; (ILL) OCLC WorldShare Interlibrary Loan; (OPAC) Innovative Interfaces, Inc; (Serials) Innovative Interfaces, Inc
Wireless access
Partic in GMILCS, Inc; New Hampshire College & University Council
Open Mon-Thurs 7:30am-Midnight, Fri 7:30am-8pm, Sat 10-5, Sun 10am-Midnight
Friends of the Library Group

Departmental Libraries:

TETI LIBRARY AT THE INSTITUTE OF ART & DESIGN, French Hall, 148 Concord St, Manchester, 03104. Tel: 603-836-2532. Web Site: libguides.nec.edu/librarywebsite/aboutusteti. *Academic & Public Services Coord,* Angie Hurshman; E-mail: ahurshman@nec.edu
Function: Computers for patron use, Photocopying/Printing, Res assist avail, Scanner
Restriction: Open by appt only

P TUCKER FREE LIBRARY*, 31 Western Ave, 03242. (Mail add: PO Box 688, 03242-0688), SAN 309-8427. Tel: 603-428-3471. FAX: 603-428-7106. E-mail: tuckerfree@comcast.net. Web Site: www.tuckerfreelibrary.org. *Dir,* Lynn Piotrowicz; E-mail: lynnpiotrowicz@tuckerfreelibrary.org; Staff 9 (MLS 1, Non-MLS 8)
Founded 1903. Pop 4,500; Circ 40,000
Library Holdings: Bk Vols 30,000; Per Subs 60
Automation Activity & Vendor Info: (Cataloging) Biblionix; (Circulation) Biblionix
Wireless access
Friends of the Library Group

HILL

P HILL PUBLIC LIBRARY*, 30 Crescent St, 03243. (Mail add: PO Box 257, 03243), SAN 309-8435. Tel: 603-934-9712. FAX: 603-934-9712. E-mail: hillpubliclibrary@comcast.net. Web Site: www.hillpubliclibrary.com. *Librn,* Lynn Christopher; Staff 1 (Non-MLS 1)
Pop 1,078; Circ 5,500
Library Holdings: Bk Titles 11,000; Videos 1,500
Wireless access
Function: Adult bk club, Audiobks via web, Bk club(s), Children's prog, Computer training, Computers for patron use, Free DVD rentals, Holiday prog, ILL available, Microfiche/film & reading machines, OverDrive digital audio bks, Photocopying/Printing, Preschool reading prog, Prog for adults, Prog for children & young adult, Story hour, Summer reading prog, VHS videos, Wheelchair accessible
Partic in New Hampshire Downloadable Books Consortium
Special Services for the Blind - Large print bks
Open Tues-Fri 10-6

Restriction: Circ to mem only, Free to mem, In-house use for visitors
Friends of the Library Group

HILLSBORO

P FULLER PUBLIC LIBRARY*, 29 School St, 03244. (Mail add: PO Box 43, 03244-0043), SAN 309-8443. Tel: 603-464-3595. FAX: 603-464-4572. E-mail: circ@fullerlibrary.info. Web Site: fullerlibrary.info. *Dir,* Samantha Gallo; E-mail: director@fullerlibrary.info
Founded 1877. Pop 6,000; Circ 35,000
Library Holdings: Bk Vols 35,090; Per Subs 62
Automation Activity & Vendor Info: (Cataloging) Follett Software; (Circulation) Follett Software
Wireless access
Open Mon & Fri 12-5, Tues & Thurs 9-8, Sat 9-1

HINSDALE

P HINSDALE PUBLIC LIBRARY*, 122 Brattleboro Rd, 03451. (Mail add: PO Box 6, 03451-0006), SAN 309-8451. Tel: 603-336-5713. E-mail: hinsdalelibrary@yahoo.com. Web Site: www.town.hinsdale.nh.us/library. *Librn,* Mary Major; *Asst Librn,* Catherine Palmatier
Pop 4,000; Circ 6,193
Library Holdings: Bk Vols 25,000; Per Subs 15
Open Mon, Wed & Thurs 12-5 & 6:30-8, Fri 10-3, Sat 10-12

HOLDERNESS

P HOLDERNESS LIBRARY, 866 US Rte 3, 03245. (Mail add: PO Box L, 03245-0712), SAN 309-846X. Tel: 603-968-7066. E-mail: holdernessfree@gmail.com, holdernesslibrary@gmail.com. Web Site: www.holdernessfreelibrary.org. *Dir,* Adam Di Filippe; *Libr Asst,* Jeanne Perkins; *ILL,* Rachel Grotheer; *Youth Serv,* Susan Seeley; E-mail: holdernessyouth@gmail.com; Staff 4 (Non-MLS 4)
Founded 1878. Pop 2,400
Library Holdings: Audiobooks 463; Bks on Deafness & Sign Lang 6; DVDs 750; e-books 1,100; Large Print Bks 81; Bk Titles 1,047; Per Subs 52
Special Collections: New Hampshire Special Coll, bks, pamphlets
Automation Activity & Vendor Info: (Acquisitions) Baker & Taylor; (Cataloging) Book Systems; (Circulation) Book Systems; (ILL) Auto-Graphics, Inc; (Media Booking) Book Systems; (OPAC) Book Systems; (Serials) Book Systems
Wireless access
Function: 24/7 Electronic res, 24/7 Online cat, Activity rm, Adult bk club, Adult literacy prog, After school storytime, Archival coll, Art exhibits, Art programs, Audio & video playback equip for onsite use, Audiobks on Playaways & MP3, Audiobks via web, AV serv, Bk club(s), Bk reviews (Group), Bks on CD, CD-ROM, Chess club, Children's prog, Computer training, Computers for patron use, E-Readers, E-Reserves, Electronic databases & coll, Equip loans & repairs, Family literacy, For res purposes, Free DVD rentals, Games & aids for people with disabilities, Govt ref serv, Health sci info serv, Holiday prog, Home delivery & serv to seniorr ctr & nursing homes, Homebound delivery serv, Homework prog, ILL available, Instruction & testing, Internet access, Laminating, Learning ctr, Life-long learning prog for all ages, Magazines, Magnifiers for reading, Mail & tel request accepted, Meeting rooms, Movies, Museum passes, Online cat, Online ref, Outreach serv, OverDrive digital audio bks, Photocopying/Printing, Preschool reading prog, Printer for laptops & handheld devices, Prof lending libr, Prog for adults, Prog for children & young adult, Ref & res, Ref serv available, Res assist avail, Res libr, Scanner, Senior computer classes, Senior outreach, Serves people with intellectual disabilities, Story hour, Study rm, Summer & winter reading prog, Summer reading prog, Tax forms, Teen prog, Telephone ref, Visual arts prog, Wheelchair accessible, Winter reading prog, Workshops, Writing prog
Partic in New Hampshire Automated Information Systems
Special Services for the Deaf - Closed caption videos
Special Services for the Blind - Bks on CD; Large print bks
Open Mon-Wed & Fri 9-5, Sat 9-2
Restriction: Non-resident fee
Friends of the Library Group

HOLLIS

P HOLLIS SOCIAL LIBRARY*, Two Monument Sq, 03049. (Mail add: PO Box 659, 03049-0659), SAN 309-8478. Tel: 603-465-7721. FAX: 603-465-3507. E-mail: helpdesk@hollislibrary.org. Web Site: www.hollislibrary.org. *Dir,* Laura Klain; E-mail: director@hollislibrary.org; Staff 9 (MLS 2, Non-MLS 7)
Founded 1799. Pop 7,603; Circ 85,632
Library Holdings: AV Mats 5,279; CDs 634; DVDs 1,549; Large Print Bks 749; Bk Vols 55,000; Per Subs 75; Talking Bks 1,625; Videos 1,471
Subject Interests: Local hist
Automation Activity & Vendor Info: (Cataloging) TLC (The Library Corporation); (Circulation) TLC (The Library Corporation); (OPAC) TLC (The Library Corporation); (Serials) TLC (The Library Corporation)
Wireless access
Publications: HSL Newsletter (Monthly)
Partic in New Hampshire Automated Information Systems
Open Mon-Thurs 10:30-8:30, Fri 10:30-5:30, Sat 10:30-5, Sun 1-5
Friends of the Library Group

HOOKSETT

P HOOKSETT PUBLIC LIBRARY*, 31 Mount Saint Mary's Way, 03106-1852. SAN 309-8486. Tel: 603-485-6092. FAX: 603-485-6193. Web Site: www.hooksettlibrary.org. *Dir,* Heather Rainier; E-mail: hrainier@hooksettlibrary.org; *Asst Dir/Ref Librn,* Dara Bradds; E-mail: dbradds@hooksettlibrary.org; *Youth Serv Librn,* Grace Larochelle; E-mail: glarochelle@hooksettlibrary.org; *Circ Supvr,* LeeAnn Chase; E-mail: lchase@hooksettlibrary.org; *Technology Spec,* Mark Glisson; E-mail: mglisson@hooksettlibrary.org; *Cataloger,* Martha Simmons; E-mail: msimmons@hooksettlibrary.org; Staff 6 (MLS 4, Non-MLS 2)
Founded 1909. Pop 13,900
Library Holdings: Bk Titles 43,000; Per Subs 100
Automation Activity & Vendor Info: (Cataloging) Innovative Interfaces, Inc; (Circulation) Innovative Interfaces, Inc; (OPAC) Innovative Interfaces, Inc
Wireless access
Partic in GMILCS, Inc
Open Mon-Wed 9-8, Thurs 11-8, Fri & Sat 9-5
Friends of the Library Group

HOPKINTON

S HOPKINTON HISTORICAL SOCIETY*, 300 Main St, 03229. SAN 326-0836. Tel: 603-746-3825. E-mail: nhas@tds.net. Web Site: www.hopkintonhistory.org. *Exec Dir,* Heather Mitchell
Library Holdings: Bk Vols 14,000
Special Collections: Primitive Portraits Costume Coll
Open Thurs & Fri 9-4, Sat 9-1

HUDSON

P GEORGE H & ELLA M RODGERS MEMORIAL LIBRARY*, Rodgers Memorial Library, 194 Derry Rd, 03051. SAN 309-8508. Tel: 603-886-6030. Interlibrary Loan Service Tel: 603-886-6030, Ext 4509. Reference Tel: 603-886-6030, Ext 4522. Automation Services Tel: 603-886-6030, Ext 4525. FAX: 603-816-4501. E-mail: askus@rodgerslibrary.org. Web Site: rodgerslibrary.org. *Dir,* Linda Pilla; E-mail: director@rodgerslibrary.org; *Syst Adminr,* Brian Hewey; E-mail: brianhewey@rodgerslibrary.org; *Tech Librn,* Vicky Sandin; E-mail: victoriasandin@rodgerslibrary.org; *Adult Serv,* Amy Friedman; E-mail: amyfriedman@rodgerslibrary.org; *Cat,* Ann Carle; Tel: 603-886-6030, Ext 4512, E-mail: anncarle@rodgerslibrary.org; *Ch Serv,* Betsey Martel; Tel: 603-886-6030, Ext 4519; *Circ,* Linda Pilla; Tel: 603-886-6030, Ext 4516, E-mail: lindapilla@rodgerslibrary.org; Staff 6 (MLS 4, Non-MLS 2)
Founded 2009. Pop 25,000; Circ 170,315
Jul 2015-Jun 2016 Income $1,016,937, City $994,672, Locally Generated Income $22,265
Library Holdings: Audiobooks 2,566; AV Mats 5,926; CDs 939; DVDs 4,987; e-books 17,360; Bk Titles 46,919; Bk Vols 49,884; Per Subs 294
Subject Interests: Genealogy, Local hist
Automation Activity & Vendor Info: (Acquisitions) Evergreen; (Cataloging) Evergreen; (Circulation) Evergreen; (ILL) Evergreen; (OPAC) Evergreen; (Serials) Evergreen
Wireless access
Function: 24/7 Electronic res, 24/7 Online cat, Activity rm, Adult bk club, After school storytime, Archival coll, Art exhibits, Audiobks via web, Bilingual assistance for Spanish patrons, Bk club(s), Bks on CD, Children's prog, Computers for patron use, Electronic databases & coll, Free DVD rentals, Genealogy discussion group, ILL available, Internet access, Magazines, Magnifiers for reading, Mail & tel request accepted, Meeting rooms, Movies, Museum passes, Music CDs, Notary serv, Online cat, OverDrive digital audio bks, Photocopying/Printing, Preschool outreach, Prog for adults, Prog for children & young adult, Ref & res, Ref serv available, Scanner, Senior computer classes, Story hour, Summer reading prog, Tax forms, Teen prog, Telephone ref, Wheelchair accessible, Workshops
Partic in Merri-Hill-Rock Library Cooperative
Special Services for the Blind - Accessible computers; Aids for in-house use; Assistive/Adapted tech devices, equip & products; Bks on CD; Home delivery serv; Large print bks
Open Mon-Thurs 9-9, Fri 9-6, Sat 9-5
Friends of the Library Group

JACKSON

P JACKSON PUBLIC LIBRARY, 125 Main St, 03846. (Mail add: PO Box 276, 03846-0276), SAN 309-8524. Tel: 603-383-9731. FAX: 603-383-9731. E-mail: jacksonpubliclibrary@gmail.com, staff@jacksonlibrary.org. Web Site: jacksonlibrarynh.org. *Libr Dir,* Lichen J Rancourt; *Ch,* Meredith Piotrow
Founded 1879. Pop 800; Circ 12,233
Library Holdings: Bk Vols 11,000
Automation Activity & Vendor Info: (Cataloging) Follett Software; (Circulation) Follett Software; (OPAC) Follett Software
Wireless access
Function: Adult bk club, ILL available, Mail & tel request accepted, Photocopying/Printing, Prog for children & young adult, Spoken cassettes & CDs, Summer reading prog, VHS videos
Open Tues & Thurs 11-6, Wed & Fri 2-5, Sat 10-2
Friends of the Library Group

JAFFREY

P JAFFREY PUBLIC LIBRARY, 38 Main St, 03452-1196. SAN 309-8532. Tel: 603-532-7301. Web Site: www.townofjaffrey.com/jaffrey-public-library. *Libr Dir,* Julie M Perrin; E-mail: jperrin@jaffreypubliclibrary.org; *Youth Serv Librn,* Andrea Connolly; E-mail: aconnolly@jaffreypubliclibrary.org; Staff 3.5 (MLS 2, Non-MLS 1.5)
Founded 1896. Pop 5,434; Circ 47,730
Library Holdings: AV Mats 1,200; Electronic Media & Resources 16; Bk Vols 30,366; Per Subs 59; Talking Bks 859
Special Collections: Amos Fortune Historical Coll; Puppet Coll
Automation Activity & Vendor Info: (Circulation) Koha
Wireless access
Function: 24/7 Electronic res, Adult bk club, Archival coll, Art exhibits, Audiobks via web, AV serv, Bk club(s), Bks on CD, Children's prog, Computers for patron use, Electronic databases & coll, Holiday prog, ILL available, Internet access, Magazines, Mail & tel request accepted, Microfiche/film & reading machines, Movies, Museum passes, Online cat, OverDrive digital audio bks, Photocopying/Printing, Prog for adults, Prog for children & young adult, Ref & res, Story hour, Summer & winter reading prog, Summer reading prog, Tax forms, Wheelchair accessible
Partic in Nubanusit Library Cooperative
Open Mon, Thurs & Fri 10-5:30, Tues & Wed 10-7, Sat 10-1
Friends of the Library Group

JEFFERSON

P JEFFERSON PUBLIC LIBRARY*, 737 Presidential Hwy, 03583. (Mail add: PO Box 27, 03583-0027), SAN 309-8540. Tel: 603-586-7791. E-mail: lookitup@ne.rr.com. Web Site: www.myjeffersonlibrary.com. *Libr Dir,* Joy McCorkhill
Pop 802; Circ 2,544
Library Holdings: AV Mats 440; Large Print Bks 50; Bk Vols 7,000; Per Subs 12; Videos 320
Subject Interests: Town hist
Wireless access
Open Tues & Thurs 2-8, Sat 10-2
Friends of the Library Group

KEENE

C ANTIOCH UNIVERSITY NEW ENGLAND LIBRARY*, 40 Avon St, 03431. SAN 309-8559. Tel: 603-283-2400. FAX: 603-357-7345. E-mail: circulation.ane@antioch.edu. Web Site: www.antioch.edu/new-england/resources/students/library. *Dir, Libr Serv,* Lisa Lepore; E-mail: llepore@antioch.edu; *Res & Instruction Librn,* Rachel Sperling; E-mail: rsperling1@antioch.edu; *Access Serv,* Abby Jones; E-mail: ajones7@antioch.edu; *Syst Serv,* Catherine Boswell; E-mail: cboswell@antioch.edu; Staff 5 (MLS 3, Non-MLS 2)
Library Holdings: Bk Vols 38,320; Per Subs 1,625
Subject Interests: Dance movement therapy, Doctoral programs in psychology, Educ, Environ studies, Experienced educators prog, Family therapy, Marriage, Organization, Psychol, Substance abuse, Waldorf educ
Automation Activity & Vendor Info: (Acquisitions) Ex Libris Group; (Cataloging) Ex Libris Group; (Circulation) Ex Libris Group; (Course Reserve) Ex Libris Group; (ILL) Ex Libris Group; (OPAC) Ex Libris Group; (Serials) Ex Libris Group
Wireless access
Open Mon-Fri 7:45am-9pm, Sat & Sun 10-6

S HISTORICAL SOCIETY OF CHESHIRE COUNTY, 246 Main St, 03431. (Mail add: PO Box 803, 03431-0803), SAN 323-9675. Tel: 603-352-1895. FAX: 603-352-9226. E-mail: hscc@hsccnh.org. Web Site: www.hsccnh.org. *Dir,* Alan Rumrill; E-mail: director@hsccnh.org; Staff 5 (MLS 2, Non-MLS 3)
Founded 1927
Library Holdings: CDs 130; Bk Titles 11,500; Spec Interest Per Sub 15; Videos 40
Special Collections: Cheshire County History, bks, ms, photog; New England Genealogy & Local History Coll. Oral History
Wireless access
Function: 24/7 Online cat, Art exhibits, For res purposes, Meeting rooms, Microfiche/film & reading machines, Online cat, Outreach serv, Photocopying/Printing, Prog for adults, Prog for children & young adult, Ref & res, Res libr, Res performed for a fee, Wheelchair accessible
Publications: Newsletter (Quarterly)
Open Tues, Thurs & Fri 9-4, Wed 9-8
Restriction: Internal use only, Not a lending libr, Open to pub for ref only

P KEENE PUBLIC LIBRARY*, 60 Winter St, 03431. SAN 309-8575. Tel: 603-352-0157. FAX: 603-283-5656. Web Site: www.keenepubliclibrary.org. *Dir,* Nancy Vincent; Tel: 603-757-1842, E-mail: nvincent@ci.keene.nh.us; *Head, Commun Serv, Head, Youth Serv,* Gail Zachariah; E-mail: gzachariah@ci.keene.nh.us; *Head, Ref, ILL Librn,* John Johnson; E-mail: jjohnson@ci.keene.nh.us; *AV Serv Librn,* Sheila Williams; *Digital Res Librn,* Cary Jardine; *Youth Librn,* Colleen Swider; E-mail: cswider@ci.keene.nh.us; *Circ Supvr,* Susan Hansmeier; *Coll Develop,* Judy Koopman; *Teen Serv,* Jay Fee
Founded 1857. Pop 23,000
Library Holdings: AV Mats 11,459; Bk Vols 116,764; Per Subs 233
Subject Interests: NH
Automation Activity & Vendor Info: (Acquisitions) Innovative Interfaces, Inc; (Cataloging) Innovative Interfaces, Inc; (Circulation) Innovative Interfaces, Inc; (ILL) Innovative Interfaces, Inc; (Media Booking) Innovative Interfaces, Inc; (OPAC) Innovative Interfaces, Inc; (Serials) Innovative Interfaces, Inc
Wireless access
Open Mon-Thurs 9-9, Fri 9-6, Sat 9-5 (9-1 Summer)
Friends of the Library Group

C KEENE STATE COLLEGE*, Wallace E Mason Library, 229 Main St, 03435-3201. SAN 309-8583. Tel: 603-358-2711. Interlibrary Loan Service Tel: 603-358-2715. Reference Tel: 603-358-2710. Administration Tel: 603-358-2723. FAX: 603-358-2745. Web Site: library.keene.edu. *Dean,* Celia Rabinowitz; E-mail: celia.rabinowitz@keene.edu; *Head, Archives & Spec Coll,* Rodney Obien; Tel: 603-358-2717, E-mail: robien@keene.edu; *Info Literacy Librn,* Elizabeth Dolinger; Tel: 603-358-2749, E-mail: edolinger@keene.edu; *Access Serv Mgr,* Jeff Kazin; Tel: 603-358-2782, E-mail: jeff.kazin@keene.edu; *Libr Syst Mgr,* Dana Clark; Tel: 603-358-2755, E-mail: dclark5@keene.edu; *ILL Coordr,* Mylynda Gill; E-mail: mylynda.gill@keene.edu; Staff 19 (MLS 10, Non-MLS 9)
Founded 1909. Enrl 5,000; Fac 198; Highest Degree: Master
Library Holdings: AV Mats 9,000; Bk Vols 200,000; Per Subs 790
Special Collections: Cohen Center for Holocaust & Genocide Studies; College Archives; K-12 Curriculum Library; New Hampshire History Coll; Orang Asli Archives. State Document Depository
Subject Interests: Curric related mat for K-12, Educ, State hist
Automation Activity & Vendor Info: (Acquisitions) Innovative Interfaces, Inc; (Cataloging) Innovative Interfaces, Inc; (Circulation) Innovative Interfaces, Inc; (Course Reserve) Innovative Interfaces, Inc; (ILL) OCLC ILLiad; (OPAC) Innovative Interfaces, Inc; (Serials) Innovative Interfaces, Inc
Wireless access
Partic in New Hampshire Automated Information Systems; New Hampshire College & University Council; OCLC Online Computer Library Center, Inc; Westchester Academic Library Directors Organization
Special Services for the Blind - Closed circuit TV magnifier; Computer with voice synthesizer for visually impaired persons; Reader equip; ZoomText magnification & reading software
Open Mon-Thurs 8am-Midnight, Fri 8am-10pm, Sat 10-10, Sun 10am-Midnight

KENSINGTON

P KENSINGTON PUBLIC LIBRARY*, 126 Amesbury Rd, 03833-5621. SAN 309-8605. Tel: 603-772-5022. FAX: 603-778-2953. E-mail: kensingtonlibrary@comcast.net. Web Site: www.kensingtonpubliclibrary.org. *Dir,* Susan Gilbert; *Children's Serv Supvr,* Kristin Berardino; *ILL Coordr,* Dana Donovan; Staff 4 (MLS 1, Non-MLS 3)
Pop 2,089
Library Holdings: Bk Vols 13,068; Per Subs 49
Special Collections: Antiques & Art Coll
Wireless access
Function: Adult bk club, Audiobks via web, Bks on cassette, Bks on CD, Children's prog, Computers for patron use, Electronic databases & coll, Free DVD rentals, ILL available, Museum passes, Music CDs, OverDrive digital audio bks, Photocopying/Printing, Prog for adults, Prog for children & young adult, Ref serv available, Story hour, Summer reading prog, VHS videos, Wheelchair accessible
Partic in New Hampshire Automated Information Systems
Open Tues 9-8, Wed & Sat 9-1, Thurs 10-6, Fri 1-5
Friends of the Library Group

KINGSTON

P KINGSTON COMMUNITY LIBRARY*, Two Library Lane, 03848. SAN 309-8613. Tel: 603-642-3521. FAX: 603-642-3135. E-mail: info@kingston-library.org. Web Site: www.kingston-library.org. *Dir,* Rebekka Mateyk; E-mail: director@kingston-library.org
Founded 1898. Circ 40,000
Library Holdings: Bk Vols 22,000; Per Subs 71
Subject Interests: Hist
Automation Activity & Vendor Info: (Cataloging) Book Systems; (Circulation) Book Systems
Wireless access
Open Mon & Fri 10-4, Tues-Thurs 10-8, Sat 9-1
Friends of the Library Group

LACONIA

P LACONIA PUBLIC LIBRARY, 695 Main St, 03246. SAN 350-5170. Tel: 603-524-4775. FAX: 603-527-1277. E-mail: info@laconialibrary.org. Web Site: laconianh.gov/336/library. *Libr Dir,* Randy Brough; E-mail: rbough@laconialibrary.org; *Ref Librn,* Deann Hunter; E-mail: dhunter@laconialibrary.org; Staff 11 (MLS 3, Non-MLS 8)
Founded 1903. Pop 17,233; Circ 129,583
Library Holdings: Audiobooks 1,745; AV Mats 5,776; CDs 951; DVDs 1,311; Large Print Bks 1,050; Bk Vols 48,106; Per Subs 130; Videos 1,728
Special Collections: State Document Depository
Automation Activity & Vendor Info: (Cataloging) TLC (The Library Corporation); (Circulation) TLC (The Library Corporation); (OPAC) TLC (The Library Corporation)
Wireless access
Publications: Browsing (Newsletter)
Partic in Urban Libr Consortia
Open Mon-Thurs 9-8, Fri 9-5, Sat 9-4
Branches: 1
LAKEPORT (OSSIAN WILBUR GOSS READING ROOM), 188 Elm St, 03246, SAN 350-5200. Tel: 603-524-3808. *Librn,* Susan Laramie; Staff 1 (Non-MLS 1)
Founded 1907. Pop 17,233
Library Holdings: Bk Vols 3,283
Open Tues & Thurs 12-5

J LAKE REGION COMMUNITY COLLEGE*, Bennett Library, 379 Belmont Rd, 03246. SAN 309-8621. Tel: 603-524-3207. Web Site: www.lrcc.edu/student-resources/bennett-library. *Libr Supvr,* Penny Garrett; Tel: 603-524-3207, Ext 6794, E-mail: pgarrett@ccsnh.edu; Staff 2 (MLS 1, Non-MLS 1)
Founded 1968. Enrl 1,150; Fac 37; Highest Degree: Associate
Library Holdings: e-books 45,000; Bk Titles 12,500; Per Subs 90
Subject Interests: Bus, Computers, Fire sci, Nursing
Automation Activity & Vendor Info: (Cataloging) TLC (The Library Corporation); (Circulation) TLC (The Library Corporation)
Wireless access
Open Mon-Thurs (Summer) 7:30-6, Fri 8-4; Mon-Fri (Fall & Spring) 8-6
Friends of the Library Group

LANCASTER

P WILLIAM D WEEKS MEMORIAL LIBRARY*, 128 Main St, 03584-3031. SAN 309-863X. Tel: 603-788-3352. FAX: 603-788-3203. E-mail: weekslib@myfairpoint.net. Web Site: www.weekslib.org. *Dir,* Barbara R Robarts; *Youth Serv Librn,* Ronnie Buckman; Staff 1 (MLS 1)
Founded 1884. Pop 3,500; Circ 4,500
Library Holdings: AV Mats 1,400; Large Print Bks 114; Bk Vols 45,000; Per Subs 150; Talking Bks 892
Subject Interests: NH
Wireless access
Open Mon, Wed & Fri 1-4:30 & 7-9, Tues & Thurs 9-4:30, Sat 10-12
Friends of the Library Group

LEBANON

P LEBANON PUBLIC LIBRARY*, Nine E Park St, 03766. SAN 350-5235. Tel: 603-448-2459. E-mail: library@leblibrary.com. Web Site: www.leblibrary.com. *Dir,* Sean Fleming; E-mail: sean.fleming@leblibrary.com; *Dep Dir,* Amy Lappin
Founded 1909. Pop 13,600; Circ 150,000
Special Collections: Local History Coll
Automation Activity & Vendor Info: (Cataloging) LibLime; (Circulation) LibLime; (OPAC) LibLime
Wireless access
Open Mon-Thurs 10-8, Fri & Sat 10-5, Sun (Sept-March) 1-5

LEE

P LEE PUBLIC LIBRARY*, Nine Mast Rd, 03861. SAN 309-8648. Tel: 603-659-2626. FAX: 603-659-2986. E-mail: leelibrary@comcast.net. Web Site: leelibrarynh.org. *Dir,* Ruth Eifert; *Circ Librn, ILL Librn,* Michelle Stevens; *Youth Serv,* Jody Belanger
Founded 1892. Pop 4,000; Circ 57,381
Library Holdings: AV Mats 629; Bks on Deafness & Sign Lang 10; Large Print Bks 91; Bk Titles 26,060; Per Subs 79; Talking Bks 794
Automation Activity & Vendor Info: (Circulation) Follett Software
Wireless access
Partic in Rochester Area Librarians
Open Mon-Wed 12-8, Thurs & Fri 10-5, Sat 10-3
Friends of the Library Group

LINCOLN

P LINCOLN PUBLIC LIBRARY*, 22 Church St, 03251. (Mail add: PO Box 98, 03251-0098), SAN 309-8656. Tel: 603-745-8159. FAX: 603-745-2037. E-mail: library@lincolnnh.org. Web Site: www.lincoln.lib.nh.us. *Dir,* Carol Riley; *Circ Librn,* Janet Peltier; *Youth Serv Librn,* Vivica Duffield; E-mail: vivyouthservices@gmail.com
Pop 1,662; Circ 11,000
Library Holdings: Bk Vols 12,000; Per Subs 40
Subject Interests: NH
Automation Activity & Vendor Info: (Acquisitions) ComPanion Corp; (Cataloging) ComPanion Corp; (Circulation) ComPanion Corp; (OPAC) ComPanion Corp
Wireless access
Function: 24/7 Online cat, Activity rm, Adult bk club, Art exhibits, Bk club(s), Bks on CD, Children's prog, Computers for patron use, Free DVD rentals, ILL available, Internet access, Magazines, Mail & tel request accepted, Meeting rooms, Movies, Museum passes, Online cat, OverDrive digital audio bks, Photocopying/Printing, Preschool outreach, Preschool reading prog, Prog for adults, Prog for children & young adult, Ref & res, Scanner, Senior outreach, Story hour, Study rm, Summer & winter reading prog, Summer reading prog, Tax forms, Teen prog, Visual arts prog, Workshops
Open Mon-Fri 10-8, Sat 10-2
Friends of the Library Group

LISBON

P LISBON PUBLIC LIBRARY, 45 School St, 03585. SAN 309-8664. Tel: 603-838-6615. FAX: 603-838-6615. Web Site: lisbonpubliclibrary.org. *Librn,* Karla Houston; E-mail: Karla@lisbonpubliclibrary.org
Founded 1864. Pop 1,543; Circ 9,200
Library Holdings: Bk Vols 9,881; Per Subs 29
Special Collections: Local Culture & History (New Hampshire Coll)
Open Mon, Wed & Fri 11-5, Thurs 2-6

LITCHFIELD

P AARON CUTLER MEMORIAL LIBRARY, 269 Charles Bancroft Hwy, 03052. SAN 309-8516. Tel: 603-424-4044. FAX: 603-424-4044. E-mail: cutler_library@comcast.net. Web Site: cutlerlibrary.blogspot.com. *Libr Dir,* Vicki Varick; E-mail: acml_director@comcast.net; *Teen & Adult Librn,* Position Currently Open; *Asst Librn,* Lynn Richardson; E-mail: acml_assistantlib@comcast.net; *Ch Serv,* Alexis Britton; E-mail: acml_childrenslibrarian@comcast.net; Staff 3 (Non-MLS 3)
Founded 1821. Pop 8,366; Circ 26,409
Jan 2021-Dec 2021. Mats Exp $18,311, Books $9,401, AV Mat $2,995, Electronic Ref Mat (Incl. Access Fees) $5,915
Library Holdings: Audiobooks 760; DVDs 1,573; Electronic Media & Resources 2; Bk Vols 13,071; Per Subs 28
Automation Activity & Vendor Info: (Acquisitions) Koha; (Cataloging) Koha; (Circulation) Koha; (OPAC) Koha; (Serials) Koha
Wireless access
Function: 24/7 Electronic res, 24/7 Online cat, Adult bk club, Audiobks via web, Bk club(s), Bks on CD, Children's prog, Computer training, Computers for patron use, Digital talking bks, Electronic databases & coll, Free DVD rentals, Holiday prog, ILL available, Internet access, Life-long learning prog for all ages, Magazines, Mango lang, Museum passes, Online cat, Online ref, OverDrive digital audio bks, Photocopying/Printing, Preschool reading prog, Printer for laptops & handheld devices, Prog for adults, Prog for children & young adult, Scanner, STEM programs, Story hour, Summer & winter reading prog, Tax forms, Teen prog, Wheelchair accessible, Workshops
Open Tues-Thurs 10-8, Fri 10-6, Sat (Sept-June) 9-12
Friends of the Library Group

LITTLETON

P LITTLETON PUBLIC LIBRARY*, 92 Main St, 03561-1238. SAN 309-8672. Tel: 603-444-5741. FAX: 603-444-1706. E-mail: littlib@gmail.com. Web Site: www.littletonpubliclibrary.org. *Dir,* Meagan Carr; Staff 5 (Non-MLS 5)
Founded 1890. Pop 5,845; Circ 36,363
Library Holdings: Bk Vols 39,870; Per Subs 77; Talking Bks 634
Special Collections: Kilburn Stereoptic Views Coll; NH History and Genealogy Coll
Automation Activity & Vendor Info: (Cataloging) Book Systems; (Circulation) Book Systems; (OPAC) Book Systems
Wireless access
Function: ILL available
Open Tues & Wed 9:30-7, Fri 9:30-5, Sat 9:30-4
Friends of the Library Group

M LITTLETON REGIONAL HEALTHCARE*, Gale Medical Library, 600 St Johnsbury Rd, 03561. SAN 377-273X. Tel: 603-444-9564. FAX: 603-444-7491. Web Site: www.littletonhospital.org/department_details.php?DeptID=16. *Dir,* Anne Conner; E-mail: aconner@lrhcares.org; Staff 1 (MLS 1)
Library Holdings: Bk Titles 400; Bk Vols 500; Per Subs 125
Special Collections: Anna Connors Patient & Family Resource Center
Wireless access
Function: Computers for patron use, Ref serv available, Scanner, Study rm, Telephone ref, Wheelchair accessible
Partic in National Network of Libraries of Medicine Region 7
Open Mon-Fri 8-4:30
Restriction: Badge access after hrs

J WHITE MOUNTAINS COMMUNITY COLLEGE*, Littleton Academic Center Library, 646 Union St, Ste 300, 03561. Tel: 603-444-1326. FAX: 603-444-0981. Web Site: www.wmcc.edu. *Dir,* Melanie Robbins; E-mail: mrobbins@ccsnh.edu
Library Holdings: Bk Vols 2,000; Per Subs 10
Wireless access
Function: ILL available
Open Mon-Thurs 8:30-8:30, Fri 8:30-3

LONDONDERRY

P LEACH LIBRARY*, 276 Mammoth Rd, 03053. SAN 309-8680. Tel: 603-432-1132. FAX: 603-437-6610. Web Site: www.londonderrynh.org/leach-library. *Libr Dir,* Barbara Ostertag-Holtkamp; E-mail: bostertag-holtkamp@londonderrynh.org; Staff 7 (MLS 7)
Founded 1880. Pop 24,209; Circ 413,446
Jul 2020-Jun 2021 Income $1,279,209
Library Holdings: Bk Vols 75,328; Per Subs 193
Special Collections: Local History Coll
Automation Activity & Vendor Info: (Cataloging) Follett Software; (Circulation) Follett Software; (OPAC) Follett Software
Wireless access
Publications: Children's Room News; Leach Library News
Partic in Merri-Hill-Rock Library Cooperative; Urban Pub Libr Consortium
Open Mon-Thurs 9-8, Fri & Sat 9-5
Friends of the Library Group

LOUDON

P MAXFIELD PUBLIC LIBRARY*, 8 Rte 129, 03307. SAN 309-8699. Tel: 603-798-5153. E-mail: maxlib@comcast.net. Web Site: www.maxfieldlibrary.com. *Dir,* Dana Norman; *Ch,* Cheryl Ingerson
Pop 5,000; Circ 28,572
Library Holdings: Bk Vols 20,000; Per Subs 54
Automation Activity & Vendor Info: (Cataloging) Book Systems
Wireless access
Publications: Newsletter (Monthly)
Partic in New Hampshire Automated Information Systems; Suncook Interlibrary Cooperative
Open Tues & Thurs 10-7:30, Mon & Wed 2-7:30, Sat 9-1

LYME

P CONVERSE FREE LIBRARY, 38 Union St, 03768-9702. SAN 350-5294. Tel: 603-795-4622. FAX: 603-795-9346. E-mail: Info@lymenhlibrary.org. Web Site: lymenhlibrary.org. *Libr Dir,* Judith G Russell; E-mail: jrussell@lymenhlibrary.org; *Asst Dir,* Margaret Caffry; E-mail: mcaffry@lymenhlibrary.org; *Circ Librn,* Brian Passeri; E-mail: bpasseri@lymenhlibrary.org
Founded 1936. Pop 1,700; Circ 15,932
Library Holdings: Bk Vols 22,000; Per Subs 30
Automation Activity & Vendor Info: (Cataloging) Follett Software; (Circulation) Follett Software; (OPAC) Follett Software
Wireless access
Open Mon 1-5, Tues & Thurs 10-5, Wed 10-8, Fri 10-3, Sat 9-12
Friends of the Library Group

LYNDEBOROUGH

P J A TARBELL LIBRARY*, 136 Forest Rd, 03082. (Mail add: PO Box 54, 03082-0054), SAN 376-5075. Tel: 603-654-6790. FAX: 603-654-6790. E-mail: jat@tellink.net. Web Site: www.jatarbelllibrary.org. *Dir,* Brenda Cassidy
Library Holdings: Bk Vols 8,800; Per Subs 29
Open Mon 12-5 & 6-8, Wed 10-6, Thurs 1-6, Sat 10-Noon
Friends of the Library Group

MADBURY

P MADBURY PUBLIC LIBRARY*, Nine Town Hall Rd, 03823. Tel: 603-743-1400. E-mail: library@madburylibrary.org. Information Services E-mail: info@madburylibrary.org. Web Site: www.madburylibrary.org. *Dir,* Susan Sinnott; E-mail: directormpl@comcast.net; *Ch,* Kayla Morin; *Asst Librn,* Peggy Wolcott
Library Holdings: AV Mats 500; Bk Vols 9,000
Automation Activity & Vendor Info: (Cataloging) Follett Software; (Circulation) Follett Software; (OPAC) Follett Software; (Serials) Follett Software
Wireless access
Partic in Rochester Area Librarians
Open Mon & Wed 10-7, Thurs 10-5, Sat 10-2
Friends of the Library Group

MADISON

P MADISON LIBRARY, 1895 Village Rd, 03849. (Mail add: PO Box 240, 03849-0240), SAN 309-8702. Tel: 603-367-8545. FAX: 603-367-4479. E-mail: librarian@madison.lib.nh.us. Web Site: madisonlibrary-nh.org/WP. *Libr Dir,* Sloane Jarell; E-mail: sjarell@madison.lib.nh.us; *Asst Librn,* Camilla Spence; E-mail: cspence@madison.lib.nh.us; *Asst Librn,* Gordon Willey; E-mail: gwilley@madison.lib.nh.us; Staff 3 (MLS 1, Non-MLS 2)
Founded 1893. Pop 2,200; Circ 16,511
Library Holdings: Bk Vols 20,000; Per Subs 40
Automation Activity & Vendor Info: (Cataloging) ByWater Solutions; (Circulation) ByWater Solutions; (OPAC) ByWater Solutions
Wireless access
Partic in New Hampshire Automated Information Systems
Open Mon 2-5, Tues & Fri 10-6, Wed & Thurs 2-7, Sat 9-1
Friends of the Library Group

MANCHESTER

S AMERICAN-CANADIAN GENEALOGICAL SOCIETY LIBRARY, One Sundial Ave, Ste 317N, 03103-7242. SAN 326-212X. Tel: 603-622-1554. E-mail: acgs@acgs.org. Web Site: www.acgs.org. *Pres,* Juliet Smith
Founded 1973
Library Holdings: Bk Titles 7,000; Bk Vols 8,843
Special Collections: Canadian Marriage Records; Digitized Drouin Microfilm Coll; Diocese of Moncton, microfilm; Drouin Index; IGI Files of the Family History Library of the Church of Jesus Christ of Latter Day Saints; Loiselle, microfilm & fiche; Manchester, New Hampshire Vitals; Massachusetts Vital Records; N B Records; State of New Hampshire Vitals; State of Vermont Vitals
Wireless access
Publications: American-Canadian Genealogist (Quarterly); Repertoires of the Marriages, Baptisms & Burials of Several New England & New York State Catholic Churches
Open Wed 9-4
Restriction: Circ to mem only

SR BROOKSIDE CONGREGATIONAL CHURCH LIBRARY*, 2013 Elm St, 03104. SAN 373-4706. Tel: 603-669-2807. FAX: 603-668-9041. E-mail: admin@brooksidecc.org. Web Site: www.brooksidecc.org. *Librn,* Sarah Merrill
Library Holdings: Bk Vols 500
Wireless access
Open Mon-Thurs 9-3:30

S CURRIER MUSEUM OF ART*, Art Reference Library & Archive, 150 Ash St, 03104. SAN 377-2446. Tel: 603-518-4927, 603-669-6144. FAX: 603-669-7194. E-mail: library@currier.org. Web Site: www.currier.org/library. *Librn & Archivist,* Meghan Petersen; Staff 1 (MLS 1)
Founded 1929
Library Holdings: Bk Vols 14,000; Per Subs 25
Subject Interests: Decorative art, European art, Photog
Restriction: Non-circulating to the pub, Open by appt only

P MANCHESTER CITY LIBRARY*, 405 Pine St, 03104-6199. SAN 309-8737. Tel: 603-624-6550. FAX: 603-624-6559. E-mail: library@manchesternh.gov. Web Site: www.manchester.lib.nh.us, www.manchesterlibrary.org. *Dir,* Denise van Zanten; E-mail: dvanzant@manchesternh.gov; *Dep Libr Dir,* Dee Santoso; E-mail: dsantoso@manchesternh.gov; *Head, Circ,* Carlos Pearman; E-mail: cpearman@manchesternh.gov; *Head, Info & Tech,* Steve Viggiano; E-mail: sviggiano@manchesternh.gov; *Head, Outreach Serv,* Caleb Moshier; E-mail: cmoshier@manchesternh.gov; *Head, Tech Serv,* Sarah St Martin; E-mail: sstmartin@manchesternh.gov; *Head, Youth Serv,* Karyn Isleb; E-mail: kisleb@manchesternh.gov; Staff 17.5 (MLS 12, Non-MLS 5.5)
Founded 1854. Pop 109,000; Circ 537,784. Sal $1,072,154 (Prof $684,306)
Library Holdings: Audiobooks 8,388; DVDs 7,005; e-books 27,773; Microforms 7,479; Per Subs 161
Special Collections: ArtBook Coll; New Hampshire History. State Document Depository; US Document Depository
Automation Activity & Vendor Info: (Acquisitions) Innovative Interfaces, Inc; (Cataloging) Innovative Interfaces, Inc; (Circulation) Innovative Interfaces, Inc; (OPAC) Innovative Interfaces, Inc; (Serials) Innovative Interfaces, Inc
Wireless access
Function: Adult bk club, Adult literacy prog, Archival coll, Audiobks via web, Bk club(s), Bks on CD, Children's prog, Computer training, Computers for patron use, Digital talking bks, Doc delivery serv, Electronic databases & coll, Family literacy, Free DVD rentals, Govt ref serv, Health sci info serv, Holiday prog, Home delivery & serv to seniorr ctr & nursing homes, Homebound delivery serv, ILL available, Magnifiers for reading, Microfiche/film & reading machines, Museum passes, Music CDs, Online cat, Orientations, OverDrive digital audio bks, Photocopying/Printing, Preschool outreach, Prog for adults, Prog for children & young adult, Ref & res, Spanish lang bks, Spoken cassettes & CDs, Story hour, Summer reading prog, Tax forms, Teen prog, Telephone ref, Wheelchair accessible
Publications: MCL Notes (Newsletter)
Partic in GMILCS, Inc
Open Mon, Tues & Thurs 8:30-8:30, Wed & Fri 8:30-5:30, Sat 9:30-2:30
Restriction: Access at librarian's discretion
Branches: 1
WEST MANCHESTER BRANCH LIBRARY, 76 N Main St, 03102-4084, SAN 377-029X. Tel: 603-624-6560. FAX: 603-628-6216. *Head, Outreach Serv,* Caleb Moshier; E-mail: cmoshier@manchesternh.gov
Library Holdings: Audiobooks 1,889; DVDs 2,693; Bk Vols 30,172; Per Subs 20
Special Services for the Deaf - Accessible learning ctr; ADA equip
Open Wed 12:30-8:30, Thurs & Fri 9:30-5:30

J MANCHESTER COMMUNITY COLLEGE LIBRARY, 1066 Front St, 03102. SAN 309-8761. Tel: 603-206-8150. E-mail: manchesterlibrary@ccsnh.edu. Web Site: library.mccnh.edu/home. *Libr Dir,* Deb Baker; E-mail: mcclibrary@ccsnh.edu; *Outreach & Instruction Librn,* Kristen Giurciullo; *Access Serv Coordr,* Mark McShane; Staff 3 (MLS 2, Non-MLS 1)
Founded 1968. Enrl 2,565; Fac 197; Highest Degree: Associate
Library Holdings: CDs 60; DVDs 500; Bk Titles 17,000; Bk Vols 18,400; Per Subs 50
Subject Interests: Bldg tech, Nursing
Automation Activity & Vendor Info: (Cataloging) TLC (The Library Corporation); (Circulation) TLC (The Library Corporation); (Course Reserve) TLC (The Library Corporation); (Discovery) EBSCO Discovery Service; (ILL) OCLC WorldShare Interlibrary Loan; (OPAC) TLC (The Library Corporation)
Wireless access
Partic in New Hampshire Automated Information Systems; New Hampshire College & University Council; OCLC Online Computer Library Center, Inc; Westchester Academic Library Directors Organization

S MANCHESTER HISTORIC ASSOCIATION LIBRARY*, 129 Amherst St, 03101. SAN 309-8745. Tel: 603-622-7531. E-mail: library@manchesterhistoric.org. Web Site: www.manchesterhistoric.org. *Exec Dir,* John Clayton; E-mail: jclayton@manchesterhistoric.org; *Fac Mgr, Res,* Daniel T Peters; E-mail: dpeters@manchesterhistoric.org
Founded 1896
Library Holdings: Bk Vols 3,500
Special Collections: Correspondence, notes & reports; Personal Files (F C Dumaine Coll); Photographs - 19th Century & early 20th; Textile Design, graphs & notes
Subject Interests: Amoskeag industries, Amoskeag Manufacturing Co (Textiles), Hist of Manchester
Publications: Guide to Amoskeag Manufacturing Company Collections in the Manchester Historic Association
Open Wed 10-4, Sat 10-3

L MCLANE MIDDLETON*, Law Library, 900 Elm St, 10th Flr, 03101. (Mail add: PO Box 326, 03105-0326), SAN 323-7133. Tel: 603-628-1428. FAX: 603-625-5650. Web Site: www.mclane.com. *Dir, Libr & Res Serv,* Jennifer M Finch; E-mail: jennifer.finch@mclane.com; Staff 1.2 (MLS 1.2)
Library Holdings: Bk Titles 2,250; Bk Vols 9,000; Per Subs 100
Special Collections: New Hampshire Legal, Legislative, Regulatory & Historical Information Coll
Automation Activity & Vendor Info: (Cataloging) CyberTools for Libraries; (Circulation) CyberTools for Libraries; (ILL) OCLC FirstSearch; (OPAC) CyberTools for Libraries; (Serials) CyberTools for Libraries
Wireless access
Restriction: Employees only

C SAINT ANSELM COLLEGE*, Geisel Library, 100 Saint Anselm Dr, 03102-1310. SAN 309-8796. Tel: 603-641-7300. Reference Tel: 603-641-7306. FAX: 603-641-7345. Web Site: www.anselm.edu/library. *Head, Coll Develop,* Melinda Malik; E-mail: mmalik@anselm.edu; *Asst Librn, Head, Tech,* John Dillon; E-mail: jdillon@anselm.edu; *Librn,* Charles Getchell; E-mail: cgetchell@anselm.edu; Staff 28 (MLS 13, Non-MLS 15)
Founded 1889. Enrl 2,000; Fac 146; Highest Degree: Bachelor
Library Holdings: CDs 2,260; DVDs 1,690; e-journals 36,000; Electronic Media & Resources 8,800; Microforms 74,790; Bk Titles 189,900; Bk Vols 239,000; Per Subs 1,100; Videos 2,210
Special Collections: Archives of College; New England History. State Document Depository; US Document Depository
Subject Interests: Hist, New England hist, Nursing, Theol
Automation Activity & Vendor Info: (Acquisitions) Innovative Interfaces, Inc; (Cataloging) Innovative Interfaces, Inc; (Circulation) Innovative Interfaces, Inc; (Serials) Innovative Interfaces, Inc
Wireless access
Publications: Friends Forum (Newsletter); Geisel Library News (Newsletter)
Partic in LYRASIS; New Hampshire College & University Council; OCLC Online Computer Library Center, Inc
Open Mon-Thurs (Winter) 8am-Midnight, Fri 8am-11pm, Sat Noon-11, Sun 11am-Midnight; Mon-Fri (Summer) 8:30-4:30
Friends of the Library Group

L SHEEHAN PHINNEY LIBRARY*, 1000 Elm St, 17th Flr, 03101. (Mail add: PO Box 3701, 03105-3701), SAN 371-568X. Tel: 603-668-0300. FAX: 603-627-8121. Web Site: www.sheehan.com.
Library Holdings: Bk Vols 10,000
Restriction: Staff use only

C SOUTHERN NEW HAMPSHIRE UNIVERSITY*, Shapiro Library, 2500 N River Rd, 03106-1045. SAN 378-486X. Tel: 603-645-9605. Circulation E-mail: circulation@snhu.edu. Interlibrary Loan Service E-mail: ill@snhu.edu. Web Site: www.snhu.edu/student-experience/campus-experience/shapiro-library. *Dean of Libr,* William A Mayer; Tel: 603-626-9100, Ext 2166, E-mail: w.mayer@snhu.edu; *Assoc Dean, Fac & Access Serv, Coll,* Steve Robichaud; Tel: 603-626-9100, Ext 2168, E-mail: s.robichaud@snhu.edu; *Archivist, Digital Initiatives Librn,* Christopher Cooper; Tel: 603-668-2211, Ext 2160, E-mail: c.cooper@snhu.edu; *Electronic Res Librn,* Sandy Srivastava; Tel: 603-645-9605, Ext 2159, E-mail: s.srivastava@snhu.edu; *Ref Librn,* Alexis Baker; E-mail: a.baker@snhu.edu; *Acq, Libr Spec,* Jessica Sheehan; Tel: 603-626-9100, Ext 2166, E-mail: j.sheehan@snhu.edu; Staff 11 (MLS 9, Non-MLS 2)
Founded 1963. Enrl 5,150; Fac 129; Highest Degree: Doctorate
Library Holdings: Bk Vols 94,042; Per Subs 755
Special Collections: AMEX & NYSE 10K & Annual Reports, fiche; Business History Coll, micro; Education Resource Coll; Social Science & History (Library of American Civilization), fiche. State Document Depository; US Document Depository
Subject Interests: Acctg, Behav sci, Bus, Econ, Educ, Hotels, Humanities, Indust, Soc sci, Tourism
Automation Activity & Vendor Info: (Acquisitions) SirsiDynix; (Cataloging) SirsiDynix; (Circulation) SirsiDynix; (Course Reserve) SirsiDynix; (OPAC) SirsiDynix; (Serials) SirsiDynix
Wireless access
Publications: Accession List (Monthly); Periodical List; Periodical Subject List
Partic in LYRASIS; New Hampshire College & University Council
Open Mon-Fri 7:30am-12:45am, Sat 10-7:45

C UNIVERSITY OF NEW HAMPSHIRE AT MANCHESTER LIBRARY, 88 Commercial St, 03101. SAN 320-6955. Tel: 603-641-4173. Interlibrary Loan Service Tel: 603-641-4183. E-mail: unhm.library@unh.edu. Web Site: manchester.unh.edu/library. *Dir,* Carolyn Gamtso; Tel: 603-641-4172, E-mail: carolyn.gamtso@unh.edu; *Sr Libr Mgr,* Cindy Tremblay; E-mail: cindy.tremblay@unh.edu; *Contract Librn,* Kathleen Norton; Tel: 603-641-4195, E-mail: kathleen.norton@unh.edu; Staff 3 (MLS 3)
Founded 1967. Enrl 790; Fac 40; Highest Degree: Master
Library Holdings: AV Mats 4,673; Bk Vols 21,092; Per Subs 259
Special Collections: Twentieth Century European Intellectual Thought
Subject Interests: Deafness, Early New Hampshire newspapers, Sign lang

Automation Activity & Vendor Info: (Cataloging) Ex Libris Group; (Circulation) Ex Libris Group; (Course Reserve) Ex Libris Group; (ILL) Clio; (OPAC) Ex Libris Group; (Serials) Ex Libris Group
Wireless access
Publications: Handbook; Library Research Guides
Partic in Boston Library Consortium, Inc; New Hampshire College & University Council
Special Services for the Deaf - Accessible learning ctr; Assistive tech; Bks on deafness & sign lang; Coll on deaf educ; TTY equip
Open Mon-Thurs 8-7, Fri 8:30-3

GM VETERANS AFFAIRS MEDICAL CENTER LIBRARY*, 718 Smyth Rd, W347, 03104-7004. SAN 309-8818. Tel: 603-624-4366, Ext 6033. FAX: 603-626-6503. Web Site: www.manchester.va.gov. *Libr Dir,* Mimi Guessferd; E-mail: mary.guessferd@va.gov; Staff 1 (MLS 1)
Founded 1950
Library Holdings: e-journals 50; Bk Titles 450
Subject Interests: Dentistry, Med, Nursing
Function: Audio & video playback equip for onsite use, Health sci info serv, ILL available, Ref serv available, Telephone ref
Partic in Health Sciences Libraries of New Hampshire & Vermont
Open Mon-Fri 8-4
Restriction: Circulates for staff only, Clients only, Employees & their associates, In-house use for visitors

MARLBOROUGH

P FROST FREE LIBRARY*, 28 Jaffrey Rd, 03455. (Mail add: PO Box 457, 03455-0457), SAN 309-8826. Tel: 603-876-4479. E-mail: library@frostfree.org. Web Site: frostfree.org. *Dir,* Kristin Readel; E-mail: kreadel@frostfree.org; *Asst Librn,* Jane Richards-Jones; Staff 3 (Non-MLS 3)
Founded 1865. Pop 2,025; Circ 12,818
Library Holdings: Bk Vols 13,286; Per Subs 47
Automation Activity & Vendor Info: (Circulation) Follett Software
Wireless access
Function: 24/7 Electronic res, 24/7 Online cat, Activity rm, Adult bk club, Art exhibits, Audiobks via web, Bks on CD, Children's prog, Computers for patron use, Electronic databases & coll, Free DVD rentals, ILL available, Internet access, Laminating, Magazines, Meeting rooms, Movies, Notary serv, Online cat, Photocopying/Printing, Preschool outreach, Scanner
Publications: Bemis History of Marlborough (Local historical information)
Partic in New England Libr Asn; Nubanusit Library Cooperative
Open Tues & Wed 2-8, Thurs & Fri 10-5, Sat 10-1
Friends of the Library Group

MARLOW

P MARLOW TOWN LIBRARY, 12 Church St, 03456. (Mail add: PO Box 64, 03456), SAN 309-8834. Tel: 603-446-3466. E-mail: marlowtownlibrary@gmail.com. Web Site: www.marlownewhampshire.org/library.php, www.marlownh.gov/library. *Librn,* Jennifer Brown; *Ch,* Tina Fava; Staff 1 (Non-MLS 1)
Founded 1889. Pop 750
Library Holdings: Bk Vols 11,000; Per Subs 15
Automation Activity & Vendor Info: (OPAC) LibraryWorld, Inc
Wireless access
Function: 24/7 Electronic res, 24/7 Online cat, Audio & video playback equip for onsite use, Audiobks via web, Bks on CD, Children's prog, Computer training, Computers for patron use, Free DVD rentals, ILL available, Instruction & testing, Internet access, Life-long learning prog for all ages, Magazines, Mail & tel request accepted, Movies, Museum passes, Online cat, OverDrive digital audio bks, Photocopying/Printing, Preschool outreach, Prog for adults, Prog for children & young adult, Scanner, Senior computer classes, Summer reading prog, Tax forms, Wheelchair accessible, Workshops
Partic in Nubanusit Library Cooperative
Open Mon 12-5 & 6-8, Wed 4-8, Sat 9-Noon
Restriction: Access at librarian's discretion, Free to mem, Non-circulating coll, Non-circulating of rare bks, Non-resident fee

MASON

P MASON PUBLIC LIBRARY*, Mann House, 16 Darling Hill Rd, 03048. SAN 309-8842. Tel: 603-878-3867. FAX: 603-878-6146. E-mail: library@masonnh.us. Web Site: masonnh.us/mason-public-library-general-information. *Dir,* Denise Ginzler
Pop 1,382; Circ 10,000
Library Holdings: AV Mats 811; Bk Vols 11,091; Per Subs 25; Videos 529
Special Collections: Video Classics Project Coll
Publications: Booklist
Open Tues 9-4 & 6-8, Wed & Thurs 9-4, Sat 9-Noon

MEREDITH

P MEREDITH PUBLIC LIBRARY*, 91 Main St, 03253. (Mail add: PO Box 808, 03253-0808), SAN 309-8850. Tel: 603-279-4303. FAX: 603-279-5352. Web Site: www.meredithlibrary.org. *Dir,* Erin Apostolos; E-mail: erin@meredithlibrary.org; *Asst Libr Dir,* Christopher Leland; E-mail: chris@meredithlibrary.org; *Circ Librn,* Matthew Gunby; E-mail: matthew@meredithlibrary.org; *Youth Serv Librn,* John Lock; E-mail: john@meredithlibrary.org; Staff 7 (MLS 2, Non-MLS 5)
Founded 1882. Pop 4,636; Circ 115,201
Library Holdings: Bk Vols 35,500; Per Subs 72
Special Collections: Oral History
Automation Activity & Vendor Info: (Cataloging) Follett Software; (Circulation) Follett Software
Wireless access
Open Tues-Thurs 9-8, Fri 9-5, Sat 9-2

MERIDEN

P PLAINFIELD PUBLIC LIBRARIES*, Meriden Library, 22 Bean Rd, 03770. (Mail add: PO Box 128, 03770-0128), SAN 309-8869. Tel: 603-469-3252. E-mail: mer-prml@plainfieldlibraries.org. Web Site: plainfieldlibraries.org. *Dir,* Mary King; *Libr Asst,* Terri Crane; *Libr Asst,* Lori Estey
Founded 1797. Pop 2,364; Circ 9,668
Library Holdings: Audiobooks 248; DVDs 277; Bk Vols 9,406
Special Collections: Boyd's History (Plainfield) 4 vols; History Coll; Plainfield Oral History
Automation Activity & Vendor Info: (Serials) Evergreen
Wireless access
Open Mon & Tues 1-7, Thurs 10-7, Sat 9-Noon
Friends of the Library Group
Branches: 1
PHILIP READ MEMORIAL LIBRARY, 1088 Rte 12A, Plainfield, 03781, SAN 309-9288. Tel: 603-675-6866. Web Site: plainfieldlibraries.org/plainfield. *Dir,* Mary King; Staff 1 (Non-MLS 1)
Founded 1920. Pop 2,450; Circ 13,622
Library Holdings: Audiobooks 1,103; AV Mats 1,791; Bks on Deafness & Sign Lang 10; Braille Volumes 26; Bk Titles 27,179; Per Subs 95
Special Collections: Local Author Book & Magazine Coll. Oral History
Subject Interests: Local author coll, Local hist, Oral hist tapes
Partic in Librarians of the Upper Valley Coop
Publications: Newsletter
Special Services for the Blind - Braille bks
Open Mon 1-8, Wed 10-8, Fri 1-5, Sat 9-12
Friends of the Library Group

MERRIMACK

P MERRIMACK PUBLIC LIBRARY*, 470 Daniel Webster Hwy, 03054-3694. SAN 309-8885. Tel: 603-424-5021. FAX: 603-424-7312. Web Site: www.merrimacklibrary.org. *Dir,* Yvette Couser; E-mail: ycouser@merrimacklibrary.org; *Head, Adult Serv,* Max Blanchette; *Head, Tech Serv,* Jennifer Stover; Staff 31 (MLS 8, Non-MLS 23)
Founded 1892. Pop 26,577; Circ 235,361
Library Holdings: Bk Titles 73,675; Per Subs 148
Automation Activity & Vendor Info: (Acquisitions) Innovative Interfaces, Inc; (Cataloging) Innovative Interfaces, Inc; (Circulation) Innovative Interfaces, Inc; (Course Reserve) Innovative Interfaces, Inc; (ILL) Innovative Interfaces, Inc; (OPAC) Innovative Interfaces, Inc; (Serials) Innovative Interfaces, Inc
Wireless access
Publications: Library Link
Partic in GMILCS, Inc
Open Mon-Thurs 10-9, Fri 10-5, Sat 9-1, Sun 1-5
Friends of the Library Group

C THOMAS MORE COLLEGE OF LIBERAL ARTS, Warren Memorial Library, Six Manchester St, 03054-4805. SAN 373-0816. Tel: 603-880-0425. FAX: 603-880-9280. Web Site: www.thomasmorecollege.edu/library. *Col Librn,* Alexis Rohlfing; E-mail: arohlfing@thomasmorecollege.edu; Staff 2 (MLS 1, Non-MLS 1)
Founded 1978. Enrl 90; Fac 8; Highest Degree: Bachelor
Library Holdings: Bk Titles 32,000; Bk Vols 40,000; Per Subs 20
Subject Interests: Biology, Hist, Lit, Philos, Relig
Wireless access
Partic in New Hampshire Automated Information Systems

MILAN

P DUMMER PUBLIC LIBRARY*, 67 Hill Rd, Dummer, 03588-9711. Tel: 603-449-0995. E-mail: dummerlibrary@gmail.com. *Dir,* Jamie Amato
Library Holdings: AV Mats 500; Bk Vols 8,000; Talking Bks 50
Automation Activity & Vendor Info: (Cataloging) JayWil Software Development, Inc; (Circulation) JayWil Software Development, Inc
Wireless access

Open Wed 4-7, Sat 9-Noon
Friends of the Library Group

P MILAN PUBLIC LIBRARY*, 20 Bridge St, 03588. (Mail add: PO Box 263, 03588-0263), SAN 309-8893. Tel: 603-449-7307. E-mail: gotmorebooks@gmail.com. Web Site: www.townofmilan.org/library.html. *Librn,* Vickie Plourde
Pop 1,370; Circ 1,500
Library Holdings: AV Mats 114; Bk Vols 7,800
Subject Interests: Local hist
Wireless access
Open Mon & Thurs 9-5

MILFORD

P WADLEIGH MEMORIAL LIBRARY, 49 Nashua St, 03055. SAN 309-8907. Tel: 603-249-0645. FAX: 603-672-6064. E-mail: wadleigh@wadleighlibrary.org. Circulation E-mail: wmlcirc@wadleighlibrary.org. Interlibrary Loan Service E-mail: wmlill@wadleighlibrary.org. Reference E-mail: refdesk@wadleighlibrary.org. Web Site: www.wadleighlibrary.org. *Libr Dir,* Betsy Solon; E-mail: director@wadleighlibrary.org; *Head, Circ,* Mary Ann Shea; E-mail: mshea@wadleighlibrary.org; *Head, Ref & Adult Serv,* Kim Gabert; E-mail: kgabert@wadleighlibrary.org; *Tech Serv,* Kathy Prevey-Levin; E-mail: techserv@wadleighlibrary.org; *YA Serv,* Katie Spofford; E-mail: wadleighya@gmail.com; Staff 10.5 (MLS 4.5, Non-MLS 6)
Founded 1868. Pop 15,099; Circ 220,967
Library Holdings: CDs 1,715; e-books 900; Bk Vols 67,494; Per Subs 180; Talking Bks 1,977; Videos 3,071
Special Collections: Hutchinson Family Singers; Local History; Local Newspapers 1800-present, microfilm
Automation Activity & Vendor Info: (Acquisitions) Innovative Interfaces, Inc; (Cataloging) Innovative Interfaces, Inc; (Circulation) Innovative Interfaces, Inc; (OPAC) Innovative Interfaces, Inc; (Serials) Innovative Interfaces, Inc
Wireless access
Function: 24/7 Electronic res, 24/7 Online cat, Adult bk club, Adult literacy prog, Archival coll, Audiobks on Playaways & MP3, Audiobks via web, BA reader (adult literacy), Bk club(s), Bks on CD, Children's prog, Computer training, Computers for patron use, Digital talking bks, Family literacy, Free DVD rentals, Health sci info serv, Home delivery & serv to seniorr ctr & nursing homes, Homebound delivery serv, ILL available, Internet access, Magazines, Magnifiers for reading, Mail & tel request accepted, Meeting rooms, Microfiche/film & reading machines, Museum passes, Music CDs, Notary serv, Online cat, Online ref, OverDrive digital audio bks, Photocopying/Printing, Preschool outreach, Prog for adults, Prog for children & young adult, Ref serv available, Scanner, Senior computer classes, Serves people with intellectual disabilities, Spoken cassettes & CDs, Spoken cassettes & DVDs, Story hour, Study rm, Summer reading prog, Tax forms, Teen prog, Telephone ref, VHS videos, Wheelchair accessible, Workshops
Partic in GMILCS, Inc
Open Mon, Tues, Thurs & Fri 9-4, Wed 9-4 & 5-7, Sat 9-1
Friends of the Library Group

MILTON

P NUTE HIGH SCHOOL & LIBRARY*, Nute Library, 22 Elm St, 03851. SAN 350-5359. Tel: 603-652-7829. FAX: 603-652-4793. E-mail: nutelibrary@gmail.com. Web Site: www.nutelibrary.com. *Librn,* Al Goodwin; *Sch Librn,* Position Currently Open; Staff 2 (MLS 1, Non-MLS 1)
Pop 4,000; Circ 15,069
Library Holdings: Bk Vols 15,000; Per Subs 15
Special Collections: Local History Coll
Automation Activity & Vendor Info: (Cataloging) Book Systems; (Circulation) Book Systems; (OPAC) Book Systems
Wireless access
Function: 24/7 Electronic res, 24/7 Online cat, Activity rm, Archival coll, Audiobks on Playaways & MP3, Bks on CD, Children's prog, Computers for patron use, Electronic databases & coll, Free DVD rentals, ILL available, Internet access, Magazines, Meeting rooms, Museum passes, Online cat, Photocopying/Printing, Story hour, Summer reading prog, Tax forms, Wheelchair accessible
Partic in New Hampshire Automated Information Systems; Rochester Area Librarians
Open Mon, Tues & Thurs 9-5, Wed 9-7, Fri 9-2:15, Sat 9-Noon

MILTON MILLS

P MILTON FREE PUBLIC LIBRARY*, 13 Main St, 03852. (Mail add: PO Box 127, 03852-0127). Tel: 603-473-8535. E-mail: mfpl@metrocast.net. Web Site: www.miltonfreepubliclibrary.org. *Dir,* Betsy Baker; *Asst Librn,* Mary Engels; *Asst Librn,* Ruth Gutman; *Asst Librn,* Amy Hampton; Staff 3 (Non-MLS 3)
Founded 1916. Pop 3,940
Library Holdings: AV Mats 100; Large Print Bks 35; Bk Vols 8,500; Talking Bks 90
Wireless access
Partic in New Hampshire Automated Information Systems; Rochester Area Librarians
Open Tues 3:30-7:30, Wed 12-7:30, Thurs 10-12 & 3:30-7:30, Fri 1-7:30, Sat 10-1
Friends of the Library Group

MONROE

P MONROE PUBLIC LIBRARY*, 19 Plains Rd, 03771. (Mail add: PO Box 67, 03771-0067), SAN 309-8915. Tel: 603-638-4736. E-mail: monroepubliclibrary@roadrunner.com. *Dir,* Jessica Sherman; *Libr Asst,* Susan Price; *Libr Asst,* Kim Ward
Pop 618; Circ 17,887
Library Holdings: Bk Vols 19,000; Per Subs 40
Special Collections: State Document Depository
Wireless access
Partic in New Hampshire Automated Information Systems
Special Services for the Deaf - Assisted listening device
Open Mon & Tues 10-1 & 4-7, Thurs 2:30-5:30, Sat 9-Noon

MONT VERNON

P DALAND MEMORIAL LIBRARY, Five N Main St, 03057. (Mail add: PO Box 335, 03057), SAN 309-8923. Tel: 603-673-7888. FAX: 603-673-7888. E-mail: dalandlibrary@comcast.net. Web Site: www.dalandlibrary.com. *Dir,* Bonnie Angulas; *Children's Dir,* JoAnn Kitchel
Founded 1892. Pop 2,600
Library Holdings: Bk Vols 14,000; Per Subs 14
Automation Activity & Vendor Info: (Circulation) Follett Software
Wireless access
Open Tues & Thurs 10-5:30, Wed 12-8, Fri 2-6, Sat 10-1
Friends of the Library Group

MOULTONBOROUGH

P MOULTONBOROUGH PUBLIC LIBRARY*, Four Holland St, 03254. (Mail add: PO Box 150, 03254-0150), SAN 309-8931. Tel: 603-476-8895. FAX: 603-476-5261. Web Site: www.moultonboroughlibrary.org. *Dir,* Nancy McCue; *Asst Dir,* Jane Rice; *Ch,* Sharon Gulla; *Tech Librn,* Anne Marie Welch; Staff 6 (MLS 1, Non-MLS 5)
Founded 1890. Pop 4,800; Circ 61,725
Library Holdings: Bk Titles 25,000; Per Subs 75
Subject Interests: Local hist
Automation Activity & Vendor Info: (Acquisitions) Follett Software; (Cataloging) Follett Software; (Circulation) Follett Software
Wireless access
Function: Computer training, Homebound delivery serv, ILL available, Magnifiers for reading, Music CDs, Photocopying/Printing, Prog for adults, Prog for children & young adult, Ref serv available, Spoken cassettes & CDs, Spoken cassettes & DVDs, Summer reading prog, Tax forms, Telephone ref, VHS videos, Wheelchair accessible
Open Mon-Thurs 10-8, Fri 10-5, Sat 10-2
Friends of the Library Group

NASHUA

J NASHUA COMMUNITY COLLEGE*, Walter R Peterson Library & Media Center, 505 Amherst St, 03063-1026. SAN 309-8974. Tel: 603-578-8905. Interlibrary Loan Service Tel: 603-578-6810. FAX: 603-882-8690. Web Site: www.nashuacc.edu/academics/library-and-media-services. *Dir,* Margaret Bero; E-mail: mbero@ccsnh.edu; *Libr Tech,* Stephanie Saxton; E-mail: ssaxton@ccsnh.edu; Staff 7 (MLS 2, Non-MLS 5)
Founded 1971. Enrl 2,000; Fac 45; Highest Degree: Associate
Library Holdings: DVDs 1,200; e-books 72,000; e-journals 35,000; Bk Titles 18,000; Per Subs 250
Subject Interests: Automotive, Computer, Drafting, Electronic tech, Liberal arts, Machining, Mat sci
Automation Activity & Vendor Info: (Cataloging) TLC (The Library Corporation); (Circulation) TLC (The Library Corporation); (OPAC) TLC (The Library Corporation); (Serials) TLC (The Library Corporation)
Publications: Handbook (User's guide); PR Materials; Reference Guides
Partic in LYRASIS; Westchester Academic Library Directors Organization
Open Mon-Thurs 8-8, Fri 8-5, Sat 9-1

P NASHUA PUBLIC LIBRARY*, Two Court St, 03060. SAN 350-5413. Tel: 603-589-4600. FAX: 603-594-3457. Web Site: www.nashualibrary.org. *Dir,* Jennifer McCormack; Tel: 603-589-4620, E-mail: jennifer.mccormack@nashualibrary.org; *Asst Dir,* Jenn Hosking; Tel:

603-589-4621; *YA Librn,* Position Currently Open; *Circ Supvr,* Loren Rosson; Tel: 603-589-4617; *Supvr, Tech Serv,* Margaret Gleeson; Tel: 603-589-4624; Staff 52 (MLS 12, Non-MLS 40)
Founded 1867. Pop 90,000; Circ 692,939
Library Holdings: AV Mats 19,608; Bks on Deafness & Sign Lang 59; Braille Volumes 16; CDs 4,816; DVDs 4,820; Electronic Media & Resources 994; Large Print Bks 4,442; Music Scores 21; Bk Vols 240,555; Per Subs 250
Special Collections: Local & State Histories (Hunt Room Coll). State Document Depository; US Document Depository
Subject Interests: Archit, Art, Music
Automation Activity & Vendor Info: (Acquisitions) SirsiDynix; (Circulation) SirsiDynix; (Media Booking) SirsiDynix; (OPAC) SirsiDynix
Wireless access
Function: Adult bk club, Art exhibits, AV serv, Bk club(s), Bus archives, Chess club, Electronic databases & coll, Govt ref serv, Health sci info serv, Home delivery & serv to seniorr ctr & nursing homes, Homebound delivery serv, Homework prog, ILL available, Internet access, Jazz prog, Large print keyboards, Mail & tel request accepted, Online ref, Orientations, Photocopying/Printing, Preschool outreach, Prog for adults, Prog for children & young adult, Ref serv available, Satellite serv, Senior computer classes, Spoken cassettes & CDs, Spoken cassettes & DVDs, Summer reading prog, Telephone ref, VHS videos, Wheelchair accessible, Workshops
Publications: Nashua Experience: History in the Making, 1673-1978
Special Services for the Deaf - TTY equip
Open Mon-Fri 9-9, Sat 9-5:30, Sun 1-5
Friends of the Library Group

R PILGRIM CONGREGATIONAL CHURCH*, Goodhue Memorial Library, Four Watson St, 03064. SAN 309-8982. Tel: 603-882-1801, FAX: 603-882-1801. E-mail: Office@pilgrimchurchnashua.org. Web Site: www.pilgrimchurchnashua.org.
Library Holdings: Bk Vols 250
Subject Interests: Congregational info, Fiction

CR RIVIER UNIVERSITY, Regina Library, 420 S Main St, 03060-5086. SAN 309-8990. Tel: 603-897-8256. FAX: 603-897-8889. E-mail: libmail@rivier.edu. Web Site: www.rivier.edu/regina-library. *Libr Dir,* Dan Speidel; Tel: 603-897-8576, E-mail: dspeidel@rivier.edu; *Asst Dir,* Samantha Cabral; Tel: 603-897-8536, E-mail: scabral@rivier.edu; *Res & Instruction Librn,* Kati MacFarline; Tel: 603-897-8673, E-mail: kmacfarline@rivier.edu; *Electronic Info Librn,* Sara Heng; Tel: 603-897-8683, E-mail: sheng@rivier.edu; *Acq & Ser Librn,* Abbie Joy; Tel: 603-897-8535, E-mail: ajoy1@rivier.edu; *Tech Serv Librn,* Elaine Bean; Tel: 603-897-8672, E-mail: ebean@rivier.edu; *Archives Asst, Tech Serv Librn,* Christine Shearman; Tel: 603-897-8671, E-mail: cshearman@rivier.edu; *ILL Coordr,* Holly Klump; Tel: 603-897-8255, E-mail: hklump@rivier.edu; *Access Serv Coordr,* Megan Doyle; Tel: 603-897-8685, E-mail: mdoyle@rivier.edu; *Educational Resource Ctr Asst,* Peter Guevin; Tel: 603-897-8463, E-mail: pguevin@rivier.edu; Staff 16 (MLS 9, Non-MLS 7)
Founded 1933. Enrl 1,562; Fac 70; Highest Degree: Doctorate
Library Holdings: AV Mats 4,500; e-books 240,000; e-journals 130,000; Bk Vols 90,000; Per Subs 135
Special Collections: Franco-American Literary Criticism (Rocheleau-Rouleau Coll); Patristics (Gilbert Coll)
Subject Interests: Educ, Nursing
Automation Activity & Vendor Info: (Acquisitions) Innovative Interfaces, Inc; (Cataloging) Innovative Interfaces, Inc; (Circulation) Innovative Interfaces, Inc; (Course Reserve) Innovative Interfaces, Inc; (Discovery) EBSCO Discovery Service; (ILL) OCLC Online; (Media Booking) Innovative Interfaces, Inc; (OPAC) Innovative Interfaces, Inc; (Serials) Innovative Interfaces, Inc
Wireless access
Function: ILL available
Partic in New Hampshire College & University Council
Special Services for the Blind - Reader equip
Open Mon-Thurs 8am-Midnight, Fri 8-8, Sat 10-6, Sun 11-11

NELSON

P OLIVIA RODHAM MEMORIAL LIBRARY*, Nelson Library, One Nelson Common Rd, 03457. SAN 324-2862. Tel: 603-847-3214. E-mail: library@townofnelson.com. Web Site: townofnelson.com/library. *Dir,* Kristine Finnegan; Staff 1 (Non-MLS 1)
Founded 1926. Pop 670
Library Holdings: Bk Vols 8,000; Per Subs 25
Wireless access
Partic in Nubanusit Library Cooperative
Open Mon & Sat 10-1, Tues-Thurs 3-7
Friends of the Library Group

NEW BOSTON

P WHIPPLE FREE LIBRARY, 67 Mont Vernon Rd, 03070. (Mail add: PO Box 237, 03070-0237), SAN 309-9016. Tel: 603-487-3391. FAX: 603-487-2886. E-mail: whipplefreelibrary@gmail.com. Web Site: www.whipplefreelibrary.org. *Dir,* Sarah Chapman; E-mail: directorwfl@gmail.com; *Ch,* Barbara Ballou; E-mail: childrenswfl@yahoo.com; *Coordr, ILL, Libr Asst, Tech,* Ken Ballou; *Tech Serv,* Ronna LaPenn
Pop 5,100
Library Holdings: Bk Vols 19,500; Per Subs 72
Automation Activity & Vendor Info: (Acquisitions) Biblionix; (Cataloging) Biblionix; (Circulation) Biblionix; (OPAC) Biblionix
Wireless access
Open Mon, Wed & Fri 10-5, Thurs 2:30-6:30
Friends of the Library Group

NEW CASTLE

P NEW CASTLE PUBLIC LIBRARY, 301 Wentworth Rd, 03854. (Mail add: PO Box 329, 03854-0329), SAN 309-9024. Tel: 603-431-6773. E-mail: nwcstle.library@comcast.net. Web Site: newcastlenh.org/library. *Libr Dir,* Christine Collins
Pop 1,100; Circ 6,500
Library Holdings: Bk Vols 10,895; Per Subs 23
Special Collections: Genealogy Coll; International Mystery Coll; Local History, bks, prints
Automation Activity & Vendor Info: (Cataloging) Follett Software; (Circulation) Follett Software
Wireless access
Open Tues, Wed & Fri 12-5, Thurs 9-3, Sat 9-Noon

NEW DURHAM

P NEW DURHAM PUBLIC LIBRARY, Two Old Bay Rd, 03855-2214. SAN 309-9032. Tel: 603-859-2201. FAX: 603-859-0216. E-mail: newdurhamlibrary@gmail.com. Web Site: newdurhamlibrary.org. *Libr Dir,* Cathy Allyn
Founded 1894. Pop 2,600; Circ 7,800
Subject Interests: Local genealogy, Local hist
Automation Activity & Vendor Info: (Cataloging) Follett Software; (Circulation) Follett Software
Wireless access
Function: 24/7 Online cat, Adult bk club, Art exhibits, Audio & video playback equip for onsite use, Bk club(s), Bks on CD, Children's prog, Computers for patron use, Free DVD rentals, Holiday prog, ILL available, Internet access, Magazines, Museum passes, Music CDs, Online cat, Outreach serv, OverDrive digital audio bks, Photocopying/Printing, Preschool outreach, Prog for adults, Prog for children & young adult, Scanner, Spanish lang bks, Story hour, Summer reading prog, Wheelchair accessible
Partic in Rochester Area Librarians
Open Mon-Thurs 1-7, Fri 10-5, Sat 10-2
Friends of the Library Group

NEW HAMPTON

P GORDON-NASH LIBRARY, 69 Main St, 03256. SAN 309-9040. Tel: 603-677-3740. FAX: 603-677-3491. E-mail: library@newhampton.org. Web Site: gordonnashlibrary.org. *Dir,* Jerrica Blackey; *Children's Prog Coordr,* Christine Hunewell; Staff 4 (Non-MLS 4)
Founded 1895. Pop 2,135; Circ 25,517
Library Holdings: Audiobooks 122; CDs 1,355; DVDs 1,087; High Interest/Low Vocabulary Bk Vols 3,077; Large Print Bks 979; Bk Titles 31,613; Per Subs 61; Videos 1,716
Automation Activity & Vendor Info: (Acquisitions) Baker & Taylor; (Cataloging) Book Systems; (Circulation) Book Systems; (Course Reserve) Book Systems; (ILL) SirsiDynix; (OPAC) Book Systems
Wireless access
Partic in New Hampshire Automated Information Systems
Open Mon-Fri 9-6
Friends of the Library Group

NEW IPSWICH

P NEW IPSWICH LIBRARY*, Six Main St, 03071. (Mail add: PO Box 320, 03071-0320). Tel: 603-878-4644. E-mail: nilibrary@comcast.net. Web Site: newipswichlibrary.wordpress.com. *Interim Dir,* Michelle Pelletier; *Librn,* Ann-Marie Howard
Library Holdings: AV Mats 400; CDs 25; DVDs 125; Large Print Bks 40; Bk Vols 15,000; Per Subs 40; Videos 75
Automation Activity & Vendor Info: (Cataloging) New Generation Technologies Inc. (LiBRARYSOFT); (Circulation) New Generation Technologies Inc. (LiBRARYSOFT); (OPAC) New Generation Technologies Inc. (LiBRARYSOFT)

Wireless access
Open Mon & Wed 2-8, Tues, Fri & Sat 9-1

NEW LONDON

C COLBY-SAWYER COLLEGE, Susan Colgate Cleveland Library & Learning Center, 541 Main St, 03257-4648. SAN 309-9067. Tel: 603-526-3685. Reference Tel: 603-526-3687. E-mail: reference@colby-sawyer.edu. Web Site: library.colby-sawyer.edu. *Col Librn,* Malia Ebel; Tel: 603-526-3375, E-mail: malia.ebel@colby-sawyer.edu; *Col Archivist,* Brantley Palmer; Tel: 603-526-3360, E-mail: brantley.palmer@colby-sawyer.edu; *Res & Instruction Librn,* Beth Krajewski; Tel: 603-526-3799, E-mail: ekrajewski@colby-sawyer.edu; *Evening Circ Supvr, Syst Coordr,* Susan Azodi; E-mail: sazodi@colby-sawyer.edu; *Weekend Supvr,* Brooke Vigliotta; E-mail: brooke.vigliotta@colby-sawyer.edu; Staff 12 (MLS 4, Non-MLS 8)
Founded 1837. Enrl 1,000; Fac 100; Highest Degree: Bachelor
Library Holdings: AV Mats 3,000; Bk Vols 98,000; Per Subs 200
Automation Activity & Vendor Info: (Cataloging) Innovative Interfaces, Inc - Sierra; (Circulation) Innovative Interfaces, Inc - Sierra; (Course Reserve) Innovative Interfaces, Inc - Sierra; (Discovery) Innovative Interfaces, Inc - Sierra; (ILL) OCLC WorldShare Interlibrary Loan; (OPAC) Innovative Interfaces, Inc - Sierra
Wireless access
Function: Photocopying/Printing
Partic in New Hampshire College & University Council; Westchester Academic Library Directors Organization
Open Mon-Thurs 8am-Midnight, Fri 8-8, Sat & Sun 10-5
Friends of the Library Group

P TRACY MEMORIAL LIBRARY*, 304 Main St, 03257-7813. SAN 309-9075. Tel: 603-526-4656. FAX: 603-526-8035. E-mail: info@tracylibrary.org. Web Site: www.tracylibrary.org. *Dir,* Sandra Licks; E-mail: slicks@tracylibrary.org; *Asst Dir,* Jo-Ann Roy; E-mail: jroy@tracylibrary.org; *Head, Youth Serv,* Lorreen Keating; E-mail: lkeating@tracylibrary.org; Staff 8 (MLS 3, Non-MLS 5)
Pop 5,000; Circ 100,000
Library Holdings: AV Mats 4,331; Large Print Bks 1,275; Bk Titles 30,068; Per Subs 125
Automation Activity & Vendor Info: (Circulation) Follett Software; (OPAC) Follett Software
Wireless access
Function: Homebound delivery serv
Partic in New Hampshire Automated Information Systems
Open Tues & Thurs 9-8, Wed & Fri 9-5, Sat 9-1
Friends of the Library Group

NEWBURY

P NEWBURY PUBLIC LIBRARY, 933 Rte 103, 03255. (Mail add: PO Box 245, 03255-0245), SAN 309-9083. Tel: 603-763-5803. FAX: 603-763-5803. E-mail: newburypubliclibrary@yahoo.com. Web Site: www.newburynhlibrary.net. *Dir,* Lea McBain; E-mail: director@newburynhlibrary.net; *Asst Dir,* Laura Pezone; E-mail: assistantdirector@newburynhlibrary.org; Staff 3 (MLS 1, Non-MLS 2)
Founded 1893
Library Holdings: Bk Titles 13,100; Per Subs 55
Automation Activity & Vendor Info: (Cataloging) Follett Software; (Circulation) Follett Software; (OPAC) Follett Software
Wireless access
Open Mon 12-8, Tues-Thurs 9:30-5:30, Sat 10-2, Sun Noon-5
Friends of the Library Group

NEWFIELDS

P PAUL MEMORIAL LIBRARY*, 76 Main St, 03856-8312. SAN 309-9091. Tel: 603-778-8169. E-mail: newpl@comcast.net. Web Site: www.paulmemoriallibrary.org. *Dir,* Carl Heidenblad; Staff 4 (MLS 1, Non-MLS 3)
Founded 1893. Pop 1,670; Circ 6,000
Library Holdings: Bk Vols 11,500; Per Subs 16
Special Collections: Butterfly Coll
Subject Interests: Newfields hist
Automation Activity & Vendor Info: (Acquisitions) Baker & Taylor; (Cataloging) Biblionix/Apollo; (Circulation) Biblionix/Apollo; (OPAC) Biblionix/Apollo
Wireless access
Function: Summer reading prog
Open Mon & Fri 12-4, Tues & Thurs 10-5, Wed 10-7, Sat 9-1
Friends of the Library Group

NEWINGTON

P LANGDON LIBRARY, 328 Nimble Hill Rd, 03801. SAN 309-9105. Tel: 603-436-5154. FAX: 603-570-2024. E-mail: info@langdonlibrary.org. Web Site: www.langdonlibrary.org. *Dir,* Lara Croft Berry; E-mail: director@langdonlibrary.org
Founded 1892. Pop 900; Circ 13,110
Library Holdings: Bk Titles 17,000; Per Subs 36
Special Collections: Historical Records & Photographs Coll
Automation Activity & Vendor Info: (Cataloging) Follett Software; (Circulation) Follett Software; (Course Reserve) Follett Software
Wireless access
Publications: Newington Neighbor (Quarterly newsletter)
Open Mon & Tues 1-8, Thurs & Fri 9-5, Sat 10-2
Friends of the Library Group

NEWMARKET

P NEWMARKET PUBLIC LIBRARY*, One Elm St, 03857-1201. SAN 309-9113. Tel: 603-659-5311. FAX: 603-659-8849.
Subject Interests: Town hist
Wireless access
Friends of the Library Group

NEWPORT

P RICHARDS FREE LIBRARY, 58 N Main St, 03773. SAN 309-9121. Tel: 603-863-3430. E-mail: rfl@newport.lib.nh.us. Web Site: www.newport.lib.nh.us. *Libr Dir,* Justine Fafara; E-mail: jfafara@newport.lib.nh.us; *Asst Dir, ILL Librn,* Sally Bernier; E-mail: sbernier@newport.lib.nh.us; *Youth Librn,* Mo Churchill-Calkins; E-mail: mchurchill@newport.lib.nh.us; Staff 6 (MLS 2, Non-MLS 4)
Founded 1888. Pop 6,200
Library Holdings: CDs 100; DVDs 200; Large Print Bks 404; Bk Vols 36,102; Per Subs 60; Talking Bks 1,372; Videos 1,700
Special Collections: Kenneth Andler NH Hist Coll; Local Newspapers (Argus Champion 1878 to present), micro; Sarah Hosepha Hale Coll
Automation Activity & Vendor Info: (Cataloging) ByWater Solutions; (Circulation) ByWater Solutions; (OPAC) ByWater Solutions
Wireless access
Function: 24/7 Electronic res, 24/7 Online cat, Activity rm, Adult bk club, Adult literacy prog, Archival coll, Bk club(s), Homebound delivery serv, ILL available, Magnifiers for reading, Prog for adults, Prog for children & young adult, Spoken cassettes & CDs, Wheelchair accessible
Open Mon 1-6, Tues & Thurs 10-8, Wed & Fri 10-6, Sat 10-2
Friends of the Library Group

NEWTON

P GALE LIBRARY*, 16 S Main St, 03858. (Mail add: PO Box 329, 03858), SAN 309-913X. Tel: 603-382-4691. FAX: 603-382-2528. E-mail: galelibraryreads@comcast.net. Web Site: www.newton-nh.gov/gale-library. *Dir,* Theresa Caswell; *Asst Dir, Ch,* Sue Mears; *Asst Librn,* Nicole Belisle-Briggs; *Libr Asst III,* Elizabeth Standling; *Libr Asst I,* Lauri Gaudet; Staff 6 (Non-MLS 6)
Pop 4,000; Circ 24,000
Library Holdings: Bk Vols 26,000; Per Subs 50
Special Collections: New Hampshire Coll
Automation Activity & Vendor Info: (Cataloging) Follett Software; (Circulation) Follett Software; (OPAC) Follett Software
Wireless access
Open Mon & Wed 12-8, Tues & Sat 9-1, Fri 10-6
Friends of the Library Group

NORTH CONWAY

M MEMORIAL HOSPITAL*, Health Sciences Library, 3073 White Mountain Hwy, 03860. SAN 377-9513. Tel: 603-356-5461. Web Site: mainehealth.org/memorial-hospital. *Mgr,* Barbara Rosman; Tel: 603-356-5461, Ext 2157, E-mail: brosman@memorialhospitalnh.org
Library Holdings: Per Subs 25
Wireless access
Open Mon-Fri 7-7
Restriction: Non-circulating

S MOUNT WASHINGTON OBSERVATORY*, Gladys Brooks Memorial Library, 2779 White Mountain Hwy, Lower Level, 03860. (Mail add: PO Box 2310, 03860-2310), SAN 371-2370. Tel: 603-356-2137, Ext 203. FAX: 603-356-0307. Web Site: www.mountwashington.org/visit-us/gladys-brooks-memorial-library.aspx. *Curator,* Peter Crane; E-mail: pcrane@mountwashington.org
Library Holdings: Bk Vols 3,000; Per Subs 10
Subject Interests: Meteorology, Polar regions, White Mountains
Automation Activity & Vendor Info: (Acquisitions) Follett Software; (Cataloging) Follett Software; (Circulation) Follett Software

Partic in New Hampshire Automated Information Systems
Restriction: Open by appt only

P NORTH CONWAY PUBLIC LIBRARY*, 2719 White Mountain Hwy, 03860. (Mail add: PO Box 409, 03860-0409), SAN 376-5083. Tel: 603-356-2961. E-mail: info@northconwaylibrary.com. Web Site: www.northconwaylibrary.com. *Libr Dir,* Andrea Masters; Staff 3 (Non-MLS 3)
Founded 1887. Pop 2,000
Jan 2013-Dec 2013 Income $90,000, City $7,500, Locally Generated Income $30,000, Parent Institution $52,500. Mats Exp $8,000, Books $6,000, Per/Ser (Incl. Access Fees) $400, AV Mat $1,000
Library Holdings: CDs 400; DVDs 1,100; Large Print Bks 50; Per Subs 18
Automation Activity & Vendor Info: (OPAC) Biblionix/Apollo
Wireless access
Function: Adult bk club, Audiobks via web, Bks on CD, Computers for patron use, E-Readers, Magazines, Photocopying/Printing, Tax forms, VHS videos
Open Tues 10-5, Wed & Thurs 12-6, Fri 12-5, Sat 10-1

NORTH HAMPTON

P NORTH HAMPTON PUBLIC LIBRARY*, 237A Atlantic Ave, 03862-2341. SAN 309-9148. Tel: 603-964-6326. FAX: 603-964-1107. Web Site: www.nhplib.org. *Dir,* Susan Grant; E-mail: nhpldirector@gmail.com; *Asst Dir, Ch & Youth Librn,* Connie Margowsky; *Adult Serv, ILL,* Elizabeth Flot; *Tech Serv,* Barbara Dewing; Staff 3 (MLS 2, Non-MLS 1)
Founded 1892. Pop 4,300; Circ 42,756
Library Holdings: CDs 1,100; DVDs 2,600; Large Print Bks 268; Per Subs 60
Automation Activity & Vendor Info: (Cataloging) Book Systems; (Circulation) Book Systems; (OPAC) Book Systems
Function: 24/7 Electronic res, 24/7 Online cat, Adult bk club, Art exhibits, Audio & video playback equip for onsite use, Audiobks on Playaways & MP3, Audiobks via web, Bk club(s), Bks on CD, Children's prog, Computers for patron use, E-Readers, E-Reserves, Electronic databases & coll, Free DVD rentals, Genealogy discussion group, Homebound delivery serv, ILL available, Internet access, Magazines, Microfiche/film & reading machines, Movies, Museum passes, Notary serv, Online cat, Online ref, OverDrive digital audio bks, Prog for adults, Prog for children & young adult, Ref serv available, Scanner, Story hour, Study rm, Summer reading prog, Tax forms, Teen prog
Open Mon & Wed 10-8, Tues, Thurs & Fri 10-5, Sat 10-2
Friends of the Library Group

NORTH HAVERHILL

P PATTEN-NORTH HAVERHILL LIBRARY, 2885 Dartmouth College Hwy, 03774-4533. SAN 309-8389. Tel: 603-787-2542. E-mail: pattenlibrary@yahoo.com. Web Site: www.haverhill-nh.com. *Librn,* Debi English; *Asst Librn,* Audrey Clough
Pop 4,416; Circ 7,000
Library Holdings: Bk Vols 25,000; Per Subs 20; Talking Bks 35; Videos 75
Open Mon 10-6, Wed 2-6

NORTH STRATFORD

P STRATFORD PUBLIC LIBRARY*, 74 Main St, 03590. (Mail add: PO Box 313, 03590-0366). Tel: 603-922-9016. E-mail: library03590@gmail.com. Web Site: www.stratfordnhlibraries.com. *Librn,* Tom McCorkhill
Library Holdings: DVDs 50; Bk Titles 10,000; Talking Bks 20
Wireless access
Open Mon 9-2, Thurs & Fri 9-5

NORTH WOODSTOCK

P MOOSILAUKE PUBLIC LIBRARY*, 165 Lost River Rd, 03262. (Mail add: PO Box 21, 03262), SAN 309-9156. Tel: 603-745-9971. E-mail: moosilpl@roadrunner.com. Web Site: www.woodstocknh.org/library. *Dir,* Wendy L Pelletier; Staff 1 (Non-MLS 1)
Founded 1896. Pop 1,380; Circ 3,299
Library Holdings: Audiobooks 25; AV Mats 398; DVDs 50; Large Print Bks 51; Bk Vols 10,302; Per Subs 30; Talking Bks 76; Videos 450
Special Collections: White Mountains & Local History
Wireless access
Open Mon & Thurs 9-8, Fri & Sat 9-5

NORTHFIELD

P HALL MEMORIAL LIBRARY*, 18 Park St, 03276. SAN 309-9717. Tel: 603-286-8971. FAX: 603-286-2278. E-mail: hallmemo@metrocast.net, hallmemojuv@metrocast.net. Web Site: www.hallmemoriallibrary.org. *Dir,* Jenna Davis; Staff 3.8 (Non-MLS 3.8)
Founded 1886. Pop 8,350; Circ 65,000
Special Collections: 19th Century; Civil War Regiment Records; Northfield History, bks, illustrations, town rpts & tax lists
Automation Activity & Vendor Info: (Cataloging) Gateway; (Circulation) Gateway; (OPAC) Gateway; (Serials) Prenax, Inc
Wireless access
Partic in New Hampshire Automated Information Systems
Open Mon & Thurs 10-8, Tues, Wed & Fri 10-6, Sat 10-2

NORTHWOOD

P CHESLEY MEMORIAL LIBRARY*, Eight Mountain Ave, 03261. SAN 309-9172. Tel: 603-942-5472. FAX: 603-942-5132. *Libr Dir,* Donna Bunker; E-mail: chesleydirector@gmail.com; Staff 1 (Non-MLS 1)
Founded 1954. Pop 4,301
Library Holdings: Audiobooks 183; CDs 148; DVDs 753; Large Print Bks 158; Per Subs 20
Automation Activity & Vendor Info: (Cataloging) Book Systems; (Circulation) Book Systems; (ILL) Auto-Graphics, Inc; (OPAC) Book Systems
Wireless access
Partic in Suncook Interlibrary Cooperative
Open Mon-Thurs 10-7, Sat 10-1
Friends of the Library Group

NOTTINGHAM

P BLAISDELL MEMORIAL LIBRARY*, 129 Stage Rd, 03290. (Mail add: PO Box 115, 03290-0115), SAN 320-8451. Tel: 603-679-8484. FAX: 603-679-6774. E-mail: blaisdellml@comcast.net. Web Site: www.nottinghamlibrary.org. *Dir,* Elizabeth Bolton
Pop 4,500; Circ 25,000
Library Holdings: Bk Vols 19,000; Per Subs 10
Wireless access
Partic in Rochester Area Librarians
Open Tues & Fri 10-5, Wed & Thurs 10-8, Sat 9-2, Sun 1-5
Friends of the Library Group

ORFORD

P ORFORD FREE LIBRARY*, 2539 Rte 25A, 03777. (Mail add: PO Box 186, 03777-0186), SAN 309-9199. Tel: 603-353-9166. FAX: 603-353-9166. E-mail: orfordfreelibrary@mytopsmail.com. *Librn,* Laurel Fulford
Founded 1893. Pop 926; Circ 2,211
Library Holdings: Bk Vols 7,755
Special Collections: Clothing; Old Snapshots
Wireless access
Partic in New Hampshire Automated Information Systems
Open Tues & Fri 3:30-7:30, Sat 9-11:30, Sun 2-5
Friends of the Library Group

P ORFORD SOCIAL LIBRARY*, 573 NH Rte 10, 03777. (Mail add: PO Box 189, 03777-0189), SAN 309-9202. Tel: 603-353-9756. E-mail: orfordsoclib@gmail.com. Web Site: oslibrary.org. *Libr Dir,* Laina Warsavage
Founded 1792. Pop 926; Circ 2,300
Library Holdings: Audiobooks 160; CDs 125; DVDs 650; Large Print Bks 50; Bk Vols 10,000; Per Subs 25
Wireless access
Open Mon & Thurs 1-8, Wed & Sat 9-1
Friends of the Library Group

PELHAM

P PELHAM PUBLIC LIBRARY*, 24 Village Green, 03076. SAN 309-9229. Tel: 603-635-7581. FAX: 603-635-6952. Web Site: www.pelhampubliclibrary.org. *Libr Dir,* Jennifer Greene; E-mail: jgreene@pelhamweb.com; *Asst Dir,* Position Currently Open; *Head, YA,* Katy Kania; *Circ/ILL Librn,* Irja Finn; E-mail: ifinn@pelhamweb.com; *Head, Children's Servx,* Betsy Vecchi; E-mail: bvecchi@pelhamweb.com; Staff 5 (MLS 1, Non-MLS 4)
Founded 1892. Pop 12,440; Circ 83,824
Library Holdings: Audiobooks 520; DVDs 1,550; Large Print Bks 791; Bk Titles 27,925; Bk Vols 28,879; Per Subs 77
Automation Activity & Vendor Info: (Cataloging) Follett Software; (Circulation) Follett Software; (OPAC) Follett Software
Wireless access
Function: Art exhibits, Audiobks via web, Bks on CD, Children's prog, Computers for patron use, Doc delivery serv, Electronic databases & coll, ILL available, Museum passes, Online cat, OverDrive digital audio bks, Photocopying/Printing, Prog for adults, Prog for children & young adult, Ref serv available, Story hour, Summer reading prog, Tax forms, Teen prog, Telephone ref, Wheelchair accessible
Open Mon-Wed 10-8, Thurs 1-8, Fri 12-5, Sat 10-2

Restriction: Non-resident fee
Friends of the Library Group

PEMBROKE

P PEMBROKE TOWN LIBRARY, 313 Pembroke St, 03275. SAN 309-9237. Tel: 603-485-7851. FAX: 603-485-3351. E-mail: pembrokenhtownlibrary@gmail.com. Web Site: www.pembroke-nh.com/library. *Dir,* Tim Sheehan; *Asst Dir,* Heather Tiddes; Staff 3 (Non-MLS 3)
Pop 6,724; Circ 23,000
Library Holdings: Bk Vols 21,000; Per Subs 78
Automation Activity & Vendor Info: (Circulation) Follett Software
Wireless access
Function: ILL available, Photocopying/Printing, Prog for adults, Prog for children & young adult, Summer reading prog, Wheelchair accessible
Partic in Suncook Interlibrary Cooperative
Open Mon, Tues & Thurs 10-5, Wed 10-7, Fri 10-4, Sat (Sept-May) 10-2
Friends of the Library Group

PETERBOROUGH

S MARIPOSA MUSEUM LIBRARY, 26 Main St, 03458. Tel: 603-924-4555. FAX: 603-924-7893. E-mail: info@mariposamuseum.org. Web Site: mariposamuseum.org. *Dir,* Karla Hostetler; *Adminr,* Tina Thaing; E-mail: tina@mariposamuseum.org
Founded 2002
Library Holdings: Bk Vols 5,000
Restriction: Open by appt only, Open to pub for ref only

S MONADNOCK CENTER FOR HISTORY & CULTURE AT PETERBOROUGH HISTORICAL SOCIETY*, Morison Library & Archives, 19 Grove St, 03458. (Mail add: PO Box 58, 03458-0058), SAN 328-1442. Tel: 603-924-3235. FAX: 603-924-3200. E-mail: director@peterboroughhistory.org. Web Site: monadnockcenter.org/library-research. *Exec Dir,* Michelle M Stahl; E-mail: director@monadnockcenter.org; Staff 2 (Non-MLS 2)
Founded 1902
Library Holdings: Bk Vols 800
Special Collections: Mills Records Coll (1796-1920); Peterborough 1796-1873 (Dr Albert Smith Coll); letters; Peterborough Photograph Coll (1860-present)
Subject Interests: Genealogy, Local hist
Wireless access
Open Wed-Sat 10-4 by appointment only

M MONADNOCK COMMUNITY HOSPITAL*, Thomas Eckfeldt Memorial Medical Library, 452 Old Street Rd, 03458. SAN 323-6277. Tel: 603-924-7191. FAX: 603-924-9586. Web Site: www.monadnockcommunityhospital.org. *Librn,* Position Currently Open; Staff 1 (MLS 1)
Founded 1970
Library Holdings: Bk Titles 200; Per Subs 35

P PETERBOROUGH TOWN LIBRARY*, Two Concord St, 03458. SAN 309-9245. Tel: 603-924-8040. FAX: 603-924-8041. E-mail: library@peterboroughnh.gov. Web Site: peterboroughtownlibrary.org. *Dir,* Corinne Chronopoulos; E-mail: corinne@peterboroughnh.gov; *Asst Dir,* Mary Hubbard; E-mail: mhubbard@peterboroughnh.gov; *Head, Youth Serv,* Lisa Bearce; E-mail: lbearce@peterboroughnh.gov; *Tech Serv Librn,* Linda Tiernan Kepner; *ILL Coordr,* Ann Harrison; Staff 7 (MLS 4, Non-MLS 3)
Founded 1833. Pop 5,883; Circ 93,073
Library Holdings: Large Print Bks 738; Bk Vols 44,030; Per Subs 172
Special Collections: Town Histories (McGilvray Coll). State Document Depository
Subject Interests: Local hist, Original art photog, State hist, Town hist
Automation Activity & Vendor Info: (Cataloging) EOS International; (Circulation) EOS International; (OPAC) EOS International
Wireless access
Publications: History of the First Free Tax-Supported Library in the World-Peterborough
Partic in OCLC Online Computer Library Center, Inc
Open Mon, Wed & Fri 10-6, Tues & Thurs 10-8, Sat 10-4
Friends of the Library Group

PIERMONT

P PIERMONT PUBLIC LIBRARY*, 130 Rte 10, 03779. (Mail add: PO Box 6, 03779-0006), SAN 309-9253. Tel: 603-272-4967. FAX: 603-272-4947. E-mail: librarian@piermontlibrary.com. Web Site: piermontlibrary.blogspot.com. *Librn,* Margaret Ladd; *Asst Librn,* Jim Meddaugh
Pop 709; Circ 12,016
Library Holdings: AV Mats 928; Bk Vols 14,039; Per Subs 16
Wireless access
Open Mon-Thurs 3-7, Sun 1-3

PITTSBURG

P BREMER POND MEMORIAL LIBRARY*, 12 School St, 03592. (Mail add: PO Box 98, 03592-0098), SAN 309-9261. Tel: 603-538-7032. *Librn,* Bill Stebbins
Pop 1,000; Circ 1,300
Library Holdings: Bk Vols 20,000; Per Subs 15
Wireless access

PITTSFIELD

P JOSIAH CARPENTER LIBRARY*, 41 Main St, 03263. SAN 309-927X. Tel: 603-435-8406. Web Site: www.pittsfieldnh.gov/josiah-carpenter-library. *Libr Dir,* Leslie Vogt; E-mail: lesliegvogt@gmail.com; *Asst Librn,* Shayla Locke; *Ch,* Heather Dunagin
Founded 1901. Pop 4,200
Subject Interests: Town hist
Automation Activity & Vendor Info: (Acquisitions) Baker & Taylor; (Cataloging) Book Systems; (Circulation) Book Systems; (OPAC) Book Systems
Wireless access
Function: 24/7 Electronic res, 24/7 Online cat, Adult bk club, After school storytime, Archival coll, Audiobks via web, Digital talking bks, Free DVD rentals, Home delivery & serv to seniorr ctr & nursing homes, Internet access, Preschool outreach, Story hour, Summer reading prog
Partic in Suncook Interlibrary Cooperative
Open Mon 2:30-5, Tues & Thurs 10-6, Wed 2:30-6:30, Fri & Sat 10-1
Restriction: Authorized patrons
Friends of the Library Group

PLAISTOW

P PLAISTOW PUBLIC LIBRARY*, 85 Main St, 03865. SAN 309-9296. Tel: 603-382-6011. FAX: 603-382-0202. E-mail: info@plaistowlibrary.com. Web Site: plaistowlibrary.com. *Dir,* Cab Vinton; E-mail: director@plaistowlibrary.com; *Head, Circ/ILL,* Kelli Lennon; E-mail: ill@plaistowlibrary.com; *Head, Youth Serv,* Jennifer Dawley; E-mail: youth@plaistowlibrary.com; *Tech Serv Librn,* Raven Gregg; E-mail: techservices@plaistowlibrary.com; Staff 9 (MLS 1, Non-MLS 8)
Founded 1897. Pop 7,800
Library Holdings: Audiobooks 1,253; CDs 252; Large Print Bks 424; Bk Titles 42,659; Per Subs 71; Videos 1,400
Automation Activity & Vendor Info: (Cataloging) Koha; (Circulation) Koha; (OPAC) Koha; (Serials) Koha
Wireless access
Open Mon-Thurs 9-7:30, Fri 9-5, Sat 9-1
Friends of the Library Group

PLYMOUTH

P PEASE PUBLIC LIBRARY*, One Russell St, 03264-1414. SAN 309-930X. Tel: 603-536-2616. FAX: 603-536-2369. Web Site: www.peasepubliclibrary.org. *Dir,* Diane Lynch; *Asst Dir, Youth Serv,* Tanya Ricker; *Cat Librn,* Allison Reilly; *ILL Librn,* Michelle Langer; Staff 6 (MLS 1, Non-MLS 5)
Founded 1874. Pop 5,800; Circ 73,000
Library Holdings: Bk Vols 25,963; Per Subs 88; Talking Bks 932
Special Collections: History-Genealogy (Eva A Speare Coll)
Subject Interests: Children's lit
Automation Activity & Vendor Info: (Cataloging) Follett Software; (Circulation) Follett Software
Wireless access
Function: Adult literacy prog, Homebound delivery serv, ILL available, Photocopying/Printing, Prog for children & young adult, Ref serv available, Summer reading prog, Telephone ref, Wheelchair accessible
Partic in Statewide Libr Network
Open Mon, Tues & Wed 10-8, Thurs & Fri 10-5, Sat 10-2
Friends of the Library Group

C PLYMOUTH STATE UNIVERSITY, Herbert H Lamson Library, 17 High St, 03264. SAN 309-9318. Tel: 603-535-2832. Web Site: library.plymouth.edu. *Library Discipline Coord,* Ann Jung-Mathews; Tel: 603-535-2833, E-mail: amjung@plymouth.edu; Staff 9 (MLS 5, Non-MLS 4)
Founded 1871. Enrl 4,004; Highest Degree: Doctorate
Library Holdings: Bk Vols 306,036; Per Subs 1,930
Special Collections: Brown Company Coll; McGoldrick Coll; Robert Frost Coll. State Document Depository
Automation Activity & Vendor Info: (Acquisitions) OCLC Worldshare Management Services; (Cataloging) OCLC Worldshare Management Services; (Circulation) OCLC Worldshare Management Services; (Course Reserve) OCLC Worldshare Management Services; (ILL) OCLC Tipasa;

(OPAC) OCLC Worldshare Management Services; (Serials) OCLC Worldshare Management Services
Wireless access
Function: Art exhibits, Doc delivery serv, Electronic databases & coll, ILL available, Photocopying/Printing
Partic in NHCUC; OCLC Online Computer Library Center, Inc
Open Mon-Thurs 7:30am-10pm, Fri 7:45-5, Sat 10-5, Sun Noon-10pm; Mon-Fri 8-5, Sat & Sun 1-5 (Summer)

PORTSMOUTH

J GREAT BAY COMMUNITY COLLEGE LIBRARY*, 320 Corporate Dr, 03801. SAN 309-9326. Tel: 603-427-7618. Reference E-mail: reference@ccsnh.edu. Web Site: www.greatbay.edu/library. *Libr Dir,* Rebecca Clerkin; E-mail: rclerkin@ccsnh.edu; Staff 2 (MLS 1, Non-MLS 1)
Founded 1970. Enrl 1,300; Fac 35
Library Holdings: Bk Vols 10,400; Per Subs 128
Automation Activity & Vendor Info: (Cataloging) TLC (The Library Corporation); (Circulation) TLC (The Library Corporation); (OPAC) TLC (The Library Corporation)
Wireless access

S PORTSMOUTH ATHENAEUM*, Research Library & Randall Library, Six-Nine Market Sq, 03801. SAN 320-2038. Tel: 603-431-2538. E-mail: info@portsmouthathenaeum.org. Web Site: portsmouthathenaeum.org. *Dir,* Thomas Hardiman; E-mail: thardiman@portsmouthathenaeum.org; *Librn,* Robin Silva; *Research Librn,* Carolyn Marvin; Staff 4 (MLS 2, Non-MLS 2)
Founded 1817
Library Holdings: Bk Titles 50,000; Per Subs 5
Special Collections: Isles of Shoals Coll; Langdon Papers Coll; Manuscripts; NH Gazette Coll; NNH Fire & Marine Insurance Company Papers, docs; Papers (church, institutional, business & family); Wendell Family Papers, photog; Wentworth-by-the Sea Hotel Coll
Subject Interests: Genealogy, Maine, Marine, Naval, New England, NH hist, Ships
Wireless access
Open Tues-Sat 1-4

P PORTSMOUTH PUBLIC LIBRARY*, 175 Parrott Ave, 03801-4452. Tel: 603-427-1540. Reference Tel: 603-766-1720. FAX: 603-433-0981. Web Site: www.cityofportsmouth.com/library. *Dir,* Steve Butzel; E-mail: skbutzel@cityofportsmouth.com; *Asst Dir,* Christine Friese; E-mail: ccfriese@cityofportsmouth.com; *Commun Relations Librn, Pub Programming Librn,* Laura Horwood-Benton; E-mail: lkhorwood-benton@cityofportsmouth.com; *Youth Serv Librn,* Gretul Macalaster; Tel: 603-766-1742, E-mail: gmmacalaster@cityofportsmouth.com; *Ref Serv Supvr,* Nicole Luongo Cloutier; E-mail: nlcoutier@cityofportsmouth.com; *Tech Serv Supvr,* Sarah Cornell; E-mail: sbcornell@cityofportsouth.com; Staff 25 (MLS 9, Non-MLS 16)
Founded 1881. Pop 21,800; Circ 488,630
Library Holdings: AV Mats 17,181; Electronic Media & Resources 58; Bk Vols 127,818; Per Subs 422
Special Collections: Municipal Document Depository; State Document Depository
Subject Interests: Local hist
Automation Activity & Vendor Info: (Acquisitions) Innovative Interfaces, Inc; (Cataloging) Innovative Interfaces, Inc; (Circulation) Innovative Interfaces, Inc; (OPAC) Innovative Interfaces, Inc; (Serials) Innovative Interfaces, Inc
Wireless access
Partic in LYRASIS; New Hampshire Automated Information Systems; New Hampshire Urban Pub Libr Consortium
Special Services for the Blind - ZoomText magnification & reading software
Open Mon-Thurs 9-9, Fri 9-5:30, Sat 9-5, Sun (Sept-May) 1-5
Friends of the Library Group

M PORTSMOUTH REGIONAL HOSPITAL*, Health Science Library, 333 Borthwick Ave, 03801. SAN 377-9394. Tel: 603-433-4094. FAX: 603-433-5144. *Librn,* Elanor Pickens; Staff 1 (MLS 1)
Founded 1987
Library Holdings: Bk Titles 80; Per Subs 140
Partic in Basic Health Sciences Library Network; CinaHL; Health Sciences Libraries of New Hampshire & Vermont; North Atlantic Health Sciences Libraries, Inc
Open Mon-Fri 8-4:30

S STRAWBERY BANKE MUSEUM*, Thayer Cumings Library & Archives, 14 Hancock St, 03801. (Mail add: PO Box 300, 03802-0300), SAN 309-9342. Tel: 603-422-7524. FAX: 603-422-7527, 603-433-1115. Web Site: www.strawberybanke.org. *Chief Curator,* Elizabeth Farish; Tel: 603-422-7526, E-mail: efarish@sbmuseum.org; Staff 1 (Non-MLS 1)
Founded 1970
Library Holdings: Bk Titles 7,000; Bk Vols 8,000; Per Subs 20
Special Collections: Manuscript Coll; Papers of Ichabod & Sarah Parker Rice Goodwin, Governor John Langdon & the Chase Family; Portsmouth Photo Coll, 1870-1970
Subject Interests: Archaeology, Archit, Art hist, Decorative art, Hort, Local hist, Presv
Publications: A Guide to the Cumings Library & Archives; Official Strawbery Banke Guide Book
Restriction: Open by appt only

S JAMES E WHALLEY MUSEUM & LIBRARY*, 351 Middle St, 03801. SAN 328-0217. Tel: 603-436-3712. Web Site: www.portsmouthfreemasons.org/james-e-whalley-masonic-library-and-museum. *Historian,* Alan M Robinson; E-mail: robinsonam@comcast.net
Founded 1962
Library Holdings: Bk Titles 3,500; Bk Vols 3,600; Per Subs 12
Restriction: Mem only

RANDOLPH

P RANDOLPH PUBLIC LIBRARY*, 130 Durand Rd, 03593. Tel: 603-466-5408. E-mail: randolphnhlibrary@gmail.com. *Dir,* Yvonne Jenkins
Library Holdings: Bk Vols 6,500; Talking Bks 100; Videos 92
Wireless access
Open Mon & Sat 10-Noon, Wed & Thurs 3-8
Friends of the Library Group

RAYMOND

P DUDLEY-TUCKER LIBRARY*, Six Epping St, 03077. (Mail add: PO Box 909, 03077-0909), SAN 309-9350. Tel: 603-895-7057. FAX: 603-895-7059. E-mail: dudleytucker@comcast.net. Web Site: www.raymondnh.gov/dudley-tucker-library. *Dir,* Kirsten Rundquist Corbett; E-mail: dudleytucker@comcast.net; *Asst Dir,* Pat Currier; *Ch,* Cathy Fancher; *Ch,* Betty Wynne; Tel: 603-895-7058; Staff 2 (MLS 1, Non-MLS 1)
Founded 1894. Pop 10,000; Circ 52,000
Library Holdings: Bk Vols 26,500; Per Subs 100
Automation Activity & Vendor Info: (Acquisitions) Biblionix/Apollo; (Cataloging) Biblionix/Apollo; (Circulation) Biblionix/Apollo; (ILL) Biblionix/Apollo; (OPAC) Biblionix/Apollo; (Serials) Biblionix/Apollo
Wireless access
Function: 24/7 Electronic res, 24/7 Online cat, Audiobks on Playaways & MP3, Bks on CD, Children's prog, E-Readers, Free DVD rentals, ILL available, Internet access, Magazines, Museum passes, OverDrive digital audio bks, Prog for adults, Prog for children & young adult, Scanner, Tax forms, Wheelchair accessible
Partic in Merri-Hill-Rock Library Cooperative
Open Mon & Thurs 12-8, Tues 10-8, Wed & Fri 10-5, Sat (Sept-May) 10-1
Friends of the Library Group

RICHMOND

P RICHMOND PUBLIC LIBRARY, 19 Winchester Rd, 03470. SAN 309-9369. Tel: 603-239-6164. E-mail: library@richmondnh.us. Web Site: www.richmond.nh.gov. *Librn,* Wendy O'Brien; *Asst Librn,* Patricia Newton
Pop 1,146; Circ 4,340
Library Holdings: Bk Vols 15,000; Per Subs 22
Automation Activity & Vendor Info: (Cataloging) Follett Software; (Circulation) Follett Software
Wireless access
Partic in Nubanusit Library Cooperative
Open Tues & Thurs 3-7, Wed 9-Noon, Sat 10-2
Friends of the Library Group

RINDGE

C FRANKLIN PIERCE UNIVERSITY LIBRARY*, Frank S DiPietro Library, 40 University Dr, 03461-3114. SAN 309-9377. Tel: 603-899-4140. Reference Tel: 603-899-1149. FAX: 603-899-4375. E-mail: library@franklinpierce.edu. Web Site: library.franklinpierce.edu. *Univ Librn,* Paul Jenkins; Tel: 603-899-4142, E-mail: jenkinsp@franklinpierce.edu; *Electronic Res Librn,* Leslie Inglis; E-mail: inglisl@franklinpierce.edu; *Ref & Instruction Librn,* Eric Shannon; E-mail: shannone@franklinpierce.edu; *Tech Serv Librn,* Melissa Stearns; E-mail: stearnsm@franklinpierce.edu; *Circ Mgr,* Jill Wixom; Staff 8 (MLS 5, Non-MLS 3)
Founded 1962. Enrl 2,347; Fac 78; Highest Degree: Doctorate
Library Holdings: Bk Titles 130,000
Subject Interests: Ecology, Graphic arts, Mass communications
Automation Activity & Vendor Info: (Acquisitions) Ex Libris Group; (Cataloging) Ex Libris Group; (Circulation) Ex Libris Group; (Course

Reserve) Ex Libris Group; (Media Booking) Ex Libris Group; (OPAC) Ex Libris Group; (Serials) Ex Libris Group
Partic in New Hampshire College & University Council
Open Mon-Wed 7:45am-Midnight, Thurs 7:45 am-11pm, Fri 7:45am-8pm, Sat 10-6, Sun Noon-Midnight
Friends of the Library Group

P INGALLS MEMORIAL LIBRARY*, 203 Main St, 03461. (Mail add: PO Box 224, 03461-0224), SAN 309-9385. Tel: 603-899-3303. FAX: 603-899-5797. E-mail: info@ingallslibrary.com. Web Site: www.rindgenh.org/towncloud/entity/Ingalls-Memorial-Library-6. *Dir,* Donna Straitiff; E-mail: donna@ingallslibrary.com; *Asst Dir, ILL Librn,* Debbie Qualey; E-mail: debbie@ingallslibrary.com; *Asst Dir,* Sheila Vanderhorst; *Ch,* Georgianna Connor; E-mail: georgi@ingallslibrary.com; *Libr Asst,* Mary McQuaid; E-mail: marybeth@ingallslibrary.com
Founded 1894. Pop 6,130; Circ 26,485
Library Holdings: Bk Vols 29,764; Per Subs 70
Subject Interests: Humanities, NH
Automation Activity & Vendor Info: (Cataloging) ByWater Solutions; (Circulation) ByWater Solutions; (OPAC) ByWater Solutions; (Serials) ByWater Solutions
Wireless access
Function: 24/7 Electronic res, 24/7 Online cat, 3D Printer, Adult bk club, After school storytime, Audiobks on Playaways & MP3, Bks on CD, Children's prog, Computers for patron use, E-Reserves, Electronic databases & coll, Free DVD rentals, Genealogy discussion group, ILL available, Internet access, Magazines, Museum passes, Music CDs, Online cat, Photocopying/Printing, Scanner, Summer reading prog, Tax forms, Wheelchair accessible
Partic in Nubanusit Library Cooperative
Open Mon, Wed & Fri 10-5, Tues & Thurs 2:30-8, Sat 9-Noon
Friends of the Library Group

ROCHESTER

M FRISBIE MEMORIAL HOSPITAL*, Medical Library, 11 Whitehall Rd, 03867. SAN 377-953X. Tel: 603-335-8419. FAX: 603-330-8946. Web Site: www.frisbiehospital.com. *Coordr, Med Staff Spec,* Kate Connor
Library Holdings: Bk Titles 200; Per Subs 50
Wireless access
Partic in Health Sciences Libraries of New Hampshire & Vermont; Medical Library Association
Restriction: Staff use only

P ROCHESTER PUBLIC LIBRARY*, 65 S Main St, 03867-2707. SAN 309-9407. Tel: 603-332-1428. Reference Tel: 603-335-7550. FAX: 603-335-7582. E-mail: RPLReference@rochesternh.net. Web Site: www.rpl.lib.nh.us. *Libr Dir,* Brian Sylvester; E-mail: brian.sylvester@rpl.lib.nh.us; *Ch Serv,* Marie Kelly; *Circ Serv,* Peggy Trout; *Ref Serv,* Elizabeth Nerbonne; *Tech Serv,* Dorinda Howard; *YA Serv,* Donna Hynes; Staff 7 (MLS 3, Non-MLS 4)
Founded 1893. Pop 29,752; Circ 276,781
Special Collections: Rochester Courier
Automation Activity & Vendor Info: (Acquisitions) Innovative Interfaces, Inc; (Cataloging) OCLC Online; (Circulation) Innovative Interfaces, Inc; (ILL) OCLC Online; (OPAC) Innovative Interfaces, Inc; (Serials) Innovative Interfaces, Inc
Wireless access
Partic in Rochester Area Librarians; Urban Pub Libr Consortium
Open Mon-Thurs 9-8:30, Fri 9-5, Sat (Winter) 9-4
Friends of the Library Group

ROLLINSFORD

P ROLLINSFORD PUBLIC LIBRARY*, Three Front St, Ste 2B, 03869. (Mail add: PO Box 70, 03869). Tel: 603-516-2665. E-mail: rollinsfordlibrary@comcast.net. Web Site: www.rollinsfordlibrary.org. *Dir,* Sarah Doucette-McLauchlin
Library Holdings: CDs 200; DVDs 150; Bk Vols 10,000; Per Subs 28; Talking Bks 150
Automation Activity & Vendor Info: (Cataloging) LibraryWorld, Inc; (Circulation) LibraryWorld, Inc; (OPAC) LibraryWorld, Inc
Wireless access
Open Mon-Wed 9-7, Thurs 9-5, Sun 1-5
Friends of the Library Group

RUMNEY

P BYRON G MERRILL LIBRARY*, Ten Buffalo Rd, 03266. SAN 309-9415. Tel: 603-786-9520. E-mail: rumneylibrary@roadrunner.com. Web Site: rumneynh.org/Library. *Dir,* Susan Turbyne; *Librn,* Rachel Anderson; Staff 2 (Non-MLS 2)
Founded 1906. Pop 1,466; Circ 9,416
Library Holdings: DVDs 458; Bk Vols 20,000; Per Subs 15
Wireless access
Open Wed & Thurs 1-5, Sat 10-1

RYE

P RYE PUBLIC LIBRARY, 581 Washington Rd, 03870. SAN 309-9423. Tel: 603-964-8401. E-mail: contact@ryepubliclibrary.org. Web Site: www.ryepubliclibrary.org. *Dir,* Andrew Richmond; E-mail: arichmond@ryepubliclibrary.org; *Asst Dir, Coll Mgr, ILL Mgr,* Lisa Houde; *Head, Youth Serv,* Jessica Ryan; *Ad,* Juliette Doherty; *Ad,* Shawna Healy; *Ad,* Gwen Putnam-Bailey; *Asst Librn, Youth Serv,* Brenda Nolette; Staff 9 (MLS 1, Non-MLS 8)
Founded 1911. Pop 5,182; Circ 80,000
Library Holdings: Bk Titles 43,000; Bk Vols 48,000; Per Subs 125
Subject Interests: Rye hist
Automation Activity & Vendor Info: (Cataloging) TLC (The Library Corporation); (Circulation) TLC (The Library Corporation); (OPAC) TLC (The Library Corporation)
Wireless access
Publications: Off the Shelf (Newsletter)
Special Services for the Blind - Bks on cassette
Open Mon & Fri 9-4, Tues-Thurs 9-7, Sat 9-2
Friends of the Library Group

SALEM

P KELLEY LIBRARY*, 234 Main St, 03079-3190. SAN 309-944X. Tel: 603-898-7064. FAX: 603-898-8583. E-mail: info@kelleylibrary.org. Web Site: www.kelleylibrary.org. *Dir,* Alison Baker; E-mail: abaker@kelleylibrary.org; *Asst Dir,* Natalie Ducharme; E-mail: nducharme@kelleylibrary.org; *Head, Adult Serv,* Karen Brown; E-mail: kbrown@kelleylibrary.org; *Head, Ref,* Paul Giblin; E-mail: pgiblin@kelleylibrary.org; *Youth Serv,* Laura Stevens; E-mail: lstevens@kelleylibrary.org; Staff 22 (MLS 5, Non-MLS 17)
Founded 1893. Pop 29,115; Circ 290,786
Library Holdings: AV Mats 14,519; Large Print Bks 1,489; Bk Titles 116,949; Per Subs 312
Special Collections: Municipal Document Depository; Oral History; State Document Depository
Automation Activity & Vendor Info: (Acquisitions) Innovative Interfaces, Inc; (Cataloging) Innovative Interfaces, Inc; (Circulation) Innovative Interfaces, Inc; (ILL) Innovative Interfaces, Inc; (OPAC) Innovative Interfaces, Inc; (Serials) Innovative Interfaces, Inc
Wireless access
Partic in GMILCS, Inc
Special Services for the Blind - Bks on cassette; Bks on CD; Home delivery serv; Large print bks
Open Mon-Fri 9-8:30, Sat 9-2

SALISBURY

P SALISBURY FREE LIBRARY*, 641 Old Turnpike Rd, 03268. (Mail add: PO Box 284, 03268-0284), SAN 309-9458. Tel: 603-648-2278. E-mail: salisburyfree@gmail.com. Web Site: salisburyfreelibrary.wordpress.com. *Libr Dir,* Katherine Bollenbach; Staff 1 (Non-MLS 1)
Pop 1,200; Circ 5,200
Library Holdings: AV Mats 900; Large Print Bks 65; Bk Titles 7,200
Wireless access
Function: ILL available, Photocopying/Printing, Prog for children & young adult, Ref serv available, Summer reading prog, Telephone ref, Wheelchair accessible
Special Services for the Blind - Magnifiers
Open Tues Mon & Sat 10-3, Tues & Thurs 1-7
Friends of the Library Group

SANBORNTON

P SANBORNTON PUBLIC LIBRARY*, 27 Meetinghouse Hill Rd, 03269. (Mail add: PO Box 88, 03269-0088), SAN 309-9466. Tel: 603-286-8288. FAX: 603-286-9544. E-mail: SPL@metrocast.net. Web Site: www.splnh.com. *Dir,* Marcia Haigh; E-mail: spl3@metrocast.net; *Tech Serv Librn,* Martha Bodwell; E-mail: spl2@metrocast.net; Staff 2.4 (MLS 1, Non-MLS 1.4)
Founded 1903. Pop 3,000; Circ 16,500
Library Holdings: Bks on Deafness & Sign Lang 10; Bk Vols 16,000; Per Subs 30
Subject Interests: NH
Function: Adult bk club, Archival coll, Art exhibits, Audiobks via web, AV serv, Bk club(s), Bks on cassette, Bks on CD, Children's prog, Computer training, Computers for patron use, Free DVD rentals, Genealogy discussion group, Homebound delivery serv, ILL available, Internet access, Museum passes, Music CDs, Online cat, Online ref, OverDrive digital audio bks, Photocopying/Printing, Prog for adults, Prog for children & young adult, Ref & res, Ref serv available, Scanner, Spoken

cassettes & CDs, Spoken cassettes & DVDs, Story hour, Summer reading prog, Telephone ref, VHS videos, Visual arts prog, Wheelchair accessible
Open Tues & Fri 9-5, Wed & Thurs 1-8, Sat 9-2

SANBORNVILLE

P GAFNEY LIBRARY, INC, 14 High St, 03872. (Mail add: PO Box 517, 03872-0517), SAN 309-975X. Tel: 603-522-3401. FAX: 603-522-7123. E-mail: gafney@gafneylibrary.org. Web Site: www.gafneylibrary.org. *Libr Dir,* Beryl Donovan; E-mail: beryl.donovan@gafneylibrary.org; Staff 4 (Non-MLS 4)
Founded 1925. Pop 7,000; Circ 15,520
Library Holdings: Bks on Deafness & Sign Lang 12; CDs 104; DVDs 507; High Interest/Low Vocabulary Bk Vols 35; Bk Titles 12,002; Per Subs 12; Talking Bks 364; Videos 414
Automation Activity & Vendor Info: (Circulation) Biblionix/Apollo
Wireless access
Function: 24/7 Electronic res, 24/7 Online cat, Adult literacy prog, Art exhibits, Chess club, Children's prog, Computers for patron use, Electronic databases & coll, Free DVD rentals, ILL available, Museum passes, Music CDs, Notary serv, OverDrive digital audio bks, Photocopying/Printing, Story hour, Summer reading prog, Tax forms
Partic in Rochester Area Librarians
Open Tues-Thurs 1-7, Fri & Sat 9-12:30
Restriction: Circ to mem only
Friends of the Library Group

SANDOWN

P SANDOWN PUBLIC LIBRARY*, 305 Main St, 03873. (Mail add: PO Box 580, 03873-0580), SAN 309-9474. Tel: 603-887-3428. FAX: 603-887-0590. E-mail: library@sandownlibrary.us. Web Site: www.sandownlibrary.us. *Libr Dir,* Deb Hoadley; E-mail: director@sandownlibrary.us; *Asst Dir, Cataloger,* Cathy Hassard; E-mail: chassard@sandownlibrary.us; *Youth Serv Dir,* Jennifer Bryant; E-mail: jbryant@sandownlibrary.us; *Libr Tech,* Julie Ball; E-mail: jball@sandownlibrary.us; *ILL, Libr Tech,* Susan Kehoe; E-mail: skehoe@sandownlibrary.us; Staff 10 (MLS 2, Non-MLS 8)
Founded 1892. Pop 6,000; Circ 65,000
Library Holdings: AV Mats 1,000; Bks on Deafness & Sign Lang 65; DVDs 750; Large Print Bks 200; Bk Titles 29,352; Bk Vols 36,000; Per Subs 67; Talking Bks 850; Videos 1,195
Special Collections: Cake Pans
Automation Activity & Vendor Info: (Circulation) Follett Software; (OPAC) Follett Software; (Serials) Follett Software
Wireless access
Function: Adult bk club, After school storytime, Audiobks via web, Bks on CD, CD-ROM, Chess club, Children's prog, Computer training, Computers for patron use, E-Reserves, Electronic databases & coll, Equip loans & repairs, ILL available, Museum passes, Music CDs, Online cat, OverDrive digital audio bks, Photocopying/Printing, Prog for adults, Prog for children & young adult, Summer reading prog, Tax forms, VHS videos, Wheelchair accessible
Partic in Merri-Hill-Rock Library Cooperative
Open Mon-Thurs 9-8, Sat 9-3
Friends of the Library Group

SEABROOK

P SEABROOK LIBRARY*, 25 Liberty Lane, 03874-4506. SAN 309-9490. Tel: 603-474-2044. FAX: 603-474-1835. E-mail: ocean@sealib.org. Web Site: www.sealib.org. *Dir,* Susan Schatvet; E-mail: sschatvet@sealib.org; *Youth Serv Librn,* Jenn Hartshorn; *Tech Serv,* Sharon Rafferty; *Circ Asst,* Diane Cira; E-mail: dcira@sealib.org; Staff 10 (MLS 5, Non-MLS 5)
Pop 7,000
Library Holdings: Bk Vols 47,000
Wireless access
Open Mon-Fri 9-5
Friends of the Library Group

SHELBURNE

P SHELBURNE PUBLIC LIBRARY*, 74 Village Rd, 03581-3209. SAN 309-9504. Tel: 603-466-2262. *Library Contact,* Bob Pinkham
Pop 385; Circ 562
Library Holdings: AV Mats 129; Bk Vols 3,505; Per Subs 10
Special Collections: Local History Coll
Wireless access
Open Mon 3-5, Thurs 2-4

SOMERSWORTH

P SOMERSWORTH PUBLIC LIBRARY, 25 Main St, 03878-3198. SAN 309-9512. Tel: 603-692-4587. E-mail: library@somersworth.com. Web Site: www.somersworth.com/somersworth-public-library. *Libr Dir,* Rebecca Whitney; *Asst Libr,* Michelle Baker; E-mail: libraryassistant@somersworth.com; Staff 2 (MLS 2)
Founded 1899. Pop 11,788
Library Holdings: Bk Titles 45,000; Per Subs 65
Special Collections: Somersworth Historical Coll
Automation Activity & Vendor Info: (Circulation) ByWater Solutions; (OPAC) ByWater Solutions
Wireless access
Function: 24/7 Electronic res, 24/7 Online cat, Adult bk club, Art exhibits, Audiobks via web, Bk club(s), Bks on CD, Children's prog, Computer training, Computers for patron use, Electronic databases & coll, Free DVD rentals, Holiday prog, Homebound delivery serv, ILL available, Instruction & testing, Internet access, Magazines, Mail & tel request accepted, Microfiche/film & reading machines, Movies, Museum passes, Online cat, OverDrive digital audio bks, Photocopying/Printing, Preschool reading prog, Printer for laptops & handheld devices, Prog for adults, Prog for children & young adult, Ref & res, Ref serv available, Story hour, Summer reading prog, Tax forms, Telephone ref
Partic in Rochester Area Librarians
Open Tues & Wed 11-7, Thurs-Sat 9-5 (Winter); Tues & Wed 11-7, Thurs & Fri 9-5, Sat 9-1 (Summer)
Restriction: Non-resident fee

SOUTH HAMPTON

P SOUTH HAMPTON PUBLIC LIBRARY, 3-1 Hilldale Ave, 03827. SAN 309-9520. Tel: 603-394-7319. FAX: 603-394-7319. E-mail: southhamptonlibrary@comcast.net. Web Site: www.southhamptonnh.org/12501. *Dir,* Lori Laverty
Pop 844; Circ 7,440
Library Holdings: AV Mats 145; Bk Vols 7,333; Per Subs 25; Videos 21
Special Collections: Al Capp Coll; Memorial Coll; New Hampshire History
Automation Activity & Vendor Info: (Circulation) Follett Software
Wireless access
Open Mon 6pm-8pm, Wed & Thurs 10-5, Fri 12-4
Friends of the Library Group

SPRINGFIELD

P LIBBIE A CASS MEMORIAL LIBRARY*, 2748 Main St, 03284. (Mail add: PO Box 89, 03284-0089), SAN 309-9539. Tel: 603-763-4381. FAX: 603-763-4381. E-mail: libbiecass@gmail.com. Web Site: libbiecass.weebly.com. *Dir,* Laura Pauling
Founded 1893. Pop 970; Circ 4,300
Library Holdings: DVDs 150; Large Print Bks 120; Bk Vols 17,000; Per Subs 12; Talking Bks 500; Videos 652
Partic in Librarians of the Upper Valley Coop
Open Mon & Thurs 12-7, Tues 9-11 & 12-7, Wed 1-5:30, Fri 3-5:30, Sat 9-11
Friends of the Library Group

STODDARD

P DAVIS PUBLIC LIBRARY, 1391 Rte 123 N, 03464. (Mail add: PO Box 749, 03464-0749), SAN 309-9571. Tel: 603-446-6251. E-mail: davispubliclibrary@gmail.com. Web Site: davislibraryassist.wixsite.com/dmpl, www.stoddardnh.org/davis-public-library. *Libr Dir,* Inga Cullen; Staff 1 (Non-MLS 1)
Pop 1,000; Circ 3,000
Library Holdings: Large Print Bks 100; Bk Vols 5,500; Talking Bks 50; Videos 300
Wireless access
Function: Adult bk club, After school storytime, Family literacy, ILL available, Preschool outreach, Prog for children & young adult, Serves people with intellectual disabilities, Spoken cassettes & CDs, Spoken cassettes & DVDs, Summer reading prog, Tax forms, VHS videos, Wheelchair accessible
Open Mon & Fri 3-7, Tues & Wed 1-5, Thurs 10-5, Sat 10-2
Friends of the Library Group

STRAFFORD

P HILL LIBRARY*, 1151 Parker Mountain Rd, 03884. (Mail add: PO Box 130, 03884), SAN 376-656X. Tel: 603-664-2800. FAX: 603-664-2800. E-mail: LibrarySupport@hilllibrary.org. Web Site: www.hilllibrary.org. *Libr Dir,* Paige Holman; E-mail: pholman@hilllibrary.org; *Admin Librn,* Larisa Molloy; *Youth Librn,* Megan Grondin; Staff 6 (MLS 1, Non-MLS 5)
Founded 1973. Pop 4,010
Library Holdings: Bk Titles 12,500; Per Subs 23
Automation Activity & Vendor Info: (Cataloging) Follett Software; (Circulation) Follett Software
Wireless access
Function: 24/7 Electronic res, 24/7 Online cat, Adult bk club, After school storytime, Archival coll, Audiobks via web, AV serv, Bk club(s), Bks on

CD, CD-ROM, Children's prog, Computer training, Computers for patron use, Digital talking bks, E-Reserves, Electronic databases & coll, Family literacy, Free DVD rentals, Homebound delivery serv, ILL available, Internet access, Laminating, Life-long learning prog for all ages, Magazines, Mail & tel request accepted, Meeting rooms, Movies, Museum passes, Notary serv, Online cat, Outside serv via phone, mail, e-mail & web, OverDrive digital audio bks, Passport agency, Photocopying/Printing, Preschool outreach, Printer for laptops & handheld devices, Prog for adults, Prog for children & young adult, Scanner, Story hour, Summer reading prog, Tax forms, Teen prog, Wheelchair accessible, Writing prog
Partic in Suncook Interlibrary Cooperative
Open Mon-Thurs 11-7, Sat 10-2
Friends of the Library Group

STRATHAM

P WIGGIN MEMORIAL LIBRARY, Ten Bunker Hill Ave, 03885. SAN 309-9601. Tel: 603-772-4346. E-mail: wigginml@comcast.net. Web Site: library.strathamnh.gov. *Dir,* Lesley Kimball; E-mail: librarydirector@wigginml.org; *Ch,* Sam Lucius; *Adult Serv Coordr,* Tricia Ryden; *Teen Librn,* Lucia von Letkemann; *Circ & ILL,* Karen Ryan
Founded 1891. Pop 7,200; Circ 90,000
Library Holdings: Bk Vols 50,000
Subject Interests: NH
Automation Activity & Vendor Info: (Circulation) ByWater Solutions
Wireless access
Function: Adult bk club, Audio & video playback equip for onsite use, Audiobks via web, Bi-weekly Writer's Group, Bk club(s), Bks on CD, Children's prog, Computer training, Computers for patron use, E-Reserves, Electronic databases & coll, Free DVD rentals, Homebound delivery serv, ILL available, Internet access, Mail & tel request accepted, Museum passes, Music CDs, Online cat, Outreach serv, OverDrive digital audio bks, Photocopying/Printing, Preschool outreach, Printer for laptops & handheld devices, Prog for adults, Prog for children & young adult, Ref serv available, Story hour, Summer reading prog, Tax forms, Teen prog, Telephone ref, VHS videos, Wheelchair accessible
Open Mon-Wed 1-6, Thurs & Fri 10-12 & 1-3
Friends of the Library Group

SUGAR HILL

P RICHARDSON MEMORIAL LIBRARY, 1411 Rte 117, 03586. SAN 309-961X. Tel: 603-823-7001. E-mail: librariansrml@gmail.com. Web Site: richardson-memorial-library.org, sugarhillnh.org/library-and-museum/richardson-memorial-library. *Librn,* Judith Weisenberger
Pop 639; Circ 3,548
Library Holdings: AV Mats 144; Bk Vols 6,664; Per Subs 11; Videos 68
Wireless access
Open Mon 4-6, Tues 1-4, Thurs 10-1, Sat 9-12

SULLIVAN

P SULLIVAN PUBLIC LIBRARY, 436 Centre St, 03445. (Mail add: PO Box 92, 03445-0092), SAN 376-7698. Tel: 603-847-3458. FAX: 603-847-9154 (Town Hall). E-mail: sullivanpubliclibrary@gmail.com. Web Site: townofsullivannh.com/library. *Librn,* Paulette Tuttle; Staff 1 (Non-MLS 1)
Founded 1894. Pop 677
Library Holdings: Audiobooks 189; CDs 30; DVDs 152; Bk Vols 6,955; Per Subs 4; Videos 634
Special Collections: Local History Coll
Automation Activity & Vendor Info: (Cataloging) LibraryWorld, Inc; (Circulation) LibraryWorld, Inc; (ILL) LibraryWorld, Inc; (OPAC) LibraryWorld, Inc
Wireless access
Function: Adult bk club, Archival coll, Bks on cassette, Bks on CD, Children's prog, Computers for patron use, Electronic databases & coll, Free DVD rentals, ILL available, Music CDs, Notary serv, OverDrive digital audio bks, Photocopying/Printing, Prog for adults, Prog for children & young adult, Ref serv available, Scanner, Serves people with intellectual disabilities, Spoken cassettes & CDs, Summer reading prog, VHS videos, Wheelchair accessible
Partic in Nubanusit Library Cooperative
Open Tues 10-4 & 6-8, Thurs 2-4 & 6-8, Sat 9-Noon
Friends of the Library Group

SUNAPEE

P ABBOTT LIBRARY*, 11 Soonipi Circle, 03782. (Mail add: PO Box 314, 03782-0314), SAN 309-9636. Tel: 603-763-5513. FAX: 603-763-8765. E-mail: info@abbottlibrary.org. Web Site: www.abbottlibrary.org. *Dir,* Melinda Atwood; E-mail: director@abbottlibrary.org; *Asst Dir,* Justin Levesque; E-mail: jlevesque@abbottlibrary.org; *Ch,* Joyce Martin
Founded 1926. Pop 3,500; Circ 56,000
Library Holdings: Bk Vols 36,000; Per Subs 77
Automation Activity & Vendor Info: (Cataloging) Koha; (Circulation) Koha; (OPAC) Koha
Open Mon & Wed 9-8, Thurs & Fri 9-6, Sat 9-1
Friends of the Library Group

SURRY

P REED FREE LIBRARY*, Eight Village Rd, 03431-8314. SAN 309-9644. Tel: 603-352-1761. Web Site: surry.nh.gov/library-2. *Librn,* Carolyn Locke
Pop 662; Circ 2,207
Library Holdings: Large Print Bks 52; Bk Vols 8,000
Special Collections: Oral History
Wireless access
Open Mon & Thurs 2-7

SWANZEY

P MOUNT CAESAR UNION LIBRARY*, 628 Old Homestead Hwy, 03446. SAN 309-9660. Tel: 603-357-0456. E-mail: mculibrary@yahoo.com. Web Site: mcul.sharepoint.com/Pages/default.aspx. *Libr Dir,* Cadigan Gregory
Founded 1885. Pop 7,000; Circ 18,354
Library Holdings: Audiobooks 520; DVDs 1,681; Bk Titles 21,157; Per Subs 17
Subject Interests: Genealogy, Local hist
Automation Activity & Vendor Info: (Circulation) ComPanion Corp
Wireless access
Publications: Newsletter
Open Mon 10-4, Tues & Thurs 10-5, Wed 2-8, Sat 10-2
Friends of the Library Group

TAMWORTH

P COOK MEMORIAL LIBRARY*, 93 Main St, 03886. SAN 309-9687. Tel: 603-323-8510. FAX: 603-323-2077. E-mail: cooklib@tamworthlibrary.org. Web Site: www.tamworthlibrary.org. *Libr Dir,* Mary Cronin; E-mail: director@tamworthlibrary.org; *Ch,* Amy Carter; *Genealogy & Hist Librn,* Christine Clyne; Staff 2.3 (MLS 0.9, Non-MLS 1.4)
Founded 1894. Pop 2,560; Circ 34,000
Library Holdings: CDs 1,000; DVDs 2,000; Bk Titles 21,000; Per Subs 45
Special Collections: Index Card File on Vital Statistics (1777-1890); Remnants of Tamworth Social Library Coll (26 vols). Oral History
Automation Activity & Vendor Info: (Cataloging) Koha; (Circulation) Koha; (OPAC) Koha
Wireless access
Function: 24/7 Online cat, Adult bk club, Archival coll, Art exhibits, Bk club(s), Bks on CD, Children's prog, Computer training, Computers for patron use, Doc delivery serv, E-Reserves, Free DVD rentals, Homebound delivery serv, ILL available, Instruction & testing, Internet access, Magazines, Meeting rooms, Museum passes, Music CDs, Online cat, Outside serv via phone, mail, e-mail & web, OverDrive digital audio bks, Photocopying/Printing, Printer for laptops & handheld devices, Prog for adults, Prog for children & young adult, Ref serv available, Story hour, Summer reading prog, Wheelchair accessible
Open Mon 10-2, Tues & Wed 10-8, Fri 10-5, Sat 10-4
Friends of the Library Group

TEMPLE

P MANSFIELD PUBLIC LIBRARY, Five Main St, 03084. (Mail add: PO Box 210, 03084-0210), SAN 309-9695. Tel: 603-878-3100. FAX: 603-878-0654. E-mail: mansfieldlibrarynh@comcast.net. Web Site: www.templenh.org/library. *Libr Dir,* Beth Crooker; *Asst Librn,* Robin Downes
Founded 1890. Pop 1,300; Circ 8,609
Library Holdings: Bk Vols 14,407; Per Subs 48
Wireless access
Open Mon & Fri 10-2, Tues 3-7, Sat 10-Noon

THORNTON

P THORNTON PUBLIC LIBRARY*, 1884 NH Rte 175, 03285. SAN 309-9709. Tel: 603-726-8981. FAX: 603-726-8985. E-mail: info@thorntonpubliclibrary.org. Web Site: www.thorntonpubliclibrary.org. *Dir,* Nina Sargent; E-mail: director@thorntonpubliclibrary.org; *Libr Asst,* Judy Cooper; Staff 2 (Non-MLS 2)
Founded 1899. Pop 2,200; Circ 2,900
Library Holdings: Bk Titles 6,500; Per Subs 14
Automation Activity & Vendor Info: (Circulation) Follett Software
Wireless access
Open Mon & Wed 9-7, Tues, Thurs & Fri 9-4
Friends of the Library Group

TROY

P GAY-KIMBALL LIBRARY, 10 S Main St, 03465. (Mail add: PO Box 837, 03465-0837), SAN 309-9725. Tel: 603-242-7743. FAX: 603-242-7743. E-mail: library@troylibrary.us. Web Site: www.troylibrary.us. *Dir,* Position Currently Open
Founded 1824. Pop 2,137; Circ 19,000
Library Holdings: DVDs 1,200; Bk Vols 23,500; Per Subs 30
Special Collections: New England Coll, local area
Automation Activity & Vendor Info: (Cataloging) ByWater Solutions; (Circulation) ByWater Solutions
Wireless access
Function: Adult bk club, After school storytime, Bks on CD, Computers for patron use, Electronic databases & coll, Free DVD rentals, ILL available, Magazines, Online cat, OverDrive digital audio bks, Photocopying/Printing, Prog for adults, Ref serv available, Scanner, Summer reading prog
Open Tues 10-7, Wed & Thurs 2-7, Sat 10-2

UNITY

P UNITY FREE PUBLIC LIBRARY*, 13 Center Rd, 03603. SAN 309-9741. Tel: 603-543-3253. E-mail: unitylibrary@yahoo.com. *Dir,* Rhoda Staff
Pop 1,621; Circ 7,870
Library Holdings: Audiobooks 246; DVDs 1,740; Large Print Bks 70; Bk Vols 5,381; Per Subs 30
Special Collections: Government Publications; Rare Book Coll; Town History
Wireless access
Function: 24/7 Online cat, Activity rm, Adult bk club, Audio & video playback equip for onsite use, Audiobks via web, Bk club(s), Bks on CD, Children's prog, Computers for patron use, Digital talking bks, E-Readers, Electronic databases & coll, Free DVD rentals, Magazines, Meeting rooms, Museum passes, Online cat, OverDrive digital audio bks, Photocopying/Printing, Printer for laptops & handheld devices, Prog for adults, Ref & res, Ref serv available, Res assist avail, Scanner, Spoken cassettes & CDs, Spoken cassettes & DVDs, Study rm, Summer & winter reading prog, Summer reading prog, Wheelchair accessible
Open Mon, Wed & Fri 12-5, Sat 9-2
Restriction: Free to mem, Open to pub for ref & circ; with some limitations
Friends of the Library Group

WAKEFIELD

P WAKEFIELD LIBRARY ASSOCIATION*, 2699 Wakefield Rd, 03872. (Mail add: PO Box 904, Sanbornville, 03872-0904), SAN 309-9768. Tel: 603-522-3032. Web Site: wakefieldlibrary.wordpress.com. *Librn,* Donna Lee Jackson; E-mail: 4jacksons@roadrunner.com
Founded 1895. Pop 4,800
Library Holdings: Audiobooks 2; Large Print Bks 3; Bk Vols 5,200
Wireless access
Partic in The Alberta Library; The Regional Automation Consortium
Open Wed (Summer) 9-4, Sat 9-3; Wed (Winter) 1-3, Sat 10-12
Friends of the Library Group

WALPOLE

P WALPOLE TOWN LIBRARY*, Bridge Memorial Library, 48 Main St, 03608. (Mail add: PO Box 487, 03608-0487), SAN 350-5626. Tel: 603-756-9806. FAX: 603-756-3140. E-mail: walpolelibrary@comcast.net. Web Site: www.walpoletownlibrary.org. *Dir,* Justine Fafara; E-mail: jfafara@walpoletownlibrary.org; *Cat Librn, Ref Librn,* Christine Burchstead; *Ch, ILL Librn,* Julie Rios; Staff 4 (MLS 1, Non-MLS 3)
Founded 1795. Pop 3,594
Library Holdings: Bk Vols 25,000; Per Subs 76
Automation Activity & Vendor Info: (Cataloging) Koha; (Circulation) Koha
Wireless access
Partic in Nubanusit Library Cooperative
Open Mon 1-8, Tues, Thurs & Fri 1-6, Wed 10-12 & 1-8, Sat 9-1
Friends of the Library Group
Branches: 1
NORTH WALPOLE, 70 Church St, North Walpole, 03609, SAN 350-5650. Tel: 603-445-5153. FAX: 603-445-5153. *Dir,* Justine Fafara; *Librn,* Rose Werden
Library Holdings: Bk Vols 6,150
Open Tues & Wed 2-4, Sat 1-4
Friends of the Library Group

WARNER

CR NORTHEAST CATHOLIC COLLEGE*, St Augustine Library, 511 Kearsarge Mountain Rd, 03278. SAN 321-7337. Tel: 603-456-2656. FAX: 603-456-2660. *Dir,* Marie A Lasher; E-mail: mlasher@NortheastCatholic.edu; Staff 1 (MLS 1)
Founded 1973. Enrl 90; Fac 12; Highest Degree: Bachelor
Library Holdings: Bk Titles 21,000; Bk Vols 27,000; Per Subs 50
Subject Interests: Humanities
Automation Activity & Vendor Info: (Acquisitions) Mandarin Library Automation; (Cataloging) Mandarin Library Automation; (Circulation) Mandarin Library Automation; (ILL) OCLC WorldShare Interlibrary Loan; (OPAC) Mandarin Library Automation
Wireless access
Partic in New Hampshire Automated Information Systems; OCLC Online Computer Library Center, Inc

P PILLSBURY FREE LIBRARY, 18 E Main St, 03278. (Mail add: PO Box 299, 03278-0299), SAN 309-9776. Tel: 603-456-2289. FAX: 603-456-3177. E-mail: info@warner.lib.nh.us. Web Site: warner.lib.nh.us. *Libr Dir,* Nancy Ladd; *Asst Dir, Ch,* Susan Matott; Staff 5 (MLS 1, Non-MLS 4)
Founded 1892. Pop 3,000; Circ 36,600
Jan 2020-Dec 2020 Income $218,854, State $275, City $187,148, Locally Generated Income $11,000, Other $1,000. Mats Exp $17,000, Books $12,200, Per/Ser (Incl. Access Fees) $1,500, AV Mat $1,500, Electronic Ref Mat (Incl. Access Fees) $1,500, Presv $300. Sal $108,626 (Prof $100,000)
Library Holdings: Audiobooks 821; AV Mats 3,000; Bks on Deafness & Sign Lang 12; CDs 300; DVDs 1,700; e-books 10; Electronic Media & Resources 14; High Interest/Low Vocabulary Bk Vols 40; Large Print Bks 130; Microforms 105; Music Scores 94; Bk Titles 27,200; Bk Vols 27,300; Per Subs 70; Talking Bks 825; Videos 1,880
Special Collections: Paul Knudson Music Score Coll, sheet music; Warner Coll, print & non-print items. Oral History
Subject Interests: Town hist
Automation Activity & Vendor Info: (Circulation) ByWater Solutions; (OPAC) ByWater Solutions; (Serials) EBSCO Online
Wireless access
Function: Adult literacy prog, Art exhibits, Audio & video playback equip for onsite use, Audiobks via web, Bks on cassette, Bks on CD, CD-ROM, Children's prog, Computer training, Computers for patron use, Digital talking bks, E-Reserves, Electronic databases & coll, Equip loans & repairs, Free DVD rentals, Holiday prog, Homebound delivery serv, ILL available, Literacy & newcomer serv, Magnifiers for reading, Mail & tel request accepted, Microfiche/film & reading machines, Museum passes, Music CDs, Online cat, OverDrive digital audio bks, Photocopying/Printing, Preschool reading prog, Printer for laptops & handheld devices, Prog for adults, Prog for children & young adult, Ref serv available, Scanner, Spoken cassettes & CDs, Spoken cassettes & DVDs, Story hour, Summer reading prog, Tax forms, Wheelchair accessible
Partic in New Hampshire Automated Information Systems
Special Services for the Deaf - Bks on deafness & sign lang; Closed caption videos
Special Services for the Blind - Accessible computers; Aids for in-house use; Audio mat; Bks on cassette; Bks on CD; Copier with enlargement capabilities; Digital talking bk; Home delivery serv; Large print bks; Magnifiers; Networked computers with assistive software
Open Mon & Wed 1-5, Tues & Thurs 9-12 & 1-8, Sat 9-2
Friends of the Library Group

WARREN

P JOSEPH PATCH LIBRARY*, 320 New Hampshire, Rte 25, 03279. SAN 309-9784. Tel: 603-764-9072. E-mail: jpatchlibrary@yahoo.com. Web Site: www.warren-nh.com/library. *Librn,* Veronica Mueller
Pop 820; Circ 4,096
Library Holdings: Audiobooks 150; AV Mats 415; CDs 50; DVDs 200; Large Print Bks 100; Bk Titles 5,000; Per Subs 25; Videos 100
Wireless access
Function: Adult bk club, Audiobks via web, AV serv, Bk club(s), Bks on cassette, Bks on CD, CD-ROM, Children's prog, Computers for patron use, Free DVD rentals, ILL available, Mail & tel request accepted, Music CDs, Online cat, OverDrive digital audio bks, Photocopying/Printing, Prog for adults, Prog for children & young adult, Story hour, Summer reading prog, VHS videos, Wheelchair accessible
Open Mon 9-1, Tues 1-5, Wed 3-7, Sat 10-1
Restriction: Open to pub for ref & circ; with some limitations
Friends of the Library Group

WASHINGTON

P SHEDD FREE LIBRARY*, 46 N Main, 03280. (Mail add: PO Box 288, 03280-0288), SAN 309-9792. Tel: 603-495-3592. FAX: 603-495-0410. Web Site: www.washingtonnh.org/library. *Dir,* James Bruno; *Asst Librn,* Susan Toczko
Founded 1869. Pop 1,100; Circ 5,514
Library Holdings: Bk Vols 8,000; Per Subs 19
Wireless access

Open Tues 10-5, Wed (May-Oct) 10-1, Thurs 1-7, Sat 10-1
Friends of the Library Group

WATERVILLE VALLEY

P OSCEOLA LIBRARY*, Two W Branch Rd, 03215. (Mail add: PO Box 500, 03215-0500), SAN 321-1029. Tel: 603-236-4369, 603-236-4730. E-mail: wvlibrary@watervillevalley.org. Web Site: www.watervillevalley.org/osceola-library. *Library Contact,* Maureen Fish
Founded 1888. Pop 305; Circ 1,566
Library Holdings: Audiobooks 180; Bk Vols 3,100
Special Collections: New Hampshire History Coll; Recreational Books; White Mountains Coll
Wireless access
Open Tues, Thurs & Sat (Winter) 3-5; Mon-Sun (Summer) 3-5

WEARE

P WEARE PUBLIC LIBRARY, Ten Paige Memorial Lane, 03281. SAN 309-9806. Tel: 603-529-2044. E-mail: wearepl@comcast.net. Web Site: weare.nh.gov/library, wearepubliclibrary.com. *Dir,* Clay Kriese; *Ch,* Karen Metcalf; *Asst Librn, ILL,* Thelma Tracy; Staff 8 (Non-MLS 8)
Founded 1892. Pop 9,000; Circ 34,974
Library Holdings: AV Mats 1,779; Bks on Deafness & Sign Lang 11; Bk Vols 19,831; Per Subs 88
Automation Activity & Vendor Info: (Cataloging) Follett Software
Wireless access
Function: Adult bk club, Children's prog, Computers for patron use, Free DVD rentals, ILL available, Museum passes, Photocopying/Printing, Prog for children & young adult, Tax forms, VHS videos
Open Mon & Thurs 10-8, Tues & Wed 10-6, Sat (Sept-June) 9-2
Friends of the Library Group

WEBSTER

P WEBSTER FREE PUBLIC LIBRARY, 947 Battle St, 03303. SAN 309-9814. Tel: 603-648-2706. E-mail: websterl@tds.net. Web Site: webster-nh.gov/webster-free-public-library. *Libr Dir,* Cathryn Clark-Dawe
Pop 1,405; Circ 9,300
Library Holdings: Bk Vols 10,500; Per Subs 14
Automation Activity & Vendor Info: (Cataloging) Follett Software; (Circulation) Follett Software
Wireless access
Open Mon 1-8, Wed 9-8, Sun 12-4

WENTWORTH

P WEBSTER MEMORIAL LIBRARY*, 20 Wentworth Village Rd, 03282. (Mail add: PO Box 105, 03282-0105), SAN 309-9822. Tel: 603-764-5818. E-mail: webstermemlib@gmail.com. *Dir,* Nance Masterson; Staff 2 (Non-MLS 2)
Founded 1917. Pop 940; Circ 2,232
Library Holdings: AV Mats 1,145; Bk Vols 11,786; Per Subs 20
Wireless access
Open Mon 1-5, Wed 11-5, Sat 9-12

WEST STEWARTSTOWN

P DENNIS JOOS MEMORIAL LIBRARY*, 888 Washington St, 03597. (Mail add: PO Box 119, 03597-0119), SAN 309-9563. Tel: 603-246-3329. FAX: 603-246-3329. *Dir,* Donna Allen
Pop 1,004
Library Holdings: Bk Vols 4,599
Open Mon & Wed 2-4, Thurs 2-6

WEST SWANZEY

P STRATTON FREE LIBRARY, Nine Main St, 03446. (Mail add: PO Box 578, 03469-0578), SAN 309-9679. Tel: 603-352-9391. E-mail: strattonfreelibrary@ne.rr.com. Web Site: www.swanzeynh.gov/community/stratton_free_library.php. *Libr Dir,* Becky Streeter; *Librn,* Carol Haley; Staff 2 (Non-MLS 2)
Founded 1885. Pop 7,200
Jan 2015-Dec 2015 Income $46,787, City $41,845, Locally Generated Income $4,942. Mats Exp $6,330. Sal $19,612
Library Holdings: Audiobooks 189; e-books 18,305; Bk Vols 13,131; Per Subs 6; Videos 519
Subject Interests: Local hist
Wireless access
Partic in New Hampshire Downloadable Books Consortium
Open Tues & Thurs 2:30-7, Fri & Sat 10-2

WESTMORELAND

P WESTMORELAND PUBLIC LIBRARY*, 33 S Village Rd, 03467. SAN 309-9830. Tel: 603-399-7750. E-mail: wpl33svr@myfairpoint.net. Web Site: wplnh.org. *Dir,* Jayne Burnett
Founded 1888. Pop 1,650; Circ 5,938
Library Holdings: Bk Titles 11,000; Per Subs 10
Wireless access
Open Tues & Thurs 10-7, Sat 9-1

WHITEFIELD

P WHITEFIELD PUBLIC LIBRARY*, Eight Lancaster Rd, 03598. SAN 309-9849. Tel: 603-837-2030. E-mail: whitefieldpl@myfairpoint.net. *Librn,* Courtney Vashaw; E-mail: cbvashaw@icloud.com
Founded 1893. Pop 1,724; Circ 13,680
Library Holdings: Bk Vols 12,000; Per Subs 40
Wireless access
Function: Activity rm, Audiobks via web, Bks on CD, Children's prog, Computers for patron use, Free DVD rentals, ILL available, Internet access, Magazines, Meeting rooms, Photocopying/Printing, Wheelchair accessible
Open Mon 9-12, Tues & Thurs 2-8, Sat 10-5
Friends of the Library Group

WILMOT

P WILMOT PUBLIC LIBRARY*, 11 N Wilmot Rd, 03287-4302. SAN 309-9857. Tel: 603-526-6804. FAX: 603-526-6804. E-mail: wilmotlibrary@comcast.net. Web Site: www.wilmotlibrary.org. *Dir,* Glynis Hart
Founded 1898. Pop 1,100
Library Holdings: Bk Vols 8,000
Open Mon, Tues & Thurs 3-7, Wed 10-7, Fri 3-5, Sat 10-12
Friends of the Library Group

WILTON

P WILTON PUBLIC & GREGG FREE LIBRARY, Seven Forest Rd, 03086. (Mail add: PO Box 420, 03086-0420), SAN 309-9865. Tel: 603-654-2581. FAX: 603-654-3674. E-mail: wiltonlibrarynh@gmail.com. Web Site: www.wiltonlibrarynh.org. *Dir,* Pat Fickett; E-mail: patf@wiltonlibrarynh.org; *Youth Serv Librn,* Bettielue Hill; E-mail: bettieluehh@wiltonlibrarynh.org; *Adult Serv Mgr,* Deb Cheney; E-mail: debc@wiltonlibrary.org; *Circ & Outreach,* Rebecca Brown; E-mail: rebeccab@wiltonlibrarynh.org; Staff 5 (MLS 2, Non-MLS 3)
Founded 1908. Pop 3,750; Circ 28,153
Library Holdings: Audiobooks 6,881; DVDs 961; e-books 7,113; Large Print Bks 200; Bk Titles 20,733; Bk Vols 22,530; Per Subs 50; Talking Bks 425
Automation Activity & Vendor Info: (Acquisitions) Biblionix; (Cataloging) Biblionix; (Circulation) Biblionix; (OPAC) Biblionix; (Serials) Biblionix
Wireless access
Open Tues-Thurs 9:30-7, Fri 1:30-5, Sat 9:30-1:30
Friends of the Library Group

WINCHESTER

P CONANT PUBLIC LIBRARY*, 111 Main St, 03470. SAN 309-9873. Tel: 603-239-4331. FAX: 603-239-4331. E-mail: interlibraryloan@conantlibrary.org. Web Site: www.conantlibrary.org. *Dir,* Abigail Storm; E-mail: director@conantlibrary.org
Founded 1892. Pop 4,223; Circ 15,746
Library Holdings: DVDs 630; Large Print Bks 228; Bk Titles 20,000; Per Subs 45
Special Collections: Keene Sentinel 1799-1999; Microfilm of Town Records 1733-1800; Winchester Star, 1895-1917
Automation Activity & Vendor Info: (Circulation) Mandarin Library Automation; (OPAC) Mandarin Library Automation
Wireless access
Open Mon, Wed & Fri 10-8, Sat 10-2

WINDHAM

P NESMITH LIBRARY, Eight Fellows Rd, 03087-1909. SAN 309-989X. Tel: 603-432-7154. FAX: 603-537-0097. E-mail: info@nesmithlibrary.org. Web Site: www.nesmithlibrary.org. *Libr Dir,* Sylvie Brikiatis; E-mail: director@nesmithlibrary.org; *Asst Dir, Head, Tech Serv,* Nancy Vigezzi; E-mail: nvigezzi@nesmithlibrary.org; *Tech Serv Librn,* Elaine Rittenhouse; E-mail: erittenhouse@nesmithlibrary.org; *Circ Mgr, Outreach Serv,* Karen Frey; E-mail: kfrey@nesmithlibrary.org; Staff 14 (MLS 4, Non-MLS 10)
Founded 1871. Pop 14,500; Circ 132,641
Library Holdings: AV Mats 4,844; Bks on Deafness & Sign Lang 14; Large Print Bks 750; Bk Titles 65,719; Per Subs 204; Spec Interest Per Sub 11
Special Collections: Chinese Coll; Parents/First Teachers Coll

Subject Interests: NH hist
Automation Activity & Vendor Info: (Cataloging) Follett Software; (Circulation) Follett Software; (OPAC) Follett Software
Wireless access
Publications: Nesmith Library News (Monthly)
Partic in GMILCS, Inc; LYRASIS; Merri-Hill-Rock Library Cooperative
Open Mon-Thurs 9-8, Fri 9-5, Sat 9-4, Sun 1-5
Friends of the Library Group

WOLFEBORO

P WOLFEBORO PUBLIC LIBRARY*, 259 S Main St, 03894. SAN 309-9903. Tel: 603-569-2428. Web Site: www.wolfeborolibrary.org. *Dir,* Cynthia L Scott; E-mail: librarydirector@wolfeboropubliclibrary.org; *Ch,* Barbara Widmer; *ILL Librn,* Helen Gallagher; *Tech Serv Librn,* Lynne Clough; Staff 7 (MLS 1, Non-MLS 6)
Founded 1900. Pop 6,306; Circ 98,395
Jan 2018-Dec 2018 Income $557,695, City $525,669, Locally Generated Income $32,026. Mats Exp $56,679, Books $32,289, AV Mat $15,274, Electronic Ref Mat (Incl. Access Fees) $9,116. Sal $293,801
Library Holdings: Audiobooks 3,891; CDs 3,772; DVDs 3,582; e-books 29,539; e-journals 25; Bk Vols 34,584; Per Subs 62; Videos 12
Special Collections: Bowers Postcard Coll - Historical NH Postcards; Fitts Postcard Coll
Automation Activity & Vendor Info: (Cataloging) Book Systems; (Circulation) Book Systems; (OPAC) Book Systems
Wireless access
Function: 24/7 Electronic res, 24/7 Online cat, Activity rm, Archival coll, Art exhibits, Audiobks via web, Bk club(s), Bk reviews (Group), Bks on CD, Children's prog, Computer training, Computers for patron use, E-Readers, Electronic databases & coll, Free DVD rentals, Genealogy discussion group, Holiday prog, ILL available, Internet access, Large print keyboards, Magazines, Mail & tel request accepted, Meeting rooms, Movies, Museum passes, Music CDs, Online cat, Outreach serv, OverDrive digital audio bks, Photocopying/Printing, Preschool outreach, Preschool reading prog, Printer for laptops & handheld devices, Prog for adults, Prog for children & young adult, Ref serv available, Scanner, Story hour, Summer reading prog, Tax forms, Telephone ref, Wheelchair accessible, Workshops
Open Mon-Thurs 9:30-8, Fri & Sat 9:30-5
Friends of the Library Group

WOODSVILLE

P WOODSVILLE FREE PUBLIC LIBRARY*, 14 School Lane, 03785. SAN 309-8400. Tel: 603-747-3483. E-mail: woodsvillelibrary@hotmail.com. *Head Librn,* Karen O'Donnell-Leach; *Asst Librn,* Position Currently Open
Pop 3,444; Circ 23,111
Library Holdings: Bk Vols 35,860; Per Subs 54
Subject Interests: Town hist
Wireless access
Publications: Local Paper
Open Tues, Thurs & Fri 1-7

NEW JERSEY

Date of Statistics: Data Year 2018
Population, 2020 Census: 8,882,371
Population Served by Public Libraries: 8,741,619
Unserved: 50,275
Total Volumes in Public Libraries: 45,819,839
Volumes Per Capita: 5.21
Digital Resources:
Total e-books: 9,555,098
Total audio items (physical and downloadable units): 7,236,933
Total video items (physical and downloadable units): 3,555,454
Total computers for use by the public: 9,306
Total annual wireless sessions: 6,811,072
Income and Expenditures:
Total Public Library Income: $577,406,115
Average Income Per Library: $2,062,165
Source of Income: Mainly public funds
Expenditures Per Capita: $52.70
Grants-in-Aid to Public Libraries:
Federal: $541,804
State Aid: $3,639,240
Number of County Libraries: 14

ABSECON

P ABSECON PUBLIC LIBRARY, 305 New Jersey Ave, 08201. SAN 309-9911. Tel: 609-646-2228. FAX: 609-383-8992. E-mail: abseconlibrary@yahoo.com. Web Site: abseconlibrary.org. *Libr Dir,* Barbara Wilson
Founded 1937. Pop 7,000; Circ 20,429
Library Holdings: Bk Vols 25,000; Per Subs 50
Automation Activity & Vendor Info: (Cataloging) SirsiDynix; (Circulation) SirsiDynix; (OPAC) SirsiDynix
Wireless access
Partic in Coalition of Independent Libraries
Open Mon-Fri 9:30-5, Sat 9:30-1

ALLENDALE

P LEE MEMORIAL LIBRARY, 500 W Crescent Ave, 07401. SAN 309-992X. Tel: 201-327-4338. Reference E-mail: aldlcirc@bccls.org. Web Site: leememoriallibrary.org. *Libr Dir,* Susan Wilkinson; E-mail: wilkinson@allendale.bccls.org; *Exec Adminir,* Patricia Durso; E-mail: patricia.durso@allendale.bccls.org; Staff 16 (MLS 2, Non-MLS 14)
Founded 1923. Pop 6,505; Circ 181,952
Library Holdings: AV Mats 8,314; Bk Vols 150,000; Per Subs 100
Wireless access
Function: Activity rm, Adult bk club, Adult literacy prog, After school storytime, Audiobks via web, AV serv, Bk club(s), Bk reviews (Group), Bks on CD, Children's prog, Computers for patron use, E-Reserves, Electronic databases & coll, Free DVD rentals, Home delivery & serv to seniorr ctr & nursing homes, Homebound delivery serv, ILL available, Internet access, Life-long learning prog for all ages, Magazines, Mail & tel request accepted, Mango lang, Movies, Museum passes, Music CDs, Notary serv, Online cat, Online ref, Outreach serv, OverDrive digital audio bks, Photocopying/Printing, Preschool outreach, Preschool reading prog, Prog for adults, Prog for children & young adult, Spoken cassettes & CDs, Spoken cassettes & DVDs, Story hour, Summer & winter reading prog, Summer reading prog, Tax forms, Teen prog, Telephone ref
Partic in Bergen County Cooperative Library System, Inc
Open Mon, Tues & Thurs 10-8, Wed, Fri & Sat 10-5 (10-2 Summer)
Friends of the Library Group

ALPHA

P W H WALTERS FREE PUBLIC LIBRARY*, 1001 East Blvd, 08865. SAN 376-0650. Tel: 908-454-1445. E-mail: alphapubliclibrary1@outlook.com. Web Site: www.alphapubliclibrary.com. *Libr Dir,* Carla Roselle
Founded 1937
Library Holdings: Bk Titles 16,000; Per Subs 14
Wireless access
Function: 24/7 Electronic res, 24/7 Online cat, Adult bk club, Audiobks via web, Bk club(s), Bks on CD, Children's prog, Computer training, Computers for patron use, Electronic databases & coll, Free DVD rentals, Holiday prog, ILL available, Life-long learning prog for all ages, Magazines, Movies, Online cat, Photocopying/Printing, Prog for adults, Prog for children & young adult, Scanner, Senior computer classes, Story hour, Summer & winter reading prog, Summer reading prog, Tax forms, Teen prog
Open Mon & Tues (April-Oct) 9:30-7, Thurs & Fri 9:30-5; Mon, Tues, Thurs & Fri 9:30-5, Sat 9:30-1

ANNANDALE

S MOUNTAINVIEW YOUTH CORRECTIONAL FACILITY LIBRARY*, Law Library, 31 Petticoat Lane, 08801-4097. Tel: 908-638-6191. *Library Contact,* Megan Harper
Library Holdings: Bk Vols 1,600; Per Subs 20
Restriction: Not open to pub

ASBURY PARK

P ASBURY PARK PUBLIC LIBRARY*, 500 First Ave, 07712. SAN 309-9938. Tel: 732-774-4221. FAX: 732-988-6101. E-mail: apl-info@asburyparklibrary.org. Web Site: asbury.ent.sirsi.net/client/en_us/default. *Dir,* Robert W Stewart; E-mail: rstewart@asburyparklibrary.org
Founded 1878. Circ 47,469
Library Holdings: Bk Titles 105,136; Bk Vols 114,399; Per Subs 406
Automation Activity & Vendor Info: (Cataloging) SirsiDynix; (Circulation) SirsiDynix; (OPAC) SirsiDynix
Wireless access
Partic in LibraryLinkNJ, The New Jersey Library Cooperative
Open Mon-Wed 11-8, Thurs & Fri 9-5, Sat 12-5

P BOROUGH OF INTERLAKEN LIBRARY*, 100 Grassmere Ave, Interlaken, 07712. Tel: 732-531-7405. FAX: 732-531-0150. Web Site: www.interlakenboro.com/library.html. *Librn,* Vicki LaBella; E-mail: vlabella@interlakenboro.com
Open Tues & Sat 2-4

ATCO

P WATERFORD TOWNSHIP PUBLIC LIBRARY*, 2204 Atco Ave, 08004. SAN 309-9954. Tel: 856-767-7727. FAX: 856-753-8998. E-mail: wtpl@njlibraries.org. Web Site: waterfordtwplibrary.org. *Libr Dir,* Tanya Finney Estrada; Tel: 856-767-7727, Ext 13, E-mail: tfestrada@njlibraries.org; Staff 9 (MLS 1, Non-MLS 8)
Founded 1964. Pop 11,000
Library Holdings: Bk Vols 25,888; Per Subs 81
Subject Interests: Parenting
Automation Activity & Vendor Info: (Circulation) Follett Software; (ILL) Auto-Graphics, Inc
Wireless access
Partic in The Library Network
Open Mon-Thurs 10-8, Fri 10-5, Sat 10-3
Friends of the Library Group

ATLANTIC CITY

P ATLANTIC CITY FREE PUBLIC LIBRARY*, One N Tennessee Ave, 08401. SAN 350-5685. Tel: 609-345-2269. Circulation Tel: 609-345-2269, Ext 3070. FAX: 609-345-5570. Web Site: www.acfpl.org. *Dir,* Robert P Rynkiewicz; E-mail: brynk@acfpl.org; *Adult Serv,* Barbara O'Hara; *Youth Serv,* Maureen Moffit; Staff 37 (MLS 9, Non-MLS 28)
Founded 1902. Pop 40,517; Circ 317,520
Library Holdings: Bk Titles 104,200; Bk Vols 135,000; Per Subs 350
Special Collections: Casino Gambling; Genealogy & Atlantic City History (Alfred M Heston Coll)
Automation Activity & Vendor Info: (Acquisitions) Innovative Interfaces, Inc - Millennium; (Cataloging) Innovative Interfaces, Inc - Millennium; (Circulation) Innovative Interfaces, Inc - Millennium
Wireless access
Publications: Atlantic City News Index; Clubs & Organizations Directory
Partic in Coalition of Independent Libraries; LibraryLinkNJ, The New Jersey Library Cooperative; OCLC Online Computer Library Center, Inc
Open Mon, Fri & Sat 9:30-5, Tues-Thurs 9:30-6:30
Branches: 1
RICHMOND AVENUE BRANCH, 4115 Ventnor Ave, 08401, SAN 350-574X. Tel: 609-340-0215. *Library Contact,* Maureen Moffit
Library Holdings: Bk Vols 5,000
Open Tues-Thurs 12-5

M ATLANTICARE REGIONAL MEDICAL CENTER*, Health Science Library, 1925 Pacific Ave, 08401. SAN 309-9962. Tel: 609-441-8966. FAX: 609-441-2137. *Dir,* Jeanne Jarensky; *Libr Asst,* Kathleen Nolan
Library Holdings: Bk Vols 2,285; Per Subs 115
Subject Interests: Med, Nursing
Partic in New Jersey Health Sciences Library Network
Open Mon-Fri 8-4

G FEDERAL AVIATION ADMINISTRATION*, William J Hughes Technical Center Library, Reference & Research Library, AJP-7200, Atlantic City International Airport, 08405. SAN 309-9970. Tel: 609-485-5124. Administration Tel: 609-485-5242. FAX: 609-485-6088. E-mail: actlibrary@faa.gov. Web Site: actlibrary.tc.faa.gov. *Chief Librn,* Robert Mast; E-mail: robert.mast@faa.gov; Staff 1 (MLS 1)
Founded 1958
Library Holdings: Bk Vols 15,000
Special Collections: Technical Reports
Subject Interests: Aeronaut, Air traffic control, Airports, Aviation safety, Communications, Navigation, Radar
Automation Activity & Vendor Info: (Cataloging) EOS International; (Circulation) EOS International; (ILL) OCLC ILLiad; (OPAC) EOS International; (Serials) EOS International
Wireless access
Function: ILL available, Photocopying/Printing, Res libr
Partic in OCLC Online Computer Library Center, Inc
Open Mon-Thurs 6am-4:30pm
Restriction: Closed stack, Non-circulating to the pub, Pub ref by request, Restricted borrowing privileges, Restricted pub use, Secured area only open to authorized personnel

AUDUBON

P FREE PUBLIC LIBRARY OF AUDUBON, 239 Oakland Ave, 08106-1598. SAN 310-0006. Tel: 856-547-8686. FAX: 856-547-0277. Web Site: www.audubonlibrary.org. *Dir,* Andrew Brenza; E-mail: abrenza@audubonlibrary.org; Staff 7 (MLS 1, Non-MLS 6)
Pop 9,205; Circ 42,000
Library Holdings: Bk Titles 24,000; Bk Vols 28,000; Per Subs 50
Publications: Newsletter
Partic in LibraryLinkNJ, The New Jersey Library Cooperative
Open Mon-Thurs 11-8, Fri 11-6, Sat (Sept-June) 10-2

AUDUBON PARK

P DORATHEA ZEOLI PUBLIC LIBRARY*, Two Rd C, 08106. Tel: 856-323-8771. E-mail: library@audubonparknj.org. Web Site: www.audubonparknj.org/serv-library.html. *Librn,* Rosemary Romeo; *Librn,* Mary Talucci; E-mail: mtalucci@audubonparknj.org
Founded 1948
Library Holdings: Bk Vols 5,000
Wireless access
Mem of Camden County Library System
Open Tues & Thurs 9-1, Wed 9-1 & 4-7

AVALON

P AVALON FREE PUBLIC LIBRARY*, 235-32nd St, 08202. SAN 378-5688. Tel: 609-967-7155. FAX: 609-967-4723. Web Site: www.avalonfreelibrary.org. *Libr Dir,* Erin Brown; E-mail: ebrown@avalonfreelibrary.org
Wireless access
Open Mon-Thurs 9-8, Fri & Sat 9-5, Sun 11-3

AVENEL

S NEW JERSEY DEPARTMENT OF CORRECTIONS*, Adult Diagnostic & Treatment Center Library, Eight Production Way, 07001. Tel: 732-574-2250, Ext 8017. FAX: 732-382-8912. Web Site: www.state.nj.us/corrections. *Educ Supvr,* Diane Patrick
Library Holdings: Bk Vols 14,000; Per Subs 25
Special Collections: Law Coll
Restriction: Not open to pub

AVON BY THE SEA

P AVON PUBLIC LIBRARY*, Garfield & Fifth Ave, 07717. SAN 310-0014. Tel: 732-502-4525. FAX: 732-775-8430. E-mail: library@avonbytheseanj.com. Web Site: www.avonbytheseanj.com/avonbythesea_library.htm. *Dir,* Sheila Watson
Founded 1916. Pop 2,163; Circ 25,174
Library Holdings: Bk Titles 21,000; Per Subs 52
Automation Activity & Vendor Info: (Cataloging) Follett Software; (Circulation) Follett Software
Wireless access
Function: ILL available
Open Mon, Wed & Thurs (Winter) 12-7, Tues & Fri 1-5, Sat 9-1; Mon-Fri (Summer) 9-1 & 6-8

BASKING RIDGE

P BERNARDS TOWNSHIP LIBRARY*, 32 S Maple Ave, 07920-1216. SAN 310-0049. Tel: 908-204-3031. FAX: 908-766-1580. Web Site: www.BernardsLibrary.org. *Libr Dir,* Ruth Lufkin; E-mail: rlufkin@bernards.org; *Supv Librn, Ch,* Ellen Ryan; E-mail: eryan@bernards.org; *Supv Librn, Circ,* Ann Babits; E-mail: ababits@bernards.org; *Supv Librn, Ref,* Karen Vaias; E-mail: kvaias@bernards.org; *Supv Librn, Tech Serv,* Marcia Lubansky; E-mail: mlubansky@bernards.org; *Emerging Tech Librn,* Karen Andriolo; E-mail: kandriolo@bernards.org; *YA Librn,* Rachel Talbert; E-mail: rtalbert@bernards.org; *Prog Coordr,* Maureen Norton; E-mail: mnorton@bernards.org; Staff 35 (MLS 9, Non-MLS 26)
Founded 1898. Pop 27,000
Library Holdings: Bk Vols 147,830; Per Subs 135
Special Collections: Local History Coll; Performing Arts Coll
Automation Activity & Vendor Info: (Cataloging) Innovative Interfaces, Inc; (Circulation) Innovative Interfaces, Inc; (OPAC) Innovative Interfaces, Inc
Wireless access
Publications: Electronic Newsletters; History of the Library in Basking Ridge
Partic in LibraryLinkNJ, The New Jersey Library Cooperative; Morris Automated Information Network; Morris-Union Federation; Raritan Valley Fedn of Librs
Open Mon-Thurs 9:30-9, Fri 9:30-5, Sat 10-5, Sun 1-4
Friends of the Library Group

S SOMERSET COUNTY PARK COMMISSION*, Environmental Education Center Library, 190 Lord Stirling Rd, 07920. SAN 321-043X. Tel: 908-722-1200, Ext 5002. FAX: 908-766-2687. Web Site: www.somersetcountyparks.org. *Mgr,* Carrie Springer; E-mail: cspringer@scparks.org; Staff 14 (Non-MLS 14)
Founded 1972
Library Holdings: Bk Titles 2,000; Per Subs 10
Subject Interests: Environ studies, Natural hist
Wireless access
Open Mon-Sun 9-5
Restriction: In-house use for visitors, Not a lending libr

BAYONNE

P FREE PUBLIC LIBRARY & CULTURAL CENTER OF BAYONNE*, 697 Avenue C, 07002. SAN 350-5774. Tel: 201-858-6970. Circulation Tel: 201-858-6971. Reference Tel: 201-858-6980. E-mail: library@bayonnelibrary.org. Web Site: www.bayonnelibrary.org. *Dir,* Sneh P Bains; E-mail: director@bayonnelibrary.org; *Head, Children's Dept,* Paula Micalizzi; E-mail: pmicalizzi@hotmail.com; *Head, Circ,* Susan Humenic; E-mail: shumenic@bayonnelibrary.org; *Ref Librn,* Lisa Attanasio; E-mail: lattanasio@bayonnelibrary.org; *Ref Librn,* Jeannette Torres-Hanley; E-mail: jtorres@bayonnelibrary.org; Staff 6 (MLS 6)
Founded 1893. Pop 63,024; Circ 190,503
Library Holdings: Audiobooks 2,777; CDs 4,964; DVDs 6,012; e-books 28,415; Large Print Bks 2,987; Bk Vols 328,527; Per Subs 129
Special Collections: Local History (New Jersey & Bayonneana). Oral History
Subject Interests: Archit, Art, Indust, Music

Automation Activity & Vendor Info: (Cataloging) SirsiDynix; (Circulation) SirsiDynix; (OPAC) SirsiDynix; (Serials) EBSCO Online
Wireless access
Publications: Newsletter (Quarterly)
Partic in LibraryLinkNJ, The New Jersey Library Cooperative
Special Services for the Blind - Computer with voice synthesizer for visually impaired persons
Open Mon-Thurs 9-9, Fri & Sat 9-5
Friends of the Library Group

BEACH HAVEN

P BEACH HAVEN PUBLIC LIBRARY*, 247 N Beach Ave, 08008-1865. SAN 310-0073. Tel: 609-492-7081. FAX: 609-492-1048. E-mail: bhpl@comcast.net. Web Site: www.beachhavenlibrary.org. *Dir,* Jean Frazier; *Principal Libr Asst,* Eileen Mitchell; *Info Tech,* Anna Serbek
Founded 1924. Pop 2,400; Circ 25,924
Library Holdings: Bk Vols 25,000; Per Subs 60
Special Collections: Local History Coll; Regional History Coll
Wireless access
Partic in LibraryLinkNJ, The New Jersey Library Cooperative
Open Mon, Wed, Fri & Sat 10-4, Tues & Thurs 10-6

BEDMINSTER

P CLARENCE DILLON PUBLIC LIBRARY, 2336 Lamington Rd, 07921. SAN 310-009X. Tel: 908-234-2325. Reference Tel: 908-234-2325, Ext 116. E-mail: ref@dillonlibrary.org. Web Site: www.dillonlibrary.org. *Libr Dir,* Marie Crenshaw; E-mail: mcrenshaw@dillonlibrary.org; *Dir, Ch Serv,* Helen Petersen; E-mail: hpetersen@dillonlibrary.org; *Tech Serv Librn,* Arthur Merchant; E-mail: amerchant@dillonlibrary.org
Pop 8,500
Special Collections: Local History (Anne O'Brien Coll)
Subject Interests: Civil War
Automation Activity & Vendor Info: (Cataloging) TLC (The Library Corporation); (Circulation) TLC (The Library Corporation)
Wireless access
Function: Homebound delivery serv
Partic in LibraryLinkNJ, The New Jersey Library Cooperative; Raritan Valley Fedn of Librs
Special Services for the Blind - Large print bks
Open Mon-Thurs 10-9, Fri & Sat 10-5 (10-3 July & Aug), Sun (Sept-May) 1-4
Friends of the Library Group

BELLEVILLE

P BELLEVILLE PUBLIC LIBRARY & INFORMATION CENTER*, 221 Washington Ave, 07109-3189. SAN 310-0103. Tel: 973-450-3434. FAX: 973-759-6731. Web Site: www.bellepl.org. *Libr Dir,* Michelle Malone; E-mail: mmalone@bellepl.org; *Ch Serv,* Shaunterria Owens; E-mail: sowens@bellepl.org; *Circ,* Mia Torres; *Ref Serv,* Louise Yan; E-mail: reference@bellepl.org; Staff 8 (MLS 3, Non-MLS 5)
Founded 1902. Pop 35,928; Circ 65,323
Library Holdings: AV Mats 5,880; Bk Titles 76,820; Bk Vols 96,447; Per Subs 156
Subject Interests: Career, City hist, State hist
Automation Activity & Vendor Info: (Cataloging) Innovative Interfaces, Inc
Wireless access
Function: After school storytime, Archival coll, Bks on CD, Children's prog, Citizenship assistance, Computer training, Computers for patron use, Electronic databases & coll, Free DVD rentals, Holiday prog, ILL available, Internet access, Museum passes, Notary serv, Online ref, Photocopying/Printing, Printer for laptops & handheld devices, Prog for adults, Prog for children & young adult, Ref & res, Ref serv available, Senior computer classes, Spanish lang bks, Story hour, Summer reading prog, Tax forms, Teen prog
Partic in LibraryLinkNJ, The New Jersey Library Cooperative
Open Mon, Tues & Thurs (Winter) 9-8, Wed, Fri & Sat 9-5; Mon (Summer) 9-8, Tues-Fri 9-5
Friends of the Library Group

S 1ST CEREBRAL PALSY OF NEW JERSEY, Dr Charles I Nadel Library, Seven Sanford Ave, 07109. SAN 375-9989. Tel: 973-751-0200. FAX: 973-751-4635. Web Site: www.cerebralpalsycenter.org. *Exec Dir,* Patrick Colligan; *Assoc Dir, Principal,* Keith Kygiel; E-mail: krygiel@cerebralpalsycenter.org
Library Holdings: Bk Titles 500; Per Subs 50
Subject Interests: Childrens' bks
Open Mon-Fri 8:30-4:30
Restriction: Employee & client use only

M CLARA MAASS MEDICAL CENTER*, Medical Library, One Clara Maass Dr, 07109. SAN 327-3601. Tel: 973-450-2294. FAX: 973-844-4390. Web Site: www.rwjbh.org. *Library Contact,* Nadine Randolphe; Staff 1 (MLS 1)
Library Holdings: Bk Titles 1,050; Per Subs 124
Subject Interests: Med, Nursing
Automation Activity & Vendor Info: (Cataloging) Professional Software; (Serials) Professional Software
Wireless access
Partic in Basic Health Sciences Library Network; LibraryLinkNJ, The New Jersey Library Cooperative
Restriction: Staff use only

BELMAR

P BELMAR PUBLIC LIBRARY, 517 Tenth Ave, 07719. SAN 310-012X. Tel: 732-681-0775. FAX: 732-280-1685. E-mail: library@belmar.com. Web Site: www.belmarlibrary.org. *Dir,* Rosemarie Korbelak; *Prog Coordr,* Margaret O'Connor; *Libr Asst,* Patricia Faugno; *Libr Asst,* Liz Griffin; *Libr Asst,* Connie Nolan; *Libr Asst,* Luis B Pulido; E-mail: lpulido@belmar.com; *Libr Asst,* Lorraine Walsh; Staff 3 (Non-MLS 3)
Founded 1911. Pop 5,900; Circ 14,000
Wireless access
Function: 24/7 Electronic res, 24/7 Online cat, Adult bk club, Archival coll, Art programs, Bk club(s), Bks on CD, Children's prog, Citizenship assistance, Computers for patron use, Electronic databases & coll, Free DVD rentals, Holiday prog, Internet access, Life-long learning prog for all ages, Magazines, Magnifiers for reading, Mail & tel request accepted, Online cat, Online ref, OverDrive digital audio bks, Photocopying/Printing, Printer for laptops & handheld devices, Prog for adults, Prog for children & young adult, STEM programs, Story hour, Summer reading prog, Wheelchair accessible, Workshops
Partic in LibraryLinkNJ, The New Jersey Library Cooperative
Open Mon, Tues & Fri 9-4, Wed & Thurs 9-7, Sat 9-1
Friends of the Library Group

BELVIDERE

S WARREN COUNTY HISTORICAL SOCIETY & GENEALOGY*, Resource Room, 313 Mansfield St, 07823-1828. (Mail add: PO Box 313, 07823-0313), SAN 375-7374. Tel: 908-475-4246. E-mail: warrencountynjhistorical@yahoo.com. Web Site: warrencountynjhistorical.org. *Pres,* Patricia Burnk; *Librn,* Lynn Moore
Library Holdings: Bk Vols 600
Open Sun 2-4

P WARREN COUNTY LIBRARY*, Two Shotwell Dr, 07823. SAN 350-5898. Tel: 908-818-1280. Administration Tel: 908-475-6320. E-mail: hqbranch@warrrenlib.org. Web Site: www.warrenlib.org. *Dir,* Maureen Baker Wilkinson; E-mail: director@warrenlib.org; *Br Mgr,* Jennifer Sidie; Staff 36 (MLS 7, Non-MLS 29)
Founded 1931. Pop 72,507; Circ 641,858
Jan 2017-Dec 2017 Income (Main & Associated Libraries) $4,665,818, State $38,506, County $4,627,312. Mats Exp $561,995, Books $335,274, AV Mat $125,463. Sal $1,543,941
Library Holdings: Audiobooks 8,940; CDs 8,501; DVDs 24,572; e-books 5,251; Bk Titles 207,954; Bk Vols 222,895; Per Subs 302
Special Collections: Local History (Warren County Library Headquarters), bks, micro, pamphlets
Automation Activity & Vendor Info: (Cataloging) TLC (The Library Corporation); (Circulation) TLC (The Library Corporation); (OPAC) TLC (The Library Corporation); (Serials) TLC (The Library Corporation)
Wireless access
Function: Audio & video playback equip for onsite use, Bk club(s), Bks on CD, Children's prog, Computer training, Computers for patron use, Digital talking bks, Electronic databases & coll, Free DVD rentals, Home delivery & serv to seniorr ctr & nursing homes, Homebound delivery serv, ILL available, Internet access, Magnifiers for reading, Mail & tel request accepted, Microfiche/film & reading machines, Museum passes, Music CDs, Online cat, Online ref, Outreach serv, OverDrive digital audio bks, Photocopying/Printing, Preschool outreach, Preschool reading prog, Printer for laptops & handheld devices, Prof lending libr, Prog for adults, Prog for children & young adult, Ref serv available, Res libr, Senior computer classes, Senior outreach, Spoken cassettes & CDs, Spoken cassettes & DVDs, Story hour, Summer reading prog, Tax forms, Teen prog, Telephone ref, Wheelchair accessible, Workshops
Open Mon-Thurs 9-9, Fri 9-6, Sat 10-4
Friends of the Library Group
Branches: 3
CATHERINE DICKSON HOFMAN BRANCH, Four Lambert Rd, Blairstown, 07825, SAN 310-0227. E-mail: cdhbranch@warrenlib.org. *Br Mgr,* Kelly Durkin
Founded 1941
Open Mon-Thurs 9-8, Fri 9-6, Sat 10-3

NORTHEAST BRANCH, 40 US Hwy 46 W, Hackettstown, 07840, SAN 377-7774. *Br Mgr,* Adam Petroski
Founded 1993
Open Mon-Thurs 9-8, Fri 9-6, Sat 10-3
Friends of the Library Group
SOUTHWEST BRANCH, 404 Rte 519, Phillipsburg, 08885. Tel: 908-818-1280. *Interim Br Mgr,* Suzanne Walzer; Staff 8 (MLS 2, Non-MLS 6)
Founded 2018. Pop 15,000
Function: 24/7 Electronic res, 24/7 Online cat, 3D Printer, Activity rm, Adult bk club, Audiobks via web, AV serv, Bks on CD, Chess club, Children's prog, Computer training, Computers for patron use, Digital talking bks, Doc delivery serv, E-Readers, E-Reserves, Electronic databases & coll, Free DVD rentals, Holiday prog, Home delivery & serv to seniorr ctr & nursing homes, Homebound delivery serv, ILL available, Internet access, Magazines, Mail & tel request accepted, Makerspace, Meeting rooms, Movies, Museum passes, Music CDs, Online cat, Online ref, Outreach serv, Outside serv via phone, mail, e-mail & web, Photocopying/Printing, Preschool reading prog, Printer for laptops & handheld devices, Prof lending libr, Prog for adults, Prog for children & young adult, Ref serv available, Res assist avail, Scanner, Senior computer classes, Senior outreach, Serves people with intellectual disabilities, STEM programs, Story hour, Summer & winter reading prog, Summer reading prog, Tax forms, Teen prog, Telephone ref, Visual arts prog, Wheelchair accessible, Workshops, Writing prog
Open Mon & Thurs 1-8, Wed & Fri 10-5, Sat 9-3
Bookmobiles: 1. Bk titles 2,400

BERGENFIELD

P BERGENFIELD PUBLIC LIBRARY*, 50 W Clinton Ave, 07621-2799. SAN 310-0146. Tel: 201-387-4040. Reference Tel: 201-387-4040, Ext 2832. FAX: 201-387-9004. E-mail: bfldcirc@bccls.org. Web Site: bergenfieldlibrary.org. *Dir,* Allison Moonitz; E-mail: amoonitz@bergenfieldlibrary.org; *Head, Circ,* Lois Alexander; E-mail: lalexander@bergenfieldlibrary.org; *Head, Ref,* John Capps; E-mail: jcapps@bergenfieldlibrary.org; *Head, Youth Serv,* Kara Gilbert; E-mail: kgilbert@bergenfieldlibrary.org; Staff 28 (MLS 4, Non-MLS 24)
Founded 1920. Pop 26,247; Circ 233,201
Library Holdings: AV Mats 10,082; Bk Vols 136,588; Per Subs 229
Special Collections: ESL Coll, New Jersey
Wireless access
Function: Adult bk club, After school storytime, Art exhibits, AV serv, Bk club(s), E-Reserves, Electronic databases & coll, Homebound delivery serv, ILL available, Mail & tel request accepted, Photocopying/Printing, Preschool outreach, Prog for adults, Prog for children & young adult, Ref & res, Spoken cassettes & CDs, Summer reading prog, Tax forms, VHS videos, Wheelchair accessible
Partic in Bergen County Cooperative Library System, Inc
Open Mon-Thurs 10-9, Fri & Sun 1-5, Sat 10-2
Friends of the Library Group

BERKELEY HEIGHTS

P BERKELEY HEIGHTS PUBLIC LIBRARY, 29 Park Ave, 07922. SAN 310-0154. Tel: 908-464-9333. FAX: 908-464-7098. Web Site: www.bhplnj.org. *Libr Dir,* Stephanie Bakos; E-mail: sbakos@bhplnj.org; *Head, Children's Servx,* Laura Fuhro; E-mail: lfuhro@bhplnj.org; *Head, Circ,* Ann Marie Sieczka; *Dept Head, Ref,* Lisa Wernett; E-mail: reference@bhplnj.org; *Head, Tech Serv,* Karen Dreitlein; Staff 3 (MLS 3)
Founded 1953. Pop 13,407; Circ 163,670
Jan 2017-Dec 2017 Income $1,068,715, State $5,730, City $1,042,985, Locally Generated Income $20,000. Mats Exp $157,500, Books $85,000, Per/Ser (Incl. Access Fees) $10,000, AV Mat $22,500, Electronic Ref Mat (Incl. Access Fees) $40,000. Sal $500,000
Library Holdings: AV Mats 3,992; DVDs 1,071; Bk Titles 70,000; Bk Vols 81,598; Per Subs 190; Talking Bks 1,696
Subject Interests: Archit, Art
Automation Activity & Vendor Info: (Acquisitions) TLC (The Library Corporation); (Cataloging) TLC (The Library Corporation); (Circulation) TLC (The Library Corporation); (OPAC) TLC (The Library Corporation)
Wireless access
Function: 24/7 Electronic res, 24/7 Online cat, Activity rm, Adult bk club, Art exhibits, Audiobks on Playaways & MP3, Audiobks via web, Bk club(s), Bks on CD, Children's prog, Computer training, Computers for patron use, Digital talking bks, E-Reserves, Electronic databases & coll, Free DVD rentals, Holiday prog, Homebound delivery serv, ILL available, Internet access, Magazines, Magnifiers for reading, Mail & tel request accepted, Meeting rooms, Movies, Music CDs, Online cat, Online ref, Outside serv via phone, mail, e-mail & web, OverDrive digital audio bks, Photocopying/Printing, Preschool reading prog, Prog for adults, Prog for children & young adult, Ref & res, Ref serv available, Scanner, Senior computer classes, Spoken cassettes & CDs, Spoken cassettes & DVDs, Story hour, Study rm, Summer reading prog, Tax forms, Telephone ref, Wheelchair accessible
Partic in Morris-Union Federation; MURAL
Open Mon-Thurs 9-9, Fri & Sat 9-5, Sun 2-5
Friends of the Library Group

BERLIN

P MARIE FLECHE MEMORIAL LIBRARY*, 49 S White Horse Pike, 08009. SAN 310-0170. Tel: 856-767-2448. FAX: 856-768-3066. E-mail: mfml@berlinborolibrary.org. Web Site: berlinborolibrary.org. *Libr Dir,* Christine Flynn; Tel: 856-787-2448, Ext 5, E-mail: director@berlinborolibrary.org; Staff 6 (MLS 1, Non-MLS 5)
Founded 1957. Pop 7,500; Circ 15,000
Library Holdings: Bk Vols 26,000; Per Subs 20
Automation Activity & Vendor Info: (Acquisitions) Book Systems; (Cataloging) Book Systems; (Circulation) Book Systems; (ILL) JerseyCat; (OPAC) Book Systems
Wireless access
Function: 24/7 Online cat, Adult bk club, Bks on CD, Children's prog, Computers for patron use, E-Readers, Electronic databases & coll, Free DVD rentals, Govt ref serv, ILL available, Internet access, Magazines, Mail & tel request accepted, Museum passes, Online cat, OverDrive digital audio bks, Photocopying/Printing, Preschool reading prog, Prog for adults, Prog for children & young adult, Story hour, Summer reading prog, Tax forms, Wheelchair accessible
Open Mon-Thurs 10-8, Fri 10-4, Sat 11-2
Restriction: Authorized patrons, Circ to mem only, In-house use for visitors, Non-resident fee
Friends of the Library Group

BERNARDSVILLE

P BERNARDSVILLE PUBLIC LIBRARY, One Anderson Hill Rd, 07924. SAN 310-0189. Tel: 908-766-0118. FAX: 908-766-2464. E-mail: librarian@bernardsvillelibrary.org. Web Site: www.bernardsvillelibrary.org. *Exec Dir,* Alexandria Arnold; *Bus Mgr,* Jill Hackett; E-mail: jhackett@bernardsvillelibrary.org; *Readers' Serv Manager,* Laura Cole; E-mail: lcole@bernardsvillelibrary.org; *Adult Programs, Youth Serv Mgr,* Meaghan Darling; E-mail: mdarling@bernardsvillelibrary.org; Staff 17 (MLS 2, Non-MLS 15)
Founded 1902. Pop 7,805; Circ 213,753
Library Holdings: AV Mats 13,412; Bks on Deafness & Sign Lang 48; Large Print Bks 428; Bk Titles 68,732; Per Subs 177
Special Collections: Family Literacy, ESL; Local History, bks, microfilm. Oral History
Automation Activity & Vendor Info: (Circulation) Innovative Interfaces, Inc
Wireless access
Function: 24/7 Electronic res, 24/7 Online cat, Adult bk club, After school storytime, Archival coll, Art exhibits, Audiobks on Playaways & MP3, Audiobks via web, Bilingual assistance for Spanish patrons, Bk club(s), Bks on CD, Children's prog, Computer training, Computers for patron use, E-Readers, Electronic databases & coll, Free DVD rentals, ILL available, Internet access, Life-long learning prog for all ages, Magazines, Meeting rooms, Movies, Museum passes, Music CDs, Online cat, Photocopying/Printing, Preschool outreach, Printer for laptops & handheld devices, Prog for adults, Prog for children & young adult, Ref & res, Ref serv available, Spanish lang bks, Story hour, Study rm, Summer reading prog, Tax forms
Publications: Bernardsville Library (Newsletter)
Partic in Morris-Union Federation; Raritan Valley Fedn of Librs
Special Services for the Deaf - Adult & family literacy prog; Bks on deafness & sign lang; Closed caption videos; TTY equip
Special Services for the Blind - Aids for in-house use; Audio mat; Bks on CD; Low vision equip; Magnifiers; Talking bks
Open Mon-Wed 10-8, Thurs 1-5, Fri 10-5, Sat 10-2, Sun 1-5
Friends of the Library Group

BEVERLY

P BEVERLY FREE LIBRARY*, 441 Cooper St, 08010. SAN 310-0197. Tel: 609-387-1259. FAX: 609-387-1259. E-mail: beverly@bcls.lib.nj.us. *Mgr,* Barbara Johnson Kelly; Staff 1 (MLS 1)
Founded 1929. Pop 10,525
Library Holdings: Bk Vols 10,830
Subject Interests: NJ
Automation Activity & Vendor Info: (Cataloging) Horizon
Mem of Burlington County Library
Open Tues & Fri 5pm-9pm, Wed & Sat 12-4

BLACKWOOD

J CAMDEN COUNTY COLLEGE LIBRARY*, Wolverton Library, College Dr, 08012. (Mail add: PO Box 200, 08012-0200), SAN 310-0200. Tel: 856-227-7200, Ext 4615. Circulation Tel: 856-227-7200, Ext 4404. Interlibrary Loan Service Tel: 856-874-6001. Reference Tel: 856-227-7200, Ext 4408. FAX: 856-374-4897. Web Site: library.camdencc.edu/. *Dir,*

Position Currently Open; *Asst Dir,* Isabel Gray; E-mail: igray@camdencc.edu; *Ref & Instruction Librn,* Olivia Nellums; Tel: 856-227-7200, Ext 4405, E-mail: onellums@camdencc.edu; *Coordr, Ref & Instrul Serv, Web Developer,* Miriam Mlynarski; Tel: 856-227-7200, Ext 4615, E-mail: mmlynarski@camdencc.edu; *Circ Serv, Tech Serv,* Lorraine Baggett-Heuser; Tel: 856-227-7200, Ext 4417, E-mail: lbaggett@camdencc.edu; *Coll Develop,* Patricia Fazio; Tel: 856-227-7200, Ext 4402, E-mail: pfazio@camdencc.edu; Staff 10.5 (MLS 6.5, Non-MLS 4)
Founded 1967. Enrl 16,000; Fac 900; Highest Degree: Associate
Library Holdings: Bks on Deafness & Sign Lang 250; CDs 600; e-books 42,000; e-journals 20,000; Bk Titles 70,000; Bk Vols 93,500; Per Subs 209; Videos 2,750
Subject Interests: Art, Judaica
Automation Activity & Vendor Info: (Cataloging) Innovative Interfaces, Inc; (Circulation) Innovative Interfaces, Inc; (Course Reserve) Innovative Interfaces, Inc; (ILL) L4U Library Software; (OPAC) Innovative Interfaces, Inc; (Serials) Innovative Interfaces, Inc
Wireless access
Partic in LibraryLinkNJ, The New Jersey Library Cooperative; LYRASIS; OCLC Online Computer Library Center, Inc; Virtual Academic Library Environment
Restriction: In-house use for visitors

BLOOMFIELD

C BLOOMFIELD COLLEGE LIBRARY*, Liberty St & Oakland Ave, 07003. SAN 310-0235. Tel: 973-748-9000, Ext 1332. FAX: 973-566-9674. Web Site: www.bloomfield.edu/academics/library. *Dir,* Dr Greg R Reid; E-mail: greg_reid@bloomfield.edu; *Fac Librn,* Mark Jackson; Tel: 973-748-9000, Ext 1714, E-mail: mark_jackson@bloomfield.edu; Staff 4 (MLS 4)
Founded 1869. Enrl 2,000; Fac 170; Highest Degree: Bachelor
Library Holdings: Bk Vols 58,000; Per Subs 600
Subject Interests: Educ, Multicultural diversity
Automation Activity & Vendor Info: (Cataloging) SirsiDynix; (Circulation) SirsiDynix; (OPAC) SirsiDynix
Wireless access
Partic in OCLC Online Computer Library Center, Inc; Proquest Dialog; Virtual Academic Library Environment
Open Mon-Thurs 7:30am-10pm, Fri 7:30-5, Sat 8-5, Sun 12-5
Departmental Libraries:
MEDIA CENTER, 80 Oakland Ave, 07003. Tel: 973-748-9000, Ext 1370. FAX: 973-566-9483. E-mail: media_center@bloomfield.edu. Web Site: www.bloomfield.edu/academics/library/media-center. *Dir,* Barbara Isacson; E-mail: barbara_isacson@bloomfield.edu
Library Holdings: AV Mats 4,000
Open Mon-Fri 8:30-4:30
Restriction: Non-circulating

P BLOOMFIELD PUBLIC LIBRARY, 90 Broad St, 07003. SAN 310-0243. Tel: 973-566-6200. Reference E-mail: reference@bloomfield.bccls.org. Web Site: www.bplnj.org. *Dir,* Holly Belli; E-mail: belli@bloomfield.bccls.org; *Head, Children's Servx,* Cheryl Locastro; E-mail: cheryl.locastro@bloomfield.bccls.org; *Head, Circ,* Jessica Osolin; E-mail: jessica.osolin@bloomfield.bccls.org; *Head, Ref,* Linda Pendergrass; E-mail: linda.pendergrass@bloomfield.bccls.org; *Librn,* Lisa Cohn; E-mail: lisa.cohn@bloomfield.bccls.org; *Supv Librn, Adult Serv,* Lisa Hoffman; E-mail: lisa.hoffman@bloomfield.bccls.org; Staff 23 (MLS 8, Non-MLS 15)
Founded 1924. Pop 48,000; Circ 201,941
Library Holdings: Bk Vols 160,000
Special Collections: Business & Labor Coll, bks, micro, per; Music Coll
Subject Interests: Labor, Local hist, Music
Automation Activity & Vendor Info: (Circulation) Infor Library & Information Solutions
Wireless access
Partic in OCLC Online Computer Library Center, Inc
Open Mon 1-8, Tues-Sat 10-5
Friends of the Library Group

S CHICAGO BRIDGE & IRON CO*, Technology Library, 1515 Broad St, 07003. SAN 310-0251. Tel: 973-893-2257. E-mail: cltb.library@cbi.com. *Librn,* Carol Schneider-Linn; Staff 1 (MLS 1)
Founded 1930
Library Holdings: Bk Vols 11,000; Per Subs 40
Special Collections: Crude Oil, bks & pamphlets
Subject Interests: Chem engr, Petrochemicals, Petroleum refining
Automation Activity & Vendor Info: (OPAC) Inmagic, Inc.; (Serials) Professional Software
Wireless access
Partic in New Jersey Library Network
Open Mon-Fri 9-2:30
Restriction: Open to pub by appt only

BLOOMINGDALE

P BLOOMINGDALE FREE PUBLIC LIBRARY, Municipal Bldg, 101 Hamburg Tpk, 07403. SAN 310-0278. Tel: 973-838-0077. FAX: 973-838-2482. E-mail: bfpl@bloomingdalelibrary.org. Web Site: www.bloomingdalelibrary.org. *Libr Dir,* Patricia Perugino; E-mail: perugino@bloomingdalelibrary.org; *Children's Prog Coordr,* Monica Galiano; E-mail: galiano@bloomingdalelibrary.org
Founded 1926. Pop 7,610; Circ 37,369
Library Holdings: Bk Titles 26,867
Subject Interests: Bloomingdale hist
Automation Activity & Vendor Info: (Cataloging) SirsiDynix; (Circulation) SirsiDynix
Wireless access
Partic in PALS Plus, The Computer Consortium of Passaic County Libraries
Open Mon-Wed 10-7, Thurs 10-5, Fri 10-2, Sat 10-1

BOGOTA

P BOGOTA PUBLIC LIBRARY*, 375 Larch Ave, 07603. SAN 310-0286. Tel: 201-488-7185. FAX: 201-342-2094. Circulation E-mail: bogtcirc@bccls.org. Web Site: www.bogotapubliclibrary.org. *Dir,* Chelsea Dodd Coleman; E-mail: director@bogota.bccls.org; Staff 7 (MLS 1, Non-MLS 6)
Founded 1916. Pop 8,507; Circ 50,395
Library Holdings: Bk Vols 36,564; Per Subs 82
Automation Activity & Vendor Info: (Cataloging) SirsiDynix; (Circulation) SirsiDynix; (OPAC) SirsiDynix
Wireless access
Function: 24/7 Electronic res, 24/7 Online cat, Adult bk club, Art exhibits, Bilingual assistance for Spanish patrons, Bk club(s), Bks on CD, Children's prog, Computers for patron use, Electronic databases & coll, Free DVD rentals, Genealogy discussion group, ILL available, Internet access, Life-long learning prog for all ages, Magazines, Mail & tel request accepted, Movies, Online cat, Online ref, Outreach serv, Outside serv via phone, mail, e-mail & web, OverDrive digital audio bks, Passport agency, Photocopying/Printing, Prog for adults, Prog for children & young adult, Ref & res, Ref serv available, Scanner, Spanish lang bks, STEM programs, Story hour, Summer reading prog, Teen prog, Telephone ref
Partic in Bergen County Cooperative Library System, Inc; NJ Regional Libr Coop, Region 2
Open Mon, Tues & Thurs 10-9, Wed & Fri 10-5, Sat 10-3
Friends of the Library Group

BOONTON

P BOONTON HOLMES PUBLIC LIBRARY*, 621 Main St, 07005. SAN 310-0308. Tel: 973-334-2980. FAX: 973-334-3917. E-mail: bhpl@boontonholmeslibrary.org. Web Site: www.boontonholmeslibrary.org. *Dir,* Stephanie Gabelmann; E-mail: stephanie.gabelmann@boontonholmeslibrary.org; *Youth Serv Librn,* Anne O'Gorman; Staff 4 (MLS 3, Non-MLS 1)
Founded 1893. Pop 8,400; Circ 49,000
Library Holdings: Bk Titles 32,000; Bk Vols 35,000; Per Subs 47
Special Collections: Boonton Newspaper Coll, microfiche; Boonton Photographs; Boonton Postcards; Boonton Yearbooks
Subject Interests: Local hist
Wireless access
Function: Adult bk club, Archival coll, Audiobks via web, Bi-weekly Writer's Group, Bk club(s), Bks on cassette, Bks on CD, Chess club, Children's prog, Computer training, Computers for patron use, Electronic databases & coll, ILL available, Internet access, Museum passes, Music CDs, Notary serv, Online cat, Online ref, OverDrive digital audio bks, Photocopying/Printing, Preschool outreach, Prog for adults, Prog for children & young adult, Scanner, Senior computer classes, Story hour, Summer reading prog, Tax forms, Teen prog, Telephone ref, VHS videos, Wheelchair accessible
Partic in LibraryLinkNJ, The New Jersey Library Cooperative; Morris Automated Information Network
Open Mon-Thurs 10-9, Fri 10-5, Sat 10-3, Sun (Sept-June) 1-5
Friends of the Library Group

BORDENTOWN

S ALBERT C WAGNER YOUTH CORRECTIONAL FACILITY LIBRARY*, 500 Ward Ave, 08505-2928. (Mail add: PO Box 500, 08505-0500). Tel: 609-298-0500. *Library Contact,* James McConnell
Library Holdings: Bk Titles 14,300
Restriction: Staff use only

BRADLEY BEACH

P BRADLEY BEACH PUBLIC LIBRARY*, 511 Fourth Ave, 07720. SAN 310-0367. Tel: 732-776-2995. FAX: 732-774-4591. Web Site: www.bradleybeachlibrary.org. *Dir,* Ashley Foglia; E-mail: ashley@bradleybeachlibrary.org; Staff 4 (MLS 1, Non-MLS 3)
Founded 1927. Pop 4,973; Circ 24,941
Library Holdings: AV Mats 1,648; Bk Titles 30,147; Bk Vols 37,334; Per Subs 51
Automation Activity & Vendor Info: (Acquisitions) Auto-Graphics, Inc; (Cataloging) Auto-Graphics, Inc; (Circulation) Auto-Graphics, Inc; (ILL) Auto-Graphics, Inc; (OPAC) Auto-Graphics, Inc; (Serials) Auto-Graphics, Inc
Wireless access
Open Mon & Fri 9-5, Tues & Thurs 9-8, Wed 9-6, Sat 9-1
Friends of the Library Group

BRIDGETON

P BRIDGETON FREE PUBLIC LIBRARY*, 150 E Commerce St, 08302-2684. SAN 310-0375. Tel: 856-451-2620. E-mail: Bpl@bridgetonlibrary.org. Web Site: www.bridgetonlibrary.org. *Dir,* Linda McFadden; Staff 2 (MLS 2)
Founded 1921. Pop 24,000; Circ 36,000
Library Holdings: Bk Titles 57,000; Bk Vols 58,000; Per Subs 45
Special Collections: American Indians (Lenni-Lenapes Coll); South Jersey History
Automation Activity & Vendor Info: (Cataloging) SirsiDynix; (Circulation) SirsiDynix; (OPAC) SirsiDynix
Wireless access
Open Tues-Thurs 10-8, Fri 9-5, Sat 9-4
Friends of the Library Group

L CUMBERLAND COUNTY LAW LIBRARY*, Cumberland County Courthouse, 1st Flr, Broad & Fayette Sts, 08302. SAN 328-1515. Tel: 856-453-4530. *Librn,* Diane Frank
Founded 1909
Library Holdings: Bk Vols 600
Wireless access
Open Mon-Fri 8:30-4:30
Restriction: Non-circulating to the pub

P CUMBERLAND COUNTY LIBRARY*, 800 E Commerce St, 08302-2295. SAN 310-0383. Tel: 856-453-2210. FAX: 856-451-1940. Web Site: www.clueslibs.org. *Dir,* Susanne Sacchetti; *IT & Security Mgr,* Myron Estelle; *Circ Supvr,* Margaret Allen; *Ref (Info Servs),* Tom Ayars; Staff 7 (MLS 7)
Founded 1963. Pop 146,438; Circ 84,306
Library Holdings: Bk Vols 100,000; Per Subs 170
Special Collections: Adult Basic Education Materials; New Jersey Materials. State Document Depository
Automation Activity & Vendor Info: (Cataloging) SirsiDynix; (Circulation) SirsiDynix; (OPAC) SirsiDynix
Wireless access
Partic in Cumberland Libraries United Electronic System; OCLC Online Computer Library Center, Inc
Special Services for the Deaf - Staff with knowledge of sign lang
Special Services for the Blind - Bks on CD
Open Mon-Wed 9-8, Thurs-Sat 9-5
Friends of the Library Group
Bookmobiles: 1. In Charge, Courtenay Reece. Bk vols 5,000

S NEW JERSEY DEPARTMENT OF CORRECTIONS*, South Woods State Prison - Facility I Library, 215 Burlington Rd S, 08302. Tel: 856-459-7000, Ext 8145. FAX: 856-459-8125. Web Site: www.state.nj.us/corrections. *Librn,* Heather Bolden; E-mail: heather.bolden@doc.nj.gov
Founded 1997
Library Holdings: Bk Titles 1,500; Bk Vols 1,800
Special Collections: Law Coll
Publications: NJ Legal Library
Restriction: Not open to pub
Branches:
SOUTH WOODS STATE PRISON - FACILITY II LIBRARY, 215 Burlington Rd S, 08302. Tel: 856-459-8249.
Library Holdings: Bk Vols 1,250
Special Collections: Law Coll
Restriction: Not open to pub
SOUTH WOODS STATE PRISON - FACILITY III LIBRARY, 215 Burlington Rd S, 08302. Tel: 856-459-8349.
Library Holdings: Bk Vols 1,250
Special Collections: Law Coll
Restriction: Not open to pub

BRIDGEWATER

L NORRIS MCLAUGHLIN*, Law Library, 400 Crossing Blvd, 8th Flr, 08807. (Mail add: PO Box 5933, 08807-5933), SAN 372-4824. Tel: 908-722-0700. FAX: 908-722-0755. Web Site: norrismclaughlin.com. *Librn,* Janice Lustiger; E-mail: jlustiger@norris-law.com
Library Holdings: Bk Vols 10,000
Restriction: Not open to pub

S SOMERSET COUNTY HISTORICAL SOCIETY, Van Horn Library, Nine Van Veghten Dr, 08807-3259. SAN 375-507X. Tel: 908-218-1281. E-mail: info@somersethistorynj.org. Web Site: somersethistorynj.org. *Librn,* Position Currently Open. Subject Specialists: *Genealogy, Local hist,* Position Currently Open; Staff 1 (MLS 1)
Founded 1882
Library Holdings: Bk Titles 900; Bk Vols 1,000
Special Collections: Archives (Somerset County NJ); Early Somerset Coll, pamphlets, photogs, newsp, clippings; Revolutionary War Research (A A Boom Coll); United States Revolution 1778-1783
Subject Interests: Genealogy, Local hist, State hist
Wireless access
Function: Res libr, Res performed for a fee
Open Tues 12-3
Restriction: Non-circulating

P SOMERSET COUNTY LIBRARY SYSTEM OF NEW JERSEY*, One Vogt Dr, 08807-2136. (Mail add: PO Box 6700, 08807-0700), SAN 351-3661. Tel: 908-458-8415. E-mail: bridgewater@sclibnj.org. Web Site: sclsnj.org. *Adminr, County Librn,* Brian Auger; Tel: 908-458-8401, E-mail: bauger@sclibnj.org; *Dir, Pub Relations, Dir, Mkt,* Carolann DeMatos; Tel: 908-458-8404, E-mail: cdematos@sclibnj.org; *Dir, Finance & Operations,* Brian Morgan; Tel: 908-458-8402, E-mail: bmorgan@sclibnj.org; *Dir, Human Res,* Deanna Rivera; Tel: 908-458-8407, E-mail: drivera@sclibnj.org; *Dir, Operations,* Lynn Hoffman; Tel: 908-458-4940, E-mail: lhoffman@sclibnj.org; *Pub Serv Dir,* Christopher Korenowsky; Tel: 908-458-4931, E-mail: ckorenowsky@sclibnj.org; *Automation Mgr,* Wendy Clarkson; Tel: 908-458-4942, E-mail: wclarkson@sclibnj.org; *Mgr, Br Serv,* Lauren Ryan; Tel: 908-458-8451, E-mail: lryan@sclibnj.org; Staff 206 (MLS 46, Non-MLS 160)
Founded 1930. Pop 176,402; Circ 3,104,862
Library Holdings: Audiobooks 22,423; DVDs 53,292; e-books 2,048; Bk Vols 708,652
Special Collections: The New Jersey Room, bks, pamphlets, maps, micro. Oral History; State Document Depository
Automation Activity & Vendor Info: (Acquisitions) Innovative Interfaces, Inc; (Cataloging) Innovative Interfaces, Inc; (Circulation) Innovative Interfaces, Inc; (ILL) Innovative Interfaces, Inc; (Media Booking) ADLiB; (OPAC) Innovative Interfaces, Inc; (Serials) Innovative Interfaces, Inc
Wireless access
Function: ILL available
Partic in OCLC Online Computer Library Center, Inc
Special Services for the Blind - Accessible computers; Assistive/Adapted tech devices, equip & products; Audiovision-a radio reading serv; Bks on CD; Bks on flash-memory cartridges; Digital talking bk; Digital talking bk machines; Home delivery serv; Info on spec aids & appliances; Large print bks; Large print bks & talking machines; Low vision equip; Newsline for the Blind; Talking bk serv referral; Talking bks; Talking bks & player equip; VisualTek equip
Open Mon-Thurs 10-8, Fri & Sat 10-6, Sun 1-5
Friends of the Library Group
Branches: 9
BRANCHBURG READING STATION, The Station House, 412 Olive St, Neshanic Station, 08853. Tel: 908-369-5355.
Library Holdings: AV Mats 30; Bk Vols 4,000
Open Mon & Thurs 6:30pm-8pm, Wed 1:30-5, Sat 10-12
Friends of the Library Group
HILLSBOROUGH PUBLIC, Hillsborough Municipal Complex, 379 S Branch Rd, Hillsborough, 08844, SAN 351-3696. Tel: 908-458-8420. E-mail: hillsborough@sclibnj.org. *Br Mgr,* Karen Pifher; E-mail: kpifher@sclibnj.org; *Head, Youth Serv,* Jessica Bauer; E-mail: jbauer@sclibnj.org; *Circ Supvr,* Ziyan Wang; E-mail: zwang@sclibnj.org; Staff 28 (MLS 10, Non-MLS 18)
Founded 1966. Pop 42,000; Circ 450,155
Library Holdings: Bk Titles 107,000; Per Subs 200
Function: Adult bk club, Adult literacy prog, Electronic databases & coll, Homework prog, ILL available, Internet access, Music CDs, Photocopying/Printing, Ref serv available, Tax forms, Wheelchair accessible
Open Mon 10-8, Tues-Fri 10-4:30
Friends of the Library Group
MARY JACOBS MEMORIAL, 64 Washington St, Rocky Hill, 08553, SAN 351-3726. Tel: 908-458-8430. E-mail: maryjacobs@sclibnj.org. *Br Mgr,* Manuela Miracle; E-mail: mmiracle@sclibnj.org; Staff 17 (MLS 4, Non-MLS 13)
Founded 1974. Pop 19,000; Circ 215,000

Library Holdings: Bk Vols 100,070; Per Subs 170
Open Mon-Thurs 10-8, Fri & Sat 10-6
Friends of the Library Group

NORTH PLAINFIELD LIBRARY, Six Rockview Ave, North Plainfield, 07060, SAN 351-3750. Tel: 908-458-8435. E-mail: northplainfield@sclibnj.org. *Br Mgr,* Christal Blue; E-mail: cblue@sclibnj.org
Pop 22,464; Circ 168,452
Library Holdings: Bk Vols 85,000; Per Subs 175
Open Mon-Thurs 10-8, Fri & Sat 10-6

PEAPACK & GLADSTONE PUBLIC, School St, Peapack, 07977, SAN 310-1819. Tel: 908-458-8440. E-mail: peapack-gladstone@sclibnj.org. *Br Mgr, Ref Serv, Ad,* Melissa Banks; E-mail: mbanks@sclibnj.org; *Head, Circ, YA Serv,* Melissa John-Williams; E-mail: mwilliams@sclibnj.org; *Ch Serv,* Jenna Galley; E-mail: jgalley@sclibnj.org; Staff 9 (MLS 9)
Founded 1936. Pop 2,433; Circ 31,000
Library Holdings: Large Print Bks 720,591; Bk Vols 37,000; Per Subs 70
Special Collections: Equestrian Coll
Publications: The Trumpet (Newsletter)
Open Mon-Thurs 10-8, Fri & Sat 10-6
Friends of the Library Group

SOMERVILLE PUBLIC LIBRARY, 35 West End Ave, Somerville, 08876, SAN 310-5091. Tel: 908-458-8445. FAX: 908-231-0608. E-mail: somerville@sclibnj.org. *Br Mgr,* Doug Poswencyk; E-mail: dposwenc@sclibnj.org
Founded 1871. Pop 12,423; Circ 66,000
Library Holdings: AV Mats 5,000; Bks on Deafness & Sign Lang 20; High Interest/Low Vocabulary Bk Vols 200; Bk Titles 53,457; Bk Vols 58,640; Per Subs 120; Talking Bks 1,010; Videos 2,600
Special Collections: New Jersey Archives Holdings; Paul Robeson-iana; Somerville & Somerset County, New Jersey Genealogical Material. Oral History
Subject Interests: City hist, Local hist, NJ, Somerset County hist
Function: Bks on cassette, Bks on CD, CD-ROM, Chess club, Children's prog, Computer training, Computers for patron use, Digital talking bks, Electronic databases & coll, Family literacy, Free DVD rentals, Holiday prog, ILL available, Magnifiers for reading, Mail & tel request accepted, Music CDs, Notary serv, Online cat, Outside serv via phone, mail, e-mail & web, OverDrive digital audio bks, Photocopying/Printing, Preschool outreach, Prog for adults, Prog for children & young adult, Senior outreach, Spoken cassettes & CDs, Spoken cassettes & DVDs, Summer reading prog, Tax forms, Teen prog, Telephone ref
Open Mon-Thurs 9:30-9, Fri & Sat 9:30-5
Restriction: Non-resident fee
Friends of the Library Group

WARREN TOWNSHIP BRANCH, 42 Mountain Blvd, Warren, 07059, SAN 351-3777. Tel: 908-458-8450. E-mail: warrentownship@sclibnj.org. *Br Mgr,* Lauren Ryan; E-mail: lryan@sclibnj.org
Pop 14,260; Circ 181,500
Library Holdings: Bk Vols 100,000; Per Subs 250
Open Mon-Thurs 10-8, Fri & Sat 10-6, Sun 1-5
Friends of the Library Group

WASHINGTON VALLEY, Washington Valley Rd, Martinsville, 08836, SAN 310-2734. Tel: 732-356-2363.
Founded 1950. Pop 3,400; Circ 4,533
Library Holdings: Bk Vols 4,800
Open Mon & Wed 2-4 & 7-9, Tues, Thurs & Fri 2-4, Sat 10-12

WATCHUNG PUBLIC, 12 Stirling Rd, Watchung, 07069, SAN 310-5814. Tel: 908-458-8455. E-mail: watchung@sclibnj.org. *Br Mgr,* Hannah Kerwin; E-mail: hkerwin@sclibnj.org; *Circ Serv,* Elaine Stringer; E-mail: estringer@sclibnj.org; *Youth Serv,* Lynn Mazur; E-mail: lmazur@sclibnj.org
Circ 85,715
Library Holdings: Bk Vols 36,595
Open Mon-Thurs 10-8, Fri & Sat 10-6
Friends of the Library Group

BRIELLE

P BRIELLE PUBLIC LIBRARY, 610 South St, 08730. SAN 310-0413. Tel: 732-528-9381. E-mail: briellelibrary@gmail.com. Web Site: www.briellelibrary.com, www.briellepubliclibrary.org. *Libr Dir,* Janet Torsney; Staff 8 (MLS 1, Non-MLS 7)
Founded 1954. Pop 4,800; Circ 58,000
Library Holdings: Bk Vols 45,000; Per Subs 81
Subject Interests: NJ hist
Automation Activity & Vendor Info: (Acquisitions) SirsiDynix; (Cataloging) SirsiDynix; (Circulation) SirsiDynix; (OPAC) SirsiDynix
Wireless access
Mem of Monmouth County Library
Partic in LibraryLinkNJ, The New Jersey Library Cooperative
Open Mon, Tues & Thurs 10-7:30, Wed & Fri 12-5, Sat 10-1

BROOKSIDE

P MENDHAM TOWNSHIP LIBRARY*, Two W Main St, 07926. (Mail add: PO Box 500, 07926-0500), SAN 310-0421. Tel: 973-543-4018. FAX: 973-543-5472. Web Site: www.mendhamtownshiplibrary.org. *Dir,* Stephanie Cotton; E-mail: stephanie.cotton@mendhamtwplib.org; Staff 6 (MLS 1, Non-MLS 5)
Pop 4,900; Circ 60,000
Library Holdings: Bk Titles 40,000; Per Subs 70
Special Collections: Bks on Tape; Gardening Coll; Local History Coll; Mysteries Coll
Automation Activity & Vendor Info: (Cataloging) SirsiDynix; (Circulation) SirsiDynix; (OPAC) SirsiDynix
Wireless access
Publications: Newsletter
Partic in Morris Automated Information Network
Special Services for the Blind - Bks on cassette
Open Mon 10-8, Tues-Thurs 9:30-8, Fri 10-6, Sat 10-3, Sun (Sept-June) 2-5
Friends of the Library Group

BROWNS MILLS

M DEBORAH HEART & LUNG CENTER*, Edith & Jack Tobin Medical Library, 200 Trenton Rd, 08015. SAN 310-043X. Tel: 609-893-6611, Ext 4397. FAX: 609-893-1566. Web Site: demanddeborah.org/healthcare-professionals/medical-library. *Dir,* Position Currently Open
Founded 1971
Library Holdings: Bk Titles 2,600; Bk Vols 3,200; Per Subs 150
Subject Interests: Cardio-pulmonary diseases
Partic in Mid-Eastern Regional Med Libr Serv
Restriction: Non-circulating to the pub, Open to pub by appt only

BUENA

S NEW KUBAN EDUCATION & WELFARE ASSOCIATION*, All Cossack Museum & Library, 228 Don Rd, 08310. (Mail add: 521 Weymouth Rd, 08310), SAN 371-9286. Tel: 856-697-2255. FAX: 856-697-2255. *Librn,* Nina Sienczenko; E-mail: nkewa@comcast.net; Staff 1 (Non-MLS 1)
Founded 1953
Library Holdings: Bk Titles 5,000
Special Collections: Cossack Culture & History Coll
Subject Interests: Russian hist, Ukrainian hist
Function: Res libr
Restriction: Non-circulating, Open by appt only

BURLINGTON

S BURLINGTON COUNTY HISTORICAL SOCIETY*, Delia Biddle-Pugh Library, 457 High St, 08016-4514. SAN 310-0456. Tel: 609-386-4773. Reference Tel: 609-386-4773, Ext 2. FAX: 609-386-4828. Web Site: www.burlingtoncountyhistoricalsociety.org. *Curator,* Anne Baker
Library Holdings: Bk Vols 4,000
Special Collections: Deeds; Historic Manuscripts; James Fenimore Cooper Coll; Photographs; Vital Statistics 1795-present
Subject Interests: Genealogy, Local hist
Wireless access
Open Wed & Thurs 1-5
Restriction: Non-circulating to the pub

P LIBRARY COMPANY OF BURLINGTON*, 23 W Union St, 08016. SAN 310-0464. Tel: 609-386-1273. Web Site: www.librarycompanyofburlington.org. *Dir,* Sharon Vincz; E-mail: svincz@bcls.lib.nj.us
Founded 1757. Pop 20,000; Circ 30,394
Jan 2017-Dec 2017. Mats Exp $6,000. Sal $61,000
Library Holdings: Audiobooks 148; Bks on Deafness & Sign Lang 8; CDs 335; DVDs 1,100; Large Print Bks 75; Bk Vols 58,770; Per Subs 54
Special Collections: Early 18th Century Vols; New Jersey History Coll
Automation Activity & Vendor Info: (Cataloging) SirsiDynix; (Circulation) SirsiDynix; (OPAC) SirsiDynix
Wireless access
Mem of Burlington County Library
Special Services for the Blind - Large print bks; Talking bks & player equip
Open Mon-Thurs 11-8, Fri (Sept-June) 1-6, Sat (Sept-June) 11-3
Friends of the Library Group

BUTLER

P BUTLER PUBLIC LIBRARY*, One Ace Rd, 07405. SAN 310-0480. Tel: 973-838-3262. FAX: 973-838-9436. Web Site: www.butlerlibrary.org. *Dir,* Luis Rodriguez; E-mail: luis.rodriguez@butlerlibrary.org
Founded 1924. Pop 7,600; Circ 37,000

Library Holdings: Bk Titles 43,000; Bk Vols 44,000; Per Subs 90
Automation Activity & Vendor Info: (Cataloging) SirsiDynix; (Circulation) SirsiDynix; (OPAC) SirsiDynix
Wireless access
Open Mon-Thurs 10-8, Fri 10-5, Sat (Sept-June) 10-3
Friends of the Library Group

CALDWELL

P CALDWELL PUBLIC LIBRARY*, 268 Bloomfield Ave, 07006-5198. SAN 310-0502. Tel: 973-226-2837. FAX: 973-403-8606. E-mail: librarian@caldwellpl.org. Web Site: www.caldwellpl.org. *Dir,* Claudine Pascale; *Youth Serv Librn,* Kristen Churchill; Staff 7 (MLS 1, Non-MLS 6)
Founded 1907. Pop 7,584; Circ 67,478
Library Holdings: Bk Titles 35,784; Bk Vols 37,708; Per Subs 85
Subject Interests: Local hist
Automation Activity & Vendor Info: (Circulation) SirsiDynix-iBistro; (OPAC) SirsiDynix-iBistro
Wireless access
Function: ILL available
Partic in Essex County Coop Librs; PALS Plus, The Computer Consortium of Passaic County Libraries
Open Mon & Fri 9-5, Tues-Thurs 9-8, Sat (Sept-June) 9-1

C CALDWELL UNIVERSITY, Jennings Library, 120 Bloomfield Ave, 07006. SAN 310-0499. Tel: 973-618-3337. Interlibrary Loan Service Tel: 973-618-3564. FAX: 973-618-3360. E-mail: library@caldwell.edu. Web Site: www.caldwell.edu/library. *Interim Head Librn,* Victoria Swanson; Tel: 973-618-3311, E-mail: viswanson@caldwell.edu; *Librn,* Christina Getaz; E-mail: cgetaz@caldwell.edu; *Archives,* Kimberly Lynch; E-mail: kalynch@caldwell.edu; *ILL,* Roseann Pennisi; E-mail: rpennisi@caldwell.edu; *Tech Serv,* Ellen Johnston; Tel: 973-618-3502, E-mail: ejohnston@caldwell.edu; Staff 10 (MLS 4, Non-MLS 6)
Founded 1939. Enrl 2,098; Fac 277; Highest Degree: Doctorate
Library Holdings: e-books 334,803; e-journals 70,690; Bk Titles 131,665; Bk Vols 146,281; Per Subs 441
Special Collections: American History (Grover Cleveland Coll)
Subject Interests: Archit, Art, Educ curric, Hist, Lit, Relig studies, Women's studies
Wireless access
Publications: General Information Brochure; Monthly New Acquisitions List; Newsletter
Partic in Essex County Coop Librs; LibraryLinkNJ, The New Jersey Library Cooperative; OCLC Online Computer Library Center, Inc; Virtual Academic Library Environment
Open Mon-Thurs 7:30am-Midnight, Fri 7:30-4:30, Sat 9-5, Sun 1-9

CALIFON

P BUNNVALE PUBLIC LIBRARY, Seven Bunnvale Rd, 07830. Tel: 908-638-8523, Ext 401. E-mail: bunnvalelibrary@gmail.com. Web Site: www.hclibrary.us/branches/bunnvale.htm, www.lebanontownship.net/services/library.aspx. *Head Librn,* Karla Drumm
Founded 1978
Library Holdings: AV Mats 240; Large Print Bks 30; Bk Vols 58,427; Per Subs 50; Talking Bks 250
Automation Activity & Vendor Info: (Cataloging) SirsiDynix; (Circulation) SirsiDynix; (OPAC) SirsiDynix
Wireless access
Mem of Hunterdon County Library
Open Wed 1-8, Thurs & Fri 9-5, Sat 9-2
Friends of the Library Group

CAMDEN

S CAMDEN COUNTY HISTORICAL SOCIETY*, Richard H Hineline Research Library, 1900 Park Blvd, 08103-3611. (Mail add: PO Box 378, Collingswood, 08108-0378), SAN 310-0529. Tel: 856-964-3333. E-mail: admin@cchsnj.org. Web Site: www.cchsnj.org. *Libr Dir,* Bonny Beth Elwell
Founded 1899
Library Holdings: Bk Titles 20,000
Special Collections: Camden Courier Newspaper Coll 1882-1959, microfilm; History of Southern New Jersey (Charles Boyer Coll), author's notes, unpublished bks & ms; Legal History of Southern New Jersey (John D Morgan Coll); South New Jersey Jewish History (Tri-County Jewish Historical Society Coll). Oral History
Subject Interests: Camden County hist, County hist, Genealogy, Genealogy for S NJ & Penn, Hist of Del River Valley, Quaker hist
Wireless access
Function: Res performed for a fee
Publications: Newsletter (Quarterly)
Open Wed-Fri 10-4:30, Sun 12-3

OUR LADY OF LOURDES

M MEDICAL CENTER LIBRARY*, 1600 Haddon Ave, 08103, SAN 350-6134. Tel: 856-757-3548. FAX: 856-757-3215. *Dir,* Susan Cleveland; Staff 1 (MLS 1)
Founded 1973
Library Holdings: Bk Titles 685; Per Subs 50
Special Collections: Hospital Archives
Subject Interests: Clinical health sci
Partic in Basic Health Sciences Library Network; LibraryLinkNJ, The New Jersey Library Cooperative; National Network of Libraries of Medicine Region 1
Open Mon-Fri 6-2:30

M SCHOOL OF NURSING LIBRARY*, 1600 Haddon Ave, 08103, SAN 350-6169. Tel: 856-757-3722. FAX: 856-757-3767. *Librn,* Donna Soultoukis; E-mail: soultoukisd@lourdesnet.org; Staff 1 (MLS 1)
Founded 1961. Fac 14; Highest Degree: Master
Library Holdings: CDs 75; DVDs 50; Bk Titles 575; Bk Vols 1,900; Per Subs 35; Videos 100
Special Collections: Nursing History Coll
Subject Interests: Nursing educ
Automation Activity & Vendor Info: (Cataloging) Follett Software; (Circulation) Follett Software; (OPAC) Follett Software
Partic in National Network of Libraries of Medicine Region 1; New Jersey Health Sciences Library Network; S Jersey Regional Libr Consortium
Open Mon-Thurs 6am-11pm, Fri 6-3:30
Restriction: Students only

RUTGERS UNIVERSITY LIBRARIES

CL CAMDEN LAW LIBRARY*, 217 N Fifth St, 08102-1203, SAN 350-6223. Tel: 856-225-6172. Web Site: lawlibrary.rutgers.edu. *Dir, Law Libr & Assoc Prof of Law,* Anne Dalesandro; Tel: 856-225-8182, E-mail: dalesand@camden.rutgers.edu; *Head, Circ, Head, Digital Planning,* John Jorgensen; Tel: 856-225-6460, E-mail: jjoerg@camden.rutgers.edu; *Head, Govt Doc & Micro, Ref & Instrul Serv Librn,* A Hays Butler; Tel: 856-225-6496, E-mail: ahbutler@camden.rutgers.edu; *Head, ILL, Ref & Instrul Serv Librn,* Eric Gilson; Tel: 856-225-6462; *Head, Ref & Res Serv,* David Batista; Tel: 856-225-6469, E-mail: batista@camden.rutgers.edu; *Head, Tech Serv,* Gloria Chao; Tel: 856-225-6457; *Intl Law Librn, Ref Librn,* Lucy Cox; Tel: 856-225-6464, E-mail: lcox@camden.rutgers.edu; Staff 19 (MLS 7, Non-MLS 12)
Founded 1926. Enrl 770; Fac 46; Highest Degree: Doctorate
Library Holdings: Bk Titles 94,635; Bk Vols 439,801; Per Subs 4,624
Automation Activity & Vendor Info: (Acquisitions) Innovative Interfaces, Inc; (Cataloging) Innovative Interfaces, Inc; (Circulation) Innovative Interfaces, Inc; (ILL) Innovative Interfaces, Inc; (OPAC) Innovative Interfaces, Inc; (Serials) Innovative Interfaces, Inc
Partic in Association of Research Libraries; Center for Research Libraries; LibraryLinkNJ, The New Jersey Library Cooperative; OCLC Research Library Partnership; Partnership for Academic Library Collaborative & Innovation; Research Libraries Information Network
Open Mon-Thurs 8am-Midnight, Fri 8am-10pm, Sat 9-8, Sun 10am-Midnight

C PAUL ROBESON LIBRARY, CAMDEN*, 300 N Fourth St, 08102-1404, SAN 350-6193. Tel: 856-225-2848, 856-225-6034. FAX: 856-225-6428. Web Site: www.libraries.rutgers.edu/robeson. *Dir,* Regina Koury; E-mail: regina.koury@rutgers.edu; *Head, Pub Serv, Ref Serv,* John Maxymuk; E-mail: maxymuk@libraries.rutgers.edu; *Coll Develop Coordr, Ref Librn,* Julie Still; E-mail: still@libraries.rutgers.edu; *Outreach Coordr, Ref & Instruction Librn,* Zara Wilkinson; *Ref,* Katie Anderson
Founded 1951. Highest Degree: Doctorate
Library Holdings: AV Mats 74; Bk Vols 255,804; Per Subs 1,464
Special Collections: State Document Depository; US Document Depository
Subject Interests: Grad educ, Undergrad educ
Special Services for the Blind - Assistive/Adapted tech devices, equip & products
Open Mon-Thurs 7:30am-10pm, Fri 7:30-5, Sat 9-5

G UNITED STATES COURT OF APPEALS*, James Hunter III Memorial Library, One J F Gerry Plaza, Fourth & Cooper, 08101. (Mail add: PO Box 1988, 08101), SAN 377-2055. Tel: 856-968-4859. FAX: 856-968-4871. *Br Librn,* Kristin Schroth; E-mail: kristin_schroth@ca3.uscourts.gov; Staff 1 (MLS 1)
Library Holdings: Bk Vols 10,000
Automation Activity & Vendor Info: (Cataloging) SirsiDynix
Wireless access
Open Mon-Fri 8:30-12:30 & 1:30-4:30

CAPE MAY COURT HOUSE

S CAPE MAY COUNTY HISTORICAL & GENEALOGICAL SOCIETY LIBRARY*, Alexander Memorial, 504 Rte 9 N, 08210. SAN 329-8663. Tel: 609-465-3535. FAX: 609-465-4274. E-mail:

cmchgslibrary@gmail.com. Web Site: www.cmcmuseum.org. *Librn,* Lois Broomell
Library Holdings: Bk Vols 800
Special Collections: Cape May County Family Documents & Bibles; Historic Maps (1872 Beer's Map)
Subject Interests: Family hist, Genealogy, Local hist
Function: Archival coll, Photocopying/Printing, Prog for adults, Ref serv available, Telephone ref
Publications: Cape May County Magazine of History & Genealogy (Annual report)
Open Wed-Fri 10-3:30
Restriction: Internal use only

P CAPE MAY COUNTY LIBRARY*, 30 Mechanic St, 08210. (Mail add: Four Moore Rd - DN2030, 08210), SAN 350-6258. Tel: 609-463-6350. Interlibrary Loan Service Tel: 609-463-6364. Reference Tel: 609-463-6352. Information Services Tel: 609-463-6357. FAX: 609-465-3895. Web Site: www.cmclibrary.org. *Dir,* Andrea Orsini; E-mail: andreao@cmclibrary.org; *ILL,* Dana McAnaney; *Ref (Info Servs),* Lisa Brownback; *Tech Serv,* Allen Jett; Staff 61 (MLS 17, Non-MLS 44)
Founded 1925. Pop 92,250; Circ 525,000
Library Holdings: Bk Titles 180,000; Bk Vols 398,000; Per Subs 700
Automation Activity & Vendor Info: (Acquisitions) Innovative Interfaces, Inc; (Cataloging) Innovative Interfaces, Inc; (Circulation) Innovative Interfaces, Inc; (OPAC) Innovative Interfaces, Inc
Wireless access
Function: 24/7 Electronic res, 24/7 Online cat, 3D Printer, Adult bk club, Audiobks on Playaways & MP3, Audiobks via web, Bk club(s), Bks on CD, Chess club, Children's prog, Computer training, Computers for patron use, Electronic databases & coll, Free DVD rentals, Holiday prog, Home delivery & serv to seniorr ctr & nursing homes, Homebound delivery serv, ILL available, Internet access, Large print keyboards, Magazines, Mango lang, Meeting rooms, Microfiche/film & reading machines, Movies, Music CDs, Online cat, Online info literacy tutorials on the web & in blackboard, Outreach serv, OverDrive digital audio bks, Photocopying/Printing, Preschool outreach, Preschool reading prog, Printer for laptops & handheld devices, Prog for adults, Prog for children & young adult, Ref & res, Scanner, Senior computer classes, Story hour, Study rm, Summer & winter reading prog, Tax forms, Teen prog, Telephone ref, Wheelchair accessible, Workshops, Writing prog
Partic in LibraryLinkNJ, The New Jersey Library Cooperative
Open Mon-Fri 8:30am-9pm, Sat 9-4:30, Sun (Oct-April) 1-5
Branches: 7
CAPE MAY CITY BRANCH, 110 Ocean St, Cape May, 08204, SAN 375-5142. Tel: 609-884-9568. *Br Mgr,* Linda Smith
Library Holdings: Bk Titles 42,000; Per Subs 32
Open Mon, Wed, Fri 9-5, Tues & Thurs 9-8, Sat 9-4
LOWER CAPE BRANCH, 2600 Bayshore Rd, Villas, 08251, SAN 350-6290. Tel: 609-886-8999. *Librn,* Edward Carson; Staff 9 (MLS 2, Non-MLS 7)
Library Holdings: Bk Titles 50,000; Per Subs 100
Open Mon, Wed & Thurs 9-8, Tues & Fri 9-5, Sat 9-4:30
SEA ISLE CITY BRANCH, 4800 Central Ave., Sea Isle City, 08243, SAN 350-6304. Tel: 609-263-8485. *Br Mgr,* Cheryl Opuszynski
Library Holdings: Bk Titles 15,000; Per Subs 54
Open Mon & Wed 9-8, Tues, Thurs-Sat 9-4:30
STONE HARBOR BRANCH, 9516 Second Ave, Stone Harbor, 08247, SAN 350-6312. Tel: 609-368-6809. *Br Mgr,* Kathryn Ridge
Library Holdings: Bk Titles 8,000; Per Subs 35
Open Mon & Thurs 9-8, Tues, Wed-Sat 9-4:30
Friends of the Library Group
UPPER CAPE BRANCH, 2050 Rte 631, Petersburg, 08270, SAN 325-4267. Tel: 609-628-2607. *Br Mgr,* Deanna Pettit; Staff 7 (MLS 1, Non-MLS 6)
Library Holdings: Bk Vols 45,000; Per Subs 80
Open Mon & Thurs 11-7, Tues, Wed, Fri 9-5, Sat 9-4:30
WILDWOOD CREST BRANCH, 6300 Atlantic Ave., Wildwood Crest, 08260, SAN 350-6282. Tel: 609-522-0564. *Br Mgr,* Sandra Carlton
Library Holdings: Bk Titles 15,000
Open Mon & Wed 9-8, Tues, Thurs, Fri, Sat 9-4:30
WOODBINE BRANCH, 800 Monroe St, Woodbine, 08270. Tel: 609-861-2501. *Br Mgr,* Michael Conley
Open Mon, Wed, Thur, Fri 9-4:30, Tues 11-6:30, Sat 9-4:30
Bookmobiles: 1

CARLSTADT

P WILLIAM E DERMODY FREE PUBLIC LIBRARY*, 420 Hackensack St, 07072. SAN 310-060X. Tel: 201-438-8866. FAX: 201-438-2733. E-mail: adultservices@carlstadt.bccls.org. Circulation E-mail: carlcirc@bccls.org. Web Site: carlstadt.bccls.org. *Dir,* Mary Disanza; E-mail: director@carlstadt.bccls.org; *Ch,* Erin Hughes; E-mail: erin.hughes@carlstadt.bccls.org; *Adult Serv,* Rebecca Spero; E-mail: rebecca.spero@carlstadt.bccls.org; Staff 3 (MLS 2, Non-MLS 1)
Founded 1936. Pop 6,127; Circ 67,170
Library Holdings: Bk Vols 30,063; Per Subs 81
Special Collections: Carlstadt Freie Press Newspaper (1873-1926 & 1936-present)
Automation Activity & Vendor Info: (Acquisitions) Baker & Taylor; (Circulation) Innovative Interfaces, Inc; (ILL) Innovative Interfaces, Inc
Wireless access
Function: Adult bk club, Audiobks via web, Bk club(s), Bks on CD, Children's prog, Computer training, Computers for patron use, E-Reserves, Electronic databases & coll, Free DVD rentals, ILL available, Literacy & newcomer serv, Magazines, Magnifiers for reading, Movies, Music CDs, Online cat, OverDrive digital audio bks, Photocopying/Printing, Preschool reading prog, Prog for adults, Prog for children & young adult, Ref serv available, Scanner, Spoken cassettes & CDs, Spoken cassettes & DVDs, Story hour, Summer reading prog, Tax forms, Teen prog
Partic in Bergen County Cooperative Library System, Inc
Open Mon-Thurs 10-9, Fri 10-5, Sat (Fall-Spring) 10-2

CARNEYS POINT

J SALEM COMMUNITY COLLEGE LIBRARY*, Michael S Cettei Memorial Library, 460 Hollywood Ave, 08069. SAN 321-6233. Tel: 856-351-2681. E-mail: Library@salemcc.edu. Web Site: www.salemcc.edu/library. *Dir, Libr & Acad Info Serv,* Jennifer Pierce
Founded 1972. Fac 18; Highest Degree: Associate
Subject Interests: Glassblowing
Automation Activity & Vendor Info: (Cataloging) SirsiDynix; (Circulation) SirsiDynix; (OPAC) SirsiDynix
Wireless access
Partic in Libraries of Gloucester, Salem & Cumberland Information Network; LibraryLinkNJ, The New Jersey Library Cooperative; Virtual Academic Library Environment
Open Mon-Thurs 8-6, Fri 8-4:30
Bookmobiles: 1. Dir, Margaret Masserini

CARTERET

P CARTERET PUBLIC LIBRARY, 100 Cooke Ave, 07008. SAN 310-0626. Tel: 732-541-3830. FAX: 732-541-6948. E-mail: library@carteret.net. Web Site: www.carteret.net/library. *Dir,* Joseph Norris; Staff 10 (MLS 2, Non-MLS 8)
Founded 1931. Pop 22,844; Circ 39,440
Library Holdings: Bk Vols 70,635; Per Subs 140
Automation Activity & Vendor Info: (Cataloging) SirsiDynix; (Circulation) SirsiDynix; (OPAC) SirsiDynix-iBistro
Wireless access
Partic in Libraries of Middlesex Automation Consortium
Open Mon-Sat 9-8; Summer, Mon-Thurs 9-8, Fri & Sat 9-5
Friends of the Library Group

CEDAR GROVE

P CEDAR GROVE FREE PUBLIC LIBRARY*, One Municipal Plaza, 07009. SAN 310-0642. Tel: 973-239-1447. FAX: 973-239-1275. Web Site: www.cedargrovenj.org/library. *Dir,* Catherine Wolverton; Tel: 973-239-1447, Ext 11, E-mail: wolverton@palsplus.org; *Admin Serv,* Francine Falcone; Tel: 973-239-1447, Ext 10, E-mail: falcone@palsplus.org; *Youth Serv,* Natalie Cheetham; Tel: 973-239-1447, Ext 15, E-mail: cheetham@palsplus.org; Staff 8 (MLS 3, Non-MLS 5)
Founded 1965. Pop 12,300; Circ 84,372
Library Holdings: Bk Titles 41,500; Bk Vols 43,000; Per Subs 105
Automation Activity & Vendor Info: (Cataloging) SirsiDynix-WorkFlows; (Circulation) SirsiDynix-WorkFlows; (OPAC) SirsiDynix-Unicorn
Wireless access
Function: ILL available
Partic in LibraryLinkNJ, The New Jersey Library Cooperative; PALS Plus, The Computer Consortium of Passaic County Libraries
Open Mon, Tues & Thurs 9-8, Wed & Fri 9-5, Sat (Sept-June) 9-1
Friends of the Library Group

CEDAR KNOLLS

S OLI SYSTEMS, INC LIBRARY*, 240 Cedar Knolls Rd, Ste 301, 07927. SAN 375-846X. Tel: 973-539-4996. FAX: 973-539-5922. Web Site: www.olisystems.com. *Exec Dir, CEO,* Marshall Rafal; Tel: 973-539-4996, Ext 21, E-mail: marshall.rafal@olisystems.com
Founded 1990
Library Holdings: Bk Titles 1,000; Per Subs 40; Spec Interest Per Sub 20
Subject Interests: Chem, Computers, Engr
Restriction: Staff use only

CHATHAM

L BLUME, FORTE, FRIED, ZERRES & MOLINARI, PC, Law Library, (Formerly Blume, Goldfaden, Berkowitz, Donnelly, Fried & Forte, PC), One Main St, 07928. SAN 371-716X. Tel: 973-635-5400, Ext 189. FAX:

973-635-9339. Web Site: www.njatty.com. *Law Librn,* Sungji Koo; E-mail: skoo@njatty.com; Staff 1 (MLS 1)
Founded 1975
Library Holdings: Bk Vols 3,000; Per Subs 58
Subject Interests: Obstetrics & gynecology, Pediatrics
Partic in New Jersey Law Librarians Association
Open Mon-Thurs 8:30-4:30

P LIBRARY OF THE CHATHAMS*, 214 Main St, 07928. SAN 310-0693. Tel: 973-635-0603. FAX: 973-635-7827. E-mail: librarian@chathamlibrary.org. Web Site: chathamlibrary.org. *Dir,* Karen Brodsky; E-mail: kbrodsky@chathamlibrary.org; *Head, Adult Serv,* Deborah R Fitzgerald; E-mail: dfitzgerald@chathamlibrary.org; *Head, Ref,* Robert Schriek; E-mail: rschriek@chathamlibrary.org; *Head, Tech Serv,* Mary Kennedy; E-mail: mkennedy@chathamlibrary.org; *Head, Youth Serv,* Jamie Sabonya; E-mail: jsabonya@chathamlibrary.org; Staff 8 (MLS 8)
Founded 1907. Pop 18,669; Circ 196,256
Library Holdings: AV Mats 7,000; CDs 3,000; DVDs 2,991; e-books 75; Bk Titles 95,000; Per Subs 220
Subject Interests: Consumer health, Earth sci, Health, Med, Psychol
Automation Activity & Vendor Info: (Cataloging) Innovative Interfaces, Inc; (Circulation) Innovative Interfaces, Inc; (ILL) Innovative Interfaces, Inc
Wireless access
Partic in LibraryLinkNJ, The New Jersey Library Cooperative; Morris Automated Information Network; Morris-Union Federation
Open Mon-Thurs 9:30-9, Fri 9:30-6, Sat 9:30-5, Sun 2-5
Friends of the Library Group

SR PRESBYTERIAN CHURCH OF CHATHAM TOWNSHIP LIBRARY*, 240 Southern Blvd, 07928. SAN 371-7178. Tel: 973-635-2340. Web Site: pcct-nj.org. *Library Contact,* Susan Tompson
Library Holdings: Bk Titles 2,800
Open Mon-Fri 9-5, Sun 8-Noon

CHERRY HILL

CAMDEN COUNTY COLLEGE LIBRARY
See Blackwood

P CHERRY HILL PUBLIC LIBRARY, 1100 Kings Hwy N, 08034. SAN 310-0715. Tel: 856-667-0300. FAX: 856-667-9503. E-mail: info@chplnj.org. Web Site: www.chplnj.org. *Dir,* Laverne Mann; E-mail: lmann@chplnj.org; *Ad,* Claire Thomas; E-mail: cthomas@chplnj.org; *Adult Serv Supvr,* Tierney Miller; E-mail: tmiller@chplnj.org; *Youth Serv Supvr,* Beth Cackowski; E-mail: bcackowski@chplnj.org; Staff 37 (MLS 34, Non-MLS 3)
Founded 1957. Pop 70,000; Circ 565,487
Library Holdings: AV Mats 11,930; Bk Vols 156,000; Per Subs 343
Special Collections: New Jersey
Subject Interests: Computers, Foreign trade, Investing, Local hist
Automation Activity & Vendor Info: (Acquisitions) SirsiDynix; (Cataloging) SirsiDynix; (Circulation) SirsiDynix; (OPAC) SirsiDynix; (Serials) SirsiDynix
Wireless access
Function: Adult bk club, Art exhibits, Audio & video playback equip for onsite use, Audiobks via web, AV serv, Bk club(s), Bk reviews (Group), Bks on CD, CD-ROM, Children's prog, Computer training, Computers for patron use, E-Reserves, Electronic databases & coll, ILL available, Instruction & testing, Internet access, Magnifiers for reading, Microfiche/film & reading machines, Music CDs, Notary serv, Online cat, Online ref, Photocopying/Printing, Preschool reading prog, Prog for adults, Prog for children & young adult, Ref serv available, Scanner, Spoken cassettes & CDs, Story hour, Summer reading prog, Tax forms, Teen prog, Wheelchair accessible
Publications: Cherry Hill Area Organizations & Agencies
Partic in OCLC Online Computer Library Center, Inc
Special Services for the Deaf - Assisted listening device; Bks on deafness & sign lang
Special Services for the Blind - Accessible computers; Aids for in-house use; Assistive/Adapted tech devices, equip & products; Bks available with recordings; Bks on CD; Closed circuit TV magnifier; Large print bks; Large screen computer & software; Low vision equip; Screen enlargement software for people with visual disabilities; Talking bk serv referral; ZoomText magnification & reading software
Open Mon & Wed 10-7, Tues & Thurs-Sat 10-4
Restriction: 24-hr pass syst for students only
Friends of the Library Group

M JEFFERSON HEALTH-NEW JERSEY*, Dr Barney A Slotkin Memorial Library, 2201 Chapel Ave W, 08002-2048. SAN 320-3948. Tel: 856-488-6500, 856-488-6865. FAX: 856-488-6467. *Librn,* Sherri Kaminski; E-mail: 28sheri@gmail.com; Staff 1 (Non-MLS 1)
Founded 1974
Library Holdings: Bk Titles 800; Per Subs 49
Subject Interests: Med, Orthopedics, Osteopathy, Psychiat
Partic in Basic Health Sciences Library Network; SW NJ Consortium

R TEMPLE BETH SHOLOM*, Adele & Terry Uhr Memorial Library, 1901 Kresson Rd, 08003. SAN 310-1967. Tel: 856-751-6663. FAX: 856-751-2369. E-mail: msiegel@tbsonline.org. Web Site: www.tbsonline.org/lifelong-learning-center. *Librn,* Minna Siegel; E-mail: Msiegel@tbsonline.org; Staff 1 (Non-MLS 1)
Founded 1948
Library Holdings: Bk Titles 6,000; Per Subs 10; Videos 300
Wireless access
Open Mon, Tues & Thurs 9:30-12:30, Wed 2-5, Sun 9-11
Restriction: Authorized patrons

R TEMPLE EMANUEL LIBRARY*, 1101 Springdale Rd, 08003. SAN 310-0723. Tel: 856-489-0029, 856-489-0035. FAX: 856-489-0032. Web Site: templeemanuel.org.
Founded 1971
Library Holdings: Bk Vols 8,000
Subject Interests: Holocaust, Judaica
Wireless access
Open Mon-Fri 9-5, Sat & Sun 9-1
Friends of the Library Group

R TRINITY PRESBYTERIAN CHURCH LIBRARY*, Norman E Hjorth Memorial Library, 499 Rte 70E, 08034. SAN 310-0731. Tel: 856-428-2050. FAX: 856-795-8471. *Librn,* Michele Strobel; Staff 2 (MLS 2)
Founded 1962
Library Holdings: AV Mats 125; Bk Titles 3,500
Special Collections: Children's Books
Subject Interests: Bible study, Christian educ
Wireless access
Open Mon-Thurs 9-4

CHESTER

P CHESTER LIBRARY, 250 W Main St, 07930. SAN 310-074X. Tel: 908-879-7612. FAX: 908-879-8695. E-mail: contactus@chesterlib.org. Web Site: chesterlib.org. *Dir,* Lesley Karczewski; E-mail: lesley.karczewski@chesterlib.org; *Asst Dir,* Terry Ferri; E-mail: terry.ferri@chesterlib.org; Staff 5 (MLS 3, Non-MLS 2)
Founded 1911. Pop 9,500; Circ 142,950
Jan 2020-Dec 2020 Income $4,000, State $4,000
Library Holdings: Per Subs 63
Automation Activity & Vendor Info: (Cataloging) Innovative Interfaces, Inc. - Polaris; (Circulation) Innovative Interfaces, Inc. - Polaris
Wireless access
Function: 24/7 Electronic res, 24/7 Online cat, Adult bk club, Archival coll, Art exhibits, Art programs, Audio & video playback equip for onsite use, Audiobks via web, AV serv, Bk club(s), Bk reviews (Group), Bks on CD, Chess club, Children's prog, Computer training, Computers for patron use, E-Reserves, Electronic databases & coll, Free DVD rentals, Holiday prog, Homework prog, ILL available, Internet access, Magazines, Mail & tel request accepted, Meeting rooms, Movies, Museum passes, Music CDs, Notary serv, Online cat, Online info literacy tutorials on the web & in blackboard, Photocopying/Printing, Printer for laptops & handheld devices, Prog for adults, Prog for children & young adult, Ref & res, Ref serv available, Res assist avail, Scanner, Spanish lang bks, Story hour, Study rm, Summer reading prog, Tax forms, Teen prog, Wheelchair accessible, Writing prog
Partic in Morris Automated Information Network
Open Mon-Thurs 9-9, Fri & Sat 9-5, Sun 1-5
Friends of the Library Group

CINNAMINSON

R JACK BALABAN MEMORIAL LIBRARY OF TEMPLE SINAI*, 2101 New Albany Rd, 08077-3536. SAN 310-0766. Tel: 856-829-0658. FAX: 856-829-0310. E-mail: TempleSinaiNJ2101@gmail.com. Web Site: www.templesinainj.com/site/library. *Librn,* Shelley Sbar
Founded 1963
Library Holdings: Bk Vols 2,300
Special Collections: Encyclopaedia Judaica; Yiddish Coll
Subject Interests: Jewish authors, Jewish content
Restriction: Not open to pub

CLARK

P CLARK PUBLIC LIBRARY*, 303 Westfield Ave, 07066. SAN 310-0774. Tel: 732-388-5999. FAX: 732-388-7866. Web Site: www.clarklibrary.org. *Dir,* Megan Kociolek; E-mail: clarklibrarydirector@gmail.com; Staff 14.8 (MLS 3.8, Non-MLS 11)
Founded 1961. Pop 14,759; Circ 110,000
Library Holdings: Bk Vols 60,000; Per Subs 190

Automation Activity & Vendor Info: (Acquisitions) TLC (The Library Corporation); (Cataloging) TLC (The Library Corporation); (Circulation) TLC (The Library Corporation); (ILL) TLC (The Library Corporation); (OPAC) TLC (The Library Corporation)
Wireless access
Function: Adult bk club, Art exhibits, Bk club(s), Chess club, Computer training, Digital talking bks, Homebound delivery serv, ILL available, Internet access, Music CDs, Online ref, Photocopying/Printing, Prog for adults, Prog for children & young adult, Ref & res, Senior computer classes, Summer reading prog, Tax forms, Telephone ref, Wheelchair accessible
Partic in LibraryLinkNJ, The New Jersey Library Cooperative; MURAL
Open Mon, Tues & Thurs 9:30-9, Wed, Fri & Sat 9:30-5
Friends of the Library Group

CLEMENTON

P CLEMENTON MEMORIAL LIBRARY*, 195 Gibbsboro Rd, 08021. SAN 310-0790. Tel: 856-783-3233. FAX: 856-784-8794. E-mail: clemlibrary2@gmail.com. *Library Contact,* Donna Rimby
Circ 7,278
Library Holdings: Bk Vols 8,000; Per Subs 15
Mem of Camden County Library System
Open Mon 11-4, Wed 11-7, Thurs 11-2, Sat 11-1

CLIFFSIDE PARK

P CLIFFSIDE PARK FREE PUBLIC LIBRARY*, 505 Palisade Ave, 07010. SAN 310-0804. Tel: 201-945-2867. FAX: 201-945-1016. Circulation E-mail: circ@cliffsideparklibrary.bccls.org. Web Site: cliffsideparklibrary.org. *Dir,* Stephanie M Bellucci; E-mail: bellucci@cliffsidepark.bccls.org; Staff 14 (MLS 4, Non-MLS 10)
Founded 1913. Pop 23,000; Circ 161,745
Library Holdings: AV Mats 5,345; Bk Titles 69,354; Per Subs 121
Automation Activity & Vendor Info: (Cataloging) SirsiDynix; (Circulation) SirsiDynix; (OPAC) SirsiDynix; (Serials) Gateway
Wireless access
Function: Ref serv available
Partic in Bergen County Cooperative Library System, Inc
Open Mon-Thurs 10-9, Fri & Sat 10-5, Sun 1-5
Friends of the Library Group

CLIFTON

P CLIFTON PUBLIC LIBRARY*, 292 Piaget Ave, 07011. SAN 350-6347. Tel: 973-772-5500. Administration FAX: 973-772-2926. E-mail: cliftoncirc@cliftonpl.org. *Libr Dir,* Justine Tomczak; E-mail: tomczak@cliftonpl.org; *Ch,* Gloria Abero; E-mail: abero@cliftonpl.org; *Librn,* Mr Pat John Ferro; E-mail: ferro@cliftonpl.org; *Librn,* Kathleen Grimshaw-Haven; E-mail: grimshaw@cliftonpl.org; Staff 37 (MLS 9, Non-MLS 28)
Founded 1920. Circ 250,000
Library Holdings: Bk Titles 150,000; Per Subs 295; Videos 9,000
Subject Interests: Local hist
Automation Activity & Vendor Info: (Cataloging) SirsiDynix; (Circulation) SirsiDynix; (OPAC) SirsiDynix
Wireless access
Function: 24/7 Electronic res, 24/7 Online cat, Adult bk club, Archival coll, Art exhibits, Bk club(s), Bks on CD, Children's prog, Computer training, Computers for patron use, Digital talking bks, Electronic databases & coll, Free DVD rentals, Home delivery & serv to seniorr ctr & nursing homes, Homebound delivery serv, Homework prog, ILL available, Internet access, Magazines, Magnifiers for reading, Meeting rooms, Microfiche/film & reading machines, Movies, Museum passes, Music CDs, Photocopying/Printing, Preschool outreach, Printer for laptops & handheld devices, Prog for adults, Prog for children & young adult, Ref & res, Ref serv available, Res assist avail, Scanner, Senior computer classes, Spanish lang bks, Story hour, Study rm, Summer reading prog, Tax forms, Teen prog, Telephone ref, Wheelchair accessible, Workshops
Partic in PALS Plus, The Computer Consortium of Passaic County Libraries
Special Services for the Deaf - Assistive tech; Bks on deafness & sign lang; TTY equip
Special Services for the Blind - Audio mat; Bks on CD; Home delivery serv; Large print bks; Talking bks
Open Mon-Thurs 10-9, Fri 10-6, Sat 9-5, Sun 1-5
Friends of the Library Group
Branches: 1
ALLWOOD BRANCH, 44 Lyall Rd, 07012, SAN 350-6371. Tel: 973-471-0555. Web Site: www.cliftonpl.org. *Br Mgr,* Barbara Altilio; Tel: 973-471-0555, E-mail: altilio@cliftonpl.org; *Ch Serv,* Heather Nilsen; E-mail: nilsen@cliftonpl.org
Open Mon-Wed 10-9, Thurs & Fri 10-6, Sat 10-5

CLINTON

S CORRECTIONAL INSTITUTION FOR WOMEN*, Edna Mahan Hall Library, PO Box 4004, 08809-4004. SAN 310-0898. Tel: 908-735-7111, Ext 3641. FAX: 908-735-0108. *Adminr,* Sarah Davis; *Supvr of Educ,* Celeste Thatcher; Staff 3 (MLS 1, Non-MLS 2)
Library Holdings: Bk Vols 8,600; Per Subs 40
Special Collections: Criminal Law; Women in Prison
Restriction: Not open to pub

S HUNTERDON DEVELOPMENTAL CENTER LIBRARY*, 40 Pittstown Rd, 08809. (Mail add: PO Box 4003, 08809-4003), SAN 325-7584. Tel: 908-735-4031, Ext 1038, 908-735-4031, Ext 1149. FAX: 908-730-1359. *Library Contact,* Elizabeth Keel; E-mail: elizabeth.keel@dhs.state.nj.us
Library Holdings: AV Mats 60; Bk Vols 5,000; Per Subs 60
Restriction: Non-circulating to the pub, Staff use only

S RED MILL MUSEUM LIBRARY*, 56 Main St, 08809. SAN 321-5970. Tel: 908-735-4101. FAX: 908-735-0914. E-mail: admin@theredmill.org. Web Site: theredmill.org. *Exec Dir,* Paul Muir; Tel: 908-735-4101, Ext 101, E-mail: director@theredmill.org; *Curator,* Elizabeth Cole; Tel: 908-735-4101, Ext 103, E-mail: ecole@theredmill.org
Library Holdings: Bk Titles 461; Bk Vols 475
Special Collections: Antique Textbooks; Daybooks
Subject Interests: Antiques, Local hist
Restriction: Open by appt only

CLOSTER

P CLOSTER PUBLIC LIBRARY*, 280 High St, 07624-1898. SAN 310-0901. Tel: 201-768-4197. FAX: 201-768-4220. Circulation E-mail: cltrcirc@bccls.org. Web Site: closterpubliclibrary.org/. *Dir & Librn,* Ruth Rando; E-mail: rando@closter.bccls.org; *Head, Circ,* Deborah Leary; E-mail: deborahleary@closter.bccls.org; *Head, Youth Serv, Librn,* Lupita O'Brien; E-mail: lupita.obrien@closter.bccls.org; *Ad,* Tim Baek; E-mail: tim.baek@closter.bccls.org; Staff 5 (MLS 3, Non-MLS 2)
Founded 1956. Pop 8,500
Library Holdings: AV Mats 7,500; CDs 842; DVDs 2,500; Large Print Bks 800; Bk Titles 56,257; Bk Vols 58,472; Per Subs 123; Talking Bks 1,500
Subject Interests: Closter hist, NJ
Automation Activity & Vendor Info: (OPAC) SirsiDynix
Wireless access
Function: 24/7 Electronic res, 24/7 Online cat, 3D Printer, Activity rm, Adult bk club, After school storytime, Art exhibits, Audiobks on Playaways & MP3, Audiobks via web, Bk club(s), Bks on CD, Chess club, Children's prog, Computer training, Computers for patron use, Digital talking bks, E-Reserves, Electronic databases & coll, Free DVD rentals, ILL available, Internet access, Literacy & newcomer serv, Magazines, Mail & tel request accepted, Meeting rooms, Movies, Museum passes, Music CDs, Notary serv, Online cat, OverDrive digital audio bks, Photocopying/Printing, Preschool outreach, Printer for laptops & handheld devices, Prog for adults, Prog for children & young adult, Ref serv available, Scanner, Spoken cassettes & CDs, Story hour, Summer & winter reading prog, Summer reading prog, Tax forms, Teen prog, Telephone ref, Wheelchair accessible, Winter reading prog
Partic in Bergen County Cooperative Library System, Inc
Open Mon-Wed 9-9, Thurs-Sat 9-5
Friends of the Library Group

COLLINGSWOOD

P COLLINGSWOOD PUBLIC LIBRARY, 771 Haddon Ave, 08108. SAN 310-091X. Tel: 856-858-0649. FAX: 856-823-1653. Web Site: www.collingswoodlib.org. *Dir,* Carissa Schanely; E-mail: cschanely@collingswoodlib.org; *Head, Access/Tech Serv,* Carol Ehret; *Ch,* Melissa Desantis; E-mail: mdesantis@collingswoodlib.org; Staff 12 (MLS 5, Non-MLS 7)
Founded 1910. Pop 14,500; Circ 70,000
Library Holdings: Bk Titles 61,000; Bk Vols 65,000; Per Subs 120
Special Collections: Southern New Jersey Coll, bks, blue prints, engravings, maps, photog, trade cat. Oral History
Automation Activity & Vendor Info: (Cataloging) Innovative Interfaces, Inc; (Circulation) Innovative Interfaces, Inc; (Media Booking) Innovative Interfaces, Inc
Wireless access
Function: 24/7 Online cat, Adult bk club, Archival coll, Audiobks on Playaways & MP3, Bk club(s), Bks on CD, Chess club, Children's prog, Computers for patron use, Electronic databases & coll, Free DVD rentals, ILL available, Internet access, Life-long learning prog for all ages, Magazines, Mango lang, Meeting rooms, Movies, Museum passes, Music CDs, Online cat, Online ref, Outside serv via phone, mail, e-mail & web, OverDrive digital audio bks, Photocopying/Printing, Preschool reading prog, Printer for laptops & handheld devices, Prog for adults, Prog for children & young adult, Ref & res, Ref serv available, Scanner, Spanish

lang bks, Spoken cassettes & CDs, Story hour, Summer reading prog, Tax forms, Teen prog, Wheelchair accessible, Writing prog
Publications: Friends of the Library (Newsletter)
Open Mon & Wed 10-8, Tues, Thurs & Fri 10-5, Sat 10-1
Friends of the Library Group

CRANBURY

P CRANBURY PUBLIC LIBRARY, 30 N Main St, 08512. SAN 310-0979. Tel: 609-799-6992. E-mail: reference@cranburypubliclibrary.org. Web Site: www.cranburypubliclibrary.org. *Dir,* Marilynn Mullen; E-mail: mullen@cranburypubliclibrary.org; *Operations Adminr,* Beth Anne Kafasis; E-mail: kafasis@cranburypubliclibrary.org; *Community Outreach, Tech Librn,* Dean Klimek; E-mail: klimek@cranburypubliclibrary.org; *Children's Spec, Educ Spec,* Laura Bonds; E-mail: bonds@cranburypubliclibrary.org; Staff 10 (MLS 2, Non-MLS 8)
Founded 1906. Pop 3,800; Circ 50,000
Jan 2020-Dec 2020 Income $607,684, State $1,672, City $606,012. Mats Exp $606,012, Books $11,000, Per/Ser (Incl. Access Fees) $100, AV Mat $7,000, Electronic Ref Mat (Incl. Access Fees) $13,600. Sal $267,669
Library Holdings: Audiobooks 735; AV Mats 70; Bks on Deafness & Sign Lang 5; DVDs 1,500; e-books 415; Electronic Media & Resources 11; Large Print Bks 200; Microforms 1; Bk Vols 15,800; Per Subs 5
Special Collections: Cranbury Press Newspaper (1886-present), digital pdfs, microfilm
Subject Interests: Local hist
Automation Activity & Vendor Info: (Cataloging) SirsiDynix-Enterprise; (Circulation) SirsiDynix-Enterprise; (ILL) JerseyCat; (OPAC) SirsiDynix-Enterprise
Wireless access
Function: 24/7 Electronic res, 24/7 Online cat, Adult bk club, Archival coll, Audiobks on Playaways & MP3, Audiobks via web, AV serv, Bk club(s), Bks on CD, Chess club, Children's prog, Computer training, Computers for patron use, Digital talking bks, Doc delivery serv, E-Readers, E-Reserves, Electronic databases & coll, Equip loans & repairs, Family literacy, Free DVD rentals, Home delivery & serv to seniorr ctr & nursing homes, Homebound delivery serv, Homework prog, ILL available, Internet access, Life-long learning prog for all ages, Literacy & newcomer serv, Magazines, Mail & tel request accepted, Museum passes, Music CDs, Notary serv, Online cat, Online ref, Outreach serv, Outside serv via phone, mail, e-mail & web, OverDrive digital audio bks, Photocopying/Printing, Preschool outreach, Preschool reading prog, Printer for laptops & handheld devices, Prog for adults, Prog for children & young adult, Ref serv available, Res assist avail, Senior computer classes, Senior outreach, Spoken cassettes & CDs, STEM programs, Story hour, Summer reading prog, Teen prog, Telephone ref, Wheelchair accessible
Partic in Libraries of Middlesex Automation Consortium; LibraryLinkNJ, The New Jersey Library Cooperative; MURAL
Special Services for the Deaf - Bks on deafness & sign lang; Closed caption videos
Special Services for the Blind - Audio mat; Bks on CD; Digital talking bk; Home delivery serv; Large print bks; Large type calculator; Playaways (bks on MP3); Recorded bks; Rental typewriters & computers; Sound rec
Open Mon-Thurs 10-8, Fri 10-5, Sat 10-2
Friends of the Library Group

CRANFORD

P CRANFORD FREE PUBLIC LIBRARY*, 224 Walnut Ave, 07016-2931. (Mail add: PO Box 400, 07016-0400), SAN 310-0987. Tel: 908-709-7272. FAX: 908-709-1658. E-mail: library@cranfordnj.org. Web Site: www.cranfordlibrary.org. *Dir,* Michael Maziekien; E-mail: m-maziekien@crandordnj.org; *Asst Dir, Ch,* Judith Klimowicz; E-mail: j-klimowicz@cranfordnj.org; *Ref Librn, Syst Adminr,* Ben Stanley; E-mail: b-stanley@cranfordnj.org; *Ch,* Lauren Antolino; E-mail: l-antolino@cranfordnj.org; *Programming Librn, YA Librn,* Stacey Shapiro; E-mail: s-shapiro@cranfordnj.org; *Ref Librn,* Ronald Gorda; E-mail: r-gorda@cranfordnj.org; Staff 12 (MLS 6, Non-MLS 6)
Founded 1910. Pop 22,625; Circ 201,781
Library Holdings: Bk Titles 100,000
Special Collections: Oral History
Automation Activity & Vendor Info: (Cataloging) Innovative Interfaces, Inc; (Circulation) Innovative Interfaces, Inc; (OPAC) Innovative Interfaces, Inc
Wireless access
Function: 24/7 Electronic res, Adult bk club, Art exhibits, Bks on cassette, Bks on CD, CD-ROM, Children's prog, Computer training, Computers for patron use, Digital talking bks, E-Readers, Electronic databases & coll, Free DVD rentals, Games & aids for people with disabilities, Homebound delivery serv, ILL available, Internet access, Magazines, Magnifiers for reading, Microfiche/film & reading machines, Movies, Museum passes, Music CDs, Notary serv, Online cat, Online info literacy tutorials on the web & in blackboard, Online ref, OverDrive digital audio bks, Photocopying/Printing, Prog for adults, Prog for children & young adult, Spanish lang bks, Spoken cassettes & CDs, Story hour, Summer & winter reading prog, Tax forms, Teen prog, Telephone ref, VHS videos, Wheelchair accessible, Winter reading prog, Workshops
Publications: Newsletter (bi-monthly)
Partic in Eastern NJ Regional Libr Coop; LibraryLinkNJ, The New Jersey Library Cooperative; Librs of Union County Consortium; MURAL
Special Services for the Deaf - High interest/low vocabulary bks
Special Services for the Blind - Home delivery serv
Open Mon-Thurs 10-9, Fri & Sat 10-5, Sat 10-2 (Summer)
Restriction: 24-hr pass syst for students only
Friends of the Library Group

S CHARLES E STEVENS AMERICAN ATHEIST LIBRARY & ARCHIVES, INC*, 225 Cristiani St, 07016. SAN 320-9016. Tel: 908-276-7300. FAX: 908-276-7402. E-mail: library@atheists.org. Web Site: www.atheists.org/about/library. *Librn,* Dr David I Orenstein; E-mail: dorenstein@atheists.org; Staff 3 (MLS 1, Non-MLS 2)
Founded 1968
Library Holdings: Bk Titles 8,500
Special Collections: Haldeman-Julius Publications; Ingersoll Coll; McCabe Coll; Robertson Coll
Subject Interests: Anarchism, Atheism, Church-state, Relig, Sci, Soc issues
Wireless access
Restriction: Open by appt only

J UNION COUNTY COLLEGE LIBRARIES*, MacKay Library, 1033 Springfield Ave, 07016. SAN 310-1029. Tel: 908-709-7623. Reference Tel: 908-709-7620. FAX: 908-709-7589. Web Site: www.ucc.edu/about/library. *Dir, Libr & Acad Learning Ctr,* Dena Leiter; E-mail: leiter@ucc.edu; *Asst Dir, Lib,* Patricia Reilly; *Acq Librn,* Karen Malnati; Tel: 908-709-7027, E-mail: malnati@ucc.edu; *Instrul Serv Librn,* Susan Goodman; E-mail: susan.goodman@ucc.edu; *Ref Serv,* Josaine Royster; E-mail: royster@ucc.edu; *Tech Serv & Automation,* William Schryba; E-mail: schryba@ucc.edu. Subject Specialists: *Educ, Psychol, Sociol,* Karen Malnati; *Engr, Hist, Philos,* Susan Goodman; *Bus,* Josaine Royster; Staff 15 (MLS 8, Non-MLS 7)
Founded 1933. Enrl 11,000; Fac 205; Highest Degree: Associate
Library Holdings: DVDs 2,545; Bk Titles 84,000; Per Subs 448
Automation Activity & Vendor Info: (Acquisitions) SirsiDynix; (Cataloging) SirsiDynix; (Circulation) SirsiDynix; (Course Reserve) SirsiDynix; (ILL) SirsiDynix; (OPAC) SirsiDynix
Wireless access
Publications: Bibliographies; Handbook Guides; Newsletter
Partic in LibraryLinkNJ, The New Jersey Library Cooperative; Librs of Union County Consortium; OCLC Online Computer Library Center, Inc; Virtual Academic Library Environment
Departmental Libraries:
KELLOGG LIBRARY, 40 W Jersey St, Elizabeth, 07202-2314. Tel: 908-965-6075. *Librn,* Margaret Deng. Subject Specialists: *English as a second lang, Nursing,* Margaret Deng; Staff 2 (MLS 1, Non-MLS 1)
Highest Degree: Associate
PLAINFIELD CAMPUS, 232 E Second St, Plainfield, 07060-1308. Tel: 908-412-3545. *Librn,* Elsa Bruguier. Subject Specialists: *Allied health, Sport mgt,* Elsa Bruguier; Staff 2 (MLS 1, Non-MLS 1)
Highest Degree: Associate

CRESSKILL

P CRESSKILL PUBLIC LIBRARY*, 53 Union Ave, 07626. SAN 310-1037. Tel: 201-567-3521. FAX: 201-567-5067. Circulation E-mail: crescirc@bccls.org. Web Site: www.cresskilllibrary.org. *Dir,* Laura Chumas; E-mail: chumas@cresskill.bccls.org; *Youth Serv Librn,* Rebecca Morel; E-mail: rebecca.morel@cresskill.bccls.org; *Asst Librn,* Kiwon Kim; E-mail: kiwon.kim@cresskill.bccls.org. Subject Specialists: *Korean lang mat,* Kiwon Kim; Staff 5 (MLS 2, Non-MLS 3)
Founded 1930. Pop 8,573; Circ 148,000
Library Holdings: Bk Titles 64,776
Wireless access
Partic in Bergen County Cooperative Library System, Inc
Open Mon, Wed & Thurs 10-8, Tues & Fri 10-5, Sat 10-3
Friends of the Library Group

CROSSWICKS

P THE CROSSWICKS LIBRARY CO*, Crosswicks Public Library, 483 Main St, 08515. (Mail add: PO Box 147, 08515), SAN 321-0537. Tel: 609-298-6271. FAX: 609-298-0510. E-mail: crosswicks@bcls.lib.nj.us. Web Site: www.bcls.lib.nj.us/crosswicks. *Dir,* Debbie Drachaman; Tel: 609-298-6271, E-mail: ddrachaman@bcls.lib.nj.us; Staff 1 (MLS 0.5, Non-MLS 0.5)
Founded 1817. Pop 8,000
Library Holdings: Bk Titles 12,346; Bk Vols 18,000
Special Collections: Oral History
Subject Interests: Antiques, Local hist, NJ hist, Quaker info

Automation Activity & Vendor Info: (Cataloging) Horizon; (Circulation) Horizon; (OPAC) Horizon
Wireless access
Mem of Burlington County Library
Open Mon & Wed 10-5, Tue & Thurs 1-8, Sat 10-2
Friends of the Library Group

DELANCO

P DELANCO PUBLIC LIBRARY*, M Joan Pearson School, 1303 Burlington Ave, 08075. SAN 310-1053. Tel: 856-461-6850. FAX: 856-461-6850. E-mail: mail@delancolibrary.org. Web Site: delancolibrary.org, www.bcls.lib.nj.us/delanco. *Dir,* Katharina Radcliffe; E-mail: kradclif@bcls.lib.nj.us; *Asst Dir,* Heather Phillips
Founded 1865. Pop 3,361; Circ 10,732
Library Holdings: Bk Vols 45,000; Per Subs 30
Automation Activity & Vendor Info: (Cataloging) SirsiDynix; (Circulation) SirsiDynix; (OPAC) SirsiDynix
Wireless access
Mem of Burlington County Library
Special Services for the Deaf - Bks on deafness & sign lang; High interest/low vocabulary bks; Spec interest per
Open Mon & Fri 10-5, Tues & Thurs 2-8, Sat 10-2
Friends of the Library Group

DEMAREST

P DEMAREST PUBLIC LIBRARY*, 90 Hardenburgh Ave, 07647. SAN 310-1061. Tel: 201-768-8714. Circulation E-mail: demacirc@bccls.org. Web Site: demarestlibrary.org. *Dir,* Edna Ortega; E-mail: ortega@demarest.bccls.org; *Head, Circ,* Patty Irizarry; E-mail: patti.irizarry@demarest.bccls.org
Founded 1965. Pop 4,950; Circ 32,494
Library Holdings: Bk Titles 26,526; Bk Vols 27,357; Per Subs 50
Automation Activity & Vendor Info: (Cataloging) SirsiDynix; (Circulation) SirsiDynix; (OPAC) SirsiDynix
Wireless access
Partic in Bergen County Cooperative Library System, Inc
Open Mon, Wed & Thurs 9-8, Tues & Fri 9-5, Sat 9-1, Sun 1-5

DENVILLE

CR ASSUMPTION COLLEGE FOR SISTERS LIBRARY, 200 A Morris Ave, 07834. SAN 310-2793. Tel: 973-957-0188. FAX: 973-957-0190. E-mail: librarian@acs350.org. Web Site: acs350.org/library. *Librn,* Mrs Leslie Monchar; Staff 1 (MLS 1)
Founded 1961. Enrl 50; Fac 20; Highest Degree: Associate
Library Holdings: AV Mats 464; CDs 72; DVDs 88; Electronic Media & Resources 1; Bk Titles 711; Bk Vols 815; Videos 304
Subject Interests: Philos, Theol
Wireless access
Function: For res purposes, ILL available, Photocopying/Printing, Ref serv available
Publications: New Books Listing (Monthly)
Partic in LibraryLinkNJ, The New Jersey Library Cooperative; Virtual Academic Library Environment
Restriction: By permission only, Employees & their associates, Open by appt only, Open to fac, students & qualified researchers, Open to pub for ref & circ; with some limitations

P DENVILLE FREE PUBLIC LIBRARY*, 121 Diamond Spring Rd, 07834. SAN 310-107X. Tel: 973-627-6555. Circulation Tel: 973-627-6555, Ext 200, 973-627-6555, Ext 201. Reference Tel: 973-627-6555, Ext 203. Administration Tel: 973-627-6555, Ext 204, 973-627-6555, Ext 207. FAX: 973-627-1913. Web Site: www.denvillelibrary.org. *Dir,* Siobhan L Koch; E-mail: siobhan.koch@denvillelibrary.org; *Adult Serv, ILL, Ref (Info Servs),* Ilene Leftokwitz; *Ch Serv,* Maryellen Liddy; Staff 6 (MLS 6)
Founded 1921. Pop 16,635; Circ 154,438
Library Holdings: Audiobooks 3,163; CDs 1,971; DVDs 1,898; e-books 320; Electronic Media & Resources 10; Bk Titles 41,990; Per Subs 173
Wireless access
Partic in Morris Automated Information Network
Open Mon-Thurs 9:30-9, Fri & Sat 9:30-5
Friends of the Library Group

DEPTFORD

P DEPTFORD FREE PUBLIC LIBRARY*, 670 Ward Dr, 08096. SAN 310-1088. Tel: 856-848-9149. FAX: 856-848-1813. Web Site: www.deptfordpubliclibrary.org. *Libr Dir,* Jenna McAndrews; E-mail: mcandrewsj@deptfordpubliclibrary.org; *Cat, Principal Libr Asst,* Bunny Jacobsen; E-mail: jacobsenb@deptfordpubliclibrary.org; *Ch,* Susann Kaback; E-mail: kabacks@deptfordpubliclibrary.org; Staff 14 (MLS 3, Non-MLS 11)
Founded 1961. Pop 30,000; Circ 200,000
Library Holdings: Bk Vols 70,000; Per Subs 209
Special Collections: Deptford History Coll
Automation Activity & Vendor Info: (Cataloging) SirsiDynix; (Circulation) SirsiDynix; (OPAC) SirsiDynix
Wireless access
Special Services for the Deaf - Bks on deafness & sign lang
Special Services for the Blind - Audio mat; Bks on CD
Open Mon-Thurs 10-9, Fri & Sat 10-4
Friends of the Library Group

DOVER

P DOVER FREE PUBLIC LIBRARY*, 32 E Clinton St, 07801. SAN 310-1096. Tel: 973-366-0172. FAX: 973-366-0175. E-mail: doverfreelibrary@yahoo.com. Web Site: www.dfpl.org. *Dir,* Diane Sebastian; Staff 8 (MLS 2, Non-MLS 6)
Founded 1912. Pop 18,000; Circ 61,000
Library Holdings: Bk Titles 46,000; Bk Vols 49,000; Per Subs 90
Subject Interests: Spanish
Wireless access
Partic in Morris Automated Information Network
Open Mon, Tues & Thurs 10-8, Wed 10-6, Fri 10-5:30, Sat 10-4
Friends of the Library Group

DUMONT

P DIXON HOMESTEAD LIBRARY*, Dumont Public Library, 180 Washington Ave, 07628. SAN 310-1118. Tel: 201-384-2030. FAX: 201-384-5878. Circulation E-mail: dumtcirc@bccls.org. Reference E-mail: dumtref@bccls.org. Web Site: dumont.bccls.org. *Interim Dir, Youth Serv Librn,* Korine Stopsky; E-mail: korine.stopsky@dumont.bccls.org; *Ref Librn,* Julie Whitehead; E-mail: julie.whitehead@dumont.bccls.org; Staff 3 (MLS 2, Non-MLS 1)
Founded 1925
Library Holdings: Per Subs 93
Automation Activity & Vendor Info: (Circulation) Innovative Interfaces, Inc
Wireless access
Function: 24/7 Electronic res, 24/7 Online cat, Adult bk club, Adult literacy prog, Audiobks via web, Bk club(s), Bks on CD, Chess club, Children's prog, Computers for patron use, Electronic databases & coll, ILL available, Internet access, Magazines, Mango lang, Movies, Museum passes, Music CDs, Notary serv, Online cat, Photocopying/Printing, Preschool reading prog, Prog for adults, Prog for children & young adult, Ref serv available, Scanner, Story hour, Summer & winter reading prog, Tax forms, Telephone ref, Wheelchair accessible
Partic in Bergen County Cooperative Library System, Inc
Open Mon-Wed 10-8, Thurs & Fri 10-5, Sat 10-2
Friends of the Library Group

DUNELLEN

P DUNELLEN PUBLIC LIBRARY, Arnold A Schwartz Memorial Library, 100 New Market Rd, 08812. SAN 310-1134. Tel: 732-968-4585. FAX: 732-424-1370. E-mail: DunellenLibraryStaff@gmail.com, info@dunellenlibrary.org. Web Site: www.dunellenlibrary.org. *Ch,* Jennifer Neely; Staff 1 (MLS 1)
Founded 1911. Pop 7,000; Circ 38,000
Library Holdings: Audiobooks 13,682; CDs 6,000; DVDs 2,000; e-books 21,968; Bk Vols 33,058; Per Subs 100; Videos 2,088
Special Collections: Disabilities Coll
Subject Interests: Autism
Automation Activity & Vendor Info: (Cataloging) SirsiDynix-WorkFlows; (Circulation) SirsiDynix-WorkFlows; (ILL) JerseyCat; (OPAC) SirsiDynix-iBistro
Wireless access
Function: Adult bk club
Partic in Libraries of Middlesex Automation Consortium
Special Services for the Blind - BiFolkal kits
Open Mon-Wed 10-8, Thurs-Sat 10-3
Friends of the Library Group

EAST BRUNSWICK

P EAST BRUNSWICK PUBLIC LIBRARY*, Two Jean Walling Civic Ctr, 08816-3599. SAN 350-6525. Tel: 732-390-6950. Interlibrary Loan Service Tel: 732-390-6785. Administration Tel: 732-390-6781. Information Services Tel: 732-390-6767. FAX: 732-390-6796. Administration FAX: 732-390-6869. Web Site: www.ebpl.org. *Dir,* Jennifer Podolsky; E-mail: jpodolsky@ebpl.org; *Adult Serv,* Stephanie Filippone; E-mail: sfilippone@ebpl.org; *Circ,* Katherine Bowden; E-mail: kbowden@ebpl.org; *Info Serv,* Karen Parry; E-mail: kparry@ebpl.org; *Info Tech,* Sascha Basista; E-mail: sbasista@ebpl.org; *Youth Serv,* Aaron Pickett; E-mail: apickett@ebpl.org; Staff 120 (MLS 20, Non-MLS 100)
Founded 1967. Pop 48,630; Circ 640,510
Library Holdings: AV Mats 27,955; Bk Vols 135,000; Per Subs 250

Special Collections: Mystery Classics; World Language (Spanish, Korean, Hindi, Arabic, Gujarati, Russian)
Automation Activity & Vendor Info: (Acquisitions) Horizon; (Cataloging) Horizon; (Circulation) Horizon; (OPAC) Horizon
Wireless access
Function: 24/7 Electronic res, 24/7 Online cat, Adult bk club, Art exhibits, BA reader (adult literacy), Bks on CD, Children's prog, Computer training, Computers for patron use, Electronic databases & coll, Homebound delivery serv, ILL available, Internet access, Large print keyboards, Magazines, Magnifiers for reading, Meeting rooms, Museum passes, Music CDs, Online cat, Outreach serv, Passport agency, Photocopying/Printing, Prog for adults, Prog for children & young adult, Ref serv available, Scanner, Spanish lang bks, Spoken cassettes & CDs, Story hour, Study rm, Summer reading prog, Telephone ref, Wheelchair accessible, Workshops, Writing prog
Publications: The Library @ East Brunswick (Bimonthly)
Partic in Libraries of Middlesex Automation Consortium
Special Services for the Deaf - Assistive tech; Closed caption videos; TDD equip; TTY equip
Special Services for the Blind - Accessible computers; Aids for in-house use; Assistive/Adapted tech devices, equip & products
Open Mon, Tues & Thurs 9-9, Wed, Fri & Sat 9-5, Sun 1-5
Friends of the Library Group

EAST HANOVER

P EAST HANOVER TOWNSHIP FREE PUBLIC LIBRARY*, 415 Ridgedale Ave, 07936. SAN 310-1169. Tel: 973-888-6095. E-mail: contactus@easthanoverlibrary.com. Web Site: www.easthanoverlibrary.com. *Dir,* Gayle B Carlson
Founded 1959. Pop 11,427; Circ 66,500
Library Holdings: AV Mats 8,000; Bk Vols 70,000; Per Subs 112
Wireless access
Partic in Morris Automated Information Network
Open Mon-Thurs 9-9, Fri 9-5, Sat 10-4, Sun (Sept-June) 1-4
Friends of the Library Group

EAST ORANGE

GM DEPARTMENT OF VETERANS AFFAIRS MEDICAL CENTER LIBRARY*, 385 Tremont Ave, 07018-1095. SAN 310-1207. Tel: 908-647-0180, Ext 4545, 973-676-1000, Ext 1969. FAX: 973-395-7234. *Med Librn,* Veronica Marie Lisa; Tel: 973-676-1000, Ext 1962, E-mail: veronica.lisa1@va.gov; *Libr Tech,* Lisa Lowman Sheppard; E-mail: lisa.lowman@va.gov; Staff 2 (MLS 1, Non-MLS 1)
Founded 1955
Library Holdings: AV Mats 300; CDs 86; DVDs 214; e-books 500; e-journals 3,500; Electronic Media & Resources 59; Bk Titles 3,306; Per Subs 47
Automation Activity & Vendor Info: (Acquisitions) LibraryWorld, Inc; (Cataloging) LibraryWorld, Inc; (Circulation) LibraryWorld, Inc; (Serials) LibraryWorld, Inc
Function: Doc delivery serv, Electronic databases & coll, ILL available, Internet access, Online ref, Photocopying/Printing
Partic in New Jersey Health Sciences Library Network
Restriction: Circulates for staff only, Med staff only

P EAST ORANGE PUBLIC LIBRARY*, 21 S Arlington Ave, 07018. SAN 350-6649. Tel: 973-266-5600. Circulation Tel: 973-266-5501. Web Site: www.eopl.org. *Dir,* Carolyn Ryan Reed; E-mail: crreed@eopl.org; *Asst Dir, Circ,* Pamela V Holmes; E-mail: pholmes@eopl.org; *Adult Serv,* Nathalia Bermudez; E-mail: nbermudez@eopl.org; *Ch Serv,* Marissa Lieberman; E-mail: mlieberman@eopl.org; *Ref (Info Servs),* Ivonne Kratz; E-mail: ikratz@eopl.org; *Tech Serv,* Jenny Tong; E-mail: jtong@eopl.org; Staff 73 (MLS 13, Non-MLS 60)
Founded 1900. Pop 69,824; Circ 336,362
Library Holdings: AV Mats 13,922; Bk Titles 256,713; Bk Vols 405,165; Per Subs 634
Special Collections: New Jerseyana. State Document Depository; US Document Depository
Subject Interests: Ethnic studies
Wireless access
Partic in LibraryLinkNJ, The New Jersey Library Cooperative
Special Services for the Deaf - High interest/low vocabulary bks; Staff with knowledge of sign lang
Open Mon-Thurs 9-9, Fri 10-6, Sat 9:30-1:30
Friends of the Library Group
Branches: 3
AMPERE, 39 Ampere Plaza, 07017, SAN 350-6673. Tel: 973-266-7047, 973-266-7048. FAX: 973-674-1991. *Librn,* Nancy Tinney
Library Holdings: Bk Vols 31,250
Open Mon-Fri 1:30-5:30
ELMWOOD, 317 S Clinton St, 07018, SAN 350-6703. Tel: 973-266-7050. *Librn,* Nancy Tinney
Library Holdings: Bk Vols 24,500
Open Tues, Thurs & Fri 1:30-5:30
FRANKLIN, 192 Dodd St, 07017, SAN 350-6738. Tel: 973-266-7053. FAX: 973-674-1991. *Librn,* Nancy Tinney
Library Holdings: Bk Vols 16,000
Open Mon & Wed 1:30-5:30

EAST RUTHERFORD

P EAST RUTHERFORD MEMORIAL LIBRARY*, 143 Boiling Springs Ave, 07073. SAN 310-1215. Tel: 201-939-3930. FAX: 201-939-1231. Circulation E-mail: erutcirc@bccls.org. Web Site: eastrutherford.bccls.org. *Dir,* Christine Hartigan; E-mail: hartigan@eastrutherford.bccls.org; Staff 1 (MLS 1)
Pop 8,940; Circ 50,000
Library Holdings: Bk Vols 27,700; Per Subs 41
Automation Activity & Vendor Info: (Acquisitions) SirsiDynix; (Circulation) SirsiDynix; (OPAC) SirsiDynix
Wireless access
Partic in Bergen County Cooperative Library System, Inc
Open Mon-Thurs 10-8, Fri 12-5, Sat 10-2 (10-4 Winter)

EATONTOWN

P EATONTOWN LIBRARY, 33 Broad St, 07724. Tel: 732-389-2665. FAX: 732-389-7665. E-mail: library@eatontownnj.com. Web Site: eatontownnj.com/library-home-page. *Libr Mgr,* Barbara Sacco
Founded 1902. Pop 14,000; Circ 43,000
Library Holdings: AV Mats 2,000; Bk Vols 25,000; Per Subs 43
Automation Activity & Vendor Info: (Cataloging) SirsiDynix; (Circulation) SirsiDynix
Wireless access
Function: Free DVD rentals, Magazines, Meeting rooms, Photocopying/Printing, Prog for children & young adult, Spoken cassettes & CDs, Story hour, Summer reading prog, Telephone ref, Wheelchair accessible
Open Mon & Fri 10-5, Tues & Thurs 10-2, Wed 10-7, Sat 10-1
Friends of the Library Group

EDGEWATER

P EDGEWATER FREE PUBLIC LIBRARY*, 49 Hudson Ave, 07020. SAN 310-1258. Tel: 201-224-6144. FAX: 201-886-3395. Web Site: www.edgewaterlibrary.org. *Dir,* Linda Corona; E-mail: corona@edgewater.bccls.org; *Sr Librn,* Andrew Paris; E-mail: andrew.paris@edgewater.bccls.org; Staff 14 (MLS 2, Non-MLS 12)
Founded 1910. Pop 11,513; Circ 81,437
Library Holdings: AV Mats 3,410; CDs 514; DVDs 1,587; e-books 420; Large Print Bks 246; Bk Vols 24,538; Per Subs 87
Special Collections: Edgewater Works Progress Administration Papers, Photos (Edgewater Library Historical Coll). Municipal Document Depository
Automation Activity & Vendor Info: (Circulation) SirsiDynix; (ILL) Auto-Graphics, Inc; (OPAC) SirsiDynix
Wireless access
Function: 24/7 Online cat, 3D Printer, Adult bk club, Art programs, Audiobks via web, Bks on CD, Children's prog, Electronic databases & coll, Holiday prog, Home delivery & serv to seniorr ctr & nursing homes, Homebound delivery serv, Homework prog, ILL available, Internet access, Mango lang, Museum passes, Music CDs, Notary serv, Online cat, Outreach serv, Prog for adults, Prog for children & young adult, Ref serv available, Senior outreach, Spanish lang bks, Story hour, Summer reading prog, Teen prog
Partic in Bergen County Cooperative Library System, Inc
Open Mon-Thurs 10-8, Fri 10-6, Sat 10-5
Friends of the Library Group

EDISON

P EDISON TOWNSHIP FREE PUBLIC LIBRARY*, 340 Plainfield Ave, 08817. SAN 350-6762. Tel: 732-287-2298. Reference Tel: 732-287-2298, Ext 226, 732-287-2298, Ext 227. FAX: 732-819-9134. TDD: 732-777-7813. E-mail: eplcomments@lmxac.org. Web Site: www.edisonpubliclibrary.net. *Dir,* Judith Mansbach; E-mail: jellmans@lmxac.org; *Asst Dir,* Evan T Davis; Tel: 732-548-3045, Fax: 732-549-5171; Staff 80 (MLS 17, Non-MLS 63)
Founded 1928. Pop 100,000; Circ 529,386
Library Holdings: AV Mats 14,065; CDs 1,984; DVDs 4,379; Bk Vols 280,866; Per Subs 146; Talking Bks 5,761; Videos 1,025
Subject Interests: Local hist
Automation Activity & Vendor Info: (Acquisitions) SirsiDynix-DRA; (Cataloging) SirsiDynix-DRA; (Circulation) SirsiDynix-DRA; (Course Reserve) SirsiDynix-DRA; (ILL) SirsiDynix-DRA; (OPAC) SirsiDynix-DRA; (Serials) SirsiDynix-DRA

Wireless access
Function: Adult bk club, Art exhibits, Bk club(s), Bks on cassette, Bks on CD, Children's prog, Citizenship assistance, Computers for patron use, E-Reserves, Electronic databases & coll, Home delivery & serv to seniorr ctr & nursing homes, Homebound delivery serv, ILL available, Music CDs, Online cat, Outreach serv, Photocopying/Printing, Prog for adults, Prog for children & young adult, Ref & res, Ref serv available, Spoken cassettes & CDs, Spoken cassettes & DVDs, Story hour, Summer reading prog, Tax forms, Teen prog, Telephone ref, VHS videos, Wheelchair accessible
Publications: Library Letter (Newsletter)
Partic in Libraries of Middlesex Automation Consortium; LibraryLinkNJ, The New Jersey Library Cooperative
Special Services for the Deaf - TTY equip
Open Mon-Wed 9:30-9, Thurs & Fri 9:30-5, Sat 10-4
Friends of the Library Group
Branches: 2
CLARA BARTON BRANCH, 141 Hoover Ave, 08837, SAN 350-6797. Tel: 732-738-0096. FAX: 732-738-8325. *Br Mgr,* Margaret Vellucci; Staff 5.5 (MLS 1.5, Non-MLS 4)
Library Holdings: AV Mats 1,814; CDs 305; DVDs 173; Bk Vols 56,923; Per Subs 99; Talking Bks 428; Videos 558
Function: Computers for patron use, ILL available, Music CDs, Online cat, Photocopying/Printing, Ref & res, Ref serv available, Spoken cassettes & CDs, Spoken cassettes & DVDs, Story hour, Summer reading prog, Tax forms, Telephone ref, VHS videos, Wheelchair accessible
Publications: The Library Letter (Newsletter)
Open Mon & Thurs 12:30-8, Tues 9-5, Fri & Sat 9:30-5
Friends of the Library Group
NORTH EDISON BRANCH, 777 Grove Ave, 08820, SAN 350-6827. Tel: 732-548-3045. FAX: 732-549-5171. *Asst Dir, Br Mgr,* Evan T Davis; E-mail: edavis@lmxac.org; *Ref Librn,* Christine Yang; *Coordr, Ch Serv,* Carolyn N Cullum; E-mail: cncullum@lmxac.org; *Ref Serv, Ad,* Cathy Denner; E-mail: cdenner@lmxac.org; Staff 8 (MLS 6, Non-MLS 2)
Founded 1971. Pop 99,523; Circ 257,377
Library Holdings: CDs 815; DVDs 1,902; Bk Vols 100,529; Per Subs 146; Talking Bks 2,194; Videos 451
Function: Prog for adults, Prog for children & young adult, Spoken cassettes & CDs, Story hour, Summer reading prog, Tax forms, Teen prog, VHS videos, Wheelchair accessible
Publications: The Library Letter (Newsletter)
Open Mon-Thurs 9:30-9, Fri 9:30-5, Sat 10-4
Friends of the Library Group
Bookmobiles: 1. Librn, Sharon Giniger. Bk vols 10,278

M JFK MEDICAL CENTER*, Medical Library, Hackensack Meridian Health, 65 James St, 08818-3059. SAN 320-6971. Tel: 732-321-7181. FAX: 732-744-5639. E-mail: jfklibrary@gmail.com. Web Site: www.jfkmc.org. *Med Librn,* Cathy Hilman
Founded 1976
Library Holdings: Bk Titles 3,000; Per Subs 250
Subject Interests: Family practice, Rehabilitation
Wireless access
Publications: Library News; Library Update (Acquisition list)
Partic in Med Resources Consortium of Cent NJ; New Jersey Health Sciences Library Network
Restriction: Open to pub by appt only

J MIDDLESEX COLLEGE LIBRARY, (Formerly Middlesex County College Library), 2600 Woodbridge Ave, 08818. SAN 310-1282. Tel: 732-906-2561. Reference Tel: 732-906-4253. FAX: 732-906-4159. E-mail: library@middlesexcc.edu. Web Site: www.middlesexcc.edu/library. *Dir,* Marilyn Ochoa; Tel: 732-906-4252, E-mail: mochoa@middlesexcc.edu; *Tech Serv Librn,* Charles Dolan; Tel: 732-906-4254, E-mail: cdolan@middlesexcc.edu
Founded 1966. Enrl 11,000; Fac 155; Highest Degree: Associate
Library Holdings: DVDs 2,602; e-books 3,204; High Interest/Low Vocabulary Bk Vols 430; Bk Titles 81,409; Bk Vols 88,173; Per Subs 100; Talking Bks 8
Subject Interests: Nursing, Paralegal
Wireless access
Publications: Fact Sheets; Research Guides
Partic in Libraries of Middlesex Automation Consortium; LibraryLinkNJ, The New Jersey Library Cooperative; LYRASIS; OCLC Online Computer Library Center, Inc; Virtual Academic Library Environment
Open Mon-Thurs 7:45am-10pm, Fri 7:45-5, Sat 9-4, Sun 12-5

ELIZABETH

P ELIZABETH PUBLIC LIBRARY*, 11 S Broad St, 07202. SAN 350-6851. Tel: 908-354-6060. FAX: 908-354-5845. Web Site: www.elizpl.org. *Libr Dir,* Mary Faith Chmiel; E-mail: mfchmiel@elizpl.org; *Asst Dir,* Andrew Luck; Staff 13 (MLS 11, Non-MLS 2)
Founded 1908. Pop 125,000; Circ 182,689
Jul 2019-Jun 2020 Income (Main & Associated Libraries) $4,295,000, State $65,000, City $4,200,000, Locally Generated Income $30,000
Library Holdings: Bk Vols 275,000; Per Subs 110
Special Collections: Digitized Elizabeth Daily Journal 1872-1922; Elizabethtown Room Coll; Elizabethtown; Elizabeth, NJ; Regina Jones Woody;. US Document Depository
Automation Activity & Vendor Info: (Cataloging) SirsiDynix; (Circulation) SirsiDynix; (ILL) SirsiDynix; (OPAC) SirsiDynix; (Serials) SirsiDynix
Wireless access
Function: 24/7 Electronic res, 24/7 Online cat, Activity rm, Adult literacy prog, Archival coll, Art exhibits, Audiobks on Playaways & MP3, Audiobks via web, BA reader (adult literacy), Bilingual assistance for Spanish patrons, Bk club(s), Bks on CD, Children's prog, Citizenship assistance, Computer training, Computers for patron use, Electronic databases & coll, Holiday prog, Home delivery & serv to seniorr ctr & nursing homes, Homebound delivery serv, Homework prog, ILL available, Instruction & testing, Internet access, Life-long learning prog for all ages, Magazines, Magnifiers for reading, Meeting rooms, Microfiche/film & reading machines, Movies, Notary serv, Online cat, Orientations, Outreach serv, OverDrive digital audio bks, Photocopying/Printing, Preschool reading prog, Prog for adults, Prog for children & young adult, Ref & res, Ref serv available, Res performed for a fee, Scanner, Spanish lang bks, Summer reading prog, Tax forms, Teen prog, Wheelchair accessible, Writing prog
Partic in Libraries of Middlesex Automation Consortium; LibraryLinkNJ, The New Jersey Library Cooperative; LUCC; MURAL
Special Services for the Deaf - Am sign lang & deaf culture
Special Services for the Blind - Accessible computers; Computer access aids; Computer with voice synthesizer for visually impaired persons; Large screen computer & software; Screen enlargement software for people with visual disabilities
Open Mon-Thurs 9-9, Fri 10-7, Sat 9-5, Sun 12-4
Branches: 3
ELIZABETH PORT, 102-110 Third St, 07206-1717. Tel: 908-289-9032. FAX: 908-289-5663. *Br Serv Mgr,* Robert Barbanell; Tel: 908-353-4820
Library Holdings: Bk Vols 9,000; Per Subs 16
Open Mon-Fri 10-6, Sat 9-5
ELMORA, 740 W Grand St, 07202. Tel: 908-353-4820. FAX: 908-353-6877. *Br Serv Mgr,* Robert Barbanell
Library Holdings: Bk Vols 12,000; Per Subs 16
Open Mon, Wed & Thurs 9-9, Tues & Sat 9-5, Fri 10-5, Sun 12-4
LACORTE, 418-424 Palmer St, 07202, SAN 377-5895. Tel: 908-469-1866. FAX: 908-820-4764. *Br Serv Mgr,* Robert Barbanell; Tel: 908-353-4820
Library Holdings: Bk Vols 8,500; Per Subs 16
Open Mon, Wed, Sat 9-5, Tues & Thurs 12-8; Fri, 10-5

M TRINITAS REGIONAL MEDICAL CENTER*, Medical Library, 225 Williamson St, 07207. SAN 310-1355. Tel: 908-994-5371. FAX: 908-994-5099. Web Site: trinitasrmc.org/medical_library.htm. *Libr Dir,* Elisabeth Marrapodi; Tel: 908-994-5488, E-mail: EMarrapodi@Trinitas.org; *Libr Asst,* Ritza Alexandre
Founded 1930
Library Holdings: Bk Vols 1,020; Per Subs 90
Subject Interests: Med, Nursing
Wireless access
Partic in Basic Health Sciences Library Network; National Network of Libraries of Medicine Region 1; New Jersey Health Sciences Library Network; New Jersey Library Network
Open Mon-Fri 7:30-4, Sat 7:30-Noon
Restriction: Open to pub by appt only

UNION COUNTY COLLEGE
See Cranford

ELMER

S ELMER LIBRARY*, 120 S Main St, 08318. (Mail add: PO Box 372, 08318), SAN 375-7382. Tel: 856-358-2014. E-mail: elmer.librarian@comcast.net. Web Site: elmerlibrarynj.org. *Libr Consult,* Mary Linda Lacotte; *Libr Asst,* Rebecca Harrison
Library Holdings: Bk Titles 11,000
Automation Activity & Vendor Info: (Cataloging) Follett Software; (Circulation) Follett Software
Wireless access
Open Mon-Thurs 10-2 & 6:30-8:30, Sat 10-Noon
Friends of the Library Group

ELMWOOD PARK

P ELMWOOD PARK PUBLIC LIBRARY*, 210 Lee St, 07407. SAN 310-1401. Tel: 201-796-8888. FAX: 201-703-1425. Circulation E-mail: elpkcirc@bccls.org. Web Site: elmwoodpark.bccls.org. *Librn,* Jennifer Lazidis; Staff 22 (MLS 5, Non-MLS 17)
Founded 1953. Pop 18,925; Circ 104,000
Library Holdings: CDs 1,450; DVDs 875; Large Print Bks 1,250; Bk Titles 59,000; Bk Vols 68,000; Per Subs 75; Talking Bks 1,950; Videos 1,750

Automation Activity & Vendor Info: (OPAC) SirsiDynix
Function: ILL available
Open Mon, Fri & Sat 10-5, Tues-Thurs 10-8, Sun (Sept-May) 1-5
Friends of the Library Group

EMERSON

P EMERSON PUBLIC LIBRARY*, 20 Palisade Ave, 07630. SAN 310-141X. Tel: 201-261-5604. FAX: 201-262-7999. Circulation E-mail: emercirc@bccls.org. Web Site: emersonlibrary.org. *Dir,* Camille Valentino; E-mail: director@emerson.bccls.org; Staff 2 (MLS 1, Non-MLS 1)
Founded 1958. Pop 7,200; Circ 32,000
Library Holdings: AV Mats 2,400; Bk Vols 30,000; Per Subs 55; Talking Bks 735
Automation Activity & Vendor Info: (Circulation) SirsiDynix; (OPAC) SirsiDynix
Open Mon, Tues & Thurs 10-9, Wed, Fri & Sat 10-5
Friends of the Library Group

ENGLEWOOD

M ENGLEWOOD HEALTH*, Dr Walter Phillips Health Sciences Library, 350 Engle St, 07631. SAN 310-1436. Tel: 201-894-3069. FAX: 201-894-9049. Web Site: www.englewoodhealth.org. *Coordr,* Lia Sabbagh; Tel: 201-894-3069, E-mail: lia.sabbagh@ehmchealth.org; Staff 1 (MLS 1)
Founded 1943
Library Holdings: Bk Titles 3,000; Per Subs 250
Subject Interests: Commun health, Consumer health, Internal med, Ophthalmology, Otolaryngology, Patient educ, Psychiat, Surgery
Wireless access
Partic in Health Sci Libr Asn of NJ; LibraryLinkNJ, The New Jersey Library Cooperative; Medical Library Association; New Jersey Health Sciences Library Network
Open Mon-Fri 8-4

P ENGLEWOOD PUBLIC LIBRARY*, 31 Engle St, 07631. SAN 310-1444. Tel: 201-568-2215. FAX: 201-568-6895. Web Site: www.englewoodlibrary.org. *Dir,* John Arthur; Tel: 201-568-2215, Ext 222, E-mail: arthur@englewood.bccls.org; *Head, Children's Servx,* Donna-Lynne Cooper; Tel: 201-568-2215, Ext 243, E-mail: donnalynne.cooper@englewood.bccls.org; *Head, Literacy,* Lance Krubner; E-mail: lance.krubner@englewood.bccls.org; *Head, Ref & Adult Serv,* Charlene Taylor; Tel: 201-568-2215, Ext 229, E-mail: charlene.taylor@englewood.bccls.org; *Head, Tech Serv,* Jay Wolf; Tel: 201-568-2215, Ext 235, E-mail: jay.wolf@englewood.bccls.org; *Sr Librn,* Monica Sanchez; E-mail: monica.sanchez@englewood.bccls.org; *Ch,* Susan Okechukwu; Tel: 201-568-2215, Ext 241, E-mail: susan.okechukwu@englewood.bccls.org; *Ref Librn,* Margery Frohlinger; E-mail: margery.frohlinger@englewood.bccls.org; *Circ Supvr,* Marguerite Sansone; Tel: 201-568-2215, Ext 226, E-mail: marguerite.sansone@englewood.bccls.org; *Sr Libr Asst/Tech Serv,* Sheila Frisch; E-mail: sheila.frisch@englewood.bccls.org; Staff 20 (MLS 10, Non-MLS 10)
Founded 1901. Pop 26,203; Circ 249,784
Library Holdings: Bk Titles 112,276; Bk Vols 124,470; Per Subs 255
Subject Interests: African-Am studies, Careers, Jazz, Judaica, Local hist
Automation Activity & Vendor Info: (Circulation) SirsiDynix
Wireless access
Publications: Newsletter (Quarterly)
Open Mon-Thurs 9-9, Fri & Sat 9-5, Sun 1-5
Friends of the Library Group

ENGLEWOOD CLIFFS

CR SAINT PETER'S UNIVERSITY*, Englewood Cliffs Campus Library, Hudson Terrace, 07632. Tel: 201-761-7488. FAX: 201-568-6614. Web Site: www.saintpeters.edu/library. *Librn,* Mark Graceffo; E-mail: mgraceffo@saintpeters.edu; *Sr Asst Librn,* Ann Marie Ziadie; Tel: 201-761-6459, E-mail: aziadie@saintpeters.edu; Staff 12 (MLS 8, Non-MLS 4)
Founded 1973
Library Holdings: Bk Vols 300,000; Per Subs 134
Subject Interests: Nursing
Automation Activity & Vendor Info: (Cataloging) Ex Libris Group; (Circulation) Ex Libris Group; (Course Reserve) Ex Libris Group; (ILL) Ex Libris Group; (OPAC) Ex Libris Group
Wireless access
Open Mon, Wed & Thurs 3pm-8pm, Tues 9-8

EWING

C THE COLLEGE OF NEW JERSEY, R Barbara Gitenstein Library, 2000 Pennington Rd, 08628-1104. (Mail add: PO Box 7718, 08628-0718), SAN 310-5520. Tel: 609-771-2311. Interlibrary Loan Service Tel: 609-771-2028. Reference Tel: 609-771-2417. FAX: 609-637-5177. Circulation E-mail: circ@tcnj.edu. Web Site: library.tcnj.edu. *Dean of Libr,* Taras Pavlovsky; Tel: 609-771-2332, E-mail: pavlovsk@tcnj.edu; *Asst Dean,* Marlena Frackowski; *Asst Dir, Pub Serv,* Erin Ackerman; *Librn,* Valerie Tucci; *Access Serv Librn,* Bethany Sewell; *Bus & Econ Librn,* Terrence Bennett; *Cataloging & Metadata Librn,* Yuji Tosaka; *Education Children's Librn,* Genevieve Innes; *Emerging Tech Librn,* Amanda Cowell; *Humanities Librn,* David Murray; *Info Literacy Librn,* John Oliver; *Music & Media Librn,* Dr Linda Dempf; *Syst Librn,* Yongming Wang; *Acq,* Forrest Link; *Archives,* Debra Shiff; *Electronic Res,* Jia Mi. Subject Specialists: *Engr, Phys sci,* Valerie Tucci; Staff 14 (MLS 14)
Founded 1855. Enrl 7,000; Fac 350; Highest Degree: Master
Library Holdings: Bk Vols 580,200; Per Subs 1,485
Special Collections: History of American Education, Historical Textbooks & Historical Children's Books; History of New Jersey. State Document Depository
Automation Activity & Vendor Info: (Acquisitions) Ex Libris Group; (Cataloging) Ex Libris Group; (Circulation) Ex Libris Group; (Course Reserve) Ex Libris Group; (ILL) Ex Libris Group; (OPAC) Ex Libris Group; (Serials) SerialsSolutions
Wireless access
Partic in LibraryLinkNJ, The New Jersey Library Cooperative; LYRASIS; OCLC Online Computer Library Center, Inc; Virtual Academic Library Environment
Open Mon-Thurs 7:30am-Midnight, Fri 7:30-6, Sat 10-7, Sun 11-11

FAIR HAVEN

P FAIR HAVEN PUBLIC LIBRARY*, 748 River Rd, 07704. SAN 310-1495. Tel: 732-747-5031, Ext 220. FAX: 732-747-6962. E-mail: fairhavenlibrary@monmouthcountylib.org. Web Site: www.fairhavenlib.org. *Dir,* Donna Powers
Founded 1933. Pop 6,000; Circ 51,000
Library Holdings: Bk Vols 25,000
Automation Activity & Vendor Info: (Cataloging) SirsiDynix; (Circulation) SirsiDynix; (OPAC) SirsiDynix
Wireless access
Mem of Monmouth County Library
Open Mon-Wed & Fri 9-5, Thurs 1-8, Sat (Sept-May) 10-1

FAIR LAWN

P MAURICE M PINE FREE PUBLIC LIBRARY*, 10-01 Fair Lawn Ave, 07410. SAN 310-1533. Tel: 201-796-3400. FAX: 201-794-6344. Web Site: www.fairlawnlibrary.org. *Dir,* Adele P Puccio; E-mail: puccio@fairlawn.bccls.org; *Ch Serv,* Kate Nafz; E-mail: kate.nafz@fairlawn.bccls.org; *Circ,* Justin Portelli; E-mail: justin.portelli@fairlawn.bccls.org; *Ref (Info Servs),* Leslie Kruegel; E-mail: leslie.kruegel@fairlawn.bccls.org; Staff 6 (MLS 6)
Founded 1933. Pop 32,229; Circ 392,894
Library Holdings: Bk Vols 179,205; Per Subs 204
Automation Activity & Vendor Info: (Cataloging) SirsiDynix; (Circulation) SirsiDynix; (OPAC) SirsiDynix
Wireless access
Open Mon-Wed 10-9, Thurs 10-6, Fri 10-5, Sat 9-5, Sun 1-5
Friends of the Library Group

FAIRFIELD

P FAIRFIELD PUBLIC LIBRARY*, Anthony Pio Costa Memorial Library, 261 Hollywood Ave, 07004. SAN 310-155X. Tel: 973-227-3575. FAX: 973-227-7305. E-mail: ffpl@ffpl.org. Web Site: www.ffpl.org. *Dir,* Brianne Colombo; E-mail: colombo@ffpl.org; Staff 5 (MLS 2, Non-MLS 3)
Founded 1962. Pop 7,800; Circ 55,000
Library Holdings: AV Mats 5,000; Bk Vols 61,000; Per Subs 130; Talking Bks 650
Wireless access
Function: Adult bk club, Bk club(s), Bks on cassette, Bks on CD, CD-ROM, Children's prog, Computers for patron use, Electronic databases & coll, Free DVD rentals, Holiday prog, ILL available, Mail & tel request accepted, Music CDs, Notary serv, Online cat, Online ref, Photocopying/Printing, Prog for adults, Prog for children & young adult, Ref serv available, Story hour, Summer reading prog, Tax forms, Teen prog, Telephone ref, Wheelchair accessible
Publications: Newsletter
Partic in PALS Plus, The Computer Consortium of Passaic County Libraries; ReBL
Open Mon-Thurs 10-9, Fri 10-5, Sat (Fall-Spring) 10-4
Friends of the Library Group

FAIRVIEW

P FAIRVIEW FREE PUBLIC LIBRARY*, 213 Anderson Ave, 07022. SAN 310-1568. Tel: 201-943-6244. FAX: 201-943-5289. Web Site: fairview.bccls.org. *Dir,* Kristin Nelson; E-mail: nelson@fairview.bccls.org
Founded 1944. Pop 13,855; Circ 46,000
Library Holdings: DVDs 2,000; e-books 4,000; Large Print Bks 300; Bk Titles 17,500; Bk Vols 21,700; Per Subs 75

Automation Activity & Vendor Info: (Acquisitions) Innovative Interfaces, Inc; (Cataloging) Innovative Interfaces, Inc; (Circulation) Innovative Interfaces, Inc; (OPAC) Innovative Interfaces, Inc
Wireless access
Partic in Bergen County Cooperative Library System, Inc
Open Mon-Thurs 10-8, Fri & Sat 10-5

FANWOOD

P FANWOOD MEMORIAL LIBRARY, Five Forest Rd, 07023. SAN 310-1576. Tel: 908-322-6400. FAX: 908-322-5590. E-mail: library@fanwoodlibrary.org. Web Site: www.fanwoodlibrary.org. *Dir,* Dan Weiss; E-mail: dweiss@fanwoodlibrary.org; *Head, Circ, Head, YA, Supv Libr Asst,* Meredith Scheiner; E-mail: mscheiner@fanwoodlibrary.org; *Ch Serv,* Position Currently Open; Staff 3 (MLS 3)
Founded 1903. Pop 7,300; Circ 49,000
Library Holdings: AV Mats 800; Bk Titles 30,000; Bk Vols 39,000; Per Subs 75; Talking Bks 250
Special Collections: Local History Coll
Automation Activity & Vendor Info: (Acquisitions) TLC (The Library Corporation); (Cataloging) TLC (The Library Corporation); (Circulation) TLC (The Library Corporation); (OPAC) TLC (The Library Corporation)
Wireless access
Partic in LibraryLinkNJ, The New Jersey Library Cooperative
Open Mon 9:30-7, Tues 12-5, Wed 9:30-4, Thurs 9:30-5, Fri 9:30-1
Friends of the Library Group

FARMINGDALE

S ALLAIRE VILLAGE INC, Research Library, 4263 Atlantic Ave, 07727. Tel: 732-919-3500. FAX: 732-938-3302. E-mail: info@allairevillage.org. Web Site: www.allairevillage.org. *Exec Dir,* Hance M Silkus
Founded 1958
Library Holdings: AV Mats 25; Electronic Media & Resources 10; Bk Titles 500
Special Collections: Historic Allaire Village Coll, bus rec, ledgers, letters, photos; Howell Iron Works Company Coll, bus rec; James P Allaire Coll, ledgers, letters, photos
Subject Interests: 19th Century, Local hist
Function: Res libr
Publications: The Village Star (Newsletter)
Restriction: Open by appt only

FLANDERS

P MOUNT OLIVE PUBLIC LIBRARY*, 202 Flanders-Drakestown Rd, 07836. SAN 310-0448. Tel: 973-691-8686. FAX: 973-691-8542. Web Site: www.mopl.org. *Dir,* Mr Mauro Magarelli; E-mail: director@mopl.org; *Electronic Res,* Timothy Gilbert; E-mail: tim.gilbert@mopl.org; Staff 25 (MLS 8, Non-MLS 17)
Founded 1974. Pop 25,540; Circ 240,000
Library Holdings: Bk Vols 72,000; Per Subs 138
Special Collections: Heritage Coll; Mount Olive History Coll; New Jersey History Coll
Automation Activity & Vendor Info: (Circulation) SirsiDynix; (ILL) SirsiDynix; (OPAC) SirsiDynix
Wireless access
Partic in NJ Libr Asn
Special Services for the Deaf - Assisted listening device; Assistive tech; Closed caption videos; TTY equip
Special Services for the Blind - Bks on cassette; Bks on CD; Closed circuit TV magnifier; Copier with enlargement capabilities; Home delivery serv; Large print bks; Large type calculator; Low vision equip; Magnifiers; PC for people with disabilities; Reader equip; Scanner for conversion & translation of mats; ZoomText magnification & reading software
Open Mon-Thurs 9-9, Fri 9-5, Sat 9-4, Sun 12-4
Friends of the Library Group

FLEMINGTON

P FLEMINGTON FREE PUBLIC LIBRARY*, 118 Main St, 08822. SAN 310-1606. Tel: 908-782-5733. FAX: 908-782-3875. E-mail: flemingtonlibrary@gmail.com. Web Site: flemingtonlibrary.org. *Dir,* Shawn Armington
Founded 1899. Pop 4,344; Circ 35,838
Library Holdings: Bk Vols 40,000; Per Subs 50
Subject Interests: Humanities
Mem of Hunterdon County Library
Open Mon, Wed & Thurs 9-9, Tues & Fri 9-5, Sat 10-3 (10-1 June-Aug)
Friends of the Library Group

S HUNTERDON COUNTY HISTORICAL SOCIETY*, Hiram E Deats Memorial Library, 114 Main St, 08822. SAN 325-9307. Tel: 908-782-1091. E-mail: hunterdonhistoryinfo@gmail.com. Web Site: hunterdonhistory.org. *Exec Dir,* Patricia E Millen; *Librn,* Pamela J Robinson; *Ms Curator,* Donald Cornelius; E-mail: hunterdonhistory@gmail.com; Staff 3 (MLS 2, Non-MLS 1)
Founded 1885
Library Holdings: Bk Vols 7,000
Subject Interests: Genealogy, Local hist
Wireless access
Function: Mail & tel request accepted, Microfiche/film & reading machines, Online cat, Res libr, Res performed for a fee, Wheelchair accessible
Restriction: Internal use only, Non-circulating coll, Off-site coll in storage - retrieval as requested

L HUNTERDON COUNTY LAW LIBRARY*, 65 Park Ave, 08822. SAN 325-7606. Tel: 908-824-9750.
Library Holdings: Bk Vols 500
Wireless access
Restriction: Non-circulating to the pub, Open by appt only

P HUNTERDON COUNTY LIBRARY*, 314 State Rte 12, Bldg 3, 08822. SAN 310-1614. Tel: 908-788-1444. Circulation Tel: 908-788-1437. Reference Tel: 908-788-1434. FAX: 908-806-4862. Reference FAX: 908-806-5179. E-mail: library@hclibrary.us. Reference E-mail: reference@hclibrary.us. Web Site: www.hclibrary.us. *Dir,* James Keehbler; *Asst Dir,* Jennifer Winberry; E-mail: jwinberry@hclibrary.us; Staff 59 (MLS 21, Non-MLS 38)
Founded 1928. Pop 112,726; Circ 1,226,223
Library Holdings: AV Mats 46,816; Bk Titles 222,208; Bk Vols 384,939; Per Subs 591
Special Collections: New Jersey (Jerseyana)
Automation Activity & Vendor Info: (Acquisitions) Innovative Interfaces, Inc; (Cataloging) Innovative Interfaces, Inc; (Circulation) Innovative Interfaces, Inc
Wireless access
Function: Adult bk club, Art exhibits, Computers for patron use, Electronic databases & coll, Large print keyboards, Online cat, OverDrive digital audio bks, Prog for adults, Prog for children & young adult
Publications: HCL Duck (Newsletter); HCL Scoop (Bimonthly)
Member Libraries: Bunnvale Public Library; Flemington Free Public Library; Frenchtown Free Public Library; High Bridge Public Library; Holland Free Public Library; Milford Public Library; Readington Township Library; Tewksbury Township Public Library; Three Bridges Public Library
Open Mon, Fri & Sat 9-5, Tues-Thurs 9-9, Sun (Sept-June) 1-5
Friends of the Library Group
Branches: 2
NORTH COUNTY BRANCH, 65 Halstead St, Clinton, 08809. Tel: 908-730-6262. Reference Tel: 908-730-6135. FAX: 908-730-6750. *Br Mgr,* Terry Edwards; E-mail: tedwards@hclibrary.us
Library Holdings: Bk Vols 98,950
Open Mon, Fri & Sat 9-5, Tues-Thurs 9-9, Sun (Sept-June) 1-5
Friends of the Library Group
SOUTH COUNTY BRANCH, 1108 Old York Rd, Ringoes, 08551. Tel: 908-968-4611. E-mail: southcounty@hclibrary.us. *Asst Dir,* Jennifer Winberry
Library Holdings: Bk Vols 19,000
Open Mon & Thurs-Sat 9-5, Tues & Wed 9-9
Friends of the Library Group
Bookmobiles: 1

M HUNTERDON MEDICAL CENTER LIBRARY*, 2100 Wescott Dr, 08822. SAN 310-1622. Tel: 908-788-6100, Ext 2579. FAX: 908-788-2537. *Librn,* Karen Wenk; E-mail: kwenk@hhsnj.org
Founded 1954
Library Holdings: Bk Vols 1,000; Per Subs 15
Partic in Health Sci Libr Asn of NJ; Med Resources Consortium of Cent NJ; New Jersey Health Sciences Library Network
Open Mon-Fri 8-4:30

FLORHAM PARK

P FLORHAM PARK PUBLIC LIBRARY*, 107 Ridgedale Ave, 07932. SAN 310-1665. Tel: 973-377-2694. FAX: 973-377-2085. Reference E-mail: reference@florhamparklib.org. Web Site: www.florhamparklib.org. *Dir,* Nancy Aravecz Shaw; E-mail: nancyashah@florhamparklib.org; *Children's/Ref Librn,* Kate Dinneny; Staff 1.8 (MLS 1.8)
Founded 1965. Pop 11,000; Circ 92,893
Library Holdings: AV Mats 4,677; CDs 1,554; DVDs 1,400; e-books 321; Bk Vols 49,270; Per Subs 150
Subject Interests: Art
Automation Activity & Vendor Info: (Cataloging) Innovative Interfaces, Inc; (Circulation) Innovative Interfaces, Inc; (ILL) Innovative Interfaces, Inc; (OPAC) Innovative Interfaces, Inc
Wireless access
Function: ILL available, Photocopying/Printing, Telephone ref
Publications: Directory of Services (Annual)
Partic in Morris Automated Information Network

Open Mon-Thurs 9:30-9, Fri 9:30-5, Sat 10-4, Sun 1-4
Friends of the Library Group

FORT LEE

P FORT LEE PUBLIC LIBRARY*, 320 Main St, 07024. SAN 310-1673. Tel: 201-592-3615. FAX: 201-585-0375. Web Site: fortleelibrary.org. *Libr Dir,* Chris Yurgelonis; E-mail: yurgelonis@fortlee.bccls.org; *Head, Coll Develop,* Morris Balacco; E-mail: morris.balacco@fortlee.bccls.org; *Admin Librn, Head, Youth Serv,* Sarah Pardi; E-mail: sarah.pardi@fortlee.bccls.org; *Ref Serv Librn, Tech Serv Librn,* Wei Guan; E-mail: wei.guan@fortlee.bccls.org; Staff 7 (MLS 7)
Founded 1930. Pop 38,000; Circ 252,682. Sal $1,231,000 (Prof $357,425)
Library Holdings: AV Mats 1,135; Bk Vols 5,743; Per Subs 310; Talking Bks 2,813
Special Collections: Books in Japanese & Korean; Silent Film Photos
Subject Interests: Feminism
Automation Activity & Vendor Info: (Acquisitions) Baker & Taylor; (Cataloging) Baker & Taylor; (Circulation) Innovative Interfaces, Inc; (OPAC) Innovative Interfaces, Inc
Wireless access
Publications: Library Looking Glass (Newsletter)
Partic in Bergen County Cooperative Library System, Inc
Open Mon-Thurs 9:30-9, Fri & Sat 9:30-5, Sun 1-5
Friends of the Library Group

FRANKLIN LAKES

P FRANKLIN LAKES FREE PUBLIC LIBRARY*, 470 DeKorte Dr, 07417. SAN 310-1681. Tel: 201-891-2224. FAX: 201-891-5102. Web Site: www.franklinlakeslibrary.org. *Dir,* Gerry McMahon; E-mail: mcmahon@franklinlakes.bccls.org; *Asst Dir,* Position Currently Open; *Ad,* Jennifer Hendricks; E-mail: jennifer.hendricks@franklinlakes.bccls.org; *Ch,* Sarah Tobias; E-mail: sara.tobias@franklinlakes.bccls.org; *Teen Serv Librn,* Donna Kurdock; E-mail: donna.kurdock@franklinlakes.bccls.org; *AV Coll,* Ken Lew; E-mail: ken.lew@franklinlakes.bccls.org; *Local Hist Librn,* Jackie Bunker-Lohrenz; E-mail: jackie.bunker-lohrenz@franklinlakes.bccls.org; Staff 25 (MLS 6, Non-MLS 19)
Founded 1968. Pop 10,422
Library Holdings: Bk Vols 80,000; Per Subs 255
Automation Activity & Vendor Info: (Cataloging) Innovative Interfaces, Inc; (Circulation) Innovative Interfaces, Inc; (OPAC) Innovative Interfaces, Inc
Wireless access
Function: Art exhibits, Bk club(s), Bks on cassette, Bks on CD, Children's prog, Computer training, Computers for patron use, Digital talking bks, Electronic databases & coll, Free DVD rentals, Holiday prog, Homework prog, ILL available, Online cat, OverDrive digital audio bks, Photocopying/Printing, Prog for adults, Prog for children & young adult, Summer reading prog, Tax forms, Teen prog, Wheelchair accessible, Workshops
Partic in Bergen County Cooperative Library System, Inc; LibraryLinkNJ, The New Jersey Library Cooperative
Open Mon-Thurs 10-9, Fri 10-6, Sat 10-5, Sun (Sept-June) 1-5
Friends of the Library Group

FRANKLINVILLE

P FRANKLIN TOWNSHIP PUBLIC LIBRARY, 1584 Coles Mill Rd, 08322. SAN 350-8625. Tel: 856-694-2833. FAX: 856-694-1708. Web Site: www.ftlnj.org. *Dir,* Deborah Riether; E-mail: driether@ftlnj.org; Staff 7 (MLS 1, Non-MLS 6)
Founded 1966. Pop 16,820
Library Holdings: Bk Titles 40,000; Per Subs 50
Special Collections: NJ Coll
Automation Activity & Vendor Info: (Circulation) SirsiDynix; (OPAC) SirsiDynix
Wireless access
Function: 24/7 Electronic res, 24/7 Online cat, Adult bk club, Audiobks on Playaways & MP3, Audiobks via web, Bk club(s), Bks on CD, Children's prog, Computers for patron use, Electronic databases & coll, Free DVD rentals, Holiday prog, ILL available, Internet access, Laminating, Life-long learning prog for all ages, Magazines, Mail & tel request accepted, Museum passes, Music CDs, Online cat, Outreach serv, OverDrive digital audio bks, Photocopying/Printing, Preschool outreach, Printer for laptops & handheld devices, Prog for adults, Prog for children & young adult, Ref & res, Scanner, STEM programs, Story hour, Summer reading prog, Teen prog, Telephone ref, Workshops
Partic in Libraries of Gloucester, Salem & Cumberland Information Network
Open Mon-Thurs 10-8, Fri 10-5, Sat 10-4:30
Restriction: ID required to use computers (Ltd hrs)
Friends of the Library Group

FREEHOLD

M CENTRASTATE HEALTHCARE SYSTEM LIBRARY*, 901 W Main St, 07728. SAN 375-5088. Tel: 732-294-2668. *Librn,* Christine Forbes; Staff 1 (MLS 1)
Library Holdings: Bk Vols 1,500; Per Subs 125
Wireless access
Partic in Basic Health Sciences Library Network; LibraryLinkNJ, The New Jersey Library Cooperative; New Jersey Health Sciences Library Network; OCLC Online Computer Library Center, Inc
Restriction: Staff use only

P FREEHOLD PUBLIC LIBRARY*, 28 1/2 E Main St, 07728. SAN 310-1703. Tel: 732-462-5135. FAX: 732-577-9598. E-mail: fplib@freeholdpubliclibrary.org. Web Site: freeholdpubliclibrary.org. *Dir,* Barbara Greenberg; Staff 7 (MLS 1, Non-MLS 6)
Founded 1903. Pop 10,742; Circ 29,914
Library Holdings: Bk Vols 23,506; Per Subs 78
Special Collections: Books on Compact Discs; DVDs; Large Print Books
Subject Interests: Local hist
Automation Activity & Vendor Info: (Circulation) Mandarin Library Automation; (ILL) Mandarin Library Automation; (OPAC) Mandarin Library Automation
Wireless access
Publications: Freehold Public Library Blog; Newsletter (Online only); Patron Brochure (Monthly newsletter)
Open Mon, Wed & Thurs 9-9, Tues & Fri 9-5, Sat 10-4
Friends of the Library Group

S MONMOUTH COUNTY HISTORICAL ASSOCIATION LIBRARY & ARCHIVES*, 70 Court St, 07728. SAN 310-172X. Tel: 732-462-1466. E-mail: library@monmouthhistory.org. Web Site: 7005.sydneyplus.com/final/Portal/Monmouth.aspx?lang=en-US. *Archivist, Research Librn,* Dana Howell. Subject Specialists: *Genealogy, Hist,* Dana Howell
Founded 1898
Special Collections: A&M Karagheusian Coll; Allaire Family Papers (Howell Iron Works); Battle of Monmouth Coll; Hartshorne Family Papers; John C Mills Maritime Coll; North American Phalanx Records; Pach Brothers Studio Coll; Philip Freneau Papers
Subject Interests: Genealogy, Hist, Revolutionary war
Wireless access
Function: 24/7 Online cat, Archival coll
Publications: Collections Book; Diary of Sarah Tabitha Reid, 1868-1873; Micah Williams: Portrait Artist; Steamboats in Monmouth County: A Gazetteer
Partic in LibraryLinkNJ, The New Jersey Library Cooperative; NJ Libr Asn
Special Services for the Blind - Magnifiers
Restriction: Non-circulating to the pub, Open by appt only

FRENCHTOWN

P FRENCHTOWN FREE PUBLIC LIBRARY*, 29 Second St, 08825. SAN 310-1746. Tel: 908-996-4788. Web Site: frenchtownboro.com/library. *Librn,* Kelly Pickering
Circ 21,514
Library Holdings: Audiobooks 50; CDs 100; DVDs 1,000; Large Print Bks 50; Bk Vols 16,000; Per Subs 30; Videos 100
Automation Activity & Vendor Info: (Cataloging) SirsiDynix; (Circulation) SirsiDynix; (OPAC) SirsiDynix
Wireless access
Mem of Hunterdon County Library
Open Mon 3:30-6:30, Tues & Wed 3:30-7:30, Thurs 9:30-12:30

GALLOWAY

C STOCKTON UNIVERSITY*, Richard E Bjork Library, 101 Vera King Farris Dr, 08205-9441. SAN 310-4362. Tel: 609-652-4343. Circulation Tel: 609-652-4346. Reference Tel: 609-652-4266. FAX: 609-652-4964. E-mail: librarian@stockton.edu. Web Site: library.stockton.edu. *Dir,* Joe Toth; *Assoc Dir, Pub Serv,* Gus Stamatopoulos; E-mail: gus.stamatopoulos@stockton.edu; Staff 9 (MLS 8, Non-MLS 1)
Founded 1971. Enrl 9,621; Fac 330; Highest Degree: Doctorate
Jul 2018-Jun 2019. Mats Exp $975,000. Sal $2,019,304
Library Holdings: Audiobooks 349; CDs 1,117; DVDs 8,236; e-books 3,645; e-journals 41,000; Music Scores 1,713; Bk Titles 195,042; Bk Vols 261,023; Per Subs 490; Videos 14,161
Special Collections: Cape May Jazz Festival Archives; Holocaust & Genocide Studies; John Henry "Pop" Lloyd Archives; New Jersey Pine Barrens; Southern New Jersey Coll. Oral History; State Document Depository; US Document Depository
Automation Activity & Vendor Info: (Acquisitions) SirsiDynix; (Cataloging) SirsiDynix; (Circulation) SirsiDynix; (Discovery) ProQuest; (ILL) OCLC ILLiad; (OPAC) SirsiDynix; (Serials) SirsiDynix
Wireless access

Partic in LYRASIS; Virtual Academic Library Environment; Westchester Academic Library Directors Organization
Open Mon-Thurs 8am-Midnight, Fri 8-8, Sat 10-10, Sun Noon-Midnight

GARFIELD

P GARFIELD PUBLIC LIBRARY, 500 Midland Ave, 07026. SAN 310-1754. Tel: 973-478-3800. FAX: 973-478-7162. Web Site: www.garfield.bccls.org. *Dir,* Mary Jo Jennings; E-mail: jennings@garfield.bccls.org; *Children/Youth Librn,* Lauren Magielnicki; Staff 7 (MLS 3, Non-MLS 4)
Founded 1923. Circ 71,406
Library Holdings: Bk Vols 62,000
Special Collections: Black History-Literature (Black History), bks
Wireless access
Function: 24/7 Electronic res, 24/7 Online cat, 3D Printer, Adult bk club
Partic in Bergen County Cooperative Library System, Inc
Open Mon, Tues & Wed 9:30-8, Thurs & Fri 9:30-5:30, Sat 9:30-5 (Winter); Mon & Tues 9:30-8, Wed-Fri 9:30-5:30 (Summer)
Friends of the Library Group

GARWOOD

P GARWOOD FREE PUBLIC LIBRARY, 411 Third Ave, 07027. SAN 310-1789. Tel: 908-789-1670. FAX: 908-317-8146. E-mail: garwoodlibrary@gmail.com. Web Site: garwood.org, www.youseemore.com/garwood. *Libr Dir,* Maryanne Duffy; Staff 4 (MLS 1, Non-MLS 3)
Founded 1933. Pop 4,210; Circ 11,500
Library Holdings: Bk Vols 28,000; Per Subs 35
Special Collections: New Jersey Coll
Automation Activity & Vendor Info: (Cataloging) TLC (The Library Corporation); (Circulation) TLC (The Library Corporation)
Wireless access
Partic in LibraryLinkNJ, The New Jersey Library Cooperative
Open Mon, Wed & Fri 9-4, Tues & Thurs 9-7, Sat 10-1

GIBBSBORO

P GIBBSBORO PUBLIC LIBRARY*, Municipal Bldg, Lower Level, 49 Kirkwood Rd, 08026. Tel: 856-783-6655, Ext 116. E-mail: gibbsborolibrary@comcast.net. Web Site: www.gibbsborotownhall.com/index.php/library. *Dir,* Jodie Favat
Library Holdings: DVDs 200; Bk Vols 5,000; Per Subs 35
Wireless access
Mem of Camden County Library System
Open Tues 10-2 & 6-8, Wed 12-3, Thurs 6-8, Sat 9-Noon

GILLETTE

P LONG HILL TOWNSHIP PUBLIC LIBRARY*, 917 Valley Rd, 07933. SAN 310-5210. Tel: 908-647-2088. FAX: 908-647-2098. E-mail: librarians@lhtlibrary.mainlib.org. Web Site: www.longhilllibrary.org. *Dir,* Pierre Rosen; E-mail: pierre.rosen@lhtlibrary.mainlib.org; Staff 10 (MLS 4, Non-MLS 6)
Founded 1957. Pop 8,777; Circ 108,460
Library Holdings: Audiobooks 1,972; DVDs 3,910; Bk Vols 59,736; Per Subs 110
Special Collections: Cooking Coll; Gardening Coll; Large Print Coll; Parenting Coll
Wireless access
Function: Audiobks via web, Bk club(s), Bks on CD, Children's prog, Computers for patron use, Internet access, Magazines, Museum passes, Photocopying/Printing, Prog for adults, Teen prog
Publications: newsletter
Partic in Morris Automated Information Network; Morris-Union Federation
Open Mon-Thurs 10-9, Fri & Sat 10-5, Sun (Sept-June) 1-5
Friends of the Library Group

GLASSBORO

C ROWAN UNIVERSITY LIBRARY*, Keith & Shirley Campbell Library, 201 Mullica Hill Rd, 08029. SAN 350-7572. Tel: 856-256-4800. Circulation Tel: 856-256-4802. Interlibrary Loan Service Tel: 856-256-4803. Reference Tel: 856-256-4801. Administration Tel: 856-256-4984. FAX: 856-256-4924. E-mail: circulation@rowan.edu. Web Site: www.lib.rowan.edu/campbell. *Assoc Provost of Libr Info Servs,* Scott P Muir; Tel: 856-256-4981, E-mail: muir@rowan.edu; Staff 42 (MLS 15, Non-MLS 27)
Founded 1923. Enrl 9,762; Fac 630; Highest Degree: Doctorate
Library Holdings: e-books 249,282; e-journals 100,814; Bk Vols 328,891; Per Subs 3,962
Special Collections: United States, New Jersey & Delaware Valley History (Stewart Coll), bks, deeds, genealogical mat, ms, papers. State Document Depository; US Document Depository
Subject Interests: Educ, Engr, Health
Automation Activity & Vendor Info: (Acquisitions) Ex Libris Group; (Cataloging) Ex Libris Group; (Circulation) Ex Libris Group; (Course Reserve) Ex Libris Group; (Discovery) ProQuest; (ILL) Atlas Systems; (OPAC) Ex Libris Group; (Serials) Ex Libris Group
Wireless access
Partic in Coalition for Networked Information; LibraryLinkNJ, The New Jersey Library Cooperative; LYRASIS; Partnership for Academic Library Collaborative & Innovation; Philadelphia Area Consortium of Special Collections Libraries; Tri-State College Library Cooperative; Virtual Academic Library Environment
Open Mon-Thurs 7:30am-Midnight, Fri 7:30am-8pm, Sat Noon-7pm, Sun 11am-Midnight
Friends of the Library Group

GLEN RIDGE

P GLEN RIDGE FREE PUBLIC LIBRARY, 240 Ridgewood Ave, 07028. SAN 310-1843. Tel: 973-748-5482. FAX: 973-748-9350. E-mail: glrgcirc@bccls.org. Web Site: www.glenridgelibrary.org. *Dir,* Tina Marie Doody; E-mail: tmdoody@glenridgelibrary.org; *Ref Librn,* Helen Beckert; E-mail: hbeckert@glenridgelibrary.org; *Principal Libr Asst/Tech Serv & Circ,* Dawn Petretti; E-mail: dpetretti@glenridgelibrary.org; *Principal Libr Asst/Youth serv,* Sydney Young; E-mail: syoung@glenridgelibrary.org; Staff 18 (MLS 2, Non-MLS 16)
Founded 1912. Pop 7,802; Circ 129,091
Jan 2020-Dec 2020 Income $689,437, State $3,294, City $647,130, Locally Generated Income $39,013. Mats Exp $65,443, Books $48,055, Per/Ser (Incl. Access Fees) $2,830, AV Mat $14,558. Sal $393,389 (Prof $140,000)
Library Holdings: Audiobooks 530; CDs 1,993; DVDs 7,094; Electronic Media & Resources 5; Bk Titles 47,871; Per Subs 56
Special Collections: Glen Ridge Historical Coll & Archive
Subject Interests: Local hist
Automation Activity & Vendor Info: (Acquisitions) Baker & Taylor; (ILL) JerseyCat
Wireless access
Function: 24/7 Electronic res, 24/7 Online cat, 3D Printer, Adult bk club, After school storytime, Archival coll, Art exhibits, Audiobks on Playaways & MP3, Audiobks via web, Bk club(s), Bks on CD, Children's prog, Computers for patron use, Digital talking bks, E-Readers, Electronic databases & coll, Free DVD rentals, Homebound delivery serv, Homework prog, ILL available, Internet access, Laminating, Life-long learning prog for all ages, Magazines, Mail & tel request accepted, Makerspace, Meeting rooms, Microfiche/film & reading machines, Movies, Museum passes, Music CDs, Notary serv, Online cat, Online ref, Orientations, Outreach serv, Outside serv via phone, mail, e-mail & web, OverDrive digital audio bks, Photocopying/Printing, Preschool reading prog, Printer for laptops & handheld devices, Prog for adults, Prog for children & young adult, Ref & res, Ref serv available, Res assist avail, Scanner, STEM programs, Story hour, Summer reading prog, Tax forms, Teen prog, Telephone ref, Wheelchair accessible, Workshops
Publications: Brochures for Library Programs; Event Flyers; Monthly Calendar; Monthly newsletter via Constant Contact
Partic in Bergen County Cooperative Library System, Inc; LibraryLinkNJ, The New Jersey Library Cooperative; ReBL
Special Services for the Blind - Home delivery serv
Open Mon-Wed 9-8, Thurs-Sat 9-5
Friends of the Library Group

GLEN ROCK

P GLEN ROCK PUBLIC LIBRARY, 315 Rock Rd, 07452. SAN 310-1851. Tel: 201-670-3970. Reference Tel: 201-670-3991. FAX: 201-445-0872. Circulation E-mail: glrkcirc@bccls.org. Web Site: www.glenrocklibrary.org. *Dir,* Ellen O'Keefe; E-mail: okeefe@glenrock.bccls.org; *Head, Circ & Adult Serv,* Theresa Sarracino; E-mail: theresa.sarracino@glenrock.bccls.org; *Ch,* Danielle Cesena; E-mail: danielle.cesena@glenrock.bccls.org; *Teen/Tech Librnb,* Kristen Rasczyk; E-mail: kristen.rasczyk@glenrock.bccls.org; Staff 25 (MLS 6, Non-MLS 19)
Founded 1922. Pop 11,500; Circ 201,000
Library Holdings: DVDs 563; Large Print Bks 1,000; Bk Titles 80,000; Bk Vols 84,750; Per Subs 100; Talking Bks 3,313; Videos 1,830
Automation Activity & Vendor Info: (Cataloging) Innovative Interfaces, Inc; (Circulation) Innovative Interfaces, Inc; (OPAC) Innovative Interfaces, Inc
Wireless access
Function: Adult bk club, Adult literacy prog, After school storytime, Art exhibits, Audiobks via web, AV serv, Bks on cassette, Bks on CD, CD-ROM, Children's prog, Computers for patron use, Digital talking bks, E-Reserves, Electronic databases & coll, Free DVD rentals, ILL available, Instruction & testing, Internet access, Magnifiers for reading, Music CDs, Online cat, Photocopying/Printing, Prog for adults, Prog for children & young adult, Ref serv available, Spoken cassettes & CDs, Spoken cassettes & DVDs, Summer reading prog, Tax forms, Teen prog, Telephone ref, VHS videos, Wheelchair accessible

Partic in Bergen County Cooperative Library System, Inc
Open Mon & Thurs 10-9, Tues , Wed & Fri 10-5, Sat 10-2
Friends of the Library Group

GLOUCESTER CITY

P GLOUCESTER CITY LIBRARY*, 50 N Railroad Ave, 08030. SAN 310-186X. Tel: 856-456-4181. FAX: 856-456-6724. E-mail: gc@gcpl.us. Web Site: www.gloucestercitylibrary.org. *Libr Dir,* Wan Gu; Staff 4 (MLS 4)
Founded 1925. Pop 11,500; Circ 50,000
Library Holdings: Bk Titles 55,000; Per Subs 75
Automation Activity & Vendor Info: (Cataloging) Innovative Interfaces, Inc; (Circulation) Innovative Interfaces, Inc; (OPAC) Innovative Interfaces, Inc
Partic in LibraryLinkNJ, The New Jersey Library Cooperative
Open Mon 12-8, Tues & Fri 9-5, Wed & Thurs 9-8, Sat (Oct-May) 10-1

GREENWICH

S CUMBERLAND COUNTY HISTORICAL SOCIETY LIBRARY, The Warren & Reba Lummis Genealogical & Historical Library, 981 Great St, 08323. (Mail add: PO Box 16, 08323), SAN 375-8427. Tel: 856-455-4055, 856-455-8580. E-mail: cchistsoc@verizon.net. Web Site: warren-and-reba-lummis-research-library.org/. *Chairperson,* Charles Viel; *Dir,* Warren Adams; *Archivist, Asst Dir,* Joseph Mathews; *Librn,* Jeanne Garrison
Library Holdings: Bk Vols 2,800
Subject Interests: Genealogy
Function: Res libr
Open Wed 10-4, Sat & Sun 1-4
Restriction: Non-circulating

HACKENSACK

S BERGEN COUNTY HISTORICAL SOCIETY LIBRARY & ARCHIVES*, 355 Main St, Rm 124, 07601. (Mail add: PO Box 55, River Edge, 07661-0055), SAN 377-3981. Tel: 201-343-9492. E-mail: contactBCHS@bergencountyhistory.org, theBCHSlibrary@gmail.com. Web Site: www.bergencountyhistory.org/Pages/librarycollections.html. *Pres,* Jim Smith; *Librn,* Lucille Bertram
Founded 1902
Library Holdings: Bk Titles 2,500; Bk Vols 3,000
Special Collections: Genealogy Coll; Manuscripts Coll; Map Coll; Photographs & Slides
Subject Interests: Colonial hist, Revolutionary war
Wireless access
Open Wed 12-5, Thurs 10-3 & by appointment

GL BERGEN COUNTY LAW LIBRARY*, Bergen County Justice Ctr, Ten Main St, 1st Flr, 07601. SAN 310-1894. Tel: 201-527-2274. FAX: 201-371-1121. *Librn,* Henry Gozdz; E-mail: henry.gozdz@njcourts.gov
Library Holdings: Bk Vols 36,000; Per Subs 10
Wireless access
Open Mon-Fri 8:30-4:30
Restriction: Non-circulating to the pub

C FAIRLEIGH DICKINSON UNIVERSITY*, Business Research Library-New Jersey Room, Dickinson Hall, 140 University Plaza Dr, 07601. Tel: 201-692-2608. FAX: 201-692-7048. Web Site: www.fdu.edu. *Head of Libr,* Maria Kocylowsky; E-mail: marialk@fdu.edu; *Librn,* Michele Nestory; E-mail: michele1@fdu.edu
Library Holdings: Bk Vols 17,000
Wireless access
Open Mon-Thurs 8:30-8:30, Fri 8:30-4:30, Sat 11-5

M HACKENSACK UNIVERSITY MEDICAL CENTER*, Samuel & Sandra Hekemian Medical Library, 30 Prospect Ave, 07601. SAN 310-1916. Tel: 501-996-2326. FAX: 501-996-2467. *Dir,* Barbara S Reich; E-mail: barbara.reich@hackensackmeridian.org
Library Holdings: Bk Titles 3,500; Per Subs 312
Subject Interests: Hist
Wireless access
Partic in Basic Health Sciences Library Network; LibraryLinkNJ, The New Jersey Library Cooperative; National Network of Libraries of Medicine Region 1; New Jersey Health Sciences Library Network; New Jersey Library Network
Open Mon-Thurs 8am-9pm, Fri 8-6

P JOHNSON FREE PUBLIC LIBRARY, 274 Main St, 07601-5797. SAN 350-7637. Tel: 201-343-4169. Reference Tel: 201-343-4781. FAX: 201-343-1395. Reference E-mail: hackref@hackensack.bccls.org. Web Site: johnsonlib.org. *Dir,* Tara Cooper; *Head, Children's Servx,* Mari Zigas; *Head, Circ,* Beverley Wyche; *Head, Per,* Keri Adams; *Head, Ref,* Deborah Bock; *Head, Tech Serv,* Michael Ferrante; *Head, YA,* Keri Adams; *Commun Relations, Outreach Librn,* Laurie Meeske; Staff 10 (MLS 10)
Founded 1901. Pop 43,010; Circ 178,831
Library Holdings: Bk Vols 158,722; Per Subs 201
Special Collections: New Jersey History Coll, bks, microfilm, per, pictures; Spanish Language Coll. State Document Depository; US Document Depository
Automation Activity & Vendor Info: (Cataloging) Innovative Interfaces, Inc; (Circulation) Innovative Interfaces, Inc; (ILL) JerseyCat; (OPAC) Innovative Interfaces, Inc
Wireless access
Partic in Bergen County Cooperative Library System, Inc
Open Mon-Thurs 9-9, Fri & Sat 9-5
Friends of the Library Group

HACKETTSTOWN

C CENTENARY UNIVERSITY*, Taylor Memorial Library, 400 Jefferson St, 07840. SAN 310-1932. Tel: 908-852-1400, Ext 2345. FAX: 908-850-9528. E-mail: library@centenaryuniversity.edu. Web Site: libguides.centenaryuniversity.edu, www.centenaryuniversity.edu/academics/library. *Dir, Univ Librn,* Maryanne Fegan; E-mail: maryanne.fegan@centenaryuniversity.edu; Staff 8 (MLS 3, Non-MLS 5)
Founded 1867. Enrl 2,551; Fac 51
Library Holdings: DVDs 800; Bk Titles 69,300; Bk Vols 73,000; Per Subs 75
Special Collections: Centenary College Historical Coll
Subject Interests: Liberal arts
Automation Activity & Vendor Info: (Cataloging) ByWater Solutions; (Circulation) ByWater Solutions; (Course Reserve) ByWater Solutions; (OPAC) ByWater Solutions; (Serials) ByWater Solutions
Wireless access
Publications: Acquisitions List; Bibliographies; Guides; Handbook for the Taylor Memorial LRC
Partic in LibraryLinkNJ, The New Jersey Library Cooperative; OCLC Online Computer Library Center, Inc; Virtual Academic Library Environment
Open Mon-Thurs 8am-10:45pm, Fri 8-4:30, Sat 9-2, Sun 1-9:30
Friends of the Library Group

P HACKETTSTOWN FREE PUBLIC LIBRARY*, 110 Church St, 07840. SAN 310-1940. Tel: 908-852-4936. FAX: 908-852-7850. E-mail: info@hackettstownlibrary.org. Web Site: www.hackettstownlibrary.org. *Dir,* Rachel Burt; E-mail: rburt@hackettstownlibrary.org; Staff 4.5 (MLS 1.5, Non-MLS 3)
Founded 1913. Pop 8,984; Circ 35,000
Library Holdings: AV Mats 4,156; CDs 525; DVDs 2,026; Bk Titles 32,000; Per Subs 60
Subject Interests: Local hist
Automation Activity & Vendor Info: (Circulation) Auto-Graphics, Inc; (OPAC) Auto-Graphics, Inc
Wireless access
Partic in New Jersey Library Network
Open Mon-Fri 9-8, Sat 9-12
Friends of the Library Group

M HACKETTSTOWN REGIONAL MEDICAL CENTER*, Dr Eddy Palmer Medical Library, 651 Willow Grove St, 07840. SAN 373-2479. Tel: 908-850-6819. FAX: 908-850-6815, 908-850-7743. Web Site: www.hrmcnj.org.
Library Holdings: Bk Vols 500; Per Subs 24
Restriction: Staff use only

HADDON HEIGHTS

P HADDON HEIGHTS PUBLIC LIBRARY*, 608 Station Ave, 08035-1907. SAN 310-1959. Tel: 856-547-7132. FAX: 856-547-2867. Web Site: www.haddonheightslibrary.com. *Dir,* Christopher S Walter; E-mail: chris@haddonheightslibrary.com; *Ch Serv, Tech Serv,* Kathleen Bernardi
Founded 1902. Pop 7,500; Circ 42,000
Library Holdings: Bk Titles 53,000; Bk Vols 54,000; Per Subs 97
Special Collections: Local History Coll; Theatrical Plays
Automation Activity & Vendor Info: (Cataloging) Koha; (Circulation) Koha; (ILL) JerseyCat; (OPAC) Koha
Wireless access
Open Mon-Fri 10-9, Sat 10-4
Friends of the Library Group

HADDONFIELD

S ARCHER & GREINER LIBRARY, One Centennial Sq, 08033. SAN 325-7681. Tel: 856-795-2121. FAX: 856-795-0574. *Librn,* Elizabeth Olson; E-mail: lolson@archerlaw.com; Staff 2 (MLS 1, Non-MLS 1)
Library Holdings: Bk Vols 1,000

Subject Interests: Law
Restriction: Not open to pub

P HADDONFIELD PUBLIC LIBRARY*, 60 Haddon Ave, 08033-2422. SAN 310-1975. Tel: 856-429-1304. Reference Tel: 856-429-1304, Ext 112. FAX: 856-429-3760. E-mail: reference@haddonfieldlibrary.org. Web Site: www.haddonfieldlibrary.org. *Libr Dir,* Eric Zino; E-mail: ezino@haddonfieldlibrary.org; *Emerging Tech Librn,* Cathy DeCampli; E-mail: cdecampli@haddonfieldlibrary.org; *Tech Serv Librn,* Kathleen Metrick; E-mail: kmetrick@haddonfieldlibrary.org; *ILL Coordr,* Cynthia Guerra; E-mail: ill@haddonfieldlibrary.org; *Ch Serv,* Jordan Bilodeau; E-mail: jbilodeau@haddonfieldlibrary.org; Staff 6 (MLS 4, Non-MLS 2)
Founded 1803. Pop 11,659; Circ 134,613
Library Holdings: Bk Titles 74,825; Bk Vols 77,801; Per Subs 153
Special Collections: Oral History
Subject Interests: Local hist
Automation Activity & Vendor Info: (Cataloging) Innovative Interfaces, Inc; (Circulation) Innovative Interfaces, Inc; (OPAC) Innovative Interfaces, Inc
Wireless access
Partic in LibraryLinkNJ, The New Jersey Library Cooperative; LYRASIS
Open Mon-Thurs 10-9, Fri 10-6, Sat 10-5, Sun 1-5
Friends of the Library Group

S HISTORICAL SOCIETY OF HADDONFIELD ARCHIVES CENTER, 343 Kings Hwy E, 08033. SAN 325-7703. Tel: 856-429-7375. E-mail: info@haddonfieldhistory.org, library@haddonfieldhistory.org. Web Site: www.haddonfieldhistory.org. *Archivist/Librn,* Position Currently Open
Founded 1914
Library Holdings: Bk Titles 900
Special Collections: Family Papers, incl Gill, Hinchman, Hopkins, Rowand, Rhoads, Tatem-Moore-Brigham & Cuthbert-Ogden
Subject Interests: Local hist
Wireless access
Function: Archival coll
Open Tues & Wed 9:30-11:30
Restriction: Non-circulating to the pub

HALEDON

P HALEDON FREE PUBLIC LIBRARY*, Municipal Bldg, 3rd Flr, 510 Bellmont Ave, 07508. SAN 310-1991. Tel: 973-790-3808. Web Site: haledonlib.org. *Dir,* Tara Morstatt; E-mail: Director@haledonlib.org; Staff 6 (Non-MLS 6)
Founded 1958. Pop 8,252; Circ 14,000
Library Holdings: AV Mats 2,100; CDs 806; DVDs 1,093; Bk Titles 15,976; Per Subs 52
Automation Activity & Vendor Info: (Cataloging) SirsiDynix-WorkFlows; (Circulation) SirsiDynix-WorkFlows; (ILL) Auto-Graphics, Inc
Function: Audio & video playback equip for onsite use, ILL available, Photocopying/Printing, Summer reading prog, Telephone ref
Partic in PALS Plus, The Computer Consortium of Passaic County Libraries
Open Mon 10-7, Tues-Thurs 10-8, Fri 10-5, Sat 10-3

HAMILTON

P HAMILTON TOWNSHIP PUBLIC LIBRARY, One Justice Samuel A Alito, Jr Way, 08619. SAN 351-4862. Tel: 609-581-4060. FAX: 609-581-4073. Web Site: www.hamiltonnjpl.org. *Dir,* Scott Chianese; E-mail: schianese@hamiltonnjpl.org; *Adult Serv Mgr,* Mary Lopez; E-mail: mlopez@hamiltonnjpl.org; *Ch Mgr,* Colleen Affrime; E-mail: caffrime@hamiltonnjpl.org; Staff 8 (MLS 8)
Founded 1923. Pop 92,000; Circ 410,236
Library Holdings: AV Mats 13,317; Large Print Bks 3,810; Bk Titles 216,959; Bk Vols 270,214; Per Subs 440; Talking Bks 3,843
Subject Interests: Local hist
Automation Activity & Vendor Info: (Acquisitions) Baker & Taylor; (Cataloging) Koha; (Circulation) Koha; (OPAC) Koha
Wireless access
Function: ILL available
Partic in LibraryLinkNJ, The New Jersey Library Cooperative; OCLC Online Computer Library Center, Inc
Special Services for the Deaf - Bks on deafness & sign lang; High interest/low vocabulary bks; Staff with knowledge of sign lang; TTY equip
Open Mon-Thurs 9-8:30, Fri & Sat 9-5
Friends of the Library Group

HARRINGTON PARK

P HARRINGTON PARK PUBLIC LIBRARY*, Ten Herring St, 07640. SAN 310-2017. Tel: 201-768-5675. FAX: 201-768-7495. E-mail: hapkcirc@bccls.org. Web Site: www.harringtonpark.bccls.org. *Dir,* Judith Heldman; E-mail: heldman@harringtonpark.bccls.org
Founded 1964. Pop 5,000; Circ 25,251
Library Holdings: Bk Vols 33,000; Per Subs 100
Automation Activity & Vendor Info: (Cataloging) SirsiDynix; (Circulation) SirsiDynix; (OPAC) SirsiDynix
Wireless access
Open Mon & Thurs 10-9, Tues & Fri 12-5, Wed 10-5, Sat 10-1, Sun 1-4
Friends of the Library Group

HARRISON

P HARRISON PUBLIC LIBRARY, 415 Harrison Ave, 07029. SAN 310-2025. Tel: 973-483-2366. FAX: 973-483-1052. E-mail: library@townofharrison.com. Web Site: www2.youseemore.com/harrisonpl. *Actg Dir,* Nelba Mejias; E-mail: nmejias@townofharrison.com; Staff 5 (Non-MLS 5)
Founded 1911. Pop 16,700; Circ 110,000
Library Holdings: Bk Vols 48,500; Per Subs 50
Automation Activity & Vendor Info: (Cataloging) TLC (The Library Corporation); (Circulation) TLC (The Library Corporation); (OPAC) TLC (The Library Corporation); (Serials) EBSCO Online
Wireless access
Function: 24/7 Online cat, Bilingual assistance for Spanish patrons, Bks on CD, Children's prog, Computers for patron use, Free DVD rentals, Holiday prog, ILL available, Internet access, Magazines, Movies, Online cat, Photocopying/Printing, Prog for children & young adult, Spanish lang bks, Spoken cassettes & CDs, Spoken cassettes & DVDs, Summer reading prog, Tax forms
Partic in LibraryLinkNJ, The New Jersey Library Cooperative; New Jersey Library Network
Open Mon-Fri 9-4:30
Restriction: Borrowing requests are handled by ILL, Circ to mem only, In-house use for visitors, Non-resident fee, Not a lending libr, Pub use on premises

HASBROUCK HEIGHTS

P FREE PUBLIC LIBRARY OF HASBROUCK HEIGHTS, 320 Boulevard, 07604. SAN 310-2033. Tel: 201-288-0484, 201-288-0488. FAX: 201-288-5467. Web Site: www.hasbrouckheightslibrary.org. *Dir,* Mimi Hui; E-mail: hui@hasbrouckheights.bccls.org; *Head, Circ,* Robin Lasky; E-mail: robin.lasky@hasbrouckheights.bccls.org; *Head, Ref,* Laura Rios; E-mail: laura.rios@hasbrouckheights.bccls.org; *Youth Serv Librn,* Maureen Herman; E-mail: maureen.herman@hasbrouckheights.bccls.org; Staff 3 (MLS 3)
Founded 1916. Pop 11,842; Circ 121,887
Library Holdings: DVDs 4,282; Large Print Bks 122; Bk Titles 58,643; Bk Vols 58,845; Per Subs 95
Special Collections: Oral History
Subject Interests: Local hist
Wireless access
Function: 24/7 Electronic res, 24/7 Online cat, Adult bk club, Bk club(s), Bks on CD, Children's prog, Computer training, Computers for patron use, Homebound delivery serv, Magnifiers for reading, Meeting rooms, Photocopying/Printing, Ref & res, Senior outreach, Study rm, Summer reading prog, Tax forms
Publications: Hasbrouck Heights: A History
Partic in Bergen County Cooperative Library System, Inc
Open Mon-Wed 10-9, Thurs-Sat 10-5 (Winter); Mon 10-5, Tues-Thurs 10-8, Fri 10-5 (Summer)
Friends of the Library Group

HAWORTH

P HAWORTH MUNICIPAL LIBRARY*, 165 Stevens Pl, 07641. SAN 310-2041. Tel: 201-384-1020. FAX: 201-385-7750. Circulation E-mail: hawhcirc@bccls.org. Web Site: www.haworthlibrary.org. *Dir,* Shinae Hyun; E-mail: hyun@haworth.bccls.org
Circ 38,000
Library Holdings: Audiobooks 1,162; CDs 1,175; DVDs 2,045; e-books 12,710; Bk Vols 22,330; Per Subs 53
Special Collections: Local History Coll
Automation Activity & Vendor Info: (Cataloging) Innovative Interfaces, Inc; (Circulation) Innovative Interfaces, Inc; (OPAC) Innovative Interfaces, Inc
Wireless access
Partic in Bergen County Cooperative Library System, Inc
Open Mon & Wed 10-9, Tues, Thurs & Fri 10-5, Sat 10-2
Friends of the Library Group

HAWTHORNE

P LOUIS BAY 2ND LIBRARY*, 345 Lafayette Ave, 07506-2546. SAN 310-205X. Tel: 973-427-5745. FAX: 973-427-5269. Web Site: hawthorne.bccls.org. *Dir,* Monica A Smith; E-mail: smith@hawthorne.bccls.org; *Head, Acq, Head, Tech Serv,* Amy Fletcher; Tel: 973-427-5745, Ext 18; *Head, Adult Serv,* Gina Gerard; Tel: 973-427-5745, Ext 19; *Head, Children's Servx,* Wendy Hollis; Tel:

973-427-5745, Ext 21; *Head, Circ,* Marilyn Rees; Tel: 973-427-5745, Ext 10; Staff 25 (MLS 9, Non-MLS 16)
Founded 1913. Pop 18,000; Circ 175,804
Library Holdings: Bks on Deafness & Sign Lang 115; High Interest/Low Vocabulary Bk Vols 250; Bk Vols 76,223; Per Subs 194; Spec Interest Per Sub 15
Special Collections: Deafness & Sign Language; Hawthorne & Passaic County Local History
Subject Interests: Cinema, Hist, Literacy, Quilting, Video
Automation Activity & Vendor Info: (Acquisitions) Baker & Taylor; (ILL) JerseyCat
Wireless access
Function: 24/7 Electronic res, 24/7 Online cat, Adult bk club, Adult literacy prog, Archival coll, Art exhibits, Audiobks via web, Bk club(s), Bks on CD, Children's prog, Computer training, Computers for patron use, Digital talking bks, E-Readers, E-Reserves, Electronic databases & coll, Free DVD rentals, Holiday prog, ILL available, Internet access, Magazines, Meeting rooms, Microfiche/film & reading machines, Movies, Music CDs, Online cat, OverDrive digital audio bks, Photocopying/Printing, Prog for adults, Prog for children & young adult, Ref & res, Ref serv available, Scanner, Spanish lang bks, Story hour, Study rm, Summer & winter reading prog, Summer reading prog, Tax forms, Telephone ref, Wheelchair accessible
Partic in Bergen County Cooperative Library System, Inc
Open Mon-Thurs 9-9, Fri 9-5:30, Sat 10-5
Restriction: ID required to use computers (Ltd hrs)
Friends of the Library Group

HIGH BRIDGE

P HIGH BRIDGE PUBLIC LIBRARY*, 71 Main St, 08829. SAN 310-2068. Tel: 908-638-8231. E-mail: library71@comcast.net. Web Site: highbridge.org/about-high-bridge/library. *Librn,* Theresa Steets
Founded 1914. Pop 3,770; Circ 10,304
Library Holdings: Bk Vols 8,500; Per Subs 52
Automation Activity & Vendor Info: (Cataloging) Innovative Interfaces, Inc; (Circulation) Innovative Interfaces, Inc; (OPAC) Innovative Interfaces, Inc
Wireless access
Mem of Hunterdon County Library
Open Mon & Wed 10-12 & 3-8, Fri 10-12 & 3-7, Sat 10-2
Friends of the Library Group

HIGHLAND PARK

P HIGHLAND PARK PUBLIC LIBRARY*, 31 N Fifth Ave, 08904. SAN 310-2076. Tel: 732-572-2750. FAX: 732-819-9046. Web Site: www.hpplnj.org. *Dir,* Kate Jaggers; E-mail: director@hpplnj.org; *Adult Serv,* Sherry Johnson; *Youth Serv,* Karen Jarzabski; Staff 8 (MLS 4, Non-MLS 4)
Founded 1922. Pop 13,396; Circ 182,000
Library Holdings: Bk Vols 60,000; Per Subs 170
Wireless access
Function: 24/7 Electronic res, 24/7 Online cat, Adult bk club, Art exhibits, Audiobks via web, Bi-weekly Writer's Group, Bk club(s), Bks on CD, Children's prog, Computers for patron use, Electronic databases & coll, Free DVD rentals, ILL available, Internet access, Life-long learning prog for all ages, Magazines, Mail & tel request accepted, Meeting rooms, Movies, Museum passes, Notary serv, Online cat, Online ref, Outreach serv, Outside serv via phone, mail, e-mail & web, OverDrive digital audio bks, Photocopying/Printing, Preschool outreach, Prog for adults, Prog for children & young adult, Ref & res, Ref serv available, Scanner, STEM programs, Story hour, Study rm, Summer reading prog, Tax forms, Teen prog, Telephone ref, Wheelchair accessible, Writing prog
Partic in Libraries of Middlesex Automation Consortium
Open Mon, Tues & Thurs 10-9, Wed, Fri & Sat 10-5 (10-2 Summer), Sun 1-5
Friends of the Library Group

HIGHLANDS

G NATIONAL MARINE FISHERIES SERVICE*, Lionel A Walford Library, Northeast Fisheries Science Ctr, 74 Magruder Rd, 07732. SAN 310-2084. Tel: 732-872-3034, 732-872-3035. FAX: 732-872-3088. Web Site: www.nefsc.noaa.gov/libraries/SH-library.html, www.nefsc.noaa.gov/nefsc/SandyHook/library. *Librn,* Sally Weiner; E-mail: Sally.Weiner@noaa.gov
Library Holdings: Bk Titles 2,500
Special Collections: NJ Sea Grant Coll
Subject Interests: Chem, Environ studies, Marine biol, Oceanography
Partic in Federal Library & Information Network; NOAA Libraries Network; OCLC-LVIS
Restriction: Open by appt only

HILLSDALE

P HILLSDALE FREE PUBLIC LIBRARY*, 509 Hillsdale Ave, 07642. SAN 310-2106. Tel: 201-358-5072. FAX: 201-358-5074. Circulation E-mail: info@hfpl.org. Web Site: hfpl.org. *Dir,* David J Franz; E-mail: franz@hillsdale.bccls.org; *Ch,* Cindy Greenwald; E-mail: cindy.greenwald@hillsdale.bccls.org; Staff 4 (MLS 2, Non-MLS 2)
Founded 1935. Pop 10,222; Circ 92,000
Library Holdings: Bk Vols 60,000; Per Subs 120
Automation Activity & Vendor Info: (Cataloging) SirsiDynix; (Circulation) SirsiDynix; (OPAC) SirsiDynix
Wireless access
Partic in Bergen County Cooperative Library System, Inc
Open Mon, Tues & Thurs 10-9, Wed 10-6, Fri & Sat 10-5, Sun 1-4
Friends of the Library Group

HILLSIDE

P HILLSIDE PUBLIC LIBRARY*, John F Kennedy Plaza, 1409 Liberty Ave, 07205. SAN 310-2122. Tel: 973-923-4413. E-mail: info@hillsidepl.org. Web Site: www.hillsidepl.org. *Libr Dir,* Kassundra Miller; E-mail: kmiller@hillsidepl.org; *Head, Circ,* Michele Mitchell; *Head, Youth Serv,* Stephanie Nesmith; Staff 12 (MLS 1, Non-MLS 11)
Founded 1947. Pop 21,200; Circ 46,372
Library Holdings: Audiobooks 333; AV Mats 3,105; CDs 428; DVDs 1,093; Large Print Bks 536; Bk Titles 94,000; Bk Vols 98,000; Per Subs 109; Videos 645
Special Collections: Ethel Smith African-American Coll; Hillside Local Newspapers Digitized from 1924
Automation Activity & Vendor Info: (Cataloging) TLC (The Library Corporation); (Circulation) TLC (The Library Corporation); (ILL) JerseyCat; (OPAC) TLC (The Library Corporation)
Wireless access
Function: Adult literacy prog, After school storytime, Bilingual assistance for Spanish patrons, Bk club(s), Bk reviews (Group), Bks on CD, Chess club, Children's prog, ILL available, Internet access, Magnifiers for reading, Notary serv, Online cat, Outside serv via phone, mail, e-mail & web, Photocopying/Printing, Prog for adults, Prog for children & young adult, Ref serv available, Spoken cassettes & CDs, Story hour, Summer reading prog, Tax forms, VHS videos, Wheelchair accessible
Publications: Info To Go (Newsletter)
Special Services for the Blind - Bks on CD; Computer with voice synthesizer for visually impaired persons
Open Mon, Wed & Thurs 10-8, Tues & Fri 10-6; Sat (Fall & Spring) 10-4:30

HOBOKEN

P HOBOKEN PUBLIC LIBRARY*, 500 Park Ave, 07030. SAN 310-2157. Tel: 201-420-2346. Circulation Tel: 201-420-2280. Reference Tel: 201-420-2347. FAX: 201-420-2299. Circulation E-mail: hobkcirc@bccls.org. Reference E-mail: reference@hobokan.bccls.org. Web Site: hoboken.bccls.org, hobokenpubliclibrary.org. *Dir,* Lina Podles; E-mail: podles@hoboken.bccls.org; *Adult Serv,* Rosary Van Ingen; *Ch Serv,* Lois Gross; Staff 19 (MLS 4, Non-MLS 15)
Founded 1890. Pop 50,050; Circ 214,000
Library Holdings: Bk Vols 74,500; Per Subs 166
Special Collections: Hoboken History Coll
Automation Activity & Vendor Info: (Cataloging) SirsiDynix; (Circulation) SirsiDynix; (ILL) SirsiDynix; (OPAC) SirsiDynix
Wireless access
Function: ILL available
Partic in Bergen County Cooperative Library System, Inc; LibraryLinkNJ, The New Jersey Library Cooperative
Open Mon 10-8, Tues & Wed 9-8, Thurs 9-9, Fri 9-5, Sat 10-5, Sun 10-3
Friends of the Library Group

C STEVENS INSTITUTE OF TECHNOLOGY*, Samuel C Williams Library, One Castle Point on Hudson, 07030. SAN 310-2165. Tel: 201-216-5200. Circulation Tel: 201-216-5327. Interlibrary Loan Service Tel: 201-216-5413. Administration Tel: 201-216-5205. FAX: 201-216-8319. E-mail: library@stevens.edu. Web Site: library.stevens.edu. *Dir,* Linda Beninghove; Tel: 201-216-5412, E-mail: linda.beninghove@stevens.edu; *Asst Admin,* Nydia Cruz; E-mail: nydia.cruz@stevens.edu; *Head, ILL & Doc Delivery,* Mary Ellen Valverde; Tel: 201-216-5408, E-mail: mary.valverde@stevens.edu; *Head, Acq & Coll Develop,* Scott Smith; Tel: 201-216-5419, E-mail: scott.smith@stevens.edu; *Head, Archives & Spec Coll,* Leah Loscutoff; Tel: 201-216-5416, E-mail: lloscuto@stevens.edu; *Mgr, Circ Serv,* John Cruz; Tel: 201-216-5334, E-mail: juan.cruz@stevens.edu; *Asst Curator,* Doris Oliver; Tel: 201-216-5415; Staff 6 (MLS 4, Non-MLS 2)
Founded 1870. Enrl 3,200; Fac 200; Highest Degree: Doctorate
Library Holdings: e-books 3,500; e-journals 30,000; Bk Titles 64,105; Bk Vols 79,950; Per Subs 120

Special Collections: Art (Leonardo da Vinci Coll), bks, drawings, micro; History (Stevens Family Archives), bks, micro; Industrial Management (Frederick Winslow Taylor Coll), bks, micro
Subject Interests: Applied sci, Engr, Natural sci
Automation Activity & Vendor Info: (Cataloging) SirsiDynix; (Circulation) SirsiDynix; (ILL) OCLC; (OPAC) SirsiDynix; (Serials) SirsiDynix
Wireless access
Partic in Metropolitan New York Library Council; OCLC Online Computer Library Center, Inc; Virtual Academic Library Environment
Open Mon-Thurs 8am-2am, Fri 8am-Midnight, Sat 9-Midnight, Sun 9am-2am
Restriction: In-house use for visitors
Friends of the Library Group

HO-HO-KUS

P WORTH PINKHAM MEMORIAL LIBRARY*, Ho-Ho-Kus Public Library, 91 Warren Ave, 07423. SAN 310-2130. Tel: 201-445-8078. FAX: 201-445-8492. Circulation E-mail: hohocirc@bccls.org. Web Site: hohokuslibrary.org. *Dir,* Gretchen Kaser; E-mail: kaser@hohokus.bccls.org; Staff 2 (MLS 2)
Founded 1924. Pop 4,078; Circ 40,948
Library Holdings: Bk Vols 27,000; Per Subs 60
Wireless access
Function: 24/7 Electronic res, 24/7 Online cat, Adult bk club, Art exhibits, Audiobks on Playaways & MP3, Audiobks via web, AV serv, Bk club(s), Bks on CD, Children's prog, Computer training, Computers for patron use, Digital talking bks, E-Reserves, Electronic databases & coll, Free DVD rentals, Holiday prog, Home delivery & serv to seniorr ctr & nursing homes, Homebound delivery serv, ILL available, Internet access, Life-long learning prog for all ages, Magazines, Magnifiers for reading, Mango lang, Movies, Museum passes, Music CDs, Notary serv, Online cat, Outreach serv, OverDrive digital audio bks, Photocopying/Printing, Preschool outreach, Preschool reading prog, Printer for laptops & handheld devices, Prog for adults, Prog for children & young adult, Ref & res, Ref serv available, Scanner, Senior computer classes, Spoken cassettes & CDs, STEM programs, Story hour, Summer reading prog, Teen prog, Telephone ref, Visual arts prog, Wheelchair accessible
Partic in Bergen County Cooperative Library System, Inc
Open Mon, Wed & Fri 10-5, Tues & Thurs 10-8, Sat 10-1

HOPEWELL

P HOPEWELL PUBLIC LIBRARY, 13 E Broad St, 08525. SAN 310-2203. Tel: 609-466-1625. FAX: 609-466-1996. E-mail: hpl@redlibrary.org. Web Site: www.redlibrary.org. *Dir,* Anne Zeman; *Staff Librn,* Norman Lee; *Staff Librn,* Barbara Merry; *Children's Coordr,* Jennifer Saltman. Subject Specialists: *Volunteer mgt,* Barbara Merry; Staff 4 (Non-MLS 4)
Founded 1914. Circ 17,500
Library Holdings: AV Mats 40; Bks on Deafness & Sign Lang 20; Large Print Bks 200; Bk Titles 15,000; Per Subs 53; Talking Bks 400
Special Collections: Local Newspaper Coll (1881-present), microfilm
Wireless access
Function: 24/7 Electronic res, 24/7 Online cat, Adult bk club, Computers for patron use, Holiday prog, ILL available, Internet access, Magazines, Movies, Online cat, Photocopying/Printing, Printer for laptops & handheld devices, Prog for adults, Prog for children & young adult, Ref serv available, Scanner
Partic in LibraryLinkNJ, The New Jersey Library Cooperative
Open Mon & Wed 10-8, Tues & Thurs 12-8, Fri 12-5, Sat 10-2
Friends of the Library Group

IRVINGTON

P IRVINGTON PUBLIC LIBRARY*, Civic Sq, 07111-2498. SAN 350-7785. Tel: 973-372-6400. FAX: 973-372-6860. E-mail: ipl@irvingtonpubliclibrary.org. Web Site: www.irvingtonpubliclibrary.org. *Libr Dir,* Jeanetta Singleton; E-mail: jsingleton@irvingtonpubliclibrary.org; Staff 31 (MLS 7, Non-MLS 24)
Founded 1914. Pop 61,018; Circ 73,242
Library Holdings: Large Print Bks 500; Bk Vols 200,000; Per Subs 150; Talking Bks 500
Special Collections: Adult Literacy; Audio Books; Large Print; Local History & Photographs. US Document Depository
Automation Activity & Vendor Info: (Cataloging) SirsiDynix; (Circulation) SirsiDynix; (OPAC) SirsiDynix
Wireless access
Partic in LibraryLinkNJ, The New Jersey Library Cooperative
Open Mon, Tues & Thurs 9-9, Wed & Fri 9-5:30, Sat 9-5
Friends of the Library Group

ISELIN

S BASF CATALYSTS TECHNICAL INFORMATION CENTER*, 25 Middlesex-Essex Tpk, 08830. SAN 310-1274. Tel: 732-205-5269, 732-205-5271. FAX: 732-205-6900. *Mgr,* Maurica Fedors; *Sr Info Spec,* Arda Agulian; E-mail: arda.agulian@basf.com; Staff 3 (MLS 3)
Library Holdings: Bk Titles 4,000; Per Subs 50
Special Collections: Catalysts
Subject Interests: Catalysis, Indust applications
Wireless access
Restriction: Employees only, External users must contact libr

JAMESBURG

P JAMESBURG PUBLIC LIBRARY, 229 Gatzmer Ave, 08831. SAN 310-222X. Tel: 732-521-0440. FAX: 732-521-6136. E-mail: jamesburglibrarynews@gmail.com. Web Site: www.jamesburglibrary.org. *Dir,* Gabriella Oakley; E-mail: jamesburg@lmxac.org; Staff 1 (MLS 1)
Founded 1882. Pop 6,000; Circ 25,000
Library Holdings: CDs 800; DVDs 1,500; e-books 1,600; Bk Vols 20,000; Per Subs 62; Talking Bks 6,675
Wireless access
Partic in Libraries of Middlesex Automation Consortium; LibraryLinkNJ, The New Jersey Library Cooperative
Open Mon & Thurs 10-8, Wed & Fri 10-5, Sat 10-3
Friends of the Library Group

JERSEY CITY

S AFRO-AMERICAN HISTORICAL SOCIETY MUSEUM LIBRARY*, Jersey City Free Library - Earl A Morgan Branch, 1841 Kennedy Blvd, 07305. Tel: 201-547-5262. FAX: 201-547-5392. Web Site: www.cityofjerseycity.org/docs/afroam.shtml. *Dir,* Neal E Brunson
Library Holdings: Bk Vols 1,500
Special Collections: Genealogy Coll; Rare Book Coll
Function: Res libr
Open Sat 9-5 or by appointment
Restriction: Non-circulating

P JERSEY CITY FREE PUBLIC LIBRARY*, Priscilla Gardner Main Library & Administrative Offices, 472 Jersey Ave, 07302-3499. SAN 350-7874. Tel: 201-547-4526. Reference Tel: 201-547-4501. FAX: 201-547-4584. Web Site: www.jclibrary.org. *Libr Dir,* Jeffrey Trzeciak; Tel: 201-547-4788, E-mail: director@jclibrary.org; *Chief Librn,* Hussein Odeh; Tel: 201-547-4304, Fax: 201-946-7379, E-mail: hodeh@jclibrary.org; *Head, Ref,* John Butler; E-mail: jbutler@jclibrary.org; *Br Mgr, Biblioteca Criolla,* Patricia Vega; Tel: 201-547-4541, Fax: 201-547-5889, E-mail: pvega@jclibrary.org; *Doc,* Sharon Tucker; Tel: 201-547-4517, E-mail: tuckers@jclibrary.org. Subject Specialists: *Fed docs,* Sharon Tucker; Staff 88 (MLS 23, Non-MLS 65)
Founded 1889. Pop 356,143; Circ 291,519
Library Holdings: CDs 3,100; DVDs 16,410; Large Print Bks 5,851; Bk Titles 289,382; Bk Vols 539,645; Per Subs 839
Special Collections: New Jersey Coll; Spanish coll. US Document Depository
Automation Activity & Vendor Info: (Acquisitions) SirsiDynix; (Cataloging) SirsiDynix; (Circulation) SirsiDynix; (OPAC) SirsiDynix
Wireless access
Partic in OCLC Online Computer Library Center, Inc
Special Services for the Deaf - Staff with knowledge of sign lang
Special Services for the Blind - Reader equip
Open Mon-Thurs 9-8, Fri & Sat 9-5
Branches: 9
GLENN D CUNNINGHAM BRANCH LIBRARY & COMMUNITY CENTER, 275 Martin Luther King Jr Dr, 07305, SAN 350-7939. Tel: 201-547-4555. FAX: 201-547-5880. *Br Mgr,* Jason Sanders; E-mail: jsander@jclibrary.org
Special Services for the Blind - Networked computers with assistive software; Screen reader software
Open Mon, Tues & Thurs 10-6, Wed 12-8, Fri & Sat 9-5
FIVE CORNERS, 678 Newark Ave, 07306, SAN 350-7963. Tel: 201-547-4543. FAX: 201-656-1517. *Br Mgr,* Susan Stewart; E-mail: sstewart@jclibrary.org
Open Mon 12-8, Tues-Thurs 10-6, Fri & Sat 9-5
THE HEIGHTS, 14 Zabriskie St, 07307, SAN 350-8021. Tel: 201-547-4556. FAX: 201-876-0092. *Br Mgr,* Mary Quinn; E-mail: mquinn@jclibrary.org
Open Mon-Wed 10-6, Thurs 12-8, Fri & Sat 9-5
LAFAYETTE, 307 Pacific Ave, 07304, SAN 350-8056. Tel: 201-547-5017. FAX: 201-547-5878. *Br Mgr,* Vanessa Benekin; E-mail: vbenekin@jclibrary.org
Open Mon-Fri 9-5

MARION, 1017 West Side Ave, 07306, SAN 350-8080. Tel: 201-547-4552. FAX: 201-547-5888. *Br Mgr,* Dolores Reyes; E-mail: dreyes@jclibrary.org
Open Mon-Fri 9-5
MILLER, 489 Bergen Ave, 07304, SAN 350-8110. Tel: 201-547-4551. FAX: 201-434-1469. *Br Mgr,* Renee Moody; E-mail: rmoody@jclibrary.org
Open Mon, Tues & Thurs 10-6, Wed Noon-8, Fri & Sat 9-5
EARL A MORGAN BRANCH, 1841 Kennedy Blvd, 07305, SAN 350-7998. Tel: 201-547-4553. FAX: 201-433-1708. *Br Mgr,* Kenneth Uko; E-mail: kuko@jclibrary.org
Open Mon, Wed & Thurs 10-6, Tues 12-8, Fri & Sat 9-5
PAVONIA, 326 Eighth St, 07302, SAN 350-8145. Tel: 201-547-4808. FAX: 201-547-5222. *Br Mgr,* Grisel Velasquez; E-mail: gvelasquez@jclibrary.org
Open Mon 12-8, Tues-Thurs 10-6, Fri 9-5
WEST BERGEN, 546 West Side Ave, 07304, SAN 350-817X. Tel: 201-547-4554. FAX: 201-547-5887. *Br Mgr,* Deborah Oriol; E-mail: doriol@jclibrary.org
Open Mon-Fri 9-5
Bookmobiles: 1. Contact, Eddie Perez

M JERSEY CITY MEDICAL CENTER LIBRARY*, 355 Grand St, 07302. SAN 373-2495. Tel: 201-915-2000, Ext 2136. FAX: 201-915-2911. *Librn,* Position Currently Open
Library Holdings: Bk Vols 800; Per Subs 180
Wireless access
Function: Res libr
Partic in New Jersey Health Sciences Library Network
Open Mon-Thurs 9-7, Fri 9-5
Restriction: Non-circulating, Open to pub upon request

C NEW JERSEY CITY UNIVERSITY*, Congressman Frank J Guarini Library, 2039 Kennedy Blvd, 07305-1597. SAN 310-2254. Tel: 201-200-3030. Interlibrary Loan Service Tel: 201-200-2183. Reference Tel: 201-200-3033. FAX: 201-200-2330, 201-200-2331. *Dir,* Frederick Smith; Tel: 201-200-3474, E-mail: fsmith@njcu.edu; Staff 12 (MLS 10, Non-MLS 2)
Founded 1927. Enrl 10,000; Fac 240; Highest Degree: Doctorate
Jul 2019-Jun 2020. Mats Exp $541,000, Books $60,000, Per/Ser (Incl. Access Fees) $50,355, AV Mat $5,000, Electronic Ref Mat (Incl. Access Fees) $400,000
Library Holdings: DVDs 4,000; e-books 150,000; e-journals 39,499; Electronic Media & Resources 152; Microforms 1,802,659; Bk Vols 300,000; Per Subs 400
Special Collections: Anthropology (Human Relations Area Files), fiche; Eric Coll. State Document Depository; US Document Depository
Subject Interests: African-Am studies, Art, Biology, Bus admin, Caribbean studies, Chem, Computer sci, Criminal justice, Econ, Educ, English, English as a second lang, Fire sci, Geog, Geoscience, Health sci, Hist, Latin Am studies, Latino studies, Media arts, Music, Nursing, Philos, Physics, Polit sci, Psychol, Relig, Security, Sociol
Automation Activity & Vendor Info: (Acquisitions) SirsiDynix
Wireless access
Function: 24/7 Electronic res
Partic in LibraryLinkNJ, The New Jersey Library Cooperative; LYRASIS; OCLC Online Computer Library Center, Inc; Virtual Academic Library Environment; Westchester Academic Library Directors Organization
Special Services for the Blind - Magnifiers; Open bk software on pub access PC; Screen reader software
Open Mon-Thurs (Winter) 7:30am-10pm, Fri 7:30-5, Sat 9-5, Sun 11-5; Mon-Thurs (Summer) 7:30am-10pm, Sun 11-5

CR SAINT PETER'S UNIVERSITY*, Theresa & Edward O'Toole Library, 99 Glenwood Ave, 07306. SAN 350-820X. Tel: 201-761-6461. Reference Tel: 201-761-6460. Administration Tel: 201-761-6464. FAX: 201-761-6451. Web Site: saintpeters.edu/library. *Dir,* Daisy DeCoster; E-mail: ddecoster@saintpeters.edu; *Exhibits Librn, Ref Librn,* Ilona MacNamara; Tel: 201-761-6465, E-mail: imacnamara@saintpeters.edu; *Col Archivist,* Mary Kinahan-Ockay; Tel: 201-761-6462, E-mail: mkinahan@saintpeters.edu; Staff 9 (MLS 9)
Founded 1872. Enrl 3,512; Fac 114; Highest Degree: Doctorate
Library Holdings: Bk Titles 180,419; Bk Vols 229,315; Per Subs 750
Special Collections: Religion, History (including local), Literature, Art, Science & Technology, Early Cinema, with Imprint Dates from the 15th to 16th Centuries
Subject Interests: Biology, Nursing, Philos, Theol
Automation Activity & Vendor Info: (Acquisitions) SirsiDynix; (Cataloging) SirsiDynix; (Circulation) SirsiDynix; (Course Reserve) SirsiDynix; (OPAC) SirsiDynix; (Serials) SirsiDynix
Wireless access
Partic in LibraryLinkNJ, The New Jersey Library Cooperative; Metropolitan New York Library Council; Virtual Academic Library Environment
Special Services for the Blind - Reader equip
Open Mon-Thurs 8am-11pm, Fri 8-5, Sat 9-5, Sun Noon-11
Friends of the Library Group

KEANSBURG

P KEANSBURG WATERFRONT PUBLIC LIBRARY*, 55 Shore Blvd, 07734. Tel: 732-787-0636. FAX: 732-787-0631. Web Site: keansburgnj.gov/residents/library. *Librn,* Sarah Armenti
Founded 1917
Wireless access
Mem of Monmouth County Library
Open Tues & Thurs 11-6, Wed 1-7, Sat Noon-4

KEARNY

P KEARNY PUBLIC LIBRARY*, 318 Kearny Ave, 07032. SAN 310-2270. Tel: 201-998-2666. FAX: 201-998-1141. Web Site: kearnylibrary.org, www.kearnynj.org/publiclibrary. *Dir,* Josh Humphrey; Tel: 201-998-2667, E-mail: jhumphrey@kearnylibrary.org; *Sr Ch,* Joanne Friedman
Founded 1906. Pop 40,513
Library Holdings: Bk Vols 70,000; Per Subs 120
Subject Interests: Local hist
Automation Activity & Vendor Info: (Acquisitions) Innovative Interfaces, Inc; (Cataloging) Innovative Interfaces, Inc; (Circulation) Innovative Interfaces, Inc; (OPAC) Innovative Interfaces, Inc
Wireless access
Open Mon, Thurs & Fri 9:30-6, Tues & Wed 9:30-8, Sat 9-1
Friends of the Library Group
Branches: 1
KEARNY BRANCH, 759 Kearny Ave, 07032, SAN 376-2513. Tel: 201-955-7988.
Library Holdings: Bk Titles 5,200; Per Subs 15
Open Mon-Thurs 1-5
Friends of the Library Group

KENILWORTH

P KENILWORTH PUBLIC LIBRARY*, 548 Blvd, 07033. SAN 310-2297. Tel: 908-276-2451. FAX: 908-276-7897. Web Site: www.kenilworthlibrary.org. *Libr Dir,* Lorraine Ruitz; E-mail: Lruiz@lmxac.org; Staff 2 (MLS 1, Non-MLS 1)
Founded 1934. Pop 7,700
Library Holdings: Audiobooks 1,000; CDs 1,500; DVDs 2,100; Large Print Bks 1,800; Bk Vols 30,000; Per Subs 67
Automation Activity & Vendor Info: (Cataloging) SirsiDynix; (Circulation) SirsiDynix; (OPAC) SirsiDynix
Wireless access
Function: Adult bk club, Art exhibits, Audiobks via web, Bks on CD, Children's prog, Computers for patron use, Digital talking bks, E-Reserves, Electronic databases & coll, Free DVD rentals, Holiday prog, ILL available, Internet access, Music CDs, Online cat, OverDrive digital audio bks, Photocopying/Printing, Prog for adults, Prog for children & young adult, Ref serv available, Story hour, Summer & winter reading prog, Tax forms, Telephone ref, Wheelchair accessible, Workshops
Partic in Libraries of Middlesex Automation Consortium; LibraryLinkNJ, The New Jersey Library Cooperative
Open Mon, Tues & Thurs 10-9, Wed 10-6, Fri 10-5, Sat 10-2
Friends of the Library Group

KEYPORT

P KEYPORT FREE PUBLIC LIBRARY*, 109 Broad St, 07735. SAN 310-2327. Tel: 732-264-0543. FAX: 732-264-0875. E-mail: info@keyportnjlib.org. Web Site: lmac.ent.sirsi.net/client/en_US/keyport. *Dir,* Janet Torsney
Founded 1914. Pop 7,500; Circ 22,000
Library Holdings: Bk Vols 49,000; Per Subs 80
Special Collections: War of the Rebellion: A Compilation of the Official Records of the Union & Confederate Armies
Wireless access
Partic in Libraries of Middlesex Automation Consortium; LibraryLinkNJ, The New Jersey Library Cooperative
Open Mon & Thurs 10-5, Tues 1-9, Wed 10-9, Fri 1-5, Sat 9-1
Friends of the Library Group

KINNELON

P KINNELON PUBLIC LIBRARY, 132 Kinnelon Rd, 07405. SAN 310-2335. Tel: 973-838-1321. FAX: 973-838-0741. Web Site: www.kinnelonlibrary.org. *Libr Dir,* Kimberly Fraone; E-mail: kimberly.fraone@kinnelonlibrary.org; *Libr Office Mgr,* Ann Ferrara; *Circ Supvr,* Tanya Lenkow; E-mail: tanya.lenkow@kinnelonlibrary.org; *Adult Serv,* Anne Mandanayake; E-mail: anne.mandanayake@kinnelonlibrary.org; *Prog Spec,* Kim Christian; E-mail: kim.christian@kinnelonlibrary.org; *Ch Serv,* Cathy Presti; *Circ,* Beate Amos; *Teen Serv,* Mary Ann O'Gorman;

E-mail: maryann.ogorman@kinnelonlibrary.org; *Tech Serv,* Jill Iannino; Staff 14 (MLS 1, Non-MLS 13)
Founded 1962. Pop 10,200; Circ 97,000
Jan 2016-Dec 2016 Income $798,500, State $4,500, City $703,000, Locally Generated Income $20,000, Other $71,000. Mats Exp $67,800. Sal $464,000
Library Holdings: CDs 1,143; DVDs 4,500; Bk Vols 65,308; Per Subs 130; Talking Bks 4,322; Videos 3,000
Automation Activity & Vendor Info: (Acquisitions) Innovative Interfaces, Inc; (Cataloging) Innovative Interfaces, Inc; (Circulation) Innovative Interfaces, Inc; (ILL) JerseyCat; (OPAC) Innovative Interfaces, Inc
Wireless access
Function: 24/7 Electronic res, Activity rm, Adult bk club, Art exhibits, Audiobks on Playaways & MP3, Audiobks via web, AV serv, Bk club(s), Bks on cassette, Bks on CD, CD-ROM, Children's prog, Computer training, Computers for patron use, Digital talking bks, E-Readers, Electronic databases & coll, Equip loans & repairs, Free DVD rentals, Holiday prog, ILL available, Instruction & testing, Internet access, Laminating, Life-long learning prog for all ages, Magazines, Magnifiers for reading, Meeting rooms, Movies, Museum passes, Music CDs, Notary serv, Online cat, Online ref, Orientations, Outside serv via phone, mail, e-mail & web, Photocopying/Printing, Preschool outreach, Preschool reading prog, Prog for adults, Prog for children & young adult, Ref serv available, Scanner, Senior computer classes, Story hour, Summer reading prog, Tax forms, Teen prog, Telephone ref, VHS videos, Wheelchair accessible
Publications: Bookmarks (Newsletter); Kinnelon Service Directory
Partic in Morris Automated Information Network
Open Mon 10-6, Tues-Thurs 10-8, Fri 10-5, Sat 10-4
Friends of the Library Group

LAKEWOOD

CR GEORGIAN COURT UNIVERSITY*, S Mary Joseph Cunningham Library, 900 Lakewood Ave, 08701-2697. SAN 310-2351. Tel: 732-987-2419. Reference Tel: 732-987-2422. Administration Tel: 732-987-2421. FAX: 732-987-2017. E-mail: reference@georgian.edu. Web Site: georgian.edu/academics/library. *Dir, Libr Serv,* Jeffrey Donnelly; Tel: 732-987-2429, Fax: 732-987-2060, E-mail: donnellyj@georgian.edu; *Bus Librn,* Barbara Herbert; Tel: 732-987-2428, E-mail: herbert@georgian.edu; *Humanities Librn,* Mary Basso; Tel: 732-987-2427, E-mail: basso@georgian.edu; *Soc Sci Librn, Tech Serv Librn,* Jaimie Donnelly; Tel: 732-987-2435, E-mail: ja_donnelly@georgian.edu; *Archivist/Librn,* Sister Barbara Williams; Tel: 732-987-2441, E-mail: williamssb@georgian.edu. Subject Specialists: *Behav sci,* Barbara Herbert; *Nursing, Sci,* Sister Barbara Williams; Staff 18 (MLS 6, Non-MLS 12)
Founded 1908. Enrl 2,257; Fac 228; Highest Degree: Master
Jul 2014-Jun 2015. Mats Exp $477,010, Books $81,500, Per/Ser (Incl. Access Fees) $224,204, AV Mat $10,800, Electronic Ref Mat (Incl. Access Fees) $160,386, Presv $120
Library Holdings: AV Mats 5,848; CDs 874; DVDs 840; e-books 550; e-journals 53,274; Large Print Bks 15; Bk Titles 112,418; Bk Vols 160,582; Per Subs 400; Videos 1,779
Special Collections: Georgian Court University Archives; Georgian Court University Special Coll; Instructional Material Center; Thomas Merton Coll (NASA Resource Center)
Subject Interests: Educ
Automation Activity & Vendor Info: (Acquisitions) OCLC; (Cataloging) OCLC; (Circulation) OCLC; (Course Reserve) OCLC; (ILL) OCLC WorldShare Interlibrary Loan; (OPAC) OCLC; (Serials) OCLC
Wireless access
Partic in LibraryLinkNJ, The New Jersey Library Cooperative; LYRASIS; New Jersey Library Network; OCLC Online Computer Library Center, Inc; Virtual Academic Library Environment; Westchester Academic Library Directors Organization
Open Mon-Thurs 8am-11pm, Fri 8-6, Sat 10-5, Sun 2-10
Restriction: Open to pub for ref & circ; with some limitations, Open to students, fac & staff

S WORTHINGTON BIOCHEMICAL CORP LIBRARY*, 730 Vassar Ave, 08701. SAN 375-7455. Tel: 732-942-1660. Toll Free Tel: 800-445-9603. FAX: 732-942-9270. *Librn,* Nancy Worthington; E-mail: nancyw@worthington-biochem.com; Staff 1 (Non-MLS 1)
Founded 1987
Library Holdings: Bk Titles 500; Spec Interest Per Sub 5
Wireless access
Restriction: Staff use only

LAMBERTVILLE

P LAMBERTVILLE FREE PUBLIC LIBRARY, Six Lilly St, 08530. SAN 310-2378. Tel: 609-397-0275. E-mail: staff@lambertvillelibrary.org. Web Site: www.lambertvillelibrary.org. *Dir,* Jennifer Sirak; Staff 11 (MLS 1, Non-MLS 10)
Founded 1881. Pop 3,868; Circ 34,000
Jan 2020-Dec 2020 Income $252,800, State $1,800, City $246,000, Locally Generated Income $5,000. Mats Exp $31,900, Books $22,000, Per/Ser (Incl. Access Fees) $2,400, AV Equip $500, AV Mat $7,000. Sal $115,000
Library Holdings: Audiobooks 945; AV Mats 2,451; CDs 373; DVDs 370; e-books 52; Large Print Bks 194; Bk Vols 20,534; Per Subs 78; Videos 2,412
Special Collections: Lambertville Beacon Coll (1860-2005), microfilm; Michael Lewis Art Coll; Regional History Coll
Subject Interests: Regional hist
Automation Activity & Vendor Info: (Cataloging) Surpass; (Circulation) Surpass; (OPAC) Surpass; (Serials) Surpass
Wireless access
Function: Art exhibits, Bi-weekly Writer's Group, Bks on CD, Computers for patron use, Free DVD rentals, Music CDs, Online cat, Photocopying/Printing, Prog for adults, Scanner, Story hour, Summer reading prog, Teen prog, Wheelchair accessible
Open Mon, Tues & Thurs 10-7, Fri 1-6, Sat 10-3
Friends of the Library Group

LAWRENCEVILLE

P MERCER COUNTY LIBRARY SYSTEM*, 2751 Brunswick Pike, 08648-4132. SAN 351-4536. Tel: 609-883-8294. Interlibrary Loan Service Tel: 609-883-0245. Reference Tel: 609-883-8292. FAX: 609-538-9238. Web Site: www.mcl.org. *Dir,* Ellen Brown; Tel: 609-883-8290, E-mail: director@mcl.org; *Supv Libr Dir,* Laurence McNamara; Tel: 609-883-6450; *Chief Financial Officer,* Richard J Cavallo; Tel: 609-883-8298; *Mgr,* James Damron; Tel: 609-883-8291; Staff 58 (MLS 18, Non-MLS 40)
Founded 1929. Pop 130,000; Circ 1,480,000
Library Holdings: Bk Titles 359,468; Per Subs 357
Special Collections: New Jersey History; Spanish & Chinese Coll
Wireless access
Function: Res libr
Partic in OCLC Online Computer Library Center, Inc
Open Mon-Thurs 9:30-9, Fri & Sat 9:30-5; Mon-Thurs 9:30-9, Fri & Sat 9:30-5, Sun 12:30-5 (Sept-May)
Friends of the Library Group
Branches: 9

EWING BRANCH, 61 Scotch Rd, Ewing, 08628, SAN 351-4595. Tel: 609-882-3130. Reference Tel: 609-882-3148. FAX: 609-538-0212. *Br Mgr,* Jackie Huff
Library Holdings: Bk Vols 103,401
Open Mon-Thurs 9-9, Fri 9-5, Sat 9:30-5; Mon-Thurs 9-9, Fri 9-5, Sat 9:30-5, Sun 12:30-5 (Sept-May)
Friends of the Library Group

HICKORY CORNER BRANCH, 138 Hickory Corner Rd, East Windsor, 08520, SAN 351-4560. Tel: 609-448-1330. Reference Tel: 609-448-0957. *Br Mgr,* Sharon Galbraith Ryer; Staff 8 (MLS 3, Non-MLS 5)
Library Holdings: Bk Vols 46,554
Open Mon-Thurs 9:30-9, Fri & Sat 9:30-5; Mon-Thurs 9:30-9, Fri & Sat 9:30-5, Sun 12:30-5 (Sept-May)
Friends of the Library Group

HIGHTSTOWN MEMORIAL, 114 Franklin St, Hightstown, 08520, SAN 351-4625. Tel: 609-448-1474. *Br Mgr,* Emily Frey; Staff 5 (MLS 2, Non-MLS 3)
Library Holdings: Bk Vols 29,916
Open Mon-Thurs 9:30-9, Fri & Sat 9:30-5
Friends of the Library Group

HOLLOWBROOK COMMUNITY CENTER, 320 Hollowbrook Dr, Trenton, 08638, SAN 328-8021. Tel: 609-883-5914. *Br Mgr,* Christine Crawford
Library Holdings: Bk Vols 11,832
Open Mon-Fri 9-12 & 1-5
Friends of the Library Group

HOPEWELL BRANCH, 245 Pennington-Titusville Rd, Pennington, 08534, SAN 351-4633. Tel: 609-737-2610. *Br Mgr,* Andrea Merrick
Library Holdings: Bk Vols 59,103
Open Mon-Thurs 9:30-9, Fri & Sat 9:30-5
Friends of the Library Group

LAWRENCE HEADQUARTERS, 2751 Brunswick Pike, 08648, SAN 351-465X. Tel: 609-882-9246. *Br Mgr,* James Damron
Circ 2,046,910
Library Holdings: Bk Vols 144,891
Open Mon-Thurs 9:30-9, Fri & Sat 9:30-5; Mon-Thurs 9:30-9, Fri & Sat 9:30-5, Sun 12:30-5 (Sept-May)
Friends of the Library Group

ROBBINSVILLE BRANCH, 42 Allentown-Robbinsville Rd, Robbinsville, 08691, SAN 351-4714. Tel: 609-259-2150. *Br Mgr,* Ann Marie Ehrenberg
Library Holdings: Bk Vols 33,752
Open Mon-Thurs 9:30-9, Fri & Sat 9:30-5
Friends of the Library Group

TWIN RIVERS BRANCH, 276 Abbington Dr, East Windsor, 08520, SAN 351-4684. Tel: 609-443-1880. Reference Tel: 609-448-0478. *Br Mgr,* Jeanne Murray
Library Holdings: Bk Vols 50,119
Open Mon-Thurs 9:30-9, Fri & Sat 9:30-5
Friends of the Library Group

WEST WINDSOR, 333 N Post Rd, Princeton Junction, 08550, SAN 351-4749. Tel: 609-799-0462. Reference Tel: 609-272-8901. *Br Mgr,* Robert Bee
Library Holdings: Bk Vols 82,079
Open Mon-Thurs 9:30-9, Fri & Sat 9:30-5; Mon-Thurs 9:30-9, Fri & Sat 9:30-5, Sun 12:30-5 (Sept-May)
Friends of the Library Group

C RIDER UNIVERSITY*, Franklin F Moore Library, 2083 Lawrenceville Rd, 08648. SAN 310-2394. Tel: 609-896-5111. Circulation Tel: 609-896-5113. Interlibrary Loan Service Tel: 609-896-5118. Reference Tel: 609-896-5115. FAX: 609-896-8029. Web Site: www.rider.edu/academics/libraries/moore. *Dean of Libr,* Richard L Riccardi; E-mail: rriccardi@rider.edu; *Dept Chair, Librn,* Robert Lackie; Tel: 609-895-5626, E-mail: rlackie@rider.edu; *Librn,* Diane K Campbell; Tel: 609-896-5729, E-mail: dcampbell@rider.edu; *Archivist, Librn,* Robert Congleton; Tel: 609-896-5248, E-mail: rcongleton@rider.edu; *Librn,* Ma Lei Hseih; Tel: 609-896-5241, E-mail: mhseih@rider.edu; *E-Resources Librn, User Serv Librn,* Sharon Whitfield; E-mail: swhitfield@rider.edu; *Acq,* Coleen Carr; E-mail: carr@rider.edu; *Cat,* Frank Gao; E-mail: lgao@rider.edu; *Cat,* Carl Rizzo; E-mail: rizzo@rider.edu; *Doc Delivery,* Rose Marie Hilgar; E-mail: hilgar@rider.edu; Staff 12 (MLS 12)
Founded 1865. Enrl 5,000; Fac 250; Highest Degree: Master
Library Holdings: Bk Titles 473,370; Bk Vols 1,545,034; Per Subs 2,300
Special Collections: Delaware Valley Newspapers (from Colonial Times to present); Dispatches of United States Envoys in Britain & France During Civil War Period, micro; Early Shorthand Works (Kendrick C Hill Coll), per; Historical Shorthand Materials (Leslie Coll); Typewriting History (Alan Lloyd Coll). State Document Depository; US Document Depository
Automation Activity & Vendor Info: (Acquisitions) Ex Libris Group; (Cataloging) Ex Libris Group; (Circulation) Ex Libris Group; (OPAC) Ex Libris Group; (Serials) Ex Libris Group
Wireless access
Partic in Dow Jones News Retrieval; NJ Regional Libr Coop; OCLC Online Computer Library Center, Inc; Proquest Dialog
Open Mon-Thurs 8:30am-Midnight, Fri 8:30am-10pm, Sat 10-7, Sun Noon-11

Departmental Libraries:

KATHARINE HOUK TALBOTT LIBRARY, Westminster Choir College, 101 Walnut Lane, Princeton, 08540-3899, SAN 351-3181. Tel: 609-921-7100, Ext 8237. Interlibrary Loan Service Tel: 609-921-7100, Ext 8337. Reference Tel: 609-921-7100, Ext 8314. Administration Tel: 609-921-7100, Ext 8304. FAX: 609-497-0243. E-mail: library@rider.edu. Web Site: www.rider.edu/talbott. *Chair,* Mi-Hye Chyun; E-mail: chyun@rider.edu; *Bibliog Control Librn,* Jane Nowakowski; Tel: 609-921-7100, Ext 8305, E-mail: nowakows@rider.edu; *Instruction, Ref & Ser Librn,* Robert Terrio; Tel: 609-921-7100, Ext 8296, E-mail: rterrio@rider.edu; *Media Librn,* Kenneth Kauffman; Tel: 609-921-7100, Ext 8338, E-mail: kkauffman@rider.edu; *Spec Coll Librn,* Amy Kimura; Tel: 609-921-7100, Ext 8375, E-mail: akimura@rider.edu; *Acq Asst,* Kylee Caldwell; Tel: 609-921-7100, Ext 8336, E-mail: carmink@rider.edu; *Cat Asst,* Frank Ferko; Tel: 609-921-7100, Ext 8297, E-mail: fferko@rider.edu; *Circ,* Rena Blakeslee; Tel: 609-921-7100, Ext 8335, E-mail: blakesle@rider.edu; *Circ,* William Vallandigham; Tel: 609-921-7100, Ext 8359, E-mail: wvallandigh@rider.edu; *Circ & ILL,* Nancy Deffeyes; E-mail: ndeffeyes@rider.edu; *Performance Coll,* Devin Mariman; Tel: 609-921-7100, Ext 8298, E-mail: dmariman@rider.edu; *Tech Asst,* Sue Nelson; Tel: 609-921-7100, Ext 8339, E-mail: snelson@rider.edu; Staff 4 (MLS 4)
Founded 1926. Enrl 500; Highest Degree: Master
Library Holdings: AV Mats 35,000; CDs 20,800; DVDs 700; e-journals 45,000; Music Scores 40,000; Bk Vols 80,000; Per Subs 150; Spec Interest Per Sub 150; Videos 400
Special Collections: Adams Coll of Dupre, memorabilia; Carl F Mueller Coll; Carl Weinrich Coll; Choral Octavo Reference File; DeWitt Wasson Research Coll; Hymnology (Erik Routley Coll); Leopold Stokowski Coll; Nathaniel Burt Coll; Organ Historical Society Archives; Robert Shaw Coll, marked scores; Tams-Witmark Coll; Tiplady Coll; Warren Marten Coll, compositions; Winfred Douglas & Walter Williams Coll, choral & liturgical music
Subject Interests: Music
Automation Activity & Vendor Info: (Acquisitions) Ex Libris Group; (Cataloging) Ex Libris Group; (Circulation) Ex Libris Group; (Course Reserve) Ex Libris Group; (Discovery) EBSCO Discovery Service; (ILL) OCLC; (OPAC) Ex Libris Group; (Serials) Ex Libris Group
Function: Audio & video playback equip for onsite use, Computers for patron use, Electronic databases & coll, ILL available, Internet access, Online cat, Online info literacy tutorials on the web & in blackboard, Online ref, Ref & res, Ref serv available
Partic in LYRASIS; OCLC Online Computer Library Center, Inc
Open Mon-Thurs 8:30am-10pm, Fri 8:30-5, Sat 10-5, Sun 3-10
Restriction: Borrowing privileges limited to fac & registered students, Borrowing requests are handled by ILL, In-house use for visitors, Open to fac, students & qualified researchers, Open to students, fac, staff & alumni
Friends of the Library Group

LEONIA

P LEONIA PUBLIC LIBRARY, 227 Fort Lee Rd, 07605. SAN 310-2408. Tel: 201-592-5770. Reference Tel: 201-592-5773. FAX: 201-592-5775. E-mail: leoncirc@bccls.org. Web Site: leonialibrary.org. *Dir,* Elysse Fink; E-mail: fink@leonia.bccls.org; *Head, Circ,* Joseph Emery; E-mail: joseph.emery@leonia.bccls.org; *Head, Youth Serv,* Lizzie Latham; E-mail: elizabeth.latham@leonia.bccls.org; Staff 3 (MLS 3)
Founded 1923. Pop 8,900; Circ 105,140
Library Holdings: Bk Titles 48,000; Bk Vols 49,000; Per Subs 100
Special Collections: Local History Coll
Automation Activity & Vendor Info: (Cataloging) SirsiDynix; (Circulation) SirsiDynix; (OPAC) SirsiDynix
Wireless access
Partic in Bergen County Cooperative Library System, Inc; LibraryLinkNJ, The New Jersey Library Cooperative
Open Mon, Wed & Thurs 10-8, Tues, Fri & Sat 10-5
Friends of the Library Group

LIBERTY CORNER

S UNITED STATES GOLF ASSOCIATION MUSEUM & ARCHIVES, 77 Liberty Corner Rd, 07938. SAN 310-1584. Tel: 908-326-1207. Web Site: www.usga.org/history/research-tools.html. *Librn,* Tara Valente; E-mail: tvalente@usga.org; Staff 1 (MLS 1)
Founded 1936
Library Holdings: Bk Titles 15,000; Bk Vols 50,000; Per Subs 100
Special Collections: Bobby Jones Coll; Golf Architecture Archive; Pamela Fox Emory Oral History Coll. Oral History
Subject Interests: Golf
Wireless access
Function: Ref serv available, Res libr, Wheelchair accessible
Open Mon-Fri 9-5
Restriction: Non-circulating, Not a lending libr

LINCOLN PARK

P LINCOLN PARK PUBLIC LIBRARY*, 12 Boonton Tpk, 07035. SAN 310-2416. Tel: 973-694-8283. FAX: 973-694-5515. Web Site: www.lincolnparklibrary.org. *Dir,* Stephanie Flood; E-mail: stephanie.iberer@lincolnparklibrary.org
Founded 1969. Pop 11,400; Circ 68,200
Library Holdings: Bk Vols 54,000; Per Subs 100
Special Collections: New Jersey Coll
Automation Activity & Vendor Info: (Acquisitions) Innovative Interfaces, Inc; (Cataloging) Innovative Interfaces, Inc; (Circulation) Innovative Interfaces, Inc; (OPAC) Innovative Interfaces, Inc; (Serials) Innovative Interfaces, Inc
Wireless access
Function: 24/7 Electronic res, 24/7 Online cat, Adult bk club, After school storytime, Art programs, Audiobks on Playaways & MP3, Audiobks via web, Bk club(s), Bks on CD, Children's prog, Computer training, Computers for patron use, Digital talking bks, Electronic databases & coll, Free DVD rentals, Health sci info serv, Holiday prog, ILL available, Internet access, Life-long learning prog for all ages, Magazines, Movies, Museum passes, Music CDs, Online cat, Photocopying/Printing, Prog for adults, Prog for children & young adult, Ref & res, Ref serv available, Res assist avail, Scanner, Serves people with intellectual disabilities, Spoken cassettes & CDs, Spoken cassettes & DVDs, Story hour, Summer & winter reading prog, Summer reading prog, Tax forms, Teen prog, Wheelchair accessible
Open Mon-Thurs (Sept-June) 10-9, Fri 10-5, Sat 9:30-4 (10-2 July-Aug), Sun (Sept-June) 12-4
Friends of the Library Group

LINCROFT

J BROOKDALE COMMUNITY COLLEGE*, Bankier Library, 765 Newman Springs Rd, 07738-1597. SAN 310-2424. Tel: 732-224-2706. FAX: 732-224-2982. Web Site: www.brookdalecc.edu/library. *Interim Dir,* Rira Lo; E-mail: rlo@brookdalecc.edu; *Prof, Ref Librn,* Shay Delcurla; Tel: 732-224-2438, E-mail: sdelcurla@brookdalecc.edu; Staff 11 (MLS 11)
Founded 1969. Enrl 15,000; Fac 251; Highest Degree: Associate
Library Holdings: Audiobooks 453; CDs 448; DVDs 1,262; e-books 4,027; Bk Titles 60,874; Bk Vols 80,592; Per Subs 425; Videos 7,381
Automation Activity & Vendor Info: (Acquisitions) Innovative Interfaces, Inc; (Cataloging) Innovative Interfaces, Inc; (Circulation) Innovative Interfaces, Inc; (Course Reserve) Innovative Interfaces, Inc; (ILL)

Innovative Interfaces, Inc; (Media Booking) Innovative Interfaces, Inc; (OPAC) Innovative Interfaces, Inc; (Serials) Innovative Interfaces, Inc
Wireless access
Partic in LibraryLinkNJ, The New Jersey Library Cooperative; LYRASIS; OCLC Online Computer Library Center, Inc; Virtual Academic Library Environment

LINDEN

P LINDEN FREE PUBLIC LIBRARY*, 31 E Henry St, 07036. SAN 350-8323. Tel: 908-298-3830. FAX: 908-486-2636. Web Site: www.lindenpl.org. *Dir,* Dennis Patrick Purves, Jr; E-mail: dpurves@lindenpl.org; Staff 24 (MLS 5, Non-MLS 19)
Founded 1925. Pop 39,000; Circ 143,539
Library Holdings: Bk Titles 87,645; Bk Vols 88,935; Per Subs 185
Special Collections: Local History Coll
Automation Activity & Vendor Info: (Cataloging) SirsiDynix; (Circulation) SirsiDynix; (OPAC) SirsiDynix
Wireless access
Publications: Library Lineup
Partic in LibraryLinkNJ, The New Jersey Library Cooperative
Open Mon & Wed 9-9, Tues & Thurs 9-6, Fri 9:30-5
Friends of the Library Group

LINDENWOLD

P LINDENWOLD PUBLIC LIBRARY, 310 E Linden Ave, 08021. SAN 310-2467. Tel: 856-784-5602. FAX: 856-566-1413. E-mail: library@lindenwold.net. Web Site: www.lindenwoldnj.gov/library. *Libr Supvr,* Brenda Roach
Pop 18,000
Library Holdings: Bks on Deafness & Sign Lang 16; DVDs 1,800; Large Print Bks 209; Bk Titles 14,244; Bk Vols 15,281; Per Subs 37
Automation Activity & Vendor Info: (Cataloging) Follett Software; (Circulation) Follett Software; (Serials) EBSCO Online
Wireless access
Function: Computers for patron use, Free DVD rentals, ILL available, Internet access, Magazines, Notary serv, Online cat, Photocopying/Printing, Spanish lang bks, Tax forms
Mem of Camden County Library System
Open Tues, Wed & Fri 9-5, Thurs 12-8, Sat 9-3
Friends of the Library Group

LINWOOD

P LINWOOD PUBLIC LIBRARY*, 301 Davis Ave, 08221. SAN 310-2475. Tel: 609-926-7991. Circulation Tel: 609-926-7991, Ext 3. FAX: 609-927-6147. E-mail: linwoodlibrary@linwoodlibrary.com. Web Site: linwoodlibrary.com. *Dir,* Maria Moss; Tel: 609-926-7991, Ext 1; *Asst Dir,* Mary Ann Branciforti
Founded 1926. Pop 6,144; Circ 31,190
Library Holdings: Bk Vols 35,000; Per Subs 77
Special Collections: New Jersey Coll
Automation Activity & Vendor Info: (Cataloging) Follett Software; (Circulation) Follett Software; (OPAC) Follett Software
Wireless access
Partic in Coalition of Independent Libraries; NJ Regional Libr Coop
Open Mon-Thurs 10-8, Fri 10-5, Sat 10-4, Sun (Winter) 11-3
Friends of the Library Group

LITTLE FALLS

P LITTLE FALLS PUBLIC LIBRARY, Eight Warren St, 07424. SAN 310-2483. Tel: 973-256-2784. FAX: 973-256-6312. Web Site: www.littlefallslibrary.org. *Dir,* Kristin Blumberg; E-mail: blumberg@littlefallslibrary.org; *Info & Tech Serv Librn,* Jennifer Larrinaga; E-mail: larrinaga@littlefallslibrary.org; *Children's & Prog Serv Spec,* Linda Belen; E-mail: belen@littlefallslibrary.org; Staff 2 (MLS 2)
Founded 1906. Circ 47,000
Jan 2014-Dec 2014 Income $584,920, State $6,273, City $559,220, County $250, Other $12,854. Mats Exp $58,969, Books $38,622, Per/Ser (Incl. Access Fees) $6,093, AV Mat $6,863, Electronic Ref Mat (Incl. Access Fees) $7,391. Sal $287,000 (Prof $127,700)
Library Holdings: Audiobooks 904; CDs 1,215; DVDs 2,479; e-books 70; Electronic Media & Resources 7; Large Print Bks 336; Bk Titles 47,583; Per Subs 125
Special Collections: Jerseyana
Subject Interests: NJ
Automation Activity & Vendor Info: (Acquisitions) SirsiDynix; (Cataloging) SirsiDynix; (Circulation) SirsiDynix; (OPAC) SirsiDynix
Wireless access
Function: Computers for patron use, Ref serv available, Story hour, Summer reading prog
Partic in PALS Plus, The Computer Consortium of Passaic County Libraries
Open Mon-Thurs (Winter) 10-9, Fri 10-5, Sat 10-3; Mon-Thurs (Summer) 10-9, Fri 10-5
Friends of the Library Group

LITTLE FERRY

P LITTLE FERRY FREE PUBLIC LIBRARY, 239 Liberty St, 07643. SAN 310-2491. Tel: 201-641-3721. Web Site: littleferry.bccls.org. *Dir,* Stephen Turro; E-mail: director@littleferry.bccls.org; Staff 8 (MLS 1, Non-MLS 7)
Founded 1929. Pop 10,626; Circ 25,661
Library Holdings: Bk Vols 52,925; Per Subs 24
Special Collections: United States Cinema History Coll
Wireless access
Function: 24/7 Electronic res, 24/7 Online cat, Children's prog, ILL available, Internet access, Magazines, Magnifiers for reading, Movies, Music CDs, Online cat, Story hour, Tax forms
Partic in Bergen County Cooperative Library System, Inc
Special Services for the Blind - Large print bks; Talking bks
Open Mon-Wed 10-8, Thurs & Fri 10-5:30, Sat 10-3
Friends of the Library Group

LITTLE SILVER

P LITTLE SILVER PUBLIC LIBRARY, 484 Prospect Ave, 07739. SAN 310-2505. Tel: 732-747-9649. Web Site: www.littlesilverlibrary.org. *Libr Dir,* Anita O'Brien; E-mail: aobrien@monmouthcountylib.org; Staff 4 (MLS 1, Non-MLS 3)
Founded 1926. Pop 6,200; Circ 31,000
Library Holdings: Bk Titles 27,000; Bk Vols 27,500; Per Subs 50
Automation Activity & Vendor Info: (Cataloging) SirsiDynix; (Circulation) SirsiDynix; (OPAC) SirsiDynix
Wireless access
Mem of Monmouth County Library
Partic in LibraryLinkNJ, The New Jersey Library Cooperative
Open Mon 12-7:30, Tues-Fri 11-4, Sat 10-1
Friends of the Library Group

LIVINGSTON

P LIVINGSTON PUBLIC LIBRARY*, Ten Robert Harp Dr, 07039. SAN 310-2513. Tel: 973-992-4600. FAX: 973-994-2346. Web Site: www.livingstonlibrary.org. *Dir,* Amy Babcock-Landry; E-mail: babcock-landry@livingston.bccls.org; *Assoc Dir,* Melissa Brisbin; E-mail: melissa.brisbin@livingston.bccls.org; *Tech Serv,* Joseph Emery; E-mail: joseph.emery@livingston.bccls.org; Staff 46 (MLS 14, Non-MLS 32)
Founded 1911. Pop 29,360; Circ 430,028
Library Holdings: Bk Titles 219,524; Per Subs 557
Special Collections: Bibliography of Dr Lyndon A Peer; Large Print Coll; New Jerseyana. Oral History
Subject Interests: Art, Holocaust
Automation Activity & Vendor Info: (Cataloging) SirsiDynix; (Circulation) SirsiDynix; (OPAC) SirsiDynix
Wireless access
Function: Bi-weekly Writer's Group
Publications: Annual Report; Archival Holdings for the Township of Livingston; Footnotes (Monthly Newsletter); Livingston Local Business Directory
Special Services for the Deaf - TDD equip
Open Mon-Thurs 10-9, Fri 10-6, Sat 10-5, Sun 1-5
Friends of the Library Group

LODI

C FELICIAN UNIVERSITY*, Lodi Campus Library, 262 S Main St, 07644-2198. SAN 310-253X. Tel: 201-559-6071. FAX: 201-559-6148. E-mail: library@felician.edu. Web Site: felician.libguides.com/libraries. *Dir, Libr Serv,* Jodi Shelly, II; Tel: 201-559-6070, E-mail: Shellyj@felician.edu; *Head, Res & Instrul Serv,* Kaitlyn Curtis; Tel: 201-559-6125, E-mail: curtisk@felician.edu; Staff 11 (MLS 4, Non-MLS 7)
Founded 1942. Enrl 1,953; Fac 152; Highest Degree: Doctorate
Jul 2012-Jun 2013 Income $682,049. Mats Exp $682,049, Books $36,924, Per/Ser (Incl. Access Fees) $11,111, AV Mat $563, Electronic Ref Mat (Incl. Access Fees) $106,602, Presv $2,158. Sal $404,199 (Prof $354,955)
Library Holdings: CDs 1,465; DVDs 110; e-books 102,011; e-journals 26,689; Microforms 89,191; Bk Titles 183,766; Bk Vols 78,766; Per Subs 364; Videos 101
Special Collections: Children's Books; Poetry (Ammons Coll); Storytelling & Folklore (Helen Robinette Coll)
Subject Interests: Arts, Bus, Educ, Nursing
Automation Activity & Vendor Info: (Cataloging) SirsiDynix; (Circulation) SirsiDynix; (Course Reserve) SirsiDynix; (ILL) JerseyCat; (OPAC) SirsiDynix
Wireless access
Publications: Faculty Guide (Library handbook); Library Handbook; Library Updates (Online only)

Partic in LibraryLinkNJ, The New Jersey Library Cooperative; LYRASIS; OCLC Online Computer Library Center, Inc; Virtual Academic Library Environment
Special Services for the Blind - Computer with voice synthesizer for visually impaired persons
Open Mon-Thurs 8:45am-Midnight, Fri 8:45-4:45, Sat 10-4, Sun Noon-Midnight
Departmental Libraries:
RUTHERFORD CAMPUS LIBRARY, 227 Montross Ave, Rutherford, 07070. Tel: 201-559-3319. *Librn,* Alison Cole; Tel: 201-559-3336, E-mail: colea@felician.edu; *Libr Asst,* Sister Mary Abysius Morgan; E-mail: morganm@felician.edu

P LODI MEMORIAL LIBRARY*, One Memorial Dr, 07644. SAN 310-2548. Tel: 973-365-4044. FAX: 973-365-0172. Reference E-mail: REFERENCE@LODI.bccls.org. Web Site: lodi.bccls.org. *Dir,* Karyn Gost; E-mail: director@lodi.bccls.org; Staff 3 (MLS 3)
Founded 1924. Pop 24,136; Circ 56,138. Sal $456,974
Library Holdings: Audiobooks 1,402; Bks on Deafness & Sign Lang 45; CDs 1,176; DVDs 2,873; e-books 2,591; Bk Vols 60,155; Per Subs 1,540; Videos 2,260
Automation Activity & Vendor Info: (Cataloging) Innovative Interfaces, Inc; (Circulation) Innovative Interfaces, Inc; (OPAC) Innovative Interfaces, Inc
Wireless access
Function: Children's prog
Partic in Bergen County Cooperative Library System, Inc
Open Mon, Tues & Thurs 12:30-8, Wed, Fri & Sat 9:30-5
Friends of the Library Group

LONG BRANCH

P LONG BRANCH FREE PUBLIC LIBRARY*, 328 Broadway, 07740. SAN 310-2564. Tel: 732-222-3900. FAX: 732-222-3799. Web Site: www.longbranchlib.org/. *Dir,* Tonya Garcia; E-mail: tgarcia.lbpl@gmail.com; *Commun Engagement Librn, Tech,* Kate Angelo; E-mail: kangelo.lbpl@gmail.com; *Adult Serv Mgr,* Janet Birckhead; E-mail: jbirckhead.lbpl@gmail.com; *Circ Mgr,* Cadene Patterson; E-mail: cpatterson.lbpl@gmail.com; *Children's & Teen Serv, Manager, Family Services,* Nekesha Marshall; E-mail: nmarshall.lbpl@gmail.com; Staff 24 (MLS 3, Non-MLS 21)
Founded 1916. Pop 31,340; Circ 169,880. Sal $923,115 (Prof $296,146)
Library Holdings: Audiobooks 8,111; AV Mats 15,314; CDs 4,812; DVDs 10,857; e-books 6,702; Large Print Bks 2,547; Bk Titles 90,061; Per Subs 126
Special Collections: Audio Books; ESL Coll; Local Newspaper, micro; Long Branch Historical Coll; Spanish & Portuguese Coll
Automation Activity & Vendor Info: (Acquisitions) Baker & Taylor; (Cataloging) SirsiDynix-iBistro; (Circulation) SirsiDynix; (Course Reserve) JerseyCat; (ILL) JerseyCat; (OPAC) SirsiDynix-iBistro; (Serials) EBSCO Online
Wireless access
Function: 24/7 Electronic res, 24/7 Online cat, Adult bk club, Adult literacy prog, After school storytime, Archival coll, Art exhibits, Audiobks via web, AV serv, BA reader (adult literacy), Bilingual assistance for Spanish patrons, Bk club(s), Bks on CD, Butterfly Garden, CD-ROM, Children's prog, Citizenship assistance, Computer training, Computers for patron use, E-Readers, E-Reserves, Electronic databases & coll, Free DVD rentals, Holiday prog, Home delivery & serv to seniorr ctr & nursing homes, Homebound delivery serv, Homework prog, ILL available, Instruction & testing, Internet access, Magazines, Mango lang, Meeting rooms, Microfiche/film & reading machines, Movies, Museum passes, Music CDs, Notary serv, Online cat, Outreach serv, Photocopying/Printing, Preschool outreach, Prog for adults, Prog for children & young adult, Ref serv available, Res assist avail, Senior outreach, Serves people with intellectual disabilities, Spanish lang bks, Story hour, Summer reading prog, Tax forms, Teen prog, Telephone ref, VHS videos, Wheelchair accessible, Workshops
Partic in Libraries of Middlesex Automation Consortium; LibraryLinkNJ, The New Jersey Library Cooperative
Open Mon-Thurs 10-8, Fri & Sat 12-5
Friends of the Library Group
Branches: 1
ELBERON BRANCH, 168 Lincoln Ave, Elberon, 07740. SAN 310-1312. Tel: 732-870-1776. *Br Mgr,* Tara Sullivan; E-mail: tsullivan.lbpl@gmail.com; Staff 1 (Non-MLS 1)
Library Holdings: Bk Vols 9,884
Open Mon, Tues & Thurs-Sat 10-5, Wed 12-8
Friends of the Library Group

M MONMOUTH MEDICAL CENTER, Altschul Medical Library, 300 Second Ave, 07740. SAN 310-2572. Tel: 732-923-6645. E-mail: MedicalLibrary.MMC@rwjbh.org. Web Site: rwjbh.org/for-healthcare-professionals/medical-education/monmouth-medical-center/medical. *Libr Dir,* Frederic C Pachman; E-mail: frederic.pachman@rwjbh.org; Staff 1 (MLS 1)
Founded 1973
Library Holdings: Bk Titles 3,500; Bk Vols 4,000; Per Subs 20
Special Collections: Monmouth Medical Center History
Subject Interests: Med, Nursing, Pediatrics
Wireless access
Publications: Newsletter (Quarterly)
Partic in Docline; LibraryLinkNJ, The New Jersey Library Cooperative; National Network of Libraries of Medicine Region 1; New Jersey Health Sciences Library Network

LONG VALLEY

P WASHINGTON TOWNSHIP FREE PUBLIC LIBRARY*, 37 E Springtown Rd, 07853. SAN 310-2580. Tel: 908-876-3596. FAX: 908-876-3541. E-mail: info@wtpl.org. Web Site: wtpl.org. *Dir,* Jacqueline Zuzzi; E-mail: jacqueline.zuzzi@wtpl.org; Staff 13.5 (MLS 4, Non-MLS 9.5)
Founded 1968. Pop 18,544; Circ 168,209
Library Holdings: AV Mats 10,580; Per Subs 161
Automation Activity & Vendor Info: (Acquisitions) Baker & Taylor; (Cataloging) Main Library Systems; (Circulation) Main Library Systems; (ILL) JerseyCat; (OPAC) Main Library Systems
Wireless access
Function: 24/7 Electronic res, 24/7 Online cat, Activity rm, Adult bk club, Art exhibits, Art programs, Audiobks on Playaways & MP3, Audiobks via web, Bi-weekly Writer's Group, Bk club(s), Bk reviews (Group), Bks on CD, Butterfly Garden, CD-ROM, Chess club, Children's prog, Computer training, Computers for patron use, Digital talking bks, E-Readers, E-Reserves, Electronic databases & coll, For res purposes, Free DVD rentals, Genealogy discussion group, Holiday prog, Home delivery & serv to seniorr ctr & nursing homes, ILL available, Internet access, Large print keyboards, Life-long learning prog for all ages, Magazines, Meeting rooms, Movies, Museum passes, Music CDs, Notary serv, Online cat, Online ref, Photocopying/Printing, Preschool outreach, Preschool reading prog, Prog for adults, Prog for children & young adult, Ref & res, Ref serv available, Scanner, STEM programs, Story hour, Study rm, Summer & winter reading prog, Summer reading prog, Tax forms, Teen prog, Telephone ref, Wheelchair accessible, Winter reading prog
Partic in Morris Automated Information Network
Open Mon-Thurs 10-9, Fri & Sat 10-5
Friends of the Library Group

S WASHINGTON TOWNSHIP HISTORICAL SOCIETY LIBRARY, Six Fairview Ave, 07853-3172. (Mail add: PO Box 189, 07853-0189), SAN 373-2509. Tel: 908-876-9696. E-mail: info@wthsnj.org. Web Site: wthsnj.org. *Co-Pres,* Sig Schorr; *Co-Pres,* Annette Sadloski
Founded 1960
Library Holdings: Bk Vols 300
Special Collections: Local Cemetery Listings; Local Church Records; New Jersey History by Henry Charlton Beck; Original Newspaper Articles; Schooley's Mountain Springs Coll
Subject Interests: Genealogy, Local hist
Open Sun 2-4

LONGPORT

P LONGPORT PUBLIC LIBRARY*, 2305 Atlantic Ave, 08403. SAN 373-1901. Tel: 609-487-7403. E-mail: library@longportpubliclibrary.org. Web Site: www.longportpubliclibrary.org. *Dir,* Richard Gerhardt
Founded 1990
Library Holdings: Bk Titles 7,000
Automation Activity & Vendor Info: (Cataloging) Innovative Interfaces, Inc
Wireless access
Open Mon & Wed-Sat 9-5, Tues 9-8

LYNDHURST

P LYNDHURST FREE PUBLIC LIBRARY*, 355 Valley Brook Ave, 07071. SAN 310-2599. Tel: 201-804-2478. FAX: 201-939-7677. Circulation E-mail: lyndcirc@bccls.org. *Dir,* Donna M Romeo; E-mail: romeo@lyndhurst.bccls.org; *Dept Head, Ref Librn,* Thomas Hilton; E-mail: lyndref@bccls.org; *Ch Serv, Librn,* Maryellen Kulzy; E-mail: lyndchild@bccls.org; *Circ Supvr,* Michelle Kelly; *Tech Serv,* Elizabeth Hughes; E-mail: lyndtech@bccls.org; Staff 11 (MLS 4, Non-MLS 7)
Founded 1914. Pop 19,400; Circ 51,000
Library Holdings: Bk Titles 56,000; Bk Vols 65,000; Per Subs 114
Special Collections: Local History Coll, slides tapes; New Jerseyana Col, bks, photog, a-tapes, slides
Automation Activity & Vendor Info: (Cataloging) SirsiDynix; (Circulation) SirsiDynix
Wireless access
Open Mon 11-8, Tues & Fri 9-5, Wed & Thurs 9-8, Sat 9-1

LYONS

DEPARTMENT OF VETERANS AFFAIRS

GM LYONS CAMPUS MEDICAL LIBRARY*, 151 Knollcroft Rd, 07939, SAN 350-8501. Tel: 908-647-0180, Ext 4545, 973-676-1000. FAX: 908-604-5837. *Librn,* Veronica Lisa; *ILL,* Kim Jaciw
Founded 1931
Library Holdings: Bk Titles 4,200; Per Subs 350
Special Collections: Patient Health Education
Subject Interests: Med, Nursing, Psychiat, Psychol
Partic in New Jersey Health Sciences Library Network
Restriction: Staff use only

GM LYONS CAMPUS PATIENT'S LIBRARY*, 151 Knollcroft Rd, 07939, SAN 350-8536. Tel: 908-647-0180, Ext 6421, 973-676-1000. FAX: 908-604-5837. *Libr Tech,* Kris Reinmann

MADISON

C DREW UNIVERSITY LIBRARY, 36 Madison Ave, 07940. SAN 310-2602. Tel: 973-408-3486. Reference Tel: 973-408-3588. Administration Tel: 973-408-3207. FAX: 973-408-3770. E-mail: library@drew.edu. Web Site: drew.edu/library. *Dir, Tech Serv, Interim Libr Dir, Syst Librn,* Guy Dobson; E-mail: gdobson@drew.edu; *Dir of Coll, Electronic Res Librn,* Kathleen Juliano; Tel: 973-408-3478, E-mail: kjuliano@drew.edu; *Head, Access Serv,* Lauren Levinson; Tel: 973-408-3875, E-mail: levinson@drew.edu; *Govt Doc/Ref Librn,* Irina Radeva; Tel: 973-408-3480, E-mail: iradeva@drew.edu; *Sci Librn,* Margery Ashmun; Tel: 973-408-3483, E-mail: mashmun@drew.edu; *Theological Librn,* Jesse Mann; Tel: 973-408-3472, E-mail: jmann@drew.edu; *Access Services Assoc,* Judy Ahlers; Tel: 973-408-3589, E-mail: jahlers@drew.edu; *Tech Serv Assoc,* Yanira Ramirez; Tel: 973-408-3672, E-mail: yramirez@drew.edu; *Mgr, Spec Coll,* Candace Reilly; Tel: 973-408-3590, E-mail: creilly1@drew.edu; *Digital Scholarship Tech Mgr,* Danielle Reay; Tel: 973-408-3855, E-mail: dreay@drew.edu; *Univ Archivist,* Matthew Beland; Tel: 973-408-3532, E-mail: mbeland@drew.edu; *Methodist Curator,* Alex Parrish; Tel: 973-408-3910, E-mail: aparrish@drew.edu; Staff 12 (MLS 7, Non-MLS 5)
Founded 1867. Enrl 2,042; Fac 260; Highest Degree: Doctorate
Library Holdings: AV Mats 6,887; e-books 313,688; Microforms 61,101; Bk Vols 750,684; Per Subs 100,375
Special Collections: 19th Century Pamphlets Coll; Carl Michalson Coll; Creamer Hymnology Coll; David Johnson Science Fiction & MAD Magazine Coll; Dornan Coll (Russian Samizdat Archive); Drew University Archives; George D Kelsey Coll; Georges Simenon Coll; Haberly Book Arts Coll; Letters of John Wesley & the Wesley Family; Maser & Prinster Prayer Book Coll; McClintock Rare Book Coll; Political & Graphic Satire (Chesler Coll); Political Journalism (Bela Kornitzer Coll); Reformation Church History (Koehler Coll); Society of Biblical Literature Archives; Theology Coll, bks, ms; United Nations Coll, bks, doc; Will Herberg Coll; Willa Cather Coll; World Methodism, archives, doc, journals, ms, papers, per, publs, rec; Zuck Botanical Coll. State Document Depository; UN Document Depository; US Document Depository
Subject Interests: Biblical studies, Liberal arts, Liturgics, Methodism, Relig hist, Theol
Automation Activity & Vendor Info: (Acquisitions) EBSCO Discovery Service; (Cataloging) EBSCO Discovery Service; (Circulation) EBSCO Discovery Service; (ILL) OCLC Tipasa
Wireless access
Function: Computers for patron use, Microfiche/film & reading machines, Photocopying/Printing, Ref serv available, Scanner, Telephone ref
Publications: Visions (Newsletter)
Partic in Amigos Library Services, Inc; LibraryLinkNJ, The New Jersey Library Cooperative; LYRASIS; Oberlin Group; Virtual Academic Library Environment; Westchester Academic Library Directors Organization
Open Mon-Thurs 9am-10pm, Fri 9-5, Sat Noon-5, Sun 2-8
Friends of the Library Group

C FAIRLEIGH DICKINSON UNIVERSITY*, Florham Campus Library, 285 Madison Ave, M-LAO-03, 07940. SAN 350-8595. Tel: 973-443-8515. Interlibrary Loan Service Tel: 973-443-8530. Reference Tel: 973-443-8516. Administration Tel: 973-443-8682. FAX: 973-443-8525. Web Site: library.fdu.edu/florham. *Assoc Univ Librn, Dir, Tech Serv,* Brigid Burke; Tel: 973-443-8520, E-mail: bburke@fdu.edu; *Actg Dir, Pub Serv,* Nicole Potdevin; Tel: 973-443-8627, E-mail: potdevin@fdu.edu; *Electronic Res Librn,* Robert Wolf; Tel: 973-443-8523, E-mail: wolfrd@fdu.edu; *Metadata Librn, Res, Tech Serv,* Position Currently Open; *Res & Instruction Librn,* Eleanor Friedl; E-mail: friedl@fdu.edu; *Res & Instruction Librn,* Nicole Potdevin; Tel: 973-443-8627, E-mail: potdevin@fdu.edu; *Res & Instruction Librn,* Robert Richlan; E-mail: richlan@fdu.edu; *Syst Librn,* Youbo Wang; E-mail: ywang@fdu.edu; *Circ Coordr,* Tracy Dante; E-mail: tldante@fdu.edu; Staff 10.5 (MLS 5, Non-MLS 5.5)
Founded 1958. Enrl 3,400; Fac 130; Highest Degree: Doctorate
Library Holdings: DVDs 2,000; e-books 138,000; Microforms 19,000; Bk Vols 135,000; Per Subs 190
Special Collections: Black Fiction Coll; Douglas Kahn Photo & Film History Coll; Lloyd Haberly Book Arts Coll
Automation Activity & Vendor Info: (Acquisitions) Ex Libris Group; (Cataloging) Ex Libris Group; (Circulation) Ex Libris Group; (Course Reserve) Ex Libris Group; (ILL) OCLC; (OPAC) Ex Libris Group; (Serials) Ex Libris Group
Wireless access
Function: 24/7 Online cat, Archival coll, Art exhibits, Audio & video playback equip for onsite use, Audiobks via web, CD-ROM, Computer training, Computers for patron use, Distance learning, Doc delivery serv, Electronic databases & coll, Free DVD rentals, ILL available, Internet access, Notary serv, Online cat, Online ref, Orientations, Outside serv via phone, mail, e-mail & web, Photocopying/Printing, Ref & res, Ref serv available, Res libr, Scanner, Telephone ref, VHS videos, Wheelchair accessible, Workshops
Partic in LibraryLinkNJ, The New Jersey Library Cooperative; OCLC Online Computer Library Center, Inc; Virtual Academic Library Environment
Open Mon-Thurs 8:30am-11pm, Fri 8:30-5, Sat 10-6, Sun 2-10
Friends of the Library Group

P MADISON PUBLIC LIBRARY*, 39 Keep St, 07940. SAN 310-2610. Tel: 973-377-0722. FAX: 973-377-3142. Web Site: madisonnjlibrary.org. *Dir,* Lynn Favreau; E-mail: lynn.favreau@mainlib.org; *Supvr, Ch Serv,* Emily Weisenstein; E-mail: emily.weisenstein@mainlib.org; *Adult Serv & Tech Serv/ILL,* Adrienne Tawil; E-mail: adrienne.tawil@mainlib.org; *Circ & ILL,* Ralph Graham; E-mail: ralph.graham@mainlib.org; Staff 19.3 (MLS 6.1, Non-MLS 13.2)
Founded 1900. Pop 15,845; Circ 226,417
Library Holdings: AV Mats 13,956; Bk Vols 132,197; Per Subs 213
Special Collections: Golden Hind Press Publications; Madison History
Subject Interests: Am lit, British lit
Automation Activity & Vendor Info: (Cataloging) Innovative Interfaces, Inc; (Circulation) Innovative Interfaces, Inc; (ILL) Innovative Interfaces, Inc; (OPAC) Innovative Interfaces, Inc
Wireless access
Function: Adult bk club, Archival coll, Art exhibits, Bks on CD, Children's prog, Computers for patron use, Electronic databases & coll, Free DVD rentals, ILL available, Microfiche/film & reading machines, Museum passes, Music CDs, Online cat, Online ref, OverDrive digital audio bks, Photocopying/Printing, Preschool reading prog, Prog for adults, Prog for children & young adult, Ref & res, Ref serv available, Story hour, Tax forms, Telephone ref, Wheelchair accessible
Publications: Newsletter (Bimonthly)
Partic in Morris-Union Federation
Open Mon-Wed 10-9, Thurs & Fri 10-6, Sat 10-5, Sun (Fall-Spring) 2-5
Restriction: Authorized patrons
Friends of the Library Group

S MUSEUM OF EARLY TRADES & CRAFTS LIBRARY, Nine Main St, 07940. SAN 377-483X. Tel: 973-377-2982, Ext 10. E-mail: info@metc.org. Web Site: www.metc.org. *Dir,* Deborah Farrar; *Curator of Collections & Exhibits,* Shelley Cathcart; E-mail: curator@metc.org
Library Holdings: Bk Vols 600
Subject Interests: Craft, Early Am hist, Tools
Open Tues-Sat 10-4, Sun 12-5 (Winter); Tues-Sat 10-4 (Summer)
Restriction: Not a lending libr

R UNITED METHODIST CHURCH, General Commission on Archives & History Library, 36 Madison Ave, 07940. SAN 312-8997. Tel: 973-408-3590. Web Site: gcah.org, www.drew.edu/library/2019/08/21/united-methodist-archives-and-history-center. *Mgr, Spec Coll,* Candace Reilly; E-mail: creilly1@drew.edu
Founded 1968
Library Holdings: Bk Titles 40,000; Bk Vols 50,000; Per Subs 600
Special Collections: Methodist/EUB/Holiness Hymnals; Missions Periodicals
Subject Interests: United Methodist Church
Automation Activity & Vendor Info: (Acquisitions) SirsiDynix; (Cataloging) SirsiDynix; (Circulation) SirsiDynix; (OPAC) SirsiDynix; (Serials) SirsiDynix
Wireless access
Open Mon-Fri 9-5
Friends of the Library Group

MAHWAH

P MAHWAH PUBLIC LIBRARY*, 100 Ridge Rd, 07430. SAN 310-2645. Tel: 201-529-7323. FAX: 201-529-9027. Circulation E-mail: info@mahwahlibrary.org. Web Site: www.mahwahlibrary.org. *Dir,* Kurt Hadeler; Tel: 201-529-7323, Ext 221, E-mail: khadeler@mahwahlibrary.org; Staff 34 (MLS 7, Non-MLS 27)
Founded 1912. Pop 24,062; Circ 176,000
Library Holdings: AV Mats 12,126; Large Print Bks 1,082; Bk Titles 80,114; Bk Vols 85,330; Per Subs 268

Subject Interests: Theatre
Wireless access
Publications: Brochures; Flyers; Monthly Calendar; Monthly Newsletter
Partic in Bergen County Cooperative Library System, Inc; LibraryLinkNJ, The New Jersey Library Cooperative
Open Mon-Thurs (Sept-June) 10-9, Fri-Sun 10-5; Mon-Wed (July-Aug) 10-9, Thurs-Sat 10-5
Friends of the Library Group

C RAMAPO COLLEGE OF NEW JERSEY*, George T Potter Library, 505 Ramapo Valley Rd, 07430-1623. SAN 310-2661. Tel: 201-684-7575. Web Site: ramapo.edu/library. *Col Librn,* Elizabeth J Siecke; E-mail: esiecke@ramapo.edu; *Circ Librn, Instruction Librn, Ref Librn,* Madel Tisi; Tel: 201-684-7510, E-mail: mtisi@ramapo.edu; *Govt Doc Librn, Instruction Librn,* Shirley Knight; Tel: 201-684-7315, E-mail: sknight@ramapo.edu; *Instruction & Emerging Tech Librn,* Christina Connor; Tel: 201-684-7581, E-mail: cconnor@ramapo.edu; *Outreach Librn, Ref & Instruction Librn,* Hilary Westgate; Tel: 201-684-7570, E-mail: switten1@ramapo.edu; *Archivist, Ref & Instruction Librn,* Susan Kurzmann; Tel: 201-684-7199, E-mail: skurzman@ramapo.edu; *Tech Serv Librn,* Marcia Sexton; Tel: 201-684-7362, E-mail: msexton@ramapo.edu; *Information Literacy Coord,* Leigh Cregan Keller; Tel: 201-684-7316, E-mail: lkeller1@ramapo.edu; Staff 27 (MLS 9, Non-MLS 18)
Founded 1968. Enrl 5,631; Fac 170; Highest Degree: Master
Library Holdings: Bk Titles 155,038; Bk Vols 178,737; Per Subs 976
Special Collections: State Document Depository
Automation Activity & Vendor Info: (Acquisitions) LibLime; (Cataloging) OCLC; (Circulation) LibLime; (Course Reserve) LibLime; (ILL) OCLC; (OPAC) LibLime
Wireless access
Partic in LibraryLinkNJ, The New Jersey Library Cooperative; NJ Col & Univ Libr Coun; Virtual Academic Library Environment

MANALAPAN

P MONMOUTH COUNTY LIBRARY*, Headquarters, 125 Symmes Dr, 07726. SAN 350-7181. Tel: 732-431-7220. FAX: 732-308-2955. TDD: 732-845-0064. Web Site: www.monmouthcountylib.org. *Libr Dir,* Judith Tolchin; E-mail: jtolchin@monmouthcountylib.org; *Asst Libr Dir,* Heidi Amici; *Br Serv Librn,* Rachel Yost Scalise; *Children's Coordr, Supv Librn,* Pat Findra; *Supv Librn,* Robyn Miller; Staff 62 (MLS 50, Non-MLS 12)
Founded 1922. Pop 415,584; Circ 3,320,308
Jan 2021-Dec 2021. Mats Exp $3,693,400, Books $2,650,000, AV Mat $625,000, Electronic Ref Mat (Incl. Access Fees) $207,000
Library Holdings: Bk Titles 1,488,627
Special Collections: New Jersey History
Wireless access
Publications: Children's Newsletter; Monthly Calendar; Municipal Government (Newsletter)
Member Libraries: Brielle Public Library; Fair Haven Public Library; Keansburg Waterfront Public Library; Little Silver Public Library; Manasquan Public Library; Monmouth Beach Library; Neptune City Library; Oceanic Free Library; Sea Bright Library; Tinton Falls Public Library; Union Beach Memorial Library
Partic in LibraryLinkNJ, The New Jersey Library Cooperative; OCLC Online Computer Library Center, Inc
Special Services for the Deaf - Assisted listening device; Bks on deafness & sign lang; Sign lang interpreter upon request for prog; TTY equip
Special Services for the Blind - Closed circuit TV magnifier
Open Mon-Thurs 9-9, Fri & Sat 9-5, Sun (Sept-June) 1-5
Friends of the Library Group
Branches: 12
ALLENTOWN BRANCH, 16 S Main St, Allentown, 08501, SAN 350-7211. Tel: 609-259-7565. FAX: 609-259-9620. *Br Mgr,* Josephine Mayer
Library Holdings: Bk Vols 20,350
Open Mon & Wed 10-5, Tues & Thurs 10-9, Fri 2-5, Sat 10-3
ATLANTIC HIGHLANDS BRANCH, 100 First Ave, Atlantic Highlands, 07716, SAN 309-9997. Tel: 732-291-1956. *Br Mgr,* Jane Reynolds
Founded 1926. Pop 4,895; Circ 34,440
Library Holdings: Bk Vols 20,000; Per Subs 50
Automation Activity & Vendor Info: (Cataloging) SirsiDynix; (Circulation) SirsiDynix; (OPAC) SirsiDynix
Function: Adult bk club, After school storytime, Bk club(s), Chess club, Electronic databases & coll, ILL available, Internet access, Online ref, Prog for adults, Prog for children & young adult, Spoken cassettes & CDs, Spoken cassettes & DVDs, Summer reading prog, Tax forms, VHS videos
Open Mon & Tues 9-4, Wed 9-6, Thurs 1-9, Fri 1-5, Sat 9-5 (9-1 July-Aug)
Friends of the Library Group
COLTS NECK BRANCH, One Winthrop Dr, Colts Neck, 07722, SAN 350-722X. Tel: 732-431-5656. FAX: 732-462-0327. *Br Mgr,* Stephanie Laurino
Library Holdings: Bk Vols 28,450
Open Mon & Wed 9-5, Tues & Thurs 1-9, Fri 1-5, Sat 9-5 (9-1 July-Aug)
EASTERN BRANCH, 1001 Rte 35, Shrewsbury, 07702, SAN 350-7246. Tel: 732-683-8980. Toll Free Tel: 866-941-8188. FAX: 732-219-0140. TDD: 732-933-1285. *Chief Librn,* Kim Avagliano
Library Holdings: Bk Vols 145,000
Special Collections: US Document Depository
Subject Interests: Art, Educ, Law, Music
Open Mon-Thurs 9-9, Fri & Sat 9-5, Sun (Sept-May) 1-5
HAZLET BRANCH, 251 Middle Rd, Hazlet, 07730, SAN 350-7270. Tel: 732-264-7164. FAX: 732-739-1556. *Br Mgr,* Mary Patterson
Library Holdings: Bk Vols 54,000
Open Mon & Wed 1-9, Tues & Thurs 9-5, Fri 1-5, Sat 9-5 (9-1 July-Aug)
HOLMDEL BRANCH, 101 Crawfords Corner Rd, Ste 2110, Holmdel, 07733, SAN 350-7300. Tel: 732-946-4118. FAX: 732-946-2980. *Br Mgr,* Karen Nealis
Library Holdings: Bk Vols 38,000
Special Collections: Township History Coll
Open Mon & Wed 1-9, Tues & Thurs 9-5, Fri 1-5, Sat 9-5 (9-1 July-Aug)
HOWELL BRANCH, 318 Old Tavern Rd, Howell, 07731, SAN 350-7335. Tel: 732-938-2300. FAX: 732-938-4739. *Br Mgr,* Beth Henderson
Library Holdings: Bk Vols 46,000
Special Collections: Township History Coll
Open Mon & Wed 10-9, Tues & Thurs 9-9, Fri 1-5, Sat 9-5 (9-1 July-Aug)
MARLBORO BRANCH, One Library Ct, Marlboro, 07746-1102, SAN 350-7394. Tel: 732-536-9406. FAX: 732-536-4708. *Br Mgr,* Stephenie Acosta
Library Holdings: Bk Vols 100,000
Subject Interests: Local hist
Open Mon, Tues & Thurs 9-9, Wed 9-6, Fri 1-5, Sat 9-5 (9-1 July-Aug)
OCEAN TOWNSHIP, 701 Deal Rd, Ocean, 07712, SAN 350-7459. Tel: 732-531-5092. FAX: 732-531-5262. *Br Mgr,* Diana Zambrano
Library Holdings: Bk Vols 64,000
Subject Interests: Local hist
Open Mon 10-9, Tues-Thurs 9-9, Fri 1-5, Sat 9-5 (9-1 July-Aug)
OCEANPORT BRANCH, Eight Iroquios Ave, Oceanport, 07757, SAN 350-7424. Tel: 732-229-2626. FAX: 732-571-0661. *Br Mgr,* Barbara Eckert
Library Holdings: Bk Vols 20,350
Open Mon 1-5 & 6-9, Tues 9-12 & 1-5, Thurs 9-12 & 1-5, Fri 1-5
WALL TOWNSHIP, 2700 Allaire Rd, Wall, 07719, SAN 350-7483. Tel: 732-449-8877. FAX: 732-449-1732. *Br Mgr,* Sue Domas
Library Holdings: Bk Vols 104,000
Special Collections: Local Hist Coll
Open Mon 10-9, Tues-Thurs 9-9, Fri 1-5, Sat 9-5 (9-1 July-Aug)
WEST LONG BRANCH, 95 Poplar Ave, West Long Branch, 07764, SAN 310-5938. Tel: 732-222-5993. FAX: 732-229-5138. *Br Mgr,* Kathleen Kenny
Library Holdings: Bk Vols 35,000; Per Subs 125
Special Collections: Monmouth County NJ History Coll
Open Mon & Thurs 10-9, Tues & Wed 9-5, Fri 1-5, Sat 9-5 (9-1 July-Aug)

MANASQUAN

P MANASQUAN PUBLIC LIBRARY*, 55 Broad St, 08736. SAN 310-2688. Tel: 732-223-1503. FAX: 732-292-0336. Circulation E-mail: mqcirc@monmouthcountylib.org. Web Site: www.manasquan.lib.nj.us. *Dir,* Carol C Mennie
Founded 1915. Pop 5,500; Circ 36,000
Library Holdings: Bk Titles 32,000; Per Subs 50
Wireless access
Mem of Monmouth County Library
Open Mon & Thurs 10-8, Tues & Fri 10-5, Sat 9:30-12:30

MANVILLE

P MANVILLE PUBLIC LIBRARY, 100 S Tenth Ave, 08835. SAN 310-2696. Tel: 908-458-8425. E-mail: manville@sclibnj.org. Web Site: sclsnj.org/about/branch-locations, www.manvillenj.org/544/Manville-Public-Library. *Br Mgr,* Nan Peterson; E-mail: npeterso@sclibnj.org; *Adult Serv,* Ashley Soulier; Staff 8 (MLS 1, Non-MLS 7)
Founded 1960. Pop 10,541; Circ 28,000
Library Holdings: CDs 325; DVDs 840; Bk Titles 50,000; Bk Vols 53,533; Per Subs 90; Videos 1,243
Subject Interests: Coal

Automation Activity & Vendor Info: (Cataloging) SirsiDynix; (Circulation) SirsiDynix; (ILL) JerseyCat
Wireless access
Publications: Monthly Calendar; Newsletter (Quarterly)
Partic in Raritan Valley Fedn of Librs
Open Mon-Thurs 10-8, Fri & Sat 10-6
Friends of the Library Group

MAPLEWOOD

P MAPLEWOOD MEMORIAL LIBRARY*, 51 Baker St, 07040-2618. SAN 350-8684. Tel: 973-762-1622. Circulation Tel: 973-762-1622, Ext 5000. FAX: 973-762-4593. E-mail: library@maplewoodlibrary.org. Web Site: www.maplewoodlibrary.org. *Dir,* Sarah Lester; E-mail: slester@maplewoodlibrary.org; *Head, Adult Serv, Head, Tech,* Barbara Laub; E-mail: blaub@maplewoodlibrary.org; *Head, Children's Servx,* Jane Folger; E-mail: jfolger@maplewoodlibrary.org; *Head, Circ & Tech Serv,* Amanda Eigen; E-mail: aeigen@maplewoodlibrary.org; *Teen Serv Librn,* Emily Witkowski; E-mail: ewitkowski@maplewoodlibrary.org; Staff 10 (MLS 9, Non-MLS 1)
Founded 1913. Pop 23,868; Circ 221,148
Library Holdings: Bk Titles 92,415; Bk Vols 131,795; Per Subs 180
Special Collections: Local History (Durand Room Coll), bks, clippings, photog, especially Asher B Durand, 1796-1886 & James A Ricalton, 1844-1929
Automation Activity & Vendor Info: (Acquisitions) Innovative Interfaces, Inc; (Cataloging) Innovative Interfaces, Inc; (Circulation) Innovative Interfaces, Inc; (ILL) Auto-Graphics, Inc; (OPAC) Innovative Interfaces, Inc
Wireless access
Publications: Maplewood Library News (co-published with Friends) (Newsletter)
Partic in LibraryLinkNJ, The New Jersey Library Cooperative; ReBL
Open Mon, Wed & Thurs 10-9, Tues 10-6, Fri & Sat 10-5; Mon, Wed & Thurs (Summer) 9-9, Tues 9-6, Fri 9-5, Sat 10-5
Friends of the Library Group
Branches: 1
HILTON, 1688 Springfield Ave, 07040-2923, SAN 350-8714. Tel: 973-762-1688. Circulation Tel: 973-762-1688, Ext 5100. *Br Head,* Irene Langlois; E-mail: ilanglois@maplewoodlibrary.org; *Ch,* Jenny Burkholder
Founded 1882
Library Holdings: Bk Titles 23,000; Bk Vols 27,000
Open Mon & Wed (Sept-June) 10-5, Tues & Thurs 12-8, Sat (Sept-June) 10-1
Friends of the Library Group

SR MORROW MEMORIAL UNITED METHODIST CHURCH*, Library & Media Center, 600 Ridgewood Rd, 07040-2161. SAN 326-2359. Tel: 973-763-7676. FAX: 973-763-6798. E-mail: opendoors@morrowchurch.org. Web Site: www.morrowchurch.org.
Pop 861
Library Holdings: Bk Titles 800; Bk Vols 1,000
Subject Interests: Archives, Art, Church hist, Fiction, Hist
Restriction: Mem only

MARGATE CITY

P MARGATE CITY PUBLIC LIBRARY*, 8100 Atlantic Ave, 08402. SAN 310-2726. Tel: 609-822-4700. FAX: 609-823-0064. Web Site: www.margatelibrary.org. *Dir,* James J Cahill, Jr; E-mail: jim@margatelibrary.org; Staff 6 (MLS 2, Non-MLS 4)
Founded 1972. Pop 9,200
Library Holdings: Bk Titles 36,593; Per Subs 120
Automation Activity & Vendor Info: (Cataloging) Innovative Interfaces, Inc - Millennium; (Circulation) Innovative Interfaces, Inc - Millennium
Wireless access
Function: Bks on CD, Computers for patron use, Digital talking bks, Electronic databases & coll, Internet access, Photocopying/Printing, Prog for adults, Prog for children & young adult, Ref serv available, Senior computer classes, Tax forms, Wheelchair accessible
Partic in Coalition of Independent Libraries; LibraryLinkNJ, The New Jersey Library Cooperative
Open Mon, Tues & Thurs 9:30-8, Wed, Fri & Sat 9:30-5, Sun 10-2
Friends of the Library Group

MATAWAN

S MADISON-OLD BRIDGE TOWNSHIP HISTORICAL SOCIETY*, Thomas Warne Museum & Library, 4216 Route 516, 07747-7032. SAN 325-7746. Tel: 732-566-2108. FAX: 732-566-6943. E-mail: info@thomas-warne-museum.com. Web Site: www.thomas-warne-museum.com. *Pres,* Richard Pucciarelli; *Library Contact,* Jeff Kagen
Founded 1964
Library Holdings: Bk Vols 1,300
Special Collections: 19th Century Tools; Handcrafts; Local History & Genealogy; Newspaper Coll, Early 1800s; Old School Coll, bks, related items; Photograph Coll, Early 19th Century, vf ref
Subject Interests: Township History
Wireless access
Function: Res libr
Publications: At the Headwaters of Cheesequake Creek (Local history book); From Groaning Board Cooks; Images of America Old Bridge; Timepiece (Newsletter)
Open Sat & Sun Noon-4
Restriction: Not a lending libr

P MATAWAN-ABERDEEN PUBLIC LIBRARY*, 165 Main St, 07747. SAN 310-2742. Tel: 732-583-9100. E-mail: info@matawanaberdeenlibrary.com. Web Site: www.matawanaberdeenlibrary.com. *Dir,* Kimberly Paone; E-mail: kpaone@lmxac.org; *Head, Adult Serv,* Jill Stafford; *Head, Circ,* Laura Beyer; *Head, Youth Serv,* Leslie Kotzas; Staff 24 (MLS 9, Non-MLS 15)
Founded 1903. Pop 27,020; Circ 73,587
Automation Activity & Vendor Info: (Circulation) SirsiDynix
Wireless access
Function: 24/7 Electronic res, 24/7 Online cat, Activity rm, Adult bk club, After school storytime, Archival coll, Art exhibits, Audiobks on Playaways & MP3, Audiobks via web, Bilingual assistance for Spanish patrons, Bk club(s), Bks on CD, Children's prog, Citizenship assistance, Computer training, Computers for patron use, Digital talking bks, E-Reserves, Electronic databases & coll, Family literacy, Free DVD rentals, Genealogy discussion group, Holiday prog, Homework prog, ILL available, Internet access, Life-long learning prog for all ages, Magazines, Mail & tel request accepted, Mango lang, Movies, Museum passes, Music CDs, Notary serv, Online cat, Online ref, Outreach serv, Outside serv via phone, mail, e-mail & web, OverDrive digital audio bks, Photocopying/Printing, Preschool outreach, Preschool reading prog, Prog for adults, Prog for children & young adult, Ref & res, Ref serv available, Scanner, Senior computer classes, Senior outreach, Serves people with intellectual disabilities, Spanish lang bks, Story hour, Summer & winter reading prog, Summer reading prog, Tax forms, Teen prog, Telephone ref, Wheelchair accessible, Winter reading prog, Workshops, Writing prog
Partic in Libraries of Middlesex Automation Consortium
Open Mon, Wed & Thurs 9-9, Tues & Fri 9-6, Sat 9-5 (9-12:30 Summer), Sun 12-5
Restriction: Non-resident fee
Friends of the Library Group

MAYS LANDING

J ATLANTIC CAPE COMMUNITY COLLEGE*, William Spangler Library, 5100 Black Horse Pike, 08330. SAN 310-2750. Tel: 609-343-4951. Circulation Tel: 609-343-4951. Reference Tel: 609-343-5665. Web Site: www.atlantic.edu/library. *Dir, Academic Support,* Janet Hauge; Tel: 609-343-4937, E-mail: jhauge@atlantic.edu; *Asst Dir, Acad Affairs,* Michael Sargente; Tel: 609-343-5631, E-mail: msargent@atlantic.edu; *Ref Serv,* Leslie Murtha; Staff 5 (MLS 3, Non-MLS 2)
Founded 1966. Enrl 5,000; Fac 71; Highest Degree: Associate
Library Holdings: e-books 5,000; Bk Vols 81,000; Per Subs 300
Special Collections: Southern New Jersey History
Automation Activity & Vendor Info: (Cataloging) SirsiDynix; (Circulation) SirsiDynix; (OPAC) SirsiDynix
Wireless access
Function: 24/7 Electronic res, 24/7 Online cat, Art exhibits, Bk club(s), Computers for patron use, Electronic databases & coll, For res purposes, ILL available, Internet access, Learning ctr, Magazines, Magnifiers for reading, Outside serv via phone, mail, e-mail & web, Photocopying/Printing, Ref & res, Ref serv available, Wheelchair accessible
Partic in LibraryLinkNJ, The New Jersey Library Cooperative; Med Libr & Info Consortium; OCLC Online Computer Library Center, Inc; Virtual Academic Library Environment
Open Mon-Thurs 8am-10pm, Fri 8-4:30, Sat 11-4

P ATLANTIC COUNTY LIBRARY SYSTEM*, 40 Farragut Ave, 08330-1750. SAN 310-4346. Tel: 609-625-2776. FAX: 609-625-8143. Web Site: www.atlanticlibrary.org. *Dir,* Regina Bell; E-mail: rbell@aclsys.org; *Asst Dir,* Kathryn Gindin; *Fiscal Officer,* Carolina Ramos; Staff 24 (MLS 24)
Founded 1926. Pop 181,307; Circ 897,590
Library Holdings: Bk Titles 248,143; Bk Vols 486,854
Special Collections: Jerseyana; Music Coll. State Document Depository
Automation Activity & Vendor Info: (Acquisitions) SirsiDynix; (Cataloging) SirsiDynix; (Circulation) SirsiDynix; (OPAC) SirsiDynix; (Serials) SirsiDynix
Wireless access
Publications: Wavelength (Newsletter)
Partic in LibraryLinkNJ, The New Jersey Library Cooperative
Special Services for the Blind - Accessible computers

Open Mon-Thurs 9-9, Fri & Sat 9-5
Friends of the Library Group
Branches: 9
BRIGANTINE BRANCH, 201 15th St S, Brigantine, 08203, SAN 321-8198. Tel: 609-266-0110. FAX: 609-266-0040. *Br Mgr,* Mary Beth Fine
Founded 1983
Open Mon, Tues, Fri & Sat 9:30-5; Wed & Thurs 9-8
Friends of the Library Group
EGG HARBOR CITY BRANCH, 134 Philadelphia Ave, Egg Harbor City, 08215. Tel: 609-804-1063. FAX: 609-804-1082. *Br Mgr,* Marci Schultz
Open Mon, Wed, Fri & Sat 9:30-5, Tues & Thurs 12-8
EGG HARBOR TOWNSHIP BRANCH, One Swift Ave, Egg Harbor Township, 08234, SAN 320-9962. Tel: 609-927-8664. FAX: 609-927-4683. *Br Mgr,* Ruth Conrad
Open Mon, Fri & Sat 9:30-5, Tues-Thurs 9-8
Friends of the Library Group
GALLOWAY BRANCH, 306 E Jimmie Leeds Rd, Galloway, 08205, SAN 328-6754. Tel: 609-652-2352. FAX: 609-652-3613. *Br Mgr,* Brandi Grosso
Founded 1970
Library Holdings: Bk Titles 8,000; Bk Vols 15,000
Open Mon, Fri & Sat 9:30-5, Tues-Thurs 9-8
Friends of the Library Group
HAMMONTON BRANCH, 451 Egg Harbor Rd, Hammonton, 08037, SAN 320-3603. Tel: 609-561-2264. FAX: 609-561-1816. *Br Mgr,* Clare Bebbington
Founded 1928
Library Holdings: Bk Vols 1,000
Open Mon, Fri & Sat 9:30-5, Tues-Thurs 9-8
Friends of the Library Group
MAYS LANDING BRANCH, 40 Farragut Ave, 08330, SAN 321-818X. Tel: 609-625-2776. FAX: 609-625-8143. *Br Mgr,* Molly Monte
Founded 1926
Open Mon, Fri & Sat 9:30-5, Tues-Thurs 9-8
Friends of the Library Group
PLEASANTVILLE BRANCH, 33 Martin L King Jr Dr, Pleasantville, 08232, SAN 322-6018. Tel: 609-641-1778. FAX: 609-641-0771. *Br Mgr,* Beth Bliss
Founded 1955
Open Mon-Thurs 9-8, Fri & Sat 9-5
Friends of the Library Group
SOMERS POINT BRANCH, 801 Shore Rd, Somers Point, 08244, SAN 310-5040. Tel: 609-927-7113. FAX: 609-926-3062. *Br Mgr,* Kevin McCabe
Founded 1906
Open Mon, Fri & Sat 9:30-5, Tues-Thurs 9-8
Friends of the Library Group
VENTNOR BRANCH, 6500 Atlantic Ave, Ventnor, 08406, SAN 320-3611. Tel: 609-823-4614. FAX: 609-823-2639. *Br Mgr,* Jaimie Vigue
Founded 1951
Open Mon, Fri & Sat 9:30-5, Tues-Thurs 9-8
Friends of the Library Group
Bookmobiles: 1

MAYWOOD

P MAYWOOD PUBLIC LIBRARY*, 459 Maywood Ave, 07607-1909. SAN 310-2777. Tel: 201-845-2915. FAX: 201-845-7387. Circulation E-mail: maywcirc@bccls.org. Web Site: www.maywoodpubliclibrary.com. *Dir,* Caitlin Hull; E-mail: hull@maywood.bccls.org
Founded 1951. Pop 9,523; Circ 84,000
Library Holdings: Bk Titles 61,140; Bk Vols 61,300; Per Subs 81
Automation Activity & Vendor Info: (Cataloging) Innovative Interfaces, Inc; (Circulation) Innovative Interfaces, Inc
Wireless access
Open Mon-Wed 10-8, Thurs & Fri 10-5:30, Sat 10-4:30 (10-2 July-Aug), Sun 1:30-4:30
Friends of the Library Group

MCGUIRE AFB

A UNITED STATES AIR FORCE*, Joint Base McGuire - Dix Lakehurst Library, 2603 Tuskegee Airmen Ave, 08641-5016. SAN 350-8560. Tel: 609-754-2079. FAX: 609-754-5108. Web Site: gomdl.com/activities/library. *Librn,* Position Currently Open
Library Holdings: Bk Vols 72,000; Per Subs 230
Special Collections: Air Force History Coll
Subject Interests: Aviation, Mil hist, Quality mgt
Wireless access
Function: ILL available
Open Mon-Thurs 10-8, Fri & Sat 12-5, Sun 1-5

MENDHAM

P MENDHAM BOROUGH LIBRARY*, Ten Hilltop Rd, 07945. SAN 321-4931. Tel: 973-543-4152. FAX: 973-543-9096. Web Site: www.mendhamboroughlibrary.org. *Dir,* Janice Perrier; E-mail: jan.perrier@mendhamboroughlibrary.org; Staff 7 (MLS 1, Non-MLS 6)
Founded 1912. Pop 5,000
Library Holdings: Audiobooks 500; DVDs 500; Large Print Bks 200; Bk Titles 25,000; Per Subs 100
Special Collections: Local History Coll
Automation Activity & Vendor Info: (Cataloging) Innovative Interfaces, Inc; (Circulation) Innovative Interfaces, Inc; (OPAC) Innovative Interfaces, Inc
Wireless access
Function: Adult bk club, After school storytime, Bks on CD, Children's prog, Computers for patron use, Electronic databases & coll, Free DVD rentals, ILL available, Internet access, Magazines, Notary serv, Photocopying/Printing, Preschool reading prog, Prog for children & young adult, Ref serv available, Scanner, Summer reading prog, Tax forms, Teen prog
Publications: Legacy Through the Lens; Library Notes (Newsletter); Mendham Poets
Partic in Morris Automated Information Network
Open Mon-Thurs 10-8, Fri 10-5, Sat 10-2
Friends of the Library Group

MERCHANTVILLE

P MERCHANTVILLE PUBLIC LIBRARY*, 130 S Centre St, 08109-2201. SAN 310-2823. Tel: 856-665-3128. FAX: 856-665-4296. Web Site: www.camdencountylibrary.org/merchantville. *Br Mgr,* Christen Orbanus; E-mail: corbanus@camdencountylibrary.org; Staff 1 (MLS 1)
Library Holdings: Bk Titles 4,500; Per Subs 60
Special Collections: Children's Materials; Local History
Automation Activity & Vendor Info: (Cataloging) Innovative Interfaces, Inc; (Circulation) Innovative Interfaces, Inc; (OPAC) Innovative Interfaces, Inc
Wireless access
Open Mon & Wed 2-9, Tues & Thurs 2-5, Sat 10:30-4
Friends of the Library Group

METUCHEN

P METUCHEN PUBLIC LIBRARY*, 480 Middlesex Ave, 08840. SAN 310-2831. Tel: 732-632-8526. FAX: 732-632-8535. E-mail: metuchenlibrary@lmxac.org. Web Site: www.metuchennj.org/library. *Libr Dir,* John Arthur; Tel: 732-632-8530, E-mail: jarthur@lmxac.org; *Principal Librn,* Hsi Hsi Chung; Tel: 732-632-8527, E-mail: hsichung@lmxac.org; *Sr Librn/Youth Serv,* Glynis Brookens; Tel: 732-632-8532, E-mail: brookens@lmxac.org; *Sr Librn,* John McBride; Tel: 732-632-8528, E-mail: jmcbride@lmxac.org; *Youth Serv,* Moira Whittington; E-mail: mwhittington@lmxac.org; *Libr Asst,* Michael Cadena; Tel: 732-632-8533, E-mail: mcadena@lmxac.org; Staff 4.5 (MLS 4.5)
Founded 1870. Pop 13,292; Circ 108,813
Library Holdings: Audiobooks 551; CDs 103; DVDs 1,355; Large Print Bks 1,200; Bk Vols 68,685; Per Subs 160; Videos 100
Special Collections: Chinese Language Coll; Large Print Coll. Oral History
Subject Interests: Genealogy, Literacy, Mystery
Automation Activity & Vendor Info: (Cataloging) SirsiDynix; (Circulation) SirsiDynix; (ILL) SirsiDynix; (OPAC) SirsiDynix
Wireless access
Function: Adult bk club, Art exhibits, Bks on CD, Children's prog, Computers for patron use, Homebound delivery serv, Mail & tel request accepted, Museum passes, Music CDs, Online cat, Photocopying/Printing, Preschool outreach, Prog for adults, Prog for children & young adult, Story hour, Summer reading prog, Teen prog, Telephone ref, Wheelchair accessible
Partic in Libraries of Middlesex Automation Consortium; LibraryLinkNJ, The New Jersey Library Cooperative
Special Services for the Deaf - Bks on deafness & sign lang; Deaf publ
Special Services for the Blind - Bks on CD; Info on spec aids & appliances; Large print bks; Magnifiers; Playaways (bks on MP3); Ref serv
Open Mon-Thurs 10-9, Fri & Sat 10-5
Friends of the Library Group

MIDDLESEX

P MIDDLESEX PUBLIC LIBRARY*, 1300 Mountain Ave, 08846. SAN 310-284X. Tel: 732-356-6602. FAX: 732-356-8420. E-mail: info@middlesexlibrarynj.org. Web Site: www.middlesexlibrarynj.org. *Dir,* Dr May Lein Ho; *Ch Serv,* Chrissy George; *Ref Serv,* Mary Ann Greczek; Staff 4 (MLS 4)
Founded 1963. Pop 13,717; Circ 74,282
Library Holdings: Bks on Deafness & Sign Lang 12; Large Print Bks 350; Bk Titles 63,000; Per Subs 147

Wireless access
Partic in Libraries of Middlesex Automation Consortium
Open Mon & Wed 11-8, Tues & Thurs 1-9, Fri 10-5, Sat 10-2
Friends of the Library Group

MIDDLETOWN

P MIDDLETOWN TOWNSHIP PUBLIC LIBRARY*, 55 New Monmouth Rd, 07748. SAN 350-8749. Tel: 732-671-3700. Reference Tel: 732-671-3700, Ext 320, 732-671-3700, Ext 321. Administration Tel: 732-671-3703, Ext 311. FAX: 732-671-5839. Web Site: mtpl.org. *Libr Dir,* Kim Rinaldi; Tel: 732-671-3700, Ext 330, E-mail: krinaldi@mtpl.org; *Adult Serv,* Megan Wianecki; Tel: 732-671-3700, Ext 317, E-mail: mwianecki@mtpl.org; *Ch Serv,* Ellie Strbo; Tel: 732-671-3700, Ext 358, E-mail: estrbo@mtpl.org; *Circ,* Eileen McGrath; Tel: 732-671-3700, Ext 310; *ILL Librn,* Annie Sansevere; Tel: 732-671-3700, Ext 318; Staff 39 (MLS 11, Non-MLS 28)
Founded 1921. Pop 67,479
Jan 2016-Dec 2016
Library Holdings: Audiobooks 7,357; CDs 9,786; DVDs 18,306; e-books 174,738; Large Print Bks 2,890; Bk Vols 189,061; Per Subs 200
Subject Interests: NJ mat
Automation Activity & Vendor Info: (Cataloging) OCLC Connexion; (Circulation) ByWater Solutions; (ILL) JerseyCat; (OPAC) ByWater Solutions; (Serials) ByWater Solutions
Wireless access
Function: 24/7 Electronic res, 24/7 Online cat, 3D Printer, Activity rm, Adult bk club, After school storytime, Archival coll, Art exhibits, Audio & video playback equip for onsite use, Audiobks on Playaways & MP3, Audiobks via web, AV serv, Bi-weekly Writer's Group, Bk club(s), Bks on CD, Children's prog, Computer training, Computers for patron use, Digital talking bks, Electronic databases & coll, Free DVD rentals, Health sci info serv, Holiday prog, Homebound delivery serv, Homework prog, ILL available, Internet access, Large print keyboards, Life-long learning prog for all ages, Magazines, Magnifiers for reading, Mail & tel request accepted, Mango lang, Meeting rooms, Microfiche/film & reading machines, Movies, Museum passes, Music CDs, Online cat, Online ref, Outreach serv, Outside serv via phone, mail, e-mail & web, OverDrive digital audio bks, Photocopying/Printing, Preschool outreach, Preschool reading prog, Printer for laptops & handheld devices, Prog for adults, Prog for children & young adult, Ref & res, Ref serv available, Scanner, Senior computer classes, Spanish lang bks, Story hour, Study rm, Summer & winter reading prog, Summer reading prog, Tax forms, Teen prog, Telephone ref, Wheelchair accessible, Winter reading prog, Workshops, Writing prog
Special Services for the Blind - Accessible computers; Assistive/Adapted tech devices, equip & products
Open Mon-Thurs 9-9, Fri & Sat 9-5, Sun (Sept-May) 1-5
Restriction: Circ to mem only, Non-resident fee
Friends of the Library Group

S MONMOUTH COUNTY PARK SYSTEM*, Elvin McDonald Horticultural Library, 352 Red Hill Rd, 07748. (Mail add: 805 Newman Springs Rd, Lincroft, 07738), SAN 323-6021. Tel: 732-671-6050. FAX: 732-671-6905. Web Site: www.monmouthcountyparks.com/page.aspx?ID=2559. *Library Contact,* Position Currently Open
Founded 1979
Library Holdings: Bk Titles 4,000; Per Subs 30; Videos 50
Subject Interests: Hort
Partic in LibraryLinkNJ, The New Jersey Library Cooperative
Open Mon-Fri 9-4, Sat 10-4
Restriction: Restricted loan policy

MIDLAND PARK

P MIDLAND PARK MEMORIAL LIBRARY*, 250 Godwin Ave, 07432. SAN 310-2858. Tel: 201-444-2390. FAX: 201-444-2813. Circulation E-mail: mipkcirc@bccls.org. Web Site: www.midlandparklibrary.org. *Dir,* Catherine Dileo; *Ch,* Emily Myhren; Staff 5 (MLS 2, Non-MLS 3)
Founded 1937. Pop 7,047
Library Holdings: Bk Vols 55,000; Per Subs 110
Wireless access
Partic in Bergen County Cooperative Library System, Inc
Open Mon, Tues & Thurs 10-9, Wed & Fri 10-5, Sat 10-5 (10-1 July-Sept)
Friends of the Library Group

MILFORD

P HOLLAND FREE PUBLIC LIBRARY, 129 Spring Mills Rd, 08848. SAN 310-2866. Tel: 908-995-4767. E-mail: thehollandlibrary@gmail.com. Web Site: www.hollandlibrary.org. *Supv Librn,* Matheson Westlake; Staff 3 (Non-MLS 3)
Founded 1965. Pop 9,600; Circ 54,339
Library Holdings: Bk Vols 22,000; Per Subs 67
Special Collections: Large Print Coll
Automation Activity & Vendor Info: (Cataloging) Innovative Interfaces, Inc; (Circulation) Innovative Interfaces, Inc; (OPAC) Re:discovery Software, Inc
Wireless access
Function: 24/7 Electronic res, 24/7 Online cat, Adult bk club, Art programs, Audiobks via web, Bks on CD, Children's prog, Computers for patron use, E-Reserves, Free DVD rentals, ILL available, Internet access, Museum passes, Online cat, OverDrive digital audio bks, Photocopying/Printing, Prog for adults, Prog for children & young adult, Scanner, Story hour
Publications: Library Links
Mem of Hunterdon County Library
Partic in Morris Automated Information Network
Open Mon, Tues, Thurs & Fri 9-12 & 3-7, Wed 9-12 & 3-6, Sat 10-1

P MILFORD PUBLIC LIBRARY*, 40 Frenchtown Rd, 08848. (Mail add: PO Box F, 08848), SAN 310-2874. Tel: 908-995-4072. E-mail: library4072@verizon.net. Web Site: www.milfordnjlibrary.org. *Librn,* Jennifer Locke
Founded 1954. Pop 1,200; Circ 6,000
Library Holdings: Audiobooks 56; CDs 102; DVDs 325; Bk Vols 16,300; Per Subs 15
Wireless access
Function: Children's prog, Computers for patron use, Free DVD rentals, ILL available, Music CDs, Photocopying/Printing, Story hour
Mem of Hunterdon County Library
Open Mon 12-7, Tues 11-5, Wed 12-8, Thurs 11-8, Fri 10-1 & 5-8, Sat 10-1

MILLBURN

P MILLBURN FREE PUBLIC LIBRARY*, 200 Glen Ave, 07041. SAN 310-2912. Tel: 973-376-1006. Circulation Tel: 973-376-1006, Ext 111. Reference Tel: 973-376-1006, Ext 191. FAX: 973-376-0104. Web Site: millburnlibrary.org. *Dir,* Michael Banick; Tel: 973-376-1006, Ext 126, E-mail: banick@millburnlibrary.org; *Head, Pub Serv,* Sarah Pardi; Tel: 973-376-1006, Ext 117, E-mail: sarah@millburnlibrary.org; *Circ,* Diane Bratton; Tel: 973-376-1006, Ext 121, E-mail: diane@millburnlibrary.org; Staff 37 (MLS 13, Non-MLS 24)
Founded 1938. Pop 20,149; Circ 229,154
Library Holdings: Bk Titles 94,000; Bk Vols 110,000; Per Subs 150; Talking Bks 4,561
Automation Activity & Vendor Info: (Cataloging) SirsiDynix; (Circulation) SirsiDynix; (ILL) SirsiDynix; (OPAC) SirsiDynix
Wireless access
Open Mon-Thurs 9:30-8:45, Fri & Sat 9:30-5:15, Sun 1-4:45
Friends of the Library Group

MILLTOWN

P MILLTOWN PUBLIC LIBRARY, 20 W Church St, 08850. SAN 310-2920. Tel: 732-247-2270. FAX: 732-745-9493. E-mail: MilltownLibraryHelp@lmxac.org. Web Site: www.lmxac.org/milltown. *Dir,* Bonnie Sterling; E-mail: bsterlin@lmxac.org; Staff 2 (MLS 2)
Founded 1896. Pop 7,000; Circ 53,000
Library Holdings: Bk Vols 45,000; Per Subs 70
Subject Interests: Local hist
Automation Activity & Vendor Info: (Cataloging) SirsiDynix; (Circulation) SirsiDynix; (ILL) SirsiDynix; (OPAC) SirsiDynix; (Serials) SirsiDynix
Wireless access
Function: 24/7 Electronic res, 24/7 Online cat, Activity rm, Adult bk club
Partic in Libraries of Middlesex Automation Consortium
Open Mon, Tues & Thurs 10-8, Wed & Fri 10-5, Sat 10-2
Friends of the Library Group

MILLVILLE

P MILLVILLE PUBLIC LIBRARY*, 210 Buck St, 08332. SAN 310-2939. Tel: 856-825-7087. FAX: 856-327-8572. E-mail: contactus@millvillepubliclibrary.org. Web Site: www.millvillepubliclibrary.org. *Dir,* Courtenay Reece
Founded 1864. Pop 28,600; Circ 64,000
Jan 2015-Dec 2015 Income $697,200, City $684,800, Other $12,400. Sal $353,400
Library Holdings: Bk Titles 56,000; Per Subs 80
Special Collections: New Jersey Coll
Automation Activity & Vendor Info: (Cataloging) Innovative Interfaces, Inc - Sierra; (Circulation) Innovative Interfaces, Inc - Sierra; (OPAC) Innovative Interfaces, Inc - Sierra
Wireless access
Partic in LibraryLinkNJ, The New Jersey Library Cooperative
Open Mon-Thurs 10-7:45, Fri 10-4:45, Sat 10-3:45
Friends of the Library Group

S MUSEUM OF AMERICAN GLASS*, Research Library, Wheaton Arts & Cultural Ctr, 1501 Glasstown Rd, 08332. SAN 370-3002. Tel: 856-825-6800, Ext 141. FAX: 856-825-2410. E-mail: dwood@wheatonarts.org. Web Site: www.wheatonarts.org. *Dir, Exhibitions & Coll,* Kristin Qualls; E-mail: kqualls@wheatonarts.org; *Curatorial Asst,* Dianne Wood; E-mail: dwood@wheatonarts.org
Library Holdings: Bk Vols 2,800
Special Collections: Charles B Gardner Coll; Glass Related Coll; Historical Documents & Photos
Subject Interests: Antiques
Restriction: Open by appt only

MONMOUTH BEACH

P MONMOUTH BEACH LIBRARY*, 18 Willow Ave, 07750. SAN 310-2947. Tel: 732-229-1187. Web Site: www.monmouthbeach.lib.nj.us. *Dir,* Judith Bakos; E-mail: jbakos@monmouthcountylib.org; Staff 1 (MLS 1)
Pop 3,595; Circ 38,763
Library Holdings: AV Mats 1,000; Bk Vols 45,000; Per Subs 33
Special Collections: New Jersey Coll
Automation Activity & Vendor Info: (Cataloging) SirsiDynix; (Circulation) SirsiDynix
Wireless access
Mem of Monmouth County Library
Open Mon & Wed 9-4:30, Tues & Thurs 9-7, Sat 9-1
Friends of the Library Group

MONMOUTH JUNCTION

P SOUTH BRUNSWICK PUBLIC LIBRARY*, 110 Kingston Lane, 08852. SAN 310-2955. Tel: 732-329-4000, Ext 7290. Reference Tel: 732-329-4000, Ext 7286. Administration Tel: 732-329-4000, Ext 7281. FAX: 732-329-0573. Web Site: www.sbpl.info. *Libr Dir,* Mr Christopher Carbone; Tel: 732-329-4000, Ext 7287, E-mail: ccarbone@sbpl.info; *Asst Dir,* Judy Pietrobono; Tel: 732-329-4000, Ext 7351, E-mail: jpietrobono@sbpl.info; *Head, Children's Dept,* Matt Kirschner; Tel: 732-329-4000, Ext 7344, E-mail: mkirschner@sbpl.info; *Head, Outreach Serv,* Barbara Battles; Tel: 732-329-4000, Ext 7637, E-mail: bbattles@sbpl.info; *Head, Info Serv, Ref,* Jill D'Amico; Tel: 732-329-4000, Ext 7638, E-mail: jdamico@sbpl.info; *Head, Tech Serv, Network Adminr,* Hai-Chin Chung; Tel: 732-329-4000, Ext 7284, E-mail: hchung@sbpl.info; *Principal Librn, YA,* Saleena Davidson; Tel: 732-329-4000, Ext 7634, E-mail: sdavidson@sbpl.info; *Principal Tech Librn,* Randy Marsola; Tel: 732-329-4000, Ext 7636, E-mail: rmarsola@sbpl.info; *Loan Serv, Supvr,* Diane Hurley; Tel: 732-329-4000, Ext 7295, E-mail: dhurley@sbpl.info; Staff 14 (MLS 14)
Founded 1967. Pop 43,417; Circ 475,540
Library Holdings: AV Mats 11,681; Bk Vols 137,045; Per Subs 263; Spec Interest Per Sub 10
Subject Interests: Chinese, Local hist
Automation Activity & Vendor Info: (Acquisitions) SirsiDynix-Unicorn; (Cataloging) SirsiDynix-Unicorn; (Circulation) SirsiDynix-Unicorn; (OPAC) SirsiDynix-iBistro
Wireless access
Function: 24/7 Electronic res, 24/7 Online cat, 3D Printer, Adult bk club, Adult literacy prog, After school storytime
Publications: Calendar of Events; Compass Newsletter
Partic in Libraries of Middlesex Automation Consortium
Open Mon-Thurs 10-9, Fri 12-6, Sat 10-5, Sun 1-5
Friends of the Library Group
Bookmobiles: 1

MONROE TOWNSHIP

P MONROE TOWNSHIP PUBLIC LIBRARY*, Four Municipal Plaza, 08831-1900. SAN 375-5061. Tel: 732-521-5000. FAX: 732-521-4766. Web Site: www.monroetwplibrary.org. *Dir,* Irene Goldberg; Tel: 732-521-5000, Ext 107, E-mail: igoldberg@monroetwplibrary.org; *Asst Dir,* Leah Wagner; Tel: 732-521-5000, Ext 108, E-mail: lwagner@monroetwplibrary.org; *Head, Circ,* MaryAnn Reiner; Tel: 732-521-5000, Ext 101, E-mail: mreiner@monroetwplibrary.org; *Ch,* Lynnette Fucci; Tel: 732-521-5000, Ext 125; *Teen Serv Librn,* Emily Mazzoni; *Virtual Br Mgr, Virtual Ref,* Karen Klapperstuck; Tel: 732-521-5000, Ext 105; *Ref (Info Servs),* Susan Grotyohann; Tel: 732-521-5000, Ext 153, E-mail: sgrot@monroetwplibrary.org; *Ref (Info Servs),* Tyler Rousseau; Tel: 732-521-5000, Ext 123; *Ref (Info Servs),* Monica Teixeira; E-mail: mteixeira@monroetwplibrary.org; Staff 31 (MLS 9, Non-MLS 22)
Founded 1989. Pop 39,132; Circ 485,603
Jan 2017-Dec 2017 Income $3,586,422. Mats Exp $312,626, Books $226,626, Per/Ser (Incl. Access Fees) $20,000, AV Mat $20,000, Electronic Ref Mat (Incl. Access Fees) $46,000. Sal $239,422
Library Holdings: AV Mats 14,000; Large Print Bks 2,300; Bk Titles 131,828; Bk Vols 104,000; Per Subs 150
Special Collections: Holocaust (Henry Ricklis Memorial Coll), AV, bks
Automation Activity & Vendor Info: (Circulation) SirsiDynix
Wireless access
Partic in Libraries of Middlesex Automation Consortium
Special Services for the Deaf - Bks on deafness & sign lang; High interest/low vocabulary bks; Staff with knowledge of sign lang; TTY equip
Special Services for the Blind - Closed circuit TV magnifier; Large screen computer & software; Reader equip
Open Mon-Thurs 9:30-9, Fri 9:30-5, Sat 10-5, Sun 1-5
Friends of the Library Group
Bookmobiles: 1. Bk vols 2,000

MONTCLAIR

M HACKENSACKUMC MOUNTAINSIDE*, Health Sciences Library, One Bay Ave, 07042-4898. SAN 350-8986. Tel: 973-429-6240, 973-429-6245. FAX: 973-680-7850. E-mail: MSH.Library@Mountainsidehosp.com, sontranscripts@mountainsidehosp.com. Web Site: mountainsidehosp.com/patients-visitors/health-sciences-library. *Med Librn,* Narmin Kurzum; Staff 1 (MLS 1)
Library Holdings: Bk Titles 2,000; Per Subs 75
Subject Interests: Med, Nursing
Automation Activity & Vendor Info: (Acquisitions) Softlink America; (Cataloging) Softlink America; (Circulation) Softlink America; (Course Reserve) Softlink America; (ILL) Softlink America; (Media Booking) Softlink America; (OPAC) Softlink America; (Serials) Softlink America
Wireless access
Partic in Basic Health Sciences Library Network; LibraryLinkNJ, The New Jersey Library Cooperative; New Jersey Health Sciences Library Network
Open Mon-Fri 8-5
Restriction: Authorized personnel only, Badge access after hrs

P MONTCLAIR PUBLIC LIBRARY*, 50 S Fullerton Ave, 07042. SAN 350-8927. Tel: 973-744-0500. Circulation Tel: 973-744-0500, Ext 2245. Reference Tel: 973-744-0500, Ext 2235. Administration Tel: 973-744-0500, Ext 2221. Web Site: www.montclairlibrary.org. *Dir,* Peter Coyl; E-mail: coyl@montclair.bccls.org; *Asst Dir,* Selwa Shamy; E-mail: shamy@montclair.bccls.org; *Libr Office Mgr,* Linda Welch; E-mail: welch@montclair.bccls.org; Staff 49 (MLS 18, Non-MLS 31)
Founded 1893. Pop 38,977; Circ 312,676
Jan 2017-Dec 2017 Income (Main & Associated Libraries) $3,884,039, State $16,000, City $3,418,039, Other $450,000
Special Collections: Montclair History, pictures & micro
Automation Activity & Vendor Info: (Acquisitions) Baker & Taylor; (Cataloging) Innovative Interfaces, Inc; (Circulation) Innovative Interfaces, Inc
Wireless access
Function: Large print keyboards, Wheelchair accessible
Partic in Bergen County Cooperative Library System, Inc; LibraryLinkNJ, The New Jersey Library Cooperative
Special Services for the Deaf - Bks on deafness & sign lang; Closed caption videos; TTY equip
Special Services for the Blind - Braille equip; Talking bks
Open Mon-Thurs 10-8, Fri & Sat 10-6, Sun 1-6
Friends of the Library Group
Branches: 1
BELLEVUE AVENUE BRANCH, 185 Bellevue Ave, 07043, SAN 350-8951. Tel: 973-744-2468. FAX: 973-744-3712.
Founded 1914
Open Mon & Thurs 10-8, Tues, Wed, Fri & Sat 2-6
Friends of the Library Group
Bookmobiles: 1

C MONTCLAIR STATE UNIVERSITY*, Harry A Sprague Library, One Normal Ave, 07043-1699. SAN 310-5628. Tel: 973-655-4301. Circulation Tel: 973-655-4288. Interlibrary Loan Service Tel: 973-655-7143. Reference Tel: 973-655-4291. FAX: 973-655-7780. Web Site: www.montclair.edu/library. *Dean,* Dr Judith Lin Hunt; E-mail: huntjl@montclair.edu; *Head, Access Serv Dept, Syst Librn,* Denise O'Shea; Tel: 973-655-2098, E-mail: oshead@montclair.edu; *Head, Cat, Metadata & Archival Serv,* Kathleen Hughes; Tel: 973-655-7077, E-mail: hughesk@montclair.edu; *Head, Coll Develop & Acq Develop,* Suxiao Hu; Tel: 973-655-7151, E-mail: hus@montclair.edu; *Head, Per,* Eduardo Gil; Tel: 973-655-5286, E-mail: gile@montclair.edu; *Cat Librn,* Mei Ling Chow; Tel: 973-655-4422, E-mail: chowm@montclair.edu; *Archivist, Cat Librn,* Paul Martinez; Tel: 973-655-3465, E-mail: martinezp@montclair.edu; *Electronic Res Librn, Multimedia,* Steven Shapiro; Tel: 973-655-4428, E-mail: shapiros@montclair.edu; *Govt Doc & Data Librn,* Darren L Sweeper; Tel: 973-655-7145, E-mail: sweeperd@montclair.edu; *Online & Outreach Serv Librn,* Catherine Baird; Tel: 973-655-7144, E-mail: bairdc@montclair.edu; *Ref Librn,* Laura Levy; Tel: 973-655-7148, E-mail: levyl@montclair.edu; *Ref Librn,* Siobhan McCarthy; Tel: 973-655-7146, E-mail: mccarthys@montclair.edu; *Ref Librn,* Carol Nurse; Tel: 973-655-7667, E-mail: nursec@montclair.edu; *ILL, Ref Librn,* Kevin Prendergast; E-mail: prendergask@montclair.edu; *Res Spec,* Karen Ramsden; Tel: 973-655-5276, E-mail: ramsdenk@montclair.edu; Staff 20 (MLS 16, Non-MLS 4)

Founded 1908. Enrl 20,000; Fac 650; Highest Degree: Doctorate
Jul 2017-Jun 2018 Income $5,729,150. Mats Exp $1,479,652, Books $235,619, Per/Ser (Incl. Access Fees) $1,193,726, Manu Arch $1,000, Electronic Ref Mat (Incl. Access Fees) $47,853, Presv $2,454. Sal $2,999,716 (Prof $2,141,657)
Library Holdings: CDs 3,929; DVDs 6,953; e-books 54,495; e-journals 1,787; Electronic Media & Resources 308,974; Microforms 1,185,675; Music Scores 7,404; Bk Titles 441,924; Bk Vols 500,014; Per Subs 2,533; Videos 9,109
Special Collections: US Document Depository
Subject Interests: Communications, Modern poetry, Music, Philos, Speech, Teacher educ
Automation Activity & Vendor Info: (Acquisitions) OCLC; (Cataloging) OCLC; (Circulation) OCLC; (Course Reserve) OCLC; (Discovery) EBSCO Discovery Service; (ILL) OCLC Tipasa; (OPAC) OCLC; (Serials) OCLC
Wireless access
Function: Archival coll, Audio & video playback equip for onsite use, E-Reserves, Electronic databases & coll, Govt ref serv, ILL available, Music CDs, Online cat, Orientations, Outside serv via phone, mail, e-mail & web, Photocopying/Printing, Res libr, VHS videos, Wheelchair accessible
Partic in OCLC Online Computer Library Center, Inc; Virtual Academic Library Environment
Special Services for the Deaf - Bks on deafness & sign lang; Closed caption videos
Open Mon-Fri 8-Midnight, Sun 12-12, Sat 9-5

R UNION CONGREGATIONAL CHURCH*, Schneidewind Library, 176 Cooper Ave, 07043. SAN 310-5636. Tel: 973-744-7424. FAX: 973-744-1364. E-mail: infoucc@unioncong.org. Web Site: www.unioncong.org/learn/books. *Librn,* Catherine Spinelli
Founded 1958
Library Holdings: Bk Vols 3,000
Subject Interests: Art, Biblical hist, Christian educ, Current affairs, Ecology, Mental health, Philos, Relig hist, Relig symbolism, Soc ethics, Theol
Wireless access
Open Mon-Fri 8-4
Restriction: Circ limited

MONTVALE

P MONTVALE FREE PUBLIC LIBRARY*, 12 Mercedes Dr, Ste 100, 07645. SAN 310-298X. Tel: 201-391-5090. FAX: 201-307-5647. Circulation E-mail: movlcirc@bccls.org. Web Site: www.montvalelibrarynj.org. *Dir,* Paul Shaver; E-mail: shaver@montvale.bccls.org; *Librn,* George R Galuschak; Staff 2 (MLS 2)
Founded 1975. Pop 7,844
Library Holdings: Bk Vols 75,180; Per Subs 134
Wireless access
Partic in Bergen County Cooperative Library System, Inc
Open Mon-Thurs 10-9, Fri & Sat 11-5, Sun 1-4
Friends of the Library Group

MONTVILLE

P MONTVILLE TOWNSHIP PUBLIC LIBRARY*, 90 Horseneck Rd, 07045-9626. SAN 310-3005. Tel: 973-402-0900. FAX: 973-402-0592. E-mail: information@montvillelibrary.org. Web Site: www.montvillelibrary.org. *Dir,* Allan M Kleiman; E-mail: akleiman@montvillelibrary.org; *Asst Dir,* Catherine LaBelle; E-mail: clabelle@montvillelibrary.org; Staff 18 (MLS 8, Non-MLS 10)
Founded 1921. Pop 20,389; Circ 200,000
Library Holdings: Bk Vols 95,000; Per Subs 150
Automation Activity & Vendor Info: (Cataloging) SirsiDynix; (Circulation) SirsiDynix; (ILL) JerseyCat; (OPAC) SirsiDynix
Wireless access
Partic in Morris Automated Information Network; New Jersey Library Network
Open Mon-Thurs 9-9, Fri 9-6, Sat 9-5, Sun 12-5

MOORESTOWN

S HISTORICAL SOCIETY OF MOORESTOWN LIBRARY*, 12 High St, 08057. (Mail add: PO Box 477, 08057-0477), SAN 372-6762. Tel: 856-235-0353. E-mail: moorestownhistory@comcast.net. Web Site: www.moorestownhistory.org. *Librn,* Stephanie Herz
Founded 1969
Library Holdings: Bk Titles 500; Bk Vols 550
Special Collections: Historic Buildings-House Index; Moorestown History & Genealogy. Oral History
Subject Interests: Manuscripts, Maps
Wireless access
Function: Photocopying/Printing
Restriction: Non-circulating

P MOORESTOWN PUBLIC LIBRARY, 111 W Second St, 08057. SAN 310-3021. Tel: 856-234-0333. FAX: 856-235-4687. Reference E-mail: reference@moorestownlibrary.org. Web Site: www.moorestownlibrary.org. *Dir,* Joan Serpico; E-mail: jserpico@moorestownlibrary.org; *Ch Serv Librn,* Jennifer Dunne; E-mail: jdunne@moorestownlibrary.org; *Adult Serv, Ref Librn,* Joanne Parra; *Teen Serv Librn,* Robin Guenther; Staff 22 (MLS 7, Non-MLS 15)
Founded 1853. Pop 20,000; Circ 180,470
Library Holdings: AV Mats 9,207; Bk Titles 119,297; Bk Vols 141,665; Per Subs 228
Subject Interests: Genealogy, NJ, Quakers
Automation Activity & Vendor Info: (Acquisitions) Innovative Interfaces, Inc; (Cataloging) Innovative Interfaces, Inc; (Circulation) Innovative Interfaces, Inc; (Discovery) EBSCO Discovery Service; (OPAC) Innovative Interfaces, Inc
Wireless access
Function: 24/7 Electronic res, 24/7 Online cat, Activity rm, Adult bk club, After school storytime, Archival coll, Art exhibits, Audiobks via web, AV serv, Bk club(s), Bks on CD, Children's prog, Computer training, Computers for patron use, Digital talking bks, Electronic databases & coll, Free DVD rentals, Holiday prog, ILL available, Internet access, Magazines, Magnifiers for reading, Mail & tel request accepted, Meeting rooms, Microfiche/film & reading machines, Movies, Museum passes, Music CDs, Notary serv, Online cat, Outreach serv, OverDrive digital audio bks, Photocopying/Printing, Preschool reading prog, Printer for laptops & handheld devices, Prog for adults, Prog for children & young adult, Ref & res, Ref serv available, Scanner, Story hour, Study rm, Summer & winter reading prog, Summer reading prog, Tax forms, Teen prog, Telephone ref, Wheelchair accessible, Winter reading prog, Workshops
Partic in LibraryLinkNJ, The New Jersey Library Cooperative
Open Mon & Wed 9:30-8:30, Tues & Thurs-Sat 9:30-4:30
Friends of the Library Group

MORGANVILLE

S NEW JERSEY SCOUT MUSEUM LIBRARY*, 705 Ginesi Dr, 07751. Tel: 732-862-1282. FAX: 732-536-2850. E-mail: curator@njsm.org. Web Site: njsm.squarespace.com. *Curator,* Steven Buckley; Staff 2 (MLS 1, Non-MLS 1)
Founded 2004
Subject Interests: Boys Scouts of Am, Girls Scouts of Am, Order of the Arrow
Function: Archival coll, Photocopying/Printing, Ref & res
Publications: New Jersey Scout Museum Newsletter
Temporarily closed for relocation 2020
Open Wed 6pm-8pm
Restriction: Authorized scholars by appt

MORRIS PLAINS

GM GREYSTONE PARK PSYCHIATRIC HOSPITAL*, Health Science Library, 59 Koch Ave, 07950. SAN 310-1886. Tel: 973-538-1800. *Librn,* Stephanie Gabelmann; Staff 1 (MLS 1)
Founded 1930
Library Holdings: Bks on Deafness & Sign Lang 13; DVDs 100; Bk Titles 2,000; Bk Vols 1,960; Per Subs 50; Spec Interest Per Sub 25; Videos 240
Subject Interests: Med, Nursing, Psychiat, Psychiat rehabilitation, Psychol
Automation Activity & Vendor Info: (Cataloging) Professional Software; (OPAC) Professional Software
Function: ILL available
Partic in Basic Health Sciences Library Network; LibraryLinkNJ, The New Jersey Library Cooperative; New Jersey Health Sciences Library Network
Restriction: Open to others by appt, Open to staff only

P MORRIS PLAINS LIBRARY*, 77 Glenbrook Rd, 07950. SAN 310-3048. Tel: 973-538-2599. FAX: 973-538-8974. *Libr Dir,* Sheila Jain; E-mail: sheila.jain@morrisplains.mainlib.org; Staff 1 (Non-MLS 1)
Founded 1881. Pop 5,700; Circ 32,947
Library Holdings: Audiobooks 75; DVDs 150; Large Print Bks 1,400; Bk Titles 22,576; Bk Vols 22,857; Per Subs 34
Wireless access
Open Tues & Thurs 10-7, Wed & Fri 10-5, Sat 10-2
Friends of the Library Group

MORRISTOWN

C COLLEGE OF SAINT ELIZABETH*, Mahoney Library, Two Convent Rd, 07960-6989. SAN 310-0936. Tel: 973-290-4237. Reference Tel: 973-290-4248. FAX: 973-290-4226. Web Site: www.steu.edu/academics/mahoney-library. *Libr Dir,* Mark Ferguson; Tel: 973-290-4238, E-mail: mferguson@steu.edu; *Librn,* Madeline M Ruggiero; E-mail: mruggiero@cse.edu; *Librn,* Helen E Wollny; E-mail: hwollny@cse.edu; *Electronic Res Librn,* Adrienne Bross; Tel: 973-290-4253, E-mail: abross@cse.edu; *Evening/Weekend Librn,* Victoria

Wollny; Tel: 973-290-4236, E-mail: vwollny@cse.edu; Staff 12 (MLS 8, Non-MLS 4)
Founded 1899. Highest Degree: Doctorate
Library Holdings: Bk Titles 108,000; Bk Vols 112,000; Per Subs 609
Special Collections: Atlases (Phillips Coll); History of Chemistry (Florence E Wall Coll); World War I (Henry C & Ann Fox Wolfe Coll), literary first & signed editions
Subject Interests: Econ, Educ, Lit, Nursing, Nutrition, Psychol, Theol
Automation Activity & Vendor Info: (Acquisitions) Ex Libris Group; (Cataloging) Ex Libris Group; (Circulation) Ex Libris Group; (Course Reserve) Ex Libris Group; (OPAC) Ex Libris Group; (Serials) Ex Libris Group
Wireless access
Partic in OCLC Online Computer Library Center, Inc; Virtual Academic Library Environment
Open Mon-Thurs 8:30am-9pm, Fri 8:30-5, Sat 10:30-5:30, Sun 2-6
Restriction: Authorized patrons, Authorized scholars by appt, Borrowing requests are handled by ILL, In-house use for visitors, Non-circulating of rare bks, Non-circulating to the pub

S IRISH-AMERICAN CULTURAL INSTITUTE LIBRARY, PO Box 1716, 07962. SAN 376-1592. Tel: 973-605-1991. FAX: 973-605-8875. E-mail: info@iaci-usa.org. Web Site: www.iaci-usa.org. *Exec Dir,* Carol Bucks; E-mail: cbuck@iaci-usa.org
Founded 1962
Library Holdings: Bk Titles 4,000; Bk Vols 4,500
Subject Interests: Culture, Irish, Irish hist, Politics, Sociol
Function: Res libr
Restriction: Non-circulating to the pub, Open by appt only

L MCELROY, DEUTSCH, MULVANEY & CARPENTER, LLP*, Law Library, 1300 Mt Kemble Ave, 07962. (Mail add: PO Box 2075, 07962-2075). Tel: 973-425-8810. FAX: 973-425-0161. Web Site: www.mdmc-law.com. *Dir, Libr Serv,* Mary Ellen Kaas; E-mail: mkaas@mdmc-law.com
Library Holdings: Bk Vols 10,000
Restriction: Not open to pub
Branches:
LAW LIBRARY, 570 Broad St, Ste 1500, Newark, 07102, SAN 372-4794. Tel: 973-622-7711, Ext 2065. FAX: 973-622-5314.
Library Holdings: Bk Vols 13,000
Restriction: Not open to pub

S MORRIS COUNTY HISTORICAL SOCIETY*, 68 Morris Ave, 07960. SAN 327-6333. Tel: 973-267-3465. FAX: 973-267-8773. E-mail: MCHSAcornHall@gmail.com. Web Site: morriscountyhistory.org. *Dir,* Amy E Curry; E-mail: directorMCHS@gmail.com
Library Holdings: DVDs 1; Bk Vols 2,700; Spec Interest Per Sub 5
Subject Interests: 19th Century life, 19th Century lit, 19th Century works of fiction & non-fiction, Morris County (NJ) hist
Open Tues-Thurs 11-4, Sun 1-4
Restriction: Fee for pub use, Mem only, Not a lending libr, Open to pub with supv only, Open to researchers by request

GL MORRIS COUNTY LAW LIBRARY*, Court House, Eight Ann St, 07963-0900. (Mail add: PO Box 910, 07963-0910), SAN 310-3110. Tel: 973-656-3917. FAX: 973-656-3949. *Librn,* Peter DeLucia; E-mail: peter.delucia@njcourts.gov
Founded 1970
Library Holdings: Bk Vols 1,000
Function: Res libr
Open Mon-Fri 8-5

P THE MORRISTOWN & MORRIS TOWNSHIP LIBRARY*, One Miller Rd, 07960. SAN 310-3099. Tel: 973-538-6161. FAX: 973-267-4064. Web Site: mmtlibrary.org, morristownmorristwplibrary.info. *Dir,* Chad Leinaweaver; E-mail: chad.leinaweaver@mmt.mainlib.org; *Asst Dir,* Mary Lynn Becza; E-mail: marylynn.becza@mmt.mainlib.org; *Genealogy Librn,* James Lewis; E-mail: james.lewis@mmt.mainlib.org; *Cat, Tech Serv,* Jim Collins; E-mail: james.collins@mmt.mainlib.org; *Ch Serv,* Arlene Sprague; E-mail: arlene.sprague@mmt.mainlib.org; *Circ,* Ruth Bensley; E-mail: ruth.bensley@mmt.mainlib.org; *Media Serv, Per,* Tim Lynch; E-mail: timothy.lynch@mmt.mainlib.org; *Ref,* Barbara Gordon; E-mail: barbara.gordon@mmt.mainlib.org
Founded 1917. Pop 40,000; Circ 213,000
Special Collections: Manuscript Coll; Printing Coll; Topography, American History Coll. Oral History
Subject Interests: Genealogy, Local NJ hist, Rare children's bks
Wireless access
Function: 24/7 Electronic res, 24/7 Online cat, Activity rm, Adult bk club, Archival coll, Art exhibits, Audiobks via web, Bk club(s), Bks on CD, Children's prog, Computer training, Computers for patron use, Digital talking bks, E-Readers, Electronic databases & coll, Free DVD rentals, ILL available, Internet access, Magazines, Meeting rooms, Microfiche/film & reading machines, Movies, Music CDs, Notary serv, Online cat, Prog for adults, Prog for children & young adult, Ref & res, Summer reading prog
Publications: Early Printing in Morristown; In Lights & Shadows: Morristown in three centuries; Men from Morris County New Jersey who served in the American Revolution; Morris Township; New Jersey; New Jersey: A Glimpse into the past; Ordinary Days
Partic in Morris Automated Information Network; Morris-Union Federation
Special Services for the Blind - Accessible computers
Open Mon-Thurs 9-9, Fri 9-6, Sat 9:30-5 (10-2 July & Aug), Sun 1-5
Friends of the Library Group
Branches: 1
NORTH JERSEY HISTORY & GENEALOGY CENTER, One Miller Rd, 07960. Tel: 973-538-3473. FAX: 973-267-4064. *Libr Dir,* Chad Leinaweaver; E-mail: chad.leinaweaver@mmt.mainlib.org; *Dept Head,* James Lewis; E-mail: james.lewis@mmt.mainlib.org. Subject Specialists: *Genealogy, NJ hist,* James Lewis; Staff 5 (MLS 5)
Library Holdings: AV Mats 33,483; Electronic Media & Resources 13; Bk Vols 60,000; Per Subs 350
Special Collections: A B Frost Coll; Archival Colls, church, club, govt, local bus, orgn & sch recs, deeds, family & personal papers, maps & atlases, landscape architecture plans, photographs/postcard coll.,hist presv res mat; Eastern US Genealogical Resources; Homer Davenport Coll; John DePol Coll; New Jersey Historical Material; Thomas Nast Coll
Function: Ref & res
Open Mon-Thurs 9-9, Fri 9-6, Sat 9:30-5 (10-2 July & Aug), Sun 1-5
Restriction: Non-circulating coll
Friends of the Library Group
Bookmobiles: 1

R MORRISTOWN JEWISH CENTER*, Beit Yisrael Library, 177 Speedwell Ave, 07960. SAN 310-3137. Tel: 973-538-9292, 973-538-9293. FAX: 973-538-3229.
Founded 1967
Library Holdings: Bk Titles 7,500
Subject Interests: Art, Biographies, Hist, Holocaust, Israel, Judaica, Lang, Relig studies
Partic in NJ NW Regional Libr Coop
Restriction: Mem only
Friends of the Library Group

M MORRISTOWN MEDICAL CENTER LIBRARY*, Shinn-Lathrope Health Sciences Library, Leonard B Kahn Pavilion, Level B, 100 Madison Ave, 07962. SAN 320-3972. Tel: 973-971-8926. FAX: 973-290-7045. E-mail: library.mmh@atlantichealth.org. Web Site: www.atlantichealth.org/atlantic/for-professionals/helpful-resources/health-sciences-libraries.html. *Mgr,* Janina Kaldan; E-mail: janina.kaldan@atlantichealth.org; Staff 3 (MLS 2, Non-MLS 1)
Founded 1952
Library Holdings: Bk Titles 5,000; Per Subs 270
Special Collections: Consumer Health
Subject Interests: Dentistry, Med, Nursing
Automation Activity & Vendor Info: (Cataloging) Softlink America; (Circulation) Softlink America
Wireless access
Partic in Basic Health Sciences Library Network; Health Sci Libr Asn of NJ; LibraryLinkNJ, The New Jersey Library Cooperative; New Jersey Health Sciences Library Network
Open Mon-Thurs 8-6, Fri 8-5

S NATIONAL PARK SERVICE*, Morristown National Historical Park Library, 30 Washington Pl, 07960-4299. SAN 310-3145. Tel: 973-539-2016, Ext 204. Web Site: www.nps.gov/morr. *Curator,* Jude Pfister; E-mail: jude_pfister@nps.gov; Staff 1 (Non-MLS 1)
Founded 1933
Oct 2015-Sept 2016. Mats Exp $1,200, Books $1,000, Presv $200
Library Holdings: Bk Titles 16,000; Bk Vols 25,000; Per Subs 12
Special Collections: Ford Papers, ms; Hessian Document Coll; Lloyd W Smith Coll; Park Coll, ms; Washington Association of New Jersey Records
Subject Interests: 18th Century Am life, 18th Century culture, Am Revolutionary War, European cultural political hist 15th-20th century, George Washington
Publications: A Guide to the Manuscript Collection of Morristown National Historical Park; Guide to Hessian Documents of the American Revolution 1776-1783; Morristown National Historical Park Library Brochure; Orderly Books of the American Revolution in the Morristown National Historical Park Library
Restriction: Non-circulating, Open by appt only
Friends of the Library Group

S PASSAIC RIVER COALITION*, Environmental Library, 330 Speedwell Ave, 07960. SAN 329-0409. Tel: 973-532-9830. FAX: 973-889-9172. E-mail: info@passaicriver.org. Web Site: passaicriver.org. *Exec Dir,* Laurie Howard

Founded 1971
Library Holdings: Bk Vols 3,500; Per Subs 40

L PORZIO, BROMBERG & NEWMAN LIBRARY*, 100 Southgate Pkwy, 07962-1997. (Mail add: PO Box 1997, 07962-1997), SAN 372-4360. Tel: 973-538-4006. FAX: 973-538-5146. Web Site: www.pbnlaw.com. *Librn,* Janice Schouten; Tel: 973-889-4368, E-mail: jmschouten@pbnlaw.com; Staff 1 (MLS 1)
Library Holdings: Bk Vols 10,000; Per Subs 75
Restriction: Not open to pub, Staff use only

C RABBINICAL COLLEGE OF AMERICA*, Hoffman Memorial Library, 226 Sussex Ave, 07960-3632. (Mail add: PO Box 1996, 07962-1996), SAN 375-8478. Tel: 973-267-9404. FAX: 973-267-5208. E-mail: info@rca.edu.
Library Holdings: Bk Vols 17,000; Per Subs 50
Special Collections: Judaica Coll, cassettes
Subject Interests: Hebrew, Talmud

L RIKER, DANZIG, SCHERER, HYLAND & PERRETTI*, Law Library, Headquarters Plaza, One Speedwell Ave, 07962-1981. SAN 372-476X. Tel: 973-538-0800. FAX: 973-538-1984. Web Site: riker.com/law-firm-offices/morristown-new-jersey. *Librn,* Anne Shulman; E-mail: ashulman@riker.com
Library Holdings: Bk Vols 5,000
Restriction: Staff use only

MOUNT ARLINGTON

P MOUNT ARLINGTON PUBLIC LIBRARY, 333 Howard Blvd, 07856-1196. SAN 310-317X. Tel: 973-398-1516. FAX: 973-398-0171. Web Site: mountarlingtonlibrary.org. *Libr Dir,* Tina Mayer; E-mail: Tina.Mayer@mtarlington.mainlib.org; Staff 1 (Non-MLS 1)
Founded 1968. Pop 5,050; Circ 19,845
Library Holdings: Bk Vols 25,000; Per Subs 50
Automation Activity & Vendor Info: (Acquisitions) Innovative Interfaces, Inc; (Cataloging) Innovative Interfaces, Inc; (Circulation) Innovative Interfaces, Inc; (OPAC) Innovative Interfaces, Inc; (Serials) Innovative Interfaces, Inc
Wireless access
Partic in Morris Automated Information Network
Open Mon-Thurs 10-6, Fri & Sat 9-3

MOUNT LAUREL

L CAPEHART & SCATCHARD, PA LIBRARY*, 8000 Midlantic Dr, Ste 300 S, 08054. SAN 323-6498. Tel: 856-234-6800, Ext 2151. FAX: 856-235-2786. Web Site: www.capehart.com. *Librn,* Francine Viden
Library Holdings: Bk Titles 367; Bk Vols 8,600; Per Subs 32
Wireless access
Restriction: Staff use only

P MOUNT LAUREL LIBRARY, 100 Walt Whitman Ave, 08054. SAN 310-3218. Tel: 856-234-7319. FAX: 856-234-6916. E-mail: refdesk@mountlaurellibrary.org. Web Site: www.mountlaurellibrary.org. *Dir,* Becky Boydston; E-mail: becky@mountlaurellibrary.org; *Head, Circ,* Arlene Toussaint; E-mail: atoussaint@mountlaurellibrary.org; *Info Serv Mgr,* Adrian Alexander; E-mail: aalexander@mountlaurellibrary.org; Staff 14 (MLS 11, Non-MLS 3)
Founded 1970. Pop 42,000; Circ 469,787
Jan 2020-Dec 2020 Income $98,350, State $18,000, Locally Generated Income $80,350
Automation Activity & Vendor Info: (Acquisitions) Horizon; (Cataloging) Horizon; (Circulation) Horizon; (Discovery) SirsiDynix-Enterprise; (ILL) Auto-Graphics, Inc; (OPAC) Horizon; (Serials) Horizon
Wireless access
Function: 24/7 Electronic res, 24/7 Online cat, 3D Printer, Activity rm, Adult bk club, Audio & video playback equip for onsite use, Audiobks on Playaways & MP3, Audiobks via web, Bk club(s), Bks on CD, Children's prog, Computers for patron use, Electronic databases & coll, Free DVD rentals, ILL available, Life-long learning prog for all ages, Magazines, Magnifiers for reading, Mail & tel request accepted, Makerspace, Mango lang, Meeting rooms, Movies, Museum passes, Music CDs, Online cat, Online ref, OverDrive digital audio bks, Photocopying/Printing, Printer for laptops & handheld devices, Prog for adults, Prog for children & young adult, Ref serv available, Scanner, STEM programs, Story hour, Study rm, Summer & winter reading prog, Tax forms, Teen prog, Telephone ref, Wheelchair accessible
Publications: Newsletter
Partic in LibraryLinkNJ, The New Jersey Library Cooperative
Open Mon-Thurs 9:30-9, Fri 9:30-7, Sat 9:30-5, Sun 12-5
Friends of the Library Group

J ROWAN COLLEGE AT BURLINGTON COUNTY LIBRARY, 900 College Circle, 08054-5308. SAN 310-4095. Tel: 856-894-9311, Ext 2100. E-mail: library@rcbc.edu. Web Site: www.rcbc.edu/library. *Dir,* David Peterson; Tel: 856-222-9311, Ext 2021; *Admin Librn,* Rachel Pieterss; Staff 6 (MLS 4, Non-MLS 2)
Founded 1969. Enrl 7,797; Fac 68; Highest Degree: Associate
Library Holdings: Bks on Deafness & Sign Lang 10; DVDs 200; e-journals 25; Electronic Media & Resources 50; High Interest/Low Vocabulary Bk Vols 100; Bk Vols 30,000; Per Subs 50
Automation Activity & Vendor Info: (Acquisitions) Innovative Interfaces, Inc. - Polaris; (Cataloging) Innovative Interfaces, Inc. - Polaris; (Circulation) Innovative Interfaces, Inc. - Polaris; (ILL) OCLC WorldShare Interlibrary Loan; (OPAC) Innovative Interfaces, Inc. - Polaris; (Serials) Innovative Interfaces, Inc. - Polaris
Wireless access
Partic in LibraryLinkNJ, The New Jersey Library Cooperative; OCLC Online Computer Library Center, Inc; Virtual Academic Library Environment
Open Mon-Thurs 9-8, Fri 9-5, Sat 11-4

MOUNTAIN LAKES

P MOUNTAIN LAKES PUBLIC LIBRARY*, Nine Elm Rd, 07046-1316. SAN 310-3226. Tel: 973-334-5095. FAX: 973-299-1622. Web Site: library.mtnlakes.org. *Dir,* Jennifer Lynch; E-mail: jennifer.lynch@mainlib.org
Founded 1914. Pop 4,256; Circ 61,413
Library Holdings: Bk Vols 42,000; Per Subs 35
Automation Activity & Vendor Info: (Cataloging) Innovative Interfaces, Inc; (Circulation) Innovative Interfaces, Inc; (OPAC) Innovative Interfaces, Inc
Wireless access
Partic in Morris Automated Information Network
Open Mon & Wed 9-9, Tues, Thurs & Fri 9-5, Sat 9-2

MOUNTAINSIDE

P MOUNTAINSIDE PUBLIC LIBRARY, One Constitution Plaza, 07092. SAN 310-3234. Tel: 908-233-0115. E-mail: info@mountainsidelibrary.org. Web Site: www.mountainsidelibrary.org. *Libr Dir,* Kathryn Brown; E-mail: mpldirector@mountainsidelibrary.org; Staff 13 (MLS 4, Non-MLS 9)
Founded 1934. Pop 6,657; Circ 75,902
Jan 2015-Dec 2015 Income $610,876, State $2,923, City $569,060, Other $38,893. Mats Exp $47,595, Books $26,718, Per/Ser (Incl. Access Fees) $8,976, AV Mat $5,487, Electronic Ref Mat (Incl. Access Fees) $1,958, Presv $4,456. Sal $291,097 (Prof $129,423)
Library Holdings: Audiobooks 1,164; CDs 2,639; DVDs 3,536; Bk Titles 55,939; Bk Vols 58,276; Per Subs 128; Talking Bks 1,164; Videos 3,536
Automation Activity & Vendor Info: (Cataloging) SirsiDynix; (Circulation) SirsiDynix; (ILL) JerseyCat; (OPAC) SirsiDynix
Wireless access
Function: 24/7 Electronic res, 24/7 Online cat, After school storytime, Bks on CD, Children's prog, Computers for patron use, Electronic databases & coll, Home delivery & serv to seniorr ctr & nursing homes, Homebound delivery serv, ILL available, Internet access, Magnifiers for reading, Music CDs, Notary serv, Online cat, OverDrive digital audio bks, Photocopying/Printing, Prog for adults, Prog for children & young adult, Ref & res, Ref serv available, Scanner, Story hour, Summer reading prog, Tax forms, Teen prog, Wheelchair accessible
Publications: Annual Report; e-Newsletter (Monthly); Friends' Newsletter (Annual)
Partic in LibraryLinkNJ, The New Jersey Library Cooperative; MURAL
Special Services for the Deaf - Closed caption videos
Special Services for the Blind - Bks on CD; Large print bks; Magnifiers; ZoomText magnification & reading software
Open Mon, Wed & Fri 10-5, Tues & Thurs 1-8, Sat (Sept-June) 10-1
Friends of the Library Group

MULLICA HILL

P GLOUCESTER COUNTY LIBRARY SYSTEM*, Mullica Hill Branch, 389 Wolfert Station Rd, 08062. SAN 321-0820. Tel: 856-223-6000. Circulation Tel: 856-223-6060. Reference Tel: 856-223-6050. FAX: 856-223-6039. Reference E-mail: reference@gcls.org. Web Site: www.gcls.org. *Head, Adult Serv,* Nancy Polhamus; Tel: 856-223-6025, E-mail: npolhamus@gcls.org; *Head, Digital Serv,* Bryan Bonfiglio; Tel: 856-223-6017, E-mail: bbonfiglio@gcls.org; *Head, Pub Serv,* Brenda Muhlbaier; Tel: 856-223-6041, E-mail: bmuhlbaier@gcls.org; *Head, Tech Serv,* Linda Gentile; Tel: 856-223-6013, E-mail: lgentile@gcls.org; *Head, Youth Serv,* Jennifer Schureman; Tel: 856-223-6027, E-mail: jschureman@gcls.org; Staff 69 (MLS 9, Non-MLS 60)
Founded 1976. Pop 84,380; Circ 504,118
Automation Activity & Vendor Info: (Acquisitions) SirsiDynix; (Cataloging) SirsiDynix; (Circulation) SirsiDynix; (Discovery) EBSCO Discovery Service; (OPAC) SirsiDynix; (Serials) SirsiDynix
Wireless access

Function: Homebound delivery serv
Partic in Libraries of Gloucester, Salem & Cumberland Information Network; LibraryLinkNJ, The New Jersey Library Cooperative
Special Services for the Deaf - Assistive tech; Closed caption videos; TDD equip
Special Services for the Blind - Audio mat; Large print bks; Talking bks
Open Mon-Thurs 10-9, Fri & Sat 10-5, Sun (Sept-May) 1-5
Friends of the Library Group
Branches: 5
GLASSBORO BRANCH, Two Center St, Glassboro, 08028, SAN 350-7513. Tel: 856-881-0001. FAX: 856-881-9338. *Br Mgr,* Loretta Lisowski; E-mail: llisowski@gcls.org; Staff 8.5 (MLS 2, Non-MLS 6.5)
Founded 1956
Open Mon-Thurs 10-9, Fri 10-5, Sat 10-2
GREENWICH TOWNSHIP BRANCH, 411 Swedesboro Rd, Gibbstown, 08027, SAN 310-1800. Tel: 856-423-0684. FAX: 856-423-1201. *Br Mgr,* Patricia Collins; E-mail: pcollins@gcls.org; Staff 5 (MLS 1, Non-MLS 4)
Pop 5,333; Circ 36,436
Open Mon-Thurs 10-9, Fri 10-5, Sat 10-2
LOGAN TOWNSHIP BRANCH, 498 Beckett Rd, Logan Township, 08085, SAN 376-9313. Tel: 856-241-0202. FAX: 856-241-0491. *Br Mgr,* Carolyn Oldt; E-mail: coldt@gcls.org; Staff 5.5 (MLS 1, Non-MLS 4.5)
Founded 1979
Open Mon-Thurs 10-9, Fri 10-5, Sat 10-2
NEWFIELD PUBLIC, 115 Catawba Ave, Newfield, 08344, SAN 310-3617. Tel: 856-697-0415. FAX: 856-697-1544. E-mail: newfieldlibrary@hotmail.com. *Mgr,* Carol Thomasson; E-mail: cthomasson@gcls.org; Staff 3 (Non-MLS 3)
Founded 1876
Library Holdings: Bk Titles 22,379; Bk Vols 23,207; Per Subs 24
Open Mon-Thurs 10-7, Fri 10-5
SWEDESBORO BRANCH, 1442 Kings Hwy, Swedesboro, 08085, SAN 310-527X. Tel: 856-467-0111. FAX: 856-241-0594. *Br Mgr,* Judith Pissano; E-mail: jpissano@gcls.org
Pop 2,000; Circ 18,592
Subject Interests: Local hist
Open Mon-Thurs 10-8, Fri 10-5, Sat 10-2

NEPTUNE

M JERSEY SHORE UNIVERSITY MEDICAL CENTER*, Booker Health Sciences Library, 1945 Route 33, 07753. SAN 310-3269. Tel: 732-776-4265. FAX: 732-776-4530. E-mail: jsumclibrary@hmhn.org. Web Site: www.jerseyshoreuniversitymedicalcenter.com/patients-visitors/hospital-amenities/booker-heal. *Dir, Med Libr,* Darlene Robertelli; Tel: 732-776-4266, E-mail: darlene.robertelli@hmhn.org; *Syst Librn,* Chunwei Ma; Tel: 732-776-4636, E-mail: chunwei.ma@hmhn.org; *Assoc Librn,* Lawren Wilkins; E-mail: lawren.wilkins@hmhn.org; Staff 3 (MLS 3)
Library Holdings: e-books 3,295; e-journals 3,275
Subject Interests: Consumer health, Med, Nursing
Automation Activity & Vendor Info: (Acquisitions) Ex Libris Group; (Cataloging) Ex Libris Group; (Circulation) Ex Libris Group; (OPAC) Ex Libris Group; (Serials) Ex Libris Group
Wireless access
Partic in Basic Health Sciences Library Network; New Jersey Health Sciences Library Network
Open Mon-Fri 9-5
Restriction: Authorized personnel only

P NEPTUNE PUBLIC LIBRARY*, 25 Neptune Blvd, 07753-1125. SAN 310-3277. Tel: 732-775-8241. FAX: 732-774-1132. E-mail: info@neptunepubliclibrary.org. Web Site: www.neptunepubliclibrary.org. *Dir,* John Bonney; E-mail: jbonney@neptunepubliclibrary.org; Staff 11 (MLS 5, Non-MLS 6)
Founded 1924. Pop 27,935; Circ 150,000
Library Holdings: Bk Vols 75,000; Per Subs 104
Special Collections: Neptune Archive (Local History). Municipal Document Depository
Automation Activity & Vendor Info: (Cataloging) SirsiDynix; (Circulation) SirsiDynix; (OPAC) SirsiDynix
Wireless access
Partic in LibraryLinkNJ, The New Jersey Library Cooperative
Special Services for the Blind - Bks on CD
Open Mon, Wed & Fri 9-5, Tues & Thurs 9-8, Sat 9-5 (9-1 Summer)
Friends of the Library Group

NEPTUNE CITY

P NEPTUNE CITY LIBRARY*, 106 W Sylvania Ave, 07753. Tel: 732-988-8866. Web Site: www.neptunecity.lib.nj.us.
Library Holdings: AV Mats 100; DVDs 850; Large Print Bks 150; Bk Vols 13,000; Videos 250
Automation Activity & Vendor Info: (Cataloging) SirsiDynix; (Circulation) SirsiDynix; (OPAC) SirsiDynix
Wireless access
Mem of Monmouth County Library
Open Mon 10-8, Tues & Thurs 1-8, Fri & Sat 10-1
Friends of the Library Group

NEW BRUNSWICK

S JEWISH HISTORICAL SOCIETY OF CENTRAL JERSEY LIBRARY*, 222 Livingston Ave, 08901. SAN 376-0529. Tel: 732-249-4894. E-mail: info.jhscj@gmail.com. Web Site: www.jewishgen.org/jhscj. *Adminr, Archivist,* Deborah Cohn; Staff 1 (MLS 1)
Founded 1977
Library Holdings: Bk Vols 807
Special Collections: NJ Jewish Organization Documents. Oral History
Subject Interests: Genealogy, Jewish hist
Function: Archival coll, For res purposes, Res libr
Publications: Newsletter (Quarterly)
Open Mon-Fri 9-1
Restriction: Not a lending libr

S MIDDLESEX COUNTY CULTURAL & HERITAGE COMMISSION*, Office of Arts & History, 75 Bayard St, 08901. SAN 375-6998. Tel: 732-745-4489. FAX: 732-745-4524. E-mail: culturalandheritage@co.middlesex.nj.us. Web Site: www.middlesexcountynj.gov. *Div Head,* Isha Vyas; Staff 17 (Non-MLS 17)
Founded 1995
Library Holdings: Bk Titles 2,000
Subject Interests: Archaeology, Archit, Art educ, Folklife, Fundraising, Historic sites, Local hist, NJ hist, Nonprofit mgt
Function: Wheelchair accessible
Special Services for the Deaf - TTY equip
Open Mon-Fri 8:30-4:15
Restriction: Open to pub for ref & circ; with some limitations

GL MIDDLESEX COUNTY LAW LIBRARY*, 56 Patterson St, 08901. SAN 310-3293. Tel: 732-519-3452. FAX: 732-519-3454. E-mail: midlawlib@yahoo.com. *Librn,* Lisa Jodide; E-mail: lisa.jodide@njcourts.gov
Library Holdings: Bk Vols 5,000
Wireless access
Open Mon-Fri 8:30-4:30
Restriction: Non-circulating to the pub

P NEW BRUNSWICK FREE PUBLIC LIBRARY, 60 Livingston Ave, 08901-2597. SAN 310-3315. Tel: 732-745-5108. Circulation Tel: 732-745-5108, Ext 25. Reference Tel: 732-745-5108, Ext 20. Administration Tel: 732-745-5108, Ext 14. FAX: 732-846-0226. E-mail: nbfpl@lmxac.org. Web Site: www.nbfpl.org. *Dir,* Robert Belvin; Tel: 732-745-5721, E-mail: bbelvin@lmxac.org; *Asst Dir,* Linda Crittenden; Tel: 732-745-5108, Ext 11, E-mail: kayser@lmxac.org; *YA Librn,* Trevor Hotalen; Tel: 732-745-5108, Ext 22, E-mail: thotalen@lmxac.org; *Ch Serv,* Karen Stuppi; Tel: 732-745-5108, Ext 15, E-mail: kstuppi@lmxac.org; *Ref Serv,* Hsien-min Chen; Tel: 732-745-5108, Ext 23; *Tech Serv,* Iren Ruschak; Tel: 732-745-5108, Ext 27, E-mail: iren@lmxac.org; Staff 11.5 (MLS 9, Non-MLS 2.5)
Founded 1883. Pop 55,000; Circ 84,000
Jan 2021-Dec 2021 Income $1,451,810, State $28,810, City $140,000, Locally Generated Income $22,000, Other $10,000. Mats Exp $120,700, Books $85,500, Per/Ser (Incl. Access Fees) $8,000, AV Mat $16,200, Electronic Ref Mat (Incl. Access Fees) $11,000. Sal $1,301,610
Library Holdings: Bk Vols 80,000; Per Subs 254
Subject Interests: Local hist
Automation Activity & Vendor Info: (Circulation) SirsiDynix; (OPAC) SirsiDynix
Wireless access
Partic in Libraries of Middlesex Automation Consortium
Open Mon-Thurs 10-9, Fri & Sat 10-5, Sun 1-5
Friends of the Library Group

R NEW BRUNSWICK THEOLOGICAL SEMINARY*, Gardner A Sage Library, 21 Seminary Pl, 08901. SAN 310-3331. Tel: 732-247-5241. FAX: 732-249-5412. Web Site: www.nbts.edu/sage-library. *Dir,* Dr T Patrick Milas; E-mail: pmilas@nbts.edu; *Pub Serv Librn,* Laura Giacobbe; E-mail: lgiacobbe@nbts.edu; Staff 4 (MLS 3, Non-MLS 1)
Founded 1784. Highest Degree: Doctorate
Library Holdings: AV Mats 269; Bk Vols 160,000; Per Subs 231
Special Collections: Archives of Reformed Church in America; Leiby Coll
Subject Interests: Biblical studies, Classics, Dutch Church hist, Theol disciplines
Automation Activity & Vendor Info: (Acquisitions) TLC (The Library Corporation); (Cataloging) TLC (The Library Corporation); (Circulation) TLC (The Library Corporation); (Course Reserve) TLC (The Library Corporation); (ILL) OCLC FirstSearch; (OPAC) TLC (The Library Corporation)
Wireless access

Function: Ref serv available
Partic in NY Area Theol Libr Asn; Southeastern Pennsylvania Theological Library Association; Virtual Academic Library Environment
Open Mon-Thurs 11-10, Fri 9-6, Sat 10-2
Restriction: Open to fac, students & qualified researchers

C RUTGERS UNIVERSITY LIBRARIES*, 169 College Ave, 08901-1163. SAN 350-9850. Tel: 848-932-7505. Interlibrary Loan Service Tel: 848-932-6005. FAX: 732-932-7637. Web Site: www.libraries.rutgers.edu. *Univ Librn,* Maloney Krisellen; E-mail: krisellen.maloney@rutgers.edu; *Asst VP, Info Servs,* Judy Cohn; Tel: 973-972-0560, E-mail: judith.s.cohn@rutgers.edu; *Dir, Finance & Planning,* Abigail Dipaolo; Tel: 848-932-5998, E-mail: adipaolo@libraries.rutgers.edu. Subject Specialists: *Bus operations,* Abigail Dipaolo; Staff 274 (MLS 83, Non-MLS 191)
Founded 1766. Enrl 68,942; Fac 4,314; Highest Degree: Doctorate
Special Collections: Oral History; State Document Depository; US Document Depository
Automation Activity & Vendor Info: (Acquisitions) SirsiDynix; (Cataloging) SirsiDynix; (Circulation) SirsiDynix; (Course Reserve) SirsiDynix; (Media Booking) SirsiDynix; (OPAC) SirsiDynix; (Serials) SirsiDynix
Wireless access
Publications: Annual Report; Collection Guides; Instructional & Informational Material; Journal of the Rutgers University Libraries; Report (Newsletter)
Partic in Association of Research Libraries; Big Ten Academic Alliance; Northeast Research Libraries Consortium; OCLC Online Computer Library Center, Inc
Open Mon-Fri 8:30-4:30

Departmental Libraries:

ARCHIBALD STEVENS ALEXANDER LIBRARY, 169 College Ave, 08901-1163, SAN 350-9885. Tel: 848-932-7851. Reference Tel: 848-932-7509. Administration Tel: 848-932-7129. FAX: 732-932-1101. Web Site: www.libraries.rutgers.edu/alexander. *Assoc Univ Librn,* Dianna Magnoni; E-mail: dee.magnoni@rutgers.edu; *Bus Mgr,* Charlene Houser; Tel: 848-932-5997, E-mail: charlene.houser@rutgers.edu; *Operations Mgr,* Douglas Allen; Tel: 848-932-6102, E-mail: doug.allen@rutgers; *Libr Supvr,* Zohreh Bonianian; Tel: 848-932-6056, E-mail: zohreh@libraries.rutgers.edu; *Libr Supvr,* Brian Stubbs; Tel: 848-932-6054, E-mail: bstubbs@libraries.rutgers.edu; *Libr Supvr,* Jeffrey Teichmann; Tel: 848-932-6057, E-mail: jteich@libraries.rutgers.edu; Staff 43 (MLS 11, Non-MLS 32)
Special Collections: Government Publications Coll. State Document Depository; US Document Depository
Subject Interests: Humanities
Special Services for the Blind - Assistive/Adapted tech devices, equip & products

ART LIBRARY, Voorhees Hall, 71 Hamilton St, 08901-1248, SAN 350-9974. Tel: 848-932-7739. Web Site: www.libraries.rutgers.edu/art. *Art Librn,* Megan Lotts; Tel: 848-932-7189, E-mail: megan.lotts@rutgers.edu; Staff 3 (MLS 1, Non-MLS 2)
Special Collections: American & Russian Art & Architecture Coll
Subject Interests: Archit hist, Art, Landscape archit, Visual arts
Open Mon-Fri 9-5
Restriction: Non-circulating

JAMES B CAREY LIBRARY, School of Management & Labor Relations, 50 Labor Center Way, 08901-8553, SAN 351-8553. Tel: 848-932-9513. Web Site: smlr.rutgers.edu/content/library. *Libr Dir,* Julie A Peters; Tel: 848-932-9608, E-mail: jpeters@smlr.rutgers.edu; *Libr Assoc,* Eugene McElroy; Tel: 848-932-9513, E-mail: mcelroy@work.rutgers.edu; Staff 2 (MLS 1, Non-MLS 1)
Special Collections: New Jersey Public Sector Collective Bargaining Contracts
Subject Interests: Human resources, Indust relations, Labor
Special Services for the Deaf - Assistive tech
Special Services for the Blind - Assistive/Adapted tech devices, equip & products
Open Mon-Thurs 8am-9pm, Fri 8-5, Sat 10-2

JAMES DICKSON CARR LIBRARY, 75 Ave E, Piscataway, 08854-8040, SAN 351-2134. Circulation Tel: 848-445-3613. Reference Tel: 848-445-3614. Web Site: www.libraries.rutgers.edu/carr. *Libr Supvr,* Barry Lipinsky; Tel: 848-445-3838, E-mail: bvl@libraries.rutgers.edu; *Libr Supvr,* Paul Young; Tel: 848-445-3607, E-mail: pjyesq@libraries.rutgers.edu; *Instrul Design Librn,* Leslin Charles; Tel: 848-445-4432, E-mail: leslin.charles@rutgers.edu; *Instrul Serv Librn, Soc Sci Librn,* Triveni Kuchi; Tel: 848-445-5733, E-mail: triveni.kuchi@rutgers.edu; *Soc Sci Librn,* Rebecca Gardner; Tel: 848-445-3605, E-mail: rgardner@rutgers.edu; Staff 12 (MLS 4, Non-MLS 8)
Founded 1969
Subject Interests: Bus, Career res, Undergrad educ
Special Services for the Blind - Assistive/Adapted tech devices, equip & products
Open Mon-Thurs 8-6, Fri 8-5

STEPHEN & LUCY CHANG SCIENCE LIBRARY, Walter E Foran Hall, 59 Dudley Rd, 08901-8520. Tel: 848-932-0305. FAX: 732-932-0311. Web Site: www.libraries.rutgers.edu/chang. *Libr Supvr,* Nita Mukherjee; Tel: 848-932-5085, E-mail: nmukherj@libraries.rutgers.edu; Staff 1 (Non-MLS 1)
Subject Interests: Agr, Animal sci, Aquaculture, Bio engr, Fisheries, Food sci, Plant sci
Special Services for the Blind - Assistive/Adapted tech devices, equip & products
Open Mon-Fri 9-5

JOHN COTTON DANA LIBRARY
See Separate Entry in Newark

MABEL SMITH DOUGLASS LIBRARY, Eight Chapel Dr, 08901-8527, SAN 351-0123. Tel: 848-932-9411. Reference Tel: 848-932-5020. FAX: 732-932-6777. Web Site: www.libraries.rutgers.edu/douglass. *Head, Educ Res Ctr,* Kayo Denda; Tel: 848-932-5023, E-mail: kayo.denda@rutgers.edu; *Music & Performing Arts Librn,* Jonathan Sauceda; Tel: 848-932-9023, E-mail: jonathan.sauceda@rutgers.edu; *Undergraduate Ed Librn,* Lilyana Todorinova; Tel: 848-932-1696, E-mail: lily.todorinova@rutgers.edu. Subject Specialists: *Women's studies,* Kayo Denda; Staff 11 (MLS 3, Non-MLS 8)
Special Collections: Elizabeth Cady Stanton Papers; Gerritsen Coll, bks & per. State Document Depository; UN Document Depository
Subject Interests: Performing arts, Undergrad educ, Women's studies
Special Services for the Blind - Assistive/Adapted tech devices, equip & products
Open Mon-Thurs 8-6, Fri 8-5

EAST ASIAN LIBRARY, Alexander Library, 169 College Ave, 08901-1163, SAN 329-3491. Web Site: www.libraries.rutgers.edu/east_asian. *Librn,* Tao Yang; Tel: 848-932-6086, E-mail: tao.yang@rutgers.edu; Staff 1 (MLS 1)
Special Collections: Chinese History, Literature, Religion & Philosophy Coll; Chinese Medicine (Professor Kuang-chung Ho Coll), bks & journals
Subject Interests: Chinese, Japanese, Korean lang mat
Open Mon-Thurs 7:45am-9pm, Fri 7:45-6, Sat 12-6, Sun 1-6

INSTITUTE OF JAZZ STUDIES
See Separate Entry in Newark

CM ROBERT WOOD JOHNSON LIBRARY OF THE HEALTH SCIENCES, One Robert Wood Johnson Pl, 08903. (Mail add: PO Box 19, 08903), SAN 320-3980. Circulation Tel: 732-235-7610. Reference Tel: 732-235-7604. FAX: 732-235-7826. Web Site: www.libraries.rutgers.edu/rwj. *Assoc Dir,* Victoria Wagner; Tel: 732-235-7606, E-mail: victoria.wagner@rutgers.edu; *Info & Educ Librn,* Pamela Hargwood; Tel: 732-235-7261, E-mail: hargwood@rutgers.edu; *Info & Educ Librn,* Yingting Zhang; Tel: 732-235-7604, E-mail: yzhang@libraries.rutgers.edu; Staff 7 (MLS 3, Non-MLS 4)
Partic in New Jersey Health Sciences Library Network
Open Mon-Thurs 8-6, Fri 8-5

BLANCHE & IRVING LAURIE PERFORMING ARTS LIBRARY, Mabel Smith Douglass Library, Eight Chapel Dr, 08901-8527, SAN 351-0255. Tel: 848-932-5038. FAX: 732-932-6777. Web Site: www.libraries.rutgers.edu/performing_arts. *Libr Assoc, Media Serv,* John Rake; E-mail: johnrake@libraries.rutgers.edu; Staff 2 (MLS 1, Non-MLS 1)
Subject Interests: Music
Special Services for the Blind - Assistive/Adapted tech devices, equip & products
Open Mon-Thurs 8-6, Fri 8-5

CM LIBRARY OF SCIENCE & MEDICINE, 165 Bevier Rd, Piscataway, 08854-8009, SAN 351-2169. Circulation Tel: 848-445-3854. FAX: 732-445-5703. Web Site: www.libraries.rutgers.edu/lsm. *Access Serv, Behav Sci Librn,* Laura Mullen; Tel: 848-445-3663, E-mail: lbmullen@rutgers.edu; *Biological Sci Librn,* Position Currently Open; *Chem & Physics Librn,* Laura Palumbo; Tel: 848-445-3558, E-mail: laura.palumbo@rutgers.edu; *Eng Res Librn,* Connie Wu; Tel: 848-445-3489, E-mail: conniewu@rutgers.edu; *Ref & Instruction Librn,* Jill Nathanson; E-mail: jill.nathanson@rutgers.edu; *Libr Assoc,* Krista Haviland; Tel: 848-445-3519, E-mail: kdandura@libraries.rutgers.edu; Staff 17 (MLS 7, Non-MLS 10)
Founded 1970
Special Collections: Patent & Trademark Resource Center. State Document Depository; US Document Depository
Subject Interests: Behav sci, Biol sci, Earth sci, Engr, Pharmaceutical sci
Partic in LYRASIS
Special Services for the Blind - Assistive/Adapted tech devices, equip & products
Open Mon-Thurs 8am-11pm, Fri 8-6, Sat 12-6, Sun 1-6

MATHEMATICAL SCIENCES & PHYSICS LIBRARY, Hill Ctr for Mathematical Sciences, 110 Frelinghuysen Rd, Piscataway, 08854-8019, SAN 351-0212. Circulation Tel: 848-445-5955. FAX: 732-445-3064. Web Site: www.libraries.rutgers.edu/math-physics. *Chem & Physics Librn,* Laura Palumbo; Tel: 848-445-3558, E-mail: laura.palumbo@rutgers.edu; *Research Librn, Sci Librn,* Mei Ling Lo;

Tel: 848-445-5914, E-mail: mlo@rutgers.edu; *Libr Assoc,* Melanie Miller; Tel: 848-445-5919, E-mail: lmmill@libraries.rutgers.edu; Staff 2 (MLS 1, Non-MLS 1)
Special Collections: Technical Reports
Subject Interests: Computer sci, Math, Statistics
Open Mon-Fri 9-5
MEDIA CENTER, Douglass Library, Eight Chapel Dr, 08901. Tel: 848-932-9783. Web Site: www.libraries.rutgers.edu/media-services. *Libr Supvr,* Jan Reinhart; Tel: 848-932-5032, E-mail: jreinhar@libraries.rutgers.edu; Staff 4 (Non-MLS 4)
PAUL ROBESON LIBRARY
See Separate Entry in Camden

CM GEORGE F SMITH LIBRARY OF THE HEALTH SCIENCES, 30 12th Ave, Newark, 07101, SAN 310-3412. Tel: 973-972-8538. Reference Tel: 973-972-4358. FAX: 973-972-7474. Web Site: www.libraries.rutgers.edu/smith. *Dir, Health Sci Libr,* Judith Cohn; Tel: 973-972-0560, E-mail: cohn@libraries.rutgers.edu; *Libr Asst,* Corisa Mobley; Tel: 973-972-6528, E-mail: corisa.mobley@rutgers.edu; *Prog Spec, Support Serv,* Ricardo Camposagrado; Tel: 973-972-5317, E-mail: camposrq@libraries.rutgers.edu; Staff 26 (MLS 9, Non-MLS 17)
Partic in New Jersey Health Sciences Library Network
Open Mon-Thurs 7:30am-2am, Fri 7:30am-10pm, Sat 9-5, Sun 10am-2am
SPECIAL COLLECTIONS & UNIVERSITY ARCHIVES, Alexander Library, 169 College Ave, 08901-1163, SAN 323-5696. Reference Tel: 848-932-6159. FAX: 732-932-7012. Web Site: www.libraries.rutgers.edu/scua. *Head, Exhibitions Prog Curator/William E Griffis Coll, Univ Archivist,* Fernanda H Perrone; Tel: 848-932-6154, E-mail: hperrone@libraries.rutgers.edu; *Head, Presv,* Timothy Corlis; Tel: 848-932-6147, E-mail: tcorlis@libraries.rutgers.edu; *Head, Pub Serv, NJ Regional Studies Librn,* Christine A Lutz; Tel: 848-932-6148, E-mail: christie.lutz@rutgers.edu; *Head, Spec Coll Cat,* Melissa DeFino; Tel: 848-445-5881, E-mail: mdefino@rutgers.edu; *Rare Bk Librn,* Michael Joseph; Tel: 848-932-6163, E-mail: mjoseph@libraries.rutgers.edu; *Archivist,* Erika Gorder; Tel: 848-932-6150, E-mail: gorder@libraries.rutgers.edu; *Archivist,* Tara Kelley; Tel: 848-932-6009, E-mail: tkelley@libraries.rutgers.edu; *Digital Archivist,* Caryn Radick; Tel: 848-932-6152, E-mail: cradick@libraries.rutgers.edu; *Ms Curator,* Albert C King; Tel: 848-932-6153, E-mail: albert.king@rutgers.edu; *Proc Archivist,* Tara Maharjan; Tel: 848-932-6158, E-mail: tara.maharjan@rutgers.edu. Subject Specialists: *AV,* Tara Kelley; Staff 16 (MLS 11, Non-MLS 5)
Founded 1946. Highest Degree: Doctorate
Special Collections: British & American Literature (18th & 19th centuries); Diaries; Dictionaries; History of Business & Labor; Manuscript Colls; Rare Book Coll (17th & 18th Century British & American Writers); Sinclair New Jersey Coll; University Archives; Westerners in Japan; William Elliot Griffis Coll. Oral History
Subject Interests: Archives, Manuscripts, New Jerseyana, Rare bks
Function: Archival coll
Publications: Bibliographies; Collection Guides; Exhibition Catalogs
Special Services for the Blind - Assistive/Adapted tech devices, equip & products
Open Mon-Thurs 9-5, Fri 9-1
Restriction: Non-circulating

M SAINT PETER'S UNIVERSITY HOSPITAL MEDICAL LIBRARY*, 254 Easton Ave, 08903. SAN 310-3358. Tel: 732-745-8545. Reference Tel: 732-745-8508. FAX: 732-937-6091. E-mail: mlibrary@saintpetersuh.com. Web Site: saintpetershcs.com/Patients/Medical-Library. *Mgr, Libr Serv,* Jeannine Creazzo; Staff 2 (MLS 2)
Founded 1907
Library Holdings: Bk Vols 25,000; Per Subs 450
Special Collections: Consumer Health Coll; Cultural Competency Coll; History of Medicine; Leadership Development Coll
Subject Interests: Gynecology, Med, Nursing, Obstetrics, Pediatrics
Wireless access
Partic in BSHL; Health Sci Libr Asn of NJ; New Jersey Health Sciences Library Network
Open Mon-Fri 9-4

NEW MILFORD

P NEW MILFORD PUBLIC LIBRARY, 200 Dahlia Ave, 07646. SAN 310-3374. Tel: 201-262-1221. FAX: 201-262-5639. Web Site: www.newmilford.njlibraries.org. *Dir,* Terrie McColl; E-mail: mccoll@newmilford.bccls.org; Staff 12 (MLS 5, Non-MLS 7)
Founded 1936. Pop 16,425; Circ 88,879
Library Holdings: CDs 1,092; DVDs 2,255; Large Print Bks 579; Bk Vols 54,441; Per Subs 105; Talking Bks 1,042; Videos 2,182
Subject Interests: Consumer info, Cooking
Wireless access
Open Mon & Tues 10-9, Wed 10-8, Thurs 10-6, Fri & Sat 1-5
Friends of the Library Group

NEW PROVIDENCE

S MCNEIL & FOSTER LIBRARY*, Reference Library, 121 Chanlon Rd, Ste G-20, 07974. SAN 330-0366. Tel: 908-219-0278. *Librn,* Elizabeth M Button; Staff 1 (Non-MLS 1)
Founded 1985
Apr 2018-Mar 2019 Income $45,000. Mats Exp $3,000
Library Holdings: CDs 35; DVDs 30; Bk Titles 17,000; Per Subs 250; Videos 200
Automation Activity & Vendor Info: (Acquisitions) Brodart
Wireless access
Partic in OCLC Online Computer Library Center, Inc
Restriction: Staff use only

S NEW PROVIDENCE HISTORICAL SOCIETY LIBRARY*, c/o Memorial Library, 377 Elkwood Ave, 07974. SAN 323-4673. Tel: 908-665-1034. Web Site: newprovidencehistorical.com. *Pres,* Linda Kale; *VPres,* Rick Anderson; E-mail: rick243@comcast.net
Founded 1966
Library Holdings: Bk Vols 200
Special Collections: Oral History
Subject Interests: Local hist
Open Tues & Thurs 10-Noon

P NEW PROVIDENCE MEMORIAL LIBRARY*, 377 Elkwood Ave, 07974. SAN 310-3382. Tel: 908-665-0311. FAX: 908-665-2319. Reference E-mail: npmlref@newprovidencelibrary.org. Web Site: www.newprovidencelibrary.org. *Dir,* Lisa Florio; Staff 14 (MLS 4, Non-MLS 10)
Founded 1921. Pop 13,308; Circ 109,206
Library Holdings: Bk Titles 75,000; Bk Vols 80,000; Per Subs 120
Automation Activity & Vendor Info: (Cataloging) TLC (The Library Corporation); (Circulation) TLC (The Library Corporation); (OPAC) TLC (The Library Corporation)
Wireless access
Function: 24/7 Electronic res, 24/7 Online cat, Adult bk club, Art exhibits, Audiobks via web, Bk club(s), Bks on CD, Butterfly Garden, Children's prog, Computers for patron use, Digital talking bks, Electronic databases & coll, ILL available, Internet access, Magazines, Meeting rooms, Movies, Museum passes, Music CDs, Online cat, Online ref, OverDrive digital audio bks, Photocopying/Printing, Prog for adults, Prog for children & young adult, Ref & res, Ref serv available, STEM programs, Story hour, Summer reading prog, Tax forms, Workshops, Writing prog
Partic in LibraryLinkNJ, The New Jersey Library Cooperative; LUCC; Morris-Union Federation; MURAL
Open Mon, Tues & Thurs 9-9, Wed, Fri & Sat 9-5, Sun (Fall-Spring) 1-5
Friends of the Library Group

NEW VERNON

P KEMMERER LIBRARY HARDING TOWNSHIP*, 19 Blue Mill Rd, 07976. (Mail add: PO Box 283, 07976-0283). Tel: 973-267-2665. E-mail: desk@hardinglibrary.org. Web Site: hardinglibrary.org. *Dir,* Alison Maxwell
Pop 3,400
Library Holdings: High Interest/Low Vocabulary Bk Vols 3,000; Bk Vols 7,000
Wireless access
Partic in Morris Automated Information Network
Open Mon-Fri 10-5, Sat 10-1
Friends of the Library Group

NEWARK

J ESSEX COUNTY COLLEGE LIBRARY*, 303 University Ave, 07102. SAN 351-0395. Tel: 973-877-3238. Circulation Tel: 973-877-3028. Reference Tel: 973-877-3241. Administration Tel: 973-877-3233. FAX: 973-877-1887. Web Site: www.essex.edu/library. *Dir,* Gwendolyn C Slaton; E-mail: slaton@essex.edu; *Ref Librn,* Dr Stephen Keister; Tel: 973-877-3286, E-mail: keister@essex.edu; *Circ,* Rita Willis; E-mail: rwillis@essex.edu; *Ref (Info Servs),* Leola Taylor-Bandele; E-mail: ltaylor@essex.edu. Subject Specialists: *Educ, Law,* Gwendolyn C Slaton; *Engr, Math, Tech,* Dr Stephen Keister; *Art, Hist, Humanities,* Rita Willis; *Biology, Chem,* Leola Taylor-Bandele; Staff 8 (MLS 4, Non-MLS 4)
Founded 1968. Enrl 12,500; Fac 150; Highest Degree: Associate
Library Holdings: AV Mats 4,909; High Interest/Low Vocabulary Bk Vols 1,146; Bk Titles 104,234; Bk Vols 114,543; Per Subs 500
Subject Interests: Nursing
Automation Activity & Vendor Info: (Acquisitions) Innovative Interfaces, Inc; (Cataloging) Innovative Interfaces, Inc; (Circulation) Innovative Interfaces, Inc; (Course Reserve) Innovative Interfaces, Inc; (ILL) Innovative Interfaces, Inc; (OPAC) Innovative Interfaces, Inc; (Serials) Innovative Interfaces, Inc
Wireless access
Function: Audio & video playback equip for onsite use, Electronic databases & coll, ILL available, Internet access, Magnifiers for reading,

Mail & tel request accepted, Orientations, Photocopying/Printing, Ref & res, Ref serv available, Telephone ref, VHS videos, Wheelchair accessible
Publications: Subject Bibliographies
Partic in Eastern NJ Regional Libr Coop; LibraryLinkNJ, The New Jersey Library Cooperative; ReBL; Virtual Academic Library Environment
Open Mon-Thurs 8:30am-9pm, Fri 8-5, Sat 8-3
Restriction: Open to pub for ref & circ; with some limitations, Open to students

Departmental Libraries:

BRANCH CAMPUS, 730 Bloomfield Ave, West Caldwell, 07007, SAN 370-0259. Tel: 973-877-1883. FAX: 973-877-6635. *Librn,* Anelia Chatterjee; E-mail: achatter@essex.edu; Staff 2 (MLS 1, Non-MLS 1)
Highest Degree: Associate
Library Holdings: Bk Vols 16,000; Per Subs 90
Open Mon-Thurs 8am-9pm, Fri 8-5, Sat 8-3

L GIBBONS PC*, Law Library, One Gateway Ctr, 07102-5310. SAN 371-5272. Tel: 973-596-4500. FAX: 973-639-6368. Web Site: www.gibbonslaw.com.
Library Holdings: Bk Titles 3,000; Bk Vols 10,000
Partic in LibraryLinkNJ, The New Jersey Library Cooperative
Restriction: Private libr

L MCCARTER & ENGLISH LIBRARY*, Four Gateway Ctr, 100 Mulberry St, 07102. SAN 310-3447. Tel: 973-622-4444. FAX: 973-624-7070.
Library Holdings: Bk Titles 29,000; Per Subs 200
Automation Activity & Vendor Info: (Cataloging) Sydney Enterprise; (Circulation) Sydney Enterprise; (Discovery) OCLC FirstSearch; (ILL) OCLC WorldShare Interlibrary Loan; (OPAC) Sydney Enterprise; (Serials) Sydney Enterprise
Wireless access
Restriction: Staff use only

S NEW JERSEY HISTORICAL SOCIETY LIBRARY*, 52 Park Pl, 07102-4302. SAN 310-348X. Tel: 973-596-8500. FAX: 973-596-6957. E-mail: library@jerseyhistory.org. Web Site: www.jerseyhistory.org. *Libr Spec,* James Amemasor; Tel: 973-596-8500, Ext 249, E-mail: jamemasor@jerseyhistory.org; Staff 4 (MLS 1, Non-MLS 3)
Founded 1845
Library Holdings: Bk Vols 65,000; Per Subs 100
Special Collections: Early New Jersey Imprints; Ephemera; Historical Newspapers; Manuscripts; Maps; Photographic Prints & Negatives; Rare Books. Oral History
Subject Interests: Am hist, NJ
Function: Archival coll, ILL available, Photocopying/Printing, Prog for adults, Prog for children & young adult, Ref serv available, Res libr, Telephone ref, Wheelchair accessible
Publications: New Jersey History
Partic in New Jersey Library Network; OCLC Online Computer Library Center, Inc
Special Services for the Deaf - Staff with knowledge of sign lang; TTY equip
Open Wed, Thurs & Sat 12-5
Restriction: Closed stack, Non-circulating to the pub, Not a lending libr, Open to pub for ref only

C NEW JERSEY INSTITUTE OF TECHNOLOGY*, Robert W Van Houten Library, 186 Central Ave, 07103. (Mail add: University Heights, 323 MLK Jr Blvd, 07102-1982), SAN 310-3498. Tel: 973-596-3206. Interlibrary Loan Service Tel: 973-596-3204. Reference Tel: 973-596-3210. Administration Tel: 973-596-5798. FAX: 973-642-7166. Web Site: library.njit.edu. *Univ Librn,* Ann D Hoang; E-mail: ahoang@njit.edu; *Assoc Univ Librn, Scholarly Communications,* Gordon Xu; Tel: 973-596-3205; *Interim Head, Circ, ILL,* Position Currently Open; *Dir, Ref,* Davida Scharf; Tel: 973-596-4397, E-mail: davida.scharf@njit.edu; *Bus Mgr,* Lucy Velez; Tel: 973-596-3207, E-mail: velez@njit.edu; *Evening Supvr,* Richard Donegan; Tel: 973-596-5586, E-mail: richard.l.donegan@njit.edu. Subject Specialists: *Technologies,* Gordon Xu; Staff 15 (MLS 13, Non-MLS 2)
Founded 1881. Enrl 12,000; Fac 489; Highest Degree: Doctorate
Library Holdings: e-books 217,000; e-journals 69,000; Bk Vols 223,000; Per Subs 194
Special Collections: Electronic Theses & Dissertation; Weston History of Science & Technology Coll
Subject Interests: Archit, Computer sci, Engr, Sci
Automation Activity & Vendor Info: (Acquisitions) Ex Libris Group; (Cataloging) Ex Libris Group; (Circulation) Ex Libris Group; (Course Reserve) Ex Libris Group; (Discovery) Ex Libris Group; (ILL) OCLC; (OPAC) Ex Libris Group; (Serials) Ex Libris Group
Wireless access
Function: 24/7 Electronic res, 24/7 Online cat, Archival coll, Computers for patron use, Distance learning, Doc delivery serv, E-Readers, E-Reserves, Electronic databases & coll, Equip loans & repairs, For res purposes, ILL available, Internet access, Magazines, Mail & tel request accepted, Meeting rooms, Microfiche/film & reading machines, Online cat, Online ref, Outside serv via phone, mail, e-mail & web, Photocopying/Printing, Printer for laptops & handheld devices, Ref & res, Ref serv available, Res assist avail, Res libr, Scanner, Study rm, Telephone ref, Wheelchair accessible, Workshops
Partic in LibraryLinkNJ, The New Jersey Library Cooperative; LYRASIS; OCLC Online Computer Library Center, Inc; Virtual Academic Library Environment
Open Mon-Thurs 7:30am-Midnight, Fri 7:30am-8pm, Sat 10-9, Sun 1-Midnight

Departmental Libraries:

BARBARA & LEONARD LITTMAN ARCHITECTURE & DESIGN LIBRARY, 456 Weston Hall, 323 King Blvd, 07102-1982. Tel: 973-596-3083. FAX: 973-643-5601. Web Site: archlib.njit.edu. *Dir,* Maya Gervits; E-mail: maya.gervits@njit.edu; *Archit/Art Librn,* Monica Kenzie; E-mail: kenzie@njit.edu; *Libr Asst I,* Cherron Bradshaw; E-mail: bradshaw@njit.edu. Subject Specialists: *Design,* Monica Kenzie; Staff 2 (MLS 2)
Founded 1975. Enrl 600; Fac 80; Highest Degree: Doctorate
Library Holdings: Bk Vols 20,000
Automation Activity & Vendor Info: (Acquisitions) Ex Libris Group; (Cataloging) Ex Libris Group; (Circulation) Ex Libris Group; (Course Reserve) Ex Libris Group; (Discovery) Ex Libris Group; (ILL) OCLC; (Serials) Ex Libris Group
Open Mon-Thurs 8am-8:30pm, Fri 8-6, Sat Noon-6, Sun 1-7

M NEWARK BETH ISRAEL MEDICAL CENTER*, Dr Victor Parsonnet Memorial Library, 201 Lyons Ave, 07112. SAN 310-3501. Tel: 973-926-7441. FAX: 973-923-4280. E-mail: nbimedlibrary@rwjbh.org. *Librn,* Laverne Davis
Founded 1900
Library Holdings: Bk Titles 2,000; Per Subs 150
Special Collections: Antique (Classic) Medical Books; Dr Aaron Parsonnet Coll, bks
Partic in Basic Health Sciences Library Network; Health Sci Libr Asn of NJ; LibraryLinkNJ, The New Jersey Library Cooperative; New Jersey Health Sciences Library Network; New Jersey Library Network
Open Mon-Fri 9-5
Restriction: Non-circulating to the pub

S NEWARK MUSEUM OF ART LIBRARY & ARCHIVES*, 49 Washington St, 07102-3176. SAN 310-3536. Tel: 973-596-6625. FAX: 973-642-0459. E-mail: wpeniston@newarkmuseumart.org. *Librn & Archivist,* William A Peniston; E-mail: wpeniston@newarkmuseum.org; Staff 1 (MLS 1)
Founded 1915
Library Holdings: AV Mats 1,500; DVDs 750; Electronic Media & Resources 4; Bk Titles 50,000; Bk Vols 60,000; Per Subs 50; Videos 750
Special Collections: History of the Newark Museum (Dana Coll); Tibet Coll
Subject Interests: African art, Am art, Asian art, Classical art, Decorative art, Natural sci, Numismatics
Wireless access
Partic in LibraryLinkNJ, The New Jersey Library Cooperative
Open Mon-Fri 9-5

P NEWARK PUBLIC LIBRARY*, Five Washington St, 07101. (Mail add: PO Box 630, 07101-0630), SAN 351-045X. Tel: 973-733-7784, 973-733-7800. Circulation Tel: 973-733-7791. Reference Tel: 973-733-7779. Administration Tel: 973-733-7758, 973-733-7780. FAX: 973-733-5648. E-mail: reference@npl.org. Web Site: www.npl.org. *Dir,* Joslyn Bowling Dixon; E-mail: director@npl.org; *Develop, Interim Asst Dir,* Kirsten Giardi; Tel: 973-424-1832, E-mail: kgiardi@npl.org; *Asst Dir, Finance & Develop,* Rodney Jefferson; Tel: 973-733-4842, E-mail: rjefferson@npl.org; *Asst Dir, Human Res, Security & Phys Plant,* Leslie Colson; Tel: 973-733-7740, E-mail: lcolson@npl.org; Staff 37 (MLS 34, Non-MLS 3)
Founded 1888. Pop 277,140; Circ 297,207
Library Holdings: AV Mats 26,351; Bks on Deafness & Sign Lang 1,208; CDs 11,092; DVDs 14,221; Electronic Media & Resources 8,211; High Interest/Low Vocabulary Bk Vols 347; Large Print Bks 1,838; Music Scores 15,879; Bk Titles 720,264; Bk Vols 1,736,140; Per Subs 1,295; Talking Bks 1,297; Videos 8,760
Special Collections: Allen Fine Prints from Puerto Rico; Art (Pictures, Prints & Popular Sheet Music); Artists Books; Autographs; Bookplates; Bruce Rogers Books & Files; Childrens Books 18th, 19th & Early 20th Century (Wilbur Macy Stone Coll); Christmas Cards; Fine Printing (R C Jenkins Coll); Historic Greeting Cards; Historic Posters; Illustrated Books; Incunabula; Japanese Ehon Coll; John Tasker Howard Music Archive; McEwen Christmas Coll; Medieval Manuscripts; New Jersey Rare Books; Newark Evening News Morgue; Original Fine Prints; Postcard Sets; Puerto Rican Reference Coll; Rabin & Kreuger Archives; Shopping Bags; The Jenkinson Coll; US Patent Coll; William Macy Stone Childrens Book Coll. Municipal Document Depository; State Document Depository; US Document Depository
Subject Interests: Art, Bus, Music, Patents

Automation Activity & Vendor Info: (Acquisitions) Innovative Interfaces, Inc; (Cataloging) Innovative Interfaces, Inc; (Circulation) Innovative Interfaces, Inc; (ILL) Innovative Interfaces, Inc; (OPAC) Innovative Interfaces, Inc; (Serials) Innovative Interfaces, Inc
Wireless access
Function: Adult literacy prog, Archival coll, Art exhibits, Bilingual assistance for Spanish patrons, Bks on CD, Bus archives, CD-ROM, Children's prog, Citizenship assistance, Computer training, Computers for patron use, E-Reserves, Electronic databases & coll, Family literacy, Free DVD rentals, Games & aids for people with disabilities, Govt ref serv, Health sci info serv, Holiday prog, Homework prog, ILL available, Instruction & testing, Internet access, Learning ctr, Magnifiers for reading, Mail & tel request accepted, Music CDs, Online ref, Orientations, Outside serv via phone, mail, e-mail & web, Photocopying/Printing, Preschool outreach, Prog for adults, Prog for children & young adult, Ref & res, Ref serv available, Res libr, Scanner, Senior computer classes, Serves people with intellectual disabilities, Spoken cassettes & CDs, Spoken cassettes & DVDs, Summer reading prog, Tax forms, Telephone ref, VHS videos, Wheelchair accessible, Workshops
Publications: A History of Fine Printing: A Special Collection in the Newark Public Library (Research guide); Black America on Stage. The Newark Public Library. 1993 (Research guide); Exposition Retrospective DeLorenzo Homar (Research guide); Hidden Treasures: Japanese Art From the Newark Public Library. The Newark Public Library. 1991 (Research guide); Homar: An Exhibition in Appreciation of Lorenzo Homar & His Graphic Works 1954-1994. Newark Public Library, 1994 (Research guide); Lasting Impressions: Greater Newark's Jewish Legacy (Research guide); Second Century (Newsletter); The Graphic Proof (Research guide); The Magic World of the Illustrated Book (College Journal) (Research guide); The Richard C Jenkinson Collection of Books: Chosen to Show the Work of the Best Printers Vol 1 (1925) & 2 (1929); Merrymount Presse (Research guide); The Story of Saga (Research guide)
Partic in LibraryLinkNJ, The New Jersey Library Cooperative; Proquest Dialog; Wilsonline
Special Services for the Deaf - Adult & family literacy prog; Assistive tech; Bks on deafness & sign lang; Deaf publ; High interest/low vocabulary bks; Interpreter on staff; Sign lang interpreter upon request for prog; Staff with knowledge of sign lang; Video & TTY relay via computer
Special Services for the Blind - Computer with voice synthesizer for visually impaired persons; Large print bks; Large screen computer & software; PC for people with disabilities; Ref serv; Spec prog; Talking bks
Open Mon, Tues & Thurs-Sat 9-5:30, Wed 9-8:30
Restriction: Non-resident fee
Friends of the Library Group
Branches: 8
BRANCH BROOK, 235 Clifton Ave, 07104. Tel: 973-733-7760. *Br Mgr,* Isabel Castro; E-mail: icastro@npl.org; Staff 6 (MLS 2, Non-MLS 4)
Circ 14,931
Library Holdings: Bk Titles 25,000; Per Subs 40
Open Tues, Thurs & Fri 9:30-5:30, Wed 1-8, Sat 11-3
Friends of the Library Group
CLINTON, 739 Bergen St, 07108, SAN 351-0514. Tel: 973-733-7757. *Br Mgr,* Paul Volpe; E-mail: pvolpe@npl.org; Staff 5 (MLS 2, Non-MLS 3)
Pop 18,693
Library Holdings: Bk Vols 39,896; Per Subs 40
Function: Children's prog, Computers for patron use, Electronic databases & coll, Holiday prog, Online cat, Online ref, Photocopying/Printing, Preschool outreach, Prog for children & young adult, Ref serv available, Story hour, Tax forms, Telephone ref
Open Tues, Thurs & Fri 9:30-5:30, Wed 1-8, Sat 11-3
Friends of the Library Group
NORTH END, 722 Summer Ave, 07104, SAN 351-0549. Tel: 973-733-7766. *Br Mgr,* Paula Baratta; E-mail: pbaratta@npl.org; Staff 5 (MLS 1, Non-MLS 4)
Library Holdings: Bk Vols 31,185; Per Subs 69
Function: Homebound delivery serv, ILL available, Large print keyboards, Photocopying/Printing, Prog for adults, Prog for children & young adult, Ref serv available, Summer reading prog, Telephone ref, Wheelchair accessible
Open Tues, Thurs & Fri 9:30-5:30, Wed 1-8, Sat 11-3
Friends of the Library Group
ROSEVILLE, 99 Fifth St, 07107, SAN 351-0573. Tel: 973-733-7770. *Br Mgr,* Position Currently Open
Library Holdings: Bk Vols 19,057; Per Subs 63
Function: ILL available, Large print keyboards, Photocopying/Printing, Prog for children & young adult, Ref serv available, Summer reading prog, Telephone ref
Temporarily closed Summer 2020-
Friends of the Library Group
SPRINGFIELD, 50 Hayes St, 07103, SAN 351-0603. Tel: 973-733-7736. *Br Mgr,* Sharon Owens; E-mail: sowens@npl.org; Staff 5 (Non-MLS 5)
Library Holdings: Bk Vols 33,866; Per Subs 70
Function: ILL available, Large print keyboards, Photocopying/Printing, Prog for adults, Prog for children & young adult, Ref serv available, Summer reading prog, Telephone ref, Wheelchair accessible
Open Tues, Thurs & Fri 9:30-5:30, Wed 1-8, Sat 11-3
Friends of the Library Group
VAILSBURG, 75 Alexander St, 07106, SAN 351-0638. Tel: 973-733-7755. *Br Mgr,* Mabel Williams; E-mail: mwilliams@npl.org; Staff 5 (MLS 2, Non-MLS 3)
Library Holdings: Bk Vols 33,866; Per Subs 66
Function: Homebound delivery serv, ILL available, Large print keyboards, Photocopying/Printing, Prog for adults, Prog for children & young adult, Ref serv available, Summer reading prog, Telephone ref, Wheelchair accessible
Open Tues, Thurs & Fri 9:30-5:30, Wed 1-8, Sat 11-3
Friends of the Library Group
VAN BUREN, 140 Van Buren St, 07105, SAN 351-0662. Tel: 973-733-7750. *Br Mgr,* Susan Lazarri; E-mail: slazarri@npl.org; Staff 5 (MLS 1, Non-MLS 4)
Library Holdings: Bk Vols 37,474; Per Subs 30
Function: ILL available, Large print keyboards, Prog for children & young adult, Ref serv available, Summer reading prog, Telephone ref, Wheelchair accessible
Open Tues, Thurs & Fri 9:30-5:30, Wed 1-8, Sat 11-3
Friends of the Library Group
WEEQUAHIC, 355 Osborne Terrace, 07112, SAN 351-0697. Tel: 973-733-7751. *Br Mgr,* Shileen Shaw; E-mail: sshaw@npl.org; Staff 4 (MLS 2, Non-MLS 2)
Library Holdings: Bk Vols 27,552; Per Subs 57
Function: ILL available, Large print keyboards, Photocopying/Printing, Prog for adults, Prog for children & young adult, Ref serv available, Summer reading prog, Telephone ref, Wheelchair accessible
Open Tues, Thurs & Fri 9:30-5:30, Wed 1-8, Sat 11-3
Friends of the Library Group

S NORTHERN STATE PRISON LIBRARY*, 168 Frontage Rd, 07114-3794. (Mail add: PO Box 2300, 07114-0300), SAN 371-5574. Tel: 973-465-0068, Ext 4521. FAX: 973-578-4393. *Librn,* Gail Gillespie; E-mail: gail.gillespie@doc.nj.gov; Staff 1 (MLS 1)
Founded 1987
Library Holdings: Bks on Deafness & Sign Lang 3; Bk Titles 4,000; Bk Vols 4,200; Per Subs 1
Partic in LibraryLinkNJ, The New Jersey Library Cooperative
Special Services for the Blind - Talking bks
Open Mon, Tues & Fri 8-10, 1-3 & 5:30-7, Wed & Thurs 8-10 & 1-3

L PRUDENTIAL FINANCIAL*, Prudential Insurance Law Library, Three Gateway Ctr, NJ -05-03-15, 100 Mulberry St, 07102. SAN 351-0751. Tel: 973-367-3175. FAX: 973-802-2298. E-mail: jbizub@prudential.com. Web Site: www.prudential.com. *Dir, Libr Serv,* Johanna C Bizub; Tel: 973-367-3175, E-mail: jbizub@prudential.com; *Knowledge Mgr, Res Assoc,* Latoya Rosario; Tel: 973-802-5289, E-mail: latyoa.rosario@prudential.com; Staff 5 (MLS 2, Non-MLS 3)
Library Holdings: Bk Titles 1,000; Bk Vols 7,500; Per Subs 100
Subject Interests: Ins, Law, Real estate, Securities
Restriction: Staff use only

RUTGERS UNIVERSITY LIBRARIES
C JOHN COTTON DANA LIBRARY*, 185 University Ave, 07102, SAN 351-0786. Tel: 973-353-5222. Circulation Tel: 973-353-5161. Interlibrary Loan Service Tel: 973-353-5902. Reference Tel: 973-353-5901. FAX: 973-353-5257. Web Site: www.libraries.rutgers.edu/dana. *Dir,* Consuella Askew; E-mail: consuella.askew@rutgers.edu; *Head, Pub Serv,* Natalie Borisovets; E-mail: natalieb@libraries.rutgers.edu; *Bus Librn, Information Literacy Coord,* Roberta Tipton; E-mail: tipton@libraries.rutgers.edu; Staff 37 (MLS 10, Non-MLS 27)
Founded 1927. Enrl 10,000; Fac 500; Highest Degree: Doctorate
Library Holdings: AV Mats 39,207; Bk Vols 346,393; Per Subs 3,223
Special Collections: State Document Depository; US Document Depository
Subject Interests: Bus, Nursing
Automation Activity & Vendor Info: (Circulation) SirsiDynix
Partic in Association of Research Libraries; Metropolitan New York Library Council; Proquest Dialog; Research Libraries Information Network; SDC
Publications: Library Guide Series, Library News Release
Open Mon-Thurs 8am-10pm, Fri 8-5, Sat 10-6
CL DON M GOTTFREDSON LIBRARY OF CRIMINAL JUSTICE*, 123 Washington St, Ste 350, 07102-3094, SAN 327-9499. Tel: 973-353-3118. FAX: 973-353-1275. Web Site: www.libraries.rutgers.edu/rul/libs/crim_just/crim_just.shtml. *Librn,* Phyllis Schultze; E-mail: pschultz@andromeda.rutgers.edu; Staff 1 (MLS 1)
Function: ILL available
Partic in Association of Research Libraries
Publications: Acquisitions List (Bimonthly)
Open Mon-Thurs 9am-10pm, Fri 9-5, Sat & Sun 12-5
Friends of the Library Group

C INSTITUTE OF JAZZ STUDIES*, John Cotton Dana Library, 185 University Ave, 4th Flr, 07102, SAN 351-0808. Tel: 973-353-5595. FAX: 973-353-5944. Web Site: www.libraries.rutgers.edu/jazz. *Exec Dir,* Wayne Winborne; Tel: 973-353-3796, E-mail: wayne.winborne@rutgers.edu; *Head, Archival Colls & Servs,* Adriana Cuervo; E-mail: adriana.cuervo@rutgers.edu
Founded 1952
Library Holdings: CDs 100,000; Bk Vols 10,000; Per Subs 150
Special Collections: Jazz Archive Coll; Memorabilia; Realia. Oral History
Subject Interests: Jazz
Publications: Annual Review of Jazz Studies; Studies in Jazz
Open Mon-Fri 9-5
Restriction: Non-circulating

CL RUTGERS UNIVERSITY LIBRARY FOR THE CENTER FOR LAW & JUSTICE*, 123 Washington St, 07102-3094. SAN 351-0816. Tel: 973-353-3121. FAX: 973-353-1574. Web Site: www.newark.rutgers.edu/center-law-justice-building-access. *Assoc Dean, Info Tech,* Wei Fang; Tel: 973-353-3061, E-mail: wfang@law.rutgers.edu; *Dep Dir,* Paul Axel-Lute; *Assoc Dir,* Caroline Young; Tel: 973-353-3151, E-mail: caroline.young@rutgers.edu; *Head, User Serv,* Lee Sims; *Ref Librn,* Marjorie E Crawford; Tel: 973-353-3144, E-mail: mcrawfrd@law.rutgers.edu; *Ref Librn,* Dennis Kim-Prieto; Tel: 973-353-3037; *Govt Doc Librn,* Susan Lyons; Staff 18 (MLS 9, Non-MLS 9)
Library Holdings: Bk Vols 381,000
Special Collections: Law Library of US Supreme Court Justice Bradley. State Document Depository; US Document Depository
Automation Activity & Vendor Info: (Acquisitions) Innovative Interfaces, Inc; (Cataloging) Innovative Interfaces, Inc; (Circulation) Innovative Interfaces, Inc; (OPAC) Innovative Interfaces, Inc; (Serials) Innovative Interfaces, Inc
Wireless access
Partic in OCLC Online Computer Library Center, Inc
Friends of the Library Group

CL SETON HALL UNIVERSITY SCHOOL OF LAW*, Peter W Rodino Jr Law Library, One Newark Ctr, 07102. SAN 310-3579. Circulation Tel: 973-642-8720. Reference Tel: 973-642-8861. Administration Tel: 973-642-8773. Administration FAX: 973-642-8748. Web Site: law.shu.edu. *Assoc Prof of Law, Dir, Law Libr,* Deborah Schander; Tel: 973-642-8773, E-mail: deborah.schander@shu.edu; *Assoc Prof, Head, Pub Serv,* Brittany Persson; Tel: 973-642-8767, E-mail: brittany.persson@shu.edu; *Assoc Dir, Digital Serv, Libr Tech,* Kristina Anderson; Tel: 973-642-8764; *Archivist, Govt Doc Librn, ILL & Ser,* Dianne Oster; Tel: 973-642-8195, E-mail: Dianne.Oster@shu.edu; *Fac Serv Librn,* Position Currently Open; Staff 11 (MLS 5, Non-MLS 6)
Founded 1950. Enrl 650; Fac 65; Highest Degree: Doctorate
Library Holdings: Bk Titles 463,572; Bk Vols 458,682
Special Collections: Rodino Archives. State Document Depository; US Document Depository
Subject Interests: Law, Policy, Res, Sci, Soc justice, Tech
Automation Activity & Vendor Info: (Acquisitions) OCLC Worldshare Management Services; (Cataloging) OCLC Worldshare Management Services; (Circulation) OCLC Worldshare Management Services; (ILL) OCLC Worldshare Management Services; (OPAC) OCLC Worldshare Management Services; (Serials) OCLC Worldshare Management Services
Wireless access
Partic in NELLCO Law Library Consortium, Inc.
Open Mon-Fri 8-6, Sat 9-5, Sun 12-7
Restriction: Restricted access

GL UNITED STATES ATTORNEY'S OFFICE LIBRARY, 970 Broad St, Rm 700, 07102. SAN 310-3595. Tel: 973-645-2851. FAX: 973-297-2007. *Librn,* Sam Li; E-mail: sam.li@us.doj.gov; Staff 4 (MLS 2, Non-MLS 2)
Library Holdings: Bk Vols 6,000
Restriction: Not open to pub
Branches:
NORTH BRANCH, 970 Broad St, Ste 700, 07102, SAN 321-4982. Tel: 973-645-2709. *Law Librn,* Sam Li
Library Holdings: Bk Vols 4,000
Restriction: Not open to pub
TRENTON BRANCH, 402 E State St, Trenton, 08608, SAN 321-4990. Tel: 973-645-2709. *Law Librn,* Sam Li
Library Holdings: Bk Vols 5,216
Restriction: Not open to pub

GL UNITED STATES COURT OF APPEALS, United States Court Library, King Courthouse, Rm 5007, 50 Walnut St, 07102. (Mail add: PO Box 1068, 07101-1068), SAN 325-7762. Tel: 973-645-3034. *Librn,* Nicole Peaks; E-mail: nicole_peaks@ca3.uscourts.gov; Staff 2 (MLS 1, Non-MLS 1)
Library Holdings: Bk Vols 18,000; Spec Interest Per Sub 15
Subject Interests: Law
Automation Activity & Vendor Info: (Acquisitions) SirsiDynix; (Cataloging) OCLC; (Circulation) SirsiDynix; (OPAC) SirsiDynix; (Serials) SirsiDynix
Open Mon-Fri 8:30-4:30
Restriction: Circulates for staff only

NEWTON

J SUSSEX COUNTY COMMUNITY COLLEGE LIBRARY*, One College Hill Rd, 07860. SAN 375-7439. Tel: 973-300-2162. Reference Tel: 973-300-2292. Administration Tel: 973-300-2161. Web Site: sussex.edu/library. *Dir,* Stephanie Cooper; E-mail: scooper@sussex.edu; *Asst to the Dir,* Lauren Jessop; E-mail: ljessop@sussex.edu; Staff 3 (MLS 3)
Founded 1989. Enrl 4,008; Fac 51; Highest Degree: Associate
Library Holdings: Bks on Deafness & Sign Lang 51; CDs 35; DVDs 22; Electronic Media & Resources 16; High Interest/Low Vocabulary Bk Vols 48; Bk Titles 36,000; Per Subs 175; Spec Interest Per Sub 145; Videos 100
Subject Interests: Juv, Law
Automation Activity & Vendor Info: (Acquisitions) SirsiDynix; (Cataloging) SirsiDynix; (Circulation) SirsiDynix; (Course Reserve) SirsiDynix; (ILL) OCLC; (OPAC) SirsiDynix
Wireless access
Function: Archival coll, Audio & video playback equip for onsite use, Computers for patron use, Electronic databases & coll, ILL available, Magnifiers for reading, Online cat, Orientations, Outside serv via phone, mail, e-mail & web, Photocopying/Printing, Wheelchair accessible
Partic in LibraryLinkNJ, The New Jersey Library Cooperative; LYRASIS; Virtual Academic Library Environment
Special Services for the Deaf - Bks on deafness & sign lang; Staff with knowledge of sign lang
Special Services for the Blind - Assistive/Adapted tech devices, equip & products; Bks on CD
Open Mon 9-6, Tues-Thurs 9-7, Fri 9-5
Restriction: Non-circulating to the pub, Open to students, fac & staff

S SUSSEX COUNTY HISTORICAL SOCIETY LIBRARY*, 82 Main St, 07860-2046. (Mail add: PO Box 913, 07860), SAN 328-1868. Tel: 973-383-6010. FAX: 973-383-6010. E-mail: sussexcountyhs@gmail.com. Web Site: www.sussexcountyhistory.org. *Library Contact,* Myra Snook
Library Holdings: Bk Titles 1,200
Wireless access
Function: Ref & res, Ref serv available, Res libr
Restriction: Mem only, Non-circulating

L SUSSEX COUNTY LAW LIBRARY*, 4347 High St, 07860. SAN 327-9456. Tel: 973-579-0702. FAX: 973-579-0679. *Head Librn,* Joe Tuttle
Library Holdings: Bk Titles 1,000
Open Mon-Fri 8:30-4:30
Friends of the Library Group

P SUSSEX COUNTY LIBRARY SYSTEM*, 125 Morris Tpk, 07860. SAN 351-0905. Tel: 973-948-3660. FAX: 973-948-2071. Web Site: www.sussexcountylibrary.org. *Libr Dir,* Will Porter; E-mail: wporter@sussexcountylibrary.org; *Chief Librn,* Ellen Callanan; E-mail: callanan@sussexcountylibrary.org; *Head, Tech Serv,* Tim Thacker; E-mail: timtcat@sussexcountylibrary.org; Staff 62 (MLS 9, Non-MLS 53)
Founded 1942. Pop 119,416; Circ 616,201
Library Holdings: Bk Titles 146,307; Per Subs 450
Special Collections: Delaware Water Gap National Recreation Area (Tocks Island Regional Advisory Council Library); Sussex County History Coll. State Document Depository; US Document Depository
Automation Activity & Vendor Info: (Circulation) Horizon
Wireless access
Partic in LibraryLinkNJ, The New Jersey Library Cooperative
Open Mon-Wed 8:30-8:30, Thurs & Fri 8:30-5, Sat 9-5
Branches: 5
E LOUISE CHILDS MEMORIAL, 21 Stanhope Sparta Rd, Stanhope, 07874, SAN 351-1022. Tel: 973-770-1000. FAX: 973-770-0094. *Br Librn,* Regina Bohn; E-mail: rbohn@sussexcountylibrary.org
Open Mon & Wed-Fri 9-5, Tues 12-8, Sat 9-1
DENNIS MEMORIAL, 101 Main St, 07860, SAN 351-0964. Tel: 973-383-4810. FAX: 973-383-1322. *Librn,* Jacqueline Oregero; E-mail: joregero@sussexcountylibrary.org
Open Mon 12-8, Tues-Fri 9-5
FRANKLIN BRANCH, 103 Main St, Franklin, 07416, SAN 351-0999. Tel: 973-827-6555. FAX: 973-827-9422. *Br Librn,* Jess Lester; E-mail: jlester@sussexcountylibrary.org; Staff 1 (MLS 1)
Open Mon-Wed & Fri 9-5, Thurs 12-8
DOROTHY E HENRY MEMORIAL, 66 Rte 94, Vernon, 07462, SAN 351-1081. Tel: 973-827-8095. FAX: 973-827-8664. *Br Librn,* Jerry Galante; E-mail: jgalante@sussexcountylibrary.org
Open Mon & Wed-Sat 9-5, Tues 12-8
Friends of the Library Group

SUSSEX-WANTAGE, 69 Rte 639, Wantage, 07461, SAN 351-1057. Tel: 973-875-3940. FAX: 973-875-1336. *Br Librn,* Sara Branagan; E-mail: sbranagan@sussexcountylibrary.org; Staff 1 (MLS 1)
Open Mon, Tues & Thurs-Sat 9-5, Wed 12-8
Friends of the Library Group

NORTH ARLINGTON

P NORTH ARLINGTON FREE PUBLIC LIBRARY*, 210 Ridge Rd, 07031. SAN 310-3633. Tel: 201-955-5640. FAX: 201-991-7850. E-mail: noarcirc@bccls.org. Web Site: northarlington.bccls.org. *Dir,* Leo Bellino; E-mail: bellino@northarlington.bccls.org; Staff 6 (MLS 3, Non-MLS 3)
Founded 1939. Pop 15,000; Circ 70,000
Library Holdings: Bk Titles 90,000; Bk Vols 95,000; Per Subs 60; Talking Bks 700
Special Collections: New Jerseyana
Automation Activity & Vendor Info: (Cataloging) OCLC; (Circulation) SirsiDynix; (OPAC) SirsiDynix
Wireless access
Partic in Bergen County Cooperative Library System, Inc
Open Mon, Tues & Thurs 9:30-8:30, Wed & Fri 9:30-5, Sat 10-1
Friends of the Library Group

NORTH BERGEN

P NORTH BERGEN FREE PUBLIC LIBRARY*, 8411 Bergenline Ave, 07047. SAN 351-1111. Tel: 201-869-4715. FAX: 201-868-0968. Web Site: www.nbpl.org. *Dir,* Mrs Sai Rao; E-mail: srao@nbpl.org; Staff 26 (MLS 6, Non-MLS 20)
Founded 1936. Pop 58,092; Circ 101,000
Library Holdings: Bk Titles 161,000; Bk Vols 166,000; Per Subs 226
Special Collections: Foreign Language Coll; Large Print Coll; Literature Coll; New Jerseyiana
Automation Activity & Vendor Info: (Cataloging) SirsiDynix; (Circulation) SirsiDynix; (OPAC) SirsiDynix
Wireless access
Partic in Bergen County Cooperative Library System, Inc; LibraryLinkNJ, The New Jersey Library Cooperative
Open Mon-Thurs 9-8, Fri & Sat 9-5
Branches: 1
KENNEDY BRANCH, 2123 Kennedy Blvd, 07047. Tel: 201-869-4715, Ext 6. *Librn,* Laura Raios
Open Mon-Thurs 9-8, Fri & Sat 9-5

NORTH BRUNSWICK

S MIDDLESEX COUNTY ADULT CORRECTION CENTER LIBRARY*, Apple Orchard Lane, Rte 130, 08902. (Mail add: PO Box 266, New Brunswick, 08903-0266). Tel: 732-297-3636, Ext 6224. *Librn,* Scott Greenberg
Library Holdings: Bk Vols 25,000
Restriction: Internal circ only, Not open to pub

P NORTH BRUNSWICK FREE PUBLIC LIBRARY*, 880 Hermann Rd, 08902. SAN 310-3668. Tel: 732-246-3545. FAX: 732-246-1341. E-mail: refdesk@northbrunswicklibrary.org. Web Site: www.northbrunswicklibrary.org. *Libr Dir,* Zoltan L Braz, Jr; E-mail: zbraz@northbrunswicklibrary.org; *Ad,* Adriana Bernstein; *Ad,* Barbara Elieff; *Ch,* Anna Shifton; *IT Librn,* Monica Shine; *YA Librn,* Andrew Gerber; Staff 23 (MLS 9, Non-MLS 14)
Founded 1966. Pop 40,000; Circ 257,000
Library Holdings: Bk Vols 100,000; Per Subs 240
Special Collections: Chinese Language Coll; Gujarati Language Coll; Hindi Language Coll; Spanish Language Coll; Telugu Language Coll; Urdu Language Coll
Automation Activity & Vendor Info: (Acquisitions) SirsiDynix; (Circulation) SirsiDynix-iBistro; (OPAC) SirsiDynix
Wireless access
Function: 24/7 Electronic res, 24/7 Online cat, Adult bk club, Audiobks via web, Bk club(s), Bks on CD, Children's prog, Computer training, Computers for patron use, E-Readers, Electronic databases & coll, Free DVD rentals, Homebound delivery serv, ILL available, Internet access, Magazines, Mail & tel request accepted, Mango lang, Museum passes, Music CDs, Notary serv, Online cat, Outreach serv, OverDrive digital audio bks, Photocopying/Printing, Printer for laptops & handheld devices, Prog for adults, Prog for children & young adult, Ref & res, Ref serv available, Res assist avail, Scanner, Senior outreach, Spanish lang bks, STEM programs, Study rm, Summer reading prog, Tax forms, Telephone ref, Wheelchair accessible
Partic in Libraries of Middlesex Automation Consortium
Open Mon-Thurs 10-9, Fri & Sat 10-5, Sun 12-5
Friends of the Library Group

NORTH HALEDON

P NORTH HALEDON FREE PUBLIC LIBRARY*, 129 Overlook Ave, 07508-2533. SAN 310-3676. Tel: 973-427-6213. FAX: 973-427-1826. Web Site: www.northhaledonlibrary.org. *Dir,* Susan Serico; E-mail: serico@northhaledonlibrary.org; Staff 1 (MLS 1)
Founded 1929. Pop 7,920; Circ 66,972
Library Holdings: AV Mats 1,210; CDs 2,178; DVDs 2,673; e-books 1,526; Bk Vols 26,341; Per Subs 71
Automation Activity & Vendor Info: (Cataloging) SirsiDynix; (Circulation) SirsiDynix; (OPAC) SirsiDynix
Wireless access
Partic in LibraryLinkNJ, The New Jersey Library Cooperative; PALS Plus, The Computer Consortium of Passaic County Libraries
Open Mon-Thurs 9-9, Fri & Sat 9-5
Friends of the Library Group

NORTHFIELD

P OTTO BRUYNS PUBLIC LIBRARY OF NORTHFIELD, 241 W Mill Rd, 08225. SAN 310-3684. Tel: 609-646-4476. Web Site: www.nflibrary.org. *Dir,* Aubrey Hiers; E-mail: ahiers@nflibrary.org; Staff 1 (Non-MLS 1)
Founded 1926. Pop 7,875; Circ 37,082
Library Holdings: Bk Vols 29,000; Per Subs 76
Special Collections: History of Northfield, monographs
Automation Activity & Vendor Info: (Cataloging) Follett Software; (Circulation) Follett Software; (OPAC) Follett Software
Wireless access
Partic in Coalition of Independent Libraries
Open Mon-Thurs 10-8, Fri & Sat 10-5
Friends of the Library Group

NORWOOD

P NORWOOD PUBLIC LIBRARY, 198 Summit St, 07648. SAN 310-3722. Tel: 201-768-9555. E-mail: nowdcirc@bccls.org. Web Site: nplnj.org. *Libr Dir,* Liz Fried; *Ch Serv,* Kena Kyqykalyu
Founded 1938. Pop 4,600; Circ 14,035
Library Holdings: Bk Titles 37,000; Per Subs 65
Automation Activity & Vendor Info: (Cataloging) Innovative Interfaces, Inc; (Circulation) Innovative Interfaces, Inc; (OPAC) Innovative Interfaces, Inc
Wireless access
Partic in Bergen County Cooperative Library System, Inc
Special Services for the Blind - Magnifiers
Open Mon, Wed & Fri 10-4, Tues & Thurs 12-6
Friends of the Library Group

NUTLEY

P NUTLEY FREE PUBLIC LIBRARY*, 93 Booth Dr, 07110. SAN 310-3749. Tel: 973-667-0405. E-mail: library@nutleynj.org. Web Site: nutleypubliclibrary.org. *Dir,* Maria LaBadia; E-mail: labadia@nutley.bccls.org; Staff 11 (MLS 6, Non-MLS 5)
Founded 1913. Pop 27,362; Circ 141,737
Library Holdings: CDs 2,951; DVDs 2,821; Bk Vols 86,208; Per Subs 215; Talking Bks 2,793
Special Collections: Harry W Chenoweth Interviews; Nutley Sun & Nutley Journal (online access & micro)
Subject Interests: Local hist
Automation Activity & Vendor Info: (Cataloging) SirsiDynix-Unicorn; (Circulation) SirsiDynix-WorkFlows; (ILL) SirsiDynix-Unicorn; (OPAC) SirsiDynix-Unicorn
Wireless access
Function: Adult bk club, Art exhibits, Audio & video playback equip for onsite use, Audiobks via web, Bilingual assistance for Spanish patrons, Bk club(s), Bks on CD, CD-ROM, Chess club, Children's prog, Computer training, Computers for patron use, E-Reserves, Electronic databases & coll, Holiday prog, Homebound delivery serv, ILL available, Internet access, Literacy & newcomer serv, Magnifiers for reading, Mail & tel request accepted, Museum passes, Music CDs, Online cat, Online ref, Outreach serv, Photocopying/Printing, Preschool outreach, Prog for adults, Prog for children & young adult, Ref serv available, Senior outreach, Story hour, Summer reading prog, Tax forms, Teen prog, Telephone ref, Wheelchair accessible, Writing prog
Partic in Bergen County Cooperative Library System, Inc; LibraryLinkNJ, The New Jersey Library Cooperative
Special Services for the Blind - Audio mat; Large print bks
Open Mon, Tues & Thurs 9-9, Wed, Fri & Sat 9-5
Friends of the Library Group

CM SETON HALL UNIVERSITY LIBRARIES*, Interprofessional Health Sciences Library, 340 Kingsland St, 07110. E-mail: ihslibrary@shu.edu. Web Site: library.shu.edu/ihs. *Assoc Dean & Dir,* Chris Duffy; Tel: 973-275-2787, E-mail: christopher.duffy1@shu.edu; *Health Sci Librn,* Andy Hickner; Tel: 973-542-6973, E-mail: andrew.hickner@shu.edu; *Libr*

Asst, Denise D'Agostino; Tel: 973-542-6969, E-mail: denise.agostino@shu.edu
Restriction: Not open to pub

OAK RIDGE

M AMERICAN RHINOLOGIC SOCIETY LIBRARY*, PO Box 269, 07438. SAN 376-1835. Tel: 973-545-2735. FAX: 973-545-2736. Web Site: www.american-rhinologic.org. *Exec Adminir,* Wendi Perez; E-mail: Wendi@american-rhinologic.org
Library Holdings: Bk Vols 500

P JEFFERSON TOWNSHIP PUBLIC LIBRARY*, 1031 Weldon Rd, 07438. SAN 320-2046. Tel: 973-208-6244. FAX: 973-697-7051. E-mail: jtpl@jeffersonlibrary.net. Web Site: www.jeffersonlibrary.net. *Dir,* Seth Stephens; Tel: 973-208-6244, Ext 207, E-mail: seth.stephens@jeffersonlibrary.net; *Asst Dir,* Sandy Cale; Tel: 973-208-6244, Ext 204, E-mail: sandy.cale@jeffersonlibrary.net; Staff 8 (MLS 1, Non-MLS 7)
Founded 1960. Pop 20,000
Library Holdings: Bk Titles 52,000; Per Subs 97
Automation Activity & Vendor Info: (Cataloging) SirsiDynix; (Circulation) SirsiDynix; (OPAC) SirsiDynix
Wireless access
Publications: Violet's Porch (Newsletter)
Partic in Morris Automated Information Network
Open Mon-Fri 9:30-9, Sat 9:30-6, Sun 1-5
Friends of the Library Group

OAKLAND

P OAKLAND PUBLIC LIBRARY*, Two Municipal Plaza, 07436. SAN 310-3773. Tel: 201-337-3742. Circulation E-mail: oaklcirc@bccls.org. Web Site: www.oaklandnjlibrary.org. *Dir,* Peter Havel; Tel: 201-337-3742, Ext 7100, E-mail: havel@oakland.bccls.org; Staff 16 (MLS 3, Non-MLS 13)
Founded 1910. Pop 11,997; Circ 95,029
Library Holdings: Bk Vols 60,500; Per Subs 180
Automation Activity & Vendor Info: (Cataloging) SirsiDynix; (Circulation) SirsiDynix; (OPAC) SirsiDynix
Wireless access
Special Services for the Blind - Magnifiers
Open Mon, Tues & Thurs 9:30-8, Wed, Fri & Sat 9:30-5
Friends of the Library Group

OAKLYN

P OAKLYN MEMORIAL LIBRARY*, 602 Newton Ave, 08107. SAN 310-3803. Tel: 856-858-8226. E-mail: oaklynmemlibrary@gmail.com. *Dir,* Andrea Cline; *Libr Asst,* Janet Larson; *Libr Asst,* Monica Rottler
Founded 1927. Pop 5,000; Circ 15,789
Library Holdings: Bk Titles 20,000; Bk Vols 25,000; Per Subs 38
Special Collections: Local History Coll; Popular Fiction Coll
Wireless access
Mem of Camden County Library System
Open Mon-Sat 10-2; Mon, Tues & Thurs (Summer) 3-7
Friends of the Library Group

OCEAN

S OCEAN TOWNSHIP HISTORICAL MUSEUM LIBRARY*, Eden Woolley House, 703 Deal Rd, 07712. (Mail add: PO Box 516, Oakhurst, 07755), SAN 377-5011. Tel: 732-531-2136. E-mail: oceanmuseum@yahoo.com. Web Site: www.oceanmuseum.org/LIBRARY.html. *Pres,* Paul Edelson; E-mail: pgedelson@aol.com
Library Holdings: Bk Vols 250
Special Collections: Oral History
Wireless access
Open Tues-Thurs 1-4

OCEAN CITY

P OCEAN CITY FREE PUBLIC LIBRARY*, 1735 Simpson Ave, Ste 4, 08226. SAN 310-382X. Tel: 609-399-2434. Circulation Tel: 609-399-2434, Ext 5221. Interlibrary Loan Service Tel: 609-399-2434, Ext 5229. Reference Tel: 609-399-2434, Ext 5231. Administration Tel: 609-399-2434, Ext 5238. Information Services Tel: 609-399-2434, Ext 5240. FAX: 609-398-0751. Web Site: www.oceancitylibrary.org. *Dir,* Karen Mahar; E-mail: director@oceancitylibrary.org; *Asst Libr Dir, Ch Serv,* Leslie Clarke; Tel: 609-399-2434, Ext 5241, E-mail: leslie@oceancitylibrary.org; *Head, Circ,* Jackie Leeds; E-mail: jackie@oceancitylibrary.org; *Adult Programming, Librn,* Julie Howard; Tel: 609-399-2434, Ext 5222, E-mail: jhoward@oceancitylibrary.org; *Ad, Circ/Acq,* Kathryn Brown; Tel: 609-399-2434, Ext 5223, E-mail: kathryn@oceancitylibrary.org; *Ref Serv Librn,* Kevin Bligh; Tel: 609-399-2434, Ext 5226, E-mail: kevin@oceancitylibrary.org; *YA Librn,* Sara Bruesehoff; Tel: 609-399-2434, Ext 5235, E-mail: sara@oceancitylibrary.org; *IT Serv,* John Ruban; E-mail: john@oceancitylibrary.org; Staff 43 (MLS 13, Non-MLS 30)
Pop 15,378; Circ 437,214
Library Holdings: Bk Vols 90,000; Per Subs 250
Subject Interests: Local hist
Automation Activity & Vendor Info: (Cataloging) Innovative Interfaces, Inc; (Circulation) Innovative Interfaces, Inc; (ILL) Innovative Interfaces, Inc; (OPAC) Innovative Interfaces, Inc
Wireless access
Function: 24/7 Electronic res, 24/7 Online cat, 3D Printer, Activity rm, Adult bk club, Adult literacy prog, After school storytime, Archival coll, Art exhibits, Art programs, Audio & video playback equip for onsite use, Audiobks on Playaways & MP3, Audiobks via web, AV serv, Bi-weekly Writer's Group, Bilingual assistance for Spanish patrons, Bk club(s), Bk reviews (Group), Bks on CD, Bus archives, Chess club, Children's prog, Citizenship assistance, Computer training, Computers for patron use, Digital talking bks, Doc delivery serv, E-Readers, E-Reserves, Electronic databases & coll, Family literacy, Genealogy discussion group, Holiday prog, Home delivery & serv to seniorr ctr & nursing homes, Homebound delivery serv, Homework prog, ILL available, Internet access, Jazz prog, Laminating, Life-long learning prog for all ages, Literacy & newcomer serv, Magazines, Magnifiers for reading, Mail & tel request accepted, Mail loans to mem, Mango lang, Meeting rooms, Movies, Museum passes, Music CDs, Online cat, Online info literacy tutorials on the web & in blackboard, Online ref, Outreach serv, OverDrive digital audio bks, Photocopying/Printing, Preschool outreach, Printer for laptops & handheld devices, Prog for adults, Prog for children & young adult, Ref & res, Ref serv available, Res assist avail, Scanner, Senior computer classes, Senior outreach, Spanish lang bks, Spoken cassettes & CDs, Spoken cassettes & DVDs, STEM programs, Story hour, Study rm, Summer & winter reading prog, Summer reading prog, Tax forms, Teen prog, Telephone ref, Wheelchair accessible, Winter reading prog, Workshops, Writing prog
Partic in Coalition of Independent Libraries; LibraryLinkNJ, The New Jersey Library Cooperative
Open Mon-Fri 9-9, Sat 9-5, Sun 11-5
Friends of the Library Group
Bookmobiles: 1. Asst Libr Dir, Leslie Clarke

S OCEAN CITY HISTORICAL MUSEUM*, Research Library, 1735 Simpson Ave, Ste #3, 08226. SAN 373-2533. Tel: 609-399-1801. FAX: 609-399-0544. E-mail: info@ocnjmuseum.org. Web Site: ocnjmuseum.org. *Dir,* Position Currently Open
Founded 1964
Library Holdings: Bk Vols 500; Per Subs 10
Subject Interests: Local hist
Function: Res libr
Open Mon-Sat 10-4

OCEAN GROVE

S HISTORICAL SOCIETY OF OCEAN GROVE*, Museums, Archives & Library, 50 Pitman Ave, 07756. (Mail add: PO Box 446, 07756), SAN 329-2991. Tel: 732-774-1869. FAX: 732-774-1685. E-mail: info@oceangrovehistory.org. Web Site: oceangrovehistory.org. *Board Pres,* Sam Olshan; Staff 2 (MLS 1, Non-MLS 1)
Founded 1970
Library Holdings: Bk Vols 250
Subject Interests: Local hist, Victorian-era hist
Wireless access
Publications: Bibliographies; Newsletters

OLD BRIDGE

P OLD BRIDGE PUBLIC LIBRARY*, One Old Bridge Plaza, 08857-2498. SAN 351-1235. Tel: 732-721-5600, Ext 5010. Administration Tel: 732-721-5600, Ext 5016. FAX: 732-607-4816. Web Site: www.oldbridgelibrary.org. *Dir,* Nancy Cohen; Tel: 732-721-5600, Ext 5042, E-mail: ncohen@oldbridgelibrary.org; *Adult Serv, Info Serv,* Nicole Dematteo; Tel: 732-721-5600, Ext 5030, E-mail: ndematteo@oldbridgelibrary.org; *Circ,* Felisha McEachern; Tel: 732-721-5600, Ext 5012, E-mail: fmceachern@oldbridgelibrary.org; *ILL,* Amy Trombetta; Tel: 732-721-5600, Ext 5033, E-mail: amygt@oldbridgelibrary.org; Staff 15 (MLS 15)
Founded 1970. Pop 60,456; Circ 345,000
Library Holdings: AV Mats 10,208; Bk Titles 131,717; Bk Vols 169,843; Per Subs 538; Talking Bks 6,900
Special Collections: Gujanati, ESL & ABR
Automation Activity & Vendor Info: (Circulation) SirsiDynix; (ILL) SirsiDynix; (OPAC) SirsiDynix
Wireless access
Publications: Bookends (Newsletter)
Partic in Libraries of Middlesex Automation Consortium
Special Services for the Blind - Braille bks
Open Mon-Fri 10-9, Sat 10-5, Sun 12-5
Friends of the Library Group

Branches: 1
LAURENCE HARBOR BRANCH, 277 Shoreland Circle, Laurence Harbor, 08879, SAN 351-126X. Tel: 732-566-2227. FAX: 732-583-8829. *Br Mgr,* Amy Trombetta
Open Mon, Wed & Sat 9:30-5, Tues & Thurs 1-8

OLD TAPPAN

P OLD TAPPAN FREE PUBLIC LIBRARY*, 56 Russell Ave, 07675. SAN 310-3854. Tel: 201-664-3499. FAX: 201-664-5999. Circulation E-mail: otpncirc@bccls.org. Web Site: oldtappan.bccls.org. *Dir,* Susan Meeske; E-mail: meeske@bccls.org
Founded 1943. Pop 4,300; Circ 25,400
Library Holdings: Bk Vols 34,000; Per Subs 50
Automation Activity & Vendor Info: (Cataloging) SirsiDynix; (Circulation) SirsiDynix; (OPAC) SirsiDynix
Wireless access
Special Services for the Blind - Magnifiers
Open Mon, Tues & Thurs 9-9, Wed & Fri 9-5, Sat 10-2; Mon, Tues & Thurs (Summer) 9-9, Wed 9-5, Fri 9-4, Sat 9-1

OLDWICK

P TEWKSBURY TOWNSHIP PUBLIC LIBRARY, 31 Old Turnpike Rd, 08858. (Mail add: PO Box 49, 08858-0049), SAN 310-3862. Tel: 908-439-3761. FAX: 908-572-7498. E-mail: thetewksburylibrary@gmail.com. Web Site: www.tewksburylibrary.org. *Libr Mgr,* Joanne Ricciardi
Circ 23,677
Library Holdings: Bk Vols 18,000; Per Subs 40
Special Collections: Art Coll
Subject Interests: Art, Gardening, Hist
Automation Activity & Vendor Info: (Cataloging) SirsiDynix; (Circulation) SirsiDynix; (ILL) SirsiDynix; (OPAC) SirsiDynix
Wireless access
Mem of Hunterdon County Library
Open Tues-Thurs 9-6, Fri 9-5, Sat 9-12
Friends of the Library Group

ORADELL

P ORADELL FREE PUBLIC LIBRARY, 375 Kinderkamack Rd, 07649-2122. SAN 310-3889. Tel: 201-262-2613. FAX: 201-262-9112. Web Site: oradell.bccls.org. *Libr Dir,* John J Trause; E-mail: trause@oradell.bccls.org; *Info Serv Librn,* Linda R Pabian; E-mail: linda.pabian@oradell.bccls.org; *Youth Serv Librn,* Carol Blakeslee; E-mail: carol.blakeslee@oradell.bccls.org; *Circ Mgr,* Donna Z Sweatlock; E-mail: Donna.sweatlock@oradell.bccls.org; Staff 23 (MLS 3, Non-MLS 20)
Founded 1913. Pop 8,219; Circ 109,107
Library Holdings: AV Mats 8,984; Bk Vols 52,132; Per Subs 68
Special Collections: Books Illustrated by Charles Livingston Bull. Oral History
Subject Interests: Bks, Local hist, Paper
Automation Activity & Vendor Info: (Acquisitions) Baker & Taylor; (ILL) JerseyCat
Wireless access
Function: 24/7 Electronic res, 24/7 Online cat, Adult bk club, Archival coll, Art exhibits, Bk club(s), Bks on CD, Children's prog, Computer training, Computers for patron use, E-Readers, E-Reserves, Electronic databases & coll, ILL available, Internet access, Magazines, Museum passes, Music CDs, Online cat, Photocopying/Printing, Prog for adults, Prog for children & young adult, Ref serv available, Scanner, Spoken cassettes & CDs, Spoken cassettes & DVDs, Story hour, Summer reading prog, Tax forms, Teen prog, Telephone ref
Publications: The Bookmark (Newsletter)
Partic in Bergen County Cooperative Library System, Inc; LibraryLinkNJ, The New Jersey Library Cooperative
Special Services for the Blind - Large print bks; Ref serv; Telesensory screen enlarger
Open Mon-Thurs 10-9, Fri & Sat 10-5, Sun 1-5
Friends of the Library Group

ORANGE

P ORANGE PUBLIC LIBRARY*, 348 Main St, 07050-2794. SAN 310-3897. Tel: 973-673-0153, Ext 10. Reference Tel: 973-673-0153, Ext 18. Administration Tel: 973-673-0153, Ext 14. FAX: 973-673-1847. Web Site: www.orangepl.org. *Libr Dir,* Timur A Davis; E-mail: tdavis@orangepl.org; *Ch,* Position Currently Open; *Ref Librn,* Alice McMillan; E-mail: amcmillan@orangepl.org; Staff 2 (MLS 2)
Founded 1884. Pop 32,868; Circ 98,781
Library Holdings: AV Mats 10,537; Bk Titles 133,000; Bk Vols 201,000; Per Subs 75
Special Collections: Black Literature & History; Orangeana
Automation Activity & Vendor Info: (Acquisitions) Baker & Taylor; (Cataloging) Auto-Graphics, Inc; (Circulation) Auto-Graphics, Inc; (ILL) JerseyCat; (OPAC) Auto-Graphics, Inc
Wireless access
Function: 24/7 Electronic res, 24/7 Online cat, Activity rm, Adult literacy prog, Archival coll, Bilingual assistance for Spanish patrons, Children's prog, Citizenship assistance, Electronic databases & coll, Free DVD rentals, Homework prog, ILL available, Internet access, Magazines, Magnifiers for reading, Mail & tel request accepted, Meeting rooms, Microfiche/film & reading machines, Movies, Music CDs, Notary serv, Photocopying/Printing, Prof lending libr, Wheelchair accessible
Partic in NJ State Libr Network; OCLC Online Computer Library Center, Inc
Open Mon 9-8, Tues & Thurs 9-6, Wed & Fri 9-7, Sat (Sept-May) 9-1
Restriction: Access at librarian's discretion, Fee for pub use

OXFORD

P OXFORD PUBLIC LIBRARY*, 42 Washington Ave, 07863-3037. (Mail add: PO Box 38, 07863-0038), SAN 376-0480. Tel: 908-453-2625. E-mail: oxfordlibrary@comcast.net. *Dir,* Eugene Bisanti
Founded 1921. Pop 2,307
Library Holdings: Bk Vols 2,500
Open Sat 10-2

S WARREN COUNTY CULTURAL & HERITAGE COMMISSION LIBRARY, Shippen Manor, Eight Belvidere Ave, 07863. SAN 376-0626. Tel: 908-453-4381. FAX: 908-453-4389, 908-453-4981. E-mail: manor@wcchc.org. Web Site: wcchc.org. *Dir,* Gina Rosseland; E-mail: grosseland@co.warren.nj.us
Library Holdings: Bk Titles 400
Special Collections: Warren County History, docs, maps
Restriction: Open by appt only

PALISADES PARK

P PALISADES PARK PUBLIC LIBRARY*, 257 Second St, 07650. SAN 310-3935. Tel: 201-585-4150. FAX: 201-585-2151. Circulation E-mail: reference@palisadespark.bccls.org. Web Site: www.palparklibrary.org. *Dir,* Katie Piano; E-mail: piano@palisadespark.bccls.org; Staff 8 (MLS 1, Non-MLS 7)
Founded 1922. Pop 19,000
Library Holdings: Bk Titles 52,875; Bk Vols 54,114; Per Subs 50
Subject Interests: Korean (Lang)
Wireless access
Function: Adult literacy prog, ILL available, Prog for children & young adult, Summer reading prog
Partic in Bergen County Cooperative Library System, Inc
Open Mon-Thurs 10:30-9, Fri 10:30-5, Sat 10:30-4

PARAMUS

S ARMENIAN MISSIONARY ASSOCIATION OF AMERICA LIBRARY*, 31 W Century Rd, 07652. Tel: 201-265-2607. FAX: 201-265-6015. E-mail: info@amaa.org. Web Site: amaa.org.
Founded 1918
Library Holdings: Bk Titles 20,000; Per Subs 16
Wireless access
Open Mon-Fri 8:30-4:30 by appointment
Restriction: Non-circulating

J BERGEN COMMUNITY COLLEGE*, Sidney Silverman Library & Learning Resource Center, 400 Paramus Rd, 07652-1595. SAN 310-3943. Tel: 201-447-7970. Reference Tel: 201-447-7436. Administration Tel: 201-447-7130. FAX: 201-493-8167. E-mail: libraryweb@bergen.edu. Web Site: www.bergen.edu/current-students/student-support-services/library. *Dean, Libr Serv,* David Marks; E-mail: dmarks1@bergen.edu; *Asst Dir, Syst & Tech,* Rong Wang; Tel: 201-612-5563, E-mail: rwang@bergen.edu; *Access Serv,* Kristen Ko; Tel: 201-879-8920, E-mail: kko1@bergen.edu; *Ref (Info Servs),* Kate McGivern; Tel: 201-447-7980, E-mail: kmcgivern@bergen.edu; *Ref (Info Servs),* Annemarie Roscello; Tel: 301-447-5569, E-mail: aroscello@bergen.edu; *Ref (Info Servs),* Lynn Schott; Tel: 201-447-8889, E-mail: lschott@bergen.edu; *Ref (Info Servs),* Paula Williams; Tel: 201-612-5299, E-mail: pwilliams@bergen.edu; *Tech Serv,* Joan Liu-DeVizio; Tel: 201-447-7653, E-mail: jliu-devizio@bergen.edu; Staff 30 (MLS 12, Non-MLS 18)
Founded 1965. Enrl 17,000; Fac 300; Highest Degree: Associate
Automation Activity & Vendor Info: (Acquisitions) Innovative Interfaces, Inc; (Cataloging) Innovative Interfaces, Inc; (Circulation) Innovative Interfaces, Inc; (Course Reserve) Innovative Interfaces, Inc; (ILL) Innovative Interfaces, Inc; (OPAC) Innovative Interfaces, Inc; (Serials) Innovative Interfaces, Inc
Wireless access
Partic in LibraryLinkNJ, The New Jersey Library Cooperative; LYRASIS; Virtual Academic Library Environment

Open Mon-Fri 7:40am-10:40pm, Sat 9-1
Friends of the Library Group

P PARAMUS PUBLIC LIBRARY*, 116 E Century Rd, 07652. SAN 351-1324. Tel: 201-599-1300. Circulation Tel: 201-599-1302. Reference Tel: 201-599-1305. FAX: 201-599-0059. Circulation E-mail: paracirc@bccls.org. Reference E-mail: pararef@bccls.org. Web Site: www.paramuslibrary.org. *Dir,* Leonard LoPinto; E-mail: lopinto@paramus.bccls.org; *Ref Librn,* Hanna Blatt; E-mail: blatt@paramus.bccls.org; *Br Coordr,* Cathy Eng; E-mail: cteng@paramus.bccls.org; *Ch Serv,* Sharon Kalman; E-mail: kalman@paramus.bccls.org; *Circ,* Valerie Danhart; E-mail: danhart@paramus.bccls.org; Staff 40 (MLS 9, Non-MLS 31)
Founded 1954. Pop 26,474; Circ 340,177
Library Holdings: Bk Vols 103,781; Per Subs 338
Special Collections: Korean, Chinese, Japanese (Foreign Language Books & Media Coll)
Automation Activity & Vendor Info: (Acquisitions) Baker & Taylor; (Cataloging) Baker & Taylor; (Circulation) SirsiDynix; (ILL) Auto-Graphics, Inc; (OPAC) SirsiDynix
Wireless access
Partic in LibraryLinkNJ, The New Jersey Library Cooperative
Open Mon-Thurs 9:30-9, Fri 9:30-6, Sat 9:30-5, Sun 1-5
Friends of the Library Group
Branches: 1
CHARLES E REID BRANCH, W 239 Midland Ave, 07652, SAN 351-1359. Tel: 201-444-4911. *Supvr,* Catherine Eng
Open Mon 10-9, Tues-Fri 10-6
Friends of the Library Group

PARK RIDGE

P PARK RIDGE PUBLIC LIBRARY*, 51 Park Ave, 07656. SAN 310-3978. Tel: 201-391-5151. FAX: 201-391-2739. Circulation E-mail: pkrdcirc@bccls.org. Web Site: parkridge.bccls.org. *Dir,* Christina Doto; Staff 9 (MLS 1, Non-MLS 8)
Pop 8,645; Circ 118,984
Library Holdings: Audiobooks 1,545; CDs 3,139; DVDs 100,866; e-books 39,674; e-journals 1,105; Electronic Media & Resources 9; Large Print Bks 2; Bk Titles 51,623; Per Subs 51
Automation Activity & Vendor Info: (Circulation) Innovative Interfaces, Inc
Wireless access
Function: 24/7 Electronic res, Adult bk club, Adult literacy prog, After school storytime, Art exhibits, Audiobks via web, Bks on CD, Children's prog, Computers for patron use, E-Readers, Electronic databases & coll, Free DVD rentals, ILL available, Internet access, Magazines, Movies, Museum passes, Music CDs, Notary serv, Online cat, OverDrive digital audio bks, Photocopying/Printing, Preschool reading prog, Printer for laptops & handheld devices, Prog for adults, Story hour, Summer reading prog, Tax forms, Wheelchair accessible
Open Mon-Thurs 9:30-8, Fri 9:30-5, Sat 9:30-3, Sun 12-4

PARLIN

P SAYREVILLE PUBLIC LIBRARY*, 1050 Washington Rd, 08859. SAN 310-3994. Tel: 732-727-0212. FAX: 732-553-0775. E-mail: SFPLlibrarian@lmxac.org. Web Site: www.sayrevillelibrary.org. *Libr Dir,* Leah Kloc; Tel: 732-727-0212, Ext 7, E-mail: lkloc@lmxac.org; Staff 6 (MLS 6)
Founded 1931. Pop 41,000; Circ 176,000
Library Holdings: AV Mats 5,339; Large Print Bks 1,250; Bk Titles 100,000; Per Subs 196; Talking Bks 1,355
Special Collections: Municipal Document Depository
Automation Activity & Vendor Info: (Cataloging) SirsiDynix; (Circulation) SirsiDynix; (ILL) Auto-Graphics, Inc; (OPAC) SirsiDynix
Wireless access
Function: Homebound delivery serv, ILL available, Internet access, Photocopying/Printing, Prog for children & young adult, Ref serv available, Summer reading prog, Telephone ref, Wheelchair accessible
Partic in Libraries of Middlesex Automation Consortium
Special Services for the Blind - Audio mat; Bks on cassette; Bks on CD; Large print bks; Talking bks; Videos on blindness & physical disabilties
Open Mon-Thurs 9:30-7:55, Fri & Sat (Sept-June) 9:30-4:55, Sun 1-4:55
Friends of the Library Group

PARSIPPANY

L DAY PITNEY LLP*, Information Resource Center, One Jefferson Rd, 07054. (Mail add: PO Box 1945, Morristown, 07962-1945), SAN 310-3153. Tel: 973-966-6300. FAX: 973-966-1015. Web Site: www.daypitney.com. *Law Librn,* Joe Williams; Staff 4 (MLS 2, Non-MLS 2)
Founded 1902
Library Holdings: Bk Titles 7,000; Bk Vols 38,000; Per Subs 150
Subject Interests: Gen law, NJ law
Automation Activity & Vendor Info: (Acquisitions) EOS International; (Cataloging) EOS International; (OPAC) EOS International; (Serials) EOS International
Restriction: Staff use only

P PARSIPPANY-TROY HILLS FREE PUBLIC LIBRARY*, 449 Halsey Rd, 07054. SAN 351-1448. Tel: 973-887-5150. Administration Tel: 973-887-8907, Ext 217. Information Services Tel: 973-887-8907, Ext 209. FAX: 973-887-0062. Web Site: parsippanylibrary.org. *Dir,* Jayne Beline; E-mail: jayne.beline@parsippanylibrary.org; *Head, Customer & Info Serv,* Aida Courtney; *Head, Tech Serv,* Bill Harrison; *Customer Serv Supvr,* Loretto Bapiran; Staff 86 (MLS 16, Non-MLS 70)
Founded 1968. Pop 50,000; Circ 450,000
Library Holdings: Bk Vols 210,000; Per Subs 210
Automation Activity & Vendor Info: (Acquisitions) SirsiDynix; (Cataloging) SirsiDynix; (Circulation) SirsiDynix; (OPAC) SirsiDynix
Wireless access
Function: AV serv, ILL available, Internet access, Photocopying/Printing, Prog for adults, Prog for children & young adult, Ref serv available, Summer reading prog, Telephone ref, Wheelchair accessible, Workshops
Partic in Morris Automated Information Network
Open Mon-Thurs 9-9, Fri & Sat 9-5, Sun (Oct-June) 1-5
Friends of the Library Group
Branches: 2
LAKE HIAWATHA BRANCH, 68 Nokomis Ave, Lake Hiawatha, 07034, SAN 351-1472. Tel: 973-335-0952. FAX: 973-335-8610. *Br Mgr,* Korin Rosenkrans
Open Mon-Thurs 10-9, Fri & Sat 10-5
Friends of the Library Group
MOUNT TABOR BRANCH, 31 Trinity Park, Mount Tabor, 07878, SAN 351-1502. Tel: 973-627-9508. *Br Mgr,* Korin Rosenkrans
Open Mon-Thurs 12:30-7:30, Fri & Sat 9-1
Friends of the Library Group

PASSAIC

P PASSAIC PUBLIC LIBRARY*, Julius Forstmann Library, 195 Gregory Ave, 07055. SAN 351-1561. Tel: 973-779-0474. FAX: 973-779-0889. Circulation E-mail: ref@passaicpubliclibrary.org. Web Site: www.passaicpubliclibrary.org. *Exec Dir,* Mario Gonzalez; E-mail: mgonzalez@passaicpubliclibrary.org; *Sr Librn,* Luba Furtak; E-mail: furtak@passaicpubliclibrary.org; *Ch,* Stephanie Fernandez; *Circ,* Dawn Rodriguez; Staff 18 (MLS 7, Non-MLS 11)
Founded 1887. Pop 70,000; Circ 210,363
Jul 2014-Jun 2015 Income (Main & Associated Libraries) $1,203,938, State $30,572, City $1,173,366
Library Holdings: Audiobooks 1,098; AV Mats 5; CDs 1,142; DVDs 6,270; Bk Vols 107,712; Per Subs 70; Videos 956
Special Collections: Local History (Passaic Coll), bks, clippings, photog
Subject Interests: Art, Cooking, Jewish studies, Literacy, Local hist
Automation Activity & Vendor Info: (Cataloging) SirsiDynix; (Circulation) SirsiDynix; (ILL) PALS; (OPAC) SirsiDynix
Wireless access
Function: Adult bk club, Art exhibits, Audiobks via web, Bilingual assistance for Spanish patrons, Bk club(s), Bks on CD, Children's prog, Computers for patron use, Electronic databases & coll, Free DVD rentals, Home delivery & serv to seniorr ctr & nursing homes, Homebound delivery serv, ILL available, Magazines, Mail & tel request accepted, Movies, Music CDs, Online cat, Outreach serv, Outside serv via phone, mail, e-mail & web, OverDrive digital audio bks, Photocopying/Printing, Preschool reading prog, Prog for adults, Prog for children & young adult, Ref & res, Ref serv available, Res performed for a fee, Spanish lang bks, Story hour, Summer reading prog, Tax forms, Teen prog, Telephone ref, VHS videos, Wheelchair accessible
Partic in LibraryLinkNJ, The New Jersey Library Cooperative; PALS Plus, The Computer Consortium of Passaic County Libraries
Open Mon-Thurs 9-9, Fri 9-6, Sat 9-5, Sun 12-5
Branches: 1
REID MEMORIAL BRANCH, 80 Third St, 07055. (Mail add: 195 Gregory Ave, 07055), SAN 351-1626. Tel: 973-777-6044. FAX: 973-779-0172.
Founded 1903. Pop 70,000
Library Holdings: Bk Vols 26,900; Per Subs 28
Special Collections: Spanish Language Books
Open Mon-Fri 1-5
Bookmobiles: 1

PATERSON

J PASSAIC COUNTY COMMUNITY COLLEGE*, Library & Learning Resources Center, One College Blvd, 07505. SAN 310-4028. Tel: 973-684-5877. Interlibrary Loan Service Tel: 973-684-6918. Reference Tel: 973-684-5888. Web Site: pccc.libguides.com/library. *Assoc Dean,* Gregory Fallon; E-mail: gfallon@pccc.edu; *Head Librn,* Mibong La; Tel:

973-684-5885, E-mail: mla@pccc.edu; *Electronic Res Librn,* Yaro Furtak; Tel: 973-684-5696, E-mail: yfurtak@pccc.edu; Staff 8 (MLS 5, Non-MLS 3)
Founded 1971. Enrl 7,000; Highest Degree: Associate
Library Holdings: AV Mats 1,500; CDs 500; Bk Titles 53,000; Bk Vols 54,064; Per Subs 230; Videos 1,200
Special Collections: Passaic County Poetry Center
Automation Activity & Vendor Info: (Cataloging) SirsiDynix; (Circulation) SirsiDynix; (Course Reserve) SirsiDynix; (ILL) SirsiDynix; (OPAC) SirsiDynix
Wireless access
Publications: LRC Handbook
Partic in LibraryLinkNJ, The New Jersey Library Cooperative; OCLC, Inc through Palinet; PALS Plus, The Computer Consortium of Passaic County Libraries; Virtual Academic Library Environment
Open Mon-Thurs 8am-10pm, Fri 8-8, Sat 8-3

S PASSAIC COUNTY HISTORICAL SOCIETY*, Elizabeth A Beam Memorial Historical Research Library, Lambert Castle, Three Valley Rd, 07503-2932. SAN 310-4036. Tel: 973-247-0085. FAX: 973-881-9434. E-mail: library@lambertcastle.org. Web Site: www.lambertcastle.org. *Librn,* Patrick Byrnes
Founded 1926
Library Holdings: Bk Titles 10,000
Special Collections: Derrom Family Coll; Haines Family Coll; Hewitt Coll; Hobart Family Coll; Industrial History (Society for Establishing Useful Manufactures Papers), mss; Manuscript Coll; New Jersey (John Reid Photo Coll), photos; Pamphlet Coll; Passaic General Hospital Coll; Paterson Orphans Asylum Records; Wright Aeronautical Coll
Function: Archival coll, Photocopying/Printing, Res libr
Publications: Castle Genie (Newsletter); The Historic County (Newsletter)
Open Wed-Fri 1-4
Restriction: Non-circulating

L PASSAIC VICINAGE LAW LIBRARY*, 77 Hamilton St, 2nd Flr, 07505-2096. SAN 310-4044. Tel: 973-247-8013. Web Site: www.njcourts.gov/courts/vicinages/passaic.html. *Librn,* Maria Vlahos
Founded 1930
Library Holdings: Bk Vols 57,220
Open Mon-Fri 8-4

P PATERSON FREE PUBLIC LIBRARY*, Danforth Memorial Library, 250 Broadway, 07501. SAN 351-1685. Tel: 973-321-1223. Administration Tel: 973-321-1216. FAX: 973-321-1205. Web Site: www.patersonpl.org. *Dir,* Corey Fleming; E-mail: fleming@patersonpl.org; *Asst Dir,* Mary Wilson; E-mail: wilson@patersonpl.org; *Adult Serv, Circ,* Shonn Burton; E-mail: burton@patersonpl.org; Staff 8 (MLS 8)
Founded 1885. Pop 146,199
Jan 2015-Dec 2015 Income $4,242,432, State $76,718, City $4,064,041, Federal $67,370, Other $34,303. Mats Exp $200,696, Books $134,177, Per/Ser (Incl. Access Fees) $15,562, AV Mat $16,010, Electronic Ref Mat (Incl. Access Fees) $34,947. Sal $1,843,187 (Prof $506,695)
Library Holdings: CDs 3,186; DVDs 12,431; e-books 11,401; Electronic Media & Resources 10; Bk Vols 186,342; Per Subs 218; Talking Bks 446
Special Collections: African American Coll; Local History Coll; Spanish Language Coll
Subject Interests: Genealogy, Local hist
Automation Activity & Vendor Info: (Acquisitions) Baker & Taylor; (Cataloging) SirsiDynix-WorkFlows; (Circulation) SirsiDynix-WorkFlows; (ILL) JerseyCat; (OPAC) SirsiDynix-iBistro
Wireless access
Function: Family literacy
Partic in LibraryLinkNJ, The New Jersey Library Cooperative; PALS Plus, The Computer Consortium of Passaic County Libraries
Open Mon-Thurs 9-8, Fri & Sat 9-5
Friends of the Library Group
Branches: 3
NORTHSIDE BRANCH, 60 Temple St, Rm 3, 07522, SAN 351-174X. Tel: 973-321-1309. *Libr Supvr,* Thomasina Duncan; E-mail: duncan@patersonpl.org
Library Holdings: Bk Vols 4,306
Open Mon, Tues & Thurs 9-5, Wed 12-8
Friends of the Library Group
SOUTH PATERSON, 930 Main St, 07503, SAN 351-1863. Tel: 973-357-3020. *Libr Supvr,* Lillian Hamilton; E-mail: hamilton@patersonpl.org
Library Holdings: Bk Vols 31,610
Special Collections: Arabic/Islamic Coll
Open Mon 12-8, Tues-Thurs & Sat 9-5
Friends of the Library Group
TOTOWA BRANCH, 405 Union Ave, 07502, SAN 351-1898. Tel: 973-942-7198. *Libr Supvr,* Susan Johnson; E-mail: johnson@patersonpl.org
Library Holdings: Bk Vols 30,892
Open Mon, Wed, Thurs & Sat 9-5, Tues 12-8
Friends of the Library Group

M SAINT JOSEPH'S REGIONAL MEDICAL CENTER*, Health Sciences Library, Xavier Bldg, 4th Flr, 703 Main St, 07503. SAN 320-5835. Tel: 973-754-3590. FAX: 973-754-3593. E-mail: library@sjhmc.org. Web Site: www.stjosephshealth.org/library. *Dir,* Patricia May; E-mail: mayp@sjhmc.org
Founded 1932
Library Holdings: Bk Vols 5,000; Per Subs 280
Partic in New Jersey Health Sciences Library Network
Open Mon, Wed & Fri 8:30-5, Tues & Thurs 8:30-8

PAULSBORO

P GILL MEMORIAL LIBRARY*, 145 E Broad St, 08066. SAN 310-4079. Tel: 856-423-5155. FAX: 856-423-9162. Web Site: www.gillmemoriallibrary.org. *Dir,* Jonathan Amey; E-mail: director@gillmemoriallibrary.org; *Asst Librn,* Leslie Baker; Staff 3 (Non-MLS 3)
Founded 1951. Pop 6,500
Library Holdings: Bk Titles 20,730; Per Subs 52
Special Collections: Database of Local High School Graduates, Marriages, Birth & Deaths; Microfilm of Local Newspapers; New Jersey Archives; New Jersey Museum Room with Local History
Automation Activity & Vendor Info: (Cataloging) SirsiDynix; (Circulation) SirsiDynix; (ILL) SirsiDynix
Wireless access
Function: ILL available
Partic in Libraries of Gloucester, Salem & Cumberland Information Network
Open Mon-Thurs 1-8, Sat 10-3

PENNINGTON

M CAPITAL HEALTH MEDICAL CENTER-HOPEWELL*, Health Sciences Library, One Capital Way, 08534. Tel: 609-303-4125. *Libr Serv Mgr,* Erica Moncrief; E-mail: emoncrief@capitalhealth.org
Wireless access
Partic in New Jersey Health Sciences Library Network
Open Mon-Fri 7-3:30

P PENNINGTON PUBLIC LIBRARY*, 30 N Main St, 08534. SAN 310-4109. Tel: 609-737-0404. FAX: 609-737-2948. Web Site: www.penningtonlibrary.org. *Libr Dir,* Kim T Ha; E-mail: kha@penningtonlibrary.org; *Prog Coordr,* Tara Russell; E-mail: TRussell@penningtonlibrary.org; Staff 2.5 (MLS 1, Non-MLS 1.5)
Founded 1875. Pop 3,035; Circ 41,590
Library Holdings: Audiobooks 773; DVDs 1,594; Bk Vols 20,353; Per Subs 34
Special Collections: Pennington Newspaper, 1897-present
Automation Activity & Vendor Info: (Cataloging) Auto-Graphics, Inc; (Circulation) Auto-Graphics, Inc; (OPAC) Auto-Graphics, Inc
Wireless access
Function: Adult bk club, Audiobks via web, Bk club(s), Bks on CD, Children's prog, Computers for patron use, Electronic databases & coll, Free DVD rentals, Holiday prog, ILL available, Internet access, Online cat, Photocopying/Printing, Prog for adults, Prog for children & young adult, Senior outreach, Story hour, Summer reading prog, Tax forms, Teen prog, Workshops
Open Mon-Thurs 10-8, Fri 10-5, Sat 10-2
Friends of the Library Group

PENNSAUKEN

P PENNSAUKEN FREE PUBLIC LIBRARY*, Rogers Library, 5605 Crescent Blvd, 08110. SAN 310-4141. Tel: 856-665-5959. FAX: 856-486-0142. E-mail: penncirculation@gmail.com. Web Site: www.pennsaukenlibrary.org. *Dir,* David Chang; E-mail: director@pennsaukenlibrary.org; Staff 21 (MLS 5, Non-MLS 16)
Founded 1959. Pop 37,500; Circ 194,000
Library Holdings: Bk Titles 72,300; Per Subs 75
Special Collections: Municipal Document Depository
Subject Interests: Local hist
Automation Activity & Vendor Info: (Acquisitions) Innovative Interfaces, Inc; (Cataloging) Innovative Interfaces, Inc; (Circulation) Innovative Interfaces, Inc; (OPAC) Innovative Interfaces, Inc; (Serials) Innovative Interfaces, Inc
Wireless access
Partic in LibraryLinkNJ, The New Jersey Library Cooperative; New Jersey Library Network
Special Services for the Deaf - Bks on deafness & sign lang
Special Services for the Blind - Extensive large print coll; Magnifiers; Reader equip; Ref serv; Spec prog; Talking bks

Open Mon-Thurs 10-9, Fri & Sat 10-6, Sun 1-5; Mon, Wed & Fri (Summer) 10-9, Tues & Fri 10-6, Sat 10-2
Friends of the Library Group

PENNSVILLE

P PENNSVILLE PUBLIC LIBRARY*, 190 S Broadway, 08070. SAN 310-415X. Tel: 856-678-5473. FAX: 856-678-8121. E-mail: pennsvillelibrary@gmail.com. Web Site: www.pennsvillelibrary.org. *Dir,* Allyson Cogan; E-mail: librarian@pennsvillelibrary.org; Staff 4 (Non-MLS 4)
Founded 1937. Pop 13,400; Circ 30,259
Library Holdings: AV Mats 350; Bk Titles 29,237; Bk Vols 32,172; Per Subs 32
Subject Interests: NJ
Automation Activity & Vendor Info: (Circulation) SirsiDynix-WorkFlows; (OPAC) SirsiDynix-WorkFlows
Wireless access
Partic in Libraries of Gloucester, Salem & Cumberland Information Network
Open Mon, Tues & Thurs 10-7, Fri 10-4, Sat 10-2
Friends of the Library Group

PERTH AMBOY

P PERTH AMBOY FREE PUBLIC LIBRARY*, 196 Jefferson St, 08861. SAN 351-2010. Tel: 732-826-2600. FAX: 732-324-8079. Web Site: www.lmxac.org, www.perthamboynj.org/library. *Bus Mgr,* Herschel Chomsky; E-mail: herschel@lmxac.org; Staff 10 (MLS 3, Non-MLS 7)
Founded 1903. Pop 51,000
Library Holdings: Bk Vols 176,236; Per Subs 444
Special Collections: Perth Amboy Historical Documents; Perth Amboy Newspaper, microfilm
Subject Interests: Local hist, Spanish (Lang)
Wireless access
Function: 24/7 Electronic res, 24/7 Online cat, Adult literacy prog, Archival coll, Home delivery & serv to seniorr ctr & nursing homes, Homebound delivery serv, ILL available, Prog for children & young adult, Summer reading prog
Partic in Libraries of Middlesex Automation Consortium
Open Mon, Tues & Thurs 9-8, Wed & Fri 9-5, Sat 9-4
Friends of the Library Group

PHILLIPSBURG

P PHILLIPSBURG FREE PUBLIC LIBRARY*, 200 Broubalow Way, 08865. SAN 310-4192. Tel: 908-454-3712. FAX: 908-859-4667. Web Site: www.pburglib.org. *Dir,* Deb Messling; E-mail: director@pburglib.org; *Ad,* Stephanie Rath-Tickle; *Ch,* Position Currently Open; Staff 17 (MLS 4, Non-MLS 13)
Founded 1923. Pop 14,950; Circ 93,849
Library Holdings: Audiobooks 1,629; CDs 816; DVDs 2,951; Large Print Bks 1,333; Bk Vols 92,339; Per Subs 165; Videos 609
Special Collections: ERIC repts on microfiche. State Document Depository; US Document Depository
Subject Interests: Educ
Automation Activity & Vendor Info: (Cataloging) Innovative Interfaces, Inc; (Circulation) Innovative Interfaces, Inc; (ILL) JerseyCat; (OPAC) Innovative Interfaces, Inc
Wireless access
Function: 24/7 Electronic res, 24/7 Online cat, Activity rm, Adult bk club, After school storytime, Audiobks via web, Bk club(s), Bks on cassette, Bks on CD, Children's prog, Computer training, Digital talking bks, Electronic databases & coll, For res purposes, Free DVD rentals, Health sci info serv, Holiday prog, Homework prog, ILL available, Instruction & testing, Internet access, Life-long learning prog for all ages, Magazines, Magnifiers for reading, Mail & tel request accepted, Meeting rooms, Microfiche/film & reading machines, Movies, Music CDs, Online cat, Outside serv via phone, mail, e-mail & web, Photocopying/Printing, Preschool outreach, Prog for adults, Prog for children & young adult, Ref & res, Ref serv available, Scanner, Senior outreach, Serves people with intellectual disabilities, Spanish lang bks, Spoken cassettes & CDs, Story hour, Study rm, Summer & winter reading prog, Summer reading prog, Tax forms, Teen prog, VHS videos, Wheelchair accessible, Winter reading prog, Workshops, Writing prog
Partic in LibraryLinkNJ, The New Jersey Library Cooperative
Special Services for the Blind - Talking bk & rec for the blind cat; Talking bks
Open Mon-Thurs 9:30-9, Fri & Sat 9:30-5
Friends of the Library Group

PICATINNY ARSENAL

A PICATINNY ARMAMENT TECHNICAL LIBRARY*, Bldg 59, Phipps Rd, 07806-5000. SAN 350-6460. Tel: 973-724-4712. FAX: 973-724-3044. *Chief Librn,* Liz Reisman; Tel: 973-724-5350, E-mail: liz.z.reisman.civ@mail.mil. Subject Specialists: *Engr,* Liz Reisman; Staff 3 (MLS 2, Non-MLS 1)
Founded 1929
Library Holdings: e-books 5,000; Bk Vols 50,000; Per Subs 50
Special Collections: Frankford Arsenal Archives, PA; Picatinny Arsenal Archives, NJ
Subject Interests: Ammunition, Armament, Explosives, Plastics, Propellants, Pyrotechnics, Weapons
Automation Activity & Vendor Info: (Cataloging) SirsiDynix; (Circulation) SirsiDynix; (ILL) OCLC; (OPAC) SirsiDynix; (Serials) OCLC
Function: Archival coll, ILL available, Ref serv available
Partic in NW Libr Network
Restriction: Circ limited, Open to others by appt

PISCATAWAY

P PISCATAWAY TOWNSHIP FREE PUBLIC LIBRARY, John F Kennedy Memorial Library, 500 Hoes Lane, 08854. SAN 351-207X. Tel: 732-463-1633. Administration Tel: 732-463-3911. Web Site: piscatawaylibrary.org. *Dir,* Heidi Cramer; E-mail: hcramer@piscatawaylibrary.org; *Assoc Dir,* Doug Baldwin; E-mail: dbaldwin@piscatawaylibrary.org; *Head, Children's Servx,* Sharlene Edwards; E-mail: sedwards@piscatawaylibrary.org; *Ad,* Carina Gonzalez; E-mail: cgonzalez@piscatawaylibrary.org; *Ad,* Joy Robinson; E-mail: jrobinson@piscatawaylibrary.org; *Ch Serv Librn,* Patty Sumner; E-mail: pasumner@piscatawaylibrary.org; *Ch Serv Librn,* Peggy Wong; E-mail: pwong@piscatawaylibrary.org; Staff 31 (MLS 13, Non-MLS 18)
Founded 1961. Pop 56,000; Circ 350,000
Library Holdings: Bk Vols 156,261; Per Subs 308
Special Collections: Piscataway Local History Coll, bks, ms, maps, newsp, oral hist tapes. Oral History
Subject Interests: Chinese lang, Local hist
Automation Activity & Vendor Info: (Acquisitions) SirsiDynix-WorkFlows; (Cataloging) SirsiDynix; (Circulation) SirsiDynix; (Course Reserve) SirsiDynix; (OPAC) SirsiDynix; (Serials) SirsiDynix
Wireless access
Partic in Libraries of Middlesex Automation Consortium; LibraryLinkNJ, The New Jersey Library Cooperative
Special Services for the Deaf - TTY equip
Open Mon-Wed 12-8, Thurs-Sat 12-4
Friends of the Library Group
Branches: 1
JOHANNA W WESTERGARD LIBRARY, 20 Murray Ave, 08854, SAN 351-210X. Tel: 732-752-1166. *Br Mgr, Teen Serv Librn,* Erica Krivopal; E-mail: ekrivopal@piscatawaylibrary.org
Special Collections: Gujrati Coll; Parenting Coll, bks, mag, newsp & videos; Spanish Coll
Open Mon-Wed 12-8, Thurs-Sat 12-4
Friends of the Library Group

PITMAN

P MCCOWAN MEMORIAL LIBRARY*, 15 Pitman Ave, 08071. SAN 310-4265. Tel: 856-589-1656. FAX: 856-582-4982. E-mail: library@mccowan-pitman.org. Web Site: www.mccowan-pitman.org. *Dir,* Andrew Coldren; E-mail: andrew.coldren@mccowan-pitman.org; *Children's Prog Coordr,* Patti Forte; E-mail: mrs.forte@mccowan-pitman.org; *Circ,* Dolores Novin; E-mail: dolores@mccowan-pitman.org; *ILL, Ref,* Margaret Ware; E-mail: margaret.ware@mccowan-pitman.org; Staff 9 (MLS 1, Non-MLS 8)
Founded 1919. Pop 9,011; Circ 75,052
Library Holdings: Bk Titles 41,950; Bk Vols 43,770; Per Subs 76
Automation Activity & Vendor Info: (Acquisitions) SirsiDynix-WorkFlows; (Cataloging) SirsiDynix-Unicorn; (Circulation) SirsiDynix-Unicorn; (Course Reserve) SirsiDynix-WorkFlows; (OPAC) SirsiDynix; (Serials) EBSCO Online
Wireless access
Partic in LibraryLinkNJ, The New Jersey Library Cooperative
Open Mon-Thurs 10-9, Fri 10-6, Sat 10-2
Friends of the Library Group

PLAINFIELD

P PLAINFIELD PUBLIC LIBRARY*, 800 Park Ave, 07060-2594. SAN 310-4303. Tel: 908-757-1111. Circulation Tel: 908-757-1111, Ext 111. Reference Tel: 908-757-1111, Ext 112. Administration Tel: 908-757-2305. FAX: 908-754-0063. E-mail: ref@plfdpl.info. Web Site: www.plainfieldlibrary.info. *Dir,* Mary Ellen Rogan; E-mail: me.rogan@plfdpl.info; *Asst Dir,* Tina Marie Doody; Tel: 908-757-1111, Ext 132, E-mail: tina.doody@plfdpl.info; *Chief Tech Officer,* Peter Rajcevic; Tel: 908-757-1111, Ext 130, E-mail: peter.rajcevic@plfdpl.info; *Head, Children's Dept,* Janice People; Tel: 908-757-1111, Ext 129; *Adult Literacy Coordr,* Scott Kuchinsky; Tel: 908-757-1111, Ext 120, E-mail: scott.kuchinsky@plfdpl.info; *ESL Coordr,* Stella Segura; Tel: 908-757-1111, Ext 121, E-mail: luz.segura@plfdpl.info; *Archivist/Head of*

Local Hist, Sarah Hull; Tel: 908-757-1111, Ext 136, E-mail: sarah.hull@plfdpl.info; Staff 38 (MLS 15, Non-MLS 23)
Founded 1881. Pop 49,808; Circ 104,650
Library Holdings: Bk Titles 136,062; Bk Vols 190,060; Per Subs 275
Special Collections: Oral History
Subject Interests: 19th Century per, Civil War, Early Am hist, Genealogy, Local hist, NJ hist, Union County hist
Automation Activity & Vendor Info: (Acquisitions) SirsiDynix; (Circulation) SirsiDynix; (OPAC) SirsiDynix
Wireless access
Function: 24/7 Electronic res, Adult literacy prog, Archival coll, Art exhibits, Audiobks via web, Bilingual assistance for Spanish patrons, Bks on CD, Children's prog, Citizenship assistance, Computer training, Computers for patron use, E-Reserves, Electronic databases & coll, Genealogy discussion group, ILL available, Internet access, Magazines, Mail & tel request accepted, Microfiche/film & reading machines, Movies, Notary serv, Online cat, OverDrive digital audio bks, Photocopying/Printing, Printer for laptops & handheld devices, Prog for adults, Prog for children & young adult, Ref serv available, Res performed for a fee, Scanner, Senior computer classes, Spanish lang bks, Story hour, Study rm, Summer reading prog, Tax forms, Telephone ref, Wheelchair accessible
Partic in MURAL
Open Mon-Thurs 9-9, Fri & Sat 9-5; Mon-Wed (Summer) 9-9, Thurs & Fri 9-5, Sat 9-1
Restriction: Researchers by appt only
Friends of the Library Group

UNION COUNTY COLLEGE
See Cranford

PLAINSBORO

P PLAINSBORO FREE PUBLIC LIBRARY*, Nine Van Doren St, 08536. SAN 326-3924. Tel: 609-275-2899. Circulation Tel: 609-275-2897. Reference Tel: 609-275-2898. FAX: 609-799-5883. E-mail: plibrary@lmxac.org. Web Site: www.lmxac.org/plainsboro. *Dir,* Carol Quick; Staff 18.5 (MLS 6.2, Non-MLS 12.3)
Founded 1964. Pop 22,999; Circ 397,159
Library Holdings: Bk Vols 113,083; Per Subs 150
Special Collections: Chinese Cultural Exchange; Gujrati Coll; Hindi Coll; JFK Coll; Large Print Coll
Automation Activity & Vendor Info: (Cataloging) TLC (The Library Corporation); (Circulation) TLC (The Library Corporation); (ILL) TLC (The Library Corporation); (OPAC) TLC (The Library Corporation)
Wireless access
Publications: Annual Report Newsletter; Plainsboro Community Directory
Partic in Libraries of Middlesex Automation Consortium; LibraryLinkNJ, The New Jersey Library Cooperative; OCLC Online Computer Library Center, Inc
Open Mon-Thurs 10-8:30, Fri-Sun 10-5
Friends of the Library Group

M PRINCETON HEALTHCARE SYSTEM*, Medical Library & Business Center, One Plainsboro Rd, 08536. SAN 326-2405. Tel: 609-853-6799. FAX: 609-853-6798. E-mail: libraryservices@hiltonpub.com. Web Site: www.princetonhcs.org/patients-visitors/support-and-educational-resources/medical-library-at-umcp. *Dir, Libr Serv,* Judy Knight; Staff 1 (MLS 1)
Founded 1953
Library Holdings: Bk Titles 2,800; Bk Vols 3,000; Per Subs 200
Subject Interests: Allied health, Med, Nursing, Psychiat, Surgery
Wireless access
Publications: AV Catalogue; Guide to the Library; Serial Holdings
Partic in Health Sci Libr Asn of NJ; Medcore; Medical Library Association
Special Services for the Deaf - Interpreter on staff
Special Services for the Blind - Assistive/Adapted tech devices, equip & products; Audio mat; Bks & mags in Braille, on rec, tape & cassette; Bks on cassette; Braille bks
Open Mon-Sun 6am-9pm
Friends of the Library Group

POMONA

M BACHARACH INSTITUTE FOR REHABILITATION*, Medical-Clinical Staff Library, 61 W Jimmie Leeds Rd, 08240. (Mail add: PO Box 723, 08240-0723), SAN 373-2541. Tel: 609-652-7000. Web Site: www.bacharach.org.
Library Holdings: Bk Vols 50; Per Subs 20
Wireless access
Open Mon-Fri 9-5
Restriction: Staff & patient use

POMPTON LAKES

P THE FREE PUBLIC LIBRARY OF THE BOROUGH OF POMPTON LAKES*, Emanuel Einstein Memorial Library, 333 Wanaque Ave, 07442. SAN 310-4370. Tel: 973-835-0482. FAX: 973-835-4767. Web Site: www.pomptonlakeslibrary.org. *Dir,* Michael Drazek; E-mail: drazek@pomptonlakeslibrary.org; *Youth Serv Librn,* Ashley Monochello; E-mail: monochello@pomptonlakeslibrary.org; *Circ & Ref,* Linda Brophy; E-mail: brophy@pomptonlakeslibrary.org; Staff 13 (MLS 1, Non-MLS 12)
Founded 1912. Pop 11,059; Circ 66,389
Library Holdings: AV Mats 1,372; Bk Vols 41,210; Per Subs 60
Special Collections: Albert Payson Terhune Coll; New Jersey History (Van Orden Coll)
Automation Activity & Vendor Info: (Cataloging) SirsiDynix; (Circulation) SirsiDynix; (OPAC) SirsiDynix
Wireless access
Function: Homebound delivery serv, ILL available, Internet access, Magnifiers for reading, Photocopying/Printing, Prog for children & young adult, Summer reading prog, Telephone ref, Wheelchair accessible
Open Mon & Wed 10-9, Tues & Thurs 10-6, Fri 10-5, Sat (Sept-May) 10-5
Friends of the Library Group

POMPTON PLAINS

M CHILTON MEMORIAL HOSPITAL*, Medical Library, 97 West Pkwy, 07444. SAN 325-9404. Tel: 973-831-5058. FAX: 973-831-5041. *Librn,* Eleanor Silverman; Staff 1 (MLS 1)
Library Holdings: Bk Vols 500
Wireless access
Partic in New Jersey Health Sciences Library Network
Open Thurs 9-1

P PEQUANNOCK TOWNSHIP PUBLIC LIBRARY*, 477 Newark Pompton Tpk, 07444. SAN 351-2223. Tel: 973-835-7460. FAX: 973-835-1928. Web Site: www.pequannocklibrary.org. *Libr Dir,* Debbie Maynard; E-mail: debbie.maynard@pequannocklibrary.org; *Asst Dir, Head, Adult Serv,* Nicholas Jackson; E-mail: nicholas.jackson@pequannocklibrary.org; Staff 20 (MLS 4, Non-MLS 16)
Founded 1962. Pop 14,000; Circ 147,617
Jan 2015-Dec 2015 Income $909,927, State $17,013, Locally Generated Income $892,914. Mats Exp $118,040, Books $98,100, Per/Ser (Incl. Access Fees) $8,050, Other Print Mats $2,590, AV Mat $9,300. Sal $700,358 (Prof $189,748)
Library Holdings: AV Mats 8,598; Large Print Bks 1,388; Bk Vols 85,305; Per Subs 200; Talking Bks 3,542
Special Collections: Landsberger Holocaust Coll
Subject Interests: Local hist
Automation Activity & Vendor Info: (Circulation) SirsiDynix
Wireless access
Publications: Quarterly Program Brochure
Partic in Morris Automated Information Network
Open Mon-Thurs 9-9, Fri 9-5:30, Sat 10-4 (10-2 Summer)
Friends of the Library Group

PRINCETON

S EDUCATIONAL TESTING SERVICE, R&D Library & Test Collection, Turnbull Hall, Mail Stop 01-R, 660 Rosedale Rd, 08541. SAN 310-4419. Tel: 609-734-5049. E-mail: librarystaff@ets.org. *Library Services, Supvr,* Charlotte Kirkby; Tel: 609-734-1148, E-mail: ckirkby@ets.org; *Knowledge Servs, Spec,* Miriam Terron-Elder; Tel: 609-734-5049, E-mail: mterron-elder@ets.org; Staff 2 (MLS 2)
Founded 1961
Library Holdings: Bk Vols 10,000; Per Subs 250
Special Collections: ETS Online Research Library, database; Test Coll, database
Subject Interests: Artificial intelligence, Behav sci, Cognitive sci, Educ, Expert systs, Internet, Measurements, Psychol, Soc sci, Statistics
Automation Activity & Vendor Info: (Cataloging) SydneyPlus; (Circulation) SydneyPlus; (Discovery) EBSCO Discovery Service; (ILL) OCLC WorldShare Interlibrary Loan; (OPAC) SydneyPlus; (Serials) SydneyPlus
Wireless access
Partic in LibraryLinkNJ, The New Jersey Library Cooperative; OCLC Online Computer Library Center, Inc
Restriction: Borrowing requests are handled by ILL, External users must contact libr, Staff use only

S HISTORICAL SOCIETY OF PRINCETON*, Museum & Research Library, Updike Farmstead, 345 Quaker Road, 08540. SAN 310-4443. Tel: 609-921-6748. FAX: 609-921-6939. Web Site: princetonhistory.org. *Res,* Stephanie Schwartz; Tel: 609-921-6748, Ext 103, E-mail: stephanie@princetonhistory.org; Staff 3 (Non-MLS 3)
Founded 1938
Library Holdings: Bk Titles 1,500

Subject Interests: Local hist, Princeton hist
Publications: Guide to Manuscripts; Princeton History Journal
Restriction: Closed stack, Non-circulating

S INSTITUTE FOR ADVANCED STUDY LIBRARIES*, One Einstein Dr, 08540. SAN 310-4451. Tel: 609-734-8000. E-mail: hslib@ias.edu, mnlib@ias.edu. Web Site: library.ias.edu. *Librn,* Emma Moore; E-mail: emoore@ias.edu; *Librn,* Marcia Tucker; E-mail: tucker@ias.edu; *Tech Serv Librn,* Dana Van Meter; E-mail: vanmeter@ias.edu; *Archivist,* Position Currently Open; E-mail: archives@ias.edu; *ILL,* Karen Downing; E-mail: kd@ias.edu. Subject Specialists: *Math, Natural sci,* Emma Moore; Staff 12 (MLS 6, Non-MLS 6)
Founded 1940
Library Holdings: Bk Vols 130,000; Per Subs 1,100
Special Collections: History of Science (Rosenwald Coll)
Subject Interests: Art, Classical archaeol, Classical studies, Hist, Math, Natural sci, Soc sci
Automation Activity & Vendor Info: (Acquisitions) SirsiDynix; (Cataloging) SirsiDynix; (OPAC) SirsiDynix; (Serials) SirsiDynix
Wireless access
Function: Archival coll, Res libr
Partic in OCLC Research Library Partnership; Philadelphia Area Consortium of Special Collections Libraries
Restriction: External users must contact libr, Limited access for the pub, Not open to pub

S INSTITUTE FOR DEFENSE ANALYSES*, Center for Communications Research Library, 805 Bunn Dr, 08540. SAN 310-446X. Tel: 609-924-4600. FAX: 609-924-3061. Web Site: www.ida.org. *Dir,* David Saltman; E-mail: saltman@idaccr.org; *Mgr, Info Serv,* Barbara Hamilton; E-mail: hamilton@idaccr.org; Staff 2 (MLS 1, Non-MLS 1)
Founded 1959
Library Holdings: Bk Vols 15,000; Per Subs 300
Subject Interests: Computer sci, Electrical engr, Linguistics, Math
Automation Activity & Vendor Info: (Acquisitions) Sydney; (Cataloging) Sydney; (Circulation) Sydney; (OPAC) Sydney; (Serials) Sydney
Publications: Acquisitions List (Biannually); Journals List; Print Catalog of Book Holdings; Staff Publications List
Restriction: Staff use only

S ROBERT WOOD JOHNSON FOUNDATION*, Information Center, 50 College Rd E, 08540. SAN 310-4478. Tel: 609-627-5895. FAX: 609-627-6421. Web Site: www.rwjf.org. *Info Coordr,* MaryBeth Kren; Staff 1 (Non-MLS 1)
Founded 1972
Library Holdings: DVDs 25; Bk Titles 4,000; Per Subs 100
Subject Interests: Access to healthcare, Health policy, Nursing, Obesity, Philanthropy, Primary health care, Pub health issues, Vulnerable pop
Wireless access
Partic in New Jersey Health Sciences Library Network
Restriction: Employees only

S MATHEMATICA INC LIBRARY*, 600 Alexander Park, 08543. SAN 376-0537. Tel: 609-945-6570. E-mail: library@mathematica-mpr.com. Web Site: www.mathematica-mpr.com. *Head, Libr Serv,* William Rafferty; E-mail: wrafferty@mathematica-mpr.com; *Info Spec,* Jeanette de Richemond; E-mail: jderichemond@mathematica-mpr.com; *Libr Asst,* Nicole Schatten; E-mail: nschatten@mathematica-mpr.com; *Libr Spec,* Georgia Mae Oates; E-mail: goates@mathematica-mpr.com; *ILL, Libr Assoc,* Jazmine Faherty; E-mail: jfaherty@mathematica-mpr.com; Staff 6 (MLS 3, Non-MLS 3)
Library Holdings: Bk Vols 60,000; Per Subs 350
Subject Interests: Soc policy
Automation Activity & Vendor Info: (Cataloging) EOS International
Wireless access
Restriction: Staff use only

G NATIONAL OCEANIC & ATMOSPHERIC ADMINISTRATION, Geophysical Fluid Dynamics Laboratory Library, Forrestal Campus, US Rte 1, 201 Forrestal Rd, 08542. SAN 310-4524. Tel: 609-452-6500. FAX: 609-987-5063. Web Site: www.gfdl.noaa.gov.
Founded 1968
Library Holdings: Bk Titles 8,000; Bk Vols 10,000; Per Subs 130
Subject Interests: Applied math, Meteorology, Oceanography
Partic in NOAA Libraries Network; OCLC Online Computer Library Center, Inc

P PRINCETON PUBLIC LIBRARY, 65 Witherspoon St, 08542. SAN 310-4540. Tel: 609-924-9529. Administration Tel: 609-924-9529, Ext 1250. Administration FAX: 609-924-7937. Web Site: www.princetonlibrary.org. *Exec Dir,* Jennifer Podolsky; E-mail: jpodolsky@princetonlibrary.org; *Asst Dir,* Erica Bess; E-mail: ebess@princetonlibrary.org; *Develop Dir,* Lisa Belshaw; E-mail: lham@princetonlibrary.org; *Dir, Mkt & Communications,* Tim Quinn; E-mail: tquinn@princetonlibrary.org; *Head, Access Serv,* Ji Hae Ju; E-mail: jju@princetonlibrary.org; *Dept Head, Lending Serv,* Sonja Vloeberghs; E-mail: svloeberghs@princetonlibrary.org; *Youth Serv Dept Head,* Susan Conlon; E-mail: sconlon@princetonlibrary.org; *Adult Programming, Mgr,* Janie Hermann; E-mail: jhermann@princetonlibrary.org; Staff 58 (MLS 18, Non-MLS 40)
Founded 1909. Pop 28,572; Circ 611,400
Jan 2020-Dec 2020 Income $5,499,610, State $15,022, City $4,448,230, Locally Generated Income $923,030, Other $102,972. Mats Exp $3,953,636, Books $192,298, Per/Ser (Incl. Access Fees) $29,418, Other Print Mats $32,024, AV Mat $29,726, Electronic Ref Mat (Incl. Access Fees) $99,812. Sal $3,953,636
Library Holdings: Audiobooks 6,426; AV Mats 8,000; CDs 6,852; DVDs 14,299; e-books 40,868; e-journals 50; Electronic Media & Resources 27; High Interest/Low Vocabulary Bk Vols 250; Large Print Bks 1,000; Microforms 500; Bk Titles 163,830; Bk Vols 218,953; Per Subs 300
Special Collections: African Genealogy (Paul Robeson Coll); Princeton History Coll
Subject Interests: Bus, Consumer health
Automation Activity & Vendor Info: (Acquisitions) Innovative Interfaces, Inc; (Cataloging) Innovative Interfaces, Inc; (Circulation) Innovative Interfaces, Inc; (ILL) OCLC; (OPAC) Innovative Interfaces, Inc
Wireless access
Publications: Connections (Newsletter)
Open Mon, Wed, Fri & Sat 10-5, Tues & Thurs 10-7, Sun 1-5
Friends of the Library Group

R PRINCETON THEOLOGICAL SEMINARY LIBRARY, 25 Library Pl, 08540. (Mail add: PO Box 821, 08542-0821), SAN 310-4559. Tel: 609-497-7940. Reference Tel: 609-497-7933. E-mail: library@ptsem.edu. Web Site: library.ptsem.edu. *Managing Dir,* Evelyn Frangakis; E-mail: evelyn.frangakis@ptsem.edu; *Head, Spec Coll & Archives,* Brian Shetler; E-mail: brian.shetler@ptsem.edu; *Ref Librn,* Kate Skrebutenas; E-mail: kate.skrebutenas@ptsem.edu
Founded 1812. Highest Degree: Doctorate
Library Holdings: Microforms 500,000; Bk Vols 533,707; Per Subs 2,000
Special Collections: Baptist Controversy; Early American Theological Pamphlets (Sprague Coll); Hymnology (Benson Coll); Puritan Literature, bks, pamphlets
Subject Interests: Theol
Automation Activity & Vendor Info: (Acquisitions) Ex Libris Group; (Cataloging) Ex Libris Group; (Circulation) Ex Libris Group; (OPAC) Ex Libris Group; (Serials) Ex Libris Group
Wireless access
Partic in OCLC Online Computer Library Center, Inc
Open Mon-Thurs 8am-9pm, Fri 8-6, Sat 9-5, Sun 2-6 (Fall-Spring); Mon-Thurs 9-5, Fri 9-1 (Summer)

C PRINCETON UNIVERSITY*, Firestone Library, One Washington Rd, 08544-2098. SAN 351-2282. Tel: 609-258-1470, 609-258-4820. Circulation Tel: 609-258-3202. Interlibrary Loan Service Tel: 609-258-3272. Reference Tel: 609-258-5964. FAX: 609-258-0441. Web Site: library.princeton.edu/firestone. *Univ Librn,* Anne Jarvis; Tel: 609-258-3170, E-mail: ajarvis@princeton.edu; *Assoc Univ Librn, Coll Develop,* David Magier; Tel: 609-258-5710, E-mail: dmagier@princeton.edu; *Assoc Univ Librn, External Engagement,* Stephen Ferguson; Tel: 609-258-3165, E-mail: ferguson@princeton.edu; *Asst Univ Librn, Coll Develop,* Patty Gaspari Bridges; Tel: 609-258-5483, E-mail: pattygb@princeton.edu; *Dir, Admin & Finance,* Jeffrey Rowlands; Tel: 609-258-4158, E-mail: rowlands@princeton.edu; Staff 321 (MLS 152, Non-MLS 169)
Founded 1756. Enrl 7,972; Fac 931; Highest Degree: Doctorate
Jan 2015-Dec 2015. Mats Exp $52,959,064
Library Holdings: e-books 1,732,373; Bk Vols 10,159,715
Special Collections: Aeronautics Coll; Ainsworth, Barrie, the Brontes, Bulwer-Lytton, Collins, Mrs Craik, Dickens, Disraeli, Dogson, George Eliot, Mrs Gaskell, Hardy, Hughes, Kingsley, Lever, Reade, Stevenson, Thackeray, Trollope (Parrish Coll of Victorian Novelists); American Historical Manuscripts; American Woodcut Illustrated Books Coll; Americana Coll; Arts; Chateaubriand Coll; Chess Coll; Civil Rights Coll; Coins; Emblem Books; Emily Dickinson Coll; English Restoration Drama; European Historical Manuscripts; European Legal Documents (11th to 19th Century); Fishing & Angling; Graphic; Halliburton, Handel, Hemingway, Horace, Leigh Hunt, Laurence Hutton, Otto H Kahn, George Kennan, Kierkegaard, Ivy Lee, C G Leland, Lilienthal, George McAneny, Thomas Mann, E L Masters, Harold R Medina, Montaigne, W V Moody, O'Neill, Coventry Patmore, H L Piozzi, Pound, Rabelais, Rowlandson, Richard Rush, Ruskin, Schweitzer, William Seymour, Shellabarger, H Alexander Smith, Samuel Southard, Adlai Stevenson, Julian Street, Symons, Tarkington, Allen Tate, Ridgeley Torrence, Carl Van Doren, Henry Van Dyke, Vergil, Viele-Griffin, Woodrow Wilson; History of Women; Horace Coll; Incunabula; Individual Colls: Louis Adamic, Elmer Adler, American Civil Liberties Union, Audubon, Bernard Baruch, Beardsley, Beauharnais (Administration of Italy & War Claims, Archives of Prince Eugene De Beauharnais), Blake, Boker, Boudinot Family, Aaron Burr Sr, M S Burt, F A R De Chateaubriand, William Cowper, J G Cozzens, Cruishank, John

Davidson, Allan Dulles, J F Duells, Jonathan Edwards, Faulkner, F S Fitzgerald, Forrestal, Goethe; Islamic Manuscripts; John Foster Dulles Project; Latin America (Spanish & English Language Documents, 16th to 19th Century); Manuscripts & Maps Coll; Medieval & Renaissance Manuscripts; Middle East Manuscripts; Montaigne Coll; Mormon History; Mountaineering; New Jersey History & Imprints; Papyrus Manuscripts; Pliny-Fisk Library of Economics & Finance; Publishers & Publishing (Doubleday, Harper, Holt, John Day, Scribner), papers; Rowlandson Coll; Sporting Books Coll; Story Magazine; Theater Coll; United Nations; Vergil Coll; Western Americana Coll. UN Document Depository; US Document Depository
Subject Interests: Ancient hist, Behav sci, China, Classics hist, Econ, Hist, Humanities, Intl law, Japan, Lit, Music, Natural sci, Near East, Relations, Soc sci
Wireless access
Function: Art exhibits, Digital talking bks, Doc delivery serv, E-Reserves, Electronic databases & coll, ILL available, Internet access, Magazines, Microfiche/film & reading machines, Notary serv, Online cat, Online ref, Photocopying/Printing, Printer for laptops & handheld devices, Prof lending libr, Ref & res, Ref serv available, Res libr, Wheelchair accessible
Publications: The Princeton University Library Chronicle
Partic in OCLC Research Library Partnership
Open Mon-Fri 8am-11:45pm, Sat & Sun 9am-11:45pm
Restriction: 24-hr pass syst for students only, Access for corporate affiliates, Borrowing privileges limited to fac & registered students, Fee for pub use, Off-site coll in storage - retrieval as requested, Open to authorized patrons, Open to employees & special libr, Open to fac, students & qualified researchers, Open to researchers by request, Open to students, Open to students, fac & staff, Open to students, fac, staff & alumni, Photo ID required for access, Restricted access, Restricted borrowing privileges, Restricted loan policy, Use of others with permission of librn
Friends of the Library Group

Departmental Libraries:

ARCHITECTURE LIBRARY, Architecture Bldg, 2nd Flr, S-204, 08544. (Mail add: One Washington Rd, 08544). Tel: 609-258-3256. E-mail: ues@princeton.edu. Web Site: library.princeton.edu/architecture. *Librn,* Gabriella Karl-Johnson; Tel: 609-258-3128, E-mail: gjk@princeton.edu; Staff 4 (MLS 1, Non-MLS 3)
Founded 1967. Enrl 120; Fac 16
Library Holdings: Bk Vols 32,000; Per Subs 300
Subject Interests: Archit hist, Landscape archit, Urban design
Open Mon-Fri 9am-11:45pm, Sat 10am-11:45pm, Sun 1-11:45
Restriction: Non-circulating

EAST ASIAN LIBRARY, 33 Frist Campus Ctr, Rm 317, 08544. (Mail add: One Washington Rd, 08544). Tel: 609-258-3182. FAX: 609-258-4573. E-mail: gestcirc@princeton.edu. Web Site: library.princeton.edu/eastasian. *Dir,* Martin Heijdra; Tel: 609-258-3183, E-mail: mheijdra@princeton.edu; *Librn,* Hyoungbae Lee; Tel: 609-258-0417, E-mail: hyoungl@princeton.edu; *Librn,* Setsuko Noguchi; Tel: 609-258-6159, E-mail: snoguchi@princeton.edu; *Librn,* Joshua Seufert; Tel: 609-258-5336, E-mail: jseufert@princeton.edu. Subject Specialists: *Korean studies,* Hyoungbae Lee; *Japanese studies,* Setsuko Noguchi; *Chinese studies,* Joshua Seufert; Staff 8 (MLS 4, Non-MLS 4)
Founded 1937
Library Holdings: Bk Vols 784,000; Per Subs 36,000
Special Collections: Gest Coll of String-bound Chinese Books, most printed prior to 18th century
Partic in East Coast Consortium of East Asian Libraries; OCLC Online Computer Library Center, Inc
Open Mon-Fri (Winter) 9am-11pm, Sat 10-5, Sun 2-11; Mon-Fri (Summer) 8:30-4:30

ENGINEERING LIBRARY, Friend Ctr, William St, 08544. (Mail add: One Washington Rd, 08544). Tel: 609-258-3200. E-mail: englib@princeton.edu. Web Site: library.princeton.edu/engineering. *Eng Librn,* Willow Dressel; Tel: 609-258-6567, E-mail: wdressel@princeton.edu; Staff 5 (MLS 1, Non-MLS 4)
Founded 1963. Enrl 1,600; Highest Degree: Doctorate
Library Holdings: Bk Vols 600,000
Automation Activity & Vendor Info: (Acquisitions) Ex Libris Group; (Cataloging) Ex Libris Group; (Circulation) Ex Libris Group; (ILL) OCLC ILLiad; (Serials) Ex Libris Group
Open Mon-Thurs 8:30am-2am, Fri 8:30am-9pm, Sat 9-9, Sun 1pm-2am

LEWIS SCIENCE LIBRARY, Washington Rd, 08544-0001. (Mail add: One Washington Rd, 08544). Tel: 609-258-6004. E-mail: lewislib@princeton.edu. Web Site: library.princeton.edu/lewis. *Head, Sci Libr,* Denise Hersey; Tel: 609-258-1187, E-mail: dhersey@princeton.edu; *Librn,* Kelee Pacion; Tel: 609-258-8601, E-mail: kpacion@princeton.edu; *Librn,* Wangyal Tsering Shawa; Tel: 609-258-6804, E-mail: shawatw@princeton.edu; *Behav Sci Librn,* Meghan Testerman; Tel: 609-258-5481, E-mail: mtesterman@princeton.edu; *Physics, Astronomy & Mat Librn,* Anya Bartelmann; Tel: 609-258-3150, E-mail: abartelm@princeton.edu. Subject Specialists: *Biology,* Kelee Pacion; *Geographic Info Syst,* Wangyal Tsering Shawa; Staff 16 (MLS 6, Non-MLS 10)
Fac 95
Library Holdings: Bk Titles 55,500; Bk Vols 128,000; Per Subs 784; Spec Interest Per Sub 680
Special Collections: 18th Century German Mathematics Dissertations; High Energy & Statistics Preprints; Rare Mathematics Texts
Subject Interests: Math, Physics, Statistics
Function: Doc delivery serv, Ref serv available
Partic in ISI
Open Mon-Thurs 8:30am-Midnight, Fri & Sat 8:30am-9pm, Sun 9am-Midnight
Friends of the Library Group

MARQUAND LIBRARY OF ART & ARCHAEOLOGY, McCormick Hall, 08544-0001. (Mail add: One Washington Rd, 08544), SAN 351-2371. Tel: 609-258-3783. FAX: 609-258-7650. E-mail: marquand@princeton.edu. Web Site: library.princeton.edu/marquand. *Head Librn,* Holly Hatheway; Tel: 609-258-5860, E-mail: hhatheway@princeton.edu; *Asst Librn,* Rebecca Friedman; Tel: 609-258-3163, E-mail: rfriedma@princeton.edu; *Spec,* Nicole Fabricand-Person; E-mail: nfperson@princeton.edu; *Spec,* Kim Wishart; E-mail: kwishart@princeton.edu. Subject Specialists: *Art, Japanese,* Nicole Fabricand-Person; *Chinese art,* Kim Wishart; Staff 8 (MLS 3, Non-MLS 5)
Founded 1908
Library Holdings: Bk Vols 500,000
Subject Interests: Archaeology, Archit, Art, Gardens, Landscaping, Photog, Rare bks
Automation Activity & Vendor Info: (Acquisitions) Ex Libris Group; (Cataloging) Ex Libris Group; (Circulation) Ex Libris Group; (OPAC) Ex Libris Group
Open Mon-Fri (Fall-Spring) 8:30am-11:45pm, Sat 10am-10:45pm, Sun 12-11:45; Mon-Thurs (Summer) 8:30am-8:45pm, Fri 8:30am-5:45pm, Sat & Sun 12-5:45
Restriction: Restricted access

MENDEL MUSIC LIBRARY, Woolworth Ctr for Musical Studies, 08544. (Mail add: One Washington Rd, 08544). Tel: 609-258-3230. E-mail: muslib@princeton.edu. Web Site: library.princeton.edu/music. *Music Librn,* Darwin Scott; Tel: 609-258-4251, E-mail: dfscott@princeton.edu; Staff 4 (MLS 1, Non-MLS 3)
Founded 1997
Library Holdings: Bk Vols 65,000
Special Collections: Old Nassau Coll (1859-1989)
Open Mon-Thurs 8:30am-11:45pm, Fri 8:30-7:45, Sat 10-7:45, Sun Noon-11:45

SEELEY G MUDD MANUSCRIPT LIBRARY, 65 Olden St, 08544. Tel: 609-258-6345. E-mail: mudd@princeton.edu. Web Site: rbsc.princeton.edu/mudd. *Interim Univ Archivist,* Sara Logue; Tel: 609-258-6345, E-mail: slogue@princeton.edu; *Digital Archivist,* Annalise Berdini; Tel: 609-258-3248, E-mail: aberdini@princeton.edu; *Rec Mgr,* Anne Marie Phillips; Tel: 609-258-3213, E-mail: ap2@princeton.edu; Staff 10 (MLS 6, Non-MLS 4)
Special Collections: Manuscripts Coll; University Archives
Subject Interests: 20th Century Am, Foreign policy, Intl develop, Journalism, Law
Function: Archival coll
Open Mon-Fri 9-4:45
Restriction: Closed stack, Non-circulating

DONALD E STOKES LIBRARY - PUBLIC & INTERNATIONAL AFFAIRS & POPULATION RESEARCH, Wallace Hall, Lower Flr, 08544. (Mail add: One Washington Rd, 08544). Tel: 609-258-5455. FAX: 609-258-6844. E-mail: piaprlib@princeton.edu. Web Site: library.princeton.edu/stokes. *Head Librn,* Seth Porter; Tel: 609-258-4782, E-mail: smporter@princeton.edu; *Population Res Librn,* Joann Donatiello; Tel: 609-258-1377, E-mail: jdonatie@princeton.edu; *Asst Population Res Librn,* Elana Broch; Tel: 609-258-5517, E-mail: ebroch@princeton.edu; Staff 6 (MLS 3, Non-MLS 3)
Library Holdings: Bk Vols 55,000; Per Subs 500
Special Collections: Ansley J Coale Population Research Coll
Subject Interests: Census, Statistics
Open Mon-Thurs (Winter) 8:30am-Midnight, Fri 8:30am-10pm, Sat 10-9, Sun Noon-Midnight; Mon-Thurs (Summer) 8:30-8, Fri 8:30-4:30, Sat & Sun 1-5

S SIEMENS CORPORATE RESEARCH, INC*, Research Library, 755 College Rd E, 08540. SAN 375-6440. Tel: 609-734-3311, 609-734-6500. *Librn,* Stephanie Hale; Staff 2 (MLS 2)
Library Holdings: Bk Titles 12,000; Per Subs 20
Subject Interests: Computer sci
Automation Activity & Vendor Info: (Cataloging) EOS International; (Circulation) EOS International; (OPAC) EOS International; (Serials) EOS International
Restriction: Not open to pub

S TOBACCO MERCHANTS ASSOCIATION OF THE UNITED STATES*, Howard S Cullman Library, 231 Clarksville Rd, 08543. (Mail add: PO Box 8019, 08543-8019), SAN 312-0929. Tel: 609-275-4900. FAX:

609-275-8379. Web Site: www.tma.org. *Library Contact,* Darryl Jason; E-mail: darryl@tma.org; Staff 2 (Non-MLS 2)
Founded 1915
Library Holdings: Bk Vols 300; Per Subs 100
Special Collections: Tobacco & Products (Trademark & Brand Files), electronic
Wireless access
Publications: Newsletters
Partic in LibraryLinkNJ, The New Jersey Library Cooperative
Restriction: Staff & mem only

RAHWAY

S EAST JERSEY STATE PRISON LIBRARY*, 1100 Woodbridge Rd, 07065. SAN 375-8451. Tel: 732-499-5010, Ext 2695. Web Site: www.state.nj.us/corrections/pages. *Supvr,* Kristen Difiore; E-mail: kristen.difiore@doc.nj.gov
Library Holdings: Bk Vols 1,000
Restriction: Not open to pub
Branches:
LAW, Lock Bag R, Woodbridge Ave, 07065. Tel: 732-499-5010, Ext 2695. *Supvr,* Kristen Difiore
Library Holdings: Bk Vols 1,000
Restriction: Not open to pub

M ROBERT WOOD JOHNSON UNIVERSITY HOSPITAL RAHWAY*, Health Sciences Library, 865 Stone St, 07065. Tel: 732-499-7929. Web Site: www.rwjuhr.com. *Librn,* Jennifer Davila; Staff 1 (MLS 1)
Library Holdings: Bk Vols 500; Per Subs 40
Automation Activity & Vendor Info: (Cataloging) LibraryWorld, Inc; (Circulation) LibraryWorld, Inc; (OPAC) LibraryWorld, Inc; (Serials) LibraryWorld, Inc
Wireless access
Partic in Basic Health Sciences Library Network

P RAHWAY PUBLIC LIBRARY*, Two City Hall Plaza, 07065. SAN 310-4648. Tel: 732-340-1551. FAX: 732-340-0393. E-mail: info@rahwaylibrary.org. Web Site: www.rahwaylibrary.org. *Dir,* Gail Miller; E-mail: gmiller@rahwaylibrary.org; Staff 8 (MLS 3, Non-MLS 5)
Founded 1858. Pop 25,760; Circ 125,341
Library Holdings: Bk Titles 75,000; Bk Vols 90,000; Per Subs 175
Subject Interests: Local hist, NJ
Automation Activity & Vendor Info: (Cataloging) TLC (The Library Corporation); (Circulation) TLC (The Library Corporation)
Wireless access
Publications: Annual Report
Partic in LibraryLinkNJ, The New Jersey Library Cooperative
Open Mon, Wed & Thurs 9-8, Tues, Fri & Sat 9-5
Friends of the Library Group

RAMSEY

P RAMSEY FREE PUBLIC LIBRARY*, 30 Wyckoff Ave, 07446. SAN 310-4656. Tel: 201-327-1445. FAX: 201-327-3687. E-mail: ramscirc@bccls.org. Web Site: www.ramseylibrary.org. *Dir,* Matthew Latham; E-mail: latham@ramsey.bccls.org; *Asst Dir,* Kathy Elwell; *Libr Asst,* Matthew Camarda; *Ref (Info Servs),* Debbie Burnette; Staff 4 (MLS 4)
Founded 1921. Pop 16,000; Circ 205,000
Library Holdings: Bk Vols 113,000; Per Subs 175
Special Collections: Sidoroff Language Learning Coll
Subject Interests: NJ hist, Spanish
Automation Activity & Vendor Info: (Cataloging) SirsiDynix; (Circulation) SirsiDynix; (OPAC) SirsiDynix
Wireless access
Publications: Ramsey Reader (Newsletter)
Partic in Bergen County Cooperative Library System, Inc; LibraryLinkNJ, The New Jersey Library Cooperative
Open Mon-Thurs 9-9, Fri 9-5, Sat 10-5, Sun 12-4
Friends of the Library Group

RANDOLPH

J COUNTY COLLEGE OF MORRIS, Sherman H Masten Learning Resource Center, 214 Center Grove Rd, 07869-2086. SAN 310-4672. Tel: 973-328-5300. Reference Tel: 973-328-5296. Administration Tel: 973-328-5282. Web Site: www.ccm.edu/learning-resource-center, www.ccm.edu/library. *Dean of Learning Resource Ctr,* Heather Craven; E-mail: hcraven@ccm.edu; *Assoc Dir,* Mark Tolleson; Tel: 973-328-5311, E-mail: mtolleson@ccm.edu; *Ref Librn,* Jane Kingsland; E-mail: jkingsland@ccm.edu; *Coordr, Instrul Serv,* Lynee Richel; E-mail: lrichel@ccm.edu; *Coordr, Tech Serv,* Regina Cannizzaro; E-mail: rcannizzaro@ccm.edu; Staff 9.2 (MLS 5.2, Non-MLS 4)
Founded 1968. Highest Degree: Associate
Library Holdings: Bk Titles 55,000
Special Collections: US Document Depository
Automation Activity & Vendor Info: (Acquisitions) OCLC Worldshare Management Services; (Cataloging) OCLC Worldshare Management Services; (Circulation) OCLC Worldshare Management Services; (Course Reserve) OCLC Worldshare Management Services; (ILL) OCLC Worldshare Management Services; (OPAC) OCLC Worldshare Management Services; (Serials) OCLC Worldshare Management Services
Wireless access
Publications: Bibliographies; Function-specific guides; In-house Catalogs
Partic in LibraryLinkNJ, The New Jersey Library Cooperative; LYRASIS; OCLC Online Computer Library Center, Inc; Virtual Academic Library Environment

P RANDOLPH TOWNSHIP FREE PUBLIC LIBRARY, 28 Calais Rd, 07869. SAN 310-4664. Tel: 973-895-3556. FAX: 973-895-4946. Web Site: www.randolphnj.org/library. *Dir,* Lore Reinhart; E-mail: director@randolphlibrary.net; *Asst Dir,* Robert Tambini; E-mail: rob.tambini@mainlib.org; Staff 4.1 (MLS 4.1)
Founded 1964. Pop 26,000; Circ 294,000
Jan 2018-Dec 2018 Income (Main Library Only) $1,530,000. Mats Exp $1,360,658, Books $130,251, Per/Ser (Incl. Access Fees) $9,110, AV Mat $35,686
Library Holdings: Audiobooks 3,510; CDs 5,000; DVDs 7,990; Large Print Bks 1,020; Bk Titles 100,000; Per Subs 130
Automation Activity & Vendor Info: (Circulation) Innovative Interfaces, Inc; (OPAC) Innovative Interfaces, Inc
Wireless access
Function: Adult bk club, After school storytime, Audiobks via web, Bk club(s), Bks on CD, CD-ROM, Children's prog, Computer training, Computers for patron use, Free DVD rentals, ILL available, Music CDs, Notary serv, Photocopying/Printing, Preschool reading prog, Prog for adults, Prog for children & young adult, Scanner, Story hour, Summer reading prog, Wheelchair accessible
Partic in LibraryLinkNJ, The New Jersey Library Cooperative; Morris Automated Information Network
Open Mon-Thurs 9-7, Fri & Sat 9-5, Sun 12-4 (Winter); Mon-Thurs 9-7, Fri 9-5, Sat 9-12 (Summer)
Friends of the Library Group

RARITAN

P RARITAN PUBLIC LIBRARY*, 54 E Somerset St, 08869. SAN 310-4702. Tel: 908-725-0413. FAX: 908-725-1832. E-mail: RaritanL@yahoo.com. Web Site: www.raritanlibrary.org. *Dir,* Mary Jane Paese
Founded 1961. Pop 5,798; Circ 39,000
Library Holdings: Bk Vols 39,000; Per Subs 100
Special Collections: Basilone Congressional Record, Tribute & Citation; Basilone History Coll; Frelinghuysen Portraits Coll
Automation Activity & Vendor Info: (Acquisitions) Follett Software; (Cataloging) Follett Software; (Circulation) Follett Software; (Serials) Follett Software
Wireless access
Publications: Raritan Library News
Partic in NW Regional Libr Coop; Raritan Valley Fedn of Librs
Open Mon-Thurs 10-8, Fri 10-5, Sat 10-3
Friends of the Library Group

RED BANK

P RED BANK PUBLIC LIBRARY*, Eisner Memorial Library, 84 W Front St, 07701. SAN 310-4710. Tel: 732-842-0690. Circulation Tel: 732-842-0690, Ext 110. Reference Tel: 732-842-0690, Ext 111. Web Site: redbanklibrary.org. *Libr Dir,* Position Currently Open; Staff 5 (MLS 4, Non-MLS 1)
Founded 1878. Pop 12,206; Circ 46,325
Library Holdings: Bk Vols 42,500; Per Subs 108
Subject Interests: NJ hist
Automation Activity & Vendor Info: (Cataloging) SirsiDynix; (Circulation) SirsiDynix; (ILL) OCLC; (OPAC) SirsiDynix
Wireless access
Function: 24/7 Electronic res, 24/7 Online cat, Adult bk club, Adult literacy prog
Partic in Libraries of Middlesex Automation Consortium; LibraryLinkNJ, The New Jersey Library Cooperative
Open Mon, Tues & Sat 10-5, Wed & Thurs 1-9, Fri 1-5
Friends of the Library Group

RIDGEFIELD

P RIDGEFIELD PUBLIC LIBRARY*, 527 Morse Ave, 07657. SAN 310-4745. Tel: 201-941-0192. FAX: 201-941-9354. Circulation E-mail: rfldcirc@bccls.org. Web Site: www.ridgefieldpubliclibrary.com. *Dir,* Jane Forte; Tel: 201-941-0192, Ext 15, E-mail: forte@ridgefield.bccls.org; *Adult Ref,* Yilin Sheng; E-mail: sheng@ridgefield.bccls.org; Staff 6 (MLS 2, Non-MLS 4)

Founded 1930. Pop 10,081; Circ 69,082
Library Holdings: Bk Vols 61,000; Per Subs 200
Special Collections: Ridgefield History Coll
Automation Activity & Vendor Info: (Cataloging) SirsiDynix; (Circulation) SirsiDynix; (ILL) SirsiDynix; (OPAC) SirsiDynix
Wireless access
Open Mon-Thurs 10-8. Fri 10-5, Sat 10-2
Friends of the Library Group

RIDGEFIELD PARK

P RIDGEFIELD PARK FREE PUBLIC LIBRARY*, 107 Cedar St, 07660. SAN 310-4753. Tel: 201-641-0689. FAX: 201-440-1058. Circulation E-mail: rfpkcirc@bccls.org. Web Site: www.ridgefieldparkpubliclibrary.org. *Dir,* Omar Khan; E-mail: khan@ridgefieldpark.bccls.org; *Head, Children's Servx,* Deborah Fagnan; E-mail: deborah.fagnan@ridgefieldpark.bccls.org; Staff 4 (MLS 2, Non-MLS 2)
Founded 1890. Pop 12,854; Circ 69,561
Library Holdings: Bk Vols 62,395; Per Subs 95
Automation Activity & Vendor Info: (Cataloging) SirsiDynix; (Circulation) SirsiDynix; (ILL) SirsiDynix; (OPAC) SirsiDynix
Wireless access
Function: Adult bk club, Adult literacy prog, After school storytime, Archival coll, Art exhibits, Audiobks via web, Bk club(s), Bks on CD, CD-ROM, Children's prog, Computer training, Computers for patron use, Digital talking bks, E-Reserves, Electronic databases & coll, Free DVD rentals, Homebound delivery serv, ILL available, Magnifiers for reading, Museum passes, Music CDs, Online cat, OverDrive digital audio bks, Photocopying/Printing, Preschool outreach, Prog for adults, Prog for children & young adult, Ref serv available, Story hour, Summer & winter reading prog, Summer reading prog, Tax forms, Teen prog, Wheelchair accessible
Open Mon-Thurs 9:30-9, Fri 9:30-5:30, Sat 9:30-4:30
Friends of the Library Group

RIDGEWOOD

P RIDGEWOOD PUBLIC LIBRARY*, 125 N Maple Ave, 07450-3288. SAN 351-336X. Tel: 201-670-5600. FAX: 201-670-0293. Web Site: www.ridgewoodlibrary.org. *Dir,* Nancy K Greene; E-mail: ngreene@ridgewoodlibrary.org; *Asst Dir,* Lorri Steinbacher; E-mail: lsteinbacher@ridgewoodlibrary.org; Staff 11 (MLS 11)
Founded 1923. Pop 27,000; Circ 502,000
Library Holdings: AV Mats 20,031; Bk Vols 148,000
Subject Interests: English as a second lang, Local hist
Wireless access
Publications: Annual Report
Partic in Bergen County Cooperative Library System, Inc
Open Mon-Thurs 9-9, Fri 9-6, Sat 9-5, Sun 1-5
Friends of the Library Group

M VALLEY HOSPITAL*, Medical Library, 223 N Van Dien Ave, 07450. SAN 322-9122. Tel: 201-447-8285. FAX: 201-447-8602. Web Site: www.valleyhealth.com. *Dir, Libr Serv,* Claudia Allocco; E-mail: callocc@valleyhealth.com; Staff 2 (MLS 1, Non-MLS 1)
Library Holdings: Bk Vols 2,000; Per Subs 100
Subject Interests: Consumer health
Partic in New Jersey Health Sciences Library Network
Open Mon-Fri 7:30-3
Restriction: Pub by appt only

RINGWOOD

P RINGWOOD PUBLIC LIBRARY, 30 Cannici Dr, 07456. SAN 310-477X. Tel: 973-962-6256. FAX: 973-962-7799. E-mail: ringwoodpl@ringwoodlibrary.org. Web Site: www.ringwoodlibrary.org. *Dir,* Daniel Parker; Tel: 973-962-6256, Ext 114, E-mail: parker@ringwoodlibrary.org; *Ad, Supv Librn,* Wendy Sandford; Tel: 973-962-6256, Ext 120, E-mail: sandford@ringwoodlibrary.org; *Youth Serv Librn,* Aleksander Brittain; Tel: 973-962-6256, Ext 115, E-mail: brittain@ringwoodlibrary.org; *Technical Services & STEM Supvr,* Heather Caldwell; Tel: 973-962-6256, Ext 121, E-mail: caldwell@ringwoodlibrary.org; Staff 15 (MLS 3, Non-MLS 12)
Founded 1960. Pop 12,454; Circ 92,213
Jan 2018-Dec 2018 Income $678,500, State $5,412, City $581,200, Locally Generated Income $79,070, Other $12,818. Mats Exp $31,913, Books $23,132, Per/Ser (Incl. Access Fees) $3,495, AV Mat $1,250, Electronic Ref Mat (Incl. Access Fees) $4,036
Library Holdings: Audiobooks 1,691; CDs 2,948; DVDs 2,826; e-books 6,230; Electronic Media & Resources 7; Bk Vols 51,152; Per Subs 25
Special Collections: Local Minutes of Public Agencies Coll; Official Repository for EPA Superfund Documents for Ringwood Mines Site; Oral History of Camp Midvale Coll; Oral History of Upper Ringwood Coll; Ringwood History Coll, bks, clippings, microfiche, pamphlets
Automation Activity & Vendor Info: (Cataloging) SirsiDynix-WorkFlows; (Circulation) SirsiDynix-WorkFlows; (ILL) JerseyCat; (OPAC) SirsiDynix-iBistro
Wireless access
Function: 24/7 Electronic res, 24/7 Online cat, 3D Printer, Adult bk club, Adult literacy prog, Archival coll, Art exhibits, Art programs, Audio & video playback equip for onsite use, Audiobks via web, AV serv, Bk club(s), Bks on CD, Children's prog, Computer training, Computers for patron use, E-Reserves, Electronic databases & coll, Free DVD rentals, Holiday prog, Homework prog, ILL available, Internet access, Large print keyboards, Life-long learning prog for all ages, Magazines, Magnifiers for reading, Mail & tel request accepted, Makerspace, Meeting rooms, Movies, Museum passes, Music CDs, Notary serv, Online cat, Online ref, Orientations, Outreach serv, OverDrive digital audio bks, Photocopying/Printing, Preschool reading prog, Prog for adults, Prog for children & young adult, Ref & res, Ref serv available, Scanner, Spoken cassettes & CDs, STEM programs, Story hour, Summer reading prog, Tax forms, Teen prog, Telephone ref, Wheelchair accessible, Workshops, Writing prog
Partic in LibraryLinkNJ, The New Jersey Library Cooperative; PALS Plus, The Computer Consortium of Passaic County Libraries
Open Mon-Thurs 10-9, Fri 10-5, Sat 10-4
Friends of the Library Group

RIVER EDGE

L PECKAR & ABRAMSON*, Law Library, 70 Grand Ave, 07661. SAN 372-4298. Tel: 201-343-3434. FAX: 201-343-6306. Web Site: www.pecklaw.com. *Librn,* David H Sloves
Library Holdings: Bk Vols 5,000; Per Subs 50
Wireless access
Partic in New Jersey Library Network
Restriction: Not open to pub

P RIVER EDGE FREE PUBLIC LIBRARY*, 685 Elm Ave, 07661. SAN 310-4788. Tel: 201-261-1663. FAX: 201-986-0214. Circulation E-mail: rivecirc@bccls.org. Web Site: www.riveredgepubliclibrary.org. *Dir,* Daragh O'Connor; E-mail: oconnor@riveredge.bccls.org; *Ref Librn,* Margaret Churley; E-mail: margaret.churley@riveredge.bccls.org; *Youth Serv Librn,* Maryanne Guiliano; E-mail: mary.anne.guiliano@riveredge.bccls.org; *Adult Serv,* Jennifer Kelemen; E-mail: jennifer.kelemen@riveredge.bccls.org; Staff 4 (MLS 4)
Founded 1953. Pop 10,946; Circ 148,000
Library Holdings: AV Mats 3,398; Bk Titles 70,000; Bk Vols 75,000; Per Subs 120; Talking Bks 685
Special Collections: Korean Coll
Automation Activity & Vendor Info: (Cataloging) SirsiDynix; (Circulation) SirsiDynix; (OPAC) SirsiDynix
Wireless access
Partic in Bergen County Cooperative Library System, Inc
Open Mon-Thurs 10-9, Fri & Sat 10-5
Friends of the Library Group

RIVER VALE

P RIVER VALE FREE PUBLIC LIBRARY*, 412 Rivervale Rd, 07675. SAN 310-4796. Tel: 201-391-2323. FAX: 201-391-6599. E-mail: reference@rivervalelibrary.org. Web Site: www.rivervalelibrary.org. *Dir,* Ann McCarthy; E-mail: mccarthy@rivervale.bccls.org; *Ref Librn,* Diane Sweatlock; *Ref/YA,* Dale Friedman; *Youth Serv Librn,* Karen Pankovcin; Staff 4 (MLS 3, Non-MLS 1)
Founded 1964. Pop 9,449; Circ 114,982
Library Holdings: Bk Vols 52,100; Per Subs 125
Automation Activity & Vendor Info: (Cataloging) SirsiDynix; (Circulation) SirsiDynix; (OPAC) SirsiDynix; (Serials) SirsiDynix
Wireless access
Partic in LibraryLinkNJ, The New Jersey Library Cooperative
Open Mon-Wed 10-9, Thurs 10-6, Fri & Sat 10-5, Sun 1-4; Mon-Wed (Summer) 10-9, Thurs 10-6, Fri 10-5, Sat 10-2
Friends of the Library Group

RIVERDALE

P RIVERDALE PUBLIC LIBRARY, 93 Newark Pompton Tpk, 07457. SAN 376-057X. Tel: 973-835-5044. FAX: 973-835-2175. Web Site: www.riverdalelibrary.org. *Dir,* Therese McClachrie; E-mail: director@riverdalelibrary.org; *Ch Serv,* Geneva Fucci; Staff 2 (MLS 1, Non-MLS 1)
Founded 2002. Pop 3,559; Circ 32,613
Library Holdings: Audiobooks 1,375; CDs 104; DVDs 2,601; Large Print Bks 652; Bk Titles 34,484; Bk Vols 34,987; Per Subs 46; Talking Bks 1,375; Videos 2,601
Automation Activity & Vendor Info: (Cataloging) Innovative Interfaces, Inc; (Circulation) Innovative Interfaces, Inc; (OPAC) Innovative Interfaces, Inc

Wireless access
Partic in Morris Automated Information Network
Open Mon, Wed & Thurs 10-8, Tues & Fri 10-5, Sat (Summer 10-2) 10-4
Friends of the Library Group

RIVERSIDE

P RIVERSIDE PUBLIC LIBRARY*, Ten Zurbrugg Way, 08075. SAN 310-480X. Tel: 856-461-6922. E-mail: riverside@bcls.lib.nj.us. *Dir,* Jean Bowker; E-mail: jbowker@bcls.lib.nj.us
Founded 1922. Pop 8,079; Circ 41,611
Library Holdings: Audiobooks 36; CDs 258; DVDs 2,244; Bk Vols 33,615; Per Subs 32
Automation Activity & Vendor Info: (Cataloging) Horizon; (Circulation) Horizon; (OPAC) Horizon
Wireless access
Open Mon & Thurs 12-5 & 6:30-8:30, Tues 12-5, Wed 10-5, Sat 10-2

ROCHELLE PARK

P ROCHELLE PARK LIBRARY*, 151 W Passaic St, 07662. Tel: 201-587-7730, Ext 8. FAX: 201-587-9855. Web Site: rplibrary.org. *Interim Dir,* Jennifer Collen; E-mail: librarydirector@rochelleparknj.gov; Staff 7 (MLS 1, Non-MLS 6)
Library Holdings: Audiobooks 165; CDs 458; Large Print Bks 205; Per Subs 32; Talking Bks 165
Automation Activity & Vendor Info: (Cataloging) SirsiDynix; (Circulation) SirsiDynix; (OPAC) SirsiDynix
Wireless access
Function: 24/7 Online cat, Activity rm, Adult bk club, Audiobks via web, Bk club(s), Bks on CD, Children's prog, Computer training, Computers for patron use, Digital talking bks, E-Reserves, Electronic databases & coll, Free DVD rentals, Holiday prog, Home delivery & serv to seniorr ctr & nursing homes, Homebound delivery serv, ILL available, Internet access, Magazines, Movies, Music CDs, Online cat, OverDrive digital audio bks, Photocopying/Printing, Prog for adults, Prog for children & young adult, Scanner, Senior computer classes, Serves people with intellectual disabilities, Spanish lang bks, Spoken cassettes & CDs, STEM programs, Summer reading prog, Tax forms, Teen prog, Telephone ref, Wheelchair accessible
Partic in Bergen County Cooperative Library System, Inc
Open Mon-Thurs 10-8, Fri 10-5, Sat 10-3, Sun 12-4
Restriction: Circ limited

ROCKAWAY

P ROCKAWAY BOROUGH PUBLIC LIBRARY*, 82 E Main St, 07866. SAN 371-5388. Tel: 973-627-5709. FAX: 973-627-5796. E-mail: circ-rcb@mainlib.org. Web Site: www.rblibrary.org. *Dir,* Edna Puleo; *Ch Serv,* Jennifer Boyle; *ILL,* Marilyn Senesicy; Staff 9 (MLS 1, Non-MLS 8)
Founded 1914. Pop 6,500
Library Holdings: Bk Titles 30,000; Bk Vols 35,000; Per Subs 80
Subject Interests: Local hist, Natural hist, NJ hist, State hist
Automation Activity & Vendor Info: (Circulation) SirsiDynix; (ILL) SirsiDynix; (OPAC) SirsiDynix
Wireless access
Publications: Rockaway Borough Library Newsletter
Partic in Morris Automated Information Network
Special Services for the Blind - Magnifiers
Open Mon & Wed 12-8, Tues, Thurs & Fri 10-6, Sat 10-2
Friends of the Library Group

P ROCKAWAY TOWNSHIP FREE PUBLIC LIBRARY, 61 Mount Hope Rd, 07866. SAN 351-3424. Tel: 973-627-2344. FAX: 973-627-7658. E-mail: rockawaytwplibrary@rtlibrary.org. Web Site: www.rtlibrary.org. *Libr Dir,* Scott Davan; E-mail: scott.davan@rtlibrary.org; *Head, Ref/IT,* Lisa Laskaris; E-mail: lisa.laskaris@rtlibrary.org; *Head, Youth Serv,* Darlene Steinhart; E-mail: darlene.steinhart@rtlibrary.org; *Ref Librn,* Rachel Franklin; E-mail: rachel.franklin@rtlibrary.org
Founded 1966. Pop 25,000
Library Holdings: AV Mats 8,160; CDs 2,325; DVDs 4,040; Bk Vols 112,000
Automation Activity & Vendor Info: (Circulation) Innovative Interfaces, Inc; (ILL) Auto-Graphics, Inc; (OPAC) Innovative Interfaces, Inc
Wireless access
Partic in Morris Automated Information Network; OCLC Online Computer Library Center, Inc
Open Mon & Wed 9-8, Tues & Thurs-Sat 9-5
Friends of the Library Group
Branches: 1
HIBERNIA BRANCH, 419 Green Pond Rd, 07866. (Mail add: 61 Mount Hope Rd, 07866), SAN 351-3459. Tel: 973-627-6872.
Open Mon 9:30-5:30, Wed Noon-8
Friends of the Library Group

ROEBLING

P FLORENCE TOWNSHIP PUBLIC LIBRARY*, 1350 Hornberger Ave, 08554. SAN 310-4842. Tel: 609-499-0143. FAX: 609-499-0551. E-mail: florence@bcls.lib.nj.us. Web Site: www.bcls.lib.nj.us/florence, www.florence-nj.gov/library.html. *Librn,* LaVonna Lawrence
Circ 12,000
Library Holdings: Bk Vols 26,000; Per Subs 78
Automation Activity & Vendor Info: (Acquisitions) Horizon; (Cataloging) Horizon; (Circulation) Horizon
Wireless access
Mem of Burlington County Library
Open Mon-Thurs 11-8, Fri 11-4, Sat (Sept-June) 10-2

ROSELAND

L CONNELL FOLEY LAW LIBRARY, 56 Livingston Ave, 07068. Tel: 973-535-0500. Interlibrary Loan Service Tel: 973-535-0500, Ext 2439. FAX: 973-535-9217. Web Site: www.connellfoley.com/offices-roseland. *Head Librn,* Aimee Sachs; E-mail: asachs@connellfoley.com; Staff 1 (MLS 1)
Founded 1936
Library Holdings: Bk Vols 22,000
Subject Interests: Banking, Corporate, Estates, NJ law, Tax, Trusts
Wireless access
Partic in LibraryLinkNJ, The New Jersey Library Cooperative
Open Mon-Fri 9-5
Restriction: Private libr, Restricted access

L LOWENSTEIN SANDLER LLP LIBRARY, One Lowenstein Dr, 07068. SAN 376-0707. Tel: 973-597-2500. FAX: 973-597-2400. E-mail: lawlibrary@lowenstein.com. *Mgr, Res Serv,* Katherine Taggart; Tel: 973-422-6442, E-mail: ktaggart@lowenstein.com; *Research Servs Librn,* Carrie Hayter; E-mail: chayter@lowenstein.com; *Research Servs Librn,* Zoraida Michaud; E-mail: zmichaud@lowenstein.com
Library Holdings: Bk Vols 25,000
Restriction: Not open to pub

L LUM, DRASCO & POSITAN LLC*, Law Library, 103 Eisenhower Pkwy, Ste 401, 07068-1049. SAN 310-3439. Tel: 973-403-9000. FAX: 973-403-9021. Web Site: www.lumlaw.com.
Founded 1869
Library Holdings: Bk Vols 19,500
Subject Interests: Banking, Corporate, Estates, Securities, Tax, Trusts
Partic in Proquest Dialog
Restriction: Staff use only

P ROSELAND FREE PUBLIC LIBRARY*, 20 Roseland Ave, 07068-1235. SAN 310-4850. Tel: 973-226-8636. FAX: 973-226-6429. Circulation E-mail: rosecirc@bccls.org. Web Site: roselandpubliclibrary.org. *Dir,* Jen Overton; E-mail: overton@roseland.bccls.org; *Operations Mgr,* Terry Gamba; E-mail: terry.gamba@roseland.bccls.org; Staff 22 (MLS 4, Non-MLS 18)
Founded 1961. Pop 5,300; Circ 88,000
Library Holdings: Bk Titles 63,000; Bk Vols 65,000; Per Subs 80
Automation Activity & Vendor Info: (Cataloging) SirsiDynix-WorkFlows; (Circulation) SirsiDynix-WorkFlows; (OPAC) SirsiDynix-Unicorn
Wireless access
Partic in Bergen County Cooperative Library System, Inc
Special Services for the Blind - Aids for in-house use; Bks on CD; Large print bks; Low vision equip
Open Mon-Thurs 9-9, Fri 9-5, (Sept-June) Sat 10-3
Friends of the Library Group

ROSELLE

P ROSELLE FREE PUBLIC LIBRARY*, 104 W Fourth Ave, 07203. SAN 310-4869. Tel: 908-245-5809. FAX: 908-298-8881. E-mail: roselle@lmxac.org. Web Site: www.rosellelibrary.org. *Libr Dir,* Jeanne Marie Ryan; E-mail: jmryan@lmxac.org; *Libr Assoc,* Marita Parham; E-mail: mparham@lmxac.org; Staff 3.2 (MLS 2.2, Non-MLS 1)
Founded 1917. Pop 21,274; Circ 65,000
Library Holdings: AV Mats 3,400; Bk Titles 52,000; Bk Vols 57,000; Per Subs 122
Automation Activity & Vendor Info: (Cataloging) SirsiDynix; (Circulation) SirsiDynix; (ILL) Auto-Graphics, Inc; (OPAC) SirsiDynix
Wireless access
Function: Adult bk club, AV serv, Bilingual assistance for Spanish patrons, Children's prog, Computers for patron use, Electronic databases & coll, ILL available, Music CDs, Notary serv, Online cat, Passport agency, Photocopying/Printing, Spoken cassettes & CDs, Summer reading prog, Tax forms, Teen prog, Wheelchair accessible
Publications: Facts About the Library (Library handbook)
Partic in Libraries of Middlesex Automation Consortium; LibraryLinkNJ, The New Jersey Library Cooperative

Open Mon 10-8, Thurs & Fri 10-5, Sat (Winter) 10-2
Friends of the Library Group

ROSELLE PARK

P ROSELLE PARK VETERANS MEMORIAL LIBRARY, 404 Chestnut St, 07204. SAN 310-4877. Tel: 908-245-2456. FAX: 908-245-9204. E-mail: library@rosellepark.net. Web Site: lmac.ent.sirsi.net/client/en_US/rospark//new. *Dir,* Jenny Lichtenwalner; E-mail: jennyl@rosellepark.net; *Tech Serv,* Kit Rubino; E-mail: krubino@rosellepark.net; Staff 4 (MLS 2, Non-MLS 2)
Founded 1930. Pop 13,281; Circ 49,500
Library Holdings: Bk Titles 50,600; Bk Vols 55,000; Per Subs 80
Special Collections: Decorating (Weissman Coll); Jones Memorial Science Coll
Wireless access
Partic in Libraries of Middlesex Automation Consortium; LUCC; Mandarin
Open Mon, Wed & Fri 10-5, Tues & Thurs 10-8
Friends of the Library Group

RUMSON

P OCEANIC FREE LIBRARY, 109 Avenue of Two Rivers, 07760. SAN 310-4885. Tel: 732-842-2692. FAX: 732-842-5713. Web Site: oceaniclib.org. *Dir,* Nanette Reis; E-mail: reisn@monmouthcountylib.org
Founded 1920. Pop 7,137; Circ 28,000
Library Holdings: Bk Vols 27,000; Per Subs 28
Special Collections: Opera Libretti, autographed bks
Automation Activity & Vendor Info: (Cataloging) SirsiDynix; (Circulation) SirsiDynix; (OPAC) SirsiDynix
Wireless access
Mem of Monmouth County Library
Open Mon-Fri 10-2
Friends of the Library Group

RUNNEMEDE

P RUNNEMEDE FREE PUBLIC LIBRARY*, Two Broadway & Black Horse Pike, 08078. (Mail add: PO Box 119, 08078-0119), SAN 320-491X. Tel: 856-939-4688. FAX: 856-939-6371. E-mail: runnemedelibrary@gmail.com. Web Site: www.runnemedepubliclibrary.com. *Dir,* Kathleen Ann Vasinda; Staff 1 (Non-MLS 1)
Founded 1975. Pop 8,533; Circ 10,583
Library Holdings: Bk Titles 25,000; Per Subs 1
Automation Activity & Vendor Info: (Acquisitions) Follett Software; (Cataloging) Follett Software; (Circulation) Follett Software
Wireless access
Open Mon & Wed 10-4, Tues 12-8, Thurs 10-6, Fri 10-3
Friends of the Library Group

RUTHERFORD

P RUTHERFORD PUBLIC LIBRARY*, 150 Park Ave, 07070. SAN 310-4907. Tel: 201-939-8600. FAX: 201-939-4108. Circulation E-mail: ruthcirc@rutherford.bccls.org. Web Site: www.rutherfordlibrary.org. *Dir,* Judah Hamer; E-mail: hamer@rutherford.bccls.org; *Head, Circ,* Ellen Carter; *Ch Serv Librn,* Jane Tarantino; *Ref Librn,* Rhoda Portugal; Staff 17 (MLS 4, Non-MLS 13)
Founded 1893. Pop 18,000; Circ 160,000
Library Holdings: Bk Vols 80,000; Per Subs 120
Special Collections: William Carlos Williams Coll
Automation Activity & Vendor Info: (Cataloging) Innovative Interfaces, Inc; (Circulation) Innovative Interfaces, Inc; (OPAC) Innovative Interfaces, Inc
Wireless access
Function: Adult bk club, Bks on CD, Computers for patron use, Microfiche/film & reading machines, Music CDs, Photocopying/Printing, Scanner, Spanish lang bks, Story hour, Tax forms, Wheelchair accessible
Partic in Bergen County Cooperative Library System, Inc
Special Services for the Blind - Braille bks
Open Mon-Wed 10-8, Thurs & Fri 10-6, Sat 10-4
Friends of the Library Group

SADDLE BROOK

P SADDLE BROOK FREE PUBLIC LIBRARY*, 340 Mayhill St, 07663. SAN 310-4915. Tel: 201-843-3287. FAX: 201-843-5512. E-mail: sabkcirc@bccls.org. Web Site: saddlebrook.bccls.org. *Dir,* Katherine Hybertsen; E-mail: director@saddlebrook.bccls.org; Staff 3 (MLS 3)
Founded 1944. Pop 13,100
Library Holdings: Bk Vols 68,000; Per Subs 85
Automation Activity & Vendor Info: (Cataloging) SirsiDynix; (Circulation) SirsiDynix; (OPAC) SirsiDynix
Wireless access
Open Mon-Thurs 10-9, Fri 10-5, Sat 10-3

SALEM

S SALEM COUNTY HISTORICAL SOCIETY*, Josephine Jaquett Memorial Library, 79-83 Market St, 08079. SAN 310-4923. Tel: 856-935-5004. FAX: 856-935-0728. E-mail: librarian@salemcountyhistoricalsociety.com. Web Site: www.salemcountyhistoricalsociety.com/research-library. *Admin Librn,* Richard Guido
Founded 1884
Library Holdings: Bk Vols 1,000; Per Subs 10
Special Collections: Family Bibles Coll; Unrecorded Deed Coll
Subject Interests: Genealogy, Hist
Wireless access
Publications: Newsletter (Quarterly)
Open Tues-Sat 12-4

P SALEM FREE PUBLIC LIBRARY, 112 W Broadway, 08079-1302. SAN 310-4931. Tel: 856-935-0526. Circulation Tel: 856-935-0526, Ext 10. FAX: 856-935-5110. E-mail: mysalemlibrary@gmail.com. Web Site: www.mysalemlibrary.org. *Mgr,* Anne Lester; Tel: 856-935-0526, Ext 11, E-mail: mysalemlibrary@gmail.com
Founded 1804. Pop 4,781; Circ 12,861
Library Holdings: Bk Titles 25,000; Per Subs 62
Special Collections: Local History (Granville S Thomas Coll), bks, pamphlets; PSEG Salem Nuclear Generating Station
Wireless access
Partic in Libraries of Gloucester, Salem & Cumberland Information Network; LibraryLinkNJ, The New Jersey Library Cooperative
Open Tues, Thurs & Fri 10-1 & 2-5, Wed & Sat 10-1
Friends of the Library Group

SCOTCH PLAINS

P SCOTCH PLAINS PUBLIC LIBRARY*, 1927 Bartle Ave, 07076-1212. SAN 310-494X. Tel: 908-322-5007. Circulation Tel: 908-322-5007, Ext 200. E-mail: library@scotlib.org. Web Site: www.scotlib.org. *Dir,* Michelle Willis; Tel: 908-322-5007, Ext 202, E-mail: director@scotlib.org; *Head, Adult Serv,* Pamela Brooks; E-mail: pbrooks@scotlib.org; *Head, Circ Serv,* Mimi Sengupta; E-mail: msengupta@scotlib.org; *Head, Tech Serv,* Linda Rosario; Staff 5.2 (MLS 5.2)
Founded 1888. Pop 22,700
Library Holdings: Bks on Deafness & Sign Lang 40; Bk Titles 67,853; Bk Vols 74,865; Per Subs 196
Special Collections: New Jersey Local & State History Coll
Automation Activity & Vendor Info: (Cataloging) TLC (The Library Corporation); (Circulation) TLC (The Library Corporation); (ILL) JerseyCat; (OPAC) TLC (The Library Corporation)
Wireless access
Function: Adult bk club, Art exhibits, Bks on CD, Chess club, Children's prog, Computers for patron use, Electronic databases & coll, Homebound delivery serv, ILL available, Magnifiers for reading, Museum passes, Music CDs, Online cat, Online ref, Passport agency, Photocopying/Printing, Prog for adults, Prog for children & young adult, Story hour, Summer reading prog, Tax forms, Teen prog, Wheelchair accessible
Partic in LibraryLinkNJ, The New Jersey Library Cooperative; Librs of Union County Consortium
Open Mon & Thurs 9-9, Tues, Fri & Sat 9-5, Wed 9-8, Sun 12-4
Friends of the Library Group

SEA BRIGHT

P SEA BRIGHT LIBRARY*, J W Ross Cultural Arts Ctr, 1104 Ocean Ave, 07760. Tel: 732-382-8092. Web Site: seabrightlibrary.org. *Dir,* Jane Farmer; E-mail: jfarmer@seabrightnj.org
Library Holdings: AV Mats 300; Bk Vols 10,000; Per Subs 40; Talking Bks 150
Wireless access
Mem of Monmouth County Library
Open Mon & Fri 1-5, Tues & Thurs 10-2, Wed 10-5, Sat 9-12
Friends of the Library Group

SEA GIRT

P SEA GIRT LIBRARY*, Railroad Station at the Plaza, 08750. (Mail add: PO Box 414, 08750-0414). Tel: 732-449-1099. FAX: 732-449-4138. E-mail: seagirtlibrary@gmail.com. Web Site: seagirtboro.com/library-3. *Librn,* Lisa Luke
Founded 1992
Library Holdings: AV Mats 250; Bk Vols 10,000; Per Subs 20; Talking Bks 150
Wireless access
Open Mon 6pm-8pm, Tues-Thurs 1-5, Sat 10-Noon

SECAUCUS

P SECAUCUS PUBLIC LIBRARY*, 1379 Patterson Plank Rd, 07094. SAN 310-4974. Tel: 201-330-2083. Web Site: www.secaucuslibrary.org. *Dir,* Jen May; Tel: 201-330-2084, Ext 4011, E-mail: may@secaucus.bccls.org; Staff 2 (MLS 2)
Founded 1957. Pop 13,500; Circ 87,367
Library Holdings: Bk Vols 57,500; Per Subs 82
Special Collections: Oral History
Subject Interests: Arts, Sci
Automation Activity & Vendor Info: (Cataloging) SirsiDynix; (Circulation) SirsiDynix; (OPAC) SirsiDynix
Wireless access
Open Mon-Fri (Winter) 9-9, Sat 9-4, Sun 12-4; Mon-Fri (Summer) 9-9, Sat & Sun 12-4
Friends of the Library Group

SEWELL

P MARGARET E HEGGAN FREE PUBLIC LIBRARY,TOWNSHIP OF WASHINGTON, 606 Delsea Dr, 08080. SAN 310-5555. Tel: 856-589-3334. FAX: 856-582-2042. Web Site: www.hegganlibrary.org. *Libr Dir,* Sheila Mikkelson; E-mail: smikkelson@hegganlibrary.org; *Head, Ref,* Debra Rosner; E-mail: drosner@hegganlibrary.org; *Ch,* Jennifer Berry; E-mail: jberry@hegganlibrary.org; *Ref Librn,* Heather Deitch; E-mail: hdeitch@hegganlibrary.org; *Ref Librn,* Jennifer Mentzer; E-mail: jmentzer@hegganlibrary.org; *Syst Librn,* Sergio Ragno; E-mail: sragno@hegganlibrary.org; *Teen Librn,* Barbara Pilling; E-mail: bpilling@hegganlibrary.org; *Circ Supvr,* Laurie Porsia; E-mail: lporsia@hegganlibrary.org; Staff 28 (MLS 8, Non-MLS 20)
Founded 1965. Pop 48,500; Circ 207,332
Jan 2021-Dec 2021 Income $1,675,048, State $21,042, City $1,635,806, Locally Generated Income $18,200. Mats Exp $214,562, Books $166,150, Per/Ser (Incl. Access Fees) $10,000, AV Mat $33,912, Electronic Ref Mat (Incl. Access Fees) $4,500. Sal $842,556 (Prof $427,225)
Library Holdings: Audiobooks 4,436; CDs 3,580; DVDs 10,456; Large Print Bks 8,500; Bk Titles 89,561; Per Subs 120
Subject Interests: NJ
Automation Activity & Vendor Info: (Cataloging) SirsiDynix-WorkFlows; (Circulation) SirsiDynix-WorkFlows; (ILL) JerseyCat
Wireless access
Function: 24/7 Electronic res, 24/7 Online cat, Activity rm, Adult bk club, After school storytime, Art exhibits, Audiobks via web, Bk club(s), Bks on CD, Children's prog, Computer training, Computers for patron use, Electronic databases & coll, Free DVD rentals, Genealogy discussion group, ILL available, Instruction & testing, Internet access, Life-long learning prog for all ages, Magazines, Mango lang, Meeting rooms, Movies, Museum passes, Music CDs, Online cat, Outreach serv, OverDrive digital audio bks, Photocopying/Printing, Preschool outreach, Preschool reading prog, Prog for adults, Prog for children & young adult, Ref & res, Ref serv available, Res assist avail, Senior computer classes, Senior outreach, Spanish lang bks, Story hour, Study rm, Summer reading prog, Teen prog, Telephone ref, Wheelchair accessible, Workshops, Writing prog
Partic in Libraries of Gloucester, Salem & Cumberland Information Network; LibraryLinkNJ, The New Jersey Library Cooperative
Open Mon-Thurs 10-9, Fri & Sat 10-5, Sun 1-5
Restriction: Limited access based on advanced application
Friends of the Library Group

J ROWAN COLLEGE OF NEW JERSEY*, Gloucester Campus Library, 1400 Tanyard Rd, 08080. SAN 310-4982. Tel: 856-415-2252. Circulation Tel: 856-415-2251. FAX: 856-464-1695. Web Site: www.rcsj.edu/library/gloucester. *Dir,* Jane Crocker; E-mail: jcrocker@rcsj.edu; *Adminr,* Amanda Fach; E-mail: afach@rcsj.edu; *Circ, ILL,* Patricia Hirsekorn; E-mail: phirseko@rcsj.edu; Staff 4 (MLS 4)
Founded 1968. Enrl 3,351; Fac 93
Library Holdings: Bk Vols 55,000; Per Subs 78
Subject Interests: Art, Nursing
Automation Activity & Vendor Info: (Cataloging) SirsiDynix; (Circulation) SirsiDynix; (OPAC) SirsiDynix
Wireless access
Partic in LibraryLinkNJ, The New Jersey Library Cooperative; Virtual Academic Library Environment
Open Mon-Thurs 8am-9pm, Fri 8-5, Sat 10-4

SOMERS POINT

S ATLANTIC COUNTY HISTORICAL SOCIETY LIBRARY*, 907 Shore Rd, 08244. (Mail add: PO Box 301, 08244), SAN 310-5032. Tel: 609-927-5218. FAX: 609-927-5218. E-mail: achsinfo@comcast.net. Web Site: www.atlanticcountyhistoricalsocietynj.org. *Librn,* Norman Goos
Founded 1913
Library Holdings: Bk Vols 8,000
Special Collections: Atlantic County Coll, glass plate negatives, lantern slides, maps, photog; Atlantic County, diaries, deeds, genealogy, letters, ms; Family Bible; New Jersey History & Genealogy, rare & out of print bks
Subject Interests: Genealogy, Local hist
Wireless access
Publications: Annual Year Book; Quarterly Newsletter
Open Wed-Sat 10-3:30

SOMERSET

P FRANKLIN TOWNSHIP FREE PUBLIC LIBRARY*, 485 DeMott Lane, 08873. SAN 351-3572. Tel: 732-873-8700. FAX: 732-873-0746. E-mail: refdesk@franklintwp.org. Web Site: www.franklintwp.org. *Dir, Libr Serv,* January Adams; *Head, Adult Serv,* Ann Smith; *Ref/YA,* Karen Bilton; *Syst Librn,* Michael Ferrante; *Circ,* Megan Ingegno; *Youth Serv,* Anne Lemay; Staff 17 (MLS 12, Non-MLS 5)
Founded 1957
Library Holdings: Bk Titles 155,231; Bk Vols 178,859
Subject Interests: African-Am, Collectibles, Local hist, Pets
Automation Activity & Vendor Info: (Acquisitions) SirsiDynix; (Cataloging) SirsiDynix; (Circulation) SirsiDynix; (ILL) SirsiDynix; (OPAC) SirsiDynix; (Serials) SirsiDynix
Wireless access
Partic in LibraryLinkNJ, The New Jersey Library Cooperative
Special Services for the Blind - Reader equip
Open Mon-Thurs (Sept-June) 10-9, Fri & Sat 10-5, Sun 1-4; Mon-Thurs (July & Aug) 10-9, Fri 10-5, Sat 10-2, Sun 1-4
Branches: 1
FRANKLIN PARK BRANCH, 3391 Rte 27 S, Ste 101, Franklin Park, 08823. Tel: 732-873-8700, Option 5. FAX: 732-297-3391. *Br Mgr,* Amanda Decker
Library Holdings: Bk Titles 8,102
Open Mon-Wed & Fri 10-5, Thurs 2-9, Sat 10-2

SOMERVILLE

J RARITAN VALLEY COMMUNITY COLLEGE, Evelyn S Field Library, Theater Bldg Branchburg, 118 Lamington Rd, 08876. (Mail add: PO Box 3300, 08876-3300), SAN 310-5083. Tel: 908-218-8865. Interlibrary Loan Service Tel: 908-429-4252. Web Site: library.raritanval.edu. *Instrul Serv Librn,* Megan Dempsey; *Tech Serv & Syst Librn,* Janelle Bitter; E-mail: janelle.bitter@raritanval.edu; *Pub Serv Coordr,* Chad Peters; E-mail: chad.peters@raritanval.edu; Staff 11 (MLS 4, Non-MLS 7)
Founded 1968. Enrl 6,117; Fac 108; Highest Degree: Associate
Library Holdings: Audiobooks 306; DVDs 1,369; e-books 10,243; Microforms 56; Bk Titles 80,530; Bk Vols 79,850; Per Subs 202; Videos 350
Automation Activity & Vendor Info: (Acquisitions) Innovative Interfaces, Inc; (Cataloging) Innovative Interfaces, Inc; (Circulation) Innovative Interfaces, Inc; (Course Reserve) Innovative Interfaces, Inc; (OPAC) Innovative Interfaces, Inc; (Serials) Innovative Interfaces, Inc
Wireless access
Partic in NJ State Libr Network; OCLC Online Computer Library Center, Inc; Virtual Academic Library Environment
Open Mon-Thurs 8am-9pm, Fri 8-5

SOUTH AMBOY

P SADIE POPE DOWDELL LIBRARY OF SOUTH AMBOY, 100 Harold G Hoffman Plaza, 08879. SAN 310-5105. Tel: 732-721-6060. FAX: 732-721-1054. E-mail: comments@dowdell.org. Web Site: www.dowdell.org. *Dir,* Elaine R Gaber; E-mail: egaber@dowdell.org; *Head, Tech,* Michael Elson; *Supv Libr Asst,* Dennis Kuhn; *Sr Libr Assoc,* Holly Smith; *Libr Assoc,* Position Currently Open; *Archives, Circ Serv,* Barbara Bringman; *Circ Serv,* Melissa Mulcahy; *Circulation Servs, Exhibitions,* Maryanne Candelora; Staff 9 (MLS 2, Non-MLS 7)
Founded 1914. Pop 7,900; Circ 65,326
Jan 2021-Dec 2021 Income $345,145, State $3,740, City $331,405, Locally Generated Income $10,000
Library Holdings: Bk Vols 69,239; Per Subs 50
Special Collections: New Jersey History Coll; Railroads Coll; South Amboy History Coll
Automation Activity & Vendor Info: (Cataloging) SirsiDynix; (Circulation) SirsiDynix-iBistro; (ILL) Auto-Graphics, Inc; (OPAC) SirsiDynix-WorkFlows
Wireless access
Function: 24/7 Electronic res, 24/7 Online cat, 3D Printer, Activity rm, Adult bk club, Adult literacy prog, After school storytime, Archival coll, Art exhibits, Art programs, Audio & video playback equip for onsite use, Audiobks on Playaways & MP3, Audiobks via web, Bilingual assistance for Spanish patrons, Bk club(s), Bks on CD, Bus archives, Children's prog, Citizenship assistance, Computer training, Computers for patron use, Digital talking bks, Distance learning, Doc delivery serv, E-Readers, E-Reserves, Electronic databases & coll, Equip loans & repairs, Family literacy, For res purposes, Free DVD rentals, Govt ref serv, Holiday prog, Home delivery & serv to seniorr ctr & nursing homes, Homebound delivery serv, Homework prog, ILL available, Instruction & testing, Internet

access, Learning ctr, Life-long learning prog for all ages, Literacy & newcomer serv, Magazines, Mail & tel request accepted, Mail loans to mem, Makerspace, Meeting rooms, Movies, Notary serv, Online cat, Online info literacy tutorials on the web & in blackboard, Online ref, Orientations, Outreach serv, Outside serv via phone, mail, e-mail & web, OverDrive digital audio bks, Photocopying/Printing, Preschool outreach, Preschool reading prog, Printer for laptops & handheld devices, Prog for adults, Prog for children & young adult, Ref & res, Ref serv available, Scanner, Senior computer classes, Senior outreach, Spanish lang bks, Spoken cassettes & CDs, Spoken cassettes & DVDs, STEM programs, Story hour, Study rm, Summer & winter reading prog, Summer reading prog, Tax forms, Teen prog, Telephone ref, Visual arts prog, Wheelchair accessible, Winter reading prog, Workshops
Publications: Annual Report; History of Dowdell Library; Magazines & Newspapers (Index to periodicals); South Amboy Archives (Archives guide)
Partic in Libraries of Middlesex Automation Consortium; LibraryLinkNJ, The New Jersey Library Cooperative
Special Services for the Blind - Talking bks
Open Mon, Tues & Thurs 10-8, Wed & Fri 10-5, Sat (Sept-May) 12-4
Restriction: Authorized patrons, Borrowing requests are handled by ILL, ID required to use computers (Ltd hrs), In-house use for visitors, Non-circulating of rare bks, Non-resident fee
Friends of the Library Group

SOUTH ORANGE

R SETON HALL UNIVERSITY*, Monsignor James C Turro Seminary Library, 400 S Orange Ave, 07079. SAN 310-1045. Tel: 973-761-9198, 973-761-9336. FAX: 973-275-2074. Web Site: library.shu.edu. *Dir,* Rev Lawrence Porter, PhD; E-mail: lawrence.porter@shu.edu; *Librn, Mgr,* Stella F Wilkins; E-mail: stella.wilkins@shu.edu; *Libr Asst,* Andrew M Brenycz; E-mail: andrew.brenycz@shu.edu; Staff 2 (MLS 1, Non-MLS 1)
Founded 1858. Enrl 246; Fac 20
Library Holdings: CDs 526; DVDs 311; Bk Vols 67,690; Per Subs 340; Videos 462
Subject Interests: Biblical, Catechism, Christian ethics, Church hist, Church ministries, Liturgy, Philos, Theol
Automation Activity & Vendor Info: (Cataloging) OCLC; (Circulation) OCLC; (ILL) JerseyCat; (OPAC) OCLC
Wireless access
Partic in NYATLA - New York Area Theological Library Association
Open Mon-Wed 9am-10pm, Thurs 9-7, Fri 9-5, Sat 10-4 (Spring & Fall)

C SETON HALL UNIVERSITY LIBRARIES, Walsh Library, Walsh Library Bldg, 400 S Orange Ave, 07079. Tel: 973-761-9005. Circulation Tel: 973-761-9443. Interlibrary Loan Service Tel: 973-761-9441. Information Services Tel: 973-761-9437. FAX: 973-761-9432. Web Site: library.shu.edu/library. *Dean, Univ Libr,* John Buschman; *Asst Dean, Info Tech, Res Acq & Description,* Elizabeth Leonard; Tel: 973-761-9445, E-mail: elizabeth.leonard@shu.edu; *Asst Dean, Pub Serv,* Sebastian Derry; Tel: 973-761-2058, E-mail: sebastian.derry@shu.edu; *Coll Develop, Head of Acq Serv, Librn,* Sulekha Kalyan; Tel: 973-761-9438, E-mail: sulekha.kalyan@shu.edu; *Head, Tech Serv,* Martha Loesch; Tel: 973-761-9296, E-mail: martha.loesch@shu.edu; *Bus Librn,* Chelsea Barrett; Tel: 973-275-2035, E-mail: chelsea.barrett@shu.edu; *Humanities Librn, Outreach Librn,* Marta Deyrup; Tel: 973-275-2223, E-mail: marta.deyrup@shu.edu; *Instruction Librn,* Brooke Duffy; Tel: 973-275-4689, E-mail: brooke.duffy@shu.edu. Subject Specialists: *Educ,* Martha Loesch; Staff 41 (MLS 16, Non-MLS 25)
Founded 1856. Enrl 9,800; Fac 430; Highest Degree: Doctorate
Jul 2012-Jun 2013 Income $4,308,000. Mats Exp $1,711,604, Books $377,912, Per/Ser (Incl. Access Fees) $429,320, AV Mat $4,966, Electronic Ref Mat (Incl. Access Fees) $899,406. Sal $2,119,000 (Prof $1,155,650)
Library Holdings: AV Mats 4,172; e-books 194,992; e-journals 25,000; Microforms 27,454; Bk Vols 425,880
Special Collections: American Civil War & Abraham Lincoln Coll; Brendan Byrne Coll; Irish Literature & History (McManus Coll); Oesterriecher Coll (Judeo-Christian Studies); Peter Rodino Coll; Richard Hughes Coll; Seton Hall Univ & Newark Archdiocesan Archives. State Document Depository; UN Document Depository; US Document Depository
Automation Activity & Vendor Info: (Acquisitions) Ex Libris Group; (Cataloging) Ex Libris Group; (Circulation) Ex Libris Group; (Course Reserve) Ex Libris Group; (ILL) OCLC ILLiad; (OPAC) Ex Libris Group; (Serials) Ex Libris Group
Wireless access
Function: Archival coll, Art exhibits, Computers for patron use, Doc delivery serv, Electronic databases & coll, Govt ref serv, ILL available, Microfiche/film & reading machines, Music CDs, Online cat, Online ref, Orientations, Photocopying/Printing, Ref & res, Ref serv available, Scanner
Partic in LibraryLinkNJ, The New Jersey Library Cooperative; Partnership for Academic Library Collaborative & Innovation; Virtual Academic Library Environment
Special Services for the Blind - Assistive/Adapted tech devices, equip & products
Restriction: Open to pub for ref only, Open to students, fac & staff, Photo ID required for access

P SOUTH ORANGE PUBLIC LIBRARY*, 65 Scotland Rd, 07079. SAN 310-5121. Tel: 973-762-0230. FAX: 973-762-1469. E-mail: librarian@sopl.org. Web Site: www.sopl.org. *Dir,* Melissa Kopecky; E-mail: mkopecky@sopl.org; *Head, Children's Servx,* Beth Halliday; E-mail: bhalliday@sopl.org; *Head, Communications & Coll,* Michael Pucci; E-mail: mpucci@sopl.org; *Head, Ref & Libr Serv,* Lindita Cani; E-mail: lcani@sopl.org; *Vols Coordr, Youth Serv,* Keisha Miller; E-mail: kmiller@sopl.org; Staff 11 (MLS 5, Non-MLS 6)
Founded 1864. Pop 16,964
Library Holdings: Audiobooks 1,789; AV Mats 7,791; CDs 2,396; DVDs 3,606; e-books 26,391; Electronic Media & Resources 18; Large Print Bks 1,362; Bk Titles 82,547; Bk Vols 83,330; Per Subs 145
Special Collections: Local History Coll
Automation Activity & Vendor Info: (Acquisitions) Baker & Taylor; (Cataloging) TLC (The Library Corporation); (Circulation) TLC (The Library Corporation); (ILL) Auto-Graphics, Inc; (OPAC) TLC (The Library Corporation)
Wireless access
Partic in LibraryLinkNJ, The New Jersey Library Cooperative
Special Services for the Blind - Accessible computers; Assistive/Adapted tech devices, equip & products; Audio mat; Bks on CD; Computer with voice synthesizer for visually impaired persons; Copier with enlargement capabilities; Internet workstation with adaptive software; Large print bks; Low vision equip; Playaways (bks on MP3); Scanner for conversion & translation of mats; Screen enlargement software for people with visual disabilities; Screen reader software; ZoomText magnification & reading software
Open Mon, Tues & Thurs 9-9, Wed & Fri 9-6, Sat 9-5, Sun 1-5
Friends of the Library Group

R TEMPLE SHAREY TEFILO-ISRAEL*, Abelson Echikson Ehrenkrantz Memorial Library, 432 Scotland Rd, 07079. SAN 325-948X. Tel: 973-763-4116. FAX: 973-763-3941. Web Site: www.tsti.org.
Library Holdings: Bk Vols 300
Partic in Asn of Jewish Librs
Open Mon-Thurs 9-5, Fri 9-4

SOUTH PLAINFIELD

P SOUTH PLAINFIELD PUBLIC LIBRARY*, 2484 Plainfield Ave, 07080. SAN 310-5156. Tel: 908-754-7885. FAX: 908-753-3846. Web Site: www.southplainfield.lib.nj.us. *Dir,* Linda Hansen; E-mail: lhansen@southplainfield.lib.nj.us; Staff 5 (MLS 5)
Founded 1935. Pop 21,810; Circ 188,513
Library Holdings: AV Mats 6,345; CDs 1,460; DVDs 3,479; Large Print Bks 387; Bk Titles 66,017; Bk Vols 75,552; Per Subs 208
Subject Interests: Chinese lang, Graphic novels, Spanish lang, Vietnamese
Automation Activity & Vendor Info: (Cataloging) Innovative Interfaces, Inc; (Circulation) Innovative Interfaces, Inc; (ILL) Innovative Interfaces, Inc; (OPAC) Innovative Interfaces, Inc
Wireless access
Function: Art exhibits, Audiobks via web, Bks on cassette, Bks on CD, CD-ROM, Children's prog, Computer training, Computers for patron use, Electronic databases & coll, Free DVD rentals, Holiday prog, Home delivery & serv to seniorr ctr & nursing homes, ILL available, Magnifiers for reading, Mail & tel request accepted, Music CDs, Notary serv, Online cat, OverDrive digital audio bks, Photocopying/Printing, Prog for adults, Prog for children & young adult, Ref serv available, Story hour, Summer reading prog, Tax forms, Telephone ref, VHS videos, Wheelchair accessible
Partic in Libraries of Middlesex Automation Consortium
Open Mon, Wed & Thurs 10-9, Tues & Fri 10-6, Sat 9-5
Friends of the Library Group

SOUTH RIVER

P SOUTH RIVER PUBLIC LIBRARY*, 55 Appleby Ave, 08882-2499. SAN 310-5164. Tel: 732-254-2488. FAX: 732-254-4116. E-mail: srpl@southriverlibrary.org. Web Site: www.southriverlibrary.org. *Dir,* Evalina Erbe; E-mail: evalina@southriverlibrary.org; *Supv Librn,* Kate Russo; E-mail: kate@southriverlibrary.org; *Youth Serv Librn,* Rita Post; E-mail: rita@southriverlibrary.org; *Circ Supvr,* Robbin Seuling; E-mail: robbin@southriverlibrary.org; Staff 4 (MLS 4)
Founded 1920. Pop 15,322; Circ 60,690
Library Holdings: Bk Titles 42,000; Bk Vols 46,000; Per Subs 75
Special Collections: Cake Pans; Children's Foreign Language Books; Foreign Films on DVD; Graphic Novels For Children and Teens; TV Series on DVD
Automation Activity & Vendor Info: (Acquisitions) SirsiDynix; (Cataloging) SirsiDynix; (Circulation) SirsiDynix

Wireless access
Function: Adult bk club, Butterfly Garden, Children's prog, Computer training, Electronic databases & coll, Holiday prog, Homebound delivery serv, ILL available, Makerspace, Mango lang, Meeting rooms, Museum passes, Music CDs, Notary serv, Online cat, Photocopying/Printing, Preschool outreach, Preschool reading prog, Printer for laptops & handheld devices, Prog for adults, Prog for children & young adult, Senior computer classes, STEM programs, Story hour, Study rm, Summer reading prog, Tax forms, Teen prog, Telephone ref, Wheelchair accessible
Partic in Libraries of Middlesex Automation Consortium
Open Mon, Wed & Fri 10-5, Tues & Thurs 12-9, Sat & Sun 10-3
Friends of the Library Group

SPARTA

P SPARTA PUBLIC LIBRARY*, 22 Woodport Rd, 07871. SAN 310-5172. Tel: 973-729-3101. FAX: 973-729-1755. Web Site: spartalibrary.com. *Dir,* David Costa; E-mail: david@spartalibrary.com; Staff 15 (MLS 2, Non-MLS 13)
Founded 1841. Circ 298,138
Library Holdings: Bk Vols 68,111; Per Subs 200
Automation Activity & Vendor Info: (Cataloging) Innovative Interfaces, Inc; (Circulation) Innovative Interfaces, Inc; (ILL) Auto-Graphics, Inc; (OPAC) Innovative Interfaces, Inc
Wireless access
Function: 24/7 Electronic res, 24/7 Online cat, 3D Printer, Adult literacy prog, Audiobks via web, Bks on CD, Computer training, Computers for patron use, Digital talking bks, Electronic databases & coll, Equip loans & repairs, Free DVD rentals, Health sci info serv, ILL available, Internet access, Magazines, Mail & tel request accepted, Makerspace, Meeting rooms, Movies, Museum passes, Music CDs, Notary serv, Online cat, Outreach serv, Photocopying/Printing, Prog for adults, Prog for children & young adult, Scanner, Senior computer classes, Spanish lang bks, Spoken cassettes & CDs, Spoken cassettes & DVDs, Story hour, Summer & winter reading prog, Summer reading prog, Tax forms, Teen prog, Wheelchair accessible
Partic in New Jersey Library Network
Open Mon-Thurs 8:30-8, Fri 8:30-5, Sat 8:30-3 (8:30-1 Summer), Sun 1-5

SPOTSWOOD

P SPOTSWOOD PUBLIC LIBRARY*, DeVoe Memorial Library, 548 Main St, 08884. SAN 310-5180. Tel: 732-251-1515. FAX: 732-251-8151. E-mail: spl@spotslibrary.org. Web Site: www.spotslibrary.org. *Libr Dir,* C L Quillen; Staff 3 (MLS 1, Non-MLS 2)
Founded 1937. Pop 8,140; Circ 32,000
Library Holdings: Bk Vols 21,000; Per Subs 35
Automation Activity & Vendor Info: (Cataloging) SirsiDynix; (Circulation) SirsiDynix; (ILL) SirsiDynix; (OPAC) SirsiDynix
Wireless access
Function: 24/7 Electronic res, 24/7 Online cat, Activity rm, Adult bk club, After school storytime, Audiobks on Playaways & MP3, Audiobks via web, AV serv, Bks on CD, Children's prog, Computers for patron use, Electronic databases & coll, Free DVD rentals, Holiday prog, ILL available, Internet access, Life-long learning prog for all ages, Magazines, Mail & tel request accepted, Meeting rooms, Movies, Museum passes, Music CDs, Online cat, OverDrive digital audio bks, Photocopying/Printing, Preschool reading prog, Prog for adults, Prog for children & young adult, Ref & res, Ref serv available, Spoken cassettes & DVDs, Story hour, Summer reading prog, Telephone ref, Wheelchair accessible, Workshops
Partic in Libraries of Middlesex Automation Consortium
Open Mon, Wed & Thurs 10-7:30, Tues & Fri 10-5, Sat 10-2
Friends of the Library Group

SPRING LAKE

P SPRING LAKE PUBLIC LIBRARY*, 1501 Third Ave, 07762. SAN 310-5199. Tel: 732-449-6654. E-mail: splklib1@gmail.com, springlakelibrary@gmail.com. Web Site: springlakelibrary.org. *Dir,* Janet Boldt
Founded 1920. Circ 28,000
Library Holdings: Bk Vols 30,000; Per Subs 50
Special Collections: Large Print Coll
Automation Activity & Vendor Info: (Acquisitions) Follett Software; (Cataloging) Follett Software; (Circulation) Follett Software; (ILL) Follett Software; (OPAC) Follett Software; (Serials) Follett Software
Partic in LibraryLinkNJ, The New Jersey Library Cooperative
Open Mon & Wed 10-8, Tues, Thurs & Fri 10-5, Sat 10-1

SPRINGFIELD

P SPRINGFIELD FREE PUBLIC LIBRARY, 66 Mountain Ave, 07081-1786. SAN 310-5202. Tel: 973-376-4930. FAX: 973-376-1334. E-mail: questions@springfieldpubliclibrary.com. Web Site: www.sfplnj.org, www.springfieldpubliclibrary.com. *Libr Dir,* Dale T Spindel; Tel: 973-376-4930, Ext 227, E-mail: dspindel@sfplnj.org; *Asst Dir,* Tommy Shaw; Tel: 973-376-4930, Ext 235, E-mail: tshaw@sfplnj.org; Staff 5 (MLS 5)
Founded 1931. Pop 15,817; Circ 127,206
Jan 2019-Dec 2019 Income $1,033,590, State $6,990, City $1,019,600
Special Collections: Local History (Sarah Bailey Coll); Local History Artifacts (Donald B Palmer Museum)
Automation Activity & Vendor Info: (Acquisitions) TLC (The Library Corporation); (Cataloging) TLC (The Library Corporation); (Circulation) TLC (The Library Corporation); (ILL) Auto-Graphics, Inc; (OPAC) TLC (The Library Corporation)
Wireless access
Function: 24/7 Electronic res, 24/7 Online cat, Activity rm, Adult bk club, Archival coll, Art exhibits, Audiobks on Playaways & MP3, Audiobks via web, AV serv, Bi-weekly Writer's Group, Bk club(s), Bks on CD, Chess club, Children's prog, Computer training, Computers for patron use, Digital talking bks, E-Reserves, Electronic databases & coll, ILL available, Internet access, Magazines, Magnifiers for reading, Mail & tel request accepted, Meeting rooms, Microfiche/film & reading machines, Movies, Museum passes, Music CDs, Online cat, Online ref, OverDrive digital audio bks, Photocopying/Printing, Printer for laptops & handheld devices, Prog for adults, Prog for children & young adult, Ref serv available, Scanner, Story hour, Study rm, Summer reading prog, Tax forms, Teen prog, Telephone ref, Wheelchair accessible, Writing prog
Partic in Libraries of Middlesex Automation Consortium; LibraryLinkNJ, The New Jersey Library Cooperative
Open Mon, Wed & Thurs 10-8, Tues, Fri & Sat 10-5
Friends of the Library Group

STANHOPE

S CANAL SOCIETY OF NEW JERSEY, Museum & Library, Waterloo Village, 07874. (Mail add: PO Box 737, Morristown, 07963-0737), SAN 375-2607. Tel: 973-292-2755. E-mail: nj-cnal@googlegroups.com. Web Site: www.canalsocietynj.org. *Pres,* Joe Macasek; *Mus Dir,* Rich Richter; E-mail: fiero87r@netscape.net
Founded 1969
Library Holdings: Bk Vols 300
Restriction: Non-circulating, Open by appt only

STRATFORD

M ROWAN UNIVERSITY SCHOOL OF OSTEOPATHIC MEDICINE*, Health Science Library, Academic Ctr, One Medical Center Dr, 08084. SAN 320-6998. Tel: 856-566-6800. FAX: 856-566-6380. Web Site: www.lib.rowan.edu/som. *Dir,* Charlie Greenberg; E-mail: greenbergc@rowan.edu; *Syst Librn,* Kevin Block; Tel: 856-566-6804, E-mail: kblock@rowan.edu; *Pub Serv, Website Mgr,* Marita Malone; Tel: 856-566-6992, E-mail: malone@rowan.edu; *ILL,* Nancy Demaris; Tel: 856-566-6808, E-mail: cottonnd@rowan.edu; Staff 11 (MLS 5, Non-MLS 6)
Founded 1970
Library Holdings: Bk Vols 30,000; Per Subs 35
Special Collections: History of Osteopathy
Subject Interests: Basic sci, Clinical med, Res
Automation Activity & Vendor Info: (Acquisitions) Ex Libris Group; (Cataloging) Ex Libris Group; (Circulation) Ex Libris Group; (ILL) OCLC ILLiad; (OPAC) Ex Libris Group; (Serials) Ex Libris Group
Wireless access
Partic in Health Sci Libr Asn of NJ; New Jersey Health Sciences Library Network; Virtual Academic Library Environment
Open Mon-Thurs 8am-Midnight, Fri 8am-9pm, Sat 9-9, Sun 9am-Midnight

P STRATFORD FREE PUBLIC LIBRARY*, 303 Union Ave, 08084. SAN 310-5229. Tel: 856-783-0602. FAX: 856-435-8757. E-mail: Library@stratfordnj.org. Web Site: www.stratfordnj.org/library.htm. *Dir,* Alfred Encarnation; Staff 1 (Non-MLS 1)
Founded 1923. Pop 7,500; Circ 30,000
Library Holdings: Bk Vols 38,000; Per Subs 25
Automation Activity & Vendor Info: (Cataloging) Winnebago Software Co; (Circulation) Winnebago Software Co
Wireless access
Open Mon, Tues & Thurs 12-8, Wed & Fri 10-4, Sat 10-1
Friends of the Library Group

SUCCASUNNA

P ROXBURY TOWNSHIP PUBLIC LIBRARY*, 103 Main St, 07876. SAN 310-5237. Tel: 973-584-2400. FAX: 973-584-5484. E-mail: comments@roxburylibrary.org. Web Site: roxburylibrary.org. *Dir,* Radwa Ali; E-mail: radwa.ali@roxburylibrary.org
Founded 1960. Pop 23,924; Circ 188,251
Library Holdings: Bk Vols 70,482; Per Subs 217
Special Collections: Children's Historical Fiction (Mary Wolfe Thompson Coll); Historical Reference (New Jersey)
Automation Activity & Vendor Info: (Circulation) SirsiDynix

Wireless access
Partic in Morris Automated Information Network
Open Mon-Thurs (Sept-May) 10-8, Fri 10-5, Sat 10-3, Sun 2-5; Mon-Thurs (June-Aug) 10-8, Fri 10-5, Sat 10-1
Friends of the Library Group

SUMMIT

M OVERLOOK MEDICAL CENTER*, Robert H Mulreany Health Sciences Library, 99 Beauvoir Ave, 07902-0220. SAN 370-1891. Tel: 908-522-2119. FAX: 908-522-2274. *Libr Mgr,* Patricia Regenberg; Staff 2 (MLS 1, Non-MLS 1)
Library Holdings: Bk Titles 6,000; Per Subs 325
Subject Interests: Consumer health, Med
Partic in Basic Health Sciences Library Network; New Jersey Health Sciences Library Network
Open Mon-Thurs 8-5:30, Fri 8-5

P SUMMIT FREE PUBLIC LIBRARY*, 75 Maple St, 07901-9984. SAN 310-5261. Tel: 908-273-0350. FAX: 908-273-0031. Web Site: www.summitlibrary.org. *Dir,* Susan Permahos; E-mail: suepermahos@summitlibrary.org; *Head, Tech Serv, Syst Adminr,* Beata P Barrasso; *Head, Adult Serv,* Abigail Brady; *Head, Circ,* Diane Hull; *Head, Youth Serv,* Ann-Marie Aymer; *Adult Programming,* Robin Carroll-Mann
Founded 1874. Pop 21,131; Circ 285,687
Library Holdings: Audiobooks 5,651; Bk Vols 107,560; Per Subs 469; Videos 1,000
Automation Activity & Vendor Info: (Cataloging) SirsiDynix; (Circulation) SirsiDynix; (OPAC) SirsiDynix
Wireless access
Function: Adult bk club, Art exhibits, Bks on cassette, Bks on CD, Bus archives, Children's prog, Computer training, Computers for patron use, ILL available, Music CDs, Online cat, Photocopying/Printing, Prog for adults, Prog for children & young adult, Tax forms, Teen prog, Telephone ref, VHS videos, Wheelchair accessible
Partic in LibraryLinkNJ, The New Jersey Library Cooperative; Morris-Union Federation; New Jersey Library Network
Open Mon-Thurs 9-9, Fri & Sat 9-5, Sun 1-5

TEANECK

C FAIRLEIGH DICKINSON UNIVERSITY*, Frank Giovatto Library, 1000 River Rd, 07666-1914. Tel: 201-692-2279. Reference Tel: 201-692-2100. Web Site: view.fdu.edu/metropolitan-campus/libraries. *Assoc Univ Librn, Dir, Pub Serv,* Kathleen Stein-Smith; Tel: 201-692-2276, E-mail: stein@fdu.edu; *Assoc Univ Librn,* Maria Kocylowsky; Tel: 201-692-2608, E-mail: marialk@fdu.edu; *Librn, Outreach Coordr,* Michelle Nestory; E-mail: michelel@fdu.edu; *Res & Instruction Librn,* Patricia Murray; Tel: 201-692-2285, E-mail: murray@fdu.edu; *Univ Archivist,* Richard Goerner; Tel: 201-692-2598, E-mail: goerner@fdu.edu; Staff 11 (MLS 9, Non-MLS 2)
Founded 1954. Enrl 5,032; Fac 365; Highest Degree: Doctorate
Library Holdings: Audiobooks 8; CDs 405; DVDs 1,320; e-books 40,137; e-journals 684; Electronic Media & Resources 82; Microforms 103,000; Bk Vols 154,000; Per Subs 430; Videos 547
Special Collections: Lincoln, Mf Coll Presidential Papers. State Document Depository; US Document Depository
Automation Activity & Vendor Info: (Acquisitions) Ex Libris Group; (Cataloging) Ex Libris Group; (Circulation) Ex Libris Group; (Course Reserve) Ex Libris Group; (ILL) OCLC; (OPAC) Ex Libris Group; (Serials) Ex Libris Group
Wireless access
Partic in LYRASIS; Metropolitan New York Library Council; OCLC Online Computer Library Center, Inc
Open Mon-Thurs 8am-11pm, Fri 8-5, Sat 10-6, Sun 12-10
Friends of the Library Group

P TEANECK PUBLIC LIBRARY*, 840 Teaneck Rd, 07666. SAN 310-5296. Tel: 201-837-4171. FAX: 201-837-0410. Circulation E-mail: teancirc@bccls.org. Web Site: teanecklibrary.org. *Libr Dir,* Allen McGinley; E-mail: mcginley@teaneck.bccls.org; *Ch Serv,* Amy Sears; E-mail: amy.sears@teaneck.bccls.org; *Circ, Tech Serv,* Jonna Davis; E-mail: jonna.davis@teaneck.bccls.org; *Ref (Info Servs),* Weilee Liu; E-mail: weilee.liu@teaneck.bccls.org; Staff 26 (MLS 8, Non-MLS 18)
Founded 1922. Pop 39,800; Circ 625,200
Jan 2017-Dec 2017 Income $3,002,700, State $20,700, City $2,900,000, Locally Generated Income $82,000. Mats Exp $348,000, Books $220,000, Per/Ser (Incl. Access Fees) $11,500, Manu Arch $500, AV Mat $97,000, Electronic Ref Mat (Incl. Access Fees) $18,000, Presv $1,000
Library Holdings: CDs 5,500; DVDs 11,500; Large Print Bks 1,075; Bk Vols 111,500; Per Subs 375; Talking Bks 3,150
Special Collections: Oral History
Subject Interests: African-Am studies, Judaica
Automation Activity & Vendor Info: (Cataloging) SirsiDynix; (Circulation) SirsiDynix; (OPAC) SirsiDynix
Wireless access
Function: 24/7 Electronic res, 24/7 Online cat, Adult literacy prog, Archival coll, Art exhibits, Audiobks via web, Bks on CD, Children's prog, Computer training, Computers for patron use, Digital talking bks, E-Reserves, Electronic databases & coll, Free DVD rentals, Holiday prog, Homebound delivery serv, ILL available, Internet access, Magazines, Mail & tel request accepted, Mango lang, Meeting rooms, Movies, Museum passes, Music CDs, Online cat, Online ref, Photocopying/Printing, Preschool outreach, Preschool reading prog, Printer for laptops & handheld devices, Prog for adults, Prog for children & young adult, Ref & res, Scanner, Spanish lang bks, Spoken cassettes & CDs, Spoken cassettes & DVDs, Story hour, Summer & winter reading prog, Summer reading prog, Tax forms, Teen prog, Telephone ref, Wheelchair accessible, Winter reading prog
Partic in Bergen County Cooperative Library System, Inc
Open Mon-Thurs 9-9, Fri 9-6, Sat 9-5, Sun 12:30-5:30
Friends of the Library Group

TENAFLY

SR KAPLEN JEWISH COMMUNITY CENTER ON THE PALISADES, Judaica Library, 411 E Clinton Ave, 07670. SAN 310-1452. Tel: 201-569-7900, Ext 1453. FAX: 201-569-7448. Web Site: www.jccotp.org. *Librn,* Freida Harris; E-mail: fharris@jccotp.org
Library Holdings: Bk Vols 3,900; Per Subs 10
Restriction: Mem only

P TENAFLY PUBLIC LIBRARY, 100 Riveredge Rd, 07670-1962. SAN 310-5318. Tel: 201-568-8680. Administration Tel: 201-568-7809. FAX: 201-568-5475. E-mail: reference@tenafly.bccls.org. Web Site: www.tenaflylibrary.org. *Dir,* Julie Marallo; E-mail: marallo@tenafly.bccls.org; *Asst Dir,* Marcia Literati; E-mail: marcia.literati@tenafly.bccls.org; *Youth Serv Librn,* Latricia Markle; E-mail: latricia.markle@tenafly.bccls.org; *Coll Develop Librn,* Rafat Ispahany; E-mail: rafat.ispahany@tenafly.bccls.org; *Emerging Tech Librn, Teen Librn,* Florence Pao; E-mail: florence.pao@tenafly.bccls.org; Staff 5 (MLS 5)
Founded 1920. Pop 156,757; Circ 271,563
Jan 2015-Dec 2015 Income $6,400, State $6,400. Mats Exp $115,300, Books $80,000, Per/Ser (Incl. Access Fees) $5,300, AV Mat $30,000
Library Holdings: AV Mats 5,091; Bk Titles 76,937; Bk Vols 84,000; Per Subs 170
Automation Activity & Vendor Info: (Circulation) Innovative Interfaces, Inc; (ILL) JerseyCat; (OPAC) Innovative Interfaces, Inc
Wireless access
Partic in Bergen County Cooperative Library System, Inc; LibraryLinkNJ, The New Jersey Library Cooperative
Special Services for the Blind - VisualTek equip
Open Mon, Tues & Thurs 10-9, Wed, Fri & Sat 10-5, Sun (Sept-May) 12-4
Friends of the Library Group

TETERBORO

S AVIATION HALL OF FAME & MUSEUM LIBRARY OF NEW JERSEY*, Teterboro Airport, 400 Fred Wehran Dr, 07608. SAN 375-7285. Tel: 201-288-6344. FAX: 201-288-5666. E-mail: njahof@verizon.net. Web Site: www.njahof.org. *Sr Librn,* Michelle Fanelli; E-mail: mfanelli@pace.edu; Staff 1 (MLS 1)
Library Holdings: Bk Titles 3,900
Special Collections: Aviation Scrapbooks, 1860-1990 (Bill Rhode Coll); Curtiss-Wright Aircraft Engines (Wright Aeronautical Coll)
Function: Res libr
Restriction: Open to pub by appt only

THREE BRIDGES

P THREE BRIDGES PUBLIC LIBRARY*, 449 Main St, 08887. (Mail add: PO Box 465, 08887-0465). Tel: 908-782-2908. E-mail: 3bridgeslibrary@gmail.com. Web Site: www.hclibrary.us/branches/threebridges.htm. *Dir,* Theresa Stoveken; Staff 2 (MLS 2)
Founded 1985
Library Holdings: AV Mats 350; Bk Vols 15,973; Per Subs 30
Automation Activity & Vendor Info: (Cataloging) Innovative Interfaces, Inc; (Circulation) Innovative Interfaces, Inc; (OPAC) Innovative Interfaces, Inc
Wireless access
Mem of Hunterdon County Library
Open Mon, Thurs & Fri 9-5, Wed 11-7, Sat (Sept-July) 9-12
Friends of the Library Group

TINTON FALLS

P TINTON FALLS PUBLIC LIBRARY*, 664 Tinton Ave, 07724. SAN 310-5342. Tel: 732-542-3110. FAX: 732-542-6755. E-mail: tflibrary@monmouthcountylib.org. Web Site: www.tintonfalls.com/content/119/671/162. *Libr Dir,* Kim James

Founded 1961. Pop 16,500; Circ 57,700
Library Holdings: AV Mats 2,337; CDs 645; DVDs 190; Electronic Media & Resources 41; Large Print Bks 110; Bk Vols 37,780; Per Subs 19; Talking Bks 696; Videos 2,702
Automation Activity & Vendor Info: (Cataloging) SirsiDynix; (Circulation) SirsiDynix
Wireless access
Publications: Snippets (Newsletter)
Mem of Monmouth County Library
Open Mon-Thurs 10-8, Fri 10-4, Sat 10-2
Friends of the Library Group

TOMS RIVER

M COMMUNITY MEDICAL CENTER*, Medical Library, 99 Hwy 37 W, 08755. SAN 375-6912. Tel: 732-557-8117. FAX: 732-557-2762. *Dir,* Reina Reisler; E-mail: rreisler@barnabashealth.org
Subject Interests: Med

J OCEAN COUNTY COLLEGE LIBRARY*, College Dr, 08754. (Mail add: PO Box 2001, 08754-2001), SAN 310-5350. Tel: 732-255-0392. Interlibrary Loan Service Tel: 732-255-0400, Ext 2247. Reference Tel: 732-255-0400, Ext 2287. FAX: 732-864-3869. Web Site: lib.ocean.edu/content/public/study-on-campus/campus-life/library.html. *Dir, Libr Serv,* Donna Rosinski-Kauz; E-mail: drosinski-kauz@ocean.edu; *Mgr, Circ Serv,* Terrence Cleary; Tel: 732-255-0400, Ext 2288, E-mail: tcleary@ocean.edu; *Tech Serv Spec,* Christopher Graham; Tel: 732-255-0400, Ext 4489, E-mail: cgraham@ocean.edu; *Libr Tech 1,* Judith Collins; Tel: 732-255-0400, Ext 2151, E-mail: jcollins@ocean.edu; *Ref & Instruction,* Janelle Bitter; Tel: 732-255-0400, Ext 2351, E-mail: jbitter@ocean.edu; *Ref & Instruction,* James Marshall; Tel: 732-255-0400, Ext 2248, E-mail: jmarshall@ocean.edu; Staff 13 (MLS 5, Non-MLS 8)
Founded 1966. Enrl 9,900; Fac 227; Highest Degree: Associate
Library Holdings: Bk Titles 77,000
Special Collections: State Document Depository; US Document Depository
Subject Interests: Undergrad studies
Automation Activity & Vendor Info: (Acquisitions) SirsiDynix; (Cataloging) SirsiDynix; (Circulation) SirsiDynix; (Course Reserve) SirsiDynix; (ILL) JerseyCat; (OPAC) SirsiDynix; (Serials) SirsiDynix
Wireless access
Function: Govt ref serv, ILL available, Magnifiers for reading, Wheelchair accessible
Partic in LibraryLinkNJ, The New Jersey Library Cooperative; LYRASIS; OCLC Online Computer Library Center, Inc; Virtual Academic Library Environment
Special Services for the Blind - Assistive/Adapted tech devices, equip & products
Open Mon-Fri (Summer-Winter) 7:45am-8pm; Mon-Thurs (Spring) 7:45am-10pm, Fri 7:45am-8pm, Sat 9-5

S OCEAN COUNTY HISTORICAL SOCIETY, Richard Lee Strickler Research Center, 26 Hadley Ave, 08753. SAN 371-6252. Tel: 732-341-1880. FAX: 732-341-4372. E-mail: oceancounty.history@verizon.net, ochs_research@verizon.net. Web Site: www.oceancountyhistory.org. *Head, Research Dept,* Janis Gibson
Founded 1980
Library Holdings: Bk Vols 1,000
Subject Interests: County genealogy, County hist
Wireless access
Open Tues & Wed 1-4
Restriction: Non-circulating

P OCEAN COUNTY LIBRARY*, 101 Washington St, 08753. SAN 351-3998. Tel: 732-349-6200. Administration FAX: 732-473-1356. Information Services FAX: 732-349-0478. Web Site: www.theoceancountylibrary.org. *Dir,* Susan Quinn; Tel: 732-914-5400, E-mail: squinn@theoceancountylibrary.org; *Asst Dir,* Sara Siegler; Tel: 732-914-5412, E-mail: ssiegler@theoceancountylibrary.org; *Chief of Br Serv,* Rita Oakes; Tel: 732-914-5409, E-mail: roakes@theoceancountylibrary.org; *Chief Librn,* Jeri Gunther; Tel: 732-914-5415, E-mail: jgunther@theoceancountylibrary.org; *Chief Librn, Hq,* Rachael LaVoe-Dohn; Tel: 732-914-5403; Staff 520 (MLS 116, Non-MLS 404)
Founded 1925. Pop 575,397; Circ 4,514,037
Jan 2015-Dec 2015. Mats Exp $1,842,782, Books $1,694,980, Per/Ser (Incl. Access Fees) $147,802. Sal $17,077,791
Library Holdings: Audiobooks 39,724; AV Mats 138,912; e-books 26,370; Bk Vols 1,060,651; Per Subs 2,701
Special Collections: Local History (New Jersey Coll). State Document Depository
Automation Activity & Vendor Info: (Acquisitions) Innovative Interfaces, Inc; (Cataloging) Innovative Interfaces, Inc; (Circulation) Innovative Interfaces, Inc; (ILL) OCLC FirstSearch; (OPAC) Innovative Interfaces, Inc; (Serials) Innovative Interfaces, Inc
Wireless access
Function: Adult bk club, After school storytime, Art exhibits, Audiobks via web, Bilingual assistance for Spanish patrons, Bk club(s), Bks on cassette, Bks on CD, Children's prog, Citizenship assistance, Computer training, Computers for patron use, Doc delivery serv, E-Reserves, Electronic databases & coll, Family literacy, Free DVD rentals, Home delivery & serv to seniorr ctr & nursing homes, Homebound delivery serv, ILL available, Music CDs, Online cat, OverDrive digital audio bks, Photocopying/Printing, Preschool outreach, Preschool reading prog, Prog for adults, Prog for children & young adult, Ref & res, Ref serv available, Scanner, Senior computer classes, Senior outreach, Serves people with intellectual disabilities, Spanish lang bks, Spoken cassettes & CDs, Spoken cassettes & DVDs, Story hour, Summer reading prog, Teen prog, Telephone ref, Wheelchair accessible
Publications: Clubs & Organizations of Ocean County, Connect Newsletter; Immigration Resource Directory; Ocean County Resource Directory; Small Business Handbook
Partic in LibraryLinkNJ, The New Jersey Library Cooperative; New Jersey Library Network; OCLC Online Computer Library Center, Inc
Special Services for the Deaf - Staff with knowledge of sign lang; TTY equip
Special Services for the Blind - Computer with voice synthesizer for visually impaired persons
Open Mon-Thurs 9-9, Fri & Sat 9-5, Sun (Sept-May) 1-5
Restriction: Co libr, Non-resident fee
Friends of the Library Group
Branches: 20

BARNEGAT BRANCH, 112 Burr St, Barnegat, 08005, SAN 351-4005. Tel: 609-698-3331. FAX: 609-698-9592. *Br Mgr,* Rachel Cantor
Open Mon, Fri & Sat 10-5, Tues-Thurs 10-9
Friends of the Library Group

BAY HEAD READING CENTER, 136 Meadow Ave, Bay Head, 08742-5080, SAN 371-4713. Tel: 732-892-0662. FAX: 732-473-1356. *Br Mgr,* Melissa Rutkowski
Open Mon & Wed 1-5, Tues & Sat 10-1, Thurs 1-5 & 7-9

BEACHWOOD BRANCH, 126 Beachwood Blvd, Beachwood, 08722-2810, SAN 351-4021. Tel: 732-244-4573. FAX: 732-736-1025. *Br Mgr,* Steven Copp
Open Mon 1-9, Tues-Fri 10-5, Sat 10-1
Friends of the Library Group

BERKELEY BRANCH, 30 Station Rd, Bayville, 08721-2198, SAN 351-403X. Tel: 732-269-2144. FAX: 732-237-2955. *Br Mgr,* Brooke Jacob
Open Mon-Thurs 9-9, Fri & Sat 9-5
Friends of the Library Group

BRICK BRANCH, 301 Chambers Bridge Rd, Brick, 08723-2803, SAN 351-4056. Tel: 732-477-4513. FAX: 732-920-9314. *Br Mgr,* Nancy Voitko
Open Mon-Thurs 9-9, Fri & Sat 9-5
Friends of the Library Group

ISLAND HEIGHTS BRANCH, 121 Central Ave, Island Heights, 08732. (Mail add: PO Box 1127, Island Heights, 08732), SAN 351-4080. Tel: 732-270-6266. FAX: 732-270-0308. *Br Mgr,* Christine Maloney
Open Mon 1-9, Tues-Fri 10-5, Sat 10-1
Friends of the Library Group

JACKSON BRANCH, Two Jackson Dr, Jackson, 08527-3601, SAN 351-4145. Tel: 732-928-4400. FAX: 732-833-0615. *Br Mgr,* Sabrina Guimaeres
Open Mon-Thurs 9-9, Fri & Sat 9-5
Friends of the Library Group

LACEY BRANCH, Ten E Lacey Rd, Forked River, 08731-3626, SAN 351-4110. Tel: 609-693-8566. FAX: 609-971-8973. *Br Mgr,* Rebecca Leopold-Bunucci
Open Mon-Thurs 9-9, Fri & Sat 9-5
Friends of the Library Group

LAKEWOOD BRANCH, 301 Lexington Ave, Lakewood, 08701, SAN 310-236X. Tel: 732-363-1435. FAX: 732-363-1438. *Br Mgr,* Cathi Sheridan
Open Mon-Thurs 9-9, Fri & Sat 9-5, Sun (Sept-May) 1-5
Friends of the Library Group

LITTLE EGG HARBOR BRANCH, 290 Mathistown Rd, Little Egg Harbor, 08087, SAN 376-8317. Tel: 609-294-1197. FAX: 609-294-1302. *Br Mgr,* Dawn Heyson
Open Mon, Fri & Sat 10-5, Tues-Thurs 10-9
Friends of the Library Group

LONG BEACH ISLAND BRANCH, 217 S Central Ave, Surf City, 08008-4800, SAN 351-417X. Tel: 609-494-2480. FAX: 609-494-7850. *Br Mgr,* Toni Smirniw
Open Mon & Wed 9-9, Tues & Thurs-Sat 9-5
Friends of the Library Group

MANCHESTER BRANCH, 21 Colonial Dr, Manchester, 08759, SAN 370-4475. Tel: 732-657-7600. FAX: 732-323-9246. *Br Mgr,* Erin DeLucia
Open Mon-Thurs 9-9, Fri & Sat 9-5
Friends of the Library Group

PLUMSTED BRANCH, 119 Evergreen Rd, New Egypt, 08533, SAN 351-420X. Tel: 609-758-7888. FAX: 609-758-6997. *Br Mgr,* Alexandra Majeski
Open Mon & Wed 1-9, Tues, Thurs & Fri 10-5, Sat 10-1
Friends of the Library Group

POINT PLEASANT BEACH BRANCH, 710 McLean Ave, Point Pleasant Beach, 08742-2522, SAN 370-4483. Tel: 732-892-4575. FAX: 732-701-1941. *Br Mgr,* Matthew Willbergh
Open Mon, Wed, Thurs & Fri (Oct-April) 10-5, Tues 1-9, Sat 10-1; Mon, Wed & Fri (May-Sept) 10-5, Tues 1-9, Thurs 10-9, Sat 10-1
Friends of the Library Group

POINT PLEASANT BOROUGH BRANCH, 834 Beaver Dam Rd, Point Pleasant Beach, 08742-3853. Tel: 732-295-1555. FAX: 732-714-1578. *Br Mgr,* Kelsey Watkoskey
Open Mon, Wed & Thurs 10-9, Tues, Fri & Sat 10-5
Friends of the Library Group

STAFFORD BRANCH, 129 N Main St, Manahawkin, 08050-2933, SAN 351-4250. Tel: 609-597-3381. FAX: 609-978-0770. *Br Mgr,* Theresa Foster
Open Mon, Wed & Thurs 9-9, Tues, Fri & Sat 9-5, Sun (Sept-May) 1-5
Friends of the Library Group

TUCKERTON BRANCH, 380 Bay Ave, Tuckerton, 08087-2557, SAN 351-4269. Tel: 609-296-1470. FAX: 609-296-6487. *Br Mgr,* Cindy Simerlink
Open Mon 1-9, Tues-Fri 10-5, Sat 10-1
Friends of the Library Group

UPPER SHORES BRANCH, 112 Jersey City Ave, Lavallette, 08735, SAN 376-8325. Tel: 732-793-3996. FAX: 732-793-4942. *Br Mgr,* Melissa Rutkowski
Open Mon, Thurs, Fri & Sat 10-5, Tues & Wed 10-9
Friends of the Library Group

WARETOWN BRANCH, 112 Main St, Waretown, 08758-9252, SAN 351-4277. Tel: 609-693-5133. FAX: 609-242-8784. *Br Mgr,* Position Currently Open
Open Mon 1-9, Tues-Fri 10-5, Sat 10-1
Friends of the Library Group

WHITING READING CENTER, Whiting Commons Shopping Ctr, 400 Lacey Rd, Ste 5, Whiting, 08759. Tel: 732-849-0391. FAX: 732-849-0283. *Br Mgr,* Erin DeLucia
Open Mon 9-7, Tues & Thurs 9-5, Wed, Fri & Sat 9-1

L OCEAN VICINAGE LEGAL RESEARCH & INFORMATION CENTER*, Ocean County Courthouse, Rm 101, 118 Washington St, 08753. SAN 325-9110. Tel: 732-506-5026, 732-929-2063, 732-929-2065. Web Site: www.njcourts.gov/courts/vicinages/ocean.html.
Library Holdings: Bk Vols 1,000
Wireless access
Open Mon-Fri 8:30-4:30

TOTOWA

P BOROUGH OF TOTOWA PUBLIC LIBRARY, Dwight D Eisenhower Public Library, 537 Totowa Rd, 07512-1699. SAN 310-5377. Tel: 973-790-3265, Ext 10. Administration Tel: 973-790-3265, Ext 11. FAX: 973-790-0306. E-mail: totawapl@gmail.com. Web Site: www.totowapl.org. *Dir,* Anne Krautheim; E-mail: krautheimanne@palsplus.org; *Ch Serv,* Annemarie Shapiola; E-mail: shapiola@palsplus.org; Staff 10 (MLS 2, Non-MLS 8)
Founded 1957. Pop 10,804; Circ 34,328
Library Holdings: Bk Titles 44,158; Bk Vols 46,647; Per Subs 250
Special Collections: Library of America (60 vol set)
Subject Interests: Lit
Automation Activity & Vendor Info: (Cataloging) SirsiDynix; (Circulation) SirsiDynix; (OPAC) SirsiDynix
Wireless access
Partic in LibraryLinkNJ, The New Jersey Library Cooperative; PALS Plus, The Computer Consortium of Passaic County Libraries
Special Services for the Deaf - Bks on deafness & sign lang; Staff with knowledge of sign lang
Open Mon, Wed & Fri 10-5, Tues & Thurs 10-6, Sat 10-2
Friends of the Library Group

TRENTON

M CAPITAL HEALTH REGIONAL MEDICAL CENTER*, Health Sciences Library, 750 Brunswick Ave, 08638. SAN 310-5407. Tel: 609-394-6065. FAX: 609-278-1882. Web Site: www.capitalhealth.org/professionals/health-science-library. *Dir, Libr Serv,* Erica Moncrief; Tel: 609-303-4125, E-mail: emoncrief@capitalhealth.org; *Librn,* Jennifer Kral; E-mail: jskral@capitalhealth.org; Staff 2 (MLS 1, Non-MLS 1)
Library Holdings: Bk Titles 3,500; Per Subs 150
Special Collections: Hist of Hospital & Nursing School
Subject Interests: Allied health, Med, Neuroscience, Nursing, Psychol
Wireless access
Partic in Basic Health Sciences Library Network; New Jersey Health Sciences Library Network
Open Mon-Fri 7:30-5
Restriction: Open to students, fac & staff

S MERCER COUNTY CORRECTION CENTER LIBRARY*, 640 S Broad St, 08650. SAN 375-7013. Tel: 609-989-6901, Ext 2308. FAX: 609-397-3290. *Prog Coordr,* Charles Peters
Library Holdings: Bk Titles 4,000
Restriction: Not open to pub

G NEW JERSEY DEPARTMENT OF ENVIRONMENTAL PROTECTION, Environmental Research Library, 432 E State St, 1st Flr, 08608. (Mail add: Mail Code 432-01, PO Box 420, 08625-0420), SAN 325-9323. Tel: 609-984-2249. Administration Tel: 609-633-2151. FAX: 609-292-3298. Web Site: www.state.nj.us/dep/dsr/irc. *Librn,* Tonia Wu; E-mail: tonia.wu@dep.nj.gov; Staff 2 (MLS 2)
Founded 1984
Library Holdings: Bk Vols 7,500; Per Subs 45
Special Collections: IARC Monographs; limited coll of NJDEP reports; USEPA documents; USGS documents; WHO Environmental Health Criteria
Automation Activity & Vendor Info: (Acquisitions) SirsiDynix; (Cataloging) OCLC Connexion; (Circulation) SirsiDynix; (ILL) OCLC FirstSearch
Function: Govt ref serv
Partic in LibraryLinkNJ, The New Jersey Library Cooperative
Restriction: Open to pub by appt only

G NEW JERSEY DEPARTMENT OF LABOR & WORKFORCE DEVELOPMENT LIBRARY, John Fitch Plaza, 4th Flr, 08611. (Mail add: PO Box 943, 08625-0943), SAN 310-544X. Tel: 609-292-2035. FAX: 609-984-5457. *Librn III,* Hing Choi Fung; E-mail: hing-choi.fung@dol.nj.gov; *Librn I,* Carlyn Hudson; Staff 2 (MLS 2)
Founded 1966
Library Holdings: Bk Vols 2,934; Per Subs 23
Subject Interests: Census, Disability ins, Econ, Employment, Labor, Labor law practices, Labor market info, Training, Unemployment ins, Vocational rehabilitation
Automation Activity & Vendor Info: (Cataloging) Koha; (Circulation) Koha; (OPAC) Koha
Function: Ref serv available
Partic in LibraryLinkNJ, The New Jersey Library Cooperative
Open Mon-Fri 8:30-4:30
Restriction: Non-circulating

GL NEW JERSEY DEPARTMENT OF LAW & PUBLIC SAFETY, Attorney General's Library, 25 Market St, West Wing, 6th Flr, 08625. (Mail add: PO Box 115, 08625-0115), SAN 310-5490. Tel: 609-292-4958, 609-376-2290. FAX: 609-633-6555. E-mail: oag.library@njoag.gov. Web Site: nj.gov/oag/library.htm. *Librn III,* Tamar Pritchard; Tel: 973-648-4849; Staff 1 (MLS 1)
Subject Interests: Criminology, NJ law, Regulatory law
Automation Activity & Vendor Info: (Acquisitions) OCLC; (Cataloging) Horizon; (Circulation) Horizon; (ILL) OCLC; (OPAC) Horizon; (Serials) Horizon
Wireless access
Function: Govt ref serv
Restriction: Authorized personnel only

S NEW JERSEY DEPARTMENT OF TRANSPORTATION*, Research Library, 1035 Parkway Ave, 08618-2309. (Mail add: PO Box 600, 08625-0600). Tel: 609-530-5289. E-mail: library@dot.nj.gov. *Librn,* Laurie Strow; Staff 2 (MLS 2)
Founded 1962
Library Holdings: AV Mats 170; CDs 220; DVDs 40; Electronic Media & Resources 100; Bk Titles 8,000; Per Subs 30; Videos 150
Special Collections: AASHTO Publications; Federal Highway Administration Publications; NJDOT Publications; Transportation Research Board Publications
Automation Activity & Vendor Info: (Acquisitions) Horizon; (Cataloging) Horizon; (Circulation) Horizon; (ILL) OCLC; (OPAC) Horizon
Publications: Selected Recent Acquisitions (Acquisition list)
Partic in Eastern Transportation Knowledge Network; LibraryLinkNJ, The New Jersey Library Cooperative
Open Mon-Fri 9-5
Restriction: In-house use for visitors

G NEW JERSEY STATE LEAGUE OF MUNICIPALITIES*, Bureau of Municipal Information, 222 W State St, 08608. SAN 323-4266. Tel: 609-695-3481. FAX: 609-695-5156. Web Site: www.njlm.org/bureau. *Innovations Mgr, Sr Res Libr Mgr,* Taran Samhammer; E-mail: tsamhammer@njlm.org

Founded 1915
Library Holdings: e-books 15,000
Special Collections: Ordinances; Shared Service Agreements
Restriction: Not open to pub

P NEW JERSEY STATE LIBRARY*, 185 W State St, 08608. (Mail add: PO Box 520, 08625-0520), SAN 351-4773. Tel: 609-278-2640. Information Services Tel: 609-278-2640, Ext 131. FAX: 609-278-2652. E-mail: refdesk@njstatelib.org. Web Site: www.njstatelib.org. *State Librn,* Mary Chute; Tel: 609-278-2640, Ext 101, E-mail: mchute@njstatelib.org; *Chief Deputy, State Librn, Dir, SLIC,* Margaret Nizolek; Tel: 609-278-2640, Ext 148, E-mail: mnizolek@njstatelib.org; *Dir, Communications, Dir, Mkt,* Tiffany McClary; Tel: 609-278-2640, Ext 122, E-mail: tmcclary@njstatelib.org; *Dep State Librn, Innovation & Outreach,* Peggy Cadigan; Tel: 609-278-2640, Ext 113, E-mail: pcadigan@njstatelib.org; *Dep State Librn, Libr Support Serv,* Kathleen Moeller-Peiffer; Tel: 609-278-2640, Ext 157, E-mail: kmoellerpeiffer@njstatelib.org; *Dep State Librn, Lifelong Learning,* Michele Stricker; Tel: 609-278-2640, Ext 164, E-mail: mstricker@njstatelib.org; *Youth Serv Spec, Lifelong Learning,* Sharon Rawlins; Tel: 609-278-2640, Ext 116, E-mail: srawlins@njstatelib.org; *Data Coordr, Libr Support Serv,* Bob Keith; Tel: 609-278-2640, Ext 192, E-mail: rkeith@njstatelib.org; Staff 93 (MLS 41, Non-MLS 52)
Founded 1796
Jul 2016-Jun 2017 Income (Main & Associated Libraries) $18,424,000. Mats Exp $993,000, Books $473,000, Per/Ser (Incl. Access Fees) $216,000, Electronic Ref Mat (Incl. Access Fees) $304,000
Library Holdings: Audiobooks 7,786; AV Mats 598; e-books 51,357; e-journals 113; Microforms 2,902,355; Bk Titles 405,256; Bk Vols 542,108; Per Subs 806; Videos 406
Special Collections: Foundations Coll; Genealogy Coll; Jerseyana; Law Coll; Maps & Atlases; New Jersey State Documents. State Document Depository; US Document Depository
Subject Interests: Educ, Genealogy, Grantsmanship, Law, Libr sci, Mgt, Pub health, Soc sci, State govt, State hist
Automation Activity & Vendor Info: (Acquisitions) SirsiDynix; (Cataloging) SirsiDynix; (Circulation) SirsiDynix; (Discovery) EBSCO Discovery Service; (ILL) OCLC ILLiad; (OPAC) SirsiDynix; (Serials) SirsiDynix
Wireless access
Publications: Library Data (Online only); New Books Lists; New Jersey Library Laws (Online only); New Jersey Public Library Statistics (Online only); NJSL Direct Newsletter (Online only); Shipping List of NJ Documents; Special Bibliographies; TBBC's Insights (Quarterly); The Link Newsletter
Partic in LibraryLinkNJ, The New Jersey Library Cooperative; LYRASIS; New Jersey Library Network; Virtual Academic Library Environment
Special Services for the Blind - Assistive/Adapted tech devices, equip & products; Audio mat; Audiovision-a radio reading serv; Bks on flash-memory cartridges; Braille alphabet card; Braille bks; Cassette playback machines; Cassettes; Children's Braille; Digital talking bk; Digital talking bk machines; Disability awareness prog; Large print bks; Large screen computer & software; Lending of low vision aids; Local mags & bks recorded; Newsletter (in large print, Braille or on cassette); Newsline for the Blind; PC for people with disabilities; Radio reading serv; Talking bks; Talking bks & player equip
Open Mon-Fri 8:30-5
Friends of the Library Group
Branches: 1

P TALKING BOOK & BRAILLE CENTER, 2300 Stuyvesant Ave, 08618. (Mail add: PO Box 501, 08625-0501), SAN 329-0131. Tel: 609-406-7179. Toll Free Tel: 800-792-8322, Ext 804, 800-792-8322, Ext 823. FAX: 609-406-7181. E-mail: tbbc@njstatelib.org. Web Site: www.njstatelib.org/talking-book-braille-center. *Dep State Librn, NJSL Talking Bk & Braille Ctr, Dir,* Adam Szczepaniak, Jr; Tel: 604-406-7179, Ext 801, E-mail: aszczepaniak@njstatelib.org; *CUL Adminr,* Gary Zonderwyk; Tel: 609-406-7179, Ext 825, E-mail: gzonderwyk@njstatelib.org; *Head, Reader Serv, Head, Youth Serv,* Elizabeth Burns; Tel: 609-406-7179, Ext 804, E-mail: eburns@njstatelib.org; *Supvr, Machine Lending,* Andy O'Rahilly; Tel: 609-406-7179, Ext 819, E-mail: aorahilly@njstatelib.org; *Assistive Tech Coordr,* Christian Riehl; Tel: 609-406-7179, Ext 821, E-mail: criehl@njstatelib.org; *Develop,* Linda Cerce; Tel: 609-406-7179, Ext 835, E-mail: lcerce@njstatelib.org; *Media Prod,* Mary Crain; Tel: 609-406-7179, Ext 809, E-mail: mcrain@njstatelib.org; Staff 6 (MLS 4, Non-MLS 2)
Founded 1968
Library Holdings: AV Mats 1,043; Braille Volumes 45,311; High Interest/Low Vocabulary Bk Vols 23; Bk Titles 125,540; Bk Vols 436,944; Per Subs 90; Talking Bks 106,669
Publications: Insights (Newsletter); Rap Sheet (Newsletter)
Special Services for the Deaf - TDD equip; TTY equip
Special Services for the Blind - Braille bks; Talking bks
Open Mon-Fri 8:30-4
Restriction: Residents only
Friends of the Library Group

S NEW JERSEY STATE MUSEUM-FINE ART BUREAU*, 205 W State St, 08625. (Mail add: PO Box 530, 08625-0530), SAN 323-5122. Tel: 609-984-3899. FAX: 609-292-7636. Web Site: www.state.nj.us/state/museum. *Exec Dir,* Margaret O'Reilly; E-mail: margaret.oreilly@sos.nj.gov; Staff 3 (Non-MLS 3)
Founded 1895
Library Holdings: Bk Vols 4,000
Subject Interests: Fine arts
Restriction: Staff use only

L NEW JERSEY STATE PRISON*, Law Library, PO Box 861, 08625. SAN 310-5539. Tel: 609-292-9700, Ext 4285. FAX: 609-777-1885. *Dir of Educ,* Jecrois Jean-Baptiste; E-mail: jecrois.jean-baptiste@doc.nj.gov
Founded 1900
Library Holdings: Bk Vols 2,000
Subject Interests: Fiction, Law, Non-fiction, Philos, Psychol

M SAINT FRANCIS MEDICAL CENTER*, Medical Library, 601 Hamilton Ave, 08629. SAN 310-5504. Tel: 609-599-5068. FAX: 609-599-5773. Web Site: www.stfrancismedical.org/Education/Library.aspx. *Med Librn,* Donna Barlow; E-mail: dbarlow@StFrancisMedical.org; Staff 1 (MLS 1)
Founded 1930
Library Holdings: Bk Vols 8,000; Per Subs 300
Subject Interests: Allied health, Health serv admin, Med, Nursing
Publications: Journal Holdings List; Library Bulletin
Partic in New Jersey Health Sciences Library Network
Open Mon-Fri 7:30-4

G STATE OF NEW JERSEY - DEPARTMENT OF BANKING & INSURANCE LIBRARY*, Roebling Building Library, 20 W State St, 08608-1206. (Mail add: PO Box 325, 08625-0325), SAN 371-7887. Tel: 609-292-5064, 609-292-7272. FAX: 609-633-8213. Web Site: www.state.nj.us/dobi. *Librn,* Marshall McKnight; E-mail: Marshall.McKnight@dobi.nj.gov
Library Holdings: Bk Titles 200; Bk Vols 600; Per Subs 75
Special Collections: New Jersey Department of Banking & Insurance Coll; New Jersey Law
Publications: Checklist of Publications
Restriction: Open by appt only

P TRENTON FREE PUBLIC LIBRARY*, 120 Academy St, 08608. SAN 351-4293. Tel: 609-392-7188. Circulation Tel: 609-392-7188, Ext 10. Reference Tel: 609-392-7188, Ext 34. FAX: 609-695-8631. Web Site: www.trentonlib.org. *Dir, Operations,* Patricia Hall; E-mail: phall@trentonlib.org; *Youth Serv Librn,* Rebecca Francomartin; Staff 36 (MLS 13, Non-MLS 23)
Founded 1750. Pop 85,403; Circ 196,949
Library Holdings: Bk Titles 300,000; Bk Vols 375,000; Per Subs 770
Special Collections: Art & Music, bks, CDs, prints, recs, scores; Trentoniana Coll, bks, pamphlets, photogs, docs. State Document Depository; US Document Depository
Automation Activity & Vendor Info: (Acquisitions) TLC (The Library Corporation); (Cataloging) TLC (The Library Corporation); (Circulation) TLC (The Library Corporation); (Course Reserve) TLC (The Library Corporation); (ILL) TLC (The Library Corporation); (Media Booking) TLC (The Library Corporation); (OPAC) TLC (The Library Corporation); (Serials) TLC (The Library Corporation)
Wireless access
Publications: Acquisitions List (Monthly); Union List of Serials
Special Services for the Deaf - Adult & family literacy prog; Bks on deafness & sign lang; Closed caption videos; High interest/low vocabulary bks
Open Mon-Thurs 9-8, Fri & Sat 9-5
Friends of the Library Group

GL US COURTS LIBRARY*, Phillip Forman Law Library, Clarkson S Fisher Judicial Complex, Rm 300, 402 E State St, 08608. SAN 377-3647. Tel: 609-989-2345. FAX: 609-989-0485. Web Site: www.ca3.uscourts.gov/circuit-libraries. *Librn,* Tom Fasching
Library Holdings: Bk Titles 7,000; Bk Vols 9,000
Automation Activity & Vendor Info: (Cataloging) SirsiDynix
Wireless access
Open Mon-Fri 8:30-4:30
Restriction: Non-circulating

UNION

C KEAN UNIVERSITY*, Nancy Thompson Library, 1000 Morris Ave, 07083. SAN 310-558X. Tel: 908-737-4629. Interlibrary Loan Service Tel: 908-737-4602. E-mail: library@kean.edu. Web Site: libguides.kean.edu/Library. *Librn,* Craig Anderson; E-mail: cjanders@kean.edu; *Librn,* Linda Cifelli; *Librn,* Janette Gonzalez; *Librn,*

Shirley Horbatt; *Librn,* Eleanor McKnight; *Librn,* Marquan Mutazz; *Librn,* Chrisler Pitts; Staff 9 (MLS 9)
Founded 1914. Enrl 15,100; Fac 400; Highest Degree: Doctorate
Library Holdings: Bk Titles 315,000; Bk Vols 379,905; Per Subs 34,000
Special Collections: History (New Jerseyana), bks, pamphlets
Subject Interests: Allied health, Computer sci, Econ, Educ, English, Occupational therapy
Automation Activity & Vendor Info: (Acquisitions) Ex Libris Group; (Cataloging) Ex Libris Group; (Circulation) Ex Libris Group; (Course Reserve) Ex Libris Group; (OPAC) Ex Libris Group; (Serials) Ex Libris Group
Wireless access
Function: Art exhibits, E-Reserves, Electronic databases & coll, ILL available, Online cat, Online info literacy tutorials on the web & in blackboard, Online ref, Photocopying/Printing, Ref serv available, Wheelchair accessible
Partic in LibraryLinkNJ, The New Jersey Library Cooperative; LYRASIS; OCLC Online Computer Library Center, Inc; Virtual Academic Library Environment; Westchester Academic Library Directors Organization
Open Mon-Thurs (Fall & Spring) 8am-2am, Fri 8-5, Sat 9-5, Sun 1-10; Mon-Thurs (Summer) 8am-2am

P UNION PUBLIC LIBRARY*, 1980 Morris Ave, 07083. SAN 351-5079. Tel: 908-851-5450. Reference Tel: 908-851-5450, Ext 3. E-mail: unionpl@uplnj.org. Web Site: www.uplnj.org. *Dir,* Karen O'Malley; E-mail: komalley@uplnj.org; Staff 32 (MLS 11, Non-MLS 21)
Founded 1927
Automation Activity & Vendor Info: (Cataloging) TLC (The Library Corporation); (Circulation) TLC (The Library Corporation); (ILL) JerseyCat; (OPAC) TLC (The Library Corporation)
Wireless access
Function: 24/7 Electronic res, 24/7 Online cat, Activity rm, Adult bk club, Adult literacy prog, After school storytime, Art exhibits, Art programs, Audiobks via web, Children's prog, Citizenship assistance, Computer training, Computers for patron use, Electronic databases & coll, Free DVD rentals, Homebound delivery serv, ILL available, Internet access, Magazines, Mango lang, Meeting rooms, Microfiche/film & reading machines, Movies, Museum passes, Music CDs, Online cat, Online ref, Outreach serv, OverDrive digital audio bks, Photocopying/Printing, Preschool outreach, Prog for adults, Prog for children & young adult, Ref serv available, Scanner, Senior outreach, Spanish lang bks, STEM programs, Summer reading prog, Tax forms, Teen prog, Wheelchair accessible, Writing prog
Partic in Librs of Union County Consortium; MURAL
Special Services for the Blind - Assistive/Adapted tech devices, equip & products; Bks on CD; Bks on flash-memory cartridges; Digital talking bk; Digital talking bk machines; Home delivery serv; Large print bks; Talking bk serv referral
Open Mon, Tues & Thurs 10-9, Wed 10-6, Fri & Sat 9-5; Mon, Tues & Thurs (Summer) 10-9, Wed 10-6, Fri 9-5
Friends of the Library Group
Branches: 1
VAUXHALL BRANCH, 123 Hilton Ave, Vauxhall, 07088, SAN 351-5133. Tel: 908-851-5451. *Dir,* Karen O'Malley; *Br Mgr,* Erica Bell
Automation Activity & Vendor Info: (Cataloging) TLC (The Library Corporation); (Circulation) TLC (The Library Corporation); (ILL) JerseyCat; (OPAC) TLC (The Library Corporation)
Function: 24/7 Electronic res, 24/7 Online cat, Activity rm, Adult bk club, Adult literacy prog, After school storytime, Audiobks via web, Bks on CD, Children's prog, Citizenship assistance, Computer training, Computers for patron use, Electronic databases & coll, Free DVD rentals, Homebound delivery serv, ILL available, Internet access, Magazines, Mango lang, Meeting rooms, Museum passes, Music CDs, Online cat, Outreach serv, OverDrive digital audio bks, Photocopying/Printing, Preschool reading prog, Prog for adults, Prog for children & young adult, Story hour, Tax forms, Teen prog, Wheelchair accessible
Special Services for the Deaf - Closed caption videos; High interest/low vocabulary bks
Special Services for the Blind - Bks on CD; Digital talking bk machines; Extensive large print coll; Home delivery serv; Info on spec aids & appliances; Large print bks & talking machines; Reader equip; Ref serv; Talking bk serv referral
Open Mon & Wed 1-9, Tues & Thurs 10-6, Sat 9-5; Fri (Summer) 9-5
Friends of the Library Group

UNION BEACH

P UNION BEACH MEMORIAL LIBRARY, 810 Union Ave, 07735. SAN 310-5601. Tel: 732-264-3792. FAX: 732-264-3318. E-mail: ublibrary07735@gmail.com. Web Site: www.sites.google.com/site/ublibrary07735/home. *Libr Mgr,* Janet Manochio; Staff 3 (MLS 3)
Library Holdings: Bk Titles 29,500
Automation Activity & Vendor Info: (Cataloging) SirsiDynix; (Circulation) SirsiDynix
Wireless access
Mem of Monmouth County Library
Open Mon, Wed & Fri 2-6, Tues, Thurs & Sat 9-1

UNION CITY

P UNION CITY PUBLIC LIBRARY*, 324 43rd St, 07087-5008. SAN 351-5168. Tel: 201-866-7500. FAX: 201-866-0962. Web Site: www.uclibrary.org. *Dir,* Rita Mann; E-mail: rmann@uclibrary.org; *Ch,* Violeta Aybar Maki; E-mail: vaybarmaki@uclibrary.org; Staff 1 (MLS 1)
Founded 1905. Pop 67,088
Library Holdings: Bk Titles 29,815; Bk Vols 42,128; Per Subs 163
Subject Interests: English lit, Film, Spanish lang
Automation Activity & Vendor Info: (Acquisitions) Follett Software; (Cataloging) Follett Software; (Circulation) Follett Software; (OPAC) Follett Software; (Serials) Follett Software
Wireless access
Open Mon, Wed & Fri 10-6, Tues & Thurs 10-8:30, Sat 10-5
Branches: 1
SUMMIT BRANCH, 1800 Summit Ave, 07087-4320, SAN 351-5192. Tel: 201-866-7503. FAX: 201-348-2635. E-mail: unioncitybranchlibrary@gmail.com. *Librn,* Carolina Bermudez; Staff 3 (Non-MLS 3)
Founded 2004. Pop 67,088
Library Holdings: Bk Titles 21,017; Bk Vols 31,806; Per Subs 72
Open Mon & Wed 12:30-8:30, Tues, Thurs & Fri 10-6, Sun 10-3
Friends of the Library Group

UPPER SADDLE RIVER

P UPPER SADDLE RIVER PUBLIC LIBRARY*, 245 Lake St, 07458. SAN 310-5644. Tel: 201-327-2583. FAX: 201-327-3966. Circulation E-mail: usdrcirc@bccls.org. Web Site: www.uppersaddleriverlibrary.org. *Dir,* Kathleen McGrail; E-mail: mcgrail@bccls.org
Founded 1959. Pop 7,700; Circ 120,000
Library Holdings: Bk Titles 69,625; Per Subs 355
Automation Activity & Vendor Info: (Circulation) SirsiDynix; (OPAC) SirsiDynix
Wireless access
Publications: Business & Residents Local Directory
Open Mon-Thurs 9:30-8:30, Fri & Sat 10-5, Sun 1-5
Friends of the Library Group

VERONA

P VERONA PUBLIC LIBRARY, 17 Gould St, 07044-1928. SAN 310-5679. Tel: 973-857-4848. FAX: 973-857-4851. E-mail: info@veronalibrary.org. Web Site: www.veronalibrary.org. *Libr Dir,* Claudine Pascale; E-mail: pascale@veronalibrary.org; *Asst Dir,* Catherine Adair Williams; E-mail: adair.williams@veronalibrary.org; *Ch,* Ryan Oxild; E-mail: oxild@veronalibrary.org; *Tech Serv Librn, Teen Serv Librn,* Precious Mack; E-mail: mack@veronalibrary.org; Staff 9 (MLS 4, Non-MLS 5)
Founded 1912. Pop 13,553; Circ 90,000
Library Holdings: Bk Titles 55,000; Bk Vols 60,000; Per Subs 175
Special Collections: Landsberger Holocaust Coll; Unico Italian Heritage Coll
Automation Activity & Vendor Info: (Cataloging) Auto-Graphics, Inc; (Circulation) Auto-Graphics, Inc; (ILL) JerseyCat; (OPAC) Auto-Graphics, Inc
Wireless access
Partic in PALS Plus, The Computer Consortium of Passaic County Libraries
Open Mon, Tues & Thurs 9-9, Wed, Fri & Sat 9-5, Sun 2-5
Friends of the Library Group

VINCENTOWN

P SALLY STRETCH KEEN MEMORIAL LIBRARY*, 94 Main St, 08088. SAN 310-5687. Tel: 609-859-3598. E-mail: vincentown@bcls.lib.nj.us. Web Site: www.vincentownlibrary.org. *Dir,* Marsha Jones
Founded 1923. Pop 10,000
Library Holdings: Bk Vols 40,000; Per Subs 20
Subject Interests: Civil War
Wireless access
Mem of Burlington County Library
Partic in LibraryLinkNJ, The New Jersey Library Cooperative
Open Mon & Wed 10-5, Tues & Thurs 10-7, Sat 10-2

VINELAND

§M INSPIRA HEALTH MEDICAL LIBRARY, 1505 W Sherman Ave, 08360. Tel: 856-641-7547. FAX: 856-575-5015. Web Site: www.inspirahealthnetwork.org/locations/inspira-medical-center-vineland. *Dir,* Emily Turnure
Partic in New Jersey Health Sciences Library Network

J ROWAN COLLEGE OF SOUTH JERSEY, Cumberland Campus Library, 3322 College Dr, 08360. (Mail add: PO Box 1500, 08362-1500), SAN 310-5709. Tel: 856-200-4623. Web Site: www.rcsj.edu. *Head Librn,* Patti Schmid; Tel: 856-200-4624, E-mail: pschmid@rscj.edu; *Librn,* Kelly Hayden; E-mail: khayden@rcsj.edu; Staff 3.5 (MLS 3.5)
Founded 1966. Enrl 3,144; Fac 50; Highest Degree: Associate
Library Holdings: Bk Titles 33,000; Bk Vols 38,000; Per Subs 50
Special Collections: Jerseyanna; Holocaust
Subject Interests: Holistic health, Mythology, Nursing
Automation Activity & Vendor Info: (Cataloging) SirsiDynix; (Circulation) SirsiDynix; (OPAC) SirsiDynix
Wireless access
Function: Computers for patron use, Electronic databases & coll, Notary serv, Online cat, Online info literacy tutorials on the web & in blackboard, Orientations, Photocopying/Printing, Ref & res, Ref serv available, Scanner, Wheelchair accessible
Publications: Student Handbook
Partic in LibraryLinkNJ, The New Jersey Library Cooperative; OCLC Online Computer Library Center, Inc; Virtual Academic Library Environment
Open Mon-Thurs 10-8, Fri 10-3, Sat 11-2
Restriction: Circ limited, In-house use for visitors, Non-resident fee, Open to pub for ref & circ; with some limitations

M VINELAND DEVELOPMENTAL CENTER HOSPITAL LIBRARY*, 1676 E Landis Ave, 08360. (Mail add: PO Box 1513, 08360-1513), SAN 376-060X. Tel: 856-696-6000. *Coordr,* Patricia Schwegel
Library Holdings: Bk Titles 950; Per Subs 36
Partic in LibraryLinkNJ, The New Jersey Library Cooperative
Open Mon-Fri 7-3

S VINELAND HISTORICAL & ANTIQUARIAN SOCIETY, 108 S Seventh St, 08360-4607. (Mail add: PO Box 35, 08362-0035), SAN 325-8998. Tel: 856-691-1111. E-mail: vinelandhistory@gmail.com. Web Site: www.discovervinelandhistory.org. *Curator,* Patricia Martinelli; Staff 1 (Non-MLS 1)
Founded 1864
Library Holdings: Bk Vols 8,000
Special Collections: Women's history
Subject Interests: Am hist, NJ hist
Wireless access
Restriction: 24-hr pass syst for students only, Badge access after hrs, Borrowing privileges limited to anthropology fac & libr staff, Borrowing privileges limited to fac & registered students, Borrowing requests are handled by ILL, Circ limited, Circ privileges for students & alumni only, Circ to mem only, Circ to mil employees only, Clients only, Closed stack, Co libr, Congregants only, Employee & client use only, Employees & their associates, Employees only

P VINELAND PUBLIC LIBRARY, 1058 E Landis Ave, 08360. SAN 310-5717. Tel: 856-794-4244. FAX: 856-691-0366. E-mail: reference@vinelandlibrary.org. Web Site: www.vinelandlibrary.org. *Dir,* Brandi Grosso; E-mail: bgrosso@vinelandlibrary.org; *Head, Youth Serv,* Helen Cowan; E-mail: hcowan@vinelandlibrary.org
Founded 1901. Pop 57,500; Circ 254,000
Jan 2019-Dec 2019 Income $1,449,354. Mats Exp $1,428,363
Library Holdings: Bk Titles 100,000; Per Subs 161
Automation Activity & Vendor Info: (Cataloging) SirsiDynix
Wireless access
Partic in Cumberland Libraries United Electronic System; LibraryLinkNJ, The New Jersey Library Cooperative
Open Mon-Thurs 11-2, Fri 11-4
Friends of the Library Group

VOORHEES

P CAMDEN COUNTY LIBRARY SYSTEM*, M Allan Vogelson Regional Branch & Headquarters, 203 Laurel Rd, 08043. SAN 351-5222. Tel: 856-772-1636. Circulation Tel: 856-772-1636, Ext 7355. Interlibrary Loan Service Tel: 856-772-1636, Ext 7316. FAX: 856-772-6105. Web Site: www.camdencountylibrary.org. *Dir,* Linda Devlin; Tel: 856-772-1636, Ext 7344, E-mail: ldevlin@camdencountylibrary.org; *Assoc Dir,* David Lisa; Tel: 856-772-1636, Ext 7338, E-mail: dlisa@camdencountylibrary.org; *Br Mgr,* William Brahms; Tel: 856-772-1636, Ext 7308, E-mail: wbrahms@camdencountylibrary.org; *Adult Serv,* Rosemary Scalese; Tel: 856-772-1636, Ext 7350, E-mail: rscalese@camdencountylibrary.org; *Ch Serv,* Emily Moore; Tel: 856-772-1636, Ext 7321, E-mail: emoore@camdencountylibrary.org; *Circ,* Chris Entwisle; Tel: 856-772-1636, Ext 7309, E-mail: centwisle@camdencountylibrary.org; *Human Res,* Lauren Callahan; Tel: 856-772-1636, Ext 7347, E-mail: lcallahan@camdencountylibrary.org; *Info Tech, Tech Serv,* Lisa Derfler; Tel: 856-772-1636, Ext 7333, E-mail: lderfler@camdencountylibrary.org; Staff 188 (MLS 43, Non-MLS 145)
Founded 1922
Library Holdings: AV Mats 35,065; Electronic Media & Resources 93; Bk Titles 177,726; Bk Vols 430,060; Per Subs 895
Subject Interests: NJ
Automation Activity & Vendor Info: (Acquisitions) Innovative Interfaces, Inc; (Cataloging) Innovative Interfaces, Inc; (Circulation) Innovative Interfaces, Inc; (ILL) Innovative Interfaces, Inc; (OPAC) Innovative Interfaces, Inc; (Serials) Innovative Interfaces, Inc
Wireless access
Member Libraries: Berlin Township Library; Clementon Memorial Library; Dorathea Zeoli Public Library; Gibbsboro Public Library; Lindenwold Public Library; Oaklyn Memorial Library
Partic in LibraryLinkNJ, The New Jersey Library Cooperative; LYRASIS; National Network of Libraries of Medicine Region 1; New Jersey Library Network; OCLC Online Computer Library Center, Inc
Special Services for the Deaf - Assisted listening device; Closed caption videos; TTY equip
Special Services for the Blind - Large print bks; ZoomText magnification & reading software
Open Mon-Fri 10-9, Sat 10-6, Sun (Sept-May) 1-5
Branches: 7
RILETTA L CREAM FERRY AVENUE BRANCH, 852 Ferry Ave, Camden, 08104. Tel: 856-342-9789. FAX: 856-342-9791. *Br Mgr,* Jane Leven; E-mail: jleven@camdencountylibrary.org
Open Mon-Thurs 10-8, Fri & Sat 10-5
NILSA I CRUZ-PEREZ DOWNTOWN BRANCH-RUTGERS, Rutgers Campus, 301 N 5th St, Camden, 08102. Tel: 856-225-6807. FAX: 856-225-6802. *Br Mgr,* Julie Tozer; E-mail: jtozer@camdencountylibrary.org
Open Mon-Thurs 10-8, Fri & Sat 10-5
GLOUCESTER TOWNSHIP-BLACKWOOD ROTARY LIBRARY, 15 S Black Horse Pike, Blackwood, 08012, SAN 351-5257. Tel: 856-228-0022. FAX: 856-228-9085. *Br Mgr,* Anne Ackroyd; E-mail: aackroyd@camdencountylibrary.org; Staff 3 (MLS 3)
Pop 76,519
Library Holdings: Bk Vols 55,130; Per Subs 50
Open Mon-Thurs 10-9, Fri & Sat 10-5
ANTHONY P INFANTI BELLMAWR BRANCH LIBRARY, 35 E Browning Rd, Bellmawr, 08031, SAN 378-1542. Tel: 856-931-1400. FAX: 856-931-5338. *Br Mgr,* Debbie Stefano; E-mail: dstefano@camdencountylibrary.org; Staff 3 (MLS 3)
Pop 27,939
Library Holdings: Bk Vols 35,000; Per Subs 96
Open Mon-Thurs 10-9, Fri & Sat 10-5
Friends of the Library Group
MERCHANTVILLE PUBLIC LIBRARY, 130 S Centre St, Merchantville, 08109. Tel: 856-665-3128. FAX: 856-665-4296. *Mgr,* Christen Orbanus; E-mail: corbanus@camdencountylibrary.org; Staff 1 (MLS 1)
Pop 7,780
Library Holdings: Bk Vols 14,125
Open Mon & Wed 2-9, Tues & Thurs 2-5, Sat 10:30-4
WILLIAM G ROHRER MEMORIAL LIBRARY - HADDON TOWNSHIP, 15 MacArthur Blvd, Westmont, 08108, SAN 351-5281. Tel: 856-854-2752. FAX: 856-854-8825. *Br Mgr,* Christina Sirianni; E-mail: csirianni@camdencountylibrary.org; Staff 3 (MLS 3)
Library Holdings: Bk Vols 57,064; Per Subs 100
Open Mon-Thurs 10-9, Fri & Sat 10-5
Friends of the Library Group
SOUTH COUNTY REGIONAL BRANCH - WINSLOW TOWNSHIP, 35 Coopers Folly Rd, Atco, 08004, SAN 351-5311. Tel: 856-753-2537. FAX: 856-753-7289. *Br Mgr,* Jennifer Druce; Tel: 856-753-2537, Ext 7404, E-mail: jdruce@camdencountylibrary.org; Staff 6 (MLS 5, Non-MLS 1)
Pop 64,086
Library Holdings: Bk Vols 77,217; Per Subs 150
Open Mon-Fri 10-9, Sat 10-6, Sun (Sept-May) 1-5

M VIRTUA HEALTH SYSTEM, VOORHEES DIVISION*, Staff Medical Library, 100 Bowman Dr, Medical Library, Garden Level Rm GD550, 08043. SAN 351-5346. Tel: 856-247-3207. FAX: 856-247-3222. Web Site: www.virtua.org. *Med Librn,* David Kruidenier; E-mail: dkruidenier@virtua.org; Staff 1 (MLS 1)
Founded 1976
Library Holdings: e-books 55; Bk Titles 200; Per Subs 100
Subject Interests: Hospital admin, Med, Nursing, Patient educ
Wireless access
Partic in Basic Health Sciences Library Network; LibraryLinkNJ, The New Jersey Library Cooperative; SW NJ Consortium

WALDWICK

P WALDWICK PUBLIC LIBRARY*, 19 E Prospect St, 07463-2099. SAN 310-5733. Tel: 201-652-5104. FAX: 201-652-6233. E-mail: waldcirc@bccls.org. Web Site: waldwick.bccls.org. *Dir,* Lori-Ann Quinn; E-mail: quinn@bccls.org; Staff 2 (MLS 2)
Founded 1954. Pop 9,622; Circ 120,809
Library Holdings: Bk Titles 43,000; Bk Vols 55,347; Per Subs 92
Special Collections: Italian-American. Oral History
Subject Interests: Local hist
Wireless access
Open Mon-Thurs 10-9, Fri & Sat 10-5
Friends of the Library Group

WALLINGTON

P JOHN F KENNEDY MEMORIAL LIBRARY, Wallington Public Library, 92 Hathaway St, 07057. SAN 310-5741. Tel: 973-471-1692. FAX: 973-471-1387. Circulation E-mail: wallcirc@bccls.org. Web Site: wallingtonpubliclibrary.org. *Dir,* Kathryn Ennist; *E-mail:* ennist@bccls.org; *Supv Libr Asst,* Susan Finch Kowalski; *Libr Asst,* Tonette Benz; Staff 7 (MLS 1, Non-MLS 6)
Founded 1964. Pop 11,500
Jan 2016-Dec 2016 Income $320,978
Library Holdings: Bk Titles 40,000; Per Subs 105
Special Collections: Polish Language Material
Automation Activity & Vendor Info: (Cataloging) Innovative Interfaces, Inc
Wireless access
Function: 24/7 Electronic res, 24/7 Online cat, Adult bk club, After school storytime, Audiobks on Playaways & MP3, Audiobks via web, Bk club(s), Bks on CD, Children's prog, Computer training, E-Reserves, Electronic databases & coll, Free DVD rentals, Holiday prog, Homebound delivery serv, ILL available, Internet access, Magazines, Magnifiers for reading, Mail & tel request accepted, Mail loans to mem, Movies, Museum passes, Music CDs, Notary serv, Online cat, Online info literacy tutorials on the web & in blackboard, Outreach serv, OverDrive digital audio bks, Photocopying/Printing, Prog for adults, Prog for children & young adult, Scanner, Story hour, Summer & winter reading prog, Wheelchair accessible
Partic in Bergen County Cooperative Library System, Inc; LibraryLinkNJ, The New Jersey Library Cooperative
Open Mon 10-6, Tues 10-8, Wed & Thurs 12-8, Fri 10-5, Sat (Sept-June) 10-4
Restriction: Borrowing requests are handled by ILL

WANAQUE

P WANAQUE PUBLIC LIBRARY*, 616 Ringwood Ave, 07465. SAN 310-575X. Tel: 973-839-4434. FAX: 973-839-8904. E-mail: wanaquelibrary@gmail.com. Web Site: www.wanaquelibrary.org. *Dir,* Mary Martin; E-mail: martin@wanaquelibrary.org; *Ch Serv,* Denise Carrozza; *Ch Serv,* Donna O'Hanlon; *Circ,* Lori Bailey; Staff 8 (MLS 1, Non-MLS 7)
Founded 1968. Pop 11,500; Circ 25,155
Library Holdings: Bk Vols 31,412; Per Subs 83
Automation Activity & Vendor Info: (Acquisitions) SirsiDynix; (Cataloging) SirsiDynix; (Circulation) SirsiDynix; (OPAC) SirsiDynix
Wireless access
Function: 24/7 Electronic res, 24/7 Online cat, Adult bk club, Audiobks via web, Bks on CD, Children's prog, Computers for patron use, Electronic databases & coll, Free DVD rentals, ILL available, Internet access, Magazines, Movies, Notary serv, Online cat, OverDrive digital audio bks, Scanner, Story hour, Summer reading prog, Tax forms
Partic in LibraryLinkNJ, The New Jersey Library Cooperative; PALS Plus, The Computer Consortium of Passaic County Libraries
Open Mon & Fri 9-5, Tues-Thurs 9-8, Sat (Sept-May) 10-3

WASHINGTON

J WARREN COUNTY COMMUNITY COLLEGE LIBRARY*, 475 Rte 57 W, 07882-4343. SAN 371-9170. Tel: 908-835-2336. *Dir, Libr Serv,* Lisa Stoll; E-mail: lstoll@warren.edu; Staff 1 (MLS 1)
Founded 1984. Enrl 1,440; Fac 40; Highest Degree: Associate
Library Holdings: Audiobooks 4; AV Mats 1,054; CDs 30; DVDs 850; e-books 132,000; Electronic Media & Resources 55; High Interest/Low Vocabulary Bk Vols 65; Bk Titles 13,754; Per Subs 5; Videos 850
Special Collections: World War II & Holocaust Research Center
Subject Interests: Humanities, Law, Nursing
Automation Activity & Vendor Info: (Acquisitions) LibLime Koha; (Cataloging) LibLime Koha; (Circulation) LibLime Koha; (ILL) OCLC WorldShare Interlibrary Loan; (OPAC) LibLime Koha; (Serials) LibLime Koha
Wireless access
Function: AV serv, Distance learning, Doc delivery serv, ILL available, Photocopying/Printing, Ref serv available, Telephone ref, Wheelchair accessible
Partic in Virtual Academic Library Environment
Special Services for the Deaf - Closed caption videos
Special Services for the Blind - Computer with voice synthesizer for visually impaired persons; ZoomText magnification & reading software
Open Mon-Thurs 8-8, Fri 8-3
Restriction: Open to pub for ref & circ; with some limitations, Open to students, fac & staff

P WASHINGTON PUBLIC LIBRARY*, 20 W Carlton Ave, 07882. SAN 310-5792. Tel: 908-689-0201. FAX: 908-835-0803. E-mail: library@washboropl.org. Web Site: www.washboropl.org. *Dir,* Usha Thampi-Lukose; Staff 1 (MLS 1)
Founded 1927. Pop 6,712; Circ 23,000
Library Holdings: Bks on Deafness & Sign Lang 25; CDs 801; DVDs 237; Electronic Media & Resources 7; High Interest/Low Vocabulary Bk Vols 400; Large Print Bks 750; Bk Vols 49,988; Per Subs 111; Videos 1,762
Special Collections: Star Gazette Newspaper Archive
Subject Interests: Local hist
Automation Activity & Vendor Info: (Cataloging) Follett Software; (Circulation) Follett Software; (ILL) Auto-Graphics, Inc; (OPAC) Follett Software
Wireless access
Special Services for the Blind - Assistive/Adapted tech devices, equip & products
Open Mon & Thurs 12:30-8, Tues & Wed 10-6, Sat 10-2

WASHINGTON TOWNSHIP

P TOWNSHIP OF WASHINGTON PUBLIC LIBRARY*, 144 Woodfield Rd, 07676. SAN 310-6047. Tel: 201-664-4586. FAX: 201-664-7331. Circulation E-mail: washcirc@bccls.org. Web Site: www.twpofwashingtonpl.org. *Dir,* Laura Rifkin; *Head, Circ,* Janet Baker; *Head, Youth Serv,* Marie Joyce; Staff 1 (MLS 1)
Founded 1963. Pop 9,245; Circ 77,100
Library Holdings: Bk Titles 38,770; Bk Vols 41,238; Per Subs 100
Special Collections: Careers; Large Print Bks
Subject Interests: Cooking, Japanese culture, Mysteries, Travel
Wireless access
Open Mon-Thurs 9-8, Fri 9-5, Sat 10-5
Friends of the Library Group

WAYNE

P WAYNE PUBLIC LIBRARY*, 461 Valley Rd, 07470. SAN 351-5494. Tel: 973-694-4272. Circulation Tel: 973-694-4272, Ext 5210. Interlibrary Loan Service Tel: 973-694-4272, Ext 5406. Reference Tel: 973-694-4272, Ext 5401. FAX: 973-692-0637. E-mail: wplcomments@waynepubliclibrary.org. Web Site: www.waynepubliclibrary.org. *Dir,* Ricardo Pino; Tel: 973-694-4272, Ext 5101; Staff 14 (MLS 11, Non-MLS 3)
Founded 1922. Pop 54,717; Circ 525,295
Jan 2018-Dec 2018 Income (Main & Associated Libraries) $3,380,489. Mats Exp $138,780, Books $85,000, Per/Ser (Incl. Access Fees) $12,000, Micro $13,000, AV Mat $10,000, Electronic Ref Mat (Incl. Access Fees) $18,780. Sal $1,673,503 (Prof $359,136)
Library Holdings: Bk Titles 202,239; Bk Vols 229,851; Per Subs 288
Special Collections: Business Reference; New Jersey History (Lockett Coll)
Subject Interests: Bus ref, NJ docs
Automation Activity & Vendor Info: (Cataloging) SirsiDynix; (Circulation) SirsiDynix; (ILL) SirsiDynix; (OPAC) SirsiDynix
Wireless access
Publications: Insights (Newsletter)
Partic in PALS Plus, The Computer Consortium of Passaic County Libraries
Open Mon-Thurs 9-9, Fri 9-5:30, Sat 10-5, Sun (Sept-May) 1-5
Friends of the Library Group

C WILLIAM PATERSON UNIVERSITY, David & Lorraine Cheng Library, 300 Pompton Rd, 07470. SAN 310-5865. Tel: 973-720-2541. Circulation Tel: 973-720-3180. Interlibrary Loan Service Tel: 973-720-2567. Reference Tel: 973-720-2116. FAX: 973-720-3171. E-mail: refdesk@wpunj.edu. Web Site: www.wpunj.edu/library. *Dean of Libr,* Dr Edward Owusu-Ansah; Tel: 973-720-3179, E-mail: owusuansahe@wpunj.edu; *Asst Dir, Access & Info Systems,* Nancy Weiner; Tel: 973-720-2161, E-mail: weinern@wpunj.edu; *Head, Bibliog Serv,* Deborah Pluss; Tel: 973-720-3143, E-mail: plussd@wpunj.edu; *Head, Libr Info Serv,* Ray Schwartz; Tel: 973-720-3192, E-mail: schwartzr2@wpunj.edu; *Head, Per,* Judy Matthew; Tel: 973-720-2346, E-mail: matthewj@wpunj.edu; *Head, Ref,* Bill Duffy; Tel: 973-720-3191, E-mail: duffyb@wpunj.edu; *Access Serv Librn,* Satasha Williams; Tel: 973-720-3190, E-mail: williamss167@wpunj.edu; *Cataloging & Metadata Librn,* Imani Hardaway; Tel: 973-720-2437, E-mail: hardawayi@wpunj.edu; *Educ Res Librn,* Neil Grimes; Tel: 973-720-3184, E-mail: grimesn@wpunj.edu; *Ref Librn & Co-Coordr of User Educ,* Cara Berg; Tel: 973-720-3189, E-mail: bergc1@wpunj.edu; *Ref Librn & Co-Coordr of User Educ,* Anthony Joachim; Tel: 973-720-3665;

Ref/Electronic Serv Librn, Richard Kearney; Tel: 973-720-2165, E-mail: kearneyr@wpunj.edu; *Syst Librn,* Linda Salvesen; Tel: 973-720-3127, E-mail: salvesen1@wpunj.edu; *Evening Supvr,* Maurice Vacca; Tel: 973-720-3181, E-mail: vaccam@wpunj.edu; *Cat,* Kristen Regula; Tel: 973-720-2295, E-mail: regulak@wpunj.edu; *Curriculum Materials,* Pat Moore; Tel: 973-720-2174, E-mail: moorep@wpunj.edu; *Electronic Res, Per,* Mohamed Hassan; Tel: 973-720-2117, E-mail: hassanm@wpunj.edu; *Info Serv,* Radha Ravichandran; Tel: 973-720-2769, E-mail: ravichandranr@wpunj.edu; *ILL,* Michael Cadena; Tel: 973-720-3186, E-mail: cadenam@wpunj.edu; *ILL,* Urooj Khan; E-mail: khanu@wpunj.edu; *Lending Servs,* Mark Pawlak; Tel: 973-720-2542, E-mail: pawlakm@wpunj.edu; *Lending Servs,* Jill Pruden; Tel: 973-720-3183, E-mail: prudenj@wpunj.edu; *Lending Servs,* Sherri Tucker; Tel: 973-720-3182, E-mail: tuckers@wpunj.edu; *Ref,* Marie Leah Zamora; Tel: 973-720-2663, E-mail: zamoral2@wpunj.edu; Staff 25 (MLS 14, Non-MLS 11)
Founded 1924. Enrl 10,000; Fac 400; Highest Degree: Doctorate
Jul 2020-Jun 2021 Income $3,728,625. Mats Exp $1,159,390, Books $103,390, Per/Ser (Incl. Access Fees) $656,000, Electronic Ref Mat (Incl. Access Fees) $400,000
Library Holdings: AV Mats 91,000; Bk Titles 564,000; Bk Vols 664,000
Special Collections: Governor William Paterson Coll; Guide to Falkner/Faulkner Family Coll, 1770s-1980s; Guide to the Letters from Louis Ginsberg to Donald Duclos & Related Press Clippings; Guide to the Papers of the Chaucer Guild; Guide to Theater & Movie-Related Artifacts in the New York/New Jersey Area; Inventory to the Records of the Student Government Association, 1961-2004; New Jersey Coll; Nicholas Martini Coll, 1931-1991; Robert A Roe Archive; William Paterson University of New Jersey Coll & Artifacts. State Document Depository
Subject Interests: Biology, Bus, Communications, Criminal justice, Educ, Kinesiology, Nursing, Psychol
Automation Activity & Vendor Info: (Acquisitions) Ex Libris Group; (Cataloging) Ex Libris Group; (Circulation) Ex Libris Group; (Media Booking) Ex Libris Group; (OPAC) Ex Libris Group; (Serials) Ex Libris Group
Wireless access
Publications: Archives Brochure; Bibliographic Series; Connections (Newsletter); Information Series; Instruction Bulletins
Partic in LibraryLinkNJ, The New Jersey Library Cooperative; LYRASIS; OCLC Online Computer Library Center, Inc; Virtual Academic Library Environment
Open Mon-Thurs 7:45am-11:45pm, Fri 7:45am-10pm, Sat 8-8, Sun Noon-11-45pm

WEEHAWKEN

P WEEHAWKEN FREE PUBLIC LIBRARY*, Multimedia Center, 49 Hauxhurst Ave, Ste 1, 07086. SAN 310-5873. Tel: 201-863-7823. FAX: 201-863-7958. Circulation E-mail: weehcirc@bccls.org. Web Site: weehawken-nj.us/library.html. *Dir,* Holly Pizzuta; E-mail: director@weehawken.bccls.org
Founded 1942. Pop 12,715; Circ 22,116
Library Holdings: Bk Vols 22,179; Per Subs 37
Partic in Bergen County Cooperative Library System, Inc
Open Mon & Wed 9-9, Tues, Thurs & Fri 9-6, Sat (Sept-June) 9-5

WENONAH

P WENONAH FREE PUBLIC LIBRARY*, 101 E Mantua Ave, 08090. SAN 310-5881. Tel: 856-468-6323. E-mail: wenonahlibrary@hotmail.com. Web Site: www.wenonahlibrary.com. *Dir,* Anne Zuber
Founded 1900. Pop 2,278; Circ 18,000
Library Holdings: Bk Vols 15,777; Per Subs 15
Automation Activity & Vendor Info: (Acquisitions) SirsiDynix; (Cataloging) SirsiDynix; (Circulation) SirsiDynix; (Course Reserve) SirsiDynix; (ILL) SirsiDynix; (Media Booking) SirsiDynix; (OPAC) SirsiDynix; (Serials) SirsiDynix
Wireless access
Partic in Libraries of Gloucester, Salem & Cumberland Information Network; LibraryLinkNJ, The New Jersey Library Cooperative
Open Mon, Tues & Thurs 3-9, Wed 9-9, Fri 1-5, Sat 10-2

WEST BERLIN

P BERLIN TOWNSHIP LIBRARY, John J McPeak Library, 201 Veterans Ave, 08091. SAN 310-589X. Tel: 856-767-0439. FAX: 856-753-6729. E-mail: library@berlintwp.com. Web Site: www.berlintwp.com/john-j-mcpeak-library. *Librn,* Dana Landolt
Founded 1965. Pop 7,500; Circ 10,092
Library Holdings: Bk Vols 10,500; Talking Bks 60
Mem of Camden County Library System
Open Mon & Wed 1-8:15, Tues & Thurs 9-10:45 & 1-8:15, Sat 10-1:45

WEST CALDWELL

P WEST CALDWELL PUBLIC LIBRARY*, 30 Clinton Rd, 07006. SAN 310-5903. Tel: 973-226-5441. FAX: 973-228-7572. Reference E-mail: mccoy@westcaldwell.bccls.org. Web Site: wcplnj.org. *Dir,* Samantha McCoy; E-mail: mccoy@westcaldwell.bccls.org; Staff 24 (MLS 8, Non-MLS 16)
Founded 1915
Wireless access
Function: 24/7 Electronic res, 24/7 Online cat, 3D Printer, Adult bk club, Adult literacy prog, After school storytime, Art exhibits, Audiobks via web, Bk club(s), Children's prog, Citizenship assistance, Computer training, Computers for patron use, E-Reserves, Electronic databases & coll, For res purposes, Free DVD rentals, Holiday prog, Home delivery & serv to seniorr ctr & nursing homes, Homebound delivery serv, ILL available, Internet access, Laminating, Life-long learning prog for all ages, Literacy & newcomer serv, Magazines, Magnifiers for reading, Mail & tel request accepted, Mango lang, Meeting rooms, Microfiche/film & reading machines, Movies, Museum passes, Music CDs, Online cat, Outreach serv, Photocopying/Printing, Preschool outreach, Printer for laptops & handheld devices, Prog for adults, Prog for children & young adult, Ref serv available, Scanner, Story hour, Study rm, Summer & winter reading prog, Summer reading prog, Tax forms, Teen prog, Winter reading prog, Workshops, Writing prog
Partic in Bergen County Cooperative Library System, Inc; ReBL
Open Mon-Thurs 9-8, Fri 9-6, Sat 9-5
Friends of the Library Group

WEST DEPTFORD

P WEST DEPTFORD FREE PUBLIC LIBRARY*, 420 Crown Point Rd, 08086. SAN 310-5326. Tel: 856-845-5593. FAX: 856-848-3689. Administration E-mail: admin@westdeptford.lib.nj.us. Web Site: www.westdeptford.lib.nj.us. *Dir,* Carolyn Wood; E-mail: cwood@westdeptford.lib.nj.us; Staff 16 (MLS 4, Non-MLS 12)
Founded 1965. Pop 19,964; Circ 121,704
Library Holdings: Audiobooks 824; CDs 1,569; DVDs 3,932; Electronic Media & Resources 9; Bk Titles 79,261; Bk Vols 86,639; Per Subs 227
Special Collections: South Jersey Environmental Information Center Coll; United Nations Environment Programme Coll
Subject Interests: Environ, Health, Nutrition
Automation Activity & Vendor Info: (Circulation) SirsiDynix
Wireless access
Function: Bks on CD, Children's prog, Computer training, Computers for patron use, Electronic databases & coll, ILL available, Music CDs, Notary serv, Online cat, OverDrive digital audio bks, Photocopying/Printing, Preschool outreach, Prog for adults, Prog for children & young adult, Senior computer classes, Spoken cassettes & CDs, Spoken cassettes & DVDs, Story hour, Summer reading prog, Tax forms, Teen prog, Telephone ref, Wheelchair accessible
Publications: Check It Out (Newsletter)
Partic in Libraries of Gloucester, Salem & Cumberland Information Network; LibraryLinkNJ, The New Jersey Library Cooperative
Special Services for the Deaf - Sign lang interpreter upon request for prog
Special Services for the Blind - Accessible computers; Bks on cassette; Bks on CD; Large print bks; Magnifiers
Open Mon-Thurs (Oct-May) 10-9, Fri 10-5, Sat 10-3, Sun 1-5; Mon-Thurs 10-9, Fri 10-5, Sat 10-1
Friends of the Library Group

WEST LONG BRANCH

C MONMOUTH UNIVERSITY LIBRARY*, Guggenheim Memorial Library, 400 Cedar Ave, 07764. SAN 310-592X. Tel: 732-571-3450. Reference Tel: 732-571-3438. FAX: 732-263-5124. Reference E-mail: referenc@monmouth.edu. Web Site: library.monmouth.edu. *Univ Librn,* Kurt Wagner; Tel: 732-571-4401, E-mail: kwagner@monmouth.edu; *Head, Circ,* Allison Shields; Tel: 732-571-4413; *Head, Tech Serv,* Aurora S Ioanid; Tel: 732-571-5364; *Instr Librn,* Lisa Iannucci; Tel: 732-571-7560, E-mail: liannucc@monmouth.edu; *Ref & Instruction Librn,* Mary Beth Meszaros; Tel: 732-571-4404, E-mail: mmeszaro@monmouth.edu; *Ref Librn,* Eleonora Dubicki; Tel: 732-571-4402, E-mail: edubicki@monmouth.edu; *Syst Librn,* Sara Margaret Rizzo; Tel: 972-571-4537, E-mail: srizzo@monmouth.edu; *Govt Doc,* Susan Bucks; Tel: 732-263-5591; *Ref Serv,* George Germek; Tel: 732-571-4403. Subject Specialists: *Art, Design, Music,* Aurora S Ioanid; *Counseling, Curric, Hist of anthrop, Interdisciplinary studies, Philos, Spec educ, Theatre arts,* Mary Beth Meszaros; *Counseling, Health, Nursing, Phys educ, Psychol, Speech pathology,* Eleonora Dubicki; *Biology, Chemistry, Computer sci, Math, Physics, Software engr,* Sara Margaret Rizzo; *Communication, Polit sci, Sociol,* Susan Bucks; *Cultures, English, World lang,* George Germek; Staff 10 (MLS 10)
Founded 1933. Enrl 6,000; Fac 188; Highest Degree: Master
Library Holdings: Bk Titles 23,500; Bk Vols 26,000; Per Subs 2,200
Special Collections: Lewis Mumford Coll; New Jersey History Coll. State Document Depository; US Document Depository

Automation Activity & Vendor Info: (Acquisitions) Innovative Interfaces, Inc; (Cataloging) Innovative Interfaces, Inc; (Circulation) Innovative Interfaces, Inc; (OPAC) Innovative Interfaces, Inc; (Serials) Innovative Interfaces, Inc
Wireless access
Partic in LibraryLinkNJ, The New Jersey Library Cooperative; LYRASIS; NJ Union List of Serials; OCLC Online Computer Library Center, Inc; Virtual Academic Library Environment
Open Mon-Thurs 8am-Midnight, Fri 8-7, Sat 10-6, Sun 11am-Midnight
Friends of the Library Group

S PREVENTION FIRST, A DIVISION OF PREFERRED BEHAVIORAL HEALTH GROUP, Prevention & Education Program Resource Center, (Formerly Prevention First), Bldg B, Ste B20, 185 Hwy 36, 07764. SAN 377-533X. Tel: 732-663-1800, Ext 2180. FAX: 732-663-1698. Web Site: www.pcofmc.org, www.preferredbehavioral.org/prevention-first. *Prog Dir,* Liza DeJesus; E-mail: ldejesus@preventionfirst.net
Library Holdings: Bk Titles 450
Wireless access
Partic in LibraryLinkNJ, The New Jersey Library Cooperative
Restriction: Open by appt only

WEST MILFORD

P WEST MILFORD TOWNSHIP LIBRARY*, 1470 Union Valley Rd, 07480. SAN 310-5946. Tel: 973-728-2820. Administration Tel: 973-728-2824. FAX: 973-728-2106. E-mail: wmtl@wmtl.org. Web Site: www.wmtl.org. Staff 5.3 (MLS 5.3)
Founded 1954. Pop 25,850; Circ 143,280
Library Holdings: Audiobooks 3,600; CDs 181; DVDs 4,929; e-books 3,591; Bk Vols 53,298; Per Subs 53
Automation Activity & Vendor Info: (Cataloging) SirsiDynix-WorkFlows; (Circulation) SirsiDynix-WorkFlows; (ILL) JerseyCat; (OPAC) SirsiDynix-iBistro
Wireless access
Function: 24/7 Electronic res, 24/7 Online cat, Activity rm, Adult bk club, Art exhibits, Audiobks on Playaways & MP3, Audiobks via web, Bk club(s), Bks on CD, Children's prog, Computers for patron use, Electronic databases & coll, Free DVD rentals, Health sci info serv, Holiday prog, ILL available, Internet access, Magazines, Meeting rooms, Movies, Online cat, Photocopying/Printing, Printer for laptops & handheld devices, Prog for adults, Prog for children & young adult, Ref & res, Ref serv available, Res assist avail, Scanner, Spoken cassettes & CDs, Story hour, Study rm, Summer reading prog, Tax forms, Teen prog, Telephone ref, Wheelchair accessible
Partic in PALS Plus, The Computer Consortium of Passaic County Libraries
Open Mon-Thurs 10-8, Fri 10-6, Sat 9-5, Sun 12-4
Friends of the Library Group

WEST NEW YORK

P WEST NEW YORK PUBLIC LIBRARY*, 425 60th St, 07093-2211. SAN 310-5954. Tel: 201-295-5135. Reference Tel: 201-295-5137. FAX: 201-662-1473. E-mail: wnypubliclibrary@gmail.com. Web Site: www.wnypl.org. *Dir,* Weiliang Lai; *Ref,* Estela Longo-Salvador; E-mail: wnyreference@gmail.com; Staff 3 (MLS 3)
Founded 1916. Pop 49,708
Library Holdings: AV Mats 1,650; CDs 310; DVDs 400; Large Print Bks 300; Bk Titles 61,000; Bk Vols 62,200; Per Subs 120; Talking Bks 190
Subject Interests: Family literacy, Jerseyana, Local hist, Parenting, Spanish
Automation Activity & Vendor Info: (Acquisitions) Innovative Interfaces, Inc; (Cataloging) Innovative Interfaces, Inc; (Circulation) Innovative Interfaces, Inc; (OPAC) Innovative Interfaces, Inc; (Serials) Innovative Interfaces, Inc
Wireless access
Partic in LibraryLinkNJ, The New Jersey Library Cooperative
Open Mon, Tues & Thurs 9-8, Wed, Fri & Sat 9-5
Friends of the Library Group

WEST ORANGE

M KESSLER FOUNDATION MEDICAL LIBRARY*, 1199 Pleasant Valley Way, 07052-1499. SAN 375-7358. Tel: 973-324-3523. FAX: 973-243-6835. Web Site: kesslerfoundation.org. *Med Librn,* Marita F Delmonico; E-mail: mdelmonico@kesslerfoundation.org; Staff 2 (MLS 1, Non-MLS 1)
Founded 1948
Library Holdings: Bk Titles 1,300; Per Subs 68
Automation Activity & Vendor Info: (Acquisitions) LibraryWorld, Inc; (Cataloging) LibraryWorld, Inc; (Circulation) LibraryWorld, Inc; (OPAC) LibraryWorld, Inc; (Serials) LibraryWorld, Inc
Function: For res purposes
Partic in Basic Health Sciences Library Network
Open Mon, Wed & Thurs 8-4
Restriction: Internal circ only

L LAW LIBRARY OF CHIESA, SHAHINIAN & GIANTOMASI*, One Boland Dr, 07052. SAN 372-414X. Tel: 973-530-2146. FAX: 973-530-2346. Web Site: www.csglaw.com. *Librn,* Rosemary Walton; E-mail: rwalton@csglaw.com
Library Holdings: Bk Vols 12,000
Wireless access
Partic in LibraryLinkNJ, The New Jersey Library Cooperative
Open Mon-Fri 9-4:30

P WEST ORANGE PUBLIC LIBRARY*, 46 Mount Pleasant Ave, 07052. SAN 351-5583. Tel: 973-736-0198. E-mail: admin@westorangelibrary.org. Web Site: www.wopl.org. *Dir,* David Cubie; E-mail: dcubie@westorangelibrary.org; *Head, Circ Serv,* Debra Sarr; E-mail: circ@westorangelibrary.org; *Head, Ref Serv,* Mary-Jean Gurzenda; E-mail: ref@westorangelibrary.org; *Head, Youth Serv,* Faith Boyle; E-mail: youth@westorangelibrary.org; Staff 7 (MLS 7)
Founded 1948. Pop 46,207; Circ 364,000
Jan 2013-Dec 2013 Income $2,334,671
Library Holdings: Audiobooks 12,918; CDs 1,993; DVDs 6,741; e-books 4,563; Large Print Bks 692; Bk Vols 143,000; Per Subs 192
Automation Activity & Vendor Info: (Acquisitions) Innovative Interfaces, Inc; (Cataloging) Innovative Interfaces, Inc; (Circulation) Innovative Interfaces, Inc; (ILL) Auto-Graphics, Inc; (OPAC) Innovative Interfaces, Inc; (Serials) Innovative Interfaces, Inc
Wireless access
Function: Adult bk club, After school storytime, Audiobks via web, Bk club(s), Bks on CD, Children's prog, Computer training, Computers for patron use, E-Reserves, Electronic databases & coll, Free DVD rentals, Homebound delivery serv, ILL available, Magnifiers for reading, Microfiche/film & reading machines, Music CDs, Online cat, Online ref, OverDrive digital audio bks, Photocopying/Printing, Preschool reading prog, Prog for adults, Prog for children & young adult, Ref serv available, Spoken cassettes & CDs, Story hour, Summer reading prog, Tax forms, Teen prog, Telephone ref
Partic in LibraryLinkNJ, The New Jersey Library Cooperative
Open Mon, Wed & Thurs 10-9, Tues & Fri 10-5:30, Sat 9-5, Sun (Winter) 1-5

WEST TRENTON

M ANN KLEIN FORENSIC CENTER*, Thomas A Hall Sr Library, Stuyvesant Ave, 08628. (Mail add: PO Box 7717, 08628-0717). Tel: 609-633-0884. *Library Contact,* Mr Q Washington; Staff 4 (MLS 1, Non-MLS 3)
Library Holdings: DVDs 50; Bk Titles 2,190; Bk Vols 2,245; Per Subs 31; Videos 200
Function: Serves people with intellectual disabilities
Partic in LibraryLinkNJ, The New Jersey Library Cooperative
Open Mon-Fri 9-3:15

WEST WINDSOR

J MERCER COUNTY COMMUNITY COLLEGE LIBRARY*, West Windsor Campus, 1200 Old Trenton Rd, 08550. SAN 351-4471. Tel: 609-570-3554, 609-570-3560. Circulation Tel: 609-570-3561. Interlibrary Loan Service Tel: 609-570-3550. FAX: 609-570-3845. E-mail: library@mccc.edu. Web Site: www.mccc.edu/student_library.shtml. *Dir, Libr Serv,* Pamela A Price; Tel: 609-570-3562, E-mail: pricep@mccc.edu; *Acq Librn,* Olivia Nellums; Tel: 609-570-3559, E-mail: nellumso@mccc.edu; *Electronic Res Librn,* Daniel Calandro; E-mail: calandrd@mccc.edu; *Ref Librn,* Martin Crabtree; Tel: 609-570-3545, E-mail: crabtrem@mccc.edu; *Libr Assoc/Circ,* Lavanya Srinath; Tel: 609-570-3558, E-mail: srinathl@mccc.edu; *Libr Tech,* Denise Niclas; Tel: 609-570-3179, E-mail: niclasd@mccc.edu; Staff 9 (MLS 6, Non-MLS 3)
Founded 1947. Enrl 6,500; Fac 145; Highest Degree: Associate
Library Holdings: CDs 153; DVDs 269; e-books 73,000; e-journals 25,000; Microforms 789; Bk Titles 54,559; Bk Vols 69,063; Per Subs 39; Videos 1,134
Special Collections: Mortuary Science Coll, disks & v-tapes
Subject Interests: Gen acad libr res
Automation Activity & Vendor Info: (Acquisitions) SirsiDynix; (Cataloging) SirsiDynix; (Circulation) SirsiDynix; (Course Reserve) SirsiDynix; (ILL) SirsiDynix; (Media Booking) SirsiDynix; (OPAC) SirsiDynix; (Serials) SirsiDynix
Wireless access
Publications: Library Annual Report
Partic in LibraryLinkNJ, The New Jersey Library Cooperative; LYRASIS; Virtual Academic Library Environment
Special Services for the Deaf - Assisted listening device; Assistive tech; Closed caption videos

Special Services for the Blind - Assistive/Adapted tech devices, equip & products
Open Mon-Thurs 8am-9pm, Fri 8-5, Sat 10-4
Departmental Libraries:
JAMES KERNEY CAMPUS, 102 N Broad St, Trenton, 08690, SAN 351-4501. Tel: 609-570-3179. FAX: 609-394-8167. *Libr Tech,* Denise Niclas; E-mail: niclasd@mccc.edu; Staff 1 (Non-MLS 1)
Founded 1975. Enrl 2,000; Fac 22; Highest Degree: Associate
Library Holdings: Bk Titles 5,800; Per Subs 63
Special Collections: African Art Books; Literacy
Subject Interests: Gen acad, High sch level res
Open Mon-Thurs 9-8, Fri 9-5, Sat 9-12
Restriction: Open to students, fac & staff, Pub use on premises

WESTAMPTON

P BURLINGTON COUNTY LIBRARY*, Five Pioneer Blvd, 08060. SAN 350-9281. Tel: 609-267-9660. Circulation Tel: 609-267-6703. FAX: 609-267-4091. TDD: 609-267-2978. Web Site: www.bcls.lib.nj.us. *Dir,* Ranjna Das; *Asst Dir,* Heather Andolsen; E-mail: handolse@bcls.lib.nj.us; Staff 150 (MLS 45, Non-MLS 105)
Founded 1921. Pop 352,917; Circ 2,184,598
Library Holdings: AV Mats 96,381; e-books 5,012; Large Print Bks 21,756; Bk Vols 756,007; Per Subs 863; Videos 64,849
Special Collections: Local Newspapers from 1835, bd & microfilm. State Document Depository
Subject Interests: Genealogy, Local hist
Automation Activity & Vendor Info: (Acquisitions) Horizon; (Cataloging) Horizon; (Circulation) Horizon; (ILL) OCLC; (OPAC) Horizon; (Serials) Horizon
Wireless access
Function: Adult bk club, Adult literacy prog, Art exhibits, Audiobks via web, AV serv, Bk club(s), Bks on cassette, Bks on CD, CD-ROM, Chess club, Children's prog, Citizenship assistance, Computer training, Computers for patron use, Digital talking bks, Doc delivery serv, E-Reserves, Electronic databases & coll, Family literacy, Free DVD rentals, Games & aids for people with disabilities, Genealogy discussion group, Govt ref serv, Holiday prog, Home delivery & serv to seniorr ctr & nursing homes, Homebound delivery serv, Homework prog, ILL available, Internet access, Literacy & newcomer serv, Magnifiers for reading, Mail & tel request accepted, Mail loans to mem, Museum passes, Music CDs, Notary serv, Online cat, Online ref, Outreach serv, Outside serv via phone, mail, e-mail & web, OverDrive digital audio bks, Passport agency, Photocopying/Printing, Preschool outreach, Prog for adults, Prog for children & young adult, Ref & res, Ref serv available, Res libr, Res performed for a fee, Scanner, Senior computer classes, Senior outreach, Spoken cassettes & CDs, Spoken cassettes & DVDs, Story hour, Summer reading prog, Tax forms, Teen prog, Telephone ref, VHS videos, Wheelchair accessible, Workshops
Member Libraries: Beverly Free Library; Burlington County Lyceum of History & Natural Sciences Library; Delanco Public Library; Florence Township Public Library; Library Company of Burlington; Sally Stretch Keen Memorial Library; The Crosswicks Library Co
Partic in LYRASIS
Special Services for the Deaf - Assisted listening device; Assistive tech; Bks on deafness & sign lang; Closed caption videos; TTY equip
Special Services for the Blind - Assistive/Adapted tech devices, equip & products; Audio mat; Bks on cassette; Bks on CD; Cassettes; Copier with enlargement capabilities; Descriptive video serv (DVS); Extensive large print coll; Home delivery serv; Large print & cassettes; Large print bks; Low vision equip; Magnifiers; Playaways (bks on MP3); Sound rec
Open Mon-Fri 9-9, Sat 9-5, Sun 1-5
Friends of the Library Group
Branches: 7
BORDENTOWN LIBRARY, 18 E Union St, Bordentown, 08505, SAN 350-9311. Tel: 609-298-0622. E-mail: bt@bcls.lib.nj.us. Web Site: www.bcls.lib.nj.us/bordentown. *Br Mgr,* Caitlin Hawe-Ndrio; Staff 14 (MLS 4, Non-MLS 10)
Library Holdings: Large Print Bks 756; Bk Vols 44,000; Per Subs 95
Special Collections: Bordentown Military Institute Yearbooks; Bordentown Regional High School Yearbooks; Bordentown Register (May 25, 1855+ on microfilm); New Jersey-Bordentown Coll
Open Mon-Thurs 10-8:30, Fri 10-5, Sat (Winter) 10-5
Friends of the Library Group
CINNAMINSON LIBRARY, 1619 Riverton Rd, Cinnaminson, 08077, SAN 350-9346. Tel: 856-829-9340. FAX: 856-829-2243. E-mail: cb@bcls.lib.nj.us. Web Site: www.bcls.lib.nj.us/cinnaminson. *Br Mgr,* Position Currently Open
Library Holdings: Bk Vols 82,537
Open Mon-Thurs 10-8:30, Fri 10-5, Sat (Winter) 10-5
Friends of the Library Group
EVESHAM LIBRARY, Evesham Municipal Complex, 984 Tuckerton Rd, Marlton, 08053, SAN 350-9370. Tel: 856-983-1444. FAX: 856-983-4939. E-mail: ev@bcls.lib.nj.us. Web Site: www.bcls.lib.nj.us/evesham. *Br Mgr,* Susan Szymanik; Staff 19 (MLS 5, Non-MLS 14)
Library Holdings: Bk Vols 100,000
Open Mon-Thurs 10-8:30, Fri & Sat 10-5, Sun (Winter) 1-5
Friends of the Library Group
MAPLE SHADE LIBRARY, 200 Stiles Ave, Maple Shade, 08052. Tel: 856-779-9767. FAX: 856-779-0033. E-mail: ma@bcls.lib.nj.us. Web Site: www.bcls.lib.nj.us/mapleshade. *Br Mgr,* Jaimie Donnelly; Staff 12 (MLS 2, Non-MLS 10)
Pop 20,000
Library Holdings: Audiobooks 1,000; DVDs 3,000; Bk Vols 53,000; Per Subs 85
Open Mon-Fri (Sept-June) 10-8:30, Sat 10-2; Mon-Thurs (July-Aug) 10-8:30, Fri 10-5, Sat 10-2
Friends of the Library Group
PINELANDS LIBRARY, 39 Allen Ave, Medford, 08055, SAN 350-9400. Tel: 609-654-6113. FAX: 609-953-2142. E-mail: mf@bcls.lib.nj.us. Web Site: www.bcls.lib.nj.us/pinelands. *Br Mgr,* Danielle Haubrich; Staff 8 (MLS 4, Non-MLS 4)
Library Holdings: Bk Vols 72,000; Per Subs 75
Special Collections: NJ Coll; Pinelands Coastal Coll
Open Mon-Thurs 10-8:30, Fri & Sat 10-5
Friends of the Library Group
RIVERTON FREE LIBRARY, 306 Main St, Riverton, 08077, SAN 310-4826. Tel: 856-829-2476. Web Site: www.bcls.lib.nj.us/riverton, www.rivertonlibrary.burlco.org. *Br Mgr,* Nancy Fort
Founded 1899. Circ 48,079
Library Holdings: AV Mats 1,500; Bk Vols 24,000; Per Subs 40
Open Mon-Thurs 10-8:30, Fri 10-2, Sat 10-5, Sun 1-5; Mon-Thurs (Winter) 10-8:30, Fri 10-2
Friends of the Library Group
PEMBERTON LIBRARY, 16 Broadway, Browns Mills, 08015, SAN 328-9281. Tel: 609-893-8262. FAX: 609-893-7547. E-mail: p@bcls.lib.nj.us. Web Site: www.bcls.lib.nj.us/pemberton. *Br Mgr,* Laurie Bowden; Staff 15 (MLS 4, Non-MLS 11)
Founded 1906. Pop 32,000; Circ 141,000
Library Holdings: Bk Vols 61,000
Special Collections: Foreign Language Coll; Literacy Coll
Function: Adult bk club, Art exhibits, Audiobks via web, Bks on cassette, Bks on CD, CD-ROM, Children's prog, Computer training, Computers for patron use, E-Reserves, Electronic databases & coll, Free DVD rentals, Holiday prog, Homebound delivery serv, ILL available, Internet access, Magnifiers for reading, Mail & tel request accepted, Music CDs, Notary serv, Online cat, Online ref, Outreach serv, OverDrive digital audio bks, Photocopying/Printing, Preschool outreach, Prog for adults, Prog for children & young adult, Ref serv available, Scanner, Spoken cassettes & CDs, Spoken cassettes & DVDs, Story hour, Summer reading prog, Tax forms, Telephone ref, VHS videos, Wheelchair accessible
Special Services for the Deaf - Adult & family literacy prog; Closed caption videos
Special Services for the Blind - Audio mat; Bks available with recordings; Bks on cassette; Bks on CD; Large print bks; Large type calculator; Low vision equip; Magnifiers; Playaways (bks on MP3)
Open Mon-Thurs (Winter) 10-8:30, Fri & Sat 10-5, Sun 1-5; Mon-Thurs (Summer) 10-8:30, Fri 10-5
Friends of the Library Group
Bookmobiles: 1. Bkmobile Coordr, Nancy Breece. Bk titles 5,189

WESTFIELD

P WESTFIELD MEMORIAL LIBRARY*, 550 E Broad St, 07090. SAN 310-6012. Tel: 908-789-4090. FAX: 908-789-0921. Web Site: www.wmlnj.org. *Dir,* Allen McGinley; E-mail: amcginley@wmlnj.org; *Asst Dir,* Kathy Muhm; Staff 19 (MLS 7, Non-MLS 12)
Founded 1872. Pop 30,291; Circ 350,000
Library Holdings: Bk Titles 159,318; Bk Vols 195,509; Per Subs 202
Special Collections: Oral History
Subject Interests: Local hist
Automation Activity & Vendor Info: (Circulation) SirsiDynix; (OPAC) SirsiDynix
Wireless access
Publications: Take Note (Newsletter)
Partic in LibraryLinkNJ, The New Jersey Library Cooperative
Open Mon-Thurs 9:30-9, Fri & Sat 9:30-5, Sun 1-5
Friends of the Library Group

WESTVILLE

P WESTVILLE PUBLIC LIBRARY*, 1035 Broadway, 08093. SAN 310-6020. Tel: 856-456-0357. FAX: 856-742-8190. E-mail: info@westvillelibrary.com. Web Site: www.westvillelibrary.com. *Dir,* Gwen Carotenuto; *Librn,* Mary Ward
Founded 1924. Pop 4,500
Library Holdings: Bk Titles 22,000; Per Subs 54
Automation Activity & Vendor Info: (Cataloging) SirsiDynix; (Circulation) SirsiDynix

Wireless access
Partic in Libraries of Gloucester, Salem & Cumberland Information Network
Open Tues & Thurs 11-8, Wed 12-5

WESTWOOD

P WESTWOOD PUBLIC LIBRARY*, 49 Park Ave, 07675. SAN 310-6055. Tel: 201-664-0583. FAX: 201-664-6088. E-mail: library@westwood.bccls.org. Web Site: www.westwoodpubliclibrary.org. *Dir,* Martha Urbiel; E-mail: urbiel@westwood.bccls.org; *Head, Circ,* Kathy Carvalho; *Ch,* Kat Vander Wende; *Ref Librn,* Janet Dunn; Staff 13 (MLS 3, Non-MLS 10)
Founded 1919. Pop 10,999; Circ 127,000
Library Holdings: Bk Titles 51,000; Bk Vols 53,086; Per Subs 90
Special Collections: Literacy Program Coll
Automation Activity & Vendor Info: (Acquisitions) SirsiDynix; (Cataloging) SirsiDynix; (Circulation) SirsiDynix; (ILL) SirsiDynix
Wireless access
Open Mon, Tues & Thurs 10-9, Wed & Fri 10-5, Sun 1-5
Friends of the Library Group

WHARTON

P WHARTON PUBLIC LIBRARY*, 15 S Main St, 07885. SAN 310-6063. Tel: 973-361-1333. E-mail: info@whartonlibrary.org. Web Site: www.whartonlibrary.org. *Dir,* Eileen Burnash; Staff 5 (MLS 1, Non-MLS 4)
Founded 1891. Pop 6,298; Circ 38,856
Library Holdings: Audiobooks 180; CDs 115; DVDs 480; Large Print Bks 88; Bk Vols 24,000; Per Subs 59; Talking Bks 354; Videos 100
Special Collections: Municipal Document Depository; Oral History
Wireless access
Partic in LibraryLinkNJ, The New Jersey Library Cooperative; Morris Automated Information Network
Open Mon-Thurs 10-8, Fri 10-5, Sat (Sept-May) 9-1
Friends of the Library Group

WHIPPANY

S JEWISH HISTORICAL SOCIETY OF NEW JERSEY*, 901 Rte 10 E, 07981. SAN 375-3123. Tel: 973-929-2994, 973-929-2995. FAX: 973-428-8327. Web Site: www.jhs-nj.org. *Archivist,* Jill Hershorin; E-mail: jhershorin@jhs-nj.org
Founded 1990
Library Holdings: AV Mats 100; Bk Titles 120
Special Collections: Late 19th Century to Present. Oral History
Subject Interests: Ethnic hist, Judaica
Wireless access
Function: Res libr
Publications: Newsletter; Technical Leaflets
Open Mon-Thurs 9-5, Fri 9-4
Restriction: Access at librarian's discretion

P MORRIS COUNTY LIBRARY, 30 E Hanover Ave, 07981. SAN 310-6098. Tel: 973-285-6930. Reference Tel: 973-285-6969. Administration Tel: 973-285-6934. Information Services Tel: 973-285-6970. Web Site: www.mclib.info. *Dir,* Darren O'Neill; E-mail: doneill@co.morris.nj.us; *Chief Librn, Head, Children's Servx, Head, Reader Serv,* Mary Sanders; E-mail: MSanders@co.morris.nj.us; *Head, ILL, Head, Ref Serv,* Laurence Ross; E-mail: lross@co.morris.nj.us; *Head, Tech Serv,* Vidya Manohar; Tel: 973-285-6955, E-mail: VManohar@co.morris.nj.us; Staff 64 (MLS 24, Non-MLS 40)
Founded 1922. Pop 492,276; Circ 519,796
Library Holdings: Audiobooks 6,000; AV Mats 39,726; Bks on Deafness & Sign Lang 307; CDs 21,598; DVDs 15,681; e-books 9,000; Large Print Bks 7,210; Microforms 300; Music Scores 2,494; Bk Vols 252,070; Per Subs 860
Special Collections: Local Newspaper 1900-Present; Morris Authors; New Adult Readers; New Jersey History; Sheet Music. State Document Depository
Subject Interests: Bus, Law, Local hist, Music
Automation Activity & Vendor Info: (Acquisitions) Innovative Interfaces, Inc; (Cataloging) Innovative Interfaces, Inc; (Circulation) Innovative Interfaces, Inc; (ILL) OCLC; (OPAC) Innovative Interfaces, Inc; (Serials) EBSCO Online
Wireless access
Function: Art exhibits, Audiobks via web, Children's prog, Computer training, Computers for patron use, Digital talking bks, Distance learning, Electronic databases & coll, Home delivery & serv to seniorr ctr & nursing homes, ILL available, Magnifiers for reading, Microfiche/film & reading machines, Museum passes, Notary serv, Online cat, Online ref, Photocopying/Printing, Preschool reading prog, Ref & res, Scanner, Summer reading prog, Tax forms
Partic in LibraryLinkNJ, The New Jersey Library Cooperative; Morris Automated Information Network; OCLC Online Computer Library Center, Inc
Special Services for the Deaf - Assisted listening device; Bks on deafness & sign lang; Captioned film dep; Closed caption videos; Coll on deaf educ; Deaf publ; High interest/low vocabulary bks; Pocket talkers; TDD equip; TTY equip
Special Services for the Blind - Accessible computers; Bks available with recordings; Bks on cassette; Bks on CD; Large print bks; Magnifiers; PC for people with disabilities; Talking bks; ZoomText magnification & reading software
Open Mon-Thurs 9-9, Fri & Sat 9-5, Sun (Sept-April) 1-5
Restriction: Non-circulating of rare bks

P WHIPPANONG LIBRARY*, 1000 Rte 10, 07981. SAN 310-6101. Tel: 973-428-2460. FAX: 973-515-3771. E-mail: general@whippanong.org. Web Site: www.whippanong.org. *Dir,* Rochelle Levin; Staff 9 (MLS 2, Non-MLS 7)
Founded 1957. Pop 12,898; Circ 72,508
Library Holdings: Audiobooks 2,527; CDs 508; DVDs 2,216; e-books 770; Bk Titles 36,821; Bk Vols 42,813; Per Subs 80
Automation Activity & Vendor Info: (Cataloging) Innovative Interfaces, Inc; (Circulation) Innovative Interfaces, Inc; (ILL) Innovative Interfaces, Inc; (OPAC) Innovative Interfaces, Inc; (Serials) Innovative Interfaces, Inc
Wireless access
Partic in Morris Info Network
Open Mon, Tues & Thurs 9-8, Wed 9-5, Fri 9-2, Sat 9-1
Friends of the Library Group

WHITEHOUSE STATION

P READINGTON TOWNSHIP LIBRARY*, 105 Rte 523, 08889. (Mail add: PO Box 87, 08889-0087). Tel: 908-534-4421. FAX: 908-534-5909. E-mail: rtlibrary@hotmail.com. Web Site: www.readingtontwp.org/library_main.html. *Librn,* Karen Konn
Library Holdings: AV Mats 1,000; Large Print Bks 125; Bk Vols 18,000; Per Subs 46; Talking Bks 150
Subject Interests: Local hist
Automation Activity & Vendor Info: (Cataloging) Innovative Interfaces, Inc; (Circulation) Innovative Interfaces, Inc; (OPAC) Innovative Interfaces, Inc
Wireless access
Mem of Hunterdon County Library
Open Mon, Wed & Fri 9-5, Tues & Thurs 12-8, Sat (Sept-July) 9-2
Friends of the Library Group

WILLIAMSTOWN

P FREE PUBLIC LIBRARY OF MONROE TOWNSHIP*, Monroe Library, 713 Marsha Ave, 08094. SAN 310-6128. Tel: 856-629-1212. Circulation Tel: 856-629-1212, Ext 210. Reference Tel: 856-629-1212, Ext 206. Administration Tel: 856-629-1212, Ext 203. FAX: 856-875-0191. Administration FAX: 856-629-5967. E-mail: info@MonroeTPL.org. Web Site: www.MonroeTPL.Org. *Libr Dir,* Samantha Snyder; Tel: 856-629-1212,Ext 200, E-mail: ssnyder@monroetpl.org; *Ad, Ref Librn,* Martha Oxley; Tel: 856-629-121, Ext 202, E-mail: MOxley@MonroeTPL.Org; *Ad,* Jennifer E Schillig; Tel: 856-629-1212, Ext 204, E-mail: JSchillig@monroetpl.org; *Ad,* Olympia Sosangelis; Tel: 856-629-1212, Ext 208, E-mail: osoangelis@monroetpl.org; *Cat Librn, Ch,* Katrina Hauserman; Tel: 856-629-1212, Ext 201, E-mail: khauserman@monroetpl.org; *Teen & Adult Librn,* Christopher DiFazio; Tel: 856-629-1212, Ext 209, E-mail: cdifazio@monroetpl.org. Subject Specialists: *Film, Music,* Jennifer E Schillig; *Computer instruction,* Olympia Sosangelis; *Children's lit,* Katrina Hauserman; Staff 14 (MLS 7, Non-MLS 7)
Founded 1969. Pop 40,274; Circ 121,400
Library Holdings: Bk Titles 71,000; Bk Vols 74,000; Per Subs 147; Talking Bks 2,500
Automation Activity & Vendor Info: (Cataloging) SirsiDynix; (Circulation) SirsiDynix; (OPAC) SirsiDynix
Wireless access
Function: 24/7 Electronic res, 24/7 Online cat, Accelerated reader prog, Adult bk club, Art exhibits, Audio & video playback equip for onsite use, Audiobks via web, AV serv, Bk club(s), Bks on CD, CD-ROM, Children's prog, Computer training, Computers for patron use, Free DVD rentals, Holiday prog, ILL available, Instruction & testing, Internet access, Jazz prog, Life-long learning prog for all ages, Magazines, Meeting rooms, Movies, Music CDs, Online cat, Photocopying/Printing, Prog for adults, Prog for children & young adult, Ref & res, Ref serv available, Story hour, Study rm, Summer reading prog, Tax forms, Teen prog, Telephone ref, Wheelchair accessible, Writing prog
Publications: Library Lines (Monthly newsletter); Monroe Teens Monthly (Newsletter); Out and About (Monthly)
Partic in Libraries of Gloucester, Salem & Cumberland Information Network; LibraryLinkNJ, The New Jersey Library Cooperative

Special Services for the Blind - Accessible computers
Open Mon-Thurs 11-9, Fri 12-5, Sat 10-3
Restriction: Circ limited, Free to mem
Friends of the Library Group

WILLINGBORO

P WILLINGBORO PUBLIC LIBRARY*, Willingboro Town Ctr, 220 Willingboro Pkwy, 08046. SAN 310-6152. Tel: 609-877-0476, 609-877-6668. FAX: 609-877-6250. E-mail: wipl@willingboro.org. Web Site: www.willingboro.org. *Dir,* Sandra L Cronce; E-mail: scronce@willingboro.org; *Syst Adminr,* Eulas Boatwright; E-mail: eboatwright@willingboro.org; *Head, Children's Servx,* Paulette Doe-Williams; E-mail: pdwillia@willingboro.org; *Head, Circ,* Sylvia Morris; E-mail: smorris@willingboro.org; *Head, Ref Serv,* Susan Hacker; *Teen Librn,* Megan Cross; E-mail: mcross@willingboro.org; Staff 14 (MLS 5, Non-MLS 9)
Founded 1960. Pop 33,008; Circ 104,000
Library Holdings: Bk Titles 75,566; Bk Vols 82,014; Per Subs 200
Special Collections: African American History Coll; Local History Coll
Automation Activity & Vendor Info: (Acquisitions) Koha; (Cataloging) Koha; (Circulation) Koha; (ILL) JerseyCat; (OPAC) Koha
Wireless access
Function: 24/7 Electronic res, 24/7 Online cat, Activity rm, Adult bk club, Adult literacy prog, Art exhibits, E-Readers, Homebound delivery serv, ILL available, Magnifiers for reading, Meeting rooms, Notary serv, Online ref, Outreach serv, Photocopying/Printing, Printer for laptops & handheld devices, Prog for adults, Prog for children & young adult, Spoken cassettes & CDs, Spoken cassettes & DVDs, Summer reading prog, Tax forms, Telephone ref, Wheelchair accessible
Partic in LibraryLinkNJ, The New Jersey Library Cooperative
Open Mon-Thurs 10-9, Sat 9-5
Friends of the Library Group

WOODBRIDGE

L GREENBAUM, ROWE, SMITH & DAVIS LLP*, Law Library, 99 Wood Ave S, 07095. SAN 323-6684. Tel: 732-549-5600. FAX: 732-549-1881. Web Site: www.greenbaumlaw.com. *Dir,* Leigh DeProspo; E-mail: ldeprospo@greenbaumlaw.com; *Asst Librn,* Madelyn Robbins; E-mail: mrobbins@greenbaumlaw.com; Staff 3 (Non-MLS 3)
Library Holdings: Bk Vols 9,000
Wireless access
Partic in LibraryLinkNJ, The New Jersey Library Cooperative; New Jersey Law Librarians Association
Open Mon-Fri 9-6

L WILENTZ, GOLDMAN & SPITZER*, Law Library, 90 Woodbridge Center Dr, 07095. SAN 372-4646. Tel: 732-855-6177. Web Site: www.wilentz.com. *Ref Librn,* Laura Valentine; Tel: 732-855-6140, Fax: 732-726-6503; Staff 3 (MLS 1, Non-MLS 2)
Founded 1919
Library Holdings: Bk Vols 20,000
Restriction: Not open to pub

P WOODBRIDGE PUBLIC LIBRARY*, One George Frederick Plaza, 07095. SAN 351-5648. Tel: 732-634-4450. Web Site: www.woodbridgelibrary.org. *Dir,* Monica Eppinger; E-mail: meppinger@woodbridgelibrary.org; *Asst Libr Dir,* Kathryn Brown; E-mail: Kbrown@woodbridgelibrary.org
Founded 1964. Pop 99,585
Special Collections: State Document Depository; US Document Depository
Subject Interests: Educ, Law
Automation Activity & Vendor Info: (Acquisitions) SirsiDynix; (Cataloging) SirsiDynix; (Circulation) SirsiDynix; (ILL) Baker & Taylor; (OPAC) SirsiDynix; (Serials) SirsiDynix
Wireless access
Function: Adult bk club, Archival coll, BA reader (adult literacy), Bk club(s), Bk reviews (Group), Bks on CD, Bus archives, CD-ROM, Children's prog, Computer training, Computers for patron use, Digital talking bks, Electronic databases & coll, Govt ref serv, Homebound delivery serv, Homework prog, ILL available, Internet access, Life-long learning prog for all ages, Magazines, Meeting rooms, Movies, Museum passes, Music CDs, Online cat, Online info literacy tutorials on the web & in blackboard, Online ref, OverDrive digital audio bks, Photocopying/Printing, Prog for adults, Prog for children & young adult, Ref & res, Ref serv available, Summer reading prog, Tax forms, Teen prog, Telephone ref, Wheelchair accessible
Partic in OCLC Online Computer Library Center, Inc
Special Services for the Blind - Talking bks
Open Mon-Thurs 9-9, Fri & Sat 9-5, Sun (Sept-May) 1-5
Friends of the Library Group

WOODBURY

S GLOUCESTER COUNTY HISTORICAL SOCIETY LIBRARY*, 17 Hunter St, 08096-4605. SAN 310-6187. Tel: 856-845-4771. E-mail: library@gchsnj.org. Web Site: www.gchsnj.org/library. *Libr Coord,* Barbara Price
Founded 1903
Library Holdings: Microforms 3,200; Bk Titles 10,000; Per Subs 12
Special Collections: Genealogical Coll, doc, ms, typescripts, vital statistics; History of Gloucester County (Gloucester County Documents 1686-1900); Local Newspapers (Howell Family Coll), microfilm; South Jersey Church, local records; US Navy in Early 19th Century (Richard Somers Coll), doc
Subject Interests: Genealogy of the Del Valley-South Jersey area, Hist
Wireless access
Function: 24/7 Electronic res, 24/7 Online cat, Archival coll, Electronic databases & coll, For res purposes, Microfiche/film & reading machines, Online cat, Online ref, Photocopying/Printing, Res libr, Res performed for a fee, Scanner
Publications: Bulletin of the Gloucester County Historical Society (Quarterly)
Open Tues 6pm-9pm, Wed-Fri 12-4
Restriction: Free to mem, Non-circulating

L GLOUCESTER COUNTY LAW LIBRARY*, 70 Hunter St, 08096. Tel: 856-686-7449.
Restriction: Mem only, Non-circulating to the pub

P WOODBURY PUBLIC LIBRARY*, 33 Delaware St, 08096. SAN 310-6209. Tel: 856-845-2611. E-mail: woodburylibrary@gmail.com. Web Site: www.woodburylibrary.org. *Dir,* Michelle Yeager; E-mail: myeager@woodburylibrary.org; *Head, Children's Servx,* Audra Bonfiglio; E-mail: abonfiglio@woodburylibrary.org; *Head, Circ/ILL,* Janet Coates; *Teen & Adult Librn,* David McMahon
Founded 1790. Pop 10,350; Circ 80,000
Library Holdings: AV Mats 5,200; Bk Vols 57,000; Per Subs 75
Automation Activity & Vendor Info: (Acquisitions) SirsiDynix; (Cataloging) SirsiDynix; (Circulation) SirsiDynix
Wireless access
Open Mon-Thurs 10:30-8, Fri & Sat 10:30-5
Friends of the Library Group

WOODLAND PARK

P ALFRED H BAUMANN FREE PUBLIC LIBRARY*, Seven Brophy Lane, 07424-2733. SAN 310-5989. Tel: 973-345-8120. FAX: 973-345-8196. E-mail: library@abwplibrary.org. Web Site: www.abwplibrary.org. *Libr Dir,* Linda Hoffman; Staff 1 (MLS 1)
Founded 1962. Pop 11,400; Circ 30,834
Library Holdings: Bk Titles 37,000; Bk Vols 43,000; Per Subs 95
Automation Activity & Vendor Info: (Cataloging) SirsiDynix; (Circulation) SirsiDynix; (OPAC) SirsiDynix
Wireless access
Partic in PALS Plus, The Computer Consortium of Passaic County Libraries
Open Mon-Thurs 10-8, Fri 10-5, Sat 10-3, Sun 12-3

J BERKELEY COLLEGE*, Walter A Brower Library, 44 Rifle Camp Rd, 07424. SAN 325-5573. Tel: 973-278-5400, Ext 1230. FAX: 973-278-9141. E-mail: library@berkeleycollege.edu. Web Site: www.berkeleycollege.edu/library. *VPres, Libr Serv,* Marlene Doty; *Libr Dir,* Laurie McFadden; E-mail: ljc@berkeleycollege.edu; Staff 3 (MLS 3)
Founded 1931. Enrl 640; Fac 25
Library Holdings: Bk Vols 5,400; Per Subs 91
Subject Interests: Bus mgt, Computers, Fashion, Humanities, Liberal arts, Mkt
Automation Activity & Vendor Info: (Cataloging) TLC (The Library Corporation); (Circulation) TLC (The Library Corporation); (OPAC) TLC (The Library Corporation)
Partic in OCLC Online Computer Library Center, Inc
Open Mon-Thurs 8am-9:30pm, Fri 8-4, Sat 9-4
Departmental Libraries:
MIDDLESEX CAMPUS, 430 Rahway Ave, Woodbridge, 07095, SAN 370-6966. Tel: 732-750-1800, Ext 2200. FAX: 732-726-9286. *Dir,* Bonnie Lafazan
Library Holdings: Bk Titles 4,500; Bk Vols 5,000; Per Subs 70
Subject Interests: Computer sci, Fashion, Legal
Open Mon-Thurs 8am-9pm, Fri 9-2
PARAMUS CAMPUS, 64 E Midland Ave, Paramus, 07652-3367, SAN 370-6958. Tel: 201-967-9667, Ext 1764. FAX: 201-265-6446. Web Site: berkeleycollege.edu/library. *Dir,* Maria Deptula; Staff 2 (MLS 1.5, Non-MLS 0.5)
Fac 2; Highest Degree: Bachelor
Library Holdings: DVDs 368; e-books 75,000; Electronic Media & Resources 17,500; Bk Titles 4,961; Bk Vols 5,205; Per Subs 48

Subject Interests: Interior design
Automation Activity & Vendor Info: (Acquisitions) TLC (The Library Corporation); (Cataloging) OCLC Connexion; (Circulation) TLC (The Library Corporation); (Course Reserve) TLC (The Library Corporation); (ILL) OCLC FirstSearch; (OPAC) TLC (The Library Corporation)
Open Mon-Thurs 8am-9pm, Fri 8-4, Sat 9-2
Restriction: Authorized patrons

WOOD-RIDGE

P WOOD-RIDGE MEMORIAL LIBRARY*, 231 Hackensack St, 07075. SAN 310-6179. Tel: 201-438-2455. FAX: 201-438-8399. Circulation E-mail: wrdgcirc@bccls.org. Web Site: woodridgememoriallibrary.org. *Dir,* Erin Hughes; E-mail: hughes@woodridge.bccls.org; Staff 2 (MLS 2)
Founded 1931. Pop 8,000; Circ 50,000
Library Holdings: Bk Vols 39,926; Per Subs 95
Special Collections: Local History Coll, (Wood-Ridge)
Automation Activity & Vendor Info: (Cataloging) SirsiDynix; (Circulation) SirsiDynix; (OPAC) SirsiDynix
Wireless access
Partic in Bergen County Cooperative Library System, Inc; LibraryLinkNJ, The New Jersey Library Cooperative
Open Mon-Thurs 10-9, Fri 10-5, Sat 10-3
Friends of the Library Group

WOODSTOWN

P WOODSTOWN-PILESGROVE PUBLIC LIBRARY*, 14 School Lane, 08098-1331. SAN 310-6217. Tel: 856-769-0098. E-mail: woodstownlibrary@gmail.com. Web Site: www.woodstownlibrary.org. *Librn,* Deborah Dietrich; Staff 1 (MLS 1)
Founded 1810. Pop 13,000; Circ 22,575
Library Holdings: Audiobooks 200; DVDs 85; Bk Vols 50,000; Per Subs 35
Special Collections: New Jersey Historical Books
Wireless access
Function: Story hour
Partic in S Jersey Regional Libr Network
Open Mon-Thurs (Sept-May) 10-12 & 2:30-4:30, Fri & Sat 10-Noon; Mon-Thurs (June-Aug) 10-12, 2:30-4:30 & 7-9
Restriction: ID required to use computers (Ltd hrs)

WYCKOFF

P WYCKOFF PUBLIC LIBRARY*, 200 Woodland Ave, 07481. SAN 310-6225. Tel: 201-891-4866. FAX: 201-891-3892. Web Site: www.wyckofflibrary.org. *Dir,* Laura Leonard; E-mail: director@wyckoff.bccls.org; *Ad,* Marilyn Force; *Ch,* Denise Marchetti; *Ref Librn,* Katie Haake; *Teen Librn/Ref,* Riley McArthur; *Circ Supvr,* Susan Valenta; Staff 21.5 (MLS 4.5, Non-MLS 17)
Founded 1921. Pop 16,508; Circ 259,376
Library Holdings: AV Mats 13,502; Bk Vols 67,952; Per Subs 95
Subject Interests: Local hist
Automation Activity & Vendor Info: (Circulation) SirsiDynix-WorkFlows
Wireless access
Partic in Bergen County Cooperative Library System, Inc
Open Mon-Thurs 9-9, Fri & Sat 10-5, Sun (1-5 Sept-June)
Friends of the Library Group

YARDVILLE

S GARDEN STATE YOUTH CORRECTIONAL FACILITY LIBRARY*, PO Box 11401, 08620-1401. SAN 375-7471. Tel: 609-298-6300, Ext 2225. *Librn,* Darlene Maggioncalda
Library Holdings: Bk Vols 16,000; Per Subs 48
Restriction: Not open to pub

NEW MEXICO

Date of Statistics: FY 2019
Population, 2020 U.S. Census: 2,106,319
Population Served by Public Libraries: 1,501,042
Unserved: 558,137
Total Number of Recognized Public Libraries: 97
Total Number of Library Visitors: 6,829,489
Digital Resources:
Total Number of Public Internet Computers: 1,813
Total Number of Public Internet Computer Sessions: 1,531,603
Average Public Internet Computer Sessions Per Library Visitor: 4.45
Total Volumes in Public Libraries: 4,072,650
Volumes Per Capita: 1.97 (state population); 2.71 (served population)
Total Public Library Collection Use: 11,814,509
Collection Use Per Capita: 5.73 (state population); 7.87 (served population)
Income and Expenditures:
Total Public Library Income: $54,293,659
Source of Income: Public funds: municipal 72.9%, county 12.4%, tribal 2.7%, state 3.2%, federal 0.36%, other 8.3%
Expenditures Per Capita: $3.48 (state population); $4.77 (served population)
Grants-in-Aid to Public Libraries: $990,000
Number of Bookmobiles in State: 3
Information provided courtesy of: Carmelita Aragon, State Data Coordinator; Library Development Services Bureau

ABIQUIU

SR GHOST RANCH LIBRARY*, 280 Private Dr 1708, 87510-9601. SAN 310-6233. Tel: 505-685-1000, Ext 4109. E-mail: library@ghostranch.org. Web Site: www.ghostranch.org/activities/ghost-ranch-library. *Dir,* Gretchen Gurtler; E-mail: gretcheng@ghostranch.org
Founded 1955
Library Holdings: AV Mats 300; Bk Titles 17,000; Per Subs 25
Special Collections: Southwest Coll
Subject Interests: Archaeology, Art, Ecology, Geol, Health, Paleontology, Relig, Spirituality, Sustainability, Theol
Automation Activity & Vendor Info: (Cataloging) Follett Software
Wireless access
Open Mon-Fri 9-4
Restriction: Authorized patrons, Non-circulating to the pub

P PUEBLO DE ABIQUIU LIBRARY & CULTURAL CENTER*, Abiquiu Public Library, Bldg 29, County Rd 187, 87510. (Mail add: PO Box 838, 87510). Tel: 505-685-4884. FAX: 505-685-0754. E-mail: abiquiupl@gmail.com. Web Site: abiquiupl.org. *Dir,* Isabel W Trujillo; *Librn,* Sharon Garcia
Library Holdings: Bk Vols 12,000
Automation Activity & Vendor Info: (Cataloging) Follett Software; (Circulation) Follett Software
Wireless access
Open Mon-Thurs & Sun 12-5

ALAMOGORDO

P ALAMOGORDO PUBLIC LIBRARY*, 920 Oregon Ave, 88310. SAN 310-6241. Tel: 575-439-4140. Reference Tel: 575-439-4148. FAX: 575-439-4108. E-mail: COAlibrary@ci.alamogordo.nm.us. Web Site: ci.alamogordo.nm.us/coa/communityservices/library.htm. *Libr Mgr,* Sharon Rowe; E-mail: srowe@ci.alamogordo.nm.us; *Youth Serv Librn,* Ami Jones; E-mail: ajones@ci.alamogordo.nm.us; *Homebound & Vols Coordr,* Becky Miller; E-mail: bmiller@ci.alamogordo.nm.us; Staff 4 (MLS 1, Non-MLS 3)
Founded 1899. Pop 62,298; Circ 265,585
Library Holdings: Audiobooks 2,819; AV Mats 11,123; Bk Titles 94,477; Per Subs 210
Special Collections: Eugene M Rhodes Coll, bks & ms; Mother Goose Editions (Lillian Maddox Coll). Oral History
Subject Interests: Lit, SW hist
Automation Activity & Vendor Info: (Acquisitions) TLC (The Library Corporation); (Cataloging) TLC (The Library Corporation); (Circulation) TLC (The Library Corporation); (OPAC) TLC (The Library Corporation)
Wireless access
Partic in OCLC Online Computer Library Center, Inc
Special Services for the Blind - Screen reader software
Open Mon-Thurs 10-8, Fri 10-5, Sat 11-5
Friends of the Library Group

S NEW MEXICO SCHOOL FOR THE BLIND & VISUALLY IMPAIRED LIBRARY*, 1900 N White Sands Blvd, 88310. SAN 320-2062. Tel: 575-437-3505. Toll Free Tel: 800-437-3505. FAX: 575-439-4454. Web Site: www.nmsbvi.k12.nm.us. *Librn,* Amy Brody; Tel: 575-437-3505, Ext 4510, E-mail: amybrody@nmsbvi.k12.nm.us; Staff 1 (Non-MLS 1)
Founded 1903
Library Holdings: Audiobooks 4,000; Braille Volumes 4,000; CDs 427; Large Print Bks 1,500; Bk Vols 12,000; Per Subs 12; Talking Bks 900; Videos 400
Special Collections: Blindness, Teaching Blind or Visually Impaired Children & Multi-Handicapped (Professional Coll); Braille, Print Braille & Large Print Recreational Reading Titles & Textbooks & Instructional Materials (Depository Coll)
Subject Interests: Gen K-12 fiction, Gen K-12 nonfiction
Automation Activity & Vendor Info: (Cataloging) Keystone Systems, Inc (KLAS); (Circulation) Keystone Systems, Inc (KLAS); (OPAC) Keystone Systems, Inc (KLAS)
Special Services for the Blind - Assistive/Adapted tech devices, equip & products; Audio mat; Bks & mags in Braille, on rec, tape & cassette; Bks on CD; Children's Braille; Descriptive video serv (DVS); Large print bks; Magnifiers; Talking bks
Open Mon-Thurs 8-5, Fri 8-Noon

J NEW MEXICO STATE UNIVERSITY AT ALAMOGORDO*, David H Townsend Library, 2400 N Scenic Dr, 88310. SAN 310-625X. Tel: 575-439-3650. FAX: 575-439-3657. E-mail: libraryNMSUA@nmsu.edu. Web Site: nmsua.edu/library. *Libr Dir,* Dr Sharon Jenkins; Tel: 575-439-3806; *Libr Coord,* Emily Anderson; E-mail: emilyt@nmsu.edu; *Libr Asst,* Wayne West; Tel: 575-439-3653, E-mail: wwphx@nmsu.edu; *Libr Spec,* Emily Tibbs; Tel: 575-439-3851, E-mail: emilyt@nmsu.edu; Staff 3 (MLS 2, Non-MLS 1)
Founded 1975. Enrl 950; Highest Degree: Associate
Library Holdings: AV Mats 1,948; e-books 35,351; Bk Vols 39,000; Per Subs 70
Special Collections: State Document Depository
Subject Interests: Allied health, Art, NMex, Nursing
Automation Activity & Vendor Info: (Acquisitions) Ex Libris Group; (Cataloging) Ex Libris Group; (Circulation) Ex Libris Group; (Course Reserve) Ex Libris Group; (ILL) Ex Libris Group; (OPAC) Ex Libris Group; (Serials) Ex Libris Group
Wireless access
Partic in Amigos Library Services, Inc; New Mexico Consortium of Academic Libraries; OCLC Online Computer Library Center, Inc
Open Mon-Fri 8-5

ALBUQUERQUE

P ALBUQUERQUE-BERNALILLO COUNTY LIBRARY SYSTEM*, 501 Copper Ave NW, 87102. SAN 351-5915. Information Services Tel: 505-768-5141. FAX: 505-768-5191. E-mail: library@cabq.gov. Web Site: abqlibrary.org. *Dir,* Dean P Smith; E-mail: dpsmith@cabq.gov; *Branch & Customer Servs,* Cindy C Burns; E-mail: cburns@cabq.gov; *Human &*

Financial Resources, Jacqueline Lauren Fernandez; Tel: 505-768-5113, E-mail: jlfernandez@cabq.gov; Staff 140 (MLS 43, Non-MLS 97)
Founded 1901. Pop 639,921; Circ 4,578,070
Library Holdings: Audiobooks 43,544; e-books 2,962; Bk Vols 1,282,378
Automation Activity & Vendor Info: (Acquisitions) Innovative Interfaces, Inc; (Cataloging) Innovative Interfaces, Inc; (Circulation) Innovative Interfaces, Inc; (OPAC) Innovative Interfaces, Inc; (Serials) Innovative Interfaces, Inc
Wireless access
Partic in OCLC Online Computer Library Center, Inc
Open Mon & Thurs-Sat 10-6, Tues & Wed 10-7
Friends of the Library Group
Branches: 17
ALAMOSA LIBRARY, 6900 Gonzales Rd SW, 87105, SAN 351-5974. Tel: 505-836-0684. FAX: 505-876-8779. E-mail: alamosalibrary@cabq.gov. Web Site: abqlibrary.org/alamosa. *Br Mgr,* Nicholas Newlin; E-mail: nnewlin@cabq.gov
Open Mon-Fri 10-6
Friends of the Library Group
RUDOLFO ANAYA NORTH VALLEY LIBRARY, 7704-B Second St NW, 87107, SAN 374-7107. Tel: 505-897-8823. FAX: 505-897-8825. E-mail: northvalley@cabq.gov. Web Site: abqlibrary.org/RudolfoAnaya. *Br Mgr,* Sue Heitz; E-mail: sheitz@cabq.gov
Founded 1994
Open Tues, Wed, Fri & Sat 10-6, Thurs 11-7
Friends of the Library Group
CHERRY HILLS LIBRARY, 6901 Barstow NE, 87111. Tel: 505-857-8321. FAX: 505-857-8323. E-mail: cherryhills@cabq.gov. Web Site: abqlibrary.org/cherryhills. *Area Mgr,* Rachel Howart; E-mail: rhowart@cabq.gov
Open Mon & Tues 10-8, Wed-Sat 10-6, Sun 1-5
Friends of the Library Group
EAST MOUNTAIN LIBRARY, 487 NM 333, Tijeras, 87059, SAN 374-7115. Tel: 505-281-8508. FAX: 505-281-8510. E-mail: eastmountain@cabq.gov. Web Site: abqlibrary.org/eastmountain. *Br Mgr,* Lynne Fothergill; E-mail: lfothergill@cabq.gov
Open Tues, Wed, Fri & Sat 10-6, Thurs 11-7
Friends of the Library Group
ERNA FERGUSSON LIBRARY, 3700 San Mateo NE, 87110, SAN 351-6008. Tel: 505-888-8100. FAX: 505-888-8109. E-mail: ernafergusson@cabq.gov. Web Site: abqlibrary.org/ernafergusson. *Area Mgr,* Kelli Murphy; E-mail: kkmurphy@cabq.gov
Open Mon-Thurs 10-8, Fri & Sat 10-6, Sun 1-5
Friends of the Library Group
TONY HILLERMAN LIBRARY, 8205 Apache Ave NE, 87110, SAN 351-6067. Tel: 505-291-6264. FAX: 505-291-6275. E-mail: wyoming@cabq.gov. Web Site: abqlibrary.org/tonyhillerman. *Br Mgr,* Laura Metzler; E-mail: lmetzler@cabq.gov
Open Tues & Wed 10-8, Thurs-Sat 10-6
Friends of the Library Group
LOMAS-TRAMWAY LIBRARY, 908 Eastridge Dr NE, 87123, SAN 329-689X. Tel: 505-291-6295. FAX: 505-291-6299. E-mail: lomastramway@cabq.gov. Web Site: abqlibrary.org/lomastramway. *Br Mgr,* Kathy Hunt; E-mail: mkhunt@cabq.gov
Open Tues & Wed 10-8, Thurs-Sat 10-6
Friends of the Library Group
LOS GRIEGOS LIBRARY, 1000 Griegos Rd NW, 87107, SAN 351-6032. Tel: 505-761-4020. FAX: 505-761-4014. E-mail: losgriegos@cabq.gov. Web Site: abqlibrary.org/losgriegos. *Br Mgr,* Lillian Byres-Richardson; E-mail: lbyres-richardson@cabq.gov
Open Tues, Fri & Sat 10-6, Wed & Thurs 11-7
Friends of the Library Group
ERNIE PYLE LIBRARY, 900 Girard Blvd SE, 87106, SAN 351-6091. Tel: 505-256-2065. FAX: 505-256-2069. E-mail: erniepyle@cabq.gov. Web Site: abqlibrary.org/erniepyle. *Site Supvr,* Lizzie Peacock; E-mail: epeacock@cabq.gov
Open Tues & Thurs-Sat 10-6, Wed 11-7
Friends of the Library Group
SAN PEDRO LIBRARY, 5600 Trumbull Ave SE, 87108, SAN 351-6121. Tel: 505-256-2067. FAX: 505-256-2064. E-mail: sanpedro@cabq.gov. Web Site: abqlibrary.org/sanpedro. *Br Mgr,* Florence Sablan; E-mail: fsablan@cabq.gov
Open Tues, Fri & Sat 10-6, Wed & Thurs 11-7
Friends of the Library Group
SOUTH BROADWAY LIBRARY, 1025 Broadway Blvd SE, 87102, SAN 373-9309. Tel: 505-764-1742. FAX: 505-764-1783. E-mail: southbroadway@cabq.gov. Web Site: abqlibrary.org/southbroadway. *Br Mgr,* Sheila Reece; E-mail: sreece@cabq.gov
Open Tues-Sat 10-6
Friends of the Library Group
SOUTH VALLEY LIBRARY, 3904 Isleta SW, 87105, SAN 329-6938. Tel: 505-877-5170. FAX: 505-877-6639. E-mail: southvalley@cabq.gov. Web Site: abqlibrary.org/southvalley. *Br Mgr,* Reanna Fox; E-mail: refox@cabq.gov
Open Tues, Wed, Fri & Sat 10-6, Thurs 11-7
Friends of the Library Group
SPECIAL COLLECTIONS LIBRARY, 423 Central Ave NE, 87102, SAN 351-6156. Tel: 505-848-1376. FAX: 505-764-1574. E-mail: specialcollections@cabq.gov. Web Site: abqlibrary.org/specialcollections. *Br Mgr,* Kathryn Seidel; E-mail: kseidel@cabq.gov; Staff 3.5 (MLS 1, Non-MLS 2.5)
Library Holdings: AV Mats 12,000; Bk Vols 32,000; Spec Interest Per Sub 300
Special Collections: Archival Coll Relating to the History & Development of the City of Albuquerque, including the Ernie Pyle Coll; History of Books & Printing, part of the Center for the Book; New Mexicana & Local, Albuquerque, History
Function: Archival coll, Art exhibits, Audio & video playback equip for onsite use, Computer training, Computers for patron use, Internet access, Life-long learning prog for all ages, Mail & tel request accepted, Online cat, Online ref, Orientations, Photocopying/Printing, Prog for adults, Ref & res, Ref serv available, Study rm, Telephone ref, Wheelchair accessible, Workshops
Open Tues, Wed, Fri & Sat 10-6, Thurs 11-7
Restriction: Internal use only, Non-circulating, Open to pub for ref & circ; with some limitations
Friends of the Library Group
JUAN TABO LIBRARY, 3407 Juan Tabo Blvd NE, 87111, SAN 351-6164. Tel: 505-291-6260. FAX: 505-291-6225. E-mail: juantabo@cabq.gov. Web Site: abqlibrary.org/juantabo. *Br Mgr,* Alima Jimenez; E-mail: ajimenez@cabq.gov
Open Tues & Wed 10-8, Thurs-Sat 10-6
Friends of the Library Group
TAYLOR RANCH LIBRARY, 5700 Bogart NW, 87120, SAN 329-6911. Tel: 505-897-8816. FAX: 505-897-8813. E-mail: taylorranch@cabq.gov. Web Site: abqlibrary.org/taylorranch. *Area Mgr,* Position Currently Open
Open Mon-Thurs 10-8, Fri & Sat 10-6, Sun 1-5
Friends of the Library Group
WESTGATE LIBRARY, 1300 Delgado SW, 87121. Tel: 505-833-6984. FAX: 505-833-6989. E-mail: westgate@cabq.gov. Web Site: abqlibrary.org/westgate. *Mgr,* Malcolm Alonzo; E-mail: malonzo@cabq.gov
Open Mon-Fri 10-6
Friends of the Library Group
CENTRAL & UNSER - PATRICK J BACA LIBRARY, 8081 Central Ave NW, 87121. Tel: 505-768-4320. E-mail: centralunserlibrary@cabq.gov. Web Site: abqlibrary.org/centralunser. *Area Mgr,* Mary Sue Houser; E-mail: mhouser@cabq.gov
Open Mon-Thurs 10-8, Fri & Sat 10-6, Sun 1-5
Friends of the Library Group
Bookmobiles: 1

S THE ALBUQUERQUE MUSEUM*, Reference Library, 2000 Mountain Rd NW, 87104. SAN 320-8664. Tel: 505-243-7255. FAX: 505-764-6546. E-mail: abqmuseum@cabq.gov. Web Site: www.cabq.gov/culturalservices/albuquerque-museum. *Asst Dir,* Cyndy Garcia; E-mail: CynthiaGarcia@cabq.gov
Founded 1967
Library Holdings: Bk Vols 12,000; Per Subs 23
Subject Interests: Hist, Middle Rio Grande valley, SW art
Wireless access
Restriction: Open by appt only

J CENTRAL NEW MEXICO COMMUNITY COLLEGE LIBRARIES*, 525 Buena Vista SE, 87106-4023. Tel: 505-224-3274. FAX: 505-224-3321. Web Site: www.cnm.edu/depts/libraries. *Dir of Libr,* Poppy Johnson-Renvall; Tel: 505-224-4435, E-mail: pjohnsonrenval@cnm.edu; *Assoc Libr Dir,* Renee Goodvin; Tel: 505-224-4000, Ext 52550, E-mail: fgoodvin@cnm.edu; *Ref/Syst Librn,* Yuqing Zhou; Tel: 505-224-4000, Ext 52540, E-mail: yzhou@cnm.edu; *Libr Mgr,* Mary Bates-Ulibani; Tel: 505-224-4000, Ext 52552, E-mail: ulimb@cnm.edu; *Ref Spec,* Wynn Harris; Tel: 505-224-4000, Ext 51498, E-mail: wharris@cnm.edu; *Libr Tech,* Leda Rizzo; Tel: 505-224-4000, Ext 52538, E-mail: lkoltinick@cnm.edu; Staff 9 (MLS 4, Non-MLS 5)
Founded 1965. Enrl 17,000; Fac 700
Library Holdings: Bk Titles 59,508; Per Subs 584
Subject Interests: Air conditioning, Alternative energy, Auto repair, Carpentry, Creativity, Culinary arts, Electronics, Hospitality, Laser optics, Law enforcement, Plumbing, Robotics, Sheet metal, Tourism, Use of tools, Welding
Automation Activity & Vendor Info: (Cataloging) OCLC WorldShare Interlibrary Loan; (Circulation) OCLC WorldShare Interlibrary Loan; (OPAC) OCLC WorldShare Interlibrary Loan
Wireless access
Partic in New Mexico Consortium of Academic Libraries
Open Mon-Thurs 7:30am-9pm, Fri 7:30-5, Sat 9-5

Departmental Libraries:
MONTOYA CAMPUS LIBRARY, 4700 Morris St NE, RB 101, 87111, SAN 320-9598. Circulation Tel: 505-224-5721. *Libr Mgr,* Bridget O'Leary-Storer; Tel: 505-224-4000, Ext 52548, E-mail: boleary@cnm.edu; *Ref Librn,* Catherine Lopez; Tel: 505-224-4000, Ext 53768, E-mail: clopez117@cmn.edu; *Ref Spec,* Allyson James-Vigil; Tel: 505-224-4000, Ext 51342, E-mail: allyson@cnm.edu. Subject Specialists: *Bus,* Allyson James-Vigil; Staff 5 (MLS 1, Non-MLS 4)
Founded 1981. Enrl 8,000; Highest Degree: Associate
Subject Interests: Laser optics
Function: For res purposes
Open Mon-Thurs 8-8, Fri 8-5, Sat 9-5
RIO RANCHO CAMPUS LIBRARY, 2601 Campus Blvd NE, Rm 112, Rio Rancho, 87144. Tel: 505-224-4953. *Libr Spec,* Carlee Philpot; E-mail: cphilpot@cnm.edu; Staff 1.5 (MLS 1.5)
Founded 2010. Enrl 1,550; Fac 50; Highest Degree: Associate
Library Holdings: AV Mats 66; High Interest/Low Vocabulary Bk Vols 22; Bk Titles 633; Per Subs 17
Subject Interests: Nursing
Function: Audio & video playback equip for onsite use, CD-ROM, Computers for patron use, Doc delivery serv, Electronic databases & coll, Free DVD rentals, ILL available, Internet access, Mail & tel request accepted, Online cat, Online info literacy tutorials on the web & in blackboard, Online ref, Photocopying/Printing, Ref & res, Ref serv available, Scanner, Tax forms, Telephone ref, VHS videos, Wheelchair accessible
Partic in LIBROS Consortium
Open Mon-Thurs 9-6, Fri 8-5
Restriction: Fee for pub use, ID required to use computers (Ltd hrs), Open to pub for ref & circ; with some limitations
SOUTH VALLEY CAMPUS LIBRARY, 525 Buena Vista Dr, 87105. *Libr Spec,* Tiffany Tomchak; Tel: 505-224-4000, Ext 53275, E-mail: ttomchak@cnm.edu
Library Holdings: AV Mats 203; e-journals 7; Electronic Media & Resources 16; Bk Vols 286; Per Subs 22
Automation Activity & Vendor Info: (Cataloging) Innovative Interfaces, Inc; (Circulation) Innovative Interfaces, Inc; (OPAC) Innovative Interfaces, Inc
Open Mon-Fri 8-5
WESTSIDE CAMPUS LIBRARY, WS1 200, 10549 Universe Blvd NW, 87114. Tel: 505-224-5423. *Libr Spec,* Martha Castillo; Tel: 505-224-4000, Ext 52990, E-mail: mcastillo114@cnm.edu
Library Holdings: AV Mats 150; DVDs 12; Bk Titles 338; Bk Vols 356; Per Subs 19; Videos 138
Automation Activity & Vendor Info: (Cataloging) Innovative Interfaces, Inc; (Circulation) Innovative Interfaces, Inc; (OPAC) Innovative Interfaces, Inc
Open Mon-Thurs 8-8, Fri 8-5

SR CENTRAL UNITED METHODIST CHURCH LIBRARY*, 201 University Blvd NE, 87106-4596. SAN 371-8476. Tel: 505-243-7834. FAX: 505-242-6986. E-mail: info@centraltolife.org. Web Site: centraltolife.org. *Librn,* Rex Allender
Library Holdings: Large Print Bks 10; Bk Vols 3,000
Special Collections: Bible, AV, bks; Methodist History, AV, bks
Publications: Acquisitions List; Bibliographies; Guides
Open Mon-Fri 9-4:30, Sun 9-Noon

R CONGREGATION B'NAI ISRAEL*, Isidore & Rose Bloch Memorial Library, 4401 Indian School Rd NE, 87110-3914. SAN 310-6322. Tel: 505-266-0155. FAX: 505-268-6136. E-mail: office@bnaiisrael-nm.org. Web Site: bnaiisrael-nm.org.
Library Holdings: Braille Volumes 1; CDs 640; DVDs 101; Music Scores 9; Bk Titles 2,280; Per Subs 1; Videos 340
Special Collections: American Jewish Music (Milken Archive); Judaica; Marilyn Bromberg-Marilyn Reinman Children's Coll; Norman Schwartz Memorial Music Coll
Open Mon 4:30-6, Thurs & Sun 9:30-Noon

R FIRST PRESBYTERIAN CHURCH LIBRARY*, 215 Locust NE, 87102. SAN 310-6349. Tel: 505-764-2900. FAX: 505-764-2940. Web Site: firstpresabq.org. *Dir, Christian Educ,* Elizabeth Libby Whiteley
Founded 1955
Library Holdings: Bk Titles 6,000; Bk Vols 7,183; Per Subs 40
Special Collections: Local History & Culture Coll; Southwest Interest Coll
Subject Interests: Biblical studies, Fiction, Personal help, Relig, Soc issues, Theol
Open Mon-Fri 8:30-5, Sun 8:45-2
Friends of the Library Group

S LOVELACE RESPIRATORY RESEARCH INSTITUTE*, Sam White Library, 2425 Ridgecrest Dr SE, 87108-5127. SAN 310-6810. Tel: 505-348-9361. FAX: 505-348-4978. E-mail: info@lrri.org. Web Site: www.lrri.org.
Founded 1974
Library Holdings: Bk Titles 10,000; Bk Vols 25,000; Per Subs 75
Subject Interests: Aerosol physics, Fossil fuels effluents, Radiation effects, Respiratory syst, Toxicology, Veterinary med
Function: ILL available, Res libr
Restriction: Employees only

S MAXWELL MUSEUM OF ANTHROPOLOGY*, Archives, University of New Mexico, 500 University Blvd NE, Hibben Ctr, Rm 123, 87131. SAN 377-3280. Tel: 505-277-4405. Web Site: maxwellmuseum.unm.edu. *Archivist,* Diane Tyink; Tel: 505-277-1549, E-mail: dtyink@unm.edu
Founded 1972
Library Holdings: Bk Titles 12,000; Per Subs 35
Function: Res libr
Restriction: Borrowing privileges limited to anthropology fac & libr staff

S MENAUL HISTORICAL LIBRARY OF THE SOUTHWEST, 301 Menaul Blvd NE, 87107. SAN 371-2249. Tel: 505-343-7480. E-mail: archives@menaulhistoricallibrary.org. Web Site: www.menaulhistoricallibrary.org. *Dir,* Olga Joyce
Founded 1974
Library Holdings: Bk Vols 3,700; Per Subs 11; Spec Interest Per Sub 20
Special Collections: Presbyterian Church History - New Mexico, Arizona & Utah, artifacts, bks, doc. Oral History
Subject Interests: Native Am, Presbyterian churches, Presbyterian hist
Function: Res libr
Open Tues-Fri 10-4
Restriction: Non-circulating

L MILLER STRATVERT PA*, Law Library, 500 Marquette Ave NW, Ste 1100, 87102. (Mail add: PO Box 25687, 87125-0687), SAN 372-4387. Tel: 505-842-1950. FAX: 505-243-4408. Web Site: mstlaw.com. *Librn,* Lee Perea; E-mail: lperea@mstlaw.com; Staff 1 (MLS 1)
Founded 1978
Library Holdings: Bk Vols 1,000; Per Subs 20

S NATIONAL HISPANIC CULTURAL CENTER LIBRARY*, 1701 Fourth St SW, 87102. SAN 370-6516. Tel: 505-383-4778. Web Site: www.nhccnm.org/learn/nhcc-library-archive. *Librn,* Cassandra Osterloh; E-mail: cassandra.osterloh@state.nm.us; Staff 1 (MLS 1)
Founded 2000
Library Holdings: Bk Titles 14,500; Per Subs 4
Automation Activity & Vendor Info: (Cataloging) OCLC Connexion
Wireless access
Function: 24/7 Online cat, Adult bk club, Archival coll, Computers for patron use, Internet access, Life-long learning prog for all ages, Microfiche/film & reading machines, Online cat, Photocopying/Printing, Prog for adults, Prog for children & young adult, Ref & res, Res assist avail, Spanish lang bks, Summer reading prog, Writing prog
Open Tues-Fri 10-5
Restriction: Circ to mem only

S NEW MEXICO CORRECTIONS DEPARTMENT*, Education Bureau, Charles S Gara Public Safety Ctr, 615 First St, NW, 87102. SAN 310-723X. Tel: 505-490-5492. Web Site: cd.nm.gov/apd/ed.html. *Bur Chief,* Position Currently Open; *Dep Adminr,* Ms Leslie Bradley; E-mail: Leslie.Bradley@state.nm.us; Staff 1 (MLS 1)
Library Holdings: Bk Vols 115,000; Per Subs 210
Special Collections: Arizona Legal Access Model
Subject Interests: Corrections, Law
Special Services for the Deaf - Captioned film dep; High interest/low vocabulary bks
Restriction: Staff & inmates only

GM NEW MEXICO VA HEALTH CARE SYSTEM*, General & Medical Library (142D), 1501 San Pedro SE, 87108. SAN 310-6489. Tel: 505-265-1711, Ext 2248. Web Site: www.albuquerque.va.gov. *Dir, Libr Serv,* Christine Fleuriel; E-mail: christine.fleuriel@va.gov; Staff 3 (MLS 2, Non-MLS 1)
Founded 1932
Library Holdings: Bk Vols 2,202; Per Subs 250
Subject Interests: Gen med, Geriatrics, Gerontology, Nursing, Psychiat, Psychol, Surgery
Automation Activity & Vendor Info: (Acquisitions) Inmagic, Inc.; (Cataloging) Inmagic, Inc.; (Circulation) Inmagic, Inc.; (OPAC) Inmagic, Inc.; (Serials) Inmagic, Inc.
Partic in N Mex Consortium of Biomedical & Hospital Libr; National Network of Libraries of Medicine Region 4
Special Services for the Deaf - Closed caption videos
Special Services for the Blind - Talking bks & player equip
Restriction: Not open to pub

M PRESBYTERIAN HOSPITAL*, Robert Shafer Memorial Library, 1100 Central Ave SE, 87125. SAN 310-6411. Tel: 505-841-1516. FAX: 505-841-1067. *Med Librn,* Amanda Okandan; E-mail: aokandan@phs.org
Founded 1962
Library Holdings: Bk Titles 900; Per Subs 120
Subject Interests: Med
Wireless access
Restriction: Staff use only

R SAINT JOHN'S EPISCOPAL CATHEDRAL*, Kadey Memorial Library, 318 Silver SW, 87102. SAN 310-642X. Tel: 505-247-1581. Web Site: stjohnsabq.org.
Founded 1975
Library Holdings: Bk Titles 1,000
Subject Interests: Biblical lit, Devotional, Devotional psychol, Liturgy, Philos, Relig studies, Theol
Restriction: Not open to pub

S SANDIA NATIONAL LABORATORIES*, Technical Library, PO Box 5800, MS 0899, 87185-0899. SAN 310-6438. Tel: 505-845-8287. FAX: 505-844-3143. Web Site: www.sandia.gov/resources/employees/technical_library. *Mgr, Tech Libr Operations,* Donald Guy; Tel: 505-284-2859, E-mail: dwguy@sandia.gov; Staff 6 (MLS 6)
Founded 1948
Library Holdings: Bk Titles 70,000
Subject Interests: Aerodynamics, Electronics, Energy res, Explosives, Nuclear safety, Nuclear waste mgt, Nuclear weapons, Ordinance, Security
Automation Activity & Vendor Info: (Cataloging) SirsiDynix; (Circulation) SirsiDynix; (OPAC) SirsiDynix
Partic in Horizon Users Group
Restriction: Staff use only

S SOUTHWEST RESEARCH & INFORMATION CENTER LIBRARY*, 105 Stanford SE, 87106-3537. (Mail add: PO Box 4524, 87106-4524), SAN 326-0089. Tel: 505-262-1862. FAX: 505-262-1864. Web Site: www.sric.org. *Adminr,* Don Hancock; E-mail: sricdon@earthlink.net; Staff 1 (Non-MLS 1)
Founded 1971
Library Holdings: Bk Titles 10,000; Per Subs 100
Wireless access
Function: Photocopying/Printing, Ref serv available
Open Mon-Fri 9-5
Restriction: Open to pub for ref only

J SOUTHWESTERN INDIAN POLYTECHNIC INSTITUTE LIBRARIES*, 9169 Coors Rd NW, 87184. SAN 310-6454. Tel: 505-792-4498. FAX: 505-346-7713. Web Site: www.sipi.edu/apps/pages/library. *Libr Tech,* Tedra Begay; Tel: 505-922-4097, E-mail: tedra.begay@bie.edu
Library Holdings: Bk Vols 30,000; Per Subs 150
Special Collections: Indian Coll, mat, tech bks
Subject Interests: Acctg electronics, Engr tech, Food tech, Mkt, Natural res, Secretarial
Automation Activity & Vendor Info: (Cataloging) Follett Software; (Circulation) Follett Software
Partic in New Mexico Consortium of Academic Libraries
Open Mon-Thurs 8:30-5:30, Fri 8-4

L SUTIN, THAYER & BROWNE*, Law Library, 6100 Uptown Blvd NE, Ste 400, 87110. SAN 372-4379. Tel: 505-883-2500. FAX: 505-888-6565. Web Site: www.sutinfirm.com. *Info & Res Mgr,* Laura Mudd; E-mail: llm@sutinfirm.com; Staff 1 (Non-MLS 1)
Library Holdings: Bk Vols 10,000; Per Subs 100
Wireless access

S TELEPHONE MUSEUM OF NEW MEXICO LIBRARY, 110 Fourth St NW, 87102. (Mail add: PO Box 16174, 87191). Tel: 505-842-2937. FAX: 505-332-4088. E-mail: telmuseum@hotmail.com. Web Site: www.museumsusa.org/museums/info/6919. *Chairperson,* Tom Baker; Tel: 505-238-1952; Staff 2 (Non-MLS 2)
Founded 1997
Library Holdings: Bk Titles 2,600; Bk Vols 3,600
Subject Interests: Telephone
Wireless access
Restriction: Not a lending libr, Open by appt only

GL US COURTS LIBRARY - TENTH CIRCUIT COURT OF APPEALS*, 333 Lomas Blvd NW, Ste 360, 87102. SAN 372-428X. Tel: 505-348-2135. FAX: 505-348-2795. *Librn,* Gregory L Townsend; E-mail: gregory_townsend@ca10.uscourts.gov; *Tech Serv,* Greg Surratt
Library Holdings: Bk Vols 19,000; Per Subs 50
Function: Res libr
Open Mon-Fri 8-12 & 1-5
Restriction: Non-circulating to the pub

C UNIVERSITY OF NEW MEXICO-UNIVERSITY LIBRARIES*, Zimmerman Library, 1900 Roma NE, 87131-0001. (Mail add: One University of New Mexico, MSC 05-3020, 87131-0001), SAN 351-6210. Interlibrary Loan Service Tel: 505-277-5617. Reference Tel: 505-277-9100. Administration Tel: 505-277-4241. Administration FAX: 505-277-7196. TDD: 505-277-4866. Web Site: library.unm.edu. *Interim Dean of Libr, Sr Assoc Dean,* Fran Wilkinson; Tel: 505-277-4241, E-mail: fwilkins@unm.edu; *Assoc Dean, Pub Serv,* Dr Mark Emmons; Tel: 505-277-4241, E-mail: emmons@unm.edu; *Dir,* Tomas Jaehn; Tel: 505-277-7107, E-mail: tjaehn@unm.edu; Staff 94 (MLS 27, Non-MLS 67)
Founded 1892. Fac 1,069; Highest Degree: Doctorate
Library Holdings: e-books 962,948; Bk Titles 3,479,955; Bk Vols 221,907
Special Collections: 19th & 20th Century Oaxaca, Mexico Pamphlets & Regional History; 19th Century Latin American Travel Narratives; Indian Affairs (Glenn Leonidas Emmons & Michael Steck Coll), papers; Indians (Doris Duke Foundation Coll AIM Archives); John Donald Robb Archive of Southwestern Music, a-tapes; Land Records (Maxwell Land Grant Co, US Soil Conservation Service Reports); Latin American Agrarian History, Agricultural Economics & Rural Sociology (T Lynn Smith Coll); Literary Manuscripts (Erna Fergusson Papers, Frank Waters Papers, Papers of Regional Hispanic Writers); New Mexicana; Papers of Public Figures (Thomas B Catron, Albert Bacon Fall, Miguel Antonio Otero, US Senators: Dennis Chavez, Pete V Domenici, Joseph M Montoya, Harrison H Schmitt, Congressman Manuel J Lujan); Photocopies Spanish, Mexican & New Mexican Archives; Pioneers Foundation Coll (Anglos); Popular Culture (Day Science Fiction Periodicals & Dime Novels); Puppetry (McPharlin Coll), bks, realia; Regional Historical Manuscripts: Business Records (Bell Ranch-Red River Valley Co, Charles Ilfeld Mercantile Co, First National Bank of Santa Fe); Regional Historical Photographs (William Henry Cobb, Charles Fletcher Lummis & Henry Schmidt Colls); Southwestern Americana; Southwestern Historical Architectural Documents (John Gaw Meem Coll); US Patent Dept. Oral History; State Document Depository; US Document Depository
Subject Interests: Hist of photog, Ibero-Am mat, SW archit
Automation Activity & Vendor Info: (Acquisitions) OCLC Worldshare Management Services; (Cataloging) OCLC Worldshare Management Services; (Circulation) OCLC Worldshare Management Services; (Course Reserve) OCLC Worldshare Management Services; (Discovery) OCLC Worldshare Management Services; (OPAC) OCLC Worldshare Management Services; (Serials) OCLC Worldshare Management Services
Wireless access
Function: Archival coll, For res purposes, Govt ref serv, Homebound delivery serv, ILL available, Internet access, Photocopying/Printing, Ref serv available, Res libr, Wheelchair accessible
Publications: Developments at University Libraries (Newsletter)
Partic in Association of Research Libraries; Greater Western Library Alliance; LIBROS Consortium; New Mexico Consortium of Academic Libraries
Special Services for the Deaf - Bks on deafness & sign lang
Special Services for the Blind - Accessible computers; Aids for in-house use; Assistive/Adapted tech devices, equip & products; Braille servs; Braille Webster's dictionary; Compressed speech equip; Reader equip; Telesensory screen enlarger & speech synthesis interface to the OPAC; VisualTek equip
Restriction: Open to students, fac & staff, Pub use on premises

Departmental Libraries:

BUREAU OF BUSINESS & ECONOMIC RESEARCH DATA BANK, 1919 Las Lomas NE, 87106. (Mail add: MSC06 3510, One University of New Mexico, 87131-0001), SAN 310-6330. Tel: 505-277-3038. Reference Tel: 505-277-6626. FAX: 505-277-2773. E-mail: dbinfo@unm.edu. Web Site: bber.unm.edu/bber_data.html. *Sr Prog Mgr,* Suzan Reagan-Kershner; E-mail: sreagan@unm.edu; *Info Spec,* Lawrence Compton; Tel: 505-277-2142, E-mail: lcompton@unm.edu. Subject Specialists: *Demographics, Econ, Statistics,* Suzan Reagan-Kershner; *Demographics, Econ, Statistics,* Lawrence Compton; Staff 2 (MLS 1, Non-MLS 1)
Founded 1967
Library Holdings: CDs 800; Bk Vols 14,000; Per Subs 45
Special Collections: New Mexico Social Statistics; New Mexico Statistics (New Mexico State & Local Government Agency Publications); New Mexico's Economy; US Census Reports
Subject Interests: Census, Demographics, Econ
Automation Activity & Vendor Info: (Cataloging) Innovative Interfaces, Inc - Millennium; (OPAC) Innovative Interfaces, Inc - Millennium
Function: For res purposes
Partic in LIBROS Consortium
Publications: New Mexico Business-Current Economic Report (Monthly)
Open Mon, Wed & Fri 8-12 & 1-5, Tues & Thurs 8-Noon
Restriction: Open to pub for ref only

CENTENNIAL SCIENCE & ENGINEERING LIBRARY, 211 Terrace St NE, 87131-0001. (Mail add: MSC05 3020, One University of New Mexico, 87131-0001). FAX: 505-277-0702. Reference E-mail: cselref@unm.edu.
Special Collections: Map Room; United States Patents

FINE ARTS & DESIGN LIBRARY, George Pearl Hall, 4th Flr, 87131. (Mail add: MSC05 3020, One University of New Mexico, 87131-0001). Reference E-mail: falref@unm.edu.
Founded 1963. Highest Degree: Doctorate
Library Holdings: e-books 68,845; Bk Vols 230,000; Per Subs 250
Special Collections: Oral History; State Document Depository; US Document Depository
Subject Interests: Latin American, SW

CM HEALTH SCIENCES LIBRARY & INFORMATICS CENTER, MSC09-5100, One University of New Mexico, 87131-0001. Tel: 505-272-2311. Interlibrary Loan Service Tel: 505-272-8052. Administration Tel: 505-272-0634. FAX: 505-272-5350. Administration FAX: 505-272-8254. E-mail: reflib@salud.unm.edu. Web Site: hslic.unm.edu. *Dir,* Holly Shipp Buchanan; E-mail: hbuchanan@salud.unm.edu; Staff 68 (MLS 11, Non-MLS 57)
Founded 1963. Enrl 1,860; Fac 935; Highest Degree: Doctorate
Library Holdings: Bk Vols 45,814; Per Subs 1,924
Special Collections: Indian Health Services Research; Southwest & New Mexico Medicine, media; UNM Health Sciences Center Archives; World Health Organization Publications. Oral History
Subject Interests: Allied health, Med, Med hist, Native Am health, Nursing, Pharm, Pub health
Automation Activity & Vendor Info: (Acquisitions) OCLC WorldShare Interlibrary Loan; (Cataloging) OCLC WorldShare Interlibrary Loan; (Circulation) OCLC WorldShare Interlibrary Loan; (Course Reserve) OCLC WorldShare Interlibrary Loan; (ILL) OCLC ILLiad; (OPAC) OCLC WorldShare Interlibrary Loan; (Serials) OCLC WorldShare Interlibrary Loan
Partic in National Network of Libraries of Medicine Region 4; New Mexico Consortium of Academic Libraries; OCLC Online Computer Library Center, Inc; South Central Academic Medical Libraries Consortium
Publications: Selected Bibliographies

CL LAW LIBRARY, 1117 Stanford Dr NE, 87131-1441, SAN 351-627X. Tel: 505-277-6236. FAX: 505-277-0068. Web Site: lawschool.unm.edu/lawlib/index.php. *Dir,* Carol Parker; E-mail: cparker@unm.edu; *Assoc Dir,* Michelle Rigual; E-mail: mrigual@unm.edu; *Law Librn,* Barbara Lah; *Law Librn,* Sherri Thomas; *Assoc Librn,* Eileen Cohen
Founded 1948. Enrl 320; Fac 30; Highest Degree: Doctorate
Library Holdings: Bk Titles 97,771; Bk Vols 412,694; Per Subs 3,168
Special Collections: Alternative Dispute Resolution; American Indian Law Coll; Land Grant Law Coll; Mexican Law Coll. US Document Depository
Automation Activity & Vendor Info: (Acquisitions) Innovative Interfaces, Inc; (Cataloging) Innovative Interfaces, Inc; (Circulation) Innovative Interfaces, Inc; (Course Reserve) Innovative Interfaces, Inc; (OPAC) Innovative Interfaces, Inc; (Serials) Innovative Interfaces, Inc
Partic in New Mexico Consortium of Academic Libraries
Open Mon-Thurs 8am-11pm, Fri 8-6, Sat 9-6, Sun Noon-11

WILLIAM J PARISH MEMORIAL BUSINESS & ECONOMICS LIBRARY, One University of New Mexico, MSC05 3020, 87131-1496. Tel: 505-277-5912. FAX: 505-277-9813. Web Site: library.unm.edu/about/libraries/pml.php. ; Staff 10 (MLS 4, Non-MLS 6)
Founded 1989. Enrl 24,000; Highest Degree: Doctorate
Library Holdings: e-books 8,000; Bk Vols 185,000; Per Subs 5,000
Subject Interests: Econ, Mgt
Function: Computers for patron use, E-Reserves, Electronic databases & coll, ILL available, Online cat, Online ref, Orientations, Ref & res, Ref serv available, Tax forms
Special Services for the Deaf - ADA equip; TTY equip

TAOS CAMPUS, 115 Civic Plaza Dr, Taos, 87571. (Mail add: 1157 County Rd 110, Ranchos de Taos, 87557). Tel: 575-737-6242. FAX: 575-737-6292. E-mail: unmtlib@unm.edu. Web Site: taos.unm.edu/library. *Libr Dir,* Kathleen Knoth; Tel: 575-737-6243, E-mail: kathk@unm.edu; *Asst Librn,* Ana Pacheco; E-mail: apache02@unm.edu; *Info Spec I,* Enrico Trujillo; E-mail: enrico@unm.edu; Staff 2.5 (MLS 1, Non-MLS 1.5)
Founded 1995. Enrl 1,700; Highest Degree: Associate
Library Holdings: AV Mats 720; Bk Vols 5,200; Per Subs 24
Automation Activity & Vendor Info: (Cataloging) Innovative Interfaces, Inc; (Circulation) Innovative Interfaces, Inc - Millennium; (ILL) OCLC WorldShare Interlibrary Loan
Function: Art exhibits, Audio & video playback equip for onsite use, Computer training, Computers for patron use, Doc delivery serv, Electronic databases & coll, For res purposes, Free DVD rentals, ILL available, Instruction & testing, Internet access, Music CDs, Online cat, Orientations, Outreach serv, Photocopying/Printing, Prog for adults, Prog for children & young adult, Ref & res, Ref serv available, Scanner, Spoken cassettes & CDs, Spoken cassettes & DVDs, VHS videos, Wheelchair accessible, Workshops
Partic in New Mexico Consortium of Academic Libraries
Open Mon-Thurs 8-8, Fri 8-5, Sat 10-4, Sun 12-5

VALENCIA CAMPUS, 280 La Entrada, Los Lunas, 87031. Tel: 505-925-8990. FAX: 505-925-8994. Web Site: www.unm.edu/~unmvclib. *Dir,* Dr Barbara Lovato; Tel: 505-925-8991, E-mail: bllovato@unm.edu; *Info Spec,* Lisa Pate; Tel: 505-925-8992, E-mail: lpate@unm.edu; *Pub Serv,* Leann Weller; Tel: 505-925-8993, E-mail: lweller1@unm.edu; Staff 2 (MLS 2)
Enrl 2,500; Highest Degree: Associate
Library Holdings: AV Mats 2,900; Bk Vols 43,500; Per Subs 150
Partic in New Mexico Consortium of Academic Libraries
Open Mon-Thurs 8am-8:30pm, Fri 10:30-5

ANGEL FIRE

P THE SHUTER LIBRARY OF ANGEL FIRE, 11 S Angel Fire Rd, 87110. (Mail add: PO Box 298, 87110-0298). Tel: 575-377-6755. E-mail: info@shuterlibrary.net. Web Site: www.shuterlibrary.net. *Libr Dir,* Melody Costa; Tel: 575-377-6755, E-mail: director@shuterlibrary.net; Staff 3 (MLS 1, Non-MLS 2)
Founded 1978. Pop 1,200
Library Holdings: AV Mats 1,944; Bk Vols 12,204
Special Collections: Southwest Coll
Automation Activity & Vendor Info: (Cataloging) Follett Software; (Circulation) Follett Software
Wireless access
Function: 24/7 Electronic res, 24/7 Online cat, Adult bk club, Audiobks via web, Bk club(s), Bks on CD, Butterfly Garden, Computer training, Computers for patron use, E-Readers, Internet access, Magazines, Meeting rooms, Online cat, OverDrive digital audio bks, Photocopying/Printing, Preschool reading prog, Prog for adults, Prog for children & young adult, Ref & res, Scanner, Spanish lang bks, Summer reading prog, Workshops
Open Tues-Fri 10-5, Sat 10-3
Friends of the Library Group

ARTESIA

S ARTESIA HISTORICAL MUSEUM & ART CENTER*, Research Facility, 505 W Richardson Ave, 88210. SAN 373-4773. Tel: 575-748-2390. FAX: 575-748-7345 (Attn: Museum). E-mail: artesiamuseum@artesianm.gov. Web Site: www.artesianm.gov/154/Museum-Art-Center. *Supvr,* Nancy Dunn; E-mail: ndunn@artesianm.gov
Founded 1970
Library Holdings: Bk Vols 500
Special Collections: City of Artesia Archives
Subject Interests: Genealogy, Local hist
Wireless access
Function: Res libr
Open Tues-Fri 9-12 & 1-5, Sat 1-5

P ARTESIA PUBLIC LIBRARY, 205 W Quay Ave, 88210. SAN 310-6500. Tel: 575-746-4252. FAX: 575-746-3075. Web Site: www.artesianm.gov/146/Library. *Libr Supvr,* Erin Loveland; E-mail: eloveland@artesianm.gov; Staff 8 (MLS 2, Non-MLS 6)
Founded 1902. Pop 11,300
Library Holdings: Bk Titles 71,000; Per Subs 200
Special Collections: Dr Glenn E Stone (Southwest Coll); Leah Kennedy (Southwest Coll)
Automation Activity & Vendor Info: (Cataloging) Follett Software; (Circulation) Follett Software
Wireless access
Function: Homebound delivery serv, ILL available, Photocopying/Printing, Prog for children & young adult, Spoken cassettes & CDs, Summer reading prog
Open Mon-Sat 9:30-6
Friends of the Library Group

AZTEC

P AZTEC PUBLIC LIBRARY*, 319 S Ash, 87410. SAN 310-6519. Tel: 505-334-7657. FAX: 505-334-7659. Web Site: www.azteclibrary.org. *Libr Dir,* Angela Watkins; E-mail: awatkins@aztecnm.gov; Staff 3 (Non-MLS 3)
Founded 1908
Library Holdings: Bk Vols 33,000; Per Subs 65
Special Collections: Audio/Video Coll (Adult & Juvenile); Local History; Southwest Coll; UFO'S
Subject Interests: Ancient astronomy, Aztec ruins, Chaco Canyon, Mesa Verde areas
Automation Activity & Vendor Info: (Acquisitions) SirsiDynix; (Cataloging) SirsiDynix; (Circulation) SirsiDynix
Wireless access
Open Mon-Fri 9-6, Sat 10-5

G NATIONAL PARK SERVICE*, Aztec Ruins National Monument Library, 725 Ruins Rd, 87410. SAN 329-0697. Tel: 505-334-6174, Ext 232. FAX: 505-334-6372. E-mail: azru_information@nps.gov. Web Site: www.nps.gov/azru. *Library Contact,* Danielle York
Founded 1923
Library Holdings: Bk Titles 700
Subject Interests: Archaeology
Function: For res purposes
Restriction: Staff use only

BAYARD

P BAYARD PUBLIC LIBRARY, 1112 Central Ave, 88023. Tel: 575-537-6244. FAX: 575-537-6246. E-mail: bayardlibrary@cityofbayardnm.com. *Dir,* Sonya Dixon; *Asst Librn,* Jenny Castanon
Library Holdings: Bk Vols 14,000; Talking Bks 150
Wireless access
Open Mon-Fri 9:30-5:30

BELEN

P BELEN PUBLIC LIBRARY, 333 Becker Ave, 87002. SAN 310-6527. Tel: 505-966-2600. E-mail: belenpubliclibrary@gmail.com. Web Site: belen.biblionix.com, www.belen-nm.gov/belen-public-library. *Dir,* Kathleen Pickering; Tel: 505-966-2604, E-mail: kathleen.pickering@belen-nm.gov; *Tech Serv Librn,* Stephanie Wallace; Tel: 505-966-2606, E-mail: stephanie.wallace@belen-nm.gov; *Libr Tech II, Outreach Serv, Youth Serv,* Alyissa Aragon; Tel: 505-966-2608, E-mail: alyissa.aragon@belen-nm.gov; *Adult/Ref Serv, Libr Tech II, Youth Serv,* Danny Garcia; Tel: 505-966-2603, E-mail: danny.garcia@belen-nm.gov; *Adult/Ref Serv, Circ Serv, Libr Tech II,* Connie Ridley; Tel: 505-966-2607, E-mail: connie.ridley@belen-nm.gov; *Computer Spec, Electronic Res,* Summer Ludwig; E-mail: summer.ludwig@belen-nm.gov. Subject Specialists: *Teen serv,* Danny Garcia; Staff 6 (Non-MLS 6)
Founded 1966. Pop 7,269; Circ 51,874
Library Holdings: Bk Vols 41,605; Per Subs 47
Subject Interests: Local hist, SW
Automation Activity & Vendor Info: (Circulation) TLC (The Library Corporation); (OPAC) TLC (The Library Corporation)
Wireless access
Function: 24/7 Electronic res, 24/7 Online cat, Activity rm, Adult bk club, Archival coll, Art exhibits, Audiobks via web, Bilingual assistance for Spanish patrons, Bk club(s), Bks on cassette, Bks on CD, CD-ROM, Chess club, Children's prog, Computer training, Computers for patron use, Digital talking bks, Distance learning, E-Reserves, Electronic databases & coll, Free DVD rentals, Holiday prog, Homebound delivery serv, Homework prog, ILL available, Internet access, Life-long learning prog for all ages, Literacy & newcomer serv, Magazines, Mail & tel request accepted, Meeting rooms, Microfiche/film & reading machines, Movies, Museum passes, Music CDs, Notary serv, Online cat, Online ref, Outreach serv, OverDrive digital audio bks, Photocopying/Printing, Preschool reading prog, Prog for adults, Prog for children & young adult, Ref serv available, Res assist avail, Senior computer classes, Senior outreach, Serves people with intellectual disabilities, Spanish lang bks, Spoken cassettes & CDs, STEM programs, Story hour, Summer reading prog, Tax forms, Teen prog, VHS videos, Wheelchair accessible
Open Mon-Fri 10-4
Restriction: Non-circulating of rare bks
Friends of the Library Group

BERNALILLO

P MARTHA LIEBERT PUBLIC LIBRARY, 124 Calle Malinche, 87004. (Mail add: PO Box 638, 87004-0638), SAN 310-6535. Tel: 505-867-1440. FAX: 505-771-3926. E-mail: toblibrary@townofbernalillo.org. Web Site: www.townofbernalillo.org/departments/public_library. *Libr Dir,* Joseph Mckenzie; E-mail: jmckenzie@townofbernalillo.org; Staff 2 (MLS 1, Non-MLS 1)
Founded 1965. Pop 9,000
Library Holdings: Audiobooks 380; DVDs 1,019; e-books 4,000; Large Print Bks 302; Bk Titles 19,000; Per Subs 26
Special Collections: Historical Coll of Southwest; Spanish Titles Coll
Wireless access
Function: Adult bk club, Adult literacy prog, After school storytime, Audio & video playback equip for onsite use, Audiobks via web, Bilingual assistance for Spanish patrons, ILL available, Internet access, Magazines, Meeting rooms, Museum passes, Online cat, Online ref, Outreach serv, Photocopying/Printing, Prog for adults, Prog for children & young adult, Ref serv available, Scanner, STEM programs, Story hour, Study rm, Summer reading prog, Teen prog, Wheelchair accessible
Special Services for the Blind - Accessible computers; Bks on CD
Open Mon-Fri 9:30-5:30, Sat 9-1
Friends of the Library Group

P SANTA ANA PUEBLO COMMUNITY LIBRARY, Two Dove Rd, 87004. Tel: 505-771-6736. FAX: 505-771-3849. Web Site: santaana-nsn.gov/library. *Dir,* Cassandra Zamora; E-mail: cassandra.zamora@santaana-nsn.gov
Pop 727
Library Holdings: AV Mats 2,000; Bk Vols 10,000; Per Subs 40
Wireless access
Open Mon-Fri 10-5

BLOOMFIELD

P BLOOMFIELD PUBLIC LIBRARY*, 333 S First St, 87413-3559. SAN 375-5207. Tel: 505-632-8315. FAX: 505-632-0876. E-mail: bloomfieldlibrary@bloomfieldnm.com. Web Site: www.bloomfieldnm.gov/library. *Dir, Libr Serv,* Mr Corey Bard; E-mail: cbard@bloomfieldnm.gov; Staff 1 (MLS 1)
Founded 1990. Pop 7,304; Circ 22,007
Library Holdings: AV Mats 300; Bk Vols 20,000; Per Subs 25; Videos 100
Automation Activity & Vendor Info: (Cataloging) Insignia Software; (Circulation) Insignia Software
Wireless access
Special Services for the Deaf - Bks on deafness & sign lang; High interest/low vocabulary bks
Special Services for the Blind - Talking bks
Open Mon 9-7:30, Tues-Thurs 9-6:30, Fri 9-12 & 1-4
Friends of the Library Group

S SAN JUAN COUNTY ARCHAEOLOGICAL RESEARCH CENTER & LIBRARY AT SALMON RUINS, Salmon Ruins Museum, 6131 US Hwy 64, 87413. (Mail add: PO Box 125, 87413-0125), SAN 326-2480. Tel: 505-632-2013. E-mail: sreducation@sisna.com. Web Site: www.salmonruins.com. *Exec Dir,* Larry L Baker; *Curator, Research Librn,* Tori L Myers. Subject Specialists: *Archaeology, Archit, Presv,* Larry L Baker; *Archaeology, Local hist,* Tori L Myers; Staff 3 (MLS 1, Non-MLS 2)
Founded 1973
Library Holdings: DVDs 10; e-books 100; Bk Titles 6,000; Per Subs 200; Spec Interest Per Sub 170; Videos 20
Special Collections: Hadlock, Rothrock & Rodgers Coll (Local Documentation of Rock Art Sites, Symbolism, Interpretation), photog, slides; Salmon Ruins Coll (Salmon Ruin Excavation & Preservation Records), photog, slides & research documentation; San Juan County Historical File (Local Information Related to Genealogy, Homesteading, Photos, Archaeological Sites, Newspaper Articles); Snyder Coll (Civilian Conservation Corps); Turbull Coll (San Juan Episcopal Mission Records); Wynhoff Coll (Native Plant Identification & Botanic Examples). Oral History
Subject Interests: Anthrop, Archaeology, Local hist, NMex, SW
Publications: San Juan County Museum Association (Documents)
Open Mon-Fri 8-5
Restriction: Authorized patrons, Authorized scholars by appt, Borrowing privileges limited to anthropology fac & libr staff, Circ to mem only, Restricted borrowing privileges, Secured area only open to authorized personnel
Friends of the Library Group

BOSQUE FARMS

P BOSQUE FARMS PUBLIC LIBRARY*, 1455 W Bosque Loop, 87068. SAN 373-8167. Tel: 505-869-2227. FAX: 505-869-3342. Web Site: bosquefarmsnm.gov/public-library, library.bosquefarmsnm.gov. *Libr Dir,* Amanda Carrasco-Vigil; E-mail: a.vigil@bosquefarmsnm.gov
Founded 1985. Pop 3,931; Circ 25,311
Library Holdings: Bk Titles 25,000
Automation Activity & Vendor Info: (Cataloging) Follett Software; (Circulation) Follett Software; (OPAC) Follett Software
Open Mon-Thurs 10-5, Fri & Sat 10-2
Friends of the Library Group

CANNON AFB

A UNITED STATES AIR FORCE, Cannon Air Force Base Library FL4855, 27 SOFSS/FSDL, 107 Albright Ave, Bldg 75, 88103-5211. SAN 351-6393. Tel: 575-784-2786. FAX: 575-784-6929. E-mail: 27sow.library@us.af.mil. Web Site: www.cannonlibrary.org. *Head Librn,* Melissa Haraughty; E-mail: melissa.haraughty.1@us.af.mil; Staff 5 (MLS 1, Non-MLS 4)
Library Holdings: Bk Vols 25,000; Per Subs 70
Automation Activity & Vendor Info: (Acquisitions) SirsiDynix; (Cataloging) SirsiDynix; (Circulation) SirsiDynix; (Serials) SirsiDynix
Wireless access
Open Mon-Thurs 9-7, Fri & Sat 9-3

CAPITAN

P CAPITAN PUBLIC LIBRARY*, 102 E Second St, 88316. (Mail add: PO Box 1169, 88316-1169). Tel: 575-354-3035. FAX: 575-354-3223. E-mail: capitanlibrary@gmail.com. Web Site: www.capitanlibrary.org. *Board Pres,* Bill Jeffrey; *Dir,* Pat Garrett; *Asst Dir,* Debra Myers; *Cataloger,* Barbara Stewart
Founded 1996. Pop 2,000; Circ 10,000
Automation Activity & Vendor Info: (Cataloging) Biblionix; (Circulation) Biblionix/Apollo
Wireless access
Function: Adult bk club, After school storytime, Art exhibits, Bi-weekly Writer's Group, Bks on CD, Children's prog, Computers for patron use, Holiday prog, ILL available, Internet access, Magazines, Meeting rooms, Museum passes, Online cat, Photocopying/Printing, Preschool outreach, Prog for adults, Prog for children & young adult, Ref & res, Satellite serv, Scanner, Senior computer classes, Summer reading prog, Tax forms, VHS videos, Wheelchair accessible
Open Tues-Thurs 10-6, Fri & Sat 10-2
Friends of the Library Group

CAPULIN

G US NATIONAL PARK SERVICE, Capulin Volcano National Monument Library, 46 Volcano Rd, 88414. (Mail add: PO Box 40, Des Moines, 88418). Tel: 575-278-2201, Ext 231. FAX: 575-278-2211. Web Site: www.nps.gov/cavo. *Library Contact,* Position Currently Open
Library Holdings: Bk Titles 1,455; Bk Vols 1,500
Open Mon-Sun 8-4:30

CARLSBAD

P CARLSBAD PUBLIC LIBRARY, 101 S Halagueno St, 88220. SAN 310-6543. Tel: 575-885-6776. E-mail: cplinfo@cityofcarlsbadnm.com. Web Site: cityofcarlsbadnm.com/departments/carlsbad-public-library. *Dir,* Sarah Jones; E-mail: sejones@cityofcarlsbadnm.com; *Asst Dir,* Position Currently Open; *Ad,* Terry Busby; E-mail: tdbusby@cityofcarlsbadnm.com; *Youth Serv Librn,* Beth Nieman; E-mail: banieman@cityofcarlsbadnm.com; Staff 6 (MLS 3, Non-MLS 3)
Founded 1897. Pop 26,000; Circ 77,206
Jul 2017-Jun 2018 Income $806,452, State $56,993, City $746,959, Locally Generated Income $2,500. Mats Exp $74,072, Books $36,994, Per/Ser (Incl. Access Fees) $1,778, AV Mat $8,727, Electronic Ref Mat (Incl. Access Fees) $26,573. Sal $419,652 (Prof $278,423)
Library Holdings: Audiobooks 2,247; Bks on Deafness & Sign Lang 62; CDs 64; DVDs 3,674; e-books 17,046; e-journals 66; Electronic Media & Resources 14; High Interest/Low Vocabulary Bk Vols 32; Large Print Bks 3,924; Bk Titles 49,688; Bk Vols 53,086; Per Subs 22
Special Collections: Children's Music; Large Print; New Mexico History; Science Projects; Spanish books for adults & children; SW Archives; Teen section
Automation Activity & Vendor Info: (Acquisitions) Biblionix/Apollo; (Cataloging) Biblionix/Apollo; (Circulation) Biblionix/Apollo; (ILL) OCLC ILLiad; (OPAC) Biblionix/Apollo; (Serials) Biblionix/Apollo
Wireless access
Function: 24/7 Electronic res, 24/7 Online cat, Accelerated reader prog, Activity rm, Archival coll, Audiobks via web, Bilingual assistance for Spanish patrons, Bks on CD, Children's prog, Computer training, Computers for patron use, Distance learning, Doc delivery serv, E-Readers, E-Reserves, Electronic databases & coll, Free DVD rentals, Holiday prog, Home delivery & serv to seniorr ctr & nursing homes, Homebound delivery serv, ILL available, Internet access, Large print keyboards, Magazines, Magnifiers for reading, Mail & tel request accepted, Mango lang, Movies, Museum passes, Music CDs, Online cat, Online info literacy tutorials on the web & in blackboard, Online ref, Outreach serv, Outside serv via phone, mail, e-mail & web, OverDrive digital audio bks, Photocopying/Printing, Preschool outreach, Preschool reading prog, Printer for laptops & handheld devices, Prog for adults, Prog for children & young adult, Scanner, Spanish lang bks, Story hour, Summer reading prog, Tax forms, Teen prog, Telephone ref, Wheelchair accessible
Publications: Friends of the Library Newletter (Quarterly)
Special Services for the Deaf - Bks on deafness & sign lang; Closed caption videos; Sign lang interpreter upon request for prog
Special Services for the Blind - Accessible computers; Aids for in-house use; Audio mat; Bks & mags in Braille, on rec, tape & cassette; Bks available with recordings; Bks on CD; Copier with enlargement capabilities; Extensive large print coll; Free checkout of audio mat; Home delivery serv; Internet workstation with adaptive software; Large print bks; Large screen computer & software; Lending of low vision aids; Magnifiers; Talking bk serv referral; ZoomText magnification & reading software
Open Mon-Thurs 9-8, Fri & Sat 9-6
Restriction: Non-circulating of rare bks
Friends of the Library Group

J SOUTHEAST NEW MEXICO COLLEGE*, Library, (Formerly New Mexico State University at Carlsbad), 1500 University Dr, 88220. SAN 310-6551. Tel: 575-234-9330. Web Site: senmc.edu/. *Libr Dir,* Samantha Villa; E-mail: svilla@senmc.edu; Staff 4 (MLS 1, Non-MLS 3)
Highest Degree: Associate
Library Holdings: Bk Titles 20,000; Per Subs 100
Wireless access
Partic in New Mexico Consortium of Academic Libraries
Open Mon-Thurs 8-8, Fri 8-5, Sat Noon-2

S TFE (TECHNICAL FIELD ENGINEERS)*, WIPP Technical Library, 4021 National Parks Hwy, 88220. (Mail add: PO Box 2078, 88221-5608), SAN 323-7605. Tel: 575-234-7618. FAX: 575-234-7076. *Library Contact,* Maelene Soto; Staff 1 (Non-MLS 1)
Library Holdings: Bk Vols 1,821; Per Subs 20
Subject Interests: Waste mgt
Wireless access
Restriction: Not open to pub

CHAMA

P ELEANOR DAGGETT PUBLIC LIBRARY, 299 W Fourth St, 87520-0786. (Mail add: PO Box 795, 87520-0795), SAN 310-6578. Tel: 575-756-2184. FAX: 575-756-2412. E-mail: chamalib64@yahoo.com. *Dir,* Yvonne Martinez; Staff 1 (Non-MLS 1)
Founded 1973. Pop 1,070; Circ 3,900
Library Holdings: Bk Vols 15,000; Per Subs 27
Special Collections: Southwest Coll
Wireless access
Function: Adult bk club, Audio & video playback equip for onsite use, Bks on cassette, Bks on CD, Children's prog, Electronic databases & coll, Free DVD rentals, ILL available, Photocopying/Printing, Preschool outreach, Spoken cassettes & CDs, Spoken cassettes & DVDs, Story hour, Summer reading prog, Tax forms, VHS videos, Wheelchair accessible
Partic in NMex Info Systs
Open Mon-Fri 8-12 & 1-5

CIMARRON

S NATIONAL SCOUTING MUSEUM*, Philmont Scout Ranch Library, Philmont Scout Ranch, 17 Deer Run Rd, 87714. SAN 310-6594. Tel: 575-376-1136, 575-376-2281, Ext 1256. FAX: 575-376-2602. Web Site: www.philmontscoutranch.org. *Dir,* David I Werhane; E-mail: david.werhane@scouting.org; *Librn,* Dee Dee Montoya; E-mail: denise.montoya@scouting.org; *Curator,* Nancy Klein; Tel: 575-376-2281, Ext 1271, E-mail: nancy.klein@scouting.org
Library Holdings: Bk Vols 7,500; Per Subs 12
Special Collections: Artifacts & Jewelry (Indian Coll); Natural History (Boy Scout Coll)
Subject Interests: SW hist
Open Mon-Fri 8-5

CLAYTON

P CLAYTON PUBLIC LIBRARY, Albert W Thompson Memorial Library, 17 Chestnut St, 88415. SAN 310-6608. Tel: 575-374-9423. FAX: 575-374-2307. E-mail: clayton.nmlibrary@gmail.com. Web Site: thompson.biblionix.com. *Librn,* Ann Reeser; Staff 1 (MLS 1)
Founded 1920. Pop 3,500; Circ 11,450
Library Holdings: Bk Titles 16,000; Bk Vols 18,300; Per Subs 15
Special Collections: New Mexico & Southwest, bks, filmstrips
Partic in NMex Info Systs
Open Mon, Wed, Fri & Sat 9-5, Tues & Thus 9-6:30

CLOUDCROFT

P MICHAEL NIVISON PUBLIC LIBRARY*, 90 Swallow Pl, 88317. (Mail add: PO Box 515, 88317-0515). Tel: 575-682-1111. FAX: 575-682-1111. E-mail: library@tularosa.net. Web Site: users.apo.nmsu.edu/~jb/library. *Dir,* Joyce Komraus
Library Holdings: AV Mats 24; CDs 50; DVDs 100; Bk Vols 13,600; Talking Bks 1,000
Automation Activity & Vendor Info: (Cataloging) Follett Software; (Circulation) Follett Software
Wireless access
Open Mon & Sat 10-3, Tues 12-5, Thurs 10-6, Fri 10-5
Friends of the Library Group

CLOVIS

P CLOVIS-CARVER PUBLIC LIBRARY, 701 N Main, 88101. SAN 310-6616. Tel: 505-769-7840. FAX: 505-769-7842. E-mail: library@cityofclovis.org. Web Site: www.cityofclovis.org/library. *Libr Dir,* Margaret Hinchee; E-mail: mhinchee@cityofclovis.org; *Libr Spec, Ref,* John Conrad Laun; E-mail: jlaun@cityofclovis.org; *Libr Spec, Ref,* Lijewski Michael; E-mail: mlijewski@cityovclovis.org; *Circ Supvr,* Scott

Jones; E-mail: sjones@cityofclovis.org; *Coord, Ad Serv, ILL,* Sara Williford; E-mail: swilliford@cityofclovis.org; Staff 15 (MLS 1, Non-MLS 14)
Founded 1949. Pop 37,000; Circ 171,029
Jul 2016-Jun 2017 Income $883,254, State $12,797, City $809,735, Locally Generated Income $60,722. Mats Exp $92,276, Books $69,635, Per/Ser (Incl. Access Fees) $4,122, AV Mat $3,965, Electronic Ref Mat (Incl. Access Fees) $14,554
Library Holdings: AV Mats 5,848; e-books 3,529; Large Print Bks 3,122; Bk Vols 124,125; Per Subs 155
Special Collections: New Mexico Documents. State Document Depository
Subject Interests: SW
Automation Activity & Vendor Info: (Cataloging) Book Systems; (Circulation) Book Systems; (ILL) OCLC WorldShare Interlibrary Loan; (OPAC) Book Systems
Wireless access
Partic in NMex Info Systs; OCLC Online Computer Library Center, Inc
Special Services for the Blind - Talking bks
Open Mon-Thurs 9-8, Fri & Sat 9-5
Friends of the Library Group

J CLOVIS COMMUNITY COLLEGE LIBRARY*, 417 Schepps Blvd, 88101. SAN 310-6624. Tel: 575-769-4080. FAX: 575-769-4190. E-mail: ccclib@clovis.edu. Web Site: www.clovis.edu. *Dean, Libr Serv,* Ms Robbie Kunkel; E-mail: robbie.kunkel@cloviscollege.edu; *Dir,* Dr Curtis Chapman; Tel: 575-769-4179; *Circ Tech,* Karen Jones; Tel: 575-769-4148, E-mail: karen.jones@clovis.edu; Staff 2 (MLS 2)
Founded 1969. Enrl 4,000; Fac 60; Highest Degree: Associate
Library Holdings: Bks on Deafness & Sign Lang 200; DVDs 300; Bk Titles 45,000; Bk Vols 70,000; Per Subs 300; Videos 1,700
Special Collections: Rare Books (Some Autographed); Southwest Coll
Subject Interests: SW Am
Automation Activity & Vendor Info: (Acquisitions) Innovative Interfaces, Inc; (Cataloging) Innovative Interfaces, Inc; (Circulation) Innovative Interfaces, Inc; (OPAC) Innovative Interfaces, Inc; (Serials) Innovative Interfaces, Inc
Wireless access
Publications: Bibliographies
Partic in Leann; New Mexico Consortium of Academic Libraries
Open Mon-Thurs 7:30am-8pm, Fri 8-4:30; Mon-Thurs 8-7, Fri 8-4:30 (Summer)

COCHITI LAKE

P IRENE S SWEETKIND PUBLIC LIBRARY*, 6515A Hoochaneetsa Blvd, 87083. SAN 375-4359. Tel: 505-465-2561. FAX: 505-465-3009. E-mail: library@cochitilake.org. Web Site: www.cochitilake.org/cv. *Libr Dir,* Mary Badarak
Library Holdings: Bk Vols 9,800
Special Collections: Southwest Coll
Subject Interests: Arizona, Colorado, NMex, Tex, Utah
Automation Activity & Vendor Info: (Cataloging) Follett Software
Wireless access
Open Mon-Wed 11-5, Thurs 2-7, Fri 2-6, Sat 10-1
Friends of the Library Group

COCHITI PUEBLO

P COCHITI PUEBLO COMMUNITY LIBRARY, 245 Cochiti St, 87072. (Mail add: PO Box 70, 87072-0070), SAN 321-7515. Tel: 505-465-3118. FAX: 505-465-2203. *Dir,* Geraldine Jojola; E-mail: geraldine_jojola@pueblodecochiti.org
Founded 1977
Library Holdings: Bk Titles 4,700
Special Collections: Cochiti History; Cochiti Pueblo Past & Present, photogs
Wireless access
Open Mon-Fri 8-5

COLUMBUS

P COLUMBUS VILLAGE LIBRARY*, 112 W Broadway Ave, 88029. (Mail add: PO Box 270, 88029-0270). Tel: 575-531-2612. E-mail: columbuslibrary@vtc.net. Web Site: columbus.biblionix.com/catalog. *Dir,* Maria Constantine; *Youth Librn,* Maggie Calderon; *Asst Librn,* Rosario Pando
Pop 1,660
Special Collections: Pancho Villa raid in 1916
Wireless access
Function: 24/7 Electronic res, 24/7 Online cat, Accelerated reader prog, Activity rm, Adult bk club, Art exhibits, Art programs, Audiobks via web, Bilingual assistance for Spanish patrons, Bk club(s), Bks on CD, Citizenship assistance, Computer training, Computers for patron use, For res purposes, Free DVD rentals, Govt ref serv, Holiday prog, ILL available, Internet access, Laminating, Magazines, Meeting rooms, Movies, Museum passes, Prog for adults, Prog for children & young adult, Spanish lang bks, Summer reading prog, Tax forms, Wheelchair accessible, Workshops
Open Mon-Fri 8-5
Friends of the Library Group

CORRALES

P CORRALES COMMUNITY LIBRARY*, 84 W La Entrada Rd, 87048. (Mail add: PO Box 1868, 87048-1868), SAN 310-6632. Tel: 505-897-0733. FAX: 505-897-0596. E-mail: info@corraleslibrary.org. Web Site: www.corraleslibrary.org. *Dir,* Marian Frear; E-mail: marian@corraleslibrary.org
Founded 1957. Pop 7,500
Library Holdings: Bk Vols 36,000; Per Subs 70
Special Collections: Southwest Coll
Automation Activity & Vendor Info: (Acquisitions) BiblioMondo; (Cataloging) BiblioMondo; (Circulation) BiblioMondo
Wireless access
Open Mon & Fri 10-5, Tues & Thurs 11-8, Wed 10-7, Sat 10-1
Friends of the Library Group

CROWNPOINT

J DINE COLLEGE*, Crownpoint Campus Library, State Hwy 371 & Navajo Service Rte 9, 87313. (Mail add: PO Box 500, 87313). Tel: 505-786-7391, Ext 7205. FAX: 505-786-5240. E-mail: library@dinecollege.edu. Web Site: library.dinecollege.edu. *Col Librn,* Herman Peterson
Library Holdings: AV Mats 300; Bk Titles 4,000; Talking Bks 100
Automation Activity & Vendor Info: (Acquisitions) Ex Libris Group; (Cataloging) Ex Libris Group; (Circulation) Ex Libris Group; (OPAC) Ex Libris Group
Open Mon-Thurs 10-7, Fri 8-5

§C NAVAJO TECHNICAL UNIVERSITY LIBRARY, Lowerpoint Rd, State Hwy 371, 87313. Tel: 505-387-7521. Web Site: www.navajotech.edu/students/library. *Circ Supvr,* Marla Price; Tel: 505-387-7469, E-mail: mprice@navajotech.edu
Wireless access
Function: ILL available, Meeting rooms
Partic in New Mexico Consortium of Academic Libraries
Open Mon-Fri 8-5

CUBA

P CUBA PUBLIC LIBRARY*, 13 E Cordova Ave, 87013. (Mail add: PO Box 426, 87013-0426), SAN 321-4680. Tel: 575-289-3100. FAX: 575-289-9187. E-mail: cubalib2001@yahoo.com. *Dir, Libr Serv Mgr,* Barbara Trujillo
Founded 1962. Pop 13,960
Library Holdings: Bk Titles 23,400; Per Subs 51
Special Collections: Southwest Coll
Automation Activity & Vendor Info: (Acquisitions) Follett Software; (Circulation) Follett Software
Wireless access
Function: Outside serv via phone, mail, e-mail & web, Prog for children & young adult, Ref serv available, Summer reading prog, Telephone ref, VHS videos, Wheelchair accessible, Workshops
Open Mon-Fri 8-5
Restriction: Circ to mem only, Open to pub for ref & circ; with some limitations, Open to pub with supv only, Open to students, fac & staff, Photo ID required for access, Pub use on premises, Restricted loan policy, Use of others with permission of librn
Friends of the Library Group
Bookmobiles: 1

DATIL

P BALDWIN CABIN PUBLIC LIBRARY*, Cibola National Forest, Forest Rd 100, 87821. (Mail add: PO Box 255, 87821-0255). Tel: 575-772-5230. Administration Tel: 575-772-5730. *Dir,* Linn Kennedy
Founded 1999. Pop 1,200; Circ 2,900
Library Holdings: AV Mats 400; Bks on Deafness & Sign Lang 3; CDs 40; DVDs 70; Large Print Bks 85; Bk Titles 20,000; Talking Bks 200
Special Collections: Cibola National Forest Coll; Southwest Coll
Function: Children's prog, Holiday prog, Prog for adults
Open Mon, Thurs & Sat 9-Noon
Friends of the Library Group

DEMING

P MARSHALL MEMORIAL LIBRARY*, 110 S Diamond St, 88030-3698. SAN 310-6640. Tel: 575-546-9202. FAX: 505-546-9649. E-mail: demingpl@cityofdeming.org. Web Site: www1.youseemore.com/marshall. *Interim Dir,* Angela Wilds; E-mail: awilds@cityofdeming.org; *Circ,* Jeannie Keeler; Staff 5 (Non-MLS 5)
Founded 1917. Pop 18,000; Circ 184,880

Library Holdings: Bk Vols 68,133; Per Subs 100
Special Collections: Southwest Coll
Subject Interests: SW US fiction
Automation Activity & Vendor Info: (Cataloging) TLC (The Library Corporation); (Circulation) TLC (The Library Corporation)
Wireless access
Function: ILL available
Publications: Information Brochure
Open Tues-Fri 8-7:45
Friends of the Library Group

DEXTER

P DEXTER PUBLIC LIBRARY*, 115 E Second St, 88230. (Mail add: PO Box 249, 88230). Tel: 575-734-5482. FAX: 575-734-6605.
Library Holdings: Bk Vols 12,000
Wireless access
Open Mon-Fri 8-12:30 & 1-4:30

DIXON

P EMBUDO VALLEY LIBRARY*, 217A Hwy 75, 87527. (Mail add: PO Box 310, 87527-0310). Tel: 505-579-9181. FAX: 505-579-9128. E-mail: librarian@embudovalleylibrary.org. Web Site: www.embudovalleylibrary.org. *Dir,* Felicity Fonseca; *Head Librn,* Minna Santos; *Asst Librn,* Shirley Atencio; Staff 3 (Non-MLS 3)
Founded 1992. Pop 1,428; Circ 12,853
Library Holdings: AV Mats 2,655; Bk Vols 12,779; Per Subs 45
Automation Activity & Vendor Info: (Acquisitions) Book Systems; (Cataloging) Book Systems; (Circulation) Book Systems; (ILL) OCLC ILLiad; (OPAC) Book Systems
Wireless access
Function: 24/7 Electronic res, 24/7 Online cat, Activity rm, Adult literacy prog, After school storytime, Archival coll, Art exhibits, Audio & video playback equip for onsite use, Audiobks via web, AV serv, Bk reviews (Group), Bks on cassette, Bks on CD, Butterfly Garden, CD-ROM, Children's prog, Computer training, Computers for patron use, Digital talking bks, Distance learning, E-Readers, E-Reserves, Electronic databases & coll, Family literacy, For res purposes, Free DVD rentals, Games & aids for people with disabilities, Govt ref serv, Health sci info serv, Holiday prog, Homework prog, ILL available, Instruction & testing, Internet access, Laminating, Learning ctr, Life-long learning prog for all ages, Literacy & newcomer serv, Magazines, Magnifiers for reading, Mail & tel request accepted, Meeting rooms, Movies, Music CDs, Notary serv, Online cat, Online ref, Outreach serv, Outside serv via phone, mail, e-mail & web, OverDrive digital audio bks, Photocopying/Printing, Preschool outreach, Preschool reading prog, Printer for laptops & handheld devices, Prog for adults, Prog for children & young adult, Ref & res, Ref serv available, Res libr, Scanner, Senior computer classes, Senior outreach, Serves people with intellectual disabilities, Spanish lang bks, Spoken cassettes & CDs, Spoken cassettes & DVDs, Story hour, Summer & winter reading prog, Summer reading prog, Tax forms, Teen prog, Telephone ref, VHS videos, Visual arts prog, Wheelchair accessible, Winter reading prog, Workshops
Open Mon-Fri 11-6, Sat 11-5

EAGLE NEST

P EAGLE NEST PUBLIC LIBRARY*, 74 N Tomboy Dr, 87718. (Mail add: PO Box 168, 87718-0168). Tel: 575-377-0657. E-mail: eaglenestlibrary@gmail.com. Web Site: eaglenestlibrary.org. *Dir,* Ron Andersen
Pop 278; Circ 2,355
Library Holdings: AV Mats 675; Bk Vols 6,000; Talking Bks 150
Wireless access
Open Mon & Tues 9:30-5:30, Thurs & Fri 9:30-5

EDGEWOOD

P EDGEWOOD COMMUNITY LIBRARY*, 171 B State Rd 344, 87015. (Mail add: PO Box 3610, 87015), SAN 375-5029. Tel: 505-281-0138. FAX: 505-286-9107. E-mail: ecl_cat@yahoo.com. Web Site: www.edgewood-nm.gov/1079/Library. *Librn,* Andrea Corvin; E-mail: acorvin@edgewood-nm.gov; *Asst Librn,* Barbara Hambek; E-mail: bhambek@edgewood-nm.gov
Founded 1991. Pop 2,700; Circ 21,372
Library Holdings: DVDs 340; Bk Titles 18,106
Automation Activity & Vendor Info: (Cataloging) Biblionix; (Circulation) Biblionix
Wireless access
Open Mon-Fri 10-6, Sat 10-3
Friends of the Library Group

EL RITO

P EL RITO PUBLIC LIBRARY*, 182 Placitas Rd, 87530. (Mail add: PO Box 5, 87530-0005). Tel: 575-581-4608. FAX: 575-581-9591. E-mail: info@elritolibrary.org. Web Site: www.elritolibrary.org. *Dir,* Lynette Gillette; *Librn,* Thomas Fortson
Founded 1986
Library Holdings: CDs 100; Bk Vols 16,000; Per Subs 15; Videos 500
Automation Activity & Vendor Info: (Cataloging) Follett Software; (Circulation) Follett Software; (Course Reserve) Follett Software
Wireless access
Open Tues-Fri 12-5, Sat 9-2

ESPANOLA

P ESPANOLA PUBLIC LIBRARY, 313 N Paseo de Onate, 87532. SAN 310-6659. Tel: 505-747-6087. Circulation Tel: 505-747-6088. FAX: 505-747-6160. E-mail: espanolalibrary@yahoo.com. Web Site: www.cityofespanola.org/165/Espaola-Public-Library. *Libr Dir,* Sherry Aragon; E-mail: saragon@espanolanm.gov; Staff 6 (Non-MLS 6)
Founded 1969. Pop 14,000; Circ 40,707
Library Holdings: AV Mats 900; Bk Vols 43,000; Per Subs 102
Special Collections: Southwest Coll; Spanish Language Coll
Automation Activity & Vendor Info: (Cataloging) TLC (The Library Corporation); (Circulation) TLC (The Library Corporation); (ILL) TLC (The Library Corporation); (OPAC) TLC (The Library Corporation); (Serials) TLC (The Library Corporation)
Wireless access
Partic in NMex Info Systs
Open Mon-Fri 8-11 & 1-4
Friends of the Library Group

J NORTHERN NEW MEXICO COLLEGE*, Ben Lujan Library, 921 Paseo de Onate, 87532. SAN 310-7108. Tel: 505-747-2100. Circulation Tel: 505-747-2243. Administration FAX: 505-747-2244. E-mail: library@nnmc.edu. Web Site: nnmc.libguides.com. *Libr Dir,* Courtney Bruch; E-mail: courtney.bruch@nnmc.edu; Staff 1 (MLS 1)
Founded 1973. Enrl 1,100
Library Holdings: Microforms 5,000; Bk Titles 40,000; Per Subs 150
Special Collections: Local History
Automation Activity & Vendor Info: (Cataloging) OCLC; (Circulation) Innovative Interfaces, Inc; (ILL) OCLC; (OPAC) Innovative Interfaces, Inc; (Serials) EBSCO Online
Wireless access
Partic in New Mexico Consortium of Academic Libraries
Open Mon-Thurs 8-7:30, Fri 8-5

P SANTA CLARA PUEBLO COMMUNITY LIBRARY*, 578 Kee St, 87532. SAN 310-6667. Tel: 505-692-6295. E-mail: sclib@santaclarapueblo.org. Web Site: santaclarapueblocommunitylibrary.com. *Librn,* Teresa Naranjo; *IT Tech,* Ron Suazo
Circ 6,984
Library Holdings: Bk Titles 7,000; Bk Vols 8,535; Per Subs 60
Special Collections: Southwest Indian Special Coll
Subject Interests: Native Am
Wireless access
Partic in New Mexico Libr Asn Round Table
Open Mon-Thurs 8-6, Fri 8-4:30

ESTANCIA

P ESTANCIA PUBLIC LIBRARY*, 601 S Tenth St, 87016. (Mail add: PO Box 166, 87016-0166), SAN 373-837X. Tel: 505-384-9655. FAX: 505-384-3023. E-mail: estanciapblib@townofestancia.com. Web Site: www.townofestancia.com/index.php?page=library. *Head Librn,* Angela Creamer; *Asst Librn,* Ivonne Chavarria; Staff 2 (Non-MLS 2)
Founded 1908. Pop 1,500; Circ 2,200
Library Holdings: Bk Vols 10,500; Per Subs 20
Special Collections: New Mexico & the Southwest (Southwest Coll)
Automation Activity & Vendor Info: (Cataloging) Follett Software
Wireless access
Open Mon-Fri 9-5

EUNICE

P EUNICE PUBLIC LIBRARY*, 1003 Ave N, 88231. (Mail add: PO Box 1629, 88231-1629), SAN 310-6675. Tel: 575-394-2336, 575-394-2338. FAX: 575-394-0970. E-mail: eunplib@valornet.com. Web Site: elinlib.org. *Libr Dir,* Tara G Parker; E-mail: tparker@elinlib.org; *Ch,* Melinda Cowan; E-mail: cowanmk@hotmail.com; *Ch Asst,* Margie Tipton; Staff 3 (Non-MLS 3)
Founded 1957. Pop 2,922; Circ 13,524
Jul 2017-Jun 2018 Income $260,851, State $5,672, City $238,000, Federal $1,796, County $10,000, Locally Generated Income $2,315, Other $3,068.

Mats Exp $17,481, Books $14,000, Per/Ser (Incl. Access Fees) $354, AV Mat $2,127, Electronic Ref Mat (Incl. Access Fees) $1,000. Sal $97,871 (Prof $43,000)
Library Holdings: Audiobooks 732; AV Mats 944; DVDs 613; Electronic Media & Resources 202; Bk Titles 23,425; Per Subs 28; Videos 50
Special Collections: Christian Books (Family Coll)
Subject Interests: Livestock, NMex, Oil field, SW
Automation Activity & Vendor Info: (Acquisitions) SirsiDynix-Unicorn; (Cataloging) OCLC CatExpress; (Circulation) SirsiDynix-WorkFlows; (OPAC) SirsiDynix-WorkFlows
Wireless access
Function: Bks on cassette, Bks on CD, Children's prog, Computers for patron use, Free DVD rentals, Homebound delivery serv, ILL available, Internet access, Notary serv, Online cat, Photocopying/Printing, Res libr, Story hour, Summer reading prog, Tax forms, Telephone ref, VHS videos
Partic in Estacado Library Information Network; NMex Libr Asn; OCLC Online Computer Library Center, Inc
Special Services for the Deaf - ADA equip; Bks on deafness & sign lang
Special Services for the Blind - Large print bks; Recorded bks; Sound rec; Talking bks
Open Mon-Thurs 8-5:30, Fri 8-5

FARMINGTON

P FARMINGTON PUBLIC LIBRARY*, 2101 Farmington Ave, 87401. SAN 310-6683. Tel: 505-599-1270. Reference Tel: 505-599-1272. FAX: 505-599-1257. Web Site: www.infoway.org. *Libr Dir,* Karen McPheeters; Tel: 505-599-1275, E-mail: kmcpheet@infoway.org; *Dep Dir,* Mary Lee Smith; Tel: 505-566-2205, E-mail: mlsmith@infoway.org; *Tech Serv Supvr,* Sharon BlueEyes; Tel: 505-599-1274, E-mail: sblueeyes@infoway.org; *Adult Serv Coordr,* Betty Decker; Tel: 505-566-2203, E-mail: bldecker2@infoway.org; *Youth Serv Coordr,* Flo Trujillo; Tel: 505-599-1261, E-mail: ftrujill@infoway.org; Staff 15 (MLS 3, Non-MLS 12)
Founded 1921. Pop 115,169; Circ 484,080
Library Holdings: Audiobooks 4,406; CDs 11,558; DVDs 7,163; e-books 13,691; Electronic Media & Resources 99; Bk Titles 163,926; Per Subs 520
Special Collections: Southwest Coll. State Document Depository; UN Document Depository; US Document Depository
Automation Activity & Vendor Info: (Cataloging) SirsiDynix; (Circulation) SirsiDynix; (Discovery) SirsiDynix-Enterprise; (ILL) OCLC ILLiad; (OPAC) SirsiDynix; (Serials) SirsiDynix
Wireless access
Function: 24/7 Electronic res, 24/7 Online cat, 3D Printer, Adult bk club, After school storytime, Audiobks via web, Bilingual assistance for Spanish patrons, Bk club(s), Bks on CD, Children's prog, Computer training, Computers for patron use, Electronic databases & coll, Family literacy, Free DVD rentals, Holiday prog, ILL available, Internet access, Life-long learning prog for all ages, Magazines, Mango lang, Microfiche/film & reading machines, Music CDs, Notary serv, Online cat, OverDrive digital audio bks, Photocopying/Printing, Preschool reading prog, Printer for laptops & handheld devices, Prog for adults, Prog for children & young adult, Ref & res, Ref serv available, Spanish lang bks, STEM programs, Story hour, Study rm, Summer & winter reading prog, Summer reading prog, Tax forms, Teen prog, Telephone ref, Wheelchair accessible
Open Mon-Thurs 9-9, Fri 9-5, Sat 10-5, Sun 1-5; Mon-Thurs (Summer) 9-7
Friends of the Library Group

J SAN JUAN COLLEGE LIBRARY*, 4601 College Blvd, 87402. SAN 310-6691. Tel: 505-566-3249. Reference Tel: 505-566-3256. Web Site: www.sanjuancollege.edu/learning/departments/library. *Dir, Libr Serv,* Christopher Schipper; Tel: 505-566-3449, E-mail: schipperc@sanjuancollege.edu; *Librn,* Danielle Burbank; Tel: 505-566-3100, E-mail: burbankd@sanjuancollege.edu; *Sr Admin Assoc,* Cindy Williams; E-mail: williams_c@sanjuancollege.edu; Staff 9 (MLS 4, Non-MLS 5)
Founded 1964. Enrl 5,000; Fac 110; Highest Degree: Associate
Jul 2012-Jun 2013 Income $688,312. Mats Exp $317,852. Sal $317,460
Library Holdings: Bk Vols 77,678; Per Subs 304
Special Collections: San Juan County Law Coll; Southwestern Americana, bks, maps, rpts; Tom Carter Petroleum Geological Coll. State Document Depository
Automation Activity & Vendor Info: (Cataloging) Ex Libris Group; (Circulation) Ex Libris Group; (OPAC) Ex Libris Group
Wireless access
Publications: Information Brochures
Partic in New Mexico Consortium of Academic Libraries; New Mexico Libr Asn Round Table; OCLC Online Computer Library Center, Inc
Open Mon-Thurs (Fall-Spring) 8am-9pm, Fri 8-5, Sat 9-5; Mon-Thurs (Summer) 9-7, Fri 8-5

FORT SUMNER

P FORT SUMNER PUBLIC LIBRARY*, 235 W Sumner Ave, 88119. (Mail add: PO Drawer D, 88119), SAN 310-6713. Tel: 575-355-2832. FAX: 575-355-7732. E-mail: fspl@plateautel.net. Web Site: fspl.booksys.net, www.fortsumner.net/library. *Dir,* Karla Hunt; *Ch,* Heather Davenport; E-mail: ftsumnerpl@plateautel.net
Pop 2,016
Library Holdings: Audiobooks 377; Bks on Deafness & Sign Lang 42; CDs 15; DVDs 208; Large Print Bks 481; Bk Vols 19,012; Per Subs 26; Talking Bks 407; Videos 475
Automation Activity & Vendor Info: (Acquisitions) Book Systems; (Cataloging) Book Systems; (Circulation) Book Systems; (ILL) OCLC ILLiad; (OPAC) Book Systems
Wireless access
Open Mon & Fri 9-5
Friends of the Library Group

GALLUP

P OCTAVIA FELLIN PUBLIC LIBRARY*, 115 W Hill Ave, 87301. SAN 351-6423. Tel: 505-863-1291, Ext 14017. Administration Tel: 505-863-1291, Ext 14016. FAX: 505-722-5090. Reference E-mail: library@GallupNM.gov. Web Site: www.gallupnm.gov/718. *Dir,* Tammi Moe; E-mail: tmoe@gallupnm.gov; *Dep Dir,* Betty Martin; E-mail: bmartin@gallupnm.gov; Staff 5 (MLS 3, Non-MLS 2)
Founded 1928
Library Holdings: AV Mats 3,000; CDs 12,000; DVDs 1,671; Large Print Bks 1,452; Bk Vols 160,000; Per Subs 150
Special Collections: Southwest Coll. Oral History; State Document Depository
Subject Interests: Art, Local hist
Automation Activity & Vendor Info: (Acquisitions) TLC (The Library Corporation); (Cataloging) TLC (The Library Corporation); (Circulation) TLC (The Library Corporation); (OPAC) TLC (The Library Corporation); (Serials) TLC (The Library Corporation)
Wireless access
Publications: Community Resource Directory: An Information & Reference Service, 1978
Partic in NMex Info Systs
Open Mon-Thurs 9-8, Fri 10-6, Sat 9-6
Branches: 1
CHILDREN'S BRANCH, 200 W Aztec Ave, 87301. (Mail add: 115 W Hill Ave, 87301). Tel: 505-726-6120. Web Site: www.gallupnm.gov/Facilities/Facility/Details/Childrens-Library-46. *Mgr, Youth Serv,* Anne Price; E-mail: aprice@gallupnm.gov; Staff 5 (MLS 3, Non-MLS 2)
Founded 1947. Pop 72,000; Circ 300,000
Automation Activity & Vendor Info: (Acquisitions) TLC (The Library Corporation); (Cataloging) TLC (The Library Corporation); (Circulation) TLC (The Library Corporation); (Course Reserve) TLC (The Library Corporation); (ILL) TLC (The Library Corporation); (Media Booking) TLC (The Library Corporation); (Serials) TLC (The Library Corporation)
Open Tues-Thurs 10-7, Fri 10-6, Sat 9-6

C UNIVERSITY OF NEW MEXICO, Zollinger Library, 705 Gurley Ave, 87301. SAN 310-6721. Tel: 505-863-7531. Administration Tel: 505-863-7608. FAX: 505-863-7624. Web Site: www.gallup.unm.edu/library. *Interim Dir,* Jim Fisk; Tel: 505-863-7616, E-mail: fiskj@unm.edu; Staff 7 (MLS 2, Non-MLS 5)
Founded 1970. Enrl 1,600
Library Holdings: Bk Titles 46,000; Per Subs 300
Subject Interests: Educ K-12, Health careers
Function: Electronic databases & coll, Orientations, Photocopying/Printing, Ref serv available, Wheelchair accessible
Partic in New Mexico Consortium of Academic Libraries
Open Mon-Thurs 8-7, Fri 8-3, Sat 10-2

GRANTS

P GRANTS PUBLIC LIBRARY, 1101 N First St, 87020-2526. SAN 310-673X. Tel: 505-287-4793. FAX: 505-285-3818. E-mail: library@grantsnm.gov. Web Site: www.cityofgrants.net/library, www.youseemore.com/whiteside. *Dir,* Nadine Jiron; E-mail: librarydir@grantsnm.gov; Staff 2 (MLS 1, Non-MLS 1)
Founded 1949
Library Holdings: Bk Titles 29,000; Per Subs 20
Subject Interests: Local hist, SW
Automation Activity & Vendor Info: (Cataloging) TLC (The Library Corporation); (Circulation) TLC (The Library Corporation)
Wireless access
Open Mon-Fri 9-5

S NEW MEXICO CORRECTIONS DEPARTMENT*, Western New Mexico Correctional Facility Library, 1121 Lobo Canyon Rd, 87020. SAN 375-4731. Tel: 505-876-8300. FAX: 505-876-8200. Web Site: cd.nm.gov/apd/wnmcf.html. *Librn,* Roxie Cooper
Founded 1975
Library Holdings: Bk Titles 6,000; Per Subs 3
Automation Activity & Vendor Info: (Acquisitions) Follett Software; (Cataloging) Follett Software; (Circulation) Follett Software
Special Services for the Deaf - Bks on deafness & sign lang; High interest/low vocabulary bks
Restriction: Not open to pub

J NEW MEXICO STATE UNIVERSITY AT GRANTS*, Library, 1500 N Third St, 87020. SAN 310-6748. Tel: 505-287-6639. FAX: 505-287-6676. Web Site: grants.nmsu.edu/library. *Dir,* Position Currently Open; *Libr Spec,* Peggy Leslie; Staff 3 (MLS 1, Non-MLS 2)
Founded 1968. Enrl 654; Fac 50; Highest Degree: Associate
Library Holdings: Bk Vols 32,000; Per Subs 35
Special Collections: New Mexico History Coll
Automation Activity & Vendor Info: (Acquisitions) Ex Libris Group; (Cataloging) Ex Libris Group; (Circulation) Ex Libris Group; (OPAC) Ex Libris Group
Wireless access
Function: Computers for patron use, Online cat, Orientations, Photocopying/Printing, Ref & res, Ref serv available, Scanner, Tax forms, Telephone ref
Partic in New Mexico Consortium of Academic Libraries
Open Mon-Thurs 8-8, Fri 8-5, Sat 10-2

HATCH

P HATCH PUBLIC LIBRARY, 530 E Hall, 87937. (Mail add: PO Box 289, 87937-0289), SAN 310-6756. Tel: 575-267-5132. Web Site: villageofhatch.org/arts_and_culture/library_and_history. *Librn,* Lisa Sue Neal; E-mail: lneal@villageofhatch.org
Founded 1946. Pop 1,640; Circ 4,000
Library Holdings: Bk Vols 9,003; Per Subs 5
Open Mon-Fri 10-6, Sat 10-2

HILLSBORO

P HILLSBORO COMMUNITY LIBRARY, 158 Elenora St, 88042. (Mail add: PO Box 205, 88042-0205). Tel: 575-895-3349. FAX: 575-895-3349. E-mail: hbolib@gmail.com. Web Site: www.hillsborocommunitylibrary.com. *Pres,* John Cornell
Pop 400; Circ 1,100
Jan 2019-Dec 2019 Income $3,949, Locally Generated Income $3,749, Other $200. Mats Exp $2,012, Books $1,968, Per/Ser (Incl. Access Fees) $44
Library Holdings: CDs 348; DVDs 1,135; e-books 12; Bk Vols 6,011; Per Subs 2
Automation Activity & Vendor Info: (Cataloging) JayWil Software Development, Inc; (Circulation) JayWil Software Development, Inc; (ILL) OCLC ILLiad; (OPAC) JayWil Software Development, Inc
Wireless access
Function: Bks on CD, Computers for patron use, Free DVD rentals, ILL available, Magazines, Meeting rooms, Music CDs, Online cat, Photocopying/Printing, Ref & res, Scanner, Spanish lang bks, Wheelchair accessible
Special Services for the Blind - Large print bks
Open Tues 3-6, Thurs 3:30-5:30, Fri 10-1, Sat 12-2
Friends of the Library Group

HOBBS

P HOBBS PUBLIC LIBRARY, 509 N Shipp St, 88240. SAN 310-6772. Tel: 575-397-9328. FAX: 575-397-1508. Reference E-mail: reference@elinlib.org. Web Site: hobbspubliclibrary.org. *Libr Dir,* Sandy Farrell; E-mail: sfarrell@elinlib.org; *Access Serv Librn/YA, Digital & Electronic Serv,* Tonya Allen; E-mail: tallen@elinlib.org; *Ch/Children's Serv,* Jamie Robertson; E-mail: jrobertson@elinlib.org; *Ref Librn/Coll Develop,* Robert Hamilton; E-mail: rhamilton@elinlib.org; *Tech Serv Librn,* Melody Maldonado; E-mail: mmaldonado@elinlib.org; Staff 16 (MLS 2, Non-MLS 14)
Founded 1939. Pop 35,000; Circ 104,522
Jul 2013-Jun 2014 Income $1,084,986, State $16,463, City $1,068,523. Mats Exp $135,925, Books $75,358, Per/Ser (Incl. Access Fees) $10,798, Other Print Mats $7,084, Micro $3,013, AV Equip $1,000, AV Mat $15,248, Electronic Ref Mat (Incl. Access Fees) $23,424
Library Holdings: Audiobooks 255; CDs 5,161; DVDs 3,966; e-books 501; e-journals 42; Electronic Media & Resources 15; High Interest/Low Vocabulary Bk Vols 115; Large Print Bks 4,425; Microforms 676; Bk Vols 134,620; Per Subs 86; Spec Interest Per Sub 3; Videos 1,170
Subject Interests: Petroleum, Spanish lang, SW
Automation Activity & Vendor Info: (Cataloging) SirsiDynix; (Circulation) SirsiDynix; (OPAC) SirsiDynix; (Serials) SirsiDynix
Wireless access
Function: Activity rm, After school storytime, Art exhibits, Bks on CD, Children's prog, Computers for patron use, E-Readers, Electronic databases & coll, Free DVD rentals, ILL available, Magazines, Mango lang, Microfiche/film & reading machines, Movies, Music CDs, Online cat, Online ref, OverDrive digital audio bks, Photocopying/Printing, Preschool reading prog, Prog for children & young adult, Spanish lang bks, Story hour, Study rm, Summer reading prog, Tax forms, Teen prog, Wheelchair accessible
Partic in Estacado Library Information Network; OCLC Online Computer Library Center, Inc
Special Services for the Blind - Audio mat; Large print bks
Open Mon 9:30-8, Tues & Wed 9:30-6, Fri & Sat 9:30-5
Friends of the Library Group

J NEW MEXICO JUNIOR COLLEGE*, Pannell Library, One Thunderbird Circle, 88240. SAN 310-6780. Tel: 575-492-2870. FAX: 575-492-2883. E-mail: library@nmjc.edu. Web Site: www.nmjc.edu/resource_service/library. *Librn,* Laurie Muffley; E-mail: lmuffley@nmjc.edu; *Ref Librn,* Kayla Kasprzak; Tel: 575-492-2874, E-mail: kkasprzak@nmjc.edu; *Libr Asst,* Brenda Davis; Tel: 575-492-2875, E-mail: bdavis@nmjc.edu; *Libr Asst,* Mandy Youngblood; E-mail: myoungblood@nmjc.edu; *Libr Tech,* Gail Drennan; E-mail: gdrennan@nmjc.edu; *Libr Tech,* Patricia Sanderson; E-mail: psanderson@nmjc.edu; *Libr Tech,* Cheri West; E-mail: cwest@nmjc.edu; Staff 2 (MLS 2)
Founded 1965. Enrl 3,200; Fac 175; Highest Degree: Associate
Library Holdings: Bk Vols 110,000; Per Subs 343
Special Collections: Oral History; US Document Depository
Subject Interests: Automotive, Humanities, Nursing, Paralegal, Petroleum
Automation Activity & Vendor Info: (Cataloging) SirsiDynix; (Circulation) SirsiDynix; (Course Reserve) SirsiDynix; (OPAC) SirsiDynix; (Serials) SirsiDynix
Wireless access
Function: Art exhibits, Bks on CD, Electronic databases & coll, Free DVD rentals, ILL available, Internet access, Jail serv, Magazines, Microfiche/film & reading machines, Movies, Online cat, Online info literacy tutorials on the web & in blackboard, Online ref, Orientations, Photocopying/Printing, Ref serv available, Scanner, Wheelchair accessible
Partic in Estacado Library Information Network; New Mexico Consortium of Academic Libraries
Open Mon-Thurs (Winter) 7:30am-9pm, Fri 7:30-5, Sat & Sun 10-2; Mon-Thurs (Summer) 7:30-7, Fri 7:30-5

C UNIVERSITY OF THE SOUTHWEST, Scarborough Memorial Library, 6610 Lovington Hwy, T-30, 88240. SAN 310-6764. Tel: 575-392-6561. Web Site: library.usw.edu. *Dir, Students Learning Resources,* Corina Madrid; E-mail: cmadrid@usw.edu
Founded 1962. Highest Degree: Master
Library Holdings: Bk Vols 55,472; Per Subs 133; Videos 1,583
Special Collections: Hatton W Sumners Coll; New Mexico Textbook Adoption Center; Southwest Heritage Room (Thelma A Webber Coll); Southwestern History & Art Literature
Subject Interests: Folklore, Free market econ, Lit, SW hist
Automation Activity & Vendor Info: (Cataloging) SirsiDynix; (Circulation) SirsiDynix; (Course Reserve) SirsiDynix; (OPAC) SirsiDynix
Wireless access
Function: 24/7 Electronic res, 24/7 Online cat
Open Mon-Fri 8-5, Sat & Sun 1-5
Restriction: Open to students, fac & staff

HOLLOMAN AFB

A UNITED STATES AIR FORCE*, Ahrens Memorial Library, 596 Fourth St, Bldg 224, 88330-8038. SAN 351-6482. Tel: 575-572-3939. FAX: 575-572-5340. E-mail: ahrens.library@us.af.mil, holloman.library@gmail.com. Web Site: myhollomanlibrary.com, www.hollomanfss.com/library. *Syst Adminr,* Steven Lavallee; E-mail: steven.lavallee2@us.af.mil; Staff 7 (MLS 1, Non-MLS 6)
Library Holdings: e-books 7,000; Bk Titles 40,000; Per Subs 60
Special Collections: Military Studies, Foreign Relations & Management
Subject Interests: Aerospace, Foreign relations, Mil studies
Automation Activity & Vendor Info: (Cataloging) SirsiDynix; (Circulation) SirsiDynix; (ILL) OCLC; (OPAC) SirsiDynix; (Serials) SirsiDynix
Wireless access
Partic in OCLC Online Computer Library Center, Inc
Open Mon-Thurs 9-7, Fri 9-5, Sat 10-4

ISLETA

P PUEBLO OF ISLETA LIBRARY*, 950 Moonlight Dr SW, 87105. (Mail add: PO Box 597, 87022-0597). Tel: 505-869-9808. FAX: 505-869-8119. E-mail: poi02002@isletapueblo.com. Web Site: isletapueblo.com/notlib.html, www.isletapueblo.com/library.html. *Librn,* Nathaniel Lujan; Staff 4 (Non-MLS 4)
Founded 1995. Pop 4,500
Library Holdings: CDs 250; Large Print Bks 90; Bk Vols 16,000; Per Subs 80; Talking Bks 350
Automation Activity & Vendor Info: (Cataloging) Follett Software; (Circulation) Follett Software
Wireless access
Function: ILL available, Music CDs, Prog for children & young adult, Summer reading prog, Wheelchair accessible
Open Mon-Thurs 8-6:30, Fri 8-4:30, Sat 9-1
Friends of the Library Group

JAL

P WOOLWORTH COMMUNITY LIBRARY, 100 E Utah Ave, 88252. (Mail add: PO Box 1249, 88252-1249), SAN 310-6802. Tel: 505-395-3268. FAX: 505-395-2138. Web Site: www.woolworth.org. *Librn,* Rosa Ellis; E-mail: rellis@elinlib.org; *Librn,* Joyce Pittam; E-mail: jpittam@elinlib.org; *Librn,* Beth Speed; E-mail: bspeed@elinlib.org
Founded 1978. Pop 1,576; Circ 26,996
Library Holdings: Bk Vols 42,000
Subject Interests: Local hist, Spanish lang, SW hist
Wireless access
Open Mon, Tues & Thurs 7-6, Fri 7-4, Sat 8-Noon

JEMEZ PUEBLO

P JEMEZ PUEBLO COMMUNITY LIBRARY & ARCHIVES, 20 Mission Rd, 87024. (Mail add: PO Box 650, 87024-0650). Tel: 575-834-9171. FAX: 575-834-9173. Web Site: www.jemezpueblo.org/government/education/library. *Librn,* Maureen Wacondo; E-mail: maureen.a.wacondo@jemezpueblo.org
Pop 3,360; Circ 589
Library Holdings: AV Mats 2,281; Bk Vols 16,810; Per Subs 50; Talking Bks 30
Automation Activity & Vendor Info: (Cataloging) Book Systems; (Circulation) Book Systems; (OPAC) Book Systems
Wireless access
Open Mon-Fri 9-12 & 1-6

JEMEZ SPRINGS

P JEMEZ SPRINGS PUBLIC LIBRARY*, 30 Jemez Plaza, 87025. (Mail add: PO Box 479, 87025-0479), SAN 320-4936. Tel: 575-829-9155. E-mail: librarian@jsplibrary.org. Web Site: jsplibrary.org. *Dir,* Janet Phillips; Staff 2 (Non-MLS 2)
Pop 1,700; Circ 2,200
Library Holdings: Bk Titles 9,500; Per Subs 22
Open Tues-Thurs 9-4, Fri & Sat 9-1
Friends of the Library Group

KIRTLAND AFB

A UNITED STATES AIR FORCE*, Phillips Site Technical Library FL2809, AFRL/RVIL, 3550 Aberdeen Ave SE Bldg 570, 87117-5776. SAN 351-6571. Tel: 505-846-4767. E-mail: afrl.rvi.librarian@us.af.mil. *Librn,* Elizabeth Luebchow; *Librn,* Heather O'Daniel; E-mail: heather.odaniel.1.ctr@us.af.mil; Staff 4 (MLS 4)
Founded 1947
Library Holdings: Bk Vols 50,000; Per Subs 800
Subject Interests: Engr with applications in directed energy & space vehicles
Automation Activity & Vendor Info: (Acquisitions) SirsiDynix; (Cataloging) SirsiDynix; (Circulation) SirsiDynix; (Course Reserve) SirsiDynix
Open Mon-Fri 7:30-4

LA JOYA

P RIO ABAJO COMMUNITY LIBRARY*, 28 Calle de Centros Sur, 87028. Tel: 505-861-8289. E-mail: raclibrary@hotmail.com. Web Site: raclibrary.us. *Libr Dir,* Position Currently Open; *Libr Asst,* Position Currently Open
Founded 1999. Circ 2,100
Library Holdings: Audiobooks 50; Bks on Deafness & Sign Lang 11; CDs 50; DVDs 203; Large Print Bks 100; Music Scores 9; Bk Vols 5,505; Per Subs 47; Spec Interest Per Sub 2; Talking Bks 212; Videos 314
Special Collections: Agriculture/Rural (This focus is for the patron base); Everything New Mexico (Items focused solely on New Mexico)
Function: 24/7 Online cat, Bks on cassette, Bks on CD, CD-ROM, Children's prog, Computer training, Computers for patron use, Electronic databases & coll, For res purposes, Free DVD rentals, Govt ref serv, Home delivery & serv to seniorr ctr & nursing homes, ILL available, Internet access, Magazines, Movies, Museum passes, Music CDs, Notary serv, Online cat, Online ref, Photocopying/Printing, Prog for children & young adult, Ref & res, Ref serv available, Res libr, Scanner, Senior outreach, Spanish lang bks, Spoken cassettes & CDs, Spoken cassettes & DVDs, Study rm, Summer reading prog, Telephone ref
Special Services for the Deaf - Am sign lang & deaf culture; Assistive tech; Bks on deafness & sign lang
Closed July 2019 for restructuring/renovations
Open Tues-Thurs 12-5:30, Fri 9-1

LAGUNA

P LAGUNA PUBLIC LIBRARY, 29 Rodeo Dr, 87026. (Mail add: PO Box 194, 87026-0194). Tel: 505-552-6280. FAX: 505-552-9388. E-mail: info.library@pol-nsn.gov. Web Site: lagunalibrary.com. *Library Contact,* Lynnelle Aragon; E-mail: laragon@pol-nsn.gov; Staff 4 (MLS 1, Non-MLS 3)
Founded 1974
Library Holdings: Audiobooks 231; CDs 62; DVDs 957; e-books 132; Electronic Media & Resources 2; Large Print Bks 150; Per Subs 33
Automation Activity & Vendor Info: (Cataloging) Book Systems; (Circulation) Book Systems; (OPAC) Book Systems
Wireless access
Function: 24/7 Electronic res, 24/7 Online cat, Archival coll, Audiobks via web, Bks on CD, Children's prog, Computer training, Computers for patron use, Family literacy, Free DVD rentals, Holiday prog, ILL available, Internet access, Laminating, Life-long learning prog for all ages, Magazines, Mango lang, Movies, Museum passes, Music CDs, Online cat, OverDrive digital audio bks, Photocopying/Printing, Preschool outreach, Preschool reading prog, Prog for adults, Prog for children & young adult, Ref & res, Scanner, Summer reading prog, Tax forms, Teen prog
Open Mon-Fri 8-6:30, Sat 9-2; Mon-Fri 8-5:30 (Winter)
Restriction: Non-circulating of rare bks

LAS CRUCES

P THOMAS BRANIGAN MEMORIAL LIBRARY, 200 E Picacho Ave, 88001-3499. SAN 310-6837. Tel: 575-528-4000. Interlibrary Loan Service Tel: 575-528-4024. Reference Tel: 575-528-4005. FAX: 575-528-4030. TDD: 575-528-4008. Web Site: library.las-cruces.org. *Libr Adminr,* Margaret M Neill; Tel: 575-528-4017, E-mail: mneill@las-cruces.org; *Libr Mgr, Public Programs,* Brita Sauer; Tel: 575-528-4085, E-mail: bsauer@las-cruces.org; *Library Mgr, Tech Services & Systems,* Steven Haydu; Tel: 575-528-4043, E-mail: shaydu@las-cruces.org; *Libr Supvr, Circ & Media,* Colleen Corgel; Tel: 575-541-2098, E-mail: ccorgel6854@las-cruces.org; Staff 39 (MLS 11, Non-MLS 28)
Founded 1935. Pop 120,001; Circ 577,657
Jul 2019-Jun 2020. Mats Exp $362,575, Books $240,307, AV Mat $35,344, Electronic Ref Mat (Incl. Access Fees) $86,924. Sal $1,744,688
Library Holdings: Audiobooks 7,866; AV Mats 12,149; Bks-By-Mail 13,928; Bks on Deafness & Sign Lang 50; DVDs 20,296; e-books 4,825; Bk Vols 127,936; Per Subs 262
Special Collections: New Mexico & Southwestern History (Helen P Caffey Coll)
Subject Interests: Archit, Art, Hist
Automation Activity & Vendor Info: (Acquisitions) Innovative Interfaces, Inc; (Cataloging) Innovative Interfaces, Inc; (Circulation) Innovative Interfaces, Inc; (Course Reserve) Innovative Interfaces, Inc; (ILL) Innovative Interfaces, Inc; (Media Booking) Innovative Interfaces, Inc; (OPAC) Innovative Interfaces, Inc; (Serials) Innovative Interfaces, Inc
Wireless access
Function: 24/7 Electronic res, 24/7 Online cat, Adult bk club, Art exhibits, Audiobks on Playaways & MP3, Audiobks via web, Bilingual assistance for Spanish patrons, Bk club(s), Bks on CD, Children's prog, Computer training, Computers for patron use, Digital talking bks, Electronic databases & coll, Free DVD rentals, Genealogy discussion group, Holiday prog, Home delivery & serv to seniorr ctr & nursing homes, Homebound delivery serv, ILL available, Internet access, Magazines, Magnifiers for reading, Makerspace, Meeting rooms, Microfiche/film & reading machines, Movies, Museum passes, Music CDs, Notary serv, Online cat, Outreach serv, Outside serv via phone, mail, e-mail & web, Photocopying/Printing, Preschool outreach, Prog for adults, Prog for children & young adult, Ref & res, Ref serv available, Senior computer classes, Senior outreach, Serves people with intellectual disabilities, Spanish lang bks, Spoken cassettes & CDs, STEM programs, Story hour, Study rm, Summer & winter reading prog, Summer reading prog, Tax forms, Teen prog, Telephone ref, Wheelchair accessible
Partic in OCLC Online Computer Library Center, Inc
Special Services for the Deaf - TTY equip; Video & TTY relay via computer

Special Services for the Blind - Accessible computers; BiFolkal kits; Bks available with recordings; Bks on CD; Large print bks; Playaways (bks on MP3); Reader equip
Open Mon-Thurs 9-8, Fri & Sat 10-6, Sun 1-5
Friends of the Library Group

§CM BURRELL COLLEGE OF OSTEOPATHIC MEDICINE, Health Sciences Library, 3501 Arrowhead Dr, 88001. Tel: 575-674-2347. FAX: 575-674-2248. E-mail: library@burrell.edu. Web Site: library.bcomnm.org. *Libr Dir,* Erin Palazzolo; Tel: 575-674-2330, E-mail: epalazzolo@burrell.edu; *Assoc Libr Dir,* Norice Lee; Tel: 575-674-2346, E-mail: nlee@burrell.edu
Wireless access
Function: Doc delivery serv, Res assist avail, Study rm
Partic in Del Norte Biosciences Library Consortium; New Mexico Consortium of Academic Libraries
Open Mon-Fri 8am-8pm, Sat & Sun 8-3

J DONA ANA COMMUNITY COLLEGE*, Espina Library, 3400 S Espina, Rm 260, 88003. Tel: 575-527-7555. Toll Free Tel: 800-903-7503. FAX: 575-527-7636. Web Site: dacc.nmsu.edu/library. *Libr Dir,* Tammy Powers; E-mail: tpowers@dacc.nmsu.edu; *AV Tech Equip Mgr,* Rodner Santos; E-mail: rosantos@dacc.nm.su.edu; *Circ Supvr,* Becky Ponce; E-mail: rponce@dacc.nmsu.edu; *Cataloger,* Kathleen DeBoy; E-mail: kdeboy@dacc.nmsu.edu
Enrl 5,828
Library Holdings: e-books 29,000; e-journals 15; Bk Titles 18,000; Per Subs 180
Automation Activity & Vendor Info: (Cataloging) Ex Libris Group; (Circulation) Ex Libris Group; (OPAC) Ex Libris Group; (Serials) Ex Libris Group
Wireless access
Partic in New Mexico Consortium of Academic Libraries
Open Mon-Thurs (Winter) 8-7, Fri 8-5, Sat 10-2; Mon-Fri (Summer) 8-5
Departmental Libraries:
EAST MESA LIBRARY, 2800 N Sonoma Ranch Blvd, 88011. Tel: 575-528-7260. FAX: 575-528-7422. *Instrul Librn,* Jose Aranda; E-mail: jaranda@dacc.nmsu.edu; *Libr Mgr,* Vita Montano; E-mail: vmontano@dacc.nmsu.edu
Open Mon-Fri (Summer) 8-5; Mon-Thurs (Winter) 8-7, Fri 8-5, Sat 10-2

S INSTITUTE OF HISTORICAL SURVEY FOUNDATION LIBRARY, 3035 S Main, 88005-3756. (Mail add: PO Box 36, Mesilla Park, 88047-0036), SAN 377-8223. Tel: 575-525-3035. FAX: 575-525-0106. E-mail: ihsf@zianet.com. *Dir,* Dr Evan Davies; *Librn,* Anne Morgan; E-mail: anmorgan@zianet.com; Staff 2 (MLS 1, Non-MLS 1)
Founded 1970
Library Holdings: Bk Titles 40,000; Bk Vols 45,000
Special Collections: Oral History
Subject Interests: Art, Aviation hist, Geog, Hist, Philos, Photog, Relig
Function: Archival coll, AV serv, Equip loans & repairs, Mail & tel request accepted, Outside serv via phone, mail, e-mail & web, Res libr, Res performed for a fee, Telephone ref
Open Mon-Fri 8-4
Restriction: Non-circulating

G NASA, White Sands Test Facility Technical Library, 12600 NASA Rd, 88012. (Mail add: PO Box 20, 88004-0020), SAN 328-0969. Tel: 575-524-5683. Web Site: www.nasa.gov/centers/wstf/home/index.html. *Mgr,* Moira Romansky; E-mail: moira.j.romansky@nasa.gov; Staff 2 (MLS 1, Non-MLS 1)
Library Holdings: Bk Titles 2,000
Partic in OCLC Online Computer Library Center, Inc; Proquest Dialog

S NEW MEXICO CORRECTIONS DEPARTMENT*, Southern New Mexico Correctional Facility Library, 1983 Joe R Silva Blvd, 88004. (Mail add: PO Box 639, 88004-0639). Tel: 575-523-3398. FAX: 575-523-3398. Web Site: cd.nm.gov/apd/snmcf.html. *Librn,* Sonia Azua; E-mail: sonia.azua@state.nm.us
Library Holdings: Bk Vols 10,500; Per Subs 40
Automation Activity & Vendor Info: (Cataloging) Winnebago Software Co; (Circulation) Winnebago Software Co
Restriction: Not open to pub

C NEW MEXICO STATE UNIVERSITY LIBRARY*, 2911 McFie Circle, 88003. (Mail add: PO Box 30006, MSC 3475, 88003-8006), SAN 351-6636. Tel: 575-646-1508. Circulation Tel: 575-646-6910. Interlibrary Loan Service Tel: 575-646-4737. Information Services Tel: 575-646-5792. Toll Free Tel: 866-835-9826. FAX: 575-646-6940. Interlibrary Loan Service FAX: 575-646-4335. Web Site: lib.nmsu.edu. *Assoc Dean, Interim Dean,* Katherine Terpis; E-mail: kterpis@nmsu.edu; *Head, Archives & Spec Coll,* Dennis Dailey; *Head, Tech Serv,* Ellen Bosman; Tel: 575-646-1723; Staff 34 (MLS 23, Non-MLS 11)
Founded 1888. Fac 629; Highest Degree: Doctorate. Sal $1,805,017 (Prof $2,786,882)
Library Holdings: AV Mats 17,059; e-books 16,183; e-journals 95,127; Microforms 1,490,144; Music Scores 8,248; Bk Vols 1,830,030; Per Subs 2,620
Special Collections: Pete V Domenici Archives (Political Papers); Rio Grande Historical Coll; University Archives. Oral History; State Document Depository; US Document Depository
Automation Activity & Vendor Info: (Acquisitions) Ex Libris Group; (Cataloging) Ex Libris Group; (Circulation) Ex Libris Group; (Course Reserve) Docutek; (ILL) OCLC ILLiad; (OPAC) Ex Libris Group; (Serials) Ex Libris Group
Wireless access
Publications: New Mexico State University Library (Newsletter)
Partic in Amigos Library Services, Inc; New Mexico Consortium of Academic Libraries
Special Services for the Deaf - TDD equip
Open Mon-Fri 8-5

R SAINT PAUL'S UNITED METHODIST CHURCH*, Ralph Johnson Memorial Library, 225 W Griggs Ave, 88005. SAN 328-1272. Tel: 575-526-6689. FAX: 575-524-7660. Web Site: www.stpaulslascruces.com. *Adminr,* Mark Ewing; Tel: 575-526-6689, Ext 1002, E-mail: mark@stpaulslascruces.com
Founded 1961
Library Holdings: Bk Vols 3,000
Wireless access
Publications: History of Church
Open Mon-Thurs 8-5, Fri & Sun 8-Noon

LAS VEGAS

P CARNEGIE PUBLIC LIBRARY*, 500 National Ave, 87701. SAN 310-6853. Tel: 505-426-3304. Web Site: www.lasvegasnm.gov/community/carnegie_library/index.php. *Libr Mgr,* Sonia Gomez; E-mail: sgomez@lasvegasnm.gov
Founded 1904. Circ 84,557
Library Holdings: Bk Vols 61,000; Per Subs 80
Special Collections: Local history; Southwest Coll
Subject Interests: SW
Automation Activity & Vendor Info: (Cataloging) Follett Software; (Circulation) Follett Software
Wireless access
Function: 24/7 Electronic res, 24/7 Online cat, Activity rm, After school storytime, Archival coll, Audio & video playback equip for onsite use, Audiobks on Playaways & MP3, Audiobks via web, Bks on CD, Children's prog, Computers for patron use, Electronic databases & coll, ILL available, Internet access, Magazines, Magnifiers for reading, Microfiche/film & reading machines, Movies, Museum passes, Music CDs, Notary serv, Online cat, Online ref, Outreach serv, OverDrive digital audio bks, Photocopying/Printing, Printer for laptops & handheld devices, Prog for children & young adult, Ref & res, Ref serv available, Res assist avail, Spanish lang bks, Spoken cassettes & CDs, Story hour, Summer reading prog, Tax forms, VHS videos, Wheelchair accessible
Partic in OCLC Online Computer Library Center, Inc
Open Mon-Fri 8-5, Sat 8-2
Friends of the Library Group

§J LUNA COMMUNITY COLLEGE, Samuel F Vigil Learning Resource Center, 366 Luna Dr, 87701. Tel: 505-454-2540. E-mail: lrc@luna.edu. Web Site: luna.edu/lrc. *Mgr,* Linda Salazar; Tel: 505-454-5333, E-mail: lsalazar@luna.edu
Automation Activity & Vendor Info: (Cataloging) TLC (The Library Corporation); (OPAC) TLC (The Library Corporation)
Wireless access
Partic in New Mexico Consortium of Academic Libraries
Open Mon-Fri 8-5

GM NEW MEXICO BEHAVIORAL HEALTH INSTITUTE AT LAS VEGAS*, Medical Library, 3695 Hot Springs Blvd, 87701. SAN 310-6861. Tel: 505-454-2108. FAX: 505-454-2136. *Library Contact,* Evelyn Lucero
Founded 1970
Library Holdings: Bk Titles 7,000
Special Collections: Psychiatry; Psychology; Social Work
Subject Interests: Gen med, Nursing
Partic in National Network of Libraries of Medicine Region 4
Restriction: Not open to pub

C NEW MEXICO HIGHLANDS UNIVERSITY*, Thomas C Donnelly Library, 802 National Ave, 87701. (Mail add: PO Box 9000, 87701), SAN 310-687X. Tel: 505-454-3401. Circulation Tel: 505-454-3403. Interlibrary Loan Service Tel: 505-454-3481. Administration Tel: 505-454-3332. Automation Services Tel: 505-454-3330. Information Services Tel: 505-454-3139. FAX: 505-454-0026. Web Site: www.nmhu.edu/library. *Dir,* Ruben F Aragon; E-mail: rubenaragon@nmhu.edu; *Head, Coll &*

Instruction Div/Librn, Leslie Broughton; Tel: 505-454-3408, E-mail: labroughton@nmhu.edu; *Head, Govt Doc & Per Div/Librn,* Josephine Sena; Tel: 505-454-3411, E-mail: jlsenag@nmhu.edu; *Head, Pub Serv Div/Librn,* April Kent; E-mail: ajkent@nmhu.edu; *Libr Assoc/Acq Section,* Beatrice Ulibarri; Tel: 505-454-3336; Staff 17.3 (MLS 6, Non-MLS 11.3)
Founded 1893. Enrl 3,208; Fac 115; Highest Degree: Master
Library Holdings: AV Mats 2,148; CDs 291; e-books 42,605; Microforms 169,296; Bk Vols 164,828; Per Subs 700
Special Collections: Fort Union Archives, mss; Government Documents Coll; Southwest History (Arrott Coll). State Document Depository; US Document Depository
Automation Activity & Vendor Info: (Acquisitions) Innovative Interfaces, Inc; (Cataloging) Innovative Interfaces, Inc; (Circulation) Innovative Interfaces, Inc; (Course Reserve) Innovative Interfaces, Inc; (ILL) OCLC; (OPAC) Innovative Interfaces, Inc; (Serials) Innovative Interfaces, Inc
Wireless access
Partic in New Mexico Consortium of Academic Libraries
Open Mon-Thurs 7:30am-10pm, Fri 7:30-5, Sun 1-10

LORDSBURG

P LORDSBURG-HIDALGO LIBRARY*, 208 E Third St, 88045. SAN 310-6888. Tel: 575-542-9646. FAX: 575-542-9646. E-mail: oldbkbuilding@yahoo.com. Web Site: www.lordsburghidalgolibrary.com. *Dir,* Alice Webb; *Ch Serv,* Rita Morris
Founded 1919. Pop 5,000; Circ 20,645
Library Holdings: Bk Vols 23,000; Per Subs 60
Wireless access
Special Services for the Deaf - Bks on deafness & sign lang
Open Mon-Fri 10-6
Friends of the Library Group

LOS ALAMOS

SR FIRST UNITED METHODIST CHURCH LIBRARY, 715 Diamond Dr, 87544. SAN 373-479X. Tel: 505-662-6277. E-mail: office@lafumc.org. Web Site: www.firstinyourheart.org.
Library Holdings: Bk Vols 1,100
Subject Interests: Theol
Wireless access
Open Mon-Fri 8-5, Sun 8-Noon

SR IMMACULATE HEART OF MARY PARISH LIBRARY*, 3700 Canyon Rd, 87544. SAN 310-690X. Tel: 505-662-6193. FAX: 505-662-5191. E-mail: ihmlib3700@gmail.com. *Librn,* Tina Szymanski
Founded 1961
Library Holdings: Bk Titles 5,000; Per Subs 20
Subject Interests: Family, Marriage, Philos, Psychol, Relig, Relig educ, Socio-econ concerns, Theol
Open Mon-Fri 8-5, Sun 9-Noon

P LOS ALAMOS COUNTY LIBRARY SYSTEM, 2400 Central Ave, 87544. SAN 370-4602. Tel: 505-662-8240. Circulation Tel: 505-662-8250. Interlibrary Loan Service Tel: 505-662-8255. Reference Tel: 505-662-8253. Automation Services Tel: 505-662-8260. FAX: 505-662-8245. Reference FAX: 505-662-8246. TDD: 505-662-8256. E-mail: libweb@lacnm.us. Web Site: www.losalamosnm.us/government/departments/community_services/library. *Libr Mgr,* Eileen Sullivan; E-mail: eileen.sullivan@lacnm.us; *Asst Libr Mgr,* Gwen Kalavaza; E-mail: gwen.kalavaza@lacnm.us; *Circ Supvr,* Eva Jacobson; E-mail: eva.jacobson@lacnm.us; *Ref Serv,* Liza Rivera; E-mail: elizabeth.rivera@lacnm.us; *Tech Serv,* Doris Logan; E-mail: doris.logan@lacnm.us; Staff 28.9 (MLS 7, Non-MLS 21.9)
Founded 1943. Pop 17,950; Circ 332,770
Jul 2019-Jun 2020 Income $2,162,358, State $35,107, County $2,119,169, Other $8,082. Mats Exp $2,162,358. Sal $1,274,353
Library Holdings: Audiobooks 11,581; AV Mats 16,356; e-books 13,866; Bk Vols 157,940
Special Collections: Southwest Americana Regional Coll bk, video
Automation Activity & Vendor Info: (Acquisitions) SirsiDynix; (Cataloging) SirsiDynix; (Circulation) SirsiDynix; (ILL) SirsiDynix; (OPAC) SirsiDynix; (Serials) SirsiDynix
Wireless access
Function: Art exhibits, Audio & video playback equip for onsite use, Audiobks via web, Bks on CD, Children's prog, Computers for patron use, Digital talking bks, E-Reserves, Electronic databases & coll, Free DVD rentals, Games & aids for people with disabilities, Govt ref serv, Home delivery & serv to seniorr ctr & nursing homes, Homework prog, ILL available, Literacy & newcomer serv, Magnifiers for reading, Music CDs, Online cat, Outreach serv, Photocopying/Printing, Preschool outreach, Prof lending libr, Prog for adults, Prog for children & young adult, Ref serv available, Story hour, Summer reading prog, Tax forms, Teen prog, Telephone ref, Wheelchair accessible
Special Services for the Deaf - TDD equip; TTY equip
Special Services for the Blind - Large print bks; Magnifiers
Open Mon-Thurs 10-9, Fri 10-6, Sat 10-5, Sun 12-5
Friends of the Library Group

S LOS ALAMOS HISTORICAL SOCIETY, Museum Archives, 1050 Bathtub Row, 87544. (Mail add: PO Box 43, 87544-0043), SAN 325-903X. Tel: 505-662-6272. E-mail: archives@losalamoshistory.org, info@losalamoshistory.org. Web Site: www.losalamoshistory.org. *Exec Dir,* Elizabeth Martineau; E-mail: execdirector@losalamoshistory.org; *Archivist,* Rebecca Collinsworth; Staff 3 (Non-MLS 3)
Founded 1976
Library Holdings: Bk Vols 900; Spec Interest Per Sub 25
Special Collections: Laura Gilpin Photographs Coll; T H Parkhurst Photographs Coll. Oral History
Subject Interests: Atomic energy, Nuclear energy
Wireless access
Function: Archival coll, Electronic databases & coll
Publications: Los Alamos Historical Society Magazine (Quarterly)
Restriction: Closed stack, Non-circulating, Open by appt only

S LOS ALAMOS NATIONAL LABORATORY*, Research Library, MS-P362, PO Box 1663, 87545-1362. SAN 351-6695. Tel: 505-667-5809. FAX: 505-665-6452. E-mail: library@lanl.gov. Web Site: www.lanl.gov/library.
Founded 1943
Library Holdings: Bk Vols 131,500; Per Subs 6,710
Special Collections: AEC period publications; Electronic Reports; LANL Technical Reports
Wireless access
Open Mon-Thurs 7:30-5, Fri 7:30-4

R UNITED CHURCH OF LOS ALAMOS LIBRARY*, 2525 Canyon Rd, 87544. SAN 310-6926. Tel: 505-662-2971. FAX: 505-662-5927. E-mail: ucoffice@unitedchurchla.org. Web Site: unitedchurchla.org.
Founded 1966
Library Holdings: Bk Vols 3,500; Per Subs 10
Subject Interests: Family life, Health, Psychol, Relig
Open Mon-Fri 8:30-4:30, Sun 9-Noon

C UNIVERSITY OF NEW MEXICO*, Los Alamos Campus Library, 4000 University Dr, 87544. SAN 326-1476. Tel: 505-662-0343. FAX: 505-662-0344. E-mail: ulalib@unm.edu. Web Site: losalamos.unm.edu/library. *Libr Dir,* Dennis Davies-Wilson; E-mail: davies@unm.edu; *Info Spec,* Joe Matthews; *Info Spec,* Alyssa Stubbs; Staff 3 (MLS 2, Non-MLS 1)
Special Collections: Southwest Coll
Subject Interests: Art
Automation Activity & Vendor Info: (Cataloging) OCLC Connexion; (Circulation) OCLC Worldshare Management Services; (Course Reserve) OCLC Worldshare Management Services; (ILL) OCLC WorldShare Interlibrary Loan; (OPAC) OCLC Worldshare Management Services
Wireless access
Partic in LIBROS Consortium; New Mexico Consortium of Academic Libraries; OCLC Online Computer Library Center, Inc
Open Mon-Thurs 8-7, Fri 8-4

LOS LUNAS

P LOS LUNAS PUBLIC LIBRARY*, 460 Main St NE, 87031. (Mail add: PO Box 1209, 87031-1209), SAN 310-6934. Tel: 505-839-3850. FAX: 505-352-3582. Web Site: www.loslunasnm.gov/103/Library. *Libr Dir,* Cynthia J Shetter; E-mail: shetterc@loslunasnm.gov; *Asst Dir,* Andrea Chavez; E-mail: chavezan@loslunasnm.gov; Staff 6 (Non-MLS 6)
Founded 1959. Pop 11,500; Circ 36,000
Library Holdings: Bk Vols 28,000
Open Mon 12-5, Tues 10-7, Wed & Fri 9-5, Thurs 9-7, Sat 9-4
Restriction: Open to pub for ref & circ; with some limitations

LOVINGTON

P LOVINGTON PUBLIC LIBRARY*, 115 S Main St, 88260. SAN 310-6950. Tel: 575-396-3144. FAX: 575-396-7189. Web Site: www.lovingtonpubliclibrary.org. *Libr Dir,* Debbie Mitchell; E-mail: dmitchell@elinlib.org
Founded 1931. Pop 11,000; Circ 96,105
Library Holdings: DVDs 1,100; e-books 75; Bk Vols 51,000; Per Subs 41
Subject Interests: Genealogy
Automation Activity & Vendor Info: (Cataloging) SirsiDynix; (Circulation) SirsiDynix; (ILL) SirsiDynix; (OPAC) SirsiDynix
Wireless access
Partic in Estacado Library Information Network
Special Services for the Deaf - Bks on deafness & sign lang; Closed caption videos
Special Services for the Blind - Cassettes; Copier with enlargement capabilities; Home delivery serv; Large print & cassettes; Large print bks; Magnifiers; ZoomText magnification & reading software

Open Mon-Fri 9:30-6
Friends of the Library Group

MAGDALENA

P MAGDALENA PUBLIC LIBRARY*, 108 N Main St, 87825. (Mail add: PO Box 145, 87825-0145). Tel: 575-854-2361. E-mail: library@villageofmagdalena.com. Web Site: www.magdalenapubliclibrary.org. *Dir,* Ivy Stover; Staff 1 (MLS 1)
Pop 1,000
Library Holdings: Audiobooks 223; DVDs 2,299; e-books 13,210; Large Print Bks 232; Bk Vols 22,067
Automation Activity & Vendor Info: (Acquisitions) Book Systems; (Cataloging) Book Systems; (Circulation) Book Systems; (Course Reserve) Book Systems; (ILL) Book Systems; (OPAC) Book Systems
Wireless access
Function: 24/7 Online cat, Adult bk club, Audiobks via web, Bks on CD, Children's prog, Electronic databases & coll, Free DVD rentals, Holiday prog, ILL available, Internet access, Movies, Museum passes, Online cat, OverDrive digital audio bks, Photocopying/Printing, Printer for laptops & handheld devices, Prog for adults, Prog for children & young adult, Scanner, Summer reading prog
Open Tues-Fri 11-5, Sat 10-3
Friends of the Library Group

MESCALERO

P MESCALERO COMMUNITY LIBRARY*, 148 Cottonwood Dr, 88340. (Mail add: PO Box 227, 88340). Tel: 505-464-5010. FAX: 505-464-5011. E-mail: mescalero_library@yahoo.com. Web Site: mescalerolibrary.org. *Librn,* Lillian Chavez
Library Holdings: Audiobooks 75; AV Mats 420; CDs 185; DVDs 235; Bk Titles 7,500; Bk Vols 3,500; Per Subs 24
Automation Activity & Vendor Info: (Acquisitions) Insignia Software; (Cataloging) Insignia Software; (Circulation) Insignia Software; (ILL) Insignia Software; (OPAC) Insignia Software
Wireless access
Open Mon-Fri 8-6:30, Sat 10-6:30

MORIARTY

P MORIARTY COMMUNITY LIBRARY, 202 S Broadway, 87035. Tel: 505-832-2513. FAX: 505-832-9286. E-mail: moriartylibrary@gmail.com. Web Site: www.moriartynm.org/info/library-museum. *Libr Dir,* Natalie Bott; *Libr Spec,* Ashley Williams; Staff 4 (Non-MLS 4)
Library Holdings: Bk Vols 20,000; Per Subs 12
Automation Activity & Vendor Info: (Cataloging) Biblionix; (Circulation) Biblionix; (Course Reserve) Biblionix
Wireless access
Open Mon-Fri 9-5
Friends of the Library Group

MOUNTAINAIR

P MOUNTAINAIR PUBLIC LIBRARY*, 109 Roosevelt Ave, 87036. (Mail add: PO Box 100, 87036-0100). Tel: 505-847-9676. E-mail: library@mountainairnm.gov. Web Site: mountainairnm.gov/index.php?page=library. *Dir,* Evelyn Walker; E-mail: ewalker97@mindspring.com
Library Holdings: AV Mats 30; Bk Vols 8,000; Per Subs 10; Talking Bks 50
Automation Activity & Vendor Info: (Cataloging) Follett Software; (Circulation) Follett Software
Wireless access
Open Mon-Wed 9-Noon, Thurs 9-12 & 2-6, Fri 10-3, Sat 9-1

G NATIONAL PARK SERVICE*, Salinas Pueblo Missions Research Library, Corner of Broadway & Ripley, PO Box 517, 87036-0517. SAN 374-5538. Tel: 505-847-2585. FAX: 505-847-2441. Web Site: www.nps.gov/sapu. *Adminr,* Loretta Moseley; E-mail: loretta_moseley@nps.gov; Staff 1 (Non-MLS 1)
Founded 1930
Library Holdings: Bk Titles 1,700
Special Collections: Archaeology; Southwest Prehistory & History. Oral History
Open Mon-Fri 8-4

NAGEEZI

G USDI NATIONAL PARK SERVICE, Chaco Culture National, PO Box 220, 87037-0220. SAN 323-9691. Tel: 505-786-7014. FAX: 505-786-7061. Web Site: www.nps.gov/chcu. *Chief of Interpretation,* Nathan Hatfield; E-mail: nathan_hatfield@nps.gov
Library Holdings: Bk Titles 5,000
Special Collections: Oral History
Open Mon-Fri 8-5

PORTALES

C EASTERN NEW MEXICO UNIVERSITY - PORTALES*, Golden Library, 1500 S Ave K, 88130-7402. (Mail add: Sta 32, 88130), SAN 351-675X. Tel: 575-562-2624. Circulation Tel: 575-562-2634. FAX: 575-562-2647. Web Site: my.enmu.edu/web/golden-library. *Dir,* Melveta Walker; Tel: 575-562-2626, E-mail: Melveta.Walker@enmu.edu; *ILL/Distance Educ Librn,* Karen Nelson; Tel: 575-562-2644, E-mail: Karen.Nelson@enmu.edu; *Govt Doc Librn,* Paul Moore; Tel: 575-562-2650, E-mail: Paul.Moore@enmu.edu; *Media Librn,* Richard Baysinger; Tel: 575-562-2602, E-mail: Richard.Baysinger@enmu.edu; *Pub Relations Librn,* Christy Ruby; Tel: 575-562-2640, E-mail: Christy.Ruby@enmu.edu; *Ser Librn,* Susan Asplund; Tel: 575-562-2629, E-mail: Susan.Asplund@enmu.edu; *Spec Coll Librn,* Gene Bundy; Tel: 575-562-2636, E-mail: Gene.Bundy@enmu.edu; *Cat,* Courtney Marshall; Tel: 575-562-2622, E-mail: Courtney.Marshall@enmu.edu; Staff 9 (MLS 8, Non-MLS 1)
Founded 1934. Enrl 5,000; Fac 173; Highest Degree: Master
Library Holdings: AV Mats 17,095; e-books 11,000; Bk Titles 270,935; Bk Vols 346,290; Per Subs 27,000; Talking Bks 540
Special Collections: Harold Runnels Coll; NMex; Textbook Review Center; Williamson Science Fiction Coll. Oral History; State Document Depository; US Document Depository
Subject Interests: Educ, Fine arts, Liberal arts
Automation Activity & Vendor Info: (Acquisitions) Innovative Interfaces, Inc; (Cataloging) Innovative Interfaces, Inc; (Circulation) Innovative Interfaces, Inc; (Course Reserve) Innovative Interfaces, Inc; (ILL) OCLC; (OPAC) Innovative Interfaces, Inc; (Serials) Innovative Interfaces, Inc
Wireless access
Partic in Llano Estacado Info Access Network; New Mexico Consortium of Academic Libraries
Open Mon-Thurs 7:30am-Midnight, Fri 7:30am-8pm, Sat 10-7, Sun Noon-Midnight

P PORTALES PUBLIC LIBRARY*, 218 S Ave B, 88130. SAN 310-6985. Tel: 505-356-3940. FAX: 505-356-3964. Web Site: www.portalesnm.gov/department/?structureid=43. *Dir,* Position Currently Open; Staff 7 (MLS 1, Non-MLS 6)
Founded 1934. Pop 15,695; Circ 68,639
Library Holdings: Bk Vols 40,000; Per Subs 85
Subject Interests: Genealogy
Wireless access
Open Mon-Wed 10-6, Thurs 10-7, Fri 10-5, Sat 10-2
Friends of the Library Group

RATON

P ARTHUR JOHNSON MEMORIAL LIBRARY*, 244 Cook Ave, 87740. SAN 310-6993. Tel: 575-445-9711. FAX: 575-445-8336. E-mail: library@cityofraton.com. Web Site: www.ratonnm.gov/139/Library. *Librn,* Thayla Wright; E-mail: twright@cityofraton.com
Founded 1912. Pop 6,584; Circ 26,765
Library Holdings: Bk Vols 48,000; Per Subs 111
Special Collections: Southwest & Local History, audio, CD, file mat, pictures, tapes, video. Oral History; State Document Depository
Partic in NMex Info Systs; OCLC Online Computer Library Center, Inc
Open Mon 1-6, Tues-Sat 10-6, Thurs 10-9
Friends of the Library Group

RED RIVER

P RED RIVER PUBLIC LIBRARY*, 702 E Main St, 87558. (Mail add: PO Box 1020, 87558-1020). Tel: 505-754-6564. FAX: 505-754-6564. Web Site: redriver.org/town/town-services/library. *Libr Dir,* Holly Snowden Fagan; E-mail: hsnowden@redriver.org
Library Holdings: Audiobooks 1,183; AV Mats 2,609; Bk Vols 13,119; Per Subs 11; Videos 1,416
Special Collections: Southwest Coll
Automation Activity & Vendor Info: (Acquisitions) Biblionix; (Cataloging) Biblionix; (Circulation) Biblionix; (OPAC) Biblionix
Wireless access
Open Mon, Tues, Fri & Sat 9:30-12 & 1-5, Thurs 5-9

RIO RANCHO

P RIO RANCHO PUBLIC LIBRARY, 755 Loma Colorado Blvd NE, 87124. SAN 321-7671. Tel: 505-891-5013. Circulation Tel: 505-891-5013, Ext 3027. Administration Tel: 505-891-5013, Ext 8818. FAX: 502-892-4782. Web Site: rrnm.gov/4217/Library-Information-Services. *Dir,* Lynette Schurdevin; Tel: 505-896-8817, E-mail: lschurdevin@rrnm.gov; *Youth Serv,* Deirdre Caparoso; E-mail: dcaparoso@rrnm.gov; Staff 14 (MLS 10, Non-MLS 4)
Founded 1974. Pop 68,000; Circ 502,024
Library Holdings: Bk Vols 149,891; Per Subs 111
Special Collections: Southwest Coll

Automation Activity & Vendor Info: (Acquisitions) Innovative Interfaces, Inc; (Cataloging) OCLC Online; (Circulation) Innovative Interfaces, Inc; (ILL) OCLC Online; (OPAC) Innovative Interfaces, Inc; (Serials) Innovative Interfaces, Inc
Wireless access
Function: After school storytime, CD-ROM, Homebound delivery serv, ILL available, Internet access, Learning ctr, Music CDs, Photocopying/Printing, Prog for adults, Prog for children & young adult, Ref serv available, Satellite serv, Spoken cassettes & CDs, Summer reading prog, Telephone ref, VHS videos, Wheelchair accessible, Workshops
Publications: Booklist (Periodical)
Special Services for the Deaf - Bks on deafness & sign lang
Special Services for the Blind - VisualTek equip
Open Mon & Wed-Sat 9-5, Tues 10-6
Friends of the Library Group
Branches: 1
ESTER BONE MEMORIAL LIBRARY, 950 Pinetree Rd SE, 87124-7616. Tel: 505-891-5012. FAX: 505-891-1396. *Br Mgr,* Position Currently Open
Open Tues 10-6, Wed-Fri 9-5

ROSWELL

C EASTERN NEW MEXICO UNIVERSITY - ROSWELL*, Learning Resource Center, 52 University Blvd, 88203. (Mail add: PO Box 6000, 88202-6000), SAN 310-7027. Tel: 575-624-7282. FAX: 575-624-7068. Web Site: www.roswell.enmu.edu. *Dir,* Rollah Aston; E-mail: rollah.aston@roswell.enmu.edu; Staff 5 (MLS 1, Non-MLS 4)
Founded 1959. Enrl 2,657; Fac 52; Highest Degree: Associate
Library Holdings: Bk Vols 45,000; Per Subs 60
Special Collections: Child Development Center; Nursing History Coll. Oral History
Automation Activity & Vendor Info: (Cataloging) OCLC WorldShare Interlibrary Loan; (Circulation) OCLC WorldShare Interlibrary Loan; (ILL) OCLC WorldShare Interlibrary Loan; (OPAC) OCLC WorldShare Interlibrary Loan
Wireless access
Partic in New Mexico Consortium of Academic Libraries
Open Mon-Thurs 7:30am-8pm, Fri 8am-Midnight, Sat 8-4

J NEW MEXICO MILITARY INSTITUTE*, Paul Horgan Library-Toles Learning Center, Toles Learning Ctr, 101 W College Blvd, 88201-5173. SAN 310-7051. Tel: 575-624-8380. Circulation Tel: 575-624-8385. Reference Tel: 575-624-8384. FAX: 575-624-8390. Web Site: www.nmmi.edu/academics/paul-horgan-library. *Dir, Learning Res Ctr,* Kalith Smith; *Head of Libr,* June Frosch; *Assoc Librn,* Joan Jump; Tel: 575-624-8387; *Asst Librn,* Emily Percell; Staff 6 (MLS 2, Non-MLS 4)
Founded 1902. Enrl 919; Fac 78; Highest Degree: Associate
Library Holdings: Bk Titles 50,000; Bk Vols 70,000; Per Subs 128
Special Collections: Henry David Thoreau Coll; Paul Horgan Writings
Subject Interests: Hist, Humanities, Mil hist (US), Napoleonic era, Natural sci, SW hist
Automation Activity & Vendor Info: (Acquisitions) Innovative Interfaces, Inc; (Cataloging) Innovative Interfaces, Inc; (Circulation) Innovative Interfaces, Inc; (Course Reserve) Innovative Interfaces, Inc; (ILL) OCLC; (OPAC) Innovative Interfaces, Inc; (Serials) Innovative Interfaces, Inc
Wireless access
Partic in New Mexico Consortium of Academic Libraries
Open Mon, Wed & Fri 7-4, Tues & Thurs 7-7; Mon-Fri (Summer) 7:30-Noon & 1-3:30

S ROSWELL MUSEUM & ART CENTER LIBRARY*, 100 W 11th St, 88201. SAN 310-7078. Tel: 575-624-6744, Ext 25. FAX: 575-624-6765. E-mail: c.jordan@roswell-nm.gov. Web Site: roswell-nm.gov/308/Roswell-Museum-Art-Center. *Exec Dir,* Caroline Brooks; Tel: 575-624-6744, Ext 12, E-mail: c.brooks@roswell-nm.gov; *Librn & Archivist,* Deborah Jordan; Tel: 575-624-6744, Ext 25, E-mail: c.jordan@roswell-nm.gov; Staff 1 (Non-MLS 1)
Jul 2016-Jun 2017 Income City $20,000. Mats Exp $2,500, Books $1,000, Per/Ser (Incl. Access Fees) $1,000, Presv $500. Sal $16,000 (Prof $16,000)
Library Holdings: AV Mats 300; CDs 15; DVDs 60; Bk Vols 8,000; Per Subs 21; Videos 444
Special Collections: Fritz Scholder Archives; Howard Cook Archives; New Mexico Artists Files; Peter Hurd Archives; Robert H Goddard Archives & Coll; Roswell Artist-in-Residence Files; Roswell Museum & Art Center Archives. Oral History
Subject Interests: Artists
Automation Activity & Vendor Info: (Cataloging) Inmagic, Inc.
Function: For res purposes
Open Tues-Fri 10-noon & 1-3
Restriction: Not a lending libr

P ROSWELL PUBLIC LIBRARY*, 301 N Pennsylvania Ave, 88201. SAN 310-7086. Tel: 575-622-7101. FAX: 575-622-7107. Reference E-mail: reference@roswell-nm.gov. Web Site: roswell-nm.gov/1260/Roswell-Public-Library. *Libr Dir,* Enid Costley; E-mail: e.costley@roswell-nm.gov; Staff 6 (MLS 4, Non-MLS 2)
Founded 1906. Pop 61,382; Circ 302,542
Library Holdings: Audiobooks 3,366; AV Mats 5,722; Bks on Deafness & Sign Lang 72; CDs 3,699; DVDs 1,155; e-books 5; Large Print Bks 5,410; Bk Titles 156,821; Bk Vols 164,018; Per Subs 178; Talking Bks 2,966; Videos 1,032
Special Collections: Southwest Coll. State Document Depository
Subject Interests: Genealogy
Automation Activity & Vendor Info: (Cataloging) SirsiDynix; (Circulation) SirsiDynix; (OPAC) SirsiDynix
Wireless access
Special Services for the Blind - Audio mat; Cassette playback machines; Cassettes; Home delivery serv; Large print bks; Reader equip; Talking bks
Open Mon-Thurs 9-8, Fri & Sat 9-6, Sun 2-6
Friends of the Library Group

RUIDOSO

§C EASTERN NEW MEXICO UNIVERSITY - RUIDOSO, Learning Commons, 709 Mechem Dr, 88345. Tel: 575-315-1135. E-mail: ruidoso.learning-commons@enmu.edu. Web Site: ruidoso.enmu.edu/library. *Libr Dir,* James Pawlak; E-mail: james.pawlak@enmu.edu; *Dir, E-Learning & Assessment,* Miriam Maske; Tel: 575-315-1136, E-mail: miriam.maske@enmu.edu
Automation Activity & Vendor Info: (Cataloging) OCLC; (OPAC) OCLC
Wireless access
Function: Computers for patron use, ILL available, Res assist avail, Study rm
Partic in New Mexico Consortium of Academic Libraries
Open Mon-Fri 9-5

P RUIDOSO PUBLIC LIBRARY*, 107 Kansas City Rd, 88345. SAN 310-7094. Tel: 575-258-3704. FAX: 575-258-4619. E-mail: library@ruidoso-nm.gov. Web Site: ruidosolibrary.org. *Dir,* Marian Royal; Staff 7 (MLS 1, Non-MLS 6)
Founded 1950. Pop 20,000; Circ 38,000
Jul 2015-Jun 2016 Income $493,150, State $7,350, City $470,800, County $10,000, Locally Generated Income $5,000. Mats Exp $39,500, Books $32,000, Per/Ser (Incl. Access Fees) $4,000, AV Mat $3,500. Sal $254,864 (Prof $65,000)
Library Holdings: Bk Vols 40,000; Per Subs 171
Automation Activity & Vendor Info: (Cataloging) TLC (The Library Corporation); (Circulation) TLC (The Library Corporation); (ILL) OCLC; (OPAC) TLC (The Library Corporation); (Serials) EBSCO Online
Wireless access
Open Mon-Fri 9-5:30, Sat 9-5
Friends of the Library Group

SAN FELIPE PUEBLO

P PUEBLO OF SAN FELIPE COMMUNITY LIBRARY, 18 Cougar Rd, 87001. (Mail add: PO Box 4339, 87001). Tel: 505-771-9970. FAX: 505-867-0320. E-mail: katishtyalibrary@gmail.com. Web Site: katishtyalibrary.wixsite.com/sfcl. *Libr Mgr,* Tracey A Charlie; E-mail: tcharlie@sfpueblo.com; *Library Contact,* Shannon Townsend; E-mail: stownsend@sfpueblo.com
Library Holdings: Bk Vols 1,500
Wireless access
Open Mon-Thurs 9-7, Fri 9-5

SAN LORENZO

S PINHOLE RESOURCE LIBRARY*, 224 Royal John Mine Rd, 88041. (Mail add: PO Box 1355, 88041), SAN 326-288X. Tel: 505-536-9942. E-mail: pinhole@gilanet.com. Web Site: www.pinholeresource.com. *Dir,* Eric Renner
Library Holdings: Bk Titles 400
Publications: Bibliography of Pinhole Optics; Bibliography of Pinhole Photography; Pinhole Journal
Partic in Soc for Photog Educ

SANTA FE

M CHRISTUS ST VINCENT REGIONAL MEDICAL CENTER LIBRARY*, 455 St Michael's Dr, 87505. SAN 375-1929. Tel: 505-820-5218. FAX: 505-989-6478.
Library Holdings: Bk Vols 2,000; Per Subs 210
Restriction: Staff use only

R CHURCH OF THE HOLY FAITH, EPISCOPAL*, Parish Library, 311 E Palace Ave, 87501. SAN 310-7124. Tel: 505-982-4447. E-mail: library@holyfaithchurchsf.org. Web Site: holyfaithchurchsf.org. *Librn,* Virginia Lopez; Tel: 505-982-4447, Ext 113
Founded 1949

Library Holdings: Bk Titles 7,000; Per Subs 6
Subject Interests: Altar, Arts, Biblical studies, Biog, Church hist, Comparative faiths, Healing, Missions, Music, Personal relig, Symbolism, Theol
Publications: Monthly Parish Magazine; Weekly Bulletin
Open Tues-Fri 9:30-4:30
Friends of the Library Group

C INSTITUTE OF AMERICAN INDIAN ARTS LIBRARY*, 83 Avan Nu Po Rd, 87508. SAN 310-7167. Tel: 505-424-5715. FAX: 505-424-3131. Web Site: iaia.edu/academics/library. *Instruction & Ref Librn,* Sara Quimby; Tel: 505-424-2399, E-mail: sara.quimby@iaia.edu; *Cat, Pub Serv Librn,* Jessica Mlotkowski; Tel: 505-424-2333, E-mail: jessica.mlotkowski@iaia.edu; *Archivist,* Ryan Flahive; Tel: 505-424-5743, E-mail: rflahive@iaia.edu; *Libr Asst,* Peggy Trujillo; E-mail: peggy.trujillo@iaia.edu; *Libr Spec,* Grace Nuvayestewa; Tel: 505-424-2398, E-mail: gnuvayestewa@iaia.edu; Staff 5 (MLS 4, Non-MLS 1)
Founded 1962. Enrl 343; Highest Degree: Bachelor
Library Holdings: CDs 700; DVDs 900; Bk Vols 39,000; Per Subs 150
Special Collections: History of the Institute (IAIA Archives); Lee & Stewart Udall Special Coll; Lloyd Kiva New Special Coll; National Anthropological Archive Photographs (Smithsonian Photo Coll of Native American People & Places); Native American Music Coll, cassettes & rec; TC Cannon Special Coll; Visual Resources Coll
Subject Interests: Art, Native Am
Automation Activity & Vendor Info: (Cataloging) Innovative Interfaces, Inc - Millennium; (Circulation) Innovative Interfaces, Inc - Millennium; (Serials) Innovative Interfaces, Inc - Millennium
Wireless access
Function: Archival coll, Electronic databases & coll, For res purposes, Online cat, Wheelchair accessible
Partic in American Indian Higher Education Consortium; New Mexico Consortium of Academic Libraries
Open Mon-Thurs 8am-9pm, Fri 8-5, Sun 12-9
Restriction: Open to students, fac & staff, Pub use on premises

G LEGISLATIVE COUNCIL SERVICE LIBRARY*, 411 State Capitol, 87501. SAN 310-7183. Tel: 505-986-4600. FAX: 505-986-4680. Web Site: www.nmlegis.gov. *Sr Legis Librn,* Joanne Vandestreek; Tel: 505-986-4656, E-mail: joanne.vandestreek@nmlegis.gov; Staff 2 (MLS 2)
Founded 1951
Library Holdings: Bk Titles 2,800; Bk Vols 4,000; Per Subs 25
Special Collections: Legislative Reports. State Document Depository
Subject Interests: Govt, Pub finance, Taxation
Wireless access
Open Mon-Fri 8-5

L MONTGOMERY & ANDREWS*, Law Library, 325 Paseo de Peralta, 87501. SAN 372-4271. Tel: 505-982-3873. FAX: 505-982-4289. Web Site: montand.com. *Librn,* Bertha Sandoval; E-mail: btrujillo@montand.com
Library Holdings: Bk Vols 15,000
Subject Interests: Commercial law
Restriction: Not open to pub

S MUSEUM OF INTERNATIONAL FOLK ART, Bartlett Library, 706 Camino Lejo, 87505. (Mail add: PO Box 2087, 87504-2087), SAN 351-6903. Tel: 505-476-1210. FAX: 505-476-1300. E-mail: bartlett.library@state.nm.us. Web Site: library.internationalfolkart.org. *Librn & Archivist,* Brian Graney; E-mail: brian.graney@state.nm.us; Staff 1 (MLS 1)
Founded 1953
Library Holdings: AV Mats 70; e-journals 10; Microforms 70; Bk Titles 21,000; Per Subs 345
Special Collections: Oral History
Subject Interests: Conserv, Craft, Folk art, Mus studies, Outsider art, Spanish colonial art, Textiles
Automation Activity & Vendor Info: (Cataloging) ByWater Solutions; (Circulation) ByWater Solutions; (ILL) OCLC WorldShare Interlibrary Loan; (OPAC) ByWater Solutions
Wireless access
Function: Ref serv available, Res libr
Partic in Amigos Library Services, Inc; OCLC Online Computer Library Center, Inc
Restriction: Non-circulating, Open by appt only

MUSEUM OF NEW MEXICO
S PALACE OF THE GOVERNORS-FRAY ANGELICO CHAVEZ HISTORY LIBRARY*, 120 Washington Ave, 87501. (Mail add: PO Box 2087, 87504), SAN 351-6814. Tel: 505-476-5090. E-mail: historylibrary@state.nm.us. Web Site: www.palaceofthegovernors.org. *Librn,* Patricia Hewitt; *Curator,* Tomas Jaehn; Staff 2 (Non-MLS 2)
Founded 1885
Library Holdings: Bk Vols 50,000; Per Subs 45
Special Collections: New Mexico, maps & ms, newsp, rare bks; Southwest (Photo Archives), prints. Oral History
Subject Interests: NMex, SW, Western Americana
Function: Ref serv available
Publications: El Palacio
Open Tues-Fri 1-5
Restriction: Open to pub for ref only

S MUSEUM OF FINE ARTS LIBRARY*, 107 W Palace Ave, 87501. (Mail add: PO Box 2087, 87504-2087), SAN 351-6873. Tel: 505-476-5061. FAX: 505-476-5076. Web Site: www.mfasantafe.org. *Librn,* Rebecca Potance; E-mail: rebecca.potance@state.nm.us
Founded 1917
Library Holdings: Bk Titles 7,500; Per Subs 35
Special Collections: Artist Biographies; Exchange Exhibition, cats; New Mexican & Southwestern Art Coll
Restriction: Open by appt only

S MUSEUM OF INDIAN ARTS & CULTURE-LABORATORY OF ANTHROPOLOGY LIBRARY*, 708 Camino Lejo, 87505. (Mail add: PO Box 2087, 87504-2087), SAN 351-6849. Tel: 505-476-1264. FAX: 505-476-1330. E-mail: LOA.Library@State.NM.US. Web Site: www.indianartsandculture.org. *Libr Dir,* Allison Colborne; E-mail: allison.colborne@state.nm.us; Staff 1 (MLS 1)
Founded 1929
Library Holdings: Bk Vols 39,300; Per Subs 70
Special Collections: LOA Library Rare Books Coll; Mesoamerican Archaeology & Ethnohistory Coll (Sylvanus G Morley Library)
Subject Interests: Indians of Cent Am, Indians of Mexico, SW anthrop, SW archaeol, SW hist, SW Indian arts, SW Indian mat culture
Automation Activity & Vendor Info: (OPAC) ByWater Solutions
Function: ILL available, Ref serv available
Publications: List of Serials Holdings
Open Mon-Fri 10-12 & 1-5
Restriction: In-house use for visitors, Open to pub for ref only

S PALACE OF THE GOVERNORS PHOTO ARCHIVES*, 120 Washington Ave, 87501. (Mail add: PO Box 2087, 87504-2087), SAN 351-6938. Tel: 505-476-5092. FAX: 505-476-5053, 505-476-5104. E-mail: photos@mnm.state.nm.us. Web Site: palaceofthegovernors.org/photoarchives.html.
Founded 1960
Library Holdings: Bk Titles 3,000
Special Collections: Photograph Coll 1850-present
Subject Interests: Agr, Anthrop, Archaeology, Australia, China, Ethnology, Hist of NMex, India, Indians, Japan, Latin Am, Middle East, Mining, New Zealand, Philippines, Railroads
Publications: Collection Guides; Photog Catalogs; Reprint Series
Open Mon-Fri 1-5
Restriction: Not a lending libr

S NEW MEXICO SCHOOL FOR THE DEAF LIBRARY*, 1060 Cerrillos Rd, 87505, SAN 310-7191. Tel: 505-476-6383. FAX: 505-476-6376. Web Site: www.nmsd.k12.nm.us/academic_programs/library___media. *Librn,* Briean Burton; E-mail: briean.burton@nmsd.k12.nm.us
Library Holdings: Bk Vols 16,000; Per Subs 40
Subject Interests: Deaf culture, Deaf educ, Deafness, Sign lang
Wireless access
Function: After school storytime, CD-ROM, Distance learning, Photocopying/Printing
Restriction: Open to students, fac & staff

P NEW MEXICO STATE LIBRARY*, 1209 Camino Carlos Rey, 87507. SAN 351-6962. Tel: 505-476-9700. Toll Free Tel: 800-477-4401. FAX: 505-476-9701. Web Site: www.nmstatelibrary.org. *Dep State Librn,* Joy Poole; Tel: 505-476-9712, E-mail: joy.poole@state.nm.us; Staff 22 (MLS 22)
Founded 1929. Pop 1,819,046
Library Holdings: Bk Vols 200,000; Per Subs 2,000
Special Collections: State Document Depository; US Document Depository
Subject Interests: Govt, Pub policy
Automation Activity & Vendor Info: (Circulation) SirsiDynix
Wireless access
Publications: Annual Report; Annual Statistical Reports; Hitchhiker; Library Directory
Partic in OCLC Online Computer Library Center, Inc
Open Mon-Fri 10-5
Branches: 1

P LIBRARY FOR THE BLIND & PHYSICALLY HANDICAPPED, 1209 Camino Carlos Rey, 87507, SAN 310-7213. Tel: 505-476-9770. Toll Free Tel: 800-456-5515. FAX: 505-476-9776. E-mail: sl.lbph@state.nm.us. Web Site: www.nmstatelibrary.org/lbph. *Regional Librn,* John Mugford; Tel: 505-476-9772, E-mail: john.mugford@state.nm.us; *Librn,* Tim Donahue; Tel: 505-476-9760, E-mail: tim.donahue@state.nm.us; Staff 6 (MLS 1.5, Non-MLS 4.5)
Founded 1967

Library Holdings: Bk Titles 72,000; Bk Vols 150,000; Talking Bks 72,000; Videos 150
Subject Interests: NMex
Automation Activity & Vendor Info: (Cataloging) Keystone Systems, Inc (KLAS); (Circulation) Keystone Systems, Inc (KLAS); (OPAC) Keystone Systems, Inc (KLAS)
Function: Bks on cassette, Digital talking bks
Publications: New Mexico State Library News of the Library for the Blind & Physically Handicapped (Newsletter)
Special Services for the Blind - Braille bks
Open Mon-Fri 10-4
Friends of the Library Group
Bookmobiles: 3

S GEORGIA O'KEEFFE MUSEUM, Michael S Engl Family Foundation Library & Archive, 217 Johnson St, 87501. Information Services Tel: 505-946-1040. E-mail: library@okeeffemuseum.org. Web Site: www.okeeffemuseum.org/research-center/library-and-archives. *Dir,* Cody Hartley; *Head, Research Collections & Services,* Elizabeth Ehrnst; E-mail: eehrnst@okeeffemuseum.org; *Res Assoc,* Tori Duggan; E-mail: tduggan@okeeffemuseum.org; *Archivist,* Ashley Baranyk; E-mail: abaranyk@okeeffemuseum.org; Staff 3 (MLS 1, Non-MLS 2)
Founded 2001
Library Holdings: Electronic Media & Resources 8,895; Bk Titles 10,162; Per Subs 30
Special Collections: American Modernism; Georgia O'Keeffe Foundation Archive; Georgia O'Keeffe Papers; Maria Chabot Archive; Rare Books
Automation Activity & Vendor Info: (Acquisitions) Koha; (Cataloging) OCLC CatExpress; (Circulation) Koha; (Discovery) Koha; (ILL) OCLC WorldShare Interlibrary Loan; (OPAC) Koha
Wireless access
Function: 24/7 Electronic res, 24/7 Online cat, Archival coll, Art exhibits, Audio & video playback equip for onsite use, Bk reviews (Group), Bus archives, CD-ROM, Computer training, Computers for patron use, Doc delivery serv, Electronic databases & coll, For res purposes, Free DVD rentals, Holiday prog, ILL available, Internet access, Magnifiers for reading, Mail & tel request accepted, Meeting rooms, Movies, Museum passes, Online cat, Online ref, Orientations, Outreach serv, Photocopying/Printing, Prog for adults, Prog for children & young adult, Ref & res, Ref serv available, Res assist avail, Res libr, Scanner, VHS videos, Wheelchair accessible, Workshops
Partic in Amigos Library Services, Inc
Restriction: Circ limited, Internal circ only, Non-circulating of rare bks, Non-circulating to the pub, Not a lending libr, Off-site coll in storage - retrieval as requested, Open to pub by appt only

P PUEBLO OF POJOAQUE PUBLIC LIBRARY*, 37 Camino del Rincon, Ste 2, 87506-9810. Tel: 505-455-7511. FAX: 505-455-0501. Web Site: www.puebloofpojoaquepubliclibrary.org. *Libr Dir,* Adam Becker; E-mail: abecker@pojoaque.org; *Circ,* Bernadette Fresquez; *Tech Serv,* Vanessa Montoya; Staff 3 (MLS 1, Non-MLS 2)
Library Holdings: AV Mats 1,500; Bk Vols 15,000; Per Subs 20
Special Collections: Southwest Coll
Wireless access
Open Mon-Thurs 9-7, Fri 9-5, Sat 10-3

C SAINT JOHN'S COLLEGE*, Meem Library, 1160 Camino Cruz Blanca, 87505. SAN 310-7248. Tel: 505-984-6042. FAX: 505-984-6004. Web Site: www.sjc.edu/academic-programs/libraries/meem-library. *Dir,* Jennifer Sprague; Tel: 505-984-6041, E-mail: jennifer.sprague@sjc.edu; *Acq, Archives,* Craig Jolly; Tel: 505-984-6043, E-mail: craig.jolly@sjc.edu; *ILL, Tech Serv,* Laura Cooley; Tel: 505-984-6045, E-mail: laura.cooley@sjc.edu; Staff 3 (MLS 2, Non-MLS 1)
Founded 1964. Enrl 355; Fac 70; Highest Degree: Master
Library Holdings: Bk Titles 35,000; Bk Vols 70,000; Per Subs 120
Special Collections: Hunt Coll; Music (Grumman, Holzman, Schmidt & White)
Subject Interests: Classics, Music, Philos
Automation Activity & Vendor Info: (Cataloging) SirsiDynix; (Circulation) SirsiDynix; (OPAC) SirsiDynix
Wireless access
Function: ILL available
Partic in New Mexico Consortium of Academic Libraries; OCLC Online Computer Library Center, Inc

J SANTA FE COMMUNITY COLLEGE LIBRARY, 6401 Richards Ave, 87508-4887. Tel: 505-428-1352. FAX: 505-428-1288. E-mail: library@sfcc.edu. Web Site: www.sfcc.edu/offices/library. *Libr Dir,* Valeria Nye; Tel: 505-428-1506, E-mail: valerie.nye@sfcc.edu; *Coll & Instruction Librn,* Laura Smith; Tel: 505-428-1368, E-mail: laura.smith@sfcc.edu; *Ref & Instruction Librn,* Sarah Hood; Tel: 505-428-1830, E-mail: sarah.hood@sfcc.edu; *Tech Serv Librn,* Harriet Meiklejohn; Tel: 505-428-1287, E-mail: harriet.meiklejohn@sfcc.edu; *Libr Tech,* Fran Lopez; Tel: 505-428-1213, E-mail: francelia.lopez@sfcc.edu; *Libr Asst,* Position Currently Open; Staff 6 (MLS 4, Non-MLS 2)
Founded 1983. Highest Degree: Associate
Library Holdings: Audiobooks 150; CDs 430; DVDs 1,700; e-journals 30,000; Bk Vols 60,000; Per Subs 200
Automation Activity & Vendor Info: (Cataloging) OCLC Worldshare Management Services; (Circulation) OCLC Worldshare Management Services; (Course Reserve) OCLC Worldshare Management Services; (ILL) OCLC WorldShare Interlibrary Loan; (OPAC) OCLC Worldshare Management Services
Wireless access
Function: 24/7 Online cat, Telephone ref
Partic in New Mexico Consortium of Academic Libraries
Open Mon-Thurs 8-7, Fri 8-5, Sat 10-4

S SANTA FE INSTITUTE LIBRARY, 1399 Hyde Park Rd, 87501. SAN 375-359X. Tel: 505-946-2707. Reference Tel: 505-946-2708. FAX: 505-982-0565. E-mail: library@santafe.edu. Web Site: www.santafe.edu/research/resources/library. *Librn,* Caroline Seigel; E-mail: cseigel@santafe.edu; Staff 2 (MLS 1, Non-MLS 1)
Founded 1984
Library Holdings: e-journals 600; Bk Vols 10,500; Per Subs 25
Special Collections: Garrett Birkhoff Coll; Stanislav Ulum Coll
Automation Activity & Vendor Info: (Circulation) Innovative Interfaces, Inc; (OPAC) Innovative Interfaces, Inc
Wireless access
Partic in OCLC Online Computer Library Center, Inc
Open Mon-Fri 10:30-2:30
Restriction: Non-circulating to the pub

P SANTA FE PUBLIC LIBRARY*, 145 Washington Ave, 87501. SAN 351-7020. Tel: 505-955-6780. Circulation Tel: 505-955-6785. Interlibrary Loan Service Tel: 505-955-6720. Reference Tel: 505-955-6781. Administration Tel: 505-955-6789. FAX: 505-955-6676. E-mail: library@santafenm.gov. Web Site: www.santafelibrary.org. *Libr Dir,* Maria Sanchez-Tucker; E-mail: metucker@santafenm.gov; *Dir, Tech Serv,* Margaret G Baca; E-mail: mgbaca@ci.santafenm.gov; Staff 19 (MLS 17, Non-MLS 2)
Founded 1896. Pop 67,947; Circ 690,308
Jul 2014-Jun 2015 Income (Main & Associated Libraries) $3,827,819, State $81,959, City $3,588,451, Federal $15,560, County $30,000, Other $141,859. Mats Exp $492,153, Books $334,411, Per/Ser (Incl. Access Fees) $25,617, Micro $6,000, AV Mat $70,159, Electronic Ref Mat (Incl. Access Fees) $55,966. Sal $1,721,150
Library Holdings: Audiobooks 7,184; Bks on Deafness & Sign Lang 182; CDs 5,919; DVDs 17,633; e-books 4,088; Electronic Media & Resources 8,641; Large Print Bks 3,597; Microforms 108; Music Scores 270; Bk Titles 168,362; Bk Vols 256,532; Per Subs 449
Special Collections: New Mexico & Santa Fe (Southwest Coll)
Automation Activity & Vendor Info: (Acquisitions) Innovative Interfaces, Inc; (Cataloging) Innovative Interfaces, Inc; (Circulation) Innovative Interfaces, Inc; (ILL) OCLC Connexion; (OPAC) Innovative Interfaces, Inc
Wireless access
Function: 24/7 Electronic res, 24/7 Online cat, Art exhibits, Audiobks via web, AV serv, Bilingual assistance for Spanish patrons, Bks on CD, Children's prog, Computers for patron use, Electronic databases & coll, Free DVD rentals, ILL available, Internet access, Magazines, Magnifiers for reading, Mango lang, Meeting rooms, Microfiche/film & reading machines, Movies, Museum passes, Music CDs, Online cat, Orientations, Outreach serv, OverDrive digital audio bks, Photocopying/Printing, Preschool outreach, Prog for adults, Prog for children & young adult, Ref serv available, Spanish lang bks, Spoken cassettes & CDs, Spoken cassettes & DVDs, Story hour, Summer reading prog, Tax forms, Teen prog, Wheelchair accessible, Workshops
Partic in OCLC Online Computer Library Center, Inc
Special Services for the Deaf - Bks on deafness & sign lang; Closed caption videos; Sign lang interpreter upon request for prog
Special Services for the Blind - Audio mat; Bks on CD; Copier with enlargement capabilities; Large print bks; Low vision equip; Magnifiers
Open Mon-Thurs 10-8, Fri & Sat 10-6, Sun 1-5
Friends of the Library Group
Branches: 2
OLIVER LA FARGE BRANCH LIBRARY, 1730 Llano St, 87505-5460, SAN 351-7101. Tel: 505-955-4860. Reference Tel: 505-955-4862. FAX: 505-955-4861.
Founded 1978
Function: After school storytime, Art exhibits, AV serv, Bk club(s), Bks on CD, Children's prog, Computers for patron use, Electronic databases & coll, Free DVD rentals, ILL available, Magazines, Magnifiers for reading, Mango lang, Music CDs, Online cat, Orientations, Outreach serv, Photocopying/Printing, Preschool reading prog, Prog for adults, Prog for children & young adult, Ref serv available, Spanish lang bks, Story hour, Summer reading prog, Tax forms, Teen prog, Telephone ref, VHS videos, Wheelchair accessible

Special Services for the Deaf - Bks on deafness & sign lang; Closed caption videos; Sign lang interpreter upon request for prog
Special Services for the Blind - Audio mat; Bks on CD; Large print bks; Large screen computer & software
Open Mon-Wed 10-8, Thurs-Sat 10-6
Friends of the Library Group

SOUTHSIDE BRANCH LIBRARY, 6599 Jaguar Dr, 85707. Tel: 505-955-2810. Reference Tel: 505-955-2820. FAX: 505-955-2811.
Function: After school storytime, Art exhibits, Bks on CD, Children's prog, Computer training, Computers for patron use, Electronic databases & coll, Free DVD rentals, ILL available, Magazines, Magnifiers for reading, Mango lang, Music CDs, Online cat, Orientations, Outreach serv, Photocopying/Printing, Preschool reading prog, Prog for adults, Prog for children & young adult, Ref serv available, Spanish lang bks, Story hour, Study rm, Summer reading prog, Tax forms, Teen prog, Telephone ref, Wheelchair accessible
Special Services for the Deaf - Bks on deafness & sign lang; Closed caption videos; Sign lang interpreter upon request for prog
Special Services for the Blind - Audio mat; Bks on cassette; Bks on CD; Cassette playback machines; Large print bks; Large screen computer & software; Text reader
Open Mon-Thurs 10:30-8, Fri & Sat 10:30-6, Sun 1-5
Friends of the Library Group

S SCHOOL FOR ADVANCED RESEARCH LIBRARY*, Catherine McElvain Library, 660 Garcia St, 87505. (Mail add: PO Box 2188, 87504-2188), SAN 310-7256. Tel: 505-954-7234. FAX: 505-954-7214. E-mail: library@sarsf.org. Web Site: sarweb.org/education/catherine-mcelvain-library. *Librn,* Katherine Wolf; E-mail: wolf@sarsf.org; Staff 1 (MLS 1)
Founded 1960
Library Holdings: Bk Titles 9,000; Per Subs 49
Special Collections: Institutional, Indian Arts Fund & Associated Individuals Archive
Subject Interests: Anthrop, Hist of anthrop, Theory & methodology
Automation Activity & Vendor Info: (Cataloging) LibLime; (Circulation) LibLime
Wireless access
Function: Res libr
Open Mon-Fri 10-12 & 1-5

C SOUTHWESTERN COLLEGE*, Quimby Memorial Library, 3960 San Felipe Rd, 87507. SAN 375-3166. Tel: 505-467-6825. Toll Free Tel: 877-471-5756, Ext 6825. FAX: 505-467-6826. E-mail: library@swc.edu. Web Site: www.swc.edu/about-the-library. *Libr Dir,* Leslie Monsalve-Jones; *Distance Educ Librn,* Larry Harkcom; E-mail: larryharkcom@swc.edu; Staff 1 (Non-MLS 1)
Founded 1963. Enrl 180; Fac 18; Highest Degree: Master
Library Holdings: AV Mats 258; Bk Titles 18,000; Per Subs 12
Subject Interests: Applied psychol, Art therapy, Comparative relig, Counseling, Experimental educ, Grief therapy, Metaphysics
Automation Activity & Vendor Info: (Acquisitions) Follett Software; (Cataloging) Follett Software; (Circulation) Follett Software; (Course Reserve) EBSCO Online; (OPAC) Follett Software
Wireless access
Function: AV serv, Res libr
Open Mon-Thurs 8:30-6, Fri 8:45-4, Sat 10-5

GL SUPREME COURT LAW LIBRARY, 237 Don Gaspar Ave, 87501. (Mail add: PO Box L, 87504-0318), SAN 310-7221. Tel: 505-827-4850. FAX: 505-827-4852. Reference E-mail: libref@nmcourts.gov. Web Site: lawlibrary.nmcourts.gov.
Founded 1853
Special Collections: US Document Depository
Subject Interests: Anglo-Am law, Pre-1850 Mexican Law
Automation Activity & Vendor Info: (Cataloging) EOS International; (Circulation) EOS International; (ILL) OCLC WorldShare Interlibrary Loan; (OPAC) EOS International
Wireless access
Function: 24/7 Online cat, Archival coll, Computers for patron use, Doc delivery serv, Electronic databases & coll, For res purposes, ILL available, Internet access, Legal assistance to inmates, Mail & tel request accepted, Microfiche/film & reading machines, Online cat, Outside serv via phone, mail, e-mail & web, Photocopying/Printing, Ref serv available, Res libr, Telephone ref
Partic in Amigos Library Services, Inc
Open Mon-Fri 8-12 & 1-5
Restriction: Badge access after hrs, Borrowing requests are handled by ILL, Circ limited, Closed stack, In-house use for visitors, Non-circulating of rare bks, Open to pub for ref & circ; with some limitations, Restricted borrowing privileges, Restricted loan policy, Secured area only open to authorized personnel

P VISTA GRANDE PUBLIC LIBRARY*, 14 Avenida Torreon, 87508-9199. (Mail add: Seven Avenida Vista Grande, B7-192, 87508). Tel: 505-466-7323. E-mail: read@vglibrary.org. Web Site: www.vglibrary.org. *Dir,* Julia Kelso; *Libr Asst,* Tracey Mitchell; Staff 1 (Non-MLS 1)
Founded 2001. Pop 5,799; Circ 35,000
Jul 2019-Jun 2020 Income $148,000, County $50,000, Locally Generated Income $90,000, Other $8,000. Mats Exp $15,225, Books $11,000, Per/Ser (Incl. Access Fees) $225, AV Mat $4,000
Library Holdings: Audiobooks 1,830; AV Mats 5; CDs 1,360; DVDs 4,330; Electronic Media & Resources 1,045; High Interest/Low Vocabulary Bk Vols 65; Large Print Bks 183; Bk Vols 24,800; Per Subs 12
Automation Activity & Vendor Info: (Cataloging) Biblionix/Apollo; (Circulation) Biblionix/Apollo; (OPAC) Biblionix/Apollo
Wireless access
Function: 24/7 Electronic res, 24/7 Online cat, Activity rm, After school storytime, Art exhibits, AV serv, Bk club(s), Bk reviews (Group), Bks on CD, Chess club, Children's prog, Computers for patron use, Digital talking bks, E-Reserves, Electronic databases & coll, Equip loans & repairs, For res purposes, Free DVD rentals, Genealogy discussion group, Health sci info serv, Holiday prog, ILL available, Internet access, Large print keyboards, Life-long learning prog for all ages, Magazines, Magnifiers for reading, Mail & tel request accepted, Meeting rooms, Movies, Museum passes, Music CDs, Notary serv, Online cat, Online info literacy tutorials on the web & in blackboard, Online ref, Photocopying/Printing, Preschool reading prog, Prog for adults, Prog for children & young adult, Ref & res, Ref serv available, Scanner, Serves people with intellectual disabilities, Spanish lang bks, Story hour, Study rm, Summer & winter reading prog, Summer reading prog, Tax forms, Wheelchair accessible, Winter reading prog
Open Tues-Fri 10-6, Sat 10-4
Restriction: Circ to mem only

S WHEELWRIGHT MUSEUM OF THE AMERICAN INDIAN*, Mary Cabot Wheelwright Research Library, 704 Camino Lejo, 87505. (Mail add: PO Box 5153, Sante Fe, 87502-5153), SAN 310-7264. Tel: 505-982-4636. Toll Free Tel: 800-607-4636. FAX: 505-989-7386. E-mail: info@wheelwright.org. Web Site: www.wheelwright.org. *Interim Dir,* Jean Higgins; E-mail: asstdir@wheelwright.org; *Chief Curator,* Andrea Hanley; E-mail: ahanley@wheelwright.org
Founded 1937
Library Holdings: Bk Vols 4,000
Subject Interests: Culture of Navajo Indians, Indians of NAm
Open Tues-Sat 10-4

SANTA ROSA

P MOISE MEMORIAL LIBRARY, 208 S Fifth St, 88435-2329. SAN 310-7272. Tel: 575-472-3101. FAX: 575-472-4101. E-mail: moiselibrary@plateautel.net. Web Site: moiselibrary.wordpress.com. *Dir & Librn,* Mary Martinez
Founded 1932. Pop 2,840; Circ 15,196
Library Holdings: Audiobooks 589; CDs 69; DVDs 388; Bk Vols 17,040; Per Subs 30; Videos 665
Special Collections: Municipal. Oral History
Wireless access
Special Services for the Deaf - Spec interest per
Open Mon-Fri 10-6, Sat 9-12
Friends of the Library Group

SANTO DOMINGO PUEBLO

P SANTO DOMINGO PUBLIC LIBRARY, Tesuque St, 87052-0160. E-mail: kewalib@yahoo.com. Web Site: santodomingotribe.org/library. *Librn,* Cynthia Aguilar; E-mail: caguilar@kewa-nsn.us
Library Holdings: Bk Vols 2,778; Per Subs 27
Automation Activity & Vendor Info: (Cataloging) Follett Software; (Circulation) Follett Software; (OPAC) Follett Software
Function: AV serv, Children's prog, Computer training, Computers for patron use, Online ref, Prog for children & young adult, Satellite serv, Summer reading prog, Wheelchair accessible
Open Mon-Fri 8-5
Restriction: Circ limited, Open evenings by appt, Open to employees & special libr, Open to pub upon request, Open to students, Pub use on premises, Use of others with permission of librn

SHIPROCK

J DINE COLLEGE*, Senator John D Pinto Library, Hwy 64 & N 570, 87420. (Mail add: PO Box 580, 87240). Tel: 505-368-3346. E-mail: library@dinecollege.edu. Web Site: library.dinecollege.edu. *Br Librn,* Phillipa Rosman; Tel: 505-368-3644, E-mail: prosman@dinecollege.edu; Staff 4 (Non-MLS 4)
Enrl 450; Highest Degree: Associate
Library Holdings: e-books 11,000; Bk Vols 25,000; Per Subs 35
Special Collections: American Indian Culture with Special Navajo Coll
Subject Interests: Geol of western US

Automation Activity & Vendor Info: (Acquisitions) Ex Libris Group; (Cataloging) Ex Libris Group; (Circulation) Ex Libris Group; (OPAC) Ex Libris Group
Wireless access
Partic in New Mexico Consortium of Academic Libraries
Open Mon-Thurs 8-6, Fri 8-5: Mon-Thurs 8-7, Fri 8-5 (Summer)

SILVER CITY

C WESTERN NEW MEXICO UNIVERSITY, J Cloyd Miller Library, 1000 W College Ave, 88062. (Mail add: PO Box 680, 88062-0680), SAN 310-7310. Tel: 575-538-6745. FAX: 575-538-6178. E-mail: libraryadmin@wnmu.edu. Web Site: library.wnmu.edu. *Univ Librn,* Dr Gilda Baeza-Ortego; Tel: 575-538-6358, E-mail: gilda.baeza-ortego@wnmu.edu; Staff 5 (MLS 4, Non-MLS 1)
Founded 1893. Enrl 4,100; Fac 120; Highest Degree: Master
Library Holdings: Bks on Deafness & Sign Lang 300; Bk Titles 150,384; Per Subs 950
Special Collections: Bruce Hayword Papers; Chino Administrative Order of Consent Repository; Dale French Papers; Empire Zinc Strike Early 1950s (Juan Chacon & Jack Cargill Coll); Fort Bayard Blueprints & Maps; History (Library of American Civilization, Indian Claims Commission, Contemporary Newspapers of the North American Indian & Western Americana History), fiche & film; Kennecott Copper Corp, Chino Division Newletters; Local Newspapers from 1886; US National Archive Records, microfilm. State Document Depository; US Document Depository
Subject Interests: Allied health, Border studies, Culture, Educ, Environ studies, Mexican-Am studies, Native American, Nursing, Rural, SW hist, Wilderness area
Automation Activity & Vendor Info: (Acquisitions) Ex Libris Group; (Cataloging) Ex Libris Group; (Circulation) Ex Libris Group; (Course Reserve) Ex Libris Group; (ILL) Ex Libris Group; (OPAC) Ex Libris Group; (Serials) Ex Libris Group
Wireless access
Partic in Amigos Library Services, Inc; National Network of Libraries of Medicine Region 4; New Mexico Consortium of Academic Libraries; OCLC Online Computer Library Center, Inc
Open Mon-Thurs 7:30am-8:30pm, Fri 7:30-5, Sat & Sun Noon-4

SOCORRO

C NEW MEXICO TECH*, Joseph R Skeen Library, 801 Leroy Pl, 87801. SAN 310-7337. Tel: 575-835-5614. Interlibrary Loan Service Tel: 575-835-6600. FAX: 575-835-5754. E-mail: nmtlib@npe.nmt.edu. Web Site: www.nmt.edu/library. *Dir,* Dr David Cox; E-mail: david.cox@nmt.edu; Staff 9 (MLS 3, Non-MLS 6)
Founded 1895. Enrl 2,000; Fac 128; Highest Degree: Doctorate
Library Holdings: DVDs 1,224; e-books 111,000; Bk Titles 242,289; Bk Vols 483,038; Per Subs 2,429
Special Collections: Congressional Papers of Joseph Skeen; Theses & Dissertations; US Bureau of Mines Publications; US Geological Survey Publications, microfiche, print. State Document Depository; US Document Depository
Subject Interests: Applied math, Astrophysics, Biology, Computer sci, Electrical engr, Environ engr, Environ sci, Geol, Petroleum engr, Physics
Automation Activity & Vendor Info: (Acquisitions) Innovative Interfaces, Inc; (Cataloging) Innovative Interfaces, Inc; (Circulation) Innovative Interfaces, Inc; (ILL) OCLC ILLiad; (OPAC) Innovative Interfaces, Inc
Wireless access
Function: Free DVD rentals, Govt ref serv, Photocopying/Printing, Wheelchair accessible
Partic in Amigos Library Services, Inc; New Mexico Consortium of Academic Libraries; Statewide California Electronic Library Consortium
Open Mon-Thurs (Winter) 8am-Midnight, Fri 8-8, Sat 10-6, Sun Noon-Midnight; Mon-Thurs (Summer) 8am-10pm, Fri 8-5, Sun Noon-8

P SOCORRO PUBLIC LIBRARY*, 401 Park St, 87801-4544. SAN 310-7345. Tel: 505-835-1114. FAX: 505-835-1182. E-mail: library@adobelibrary.org. Web Site: www.adobelibrary.org. *Dir,* Donald Padilla; *Ad,* Chelsea Lyons; E-mail: spladult@adobelibrary.org; *Youth Serv,* Britta Herweg-Samuels; E-mail: splyouth@adobelibrary.org; Staff 8 (MLS 2, Non-MLS 6)
Founded 1924. Pop 9,000; Circ 78,064
Library Holdings: Bk Titles 50,000; Per Subs 100
Subject Interests: Adult basic reading, Local hist, SW hist
Wireless access
Function: 24/7 Online cat, Adult bk club, Adult literacy prog, Audio & video playback equip for onsite use, Audiobks via web, Bks on CD, Children's prog, Citizenship assistance, Computer training, Computers for patron use, Doc delivery serv, E-Readers, E-Reserves, Electronic databases & coll, Free DVD rentals, Holiday prog, ILL available, Internet access, Jail serv, Life-long learning prog for all ages, Literacy & newcomer serv, Magazines, Mango lang, Meeting rooms, Microfiche/film & reading machines, Museum passes, Music CDs, Online cat, Photocopying/Printing, Preschool reading prog, Prog for adults, Prog for children & young adult, Ref & res, Scanner, Senior computer classes, Senior outreach, Serves people with intellectual disabilities, Spanish lang bks, Summer & winter reading prog, Summer reading prog, Tax forms, Teen prog, Winter reading prog, Workshops
Publications: Friends of the Socorro Public Library (Newsletter)
Partic in NMex Info Systs
Open Mon-Thurs 9-6, Fri 9-5, Sat 9-2
Friends of the Library Group

SPRINGER

P FRED MACARON LIBRARY, 600 Colbert, 87747. (Mail add: PO Box 726, 87747-0726), SAN 310-7353. Tel: 575-483-2848. FAX: 575-483-2471. E-mail: macaronlibrary@qwestoffice.net. Web Site: macaron.biblionix.com. *Librn,* Norma Vigil
Circ 11,043
Library Holdings: Bk Vols 26,069; Per Subs 20
Wireless access
Open Mon-Fri 10-6

SUNLAND PARK

P SUNLAND PARK COMMUNITY LIBRARY*, 984 McNutt Rd, 88063-9039. Tel: 575-874-0873. Web Site: sunland.biblionix.com/catalog. *Libr Dir,* Crystal Jaime; E-mail: crystal.jaime@sunlandpark-nm.gov; *Libr Asst,* Lilia Rojas; E-mail: lilia.rojas@sunlandpark-nm.gov
Founded 2000
Automation Activity & Vendor Info: (Circulation) Innovative Interfaces, Inc; (OPAC) Innovative Interfaces, Inc
Wireless access
Function: 24/7 Online cat, Adult literacy prog, Art exhibits, Children's prog, Computer training, Computers for patron use, Electronic databases & coll, Family literacy, Homework prog, Internet access, Life-long learning prog for all ages, Museum passes, Music CDs, Online cat, Outreach serv, Outside serv via phone, mail, e-mail & web, Photocopying/Printing, Preschool outreach, Preschool reading prog, Prog for adults, Prog for children & young adult, Ref serv available, Spanish lang bks, Story hour, Summer reading prog, Tax forms, Teen prog, Telephone ref, Workshops
Open Mon-Fri 8-5
Restriction: Circ to mem only, Circulates for staff only, In-house use for visitors

TAOS

P TAOS PUBLIC LIBRARY*, 402 Camino de La Placita, 87571. SAN 310-7388. Tel: 575-758-3063. Circulation Tel: 575-737-2591. Interlibrary Loan Service Tel: 575-737-2593. Reference Tel: 575-737-2590. Web Site: www.taoslibrary.org. *Dir,* Shirley Fernandez; Tel: 575-737-2594, E-mail: sfernandez@taosgov.com; Staff 10 (Non-MLS 10)
Founded 1923. Pop 32,000
Library Holdings: Audiobooks 1,364; CDs 687; DVDs 1,952; Large Print Bks 1,074; Bk Titles 69,029; Bk Vols 73,702; Per Subs 110; Videos 2,384
Special Collections: D H Lawrence Coll; Frank Waters Coll; Scottish Clan MacLeod Coll; Taos-Specific Coll. Oral History
Subject Interests: Fine arts, Indigenous people, SW
Automation Activity & Vendor Info: (Cataloging) TLC (The Library Corporation); (Circulation) TLC (The Library Corporation); (OPAC) TLC (The Library Corporation)
Wireless access
Function: 24/7 Online cat, Archival coll, Audiobks via web, Bks on CD, Children's prog, Computers for patron use, Free DVD rentals, ILL available, Magazines, Mango lang, Museum passes, Online cat, OverDrive digital audio bks, Photocopying/Printing, Spanish lang bks, Story hour, Summer reading prog, Teen prog
Publications: Newsletter (Quarterly)
Partic in NMex Libr Asn
Special Services for the Blind - Magnifiers
Open Mon-Fri 10-6, Sat 10-5
Restriction: Authorized patrons, Non-resident fee
Friends of the Library Group

TATUM

P TATUM COMMUNITY LIBRARY, 323 E Broadway, 88267. (Mail add: PO Box 156, 88267-0156), SAN 310-7396. Tel: 575-398-4822. FAX: 575-398-4823. E-mail: tatumcommunitylibrary@leaco.net. *Libr Dir,* Crystal Weigel; *Librn,* Pam Dallas
Founded 1964. Pop 798
Jul 2018-Jun 2019 Income $71,210, State $12,885, City $58,325
Library Holdings: Audiobooks 501; CDs 9; DVDs 271; Electronic Media & Resources 49; Large Print Bks 720; Bk Titles 13,887; Per Subs 32; Videos 470
Automation Activity & Vendor Info: (Cataloging) Biblionix/Apollo
Wireless access
Function: 24/7 Online cat, Bks on CD, Computers for patron use, Free DVD rentals, ILL available, Internet access, Laminating, Magazines,

Museum passes, Notary serv, Online cat, Photocopying/Printing, Ref serv available, Res assist avail, Scanner, Spanish lang bks, Summer reading prog, Tax forms, VHS videos
Open Mon-Thurs 8:30-5:30, Fri 8:30-1:30

TRUCHAS

P TRUCHAS COMMUNITY LIBRARY, 60 County Rd 75, 87578. (Mail add: PO Box 330, 87578-0330). Tel: 505-689-2683. FAX: 505-689-1155. E-mail: truchas@cybermesa.com. Web Site: truchasservicescenter.org/library. *Libr Dir,* Julie C Trujillo; *Head Librn,* Virginia Padilla; *Librn,* Patricia Putnam
Pop 1,200
Library Holdings: AV Mats 42; CDs 275; DVDs 150; Large Print Bks 150; Bk Vols 6,274; Per Subs 26; Talking Bks 25; Videos 150
Automation Activity & Vendor Info: (ILL) LAC Group
Wireless access
Function: ILL available
Open Mon-Thurs 2-7, Fri 1-6, Sat 12-4

TRUTH OR CONSEQUENCES

P TRUTH OR CONSEQUENCES PUBLIC LIBRARY*, 325 Library Lane, 87901-2375. SAN 310-7418. Tel: 505-894-3027. FAX: 505-894-2068. E-mail: torclibrary@torcnm.org. Web Site: torcnm.org/departments/library/index.php. *Dir,* Pat O'Hanlon; Staff 4 (Non-MLS 4)
Founded 1933. Pop 7,200; Circ 58,000
Library Holdings: Audiobooks 1,550; AV Mats 3,065; Bk Titles 50,801; Per Subs 75
Subject Interests: SW
Wireless access
Function: 24/7 Online cat, Activity rm, Adult bk club
Partic in NMex Info Systs; OCLC Online Computer Library Center, Inc
Open Mon-Fri 9-5, Sat 9-Noon
Friends of the Library Group
Branches: 1
DOWNTOWN, 401 N Foch St, 87901. Tel: 505-894-7821. *Dir,* Pat O'Hanlon; *Asst Dir,* Denise Beard
Library Holdings: Bk Vols 3,500
Open Mon-Fri 9-12
Friends of the Library Group

TUCUMCARI

§J MESALANDS COMMUNITY COLLEGE LIBRARY, 911 S Tenth St, Bldg A, 88401. Tel: 575-461-4413, Ext 121. FAX: 575-461-1901. Web Site: www.mesalands.edu/current-students/support-services/library. *Dir,* Todd Morris; E-mail: toddm@mesalands.edu; *Libr Tech,* Nikki Vazquez; E-mail: nikkiv@mesalands.edu
Wireless access
Partic in New Mexico Consortium of Academic Libraries
Open Mon-Thurs 8am-8pm, Fri 8-5

P TUCUMCARI PUBLIC LIBRARY, 602 S Second, 88401-2899. SAN 310-7434. Tel: 505-461-0295. FAX: 505-461-0297. E-mail: library@cityoftucumcari.com. Web Site: www.cityoftucumcari.com/library.html, www.youseemore.com/tucumcari. *Dir,* Linda Gonzalez; *Librn,* Angelaica Gray
Founded 1927. Pop 10,155; Circ 65,876
Library Holdings: Bk Vols 35,000; Per Subs 62
Wireless access
Open Mon 9:30-7, Tues-Fri 9:30-5:30, Sat 9-1

VAUGHN

P VAUGHN PUBLIC LIBRARY*, 667 Victory Ct, 88353. Tel: 575-584-2580. *Librn,* Diana Gallegos
Pop 539
Library Holdings: Bk Vols 12,000
Open Mon, Wed & Fri 4:30-8:30

VIRDEN

P VIRDEN PUBLIC LIBRARY*, 209 Church St, 88045. Tel: 575-358-2544. FAX: 575-358-2544. E-mail: virdenlibrary@gmail.com. Web Site: www.villageofvirden.com/p/virden-public-library.html. *Librn,* Charlene Jones
Pop 142
Library Holdings: AV Mats 100; Bk Titles 7,000
Wireless access
Open Wed 9-5, Fri 10-12
Friends of the Library Group

WHITE SANDS MISSILE RANGE

A UNITED STATES ARMY*, Consolidated Library, Bldg 465, Rm 113, 88002-5039. SAN 351-711X. Tel: 575-678-5820. FAX: 575-678-2270. Web Site: whitesands.armymwr.com/programs/post-library. *Supvry Librn,* Colin R O'Hanlon, Sr; E-mail: colin.r.ohanlon.civ@mail.mil; Staff 4 (MLS 2, Non-MLS 2)
Founded 1950
Library Holdings: Audiobooks 300; AV Mats 500; Bks on Deafness & Sign Lang 12; CDs 360; DVDs 175; e-books 700; e-journals 300; High Interest/Low Vocabulary Bk Vols 50; Large Print Bks 100; Microforms 1,000; Bk Titles 52,300; Bk Vols 55,400; Per Subs 45; Spec Interest Per Sub 12; Talking Bks 300; Videos 100
Special Collections: Military Science Coll; Southwest Coll; Technical Documents Coll
Subject Interests: SW region, US Mil
Automation Activity & Vendor Info: (Cataloging) EOS International; (Circulation) EOS International; (Course Reserve) EOS International; (Media Booking) EOS International; (OPAC) EOS International
Wireless access
Function: Archival coll, Art exhibits, Bks on cassette, Bks on CD, Computers for patron use, Digital talking bks, Electronic databases & coll, Govt ref serv, Holiday prog, ILL available, Internet access, Mail & tel request accepted, Online cat, Online ref, Outside serv via phone, mail, e-mail & web, Photocopying/Printing, Ref & res, Ref serv available, Spoken cassettes & CDs, Spoken cassettes & DVDs, Tax forms, Telephone ref, Wheelchair accessible
Partic in OCLC Online Computer Library Center, Inc
Restriction: Authorized patrons, Govt use only, Mil, family mem, retirees, Civil Serv personnel NAF only, Not open to pub, Open to mil & govt employees only, Photo ID required for access

ZIA PUEBLO

P ZIA ENRICHMENT LIBRARY*, 162B Zia Blvd, 87053-6002. Tel: 505-867-3304. FAX: 505-867-3308. *Dir,* Joyce Medina
Pop 646; Circ 1,500
Library Holdings: AV Mats 100; Bk Vols 8,589; Per Subs 12
Automation Activity & Vendor Info: (Cataloging) Follett Software; (Circulation) Follett Software
Wireless access
Open Mon-Fri 8-7

ZUNI

P ZUNI PUBLIC LIBRARY, 27 E Chavez Circle, 87327. (Mail add: PO Box 339, 87327-0339). Tel: 505-782-4575. E-mail: zunilibrary@ashiwi.org. Web Site: zunipubliclibrary.org. *Actg Librn,* Sonya Quam; E-mail: sonya.quam@ashiwi.org
Library Holdings: AV Mats 3,760; Bk Vols 11,863
Automation Activity & Vendor Info: (Cataloging) Follett Software; (Circulation) Follett Software
Wireless access
Open Mon-Fri 8-5

NEW YORK

Date of Statistics: FY 2019-2020
Population, 2020 U.S. Census: 19,378,102
Population Served by Public Libraries: 19,378,102
Total Materials in Public Libraries: 167,337,213
Materials Per Capita: 8.64
Total Volumes in Public Libraries: 63,298,473
Volumes Per Capita: 3.27
Total Public Library Circulation: 112,222,958
Circulation Per Capita: 5.79
Digital Resources:
Total e-books: 38,646,565
Total audio items (physical and downloadable units): 12,985,821
Total video items (physical and downloadable units): 6,092,180
Total computers for use by the public: 19,426
Income and Expenditures:
Total Public Library Income (including Capital & Grant-in-Aid): $1,618,897,730
Source of Income: Mainly public funds
Expenditure Per Capita: $74,93
Grants-in-Aid to Public Libraries:
Federal (Library Services & Technology Act): $2,633,022
State Aid: $89,745,894
Formula for Apportionment Intent: Formation of Library System to serve given area
Operation: Payment on basis of population, service, and square mileage (includes fixed annual grant)
State Library's Share from Federal Sources: $5,568,148
Number of County or Multi-county (Regional) Libraries: 23
Counties Served: 62
Number of Bookmobiles in State: 12
Information provided courtesy of: Adriana Mastroianni, Education Program Assistant ; New York State Library

ADAMS

P ADAMS FREE LIBRARY, Two N Main St, 13605. (Mail add: PO Box 58, 13605-0058), SAN 376-3102. Tel: 315-232-2265. FAX: 315-232-2265. E-mail: admlib@ncls.org. Web Site: www.adamsfreelibrary.org. *Dir,* Samantha Morgan; *Libr Asst,* Priscilla King; Staff 1 (Non-MLS 1)
Founded 1902. Pop 1,624; Circ 8,026
Library Holdings: Bk Titles 9,568; Talking Bks 145
Automation Activity & Vendor Info: (Cataloging) SirsiDynix; (Circulation) SirsiDynix; (OPAC) SirsiDynix; (Serials) SirsiDynix
Wireless access
Mem of North Country Library System
Open Mon, Wed & Fri 12-6, Tues & Thurs 10-2, Sat 10-Noon

ADAMS CENTER

P ADAMS CENTER FREE LIBRARY, 18267 State Rte 177, 13606. SAN 310-7442. Tel: 315-583-5501. FAX: 315-583-6242. E-mail: adclib@ncls.org. Web Site: www.adamscenterfreelibrary.org. *Dir,* Mrs Jaye Worden
Library Holdings: Bk Vols 9,000
Automation Activity & Vendor Info: (Cataloging) SirsiDynix; (Circulation) SirsiDynix; (OPAC) SirsiDynix; (Serials) SirsiDynix
Wireless access
Mem of North Country Library System
Open Mon 3-6:30, Tues, Wed & Thurs 3-5:30, Fri 12-4:30, Sat 10-12:30

ADDISON

P ADDISON PUBLIC LIBRARY*, Six South St, 14801. SAN 310-7450. Tel: 607-359-3888. FAX: 607-359-3611. *Dir,* Lori Patterson; E-mail: pattersonl@stls.org
Founded 1893. Pop 2,734; Circ 19,077
Library Holdings: Bk Vols 16,500; Per Subs 30
Automation Activity & Vendor Info: (Cataloging) SirsiDynix; (Circulation) SirsiDynix; (OPAC) SirsiDynix; (Serials) SirsiDynix
Wireless access
Mem of Southern Tier Library System
Open Mon & Wed 2-8, Thurs 10-6, Fri 12-5

AFTON

P AFTON FREE LIBRARY, 105A Main St, 13730. (Mail add: PO Box 48, 13730-0048), SAN 310-7469. Tel: 607-639-1212. FAX: 607-639-1557. E-mail: af.ill@4cls.org. Web Site: libraries.4cls.org/afton. *Libr Mgr,* Ramona Bogart
Founded 1933. Pop 2,851; Circ 10,200
Library Holdings: AV Mats 154; Bk Vols 15,118; Per Subs 47
Automation Activity & Vendor Info: (Cataloging) SirsiDynix; (Circulation) SirsiDynix; (OPAC) SirsiDynix
Wireless access
Mem of Four County Library System
Open Mon & Tues 12-5, Thurs 12-7, Fri 9-5, Sat 9-1

AKRON

P NEWSTEAD PUBLIC LIBRARY*, Akron Library, 33 Main St, 14001-1020. SAN 310-7477. Tel: 716-542-2327. FAX: 716-542-3703. Web Site: www.buffalolib.org/content/library-locations/newstead. *Dir,* Kristine Sutton; E-mail: suttonk@buffalolib.org; Staff 3 (MLS 1, Non-MLS 2)
Founded 1942. Pop 7,440; Circ 32,507
Library Holdings: Bk Titles 17,000; Per Subs 99
Automation Activity & Vendor Info: (Acquisitions) SirsiDynix
Wireless access
Mem of Buffalo & Erie County Public Library System
Open Mon & Wed (Winter) 1-8, Tues, Fri & Sat 10-5; Mon & Wed (Summer) 10-8, Tues 10-6, Fri 10-5
Friends of the Library Group

ALBANY

C ALBANY COLLEGE OF PHARMACY & HEALTH SCIENCES*, George & Leona Lewis Library, 106 New Scotland Ave, 12208. SAN 324-7503. Tel: 518-694-7270. FAX: 518-694-7300. E-mail: library@acphs.edu. Web Site: libraryservices.acphs.edu. *Interim Dir, Libr Serv,* Kimberly Mitchell; Tel: 518-694-7124, E-mail: kimberly.mitchell@acphs.edu; *Head Librn,* Lisa Shaffer; E-mail: lisa.shaffer@acphs.edu; Staff 4 (MLS 2, Non-MLS 2)
Founded 1960. Enrl 1,148; Fac 83; Highest Degree: Doctorate
Subject Interests: Pharm
Automation Activity & Vendor Info: (Cataloging) SirsiDynix; (Circulation) SirsiDynix; (Course Reserve) SirsiDynix; (OPAC) SirsiDynix
Wireless access
Partic in Cap District Libr Coun for Ref & Res Resources

S ALBANY INSTITUTE OF HISTORY & ART*, 125 Washington Ave, 12210-2296. SAN 310-7493. Tel: 518-463-4478. FAX: 518-462-1522. E-mail: AIHAlibrary@albanyinstitute.org. Web Site: www.albanyinstitute.org. *Exec Dir,* Tammis Groft; Tel: 518-463-4478, Ext 423, E-mail: grofttk@albanyinstitute.org; *Chief Curator,* W Douglas McCombs, PhD; Tel: 518-463-4478, Ext 428, E-mail: mccombsd@albanyinstitute.org; *Librn & Archivist,* Hannah Cox; E-mail: coxh@albanyinstitute.org. Subject Specialists: *Archives, Manuscripts,* Tammis Groft; Staff 1 (MLS 1)
Founded 1791
Library Holdings: Bk Vols 14,000; Per Subs 50
Special Collections: Albany imprints, almanacs, maps, photographs, manuscripts, broadsides, archives, architectural drawings, ephemera, scrapbooks; Albany Social, Political & Business History, 18th & 19th Centuries, maps, ms, photog; American Painters & Sculptors, ms, photog; Broadsides (including DeWitt Clinton Coll of 18th & Early 19th Century); Dutch in The Upper Hudson Valley, 17th & 18th Centuries, maps, ms; Political Broadsides
Subject Interests: Art, Hist, Local hist, Upper Hudson valleys
Automation Activity & Vendor Info: (OPAC) Follett Software
Partic in Capital District Library Council
Open Thurs 1-4:30

CL ALBANY LAW SCHOOL, Schaffer Law Library, 80 New Scotland Ave, 12208. SAN 310-7507. Circulation Tel: 518-445-2340. Circulation E-mail: circ@albanylaw.edu. Reference E-mail: reference@albanylaw.edu. Web Site: www.albanylaw.edu/Student-experience-support/schaffer-law-library. *Dir,* David Walker; E-mail: dwalk@albanylaw.edu; *Access Serv Librn, ILL Spec,* Pegeen Lorusso; E-mail: ploru@albanylaw.edu; *Cataloging & Govt Info Librn,* Leslie Cunningham; E-mail: lcunn@albanylaw.edu; *Research Instruction & Acquisitions Librn,* Thomas Hemstock; E-mail: thems@albanylaw.edu; *Tech Serv Librn,* Elizabeth Rice; E-mail: epora@albanylaw.edu; *Circ Mgr,* Lisa Suto; E-mail: lsuto@albanylaw.edu; *Cataloging & Continuing Resources Specialist,* Brianna Pulver; E-mail: bpulv@albanylaw.edu; Staff 14 (MLS 8, Non-MLS 6)
Founded 1851. Enrl 396; Fac 42; Highest Degree: Doctorate
Library Holdings: Microforms 2,335,132; Bk Titles 100,000; Bk Vols 290,000
Special Collections: State Document Depository; US Document Depository
Automation Activity & Vendor Info: (Cataloging) OCLC Online; (Circulation) SirsiDynix; (Course Reserve) SirsiDynix; (ILL) OCLC Online; (OPAC) SirsiDynix; (Serials) SirsiDynix
Wireless access
Partic in Capital District Library Council; NELLCO Law Library Consortium, Inc.; OCLC Online Computer Library Center, Inc
Open Mon-Thurs 8am-Midnight, Fri 8am-10pm, Sat 9-9, Sun 10am-Midnight

CM ALBANY MEDICAL COLLEGE*, Schaffer Library of Health Sciences, 47 New Scotland Ave, MC 63, 12208. SAN 351-7985. Tel: 518-262-5530. Reference Tel: 518-262-5532. Administration Tel: 518-262-5586. FAX: 518-262-5820. E-mail: library@mail.amc.edu. Web Site: www.amc.edu/academic/schaffer/index.html. *Assoc Dean, Dir, Info Tech,* Enid Geyer; E-mail: geyere@mail.amc.edu; *Asst Dir,* Elizabeth Irish; Tel: 518-262-4980, E-mail: irishe@mail.amc.edu; *Access Serv,* Debra Wellspeak; Tel: 518-262-6460, E-mail: wellspd@mail.amc.edu; Staff 35 (MLS 9, Non-MLS 26)
Founded 1928. Enrl 1,490; Fac 417; Highest Degree: Doctorate
Library Holdings: Bk Titles 42,368; Bk Vols 148,664; Per Subs 3,810
Special Collections: Archives of Albany Medical College
Subject Interests: Med sci
Automation Activity & Vendor Info: (Cataloging) SirsiDynix; (Circulation) SirsiDynix; (Course Reserve) SirsiDynix; (OPAC) SirsiDynix; (Serials) SirsiDynix
Publications: Fact Sheets
Partic in Cap District Libr Coun for Ref & Res Resources; National Network of Libraries of Medicine Region 7; OCLC Online Computer Library Center, Inc
Open Mon-Fri 8-6

P ALBANY PUBLIC LIBRARY*, 161 Washington Ave, 12210. SAN 351-7209. Tel: 518-427-4300. Reference Tel: 518-427-4303. FAX: 518-449-3386. Interlibrary Loan Service E-mail: washingtonave@albanypubliclibrary.org. Web Site: www.albanypubliclibrary.org. *Exec Dir,* Scott Jarzombek; *Asst Libr Dir,* Melanie Metzger; E-mail: metzgerm@albanypubliclibrary.org; *Head, Br Libr,* Sarah Clark; *Head, Br Libr,* Mary Coon; *Head, Br Libr,* Rebecca Lubin; Staff 61 (MLS 24, Non-MLS 37)
Founded 1833. Pop 95,000; Circ 991,442
Library Holdings: AV Mats 40,873; Large Print Bks 1,692; Bk Vols 190,432; Per Subs 720
Special Collections: Local History (Pruyn Coll), bks, pamphlets, clippings, newspr, photog. Oral History
Automation Activity & Vendor Info: (Acquisitions) Horizon; (Cataloging) Horizon; (Circulation) Horizon; (ILL) Horizon; (OPAC) Horizon; (Serials) Horizon
Wireless access
Mem of Upper Hudson Library System
Partic in OCLC Online Computer Library Center, Inc
Special Services for the Blind - Micro-computer access & training; Reader equip
Open Mon-Wed 10-8, Thurs & Fri 10-6, Sat 10-5, Sun (Sept-June) 1-5
Friends of the Library Group
Branches: 6
ARBOR HILL/WEST HILL BRANCH, 148 Henry Johnson Blvd, 12210. Tel: 518-694-0596. E-mail: arborhillwest@albanypubliclibrary.org.
Open Mon & Wed 10-6, Tues & Thurs 12-8, Fri 12-6, Sat 12-5
JOHN J BACH BRANCH, 455 New Scotland Ave, 12208, SAN 351-7322. Tel: 518-482-2154. E-mail: bach@albanypubliclibrary.org.
Open Mon & Wed 10-6, Tues & Thurs 12-8, Fri 12-6, Sat 12-5
DELAWARE BRANCH, 331 Delaware Ave, 12209, SAN 351-7268. Tel: 518-463-0254. E-mail: delaware@albanypubliclibrary.org.
Open Mon & Wed 10-6, Tues & Thurs 12-8, Fri 12-6, Sat 12-5
JOHN HOWE LIBRARY, 105 Schuyler St, 12202, SAN 351-7292. Tel: 518-472-9485. FAX: 518-472-9406. E-mail: howe@albanypubliclibrary.org.
Open Mon & Wed 12-8, Tues 10-6, Thurs & Fri 12-6, Sat 12-5
NORTH ALBANY BRANCH, 616 N Pearl St, 12204. Tel: 518-463-1581. E-mail: northalbany@albanypubliclibrary.org.
Open Mon & Tues 10-6, Wed 12-8, Thurs & Fri 12-6, Sat 10-3
PINE HILLS, 517 Western Ave, 12203, SAN 351-7357. Tel: 518-482-7911. FAX: 518-482-7916. E-mail: pinehills@albanypubliclibrary.org.
Open Mon & Wed 12-8, Tues 10-6, Thurs & Fri 12-6, Sat 12-5
Bookmobiles: 1. Outreach, Patrice Hollman. Bk titles 3,000

J BRYANT & STRATTON COLLEGE LIBRARY*, 1259 Central Ave, 12205. SAN 310-7485. Tel: 518-437-1802. FAX: 518-437-1048. Web Site: www.bryantstratton.edu. *Librn,* Casey Wayman; E-mail: cawayman@bryantstratton.edu; Staff 1 (MLS 1)
Founded 1988. Enrl 610; Fac 45; Highest Degree: Associate
Library Holdings: Bk Titles 4,700; Bk Vols 4,900; Per Subs 52
Subject Interests: Bus, Data proc, Econ, Law, Med asst, Mgt, Mkt, Off procedures, Travel
Automation Activity & Vendor Info: (Acquisitions) Follett Software; (Cataloging) Follett Software; (Circulation) Follett Software; (Course Reserve) Follett Software; (ILL) Follett Software; (OPAC) Follett Software; (Serials) Follett Software
Wireless access
Partic in Cap District Libr Coun for Ref & Res Resources
Open Mon-Thurs 8am-9:30pm, Fri 8-Noon

C COLLEGE OF SAINT ROSE*, Neil Hellman Library, 432 Western Ave, 12203. SAN 310-7515. Tel: 518-454-5183. Interlibrary Loan Service Tel: 518-454-2155. Reference Tel: 518-454-5181. FAX: 518-454-2897. Web Site: library.strose.edu. *Dir,* Drew Urbanek; Tel: 518-485-3731, E-mail: urbaneka@strose.edu; *Head, Ref, Outreach Librn,* Kate Moss; Tel: 518-454-2154, E-mail: mossk@strose.edu; *Cataloger, Ref Librn,* Mary Lindner; Tel: 518-337-4693, E-mail: lindnerm@strose.edu; Staff 17 (MLS 7, Non-MLS 10)
Founded 1920. Enrl 3,145; Fac 172; Highest Degree: Master
Library Holdings: Bk Vols 202,000; Per Subs 925
Special Collections: College Archives; Curriculum Library
Subject Interests: Educ
Automation Activity & Vendor Info: (Acquisitions) Ex Libris Group; (Cataloging) Ex Libris Group; (Circulation) Ex Libris Group; (Course Reserve) Ex Libris Group; (ILL) Ex Libris Group; (OPAC) Ex Libris Group; (Serials) Ex Libris Group
Wireless access
Publications: Guide to the Neil Hellman Library
Partic in Capital District Library Council; OCLC Online Computer Library Center, Inc

G EMPIRE STATE DEVELOPMENT LIBRARY*, 625 Broadway, 8th Flr, 12245. SAN 310-7639. Tel: 518-292-5235. FAX: 518-292-5810. E-mail: esdlibrary@esd.ny.gov. *Dir,* Victoria Larson; E-mail: victoria.larson@esd.ny.gov; Staff 2 (MLS 1, Non-MLS 1)
Founded 1944
Library Holdings: AV Mats 40; CDs 75; DVDs 30; Bk Vols 2,500; Per Subs 70; Videos 12
Subject Interests: Bus, Econ develop, Intl trade
Automation Activity & Vendor Info: (Cataloging) Inmagic, Inc.; (ILL) OCLC; (Serials) Inmagic, Inc.
Function: ILL available
Partic in Cap District Libr Coun for Ref & Res Resources; New York State Interlibrary Loan Network
Open Mon-Fri 9-5:30

S FIRST UNITARIAN UNIVERSALIST SOCIETY OF ALBANY*, Charles R Joy Library, 405 Washington Ave, 12206. SAN 323-5459. E-mail: joylibrary@albanyuu.org. Web Site: members.albanyuu.org/wp/about-us/joy-library. *Co-Chair,* Melanie Axel-Lute; *Co-Chair,* Paul Axel-Lute; Staff 2 (MLS 2)
Jul 2018-Jun 2019 Income $400. Mats Exp $398
Library Holdings: Bk Titles 1,665
Special Collections: Ed Ryman Coll on Buddhism and Taoism
Subject Interests: Bible study, Ethics, Philos, Soc issues, Theol, Traditions, Unitarian Universalism
Wireless access
Function: 24/7 Online cat

J MARIA COLLEGE LIBRARY*, 700 New Scotland Ave, 12208. SAN 310-7574. Tel: 518-861-2515. FAX: 518-453-1366. E-mail: library@mariacollege.edu. Web Site: mariacollege.libguides.com/library. *Libr Dir,* Krista Robben; E-mail: krobben@mariacollege.edu; Staff 3 (MLS 1, Non-MLS 2)
Founded 1958. Enrl 700
Library Holdings: Bk Vols 61,000; Per Subs 225
Subject Interests: Allied health, Early childhood
Wireless access

Partic in Capital District Library Council
Open Mon-Thurs 10-6, Fri 10-4, Sat & Sun 9-5

GL NEW YORK STATE COURT OF APPEALS LIBRARY*, 20 Eagle St, 12207. SAN 310-7604. Tel: 518-455-7700, 518-455-7770. Web Site: www.nycourts.gov/ctapps. *Librn,* Marissa Mason
Founded 1870
Subject Interests: Law
Wireless access
Restriction: Staff use only

S NEW YORK STATE DEPARTMENT OF CORRECTIONAL SERVICES, Division of Library Services, Harriman State Campus, 1220 Washington Ave, 12226-2050. SAN 323-9772. Tel: 518-485-7109. FAX: 518-485-9629. Web Site: nysl.nysed.gov/libdev/outreach/corr.htm. *Dir, Libr Serv,* Corinne Leone; E-mail: corinne.leone@doccs.ny.gov; *Sr Librn,* Regina Torian
Restriction: Not open to pub

GM NEW YORK STATE DEPARTMENT OF HEALTH, Herbert W Dickerman Library, Wadsworth Ctr-NYS Department of Health, Empire State Plaza, 12237. SAN 310-7655. Tel: 518-474-3623. E-mail: dohlib@health.ny.gov. Web Site: hwd.wc.daphnis.opalsinfo.net/bin/home. *Mgr,* Ann Marie L'Hommedieu; E-mail: ann.lhommedieu@health.ny.gov; Staff 2 (MLS 1, Non-MLS 1)
Founded 1914
Library Holdings: e-journals 10,000; Bk Vols 40,000; Per Subs 1,100
Subject Interests: Clinical labs, Environ health, Epidemiology, Health policy, Infectious diseases, Molecular biol, Molecular genetics, Pub health, Radiological health, Toxicology, Veterinary med
Automation Activity & Vendor Info: (OPAC) Innovative Interfaces, Inc; (Serials) Innovative Interfaces, Inc
Wireless access
Partic in OCLC Online Computer Library Center, Inc
Restriction: Not open to pub

G NEW YORK STATE LEGISLATIVE LIBRARY*, State Capitol, Rm 337, 12224-0345. SAN 372-431X. Tel: 518-455-2468. FAX: 518-426-6901. *Librn,* James Giliberto; E-mail: gilibert@nysenate.gov; Staff 6 (MLS 2, Non-MLS 4)
Library Holdings: Bk Titles 100,000; Per Subs 100
Special Collections: History of New York Laws; Legislative Reports; New York State Agency Reports
Subject Interests: Law, Legislation
Automation Activity & Vendor Info: (Cataloging) EOS International
Wireless access
Open Mon-Fri 9-5

P NEW YORK STATE LIBRARY, State Education Department, Cultural Education Ctr, 222 Madison Ave, Empire State Plaza, 12230. SAN 351-756X. Tel: 518-474-5961. Circulation Tel: 518-473-7895. Interlibrary Loan Service Tel: 518-474-5383. Administration Tel: 518-473-1189, 518-474-5930. FAX: 518-474-5786. Administration FAX: 518-486-6880. E-mail: nyslweb@mail.nysed.gov. Circulation E-mail: circ@mail.nysed.gov. Web Site: www.nysl.nysed.gov. *State Librn,* Lauren Moore; E-mail: statelibrarian@nysed.gov; *Coordr, Libr Serv,* Carol Ann Desch; E-mail: Carol.Desch@nysed.gov; Staff 582 (MLS 32, Non-MLS 550)
Founded 1818
Library Holdings: Bk Vols 2,500,000; Per Subs 13,796
Special Collections: Broadsides; Cartographic Coll; Dutch Colonial Records; New York State Documents; New York State Historical Newspapers; New York State History Manuscripts; New York State Political & Social History; Shaker Coll. State Document Depository; US Document Depository
Automation Activity & Vendor Info: (Acquisitions) SirsiDynix; (Cataloging) SirsiDynix; (Circulation) SirsiDynix; (ILL) SirsiDynix; (OPAC) SirsiDynix; (Serials) SirsiDynix
Wireless access
Function: Archival coll, CD-ROM, Doc delivery serv, For res purposes, Govt ref serv, Health sci info serv, Homebound delivery serv, ILL available, Internet access, Orientations, Outside serv via phone, mail, e-mail & web, Photocopying/Printing, Ref serv available, Res libr, Spoken cassettes & CDs, Telephone ref, Wheelchair accessible
Partic in Association of Research Libraries; OCLC Online Computer Library Center, Inc; OCLC Research Library Partnership
Special Services for the Blind - Assistive/Adapted tech devices, equip & products
Open Mon-Sat 9:30-5
Restriction: Closed stack
Friends of the Library Group
Branches: 1
TALKING BOOK & BRAILLE LIBRARY
See Separate Entry

P NEW YORK STATE LIBRARY*, Talking Book & Braille Library, Cultural Education Ctr, 222 Madison Ave, 12230-0001. SAN 310-7744. Tel: 518-474-5935. Toll Free Tel: 800-342-3688. FAX: 518-474-7041. E-mail: tbbl@nysed.gov. Web Site: www.nysl.nysed.gov/tbbl. *Dir,* Sharon B Phillips; E-mail: Sharon.Phillips@nysed.gov; Staff 2 (MLS 2)
Founded 1896. Pop 14,700; Circ 500,000
Library Holdings: Braille Volumes 20,000; Bk Titles 50,000; Bk Vols 780,000; Talking Bks 15,000
Automation Activity & Vendor Info: (Acquisitions) Keystone Systems, Inc (KLAS); (Cataloging) Keystone Systems, Inc (KLAS); (Circulation) Keystone Systems, Inc (KLAS); (Course Reserve) Keystone Systems, Inc (KLAS); (ILL) Keystone Systems, Inc (KLAS); (Media Booking) Keystone Systems, Inc (KLAS); (OPAC) Keystone Systems, Inc (KLAS); (Serials) Keystone Systems, Inc (KLAS)
Wireless access
Publications: Bibliographies; Newsletters
Special Services for the Blind - Assistive/Adapted tech devices, equip & products; Braille bks; Digital talking bk; Digital talking bk machines
Open Mon-Fri 9-4:30

G NEW YORK STATE OFFICE OF THE STATE COMPTROLLER LIBRARY*, OSC Library, 110 State St, 15th Flr, 12236. SAN 310-7612. Tel: 518-473-5960. E-mail: osclibrary@osc.ny.gov. *Librn,* Rosemary A Del Vecchio; Tel: 518-473-5960, E-mail: rdelvecchio@osc.ny.gov; *Librn,* Stephanie Young; Tel: 518-473-4206, E-mail: syoung@osc.ny.gov; Staff 2 (MLS 2)
Library Holdings: e-books 5,000; e-journals 100; Bk Vols 5,000; Per Subs 25
Subject Interests: Govt, Law, Municipal
Automation Activity & Vendor Info: (Cataloging) SydneyPlus; (ILL) OCLC ILLiad; (OPAC) Inmagic, Inc.
Wireless access
Restriction: Authorized personnel only, Employees only, Govt use only, In-house use for visitors, Internal circ only, Lending to staff only, Not a lending libr, Not open to pub

GL NEW YORK SUPREME COURT APPELLATE DIVISION*, Third Department Library, Robert Abrams Bldg for Law & Justice, State St, 12223. (Mail add: Capitol Station, PO Box 7288, 12224-0288), SAN 310-7752. Tel: 518-471-4713, 518-471-4777. FAX: 518-471-4750. Web Site: www.nycourts.gov/ad3. *Library Contact,* Marcus Hauf
Library Holdings: Bk Vols 22,500
Wireless access
Open Mon-Fri 8:30-5

S NYS SMALL BUSINESS DEVELOPMENT CENTER RESEARCH NETWORK*, Ten N Pearl St, 12246. SAN 377-5763. Tel: 518-944-2840. Toll Free Tel: 800-732-7232 (NY Only). FAX: 518-443-5275. E-mail: sbdcrn@nyssbdc.org. Web Site: www.nyssbdc.org. *Dir,* Darrin Conroy; E-mail: darrin.conroy@nyssbdc.org; *Asst Dir,* Amelia Birdsall; E-mail: amelia.birdsall@nyssbdc.org; *Libr & Info Spec,* Josee Fonseca; *Libr & Info Spec,* Roger Green; Staff 5 (MLS 5)
Founded 1991
Library Holdings: Bk Titles 1,100; Per Subs 35
Special Collections: SBA Publications; SBDC/ASBDC Publications; US EPA/NYS DEC Publications. State Document Depository
Subject Interests: Bus
Function: For res purposes
Partic in Proquest Dialog
Restriction: Open by appt only

C THE SAGE COLLEGES*, Albany Campus Library, 140 New Scotland Ave, 12208. SAN 310-7787. Tel: 518-292-1721. Interlibrary Loan Service Tel: 518-292-1742. E-mail: libref@sage.edu. Web Site: library.sage.edu. *Dir of Libr,* Lisa Brainard; Tel: 518-292-1959, E-mail: brainl@sage.edu; *Coll Develop Librn, Tech Serv Librn,* Terrance Wasielewski; Tel: 518-244-2435, E-mail: wasiet@sage.edu; *Info Literacy Librn, Ref & Circ Librn,* Regina Vertone; Tel: 518-292-1945, E-mail: verton@sage.edu; *ILL Librn, Syst Librn,* Christopher White; Tel: 518-244-4521, E-mail: whitec2@sage.edu; *Ser & Electronic Res Librn,* Jennifer Anderson; Tel: 518-292-1701, E-mail: anderj6@sage.edu; *Circ, Sr Libr Spec,* Erik Riley; E-mail: rileye3@sage.edu; *ILL, Sr Libr Spec,* Brianna Pulver; E-mail: pulveb@sage.edu; Staff 9 (MLS 4, Non-MLS 5)
Founded 1957. Enrl 1,000; Fac 150; Highest Degree: Doctorate
Library Holdings: AV Mats 25,722; e-books 10,000; e-journals 50,000; Microforms 1,251; Bk Titles 58,850; Bk Vols 62,714; Per Subs 119
Subject Interests: Graphic arts, Legal studies, Mgt
Automation Activity & Vendor Info: (Acquisitions) SirsiDynix; (Cataloging) OCLC Online; (Circulation) SirsiDynix; (Course Reserve) SirsiDynix; (ILL) OCLC ILLiad; (OPAC) SirsiDynix; (Serials) SirsiDynix
Wireless access
Partic in Cap District Libr Coun for Ref & Res Resources; OCLC Online Computer Library Center, Inc; Westchester Academic Library Directors Organization
Open Mon-Thurs 7:30am-8pm, Fri 7:30-5

M SAINT PETER'S HOSPITAL*, Medical Library, 315 S Manning Blvd, 12208. Tel: 518-525-1490.
Restriction: Authorized personnel only

M SAINT PETER'S HOSPITAL COLLEGE OF NURSING*, Health Sciences Library, Marian Hall, Rm 111, 714 New Scotland Ave, 12208. SAN 310-7582. Tel: 518-268-5036, 518-525-1490. *Librn,* Kathy Kindness; E-mail: kathy.kindness@sphp.com; Staff 3 (MLS 1, Non-MLS 2)
Founded 1960
Library Holdings: Bk Titles 3,200; Bk Vols 3,500; Per Subs 100
Subject Interests: Med, Nursing
Wireless access
Open Mon, Wed & Thurs 8-7, Tues & Fri 8-4, Sun 12-5

C UNIVERSITY AT ALBANY, STATE UNIVERSITY OF NEW YORK*, University Libraries, 1400 Washington Ave, 12222-0001. SAN 351-7896. Tel: 518-442-3568. Circulation Tel: 518-442-3600. Interlibrary Loan Service Tel: 518-442-3613. Reference Tel: 518-442-3558. FAX: 518-442-3088. Web Site: library.albany.edu. *Interim Dean of Libr, Interim Dir,* Rebecca Frances Mugridge; E-mail: rmugridge@albany.edu; *Assoc Dir, Coll Develop,* Mary Van Ullen; Tel: 518-442-3559, E-mail: mvanullen@albany.edu; *Assoc Dir, Pub Serv,* Mary Jane Brustman; Tel: 518-442-3540, E-mail: mbrustman@albany.edu; *Assoc Dir, Tech Serv & Syst,* Heather Miller; Tel: 518-442-3631, E-mail: hmiller@albany.edu; *Asst Dir, Finance/Admin,* Peter Recore-Migirditch; Tel: 518-442-3563, Fax: 518-442-3663, E-mail: prm@albany.edu; *Head, Circ,* Kabel Stanwicks; Tel: 518-442-3578, E-mail: kstanwicks@albany.edu; *Head, Spec Coll & Archives,* Brian Keough; Tel: 518-437-3931, E-mail: bkeough@albany.edu; Staff 60.1 (MLS 32.5, Non-MLS 27.6)
Founded 1844. Enrl 17,578; Fac 1,000; Highest Degree: Doctorate
Library Holdings: AV Mats 13,178; CDs 1,915; DVDs 3,256; e-books 24,760; e-journals 38,372; Microforms 2,938,467; Bk Vols 2,223,325; Per Subs 4,199; Talking Bks 953; Videos 5,088
Special Collections: Archives for Public Affairs & Policy; Children's Historical Literature Coll; Death Penalty Archives; German Intellectual Emigre Coll. State Document Depository; US Document Depository
Subject Interests: Criminal justice, Educ, Soc sci
Automation Activity & Vendor Info: (Acquisitions) Ex Libris Group; (Cataloging) Ex Libris Group; (Circulation) Ex Libris Group; (Course Reserve) Atlas Systems; (ILL) OCLC ILLiad; (OPAC) Ex Libris Group; (Serials) Ex Libris Group
Wireless access
Partic in Association of Research Libraries; Capital District Library Council; New York State Interlibrary Loan Network; OCLC Online Computer Library Center, Inc; SUNYConnect

Departmental Libraries:

THOMAS E DEWEY GRADUATE LIBRARY, 135 Western Ave, 12222, SAN 370-3320. Tel: 518-442-3696. Circulation Tel: 518-442-3693. Reference Tel: 518-442-3691. FAX: 518-442-3474. Reference E-mail: dewref@albany.edu. Web Site: library.albany.edu/dewey. *Head of Libr,* Deborah Bernnard; Tel: 518-442-3699, E-mail: dbernnard@albany.edu; *Assoc Librn, Research Impact & Social Welfare,* Elaine M Lasda; E-mail: elasda@albany.edu; Staff 4 (MLS 3, Non-MLS 1)
Subject Interests: Criminal justice, Info sci, Libr sci, Pub admin, Soc welfare

SCIENCE LIBRARY, 1400 Washington Ave, 12222. Tel: 518-437-3948. Reference Tel: 518-437-3945. FAX: 518-437-3952. Web Site: library.albany.edu/science. *Head, Circ,* Kabel Stanwicks; Tel: 518-442-3578, E-mail: kstanwicks@albany.edu; *Digital Initiatives Librn,* Lorre Smith; E-mail: lsmith@albany.edu; *Outreach & Instruction Librn, Ref Librn,* Irina Holden; E-mail: iholden@albany.edu; *Bibliographer, Ref Librn,* Sue Kaczor; E-mail: skaczor@albany.edu; *Bibliographer, Ref Librn,* Michael Knee; E-mail: mknee@albany.edu; Staff 5 (MLS 4, Non-MLS 1)
Founded 1999
Open Mon-Thurs 8am-11pm, Fri 8-6, Sat 9-5, Sun 11-11

P UPPER HUDSON LIBRARY SYSTEM*, 28 Essex St, 12206. SAN 310-7817. Tel: 518-437-9880. FAX: 518-437-9884. Web Site: www.uhls.org. *Exec Dir,* Timothy Burke; Tel: 518-437-9880, Ext 222, E-mail: tim.burke@uhls.lib.ny.us; *Admin Mgr,* Jona Favreau; E-mail: jona.favreau@uhls.lib.ny.us; *Syst Adminr,* Rawdon Cheng; Tel: 518-437-9880, Ext 233, E-mail: rawdon@uhls.lib.ny.us; *Mgr, Youth & Family Serv,* Mary Fellows; Tel: 518-437-9880, Ext 228, E-mail: mary@uhls.lib.ny.us; *Mgr, Ad Serv, Mgr, Outreach Serv,* Natalie Hurteau; Tel: 518-437-9880, Ext 225, E-mail: natalie.hurteau@uhls.lib.ny.us; *Mgr, Automation Serv,* Joseph Thornton; Tel: 518-437-9880, Ext 230, E-mail: jthornton@uhls.lib.ny.us; Staff 10 (MLS 5, Non-MLS 5)
Founded 1960. Pop 447,103
Library Holdings: AV Mats 7,565; CDs 2,249; DVDs 1,123; e-books 557; Large Print Bks 1,894; Bk Vols 9,261; Per Subs 15; Videos 2,303
Automation Activity & Vendor Info: (Acquisitions) SirsiDynix; (Cataloging) SirsiDynix; (Circulation) SirsiDynix; (OPAC) SirsiDynix; (Serials) SirsiDynix
Wireless access
Publications: The Latest Edition (Newsletter)
Member Libraries: Albany Public Library; Altamont Free Library; Arvilla E Diver Memorial Library; Berlin Free Town Library; Berne Public Library; Bethlehem Public Library; Brunswick Community Library; Castleton Public Library; Cheney Library; Cohoes Public Library; East Greenbush Community Library; Grafton Community Library; Guilderland Public Library; Menands Public Library; Nassau Free Library; North Greenbush Public Library; Petersburgh Public Library; Poestenkill Public Library; RCS Community Library; Rensselaer Public Library; Rensselaerville Library; Sand Lake Town Library; Stephentown Memorial Library; The William K Sanford Town Library; Troy Public Library; Valley Falls Free Library; Voorheesville Public Library; Watervliet Public Library; Westerlo Public Library
Partic in Cap District Libr Coun for Ref & Res Resources; NY Libr Asn
Special Services for the Deaf - TTY equip
Special Services for the Blind - Bks on CD; Large print bks; Talking bks
Open Mon-Fri 8:30-5

S VAN RENSSELEAR - RANKIN FAMILY HISTORIC CHERRY HILL MUSEUM & LIBRARY*, 523 1/2 S Pearl St, 12202. SAN 327-7461. Tel: 518-434-4791. FAX: 518-434-4806. E-mail: info@historiccherryhill.org. Web Site: www.historiccherryhill.org. *Dir,* Liselle LaFrance; E-mail: liselle@historiccherryhill.org; *Curator,* Deborah Emmons-Andarawis; E-mail: deborah@historiccherryhill.org
Library Holdings: Bk Vols 5,000
Restriction: Open by appt only

ALBERTSON

S NATIONAL BUSINESS & DISABILITY COUNCIL AT THE VISCARDI CENTER*, 201 IU Willets Rd, 11507. SAN 310-7833. Tel: 516-465-1400. E-mail: info@viscardicenter.org. Web Site: viscardicenter.org/nbdc. *Mgr,* Christina Eisenberg; E-mail: ceisenberg@viscardicenter.org
Founded 1961
Library Holdings: Bk Vols 2,500; Per Subs 250
Subject Interests: Adjustment, Independent living for disabled personnel, Vocational rehabilitation, Work evaluation
Partic in Long Island Library Resources Council; Proquest Dialog
Open Mon-Fri 8:30-4:30

P SHELTER ROCK PUBLIC LIBRARY*, 165 Searingtown Rd, 11507. SAN 310-7841. Tel: 516-248-7343. Reference FAX: 516-248-4897. Administration FAX: 516-248-7968. TDD: 516-248-2367. E-mail: shelterrock@srpl.org. Web Site: www.srpl.org. *Libr Dir,* Andrea Meluskey; *Asst Libr Dir,* Susan A Santa; *Head, Ad Ref Serv,* Ellen Miller; *Head, Children's Servx,* Susan Nolan; *Librn, YA Serv,* Toni Ann Kaminski; Staff 11.3 (MLS 11.3)
Founded 1962. Pop 27,188
Automation Activity & Vendor Info: (Acquisitions) Innovative Interfaces, Inc; (Circulation) Innovative Interfaces, Inc; (OPAC) Innovative Interfaces, Inc
Wireless access
Function: 24/7 Electronic res, 24/7 Online cat, Adult literacy prog
Publications: The Scene (Monthly)
Mem of Nassau Library System
Special Services for the Deaf - TDD equip; TTY equip
Open Mon, Tues & Thurs 10-9, Wed 11-9, Fri 10-6, Sat 9-5, Sun 1-5

ALBION

P HOAG LIBRARY*, 134 S Main St, 14411. SAN 310-785X. Tel: 585-589-4246. FAX: 585-589-2473. E-mail: hoag_library@yahoo.com. Web Site: www.hoaglibrary.org. *Dir,* Betty Sue Miller; *Ch Serv,* Nicole Struble; *Ref (Info Servs),* Cheryle Mowatt
Founded 1899. Pop 15,000; Circ 41,335
Library Holdings: Bk Vols 43,464; Per Subs 131; Talking Bks 900; Videos 1,200
Special Collections: Lillian Achilles Doll Coll; Local History, bks, pamphlets, photogs; Rare Books; Stuart Flintham Egg Coll; William G Curtis Civil War Library
Subject Interests: Genealogy
Automation Activity & Vendor Info: (Cataloging) SirsiDynix-WorkFlows; (Circulation) SirsiDynix-WorkFlows; (ILL) SirsiDynix-WorkFlows; (OPAC) SirsiDynix-WorkFlows; (Serials) SirsiDynix-WorkFlows
Wireless access
Publications: Annual Report Brochure; Books & Money; History of Swan Library; Hours & Services, Welcome to Swan Library; Swan Library News
Mem of Nioga Library System
Partic in Western New York Library Resources Council
Open Mon-Thurs 10-8, Fri & Sat 10-5
Friends of the Library Group

S NEW YORK STATE DEPARTMENT OF CORRECTIONAL SERVICES*, Albion Correctional Facility General Library, 3595 State School Rd, 14411. SAN 327-1129. Tel: 585-589-5511, Ext 4600. *Sr Librn,* Eugene S Veress; Staff 1.5 (MLS 1, Non-MLS 0.5)
Library Holdings: AV Mats 409; Bk Titles 11,052; Per Subs 42
Automation Activity & Vendor Info: (Cataloging) Follett Software; (Circulation) Follett Software
Wireless access
Open Mon & Thurs 1-9, Tues, Wed & Fri 8-4

S ORLEANS CORRECTIONAL FACILITY LIBRARY*, 3531 Gaines Basin Rd, 14411. SAN 327-2478. Tel: 585-589-6820. *Sr Librn,* James Trinder; Staff 1 (MLS 1)
Library Holdings: Bk Titles 10,000; Per Subs 22
Automation Activity & Vendor Info: (Cataloging) Follett Software; (Circulation) Follett Software; (OPAC) Follett Software
Restriction: Not open to pub

ALDEN

P ALDEN-EWELL FREE LIBRARY, 13280 Broadway, 14004. SAN 310-7868. Tel: 716-937-7082. FAX: 716-937-7082. E-mail: ALD@buffalolib.org. Web Site: www.buffalolib.org/content/library-locations/ewell. *Pres,* Susan Sabers Chapman; E-mail: sschapman1@gmail.com; *Dir,* Rebecca Moe
Founded 1902. Pop 7,500; Circ 50,000
Library Holdings: Bk Vols 17,000; Per Subs 52
Wireless access
Function: Photocopying/Printing
Mem of Buffalo & Erie County Public Library System
Open Mon & Wed 9-4, Tues & Thurs 12-8, Sat 9-2

S WENDE CORRECTIONAL FACILITY LIBRARY*, 3040 Wende Rd, 14004. (Mail add: PO Box 1187, 14004-1187), SAN 327-2346. Tel: 716-937-4000. *Librn,* Sandra Blackman
Library Holdings: Bk Titles 12,000; Per Subs 50
Restriction: Not open to pub

ALEXANDRIA BAY

P MACSHERRY LIBRARY, 112 Walton St, 13607. SAN 310-7876. Tel: 315-482-2241. FAX: 315-482-2241. Web Site: www.macsherrylibrary.org. *Dir,* Ceil Cunningham; E-mail: ccunningham@ncls.org; *Asst Librn,* Luann Elizabeth; *Asst Librn,* Cindy Hutchinson; *Asst Librn,* Kathryn Stevens; Staff 4 (Non-MLS 4)
Founded 1896. Pop 1,078; Circ 24,000
Library Holdings: AV Mats 1,133; Bk Vols 17,503; Per Subs 23; Talking Bks 1,526; Videos 1,610
Automation Activity & Vendor Info: (Acquisitions) Baker & Taylor; (Cataloging) SirsiDynix-WorkFlows; (Circulation) SirsiDynix-WorkFlows; (ILL) SirsiDynix-WorkFlows; (OPAC) SirsiDynix-Unicorn
Wireless access
Mem of North Country Library System
Open Mon & Wed-Sat 9-2, Tues 2-7
Friends of the Library Group

ALFRED

ALFRED UNIVERSITY
C HERRICK MEMORIAL LIBRARY*, One Saxon Dr, 14802, SAN 351-8043. Tel: 607-871-2184. FAX: 607-871-2299. Web Site: herrick.alfred.edu. *Dir,* Steve Crandall; Tel: 607-871-2987, E-mail: fcrandall@alfred.edu; *Instrul Librn,* Brian Sullivan; Tel: 607-871-2268, E-mail: sullivan@alfred.edu; *Access Serv, Archivist,* Laurie McFadden; Tel: 607-871-2385, E-mail: fmcfadden@alfred.edu; *Info Syst,* Ellen Bahr; Tel: 607-871-2976, E-mail: bahr@alfred.edu; Staff 11 (MLS 4, Non-MLS 7)
Founded 1857. Enrl 2,228; Fac 175; Highest Degree: Doctorate
Library Holdings: AV Mats 1,100; e-books 27,000; e-journals 28,000; Bk Titles 127,500; Bk Vols 150,000; Per Subs 550
Special Collections: British Literature & History (Openhym Coll); William Dean Howells (Howells-Frechette Coll)
Subject Interests: Behav sci, Soc sci
Automation Activity & Vendor Info: (Cataloging) Ex Libris Group; (Circulation) Ex Libris Group; (Course Reserve) Docutek; (OPAC) Ex Libris Group; (Serials) Ex Libris Group
Partic in OCLC Online Computer Library Center, Inc; S Cent Libr Res Coun; South Central Regional Library Council; Westchester Academic Library Directors Organization
Publications: Research Guides
Special Services for the Blind - Assistive/Adapted tech devices, equip & products
Restriction: In-house use for visitors

C SCHOLES LIBRARY OF CERAMICS*, New York State College of Ceramics at Alfred University, Two Pine St, 14802-1297, SAN 351-8078. Circulation Tel: 607-871-2492. Interlibrary Loan Service Tel: 607-871-2947. Reference Tel: 607-871-2951. Administration Tel: 607-871-2494. Administration FAX: 607-871-2349. Web Site: scholes.alfred.edu. *Dir, Libr Serv,* Mark A Smith; E-mail: msmith@alfred.edu; *Pub Serv Librn,* Beverly J Crowell; Tel: 607-871-2950, E-mail: crowellb@alfred.edu; *Sci/Eng Librn,* Patricia C LaCourse; Tel: 607-871-2943, E-mail: lacourpc@alfred.edu; *Asst Librn,* Fang Wan; *Archivist,* Elizabeth Gulacsy; Tel: 607-871-2948, E-mail: gulacsy@alfred.edu; *Visual Res Curator,* John Hosford. Subject Specialists: *Engr,* Patricia C LaCourse; *Emerging tech, Engr,* Fang Wan; *Archives, Art,* Elizabeth Gulacsy; Staff 5 (MLS 5)
Founded 1947. Enrl 761; Fac 61; Highest Degree: Doctorate
Library Holdings: AV Mats 166,873; Bk Titles 87,459; Bk Vols 104,271; Per Subs 699
Special Collections: Charles Fergus Binns Papers; NCECA Archives; NYS College of Ceramics Archives
Subject Interests: Art, Biomed res, Ceramic art, Ceramic engr, Ceramic hist, Design, Electronic art media, Engr, Glass, Glass art, Glass sci, Mat sci, Photog, Sculpture
Automation Activity & Vendor Info: (Cataloging) Ex Libris Group; (Circulation) Ex Libris Group; (Course Reserve) Docutek; (ILL) OCLC; (OPAC) Ex Libris Group; (Serials) Ex Libris Group
Function: Archival coll, AV serv, Doc delivery serv, ILL available, Ref serv available, Res libr
Partic in SUNYConnect
Publications: Annual Statistics
Special Services for the Blind - Assistive/Adapted tech devices, equip & products
Open Mon-Thurs 8am-Midnight, Fri 8-8, Sat 10-6, Sun Noon-Midnight
Restriction: Open to students, fac & staff, Pub use on premises, Restricted borrowing privileges

C STATE UNIVERSITY OF NEW YORK, COLLEGE OF TECHNOLOGY*, Walter C Hinkle Memorial Library, Upper College Dr, 14802. SAN 351-8108. Tel: 607-587-4313. FAX: 607-587-4351. Web Site: alfredstate.libguides.com/c.php?g=372677. *Dir of Libr,* Joseph Petrick; E-mail: petricja@alfredstate.edu; *Assoc Librn,* Jane Vavala; E-mail: vavalaja@alfredstate.edu; *Ref Librn,* Barbara Greil; E-mail: greilbj@alfredstate.edu; *Librn,* Ronald Foster; Staff 7 (MLS 6, Non-MLS 1)
Founded 1911. Enrl 3,500; Fac 170; Highest Degree: Bachelor
Jul 2014-Jun 2015 Income $539,129. Mats Exp $108,891, Books $32,636, Per/Ser (Incl. Access Fees) $12,600, AV Mat $7,164, Electronic Ref Mat (Incl. Access Fees) $51,665, Presv $4,826. Sal $388,129 (Prof $261,678)
Library Holdings: Bk Titles 38,488; Bk Vols 54,671; Per Subs 136; Videos 3,552
Special Collections: Western New York State Historical Coll, bks, maps, artifacts
Subject Interests: Agr, Allied health, Engr, Vocational
Automation Activity & Vendor Info: (Circulation) Ex Libris Group
Wireless access
Function: ILL available
Partic in South Central Regional Library Council; SUNYConnect
Open Mon-Thurs 7:30am-10pm, Fri 7:30-7, Sat 1-7, Sun 1-10

ALLEGANY

P ALLEGANY PUBLIC LIBRARY*, 90 W Main St, 14706-1204. SAN 310-7884. Tel: 716-373-1056. FAX: 716-373-1056. Web Site: www.alleganylibrary.org. *Dir,* Nate Austin; E-mail: director@alleganylibrary.org
Founded 1965. Pop 2,078
Library Holdings: Bk Titles 20,950; Per Subs 30
Special Collections: Freedom Shrine
Wireless access
Mem of Chautauqua-Cattaraugus Library System
Partic in OCLC Online Computer Library Center, Inc
Open Mon-Fri 10-6, Sat 10-1

ALMOND

P TWENTIETH CENTURY CLUB LIBRARY, 49 N Main St, 14804. (Mail add: PO Box D, 14804), SAN 310-7892. Tel: 607-276-6311. FAX: 607-276-6311. E-mail: almondlibrary@gmail.com. Web Site: almondlibrary.org. *Dir,* Mary Jo Murray
Founded 1912. Circ 9,530
Library Holdings: Bk Vols 14,500; Per Subs 22
Special Collections: Children's Coll
Subject Interests: Local hist, Quilting
Automation Activity & Vendor Info: (Cataloging) SirsiDynix; (Circulation) SirsiDynix; (Media Booking) SirsiDynix
Wireless access
Mem of Southern Tier Library System

Open Tues-Fri 2-7, Sat 11-3
Friends of the Library Group

ALTAMONT

P ALTAMONT FREE LIBRARY, 179 Main St, 12009. (Mail add: PO Box 662, 12009-0662), SAN 310-7906. Tel: 518-861-7239. FAX: 518-595-4679. Web Site: www.altamontfreelibrary.org. *Dir,* Joseph P Burke; E-mail: director@altamontfreelibrary.org; Staff 6 (MLS 1, Non-MLS 5)
Founded 1916. Pop 2,074; Circ 19,368
Library Holdings: High Interest/Low Vocabulary Bk Vols 60; Bk Titles 10,900; Bk Vols 13,607; Per Subs 50
Automation Activity & Vendor Info: (Circulation) SirsiDynix; (ILL) SirsiDynix; (OPAC) SirsiDynix
Wireless access
Function: Homebound delivery serv, ILL available, Internet access, Photocopying/Printing, Prog for adults, Prog for children & young adult, Ref serv available, Summer reading prog, Telephone ref
Mem of Upper Hudson Library System
Open Mon-Fri 11-6
Friends of the Library Group

ALTONA

P ALTONA READING CENTER*, 3124 Miner Farm Rd, 12910. Tel: 518-236-7621, Ext 109. FAX: 518-236-7621. Web Site: www.townofaltonany.com/reading-center.html. *Dir,* Joyce Boire
Library Holdings: Bk Vols 9,000
Mem of Clinton-Essex-Franklin Library System
Open Mon-Fri 8-4

S NEW YORK STATE DEPARTMENT OF CORRECTIONS & COMMUNITY SUPERVISION*, Altona Correctional Facility Library, 555 Devils Den Rd, 12910. SAN 328-0144. Tel: 518-236-7841, Ext 4560. Web Site: doccs.ny.gov/location/altona-correctional-facility. *Sr Libm,* Christen Cardina; E-mail: christen.cardina@doccs.ny.gov; Staff 1 (MLS 1)
Apr 2016-Mar 2017 Income $3,900. Mats Exp $3,900, Books $1,000, Per/Ser (Incl. Access Fees) $2,900
Library Holdings: High Interest/Low Vocabulary Bk Vols 50; Bk Titles 6,000; Bk Vols 6,500; Per Subs 16
Automation Activity & Vendor Info: (Acquisitions) Follett Software
Mem of Clinton-Essex-Franklin Library System
Restriction: Staff & inmates only

AMAGANSETT

P AMAGANSETT FREE LIBRARY*, 215 Main St, 11930. (Mail add: PO Box 2550, 11930), SAN 310-7922. Tel: 631-267-3810. FAX: 631-267-0087. E-mail: info@amagansettlibrary.org. Web Site: amagansettlibrary.org. *Dir,* Lauren Nichols; E-mail: director@amaglibrary.org
Pop 3,000; Circ 20,000
Library Holdings: Bk Vols 38,500; Per Subs 55
Automation Activity & Vendor Info: (Cataloging) Innovative Interfaces, Inc; (Circulation) Innovative Interfaces, Inc; (OPAC) Innovative Interfaces, Inc; (Serials) Innovative Interfaces, Inc
Wireless access
Mem of Suffolk Cooperative Library System
Open Mon-Sat 10-5

AMENIA

P AMENIA FREE LIBRARY, 3309 Rte 343, 12501. (Mail add: PO Box 27, 12501-0027), SAN 310-7930. Tel: 845-373-8273. FAX: 845-373-8273. Web Site: amenialibrary.org. *Dir,* Victoria Herow; E-mail: director@amenialibrary.org
Founded 1938
Jan 2019-Dec 2019 Income $140,344, State $7,523, Federal $125,000, Other $7,821. Mats Exp $100,309, Books $11,373, Other Print Mats $11,834, AV Equip $461
Library Holdings: Bk Titles 10,600; Per Subs 15
Wireless access
Mem of Mid-Hudson Library System
Open Mon, Thurs & Fri 12-5, Tues 11-5, Sat 10-2

AMHERST

P AMHERST PUBLIC LIBRARY*, Main Library at Audubon, 350 John James Audubon Pkwy, 14228. SAN 354-4117. Tel: 716-689-4922. Administration Tel: 716-688-4919. FAX: 716-689-6116. E-mail: aud@buffalolib.org. Web Site: www.buffalolib.org/locations-hours/audubon-branch. *Dir,* Roseanne Butler-Smith; E-mail: butlersmithr@buffalolib.org
Founded 1842. Pop 116,510; Circ 1,168,400
Library Holdings: Bk Vols 298,000
Special Collections: Library Limelight Television Show, V-tapes
Wireless access
Mem of Buffalo & Erie County Public Library System
Partic in Ohio Public Library Information Network
Open Mon-Thurs 10-9, Fri & Sat 10-6
Friends of the Library Group
Branches: 3
CLEARFIELD, 770 Hopkins Rd, Williamsville, 14221, SAN 354-4141. Tel: 716-688-4955. FAX: 716-688-0281. E-mail: cfd@buffalolib.org.
Open Mon, Wed & Fri 10-8, Tues, Thurs & Sat 10-5
Friends of the Library Group
EGGERTSVILLE-SNYDER BRANCH, 4622 Main St, Synder, 14226, SAN 354-4176. Tel: 716-839-0700. FAX: 716-839-4277. E-mail: egg@buffalolib.org.
Open Mon & Wed 12-7, Tues, Thurs & Fri 10-6, Sat 11-3
Friends of the Library Group
WILLIAMSVILLE, 5571 Main St, Williamsville, 14221, SAN 354-4206. Tel: 716-632-6176. FAX: 716-634-2927. E-mail: wil@buffalolib.org.
Open Mon & Wed 10-2, Tues & Thurs 1-8, Fri 1-5
Friends of the Library Group

C DAEMEN COLLEGE LIBRARY*, Research & Information Commons, 4380 Main St, 14226-3592. SAN 351-8167. Tel: 716-839-8243. FAX: 716-839-8475. Web Site: www.daemen.edu/library. *Dir,* Melissa Peterson; E-mail: mpeters2@daemen.edu; *Asst Dir, Circ, ILL,* Kara McGuire; *Head, Ref & Instruction,* Andrea Sullivan; E-mail: asulliv1@daemen.edu; *Ref & Instruction Librn,* Rebecca Bley; E-mail: rbley@daemen.edu; *Ref & Instruction Librn,* Justin Dise; E-mail: jdise@daemen.edu; *Ref & Instruction Librn,* Jocelyn Swick-Jemison; E-mail: jswickje@daemen.edu; *Tech Serv Librn,* Randolph Chojecki; E-mail: rchojeck@daemen.edu; Staff 7 (MLS 7)
Founded 1948. Enrl 2,776; Fac 297; Highest Degree: Doctorate
Jun 2015-May 2016 Income $100,350, State $5,442, Parent Institution $94,908. Mats Exp $521,474, Books $24,115, Per/Ser (Incl. Access Fees) $275,970, AV Mat $500, Electronic Ref Mat (Incl. Access Fees) $220,889. Sal $331,509
Library Holdings: DVDs 329; e-books 138,085; Bk Titles 85,205; Bk Vols 98,158; Per Subs 488
Subject Interests: Humanities, Liberal arts, Nursing, Phys therapy, Physicians assistance studies
Automation Activity & Vendor Info: (Cataloging) Innovative Interfaces, Inc; (Circulation) Innovative Interfaces, Inc; (Course Reserve) Innovative Interfaces, Inc; (ILL) OCLC; (OPAC) Innovative Interfaces, Inc; (Serials) Innovative Interfaces, Inc
Wireless access
Partic in OCLC Online Computer Library Center, Inc; Westchester Academic Library Directors Organization; Western New York Library Resources Council
Open Mon-Thurs 7am-1am, Fri 7am-11pm, Sat 9am-11-pm, Sun 10am-1am

AMITYVILLE

P AMITYVILLE PUBLIC LIBRARY*, 19 John St, 11701. SAN 310-7949. Tel: 631-264-0567. FAX: 631-264-2006. E-mail: info@amityvillepubliclibrary.org. Web Site: www.amityvillepubliclibrary.org. *Libr Dir,* Monica Powers; *Head, Children's Servx,* Celine Lieffrig; *Coll Develop,* Grace Marsilla; *Tech Serv,* Mary Gordon; *YA Serv,* Linda Ferraro; Staff 7.5 (MLS 7.5)
Founded 1907. Pop 25,476; Circ 211,050
Library Holdings: Bk Titles 101,000; Bk Vols 112,000; Per Subs 255
Automation Activity & Vendor Info: (Cataloging) Innovative Interfaces, Inc; (Circulation) Innovative Interfaces, Inc; (Course Reserve) Innovative Interfaces, Inc; (ILL) Innovative Interfaces, Inc; (Media Booking) Innovative Interfaces, Inc - Millennium; (OPAC) Innovative Interfaces, Inc
Wireless access
Publications: Library Browser (Quarterly newsletter)
Mem of Suffolk Cooperative Library System
Open Mon-Thurs 10-7, Fri 10-5, Sat 10-4

AMSTERDAM

P AMSTERDAM FREE LIBRARY*, 28 Church St, 12010. SAN 310-7973. Tel: 518-842-1080. FAX: 518-842-1169. Web Site: www.amsterdamlibrary.com. *Dir,* Nicole Hemsley; E-mail: nhemsley@mvls.info; Staff 10 (MLS 1, Non-MLS 9)
Founded 1891. Pop 24,186; Circ 54,526
Library Holdings: Bk Vols 49,500; Per Subs 400
Special Collections: Civil War, Military History
Subject Interests: Job info, Local hist, Spanish lang
Automation Activity & Vendor Info: (Cataloging) Innovative Interfaces, Inc; (Circulation) Innovative Interfaces, Inc; (OPAC) Innovative Interfaces, Inc; (Serials) Innovative Interfaces, Inc
Wireless access

Function: 24/7 Electronic res, 24/7 Online cat, 3D Printer, Adult bk club, Art exhibits, Audiobks on Playaways & MP3, Audiobks via web, Bk club(s), Bks on CD, Children's prog, Computer training, Computers for patron use, Electronic databases & coll, Free DVD rentals, Genealogy discussion group, Holiday prog, Home delivery & serv to seniorr ctr & nursing homes, Homebound delivery serv, ILL available, Internet access, Life-long learning prog for all ages, Magazines, Magnifiers for reading, Microfiche/film & reading machines, Movies, Online cat, Outreach serv, OverDrive digital audio bks, Photocopying/Printing, Preschool reading prog, Printer for laptops & handheld devices, Prog for adults, Prog for children & young adult, Ref & res, Scanner, Senior computer classes, Senior outreach, Serves people with intellectual disabilities, Spanish lang bks, Story hour, Summer reading prog, Tax forms, Teen prog, Wheelchair accessible, Workshops
Mem of Mohawk Valley Library System
Open Mon & Thurs 9-8, Tues, Wed & Fri 9-5:30, Sat (Sept-June) 10-1
Friends of the Library Group

S WALTER ELWOOD MUSEUM LIBRARY*, 100 Church St, 12010-2228. SAN 329-1863. Tel: 518-843-5151. FAX: 518-843-6098. Web Site: www.walterelwoodmuseum.org. *Dir,* Ann Peconie; Staff 3 (MLS 1, Non-MLS 2)
Founded 1939
Library Holdings: Bk Titles 2,000
Special Collections: Bibles & Other Religious Tracts; Mohawk Valley & New York State; Natural History, old school bks
Wireless access
Function: Archival coll, Art exhibits, For res purposes, Prog for adults, Prog for children & young adult, Ref serv available, Res performed for a fee, Summer reading prog, Winter reading prog, Workshops
Open Mon-Fri 9-3
Restriction: Authorized patrons, Authorized personnel only, Authorized scholars by appt, By permission only, Circ to mem only, Free to mem, Non-circulating of rare bks, Open to pub for ref only, Pub ref by request, Use of others with permission of librn

P FORT HUNTER FREE LIBRARY*, 167 Fort Hunter Rd, 12010. SAN 311-2128. Tel: 518-829-7248. E-mail: forthunterfreelibrary@gmail.com. Web Site: www.forthunterfreelibrary.com. *Dir,* Judi Steiger
Library Holdings: Bk Titles 11,000; Per Subs 12
Automation Activity & Vendor Info: (Circulation) Innovative Interfaces, Inc; (OPAC) Innovative Interfaces, Inc
Wireless access
Mem of Mohawk Valley Library System
Open Mon & Wed 3-8, Tues, Thurs & Fri 9:30-2:30, Sat 9-1

ANDES

P ANDES PUBLIC LIBRARY*, 242 Main St, 13731. (Mail add: PO Box 116, 13731-0016), SAN 310-799X. Tel: 845-676-3333. FAX: 845-676-3333. E-mail: an.ill@4cls.org. Web Site: www.andeslibrary.org. *Dir,* Pamela West-Finkle
Founded 1922. Pop 372; Circ 1,200
Library Holdings: Bk Vols 5,600; Per Subs 14
Wireless access
Mem of Four County Library System
Open Mon & Wed 11-4, Tues 1-6, Thurs 4-7, Fri 1-5, Sat 10-Noon
Friends of the Library Group

ANDOVER

P ANDOVER FREE LIBRARY*, 40 Main St, 14806. (Mail add: PO Box 745, 14806-0745), SAN 310-8007. Tel: 607-478-8442. FAX: 607-478-5056. *Dir,* Linda Adams Hilliard; E-mail: adamsl@stls.org; *Ch Serv,* Cindy Glover; E-mail: gloverl@stls.org
Founded 1912. Circ 11,673
Library Holdings: Bks on Deafness & Sign Lang 6; CDs 94; Large Print Bks 425; Bk Titles 6,700; Bk Vols 7,000; Per Subs 15; Spec Interest Per Sub 3
Automation Activity & Vendor Info: (Cataloging) SirsiDynix-WorkFlows; (Circulation) SirsiDynix-WorkFlows; (OPAC) SirsiDynix-WorkFlows
Wireless access
Mem of Southern Tier Library System
Open Tues & Thurs 11-7, Wed 9:30-1:30
Friends of the Library Group

ANGELICA

P ANGELICA FREE LIBRARY, 55 W Main St, 14709. (Mail add: PO Box 660, 14709-0660), SAN 310-8015. Tel: 585-466-7860. Web Site: angelicafreelibrary.org. *Dir,* Ms Chris Gallmann; E-mail: gallmannc@stls.org
Founded 1900. Pop 1,000
Library Holdings: CDs 10; Large Print Bks 400; Bk Vols 15,200; Per Subs 58; Talking Bks 40; Videos 50
Wireless access
Mem of Southern Tier Library System
Special Services for the Blind - Talking bks
Open Tues & Thurs 12-8, Sat 9:30-1:30
Friends of the Library Group

ANGOLA

P ANGOLA PUBLIC LIBRARY*, 34 N Main St, 14006. SAN 310-8023. Tel: 716-549-1271. FAX: 716-549-3954. E-mail: ang@buffalolib.org. Web Site: www.buffalolib.org/content/library-locations/angola. *Mgr,* Jennifer Page
Founded 1924. Pop 2,693; Circ 55,626
Library Holdings: Bk Vols 20,337; Per Subs 45
Mem of Buffalo & Erie County Public Library System
Open Mon 12-8, Tues & Fri 10-6, Wed & Thurs 3-8, Sat 11-3
Friends of the Library Group

ANNANDALE-ON-HUDSON

C BARD COLLEGE*, Charles P Stevenson Jr Library, One Library Rd, 12504. (Mail add: PO Box 5000, 12504-5000), SAN 310-8031. Tel: 845-758-6822. Circulation Tel: 845-758-7359; 845-758-7620. Interlibrary Loan Service Tel: 845-758-7409. Reference Tel: 845-758-7281. FAX: 845-758-7170. Web Site: www.bard.edu/library. *Dir of Libr,* Betsy Cawley; E-mail: cawley@bard.edu; *Assoc Dir for Library Writing Support,* Jane E Smith; Tel: 845-758-7892, E-mail: jesmith@bard.edu; *Acq Librn,* Susan Decker-Herman; Tel: 845-785-7617, E-mail: herman@bard.edu; *Digital Tech Librn,* Jeremiah Hall; Tel: 845-785-7675, E-mail: jhall@bard.edu; *ILL Librn,* Alexa Murphy; E-mail: amurphy@bard.edu; *Metadata Librn, Syst Librn,* Amber Billey; Tel: 845-758-7619, E-mail: abilley@bard.edu; *Archivist,* Helene Tieger; Tel: 845-758-7396, E-mail: tieger@bard.edu; *Coll Develop,* Kate Laing; Tel: 845-758-7312, E-mail: claing@bard.edu; *Visual Res Curator,* Amy Herman; Tel: 845-758-7304, E-mail: aherman@bard.edu; Staff 18 (MLS 9, Non-MLS 9)
Founded 1860. Enrl 1,100; Fac 140; Highest Degree: Master
Library Holdings: e-journals 22,000; Bk Titles 165,065; Bk Vols 280,000; Per Subs 1,000
Special Collections: Bardiana, publications by Bard faculty & alumnae; Hannah Arendt & Heinrich Bluecher Coll; Hudson Valley History; Sussman Rare Book Coll
Wireless access
Partic in ConnectNY, Inc; Oberlin Group; Southeastern New York Library Resources Council
Open Mon-Thurs 8am-1am, Fri 8am-10pm, Sat 10-10, Sun 10am-1am
Restriction: Circ limited, Non-circulating to the pub

Departmental Libraries:

CENTER FOR CURATORIAL STUDIES, PO Box 5000, 12504-5000. Tel: 845-758-7567. FAX: 845-758-2442. E-mail: ccslib@bard.edu. Web Site: www.bard.edu/ccs/study/library-archives. *Dir, Libr & Archives,* Ann Butler; Tel: 845-758-7566, E-mail: butler@bard.edu; *Assoc Librn,* Bronwen Bitetti; Tel: 845-752-2395, E-mail: bbitetti@bard.edu; Staff 2 (MLS 2)
Founded 1990
Library Holdings: Bk Vols 25,000; Per Subs 60
Special Collections: Curating in the 20th & 21st Century Archives
Open Mon & Tues (Fall & Spring) 9:30-8, Wed & Thurs 9:30-7, Fri 9:30-5, Sat 1-6, Sun 1-7; Mon-Fri (Summer) 10-5
Restriction: Non-circulating, Open to fac, students & qualified researchers

LEVY ECONOMICS INSTITUTE LIBRARY, Blithewood Ave, 12504. Tel: 845-758-7729. FAX: 845-758-1149. Web Site: www.levyinstitute.org. *Librn,* Willis C Walker; E-mail: wwalker@levy.org. Subject Specialists: *Bus, Econ, Finance,* Willis C Walker; Staff 1 (MLS 1)
Founded 1987
Library Holdings: Bk Vols 12,000; Per Subs 70
Function: Archival coll, Online cat, Wheelchair accessible
Restriction: Closed stack, Open by appt only, Open to fac, students & qualified researchers

ANTWERP

P CROSBY PUBLIC LIBRARY*, 59 Main St, 13608-4157. SAN 310-804X. Tel: 315-659-8564. FAX: 315-659-8564. E-mail: antlib@ncls.org. Web Site: www.crosbylibrary.org. *Dir,* Myra Laclair
Founded 1917. Pop 1,856; Circ 4,148
Library Holdings: Bk Titles 6,595; Per Subs 33
Wireless access
Mem of North Country Library System
Partic in OCLC Online Computer Library Center, Inc
Open Mon & Fri 1-6, Wed 2-7, Thurs 3-7, Sat 10-2

APALACHIN

P APALACHIN LIBRARY*, 719 Main St, 13732. Tel: 607-625-3333. FAX: 607-625-3333. E-mail: alibrary1@stny.rr.com. Web Site: www.apalachinlibrary.org. *Dir,* Cathy Sorbor
Mem of Finger Lakes Library System

ARCADE

P ARCADE FREE LIBRARY*, 365 W Main St, 14009. SAN 310-8058. Tel: 585-492-1297. FAX: 585-492-3305. E-mail: arcadelibrarydirector@owwl.org. Web Site: arcadelibrary.blogspot.com, pls-net.org/library/arcade. *Dir,* Sue Reding; E-mail: sreding@pls-net.org; Staff 6 (MLS 1, Non-MLS 5)
Founded 1912. Pop 4,100; Circ 55,623
Library Holdings: Bk Titles 25,950; Bk Vols 27,100; Per Subs 75
Special Collections: Lone Ranger Coll
Wireless access
Mem of Pioneer Library System
Open Mon, Tues & Thurs Noon-8, Wed 9-1, Fri 9-5, Sat 10-2
Friends of the Library Group

ARDSLEY

P ARDSLEY PUBLIC LIBRARY, Nine American Legion Dr, 10502. SAN 310-8066. Tel: 914-693-6636. FAX: 914-693-6837. E-mail: APL@wlsmail.org. Web Site: www.ardsleylibrary.org. *Dir,* Angela Groth; E-mail: agroth@wlsmail.org; Staff 8 (MLS 2, Non-MLS 6)
Founded 1972. Pop 4,452; Circ 108,541
Library Holdings: DVDs 1,000; Large Print Bks 350; Bk Vols 50,000; Per Subs 70; Talking Bks 1,700; Videos 1,000
Subject Interests: Best sellers, Computers, Cooking, Local hist, Parenting, Travel
Automation Activity & Vendor Info: (Cataloging) SirsiDynix; (Circulation) SirsiDynix
Wireless access
Publications: The Bookmark (Newsletter)
Mem of Westchester Library System
Open Mon-Wed & Fri 10-5:30, Thurs 1-8, Sat 10-1
Friends of the Library Group

ARGYLE

P ARGYLE FREE LIBRARY, 21 Sheridan St, 12809. (Mail add: PO Box 238, 12809-0238), SAN 310-8082. Tel: 518-638-8911. FAX: 518-638-8911. Web Site: argylelibrary.sals.edu. *Dir,* Faith St John; E-mail: arg-director@sals.edu
Founded 1920. Pop 9,972; Circ 13,569
Library Holdings: AV Mats 556; Bk Vols 11,000; Per Subs 16
Wireless access
Mem of Southern Adirondack Library System
Open Mon & Wed 11-5, Tues & Thurs 3-7, Fri 4-7, Sat 10-3
Friends of the Library Group

ARMONK

P NORTH CASTLE PUBLIC LIBRARY*, 19 Whippoorwill Rd E, 10504. SAN 310-8104. Tel: 914-273-3887. FAX: 914-273-5572. Web Site: www.northcastlelibrary.org. *Dir,* Edie Martimucci; E-mail: ediem@wlsmail.org; *Ref Librn,* Mary Johnson; Staff 6 (MLS 6)
Founded 1938. Pop 10,849; Circ 196,731
Library Holdings: AV Mats 12,041; Bk Titles 71,256; Per Subs 157
Automation Activity & Vendor Info: (Acquisitions) SirsiDynix; (Cataloging) SirsiDynix; (Circulation) SirsiDynix; (Course Reserve) SirsiDynix; (ILL) SirsiDynix; (Media Booking) SirsiDynix; (OPAC) SirsiDynix; (Serials) SirsiDynix
Wireless access
Mem of Westchester Library System
Open Mon-Thurs 10-8, Fri 10-5:30, Sat 10-5, Sun 12-5
Friends of the Library Group
Branches: 1
NORTH WHITE PLAINS BRANCH, Ten Clove Rd, North White Plains, 10603. Tel: 914-948-6359. FAX: 914-948-6359. *Br Mgr,* Susan Grecco
Library Holdings: Bk Vols 25,000
Open Mon & Wed 10-6, Tues & Thurs 10-8, Fri 10-5:30, Sat 10-5, Sun 12-5

ASHVILLE

P ASHVILLE FREE LIBRARY*, 2200 N Maple St, 14710. SAN 310-8112. Tel: 716-763-9906. FAX: 716-763-9906. E-mail: ashvillelib@stny.rr.com. Web Site: ashvillelibrary.com. *Dir,* Tabetha Butler; E-mail: director@ashvillelibrary.com
Founded 1914. Pop 2,602; Circ 14,000
Library Holdings: Bk Titles 20,000; Per Subs 33
Special Collections: New York State, bks, pamphlets
Subject Interests: Local hist
Automation Activity & Vendor Info: (Cataloging) SirsiDynix; (Circulation) SirsiDynix; (OPAC) SirsiDynix; (Serials) SirsiDynix
Wireless access
Function: Bks on cassette, Bks on CD, Computer training, ILL available
Mem of Chautauqua-Cattaraugus Library System
Open Mon-Fri 9:30-5 & 6:30-8:30, Sat 10-1

ATHENS

P D R EVARTS LIBRARY*, 80 Second St, 12015. SAN 310-8120. Tel: 518-945-1417. FAX: 518-945-1725. Web Site: drevartslibrary.org. *Dir,* Sam Gruber; E-mail: director@drevartslibrary.org
Founded 1907. Pop 3,700; Circ 7,322
Library Holdings: AV Mats 512; Bk Vols 12,997; Per Subs 23
Automation Activity & Vendor Info: (Cataloging) Innovative Interfaces, Inc; (Circulation) Innovative Interfaces, Inc; (OPAC) Innovative Interfaces, Inc
Wireless access
Open Mon 12-8, Tues-Fri 12-6, Sat 10-4
Friends of the Library Group

ATLANTA

P E J COTTRELL MEMORIAL LIBRARY, 30 W Main St, 14808-0192. SAN 310-8139. Tel: 585-534-5030. FAX: 585-534-9316. Web Site: atlanta.stls.org. *Dir,* Belinda Schuler; E-mail: schulerb@stls.org
Founded 1921. Circ 2,700
Library Holdings: Bk Vols 10,000; Per Subs 10
Automation Activity & Vendor Info: (Cataloging) SirsiDynix; (Circulation) SirsiDynix; (OPAC) SirsiDynix
Wireless access
Mem of Southern Tier Library System
Open Mon & Tues 10-8, Wed-Fri 10-5

ATTICA

P STEVENS MEMORIAL COMMUNITY LIBRARY, 146 Main St, 14011-1243. SAN 310-8147. Tel: 585-591-2733. FAX: 585-591-3855. Web Site: attica.owwl.org, owwl.org/library/attica. *Dir,* Karen Rosolowski; E-mail: atticalibrarydirector@owwl.org; Staff 5 (MLS 1, Non-MLS 4)
Founded 1893. Pop 13,793
Library Holdings: Bk Titles 29,770; Per Subs 35
Special Collections: Attica Prison Riot Coll (1971)
Subject Interests: Civil War, Local hist, NY hist, Railroading, World War II
Automation Activity & Vendor Info: (Acquisitions) SirsiDynix; (Cataloging) SirsiDynix; (Circulation) SirsiDynix; (Course Reserve) SirsiDynix; (ILL) SirsiDynix; (Media Booking) SirsiDynix; (OPAC) SirsiDynix; (Serials) SirsiDynix
Wireless access
Mem of Pioneer Library System
Special Services for the Blind - ZoomText magnification & reading software
Open Mon & Wed 12-8, Tues & Thurs 10-7, Fri 12-4, Sat 10-1
Friends of the Library Group

S WYOMING CORRECTIONAL FACILITY GENERAL LIBRARY*, 3203 Dunbar Rd, 14011. (Mail add: PO Box 501, 14011-0501), SAN 327-2516. Tel: 585-591-1010. FAX: 585-591-1010. *Librn,* David Collins
Library Holdings: Bk Titles 15,000; Per Subs 70
Automation Activity & Vendor Info: (Cataloging) Follett Software; (Circulation) Follett Software; (OPAC) Follett Software; (Serials) Follett Software
Restriction: Staff & inmates only

AU SABLE FORKS

P AU SABLE FORKS FREE LIBRARY, Nine Church Lane, 12912-4400. (Mail add: PO Box 179, 12912-0179), SAN 310-8155. Tel: 518-647-5596. FAX: 518-647-5753. E-mail: ausablelibrary@gmail.com. Web Site: www.ausableforksfreelibrary.com. *Dir,* Alison Follos; Staff 2 (Non-MLS 2)
Founded 1962. Pop 2,100; Circ 22,000
Library Holdings: Bk Titles 20,000; Bk Vols 22,000; Per Subs 25
Special Collections: The Adirondack Coll
Automation Activity & Vendor Info: (Cataloging) Horizon; (Circulation) Horizon; (OPAC) Horizon; (Serials) Horizon
Wireless access
Function: ILL available
Mem of Clinton-Essex-Franklin Library System
Open Mon 10-2, Tues 9-2, Wed 9-1, Thurs 1-5:30, Fri 1-4:30, Sat 9:30-1:30

AUBURN

S AUBURN CORRECTIONAL FACILITY LIBRARY*, 135 State St, 13024-9000. SAN 328-5065. Tel: 315-253-8401, Ext 4650. FAX: 315-253-8401, Ext 2099. Web Site: doccs.ny.gov/location/auburn-correctional-facility. *Library Contact,* Jean Sears; E-mail: jean.sears@doccs.ny.gov; Staff 1 (MLS 1)
Library Holdings: AV Mats 1,700; High Interest/Low Vocabulary Bk Vols 500; Large Print Bks 50; Bk Titles 14,000; Per Subs 35
Special Collections: Spanish Language
Subject Interests: Law
Automation Activity & Vendor Info: (Acquisitions) Brodart; (Cataloging) Brodart; (Circulation) Brodart; (OPAC) Brodart
Restriction: Not open to pub

J CAYUGA COUNTY COMMUNITY COLLEGE, Bourke Memorial Library, 197 Franklin St, 13021. SAN 310-8171. Tel: 315-294-8596. Reference Tel: 315-294-8599. FAX: 315-255-2050. E-mail: cay_ref@cayuga-cc.edu. Web Site: www.cayuga-cc.edu/library. *Libr Dir,* Sara Davenport; E-mail: davenport@cayuga-cc.edu; *Acq, Circ,* Rosanne Bourke; E-mail: bourker@cayuga-cc.edu; *Syst/Tech Serv,* Michael Schillace; E-mail: mschilla1@cayuga-cc.edu; *Syst/Tech Serv,* Renee Schmidt; E-mail: renee.schmidt@cayuga-cc.edu; *Syst/Tech Serv,* Everitt Waldron; E-mail: patrick.waldron@cayuga-cc.edu; Staff 9 (MLS 5, Non-MLS 4)
Founded 1953. Enrl 2,568; Fac 246; Highest Degree: Associate
Library Holdings: CDs 1,265; Bk Titles 78,922; Bk Vols 81,774; Per Subs 250; Talking Bks 112; Videos 2,537
Special Collections: College Archives; Local History
Automation Activity & Vendor Info: (Cataloging) OCLC Connexion; (Circulation) Ex Libris Group; (ILL) OCLC ILLiad; (OPAC) Ex Libris Group; (Serials) Ex Libris Group
Wireless access
Function: 24/7 Electronic res, Audio & video playback equip for onsite use, Bks on CD, Computers for patron use, Distance learning, Electronic databases & coll, Photocopying/Printing, Printer for laptops & handheld devices, Wheelchair accessible
Partic in OCLC Online Computer Library Center, Inc; South Central Regional Library Council
Open Mon, Tues, Thurs & Fri 8-4:30, Wed 8-7:30
Restriction: 24-hr pass syst for students only

G CAYUGA COUNTY HISTORIAN'S OFFICE*, Research Library, Ten Court St, 13021. SAN 371-5469. Tel: 315-253-1300. E-mail: historian@cayugacounty.us. Web Site: www.cayugacounty.us/234/County-Historian-Office. *County Historian,* Ruth Bradley
Founded 1969
Library Holdings: Bk Titles 3,000; Per Subs 20
Special Collections: African-Am census 1800-1870;; Local Churches coll; Newspapers 1811-2006; US Park Systems Network to Freedom Underground Railroad Repository, photog coll, local map coll, hist homes survey. Oral History; US Document Depository
Subject Interests: Local hist archives
Function: Res libr
Open Mon, Tues, Thurs & Fri 9-5
Restriction: Not a lending libr

GL NEW YORK SUPREME COURT, Seventh District Law Library, Cayuga County Court House, 152 Genesee St, 13021-3476. SAN 310-8201. Tel: 315-237-6122. FAX: 315-237-6451. *Law Libr Asst,* Sean Clancy; E-mail: ssclancy@nycourts.gov; Staff 1 (Non-MLS 1)
Library Holdings: Bk Titles 7,500; Per Subs 1
Wireless access
Open Mon-Fri 9-5 (8-4 Summer)

S THE SEWARD HOUSE MUSEUM*, 33 South St, 13021-3929. SAN 310-8198. Tel: 315-252-1283. FAX: 315-253-3351. E-mail: info@sewardhouse.org. Web Site: www.sewardhouse.org. *Exec Dir,* Billye Chabot; E-mail: director@sewardhouse.org
Founded 1955
Library Holdings: Bk Vols 1,000
Subject Interests: Alaska, Civil War, Genealogy, Local hist
Wireless access
Open Tues-Sat 10-5, Sun (June-Aug) 1-5

P SEYMOUR PUBLIC LIBRARY DISTRICT*, 176-178 Genesee St, 13021. SAN 310-821X. Tel: 315-252-2571. FAX: 315-252-7985. Web Site: seymourlibrary.org. *Dir,* Lisa Carr; E-mail: lcarr@seymourlib.org; *Asst Dir,* Danette Davis; E-mail: ddavis@seymourlib.org; *Librn,* Mary Lovell; E-mail: mlovell@seymourlib.org; *Librn,* Leigh Romano; E-mail: lromano@seymourlib.org; *Youth Serv Librn,* Jill Hand; E-mail: jhand@seymourlib.org; *Commun Serv Coordr,* Jackie Kolb; E-mail: jkolb@seymourlib.org. Subject Specialists: *Tech,* Mary Lovell; *Reading,* Leigh Romano; *Youth activities,* Jill Hand; Staff 15 (MLS 5, Non-MLS 10)
Founded 1876. Pop 35,000; Circ 165,200
Library Holdings: Bk Titles 65,000; Per Subs 224
Special Collections: Auburn Imprints; Auburn Prison; Harriet Tubman Coll, bks, newsp
Automation Activity & Vendor Info: (Acquisitions) Innovative Interfaces, Inc; (Cataloging) Innovative Interfaces, Inc; (Circulation) Innovative Interfaces, Inc; (OPAC) Innovative Interfaces, Inc
Wireless access
Function: 24/7 Electronic res, 24/7 Online cat, Adult bk club, Audiobks on Playaways & MP3, Bk club(s), Bks on CD, Butterfly Garden, Chess club, Children's prog, Computers for patron use, Electronic databases & coll, ILL available, Internet access, Large print keyboards, Life-long learning prog for all ages, Magazines, Magnifiers for reading, Mango lang, Microfiche/film & reading machines, Museum passes, Online cat, OverDrive digital audio bks, Photocopying/Printing, Preschool outreach, Prog for adults, Prog for children & young adult, Scanner, Senior outreach, STEM programs, Story hour, Tax forms, Workshops
Mem of Finger Lakes Library System
Partic in OCLC Online Computer Library Center, Inc
Open Mon, Tues & Wed 9-8, Thurs & Fri 9-6, Sat 10-4
Friends of the Library Group

AURORA

P AURORA FREE LIBRARY*, 370 Main St, 13026. SAN 376-303X. Tel: 315-364-8074. FAX: 315-364-8074. E-mail: aurorali@rochester.rr.com. Web Site: www.aurorafreelibrary.org. *Librn,* Sandy Groth; *Asst Librn,* Susan MacCormick; E-mail: susancmac@mac.com
Pop 637
Library Holdings: Bk Vols 7,000
Automation Activity & Vendor Info: (Cataloging) Innovative Interfaces, Inc; (Circulation) Innovative Interfaces, Inc; (ILL) Innovative Interfaces, Inc; (OPAC) Innovative Interfaces, Inc; (Serials) Innovative Interfaces, Inc
Wireless access
Mem of Finger Lakes Library System
Open Mon & Fri 3-8, Wed 10-12 & 3-8, Sat 10-3

C WELLS COLLEGE*, Louis Jefferson Long Library, 170 Main St, 13026. SAN 310-8228. Tel: 315-364-3351. E-mail: library@wells.edu. Web Site: www.wells.edu/library. *Actg Libr Dir,* Tiffany Raymond; Tel: 315-364-3352, E-mail: traymond@wells.edu; *Librn,* Susan Gloss; Tel: 315-364-3354, E-mail: sgloss@wells.edu; Staff 4 (MLS 3, Non-MLS 1)
Founded 1868. Enrl 535; Fac 60; Highest Degree: Bachelor
Library Holdings: Bk Vols 186,000; Per Subs 316
Special Collections: Chemistry-Physics; Economics (Weld Coll); Fine Arts (Morgan Coll); History (Lowe Coll); Philosophy (Lowenberg Coll); Pierce W Gaines Americana Coll; Wells Fargo Express Co, CA 1825-80, ms, personal papers
Automation Activity & Vendor Info: (Acquisitions) EOS International; (Cataloging) EOS International; (Circulation) EOS International; (Course Reserve) EOS International; (ILL) EOS International; (OPAC) EOS International; (Serials) EOS International
Wireless access
Function: 24/7 Electronic res, Archival coll, Art exhibits, Computers for patron use, Doc delivery serv, E-Reserves, Electronic databases & coll, ILL available, Instruction & testing, Internet access, Literacy & newcomer serv, Magazines, Online cat, Online ref, Orientations, Outreach serv, Photocopying/Printing, Ref & res, Ref serv available, Workshops
Partic in OCLC Online Computer Library Center, Inc; South Central Regional Library Council
Open Mon-Thurs 8:30am-Midnight, Fri 8:30-6, Sat 10-6, Sun 11am-Midnight

AVERILL PARK

P SAND LAKE TOWN LIBRARY*, 8428 Miller Hill Rd, 12018. Tel: 518-674-5050. FAX: 518-674-5050. E-mail: info@sandlaketownlibrary.org. Web Site: www.sandlaketownlibrary.org. *Dir,* Melinda Fowler; *Asst Dir,* Mary Klimack
Founded 1987. Pop 7,900; Circ 56,600
Library Holdings: AV Mats 3,400; Bk Vols 32,000; Per Subs 51
Subject Interests: Adult literacy, Local hist, Parenting
Wireless access
Function: Wheelchair accessible
Mem of Upper Hudson Library System
Open Mon-Thurs 11-8, Fri 11-6, Sat 11-4, Sun (Oct-May) 1-4
Friends of the Library Group

AVOCA

P AVOCA FREE LIBRARY*, 18 N Main St, 14809. (Mail add: PO Box S, 14809-0519), SAN 376-3056. Tel: 607-566-9279. FAX: 607-566-9279. Web Site: avoca.stls.org. *Dir,* Justin Zeh; E-mail: zehj@stls.org; *Libr Asst,* Alissa Carlson

Library Holdings: Audiobooks 55; CDs 130; DVDs 285; Large Print Bks 150; Bk Vols 18,000; Per Subs 53; Videos 1,802
Wireless access
Mem of Southern Tier Library System
Open Mon 9-7, Tues & Thurs 2-7, Fri & Sat 9-2

AVON

P AVON FREE LIBRARY, 143 Genesee St, 14414. SAN 310-8244. Tel: 585-226-8461. FAX: 585-226-6615. Web Site: avonfreelibrary.org. *Dir,* Rebecca Budinger-Mulhearn; E-mail: AvonLibraryDirector@owwl.org
Pop 7,064; Circ 53,700
Library Holdings: Bk Titles 30,850; Bk Vols 32,000; Per Subs 60
Wireless access
Mem of Pioneer Library System
Open Mon & Thurs 10-8, Tues, Wed & Fri 10-6, Sat 10-3
Friends of the Library Group

BABYLON

P BABYLON PUBLIC LIBRARY, 24 S Carll Ave, 11702. SAN 310-8260. Tel: 631-669-1624. FAX: 631-893-3044. E-mail: info@babylonlibrary.org. Web Site: www.babylonlibrary.org. *Dir,* Victoria Lever; Staff 39 (MLS 12, Non-MLS 27)
Founded 1895. Pop 55,117; Circ 75,594
Library Holdings: Bk Vols 65,626; Per Subs 4,157
Special Collections: Large Print; Long Island History; Parenting
Subject Interests: Babylon hist
Automation Activity & Vendor Info: (Acquisitions) Innovative Interfaces, Inc; (Cataloging) Innovative Interfaces, Inc; (Circulation) Innovative Interfaces, Inc; (ILL) Innovative Interfaces, Inc; (OPAC) Innovative Interfaces, Inc; (Serials) Innovative Interfaces, Inc
Wireless access
Publications: Small Talk (Newsletter); The Anchor (Newsletter)
Mem of Suffolk Cooperative Library System
Partic in Partnership of Automated Librs in Suffolk
Special Services for the Deaf - TTY equip
Special Services for the Blind - Closed circuit TV; ZoomText magnification & reading software
Open Mon-Thurs 9:30-7, Fri & Sat 9:30-5
Friends of the Library Group

BAINBRIDGE

P BAINBRIDGE FREE LIBRARY, 13 N Main St, 13733. SAN 310-8279. Tel: 607-967-5305. FAX: 607-967-5305. E-mail: ba.ill@4cls.org. Web Site: libraries.4cls.org/bainbridge. *Dir,* Michelle Arnold
Founded 1908. Pop 3,331; Circ 9,048
Library Holdings: Bk Vols 15,510; Per Subs 24
Wireless access
Mem of Four County Library System
Open Tues & Wed 10-5, Thurs 10-6, Sat 10-1

BALDWIN

P BALDWIN PUBLIC LIBRARY, 2385 Grand Ave, 11510-3289. SAN 310-8287. Tel: 516-223-6228. FAX: 516-623-7991. E-mail: info@baldwinpl.org. Web Site: www.baldwinpl.org. *Dir,* Elizabeth Olesh; *Asst Dir,* Kaysha Watson-Phillips; *Head, Ad Ref Serv,* Edward Daly; *Head, Adult Serv,* Wendy Rathjens; *Head, Children's Servx,* Martha Garvey; *Head, Circ,* Bianca Roberto; *Head, Info Tech,* Jason VonButtgereit; *Head, YA,* Jill Holleufer; *Bus Mgr,* Colleen Hughes
Founded 1922. Pop 32,837
Library Holdings: AV Mats 21,959; Videos 13,265
Subject Interests: Career, City hist, Fr, Law, Local hist, Spanish, Spec educ, Testing, Travel
Automation Activity & Vendor Info: (Circulation) Innovative Interfaces, Inc; (OPAC) Innovative Interfaces, Inc
Wireless access
Publications: Piper (Newsletter)
Mem of Nassau Library System
Partic in The Library Network
Special Services for the Blind - Magnifiers
Open Mon-Wed 9-9, Thurs 11-9, Fri & Sat 9-5, Sun 1-5 (Sept-June); Mon-Wed 9-9, Thurs 11-9, Fri 9-5, Sat 9-1 (July-Aug)
Friends of the Library Group

BALDWINSVILLE

P BALDWINSVILLE PUBLIC LIBRARY*, 33 E Genesee St, 13027-2575. SAN 310-8295. Tel: 315-635-5631. FAX: 315-635-6760. E-mail: info@bville.lib.ny.us. Web Site: www.bville.lib.ny.us. *Libr Dir,* Margaret A Van Patten; E-mail: megv@bville.lib.ny.us; *Librn,* Diane Holbert; E-mail: dianeh@bville.lib.ny.us; *Ch Serv Librn,* Meghin Roberts; E-mail: meghinr@bville.lib.ny.us; *Experiential Learning Librn,* Julia Schult; E-mail: julias@bville.lib.ny.us; *Outreach Librn, Pub Relations Librn,* Nancy Howe; E-mail: nancyh@bville.lib.ny.us; *Syst Librn,* Robert Loftus; E-mail: robertl@bville.lib.ny.us; *YA Librn,* Dania Souid; E-mail: danias@bville.lib.ny.us. Subject Specialists: *Commun, Mgt,* Margaret A Van Patten; *Adult non-fiction, Non-fiction,* Diane Holbert; *Adult fiction, Commun,* Nancy Howe; *Networks, Tech,* Robert Loftus; Staff 10 (MLS 10)
Founded 1948. Pop 32,300; Circ 432,305
Library Holdings: AV Mats 6,134; DVDs 9,210; e-books 3,502; Electronic Media & Resources 159; Bk Vols 107,627; Per Subs 258
Special Collections: Newspaper Coll (1846-present), micro
Subject Interests: Local hist
Automation Activity & Vendor Info: (Cataloging) Innovative Interfaces, Inc; (Circulation) Innovative Interfaces, Inc; (OPAC) Innovative Interfaces, Inc
Wireless access
Function: Adult bk club, Adult literacy prog, Art exhibits, Audio & video playback equip for onsite use, Audiobks via web, Bi-weekly Writer's Group, Bk club(s), Bks on cassette, Bks on CD, Children's prog, Computer training, Computers for patron use, Digital talking bks, E-Reserves, Electronic databases & coll, Free DVD rentals, Genealogy discussion group, Health sci info serv, Holiday prog, Home delivery & serv to seniorr ctr & nursing homes, ILL available, Internet access, Large print keyboards, Magnifiers for reading, Mail & tel request accepted, Microfiche/film & reading machines, Music CDs, Notary serv, Online cat, Online ref, Orientations, Outreach serv, Outside serv via phone, mail, e-mail & web, OverDrive digital audio bks, Photocopying/Printing, Preschool outreach, Preschool reading prog, Printer for laptops & handheld devices, Prog for adults, Prog for children & young adult, Ref serv available, Scanner, Senior computer classes, Senior outreach, Spoken cassettes & CDs, Spoken cassettes & DVDs, Story hour, Summer reading prog, Tax forms, Teen prog, Telephone ref, Wheelchair accessible, Workshops, Writing prog
Publications: Activities Calendar (Monthly); Annual report; Library Services Guide (Brochure)
Mem of Onondaga County Public Libraries
Special Services for the Deaf - Assisted listening device; Bks on deafness & sign lang; Sign lang interpreter upon request for prog
Special Services for the Blind - Accessible computers; Aids for in-house use; Audio mat; Bks available with recordings; Bks on CD; Large print bks; Large print bks & talking machines; Large screen computer & software; Low vision equip; Playaways (bks on MP3); Rec & flexible discs; Recorded bks; Ref serv; Screen enlargement software for people with visual disabilities; Sound rec; Talking bk serv referral; Talking bks & player equip; VisualTek equip
Open Mon-Thurs 9-9, Fri 9-5, Sat 10-4, Sun 1-5
Friends of the Library Group

BALLSTON SPA

P BALLSTON SPA PUBLIC LIBRARY*, 21 Milton Ave, 12020. SAN 310-8309. Tel: 518-885-5022. Web Site: bspl.sals.edu. *Dir & Librn,* Andrea Simmons; E-mail: bal-director@sals.edu; Staff 7 (MLS 2, Non-MLS 5)
Founded 1893. Pop 4,937; Circ 81,565
Library Holdings: Bk Vols 45,000; Per Subs 73
Special Collections: Literacy Center; Parenting Center; Saratoga County (Bruce M Manzer Coll), bks, per
Wireless access
Function: Art exhibits, Audio & video playback equip for onsite use, Computers for patron use, ILL available, Meeting rooms, Prog for children & young adult, Tax forms
Mem of Southern Adirondack Library System
Open Tues-Thurs 10-7, Fri 10-5, Sat 10-3
Friends of the Library Group

BARKER

P BARKER PUBLIC LIBRARY*, 8706 Main St, 14012. (Mail add: PO Box 261, 14012-0261), SAN 310-8317. Tel: 716-795-3344. FAX: 716-795-3344. Web Site: www.barkerfreelibrary.com. *Dir,* Lisa Thompson; E-mail: lthom@nioga.org; Staff 3 (MLS 1, Non-MLS 2)
Founded 1935. Pop 2,655; Circ 12,159
Library Holdings: High Interest/Low Vocabulary Bk Vols 34; Bk Vols 15,300; Per Subs 15
Subject Interests: Adult literacy, GED programs, Local hist
Automation Activity & Vendor Info: (Acquisitions) SirsiDynix; (Cataloging) SirsiDynix; (Circulation) SirsiDynix; (Course Reserve) SirsiDynix; (ILL) SirsiDynix; (Media Booking) SirsiDynix; (OPAC) SirsiDynix; (Serials) SirsiDynix
Wireless access
Mem of Nioga Library System
Special Services for the Blind - Bks on cassette
Open Mon & Fri 10-5, Tues & Thurs 10-8, Sat 10-1
Friends of the Library Group

BARNEVELD

P BARNEVELD FREE LIBRARY*, 118 Boon St, 13304. (Mail add: PO Box 306, 13304-0306), SAN 310-8325. Tel: 315-896-2096. Web Site: www.midyorklib.org/barneveld. *Librn,* Greta Madore; E-mail: gmadore@midyork.org
Founded 1874. Pop 2,499; Circ 7,556
Library Holdings: Bk Vols 9,500; Per Subs 26
Wireless access
Mem of Mid-York Library System
Open Mon 7pm-9pm, Tues 1-5, Wed 10-12, Thurs 1-6, Fri 12-4, Sat 8:30am-10:30am

BATAVIA

J GENESEE COMMUNITY COLLEGE*, Alfred C O'Connell Library, One College Rd, 14020-9704. SAN 310-8333. Tel: 585-343-0055, Ext 6350. Circulation Tel: 585-345-6834. Reference Tel: 585-343-0055, Ext 6419. FAX: 585-345-6933. Web Site: www.genesee.edu/library. *Dir, Libr Serv,* Jessica R Olin; Tel: 585-343-0055, Ext 6256, E-mail: jrolin@genesee.edu; *Coll Develop, Prof,* Cindy A Francis; Tel: 585-343-0055, Ext 6126, E-mail: cafrancis@genesee.edu; *Instrul Serv Librn, Prof,* Nicki Lerczak; Tel: 585-343-0055, Ext 6418, E-mail: njlerczak@genesee.edu; *Asst Prof, Ref Serv Librn,* Cindy S Hagelberger; Tel: 585-343-0055, Ext 6231, E-mail: cshagelberger@genesee.edu; *Assoc Prof, Syst/Electronic Serv Librn,* Michelle Eichelberger; Tel: 585-343-0055, Ext 6458, E-mail: maeichelberger@genesee.edu; Staff 8 (MLS 5, Non-MLS 3)
Founded 1966. Enrl 7,030; Fac 72; Highest Degree: Associate
Library Holdings: Audiobooks 390; CDs 1,900; DVDs 859; e-books 3,000; Bk Titles 70,866; Bk Vols 81,967; Per Subs 177; Videos 43
Automation Activity & Vendor Info: (Cataloging) Ex Libris Group; (Circulation) Ex Libris Group; (Discovery) EBSCO Discovery Service; (ILL) OCLC ILLiad; (OPAC) Ex Libris Group
Wireless access
Function: 24/7 Online cat, Archival coll, Art exhibits, Audio & video playback equip for onsite use, Bks on CD, Computers for patron use, Distance learning, Doc delivery serv, Electronic databases & coll, ILL available, Instruction & testing, Internet access, Magazines, Mango lang, Microfiche/film & reading machines, Music CDs, Online cat, Online ref, Orientations, Outside serv via phone, mail, e-mail & web, Photocopying/Printing, Preschool outreach, Preschool reading prog, Ref & res, Ref serv available, Scanner, Study rm, Wheelchair accessible
Partic in SUNYConnect; Western New York Library Resources Council
Special Services for the Blind - VisualTek equip
Open Mon-Thurs (Fall & Spring) 7:30am-9:30pm, Fri 7:30-4:30, Sat Noon-5, Sun Noon-6; Mon-Fri (Summer) 8:30-4:30

S GENESEE COUNTY HISTORY DEPARTMENT*, Research Library, 3837 West Main Street Rd, County Bldg 2, 14020-2021. SAN 326-2626. Tel: 585-815-7904. E-mail: history@co.genesee.ny.us. Web Site: www.co.genesee.ny.us/departments/history. *County Historian, Rec Mgt Officer,* Dr Michael Eula; *Res Asst,* Judy Stiles; E-mail: Judy.Stiles@co.genesee.ny.us; Staff 2 (Non-MLS 2)
Founded 1941
Library Holdings: Bk Titles 3,000
Special Collections: County Coll; Genealogy Coll, bks & files; Local History Coll, bks & files
Function: Archival coll, Microfiche/film & reading machines, Res assist avail, Res libr, Wheelchair accessible
Open Mon-Fri 10-12 & 1-4:30
Restriction: Lending to staff only, Non-circulating, Not a lending libr
Friends of the Library Group

P RICHMOND MEMORIAL LIBRARY*, 19 Ross St, 14020. SAN 310-8341. Tel: 585-343-9550. FAX: 585-344-4651. Web Site: www.batavialibrary.org. *Libr Dir,* Robert Conrad; *Dir, Prog & Serv,* Lucine Kauffman; *Ad, Commun Outreach Librn,* Samantha Stryker; *Media Serv Librn,* Rita McCormack; *Ref & Ad Serv Librn,* Michael Boedicker; *Youth Serv Librn,* Jennifer Potter. Subject Specialists: *Fiction, Local hist,* Samantha Stryker; *Non-fiction, Tech,* Michael Boedicker; Staff 9 (MLS 5, Non-MLS 4)
Founded 1889. Pop 19,244; Circ 276,533
Library Holdings: Bk Titles 105,000; Per Subs 171
Subject Interests: Genealogy, Local hist
Automation Activity & Vendor Info: (Cataloging) SirsiDynix; (Circulation) SirsiDynix; (OPAC) SirsiDynix
Wireless access
Mem of Nioga Library System
Open Mon-Thurs 9-9, Fri & Sat 9-5
Friends of the Library Group

M UNITED MEMORIAL MEDICAL CENTER*, Medical Library, 127 North St, 14020-1697. SAN 326-5374. Tel: 585-344-5273. FAX: 585-344-7461. Web Site: www.rochesterregional.org/Locations/United-Memorial-Medical-Center.
Founded 1958
Library Holdings: e-books 63; e-journals 418; Electronic Media & Resources 2; Bk Titles 300; Bk Vols 525; Per Subs 2
Partic in Library Consortium of Health Institutions in Buffalo; National Network of Libraries of Medicine Region 7; Western New York Library Resources Council
Restriction: Circulates for staff only, In-house use for visitors, Not open to pub

BATH

P DORMANN LIBRARY, 101 W Morris St, 14810. SAN 310-8368. Tel: 607-776-4613. FAX: 607-776-6693. E-mail: bath@stls.org. Web Site: dormannlibrary.org. *Dir,* LeighAnn Rumsey; E-mail: rumseyl@stls.org
Founded 1869. Pop 11,819; Circ 63,607
Library Holdings: Bk Vols 35,000; Per Subs 65
Special Collections: Local History
Automation Activity & Vendor Info: (Cataloging) SirsiDynix; (Circulation) SirsiDynix; (OPAC) SirsiDynix
Wireless access
Mem of Southern Tier Library System
Open Mon-Fri 10-6, Sat 10-2
Friends of the Library Group

GL NEW YORK SUPREME COURT, Seventh Judicial District Law Library, Three E Pulteney Sq, 14810. SAN 310-8376. Tel: 607-622-8190. Web Site: www.nycourts.gov/lawlibraries/publicaccess.shtml. *Librn,* Kristine Gilbert; Tel: 607-622-8190, E-mail: kgilbert@nycourts.gov
Library Holdings: Bk Vols 7,500
Subject Interests: Agr, Bankruptcy, NYS statutes
Open Mon-Fri 9-5

BAYSIDE

J QUEENSBOROUGH COMMUNITY COLLEGE, CITY UNIVERSITY OF NEW YORK*, Kurt R Schmeller Library, 222-05 56th Ave, 11364-1497. SAN 310-8414. Tel: 718-631-6227. Interlibrary Loan Service Tel: 718-281-5067. Reference Tel: 718-631-6241. FAX: 718-281-5012. Interlibrary Loan Service FAX: 718-281-5118. Web Site: qcc.libguides.com/libraryhome. *Chief Librn,* Jeanne Galvin; Tel: 718-631-6220, E-mail: jgalvin@qcc.cuny.edu; *Dep Chief Librn/Fac Outreach Librn,* Devin McKay; Tel: 718-281-5032, E-mail: dmckay@qcc.cuny.edu; *Head, Ref & Ser,* Barbara Bonous-Smit; Tel: 718-281-5010, E-mail: bbonoussmit@qcc.cuny.edu; *Electronic Res, Scholarly Communications Librn,* William Blick; Tel: 718-281-5778, E-mail: wblick@qcc.cuny.edu; *Emerging Tech Librn,* Leslie Ward; Tel: 718-631-5795, E-mail: LWard@qcc.cuny.edu; *Reserves & Syst Librn,* Peijun Jeffrey Jia; Tel: 718-281-5594, E-mail: jjia@qcc.cuny.edu; *Sci Librn,* Mi-Seon Kim; Tel: 718-631-5721, E-mail: mkim@qcc.cuny.edu; *ILL Librn, Ref & Instruction,* Neera Mohess; Tel: 718-281-5067, E-mail: nmohees@qcc.cuny.edu; *Col Archivist, Coordr, Circ,* Constance Williams; Tel: 718-631-6567, E-mail: cwilliams@qcc.cuny.edu; *Coordr, Libr Pub Relations,* Sandra Marcus; Tel: 718-281-5072, E-mail: smarcus@qcc.cuny.edu; *Coordr, Pub Serv & Info Literacy,* Richard Mako; Tel: 718-631-6601, E-mail: rmako@qcc.cuny.edu; *Acq, Coordr, Tech Serv,* Sheila Beck; Tel: 718-631-5711, E-mail: sbeck@qcc.cuny.edu; *Cataloger,* Jung Cho; Tel: 718-631-6218, E-mail: jcho@qcc.cuny.edu; *Sr Col Lab Tech,* Lawrence Chan; Tel: 718-281-5595, E-mail: lchan@qcc.cuny.edu; *Col Lab Tech,* Danny Li; Tel: 718-631-6672, E-mail: dli@qcc.cuny.edu; Staff 29.5 (MLS 15.5, Non-MLS 14)
Founded 1960. Enrl 16,000; Fac 530; Highest Degree: Associate
Library Holdings: AV Mats 8,912; e-books 97,066; e-journals 59,766; Microforms 3,500; Bk Titles 132,751; Bk Vols 152,800; Per Subs 90
Wireless access
Publications: APA, MLA, Chicago Citation Style Handbooks; Glossary of Library Terms; Guide to the Library of Congress Classification System; How to Guides; Library Scene (Newsletter); Periodical Directory; Primary vs. Secondary Sources; Student Library Handbook; Student Self-Guided Library Orientation Tour; Subject Guides; The Research Process
Partic in Metropolitan New York Library Council
Open Mon-Thurs 7:30-8:45, Fri 7:30-4:45, Sat 10-3:45, Sun 10-2:45
Friends of the Library Group

BAYVILLE

P BAYVILLE FREE LIBRARY, 34 School St, 11709. SAN 310-8422. Tel: 516-628-2765. FAX: 516-628-2738. E-mail: abirbal@bayvillefreelibrary.org. *Dir,* Ashley Birbal
Circ 71,351
Library Holdings: Bk Vols 55,872; Per Subs 70
Automation Activity & Vendor Info: (Acquisitions) Baker & Taylor; (Cataloging) Baker & Taylor
Wireless access
Mem of Nassau Library System
Open Mon-Thurs 9-7, Fri & Sat 10-5
Friends of the Library Group

BEACON

S FISHKILL CORRECTIONAL FACILITY LIBRARY, Bldg 13, 12508. (Mail add: PO Box 307, 12508-0307), SAN 310-8430. Tel: 845-831-4800, Ext 4600. *Librn,* Cheryl Bennin; E-mail: Cheryl.Bennin@doccs.ny.gov
Library Holdings: Bk Vols 15,000; Per Subs 40
Subject Interests: African-Am culture, Hispanic
Automation Activity & Vendor Info: (Cataloging) Follett Software; (Circulation) Follett Software; (OPAC) Follett Software
Mem of Mid-Hudson Library System
Restriction: Staff & inmates only

P HOWLAND PUBLIC LIBRARY*, 313 Main St, 12508. SAN 310-8449. Tel: 845-831-1134. FAX: 845-831-1165. E-mail: howland@beaconlibrary.org. Web Site: beaconlibrary.org. *Dir,* Kristen Salierno; E-mail: director@beaconlibrary.org; *Ref Librn,* Peter McGivney; E-mail: reference@beaconlibrary.org; *Youth Serv Librn,* Ginny Figlia; E-mail: youth@beaconlibrary.org
Founded 1872. Pop 24,000; Circ 55,800
Library Holdings: Bk Titles 40,088; Per Subs 123
Special Collections: Chinese Coll, bks, rec; Handicapped Coll, bks, kits, VF; Spanish Language (Libros Coll), bks, rec
Subject Interests: Ethnic studies, Local hist
Automation Activity & Vendor Info: (Circulation) Innovative Interfaces, Inc - Millennium
Wireless access
Mem of Mid-Hudson Library System
Open Mon, Wed & Fri 9:30-4:30, Tues & Thurs 9:30-6:30
Friends of the Library Group

BEAR MOUNTAIN

S BEAR MOUNTAIN TRAILSIDE MUSEUMS LIBRARY, Bear Mountain State Park, 10911. (Mail add: PO Box 427, 10911-0427), SAN 371-2095. Tel: 845-786-2701. FAX: 845-786-0496. Web Site: www.trailsidemuseumsandzoo.org. *Dir,* Edwin McGowan; Tel: 845-786-2701, Ext 263, E-mail: edwin.mcgowan@parks.ny.gov
Library Holdings: Bk Vols 500
Wireless access
Restriction: Open by appt only

BEAVER FALLS

P BEAVER FALLS LIBRARY, 9607 Lewis St, 13305. (Mail add: PO Box 75, 13305-0075), SAN 310-8473. Tel: 315-346-6216. FAX: 315-346-6216. E-mail: bvflib@ncls.org. Web Site: www.beaverfallslibrary.org. *Dir,* Laurie Kirkwood
Founded 1920. Pop 1,377; Circ 4,730
Library Holdings: Bk Vols 4,600; Per Subs 5
Wireless access
Mem of North Country Library System
Open Mon 10-4, Tues 12-6, Thurs 10-4 & 6-8

BEDFORD

P BEDFORD FREE LIBRARY*, 32 Village Green, 10506. (Mail add: PO Box 375, 10506-0375), SAN 310-8481. Tel: 914-234-3570. FAX: 914-234-0546. Web Site: www.bedfordfreelibrary.org. *Dir,* Ann Cloonan; E-mail: acloonan@wlsmail.org; *Ch,* Shodie Alcorn; E-mail: salcorn@wlsmail.org; *YA Librn,* Maureen McManus; E-mail: mmcmanus@wlsmail.com
Founded 1903. Pop 6,000; Circ 45,000
Library Holdings: Bk Titles 30,000; Bk Vols 35,000; Per Subs 38
Subject Interests: Biog, Local hist
Automation Activity & Vendor Info: (Acquisitions) SirsiDynix; (Cataloging) SirsiDynix; (Circulation) SirsiDynix; (Course Reserve) SirsiDynix; (ILL) SirsiDynix; (Media Booking) SirsiDynix; (OPAC) SirsiDynix; (Serials) SirsiDynix
Wireless access
Mem of Westchester Library System
Open Mon- Fri 10-6, Sat 10-2
Friends of the Library Group

BEDFORD HILLS

P BEDFORD HILLS FREE LIBRARY, 26 Main St, 10507-1832. SAN 310-849X. Tel: 914-666-6472. FAX: 914-666-6473. E-mail: bedfordhillsfreelibrary@gmail.com. Web Site: www.bedfordhillsfreelibrary.org. *Exec Dir,* Mary Esbjornson; E-mail: mesbjornson@wlsmail.org; *Acq,* Eileen Baer
Founded 1915. Pop 6,397; Circ 35,073
Library Holdings: Bk Vols 41,517; Per Subs 99
Automation Activity & Vendor Info: (Acquisitions) SirsiDynix; (Cataloging) SirsiDynix; (Circulation) SirsiDynix; (OPAC) SirsiDynix; (Serials) SirsiDynix
Wireless access
Mem of Westchester Library System
Open Mon & Wed-Fri 10-3, Tues 10-6, Sat 10-2

S NEW YORK DEPARTMENT OF CORRECTIONAL SERVICES*, Bedford Hills Correctional Facility Library, 247 Harris Rd, 10507-2499. SAN 327-1218. Tel: 914-241-3100, Ext 4540. FAX: 914-241-3100. *Librn,* R Lim; Staff 1 (MLS 1)
Library Holdings: DVDs 274; Bk Vols 12,600; Per Subs 40
Automation Activity & Vendor Info: (Cataloging) Follett Software; (Circulation) Follett Software
Restriction: Staff & inmates only

BELFAST

P BELFAST PUBLIC LIBRARY*, 75 S Main St, 14711-8605. (Mail add: PO Box 455, 14711-0455), SAN 310-8503. Tel: 585-365-2072. FAX: 585-365-2072. E-mail: belfastpubliclibrary@gmail.com. Web Site: www.belfastpubliclibrary.org. *Dir,* Janine Preston
Pop 2,154; Circ 12,500
Library Holdings: Bk Vols 10,277; Per Subs 30
Wireless access
Mem of Southern Tier Library System
Open Mon & Sat 10-1, Tues & Thurs 3-7, Wed 10-1 & 3-7

BELLEVILLE

P BELLEVILLE PHILOMATHEAN FREE LIBRARY*, 8086 County Rte 75, 13611. (Mail add: PO Box 27, 13611-0027), SAN 310-8511. Tel: 315-846-5103. FAX: 315-846-5103. E-mail: bellib@ncls.org. Web Site: www.bellevillefreelibrary.org. *Dir,* Linda Strader
Founded 1904. Pop 225; Circ 1,375
Jan 2017-Dec 2017 Income $33,035, State $3,600, County $1,695, Locally Generated Income $27,740. Mats Exp $3,439, Books $3,253, Per/Ser (Incl. Access Fees) $20, Other Print Mats $166. Sal $8,600
Library Holdings: Audiobooks 1,281; DVDs 193; e-books 5,927; Electronic Media & Resources 24; Large Print Bks 185; Bk Titles 4,522; Per Subs 8
Automation Activity & Vendor Info: (Cataloging) SirsiDynix; (OPAC) SirsiDynix
Wireless access
Function: 24/7 Electronic res, 24/7 Online cat
Mem of North Country Library System
Open Mon 10-2, Wed & Fri 1-6

BELLMORE

P BELLMORE MEMORIAL LIBRARY*, 2288 Bedford Ave, 11710. SAN 310-852X. Tel: 516-785-2990. E-mail: ask@bellmorelibrary.org. Web Site: www.bellmorelibrary.org. *Dir,* Elaine Cummings-Young; *Adult Serv,* Valerie Acklin; *Ch Serv,* J Premuto; *Outreach Serv,* M DiVittorio; *YA Serv,* Michael Stamberg; Staff 8 (MLS 8)
Founded 1948. Pop 12,900
Library Holdings: AV Mats 14,585; Bk Vols 102,000; Per Subs 295
Wireless access
Publications: Bellmore Memorial Library (Newsletter)
Mem of Nassau Library System
Special Services for the Deaf - Closed caption videos; TTY equip
Special Services for the Blind - Accessible computers; Computer with voice synthesizer for visually impaired persons
Open Mon, Tues & Thurs 9:30-9, Wed 10:30-9, Fri 9:30-5:30, Sat 9:30-5 (9:30-1:30 Summer), Sun 1-5

BELLPORT

P SOUTH COUNTRY LIBRARY*, 22 Station Rd, 11713. SAN 310-8538. Tel: 631-286-0818. FAX: 631-286-4873. E-mail: sctyref@sctylib.org. Web Site: sctylib.org. *Dir,* Kristina Sembler; *Asst Dir,* Patrick O'Leary; Staff 50 (MLS 9, Non-MLS 41)
Founded 1921. Pop 26,400; Circ 345,000
Library Holdings: AV Mats 26,373; Bk Titles 105,956; Per Subs 2,984
Subject Interests: Art, Boating, Gardening, Hispanic, Local hist, Mysteries
Wireless access
Publications: Newsletter (Bimonthly)
Mem of Suffolk Cooperative Library System
Open Mon-Fri 9:30-9, Sat 9:30-5, Sun (Sept-June) 12-4
Friends of the Library Group

P SUFFOLK COOPERATIVE LIBRARY SYSTEM*, 627 N Sunrise Service Rd, 11713. (Mail add: PO Box 9000, 11713-9000), SAN 351-837X. Tel: 631-286-1600. FAX: 631-286-1647. TDD: 631-286-4546. Web Site: portal.suffolklibrarysystem.org, www.talkingbooks.nypl.org. *Dir,* Kevin Verbesey; E-mail: kevin@suffolknet.org; *Asst Dir, Tech,* Ruth Westfall; E-mail: ruth@suffolknet.org; *Asst Dir, Bus Operations,* Roger Reyes; E-mail: roger@suffolknet.org; *Youth Serv Librn,* Derek Ivie; E-mail: derek@suffolknet.org; Staff 50 (MLS 14, Non-MLS 36)
Founded 1961. Pop 1,499,157; Circ 17,128,500

Special Collections: Adult New Readers (literacy); Auto & Home Appliance Repair Manuals; Disability Reference Coll. State Document Depository
Automation Activity & Vendor Info: (Acquisitions) Innovative Interfaces, Inc - Sierra; (Cataloging) Innovative Interfaces, Inc - Sierra; (Circulation) Innovative Interfaces, Inc - Sierra; (Course Reserve) Innovative Interfaces, Inc - Sierra; (ILL) Innovative Interfaces, Inc - Sierra; (OPAC) Innovative Interfaces, Inc - Sierra; (Serials) Innovative Interfaces, Inc - Sierra
Wireless access
Member Libraries: Amagansett Free Library; Amityville Public Library; Babylon Public Library; Baiting Hollow Free Library; Bay Shore-Brightwaters Public Library; Bayport-Blue Point Public Library; Brentwood Public Library; Brookhaven Free Library; Center Moriches Free Public Library; Central Islip Public Library; Cold Spring Harbor Library; Commack Public Library; Comsewogue Public Library; Connetquot Public Library; Copiague Memorial Public Library; Cutchogue-New Suffolk Free Library; Deer Park Public Library; East Hampton Library; East Islip Public Library; Elwood Public Library; Emma S Clark Memorial Library; Fishers Island Library; Floyd Memorial Library; Half Hollow Hills Community Library; Hampton Bays Public Library; Harborfields Public Library; Hauppauge Public Library; Islip Public Library; John Jermain Memorial Library; Lindenhurst Memorial Library; Longwood Public Library; Mastics-Moriches-Shirley Community Library; Mattituck-Laurel Library; Middle Country Public Library; Montauk Library; North Babylon Public Library; North Shore Public Library; Northport-East Northport Public Library; Patchogue-Medford Library; Port Jefferson Free Library; Quogue Library; Riverhead Free Library; Rogers Memorial Library; Sachem Public Library; Sayville Library; Shelter Island Public Library; Smithtown Library; South Country Library; South Huntington Public Library; Southold Free Library; The Hampton Library; West Babylon Public Library; West Islip Public Library; Westhampton Free Library; Wyandanch Public Library
Special Services for the Blind - Accessible computers; Assistive/Adapted tech devices, equip & products; BiFolkal kits; Braille equip; Closed circuit TV magnifier; Low vision equip; Screen reader software; ZoomText magnification & reading software
Open Mon-Fri 9-5
Branches: 1

P LONG ISLAND TALKING BOOK LIBRARY, 627 N Sunrise Service Rd, 11713. (Mail add: PO Box 9000, 11713-9000), SAN 351-840X. Tel: 631-286-1600. Toll Free Tel: 866-833-1122 (Nassau/Suffolk Counties only). FAX: 631-286-1647. TDD: 631-286-4546. E-mail: outreach@suffolknet.org. *Adminr, Librn,* Valerie Lewis; E-mail: valerie@suffolknet.org; Staff 2 (MLS 1, Non-MLS 1)
Founded 1972
Special Collections: Blindness & Other Disabilities Reference Materials; Print-Braille Books for Children
Special Services for the Blind - Accessible computers; BiFolkal kits; Braille equip; Braille paper
Open Mon-Fri 9-5

BELMONT

S ALLEGANY COUNTY HISTORICAL MUSEUM LIBRARY*, Five Courthouse Court St, 14813-1089. SAN 310-8546. Tel: 585-268-9293. FAX: 585-268-9446. E-mail: historian@alleganyco.com. *County Historian,* Craig Braack
Founded 1972
Library Holdings: Bk Titles 1,000
Special Collections: Philip Church Records
Subject Interests: 19th Century Allegany County genealogical records, 20th Century Allegany County genealogical records, Land records
Restriction: Open to pub by appt only

P BELMONT LITERARY & HISTORICAL SOCIETY FREE LIBRARY, Two Willets Ave, 14813. SAN 310-8554. Tel: 585-268-5308. FAX: 585-268-5308. Web Site: www.belmontfreelibrary.org. *Dir,* Carrie Jefferds; E-mail: jefferdsc@stls.org; Staff 2 (Non-MLS 2)
Founded 1885. Pop 2,245; Circ 25,000
Library Holdings: Bk Titles 16,000; Per Subs 35
Special Collections: Local Newspaper Coll
Automation Activity & Vendor Info: (Acquisitions) SirsiDynix-WorkFlows; (Cataloging) SirsiDynix-WorkFlows; (Circulation) SirsiDynix-WorkFlows; (Course Reserve) SirsiDynix-WorkFlows; (ILL) SirsiDynix-WorkFlows; (Media Booking) SirsiDynix-WorkFlows; (OPAC) SirsiDynix-WorkFlows; (Serials) SirsiDynix-WorkFlows
Wireless access
Mem of Southern Tier Library System
Open Tues & Fri 1-7, Thurs 9-1, Sat 1-5

BEMUS POINT

P BEMUS POINT PUBLIC LIBRARY*, 13 Main St, 14712. (Mail add: PO Box 428, 14712-0428), SAN 310-8562. Tel: 716-386-2274. FAX: 716-386-2176. E-mail: bemuslibrary@stny.rr.com. Web Site: bemuspointlibrary.org. *Dir,* Shannon Donovan
Founded 1908. Pop 444; Circ 28,279
Library Holdings: Bk Vols 13,882
Subject Interests: Local hist
Wireless access
Mem of Chautauqua-Cattaraugus Library System
Open Mon, Tues & Fri 10-5, Wed 1-5, Thurs 10-7, Sat 10-2
Friends of the Library Group

BERGEN

P BYRON-BERGEN PUBLIC LIBRARY*, 13 S Lake Ave, 14416-9420. (Mail add: PO Box 430, 14416-0430), SAN 370-6435. Tel: 585-494-1120. FAX: 585-494-2339. E-mail: byrbgn@nioga.org. Web Site: www.byron-bergenpubliclibrary.org. *Libr Mgr,* Nancy Bailey; E-mail: nbail@nioga.org; Staff 3 (Non-MLS 3)
Founded 1962. Pop 5,483; Circ 37,658
Library Holdings: Bk Titles 10,000; Bk Vols 19,198; Per Subs 25
Subject Interests: Local hist
Automation Activity & Vendor Info: (Cataloging) SirsiDynix; (Circulation) SirsiDynix; (OPAC) SirsiDynix
Wireless access
Mem of Nioga Library System
Special Services for the Deaf - Bks on deafness & sign lang
Open Tues, Wed & Fri 10-5, Thurs 10-1 & 2-7
Friends of the Library Group

BERKSHIRE

P BERKSHIRE FREE LIBRARY*, 12519 State Rte 38, 13736. (Mail add: PO Box 151, 13736-0151), SAN 310-8570. Tel: 607-657-4418. FAX: 607-657-5110. E-mail: bfl@htva.net. Web Site: berkshirefreelibrary.org. *Dir,* Fran Miller; *Libr Asst,* Lena Sherwood; Staff 2 (Non-MLS 2)
Founded 1926. Pop 2,536; Circ 7,717
Jan 2013-Dec 2013 Income $20,653, State $1,682, City $7,500, County $8,971, Other $2,500. Sal $13,160
Library Holdings: Audiobooks 94; DVDs 254; e-books 50; Bk Titles 6,181; Per Subs 18; Videos 454
Automation Activity & Vendor Info: (Acquisitions) Innovative Interfaces, Inc; (Cataloging) Innovative Interfaces, Inc; (Circulation) Innovative Interfaces, Inc; (Course Reserve) Innovative Interfaces, Inc; (ILL) OCLC WorldShare Interlibrary Loan; (Media Booking) Innovative Interfaces, Inc; (OPAC) Innovative Interfaces, Inc; (Serials) Innovative Interfaces, Inc
Wireless access
Function: ILL available, Internet access, Photocopying/Printing, Ref serv available, Summer reading prog, Wheelchair accessible
Mem of Finger Lakes Library System
Open Tues 12-5, Wed & Fri 1:30-7, Thurs 1-5, Sat 9-2

BERLIN

P BERLIN FREE TOWN LIBRARY*, Whitehouse Memorial Bldg, 47 S Main St, 12022. (Mail add: PO Box 6, 12022), SAN 310-8589. Tel: 518-658-2231. FAX: 518-658-9565. E-mail: library@bftl.org. Web Site: www.bftl.org. *Dir,* Sharon Vogel
Founded 1895. Pop 1,929; Circ 19,616
Library Holdings: Bks on Deafness & Sign Lang 10; Bk Titles 10,233; Bk Vols 11,000; Per Subs 10
Subject Interests: Civil War, Hist
Automation Activity & Vendor Info: (Acquisitions) Horizon; (Cataloging) Horizon; (Circulation) Horizon; (Course Reserve) Horizon; (ILL) Horizon; (Media Booking) Horizon; (OPAC) Horizon; (Serials) Horizon
Wireless access
Mem of Upper Hudson Library System
Open Mon & Sat 10-1, Tues & Thurs 2-5 & 7-9, Wed & Fri 2-5

BERNE

P BERNE PUBLIC LIBRARY*, 1763 Helderberg Trail, 12023. (Mail add: PO Box 209, 12023-0209), SAN 310-8597. Tel: 518-872-1246. FAX: 518-872-1246. Web Site: www.bernepubliclibrary.org. *Dir,* Kathy Stempel; E-mail: director@bernepubliclibrary.org; Staff 1 (Non-MLS 1)
Founded 1962. Pop 2,794; Circ 13,105
Jan 2016-Dec 2016 Income $43,095, State $1,100, City $39,085, Federal $485, Locally Generated Income $1,965. Mats Exp $5,490, Books $4,152, Per/Ser (Incl. Access Fees) $336, AV Mat $1,002. Sal $39,750
Library Holdings: Audiobooks 169; CDs 169; DVDs 1,330; e-books 30; High Interest/Low Vocabulary Bk Vols 15; Large Print Bks 105; Bk Titles 12,970; Per Subs 23
Special Collections: Cake Pan Coll; STEAM Kits

Automation Activity & Vendor Info: (Circulation) Innovative Interfaces, Inc - Sierra
Wireless access
Function: Adult bk club, Bks on CD, Computer training, Computers for patron use, ILL available, Music CDs, Online cat, Outreach serv, OverDrive digital audio bks, Photocopying/Printing, Preschool outreach, Preschool reading prog, Prog for adults, Prog for children & young adult, Scanner, Story hour, Summer reading prog, Tax forms, Wheelchair accessible
Mem of Upper Hudson Library System
Special Services for the Blind - Braille bks; Talking bks & player equip
Open Mon & Thurs 2-8, Tues 10-8, Wed 12-8, Fri 2-6, Sat 9-3
Friends of the Library Group

BETHPAGE

P BETHPAGE PUBLIC LIBRARY*, 47 Powell Ave, 11714. SAN 310-8600. Tel: 516-931-3907. FAX: 516-931-3926. Web Site: www.bethpagelibrary.info. *Librn, Youth Serv,* Lisa Dobra; E-mail: ldobra@bethpagelibrary.info; *Head, Adult Programming,* Ed Hale; *Head, Children's Servx,* Michelle Ahearn; *Head, Circ,* Raissa Lai; Staff 16 (MLS 6.5, Non-MLS 9.5)
Founded 1927. Pop 19,498; Circ 219,569
Library Holdings: AV Mats 11,698; Bk Vols 186,026; Per Subs 309
Special Collections: Italian Genealogy Society
Wireless access
Publications: Newsletter (Bimonthly)
Mem of Nassau Library System
Partic in Long Island Library Resources Council
Open Mon-Fri 9-9, Sat 9-5, Sun (Sept-June) 12-4
Friends of the Library Group

BINGHAMTON

S BROOME COUNTY HISTORICAL SOCIETY LIBRARY*, Local History Center, Broome County Public Library, 185 Court St, 13901. SAN 310-8643. Tel: 607-778-3572. FAX: 607-778-6429. E-mail: broomhistorical@gmail.com. Web Site: broomehistory.org. *Historian,* Roger L Luther; Tel: 607-778-2076, Fax: 607-778-6249, E-mail: rluther@co.broome.ny.us; Staff 1 (Non-MLS 1)
Founded 1919
Library Holdings: CDs 250; Bk Vols 7,500; Per Subs 12
Special Collections: Civil War (Mattoon Coll), mss; Daniel S Dickinson, mss; Photographic Coll; Stillson Coll; Uriah Gregory Coll; Whitney Family, papers & mss; William Bingham, mss; William L Ford Coll, 1850-1870
Subject Interests: Archit, Broome County culture, Decorative art, Genealogy, Hist, Histories of NY, New England, Penn, William Bingham
Automation Activity & Vendor Info: (Cataloging) SirsiDynix; (OPAC) SirsiDynix
Wireless access
Open Mon-Thurs 10-8, Fri & Sat 10-4

P BROOME COUNTY PUBLIC LIBRARY*, 185 Court St, 13901. SAN 351-8493. Tel: 607-778-6400. Circulation Tel: 607-778-6454. Reference Tel: 607-778-6451. E-mail: bcpl@co.broome.ny.us. Web Site: www.bclibrary.info. *Interim Dir,* Sherry Kowalski; E-mail: sherry.kowalski@broomecounty.us; Staff 24 (MLS 6, Non-MLS 18)
Founded 1902. Pop 200,600; Circ 343,000
Library Holdings: Bk Vols 196,207
Special Collections: State Document Depository
Subject Interests: Local hist
Automation Activity & Vendor Info: (Acquisitions) SirsiDynix; (Cataloging) SirsiDynix-WorkFlows; (Circulation) SirsiDynix; (ILL) OCLC; (OPAC) SirsiDynix; (Serials) SirsiDynix
Wireless access
Function: 24/7 Electronic res
Publications: Bibliographies; Calendar of Events
Mem of Four County Library System
Partic in OCLC Online Computer Library Center, Inc; South Central Regional Library Council
Special Services for the Deaf - Adult & family literacy prog; Bks on deafness & sign lang; Sorenson video relay syst
Special Services for the Blind - Bks on CD
Open Mon-Thurs 9-8, Fri & Sat 9-5
Restriction: External users must contact libr
Friends of the Library Group

P FENTON FREE LIBRARY*, 1062 Chenango St, 13901-1736. SAN 310-8651. Tel: 607-724-8649. E-mail: fentonfreelibrary@gmail.com. Web Site: libraries.4cls.org/fenton, www.townoffenton.com/Library/Fentonlibrary.htm. *Dir,* Korin Spencer
Founded 1936. Pop 7,040; Circ 74,948
Library Holdings: Bk Vols 17,769
Wireless access
Publications: Dictionary Guide to Services Offered at the Moody Memorial Library; What's New (Newsletter)
Mem of Four County Library System
Open Mon, Tues & Thurs 1-8, Wed, Fri & Sat 10-4

GL NYS SUPREME COURT LIBRARY - BINGHAMTON*, Broome County Courts Law Library, Broome County Courthouse, First Flr, 92 Court St, 13901-3301. SAN 310-8716. Tel: 607-240-5786. Web Site: ww2.nycourts.gov/LIBRARY/6JD/broome. *Law Librn,* Christopher Lund; E-mail: clund@nycourts.gov; Staff 3 (MLS 1, Non-MLS 2)
Founded 1859
Library Holdings: Bk Titles 7,500; Bk Vols 60,000; Per Subs 270
Subject Interests: Bankruptcy, Criminal, Criminal practice & procedure, Domestic relations, NY Fed case law, NYS & Fed statutory law
Automation Activity & Vendor Info: (Acquisitions) SirsiDynix; (Cataloging) SirsiDynix; (Circulation) SirsiDynix; (OPAC) SirsiDynix; (Serials) SirsiDynix
Wireless access
Partic in South Central Regional Library Council
Open Mon-Fri 8:30-4:30

M OUR LADY OF LOURDES MEMORIAL HOSPITAL LIBRARY, Lourdes Library, 169 Riverside Dr, 13905. SAN 373-5990. Tel: 607-798-5290. FAX: 607-798-5989. E-mail: lourdeslib@gmail.com. Web Site: www.lourdes.com. *Med Librn,* Jean Jenkins; E-mail: jjenkins@ascension.org; Staff 1 (MLS 1)
Library Holdings: AV Mats 10; e-books 1,900; e-journals 2,000; Bk Titles 1,000; Per Subs 1
Automation Activity & Vendor Info: (Cataloging) CyberTools for Libraries; (Circulation) CyberTools for Libraries; (Discovery) TDNet; (ILL) Atlas Systems; (OPAC) CyberTools for Libraries; (Serials) CyberTools for Libraries
Wireless access
Partic in Basic Health Sciences Library Network; Health Sci Libr Asn of NJ; National Network of Libraries of Medicine Region 7; OCLC-LVIS; South Central Regional Library Council
Open Mon-Fri 6am-5pm

C STATE UNIVERSITY OF NEW YORK AT BINGHAMTON*, University Libraries, 4400 Vestal Pkwy E, 13902. (Mail add: PO Box 6012, 13902-6012), SAN 351-8671. Circulation Tel: 607-777-2194. Interlibrary Loan Service Tel: 607-777-4985. Reference Tel: 607-777-2345. Administration Tel: 607-777-4841. FAX: 607-777-4848. Interlibrary Loan Service FAX: 607-777-4347. Web Site: www.binghamton.edu/libraries. *Dean of Libr,* Curtis Kendrick; Tel: 607-777-4550, E-mail: kendrick@binghamton.edu; *Sr Exec Dir of Libraries,* Cindy D Olbrys; Tel: 607-777-4607, E-mail: colbrys@binghamton.edu; Staff 66 (MLS 29, Non-MLS 37)
Founded 1946. Enrl 18,124; Fac 1,074; Highest Degree: Doctorate
Jul 2017-Jun 2018 Income (Main & Associated Libraries) $12,825,942. Mats Exp $6,901,672. Sal $5,556,669
Library Holdings: e-books 817,118; e-journals 175,748; Microforms 1,877,590; Bk Titles 1,481,602; Bk Vols 1,666,697
Special Collections: Civil War Coll; Edwin A & Marion Clayton Link Coll; Frances R Conole Archive of Recorded Sound; Max Reinhardt Archives & Library; Vera Beaudin Saeedpour Kurdish Library & Museum Coll; William J Haggerty Coll of French Colonial History; Yi-t'ung Wang Coll & East Asian Coll. State Document Depository; US Document Depository
Automation Activity & Vendor Info: (Acquisitions) Ex Libris Group; (Cataloging) Ex Libris Group; (Circulation) Ex Libris Group; (Course Reserve) Blackboard Inc; (ILL) OCLC ILLiad; (OPAC) Ex Libris Group; (Serials) Ex Libris Group
Wireless access
Partic in Information Delivery Services Project; Inter-University Consortium for Political & Social Research; Northeast Research Libraries Consortium; OCLC Research Library Partnership; Scholarly Publ & Acad Resources Coalition; South Central Regional Library Council; SUNYConnect; Westchester Academic Library Directors Organization
Special Services for the Blind - Premier adaptive tech software; Reader equip; ZoomText magnification & reading software
Departmental Libraries:
LIBRARY ANNEX AT CONKLIN, 400 Corporate Pkwy, Conklin, 13748. Tel: 607-775-8364. FAX: 607-775-8339. *Asst Head, Reader Services, Stacks & Media,* Carrie Blabac-Myers; Tel: 607-777-5787, E-mail: cmyers@binghamton.edu
SCIENCE LIBRARY, Vestal Pkwy E, 13902, SAN 351-8760. Tel: 607-777-2166. FAX: 607-777-2274. *Head, Br Librn,* David Vose; Tel: 607-777-4903, E-mail: dvose@binghamton.edu; *Asst Head, Science Library,* Andrea Melione; Tel: 607-777-6323, E-mail: amelione@binghamton.edu

UNIVERSITY DOWNTOWN CENTER LIBRARY INFORMATION COMMONS & SERVICES, 67 Washington St, 13902-6000. Tel: 607-777-9225. FAX: 607-777-9136. *Head, Br Libr,* David Vose; Tel: 607-777-9275, E-mail: dvose@binghamton.edu; *Coordr, Reader Serv,* Sharon Fisher; Tel: 607-777-9396, E-mail: sfisher@binghamton.edu

J SUNY BROOME COMMUNITY COLLEGE*, Cecil C Tyrrell Learning Resource Center, 907 Front St, 13905-1328. SAN 310-8635. Tel: 607-778-5020. Interlibrary Loan Service Tel: 607-778-5376. Reference Tel: 607-778-5043. Administration Tel: 607-778-5045, 607-778-5201. FAX: 607-778-5108. E-mail: reference@sunybroome.edu. Web Site: sunybroome.info/library. *Dir, LRC/LAD,* Robin Petrus; E-mail: petrusre@sunybroome.edu; *Electronic Res Librn,* Noah Roth; Tel: 607-778-5528, E-mail: rothnw@sunybroome.edu; *Health Sci Ref Librn,* Karen Pitcher; Tel: 607-778-5468, E-mail: pitcherkl@sunybroome.edu; *Instruction & Outreach Librn,* Paul Bond; Tel: 607-778-5239, E-mail: bondph@sunybroome.edu; *Ref Librn,* Dana Curtin; Tel: 607-778-5249, E-mail: curtindj@sunybroome.edu; *Syst Librn,* Amanda Hollister; Tel: 607-778-5609, E-mail: hollisteraj@sunybroome.edu. Subject Specialists: *Engr,* Robin Petrus; *Hist,* Noah Roth; *Anthrop, Liberal arts,* Dana Curtin; *Chem, Sports,* Amanda Hollister; Staff 6 (MLS 6)
Founded 1947. Enrl 5,700; Fac 141; Highest Degree: Associate
Library Holdings: CDs 560; DVDs 800; e-books 70,676; Bk Vols 58,000; Per Subs 174; Talking Bks 268; Videos 2,847
Special Collections: Community College Education
Subject Interests: Engr, Health sci, Liberal arts, Tech
Automation Activity & Vendor Info: (Cataloging) Ex Libris Group; (Circulation) Ex Libris Group; (Course Reserve) Ex Libris Group; (ILL) Ex Libris Group; (OPAC) Ex Libris Group
Wireless access
Function: 24/7 Electronic res, Chess club, Computers for patron use, E-Reserves, Electronic databases & coll, Online cat, Photocopying/Printing, Wheelchair accessible
Partic in South Central Regional Library Council; SUNYConnect; Westchester Academic Library Directors Organization
Special Services for the Deaf - Assistive tech; Closed caption videos; Sign lang interpreter upon request for prog; Video & TTY relay via computer
Open Mon-Thurs 7:30am-10pm, Fri 7:30-5, Sat 1-5, Sun 3-7
Restriction: Co libr, ID required to use computers (Ltd hrs), Open to pub for ref & circ; with some limitations, Open to students, fac & staff

BLACK RIVER

P SALLY PLOOF HUNTER MEMORIAL LIBRARY*, 101 Public Works Dr, 13612. (Mail add: PO Box 253, 13612), SAN 310-8732. Tel: 315-773-5163. FAX: 315-775-1224. E-mail: blrlib@ncls.org. Web Site: www.sallyploofhunterlibrary.org. *Dir,* Mary Louise Hunt
Founded 1915. Pop 1,349; Circ 23,247
Library Holdings: Bk Titles 6,100; Bk Vols 6,700
Automation Activity & Vendor Info: (Circulation) SirsiDynix
Wireless access
Mem of North Country Library System
Open Mon-Thurs 10-7, Fri 10-5, Sat 10-3

BLAUVELT

P BLAUVELT FREE LIBRARY, 541 Western Hwy, 10913. SAN 310-8740. Tel: 845-359-2811. FAX: 845-398-0017. E-mail: blv@rcls.org. Web Site: blauveltfreelibrary.org. *Dir,* Laura Grunwerg; E-mail: lgrunwerg@rcls.org; *Asst Dir, Ref Serv,* Tonie Ann D'Angelo; E-mail: tdangelo@rcls.org; *Head, Circ, Tech Serv,* Theresa DeGraw; *Head, Youth Serv,* Marybeth Darnobid; *Mgr, Public Relations,* Barry Koch; *Info Tech, Spec Projects,* Charlie Boone. Subject Specialists: *Graphic design,* Barry Koch; Staff 13 (MLS 4, Non-MLS 9)
Founded 1909. Pop 5,602; Circ 62,381
Library Holdings: Bk Titles 63,000; Per Subs 417; Talking Bks 1,023
Special Collections: Area History; Blauvelt Family History; Genealogy (Blauvelt); Local History (Budke Coll)
Automation Activity & Vendor Info: (Cataloging) Horizon; (Circulation) Horizon; (OPAC) Horizon; (Serials) Horizon
Wireless access
Mem of Ramapo Catskill Library System
Open Mon-Thurs 9-9, Fri 9-5, Sat 11-5, Sun (Sept-May) 1-5
Friends of the Library Group

C DOMINICAN COLLEGE LIBRARY*, Sullivan Library, 480 Western Hwy, 10913-2000. SAN 310-8759. Tel: 845-848-7505. Web Site: dc.edu/sullivan-library. *Head Librn,* Mary-Elizabeth Schaub; Tel: 845-848-7500, E-mail: m.schaub@dc.edu; *Asst Librn, Tech Serv,* Judy Gitlin; *Asst Librn, Info serv, Literacy Serv,* Ellie Horowitz; *Access Serv, Asst Librn,* Heather Alexander; Staff 12 (MLS 5, Non-MLS 7)
Founded 1957. Enrl 1,868; Fac 76; Highest Degree: Doctorate
Library Holdings: Bk Vols 74,492; Per Subs 609
Automation Activity & Vendor Info: (Cataloging) SirsiDynix; (Circulation) SirsiDynix; (Course Reserve) SirsiDynix; (Discovery) EBSCO Discovery Service; (ILL) OCLC ILLiad; (OPAC) SirsiDynix
Wireless access
Partic in Southeastern New York Library Resources Council
Open Mon-Thurs 8am-Midnight, Fri 8-7, Sat & Sun 12-7

BLISS

P EAGLE FREE LIBRARY*, 3413 School St, 14024. (Mail add: PO Box 126, 14024-0126), SAN 310-8767. Tel: 585-322-7701. FAX: 585-322-7701. Web Site: eaglefreelibrary.org. *Dir,* Jody Glaser
Pop 1,192; Circ 8,375
Library Holdings: Bk Vols 10,000
Automation Activity & Vendor Info: (Cataloging) SirsiDynix; (Circulation) SirsiDynix; (OPAC) SirsiDynix
Wireless access
Mem of Pioneer Library System
Open Tues, Wed & Fri 3-7, Thurs & Sat 10-2

BLOOMFIELD

P ALLENS HILL FREE LIBRARY*, 3818 County Rd 40, 14469. SAN 311-3191. Tel: 585-229-5636. FAX: 585-229-5636. Web Site: allenshillfreelib.wixsite.com/allenshill. *Dir,* Emily Pecora; E-mail: AllenshillLibraryDirector@owwl.org
Founded 1883. Pop 311; Circ 5,933
Library Holdings: Audiobooks 376; e-books 5; Electronic Media & Resources 26; Bk Titles 7,921; Per Subs 45; Videos 759
Wireless access
Mem of Pioneer Library System
Open Tues 2-5:30, Wed 6-8, Fri 2:30-8, Sat 1-4, Sun (Oct-April) 12-3

P BLOOMFIELD PUBLIC LIBRARY, Nine Church St, 14469. SAN 311-1385. Tel: 585-657-6264. FAX: 585-657-6038. Web Site: bloomfieldpubliclibrary.org. *Dir,* Margo Park; E-mail: bloomfieldlibrarydirector@owwl.org; Staff 3 (Non-MLS 3)
Founded 1968. Pop 6,564; Circ 23,361
Library Holdings: Audiobooks 440; DVDs 5,299; Bk Vols 19,470; Per Subs 641; Talking Bks 740; Videos 1,191
Automation Activity & Vendor Info: (Circulation) SirsiDynix; (OPAC) SirsiDynix
Wireless access
Function: ILL available, Photocopying/Printing, Prog for adults, Prog for children & young adult, Ref serv available, Serves people with intellectual disabilities, Summer reading prog, Telephone ref, Wheelchair accessible
Mem of Pioneer Library System
Open Mon & Wed 2-8, Tues & Thurs 10-8, Fri 2-7, Sat 10-2
Friends of the Library Group

BLUE MOUNTAIN LAKE

S ADIRONDACK EXPERIENCE, THE MUSEUM ON BLUE MOUNTAIN LAKE LIBRARY, 9097 State Rte 30, 12812. (Mail add: PO Box 99, 12812), SAN 310-8783. Tel: 518-352-7311. FAX: 518-352-7603. E-mail: info@theadkx.org. Web Site: theadkx.org/research/library. *Libr Dir,* Ivy Gocker; Tel: 518-352-7311, Ext 108, E-mail: igocker@theadkx.org
Founded 1956
Library Holdings: Bk Vols 11,000; Per Subs 400
Special Collections: Adirondack Park Agency Coll; Association for the Protection of the Adirondacks Archives; Augustus D Shephard Architectural Plans & Drawings; Emporium Co Forestry Coll; McIntyre Iron Co Papers; Photographs Coll; W H H Adirondack Murray Papers
Subject Interests: Art, Conserv, Early 20th Centuries, Ecology, Econ life, Emphasis on 19th centuries, Lumbering, Parks, Recreation, Soc
Restriction: Open by appt only

BLUE POINT

P BAYPORT-BLUE POINT PUBLIC LIBRARY, 203 Blue Point Ave, 11715-1217. SAN 310-8791. Tel: 631-363-6133. FAX: 631-868-3520. E-mail: ContactUs@bbplibrary.org. Web Site: www.bayportbluepointlibrary.org. *Dir,* Michael Firestone; *Head, Circ,* Gerald Sullivan; *Head, Ref,* Wendy Bennett; *Head, YA,* Kelly Sheridan; *Ch Serv,* Gail Silsbe; Staff 9 (MLS 8, Non-MLS 1)
Founded 1938. Pop 13,355; Circ 172,471
Library Holdings: Bk Vols 110,412; Per Subs 378
Subject Interests: Local hist
Automation Activity & Vendor Info: (Acquisitions) Innovative Interfaces, Inc; (Cataloging) Innovative Interfaces, Inc; (Circulation) Innovative Interfaces, Inc; (OPAC) Innovative Interfaces, Inc
Wireless access
Publications: Newsletter (bi-monthly)
Mem of Suffolk Cooperative Library System
Open Mon-Fri 10-9, Sat 10-5, Sun (Sept-June) 1-5
Friends of the Library Group

BOHEMIA

P CONNETQUOT PUBLIC LIBRARY, 760 Ocean Ave, 11716. SAN 310-8805. Tel: 631-567-5079. FAX: 631-567-5137. Web Site: www.connetquotlibrary.org. *Exec Dir,* Kimberly DeCristofaro; E-mail: Kim@connetquotlibrary.org; *Asst Dir,* Jason Ladick; E-mail: jrladick@connetquotlibrary.org; Staff 54 (MLS 22, Non-MLS 32)
Founded 1974. Pop 40,162; Circ 262,894
Jul 2021-Jun 2022 Income $6,605,000
Library Holdings: Bk Vols 153,155; Per Subs 231
Automation Activity & Vendor Info: (Cataloging) SirsiDynix; (Circulation) SirsiDynix; (Discovery) SirsiDynix; (OPAC) SirsiDynix; (Serials) SirsiDynix
Wireless access
Function: 24/7 Electronic res, 24/7 Online cat, 3D Printer, Activity rm, Adult bk club, Adult literacy prog, After school storytime, Audiobks via web, Bk club(s), Bks on CD, Children's prog, Citizenship assistance, Computer training, Computers for patron use, Digital talking bks, Electronic databases & coll, Free DVD rentals, Health sci info serv, Home delivery & serv to seniorr ctr & nursing homes, Homebound delivery serv, Homework prog, ILL available, Internet access, Jail serv, Life-long learning prog for all ages, Magazines, Mail & tel request accepted, Mango lang, Meeting rooms, Microfiche/film & reading machines, Movies, Museum passes, Music CDs, Online cat, Online ref, Outreach serv, OverDrive digital audio bks, Passport agency, Photocopying/Printing, Printer for laptops & handheld devices, Prog for adults, Prog for children & young adult, Ref & res, Ref serv available, Scanner, Senior computer classes, Senior outreach, STEM programs, Story hour, Study rm, Summer & winter reading prog, Tax forms, Teen prog, Telephone ref, Wheelchair accessible, Workshops, Writing prog
Publications: Newsletter (Quarterly)
Mem of Suffolk Cooperative Library System
Open Mon-Fri 9-9, Sat 9-5, Sun (Sept-May) 1-5

BOLIVAR

P BOLIVAR FREE LIBRARY*, 390 Main St, 14715. SAN 310-8813. Tel: 585-928-2015. FAX: 585-928-2015. Web Site: bolivarfreelibrary.org. *Libr Dir,* Cathy Fuller; *Asst Dir,* Chris Evans
Founded 1898. Pop 1,200; Circ 15,000
Library Holdings: Bk Vols 10,000
Special Collections: 19th Century New York & Pennsylvania Oilfield Histories; Local Newspaper, 1892-1965
Subject Interests: Contemporary, Fiction, Mystery, Romances
Wireless access
Mem of Southern Tier Library System
Special Services for the Blind - Bks on cassette; Bks on CD; Large print & cassettes
Open Mon, Wed & Thurs 6pm-8pm, Tues & Fri 9:30-4:30
Friends of the Library Group
Bookmobiles: 1

BOLTON LANDING

P BOLTON FREE LIBRARY, 4922 Lakeshore Dr, 12814. (Mail add: PO Box 389, 12814-0389). Tel: 518-644-2233. FAX: 518-644-2234. Web Site: www.boltonfreelibrary.org. *Dir,* Megan W Baker; E-mail: mbaker@sals.edu; Staff 1 (Non-MLS 1)
Founded 1906. Pop 2,100; Circ 55,000
Jan 2021-Dec 2021 Income $101,600, Provincial $1,600, City $65,000, County $5,000, Other $30,000. Mats Exp $12,000, Books $10,000, Per/Ser (Incl. Access Fees) $1,000, AV Mat $1,000. Sal $45,000
Library Holdings: AV Mats 2,550; Bk Titles 19,000; Per Subs 5
Special Collections: Adirondack Books (Roden Coll); Art Books (David Smith Coll)
Automation Activity & Vendor Info: (Cataloging) Innovative Interfaces, Inc; (Circulation) Innovative Interfaces, Inc; (OPAC) Innovative Interfaces, Inc; (Serials) Innovative Interfaces, Inc
Wireless access
Function: Adult bk club, Audiobks via web, AV serv, Bk club(s), Bks on cassette, Bks on CD, Children's prog, Computer training, Computers for patron use, E-Reserves, Electronic databases & coll, Free DVD rentals, Home delivery & serv to seniorr ctr & nursing homes, Homebound delivery serv, ILL available, Internet access, Magnifiers for reading, Mail & tel request accepted, Mail loans to mem, Online cat, Online info literacy tutorials on the web & in blackboard, Online ref, Outside serv via phone, mail, e-mail & web, Photocopying/Printing, Preschool outreach, Prog for adults, Prog for children & young adult, Ref & res, Ref serv available, Spoken cassettes & CDs, Spoken cassettes & DVDs, Summer reading prog, Tax forms, Telephone ref, VHS videos, Wheelchair accessible, Workshops
Mem of Southern Adirondack Library System
Open Tues, Wed & Fri 10-5, Thurs 10-8, Sat 10-4

BOONVILLE

P ERWIN LIBRARY & INSTITUTE, 104 Schuyler St, 13309-1005. SAN 310-883X. Tel: 315-942-4834. FAX: 315-942-5629. E-mail: boonville@midyork.org. Web Site: erwinlibrary.org. *Dir,* Patricia Thomas; E-mail: pthomas@midyork.org
Founded 1885. Pop 2,100; Circ 25,700
Library Holdings: Bk Titles 20,100; Per Subs 59
Special Collections: Edmund Wilson Children's Books; Edmund Wilson Puppet Coll; Walter D Edmond's Film & Book Coll
Automation Activity & Vendor Info: (Cataloging) SirsiDynix; (Circulation) SirsiDynix; (OPAC) SirsiDynix
Wireless access
Mem of Mid-York Library System
Open Mon, Tues & Thurs 10-5, Fri 10-5 & 7-9, Sat 10-2

BOSTON

P BOSTON FREE LIBRARY*, 9475 Boston State Rd, 14025-9768. (Mail add: PO Box 200, 14025-0200), SAN 310-8848. Tel: 716-941-3516. FAX: 716-941-0941. E-mail: bos@buffalolib.org. Web Site: www.buffalolib.org. *Librn,* Lydia Herren
Pop 8,000; Circ 42,183
Library Holdings: Audiobooks 900; CDs 900; DVDs 4,729; Bk Vols 15,256; Per Subs 169
Wireless access
Function: 24/7 Electronic res, 24/7 Online cat, 3D Printer, Art exhibits, Art programs, Audio & video playback equip for onsite use, Audiobks via web, AV serv, Bks on CD, Children's prog, Computer training, Computers for patron use, Electronic databases & coll, Free DVD rentals, ILL available, Internet access, Magazines, Meeting rooms, Music CDs, Online cat, Online info literacy tutorials on the web & in blackboard, Online ref, Outreach serv, OverDrive digital audio bks, Photocopying/Printing, Preschool outreach, Preschool reading prog, Prog for adults, Prog for children & young adult, Ref & res, Res assist avail, Senior computer classes, Story hour, Summer & winter reading prog, Summer reading prog, Tax forms, Teen prog, Wheelchair accessible, Winter reading prog, Workshops
Mem of Buffalo & Erie County Public Library System
Open Mon & Thurs 10-7, Tues 12-8, Fri 12-5, Sat 10-2
Friends of the Library Group

BOVINA CENTER

P BOVINA PUBLIC LIBRARY*, 33 Maple Ave, 13740. (Mail add: PO Box 38, 13740-0038), SAN 310-8856. Tel: 607-832-4884. FAX: 607-832-4884. E-mail: bovinalib@delhitel.net. Web Site: bovinalibrary.org. *Libr Dir,* Annette Robbins
Founded 1918. Pop 550; Circ 3,938
Library Holdings: Bk Vols 8,000; Per Subs 50
Wireless access
Mem of Four County Library System
Open Tues (Summer) 10-3, Wed & Thurs 1-7, Sat 10-1; Tues (Winter) 10-5, Wed 1-7, Thurs 1-5, Sat 10-1

BRANCHPORT

P MODESTE BEDIENT MEMORIAL LIBRARY*, Branchport Library, 3699 State Rte 54A, 14418. SAN 310-8864. Tel: 315-595-2899. FAX: 315-595-2899. Web Site: www.branchportlibrary.org. *Dir,* Karen McKerlie; E-mail: mckerliek@stls.org
Founded 1913. Pop 3,908; Circ 7,353
Library Holdings: DVDs 300; Large Print Bks 800; Bk Vols 9,366
Automation Activity & Vendor Info: (Cataloging) SirsiDynix; (Circulation) SirsiDynix; (OPAC) SirsiDynix; (Serials) SirsiDynix
Wireless access
Mem of Southern Tier Library System
Open Tues 12-6, Wed 1-8, Fri 10-6, Sat 9-1

BRANT LAKE

P HORICON FREE PUBLIC LIBRARY, 6604 State Rte 8, 12815. (Mail add: PO Box 185, 12815-0185), SAN 376-3153. Tel: 518-494-4189. FAX: 518-494-3852. Web Site: horiconny.gov/horicon-public-library. *Dir,* Kawana Smith; E-mail: brl-director@sals.edu
Library Holdings: Bk Vols 11,568; Per Subs 15
Special Collections: Adirondacks
Wireless access
Mem of Southern Adirondack Library System
Open Mon & Thurs 2-8, Tues 12-5, Sat 10-1
Friends of the Library Group

BRENTWOOD

P BRENTWOOD PUBLIC LIBRARY*, 34 Second Ave, 11717. SAN 310-8872. Tel: 631-273-7883. Circulation Tel: 631-273-7883, Ext 101. FAX: 631-273-7896. E-mail: info@brentwoodnylibrary.org. Web Site: brentwoodnylibrary.org. *Dir,* Thomas A Tarantowicz; Staff 23 (MLS 23)
Founded 1937. Pop 70,000
Library Holdings: Large Print Bks 3,504; Bk Titles 279,778; Per Subs 553
Special Collections: Brentwood History (Verne Dyson Historical Coll), bks, ms, photogs
Automation Activity & Vendor Info: (Acquisitions) Innovative Interfaces, Inc; (Cataloging) Innovative Interfaces, Inc; (Circulation) Innovative Interfaces, Inc; (OPAC) Innovative Interfaces, Inc
Wireless access
Publications: Newsletter
Mem of Suffolk Cooperative Library System
Special Services for the Deaf - High interest/low vocabulary bks; TTY equip
Open Mon-Fri 9-9, Sat 9-5, Sun (Oct-May) 12-4

J SUFFOLK COUNTY COMMUNITY COLLEGE*, Grant Campus Library, 1001 Crooked Hill Rd, 11717. SAN 351-8825. Tel: 631-851-6740. FAX: 631-851-6509. Web Site: www.sunysuffolk.edu/libraries/3499.asp. *Head Librn,* Mary Ann Olivia; Tel: 631-851-6746, E-mail: olivam@sunysuffolk.edu; *Circ, Per, Ref,* Kerry Carlson; Tel: 631-851-6349, E-mail: carlsoke@sunysuffolk.edu; *Media Serv,* Kevin Peterman; Tel: 631-851-6747, E-mail: petermk@sunysuffolk.edu; Staff 6 (MLS 6)
Founded 1974. Enrl 7,100; Fac 125
Library Holdings: Bk Titles 47,000; Per Subs 300
Publications: Faculty handbook, newsletter, student handbook
Partic in Long Island Library Resources Council; New York State Interlibrary Loan Network
Open Mon-Thurs 8am-10pm, Fri 8-7:30, Sat 8:30-4, Sun 11:30-4

BREWSTER

P BREWSTER PUBLIC LIBRARY, 79 Main St, 10509. SAN 310-8899. Tel: 845-279-6421. FAX: 845-279-0043. E-mail: library@brewsterlibrary.org. Web Site: www.brewsterlibrary.org. *Dir,* Gina Loprinzo; E-mail: director@brewsterlibrary.org; Staff 6 (MLS 1, Non-MLS 5)
Founded 1896. Pop 18,400; Circ 54,000
Library Holdings: Bk Vols 29,000; Per Subs 100
Special Collections: Oral History
Wireless access
Mem of Mid-Hudson Library System
Open Mon & Wed 9-7, Tues & Thurs 12-7, Fri 9-4, Sat 10-3
Friends of the Library Group

BRIARCLIFF MANOR

P BRIARCLIFF MANOR PUBLIC LIBRARY, One Library Rd, 10510. SAN 310-8910. Tel: 914-941-7072. FAX: 914-941-7091. E-mail: bmplibrarycirc@gmail.com. Web Site: www.briarcliffmanorlibrary.org. *Libr Dir,* Donna Pesce; E-mail: dpesce@wlsmail.org; *Ch, Teen Librn,* Amy Kaplan; E-mail: abgkaplan@gmail.com; *Ref Librn,* Shelley Glick; E-mail: sglick@wlsmail.org; *Libr Asst,* Ricki Goe; E-mail: egoe@briarcliffmanor.org
Founded 1959. Pop 7,867; Circ 83,506
Library Holdings: AV Mats 2,500; Large Print Bks 550; Bk Titles 36,070; Per Subs 72; Talking Bks 700
Subject Interests: Art
Automation Activity & Vendor Info: (Cataloging) SirsiDynix; (Circulation) SirsiDynix; (OPAC) SirsiDynix; (Serials) SirsiDynix
Wireless access
Function: AV serv, ILL available, Photocopying/Printing, Prog for adults, Prog for children & young adult, Ref serv available, Summer reading prog, Telephone ref, Workshops
Mem of Westchester Library System
Friends of the Library Group

BRIDGEHAMPTON

P THE HAMPTON LIBRARY*, 2478 Main St, 11932. (Mail add: PO Box 3025, 11932-3025), SAN 310-8945. Tel: 631-537-0015. FAX: 631-537-7229. E-mail: info@hamptonlibrary.org. Web Site: www.hamptonlibrary.org. *Libr Dir,* Kelly Harris; E-mail: kharris@hamptonlibrary.org; Staff 8 (MLS 2, Non-MLS 6)
Founded 1877. Pop 1,866; Circ 58,452
Library Holdings: AV Mats 4,431; Electronic Media & Resources 67; Bk Vols 33,671; Per Subs 71; Talking Bks 1,609
Special Collections: Long Island Coll
Automation Activity & Vendor Info: (Acquisitions) Innovative Interfaces, Inc - Millennium; (Cataloging) PALS; (Circulation) PALS; (Course Reserve) Innovative Interfaces, Inc; (ILL) PALS; (OPAC) PALS
Wireless access
Function: Audio & video playback equip for onsite use, Audiobks via web, Bk club(s), Bk reviews (Group), Bks on CD, Children's prog, Computer training, Computers for patron use, Digital talking bks, E-Reserves, Free DVD rentals, Holiday prog, Homebound delivery serv, ILL available, Music CDs, Online ref, OverDrive digital audio bks, Photocopying/Printing, Prog for adults, Prog for children & young adult, Scanner, Story hour, Summer reading prog, Tax forms, Teen prog
Mem of Suffolk Cooperative Library System
Open Mon-Thurs 9:30-9, Fri 9:30-6, Sat 9:30-5, Sun 1-5
Friends of the Library Group

BRIDGEWATER

P BRIDGEWATER FREE LIBRARY, 408 State Rte 8, 13313. (Mail add: PO Box 372, 13313-0372), SAN 310-8953. Tel: 315-822-6475. E-mail: bridgewater@midyork.org. Web Site: www.midyorklib.org/bridgewater. *Dir,* Janet Tilbe
Pop 1,052; Circ 3,000
Library Holdings: Bk Vols 4,056
Wireless access
Mem of Mid-York Library System
Open Tues & Thurs 10-12, 1-3 & 6-8:30, Wed 10-12 & 1-3, Sat 9-12

BRIGHTWATERS

P BAY SHORE-BRIGHTWATERS PUBLIC LIBRARY, One S Country Rd, 11718-1517. SAN 310-8961. Tel: 631-665-4350. Information Services Tel: 631-665-0100. FAX: 631-665-4958. E-mail: staff@bsbwlibrary.org. Web Site: www.bsbwlibrary.org. *Dir,* Michael Squillante; Staff 10 (MLS 10)
Founded 1901. Pop 33,300; Circ 175,500
Library Holdings: Bk Titles 128,178; Bk Vols 139,252; Per Subs 620
Special Collections: Long Island, ESL Coll
Subject Interests: Compact discs, Music scores
Automation Activity & Vendor Info: (Acquisitions) TLC (The Library Corporation); (Cataloging) TLC (The Library Corporation); (Circulation) TLC (The Library Corporation); (Course Reserve) TLC (The Library Corporation); (ILL) TLC (The Library Corporation); (Media Booking) TLC (The Library Corporation); (OPAC) TLC (The Library Corporation); (Serials) TLC (The Library Corporation)
Wireless access
Mem of Suffolk Cooperative Library System
Special Services for the Blind - Bks on cassette
Open Mon-Thurs 9:30-9, Fri 9:30-6, Sat 9:30-5, Sun (Oct-May) 12-4
Friends of the Library Group

BROCKPORT

P SEYMOUR LIBRARY*, 161 East Ave, 14420. SAN 310-8996. Tel: 585-637-1050. FAX: 585-637-1051. E-mail: seymour.library@libraryweb.org. Web Site: www.seymourlibraryweb.org. *Dir,* Position Currently Open; *Ch,* Natalie Burch; E-mail: natalie.burch@libraryweb.org; *Teen Serv Librn,* Stephanie Blando; Staff 13 (MLS 1, Non-MLS 12)
Founded 1936. Pop 19,788
Library Holdings: AV Mats 8,877; Bk Titles 65,371; Per Subs 100
Special Collections: Books on the Erie Canal
Automation Activity & Vendor Info: (Circulation) CARL.Solution (TLC); (OPAC) CARL.Solution (TLC)
Wireless access
Function: Archival coll, AV serv, For res purposes, Games & aids for people with disabilities, Govt ref serv, ILL available, Photocopying/Printing, Prog for children & young adult, Ref serv available, Serves people with intellectual disabilities, Summer reading prog, Wheelchair accessible
Mem of Monroe County Library System
Open Mon-Thurs 10-8, Fri 10-6, Sat 10-3 (10-1 July-Aug)
Friends of the Library Group

C STATE UNIVERSITY OF NEW YORK COLLEGE AT BROCKPORT*, Drake Memorial Library, 350 New Campus Dr, 14420-2997. SAN 351-885X. Tel: 585-395-2140. FAX: 585-395-5651. Web Site: www.brockport.edu/library. *Dir,* Diane Fulkerson; E-mail: dfulkerson@brockport.edu; *Chief Info Officer,* Robert Cushman; Tel: 585-395-2032, E-mail: rcushman@brockport.edu; *Head, Libr Operations,* Ms Erin Sharwell; Tel: 585-395-2142, E-mail: esharwell@brockport.edu; *Assoc Librn, Coll & Scholarly Communications,* Pamela O'Sullivan; Tel: 585-395-5688, E-mail: posulliv@brockport.edu; *Assoc Librn, Discovery & Colls,* Jennifer Smathers; Tel: 585-395-2151, E-mail: jsmather@brockport.edu; *Assoc Librn, Instrul Serv,* Logan Rath; Tel: 585-395-2568, E-mail: lrath@brockport.edu; Staff 15 (MLS 15)
Founded 1835. Enrl 8,492; Fac 301; Highest Degree: Master
Library Holdings: e-books 3,690; e-journals 14,822; Bk Vols 642,650; Per Subs 1,910; Videos 7,678
Special Collections: State Document Depository
Subject Interests: Dance, Educ, English lit, Hist

Automation Activity & Vendor Info: (Acquisitions) Ex Libris Group; (Cataloging) Ex Libris Group; (Circulation) Ex Libris Group; (Course Reserve) Ex Libris Group; (OPAC) Ex Libris Group; (Serials) SerialsSolutions
Wireless access
Partic in OCLC Online Computer Library Center, Inc; Rochester Regional Library Council; SUNYConnect
Open Mon-Thurs 7:30am-1:30am, Fri 7:30-5, Sat 10-6, Sun Noon-1:30am
Friends of the Library Group

BROCTON

P AHIRA HALL MEMORIAL LIBRARY, 37 W Main St, 14716-9747. (Mail add: PO Box Q, 14716-0676), SAN 310-9003. Tel: 716-792-9418. FAX: 716-792-7334. Web Site: AhiraHall.org. *Dir,* Julie Morrison Putcher; E-mail: Director@AhiraHall.org; *Asst Dir,* Merrie Hanmann; *Libr Asst,* MariBeth Patterson
Founded 1903. Circ 23,600
Library Holdings: Bk Vols 15,000; Per Subs 30
Wireless access
Function: 24/7 Electronic res, 24/7 Online cat, Adult bk club, After school storytime, Art exhibits, Audiobks via web, Bi-weekly Writer's Group, Bks on CD, Children's prog, Computer training, Computers for patron use, Digital talking bks, Electronic databases & coll, Family literacy, Free DVD rentals, Health sci info serv, Home delivery & serv to seniorr ctr & nursing homes, Homebound delivery serv, ILL available, Internet access, Laminating, Life-long learning prog for all ages, Magnifiers for reading, Mail & tel request accepted, Makerspace, Movies, Museum passes, Music CDs, Online cat, Online ref, Outreach serv, Photocopying/Printing, Preschool reading prog, Prog for adults, Prog for children & young adult, Ref & res, Ref serv available, Scanner, Senior computer classes, Serves people with intellectual disabilities, STEM programs, Story hour, Summer & winter reading prog, Summer reading prog, Tax forms, Teen prog, Wheelchair accessible, Workshops, Writing prog
Mem of Chautauqua-Cattaraugus Library System
Open Mon & Wed 1-8, Tues & Thurs 10-5, Fri 1-5, Sat 10-1

BRONX

M ALBERT EINSTEIN COLLEGE OF MEDICINE*, D Samuel Gottesman Library, Jack & Pearl Resnick Campus, 1300 Morris Park Ave, 10461-1924. SAN 351-8884. Tel: 718-430-3108. Circulation Tel: 718-430-3111. Interlibrary Loan Service Tel: 718-430-3122. Reference Tel: 718-430-3104. FAX: 718-430-8795. E-mail: askref@einstein.yu.edu. Web Site: library.einsteinmed.org. *Dir,* Racheline Habousha; Tel: 718-430-3115, E-mail: racheline.habousha@einsteinmed.org; *Assoc Dir,* Florence Schreibstein; Tel: 718-430-3110, E-mail: florence.schreibstein@einstein.yu.edu; *Asst Dir,* Nancy Glassman; E-mail: Nancy.Glassman@einstein.yu.edu; *Archivist, Head, Ref,* Aurelia Minuti; E-mail: Aurelia.Minuti@einstein.yu.edu; *Cat,* Lydia Boyce; Tel: 718-430-3114, E-mail: Lydia.Boyce@einstein.yu.edu; Staff 25 (MLS 9, Non-MLS 16)
Founded 1955. Enrl 1,100; Fac 1,500; Highest Degree: Doctorate
Library Holdings: e-books 6,500; e-journals 7,000; Bk Vols 120,038
Subject Interests: Behav sci, Med, Psychol
Automation Activity & Vendor Info: (Acquisitions) Innovative Interfaces, Inc; (Cataloging) Innovative Interfaces, Inc; (Circulation) Innovative Interfaces, Inc; (Course Reserve) Innovative Interfaces, Inc; (OPAC) Innovative Interfaces, Inc; (Serials) Innovative Interfaces, Inc
Wireless access
Partic in National Network of Libraries of Medicine Region 7; OCLC Online Computer Library Center, Inc
Restriction: By permission only

J BRONX COMMUNITY COLLEGE LIBRARY*, 2115 University Ave, NL 252A, 10453. SAN 310-902X. Tel: 718-289-5431. Reference Tel: 718-289-5974. Information Services Tel: 718-289-5439. FAX: 718-289-6063. E-mail: library@bcc.cuny.edu. Web Site: www.bcc.cuny.edu/library. *Chief Librn,* Michael Miller; E-mail: michael.miller@bcc.cuny.edu; *Interim Head, Access Serv,* Katherine Parsons; E-mail: katherine.parsons@bcc.cuny.edu; *Head, Archives,* Cynthia Tobar; Tel: 718-289-5436, E-mail: cynthia.tobar@bcc.cuny.edu; *Head, Learning Serv,* LaRoi Lawton; Tel: 718-289-5348, E-mail: laroi.lawton@bcc.cuny.edu; *Head, Tech Serv,* Joanne Canales; Tel: 718-289-5100, Ext 3616, E-mail: joanne.canales@bcc.cuny.edu; Staff 10 (MLS 10)
Founded 1957. Enrl 12,000; Fac 200; Highest Degree: Associate
Library Holdings: AV Mats 3,684; e-books 600; Bk Vols 106,761; Per Subs 355
Automation Activity & Vendor Info: (Acquisitions) Ex Libris Group; (Cataloging) Ex Libris Group; (Circulation) Ex Libris Group; (Course Reserve) Ex Libris Group; (ILL) Ex Libris Group; (Media Booking) Ex Libris Group; (OPAC) Ex Libris Group; (Serials) Ex Libris Group
Function: 24/7 Electronic res, 24/7 Online cat, Archival coll
Partic in Metropolitan New York Library Council; OCLC Online Computer Library Center, Inc
Open Mon-Thurs 8am-10pm, Fri 8-5, Sat & Sun 10-5
Restriction: Authorized patrons, Authorized personnel only

S BRONX COUNTY HISTORICAL SOCIETY*, Research Library & Archives, 3309 Bainbridge Ave, 10467. SAN 310-9127. Tel: 718-881-8900, Ext 105. FAX: 718-881-4827. Web Site: bronxhistoricalsociety.org. *Exec Dir,* Dr Gary Hermalyn; *Librn,* Steven Payne; E-mail: spayne@bronxhistoricalsociety.org
Founded 1955
Library Holdings: AV Mats 825; CDs 45; DVDs 109; Bk Titles 15,000; Per Subs 150; Videos 600
Special Collections: Birds of the Bronx; Bronx Congressmen Records, Bronx Chamber of Commerce Records; Bronx Cookbooks; Bronx County Archives (Chamber of Commerce Records); Bronx Home News 1907-1948, micro; Edgar Allan Poe Coll; Local Newspaper (all current); Maps & Atlases; Photograph Coll. Oral History
Subject Interests: Bronx hist, Communities, Life
Publications: Annotated Primary Resources; Bicentennial of the United States Constitution Commemorative Issue; Blacks in the Colonial Era; Bronx Cookbooks; By The El: Third Avenue & Its El at Mid-Century; Edgar Allan Poe at Fordham Teachers Guide & Workbook; Edgar Allen Poe: A Short Biography; Elected Public Officials of the Bronx Since 1898; Genealogy of the Bronx: An Annotated Guide to Sources of Information; History in Asphalt: The Origin of Bronx Street & Place Names; History of the Morris Park Racecourse & the Morris Family; Landmarks of the Bronx; Legacy of the Revolution: The Valentine-Varian House; Morris High School & the Creation of the New York City Public High School System; Poems of Edgar Allan Poe at Fordham; Presidents of the United States; The Beautiful Bronx, 1920-1950; The Birth of The Bronx, 1609-1900; The Bronx County Historical Society Journal; The Bronx in Print: An Annotated Catalogue of Books & Pamphlets About the Bronx; The Bronx in the Frontier Era; The Bronx in the Innocent Years, 1890-1925; The Bronx It Was Only Yesterday, 1935-1965; The Bronx Triangle: A Portrait of Norwood; The Bronx: Then & Now; The Northern Borough: A History of The Bronx; The Study & Writing of History; Yankee Stadium: 1923-2008, Images of Baseball
Restriction: Open by appt only
Friends of the Library Group

M CALVARY HOSPITAL, Medical Library, 1740 Eastchester Rd, 10461. SAN 351-9066. Tel: 718-518-2229. FAX: 718-518-2686. *Med Librn,* Irina Pulatova; E-mail: ipulatova@calvaryhospital.org; Staff 2 (MLS 1, Non-MLS 1)
Founded 1966
Jan 2021-Dec 2021. Mats Exp $45,000. Sal $65,000
Library Holdings: Bk Titles 1,538; Bk Vols 1,623; Per Subs 110
Special Collections: Patient & Family Education Coll
Subject Interests: Bereavement, Cancer, Death, Dying, Med, Nursing, Nutrition, Oncology, Palliative care
Automation Activity & Vendor Info: (Cataloging) Marcive, Inc; (Serials) Prenax, Inc
Wireless access
Partic in Basic Health Sciences Library Network; Brooklyn-Queens-Staten Island-Manhattan-Bronx Health Sciences Librarians; Metropolitan New York Library Council; National Network of Libraries of Medicine Region 7
Restriction: Not open to pub

C COLLEGE OF MOUNT SAINT VINCENT, Elizabeth Seton Library, 6301 Riverdale Ave, 10471-1046. SAN 310-9054. Tel: 718-405-3394. Reference E-mail: reference@mountsaintvincent.edu. Web Site: www.mountsaintvincent.edu/academics/resources/library. *Dir,* Joseph Levis; E-mail: joseph.levis@mountsaintvincent.edu; *Cat,* Lina Ip
Founded 1910. Highest Degree: Master
Library Holdings: Bk Vols 125,000; Per Subs 800
Subject Interests: Biology, Communications, Irish hist, Lit, Nursing
Automation Activity & Vendor Info: (Cataloging) LibLime; (Circulation) LibLime; (OPAC) LibLime
Wireless access
Publications: Discover Resources Bulletins; Library Guides; Library Lines
Partic in OCLC Online Computer Library Center, Inc; Westchester Academic Library Directors Organization
Open Mon-Thurs 8am-11pm, Fri 8-4:30, Sat 10-5, Sun 2-10

GM DEPARTMENT OF VETERANS AFFAIRS*, James J Peters VA Medical Center Library, 130 W Kingsbridge Rd, 10468. SAN 310-9194. Tel: 718-584-9000, Ext 6924. FAX: 718-741-4608. Web Site: www.bronx.va.gov. *Chief Librn,* Judy Steever; Tel: 718-741-4229; Staff 2 (MLS 1, Non-MLS 1)
Library Holdings: AV Mats 854; Bk Titles 2,700; Per Subs 100
Subject Interests: Cancer, Clinical, Dietetics, Nuclear med, Rehabilitation, Spinal cord injury
Partic in Metropolitan New York Library Council

C FORDHAM UNIVERSITY LIBRARIES*, Walsh Library at Rose Hill, 441 E Fordham Rd, 10458-5151. SAN 351-9120. Tel: 718-817-3570. Circulation Tel: 718-817-3578. Interlibrary Loan Service Tel: 718-817-3510. Reference Tel: 718-817-3586. FAX: 718-817-3582. Web Site: www.fordham.edu/info/27156/libraries. *Dir of Libr,* Linda LoSchiavo; E-mail: loschiavo@fordham.edu; *Dir, Info Tech,* Michael Considine; E-mail: considine@fordham.edu; *Asst Dir, Tech Serv,* Michael Wares; *Head, Acq,* Betty Garity; E-mail: garity@fordham.edu; *Head, Cat,* John Williams; *Head, Circ,* John D'Angelo; E-mail: jdangelo@fordham.edu; *Head, ILL,* Charlotte Labbe; E-mail: labbe@fordham.edu; *Head, Ref & Info Serv,* Jane Suda; *Head, Ser & Electronic Res,* Lynn Parliman; *Head, Spec Coll & Archives,* Position Currently Open; *Conserv Librn, Presv Librn,* Vivian Shen; *Govt Doc,* Tom Giangreco; *Reserves,* William Milite; Staff 27 (MLS 23, Non-MLS 4)
Founded 1841. Enrl 16,037; Fac 735; Highest Degree: Doctorate
Jul 2017-Jun 2018. Mats Exp $2,050,000, Books $750,000, Electronic Ref Mat (Incl. Access Fees) $1,225,000, Presv $75,000. Sal $4,685,000 (Prof $2,720,000)
Library Holdings: CDs 12,500; DVDs 14,900; e-books 720,000; e-journals 90,000; Bk Titles 960,000; Bk Vols 1,900,000; Per Subs 2,300; Videos 50,500
Special Collections: 9/11 Coll; American Revolution & Early Federal Americana (Charles Allen Munn Coll); Arts & Architecture (Gambosville Coll); Crimes & Criminals (McGarry Coll); Detective & Mystery Fiction (Maurer Mystery Coll); French Revolution (Joseph Givernaud Coll); Gaelic (McGuire-McLees Coll); Hudson River Coll; Liturgical manuscripts & books (James Leach Coll); The Jesuits (Jesuitica Coll); Vatican (Barberini Coll), microfilm; William Cobbett Coll. US Document Depository
Subject Interests: Behav sci, Bus admin, Educ, Humanities, Natural sci, Soc
Automation Activity & Vendor Info: (Acquisitions) SirsiDynix; (Cataloging) SirsiDynix; (Circulation) SirsiDynix; (Course Reserve) SirsiDynix; (Discovery) EBSCO Discovery Service; (ILL) OCLC; (OPAC) SirsiDynix; (Serials) SirsiDynix
Wireless access
Function: 24/7 Electronic res, 24/7 Online cat
Publications: Fordham University Library Handbook; Research guides
Partic in Metropolitan New York Library Council; OCLC Online Computer Library Center, Inc; OCLC Research Library Partnership; Westchester Academic Library Directors Organization
Restriction: Open to students, fac & staff
Friends of the Library Group

Departmental Libraries:

FORDHAM WESTCHESTER LIBRARY, 400 Westchester Ave, West Harrison, 10604, SAN 312-5572. Tel: 914-367-3426. Circulation Tel: 914-367-3060. Reference Tel: 914-367-3061. ; Staff 4 (MLS 2, Non-MLS 2)
Founded 2008. Enrl 2,472; Fac 173; Highest Degree: Master
Library Holdings: Bk Titles 22,029; Bk Vols 23,071
Automation Activity & Vendor Info: (Acquisitions) SirsiDynix; (Cataloging) SirsiDynix; (Circulation) SirsiDynix; (ILL) OCLC ILLiad; (OPAC) SirsiDynix; (Serials) SirsiDynix
Function: For res purposes
Partic in Metropolitan New York Library Council; Westchester Academic Library Directors Organization
Restriction: Open to students, fac & staff

QUINN LIBRARY AT LINCOLN CENTER, Lincoln Ctr, 113 W 60th St, New York, 10023, SAN 311-7731. Tel: 212-636-6050. Circulation Tel: 212-636-6062. FAX: 212-636-6766. Web Site: www.library.fordham.edu. *Dir of Libr,* Linda LoSchiavo; Tel: 718-817-3570, E-mail: loschiavo@fordham.edu; *Asst Dir,* Robert Allen; Tel: 212-636-6058, E-mail: rallen@fordham.edu; *Head, Info Access Serv,* Nicholas Alongi; *Ref & Info Serv,* Bethany Jarret; *Ref Librn,* David Vassar; Staff 6 (MLS 6)
Founded 1969. Enrl 6,841; Fac 262; Highest Degree: Doctorate
Library Holdings: Bk Vols 450,000; Per Subs 30,000; Videos 11,000
Special Collections: Education (ERIC Documents); Holocaust. US Document Depository
Subject Interests: Bus, Educ, Soc serv
Automation Activity & Vendor Info: (Circulation) SirsiDynix; (OPAC) SirsiDynix
Partic in Metropolitan New York Library Council; Westchester Academic Library Directors Organization
Publications: Inside Fordham Libraries (Semi-annual)
Open Mon-Thurs 9am-11pm, Fri & Sat 9-8, Sun Noon-11

J HOSTOS COMMUNITY COLLEGE LIBRARY*, Shirley J Hinds Allied Health & Science Bldg, 475 Grand Concourse, Rm A308, 10451. SAN 310-9097. Tel: 718-518-4222. Reference Tel: 718-518-4215. Administration Tel: 718-518-4203. FAX: 718-518-4206. E-mail: reflibrarian@hostos.cuny.edu. Web Site: commons.hostos.cuny.edu/library. *Chief Librn,* Madeline Ford; Tel: 718-518-4211, E-mail: mford@hostos.cuny.edu; *Head, Access Serv,* Rhonda Johnson; Tel: 718-518-4214, E-mail: rhjohnson@hostos.cuny.edu; *Instruction & Ref Librn,* Dr Miriam Laskin; Tel: 718-518-4207, E-mail: mlaskin@hostos.cuny.edu; *IT Librn, Ref Serv,* Kate Lyons; Tel: 718-518-4213, E-mail: clyons@hostos.cuny.edu; *Acq, Outreach Librn,* Jennifer Tang; Tel: 718-518-4298, E-mail: jtang@hostos.cuny.edu; *Reserves Mgr,* Santa Ojeda; Tel: 718 518-4224, E-mail: sojeda@hostos.cuny.edu; *Instruction & Archives,* William Casari; Tel: 718-518-4220, E-mail: wcasari@hostos.cuny.edu. Subject Specialists: *Allied health,* Madeline Ford; *Polit sci,* Rhonda Johnson; *Engr, Lit, Writing,* Dr Miriam Laskin; *Bus, Computer sci, Info tech,* Kate Lyons; *Educ, Lit,* Jennifer Tang; *Archival mgt, Communications, Hist,* William Casari; Staff 13 (MLS 8, Non-MLS 5)
Founded 1968. Enrl 4,500; Fac 160; Highest Degree: Associate
Library Holdings: Bk Vols 65,000; Per Subs 330
Special Collections: Allied Health; Black & Latino Studies; College Archives; Hostos Digital Coll; Spanish American Literature
Subject Interests: Bilingual educ, Caribbean studies, Ethnic studies, Latin Am studies, Latino art, music & women writers, Spanish lit
Automation Activity & Vendor Info: (Acquisitions) Ex Libris Group; (Cataloging) Ex Libris Group; (Circulation) Ex Libris Group; (Course Reserve) Docutek; (OPAC) Ex Libris Group; (Serials) Ex Libris Group
Wireless access
Function: Archival coll, Health sci info serv, ILL available, Photocopying/Printing, VHS videos, Workshops
Publications: Escriba! (College journal); Liaison Update (Current awareness service); Newsletter (Biannually); Recent Acquisitions (Acquisition list)
Partic in Metropolitan New York Library Council; OCLC Online Computer Library Center, Inc
Special Services for the Deaf - ADA equip; Assistive tech
Special Services for the Blind - Assistive/Adapted tech devices, equip & products; ZoomText magnification & reading software

S HUNTINGTON FREE LIBRARY*, Nine Westchester Sq, 10461-3513. SAN 310-9135. Tel: 718-829-7770. E-mail: info@huntingtonfreelibrary.org. Web Site: huntingtonfreelibrary.org. *Librn,* Catherine McChesney; Staff 4 (MLS 1, Non-MLS 3)
Founded 1892
Library Holdings: Bk Titles 1,000; Per Subs 2
Special Collections: Bronx History; Turn of Century-Genealogy
Wireless access
Restriction: Open by appt only

C LEHMAN COLLEGE, CITY UNIVERSITY OF NEW YORK*, Leonard Lief Library, 250 Bedford Park Blvd W, 10468. SAN 310-9089. Tel: 718-960-8577. Circulation Tel: 718-960-8576. Interlibrary Loan Service Tel: 718-960-7762. Reference Tel: 718-960-8580. FAX: 718-960-8952. Web Site: www.lehman.cuny.edu/library. *Chief Librn,* Kenneth Schlesinger; E-mail: kenneth.schlesinger@lehman.cuny.edu; *Head, Per,* Edwin Wallace; Tel: 718-960-7757, E-mail: edwin.wallace@lehman.cuny.edu; *Head, Ref,* Vanessa Arce Senati; Tel: 718-960-7765, E-mail: vanessa.arcesenati@lehman.cuny.edu; *Head, Tech Serv,* Joan Jocson-Singh; Tel: 718-960-8428, E-mail: joan.jocsonsingh@lehman.cuny.edu; *Access Serv Librn,* Stephen Walker; Tel: 718-960-7773, E-mail: stephen.walker@gov.nt.ca; *Govt Doc Librn,* Rebecca Arzola; Tel: 718-960-8831, E-mail: rebecca.arzola@lehman.cuny.edu; *Online Learning Librn, Web Serv Librn,* John DeLooper; *Spec Coll & Archives Librn,* Dr Janet B Munch; Tel: 718-960-8603, E-mail: janet.munch@lehman.cuny.edu; *Information Literacy Coord, Libr Assessment Coordr,* Robert Farrell; Tel: 718-960-7761, E-mail: robert.farrell@lehman.cuny.edu; *Tech Coordr,* Raymond Diaz; Tel: 718-960-7772, E-mail: raymond.diaz@lehman.cuny.edu; *ILL,* Eugene Laper; E-mail: eugene.laper@lehman.cuny.edu. Subject Specialists: *Journalism, Speech comm, Theatre,* Kenneth Schlesinger; *Hist,* Dr Janet B Munch; *Lit,* Robert Farrell; *Lit,* Raymond Diaz; Staff 47 (MLS 10, Non-MLS 37)
Founded 1968. Enrl 9,074; Fac 667; Highest Degree: Master
Library Holdings: Bk Titles 384,482; Bk Vols 577,314; Per Subs 1,826
Special Collections: Basic Liberal Arts Coll; Bronx History; Bronz Institute Archives (Oral History Coll); Spanish Civil War (Ponce de Leon Coll). Oral History; State Document Depository; US Document Depository
Subject Interests: Botanical sci, Educ, Ethnic studies
Automation Activity & Vendor Info: (Acquisitions) Ex Libris Group; (Cataloging) Ex Libris Group; (Circulation) Ex Libris Group; (ILL) OCLC; (OPAC) Ex Libris Group; (Serials) Ex Libris Group
Wireless access
Function: Doc delivery serv
Partic in Metropolitan New York Library Council; Proquest Dialog
Special Services for the Deaf - Assistive tech
Special Services for the Blind - Assistive/Adapted tech devices, equip & products
Open Mon-Thurs 8am-11pm, Fri 8-9, Sat 11-9, Sun 11-8
Restriction: In-house use for visitors, Open to students, fac & staff
Friends of the Library Group

M LINCOLN MEDICAL CENTER*, Health Sciences Library, 234 Eugenio Maria De Hostos Blvd, 10451. SAN 327-4659. Tel: 718-579-5000, 718-579-5745. FAX: 718-579-5170. Web Site: www.nychealthandhospitals.org/lincoln. *Librn,* Position Currently Open
Founded 1971
Library Holdings: Bk Titles 2,000; Bk Vols 13,000; Per Subs 200
Subject Interests: Health sci
Automation Activity & Vendor Info: (Cataloging) Professional Software; (Circulation) Professional Software; (OPAC) Professional Software
Wireless access
Partic in Metropolitan New York Library Council
Restriction: Staff use only

S THE LUESTHER T MERTZ LIBRARY*, The New York Botanical Garden, 2900 Southern Blvd, 10458-5126. SAN 310-9143. Tel: 718-817-8728. Circulation Tel: 718-817-8560. Reference Tel: 718-817-8604. Web Site: willow.nybg.org. *Dir,* Position Currently Open; *Actg Head, Tech Serv, Head, Conserv & Presv,* Olga Marder; Tel: 718-817-8746, E-mail: omarder@nybg.org; *Actg Head, Pub Serv, Ref Librn,* Samantha D'Acunto; E-mail: sdacunto@nybg.org; *Syst Librn,* Susan Lynch; Tel: 718-817-8536, E-mail: slynch@nybg.org; *Acq, Coll Develop Mgr,* Position Currently Open; *Archives, Curator, Spec Coll, Res,* Stephen Sinon; E-mail: ssinon@nybg.org. Subject Specialists: *Conserv,* Olga Marder; Staff 12 (MLS 12)
Founded 1899
Library Holdings: e-journals 50,184; Microforms 1,200; Bk Titles 590,000; Per Subs 1,300
Special Collections: Botanical Art Coll; Collector Field Notes; Cookbooks; Darwiniana; Lantern slides; Lord & Burnham Coll; NYBG Archives; postcards; Scientific Reprints; Seed & Nursery Catalogs. Oral History
Subject Interests: Bibliog, Biog, Botany, Floral design, Hort, Landscape design, Mycology, Plant sci, Taxonomy
Automation Activity & Vendor Info: (Acquisitions) Innovative Interfaces, Inc - Sierra; (Cataloging) Innovative Interfaces, Inc - Sierra; (Circulation) Innovative Interfaces, Inc - Sierra; (Discovery) Innovative Interfaces, Inc - Sierra; (OPAC) Innovative Interfaces, Inc; (Serials) Innovative Interfaces, Inc - Sierra
Wireless access
Function: Archival coll, Art exhibits, Computers for patron use, Electronic databases & coll, ILL available, Internet access, Mail & tel request accepted, Microfiche/film & reading machines, Online cat, Outside serv via phone, mail, e-mail & web, Photocopying/Printing, Prog for adults, Ref serv available, Res assist avail, Res libr, Scanner, Study rm, Wheelchair accessible
Publications: A Reader's Guide to the LuEsther T Mertz Library; Architectural Photo Reproductions: A Manual for Identification & Care; Darwin's Garden: an Evolutionary Adventure; Emily Dickinson's Garden: The Poetry of Flowers; European Pleasure Gardens: Rare Books & Prints of Historic Design from the Elizabeth K Reilley Collection; Flora Illustrata; Glasshouses: The Architecture of Light & Air; Kiku: The Art of the Japanese Chrysanthemum; Monet's Garden; Plants & Gardens Portrayed: Rare & Illustrated Books from the LuEsther T Mertz Library; The Renaissance Herbal
Partic in Council on Botanical & Horticultural Libraries, Inc; Metropolitan New York Library Council; Nat Libr of Med Regional Med Libr Prog; OCLC Online Computer Library Center, Inc
Open Mon & Fri 10-5, Tues, Wed & Thurs 10-6
Restriction: Closed stack, Open to pub for ref & circ; with some limitations

C MONROE COLLEGE*, Thomas P Schnitzler Library, Jerome Hall, Lower Level, 2468 Jerome Ave, 10468. Tel: 646-393-8333, 718-933-6700. Circulation Tel: 718-933-6700, Ext 333. E-mail: library@monroecollege.edu. Web Site: www.monroecollege.edu. *Libr Dir,* Jeanette Madera; Tel: 718-933-6700, Ext 8342, E-mail: jmadera@monroecollege.edu; Staff 6 (MLS 4, Non-MLS 2)
Enrl 5,200; Highest Degree: Master
Library Holdings: Bk Titles 92,000; Bk Vols 1,000,000; Per Subs 350
Automation Activity & Vendor Info: (Cataloging) LibraryWorld, Inc; (Circulation) LibraryWorld, Inc; (OPAC) LibraryWorld, Inc
Wireless access
Partic in Westchester Academic Library Directors Organization
Open Mon-Thurs 8am-8:30pm, Fri & Sat 9-4

M MONTEFIORE MEDICAL CENTER*, Tishman Learning Center Health Sciences Library, Moses Research Tower, 2nd Flr, 111 E 210th St, 10467. SAN 351-9457. Tel: 718-920-4666. FAX: 718-920-4658. E-mail: medlib@montefiore.org. Web Site: www.montefiore.org. *Dir,* Sheigla Smalling; E-mail: ssmallin@montefiore.org; *Assoc Dir,* Marie Irma Elias; E-mail: melias@montefiore.org; Staff 6 (MLS 2, Non-MLS 4)
Founded 1926
Library Holdings: e-books 1,250; e-journals 3,000
Special Collections: Archives Materials
Subject Interests: Internal med
Automation Activity & Vendor Info: (Cataloging) OCLC; (Circulation) Innovative Interfaces, Inc; (Course Reserve) Innovative Interfaces, Inc; (Media Booking) Innovative Interfaces, Inc; (OPAC) Innovative Interfaces, Inc; (Serials) Innovative Interfaces, Inc
Wireless access
Partic in RML
Restriction: Employees & their associates

M SAINT BARNABAS HOSPITAL*, Medical Library, 4487 Third Ave, 10457-2594. SAN 351-9511. Tel: 718-960-6113. E-mail: stmedlib@sbhny.org. Web Site: sbhny.libguides.com/medicallibrary. *Dir, Libr Serv,* Deborah Bonelli; Tel: 718-960-6113, Ext 6466, E-mail: dbonelli@sbhny.org
Library Holdings: Per Subs 282
Publications: Quarterly Newsletter
Partic in National Network of Libraries of Medicine Region 7
Open Mon-Fri 8-4

C STATE UNIVERSITY OF NEW YORK MARITIME COLLEGE*, Stephen B Luce Library, Six Pennyfield Ave, Fort Schuyler, 10465. SAN 310-9186. Tel: 718-409-7231. FAX: 718-409-4680. E-mail: library@sunymaritime.edu. Web Site: stephenbluce.sunymaritime.edu/academics/stephen-b-luce-library. *Libr Dir,* Jillian Kehoe; E-mail: jkehoe@sunymaritime.edu; Staff 8 (MLS 6, Non-MLS 2)
Founded 1946. Enrl 1,100; Highest Degree: Master
Library Holdings: AV Mats 1,934; Bk Titles 72,120; Bk Vols 84,929; Spec Interest Per Sub 200
Special Collections: Marine Casualty Reports; Maritime History; Maritime Research, Technical Reports. US Document Depository
Subject Interests: Marine engr, Merchant marine, Nautical sci, Naval archit, Navigation, Shipping, Ships, Transportation mgt
Automation Activity & Vendor Info: (Cataloging) Ex Libris Group; (Circulation) Ex Libris Group; (OPAC) Ex Libris Group; (Serials) Ex Libris Group
Wireless access
Function: Photocopying/Printing, Ref serv available, Telephone ref
Publications: New Accessions (Accession list)
Partic in Metropolitan New York Library Council; SUNYConnect
Open Mon-Thurs (Winter) 8am-10pm, Fri 8-4:30, Sat 10-5, Sun 4-9; Mon-Fri (Summer) 8:30-12 & 1-4:30
Friends of the Library Group

S WILDLIFE CONSERVATION SOCIETY LIBRARY*, 2300 Southern Blvd, 10460. SAN 310-916X. Tel: 718-220-5100. E-mail: library@wcs.org. Web Site: library.wcs.org. *Archives Dir, Libr Dir,* Madeleine Thompson; Staff 2 (MLS 2)
Founded 1899
Library Holdings: e-journals 800; Bk Titles 8,000; Bk Vols 10,000; Per Subs 170
Special Collections: WCS Archives
Subject Interests: Wildlife conserv, Zoo biol
Automation Activity & Vendor Info: (Cataloging) Innovative Interfaces, Inc - Millennium; (Circulation) Innovative Interfaces, Inc - Millennium; (ILL) OCLC FirstSearch; (OPAC) Innovative Interfaces, Inc - Millennium; (Serials) Innovative Interfaces, Inc - Millennium
Wireless access
Function: Archival coll, ILL available
Publications: Guide to the Archives of the New York Zoological Society
Partic in Metropolitan New York Library Council; OCLC Online Computer Library Center, Inc
Restriction: Borrowing requests are handled by ILL, Open to researchers by request

BRONXVILLE

P BRONXVILLE PUBLIC LIBRARY, 201 Pondfield Rd, 10708. SAN 310-9208. Tel: 914-337-7680. FAX: 914-337-0332. Web Site: www.bronxvillelibrary.org. *Dir,* Gregory Wirszyla; E-mail: bronxvilledirector@wlsmail.org; *Head, Circ,* Marianne Wingertzahn; E-mail: mwingertzahn@wlsmail.org; *Head, Ref Serv,* Christine Utchel; E-mail: cutchel@wlsmail.org; *Head, Youth Serv,* Ellen Mctyre; E-mail: emctyre@wlsmail.org; *Ref Librn,* Tessymol John; E-mail: tessyj@wlsmail.org; Staff 10 (MLS 5, Non-MLS 5)
Founded 1906. Pop 6,300; Circ 150,000
Library Holdings: AV Mats 10,530; Bk Titles 64,800; Per Subs 112
Special Collections: Bronxville History Coll
Automation Activity & Vendor Info: (Acquisitions) SirsiDynix; (Circulation) SirsiDynix; (ILL) SirsiDynix
Wireless access
Publications: Friends of the Bronxville Library (Newsletter)
Mem of Westchester Library System

Open Mon, Wed & Fri 9:30-5:30, Tues & Thurs 1-9, Sat 9:30-5 (Winter); Mon, Wed & Fri 9:30-5:30, Tues 1-9, Thurs 1-5:30, Sat 9:30-1 (Summer)
Friends of the Library Group

C SARAH LAWRENCE COLLEGE*, Esther Raushenbush Library, One Mead Way, 10708. SAN 351-9570. Tel: 914-395-2474. Interlibrary Loan Service Tel: 914-395-2479. Reference Tel: 914-395-2225. Administration Tel: 914-395-2472. FAX: 914-395-2473. E-mail: reference@sarahlawrence.edu. Web Site: www.sarahlawrence.edu/library. *Libr Dir,* Bobbie Smolow; Tel: 914-395-2471, E-mail: bsmolow@sarahlawrence.edu; *Head, ILL/Access Serv Librn,* Geoffrey Danisher; E-mail: gdanishe@sarahlawrence.edu; *Col Archivist, Head, Ref,* Lauren Maclean; Tel: 914-395-2480, E-mail: lmaclean@sarahlawrence.edu; *Govt Doc Librn, Ser Librn,* Angelica Freitas; Tel: 914-395-2478, E-mail: afreitas@sarahlawrence.edu; *Res & Instruction Librn,* Mia Bruner; Tel: 914-395-2225, E-mail: mbruner@sarahlawrence.edu
Founded 1926. Enrl 1,574; Fac 219; Highest Degree: Master
Library Holdings: Bk Vols 300,000; Per Subs 831
Special Collections: Bessie Schoenberg Dance Coll; Sarah Lawrence College Faculty Coll. US Document Depository
Subject Interests: Art, Human genetics, Music, Psychol, Women's hist
Automation Activity & Vendor Info: (Acquisitions) LibLime; (Cataloging) LibLime; (Circulation) LibLime; (Course Reserve) LibLime; (ILL) OCLC FirstSearch; (OPAC) LibLime; (Serials) LibLime
Wireless access
Partic in Metropolitan New York Library Council; OCLC Online Computer Library Center, Inc; Westchester Academic Library Directors Organization
Open Mon-Thurs 8:30am-1am, Fri 8:30am-Midnight, Sat 11am-Midnight, Sun 11am-1am; Mon-Fri (Summer) 9-4:30
Friends of the Library Group

Departmental Libraries:

WILLIAM SCHUMAN MUSIC LIBRARY, One Mead Way, 10708. Tel: 914-395-2375. FAX: 914-395-2507. Web Site: www.sarahlawrence.edu/library/music-library.
Enrl 2,000; Highest Degree: Bachelor
Library Holdings: CDs 5,720; Music Scores 8,246; Bk Titles 4,555; Bk Vols 6,050
Open Mon-Thurs 9-9, Fri 9-5

BROOKHAVEN

P BROOKHAVEN FREE LIBRARY, 273 Beaver Dam Rd, 11719. SAN 310-9232. Tel: 631-286-1923. FAX: 631-286-0120. E-mail: bfl@brookhavenfreelibrary.org. Web Site: www.brookhavenfreelibrary.org. *Dir,* Jamie Papandrea; Staff 12 (MLS 1, Non-MLS 11)
Founded 1912. Pop 26,400
Library Holdings: Bk Vols 30,239; Per Subs 130
Special Collections: Long Island History; Nautical (Bolt Coll)
Automation Activity & Vendor Info: (Cataloging) Innovative Interfaces, Inc; (Circulation) Innovative Interfaces, Inc; (ILL) Innovative Interfaces, Inc; (OPAC) Innovative Interfaces, Inc
Wireless access
Function: CD-ROM, Homebound delivery serv, Internet access, Music CDs, Photocopying/Printing, Prog for adults, Prog for children & young adult, Ref serv available, Spoken cassettes & CDs, Summer reading prog, VHS videos
Publications: Brookhaven Free Library News (Newsletter)
Mem of Suffolk Cooperative Library System
Open Mon, Tues, Thurs & Fri 9:30-5, Wed 9:30-7, Sat 9:30-1
Friends of the Library Group

BROOKLYN

C BORICUA COLLEGE*, Special Collections Library, 186 N Sixth St, 11211. SAN 375-2348. Tel: 718-782-2200. FAX: 718-782-2050. Web Site: www.boricuacollege.edu. *Dir, Libr & Learning Res,* Liza Rivera; E-mail: lrivera@boricuacollege.edu
Special Collections: Special Puerto Rico Coll
Automation Activity & Vendor Info: (Cataloging) JayWil Software Development, Inc
Wireless access
Open Mon-Fri 10-6:30

M BROOKDALE UNIVERSITY HOSPITAL & MEDICAL CENTER, Marie Smith Schwartz Medical Library, Schulman Institute, 1st Flr, 555 Rockaway Pkwy, 11212. SAN 328-5642. Tel: 718-240-5312. FAX: 718-240-5030. E-mail: medicallibrary@bhmcny.edu. Web Site: www.brookdalehospital.org. *Dir,* Timothy O'Mara; E-mail: tomara@bhmcny.org; Staff 2 (MLS 1, Non-MLS 1)
Library Holdings: Bk Titles 2,000; Per Subs 336
Subject Interests: Med, Nursing
Automation Activity & Vendor Info: (Cataloging) Professional Software; (Circulation) Professional Software; (OPAC) Professional Software; (Serials) Professional Software
Wireless access
Partic in Basic Health Sciences Library Network
Restriction: Staff use only

L BROOKLYN BAR ASSOCIATION FOUNDATION INC LIBRARY*, 123 Remsen St, 2nd flr, 11201. SAN 310-9283. Tel: 718-624-0868. FAX: 718-797-1713. Web Site: www.brooklynbar.org/foundation. *Exec Dir,* Avery Eli Okin; E-mail: aokin@brooklynbar.org
Founded 1872
Library Holdings: Bk Titles 4,000
Subject Interests: Law related govt publications
Wireless access
Restriction: Mem only

S BROOKLYN BOTANIC GARDEN LIBRARY*, 1000 Washington Ave, 11225. SAN 310-9291. Tel: 718-623-7270. Administration Tel: 718-623-7303. FAX: 718-857-2430. E-mail: library@bbg.org. Web Site: www.bbg.org/gardening/library. *Head Librn,* Kathy Crosby; Staff 5 (MLS 1, Non-MLS 4)
Founded 1911
Library Holdings: Bk Titles 30,000; Bk Vols 55,000; Per Subs 553
Special Collections: Botanical Art; Glass Plate Negatives; Lantern Slides
Subject Interests: Botany, Ecology, Garden design, Hort, Landscaping, Systematics
Automation Activity & Vendor Info: (Cataloging) Sydney; (Circulation) Sydney; (OPAC) Sydney; (Serials) Sydney
Wireless access
Function: ILL available, Res libr
Partic in Metropolitan New York Library Council; OCLC Online Computer Library Center, Inc
Open Tues & Fri 10-4:30, Wed 10-8

C BROOKLYN COLLEGE LIBRARY, 2900 Bedford Ave, 11210. SAN 351-9694. Tel: 718-951-5335. Circulation Tel: 718-951-5335. Interlibrary Loan Service Tel: 718-951-4414. Reference Tel: 718-951-5628. Administration Tel: 718-951-5342. FAX: 718-951-4540. Administration FAX: 718-951-4557. Interlibrary Loan Service E-mail: ill@brooklyn.cuny.edu. Reference E-mail: refdesk@brooklyn.cuny.edu. Web Site: library.brooklyn.cuny.edu. *Chief Librn, Exec Dir,* Mary Mallery; E-mail: mary.mallery@brooklyn.cuny.edu; *Dir, Libr Tech Serv, Director, Systems & Network Support,* Alex Rudshteyn; E-mail: alex@brooklyn.cuny.edu; *IT Dir,* Dr Howard Spivak; E-mail: howards@brooklyn.cuny.edu; *Head, Ser,* Sally Bowdoin; Tel: 718-951-5339, E-mail: sbowdoin@brooklyn.cuny.edu; *Info Serv Librn,* Helen Georgas; Tel: 718-758-8207, E-mail: hgeorgas@brooklyn.cuny.edu; *Ref Librn,* Emma Lee Yu; Tel: 718-758-8204, E-mail: eyu@brooklyn.cuny.edu; *Assoc Librn, Access Serv,* Miriam Deutch; Tel: 718-951-5221, E-mail: miriamd@brooklyn.cuny.edu; *Assoc Librn, Info Serv,* Mariana Regalado; Tel: 718-758-8215, E-mail: regalado@brooklyn.cuny.edu; *Assoc Librn, Tech Serv,* Judith Wild; Tel: 718-951-5426, E-mail: jwild@brooklyn.cuny.edu; *Evening & Weekend Manager, Media Spec,* Harold Wilson; Tel: 718-951-5327, E-mail: hwilson@brooklyn.cuny.edu; *Network & Systems Manager,* James Liu; Tel: 718-951-4868, E-mail: jliu@brooklyn.cuny.edu; *Govt Info Spec,* Jane Cramer; Tel: 718-951-5332, E-mail: janec@brooklyn.cuny.edu; *Assoc Archivist,* Marianne LaBatto; Tel: 718-758-8221, E-mail: marianne@brooklyn.cuny.edu; *Conservator,* Vyacheslav Polishchuk; Tel: 718-951-5346, E-mail: slavap@brooklyn.cuny.edu; *Electronic Serv,* Beth Evans; Tel: 718-758-8206, E-mail: bevans@brooklyn.cuny.edu; *Multimedia/Instruction Designer,* Carlos Cruz; Tel: 718-951-4667, E-mail: carlosa@brooklyn.cuny.edu; *Music Cataloger,* Marguerite Iskenderian; Tel: 718-951-5347, E-mail: iskender@brooklyn.cuny.edu. Subject Specialists: *Am studies, Modern lang, Theatre,* Helen Georgas; *Art, Hist, Scholarly communications,* Miriam Deutch; *Anthrop, Communication, Immigration,* Mariana Regalado; *Journalism, Polit sci,* Jane Cramer; *Africana studies, Latino studies, Puerto Rican studies,* Beth Evans; Staff 88 (MLS 20, Non-MLS 68)
Founded 1930. Enrl 17,000; Fac 952; Highest Degree: Master
Library Holdings: AV Mats 22,431; e-books 45,000; Bk Vols 1,449,388; Per Subs 44,470
Special Collections: Academic Freedom Coll; Alan Dershowitz Coll; Brooklyn College Archives; Colonial Ethiopia & Horn of Africa (Robert L Hess Coll); Hank Kaplan Boxing Coll; Middle East & North Africa (Stuart Schaar Coll), bks. ms & pers; William Alfred Coll. Oral History; State Document Depository; US Document Depository
Automation Activity & Vendor Info: (Acquisitions) Ex Libris Group; (Cataloging) Ex Libris Group; (Circulation) Ex Libris Group; (ILL) OCLC WorldShare Interlibrary Loan; (OPAC) Ex Libris Group; (Serials) Ex Libris Group
Wireless access
Function: AV serv, Distance learning, Doc delivery serv, For res purposes, Govt ref serv, ILL available, Large print keyboards, Photocopying/Printing, Ref serv available, Wheelchair accessible
Partic in Academic Libraries of Brooklyn; Metropolitan New York Library Council; OCLC Online Computer Library Center, Inc
Special Services for the Deaf - Assistive tech

Special Services for the Blind - Assistive/Adapted tech devices, equip & products; Computer with voice synthesizer for visually impaired persons
Restriction: Open to students, fac & staff
Friends of the Library Group
Departmental Libraries:
WALTER W GERBOTH MUSIC LIBRARY, 2900 Bedford Ave, 2nd Flr, 11210, SAN 351-9724. Tel: 718-951-5844. Web Site: libguides.brooklyn.cuny.edu/music. *Music Librn,* Honora Raphael; Tel: 718-951-5845, E-mail: honorar@brooklyn.cuny.edu
Library Holdings: CDs 10,000; Music Scores 30,000; Videos 500
Friends of the Library Group

S BROOKLYN HISTORICAL SOCIETY OTHMER LIBRARY*, 128 Pierrepont St, 11201-2711. SAN 310-9402. Tel: 347-381-3708, 718-222-4111. FAX: 718-222-3794. E-mail: library@brooklynhistory.org. Web Site: www.brooklynhistory.org/library. *Ref Librn,* Cecily Dyer; E-mail: cdyer@brooklynhistory.org; Staff 3 (MLS 3)
Founded 1863
Library Holdings: Bk Vols 150,000
Special Collections: 19th Century Paintings & Prints Coll; Archives & Manuscripts; Brooklyn, Long Island & New York City History Coll; Decorative Arts; Family History Coll; Genealogy Coll; Historic Photographs & Postcards; Historical Brooklyn & Long Island Atlases; Newspaper Clipping Index
Wireless access
Partic in Metropolitan New York Library Council
Open Wed-Sat 1-5
Restriction: Non-circulating

M BROOKLYN HOSPITAL CENTER*, Medical Library, 121 DeKalb Ave, 3rd Flr, 11201. SAN 310-9313. Tel: 718-250-6943, 718-250-8000. FAX: 718-250-6428. Web Site: www.tbh.org. *Libr Mgr,* Laurel Wellington
Founded 1928
Library Holdings: Bk Titles 1,500; Bk Vols 3,300; Per Subs 100
Wireless access
Restriction: Not open to pub, Staff use only

CL BROOKLYN LAW SCHOOL LIBRARY, 250 Joralemon St, 11201. SAN 310-9321. Tel: 718-780-7973. Reference Tel: 718-780-7567. FAX: 718-780-7562. E-mail: askthelibrary@brooklaw.edu. Web Site: www.brooklaw.edu/library. *Libr Dir,* Janet Sinder; Tel: 718-780-7975, E-mail: janet.sinder@brooklaw.edu; *Intl Law Librn,* Jean Davis; Tel: 718-780-7534, E-mail: jean.davis@brooklaw.edu; *Ref Librn,* Carolyn Brown; Tel: 718-780-7907, E-mail: carolyn.brown@brooklaw.edu; *Ref Librn,* Loreen Peritz; Tel: 718-780-7538, E-mail: loreen.peritz@brooklaw.edu; *Ref Librn,* Sue Silverman; Tel: 718-780-0678, E-mail: sue.silverman@brooklaw.edu; *Ref & Access Serv Librn,* Eric Yap; Tel: 718-780-7580, E-mail: eric.yap@brooklaw.edu; *Assoc Librn, Pub Serv,* Kathleen Darvil; Tel: 718-780-7544, E-mail: kathleen.darvil@brooklaw.edu; *Legal & Educational Tech Specialist,* Paul Jang; Tel: 718-780-7927, E-mail: paul.jang@brooklaw.edu; *Cataloger,* Judy Baptiste-Joseph; Tel: 718-780-0670, E-mail: judy.joseph@brooklaw.edu; *Acq,* Jeff Gabel; Tel: 718-780-7978, E-mail: jeff.gabel@brooklaw.edu; *Govt Doc, ILL,* Tamika Curtle; Tel: 718-780-7526, E-mail: tamika.curtle@brooklaw.edu; Staff 20 (MLS 10, Non-MLS 10)
Founded 1901. Enrl 1,200; Fac 65; Highest Degree: Doctorate
Special Collections: US Document Depository
Subject Interests: Am law, Comparative law, Foreign law, Intl law
Automation Activity & Vendor Info: (Acquisitions) Koha; (Cataloging) Koha; (Circulation) Koha; (Discovery) EBSCO Discovery Service; (ILL) OCLC Tipasa; (OPAC) Koha
Wireless access
Function: Res libr
Partic in Metropolitan New York Library Council; NELLCO Law Library Consortium, Inc.; OCLC Online Computer Library Center, Inc
Open Mon-Fri 8am-Midnight, Sat 9am-10pm, Sun 10am-Midnight
Restriction: Authorized patrons, Open to students, fac, staff & alumni

S BROOKLYN MUSEUM LIBRARIES & ARCHIVES*, 200 Eastern Pkwy, 11238, SAN 351-9759. Tel: 718-501-6307. FAX: 718-501-6125. E-mail: library@brooklynmuseum.org. Web Site: www.brooklynmuseum.org. *Principal Librn,* Deirdre E Lawrence; Staff 8 (MLS 4, Non-MLS 4)
Founded 1823
Library Holdings: Bk Vols 250,000; Per Subs 2,000
Special Collections: Artists' Books; Artists' Files; Costume & Fashion Sketches (1900-1950); Documentary Photographs; Museum Archives; Rare Books
Subject Interests: Anthrop, Archaeology, Art, Art of the Americas, Arts of Africa, Asian art, Costumes, Decorative art, Drawings, Egyptology, Islamic art, Museology, Painting, Photog, Prints, Sculpture, Textiles
Automation Activity & Vendor Info: (Acquisitions) Innovative Interfaces, Inc - Millennium; (Cataloging) Innovative Interfaces, Inc - Millennium; (Circulation) Innovative Interfaces, Inc - Millennium; (OPAC) Innovative Interfaces, Inc - Millennium; (Serials) Innovative Interfaces, Inc - Millennium
Partic in Research Libraries Information Network
Open Wed-Fri 10-4:30
Restriction: Open to pub for ref only

S WILBOUR LIBRARY OF EGYPTOLOGY*, 200 Eastern Pkwy, 11238, SAN 351-9783. Tel: 718-501-6219. FAX: 718-501-6125. E-mail: library@brooklynmuseum.org. Web Site: www.brooklynmuseum.org. *Chief Curator,* Kevin Stayton; Staff 3 (MLS 1, Non-MLS 2)
Founded 1934
Library Holdings: Bk Titles 50,000
Special Collections: Egyptology (Seyffarth Coll), mss, rare bks
Subject Interests: Archaeology, Art, Geog, Geol, Nubiology, Philology, Relig, Travel
Automation Activity & Vendor Info: (Acquisitions) Innovative Interfaces, Inc; (OPAC) Innovative Interfaces, Inc; (Serials) Innovative Interfaces, Inc
Partic in New York Art Resources Consortium; Research Libraries Information Network
Open Wed-Fri 11-4:30

P BROOKLYN PUBLIC LIBRARY*, Ten Grand Army Plaza, 11238. SAN 351-9813. Tel: 718-230-2100. Interlibrary Loan Service Tel: 718-230-2187. Information Services Tel: 718-230-2299. Web Site: www.bklynlibrary.org. *Pres & Chief Exec Officer,* Linda E Johnson; E-mail: ljohnson@bklynlinrary.org; *Chief Librn,* Nick Higgins; E-mail: nhiggins@bklynlibrary.org; *Chief Strategy Officer,* David Giles; E-mail: dgiles@bklynlibrary.org; *Libr Dir,* Jesse Montero; E-mail: jmontero@bklynlibrary.org; *Dir, Govt & Commun Affairs,* Steven Schechter; E-mail: sshecter@bklynlibrary.org; *Dir, Neighborhood Libr,* Sheila Schofer; E-mail: sschofer@bklynlibrary.org
Founded 1897. Pop 2,465,326; Circ 19,579,270
Jan 2013-Dec 2013 Income $113,291,775, State $9,941,267, City $85,704,523, Federal $2,114,323, Locally Generated Income $4,177,106, Other $11,354,556. Mats Exp $6,208,015, Books $3,939,697, Per/Ser (Incl. Access Fees) $209,151, AV Equip $194,561, AV Mat $746,882, Electronic Ref Mat (Incl. Access Fees) $1,117,724. Sal $50,879,676
Library Holdings: Bk Vols 3,729,803
Special Collections: Brooklyn Coll
Automation Activity & Vendor Info: (OPAC) Infor Library & Information Solutions
Wireless access
Open Mon-Thurs 9-9, Fri & Sat 9-6, Sun 1-5
Friends of the Library Group
Branches: 60
ARLINGTON, 203 Arlington Ave, 11207, SAN 351-9872. Tel: 718-277-6105. *Managing Librn,* Sandra Eddie; E-mail: seddie@bklynlibrary.org
Library Holdings: Bk Vols 77,436
Open Mon, Tues & Fri 10-6, Wed 1-8, Thurs 10-8, Sat 10-5
BAY RIDGE, 7223 Ridge Blvd, 11209, SAN 351-9902. Tel: 718-748-5709. FAX: 718-748-7095. *Managing Librn,* Yvonne Zhou; E-mail: yzhou@bklynlibrary.org
Library Holdings: Bk Vols 101,792
Open Mon, Tues & Fri 10-6, Wed 10-8, Thurs 1-8, Sat 10-5
Friends of the Library Group
BEDFORD, 496 Franklin Ave, 11238, SAN 351-9937. Tel: 718-623-0012. FAX: 718-638-4271. *Managing Librn,* Alicia Pritchard; E-mail: apritchard@bklynlibrary.org
Library Holdings: Bk Vols 61,947
Open Mon & Fri 10-6, Tues & Sat 10-5, Wed 1-8, Thurs 10-8
Friends of the Library Group
BOROUGH PARK, 1265 43rd St, 11219, SAN 351-9961. Tel: 718-437-4085. FAX: 718-437-3021. *Managing Librn,* Lina Ding; E-mail: lding@bklynlibrary.org
Library Holdings: Bk Vols 119,384
Open Mon, Wed & Fri 10-6, Tues & Thurs 10-8, Sun 1-5
Friends of the Library Group
BRIGHTON BEACH, 16 Brighton First Rd, 11235, SAN 351-9996. Tel: 718-946-2917. FAX: 718-946-6176. *Managing Librn,* Adriana Mitchell; E-mail: amitchell@bklynlibrary.org
Library Holdings: Bk Vols 88,438
Open Mon, Thurs & Fri 10-6, Tues 1-8, Wed 10-8, Sat 10-5
Friends of the Library Group
BROOKLYN HEIGHTS, 109 Remsen St, 11201, SAN 352-0021. Tel: 718-623-7100. FAX: 718-222-5681. *Managing Librn,* Alexander Tretiak; E-mail: atretiak@bklynlibrary.org
Library Holdings: Bk Vols 100,726
Open Mon & Fri 10-6, Tues-Thurs 10-8, Sat 10-5
Friends of the Library Group
BROWER PARK, 725 Saint Marks Ave, 11216, SAN 352-0056. Tel: 718-773-7208. FAX: 718-773-7838. *Managing Librn,* Morris Denmark; E-mail: mdenmark@bklynlibrary.org
Library Holdings: Bk Vols 52,783

Open Mon, Tues & Fri 10-6, Wed 10-8, Thurs 1-8, Sat 10-5
Friends of the Library Group
BROWNSVILLE, 61 Glenmore Ave, 11212, SAN 352-0080. Tel: 718-498-9721. FAX: 718-498-4071. *Managing Librn,* Paul Levy; E-mail: plevy@bklynlibrary.org
Library Holdings: Bk Vols 45,221
Open Mon, Thurs & Fri 10-6, Tues 1-8, Wed 10-8, Sat 10-5
BUSHWICK, 340 Bushwick Ave, 11206, SAN 352-0110. Tel: 718-602-1348. *Managing Librn,* Marc Waldron; E-mail: mwaldron@bklynlibrary.org
Library Holdings: Bk Vols 81,708
Open Mon, Tues & Fri 10-6, Wed 10-8, Thurs 1-8, Sat 10-5
BUSINESS & CAREER CENTER, Ten Grand Army Plaza, 11238, SAN 352-0145. Tel: 718-623-7000. *Mgr,* Maud Andrew; Staff 12 (MLS 12)
Founded 1943
Library Holdings: Bk Vols 139,276; Spec Interest Per Sub 1,200
Special Collections: US Document Depository
Open Mon-Thurs 9-9, Fri & Sat 9-6, Sun 1-5
CANARSIE, 1580 Rockaway Pkwy, 11236, SAN 352-017X. Tel: 718-257-6547. FAX: 718-257-6557. *Managing Librn,* Tom Muller; E-mail: tmuller@bklynlibrary.org
Library Holdings: Bk Vols 71,750
Open Mon & Fri 10-6, Tues-Thurs 10-8, Sat 10-5
CARROLL GARDENS, 396 Clinton St, 11231, SAN 352-020X. Tel: 718-596-6972. FAX: 718-596-0370. *Managing Librn,* John Leighton; E-mail: jleighton@bklynlibrary.org
Library Holdings: Bk Vols 79,802
Open Mon, Thurs & Fri 10-6, Tues 10-8, Wed 1-8, Sat 10-5
Friends of the Library Group
CLARENDON, 2035 Nostrand Ave, 11210, SAN 352-0234. Tel: 718-421-1159. FAX: 718-421-1244. *Managing Librn,* Sara Demian; E-mail: sdemian@bklynlibrary.org
Library Holdings: Bk Vols 59,443
Open Mon, Thurs & Fri 10-6, Wed 10-8, Sat 10-5
CLINTON HILL, 380 Washington Ave, 11238, SAN 352-0269. Tel: 718-398-8713. FAX: 718-398-8715. *Managing Librn,* Tracey Mantrone; E-mail: tmantrone@bklynlibrary.org
Library Holdings: Bk Vols 63,734
Open Mon, Thurs & Fri 10-6, Tues 10-8, Wed 1-8, Sat 10-5
Friends of the Library Group
CONEY ISLAND, 1901 Mermaid Ave, 11224, SAN 352-0293. Tel: 718-265-3220. FAX: 718-265-5026. *Managing Librn,* Boris Ioselev; E-mail: bioselev@bklynlibrary.org
Library Holdings: Bk Vols 56,933
Open Mon, Tues & Fri 10-6, Wed & Thurs 10-8, Sat 10-5
CORTELYOU, 1305 Cortelyou Rd, 11226, SAN 352-0315. Tel: 718-693-7763. FAX: 718-693-7874. *Managing Librn,* Position Currently Open
Library Holdings: Bk Vols 95,150
Open Mon, Thurs & Fri 10-6, Tues 1-8, Wed 10-8, Sat 10-5
Friends of the Library Group
CROWN HEIGHTS, 560 New York Ave, 11225, SAN 352-0323. Tel: 718-773-1180. FAX: 718-773-0144. *Managing Librn,* Janelle Welch; E-mail: mwelch@bklynlibrary.org
Library Holdings: Bk Vols 85,101
Open Mon, Thurs & Fri 10-6, Tues 1-8, Wed 10-8, Sat 10-5
CYPRESS HILLS, 1197 Sutter Ave, 11208, SAN 352-0358. Tel: 718-277-6004. FAX: 718-277-6009. *Managing Librn,* Rowshon A Perveen; E-mail: rperveen@bklynlibrary.org
Library Holdings: Bk Vols 77,432
Open Mon, Thurs & Fri 10-6, Tues 1-8, Wed 10-8, Sat 10-5
Friends of the Library Group
DEKALB BRANCH, 790 Bushwick Ave, 11221, SAN 352-0382. Tel: 718-455-3898. FAX: 718-455-4071. *Managing Librn,* Tom Brogan; E-mail: mbrogan@bklynlibrary.org
Library Holdings: Bk Vols 85,086
Open Mon, Thurs & Fri 10-6, Tues 10-8, Wed 1-8, Sat 10-5
DYKER, 8202 13th Ave, 11228, SAN 352-0412. Tel: 718-748-6261. FAX: 718-748-6370. *Managing Librn,* Ali Huang; E-mail: ahuang@bklynlibrary.org
Library Holdings: Bk Vols 53,934
Open Mon, Wed & Fri 10-6, Tues 1-8, Thurs 10-8, Sat 10-5
Friends of the Library Group
EAST FLATBUSH, 9612 Church Ave, 11212, SAN 352-0447. Tel: 718-922-0927. FAX: 718-922-2394. *Managing Librn,* Larissa Larrier; E-mail: llarrier@bklynlibrary.org
Library Holdings: Bk Vols 67,251
Closed for renovation 2021-
EASTERN PARKWAY, 1044 Eastern Pkwy, 11213, SAN 352-0471. Tel: 718-953-4225. FAX: 718-953-3970. *Managing Librn,* Josephine Evans; E-mail: mevans@bklynlibrary.org
Library Holdings: Bk Vols 76,606
Open Mon, Wed & Fri 10-6, Tues 1-8, Thurs 10-8, Sat 10-5
FLATBUSH, 22 Linden Blvd, 11226, SAN 352-0501. Tel: 718-856-0813. FAX: 718-856-0899. *Managing Librn,* Negla Ross-Paris; E-mail: nrossparis@bklynlibrary.org
Library Holdings: Bk Vols 69,920
Open Mon, Wed & Fri 10-6, Tues 1-8, Thurs 10-8, Sat 10-5
FLATLANDS, 2065 Flatbush Ave, 11234, SAN 352-0536. Tel: 718-253-4409. FAX: 718-253-5018. *Managing Librn,* Laura O'Leary; E-mail: loleary@bklynlibrary.org
Library Holdings: Bk Vols 83,574
Open Mon, Wed & Fri 10-6, Tues 1-8, Thurs 10-8, Sat 10-5
Friends of the Library Group
FORT HAMILTON, 9424 Fourth Ave, 11209, SAN 352-0560. Tel: 718-748-6919. FAX: 718-748-7335. *Managing Librn,* Jay Filan; E-mail: jfilan@bklynlibrary.org
Library Holdings: Bk Vols 58,579
Open Mon, Thurs & Fri 10-6, Tues 1-8, Wed 10-8, Sat 10-5
GERRITSEN BEACH, 2808 Gerritsen Ave, 11229. Tel: 718-368-1435. FAX: 718-368-1506. *Managing Librn,* Sunitha Jonathan; E-mail: sjonathan@bklynlibrary.org
Library Holdings: Bk Vols 66,432
Open Mon, Wed & Fri 10-6, Tues 1-8, Thurs 10-8, Sat 10-5
Friends of the Library Group
GRAVESEND, 303 Ave X, 11223, SAN 352-0625. Tel: 718-382-5792. FAX: 718-382-5926. *Managing Librn,* Mirian Rivera-Shapiro; E-mail: mriverashapiro@bklynlibrary.org
Founded 1962. Circ 335,659
Library Holdings: Bk Vols 73,500
Open Mon, Wed & Fri 10-6, Tues 1-8, Thurs 10-8, Sat 10-5
GREENPOINT, 107 Norman Ave, 11222, SAN 352-065X. Tel: 718-349-8504. FAX: 718-349-8790. *Managing Librn,* Alexa Orr; E-mail: aorr@bklynlibrary.org
Library Holdings: Bk Vols 78,100
Closed for renovation summer 2019-
Friends of the Library Group
HIGHLAWN, 1664 W 13th St, 11223, SAN 352-0684. Tel: 718-234-7208. FAX: 718-234-7238. *Managing Librn,* Danielle Shapiro; E-mail: dshapiro@bklynlibrary.org
Library Holdings: Bk Vols 72,309
Open Mon, Wed & Fri 10-6, Tues 10-8, Thurs 1-8, Sat 10-5
HOMECREST, 2525 Coney Island Ave, 11223, SAN 352-0714. Tel: 718-382-5924. FAX: 718-382-5955. *Managing Librn,* Angela Barnes; E-mail: abarnes@bklynlibrary.org
Library Holdings: Bk Vols 76,315
Open Mon, Thurs & Fri 10-6, Tues 10-8, Wed 1-8, Sat 10-5
Friends of the Library Group
JAMAICA BAY, 9727 Seaview Ave, 11236, SAN 352-0749. Tel: 718-241-3571. FAX: 718-241-1981. *Managing Librn,* Zahid Shah; E-mail: zshah@bklynlibrary.org
Library Holdings: Bk Vols 62,253
Open Mon, Tues & Fri 10-6, Wed 1-8, Thurs 10-8, Sat 10-5
Friends of the Library Group
KENSINGTON, 4207 18th Ave, 11218, SAN 352-0773. Tel: 718-436-0545. *Managing Librn,* William Lewnes; E-mail: wlewnes@bklynlibrary.org
Library Holdings: Bk Vols 72,000
Open Mon, Wed & Fri 10-6, Tues 10-8, Thurs 1-8, Sat 10-5
Friends of the Library Group
KINGS BAY, 3650 Nostrand Ave, 11229, SAN 352-0803. Tel: 718-368-1709. FAX: 718-368-1410. *Managing Librn,* Liana Alaverdova; E-mail: lalaverdova@bklynlibrary.org
Library Holdings: Bk Vols 120,335
Open Mon, Wed & Fri 10-6, Tues 10-8, Thurs 1-8, Sat 10-5
Friends of the Library Group
KINGS HIGHWAY, 2115 Ocean Ave, 11229, SAN 352-0811. Tel: 718-375-3037. *Managing Librn,* Dennis Stewart; E-mail: dstewart@bklynlibrary.org
Library Holdings: Bk Vols 132,760
Open Mon & Fri 10-6, Tues-Thurs 10-8, Sat 10-5, Sun 1-5
Friends of the Library Group
LEONARD, 81 Devoe St, 11211, SAN 352-0838. Tel: 718-486-6006. FAX: 718-486-3370. *Managing Librn,* Lauren Comito; E-mail: lcomito@bklynlibrary.org
Library Holdings: Bk Vols 65,000
Open Mon, Wed & Fri 10-6, Tues 1-8, Thurs 10-8, Sat 10-5
Friends of the Library Group
MACON, 361 Lewis Ave, 11233, SAN 352-0897. Tel: 718-573-5606. FAX: 718-573-5817. *Managing Librn,* LaMeane Isaac; E-mail: lisaac@bklynlibrary.org
Library Holdings: Bk Vols 56,003
Open Mon & Fri 10-6, Tues-Thurs 10-8, Sat 10-5, Sun 1-5
Friends of the Library Group

MAPLETON, 1702 60th St, 11204, SAN 352-0927. Tel: 718-256-2117. FAX: 718-256-1487. *Managing Librn,* Anthony Loum; E-mail: aloum@bklynlibrary.org
Library Holdings: Bk Vols 11,000
Open Mon, Tues & Fri 10-6, Wed 10-8, Thurs 1-8, Sat 10-5, Sun 1-5

MARCY, 617 DeKalb Ave, 11216, SAN 352-0951. Tel: 718-935-0032. FAX: 718-935-0045. *Managing Librn,* Marcia McGibbon; E-mail: mmcgibbon@bklynlibrary.org
Library Holdings: Bk Vols 64,430
Open Mon, Wed & Fri 10-6, Tues 1-8, Thurs 10-8, Sat 10-5

MCKINLEY PARK, 6802 Fort Hamilton Pkwy, 11219, SAN 352-0862. Tel: 718-230-2267. FAX: 718-748-7746. *Managing Librn,* John Grochalski; E-mail: jgrochalski@bklynlibrary.org
Library Holdings: Bk Vols 87,500
Open Mon, Tues & Fri 10-6, Wed 1-8, Thurs 10-8, Sat 10-5
Friends of the Library Group

MIDWOOD, 975 E 16th St, 11230, SAN 352-0986. Tel: 718-252-0967. FAX: 718-252-1263. *Managing Librn,* Steven Rosenberg; E-mail: srosenberg@bklynlibrary.org
Library Holdings: Bk Vols 99,781
Open Mon, Wed & Fri 10-6, Tues & Thurs 10-8, Sun 1-5
Friends of the Library Group

MILL BASIN, 2385 Ralph Ave, 11234, SAN 352-101X. Tel: 718-241-3973. FAX: 718-241-1957. *Managing Librn,* Lauren Comito; E-mail: lcomito@bklynlibrary.org
Library Holdings: Bk Vols 68,000
Open Mon, Tues, & Fri 10-6, Wed 10-8, Thurs 1-8, Sat 10-5
Friends of the Library Group

NEW LOTS, 665 New Lots Ave, 11207, SAN 352-1044. Tel: 718-649-0311. FAX: 718-649-0719. *Managing Librn,* Lea Salem; E-mail: lsalem@bklynlibrary.org
Library Holdings: Bk Vols 83,003
Open Mon & Fri 10-6, Tues-Thurs 10-8, Sat 10-5, Sun 1-5
Friends of the Library Group

NEW UTRECHT, 1743 86th St, 11214, SAN 352-1079. Tel: 718-236-4086. FAX: 718-234-7702. *Managing Librn,* Tambe-Tysha John; E-mail: tjohn@bklynlibrary.org
Library Holdings: Bk Vols 87,742
Open Mon & Fri 10-6, Tues-Thurs 10-8, Sat 10-5
Friends of the Library Group

PACIFIC, 25 Fourth Ave, 11217, SAN 352-1109. Tel: 718-638-1531. FAX: 718-638-1580. *Managing Librn,* Candace Vasquez; E-mail: cvasquez@bklynlibrary.org
Library Holdings: Bk Vols 62,000
Open Mon, Tues & Fri 10-6, Wed 1-8, Thurs 10-8, Sat 10-5
Friends of the Library Group

PAERDEGAT, 850 E 59th St, 11234, SAN 352-1133. Tel: 718-241-3994. FAX: 718-241-1335. *Managing Librn,* Yong-Le Yau; E-mail: yyau@bklynlibrary.org
Library Holdings: Bk Vols 65,563
Open Mon, Thurs & Fri 10-6, Tues 10-8, Wed 1-8, Sat 10-5
Friends of the Library Group

PARK SLOPE, 431 Sixth Ave, 11215, SAN 352-1168. Tel: 718-832-1853. FAX: 718-832-9024. *Managing Librn,* Stephanie Brueckel; E-mail: sbrueckel@bklynlibrary.org
Library Holdings: Bk Vols 79,981
Open Mon, Thurs & Fri 10-6, Tues 1-8, Wed 10-8, Sat 10-5
Friends of the Library Group

RED HOOK, Seven Wolcott St, 11231, SAN 352-1192. Tel: 718-935-0203. FAX: 718-935-0160. *Managing Librn,* Sandra Sutton; E-mail: ssutton@bklynlibrary.org
Library Holdings: Bk Vols 61,010
Open Mon, Wed & Fri 10-6, Tues 1-8, Thurs 10-8, Sat 10-5
Friends of the Library Group

RUGBY, 1000 Utica Ave, 11203, SAN 352-1222. Tel: 718-566-0053. FAX: 718-566-0059. *Managing Librn,* Robert Nerboso; E-mail: rnerboso@bklynlibrary.org
Library Holdings: Bk Vols 68,906
Closed for Renovation 2019-
Friends of the Library Group

RYDER, 5902 23rd Ave, 11204, SAN 352-1257. Tel: 718-331-2962. FAX: 718-331-3445. *Managing Librn,* Tisha Williams; E-mail: twilliams@bklynlibrary.org; Staff 8 (MLS 3, Non-MLS 5)
Founded 1970
Function: Adult bk club
Open Mon, Wed & Fri 10-6, Tues & Thurs 10-8, Sun 1-5

SARATOGA, Eight Thomas S Boyland St, @ Macon St, 11233, SAN 352-1281. Tel: 718-573-5224. FAX: 718-573-5402. *Managing Librn,* Monica D Williams; E-mail: mwilliams@bklynlibrary.org
Library Holdings: Bk Vols 87,346
Open Mon, Thurs & Fri 10-6, Tues 10-8, Wed 1-8, Sat 10-5
Friends of the Library Group

SERVICES FOR OLDER ADULTS, 1743 86th St, 11214, SAN 352-1273. Tel: 718-236-1760. E-mail: seniors@brooklynpubliclibrary.org. *Coordr, Outreach Serv,* Taina Evans
Open Mon-Fri 9-5
Friends of the Library Group

SHEEPSHEAD BAY, 2636 E 14th St, 11235, SAN 352-1311. Tel: 718-368-1815. FAX: 718-368-1872. *Managing Librn,* Svetlana Negrimovskaya; E-mail: snegrimovskaya@bklynlibrary.org
Library Holdings: Bk Vols 83,780
Open Mon, Tues & Fri 10-6, Wed 10-8, Thurs 1-8, Sat 10-5

SPRING CREEK, 12143 Flatlands Ave, 11207, SAN 352-1346. Tel: 718-257-6571. FAX: 718-257-6588. *Managing Librn,* Benita McCray; E-mail: bmccray@bklynlibrary.org
Library Holdings: Bk Vols 66,988
Open Mon, Tues & Fri 10-6, Wed 1-8, Thurs 10-8, Sat 10-5
Friends of the Library Group

STONE AVENUE, 581 Mother Gaston Blvd, 11212, SAN 352-1370. Tel: 718-485-8347. FAX: 718-342-0748. *Managing Librn,* Jocelyn Maynard; E-mail: jmaynard@bklynlibrary.org
Founded 1914
Library Holdings: Bk Vols 100,000
Open Mon, Tues, & Fri 10-6, Wed 1-8, Thurs 10-8, Sat 10-5
Friends of the Library Group

SUNSET PARK, 4201 Fourth Ave, 11220, SAN 352-1400. Tel: 718-435-3648. FAX: 718-567-2810. *Managing Librn,* Roxana Benavides; E-mail: rbenavides@bklynlibrary.org
Library Holdings: Bk Vols 98,200
Open Mon & Fri 10-6, Tues-Thurs 10-8, Sat 10-5
Friends of the Library Group

ULMER PARK, 2602 Bath Ave, 11214, SAN 352-1435. Tel: 718-265-3443. FAX: 718-265-5115. *Managing Librn,* Edward Flanagan; E-mail: eflanagan@bklynlibrary.org
Library Holdings: Bk Vols 72,000
Open Mon, Wed & Fri 10-6, Tues 1-8, Thurs 10-8, Sat 10-5

WASHINGTON IRVING BRANCH, 360 Irving Ave, 11237, SAN 352-1494. Tel: 718-628-8378. FAX: 718-628-8439. *Managing Librn,* Boniface N Wewe; E-mail: bwewe@bklynlibrary.org
Library Holdings: Bk Vols 60,700
Open Mon, Tues & Fri 10-6, Wed 10-8, Thurs 1-8, Sat 10-5

WALT WHITMAN BRANCH, 93 Saint Edwards St, 11205, SAN 352-146X. Tel: 718-935-0244. FAX: 718-935-0284. *Neighborhood Libr Supvr,* Janet Conton; E-mail: jconton@bklynlibrary.org
Library Holdings: Bk Vols 52,341
Open Mon, Thurs & Fri 10-6, Tues 10-8, Wed 1-8, Sat 10-5
Friends of the Library Group

WILLIAMSBURGH, 240 Division Ave, 11211, SAN 352-1524. Tel: 718-302-3485. FAX: 718-387-6972. *Managing Librn,* Catherine Skrzypek; E-mail: cskrzypek@bklynlibrary.org
Library Holdings: Bk Vols 119,489
Open Mon, Wed & Fri 10-6, Tues 1-8, Thurs 10-8, Sat 10-5

WINDSOR TERRACE, 160 E Fifth St, 11218, SAN 352-1559. Tel: 718-686-9707. FAX: 718-686-0162. *Managing Librn,* Ianthee Williams; E-mail: iwilliams@bklynlibrary.org
Library Holdings: Bk Vols 57,787
Closed for renovation 2019-
Friends of the Library Group

Bookmobiles: 4. Bk vols 6,000

S CENTER FOR FICTION*, 15 Lafayette Ave, 11217. SAN 311-8908. Tel: 212-755-6710. E-mail: info@centerforfiction.org. Web Site: www.centerforfiction.org. *Exec Dir,* Noreen Tomassi; E-mail: noreen@centerforfiction.org; *Head Librn,* Allison Escoto; E-mail: allison@centerforfiction.org; Staff 6 (MLS 1, Non-MLS 5)
Founded 1820
Library Holdings: Bk Vols 75,000; Per Subs 66
Special Collections: 19th Century Fiction & Nonfiction
Subject Interests: Lit
Wireless access
Publications: Newsletter (Bimonthly)
Open Mon 10:30-6, Tues-Sun 10:30-10
Restriction: Circ to mem only
Friends of the Library Group

M CONEY ISLAND HOSPITAL*, Harold Fink Memorial Library, 2601 Ocean Pkwy, 11235. SAN 352-1583. Tel: 718-616-3000, 718-616-4158. FAX: 718-616-4178. *Libr Dir,* Stacy Difazio; Tel: 718-616-4159, E-mail: difazios@nychhc.org; Staff 1 (MLS 1)
Library Holdings: Bk Titles 3,000; Per Subs 96
Subject Interests: Gynecology, Med, Med hospital admin, Nursing, Obstetrics, Pediatrics, Pharm, Podiatry, Surgery
Publications: Journal Holdings; Library News
Partic in Basic Health Sciences Library Network; Brooklyn-Queens-Staten Island-Manhattan-Bronx Health Sciences Librarians; Metropolitan New York Library Council; National Network of Libraries of Medicine Region 7
Restriction: Staff use only

GM DEPARTMENT OF VETERANS AFFAIRS*, Medical Center Library Service, 800 Poly Pl, 11209. SAN 310-9534. Tel: 718-836-6600, Ext 3559. FAX: 718-630-3573. Web Site: www.nyharbor.va.gov/services/library.asp. *Chief Librn,* Francine Tidona; Staff 4 (MLS 2, Non-MLS 2)
Library Holdings: e-journals 3,500; Bk Vols 5,000; Per Subs 50
Subject Interests: Allied health, Health admin, Med, Nursing, Patient educ, Psychol, Surgery
Automation Activity & Vendor Info: (Cataloging) EOS International
Open Mon-Fri 8-4:30

J KINGSBOROUGH COMMUNITY COLLEGE*, Robert J Kibbee Library, 2001 Oriental Blvd, 11235. SAN 310-9372. Tel: 718-368-5632. Circulation Tel: 718-368-5442. Interlibrary Loan Service Tel: 718-368-5971. FAX: 718-368-5482. Web Site: www.kbcc.cuny.edu/kcclibrary. *Chief Librn,* Josephine Murphy; Tel: 718-368-5584, E-mail: josephine.murphy@kbcc.cuny.edu; *Ref/Electronic Serv Librn,* Elizabeth Tompkins; Tel: 718-368-6541, E-mail: ethompkins@kbcc.cuny.edu; *Reader Serv Librn,* Mark Eaton; Tel: 718-368-6557, E-mail: Mark.Eaton@kbcc.cuny.edu; *Acq,* Cecilia Salber; Tel: 718-368-5430, E-mail: csalber@kbcc.cuny.edu; *Access Serv,* Jennifer Noe; Tel: 718-368-5438, E-mail: Jennifer.Noe@kbcc.cuny.edu; *Archives, ILL,* Julia Furay; E-mail: Julia.Furay@kbcc.cuny.edu; *Bibliog Instr,* Reabeka King; Tel: 718-368-5429, E-mail: rking@kbcc.cuny.edu; *Cat, Per, Tech Serv,* Roberta A Pike; Tel: 718-368-5639, E-mail: rpike@kbcc.cuny.edu; *Mkt, Webmaster,* Carlos Arguelles; Tel: 718-368-4674, E-mail: Carlos.Arguelles@kbcc.cuny.edu; *Reader Serv,* Michael Rosson; Tel: 718-368-5146, E-mail: Michael.Rosson@kbcc.cuny.edu; Staff 14 (MLS 11, Non-MLS 3)
Founded 1964. Enrl 14,400; Fac 293; Highest Degree: Associate
Library Holdings: Per Subs 523
Special Collections: Kingsborough Community College Coll, admin rpts, col cats, yearbks; Kingsborough Historical Society Coll, bks, memorabilia, music, newsp & photogs; Manhattan Beach (Herman Field Coll), photogs
Subject Interests: Fisheries & marine tech, Nursing, Travel & tourism
Automation Activity & Vendor Info: (Acquisitions) Ex Libris Group; (Cataloging) Ex Libris Group; (Circulation) Ex Libris Group; (Course Reserve) Ex Libris Group; (OPAC) Ex Libris Group; (Serials) Ex Libris Group
Wireless access
Publications: Bibliographic Instruction Sheets; Faculty Library Handbook; Guide to Kingsborough Community College Library; Using CUNY PLUS & Finding Books in CUNY PLUS
Partic in Metropolitan New York Library Council
Open Mon-Thurs 8am-11pm, Fri 8-5, Sat & Sun 10-3

M KINGSBROOK JEWISH MEDICAL CENTER*, Medical Library, 585 Schenectady Ave, 11203. SAN 310-9399. Interlibrary Loan Service Tel: 718-604-5690. FAX: 718-604-5539. *Dir, Med Libr,* Liza Zigelbaum; Tel: 718-504-5689, E-mail: lzigelbaum@kingsbrook.org; Staff 1 (MLS 1)
Founded 1925
Library Holdings: Bk Titles 2,000
Subject Interests: Internal med, Orthopedics, Phys med, Rehabilitation
Automation Activity & Vendor Info: (Cataloging) LibraryWorld, Inc; (Circulation) LibraryWorld, Inc; (OPAC) LibraryWorld, Inc; (Serials) LibraryWorld, Inc
Wireless access
Partic in Basic Health Sciences Library Network; Metropolitan New York Library Council
Restriction: Not open to pub

S LESBIAN HERSTORY ARCHIVES, Lesbian Herstory Educational Foundation Inc, 484 14th St, 11215. SAN 325-9250. Tel: 718-768-3953. FAX: 718-768-4663. E-mail: lesbianherstoryarchives@gmail.com. Web Site: lesbianherstoryarchives.org. *Chief Librn, Dir, Acad Tech,* Amy Beth; *Coordr,* Deborah Edel
Founded 1974
Library Holdings: Audiobooks 10; CDs 1,000; DVDs 1,500; Bk Titles 18,000; Per Subs 100; Spec Interest Per Sub 60; Videos 1,500
Special Collections: Lesbian Autobiographical Memoirs. Oral History
Subject Interests: Lesbian culture & hist
Wireless access
Open Tues-Thurs 1-5, Sat 10-5
Friends of the Library Group

C LONG ISLAND UNIVERSITY*, Brooklyn Library, One University Plaza, 11201. SAN 352-1737. Tel: 718-780-4513. FAX: 718-780-4057. E-mail: libref@brooklyn.liu.edu. Web Site: liu.edu/Brooklyn/Brooklyn-Campus-Library. *Dean, Univ Libr,* Ingrid Wang; E-mail: ingrid.wang@liu.edu; *Acq Librn, Head, Cat,* Patricia Keogh; E-mail: patricia.keogh@liu.edu; *Electronic Serv Librn,* Martin Zimerman; E-mail: martin.zimerman@liu.edu; *Coordr, Libr Instruction,* Katelyn Angell; E-mail: katelyn.angell@liu.edu; *Serials/Database Coor,* Edward Keane; E-mail: edward.keane@liu.edu
Founded 1927. Highest Degree: Doctorate
Library Holdings: AV Mats 9,610; Bk Titles 175,981; Bk Vols 273,917; Per Subs 1,412
Special Collections: 19th & 20th Century Black Social & Economic Documents (Eato Aid Society Coll, William Hamilton Relief Society Coll & New York African Society for Mutual Relief Coll); Urban Architecture & City Planning (Robert Weinberg Coll), bks, correspondence, drawings, papers, artists' bks
Subject Interests: Archives, Artists bks
Automation Activity & Vendor Info: (Acquisitions) Innovative Interfaces, Inc; (Cataloging) Innovative Interfaces, Inc; (Circulation) Innovative Interfaces, Inc; (OPAC) Innovative Interfaces, Inc; (Serials) Innovative Interfaces, Inc
Wireless access
Function: Archival coll, AV serv, ILL available, Internet access, Large print keyboards, Magnifiers for reading, Photocopying/Printing
Publications: Library Leaves (Newsletter)
Partic in Academic Libraries of Brooklyn; Metropolitan New York Library Council; OCLC Online Computer Library Center, Inc; Proquest Dialog; Westchester Academic Library Directors Organization
Restriction: Open to fac, students & qualified researchers

M MAIMONIDES MEDICAL CENTER*, George A Degenshein MD Memorial Library, Admin Bldg, Fifth Flr, 4802 Tenth Ave, 11219. SAN 310-9429. Tel: 718-283-7406. FAX: 718-283-7063. E-mail: library@maimonidesmed.org. Web Site: www.maimonidesmed.org/medical-education/medical-library. *Dir,* Lydia Friedman; E-mail: lfriedman@maimonidesmed.org; *Libr Asst,* Svetlana Fridman; Staff 4 (MLS 1, Non-MLS 3)
Founded 1952
Library Holdings: e-books 2,000; e-journals 7,000
Special Collections: Judaica Coll
Subject Interests: Dentistry, Med, Nursing
Automation Activity & Vendor Info: (Cataloging) Professional Software; (Circulation) Professional Software; (ILL) SERHOLD; (OPAC) Professional Software; (Serials) Prenax, Inc
Wireless access
Function: Wheelchair accessible
Partic in Basic Health Sciences Library Network; Brooklyn-Queens-Staten Island-Manhattan-Bronx Health Sciences Librarians; Metropolitan New York Library Council
Open Mon-Thurs 8am-9pm, Fri 8-7, Sun 1-5
Restriction: Lending to staff only, Open to authorized patrons, Use of others with permission of librn

C MEDGAR EVERS COLLEGE*, Charles Evans Inniss Memorial Library, 1650 Bedford Ave, 11225. SAN 310-9437. Tel: 718-270-4873. Interlibrary Loan Service Tel: 718-270-4997. Reference Tel: 718-270-4802. Administration Tel: 718-270-4880. Automation Services Tel: 718-270-4867. FAX: 718-270-5182. E-mail: CEIML@mec.cuny.edu. Web Site: www.mec.cuny.edu/library. *Chief Librn,* David Orenstein; Tel: 718-270-4883, E-mail: dorenstein@mec.cuny.edu; *Deputy Chair, Ref Librn,* Alexei Oulanov; Tel: 718-270-4817, E-mail: aoulanov@mec.cuny.edu; *Acq,* Ching Chang; Tel: 718-270-4865, Fax: 718-270-4908, E-mail: chingchang@mec.cuny.edu; *Info Literacy,* Karl Madden; E-mail: kmadden@mec.cuny.edu; *Ser Librn,* Eric Pellerin; Tel: 718-270-4818, E-mail: epellerin@mec.cuny.edu. Subject Specialists: *Computer info syst, Econ, Finance,* Alexei Oulanov; *Acctg, Bus admin,* Ching Chang; *Mass communications, Music, Sociol,* Karl Madden; Staff 18 (MLS 12, Non-MLS 6)
Founded 1970. Enrl 3,389; Fac 355; Highest Degree: Bachelor
Library Holdings: Bk Titles 98,345; Bk Vols 116,793; Per Subs 450
Special Collections: African American History & Literature (Dorothy Porter Coll); American Civilization; American Culture Series (PCMI Coll), ultrafiche; American Fiction Series; American Periodicals Series; Black History & Culture (Arthur A Schomburg Coll Series I), microfilm; Library of American Civilization Coll, microfiche; National Black Writers Conference Coll; Southern Africa Coll
Subject Interests: African-Am studies, Caribbean studies, Lit, Women's studies
Wireless access
Publications: Acquisitions List; Library Handbook; Library Newsletter
Partic in Metropolitan New York Library Council
Special Services for the Blind - Computer with voice synthesizer for visually impaired persons
Open Mon-Thurs 8am-11pm, Fri 8-6, Sat & Sun 10-6
Friends of the Library Group

S NEW YORK AQUARIUM, Aquarium for Wildlife Conservation, Osborn Laboratories of Marine Science Library, W Eighth St & Surf Ave, 11224. SAN 310-9461. Tel: 718-265-3437. E-mail: library@wcs.org. Web Site: www.wcs.org. *Dir, Libr & Archives,* Madeleine Thompson
Founded 1967
Library Holdings: Electronic Media & Resources 100,000; Bk Titles 4,000; Bk Vols 4,600; Per Subs 56
Subject Interests: Marine biol

Publications: Wildlife Conservation
Restriction: Open to others by appt, Staff use only

J NEW YORK CITY COLLEGE OF TECHNOLOGY*, Ursula C Schwerin Library, 300 Jay St, 11201. SAN 352-1885. Circulation Tel: 718-260-5470, 718-260-5482. Interlibrary Loan Service Tel: 718-260-5792. Reference Tel: 718-260-5485. FAX: 718-260-5497. Web Site: library.citytech.cuny.edu. *Chief Librn,* Maura Smale; E-mail: msmale@citytech.cuny.edu; Staff 12 (MLS 12)
Founded 1946. Enrl 17,000; Fac 400
Library Holdings: AV Mats 5,500; Bk Titles 132,000; Bk Vols 186,000; Per Subs 600
Special Collections: College Archives; Hotel & Restaurant Management (Menu File)
Subject Interests: Dental hygiene, Engr tech, Hotel mgt, Ophthalmic dispensing, Radiologic tech, Restaurant mgt
Automation Activity & Vendor Info: (Cataloging) Ex Libris Group
Wireless access
Publications: Library Notes
Partic in Academic Libraries of Brooklyn; Metropolitan New York Library Council; OCLC Online Computer Library Center, Inc

M NEW YORK PRESBYTERIAN BROOKLYN METHODIST HOSPITAL*, Health Sciences Library, Wesley House, Rm 2H, 501 Sixth St, 11215. (Mail add: 506 Sixth St, 11215), SAN 352-1796. Tel: 718-780-5197. FAX: 718-780-7357. E-mail: library@nyp.org. Web Site: www.nyp.org/brooklyn/medical-education/health-sciences-library-for-clinicians. *Dir,* Arpita Bose; E-mail: arb9027@nyp.org; Staff 3 (MLS 1, Non-MLS 2)
Library Holdings: AV Mats 100; e-books 60; e-journals 70; Bk Titles 2,500; Per Subs 160
Special Collections: History of Methodist Hospital; Methodist Hospital Annual Reports
Subject Interests: Med, Nursing, Surgery
Wireless access
Partic in Brooklyn-Queens-Staten Island-Manhattan-Bronx Health Sciences Librarians; Nat Libr of Med Regional Med Libr Prog; New York State Interlibrary Loan Network
Open Mon-Fri 9-8:55, Sat 10-1 & 2-5:55, Sun 10-1 & 2-4:55

GL NEW YORK STATE SUPREME COURT*, Appellate Division Second Department Library, 45 Monroe Pl, 11201. SAN 310-9267. Tel: 718-722-6356. FAX: 646-963-6419. Web Site: www.courts.state.ny.us/courts/ad2. *Principal Law Librn,* Helen Akulich; E-mail: hakulich@nycourts.gov; Staff 2 (MLS 1, Non-MLS 1)
Library Holdings: Bk Vols 35,000
Special Collections: Law Coll
Automation Activity & Vendor Info: (Acquisitions) EOS International; (Cataloging) EOS International; (Circulation) EOS International; (Serials) EOS International
Wireless access
Restriction: Not open to pub

GL NEW YORK STATE SUPREME COURT LIBRARY, BROOKLYN*, Supreme Court Bldg, Rm 349, 360 Adams St, 11201-3782. SAN 310-9488. Tel: 347-296-1144. FAX: 718-643-2412. E-mail: KSC_LAW_Library@nycourts.gov. Web Site: www.nycourts.gov/library/brooklyn. *Sr Librn,* Brenda Pantell; *Librn,* Anton Mateika
Founded 1850
Library Holdings: Bk Vols 250,000
Special Collections: Records & Briefs of the Four Appellate Courts, the Court of Appeals of the State of New York
Subject Interests: Criminal law
Wireless access
Open Mon-Fri 9-4:45
Restriction: Non-circulating

M NYU LANGONE HOSPITAL*, Health Sciences Library, 150 55th St, LB 2104, 11220. SAN 310-9410. Tel: 718-630-7200. FAX: 718-630-8918. Web Site: www.nyulangone.org. *Dir,* Irina Meyman; Staff 1 (MLS 1)
Founded 1893
Library Holdings: Bk Titles 6,250; Per Subs 232
Subject Interests: Dentistry, Family practice, Internal med, Nursing, Obstetrics & gynecology, Pathology, Pediatrics, Radiology, Surgery
Automation Activity & Vendor Info: (Cataloging) LibraryWorld, Inc; (Circulation) LibraryWorld, Inc; (OPAC) LibraryWorld, Inc
Wireless access
Partic in Basic Health Sciences Library Network
Open Mon-Fri 8-8, Sat 9-5, Sun 9-1

C THE NYU TANDON SCHOOL OF ENGINEERING*, Bern Dibner Library of Science & Technology, Five MetroTech Ctr, 11201-3840. SAN 352-1915. Tel: 718-260-3530. FAX: 718-260-3756. E-mail: dibner.library@nyu.edu. Web Site: library.nyu.edu/locations/bern-dibner-library. *Dir,* Samuel Putnam; E-mail: sp6722@nyu.edu; *Head, Sci & Eng,* Kara Whatley; Tel: 646-997-3164; Staff 9 (MLS 3, Non-MLS 6)
Founded 1854. Highest Degree: Doctorate
Library Holdings: Bk Titles 144,805; Bk Vols 185,261
Special Collections: History of Science & Technology; Paint & Surface Coatings (Mathiello Memorial Coll)
Subject Interests: Computer sci, Engr, Environ studies
Automation Activity & Vendor Info: (Cataloging) OCLC; (ILL) OCLC
Wireless access
Partic in Academic Libraries of Brooklyn; Long Island Library Resources Council; Metropolitan New York Library Council; OCLC Online Computer Library Center, Inc
Open Mon-Fri 9am-11pm, Sat & Sun 10-9
Friends of the Library Group

S PILSUDSKI INSTITUTE OF AMERICA LIBRARY*, 138 Greenpoint Ave, 11222. SAN 325-9358. Tel: 212-505-9077. FAX: 212-505-9052. E-mail: office@pilsudski.org. Web Site: www.pilsudski.org/pl/zbiory/kolekcje/147-biblioteka-instytutu. *Archivist/Librn,* Tomasz Kalata; *Archivist,* Iwona Korga
Library Holdings: Bk Vols 22,000
Wireless access
Open Mon-Fri 9-5

C PRATT INSTITUTE LIBRARIES, 200 Willoughby Ave, 11205-3897. SAN 352-194X. Tel: 718-399-4223. Circulation Tel: 718-636-3420. Interlibrary Loan Service Tel: 718-230-6841. Information Services Tel: 718-636-3704. FAX: 718-399-4401. Reference E-mail: libref@pratt.edu. Web Site: library.pratt.edu. *Dir,* Russell Abell; E-mail: rabell@pratt.edu; *Dir, Visual & Multimedia Serv,* Chris Arabadjis; Tel: 718-399-4437, E-mail: carabadj@pratt.edu; *Head, Tech Serv,* John Maier; Tel: 718-636-3659, E-mail: jmaier1@pratt.edu; *Digital Learning Librn,* Nicholas Dease; E-mail: ndease@pratt.edu; Staff 20 (MLS 17, Non-MLS 3)
Founded 1887. Enrl 4,500; Highest Degree: Master
Library Holdings: AV Mats 6,000; Bk Vols 212,934; Per Subs 800
Subject Interests: Archit, Art, Design, Libr sci
Automation Activity & Vendor Info: (Acquisitions) Innovative Interfaces, Inc - Millennium; (Cataloging) Innovative Interfaces, Inc - Millennium; (Circulation) Innovative Interfaces, Inc - Millennium; (Course Reserve) Innovative Interfaces, Inc - Millennium; (ILL) OCLC; (OPAC) Innovative Interfaces, Inc - Millennium; (Serials) Innovative Interfaces, Inc - Millennium
Wireless access
Function: Art exhibits, Audio & video playback equip for onsite use, AV serv, Computers for patron use, E-Reserves, Electronic databases & coll, Equip loans & repairs, Free DVD rentals, ILL available, Online cat, Orientations, Photocopying/Printing, Ref & res, Scanner, VHS videos, Visual arts prog, Wheelchair accessible
Partic in Academic Libraries of Brooklyn; Metropolitan New York Library Council; OCLC Online Computer Library Center, Inc
Open Mon-Thurs 8:30am-10pm, Fri 8:30-6, Sat & Sun Noon-7:30
Restriction: Authorized patrons, Authorized scholars by appt
Friends of the Library Group

Departmental Libraries:

PRATT MANHATTAN LIBRARY, 144 W 14th St, Rm 410, New York, 10011-7301, SAN 373-501X. Tel: 212-647-7546. FAX: 646-336-8797. *Coordr, Info Serv,* Harsh Taggar; E-mail: htaggar@pratt.edu; Staff 1 (MLS 1)
Library Holdings: Bk Vols 14,000; Per Subs 273
Open Mon-Thurs 10-10, Fri-Sun 10-6
Restriction: Authorized patrons, Authorized scholars by appt

C ST FRANCIS COLLEGE LIBRARY*, 180 Remsen St, 11201. SAN 352-1974. Tel: 718-489-5205. FAX: 718-489-3402. E-mail: library@sfc.edu. Web Site: library.sfc.edu. *Dir, Libr Serv,* Mona Wasserman; Tel: 718-489-5305, E-mail: mwasserman@sfc.edu; *Instruction Librn, Tech Serv,* Alex Kustanovich; Tel: 718-489-5206, E-mail: akustanovich@sfc.edu; Staff 18 (MLS 8, Non-MLS 10)
Founded 1884. Enrl 2,499; Fac 121; Highest Degree: Master
Library Holdings: Bk Titles 125,999; Per Subs 573
Special Collections: Curriculum Library
Subject Interests: Behav sci, Econ, Educ, English lit, Health mgt, Philos, Relig, Sci, Soc sci
Automation Activity & Vendor Info: (Acquisitions) Ex Libris Group; (Cataloging) Ex Libris Group; (Circulation) Ex Libris Group; (Course Reserve) Ex Libris Group; (OPAC) Ex Libris Group; (Serials) Ex Libris Group
Wireless access
Function: ILL available
Partic in Academic Libraries of Brooklyn; Metropolitan New York Library Council; OCLC Online Computer Library Center, Inc; Westchester Academic Library Directors Organization
Restriction: In-house use for visitors

C SAINT JOSEPH'S COLLEGE, McEntegart Hall Library, 222 Clinton Ave, 11205-3697. SAN 352-2032. Circulation Tel: 718-940-5878. Reference Tel: 718-940-5880. E-mail: mcentegart@sjcny.edu. Web Site: sjcny.libguides.com/libraries, www.sjcny.edu/libraries. *Executive Dir of Libr,* Elizabeth Pollicino Murphy; Tel: 631-687-2630, E-mail: epollicinomurphy@sjcny.edu; *Archivist, Ref & Instruction Librn,* Mayumi Miyaoka; Tel: 718-940-5883, E-mail: mmiyaoka@sjcny.edu; *Ref & Instruction Librn,* Rebecca Toolsidass; Tel: 718-940-5877, E-mail: rtoolsidass@sjcny.edu; Staff 11 (MLS 6, Non-MLS 5)
Founded 1916. Fac 592; Highest Degree: Master
Library Holdings: e-books 100,000
Special Collections: History of Education Rare Books Coll; Local New York History Coll, 1800s-present
Subject Interests: Acctg, Child study, Commun health, Educ, Health admin, Liberal arts, Nursing
Automation Activity & Vendor Info: (Acquisitions) Ex Libris Group; (Cataloging) Ex Libris Group; (Circulation) Ex Libris Group; (Course Reserve) Docutek; (ILL) OCLC; (OPAC) Ex Libris Group; (Serials) EBSCO Online
Wireless access
Function: 24/7 Online cat, Archival coll, Audio & video playback equip for onsite use, Bks on CD, CD-ROM, Computers for patron use, Distance learning, Doc delivery serv, E-Reserves, Electronic databases & coll, Equip loans & repairs, Free DVD rentals, ILL available, Instruction & testing, Internet access, Learning ctr, Magazines, Mail & tel request accepted, Mail loans to mem, Meeting rooms, Movies, Music CDs, Online cat, Online info literacy tutorials on the web & in blackboard, Online ref, Orientations, Outreach serv, Outside serv via phone, mail, e-mail & web, Photocopying/Printing, Printer for laptops & handheld devices, Ref & res, Ref serv available, Res libr, Scanner, Study rm, Telephone ref, Wheelchair accessible, Workshops
Publications: Library News; New Acquisitions Quarterly; Periodical Holdings - 2002-2003
Partic in Academic Libraries of Brooklyn; Metropolitan New York Library Council; OCLC Online Computer Library Center, Inc; Westchester Academic Library Directors Organization
Special Services for the Deaf - Bks on deafness & sign lang
Restriction: Access at librarian's discretion, Authorized patrons, Authorized scholars by appt, Borrowing privileges limited to fac & registered students, Borrowing requests are handled by ILL, Circ privileges for students & alumni only, Limited access for the pub, Non-circulating of rare bks, Not open to pub, Open to fac, students & qualified researchers, Open to students, fac, staff & alumni, Photo ID required for access, Restricted pub use, Use of others with permission of librn

C STATE UNIVERSITY OF NEW YORK*, Brooklyn Educational Opportunity Center, 111 Livingston St, Ste 306, 11201. SAN 310-950X. Tel: 718-802-3300, 718-802-3314. *Librn,* Joyce Bavlinka; E-mail: bavlinkaj@beoc.cuny.edu
Founded 1968
Library Holdings: Bk Vols 10,500; Per Subs 25
Subject Interests: African-Am hist
Publications: BEOC Voice (Newsletter)
Partic in Central New York Library Resources Council; SUNYConnect
Open Mon-Thurs 10-7, Fri 9-5, Sat 9-1

CM STATE UNIVERSITY OF NEW YORK DOWNSTATE HEALTH SCIENCES UNIVERSITY, The Medical Research Library of Brooklyn, 395 Lenox Rd, 11203. (Mail add: 450 Clarkson Ave, PO Box 14, 11203), SAN 322-855X. Tel: 718-270-7400. Circulation Tel: 718-270-7401. Reference Tel: 718-270-7450. FAX: 718-270-7468. Web Site: library.downstate.edu. *Interim Dir,* Mohamed Hussain; Tel: 718-270-7411, E-mail: mohamed.hussain@downstate.edu; *Director of EPIC,* Andrea Markinson; *Adminr,* Tanya McPherson; *Head, Access Serv,* Juannetta LeGree; *Head, Library Resources Mgmt Servs,* Violet Price; *Soc Media Librn,* Gregg Headrick; *Web Coordr,* Christopher Stewart; Staff 38 (MLS 10, Non-MLS 28)
Founded 1860. Enrl 1,963; Fac 306; Highest Degree: Doctorate
Library Holdings: Bks on Deafness & Sign Lang 12; e-books 60,291; e-journals 74,681; Bk Vols 50,476; Per Subs 1,116
Special Collections: The History of Medicine in the County of Kings. US Document Depository
Subject Interests: Allied health, Clinical health sci, Med, Nursing
Automation Activity & Vendor Info: (Acquisitions) Ex Libris Group; (Cataloging) Ex Libris Group; (Circulation) Ex Libris Group; (ILL) Ex Libris Group; (OPAC) Ex Libris Group; (Serials) Ex Libris Group
Wireless access
Function: Telephone ref
Partic in Metrop Regional Res & Ref Librs; OCLC Online Computer Library Center, Inc
Open Mon-Thurs 8am-9pm, Fri 8-5, Sat 9-5, Sun Noon-9

M WYCKOFF HEIGHTS MEDICAL CENTER, Medical Library, 374 Stockholm St, 11237. SAN 329-8000. Tel: 718-963-7198. Interlibrary Loan Service Tel: 718-963-7197. FAX: 718-497-7649. Web Site: www.wyckoffhospital.org/patients-visitors/health-library. *Libr Asst,* Lyudmila Frumkina; E-mail: lfrumkina@wyckoffhospital.org; Staff 1 (Non-MLS 1)
Founded 1965
Library Holdings: e-journals 300; Bk Titles 1,000; Per Subs 26
Subject Interests: Dentistry, Internal med, Nursing, Obstetrics & gynecology, Pediatrics, Podiatry, Surgery
Partic in Basic Health Sciences Library Network; Metropolitan New York Library Council
Restriction: Open to hospital affiliates only

BROOKVILLE

C LONG ISLAND UNIVERSITY POST, B Davis Schwartz Memorial Library, 720 Northern Blvd, 11548. SAN 311-2756. Tel: 516-299-2307. Circulation Tel: 516-299-2303. Interlibrary Loan Service Tel: 516-299-2898. Reference Tel: 516-299-2305, 516-299-2306. FAX: 516-299-4169. Reference FAX: 516-299-4170. Reference E-mail: post-ref@liu.edu. Web Site: liu.edu/post-library. *Dean, Univ Libr,* Ingrid Wang; Tel: 516-299-2764, E-mail: ingrid.wang@liu.edu; *Cat Librn,* Selenay Aytac, PhD; Tel: 516-299-3443, E-mail: selenay.aytac@liu.edu; *ILL Librn,* Louis Pisha; Tel: 516-299-4143, E-mail: louis.pisha@liu.edu; *Ref Librn,* Mary Kate Boyd-Byrnes; Tel: 516-299-4145, E-mail: marykate.boyd-byrnes@liu.edu; Staff 44 (MLS 23, Non-MLS 21)
Founded 1955. Enrl 8,623; Fac 253; Highest Degree: Doctorate
Library Holdings: AV Mats 4,500; e-books 188,435; Microforms 406,803; Per Subs 268; Spec Interest Per Sub 470
Special Collections: American Juvenile Coll; Architectural Library of H T Lindeberg; Archival Letters of Henry James'to His Publisher William Heineman; Archive of Architectural Plans of LIU/Post; Archive of Artist Ray Johnson: A Bad Archive; Archive of Circus & Buffalo Bill Materials; Archive of George Bernard Shaw Theatre Programs; Archive of Joan & John Digby; Archive of Joseph Cameron Cross Theatrical Coll; Archive of LIU/Post – (Main Campus Archives & Ephemera); Archive of LIU/Post's "WCWP" Radio Station; Archive of Maps from the Nassau County Research Library; Archive of Original Movie Poster Research Coll; Archive of Shogo Myaida; Archive of Southampton Campus; Archive of the Cedar Swamp Historical Society Coll; Archive of the Long Island Book Collectors; Archive of the Long Island Museum Association; Archive of the Theodore Roosevelt Society Association; Archive of Tilles Center Theatrical Programs; Archive of William E Hutton II/Joan Chapin Families; Archives of American Theatrical Programs; Archives of the Metropolitan New York College Career Planning Officer's Association; Art Archives of William Randolph Hearst; Beat Generation Coll of Karl Otto Patel; Dorothy Dayton Sorzano Theatre Coll; Eugene & Carlotta O'Neill Library; Franklin B Lord Hunting & Fishing Coll; French & Irish Literature (Winthrop Palmer Coll); Henry James Coll, bks, letters; Illuminated Manuscript Facsimiles; Joan Hoerger Fern Place Elementary School "Letters to Authors Project"; LIU/Post Campus Authors; Rare Book Coll; Saidie Scudder Archival Coll of Pre-Publication Illustrations; Samuel Beckett Archives, announcements, photog, posters, theatrical programs; Theodore Roosevelt Association Coll; Underhill Quaker Coll. US Document Depository
Subject Interests: Libr & info sci
Automation Activity & Vendor Info: (Acquisitions) Innovative Interfaces, Inc - Millennium; (Cataloging) Innovative Interfaces, Inc - Millennium; (Circulation) Innovative Interfaces, Inc - Millennium; (Course Reserve) Innovative Interfaces, Inc - Millennium; (ILL) OCLC ILLiad; (OPAC) Innovative Interfaces, Inc - Millennium; (Serials) Innovative Interfaces, Inc - Millennium
Wireless access
Function: Archival coll, Art exhibits, Computers for patron use, E-Reserves, Electronic databases & coll, ILL available, Instruction & testing, Internet access, Mail & tel request accepted, Microfiche/film & reading machines, Music CDs, Online cat, Online ref, Orientations, Photocopying/Printing, Ref & res, Ref serv available, VHS videos, Wheelchair accessible
Publications: Post Library Association Report
Partic in Long Island Library Resources Council
Restriction: Authorized patrons, Borrowing requests are handled by ILL
Friends of the Library Group

BROWNVILLE

P BROWNVILLE-GLEN PARK LIBRARY*, 216 Brown Blvd, 13615. (Mail add: PO Box 510, 13615-0510), SAN 310-9550. Tel: 315-788-7889. FAX: 315-788-9014. E-mail: brolib@ncls.org. Web Site: www.brownvillelibrary.org. *Dir,* Candace Wilde
Pop 1,600; Circ 7,951
Library Holdings: Bk Vols 5,219; Per Subs 30
Special Collections: Local Historical materials
Wireless access
Mem of North Country Library System
Open Tues & Wed 10-5, Fri 1-8, Sat 10-2

BUFFALO

S ALBRIGHT-KNOX ART GALLERY*, G Robert Strauss Jr Memorial Library, 1285 Elmwood Ave, 14222-1096. SAN 310-9577. Tel: 716-270-8240. FAX: 716-882-6213. Web Site: akat.albrightknox.org, www.albrightknox.org. *Librn,* Position Currently Open; Staff 1 (MLS 1)
Founded 1905
Library Holdings: AV Mats 100; Bk Titles 50,000; Per Subs 100
Subject Interests: Artists bks, Contemporary art, Illustrated bks, Modern art, Rare bks
Automation Activity & Vendor Info: (Acquisitions) Ex Libris Group; (Cataloging) Ex Libris Group; (Circulation) Ex Libris Group; (ILL) OCLC WorldShare Interlibrary Loan; (OPAC) Ex Libris Group; (Serials) Ex Libris Group
Wireless access
Function: Archival coll, Res libr
Publications: A Guide to the Archives of the Albright-Knox Art Gallery
Partic in Western New York Library Resources Council
Restriction: Authorized personnel only, Circulates for staff only, Internal circ only, Restricted access

L BARCLAY DAMON, LLP*, Law Library, 200 Delaware Ave., 14203. SAN 372-4603. Tel: 716-856-5500. FAX: 716-846-1222. Web Site: www.barclaydamon.com. *Dir, Info Res,* Elaine Knecht; Staff 2 (MLS 2)
Wireless access
Restriction: Employees only

J BRYANT & STRATTON BUSINESS COLLEGE*, Library Learning Center, 465 Main St, Ste 400, 14203. SAN 310-9607. Tel: 716-884-9120, Ext 261. FAX: 716-884-0091. Web Site: bryanstratton.libguides.com/buffalo. *Syst Dir of Libr,* Bennett Guy; *Librn,* Amy Joyce; E-mail: apjoyce@bryantstratton.edu; *Librn,* Christopher Dale; Staff 11 (MLS 2, Non-MLS 9)
Founded 1867. Enrl 650
Library Holdings: Bk Titles 3,702; Bk Vols 3,900; Per Subs 130
Special Collections: Bryant & Stratton historical materials
Subject Interests: Acctg, Criminal justice, Info tech, Med admin
Automation Activity & Vendor Info: (Cataloging) Follett Software; (Circulation) Follett Software; (OPAC) Follett Software; (Serials) EBSCO Online
Wireless access
Function: Res libr
Publications: Echo (Newsletter)
Partic in Western New York Library Resources Council
Open Mon-Thurs 9-9, Fri & Sat 9-1

P BUFFALO & ERIE COUNTY PUBLIC LIBRARY SYSTEM*, Downtown Central Library, One Lafayette Sq, 14203-1887. SAN 352-2180. Tel: 716-858-8900. FAX: 716-845-9053. Web Site: www.buffalolib.org. *Dir,* Mary Jean Jakubowski; E-mail: jakubowskim@buffalolib.org; *Dep Dir-Chief Financial Officer,* Kenneth H Stone; E-mail: stonek@buffalolib.org; *Chief Operating Officer,* Jeannine M Doyle; E-mail: DoyleJ@buffalolib.org; *Asst Deputy Dir-Development & Communications,* Joy Testa Cinquino; E-mail: testaj@buffalolib.org; *Asst Deputy Dir-Public Services,* Dorinda Darden; E-mail: dardend@buffalolib.org; Staff 74 (MLS 58, Non-MLS 16)
Founded 1836. Pop 919,040; Circ 8,097,152
Library Holdings: CDs 77,243; DVDs 61,090; e-books 4,727; Electronic Media & Resources 4,306; Bk Vols 1,401,318; Per Subs 1,339
Special Collections: Foundations; Genealogy Coll; Local History Coll; Maps; Mark Twain Coll; Niagara Falls Prints; Patents; Sheet Music; World War I & II Posters. State Document Depository; US Document Depository
Subject Interests: Art, Bus, Foundations, Genealogy, Hist, Lit, Local hist, Maps, Music, Natural sci, Patents, Sheet music
Automation Activity & Vendor Info: (Acquisitions) SirsiDynix; (Cataloging) SirsiDynix; (Circulation) SirsiDynix; (OPAC) SirsiDynix; (Serials) SirsiDynix
Wireless access
Function: 24/7 Electronic res, 24/7 Online cat, 3D Printer, Adult literacy prog, Archival coll, Art exhibits, Audiobks via web, AV serv, Bk club(s), Bks on CD, Chess club, Children's prog, Computer training, Computers for patron use, Digital talking bks, Distance learning, Electronic databases & coll, Family literacy, For res purposes, Free DVD rentals, Genealogy discussion group, Govt ref serv, Health sci info serv, Holiday prog, ILL available, Internet access, Jail serv, Life-long learning prog for all ages, Literacy & newcomer serv, Magazines, Mail & tel request accepted, Makerspace, Meeting rooms, Microfiche/film & reading machines, Movies, Music CDs, Online cat, Online info literacy tutorials on the web & in blackboard, Online ref, Outreach serv, OverDrive digital audio bks, Photocopying/Printing, Prog for adults, Prog for children & young adult, Ref & res, Ref serv available, Res assist avail, Res libr, Senior computer classes, Spanish lang bks, STEM programs, Story hour, Study rm, Summer & winter reading prog, Summer reading prog, Tax forms, Teen prog, Telephone ref, VHS videos, Visual arts prog, Wheelchair accessible, Winter reading prog, Workshops, Writing prog
Publications: Annual Report of Director; Message from the Director - Updates (Online only)
Member Libraries: Alden-Ewell Free Library; Amherst Public Library; Angola Public Library; Aurora Town Public Library; Boston Free Library; Cheektowaga Public Library; City of Tonawanda Public Library; Clarence Public Library; Collins Public Library; Eden Library; Elma Public Library; Grand Island Memorial Library; Hamburg Public Library; Hulbert Public Library of the Town of Concord; Lackawanna Public Library; Lancaster Public Library; Marilla Free Library; Newstead Public Library; Orchard Park Public Library; Town of North Collins Public Library; Town of Tonawanda Public Library; West Seneca Public Library
Partic in OCLC Online Computer Library Center, Inc; Western New York Library Resources Council
Special Services for the Blind - Computer with voice synthesizer for visually impaired persons; Descriptive video serv (DVS); Dragon Naturally Speaking software; Magnifiers; Radio reading serv; Reader equip; Talking bks; ZoomText magnification & reading software
Open Mon-Wed, Fri & Sat 8:30-6, Thurs 8:30-8
Branches: 10
LEROY R COLES JR BRANCH LIBRARY, 1187 E Delavan Ave, 14215-3801, SAN 352-2334. Tel: 716-896-4433. FAX: 716-896-4433. E-mail: edl@buffalolib.org. *Librn,* John Stone
Circ 71,503
Library Holdings: CDs 1,460; DVDs 3,752; Bk Vols 12,966
Open Mon & Tues 12-8, Thurs & Fri 10-6, Sat 9-5
Friends of the Library Group
CRANE, 633 Elmwood Ave, 14222, SAN 352-2245. Tel: 716-883-6651. FAX: 716-883-6651. E-mail: cra@buffalolib.org. *Librn,* Joseph Mitch
Circ 148,524
Library Holdings: CDs 3,441; DVDs 4,066; Bk Vols 17,679
Open Mon & Thurs 12-8, Tues, Fri & Sat 10-6
Friends of the Library Group
DUDLEY, 2010 S Park Ave, 14220-1894, SAN 352-227X. Tel: 716-823-1854. FAX: 716-823-1854. E-mail: dud@buffalolib.org. *Librn,* Daniel Lewanbowski
Circ 121,764
Library Holdings: CDs 3,344; DVDs 4,816; Bk Vols 18,078
Open Mon, Wed & Sat 10-6, Tues & Thurs 12-8
Friends of the Library Group
EAST CLINTON, 1929 Clinton St, 14206-3214, SAN 352-230X. Tel: 716-823-5626. FAX: 716-823-5626. E-mail: ecl@buffalolib.org. *Br Mgr,* Catherine Shea
Circ 62,239
Library Holdings: CDs 1,618; DVDs 3,642; Bk Vols 11,574
Open Mon & Wed 12-8, Fri 10-6, Sat 9-5
Friends of the Library Group
ERIE COUNTY CORRECTIONAL FACILITY, 11581 Walden Ave, Alden, 14004-0300, SAN 352-2318. Tel: 716-858-5578. *Institutional Serv Mgr,* Daniel Caufield
Circ 145,208
Restriction: Not open to pub
ERIE COUNTY HOLDING CENTER, 40 Delaware Ave, 14202-3999, SAN 352-2342. Tel: 716-858-8909. *Mgr,* Daniel Caufield
Circ 44,386
Restriction: Not open to pub
ISAIAS GONZALEZ-SOTO BRANCH LIBRARY, 280 Porter Ave, 14201-1030, SAN 352-2601. Tel: 716-882-1537. FAX: 716-882-1537. E-mail: nia@buffalolib.org. *Librn,* Linda Rizzo
Circ 83,014
Library Holdings: CDs 2,348; DVDs 4,274; Bk Vols 17,016
Subject Interests: Spanish lang
Open Mon-Thurs 12-8, Fri & Sat 9-5
Friends of the Library Group
FRANK E MERRIWEATHER JR LIBRARY, 1324 Jefferson Ave, 14208, SAN 352-2636. Tel: 716-883-4418. FAX: 716-883-4418. E-mail: mrw@buffalolib.org. *Librn,* Linda Rizzo
Circ 104,137
Library Holdings: CDs 2,384; DVDs 4,281; Bk Vols 30,040
Special Collections: Black History Reference
Open Mon-Thurs 12-8, Fri & Sat 10-6, Sun 12-5
Friends of the Library Group
NORTH PARK, 975 Hertel Ave, 14216, SAN 352-2660. Tel: 716-875-3748. FAX: 716-875-3748. E-mail: npk@buffalolib.org. *Mgr,* Paul Guminski
Circ 77,486
Library Holdings: CDs 1,771; DVDs 2,065; Bk Vols 8,820
Open Mon & Sat 10-6, Wed & Fri 12-8
Friends of the Library Group
ELAINE M PANTY BRANCH LIBRARY, 820 Tonawanda St, 14207-1448, SAN 352-2725. Tel: 716-875-0562. E-mail: riv@buffalolib.org. *Br Mgr,* Rosalyn Damico; Tel: 716-875-0562
Circ 89,534
Library Holdings: CDs 1,905; DVDs 4,375; Bk Vols 16,818
Open Mon & Thurs 12-8, Tues, Wed & Sat 10-6

Friends of the Library Group
Bookmobiles: Librn, Samantha Pupora. Bk vols 3,000

S BUFFALO HISTORY MUSEUM RESEARCH LIBRARY, One Museum Ct, 14216-3199. SAN 310-9615. Tel: 716-873-9644. E-mail: library@buffalohistory.org. Web Site: buffalohistory.org/library-collections. *Dir, Libr & Archives,* Cynthia M Van Ness; *Asst Librn,* Position Currently Open. Subject Specialists: *Local hist,* Cynthia M Van Ness; Staff 2.2 (MLS 2, Non-MLS 0.2)
Founded 1862
Library Holdings: Electronic Media & Resources 130; Microforms 6,500; Bk Vols 25,000; Per Subs 200
Special Collections: Iconographic Coll, bulk 1870-1980, images; Larkin Company photographs & business records; Manuscripts Coll; Millard Fillmore papers; Oversized Works on Paper Coll, drawings, prints, plans & broadsides; Photographs Coll; War of 1812 Coll, bks, govt doc, ms, sermons; Wilbur Porterfield photographs
Subject Interests: Local hist, Maps
Automation Activity & Vendor Info: (Cataloging) OCLC Connexion; (OPAC) LibraryWorld, Inc
Wireless access
Function: 24/7 Online cat, Archival coll, Bus archives, Mail & tel request accepted, Microfiche/film & reading machines, Online cat, Online ref, Photocopying/Printing, Ref serv available, Res libr, Telephone ref, Workshops
Partic in OCLC Online Computer Library Center, Inc; Western New York Library Resources Council
Restriction: Closed stack, Free to mem, In-house use for visitors, Non-circulating, Not a lending libr, Off-site coll in storage - retrieval as requested, Open by appt only, Pub use on premises

S BUFFALO MUSEUM OF SCIENCE, Research Library, 1020 Humboldt Pkwy, 14211. SAN 310-964X. Tel: 716-896-5200. FAX: 716-897-6723. Web Site: www.sciencebuff.org. *Dir of Coll,* Kathryn H Leacock; E-mail: kleacock@sciencebuff.org; Staff 1 (MLS 1)
Founded 1861
Library Holdings: Bk Titles 15,000; Bk Vols 45,000; Per Subs 500
Special Collections: Oriental Art & Archaelogy (Elizabeth W Hamlin Coll); Tifft Farm Oral History Coll
Subject Interests: Anthrop, Astronomy, Botany, Far Eastern archaeol, Far Eastern art, Geol, Invertebrate zool, Mineralogy, Mycology, Near Eastern archaeol, Near Eastern art, Paleontology, Vertebrate zool
Automation Activity & Vendor Info: (Cataloging) Follett Software
Wireless access
Publications: Milestones of Science
Partic in Western New York Library Resources Council
Restriction: Open by appt only

C BUFFALO STATE UNIVERSITY OF NEW YORK*, E H Butler Library, 1300 Elmwood Ave, 14222. SAN 310-9879. Tel: 716-878-6314. Circulation Tel: 716-878-6303. Interlibrary Loan Service Tel: 716-878-6310. Reference Tel: 716-878-6300. FAX: 716-878-3134. Web Site: library.buffalostate.edu. *Interim Libr Dir,* Marc Dewey Bayer; Tel: 716-878-6305, E-mail: bayermd@buffalostate.edu; *Head, Archives & Spec Coll,* Daniel DiLandro; Tel: 716-878-6308, E-mail: dilanddm@buffalostate.edu; *Assoc Librn, Curator,* Wanda M Slawinska; Tel: 716-878-6208, E-mail: slawinwm@buffalostate.edu; *Info Syst Librn,* Joseph W Riggie; Tel: 716-878-6320, E-mail: riggiejw@buffalostate.edu. Subject Specialists: *Hist,* Daniel DiLandro; Staff 43 (MLS 19, Non-MLS 24)
Founded 1910. Enrl 9,413; Fac 425; Highest Degree: Master
Library Holdings: AV Mats 9,868; CDs 2,144; DVDs 7,609; e-books 124,095; Microforms 409,107; Bk Titles 472,458; Bk Vols 670,330; Per Subs 61,171
Special Collections: Children's Author Lois Lenski Coll, bks, illustrations; Courier Express Coll; Creative Education (Creative Studies Coll), bks, microfilm; Elementary & Secondary Curriculum Coll; Francis E Fronczak Coll Inventory, cats; Historical Children's Books (Hertha Ganey Coll); Historical Textbooks (Kempke-Root Coll); Isaac Klein Papers; Jazz (William H Talmadge Coll); Lester Glassner Coll; Local Polish Community (Fronczak Coll); Lois Lenski Children's Coll; Selig Adler Jewish Archives; Tom Fontana Coll
Subject Interests: African, African-Am, Applied arts, Criminal justice, Educ, Exceptional children educ, Fine arts, Local hist
Automation Activity & Vendor Info: (Acquisitions) Ex Libris Group; (Cataloging) Ex Libris Group; (Circulation) Ex Libris Group; (Course Reserve) Ex Libris Group; (ILL) OCLC ILLiad; (OPAC) Ex Libris Group; (Serials) SerialsSolutions
Wireless access
Function: Archival coll, Art exhibits, Audio & video playback equip for onsite use, AV serv, Computer training, Computers for patron use, Distance learning, Doc delivery serv, Electronic databases & coll, Equip loans & repairs, Games & aids for people with disabilities, Health sci info serv, ILL available, Internet access, Learning ctr, Magnifiers for reading, Mail & tel request accepted, Music CDs, Online cat, Online ref, Photocopying/Printing, Ref serv available, Scanner, VHS videos, Wheelchair accessible, Workshops
Partic in OCLC Online Computer Library Center, Inc; SUNYConnect; Westchester Academic Library Directors Organization; Western New York Library Resources Council
Special Services for the Deaf - Assistive tech; Bks on deafness & sign lang; Coll on deaf educ; High interest/low vocabulary bks
Special Services for the Blind - Assistive/Adapted tech devices, equip & products; Audio mat; Computer with voice synthesizer for visually impaired persons; Duplicating spec requests; Micro-computer access & training; Networked computers with assistive software; Reader equip; Ref serv; Screen enlargement software for people with visual disabilities; Talking bks; Telesensory screen enlarger & speech synthesis interface to the OPAC; ZoomText magnification & reading software
Restriction: Open to pub for ref & circ; with some limitations, Open to students, fac & staff
Friends of the Library Group

S BURCHFIELD PENNEY ART CENTER, Archives & Library, Buffalo State College, 1300 Elmwood Ave, 14222. SAN 375-2321. Tel: 716-878-3216, 716-878-6011. FAX: 716-878-6003. E-mail: burchfld@buffalostate.edu. Web Site: www.burchfieldpenney.org. *Curator, Exhibitions Mgr,* Tullis Johnson; E-mail: johnsote@buffalostate.edu; *Archivist,* Heather Gring; E-mail: gringha@buffalostate.edu; *Curator,* Nancy Weekly; E-mail: weeklyns@buffalostate.edu; Staff 3 (MLS 1, Non-MLS 2)
Founded 1966
Library Holdings: Bk Vols 3,500
Special Collections: Art Institute of Buffalo; Artpark Archive; Buffalo Society of Artists Archive; Charles Cary Rumsey Archive; Charles E Burchfield Archive; Frank K M Rehn Galleries Archive; Hollis Frampton Archive; Martha Visser't Hooft Archive; Milton Rogovin Archive; Patteran Society Archive; Paul Sharits Archive; Virgina Cuthbert/Philip Eliot Archive; Western New York Art Archives. Municipal Document Depository; Oral History; US Document Depository
Wireless access
Function: Archival coll, Art exhibits, Res libr
Partic in Western New York Library Resources Council
Restriction: Non-circulating coll, Non-circulating of rare bks, Not a lending libr, Open by appt only

C CANISIUS COLLEGE, Andrew L Bouwhuis Library, 2001 Main St, 14208-1098. SAN 310-9674. Tel: 716-888-8411. E-mail: library@canisius.edu, libweb@canisius.edu. Web Site: library.canisius.edu. *Libr Dir,* Kristine E Kasbohm; Tel: 716-888-8410, E-mail: kasbohmk@canisius.edu; *Collections & Instructional Services Librn,* Lisa Sullivan; Tel: 716-888-8403, E-mail: sullival@canisius.edu; *Archivist, Ref Librn,* Kathleen DeLaney; Tel: 716-888-8421, E-mail: delaneyk@canisius.edu; *Syst Librn,* Jeff Proehl; Tel: 716-888-8405, E-mail: proehlj@canisius.edu; Staff 8 (MLS 7, Non-MLS 1)
Founded 1870. Enrl 3,503; Fac 406; Highest Degree: Master
Library Holdings: AV Mats 11,297; e-books 38,092; e-journals 52,129; Bk Titles 242,144; Bk Vols 297,916; Per Subs 217
Special Collections: Jesuitica Coll
Subject Interests: Philos, Relig
Wireless access
Partic in ConnectNY, Inc; Westchester Academic Library Directors Organization; Western New York Library Resources Council
Open Mon-Thurs 8am-Midnight, Fri 8-4, Sat 10-2, Sun 2pm-Midnight

S COLLECTOR CAR APPRAISERS ASSOCIATION LIBRARY, 24 Myrtle Ave, 14204. SAN 322-757X. Tel: 716-855-1931. E-mail: jts1944@gmail.com. *Librn,* Mary Ann Sandoro
Library Holdings: Bk Titles 2,400; Bk Vols 3,000; Per Subs 125
Subject Interests: Autos, Bikes, Motorcycles
Restriction: Open by appt only

C D'YOUVILLE COLLEGE*, Montante Family Library, 320 Porter Ave, 14201-1084. SAN 310-9690. Tel: 716-829-7618. Reference Tel: 716-829-7747. E-mail: refdesk@dyc.edu. Web Site: library.dyc.edu. *Libr Dir,* Rand Bellavia; Tel: 716-829-7616, E-mail: bellavia@dyc.edu; *Database Librn, ILL Librn, Ser Librn,* Jill Church; Tel: 716-829-8107, E-mail: churchj@dyc.edu; *Digital Serv Librn,* Ted Sherman; E-mail: shermant@dyc.edu; *Online Learning Librn,* BreeAna Baker; Tel: 716 597-6803, E-mail: bakerb@dyc.edu; *Res & Instruction Librn,* Debra Lucas-Alieri; Tel: 716-829-7764, E-mail: lucasd@dyc.edu; *Tech Serv Librn,* Mark Bialkowski; Tel: 716 829-8106, E-mail: bialkowm@dyc.edu; Staff 7 (MLS 7)
Founded 1908. Enrl 2,400; Fac 95; Highest Degree: Doctorate
Library Holdings: AV Mats 2,500; e-books 80,000; e-journals 100,000; Bk Titles 52,000; Bk Vols 68,000; Per Subs 100
Subject Interests: Nursing, Occupational therapy, Phys therapy

Automation Activity & Vendor Info: (Acquisitions) Koha; (Cataloging) Koha; (Circulation) Koha; (Course Reserve) Koha; (Discovery) EBSCO Discovery Service; (ILL) OCLC Tipasa; (OPAC) Koha; (Serials) Koha
Wireless access
Partic in OCLC Online Computer Library Center, Inc; Western New York Library Resources Council
Special Services for the Blind - Reader equip

J ERIE COMMUNITY COLLEGE-CITY CAMPUS*, Library Resource Center, 121 Ellicott St, Rm 101, 14203. SAN 320-0558. Tel: 716-851-1074. FAX: 716-270-5987. Web Site: www.ecc.edu/library. *Col Librn,* Emily Carlin; Tel: 716-851-1774, E-mail: carlin@ecc.edu; Staff 5 (MLS 5)
Founded 1971
Library Holdings: Bk Vols 26,000; Per Subs 210
Automation Activity & Vendor Info: (Cataloging) Ex Libris Group; (Circulation) Ex Libris Group; (ILL) OCLC; (OPAC) Ex Libris Group
Wireless access
Partic in OCLC Online Computer Library Center, Inc; SUNYConnect; Western New York Library Resources Council
Open Mon-Thurs 8am-8:45pm, Fri 8-4, Sat 9-3

M ERIE COUNTY MEDICAL CENTER*, W Yerby Jones Memorial Library, 462 Grider St, 14215. SAN 310-9720. Tel: 716-898-3939. FAX: 716-898-3291. E-mail: library@ecmc.edu. Web Site: www.ecmc.edu. *Librn,* Susan Forrest
Founded 1921
Library Holdings: DVDs 200; e-books 150; e-journals 2,700; Bk Titles 2,400; Bk Vols 2,500; Per Subs 185; Videos 50
Subject Interests: Burns, Kidney transplant, Med, Nursing, Surgery, Trauma
Automation Activity & Vendor Info: (Acquisitions) SirsiDynix; (Cataloging) SirsiDynix; (Circulation) SirsiDynix; (OPAC) SirsiDynix; (Serials) SirsiDynix
Wireless access
Partic in Library Consortium of Health Institutions in Buffalo; OCLC Online Computer Library Center, Inc; Western New York Library Resources Council
Restriction: Staff use only

L HODGSON RUSS LLP*, Law Library, 140 Pearl St, Ste 100, 14202-4040. SAN 372-4158. Tel: 716-848-1282, 716-856-4000. FAX: 716-849-0349. Web Site: www.hodgsonruss.com. *Librn,* Jeanne Seeds; E-mail: jseeds@hodgsonruss.com
Library Holdings: Bk Vols 15,000
Automation Activity & Vendor Info: (Cataloging) EOS International; (Circulation) EOS International; (OPAC) EOS International
Wireless access
Open Mon-Fri 8:30-5

M KALEIDA HEALTH - BUFFALO GENERAL MEDICAL CENTER, A H Aaron Health Sciences Library, Bldg D, 4th Flr, 100 High St, 14203. SAN 352-2784. Tel: 716-859-2878. FAX: 716-859-1527. Web Site: www.kaleidahealth.org/bgmc. *Circuit Librn,* Adrienne Doepp; E-mail: adoepp@wnylrc.org; Staff 0.5 (MLS 0.5)
Founded 1920
Subject Interests: Allied health, Hospital admin, Med, Nursing
Wireless access
Partic in Library Consortium of Health Institutions in Buffalo; Western New York Library Resources Council
Open Tues & Wed 9-4

C MEDAILLE COLLEGE LIBRARY*, 18 Agassiz Circle, 14214. SAN 310-9771. Tel: 716-880-2283. FAX: 716-884-9638. E-mail: library@medaille.edu. Web Site: library.medaille.edu. *Libr Dir,* Andrew Yeager; E-mail: ayeager@medaille.edu; *Adult & Grad Studies Librn,* Thomas Orrange; E-mail: tmo39@medaille.edu; *Ref & Instruction Librn,* Deborah Ceppaglia; E-mail: dceppaglia@medaille.edu; *Syst Spec,* Chris McDermott; E-mail: cmcdermott@medaille.edu; Staff 3 (MLS 3)
Founded 1937. Enrl 2,500; Fac 80; Highest Degree: Master
Library Holdings: DVDs 250; e-books 20,000; Bk Titles 55,000; Bk Vols 57,000; Per Subs 320
Special Collections: Elementary Education (Donna Phillips Coll); Rare Books on Buffalo History; Veterinary Technology
Subject Interests: Bus mgt systs, Children's lit, Educ, Media, Psychol, Veterinary sci
Automation Activity & Vendor Info: (Cataloging) Innovative Interfaces, Inc - Millennium; (Circulation) Innovative Interfaces, Inc - Millennium; (OPAC) Innovative Interfaces, Inc - Millennium
Wireless access
Partic in Western New York Library Resources Council
Open Mon-Thurs 7:30am-Midnight, Fri 7:30-6, Sat 11-4, Sun 11-9

GL NEW YORK SUPREME COURT, Eighth Judicial District Library, 77 W Eagle St, 14202. SAN 310-981X. Tel: 716-845-9400. FAX: 716-852-3454. E-mail: sclbuff@courts.state.ny.us. Web Site: ww2.nycourts.gov/library/buffalo/index.shtml. *Librn,* Angela Patti; Tel: 716-845-9391; Staff 7 (MLS 2, Non-MLS 5)
Founded 1863
Library Holdings: Bk Titles 6,500; Bk Vols 350,000; Per Subs 226
Special Collections: Court of Appeals Records & Briefs; Law Reports (Old English & Canadian Reports Coll); New York Nominatives; NYCRR Backfile
Subject Interests: Law
Wireless access
Partic in LRS; OCLC Online Computer Library Center, Inc
Open Mon-Fri 8:30-5

L PHILLIPS, LYTLE LLP LIBRARY*, 125 Main St, 14203-2887. SAN 310-9836. Tel: 716-847-5470. Reference Tel: 716-847-5471. FAX: 716-852-6100. E-mail: info@phillipslytle.com. Web Site: phillipslytle.com/location/buffalo. *Info Serv Mgr,* Kristine Westphal
Library Holdings: Bk Titles 25,000; Per Subs 120
Subject Interests: Law, Legislation
Restriction: Staff use only

GM ROSWELL PARK COMPREHENSIVE CANCER CENTER*, Dr Edwin A Mirand Library, Elm & Carlton Sts, 14263. SAN 310-9844. Tel: 716-845-5966. FAX: 716-845-8699. E-mail: ill.library@roswellpark.org. Web Site: www.roswellpark.org/education/library. *Librn,* Gayle Ablove; *Librn,* Lauren Alessi; *Librn,* Lisabeth Becker; *Asst Med Librn,* Danielle Glynn; Staff 4 (MLS 4)
Founded 1898
Library Holdings: Bk Vols 92,000; Per Subs 1,200
Subject Interests: Chem, Genetics, Molecular biol, Oncology, Pharmacology
Automation Activity & Vendor Info: (Cataloging) OCLC Worldshare Management Services; (Circulation) OCLC Worldshare Management Services; (ILL) OCLC ILLiad; (OPAC) OCLC Worldshare Management Services
Wireless access
Function: Doc delivery serv, Electronic databases & coll, ILL available, Online cat, Photocopying/Printing
Partic in National Network of Libraries of Medicine Region 7; OCLC Online Computer Library Center, Inc; Western New York Library Resources Council
Restriction: Open to fac, students & qualified researchers, Pub use on premises, Restricted borrowing privileges, Restricted loan policy

S SAINT MARY'S SCHOOL FOR THE DEAF LIBRARY*, 2253 Main St, 14214. SAN 310-9852. Tel: 716-834-7200, Ext 152. Web Site: www.smsdk12.org/domain/117. *Librn,* Heather Karas; E-mail: heatherk@smsdk12.org; Staff 1 (MLS 1)
Founded 1964. Fac 1; Highest Degree: Master
Library Holdings: Bk Titles 25,000; Per Subs 75
Subject Interests: Audiology, Deaf, Deaf culture, Deaf studies, Sign lang, Spec educ with emphasis on deafness
Automation Activity & Vendor Info: (Acquisitions) Follett Software; (Cataloging) Follett Software; (Circulation) Follett Software; (Course Reserve) Follett Software; (ILL) Follett Software; (Media Booking) Follett Software; (Serials) Follett Software
Wireless access
Function: Computers for patron use, Electronic databases & coll, Family literacy, Free DVD rentals, Games & aids for people with disabilities, Magazines, Photocopying/Printing, Printer for laptops & handheld devices, Prog for children & young adult
Partic in Western New York Library Resources Council
Open Mon-Thurs 8:20-3
Restriction: Authorized patrons

M SISTERS OF CHARITY HOSPITAL*, Medical Staff Library, 2157 Main St, 14215. SAN 320-3999. Tel: 716-862-1256. *Librn,* Olivia Helfer; E-mail: ohelfer@chbuffalo.org; Staff 2 (MLS 1, Non-MLS 1)
Founded 1960
Library Holdings: Bk Titles 1,053
Partic in Kentucky Medical Library Association; National Network of Libraries of Medicine Region 7

M SISTERS OF CHARITY HOSPITAL MEDICAL LIBRARY*, 2157 Main St, 6th Flr, 14214. SAN 310-9860. Tel: 716-862-1256. FAX: 716-862-1883. Web Site: www.chsbuffalo.org/sisters-charity-hospital. *Med Librn,* Olivia Helfer; E-mail: ohelfer@chsbuffalo.org; Staff 1 (MLS 1)
Founded 1948
Library Holdings: Bk Titles 125; Bk Vols 300
Special Collections: Spiritual Care
Wireless access
Open Mon-Fri 8-4

R TEMPLE BETH ZION*, Aaron & Bertha Broder Center for Jewish Education, 700 Sweet Home Rd, 14226. SAN 352-3292. Tel: 716-836-6565. FAX: 716-831-1126. Web Site: www.tbz.org.
Founded 1915
Library Holdings: Bk Vols 20,000; Per Subs 22
Special Collections: Children's Judaica
Subject Interests: Judaica
Wireless access
Publications: American Jewish Odyssey, Annotated Bibliography of the Jewish Experience in America; Jewish Children's Literature, Annotated Bibliography of Books on Judaism & Jewish History; Lest We Forget, A Selected Annotated List of Books on the Holocaust

JR TROCAIRE COLLEGE LIBRARY, Rachel R Savarino Library, 360 Choate Ave, 14220-2094. SAN 310-9887. Tel: 716-827-2434. Administration Tel: 716-827-2436. Automation Services Tel: 716-827-2447. FAX: 716-828-6102. E-mail: libraryhelp@trocaire.edu. Web Site: library.trocaire.edu. *Interim Libr Mgr,* Michele Brancato; E-mail: brancatom@trocaire.edu; *Ref Librn,* Jessica Gavin; E-mail: gavinj@trocaire.edu; Staff 4.5 (MLS 4.5)
Founded 1958. Enrl 1,006; Fac 3; Highest Degree: Bachelor
Library Holdings: CDs 18; DVDs 422; e-books 998; e-journals 3; Electronic Media & Resources 37; Bk Titles 13,350; Bk Vols 14,200; Per Subs 85; Videos 37
Subject Interests: Allied health, Computer network, Hospitality, Liberal arts, Nursing
Automation Activity & Vendor Info: (Acquisitions) ComPanion Corp; (Cataloging) ComPanion Corp; (Circulation) ComPanion Corp; (OPAC) ComPanion Corp; (Serials) SerialsSolutions
Wireless access
Function: Archival coll, Computers for patron use, Distance learning, E-Reserves, Electronic databases & coll, ILL available, Internet access, Orientations, Ref & res
Partic in Western New York Library Resources Council
Open Mon-Thurs 8-8, Fri 8-4, Sat 9-2
Restriction: Fee for pub use, Open to students, fac, staff & alumni

A UNITED STATES ARMY, Corps of Engineers Buffalo District Technical Library, 1776 Niagara St, 14201-3199. SAN 352-3357. Tel: 716-879-4178. FAX: 716-879-6468. E-mail: buffalo-library@usace.army.mil. Web Site: www.lrb.usace.army.mil. *Librn,* Eric N Kolber
Founded 1976
Library Holdings: Bk Titles 15,000; Per Subs 70
Special Collections: Aerial Photography; Government Documents; Great Lakes Research; Microcomputer Software Bank; Nuclear Waste Disposal; Radioactive Waste Isolation
Subject Interests: Chem, Construction, Econ, Engr, Environ studies, Geol, Hydrol, Water res develop
Automation Activity & Vendor Info: (Cataloging) OCLC; (ILL) OCLC
Wireless access
Publications: Buffalo District Technical Library
Partic in OCLC Online Computer Library Center, Inc; Proquest Dialog
Open Mon-Fri 8-4:30

C UNIVERSITY AT BUFFALO LIBRARIES-STATE UNIVERSITY OF NEW YORK*, University Libraries, 433 Capen Hall, 14260-1625. SAN 352-2903. Tel: 716-645-2965. E-mail: library@buffalo.edu. Web Site: library.buffalo.edu. *Vice Provost for Libr,* Eviava Weinraub Lajoie; E-mail: evvivawe@buffalo.edu; Staff 160 (MLS 102, Non-MLS 58)
Founded 1922. Enrl 28,192; Fac 90; Highest Degree: Doctorate
Library Holdings: e-books 725,000; e-journals 48,400; Microforms 6,100,000; Bk Vols 3,852,074; Per Subs 80,431
Special Collections: Archives (University Archives & Manuscripts Coll); Frank Lloyd Wright/Darwin Martin House Coll; George Kelley Paperback & Pulp Fiction Coll; History of Medicine Coll; James Joyce Coll; Love Canal Coll; Poetry Coll-First Editions & Manuscripts Coll (Robert Graves, Robert Duncan,William Carlos Williams, Dylan Thomas); Polish Coll; Rare Books Coll (19th & 20th Century). Canadian and Provincial; State Document Depository; UN Document Depository; US Document Depository
Automation Activity & Vendor Info: (Acquisitions) Ex Libris Group; (Cataloging) Ex Libris Group; (Circulation) Ex Libris Group; (Course Reserve) Ex Libris Group; (ILL) OCLC ILLiad; (OPAC) Ex Libris Group; (Serials) Ex Libris Group
Wireless access
Publications: Progress Report (Annual); UB Libraries Today (Newsletter)
Partic in Association of Research Libraries; Center for Research Libraries; National Network of Libraries of Medicine Region 7; NELLCO Law Library Consortium, Inc.; OCLC Online Computer Library Center, Inc; SUNYConnect; Western New York Library Resources Council
Friends of the Library Group

Departmental Libraries:

ARCHITECTURE & PLANNING, 303 Abbott Hall, 3435 Main St, 14214-3087, SAN 352-2938. Tel: 716-829-5682. Reference Tel: 716-645-1325. FAX: 716-829-2780. E-mail: library@buffalo.edu. *Assoc Librn,* Rose Orcutt; E-mail: rmorcutt@buffalo.edu; Staff 1 (MLS 1)
Fac 1
Library Holdings: Bk Vols 40,000
Special Collections: Rudy Bruner Award for Urban Excellence Archives
Friends of the Library Group

CM HEALTH SCIENCES LIBRARY, Abbott Hall, 3435 Main St, Bldg 28, 14214-3002, SAN 352-2997. Tel: 716-829-3900. FAX: 716-829-2211. E-mail: askhsl@buffalo.edu. Web Site: library.buffalo.edu/hsl. *Interim Dir,* Amy Lyons; Tel: 716-829-5719, E-mail: alyons@buffalo.edu; *Assoc Librn,* Dr Diane Rein; Tel: 716-829-5749, E-mail: drein@buffalo.edu; *Clinical Librn,* Elizabeth M Stellrecht; Tel: 716-829-5734, E-mail: thomann4@buffalo.edu; *Outreach Librn,* Ophelia Morey; Tel: 716-829-5748, E-mail: otmorey@buffalo.edu; *Sr Asst Librn,* Nell Aronoff; Tel: 716-829-5735, E-mail: naronoff@buffalo.edu; *Ref Librn/Health Sci Liaison,* Deborah Chiarella; Tel: 716-829-5753, E-mail: dtc3@buffalo.edu; *Ref Librn/Health Sci Liaison,* Michelle Zafron; Tel: 716-829-5746, E-mail: mlzafron@buffalo.edu; *Curator,* Linda Lohr; Tel: 716-829-5737, E-mail: lalohr@buffalo.edu; *Coll Mgt,* Amanda Start; Tel: 716-829-5736, E-mail: start@buffalo.edu. Subject Specialists: *Bioinformatics,* Dr Diane Rein; *Dentistry,* Elizabeth M Stellrecht; *Pharm,* Deborah Chiarella; *Health related professions, Pub health,* Michelle Zafron; *Hist of med,* Linda Lohr; Staff 18.7 (MLS 12.7, Non-MLS 6)
Founded 1846. Enrl 27,500; Highest Degree: Doctorate
Library Holdings: e-journals 825; Bk Vols 358,880; Per Subs 453
Special Collections: History of Medicine Coll; Media Resources Center
Subject Interests: Dentistry, Health related professions, Med, Nursing, Pharm
Automation Activity & Vendor Info: (Acquisitions) Ex Libris Group; (Cataloging) Ex Libris Group; (Circulation) Ex Libris Group; (Course Reserve) Ex Libris Group; (ILL) OCLC ILLiad; (Media Booking) Ex Libris Group; (OPAC) Ex Libris Group; (Serials) Ex Libris Group
Partic in Library Consortium of Health Institutions in Buffalo; State Univ of NY at Buffalo; SUNYConnect
Publications: Library Guide
Friends of the Library Group

LOCKWOOD MEMORIAL LIBRARY, 235 Lockwood Library, North Campus, 14260-2200, SAN 352-3055. Tel: 716-645-2814. Circulation Tel: 716-645-2815. Reference Tel: 716-645-2820. Administration Tel: 716-645-7744. FAX: 716-645-3859. Web Site: library.buffalo.edu/lml. *Dir, Emeritus,* Margaret Wells; E-mail: mwells@buffalo.edu; *Bus Officer,* Ashley Kravitz; E-mail: amkravit@buffalo.edu
Special Collections: East Asian Coll; Government Documents; Graphic Novel Coll; International Leisure Reading Coll; Juvenile Coll; Polish Room. State Document Depository; US Document Depository

MUSIC LIBRARY, 112 Baird Hall, 14260-4750, SAN 352-311X. Tel: 716-645-2923. FAX: 716-645-3906. E-mail: musique@buffalo.edu. Web Site: library.buffalo.edu/music. *Assoc Librn,* John Bewley; E-mail: jmbewley@buffalo.edu; Staff 4 (MLS 3, Non-MLS 1)
Library Holdings: CDs 18,300; DVDs 650; Microforms 8,000; Music Scores 93,600; Bk Vols 41,800; Videos 1,000
Special Collections: Archive of the Center of the Creative & Performing Arts, 1964-1980; Buffalo Musicians' Association Records, 1889-2002; Irene Haupt Photographs of Musicians in Buffalo, ca. 1978-1999; J. Warren Perry Coll of Photographs; Jan Williams Images Coll; Morton Feldman Photographs, 1939-1987; Music Librarianship Archive; North American New Music Festival Archive

CL CHARLES B SEARS LAW LIBRARY, 217 John Lord O'Brian Hall, 14260-1110. (Mail add: 211 O'Brian Hall, 14260), SAN 352-2962. Tel: 716-645-6765. Interlibrary Loan Service Tel: 716-645-2347. Reference Tel: 716-645-2047. FAX: 716-645-3860. E-mail: asklaw@buffalo.edu. Web Site: law.lib.buffalo.edu. *Dir, Law Libr, Vice Dean, Legal Info Serv,* Elizabeth Adelman; Tel: 716-645-2089, E-mail: eadelman@buffalo.edu; *Assoc Dir & Head M Robert Koren AV Ctr,* Terrence McCormack; Tel: 716-645-2831, E-mail: cormack@buffalo.edu; *Head, Access Serv,* John Mondo; E-mail: jamondo@buffalo.edu; *Head, Cat,* Ellen McGrath; Tel: 716-645-2254, E-mail: emcgrath@buffalo.edu; *Head, Circ,* Melissa Bednarz; Tel: 716-645-2301, E-mail: mmt@buffalo.edu; *Head, Coll Mgt,* Theodora Belniak; Tel: 716-645-8504, E-mail: tbelniak@buffalo.edu; *Head, Info Serv,* Marcia Zubrow; Tel: 716-645-2160, E-mail: llmarcia@buffalo.edu; *Foreign & Intl Law Librn,* Nina Cascio; Tel: 716-645-2633, E-mail: ncascio@buffalo.edu; *Ref Librn,* Joseph Gerken; Tel: 716-645-6769, E-mail: gerken@buffalo.edu; *Student Serv Librn,* Brian Detweiler; Tel: 716-645-2384, E-mail: briandet@buffalo.edu; *Cataloger,* Nancy Babb; E-mail: babb@buffalo.edu; *Instrul Support Tech,* Anne Marie Swartz; Tel: 716-645-7949, E-mail: amswartz@buffalo.edu; *Passport Serv, Student Serv, Circ,* Peggy Lyons; Tel: 716-645-0395, E-mail: peglyons@buffalo.edu. Subject Specialists: *Foreign law, Intl law,* Nina Cascio; Staff 16 (MLS 14, Non-MLS 2)
Founded 1887. Enrl 720; Fac 60; Highest Degree: Doctorate
Library Holdings: Microforms 285,936; Bk Vols 296,539; Per Subs 7,207

Special Collections: John Lord O'Brian Coll, bks, papers
Function: Passport agency
Open Mon-Thurs 7:30am-11pm, Fri 7:30-5, Sat 9-7, Sun 10am-11pm
OSCAR A SILVERMAN LIBRARY, University at Buffalo, 116 Capen Hall, 14260-1672, SAN 352-3233. Tel: 716-645-1328. FAX: 716-645-3714. Web Site: library.buffalo.edu/silverman. *Dir, Emeritus,* Margaret Wells; Tel: 716-645-7744, E-mail: mwells@buffalo.edu; *Bus Officer,* Ashley Kravitz; E-mail: amkravit@buffalo.edu
Special Collections: Map Coll; Multimedia Center; Science & Engineering Information Center
Subject Interests: Biology, Chem, Computer sci, Engr, Geol, Math, Phys geog, Physics

CR VILLA MARIA COLLEGE LIBRARY*, 240 Pine Ridge Rd, 14225. SAN 310-9917. Tel: 716-961-1862. FAX: 716-896-0705. Web Site: www.villa.edu/academics/library. *Dir, Libr Serv,* Lucy Waite; Tel: 716-961-1863, E-mail: lwaite@villa.edu; *Resource Librn,* Susan Abel-Smith; Tel: 716-961-1864, E-mail: sabelsmith@villa.edu; Staff 2 (MLS 2)
Founded 1961. Enrl 500; Fac 50; Highest Degree: Bachelor
Library Holdings: AV Mats 5,000; Bk Vols 20,000; Per Subs 70
Subject Interests: Animation, Art, Fashion design, Graphic design, Interior design, Lit, Photog, Poland, Relig studies
Automation Activity & Vendor Info: (Cataloging) ComPanion Corp; (Circulation) ComPanion Corp; (OPAC) ComPanion Corp
Wireless access
Partic in Western New York Library Resources Council

BURNT HILLS

P TOWN OF BALLSTON COMMUNITY LIBRARY*, Burnt Hills-Ballston Lake, Two Lawmar Lane, 12027. SAN 310-9933. Tel: 518-399-8174. Circulation Tel: 518-399-8174, Ext 2. FAX: 518-399-1687. E-mail: bur-director@sals.edu. Web Site: burnthills.sals.edu. *Dir,* Colleen Smith; E-mail: csmith@sals.edu; *Youth Serv Librn,* Rebecca Darling; Staff 2 (MLS 2)
Founded 1952. Pop 8,200; Circ 184,850
Library Holdings: AV Mats 8,919; Bk Vols 58,805
Special Collections: Town of Ballston History, software
Subject Interests: Local hist
Automation Activity & Vendor Info: (Acquisitions) Innovative Interfaces, Inc; (Cataloging) Innovative Interfaces, Inc; (Circulation) Innovative Interfaces, Inc; (ILL) Innovative Interfaces, Inc; (OPAC) Innovative Interfaces, Inc
Wireless access
Function: Adult bk club, Art exhibits, Computer training, ILL available, Photocopying/Printing, Preschool outreach, Prog for adults, Prog for children & young adult, Spoken cassettes & CDs, Tax forms, VHS videos
Publications: Annual Report
Mem of Southern Adirondack Library System
Partic in Capital District Library Council
Open Mon-Thurs 10-8, Fri 10-5, Sat 10-2
Friends of the Library Group

CAIRO

P CAIRO PUBLIC LIBRARY, 15 Railroad Ave, 12413. (Mail add: PO Box 720, 12413-0720), SAN 310-995X. Tel: 518-622-9864. FAX: 518-622-9874. E-mail: cairolibrary720@gmail.com. Web Site: cairolibrary.org. *Dir,* Debra Kamecke; Staff 3 (MLS 1, Non-MLS 2)
Founded 1963. Pop 6,700; Circ 47,700
Library Holdings: Bk Vols 24,700; Per Subs 39
Subject Interests: Local hist
Automation Activity & Vendor Info: (Cataloging) Innovative Interfaces, Inc; (Circulation) Innovative Interfaces, Inc; (OPAC) Innovative Interfaces, Inc; (Serials) Innovative Interfaces, Inc
Wireless access
Mem of Mid-Hudson Library System
Open Mon-Wed 10-5, Thurs 2-8, Fri & Sat 10-2
Friends of the Library Group

CALEDONIA

P CALEDONIA LIBRARY, 3108 Main St, 14423. SAN 310-9968. Tel: 585-538-4512. Web Site: www.caledonialibrary.org. *Dir,* Renate Goff; E-mail: CaldoniaLibraryDirector@owwl.org
Pop 4,030; Circ 17,847
Library Holdings: Bk Vols 16,701; Per Subs 43
Automation Activity & Vendor Info: (Cataloging) SirsiDynix; (Circulation) SirsiDynix; (OPAC) SirsiDynix; (Serials) SirsiDynix
Wireless access
Mem of Pioneer Library System
Open Mon & Thurs 2-5:30 & 7-9, Tues 9-1 & 2-5:30, Fri 2-5:30, Sat 9-1

CALVERTON

P BAITING HOLLOW FREE LIBRARY*, Four Warner Dr, 11933. SAN 310-9984. Tel: 631-727-8765. E-mail: baitinghollowfreelibrary@gmail.com. Web Site: bhflibrary.wordpress.com. *Librn,* Peggy Perrone
Founded 1903. Pop 475; Circ 1,392
Library Holdings: Bk Vols 4,800
Subject Interests: Long Island hist
Wireless access
Mem of Suffolk Cooperative Library System
Open Thurs & Sat 9-3

CAMBRIDGE

P CAMBRIDGE PUBLIC LIBRARY, 21 W Main St, 12816. SAN 311-0001. Tel: 518-677-2443. FAX: 518-677-2443. Web Site: cambridge.sals.edu. *Dir,* Christina Becker; E-mail: cam-director@sals.edu; *Asst Librn,* Julie Wetherby
Pop 1,870; Circ 33,232
Library Holdings: Bk Vols 17,060; Per Subs 45
Automation Activity & Vendor Info: (Circulation) Innovative Interfaces, Inc
Wireless access
Mem of Southern Adirondack Library System
Open Mon & Wed 10-2 & 5:30-8:30, Tues & Thurs 2-6, Fri & Sat 10-2
Friends of the Library Group

CAMDEN

P CAMDEN PUBLIC LIBRARY*, 57 Second St, 13316. SAN 311-001X. Tel: 315-245-1980. FAX: 315-245-1980. Web Site: www.midyorklib.org/camden. *Dir,* Linda Frenzel; Staff 4 (Non-MLS 4)
Founded 1890. Pop 2,667; Circ 45,000
Library Holdings: Bk Titles 20,000; Per Subs 46
Special Collections: News (Camden Advance Journal Coll)
Automation Activity & Vendor Info: (Acquisitions) SirsiDynix; (Cataloging) SirsiDynix; (Circulation) SirsiDynix; (Course Reserve) SirsiDynix; (ILL) SirsiDynix; (Media Booking) SirsiDynix; (OPAC) SirsiDynix; (Serials) SirsiDynix
Wireless access
Publications: Queen Central News
Mem of Mid-York Library System
Open Tues 10-6, Wed & Thurs 2-8, Fri 10-5, Sat (Winter) 10-3

CAMILLUS

P MAXWELL MEMORIAL LIBRARY, 14 Genesee St, 13031. SAN 311-0036. Tel: 315-672-3661. FAX: 315-672-5514. E-mail: maxwell@maxwellmemoriallibrary.org. Web Site: www.maxwellmemoriallibrary.org. *Dir,* Alyssa Ali; E-mail: director@maxwellmemoriallibrary.org; Staff 1 (MLS 1)
Founded 1918. Pop 16,143; Circ 83,270
Library Holdings: Bk Vols 25,000; Per Subs 85
Automation Activity & Vendor Info: (Cataloging) Innovative Interfaces, Inc; (Circulation) Innovative Interfaces, Inc; (OPAC) Innovative Interfaces, Inc; (Serials) Innovative Interfaces, Inc
Wireless access
Mem of Onondaga County Public Libraries
Open Mon-Thurs 10-8, Fri 10-5, Sat 10-3
Friends of the Library Group

CANAJOHARIE

P CANAJOHARIE LIBRARY, Two Erie Blvd, 13317. SAN 311-0052. Tel: 518-673-2314. FAX: 518-673-5243. E-mail: canlib@sals.edu. Web Site: www.canajoharielibrary.org. *Chief Curator, Exec Dir,* Suzan Friedlander; E-mail: sfriedlander@arkellmuseum.org
Founded 1914. Pop 6,196; Circ 40,000
Library Holdings: Bk Vols 30,100; Per Subs 75
Special Collections: American Art Originals, Colonial Times to Present; Art (Gilbert Stuart, Georgia O'Keefe, Winslow Homer)
Subject Interests: Archit, Art, Local indust hist
Automation Activity & Vendor Info: (Acquisitions) Innovative Interfaces, Inc; (Circulation) Innovative Interfaces, Inc; (OPAC) Innovative Interfaces, Inc
Wireless access
Publications: Fire (History of Local Volunteer Fire Department); Masterpieces of American Art; The Permanent Collection; Walking Tour of Canajoharie
Mem of Mohawk Valley Library System
Open Tues & Thurs-Fri 10-5, Wed 10-6, Sat & Sun 12-5
Friends of the Library Group

CANANDAIGUA

P BRISTOL LIBRARY, 6750 County Rd 32, 14424. SAN 310-897X. Tel: 585-229-5862. E-mail: bricirc@pls-net.org. Web Site: thebristollibrary.com. *Libr Mgr,* Kimberlee Petrino; E-mail: Kpetrino@pls-net.org
Pop 1,802; Circ 5,700
Library Holdings: Bk Vols 8,000; Per Subs 35
Automation Activity & Vendor Info: (Cataloging) SirsiDynix; (Circulation) SirsiDynix; (OPAC) SirsiDynix; (Serials) SirsiDynix
Wireless access
Mem of Pioneer Library System
Open Mon, Wed & Thurs 3-7, Tues & Sat 10-2

J FINGER LAKES COMMUNITY COLLEGE*, Charles J Meder Library, 3325 Marvin Sands Dr, 14424-8405. SAN 311-0060. Tel: 585-785-1371. Reference Tel: 585-785-1432. FAX: 585-394-8826. Web Site: library.flcc.edu. *Dir,* Sarah Moon; E-mail: sarah.moon@flcc.edu; *Automated Syst & Serv Librn,* Jenny Burnett; E-mail: jenny.burnett@flcc.edu; *Librn,* Wally Babcock; *Sr Libr Assoc,* Karen Clement
Founded 1968. Enrl 4,723; Fac 95
Library Holdings: Bk Titles 51,692; Bk Vols 76,660; Per Subs 365
Special Collections: Canandaigua Lake Pure Waters Association Archives
Subject Interests: Environ conserv, Hort, Nursing, Paralegal, Tourism, Travel
Automation Activity & Vendor Info: (Cataloging) Ex Libris Group; (Circulation) Ex Libris Group; (OPAC) Ex Libris Group; (Serials) Ex Libris Group
Wireless access
Publications: Periodicals Guide
Partic in OCLC Online Computer Library Center, Inc; Rochester Regional Library Council; SUNYConnect
Special Services for the Deaf - Captioned film dep
Special Services for the Blind - Cassette playback machines; Integrated libr/media serv; Textbks on audio-cassettes
Open Mon-Thurs (Winter) 7:30am-9pm, Fri 7:30-4, Sat & Sun 12-4: Mon-Thurs (Summer) 8am-9pm, Fri 8-4

S ONTARIO COUNTY HISTORICAL SOCIETY LIBRARY, 55 N Main St, 14424. SAN 311-0079. Tel: 585-394-4975. FAX: 585-394-9351. Web Site: www.ochs.org/archives-and-library. *Exec Dir,* Cody Grabhorn; E-mail: director@ochs.org; *Librn,* Linda Alexander; *Curator,* Wilma Townsend; E-mail: curator@ochs.org; Staff 3 (Non-MLS 3)
Founded 1902
Library Holdings: Bk Titles 4,700; Per Subs 700
Special Collections: Civil War Library of Major Charles Richardson NY126 Vol; Local Imprints Coll; Manchester Subscription Library ca 1800; Western New York Land Sales (Oliver Phelps Coll), mss
Subject Interests: Ont county hist
Wireless access
Publications: An Illustrated History of the LISK Manufacturing Co; Backyards to Big Leagues; Early Canandaigua Architecture; Evolution of Seneca Point; Forgotten Stories of the Finger Lakes; Saving a Masterpiece - The Untold Story of Sonnenberg Gardens
Open Tues-Fri 10-4:30, Sat 11-3
Restriction: Non-circulating to the pub, Pub ref by request

P PIONEER LIBRARY SYSTEM*, 2557 State Rte 21, 14424. SAN 312-1593. Tel: 585-394-8260. FAX: 585-394-1935. Web Site: www.pls-net.org. *Exec Dir,* Ron Kirsop; Tel: 585-394-8260, Ext 1103, E-mail: rkirsop@pls-net.org; Staff 12 (MLS 5, Non-MLS 7)
Founded 1990. Pop 301,741
Library Holdings: Bk Vols 2,845
Automation Activity & Vendor Info: (Cataloging) Evergreen; (Circulation) Evergreen; (OPAC) Evergreen
Wireless access
Publications: Directories; Pioneer Pathfinder (Newsletter)
Member Libraries: Allens Hill Free Library; Arcade Free Library; Avon Free Library; Bell Memorial Library; Bloomfield Public Library; Bristol Library; Caledonia Library; Clifton Springs Library; Clyde-Savannah Public Library; Cordelia A Greene Library; Dansville Public Library; Eagle Free Library; Gainesville Public Library; Geneva Public Library; Gorham Free Library; Honeoye Public Library; Lima Public Library; Livonia Public Library; Lyons Public Library; Macedon Public Library; Marion Public Library; Mount Morris Library; Naples Library; Newark Public Library; Ontario Public Library; Palmyra Community Library; Perry Public Library; Phelps Library; Pike Library; Red Creek Free Library; Red Jacket Community Library; Rose Free Library; Sodus Community Library; Stevens Memorial Community Library; Victor Farmington Library; Wadsworth Library; Walworth-Seely Public Library; Warsaw Public Library; Williamson Public Library; Wolcott Civic Free Library; Wood Library Association; Wyoming Free Circulating Library
Partic in OCLC Online Computer Library Center, Inc; Rochester Regional Library Council

P WOOD LIBRARY ASSOCIATION*, 134 N Main St, 14424-1295. SAN 311-0095. Tel: 585-394-1381. E-mail: woodlibrary@owwl.org. Web Site: woodlibrary.org. *Exec Dir,* Jenny Goodemote; Tel: 585-394-1381, Ext 306, E-mail: jgoodemote@pls-net.org; *Ad,* Alexis Lawrence; Tel: 585-394-1381 Ext 314, E-mail: alawrence@pls-net.org; *Ch Serv Librn,* Mary Ferris; Tel: 585-394-1381, Ext 304, E-mail: mferris@pls-net.org; *Teen Serv Librn,* Katie Smith; Tel: 585-394-1381, Ext 302, E-mail: ksmith@pls-net.org; *Executive Asst,* Cyndi Fordham; Tel: 585-394-1381, Ext 313, E-mail: cfordham@pls-net.org; Staff 20 (MLS 4, Non-MLS 16)
Founded 1857. Pop 23,796; Circ 273,897
Library Holdings: Bk Titles 72,013; Per Subs 141
Wireless access
Function: 24/7 Electronic res, 24/7 Online cat, Activity rm, Adult bk club, After school storytime, Art exhibits, Bk club(s), Bks on CD, Computer training, Computers for patron use, Electronic databases & coll, Holiday prog, Home delivery & serv to seniorr ctr & nursing homes, Homebound delivery serv, ILL available, Internet access, Life-long learning prog for all ages, Magazines, Meeting rooms, Movies, Museum passes, Notary serv, Online cat, Online ref, Outreach serv, OverDrive digital audio bks, Photocopying/Printing, Preschool outreach, Preschool reading prog, Printer for laptops & handheld devices, Prog for adults, Prog for children & young adult, Ref serv available, Scanner, Senior computer classes, Senior outreach, Story hour, Study rm, Summer reading prog, Teen prog, Wheelchair accessible, Workshops, Writing prog
Publications: Annual Report & Annual Plan of Service
Mem of Pioneer Library System
Open Mon-Thurs 10-9, Fri & Sat 10-5
Friends of the Library Group

CANASERAGA

P ESSENTIAL CLUB FREE LIBRARY*, 11 Pratt St, 14822. Tel: 607-545-6443. FAX: 607-545-6443. Web Site: canaseraga.stls.org. *Libr Dir,* Lois Phillips; E-mail: phillipsl@stls.org
Founded 1897
Library Holdings: Audiobooks 200; AV Mats 500; Large Print Bks 200; Bk Vols 10,000
Automation Activity & Vendor Info: (Cataloging) SirsiDynix; (Circulation) SirsiDynix; (OPAC) SirsiDynix
Wireless access
Function: Adult literacy prog, Homebound delivery serv, Prog for children & young adult, Summer reading prog
Mem of Southern Tier Library System
Special Services for the Blind - Large print bks; Talking bks; Videos on blindness & physical disabilties
Open Mon 10-12:30 & 1-5, Wed 10-12:30, 1-5 & 7-9, Thurs 2-6, Sat 10-1
Friends of the Library Group

CANASTOTA

P CANASTOTA PUBLIC LIBRARY*, 102 W Center St, 13032. SAN 311-0117. Tel: 315-697-7030. FAX: 315-697-8653. E-mail: canastota@midyork.org. Web Site: www.canastotalibrary.org. *Dir,* Elizabeth Metzger; E-mail: lmetzger@midyork.org; Staff 1 (MLS 1)
Founded 1896. Pop 9,917; Circ 63,654
Library Holdings: Audiobooks 1,125; CDs 182; DVDs 1,713; Bk Titles 24,886; Per Subs 64
Special Collections: Children's Books for Parents (Dorothy Canfield Fisher Award Coll)
Automation Activity & Vendor Info: (Circulation) SirsiDynix; (ILL) OCLC WorldShare Interlibrary Loan
Wireless access
Function: 24/7 Electronic res, 24/7 Online cat, Adult bk club, Adult literacy prog, Archival coll, Art exhibits, Bks on CD, ILL available, Internet access, Magazines, Meeting rooms, Music CDs, Online cat, Photocopying/Printing, Prog for adults, Prog for children & young adult, Ref serv available, Scanner, Summer reading prog, Tax forms, Wheelchair accessible, Writing prog
Mem of Mid-York Library System
Open Mon-Thurs 9-8, Fri 9-5, Sat 9-1

CANDOR

P CANDOR FREE LIBRARY*, Two Bank St, 13743-1510. (Mail add: PO Box 104, 13743-0104), SAN 311-0125. Tel: 607-659-7258. FAX: 607-659-7500. E-mail: candorli@twcny.rr.com. Web Site: candorfreelibrary.org. *Librn,* Marcia Enright; E-mail: director@candorfreelibrary.org
Founded 1931. Pop 869; Circ 17,529
Library Holdings: Bk Vols 18,440; Per Subs 29
Subject Interests: Adult fiction, Hist, Mystery, Sci fict, Western
Automation Activity & Vendor Info: (Cataloging) SirsiDynix; (Circulation) SirsiDynix
Wireless access
Mem of Finger Lakes Library System

Open Mon, Wed & Fri 2-5, Tues & Thurs 10-12, 2-5 & 6-8, Sat 10-12 & 2-4
Friends of the Library Group

CANISTEO

P WIMODAUGHSIAN FREE LIBRARY*, 19 W Main St, 14823-1005. SAN 311-0133. Tel: 607-698-4445. FAX: 607-698-4445. Web Site: wimodaughsianlibrary.org. *Dir,* Heidi Robinson; E-mail: robinsonh@stls.org
Founded 1898. Pop 3,600; Circ 25,714
Library Holdings: Bk Vols 16,226; Per Subs 40
Special Collections: Bethesda Health & Wellness Coll; History (Steuben County Coll), bk, doc, clippings, pamphlets
Subject Interests: Gardening, Railroad hist
Automation Activity & Vendor Info: (Cataloging) SirsiDynix-WorkFlows; (Circulation) SirsiDynix-WorkFlows; (OPAC) SirsiDynix-WorkFlows; (Serials) SirsiDynix-WorkFlows
Wireless access
Function: Homebound delivery serv, Photocopying/Printing
Mem of Southern Tier Library System
Open Mon, Wed & Fri 12-6, Tues & Thurs 1-8, Sat 9-12
Friends of the Library Group

CANTON

P CANTON FREE LIBRARY*, Eight Park St, 13617. (Mail add: PO Box 150, 13617-0150), SAN 311-0141. Tel: 315-386-3712. FAX: 315-386-4131. E-mail: canlib@ncls.org. Web Site: www.cantonfreelibrary.org. *Dir,* Emily Owen Hasting; E-mail: eowen@ncls.org; *Br Librn,* Agnes Hoey; *Youth Serv Spec,* Valerie White
Founded 1896. Pop 10,995; Circ 53,794
Library Holdings: Bk Titles 49,913; Per Subs 139
Special Collections: Adirondacks (Menard Memorial); Canton Local Scrapbooks; Hazel Tyrell's Bird Carvings; Tyrell Handcarved Birds Coll
Subject Interests: Genealogy, Local hist
Automation Activity & Vendor Info: (Circulation) SirsiDynix
Wireless access
Function: Telephone ref
Publications: At Your Library (Newsletter)
Mem of North Country Library System
Open Mon & Wed 9:30-8, Tues, Thurs & Fri 9:30-5
Friends of the Library Group
Branches: 2
MORLEY BRANCH, 7230 County Rte 27, 13617, SAN 321-138X. Tel: 315-379-0066. E-mail: morlib@ncls.org. *Libr Mgr,* Agnes Hoey
Library Holdings: Bk Vols 3,248; Per Subs 18
Open Mon 5pm-7:30pm, Tues 1-3:30, Thurs 1:30-5:30
Friends of the Library Group
RENSSELAER FALLS BRANCH, 212 Rensselaer St, Rensselaer Falls, 13680. Tel: 315-344-4155. E-mail: reflib@ncls.org. *Libr Mgr,* Agnes Hoey
Function: Meeting rooms, Photocopying/Printing
Special Services for the Blind - Braille bks; Large print bks
Open Mon 1-3:30, Tues 5pm-7:30pm, Wed 1:30-5:30
Friends of the Library Group

S SAINT LAWRENCE COUNTY HISTORICAL ASSOCIATION ARCHIVES*, Three E Main St, 13617-1416. (Mail add: PO Box 8, 13617-0008), SAN 311-015X. Tel: 315-386-8133. E-mail: info@slcha.org. Web Site: www.slcha.org. *Exec Dir,* Sue Longshore; *Archivist,* Jean Marie Martello; E-mail: archives@slcha.org; Staff 2 (Non-MLS 2)
Founded 1947
Library Holdings: Bk Titles 2,000
Special Collections: Silas Wright (Governor Silas Wright & Family Coll), bks, doc, letters & transcripts
Subject Interests: County hist, Genealogy, Northern NY hist, St Lawrence County hist
Wireless access
Publications: The Quarterly (Periodical)
Partic in Northern New York Library Network
Open Tues-Thurs 12-4, Fri 12-6, Sat 10-4
Restriction: Non-circulating to the pub

L ST LAWRENCE SUPREME COURT*, Law Library, Courthouse, 2nd Flr, Rm 281, 48 Court St,, 13617. Tel: 315-379-2279. E-mail: 4JDLawLibrary@nycourts.gov. Web Site: ww2.nycourts.gov/library/4jd/4JD-Library-StLawrence.shtml. *Librn,* Tammy Lomaki
Library Holdings: Bk Vols 14,000
Subject Interests: Legal ref
Wireless access
Open Mon-Fri 9-5

C ST LAWRENCE UNIVERSITY, Owen D Young Library, 23 Romoda Dr, 13617. SAN 311-0168. Tel: 315-229-5451. Interlibrary Loan Service Tel: 315-229-5485. Reference Tel: 315-229-5477. FAX: 315-229-5729. Web Site: library.stlawu.edu/owen-d-young-library. *Dir of Libr,* John Payne; Tel: 315-229-5424, E-mail: jpayne@stlawu.edu; *Director, Research & Digital Scholarship,* Eric Williams-Bergen; Tel: 315 299-5453, E-mail: ewilliamsbergen@stlawu.edu; *Archives Librn, Spec Coll Librn,* Paul Doty; Tel: 315-229-5483, E-mail: pdoty@stlawu.edu; *Coll Develop & Acq Librn,* Michelle Gillie; Tel: 315-229-5834, E-mail: mgillie@stlawu.edu; *Maps Librn,* Carol Cady; Tel: 315-229-5824, E-mail: ccady@stlawu.edu; *Res & Instruction Librn,* Rhonda Courtney; Tel: 315-229-5479, E-mail: rcourtney@stlawu.edu; Staff 8 (MLS 8)
Founded 1856. Enrl 2,200; Highest Degree: Master
Library Holdings: Electronic Media & Resources 126; Microforms 598,500; Bk Vols 594,300; Per Subs 5,300
Special Collections: David Parish & Family, letters, papers; Edwin Arlington Robinson Coll; Frederic Remington Coll, bks, letters, prints; Irving Bacheller Coll; Nathaniel Hawthorne (Milburn Coll), bks, letters; Northern New York History, bks, doc, letters, maps; Owen D Young Papers; Poetry (Benet Coll); Rabbi Dr Seymour Siegel Coll, bks, writings; Robert Frost Coll. US Document Depository
Wireless access
Publications: Bulletin of the Friends of Owen D Young Library; Odyssey: A Newsletter of the SLU Libraries
Partic in Associated Colleges of the Saint Lawrence Valley; Northern New York Library Network; OCLC Online Computer Library Center, Inc
Open Mon-Thurs 8am-1am, Fri 8-8, Sat Noon-8, Sun 11am-1am
Friends of the Library Group
Departmental Libraries:
LAUNDERS SCIENCE LIBRARY, Fox Hall, 23 Romoda Dr, 13617. Tel: 315-229-5404. FAX: 315-229-7291. Web Site: library.stlawu.edu/launders-science-library. *Sci Librn,* Gwendolyn Cunningham; E-mail: gcunningham@stlawu.edu; Staff 2 (MLS 1, Non-MLS 1)
Open Mon-Thurs 8am-1am, Fri 8-8, Sat Noon-8, Sun 11am-1am
MUSIC LIBRARY, 21 Romoda Dr, 13617. Tel: 315-229-5799. Web Site: library.stlawu.edu/music-library. *Arts Metadata Tech, Music Libr Supvr,* Arline Wolfe; E-mail: awolfe@stlawu.edu
Library Holdings: CDs 3,000; Music Scores 3,500; Bk Titles 100; Videos 800
Open Mon-Thurs 4pm-11pm, Sun 2pm-11pm

C SUNY CANTON, Southworth Library, 34 Cornell Dr, 13617. SAN 311-0176. Tel: 315-386-7228. E-mail: library@canton.edu. Web Site: www.canton.edu/library. *Dir, Libr Serv,* Cori Wilhelm; E-mail: wilhelmc@canton.edu; *Access Serv Librn,* Halie Kerns; Tel: 315-386-7056, E-mail: kernsh@canton.edu; *Electronic Res Librn, Tech Serv,* Jessica Spooner; Tel: 315-386-7054, E-mail: spoonerj@canton.edu; *Instruction & Outreach Librn,* Leah Fitzgerald; Tel: 315-386-7057, E-mail: fitzgeraldl@canton.edu; Staff 2 (Non-MLS 2)
Founded 1948. Enrl 2,987; Fac 176; Highest Degree: Bachelor
Library Holdings: e-books 273,000; Bk Titles 25,000
Automation Activity & Vendor Info: (Acquisitions) Ex Libris Group; (Cataloging) Ex Libris Group; (Circulation) Ex Libris Group; (Course Reserve) Ex Libris Group; (ILL) OCLC; (OPAC) Ex Libris Group; (Serials) Ex Libris Group
Wireless access
Partic in Associated Colleges of the Saint Lawrence Valley; Northern New York Library Network; SUNYConnect
Open Mon-Thurs 7:30am-Midnight, Fri 7:30am-10pm, Sat Noon-10, Sun Noon-Midnight

CAPE VINCENT

P CAPE VINCENT COMMUNITY LIBRARY, 157 N Real St, 13618. (Mail add: PO Box 283, 13618-0283), SAN 311-0184. Tel: 315-654-2132. FAX: 315-654-2132. E-mail: cavlib@ncls.org. Web Site: www.capevincentlibrary.org. *Libr Dir,* Amy Pond
Pop 2,700; Circ 16,800
Library Holdings: Bk Vols 14,500; Per Subs 32
Automation Activity & Vendor Info: (Cataloging) SirsiDynix-WorkFlows; (Circulation) SirsiDynix-WorkFlows; (Course Reserve) SirsiDynix-WorkFlows; (ILL) SirsiDynix-WorkFlows; (OPAC) SirsiDynix-WorkFlows; (Serials) SirsiDynix-WorkFlows
Wireless access
Mem of North Country Library System
Open Tues & Thurs 9-6, Wed 9-5, Fri & Sat 9-3
Friends of the Library Group

CARMEL

GL NEW YORK STATE SUPREME COURT NINTH JUDICIAL DISTRICT*, Putnam County Supreme Court Law Library, 20 County Center, Ground Flr, 10512. Tel: 845-208-7804. E-mail: 9JDLawLibrary@nycourts.gov. *Law Libr Asst,* Gustavo Armaza

Wireless access
Open Tues, Wed & Thurs 9-12:30 & 1:30-4:45, Fri 9-12:30 & 1:30-4:30

P REED MEMORIAL LIBRARY, 1733 Rte 6, 10512. SAN 311-0206. Tel: 845-225-2439. FAX: 845-225-1436. Web Site: carmellibrary.org. *Dir,* Jeanne Buck; E-mail: jbuck@carmellibrary.org
Founded 1914. Pop 8,150; Circ 50,000
Library Holdings: Bk Vols 20,000; Per Subs 75
Wireless access
Mem of Mid-Hudson Library System
Open Mon, Wed & Fri 10-5, Tues & Thurs 1-7, Sat 10-1

CARTHAGE

P CARTHAGE FREE LIBRARY, 412 Budd St, 13619. SAN 352-3381. Tel: 315-493-2620. FAX: 315-493-2620. E-mail: carlib@ncls.org. Web Site: www.carthagefreelibrary.org. *Interim Dir,* Christina Bamberg; E-mail: cbamberg@ncls.org; Staff 1 (Non-MLS 1)
Founded 1910. Pop 5,936; Circ 30,999
Library Holdings: Bk Vols 17,000; Per Subs 40
Special Collections: Local History (New York State History Coll), ms, monographs
Automation Activity & Vendor Info: (Cataloging) SirsiDynix; (Circulation) SirsiDynix; (OPAC) SirsiDynix; (Serials) SirsiDynix
Wireless access
Function: 24/7 Electronic res, 24/7 Online cat, Activity rm, Adult bk club, Art programs, Bks on CD, Children's prog, Computer training, Computers for patron use, Genealogy discussion group, ILL available, Internet access, Laminating, Magazines, Magnifiers for reading, Mail & tel request accepted, Microfiche/film & reading machines, Movies, Museum passes, Online cat, OverDrive digital audio bks, Photocopying/Printing, Printer for laptops & handheld devices, Prog for adults, Prog for children & young adult, Scanner, Senior computer classes, Serves people with intellectual disabilities, STEM programs, Story hour, Summer & winter reading prog, Tax forms, Teen prog, Wheelchair accessible
Mem of North Country Library System
Partic in Northern New York Library Network
Open Mon-Thurs 10-7, Fri 10-4, Sat 12-4
Restriction: Circ to mem only
Friends of the Library Group

CASTILE

S CORDELIA A GREENE LIBRARY*, 11 S Main St, 14427. SAN 311-0214. Tel: 585-493-5466. FAX: 585-493-5782. Web Site: castilelibrary.blogspot.com. *Dir,* Erin Robinson; E-mail: castilelibrarydirector@owwl.org; Staff 2 (Non-MLS 2)
Founded 1897
Library Holdings: Audiobooks 300; Bks on Deafness & Sign Lang 10; CDs 270; DVDs 260; High Interest/Low Vocabulary Bk Vols 200; Large Print Bks 20; Bk Vols 15,000; Per Subs 70; Videos 240
Special Collections: Dr Cordelia A Greene Coll; Frances Willard Coll
Subject Interests: Local hist
Automation Activity & Vendor Info: (Cataloging) SirsiDynix; (Circulation) SirsiDynix; (OPAC) SirsiDynix
Wireless access
Function: Ref serv available
Mem of Pioneer Library System
Open Mon & Wed 2-8, Tues & Thurs 10-3, Sat 10-2
Friends of the Library Group

CASTLETON-ON-HUDSON

P CASTLETON PUBLIC LIBRARY*, 85 S Main St, 12033. SAN 373-8353. Tel: 518-732-0879. FAX: 518-732-0835. Web Site: www.castletonpubliclibrary.org. *Dir,* Melissa Tacke; E-mail: director@castletonpubliclibrary.org; Staff 1 (MLS 1)
Library Holdings: DVDs 1,500; Bk Titles 12,000; Bk Vols 13,000; Per Subs 14
Special Collections: Castleton-on-Hudson, bks & photogs
Wireless access
Mem of Upper Hudson Library System
Special Services for the Deaf - Bks on deafness & sign lang; Closed caption videos; High interest/low vocabulary bks
Special Services for the Blind - Audio mat; Bks available with recordings; Bks on cassette; Bks on CD
Open Mon-Wed 12-8, Thurs & Fri 10-6, Sat 10-4
Friends of the Library Group

CATO

P STEWART B LANG MEMORIAL LIBRARY*, Lang Memorial Library, 2577 E Main St, 13033. (Mail add: PO Box 58, 13033), SAN 311-0249. Tel: 315-626-2101. FAX: 315-626-3249. E-mail: librarian@langlibrary.org. Web Site: www.langlibrary.org. *Libr Dir,* Caroline Chatterton
Founded 1927. Pop 4,700; Circ 23,000
Jan 2015-Dec 2015 Income $84,000, Locally Generated Income $50,000, Other $34,000. Mats Exp $10,800, Books $9,000, Per/Ser (Incl. Access Fees) $1,000, AV Mat $800. Sal $43,000 (Prof $26,500)
Library Holdings: Audiobooks 400; DVDs 1,200; Large Print Bks 250; Bk Titles 12,000; Bk Vols 12,200; Per Subs 43; Talking Bks 238
Subject Interests: Cayuga County hist
Automation Activity & Vendor Info: (Cataloging) Innovative Interfaces, Inc; (Circulation) Innovative Interfaces, Inc
Wireless access
Publications: Booklist
Mem of Finger Lakes Library System
Open Mon & Wed 1-7, Tues & Thurs 9:30-8:30, Fri 1-5, Sat 11-3

CATSKILL

P CATSKILL PUBLIC LIBRARY, One Franklin St, 12414-1496. SAN 352-3470. Tel: 518-943-4230. FAX: 518-943-1439. Web Site: catskillpubliclibrary.org. *Dir,* Susan Ray; E-mail: director@catskillpubliclibrary.org; Staff 3 (MLS 3)
Founded 1893. Pop 12,608; Circ 42,015
Special Collections: Daily Mail, microfilm; Hudson River Steamboats (Saunders Coll)
Automation Activity & Vendor Info: (Acquisitions) Innovative Interfaces, Inc; (Cataloging) Innovative Interfaces, Inc; (Circulation) Innovative Interfaces, Inc; (OPAC) Innovative Interfaces, Inc
Wireless access
Mem of Mid-Hudson Library System
Open Tues, Thurs & Fri 11-5, Wed 11-7, Sat 11-3
Branches: 1
PALENVILLE BRANCH, 3303 Rte 23A, Palenville, 12463, SAN 352-3500. Tel: 518-678-3357. FAX: 518-678-9251. *Br Mgr,* Bathsheba Orlando; E-mail: borlando@catskillpubliclibrary.org
Open Tues & Fri 11-3, Thurs 11-7, Sat 11-1

L NEW YORK STATE SUPREME COURT LIBRARY*, Emory A Chase Memorial Law Library, Greene County Courthouse, 320 Main St, 12414. SAN 311-0257. Tel: 518-625-3197. FAX: 518-625-3198. E-mail: greenelawlibrary@nycourts.gov. Web Site: www.nycourts.gov/lawlibraries/publicaccess.shtml. *Librn,* Angelina Knott
Founded 1908
Library Holdings: Bk Vols 14,000
Special Collections: Van Orden Survey Coll
Subject Interests: NY State law
Wireless access
Partic in South Central Regional Library Council; Southeastern New York Library Resources Council
Open Mon-Fri 9-4:30

CATTARAUGUS

P CATTARAUGUS FREE LIBRARY*, 21 Main St, 14719. SAN 311-0265. Tel: 716-257-9500. FAX: 716-257-9500. E-mail: cattfl@yahoo.com. Web Site: www.cattaraugusfreelibrary.com. *Dir,* Erin Wagatha-Heitzenrater; Staff 2 (Non-MLS 2)
Founded 1926. Circ 21,238
Library Holdings: Bk Vols 12,384; Per Subs 16
Wireless access
Mem of Chautauqua-Cattaraugus Library System
Open Mon, Thurs & Fri 12-6, Tues 10-8, Sat 10-2
Friends of the Library Group

CAZENOVIA

C CAZENOVIA COLLEGE*, Daniel W Terry Witherill Library, Lincklaen St, 13035. (Mail add: 22 Sullivan St, 13035), SAN 311-0273. Tel: 315-655-7240. Reference Tel: 315-655-7282. Administration Tel: 315-655-7132. FAX: 315-655-8675. Web Site: www.cazenovia.edu/academics/witherill-library. *Libr Dir,* Heather Whalen Smith; E-mail: hcwhalensmith@cazenovia.edu; *Archivist,* John Robert Greene; E-mail: rgreene@cazenovia.edu; *ILL, Ref Serv,* Judy Azzoto; E-mail: jazzoto@cazenovia.edu; *ILL, Ref Serv,* Lauren Michel; E-mail: ldmichel@cazenovia.edu; Staff 13 (MLS 4, Non-MLS 9)
Founded 1824. Enrl 825; Highest Degree: Bachelor
Library Holdings: Bk Titles 63,000; Bk Vols 73,000; Per Subs 430; Videos 2,177
Subject Interests: Women's studies
Automation Activity & Vendor Info: (Acquisitions) Innovative Interfaces, Inc; (Cataloging) Innovative Interfaces, Inc; (Circulation) Innovative Interfaces, Inc; (ILL) Innovative Interfaces, Inc; (OPAC) Innovative Interfaces, Inc; (Serials) Innovative Interfaces, Inc
Wireless access
Function: ILL available
Publications: Acquisition Lists; Annual Report
Partic in Central New York Library Resources Council; ConnectNY, Inc; OCLC Online Computer Library Center, Inc
Open Mon-Thurs 7:45am-Midnight, Fri 7:45-5, Sat 1-5, Sun 2-Midnight

P CAZENOVIA PUBLIC LIBRARY*, 100 Albany St, 13035. SAN 311-0281. Tel: 315-655-9322. E-mail: cazenovia@midyork.org. Web Site: www.cazenoviapubliclibrary.org. *Dir,* Betsy Kennedy; Staff 8 (MLS 1, Non-MLS 7)
Founded 1886. Pop 6,500; Circ 167,000
Library Holdings: AV Mats 6,927; Bk Titles 46,199; Bk Vols 53,143; Per Subs 75
Subject Interests: Local hist
Automation Activity & Vendor Info: (Cataloging) SirsiDynix; (Circulation) SirsiDynix; (OPAC) SirsiDynix
Wireless access
Function: 24/7 Electronic res, 24/7 Online cat, Activity rm, Adult bk club, Adult literacy prog, Archival coll, Art exhibits, Audiobks via web, Bk club(s), Bks on cassette, Bks on CD, Children's prog, Computer training, Computers for patron use, E-Reserves, Electronic databases & coll, Family literacy, For res purposes, Free DVD rentals, ILL available, Internet access, Literacy & newcomer serv, Magazines, Mail & tel request accepted, Meeting rooms, Movies, Museum passes, Music CDs, Online cat, Online ref, OverDrive digital audio bks, Photocopying/Printing, Preschool outreach, Preschool reading prog, Prog for adults, Prog for children & young adult, Ref & res, Ref serv available, Res assist avail, Scanner, Senior outreach, Story hour, Summer reading prog, Tax forms, Telephone ref, VHS videos, Wheelchair accessible, Workshops
Mem of Mid-York Library System
Partic in Association for Rural & Small Libraries
Open Mon-Fri 9-9, Sat 10-5
Friends of the Library Group

S NEW YORK STATE DIVISION FOR HISTORIC PRESERVATION*, Lorenzo State Historic Site, 17 Rippleton Rd, 13035. SAN 311-029X. Tel: 315-655-3200. FAX: 315-655-4304. Web Site: www.friendsoflorenzo.org. *Assoc Curator,* Jackie Roshia; E-mail: jacqueline.roshia@parks.ny.gov; *Assoc Archivist,* Sharon Cooney; E-mail: sharon.cooney@parks.ny.gov
Founded 1968
Library Holdings: Bk Vols 4,000
Special Collections: Cazenovia Newspapers, 1800-1960, microfilm; Cazenovia, New York & Vicinity (Land Company Material from Amsterdam, Municipal Archives), microfilm; Childs, Fairchild & Stebbins Family Papers (Helen Kennard Coll); Ledyard, Hubbard, Burr & Allied Family Papers & Photographs; Personal & Land Accounts of John Lincklaen & Successors (Lorenzo Library Coll), bks, doc, microfilm; Store Records & Correspondence (Samuel S Forman Papers), doc, microfilm
Subject Interests: Allied families, Doc hist of Cazenovia, Holland Land Co, Lincklaen-Ledyard, Third great Western Turnpike
Restriction: Open by appt only

CENTER MORICHES

P CENTER MORICHES FREE PUBLIC LIBRARY*, 235 Main St, 11934. SAN 311-0303. Tel: 631-878-0940. FAX: 631-878-5218. E-mail: cmorlib@centermoricheslibrary.org. Web Site: www.centermoricheslibrary.org. *Dir,* Marcie Litjens; Staff 21 (MLS 6, Non-MLS 15)
Founded 1920. Circ 222,529
Library Holdings: e-journals 5; Bk Vols 98,057; Per Subs 184
Special Collections: Local History (LI Coll) bks, records & tapes. Oral History
Automation Activity & Vendor Info: (Cataloging) Innovative Interfaces, Inc; (Circulation) Innovative Interfaces, Inc; (OPAC) Innovative Interfaces, Inc
Wireless access
Publications: Index to Moriches Bay Tide 1955 to date (local newspaper); Index to the Center Moriches Record; The Library (Newsletter)
Mem of Suffolk Cooperative Library System
Open Mon-Fri 9:30-8:30, Sat 9:30-5, Sun 12-5
Friends of the Library Group

CENTEREACH

P MIDDLE COUNTRY PUBLIC LIBRARY*, 101 Eastwood Blvd, 11720. SAN 352-3535. Tel: 631-585-9393. FAX: 631-585-5035. E-mail: info@mcpl.lib.ny.us. Web Site: www.mcplibrary.org. *Dir,* Sophia Serlis-McPhillips; Tel: 631-585-9393, Ext 219, E-mail: serlis-mcphillipssop@mcpl.lib.ny.us; Staff 41.3 (MLS 40, Non-MLS 1.3)
Founded 1960. Pop 62,562; Circ 1,250,840
Library Holdings: AV Mats 90,393; CDs 19,243; DVDs 56,102; e-books 5,740; Electronic Media & Resources 121; Large Print Bks 4,546; Microforms 4,722; Bk Vols 334,255; Per Subs 104,112; Videos 7,921
Special Collections: Business & Finance Coll; Career Information Center Services & Coll; Catastrophe Readiness Clearinghouse; Children's Braille Coll; Children's Foreign Language Coll; Civil Service Manuals; Dual Vision & Sign Language Coll; Employment Coll; Family Education Professional Materials, Large Print Books, Adult Reader Coll (High Interest/Low Vocabulary); Health & Medical Coll; Heritage Coll; Large Print Coll; Law Coll; Local History Coll; Long Island Literary Fiction; Miller Business Coll; Multilanguage Coll; Museum Corner; Not-for-profit Coll; Parents Center; Parents Coll; Read Coll; Serials on Microfilm; Suffolk Education Clearinghouse; Tax Services Coll; Telephone Directories; Test Books; WISE Center (World of Information for Seniors & the Elderly)
Automation Activity & Vendor Info: (Acquisitions) Innovative Interfaces, Inc; (Circulation) Innovative Interfaces, Inc; (Serials) Innovative Interfaces, Inc
Wireless access
Function: Adult bk club, Adult literacy prog, Archival coll, Art exhibits, Audiobks via web, BA reader (adult literacy), Bilingual assistance for Spanish patrons, Bk club(s), Bk reviews (Group), Bks on cassette, Bks on CD, CD-ROM, Chess club, Children's prog, Citizenship assistance, Computer training, Computers for patron use, Electronic databases & coll, Free DVD rentals, Homebound delivery serv, ILL available, Internet access, Large print keyboards, Music CDs, Notary serv, Online cat, Online ref, OverDrive digital audio bks, Photocopying/Printing, Prog for adults, Prog for children & young adult, Ref & res, Senior outreach, Summer reading prog, Tax forms, Teen prog, VHS videos, Wheelchair accessible, Writing prog
Publications: Exploring Careers in Business (Bibliographies); Exploring Careers in Construction and the Trades (Bibliographies); Exploring Careers in Education & Human Services (Bibliographies); Exploring Careers in Healthcare Services (Bibliographies); Hamlet of Selden (Documents); Italian-American Bibliography; Just Getting Started (Bibliographies); Long Island Bibliography; MCPL Newsletter; MCPL Program Catalog; Menu for Mealtime (Bibliographies); Miller Center in the News (Documents); Networking Resources for Women (Bibliographies); On the Go: A List of Local Places to Visit & Activities to do with Preschool Children (Bibliographies); Parenting & Early Childhood Services (Documents); Reaching the Teen Market (Reference guide); Reflections on 1788: Long Island & the Constitution (Documents); Resources to Grow Your Business (Bibliographies); Resume Books for Individuals Without College Degrees (Bibliographies); The Countdown to College (Reference guide); Toys to Go (Index to educational materials)
Mem of Suffolk Cooperative Library System
Special Services for the Deaf - Assisted listening device; Bks on deafness & sign lang; Closed caption videos; Sign lang interpreter upon request for prog
Special Services for the Blind - Accessible computers; Audio mat; BiFolkal kits; Bks & mags in Braille, on rec, tape & cassette; Bks on cassette; Bks on CD; Cassettes; Home delivery serv; Large print & cassettes; Large print bks; Magnifiers; Suffolk Family Educ Clearinghouse; Talking bks; Talking bks & player equip; Text reader; ZoomText magnification & reading software
Open Mon-Fri 9:30-9, Sat 9:30-5, Sun (Sept-June) 1-5
Friends of the Library Group
Branches: 1
SELDEN BRANCH, 575 Middle Country Rd, Selden, 11784, SAN 352-356X. *Dir,* Sophia Serlis-McPhillips
Automation Activity & Vendor Info: (Cataloging) Innovative Interfaces, Inc
Open Mon-Thurs 9:30-9, Fri & Sat 9:30-5, Sun (Sept-June) 1-5
Friends of the Library Group

CENTERPORT

S SUFFOLK COUNTY VANDERBILT MUSEUM LIBRARY*, 180 Little Neck Rd, 17721. (Mail add: PO Box 0605, 11721-0605), SAN 373-7381. Tel: 631-854-5508, 631-854-5551. FAX: 631-854-5594. Web Site: www.vanderbiltmuseum.org. *Curator,* Stephanie Gress; E-mail: stephanie@vanderbiltmuseum.org
Founded 1950
Special Collections: W K Vanderbilt II Coll, bks, photo albums & scrapbks

CENTRAL ISLIP

P CENTRAL ISLIP PUBLIC LIBRARY, 33 Hawthorne Ave, 11722. SAN 311-0311. Tel: 631-234-9333. FAX: 631-234-9386. E-mail: information@centralisliplibrary.org. Web Site: centralisliplibrary.org. *Dir,* Tara Kohles; Staff 34 (MLS 9, Non-MLS 25)
Founded 1952. Pop 32,611; Circ 107,111
Library Holdings: Electronic Media & Resources 1; Bk Vols 116,000; Per Subs 269
Automation Activity & Vendor Info: (Cataloging) Innovative Interfaces, Inc; (Circulation) Innovative Interfaces, Inc; (OPAC) Innovative Interfaces, Inc
Wireless access
Mem of Suffolk Cooperative Library System
Open Mon-Fri (Winter) 10-9, Sat 10-5, Sun 1-5; Mon-Thurs (Summer) 10-9, Fri 10-5, Sat 10-5
Friends of the Library Group

L TENTH JUDICIAL DISTRICT SUPREME COURT LAW LIBRARY*, Cohalan Supreme Court Library, 400 Carleton Ave, 11722-9079. SAN 373-9295. Tel: 631-740-3961. FAX: 631-853-7533. Web Site: www.nycourts.gov/courts/10jd/suffolk/lawlibrary.shtml. *Sr Law Librn,* John Hadler
Wireless access

C TOURO COLLEGE*, Jacob D Fuchsberg Law Center Library, 225 Eastview Dr, 11722-4539. SAN 326-7334. Tel: 631-761-7000, 631-761-7150. FAX: 631-761-7159. Web Site: www.tourolaw.edu. *Interim Dir,* Irene Crisci; *Assoc Dir,* Beth Mobley; *Head, Tech Serv,* Beth Chamberlain; *Evening & Weekend Circ Mgr, Govt Doc Librn,* Michael Tattonetti; *Ref,* Laura Ross; Staff 18 (MLS 9, Non-MLS 9)
Enrl 650; Fac 35
Library Holdings: Bk Titles 56,000; Bk Vols 415,000; Per Subs 1,300
Special Collections: Foreign & International Law; Jewish Law. State Document Depository; US Document Depository
Automation Activity & Vendor Info: (Acquisitions) Innovative Interfaces, Inc; (Cataloging) Innovative Interfaces, Inc; (Circulation) Innovative Interfaces, Inc; (OPAC) Innovative Interfaces, Inc; (Serials) Innovative Interfaces, Inc
Wireless access
Partic in Law Library Microform Consortium; Long Island Library Resources Council; OCLC Online Computer Library Center, Inc
Restriction: Not open to pub
Friends of the Library Group

CENTRAL SQUARE

P CENTRAL SQUARE LIBRARY*, 637 S Main St, 13036. (Mail add: PO Box 513, 13036-0513), SAN 311-032X. Tel: 315-668-6104. FAX: 315-668-6104. E-mail: csqlib@ncls.org. Web Site: www.centralsquarelibrary.org. *Dir,* Cindy Partrick
Pop 1,646; Circ 15,019
Library Holdings: Bk Vols 28,000
Wireless access
Function: Adult bk club, Bks on CD, Computers for patron use, Digital talking bks, Free DVD rentals, ILL available, Internet access, Music CDs, Online cat, Photocopying/Printing, Scanner, Tax forms, VHS videos, Wheelchair accessible
Mem of North Country Library System
Open Mon, Wed & Fri 11-7, Tues, Thurs & Sat 11-4
Friends of the Library Group

CENTRAL VALLEY

P WOODBURY PUBLIC LIBRARY*, Ida Cornell Branch, 23 Smith Clove Rd, 10917. (Mail add: PO Box 38, 10917-0038), SAN 373-7047. Tel: 845-928-2114. FAX: 845-928-8867. *Library Contact,* Grainne O'Connor
Wireless access
Open Mon, Tues & Thurs 8:30-6, Wed 8:30-8, Fri 8:30-5, Sat 11-4

CHAMPLAIN

P CHAMPLAIN MEMORIAL LIBRARY, 148 Elm St, 12919-5317. (Mail add: PO Box 279, 12919-0297), SAN 311-0354. Tel: 518-298-8620. FAX: 518-298-8620. E-mail: champlib1970@gmail.com. Web Site: www.cefls.org/libraries/champlain. *Dir,* Alison M Mandeville; Staff 1 (Non-MLS 1)
Founded 1925. Pop 1,273; Circ 12,291
Library Holdings: Bk Vols 9,500
Wireless access
Mem of Clinton-Essex-Franklin Library System
Open Tues-Thurs 11:30-5:30, Sat 10-1

CHAPPAQUA

P CHAPPAQUA PUBLIC LIBRARY*, 195 S Greeley Ave, 10514. SAN 311-0362. Tel: 914-238-4779. FAX: 914-238-3597. E-mail: chappaweb@westchesterlibraries.org. Web Site: www.chappaqualibrary.org. *Dir,* Pamela Thornton; Tel: 914-238-4779, Ext 208, E-mail: thornton@wlsmail.org; *Asst Libr Dir, Head, Ref Serv,* Martha Alcott; E-mail: malcott@wlsmail.org; *Head, Children's Servx,* Teresa Bueti; E-mail: tcbueti@gmail.com; *Head, Circ,* Marjorie Perlin; Tel: 914-238-4779, Ext 201; *Head, Tech Serv,* Sally Scudo; *Head, Teen Serv,* Cathy Paulsen; E-mail: cpaulsen@wlsmail.org; *Ch,* Robbin Friedman; *Ch,* Mercy Garland; *Ch,* Julie Ann Polasko; *Ref Librn,* Vicki Fuqua; *Ref Librn,* Alan Houston; *Ref Librn,* Denise Mincin; *Ref Librn,* Cathy Paulsen; *Ref Librn,* Rebecca Rogan; Staff 32 (MLS 11, Non-MLS 21)
Founded 1922. Pop 16,126; Circ 340,594
Jul 2017-Jun 2018 Income $3,085,869, State $5,000, Locally Generated Income $3,026,269, Other $52,600. Mats Exp $715,411, Books $77,000, Per/Ser (Incl. Access Fees) $15,225, AV Mat $45,501, Electronic Ref Mat (Incl. Access Fees) $55,000. Sal $1,619,614 (Prof $1,026,192)
Library Holdings: AV Mats 19,115; e-books 28,515; Bk Vols 95,805; Per Subs 238
Subject Interests: Local hist
Automation Activity & Vendor Info: (Cataloging) Evergreen; (Circulation) Evergreen; (ILL) Evergreen; (OPAC) Evergreen
Wireless access
Function: 24/7 Electronic res, 24/7 Online cat, Adult bk club, Art exhibits, Audiobks via web, Bi-weekly Writer's Group, Bk club(s), Bks on CD, Children's prog, Computer training, Computers for patron use, Electronic databases & coll, Free DVD rentals, ILL available, Internet access, Learning ctr, Magazines, Mail & tel request accepted, Mango lang, Meeting rooms, Microfiche/film & reading machines, Movies, Museum passes, Music CDs, Notary serv, Online cat, OverDrive digital audio bks, Photocopying/Printing, Prog for adults, Prog for children & young adult, Ref serv available, Scanner, Story hour, Study rm, Tax forms, Teen prog, Writing prog
Publications: Annual Report; Community Organizations; Program Calendar (Bimonthly); Welcome (Brochure)
Mem of Westchester Library System
Partic in Westlynx
Open Mon-Thurs 9-8, Fri 9-6, Sat 9-5, Sun 1-5
Friends of the Library Group

CHATEAUGAY

P CHATEAUGAY MEMORIAL LIBRARY*, Four John St, 12920. (Mail add: PO Box 10, 12920-0010), SAN 311-0370. Tel: 518-497-0400. FAX: 518-497-0400. E-mail: chatlib@gmail.com. Web Site: cefls.org/libraries/chateaugay, www.chateaugayny.org/library. *Dir,* Melissa Erhardt
Founded 1946. Pop 3,204; Circ 9,497
Library Holdings: Bk Titles 7,145; Bk Vols 7,544; Per Subs 15
Special Collections: American Indian Coll; North Country History; Wilder, Laura Ingalls & Almonzo Coll
Subject Interests: Adirondacks
Automation Activity & Vendor Info: (Cataloging) Horizon; (Circulation) Horizon; (OPAC) Horizon
Wireless access
Function: Ref serv available
Mem of Clinton-Essex-Franklin Library System
Special Services for the Deaf - Closed caption videos
Special Services for the Blind - Audio mat; Bks on CD
Open Mon & Wed 9-6, Tues 9-1, Sat 12:30-3:30

CHATHAM

P CHATHAM PUBLIC LIBRARY*, 11 Woodbridge Ave, 12037-1399. SAN 311-0389. Tel: 518-392-3666. FAX: 518-392-1546. E-mail: chathampubliclibrary@chatham.k12.ny.us. Web Site: chatham.lib.ny.us. *Dir,* Julie DeLisle
Founded 1905. Pop 8,841; Circ 84,986
Library Holdings: Bk Vols 64,163; Per Subs 60
Subject Interests: Local hist
Automation Activity & Vendor Info: (Cataloging) Inmagic, Inc.; (Circulation) Innovative Interfaces, Inc; (OPAC) Innovative Interfaces, Inc
Wireless access
Mem of Mid-Hudson Library System
Open Mon & Wed 10-8, Tues & Fri 10-5, Thurs 11-5, Sat 10-3
Friends of the Library Group
Branches: 1
CANAAN BRANCH, 1647 County Rte 5, Canaan, 12029-3017, SAN 325-3430. Tel: 518-781-3392. E-mail: canaanlibrary@taconic.net. *Dir,* Julie Delisle; *Library Contact,* Joanne Hanson
Founded 1895
Open Wed & Fri 1-4
Friends of the Library Group

CHAUMONT

P LYME FREE LIBRARY*, 12165 Main St, 13622-9603. SAN 311-0397. Tel: 315-649-5454. FAX: 315-649-2911. E-mail: chalib@ncls.org. Web Site: www.lymefreelibrary.org. *Dir,* Patti Hughes
Founded 1923. Pop 1,695
Library Holdings: Bk Vols 16,000; Per Subs 17
Special Collections: Viet Nam (John La Comb Coll)
Automation Activity & Vendor Info: (Acquisitions) SirsiDynix-WorkFlows; (Cataloging) SirsiDynix-WorkFlows; (Circulation) SirsiDynix-WorkFlows; (Course Reserve) SirsiDynix-WorkFlows; (ILL) SirsiDynix-WorkFlows; (OPAC) SirsiDynix-WorkFlows; (Serials) SirsiDynix-WorkFlows
Wireless access
Mem of North Country Library System
Open Mon & Sat 10-4, Tues & Fri 10-8, Wed 10-6
Friends of the Library Group

CHAUTAUQUA

P SMITH MEMORIAL LIBRARY*, Chautauqua Institution Library, 21 Miller Ave, 14722. SAN 311-0400. Tel: 716-357-6296. E-mail: library@chq.org. Web Site: chq.org/about-us/community/smith-memorial-library. *Libr Dir,* Scott Ekstrom; E-mail: sekstrom@chq.org; Staff 4 (MLS 1, Non-MLS 3)
Founded 1907. Pop 2,000; Circ 40,310
Library Holdings: AV Mats 4,803; Large Print Bks 1,082; Bk Titles 31,032; Per Subs 100
Automation Activity & Vendor Info: (Cataloging) SirsiDynix; (Circulation) SirsiDynix; (OPAC) SirsiDynix
Wireless access
Mem of Chautauqua-Cattaraugus Library System
Open Mon 12-6, Wed & Fri 10-5, Sat 12-3
Friends of the Library Group

CHAZY

P CHAZY PUBLIC LIBRARY, 1329 Fiske Rd, 12921. (Mail add: PO Box 88, 12921-0088), SAN 311-0419. Tel: 518-846-7676. FAX: 518-846-7676. E-mail: director@chazypubliclibrary.org. Web Site: cefls.org/libraries/chazy. *Dir,* Blake Andrew; Staff 1 (Non-MLS 1)
Founded 1901. Pop 3,067; Circ 3,380
Library Holdings: Audiobooks 196; AV Mats 4,857; CDs 83; Bk Titles 7,000; Per Subs 25
Special Collections: Adirondack Coll/Local
Automation Activity & Vendor Info: (Cataloging) Horizon; (Circulation) Horizon; (OPAC) Horizon
Wireless access
Function: Activity rm, Art exhibits, Bks on CD, Children's prog, Computers for patron use, Free DVD rentals, ILL available, Magazines, Museum passes, Music CDs, Online cat, Photocopying/Printing, Preschool outreach, Printer for laptops & handheld devices, Scanner, Story hour, Study rm, Summer reading prog, Tax forms, Wheelchair accessible
Mem of Clinton-Essex-Franklin Library System
Open Tues & Thurs 12:30-7, Wed 10-5, Sat 9-2
Friends of the Library Group

S WILLIAM H MINER AGRICULTURAL RESEARCH INSTITUTE*, James A FitzPatrick Library, 596 Ridge Rd, 12921. (Mail add: PO Box 100, 12921-0100), SAN 326-4386. Tel: 518-846-7121, Ext 149. FAX: 518-846-7774. E-mail: library@whminer.com. Web Site: www.whminer.org. *Dir,* Amy T Bedard; Staff 1 (MLS 1)
Founded 1951
Subject Interests: Environ, Gen agr
Automation Activity & Vendor Info: (OPAC) OPALS (Open-source Automated Library System)
Wireless access
Partic in Northern New York Library Network

CHEEKTOWAGA

P CHEEKTOWAGA PUBLIC LIBRARY, Julia Boyer-Reinstein Library, 1030 Losson Rd, 14227. SAN 376-8694. Tel: 716-668-4991. FAX: 716-668-4806. E-mail: askus@buffalolib.org. *Dir,* Glenn Luba; E-mail: lubag@buffalolib.org; Staff 21.5 (MLS 6, Non-MLS 15.5)
Founded 1938. Pop 94,019; Circ 586,259
Jan 2015-Dec 2015 Income $1,296,679, State $26,169, County $1,192,873, Other $77,637. Mats Exp $255,112. Sal $596,154
Library Holdings: Bk Vols 158,643; Per Subs 499
Special Collections: Local History (Anna M Reinstein Special Local History Reference Coll)
Automation Activity & Vendor Info: (Circulation) SirsiDynix
Wireless access
Mem of Buffalo & Erie County Public Library System
Open Mon & Thurs 11-7, Tues, Wed & Fri 9-5, Sat 9-3
Branches: 1
ANNA REINSTEIN MEMORIAL, 2580 Harlem Rd, 14225, SAN 328-9915. Tel: 716-892-8089. FAX: 716-892-3370. *Dir,* Glenn Luba
Library Holdings: Bk Vols 57,801; Per Subs 224
Open Mon & Wed 2-8, Tues & Sat 9-3, Thurs 12-6

CHERRY VALLEY

P CHERRY VALLEY MEMORIAL LIBRARY, 61 Main St, 13320. (Mail add: PO Box 25, 13320-0025), SAN 311-0443. Tel: 607-264-8214. FAX: 607-264-8214. E-mail: cv.ill@4cls.org. Web Site: cherryvalleylibrary.org. *Libr Mgr,* Claire Ottman; Staff 1 (Non-MLS 1)
Founded 1907. Pop 1,223; Circ 3,067
Jan 2020-Dec 2020 Income $18,912, Locally Generated Income $11,950, Other $6,962. Mats Exp $2,775, Books $1,943, Electronic Ref Mat (Incl. Access Fees) $832. Sal $22,490
Library Holdings: Audiobooks 32; CDs 27; DVDs 19; e-books 12,238; Electronic Media & Resources 26; Bk Vols 6,446; Per Subs 28
Automation Activity & Vendor Info: (Acquisitions) SirsiDynix-WorkFlows; (Cataloging) SirsiDynix-WorkFlows; (Circulation) SirsiDynix-WorkFlows; (ILL) SirsiDynix-WorkFlows; (OPAC) SirsiDynix-Enterprise
Wireless access
Function: 24/7 Electronic res, 24/7 Online cat, Audiobks via web, Bks on CD, Computers for patron use, Free DVD rentals, ILL available, Internet access, Magazines, Mail & tel request accepted, Online cat, OverDrive digital audio bks, Photocopying/Printing, Summer reading prog, Tax forms
Mem of Four County Library System
Open Mon & Thurs 9-12 & 2-7, Sat 9-1
Restriction: Open to pub for ref & circ; with some limitations

CHESTER

P CHESTER PUBLIC LIBRARY, 1784 Kings Hwy, 10918. SAN 311-046X. Tel: 845-469-4252. Reference E-mail: chsref@rcls.org. Web Site: chesternypubliclibrary.com. *Dir,* Maureen Jagos; E-mail: mjagos@rcls.org; Staff 9 (MLS 1, Non-MLS 8)
Pop 12,140; Circ 95,981
Library Holdings: Bk Vols 55,000; Per Subs 120
Subject Interests: Cookery, Local hist
Automation Activity & Vendor Info: (Cataloging) SirsiDynix; (Circulation) SirsiDynix; (OPAC) SirsiDynix
Wireless access
Mem of Ramapo Catskill Library System
Open Mon-Thurs 10-8, Fri & Sat 10-5, Sun (Sept-June) 12-4
Friends of the Library Group

CHESTERTOWN

P TOWN OF CHESTER PUBLIC LIBRARY*, 6307 State Rte 9, 12817. (Mail add: PO Box 451, 12817-0451). Tel: 518-494-5384. FAX: 518-491-5171. E-mail: library@chesterlibrary.org. Web Site: www.chesterlibrary.org. *Dir,* Alma Alvarez; *Asst Dir,* Wendy Joy Hayes
Library Holdings: AV Mats 2,600; Bk Titles 16,600; Per Subs 900
Automation Activity & Vendor Info: (Cataloging) Innovative Interfaces, Inc; (Circulation) Innovative Interfaces, Inc; (OPAC) Innovative Interfaces, Inc
Wireless access
Mem of Southern Adirondack Library System
Open Tues & Sat 9-1, Wed & Fri 9-6, Thurs 1-6; Mon, Tues & Sat 9-1, Wed & Fri 9-6, Thurs 1-6 (Summer)
Friends of the Library Group

CHITTENANGO

P SULLIVAN FREE LIBRARY*, Chittenango Public Library, 101 Falls Blvd, 13037. (Mail add: PO Box 310, 13037-0310), SAN 352-3748. Tel: 315-687-6331. FAX: 315-687-6512. E-mail: Chittenango@midyork.org. Web Site: www.sullivanfreelibrary.org. *Exec Dir,* Karen Fauls-Traynor; *Asst Dir,* Patti Newell
Founded 1947. Pop 14,622; Circ 75,213
Library Holdings: Bk Titles 56,000; Per Subs 42
Wireless access
Mem of Mid-York Library System
Open Mon-Thurs 10-8, Fri 10-6, Sat 10-2
Friends of the Library Group
Branches: 1
BRIDGEPORT BRANCH, 8979 North Rd, Bridgeport, 13030. (Mail add: PO Box 337, Bridgeport, 13030-0337), SAN 352-3772. Tel: 315-633-2253. FAX: 315-633-2945. E-mail: Bridgeport@midyork.org. *Libr Mgr,* Della Detore
Open Mon-Thurs 10-8, Fri 10-6, Sat 10-4
Friends of the Library Group

CHURCHVILLE

P NEWMAN RIGA LIBRARY, One South Main St, 14428. SAN 311-0486. Tel: 585-293-2009. FAX: 585-293-0932. Web Site: newmanrigalibrary.org. *Dir,* Lynn Brown; E-mail: lbrown@libraryweb.org; Staff 2.3 (MLS 1, Non-MLS 1.3)
Founded 1921. Pop 5,000; Circ 28,000
Library Holdings: Bk Vols 18,000; Per Subs 20
Automation Activity & Vendor Info: (Acquisitions) CARL.Solution (TLC); (Cataloging) CARL.Solution (TLC); (Circulation) CARL.Solution (TLC); (OPAC) CARL.Solution (TLC)
Wireless access
Mem of Monroe County Library System
Open Mon, Wed & Fri 11-5, Tues & Thurs 11-8, Sat 10-2

CICERO

P NORTHERN ONONDAGA PUBLIC LIBRARY*, Cicero Branch, 8686 Knowledge Lane, 13039. SAN 311-0494. Tel: 315-699-2032. Administration Tel: 315-699-2534. FAX: 315-699-2034. Web Site:

www.nopl.org. *Dir,* Amanda Travis; E-mail: atravis@nopl.org; *Mgr,* Jill Youngs; E-mail: jyoungs@nopl.org
Founded 1924. Pop 7,500; Circ 24,742
Library Holdings: Bk Titles 12,400; Per Subs 62
Wireless access
Mem of Onondaga County Public Libraries
Open Mon-Thurs 9:30-8, Fri & Sat 9:30-5
Friends of the Library Group
Branches: 2
BREWERTON BRANCH, 5440 Bennett St, Brewerton, 13029, SAN 310-8880. Tel: 315-676-7484. FAX: 315-676-7463. *Mgr,* Alissa Borelli; E-mail: aborelli@nopl.org
Pop 6,000; Circ 60,000
Subject Interests: Genealogy, Local hist
Open Mon-Thurs 9:30-8, Fri & Sat 9:30-5
Friends of the Library Group
NORTH SYRACUSE, 100 Trolley Barn Lane, North Syracuse, 13212, SAN 377-8398. Tel: 315-458-6184. FAX: 315-458-7026. *Asst Dir, Mgr,* William Hastings; E-mail: whastings@nopl.org
Founded 1929. Pop 51,000; Circ 244,902
Automation Activity & Vendor Info: (Acquisitions) SirsiDynix; (Cataloging) SirsiDynix; (Circulation) SirsiDynix; (Course Reserve) SirsiDynix; (ILL) SirsiDynix; (Media Booking) SirsiDynix; (OPAC) SirsiDynix
Open Mon-Thurs 9:30-8, Fri & Sat 9:30-5
Friends of the Library Group

CINCINNATUS

P KELLOGG FREE LIBRARY, 5681 Telephone Rd Extension, 13040. (Mail add: PO Box 150, 13040-0150), SAN 311-0508. Tel: 607-863-4300. FAX: 607-863-3430. Web Site: kelloggfreelibrary.org. *Dir,* Martha Nettleton; E-mail: director@kelloggfreelibrary.org; *Ch Serv,* Tina Harvey
Founded 1930. Pop 1,051; Circ 24,800
Library Holdings: AV Mats 1,000; Bk Titles 14,070; Bk Vols 19,500; Per Subs 81
Automation Activity & Vendor Info: (Cataloging) Innovative Interfaces, Inc; (Circulation) Innovative Interfaces, Inc; (OPAC) Innovative Interfaces, Inc
Wireless access
Mem of Finger Lakes Library System
Open Tues & Thurs 1-8, Wed & Fri 1-5, Sat 9-1

CLARENCE

P CLARENCE PUBLIC LIBRARY, Three Town Pl, 14031. SAN 311-0524. Tel: 716-741-2650. FAX: 716-741-1243. Web Site: www.buffalolib.org/locations-hours/clarence-public-library. *Dir,* Monica Mooney; E-mail: mooneym@buffalolib.org; *Librn,* David Fairlie
Founded 1933. Pop 30,700; Circ 288,200
Library Holdings: Bk Vols 64,000
Automation Activity & Vendor Info: (Cataloging) SirsiDynix; (Circulation) SirsiDynix; (OPAC) SirsiDynix
Wireless access
Mem of Buffalo & Erie County Public Library System
Open Mon, Tues & Thurs 10-9, Wed 10-6, Fri & Sat 10-5
Friends of the Library Group

CLAVERACK

P CLAVERACK FREE LIBRARY*, 629 Rte 23B, 12513. (Mail add: PO Box 417, 12513-0417), SAN 311-0532. Tel: 518-851-7120. FAX: 518-851-7120. E-mail: info@claveracklibrary.org. Web Site: claveracklibrary.org. *Dir,* Thea Schoep; E-mail: director@claveracklibrary.org
Circ 29,000
Library Holdings: Bk Vols 27,000; Per Subs 50
Automation Activity & Vendor Info: (Cataloging) Innovative Interfaces, Inc; (Circulation) Innovative Interfaces, Inc; (OPAC) Innovative Interfaces, Inc
Wireless access
Mem of Mid-Hudson Library System
Open Mon & Wed 12-8, Tues & Sat 10-2, Thurs & Fri 12-5

CLAYTON

S ANTIQUE BOAT MUSEUM, Lou Smith Library, 750 Mary St, 13624. SAN 327-6473. Tel: 315-686-4104. Reference Tel: 315-686-4104, Ext 233. FAX: 315-686-2775. Web Site: www.abm.org/index.php/collections-2/submit-a-research-request. *Colls Mgr, Curator,* Matt Macvittie; E-mail: mattmacvittie@abm.org; Staff 1 (Non-MLS 1)
Founded 1983
Library Holdings: Bk Titles 1,500; Bk Vols 1,600; Per Subs 33; Spec Interest Per Sub 25
Special Collections: 1000 Islands History; Fresh Water Nautical Coll, boats, mechanical artifacts, charts, maps, boat plans, photos, boat & engine catalogs & manuals; Freshwater Pleasure Boating History; Local Boat Builders. Oral History
Function: Outside serv via phone, mail, e-mail & web, Photocopying/Printing, Res libr
Publications: Gazette & Gazette Annual (Museum News to Membership)
Open Mon-Fri 9-Noon or by appointment
Restriction: Non-circulating to the pub

P HAWN MEMORIAL LIBRARY*, 220 John St, 13624-1107. SAN 311-0540. Tel: 315-686-3762. FAX: 315-686-6028. E-mail: clalib@ncls.org. Web Site: www.hawnmemoriallibrary.org. *Dir,* Kathy Jewsbury; Staff 1 (Non-MLS 1)
Founded 1904. Pop 4,225; Circ 36,120
Library Holdings: Audiobooks 690; e-books 1,669; Bk Vols 16,008; Per Subs 29; Videos 756
Subject Interests: Local hist
Automation Activity & Vendor Info: (Acquisitions) SirsiDynix; (Cataloging) SirsiDynix; (Circulation) SirsiDynix; (Course Reserve) SirsiDynix; (ILL) SirsiDynix; (Media Booking) SirsiDynix; (OPAC) SirsiDynix; (Serials) SirsiDynix
Wireless access
Mem of North Country Library System
Open Mon, Wed & Fri 9-5, Tues & Thurs 9-7, Sat 9-2
Friends of the Library Group

CLAYVILLE

P CLAYVILLE LIBRARY ASSOCIATION*, 2265 Oneida St, 13322. (Mail add: PO Box 282, 13322-0282), SAN 376-3021. Tel: 315-839-5893. FAX: 315-839-5070. E-mail: clayville@midyork.org. Web Site: midyorklib.org/clayville. *Dir,* Becky Hassett
Founded 1926
Library Holdings: CDs 300; DVDs 1,300; Bk Vols 9,800; Per Subs 25; Videos 20
Automation Activity & Vendor Info: (Cataloging) SirsiDynix; (Circulation) SirsiDynix; (OPAC) SirsiDynix
Wireless access
Mem of Mid-York Library System
Open Tues & Thurs 3-8, Wed 10-8, Fri 1-6, Sat 11-2

CLIFTON PARK

P CLIFTON PARK-HALFMOON PUBLIC LIBRARY, 475 Moe Rd, 12065-3808. SAN 311-0567. Tel: 518-371-8622. FAX: 518-371-3799. Web Site: www.cphlibrary.org. *Dir,* Alexandra Gutelius; E-mail: agutelius@sals.edu; Staff 29 (MLS 10, Non-MLS 19)
Founded 1969. Pop 55,000; Circ 900,800
Library Holdings: AV Mats 25,000; Bk Vols 160,000; Per Subs 264
Special Collections: Job, Business & Finance Information; Local History (Howard I Becker Memorial Coll)
Automation Activity & Vendor Info: (Acquisitions) Innovative Interfaces, Inc; (Cataloging) Innovative Interfaces, Inc; (Circulation) Innovative Interfaces, Inc; (OPAC) Innovative Interfaces, Inc
Wireless access
Publications: Annual Report; Newsletter (Quarterly)
Mem of Southern Adirondack Library System
Open Mon-Thurs 9-7, Fri 9-6, Sat 10-4
Friends of the Library Group

CLIFTON SPRINGS

P CLIFTON SPRINGS LIBRARY*, Four Railroad Ave, 14432. SAN 311-0583. Tel: 315-462-7371. FAX: 315-462-2131. E-mail: CliftonLibrary@Owwl.org. Web Site: cliftonspringslibrary.com. *Libr Dir,* Phil Trautman; E-mail: ptrautman@pls-net.org
Founded 1895. Pop 2,500; Circ 31,800
Library Holdings: Audiobooks 800; DVDs 1,400; Bk Vols 20,000; Per Subs 55
Automation Activity & Vendor Info: (Cataloging) SirsiDynix; (Circulation) SirsiDynix; (OPAC) SirsiDynix
Wireless access
Function: Meeting rooms, Telephone ref
Mem of Pioneer Library System
Open Mon, Wed & Fri 10-5, Tues & Thurs 12-8, Sat 10-1
Friends of the Library Group

CLINTON

C HAMILTON COLLEGE*, Burke Library, 198 College Hill Rd, 13323. SAN 352-3802. Tel: 315-859-4181. Circulation Tel: 315-859-4479. Interlibrary Loan Service Tel: 315-859-4478. Reference Tel: 315-859-4735. FAX: 315-859-4185, 315-859-4578. Reference E-mail: helpdesk@hamilton.edu. Web Site: www.hamilton.edu/offices/lits. *VPres, Libr & Info Tech,* Joseph Shelley; E-mail: jshelley@hamilton.edu; *Dir,*

Archives & Spec Coll, Christian Goodwillie; Tel: 315-859-4447, E-mail: cgoodwil@hamilton.edu; *Dir, Jazz Archives,* Monk Rowe; Tel: 315-859-4071, E-mail: mrowe@hamilton.edu; *Dir, Metadata & Digital Strategies,* Shay Foley; Tel: 315-859-4487, E-mail: sfoley@hamilton.edu; *Dir, Res & Learning Serv,* Beth Bohstedt; Tel: 315-859-4485, E-mail: bbohsted@hamilton.edu; *Asst Dir, Cat & Metadata,* Jean Williams; Tel: 315-859-4383, E-mail: jfwillia@hamilton.edu; *Asst Dir, Cat & Metadata, Scholarly Communications & Res Serv Librn,* Reid Larson; Tel: 315-859-4480, E-mail: rslarson@hamilton.edu; *Acq/Ser Librn,* Barbara Swetman; Tel: 315-859-4470, E-mail: bswetman@hamilton.edu; *Engagement Librn,* Kristin Strohmeyer; Tel: 315-859-4481, E-mail: kstrohme@hamilton.edu; *Metadata Librn,* Lisa McFall; Tel: 315-859-4788, E-mail: lmcfall@hamilton.edu; *Instruction Coordr, Research Librn,* Glynis Asu; Tel: 315-859-4482, E-mail: gasu@hamilton.edu; *Res & Electronic Resources Librn,* Lynn Mayo; Tel: 315-859-4746, E-mail: lmayo@hamilton.edu; *Archivist,* Katherine Collett; Tel: 315-859-4471, E-mail: kcollett@hamilton.edu; Staff 30 (MLS 10, Non-MLS 20)
Founded 1812. Enrl 1,890; Fac 208; Highest Degree: Bachelor
Jul 2015-Jun 2016 Income (Main & Associated Libraries) $3,617,000. Mats Exp $3,617,000, Books $236,000, Per/Ser (Incl. Access Fees) $920,000, AV Mat $20,000, Electronic Ref Mat (Incl. Access Fees) $353,000, Presv $52,000. Sal $1,500,000 (Prof $1,040,000)
Library Holdings: Bk Vols 500,000; Per Subs 3,400
Special Collections: Adirondacks; Almanacs; Book Arts; Civil War Regimental Histories; Communal Societies; Cruickshankiana; Ezra Pound Coll, bk, ms; Hamiltoniana (Hamilton & Alumni Coll), bks, ms; Kirklandiana, bk, ms; Lesser Antilles (Beinecke Coll), bk, ms; Munsell Coll; Provencal; Utica (NY) Imprints; Women (McIntosh Coll). Oral History
Subject Interests: Civil War, Contemporary poetry, Feminism, Govt, Hist, Relig studies
Automation Activity & Vendor Info: (Acquisitions) Ex Libris Group; (Cataloging) Ex Libris Group; (Circulation) Ex Libris Group; (Course Reserve) Ex Libris Group; (ILL) OCLC ILLiad; (OPAC) Ex Libris Group; (Serials) Ex Libris Group
Wireless access
Publications: American Communal Societies (Quarterly)
Partic in Central New York Library Resources Council; OCLC Online Computer Library Center, Inc
Open Mon-Thurs 8am-2am, Fri 8am-10pm, Sat 10-10, Sun 10am-2am; Mon-Fri (Summer) 8-5

Departmental Libraries:

MUSIC, McEwen Hall, 198 College Hill Rd, 13323-1299. Tel: 315-859-4349. Web Site: www.hamilton.edu/offices/lits/rc/policies-music-library-policies. *Dir, Access Services & Coll Strategies,* Beth Bohstedt; Tel: 315-859-4485, E-mail: bbohsted@hamilton.edu; *Music Library Coord,* Elizabeth Brotherton; Tel: 315-859-4479, E-mail: ebrother@hamilton.edu; Staff 1 (Non-MLS 1)
Library Holdings: Music Scores 12,482

P KIRKLAND TOWN LIBRARY*, 55 1/2 College St, 13323. SAN 311-0605. Tel: 315-853-2038. FAX: 315-853-1785. E-mail: clinton@midyork.org. Web Site: www.kirklandtownlibrary.org. *Dir,* Anne Debraggio; Staff 6.5 (MLS 2, Non-MLS 4.5)
Founded 1901. Pop 10,300; Circ 123,000
Library Holdings: AV Mats 3,000; CDs 1,600; DVDs 1,300; Large Print Bks 1,400; Bk Titles 24,000; Bk Vols 24,500; Per Subs 126; Talking Bks 1,700; Videos 200
Subject Interests: NY hist
Automation Activity & Vendor Info: (Circulation) SirsiDynix; (OPAC) SirsiDynix
Wireless access
Function: 24/7 Electronic res, 24/7 Online cat, Adult bk club, After school storytime, Art exhibits, Audiobks on Playaways & MP3, Audiobks via web, Bk club(s), Bks on CD, Children's prog, Computer training, Computers for patron use, E-Reserves, Electronic databases & coll, Free DVD rentals, Holiday prog, Home delivery & serv to seniorr ctr & nursing homes, Homebound delivery serv, ILL available, Internet access, Life-long learning prog for all ages, Magazines, Meeting rooms, Movies, Music CDs, Notary serv, Online cat, OverDrive digital audio bks, Photocopying/Printing, Preschool outreach, Prog for adults, Prog for children & young adult, Ref serv available, Serves people with intellectual disabilities, Summer reading prog, Tax forms, Teen prog, Wheelchair accessible, Workshops
Mem of Mid-York Library System
Open Mon-Thurs 10-9, Fri 10-6, Sat 10-2
Friends of the Library Group

CLYDE

P CLYDE-SAVANNAH PUBLIC LIBRARY*, 204 Glasgow St, 14433. SAN 311-0613. Tel: 315-923-7767. FAX: 315-923-9315. E-mail: clydelibrary@owwl.org. Web Site: sites.google.com/site/clydesavannahpubliclibrary. *Dir,* Elizabeth Bowlby; Staff 1 (Non-MLS 1)
Founded 1931. Pop 6,500; Circ 104,521
Library Holdings: AV Mats 7,640; CDs 1,640; DVDs 5,000; Large Print Bks 480; Bk Vols 37,564; Per Subs 49; Videos 1,000
Special Collections: Genealogy (local families only)
Automation Activity & Vendor Info: (Cataloging) SirsiDynix; (Circulation) SirsiDynix; (OPAC) SirsiDynix
Wireless access
Mem of Pioneer Library System
Open Mon & Wed 1-8, Tues & Thurs 10-6, Fri 1-6, Sat (Sept-June) 10-1
Friends of the Library Group

CLYMER

P CLYMER-FRENCH CREEK FREE LIBRARY*, 564 Clymer-Sherman Rd, 14724. (Mail add: PO Box 68, 14724-0068), SAN 311-0621. Tel: 716-355-8823. FAX: 716-355-8824. E-mail: cfcplibrary@stny.rr.com. Web Site: cclslib.ent.sirsi.net/client/en_US/clymerlibrary. *Librn,* Pauleen Cochran
Circ 8,745
Library Holdings: Bk Titles 13,919; Per Subs 27
Mem of Chautauqua-Cattaraugus Library System
Open Wed 9-12 & 1-6, Thurs 10-3, Fri 9-1 & 3-6, Sat 9-2

COBLESKILL

P COMMUNITY LIBRARY*, 110 Union St, 12043-3830. (Mail add: PO Box 219, 12043-0219), SAN 311-063X. Tel: 518-234-7897. FAX: 518-234-1163. E-mail: coblib@mvls.info. Web Site: communitylibrary.mvls.info. *Dir,* Kimberly Zimmer
Founded 1921. Pop 11,000; Circ 35,000
Library Holdings: Bk Vols 24,000; Per Subs 43
Special Collections: JFK Assassination Research
Subject Interests: Genealogy, Local hist
Automation Activity & Vendor Info: (Cataloging) Innovative Interfaces, Inc; (Circulation) Innovative Interfaces, Inc; (OPAC) Innovative Interfaces, Inc
Wireless access
Function: Bk club(s), Children's prog, ILL available, Meeting rooms, Music CDs
Mem of Mohawk Valley Library System
Partic in Ohio Public Library Information Network
Open Tues & Thurs 10:30-8, Wed & Fri 10:30-6, Sat 10-1
Friends of the Library Group

C STATE UNIVERSITY OF NEW YORK COLLEGE OF AGRICULTURE & TECHNOLOGY*, Van Wagenen Library, 142 Schenectady Ave, 12043. SAN 311-0648. Tel: 518-255-5841. Reference Tel: 518-255-5866. FAX: 518-255-5843. E-mail: library@cobleskill.edu. Web Site: www.cobleskill.edu/library. *Dean,* Elizabeth Orgeron; *Interim Dir,* Peter Barvoets; E-mail: barvoepd@cobleskill.edu; *Head, Pub Serv, Head, Tech Serv,* April Davies; E-mail: daviesac@cobleskill.edu; *Archives Librn, ILL Librn,* Katherine Brent; E-mail: brentke@robleskill.edu; Staff 5.5 (MLS 5.5)
Founded 1920. Enrl 2,440; Fac 141; Highest Degree: Bachelor
Library Holdings: Bk Vols 65,000; Per Subs 200
Special Collections: County History; Historical Material Related to Agriculture & Food Service
Subject Interests: Agr, Culinary arts, Early childhood educ
Automation Activity & Vendor Info: (Acquisitions) Ex Libris Group; (Cataloging) OCLC; (Circulation) Ex Libris Group; (Course Reserve) Ex Libris Group; (ILL) OCLC ILLiad; (OPAC) Ex Libris Group; (Serials) Ex Libris Group
Wireless access
Publications: Library Link (Newsletter)
Partic in Capital District Library Council; SUNYConnect
Open Mon-Thurs 7am-10pm, Fri 7-5, Sat 10-4, Sun (Sept-May) 2-10

COHOCTON

P COHOCTON PUBLIC LIBRARY, Eight Maple Ave, 14826. (Mail add: PO Box 105, 14826-0105). Tel: 585-384-5170. FAX: 585-384-9044. E-mail: cohocton@stls.org. Web Site: cohoctonlibrary.org. *Dir,* Jessie Zeh
Founded 1977
Library Holdings: AV Mats 1,000; Large Print Bks 200; Bk Vols 14,500
Automation Activity & Vendor Info: (Cataloging) SirsiDynix-Enterprise; (Circulation) SirsiDynix-Enterprise; (OPAC) SirsiDynix-Enterprise
Wireless access
Mem of Southern Tier Library System
Open Mon, Wed & Fri 1-7, Tues & Thurs 10-7, Sat 10-2

COHOES

P COHOES PUBLIC LIBRARY, 169 Mohawk St, 12047. SAN 311-0656. Tel: 518-235-2570. FAX: 518-237-4195. Web Site: www.cohoespubliclibrary.org. *Dir,* Hannah Stahl; E-mail: director@cohoespubliclibrary.org; Staff 4 (MLS 1, Non-MLS 3)
Founded 1969. Pop 16,000; Circ 31,800
Library Holdings: Bk Vols 32,000; Per Subs 70
Special Collections: Cohoes School Yearbooks; Local Authors
Automation Activity & Vendor Info: (Cataloging) Horizon; (Circulation) Horizon; (Media Booking) Horizon
Wireless access
Mem of Upper Hudson Library System
Open Mon & Wed 10-8, Tues & Thurs 10-6, Sat 10-2
Friends of the Library Group

COLD SPRING

P JULIA L BUTTERFIELD MEMORIAL LIBRARY*, Ten Morris Ave, 10516. SAN 311-0664. Tel: 845-265-3040. FAX: 845-265-4852. E-mail: jblstaff@gmail.com. Web Site: www.butterfieldlibrary.org. *Libr Dir,* Gillian Thorpe; E-mail: jbldirector@gmail.com
Pop 2,583; Circ 17,300
Library Holdings: Bk Vols 32,381
Subject Interests: Local hist
Automation Activity & Vendor Info: (Acquisitions) Innovative Interfaces, Inc; (Cataloging) Innovative Interfaces, Inc; (Circulation) Innovative Interfaces, Inc; (Course Reserve) Innovative Interfaces, Inc; (ILL) Innovative Interfaces, Inc; (Media Booking) Innovative Interfaces, Inc; (OPAC) Innovative Interfaces, Inc; (Serials) Innovative Interfaces, Inc
Wireless access
Mem of Mid-Hudson Library System
Open Mon & Wed 10-8, Tues, Thurs, Fri & Sat 10-5, Sun 12-3
Friends of the Library Group

S PUTNAM HISTORICAL MUSEUM*, Research Library, 63 Chestnut St, 10516. SAN 311-0672. Tel: 845-265-4010, Ext 17. FAX: 845-265-2884. E-mail: library@putnamhistorymuseum.org. Web Site: putnamhistorymuseum.org. *Exec Dir,* Mindy Krazmien
Founded 1906
Library Holdings: Bk Vols 3,000
Special Collections: Genealogy (Haida Davenport & Nelson Warren Coll), scrapbooks; Local Newspapers 1867-1913, microfilm
Subject Interests: Local hist
Wireless access
Function: Res libr
Open Wed 11-3

COLD SPRING HARBOR

S COLD SPRING HARBOR LABORATORY, Library & Archives, One Bungtown Rd, 11724-2203. SAN 311-0680. Tel: 516-367-6872, 516-367-8414. Interlibrary Loan Service Tel: 516-367-8352. FAX: 516-367-6843. E-mail: archives@cshl.edu, libraryhelp@cshl.edu. Web Site: cshl.edu/cshl-library. *Dir,* Ludmila Pollock; E-mail: pollock@cshl.edu; Staff 9 (MLS 5, Non-MLS 4)
Founded 1890
Library Holdings: e-journals 900; Bk Titles 27,000; Per Subs 100
Special Collections: Historical Genetics-Eugenics Coll; History of Cold Spring Harbor Science. Oral History
Subject Interests: Biochem, Bioinformatics, Cancer res, Cell biol, Genetics, Molecular biol, Neurobiology, Plant genetics, Virology
Automation Activity & Vendor Info: (Cataloging) SirsiDynix; (OPAC) SirsiDynix
Wireless access
Publications: Bibliographies; Newsletter
Partic in Long Island Library Resources Council; Medical & Scientific Libraries of Long Island; MLC; OCLC Online Computer Library Center, Inc; OCLC Research Library Partnership
Restriction: Open by appt only

P COLD SPRING HARBOR LIBRARY*, 95 Harbor Rd, 11724. SAN 311-0699. Tel: 631-692-6820. FAX: 631-692-6827. E-mail: askref@cshlibrary.org. Web Site: www.cshlibrary.org. *Exec Dir,* Dr Roger Podell; *Asst Dir,* Diane Scinta; E-mail: dscinta@cshlibrary.org; Staff 29 (MLS 17, Non-MLS 12)
Founded 1886. Pop 8,349; Circ 120,000
Library Holdings: CDs 2,374; DVDs 6,376; e-books 1,664; Electronic Media & Resources 27,110; Large Print Bks 671; Bk Titles 67,415; Per Subs 256; Talking Bks 2,547
Special Collections: Environmental Center
Subject Interests: Local hist
Automation Activity & Vendor Info: (Acquisitions) Innovative Interfaces, Inc; (Cataloging) Innovative Interfaces, Inc; (Circulation) Innovative Interfaces, Inc; (ILL) Innovative Interfaces, Inc; (OPAC) Innovative Interfaces, Inc; (Serials) Innovative Interfaces, Inc
Wireless access
Mem of Suffolk Cooperative Library System
Open Mon-Thurs 9:30-9, Fri & Sat 9:30-5, Sun (Sept-June) 1-5
Restriction: Residents only
Friends of the Library Group

S COLD SPRING HARBOR WHALING MUSEUM LIBRARY*, 301 Main St, 11724. (Mail add: PO Box 25, 11724-0025), SAN 327-6511. Tel: 631-367-3418. FAX: 631-692-7037. Web Site: www.cshwhalingmuseum.org. *Exec Dir,* Nomi Dayan; Tel: 631-637-3418, Ext 17, E-mail: ndayan@cshwhalingmuseum.org
Library Holdings: Bk Vols 1,200
Special Collections: Whale Coll; Whale Conservation Coll
Subject Interests: Local hist, Maritime hist
Open Mon-Sun 11-5

COLLINS

S COLLINS CORRECTIONAL FACILITY LIBRARY*, Middle Rd, 14034. SAN 327-2419. Tel: 716-532-4588. *Sr Librn,* Cara Bradberry
Library Holdings: AV Mats 353; High Interest/Low Vocabulary Bk Vols 376; Large Print Bks 250; Bk Vols 23,932; Per Subs 66
Automation Activity & Vendor Info: (Cataloging) Follett Software; (Circulation) Follett Software
Function: Accelerated reader prog, Words travel prog, Writing prog
Restriction: Staff & inmates only

P COLLINS PUBLIC LIBRARY*, 2341 Main St, 14034. (Mail add: PO Box 470, 14034-0470), SAN 311-0729. Tel: 716-532-5129. FAX: 716-532-6210. E-mail: col@buffalolib.org. Web Site: www.buffalolib.org/content/library-locations/collins. *Dir,* Abigail Barten-McGrowen; Staff 7 (MLS 1, Non-MLS 6)
Pop 8,307; Circ 63,409
Library Holdings: AV Mats 3,500; Bk Vols 22,000; Per Subs 120
Automation Activity & Vendor Info: (Cataloging) SirsiDynix; (Circulation) SirsiDynix; (OPAC) SirsiDynix
Wireless access
Function: Photocopying/Printing, Prog for children & young adult, Summer reading prog, Wheelchair accessible
Mem of Buffalo & Erie County Public Library System
Open Mon, Tues & Thurs 2-8, Wed & Fri 10:30-5, Sat 10-2
Friends of the Library Group

COLTON

P HEPBURN LIBRARY OF COLTON, 84 Main St, 13625. (Mail add: PO Box 7, 13625-0007), SAN 311-0737. Tel: 315-262-2310. FAX: 315-262-2182. E-mail: collib@ncls.org. Web Site: www.coltonhepburnlibrary.org. *Dir,* Dennis Eickhoff
Pop 1,453; Circ 19,378
Library Holdings: Bk Vols 23,897
Special Collections: Genealogy Department
Automation Activity & Vendor Info: (Serials) SirsiDynix-iBistro
Wireless access
Mem of North Country Library System
Open Mon & Wed 1-7, Thurs 1-5, Fri 9-12, Sat 9-12 & 1-4
Friends of the Library Group

COMMACK

P COMMACK PUBLIC LIBRARY*, 18 Hauppauge Rd, 11725-4498. SAN 311-0745. Tel: 631-499-0888. FAX: 631-499-0591. E-mail: cpl@commackpubliclibrary.org. Web Site: www.commackpubliclibrary.org. *Dir,* Laurie Rosenthal; E-mail: laurie@commackpubliclibrary.org; *Asst Dir,* Joanne Albano; E-mail: jalbano@commackpubliclibrary.org; Staff 49 (MLS 13, Non-MLS 36)
Founded 1969. Pop 15,346
Library Holdings: Audiobooks 2,463; AV Mats 8,549; CDs 3,712; DVDs 8,409; Large Print Bks 2,210; Bk Vols 58,797; Per Subs 189
Automation Activity & Vendor Info: (Acquisitions) Innovative Interfaces, Inc; (Cataloging) Innovative Interfaces, Inc; (Circulation) Innovative Interfaces, Inc; (Course Reserve) Innovative Interfaces, Inc; (ILL) Innovative Interfaces, Inc; (OPAC) Innovative Interfaces, Inc
Wireless access
Function: 24/7 Electronic res, 24/7 Online cat, Activity rm, Adult bk club, After school storytime, Art exhibits, Art programs, Audiobks on Playaways & MP3, Audiobks via web, Bks on CD, Children's prog, Computers for patron use, E-Readers, E-Reserves, Electronic databases & coll, Free DVD rentals, Home delivery & serv to seniorr ctr & nursing homes, Homebound delivery serv, ILL available, Internet access, Life-long learning prog for all ages, Magazines, Magnifiers for reading, Meeting rooms, Movies, Museum passes, Music CDs, Notary serv, Online cat, Outreach serv, OverDrive digital audio bks, Photocopying/Printing, Preschool outreach, Preschool

reading prog, Printer for laptops & handheld devices, Prog for adults, Prog for children & young adult, Ref & res, Ref serv available, Res assist avail, Scanner, Senior outreach, Serves people with intellectual disabilities, STEM programs, Story hour, Study rm, Summer & winter reading prog, Summer reading prog, Tax forms, Teen prog, Telephone ref, Wheelchair accessible, Winter reading prog, Workshops
Publications: Colophon (Newsletter); Internet Gazette (Newsletter)
Mem of Suffolk Cooperative Library System
Open Mon-Thurs 9-9, Fri 9-6, Sat 9-5, Sun 1-5
Friends of the Library Group

SR PRESBYTERY OF LONG ISLAND*, Resource Center, 42 Hauppauge Rd, 11725. SAN 327-6538. Tel: 631-499-7171. FAX: 631-499-7063. Web Site: www.presbyteryofli.com. *Exec Dir,* Charlaine Apsel; E-mail: charlaine@prcli.org
Library Holdings: Bk Titles 2,000; Per Subs 50
Wireless access
Open Mon-Thurs (Winter) 10-4; Mon-Thurs (Summer) 10-3

COMSTOCK

S GREAT MEADOW CORRECTIONAL FACILITY LIBRARY, 11739 State Rte 22, 12821. (Mail add: PO Box 51, 12821), SAN 311-0761. Tel: 518-639-5516. *Librn,* Heather Larrow; E-mail: heather.larrow@doccs.ny.gov; Staff 1 (MLS 1)
Founded 1971
Library Holdings: High Interest/Low Vocabulary Bk Vols 300; Bk Titles 11,000; Bk Vols 11,895; Per Subs 50
Subject Interests: African-Am studies, Spanish lang
Automation Activity & Vendor Info: (Circulation) Follett Software
Mem of Southern Adirondack Library System

S WASHINGTON CORRECTIONAL FACILITY LIBRARY*, 72 Lock Eleven Lane, 12821. (Mail add: PO Box 180, 12821-0180), SAN 327-2494. Tel: 518-639-4486. FAX: 518-639-3299. *Librn,* Donald Cartmell
Library Holdings: Bk Vols 10,000
Wireless access
Mem of Southern Adirondack Library System
Restriction: Staff & inmates only

CONSTABLEVILLE

P CONSTABLEVILLE VILLAGE LIBRARY, 3158 Main St, 13325. (Mail add: PO Box 376, 13325-0376), SAN 311-077X. Tel: 315-397-2801. FAX: 315-397-2801. E-mail: cvllib@ncls.org. Web Site: www.cvillelibrary.org. *Dir,* Brandi Lewis
Library Holdings: Bk Vols 4,100; Per Subs 35
Wireless access
Mem of North Country Library System
Open Mon & Wed 12-4, Thurs 1-3 & 5-7, Sat 9-11
Friends of the Library Group

COOPERSTOWN

M BASSETT MARY IMOGENE HOSPITAL*, Bassett Learning Commons & Mackenzie Medical Library, Bassett Medical Ctr, One Atwell Rd, 13326. SAN 311-0788. Tel: 607-547-3115. FAX: 607-547-3006. E-mail: medical.library@bassett.org. Web Site: www.bassett.org. *Mgr,* Laura Dixon; E-mail: laura.dixon@bassett.org; *Educ Tech Spec,* Matthew Roslund; E-mail: matthew.roslund@bassett.org; Staff 2 (MLS 2)
Founded 1936
Subject Interests: Clinical med
Automation Activity & Vendor Info: (Cataloging) CyberTools for Libraries; (Circulation) CyberTools for Libraries; (OPAC) CyberTools for Libraries
Wireless access
Partic in New York State Interlibrary Loan Network
Open Mon-Fri 8-4:30

S FENIMORE ART MUSEUM*, Research Library, 5798 State Hwy 80, 13326. (Mail add: PO Box 800, 13326-0800), SAN 311-0818. Tel: 607-547-1470. Toll Free Tel: 888-547-1450. FAX: 607-547-1405. E-mail: library@fenimoreart.org. Web Site: www.fenimoreartmuseum.org/collections. *Dir of Coll,* Erin Richardson; E-mail: e.richardson@fenimoreart.org; Staff 6 (MLS 3, Non-MLS 3)
Founded 1899
Library Holdings: Bk Vols 89,000; Per Subs 320
Special Collections: New York State & Local History Coll, mss
Subject Interests: Am cultural hist, Am social, Decorative art, Mus studies, Native North American Indian art, NY genealogy, NY hist
Automation Activity & Vendor Info: (Cataloging) Innovative Interfaces, Inc; (OPAC) Innovative Interfaces, Inc; (Serials) Innovative Interfaces, Inc
Wireless access
Function: Archival coll, Art exhibits, Computers for patron use, ILL available, Photocopying/Printing, Ref & res, Res performed for a fee, Workshops
Partic in South Central Regional Library Council
Open Mon-Fri 10-5
Restriction: Authorized scholars by appt, Borrowing privileges limited to fac & registered students, Borrowing requests are handled by ILL, Circulates for staff only, Fee for pub use, Internal circ only, Lending to staff only, Non-circulating of rare bks, Non-circulating to the pub
Friends of the Library Group

S NATIONAL BASEBALL HALL OF FAME & MUSEUM, INC*, Library & Archives, 25 Main St, 13326. SAN 311-080X. Tel: 607-547-0330, 607-547-0335. FAX: 607-547-4094. E-mail: research@baseballhall.org. Web Site: baseballhall.org/discover-more/education/research. *Libr Dir,* Position Currently Open; *Dir, Giamatti Res Ctr,* Cassidy Lent; E-mail: clent@baseballhall.org; Staff 4 (MLS 3, Non-MLS 1)
Founded 1939
Library Holdings: AV Mats 12,000; Bk Titles 30,000; Bk Vols 35,000; Per Subs 150
Special Collections: American League & National League Performance Statistics; Archives; Box Scores (1876-present); Schedules. Oral History
Subject Interests: Baseball, Econ, Sociol of baseball, Sports hist
Automation Activity & Vendor Info: (Acquisitions) Innovative Interfaces, Inc - Millennium; (Cataloging) Innovative Interfaces, Inc - Millennium
Wireless access
Publications: Hall of Fame Yearbook; Memories & Dreams
Open Mon-Fri 9-5
Restriction: Fee for pub use, Free to mem, Non-circulating coll

P VILLAGE LIBRARY OF COOPERSTOWN*, 22 Main St, 13326. SAN 311-0826. Tel: 607-547-8344. Web Site: www.villagelibraryofcooperstown.org. *Dir,* Heather Urtz; E-mail: co.heather@4cls.org; Staff 4 (MLS 1, Non-MLS 3)
Pop 4,000; Circ 38,000
Library Holdings: CDs 50; DVDs 220; Large Print Bks 1,200; Bk Vols 22,000; Per Subs 30; Talking Bks 800; Videos 30
Automation Activity & Vendor Info: (Cataloging) SirsiDynix-iBistro; (Circulation) SirsiDynix-iBistro; (OPAC) SirsiDynix-iBistro
Wireless access
Mem of Four County Library System
Open Mon & Wed 9-8, Tues, Thurs & Fri 9-5, Sat 10-2, Sun 1-4
Friends of the Library Group

COPIAGUE

P COPIAGUE MEMORIAL PUBLIC LIBRARY*, 50 Deauville Blvd, 11726. SAN 311-0834. Tel: 631-691-1111. FAX: 631-691-5098. E-mail: information@copiaguelibrary.org. Web Site: www.copiaguelibrary.org. *Libr Dir,* Kenneth S Miller; Staff 50 (MLS 7, Non-MLS 43)
Founded 1961. Pop 25,758; Circ 332,121
Library Holdings: AV Mats 23,799; Large Print Bks 1,587; Bk Titles 70,962; Bk Vols 78,099; Per Subs 257
Wireless access
Publications: Newsletter (Bimonthly)
Mem of Suffolk Cooperative Library System
Open Mon-Thurs 10-7, Fri 10-6, Sat 9:30-4:30
Friends of the Library Group

CORFU

P CORFU FREE LIBRARY*, Seven Maple Ave, 14036. (Mail add: PO Box 419, 14036-0419), SAN 311-0850. Tel: 585-599-3321. FAX: 585-599-3321. E-mail: corfulibrary@nioga.org. Web Site: corfulibrary.org. *Libr Dir,* Diana Reding; *Ch Serv,* Josselyn Borowiec; Staff 2 (Non-MLS 2)
Founded 1920. Pop 755; Circ 14,451
Library Holdings: Bk Vols 75,000; Per Subs 25
Automation Activity & Vendor Info: (Cataloging) SirsiDynix; (Circulation) SirsiDynix; (OPAC) SirsiDynix
Wireless access
Function: ILL available
Mem of Nioga Library System
Open Mon & Wed 9-4, Tues, Thurs & Fri 1-8
Friends of the Library Group

CORINTH

P CORINTH FREE LIBRARY, 89 Main St, 12822. SAN 311-0869. Tel: 518-654-6913. FAX: 518-654-6913. Web Site: corinth.sals.edu. *Dir,* Rebecca Fasulo; E-mail: rfasulo@sals.edu; *Ch Serv,* Michael Hadfield; E-mail: mhadfield@sals.edu
Founded 1926. Pop 6,490; Circ 24,500
Library Holdings: AV Mats 800; Bk Vols 19,802; Per Subs 16

Automation Activity & Vendor Info: (Cataloging) Innovative Interfaces, Inc; (Circulation) Innovative Interfaces, Inc; (OPAC) Innovative Interfaces, Inc
Wireless access
Mem of Southern Adirondack Library System
Open Mon & Tues 10-5 & 7-8:30, Thurs 10-5, Fri 10-4, Sat 10-3
Friends of the Library Group

CORNING

S CORNING MUSEUM OF GLASS*, Juliette K & Leonard S Rakow Research Library, Five Museum Way, 14830. SAN 311-0907. Tel: 607-438-5300. FAX: 607-438-5392, 607-438-5394. E-mail: rakow@cmog.org. Web Site: www.cmog.org/library. *Chief Librn,* Kevin Reynolds; E-mail: reynoldsk@cmog.org; Staff 17.5 (MLS 8.5, Non-MLS 9)
Founded 1950
Library Holdings: AV Mats 230,000; DVDs 1,400; Electronic Media & Resources 12; Microforms 20,000; Bk Titles 50,000; Bk Vols 55,000; Per Subs 1,000; Videos 1,500
Special Collections: Antiquarian & Rare Books Coll; Auction Catalog Coll; Design Drawings & Art on Paper; Emphera Coll; Film, Video & DVD Coll; Microform Coll; Personal & Corporate Archives; Slide Coll; Trade Catalog Coll
Subject Interests: Archaeology, Glass art, Glassware, Hist of glass, Manufacturing of glass before 1930
Automation Activity & Vendor Info: (Acquisitions) Ex Libris Group; (Cataloging) Ex Libris Group; (Circulation) Ex Libris Group; (ILL) OCLC; (OPAC) Ex Libris Group; (Serials) Ex Libris Group
Wireless access
Partic in OCLC Online Computer Library Center, Inc; South Central Regional Library Council
Open Mon-Sun 9-5

P SOUTHEAST STEUBEN COUNTY LIBRARY*, 300 Nasser Civic Center Plaza, Ste 101, 14830. SAN 311-0915. Tel: 607-936-3713. Circulation Tel: 607-936-3713, Ext 501. Reference Tel: 607-936-3713, Ext 502. Administration Tel: 607-936-3713, Ext 205. FAX: 607-936-1714. Web Site: ssclibrary.org. *Dir,* Pauline Emery; E-mail: emeryp@stls.org; *Asst Dir,* Brad Turner; Tel: 607-936-3713, Ext 208, E-mail: turnerb@stls.org; *Ch,* Sue McConnell; Tel: 607-936-3713, Ext 503, E-mail: mcconnells@stls.org; Staff 17 (MLS 3, Non-MLS 14)
Founded 2000. Pop 34,141; Circ 150,203
Library Holdings: Bk Vols 118,438; Per Subs 125
Special Collections: Caldecott & Newbery Winners & Honors Coll; Foreign, Independent & Classic Films Coll; Foundation Center Coll
Subject Interests: Glass, Literacy, Local hist
Automation Activity & Vendor Info: (Acquisitions) SirsiDynix; (Cataloging) SirsiDynix; (Circulation) SirsiDynix
Wireless access
Mem of Southern Tier Library System
Open Mon, Wed & Fri 10-6, Tues & Thurs 10-8, Sat 10-4, Sun 11-5
Friends of the Library Group

J SUNY CORNING COMMUNITY COLLEGE*, Arthur A Houghton, Jr Library, One Academic Dr, 14830. SAN 311-0885. Tel: 607-962-9251. FAX: 607-962-9466. E-mail: library@corning-cc.edu. Web Site: corning-cc.edu/academics/library.php. *Libr Dir,* Amy Dibble; E-mail: adibble1@corning-cc.edu; *Acq,* Eileen Goltry; E-mail: goltry@corning-cc.edu; *Cat,* Rosanne Darcangelo; E-mail: darcanrm@corning-cc.edu; *Instruction & Outreach,* Erin Wilburn; E-mail: ewilburn@corning-cc.edu; Staff 4.5 (MLS 2, Non-MLS 2.5)
Founded 1957. Enrl 2,700; Fac 89; Highest Degree: Associate
Library Holdings: Bk Vols 25,000
Automation Activity & Vendor Info: (Acquisitions) Ex Libris Group; (Cataloging) Ex Libris Group; (Circulation) Ex Libris Group; (Course Reserve) Ex Libris Group; (Discovery) Ex Libris Group; (ILL) OCLC ILLiad; (OPAC) Ex Libris Group; (Serials) Ex Libris Group
Wireless access
Partic in SUNYConnect
Open Mon-Thurs (Fall & Spring) 7:30am-8pm, Fri 7:30-4, Sun 2-6; Mon-Fri (Winter) 8-4:30; Mon-Fri (June & July) 8-4

CORNWALL

P CORNWALL PUBLIC LIBRARY*, 395 Hudson St, 12518. SAN 352-4108. Tel: 845-534-8282. FAX: 845-534-3827. E-mail: cor@rcls.org. Web Site: www.cornwallpubliclibrary.org. *Dir,* Mary Lou Carolan; Staff 3 (MLS 3)
Pop 14,289; Circ 112,000
Library Holdings: Bk Vols 35,500; Per Subs 165
Special Collections: Biography & Literature (Local Authors Coll); Local History; The Cornwall Local, microfilm & CD
Automation Activity & Vendor Info: (Cataloging) Horizon; (Circulation) Horizon; (OPAC) Horizon
Wireless access
Function: Homebound delivery serv
Publications: Friends of the Cornwall Public Library (Newsletter); Library Newsletter
Mem of Ramapo Catskill Library System
Open Mon-Thurs 9-8, Fri 9-6, Sat 9-4, Sun 1-4
Friends of the Library Group

CORTLAND

S CORTLAND COUNTY HISTORICAL SOCIETY*, Kellogg Memorial Research Library, 25 Homer Ave, 13045. SAN 311-094X. Tel: 607-756-6071. Web Site: cortlandhistory.com/Kellogg.aspx. *Dir,* Tabitha Scoville; E-mail: tscoville@cortlandhistory.org
Founded 1925
Library Holdings: Bk Titles 4,000
Special Collections: Genealogy & History of Cortland County, ms, archives
Open Tues-Sat 1-5

P CORTLAND FREE LIBRARY*, 32 Church St, 13045. SAN 311-0958. Tel: 607-753-1042. FAX: 607-758-7329. E-mail: ref@cortlandfreelibrary.org. Web Site: cortlandfreelibrary.org. *Dir,* Raachel Hoff; E-mail: dir@cortlandfreelibrary.org; Staff 12 (MLS 2, Non-MLS 10)
Founded 1886. Pop 28,906; Circ 101,786. Sal $230,000 (Prof $121,050)
Library Holdings: Audiobooks 1,400; CDs 210; DVDs 1,200; Large Print Bks 1,400; Bk Titles 68,152; Bk Vols 73,344; Per Subs 167; Videos 135
Subject Interests: Local hist
Automation Activity & Vendor Info: (Acquisitions) Innovative Interfaces, Inc; (Cataloging) Baker & Taylor; (Circulation) Innovative Interfaces, Inc; (ILL) Innovative Interfaces, Inc; (Serials) Innovative Interfaces, Inc
Wireless access
Function: Art exhibits, Audiobks via web, Bk club(s), Bks on cassette, Bks on CD, Children's prog, Computer training, Computers for patron use, E-Reserves, Electronic databases & coll, Free DVD rentals, Health sci info serv, Homebound delivery serv, Homework prog, ILL available, Instruction & testing, Internet access, Literacy & newcomer serv, Magnifiers for reading, Music CDs, Online cat, Online ref, OverDrive digital audio bks, Photocopying/Printing, Preschool outreach, Prog for children & young adult, Ref serv available, Senior computer classes, Spoken cassettes & CDs, Spoken cassettes & DVDs, Story hour, Summer & winter reading prog, Tax forms, Teen prog, VHS videos, Wheelchair accessible
Publications: Cortland Free Library News (Newsletter)
Mem of Finger Lakes Library System
Open Mon-Thurs 9:30-8, Fri 9:30-5:30, Sat 9:30-4:30; Mon & Thurs (Summer) 9:30-8, Tues, Wed & Fri 9:30-5:30, Sat 9:30-1:30
Restriction: Authorized patrons

COXSACKIE

S COXSACKIE CORRECTIONAL FACILITY LIBRARY, 11260 Rte 9W, 12051. (Mail add: PO Box 200, 12051-0200), SAN 327-1323. Tel: 518-731-2781. FAX: 518-731-2099. Web Site: doccs.ny.gov/location/coxsackie-correctional-facility. *Sr Librn,* B Rowzee; Staff 1 (MLS 1)
Founded 1935
Library Holdings: Audiobooks 45; High Interest/Low Vocabulary Bk Vols 87; Bk Titles 11,000; Per Subs 33
Automation Activity & Vendor Info: (Cataloging) Follett Software; (Circulation) Follett Software
Function: ILL available
Restriction: Not open to pub

S GREENE CORRECTIONAL FACILITY*, General Library, 165 Plank Rd, 12051. SAN 327-2532. Tel: 518-731-2741, Ext 4600. *Sr Librn,* Ben Knowles
Library Holdings: Bk Titles 15,000; Per Subs 70
Automation Activity & Vendor Info: (Cataloging) Follett Software; (Circulation) Follett Software
Open Mon 8-4, Tues & Thurs 11-7, Wed & Fri 8am-9pm, Sat 12-7

S GREENE COUNTY HISTORICAL SOCIETY*, Vedder Research Library, 90 County Rte 42, 12051-3022. SAN 311-0990. Tel: 518-731-1033. E-mail: gchsvedderlibrary@gmail.com. Web Site: www.vedderlibrary.org, www.vedderresearchlibrary.org. *Head Archivist,* Jonathan Palmer
Founded 1994
Library Holdings: Bk Vols 10,000
Special Collections: County Maps; County Newspapers from 1792; Family Papers; Genealogy Coll; Greene County Surrogate Court Records; Postcards; Scrapbooks
Subject Interests: Catskills, Greene County, Mid-Hudson valley
Wireless access
Publications: Quarterly journal - indexed each five years
Open Tues & Wed 10-4, Sat 9-Noon

P HEERMANCE MEMORIAL LIBRARY, One Ely St, 12051. SAN 311-1008. Tel: 518-731-8084. FAX: 518-731-8264. E-mail: heermancelibrary@heermancelibrary.org. Web Site: heermancelibrary.org. *Dir,* Catherine Benson; E-mail: director@heermancelibrary.org; Staff 3.5 (MLS 1, Non-MLS 2.5)
Founded 1908. Pop 8,198; Circ 55,800
Jan 2015-Dec 2015. Mats Exp $18,654. Sal $116,811
Library Holdings: Audiobooks 700; DVDs 2,000; e-books 14,000; Electronic Media & Resources 20; Large Print Bks 1,050; Bk Titles 15,420; Bk Vols 18,600; Per Subs 45; Talking Bks 528
Subject Interests: Local hist
Automation Activity & Vendor Info: (Cataloging) Innovative Interfaces, Inc; (Circulation) Innovative Interfaces, Inc; (OPAC) Innovative Interfaces, Inc; (Serials) EBSCO Online
Wireless access
Function: Adult bk club, Audiobks via web, Bk club(s), Bks on CD, Children's prog, Computer training, Computers for patron use, Electronic databases & coll, Equip loans & repairs, Family literacy, Free DVD rentals, Health sci info serv, Home delivery & serv to seniorr ctr & nursing homes, Homebound delivery serv, Homework prog, ILL available, Internet access, Literacy & newcomer serv, Magazines, Mango lang, Museum passes, Music CDs, Online cat, Photocopying/Printing, Prog for adults, Prog for children & young adult, Ref serv available, Scanner, Senior outreach, Serves people with intellectual disabilities, Story hour, Summer reading prog, Tax forms, Telephone ref, Wheelchair accessible, Workshops, Writing prog
Mem of Mid-Hudson Library System
Open Mon, Tues, Thurs & Fri 10-4, Wed 10-6, Sat 10-2
Friends of the Library Group

CRANBERRY LAKE

P CLIFTON COMMUNITY LIBRARY*, 7171 Rte 3, 12927. (Mail add: PO Box 678, 12927), SAN 311-1024. Tel: 315-848-3256. FAX: 315-848-3554. E-mail: clklib@ncls.org. Web Site: www.cliftoncomlib.org. *Libr Dir,* Kate Kosior; Staff 3 (MLS 1, Non-MLS 2)
Founded 1975. Pop 1,005; Circ 6,675
Library Holdings: Audiobooks 125; AV Mats 298; CDs 117; DVDs 150; Large Print Bks 150; Bk Vols 7,994; Per Subs 30; Talking Bks 160; Videos 227
Special Collections: Adirondack Memorial Coll
Subject Interests: Adirondack, Local hist
Wireless access
Function: Adult bk club, Bks on cassette, Bks on CD, Computers for patron use, ILL available, Music CDs, Photocopying/Printing, Satellite serv, VHS videos
Mem of North Country Library System
Open Mon & Wed 10-3 & 6-9, Fri & Sat 10-3
Restriction: Non-circulating of rare bks
Friends of the Library Group

CROGHAN

P CROGHAN FREE LIBRARY*, 9794 State Rte 812, 13327. (Mail add: PO Box 8, 13327-0008), SAN 311-1032. Tel: 315-346-6521. FAX: 315-346-6521. E-mail: crolib@ncls.org. Web Site: www.croghanfreelibrary.org. *Dir,* Eileen Mathys
Circ 8,694
Library Holdings: Bk Vols 12,000; Per Subs 40
Wireless access
Mem of North Country Library System
Open Mon & Fri 10-6, Wed 10-8

CROTON-ON-HUDSON

P CROTON FREE LIBRARY, 171 Cleveland Dr, 10520. SAN 311-1040. Tel: 914-271-6612. FAX: 914-271-0931. E-mail: crotonref@wlsmail.org. Web Site: www.crotonfreelibrary.org. *Libr Dir,* Jesse G Bourdon; E-mail: jbourdon@wlsmail.org; *Head of Coll Dev & User Engagement,* Gwen Glazer; E-mail: gglazer@wlsmail.org; *Head, Children's/Youth Serv,* Lauren E Dorien; E-mail: ldorien@wlsmail.org; *Head, Tech Serv,* Lori Phillips; E-mail: lphillips@wlsmail.org; Staff 26 (MLS 8, Non-MLS 18)
Founded 1937. Pop 8,125; Circ 170,000
Library Holdings: AV Mats 6,622; DVDs 4,454; Bk Vols 75,771; Per Subs 166
Special Collections: Railroad Coll
Automation Activity & Vendor Info: (Acquisitions) Evergreen; (Cataloging) Evergreen; (Circulation) Evergreen; (OPAC) Evergreen
Wireless access
Function: 24/7 Electronic res, 24/7 Online cat, 3D Printer, Adult bk club, Art exhibits, Bks on CD, Electronic databases & coll, Free DVD rentals, Internet access, Magazines, Makerspace, Museum passes, Music CDs, Online cat, OverDrive digital audio bks, Photocopying/Printing, Ref serv available, Tax forms, Wheelchair accessible
Mem of Westchester Library System
Open Mon 1-9, Tues & Thurs 10-9, Wed & Fri 10-5:30, Sat 10-5 (10-1 Summer), Sun 1-5
Friends of the Library Group

CROWN POINT

P HAMMOND LIBRARY OF CROWN POINT NY, 2732 Main St, 12928. (Mail add: PO Box 245, 12928-0245), SAN 311-1075. Tel: 518-597-3616. FAX: 518-597-3616. E-mail: hammondlibrary@nycap.rr.com. *Dir,* Wendy L Terbeek; Staff 1 (Non-MLS 1)
Founded 1899. Pop 2,000; Circ 6,000
Library Holdings: CDs 48; DVDs 160; Electronic Media & Resources 1; Large Print Bks 437; Bk Titles 8,900; Per Subs 25; Talking Bks 346; Videos 1,105
Wireless access
Mem of Clinton-Essex-Franklin Library System
Special Services for the Blind - Audio mat; Bks on cassette; Bks on CD
Open Wed 2-5:30, Thurs 2-7:30

CUBA

P CUBA CIRCULATING LIBRARY*, 39 E Main St, 14727. SAN 311-1083. Tel: 585-968-1668. FAX: 585-968-3004. E-mail: cuba@stls.org. Web Site: www.cubalibrary.org. *Dir,* Leah Weber; E-mail: vooysl@stls.org@stls.org; *Children's Coordr,* Tina Dalton; E-mail: daltont@stls.org; Staff 2 (Non-MLS 2)
Founded 1872. Pop 4,672; Circ 48,475
Library Holdings: AV Mats 2,791; Bks on Deafness & Sign Lang 30; CDs 250; High Interest/Low Vocabulary Bk Vols 100; Large Print Bks 300; Bk Vols 18,202; Per Subs 48
Subject Interests: Allegany County, Cuba hist, Genealogy
Automation Activity & Vendor Info: (Acquisitions) SirsiDynix; (Cataloging) SirsiDynix; (Circulation) SirsiDynix; (ILL) SirsiDynix; (OPAC) SirsiDynix
Wireless access
Mem of Southern Tier Library System
Open Mon-Thurs 9:30-8, Sat 9:30-3:30
Friends of the Library Group

CUTCHOGUE

P CUTCHOGUE-NEW SUFFOLK FREE LIBRARY*, 27550 Main Rd, 11935. (Mail add: PO Box 935, 11935-0935), SAN 311-1091. Tel: 631-734-6360. FAX: 631-734-7010. E-mail: cutclib@cnsfl.org. Web Site: www.cutchoguelibrary.org. *Libr Dir,* Rosemary Martilotta; Staff 14 (MLS 4, Non-MLS 10)
Founded 1841. Pop 3,392; Circ 117,004
Library Holdings: AV Mats 13,660; Bk Vols 33,161; Per Subs 223
Subject Interests: Local hist
Automation Activity & Vendor Info: (Cataloging) Innovative Interfaces, Inc; (Circulation) Innovative Interfaces, Inc; (ILL) Innovative Interfaces, Inc; (OPAC) Innovative Interfaces, Inc
Wireless access
Function: Adult bk club, Archival coll, ILL available, Magnifiers for reading, Photocopying/Printing, Prog for adults, Prog for children & young adult, Ref serv available, Senior computer classes, Spoken cassettes & CDs, Summer reading prog, VHS videos
Mem of Suffolk Cooperative Library System
Open Mon-Fri 9:30-8, Sat 9:30-5, Sun (Nov-Mar) 1-5
Restriction: Open to pub for ref & circ; with some limitations
Friends of the Library Group

DANNEMORA

S CLINTON CORRECTIONAL FACILITY LIBRARY*, 1156 Rte 374, 12929. (Mail add: PO Box 2000, 12929-2000), SAN 328-7955. Tel: 518-492-2511. *Librn,* Kristen Delisle
Library Holdings: Bk Titles 8,000; Per Subs 60

P DANNEMORA FREE LIBRARY*, Village Community Ctr, 40 Emmons St, 12929. (Mail add: PO Box 730, 12929-0730), SAN 352-4345. Tel: 518-492-7005. FAX: 518-492-7005. E-mail: dannemorafreelibrary@yahoo.com. Web Site: www.dannemorafreelibrary.org. *Dir,* Eileen Cody; Staff 1 (Non-MLS 1)
Founded 1940. Pop 2,006; Circ 22,943
Library Holdings: Audiobooks 414; AV Mats 194; e-books 2,600; Large Print Bks 80; Bk Vols 6,486; Per Subs 22
Automation Activity & Vendor Info: (Cataloging) Horizon; (Circulation) Horizon; (OPAC) Horizon
Function: ILL available
Mem of Clinton-Essex-Franklin Library System
Open Mon & Wed 11-4, Tues & Thurs 2:30-8

DANSVILLE

P DANSVILLE PUBLIC LIBRARY*, Shepard Memorial Library, 200 Main St, 14437. SAN 311-1105. Tel: 585-335-6720. FAX: 585-335-6133, Web Site: www.dansvillelibrary.org. *Dir,* Teresa A Dearing; E-mail: director@dansville.lib.ny.us; Staff 1 (MLS 1)
Founded 1872. Pop 10,145; Circ 67,407. Sal $193,892 (Prof $65,750)
Library Holdings: CDs 1,396; DVDs 1,071; e-books 166; Microforms 1,465; Bk Vols 29,911; Per Subs 130; Talking Bks 50; Videos 25
Subject Interests: Local hist
Automation Activity & Vendor Info: (Circulation) Evergreen
Wireless access
Function: Art exhibits, Audiobks via web, Bks on cassette, Bks on CD, Children's prog, Computers for patron use, E-Reserves, Electronic databases & coll, Homebound delivery serv, ILL available, Mail & tel request accepted, Online cat, Orientations, OverDrive digital audio bks, Photocopying/Printing, Prog for adults, Prog for children & young adult, Scanner, Spoken cassettes & CDs, Spoken cassettes & DVDs, Story hour, Summer reading prog, Tax forms, Teen prog, VHS videos, Wheelchair accessible, Workshops
Mem of Pioneer Library System
Open Mon-Thurs 10-8, Fri 10-6, Sat 10-2
Friends of the Library Group

DEER PARK

P DEER PARK PUBLIC LIBRARY*, 44 Lake Ave, 11729. SAN 311-113X. Tel: 631-586-3000. FAX: 631-586-3006. E-mail: mail@deerparklibrary.org. Web Site: www.deerparklibrary.org. *Libr Dir,* Richard Rapecis; *Asst Dir,* Lisa Shumicky
Founded 1964. Pop 25,760; Circ 204,544
Library Holdings: e-journals 10,470; Bk Vols 102,025; Per Subs 250
Automation Activity & Vendor Info: (Cataloging) Innovative Interfaces, Inc; (Circulation) Innovative Interfaces, Inc; (OPAC) Innovative Interfaces, Inc
Wireless access
Publications: Newsletter
Mem of Suffolk Cooperative Library System
Open Mon-Thurs 9-9, Fri 9-6, Sat 9-5

DELEVAN

P DELEVAN-YORKSHIRE PUBLIC LIBRARY*, 28 School St, 14042. (Mail add: PO Box 185, 14042-0185), SAN 311-1148. Tel: 716-492-1961. FAX: 716-492-3398. E-mail: delyorkpublib@yahoo.com. Web Site: www.delevanlibrary.com. *Libr Dir,* Gwen Bixby; E-mail: gbixby@pioneercsd.org; Staff 4 (MLS 1, Non-MLS 3)
Circ 19,336
Library Holdings: Bk Vols 19,000; Per Subs 40
Automation Activity & Vendor Info: (Cataloging) SirsiDynix; (Circulation) SirsiDynix; (OPAC) SirsiDynix
Wireless access
Mem of Chautauqua-Cattaraugus Library System
Open Mon & Wed 1-8, Tues 9-12 & 2-8, Thurs 12-8, Fri 1-6, Sat 9-1; Mon & Wed (Summer) 1-8, Tues & Thurs 9-9, Fri 1-6, Sat 9-1
Friends of the Library Group

DELHI

P CANNON FREE LIBRARY*, 40 Elm St, 13753. SAN 311-1156. Tel: 607-746-2662. FAX: 607-746-2662. E-mail: di.ill@4cls.org. Web Site: libraries.4cls.org/delhi. *Libr Mgr,* Susan Mosher Frisbee; E-mail: di.susan@4cls.org; Staff 8 (Non-MLS 8)
Founded 1918. Pop 5,117
Jan 2019-Dec 2019. Mats Exp $10,255, Per/Ser (Incl. Access Fees) $23, AV Mat $934, Electronic Ref Mat (Incl. Access Fees) $9,298
Library Holdings: Audiobooks 450; DVDs 478; Large Print Bks 411; Bk Titles 16,967; Bk Vols 16,982; Per Subs 23
Special Collections: Delaware County Hist Coll
Automation Activity & Vendor Info: (Cataloging) SirsiDynix; (Circulation) SirsiDynix; (OPAC) SirsiDynix
Wireless access
Function: 24/7 Electronic res, 24/7 Online cat, Activity rm, Adult bk club, Archival coll, Bk club(s), Bks on CD, Children's prog, Computers for patron use, Free DVD rentals, Holiday prog, ILL available, Internet access, Magazines, Mail & tel request accepted, Microfiche/film & reading machines, Online cat, Online ref, OverDrive digital audio bks, Photocopying/Printing, Printer for laptops & handheld devices, Prog for adults, Prog for children & young adult, Ref & res, Story hour, Summer reading prog, Tax forms, Wheelchair accessible, Writing prog
Mem of Four County Library System
Open Tues & Thurs 9:30-7, Wed & Fri 9:30-5, Sat (Nov-March) 10-1

GL DELAWARE COUNTY SUPREME COURT LAW LIBRARY*, Three Court St, 13753. SAN 311-1164. Tel: 607-376-5429. FAX: 646-963-6401. Web Site: www.nycourts.gov/library/6jd/delaware. *Librn,* Laurie Burpoe
Founded 1880
Library Holdings: Bk Vols 8,500
Open Mon & Tues 9-2, Wed 8:30-4:30

C STATE UNIVERSITY OF NEW YORK COLLEGE OF TECHNOLOGY*, Louis & Mildred Resnick Library, Bush Hall, 454 Delhi Dr, 13753. SAN 311-1172. Tel: 607-746-4635. FAX: 607-746-4327. E-mail: library@delhi.edu. Web Site: www.delhi.edu/academics/library. *Dir,* Carrie Fishner; Tel: 607-746-4648, E-mail: fishnecj@delhi.edu; *Electronic Res & Instruction Librn,* Amanda Calabrasa; Tel: 607-746-4734, E-mail: mitcheag@delhi.ed; *Ref & Instruction Librn,* Steve G Dixon; Tel: 607-746-4642, E-mail: dixonsg@delhi.edu; *Acq Mgr,* Bradley Post; Tel: 607-746-4640, E-mail: postbj@delhi.edu; Staff 7 (MLS 4, Non-MLS 3)
Founded 1915. Enrl 3,000; Fac 139; Highest Degree: Bachelor
Library Holdings: Bk Titles 50,000; Bk Vols 60,000; Per Subs 265
Special Collections: College Archives (yearbooks, photographs, student newspapers & other college publications)
Subject Interests: Culinary, Golf, Nursing, Turf mgt, Veterinary sci
Automation Activity & Vendor Info: (Acquisitions) Ex Libris Group; (Cataloging) Ex Libris Group; (Circulation) Ex Libris Group; (Course Reserve) Ex Libris Group; (ILL) Ex Libris Group; (OPAC) Ex Libris Group
Wireless access
Function: ILL available
Publications: Library Instruction Materials; Library Rules & Regulations; Pathfinders; Staff Handbooks; Student Handbook
Partic in OCLC Online Computer Library Center, Inc; SUNYConnect
Open Mon-Thurs 7:30am-Midnight, Fri 7:30-5, Sat 12-5, Sun 2-Midnight

DELMAR

P BETHLEHEM PUBLIC LIBRARY*, 451 Delaware Ave, 12054-3042. SAN 311-1180. Tel: 518-439-9314, Administration Tel: 518-439-9314, Ext 3022. Information Services Tel: 518-439-9314, Ext 3009. FAX: 518-478-0901. Web Site: www.bethlehempubliclibrary.org. *Dir,* Geoffrey Kirkpatrick; E-mail: director@bethlehempubliclibrary.org; Staff 16 (MLS 16)
Founded 1913. Pop 25,965; Circ 627,987
Library Holdings: Bk Titles 124,848; Per Subs 289
Special Collections: Local History & Genealogy Book Coll
Automation Activity & Vendor Info: (Circulation) Innovative Interfaces, Inc - Sierra; (ILL) OCLC; (OPAC) Innovative Interfaces, Inc - Sierra
Wireless access
Publications: Footnotes (Newsletter)
Mem of Upper Hudson Library System
Partic in Cap District Libr Coun for Ref & Res Resources
Open Mon-Fri 9-9, Sat 10-5, Sun (Sept-June) 12-5
Friends of the Library Group

DEPAUVILLE

P DEPAUVILLE FREE LIBRARY*, 32333 County Rte 179, 13632. (Mail add: PO Box 239, 13632-0239), SAN 311-1199. Tel: 315-686-3299. FAX: 315-686-3299. E-mail: deplib@ncls.org. Web Site: www.depauvillefreelibrary.org. *Dir,* Kate Hamlin Wehrle; Staff 3 (MLS 1, Non-MLS 2)
Founded 1954. Pop 5,153
Jan 2016-Dec 2016 Income $71,055, State $1,495, City $10,000, County $1,056, Locally Generated Income $44,484, Other $14,020. Sal $41,699 (Prof $34,067)
Library Holdings: Audiobooks 1,170; e-books 5,272; Large Print Bks 203; Bk Vols 5,438; Per Subs 24
Wireless access
Function: 24/7 Electronic res, 24/7 Online cat, Activity rm, Adult bk club, Adult literacy prog, Art exhibits, Bi-weekly Writer's Group, Bk club(s), Chess club, Children's prog, Computer training, Computers for patron use, Electronic databases & coll, ILL available, Internet access, Life-long learning prog for all ages, Magazines, Magnifiers for reading, Meeting rooms, Online cat, Online ref, Photocopying/Printing, Preschool outreach, Preschool reading prog, Printer for laptops & handheld devices, Prog for adults, Prog for children & young adult, Ref & res, Ref serv available, Scanner, Senior computer classes, Story hour, Study rm, Summer & winter reading prog, Summer reading prog, Tax forms, Teen prog, Telephone ref, Visual arts prog, Wheelchair accessible, Winter reading prog, Workshops, Writing prog
Mem of North Country Library System
Open Mon 9-4, Tues & Wed 10-7, Thurs 9-7, Fri & Sat 10-2

DEPOSIT

P DEPOSIT FREE LIBRARY*, 159 Front St, 13754. SAN 311-1202. Tel: 607-467-2577. FAX: 607-467-1466. Web Site: depositfreelibrary.org. *Dir,* Deborah Stever; E-mail: de.deborah@4cls.org
Pop 3,888; Circ 17,522
Library Holdings: Bk Titles 15,801; Per Subs 25
Automation Activity & Vendor Info: (Cataloging) SirsiDynix; (Circulation) SirsiDynix; (OPAC) SirsiDynix
Wireless access
Mem of Four County Library System
Open Tues-Thurs 12-8, Fri & Sat 9-3

DERUYTER

P DERUYTER FREE LIBRARY*, 735 Utica St, 13052-9613. (Mail add: PO Box 399, 13052-0399), SAN 325-1543. Tel: 315-852-6262. FAX: 315-852-6262. E-mail: deruyter@midyork.org. Web Site: deruyterlibrary.org/. *Dir,* Amanda Ladd; E-mail: aladd@midyork.org
Pop 1,458; Circ 25,000
Library Holdings: Bk Titles 19,500; Per Subs 30
Automation Activity & Vendor Info: (Cataloging) SirsiDynix; (Circulation) SirsiDynix; (OPAC) SirsiDynix
Wireless access
Mem of Mid-York Library System
Open Mon 9-5, Tues & Thurs 9-7, Sat 9-1

DEWITT

P COMMUNITY LIBRARY OF DEWITT & JAMESVILLE, 5110 Jamesville Rd, 13214. SAN 311-1229. Tel: 315-446-3578. FAX: 315-446-1955. Reference E-mail: reference@cldandj.org. Web Site: www.cldandj.org. *Exec Dir,* Charles Diede; E-mail: cdiede@cldandj.org; *Asst Dir, Patron Serv,* Luke Connor; E-mail: lconnor@cldandj.org; *Asst Dir, Tech,* Erin Cassidy; E-mail: ecassidy@cldandj.org; Staff 9 (MLS 6, Non-MLS 3)
Founded 1962. Pop 35,333; Circ 195,139
Library Holdings: Audiobooks 2,000; CDs 2,800; DVDs 7,600; Electronic Media & Resources 124; Bk Titles 62,000; Per Subs 60
Special Collections: Local Interest
Automation Activity & Vendor Info: (Cataloging) Innovative Interfaces, Inc; (Circulation) Innovative Interfaces, Inc; (OPAC) Innovative Interfaces, Inc
Wireless access
Function: Adult bk club, Audiobks on Playaways & MP3, Audiobks via web, Bks on CD, Children's prog, Computer training, Computers for patron use, Electronic databases & coll, Free DVD rentals, Holiday prog, Homebound delivery serv, ILL available, Life-long learning prog for all ages, Magazines, Magnifiers for reading, Mail & tel request accepted, Meeting rooms, Movies, Music CDs, Notary serv, Online cat, Online ref, Orientations, Outreach serv, Outside serv via phone, mail, e-mail & web, OverDrive digital audio bks, Photocopying/Printing, Prog for adults, Prog for children & young adult, Ref serv available, Senior outreach, Serves people with intellectual disabilities, Story hour, Study rm, Summer reading prog, Tax forms, Teen prog, Telephone ref, Wheelchair accessible, Workshops, Writing prog
Publications: Dewitt Community Library (Newsletter)
Mem of Onondaga County Public Libraries
Open Mon-Thurs 10-9, Fri & Sat 10-5, Sun 1-5 (Winter); Mon-Thurs 10-9, Fri 10-5, Sat 10-2 (Summer)
Friends of the Library Group

DEXTER

P DEXTER FREE LIBRARY*, 120 E Kirby St, 13634. (Mail add: P O Box 544, 13634-0544), SAN 311-1237. Tel: 315-639-6785. FAX: 315-639-6785. E-mail: dexlib@ncls.org. Web Site: www.dexterfreelibrary.org. *Dir,* Jennifer Thomas
Founded 1924. Pop 1,120; Circ 5,750
Library Holdings: Bk Vols 6,395; Per Subs 30
Automation Activity & Vendor Info: (Cataloging) SirsiDynix; (Circulation) SirsiDynix; (OPAC) SirsiDynix
Wireless access
Function: After school storytime, Meeting rooms, Photocopying/Printing
Mem of North Country Library System
Open Tues 12-8, Wed 9-6, Thjurs 11-6, Sat 9-Noon
Friends of the Library Group

DIAMOND POINT

P HILLVIEW FREE LIBRARY*, 3717 Lake Shore Dr, 12824. (Mail add: PO Box 95, 12824). Tel: 518-668-3012. FAX: 518-668-3012. E-mail: hillviewfreelib@gmail.com. Web Site: hillviewfreelibrary.org. *Dir,* Virginia W Graves; *Libr Asst,* Louise Higgens; Staff 2 (Non-MLS 2)
Founded 1899. Pop 991
Library Holdings: AV Mats 150; Large Print Bks 30; Bk Vols 15,000; Per Subs 15
Special Collections: Adirondack Coll. UN Document Depository; US Document Depository
Wireless access
Function: Children's prog, Computer training, Computers for patron use, Free DVD rentals, Holiday prog, Internet access, Magazines, Movies, Museum passes, Outreach serv, Photocopying/Printing, Printer for laptops & handheld devices, Prog for adults, Prog for children & young adult, Ref & res, Ref serv available, Res assist avail, Scanner, Senior computer classes, Story hour, Teen prog, Telephone ref, Wheelchair accessible
Open Mon, Thurs & Sat (June-Aug) 10-5; Mon-Tues & Thurs-Sat (Sept-May) 10-5, Wed 10-9
Restriction: Circ to mem only, Not a lending libr, Private libr

DIX HILLS

C FIVE TOWNS COLLEGE LIBRARY*, 305 N Service Rd, 11746. SAN 311-4899. Tel: 631-656-3187. E-mail: ftclibrary@ftc.edu. Web Site: www.ftc.edu/academics/libraries. *Libr Dir,* John Vansteen; Tel: 631-656-3187; *Acad Librn, Music Librn,* Matthew Dineiro; *Librn,* Robbi Schweigert; Staff 3 (MLS 3)
Founded 1972. Enrl 650; Fac 154; Highest Degree: Doctorate
Library Holdings: AV Mats 12,000; CDs 4,000; DVDs 3,500; e-books 180,000; Music Scores 12,000; Bk Titles 25,000; Bk Vols 25,000; Videos 3,500
Special Collections: Archival Sheet Music; Popular/Classic Songbooks
Subject Interests: Educ, Film, Music, Music bus, Theatre, Video
Automation Activity & Vendor Info: (Acquisitions) EOS International; (Cataloging) EOS International; (Circulation) EOS International; (Media Booking) OCLC WorldShare Interlibrary Loan; (OPAC) EOS International
Wireless access
Function: 24/7 Electronic res, 24/7 Online cat, Computers for patron use, Electronic databases & coll, Free DVD rentals, ILL available, Internet access, Magazines, Microfiche/film & reading machines, Movies, Music CDs, Online cat, Photocopying/Printing, Res libr, Scanner, VHS videos
Partic in Long Island Library Resources Council
Open Mon-Thurs 8-8 Fri 8-4, Sat 10-3
Restriction: Borrowing privileges limited to fac & registered students

P HALF HOLLOW HILLS COMMUNITY LIBRARY, Chestnut Hill School, 600 S Service Rd, 11746. SAN 352-440X. Tel: 631-421-4530. FAX: 631-423-8946. E-mail: hhhcl@hhhlibrary.org. Web Site: hhhlibrary.org. *Exec Dir,* Helen Crosson; E-mail: hcrosson@hhhlibrary.org; *Asst Dir,* Charlene Muhr; E-mail: cmuhr@hhhlibrary.org; Staff 40 (MLS 31, Non-MLS 9)
Founded 1959
Subject Interests: Econ, Relig studies
Automation Activity & Vendor Info: (Acquisitions) Innovative Interfaces, Inc; (Cataloging) Innovative Interfaces, Inc; (Circulation) Innovative Interfaces, Inc; (ILL) Innovative Interfaces, Inc; (OPAC) Innovative Interfaces, Inc; (Serials) Innovative Interfaces, Inc
Wireless access
Publications: Business Link Newsletter (Periodical); The First R (Newsletter)
Mem of Suffolk Cooperative Library System
Partic in Long Island Library Resources Council
Open Mon-Fri 9:30-9, Sat 9:30-5
Branches: 1
MELVILLE BRANCH, 510 Sweet Hollow Rd, Melville, 11747, SAN 352-4434. Tel: 631-421-4535. *Br Librn,* Margie Hartough; E-mail: mhartough@hhhlibrary.org
Open Mon-Fri 9:30-9, Sat 9:30-5

DOBBS FERRY

P DOBBS FERRY PUBLIC LIBRARY*, 55 Main St, 10522. SAN 311-1253. Tel: 914-693-6614. FAX: 914-693-4671. E-mail: dobref@wlsmail.org. Web Site: www.dobbsferrylibrary.org. *Libr Dir,* Elizabeth Hobson; Tel: 914-231-3051, E-mail: ehobson@wlsmail.org; *Asst Dir, Head, Circ, Head, Tech Serv,* Edward Canora; Tel: 914-231-3055, E-mail: ecanora@wlsmail.org; *Adult Ref Librn, Head, Ad Ref Serv,* Sara Rodgers; Tel: 914-231-3057, E-mail: srodgers@wlsmail.org; *Ch,* Cheryl Matthews; Tel: 914-693-6615, E-mail: cmatthews@wlsmail.org; Staff 9 (MLS 7, Non-MLS 2)
Founded 1909. Pop 10,845; Circ 111,522
Jun 2012-May 2013 Income $774,334, State $2,695, City $754,923, Other $16,716. Mats Exp $88,627, Books $37,981, AV Mat $9,926, Electronic Ref Mat (Incl. Access Fees) $40,720. Sal $466,572 (Prof $337,043)
Library Holdings: Audiobooks 3,710; CDs 1,980; DVDs 2,890; e-books 42,320; Large Print Bks 625; Bk Vols 41,037; Per Subs 70; Videos 50
Automation Activity & Vendor Info: (Acquisitions) Evergreen; (Cataloging) Evergreen; (Circulation) Evergreen; (ILL) Evergreen; (OPAC) Evergreen; (Serials) Evergreen
Wireless access

Function: 24/7 Electronic res, 24/7 Online cat, 3D Printer, Adult bk club, Adult literacy prog, Art exhibits, Audiobks on Playaways & MP3, Audiobks via web, Bk club(s), Bks on CD, Children's prog, Computer training, Computers for patron use, Doc delivery serv, E-Reserves, Electronic databases & coll, Free DVD rentals, Govt ref serv, Holiday prog, Home delivery & serv to seniorr ctr & nursing homes, Homebound delivery serv, Homework prog, ILL available, Instruction & testing, Internet access, Life-long learning prog for all ages, Magazines, Magnifiers for reading, Mail & tel request accepted, Makerspace, Meeting rooms, Movies, Museum passes, Music CDs, Notary serv, Online cat, Online info literacy tutorials on the web & in blackboard, Online ref, Outreach serv, OverDrive digital audio bks, Passport agency, Photocopying/Printing, Printer for laptops & handheld devices, Prog for adults, Prog for children & young adult, Ref & res, Ref serv available, Res assist avail, Scanner, Senior computer classes, STEM programs, Story hour, Summer reading prog, Tax forms, Teen prog, Wheelchair accessible, Workshops, Writing prog
Mem of Westchester Library System
Open Mon & Wed 10-8, Tues & Thurs 10-6, Fri & Sat 10-5, Sun (Oct-Apr) 1-5
Friends of the Library Group

C MERCY COLLEGE LIBRARIES, 555 Broadway, 10522. SAN 311-1261. Tel: 914-674-7256. Interlibrary Loan Service Tel: 914-674-7580. Reference Tel: 914-674-7257. FAX: 914-674-7581. E-mail: libcirc@mercy.edu. Reference E-mail: refq@mercy.edu. Web Site: www.mercy.edu/academics/academic-centers-libraries/libraries. *Interim Libr Dir,* Moddie Breland; E-mail: mbreland@mercy.edu; *Coll Serv Librn,* Maureen Clements; Tel: 914-674-7326, E-mail: mclements2@mercy.edu; *Ref & Instruction Librn, Webmaster,* Susan Gaskin-Noel; Tel: 914-674-7672, E-mail: sgaskinnoel@mercy.edu; *ILL Supvr,* Gilda McKenna; Tel: 914-674-7580, E-mail: gmckenna2@mercy.edu; Staff 15 (MLS 15)
Founded 1950. Enrl 11,600; Fac 231; Highest Degree: Master
Library Holdings: e-books 100,000; e-journals 66,000; Bk Titles 75,000; Bk Vols 134,483; Per Subs 369
Special Collections: Eric doc. US Document Depository
Automation Activity & Vendor Info: (Acquisitions) Ex Libris Group; (Cataloging) Ex Libris Group; (Circulation) Ex Libris Group; (OPAC) Ex Libris Group; (Serials) Ex Libris Group
Wireless access
Partic in Metropolitan New York Library Council; Westchester Academic Library Directors Organization
Open Mon-Thurs 8am-11pm, Fri 8am-9pm, Sat 8:30am-9pm, Sun 11-9
Departmental Libraries:
BRONX CAMPUS, 1200 Waters Pl, Bronx, 10461, SAN 310-9100. Tel: 718-678-8850. Reference Tel: 718-678-8391. Circulation FAX: 718-678-8668. *Head Librn, Ref & Instruction,* Moddie Breland; E-mail: mbreland@mercy.edu; *Circ Supvr,* David Quiles; Tel: 718-678-8390, E-mail: dquiles@mercy.edu; Staff 2 (MLS 2)
Library Holdings: Bk Vols 30,000
Special Collections: Eye on the Bronx Coll
Open Mon-Fri 8:30-4:45, Sat & Sun 8:30-2:45
MANHATTAN CAMPUS, 47 W 34th St, New York, 10001. Tel: 212-615-3362. Reference Tel: 212-615-3336. FAX: 212-967-6330. *Head Librn, Ref & Instruction,* Yvette Page; Tel: 212-615-3364, E-mail: ypage@mercy.edu; Staff 4 (MLS 4)
Fac 3
Open Mon-Thurs 9-9, Fri 9-4, Sat 10-5:45

DOLGEVILLE

P DOLGEVILLE-MANHEIM PUBLIC LIBRARY*, 24 N Main St, 13329. SAN 311-1288. Tel: 315-429-3421. FAX: 315-429-3421. E-mail: dolgeville@midyork.org. Web Site: www.midyorklib.org/dolgeville. *Dir,* Marge Balder; Staff 1 (Non-MLS 1)
Founded 1890. Pop 3,527; Circ 21,937
Library Holdings: Bk Vols 8,369; Per Subs 12
Wireless access
Function: 24/7 Electronic res, 24/7 Online cat, Activity rm, Adult bk club, Adult literacy prog, Audiobks via web, Bks on CD, Computers for patron use, Digital talking bks, Electronic databases & coll, Family literacy, Free DVD rentals, Internet access, Laminating, Magazines, Meeting rooms, Movies, Music CDs, Online cat, OverDrive digital audio bks, Photocopying/Printing, Preschool reading prog, Prog for adults, Prog for children & young adult, Ref serv available, Senior outreach, Summer reading prog, Tax forms, Workshops
Mem of Mid-York Library System
Special Services for the Blind - Talking bks
Open Mon-Wed & Fri (Summer) 11-5, Thurs 11-8; Tues, Wed & Fri (Winter) 11-5, Thurs 11-8
Friends of the Library Group

DRYDEN

P SOUTHWORTH LIBRARY ASSOCIATION*, 24 W Main St, 13053. (Mail add: PO Box 45, 13053-0045), SAN 311-1318. Tel: 607-844-4782. FAX: 607-844-5310. E-mail: southworthlibrary@gmail.com. Web Site: southworthlibrary.org. *Libr Dir,* Diane Pamel; E-mail: director@southworthlibrary.org
Founded 1883. Pop 12,156; Circ 32,000
Library Holdings: Bk Titles 25,000; Per Subs 45
Special Collections: Rare Books (John Dryden Coll)
Subject Interests: Local hist, Rare bks
Automation Activity & Vendor Info: (Cataloging) Innovative Interfaces, Inc; (Circulation) Innovative Interfaces, Inc; (OPAC) Innovative Interfaces, Inc; (Serials) Innovative Interfaces, Inc
Wireless access
Mem of Finger Lakes Library System
Open Mon, Wed & Fri 2-7, Tues & Thurs 11-5, Sat 10-2
Friends of the Library Group

J TOMPKINS CORTLAND COMMUNITY COLLEGE LIBRARY*, Baker Commons, 2nd Flr, 170 North St, 13053-8504. (Mail add: PO Box 139, 13503-0139), SAN 311-1326. Tel: 607-844-8222, Ext 4360. Circulation Tel: 607-844-8222, Ext 4361. Administration Tel: 607-844-8222, Ext 4354. Toll Free Tel: 888-567-8211, Ext 4363. FAX: 607-844-6540. E-mail: tc3library@tomkinscortland.edu. Web Site: www.tompkinscortland.edu/library. *Libr Dir,* Gregg Kiehl; E-mail: grjk@tompkinscortland.edu; *Librn,* Karla Block; E-mail: kjb@tomkinscortland.edu; *Acq Librn,* Susanna Vant Sant; E-mail: sv1@tomkinscortland.edu; *Instrul Serv Librn,* Barbara Kobritz; Tel: 607-844-8222, Ext 4362, E-mail: kobritb@tomkinscortland.edu; *Libr Serv Librn,* Eric Jenes; E-mail: EJ1@tomkinscortland.edu; *Circ Serv Coordr,* Lucy Yang; Tel: 607-844-8222, Ext 4361, E-mail: vangl@tomkinscortland.edu; Staff 9 (MLS 5, Non-MLS 4)
Founded 1968. Enrl 3,000; Fac 75; Highest Degree: Associate
Library Holdings: Bk Titles 43,015; Bk Vols 51,709; Per Subs 350
Special Collections: State Document Depository
Subject Interests: Allied health, Bus computing, Nursing
Automation Activity & Vendor Info: (Acquisitions) Ex Libris Group; (Cataloging) Ex Libris Group; (Circulation) Ex Libris Group; (Course Reserve) Ex Libris Group
Wireless access
Partic in OCLC Online Computer Library Center, Inc; South Central Regional Library Council; SUNYConnect
Special Services for the Deaf - Assistive tech
Special Services for the Blind - Assistive/Adapted tech devices, equip & products; Reader equip; Scanner for conversion & translation of mats
Open Mon-Thurs 8am-9pm, Fri 8-4, Sun 1-5

DUNDEE

P DUNDEE LIBRARY*, 32 Water St, 14837. SAN 311-1334. Tel: 607-243-5938. FAX: 607-243-7733. E-mail: dundee@stls.org. Web Site: www.stls.org/dundee. *Libr Dir,* Segrid Dombroski; Staff 4 (Non-MLS 4)
Founded 1908. Pop 6,524; Circ 55,000
Library Holdings: Audiobooks 797; Bks on Deafness & Sign Lang 20; DVDs 1,315; High Interest/Low Vocabulary Bk Vols 200; Large Print Bks 1,500; Bk Vols 22,500; Per Subs 35; Videos 550
Special Collections: Monroe Railroad Coll
Subject Interests: Local hist, Trains
Automation Activity & Vendor Info: (Cataloging) SirsiDynix; (Circulation) SirsiDynix; (OPAC) SirsiDynix
Wireless access
Function: 24/7 Online cat, ILL available, Photocopying/Printing, Ref serv available, Telephone ref
Mem of Southern Tier Library System
Special Services for the Blind - Bks available with recordings
Open Mon-Wed 1-6, Thurs & Fri 10-6, Sat 10-2

DUNKIRK

P DUNKIRK PUBLIC LIBRARY*, 536 Central Ave, 14048. SAN 311-1342. Tel: 716-366-2511. FAX: 716-366-2525. E-mail: info@dunkirklibrary.org. Web Site: dunkirklibrary.org. *Dir,* Janice Dekoff; Staff 1 (MLS 1)
Founded 1904. Pop 15,310; Circ 136,208
Wireless access
Function: Wheelchair accessible
Mem of Chautauqua-Cattaraugus Library System
Special Services for the Blind - Braille servs
Open Mon-Thurs 10-8, Fri & Sat 10-5

EARLVILLE

P EARLVILLE FREE LIBRARY*, Four N Main St, 13332. (Mail add: PO Box 120, 13332-0120), SAN 311-1350. Tel: 315-691-5931. FAX: 315-691-5931. E-mail: earlville@midyork.org. Web Site:

www.earlvillefreelibrary.org. *Dir,* Shari Taylor; E-mail: staylor@midyork.org
Founded 1917. Pop 980; Circ 33,360
Library Holdings: Bk Vols 23,318; Per Subs 14
Special Collections: New York Indian Heroes (Ologan Coll); Wood Artifacts (Conger Coll)
Wireless access
Function: 24/7 Electronic res, 24/7 Online cat
Mem of Mid-York Library System
Open Mon-Wed 1-8, Thurs & Fri 10-5, Sat 10-1:30
Friends of the Library Group

EAST AURORA

P AURORA TOWN PUBLIC LIBRARY*, East Aurora Library, 550 Main St, 14052. SAN 351-8280. Tel: 716-652-4440. FAX: 716-655-5875. E-mail: eau@buffalolib.org. Web Site: www.buffalolib.org/content/library-locations/aurora. *Dir,* Robert Alessi
Library Holdings: AV Mats 8,145; Bk Vols 46,957
Subject Interests: Roycroft Craft Movement
Automation Activity & Vendor Info: (Cataloging) SirsiDynix; (Circulation) SirsiDynix; (OPAC) SirsiDynix; (Serials) SirsiDynix
Wireless access
Mem of Buffalo & Erie County Public Library System
Partic in Western New York Library Resources Council
Open Mon & Thurs (Winter) 1-8, Tues 10-8, Wed 12-6, Fri 10-6, Sat 10-3; Mon & Thurs (Summer) 1-8, Tues 10-8, Wed & Fri 10-6
Friends of the Library Group

R CHRIST THE KING SEMINARY LIBRARY, 711 Knox Rd, 14052. (Mail add: PO Box 607, 14052-0607), SAN 311-1369. Tel: 716-652-8900. FAX: 716-652-8903. Web Site: www.cks.edu/library. *Dir,* Teresa Lubienecki; Tel: 716-655-7098, E-mail: tlubienecki@cks.edu; *Per/Circ Librn,* Sister Jane Brady; Staff 4 (MLS 3, Non-MLS 1)
Founded 1951. Enrl 96; Fac 11; Highest Degree: Master
Library Holdings: AV Mats 1,380; Bk Vols 200,000; Per Subs 437
Special Collections: Early French Canadian & Niagara Frontier History (Msgr James Bray Coll)
Subject Interests: Philos, Relig, Theol
Automation Activity & Vendor Info: (Cataloging) ComPanion Corp; (Circulation) ComPanion Corp
Partic in OCLC Online Computer Library Center, Inc; Western New York Library Resources Council

EAST ELMHURST

S ERIC M TAYLOR CENTER*, Law Library, 10-10 Hazen St, 11370. SAN 352-4523. Tel: 718-546-7359. FAX: 718-546-7357. *Dir,* Karen Powell; E-mail: karen.powell@doc.nyc.gov
Library Holdings: e-books 5,000; Bk Vols 75
Restriction: Staff use only

EAST GREENBUSH

P EAST GREENBUSH COMMUNITY LIBRARY*, Ten Community Way, 12061. SAN 352-4469. Tel: 518-477-7476. FAX: 518-477-6692. Web Site: www.eastgreenbushlibrary.org. *Dir,* Jill Dugas Hughes; E-mail: director@eglibrary.org; Staff 43 (MLS 18, Non-MLS 25)
Founded 1948. Pop 15,560; Circ 392,324
Jan 2019-Dec 2019 Income $2,104,899, State $4,800, City $1,680,206, Locally Generated Income $108,580, Other $311,313. Mats Exp $129,135, Books $62,200, Per/Ser (Incl. Access Fees) $5,000, Other Print Mats $1,000, AV Mat $27,575, Electronic Ref Mat (Incl. Access Fees) $31,385, Presv $1,975. Sal $1,049,456
Automation Activity & Vendor Info: (Cataloging) Innovative Interfaces, Inc; (Circulation) Innovative Interfaces, Inc - Sierra; (ILL) OCLC; (OPAC) Innovative Interfaces, Inc - Sierra; (Serials) Innovative Interfaces, Inc - Sierra
Wireless access
Function: 24/7 Electronic res, 24/7 Online cat, Activity rm, Adult bk club, Adult literacy prog, Art exhibits, Art programs, Audio & video playback equip for onsite use, Audiobks on Playaways & MP3, Audiobks via web, AV serv, Bk club(s), Bks on CD, Children's prog, Computer training, Computers for patron use, Digital talking bks, E-Readers, Electronic databases & coll, Equip loans & repairs, Family literacy, Free DVD rentals, Games & aids for people with disabilities, Genealogy discussion group, Health sci info serv, Holiday prog, Home delivery & serv to seniorr ctr & nursing homes, Homebound delivery serv, Homework prog, ILL available, Internet access, Learning ctr, Life-long learning prog for all ages, Magazines, Magnifiers for reading, Mail & tel request accepted, Mango lang, Meeting rooms, Movies, Museum passes, Music CDs, Notary serv, Online cat, Online info literacy tutorials on the web & in blackboard, Outreach serv, OverDrive digital audio bks, Photocopying/Printing, Preschool outreach, Preschool reading prog, Printer for laptops & handheld devices, Prof lending libr, Prog for adults, Prog for children & young adult, Ref & res, Ref serv available, Scanner, Serves people with intellectual disabilities, STEM programs, Story hour, Study rm, Summer & winter reading prog, Summer reading prog, Tax forms, Teen prog, Telephone ref, Visual arts prog, Wheelchair accessible, Winter reading prog, Workshops, Writing prog
Publications: Greenbush Bookmark (Newsletter)
Mem of Upper Hudson Library System
Open Mon-Thurs 9-9, Fri 9-6, Sat 10-5, Sun 1-5
Friends of the Library Group

EAST HAMPTON

P EAST HAMPTON LIBRARY*, 159 Main St, 11937. SAN 311-1415. Tel: 631-324-0222. FAX: 631-329-5947. E-mail: info@easthamptonlibrary.org. Web Site: www.easthamptonlibrary.org. *Dir,* Dennis Fabiszak; Tel: 631-324-0222, Ext 7, E-mail: dennis@easthamptonlibrary.org; Staff 39 (MLS 13, Non-MLS 26)
Founded 1897. Pop 15,210; Circ 158,000
Library Holdings: Bks on Deafness & Sign Lang 10; High Interest/Low Vocabulary Bk Vols 100; Bk Titles 59,000; Bk Vols 63,719; Per Subs 96
Special Collections: Digital Long Island Coll; Long Island History, Biography & Genealogy (Pennypacker Coll), bks, microflm, memorabilia; Thomas Moran Biographical Art Coll. Oral History
Automation Activity & Vendor Info: (Cataloging) Innovative Interfaces, Inc - Millennium; (Circulation) Innovative Interfaces, Inc - Millennium; (ILL) Innovative Interfaces, Inc - Millennium; (OPAC) Innovative Interfaces, Inc - Millennium
Wireless access
Function: Adult bk club, Adult literacy prog, Archival coll, Art exhibits, Audio & video playback equip for onsite use, Audiobks via web, AV serv, Bi-weekly Writer's Group, Bilingual assistance for Spanish patrons, Bk club(s), Bk reviews (Group), Bks on cassette, Bks on CD, CD-ROM, Children's prog, Citizenship assistance, Computer training, Computers for patron use, Digital talking bks, E-Readers, E-Reserves, Electronic databases & coll, Family literacy, For res purposes, Free DVD rentals, Holiday prog, Homebound delivery serv, Homework prog, ILL available, Instruction & testing, Internet access, Life-long learning prog for all ages, Literacy & newcomer serv, Magazines, Magnifiers for reading, Mail & tel request accepted, Microfiche/film & reading machines, Movies, Music CDs, Online cat, Online ref, Orientations, Outside serv via phone, mail, e-mail & web, OverDrive digital audio bks, Photocopying/Printing, Preschool outreach, Preschool reading prog, Printer for laptops & handheld devices, Prog for adults, Prog for children & young adult, Ref & res, Ref serv available, Res libr, Scanner, Senior computer classes, Senior outreach, Serves people with intellectual disabilities, Spanish lang bks, Spoken cassettes & CDs, Spoken cassettes & DVDs, Story hour, Summer & winter reading prog, Summer reading prog, Tax forms, Teen prog, Telephone ref, VHS videos, Wheelchair accessible, Winter reading prog, Workshops, Writing prog
Mem of Suffolk Cooperative Library System
Open Mon-Thurs 9-7, Fri & Sat 9-5, Sun 1-5

EAST ISLIP

P EAST ISLIP PUBLIC LIBRARY*, 381 E Main St, 11730-2896. SAN 311-1423. Tel: 631-581-9200. FAX: 631-581-2245. E-mail: info@eipl.org. Web Site: eipl.org. *Dir,* Guy P Edwards; Tel: 631-581-9200, Ext 7, E-mail: gedwards@eipl.org; *Head, Adult Serv,* Jo-Ann Carhart; *Head, Children's Servx,* Lauren Scottaline; *Head, Circ,* Pamela Fitzsimons; *Head, Tech Serv,* Deborah Russin; *YA Librn,* Kassia Worst; Staff 33 (MLS 11, Non-MLS 22)
Founded 1960. Pop 25,796; Circ 222,286
Jul 2018-Jun 2019 Income $4,160,000, State $7,400, Locally Generated Income $4,017,689, Other $134,911
Library Holdings: AV Mats 48,500; Bk Vols 190,000; Per Subs 400
Special Collections: Art Originals Coll; Francis Hopkinson Smith Coll; Irish Heritage; Lighthouses Coll; Local History Coll. US Document Depository
Automation Activity & Vendor Info: (Circulation) Innovative Interfaces, Inc; (ILL) Innovative Interfaces, Inc; (OPAC) Innovative Interfaces, Inc
Wireless access
Function: Ref serv available
Publications: East of Islip (Local History); Librafax; Little Librafax
Mem of Suffolk Cooperative Library System
Partic in Partnership of Automated Librs in Suffolk
Special Services for the Blind - Low vision equip
Open Mon-Thurs 9-9, Fri 9-6, Sat 9-5, Sun 1-5

EAST MEADOW

P EAST MEADOW PUBLIC LIBRARY*, 1886 Front St, 11554-1705. SAN 311-1431. Tel: 516-794-2570. FAX: 516-794-1272. Administration FAX: 516-794-8536. TDD: 516-794-2949. E-mail: contactus@eastmeadow.info. Web Site: www.eastmeadow.info. *Dir,* Carol Probeyahn; *Asst Dir,* Rocco Cassano; *Ch Serv,* Gail Goldfarb; *Circ Serv,* Christina Hirsch; *Media Serv,* Karen Shaw Widman; *Reader Serv,* Marcia Blackman; *Ref Serv,* Stephanie Dwyer; *YA Serv,* Paula DeVito; Staff 65 (MLS 20, Non-MLS 45)

Founded 1955. Pop 52,102; Circ 387,697
Jul 2018-Jun 2019 Income $7,699,529, State $10,000, Locally Generated Income $7,337,829, Other $351,700. Mats Exp $544,100, Books $228,850, Per/Ser (Incl. Access Fees) $75,000, Micro $20,000, AV Mat $85,250, Electronic Ref Mat (Incl. Access Fees) $135,000. Sal $4,271,594 (Prof $2,289,804)
Library Holdings: DVDs 14,712; e-books 68,287; Bk Vols 223,772; Per Subs 641
Special Collections: Literary Criticism; Long Island History
Subject Interests: Behav sci, Civil serv, Relig studies, Repair manuals, Repair per, Soc sci
Automation Activity & Vendor Info: (Cataloging) Innovative Interfaces, Inc; (Circulation) Innovative Interfaces, Inc; (OPAC) Innovative Interfaces, Inc; (Serials) SerialsSolutions
Wireless access
Function: Adult bk club, Art exhibits, Audiobks via web, AV serv, Bk club(s), Bks on CD, Chess club, Children's prog, Computer training, Computers for patron use, Digital talking bks, Electronic databases & coll, Free DVD rentals, Homebound delivery serv, ILL available, Magnifiers for reading, Microfiche/film & reading machines, Museum passes, Music CDs, Notary serv, Online cat, Online ref, OverDrive digital audio bks, Photocopying/Printing, Prog for adults, Prog for children & young adult, Scanner, Senior computer classes, Story hour, Summer reading prog, Tax forms, Telephone ref, Wheelchair accessible
Publications: East Meadow: Past & Present (Local historical information); Who's Who in East Meadow (Annual)
Mem of Nassau Library System
Partic in Long Island Library Resources Council
Special Services for the Deaf - Assisted listening device; Described encaptioned media prog; TTY equip
Special Services for the Blind - Large print bks; Recorded bks; Talking bks
Open Mon, Tues, Thurs & Fri 9-9, Wed 11-9, Sat 9-5, Sun (Winter) 1-5
Friends of the Library Group

M NASSAU UNIVERSITY MEDICAL CENTER*, Peter Addiego Health Sciences Library, 2201 Hempstead Tpk, 11554. SAN 311-144X. Tel: 516-572-8742. Interlibrary Loan Service Tel: 516-572-5606. Administration Tel: 516-572-8745. FAX: 516-572-3009. Web Site: www.numc.edu/education/health-sciences-library. *Med Librn,* Rimma Perelman; E-mail: rperelma@numc.edu; Staff 2 (MLS 1, Non-MLS 1)
Library Holdings: Bk Titles 6,000; Per Subs 1,000
Subject Interests: Allied health sci, Behav health, Health sci, Nursing
Automation Activity & Vendor Info: (Acquisitions) EOS International; (Cataloging) EOS International; (Circulation) EOS International; (Discovery) TDNet; (OPAC) EOS International; (Serials) EOS International
Wireless access
Partic in Basic Health Sciences Library Network; Long Island Library Resources Council; Medical & Scientific Libraries of Long Island
Restriction: Authorized patrons, Authorized personnel only, Circ limited, Circulates for staff only, Hospital employees & physicians only, Internal circ only, Internal use only, Lending to staff only, Med staff & students, Not open to pub

EAST NORTHPORT

P ELWOOD PUBLIC LIBRARY*, 1929 Jericho Tpk, 11731. SAN 378-410X. Tel: 631-499-3722. Reference E-mail: reference@elwoodlibrary.org. Web Site: elwoodlibrary.org. *Dir,* Susan Goldberg
Founded 2002
Library Holdings: AV Mats 9,092; Bk Vols 18,078; Per Subs 110
Automation Activity & Vendor Info: (Acquisitions) Innovative Interfaces, Inc; (Cataloging) Innovative Interfaces, Inc; (Circulation) Innovative Interfaces, Inc; (ILL) Innovative Interfaces, Inc; (OPAC) Innovative Interfaces, Inc
Wireless access
Mem of Suffolk Cooperative Library System
Open Mon-Thurs 9:30-9, Fri & Sat 9:30-5
Friends of the Library Group

EAST ROCHESTER

P EAST ROCHESTER PUBLIC LIBRARY, 317 Main St, 14445. SAN 311-1466. Tel: 585-586-8302. Web Site: eastrochester.org/Departments/Public-Library/Public-Library-Home. *Dir,* Meredith Fraser; E-mail: mefraser@libraryweb.org
Pop 6,932; Circ 73,000
Library Holdings: Bk Titles 47,799; Per Subs 60
Automation Activity & Vendor Info: (Acquisitions) TLC (The Library Corporation); (Cataloging) TLC (The Library Corporation); (Circulation) TLC (The Library Corporation); (Course Reserve) TLC (The Library Corporation); (ILL) TLC (The Library Corporation); (Media Booking) TLC (The Library Corporation); (OPAC) TLC (The Library Corporation); (Serials) TLC (The Library Corporation)
Wireless access
Mem of Monroe County Library System
Open Mon-Thurs 9:30-7, Fri 9:30-5, Sat 10-2
Friends of the Library Group

EAST ROCKAWAY

P EAST ROCKAWAY PUBLIC LIBRARY*, 477 Atlantic Ave, 11518. SAN 311-1474. Tel: 516-599-1664. FAX: 516-596-0154. E-mail: reference@eastrockawaylibrary.org. Web Site: www.eastrockawaylibrary.org. *Dir,* Mary Thorpe; Staff 4 (MLS 4)
Founded 1903. Pop 12,714; Circ 105,091
Library Holdings: Bk Vols 63,900; Per Subs 95
Automation Activity & Vendor Info: (Circulation) Innovative Interfaces, Inc; (OPAC) Innovative Interfaces, Inc
Wireless access
Mem of Nassau Library System
Open Mon-Thurs 10-8, Fri 10-6, Sat 10-5 (Summer 9-1), Sun 1-4

EAST SYRACUSE

P EAST SYRACUSE FREE LIBRARY*, 4990 James St, 13057. SAN 311-1490. Tel: 315-437-4841. Web Site: www.eastsyracusefreelibrary.org. *Dir,* Laurie Rachetta; E-mail: lrachetta@onlib.org; Staff 11 (Non-MLS 11)
Founded 1924. Pop 3,084; Circ 77,000
Jan 2014-Dec 2014 Income $296,514. Sal $37,389
Library Holdings: Large Print Bks 1,024; Bk Titles 27,445; Per Subs 112
Special Collections: Quilting Coll; Railroad Coll
Subject Interests: Local hist
Automation Activity & Vendor Info: (Cataloging) Innovative Interfaces, Inc; (Circulation) Innovative Interfaces, Inc; (OPAC) Innovative Interfaces, Inc
Wireless access
Function: Story hour, Summer reading prog, Tax forms, Telephone ref, Wheelchair accessible
Mem of Onondaga County Public Libraries
Special Services for the Deaf - Closed caption videos
Open Mon-Thurs 10-8, Fri 10-6, Sat (Sept-May) 10-2

EAST WILLISTON

P EAST WILLISTON PUBLIC LIBRARY*, Two Prospect St, 11596. SAN 311-1504. Tel: 516-741-1213. E-mail: ewpl@ewlibrary.org. Web Site: www.ewlibrary.org. *Dir,* Emily Willis; Staff 3 (Non-MLS 3)
Founded 1937. Pop 2,515; Circ 20,000
Library Holdings: Bk Vols 18,000; Per Subs 26
Subject Interests: Local hist
Automation Activity & Vendor Info: (Cataloging) Innovative Interfaces, Inc; (Circulation) Innovative Interfaces, Inc; (OPAC) Innovative Interfaces, Inc
Wireless access
Publications: East Williston Library; East Williston Public Library Online: Monthly Website Update; East Williston Reports; Williston Times Weekly Column
Mem of Nassau Library System
Open Mon-Fri 11-7:30, Sat 10:30-3
Friends of the Library Group

EASTCHESTER

P EASTCHESTER PUBLIC LIBRARY*, 11 Oakridge Pl, 10709-2012. SAN 311-1512. Tel: 914-793-5055. Reference Tel: 914-721-8103. Administration Tel: 914-721-8101. FAX: 914-793-7862. Web Site: eastchesterlibrary.org. *Dir,* Tracy J Wright; E-mail: twright@wlsmail.org; Staff 19 (MLS 5, Non-MLS 14)
Founded 1947. Pop 18,537; Circ 245,110
Library Holdings: Bk Vols 93,853; Per Subs 200
Subject Interests: Archit, Art, Motion picture hist, Music, Mystery novels, Travel
Automation Activity & Vendor Info: (Cataloging) SirsiDynix; (Circulation) SirsiDynix; (OPAC) SirsiDynix
Wireless access
Function: Ref serv available
Mem of Westchester Library System
Open Mon & Wed 9-9, Tues & Thurs-Sat 9-5, Sun (Oct-May) 1-5
Friends of the Library Group

EDEN

P EDEN LIBRARY, 2901 E Church St, 14057. SAN 311-1520. Tel: 716-992-4028. FAX: 716-992-4340. E-mail: edn@buffalolib.org. Web Site: www.buffalolib.org/locations-hours/eden-library. *Dir,* Donna-Jo Webster; Staff 1 (MLS 1)
Founded 1911. Pop 7,688; Circ 28,685
Library Holdings: AV Mats 5,663; Electronic Media & Resources 56; Bk Vols 24,267; Per Subs 51
Special Collections: Eden High School Yearbooks, 1938-present

Wireless access
Function: Adult bk club, Audiobks via web, Bks on CD, Children's prog, Computers for patron use, E-Reserves, Electronic databases & coll, Free DVD rentals, Games & aids for people with disabilities, Holiday prog, ILL available, Magnifiers for reading, Music CDs, Online cat, Photocopying/Printing, Prog for adults, Prog for children & young adult, Scanner, Spoken cassettes & CDs, Story hour, Summer reading prog, Tax forms, Teen prog, Wheelchair accessible
Mem of Buffalo & Erie County Public Library System
Open Mon, Tues & Thurs 11-6, Wed 2-7, Fri 11-5, Sat 11-2
Friends of the Library Group

EDMESTON

S EDMESTON FREE LIBRARY*, Six West St, 13335. (Mail add: PO Box 167, 13335), SAN 311-1539. Tel: 607-965-8208. FAX: 607-965-8208. E-mail: edmestonfreelibrary@gmail.com. Web Site: libraries.4cls.org/edmeston. *Dir,* Toni Zaleski
Library Holdings: Bks on Deafness & Sign Lang 3; High Interest/Low Vocabulary Bk Vols 175; Large Print Bks 200; Bk Vols 18,000
Mem of Four County Library System
Open Mon-Wed 1-6, Sat 10-3

EDWARDS

P HEPBURN LIBRARY OF EDWARDS*, 205 Main St, 13635. (Mail add: PO Box 9, 13635-0009), SAN 311-1547. Tel: 315-562-3521. FAX: 315-562-2600. E-mail: edwlib@ncls.org. Web Site: www.hepburnlibrary.org. *Dir,* Michelle Whitford
Circ 11,669
Library Holdings: Bk Vols 8,962; Per Subs 28
Wireless access
Function: Notary serv, Photocopying/Printing, Prog for children & young adult, Scanner
Mem of North Country Library System
Open Mon 12-7, Tues & Thurs 12-5, Wed 9-3
Friends of the Library Group

ELBRIDGE

P ELBRIDGE FREE LIBRARY*, 241 E Main St, 13060. SAN 311-1555. Tel: 315-689-7111. FAX: 315-689-9448. Web Site: www.elbridgelibrary.org. *Dir,* Karen P White; E-mail: myagentkarenwhite@yahoo.com
Founded 1922. Pop 1,098; Circ 25,000
Library Holdings: Bk Vols 22,000; Per Subs 75
Special Collections: Local Newspaper (Advocate)
Automation Activity & Vendor Info: (Cataloging) Innovative Interfaces, Inc; (Circulation) Innovative Interfaces, Inc; (OPAC) Innovative Interfaces, Inc
Wireless access
Mem of Onondaga County Public Libraries
Open Mon 12-8, Tues, Thurs & Fri 12-6, Wed 9-8, Sat 12-4

ELDRED

P SUNSHINE HALL FREE LIBRARY, 14 Proctor Rd, 12732-5207. (Mail add: PO Box 157, 12732-0157), SAN 311-1563. Tel: 845-557-6258. FAX: 845-557-0578. E-mail: eld@rcls.org. Web Site: sunshinehallfreelibrary.org. *Dir,* Patricia Kennedy
Founded 1916. Circ 13,000
Library Holdings: Bk Vols 20,000; Per Subs 20
Automation Activity & Vendor Info: (Cataloging) Horizon; (Circulation) Horizon; (ILL) Horizon; (OPAC) Horizon
Wireless access
Mem of Ramapo Catskill Library System
Open Tues, Wed & Thurs 12-4, Fri 11-7, Sat 10-3
Friends of the Library Group

ELIZABETHTOWN

P ELIZABETHTOWN LIBRARY ASSOCIATION, 8256 River St, 12932. (Mail add: PO Box 7, 12932-0007), SAN 311-1571. Tel: 518-873-2670. FAX: 518-873-2670. E-mail: elizabethtownlibrary@gmail.com. Web Site: cefls.org/libraries/elizabethtown-2, elizabethtownlibra.wixsite.com/library. *Dir,* Stephanie Carman; Staff 3 (Non-MLS 3)
Founded 1884. Pop 1,497
Library Holdings: Audiobooks 225; Large Print Bks 280; Bk Vols 6,438
Automation Activity & Vendor Info: (Cataloging) Horizon; (Circulation) Horizon; (OPAC) Horizon
Wireless access
Function: ILL available, Photocopying/Printing, Preschool outreach, Prog for children & young adult, Spoken cassettes & CDs, Spoken cassettes & DVDs, Summer reading prog, VHS videos
Mem of Clinton-Essex-Franklin Library System
Open Mon, Wed & Fri 10-5, Sat 10-2

S ESSEX COUNTY HISTORICAL SOCIETY / ADIRONDACK HISTORY MUSEUM*, O B Brewster Memorial Library, 7590 Court St, 12932. (Mail add: PO Box 428, 12932-0428), SAN 311-158X. Tel: 518-873-6466. E-mail: echs@adkhistorycenter.org, research@adkhistorycenter.org. Web Site: www.adkhistorycenter.org. *Dir,* Aurora McCaffrey; *Archivist/Librn,* Andrea Anesi; Staff 5 (Non-MLS 5)
Founded 1956
Library Holdings: Bk Titles 1,693; Bk Vols 8,143; Per Subs 75
Special Collections: Essex County Cemetery Records, cards, ms; Essex County Place Names, cards; Genealogical Family Files; History of Essex County Towns (Smith Archive), ms, pamphlets, transcripts; Newspaper Articles, cards; North County Index, cards, local bks; North County Pamphlets; Photograph File
Wireless access
Function: Res libr
Publications: Index to a History of Westport, Essex County, NY
Restriction: Non-circulating, Open by appt only

ELLENBURG DEPOT

P SARAH A MUNSIL FREE LIBRARY*, 5139 Rte 11, 12935. (Mail add: PO Box 22, 12935-0022). Tel: 518-594-7314. E-mail: esamfl@gmail.com. Web Site: www.cefls.org/munsil.htm. *Dir,* Kristie Drown
Founded 1948. Pop 1,800
Library Holdings: AV Mats 25; Bk Vols 2,462
Wireless access
Mem of Clinton-Essex-Franklin Library System
Open Mon, Tues. Thurs & Fri 4-8, Sat 8-4

ELLENVILLE

P ELLENVILLE PUBLIC LIBRARY & MUSEUM*, 40 Center St, 12428-1396. SAN 311-1598. Tel: 845-647-5530. FAX: 845-647-3554. E-mail: epl@rcls.org. Web Site: eplm.org. *Dir,* Pamela Stocking; *Ch, Ref Librn,* Susan Mangan; Staff 4 (MLS 2, Non-MLS 2)
Founded 1893. Pop 12,563; Circ 92,973
Library Holdings: AV Mats 3,399; Bk Vols 49,436; Per Subs 90
Subject Interests: Local hist
Publications: Napanoch; Remembering Clayton's; Sampler of Old Houses
Mem of Ramapo Catskill Library System
Open Mon-Wed 9:30-8, Thurs & Fri 9:30-6, Sat 9:30-3

ELLICOTTVILLE

P ELLICOTTVILLE MEMORIAL LIBRARY*, 6499 Maples Rd, 14731. (Mail add: PO Box 1226, 14731-1226), SAN 311-1601. Tel: 716-699-2842. FAX: 716-699-5597. Web Site: www.ellicottvillelibrary.org. *Dir,* Laura Flanagan; E-mail: director@ellicottvillelibrary.org; Staff 1.5 (Non-MLS 1.5)
Founded 1961. Pop 3,462
Jan 2019-Dec 2019 Income $107,450, State $7,500, City $65,142, Locally Generated Income $29,801, Parent Institution $5,007. Mats Exp $7,750, Books $4,382, AV Mat $368, Electronic Ref Mat (Incl. Access Fees) $3,000. Sal $63,562 (Prof $50,700)
Library Holdings: Audiobooks 585; DVDs 2,332; e-books 16,298; Large Print Bks 233; Microforms 41; Per Subs 32
Automation Activity & Vendor Info: (Acquisitions) SirsiDynix; (Cataloging) SirsiDynix; (Circulation) SirsiDynix; (OPAC) SirsiDynix
Wireless access
Function: 24/7 Electronic res, 24/7 Online cat, Activity rm, Adult bk club, Art exhibits, Art programs, Audiobks via web, Bk club(s), Bks on CD, Children's prog, Computers for patron use, E-Readers, Electronic databases & coll, Free DVD rentals, Homebound delivery serv, ILL available, Internet access, Laminating, Magazines, Magnifiers for reading, Mail & tel request accepted, Meeting rooms, Movies, Museum passes, Online cat, Online ref, Outside serv via phone, mail, e-mail & web, OverDrive digital audio bks, Photocopying/Printing, Preschool reading prog, Printer for laptops & handheld devices, Prog for adults, Prog for children & young adult, Ref serv available, Scanner, Spoken cassettes & CDs, Spoken cassettes & DVDs, Story hour, Study rm, Summer & winter reading prog, Summer reading prog, Tax forms, Wheelchair accessible, Workshops, Writing prog
Mem of Chautauqua-Cattaraugus Library System
Open Mon & Thurs-Sat 10-5, Tues & Wed 10-8

ELLINGTON

P ELLINGTON FARMAN LIBRARY, 760 Thornten Rd, 14732. (Mail add: PO Box 26, 14732-0026), SAN 311-161X. Tel: 716-287-2945. FAX: 716-287-3694. E-mail: info@ellingtonlibrary.org. Web Site: www.ellingtonlibrary.org. *Dir,* Judith Whittaker; E-mail: director@ellingtonlibrary.org
Pop 1,632; Circ 9,862
Library Holdings: Bk Vols 14,000; Per Subs 25

Automation Activity & Vendor Info: (Cataloging) SirsiDynix; (Circulation) SirsiDynix; (OPAC) SirsiDynix
Wireless access
Mem of Chautauqua-Cattaraugus Library System
Open Mon-Thurs 11-7, Sat 10-1

ELLISBURG

P ELLISBURG FREE LIBRARY*, 12117 NY-193, 13636. SAN 311-1628. Tel: 315-846-5087. FAX: 315-846-5087. E-mail: elllib@ncls.org. Web Site: ellisburglibrary.org. *Dir,* Sheila Bettinger
Library Holdings: Bk Vols 4,900; Per Subs 32
Wireless access
Mem of North Country Library System
Open Tues & Fri 6-9, Wed & Sat 9-12

ELMA

P ELMA PUBLIC LIBRARY*, 1860 Bowen Rd, 14059. SAN 311-1636. Tel: 716-652-2719. FAX: 716-652-0381. E-mail: elm@buffalolib.org. Web Site: www.buffalolib.org/locations-hours/elma-public-library. *Dir,* Thomas Carloni; Staff 3 (MLS 2, Non-MLS 1)
Founded 1941. Pop 11,304; Circ 139,040
Library Holdings: AV Mats 7,000; Bk Vols 31,000; Per Subs 182
Automation Activity & Vendor Info: (Cataloging) SirsiDynix; (Circulation) SirsiDynix; (OPAC) SirsiDynix
Wireless access
Mem of Buffalo & Erie County Public Library System
Open Mon & Wed 12-8, Tues, Thurs & Fri 10-6, Sat 10-4
Friends of the Library Group

ELMHURST

M ELMHURST HOSPITAL CENTER*, Health Sciences Library, 79-01 Broadway, D3-52A, 11373. SAN 311-1644. Tel: 718-334-2040. FAX: 718-334-5690. E-mail: ehc-library@nychhc.org. *Dir,* Ramer Sheryl; E-mail: ramers@nychhc.org; *Asst Dir,* Barbara Gugliuzza; Staff 1 (MLS 1)
Founded 1965
Library Holdings: e-journals 750; Bk Vols 7,500; Per Subs 200
Subject Interests: Basic sci, Educ, Med
Automation Activity & Vendor Info: (Cataloging) CyberTools for Libraries; (Circulation) CyberTools for Libraries
Open Mon-Fri 9am-10pm, Sat 9-5, Sun 12-5
Restriction: Staff use only

ELMIRA

M ARNOT OGDEN MEDICAL CENTER - SCHOOL OF NURSING*, Wey Memorial Library, L D Clute Educ Bldg, 600 Roe Ave, 14905. SAN 311-1660. Tel: 607-737-4100. FAX: 607-737-4207. Web Site: www.arnothealthson.org/facilities/#wey-memorial-library. *Med Librn,* Position Currently Open
Founded 1934
Library Holdings: Bk Titles 4,000; Bk Vols 5,000; Per Subs 310
Subject Interests: Allied health, Med, Nursing
Partic in National Network of Libraries of Medicine Region 7
Open Mon-Fri 8-8, Sat 9-4

S CHEMUNG COUNTY HISTORICAL SOCIETY, INC, Mrs Arthur W Booth Library, 415 E Water St, 14901. SAN 326-2154. Tel: 607-734-4167, Ext 207. FAX: 607-734-1565. E-mail: archivist@chemungvalleymuseum.org. Web Site: www.chemungvalleymuseum.org/booth-library. *Archivist,* Rachel Dworkin; Staff 1 (Non-MLS 1)
Founded 1956
Library Holdings: Bk Titles 4,500
Special Collections: Elmira History Coll; Elmira Prison Camp Coll; Hal Roach Coll; Mark Twain Coll; Peary Arctic Exploration Coll. Oral History
Subject Interests: Genealogy, Local hist, Mil hist
Wireless access
Function: Archival coll
Mem of Southern Tier Library System
Open Mon-Fri 1-5
Restriction: Non-circulating

P CHEMUNG COUNTY LIBRARY DISTRICT*, Steele Memorial Library, 101 E Church St, 14901. SAN 311-1725. Tel: 607-733-9173. Interlibrary Loan Service Tel: 607-733-8603. Reference Tel: 607-733-9175. Administration Tel: 607-733-8607. FAX: 607-733-9176. Web Site: www.ccld.lib.ny.us. *Dir,* Ronald Shaw; Tel: 607-733-8611, E-mail: shawr@stls.org; *Head Ref Librn,* Connie Ogilvie; E-mail: ogilviec@stls.org; *Ref Librn,* Caroline Poppendeck; E-mail: poppendeckc@stls.org; *Admin Serv,* Joan Santulli; E-mail: santullij@stls.org; Staff 8 (MLS 8)
Founded 1893. Pop 91,070; Circ 412,554
Library Holdings: AV Mats 38,739; e-books 14,558; Electronic Media & Resources 3,350; Bk Vols 215,032; Per Subs 335
Special Collections: Oral History
Subject Interests: Art, Census, Genealogy
Automation Activity & Vendor Info: (Cataloging) SirsiDynix; (Circulation) SirsiDynix; (OPAC) SirsiDynix
Wireless access
Function: 24/7 Electronic res, 24/7 Online cat, 3D Printer, Adult bk club
Publications: Newsletter
Mem of Southern Tier Library System
Partic in South Central Regional Library Council
Open Mon-Thurs (Winter) 9-9, Fri & Sat 9-5; Mon-Thurs (Summer) 9-9, Fri 9-5
Friends of the Library Group
Branches: 4
BIG FLATS LIBRARY, 78 Canal St, Big Flats, 14814, SAN 378-1305. Tel: 607-562-3300. *Br Supvr,* Glenice Peel
Open Mon & Fri 12-5, Tues 12-8, Wed & Thurs 10-6
HORSEHEADS FREE LIBRARY, 405 S Main St, Horseheads, 14845, SAN 311-3299. Tel: 607-739-4581. FAX: 607-739-4592. *Head Librn,* Owen Frank; Staff 1 (MLS 1)
Founded 1944. Pop 27,535; Circ 123,594
Open Mon & Tues 9-8, Wed 12-8, Thurs-Sat 9-5
Friends of the Library Group
VAN ETTEN LIBRARY, 83 Main St, Van Etten, 14889, SAN 374-812X. Tel: 607-589-4755. *Library Contact,* Owen Frank
Open Mon 1-5, Wed 1-7, Fri 11-5
Friends of the Library Group
WEST ELMIRA LIBRARY, 1231 W Water St, 14905, SAN 378-1364. Tel: 607-733-0541. *Br Mgr,* Michelle Barrett
Open Mon 12-8, Tues & Fri 12-5, Wed & Thurs 10-6
Friends of the Library Group
Bookmobiles: 1

C ELMIRA COLLEGE*, Gannett-Tripp Library, One Park Pl, 14901. SAN 311-1679. Tel: 607-735-1862. Interlibrary Loan Service Tel: 607-735-1868. FAX: 607-735-1158. E-mail: gtl@elmira.edu. Web Site: libguides.elmira.edu. *Libr Dir,* Margaret Kappanadze; Tel: 607-735-1867, E-mail: mkappanadze@elmira.edu; *Accreditation & Info Literacy Librn,* Martha Smith; Tel: 607-735-1866, E-mail: msmith@elmira.edu; *Archivist, Curator,* Nathaniel Ball; Tel: 607-735-1869, E-mail: nball@elmira.edu. Subject Specialists: *Mark Twain,* Nathaniel Ball; Staff 8 (MLS 3, Non-MLS 5)
Founded 1855. Enrl 1,200; Highest Degree: Master
Library Holdings: DVDs 1,487; e-books 166,003; Microforms 26,657; Bk Titles 96,240; Bk Vols 106,211; Per Subs 5
Special Collections: American & English Rare Books (Lande); American Literature (Mark Twain Archives), artifacts, bks, letters on microfilm, mixed media, ms, photog; American Music (Charles Tomlinson Griffes: papers, ms & bks); Elmira College Regional History (Elmira College Archives), bks, photog; New York State Local History (Julia Boyer Reinstein Coll); New York State Women's History (New York Federation of Women's Clubs), bks, papers; Women's Education
Automation Activity & Vendor Info: (Cataloging) Innovative Interfaces, Inc - Millennium; (Circulation) Innovative Interfaces, Inc - Millennium; (Course Reserve) Innovative Interfaces, Inc - Millennium; (Discovery) EBSCO Discovery Service; (ILL) OCLC ILLiad; (Media Booking) Innovative Interfaces, Inc - Millennium; (OPAC) Innovative Interfaces, Inc - Millennium; (Serials) Innovative Interfaces, Inc - Millennium
Wireless access
Partic in OCLC-LVIS; South Central Regional Library Council
Open Mon-Thurs 7:30am-1am, Fri 7:30am-9pm, Sat 10-9, Sun 10am-1am

S NATIONAL SOARING MUSEUM, Joseph C Lincoln Memorial Library & Ralph S Barnaby Archives, Harris Hill, 51 Soaring Hill Dr, 14903-9204. SAN 373-4838. Tel: 607-734-3128. FAX: 607-732-6745. E-mail: info@soaringmuseum.org. Web Site: www.soaringmuseum.org.
Founded 1969
Library Holdings: Bk Titles 1,500; Bk Vols 2,500; Per Subs 20
Special Collections: Elmira Area Soaring Corp & Harris Hill Soaring Corp Archives; Paul A Schweizer Coll; Ralph S Barnaby Aviation Library, Archive & Artifact Coll; Soaring Society of America Archives
Function: For res purposes
Publications: NSM Historical Journal (Research guide); NSM News (Newsletter)
Restriction: Open by appt only

S NEW YORK STATE DEPARTMENT OF CORRECTIONAL SERVICES*, Elmira Correctional Facility Library, 1879 Davis St, 14901-1042. (Mail add: PO Box 500, 14902-0500), SAN 321-0014. Tel: 607-734-3901, Ext 4600. *Librn,* Greg Harris; Staff 3 (MLS 1, Non-MLS 2)
Founded 1860
Library Holdings: High Interest/Low Vocabulary Bk Vols 200; Large Print Bks 300; Bk Titles 9,500; Bk Vols 11,000; Per Subs 90
Special Collections: Vocational Guidance Coll. Oral History

Subject Interests: African-Am, Fiction, Gen fiction
Automation Activity & Vendor Info: (Cataloging) Follett Software; (Circulation) Follett Software; (OPAC) Follett Software
Publications: Summary: A Penitentiary Periodical Newsletter

GL CHARLES B SWARTWOOD SUPREME COURT LIBRARY*, Hazelett Bldg, 1st Flr, 203-205 Lake St, 14901. (Mail add: PO Box 588, 14902-0588), SAN 311-1733. Tel: 607-873-9443. FAX: 212-401-9101. E-mail: elmlawlib@courts.state.ny.us. Web Site: www.nycourts.gov/LIBRARY/6jd/Chemung. *Law Librn,* Jennifer Cartwright
Founded 1895
Library Holdings: Bk Titles 15,000; Per Subs 125
Subject Interests: NY Fed law, NY State
Automation Activity & Vendor Info: (Acquisitions) Horizon; (Cataloging) Horizon; (Circulation) Horizon
Partic in OCLC Online Computer Library Center, Inc; South Central Regional Library Council
Open Mon-Fri 8:30-4:30

ELMONT

P ELMONT MEMORIAL LIBRARY*, 700 Hempstead Tpk, 11003-1896. SAN 352-4582. Tel: 516-354-5280. FAX: 516-354-3276. E-mail: info@elmontlibrary.org. Web Site: www.elmontlibrary.org. *Dir,* Jean Simpson; E-mail: jsimpson@elmontlibrary.org; *Ch,* Nadine Spano; E-mail: nspano@elmontlibrary.org; Staff 8 (MLS 8)
Founded 1939. Pop 50,010; Circ 353,924
Library Holdings: Audiobooks 17,122; Electronic Media & Resources 508; Bk Vols 212,064; Per Subs 306
Special Collections: Municipal Document Depository
Subject Interests: Local hist
Automation Activity & Vendor Info: (Cataloging) Innovative Interfaces, Inc; (Circulation) Innovative Interfaces, Inc; (OPAC) Innovative Interfaces, Inc
Wireless access
Mem of Nassau Library System
Open Mon,Tues & Thurs 9:30-8:45,Wed 10-8:45, Fri 9:30-5:45, Sat 9:30-4:45, Sun 12-5

ELMSFORD

P GREENBURGH PUBLIC LIBRARY, 300 Tarrytown Rd, 10523. SAN 311-175X. Tel: 914-721-8200. Circulation Tel: 914-721-8204. FAX: 914-721-8201. Web Site: www.greenburghlibrary.org. *Exec Dir,* John Sexton; E-mail: director@greenburghlibrary.org; *Asst Dir,* Christina Linder; *Asst to the Dir,* Cory Deitchman; Staff 35 (MLS 15, Non-MLS 20)
Founded 1962. Pop 42,800; Circ 281,445
Jan 2020-Dec 2020 Income $4,373,273. Mats Exp $4,523,215. Sal $1,837,835
Library Holdings: AV Mats 41,551; CDs 16,002; DVDs 15,392; e-books 50,622; Bk Titles 123,650; Per Subs 124
Subject Interests: Local hist
Automation Activity & Vendor Info: (Acquisitions) SirsiDynix; (Circulation) SirsiDynix; (OPAC) SirsiDynix
Wireless access
Publications: Calendar of Events (Monthly)
Mem of Westchester Library System
Partic in Westlynx
Open Mon & Thurs-Sat 10-5:30, Tues & Wed 10-9, Sun 1-5
Friends of the Library Group

S WESTCHESTER COUNTY HISTORICAL SOCIETY LIBRARY, 2199 Saw Mill River Rd, 10523. SAN 312-584X. Tel: 914-231-1401. FAX: 914-231-1510. E-mail: info@westchesterhistory.com. Web Site: westchesterhistory.com. *Librn,* Patrick Raftery; Staff 1 (MLS 1)
Founded 1874
Library Holdings: Bk Titles 10,000
Special Collections: Westchester County Historical Materials, Almhouse rec, bks, doc, files, ledgers, maps, photog
Subject Interests: Genealogy, Westchester County hist
Wireless access
Publications: The Westchester Historian
Restriction: Open by appt only

P WESTCHESTER LIBRARY SYSTEM, 570 Taxter Rd, Ste 400, 10523-2337. SAN 311-2942. Tel: 914-674-3600. FAX: 914-674-4185. Web Site: www.westchesterlibraries.org. *Exec Dir,* Terry Kirchner; Tel: 914-231-3223, E-mail: tkirchner@wlsmail.org; *Chief Financial Officer,* Rob Caluori; Tel: 914-231-3207, E-mail: robc@wlsmail.org; *Dir, Info Tech,* Wilson Arana; Tel: 914-231-3248, E-mail: warana@westchesterlibraries.org; *Dir, Public Innovation & Engagement,* Elena Falcone; Tel: 914-231-3240, E-mail: elena@wlsmail.org; *Mgr, Cat Serv,* Douglas Wray; Tel: 914-231-3243, Fax: 914-674-4186, E-mail: dwray@westchesterlibraries.org
Founded 1958
Automation Activity & Vendor Info: (Acquisitions) Evergreen; (Cataloging) OCLC; (Circulation) Evergreen; (ILL) OCLC ILLiad; (OPAC) Evergreen
Wireless access
Publications: Assorted Bookmarks & Brochures Describing Specific Services & Bibliographies; WLS Members Directory; WLS Members Library Statistics (Annual)
Member Libraries: Ardsley Public Library; Bedford Free Library; Bedford Hills Free Library; Briarcliff Manor Public Library; Bronxville Public Library; Chappaqua Public Library; Croton Free Library; Dobbs Ferry Public Library; Eastchester Public Library; Greenburgh Public Library; Hastings-on-Hudson Public Library; Hendrick Hudson Free Library; Irvington Public Library; John C Hart Memorial Library; Katonah Village Library; Larchmont Public Library; Lewisboro Library; Mamaroneck Public Library District; Mount Kisco Public Library; Mount Pleasant Public Library; Mount Vernon Public Library; New Rochelle Public Library; North Castle Public Library; Ossining Public Library; Port Chester-Rye Brook Public Library; Pound Ridge Library; Purchase Free Library; Ruth Keeler Memorial Library; Rye Free Reading Room; Scarsdale Public Library; Somers Library; The Field Library; Town of Pelham Public Library; Tuckahoe Public Library; Warner Library; White Plains Public Library; Yonkers Public Library
Partic in Coop Libr Agency for Syst & Servs; Metropolitan New York Library Council; New York State Interlibrary Loan Network; OCLC Online Computer Library Center, Inc
Open Mon-Fri 9-5

ENDICOTT

P GEORGE F JOHNSON MEMORIAL LIBRARY, 1001 Park St, 13760. SAN 311-1784. Tel: 607-757-5350. FAX: 607-757-2491. E-mail: en.web@4cls.org. Web Site: www.gfjlibrary.org. *Libr Dir,* Seth Aaron Jacobus; E-mail: en.seth@4cls.org; *Head, Adult Serv,* Cathy Seary; E-mail: en.cathy@4cls.org; *Head, Youth Serv,* Sara-Jo Sites; E-mail: en.sarajo@4cls.org; *YA Librn,* Kenny Roman; E-mail: en.roman@4cls.org; *Youth Serv Librn,* Brooke Butler; E-mail: en.brooke@4cls.org; *Youth Serv Librn,* Suzanne Johnson; E-mail: en.suzanne@4cls.org; *Youth Serv Librn,* Erin Singleton; E-mail: en.erin@4cls.org; *Circ Mgr,* Kathy Mills; E-mail: en.kathy@4cls.org; *Libr Asst,* James Ingram; E-mail: en.james@4cls.org; *ILL,* Janet Krisko; E-mail: en.ill@4cls.org; Staff 23 (MLS 6, Non-MLS 17)
Founded 1915. Pop 13,571; Circ 196,266
Jun 2018-May 2019 Income $1,188,026, State $24,801, Locally Generated Income $1,163,225. Mats Exp $1,010,561, Books $85,000, Per/Ser (Incl. Access Fees) $13,362, AV Mat $20,024, Electronic Ref Mat (Incl. Access Fees) $3,000. Sal $539,955 (Prof $289,250)
Library Holdings: Audiobooks 2,326; AV Mats 8,627; CDs 3,054; DVDs 5,221; High Interest/Low Vocabulary Bk Vols 100; Large Print Bks 1,092; Bk Vols 93,778; Per Subs 152
Special Collections: Digitized newspapers (1856-1960); Local Historical Photographs
Automation Activity & Vendor Info: (Circulation) SirsiDynix; (OPAC) SirsiDynix
Wireless access
Function: 24/7 Electronic res, Adult bk club, Art exhibits, Audio & video playback equip for onsite use, Audiobks on Playaways & MP3, Audiobks via web, AV serv, Bk club(s), Bk reviews (Group), Bks on CD, Children's prog, Computer training, Computers for patron use, Digital talking bks, E-Reserves, Electronic databases & coll, Free DVD rentals, ILL available, Internet access, Large print keyboards, Magazines, Magnifiers for reading, Mail & tel request accepted, Mango lang, Meeting rooms, Microfiche/film & reading machines, Movies, Museum passes, Music CDs, Online cat, Orientations, OverDrive digital audio bks, Photocopying/Printing, Preschool outreach, Preschool reading prog, Printer for laptops & handheld devices, Prog for adults, Prog for children & young adult, Ref serv available, Scanner, Senior computer classes, Serves people with intellectual disabilities, Spoken cassettes & CDs, Story hour, Study rm, Summer & winter reading prog, Tax forms, Teen prog, Telephone ref, Wheelchair accessible
Publications: Curious George F News (Newsletter)
Mem of Four County Library System
Partic in S Cent Libr Res Coun
Open Mon-Thurs 9-9, Fri 9-5, Sat (Sept-May) 9-5
Restriction: Authorized patrons, Non-resident fee
Friends of the Library Group

ESSEX

P BELDON NOBLE MEMORIAL LIBRARY*, 2759 Essex Rd, 12936. (Mail add: PO Box 339, 12936-0339), SAN 311-1806. Tel: 518-963-8079. FAX: 518-963-8079. E-mail: beldennoblelibrary@gmail.com. Web Site: www.cefls.org/essex.htm. *Libr Dir,* Tom Mangano
Founded 1899
Library Holdings: Bk Vols 5,000; Per Subs 24
Subject Interests: Art

Wireless access
Mem of Clinton-Essex-Franklin Library System
Open Mon-Wed (Summer) 2-4, Thurs 1-6, Fri 12-5, Sat 10-5; Mon (Winter) 1-4, Thurs 1-6, Fri 12-5, Sat 10-5

EVANS MILLS

P EVANS MILLS PUBLIC LIBRARY*, 8706 Noble St, 13637. SAN 311-1814. Tel: 315-629-4483. FAX: 315-629-5198. E-mail: evmlib@ncls.org. Web Site: www.evansmillspubliclibrary.org. *Libr Mgr,* Helen Tooley
Founded 1956. Circ 7,880
Library Holdings: Bk Vols 4,132; Per Subs 22; Talking Bks 48; Videos 21
Wireless access
Mem of North Country Library System
Open Mon & Tues 1-5 & 7-8:30, Wed 3-8:30, Thurs 1-5, Sat 9-Noon
Friends of the Library Group

FAIR HAVEN

P FAIR HAVEN PUBLIC LIBRARY, 14426 Richmond Ave, 13064. (Mail add: PO Box 602, 13064-0602), SAN 320-4952. Tel: 315-947-5851. E-mail: fairhave@twcny.rr.com. Web Site: www.fairhavenlibrary.org. *Libr Dir,* Allen R Tompkins
Founded 1976. Pop 900
Library Holdings: Bk Titles 10,348; Bk Vols 11,915; Per Subs 11
Subject Interests: Ecology, Environ conserv, Local hist, Sailing, Water sports
Automation Activity & Vendor Info: (Cataloging) Innovative Interfaces, Inc; (Circulation) Innovative Interfaces, Inc; (OPAC) Innovative Interfaces, Inc
Wireless access
Mem of Finger Lakes Library System
Open Mon, Wed & Fri 2-5, Tues 6-8, Thurs 2-5 & 6-8, Sat 9-Noon

FAIRPORT

P FAIRPORT PUBLIC LIBRARY*, One Fairport Village Landing, 14450. SAN 311-1822. Tel: 585-223-9091. FAX: 585-223-3998. Web Site: www.fairportlibrary.org. *Dir,* Carl Gouveia; E-mail: carl.gouveia@fairportlibrary.org; Staff 33.5 (MLS 10, Non-MLS 23.5)
Founded 1906. Pop 40,055; Circ 825,737
Library Holdings: AV Mats 24,094; Electronic Media & Resources 34; Microforms 1,858; Bk Vols 99,661; Per Subs 324
Automation Activity & Vendor Info: (Cataloging) TLC (The Library Corporation); (Circulation) TLC (The Library Corporation); (OPAC) TLC (The Library Corporation)
Wireless access
Function: Adult bk club, AV serv, Bk club(s), Bks on cassette, Bks on CD, Children's prog, Computer training, Computers for patron use, Electronic databases & coll, Free DVD rentals, Holiday prog, ILL available, Mail & tel request accepted, Museum passes, Music CDs, Online cat, Online ref, OverDrive digital audio bks, Photocopying/Printing, Preschool outreach, Prog for adults, Prog for children & young adult, Ref & res, Ref serv available, Spoken cassettes & CDs, Spoken cassettes & DVDs, Story hour, Summer reading prog, Tax forms, Teen prog, Telephone ref, VHS videos, Wheelchair accessible, Workshops
Mem of Monroe County Library System
Restriction: Non-resident fee
Friends of the Library Group

FALCONER

P FALCONER PUBLIC LIBRARY, 101 W Main St, 14733. SAN 311-1830. Tel: 716-665-3504. FAX: 716-665-5320. Web Site: www.falconerlibrary.org. *Dir, Libr Mgr,* Laurie Becker; E-mail: director@falconerlibrary.org; *Outreach Coordr,* Sue Seamans
Founded 1921. Pop 2,500; Circ 101,000
Library Holdings: Audiobooks 200; Bks on Deafness & Sign Lang 47; Large Print Bks 1,500; Bk Vols 20,900; Per Subs 121
Automation Activity & Vendor Info: (Cataloging) SirsiDynix; (Circulation) SirsiDynix; (OPAC) SirsiDynix
Wireless access
Mem of Chautauqua-Cattaraugus Library System
Special Services for the Blind - Braille bks; Talking bks
Open Mon-Wed 9-6, Thurs & Fri 9-5, Sat 9-1

FALLSBURG

S SULLIVAN CORRECTIONAL FACILITY LIBRARY, 325 Riverside Dr, 12733. (Mail add: PO Box 116, 12733-0116), SAN 327-3245. Tel: 845-434-2080. *Sr Librn,* Leslie Fishman
Library Holdings: Bk Titles 13,000; Per Subs 80; Videos 180
Automation Activity & Vendor Info: (Circulation) Follett Software

FAR ROCKAWAY

M SAINT JOHN'S EPISCOPAL HOSPITAL-SOUTH SHORE DIVISION*, Medical Library, 327 Beach 19th St, 11691. SAN 311-1857. Tel: 718-869-7699. FAX: 718-869-8528. Web Site: www.ehs.org. *Dir,* Kalpana Desai; E-mail: kdesai@ehs.org; *Asst Librn,* Curtis Carson; E-mail: ccarson@ehs.org
Library Holdings: Bk Vols 3,000; Per Subs 180
Subject Interests: Gynecology, Med, Nursing, Obstetrics, Psychiat
Partic in Basic Health Sciences Library Network; Brooklyn-Queens-Staten Island-Manhattan-Bronx Health Sciences Librarians; Medical & Scientific Libraries of Long Island; Metropolitan New York Library Council

FARMINGDALE

P FARMINGDALE PUBLIC LIBRARY*, 116 Merritts Rd, 11735. SAN 311-1881. Tel: 516-249-9090. FAX: 516-694-9697. Reference E-mail: falmail@nassaulibrary.org. Web Site: www.farmingdalelibrary.org. *Dir,* Debbie Podolski; Tel: 516-249-9090, Ext 209; *Asst Dir,* Christa Lucareli; Tel: 516-249-9090, Ext 226; *Head, Ref,* Stuart Schaeffer; Tel: 516-249-9090, Ext 203; Staff 65 (MLS 19, Non-MLS 46)
Founded 1923. Pop 40,000; Circ 401,262
Library Holdings: Bk Vols 226,430; Per Subs 381
Subject Interests: Local hist
Automation Activity & Vendor Info: (Cataloging) Innovative Interfaces, Inc; (Circulation) Innovative Interfaces, Inc; (Course Reserve) Innovative Interfaces, Inc; (OPAC) Innovative Interfaces, Inc
Wireless access
Publications: Community Directory; Inside Your Library
Mem of Nassau Library System
Open Mon, Tues & Thurs 9-9, Wed 10-9, Fri 9-6, Sat 9-5 (9-1 July-Aug), Sun 1-5
Friends of the Library Group

C FARMINGDALE STATE COLLEGE OF NEW YORK, Thomas D Greenley Library, 2350 Broadhollow Rd, 11735-1021. SAN 311-1903. Tel: 934-420-2040. Circulation Tel: 934-420-2183. Reference Tel: 934-420-2184. FAX: 934-420-2473. E-mail: reference@farmingdale.edu. Web Site: www.farmingdale.edu/library. *Dir,* Karen Gelles; E-mail: gelleska@farmingdale.edu; *Access Serv,* Jessica Mcgivney; *Electronic Res, Per,* Kathryn Machin; *Ref & Instruction,* Meghan Marchese; *Ref & Instruction,* Theresa Zahor; *Scholarly Communications,* Danielle Apfelbaum; *Tech Serv,* April Earle; *Tech Serv,* Fatoma Rad; Staff 16 (MLS 8, Non-MLS 8)
Founded 1912. Enrl 8,600; Fac 350; Highest Degree: Master
Library Holdings: Bk Titles 90,000; Per Subs 150
Special Collections: US Document Depository
Subject Interests: Aviation, Biology, Bus, Communication, Dental health, Engr, Hort, Med lab tech, Nursing, Psychol
Automation Activity & Vendor Info: (Acquisitions) Ex Libris Group; (Cataloging) Ex Libris Group; (Circulation) Ex Libris Group; (Course Reserve) Ex Libris Group; (ILL) OCLC; (OPAC) Ex Libris Group; (Serials) Ex Libris Group
Wireless access
Partic in OCLC Online Computer Library Center, Inc; SUNYConnect
Open Mon-Thurs 7:45am-11pm, Fri 7:45-5, Sat 9-5, Sun 1-9

FAYETTEVILLE

P FAYETTEVILLE FREE LIBRARY*, 300 Orchard St, 13066-1386. SAN 311-1911. Tel: 315-637-6374. FAX: 315-637-2306. Web Site: www.fflib.org. *Exec Dir,* Position Currently Open; Staff 8 (MLS 5, Non-MLS 3)
Founded 1906. Pop 10,250
Library Holdings: AV Mats 4,568; Bks on Deafness & Sign Lang 100; High Interest/Low Vocabulary Bk Vols 100; Large Print Bks 500; Bk Vols 44,820; Per Subs 115
Special Collections: American Popular Sheet Music Coll; Local History Coll (Titles from 1860)
Subject Interests: 19th Century women's hist
Automation Activity & Vendor Info: (Cataloging) Innovative Interfaces, Inc; (Circulation) Innovative Interfaces, Inc; (OPAC) Innovative Interfaces, Inc
Wireless access
Mem of Onondaga County Public Libraries
Partic in OCLC Online Computer Library Center, Inc
Special Services for the Blind - Text reader
Open Mon-Thurs (Winter) 9-9, Fri & Sat 10-5, Sun 1-5; Mon-Thurs (Summer) 9-9, Fri 10-5, Sat 10-2
Friends of the Library Group

FILLMORE

P WIDE AWAKE CLUB LIBRARY*, 22 Genesee St, 14735. (Mail add: PO Box 199, 14735-0199), SAN 311-1938. Tel: 585-567-8301. FAX: 585-567-8351. E-mail: fillmore@stls.org. Web Site:

www.fillmorelibrary.com. *Libr Dir,* Roxanne Baker; E-mail: bakerro@stls.org; *Libr Mgr,* Joan Tavernier
Founded 1897. Pop 5,179; Circ 21,139
Library Holdings: Bks on Deafness & Sign Lang 10; High Interest/Low Vocabulary Bk Vols 500; Bk Vols 14,000; Per Subs 23
Subject Interests: Hist
Automation Activity & Vendor Info: (Cataloging) SirsiDynix-iBistro; (Circulation) SirsiDynix-iBistro; (ILL) SirsiDynix-iBistro; (OPAC) SirsiDynix-iBistro
Wireless access
Function: Adult literacy prog, Homebound delivery serv, ILL available, Internet access, Photocopying/Printing, Prog for adults, Prog for children & young adult, Summer reading prog
Mem of Southern Tier Library System
Special Services for the Deaf - TTY equip
Special Services for the Blind - Talking bks
Open Mon, Wed & Fri 9-5, Tues & Thurs 9-7, Sat 9-12

FINDLEY LAKE

P ALEXANDER FINDLEY COMMUNITY LIBRARY, 2883 North Rd, 14736. (Mail add: PO Box 74, 14736). Tel: 716-769-6568. FAX: 716-769-6568. E-mail: info@findleylibrary.org. Web Site: findleylibrary.org. *Mgr,* Cala Glatz; E-mail: manager@findleylibrary.org
Founded 2000. Pop 1,100; Circ 4,000
Library Holdings: AV Mats 150; DVDs 700; e-books 11,700; Bk Vols 11,600; Per Subs 27; Talking Bks 35
Automation Activity & Vendor Info: (Cataloging) Koha; (Circulation) Koha; (OPAC) Koha; (Serials) Koha
Wireless access
Mem of Chautauqua-Cattaraugus Library System
Open Mon & Sat 9-2, Tues & Thurs 1-7
Friends of the Library Group

FISHERS ISLAND

P FISHERS ISLAND LIBRARY, 988 Oriental Ave, 06390. (Mail add: PO Box 366, 06390-0366), SAN 311-1946. Tel: 631-788-7362. FAX: 631-788-7362. Web Site: www.filibrary.org. *Librn,* Ann Banks; E-mail: filibrarian@fishersisland.net
Founded 1904. Circ 3,503
Library Holdings: Audiobooks 570; DVDs 30; e-books 280,183; Bk Vols 27,368; Per Subs 15; Videos 900
Wireless access
Mem of Suffolk Cooperative Library System
Open Mon-Tues & Thurs-Fri 9-12 & 1:30-5, Wed & Sat 9-Noon
Friends of the Library Group

FISHKILL

P BLODGETT MEMORIAL LIBRARY*, 37 Broad St, 12524-1836. SAN 311-1954. Tel: 845-896-9215. FAX: 845-896-9243. E-mail: blodmem@gmail.com. Web Site: blodgettmemoriallibrary.org. *Dir, Libr Serv,* Julie Spann; Staff 2 (MLS 2)
Founded 1934. Pop 15,506; Circ 80,749
Library Holdings: Bk Vols 50,000
Subject Interests: Local hist
Automation Activity & Vendor Info: (Cataloging) Innovative Interfaces, Inc - Millennium; (Circulation) Innovative Interfaces, Inc - Millennium; (OPAC) Innovative Interfaces, Inc - Millennium
Wireless access
Mem of Mid-Hudson Library System
Open Mon-Fri 10:30-7:30, Sat & Sun 12-4

FLEISCHMANNS

P SKENE MEMORIAL LIBRARY*, 1017 Main St, 12430. (Mail add: PO Box 189, 12430-0189), SAN 311-1962. Tel: 845-254-4581. FAX: 845-254-4581. E-mail: librarian@skenelib.org. Web Site: www.skenelib.org. *Dir,* Linda Rodgers; *Computer Serv, Network Serv,* Fred Herzog
Founded 1901. Pop 434; Circ 13,532
Library Holdings: Bk Vols 17,000
Wireless access
Mem of Four County Library System
Open Tues-Fri (Winter) 1-5, Sat 10-2; Mon (Summer) 1-6, Tues-Fri 10-3, Sat 10-1

FLORAL PARK

P FLORAL PARK PUBLIC LIBRARY*, 17 Caroline Pl, 11001. SAN 311-1970. Tel: 516-326-6330. FAX: 516-437-6959. E-mail: floralpark@nassaulibrary.org. Web Site: floralparklibrary.org. *Dir,* Patricia D Eren; *Ch Serv Librn,* Kathy Guidal; *Ref (Info Servs),* Edwina Van Dam; *YA Serv,* Jane Zuckerman; E-mail: jzuckerman@nassaulibrary.org
Founded 1923
Library Holdings: AV Mats 5,446; Bk Titles 89,451; Per Subs 172
Subject Interests: Gardening, Local hist
Automation Activity & Vendor Info: (Circulation) Innovative Interfaces, Inc; (OPAC) Innovative Interfaces, Inc
Wireless access
Publications: Monthly Calendar of Events; Newsletter
Mem of Nassau Library System
Open Mon, Tues & Thurs 10-9, Wed & Fri 10-6, Sat 9-5, Sun 1-5
Friends of the Library Group

FLORIDA

P FLORIDA PUBLIC LIBRARY, Four Cohen Circle, 10921-1514. SAN 311-1989. Tel: 845-651-7659. FAX: 845-651-7689. E-mail: fpl@rcls.org. Web Site: www.floridapubliclibrary.org. *Dir,* Meg Sgombick; E-mail: msgombick@rcls.org
Founded 1958. Pop 4,724; Circ 7,621
Library Holdings: Bk Vols 5,000
Automation Activity & Vendor Info: (Circulation) SirsiDynix; (OPAC) SirsiDynix
Wireless access
Mem of Ramapo Catskill Library System
Open Mon-Thurs 10-8, Fri & Sat 10-5, Sun (Sept-June) 12-5
Friends of the Library Group

FLUSHING

M FLUSHING HOSPITAL MEDICAL CENTER*, Medical Library, 45th Ave at Parsons Blvd, 11355. SAN 311-2020. Tel: 718-670-5653. FAX: 718-670-3089. Web Site: flushinghospital.org/general-information/medical-library. *Dir,* Robin L Dornbaum; Staff 1.5 (MLS 1, Non-MLS 0.5)
Founded 1942
Library Holdings: e-books 30; e-journals 230; Bk Vols 5,124
Subject Interests: Gynecology, Internal med, Obstetrics, Pediatrics, Surgery
Automation Activity & Vendor Info: (Cataloging) Professional Software
Wireless access
Open Mon-Fri 9-5

QUEENS COLLEGE

C AARON COPLAND SCHOOL OF MUSIC LIBRARY*, 65-30 Kissena Blvd, 11367. Tel: 718-997-3900. FAX: 718-997-3928. Web Site: qcpages.qc.cuny.edu/Library/music_library. *Assoc Prof, Head Music Libr,* Dr Jennifer Oates; Staff 4 (MLS 1, Non-MLS 3)
Highest Degree: Master
Library Holdings: CDs 20,000; DVDs 125; e-journals 100; Music Scores 40,000; Bk Vols 35,000; Per Subs 225; Videos 175
Partic in CUNYPLUS
Open Mon-Thurs (Fall) 10-6:45, Fri 10-4:45; Mon-Thurs (Summer) 10-4:45

C BENJAMIN S ROSENTHAL LIBRARY*, 65-30 Kissena Blvd, 11367-0904, SAN 311-2039. Tel: 718-997-3700. Reference Tel: 718-997-3701. FAX: 718-997-3753. Web Site: www.qc.edu/Library. *Chief Librn,* Robert Shaddy; *Assoc Librn,* Shoshana Kaufmann; *Syst Coordr,* A Ben Chitty; *Acq, Govt Doc,* Nancy Macomber; *Access Serv, ILL,* Evelyn Silverman; *Coll Develop,* Richard Wall; *Instrul Serv Librn,* Alexandra De Luise; *Instrul Serv Librn, Ref Serv,* Subash Gandhi; *Ref (Info Servs),* Manuel Sanudo; *Web Coordr,* Rolf Swensen; Staff 53 (MLS 22, Non-MLS 31)
Founded 1937. Enrl 15,686; Fac 1,103; Highest Degree: Master
Library Holdings: e-books 5,000; Bk Titles 515,000; Bk Vols 780,500; Per Subs 5,820
Special Collections: Louis Armstrong Archives, mss, personal papers, photographs, rec, scrapbks & tapes; Theater & Film Coll (through 1960), posters, programs, scrapbks, scripts, stills. US Document Depository
Automation Activity & Vendor Info: (Acquisitions) Ex Libris Group; (Cataloging) Ex Libris Group; (Circulation) Ex Libris Group; (Course Reserve) Docutek; (ILL) OCLC; (OPAC) Ex Libris Group; (Serials) Ex Libris Group
Partic in Metropolitan New York Library Council; OCLC Online Computer Library Center, Inc
Publications: PageDown (Newsletter)
Special Services for the Blind - Assistive/Adapted tech devices, equip & products
Open Mon-Thurs 9am-10pm, Fri 9-5, Sat & Sun 12-6
Friends of the Library Group

C VAUGHN COLLEGE LIBRARY*, 8601 23rd Ave, 11369. SAN 311-1407. Tel: 718-429-6600, Ext 184. FAX: 718-478-7066. Web Site: www.vaughn.edu/library. *Dir, Libr Serv,* Curt Friehs; E-mail: curt.friehs@vaughn.edu; *Libr Assoc,* Pamela Sookralli; E-mail: pamela.sookralli@vaughn.edu; Staff 3 (MLS 2, Non-MLS 1)
Founded 1932. Enrl 1,462; Fac 93
Library Holdings: Audiobooks 166; AV Mats 3,500; e-books 44,000; e-journals 12,000; Bk Titles 41,000; Per Subs 1,058

Special Collections: Aircraft Maintenance Manuals; NACA & Other Annual Reports, bd vols; NASA Reports; SAE Reports
Subject Interests: Aeronaut, Avionics, Electronics, Mgt
Automation Activity & Vendor Info: (Cataloging) Follett Software; (Circulation) Follett Software; (ILL) OCLC; (OPAC) Follett Software
Wireless access
Publications: Library handbook
Partic in Metropolitan New York Library Council
Open Mon & Tues 7:30am-11pm, Wed & Thurs 7:30am-9pm, Fri 7:30-6, Sat 8-5, Sun 12-5

FLY CREEK

S NEW YORK CENTER FOR AGRICULTURAL MEDICINE & HEALTH LIBRARY, NEC/NYCAMH Library, 6160 State Hwy 28, 13337. (Mail add: One Atwell Rd, Cooperstown, 13326), SAN 374-4965. Tel: 607-547-6023, Ext 2207. Toll Free Tel: 800-343-7527, Ext 2207. FAX: 607-547-6087. Web Site: www.necenter.org, www.nycamh.org. *Research Librn,* Deborah Dalton; E-mail: deborah.dalton@bassett.org; Staff 1 (MLS 1)
Founded 1989
Library Holdings: Bk Titles 2,000; Per Subs 40
Special Collections: Agricultural Health & Safety Coll; Injury
Subject Interests: Occupational health
Automation Activity & Vendor Info: (ILL) OCLC
Partic in South Central Regional Library Council
Restriction: Open by appt only

FONDA

P FROTHINGHAM FREE LIBRARY*, 28 W Main St, 12068. (Mail add: PO Box 746, 12068-0746), SAN 311-2071. Tel: 518-853-3016. FAX: 518-853-3016. Web Site: fonlib.blogspot.com. *Interim Dir,* Linda Bell; E-mail: fon-director@mvls.info
Founded 1942. Pop 6,559; Circ 18,074
Library Holdings: Large Print Bks 479; Bk Vols 16,697; Per Subs 14
Wireless access
Mem of Mohawk Valley Library System
Open Mon-Wed 11-7, Fri 12-7, Sat 9-1

G MONTGOMERY COUNTY DEPARTMENT OF HISTORY & ARCHIVES*, Research Library, Nine Park St, 12068. (Mail add: Old Courthouse, PO Box 1500, 12068-1500), SAN 325-5336. Tel: 518-853-8186. FAX: 518-853-8392. Web Site: www.co.montgomery.ny.us. *County Historian,* Kelly Yacobucci Farquhar; E-mail: kfarquhar@co.montgomery.ny.us
Founded 1934
Library Holdings: Bk Titles 8,500
Special Collections: Archival Records (early 1700-present); Extensive Genealogical & Historical Coll
Subject Interests: Genealogy, Local hist
Function: 24/7 Online cat, Archival coll, For res purposes, Photocopying/Printing, Res libr, Res performed for a fee
Publications: Catalogue of Historical & Genealogical Materials (Collection catalog)
Open Mon-Fri (Sept-June) 8:30-4; Mon-Fri (July & Aug) 9-4
Restriction: Not a lending libr
Friends of the Library Group

FORT DRUM

A UNITED STATES ARMY*, Robert C McEwen Library, 4300 Camp Hale Rd, 13602. SAN 354-3579. Tel: 315-772-6005. Circulation Tel: 315-772-9099. Administration Tel: 315-772-4735. FAX: 315-772-4906. E-mail: usarmy.ftdrum.mwr.library@mail.mil. Web Site: drum.armymwr.com/programs/library. *Chief Librn,* Allen R Goudie; Tel: 315-772-4502; *Ref (Info Servs),* Wendy A Newell; Staff 9 (MLS 3, Non-MLS 6)
Founded 1941
Library Holdings: Audiobooks 6,011; AV Mats 5,000; Bk Vols 60,000
Subject Interests: Job hunting, Self defense
Automation Activity & Vendor Info: (Acquisitions) Innovative Interfaces, Inc; (Cataloging) Innovative Interfaces, Inc; (Circulation) Innovative Interfaces, Inc; (OPAC) Innovative Interfaces, Inc; (Serials) Innovative Interfaces, Inc
Wireless access
Function: Govt ref serv, ILL available, Prog for children & young adult, Summer reading prog, Wheelchair accessible
Open Mon-Fri 9-8, Sat & Sun 10:30-6
Restriction: Open to fac, students & qualified researchers

FORT EDWARD

P FORT EDWARD FREE LIBRARY*, 23 East St, 12828. SAN 311-211X. Tel: 518-747-6743. FAX: 518-747-6743. Web Site: fortedwardlibrary.sals.edu. *Dir,* Victoria Plude; E-mail: vplude@sals.edu
Founded 1914. Pop 3,561; Circ 6,396
Library Holdings: Bk Vols 14,000; Per Subs 30
Wireless access
Mem of Southern Adirondack Library System
Open Mon (Winter) 1-5 & 6-8, Tues & Wed 12-6, Thurs & Fri 1-5, Sat 9-Noon; Mon (Summer) 1-5 & 6-8, Tues & Wed 12-6, Thurs 1-5, Fri 10-5

FORT PLAIN

P FORT PLAIN FREE LIBRARY*, 19 Willett St, 13339-1130. SAN 311-2136. Tel: 518-993-4646. FAX: 518-993-2455. E-mail: fpfl@mvls.info. Web Site: www.fortplainfreelibrary.org. *Dir,* Whitney Hubbard; E-mail: whubbard@mvls.info; Staff 1.8 (MLS 0.8, Non-MLS 1)
Founded 1894. Circ 27,327
Library Holdings: Bk Vols 20,965; Per Subs 41
Subject Interests: Local hist
Automation Activity & Vendor Info: (Circulation) Innovative Interfaces, Inc; (OPAC) Innovative Interfaces, Inc; (Serials) Innovative Interfaces, Inc
Wireless access
Mem of Mohawk Valley Library System
Open Mon-Fri 10-5, Sat 9-12

FRANKFORT

P FRANKFORT FREE LIBRARY*, 123 S Frankfort St, 13340. SAN 311-2144. Tel: 315-894-9611. FAX: 315-894-9611. E-mail: frankfort@midyork.org. Web Site: frankfortfreelibrary.org. *Dir,* Melissa Wohler
Pop 7,200; Circ 15,281
Library Holdings: Bk Vols 10,000; Per Subs 21
Automation Activity & Vendor Info: (Cataloging) SirsiDynix; (Circulation) SirsiDynix; (OPAC) SirsiDynix
Wireless access
Mem of Mid-York Library System
Open Mon & Wed 2-8, Tues & Thurs 11-8, Fri 2-6, Sat 10-1

FRANKLIN

P FRANKLIN FREE LIBRARY*, 334 Main St, 13775. (Mail add: PO Box 947, 13775-0947), SAN 311-2152. Tel: 607-829-2941. E-mail: fr.ill@4cls.org. Web Site: www.franklinfreelibrary.org. *Dir & Librn,* Wendy Barckhaus; *Asst Dir,* Xina Sheehan; Staff 1 (MLS 1)
Founded 1827. Pop 2,440; Circ 8,000
Library Holdings: Bk Vols 10,000; Per Subs 35
Special Collections: 200 Historic Scrapbooks (indexed); Civil War Coll; Local Newspapers on Microfilm 1857-1952; Town & Village Board Meetings 1792 -
Automation Activity & Vendor Info: (OPAC) SirsiDynix
Wireless access
Function: Adult bk club, After school storytime, Audiobks via web, Bks on CD, Children's prog, Computers for patron use, Online cat, Photocopying/Printing
Mem of Four County Library System
Open Tues 9-12, 1-5 & 7-9, Wed & Sat 10-2, Thurs 9-12 & 1-5
Friends of the Library Group

FRANKLIN SQUARE

P FRANKLIN SQUARE PUBLIC LIBRARY, 19 Lincoln Rd, 11010. SAN 311-2160. Tel: 516-488-3444. FAX: 516-354-3368. E-mail: contactus@franklinsquarepl.org. Web Site: www.franklinsquarepl.org. *Dir,* Aviva Kane; E-mail: akane@franklinsquarepl.org; *Asst Dir,* Irene Winkler; E-mail: iwinkler@franklinsquarepl.org; Staff 35 (MLS 12, Non-MLS 23)
Founded 1938. Pop 26,000; Circ 125,708
Library Holdings: AV Mats 12,406; Bk Vols 118,437; Per Subs 153
Automation Activity & Vendor Info: (Circulation) Innovative Interfaces, Inc - Sierra; (OPAC) Innovative Interfaces, Inc - Sierra
Wireless access
Function: 24/7 Electronic res, 24/7 Online cat, Accelerated reader prog, Adult bk club, After school storytime, Audiobks on Playaways & MP3, Audiobks via web, Bk club(s), Bks on CD, Children's prog, Citizenship assistance, Computer training, Computers for patron use, E-Reserves, Electronic databases & coll, Free DVD rentals, Holiday prog, Home delivery & serv to seniorr ctr & nursing homes, Homebound delivery serv, ILL available, Internet access, Life-long learning prog for all ages, Magazines, Meeting rooms, Movies, Museum passes, Music CDs, Notary serv, Online cat, Online ref, Outreach serv, Outside serv via phone, mail, e-mail & web, OverDrive digital audio bks, Photocopying/Printing, Preschool outreach, Preschool reading prog, Prog for adults, Prog for children & young adult, Ref & res, Ref serv available, Scanner, STEM

programs, Story hour, Summer reading prog, Tax forms, Teen prog, Telephone ref, Wheelchair accessible
Publications: Community Directory; Newsletter
Mem of Nassau Library System
Open Mon-Thurs 10-9, Fri 10-6, Sat 10-5 (10-1 Summer)
Friends of the Library Group

FRANKLINVILLE

P BLOUNT LIBRARY, INC, Five N Main St, 14737-1015. SAN 311-2179. Tel: 716-676-5715. FAX: 716-676-5719. Web Site: www.franklinvillelibrary.org. *Dir,* Jessica Frank; E-mail: director@franklinvillelibrary.org; Staff 2 (Non-MLS 2)
Founded 1899. Pop 4,817; Circ 13,503
Library Holdings: Bk Vols 20,980
Subject Interests: Local hist
Wireless access
Mem of Chautauqua-Cattaraugus Library System
Open Mon & Thurs 9-6, Tues, Wed & Fri 9-4
Friends of the Library Group

FREDONIA

P DARWIN R BARKER LIBRARY ASSOCIATION, Seven Day St, 14063-1891. SAN 311-2187. Tel: 716-672-8051. FAX: 716-679-3547. E-mail: info@barkerlibrary.org. Web Site: www.barkerlibrary.org. *Dir,* Graham Tesdesco-Blair; E-mail: director@barkerlibrary.org; *Librn,* Sara Hart
Pop 11,230; Circ 80,100
Library Holdings: Bk Titles 55,472; Per Subs 88
Automation Activity & Vendor Info: (Cataloging) SirsiDynix; (Circulation) SirsiDynix; (OPAC) SirsiDynix
Wireless access
Mem of Chautauqua-Cattaraugus Library System
Open Mon-Thurs 10-8, Fri & Sat 10-5
Friends of the Library Group

C STATE UNIVERSITY OF NEW YORK AT FREDONIA*, Daniel A Reed Library, 280 Central Ave, 14063. SAN 311-2195. Tel: 716-673-3184. Interlibrary Loan Service Tel: 716-673-3180. Reference Tel: 716-673-3222. Administration Tel: 718-673-3181. FAX: 716-673-3185. E-mail: reedref@fredonia.edu. Web Site: fredonia.libguides.com. *Libr Dir,* Randy Gadikian; E-mail: randolph.gadikian@fredonia.edu; *Music Librn, Syst Librn,* Kevin Michki; Tel: 716-673-3117, E-mail: kevin.michki@fredonia.edu; *Archivist,* Pat Cummings-Witter; Tel: 716-673-3191, E-mail: patricia.cummings-witter@fredonia.edu; *ILL,* Linda Mull; Tel: 716-673-3180, E-mail: linda.mull@fredonia.edu; *Tech Serv,* Maribeth Patterson; Tel: 716-673-3192, E-mail: maribeth.patterson@fredonia.edu. Subject Specialists: *Music,* Kevin Michki; Staff 11 (MLS 9, Non-MLS 2)
Founded 1826. Enrl 5,200; Fac 300; Highest Degree: Master
Library Holdings: AV Mats 28,700; Bks on Deafness & Sign Lang 121; Braille Volumes 4; CDs 5,072; DVDs 406; e-books 1,988; e-journals 40,000; Electronic Media & Resources 447; Music Scores 33,548; Bk Vols 389,320; Per Subs 260; Videos 1,601
Special Collections: Chautauqua & Cattaraugus Counties' History Coll, bks, ms, micro; Holland Land Company Coll; Seneca/Iroquois History Coll, bks, ms, micro; Sigurd Rascher Coll; Stephan Zweig Coll, bks, ms, micro; West Valley Project Coll. State Document Depository
Automation Activity & Vendor Info: (Acquisitions) Ex Libris Group; (Cataloging) Ex Libris Group; (Circulation) Ex Libris Group; (Course Reserve) Ex Libris Group; (OPAC) Ex Libris Group; (Serials) Ex Libris Group
Wireless access
Function: Audio & video playback equip for onsite use, E-Reserves, Electronic databases & coll, Internet access, Music CDs, Online ref, Photocopying/Printing, Wheelchair accessible
Publications: Annual Report
Partic in New York Online Virtual Electronic Library; SUNYConnect; Western New York Library Resources Council
Open Mon-Thurs 7:30am-Midnight, Fri 7:30am-8pm, Sat Noon-8
Friends of the Library Group

FREEPORT

P FREEPORT MEMORIAL LIBRARY, 144 W Merrick Rd, 11520. SAN 311-2209. Tel: 516-379-3274. FAX: 516-868-9741. E-mail: ask@freeportlibrary.info. Web Site: freeportlibrary.info. *Dir,* Ken Bellafiore; E-mail: kbellafiore@freeportlibrary.info; Staff 15 (MLS 15)
Founded 1884. Pop 40,976; Circ 232,000
Library Holdings: Audiobooks 22,086; CDs 7,166; DVDs 9,775; e-books 126,148; Bk Vols 135,064; Per Subs 319
Special Collections: Long Island history; Vocational & careers
Subject Interests: Careers, Ethnic studies, Investment lit
Automation Activity & Vendor Info: (Cataloging) Innovative Interfaces, Inc; (Circulation) Innovative Interfaces, Inc; (ILL) Innovative Interfaces, Inc; (OPAC) Innovative Interfaces, Inc
Wireless access
Function: AV serv, Res libr
Publications: Freeport Memorial Library Newsletter
Mem of Nassau Library System
Special Services for the Deaf - Assisted listening device; High interest/low vocabulary bks; TDD equip; TTY equip
Special Services for the Blind - Audio mat; Bks on cassette; Bks on CD; Children's Braille; Home delivery serv; Large print bks; Talking bks; ZoomText magnification & reading software
Open Mon, Tues, Thurs & Fri (Fall & Spring) 9-9, Wed 10-9, Sat 9-5, Sun 1-5; Mon, Tues, Thurs & Fri (Summer) 9-9, Wed 10-9, Sat 9-1
Friends of the Library Group

FREWSBURG

P MYERS MEMORIAL LIBRARY, Six Falconer St, 14738. (Mail add: PO Box 559, 14738-0559), SAN 311-2217. Tel: 716-569-5515. FAX: 716-569-2605. E-mail: info@myerslibrary.org. Web Site: www.myerslibrary.org. *Dir,* Izabela Nowak; E-mail: director@myerslibrary.org; Staff 1 (Non-MLS 1)
Founded 1923. Pop 3,500; Circ 20,100
Library Holdings: Bks on Deafness & Sign Lang 10; CDs 75; DVDs 50; High Interest/Low Vocabulary Bk Vols 104; Large Print Bks 250; Bk Vols 18,000; Per Subs 50; Talking Bks 400; Videos 450
Special Collections: History (Robert H Jackson Coll), bks, letters; J J Myers Coll, bks
Wireless access
Function: Photocopying/Printing
Mem of Chautauqua-Cattaraugus Library System
Open Mon-Fri 10-1 & 3-6, Sat 10-1

FRIENDSHIP

P FRIENDSHIP FREE LIBRARY*, 40 W Main St, 14739-8701. (Mail add: PO Box 37, 14739-0037), SAN 311-2225. Tel: 585-973-7724. FAX: 585-973-7724. E-mail: friendshipfreelibrary@gmail.com. Web Site: friendshipfreelibrary.org. *Dir,* Michelle Hill; E-mail: hillm@stls.org
Founded 1898. Circ 7,518
Library Holdings: DVDs 200; Large Print Bks 800; Bk Titles 13,000; Per Subs 15; Talking Bks 100; Videos 1,000
Automation Activity & Vendor Info: (Cataloging) SirsiDynix; (Circulation) SirsiDynix; (OPAC) SirsiDynix
Wireless access
Publications: Newsletter (annual)
Mem of Southern Tier Library System
Open Tues & Thurs 12:30-7, Wed 9-8, Sat 10-1

FULTON

J CAYUGA COMMUNITY COLLEGE*, Fulton Campus Library, 11 River Glenn Dr, 13069. Tel: 315-593-9319. FAX: 315-598-1240. E-mail: cay_ref@cayuga-cc.edu. Web Site: www.cayuga-cc.edu/library. *Libr Dir,* Sara Davenport; E-mail: davenport@cayuga-cc.edu; Staff 3 (MLS 2, Non-MLS 1)
Highest Degree: Associate
Automation Activity & Vendor Info: (Cataloging) Ex Libris Group; (Circulation) Ex Libris Group; (Course Reserve) Ex Libris Group; (OPAC) Ex Libris Group; (Serials) Ex Libris Group
Wireless access
Partic in SUNYConnect
Open Mon 9-7, Tues-Thurs 9-4, Fri 9-3

P FULTON PUBLIC LIBRARY*, 160 S First St, 13069. SAN 311-2233. Tel: 315-592-5159. FAX: 315-592-4504. E-mail: fullib@ncls.org. Web Site: fultonpubliclibrary.org. *Dir,* Caroline Chatterton; Staff 7.5 (MLS 1.5, Non-MLS 6)
Founded 1895. Pop 20,616; Circ 43,479
Jul 2017-Jun 2018 Income $416,171, State $5,000, County $5,000, Locally Generated Income $393,971, Other $12,200. Mats Exp $31,300, Books $25,000, Per/Ser (Incl. Access Fees) $1,000, AV Mat $4,300, Electronic Ref Mat (Incl. Access Fees) $1,000. Sal $111,411 (Prof $95,702)
Library Holdings: Audiobooks 657; Braille Volumes 6; e-books 936; Electronic Media & Resources 18; Bk Vols 27,520; Per Subs 40; Videos 2,272
Subject Interests: Local hist
Automation Activity & Vendor Info: (Circulation) SirsiDynix; (OPAC) SirsiDynix
Wireless access
Function: 24/7 Electronic res, 24/7 Online cat, Adult bk club, Archival coll, Audiobks via web, Bi-weekly Writer's Group, Bk club(s), Bks on CD, Children's prog, Digital talking bks, E-Reserves, Electronic databases & coll, Free DVD rentals, ILL available, Internet access, Magazines, Mail &

tel request accepted, Movies, Music CDs, Online cat, Outreach serv, OverDrive digital audio bks, Photocopying/Printing, Preschool outreach, Prog for adults, Prog for children & young adult, Ref serv available, Scanner, Spoken cassettes & CDs, Spoken cassettes & DVDs, Summer reading prog, Tax forms, Telephone ref, Wheelchair accessible
Mem of North Country Library System
Open Mon, Fri & Sat 9-5, Tues-Thurs 9-7

GALWAY

P GALWAY PUBLIC LIBRARY, 2112 East St, 12074-2341. (Mail add: PO Box 207, 12074-0207). Tel: 518-882-6385. FAX: 518-882-2297. Web Site: www.galwaypubliclibrary.org. *Libr Dir,* Debra Flint; E-mail: gal-director@sals.edu; Staff 8 (MLS 1, Non-MLS 7)
Founded 1997. Pop 7,029
Jul 2020-Jun 2021 Income Locally Generated Income $201,400
Library Holdings: AV Mats 5,352; e-books 11,809; Bk Vols 26,846; Per Subs 42
Automation Activity & Vendor Info: (Cataloging) Innovative Interfaces, Inc; (Circulation) Innovative Interfaces, Inc; (OPAC) Innovative Interfaces, Inc
Wireless access
Function: 24/7 Electronic res, 24/7 Online cat, Activity rm, Adult bk club, After school storytime, Archival coll, Art exhibits, Art programs, Audiobks on Playaways & MP3, Bks on CD, Children's prog, Computer training, Computers for patron use, Digital talking bks, E-Readers, E-Reserves, Electronic databases & coll, Free DVD rentals, ILL available, Internet access, Magazines, Magnifiers for reading, Mail & tel request accepted, Mail loans to mem, Makerspace, Meeting rooms, Movies, Museum passes, Music CDs, Notary serv, Online cat, OverDrive digital audio bks, Photocopying/Printing, Preschool reading prog, Prog for adults, Prog for children & young adult, Scanner, STEM programs, Story hour, Summer reading prog, Tax forms, Teen prog, Telephone ref, Visual arts prog, Wheelchair accessible, Writing prog
Mem of Southern Adirondack Library System
Open Mon & Tues 10-6, Wed & Thurs 2-8, Fri 2-6, Sat 10-2
Friends of the Library Group

GARDEN CITY

C ADELPHI UNIVERSITY*, Swirbul Library, One South Ave, 11530. (Mail add: PO Box 701, 11530-0701), SAN 352-4701. Tel: 516-877-3549. Circulation Tel: 516-877-3570. Interlibrary Loan Service Tel: 516-877-3571. Reference Tel: 516-877-3574. Administration Tel: 516-877-3520. Administration FAX: 516-877-3673. Web Site: libraries.adelphi.edu. *Dean, Univ Libr,* Violeta Ilik; E-mail: vilik@adelphi.edu; *Assoc Dean, Automated Serv, Digital Initiatives,* Ken Herold; Tel: 516-877-3531, E-mail: kherold@adelphi.edu; *Assoc Dean, User Serv,* Ann Minutella; Tel: 516-877-3518, E-mail: minutell@adelphi.edu; *Head, Archives & Spec Coll,* David Ranzan; Tel: 516-877-3543, E-mail: dranzan@adelphi.edu; *Coll Strategist Librn,* Debbi Smith; Tel: 516-877-3522, E-mail: smith8@adelphi.edu; *Curric Mat Librn, Ref Librn,* Amrita Madray; Tel: 516-877-3579, E-mail: amadray@adelphi.edu; *Ref Librn,* Aditi Bandyopadhyay; Tel: 516-877-4166, E-mail: bandyopa@adelphi.edu; *Ref/Electronic Res Librn,* Lois O'Neill; Tel: 516-877-3581, E-mail: oneill@adelphi.edu; *Asst Archivist, Spec Coll Librn,* Brian McDonald; Tel: 516-877-3818, E-mail: BMcDonald@adelphi.edu; *Prof Emeritus,* Gary Cantrell; Tel: 516-877-3574, E-mail: cantrell@adelphi.edu; *Emerging Tech Coord,* Rachel Isaac-Menard; Tel: 516-877-3578, E-mail: isaac-menard@adelphi.edu; *Coordr, Instrul Serv,* Jason Byrd; Tel: 516-877-3584, E-mail: jbyrd@adelphi.edu; *Coordr of Ref Serv,* Victor Oliva; Tel: 516-877-3587, E-mail: oliva@adelphi.edu. Subject Specialists: *Bus, Info sci, Libr sci,* Debbi Smith; *Educ,* Amrita Madray; *Computer sci, Math, Sci,* Aditi Bandyopadhyay; *Health studies, Nursing,* Lois O'Neill; *Communications, Dance, Music,* Gary Cantrell; *Hist, Polit sci,* Victor Oliva; Staff 62.5 (MLS 30, Non-MLS 32.5)
Founded 1896. Enrl 6,897; Fac 1,003; Highest Degree: Doctorate
Sept 2012-Aug 2013 Income $6,672,826, State $10,200, Parent Institution $6,622,222, Other $40,404. Mats Exp $2,436,508, Books $467,984, Per/Ser (Incl. Access Fees) $839,676, Manu Arch $6,073, Other Print Mats $133,063, Micro $14,483, AV Equip $28,634, AV Mat $21,832, Electronic Ref Mat (Incl. Access Fees) $904,751, Presv $20,012. Sal $2,929,727 (Prof $2,029,120)
Library Holdings: AV Mats 35,276; Bks on Deafness & Sign Lang 268; CDs 2,289; DVDs 6,361; e-books 127,938; e-journals 80,600; Electronic Media & Resources 252; Large Print Bks 134; Microforms 789,749; Music Scores 7,053; Bk Vols 609,568; Per Subs 929; Videos 2,912
Special Collections: Adelphi Authors Coll; Adelphiana; Americana Coll; Andres Coll; Blake Coll; Blodgett Coll; Children's Illustrated Literature Coll; Cobbett Coll; Cuala Press Coll; Dakin Coll; DePol Coll; Expatriate Coll; Hauptmann Coll; Hone Coll; Kraus-Boelte Early Childhood Education Coll; Loening Coll; Long Island Coll; McMillan Coll; Modern Chapbook Coll; Morley Coll; New York City Coll; New York State Coll; Ormont Literary Coll; Ormont Psychology Coll; Ornstein Coll; Panama Canal Coll; Rare Book Coll; Small Press Coll; Spanish Civil War Coll; St Denis Coll; Stoelzer Coll; Whitman Coll; Woodruff Coll. US Document Depository
Subject Interests: Children's lit, Lit, Panama Canal, Performing arts, Political cartoons, Spanish Civil War
Automation Activity & Vendor Info: (Acquisitions) Innovative Interfaces, Inc; (Cataloging) Innovative Interfaces, Inc; (Circulation) Innovative Interfaces, Inc; (Course Reserve) Innovative Interfaces, Inc; (ILL) OCLC ILLiad; (OPAC) Innovative Interfaces, Inc; (Serials) Innovative Interfaces, Inc
Wireless access
Publications: Guides & Catalogs to Special Collections
Partic in ConnectNY, Inc; Long Island Library Resources Council; Metropolitan New York Library Council; OCLC Online Computer Library Center, Inc; Southeastern New York Library Resources Council; Westchester Academic Library Directors Organization
Special Services for the Deaf - ADA equip; Am sign lang & deaf culture; Assistive tech; Bks on deafness & sign lang; Closed caption videos; Coll on deaf educ; Deaf publ; Spec interest per; Staff with knowledge of sign lang; TTY equip; Videos & decoder
Special Services for the Blind - Accessible computers; Assistive/Adapted tech devices, equip & products; Closed circuit TV; Computer with voice synthesizer for visually impaired persons; Copier with enlargement capabilities; IBM screen reader; Large print bks; Magnifiers; PC for people with disabilities; Scanner for conversion & translation of mats; Screen enlargement software for people with visual disabilities; Screen reader software; Text reader; ZoomText magnification & reading software
Open Mon-Thurs 8am-Midnight, Fri & Sat 8-8, Sun 10am-Midnight
Friends of the Library Group

P GARDEN CITY PUBLIC LIBRARY*, 60 Seventh St, 11530. SAN 311-2276. Tel: 516-742-8405. FAX: 516-742-2675. Web Site: www.gardencitypl.org. *Libr Dir,* Marianne Malagon; E-mail: gcdirector@gardencitypl.org; *Ch Serv,* Donna Furey; *Ch Serv,* Barbara Grace; *Circ,* Jeanette Nicoletti; *Computer Serv,* Joseph Agolia; *Ref Serv,* Martin Bowe; *Ref Serv,* Laura Flanagan; *Ref Serv,* Ann Garnett; *Tech Serv,* Nancy Sherwood; *YA Serv,* Laura Guinta; Staff 12 (MLS 12)
Founded 1952. Pop 21,672; Circ 336,923
Library Holdings: Bk Vols 143,613; Per Subs 440
Special Collections: Garden City Archives; Long Island History
Automation Activity & Vendor Info: (Circulation) Innovative Interfaces, Inc; (OPAC) Innovative Interfaces, Inc
Wireless access
Function: Archival coll, Art exhibits, Bks on CD, CD-ROM, Children's prog, Computers for patron use, Free DVD rentals, Homebound delivery serv, ILL available, Museum passes, Music CDs, Notary serv, Online cat, OverDrive digital audio bks, Photocopying/Printing, Prog for adults, Prog for children & young adult, Ref serv available, Story hour, Summer reading prog, Tax forms, Telephone ref, Wheelchair accessible
Publications: Newsletter
Mem of Nassau Library System
Special Services for the Deaf - Assistive tech
Open Mon-Thurs 9:30-9, Fri & Sat 9:30-5, Sun 1-5
Friends of the Library Group

SR GEORGE MERCER JR MEMORIAL SCHOOL OF THEOLOGY, Mercer Theological Library, 65 Fourth St, 11530. SAN 311-2284. Tel: 516-248-4800, Ext 139. FAX: 516-248-4883. Web Site: www.mercerschool.org/library-use.html. *Librn,* Jane Herbst; E-mail: jherbst@dioceseli.org; Staff 1 (MLS 1)
Founded 1955. Enrl 20; Fac 1
Library Holdings: e-books 40; Bk Titles 38,000; Per Subs 20
Subject Interests: Church hist, Relig educ, Theol
Automation Activity & Vendor Info: (Cataloging) CARL.Solution (TLC); (Circulation) CARL.Solution (TLC); (OPAC) CARL.Solution (TLC)
Wireless access
Function: Archival coll, Art exhibits, CD-ROM, ILL available
Open Tues-Fri 9-4:30, Sat 8:30-3
Restriction: Access at librarian's discretion

L MEYER, SUOZZI, ENGLISH & KLEIN*, Law Library, 990 Stewart Ave, Ste 300, 11530. (Mail add: PO Box 9194, 11530), SAN 372-4344. Tel: 516-741-6565. FAX: 516-741-6706. Web Site: www.msek.com. *Library Contact,* Laura Fried
Library Holdings: Bk Titles 8,000
Wireless access
Restriction: Not open to pub

J NASSAU COMMUNITY COLLEGE*, A Holly Patterson Library, One Education Dr, 11530-6793. SAN 311-2306. Tel: 516-572-7400, 516-572-7401. Interlibrary Loan Service Tel: 516-572-7401, Ext 26035. FAX: 516-572-7846. E-mail: ask@ncc.libanswers.com. Web Site: library.ncc.edu. *Chair,* Nancy Williamson; Tel: 516-572-7400, Ext 4206; *Head, Acq,* Sharon Russin; *Head, Automation,* Sonel Emin; *Head, Cat,*

Katrina Frazier; *Head, Circ,* Richard Erben; *Head, Ref,* Charles Owusu; Staff 18 (MLS 14, Non-MLS 4)
Founded 1959. Enrl 20,000; Fac 700
Library Holdings: Bk Titles 161,000; Bk Vols 179,000; Per Subs 400
Special Collections: Dozenal Society; G Wilson Knight Interdisciplinary Society
Subject Interests: Fashion, Long Island hist
Wireless access
Publications: From the Stacks; Library Newsletter
Partic in Long Island Library Resources Council; SUNYConnect
Special Services for the Blind - Computer with voice synthesizer for visually impaired persons; VisualTek equip
Open Mon-Thurs 8am-9pm, Fri 8-8, Sat 12-4:30

GARDINER

P GARDINER LIBRARY*, 133 Farmer's Tpk, 12525-5517. (Mail add: PO Box 223, 12525-0223), SAN 376-3145. Tel: 845-255-1255. FAX: 845-255-1265. Web Site: www.gardinerlibrary.org. *Dir,* Nicole Lane; E-mail: nlane@rcls.org
Library Holdings: Bk Titles 13,500; Per Subs 40
Automation Activity & Vendor Info: (Cataloging) SirsiDynix; (Circulation) SirsiDynix; (Course Reserve) SirsiDynix; (ILL) SirsiDynix; (OPAC) SirsiDynix; (Serials) SirsiDynix
Wireless access
Mem of Ramapo Catskill Library System
Open Tues-Thurs 11-8, Fri 11-6, Sat 11-4, Sun 12-4
Friends of the Library Group

GARNERVILLE

P HAVERSTRAW KINGS DAUGHTERS PUBLIC LIBRARY*, 10 W Ramapo Rd, 10923. SAN 352-5244. Tel: 845-786-3800. FAX: 845-786-3791. E-mail: information@hkdpl.org. Web Site: www.hkdpl.org. *Dir,* Claudia Depkin; E-mail: cdepkin@rcls.org; *Head, Adult Serv,* Naomi Goldberg-Honor; E-mail: nhonor@rcls.org; *Head, Circ,* Debbie DiBernardo; E-mail: ddibernardo@rcls.org; *Head, Tech Serv,* Terry Eagle; E-mail: teagle@rcls.org; *Head, Youth Serv,* Tara Morris; E-mail: tmorris@rcls.org; Staff 40 (MLS 14, Non-MLS 26)
Founded 1895. Pop 32,540; Circ 336,745. Sal $1,267,322 (Prof $971,768)
Library Holdings: Audiobooks 2,996; CDs 5,100; DVDs 11,853; Large Print Bks 1,840; Bk Vols 112,441; Per Subs 136; Videos 2,487
Special Collections: Local History Coll (focus on Haverstraw & the Hudson Valley); Spanish Language Material
Automation Activity & Vendor Info: (Cataloging) SirsiDynix; (Circulation) SirsiDynix; (ILL) SirsiDynix; (OPAC) SirsiDynix
Wireless access
Function: 24/7 Electronic res, 24/7 Online cat, Adult bk club, Adult literacy prog, Art exhibits, Audiobks on Playaways & MP3, Audiobks via web, Bilingual assistance for Spanish patrons, Bk club(s), Bks on CD, CD-ROM, Children's prog, Computer training, Computers for patron use, Distance learning, E-Readers, E-Reserves, Electronic databases & coll, Free DVD rentals, Holiday prog, Homebound delivery serv, ILL available, Internet access, Magazines, Magnifiers for reading, Mail & tel request accepted, Meeting rooms, Microfiche/film & reading machines, Movies, Museum passes, Music CDs, Notary serv, Online cat, Outreach serv, Outside serv via phone, mail, e-mail & web, OverDrive digital audio bks, Photocopying/Printing, Preschool outreach, Prof lending libr, Prog for adults, Prog for children & young adult, Ref & res, Ref serv available, Scanner, Senior computer classes, Serves people with intellectual disabilities, Spanish lang bks, Story hour, Study rm, Summer reading prog, Tax forms, Teen prog, Telephone ref, VHS videos, Wheelchair accessible, Workshops
Mem of Ramapo Catskill Library System
Special Services for the Deaf - Bks on deafness & sign lang; TTY equip
Special Services for the Blind - Bks on cassette; Bks on CD; Talking bks
Open Mon-Thurs 9-9, Fri 9-5:30, Sat 10-5, Sun 1-5
Branches: 1
VILLAGE BRANCH, 85 Main St, Haverstraw, 10927, SAN 352-521X. Tel: 845-429-3445. FAX: 845-429-7313. *Br Mgr,* Charlotte Van Hein; Staff 19 (MLS 19)
Founded 1895. Pop 28,942; Circ 219,368
Special Collections: Haverstraw Bay Photo Archives; North Rockland History Coll
Subject Interests: Career, Local hist, Spanish (Lang)
Automation Activity & Vendor Info: (Circulation) Horizon; (ILL) Horizon; (OPAC) Horizon
Publications: Bibliographies (Reference guide); Bookmarks (Consumer guide); Computer Orientation Booklet (Consumer guide)
Special Services for the Deaf - Bks on deafness & sign lang; Video & TTY relay via computer
Special Services for the Blind - Bks on CD; Magnifiers
Open Mon 12-8, Tues-Thurs 10-6, Fri 10-5:30, Sat 10-5

GARRISON

S ALICE CURTIS DESMOND & HAMILTON FISH LIBRARY*, 472 Rte 403, 10524. (Mail add: PO Box 265, 10524). Tel: 845-424-3020. FAX: 845-424-4061. E-mail: dflstaff@highlands.com. Web Site: desmondfishlibrary.org. *Dir,* Jen McCreery; E-mail: desmondfishdirector@gmail.com
Founded 1977. Pop 6,900; Circ 61,994
Library Holdings: AV Mats 7,195; Bk Vols 29,568; Per Subs 80; Talking Bks 2,394
Special Collections: Hudson River School Art Reference Coll, slides
Automation Activity & Vendor Info: (Circulation) Innovative Interfaces, Inc; (OPAC) Innovative Interfaces, Inc
Wireless access
Mem of Mid-Hudson Library System
Open Mon, Wed & Fri 10-5, Tues & Thurs 2-9, Sat 10-4, Sun 1-5
Friends of the Library Group

S THE HASTINGS CENTER*, Robert S Morison Memorial Library, 21 Malcolm Gordon Rd, 10524-5555. SAN 326-1530. Tel: 845-424-4040, Ext 256. FAX: 845-424-4545. E-mail: mail@thehastingscenter.org. Web Site: www.thehastingscenter.org.
Founded 1969
Library Holdings: Bk Titles 8,000; Per Subs 220
Subject Interests: Bioethics, Environ med, Med, Med ethics
Publications: Hastings Center Report; Hastings Center Studies in Ethics; IRB: A Review of Ethics & Human Resources
Partic in Southeastern New York Library Resources Council
Restriction: Open to others by appt, Staff use only

GENESEO

C STATE UNIVERSITY OF NEW YORK COLLEGE, Milne Library, SUNY Geneseo, One College Circle, 14454-1498. SAN 352-4825. Tel: 585-245-5594. Interlibrary Loan Service Tel: 585-245-5589. Administration Tel: 585-245-5591. Web Site: www.geneseo.edu/library. *Libr Dir,* Corey Ha; E-mail: ha@geneseo.edu; *Head, Info Tech Serv,* Steve Dresbach; E-mail: dresbach@geneseo.edu; *Head, Coll Mgt,* Alana Nuth; E-mail: nuth@geneseo.edu; *Head, Access Serv,* Dan Ross; E-mail: rossd@geneseo.edu; *Dir, Info & Delivery Services,* Mark Sullivan; E-mail: sullivm@geneseo.edu; *Head, Instruction & Res,* Brandon West; E-mail: westb@geneseo.edu; Staff 23 (MLS 11, Non-MLS 12)
Founded 1871. Enrl 4,572; Fac 329; Highest Degree: Master
Library Holdings: e-books 7,930; Bk Vols 637,100; Per Subs 828
Special Collections: Aldous Huxley Coll; American Architecture (Carl F Schmidt Coll), mss, bd; Children's Literature (Juvenile & Young Adult Coll); Regional History (Genesee Valley Historical Coll) bk, mss; State University of New York College at Geneseo Archives, mss, bk; Wadsworth Family (Wadsworth Homestead Papers, 1800-1950), mss. State Document Depository; US Document Depository
Subject Interests: Educ, Music
Automation Activity & Vendor Info: (Course Reserve) Ex Libris Group; (ILL) OCLC ILLiad; (OPAC) Ex Libris Group; (Serials) Ex Libris Group
Wireless access
Publications: Guide to the College Libraries (Newsletter); Serials Holdings List
Partic in OCLC Online Computer Library Center, Inc; Rochester Regional Library Council; SUNYConnect
Open Mon-Thurs 7:30am-1am, Fri 7:30am-9pm, Sat 10-9, Sun 10am-1am
Friends of the Library Group

P WADSWORTH LIBRARY*, 24 Center St, 14454. SAN 311-2349. Tel: 585-243-0440. FAX: 585-243-0429. E-mail: geneseolibrary@owwl.org. Web Site: www.wadslib.com. *Dir,* Debby Emerson; E-mail: demerson@pls-net.org; *Ch Serv,* Sarah Matthews; Staff 5 (MLS 2, Non-MLS 3)
Founded 1842. Pop 11,525; Circ 84,650
Jul 2017-Jun 2018 Income $440,431, County $13,300, Locally Generated Income $404,406, Other $22,725. Mats Exp $59,500, Books $39,000, Per/Ser (Incl. Access Fees) $1,500, AV Mat $19,000. Sal $189,496 (Prof $96,896)
Library Holdings: CDs 1,641; DVDs 2,698; e-books 722; Electronic Media & Resources 21; Bk Vols 22,592; Per Subs 63
Special Collections: Local History; NY Law Library
Subject Interests: Parenting
Automation Activity & Vendor Info: (Acquisitions) Evergreen; (Cataloging) Evergreen; (Circulation) Evergreen; (ILL) Evergreen; (OPAC) Evergreen; (Serials) Evergreen
Wireless access
Function: 24/7 Online cat, Activity rm, Adult bk club, Audiobks via web, Bk reviews (Group), Bks on CD, Children's prog, Computers for patron use, Digital talking bks, Free DVD rentals, Games & aids for people with disabilities, Holiday prog, Homebound delivery serv, ILL available, Internet access, Life-long learning prog for all ages, Magazines, Magnifiers for reading, Mail & tel request accepted, Mango lang, Meeting rooms, Movies,

Music CDs, Online cat, Orientations, Outreach serv, OverDrive digital audio bks, Photocopying/Printing, Preschool outreach, Preschool reading prog, Prog for adults, Prog for children & young adult, Ref serv available, Scanner, Spanish lang bks, Story hour, Summer reading prog, Tax forms, Telephone ref, Wheelchair accessible, Workshops
Mem of Pioneer Library System
Special Services for the Deaf - ADA equip; Spec interest per
Special Services for the Blind - Bks available with recordings; Bks on cassette; Bks on CD; Computer access aids; Copier with enlargement capabilities; Home delivery serv; Info on spec aids & appliances; Large screen computer & software; Lending of low vision aids
Open Mon-Thurs 10-8:30, Fri 1:30-6, Sat 10-3
Friends of the Library Group

GENEVA

P GENEVA PUBLIC LIBRARY*, 244 Main St, 14456. SAN 311-2365. Tel: 315-789-5303. FAX: 315-789-9835. E-mail: genevaref@pls-net.org. Web Site: genevapubliclibrary.net. *Libr Dir,* Chris Finger; E-mail: cfinger@pls-net.org; *Asst Dir,* Tanya Taylor; E-mail: ttaylor@pls-net.org; *Ref & Tech Librn,* Kelsy Hibbard-Baker; E-mail: khibbardbaker@pls-net.org; Staff 20 (MLS 4, Non-MLS 16)
Founded 1905. Pop 17,500; Circ 160,000
Library Holdings: AV Mats 5,400; Bk Vols 77,500; Per Subs 137
Subject Interests: Local hist
Automation Activity & Vendor Info: (Circulation) SirsiDynix
Wireless access
Mem of Pioneer Library System
Open Mon & Tues 9-8, Wed & Thurs 9-7, Fri 9-6, Sat 9-2
Friends of the Library Group

C HOBART & WILLIAM SMITH COLLEGES, Warren Hunting Smith Library, 334 Pulteney St, 14456. SAN 311-2381. Tel: 315-781-3550. Reference Tel: 315-781-3552. FAX: 315-781-3560. Web Site: library.hws.edu. *Col Librn,* Vincent Boisselle; *Archivist & Spec Coll Librn,* Tricia McEldowney; *Assoc Librn, Coll,* Sara Greenleaf; *Asst Librn, Research Servs,* Jennifer Nace; Staff 18 (MLS 8, Non-MLS 10)
Founded 1824. Enrl 1,812; Fac 187; Highest Degree: Bachelor
Library Holdings: AV Mats 28,787; e-books 353,800; e-journals 93,890; Microforms 47,701; Bk Vols 397,389; Per Subs 1,528
Special Collections: Adaline Glasheen Coll; Alexander Campbell Coll; Arch Merrill Coll; David Bates Douglass Coll; E E Griffith Coll; George M B Hawley Coll; Leo Srole Coll
Subject Interests: Behav sci, English lit, Feminism, Hist, Local hist, Soc sci
Automation Activity & Vendor Info: (Acquisitions) Ex Libris Group; (Cataloging) Ex Libris Group; (Circulation) Ex Libris Group; (Course Reserve) Atlas Systems; (Discovery) Ex Libris Group; (ILL) OCLC ILLiad; (Serials) Ex Libris Group
Wireless access
Partic in Information Delivery Services Project; OCLC Online Computer Library Center, Inc; Rochester Regional Library Council

GERMANTOWN

P GERMANTOWN LIBRARY, 31 Palatine Park Rd, 12526-5309. SAN 376-5830. Tel: 518-537-5800. FAX: 518-537-5928. Web Site: www.germantownlibrary.org. *Dir,* Lynn Place; E-mail: director@germantownlibrary.org
Founded 1948. Pop 2,010
Library Holdings: Bk Titles 18,000; Per Subs 14
Subject Interests: Gardening, Local hist
Automation Activity & Vendor Info: (Acquisitions) Innovative Interfaces, Inc - Sierra; (Cataloging) Innovative Interfaces, Inc - Sierra; (Circulation) Innovative Interfaces, Inc - Sierra; (Course Reserve) Innovative Interfaces, Inc - Sierra; (ILL) Innovative Interfaces, Inc - Sierra; (Media Booking) Innovative Interfaces, Inc - Sierra; (OPAC) Innovative Interfaces, Inc - Sierra; (Serials) Innovative Interfaces, Inc - Sierra
Wireless access
Function: ILL available, Photocopying/Printing
Mem of Mid-Hudson Library System
Special Services for the Blind - Audio mat; Large print bks; Talking bks
Open Tues 9-7, Wed & Fri 9-4, Thurs 12-7, Sat 10-2

GILBERTSVILLE

P GILBERTSVILLE FREE LIBRARY*, 17 Commercial St, 13776. (Mail add: PO Box 332, 13776-0332), SAN 311-239X. Tel: 607-783-2832. FAX: 607-783-2832. Web Site: www.gilbertsvillefreelibrary.org. *Dir,* Jacqueline Foster; *Archivist,* Leigh Eckmair; E-mail: archivist@gilbertsvillefreelibrary.org
Founded 1889. Pop 388
Library Holdings: Bk Titles 9,000; Per Subs 22
Subject Interests: Local hist
Wireless access
Mem of Four County Library System
Open Mon, Wed & Fri 1-5, Tues & Sat 9-1

GLEN COVE

P GLEN COVE PUBLIC LIBRARY*, Four Glen Cove Ave, 11542-2885. SAN 311-242X. Tel: 516-676-2130. FAX: 516-676-2788. Administration FAX: 516-676-2094. Web Site: www.glencovelibrary.org. *Dir,* Kathie Flynn; E-mail: director@glencovelibrary.org; *Asst Dir,* Joanna Cabo; *Head, Adult Serv,* Elizabeth Hogan; *Head, Youth Serv,* Carol Cowan; *Tech Serv Supvr,* Josephine Valensisi; Staff 35 (MLS 13, Non-MLS 22)
Founded 1894. Pop 26,622; Circ 142,178
Library Holdings: AV Mats 9,437; Bk Vols 136,226; Per Subs 250
Special Collections: Long Island & Glen Cove History Coll
Automation Activity & Vendor Info: (Acquisitions) Innovative Interfaces, Inc - Millennium; (Cataloging) Innovative Interfaces, Inc - Millennium; (Circulation) Innovative Interfaces, Inc - Millennium; (OPAC) Innovative Interfaces, Inc
Wireless access
Function: Archival coll, Art exhibits, AV serv, Bi-weekly Writer's Group, CD-ROM, Home delivery & serv to seniorr ctr & nursing homes, Homebound delivery serv, ILL available, Internet access, Magnifiers for reading, Music CDs, Orientations, Photocopying/Printing, Prog for adults, Prog for children & young adult, Ref serv available, Spoken cassettes & CDs, Summer reading prog, Telephone ref, VHS videos, Wheelchair accessible, Workshops
Publications: Newsletter (Bimonthly)
Mem of Nassau Library System
Special Services for the Deaf - Assisted listening device; Bks on deafness & sign lang; Sign lang interpreter upon request for prog
Special Services for the Blind - Bks on cassette; Bks on CD
Open Mon-Thurs 9-9, Fri & Sat 9-5, Sun 1-5
Restriction: Open to pub for ref & circ; with some limitations, Pub use on premises
Friends of the Library Group

S HOLOCAUST MEMORIAL & TOLERANCE CENTER OF NASSAU COUNTY*, Louis Posner Memorial Library, Welwyn Preserve, 100 Crescent Beach Rd, 11542. SAN 377-2071. Tel: 516-571-8040, Ext 102, 516-571-8040, Ext 104. E-mail: info@hmtcli.org. Web Site: www.hmtcli.org/education/posner-library. *Sr Dir,* Beth Lilach; Tel: 516-571-8040, Ext 105, E-mail: bethlilach@hmtcli.org; *Develop, Programming,* Deborah Lom; Tel: 516-571-8040, Ext 107, E-mail: dlom@hmtcli.org; Staff 6 (MLS 6)
Founded 1994
Library Holdings: Bk Titles 6,000; Videos 300
Special Collections: Holocaust Curricula & Graphics. Oral History
Subject Interests: Holocaust
Automation Activity & Vendor Info: (Acquisitions) Follett Software; (Cataloging) Follett Software; (Circulation) Follett Software; (Course Reserve) Follett Software; (ILL) Follett Software; (Media Booking) Follett Software; (OPAC) Follett Software; (Serials) Follett Software
Function: Ref serv available
Restriction: Circ limited, Open by appt only

C WEBB INSTITUTE*, Livingston Library, 298 Crescent Beach Rd, 11542. SAN 311-2446. Tel: 516-671-0439. FAX: 516-674-9838. E-mail: library@webb.edu. Web Site: www.webb.edu/livingston-library. *Libr Dir,* Patricia M Prescott; E-mail: pprescott@webb.edu; Staff 1 (MLS 1)
Founded 1932. Enrl 83; Fac 14; Highest Degree: Master
Library Holdings: Bk Titles 45,000; Per Subs 255
Special Collections: Marine Engineering; Marine History; Naval Architecture
Automation Activity & Vendor Info: (Acquisitions) Ex Libris Group; (Cataloging) Ex Libris Group; (Circulation) Ex Libris Group; (Course Reserve) Ex Libris Group; (ILL) Ex Libris Group; (OPAC) Ex Libris Group; (Serials) Ex Libris Group
Wireless access
Publications: Acquisitions List
Partic in Long Island Library Resources Council; OCLC Online Computer Library Center, Inc
Restriction: Open to pub by appt only

GLEN HEAD

P GOLD COAST PUBLIC LIBRARY*, 50 Railroad Ave, 11545. SAN 378-4517. Tel: 516-759-8300. FAX: 516-759-8308. Web Site: www.goldcoastlibrary.org. *Dir,* Michael Morea; E-mail: mmorea@goldcoastlibrary.org; Staff 4 (MLS 4)
Founded 2005. Pop 10,974; Circ 79,489
Jan 2019-Dec 2019 Income $1,680,000
Library Holdings: AV Mats 1,406; Bk Vols 10,100; Per Subs 50
Automation Activity & Vendor Info: (Cataloging) Innovative Interfaces, Inc; (Circulation) Innovative Interfaces, Inc; (OPAC) Innovative Interfaces, Inc

Wireless access
Mem of Nassau Library System
Open Mon-Thurs 9-9, Fri & Sat 10-6, Sun (Sept-May) 12-5
Friends of the Library Group

GLENS FALLS

P CRANDALL PUBLIC LIBRARY*, 251 Glen St, 12801-3546. SAN 311-2470. Tel: 518-792-6508. Circulation Tel: 518-792-6508, Ext 2. Reference Tel: 518-792-6508, Ext 3. FAX: 518-792-5251. E-mail: crandallinfo@sals.edu. Web Site: www.crandalllibrary.org. *Dir,* Kathleen Naftaly; E-mail: knaftaly@sals.edu; *Dir of Develop,* Michelle Chandler; *Asst Dir,* Guinevere Forshey; *Head, Adult Serv,* Jenn Boyer; *Head, Children's Servx,* Pamela Frazier; *Head, Circ,* Sue Laing; *Teen Librn,* Frieda Toth; Staff 30 (MLS 13, Non-MLS 17)
Founded 1892. Pop 57,329; Circ 583,173
Jan 2020-Dec 2020 Income $4,823,195, Locally Generated Income $3,717,512, Other $1,105,683. Mats Exp $391,850. Sal $2,103,220
Library Holdings: AV Mats 35,312; Bk Vols 154,839; Per Subs 272
Special Collections: Americana; Consumer Health Information; Family Focus Center Coll; Folklife & Local History of Northern New York Adirondacks & Upper Hudson Valley, bks, clippings, genealogy, ms, photogs & serials
Automation Activity & Vendor Info: (Acquisitions) Innovative Interfaces, Inc; (Cataloging) Innovative Interfaces, Inc; (Circulation) Innovative Interfaces, Inc; (OPAC) Innovative Interfaces, Inc
Wireless access
Function: 24/7 Electronic res, 24/7 Online cat, 3D Printer, Activity rm, After school storytime, Archival coll, Art exhibits, Art programs, Audiobks on Playaways & MP3, Audiobks via web, Bks on CD, Children's prog, Computer training, Computers for patron use, Digital talking bks, Doc delivery serv, Electronic databases & coll, For res purposes, Free DVD rentals, Genealogy discussion group, Health sci info serv, Holiday prog, Home delivery & serv to seniorr ctr & nursing homes, Homebound delivery serv, Homework prog, ILL available, Instruction & testing, Internet access, Large print keyboards, Life-long learning prog for all ages, Magazines, Magnifiers for reading, Mail & tel request accepted, Mail loans to mem, Meeting rooms, Microfiche/film & reading machines, Movies, Museum passes, Music CDs, Notary serv, Online cat, Online info literacy tutorials on the web & in blackboard, Online ref, Outreach serv, OverDrive digital audio bks, Photocopying/Printing, Printer for laptops & handheld devices, Prof lending libr, Prog for adults, Prog for children & young adult, Ref & res, Ref serv available, Res assist avail, Senior outreach, Serves people with intellectual disabilities, STEM programs, Story hour, Summer & winter reading prog, Summer reading prog, Tax forms, Teen prog, Telephone ref, VHS videos, Wheelchair accessible, Winter reading prog
Publications: Annual Report; Budget Flyer; Film Flyer; Folklife Center Program Booklets; Fundraising Brochures
Mem of Southern Adirondack Library System
Open Mon-Thurs 9-9, Fri 9-6, Sat 9-5, Sun (Sept-June) 1-5
Friends of the Library Group

S GLENS FALLS-QUEENSBURY HISTORICAL ASSOCIATION*, Chapman Historical Museum Library, 348 Glen St, 12801. SAN 327-7178. Tel: 518-793-2826. FAX: 518-793-2831. E-mail: ContactUs@ChapmanMuseum.org. Web Site: chapmanmuseum.org. *Exec Dir,* Timothy Weidner; E-mail: director@chapmanmuseum.org; *Curator,* Jillian Mulder; E-mail: curator@chapmanmuseum.org
Founded 1967
Library Holdings: Bk Vols 30,000
Special Collections: Seneca Ray Stoddard Coll 1864-1917, Ephemera, ms, photos, family papers & letters, business letters
Subject Interests: Genealogy, Local hist
Wireless access
Open Tues-Sat 10-4
Restriction: Closed stack

S HYDE COLLECTION LIBRARY*, 161 Warren St, 12801. SAN 311-2489. Tel: 518-792-1761. FAX: 518-792-9197. E-mail: info@hydecollection.org. Web Site: www.hydecollection.org. *Interim Dir,* Annie Saile
Founded 1963
Library Holdings: Bk Vols 1,080
Subject Interests: Art, Classics, First edition, Hist, Rare bks, Relig
Wireless access
Function: Res libr
Restriction: Open by appt only

GLOVERSVILLE

P GLOVERSVILLE PUBLIC LIBRARY*, 58 E Fulton St, 12078. SAN 311-2519. Tel: 518-725-2819. FAX: 518-773-0292. E-mail: gpl@mvls.info. Web Site: www.gloversvillelibrary.org. *Libr Dir,* Valerie Acklin; Staff 10 (MLS 2, Non-MLS 8)
Founded 1880. Pop 15,413; Circ 64,924
Library Holdings: AV Mats 4,000; Bk Vols 44,844; Per Subs 109
Subject Interests: Local hist
Automation Activity & Vendor Info: (Cataloging) Innovative Interfaces, Inc; (Circulation) Innovative Interfaces, Inc; (OPAC) Innovative Interfaces, Inc; (Serials) Innovative Interfaces, Inc
Wireless access
Publications: Friends of the Library (Newsletter)
Mem of Mohawk Valley Library System
Open Mon 3-8, Tues & Wed 10-7, Thurs & Fri 10-6, Sat 10-4; Mon (Summer) 3-8, Tues-Fri 9-7
Friends of the Library Group

R KNESSETH ISRAEL SYNAGOGUE LIBRARY*, 34 E Fulton St, 12078. SAN 311-2527. Tel: 518-725-0649. Web Site: www.knessethisrael.net. *Library Contact,* Debbie Finkle
Founded 1975
Library Holdings: Bk Titles 685; Per Subs 4
Subject Interests: Judaica
Restriction: Mem only

GORHAM

P GORHAM FREE LIBRARY, 2664 Main St, 14461. (Mail add: PO Box 211, 14461-0211), SAN 311-2535. Tel: 585-526-6655. FAX: 585-526-6995. Web Site: gorhamfreelibrary.wordpress.com. *Dir,* Ruth Freier; E-mail: GorhamLibraryDirector@owwl.org
Founded 1913. Pop 6,900; Circ 24,000
Library Holdings: Bk Vols 18,000; Per Subs 40
Automation Activity & Vendor Info: (Cataloging) SirsiDynix; (Circulation) SirsiDynix; (OPAC) SirsiDynix
Wireless access
Mem of Pioneer Library System
Open Mon & Fri 12-6, Tues & Thurs 2-8, Wed 9-5, Sat 9-1, Sun 2-4

GOSHEN

P GOSHEN PUBLIC LIBRARY & HISTORICAL SOCIETY*, 366 Main St, 10924. SAN 311-2551. Tel: 845-294-6606. FAX: 845-294-7158. Web Site: www.goshenpubliclibrary.org. *Dir,* Matthew Gomm; E-mail: mattg@goshenpubliclibrary.org; *Asst Dir, Head, Youth Serv,* Michelle Muller; E-mail: michelle@goshenpubliclibrary.org; Staff 8 (MLS 6, Non-MLS 2)
Founded 1894. Pop 16,784; Circ 141,535
Library Holdings: AV Mats 218; Large Print Bks 1,455; Bk Vols 41,768; Per Subs 103; Talking Bks 2,374; Videos 3,927
Subject Interests: Local hist
Automation Activity & Vendor Info: (Cataloging) SirsiDynix; (Circulation) SirsiDynix; (ILL) SirsiDynix; (OPAC) SirsiDynix; (Serials) SirsiDynix
Wireless access
Function: Adult bk club, Computer training, E-Reserves, Electronic databases & coll, Homebound delivery serv, ILL available, Mail & tel request accepted, Music CDs, Photocopying/Printing, Prog for adults, Prog for children & young adult, Summer reading prog, Tax forms, Telephone ref, VHS videos
Publications: A Guide to the Manuscript Collection of the Goshen Library & Historical Society; History of the Goshen Public Library
Mem of Ramapo Catskill Library System
Open Mon-Tues 9-8, Fri 10-5, Sat 9-5, Sun 1-5
Friends of the Library Group

S HARNESS RACING MUSEUM & HALL OF FAME*, Peter D Haughton Memorial Library, 240 Main St, 10924-2157. SAN 311-256X. Tel: 845-294-6330. FAX: 845-294-3463. E-mail: library@harnessmuseum.com. Web Site: www.harnessmuseum.com/library-research. *Dir,* Janet Terhune; *Mgr, Info & Libr Serv,* Paul Wilder; Staff 1 (MLS 1)
Founded 1951
Library Holdings: AV Mats 2,500; Bk Titles 523; Bk Vols 1,600; Per Subs 12
Special Collections: Currier & Ives Travelling Exhibit; Standard Bred Horse & Harness Racing Coll, hist
Subject Interests: Art of the Am trotting horse breed, Harness racing, Hist of the Am trotting horse breed
Open Tues-Sun 10-4
Restriction: By permission only, Mem only
Friends of the Library Group

GL NEW YORK STATE SUPREME COURT NINTH JUDICIAL DISTRICT, Orange County Supreme Court Law Library, Supreme Court Law Library, 2nd Flr, Rm 2002, 285 Main St, 10924. SAN 311-2578. Tel: 845-476-3473. FAX: 845-291-2595. E-mail: 9JDLawLibrary@nycourts.gov. Web Site: www.nycourts.gov/courts/9jd/orange/orangelibrary.shtml. *Library Contact,* Pasquale Porpora; Staff 1 (MLS 1)
Library Holdings: Bk Titles 350; Bk Vols 24,000; Per Subs 10
Wireless access
Function: For res purposes

Open Mon-Fri 9-1 & 2-5
Restriction: Not a lending libr

GOUVERNEUR

S GOUVERNEUR CORRECTIONAL FACILITY, General Library, 112 Scotch Settlement Rd, 13642. (Mail add: PO Box 370, 13642-0370). Tel: 315-287-7351. FAX: 315-287-7351, Ext 3299. Web Site: doccs.ny.gov/location/gouverneur-correctional-facility. *Librn,* Krista Briggs; E-mail: krista.briggs@doccs.ny.gov
Library Holdings: Bk Vols 20,000
Automation Activity & Vendor Info: (Cataloging) Follett Software; (Circulation) Follett Software; (OPAC) Follett Software

P READING ROOM ASSOCIATION OF GOUVERNEUR*, 60 Church St, 13642. SAN 311-2594. Tel: 315-287-0191. FAX: 315-287-0191. E-mail: goulib@ncls.org. Web Site: www.gouverneurlibrary.org. *Libr Dir,* Linda Adams; Staff 1 (Non-MLS 1)
Founded 1886
Library Holdings: AV Mats 663; Bk Titles 16,484; Per Subs 34; Talking Bks 738
Automation Activity & Vendor Info: (Circulation) SirsiDynix
Wireless access
Function: Photocopying/Printing
Mem of North Country Library System
Open Mon, Tues & Thurs 12-8, Wed 9-5, Fri 12-5, Sat 10-12
Friends of the Library Group

GOWANDA

P GOWANDA FREE LIBRARY*, 56 W Main St, 14070-1390. SAN 311-2608. Tel: 716-532-3451. FAX: 716-532-3415. Web Site: enchantedmountains.com/place/gowanda-free-library, www.gowandalibrary.org. *Dir,* Hayley Wilkins; E-mail: director@gowandalibrary.org; *Mgr,* Cathy Lynn Walsh
Founded 1900. Pop 2,842; Circ 20,212
Library Holdings: DVDs 170; Bk Titles 24,770; Per Subs 36; Talking Bks 832; Videos 1,083
Special Collections: Indian Book Coll
Automation Activity & Vendor Info: (Circulation) SirsiDynix; (OPAC) SirsiDynix
Wireless access
Mem of Chautauqua-Cattaraugus Library System
Open Mon, Tues, Thurs & Fri 12:30-6:30, Sat 10-2

GRAFTON

P GRAFTON COMMUNITY LIBRARY*, 2455 NY Rte 2, 12082. (Mail add: PO Box H, 12082), SAN 311-2616. Tel: 518-279-0580. FAX: 518-279-0580. Web Site: www.graftoncommunitylibrary.org. *Dir,* Natalie Hurteau; E-mail: director@graftoncommunitylibrary.org; *Libr Asst,* Amy Hart; Staff 2 (Non-MLS 2)
Founded 1946. Pop 1,989; Circ 14,935
Library Holdings: Bk Vols 11,918
Automation Activity & Vendor Info: (Cataloging) Horizon; (Circulation) Horizon; (OPAC) Horizon; (Serials) Horizon
Wireless access
Mem of Upper Hudson Library System
Open Mon & Tues 3-7, Wed & Sat 10-1, Thurs & Fri 3-8

GRAHAMSVILLE

P DANIEL PIERCE LIBRARY*, 328 Main St, 12740. (Mail add: PO Box 268, 12740-0268), SAN 311-2624. Tel: 845-985-7233. FAX: 845-985-0135. E-mail: dpl@rcls.org. Web Site: www.danielpiercelibrary.org. *Dir,* Jessica Dymond
Founded 1898. Pop 6,402; Circ 53,861
Library Holdings: Electronic Media & Resources 135,024; Bk Vols 35,026; Per Subs 103
Automation Activity & Vendor Info: (Cataloging) SirsiDynix; (Circulation) SirsiDynix; (OPAC) SirsiDynix
Wireless access
Mem of Ramapo Catskill Library System
Open Mon 11-1, Tues-Fri 11-4
Friends of the Library Group

GRAND ISLAND

P GRAND ISLAND MEMORIAL LIBRARY*, 1715 Bedell Rd, 14072. SAN 311-2632. Tel: 716-773-7124. FAX: 716-774-1146. E-mail: gri@buffalolib.org. Web Site: www.buffalolib.org/content/library-locations/grandisland. *Dir,* Bridgette Heintz
Pop 18,621; Circ 164,331
Library Holdings: AV Mats 11,372; Bk Titles 42,358; Bk Vols 49,416; Per Subs 114; Talking Bks 5,209
Automation Activity & Vendor Info: (Acquisitions) Baker & Taylor; (Circulation) SirsiDynix
Wireless access
Mem of Buffalo & Erie County Public Library System
Friends of the Library Group

GRANVILLE

P PEMBER LIBRARY & MUSEUM OF NATURAL HISTORY*, 33 W Main St, 12832. SAN 311-2667. Tel: 518-642-2525. FAX: 518-642-2525. Web Site: thepember.org. *Dir,* Ardyce Bresett; E-mail: gra-director@sals.edu; Staff 4 (MLS 1, Non-MLS 3)
Founded 1909. Pop 2,644; Circ 38,140
Library Holdings: AV Mats 2,931; DVDs 300; Electronic Media & Resources 231; Bk Vols 19,045; Per Subs 85; Talking Bks 1,439; Videos 1,043
Subject Interests: Local hist
Automation Activity & Vendor Info: (Cataloging) Innovative Interfaces, Inc; (Circulation) Innovative Interfaces, Inc; (OPAC) Innovative Interfaces, Inc; (Serials) Innovative Interfaces, Inc
Wireless access
Function: Adult bk club, Archival coll, Audiobks via web, Bks on cassette, Bks on CD, Children's prog, Computers for patron use, Electronic databases & coll, Free DVD rentals, ILL available, Internet access, Online cat, Online ref, OverDrive digital audio bks, Photocopying/Printing, Ref serv available, VHS videos, Wheelchair accessible
Mem of Southern Adirondack Library System
Special Services for the Blind - Large print bks; Talking bks
Open Tues 9-5, Wed 1-8, Fri 12-5, Sat 10-3
Friends of the Library Group

GREAT NECK

P GREAT NECK LIBRARY*, 159 Bayview Ave, 11023. SAN 352-4884. Tel: 516-466-8055. FAX: 516-439-4837. Administration FAX: 516-439-4834. E-mail: comments@greatnecklibrary.org. Web Site: www.greatnecklibrary.org. *Actg Dir,* Tracy Van Dyne; Tel: 516-466-8055, Ext 212, E-mail: tvandyne@greatnecklibrary.org; *Head, Children's Servx,* Deidre Goode; Tel: 516-466-8055, Ext 210, E-mail: dgoode@greatnecklibrary.org; *Head, Ref,* Margery Chodosch; Tel: 516-466-8055, Ext 220, E-mail: mchodosch@greatnecklibrary.org; *Mgr,* Jamie LaGasse; Tel: 516-466-8055, Ext 216, E-mail: jlagasse@greatnecklibrary.org; *Circ Mgr,* Nick Camastro; Tel: 516-466-8055, Ext 207, E-mail: ncamastro@greatnecklibrary.org; *Prog Coordr,* Donna Litke; Tel: 516-466-8055, Ext 254, E-mail: dlitke@greatnecklibrary.org; Staff 102 (MLS 33, Non-MLS 69)
Founded 1889. Pop 43,426; Circ 647,767
Library Holdings: Bk Titles 197,442; Bk Vols 394,036; Per Subs 996
Subject Interests: Archit, Art, Behav sci, Soc sci
Automation Activity & Vendor Info: (Acquisitions) Innovative Interfaces, Inc; (Circulation) Innovative Interfaces, Inc; (OPAC) Innovative Interfaces, Inc
Wireless access
Function: 24/7 Electronic res, 24/7 Online cat, Activity rm, Adult bk club, Adult literacy prog, After school storytime, Archival coll, Art exhibits, Audiobks on Playaways & MP3, Audiobks via web, AV serv, Bilingual assistance for Spanish patrons, Bk club(s), Chess club, Children's prog, Computer training, Computers for patron use, Digital talking bks, Doc delivery serv, E-Readers, E-Reserves, Electronic databases & coll, Family literacy, For res purposes, Free DVD rentals, Games & aids for people with disabilities, Health sci info serv, Holiday prog, Home delivery & serv to seniorr ctr & nursing homes, Homebound delivery serv, Homework prog, ILL available, Instruction & testing, Internet access, Jazz prog, Life-long learning prog for all ages, Literacy & newcomer serv, Magazines, Mail & tel request accepted, Meeting rooms, Microfiche/film & reading machines, Movies, Museum passes, Music CDs, Notary serv, Online cat, Online ref, Orientations, Outreach serv, Outside serv via phone, mail, e-mail & web, OverDrive digital audio bks, Photocopying/Printing, Preschool outreach, Preschool reading prog, Printer for laptops & handheld devices, Prog for adults, Prog for children & young adult, Ref & res, Ref serv available, Res assist avail, Scanner, Senior computer classes, Senior outreach, Serves people with intellectual disabilities, Spanish lang bks, Spoken cassettes & CDs, Spoken cassettes & DVDs, Story hour, Study rm, Summer & winter reading prog, Summer reading prog, Tax forms, Teen prog, Telephone ref, Visual arts prog, Wheelchair accessible, Winter reading prog, Workshops, Writing prog
Publications: Bimonthly Newsletter
Mem of Nassau Library System
Special Services for the Deaf - Assistive tech; TTY equip
Special Services for the Blind - Closed circuit TV magnifier; Vantage closed circuit TV magnifier
Open Mon, Tues, Thurs & Fri 9-9, Wed 10-9, Sat 10-6, Sun (Sept-June) 1-5

Branches: 3
LAKEVILLE, 475 Great Neck Rd, 11021, SAN 352-4914. Tel: 516-466-8055, Ext 231, 516-466-8055, Ext 232. FAX: 516-466-7863. Web Site: www.greatnecklibrary.org/branches/lake.php. *Br Head,* Alana Mutum; E-mail: amutum@greatnecklibrary.org
Library Holdings: Bk Vols 24,300; Per Subs 30
Open Mon, Tues, Fri & Sat 10-6, Wed & Thurs 10-9
PARKVILLE, Ten Campbell St, New Hyde Park, 11040, SAN 352-4949. Tel: 516-466-8055, Ext 273. FAX: 516-437-1929. Web Site: www.greatnecklibrary.org/branches/park.php. *Br Mgr,* Position Currently Open; Staff 10 (MLS 3, Non-MLS 7)
Open Mon & Wed 10-9, Tues & Thurs 9-9, Fri & Sat 10-6, Sun (Sept-June) 1-5
STATION, 26 Great Neck Rd, 11021, SAN 352-4973. Tel: 516-466-8055, Ext 233, 516-466-8055, Ext 234, 516-466-8055, Ext 235. FAX: 516-466-4917. Web Site: www.greatnecklibrary.org/branches/station.php. *Br Mgr,* Justin Crossfox; E-mail: jcrossfox@greatnecklibrary.org; Staff 10 (MLS 2, Non-MLS 8)
Open Mon & Thurs 9-9, Tues & Wed 10-9, Fri & Sat 10-6

GREECE

P GREECE PUBLIC LIBRARY*, Two Vince Tofany Blvd, 14612. SAN 353-9946. Tel: 585-225-8951. FAX: 585-225-2777. E-mail: grwebmst@libraryweb.org. Web Site: www.greecelibrary.org. *Dir,* Cassie Guthrie; Tel: 585-720-4103, E-mail: cguthrie@libraryweb.org; *Asst Dir,* Keith Suhr; Tel: 585-723-2480; *Outreach & Prog Coordr,* Catherine Henderson; Staff 7 (MLS 7)
Founded 1958. Pop 94,141; Circ 672,463
Library Holdings: Bk Vols 97,394
Wireless access
Mem of Monroe County Library System
Open Mon-Thurs 9-9, Fri & Sat 9-5
Friends of the Library Group
Branches: 1
BARNARD CROSSING, 2780 Dewey Ave, Rochester, 14616, SAN 353-9954. Tel: 585-663-3357. FAX: 585-663-5587. *Br Mgr,* Katherine Allen Patterson; Staff 6 (MLS 1, Non-MLS 5)
Circ 100,000
Library Holdings: Bk Vols 12,856
Open Mon & Tues 1-8, Wed-Fri 10-5; Sat(Sept-May) 10-2
Friends of the Library Group

GREENE

P MOORE MEMORIAL LIBRARY, 59 Genesee St, 13778-1298. SAN 311-2691. Tel: 607-656-9349. FAX: 607-656-9349. Web Site: greenenylibrary.org. *Dir,* Gary Quarella; E-mail: gr.gary@4cls.org; Staff 1 (Non-MLS 1)
Founded 1902. Pop 5,604; Circ 43,684
Library Holdings: Audiobooks 550; CDs 900; DVDs 1,600; Bk Vols 38,200; Per Subs 45; Videos 1,000
Special Collections: Cemetery Records; Chenango American 1855-present
Automation Activity & Vendor Info: (Acquisitions) SirsiDynix; (Cataloging) SirsiDynix; (Circulation) SirsiDynix; (ILL) SirsiDynix; (Media Booking) SirsiDynix; (OPAC) SirsiDynix; (Serials) SirsiDynix
Wireless access
Function: 24/7 Electronic res, 24/7 Online cat, Activity rm, Adult bk club, Audiobks via web, Bk club(s), Bks on CD, Children's prog, Computer training, Computers for patron use, Electronic databases & coll, Free DVD rentals, Holiday prog, ILL available, Internet access, Large print keyboards, Magazines, Meeting rooms, Microfiche/film & reading machines, Movies, Music CDs, OverDrive digital audio bks, Photocopying/Printing, Preschool outreach, Printer for laptops & handheld devices, Prog for adults, Prog for children & young adult, Scanner, Senior computer classes, Story hour, Summer reading prog, Tax forms, Teen prog, Wheelchair accessible, Workshops
Mem of Four County Library System
Open Mon-Thurs 9:30-8, Fri 9:30-5, Sat 9-1

GREENLAWN

P HARBORFIELDS PUBLIC LIBRARY, 31 Broadway, 11740. SAN 311-2705. Tel: 631-757-4200. FAX: 631-757-7216. Administration FAX: 631-757-4266. E-mail: info@harborfieldslibrary.org. Web Site: harborfieldslibrary.org. *Dir,* Ryan Athanas; E-mail: rathanas@harborfieldslibrary.org; *Head, Children's Servx,* Patty Moisan; *Head, Circ,* Donna Wickers; *Head, Tech Serv,* Sarah Schnepp; *Adult Ref,* Susan Mathews; *YA Serv,* Linda Meglio; Staff 15 (MLS 14, Non-MLS 1)
Founded 1970. Pop 18,720; Circ 307,030
Library Holdings: Bk Vols 154,800; Per Subs 1,138
Subject Interests: Career, Consumer info, Health, Parenting, Teacher, Travel
Automation Activity & Vendor Info: (Acquisitions) Innovative Interfaces, Inc; (Cataloging) Innovative Interfaces, Inc; (Circulation) Innovative Interfaces, Inc; (Course Reserve) Innovative Interfaces, Inc; (ILL) Innovative Interfaces, Inc; (OPAC) Innovative Interfaces, Inc; (Serials) Innovative Interfaces, Inc
Wireless access
Publications: Monthly newsletter
Mem of Suffolk Cooperative Library System
Partic in Partnership of Automated Librs in Suffolk
Special Services for the Blind - Descriptive video serv (DVS)
Open Mon-Thurs 10-9, Fri & Sat 10-5, Sun (Winter) 1-5
Friends of the Library Group

GREENPORT

P FLOYD MEMORIAL LIBRARY*, 539 First St, 11944-1399. SAN 311-273X. Tel: 631-477-0660. FAX: 631-477-2647. E-mail: floydmemoriallibrary@gmail.com. Web Site: floydmemoriallibrary.org. *Dir,* Tom Vitale; E-mail: director@floydmemoriallibrary.org; *Asst Dir,* Priscilla Johnson; E-mail: poppyjohnson@floydmemoriallibrary.org; *Head, Children's Servx,* Joseph Cortale; E-mail: joe.cortale@gmail.com; *Head, Circ,* Jeane Payne; *YA Librn,* Tracey Moloney; E-mail: tmoloney45@gmail.com; *Tech Coordr,* Position Currently Open; Staff 9 (MLS 4, Non-MLS 5)
Founded 1904. Pop 6,089; Circ 99,000
Jan 2016-Dec 2016 Income $1,049,081, State $1,541, Locally Generated Income $1,028,340, Other $19,200. Mats Exp $73,500, Books $29,000, Per/Ser (Incl. Access Fees) $7,000, AV Mat $13,500, Electronic Ref Mat (Incl. Access Fees) $24,000. Sal $574,754 (Prof $312,865)
Library Holdings: Audiobooks 1,700; CDs 1,000; DVDs 5,920; e-books 145,979; Electronic Media & Resources 131; Large Print Bks 5,700; Bk Titles 38,074; Bk Vols 39,000; Per Subs 168
Special Collections: Historic Preservation; Shakespeare Coll
Subject Interests: English as a second lang, Literacy, Local hist, Sailing
Automation Activity & Vendor Info: (Cataloging) Innovative Interfaces, Inc - Sierra; (Circulation) Innovative Interfaces, Inc; (ILL) Innovative Interfaces, Inc; (OPAC) Innovative Interfaces, Inc - Sierra
Wireless access
Function: 24/7 Electronic res, 24/7 Online cat, Activity rm, Adult bk club, Archival coll, Art exhibits, Audiobks on Playaways & MP3, Audiobks via web, Bilingual assistance for Spanish patrons, Bks on CD, Children's prog, Citizenship assistance, Computer training, Computers for patron use, Digital talking bks, Distance learning, Electronic databases & coll, Free DVD rentals, Holiday prog, Home delivery & serv to seniorr ctr & nursing homes, Homebound delivery serv, Homework prog, ILL available, Internet access, Life-long learning prog for all ages, Literacy & newcomer serv, Magazines, Magnifiers for reading, Mail loans to mem, Meeting rooms, Movies, Music CDs, Online cat, Outreach serv, OverDrive digital audio bks, Photocopying/Printing, Preschool outreach, Prof lending libr, Prog for adults, Prog for children & young adult, Ref & res, Ref serv available, Scanner, Senior outreach, Spanish lang bks, Story hour, Study rm, Summer reading prog, Tax forms, Teen prog, Telephone ref, Wheelchair accessible
Publications: Newsletter
Mem of Suffolk Cooperative Library System
Partic in Partnership of Automated Librs in Suffolk
Special Services for the Blind - Assistive/Adapted tech devices, equip & products; Audio mat
Open Mon-Fri 9:30-8, Sat 9:30-5, Sun 1-5
Friends of the Library Group

S PARAPSYCHOLOGY FOUNDATION INC*, Eileen J Garrett Library, 308 Front St, 11944. (Mail add: PO Box 1562, New York, 10021-0043), SAN 311-9866. Tel: 212-628-1550, 631-477-2560. FAX: 212-628-1559. E-mail: office@parapsychology.org. Web Site: www.parapsychology.org/library. *Pres,* Lisette Coly; E-mail: lisettecoly@parapsychology.org
Founded 1951
Library Holdings: Bk Titles 10,000; Per Subs 100
Special Collections: Audio-Visual Archive
Subject Interests: Parapsychol
Publications: Guide to Sources of Information on Parapsychology (revised annually); International Conference Proceedings; International Journal of Parapsychology; Pamphet Series; Scholarly Monograph Series
Restriction: Open to pub by appt only

GREENVILLE

P GREENVILLE PUBLIC LIBRARY*, 11177 Rte 32, 12083. (Mail add: PO Box 8, 11177 Rte 32, 12083-0008), SAN 311-2764. Tel: 518-966-8205. FAX: 518-966-4822. E-mail: greenvillelibrary@outlook.com. Web Site: www.greenville.lib.ny.us. *Dir,* Barbara Flach; E-mail: bflach@francomm.com; Staff 4 (Non-MLS 4)
Founded 1928. Pop 3,316; Circ 79,675
Library Holdings: Audiobooks 1,953; AV Mats 2,054; e-books 224; Bk Vols 24,941; Per Subs 57
Automation Activity & Vendor Info: (Cataloging) Innovative Interfaces, Inc - Millennium; (Circulation) Innovative Interfaces, Inc - Millennium; (OPAC) Innovative Interfaces, Inc - Millennium
Wireless access

Mem of Mid-Hudson Library System
Open Mon 9-5, Tues & Thurs 9-6, Wed 9-8, Fri 12-5, Sat 9-1
Friends of the Library Group

GREENWICH

P EASTON LIBRARY, 1074 State Rte 40, 12834-9518. SAN 312-1844. Tel: 518-692-2253. FAX: 518-692-2253. Web Site: easton.sals.edu. *Dir,* Jennifer A DeCarlo; E-mail: eas-director@sals.edu
Founded 1879. Pop 2,480; Circ 12,274
Library Holdings: AV Mats 5,055; Electronic Media & Resources 43; Bk Vols 14,834; Per Subs 25
Subject Interests: Local hist
Automation Activity & Vendor Info: (Acquisitions) Innovative Interfaces, Inc; (Cataloging) Innovative Interfaces, Inc; (Circulation) Innovative Interfaces, Inc; (OPAC) Innovative Interfaces, Inc
Wireless access
Mem of Southern Adirondack Library System
Open Mon 1-5, Tues & Thurs 4-8, Wed 9:30-12 & 1-5, Sat 10-4
Friends of the Library Group

P GREENWICH FREE LIBRARY*, 148 Main St, 12834. SAN 311-2772. Tel: 518-692-7157. FAX: 518-692-7152. Web Site: www.greenwichfreelibrary.com. *Dir,* Annie Miller; E-mail: amiller@sals.edu
Founded 1902. Pop 4,942; Circ 40,517
Library Holdings: Bk Vols 38,417; Per Subs 39
Automation Activity & Vendor Info: (Acquisitions) Innovative Interfaces, Inc; (Cataloging) Innovative Interfaces, Inc; (Circulation) Innovative Interfaces, Inc; (Course Reserve) Innovative Interfaces, Inc; (ILL) Innovative Interfaces, Inc; (Media Booking) Innovative Interfaces, Inc; (OPAC) Innovative Interfaces, Inc; (Serials) Innovative Interfaces, Inc
Wireless access
Function: Archival coll, Art exhibits, Audiobks via web, Bks on CD, Children's prog, Computer training, Computers for patron use, E-Reserves, Electronic databases & coll, Family literacy, Free DVD rentals, ILL available, Internet access, Magnifiers for reading, Microfiche/film & reading machines, Music CDs, Online cat, OverDrive digital audio bks, Photocopying/Printing, Preschool reading prog, Prog for adults, Prog for children & young adult, Scanner, Senior computer classes, Story hour, Summer reading prog, Tax forms, Teen prog, Telephone ref, Wheelchair accessible, Workshops
Mem of Southern Adirondack Library System
Partic in OCLC Online Computer Library Center, Inc
Open Mon & Fri 10-5, Tues-Thurs 10-8, Sat 10-1
Friends of the Library Group

GREENWOOD

S GREENWOOD READING CENTER*, Greenwood Town Municipal Bldg, 2684 Main St, SR 248, 14839. (Mail add: PO Box 835, 14839), SAN 328-9877. Tel: 607-225-4553. *Dir,* Betty Jean Hink; E-mail: hinkb@stls.org
Library Holdings: Bk Vols 5,000
Wireless access
Function: Homebound delivery serv
Mem of Southern Tier Library System
Open Mon & Tues 4-7, Thurs 10-4

GREENWOOD LAKE

P GREENWOOD LAKE PUBLIC LIBRARY*, 79 Waterstone Rd, 10925. (Mail add: PO Box 1139, 10925-1139), SAN 311-2780. Tel: 845-477-8377. FAX: 845-477-8397. Administration FAX: 845-477-2053. E-mail: glpl@gwllibrary.org. Web Site: www.gwllibrary.org. *Libr Dir,* Jill Cronin; E-mail: jillcronin@gwllibrary.org
Founded 1932. Pop 6,565; Circ 81,977
Library Holdings: AV Mats 3,172; Bk Titles 30,460; Bk Vols 32,460; Per Subs 140; Talking Bks 2,881
Subject Interests: Local hist
Wireless access
Function: ILL available
Mem of Ramapo Catskill Library System
Open Mon & Fri 9-5, Tues-Thurs 9-9, Sat 10-4, Sun 11-3
Friends of the Library Group

GREIG

P BRANTINGHAM GREIG READING & TECHNOLOGY CENTER*, 5186 Greig Rd, 13345. Tel: 315-348-8272, Ext 5. E-mail: bhmlib@ncls.org. Web Site: www.bhmgreads.org. *Dir,* Mary Lee O'Brien
Mem of North Country Library System

GROTON

P GROTON PUBLIC LIBRARY*, 112 E Cortland St, 13073. SAN 311-2799. Tel: 607-898-5055. FAX: 607-898-5055. Web Site: grotonpubliclibrary.net. *Dir,* Sara L Knobel; E-mail: director@grotonpubliclibrary.org; Staff 1 (Non-MLS 1)
Founded 1896. Pop 5,843; Circ 35,000
Automation Activity & Vendor Info: (Acquisitions) Innovative Interfaces, Inc; (Cataloging) Innovative Interfaces, Inc; (Circulation) Innovative Interfaces, Inc; (Course Reserve) Innovative Interfaces, Inc; (ILL) Innovative Interfaces, Inc; (Media Booking) Innovative Interfaces, Inc; (OPAC) Innovative Interfaces, Inc; (Serials) Innovative Interfaces, Inc
Wireless access
Mem of Finger Lakes Library System
Special Services for the Blind - Bks on cassette; Bks on CD; Large print bks
Open Mon-Thurs 2-9, Fri 10-7, Sat 10-2
Friends of the Library Group

GUILDERLAND

P GUILDERLAND PUBLIC LIBRARY*, 2228 Western Ave, 12084. SAN 310-754X. Tel: 518-456-2400. FAX: 518-456-0923. E-mail: info@guilpl.org. Web Site: guilderlandlibrary.org. *Libr Dir,* Tim Wiles; Tel: 518-456-2400, Ext 113, E-mail: wilest@guilderlandlibrary.org; *Head, Ad Ref Serv, Head, Prog,* Maria Buhl; Tel: 518-456-2400, Ext 142, E-mail: buhlm@guilderlandlibrary.org; *Head, Cat & Coll,* Lisa Pitkin; Tel: 518-456-2400, Ext 118, E-mail: pitkinl@guilderlandlibrary.org; *Head, Info Tech,* Sean Silvernail; Tel: 518-456-2400, Ext 199, E-mail: silvernails@guilderlandlibrary.org; *Head, Youth Serv,* Beth Rienti; Tel: 518-456-2400, Ext 152, E-mail: rientib@guilderlandlibrary.org; *Pub Info Officer,* Luanne Nicholson; Tel: 518-456-2400, Ext 112, E-mail: nicholsonl@guilderlandlibrary.org; Staff 48 (MLS 18, Non-MLS 30)
Founded 1957. Pop 35,000; Circ 489,622
Library Holdings: Bk Vols 185,132; Per Subs 270
Special Collections: Altamont Enterprise microfilm, 1892 current
Automation Activity & Vendor Info: (Acquisitions) Horizon; (Cataloging) Horizon; (Circulation) Horizon; (OPAC) Horizon; (Serials) Horizon
Wireless access
Function: Activity rm, Adult bk club, Adult literacy prog, After school storytime, Art exhibits, Audio & video playback equip for onsite use, Audiobks via web, Bk club(s), Bks on CD, Bus archives, CD-ROM, Children's prog, Citizenship assistance, Computer training, Computers for patron use, Digital talking bks, E-Readers, E-Reserves, Electronic databases & coll, Family literacy, Free DVD rentals, Genealogy discussion group, Govt ref serv, Health sci info serv, Holiday prog, Home delivery & serv to seniorr ctr & nursing homes, Homebound delivery serv, ILL available, Internet access, Jazz prog, Life-long learning prog for all ages, Literacy & newcomer serv, Magazines, Magnifiers for reading, Mail & tel request accepted, Mango lang, Movies, Museum passes, Music CDs, Notary serv, Online cat, Online ref, Outreach serv, OverDrive digital audio bks, Photocopying/Printing, Preschool reading prog, Prog for adults, Prog for children & young adult, Ref & res, Ref serv available, Senior outreach, Serves people with intellectual disabilities, Spanish lang bks, Spoken cassettes & CDs, Spoken cassettes & DVDs, Story hour, Study rm, Summer & winter reading prog, Summer reading prog, Tax forms, Teen prog, Telephone ref, Wheelchair accessible, Winter reading prog, Workshops
Publications: eNews; Guilderland Public Library News (Quarterly newsletter)
Mem of Upper Hudson Library System
Partic in Capital District Library Council; OCLC Online Computer Library Center, Inc
Open Mon, Wed & Fri 11-3, Tues & Thurs 3-7
Friends of the Library Group

HAMBURG

P HAMBURG PUBLIC LIBRARY*, 102 Buffalo St, 14075-5097. SAN 352-5066. Tel: 716-649-4415. Administration Tel: 716-649-4836. FAX: 716-649-4160. Web Site: www.buffalolib.org/locations-hours/hamburg-public-library. *Dir,* Brian Hoth; E-mail: hothb@buffalolib.org; Staff 7 (MLS 4, Non-MLS 3)
Founded 1897. Pop 56,259; Circ 430,007
Library Holdings: AV Mats 7,500; Bk Vols 75,000; Per Subs 120
Subject Interests: Antiques, Art
Automation Activity & Vendor Info: (Acquisitions) SirsiDynix; (Circulation) SirsiDynix; (OPAC) SirsiDynix; (Serials) SirsiDynix
Wireless access
Function: ILL available, Magnifiers for reading, Photocopying/Printing, Prog for children & young adult, Ref serv available, Serves people with intellectual disabilities, Summer reading prog, Telephone ref, Wheelchair accessible
Mem of Buffalo & Erie County Public Library System

Special Services for the Blind - Bks on cassette; Bks on CD; Large print bks; Radio reading serv; Talking bks; VisualTek equip; ZoomText magnification & reading software
Open Mon 10-5, Wed & Fri 9-5, Sat 9-3
Friends of the Library Group
Branches: 1
LAKE SHORE, S-4857 Lake Shore Rd, 14075, SAN 352-5120. Tel: 716-627-3017. FAX: 716-627-6505. E-mail: lsh@buffalolib.org. Web Site: www.buffalolib.org/locations-hours/lake-shore-branch-library. *Br Mgr, Librn,* Stephanie Molnar; Staff 3 (Non-MLS 3)
Pop 56,259; Circ 113,920
Library Holdings: AV Mats 3,250; Bk Vols 32,176; Per Subs 127
Function: ILL available, Photocopying/Printing, Prog for children & young adult, Ref serv available, Telephone ref, Wheelchair accessible
Special Services for the Blind - Bks on cassette; Bks on CD; Copier with enlargement capabilities; Large print bks; Radio reading serv; Talking bks; ZoomText magnification & reading software
Open Mon & Wed 12-8, Tues, Thurs & Sat 9-5
Friends of the Library Group

C HILBERT COLLEGE, McGrath Library, 5200 S Park Ave, 14075. SAN 311-2829. Tel: 716-926-8913. FAX: 716-648-6530. E-mail: askus@hilbert.edu. Web Site: www.hilbert.edu/academics/library. *Interim Libr Dir,* Chloe Santangelo; Tel: 716-649-7900, Ext 365, E-mail: csantangelo@hilbert.edu; *Ref & Instruction Librn,* Melissa Laidman; Tel: 716-649-7900, Ext 245, E-mail: mlaidman@hilbert.edu; *Evening/Weekend Supvr,* Catherine McGrath; E-mail: cmcgrath@hilbert.edu; *Evening/Weekend Supvr,* Dianna Urbanski; E-mail: durbanski@hilbert.edu; Staff 5 (MLS 4, Non-MLS 1)
Founded 1955. Enrl 940; Fac 97; Highest Degree: Bachelor
Library Holdings: AV Mats 480; Bk Titles 33,212; Bk Vols 36,311; Per Subs 337; Talking Bks 102; Videos 400
Automation Activity & Vendor Info: (Cataloging) TLC (The Library Corporation); (Circulation) TLC (The Library Corporation); (OPAC) TLC (The Library Corporation)
Wireless access
Publications: Acquisitions List; Periodical Holdings Catalog; Student Information Sheets; Video Catalog
Partic in Western New York Library Resources Council
Open Mon-Thurs 8am-10pm, Fri 8-7, Sat & Sun 10-3; Mon-Thurs (Summer) 8-4:30, Fri 8-4
Friends of the Library Group

HAMILTON

C COLGATE UNIVERSITY*, Everett Needham Case Library, 13 Oak Dr, 13346-1398. SAN 311-2845. Tel: 315-228-7300. Interlibrary Loan Service Tel: 315-228-7597. FAX: 315-228-7934. Web Site: cul.colgate.edu. *Univ Librn,* Courtney Young; Tel: 315-228-7362, E-mail: clyoung@colgate.edu; *Assoc Univ Librn,* Steve Black; Tel: 315-228-6544, E-mail: seblack@colgate.edu; *Head, Coll Mgt,* Mike Poulin; Tel: 315-228-7025, E-mail: mpoulin@colgate.edu; *Head, Spec Coll, Univ Archivist,* Sarah Keen; Tel: 315-228-7305, E-mail: skeen@colgate.edu; *Syst Librn,* Mark Sandford; Tel: 315-228-7363, E-mail: msandford@colgate.edu; *Mgr, Borrower Serv,* Rob Capuano; Tel: 315-228-7301, E-mail: rcapuano@colgate.edu; *Cat Mgr,* Adger Williams; Tel: 315-228-7310, E-mail: awilliams@colgate.edu; *Govt Doc Coordr,* Sergi Domashenko; Tel: 315-228-7508, E-mail: sdomashenko@colgate.edu; Staff 34 (MLS 14, Non-MLS 20)
Founded 1819. Enrl 2,758; Fac 245; Highest Degree: Master
Library Holdings: AV Mats 16,184; e-journals 29,114; Bk Vols 721,189; Per Subs 1,698
Special Collections: 17th Century British Religious & Political Tracts; 19th-20th Century American & British Literature; George Bernard Shaw Coll; Gertrude Stein Coll; James Joyce Coll; John Masefield Coll; Joseph Conrad Coll; Photography (Edward Stone Coll); Private Press & Fine Printing, incunabula; T S Eliot Coll; University Archives; World War I & II Posters. State Document Depository; UN Document Depository; US Document Depository
Automation Activity & Vendor Info: (Acquisitions) Innovative Interfaces, Inc; (Cataloging) Innovative Interfaces, Inc; (Circulation) Innovative Interfaces, Inc; (Course Reserve) Innovative Interfaces, Inc; (ILL) Innovative Interfaces, Inc; (OPAC) Innovative Interfaces, Inc; (Serials) SerialsSolutions
Wireless access
Function: Doc delivery serv, For res purposes, Ref serv available
Partic in Central New York Library Resources Council; ConnectNY, Inc; OCLC Online Computer Library Center, Inc
Open Mon-Thurs 8am-Midnight, Fri 8am-10pm, Sat 9am-10pm, Sun 9am-Midnight; Mon-Fri (Summer) 8-5
Restriction: Access at librarian's discretion

Departmental Libraries:
GEORGE R COOLEY SCIENCE LIBRARY, 13 Oak Dr, 13346-1338. Tel: 315-228-7312. *Sci Librn,* Peter Tagtmeyer; Tel: 315-228-7402, E-mail: ptagtmeyer@colgate.edu; Staff 2 (MLS 1, Non-MLS 1)
Founded 1979. Highest Degree: Master
Library Holdings: Bk Vols 46,000; Per Subs 1,000
Automation Activity & Vendor Info: (Cataloging) Innovative Interfaces, Inc; (Circulation) Innovative Interfaces, Inc; (ILL) Innovative Interfaces, Inc; (OPAC) Innovative Interfaces, Inc; (Serials) Innovative Interfaces, Inc
Open Mon-Thurs 8am-Midnight, Fri 8am-11pm, Sat 9am-11pm

P HAMILTON PUBLIC LIBRARY, 13 Broad St, 13346. SAN 311-2853. Tel: 315-824-3060. FAX: 315-824-8420. E-mail: hamilton@midyork.org. Web Site: www.hamiltonlibrary.org. *Dir,* Travis Olivera; E-mail: tolivera@midyork.org; *Asst Dir,* Liza Taylor; E-mail: ltaylor@midyork.org
Founded 1903. Pop 4,109; Circ 60,186
Library Holdings: Bk Vols 38,500; Per Subs 50
Special Collections: Biographical Review of Madison County; History of Chenango & Madison Counties, 1784-1880 (James H Smith Coll); Madison County Cemetery Records (Genealogical Records Committee of the James Madison Chapter of the Daughters of the American Revolution, 1801-1900)
Subject Interests: Archit, Cookery, Gardening, Hist, Natural sci
Automation Activity & Vendor Info: (Acquisitions) SirsiDynix; (Cataloging) SirsiDynix; (Circulation) SirsiDynix; (Course Reserve) SirsiDynix; (ILL) SirsiDynix; (Media Booking) SirsiDynix; (OPAC) SirsiDynix; (Serials) SirsiDynix
Wireless access
Mem of Mid-York Library System
Open Mon-Thurs 10-7, Fri 10-5, Sat 9-3
Friends of the Library Group

HAMLIN

P HAMLIN PUBLIC LIBRARY*, 1680 Lake Rd, 14464. Tel: 585-964-2320. FAX: 585-964-2374. E-mail: hamlinpublib@gmail.com. Web Site: hamlinlibraryny.org. *Dir,* Katherine Hughes-Dennett; *Ad,* Adrienne Kirby; Staff 1.3 (MLS 1.3)
Founded 2000. Pop 9,050; Circ 72,126
Library Holdings: AV Mats 4,924; Bk Vols 22,701
Automation Activity & Vendor Info: (Cataloging) CARL.Solution (TLC); (Circulation) CARL.Solution (TLC); (Course Reserve) CARL.Solution (TLC); (ILL) CARL.Solution (TLC); (OPAC) CARL.Solution (TLC); (Serials) CARL.Solution (TLC)
Wireless access
Function: Adult bk club, Audiobks via web, Bks on CD, Children's prog, Computers for patron use, Digital talking bks, E-Reserves, Electronic databases & coll, Free DVD rentals, ILL available, Internet access, Mail & tel request accepted, Music CDs, Online cat, Outside serv via phone, mail, e-mail & web, Photocopying/Printing, Preschool outreach, Prog for adults, Prog for children & young adult, Ref serv available, Scanner, Story hour, Summer & winter reading prog, Tax forms, Wheelchair accessible
Mem of Monroe County Library System
Open Mon & Wed 10-6, Tues & Thurs 10-8, Fri 10-4, Sat 10-2
Friends of the Library Group

HAMMOND

P HAMMOND FREE LIBRARY, 17 N Main St, 13646. (Mail add: PO Box 229, 13646-0229), SAN 311-2861. Tel: 315-324-5139. FAX: 315-324-5302. E-mail: hamlib@ncls.org. Web Site: www.hammondfreelibrary.org. *Dir,* Sherrie Moquin; Staff 1 (Non-MLS 1)
Founded 1922. Pop 1,207; Circ 7,944
Library Holdings: Bk Vols 5,979
Wireless access
Mem of North Country Library System
Open Mon 4-6, Tues-Thurs 12-5, Sat 9-Noon

HAMMONDSPORT

S GLENN H CURTISS MUSEUM OF LOCAL HISTORY*, Minor Swarthout Memorial Library, 8419 State Rte 54, 14840-0326. SAN 326-0356. Tel: 607-569-2160. FAX: 607-569-2040. Web Site: www.glennhcurtissmuseum.org. *Curator,* Rick Leisenring; E-mail: curator@glennhcurtissmuseum.org; Staff 6 (Non-MLS 6)
Founded 1992
Library Holdings: Bk Titles 4,000
Special Collections: Oral History
Subject Interests: Aviation, Local hist
Function: Res libr
Restriction: Open by appt only

P FRED & HARRIETT TAYLOR MEMORIAL LIBRARY*, 21 William St, 14840. (Mail add: PO Box 395, 14840-0395), SAN 311-287X. Tel: 607-569-2045. FAX: 607-569-3340. E-mail: hammondsport@stls.org. Web

Site: hammondsportlibrary.org. *Dir,* Sally Jacoby Murphy; E-mail: murphys@stls.org
Founded 1876. Pop 2,807; Circ 27,798
Library Holdings: AV Mats 3,155; Bk Vols 26,000; Per Subs 25
Special Collections: Aircraft Coll, bks & pictures
Subject Interests: Local hist
Automation Activity & Vendor Info: (Acquisitions) SirsiDynix; (Cataloging) SirsiDynix; (Circulation) SirsiDynix; (Course Reserve) SirsiDynix; (ILL) SirsiDynix; (Media Booking) SirsiDynix; (OPAC) SirsiDynix; (Serials) SirsiDynix
Wireless access
Mem of Southern Tier Library System
Special Services for the Deaf - TTY equip
Open Mon & Wed 10-6, Tues & Thurs 2-6, Fri 10-5, Sat 10-2

HAMPTON BAYS

P HAMPTON BAYS PUBLIC LIBRARY*, 52 Ponquogue Ave, 11946. SAN 311-2888. Tel: 631-728-6241. FAX: 631-728-0166. E-mail: contact@hamptonbayslibrary.org. Web Site: hamptonbayslibrary.org. *Libr Dir,* Susan LaVista; E-mail: slavista@hamptonbayslibrary.org; *Ch,* Christine Fitzgerald; E-mail: cfitzgerald@hamptonbayslibrary.org; *Head, Circ,* Nancy Cariello; Staff 38 (MLS 13, Non-MLS 25)
Founded 1960. Pop 11,992; Circ 117,755
Library Holdings: AV Mats 7,236; Bk Vols 65,029; Per Subs 6,334
Special Collections: Long Island History
Subject Interests: Archit, Art
Automation Activity & Vendor Info: (Cataloging) Innovative Interfaces, Inc; (Circulation) Innovative Interfaces, Inc; (ILL) Innovative Interfaces, Inc; (OPAC) Innovative Interfaces, Inc
Wireless access
Mem of Suffolk Cooperative Library System
Open Mon-Thurs 10-9, Fri 10-7, Sat 10-5, Sun 1-5
Friends of the Library Group

HANCOCK

P LOUISE ADELIA READ MEMORIAL LIBRARY, 104 Read St, 13783. SAN 311-2896. Tel: 607-637-2519. FAX: 607-637-3377. E-mail: ha.ill@4cls.org. Web Site: libraries.4cls.org/hancock. *Dir,* Joann Haberli
Founded 1955. Pop 2,724; Circ 13,000
Library Holdings: Bk Vols 25,000; Per Subs 45
Automation Activity & Vendor Info: (Cataloging) SirsiDynix-WorkFlows; (Circulation) SirsiDynix-WorkFlows; (OPAC) SirsiDynix-WorkFlows; (Serials) SirsiDynix-WorkFlows
Wireless access
Mem of Four County Library System
Open Tues & Thurs 11-7, Wed & Fri 11-4, Sat 12-4

HANNIBAL

P HANNIBAL FREE LIBRARY*, 162 Oswego St, 13074. SAN 311-2918. Tel: 315-564-5471. FAX: 315-564-5471. E-mail: hanlib@ncls.org. Web Site: www.hannibalfreelibrary.org. *Dir,* Shelly Stanton; E-mail: sstanton@ncls.org
Pop 4,027; Circ 12,000
Library Holdings: Bk Vols 8,100; Per Subs 14
Automation Activity & Vendor Info: (Cataloging) SirsiDynix; (Circulation) SirsiDynix; (OPAC) SirsiDynix; (Serials) SirsiDynix
Wireless access
Mem of North Country Library System
Open Mon, Wed & Fri 10-4:30, Tues & Thurs 10-8, Sat 9-3
Friends of the Library Group

HARRISON

P HARRISON PUBLIC LIBRARY*, Two Bruce Ave, 10528. SAN 352-5155. Tel: 914-835-0324. FAX: 914-835-1564. Web Site: www.harrisonpl.org. *Dir,* Galina Chernykh; E-mail: gchernykh@wlsmail.org
Founded 1905. Pop 24,154; Circ 238,731
Library Holdings: Bk Vols 122,857
Special Collections: Spanish & Japanese Language Coll
Automation Activity & Vendor Info: (Cataloging) SirsiDynix; (Circulation) SirsiDynix; (OPAC) SirsiDynix
Wireless access
Open Mon & Wed 9:30-9, Tues, Thurs & Fri 9:30-5:30, Sat (Sept-June) 9:30-5:30, (9:30-12:30 July-Aug), Sun (Sept-June) 1-5
Friends of the Library Group
Branches: 1
WEST HARRISON BRANCH, Two E Madison St, West Harrison, 10604, SAN 352-518X. Tel: 914-948-2092. FAX: 914-948-4350. Web Site: www.westchesterlibraries.org. *Ch Serv,* Liz Karkoff
Special Collections: Italian Language Coll
Friends of the Library Group

HARRISVILLE

P HARRISVILLE FREE LIBRARY, 8209 Main St, 13648. (Mail add: PO Box 207, 13648-0207), SAN 311-2934. Tel: 315-543-2577. FAX: 315-543-2577. E-mail: harlib@ncls.org. Web Site: www.harrisvillefreelibrary.org. *Dir,* Nicole Spencer; *Librn,* Pam Conlin
Pop 703; Circ 7,984
Library Holdings: Bk Vols 7,000; Per Subs 5
Wireless access
Mem of North Country Library System
Open Mon-Fri 10-6
Friends of the Library Group

HARTWICK

P KINNEY MEMORIAL LIBRARY*, 3140 County Hwy 11, 13348-3007. (Mail add: PO Box 176, 13348-0176), SAN 311-2950. Tel: 607-293-6600. FAX: 607-293-6600. E-mail: kinymlib@gmail.com. Web Site: libraries.4cls.org/hartwick. *Dir,* Barbara Porter
Founded 1961. Pop 3,255; Circ 12,976
Library Holdings: Bk Vols 21,433; Per Subs 20
Special Collections: Historical Artifacts, Books & Photos
Subject Interests: Genealogy
Automation Activity & Vendor Info: (Acquisitions) SirsiDynix; (Cataloging) SirsiDynix; (Circulation) SirsiDynix; (Course Reserve) SirsiDynix; (ILL) SirsiDynix; (Media Booking) SirsiDynix; (OPAC) SirsiDynix; (Serials) SirsiDynix
Wireless access
Mem of Four County Library System
Open Mon 9-1 & 7-9, Wed 11-4 & 7-9, Fri & Sat 1-5
Friends of the Library Group

HASTINGS-ON-HUDSON

P HASTINGS-ON-HUDSON PUBLIC LIBRARY*, Seven Maple Ave, 10706. SAN 311-2969. Tel: 914-478-3307. FAX: 914-478-4813. E-mail: has@westchesterlibraries.org. Web Site: www.hastingslibrary.org. *Libr Dir,* Debbie Quinn; E-mail: dquinn@wlsmail.org; *Adult Serv,* Michael McCoy
Founded 1913. Pop 7,750; Circ 140,000
Library Holdings: AV Mats 15,000; Bk Titles 55,000; Per Subs 125
Automation Activity & Vendor Info: (Cataloging) SirsiDynix; (Circulation) SirsiDynix; (OPAC) SirsiDynix
Wireless access
Mem of Westchester Library System
Open Mon, Tues & Thurs (Winter) 9:30-8:30, Wed 9:30-6, Fri & Sat 9:30-5, Sun 1-5; Mon, Tues & Thurs (Summer) 9:30-8:30, Wed 9:30-6, Fri & Sat 9:30-2
Friends of the Library Group

HAUPPAUGE

C ADELPHI UNIVERSITY*, Hauppauge Center Library, 55 Kennedy Dr, 11788-4001. Tel: 516-237-8611. FAX: 516-237-8613. Web Site: libguides.adelphi.edu/hauppauge, libraries.adelphi.edu. *Library Contact,* AnnMarie Barbieri; Tel: 516-237-8610, E-mail: ABarbieri@adelphi.edu; Staff 1 (MLS 1)
Fac 2
Library Holdings: Bk Vols 4,000; Per Subs 5
Wireless access
Open Mon-Thurs 3-9, Fri 9-2, Sat 9-1

P HAUPPAUGE PUBLIC LIBRARY*, 1373 Veterans Memorial Hwy, Ste 1, 11788. SAN 378-407X. Tel: 631-979-1600. FAX: 631-979-4018. E-mail: info@hauppaugelibrary.org. Web Site: www.hauppaugelibrary.org. *Chief Exec Officer,* Matthew Bollerman; E-mail: matthew@hauppaugelibrary.org
Founded 2000. Pop 10,900
Library Holdings: AV Mats 20,069; Bk Vols 40,981; Per Subs 164
Automation Activity & Vendor Info: (Acquisitions) Innovative Interfaces, Inc; (Cataloging) Innovative Interfaces, Inc; (OPAC) Innovative Interfaces, Inc
Wireless access
Function: 24/7 Electronic res, 24/7 Online cat, 3D Printer, Activity rm, Adult bk club, Adult literacy prog, Art exhibits, Art programs, Audio & video playback equip for onsite use, Audiobks via web, AV serv, Bk club(s), Bks on CD, Chess club, Children's prog, Computer training, Computers for patron use, Digital talking bks, Distance learning, Doc delivery serv, E-Readers, Electronic databases & coll, Equip loans & repairs, Family literacy, For res purposes, Free DVD rentals, Games & aids for people with disabilities, Govt ref serv, Health sci info serv, Holiday prog, Home delivery & serv to seniorr ctr & nursing homes, Homebound delivery serv, Homework prog, ILL available, Instruction & testing, Internet access, Learning ctr, Life-long learning prog for all ages, Literacy & newcomer serv, Magazines, Magnifiers for reading, Meeting rooms, Movies, Museum passes, Music CDs, Online cat, Online info literacy tutorials on the web & in blackboard, Online ref, Outreach serv, Outside serv via phone, mail, e-mail & web, OverDrive digital audio bks,

Photocopying/Printing, Preschool outreach, Preschool reading prog, Printer for laptops & handheld devices, Prog for adults, Prog for children & young adult, Ref & res, Ref serv available, Res assist avail, Scanner, Senior computer classes, Senior outreach, Serves people with intellectual disabilities, STEM programs, Story hour, Study rm, Summer & winter reading prog, Summer reading prog, Tax forms, Teen prog, Telephone ref, Visual arts prog, Wheelchair accessible, Winter reading prog, Workshops, Writing prog
Publications: Hauppauge Library (Newsletter)
Mem of Suffolk Cooperative Library System
Open Mon-Fri 9:30-9, Sat 9:30-5, Sun 1-9
Friends of the Library Group

HECTOR

P ELIZABETH B PERT LIBRARY, Valois-Logan-Hector Fire House, 5736 Rte 414, 14841. (Mail add: PO Box 82, 14841-0082), SAN 352-4078. Tel: 607-546-2605. *Dir,* Roberta Beckhorn; E-mail: beckhornb@stls.org; Staff 1 (Non-MLS 1)
Pop 5,045
Library Holdings: Bk Vols 8,000
Wireless access
Function: Homebound delivery serv
Mem of Southern Tier Library System
Open Tues 12-8, Wed 9-12, Thurs 2-8, Sat 9-12
Friends of the Library Group

HEMPSTEAD

P HEMPSTEAD PUBLIC LIBRARY, 115 James A Garner Way, 11550. SAN 311-2993. Tel: 516-481-6990. FAX: 516-481-6719. Reference E-mail: ReferenceDesk@HempsteadLibrary.info. Web Site: www.hempsteadlibrary.info. *Dir,* Irene A Duszkiewicz; *Head Ref Librn,* Erica Lang; *Tech Serv,* Andrea Smernoff; Staff 36 (MLS 16, Non-MLS 20)
Founded 1889. Pop 56,554; Circ 265,268
Library Holdings: Bk Vols 212,368; Per Subs 331
Special Collections: Adult Multi-Media; Black Studies Coll; Early American Textbooks; Hispanic Studies Coll; Job & Education Information Center; LI Photography Coll; Literacy Materials; Long Island Coll; Walt Whitman Coll; World Language Coll for Adults & Children
Subject Interests: Ethnic studies, Hist
Automation Activity & Vendor Info: (Cataloging) Innovative Interfaces, Inc - Sierra; (Circulation) Innovative Interfaces, Inc - Sierra; (OPAC) Innovative Interfaces, Inc - Sierra; (Serials) Innovative Interfaces, Inc - Sierra
Wireless access
Publications: ALC Resources Bibliography; Black Studies Bibliography; Community Directory; Hispanic Studies Bibliography; Newsletter; World Language Bibliography
Mem of Nassau Library System
Partic in Libraries Online, Inc; Long Island Library Resources Council; Vutext
Open Mon-Wed 10-8, Thurs & Fri 10-6, Sat (Sept-June) 9-5

C HOFSTRA UNIVERSITY*, Joan & Donald E Axinn Library, 123 Hofstra University, 11549. SAN 352-5279. Circulation Tel: 516-463-5952. Interlibrary Loan Service Tel: 516-463-5946. Reference Tel: 516-463-5962. Administration Tel: 516-463-5940. Circulation FAX: 516-463-4309. Reference FAX: 516-463-7485. Administration FAX: 516-463-6387. Web Site: www.hofstra.edu/library. *Assoc Dean, Libr Serv,* Howard Graves; Tel: 516 463-6429, E-mail: howard.e.graves@hofstra.edu; *Chair, Ref Serv & Coll Develop,* Annmarie Boyle; Tel: 516 463-6529, E-mail: annmarie.b.boyle@hofstra.edu; *Coll Serv, Dir, Film & Media Library, Head, Res,* Sarah McCleskey; Tel: 516-463-5076, E-mail: sarah.e.mccleskey@hofstra.edu; *Mgr, Off of the Dean of Libr & Info Serv,* Carol Sasso; Tel: 516-463-5943, E-mail: carol.a.sasso@hofstra.edu; Staff 68 (MLS 30, Non-MLS 38)
Founded 1935. Enrl 11,145; Fac 1,181; Highest Degree: Doctorate
Sept 2016-Aug 2017 Income $8,649,316. Mats Exp $2,093,402, Books $2,584,160, Per/Ser (Incl. Access Fees) $1,095,634, Manu Arch $5,114, Other Print Mats $86,464, AV Mat $33,267, Electronic Ref Mat (Incl. Access Fees) $613,571, Presv $934. Sal $4,428,680 (Prof $2,416,657)
Library Holdings: AV Mats 16,709; e-books 182,883; e-journals 8,378; Electronic Media & Resources 34,016; Microforms 3,426,863; Music Scores 1,441; Bk Vols 620,237; Per Subs 8,757
Special Collections: Art of the book; Authors Coll of Late 19th & Early 20th Century; Harry Wachtel Coll; Henry Kroul Coll of Nazi Culture & Propoganda; History of Hofstra Univ; Long Island Develop Coll; Long Island Newspapers; Physicians for Social Responsibility of Nassau County Coll; Private Press Coll; Spinzia Coll of Long Island Estates History; Utopian Communities; Weingrow Coll of Avant-Garde Art & Literature. State Document Depository; US Document Depository
Automation Activity & Vendor Info: (Acquisitions) Innovative Interfaces, Inc; (Cataloging) Innovative Interfaces, Inc; (Circulation) Innovative Interfaces, Inc; (Course Reserve) Docutek; (Discovery) EBSCO Discovery Service; (ILL) OCLC ILLiad; (OPAC) Innovative Interfaces, Inc - Sierra; (Serials) Innovative Interfaces, Inc
Wireless access
Partic in Long Island Library Resources Council; LYRASIS; OCLC Online Computer Library Center, Inc; Westchester Academic Library Directors Organization
Special Services for the Blind - Reader equip; ZoomText magnification & reading software
Open Mon-Thurs 8am-2am, Fri 8am-9pm, Sat 9-9, Sun 10am-11pm
Departmental Libraries:
SPECIAL COLLECTIONS/LONG ISLAND STUDIES INSTITUTE, 032 Axinn Library, 123 Hofstra University, 11549-1230. Tel: 516-463-6404, 516-463-6411. FAX: 516-463-6442. E-mail: lisi@hofstra.edu. Web Site: www.hofstra.edu/libraries. *Asst Dean,* Geri Solomon; *Curator,* Michael O'Connor; *Acq,* Bronwyn Hannon; Staff 3 (MLS 1, Non-MLS 2)
Founded 1935
Special Collections: Long Island Studies; Rare Books & Manuscripts Coll; University Archives
Open Mon-Fri 9-4:45
Restriction: Closed stack

CL HOFSTRA UNIVERSITY LAW LIBRARY, Barbara & Maurice A Deane Law Library, 122 Hofstra University, 11549-1220. Tel: 516-463-5898. Reference Tel: 516-463-5908. Administration Tel: 516-463-5900. FAX: 516-463-5129. Web Site: law.hofstra.edu/library. *Interim Dir,* Lisa Spar; E-mail: lisa.a.spar@hofstra.edu; Staff 11 (MLS 10, Non-MLS 1)
Library Holdings: Bk Titles 240,322; Bk Vols 534,000
Automation Activity & Vendor Info: (Cataloging) OCLC
Wireless access
Partic in Long Island Library Resources Council
Open Mon-Thurs 8-8, Fri 8-5, Sat & Sun 10-6

HENDERSON

P HENDERSON FREE LIBRARY*, 8939 New York State Rte 178, 13650. SAN 311-3019. Tel: 315-938-7169. FAX: 315-938-7038. E-mail: henlib@ncls.org. Web Site: www.hendersonfreelibrary.org. *Dir,* Mary Bidwell; Staff 1 (Non-MLS 1)
Founded 1951. Pop 1,377; Circ 11,600
Library Holdings: Bk Vols 12,343; Per Subs 52
Special Collections: State Document Depository
Automation Activity & Vendor Info: (Acquisitions) SirsiDynix-WorkFlows
Wireless access
Function: Bk club(s), Bks on cassette, Bks on CD, Children's prog, Computers for patron use, E-Reserves, Electronic databases & coll, Free DVD rentals, ILL available, Mail & tel request accepted, Music CDs, Online cat, Photocopying/Printing, Preschool outreach, Scanner, Story hour, Summer reading prog, VHS videos, Wheelchair accessible
Mem of North Country Library System
Open Mon & Wed 10-5, Tues, Thurs & Sat 9-1

HERKIMER

P FRANK J BASLOE LIBRARY, 245 N Main St, 13350-1918. SAN 311-3027. Tel: 315-866-1733. FAX: 315-866-0395. E-mail: herkimer@midyork.org. Web Site: www.herkimerbasloelibrary.org. *Dir,* Christine Fleischer; Staff 2 (MLS 1, Non-MLS 1)
Founded 1895. Circ 101,422
Library Holdings: AV Mats 2,517; Bk Vols 40,250; Per Subs 94
Special Collections: NYS Coll. State Document Depository
Subject Interests: Genealogy
Automation Activity & Vendor Info: (Cataloging) SirsiDynix; (Circulation) SirsiDynix; (OPAC) SirsiDynix; (Serials) SirsiDynix
Wireless access
Mem of Mid-York Library System
Open Mon-Wed 9-8, Thurs & Fri 9-5, Sat 9-3
Friends of the Library Group

J HERKIMER COLLEGE LIBRARY*, 100 Reservoir Rd, 13350. SAN 311-3035. Tel: 315-866-0300, Ext 8270. Circulation Tel: 315-866-0300, Ext 8272. Reference Tel: 315-866-0300, Ext 8394. Toll Free Tel: 844-464-4375 (NY State only). FAX: 315-866-1806. E-mail: library@herkimer.edu. Web Site: www.herkimer.edu/library. *Dir, Libr Serv,* Fred Berowski; Tel: 315-866-0300, Ext 8345, E-mail: berowskfj@herkimer.edu; *Pub Serv,* Stephanie Conley; *Tech Serv,* Valerie Prescott; Staff 4 (MLS 4)
Founded 1967. Enrl 2,600; Fac 90; Highest Degree: Associate
Library Holdings: High Interest/Low Vocabulary Bk Vols 150; Bk Titles 69,000; Per Subs 218
Subject Interests: Art, Behav sci, Criminal justice, Educ, Law, Soc sci, Tourism
Automation Activity & Vendor Info: (Cataloging) Ex Libris Group; (Circulation) Ex Libris Group; (OPAC) Ex Libris Group; (Serials) Ex Libris Group

Wireless access
Publications: Faculty library handbook; Library handbook; Monthly acquisitions list; Periodicals holdings list
Partic in Central New York Library Resources Council; SUNYConnect
Open Mon-Thurs 8am-9pm, Fri 8-4, Sun 4-9

S HERKIMER COUNTY HISTORICAL SOCIETY LIBRARY*, Eckler Bldg, 406 N Main St, 13350. (Mail add: 400 N Main St, 13350), SAN 311-3043. Tel: 315-866-6413. E-mail: herkimerhistory@yahoo.com. Web Site: www.herkimercountyhistory.org. *Dir,* Susan R Perkins
Founded 1896
Library Holdings: Bk Vols 4,000
Special Collections: Herkimer County, New York Artifacts
Subject Interests: County hist
Wireless access
Publications: Local Genealogy; Local History
Open Mon-Fri 10-3
Restriction: Not a lending libr

GL HERKIMER COUNTY LAW LIBRARY*, 301 N Washington St, Ste 5511, 13350-1299. SAN 311-3051. Tel: 315-614-3404. FAX: 315-266-4619. *Law Libr Asst,* Lisa M Liskiewicz; E-mail: lliskiew@nycourts.gov
Founded 1941
Library Holdings: Bk Titles 500; Bk Vols 14,000
Special Collections: Legal Reference Coll

HERMON

P HEPBURN LIBRARY OF HERMON*, 105 Main St, 13652-3100. (Mail add: PO Box A, 13652-0400), SAN 311-306X. Tel: 315-347-2285. FAX: 315-347-5058. E-mail: herlib@ncls.org. Web Site: www.hermonhepburnlibrary.org. *Dir,* Kelly Hamilton
Pop 1,080; Circ 25,333
Library Holdings: Bk Vols 14,000; Per Subs 41
Automation Activity & Vendor Info: (Cataloging) SirsiDynix; (Circulation) SirsiDynix; (OPAC) SirsiDynix
Wireless access
Mem of North Country Library System
Open Mon 12-4 & 6-8, Tues, Thurs & Fri 9-1, Wed 9-3 & 6-8, Sat 10-2

HEUVELTON

P HEUVELTON FREE LIBRARY, 57 State St, 13654. (Mail add: PO Box 346, 13654-0346), SAN 311-3078. Tel: 315-344-6550. FAX: 315-344-6550. E-mail: heulib@ncls.org. Web Site: www.heuveltonfreelibrary.org. *Dir,* Lora Martin
Founded 1912. Pop 714; Circ 8,450
Library Holdings: Bk Titles 5,295; Bk Vols 8,100; Per Subs 58
Automation Activity & Vendor Info: (Cataloging) SirsiDynix-WorkFlows; (Circulation) SirsiDynix-WorkFlows; (ILL) SirsiDynix-WorkFlows
Wireless access
Mem of North Country Library System
Open Mon 6-8, Tues 1-5, Wed 1-5 & 6-8, Fri 11-3 & 4-7, Sat 2-5

HEWLETT

P HEWLETT-WOODMERE PUBLIC LIBRARY*, 1125 Broadway, 11557-0903. SAN 311-3086. Tel: 516-374-1967. E-mail: hewlett@hwpl.org. Web Site: www.hwpl.org. *Dir,* William Ferro; *Asst Dir,* Catherine Nashak; *Head, Tech, Head, User Experience,* James Hartmann; Staff 15 (MLS 15)
Founded 1947. Pop 20,265; Circ 266,281
Library Holdings: AV Mats 46,271; Bk Vols 204,106; Per Subs 429
Special Collections: Art Coll, bks, flm, slides; Music Coll, bks, cassettes, recs, scores, song indexes, tapes
Subject Interests: Art, Music
Automation Activity & Vendor Info: (Acquisitions) Innovative Interfaces, Inc; (Circulation) Innovative Interfaces, Inc; (OPAC) Innovative Interfaces, Inc
Wireless access
Function: Art exhibits, Audio & video playback equip for onsite use
Publications: Index to Art Reproductions in Books; Music & Art Catalogs; Overleaf (Newsletter); Overleaf, Jr (Newsletter)
Mem of Nassau Library System
Partic in Long Island Library Resources Council
Open Mon-Thurs 9-9, Fri 9-6, Sat 9-5, Sun 12:30-5
Friends of the Library Group

HICKSVILLE

P HICKSVILLE PUBLIC LIBRARY*, 169 Jerusalem Ave, 11801. SAN 311-3108. Tel: 516-931-1417. FAX: 516-822-5672. E-mail: hplinfo@hicksvillelibrary.org. Web Site: hicksvillelibrary.org. *Dir,* Christine Edwins; E-mail: cedwins@hicksvillelibrary.org; *Asst Dir,* Joanne Gramaglia; Staff 10 (MLS 10)
Founded 1926. Pop 39,330; Circ 260,000
Library Holdings: Bk Vols 150,000; Per Subs 400
Special Collections: Oral History
Subject Interests: Local hist
Wireless access
Mem of Nassau Library System
Partic in Long Island Library Resources Council
Special Services for the Deaf - TDD equip
Open Mon, Tues & Thurs 9-9, Wed 10-9, Fri & Sat 9-5, Sun (Oct-May) 1-5

HIGHLAND

P HIGHLAND PUBLIC LIBRARY*, 14 Elting Pl, 12528. (Mail add: PO Box 1556, 12528), SAN 311-3124. Tel: 845-691-2275. FAX: 845-691-6302. Web Site: highlandlibrary.org. *Dir,* Julie Kelsall-Dempsey; E-mail: jkelsall@highlandlibrary.org; *Asst Dir, Ch,* Holly Sgro; Staff 12 (MLS 2, Non-MLS 10)
Founded 1915. Pop 12,715; Circ 62,433
Library Holdings: Bk Titles 32,865; Per Subs 51
Automation Activity & Vendor Info: (Acquisitions) Innovative Interfaces, Inc
Wireless access
Publications: Highland Public Library Events
Mem of Mid-Hudson Library System
Open Mon & Fri 10-5, Wed 10-8, Tues & Thurs 1-8, Sat 10-4
Friends of the Library Group
Branches: 1
CLINTONDALE BRANCH, Crescent at Maple, Clintondale, 12515, SAN 372-560X. Tel: 845-883-5015. *Br Mgr,* Arlene McMahon; Tel: 845-691-2275, Ext 206
Automation Activity & Vendor Info: (Cataloging) Innovative Interfaces, Inc; (Circulation) Innovative Interfaces, Inc
Open Tues 10-12, Wed & Thurs 4-7

HIGHLAND FALLS

P HIGHLAND FALLS LIBRARY, 298 Main St, 10928. SAN 352-5392. Tel: 845-446-3113. FAX: 845-446-1109. E-mail: hfl@rcls.org. Web Site: highlandfallslibrary.org. *Dir,* Marie-Elena Ortiz; Staff 1 (Non-MLS 1)
Founded 1884. Pop 3,900; Circ 28,091
Library Holdings: CDs 1,130; DVDs 700; Electronic Media & Resources 49,000; Bk Vols 31,200; Per Subs 40; Videos 1,000
Special Collections: Hudson River; West Point
Subject Interests: Local authors, Local hist
Automation Activity & Vendor Info: (Acquisitions) SirsiDynix; (Cataloging) SirsiDynix; (Circulation) SirsiDynix; (Course Reserve) SirsiDynix; (ILL) SirsiDynix; (Media Booking) SirsiDynix; (OPAC) SirsiDynix; (Serials) SirsiDynix
Wireless access
Mem of Ramapo Catskill Library System
Open Mon-Fri 10:30-4:30, Sat 10:30-12:30
Friends of the Library Group

HIGHLAND MILLS

P WOODBURY PUBLIC LIBRARY*, Rushmore Memorial Branch, 16 County Rte 105, 10930. SAN 311-3140. Tel: 845-928-6162. Administration Tel: 845-928-7837. FAX: 845-928-3079. E-mail: wpl@rcls.org. Web Site: www.woodburypubliclibrary.org/home/rushmore-memorial-public-library. *Libr Dir,* Sara Johnson; Staff 2 (MLS 1, Non-MLS 1)
Founded 1923. Pop 11,353
Library Holdings: Bk Vols 43,991; Per Subs 107
Special Collections: Historical Coll-Town of Woodbury
Automation Activity & Vendor Info: (Cataloging) SirsiDynix; (Circulation) SirsiDynix; (OPAC) SirsiDynix
Wireless access
Mem of Ramapo Catskill Library System
Partic in Bibliomation Inc
Open Mon, Wed & Thurs 10-1, Tues 4:30-7:30
Friends of the Library Group

HILLSDALE

P ROELIFF JANSEN COMMUNITY LIBRARY ASSOCIATION, INC, 9091 Rte 22, 12529. (Mail add: PO Box 669, 12529-0669), SAN 311-3159. Tel: 518-325-4101. FAX: 518-325-4105. Web Site: roejanlibrary.org. *Libr Dir,* Tamara Gaskell; E-mail: director@roejanlibrary.org; *Libr Assoc,* Fran Colombo; E-mail: outreach@roejanlibrary.org; *Circ Librn,* Robin Gottlieb; E-mail: circulation@roejanlibrary.org; *Children's & Youth Serv,* Tia Maggio; E-mail: youth@roejanlibrary.org; *Communications Mgr, Libr Assoc,* Ingrid Kildiss; E-mail: communications@roejanlibrary.org
Founded 1913. Pop 7,115; Circ 42,694
Jan 2020-Dec 2020 Income $420,197, State $14,465, Locally Generated Income $121,815, Other $283,917

Library Holdings: Audiobooks 4,899; CDs 2,154; DVDs 3,115; e-books 13,525; Electronic Media & Resources 85; Bk Vols 20,186; Videos 1,706
Wireless access
Function: 24/7 Electronic res, 24/7 Online cat, Activity rm, Adult bk club, Art exhibits, Art programs, Audiobks on Playaways & MP3, Audiobks via web, Bi-weekly Writer's Group, Bk club(s), Bks on CD, Children's prog, Computer training, Computers for patron use, Electronic databases & coll, Equip loans & repairs, Free DVD rentals, Holiday prog, Home delivery & serv to seniorr ctr & nursing homes, Homebound delivery serv, ILL available, Internet access, Life-long learning prog for all ages, Magazines, Magnifiers for reading, Mango lang, Meeting rooms, Microfiche/film & reading machines, Movies, Museum passes, Music CDs, Notary serv, Online cat, Outreach serv, OverDrive digital audio bks, Photocopying/Printing, Preschool outreach, Prog for adults, Prog for children & young adult, Scanner, Senior computer classes, Serves people with intellectual disabilities, Spanish lang bks, Spoken cassettes & DVDs, Story hour, Summer reading prog, Tax forms, Wheelchair accessible, Workshops, Writing prog
Mem of Mid-Hudson Library System
Open Mon-Wed & Fri 10-5, Thurs 10-8, Sat 10-4
Friends of the Library Group

HILTON

P PARMA PUBLIC LIBRARY*, Seven West Ave, 14468-1214. SAN 311-3167. Tel: 585-392-8350. FAX: 585-392-9870. E-mail: parmapubliclibrary@gmail.com. Web Site: www.parmapubliclibrary.org. *Libr Dir,* Amy Hogue; E-mail: amy.hogue@libraryweb.org; Staff 13 (MLS 3, Non-MLS 10)
Founded 1885. Pop 15,633; Circ 140,267
Subject Interests: Local hist
Automation Activity & Vendor Info: (Acquisitions) CARL.Solution (TLC); (Cataloging) CARL.Solution (TLC); (Circulation) CARL.Solution (TLC); (OPAC) CARL.Solution (TLC)
Wireless access
Function: Adult bk club, After school storytime, Art exhibits, Audiobks via web, Bk club(s), Bks on CD, Children's prog, Computer training, Computers for patron use, Electronic databases & coll, Family literacy, Free DVD rentals, Holiday prog, Homebound delivery serv, Magazines, Magnifiers for reading, Mail & tel request accepted, Movies, Museum passes, Music CDs, Online cat, Outreach serv, Outside serv via phone, mail, e-mail & web, OverDrive digital audio bks, Photocopying/Printing, Preschool outreach, Prog for adults, Prog for children & young adult, Ref & res, Ref serv available, Scanner, Senior outreach, Serves people with intellectual disabilities, Story hour, Summer reading prog, Tax forms, Teen prog, Telephone ref, Wheelchair accessible, Writing prog
Mem of Monroe County Library System
Open Mon-Thurs 10-9, Fri 10-6, Sat 10-4
Friends of the Library Group

HOGANSBURG

S AKWESASNE CULTURAL CENTER LIBRARY*, 321 State Rte 37, 13655. SAN 311-3175. Tel: 518-358-2240. FAX: 518-358-2649. E-mail: akwlibr@northnet.org. Web Site: www.akwesasneculturalcenter.org/library. *Dir,* Gloria Cole
Library Holdings: Bk Titles 28,000; Per Subs 51
Special Collections: American Indian Coll
Automation Activity & Vendor Info: (Cataloging) Horizon; (Circulation) Horizon; (OPAC) Horizon
Wireless access
Function: Photocopying/Printing, Wheelchair accessible
Mem of Clinton-Essex-Franklin Library System
Partic in Northern New York Library Network
Open Mon & Fri (Winter) 9-5, Tues & Thurs 9-5:30, Wed 9-6, Sat 10-2; Mon & Fri (Summer) 9-5, Tues & Thurs 9-5:30, Wed 9-6

HOLBROOK

P SACHEM PUBLIC LIBRARY, 150 Holbrook Rd, 11741. SAN 311-3183. Tel: 631-588-5024. FAX: 631-588-5064. Administration E-mail: administration@sachemlibrary.org. Web Site: sachemlibrary.org. *Dir,* Neely McCahey; E-mail: neely.mccahey@sachemlibrary.org; *Asst Dir,* Kristen Stroh; E-mail: kristen.stroh@sachemlibrary.org; *Head of Digital Services, IT & Makerspace,* Christopher DeCristofaro; *Head, Children's Servx,* Amy Johnston; *Head, Community Engagement,* Kelly Sulima; *Head, Library Programs & Newsletter,* Alexandra Mercado; *Head, Ref,* Cara Perry; *Head, Teen Serv,* Laura Panter; *Circ Serv Coordr,* Danielle Krause; *Patron Serv,* Denise Scarbeck; Staff 33.5 (MLS 28, Non-MLS 5.5)
Founded 1961. Pop 83,196; Circ 982,561
Jul 2021-Jun 2022 Income $10,864,917. Mats Exp $3,872,931, Books $3,563,837, Per/Ser (Incl. Access Fees) $60,311, Micro $4,459, AV Mat $183,802, Electronic Ref Mat (Incl. Access Fees) $60,522. Sal $3,957,901 (Prof $2,695,926)
Library Holdings: AV Mats 55,619; Electronic Media & Resources 7,861; Bk Vols 266,519; Per Subs 572
Special Collections: Homeschooling Coll; Senior Coll; SEPTA; Virtual Reference Coll
Subject Interests: Genealogy, Local hist
Automation Activity & Vendor Info: (Acquisitions) Innovative Interfaces, Inc; (Cataloging) Innovative Interfaces, Inc; (Circulation) Innovative Interfaces, Inc; (ILL) Innovative Interfaces, Inc; (OPAC) Innovative Interfaces, Inc; (Serials) Innovative Interfaces, Inc
Wireless access
Publications: Local Directory; Newsletter; Periodicals List
Mem of Suffolk Cooperative Library System
Special Services for the Blind - Bks on cassette; Closed circuit TV magnifier; Extensive large print coll
Open Mon-Fri 9:30-9, Sat 9:30-5, Sun (Oct-May) 12-4
Friends of the Library Group

HOLLAND PATENT

P HOLLAND PATENT FREE LIBRARY, 9580 Main St, 13354-3819. (Mail add: PO Box 187, 13354-0187), SAN 311-3205. Tel: 315-865-5034. FAX: 315-865-5034. E-mail: hollandpatent@midyork.org. Web Site: hollandpatentlibrary.org. *Dir,* Cindy McVoy
Founded 1916. Circ 20,465
Library Holdings: Bk Vols 16,888; Per Subs 40
Wireless access
Mem of Mid-York Library System
Open Mon & Tues 2-5, Wed & Thurs 2-6, Fri & Sat 10-1 (Winter); Mon & Tues 1-5, Wed & Thurs 2-6, Fri 10-2 (Summer)
Friends of the Library Group

HOLLEY

P COMMUNITY FREE LIBRARY, 86 Public Sq, 14470. SAN 311-3213. Tel: 585-638-6987. FAX: 585-638-7436. Web Site: www.holleylibrary.org. *Dir,* Sandra Shaw; E-mail: sshaw@nioga.org
Pop 8,563; Circ 27,966
Library Holdings: Bk Vols 26,300; Per Subs 45
Subject Interests: Local hist
Automation Activity & Vendor Info: (Cataloging) SirsiDynix; (Circulation) SirsiDynix; (OPAC) SirsiDynix
Wireless access
Mem of Nioga Library System
Open Mon & Wed 10-1 & 4-8, Tues, Thurs & Fri 10-5, Sat 10-2

HOMER

P PHILLIPS FREE LIBRARY*, 37 S Main St, 13077-1323. (Mail add: PO Box 7, 13077-0007), SAN 311-3221. Tel: 607-749-4616. FAX: 607-749-4616. Circulation E-mail: circ@phillipsfreelibrary.org. Web Site: www.phillipsfreelibrary.org. *Dir,* Priscilla Berggren-Thomas; Staff 2 (MLS 1, Non-MLS 1)
Founded 1902. Pop 12,500; Circ 45,000
Library Holdings: DVDs 340; Bk Vols 20,000; Per Subs 36; Talking Bks 630; Videos 210
Automation Activity & Vendor Info: (Circulation) Innovative Interfaces, Inc; (OPAC) Innovative Interfaces, Inc
Wireless access
Mem of Finger Lakes Library System
Open Mon 10-6, Tues & Thurs 2-8, Wed 10-8, Fri 2-6, Sat 10-2
Friends of the Library Group

HONEOYE

P HONEOYE PUBLIC LIBRARY, 8708 Main St, 14471. (Mail add: PO Box 70, 14471-0070), SAN 311-323X. Tel: 585-229-5020. FAX: 585-229-5881. Web Site: honeoye.owwl.org. *Dir,* Janelle Speca; E-mail: honeoyelibrarydirector@owwl.org
Circ 39,618
Library Holdings: Bk Vols 16,000; Per Subs 23
Automation Activity & Vendor Info: (Cataloging) SirsiDynix-DRA; (Circulation) SirsiDynix-DRA; (OPAC) SirsiDynix-DRA
Wireless access
Mem of Pioneer Library System
Open Mon 12-6, Tues & Thurs 2-8, Wed 10-2, Sat 9-1

HONEOYE FALLS

P MENDON PUBLIC LIBRARY, 22 N Main St, 14472. SAN 311-3248. Tel: 585-624-6067. FAX: 585-624-4255. Web Site: mendonlibrary.org. *Dir,* Laurie Guenther; E-mail: laurie.guenther@libraryweb.org; Staff 1 (MLS 1)
Pop 9,150; Circ 96,050
Library Holdings: Bk Vols 39,500; Per Subs 42
Wireless access
Mem of Monroe County Library System
Open Mon-Thurs 9-8, Fri 9-3, Sat (Winter) 10-3
Friends of the Library Group

HOOSICK FALLS

P CHENEY LIBRARY*, 73 Classic St, 12090-1326. Tel: 518-686-9401. FAX: 518-686-9401. Web Site: www.cheneylibrary.org. *Dir,* Sara Yetto; E-mail: director@cheneylibrary.org
Founded 1926. Circ 19,304
Library Holdings: Bk Titles 14,732; Per Subs 24
Automation Activity & Vendor Info: (Cataloging) SirsiDynix; (Circulation) SirsiDynix; (OPAC) SirsiDynix
Wireless access
Function: Activity rm, Adult bk club, Archival coll, Audiobks on Playaways & MP3, Audiobks via web, AV serv, Bk club(s), Bks on CD, CD-ROM, Children's prog, Computers for patron use, Family literacy, Free DVD rentals, Holiday prog, Home delivery & serv to seniorr ctr & nursing homes, Homebound delivery serv, ILL available, Internet access, Life-long learning prog for all ages, Magazines, Mail & tel request accepted, Mango lang, Meeting rooms, Movies, Museum passes, Music CDs, Online cat, Outreach serv, OverDrive digital audio bks, Photocopying/Printing, Preschool reading prog, Prog for adults, Prog for children & young adult, Ref serv available, Senior computer classes, Senior outreach, Serves people with intellectual disabilities, Spoken cassettes & CDs, Story hour, Study rm, Summer & winter reading prog, Summer reading prog, Tax forms, Teen prog, Visual arts prog, Wheelchair accessible, Workshops
Mem of Upper Hudson Library System
Open Mon & Wed 1-8, Tues 10-5, Thurs 10-8, Fri 11-5, Sat 9-1
Friends of the Library Group

HOPEWELL JUNCTION

P BEEKMAN LIBRARY*, 11 Town Center Blvd, 12533. (Mail add: PO Box 697, Poughquag, 12570-0697), SAN 376-3013. Tel: 845-724-3414. FAX: 845-724-3941. E-mail: BEEKLIB@BEEKMANLIBRARY.ORG. Web Site: beekmanlibrary.org. *Exec Dir,* Carol Fortier; E-mail: cfortier@beekmanlibrary.org; Staff 7.3 (MLS 1, Non-MLS 6.3)
Founded 1965. Pop 13,655; Circ 68,477
Library Holdings: AV Mats 2,977; Bk Titles 20,443; Per Subs 91; Talking Bks 565
Subject Interests: Irish, Local hist
Automation Activity & Vendor Info: (Cataloging) Innovative Interfaces, Inc - Millennium; (OPAC) Innovative Interfaces, Inc
Wireless access
Mem of Mid-Hudson Library System
Open Mon 2-7, Tues-Fri 10-4, Sat 10-2
Friends of the Library Group

P EAST FISHKILL COMMUNITY LIBRARY*, 348 Rte 376, 12533-6075. SAN 312-6269. Tel: 845-221-9943. FAX: 845-226-1404. Web Site: www.eastfishkilllibrary.org. *Dir,* Gloria W Goverman; Tel: 845-221-9943, Ext 227, E-mail: goverman@eflibrary.org; *Ad,* Amanda Assenza; Tel: 845-221-9943, Ext 225, E-mail: assenza@eflibrary.org; *Youth Serv Librn,* Cathy Nuding; Tel: 845-221-9943, Ext 233, E-mail: nuding@eflibrary.org; *Circ Supvr,* Catherine Swierat; Tel: 845-221-9943, Ext 228, E-mail: swierat@eflibrary.org; *Tech Serv Supvr,* Kristie Simco; Tel: 845-221-9943, Ext 222, E-mail: simco@eflibrary.org; Staff 12.6 (MLS 3.7, Non-MLS 8.9)
Founded 1938. Pop 25,589; Circ 238,674
Library Holdings: Audiobooks 1,901; DVDs 3,779; Bk Titles 63,000; Per Subs 134
Automation Activity & Vendor Info: (Acquisitions) Innovative Interfaces, Inc; (Cataloging) Innovative Interfaces, Inc; (Circulation) Innovative Interfaces, Inc; (OPAC) Innovative Interfaces, Inc
Wireless access
Mem of Mid-Hudson Library System
Open Mon-Thurs 10-8, Fri 10-6, Sat 10-5
Friends of the Library Group

HOPKINTON

P HOPKINTON TOWN LIBRARY*, Seven Church St, 12965. Tel: 315-328-4113. FAX: 315-328-4113. E-mail: hoplib@ncls.org. Web Site: www.hopkintonnylibrary.org. *Dir,* Jan Keller
Wireless access
Mem of North Country Library System
Open Mon & Wed 10-12 & 3:30-5:30, Thurs 3:30-5:30, Fri & Sat 10-Noon

HORNELL

P HORNELL PUBLIC LIBRARY*, 64 Genesee St, 14843-1651. SAN 311-3280. Tel: 607-324-1210. FAX: 607-324-2570. Web Site: hornellpubliclibrary.org. *Dir,* Alice Marie Taychert; E-mail: taycherta@stls.org; Staff 2 (MLS 2)
Founded 1868. Pop 9,019; Circ 58,646
Apr 2017-Mar 2018. Mats Exp $264,809, Books $18,500, Per/Ser (Incl. Access Fees) $3,000, AV Mat $4,000. Sal $134,500 (Prof $51,409)
Library Holdings: Audiobooks 1,195; DVDs 23,348; Bk Vols 44,975; Per Subs 42; Spec Interest Per Sub 1,718; Videos 564
Special Collections: Erie Railroad
Subject Interests: Civil War, Local hist, Railroads
Automation Activity & Vendor Info: (Acquisitions) SirsiDynix; (Circulation) SirsiDynix; (ILL) SirsiDynix; (OPAC) SirsiDynix
Wireless access
Mem of Southern Tier Library System
Special Services for the Blind - Home delivery serv
Open Mon-Thurs 10-8, Fri 10-5, Sat 10-2
Friends of the Library Group

P HOWARD PUBLIC LIBRARY, 3607 County Rte 70A, 14843. SAN 310-8236. Tel: 607-566-2412. FAX: 607-566-3679. Web Site: howard.stls.org. *Mgr,* Lorraine Nelson; E-mail: nelsonl@stls.org
Founded 1911. Pop 1,331; Circ 16,000
Library Holdings: AV Mats 1,190; DVDs 172; Bk Titles 10,154; Bk Vols 11,000; Per Subs 28; Talking Bks 154; Videos 618
Automation Activity & Vendor Info: (Cataloging) SirsiDynix; (Circulation) SirsiDynix; (OPAC) SirsiDynix; (Serials) SirsiDynix
Wireless access
Mem of Southern Tier Library System
Open Mon & Thurs 2-7, Tues 12-7, Sat 9-1

HOUGHTON

C HOUGHTON COLLEGE*, Willard J Houghton Library, One Willard Ave, 14744. SAN 352-5457. Tel: 585-567-9242. Interlibrary Loan Service Tel: 585-567-9256. Reference Tel: 585-567-9241. FAX: 585-567-9248. Web Site: libguides.houghton.edu/WJHL. *Libr Dir,* David Stevick; E-mail: David.Stevick@houghton.edu; *Cat Librn, Instruction & Ref Librn,* Bradley Wilber; Tel: 585-567-9607, E-mail: Bradley.Wilber@houghton.edu; *Electronic Res Librn, Ref & Instruction Librn,* Doyin Adenuga; Tel: 585-567-9615, E-mail: Doyin.Adenuga@houghton.edu; *Cat Spec, Circ Spec,* Laura Dibble; Tel: 585-567-9244, E-mail: Laura.Dibble@houghton.edu. Subject Specialists: *Music,* Bradley Wilber; Staff 9 (MLS 4, Non-MLS 5)
Founded 1883. Enrl 1,000; Highest Degree: Master
Library Holdings: AV Mats 47,000; CDs 9,800; DVDs 6,000; e-books 21,000; e-journals 47,000; Bk Vols 226,650; Per Subs 400
Special Collections: John & Charles Wesley & Methodism Coll
Subject Interests: Biblical studies, Intercultural studies, Music, Relig, Theol
Automation Activity & Vendor Info: (Acquisitions) SirsiDynix; (Cataloging) SirsiDynix; (Circulation) SirsiDynix; (Course Reserve) SirsiDynix; (ILL) SirsiDynix; (Media Booking) SirsiDynix; (OPAC) SirsiDynix; (Serials) SirsiDynix
Wireless access
Function: ILL available
Partic in South Central Regional Library Council; Westchester Academic Library Directors Organization
Open Mon-Thurs 7:45am-11pm, Fri 7:45-5, Sat 10-6

HOWES CAVE

S IROQUOIS INDIAN MUSEUM LIBRARY*, 324 Caverns Rd, 12092. (Mail add: PO Box 7, 12092-0007), SAN 376-2025. Tel: 518-296-8949. FAX: 518-296-8955. E-mail: info@iroquoismuseum.org. Web Site: www.iroquoismuseum.org. *Dir,* Stephanie Shultes. Subject Specialists: *Anthrop,* Stephanie Shultes
Founded 1980
Library Holdings: Bk Vols 1,200
Subject Interests: Iroquois, Local hist, Native Am
Wireless access
Open Tues-Sat 10-5, Sun 12-5 (April-Dec)

HUDSON

S ANTHROPOSOPHICAL SOCIETY IN AMERICA, Rudolf Steiner Library, 351 Fairview Ave Ste 610, 12534-1259. SAN 373-1197. Tel: 518-944-7007. E-mail: rsteinerlibrary@gmail.com. Web Site: rudolfsteinerlibrary.org.
Founded 1928
Library Holdings: Bk Vols 27,000; Spec Interest Per Sub 30
Subject Interests: Anthroposophy, Liberal arts, Waldorf educ, World spirituality
Automation Activity & Vendor Info: (OPAC) OPALS (Open-source Automated Library System)
Wireless access
Function: 24/7 Online cat, ILL available, Mail loans to mem, Online cat, Photocopying/Printing, Res libr, Scanner, Spoken cassettes & CDs, VHS videos, Wheelchair accessible
Partic in Capital District Library Council
Open Wed-Sat 10-3
Restriction: Circ to mem only, In-house use for visitors
Friends of the Library Group

J COLUMBIA-GREENE COMMUNITY COLLEGE LIBRARY*, 4400 Rte 23, 12534. SAN 311-3310. Tel: 518-828-4181, Ext 3286. FAX: 518-828-4396. Web Site: www.sunycgcc.edu/academics/library-media-services. *Chairperson, Librn,* Geralynn Demarest; Tel: 518-828-4181, Ext 3290, E-mail: demarest@sunycgcc.edu; *Libr Serv Librn, Media Serv Librn,* Barbara Pilatich; E-mail: Pilatich@sunycgcc.edu; *Ref & Circ Librn,* John Santana; Tel: 518-828-4181, Ext 3287, E-mail: john.santana@sunycgcc.edu; *Coordr, Multimedia Ctr,* Carl Nabozny; Tel: 518-828-4181, Ext 3294, E-mail: nabozny@sunycgcc.edu; *Sr Libr Asst,* Tina Santiago; Tel: 518-828-4181, Ext 3284, E-mail: santiago@sunycgcc.edu; *Tech Asst III,* Lynn Erceg; Tel: 518-828-4181, Ext 3289, E-mail: erceg@sunycgcc.edu; Staff 6 (MLS 2, Non-MLS 4)
Founded 1969. Enrl 1,500; Fac 49; Highest Degree: Associate
Library Holdings: Bk Titles 60,644; Bk Vols 63,817; Per Subs 130
Special Collections: Ettelt Children's Coll; Map Coll
Automation Activity & Vendor Info: (Circulation) Ex Libris Group
Wireless access
Partic in Southeastern New York Library Resources Council; SUNYConnect
Open Mon-Thurs 8am-9pm, Fri 8-4:30, Sat & Sun (Fall & Spring) 1-5

P HUDSON AREA LIBRARY*, 51 N Fifth St, 12534. SAN 311-3337. Tel: 518-828-1792. E-mail: info@hudsonarealibrary.org. Web Site: hudsonarealibrary.org. *Libr Dir,* Emily Chameides
Founded 1959
Subject Interests: Local hist
Wireless access
Mem of Mid-Hudson Library System
Open Tues & Wed 9-8, Thurs & Fri 9-5, Sat 10-3
Friends of the Library Group

S NEW YORK STATE DEPARTMENT OF CORRECTIONAL SERVICES*, Hudson Correctional Facility Library, 50 E Court St, 12534-2429. (Mail add: PO Box 576, 12534-0576), SAN 327-1579. Tel: 518-828-4311, Ext 4600. *Sr Librn,* Suzanne Hermans
Library Holdings: Bk Titles 9,000; Per Subs 55
Automation Activity & Vendor Info: (Cataloging) Follett Software; (Circulation) Follett Software
Open Mon & Wed-Fri 8:30-3:30, Tues 12-8

HUDSON FALLS

P HUDSON FALLS FREE LIBRARY*, 220 Main St, 12839. SAN 311-3345. Tel: 518-747-6406. FAX: 518-747-6406. Web Site: hudsonfalls.sals.edu. *Libr Dir,* Kay Hafner; E-mail: hud-director@sals.edu; Staff 6 (MLS 1, Non-MLS 5)
Founded 1910. Pop 15,389; Circ 30,703
Library Holdings: Audiobooks 3,311; AV Mats 1,228; Bks on Deafness & Sign Lang 15; CDs 250; DVDs 320; e-books 1,461; Large Print Bks 500; Bk Titles 27,500; Bk Vols 28,130; Per Subs 21; Talking Bks 850; Videos 200
Subject Interests: Fiction, Local hist
Automation Activity & Vendor Info: (Acquisitions) SirsiDynix; (Cataloging) SirsiDynix; (Circulation) SirsiDynix; (ILL) SirsiDynix; (Media Booking) SirsiDynix; (OPAC) SirsiDynix; (Serials) SirsiDynix
Wireless access
Publications: Newsletters (Monthly)
Mem of Southern Adirondack Library System
Open Mon & Tues 2:30-8, Wed-Fri 10-5, Sat 10-1

HUNTER

P HUNTER PUBLIC LIBRARY, 7965 Main St, 12442. (Mail add: PO Box 76, 12442), SAN 311-3353. Tel: 518-263-4655. FAX: 518-263-4655. E-mail: hunterpubliclibrary@gmail.com. Web Site: hunterlib.org. *Libr Mgr,* Stephanie Pushman; E-mail: directorhunterlibrary@gmail.com
Pop 3,719; Circ 12,175
Library Holdings: Bk Titles 13,000; Per Subs 27
Wireless access
Mem of Mid-Hudson Library System
Special Services for the Blind - Talking bks
Open Mon, Tues & Fri 10-4, Wed & Sat 12-4, Thurs 12-6

HUNTINGTON

S HUNTINGTON HISTORICAL SOCIETY, Archives & Resource Center, 209 Main St, 11743. SAN 311-337X. Tel: 631-427-7045, Ext 406. FAX: 631-427-7056. E-mail: archives@huntingtonhistoricalsociety.org. Web Site: www.huntingtonhistoricalsociety.org/archives. *Archivist,* Karen Martin; E-mail: kmartin@huntingtonhistoricalsociety.org; Staff 1 (Non-MLS 1)
Founded 1903
Library Holdings: Bk Titles 5,000; Per Subs 19
Special Collections: Long Island Genealogy (Nellie Ritch Scudder Coll), bks, bus recs, church recs, family papers, ms, photog, recs; New York State Census (Kings, Queens, Nassau & Suffolk Counties, 1915-1925), microfilm; US Federal Census (Suffolk County, 1790-1920), microfilm. Oral History
Subject Interests: Am decorative arts, Genealogies of Huntington, Local hist of town, Long Island, Long Island families
Restriction: Open by appt only

P HUNTINGTON PUBLIC LIBRARY*, 338 Main St, 11743. SAN 352-5481. Tel: 631-427-5165. FAX: 631-421-7131. Web Site: www.myhpl.org. *Libr Dir,* Joanne Adam; Tel: 631-427-5765, Ext 206, E-mail: joanne_adam@huntlib.org; *Asst Dir,* Kristine Casper; Tel: 631-427-5765, Ext 203, E-mail: kristine_casper@huntlib.org; *Asst Dir,* Teresa Schwind; Tel: 631-427-5765, Ext 202, E-mail: teresa_schwind@huntlib.org; *Head, Customer Serv,* John Mulhern; *Head, Ref & Adult Serv,* Therese Nielsen; E-mail: therese_nielsen@huntlib.org; *Head, Tech Serv,* Tom Cohn; *Head, Youth Serv,* Laura Giuliani; Staff 17 (MLS 17)
Founded 1875. Pop 34,000; Circ 408,181
Library Holdings: Bk Titles 184,391; Per Subs 610
Special Collections: Heckscher Art Museum Coll; Long Island History; Walt Whitman Coll
Automation Activity & Vendor Info: (Circulation) Innovative Interfaces, Inc
Wireless access
Publications: Newsletter (Bimonthly)
Open Mon-Fri 9-9, Sat 9-5, Sun 1-5
Friends of the Library Group
Branches: 1
HUNTINGTON STATION BRANCH, 1335 New York Ave, Huntington Station, 11746, SAN 352-5511. Tel: 631-421-5053. Reference Tel: 631-427-5156, Ext 123. FAX: 631-421-3488. E-mail: station@huntlib.org. *Br Mgr,* Mary Kelly; Tel: 631-421-5165, Ext 126
Open Mon-Thurs 9-8, Fri & Sat 9-5, Sun 1-5
Friends of the Library Group

R SEMINARY OF THE IMMACULATE CONCEPTION LIBRARY*, 440 W Neck Rd, 11743. SAN 373-1189. Tel: 631-423-0483, Ext 141. E-mail: libraryweb@icseminary.edu. Web Site: www.icseminary.edu/library. *Dir,* Elyse Hayes; E-mail: ehayes@icseminary.edu; *Cat Librn,* Mary Kate Breen; E-mail: mkbreen@icseminary.edu; Staff 2 (MLS 1, Non-MLS 1)
Library Holdings: Bk Vols 46,277; Per Subs 368
Subject Interests: Church hist, Scripture, Theol
Automation Activity & Vendor Info: (Acquisitions) LibLime; (Cataloging) LibLime; (Circulation) LibLime; (OPAC) LibLime
Wireless access
Partic in Long Island Library Resources Council
Restriction: Open to pub by appt only

HUNTINGTON STATION

P SOUTH HUNTINGTON PUBLIC LIBRARY*, 145 Pidgeon Hill Rd, 11746. SAN 311-3426. Tel: 631-549-4411. FAX: 631-547-6912. E-mail: contactus@shpl.info. Web Site: shpl.info. *Dir,* Janet Scherer; E-mail: jscherer@shpl.info; *Asst Dir,* Nick Tanzi; E-mail: ntanzi@shpl.info; *Youth Serv,* Beth Pereira; E-mail: bpereira@shpl.info; *Ch Prog, Youth Serv,* Sally Nikolis; E-mail: snikolis@shpl.info; *Adult Serv,* Howard Spiegelglass; E-mail: hspiegelglass@shpl.info; Staff 17 (MLS 17)
Founded 1961. Pop 37,045
Library Holdings: AV Mats 22,611; Bk Vols 252,642; Per Subs 300
Subject Interests: Educ
Automation Activity & Vendor Info: (Acquisitions) Innovative Interfaces, Inc; (Cataloging) Innovative Interfaces, Inc; (Circulation) Innovative Interfaces, Inc; (ILL) Innovative Interfaces, Inc; (OPAC) Innovative Interfaces, Inc
Wireless access
Publications: Newsletter
Mem of Suffolk Cooperative Library System
Open Mon, Tues, Thurs & Fri 9-9, Wed 10-9, Sat 9-5, Sun (Sept-May) 1-5
Friends of the Library Group

S WALT WHITMAN BIRTHPLACE ASSOCIATION*, Research Library, 246 Old Walt Whitman Rd, 11746-4148. SAN 311-3434. Tel: 631-427-5240. FAX: 631-427-5247. Web Site: www.waltwhitman.org. *Dir,* Cynthia Shor; E-mail: director@waltwhitman.org
Founded 1949
Library Holdings: Music Scores 10; Bk Vols 650; Per Subs 3
Special Collections: Foreign Language Translations; Walt Whitman Coll, biog, studies, hist, editions of poetry, collected writings
Wireless access
Open Wed-Fri (Winter) 1-4, Sat & Sun 11-4; Mon-Fri (Summer) 11-4, Sat & Sun 11-5
Friends of the Library Group

HURLEY

P HURLEY LIBRARY, 48 Main St, 12443. (Mail add: PO Box 660, 12443), SAN 311-3442. Tel: 845-338-2092. FAX: 845-338-2092. E-mail: hurleylibrary@gmail.com. Web Site: hurleylibrary.org. *Libr Mgr,* Kristen Campbell; Staff 5 (MLS 1, Non-MLS 4)
Founded 1958. Circ 20,388
Library Holdings: AV Mats 500; Bk Vols 13,000; Per Subs 19
Subject Interests: Local hist
Automation Activity & Vendor Info: (Acquisitions) Innovative Interfaces, Inc; (Cataloging) Innovative Interfaces, Inc; (Circulation) Innovative Interfaces, Inc
Wireless access
Mem of Mid-Hudson Library System
Open Mon & Wed 10-5, Tues, Thurs & Fri 12-6, Sat 10-3

HYDE PARK

C CULINARY INSTITUTE OF AMERICA*, Conrad N Hilton Library, 1946 Campus Dr, 12538-1499. SAN 311-3450. Tel: 845-451-1747. E-mail: library@culinary.edu. Web Site: library.culinary.edu. *Dir, Libr & Info Serv,* Jon Grennan; Tel: 845-451-1323, E-mail: Jon.Grennan@culinary.edu; *Ref & Info Literacy Librn,* Raven Fonfa; Tel: 845-451-1757, E-mail: Raven.Fonfa@culinary.edu; *Tech Serv Librn,* Elizabeth Miller; Tel: 845-451-1373, E-mail: Elizabeth.Miller@culinary.edu; *Archive Spec, Digital Spec,* Nicole Semenchuk; Tel: 845-451-1270, E-mail: Nicole.Semenchuk@culinary.edu; Staff 7 (MLS 3, Non-MLS 4)
Founded 1973. Enrl 2,300; Fac 132; Highest Degree: Bachelor
Library Holdings: AV Mats 4,304; Bk Titles 59,906; Bk Vols 63,000; Per Subs 200; Videos 1,500
Special Collections: Menus
Subject Interests: Cookery, Culinary arts, Liberal arts, Rare bks, Restaurant mgt, Spirits, Wines
Automation Activity & Vendor Info: (Acquisitions) Innovative Interfaces, Inc; (Cataloging) Innovative Interfaces, Inc; (Circulation) Innovative Interfaces, Inc; (Course Reserve) Innovative Interfaces, Inc; (OPAC) Innovative Interfaces, Inc; (Serials) Innovative Interfaces, Inc
Wireless access
Partic in Southeastern New York Library Resources Council
Open Mon-Thurs 7:30am-11pm, Fri 7:30-7, Sat 10-5, Sun Noon-11

P HYDE PARK FREE LIBRARY*, Two Main St, 12538. Tel: 845-229-7791. E-mail: hplibrary@hydeparkfreelibrary.org. Web Site: hydeparkfreelibrary.org. *Dir,* Gregory Callahan
Founded 1927
Library Holdings: AV Mats 834; Bk Vols 30,692; Per Subs 56; Talking Bks 834
Automation Activity & Vendor Info: (Cataloging) Innovative Interfaces, Inc; (Circulation) Innovative Interfaces, Inc; (ILL) Innovative Interfaces, Inc; (OPAC) Innovative Interfaces, Inc; (Serials) Innovative Interfaces, Inc
Mem of Mid-Hudson Library System
Open Mon, Tues & Thurs 12-7, Wed 12-4, Fri 12-5, Sat 10-3

S NATIONAL ARCHIVES & RECORDS ADMINISTRATION*, Franklin D Roosevelt Presidential Library, 4079 Albany Post Rd, 12538. SAN 311-3469. Tel: 845-486-7770. Reference Tel: 845-486-1142. Toll Free Tel: 800-337-8474. FAX: 845-486-1147. E-mail: roosevelt.library@nara.gov. Web Site: www.fdrlibrary.org. *Dir,* Paul M Sparrow; Tel: 845-486-7741, E-mail: paul.sparrow@nara.gov; *Supvry Archivist,* Kirsten Carter; *Curator,* Herman Eberhardt
Founded 1941
Library Holdings: Bk Titles 32,000; Bk Vols 47,000; Per Subs 12
Special Collections: Early Juveniles Coll; Franklin D Roosevelt & Foreign Affairs, 1935-39 (seventeen volumes); Historical Materials in the Franklin D Roosevelt Library; Hudson River Valley History Coll; The Era of Franklin D Roosevelt: A Selected Bibliography of Periodicals, Essays & Dissertation Literature, 1945-1971; US Naval Hist Coll
Subject Interests: Eleanor Roosevelt, Franklin Roosevelt, Hudson River Valley hist, NY Colonial hist, Politics from 1913-1945, US Naval hist
Wireless access
Partic in Southeastern New York Library Resources Council
Open Mon-Sun (Nov-March) 9-5; Mon-Sun (April-Oct) 9-6

ILION

P ILION FREE PUBLIC LIBRARY*, 78 West St, 13357-1797. SAN 311-3485. Tel: 315-894-5028. FAX: 315-894-9980. E-mail: ilion@midyork.org. Web Site: www.midyorklib.org/ilion. *Dir,* Travis Olivera; Staff 7 (MLS 1, Non-MLS 6)
Founded 1893. Pop 8,610; Circ 75,000
Library Holdings: Bk Titles 53,000; Per Subs 98
Special Collections: Ilion, New York (Seamans Coll), photog, slides. Oral History
Automation Activity & Vendor Info: (Cataloging) SirsiDynix; (Circulation) SirsiDynix; (OPAC) SirsiDynix
Wireless access
Mem of Mid-York Library System
Open Mon, Tues & Thurs 10-8, Wed & Fri 10-6, Sat (Sept-May) 10-1
Friends of the Library Group

INDIAN LAKE

P INDIAN LAKE PUBLIC LIBRARY, 113 Pelon Rd, 12842. (Mail add: PO Box 778, 12842-0778), SAN 311-3493. Tel: 518-648-5444. FAX: 518-648-5444. Web Site: indianlake.sals.edu. *Dir,* Susan Rollings; E-mail: ind-director@sals.edu
Pop 1,410; Circ 28,407
Library Holdings: Bk Vols 26,000; Per Subs 55
Wireless access
Mem of Southern Adirondack Library System
Open Mon & Wed 12-6, Tues & Thurs 10-4, Fri 10-6, Sat 10-1
Friends of the Library Group

INLET

P TOWN OF INLET PUBLIC LIBRARY, 168 N Rte 28, 13360. (Mail add: PO Box 274, 13360-0274). Tel: 315-357-6494. FAX: 315-357-6494. Web Site: InletLibrary.sals.edu. *Dir,* Joanne Kelly; E-mail: ilt-director@sals.edu; Staff 2 (Non-MLS 2)
Library Holdings: AV Mats 969; Bk Titles 8,101; Per Subs 30; Talking Bks 446
Wireless access
Mem of Southern Adirondack Library System
Open Mon, Wed & Fri 10-2, Sat 10-Noon; Mon-Fri 10-3, Sat 10-1 (Summer)
Friends of the Library Group

INTERLAKEN

P INTERLAKEN PUBLIC LIBRARY, 8390 Main St, 14847. (Mail add: PO Box 317, 14847-0317), SAN 311-3507. Tel: 607-532-4341. Web Site: www.interlakenpubliclibrary.org. *Dir,* Chelsea Hastings; E-mail: director@interlakenpubliclibrary.org
Founded 1902. Pop 2,200; Circ 9,801
Library Holdings: Bk Vols 11,800; Per Subs 50
Subject Interests: Hist of the town of Interlaken, Seneca County
Wireless access
Mem of Finger Lakes Library System
Open Mon, Wed & Fri 9-1, Tues & Thurs 1-7, Sat 9-Noon
Friends of the Library Group

IRVINGTON

P IRVINGTON PUBLIC LIBRARY*, Guiteau Foundation Library, 12 S Astor St, 10533. SAN 311-3523. Tel: 914-591-7840. FAX: 914-591-0347. Reference E-mail: irvref@wlsmail.org. Web Site: www.irvingtonlibrary.org. *Dir,* Rosemarie Gatzek; E-mail: irvdirector@wlsmail.org; *Asst Dir,* Pamela Bernstein; *Ch Serv,* Carolyn Gallagher; *Ch Serv,* Lois Izes; Staff 6 (MLS 3, Non-MLS 3)
Founded 1866. Pop 6,631; Circ 105,846
Library Holdings: AV Mats 6,226; e-books 767; Bk Vols 57,068; Per Subs 120; Videos 1,525
Subject Interests: Local hist
Automation Activity & Vendor Info: (Circulation) SirsiDynix; (OPAC) SirsiDynix
Wireless access
Mem of Westchester Library System
Open Mon, Wed, Fri & Sat 10-5, Tues & Thurs 10-9
Friends of the Library Group

ISLAND PARK

P ISLAND PARK PUBLIC LIBRARY*, 176 Long Beach Rd, 11558. SAN 311-3531. Tel: 516-432-0122. FAX: 516-889-3584. Web Site: www.islandparklibrary.org. *Dir,* Jessica Koenig; E-mail: jkoenig@islandparklibrary.org; Staff 10 (MLS 4, Non-MLS 6)
Founded 1938. Pop 8,857; Circ 43,466
Library Holdings: Bk Vols 70,000; Per Subs 60
Automation Activity & Vendor Info: (Acquisitions) Innovative Interfaces, Inc - Millennium; (Cataloging) Innovative Interfaces, Inc - Millennium; (Circulation) Innovative Interfaces, Inc - Millennium; (OPAC) Innovative Interfaces, Inc - Millennium
Wireless access
Mem of Nassau Library System
Open Mon-Thurs 9:30-9, Fri & Sat 10-5

ISLIP

P ISLIP PUBLIC LIBRARY*, 71 Monell Ave, 11751. SAN 311-354X. Tel: 631-581-5933. FAX: 631-277-8429. Reference E-mail: reference@isliplibrary.org. Web Site: isliplibrary.org. *Dir,* Mary Schubart;

E-mail: mary@isliplibrary.org; *Asst Dir,* Lauraine Farr; E-mail: lfarr@isliplibrary.org; Staff 20 (MLS 20)
Founded 1924. Pop 20,968; Circ 248,375
Special Collections: Local History Coll
Automation Activity & Vendor Info: (Cataloging) Innovative Interfaces, Inc - Sierra; (Circulation) Innovative Interfaces, Inc - Sierra; (Course Reserve) Innovative Interfaces, Inc - Sierra; (ILL) Innovative Interfaces, Inc - Sierra; (OPAC) Innovative Interfaces, Inc - Sierra; (Serials) Innovative Interfaces, Inc - Sierra
Wireless access
Publications: Tidings (Newsletter)
Mem of Suffolk Cooperative Library System
Special Services for the Deaf - Assistive tech
Special Services for the Blind - Closed circuit TV magnifier
Open Mon-Thurs 9-9, Fri & Sat 9-5, Sun (Sept-May) 12-4

ITHACA

M CAYUGA MEDICAL CENTER AT ITHACA*, Robert Broad Medical Library, 101 Dates Dr, 14850. SAN 327-6953. Tel: 607-274-4226. FAX: 607-274-4587. *Med Librn,* Cassey Cornish; E-mail: ccornish@cayugamed.org
Library Holdings: Bk Vols 250; Per Subs 30
Wireless access
Partic in South Central Regional Library Council
Open Mon-Fri 10-3

C CORNELL UNIVERSITY LIBRARY*, 201 Olin Library, 14853. SAN 352-5546. Tel: 607-255-4144. Interlibrary Loan Service Tel: 607-255-9564. Administration Tel: 607-255-3393. FAX: 607-255-6788. Circulation FAX: 607-254-8602. E-mail: libadmin@cornell.edu. Web Site: www.library.cornell.edu. *Univ Librn,* Gerald R Beasley; E-mail: grb77@cornell.edu; *Dir, Admin & Finance,* Ezra Delaney; Tel: 607-254-5257, E-mail: ezra.delaney@cornell.edu; *Dir, Informational Serv, Interim Assoc Univ Librn,* Simeon Warner; *Assoc Univ Librn,* Tamar Evangelestia-Dougherty; E-mail: td372@cornell.edu; *Assoc Univ Librn,* Xin Li; Tel: 607-255-7026, E-mail: xl49@cornell.edu; *Assoc Univ Librn,* Danianne Mizzy; Tel: 607-254-5257, E-mail: mizzy@cornell.edu
Founded 1868. Highest Degree: Doctorate
Special Collections: UN Document Depository; US Document Depository
Wireless access
Partic in OCLC Online Computer Library Center, Inc; S Cent Libr Res Coun
Friends of the Library Group

Departmental Libraries:

ADELSON LIBRARY, LABORATORY OF ORNITHOLOGY, 159 Sapsucker Woods Rd, 14850-1999, SAN 352-6003. Tel: 607-254-2165. E-mail: adelson_lib@cornell.edu. Web Site: www.birds.cornell.edu/home/visit/adelson-library. *Coordr,* Leo Sack; E-mail: lts55@cornell.edu; Staff 1 (Non-MLS 1)
Founded 2004
Library Holdings: Bk Vols 13,000; Per Subs 150
Special Collections: Books Illustrated by Louis A Fuertes; Falconry
Subject Interests: Ornithology
Automation Activity & Vendor Info: (Cataloging) Ex Libris Group
Function: Res libr
Open Mon-Fri 10-4

MARTIN P CATHERWOOD INDUSTRIAL & LABOR RELATIONS LIBRARY, 229 Ives Hall, Tower Rd, 14853, SAN 352-5961. Tel: 607-255-2277. Reference Tel: 607-254-5370. E-mail: ilrref@cornell.edu. Web Site: catherwood.library.cornell.edu, www.library.cornell.edu/libraries/ilr. *Dir,* Curtis Lyons; E-mail: lyons@cornell.edu
Founded 1945. Enrl 1,003; Fac 53
Library Holdings: Microforms 48,834; Bk Vols 178,689
Open Mon-Thurs 8am-11pm, Fri 8-5, Sun 2-11

JOHN HENRIK CLARKE AFRICANA LIBRARY, 310 Triphammer Rd, 14850, SAN 352-5821. Tel: 607-255-3822. E-mail: afrlib@cornell.edu. Web Site: www.library.cornell.edu/libraries/africana. *Head of Libr,* Eric Kofi Acree; Tel: 607-255-5229, E-mail: ea18@cornell.edu; Staff 3 (MLS 1, Non-MLS 2)
Founded 1969
Library Holdings: CDs 50; DVDs 425; Microforms 18,475; Bk Vols 22,278; Per Subs 75; Videos 1,000
Open Mon-Thurs 9am-11pm, Fri 9-5, Sat 1-5, Sun 4-11

SIDNEY COX LIBRARY OF MUSIC & DANCE, 220 Lincoln Hall, 14853, SAN 352-5724. Tel: 607-255-4011. FAX: 607-254-2877. Reference E-mail: musicref@cornell.edu. Web Site: music.library.cornell.edu, www.library.cornell.edu/libraries/music. *Instruction Librn, Music Cat Librn,* Tracey Snyder; Tel: 607-255-6160, E-mail: tls224@cornell.edu; *Music Librn,* Lenora Schneller; Tel: 607-255-7126, E-mail: ls258@cornell.edu; Staff 6 (MLS 2, Non-MLS 4)
Library Holdings: AV Mats 70,700; Microforms 8,578; Bk Vols 145,390; Per Subs 400
Special Collections: 18th Century Chamber Music; 18th-21st Century American Music Coll; 19th Century Opera; A Scarlatti Operas; Archive of Field Recordings; Early 16th Century Music Coll
Subject Interests: Dance, Music
Open Mon-Thurs 9am-10pm, Fri 9-5, Sat 12-5, Sun 2-10

DIVISION OF ASIA COLLECTIONS (CARL A KROCH LIBRARY), Kroch Library, Level 1, 14853. Tel: 607-255-8199. E-mail: asiaref@cornell.edu. Web Site: asia.library.cornell.edu, www.library.cornell.edu/libraries/asia. *Assoc Univ Librn,* Tamar Evangelestia-Dougherty; Tel: 607-255-3393, E-mail: td372@cornell.edu
Library Holdings: Microforms 564,220; Bk Vols 799,298

DIVISION OF RARE & MANUSCRIPT COLLECTIONS (CARL A KROCH LIBRARY), 2B Carl A Kroch Library, 14853, SAN 377-810X. Tel: 607-255-3530. FAX: 607-255-9524. E-mail: rareref@cornell.edu. Web Site: rare.library.cornell.edu, www.library.cornell.edu/libraries/rmc. *Asst Dir, Curator,* Katherine Reagan; E-mail: kr33@cornell.edu; *Univ Archivist,* Evan Earle; E-mail: efe4@cornell.edu
Library Holdings: Bk Vols 433,858
Special Collections: 18th & 19th Century French History; American History; Anglo-American Literature; Dante; Food History; G B Shaw Coll; History of Science; Icelandic Literature & Culture; Native American History; Petrarch; Sexuality; Theater; Witchcraft; Wordsworth
Open Mon-Fri 10-4
Restriction: Non-circulating

CM FLOWER-SPRECHER VETERINARY LIBRARY, S1 201 Veterinary Education Ctr, 14853-6401, SAN 352-602X. Tel: 607-253-3510. Reference Tel: 607-253-3499. FAX: 607-253-3080. E-mail: vetref@cornell.edu. Circulation E-mail: vetcirc@cornell.edu. Web Site: vet.library.cornell.edu. *Head of Libr,* Erin Eldermire; Tel: 607-253-3499, E-mail: erb29@cornell.edu; *Head, User Serv,* Chris Dunham; Tel: 607-253-3512, E-mail: cd332@cornell.edu; *Info Res Librn, Outreach Librn,* Kelly Johnson; Tel: 607-253-3515, E-mail: kaj98@cornell.edu; Staff 7 (MLS 3, Non-MLS 4)
Founded 1897. Enrl 321; Fac 172; Highest Degree: Doctorate
Library Holdings: Microforms 25,985; Bk Vols 101,000; Per Subs 800
Subject Interests: Human med, Immunology, Microbiology, Parasitology, Pharmacology, Physiology, Veterinary med
Automation Activity & Vendor Info: (Acquisitions) Ex Libris Group; (Cataloging) Ex Libris Group; (Circulation) Ex Libris Group; (Course Reserve) Ex Libris Group; (ILL) Innovative Interfaces, Inc; (OPAC) Ex Libris Group; (Serials) Ex Libris Group
Partic in Center for Research Libraries; NELLCO Law Library Consortium, Inc.; OCLC Research Library Partnership
Publications: Newsletter (Quarterly)
Open Mon-Thurs 7:30am-11pm, Fri 7:30am-8pm, Sat 10-8, Sun 10am-11pm

MUI HO FINE ARTS LIBRARY, Rand Hall, 921 University Ave, #235, 14853, SAN 352-5902. Tel: 607-255-3710. Reference Tel: 607-255-6716. E-mail: fineartsref@cornell.edu. Circulation E-mail: fineartscirc@cornell.edu. Web Site: finearts.library.cornell.edu, www.library.cornell.edu/libraries/finearts. *Dir,* Martha Walker; E-mail: maw6@cornell.edu
Library Holdings: Bk Vols 104,000
Subject Interests: Art & archit, Art hist, City planning, Landscape archit, Regional planning
Open Mon-Thurs 9am-10pm, Fri 9-5, Sat 12-5, Sun 1-11

CL LAW LIBRARY, Myron Taylor Hall, 524 College Ave, 14853-4901, SAN 352-5996. Tel: 607-255-7236. Interlibrary Loan Service Tel: 607-255-5750. Reference Tel: 607-255-9577. E-mail: lawlib@cornell.edu. Web Site: law.library.cornell.edu, www.library.cornell.edu/libraries/law. *Dir,* Kim Nayyer; E-mail: kpn32@cornell.edu; Staff 10 (MLS 8, Non-MLS 2)
Founded 1887. Enrl 646; Fac 46; Highest Degree: Doctorate
Library Holdings: DVDs 50; e-books 588; e-journals 500; Microforms 1,006,433; Bk Titles 216,264; Bk Vols 542,912; Per Subs 5,000; Videos 225
Special Collections: 19th Century Trials; Bennett Coll of Statutory Materials; Donovan Coll of Nuremberg Trials. US Document Depository
Subject Interests: Foreign law, Intl law, Law, Rare bks
Partic in Northeast Foreign Law Libraries Cooperative Group; Research Libraries Information Network
Publications: InSITE (Bimonthly); The Primary Source (Newsletter)
Open Mon-Thurs 8-8, Fri 8-5, Sat 11-5, Sun 11-8

LIBRARY ANNEX, Palm Rd, 14853. Tel: 607-253-3431. E-mail: libannex@cornell.edu. Web Site: www.library.cornell.edu/libraries/annex. *Admin Supvr,* Cammie Wyckoff; Tel: 607-253-3514, E-mail: cjh8@cornell.edu
Library Holdings: Microforms 1,874,317; Bk Vols 2,543,622
Open Mon-Fri 8-5, Sat 8-12:30

ALBERT R MANN LIBRARY, Mann Library, 237 Mann Dr, 14853-4301, SAN 378-3987. Tel: 607-255-5406. Circulation Tel: 607-255-3296. Interlibrary Loan Service Tel: 607-255-7754. Reference E-mail: mann-ref@cornell.edu. Web Site: mannlib.cornell.edu, www.library.cornell.edu/libraries/mann. *Dir,* Position Currently Open

Library Holdings: Microforms 858,678; Bk Vols 1,048,053; Per Subs 3,700
Special Collections: Beekeeping (Everett Franklin Phillips Coll); James E Rice Poultry Library; Lace & Lacemaking (Elizabeth C Kackenmeister Coll); Language of Flowers. US Document Depository
Subject Interests: Agr, Biol sci, Educ, Human ecology, Nutrition, Psychol
Partic in SUNYConnect
Publications: Catalogs & Indexes
Open Mon-Thurs 8-Midnight, Fri 8-6, Sat 12-7, Sun Noon-Midnight

MATHEMATICS, 420 Malott Hall, 14853-4201, SAN 352-5694. Tel: 607-255-5076. FAX: 607-254-5023. E-mail: mathlib@cornell.edu. Web Site: mathematics.library.cornell.edu, www.library.cornell.edu/libraries/math. *Dir,* Henrik Spoon; Tel: 607-255-5268, E-mail: h.spoon@cornell.edu; *Pub Serv Mgr,* Natalie Sheridan; Tel: 607-254-3568, E-mail: nas20@cornell.edu; Staff 3 (MLS 2, Non-MLS 1)
Founded 1865
Library Holdings: e-books 15,000; Bk Vols 68,300; Per Subs 730
Special Collections: Chemistry, Physics (high use chemistry & physics volumes)
Subject Interests: Math, Statistics
Automation Activity & Vendor Info: (Acquisitions) Ex Libris Group; (Cataloging) Ex Libris Group; (Circulation) Ex Libris Group
Open Mon-Thurs 8-8, Fri 8-5, Sat Noon-5, Sun 4-8

OLIN & URIS LIBRARIES, 161 Ho Plaza, 14853, SAN 352-5562. Tel: 607-255-4144. Circulation Tel: 604-255-3537 (Uris), 607-255-4245 (Olin). E-mail: libpublicservices@cornell.edu. Reference E-mail: okuref@cornell.edu. Web Site: olinuris.library.cornell.edu, www.library.cornell.edu/libraries/olin, www.library.cornell.edu/libraries/uris. *Dir of Libr,* Bonna Boettcher; Tel: 607-255-5998, E-mail: bjb57@cornell.edu
Library Holdings: Bk Vols 171,683
Subject Interests: Asian studies, Humanities, Soc sci
Open Mon-Fri 8-5, Sat 12-5

CM SAMUEL J WOOD LIBRARY & C V STARR BIOMEDICAL INFORMATION CENTER, 1300 York Ave, C115, Box 67, New York, 10065-4896, SAN 311-7111. Tel: 646-962-2570. Interlibrary Loan Service Tel: 646-962-2559. E-mail: infodesk@med.cornell.edu. Web Site: library.weill.cornell.edu. *Dir,* Terry Wheeler; Tel: 646-962-2469, E-mail: tew2004@med.cornell.edu; *Assoc Dir, Clinical Informationist Serv, Assoc Dir, Edu Servs,* Diana Delgado; Tel: 646-962-2550, E-mail: did2005@med.cornell.edu; *Assoc Dir, Res Serv,* Peter Oxley; Tel: 646-962-2576, E-mail: pro2004@med.cornell.edu; *Head, Archives,* Nicole Milano; Tel: 646-746-6072, E-mail: njm4001@med.cornell.edu; *Clinical Librn,* Becky Baltich Nelson; Tel: 646-962-2555, E-mail: blb2008@med.cornell.edu; *Clinical Librn,* Keith Mages; Tel: 646-962-2880, E-mail: kcm2001@med.cornell.edu; *Consumer Health Librn,* Antonio DeRosa; Tel: 646-962-5727, E-mail: apd2004@med.cornell.edu; *Scholarly Communications Librn,* Drew Wright; Tel: 646-962-2554, E-mail: drw2004@med.cornell.edu; *Circ Mgr,* Loretta Merlo; Tel: 646-962-2557, E-mail: lamerlo@med.cornell.edu; *Archivist,* Elizabeth Shepard; Tel: 646-962-6072, E-mail: ems2001@med.cornell.edu; Staff 40 (MLS 10, Non-MLS 30)
Founded 1899. Enrl 725; Fac 3,479; Highest Degree: Doctorate
Library Holdings: e-journals 5,713; Bk Titles 72,055; Bk Vols 190,672; Per Subs 321
Subject Interests: Biomed, Nursing, Psychiat
Automation Activity & Vendor Info: (Acquisitions) Innovative Interfaces, Inc; (Cataloging) Innovative Interfaces, Inc; (Circulation) Innovative Interfaces, Inc; (OPAC) Innovative Interfaces, Inc; (Serials) Innovative Interfaces, Inc
Function: Health sci info serv, ILL available, Internet access, Photocopying/Printing, Ref serv available
Partic in Metropolitan New York Library Council; National Network of Libraries of Medicine Region 7
Open Mon-Thurs 8am-Midnight, Fri 8-8, Sat 10-8, Sun Noon-2am
Restriction: Open to students, fac & staff, Private libr

S DURLAND ALTERNATIVES LIBRARY*, Anne Carry Durland Memorial Library, 130 Anabel Taylor Hall, 14853-1001. SAN 352-5589. Tel: 607-255-6486. FAX: 607-255-9985. Web Site: www.alternativeslibrary.org. *Dir,* Ryan Clover-Owens; E-mail: ryan@alternativeslibrary.org; *Asst Dir,* Gary Fine; E-mail: gmf5@cornell.edu; Staff 3 (MLS 1, Non-MLS 2)
Founded 1973
Library Holdings: Audiobooks 150; CDs 1,200; DVDs 800; Bk Vols 8,000; Per Subs 300; Videos 1,200
Special Collections: African Cinema & Literature; Native American Archives-Contemporary Culture
Subject Interests: Culture, Ecology, Human rights, Politics, Psychol, Sexuality
Automation Activity & Vendor Info: (Cataloging) Innovative Interfaces, Inc; (Circulation) Innovative Interfaces, Inc; (ILL) Innovative Interfaces, Inc; (OPAC) Innovative Interfaces, Inc; (Serials) Innovative Interfaces, Inc
Wireless access
Open Mon-Fri 11-8, Sat 11-5, Sun 7pm-11pm

P FINGER LAKES LIBRARY SYSTEM*, 1300 Dryden Rd, 14850. SAN 311-3566. Tel: 607-273-4074. Toll Free Tel: 800-909-3557. FAX: 607-273-3618. Web Site: www.flls.org. *Exec Dir,* Sarah Glogowski; Tel: 607-273-4074, Ext 222, E-mail: sglogowski@flls.org; *Mem Serv Librn,* Nora Burrows; Tel: 607-273-4074, Ext 227, E-mail: nburrows@flls.org; *Bus Mgr,* James Stebbins; Tel: 607-273-4074, Ext 225, E-mail: jstebbins@flls.org; *ILL Assoc,* Sam Norton; Tel: 607-273-4074, Ext 229, E-mail: snorton@flls.org; Staff 21 (MLS 6, Non-MLS 15)
Founded 1958. Pop 312,189
Library Holdings: Bk Titles 79,025; Bk Vols 89,079; Per Subs 52
Automation Activity & Vendor Info: (Cataloging) Innovative Interfaces, Inc; (Circulation) Innovative Interfaces, Inc; (ILL) Innovative Interfaces, Inc; (OPAC) Innovative Interfaces, Inc
Wireless access
Publications: Directory (Annual); Newsletter (Quarterly)
Member Libraries: Apalachin Library; Aurora Free Library; Berkshire Free Library; Candor Free Library; Coburn Free Library; Cortland Free Library; Edith B Ford Memorial Library; Elizabeth Garnsey Delavan Library; Fair Haven Public Library; George P & Susan Platt Cady Library; Groton Public Library; Hazard Library Association; Interlaken Public Library; Kellogg Free Library; Lamont Memorial Free Library; Lansing Community Library; Newfield Public Library; Peck Memorial Library; Phillips Free Library; Port Byron Library; Powers Library; Seneca Falls Library; Seymour Public Library District; Southworth Library Association; Spencer Library; Springport Free Library; Stewart B Lang Memorial Library; Tappan-Spaulding Memorial Library; Tompkins County Public Library; Ulysses Philomathic Library; Waterloo Library & Historical Society; Waverly Free Library; Weedsport Library
Partic in OCLC Online Computer Library Center, Inc; South Central Regional Library Council
Special Services for the Deaf - TDD equip
Special Services for the Blind - Bks on cassette; Large print bks
Open Mon-Fri 8-4

S THE HISTORY CENTER IN TOMPKINS COUNTY*, Library & Archives, 110 N Tioga St, 2nd Flr, 14850. SAN 321-0839. Tel: 607-273-8284. Web Site: www.thehistorycenter.net. *Archivist, Dir, Res Serv,* Donna Eschenbrenner; E-mail: archives@thehistorycenter.net; Staff 1 (Non-MLS 1)
Founded 1935
Library Holdings: Bk Vols 4,000
Special Collections: Local History (Ithaca Imprints), photos
Subject Interests: Genealogy, Tompkins County hist
Wireless access
Partic in South Central Regional Library Council
Open Tues-Sat 11-5

C ITHACA COLLEGE LIBRARY, 953 Danby Rd, 14850-7060. SAN 311-3574. Tel: 607-274-3206. Interlibrary Loan Service Tel: 607-274-3891. Reference Tel: 607-274-3890. Administration Tel: 607-274-3182. Automation Services Tel: 607-274-3553. FAX: 607-274-1539. E-mail: libweb@ithaca.edu. Web Site: www.ithaca.edu/library. *Interim Librn,* Karin Wikoff; Tel: 607-274-3821, E-mail: kwikoff@ithaca.edu; *Electronic Res Librn,* Terri Ann Coronel; Tel: 607-274-1892, E-mail: tcoronel@ithaca.edu; *Music Librn,* Kristina Shanton; E-mail: kshanton@ithaca.edu; *Web Serv Librn,* Ron Gilmour; *Mgr, Access Serv,* Ben Hogben; Tel: 607-274-1689, E-mail: bhogben@ithaca.edu; *Mgr, Libr Media Serv,* Kelly Merritt; Tel: 607-274-3880, E-mail: kmerritt@ithaca.edu; *Libr Tech Spec,* Dan Taylor; E-mail: dtaylor@ithaca.edu; *Acq,* Terri Beth Ledbetter; E-mail: tledbetter@ithaca.edu; *ILL,* Sarah Shank; E-mail: sshank@ithaca.edu; Staff 33 (MLS 14, Non-MLS 19)
Founded 1892. Enrl 6,600; Fac 450; Highest Degree: Master
Jul 2021-Jun 2022 Income $3,901,054, Locally Generated Income $3,901,054. Mats Exp $1,256,711, Books $127,930, Per/Ser (Incl. Access Fees) $262,834, Manu Arch $2,400, Micro $1,000, AV Mat $34,891, Electronic Ref Mat (Incl. Access Fees) $818,566, Presv $9,000. Sal $1,363,816 (Prof $774,771)
Library Holdings: AV Mats 33,540; e-books 151,885; e-journals 72,576; Microforms 19,603; Music Scores 6,000; Bk Titles 285,600; Bk Vols 304,003; Per Subs 20,000
Special Collections: College Oral History Project; Digitized Historical Issues of the Ithacan Newspaper; Ithaca College Digitized Photographs (C Hadley Smith Coll); Twilight Zone (Rod Serling Coll); Wharton Studio Set Designs. Oral History
Automation Activity & Vendor Info: (Acquisitions) Ex Libris Group; (Cataloging) Ex Libris Group; (Circulation) Ex Libris Group; (Course Reserve) Ex Libris Group; (ILL) Ex Libris Group; (OPAC) Ex Libris Group; (Serials) Ex Libris Group
Wireless access
Function: Doc delivery serv, ILL available, Internet access, Magnifiers for reading, Music CDs, Orientations, Outside serv via phone, mail, e-mail &

web, Photocopying/Printing, Ref serv available, Spoken cassettes & CDs, Telephone ref, VHS videos, Wheelchair accessible, Workshops
Partic in OCLC Online Computer Library Center, Inc; South Central Regional Library Council
Restriction: Open to pub for ref & circ; with some limitations

S PALEONTOLOGICAL RESEARCH INSTITUTION LIBRARY*, 1259 Trumansburg Rd, 14850. SAN 311-3582. Tel: 607-273-6623, Ext 320. FAX: 607-273-6620. Web Site: www.priweb.org/research-and-collections/library-and-archives. *Dir,* Dr Warren Allmon; E-mail: allmon@priweb.org; *Library Contact,* Dr Jonathan Hendricks; E-mail: hendricks@priweb.org. Subject Specialists: *Earth sci, Paleontology,* Dr Warren Allmon
Founded 1932
Library Holdings: Bk Titles 60,000; Bk Vols 60,145; Per Subs 75
Subject Interests: Geol, Natural hist, Paleontology (invertebrate), Taxonomy
Wireless access
Publications: Library Serials List
Partic in South Central Regional Library Council
Restriction: Not open to pub

P TOMPKINS COUNTY PUBLIC LIBRARY*, 101 E Green St, 14850-5613. SAN 311-3590. Tel: 607-272-4557. Reference Tel: 607-272-4556. FAX: 607-272-8111. Reference E-mail: reference@tcpl.org. Web Site: tcpl.org. *Dir,* Annette Birdsall; E-mail: abirdsall@tcpl.org; *Circ Serv, Head, Access Serv,* Jennifer Schlossberg; Tel: 607-272-4557,Ext 254, E-mail: jschlossberg@tcpl.org; *Head, Info Serv,* Amy Humber; Tel: 607-272-4557, Ext 247, E-mail: shumber@tcpl.org; *Head, Tech Serv,* Melanie Pacelli; Tel: 607-272-4557, Ext 246, E-mail: mpacelli@tcpl.org; *Head, Youth Serv,* Sarah O'Shea; Tel: 607-272-4557, Ext 262, E-mail: soshea@tcpl.org; Staff 42.7 (MLS 14.4, Non-MLS 28.3)
Founded 1864. Pop 101,590; Circ 830,165
Library Holdings: Bk Vols 257,663; Per Subs 334
Special Collections: Central Book Aid Coll (Finger Lakes Library System)
Automation Activity & Vendor Info: (Acquisitions) Innovative Interfaces, Inc; (Cataloging) Innovative Interfaces, Inc; (Circulation) Innovative Interfaces, Inc; (OPAC) Innovative Interfaces, Inc
Wireless access
Function: 24/7 Electronic res, 24/7 Online cat, 3D Printer, Activity rm, Adult bk club, Adult literacy prog, After school storytime, Archival coll, Art exhibits, Audiobks on Playaways & MP3, Audiobks via web, AV serv, Bi-weekly Writer's Group, Bilingual assistance for Spanish patrons, Bk club(s), Bks on CD, Children's prog, Computer training, Computers for patron use, Digital talking bks, Distance learning, E-Readers, Electronic databases & coll, Family literacy, For res purposes, Free DVD rentals, Govt ref serv, Health sci info serv, Holiday prog, Homework prog, ILL available, Instruction & testing, Internet access, Laminating, Life-long learning prog for all ages, Literacy & newcomer serv, Magazines, Mail & tel request accepted, Mango lang, Meeting rooms, Microfiche/film & reading machines, Movies, Music CDs, Notary serv, Online cat, Online ref, Orientations, Outreach serv, Outside serv via phone, mail, e-mail & web, OverDrive digital audio bks, Photocopying/Printing, Preschool outreach, Preschool reading prog, Printer for laptops & handheld devices, Prog for adults, Prog for children & young adult, Ref & res, Ref serv available, Res performed for a fee, Satellite serv, Scanner, Senior computer classes, Senior outreach, Serves people with intellectual disabilities, Spanish lang bks, Spoken cassettes & CDs, Spoken cassettes & DVDs, Story hour, Study rm, Summer & winter reading prog, Summer reading prog, Tax forms, Teen prog, Telephone ref, Visual arts prog, Wheelchair accessible, Winter reading prog, Workshops, Writing prog
Publications: The Library Connection
Mem of Finger Lakes Library System
Partic in South Central Regional Library Council
Open Mon-Thurs 9:30-8:30, Fri 9:30-6, Sat 9:30-5, Sun (Sept-May) 1-5
Friends of the Library Group

JAMAICA

M JAMAICA HOSPITAL MEDICAL CENTER*, Medical Library, Axel Bldg, 4th Flr, 8900 Van Wyck Expressway, 11418-2832. SAN 311-3639. Tel: 718-206-8450. Administration Tel: 718-206-8451. FAX: 718-206-8460. Web Site: jamaicahospital.org/medical-library. *Dir, Ref,* Carol Cave-Davis; E-mail: cdavis@jhmc.org; *Circ & ILL,* Kathy Kruger; E-mail: kkruger@jhmc.org; Staff 2 (MLS 1, Non-MLS 1)
Founded 1963
Library Holdings: Bk Titles 2,000; Per Subs 175
Automation Activity & Vendor Info: (Cataloging) Rasco; (Circulation) Professional Software; (ILL) Professional Software; (OPAC) Professional Software; (Serials) Professional Software
Wireless access
Function: Computers for patron use, Doc delivery serv, Electronic databases & coll, ILL available, Photocopying/Printing, Ref serv available
Partic in Association of Mental Health Libraries; Basic Health Sciences Library Network; Brooklyn-Queens-Staten Island-Manhattan-Bronx Health Sciences Librarians; National Network of Libraries of Medicine Region 7
Restriction: Hospital employees & physicians only, Med staff & students, Vols & interns use only

M MOUNT SINAI SERVICES-QUEENS HOSPITAL CENTER AFFILIATION*, Health Sciences Library, 82-68 164th St, 11432. SAN 325-1500. Tel: 718-883-4020. FAX: 718-883-6125. Web Site: www.mountsinai.org/locations/queens. *Dir,* Deborah Goss; Tel: 718-883-4019; *Asst Dir,* Virginia Gilea; Staff 3 (MLS 2, Non-MLS 1)
Founded 1960
Library Holdings: e-journals 270; Bk Vols 18,000; Per Subs 300
Wireless access
Partic in Metropolitan New York Library Council; MLC; National Network of Libraries of Medicine Region 7
Restriction: Staff use only

GL QUEENS COUNTY SUPREME COURT LIBRARY, General Court House, 88-11 Sutphin Blvd, 11435. SAN 311-3655. Tel: 718-298-1206. FAX: 718-298-1189. E-mail: law_library_queens@nycourts.gov. Web Site: www.nycourts.gov/library/queens. *Sr Law Librn,* Kellie Adams; E-mail: kadams@nycourts.gov; *Sr Law Librn,* Denise Naya; E-mail: dnaya@nycourts.gov; Staff 3 (MLS 2, Non-MLS 1)
Founded 1911
Library Holdings: Bk Titles 10,000; Bk Vols 125,000; Per Subs 100
Subject Interests: State law
Automation Activity & Vendor Info: (Acquisitions) SirsiDynix; (Cataloging) SirsiDynix; (Circulation) SirsiDynix; (Course Reserve) SirsiDynix; (ILL) SirsiDynix; (Media Booking) SirsiDynix; (OPAC) SirsiDynix; (Serials) SirsiDynix
Wireless access
Partic in NY State Libr; OCLC Online Computer Library Center, Inc
Restriction: Non-circulating to the pub
Branches:
KEW GARDENS BRANCH, 125-01 Queens Blvd, 7th Flr, Kew Gardens, 11415, SAN 321-4214. Tel: 718-298-1327. FAX: 718-520-4661.
Library Holdings: Bk Vols 25,000
Subject Interests: Criminal law of NY

P QUEENS LIBRARY*, Central Library, 89-11 Merrick Blvd, 11432. SAN 352-6054. Tel: 718-990-0700. Reference Tel: 718-990-0728. Administration Tel: 718-990-0794. TDD: 718-990-0809. Web Site: www.queenslibrary.org. *Pres & Chief Exec Officer,* Dennis M Walcott; E-mail: dwalcott@queenslibrary.org; *Chief Librn,* Nick Buron; E-mail: nburon@queenslibrary.org; *Dir, Commun Engagement,* Kim McNeil-Capers; *Commun Libr Mgr,* Nelson Lu; *Coll Develop Coordr,* Hong Yao; E-mail: hyao@queenslibrary.org; Staff 1165 (MLS 416, Non-MLS 749)
Founded 1896. Pop 2,273,000; Circ 17,500,000
Jul 2012-Jun 2013 Income (Main & Associated Libraries) $128,147,000, State $9,228,000, City $88,860,000, Federal $5,144,000, Other $24,915,000. Mats Exp $4,061,000. Sal $79,497,000
Library Holdings: Bks-By-Mail 13,460; CDs 178,230; DVDs 295,000; Bk Titles 1,081,536; Bk Vols 5,677,050; Per Subs 8,032; Videos 100,894
Special Collections: Long Island History. State Document Depository; US Document Depository
Subject Interests: Behav sci, Costumes, Ethnic studies, Soc sci
Automation Activity & Vendor Info: (Cataloging) Innovative Interfaces, Inc; (Circulation) Innovative Interfaces, Inc; (ILL) OCLC; (OPAC) Innovative Interfaces, Inc; (Serials) Innovative Interfaces, Inc
Wireless access
Publications: Library Matters
Partic in Dranet; Metropolitan New York Library Council; OCLC Online Computer Library Center, Inc; Proquest Dialog; Vutext
Special Services for the Deaf - Bks on deafness & sign lang; High interest/low vocabulary bks; Spec interest per; TTY equip
Special Services for the Blind - Reader equip; Volunteer serv
Open Mon-Thurs 9-8:45, Fri 9-6:45, Sat 10-4:45, Sun 12-4:45
Friends of the Library Group
Branches: 64
THE ARCHIVES AT QUEENS LIBRARY, 89-11 Merrick Blvd, 11432. Tel: 718-990-0770. FAX: 718-658-8312. *Mgr,* Judith Todman; Staff 6 (MLS 4, Non-MLS 2)
Library Holdings: Bk Vols 28,000; Per Subs 78
Special Collections: Long Island History & Culture, maps, newspaper & photogs
ARVERNE COMMUNITY LIBRARY, 312 Beach 54th St, Arverne, 11692, SAN 352-6119. Tel: 718-634-4784. FAX: 718-318-2757. *Br Mgr,* Nicole Gordon
Library Holdings: CDs 1,600; Bk Vols 45,087
Open Mon & Thurs 12-8, Tues 1-6, Wed & Fri 10-6, Sat 10-5
Friends of the Library Group

ASTORIA COMMUNITY LIBRARY, 14-01 Astoria Blvd, Long Island City, 11102, SAN 352-6143. Tel: 718-278-2220.
Library Holdings: CDs 1,332; Bk Vols 37,229; Videos 3,128
Open Mon & Thurs 12-8, Tues 1-6, Wed & Fri 10-6, Sat 10-5
Friends of the Library Group

AUBURNDALE COMMUNITY LIBRARY, 25-55 Francis Lewis Blvd, Flushing, 11358, SAN 352-6178. Tel: 718-352-2027. *Commun Libr Mgr,* Yen Tao
Library Holdings: CDs 1,600; Bk Vols 80,900; Videos 4,170
Open Mon & Thurs 12-8, Tues 1-6, Wed & Fri 10-6, Sat 10-5
Friends of the Library Group

BAISLEY PARK COMMUNITY LIBRARY, 117-11 Sutphin Blvd, 11436, SAN 352-6208. Tel: 718-529-1590. *Commun Libr Mgr,* Bella Barclay
Library Holdings: CDs 1,087; Bk Vols 42,250; Videos 1,520
Friends of the Library Group

BAY TERRACE COMMUNITY LIBRARY, 18-36 Bell Blvd, Bayside, 11360, SAN 352-6240. Tel: 718-423-7004. FAX: 718-746-1794. *Commun Libr Mgr,* Eve Hammer
Library Holdings: CDs 1,343; Bk Vols 56,939; Videos 1,298
Open Mon & Thurs 12-8, Tues 1-6, Wed & Fri 10-6, Sat 10-5
Friends of the Library Group

BAYSIDE COMMUNITY LIBRARY, 214-20 Northern Blvd, Bayside, 11361, SAN 352-6232. Tel: 718-229-1834. FAX: 718-225-8547. *Commun Libr Mgr,* Chu Chin Lee
Library Holdings: Audiobooks 430; CDs 3,760; DVDs 22,823; Bk Vols 122,699
Open Mon 9-8, Tues 1-6, Wed & Fri 10-6, Thurs 12-8, Sat 10-5
Friends of the Library Group

BELLEROSE COMMUNITY LIBRARY, 250-06 Hillside Ave, Bellerose, 11426, SAN 352-6267. Tel: 718-831-8644. *Commun Libr Mgr,* Ronglin Wan
Library Holdings: CDs 2,130; Bk Vols 82,926; Videos 169
Open Mon & Thurs 12-8, Tues 1-6, Wed & Fri 10-6, Sat 10-5
Friends of the Library Group

BRIARWOOD COMMUNITY LIBRARY, 85-12 Main St, Briarwood, 11435, SAN 352-6291. Tel: 718-658-1680. *Commun Libr Mgr,* Shu Ching Chang
Library Holdings: CDs 6,043; DVDs 6,050; Bk Vols 68,922
Open Mon & Thurs 12-8, Tues 1-6, Wed & Fri 10-6, Sat 10-5
Friends of the Library Group

BROAD CHANNEL COMMUNITY LIBRARY, 16-26 Cross Bay Blvd, Broad Channel, 11693, SAN 372-0268. Tel: 718-318-4943. *Commun Libr Mgr,* Carol Eich
Library Holdings: Audiobooks 200; CDs 848; DVDs 1,200; Large Print Bks 100; Bk Vols 21,743; Per Subs 70
Open Mon & Thurs 12-8, Tues 1-6, Wed & Fri 10-6, Sat 10-5
Friends of the Library Group

BROADWAY COMMUNITY LIBRARY, 40-20 Broadway, Long Island City, 11103, SAN 352-6321. Tel: 718-721-2462. *Commun Libr Mgr,* Lubomira Kierkosza
Library Holdings: CDs 2,577; Bk Vols 107,648; Videos 2,218
Open Mon 9-8, Tues 1-6, Wed & Fri 10-6, Thurs 12-8, Sat 10-5
Friends of the Library Group

CAMBRIA HEIGHTS COMMUNITY LIBRARY, 218-13 Linden Blvd, Cambria Heights, 11411, SAN 352-6356. Tel: 718-528-3535. *Commun Libr Mgr,* Kacper Jarecki
Library Holdings: CDs 804; DVDs 1,425; Bk Vols 44,661
Open Mon 9-8, Tues 1-6, Wed & Fri 10-6, Thurs 12-8, Sat 10-5
Friends of the Library Group

CORONA COMMUNITY LIBRARY, 38-23 104th St, Corona, 11368, SAN 352-6380. Tel: 718-426-2844. *Commun Libr Mgr,* Vilma Daza
Library Holdings: CDs 379; Bk Vols 22,980; Videos 607
Open Mon & Thurs 12-8, Tues 1-6, Wed & Fri 10-6, Sat 10-5
Friends of the Library Group

DOUGLASTON-LITTLE NECK COMMUNITY LIBRARY, 249-01 Northern Blvd, Little Neck, 11363, SAN 352-6410. Tel: 718-225-8414. FAX: 718-631-8829.
Library Holdings: CDs 1,917; Bk Vols 52,250; Videos 1,120
Open Mon & Thurs 12-8 Tues 1-6, Wed & Fri 9-6, Sat 10-5
Friends of the Library Group

EAST ELMHURST COMMUNITY LIBRARY, 95-06 Astoria Blvd, East Elmhurst, 11369, SAN 352-6445. Tel: 718-424-2619. FAX: 718-651-7045. *Commun Libr Mgr,* Margaret Gibson
Library Holdings: CDs 2,981; Bk Vols 51,576; Videos 1,162
Open Mon & Thurs 12-8, Tues 1-6, Wed & Fri 10-6, Sat 10-5
Friends of the Library Group

EAST FLUSHING COMMUNITY LIBRARY, 196-36 Northern Blvd, Flushing, 11358, SAN 352-650X. Tel: 718-357-6643. *Commun Libr Mgr,* Ledina Hysa; Staff 7 (MLS 3, Non-MLS 4)
Library Holdings: CDs 1,400; Bk Vols 55,821; Videos 500
Open Mon & Thurs 12-8, Tues 1-6, Wed & Fri 10-6, Sat 10-5
Friends of the Library Group

ELMHURST COMMUNITY LIBRARY, 86-07 Broadway, Elmhurst, 11373, SAN 352-647X. Tel: 718-271-1020. FAX: 718-699-8069. *Commun Libr Mgr,* Yasha Hu
Library Holdings: CDs 3,440; Bk Vols 134,851; Videos 2,202
Open Mon 9-8, Tues 1-6, Wed & Fri 10-6, Thurs 12-8, Sat 10-5
Friends of the Library Group

FAR ROCKAWAY COMMUNITY LIBRARY, 1637 Central Ave, Far Rockaway, 11691, SAN 352-6534. Tel: 718-327-2549. FAX: 718-337-4184. *Commun Libr Mgr,* Sharon Anderson
Library Holdings: CDs 1,157; Bk Vols 71,525; Videos 1,944
Open Mon 9-8, Tues 1-6, Wed & Fri 10-6, Thurs 12-8, Sat 10-5
Friends of the Library Group

FLUSHING LIBRARY, 41-17 Main St, Flushing, 11355, SAN 352-6569. Tel: 718-661-1200. FAX: 718-661-1290. *Dir,* Yang Zeng
Library Holdings: CDs 9,259; Bk Vols 346,320; Videos 7,024
Open Mon-Thurs 9-9, Fri 9-7, Sat 10-5, Sun 12-5
Friends of the Library Group

FOREST HILLS COMMUNITY LIBRARY, 108-19 71st Ave, Forest Hills, 11375, SAN 352-6593. Tel: 718-268-7934. FAX: 718-268-1614. *Commun Libr Mgr,* Hwai-Min Chen-Wood
Library Holdings: CDs 2,642; Bk Vols 111,790; Videos 1,180
Open Mon 9-8, Tues 1-6, Wed & Fri 10-6, Thurs 12-8, Sat 10-5
Friends of the Library Group

FRESH MEADOWS COMMUNITY LIBRARY, 193-20 Horace Harding Expressway, Fresh Meadows, 11365, SAN 352-6623. Tel: 718-454-7272. FAX: 718-454-5820. *Commun Libr Mgr,* Jiangjing Xie
Library Holdings: CDs 2,200; DVDs 7,000; Bk Vols 155,003
Open Mon 9-8, Tues 1-6, Wed & Fri 10-6, Thurs 12-8, Sat 10-5
Friends of the Library Group

GLEN OAKS COMMUNITY LIBRARY, 256-04 Union Tpk, Glen Oaks, 11004, SAN 352-6658. Tel: 718-831-8636. FAX: 718-831-8635. *Commun Libr Mgr,* Youshin Kim
Library Holdings: CDs 1,200; Bk Vols 63,797; Videos 2,500
Open Mon & Thurs 12-8, Tues 1-6, Wed & Fri 10-6, Sat 10-5
Friends of the Library Group

GLENDALE COMMUNITY LIBRARY, 78-60 73rd Pl, Glendale, 11385, SAN 352-6682. Tel: 718-821-4980. FAX: 718-821-7160. *Commun Libr Mgr,* Ann-Marie Josephs
Library Holdings: CDs 1,297; Bk Vols 52,321; Videos 1,051
Open Mon & Thurs 12-8, Tues 1-6, Wed & Fri 10-6, Sat 10-5
Friends of the Library Group

HILLCREST COMMUNITY LIBRARY, 187-05 Union Tpk, Flushing, 11366, SAN 352-6704. Tel: 718-454-2786. *Commun Libr Mgr,* Francesca Bishop
Library Holdings: CDs 2,298; Bk Vols 79,212; Videos 1,682
Open Mon 9-8, Tues 1-6, Wed & Fri 10-6, Thurs 12-8, Sat 10-5
Friends of the Library Group

HOLLIS COMMUNITY LIBRARY, 202-05 Hillside Ave, Hollis, 11423, SAN 352-6712. Tel: 718-465-7355. FAX: 718-264-3248. *Commun Libr Mgr,* Abdullah Zahid
Library Holdings: CDs 1,718; Bk Vols 67,655; Videos 1,919
Open Mon & Thurs 12-8, Tues 1-6, Wed & Fri 10-6, Sat 10-5
Friends of the Library Group

HOWARD BEACH COMMUNITY LIBRARY, 92-06 156th Ave, Howard Beach, 11414, SAN 352-6747. Tel: 718-641-7086. *Commun Libr Mgr,* Sharla Emery
Library Holdings: CDs 1,273; Bk Vols 60,280; Videos 1,335
Open Mon & Thurs 12-8, Tues 1-6, Wed & Fri 10-6, Sat 10-5
Friends of the Library Group

LANGSTON HUGHES COMMUNITY LIBRARY, 100-01 Northern Blvd, Corona, 11368, SAN 329-6458. Tel: 718-651-1100. FAX: 718-651-6258. *Exec Dir,* Shakira Smalls
Founded 1969
Library Holdings: CDs 1,091; Bk Vols 39,786; Videos 3,591
Open Mon 9-8, Tues 1-6, Wed & Fri 10-6, Thurs 12-8, Sat 10-5

INFORMATION SERVICES, 89-11 Merrick Blvd, 11432. Tel: 718-990-0788. Circulation Tel: 718-990-0771. Reference Tel: 718-990-0714.
Founded 1896. Pop 2,200,000; Circ 23,000,000
Library Holdings: Per Subs 1,350
Special Collections: State Document Depository
Open Mon-Thurs 9-8:45, Fri 9-6:45, Sat 10-4:45, Sun 12-4:45

JACKSON HEIGHTS COMMUNITY LIBRARY, 35-51 81st St, Jackson Heights, 11372, SAN 352-6771. Tel: 718-899-2500. FAX: 718-899-7003. *Commun Libr Mgr,* Weiqing Dai; Staff 17 (MLS 8, Non-MLS 9)
Library Holdings: CDs 28,385; Bk Vols 176,367; Videos 2,204
Open Mon 9-8, Tues 1-6, Wed & Fri 10-6, Thurs 12-8, Sat 10-5
Friends of the Library Group

KEW GARDENS HILLS COMMUNITY LIBRARY, 72-33 Vleigh Pl, Flushing, 11367, SAN 352-7581. Tel: 718-261-6654. *Commun Libr Mgr,* Susan Paredes
Library Holdings: CDs 3,000; DVDs 5,000; Bk Vols 101,480
Open Mon & Thurs 12-8, Tues 1-6, Wed & Fri 10-6, Sun 12-5
Friends of the Library Group

LAURELTON COMMUNITY LIBRARY, 134-26 225th St, Laurelton, 11413, SAN 352-6801. Tel: 718-528-2822. FAX: 718-723-6837. *Commun Libr Mgr,* Dave Wang; Staff 9 (MLS 4, Non-MLS 5)
Library Holdings: CDs 1,383; DVDs 2,500; Bk Vols 60,361; Videos 60
Open Mon & Thurs 12-8, Tues 1-6, Wed & Fri 10-6, Sat 10-5
Friends of the Library Group

LEFFERTS COMMUNITY LIBRARY, 103-34 Lefferts Blvd, Richmond Hill, 11419, SAN 352-6836. Tel: 718-843-5950. *Commun Libr Mgr,* David Booker, III
Library Holdings: CDs 2,425; Bk Vols 65,000; Videos 4,500
Open Mon 9-8, Tues 1-6, Wed & Fri 10-6, Thurs 12-8, Sat 10-5
Friends of the Library Group

LEFRAK CITY COMMUNITY LIBRARY, 98-30 57th Ave, Corona, 11368, SAN 352-6860. Tel: 718-592-7677. *Commun Libr Mgr,* Greg Gao
Library Holdings: CDs 1,800; Bk Vols 65,000; Videos 150
Open Mon & Thurs 12-8, Tues 1-6, Wed & Fri 10-6, Sat 10-5
Friends of the Library Group

LONG ISLAND CITY COMMUNITY LIBRARY, 37-44 21 St, Long Island City, 11101. Tel: 718-752-3700. *Commun Libr Mgr,* Tienya Smith; Staff 9 (MLS 4, Non-MLS 5)
Library Holdings: CDs 2,272; DVDs 4,543; Bk Vols 50,388
Open Mon 9-8, Tues 1-6, Wed & Fri 10-6, Thurs 12-8, Sat 10-5
Friends of the Library Group

MASPETH COMMUNITY LIBRARY, 69-70 Grand Ave, Maspeth, 11378, SAN 352-6925. Tel: 718-639-5228. *Commun Libr Mgr,* Usha Pinto
Library Holdings: CDs 1,446; Bk Vols 71,033; Videos 2,066
Open Mon & Thurs 12-8, Tues 1-6, Wed & Fri 10-6, Sat 10-5
Friends of the Library Group

MCGOLDRICK COMMUNITY LIBRARY, 155-06 Roosevelt Ave, Flushing, 11354, SAN 352-6895. Tel: 718-461-1616. *Commun Libr Mgr,* Indra Balasubramanian; Staff 9 (MLS 3, Non-MLS 6)
Library Holdings: CDs 6,581; DVDs 7,000; Bk Vols 87,833
Open Mon & Thurs 12-8, Tues 1-6, Wed & Fri 10-6, Sat 10-5
Friends of the Library Group

MIDDLE VILLAGE COMMUNITY LIBRARY, 72-31 Metropolitan Ave, Middle Village, 11379, SAN 352-695X. Tel: 718-326-1390. *Commun Libr Mgr,* Vesna Simon; Staff 4 (MLS 2, Non-MLS 2)
Library Holdings: CDs 1,149; Bk Vols 54,197
Open Mon & Thurs 12-8, Tues 1-6, Wed & Fri 10-6, Sat 10-5
Friends of the Library Group

MITCHELL-LINDEN COMMUNITY LIBRARY, 31-32 Union St, Flushing, 11354, SAN 352-6984. Tel: 718-539-2330. *Commun Libr Mgr,* Farzaneh Momeni
Library Holdings: CDs 1,838; Bk Vols 65,809; Videos 2,060
Open Mon & Thurs 12-8, Tues 1-6, Wed & Fri 10-6, Sat 10-5
Friends of the Library Group

NORTH FOREST PARK COMMUNITY LIBRARY, 98-27 Metropolitan Ave, Forest Hills, 11375, SAN 352-700X. Tel: 718-261-5512. *Commun Libr Mgr,* Frances Tobin
Library Holdings: CDs 968; Bk Vols 61,356; Videos 1,011
Open Mon & Thurs 12-8, Tues 1-6, Wed & Fri 10-6, Sat 10-5
Friends of the Library Group

NORTH HILLS COMMUNITY LIBRARY, 57-04 Marathon Pkwy, Little Neck, 11362, SAN 352-7018. Tel: 718-225-3550. *Commun Libr Mgr,* Tina Holinski; Staff 5 (MLS 3, Non-MLS 2)
Library Holdings: CDs 1,450; Bk Vols 46,300; Videos 3,750
Open Mon & Thurs 12-8, Tues 1-6, Wed & Fri 10-6, Sat 10-5
Friends of the Library Group

OZONE PARK COMMUNITY LIBRARY, 92-24 Rockaway Blvd, Ozone Park, 11417, SAN 352-7042. Tel: 718-845-3127. FAX: 718-848-1082. *Commun Libr Mgr,* Jerome Myers
Library Holdings: CDs 1,143; Bk Vols 71,525; Videos 1,509
Open Mon & Thurs 12-8, Tues 1-6, Wed & Fri 10-6, Sat 10-5
Friends of the Library Group

PENINSULA COMMUNITY LIBRARY, 92-25 Rockaway Beach Blvd, Rockaway Beach, 11693, SAN 352-7077. Tel: 718-634-1110. *Commun Libr Mgr,* Matthew Allison
Library Holdings: Bk Vols 60,417; Per Subs 1,451; Videos 1,353
Open Mon 9-8, Tues 1-6, Wed & Fri 10-6, Thurs 12-8, Sat 10-5
Friends of the Library Group

POMONOK COMMUNITY LIBRARY, 158-21 Jewel Ave, Flushing, 11365, SAN 352-7107. Tel: 718-591-4343. *Commun Libr Mgr,* Andrew Gibson
Library Holdings: Audiobooks 75; CDs 1,194; DVDs 2,500; Large Print Bks 300; Bk Vols 52,159
Open Mon & Thurs 12-8, Tues 1-6, Wed & Fri 10-6, Sat 10-5
Friends of the Library Group

POPPENHUSEN COMMUNITY LIBRARY, 121-23 14th Ave, College Point, 11356, SAN 352-7131. Tel: 718-359-1102. FAX: 718-353-8894. *Commun Libr Mgr,* Basanda Rakhminova
Library Holdings: CDs 1,500; Bk Vols 56,150; Videos 2,350
Open Mon & Thurs 12-8, Tues 1-6, Wed & Fri 10-6, Sat 10-5
Friends of the Library Group

QUEENS LIBRARY FOR TEENS, 2002 Cornaga Ave, Far Rockaway, 11691. Tel: 718-471-2573. *Br Mgr,* Brandon Jeffries
Open Mon-Fri 2:30-6

QUEENS VILLAGE COMMUNITY LIBRARY, 94-11 217th St, Queens Village, 11428, SAN 352-7190. Tel: 718-776-6800. FAX: 718-479-4609. *Commun Libr Mgr,* Brian Morell
Library Holdings: CDs 6,956; DVDs 7,000; Bk Vols 97,102
Open Mon & Thurs 12-8, Tues 1-6, Wed & Fri 10-6, Sat 10-5
Friends of the Library Group

QUEENSBORO HILL COMMUNITY LIBRARY, 60-05 Main St, Flushing, 11355, SAN 352-714X. Tel: 718-359-8332. *Commun Libr Mgr,* Lisa Caputo
Library Holdings: CDs 880; Bk Vols 29,700; Videos 2,860
Open Mon & Thurs 12-8, Tues 1-6, Wed & Fri 10-6, Sat 10-5
Friends of the Library Group

REGO PARK COMMUNITY LIBRARY, 91-41 63rd Dr, Rego Park, 11374, SAN 352-7255. Tel: 718-459-5140. *Commun Libr Mgr,* Joseph Grosso
Library Holdings: CDs 1,091; Bk Vols 79,786; Videos 3,591
Open Mon & Thurs 12-8, Tues 1-6, Wed & Fri 10-6, Sat 10-5
Friends of the Library Group

RICHMOND HILL COMMUNITY LIBRARY, 118-14 Hillside Ave, Richmond Hill, 11418, SAN 352-728X. Tel: 718-849-7150. FAX: 718-849-4717. *Commun Libr Mgr,* Rebecca Babirye-Alibatya
Library Holdings: CDs 2,116; Bk Vols 75,862; Videos 2,055
Open Mon & Thurs 12-8, Tues 1-6, Wed & Fri 10-6, Sat 10-5
Friends of the Library Group

RIDGEWOOD COMMUNITY LIBRARY, 20-12 Madison St, Ridgewood, 11385, SAN 352-731X. Tel: 718-821-4770. FAX: 718-628-6263. *Commun Libr Mgr,* Thomas Maxheimer
Library Holdings: CDs 1,788; Bk Vols 77,069; Videos 1,317
Open Mon 9-8, Tues 1-6, Wed & Fri 10-6, Thurs 12-8, Sat 10-5
Friends of the Library Group

ROCHDALE VILLAGE COMMUNITY LIBRARY, 169-09 137th Ave, 11434, SAN 352-7344. Tel: 718-723-4440. *Commun Libr Mgr,* Jasmine Harrison
Library Holdings: CDs 1,288; Bk Vols 43,823; Videos 1,392
Open Mon 9-8, Tues 1-6, Wed & Fri 10-6, Thurs 12-8, Sat 10-5
Friends of the Library Group

ROSEDALE COMMUNITY LIBRARY, 144-20 243rd St, Rosedale, 11422, SAN 352-7379. Tel: 718-528-8490. *Commun Libr Mgr,* Elizabeth Eshun; Staff 3 (MLS 3)
Library Holdings: CDs 1,070; Bk Vols 42,581; Videos 2,500
Open Mon & Thurs 12-8, Tues 1-6, Wed & Fri 10-6, Sat 10-5
Friends of the Library Group

SAINT ALBANS COMMUNITY LIBRARY, 191-05 Linden Blvd, Saint Albans, 11412, SAN 352-7409. Tel: 718-528-8196. *Commun Libr Mgr,* Michael Brice
Library Holdings: CDs 1,174; Bk Vols 43,029; Videos 910
Open Mon & Thurs 12-8, Tues 1-6, Wed & Fri 10-6, Sat 10-5
Friends of the Library Group

SEASIDE COMMUNITY LIBRARY, 116-15 Rockaway Beach Blvd, Rockaway Park, 11694, SAN 352-7425. Tel: 718-634-1876. FAX: 718-634-8711. *Commun Libr Mgr,* Dela Cruz Jay
Library Holdings: CDs 1,411; Bk Vols 61,087; Videos 1,409
Open Mon & Thurs 12-8, Tues 1-6, Wed & Fri 10-6, Sat 10-5
Friends of the Library Group

SOUTH HOLLIS COMMUNITY LIBRARY, 204-01 Hollis Ave, South Hollis, 11412, SAN 352-7433. Tel: 718-465-6779. *Commun Libr Mgr,* Reginald Fort
Library Holdings: CDs 1,385; Bk Vols 43,675; Videos 1,410
Open Mon & Thurs 12-8, Tues 1-6, Wed & Fri 10-6, Sat 10-5
Friends of the Library Group

SOUTH JAMAICA COMMUNITY LIBRARY, 108-41 Guy R Brewer Blvd, 11433, SAN 352-7468. Tel: 718-739-4088. *Commun Libr Mgr,* Danielle Walsh
Library Holdings: CDs 550; Bk Vols 42,403; Videos 875
Open Mon & Thurs 12-8, Tues 1-6, Wed & Fri 10-6, Sat 10-5
Friends of the Library Group

SOUTH OZONE PARK COMMUNITY LIBRARY, 128-16 Rockaway Blvd, South Ozone Park, 11420, SAN 352-7492. Tel: 718-529-1660. *Commun Libr Mgr,* Mildred Said
Library Holdings: CDs 1,289; Bk Vols 63,446; Videos 1,434
Open Mon & Thurs 12-8, Tues 1-6, Wed & Fri 10-6, Sat 10-5
Friends of the Library Group

STEINWAY COMMUNITY LIBRARY, 21-45 31st St, Long Island City, 11105, SAN 352-7522. Tel: 718-728-1965. FAX: 718-956-3575. *Commun Libr Mgr,* Position Currently Open
Library Holdings: CDs 2,105; Bk Vols 75,952; Videos 1,706
Closed for renovation as of Aug 2018-
Friends of the Library Group

SUNNYSIDE COMMUNITY LIBRARY, 43-06 Greenpoint Ave, Long Island City, 11104, SAN 352-7557. Tel: 718-784-3033. *Commun Libr Mgr,* Joseph Schiavone
Library Holdings: CDs 3,000; Bk Vols 80,892; Videos 6,000

Open Mon 9-8, Tues 1-6, Wed & Fri 10-6, Thurs 12-8, Sat 10-5
Friends of the Library Group
WHITESTONE COMMUNITY LIBRARY, 151-10 14th Rd, Whitestone, 11357, SAN 352-7611. Tel: 718-767-8010. FAX: 718-357-3086. *Commun Libr Mgr,* Nonyem Illoabachie
Library Holdings: CDs 1,196; Bk Vols 59,131; Videos 1,160
Open Mon & Thurs 12-8, Tues 1-6, Wed & Fri 10-6, Sat 10-5
Friends of the Library Group
WINDSOR PARK COMMUNITY LIBRARY, 79-50 Bell Blvd, Bayside, 11364, SAN 352-7646. Tel: 718-468-8300. FAX: 718-264-0376. *Commun Libr Mgr,* Julia Tan; Staff 7 (MLS 3, Non-MLS 4)
Library Holdings: CDs 2,200; DVDs 3,200; Bk Vols 58,260
Open Mon & Thurs 12-8, Tues 1-6, Wed & Fri 10-6, Sat 10-5
Friends of the Library Group
WOODHAVEN COMMUNITY LIBRARY, 85-41 Forest Pkwy, Woodhaven, 11421, SAN 352-7662. Tel: 718-849-1010. *Commun Libr Mgr,* Jiang Liu
Library Holdings: CDs 1,307; Bk Vols 53,685; Videos 1,054
Open Mon & Thurs 12-8, Tues 1-6, Wed & Fri 10-6, Sat 10-5
Friends of the Library Group
WOODSIDE COMMUNITY LIBRARY, 54-22 Skillman Ave, Woodside, 11377, SAN 352-7670. Tel: 718-429-4700. *Commun Libr Mgr,* Jingru Pei
Library Holdings: Audiobooks 50; CDs 1,000; DVDs 1,200; Large Print Bks 600; Bk Vols 100,000; Per Subs 120
Open Mon & Thurs 12-8, Tues 1-6, Wed & Fri 10-6, Sat 10-5
Friends of the Library Group
Bookmobiles: 1. In Charge, Madlyn Schneider. Bk titles 3,000

C ST JOHN'S UNIVERSITY LIBRARY, St Augustine Hall, 8000 Utopia Pkwy, 11439. SAN 352-7700. Tel: 718-990-6201. Circulation Tel: 718-990-6850. Interlibrary Loan Service Tel: 718-990-6441. Reference Tel: 718-990-6727. E-mail: eservices@stjohns.edu. Web Site: www.stjohns.edu. *Dean of Libr,* Caroline Fuchs; Tel: 718-990-5050, E-mail: fuchsc@stjohns.edu; *Assoc Dir, Emerging Technologies,* Shilpa Karnik; Tel: 718-990-5819, E-mail: karniks@stjohns.edu; *Head, Info Mgt,* Cynthia Chambers; Tel: 718-990-1355, E-mail: chamberc@stjohns.edu; *Head, Ref,* Lucy Heckman; Tel: 718-990-6571, E-mail: heckmanl@stjohns.edu; *Head, Serials Management,* Tian Zhang; Tel: 718-990-5082, E-mail: zhangt@stjohns.edu; *Circ Supvr,* Marilyn Narson; Tel: 718-990-6202, E-mail: narsonm@stjohns.edu; *Library Budget & Planning Analyst,* Vicky Vagenas; Tel: 718-990-6714, E-mail: vagenasv@stjohns.edu; *Spec Coll, Univ Archivist,* Pia DiBari; Tel: 718-990-1465, E-mail: dibarip@stjohns.edu; Staff 18 (MLS 18)
Founded 1870. Enrl 20,881; Fac 627; Highest Degree: Doctorate
Library Holdings: e-books 548,389; e-journals 549,141; Bk Titles 360,629; Bk Vols 517,873; Per Subs 605
Special Collections: Alfred Politz Papers (1942-83); American Friends of Irish Neutrality Records (1938-41); American League for an Undivided Ireland Records (1947-63); Art Exhibition Catalogs; Asian Art Coll; Chin Ying Asian Library; Edward Carofano Apothecary Jar Coll; Joseph C Meyer Accounting Coll; Paul O'Dwyer Coll; Rare & Limited Edition Books; Saul Heller Shorthand Coll; Sen James L Buckley Papers (1970-71); University Archives; Wm M Fischer Lawn Tennis Coll
Subject Interests: Humanities, Pharm, Relig studies, Sciences, Soc sci
Automation Activity & Vendor Info: (Acquisitions) LibLime; (Cataloging) LibLime; (Circulation) LibLime; (Course Reserve) LibLime; (ILL) OCLC ILLiad; (Media Booking) LibLime; (OPAC) LibLime; (Serials) LibLime
Wireless access
Publications: Campus Guides; Library Guides
Partic in Metropolitan New York Library Council
Friends of the Library Group
Departmental Libraries:
KATHRYN & SHELBY CULLOM DAVIS LIBRARY, 101 Astor Pl, 2nd Flr, New York, 10003. Tel: 212-277-5135. E-mail: davislibrary@stjohns.edu. Web Site: www.stjohns.edu/libraries/about-libraries/campus-libraries. *Dir,* Ismael Rivera-Sierra; E-mail: riverasi@stjohns.edu; *Asst Dir, Access & Digital Services,* Richard Waller; Tel: 212-277-5136, E-mail: wallerr@stjohns.edu; *Asst Dir, Tech Serv,* Andy Seville; E-mail: sevillea@stjohns.edu; Staff 4 (MLS 3, Non-MLS 1)
Founded 1901. Enrl 400; Fac 8; Highest Degree: Master
Library Holdings: Microforms 500; Bk Vols 100,000; Per Subs 290
Special Collections: Actuarial Science; American Academy of Insurance Medicine, rec, 1889 to present; Automatic Fire Sprinkler Coll (19th Century to present); Children's Risks Coll; Disaster Images Coll; Fire Marks; Heber B Churchill Earthquake Coll; Insurance (1569 to present); Insurance Company Signages (19th Century to present); Insurance Policies (17th Century to present); Marine Insurance (Winter Coll). US Document Depository
Subject Interests: Actuarial sci, Ins, Risk mgt
Automation Activity & Vendor Info: (Acquisitions) Horizon; (Cataloging) Horizon; (Circulation) Horizon; (Course Reserve) Horizon; (ILL) OCLC; (OPAC) Horizon; (Serials) Horizon
Function: Archival coll, For res purposes, ILL available, Online cat, Res libr
Restriction: Access for corporate affiliates, Authorized patrons, Authorized scholars by appt, Borrowing privileges limited to fac & registered students, Borrowing requests are handled by ILL, Circ to mem only, External users must contact libr, Not open to pub, Open to fac, students & qualified researchers, Open to qualified scholars
LORETTO MEMORIAL LIBRARY
See Separate Entry in Staten Island

CL RITTENBERG LAW LIBRARY, 8000 Utopia Pkwy, 11439, SAN 352-776X. Circulation Tel: 718-990-1580. Reference Tel: 718-990-6651. FAX: 718-990-6649. E-mail: sjulawcirculation@gmail.com, sjulawreference@gmail.com. Web Site: www.stjohns.edu/law/rittenberg-law-library. *Assoc Dean, Libr Serv,* Courtney Selby; *Collection Servs & Digital Initiatives Librarian,* Christopher Anderson; Tel: 718-990-5074, E-mail: andersc1@stjohns.edu; *Ref & Access Serv Librn,* Josh LaPorte; Tel: 718-990-6826, E-mail: laportej@stjohns.edu; *Reference & Scholarly Servs Librn,* Saadia Iqbal; Tel: 718-990-1578, E-mail: iqbals@stjohns.edu; *Access & Collection Services Specialist,* Amber Clarke; Tel: 718-990-6825, E-mail: clarkea1@stjohns.edu; *Access & Collection Services Specialist,* Mary Ann Monaghan; Tel: 718-990-6829, E-mail: monagham@stjohns.edu; *Collection Servs & Digital Initiatives Spec,* Jeff Munoz; Tel: 718-990-6660, E-mail: munozj@stjohns.edu
Founded 1925. Highest Degree: Master
Library Holdings: Bk Titles 344,440; Bk Vols 379,456; Per Subs 14,277
Special Collections: State Document Depository; UN Document Depository; US Document Depository
Automation Activity & Vendor Info: (Acquisitions) Innovative Interfaces, Inc; (Cataloging) Innovative Interfaces, Inc; (Circulation) Innovative Interfaces, Inc; (Course Reserve) Innovative Interfaces, Inc; (ILL) Innovative Interfaces, Inc; (Media Booking) Innovative Interfaces, Inc; (OPAC) Innovative Interfaces, Inc; (Serials) Innovative Interfaces, Inc
Open Mon-Fri 7am-11pm, Sta & Sun 8am-11pm
Restriction: Open to students, fac & staff

R ST PAUL OF THE CROSS PROVINCE*, Passionist Monastery Library, 86-45 Edgerton Blvd, 11432-0024. SAN 311-3620. Tel: 718-739-6502. FAX: 718-739-3910. *Library Contact,* Fr Thomas Brislin; E-mail: tbrislin@cpprov.org; Staff 3 (MLS 1, Non-MLS 2)
Founded 1930
Library Holdings: AV Mats 700; DVDs 100; Bk Titles 40,000; Per Subs 27; Videos 500
Special Collections: Italian Encyclopedia; Patrologiae; Spanish Encyclopedia
Subject Interests: Hist of US, NY City, Philos, Preaching, Scripture liturgy, Spirituality, Theol
Restriction: Not open to pub

C YORK COLLEGE LIBRARY, 94-20 Guy R Brewer Blvd, 11451. SAN 311-3671. Tel: 718-262-2034. Circulation Tel: 718-262-2033. Administration Tel: 718-262-2021, 718-262-2026. FAX: 718-262-2997. Reference E-mail: reference@york.cuny.edu. Web Site: www.york.cuny.edu/library. *Chief Librn, Dept Chair,* Njoki Kinyatti; E-mail: nkinyatti@york.cuny.edu; *Head, Acq & Coll Develop, Webmaster,* John A Drobnicki; Tel: 718-262-2025, E-mail: jdrobnicki@york.cuny.edu; *Head, Archives, Head, Circ & Reserves,* Scott Sheidlower; Tel: 718-262-2017, E-mail: ssheidlower@york.cuny.edu; *Head, Cat & Ser,* Junli Diao; Tel: 718-262-2302, E-mail: jdiao@york.cuny.edu; *Head, Electronic Res,* Meredith Powers; Tel: 718-262-2018, E-mail: MPowers@york.cuny.edu; *Head, ILL, Head, Info Literacy,* Di Su; Tel: 718-262-2031, E-mail: DSu@york.cuny.edu; *Head, Ref,* Todd Simpson; Tel: 718-262-2022, E-mail: tsimpson3@york.cuny.edu; *Sci Librn,* Stefka Tzanova; Tel: 718-262-2037, E-mail: STzanova@york.cuny.edu; Staff 19 (MLS 11, Non-MLS 8)
Founded 1967. Enrl 8,337; Fac 196; Highest Degree: Master
Jul 2019-Jun 2020. Mats Exp $593,836, Books $94,336, Per/Ser (Incl. Access Fees) $494,982. Sal $1,438,196 (Prof $920,642)
Library Holdings: DVDs 105; e-books 1,090,823; e-journals 220,467; Microforms 148,700; Bk Titles 240,000; Bk Vols 343,336; Per Subs 44
Special Collections: American History & Literature (Library of American Civilization), ultrafiche; Books in Hebrew & Yiddish (Bassin Coll); Papers of the NAACP, film; Papers of the United Negro College Fund, fiche; Special American & Foreign Newspaper Coll, film
Subject Interests: Health, Humanities, Sci, Soc sci
Automation Activity & Vendor Info: (Acquisitions) Ex Libris Group; (Cataloging) Ex Libris Group; (Circulation) Ex Libris Group; (Course Reserve) Ex Libris Group; (Discovery) Ex Libris Group; (ILL) OCLC; (OPAC) Ex Libris Group; (Serials) Ex Libris Group
Wireless access
Publications: LibWire (Newsletter)
Partic in Metropolitan New York Library Council

Special Services for the Blind - Dragon Naturally Speaking software; Large screen computer & software; Scanner for conversion & translation of mats; Screen enlargement software for people with visual disabilities
Open Mon-Thurs 8:30am-10pm, Fri 8:30-8, Sat 9-5

JAMESTOWN

P CHAUTAUQUA-CATTARAUGUS LIBRARY SYSTEM, 106 W Fifth St, 14701. SAN 311-368X. Tel: 716-664-6675. FAX: 716-484-1205. Web Site: www.cclsny.org. *Exec Dir,* Janice Dekoff; Tel: 716-484-7135, Ext 228, E-mail: jdekoff@cclsny.org; *Digital Serv Librn,* Megan Disbro; Tel: 716-484-7135, Ext 251, E-mail: mdisbro@cclsny.org; *Tech Serv Librn,* Chris Spink; Tel: 716-484-7135, Ext 248, E-mail: cspink@cclsny.org; *Outreach Coordr, Youth Serv Consult,* L J Martin; Tel: 716-664-6675, Ext 243, E-mail: ljmartin@cclsny.org; *Data Spec, ILL,* Carolyn Hughesman; Tel: 716-484-7135, Ext 259, E-mail: chughesman@cclsny.org; Staff 13 (MLS 4, Non-MLS 9)
Founded 1960. Pop 223,705; Circ 314,913
Library Holdings: AV Mats 23,630; Bk Vols 148,135; Per Subs 16
Automation Activity & Vendor Info: (Acquisitions) ByWater Solutions; (Cataloging) ByWater Solutions; (Circulation) ByWater Solutions; (ILL) OCLC WorldShare Interlibrary Loan; (OPAC) ByWater Solutions
Wireless access
Function: Children's prog, Computer training, Doc delivery serv, E-Reserves, Electronic databases & coll, Equip loans & repairs, Free DVD rentals, Magnifiers for reading, Preschool outreach, Prof lending libr, Serves people with intellectual disabilities, Summer reading prog, VHS videos, Wheelchair accessible, Workshops
Publications: Newsletter
Member Libraries: Ahira Hall Memorial Library; Alexander Findley Community Library; Allegany Public Library; Anderson-Lee Library; Ashville Free Library; Bemus Point Public Library; Blount Library, Inc; Cattaraugus Free Library; Clymer-French Creek Free Library; Darwin R Barker Library Association; Delevan-Yorkshire Public Library; Dunkirk Public Library; Ellicottville Memorial Library; Ellington Farman Library; Falconer Public Library; Fluvanna Free Library; Gowanda Free Library; Hazeltine Public Library; James Prendergast Library; Kennedy Free Library; King Memorial Library; Lakewood Memorial Library; Mary E Seymour Memorial Free Library; Mayville Library; Memorial Library of Little Valley; Minerva Free Library; Myers Memorial Library; Olean Public Library; Patterson Library; Portville Free Library; Randolph Free Library; Ripley Public Library; Salamanca Public Library; Seneca Nation Libraries; Sinclairville Free Library; Smith Memorial Library
Partic in Western New York Library Resources Council
Open Mon-Fri 9-5

S FENTON HISTORY CENTER-LIBRARY*, 73 Forest Ave, 14701. (Mail add: 67 Washington St, 14701), SAN 311-3698. Tel: 716-664-6256. FAX: 716-483-7524. E-mail: library@fentonhistorycenter.org. Web Site: www.fentonhistorycenter.org/research-center. *Dir,* Noah Goodling; *Archivist,* Karen Livsey; Tel: 716-664-6256, Ext 106, E-mail: Karen@fentonhistorycenter.org; *Researcher,* Barbara Cessna; Tel: 716-664-6256, Ext 104, E-mail: researcher@fentonhistorycenter.org; Staff 2 (MLS 1, Non-MLS 1)
Founded 1964
Library Holdings: Bk Titles 5,400; Per Subs 27
Special Collections: Census Reports Coll; Genealogy File, card file; Local History (Manuscript Coll); Local Newspapers, incl Deaths & Marriages
Subject Interests: Civil War period, Genealogy, Local hist, Reuben E Fenton
Wireless access
Open Mon-Sat 10-4

P FLUVANNA FREE LIBRARY*, 3532 Fluvanna Ave Ext, 14701. SAN 311-2063. Tel: 716-487-1773. FAX: 716-708-4296. E-mail: flulib@stny.rr.com. Web Site: www.fluvannalibrary.org. *Dir,* Lynn Grundstrom
Founded 1914. Pop 3,150; Circ 20,000
Subject Interests: Local genealogy
Wireless access
Mem of Chautauqua-Cattaraugus Library System
Open Mon-Fri 10-6

P HAZELTINE PUBLIC LIBRARY*, 891 Busti-Sugar Grove Rd, 14701. SAN 310-9941. Tel: 716-487-1281. FAX: 716-487-0760. Web Site: www.hazeltinelibrary.org. *Libr Dir,* Katie Smith; E-mail: director@hazeltinelibrary.org; *Libr Asst,* Susan Brooks
Founded 1924. Pop 4,502; Circ 18,758
Library Holdings: AV Mats 959; Large Print Bks 105; Bk Titles 15,515; Bk Vols 17,000; Per Subs 72
Subject Interests: Antiques
Automation Activity & Vendor Info: (Cataloging) Koha; (Circulation) Koha; (ILL) Koha; (OPAC) Koha; (Serials) Koha
Wireless access
Mem of Chautauqua-Cattaraugus Library System
Open Mon, Wed & Fri 1-5 & 6:30-8:30, Tues & Thurs 10-5, Sat 10-1

J JAMESTOWN COMMUNITY COLLEGE*, Hultquist Library, 525 Falconer St, 14702. (Mail add: PO Box 20, 14702-0020), SAN 311-3701. Tel: 716-376-1000. Circulation Tel: 716-338-1008. Toll Free Tel: 800-388-8557. Web Site: www.sunyjcc.edu/library. *Dir of Libr,* Tim Arnold; Tel: 716-338-1125, E-mail: timothyarnold@mail.sunyjcc.edu; Staff 5 (MLS 2, Non-MLS 3)
Founded 1950. Enrl 3,660; Fac 70; Highest Degree: Associate
Library Holdings: AV Mats 4,762; e-books 2,000; Bk Titles 60,000; Bk Vols 66,500; Per Subs 220; Talking Bks 100
Special Collections: Scandinavian Studies
Subject Interests: Criminal justice, Nursing
Automation Activity & Vendor Info: (Cataloging) Ex Libris Group; (Circulation) Ex Libris Group; (Course Reserve) Ex Libris Group; (OPAC) Ex Libris Group; (Serials) EBSCO Online
Wireless access
Publications: Acquisitions List; Bibliographies; Newsletter; STV Alert (Monthly); TV Alert (Monthly)
Partic in OCLC Online Computer Library Center, Inc; SUNYConnect; Western New York Library Resources Council
Open Mon-Thurs 8-8, Fri 8-4, Sun 1-4
Departmental Libraries:
CATTARAUGUS COUNTY, 260 N Union St, Olean, 14760. (Mail add: PO Box 5901, Olean, 14760-5901), SAN 329-3521. Tel: 716-376-7517. *Ref Librn,* Kassandra Wegner; Staff 2 (MLS 1, Non-MLS 1)
Enrl 900; Fac 20; Highest Degree: Associate
Library Holdings: AV Mats 1,000; Bk Titles 20,000; Per Subs 160
Subject Interests: Criminal justice, Nursing
Function: ILL available, Ref serv available
Publications: Acquisition Lists
Open Mon-Thurs (Winter) 8-8, Fri 8-4, Sat 9-12; Mon-Thurs (Summer) 8:30-6

P JAMES PRENDERGAST LIBRARY*, 509 Cherry St, 14701. SAN 311-371X. Tel: 716-484-7135. E-mail: info@prendergastlibrary.org, reference@prendergastlibrary.org. Web Site: www.prendergastlibrary.org. *Exec Dir,* Annie Greene; E-mail: agreene@cclslib.org; Staff 15 (MLS 4, Non-MLS 11)
Founded 1880. Pop 31,146
Special Collections: City of Jamestown Founding Family Coll; Historic Prendergast Family Portraits
Subject Interests: City hist
Automation Activity & Vendor Info: (Acquisitions) Koha; (Cataloging) Koha; (Circulation) Koha; (OPAC) Koha
Wireless access
Function: 24/7 Electronic res, 24/7 Online cat, 3D Printer, Adult bk club, Adult literacy prog, Art exhibits, Art programs, Audiobks via web, BA reader (adult literacy), Bk club(s), Bks on cassette, Bks on CD, CD-ROM, Children's prog, Computer training, Computers for patron use, E-Readers, Electronic databases & coll, Family literacy, Free DVD rentals, Health sci info serv, Holiday prog, ILL available, Internet access, Large print keyboards, Life-long learning prog for all ages, Magazines, Magnifiers for reading, Mail & tel request accepted, Makerspace, Meeting rooms, Microfiche/film & reading machines, Movies, Museum passes, Music CDs, Notary serv, Online cat, Online ref, Outreach serv, OverDrive digital audio bks, Photocopying/Printing, Preschool outreach, Prog for adults, Prog for children & young adult, Ref & res, Ref serv available, Res assist avail, Res libr, Res performed for a fee, Scanner, Senior computer classes, Senior outreach, Spanish lang bks, Spoken cassettes & CDs, Spoken cassettes & DVDs, STEM programs, Story hour, Study rm, Summer reading prog, Tax forms, Teen prog, Telephone ref, VHS videos, Wheelchair accessible
Mem of Chautauqua-Cattaraugus Library System
Special Services for the Deaf - Assisted listening device
Special Services for the Blind - Accessible computers
Open Mon-Thurs 10-8:30, Fri 10-5, Sat 10-4

JASPER

P JASPER FREE LIBRARY, 3807 Preacher St, 14855. SAN 311-3728. Tel: 607-792-3494. FAX: 607-792-3494. E-mail: jasperfreelibrary.events@gmail.com. *Dir,* Debbie Stephens; E-mail: stephensd@stls.org
Pop 1,500; Circ 7,000
Library Holdings: Bk Titles 4,000; Bk Vols 5,100; Per Subs 25
Wireless access
Mem of Southern Tier Library System
Open Mon 6:30pm-9pm, Tues & Thurs 9-12:30 & 1-4:30, Sat 8:30-12

JEFFERSONVILLE

P WESTERN SULLIVAN PUBLIC LIBRARY*, Jeffersonville Headquarters Branch, 19 Center St, 12748. (Mail add: PO Box 594, 12748-0594), SAN 376-6950. Tel: 845-482-4350. FAX: 845-482-3092. E-mail: jef@rcls.org,

wsplprograms@rcls.org. Web Site: www.wsplonline.org. *Dir,* Audra Everett; E-mail: wspldirector@rcls.org; *Br Mgr,* Jennifer Olsen; *Adult Programs,* Claudine Luchsinger; *Children's Prog,* Kristen Dasenbrock; Staff 4 (MLS 1, Non-MLS 3)
Library Holdings: AV Mats 6,850; Electronic Media & Resources 78,041; Bk Vols 60,447; Per Subs 383
Automation Activity & Vendor Info: (Cataloging) SirsiDynix; (Circulation) SirsiDynix; (OPAC) SirsiDynix; (Serials) SirsiDynix
Wireless access
Open Tues & Wed 10-8, Thurs & Fri 10-5, Sat 10-2
Friends of the Library Group
Branches: 2
DELAWARE FREE BRANCH, 45 Lower Main St, Callicoon, 12723. (Mail add: PO Box 245, Callicoon, 12723-0245), SAN 310-9976. Tel: 845-887-4040. FAX: 845-887-8957. E-mail: del@rcls.org. *Br Mgr,* Melissa Reid
Founded 1951. Circ 12,492
Library Holdings: Bk Vols 15,206
Special Collections: Sullivan County Democrat Coll, microfilm
Subject Interests: Local hist, Mysteries
Mem of Ramapo Catskill Library System; Ramapo Catskill Library System
Special Services for the Blind - Bks on cassette; Bks on CD; Home delivery serv; Large print bks; Radio reading serv
Open Mon, Wed & Thurs 10-5, Tues 3-7, Fri 10-6, Sat 11:30-4
Friends of the Library Group
TUSTEN-COCHECTON BRANCH, 198 Bridge St, Narrowsburg, 12764-6402. (Mail add: PO Box 129, Narrowsburg, 12764-0129), SAN 376-6985. Tel: 845-252-3360. FAX: 845-252-3331. E-mail: nar@rcls.org. *Br Mgr,* Penelope Lohr
Library Holdings: Bk Vols 13,700; Per Subs 30
Subject Interests: Local hist
Open Mon 10-8, Tues 9:30-2, Wed & Fri 10-7, Sat 9:30-2
Friends of the Library Group

JERICHO

P JERICHO PUBLIC LIBRARY, One Merry Lane, 11753. SAN 311-3736. Tel: 516-935-6790. FAX: 516-433-9581. E-mail: info@jericholibrary.org. Web Site: www.jericholibrary.org. *Dir,* Angela Cinquemani; *Head, Children's Servx,* Barbara Barrett; *Head, Circ,* Vanessa Jambrone; *Head, Processing Services,* Jean Murphy; *Head, Ref (Info Serv),* Sarah Okano; *Head, Tech Serv,* Carlos Munozospina; Staff 38.1 (MLS 12, Non-MLS 26.1)
Founded 1964. Pop 17,348; Circ 361,368
Library Holdings: Audiobooks 9,109; AV Mats 23,446; Per Subs 313
Special Collections: Local History Coll, multi-media
Automation Activity & Vendor Info: (Acquisitions) Baker & Taylor; (Circulation) Innovative Interfaces, Inc; (OPAC) Innovative Interfaces, Inc
Wireless access
Function: 24/7 Electronic res, 24/7 Online cat, Computers for patron use, Internet access, Ref serv available, Scanner
Publications: Newsletter (Bimonthly)
Mem of Nassau Library System
Open Mon, Tues & Thurs 9-9, Wed 10-9, Fri 9-6, Sat 9-5, Sun 12-5

JOHNSON CITY

M UHS WILSON MEDICAL CENTER*, Medical Library, 33-57 Harrison St, 13790. SAN 311-3744. Tel: 607-763-6030. FAX: 607-763-5992. E-mail: medical_library@uhs.org. *Libr Mgr,* Position Currently Open; *Libr Serv Coordr,* Catherine Knapp; E-mail: catherine_knapp@uhs.org; Staff 2 (MLS 1, Non-MLS 1)
Founded 1935
Library Holdings: e-journals 25; Bk Vols 6,700; Per Subs 388
Subject Interests: Healthcare admin, Med, Nursing
Wireless access
Partic in South Central Regional Library Council
Restriction: Open to pub for ref only

P YOUR HOME PUBLIC LIBRARY*, Johnson City Library, 107 Main St, 13790. SAN 311-3752. Tel: 607-797-4816. FAX: 607-798-8895. E-mail: jc.lib@4cls.org. Web Site: www.yhpl.org. *Dir,* Ben Lainhart; E-mail: jc.benjamin@4cls.org; *Youth Serv Librn,* Maryse Quinn; Staff 8 (MLS 3, Non-MLS 5)
Founded 1917. Pop 16,578; Circ 93,609
Library Holdings: Bk Titles 46,414; Bk Vols 54,000; Per Subs 54
Automation Activity & Vendor Info: (Acquisitions) SirsiDynix; (Circulation) SirsiDynix; (OPAC) SirsiDynix
Wireless access
Mem of Four County Library System
Open Mon-Thurs 9-8:30, Fri 9-5, Sat (Sept-June) 9-5
Friends of the Library Group

JOHNSTOWN

J FULTON-MONTGOMERY COMMUNITY COLLEGE*, Evans Library, 2805 State Hwy 67, 12095-3790. SAN 311-3760. Tel: 518-736-3622, Ext 8058. Interlibrary Loan Service Tel: 518-736-3622, Ext 8054. E-mail: libinfo@fmcc.edu. Web Site: library.fmcc.edu. *Librn,* Daniel Towne; E-mail: daniel.towne@fmcc.edu; Staff 3 (MLS 3)
Founded 1964. Enrl 1,900; Fac 157
Library Holdings: Bk Vols 35,000; Per Subs 150
Subject Interests: Applied sci, Regional hist
Automation Activity & Vendor Info: (Cataloging) MultiLIS; (Circulation) MultiLIS; (Course Reserve) MultiLIS; (OPAC) MultiLIS
Wireless access
Publications: Handbook
Partic in OCLC Online Computer Library Center, Inc; SUNYConnect

P JOHNSTOWN PUBLIC LIBRARY*, 38 S Market St, 12095. SAN 311-3779. Tel: 518-762-8317. Web Site: www.johnstownpubliclibrary.info. *Dir,* Erica Wing; E-mail: ewing@mvls.info
Founded 1901. Pop 8,743; Circ 88,582
Library Holdings: Bk Vols 35,892; Per Subs 70
Subject Interests: Genealogy, NY local hist
Automation Activity & Vendor Info: (Cataloging) Innovative Interfaces, Inc; (Circulation) Innovative Interfaces, Inc; (Course Reserve) Innovative Interfaces, Inc; (ILL) Innovative Interfaces, Inc; (OPAC) Innovative Interfaces, Inc
Wireless access
Publications: Friends of the Library Newsletter (Quarterly)
Mem of Mohawk Valley Library System
Open Tues-Thurs 10-6, Fri 10-4, Sat 10-1
Friends of the Library Group

JORDAN

P JORDAN BRAMLEY LIBRARY, 15 Mechanic St, 13080. (Mail add: PO Box 923, 13080-0923), SAN 311-3787. Tel: 315-689-3296. FAX: 315-689-1231. E-mail: jordanlibrary@yahoo.com. Web Site: jordanbramleylibrary.org. *Dir,* Linda Byrnes; Staff 6 (Non-MLS 6)
Library Holdings: Bk Vols 27,600; Per Subs 30
Wireless access
Mem of Onondaga County Public Libraries
Open Mon-Thurs 11-7, Fri 11-4
Friends of the Library Group
Bookmobiles: 1

JORDANVILLE

CR HOLY TRINITY ORTHODOX SEMINARY LIBRARY*, 1407 Robinson Rd, 13361-0036. (Mail add: PO Box 36, 13361-0036), SAN 311-3795. Tel: 315-858-3116. Administration Tel: 315-858-0945. FAX: 315-858-0945. E-mail: library@hts.edu. Web Site: www.hts.edu. *Dir, Libr Serv,* Vladimir Tsurikov; *Curator, Librn,* Michael Perekrestov; *Libr Mgr,* Andrei Lyubimov; *Cataloger,* Michael Herrick; Staff 4 (MLS 2, Non-MLS 2)
Founded 1948. Enrl 35; Fac 15; Highest Degree: Bachelor
Library Holdings: Bk Vols 45,000; Per Subs 75
Subject Interests: Byzantine studies, Church hist, Russian (Lang), Russian lit, Russian orthodox theology, Sacred art
Automation Activity & Vendor Info: (Cataloging) Softlink America; (Circulation) Softlink America; (ILL) OCLC; (OPAC) Softlink America; (Serials) Softlink America
Wireless access
Open Mon-Fri 2-4
Restriction: Authorized patrons, Authorized scholars by appt, Borrowing privileges limited to fac & registered students, Open to researchers by request, Restricted pub use

P JORDANVILLE PUBLIC LIBRARY*, 189 Main St, 13361. SAN 311-3809. Tel: 315-858-2874. FAX: 315-858-2874. E-mail: jordanville@midyork.org. Web Site: jordanvillelibrary.org. *Libr Mgr,* Melinda Supp; Staff 2 (Non-MLS 2)
Founded 1908. Circ 9,612
Library Holdings: Bk Vols 4,068; Per Subs 17
Special Collections: Roosevelt Robinson NY State Coll
Wireless access
Publications: Historical Booklet
Mem of Mid-York Library System
Open Mon, Wed & Fri 3-7, Tues & Thurs 9-1
Friends of the Library Group

KATONAH

P KATONAH VILLAGE LIBRARY*, 26 Bedford Rd, 10536-2121. SAN 311-3833. Tel: 914-232-3508. FAX: 914-232-0415. Reference E-mail: katref@wlsmail.org. Web Site: www.katonahlibrary.org. *Dir,* Mary Kane;

E-mail: mkane@katonahlibrary.org; *Asst Dir,* Virginia Fetscher; *Librn, Spec Projects,* Michael Robin; Staff 10 (MLS 4, Non-MLS 6)
Founded 1880. Pop 7,003; Circ 137,000
Library Holdings: Bks on Deafness & Sign Lang 10; High Interest/Low Vocabulary Bk Vols 30; Large Print Bks 200; Bk Titles 50,000; Bk Vols 69,000; Per Subs 196; Spec Interest Per Sub 25; Talking Bks 300
Subject Interests: Art, Fishing, Lit, Poetry
Automation Activity & Vendor Info: (Cataloging) SirsiDynix; (Circulation) SirsiDynix; (Serials) EBSCO Online
Wireless access
Mem of Westchester Library System
Open Mon & Wed 10-8, Tues & Thurs 10-6, Fri 10-5:30, Sat 10-5
Friends of the Library Group

S NEW YORK STATE OFFICE OF PARKS, RECREATION & HISTORIC PRESERVATION*, John Jay Homestead State Historic Site Library, 400 Rte 22, 10536. (Mail add: PO Box 832, 10536-0832), SAN 311-3817. Tel: 914-232-5651. FAX: 914-232-8085. Web Site: johnjayhomestead.org. *Educ Dir,* Ariana Scecchitano; Tel: 914-232-5651, Ext 101; Staff 1 (Non-MLS 1)
Founded 1958
Library Holdings: Bk Titles 4,000
Special Collections: Papers of Ancestors & Descendants of John Jay, 1686-1953
Subject Interests: Abolitionism, Hist, Polit sci, Relig, Slavery
Restriction: Open by appt only
Friends of the Library Group

KEENE

P KEENE PUBLIC LIBRARY*, Main St, 12942. (Mail add: PO Box 206, 12942-0206), SAN 311-3841. Tel: 518-576-2200. FAX: 518-576-2200. E-mail: keenepubliclibrary@outlook.com. Web Site: cefls.org/libraries/keene. *Dir,* Aaron Miller
Pop 920; Circ 9,044
Library Holdings: Bk Vols 10,000; Per Subs 20
Wireless access
Mem of Clinton-Essex-Franklin Library System
Open Mon (Winter) 9-5 & 6-8, Wed 9-5, Sat 9-1; Mon & Wed (Summer) 9-5

KEENE VALLEY

P KEENE VALLEY LIBRARY ASSOCIATION*, 1796 Rte 73, 12943. (Mail add: PO Box 86, 12943-0086), SAN 311-385X. Tel: 518-576-4335. FAX: 518-576-4693. E-mail: kvla.library@gmail.com. Web Site: www.keenevalleylibrary.org. *Dir,* Karen Glass; *Archivist,* Nina Allen; Staff 2 (MLS 2)
Founded 1888. Pop 450; Circ 13,000
Library Holdings: Bk Titles 17,000; Per Subs 30
Special Collections: Fishing (Pickard Coll); Local History (Loomis Room Coll); Mountain (Alpine Coll)
Subject Interests: Art, Mountaineering
Automation Activity & Vendor Info: (Acquisitions) SirsiDynix; (Cataloging) SirsiDynix; (Circulation) SirsiDynix; (ILL) SirsiDynix; (OPAC) SirsiDynix
Wireless access
Mem of Clinton-Essex-Franklin Library System
Open Tues & Thurs (Winter) 9-12, 1-5 & 6-8, Sat 10-12 & 1-4; Mon, Wed & Fri (Summer) 10-5, Tues & Thurs 9-5 & 6-8, Sat 10-4

KEESEVILLE

P KEESEVILLE FREE LIBRARY*, 1721 Front St, 12944. SAN 311-3868. Tel: 518-834-9054. FAX: 518-834-9054. E-mail: keesevillelibrary@gmail.com. *Dir,* Laura Anne Thompson
Founded 1935. Pop 2,000; Circ 17,000
Library Holdings: Bk Titles 8,000; Per Subs 30
Automation Activity & Vendor Info: (Acquisitions) Horizon; (Cataloging) Horizon; (Circulation) Horizon; (Course Reserve) Horizon; (ILL) Horizon; (Media Booking) Horizon; (OPAC) Horizon; (Serials) Horizon
Wireless access
Mem of Clinton-Essex-Franklin Library System
Open Mon (Winter) 1-7, Tues & Wed 10-12 & 1-5, Fri 1-5, Sat 9-3; Mon (Summer) 10-12 & 1-7, Tues & Thurs 11-5, Wed & Fri 10-12 & 1-5

KENMORE

P TOWN OF TONAWANDA PUBLIC LIBRARY*, Kenmore Branch, 160 Delaware Rd, 14217. SAN 352-7824. Tel: 716-873-2842. FAX: 716-873-8416. E-mail: knm@buffalolib.org. Web Site: www.buffalolib.org/content/library-locations/kenmore. *Dir,* Dorinda Darden; E-mail: dardend@buffalolib.org
Founded 1925. Pop 82,000; Circ 967,880
Library Holdings: Bk Vols 111,441
Special Collections: Newspapers, micro
Automation Activity & Vendor Info: (Acquisitions) SirsiDynix; (Cataloging) SirsiDynix; (Circulation) SirsiDynix; (ILL) SirsiDynix; (OPAC) SirsiDynix; (Serials) SirsiDynix
Wireless access
Mem of Buffalo & Erie County Public Library System
Open Mon 10-6, Tues-Thurs 10-9, Fri & Sat 10-5, Sun (Sept-May) 12-5
Friends of the Library Group
Branches: 1
KENILWORTH, 318 Montrose Ave, Buffalo, 14223, SAN 352-7913. Tel: 716-834-7657. FAX: 716-834-4695. Web Site: www.buffalolib.org/content/library-locations/kenilworth. *Dir,* Dorinda Darden
Library Holdings: Bk Vols 22,500
Open Mon, Wed & Fri 12-8, Tues & Tours 10-8

KENNEDY

P KENNEDY FREE LIBRARY, 649 Second St, 14747. (Mail add: PO Box 8, 14747-0008), SAN 311-3876. Tel: 716-267-4265. FAX: 716-267-2049. E-mail: kennedyfreelibrary@gmail.com. Web Site: www.kennedyfreelibrary.org. *Dir,* Dawn Swanson; *Asst Librn,* Diane Carey
Pop 2,350; Circ 10,400
Library Holdings: Bk Vols 15,500; Per Subs 40
Automation Activity & Vendor Info: (Cataloging) SirsiDynix; (OPAC) SirsiDynix
Wireless access
Mem of Chautauqua-Cattaraugus Library System
Open Mon 2-7, Tues & Wed 10-7, Thurs 3-7, Sat 10-1
Friends of the Library Group

KENT LAKES

P KENT PUBLIC LIBRARY*, 17 Sybil's Crossing, 10512. SAN 311-0192. Tel: 845-225-8585. FAX: 845-225-8549. E-mail: library@kentlibrary.org. Web Site: kentlibrary.org. *Dir,* Carol Donick; E-mail: cdonick@kentlibrary.org
Circ 100,000
Library Holdings: AV Mats 4,000; Bk Vols 36,000; Per Subs 70
Automation Activity & Vendor Info: (Acquisitions) Innovative Interfaces, Inc; (Cataloging) Innovative Interfaces, Inc; (Circulation) Innovative Interfaces, Inc; (OPAC) Innovative Interfaces, Inc
Wireless access
Mem of Mid-Hudson Library System
Open Mon-Wed 10-8, Thurs & Fri 10-5, Sat 10-3
Friends of the Library Group

KEUKA PARK

C KEUKA COLLEGE, Lightner Library, 141 Central Ave, 14478. SAN 311-3884. Tel: 315-279-5632. Reference Tel: 315-279-5473. Web Site: www.keuka.edu/library. *Dir,* Linda Park; Tel: 315-279-5208, E-mail: lpark@keuka.edu; *Digital Literacy & Services Librn,* Dr Nancy Marksbury; Tel: 315-279-5269, E-mail: nmarksbury@keuka.edu; *Circ Supvr, ILL, Tech Serv Asst,* Judith Jones; Tel: 315-279-5340, E-mail: jjones@keuka.edu; Staff 3 (MLS 2, Non-MLS 1)
Founded 1923. Enrl 1,076; Fac 62; Highest Degree: Master
Library Holdings: Bk Vols 85,782
Subject Interests: Behav sci, Biology, Criminal justice, Local hist, Nursing, Occupational therapy, Psychol, Secondary educ, Sign lang, Soc sci
Automation Activity & Vendor Info: (Acquisitions) Innovative Interfaces, Inc; (Cataloging) Innovative Interfaces, Inc; (Circulation) Innovative Interfaces, Inc; (ILL) Innovative Interfaces, Inc; (OPAC) Innovative Interfaces, Inc; (Serials) Innovative Interfaces, Inc
Wireless access
Publications: Journal Holdings List; Keuka Library Handbook
Partic in South Central Regional Library Council
Open Mon-Fri 8:30-4:30
Friends of the Library Group

KINDERHOOK

S COLUMBIA COUNTY HISTORICAL SOCIETY LIBRARY*, Barbara P Rielly Memorial Research Library, CCHS Museum & Library, Five Albany Ave, 12106. (Mail add: PO Box 311, 12106), SAN 311-3892. Tel: 518-758-9265. E-mail: Library@cchsny.org. Web Site: www.cchsny.org/library.html. *Sr Librn,* Jim Benton; *Colls Mgr,* Position Currently Open. Subject Specialists: *Columbia County, Genealogy, NY State,* Jim Benton
Founded 1916
Library Holdings: Bk Vols 3,000
Special Collections: Columbia County, NY; Dutch & Palatine Cultures; Family Histories & Genealogies Coll; New York Colonial History Coll; Photog Coll; Town History Material Coll
Subject Interests: County, Genealogy, Regional hist

Wireless access
Open Tues, Sat & Sun 12-4

P KINDERHOOK MEMORIAL LIBRARY*, 18 Hudson St, 12106-2003. (Mail add: PO Box 293, 12106-0293), SAN 311-3906. Tel: 518-758-6192. E-mail: info@kinderhooklibrary.org. Web Site: www.kinderhooklibrary.org. *Dir,* AnnaLee Giraldo; E-mail: annalee.giraldo@kinderhooklibrary.org; Staff 7 (MLS 3, Non-MLS 4)
Founded 1928. Pop 6,486; Circ 54,000
Library Holdings: Bk Titles 26,000
Special Collections: Columbia County & Kinderhook; Gardening; Handicrafts
Automation Activity & Vendor Info: (Cataloging) Innovative Interfaces, Inc; (Circulation) Innovative Interfaces, Inc; (ILL) Innovative Interfaces, Inc; (OPAC) Innovative Interfaces, Inc
Wireless access
Function: ILL available
Mem of Mid-Hudson Library System
Open Tues-Thurs 10-8, Fri 10-5, Sat 10-4, Sun 12-4

KINGS POINT

C UNITED STATES MERCHANT MARINE ACADEMY, Schuyler Otis Bland Memorial Library, 300 Steamboat Rd, 11024. SAN 311-3922. Tel: 516-726-5751. Interlibrary Loan Service Tel: 516-726-5748. FAX: 516-726-5616. E-mail: librarycirc@usmma.edu. Web Site: www.usmma.edu/library. *Libr Dir,* Dr Donna Selvaggio; E-mail: selvaggiod@usmma.edu; *Reader Serv Librn,* Jeremy Lauber; E-mail: lauberj@usmma.edu; *Tech Serv Librn,* Jan M Edmiston; Tel: 516-726-5749, E-mail: edmistonj@usmma.edu; Staff 5 (MLS 5)
Founded 1942. Enrl 900; Fac 80; Highest Degree: Master
Library Holdings: Audiobooks 315; CDs 967; DVDs 360; Bk Titles 187,000; Bk Vols 224,000; Per Subs 850; Videos 260
Special Collections: Marad Technical Report Coll. US Document Depository
Subject Interests: Merchant marine
Automation Activity & Vendor Info: (Cataloging) OCLC; (Circulation) OCLC Worldshare Management Services; (Course Reserve) OCLC Worldshare Management Services; (Discovery) OCLC; (ILL) OCLC Tipasa; (OPAC) OCLC Worldshare Management Services; (Serials) OCLC Worldshare Management Services
Wireless access
Publications: Acquisitions List; Bibliography Series; Library Handbook; Newsletter; Periodicals Holdings List
Partic in Long Island Library Resources Council; OCLC Online Computer Library Center, Inc; Westchester Academic Library Directors Organization
Open Mon-Fri 8-4

KINGSTON

M HEALTHALLIANCE HOSPITAL - BROADWAY CAMPUS*, Medical Library, 396 Broadway, 12401. SAN 311-3965. Tel: 845-334-2786. Web Site: www.hahv.org. *Librn,* Tracey Fortich; E-mail: Tracey.Fortich@hahv.org; Staff 1 (MLS 1)
Founded 1956
Library Holdings: Bk Titles 1,378; Per Subs 138
Subject Interests: Hospital admin, Med, Nursing, Surgery
Automation Activity & Vendor Info: (Cataloging) Mandarin Library Automation
Wireless access
Function: Health sci info serv
Partic in Basic Health Sciences Library Network; Greater NE Regional Med Libr Program; Health Info Librs of Westchester; National Network of Libraries of Medicine Region 7; Southeastern New York Library Resources Council
Restriction: Staff use only

P KINGSTON LIBRARY, 55 Franklin St, 12401. SAN 311-3957. Tel: 845-331-0507. Administration Tel: 845-339-4260. FAX: 845-331-7981. E-mail: circulation@kingstonlibrary.org. Web Site: www.kingstonlibrary.org. *Dir,* Margie Menard; Tel: 845-339-4260, Ext 14, E-mail: director@kingstonlibrary.org; *Circ Mgr,* L J Cormier; *Ch Serv,* Stephanie Morgan; *Tech Serv,* Mary Lou Decker; Staff 4 (MLS 2, Non-MLS 2)
Founded 1899. Pop 23,893; Circ 94,253
Library Holdings: Audiobooks 4,150; AV Mats 6,587; CDs 1,995; DVDs 5,845; Electronic Media & Resources 15,200; Bk Titles 71,617; Bk Vols 90,201; Per Subs 60
Special Collections: Local Newspapers 1820-Present, micro
Automation Activity & Vendor Info: (Cataloging) Innovative Interfaces, Inc; (Circulation) Innovative Interfaces, Inc; (OPAC) Innovative Interfaces, Inc
Wireless access
Mem of Mid-Hudson Library System
Partic in Southeastern New York Library Resources Council
Open Mon, Tues, Thurs & Fri 10-6, Wed 12-8, Sat 9-5
Friends of the Library Group

G NEW YORK STATE OFFICE OF PARKS RECREATION & HISTORIC, Senate House State Historic Site, 312 Fair St, 12401. (Mail add: 296 Fair St, 12401-3836), SAN 311-3973. Tel: 845-338-2786. FAX: 845-334-8173. Web Site: parks.ny.gov/. *Library Contact,* Deana Preston; E-mail: deana.preston@parks.ny.gov
Founded 1927
Library Holdings: Bk Titles 700; Bk Vols 1,200
Special Collections: DeWitt Family Correspondence, ms; Ulster County Coll, doc; Van Gaasbeek Family Papers, ms; Vanderlyn Correspondence, ms
Subject Interests: NY from 17th through mid-20th centuries
Wireless access
Restriction: Open by appt only
Friends of the Library Group

GL NEW YORK STATE SUPREME COURT THIRD JUDICIAL DISTRICT, Ulster County Law Library, Hon John L Larkin Memorial Law Library, Ulster County Courthouse, 285 Wall St, 12401. SAN 311-3981. Tel: 845-481-9391. FAX: 845-340-3773. E-mail: ulsterlawlibrary@nycourts.gov. Web Site: www.nycourts.gov/courts/3jd/ulster/3JD-Ulster%20Courty%20Law%20Library.shtml. *Librn,* Charles Redmond
Library Holdings: Bk Vols 17,000
Wireless access
Open Mon-Fri 9-4:45

P TOWN OF ULSTER PUBLIC LIBRARY*, 860 Ulster Ave, 12401. SAN 312-5726. Tel: 845-338-7881. FAX: 845-338-7884. Web Site: townofulsterlibrary.org. *Dir,* Tracy Priest; E-mail: director@townofulsterlibrary.org; Staff 7 (MLS 1, Non-MLS 6)
Founded 1962
Library Holdings: Bk Titles 43,000; Bk Vols 44,000; Per Subs 57
Subject Interests: Local hist
Automation Activity & Vendor Info: (Cataloging) Innovative Interfaces, Inc; (Circulation) Innovative Interfaces, Inc; (OPAC) Innovative Interfaces, Inc
Wireless access
Publications: Quarterly newsletter
Mem of Mid-Hudson Library System
Open Mon, Wed & Fri 10-5, Tues & Thurs 12-8, Sat 10-3
Friends of the Library Group

G ULSTER COUNTY PLANNING BOARD LIBRARY*, County Office Bldg, 3rd Flr, 244 Fair St, 12402. SAN 327-6996. Tel: 845-340-3340. FAX: 845-340-3429. E-mail: planning@co.ulster.ny.us. Web Site: ulstercountyny.gov/planning. *Dir,* Dennis Doyle
Library Holdings: Bk Vols 120
Wireless access
Open Mon-Fri 9-5
Restriction: Open to pub for ref only

LA FARGEVILLE

P ORLEANS PUBLIC LIBRARY*, 36263 SR 180, 13656. (Mail add: PO Box 139, 13656-0139), SAN 311-399X. Tel: 315-658-2271. FAX: 315-658-2703. E-mail: laflib@ncls.org. Web Site: lafargevillelibrary.org. *Dir,* Stacy Snyder-Morse
Founded 1942. Circ 9,200
Library Holdings: Bk Vols 7,000; Per Subs 12
Wireless access
Mem of North Country Library System
Open Mon, Wed & Thurs 8:30-4:30, Tues 6-8, Sat 9am-11am

LACKAWANNA

P LACKAWANNA PUBLIC LIBRARY*, 560 Ridge Rd, 14218. SAN 311-4007. Tel: 716-823-0630. FAX: 716-827-1997. E-mail: lcw@buffalolib.org. Web Site: www.buffalolib.org/content/library-locations/lackawanna. *Dir,* Jennifer Johnston
Founded 1922. Pop 19,064; Circ 63,294
Library Holdings: AV Mats 4,982; Bk Vols 30,153; Per Subs 62
Subject Interests: Local hist
Wireless access
Mem of Buffalo & Erie County Public Library System
Special Services for the Blind - Talking bks
Open Mon & Wed (Summer) 12-8, Tues & Thurs 10-8, Fri 10-4; Mon & Wed (Winter) 12-8, Tues & Thurs 10-8, Sat 10-4
Friends of the Library Group

LAFAYETTE

P LAFAYETTE PUBLIC LIBRARY*, Town Commons, 2577 Rte 11 N, 13084. (Mail add: PO Box 379, 13084), SAN 311-4015. Tel: 315-677-3782. FAX: 315-677-0211. E-mail: lfstaff@onlib.org. Web Site: www.lafayettelibrary.org. *Libr Dir,* Scott Kushner; Staff 1 (MLS 1)
Pop 5,105; Circ 52,320
Library Holdings: Bk Vols 22,524; Per Subs 80
Automation Activity & Vendor Info: (Cataloging) Innovative Interfaces, Inc; (Circulation) Innovative Interfaces, Inc; (OPAC) Innovative Interfaces, Inc
Wireless access
Mem of Onondaga County Public Libraries
Open Mon, Tues & Thurs 10-6:30, Wed & Fri 10-4:30, Sat (Sept-May) 10-2

LAGRANGEVILLE

P LA GRANGE ASSOCIATION LIBRARY, 1110 Route 55, 2nd Flr, 12540. SAN 376-5849. Tel: 845-452-3141. FAX: 845-452-1974. E-mail: lagrangelibrary@laglib.org. Web Site: www.laglib.org. *Libr Dir,* Mary De Bellis; E-mail: mdebellis@laglib.org; *Head, Circ,* Lisa Sassi; E-mail: lsassi@laglib.org; *Teen & Adult Librn,* Anna Areson; E-mail: aareson@laglib.org; *Prog Asst,* Danielle Haight-Mueller; E-mail: dhaightmueller@laglib.org; *Webmaster,* Sherri Smith; E-mail: ssmith@laglib.org; *Youth Programmer,* Mary Wickham; E-mail: mwickham@laglib.org; Staff 6 (MLS 2, Non-MLS 4)
Founded 1983
Library Holdings: Bk Vols 77,000
Automation Activity & Vendor Info: (Acquisitions) Baker & Taylor; (Cataloging) Innovative Interfaces, Inc; (Circulation) Innovative Interfaces, Inc; (OPAC) Innovative Interfaces, Inc; (Serials) Innovative Interfaces, Inc
Wireless access
Function: 24/7 Electronic res, 24/7 Online cat, Activity rm, Adult bk club, After school storytime, Audiobks via web, Bk club(s), Bks on CD, Children's prog, Computers for patron use, Digital talking bks, Electronic databases & coll, Free DVD rentals, Homebound delivery serv, ILL available, Internet access, Life-long learning prog for all ages, Magazines, Mail & tel request accepted, Mango lang, Meeting rooms, Movies, Museum passes, Music CDs, Notary serv, Online cat, OverDrive digital audio bks, Passport agency, Photocopying/Printing, Preschool outreach, Preschool reading prog, Prog for adults, Prog for children & young adult, Ref serv available, Res assist avail, Senior outreach, Serves people with intellectual disabilities, STEM programs, Story hour, Summer reading prog, Tax forms, Teen prog, Telephone ref, Wheelchair accessible
Mem of Mid-Hudson Library System
Open Mon & Wed 9:30-8, Tues & Thurs 9:30-5, Fri 2-8, Sat 9:30-2
Friends of the Library Group

LAKE GEORGE

P CALDWELL-LAKE GEORGE LIBRARY*, 336 Canada St, 12845-1118. SAN 325-5824. Tel: 518-668-2528. FAX: 518-668-2528. *Libr Dir,* Barbara Durkish; E-mail: bdurkish@sals.edu; *Interim Dir,* Laura Burrows; E-mail: lburrows@sals.edu; *Asst Librn,* Matt Nelson; Staff 2 (Non-MLS 2)
Founded 1906. Pop 3,578
Library Holdings: Bk Vols 17,000; Per Subs 17
Automation Activity & Vendor Info: (Cataloging) Innovative Interfaces, Inc; (Circulation) Innovative Interfaces, Inc; (ILL) Innovative Interfaces, Inc; (OPAC) Innovative Interfaces, Inc; (Serials) Innovative Interfaces, Inc
Wireless access
Mem of Southern Adirondack Library System
Open Mon, Tues, Thurs & Fri 10-5, Wed 10-8, Sat 10-2
Friends of the Library Group

LAKE LUZERNE

P HADLEY-LUZERNE PUBLIC LIBRARY*, 19 Main St, 12846. (Mail add: PO Box 400, 12846-0400), SAN 311-4058. Tel: 518-696-3423. FAX: 518-696-4263. E-mail: luz-director@sals.edu. Web Site: hadluz.sals.edu. *Dir,* Courtney A Keir; E-mail: ckeir@sals.edu; Staff 3 (MLS 1, Non-MLS 2)
Founded 1969. Pop 4,444; Circ 23,725
Library Holdings: High Interest/Low Vocabulary Bk Vols 200; Bk Vols 17,487; Per Subs 24; Spec Interest Per Sub 24
Automation Activity & Vendor Info: (Acquisitions) Innovative Interfaces, Inc; (Cataloging) Innovative Interfaces, Inc; (Circulation) Innovative Interfaces, Inc; (ILL) Innovative Interfaces, Inc
Wireless access
Function: 24/7 Electronic res, 24/7 Online cat, Audiobks on Playaways & MP3, Audiobks via web, Bk club(s), Doc delivery serv, Electronic databases & coll, Holiday prog, ILL available, Internet access, Magazines, Meeting rooms, Music CDs, Online cat, Online ref, Photocopying/Printing, Ref & res, Ref serv available, Summer reading prog, Telephone ref, Wheelchair accessible
Mem of Southern Adirondack Library System
Partic in Capital District Library Council
Special Services for the Blind - Bks on cassette; Videos on blindness & physical disabilties
Open Wed & Fri 9-4, Tues & Thurs 9-7, Sat 9-2

LAKE PLACID

P LAKE PLACID PUBLIC LIBRARY*, 2471 Main St, 12946. SAN 311-4074. Tel: 518-523-3200. FAX: 518-523-3200. E-mail: librarian@lakeplacidlibrary.org. Web Site: www.lakeplacidlibrary.org. *Dir,* Bambi Pedu; *Asst Librn,* Linda Blair
Pop 5,000; Circ 28,884
Library Holdings: Bk Vols 24,000; Per Subs 30
Special Collections: Adirondack, Olympic Coll; Lake Placid Club Archives
Subject Interests: Local hist
Automation Activity & Vendor Info: (Cataloging) Horizon; (Circulation) Horizon; (OPAC) Horizon
Wireless access
Mem of Clinton-Essex-Franklin Library System
Open Mon, Wed & Fri 10-5:30, Tues & Thurs 10-7, Sat 10-4

LAKE PLEASANT

P TOWN OF LAKE PLEASANT PUBLIC LIBRARY*, 2864 State Hwy 8, 12108. Tel: 518-548-4411. FAX: 518-548-8395. Web Site: lakepleasantlibrary.sals.edu. *Dir,* Sherry Matthews; E-mail: Smatthews@sals.edu
Library Holdings: Bk Vols 14,000
Automation Activity & Vendor Info: (Acquisitions) Innovative Interfaces, Inc; (Cataloging) Innovative Interfaces, Inc; (Circulation) Innovative Interfaces, Inc; (Course Reserve) Innovative Interfaces, Inc; (ILL) Innovative Interfaces, Inc; (Media Booking) Innovative Interfaces, Inc; (OPAC) Innovative Interfaces, Inc; (Serials) Innovative Interfaces, Inc
Wireless access
Mem of Southern Adirondack Library System
Open Mon, Wed & Fri 1-4 & 7-9, Tues, Thurs & Sat 10-2

LAKEWOOD

P LAKEWOOD MEMORIAL LIBRARY*, 12 W Summit St, 14750. SAN 311-4120. Tel: 716-763-6234. FAX: 716-763-3624. Web Site: www.lakewoodlibrary.org. *Libr Dir,* Mary Miller; E-mail: director@lakewoodlibrary.org; Staff 1 (MLS 1)
Founded 1960. Pop 7,351; Circ 30,647
Library Holdings: Audiobooks 458; Electronic Media & Resources 13,756; Bk Vols 28,923; Per Subs 35; Videos 2,852
Subject Interests: Local hist
Automation Activity & Vendor Info: (Cataloging) SirsiDynix; (Circulation) SirsiDynix; (OPAC) SirsiDynix
Wireless access
Function: 24/7 Online cat, Activity rm, Adult bk club, Art exhibits, Audiobks via web, Bk club(s), Bks on CD, Children's prog, Computer training, Computers for patron use, E-Reserves, Electronic databases & coll, Free DVD rentals, Homebound delivery serv, ILL available, Internet access, Magazines, Mail & tel request accepted, Meeting rooms, Movies, Museum passes, Online cat, Outreach serv, Outside serv via phone, mail, e-mail & web, OverDrive digital audio bks, Photocopying/Printing, Preschool outreach, Preschool reading prog, Prog for adults, Prog for children & young adult, Ref & res, Ref serv available, Scanner, Senior computer classes, Senior outreach, Serves people with intellectual disabilities, Spoken cassettes & CDs, Spoken cassettes & DVDs, STEM programs, Story hour, Summer & winter reading prog, Summer reading prog, Teen prog, Telephone ref, Wheelchair accessible, Winter reading prog, Workshops
Mem of Chautauqua-Cattaraugus Library System
Partic in New York Online Virtual Electronic Library
Open Mon, Wed & Fri 9:30-5, Tues & Thurs 9:30-7, Sat 9:30-1

LANCASTER

P LANCASTER PUBLIC LIBRARY, 5466 Broadway, 14086. SAN 352-8006. Tel: 716-683-1120. FAX: 716-686-0749. E-mail: LNC@buffalolib.org. Web Site: www.buffalolib.org/locations-hours/lancaster-public-library. *Dir,* Kara Stock; *Youth Serv Librn,* Meagan Carr; Staff 2 (MLS 2)
Founded 1821. Pop 41,604; Circ 145,013
Library Holdings: Bk Vols 58,900; Per Subs 103
Special Collections: Local History; Parenting Resource Center
Wireless access
Function: 24/7 Electronic res, 24/7 Online cat, Activity rm, Adult bk club, Adult literacy prog, After school storytime, Archival coll, Art exhibits, Audiobks via web, Bk club(s), Bks on CD, CD-ROM, Chess club, Children's prog, Computer training, Computers for patron use, Digital talking bks, E-Readers, Electronic databases & coll, For res purposes, Free DVD rentals, Holiday prog, Home delivery & serv to seniorr ctr & nursing

homes, Homebound delivery serv, ILL available, Internet access, Magazines, Magnifiers for reading, Mail & tel request accepted, Meeting rooms, Movies, Music CDs, Notary serv, Online cat, Outreach serv, OverDrive digital audio bks, Photocopying/Printing, Preschool reading prog, Prog for adults, Prog for children & young adult, Ref & res, Scanner, Senior computer classes, Serves people with intellectual disabilities, Story hour, Summer reading prog, Tax forms, Teen prog, Telephone ref, Wheelchair accessible, Workshops
Mem of Buffalo & Erie County Public Library System
Partic in LYRASIS
Open Mon 10-6, Tues-Thurs 10-9, Fri & Sat 10-5, Sun (Sept-May) 12-5
Friends of the Library Group

LANSING

P LANSING COMMUNITY LIBRARY*, 27 Auburn Rd, 14882. Tel: 607-533-4939. FAX: 607-533-7196. E-mail: libadmin@lansinglibrary.org. Web Site: www.lansinglibrary.org. *Libr Dir,* Susie Gutenberger; E-mail: manager@lansinglibrary.org
Founded 2001
Library Holdings: Bk Titles 12,000
Automation Activity & Vendor Info: (Cataloging) Innovative Interfaces, Inc; (Circulation) Innovative Interfaces, Inc
Wireless access
Mem of Finger Lakes Library System
Open Mon-Wed 10-8, Thurs 10-6, Fri & Sat 10-2
Friends of the Library Group

LARCHMONT

P LARCHMONT PUBLIC LIBRARY*, 121 Larchmont Ave, 10538. SAN 311-4139. Tel: 914-834-2281. Web Site: www.larchmontlibrary.org. *Libr Dir,* Laura Eckley; E-mail: leckley@wlsmail.org; *Head, Ref,* William Hegarty; E-mail: whegarty@wlsmail.org; *Head, Youth Serv,* Rebecca Teglas; E-mail: rteglas@wlsmail.org; *Ch,* Linnea Moosmann; E-mail: lmoosmann@wlsmail.org; *Programming Librn,* June Hesler; E-mail: jhesler@wlsmail.org; *Ref Librn,* Frank Connelly; E-mail: fconnelly@wlsmail.org; *Ref Librn,* Paul Doherty; E-mail: pdoherty@wlsmail.org; *Ref Librn,* Alexandra Gaete Naceda; E-mail: agaete@wlsmail.org; *Teen Librn,* Kim Larsen; E-mail: klarsen@wlsmail.org; Staff 19.9 (MLS 7.5, Non-MLS 12.4)
Founded 1926. Pop 17,670; Circ 357,889
Jun 2019-May 2020 Income $2,366,336, State $5,125, City $2,245,311, Locally Generated Income $57,889. Mats Exp $147,500. Sal $1,238,000
Library Holdings: Audiobooks 7,914; DVDs 7,943; Large Print Bks 1,583; Bk Titles 92,000; Per Subs 126
Subject Interests: Local hist
Automation Activity & Vendor Info: (Acquisitions) Evergreen; (Cataloging) Evergreen; (Circulation) Evergreen; (ILL) Evergreen; (OPAC) Evergreen
Wireless access
Function: 24/7 Electronic res, 24/7 Online cat, Activity rm, Adult bk club, After school storytime, Archival coll, Art exhibits, Art programs, Audiobks on Playaways & MP3, Audiobks via web, Bk club(s), Bks on CD, Butterfly Garden, CD-ROM, Chess club, Children's prog, Computer training, Computers for patron use, Digital talking bks, Electronic databases & coll, Free DVD rentals, Genealogy discussion group, Holiday prog, Homebound delivery serv, ILL available, Internet access, Life-long learning prog for all ages, Magazines, Meeting rooms, Movies, Museum passes, Music CDs, Notary serv, Online cat, Online ref, Outreach serv, OverDrive digital audio bks, Photocopying/Printing, Preschool outreach, Printer for laptops & handheld devices, Prog for adults, Prog for children & young adult, Ref serv available, Scanner, STEM programs, Story hour, Study rm, Summer & winter reading prog, Summer reading prog, Tax forms, Teen prog, Telephone ref, Visual arts prog, Wheelchair accessible, Winter reading prog, Workshops, Writing prog
Publications: Friends of Larchmont Public Library (Newsletter)
Mem of Westchester Library System
Special Services for the Blind - Assistive/Adapted tech devices, equip & products
Open Mon & Thurs 9-9, Tues & Wed 9-6, Fri & Sat 9-5, Sun (Sept-June) 12-5
Friends of the Library Group

LAWRENCE

P PENINSULA PUBLIC LIBRARY, 280 Central Ave, 11559. SAN 311-4155. Tel: 516-239-3262. FAX: 516-239-3769. E-mail: ppl@peninsulapublic.org. Web Site: peninsulapublic.org. *Dir,* Carolynn Matulewicz; Tel: 516-239-3262, Ext 214, E-mail: ppldirector@nassaulibrary.org; *Asst Dir,* Rhonda Todtman; *Prog Coordr,* Janet Schneider; Tel: 516-239-3262, Ext 216, E-mail: programming@peninsulapublic.org; Staff 24 (MLS 10, Non-MLS 14)
Founded 1951. Pop 33,988; Circ 81,846
Library Holdings: Bk Titles 105,300; Bk Vols 126,050; Per Subs 900
Special Collections: Judaica Coll
Automation Activity & Vendor Info: (Circulation) Innovative Interfaces, Inc - Millennium; (OPAC) Innovative Interfaces, Inc - Millennium
Wireless access
Publications: Peninsula Public Library Newsletter (Quarterly)
Mem of Nassau Library System
Open Mon-Thurs 9-9, Fri & Sat 9-5, Sun 12-5 (Winter); Mon-Thurs 9-9, Fri 9-5, Sat & Sun 9-1 (Summer)

LEROY

S LEROY HISTORICAL SOCIETY LIBRARY*, 23 E Main St, 14482-1210. (Mail add: PO Box 176, 14482-0176), SAN 327-7011. Tel: 585-768-7433. FAX: 585-768-7579. Web Site: www.leroyhistoricalsociety.org. *Dir,* Lynne Belluscio; E-mail: jellodirector@frontiernet.net
Founded 1940
Library Holdings: Bk Vols 4,000
Special Collections: Ingham University Archives; Lampson Papers
Subject Interests: Genealogy
Open Mon-Sat 10-4, Sun 1-4

P WOODWARD MEMORIAL LIBRARY*, Seven Wolcott St, 14482. SAN 311-4198. Tel: 585-768-8300. FAX: 585-768-4768. E-mail: wmlib@nioga.org. Web Site: www.woodwardmemoriallibrary.org. *Dir,* Sue Border; E-mail: sbord@nioga.org; *Children's & YA Librn,* Elisabeth Halvorsen; Staff 3 (MLS 3)
Library Holdings: Bk Vols 43,000
Special Collections: Literature (Woodward Coll)
Automation Activity & Vendor Info: (Cataloging) SirsiDynix; (Circulation) SirsiDynix; (OPAC) SirsiDynix; (Serials) SirsiDynix
Wireless access
Mem of Nioga Library System
Open Mon-Thurs (Winter) 9-8:30, Fri 9-5, Sat 10-4; Mon-Thurs (Summer) 10-8:30, Fri 10-5, Sat 10-4
Friends of the Library Group

LEVITTOWN

P ISLAND TREES PUBLIC LIBRARY, 38 Farmedge Rd, 11756. SAN 311-4201. Tel: 516-731-2211. FAX: 516-731-2395, 516-731-3798. Web Site: www.islandtreespubliclibrary.org. *Libr Dir,* Michelle Young; E-mail: islandtreesdirector@gmail.com; *Head, Ch, Head, Circ,* Elizabeth Spoto; E-mail: lspoto@islandtreespubliclibrary.org; *Adult Programs, Head Ref Librn,* Marilyn Adamo; E-mail: madamo@islandtreespubliclibrary.org
Founded 1967. Pop 16,000; Circ 62,304
Library Holdings: Bk Titles 42,646; Per Subs 113
Automation Activity & Vendor Info: (Cataloging) Innovative Interfaces, Inc; (Circulation) Innovative Interfaces, Inc; (OPAC) Innovative Interfaces, Inc
Wireless access
Publications: Island Trees Newsletter (Bimonthly)
Mem of Nassau Library System
Open Mon-Fri 10-5, Sat 10-2

P LEVITTOWN PUBLIC LIBRARY, One Bluegrass Lane, 11756-1292. SAN 311-421X. Tel: 516-731-5728. FAX: 516-735-3168, Administration FAX: 516-520-5745. E-mail: levtown@nassaulibrary.org. Web Site: www.levittownpl.org. *Dir,* Trina Reed; *Asst Dir,* Maryann Ferro; Staff 57 (MLS 17, Non-MLS 40)
Founded 1950. Pop 47,552; Circ 370,500
Library Holdings: CDs 17,502; e-books 429; Electronic Media & Resources 24,948; Bk Vols 243,014; Per Subs 660; Videos 10,031
Special Collections: Oral History
Subject Interests: Local hist, Natural sci
Automation Activity & Vendor Info: (Acquisitions) Innovative Interfaces, Inc; (Cataloging) Innovative Interfaces, Inc; (Circulation) Innovative Interfaces, Inc; (Course Reserve) Innovative Interfaces, Inc; (ILL) Innovative Interfaces, Inc; (Media Booking) Innovative Interfaces, Inc; (OPAC) Innovative Interfaces, Inc; (Serials) Innovative Interfaces, Inc
Wireless access
Publications: Directory of Community Organizations; Going On: Calendar of Events
Mem of Nassau Library System
Special Services for the Deaf - TDD equip; TTY equip
Open Mon-Fri 9-9, Sat 9-5, Sun (Oct-July) 1-5

LEWISTON

P LEWISTON PUBLIC LIBRARY*, 305 S Eighth St, 14092. SAN 311-4228. Tel: 716-754-4720. FAX: 716-754-7386. E-mail: lewlib@nioga.org. Web Site: www.lewistonpubliclibrary.org. *Dir,* Jill C Palermo; E-mail: jpale@nioga.org; Staff 1 (MLS 1)
Founded 1902. Pop 13,458; Circ 109,988
Library Holdings: Audiobooks 1,301; CDs 2,394; DVDs 1,945; Large Print Bks 1,712; Bk Titles 65,212; Per Subs 91; Videos 539

Special Collections: Early Lewiston Houses (Bjorne Klaussen Coll), original acrylic & oil paintings; Old Village History. Oral History
Automation Activity & Vendor Info: (Circulation) SirsiDynix-WorkFlows; (OPAC) SirsiDynix-WorkFlows
Wireless access
Function: Children's prog, Computer training, Computers for patron use, ILL available, Online cat, Ref serv available
Publications: Lewiston - A Self-Guided Tour
Open Mon, Wed & Fri 1-5, Tues 3-7, Thurs 10-2
Friends of the Library Group

LIBERTY

P LIBERTY PUBLIC LIBRARY, 189 N Main St, 12754-1828. Tel: 845-292-6070. FAX: 845-292-5609. E-mail: lib@rcls.org. Web Site: www.libertypubliclibrary.org. *Dir,* Marjorie Linko; Staff 1 (MLS 1)
Founded 1894. Pop 10,483
Library Holdings: AV Mats 1,135; Bk Titles 20,792; Per Subs 21
Automation Activity & Vendor Info: (Cataloging) SirsiDynix; (Circulation) SirsiDynix; (ILL) SirsiDynix; (OPAC) SirsiDynix; (Serials) SirsiDynix
Wireless access
Mem of Ramapo Catskill Library System
Open Mon, Wed & Fri 10-5, Tues & Thurs 10-6:30, Sat 10-4
Friends of the Library Group

LIMA

P LIMA PUBLIC LIBRARY*, 1872 Genesee St, 14485. (Mail add: PO Box 58A, 14485-0858), SAN 311-4244. Tel: 585-582-1311. FAX: 585-582-1701. Web Site: www.lima.pls-net.org. *Dir,* Megan McLaughlin; E-mail: limalibrarydirector@owwl.org; Staff 2 (Non-MLS 2)
Founded 1910. Pop 4,541
Library Holdings: Bk Vols 29,000
Special Collections: Local History, articles, bks, pamphlets
Automation Activity & Vendor Info: (Acquisitions) Evergreen; (Cataloging) Evergreen; (Circulation) Evergreen; (Course Reserve) Evergreen; (ILL) Evergreen; (Media Booking) Evergreen; (OPAC) Evergreen; (Serials) Evergreen
Wireless access
Mem of Pioneer Library System
Partic in OhioNET
Open Mon, Tues & Thurs 1-8:30, Wed 10-12 & 1-5, Fri 1-5, Sat 9-Noon
Friends of the Library Group

LINDENHURST

P LINDENHURST MEMORIAL LIBRARY*, One Lee Ave, 11757-5399. SAN 311-4252. Tel: 631-957-7755. FAX: 631-957-7114. Reference FAX: 631-957-0993. E-mail: info@lindenhurstlibrary.org. Web Site: www.lindenhurstlibrary.org. *Dir,* Lisa Kropp; E-mail: lkropp@lindenhurstlibrary.org; *Computer Serv Librn,* Craig Pullen; *AV,* Peter Muhr; *Cat, Coll Develop, Ref (Info Servs),* Eileen Feynman; *Ch Serv,* Andrea Malchiodi; E-mail: amalchiodi@lindenhurstlibrary.org; *Circ,* Paula Bornstein; *YA Serv,* Amanda Lotito; Staff 13 (MLS 13)
Founded 1946. Pop 42,597; Circ 408,896
Library Holdings: AV Mats 28,795; CDs 5,239; DVDs 16,939; Bk Vols 231,058; Per Subs 520
Special Collections: History of Lindenhurst
Automation Activity & Vendor Info: (Acquisitions) Innovative Interfaces, Inc; (Cataloging) Innovative Interfaces, Inc; (Circulation) Innovative Interfaces, Inc; (OPAC) Innovative Interfaces, Inc; (Serials) Innovative Interfaces, Inc
Wireless access
Publications: Newsletter
Mem of Suffolk Cooperative Library System
Partic in Partnership of Automated Librs in Suffolk
Special Services for the Deaf - Bks on deafness & sign lang
Open Mon-Thurs 9-9, Fri 9-6, Sat 9-5, Sun 1-5

LISBON

P HEPBURN LIBRARY OF LISBON, 6899 County Rte 10, 13658-4242. SAN 311-4260. Tel: 315-393-0111. FAX: 315-393-0111. E-mail: lislib@ncls.org. Web Site: www.hepburnlibraryoflisbon.org. *Dir,* Michelle A McLagan; Staff 1 (Non-MLS 1)
Founded 1920. Pop 4,102
Library Holdings: DVDs 2,200; Bk Vols 20,000; Per Subs 50
Wireless access
Function: 24/7 Electronic res, 24/7 Online cat, Accelerated reader prog, Activity rm, Adult bk club, After school storytime, Art programs, Audiobks via web, Bk club(s), Bks on CD, Children's prog, Computers for patron use, Digital talking bks, Electronic databases & coll, Family literacy, Free DVD rentals, Holiday prog, Home delivery & serv to seniorr ctr & nursing homes, Homebound delivery serv, ILL available, Internet access, Laminating, Magazines, Mail & tel request accepted, Makerspace, Meeting rooms, Movies, Museum passes, Online cat, Online ref, Outreach serv, OverDrive digital audio bks, Photocopying/Printing, Preschool reading prog, Prog for adults, Prog for children & young adult, Scanner, STEM programs, Story hour, Study rm, Summer & winter reading prog, Summer reading prog, Teen prog, Visual arts prog, Wheelchair accessible, Winter reading prog, Workshops
Mem of North Country Library System
Open Mon, Tues & Thurs 3-8, Wed & Fri 9-5

LISLE

P LISLE FREE LIBRARY, 8998 Main St, 13797. (Mail add: PO Box 305, 13797-0305), SAN 311-4279. Tel: 607-692-3115. FAX: 607-692-3115. E-mail: lislefreelibrary@gmail.com. Web Site: libraries.4cls.org/lisle. *Dir,* Cheridan Douglas
Founded 1922. Pop 2,707
Library Holdings: Bk Vols 12,000; Per Subs 34
Wireless access
Mem of Four County Library System
Open Mon-Fri 11-7, Sat 9-1

LITTLE FALLS

P LITTLE FALLS PUBLIC LIBRARY*, Ten Waverly Pl, 13365. SAN 311-4287. Tel: 315-823-1542. FAX: 315-823-2995. E-mail: littlefalls@midyork.org. Web Site: www.lflibrary.org. *Libr Dir,* Anne Nassar; E-mail: anassar@midyork.org
Founded 1911. Pop 5,929; Circ 88,572
Library Holdings: Bk Titles 25,285; Per Subs 75
Wireless access
Mem of Mid-York Library System
Open Mon-Thurs 9-8, Fri 9-5, Sat (Sept-June) 10-3

LITTLE GENESEE

P GENESEE LIBRARY*, 8351 State Rte 417, 14754. Tel: 585-928-1915. FAX: 585-928-1915. E-mail: geneseelibrary@gmail.com. Web Site: genesee.stls.org. *Libr Dir,* Raeanne Smith
Founded 1908. Circ 1,440
Library Holdings: Bk Vols 5,000
Wireless access
Function: 24/7 Electronic res, 24/7 Online cat, Activity rm, Adult literacy prog, After school storytime, Art programs, Audio & video playback equip for onsite use, Audiobks via web, Bks on CD, Children's prog, Computer training, Computers for patron use, Digital talking bks, Electronic databases & coll, For res purposes, Free DVD rentals, Holiday prog, Homework prog, ILL available, Internet access, Life-long learning prog for all ages, Literacy & newcomer serv, Magazines, Makerspace, Meeting rooms, Movies, OverDrive digital audio bks, Photocopying/Printing, Printer for laptops & handheld devices, Prog for adults, Prog for children & young adult, Ref serv available, Scanner, Senior computer classes, Senior outreach, Spoken cassettes & CDs, STEM programs, Story hour, Summer & winter reading prog, Summer reading prog, Teen prog
Mem of Southern Tier Library System

LITTLE VALLEY

P MEMORIAL LIBRARY OF LITTLE VALLEY*, 110 Rock City St, 14755. SAN 311-4309. Tel: 716-938-6301. FAX: 716-938-6301. E-mail: memliblv@atlanticbb.net. Web Site: littlevalleyny.com/memorial_library_of_little_valley.html. *Dir,* Linda McCubbin; E-mail: director@littlevalleylibrary.org; Staff 1 (Non-MLS 1)
Founded 1923. Pop 1,830; Circ 12,750
Library Holdings: Bk Vols 18,000; Per Subs 42
Subject Interests: Local hist
Wireless access
Function: BA reader (adult literacy), Computers for patron use, Homebound delivery serv, Music CDs, Photocopying/Printing, Preschool outreach, Serves people with intellectual disabilities, Spoken cassettes & CDs, Spoken cassettes & DVDs, VHS videos, Wheelchair accessible, Workshops
Mem of Chautauqua-Cattaraugus Library System
Open Mon, Tues & Thurs 10-8, Fri 10-5, Sat (Sept-June) 10-12
Friends of the Library Group

LIVERPOOL

P LIVERPOOL PUBLIC LIBRARY*, 310 Tulip St, 13088-4997. SAN 311-4317. Tel: 315-457-0310. FAX: 313-457-3144. E-mail: info@LPL.org. Web Site: www.lpl.org. *Dir,* Glenna W Wisniewski; E-mail: glenna.wisniewski@lpl.org; *Asst Dir,* Susan Reckhow; *Bus Mgr,* Sheila Smith; *Communications Coordr,* Diane Towlson; *Childrens & Family Services,* Joellyn Murry; *Circ Serv,* Margaret Sanchez; *Info Tech,* Heather Highfield; Staff 20 (MLS 16, Non-MLS 4)
Founded 1893. Pop 55,000; Circ 507,395
Library Holdings: AV Mats 21,470; Bk Vols 103,145; Per Subs 340

Special Collections: Local History Video Coll
Subject Interests: Local hist
Automation Activity & Vendor Info: (Cataloging) Innovative Interfaces, Inc; (Circulation) Innovative Interfaces, Inc; (Course Reserve) Innovative Interfaces, Inc; (ILL) Innovative Interfaces, Inc; (Media Booking) Innovative Interfaces, Inc; (OPAC) Innovative Interfaces, Inc; (Serials) Innovative Interfaces, Inc
Wireless access
Mem of Onondaga County Public Libraries
Open Mon-Thurs 9-9, Fri 9-6, Sat 10-5, Sun Noon-5
Friends of the Library Group

LIVINGSTON

P LIVINGSTON FREE LIBRARY*, 90 Old Post Rd, 12541. (Mail add: PO Box 105, 12541-0105), SAN 311-4325. Tel: 518-851-2270. FAX: 518-851-2466. E-mail: livingstonlibrary105@gmail.com. Web Site: livingston.lib.ny.us. *Dir,* Wendy Tremper Wollerton
Founded 1906. Circ 1,460
Library Holdings: Bk Vols 2,900; Per Subs 15
Automation Activity & Vendor Info: (Cataloging) Innovative Interfaces, Inc; (Circulation) Innovative Interfaces, Inc; (OPAC) Innovative Interfaces, Inc
Wireless access
Mem of Mid-Hudson Library System
Open Mon & Wed 3-7, Fri 4-7, Sat 9-12

LIVINGSTON MANOR

P LIVINGSTON MANOR FREE LIBRARY, 92 Main St, 12758-5113. SAN 311-4333. Tel: 845-439-5440. FAX: 845-439-3141. E-mail: livcirc@rcls.org. Web Site: livingstonmanorlibrary.org. *Dir,* Stacey Tromblee
Founded 1938. Pop 3,450; Circ 14,732
Library Holdings: Bk Vols 12,087; Per Subs 138
Automation Activity & Vendor Info: (Cataloging) Horizon; (Circulation) Horizon; (OPAC) Horizon
Wireless access
Mem of Ramapo Catskill Library System
Open Mon, Tues & Fri 10-4, Wed & Thurs 10-5, Sat 10-1

LIVONIA

P LIVONIA PUBLIC LIBRARY*, Two Washington St, 14487. SAN 311-4341. Tel: 585-346-3450. FAX: 585-346-5911. E-mail: livonialibrary@owwl.org. Web Site: www.livonialibrary.org. *Dir,* Frank Sykes; E-mail: fsykes@pls-net.org; Staff 4 (MLS 1, Non-MLS 3)
Founded 1917. Pop 7,286; Circ 72,175
Library Holdings: AV Mats 2,251; Bk Vols 20,086; Per Subs 91; Talking Bks 1,671; Videos 1,235
Special Collections: Livonia Hist Coll
Subject Interests: Local hist
Automation Activity & Vendor Info: (Circulation) SirsiDynix; (ILL) SirsiDynix; (OPAC) SirsiDynix
Wireless access
Mem of Pioneer Library System
Partic in The Library Network
Open Mon-Thurs 1-8, Fri 10-6, Sat 10-3
Friends of the Library Group

LOCH SHELDRAKE

J SULLIVAN COUNTY COMMUNITY COLLEGE*, Hermann Memorial Library, 112 College Rd, 12759. SAN 311-435X. Tel: 845-434-5750, Ext 4226. E-mail: library@sunysullivan.edu. Web Site: sunysullivan.libguides.com/LibraryHome. *Tech Asst,* Aaron Smith; E-mail: asmith@sunysullivan.edu; Staff 3 (MLS 3)
Founded 1964. Enrl 980; Fac 60; Highest Degree: Associate
Library Holdings: e-books 140,000; Bk Vols 52,000; Per Subs 110; Videos 70
Subject Interests: Culinary arts, Graphic arts
Automation Activity & Vendor Info: (Cataloging) Ex Libris Group; (Circulation) Ex Libris Group; (Course Reserve) Ex Libris Group; (ILL) OCLC ILLiad; (OPAC) Ex Libris Group
Wireless access
Function: Accelerated reader prog
Publications: Newsletter; Subject Bibliographies
Partic in Southeastern New York Library Resources Council; SUNYConnect
Open Mon-Thurs 8:30-8:30, Fri 8:30-5, Sun 12-5

LOCKPORT

P LOCKPORT PUBLIC LIBRARY*, 23 East Ave, 14094. (Mail add: PO Box 475, 14095-0475), SAN 311-4376. Tel: 716-433-5935. FAX: 716-439-0198. Web Site: lockportlibrary.org. *Dir,* Beverly J Federspiel; E-mail: federspiel@nioga.org; Staff 15 (MLS 6, Non-MLS 9)
Founded 1897. Pop 37,071; Circ 419,917
Library Holdings: AV Mats 25,082; e-journals 5; Bk Vols 150,645; Per Subs 184
Special Collections: Freemasonry & Anti-Masonic, bks, micro
Automation Activity & Vendor Info: (Cataloging) SirsiDynix-WorkFlows; (Circulation) SirsiDynix-WorkFlows; (Course Reserve) SirsiDynix-WorkFlows; (OPAC) SirsiDynix-WorkFlows
Wireless access
Mem of Nioga Library System
Open Mon-Thurs 9-8, Fri 9-5, Sat 10-5
Friends of the Library Group

S NIAGARA COUNTY GENEALOGICAL SOCIETY LIBRARY*, 215 Niagara St, 14094-2605. SAN 326-131X. Tel: 716-433-1033. E-mail: comments@niagaragenealogy.org. Web Site: www.niagaragenealogy.org.
Jan 2017-Dec 2017 Income $15,000. Mats Exp $1,150, Books $400, Per/Ser (Incl. Access Fees) $400, Electronic Ref Mat (Incl. Access Fees) $350
Library Holdings: Bk Vols 1,450; Per Subs 10
Special Collections: Skinner Family Genealogies
Subject Interests: Genealogy, Local hist
Wireless access
Function: Res libr
Publications: Newsletter (Quarterly)
Open Thurs-Sat 1-5
Restriction: Non-circulating to the pub

P NIOGA LIBRARY SYSTEM*, 6575 Wheeler Rd, 14094. SAN 311-4384. Tel: 716-434-6167. FAX: 716-434-8231. Web Site: www.nioga.org, www.niogalibrary.org. *Syst Dir,* Thomas C Bindeman; Tel: 716-434-6167, Ext 24, E-mail: bindeman@nioga.org; *Outreach Serv Librn,* Lisa Erickson; Tel: 716-434-6167, Ext 33; *Syst Coordr,* Justin Genter; Tel: 716-434-6167, Ext 11, E-mail: jgent@nioga.org; *Cat,* Margaret Stein; Tel: 716-434-6167, Ext 18
Founded 1959
Automation Activity & Vendor Info: (Cataloging) SirsiDynix-WorkFlows; (Circulation) SirsiDynix-WorkFlows; (OPAC) SirsiDynix
Function: 24/7 Electronic res, 24/7 Online cat
Member Libraries: Barker Public Library; Byron-Bergen Public Library; Community Free Library; Corfu Free Library; Haxton Memorial Library; Hoag Library; Hollwedel Memorial Library; Lee-Whedon Memorial Library; Lockport Public Library; Newfane Public Library; Niagara Falls Public Library; North Tonawanda Public Library; Ransomville Free Library; Richmond Memorial Library; Royalton Hartland Community Library; Sanborn-Pekin Free Library; Wilson Community Library; Woodward Memorial Library; Yates Community Library; Youngstown Free Library
Partic in Association for Rural & Small Libraries; OCLC Online Computer Library Center, Inc; Western New York Library Resources Council

LOCUST VALLEY

P LOCUST VALLEY LIBRARY*, 170 Buckram Rd, 11560-1999. SAN 311-4392. Tel: 516-671-1837. FAX: 516-676-8164. E-mail: info@locustvalleylibrary.org. Web Site: www.locustvalleylibrary.org. *Dir,* Kathleen Ray Smith; E-mail: ksmith@locustvalleylibrary.org; *Head, Circ,* Kathy Jones; *Head, Youth Serv,* Leslie Armstrong; *Ref (Info Servs),* Jennifer Santo; Staff 6 (MLS 6)
Founded 1910. Pop 7,040; Circ 104,000
Library Holdings: Bk Vols 71,061; Per Subs 136
Special Collections: Parenting (Carol Tilliston Holmboe Coll)
Subject Interests: Local hist
Automation Activity & Vendor Info: (Acquisitions) Innovative Interfaces, Inc - Millennium; (Cataloging) Innovative Interfaces, Inc - Millennium; (Circulation) Innovative Interfaces, Inc - Millennium; (Course Reserve) Innovative Interfaces, Inc - Millennium; (ILL) Innovative Interfaces, Inc - Millennium; (Media Booking) Innovative Interfaces, Inc - Millennium; (OPAC) Innovative Interfaces, Inc - Millennium; (Serials) Innovative Interfaces, Inc - Millennium
Wireless access
Publications: Library Letter (Newsletter)
Mem of Nassau Library System
Open Mon-Thurs 9:15-9, Fri & Sat 9:15-5, Sun (Winter) 1-5
Friends of the Library Group

LODI

P ELIZABETH GARNSEY DELAVAN LIBRARY*, 8484 S Main St, 14860. (Mail add: PO Box 208, 14860), SAN 311-4406. Tel: 607-582-6218. FAX: 607-582-6219. Web Site: lodilibrary.net. *Dir,* Amy B May; E-mail: director@lodilibrary.net
Circ 3,035
Library Holdings: Bk Vols 10,000; Per Subs 24
Automation Activity & Vendor Info: (Circulation) Innovative Interfaces, Inc; (OPAC) Innovative Interfaces, Inc
Wireless access
Mem of Finger Lakes Library System
Open Tues & Sat 9-Noon, Wed 4-8, Thurs & Fri 1-6

LONG BEACH

P LONG BEACH PUBLIC LIBRARY*, 111 W Park Ave, 11561-3326. SAN 352-8065. Tel: 516-432-7201. Circulation Tel: 516-432-7201, Ext 224. Administration Tel: 516-432-7258. FAX: 516-889-4641. Administration FAX: 516-432-1477. E-mail: info@longbeachlibrary.org. Web Site: www.longbeachlibrary.org. *Dir,* Tara Lennen-Stanton; E-mail: director@longbeachlibrary.org; *Head, Prog,* Edie Kalickstein; E-mail: ekalickstein@longbeachlibrary.org; *Head, Youth Serv,* Jennifer Firth; E-mail: jfirth@longbeachlibrary.org; Staff 16 (MLS 12, Non-MLS 4)
Founded 1928. Pop 38,655; Circ 327,654
Jul 2012-Jun 2013 Income (Main & Associated Libraries) $3,366,868. Mats Exp $313,784, Books $171,320, Per/Ser (Incl. Access Fees) $16,772, Micro $494, AV Mat $89,845, Electronic Ref Mat (Incl. Access Fees) $35,353. Sal $1,747,535 (Prof $767,876)
Library Holdings: Audiobooks 2,298; AV Mats 38,264; CDs 13,611; DVDs 8,179; Microforms 56,604; Bk Titles 134,334; Bk Vols 172,410; Per Subs 160; Videos 3,374
Special Collections: Congressman Allard K Lowenstein Memorabilia Coll; Foreign Language (Spanish, Russian); Long Beach Historical Coll, bks, clippings, prints; Long Beach Photographs
Subject Interests: Holocaust, Local hist
Automation Activity & Vendor Info: (Acquisitions) Innovative Interfaces, Inc; (Cataloging) Innovative Interfaces, Inc; (Circulation) Innovative Interfaces, Inc; (OPAC) Innovative Interfaces, Inc
Wireless access
Publications: Channels Long Beach Public Library (Monthly newsletter); Senior Citizen Directory
Mem of Nassau Library System
Special Services for the Deaf - ADA equip; Adult & family literacy prog; Assisted listening device; Assistive tech; Bks on deafness & sign lang; Closed caption videos; Described encaptioned media prog; Lecture on deaf culture; Sign lang interpreter upon request for prog; Staff with knowledge of sign lang
Special Services for the Blind - Bks & mags in Braille, on rec, tape & cassette
Open Mon, Wed & Thurs 9-9, Tues 11-9, Fri 9-6, Sat 9-5, Sun (Sept-June) 1-5
Friends of the Library Group
Branches: 2
POINT LOOKOUT BRANCH, 79 Lido Blvd, Point Lookout, 11569, SAN 352-809X. Tel: 516-432-3409. *Library Contact,* Ingrid Stillwagon
Founded 1967. Pop 1,553; Circ 16,237
Library Holdings: Audiobooks 1,578; DVDs 1,807; Bk Titles 8,627; Per Subs 11
Open Mon 4-8, Tues & Thurs 1-5, Fri & Sat 10-2
WEST END, 810 W Beech St, 11561, SAN 352-812X. Tel: 516-432-2704. *Library Contact,* Patricia Witzki
Founded 1968
Library Holdings: AV Mats 1,730; Bk Vols 7,075
Function: Family literacy
Open Tues & Wed 1-5, Thurs 4-8, Fri & Sat 10-2
Restriction: Mil, family mem, retirees, Civil Serv personnel NAF only
Friends of the Library Group

LONG ISLAND CITY

S AMERICAN FOLK ART MUSEUM, Shirley K Schlafer Library, Collection & Education Ctr, 47-29 32nd Pl, 11101. SAN 311-905X. Tel: 646-856-8917. FAX: 718-729-3535. E-mail: library@folkartmuseum.org. *Librn,* Louise Masarof; E-mail: lmasarof@folkartmuseum.org; Staff 1 (MLS 1)
Founded 1961
Library Holdings: Bk Titles 12,103; Per Subs 482; Videos 223
Special Collections: Rare books, Clarion/Folk Art Magazine, Periodical: Quilt Connection, Bulletin of the Association for Gravestone Studies
Subject Interests: Folk art, Self taught artists
Automation Activity & Vendor Info: (Cataloging) LibraryWorld, Inc
Wireless access
Function: 24/7 Online cat
Restriction: Authorized patrons, Authorized scholars by appt, Open by appt only

J FIORELLO H LAGUARDIA COMMUNITY COLLEGE LIBRARY*, Library Media Resources Center, 31-10 Thomson Ave, 11101. SAN 311-4422. Tel: 718-482-5421. Circulation Tel: 718-482-5426. Interlibrary Loan Service Tel: 718-482-5428. Reference Tel: 718-482-5425. FAX: 718-609-2011. Web Site: library.laguardia.edu. *Chief Librn,* Scott White; *Dep Chief Librn,* Steven Ovadia; Tel: 718-482-6022, E-mail: sovadia@lagcc.cuny.edu; *Head, ILL,* Clementine Lewis; E-mail: clement@lagcc.cuny.edu; *Head, Ref & Pub Serv,* Alexandra Rojas; Tel: 718-482-6020, E-mail: arojas@lagcc.cuny.edu; *Access Serv Librn,* Chris McHale; Tel: 718-482-5441, E-mail: cmchale@lagcc.cuny.edu; *Coll Develop Librn,* Louise Fluk; Tel: 718-482-5424, E-mail: fluk@lagcc.cuny.edu; *Electronic Res Librn,* Anne O'Reilly; Tel: 718-482-6021, E-mail: moreilly@lagcc.cuny.edu; *First Year Experience Librn,* Silvia Lin Hanick; E-mail: slinhanick@lagcc.cuny.edu; *Web Serv Librn,* Derek Stadler; Tel: 718-482-5031, E-mail: dstadler@lagcc.cuny.edu; *Instruction Coordr,* Ian McDermott; Tel: 718-482-5430, E-mail: imcdermott@lagcc.cuny.edu; *Coordr, Tech Serv,* Francine Egger-Sider; Tel: 718-482-5423, E-mail: fegger@lagcc.cuny.edu; *Archivist,* Thomas Cleary; Tel: 718-482-5434, E-mail: tcleary@lagcc.cuny.edu; *Instrul Serv,* Charles Keyes; Tel: 718-482-6018, E-mail: ckeyes@lagcc.cuny.edu; Staff 19 (MLS 16, Non-MLS 3)
Founded 1973. Enrl 15,080; Fac 19; Highest Degree: Associate
Jul 2013-Jun 2014 Income $2,170,739
Library Holdings: AV Mats 3,080; CDs 1,511; DVDs 589; Bk Titles 117,330; Bk Vols 135,583; Per Subs 525
Subject Interests: Nursing, Nutrition, Occupational therapy, Veterinary med
Automation Activity & Vendor Info: (Acquisitions) Ex Libris Group
Wireless access
Function: ILL available
Publications: Library Notes (Newsletter); Periodical list
Partic in OCLC Online Computer Library Center, Inc
Restriction: Authorized patrons

LONG LAKE

P LONG LAKE PUBLIC LIBRARY, 1195 Main St, 12847. Tel: 518-624-3825. FAX: 518-624-2172. Web Site: longlake.sals.edu. *Libr Mgr,* Kristel Guimara; E-mail: lgl-director@sals.edu
Library Holdings: Bk Titles 13,000
Automation Activity & Vendor Info: (Cataloging) Innovative Interfaces, Inc; (Circulation) Innovative Interfaces, Inc; (OPAC) Innovative Interfaces, Inc
Wireless access
Mem of Southern Adirondack Library System
Open Tues (Winter) 1-7, Wed 9-1, Thurs 3-7, Fri 9-5, Sat 9-3; Mon (Summer) 11-4, Tues & Thurs 11-7, Wed 9-1, Fri 9-5, Sat 9-3
Friends of the Library Group

LOUDONVILLE

P THE WILLIAM K SANFORD TOWN LIBRARY, Town of Colonie Library, 629 Albany Shaker Rd, 12211-1196. SAN 311-4449. Tel: 518-458-9274. Reference Tel: 518-810-0314. Administration Tel: 518-810-0311. FAX: 518-438-0988. E-mail: info@colonielibrary.org. Web Site: colonielibrary.org. *Dir,* Evelyn Neale; E-mail: director@colonielibrary.org; *Adult Serv, Coll Develop,* Peggy Mello; *Coll Develop, Youth Serv,* Ann Marie Heldorfer; *Circ,* Debbie LaRose; *Circ,* Cindy Seim; *Info Tech,* Connie Weils; *ILL,* Jennifer Soucy; *YA Serv,* Elissa Valente; *Youth Serv,* Ann-Marie Helldorfer; Staff 18 (MLS 6, Non-MLS 12)
Founded 1963. Pop 82,000; Circ 734,789
Jan 2014-Dec 2014 Income $2,602,709, State $22,000, City $2,480,709, Locally Generated Income $100,000. Mats Exp $274,300, Books $220,000, Per/Ser (Incl. Access Fees) $10,000, AV Mat $32,000, Electronic Ref Mat (Incl. Access Fees) $12,300. Sal $1,432,000 (Prof $481,295)
Library Holdings: Audiobooks 3,781; AV Mats 19,261; Large Print Bks 4,686; Bk Vols 188,652; Per Subs 250; Videos 11,433
Special Collections: Basic Education & English as a Second Language Coll; Business & Finance Coll; Job Education Coll; Large Print; Local History; National & Local Telephone Books; NYS Job Bank Outlet; Parent/Teacher
Automation Activity & Vendor Info: (Cataloging) Horizon; (Circulation) Horizon; (OPAC) Horizon
Wireless access
Function: 24/7 Online cat, Activity rm, Adult bk club, Adult literacy prog, After school storytime, Art exhibits, Audio & video playback equip for onsite use, Audiobks via web, Bilingual assistance for Spanish patrons, Bk club(s), Bk reviews (Group), Bks on cassette, Bks on CD, Bus archives, Chess club, Children's prog, Citizenship assistance, Computer training, Computers for patron use, Digital talking bks, E-Reserves, Electronic databases & coll, Free DVD rentals, Holiday prog, ILL available, Internet access, Magazines, Magnifiers for reading, Mail & tel request accepted, Mango lang, Microfiche/film & reading machines, Movies, Museum passes,

Music CDs, Notary serv, Online cat, Online ref, Orientations, Outside serv via phone, mail, e-mail & web, OverDrive digital audio bks, Photocopying/Printing, Preschool outreach, Preschool reading prog, Prog for adults, Prog for children & young adult, Ref & res, Ref serv available, Scanner, Senior computer classes, Spoken cassettes & CDs, Spoken cassettes & DVDs, Story hour, Summer & winter reading prog, Summer reading prog, Tax forms, Teen prog, Telephone ref, VHS videos, Wheelchair accessible, Winter reading prog, Workshops
Publications: Annual Report; Bibliographies; Calendar (Monthly); Preschool Directory; Town of Colonie Dept Directory
Mem of Upper Hudson Library System
Open Mon-Thurs 9-8, Fri 9-6, Sat 9-5, Sun 1-5
Restriction: Closed stack
Friends of the Library Group

C SIENA COLLEGE*, J Spencer & Patricia Standish Library, 515 Loudon Rd, 12211-1462. SAN 311-4457. Tel: 518-783-6717. Interlibrary Loan Service Tel: 518-783-2518. Reference Tel: 518-783-2988. Administration Tel: 518-783-2550. FAX: 518-783-2570. Web Site: lib.siena.edu. *Dir,* Loretta Ebert; E-mail: Lebert@siena.edu; *Head, Cat & Metadata Serv,* Jennifer Fairall; Tel: 518-783-2591, E-mail: jfairall@siena.edu; *Archives & Rec Mgr,* Patricia Markley; Tel: 518-783-4196, E-mail: markley@siena.edu; *Ser Mgt,* Alison Larsen; Tel: 518-782-6765, E-mail: alarsen@siena.edu; *Info Literacy/Instruction Coordr,* Catherine Crohan; Tel: 518-782-6731, E-mail: crohan@siena.edu; *Access Serv,* John Raymond; Tel: 518-783-2522, E-mail: jraymond@siena.edu; *AV,* Sean Conley; Tel: 518-783-2539, E-mail: sconley@siena.edu; *Ref Serv,* Kelly MacWatters; Tel: 518-783-2588, E-mail: kmacwatters@siena.edu; Staff 11.5 (MLS 10.5, Non-MLS 1)
Founded 1937. Enrl 3,069; Fac 273; Highest Degree: Master
Jun 2012-May 2013 Income $1,737,135, State $6,041, Parent Institution $1,721,960, Other $9,134. Mats Exp $1,737,135, Books $201,359, Per/Ser (Incl. Access Fees) $247,902, Manu Arch $609, Micro $829, AV Equip $5,580, AV Mat $10,073, Electronic Ref Mat (Incl. Access Fees) $215,976, Presv $19,368. Sal $892,920
Library Holdings: AV Mats 6,223; CDs 2,035; DVDs 2,401; e-books 18,401; e-journals 29,627; Electronic Media & Resources 98; Microforms 26,655; Music Scores 67; Bk Titles 247,712; Bk Vols 321,764; Per Subs 275; Videos 1,792
Special Collections: Franciscana Coll; Medieval & Early Modern Studies Coll; T E Lawrence Coll
Subject Interests: Mil hist, Multicultural studies, Relig studies
Automation Activity & Vendor Info: (Acquisitions) Innovative Interfaces, Inc; (Cataloging) Innovative Interfaces, Inc; (Circulation) Innovative Interfaces, Inc; (Course Reserve) Docutek; (ILL) OCLC ILLiad; (OPAC) Innovative Interfaces, Inc; (Serials) Innovative Interfaces, Inc
Wireless access
Function: Archival coll, Art exhibits, Audio & video playback equip for onsite use, AV serv, Computers for patron use, E-Reserves, Electronic databases & coll, ILL available, Instruction & testing, Internet access, Microfiche/film & reading machines, Photocopying/Printing, Ref & res, Scanner, VHS videos, Wheelchair accessible
Partic in Cap District Libr Coun for Ref & Res Resources; ConnectNY, Inc; Libraries Interested in Theology across New York; LYRASIS
Special Services for the Blind - Assistive/Adapted tech devices, equip & products; Braille equip
Open Mon-Thurs 7:45am-1am, Fri 7:45-6, Sat 10-6, Sun 10am-1am
Restriction: Authorized patrons, Circ privileges for students & alumni only, ID required to use computers (Ltd hrs), In-house use for visitors, Non-circulating of rare bks, Restricted borrowing privileges

LOWVILLE

L LEWIS COUNTY LAW LIBRARY*, Lewis County Courthouse, 7660 N State St, 2nd Flr, 13367. Tel: 315-376-2036, 315-376-5317. FAX: 315-376-1657. Web Site: www.nycourts.gov/library/lewis. *Law Librn,* Ann Marie Hill; E-mail: amhill@courts.state.ny.us
Library Holdings: Bk Vols 6,000
Subject Interests: Legal ref
Wireless access
Function: ILL available
Open Mon-Fri 8:30-4:30
Restriction: Non-circulating

P LOWVILLE FREE LIBRARY*, 5387 Dayan St, 13367. SAN 311-4465. Tel: 315-376-2131. FAX: 315-376-2131. E-mail: lowlib@ncls.org. Web Site: www.lowvillefreelibrary.org. *Dir,* Meghan Harney; E-mail: dmyers@ncls.org
Founded 1903. Pop 4,548; Circ 33,502
Library Holdings: AV Mats 1,389; Bk Titles 17,344; Per Subs 19
Special Collections: State Document Depository
Subject Interests: Genealogy, Local hist
Wireless access
Mem of North Country Library System
Friends of the Library Group

LYNBROOK

P LYNBROOK PUBLIC LIBRARY*, 56 Eldert St, 11563. SAN 311-4473. Tel: 516-599-8630. FAX: 516-596-1312. Web Site: lynbrooklibrary.org. *Libr Dir,* Robyn Gilloon; E-mail: lpldirector@lynbrooklibrary.org; *Asst Dir, Head, Ref,* Kathy Buchsbaum; E-mail: Kbuchsbaum@lynbrooklibrary.org; Staff 17.6 (MLS 3.8, Non-MLS 13.8)
Founded 1929. Pop 19,427; Circ 109,497
Library Holdings: Audiobooks 3,188; AV Mats 3,693; Bk Vols 81,660; Per Subs 118
Automation Activity & Vendor Info: (Cataloging) Innovative Interfaces, Inc; (Circulation) Innovative Interfaces, Inc; (OPAC) Innovative Interfaces, Inc
Wireless access
Function: 24/7 Electronic res, 24/7 Online cat
Publications: Newsletter (Quarterly)
Mem of Nassau Library System
Special Services for the Blind - Closed circuit TV magnifier
Open Mon, Wed & Thurs 10-9, Tues 1-9, Fri 10-5, Sat (Sept-June) 10-5 (9-1 July & Aug)
Friends of the Library Group

R TEMPLE AM ECHAD*, Malcolm Eisman Memorial Library, One Saperstein Plaza, 11563. SAN 311-4481. Tel: 516-593-4004. FAX: 516-593-2739. Web Site: am-echad.org. *Co-Chair,* Carole Schrager; *Librn,* Bryna Pasoff. Sal $27,000
Library Holdings: Bk Vols 5,000; Per Subs 12
Special Collections: Holocaust
Subject Interests: Jewish bks
Restriction: Not open to pub

LYNDONVILLE

P YATES COMMUNITY LIBRARY*, 15 N Main St, 14098. (Mail add: PO Box 485, 14098-0485). Tel: 585-765-9041. FAX: 585-765-9527. Web Site: www.yateslibrary.org. *Libr Dir,* Emily Cebula; E-mail: ecebula@nioga.org
Founded 1949. Pop 2,371; Circ 16,371
Library Holdings: Bk Vols 16,500; Per Subs 30
Special Collections: Lyndonville Enterprise Newspaper 1906-1962, micro
Automation Activity & Vendor Info: (Cataloging) SirsiDynix; (Circulation) SirsiDynix; (OPAC) SirsiDynix
Wireless access
Mem of Nioga Library System
Open Mon, Tues & Thurs 10-8, Fri 10-5, Sat 10-2

LYONS

P LYONS PUBLIC LIBRARY*, 122 Broad St, 14489. SAN 311-4503. Tel: 315-946-9262. FAX: 315-946-3320. Web Site: lyonspubliclibrary.org. *Libr Dir,* Theresa Streb; E-mail: LyonsLibraryDirector@owwl.org
Founded 1956. Pop 6,746; Circ 40,000
Library Holdings: Bk Vols 25,589; Per Subs 60
Subject Interests: Fiction, Law, Local hist
Automation Activity & Vendor Info: (Circulation) SirsiDynix; (OPAC) SirsiDynix
Wireless access
Mem of Pioneer Library System
Open Mon-Thurs 10-8:30, Fri 10-5, Sat 9-1
Friends of the Library Group

S WAYNE COUNTY HISTORICAL SOCIETY MUSEUM LIBRARY*, 21 Butternut St, 14489. SAN 328-3666. Tel: 315-946-4943. FAX: 315-946-0069. E-mail: info@waynehistory.org. Web Site: www.waynehistory.org. *Exec Dir,* Rhea Hayes
Founded 1949
Library Holdings: Bk Titles 3,119
Wireless access
Open Tues-Fri 10-4, Sat (June-Aug) 10-4

LYONS FALLS

P LYONS FALLS LIBRARY, 3918 High St, 13368. (Mail add: PO Box 618, 13368), SAN 311-4511. Tel: 315-348-6180. FAX: 315-348-6180. E-mail: lyflib@ncls.org. Web Site: www.lyonsfallslibrary.org. *Dir,* Megan Honey
Founded 1923. Pop 755; Circ 9,495
Library Holdings: Bk Vols 7,500; Per Subs 12
Subject Interests: Educ, Environ studies, Indust
Automation Activity & Vendor Info: (OPAC) SirsiDynix
Wireless access
Mem of North Country Library System
Open Tues & Wed 3-7, Thurs & Fri 1-5, Sat 8-12
Friends of the Library Group

MACEDON

P MACEDON PUBLIC LIBRARY*, 30 Main St, 14502-9101. SAN 311-452X. Tel: 315-986-5932. FAX: 315-986-2952. E-mail: macedonlibrarydirector@owwl.org. Web Site: macedonpubliclibrary.org. *Dir,* Stacey Wicksall; Staff 10 (MLS 1, Non-MLS 9)
Pop 9,160; Circ 100,000
Library Holdings: Bk Vols 42,000; Per Subs 50
Special Collections: Bullis Family Library Coll
Automation Activity & Vendor Info: (Cataloging) Evergreen; (Circulation) Evergreen; (Discovery) Evergreen; (ILL) Evergreen; (OPAC) Evergreen
Wireless access
Function: 24/7 Electronic res, 24/7 Online cat, Accelerated reader prog, Activity rm, Adult bk club, Adult literacy prog, After school storytime, Archival coll, Audio & video playback equip for onsite use, Audiobks via web, Bks on CD, Children's prog, Computer training, Computers for patron use, Digital talking bks, Electronic databases & coll, Family literacy, For res purposes, Free DVD rentals, Genealogy discussion group, Holiday prog, Home delivery & serv to seniorr ctr & nursing homes, Homebound delivery serv, ILL available, Internet access, Laminating, Life-long learning prog for all ages, Literacy & newcomer serv, Magazines, Magnifiers for reading, Mango lang, Meeting rooms, Microfiche/film & reading machines, Movies, Music CDs, Notary serv, Online cat, Orientations, Outreach serv, Outside serv via phone, mail, e-mail & web, OverDrive digital audio bks, Photocopying/Printing, Preschool outreach, Preschool reading prog, Prog for adults, Prog for children & young adult, Ref & res, Ref serv available, Scanner, Senior outreach, Story hour, Study rm, Summer & winter reading prog, Summer reading prog, Tax forms, Teen prog, Telephone ref, Visual arts prog, Wheelchair accessible, Winter reading prog, Workshops, Writing prog
Mem of Pioneer Library System
Partic in Rochester Regional Library Council
Special Services for the Deaf - ADA equip; Bks on deafness & sign lang; Captioned film dep
Special Services for the Blind - Aids for in-house use; Bks on CD; Digital talking bk machines; Home delivery serv; Large print bks; Lending of low vision aids; Magnifiers; Recorded bks; Talking bk & rec for the blind cat; Talking bk serv referral; Talking bks & player equip
Open Mon-Thurs 10-8, Fri & Sat 1-5
Friends of the Library Group

MACHIAS

G CATTARAUGUS COUNTY MUSEUM & RESEARCH LIBRARY*, 9824 Rte 16, 1st Flr, 14101. (Mail add: PO Box 352, 14101-0352), SAN 326-2030. Tel: 716-353-8200. Web Site: www.cattco.org/museum. *Historian,* Sharon Fellows; Staff 2 (Non-MLS 2)
Founded 1914
Library Holdings: Bk Titles 1,000; Bk Vols 1,200
Special Collections: New York State & Federal Census Records; World War II Oral History. Oral History
Subject Interests: Local hist
Open Mon-Thurs 9-4

P KING MEMORIAL LIBRARY, 9538 Rte 16, 14101. (Mail add: PO Box 509, 14101-0509), SAN 311-4554. Tel: 716-353-9915. FAX: 716-353-4774. E-mail: kingmemoriallibrary@gmail.com. Web Site: www.machiaslibrary.org. *Dir,* Ann Parker; E-mail: director@machiaslibrary.org
Founded 1941. Pop 2,370; Circ 6,500
Library Holdings: Bk Vols 13,670
Automation Activity & Vendor Info: (Cataloging) SirsiDynix; (Circulation) SirsiDynix; (OPAC) SirsiDynix; (Serials) SirsiDynix
Wireless access
Mem of Chautauqua-Cattaraugus Library System
Open Mon 12-5 & 6-8, Tues 9:30-3:30, Wed 12-5 & 5:30-7:30, Thurs 9-12 & 1:30-8, Fri 9:30-3:30, Sat 9-1:30

MADRID

P HEPBURN LIBRARY OF MADRID, 11 Church St, 13660. SAN 311-4562. Tel: 315-322-5673. FAX: 315-322-4682. E-mail: madlib@ncls.org. Web Site: www.hepburnlibraryofmadrid.org. *Dir,* Deborah Chase-Lauther
Founded 1917. Pop 1,600; Circ 11,511
Library Holdings: Bk Vols 10,000; Per Subs 56
Automation Activity & Vendor Info: (Cataloging) SirsiDynix; (Circulation) SirsiDynix; (OPAC) SirsiDynix
Wireless access
Mem of North Country Library System
Open Mon & Wed 2-7, Tues & Thurs 11-2, Fri 10-2
Friends of the Library Group

MAHOPAC

P MAHOPAC PUBLIC LIBRARY*, 668 Rte 6, 10541. SAN 311-4570. Tel: 845-628-2009. Circulation Tel: 845-628-2009, Ext 133. Reference Tel: 845-628-2009, Ext 130. Information Services Tel: 845-628-2009, Ext 100. FAX: 845-628-0672. E-mail: library@mahopaclibrary.org. Web Site: mahopaclibrary.org. *Dir,* Michele Capozzella; E-mail: mcapozzella@mahopaclibrary.org; *Asst Dir,* Rita Covelli; E-mail: rcovelli@mahopaclibrary.org; Staff 32 (MLS 10, Non-MLS 22)
Founded 1952. Pop 26,485; Circ 308,925
Library Holdings: AV Mats 13,201; Electronic Media & Resources 4,384; Bk Vols 110,844; Per Subs 263
Special Collections: Autism Resource Center; Foundation Center; Health Info Center; Job & Education Info Center; Land Use Center; Local History Coll; Parenting Coll; Putnam County Reference Center
Automation Activity & Vendor Info: (Cataloging) Innovative Interfaces, Inc; (Circulation) Innovative Interfaces, Inc; (ILL) Innovative Interfaces, Inc; (OPAC) Innovative Interfaces, Inc
Wireless access
Publications: Calendar (Monthly); e-Newsletter (Monthly); Newsletter (Quarterly)
Mem of Mid-Hudson Library System
Partic in Southeastern New York Library Resources Council
Special Services for the Deaf - TDD equip
Special Services for the Blind - Ednalite Hi-Vision scope; Talking bks
Open Mon-Thurs (Sept-June) 9:30-9, Fri 9:30-7, Sat 9:30-3, Sun 1-5; Mon-Thurs (July & Aug) 9:30-9, Fri 9:30-7, Sat 9:30-3
Friends of the Library Group

MALONE

S BARE HILL CORRECTIONAL FACILITY LIBRARY*, Caller Box 20, 181 Brand Rd, 12953-0020. Tel: 518-483-8411. Web Site: doccs.ny.gov/location/bare-hill-correctional-facility. *Librn,* Bridget Schack; E-mail: bridget.schack@doccs.ny.gov
Library Holdings: Bk Vols 25,000; Per Subs 78
Automation Activity & Vendor Info: (Cataloging) Follett Software; (Circulation) Follett Software; (OPAC) Follett Software
Restriction: Not open to pub

S FRANKLIN CORRECTIONAL FACILITY LIBRARY, 62 Bare Hill Rd, 12953. (Mail add: PO Box 10, 12953-0010). Tel: 518-483-6040. Web Site: doccs.ny.gov/location/franklin-correctional-facility. *Librn,* Alisha Wheeler; E-mail: alisha.wheeler@doccs.ny.gov
Library Holdings: Bk Vols 5,708
Automation Activity & Vendor Info: (Cataloging) Follett Software; (Circulation) Follett Software
Restriction: Staff & inmates only

P WEAD LIBRARY, 64 Elm St, 12953. SAN 311-4589. Tel: 518-483-5251. FAX: 581-483-5255. E-mail: vnplib@nnyln.org. Web Site: cefls.org/libraries/malone, weadlib.wordpress.com.
Founded 1881. Pop 20,220; Circ 72,892
Library Holdings: Audiobooks 1,005; DVDs 110; Bk Vols 46,209; Per Subs 105
Special Collections: State Document Depository
Subject Interests: Genealogy, State hist
Automation Activity & Vendor Info: (Cataloging) SirsiDynix; (Circulation) SirsiDynix; (ILL) SirsiDynix; (OPAC) SirsiDynix
Wireless access
Function: Bks on CD, Computers for patron use, ILL available, Internet access, Online cat, Story hour, Wheelchair accessible
Mem of Clinton-Essex-Franklin Library System
Partic in Northern New York Library Network
Special Services for the Deaf - Bks on deafness & sign lang
Special Services for the Blind - Audio mat; Bks on CD; Large print bks; Magnifiers; Talking bk serv referral
Open Mon-Fri 10-8, Sat 10-3 (Winter); Mon-Wed 10-6, Thurs 10-8, Sat 10-3 (Summer)

MALVERNE

P MALVERNE PUBLIC LIBRARY, 61 Saint Thomas Pl, 11565. SAN 311-4597. Tel: 516-599-0750. FAX: 516-599-3320. Web Site: www.malvernelibrary.org. *Libr Dir,* Carol Lagos; E-mail: director@malvernelibrary.org; Staff 12 (MLS 4, Non-MLS 8)
Founded 1928. Pop 8,600; Circ 44,076
Library Holdings: Bk Vols 55,000; Per Subs 107
Automation Activity & Vendor Info: (Acquisitions) Innovative Interfaces, Inc - Millennium; (Cataloging) Innovative Interfaces, Inc - Millennium; (Circulation) Innovative Interfaces, Inc - Millennium; (OPAC) Innovative Interfaces, Inc - Millennium
Wireless access
Mem of Nassau Library System

Open Mon, Wed & Thurs 9:30-7, Tues & Fri 9:30-7, Sat (Sept-June) 9:30-5
Friends of the Library Group

MAMARONECK

P MAMARONECK PUBLIC LIBRARY DISTRICT*, 136 Prospect Ave, 10543. SAN 311-4600. Tel: 914-698-1250. Circulation Tel: 914-698-1250, Ext 5. Reference Tel: 914-698-1250, Ext 3. FAX: 914-381-3088. Web Site: www.mamaronecklibrary.org. *Libr Dir,* Jennifer ONeill; Tel: 914-698-1250, Ext 8, E-mail: joneill@wlsmail.org; *Head, Adult Serv,* Lori Friedli; E-mail: lfriedli@wlsmail.org; *Head, Circ,* Teresa Beebe; E-mail: tbeebe@wlsmail.org; *Head, Youth Serv,* Terry Numa; E-mail: tnuma@wlsmail.org; *Ref Librn,* Patricia (Trish) Byrne; E-mail: tbyrne@wlsmail.org; *Ref Librn,* Jack Weiss; E-mail: jweiss@wlsmail.org; *Tech Serv Librn,* Hilary Hertzoff; E-mail: hhertzoff@wlsmail.org; *Youth Serv Librn,* Michelle Magnotta; E-mail: mmagnotta@wlsmail.org; *YA Librn,* Ellen McTyre; E-mail: emctyre@wlsmail.org; *Youth Serv Librn,* Kathy Palovick; E-mail: kpalovick@wlsmail.org; *Youth Serv Librn,* Marie Pierre; E-mail: mpierre@wlsmail.org; *Bus Mgr,* Mary Soto; E-mail: msoto@wlsmail.org; *Prog Coordr,* Linda Bhandari; E-mail: lbhandari@wlsmail.org; Staff 31 (MLS 10, Non-MLS 21)
Founded 1922. Pop 18,752; Circ 204,278
Automation Activity & Vendor Info: (Cataloging) SirsiDynix; (Circulation) SirsiDynix; (OPAC) SirsiDynix
Wireless access
Function: 24/7 Electronic res, 24/7 Online cat, 3D Printer, Accelerated reader prog, Activity rm, Adult bk club, Adult literacy prog, After school storytime
Mem of Westchester Library System
Open Mon & Wed 10-8, Tues & Thurs 10-6, Fri & Sat 10-5, Sun (Sept-June) 1-4:30
Friends of the Library Group

MANHASSET

P MANHASSET PUBLIC LIBRARY*, 30 Onderdonk Ave, 11030. SAN 311-4619. Tel: 516-627-2300. Circulation Tel: 516 627-2300, Ext 101. Administration Tel: 516 365-2300, Ext 348. FAX: 516-627-4339. Administration FAX: 516-365-3466. Web Site: manhassetlibrary.org. *Dir,* Maggie Gough; E-mail: maggiegough@manhassetlibrary.org; *Asst to the Dir,* Ellen Marjorana; Tel: 516 627-2300, Ext 345, E-mail: emarjorana@manhassetlibrary.org; *Adult Serv Supvr,* Sharon Rappaport; Tel: 516 627-2300, Ext 209, E-mail: srappaport@manhassetlibrary.org; *Circ,* Nancy McGoldrick; Tel: 516-627-2300, Ext 106, E-mail: nmcgoldrick@manhassetlibrary.org; *Commun Relations,* Debbie Dellis-Quinn; Tel: 512-627-2300, Ext 150, E-mail: ddellis-quinn@manhassetlibrary.org
Founded 1945. Pop 15,961; Circ 188,457
Library Holdings: Audiobooks 3,995; AV Mats 18,603; CDs 4,694; DVDs 8,968; Large Print Bks 1,692; Microforms 3,930; Bk Vols 116,094; Per Subs 309; Videos 2,971
Special Collections: Benedetto/Rainone Puppet Coll; Books for the Bibliophile; Career Center; Frances Hodgson Burnett Archival Coll; Long Island Coll; Manhasset Authors (local oral archives); New York Coll; Poetry for Children (Kelly Miscall Coll). Oral History
Automation Activity & Vendor Info: (Cataloging) Innovative Interfaces, Inc; (Circulation) Innovative Interfaces, Inc; (ILL) OCLC; (OPAC) Innovative Interfaces, Inc
Wireless access
Publications: Quarterly Newsletter
Mem of Nassau Library System
Special Services for the Blind - Closed circuit TV
Open Mon & Wed-Fri 9-9, Tues 11-9, Sat 9-5, Sun (July-Aug) 1-5
Friends of the Library Group

M NORTH SHORE UNIVERSITY HOSPITAL*, Daniel Carroll Payson Medical Library, 300 Community Dr, 11030. SAN 311-4627. Tel: 516-562-4324. FAX: 516-562-2865. Web Site: nsuh.northwell.edu. *Librn,* Tanya Shkolnikov; *Sr Librn,* Jaclyn Vialet; E-mail: jvialet@northwell.edu; Staff 7 (MLS 4, Non-MLS 3)
Founded 1954
Library Holdings: Bk Titles 2,000; Per Subs 500
Subject Interests: Clinical med, Hist of med, Laboratory med, Nursing
Automation Activity & Vendor Info: (Cataloging) SirsiDynix; (Circulation) SirsiDynix; (OPAC) SirsiDynix
Wireless access
Open Mon-Fri 8-6

MANLIUS

P MANLIUS LIBRARY, One Arkie Albanese Ave, 13104. SAN 311-4635. Tel: 315-682-6400. FAX: 315-682-4490. Web Site: www.manliuslibrary.org. *Dir,* Jennifer Milligan; *Bus Mgr,* Kerstin Spina; E-mail: kspina@manliuslibrary.org; *Operations Mgr,* Marcia Short; E-mail: mshort@manliuslibrary.org; Staff 20 (MLS 8, Non-MLS 12)
Founded 1915. Pop 11,500; Circ 307,851
Library Holdings: AV Mats 11,300; Bks on Deafness & Sign Lang 42; Large Print Bks 800; Bk Titles 40,000; Bk Vols 47,022; Per Subs 146
Special Collections: Audubon Art Gallery & Reference Coll, bks, prints
Automation Activity & Vendor Info: (Circulation) Innovative Interfaces, Inc; (OPAC) Innovative Interfaces, Inc
Wireless access
Function: 24/7 Electronic res, 24/7 Online cat, Activity rm, Adult bk club, Adult literacy prog, After school storytime, Art exhibits, Audio & video playback equip for onsite use, Audiobks on Playaways & MP3, Audiobks via web, AV serv, Bi-weekly Writer's Group, Bk club(s), Bks on CD, Butterfly Garden, Children's prog, Computer training, Computers for patron use, E-Readers, E-Reserves, Electronic databases & coll, Equip loans & repairs, Family literacy, Free DVD rentals, Genealogy discussion group, Health sci info serv, Holiday prog, Homework prog, ILL available, Internet access, Life-long learning prog for all ages, Literacy & newcomer serv, Magazines, Mail & tel request accepted, Mango lang, Meeting rooms, Movies, Museum passes, Music CDs, Notary serv, Online cat, Online info literacy tutorials on the web & in blackboard, Online ref, Outreach serv, Outside serv via phone, mail, e-mail & web, OverDrive digital audio bks, Photocopying/Printing, Preschool outreach, Preschool reading prog, Printer for laptops & handheld devices, Prog for adults, Prog for children & young adult, Ref & res, Ref serv available, Res assist avail, Scanner, Senior computer classes, Senior outreach, Spanish lang bks, Spoken cassettes & CDs, Spoken cassettes & DVDs, STEM programs, Story hour, Study rm, Summer & winter reading prog, Summer reading prog, Tax forms, Teen prog, Telephone ref, Visual arts prog, Wheelchair accessible, Winter reading prog, Workshops, Writing prog
Mem of Onondaga County Public Libraries
Partic in Central New York Library Resources Council
Open Mon-Thurs 10-9, Fri & Sat 10-5, Sun 1-5

MANNSVILLE

P MANNSVILLE FREE LIBRARY, 106 Lilac Park Dr, 13661. SAN 311-4643. Tel: 315-465-4049. FAX: 315-465-4049. E-mail: manlib@ncls.org. Web Site: www.mannsvillelibrary.org. *Libr Mgr,* Jean Appleby
Circ 6,595
Library Holdings: Bk Vols 6,123; Per Subs 31
Wireless access
Mem of North Country Library System
Open Mon, Tues & Thurs 12-5, Wed 11-4

MARATHON

P PECK MEMORIAL LIBRARY*, 24 Main St, 13803. (Mail add: PO Box 325, 13803-0325), SAN 311-466X. Tel: 607-849-6135. FAX: 607-849-3799. Web Site: peckmemoriallibrary.org. *Libr Dir,* Mary Ann Frank; E-mail: director@peckmemoriallibrary.org
Founded 1895. Pop 1,063; Circ 16,516
Library Holdings: Bk Vols 16,000; Per Subs 26
Automation Activity & Vendor Info: (Cataloging) Innovative Interfaces, Inc; (Circulation) Innovative Interfaces, Inc; (OPAC) Innovative Interfaces, Inc
Wireless access
Function: 24/7 Electronic res, 24/7 Online cat, 3D Printer, Activity rm, Adult bk club, Art exhibits, Audiobks on Playaways & MP3, Audiobks via web, Bk club(s), Bks on cassette, Bks on CD, CD-ROM, Children's prog, Computer training, Computers for patron use, Electronic databases & coll, Free DVD rentals, Home delivery & serv to seniorr ctr & nursing homes, ILL available, Movies, Museum passes, Music CDs, Online cat, Online ref, Photocopying/Printing, Preschool outreach, Prog for adults, Prog for children & young adult, Scanner, Spoken cassettes & CDs, Spoken cassettes & DVDs, Story hour, Summer reading prog, Tax forms, Winter reading prog, Workshops
Mem of Finger Lakes Library System
Open Mon & Fri 1-5, Tues 9-12 & 1-7, Wed & Thurs 1-7, Sat (Sept-June) 9-Noon
Friends of the Library Group

MARCELLUS

P MARCELLUS FREE LIBRARY, 32 Maple St, 13108. SAN 311-4678. Tel: 315-673-3221. FAX: 315-673-0148. E-mail: marcellus@onlib.org. Web Site: www.marcelluslibrary.org. *Libr Dir,* Jacob Widrick; E-mail: jwidrick@onlib.org; Staff 5 (MLS 1, Non-MLS 4)
Founded 1913. Pop 6,319; Circ 60,000
Jan 2020-Dec 2020 Income $624,086. Mats Exp $644,642
Library Holdings: Bk Titles 30,000; Per Subs 60; Talking Bks 1,200; Videos 1,700
Special Collections: Chorale Music (Marcellus Chorale Coll), sheets
Automation Activity & Vendor Info: (Circulation) Innovative Interfaces, Inc; (OPAC) Innovative Interfaces, Inc

Wireless access
Function: AV serv, ILL available, Photocopying/Printing, Prog for children & young adult, Summer reading prog, Telephone ref, Wheelchair accessible
Mem of Onondaga County Public Libraries
Open Mon, Tues, Thurs & Fri 10-5, Wed 10-7, Sat 10-2
Friends of the Library Group

MARGARETVILLE

P FAIRVIEW PUBLIC LIBRARY*, 43 Walnut St, 12455. (Mail add: PO Box 609, 12455-0609), SAN 310-8090. Tel: 845-586-3791. FAX: 845-586-3791. E-mail: mail@fairviewpubliclibrary.org. Web Site: fairviewlibrary.org. *Dir,* Doris Warner; E-mail: director@fairviewlibrary.org
Founded 1974. Pop 4,015; Circ 12,808
Library Holdings: Bk Vols 10,000; Per Subs 10
Wireless access
Mem of Four County Library System
Open Tues, Thurs & Fri 11-5, Wed 11-7, Sat 10-3

MARILLA

P MARILLA FREE LIBRARY, 11637 Bullis Rd, 14102-9727. SAN 311-4686. Tel: 716-652-7449. FAX: 716-652-7449. E-mail: mar@buffalolib.org. Web Site: www.buffalolib.org/locations-hours/marilla-free-library. *Dir,* Shannon Thompson; E-mail: thompsons@buffalolib.org
Pop 4,864; Circ 22,244
Library Holdings: Audiobooks 1,667; Bk Vols 17,942; Per Subs 35; Videos 7,458
Automation Activity & Vendor Info: (Cataloging) SirsiDynix; (Circulation) SirsiDynix; (OPAC) SirsiDynix
Wireless access
Mem of Buffalo & Erie County Public Library System
Open Mon & Wed 10-6, Tues & Thurs 1-8, Sat 10-3
Friends of the Library Group

MARION

P MARION PUBLIC LIBRARY*, 4036 Maple Ave, 14505. (Mail add: PO Box 30, 14505-0030), SAN 311-4694. Tel: 315-926-4933. FAX: 315-926-7038. Web Site: marionlib.org. *Dir,* Tracy Whitney; E-mail: twhitney@pls-net.org; *Asst Librn,* Adrienne VanHorn
Founded 1910. Circ 46,615
Library Holdings: Bk Vols 17,000; Per Subs 30
Automation Activity & Vendor Info: (Acquisitions) SirsiDynix; (Cataloging) SirsiDynix; (Circulation) SirsiDynix; (ILL) SirsiDynix
Wireless access
Mem of Pioneer Library System
Open Mon & Wed 10-8, Tues, Thurs & Fri 2-6, Sat 9-Noon
Friends of the Library Group

MARLBORO

P MARLBORO FREE LIBRARY, 1251 Rte 9W, 12542. (Mail add: PO Box 780, 12542-0780), SAN 311-4708. Tel: 845-236-7272. FAX: 845-236-7635. E-mail: staff@marlborolibrary.org. Web Site: www.marlborolibrary.org. *Dir,* Christina Jennerich; Staff 4 (MLS 3, Non-MLS 1)
Founded 1911. Pop 11,634
Library Holdings: Bk Titles 38,466; Per Subs 210
Special Collections: Frederick W Goudy Coll. Oral History
Subject Interests: Local hist
Automation Activity & Vendor Info: (Circulation) Innovative Interfaces, Inc; (OPAC) Innovative Interfaces, Inc
Wireless access
Publications: The Inside Story (Newsletter)
Mem of Mid-Hudson Library System
Open Mon 2-8, Tues-Thurs 10-8, Fri 10-5, Sat 11-5
Friends of the Library Group

MARTINSBURG

P WILLIAM H BUSH MEMORIAL LIBRARY, 5605 Whitaker Rd, 13404. SAN 311-4716. Tel: 315-376-7490. FAX: 315-376-3096. E-mail: marlib@ncls.org. Web Site: www.martinsburglibrary.org. *Dir,* Brandie Rogers
Founded 1913. Pop 350; Circ 8,393
Library Holdings: Bk Vols 15,660; Per Subs 56
Special Collections: Local Scrapbooks & Diaries
Subject Interests: Hist
Wireless access
Mem of North Country Library System
Open Mon, Wed & Fri 10-6, Sat 10-Noon

MASSAPEQUA

P PLAINEDGE PUBLIC LIBRARY*, 1060 Hicksville Rd, 11758. SAN 311-4759. Tel: 516-735-4133. FAX: 516-735-4192. E-mail: pplained@nassau.cv.net. Web Site: www.nassaulibrary.org/plnedge. *Libr Dir,* Marilyn Kappenberg; E-mail: directorpel@nassaulibrary.org; *Asst Dir,* Judith Nilsen; *Ch Serv,* Peggy Gorman; Staff 14 (MLS 14)
Founded 1963. Pop 22,097; Circ 200,111
Library Holdings: Audiobooks 860; AV Mats 7,000; Bks on Deafness & Sign Lang 230; CDs 5,332; DVDs 5,532; Large Print Bks 600; Bk Titles 135,200; Per Subs 215; Talking Bks 4,000; Videos 500
Automation Activity & Vendor Info: (Acquisitions) Baker & Taylor; (Circulation) Innovative Interfaces, Inc; (OPAC) Innovative Interfaces, Inc; (Serials) EBSCO Online
Wireless access
Function: ILL available, Photocopying/Printing, Ref serv available
Publications: Newsletter (Monthly)
Mem of Nassau Library System
Special Services for the Blind - Large screen computer & software; Magnifiers; Screen enlargement software for people with visual disabilities
Open Mon-Fri 9-9, Sat 9-5, Sun 1-5

MASSAPEQUA PARK

P MASSAPEQUA PUBLIC LIBRARY*, Bar Harbour Bldg, 40 Harbor Lane, 11762. SAN 352-8189. Tel: 516-799-0770. FAX: 516-799-1532. E-mail: bhlibrary@massapequalibrary.org. Web Site: www.massapequalibrary.org. *Dir,* Janis A Schoen; E-mail: jaschoen@massapequalibrary.org; *Asst Dir,* Michael Matuszewski; E-mail: mmatuszewski@massapequalibrary.org; *Adult Ref Librn,* Lisa Quinn; E-mail: lquinn@massapequalibrary.org; *Tech Coordr,* Carol Santillo; E-mail: csantillo@massapequalibrary.org; *Ch Serv,* Mary McGrath; E-mail: mmcgrath@massapequalibrary.org; *Circ,* Maryetta Garrone; E-mail: mgarrone@massapequalibrary.org; *YA Serv,* Lisa Zuena; E-mail: lzuena@massapequalibrary.org; Staff 18 (MLS 18)
Founded 1952. Pop 48,931; Circ 446,292
Library Holdings: AV Mats 14,599; Bk Vols 189,442; Per Subs 590
Automation Activity & Vendor Info: (Cataloging) Innovative Interfaces, Inc; (Circulation) Innovative Interfaces, Inc; (ILL) Innovative Interfaces, Inc; (OPAC) Innovative Interfaces, Inc; (Serials) Innovative Interfaces, Inc
Wireless access
Function: Adult bk club, Computer training, Prog for adults, Prog for children & young adult, Summer reading prog, Wheelchair accessible
Publications: Monthly Calendar; Newsletter (Quarterly)
Mem of Nassau Library System
Open Mon-Thurs 9-9, Fri 9-6, Sat 9-5, Sun (Sept-June) 12-4
Branches: 1
CENTRAL AVENUE, 523 Central Ave, Massapequa, 11758, SAN 352-8154. Tel: 516-798-4607. FAX: 516-798-2804. E-mail: calibrary@massapequalibrary.org. *Adult Ref Librn,* Maris Job; E-mail: mjob@massapequalibrary.org; *Ch Serv,* Germaine Booth; E-mail: gbooth@massapequalibrary.org; *Circ,* Mary Dougherty; E-mail: mdougherty@massapequalibrary.org
Open Mon-Thurs 9-9, Fri 9-6, Sat 9-5, Sun (Sept-June) 1-5

MASSENA

M MASSENA MEMORIAL HOSPITAL LIBRARY*, One Hospital Dr, 13662. SAN 328-428X. Tel: 315-764-1711. FAX: 315-769-4780. *Library Contact,* Karen Wilkins; E-mail: kwilkins@massenahospital.org
Library Holdings: Bk Vols 306
Restriction: Staff use only

P MASSENA PUBLIC LIBRARY*, Warren Memorial Library, 41 Glenn St, 13662. SAN 311-4767. Tel: 315-769-9914. FAX: 315-769-5978. E-mail: maslib@ncls.org. Web Site: www.massenapubliclibrary.org. *Dir,* Elaine Dunne; Staff 3 (MLS 2, Non-MLS 1)
Founded 1897. Pop 13,100; Circ 95,800
Library Holdings: Bk Vols 68,000; Per Subs 156; Talking Bks 800
Automation Activity & Vendor Info: (Circulation) SirsiDynix; (OPAC) SirsiDynix
Wireless access
Publications: Books & Beyond (Bimonthly library activities)
Mem of North Country Library System
Open Mon, Wed, Fri & Sat 9:30-5, Tues & Thurs 9-8:30
Friends of the Library Group
Branches: 1
BADENHAUSEN BRANCH LIBRARY, Four Main St, Brasher Falls, 13613. Tel: 313-389-5033. FAX: 315-389-5507.
Open Mon & Fri 9-1, Tues 10-2, Wed 11-6, Thurs 3:30-7:30

MATTITUCK

P MATTITUCK-LAUREL LIBRARY, 13900 Main Rd, 11952. (Mail add: PO Box 1437, 11952-0991), SAN 311-4775. Tel: 631-298-4134. FAX: 631-298-4764. E-mail: mattitucklibrary@gmail.com. Web Site: mattitucklaurellibrary.org. *Dir,* Jeff Walden; Staff 5 (MLS 5)

Founded 1903. Pop 5,093; Circ 110,291
Library Holdings: Bk Vols 54,000; Per Subs 300
Automation Activity & Vendor Info: (Acquisitions) Innovative Interfaces, Inc; (Cataloging) Innovative Interfaces, Inc; (Circulation) Innovative Interfaces, Inc; (OPAC) Innovative Interfaces, Inc
Wireless access
Mem of Suffolk Cooperative Library System
Open Mon-Fri 9-8, Sat 10-4, Sun (Sept-June) 1-4
Friends of the Library Group

MATTYDALE

P SALINA LIBRARY*, 100 Belmont St, 13211. SAN 311-4783. Tel: 315-454-4524. FAX: 315-454-3466. E-mail: info@salinalibrary.org. Web Site: www.salinalibrary.org. *Dir,* Jeannine Chubon; E-mail: jchubon@salinalibrary.org; Staff 12 (MLS 2, Non-MLS 10)
Founded 1942. Pop 11,616; Circ 99,812
Library Holdings: Bk Vols 34,000
Automation Activity & Vendor Info: (Circulation) Innovative Interfaces, Inc; (OPAC) Innovative Interfaces, Inc
Wireless access
Function: Adult bk club, Art exhibits, Audiobks via web, Bks on CD, Children's prog, Computer training, Computers for patron use, Electronic databases & coll, Free DVD rentals, Genealogy discussion group, Holiday prog, ILL available, Magnifiers for reading, Music CDs, Online cat, OverDrive digital audio bks, Photocopying/Printing, Prog for adults, Prog for children & young adult, Summer reading prog, Tax forms
Mem of Onondaga County Public Libraries
Open Mon-Thurs 10-8, Fri 1-5, Sat 10-4
Friends of the Library Group

MAYVILLE

P MAYVILLE LIBRARY*, 92 S Erie St, 14757. SAN 311-4791. Tel: 716-753-7362. FAX: 716-753-7360. E-mail: mayvillelibrary@gmail.com. Web Site: www.mayvillelibrary.com. *Dir,* Melissa Bartok
Pop 4,666; Circ 21,000
Library Holdings: Bk Vols 19,466; Per Subs 42
Wireless access
Mem of Chautauqua-Cattaraugus Library System
Open Mon & Tues 10-7, Wed & Fri 10-5, Thurs 10-8, Sat 10-2

MCGRAW

P LAMONT MEMORIAL FREE LIBRARY*, Five Main St, 13101. (Mail add: PO Box 559, 13101-0559), SAN 311-4546. Tel: 607-836-6767. FAX: 607-836-8866. E-mail: lmemoria@twcny.rr.com. *Dir,* Heather M Cobb; Staff 2 (Non-MLS 2)
Founded 1906. Pop 1,053
Automation Activity & Vendor Info: (Cataloging) Innovative Interfaces, Inc
Wireless access
Function: Children's prog, Computers for patron use, Free DVD rentals, ILL available, Magazines, Photocopying/Printing, Summer reading prog
Mem of Finger Lakes Library System
Open Mon, Tues & Thurs 2-8, Fri 10-12 & 2-5, Sat 10-1

MECHANICVILLE

P MECHANICVILLE DISTRICT PUBLIC LIBRARY*, 190 N Main St, 12118. SAN 311-4805. Tel: 518-664-4646. FAX: 518-664-8641. E-mail: mec-director@sals.edu. Web Site: www.mechanicville.sals.edu. *Libr Dir,* Michelle Duell; E-mail: Mduell@sals.edu; Staff 8 (MLS 1, Non-MLS 7)
Founded 1966. Pop 8,437; Circ 72,895
Library Holdings: AV Mats 1,449; Bk Vols 25,570; Per Subs 51; Talking Bks 1,430
Special Collections: Coach Wiegel Sports Coll; Ellsworth Coll; Local World War & Korean War Veterans Picture Coll
Subject Interests: Local hist
Automation Activity & Vendor Info: (Cataloging) SirsiDynix
Wireless access
Mem of Southern Adirondack Library System
Open Mon & Wed 11-8, Tues, Thurs & Fri 11-6, Sat 9-1
Friends of the Library Group

MEDINA

P LEE-WHEDON MEMORIAL LIBRARY, 620 West Ave, 14103. SAN 311-4813. Tel: 585-798-3430. FAX: 585-798-4398. E-mail: info@medinalibrary.org. Web Site: leewhedon.org. *Dir,* Kristine Mostyn; *Asst Dir,* Samantha Covis; Staff 5 (MLS 2, Non-MLS 3)
Founded 1928. Pop 11,720; Circ 85,000
Library Holdings: Bk Titles 51,534; Bk Vols 59,998; Per Subs 134
Automation Activity & Vendor Info: (Cataloging) SirsiDynix-WorkFlows; (Circulation) SirsiDynix-WorkFlows
Wireless access
Function: 24/7 Electronic res, 24/7 Online cat, Adult bk club, After school storytime, Audiobks on Playaways & MP3, Audiobks via web, Bks on CD, Children's prog, Computer training, Computers for patron use, Electronic databases & coll, Family literacy, Free DVD rentals, Holiday prog, ILL available, Magazines, Meeting rooms, Microfiche/film & reading machines, Movies, Museum passes, Music CDs, Notary serv, Online cat, Online ref, Outreach serv, OverDrive digital audio bks, Photocopying/Printing, Printer for laptops & handheld devices, Prog for adults, Prog for children & young adult, Ref & res, Ref serv available, Scanner, Spanish lang bks, STEM programs, Story hour, Summer & winter reading prog, Summer reading prog, Tax forms, Teen prog, Telephone ref, Wheelchair accessible, Winter reading prog
Mem of Nioga Library System
Open Mon-Thurs 10-8, Fri & Sat 10-5
Restriction: Open to pub for ref & circ; with some limitations
Friends of the Library Group

MELVILLE

S NEWSDAY, INC LIBRARY*, 235 Pinelawn Rd, 11747-4250. SAN 311-2314. Tel: 631-843-2333. FAX: 631-843-2065. Web Site: www.newsday.com. *Mgr,* Dorothy Levin; E-mail: dorothy.levin@newsday.com; Staff 18 (MLS 4, Non-MLS 14)
Founded 1940
Library Holdings: Bk Titles 20
Special Collections: Newsday Clipping & Photo File, 1940-to present
Wireless access
Restriction: Not open to pub, Staff use only, Use of others with permission of librn

MENANDS

P MENANDS PUBLIC LIBRARY*, Four N Lyons Ave, 12204. SAN 311-4880. Tel: 518-463-4035. FAX: 518-449-3863. Web Site: www.menandslibrary.org. *Dir,* Leonard Zapala; E-mail: zapalal@uhls.lib.ny.us; *Youth Serv,* Sherry Bhatti; Staff 1 (MLS 1)
Founded 1923. Pop 4,500
Library Holdings: Bk Vols 10,400; Per Subs 43
Automation Activity & Vendor Info: (Cataloging) SirsiDynix; (OPAC) SirsiDynix
Wireless access
Mem of Upper Hudson Library System
Open Mon, Wed & Fri 12-3, Tues & Thurs 6-8, Sat 10-1

MERRICK

P MERRICK LIBRARY*, 2279 Merrick Ave, 11566-4398. SAN 311-4902. Tel: 516-377-6112. Circulation Tel: 516-277-6112, Ext 100. Interlibrary Loan Service Tel: 516-377-6112, Ext 112. Administration Tel: 516-377-6112, Ext 118. FAX: 516-377-1108. E-mail: merricklibrary@merricklibrary.org. Web Site: www.merricklibrary.org. *Dir,* Dan Chuzmir; E-mail: dchuzmir@merricklibrary.org; *Asst Dir,* Marisa Crowley; *Head, Children's Servx,* Susan Goodwin; *Head, Ref,* Diane Bondi; Tel: 516-377-6112, Ext 102, E-mail: dianebondi@merricklibrary.org; *Ref Librn,* Kristine Dugan; *Ref Librn,* Jill Moretto; *Ref Librn,* Carol Ann Tack; *YA Librn,* Luisa Munoz; *Ch Serv,* Laurie Fensterstock; *Ch Serv,* Elizabeth Maynard
Founded 1891. Pop 19,040; Circ 259,000
Subject Interests: Local hist
Automation Activity & Vendor Info: (Acquisitions) Innovative Interfaces, Inc - Sierra; (Circulation) Innovative Interfaces, Inc - Sierra; (ILL) OCLC; (OPAC) Innovative Interfaces, Inc - Sierra
Wireless access
Function: 24/7 Electronic res, 24/7 Online cat, 3D Printer, Adult bk club, Adult literacy prog, After school storytime, Archival coll, Art exhibits, Audiobks via web, Bk club(s), Bks on CD, Children's prog, Computer training, Computers for patron use, E-Readers, Electronic databases & coll, Free DVD rentals, Holiday prog, Homebound delivery serv, ILL available, Internet access, Jazz prog, Life-long learning prog for all ages, Magazines, Magnifiers for reading, Meeting rooms, Movies, Museum passes, Music CDs, Online cat, Online ref, OverDrive digital audio bks, Photocopying/Printing, Printer for laptops & handheld devices, Prog for adults, Prog for children & young adult, Ref & res, Ref serv available, Scanner, Senior computer classes, Study rm, Summer reading prog, Teen prog, Telephone ref
Publications: Children's Newsletter; Library Newsletter (Quarterly)
Mem of Nassau Library System
Partic in Long Island Library Resources Council
Friends of the Library Group

MEXICO

P MEXICO PUBLIC LIBRARY*, 3269 Main St, 13114. (Mail add: PO Box 479, 13114-0479), SAN 311-4910. Tel: 315-963-3012. FAX: 315-963-7317. E-mail: mexlib@ncls.org. Web Site: www.mexicopubliclibrary.org. *Dir,* Dorothy Dineen

Library Holdings: Bk Titles 8,880; Per Subs 26
Automation Activity & Vendor Info: (Circulation) SirsiDynix-WorkFlows; (OPAC) SirsiDynix-WorkFlows
Wireless access
Mem of North Country Library System
Open Mon & Wed 10:30-8, Tues, Thurs & Fri 10:30-5, Sat 9-12
Friends of the Library Group

MIDDLE ISLAND

P LONGWOOD PUBLIC LIBRARY*, 800 Middle Country Rd, 11953. SAN 311-4929. Tel: 631-924-6400. FAX: 631-924-7538. Web Site: www.longwoodlibrary.org. *Dir,* Lisa Jacobs; E-mail: lisa@longwoodlibrary.org; Staff 26.5 (MLS 26.5)
Founded 1953. Pop 57,739; Circ 856,562
Library Holdings: Bk Titles 256,886; Per Subs 449
Special Collections: Thomas R Bayles Historical Coll
Automation Activity & Vendor Info: (Acquisitions) Innovative Interfaces, Inc; (Cataloging) Innovative Interfaces, Inc; (Circulation) Innovative Interfaces, Inc; (Course Reserve) Innovative Interfaces, Inc; (ILL) Innovative Interfaces, Inc; (Media Booking) Innovative Interfaces, Inc; (OPAC) Innovative Interfaces, Inc; (Serials) Innovative Interfaces, Inc
Wireless access
Publications: Newsletter
Mem of Suffolk Cooperative Library System
Friends of the Library Group

MIDDLEBURGH

P MIDDLEBURGH LIBRARY*, 323 Main St, 12122. (Mail add: PO Box 670, 12122), SAN 311-4937. Tel: 518-827-5142. FAX: 518-827-5148. Web Site: www.middleburghlibrary.info. *Libr Dir,* Teresa Pavoldi; E-mail: tpavoldi@sals.edu; Staff 3 (MLS 1, Non-MLS 2)
Pop 2,980; Circ 24,404
Library Holdings: Bk Titles 16,000; Per Subs 55
Special Collections: Genealogy (Frances B Spencer Coll)
Automation Activity & Vendor Info: (Circulation) Innovative Interfaces, Inc; (OPAC) Innovative Interfaces, Inc
Wireless access
Mem of Mohawk Valley Library System
Open Mon 1:30-8:30, Tues & Thurs 10-8:30, Wed 10-5, Sat 9-2
Friends of the Library Group

MIDDLEPORT

P ROYALTON HARTLAND COMMUNITY LIBRARY, 9 South Vernon St, 14105. SAN 311-4953. Tel: 716-735-3281. FAX: 716-735-3281. E-mail: mdtrpt@nioga.org. Web Site: royhartcommunitylibrary.com. *Libr Dir,* Gretchen Schweigert; E-mail: gschweigert@nioga.org; Staff 1 (MLS 1)
Founded 1930. Pop 9,071; Circ 26,681
Jul 2016-Jun 2017 Income (Main Library Only) $103,000. Mats Exp $15,000, Books $10,000, Per/Ser (Incl. Access Fees) $2,000, AV Mat $3,000
Library Holdings: Audiobooks 410; AV Mats 1,020; CDs 220; DVDs 1,020; e-books 2,642; e-journals 104; Electronic Media & Resources 30; Large Print Bks 215; Bk Vols 20,253; Per Subs 73
Special Collections: Local History
Automation Activity & Vendor Info: (Cataloging) SirsiDynix-WorkFlows; (Circulation) SirsiDynix-WorkFlows; (OPAC) SirsiDynix
Wireless access
Function: 24/7 Electronic res, 24/7 Online cat, Activity rm, Adult bk club, After school storytime, Archival coll, Audiobks on Playaways & MP3, Audiobks via web, Bk club(s), Chess club, Children's prog, Computer training, Computers for patron use, E-Reserves, Electronic databases & coll, Free DVD rentals, Govt ref serv, Health sci info serv, Holiday prog, ILL available, Internet access, Magazines, Meeting rooms, Movies, Music CDs, Online cat, Online ref, Outreach serv, Outside serv via phone, mail, e-mail & web, OverDrive digital audio bks, Photocopying/Printing, Preschool outreach, Preschool reading prog, Prog for adults, Prog for children & young adult, Ref & res, Ref serv available, Scanner, Senior computer classes, Serves people with intellectual disabilities, Spoken cassettes & CDs, Spoken cassettes & DVDs, Story hour, Summer reading prog, Tax forms, Teen prog, Telephone ref, Wheelchair accessible, Workshops, Writing prog
Mem of Nioga Library System
Open Mon-Thur 12-7, Sat 11-4
Restriction: Authorized patrons
Friends of the Library Group

MIDDLESEX

P MIDDLESEX READING CENTER*, 1216 Rte 245, 14507. (Mail add: PO Box 147, 14507-0147), SAN 352-3896. Tel: 585-554-3607. Administration Tel: 585-554-6945. FAX: 585-554-4615. Web Site: www.middlesexny.org/Library.php. *Dir,* Sabra Dunton; E-mail: sdunton@middlesexny.org
Library Holdings: Bk Titles 5,000
Wireless access
Function: Homebound delivery serv, Wheelchair accessible
Mem of Southern Tier Library System
Special Services for the Blind - Bks on cassette; Bks on CD; Large print bks
Open Mon & Wed 4-7, Sat 10-2

MIDDLETOWN

P MIDDLETOWN THRALL LIBRARY, 11-19 Depot St, 10940. SAN 311-5003. Tel: 845-341-5454. Reference Tel: 845-341-5461. Reference E-mail: thrall2@warwick.net. Web Site: www.thrall.org. *Dir,* Matthew Pfisterer; E-mail: thrall7@warwick.net; Staff 29 (MLS 9, Non-MLS 20)
Founded 1901. Circ 280,566
Library Holdings: Bk Titles 151,000; Bk Vols 174,600; Per Subs 654
Special Collections: Orange County History Coll. US Document Depository
Automation Activity & Vendor Info: (Acquisitions) SirsiDynix; (Cataloging) SirsiDynix; (Circulation) SirsiDynix; (Course Reserve) SirsiDynix; (ILL) SirsiDynix; (Media Booking) SirsiDynix; (OPAC) SirsiDynix; (Serials) SirsiDynix
Wireless access
Publications: Newsletter
Mem of Ramapo Catskill Library System
Partic in Southeastern New York Library Resources Council
Open Mon & Fri 9-6, Tues-Thurs 9-8, Sat 10-5 (10-2 Summer)
Friends of the Library Group

J ORANGE COUNTY COMMUNITY COLLEGE LIBRARY*, 115 South St, 10940. SAN 311-4996. Tel: 845-341-4855. Interlibrary Loan Service Tel: 845-341-4254. Reference Tel: 845-341-4620. FAX: 845-341-4424. E-mail: library@sunyorange.edu. Web Site: www.sunyorange.edu/lrc. *Librn,* John Klingner; E-mail: john.klingner@sunyorange.edu; *Cat/Syst Librn,* William Worford; Tel: 845-341-4256, E-mail: william.worford@sunyorange.edu; *Ref Librn,* Deborah Canzano; E-mail: deborah.canzano@sunyorange.edu; *Circ, Ref Librn,* Amy Hillick; E-mail: amy.hillick@sunyorange.edu; *Electronic Serv,* Andrew Heiz; Tel: 845-341-4253, E-mail: andrew.heiz@sunyorange.edu; *Archives Librn, Libr Instruction,* Nancy Murillo; Tel: 845-341-4258, E-mail: nancy.murillo@sunyorange.edu; *User Serv Librn,* Lara Patel; Tel: 845-341-9051, E-mail: lara.patel@sunyorange.edu; Staff 24 (MLS 8, Non-MLS 16)
Founded 1950. Enrl 4,969; Fac 149; Highest Degree: Associate
Sept 2016-Aug 2017 Income (Main & Associated Libraries) $210,881. Mats Exp $210,881, Books $65,223, Per/Ser (Incl. Access Fees) $22,032, Electronic Ref Mat (Incl. Access Fees) $62,839, Presv $1,500. Sal $882,890
Library Holdings: Bk Vols 225,235; Per Subs 125
Special Collections: Orange County History & Heritage
Automation Activity & Vendor Info: (Acquisitions) Ex Libris Group; (Cataloging) OCLC; (Circulation) Ex Libris Group; (Course Reserve) Ex Libris Group; (Discovery) EBSCO Discovery Service; (ILL) OCLC ILLiad; (OPAC) Ex Libris Group
Wireless access
Partic in OCLC Online Computer Library Center, Inc; Southeastern New York Library Resources Council; SUNYConnect
Open Mon-Fri (Fall & Spring) 8am-9pm, Sat 9-3; Mon & Thurs (Summer) 9-7, Tues & Wed 9-9, Fri 9-5

Departmental Libraries:

NEWBURGH CAMPUS, One Washington Ctr, Newburgh, 12550. Tel: 845-562-4542. *Ref Librn,* Deborah Canzano; *User Serv Librn,* Lara Patel; Tel: 845-341-9051, E-mail: lara.patel@sunyorange.edu; *Librn,* Porter Barber; Tel: 845-341-9049, E-mail: porter.barber@sunyorange.edu; Staff 6 (MLS 3, Non-MLS 3)
Highest Degree: Associate

P RAMAPO CATSKILL LIBRARY SYSTEM*, 619 Rte 17M, 10940-4395. SAN 352-8219. Tel: 845-243-3747. FAX: 845-243-3739. Web Site: www.rcls.org. *Exec Dir,* Position Currently Open; *Asst Dir, Interim Exec Dir, Outreach Coordr,* Grace Riario; Tel: 845-343-1131, Ext 233, E-mail: griario@rcls.org; *ANSER Mgr & Network Adminr,* John Hurley; Tel: 845-343-1131, Ext 228, E-mail: jhurley@rcls.org; *ILL/Tech Serv Librn,* Dan Donohue; Tel: 845-243-3747, Ext 237, E-mail: ddonohue@rcls.org; *Fiscal Officer,* Stephen Hoefer; Tel: 845-343-1131, Ext 223, E-mail: shoefer@rcls.org; *Electronic Res Consult,* Jerry Kuntz; Tel: 845-343-1131, Ext 246, E-mail: jkuntz@rcls.org; *Youth Serv Consult,* Joanna Goldfarb; Tel: 845-343-1131, Ext 240, E-mail: jgoldfarb@rcls.org; Staff 25 (MLS 5, Non-MLS 20)
Founded 1959
Library Holdings: Bk Vols 2,500; Per Subs 100
Subject Interests: Electronic databases, Personnel mgt, Prof libr sci mgt
Automation Activity & Vendor Info: (Acquisitions) SirsiDynix-WorkFlows; (Cataloging) SirsiDynix-WorkFlows; (Circulation)

SirsiDynix-WorkFlows; (Discovery) EBSCO Discovery Service; (ILL) SirsiDynix-WorkFlows; (OPAC) SirsiDynix
Publications: RCLS Weekly Memo (Newsletter); Trustee FYI (Newsletter)
Member Libraries: Albert Wisner Public Library; Blauvelt Free Library; Chester Public Library; Cornwall Public Library; Cragsmoor Free Library; Daniel Pierce Library; Dennis P McHugh Piermont Public Library; Ellenville Public Library & Museum; Ethelbert B Crawford Public Library; Fallsburg Library Inc; Finkelstein Memorial Library; Florida Public Library; Gardiner Library; Goshen Public Library & Historical Society; Greenwood Lake Public Library; Haverstraw Kings Daughters Public Library; Highland Falls Library; Josephine-Louise Public Library; Liberty Public Library; Livingston Manor Free Library; Middletown Thrall Library; Moffat Library of Washingtonville; Monroe Free Library; Montgomery Free Library; Nanuet Public Library; New City Library; Newburgh Free Library; Orangeburg Library; Palisades Free Library; Pearl River Public Library; Pine Bush Area Library; Port Jervis Free Library; Roscoe Free Library; Rose Memorial Library; Sloatsburg Public Library; Suffern Free Library; Sunshine Hall Free Library; Tappan Library; The Nyack Library; Tomkins Cove Public Library; Tuxedo Park Library; Valley Cottage Free Library; Wallkill Public Library; West Nyack Free Library; Western Sullivan Public Library; Woodbury Public Library
Open Mon-Fri 8-4

MIDDLEVILLE

P MIDDLEVILLE FREE LIBRARY*, One S Main St, 13406. (Mail add: PO Box 155, 13406-0155), SAN 311-5011. Tel: 315-891-3655. FAX: 315-891-3655. E-mail: middleville@midyork.org. Web Site: middlevillelibrary.org. *Dir,* Sandra Zaffarano
Founded 1915. Pop 550; Circ 8,000
Library Holdings: Bk Vols 10,500; Per Subs 12
Wireless access
Mem of Mid-York Library System
Open Mon & Wed 4-8, Tues, Thurs & Fri 10-12 & 2-6, Sat 10-12

MILFORD

P MILFORD FREE LIBRARY*, 64 S Main St, 13807. (Mail add: PO Box 118, 13807), SAN 311-502X. Tel: 607-286-9076. *Dir,* Barbara Campbell
Founded 1923. Circ 8,900
Library Holdings: Bk Vols 8,000; Per Subs 20
Subject Interests: Local hist
Wireless access
Mem of Four County Library System
Open Tues & Thurs 1-9, Sat 10-2

MILLBROOK

S CARY INSTITUTE OF ECOSYSTEM STUDIES LIBRARY, Ecosystem Science Bldg, 2801 Sharon Tpk, 12545. (Mail add: PO Box AB, 12545-0129), SAN 311-5046. Tel: 845-677-7600. FAX: 845-677-5976. Web Site: www.caryinstitute.org. *Dir, Libr & Info Serv,* Amy C Schuler; Tel: 845-677-7600, Ext 164, E-mail: schulera@caryinstitute.org; Staff 1 (MLS 1)
Founded 1985
Library Holdings: Bk Titles 9,100; Per Subs 175
Special Collections: Institutional Archives; Maps; Staff Reprints; Theses; Vertical File
Subject Interests: Ecology, Nutrient cycling, Plant-animal interactions
Automation Activity & Vendor Info: (Cataloging) LibLime; (Circulation) LibLime; (ILL) OCLC; (OPAC) LibLime; (Serials) LibLime
Wireless access
Function: Res libr
Partic in Southeastern New York Library Resources Council
Restriction: Open by appt only

P MILLBROOK LIBRARY, Three Friendly Lane, 12545. (Mail add: PO Box 286, 12545-0286), SAN 311-5038. Tel: 845-677-3611. FAX: 845-677-5127. Web Site: millbrooklibrary.org. *Dir,* Courtney Tsahalis; E-mail: director@millbrooklibrary.org; *Head, Circ,* Tom Finnigan; E-mail: tfinnigan@millbrooklibrary.org; Staff 2 (MLS 1, Non-MLS 1)
Founded 1901
Wireless access
Function: 24/7 Electronic res, 24/7 Online cat, Adult bk club, Adult literacy prog, Art exhibits, Art programs, Audiobks via web, Bk club(s), Bks on CD, Children's prog, Computer training, Computers for patron use, Digital talking bks, E-Reserves, Electronic databases & coll, Family literacy, For res purposes, Free DVD rentals, Health sci info serv, Holiday prog, Home delivery & serv to seniorr ctr & nursing homes, Homebound delivery serv, Homework prog, ILL available, Internet access, Life-long learning prog for all ages, Literacy & newcomer serv, Magazines, Magnifiers for reading, Mango lang, Meeting rooms, Movies, Music CDs, Notary serv, Online cat, Online ref, Outreach serv, OverDrive digital audio bks, Photocopying/Printing, Preschool reading prog, Printer for laptops & handheld devices, Prog for adults, Prog for children & young adult, Ref & res, Ref serv available, Res assist avail, Scanner, Senior computer classes, Senior outreach, Spanish lang bks, Spoken cassettes & CDs, STEM programs, Story hour, Study rm, Summer reading prog, Tax forms, Teen prog, Telephone ref, Visual arts prog, Wheelchair accessible, Workshops, Writing prog
Mem of Mid-Hudson Library System
Open Mon & Fri 12-6, Tues & Thurs 10-6, Wed 12-8, Sat 10-4
Restriction: Registered patrons only
Friends of the Library Group

MILLERTON

P NORTHEAST-MILLERTON LIBRARY*, 75 Main St, 12546. (Mail add: PO Box 786, 12546-0786), SAN 311-5054. Tel: 518-789-3340. FAX: 518-789-6802. E-mail: info@nemillertonlibrary.org. Web Site: nemillertonlibrary.org. *Dir,* Rhiannon Leo-Jameson; Staff 1 (MLS 1)
Founded 1927. Pop 3,032; Circ 28,826
Library Holdings: DVDs 1,279; Bk Titles 22,000; Per Subs 30; Talking Bks 2,200
Automation Activity & Vendor Info: (Acquisitions) Innovative Interfaces, Inc; (Cataloging) Innovative Interfaces, Inc; (Circulation) Innovative Interfaces, Inc; (Course Reserve) Innovative Interfaces, Inc; (ILL) Innovative Interfaces, Inc; (Media Booking) Innovative Interfaces, Inc; (OPAC) Innovative Interfaces, Inc; (Serials) Innovative Interfaces, Inc
Wireless access
Function: Adult bk club, Adult literacy prog, Digital talking bks, Homebound delivery serv, ILL available, Prog for children & young adult, Spoken cassettes & CDs, VHS videos, Wheelchair accessible
Mem of Mid-Hudson Library System
Special Services for the Blind - Bks on cassette; Bks on CD; Large print bks; Talking bks
Open Tues-Fri 11-6, Sat 10-3

MILTON

P SARAH HULL HALLOCK FREE LIBRARY, Milton Library, 56-58 Main St, 12547. (Mail add: PO Box 802, 12547-0802), SAN 311-5062. Tel: 845-795-2200. FAX: 845-795-1005. E-mail: miltonlibrary@live.com. Web Site: miltonlib.org. *Pres,* Rosemary Wein; *Dir,* Lois H Skelly; *VPres,* Jennifer Wrage; Staff 2 (MLS 1, Non-MLS 1)
Founded 1887. Circ 12,943
Library Holdings: Bk Vols 18,849; Per Subs 41
Wireless access
Mem of Mid-Hudson Library System
Open Mon-Fri 12-7

MINEOLA

P MINEOLA MEMORIAL LIBRARY*, 195 Marcellus Rd, 11501. SAN 311-5089. Tel: 516-746-8488. FAX: 516-294-6459. E-mail: mineola@nassaulibrary.org. Web Site: www.mineolalibrary.info. *Dir,* Charles Sleefe; *Ch Serv,* Meredith Minkoff; *Ref Serv,* Cathy Sagevick
Pop 20,757; Circ 77,219
Library Holdings: Bk Vols 85,000; Per Subs 150
Automation Activity & Vendor Info: (Acquisitions) Innovative Interfaces, Inc; (Cataloging) Innovative Interfaces, Inc; (Circulation) Innovative Interfaces, Inc; (ILL) Innovative Interfaces, Inc; (Media Booking) Innovative Interfaces, Inc; (OPAC) Innovative Interfaces, Inc; (Serials) Innovative Interfaces, Inc
Wireless access
Mem of Nassau Library System
Open Mon, Wed & Thurs 10-9, Tues & Fri 10-5:30, Sat (Winter) 10-5
Friends of the Library Group

GL NASSAU COUNTY SUPREME COURT*, Law Library, 100 Supreme Court Dr, 2nd Flr, 11501. SAN 352-8243. Tel: 516-442-8580. FAX: 516-442-8578. *Principal Law Librn,* Jean-Paul Vivian; E-mail: jvivian@courts.state.ny.us; Staff 4 (MLS 1, Non-MLS 3)
Founded 1902
Library Holdings: Bk Vols 408,782
Special Collections: Four Departments of the Appellate & Court of Appeals Records & Briefs
Wireless access
Function: Computers for patron use, Microfiche/film & reading machines, Photocopying/Printing, Scanner
Partic in Long Island Library Resources Council
Open Mon-Fri 9-5
Restriction: Lending to staff only, Open to pub for ref only

M NYU LONG ISLAND SCHOOL OF MEDICINE, Hollis Health Sciences Library, (Formerly NYU Winthrop Hospital), 259 First St, 11501. SAN 311-5100. Tel: 516-663-2802. FAX: 516-663-8171. Web Site: nyuwinthrop.org/medical-education/hollis-health-sciences-library. *Dir,* Barnaby Nicolas; Tel: 516-663-2783, E-mail: Barnaby.Nicolas@nyulangone.org; Staff 5 (MLS 4, Non-MLS 1)
Founded 1925

Library Holdings: Bk Titles 5,000; Per Subs 500
Subject Interests: Allied health, Computer instruction, Med, Nursing, Surgery
Automation Activity & Vendor Info: (OPAC) SirsiDynix
Wireless access
Publications: Acquisition List (Quarterly)
Partic in Long Island Library Resources Council
Open Mon-Thurs 8:30am-9pm, Fri 8:30-5, Sat 10-6
Restriction: Staff use only

MINOA

P MINOA LIBRARY*, 242 N Main St, 13116. SAN 311-5119. Tel: 315-656-7401. FAX: 315-656-7033. Web Site: www.minoalibrary.org. *Dir,* Laura Ravera; E-mail: lpravera@gmail.com; Staff 7 (Non-MLS 7)
Founded 1936. Pop 3,640; Circ 38,569
Library Holdings: DVDs 222; Large Print Bks 200; Bk Titles 15,318; Bk Vols 16,325; Per Subs 55; Talking Bks 322; Videos 689
Automation Activity & Vendor Info: (Cataloging) Innovative Interfaces, Inc; (Circulation) Innovative Interfaces, Inc; (OPAC) Innovative Interfaces, Inc
Wireless access
Mem of Onondaga County Public Libraries
Open Mon-Thurs 10-8, Fri 10-5, Sat 10-3

MODENA

P PLATTEKILL PUBLIC LIBRARY*, 2047 State Rte 32, 12548. SAN 376-6977. Tel: 845-883-7286. FAX: 845-883-7295. E-mail: plattekill_lib@hotmail.com. Web Site: plattekill.lib.ny.us. *Dir,* Darren Lanspery; *Circ Supvr,* Donna Ebanks; Staff 9 (MLS 1, Non-MLS 8)
Founded 1972. Pop 10,500; Circ 14,000
Library Holdings: Audiobooks 271; Bks on Deafness & Sign Lang 50; Braille Volumes 12; CDs 455; DVDs 2,000; High Interest/Low Vocabulary Bk Vols 190; Large Print Bks 600; Bk Titles 19,910; Per Subs 100; Talking Bks 794; Videos 821
Special Collections: Library of America Books
Subject Interests: Careers, Parenting, Regional, Spanish (Children & Adults)
Automation Activity & Vendor Info: (Acquisitions) Innovative Interfaces, Inc - Sierra; (Cataloging) Innovative Interfaces, Inc - Sierra; (Circulation) Innovative Interfaces, Inc - Sierra; (OPAC) Innovative Interfaces, Inc
Wireless access
Function: 24/7 Electronic res, 24/7 Online cat, Adult bk club, After school storytime, Audiobks via web, Bilingual assistance for Spanish patrons, Bk club(s), Bks on CD, CD-ROM, Children's prog, Computer training, Computers for patron use, Digital talking bks, Electronic databases & coll, Free DVD rentals, Homework prog, ILL available, Internet access, Magazines, Mail & tel request accepted, Mango lang, Movies, Music CDs, Online cat, OverDrive digital audio bks, Photocopying/Printing, Preschool outreach, Prog for adults, Prog for children & young adult, Ref serv available, Senior computer classes, Senior outreach, Spoken cassettes & CDs, Story hour, Summer reading prog, Teen prog, Workshops
Mem of Mid-Hudson Library System
Special Services for the Deaf - Bks on deafness & sign lang; Closed caption videos; Deaf publ; High interest/low vocabulary bks; Sign lang interpreter upon request for prog
Special Services for the Blind - Accessible computers; Assistive/Adapted tech devices, equip & products; Audio mat; Bks & mags in Braille, on rec, tape & cassette; Bks on CD; Braille bks; Children's Braille; Copier with enlargement capabilities; Large print bks; Large screen computer & software; Screen enlargement software for people with visual disabilities; Text reader
Open Mon 12-6, Tues-Thurs 10-8, Fri 10-6, Sat 10-3
Restriction: ID required to use computers (Ltd hrs)
Friends of the Library Group

MOHAWK

P WELLER PUBLIC LIBRARY, 41 W Main St, 13407. SAN 311-5127. Tel: 315-866-2983. E-mail: mohawk@midyork.org. Web Site: wellerlibrary.org/about-us. *Libr Mgr,* Anne-Marie Belinfante
Circ 22,295
Library Holdings: Bk Vols 33,000; Per Subs 4
Wireless access
Mem of Mid-York Library System
Open Mon, Tues, Thurs & Fri 12-6, Wed 12-7

MONROE

P MONROE FREE LIBRARY*, 44 Millpond Pkwy, 10950. SAN 311-5135. Tel: 845-783-4411. FAX: 845-782-4707. E-mail: info@monroefreelibrary.org. Web Site: www.monroefreelibrary.org. *Exec Dir,* Amanda Primiano; *Asst Dir,* Mary Duffy; *Head, Ref & Adult Prog,* Catina Strauss; *Head, Children's Servx,* Melissa Quarles; *Automation Syst Coordr, Head, Circ & Tech Serv,* Carol Bezkorowajny
Founded 1908. Pop 23,035; Circ 115,000
Library Holdings: AV Mats 3,637; Bk Vols 50,106; Per Subs 135
Subject Interests: Local hist
Automation Activity & Vendor Info: (Acquisitions) SirsiDynix; (Cataloging) SirsiDynix; (Circulation) SirsiDynix; (ILL) SirsiDynix; (Media Booking) SirsiDynix; (OPAC) SirsiDynix; (Serials) SirsiDynix
Wireless access
Publications: Annual Report; Calendar of Events (Monthly); Newsletter (Quarterly)
Mem of Ramapo Catskill Library System
Open Mon, Tues & Thurs 9:30-8, Wed 1-9, Fri 9:30-5, Sat 9:30-4, Sun 12-5
Friends of the Library Group

MONTAUK

P MONTAUK LIBRARY*, 871 Montauk Hwy, 11954. (Mail add: PO Box 700, 11954-0500), SAN 325-5204. Tel: 631-668-3377. FAX: 631-668-3468. E-mail: info@montauklibrary.org. Web Site: montauklibrary.org. *Dir,* Denise DiPaolo; E-mail: ddipaolo@montauklibrary.org; Staff 2 (MLS 1, Non-MLS 1)
Founded 1980. Pop 3,848; Circ 33,648
Jul 2012-Jun 2013 Income $710,880, State $1,200, City $684,800, Locally Generated Income $7,680, Other $17,200. Mats Exp $60,638, Books $18,225, Per/Ser (Incl. Access Fees) $7,964, Other Print Mats $619, AV Equip $11,591, AV Mat $11,567, Electronic Ref Mat (Incl. Access Fees) $10,672. Sal $299,504 (Prof $91,847)
Library Holdings: Audiobooks 1,223; AV Mats 202; Bks on Deafness & Sign Lang 16; CDs 323; DVDs 1,844; e-books 56,141; Large Print Bks 686; Bk Titles 33,100; Bk Vols 33,550; Per Subs 63; Talking Bks 870; Videos 696
Special Collections: Archival Rm; Long Island Coll; Shakespeare Coll. Oral History
Automation Activity & Vendor Info: (Cataloging) Innovative Interfaces, Inc; (Circulation) Innovative Interfaces, Inc - Millennium; (ILL) Innovative Interfaces, Inc; (OPAC) Innovative Interfaces, Inc
Wireless access
Function: Adult bk club, Archival coll, Art exhibits, Bk club(s), Bks on CD, Children's prog, Computers for patron use, Homebound delivery serv, ILL available, Mail & tel request accepted, Microfiche/film & reading machines, Museum passes, Music CDs, Online cat, OverDrive digital audio bks, Photocopying/Printing, Preschool reading prog, Printer for laptops & handheld devices, Prog for adults, Spanish lang bks, Story hour, Summer reading prog, Tax forms, Wheelchair accessible
Mem of Suffolk Cooperative Library System
Partic in Association for Rural & Small Libraries
Open Mon & Tues 10-6, Wed-Fri 10-8, Sat 10-5, Sun 1-5
Friends of the Library Group

MONTGOMERY

P MONTGOMERY FREE LIBRARY*, 133 Clinton St, 12549-1195. SAN 311-5151. Tel: 845-457-5616. FAX: 845-457-5616. Web Site: montgomerynylib.org. *Dir,* Betsy Comizio; *Asst Dir,* Barbara Meyer
Founded 1911. Pop 2,318; Circ 17,219
Library Holdings: Bk Vols 18,393
Automation Activity & Vendor Info: (Acquisitions) SirsiDynix; (Cataloging) SirsiDynix; (Circulation) SirsiDynix; (ILL) SirsiDynix; (Media Booking) SirsiDynix; (OPAC) SirsiDynix; (Serials) SirsiDynix
Wireless access
Mem of Ramapo Catskill Library System
Open Mon-Fri 10-6, Sat 10-1
Friends of the Library Group

MONTICELLO

P ETHELBERT B CRAWFORD PUBLIC LIBRARY*, 479 Broadway, 12701. SAN 311-516X. Tel: 845-794-4660. FAX: 845-794-4602. Web Site: ebcpl.org. *Dir,* Mary Paige Lang-Clouse; E-mail: langclouse@rcls.org; Staff 6 (MLS 1, Non-MLS 5)
Pop 21,000; Circ 85,301
Library Holdings: Bk Vols 25,100
Automation Activity & Vendor Info: (Cataloging) Horizon; (Circulation) Horizon; (OPAC) Horizon
Wireless access
Mem of Ramapo Catskill Library System
Open Mon-Thurs 9:30-7, Fri 9:30-6:30, Sat 10-4
Friends of the Library Group

MONTOUR FALLS

P MONTOUR FALLS MEMORIAL LIBRARY*, 406 W Main St, 14865. (Mail add: PO Box 486, 14865-0486), SAN 376-3048. Tel: 607-535-7489. FAX: 607-535-7489. Web Site: www.montourfallslibrary.org. *Dir,* Roxanne Leyes; E-mail: roxanne@montourfallslibrary.org; *Asst Libr Dir,* Kelly Povero; E-mail: kelly@montourfallslibrary.org

Founded 1901
Library Holdings: Large Print Bks 200; Bk Vols 4,000; Per Subs 40
Wireless access
Mem of Southern Tier Library System
Open Mon-Fri 10-7, Sat 8-Noon

MONTROSE

P HENDRICK HUDSON FREE LIBRARY*, 185 Kings Ferry Rd, 10548. SAN 311-5186. Tel: 914-739-5654. FAX: 914-739-5659. Web Site: www.henhudfreelibrary.org. *Libr Dir,* Jill Davis; E-mail: jdavis@wlsmail.org; *Head, Ref, Teen Librn,* Elise Landesberg; E-mail: elandesberg@wlsmail.org; *Ch,* Terri Jersey; E-mail: tjersey@wlsmail.org; *Adult Programs, Ref Librn,* Cheri Morreale; E-mail: cmorreale@wlsmail.org; *Bus Mgr,* Jenny Kolesar; E-mail: jkolesar@wlsmail.org; Staff 28 (MLS 8, Non-MLS 20)
Founded 1937. Pop 15,642; Circ 229,642
Jul 2014-Jun 2015 Income $1,415,170, State $4,000, Locally Generated Income $821,978, Other $589,192. Mats Exp $112,500, Books $85,000, Per/Ser (Incl. Access Fees) $6,500, AV Mat $21,000. Sal $571,620
Library Holdings: CDs 4,805; DVDs 4,073; e-books 150; Bk Vols 53,801; Per Subs 99
Automation Activity & Vendor Info: (Cataloging) SirsiDynix; (Circulation) SirsiDynix; (ILL) SirsiDynix; (OPAC) SirsiDynix
Wireless access
Function: Homebound delivery serv, ILL available, Internet access, Prog for adults, Prog for children & young adult, Summer reading prog, Wheelchair accessible
Publications: Newsletter
Mem of Westchester Library System
Open Mon-Thurs 9-8, Fri 9-6, Sat 9-5, Sun 1-5

MOOERS

P MOOERS FREE LIBRARY, 25 School St, 12958. (Mail add: PO Box 286, 12958-0286), SAN 311-5208. Tel: 518-236-7744. FAX: 518-236-7744. E-mail: mooersfreelibrary@gmail.com. Web Site: cefls.org/libraries/mooers, mooerslibrary.org. *Dir,* Jenny C Lavigne
Founded 1917. Circ 6,911
Library Holdings: Audiobooks 5,350; CDs 208; DVDs 337; e-books 2,237; e-journals 5; Large Print Bks 118; Bk Titles 6,734; Per Subs 47; Talking Bks 10; Videos 50
Special Collections: Local History (Information on Mooers); Local History (Towns in Clinton County)
Subject Interests: Adirondack, Andrew Wyeth, Genealogy, Local hist
Automation Activity & Vendor Info: (Cataloging) Horizon; (OPAC) Horizon
Wireless access
Mem of Clinton-Essex-Franklin Library System
Open Mon 10-5, Tues & Fri 11-6, Sat 9-1
Friends of the Library Group

MORAVIA

P POWERS LIBRARY, 29 Church St, 13118. (Mail add: PO Box 71, 13118-0071), SAN 311-5216. Tel: 315-497-1955. FAX: 315-497-3284. E-mail: powerslibrary@hotmail.com. *Dir,* Lori A Cochran
Founded 1880. Circ 24,000
Library Holdings: Bk Vols 23,000
Wireless access
Mem of Finger Lakes Library System
Open Mon & Wed 1-7, Tues & Fri 10-5; Mon & Wed 12-6 (Dec-March)

MORRIS

P VILLAGE LIBRARY OF MORRIS*, 152 Main St, 13808. (Mail add: PO Box 126, 13808), SAN 311-5224. Tel: 607-263-2080. FAX: 607-263-2080. E-mail: mo.ill@4cls.org. Web Site: libraries.4cls.org/morris. *Mgr,* Gary Norman
Founded 1919. Pop 2,800; Circ 7,943
Library Holdings: Audiobooks 25; DVDs 79; Large Print Bks 320; Bk Titles 7,100; Bk Vols 7,138; Per Subs 12; Videos 400
Subject Interests: Local hist
Wireless access
Mem of Four County Library System
Open Mon, Wed, Fri & Sat 1-5, Tues & Thurs 1-7

MORRISTOWN

P MORRISTOWN PUBLIC LIBRARY*, 200 Main St, 13664. (Mail add: PO Box 206, 13664-0206). Tel: 315-375-8833. FAX: 315-375-8266. E-mail: mtnlib@ncls.org. Web Site: www.morristownpubliclibrary.org. *Dir,* Bridget Whalen-Nevin
Library Holdings: AV Mats 50; Bk Vols 8,000; Talking Bks 40
Wireless access
Mem of North Country Library System
Open Mon & Wed 1-8, Tues 10-5, Thurs 11-5, Sat 9-1
Friends of the Library Group

MORRISVILLE

P MORRISVILLE PUBLIC LIBRARY, 83 E Main St, 13408. (Mail add: PO Box 37, 13408-0037), SAN 311-5240. Tel: 315-684-9130. FAX: 315-684-9132. Web Site: www.morrisvillepubliclibrary.org. *Libr Mgr,* Michelle Rounds; E-mail: mrounds@midyork.org; Staff 5 (Non-MLS 5)
Founded 1903. Pop 6,137; Circ 35,587
Library Holdings: Bk Vols 15,810; Per Subs 45
Automation Activity & Vendor Info: (Cataloging) SirsiDynix-WorkFlows; (Circulation) SirsiDynix-WorkFlows; (OPAC) SirsiDynix-WorkFlows
Wireless access
Mem of Mid-York Library System
Open Mon-Fri Noon-7

C STATE UNIVERSITY OF NEW YORK*, Morrisville State College Donald G Butcher Library, PO Box 901, 13408. SAN 311-5259. Tel: 315-684-6055. FAX: 315-684-6115. Web Site: www.morrisville.edu/library. *Dir of Libr,* Christine Rudecoff; E-mail: rudecoc@morrisville.edu; *Assoc Librn, Electronic Res & Syst Librn,* Angela Rhodes; E-mail: rhodesam@morrisville.edu; *Instrul Serv Librn,* Michelle K Mitchell; E-mail: mitchemk@morrisville.edu; Staff 7 (MLS 4, Non-MLS 3)
Founded 1908. Enrl 3,000; Highest Degree: Bachelor
Library Holdings: Audiobooks 331; DVDs 2,520; e-books 14,080; e-journals 6,055; Electronic Media & Resources 50; Microforms 6,762; Bk Titles 88,725; Bk Vols 110,000; Per Subs 223
Special Collections: New York State Historical Coll
Subject Interests: Agr, Animal husbandry-horses, Automotive tech, Environ studies, Hort, Journalism, Natural res, Nursing, Renewable energy
Automation Activity & Vendor Info: (Cataloging) OCLC; (Circulation) Ex Libris Group; (Course Reserve) Docutek; (ILL) OCLC; (OPAC) Ex Libris Group; (Serials) Ex Libris Group
Wireless access
Function: Art exhibits, Computers for patron use, E-Reserves, Electronic databases & coll, Internet access, Online cat, Online info literacy tutorials on the web & in blackboard, Online ref, Photocopying/Printing, Ref serv available, Telephone ref
Partic in OCLC Online Computer Library Center, Inc; SUNYConnect
Open Mon-Thurs (Winter) 8am-Midnight, Fri 8-5, Sat 1-6, Sun 1-10; Mon-Fri (Summer) 8-4

MOUNT KISCO

P MOUNT KISCO PUBLIC LIBRARY*, 100 E Main St, 10549. SAN 311-5267. Tel: 914-666-8041. FAX: 914-666-3899. Web Site: www.mountkiscolibrary.org. *Dir,* Kathryn Feeley; Tel: 914-666-0935, E-mail: kfeeley@wlsmail.org; *Head, Adult Serv,* Martha Iwan; Tel: 914-864-0136, E-mail: miwan@wlsmail.org; *Head, Circ,* Coleen Carpenter; Tel: 914-864-0131, E-mail: ccarpenter@wlsmail.org; *Head, Youth Serv,* Linda Surovich; Tel: 914-864-0039, E-mail: lsurovich@wlsmail.org; *Bus Mgr,* Lisa Ann Graziade; Tel: 914-864-0043, E-mail: lgraziadei@wlsmail.org; Staff 17 (MLS 5, Non-MLS 12)
Founded 1913. Pop 10,000
Library Holdings: AV Mats 6,096; Electronic Media & Resources 33; Large Print Bks 200; Bk Vols 74,292; Per Subs 148; Talking Bks 500; Videos 2,402
Special Collections: State Document Depository
Subject Interests: Job info, Local hist
Automation Activity & Vendor Info: (Cataloging) SirsiDynix; (Circulation) SirsiDynix; (OPAC) SirsiDynix
Wireless access
Mem of Westchester Library System
Open Mon & Tues 10-5, Wed & Thurs 10-6, Fri & Sat 10-4, Sun 12-3
Friends of the Library Group

M NORTHERN WESTCHESTER HOSPITAL*, Hal Federman, MD Health Sciences Library, Wallace Pavilion, 1st Flr, 400 E Main St, 10549-0802. SAN 311-5275. Tel: 914-666-1259. FAX: 914-666-1259. Web Site: www.nwhc.net/wellness-and-prevention/health-library. *Dir,* Janie Kaplan; E-mail: JKaplan1@nwhc.net; Staff 1 (MLS 1)
Founded 1960
Library Holdings: e-books 35; e-journals 200; Bk Titles 600; Bk Vols 800; Per Subs 90
Subject Interests: Clinical med, Med libr
Automation Activity & Vendor Info: (OPAC) Professional Software; (Serials) TDNet
Wireless access
Partic in Basic Health Sciences Library Network; Health Info Librs of Westchester; Metropolitan New York Library Council
Restriction: Open by appt only

MOUNT MORRIS

P MOUNT MORRIS LIBRARY*, 121 Main St, 14510-1596. SAN 311-5283. Tel: 585-658-4412. FAX: 585-658-3642. Web Site: mountmorrislibrary.org. *Dir,* Sharon Stanley; E-mail: MtMorrisLibraryDirector@owwl.org
Founded 1910. Pop 4,478; Circ 25,412
Library Holdings: Bk Titles 17,923; Per Subs 24
Subject Interests: English as a second lang
Wireless access
Mem of Pioneer Library System
Open Mon & Fri 2-5, Tues 9-12 & 2-8, Thurs 2-8, Sat 11-3
Friends of the Library Group

MOUNT VERNON

P MOUNT VERNON PUBLIC LIBRARY, 28 S First Ave, 10550. SAN 311-5313. Tel: 914-668-1840. Circulation Tel: 914-668-1840, Ext 216. Administration Tel: 914-668-1840, Ext 223. FAX: 914-668-1018. Web Site: www.mountvernonpubliclibrary.org. *Libr Dir,* Timur Davis; E-mail: timurd@wlsmail.org; *Head, Circ,* Doris Hackett; E-mail: dhackett@wlsmail.org; *Head, Coll, Head, Electronic Res,* Nishan Stepak; Tel: 914-668-1840, Ext 228, E-mail: nstepak@wlsmail.org; *Head, Per,* Maxine Grandison; Tel: 914-668-1840, Ext 206, E-mail: mgrandison@wlsmail.org; *Head, Ref,* Gary Newman; Tel: 914-668-1840, Ext 209, E-mail: newman@wlsmail.org; *Community Outreach,* Catherine Webb; Tel: 914-668-1840, Ext 236, E-mail: cwebb@wlsmail.org; Staff 13 (MLS 13)
Founded 1854. Pop 67,153; Circ 239,186
Jul 2014-Jun 2015 Income $4,350,000. Mats Exp $250,000
Library Holdings: Bk Vols 615,000; Per Subs 4,320
Special Collections: Black Heritage (Haines Coll); Mills Law Coll. Oral History; State Document Depository; US Document Depository
Subject Interests: African-Am hist, Behav sci, Foreign lang, Law, Local hist, Music, Soc sci
Automation Activity & Vendor Info: (Acquisitions) SirsiDynix; (Cataloging) SirsiDynix; (Circulation) SirsiDynix; (ILL) SirsiDynix; (Media Booking) SirsiDynix; (OPAC) SirsiDynix; (Serials) SirsiDynix
Wireless access
Mem of Westchester Library System
Open Mon-Thurs 10-8:30, Fri 10-6, Sat 10-5 (9-1 Summer)
Friends of the Library Group

NANUET

P NANUET PUBLIC LIBRARY*, 149 Church St, 10954. SAN 311-5364. Tel: 845-623-4281. FAX: 845-623-2415. E-mail: nan@rcls.org. Web Site: www.nanuetpubliclibrary.org. *Dir,* Jessica Bowen; Tel: 845-623-4281, Ext 116; *Adult Serv,* Kim Maples; Tel: 845-623-4281, Ext 127; *Ch Serv,* Lauren Banks; Tel: 845-623-4281, Ext 112
Founded 1894. Pop 13,000; Circ 274,238
Library Holdings: AV Mats 15,402; Bk Titles 135,000; Per Subs 200
Automation Activity & Vendor Info: (Acquisitions) SirsiDynix; (Cataloging) SirsiDynix; (Circulation) SirsiDynix; (Course Reserve) SirsiDynix; (ILL) SirsiDynix; (Media Booking) SirsiDynix; (OPAC) SirsiDynix; (Serials) SirsiDynix
Wireless access
Mem of Ramapo Catskill Library System
Open Mon-Thurs 10-8, Fri & Sat 10-4
Friends of the Library Group

NAPANOCH

S EASTERN CORRECTIONAL FACILITY LIBRARY*, 30 Institution Rd, 12458. SAN 325-8955. Tel: 845-647-7400. FAX: 845-647-7400. *Librn,* Gabriel Wasserman; Staff 1 (MLS 1)
Library Holdings: Bk Vols 11,000; Per Subs 88
Automation Activity & Vendor Info: (Cataloging) Follett Software; (Circulation) Follett Software
Special Services for the Blind - Audio mat
Open Mon-Fri 8am-9:30pm

NAPLES

P NAPLES LIBRARY*, 118 S Main, 14512. SAN 311-5372. Tel: 585-374-2757. FAX: 585-374-6493. Web Site: napleslibrary.org. *Libr Dir,* Judy Schewe; E-mail: napleslibrarydirector@owwl.org
Founded 1962. Pop 3,563; Circ 17,367
Library Holdings: Bk Titles 17,000; Per Subs 50
Automation Activity & Vendor Info: (Acquisitions) SirsiDynix; (Cataloging) SirsiDynix; (Circulation) SirsiDynix; (Course Reserve) SirsiDynix; (ILL) SirsiDynix; (Media Booking) SirsiDynix; (OPAC) SirsiDynix; (Serials) SirsiDynix
Wireless access
Mem of Pioneer Library System
Open Mon-Fri 10-5, Sat 10-2
Friends of the Library Group

NASSAU

P NASSAU FREE LIBRARY*, 18 Church St, 12123. (Mail add: PO Box 436, 12123-0436), SAN 311-5380. Tel: 518-766-2715. FAX: 518-766-2715. E-mail: director@nassaufreelibrary.org. Web Site: www.nassaufreelibrary.org. *Dir,* Laurenne Teachout; E-mail: director@nassaufreelibrary.org; *Asst Dir,* Tracey Clague; Staff 1 (MLS 1)
Founded 1893. Pop 4,800; Circ 19,249
Library Holdings: Bk Vols 20,442
Automation Activity & Vendor Info: (Cataloging) Innovative Interfaces, Inc - Sierra; (Circulation) Innovative Interfaces, Inc - Sierra; (ILL) Innovative Interfaces, Inc - Sierra; (OPAC) Innovative Interfaces, Inc - Sierra; (Serials) Innovative Interfaces, Inc - Sierra
Wireless access
Function: Activity rm, Adult bk club, Archival coll, Art exhibits, Audiobks on Playaways & MP3, Audiobks via web, Bks on CD, Children's prog, Computer training, Computers for patron use, Digital talking bks, E-Readers, Electronic databases & coll, Family literacy, Free DVD rentals, Govt ref serv, Health sci info serv, Holiday prog, ILL available, Internet access, Life-long learning prog for all ages, Magazines, Magnifiers for reading, Mail & tel request accepted, Mango lang, Meeting rooms, Movies, Museum passes, Music CDs, Online cat, Online ref, Outreach serv, Outside serv via phone, mail, e-mail & web, OverDrive digital audio bks, Photocopying/Printing, Preschool outreach, Preschool reading prog, Prog for adults, Prog for children & young adult, Ref serv available, Scanner, Senior computer classes, Senior outreach, Serves people with intellectual disabilities, Spanish lang bks, Spoken cassettes & CDs, Spoken cassettes & DVDs, Story hour, Summer reading prog, Tax forms, Teen prog, Telephone ref, Wheelchair accessible, Workshops
Mem of Upper Hudson Library System
Open Mon, Tues, Thurs & Fri 2-8, Wed 10-12 & 2-8, Sat 10-1
Friends of the Library Group

NEW BERLIN

P NEW BERLIN LIBRARY, 15 S Main St, 13411. (Mail add: PO Box J, 13411-0610), SAN 311-5399. Tel: 607-847-8564. FAX: 607-847-8564. Web Site: libraries.4cls.org/newberlin. *Dir,* Michelle Priola; E-mail: nb.michelle@4cls.org
Founded 1896. Pop 4,519; Circ 24,362
Library Holdings: CDs 150; DVDs 200; Large Print Bks 300; Bk Titles 32,000; Per Subs 100; Talking Bks 250; Videos 300
Special Collections: Literacy Service Center Museum; New Berlin Gazettes, microfilm; Oral History Project
Subject Interests: Genealogy, Local hist
Automation Activity & Vendor Info: (Cataloging) SirsiDynix; (Circulation) SirsiDynix
Wireless access
Mem of Four County Library System
Special Services for the Blind - Talking bks
Open Mon & Wed 10-8, Tues, Thurs & Fri 10-5, Sat 10-Noon

NEW CITY

S HISTORICAL SOCIETY OF ROCKLAND COUNTY LIBRARY*, 20 Zukor Rd, 10956. SAN 328-4271. Tel: 845-634-9629. FAX: 845-634-8690. E-mail: info@rocklandhistory.org. Web Site: www.rocklandhistory.org. *Exec Dir,* Susan Deeks; E-mail: director@rocklandhistory.org
Library Holdings: AV Mats 20; Bk Vols 1,200
Special Collections: Oral History
Subject Interests: Local genealogy, Local hist
Function: Ref serv available, Res libr
Publications: South of the Mountain (Quarterly)
Restriction: Non-circulating, Not open to pub, Open by appt only

P NEW CITY LIBRARY*, 220 N Main St, 10956. SAN 311-5402. Tel: 845-634-4997. Circulation Tel: 845-634-4997, Ext 124. Reference Tel: 845-634-4997, Ext 126. Administration Tel: 845-634-4997, Ext 112. Reference FAX: 845-634-4401. Administration FAX: 845-634-0173. Web Site: www.newcitylibrary.org. *Dir,* Marianne Silver; E-mail: msilver@rcls.org; *Head, Adult Serv,* Marianne Silver; E-mail: msilver@rcls.org; *Head, Children's Servx,* Janet Makoujy; E-mail: jmakoujy@rcls.org; *Head, Circ,* Gail Seidenfrau; *Head, Tech Serv,* Sue Telesca; E-mail: stelesca@rcls.org; *Ch,* Kathy Bachor; E-mail: kbachor@rcls.org; *Coll Develop Librn,* Nancy Moskowitz; E-mail: nmoskowi@rcls.org; *Coll Develop Librn,* Karen Ostertag; E-mail: kosterta@rcls.org; *Coll Develop Librn,* Harriet Wollenberg; E-mail: hwollenb@rcls.org; *Teen Serv Librn,* Mary Phillips; E-mail: mphillip@rcls.org; *Coordr, Commun Relations,* Veronica Reynolds; E-mail: vreynolds@rcls.org; Staff 47 (MLS 14, Non-MLS 33)
Founded 1933. Pop 46,708; Circ 589,876
Library Holdings: AV Mats 28,574; CDs 5,480; DVDs 3,683; Electronic Media & Resources 49,479; Large Print Bks 3,479; Bk Vols 171,209; Per Subs 634; Talking Bks 4,979; Videos 6,959
Special Collections: Rockland County (NY) Information & Genealogy

Subject Interests: Korean (Lang), Local hist, Russian (Lang), Spanish (Lang)
Automation Activity & Vendor Info: (Cataloging) SirsiDynix; (Circulation) SirsiDynix; (OPAC) SirsiDynix
Wireless access
Function: Adult bk club, Art exhibits, Audiobks via web, AV serv, Bk club(s), Bks on cassette, Bks on CD, Children's prog, Computer training, Computers for patron use, Digital talking bks, E-Reserves, Electronic databases & coll, Free DVD rentals, Genealogy discussion group, Health sci info serv, Holiday prog, ILL available, Mail & tel request accepted, Museum passes, Music CDs, Notary serv, OverDrive digital audio bks, Photocopying/Printing, Prog for adults, Prog for children & young adult, Ref serv available, Summer reading prog, Tax forms, Teen prog, Telephone ref, VHS videos
Publications: Fine Print (Newsletter)
Mem of Ramapo Catskill Library System
Open Mon-Thurs 9-9, Fri 11-6, Sat 9-5, Sun 12-5; Mon-Thurs (Summer) 9-9, Fri 12-6, Sat 11-3

GL NEW YORK STATE SUPREME COURT NINTH JUDICIAL DISTRICT*, Rockland County Supreme Court Law Library, One S Main St, 2nd Flr, Ste 234, 10956. Tel: 845-483-8399. E-mail: 9JDLawLibrary@nycourts.gov.
Open Mon-Fri 9-1 & 2-5

NEW HAMPTON

G MID-HUDSON FORENSIC PSYCHIATRIC CENTER LIBRARY*, 2834 Rte 17M, 10958. (Mail add: PO Box 158, 10958-0158), SAN 327-8700. Tel: 845-374-8700, Ext 3625. FAX: 845-374-8700, Ext 3622. Web Site: omh.ny.gov/omhweb/facilities/mhpc. *Librn,* Elizabeth Horvath; Staff 1 (MLS 1)
Library Holdings: Bk Vols 9,000; Per Subs 60
Partic in Southeastern New York Library Resources Council
Restriction: Not open to pub

NEW HARTFORD

P NEW HARTFORD PUBLIC LIBRARY*, Two Library Lane, 13413-2815. SAN 326-5358. Tel: 315-733-1535. FAX: 315-733-0795. E-mail: newhartford@midyork.org. Web Site: www.newhartfordpubliclibrary.org. *Interim Dir,* Anne DuRoss; E-mail: aduross@midyork.org; *Ref Librn,* Jack Henke; E-mail: jhenke@midyork.org; *Ref Librn,* Margaret Preston; E-mail: mpreston@midyork.org; *Children's Programmer,* Ashlyn Samargia; E-mail: asamargia@midyork.org; *Info Tech,* Roy Senn; E-mail: rsenn@midyork.org; Staff 20.5 (MLS 2.5, Non-MLS 18)
Founded 1976. Pop 22,166; Circ 166,409
Jan 2013-Dec 2013 Income $504,280, State $5,187, City $400,000, County $19,934, Other $79,159. Mats Exp $494,499. Sal $337,101
Library Holdings: AV Mats 7,844; e-books 649; Bk Vols 74,532; Per Subs 67
Automation Activity & Vendor Info: (Acquisitions) SirsiDynix; (Cataloging) SirsiDynix; (Circulation) SirsiDynix; (Course Reserve) SirsiDynix; (ILL) SirsiDynix; (Media Booking) SirsiDynix; (OPAC) SirsiDynix; (Serials) SirsiDynix
Wireless access
Function: Adult bk club, Art exhibits, Audiobks via web, Bks on cassette, Bks on CD, Children's prog, Homebound delivery serv, Photocopying/Printing, Senior computer classes, Summer reading prog
Mem of Mid-York Library System
Open Mon & Tues 10-9, Thurs & Fri 10-6, Sat 10-5
Friends of the Library Group

NEW HYDE PARK

P HILLSIDE PUBLIC LIBRARY*, 155 Lakeville Rd, 11040-3003. SAN 311-5453. Tel: 516-355-7850. FAX: 516-355-7855. Reference E-mail: contact-us@hillsidelibrary.info. Web Site: hillsidelibrary.info. *Libr Dir,* Charlene Noll; Staff 38 (MLS 11, Non-MLS 27)
Founded 1962. Pop 22,000; Circ 153,071
Library Holdings: Audiobooks 1,430; AV Mats 192; CDs 1,763; DVDs 3,839; Large Print Bks 2,451; Bk Titles 104,876; Per Subs 110; Videos 426
Special Collections: Career Resource Center; Greater New Hyde Park Chamber of Commerce Coll; Palma Pursino New Fiction Coll; Patricia Ching Science Fiction Coll; Stanley L. Itkin War Memorial Coll; Teachers' Resource Center
Automation Activity & Vendor Info: (Acquisitions) Baker & Taylor; (Cataloging) Innovative Interfaces, Inc; (Circulation) Innovative Interfaces, Inc; (ILL) Innovative Interfaces, Inc; (OPAC) Innovative Interfaces, Inc; (Serials) Innovative Interfaces, Inc
Wireless access
Function: 24/7 Electronic res, 24/7 Online cat, Activity rm, Adult bk club, Adult literacy prog, After school storytime, Audiobks on Playaways & MP3, Audiobks via web, Bk club(s), Bks on CD, Children's prog, Citizenship assistance, Computer training, Computers for patron use, Digital talking bks, E-Reserves, Electronic databases & coll, For res purposes, Free DVD rentals, Holiday prog, ILL available, Internet access, Literacy & newcomer serv, Magazines, Mail & tel request accepted, Movies, Museum passes, Music CDs, Notary serv, Online cat, Online ref, Outreach serv, Outside serv via phone, mail, e-mail & web, OverDrive digital audio bks, Photocopying/Printing, Preschool outreach, Preschool reading prog, Prog for adults, Prog for children & young adult, Ref & res, Ref serv available, Senior computer classes, Senior outreach, Spoken cassettes & DVDs, Story hour, Summer & winter reading prog, Summer reading prog, Tax forms, Teen prog, Telephone ref, Wheelchair accessible, Winter reading prog, Workshops
Mem of Nassau Library System
Open Mon-Fri (Winter) 10-8:45, Sat 10-4:45, Sun 12-3:45; Mon-Fri (Summer) 10-8:45, Sat 10-2
Restriction: ID required to use computers (Ltd hrs)
Friends of the Library Group

M LONG ISLAND JEWISH MEDICAL CENTER*, Health Sciences Library, Schwartz Research Bldg, 270-05 76th Ave, 11040. SAN 311-5461. Tel: 718-470-7070. FAX: 718-470-6150. Web Site: www.northwell.edu. *Ref & Educ Librn,* Janice Lester; Tel: 718-470-7071, E-mail: jlester1@nshs.edu; *Project Coordr,* Raquel Fereres-Moskowitz; Tel: 718-470-7356, E-mail: rfereres@nshs.edu; Staff 4 (MLS 3, Non-MLS 1)
Founded 1954
Subject Interests: Dentistry, Geriatrics, Med, Nursing, Pharm
Automation Activity & Vendor Info: (Cataloging) SirsiDynix; (Circulation) SirsiDynix; (OPAC) SirsiDynix; (Serials) SirsiDynix
Wireless access
Partic in Metropolitan New York Library Council
Open Mon-Fri 8:30-6:30

NEW LEBANON

P NEW LEBANON LIBRARY*, 550 State Rte 20, 12125. SAN 311-418X. Tel: 518-794-8844. E-mail: leb@taconic.net. Web Site: newlebanonlibrary.org. *Libr Dir,* Moriah Sears; *Asst Dir,* Michelle Hoffman; Staff 1.8 (MLS 1, Non-MLS 0.8)
Founded 1804. Pop 2,271; Circ 27,000
Dec 2019-Nov 2020 Income $176,400, Locally Generated Income $135,000, Parent Institution $1,500, Other $39,900. Mats Exp $15,000, Books $15,000. Sal $102,300
Library Holdings: Audiobooks 597; AV Mats 551; CDs 219; DVDs 2,107; Large Print Bks 838; Bk Vols 17,063; Per Subs 38
Special Collections: Local History Coll; Notes from New Lebanon; Shaker Coll; STEAM Kits Coll
Automation Activity & Vendor Info: (Acquisitions) Baker & Taylor; (Cataloging) Baker & Taylor; (Circulation) Innovative Interfaces, Inc; (ILL) Innovative Interfaces, Inc
Wireless access
Function: 24/7 Electronic res, 24/7 Online cat, Activity rm, Adult bk club, Adult literacy prog, Bks on CD, CD-ROM, Children's prog, Computer training, Computers for patron use, Electronic databases & coll, Family literacy, Free DVD rentals, Holiday prog, ILL available, Internet access, Magazines, Mango lang, Meeting rooms, Movies, Museum passes, Music CDs, Online cat, Online ref, Outreach serv, Outside serv via phone, mail, e-mail & web, OverDrive digital audio bks, Photocopying/Printing, Preschool outreach, Printer for laptops & handheld devices, Prog for adults, Prog for children & young adult, Senior outreach, STEM programs, Story hour, Summer & winter reading prog, Tax forms, Teen prog, Wheelchair accessible, Workshops
Mem of Mid-Hudson Library System
Open Mon-Wed & Fri 10-6, Thurs 10-7, Sat 10-1
Restriction: In-house use for visitors

NEW PALTZ

P ELTING MEMORIAL LIBRARY*, 93 Main St, 12561-1593. SAN 311-5488. Tel: 845-255-5030. Web Site: www.eltinglibrary.org. *Dir,* John A Giralico; E-mail: jgiralico@eltinglibrary.org; Staff 4 (MLS 1, Non-MLS 3)
Founded 1909. Pop 14,000; Circ 100,000
Library Holdings: Audiobooks 325; CDs 1,000; DVDs 2,000; Large Print Bks 1,500; Bk Titles 50,000; Per Subs 75; Videos 800
Special Collections: Mid-Hudson History (Haviland-Heidgerd Coll). Municipal Document Depository; Oral History
Automation Activity & Vendor Info: (Acquisitions) Baker & Taylor; (Circulation) Innovative Interfaces, Inc - Millennium; (OPAC) Innovative Interfaces, Inc - Millennium; (Serials) EBSCO Online
Wireless access
Mem of Mid-Hudson Library System
Open Mon, Wed & Fri 10-8, Tues & Thurs 12-7, Sat 10-4, Sun 12-4
Friends of the Library Group

S HISTORIC HUGUENOT STREET LIBRARY & ARCHIVES*, Schoonmaker Library, 88 Huguenot St, 12561. SAN 311-5496. Tel: 845-255-1660. FAX: 845-255-0376. E-mail: library@huguenotstreet.org.

Web Site: www.huguenotstreet.org/research-library. *Librn & Archivist,* Carrie Allmendinger; Staff 1 (MLS 1)
Founded 1974
Library Holdings: Bk Titles 2,300; Per Subs 11
Special Collections: Bible Coll; Ciphering Book Coll; Map Coll; Personal & Family Papers Coll; Photograph Coll; Rare Books Coll; Town of New Paltz Coll
Subject Interests: Dutch hist, Fr hist, Genealogy, Huguenot hist, Immigration to Am, 17th-19th centuries, Local hist, NY State hist, Vernacular archit
Wireless access
Function: For res purposes, Online ref, Ref serv available, Res libr
Restriction: Lending to staff only, Non-circulating, Not a lending libr, Open by appt only, Open to pub by appt only, Open to pub upon request, Open to researchers by request, Pub by appt only, Researchers by appt only

C STATE UNIVERSITY OF NEW YORK AT NEW PALTZ*, Sojourner Truth Library, 300 Hawk Dr, 12561-2493. SAN 311-550X. Tel: 845-257-3700. Circulation Tel: 845-257-3714. Interlibrary Loan Service Tel: 845-257-3680. Reference Tel: 845-257-3710. Administration Tel: 845-257-3719. Interlibrary Loan Service FAX: 845-257-3670. Administration FAX: 845-257-3718. Web Site: library.newpaltz.edu. *Dean,* William Mark Colvson; E-mail: colvsonm@newpaltz.edu; *Head, Info Syst,* Kristy Lee; Tel: 845-257-3769, E-mail: leek@newpaltz.edu; *Assoc Librn, Coll Develop,* Valerie Mittenberg; Tel: 845-257-3703, E-mail: mittenbv@newpaltz.edu; *Ser/Accounts Librn,* Elizabeth Strickland; Tel: 845-257-3662, E-mail: strickle@newpaltz.edu; Staff 28 (MLS 15, Non-MLS 13)
Founded 1886. Enrl 7,600; Fac 350; Highest Degree: Master
Jul 2013-Jun 2014 Income $2,670,520, State $2,362,471, Other $308,049. Mats Exp $803,077, Books $204,666, Per/Ser (Incl. Access Fees) $86,084, Electronic Ref Mat (Incl. Access Fees) $507,024, Presv $5,303. Sal $1,461,028 (Prof $850,306)
Library Holdings: AV Mats 3,000; CDs 1,233; DVDs 1,370; e-books 122,481; e-journals 83,863; Microforms 40,821; Bk Vols 399,762; Per Subs 410
Special Collections: State Document Depository; US Document Depository
Automation Activity & Vendor Info: (Acquisitions) Ex Libris Group; (Cataloging) Ex Libris Group; (Circulation) Ex Libris Group; (Course Reserve) Ex Libris Group; (ILL) OCLC ILLiad; (OPAC) Ex Libris Group; (Serials) Ex Libris Group
Wireless access
Publications: The Latest @ The Library (Newsletter)
Partic in SUNYConnect
Open Mon-Thurs 8am-12:30am, Fri 8am-9pm, Sat 10-9, Sun 1-12:30
Friends of the Library Group

NEW ROCHELLE

C THE COLLEGE OF NEW ROCHELLE*, Gill Library, 29 Castle Pl, 10805-2308. SAN 311-5518. Tel: 914-654-5345. Circulation Tel: 914-654-5340. Interlibrary Loan Service Tel: 914-654-5491. Reference Tel: 914-654-5342. FAX: 914-654-5884. E-mail: gillrefdesk@cnr.edu. Web Site: library.cnr.edu. *Dean,* Ana E Fontoura; *Librn, Ref Serv,* Roslyn Grandy; *Coordr, Libr Serv,* Yvette Page; *Learning Commons Coord, Ref Serv,* Carlo Minchillo; *Archivist,* Martha Counihan; *ILL, Ref (Info Servs),* Jillian Kehoe; Tel: 914-654-5419; Staff 15 (MLS 14, Non-MLS 1)
Founded 1904. Enrl 5,811; Fac 799; Highest Degree: Master
Library Holdings: Bk Vols 150,000; Per Subs 1,100
Special Collections: Early English Text Society; English Literature (Thomas More); James Joyce; Religious History (Ursuline Coll)
Subject Interests: Educ, Psychol
Automation Activity & Vendor Info: (Acquisitions) Innovative Interfaces, Inc; (Cataloging) OCLC; (Circulation) Innovative Interfaces, Inc; (Course Reserve) Innovative Interfaces, Inc; (ILL) OCLC; (OPAC) Innovative Interfaces, Inc; (Serials) Innovative Interfaces, Inc
Wireless access
Publications: Acquisitions List
Partic in Metropolitan New York Library Council; OCLC Online Computer Library Center, Inc; Westchester Academic Library Directors Organization
Open Mon-Thurs 8am-11pm, Fri 8-5, Sat 10-6, Sun 1-11

Departmental Libraries:

BROOKLYN CAMPUS, 1368 Fulton St, Brooklyn, 11216. Tel: 718-638-2500. FAX: 914-654-5080. *Librn,* Lilith Newby; *Librn,* Marie Octobre
Library Holdings: Bk Vols 1,000; Per Subs 25
Open Mon-Thurs 10-9, Fri 10-3, Sat 11-4

CARDINAL JOHN O'CONNOR CAMPUS, 332 E 149 St, Bronx, 10451. Tel: 718-665-1310. FAX: 718-292-2906. *Librn,* Yvette Page
Open Mon-Thurs 10-9, Fri 10-4, Sat 10-2

CO-OP CITY CAMPUS, 755 Co-op City Blvd, Bronx, 10475. Tel: 718-320-0300, Ext 232. FAX: 718-379-1680. *Librn,* Yvonne Hamilton
Library Holdings: Bk Vols 3,000
Open Mon-Thurs 10-9, Fri 10-3, Sat 10-2

ROSA PARKS CAMPUS, 144 W 125th St, New York, 10027. Tel: 212-662-7500. FAX: 212-864-9469. *Librn,* Mario A Charles
Library Holdings: Bk Vols 1,000
Open Mon-Thurs 10-9, Fri 10-6, Sat 11-3

C COLLEGE OF NEW ROCHELLE*, Irene Gill Library, 29 Castle Pl, 10805. Tel: 212-815-1699. Web Site: library2.cnr.edu. *Dean of Libr,* Ana Fontoura; E-mail: afontoura@cnr.edu; *Librn,* Natalia Sucre; E-mail: nsucre@cnr.edu
Library Holdings: Bk Vols 12,000; Per Subs 50
Special Collections: Harry Gray Labor Coll
Automation Activity & Vendor Info: (Cataloging) Follett Software; (Circulation) Follett Software; (OPAC) Follett Software
Open Mon-Thurs 1-9, Fri 10:30-6:30

C IONA COLLEGE*, Ryan Library, 715 North Ave, 10801-1890. SAN 311-5534. Tel: 914-633-2351. Circulation Tel: 914-633-2343. Interlibrary Loan Service Tel: 914-633-2352. Reference Tel: 914-637-7716. FAX: 914-633-2136. Web Site: www.iona.edu/libraries. *Dir of Libr,* Richard L Palladino; E-mail: rpalladino@iona.edu; *Asst Dir, Lib,* Natalka Sawchuk; Tel: 914-633-2220, E-mail: nsawchuk@iona.edu; *Digital Colls, Fac Librn, Mgr,* Anthony Iodice; Tel: 914-633-2347, E-mail: aiodice@iona.edu; *Info Literacy, Instruction Librn,* Callie Bergeris; Tel: 914-633-2227, E-mail: cbergeris@iona.edu; *Coll Develop, Coordr, Tech Serv,* Diana Kiel; Tel: 914-633-2417, E-mail: dkiel@iona.edu; *Media & Digital Res Librn,* Jill Gross; Tel: 914-633-2353, E-mail: jgross@iona.edu; *Ref & Instrul Serv Librn,* Cynthia Denesevich; Tel: 914-633-2525, E-mail: cdenesevich@iona.edu; *Ser Librn,* Valerie Masone; Tel: 914-633-2449, E-mail: vmasone@iona.edu; *Asst Help Desk Mgr/Circ Supvr,* Kathleen Pascuzzi; E-mail: kpascuzzi@iona.edu; *Doc Delivery Spec,* Ed Helmrich; E-mail: ehelmrich@iona.edu; Staff 8 (MLS 8)
Founded 1940. Highest Degree: Master
Special Collections: Br. Charles B. Quinn Irish Coll; Brother Edmund Rice Coll; Michael J. O'Brien Coll; Msgr. Loughman (St. Theresa of Lisieux) Coll; Sean MacBride Coll; Thanhouser Studio Archive; Thomas Paine National Historical Association Coll (TPNHA); William York Tindall Coll
Subject Interests: Bus, Hist, Irish lang, Lit, Relig studies
Automation Activity & Vendor Info: (Acquisitions) OCLC WorldShare Interlibrary Loan; (Cataloging) OCLC; (Circulation) OCLC; (ILL) Clio; (OPAC) OCLC; (Serials) OCLC
Wireless access
Function: 24/7 Electronic res, 24/7 Online cat
Partic in Metropolitan New York Library Council; OCLC Online Computer Library Center, Inc; Westchester Academic Library Directors Organization; Worldcat
Open Mon-Thurs 8am-Midnight, Fri 8-8, Sat 9-8, Sun 10am-Midnight

Departmental Libraries:

HELEN T ARRIGONI LIBRARY-TECHNOLOGY CENTER, 715 North Ave, 10801-1890. Tel: 914-637-2791. FAX: 914-633-2136. *Supvr, Pub Serv,* Manuel Alvia; Tel: 914-633-2000, Ext 4165, E-mail: malvia@iona.edu; Staff 2 (MLS 1, Non-MLS 1)
Subject Interests: Computer sci, Educ, Mass communications

M MONTEFIORE MEDICAL CENTER*, Medical Library, 16 Guion Pl, 10802. SAN 311-5550. Tel: 914-365-3566. FAX: 914-365-5229. Web Site: www.montefiorehealthsystem.org. *Dir,* Shiegla Smalling; E-mail: ssmallin@montefiore.org; *Assoc Librn,* Marie Elias; E-mail: melias@montefiore.org; Staff 1 (MLS 1)
Founded 1950. Highest Degree: Doctorate
Library Holdings: Bk Vols 1,000; Per Subs 75
Subject Interests: Allied health, Med, Nursing
Automation Activity & Vendor Info: (Acquisitions) Prenax, Inc; (Cataloging) Professional Software; (Circulation) Professional Software; (Course Reserve) Aurora Information Technology; (Serials) Prenax, Inc
Wireless access
Function: Computers for patron use, Electronic databases & coll, Internet access, Outside serv via phone, mail, e-mail & web, Ref & res
Publications: New York State Database (Index to periodicals); Newsletter (Online only)
Partic in National Network of Libraries of Medicine Region 7; Regional Med Libr
Restriction: Authorized patrons

P NEW ROCHELLE PUBLIC LIBRARY*, One Library Plaza, 10801. SAN 352-8308. Tel: 914-632-7878. Reference Tel: 914-813-3737. Administration Tel: 914-632-8509. FAX: 914-632-0262. Web Site: www.nrpl.org. *Dir,* Tom Geoffino; Tel: 914-632-7879, E-mail: tgeoffino@nrpl.org; Staff 34 (MLS 16, Non-MLS 18)
Founded 1894. Pop 72,182; Circ 498,412

Library Holdings: Bk Vols 270,989; Per Subs 3,055
Special Collections: Fine Art Books (Retrospective); Libretti Scores; Local History Coll; Local Newspapers from 1861; Opera; Picture Coll
Automation Activity & Vendor Info: (Cataloging) SirsiDynix; (Circulation) SirsiDynix; (ILL) SirsiDynix; (OPAC) SirsiDynix
Wireless access
Publications: Bi-Monthly Newsletter; Monthly Calendar
Mem of Westchester Library System
Open Mon, Tues & Thurs 9-8, Wed 10-6, Fri 9-5, Sat 10-2
Friends of the Library Group
Branches: 1
HUGUENOT CHILDREN'S LIBRARY, 794 North Ave, 10801, SAN 377-6484. Tel: 914-632-8954. *Mgr,* Susan Moorhead; *Head, Children's Servx,* Kathleen Cronin; Tel: 914-632-7878, Fax: 914-632-0262, E-mail: kcronin@wlsmail.org; Staff 2 (MLS 1, Non-MLS 1)
Library Holdings: Bk Titles 4,000; Bk Vols 4,400
Automation Activity & Vendor Info: (Circulation) SirsiDynix-WorkFlows
Open Mon & Thurs 10-6, Tues, Fri & Sat 10-5, Wed 10-8

R TEMPLE ISRAEL OF NEW ROCHELLE*, Edith H Handelman Library, 1000 Pinebrook Blvd, 10804. SAN 311-5569. Tel: 914-235-1800. FAX: 914-235-1854. Web Site: www.tinr.org. *Librn,* Stephanie Krasner; Tel: 914-636-1204, E-mail: stephkras11@gmail.com; Staff 1 (Non-MLS 1)
Library Holdings: Bk Titles 7,500; Bk Vols 7,300; Spec Interest Per Sub 5
Special Collections: Judaica
Automation Activity & Vendor Info: (Cataloging) Surpass; (Circulation) Surpass
Wireless access
Function: Adult bk club, Art exhibits, Bk club(s), Children's prog, Electronic databases & coll, Family literacy, Holiday prog, Magazines, Prog for children & young adult, Wheelchair accessible
Open Mon-Fri 10-4, Sun 10-Noon
Restriction: Authorized patrons, Borrowing privileges limited to fac & registered students, Congregants only, Open to authorized patrons, Open to fac, students & qualified researchers, Open to students, fac & staff
Friends of the Library Group

NEW WOODSTOCK

P NEW WOODSTOCK FREE LIBRARY*, 2106 Main St, 13122-8718. (Mail add: PO Box 340, 13122-0340), SAN 311-5577. Tel: 315-662-3134. FAX: 315-662-3096. E-mail: newwoodstock@midyork.org. Web Site: www.midyorklib.org/newwoodstock. *Dir,* Norm Parry; *Libr Mgr,* Renee Beardsley; *Coordr, Ch Serv,* Kelly Roberts
Founded 1939
Library Holdings: Bk Vols 30,000
Wireless access
Mem of Mid-York Library System
Open Mon 1-9, Tues, Thurs & Fri 1-5, Wed 1-5 & 7-9, Sat 10-1

NEW YORK

C ADELPHI UNIVERSITY, Manhattan Center Library, 75 Varick St, 10013. SAN 352-4787. Tel: 212-965-8340. FAX: 646-315-8969. E-mail: manhattanlibrary@adelphi.edu. Web Site: www.adelphi.edu/libraries. *Dean, Univ Libr,* Violeta Ilik; Tel: 516-877-3520, E-mail: vilik@adelphi.edu; *Adjunct Fac Librn,* James McAleese; Tel: 212-965-8365, E-mail: mcaleese@adelphi.edu; Staff 1 (MLS 1)
Library Holdings: Bk Vols 7,451; Per Subs 117
Subject Interests: Educ, Intl bus, Psychol, Soc work, Speech, Sports management
Automation Activity & Vendor Info: (Acquisitions) Ex Libris Group; (Cataloging) Ex Libris Group; (Circulation) Ex Libris Group; (Course Reserve) Ex Libris Group; (OPAC) Ex Libris Group; (Serials) Ex Libris Group
Wireless access
Partic in Metropolitan New York Library Council
Open Mon-Thurs Noon-10pm, Fri-Sun 11-4
Restriction: Open to students, fac & staff
Friends of the Library Group

S AESTHETIC REALISM FOUNDATION LIBRARY*, 141 Greene St, 10012. SAN 328-8706. Tel: 212-777-4490. FAX: 212-777-4426. Web Site: aestheticrealism.org. *Librn,* Richita Anderson
Founded 1973
Library Holdings: Bk Vols 4,800
Special Collections: Books & Periodicals Containing Poems, Essays, Lectures by Eli Siegel & Works by Aesthetic Realism Consultants
Subject Interests: Aesthetics, Art, Drama, Lit, Poetry, Soc sci
Wireless access
Publications: The Right of Aesthetic Realism To Be Known (Periodical)
Restriction: Open to fac, students & qualified researchers
Branches:
ELI SIEGEL COLLECTION, 141 Greene St, 10012-3201, SAN 328-8722. Tel: 212-777-4490. FAX: 212-777-4426. Web Site: www.aestheticrealism.org. *Librn,* Richita Anderson; Staff 3 (Non-MLS 3)
Founded 1982
Library Holdings: Bk Vols 25,000; Per Subs 500
Special Collections: 19th Century Periodical Literature; British & American Poetry; Early American History; French, German & Spanish Literature; Lessons & Lectures by Eli Siegel, Founder of Aesthetic Realism; Poetry & Prose of Eli Siegel, original ms, holograph
Subject Interests: Art, Econ, Hist, Labor, Literary criticism, Philos, Poetry, Sciences
Restriction: Open to fac, students & qualified researchers

L ALSTON & BIRD, LLP LIBRARY*, 90 Park Ave, 12th Flr, 10016. SAN 325-5255. Tel: 212-210-9526. Interlibrary Loan Service Tel: 212-210-9531. FAX: 212-210-9444. Web Site: www.alston.com/en/offices/new-york. *Libr Mgr,* John H Davey; E-mail: john.davey@alston.com; *Ref Librn,* Tina Zoccali; E-mail: tina.zoccali@alston.com; Staff 2 (MLS 2)
Library Holdings: Bk Vols 15,000
Special Collections: German Law Materials
Automation Activity & Vendor Info: (Acquisitions) SydneyPlus; (Cataloging) SydneyPlus; (Circulation) SydneyPlus; (ILL) SydneyPlus; (OPAC) SydneyPlus; (Serials) SydneyPlus
Open Mon-Fri 9-5

S AMERICAN ACADEMY OF ARTS & LETTERS LIBRARY*, 633 W 155th St, 10032. SAN 311-564X. Tel: 212-368-5900. E-mail: academy@artsandletters.org. Web Site: artsandletters.org. *Exec Dir,* Cody Upton; Staff 10 (MLS 10)
Library Holdings: Bk Vols 25,000
Subject Interests: Art, Lit, Manuscripts, Memorabilia, Music
Wireless access
Restriction: Not open to pub

S AMERICAN ACADEMY OF DRAMATIC ARTS LIBRARY*, 120 Madison Ave, 10016. SAN 311-5658. Tel: 212-686-9244, Ext 337. Web Site: www.aada.org. *Librn,* Deborah Picone; Staff 1 (MLS 1)
Founded 1978
Library Holdings: Bk Titles 8,000
Wireless access
Partic in Metropolitan New York Library Council

S AMERICAN ASSOCIATION OF ADVERTISING AGENCIES*, Research Services, 1065 Avenue of the Americas, 16th Flr, 10018. SAN 311-5690. Tel: 212-682-2500. E-mail: research@aaaa.org. Web Site: www.aaaa.org. *Sr VPres,* Marsha Appel; *Asst Mgr,* Marge Morris; *Mgr, Online Serv & Tech,* Julie Zilavy; Staff 9 (MLS 9)
Founded 1938
Library Holdings: Bk Titles 900; Bk Vols 1,000; Per Subs 100
Subject Interests: Advertising, Advertising agency bus, Mkt
Publications: Index to AAAA Bulletins, Newsletters & Press Releases
Open Mon-Fri 8:30-5:30

S AMERICAN HUNGARIAN LIBRARY & HISTORICAL SOCIETY*, 215 E 82nd St, 10028. SAN 375-7277. Tel: 646-340-4172. E-mail: info@americanhungarianlibrary.org. Web Site: www.hungarianlibrary.org. *Libr Mgr,* Olivia Olah
Founded 1955
Library Holdings: DVDs 30; Bk Titles 6,000; Per Subs 1
Special Collections: Hungarian Subject Matters & Fiction in English
Subject Interests: Hungarian culture, Hungarian hist, Hungarian lit
Automation Activity & Vendor Info: (Cataloging) Inmagic, Inc.
Wireless access
Open Sat 10-1, Thurs 4-8
Friends of the Library Group

S AMERICAN IRISH HISTORICAL SOCIETY LIBRARY*, 991 Fifth Ave, 10028. SAN 311-5860. Tel: 212-288-2263. FAX: 212-628-7927. E-mail: library@aihs.org. Web Site: aihs.org/library. *Librn,* Georgette Keane
Founded 1897
Library Holdings: Bk Vols 10,000
Special Collections: Daniel Cohalan Papers; Friends of Irish Freedom Papers
Subject Interests: Am Irish, Gaelic lit, Irish hist, Lit
Publications: Newsletter (Quarterly); The Recorder (Semi-annual)
Restriction: Open by appt only

S AMERICAN KENNEL CLUB INC LIBRARY*, 260 Madison Ave, 4th Flr, 10016. SAN 311-5895. Tel: 212-696-8216. E-mail: library@akc.org. Web Site: www.akc.org/about/archive. *Archivist,* Brynn White; E-mail: bew@akc.org; Staff 1 (MLS 1)
Founded 1934
Library Holdings: Bk Vols 18,000; Per Subs 300; Videos 350

Subject Interests: Art about dogs, Breeding, Care, Domestic, Foreign studies bks, Training of dogs
Automation Activity & Vendor Info: (Cataloging) OCLC CatExpress; (OPAC) EOS International
Wireless access
Function: Ref serv available, Res libr
Partic in Metropolitan New York Library Council
Open Mon-Fri 9:30-4:30
Restriction: Not a lending libr

S AMERICAN MUSEUM OF NATURAL HISTORY LIBRARY, Research Library, 79th St & Central Park W, 10024-5192. SAN 352-8510. Tel: 212-769-5400. Interlibrary Loan Service Tel: 212-769-5404. FAX: 212-769-5009. Reference E-mail: libref@amnh.org. Web Site: www.amnh.org/our-research/research-library. *Harold Boeschenstein Dir,* Tom Baione; Tel: 212-769-5417, E-mail: tbaione@amnh.org; *Asst Dir, Acq,* Matthew Bolin; Tel: 212-769-5409, E-mail: mbolin@amnh.org; Staff 15 (MLS 9, Non-MLS 6)
Founded 1869
Library Holdings: Bk Titles 153,000; Bk Vols 550,000; Per Subs 4,004
Special Collections: Art & Memorabilia; Natural History Film Archives; Photograph & Archives Coll; Rare Books & Manuscripts Coll
Subject Interests: Anthrop, Astronomy, Biology, Expedition, Geol, Hist of sci, Mineralogy, Museology, Paleontology, Travel, Zoology
Wireless access
Function: Archival coll, Art exhibits, Computers for patron use, Electronic databases & coll, ILL available, Internet access, Online cat, Online ref, Photocopying/Printing, Ref serv available, Scanner, Telephone ref, Wheelchair accessible
Publications: Anthropological Papers; Bull of the American Museum of Natural History Library; James Arthur Lecture Series; Novitates, Natural History
Partic in Med Libr Consortium; OCLC Online Computer Library Center, Inc
Open Tues-Thurs 2-5:30
Restriction: Authorized scholars by appt, Circulates for staff only, Open to qualified scholars
Branches:
BASHFORD DEAN MEMORIAL LIBRARY, 79th St at Central Park W, 10024-5192, SAN 352-857X. Tel: 212-769-5798. FAX: 212-769-5009. Web Site: research.amnh.org/ichthyology. *Curator,* Melanie Stiassny; Tel: 212-769-5796, Fax: 212-769-5642, E-mail: mljs@amnh.org
Subject Interests: Biol of fishes
Restriction: Staff use only
HENRY FAIRFIELD OSBORN LIBRARY, Central Park W at 79th St, 10024, SAN 352-8545. Tel: 212-769-5803. Administration Tel: 212-769-5821. *Adminr,* Susan K Bell; Fax: 212-769-5842, E-mail: skbell@amnh.org
Founded 1908
Library Holdings: Bk Vols 4,500
Subject Interests: Vertebrate paleontology
Restriction: Open by appt only

S AMERICAN NUMISMATIC SOCIETY LIBRARY*, The Harry W Bass Jr Library, 75 Varick St, 10013. SAN 311-5941. Tel: 212-571-4470, Ext 170. FAX: 212-571-4479. E-mail: library@numismatics.org. Web Site: www.numismatics.org. *Head Librn,* David Hill; E-mail: hill@numismatics.org; Staff 1.5 (MLS 1.5)
Founded 1858
Library Holdings: Bk Titles 100,000; Per Subs 27
Special Collections: Auction catalogs; Numismatics
Automation Activity & Vendor Info: (Cataloging) Koha; (Circulation) Koha; (OPAC) Koha
Wireless access
Open Mon-Fri 9:30-4:30

S AMERICAN SOCIETY FOR PSYCHICAL RESEARCH INC LIBRARY & ARCHIVES, Five W 73rd St, 10023. SAN 311-5984. Tel: 212-799-5050. FAX: 212-496-2497. E-mail: aspr@aspr.com. Web Site: aspr.com. *Exec Dir,* Patrice Keane; E-mail: patricekeane@aspr.com
Founded 1885
Library Holdings: Bk Vols 10,000; Per Subs 300
Subject Interests: Alternative med, Parapsychol, Philos, Psychol, Relig studies, Spiritualism
Automation Activity & Vendor Info: (Cataloging) Inmagic, Inc.; (Circulation) Inmagic, Inc.
Restriction: Open by appt only

L ANDERSON KILL PC*, Law Library, 1251 Avenue of the Americas, 10020-1182. SAN 325-5026. Tel: 212-278-1069. FAX: 212-278-1733. E-mail: library@andersonkill.com. Web Site: andersonkill.com. *Librn,* Evgenia Nikolopoulou; E-mail: enikolopoulou@andersonkill.com; Staff 2 (Non-MLS 2)
Founded 1969
Library Holdings: Bk Titles 2,500; Bk Vols 20,100; Per Subs 150
Wireless access
Restriction: Staff use only

S ANTHOLOGY FILM ARCHIVES*, Jerome Hill Reference Library, 32 Second Ave, 10003. SAN 321-9003. Tel: 212-505-5181. FAX: 212-477-2714. Web Site: anthologyfilmarchives.org. *Dir,* John Mhiripiri; E-mail: john@anthologyfilmarchives.org; Staff 1 (MLS 1)
Founded 1970
Library Holdings: Bk Titles 12,000; Per Subs 250
Subject Interests: Avant garde film, Avant garde video
Publications: Legend of Maya Deren
Restriction: Closed stack, Open by appt only

S ANTI-DEFAMATION LEAGUE*, Rita & Leo Greenland Library & Archive, 605 Third Ave, 10158. SAN 311-6050. Tel: 212-885-5844, 212-885-7823. FAX: 212-885-5882. Web Site: www.adl.org. *Librn,* Marianne Benjamin; E-mail: mbenjamin@adl.org; Staff 3 (MLS 1, Non-MLS 2)
Founded 1939
Library Holdings: Bk Titles 10,000; Bk Vols 15,000; Per Subs 300
Special Collections: Anti-Defamation League Historic & Research Materials
Subject Interests: Anti-Semitism, Civil rights, Discrimination, Human relations, Intergroup relations, Political extremism
Automation Activity & Vendor Info: (Acquisitions) Inmagic, Inc.; (Cataloging) Inmagic, Inc.; (Circulation) Inmagic, Inc.; (OPAC) Inmagic, Inc.; (Serials) Inmagic, Inc.
Function: Archival coll
Restriction: Staff use only

L ARNOLD & PORTER KAYE SCHOLER LLP*, Information Resource Center, 250 W 55th St, 10019-9710. SAN 311-8479. Tel: 212-836-8000, 212-836-8312. FAX: 212-836-8689.
Subject Interests: Banking, Bankruptcy, Copyright, Corporate, Emerging markets, Estates, Labor, Latin Am, Law antitrust, Real estate, Tax, Trademarks, Wills
Automation Activity & Vendor Info: (Acquisitions) EOS International; (Cataloging) EOS International; (Circulation) EOS International; (Course Reserve) EOS International; (ILL) EOS International; (Media Booking) EOS International; (OPAC) EOS International; (Serials) EOS International
Wireless access
Restriction: Open by appt only

L ASSOCIATION OF THE BAR OF THE CITY OF NEW YORK LIBRARY*, 42 W 44th St, 10036. SAN 311-6166. Tel: 212-382-6666, 212-382-6711. FAX: 212-382-6790. E-mail: library@nycbar.org. Web Site: www.abcny.org/library. *Dir,* Richard Tuske; E-mail: rtuske@nycbar.org
Founded 1870
Library Holdings: Bk Titles 200,000; Bk Vols 600,000; Per Subs 2,500
Special Collections: Major coll of legal materials including appellate court records & briefs, domestic law, early Am session laws, foreign & int law
Wireless access
Open Mon-Thurs 9-9, Fri 9-7
Restriction: Mem only

S AUSTRIAN CULTURAL FORUM LIBRARY*, 11 E 52nd St, 10022. SAN 311-6204. Tel: 212-319-5300. FAX: 212-644-8660. E-mail: library@acfny.org. Web Site: www.acfny.org/library. *Librn,* Alexandra Riener; E-mail: alexandra.riener@bmeia.gv.at
Founded 1962
Library Holdings: Bk Vols 10,000; Per Subs 22
Special Collections: Austriaca Coll
Subject Interests: Archit, Art, Educ, Hist, Lit, Music, Performing arts
Wireless access
Open Mon-Fri 10-1 & 2-5

L BAKER & MCKENZIE LLP*, 452 Fifth Ave, 10018. SAN 311-6263. Tel: 212-626-4100. FAX: 212-310-1600. Web Site: www.bakermckenzie.com.
Founded 1971
Library Holdings: Bk Titles 4,500; Bk Vols 25,000; Per Subs 70
Subject Interests: Arbitration, Banking, Captive ins, Corporate law, Intellectual property, Securities, Tax
Automation Activity & Vendor Info: (Acquisitions) Sydney; (Cataloging) Sydney; (Circulation) Sydney; (OPAC) Sydney; (Serials) Sydney
Wireless access
Publications: TOC Bulletin
Restriction: Not open to pub

C BANK STREET COLLEGE OF EDUCATION LIBRARY*, 610 W 112th St, 5th Flr, 10025. SAN 311-628X. Tel: 212-875-4455. Interlibrary Loan Service Tel: 212-875-4458. Reference Tel: 212-875-4456. FAX: 212-875-4558. E-mail: librarian@bankstreet.edu. Web Site: www.bankstreet.edu/library. *Dir, Libr Serv,* Kristin Freda; E-mail:

kfreda@bankstreet.edu; *Dir, Ctr for Children's Lit,* Dr Cindy Weill; E-mail: cweill@bankstreet.edu; *Acq & Electronic Reserves Librn,* Nora Gaines; Tel: 212-875-4457, E-mail: ngaines@bankstreet.edu; *Archivist & Spec Coll Librn,* Lindsey Wyckoff; E-mail: lwyckoff@bankstreet.edu; *Ch,* Allie Jane Bruce; E-mail: abruce@bankstreet.edu; *Ref Librn,* Peter Hare; E-mail: phare@bankstreet.edu; *Tech Serv Librn,* Jackie DeQuinzio; *Acq Asst,* Debbie Taybron; *Circ Asst,* Alex Iwachiw; *Tech Serv Asst,* Audrey Pryce; Staff 10.5 (MLS 5.5, Non-MLS 5)
Founded 1916. Enrl 1,007; Fac 125; Highest Degree: Master
Library Holdings: Bk Titles 85,168; Bk Vols 150,000; Per Subs 325; Talking Bks 400; Videos 647
Subject Interests: Adolescence, Bilingual educ, Children's lit, Early childhood educ, Spec educ
Automation Activity & Vendor Info: (Acquisitions) SirsiDynix; (Cataloging) SirsiDynix; (Circulation) SirsiDynix; (ILL) OCLC; (OPAC) SirsiDynix; (Serials) SirsiDynix
Wireless access
Function: Archival coll, ILL available, Online ref, Orientations, Photocopying/Printing, Telephone ref, Wheelchair accessible
Publications: Multicultural Education: A Bibliographic Essay & AIDS Education
Partic in Metropolitan New York Library Council
Open Mon-Thurs 8:30am-9:45pm, Fri 8:30-5, Sat 10-5
Restriction: In-house use for visitors, Open to pub by appt only

C BARD GRADUATE CENTER LIBRARY*, 38 W 86th St, 10024. SAN 374-5848. Tel: 212-501-3025. FAX: 212-501-3098. Reference E-mail: reference@bgc.bard.edu. Web Site: www.bgc.bard.edu/library. *Libr Dir,* Heather Topcik; Tel: 212-501-3036, E-mail: heather.topcik@bgc.bard.edu; *Reader Serv Librn,* Anna Helgeson; Tel: 212-501-3035, E-mail: anna.helgeson@bgc.bard.edu; *Syst Librn, Tech Serv Librn,* Seth Persons; Tel: 212-501-3037, E-mail: seth.persons@bgc.bard.edu; Staff 6.5 (MLS 3, Non-MLS 3.5)
Founded 1992. Enrl 60; Highest Degree: Doctorate
Library Holdings: Bk Titles 35,000; Per Subs 190
Subject Interests: Decorative art, Design, Mat culture
Automation Activity & Vendor Info: (Acquisitions) Innovative Interfaces, Inc; (Cataloging) Innovative Interfaces, Inc; (Course Reserve) Innovative Interfaces, Inc; (OPAC) Innovative Interfaces, Inc; (Serials) Innovative Interfaces, Inc
Wireless access
Function: Res libr
Publications: Exhibition Catalogs
Partic in Metropolitan New York Library Council; OCLC Online Computer Library Center, Inc; OCLC Research Library Partnership
Restriction: Open to fac, students & qualified researchers, Open to pub by appt only, Open to researchers by request

C BARNARD COLLEGE*, Wollman Library, 3009 Broadway, 10027-6598. SAN 353-037X. Tel: 212-854-3953. E-mail: refdesk@barnard.edu. Web Site: library.barnard.edu. *Dean,* Lisa Norberg; *Res & Instruction Librn,* Lois Coleman; Tel: 212-854-9095, E-mail: lcoleman@barnard.edu; *Res & Instruction Librn,* Jenna Freedman; Tel: 212-854-4615, E-mail: jfreedma@barnard.edu; *Res & Instruction Librn,* Vani Natarajan; Tel: 212-854-8595; *Res & Instruction Librn,* Heather Van Volkingburg; Tel: 212-851-9692; *Res & Instruction Librn,* Megan Wacha; Tel: 212-854-7652; *Res & Instruction Librn,* Heidi Winston; Tel: 212-854-9096; *Archives,* Shannon O'Neill; Tel: 212-854-4079, E-mail: soneill@barnard.edu; *Tech Serv,* Michael Elmore; E-mail: melmore@barnard.edu. Subject Specialists: *Info serv,* Lisa Norberg; *Engr, Math, Sci, Tech,* Lois Coleman; *Gender studies, Women's studies,* Jenna Freedman; *Humanities,* Vani Natarajan; *Psychol, Soc sci,* Heather Van Volkingburg; *Media, Performing arts,* Megan Wacha; *Archit, Fine arts, Urban studies,* Heidi Winston; Staff 9.5 (MLS 9.5)
Founded 1889. Enrl 2,295; Fac 240; Highest Degree: Bachelor
Library Holdings: AV Mats 19,747; Microforms 18,780; Bk Titles 157,835; Bk Vols 209,883; Per Subs 419
Special Collections: American Women Writers (Overbury Coll); Zines
Automation Activity & Vendor Info: (Acquisitions) Ex Libris Group; (Cataloging) Ex Libris Group; (Circulation) Ex Libris Group; (Course Reserve) Ex Libris Group; (OPAC) Ex Libris Group; (Serials) EBSCO Online
Wireless access
Function: Archival coll, Art exhibits, Audio & video playback equip for onsite use, AV serv, Electronic databases & coll, Equip loans & repairs, ILL available, Photocopying/Printing, Scanner, Wheelchair accessible
Partic in Metropolitan New York Library Council; New York State Interlibrary Loan Network
Restriction: Access at librarian's discretion, Authorized patrons, Authorized scholars by appt, Open to students, fac & staff

C BARUCH COLLEGE-CUNY*, William & Anita Newman Library, 151 E 25th St, Box H-0520, 10010-2313. SAN 311-6395. Tel: 646-312-1610. Circulation Tel: 646-312-1660. Interlibrary Loan Service Tel: 646-312-1674. Administration Tel: 646-312-1655. Circulation FAX: 646-312-1662. Administration FAX: 646-312-1651. Information Services FAX: 646-312-1601. Web Site: library.baruch.cuny.edu. *Chief Librn,* Dr Arthur Downing; Tel: 646-312-1026, E-mail: arthur.downing@baruch.cuny.edu; *Head, Archives & Spec Coll,* Sandra Roff; Tel: 646-312-1623, E-mail: sandra.roff@baruch.cuny.edu; *Head, Coll Mgt,* Michael Waldman; Tel: 646-312-1689, Fax: 646-312-1691, E-mail: michael.waldman@baruch.cuny.edu; *Grad Serv Librn,* Linda Rath; Tel: 646-312-1622, E-mail: Linda.Rath@baruch.cuny.edu; *Info Serv Librn,* Rita Ormsby; *Mgr, Access Serv,* Monique Prince; Tel: 646-312-1670, E-mail: monique.prince@baruch.cuny.edu; *Coordr of Ref Serv,* Harold Gee; Tel: 646 312-1625, E-mail: Harold.Gee@baruch.cuny.edu. Subject Specialists: *Math, Statistics,* Dr Arthur Downing; *Hist,* Sandra Roff; *Communication studies, Healthcare admin, Polit sci,* Michael Waldman; *Anthrop, Sociol, Women's studies,* Linda Rath; Staff 52 (MLS 25, Non-MLS 27)
Founded 1968. Enrl 18,286; Fac 513; Highest Degree: Master
Jul 2016-Jun 2017. Mats Exp $1,914,761. Sal $3,565,290 (Prof $2,714,039)
Library Holdings: DVDs 2,001; e-books 515,356; e-journals 107,721; Electronic Media & Resources 4,133; Microforms 2,066,739; Bk Titles 284,482; Bk Vols 333,250; Per Subs 6,429
Subject Interests: Financial, Tax serv
Automation Activity & Vendor Info: (Acquisitions) Ex Libris Group; (Cataloging) Ex Libris Group; (Circulation) Ex Libris Group; (Course Reserve) Docutek; (ILL) OCLC; (OPAC) Ex Libris Group; (Serials) Ex Libris Group
Wireless access
Special Services for the Blind - Assistive/Adapted tech devices, equip & products
Restriction: 24-hr pass syst for students only, Circ privileges for students & alumni only, Open to students, fac, staff & alumni
Friends of the Library Group

M BELLEVUE MEDICAL LIBRARY*, Clarence E de la Chapelle Medical Library, 462 First Ave & 27th St, 14N12, 10016. SAN 352-8812. Tel: 212-562-6535. *Asst Dir, Archives & Spec Coll,* Sushan Chin; Tel: 212-263-8280, E-mail: sushan.chin@nyulangone.org. Subject Specialists: *Med,* Sushan Chin; Staff 2.4 (MLS 1, Non-MLS 1.4)
Founded 1941
Library Holdings: Bk Titles 3,000
Subject Interests: Allied health, Med, Nursing
Partic in Basic Health Sciences Library Network
Restriction: Hospital employees & physicians only
Branches:
PATIENTS LIBRARY, 462 First Ave & 27th St, 10016. Tel: 212-263-8925. *Patient Educ Librn,* Sallie Wilcox
Library Holdings: Bk Vols 5,000; Per Subs 50
Open Mon-Fri 8-4

C BERKELEY COLLEGE, New York City Campus Library, Three E 43rd St, 7th Flr, 10017. SAN 329-9260. Tel: 212-986-4343, Ext 4232. FAX: 212-661-2940. Web Site: berkeleycollege.libguides.com/library. *Exec Dir,* William McNelis; Tel: 212-986-4343, Ext 4228, E-mail: wjn@berkeleycollege.edu; Staff 4 (MLS 3, Non-MLS 1)
Founded 1936. Fac 100; Highest Degree: Bachelor
Library Holdings: AV Mats 1,200; e-books 4,000; Electronic Media & Resources 21; Bk Vols 18,000; Per Subs 100
Subject Interests: Acctg, Bus admin, Fashion mkt, Info syst mgt, Mgt, Mkt
Automation Activity & Vendor Info: (Cataloging) TLC (The Library Corporation); (Circulation) TLC (The Library Corporation); (OPAC) TLC (The Library Corporation)
Wireless access
Partic in OCLC Online Computer Library Center, Inc
Open Mon-Thurs 10-8

C BORICUA COLLEGE, Library & Learning Resources Center, 3755 Broadway, 10032. Tel: 212-694-1000, Ext 666. FAX: 212-694-1015. Web Site: www.boricuacollege.edu. *Dir,* Liza Rivera; Staff 1 (MLS 1)
Founded 1974. Enrl 1,095; Fac 50; Highest Degree: Master
Library Holdings: Bk Vols 121,000
Special Collections: Baoillo Papers; Puerto Rican Repository
Subject Interests: Latin Am, Maps, Music, Puerto Rico
Automation Activity & Vendor Info: (Cataloging) JayWil Software Development, Inc; (OPAC) JayWil Software Development, Inc
Wireless access
Partic in Metrop Regional Res & Ref Librs; Metropolitan New York Library Council

J BOROUGH OF MANHATTAN COMMUNITY COLLEGE LIBRARY, A Philip Randolph Memorial Library, 199 Chambers St, S410, 10007. SAN 311-6484. Tel: 212-220-1442. Reference Tel: 212-220-8139. FAX: 212-748-7466. Web Site: lib1.bmcc.cuny.edu. *Chief Librn,* Kathleen Dreyer; Tel: 212-220-1499, E-mail: kdreyer@bmcc.cuny.edu; *Head, Access & Delivery Serv,* Phyllis Niles; Tel: 212-220-1450, E-mail:

pniles@bmcc.cuny.edu; *Head, Pub Serv,* Robin Brown; Tel: 212-220-1445, E-mail: rbrown@bmcc.cuny.edu; *Head, Tech Serv,* Taian Zhao; Tel: 212-220-1452, E-mail: tzhao@bmcc.cuny.edu; *Acq Librn,* Linda Wadas; Tel: 212-220-1443, E-mail: lwadas@bmcc.cuny.edu; *Coll Develop Librn,* Joanna Bevacqua; Tel: 212-220-1446, E-mail: jbevacqua@bmcc.cuny.edu; *E-Learning Librn, Instruction Librn,* Lane Glisson; Tel: 212-220-8000, Ext 7112, E-mail: lglisson@bmcc.cuny.edu; *Electronic Res Librn,* Kanu Nagra; Tel: 212-220-8000, Ext 7487, E-mail: knagra@bmcc.cuny.edu; *Faculty Res Librn, Scholarly Communications Librn,* Dorothea Coiffe; Tel: 212-220-1444, E-mail: dcoiffe@bmcc.cuny.edu; *Outreach Librn,* Jean Amaral; Tel: 212 220-8000, Ext 5114, E-mail: jamaral@bmcc.cuny.edu; *Ref Librn,* Barbara Linton; Tel: 212-220-1448, E-mail: blinton@bmcc.cuny.edu; *Ref Librn,* Dr Wambui Mbugua; Tel: 212-220-1447, E-mail: wmbugua@bmcc.cuny.edu; *Syst Librn, Web Librn,* Rebecca Hyams; E-mail: rhyams@bmcc.cuny.edu; *ILL & Reserves Coordr,* Guerda Baucicaut; Tel: 212-220-8000, Ext 7211, E-mail: gbaucicaut@bmcc.cuny.edu; Staff 15 (MLS 14, Non-MLS 1)
Founded 1964. Enrl 26,606; Fac 2,007; Highest Degree: Associate
Library Holdings: DVDs 992; e-books 220,000; e-journals 73,583; Microforms 18,445; Bk Titles 102,669; Bk Vols 132,305; Per Subs 261; Videos 1,394
Subject Interests: Allied health, Computer info syst, Educ, Ethnic studies, Med, Nursing
Automation Activity & Vendor Info: (Acquisitions) Ex Libris Group; (Cataloging) Ex Libris Group; (Circulation) Ex Libris Group; (Course Reserve) Ex Libris Group; (ILL) Ex Libris Group; (OPAC) Ex Libris Group; (Serials) Ex Libris Group
Wireless access
Function: E-Reserves, Electronic databases & coll, ILL available, Magazines, Online cat, Photocopying/Printing, Ref serv available, Scanner, Study rm, Telephone ref, VHS videos, Wheelchair accessible
Partic in Metropolitan New York Library Council
Special Services for the Blind - Reader equip
Open Mon-Thurs 8am-10pm, Fri 8-7, Sat 10-6, Sun 12-5
Restriction: Open to students, fac & staff

L BRYAN CAVE LEIGHTON PAISNER LLP*, Law Library, 1290 Avenue of the Americas, 10104. SAN 324-1157. Tel: 212-541-2165. Interlibrary Loan Service Tel: 212-541-2166. Reference Tel: 212-541-2167. FAX: 212-541-1465. Web Site: www.bryancave.com. *Mgr, Libr Serv,* Christine M Wierzba; Staff 5 (MLS 3, Non-MLS 2)
Founded 1873
Library Holdings: Bk Titles 3,500; Bk Vols 10,000; Per Subs 300
Subject Interests: Law
Automation Activity & Vendor Info: (Cataloging) Inmagic, Inc.; (Serials) Inmagic, Inc.
Wireless access
Partic in Amigos Library Services, Inc; Research Libraries Information Network
Open Mon-Fri 9-5

L CADWALADER, WICKERSHAM & TAFT LIBRARY*, 200 Liberty St, 10281. SAN 311-6670. Tel: 212-504-6000. FAX: 212-504-6666. E-mail: library@cwt.com. Web Site: www.cadwalader.com. *Asst Dir, Head, Ref,* Joseph L Biagiotti; E-mail: joe.biagiotti@cwt.com; Staff 14 (MLS 6, Non-MLS 8)
Subject Interests: Banking, Commodities, Gen corp, Healthcare, Insolvency, Litigation, Mergers, Project finance, Real estate, Securities, Tax
Restriction: Staff use only

L CAHILL, GORDON & REINDEL LIBRARY*, 80 Pine St, 10005. SAN 311-6689. Tel: 212-701-3542. FAX: 212-269-5420. Web Site: www.cahill.com. *Dir, Libr & Res Serv,* Gina Cartusciello; Tel: 212-701-3541, E-mail: gcartusciello@cahill.com
Library Holdings: Bk Vols 45,000
Special Collections: Legislative Histories & Law Reports Coll
Subject Interests: Antitrust, Corporate, Corporate finance, Securities, Tax law
Open Mon-Fri 9-5

S CARIBBEAN CULTURAL CENTER LIBRARY, 120 E 125th St, 10035. SAN 371-2419. Tel: 212-307-7420. FAX: 212-315-1086. E-mail: info@cccadi.org. Web Site: www.cccadi.org. *Exec Dir,* Melody Capote; E-mail: mcapote@cccadi.org
Library Holdings: Bk Vols 1,075
Automation Activity & Vendor Info: (Cataloging) ComPanion Corp
Wireless access
Open Mon-Fri 10-5

L CARTER, LEDYARD & MILBURN LIBRARY*, Two Wall St, 15th Flr, 10005. SAN 311-6727. Tel: 212-238-8851. FAX: 212-732-3232. *Libr Dir,* Emily Moog; E-mail: moog@clm.com; *Asst Librn,* Jeanine McPartlin; Tel: 212-238-8691, E-mail: mcpartlin@clm.com. Subject Specialists: *Law,* Emily Moog; Staff 2 (MLS 2)
Library Holdings: Bk Vols 20,000; Per Subs 30
Wireless access
Open Mon-Fri 9:30-5:30

S CBS NEWS REFERENCE LIBRARY*, 524 W 57th St, Ste 533/2, 10019. SAN 311-6654. Tel: 212-975-2877, 212-975-2879. FAX: 212-975-3940. *Mgr,* Carole D Parnes; Staff 2 (MLS 2)
Founded 1940
Library Holdings: Bk Titles 24,000; Bk Vols 31,000; Per Subs 250
Special Collections: Transcripts of CBS News Broadcasts
Subject Interests: Broadcasting, Current events, Govt, Hist, Politics
Automation Activity & Vendor Info: (Acquisitions) EOS International; (Cataloging) EOS International; (Circulation) EOS International; (ILL) EOS International; (OPAC) EOS International; (Serials) EOS International
Restriction: Open by appt only

S CENTER FOR JEWISH HISTORY, Leo Baeck Institute Library, 15 W 16 St, 10011. SAN 311-6255. Tel: 212-294-8340, 212-744-6400. Web Site: www.lbi.org. *Exec Dir,* Dr William Weitzer; E-mail: wweitzer@lbi.cjh.org; *Dir of Coll,* Renate Evers; E-mail: revers@lbi.cjh.org; *Chief Archivist, Dir, Res,* Dr Frank Mecklenburg; E-mail: fmecklenburg@lbi.cjh.org; *Head Archivist,* Hermann Teifer; E-mail: hteifer@lbi.cjh.org; *Acq Librn,* Elizabeth Fedden; *Assoc Librn, Cataloging & Periodicals,* Tracey Felder; E-mail: tfelder@lbi.cjh.org; *Coll Mgr, Registrar,* Lauren Paustian; E-mail: lpaustian@lbi.cjh.org
Founded 1955
Library Holdings: Bk Vols 80,000; Per Subs 200
Special Collections: Archives of German-speaking Jewry of Central Europe, 18th-20th Century; Art & Object Coll; Comprehensive Library coll related to German-Jewish history & culture; Memoir coll of German & Austrian Jewish emigrants; Oral history coll of interviews with German & Austrian Jewish emigrants
Automation Activity & Vendor Info: (Acquisitions) Ex Libris Group; (Cataloging) Ex Libris Group; (Circulation) Ex Libris Group; (OPAC) Ex Libris Group; (Serials) Ex Libris Group
Wireless access
Publications: Exhibition Catalogs; Judischer Almanach des Leo Baeck Institute; LBI News; Leo Baeck Institute Yearbook; Memorial Lectures; Schriftenreihe Wissenschaftlicher Abhandlungen des Leo Baeck Instituts
Partic in Asn of Jewish Librs; Metropolitan New York Library Council; OCLC Online Computer Library Center, Inc
Restriction: Closed stack
Friends of the Library Group

S CENTER FOR MODERN PSYCHOANALYTIC STUDIES LIBRARY*, 16 W Tenth St, 10011. SAN 320-2119. Tel: 212-260-7050, Ext 15. FAX: 212-228-6410. Web Site: www.cmps.edu/library. *Librn,* Laura Covino; E-mail: librarian@cmps.edu; Staff 1 (MLS 1)
Founded 1972
Library Holdings: Bk Titles 2,500; Bk Vols 2,800; Per Subs 10
Special Collections: Psychoanalysts Research Projects Coll
Subject Interests: Psychiat, Psychoanalysis, Psychol, Sociol
Automation Activity & Vendor Info: (Cataloging) LibraryWorld, Inc; (Circulation) LibraryWorld, Inc; (ILL) OCLC FirstSearch; (OPAC) LibraryWorld, Inc; (Serials) LibraryWorld, Inc
Wireless access
Function: Res libr
Partic in Metropolitan New York Library Council
Restriction: Borrowing privileges limited to fac & registered students, Open to others by appt
Friends of the Library Group

S THE CENTURY ASSOCIATION LIBRARY, Seven W 43rd St, 10036. SAN 311-6778. Tel: 212-944-0090. E-mail: library@thecentury.org. Web Site: www.thecentury.org. *Library Contact,* Karen Crane
Founded 1847
Library Holdings: Bk Titles 25,000
Wireless access
Partic in Metropolitan New York Library Council
Restriction: Mem only

S CHANCELLOR ROBERT R LIVINGSTON MASONIC LIBRARY OF GRAND LODGE*, 71 W 23rd St, 14th Flr, 10010-4171. SAN 311-7901. Tel: 212-337-6620. FAX: 212-633-2639. E-mail: info@nymasoniclibrary.org. Web Site: nymasoniclibrary.org. *Interim Librn,* Joseph Patzner; Tel: 212-337-6623, E-mail: Digital@nymasoniclibrary.org; *Curator,* Catherine Walter; E-mail: cwalter@nymasoniclibrary.org; *Cat,* Georgia Hershfeld; E-mail: ghershfeld@nymasoniclibrary.org. Subject Specialists: *Anthrop,* Catherine Walter; Staff 4 (MLS 1, Non-MLS 3)
Founded 1856
Library Holdings: Bk Titles 16,000; Bk Vols 60,000; Per Subs 150
Special Collections: 18th & 19th Century Freemasons (Charles Looney Coll), engravings; Early 19th Century Anti-Masonic Movement (Victory

Birdseye Coll); Early 20th Century African American Freemasonry (Edward Cusick Coll), docs
Subject Interests: Comparative relig, Freemasonry
Automation Activity & Vendor Info: (Cataloging) Follett Software
Wireless access
Function: 24/7 Online cat, Archival coll, Bk club(s), Internet access, Online cat, Ref & res, Ref serv available, Res assist avail
Partic in Metropolitan New York Library Council
Open Mon & Wed-Fri 8:30-4:30, Tues 12-8
Restriction: Closed stack, Non-circulating to the pub, Open to pub for ref only

G CITIZENS UNION FOUNDATION LIBRARY*, 299 Broadway, Ste 700, 10007. SAN 323-6013. Tel: 212-227-0342. FAX: 212-227-0345. E-mail: info@citizensunionfoundation.org. Web Site: www.citizensunion.org.
Founded 1948
Library Holdings: Bk Titles 400; Bk Vols 1,000
Special Collections: NY City Charter Revision Commission
Restriction: Open by appt only

C CITY COLLEGE OF THE CITY UNIVERSITY OF NEW YORK*, Morris Raphael Cohen Library, North Academic Ctr, 160 Convent Ave, 10031. SAN 352-9177. Tel: 212-650-7155, 212-650-7292. Interlibrary Loan Service Tel: 212-650-7616. Reference Tel: 212-650-7611, 212-650-7612. Administration Tel: 212-650-7271. FAX: 212-650-7604. Interlibrary Loan Service FAX: 212-650-7648. Reference E-mail: reference@ccny.cuny.edu. Web Site: library.ccny.cuny.edu. *Interim Chief Librn,* Daisy Dominquez; E-mail: Dominguez@ccny.cuny.edu; *Cat Chief,* Yoko Inagi Ferguson; Tel: 212-650-7623, E-mail: yinagi@ccny.cuny.edu; *Actg Chief, Tech Serv,* Robert Laurich; Tel: 212-650-7153, E-mail: rlaurich@ccny.cuny.edu; *Head, Info Serv,* Amrita Dhawan; Tel: 212-650-5763, E-mail: adhawan@ccny.cuny.edu; *Head, Ref,* Sarah Cohn; E-mail: scohn@ccny.cuny.edu; *Access Serv Librn,* Trevar Riley-Reid; Tel: 212-650-7601, Fax: 212-650-7388, E-mail: trileyreid@ccny.cuny.edu; *Archivist,* Sydney Van Nort; Tel: 212-650-7609, E-mail: svannort@ccny.cuny.edu; *Curator of Archival Coll,* William Gibbons; Tel: 212-650-7602, E-mail: wgibbons@ccny.cuny.edu; Staff 21.4 (MLS 19.1, Non-MLS 2.3)
Founded 1847. Enrl 16,544; Fac 555; Highest Degree: Doctorate
Library Holdings: AV Mats 1,292,000; CDs 19,825; DVDs 8,013; e-books 1,092,098; e-journals 118,040; Electronic Media & Resources 88,017; Microforms 1,081,268; Music Scores 7,158; Bk Titles 741,370; Bk Vols 967,161; Per Subs 2,476
Special Collections: 18th & Early 19th Century Plays; Astronomy (Newcomb Coll); Costume Coll; English Civil War Pamphlets; Harlem Development Archive; Metropolitan Applied Research Center (MARC) Archives; Poetry (Library of Contemporary Poets: Readings from 1932-1941), rec; Robert A. Olmstead Papers on Transportation Policy; Russell Sage Coll; Socio-Economic Broadsides before 1800 (Gitelson Coll), microfilm. Oral History; State Document Depository; US Document Depository
Subject Interests: Educ, Humanities
Automation Activity & Vendor Info: (Acquisitions) Ex Libris Group; (Cataloging) Ex Libris Group; (Circulation) Ex Libris Group; (Course Reserve) Docutek; (ILL) OCLC ILLiad; (OPAC) Ex Libris Group; (Serials) SerialsSolutions
Wireless access
Function: Archival coll, Art exhibits, Doc delivery serv, Govt ref serv, ILL available, Internet access, Magnifiers for reading, Music CDs, Orientations, Outside serv via phone, mail, e-mail & web, Photocopying/Printing, Ref serv available, Res libr, Telephone ref, VHS videos, Wheelchair accessible
Publications: Circumspice (Newsletter)
Partic in Metropolitan New York Library Council; New York Online Virtual Electronic Library; OCLC Online Computer Library Center, Inc
Special Services for the Deaf - Accessible learning ctr; Assisted listening device
Special Services for the Blind - Accessible computers; Braille equip; Braille servs; Computer with voice synthesizer for visually impaired persons; Magnifiers; Networked computers with assistive software; Reader equip; Screen reader software
Open Mon-Fri 7am-Midnight, Sat 9-5, Sun 12-5
Restriction: Authorized patrons, Limited access for the pub, Photo ID required for access
Friends of the Library Group

Departmental Libraries:

ARCHITECTURE LIBRARY, Spitzer Bldg, Rm 101, 160 Convent Ave, 10031, SAN 352-9207. Tel: 212-650-8768. FAX: 212-650-7214. Web Site: library.ccny.cuny.edu/main/?page_id=6. *Librn,* Nilda Sanchez; E-mail: nsanchez@ccny.cuny.edu. Subject Specialists: *Archit,* Nilda Sanchez; Staff 2 (MLS 1, Non-MLS 1)
Subject Interests: Archit, Art, Urban landscape planning, Urban planning
Open Mon, Wed & Thurs 10-8, Tues 12-8, Fri 10-5, Sat 12-5
Friends of the Library Group

ARCHITECTURE VISUAL RESOURCES LIBRARY, Spitzer 104, 160 Convent Ave, 10031. Tel: 212-650-8754. FAX: 212-650-7604. E-mail: archimage@ccny.cuny.edu. Web Site: library.ccny.cuny.edu/main/?page_id=47. *Visual Res Librn,* Dr Ching-Jung Chen; E-mail: cchen@ccny.cuny.edu; Staff 1 (MLS 0.5, Non-MLS 0.5)
Open Mon-Thurs 9-6, Fri 9-5

CENTER FOR WORKER EDUCATION LIBRARY, 25 Broadway, 7-28, 10004. Tel: 212-925-6625, Ext 228. FAX: 212-925-0963. Web Site: library.ccny.cuny.edu/main/?page_id=134. *Librn,* Seamus Scanlon; E-mail: seamus@ccny.cuny.edu; Staff 1 (MLS 1)
Open Mon-Fri 12-8, Sat 10-5
Friends of the Library Group

COLLEGE ARCHIVES & SPECIAL COLLECTIONS, North Academic Ctr-Cohen Library, 160 Convent Ave, 10031, SAN 352-9231. Tel: 212-650-7609. FAX: 212-650-7604. E-mail: archives@ccny.cuny.edu. Web Site: library.ccny.cuny.edu/main/?page_id=9. *Archivist,* Sydney Van Nort; E-mail: svannort@ccny.cuny.edu; Staff 2 (MLS 1, Non-MLS 1)
Special Collections: First Editions & Rare Books; Harlem Development Archive; Harlem Development Archive; Papers of Cleveland Abbe, R R Bowker, Townsend Harris, J H Finley, Waldemar Kaempffert, L F Mott, Edward M Shepard, Alexander Webb & Everett Wheeler; Source Material Relating to Free Higher Education in New York since 1847; William Butler Yeats Coll, printed editions
Friends of the Library Group

DOMINICAN STUDIES INSTITUTE RESEARCH LIBRARY & ARCHIVES, NAC 2/202, 160 Convent Ave, 10031. Tel: 212-650-7170, 212-650-7496. FAX: 212-650-7489. E-mail: dsi@ccny.cuny.edu. Web Site: www.ccny.cuny.edu/dsi/dominican-library. *Librn,* Sarah Aponte; E-mail: aponte@ccny.cuny.edu; *Archivist,* Idilio Garcia-Pena; E-mail: igpconsulting@gmail.com; Staff 2 (MLS 1, Non-MLS 1)
Founded 1994
Library Holdings: Bk Vols 15,500
Open Mon & Thurs 9-8:30, Tues, Wed & Fri 9-5, Sat 12-5
Friends of the Library Group

MUSIC LIBRARY, Shepard Hall, Rm 160, 160 Convent Ave, 10031, SAN 352-9355. Tel: 212-650-7174. FAX: 212-650-7231. Web Site: library.ccny.cuny.edu/main/?page_id=138. *Chief, Music Librn,* Michael Crowley; Tel: 212-650-7120, E-mail: mcrowley@ccny.cuny.edu; Staff 2 (MLS 1, Non-MLS 1)
Open Mon 10-6, Tues-Thurs 10-7, Fri 10-5
Friends of the Library Group

SCIENCE-ENGINEERING, Marshak Bldg, Rm J29, 160 Convent Ave, 10031, SAN 352-938X. Tel: 212-650-8246. Reference Tel: 212-650-5712. FAX: 212-650-7626. Web Site: library.ccny.cuny.edu/main/?page_id=105. *Div Chief,* Loren Mendelsohn; Tel: 212-650-8244, E-mail: lmend@ccny.cuny.edu; *Ref Librn,* Philip Barnett; Tel: 212-650-8243, E-mail: pbarnett@ccny.cuny.edu; *Ref Librn,* Claudia Lascar; Tel: 212-650-6826, E-mail: clascar@ccny.cuny.edu; Staff 5 (MLS 3, Non-MLS 2)
Subject Interests: Atmospheric sci, Biochem, Biology, Chem, Computer sci, Earth sci, Engr, Magnetic resonance imaging, Math, Spectroscopy, Transportation, Waste treatment
Open Mon-Thurs 9am-11pm, Fri & Sat 9-6, Sun 12-6
Friends of the Library Group

S CITY OF NEW YORK DEPARTMENT OF RECORDS & INFORMATION SERVICES*, City Hall Library, 31 Chambers St, Rm 112, 10007. SAN 353-202X. Tel: 212-788-8590. FAX: 212-788-8589. Web Site: www1.nyc.gov/site/records/index.page. *Supv Librn,* Christine Bruzzese; E-mail: cbruzz@records.nyc.gov; Staff 2 (MLS 1, Non-MLS 1)
Founded 1913
Library Holdings: Bk Vols 66,000; Per Subs 10
Special Collections: Municipal Document Depository; State Document Depository
Subject Interests: Civil serv, Consul studies, Hist of NY City, Legislation, Local govt, Municipal mgt, Politicians, Pub health, State doc, Urban affairs
Automation Activity & Vendor Info: (Cataloging) Mandarin Library Automation; (OPAC) Mandarin Library Automation
Open Mon-Wed & Fri 9-4:30, Thurs 9-6:30

C CITY UNIVERSITY OF NEW YORK*, Mina Rees Library of Graduate School & University Center, 365 Fifth Ave, 10016-4309. SAN 311-6883. Tel: 212-817-7040. Circulation Tel: 212-817-7083. Reference Tel: 212-817-7077. FAX: 212-817-2982. Web Site: library.gc.cuny.edu. *Actg Chief Librn,* Polly Thistlethwaite; E-mail: pthistlethwaite@gc.cuny.edu; *Head, Circ & Reserves,* Matthew Curtis; E-mail: mcurtis@gc.cuny.edu; *Head, Ref Serv,* Shawn(ta) Smith-Cruz; Tel: 212-817-7053, E-mail: ssmith4@gc.cuny.edu; *Head, Resource Sharing,* Beth Posner; Tel: 212-817-7051, E-mail: bposner@gc.cuny.edu; *Adjunct Ref Librn,* Elvis Bakaitis; E-mail: ebakaitis@gc.cuny.edu; *Adjunct Ref Librn,* Donna Davey; E-mail: ddavey@gc.cuny.edu; *Assoc Librn, Pub Serv,* Jill Cirasella; Tel: 212-817-7046, E-mail: jcirasella@gc.cuny.edu; *Assoc Librn, Coll,* Alycia Sellie; Tel: 212-817-7078, E-mail: asellie@gc.cuny.edu; *Digital Scholarship Librn,* Stephen Zweibel; Tel: 212-817-7067, E-mail: szweibel@gc.cuny.edu; *Digital Serv Librn,* Stephen Klein; Tel:

212-817-7074, E-mail: sklein@gc.cuny.edu; *Institutional Repository Librn,* Adriana Palmer; Tel: 212-817-7055, E-mail: apalmer@gc.cuny.edu; *Outreach Librn, Ref,* Wanett Clyde; E-mail: wclyde@gc.cuny.edu; *Research Librn,* Roxanne Shirazi; Tel: 212-817-7069, E-mail: rshirazi@gc.cuny.edu; *Acq, Mgr, Reserves, Ser,* Melissa Longhi; Tel: 212-817-7079, E-mail: mlonghi@gc.cuny.edu; *Coll Mgt Spec,* Mike Handis; Tel: 212-817-7075, E-mail: mhandis@gc.cuny.edu; *ILL Supvr,* J Silvia Cho; Tel: 212-817-7045, E-mail: jcho@gc.cuny.edu; *Acq Asst,* Rose Ochoa; Tel: 212-817-7061, E-mail: rochoa@gc.cuny.edu; *Cat Asst,* Joel Singer; Tel: 212-817-7072, E-mail: jsinger@gc.cuny.edu; *Circ Asst,* Nancy Seda; Tel: 212-817-7043, E-mail: nseda@gc.cuny.edu; *Cataloger,* Suzanne Bernard; E-mail: sbernard@gc.cuny.edu; *Libr Asst,* Margaret O'Garro; Tel: 212-817-7072, E-mail: mogarro@gc.cuny.edu; *Ref (Info Servs),* Michael Adams; Tel: 212-817-7055, E-mail: madams@gc.cuny.edu; Staff 21 (MLS 17, Non-MLS 4)
Founded 1964. Enrl 4,000; Fac 130; Highest Degree: Doctorate
Library Holdings: Bk Vols 285,000; Per Subs 11,000
Special Collections: American History (US Presidential Papers), microfilm; City University of New York; Old York Library (Seymour Durst Coll)
Automation Activity & Vendor Info: (Acquisitions) Ex Libris Group; (Cataloging) Ex Libris Group; (Circulation) Ex Libris Group; (Course Reserve) Docutek; (ILL) OCLC ILLiad; (OPAC) Ex Libris Group; (Serials) Ex Libris Group
Wireless access
Function: 24/7 Electronic res, 24/7 Online cat, Archival coll, AV serv, Computers for patron use, Doc delivery serv, Electronic databases & coll, Equip loans & repairs, For res purposes, Free DVD rentals, Govt ref serv, Health sci info serv, ILL available, Instruction & testing, Internet access, Magnifiers for reading, Online cat, Online ref, Orientations, Outreach serv, Outside serv via phone, mail, e-mail & web, Photocopying/Printing, Printer for laptops & handheld devices, Prof lending libr, Ref & res, Ref serv available, Res libr, Scanner, Study rm, Telephone ref, VHS videos, Workshops
Partic in Metropolitan New York Library Council; OCLC Research Library Partnership; Westchester Academic Library Directors Organization
Special Services for the Deaf - Assistive tech
Special Services for the Blind - Assistive/Adapted tech devices, equip & products; Computer with voice synthesizer for visually impaired persons
Restriction: Not open to pub, Open to students, fac & staff
Friends of the Library Group

L CLEARY, GOTTLIEB, STEEN & HAMILTON LLP LIBRARY*, One Liberty Plaza, 10006. SAN 311-6913. Tel: 212-225-3444. *Research Librn,* Courtney Toiaivao; Staff 12 (MLS 6, Non-MLS 6)
Library Holdings: Bk Titles 22,000
Subject Interests: Foreign, Intl law, Intl taxation
Automation Activity & Vendor Info: (Cataloging) SirsiDynix; (OPAC) SirsiDynix
Restriction: Not open to pub, Staff use only

L CLIFFORD CHANCE US LLP LIBRARY, 31 W 52nd St, 10019. SAN 312-0368. Web Site: www.cliffordchance.com.
Automation Activity & Vendor Info: (Acquisitions) SydneyPlus; (Cataloging) SydneyPlus; (Circulation) SydneyPlus; (OPAC) SydneyPlus; (Serials) SydneyPlus
Wireless access
Restriction: Staff use only

M COLER-GOLDWATER MEMORIAL HOSPITAL*, Patients Library, 900 Main, Roosevelt Island, 10001. SAN 311-7898. Tel: 212-848-5849. *Dept Head,* Jovemay Santos; E-mail: jovemay.santos@nychhc.org
Founded 1939
Library Holdings: Bk Vols 13,680; Per Subs 386
Subject Interests: Chronic disease, Geriatrics, Hearing, Med, Rehabilitation med, Speech
Wireless access
Publications: Acquisition List
Partic in Metropolitan New York Library Council; OCLC Online Computer Library Center, Inc
Restriction: Open by appt only

S COLLECTORS CLUB LIBRARY, 22 E 35th St, 10016-3806. SAN 311-6948. Tel: 212-683-0559. FAX: 212-481-1269. E-mail: info@collectorsclub.org. Web Site: www.collectorsclub.org/the-collectors-club-library. *Committee Chair,* Robert Gray; *Librn,* Andrea Matura; E-mail: readingroom@collectorsclub.org. Subject Specialists: *Philately,* Robert Gray
Founded 1896
Library Holdings: Bk Titles 30,000; Per Subs 100
Subject Interests: Philately
Publications: Collectors Club Philatelist
Open Mon-Fri 10-5

C COLUMBIA UNIVERSITY*, Butler Library, 535 W 114th St, 10027. SAN 352-941X. Tel: 212-854-7309. Circulation Tel: 212-854-2235. Interlibrary Loan Service Tel: 212-854-7535. Reference Tel: 212-854-2241. FAX: 212-854-9099. E-mail: butler@library.columbia.edu, lio@columbia.edu. Web Site: library.columbia.edu. *Vice Provost & Univ Librn,* Ann T Thornton; E-mail: adt2138@columbia.edu; *Associate VP, Admin, Finance & Human Resources,* Kris Kavanaugh; E-mail: kavanaug@columbia.edu; *Assoc VPres, Presv, Tech,* Robert Cartolano; E-mail: rtc@columbia.edu; *Assoc Univ Librn, Coll,* Christopher J Cronin; E-mail: cjc2260@columbia.edu; *Assoc Univ Librn, Res & Learning,* Barbara A Rockenbach; E-mail: brockenbach@columbia.edu; Staff 328 (MLS 328)
Founded 1761. Enrl 23,422; Fac 1,401; Highest Degree: Doctorate
Library Holdings: Bk Vols 10,296,816
Special Collections: Oral History; State Document Depository; UN Document Depository; US Document Depository
Automation Activity & Vendor Info: (Acquisitions) Ex Libris Group; (Cataloging) Ex Libris Group; (Circulation) Ex Libris Group
Wireless access
Partic in Association of Research Libraries; Metropolitan New York Library Council; NELLCO Law Library Consortium, Inc.; Northeast Research Libraries Consortium; OCLC Research Library Partnership
Friends of the Library Group

Departmental Libraries:

ACCESS SERVICES, Butler Library, 535 W 114th St, 10027. Tel: 212-854-2245. Circulation Tel: 212-854-4734. *Dir, Access Serv,* Francie Mrkich; E-mail: mfm2123@columbia.edu

AFRICAN STUDIES, Lehman Library, 420 W 118th St, 10027, SAN 377-0044. Tel: 212-854-8045. FAX: 212-854-3834. E-mail: africa@library.columbia.edu. Web Site: library.columbia.edu/locations/global/africa. *Librn,* Yuusuf S Caruso, PhD; E-mail: caruso@columbia.edu

ARCHIVES, Butler Library, 6th Flr, 535 W 114th St, MC 1127, 10027, SAN 353-0191. Tel: 212-854-3786. FAX: 212-854-1365. E-mail: uarchives@library.columbia.edu. Web Site: library.columbia.edu/locations/cuarchives. *Univ Archivist,* Jocelyn K Wilk; Tel: 212-854-1338, E-mail: jkw19@columbia.edu; *Rec Mgr,* Joanna Rios; Tel: 212-854-1331, E-mail: jmr2196@columbia.edu; Staff 3 (MLS 2, Non-MLS 1)
Founded 1883
Library Holdings: Bk Vols 45,000
Function: Archival coll
Open Mon 9-7:45, Tues-Fri 9-4:45
Restriction: Non-circulating

AVERY ARCHITECTURAL & FINE ARTS LIBRARY, 300 Avery Hall, 1172 Amsterdam Ave, MC 0301, 10027. Tel: 212-854-6199. E-mail: avery@library.columbia.edu. Web Site: library.columbia.edu/locations/avery. *Actg Dir,* Chris Cronin; Tel: 212-854-5585, E-mail: cjc2260@columbia.edu; *Assoc Dir, Head, Access Serv,* Kitty Chibnik; Tel: 212-854-3506, E-mail: krc1@columbia.edu; *Archit Librn,* Christine Sala; *Digital Content Librn, Registrar,* Margaret Smithglass; *Access Serv Supvr,* Zachary Rouse; *Archivist,* Shelley Hayreh; *Curator,* Teresa Harris; *Indexer,* Jeffrey Ross; Staff 21 (MLS 9, Non-MLS 12)
Founded 1890
Library Holdings: Bk Vols 450,000; Per Subs 1,700
Open Mon-Thurs 9-9, Fri 9-5, Sat 11-6
Restriction: Non-circulating, Open to students, fac & staff

CR THE BURKE LIBRARY AT UNION THEOLOGICAL SEMINARY, 3041 Broadway, 10027, SAN 312-1054. Tel: 212-851-5606. Administration Tel: 212-851-5611. FAX: 212-851-5613. E-mail: burke@library.columbia.edu. Web Site: library.columbia.edu/locations/burke. *Head Librn,* Matthew Baker; E-mail: matthew.baker@columbia.edu; *Coll Serv Librn,* Jeffrey Wayno; Tel: 212-851-5608, E-mail: jeffrey.wayno@columbia.edu; *Pub Serv Librn,* Carolyn Bratnober; E-mail: c.bratnober@columbia.edu; Staff 4 (MLS 4)
Founded 1836. Enrl 226; Fac 20; Highest Degree: Doctorate
Library Holdings: AV Mats 1,781; Music Scores 1,812; Bk Vols 604,361; Per Subs 1,719; Videos 34
Special Collections: Americana Coll; Archive of Women in Theology; Archives; Auburn Coll; Bonhoeffer Coll; British History & Theology (McAlpin Coll); Christian Science Coll; Ecumenics & Church Union (William Adams Brown Coll); Gillett Coll; Hymnology; Missionary Research Library Coll; Reformation Tracts; Thompson; Van Ess Coll
Subject Interests: Bible, Christian ethics, Church hist, Communication, Ecumenics, Missions
Automation Activity & Vendor Info: (Cataloging) Ex Libris Group; (Circulation) Ex Libris Group; (Course Reserve) Ex Libris Group; (OPAC) Ex Libris Group; (Serials) Ex Libris Group
Partic in New York State Interlibrary Loan Network; OCLC Online Computer Library Center, Inc; Research Libraries Information Network
Friends of the Library Group

BUTLER LIBRARY RESEARCH SERVICES, 301 Butler Library, 535 W 114th St, 10027, SAN 352-9568. Tel: 212-854-2241. Reference E-mail: ref-ref@columbia.edu. Web Site: library.columbia.edu/locations/butler-reference. *Humanities Librn, Research Servs Librn,* Ian G Beilin; E-mail: igb4@columbia.edu; Staff 12 (MLS 10, Non-MLS 2)
Library Holdings: Bk Vols 57,981

CL ARTHUR W DIAMOND LAW LIBRARY, 435 W 116th St, 10027, SAN 353-0256. Tel: 212-854-3922. Reference Tel: 212-854-3743. Web Site: www.law.columbia.edu/library. *Dir,* Kent McKeever; Tel: 212-854-4228, E-mail: mckeever@law.columbia.edu; *Assoc Dir,* Jody Armstrong; Tel: 212-854-1308, E-mail: jdsa@law.columbia.edu; *Head, Pub Serv,* R Martin Witt; *Head, Tech Serv,* Mary Burgos; *Pub Serv Librn, Spec Coll Librn,* Heath Mayhew; *Ref Librn,* Dana Neacsu; *Ref Librn,* Hunter Whaley; Staff 41 (MLS 18, Non-MLS 23)
Library Holdings: e-journals 26,742; Microforms 24,694; Bk Titles 398,028; Bk Vols 1,197,430; Per Subs 6,103
Special Collections: UN Document Depository; US Document Depository
Subject Interests: Foreign law, Intl law
Partic in Northeast Foreign Law Libraries Cooperative Group
Open Mon-Fri (Winter) 8am-Midnight, Sat 10-8, Sun 10am-Midnight; Mon-Fri (Summer) 9-5

GLOBAL STUDIES, Lehman Library, International Affairs Bldg, 420 W 118th St, 10027, SAN 377-0141. Tel: 212-854-3630. FAX: 212-854-3834. E-mail: global@library.columbia.edu. Web Site: library.columbia.edu/locations/global. *Dir,* Pamela Graham, PhD; E-mail: graham@columbia.edu; *Librn,* Michelle Chesner; *Librn,* Yuusuf Curuso; *Librn,* Robert H Davis, Jr; *Librn,* Gary Hausman; *Librn,* Peter Magierski. Subject Specialists: *Jewish studies,* Michelle Chesner; *African studies,* Yuusuf Curuso; *European studies,* Robert H Davis, Jr; *S Asia,* Gary Hausman; *Middle East & Islamic studies,* Peter Magierski

LATIN AMERICAN & IBERIAN STUDIES, 309 Lehman Library, International Affairs Bldg, 420 W 118th St, 10027, SAN 377-0060. Tel: 212-854-1679. FAX: 212-854-3834. E-mail: latam@library.columbia.edu. Web Site: library.columbia.edu/locations/global/latinamerica. *Librn,* Sócrates Silvia; E-mail: ss5000@columbia.edu

LEHMAN SOCIAL SCIENCES LIBRARY, 300 International Affairs Bldg, 420 W 118th St, 10027, SAN 377-0125. Tel: 212-854-3794. FAX: 212-854-2495. E-mail: lehman@library.columbia.edu. Web Site: library.columbia.edu/locations/lehman. *Head, Libr Operations,* Peguy Jean-Pierre; E-mail: jp43@columbia.edu; *Head, Data Serv, Res,* Jeremiah Trinidad-Christensen; E-mail: jt2118@columbia.edu; *Metadata Librn,* Eric Glass; E-mail: ecg2104@columbia.edu
Founded 1971

CM AUGUSTUS C LONG HEALTH SCIENCES LIBRARY, 701 W 168th St, Lobby Level, 10032, SAN 353-0221. Tel: 212-305-3605. FAX: 212-234-0595. E-mail: hs-library@columbia.edu. Web Site: library.cumc.columbia.edu. *Exec Dir,* Anna Getselman; Tel: 212-305-1406, E-mail: ag3353@cumc.columbia.edu; *Dir of Libr Operations,* Michael Koehn; Tel: 212-305-9216, E-mail: mdk2126@cumc.columbia.edu; *Head, Archives & Spec Coll,* Stephen Novak; E-mail: sen13@cumc.columbia.edu
Library Holdings: Bk Vols 551,000; Per Subs 4,416
Special Collections: Anatomy (Huntington Coll); Cancer Research; Physiology (Curtis Coll); Plastic Surgery (Jerome P Webster Coll)
Automation Activity & Vendor Info: (Acquisitions) Ex Libris Group; (Cataloging) Ex Libris Group; (Circulation) Ex Libris Group; (Course Reserve) Ex Libris Group; (OPAC) Ex Libris Group; (Serials) Ex Libris Group
Function: Distance learning, Doc delivery serv, ILL available, Photocopying/Printing, Ref serv available
Open Mon-Thurs 9-7, Fri 9-5, Sun Noon-8

MATHEMATICS, 303 Mathematics, 2990 Broadway, MC 4702, 10027, SAN 352-9894. Tel: 212-854-4712. E-mail: math@library.columbia.edu. Web Site: library.columbia.edu/locations/math. *Tech Serv Supvr,* Jim Babcock; Tel: 212-854-4181, E-mail: jrb55@columbia.edu; *Libr Asst,* Wendy Zhang; Tel: 212-854-4713, E-mail: wz2108@columbia.edu
Library Holdings: Bk Vols 126,004

MIDDLE EAST & ISLAMIC STUDIES, International Affairs Bldg, 420 W 118th St, 10027, SAN 377-0087. Tel: 212-854-3995. FAX: 212-854-3834. E-mail: mideast@libraries.cul.columbia.edu, mideast@library.columbia.edu. Web Site: library.columbia.edu/locations/global/mideast. *Librn,* Peter Magierski; E-mail: pm2650@columbia.edu. Subject Specialists: *Middle East & Islamic studies,* Peter Magierski
Library Holdings: CDs 300; DVDs 100; e-books 1,000; e-journals 300; Bk Titles 300,000; Bk Vols 500,000; Per Subs 400; Videos 300
Special Collections: Oral History; US Document Depository
Friends of the Library Group

PHILIP L MILSTEIN FAMILY COLLEGE LIBRARY, 208 Butler Library, 2nd, 3rd & 4th Flrs, 535 W 114th St, 10027, SAN 352-9479. Tel: 212-854-0520. E-mail: undergrad@library.columbia.edu. Web Site: library.columbia.edu/locations/undergraduate. *Undergrad Serv Librn,* Anice Mills; E-mail: amills@columbia.edu; *Supvr,* Insaf M Ali; E-mail: ima2104@columbia.edu; Staff 2 (MLS 1, Non-MLS 1)
Founded 1998
Library Holdings: Bk Vols 92,000
Friends of the Library Group

ORIGINAL & SPECIAL MATERIALS CATALOGING, 102 Butler Library, 535 W 114th St, 10027, SAN 352-9487. Tel: 212-854-2714. FAX: 212-854-5167. Web Site: library.columbia.edu/bts/cataloging. *Dir,* Kate Harcourt; E-mail: kh33@columbia.edu

RARE BOOK & MANUSCRIPT, Butler Library, 6th Flr E, 535 W 114th St, 10027, SAN 353-0167. Tel: 212-854-5590. Information Services Tel: 212-854-5153. FAX: 212-854-1365. E-mail: rbml@library.columbia.edu. Web Site: library.columbia.edu/locations/rbml. *Dir,* Sean Quimby; Tel: 212-854-2232, E-mail: smq2109@columbia.edu; *Univ Archivist,* Jocelyn Wilk; Tel: 212-854-1338, E-mail: jkw19@columbia.edu; *Head, Pub Serv,* Tara Craig; Tel: 212-854-4051, E-mail: tcc46@columbia.edu; *Archivist,* David A Olson; E-mail: dao2118@columbia.edu; *Bibliog Serv, Rare Bk Librn,* Jane Rogers Siegel; Tel: 212-854-8482, E-mail: jrs19@columbia.edu; *Curator, Bakhmeteff Archives,* Tanya Chebotarev; Tel: 212-854-3986, E-mail: tc241@columbia.edu; *Curator, Performing Arts & Exhibitions,* Jennifer B Lee; Tel: 212-854-4048, E-mail: jbl100@columbia.edu; *Lehman Curator, Am Hist,* Thai Jones; Tel: 212-854-9616, E-mail: tsj2001@columbia.edu. Subject Specialists: *Oral hist,* David A Olson; *Russian,* Tanya Chebotarev; Staff 14 (MLS 8, Non-MLS 6)
Special Collections: Carnegie Coll; Columbia Center for Oral History; Columbia University Archives; Herbert H Lehman Coll; Manuscripts Coll; Rare Book Coll; Russian & East European History & Culture (Bakhmeteff Archive). Oral History
Function: Res libr
Restriction: Non-circulating coll
Friends of the Library Group

RUSSIAN, EURASIAN & EAST EUROPEAN STUDIES, 306 International Affairs Bldg, 420 W 118th St, 10027, SAN 377-0109. Tel: 212-854-4701. FAX: 212-854-3834. E-mail: slavic@library.columbia.edu. Web Site: library.columbia.edu/locations/global/slavic. *Librn,* Robert H Davis, Jr; E-mail: rhd2106@columbia.edu

SCIENCE & ENGINEERING LIBRARY, 401 Northwest Corner Bldg, 550 W 120th St, 10027, SAN 352-9800. Tel: 212-854-2950. FAX: 212-854-3323. E-mail: scieng@library.columbia.edu. Web Site: library.columbia.edu/locations/science-engineering. *Dir,* Kelly Barrick; Tel: 212-854-7803, E-mail: kb2880@columbia.edu

SOCIAL WORK LIBRARY, School of Social Work, 2nd Flr, 1255 Amsterdam Ave, 10027, SAN 353-0078. Tel: 212-851-2194. Reference Tel: 212-851-2196. FAX: 212-851-2199. E-mail: socwk@library.columbia.edu. Web Site: library.columbia.edu/locations/social-work. *Head of Libr,* Sophia Leveque; Tel: 212-851-2195, E-mail: scl2162@columbia.edu; *Libr Supvr,* James Morris; Tel: 212-851-2197, E-mail: jbm2111@columbia.edu; Staff 4 (MLS 1, Non-MLS 3)
Highest Degree: Doctorate
Special Collections: Gerontology (Brookdale Memorial Coll); Social Work Agency Coll
Function: AV serv, ILL available, Ref serv available, Res libr, Telephone ref, Wheelchair accessible, Workshops
Open Mon-Thurs 10-9, Fri 10-6, Sun 12-8
Restriction: Open to students, fac & staff
Friends of the Library Group

C V STARR EAST ASIAN LIBRARY, 300 Kent Hall, MC 3901, 1140 Amsterdam Ave, 10027, SAN 353-0132. Tel: 212-854-4318. FAX: 212-662-6286. E-mail: starr@library.columbia.edu. Web Site: library.columbia.edu/locations/eastasian. *Dir,* Jim Cheng; Tel: 212-854-1508, E-mail: jc3685@columbia.edu; *Head, Pub Serv,* Ria Koopmans-de Bruijn; *Head, Tech Serv,* Sarah S Elman; *Mgr, Access Serv,* Kenneth Harlin; *Evening/Weekend Supvr,* Rongxiang Zhang; Staff 14 (MLS 10, Non-MLS 4)
Founded 1902
Library Holdings: Bk Vols 1,000,000; Per Subs 7,500
Special Collections: Rare Book Coll
Subject Interests: Humanities, Lang, Lit, Soc sci

TEACHERS COLLEGE, GOTTESMAN LIBRARIES
See Separate Entry under Teachers College, Columbia University

THOMAS J WATSON LIBRARY OF BUSINESS & ECONOMICS, 130 Uris Hall, 3022 Broadway, 10027, SAN 352-9983. Tel: 212-854-7804. Reference Tel: 212-854-3383. FAX: 212-854-5723. E-mail: business@library.columbia.edu. Web Site: library.columbia.edu/locations/business. *Head, Access & Operations,* Michael Lillard; Tel: 212-854-4864, E-mail: ml1053@columbia.edu; *Supvr,* Paul Haughton; E-mail: pwh2112@columbia.edu; Staff 23 (MLS 5, Non-MLS 18)
Highest Degree: Doctorate
Library Holdings: Bk Vols 400,000
Subject Interests: Bus, Econ
Function: Res libr
Restriction: Open to pub upon request, Residents only

THE GABE M WIENER MUSIC & ARTS LIBRARY, 701 Dodge Hall, 2960 Broadway, 10027, SAN 352-9657. Tel: 212-854-4711. FAX: 212-854-4748. E-mail: music@library.columbia.edu. Web Site: library.columbia.edu/locations/music. *Head Librn,* Elizabeth Davis; Tel: 212-854-7604, E-mail: davise@columbia.edu; *Music Librn,* Nick Patterson; Tel: 212-854-8523, E-mail: njp2@columbia.edu
Library Holdings: Bk Vols 80,000
Open Mon-Fri 9-5

S CONDE NAST PUBLICATIONS LIBRARY*, One World Trade Ctr, 10007. SAN 311-7022. Tel: 212-286-2860. E-mail: library@condenast.com. Web Site: www.condenast.com. *Dir,* Cynthia Cathcart; *Librn,* Stanford Friedman; *Librn,* Deirdre Nolan
Founded 1935
Library Holdings: Bk Titles 3,000; Bk Vols 3,500; Per Subs 150
Subject Interests: Fashion
Automation Activity & Vendor Info: (Cataloging) TLC (The Library Corporation)
Wireless access
Restriction: Open by appt only

S CONDON & FORSYTH LLP LIBRARY*, Seven Times Sq, 18th Flr, 10036. SAN 326-1875. Tel: 212-490-9100. FAX: 212-370-4453. E-mail: info@condonlaw.com. Web Site: www.condonlaw.com. *Librn,* Antonietta Tatta
Founded 1922
Library Holdings: Bk Vols 10,000; Per Subs 76
Subject Interests: Aviation, Ins, Law
Restriction: Staff use only

R CONGREGATION EMANU-EL OF THE CITY OF NEW YORK*, Ivan M Stettenheim Library, One E 65th St, 10065. SAN 312-0864. Tel: 212-507-9560, 212-744-1400. FAX: 212-570-0826. Web Site: www.emanuelnyc.org/library. *Librn,* Marjorie Shuster; E-mail: mshuster@emanuelnyc.org; Staff 1 (MLS 1)
Founded 1906
Library Holdings: Bk Vols 11,000; Per Subs 45; Spec Interest Per Sub 45; Talking Bks 75
Subject Interests: Judaica
Automation Activity & Vendor Info: (Acquisitions) Mandarin Library Automation; (Cataloging) Mandarin Library Automation; (Circulation) Mandarin Library Automation; (Course Reserve) Mandarin Library Automation; (Media Booking) Mandarin Library Automation; (OPAC) Mandarin Library Automation; (Serials) Mandarin Library Automation
Special Services for the Blind - Audio mat; Bks available with recordings; Bks on cassette; Bks on CD; Cassette playback machines; Cassettes; Large print bks; Sound rec; Soundproof reading booth
Open Mon 12-7, Tues & Thurs 10-5, Wed 12-5
Restriction: Non-circulating to the pub

L COOLEY LLP*, New York Office Law Library, 55 Hudson Yards, 10001-2157. SAN 372-2457. Tel: 212-479-6000. Interlibrary Loan Service Tel: 212-479-6025. FAX: 212-479-6000. Web Site: www.cooley.com. *Sr Res Serv Librn,* Rafael Sanchez; E-mail: rsanchez@cooley.com; Staff 2 (Non-MLS 2)
Library Holdings: Bk Titles 2,000; Bk Vols 5,000; Per Subs 100
Automation Activity & Vendor Info: (Acquisitions) Softlink America; (Cataloging) Softlink America; (Serials) Softlink America
Wireless access
Restriction: Staff use only

C COOPER UNION FOR ADVANCEMENT OF SCIENCE & ART LIBRARY, Seven E Seventh St, 10003. SAN 311-7081. Tel: 212-353-4186. Circulation Tel: 212-353-4188. Interlibrary Loan Service Tel: 212-353-4189. FAX: 212-353-4017. Web Site: library.cooper.edu. *Libr Dir,* Lisa Norberg; Tel: 212-353-4187, E-mail: lisa.norberg@cooper.edu; *Librn,* Julie Castelluzzo; Tel: 212-353-4178, E-mail: juliec@cooper.edu; *Librn,* Claire Gunning; E-mail: gunning@cooper.edu; *Librn,* Thomas Micchelli; E-mail: micche@cooper.edu; *Libr & Archives Asst,* Katie Blumenkrantz; Tel: 212-353-4184, E-mail: blumenkr@cooper.edu. Subject Specialists: *Computer sci, Electrical engr,* Julie Castelluzzo; *Archit, Art,* Claire Gunning; *Art,* Thomas Micchelli; *Archives,* Katie Blumenkrantz; Staff 8 (MLS 5, Non-MLS 3)
Founded 1859. Enrl 967; Fac 58; Highest Degree: Master
Library Holdings: Bk Vols 136,711; Per Subs 170
Special Collections: Cooperana, bk & ms. US Document Depository
Subject Interests: Archit, Art, Engr
Automation Activity & Vendor Info: (Circulation) Ex Libris Group; (Course Reserve) Ex Libris Group; (OPAC) Ex Libris Group
Wireless access
Publications: Acquisitions Lists; Databases List; Faculty Guide
Partic in Metropolitan New York Library Council
Open Mon-Thurs 8:45am-9pm, Fri 9-6, Sat 11-5, Sun 12-5
Friends of the Library Group

S COUNCIL ON FOREIGN RELATIONS LIBRARY*, 58 E 68th St, 10065. SAN 311-7154. Tel: 212-434-9400. Web Site: www.cfr.org. *Dir,* Alysse Jordan; Staff 6 (MLS 4, Non-MLS 2)
Founded 1930
Library Holdings: Bk Titles 11,000; Per Subs 210
Subject Interests: Econ, Hist, Intl law, Intl relations, Polit sci
Automation Activity & Vendor Info: (Cataloging) Softlink America
Partic in LYRASIS; Metropolitan New York Library Council; OCLC Online Computer Library Center, Inc
Restriction: Staff use only

L CRAVATH, SWAINE & MOORE LLP*, Law Library, Worldwide Plaza, 825 Eighth Ave, 10019. SAN 311-7162. Tel: 212-474-3500. FAX: 212-474-3556. Web Site: www.cravath.com. *Libr Dir,* Deborah Panella
Founded 1819
Library Holdings: Bk Vols 10,000; Per Subs 400
Subject Interests: Antitrust, Corporate, Litigation, Tax
Automation Activity & Vendor Info: (Acquisitions) EOS International; (Cataloging) EOS International; (Circulation) EOS International; (Serials) EOS International
Restriction: By permission only

L CURTIS, MALLET-PREVOST, COLT & MOSLE LIBRARY*, 101 Park Ave, 10178-0061. SAN 311-7197. Tel: 212-696-6138. FAX: 212-697-1559. Web Site: www.curtis.com. *Librn,* Heather Striebel; E-mail: hstriebel@curtis.com
Founded 1900
Library Holdings: Bk Vols 16,000
Special Collections: Central & South American Law
Automation Activity & Vendor Info: (Cataloging) SydneyPlus
Wireless access
Restriction: Staff use only

S DANCE NOTATION BUREAU LIBRARY*, 178 E 109th St, No 5, 10029. SAN 324-8054. Tel: 212-571-7011. E-mail: library@dancenotation.org. Web Site: www.dancenotation.org. *Dir, Libr Serv,* Mei-Chen Lu; Staff 1 (Non-MLS 1)
Founded 1940
Library Holdings: CDs 400; DVDs 600; Music Scores 150; Bk Titles 830; Videos 300
Special Collections: Audiotapes for Notated Dances; Benesh Notation Scores; Isaac Archive (Original Pencil Labanotation Scores); Notated Theatrical Dances Coll; Technical Papers on Labanotation
Subject Interests: Dance notation, Labanotation
Function: Archival coll, Mail & tel request accepted, Ref serv available
Publications: Notated Theatrical Dances: A Listing of Theatrical Dance Scores Housed at the Dance Notation Bureau (free catalogue)
Restriction: Open by appt only

L DAVIS POLK & WARDWELL LLP LIBRARY*, 450 Lexington Ave, 10017. SAN 311-7235. Tel: 212-450-4000. FAX: 212-701-5800. *Dir, Libr Serv,* Joseph Florio; E-mail: joseph.florio@davispolk.com; *Assoc Librn,* Laurie Wilson; E-mail: laurie.wilson@davispolk.com; Staff 11 (MLS 8, Non-MLS 3)
Founded 1891
Library Holdings: Bk Titles 4,500
Special Collections: International Law; Legislature
Subject Interests: Antitrust, Banking, Securities, Taxation
Automation Activity & Vendor Info: (Acquisitions) Sydney Enterprise; (Cataloging) Sydney Enterprise; (Circulation) Sydney Enterprise
Wireless access
Partic in OCLC Online Computer Library Center, Inc
Restriction: Authorized patrons, Borrowing requests are handled by ILL, Open to authorized patrons

L DEBEVOISE & PLIMPTON*, Law Library, 919 Third Ave, 10022. SAN 311-7251. Tel: 212-909-6275. FAX: 212-909-1025. Web Site: www.debevoise.com. *Dir, Libr Serv,* Steven A Lastres
Library Holdings: Bk Vols 30,000; Per Subs 150
Subject Interests: Aviation, Corporate law, Litigation, Real estate, Securities, Taxation law
Automation Activity & Vendor Info: (Acquisitions) EOS International; (Cataloging) EOS International; (Circulation) EOS International; (ILL) EOS International; (OPAC) EOS International; (Serials) EOS International
Wireless access
Function: For res purposes
Restriction: Staff use only

L DECHERT LAW LIBRARY*, 1095 Avenue of the Americas, 30th Flr, 10036. SAN 372-4549. Tel: 212-698-3500. FAX: 212-698-3599. Web Site: www.dechert.com. *Librn,* Brian Deaver; Tel: 212-698-3515, E-mail: brian.deaver@dechert.com; Staff 3 (MLS 2, Non-MLS 1)
Library Holdings: Bk Titles 1,500; Per Subs 150

Subject Interests: Corporate securities
Automation Activity & Vendor Info: (Cataloging) SirsiDynix; (Serials) SirsiDynix
Restriction: Staff use only

L DENTONS US*, Law Library, 1221 Avenue of the Americas, 24th Flr, 10020-1089. SAN 372-2473. Tel: 212-768-6700. FAX: 212-768-6800. *Head Librn,* Alex Stubbs-Trevino; E-mail: alex.stubbs-trevino@dentons.com
Library Holdings: Bk Vols 4,500; Per Subs 15
Restriction: Staff use only

GM DEPARTMENT OF VETERANS AFFAIRS, NEW YORK HARBOR HEALTHCARE*, Learning Resources Center, 423 E 23rd St, 10010. SAN 353-829X. Tel: 212-686-7500, Ext 7682. *Chief, Learning Resources,* Peter Cole; Tel: 212-686-7500, Ext 7684, E-mail: peter.cole@va.gov; *Patient Educ Librn,* Julia Segal; Tel: 212-686-7500, Ext 7681; Staff 4 (MLS 2, Non-MLS 2)
Founded 1956
Library Holdings: Bk Titles 10,000; Per Subs 420
Subject Interests: Patient health educ
Automation Activity & Vendor Info: (Acquisitions) EBSCO Online; (Cataloging) EOS International; (Circulation) EOS International; (ILL) OCLC WorldShare Interlibrary Loan; (OPAC) EOS International
Partic in Metropolitan New York Library Council
Special Services for the Blind - Reader equip
Open Mon-Fri 9-4

L DLA PIPER US LLP*, Law Library, 1251 Avenue of Americas, 27th Flr, 10020-1104. SAN 372-4395. Tel: 212-776-3732. Web Site: www.dlapiper.com. *Head Librn,* Mark Pellis; E-mail: mark.pellis@dlapiper.com
Library Holdings: Bk Vols 8,000; Per Subs 50
Automation Activity & Vendor Info: (Acquisitions) Innovative Interfaces, Inc; (Cataloging) Innovative Interfaces, Inc; (Serials) Innovative Interfaces, Inc
Wireless access
Restriction: Staff use only

S ENGLISH-SPEAKING UNION, Ruth M Shellens Memorial Library, 144 E 39th St, 10016. SAN 311-7510. Tel: 212-818-1200. FAX: 212-202-5031. E-mail: info@esuus.org. Web Site: www.esuus.org. *Exec Dir,* Karen Karpowich; Tel: 212-818-1200, Ext 222, E-mail: kkarpowich@esuus.org
Founded 1944
Library Holdings: Bk Titles 8,000
Special Collections: Ambassador Book Awards Winners; Biographies & Autobiographies of British & American Authors, 1900-1964 (Winifred Nerney Coll)
Subject Interests: Britain, United Kingdom
Restriction: Mem only

G ENVIRONMENTAL PROTECTION AGENCY, Region 2 Library, 290 Broadway, 16th Flr, 10007-1866. SAN 311-7529. Tel: 212-637-3185. FAX: 212-637-3086. E-mail: region2_library@epa.gov. Web Site: www.epa.gov/libraries/region-2-library-services. *Regional Adminr,* Walter Mugdan; E-mail: mugdan.walter@epa.gov; Staff 2 (MLS 2)
Founded 1965
Library Holdings: CDs 58; Bk Titles 50,000; Videos 44
Special Collections: Hazardous Waste Coll
Subject Interests: Chem risk assessment, Drinking water, Environ law, Groundwater protection, Hazardous waste, Pesticides, Superfund, Toxic substance, Wetlands
Partic in OCLC Online Computer Library Center, Inc; Proquest Dialog
Open Mon-Thurs 9-4
Restriction: Circulates for staff only, In-house use for visitors

L EPSTEIN, BECKER & GREEN*, Law Library, 250 Park Ave, 12th Flr, 10177. SAN 372-2414. Tel: 212-351-4500. FAX: 212-878-8600. Web Site: www.ebglaw.com. *Librn,* Esther Quiles; E-mail: equiles@ebglaw.com
Library Holdings: Bk Vols 7,000; Per Subs 100
Automation Activity & Vendor Info: (Cataloging) Inmagic, Inc.; (Circulation) Inmagic, Inc.
Restriction: Staff use only

S THE EXPLORERS CLUB*, Research Collections & James B Ford Library, 46 E 70th St, 10021. SAN 311-7553. Tel: 212-628-8383. FAX: 212-288-4449. E-mail: researchcollections@explorers.org. Web Site: www.explorers.org. *Archivist & Curator of Res Col, Librn,* Lacey Flint; E-mail: lflint@explorers.org; Staff 1 (Non-MLS 1)
Founded 1904
Library Holdings: Bk Titles 13,000; Per Subs 50
Special Collections: 18th - 20th Century Travel Coll; Polar Exploration Coll
Subject Interests: Exploration, Geog, Travel
Wireless access
Function: Ref serv available
Restriction: Not a lending libr, Open to pub by appt only

C FASHION INSTITUTE OF TECHNOLOGY-SUNY, Gladys Marcus Library, Seventh Ave at 27th St, 227 W 27th St, 10001-5992. SAN 311-7596. Tel: 212-217-4340. Circulation Tel: 212-217-4360. Interlibrary Loan Service Tel: 212-217-4364. Reference Tel: 212-217-4400. Administration Tel: 212-217-4370. FAX: 212-217-4371. Web Site: fitnyc.edu/library. *Dir,* Greta Earnest; E-mail: greta_earnest@fitnyc.edu; *Head, Acquisitions & Metadata Servs,* Leslie Preston; Tel: 212-217-4346, E-mail: leslie_preston@fitnyc.edu; *Head, Res & Instrul Serv,* Carli Spina; Tel: 212-217-4396, E-mail: carli_spina@fitnyc.edu; *Head, Spec Coll & Archives,* Karen J Trivette; Tel: 212-217-4386, E-mail: karen_trivette@fitnyc.edu; *Digital Initiatives Librn,* Joseph Anderson; E-mail: joseph_anderson@fitnyc.edu; *Electronic Res & Per Librn,* Lana Bittman; Tel: 212-217-4382, E-mail: lana_bittman@fitnyc.edu; *Emerging Tech Librn,* Helen T Lane; Tel: 212-217-4407, E-mail: Helen_lane@fitnyc.edu; *Res & Instrul Serv Librn,* Miyo Sandlin; E-mail: miyo_sandlin@fitnyc.edu; *Access Serv Mgr/Day,* Jennifer Mak; Tel: 212-217-4363, E-mail: Jennifer_mak@fitnyc.edu; *ILL Access & Serv Mgr/Evening,* Paul Lajoie; Tel: 212-217-4362, E-mail: paul_lajoie@fitnyc.edu; *Res Serv,* Maria Rothenberger; E-mail: maria_rothenberger@fitnyc.edu; Staff 37 (MLS 12, Non-MLS 25)
Founded 1944. Enrl 9,500; Fac 989; Highest Degree: Master
Library Holdings: Bk Vols 188,780; Per Subs 500; Videos 3,684
Special Collections: Fashion (sketch bks of fashion designs); Interviews of Members of the Fashion Industry. Oral History
Subject Interests: Fashion design, Fine arts, Gallery, Merchandising, Mus studies, Retail art admin
Automation Activity & Vendor Info: (Cataloging) Ex Libris Group; (Circulation) Ex Libris Group; (ILL) OCLC ILLiad; (OPAC) Ex Libris Group; (Serials) EBSCO Online
Wireless access
Publications: Brochures/Pathfinders; CONNECTED (Newsletter); Faculty Handbook; LibGuides (Research guide); Subject Heading Brochures
Partic in Ex Libris Aleph; Metropolitan New York Library Council; OCLC Online Computer Library Center, Inc; SUNYConnect
Restriction: Open to students, fac, staff & alumni, Photo ID required for access, Pub by appt only, Visitors must make appt to use bks in the libr

CL FORDHAM UNIVERSITY SCHOOL OF LAW, The Maloney Library, 150 W 62nd St, 10023. SAN 311-7723. Circulation Tel: 212-636-7820. Interlibrary Loan Service Tel: 212-636-6902. Reference Tel: 212-636-6908. Administration Tel: 212-636-6904. FAX: 212-930-8818. Interlibrary Loan Service FAX: 212-636-7192. E-mail: refdesk@law.fordham.edu. Web Site: library.law.fordham.edu. *Dir,* Todd G E Melnick; Tel: 212-636-7677, E-mail: tmelnick@law.fordham.edu; *Dep Dir,* Alissa Black-Dorward; Tel: 212-636-7968, E-mail: blackdorward@law.fordham.edu; *Assoc Librn, Tech Serv,* Yael Mandelstam; Tel: 212-636-7971, E-mail: ymandelstam@law.fordham.edu; *Head, Ref,* Kelly Leong; Tel: 212-636-6915, E-mail: kleong4@law.fordham.edu; *Instrul Serv Librn,* Alyson Drake; E-mail: adrake4@law.fordham.edu; *Circ Librn,* Position Currently Open; *Foreign & Intl Law Librn,* Janet Kearney; Tel: 212-636-6913, E-mail: jkearney15@law.fordham.edu; *Ref Librn,* Gail McDonald; Tel: 212-636-7005, E-mail: gmcdonald5@law.fordham.edu; *Fac Serv Librn,* Nathan Delmar; Tel: 212-636-6903, E-mail: ndelmar@law.fordham.edu; *Assoc Librn, Pub Serv,* Position Currently Open; *Mgr, Syst & Tech,* Thomas Kaczorowski; Tel: 212-636-6907, E-mail: tkaczorowski@law.fordham.edu; *Coll Mgt Librn,* Jennifer Dixon; Tel: 212-636-6705, E-mail: jdixon22@law.fordham.edu; *Cat Librn,* Angela Sinhart; Tel: 212-636-7041, E-mail: asinhart@law.fordham.edu. Subject Specialists: *Advan legal res, Copyright, Legal res,* Todd G E Melnick; *Advan legal res, Legal res,* Kelly Leong; *Advan legal res, Legal res,* Alyson Drake; *Advan legal res, Intl law, Intl trade,* Janet Kearney; *Advan legal res, Legal res,* Gail McDonald; *Legal res,* Nathan Delmar; Staff 13 (MLS 9, Non-MLS 4)
Founded 1905. Enrl 1,346; Fac 66; Highest Degree: Doctorate
Jul 2016-Jun 2017. Mats Exp $1,741,940, Books $179,547, Per/Ser (Incl. Access Fees) $1,008,339, Micro $13,248, Electronic Ref Mat (Incl. Access Fees) $540,806. Sal $1,972,586 (Prof $1,548,219)
Special Collections: US Document Depository
Subject Interests: Antitrust law, Banking law, Comparative law, Corporate law, European commun law, Foreign law, Human rights, Intl law, Legal ethics, Securities law
Automation Activity & Vendor Info: (Acquisitions) Innovative Interfaces, Inc - Sierra; (Cataloging) Innovative Interfaces, Inc - Sierra; (Circulation) Innovative Interfaces, Inc - Sierra; (Course Reserve) Innovative Interfaces, Inc - Sierra; (ILL) OCLC ILLiad; (OPAC) Innovative Interfaces, Inc - Sierra; (Serials) Innovative Interfaces, Inc - Sierra
Wireless access
Function: Art exhibits, ILL available, Online cat, Photocopying/Printing, Ref serv available, Scanner
Publications: LibGuides (Reference guide)

Partic in American Association of Law Libraries; Association of Jesuit Colleges & Universities; Legal Information Preservation Alliance; NELLCO Law Library Consortium, Inc.; OCLC Online Computer Library Center, Inc; Westchester Academic Library Directors Organization
Open Mon-Sun 8am-1am
Restriction: Borrowing privileges limited to fac & registered students, Open to students, fac, staff & alumni

S FRENCH INSTITUTE-ALLIANCE FRANCAISE LIBRARY*, Haskell Library, 22 E 60th St, 10022-1011. SAN 311-7774. Tel: 212-355-6100. Circulation Tel: 646-388-6655. FAX: 212-935-4119. E-mail: library@fiaf.org. Web Site: www.fiaf.org. *VPres, Libr Serv,* Katharine Branning; Tel: 646-388-6614, E-mail: kbranning@fiaf.org; *Dir of Libr/Media Serv,* Ronda Murdock; Tel: 646-388-6636, E-mail: rmurdock@fiaf.org; *Lit Develop Assoc,* Yann Carmona; Tel: 646-388-6639, E-mail: ycarmona@fiaf.org; Staff 3 (MLS 1, Non-MLS 2)
Founded 1911
Library Holdings: AV Mats 9,000; CDs 2,500; Large Print Bks 500; Bk Vols 45,000; Per Subs 102; Videos 2,500
Subject Interests: Archit, Art, Civilization, Fr speaking countries, Geog, Hist, Lit, Philos, Tourism
Automation Activity & Vendor Info: (Acquisitions) BiblioMondo; (Cataloging) BiblioMondo; (Circulation) BiblioMondo; (Course Reserve) BiblioMondo; (ILL) BiblioMondo; (Media Booking) BiblioMondo; (OPAC) BiblioMondo; (Serials) BiblioMondo
Wireless access
Function: 24/7 Electronic res, 24/7 Online cat, Adult bk club
Publications: Acquisitions List; Newsletter
Open Mon 4-8, Tues, Wed & Thurs 11:30-8, Fri 11:30-3, Sat 9:30-3
Restriction: Circ to mem only, Open to pub for ref only
Friends of the Library Group

L FRESHFIELDS BRUCKHAUS DERINGER US LLP*, 601 Lexington Ave, 31st Flr, 10022. Tel: 212-277-4000.
Founded 1999
Function: Online cat, Ref serv available, Res performed for a fee
Restriction: Authorized patrons, Borrowing requests are handled by ILL, Circ limited, Co libr, Employees & their associates, External users must contact libr, Internal circ only, Not open to pub, Private libr, Use of others with permission of librn

S THE FRICK COLLECTION*, Frick Art Reference Library, Ten E 71st St, 10021. SAN 311-7782. Tel: 212-288-0641. E-mail: library@frick.org. Web Site: www.frick.org/research/library. *Chief Librn,* Stephen Bury; Staff 21 (MLS 12, Non-MLS 9)
Founded 1920
Jul 2015-Jun 2016 Income $718,000. Mats Exp $478,000, Books $250,000, Per/Ser (Incl. Access Fees) $40,000, Electronic Ref Mat (Incl. Access Fees) $38,000, Presv $150,000. Sal $2,400,000 (Prof $1,800,000)
Library Holdings: CDs 350; e-books 28,000; e-journals 130; Electronic Media & Resources 70; Microforms 170; Bk Titles 450,000; Bk Vols 453,000; Per Subs 530
Special Collections: Artist Files; Auction Catalogs; Exhibition Catalogs. Oral History
Subject Interests: Decorative art, Drawing, Hist of collecting, Hist of painting, Sculpture
Automation Activity & Vendor Info: (Acquisitions) Innovative Interfaces, Inc; (Cataloging) Innovative Interfaces, Inc; (Circulation) Innovative Interfaces, Inc; (ILL) OCLC; (OPAC) Innovative Interfaces, Inc; (Serials) Innovative Interfaces, Inc
Wireless access
Function: Res libr
Publications: Frick Art Reference Library Original Index to Art Periodicals (1983); Frick Art Reference Library Sales Catalogue Index (1992); Spanish Artists from the Fourth to the Twentieth Century; The Story of the Frick Art Reference Library: The Early Years (1979); Vol 1 (A-F) (1993)
Partic in Metropolitan New York Library Council; New York Art Resources Consortium; OCLC Research Library Partnership
Open Mon-Fri 10-5 (Sept-May) 10-5, Sat 10-2; Mon-Fri (June-July) 10-5; Tues-Thurs (Aug) 10-5
Restriction: Closed stack, Non-circulating, Photo ID required for access

L FRIED, FRANK, HARRIS, SHRIVER & JACOBSON LIBRARY*, One New York Plaza, 10004. SAN 311-7790. Tel: 212-859-8901. FAX: 212-859-8000. E-mail: nylibrary@ffhsj.com. Web Site: www.friedfrank.com. *Dir,* Nancy Rine
Founded 1960
Library Holdings: Bk Vols 30,000; Per Subs 110
Subject Interests: Corporate, Fed, Securities, State law
Restriction: Not open to pub

CM HELENE FULD COLLEGE OF NURSING, Peggy Wines Memorial Library, 24 E 120th St, 10035. SAN 327-1919. Tel: 212-616-7200, 212-616-7269. E-mail: library@helenefuld.edu. Web Site: www.helenefuld.edu/about-the-library. *Dir,* Indrajeet Singh
Library Holdings: AV Mats 688; Bk Vols 6,000; Per Subs 101
Automation Activity & Vendor Info: (Cataloging) Surpass; (Circulation) Surpass
Wireless access
Open Mon-Fri 9-5

S THE GENERAL SOCIETY OF MECHANICS & TRADESMEN LIBRARY*, 20 W 44th St, 10036. SAN 311-7839. Tel: 212-840-1840, Ext 2. E-mail: library@generalsociety.org. Web Site: generalsociety.org/?page_id=103. *Archivist,* Angelo Vigorito; E-mail: avigorito@generalsociety.org
Founded 1820
Library Holdings: Bk Titles 110,000; Per Subs 30
Special Collections: General Society of Mechanics & Tradesmen Archives
Subject Interests: Archit, Arts, Construction, Hist of work & tech, Labor hist, NY, Urban trades & crafts
Automation Activity & Vendor Info: (Acquisitions) Softlink America; (Cataloging) Softlink America; (Circulation) Softlink America; (OPAC) Softlink America
Wireless access
Function: Archival coll, Photocopying/Printing, Res libr
Partic in Metropolitan New York Library Council
Friends of the Library Group

SR GENERAL THEOLOGICAL SEMINARY*, Christoph Keller Jr Library, 440 West 21st St, 10011. SAN 311-7847. Tel: 646-717-9784. E-mail: library@gts.edu. Web Site: library.gts.edu. *Libr Mgr, Tech Serv,* Patrick Cates; E-mail: cates@gts.edu; *Ref Librn,* Melissa Chim; Tel: 646-717-9747, E-mail: aaronberg@gts.edu; Staff 2 (MLS 2)
Founded 1819. Enrl 50; Fac 10; Highest Degree: Doctorate
Library Holdings: Bk Titles 170,000; Bk Vols 180,000; Per Subs 180
Special Collections: Clement Clarke Moore Coll; Early English Theology Coll; Episcopal Church Hist (coll on the Protestant Episcopal Church in the United States); Latin Bible Coll; Liturgics
Subject Interests: Anglican, Christian hist, Liturgics, Spirituality, Theol
Automation Activity & Vendor Info: (Acquisitions) ByWater Solutions; (Cataloging) ByWater Solutions; (Circulation) ByWater Solutions; (Course Reserve) ByWater Solutions; (ILL) OCLC WorldShare Interlibrary Loan; (OPAC) ByWater Solutions; (Serials) ByWater Solutions
Wireless access
Function: 24/7 Electronic res, 24/7 Online cat, Archival coll, Art exhibits, Audio & video playback equip for onsite use, Computers for patron use, Electronic databases & coll, ILL available, Internet access, Microfiche/film & reading machines, Online cat, Photocopying/Printing, Res libr, Study rm, Writing prog
Partic in Metropolitan New York Library Council; NY Area Theol Libr Asn; OCLC Online Computer Library Center, Inc
Open Mon-Fri 11-5
Restriction: Borrowing privileges limited to fac & registered students, Non-circulating of rare bks, Non-circulating to the pub, Open to pub for ref only, Open to qualified scholars, Open to researchers by request, Open to students, fac, staff & alumni, Secured area only open to authorized personnel
Friends of the Library Group

S HENRY GEORGE SCHOOL OF SOCIAL SCIENCE*, Research Library, 149 E 38th St, 10016. SAN 374-5767. Tel: 212-889-8020. E-mail: info@hgsss.org. Web Site: www.hgsss.org. *Librn,* Vesa Nelson
Founded 1937
Library Holdings: Bk Titles 5,000
Special Collections: Henry George & Family, bks (incl rare ed), clippings, letters; Land Value Tax/Single Tax (Georgist Authors Coll), bks, journal-art, clippings, theses
Automation Activity & Vendor Info: (Cataloging) JayWil Software Development, Inc; (Circulation) JayWil Software Development, Inc
Wireless access
Open Mon-Fri 9-5

L GIBSON, DUNN & CRUTCHER*, Research & Information Management Department, 200 Park Ave, 48th Flr, 10166-0193. SAN 323-5688. Tel: 212-351-4005. Interlibrary Loan Service Tel: 212-351-4006. FAX: 212-351-6262. E-mail: nylibrary@gibsondunn.com. Web Site: www.gibsondunn.com. *Mgr,* Steven Raber; E-mail: sraber@gibsondunn.com; Staff 3 (MLS 3)
Founded 1987
Library Holdings: Bk Titles 600
Subject Interests: Litigation, Securities
Automation Activity & Vendor Info: (OPAC) EOS International
Wireless access

Partic in American Association of Law Libraries; Law Library Association of Greater New York
Restriction: Staff use only

S GLOBAL INTELLIGENCE*, Young & Rubicam Group, Three Columbus Circle, 10019. SAN 312-150X. Tel: 212-210-3983. FAX: 212-210-3918. E-mail: global.intelligence@yrgrp.com. *Dir,* Stephen Fleming; *Res Spec,* Susan Hoover; Staff 4 (MLS 3, Non-MLS 1)
Founded 1953
Library Holdings: Bk Titles 100; Per Subs 50
Subject Interests: Advertising, Mkt
Wireless access
Restriction: Staff use only

S GODDARD RIVERSIDE COMMUNITY CENTER*, Star Learning Center, 26 W 84th St, 10024. SAN 320-2151. Tel: 212-799-2369, Ext 4702. *Dir,* Monica Enciso; E-mail: menciso@goddard.org
Founded 1971
Library Holdings: Bk Vols 11,000
Subject Interests: Children's lit, Remedial reading
Wireless access
Restriction: Not open to pub

S GOETHE-INSTITUT NEW YORK*, German Cultural Center Library, 30 Irving Pl, 10003. SAN 311-7871. Tel: 212-439-8688. Toll Free Tel: 877-463-8431. FAX: 212-439-8705. Circulation E-mail: library-newyork@goethe.de. Web Site: www.goethe.de/newyork. *Libr Dir,* Katherine Lorimer; *Librn,* Walter Schlect; Staff 2 (MLS 2)
Founded 1957
Library Holdings: CDs 785; DVDs 885; e-books 10,000; e-journals 35; Bk Vols 5,300; Per Subs 10
Subject Interests: German (Lang)
Automation Activity & Vendor Info: (Circulation) Koha; (ILL) OCLC WorldShare Interlibrary Loan; (OPAC) Koha
Wireless access
Function: 24/7 Online cat, Activity rm, Adult bk club, Art exhibits, Audio & video playback equip for onsite use, Bks on CD, Computers for patron use, ILL available, Magazines, Magnifiers for reading, Mail & tel request accepted, Mail loans to mem, Movies, Music CDs, Online cat, Online ref, Photocopying/Printing, Prof lending libr, Ref serv available, Spoken cassettes & CDs, Spoken cassettes & DVDs, Telephone ref
Open Mon-Fri 1-6:30
Restriction: Circ to mem only, In-house use for visitors, Open to pub for ref & circ; with some limitations, Open to students

L GREENBERG TRAURIG LLP*, Research Center Law Library, MetLife Bldg, 200 Park Ave, 10166. SAN 372-4476. Tel: 212-801-9200. FAX: 212-801-6400. Web Site: www.gtlaw.com. *Librn,* Amy Carr
Library Holdings: Bk Vols 10,000
Automation Activity & Vendor Info: (Acquisitions) Ex Libris Group; (Cataloging) Ex Libris Group; (Circulation) Ex Libris Group; (Course Reserve) Ex Libris Group; (ILL) Ex Libris Group; (Media Booking) Ex Libris Group; (OPAC) Ex Libris Group; (Serials) Ex Libris Group
Open Mon-Fri 9-8

S GROLIER CLUB OF NEW YORK LIBRARY*, 47 E 60th St, 10022. SAN 311-7952. Tel: 212-838-6690, Ext 5. FAX: 212-838-2445. Web Site: www.grolierclub.org. *Librn,* Meghan Constantinou; E-mail: mconstantinou@grolierclub.org; Staff 3 (MLS 3)
Founded 1884
Library Holdings: Bk Vols 100,000; Per Subs 200
Special Collections: Archives of Book Collectors, Bookish Societies & Antiquarian Bookdealers; Book Trade & Auction Catalogs; Examples of Fine Printing & Binding; History of Printing & Book Collecting; Inventories of Private Libraries; Portraits of Authors, Printers & Artists; Rare Bibliography
Automation Activity & Vendor Info: (Cataloging) Innovative Interfaces, Inc; (OPAC) Innovative Interfaces, Inc
Wireless access
Partic in Metropolitan New York Library Council
Restriction: Open by appt only

S THE HAMPDEN-BOOTH THEATRE LIBRARY, 16 Gramercy Park S, 10003. SAN 312-0015. Tel: 212-228-1861. E-mail: hampdenboo@gmail.com. Web Site: www.hampdenbooth.org. *Curator, Librn,* Raymond Wemmlinger
Founded 1957
Library Holdings: Bk Titles 10,000
Special Collections: 18th-19th Century English Playbills (William Henderson Coll); Burlesque (Chuck Callahan Coll); Cabinet; Edwin Booth; Franklin; George M Cohan; Heller; La Mama Experimental Theatre Club Coll, playbills, doc; Maurice Evans; Off-Off Broadway Theatre; Photographs; Pipenight; Robert B Mantell; Stage Charities (British Actors Orphanage Fund Coll), correspondence, doc; The Players; Union Square Theatre; Walter Hampden
Subject Interests: Hist of Am stage, Hist of English stage
Restriction: Open by appt only

S HARVARD CLUB OF NEW YORK LIBRARY, 35 W 44th St, 2nd Flr, 10036. SAN 311-8002. Tel: 212-827-1246. FAX: 212-827-1270. E-mail: library@hcny.com. Web Site: hcny.com/join-z/amenities.
Founded 1978
Library Holdings: Bk Vols 30,000; Per Subs 100
Special Collections: Harvardiana
Open Mon-Fri 10-9, Sat 10-6 (Winter); Mon-Fri 10-8 (Summer)

L HAWKINS, DELAFIELD & WOOD*, Law Library, Seven World Trade Center, 250 Greenwich St, 10007. SAN 311-8010. Tel: 212-820-9300, 212-820-9444. *Law Librn,* Johanne Levy; Staff 2 (MLS 2)
Library Holdings: Bk Vols 8,000; Per Subs 20
Automation Activity & Vendor Info: (Cataloging) Inmagic, Inc.; (Circulation) Inmagic, Inc.; (OPAC) Inmagic, Inc.
Restriction: Not open to pub

CR HEBREW UNION COLLEGE-JEWISH INSTITUTE OF RELIGION*, Klau Library, Brookdale Ctr, HUC-JIR, One W Fourth St, 10012. SAN 353-1120. Tel: 212-824-2258. Reference Tel: 212-824-2221. FAX: 212-388-1720. Web Site: huc.edu/libraries/NY. *Dir of Libr,* Yoram Bitton; Tel: 212-674-2261, E-mail: ybitton@huc.edu; *Asst Librn,* Eli Lieberman; E-mail: elieberman@huc.edu; Staff 3 (MLS 2, Non-MLS 1)
Founded 1922
Library Holdings: Bk Titles 135,000; Per Subs 250
Subject Interests: Hebrew lit, Hist, Relig studies
Automation Activity & Vendor Info: (Cataloging) Innovative Interfaces, Inc; (Circulation) Innovative Interfaces, Inc; (OPAC) Innovative Interfaces, Inc; (Serials) Innovative Interfaces, Inc
Wireless access
Open Mon-Thurs 9-5, Fri 9-3

S HISPANIC SOCIETY OF AMERICA LIBRARY*, 613 W 155th St, 10032. SAN 311-8061. Tel: 212-926-2234, Ext 229. Reference Tel: 212-926-2234, Ext 260. FAX: 212-690-0743. E-mail: library@hispanicsociety.org. Web Site: hispanicsociety.org/library. *Curator,* Dr John O'Neill; Tel: 212-926-2234, Ext 251, E-mail: oneill@hispanicsociety.org; *Asst Librn,* William Delgado; *Asst Curator,* Vanessa Pintado; E-mail: pintado@hispanicsociety.org; *Asst Curator,* Edwin Xavier Rolon; Tel: 212-926-2234, Ext 262, E-mail: rolon@hispanicsociety.org. Subject Specialists: *Manuscripts, Rare bks,* Dr John O'Neill; *Rare bks,* Vanessa Pintado; *Modern bks,* Edwin Xavier Rolon; Staff 6 (MLS 3, Non-MLS 3)
Founded 1904
Library Holdings: Bk Vols 300,000; Per Subs 142
Special Collections: Golden Age Drama Manuscript Coll; Medieval Manuscripts Coll; Rare Book Coll
Subject Interests: Archaeology, Art, Customs, Hist, Lit
Automation Activity & Vendor Info: (Acquisitions) Mandarin Library Automation; (Cataloging) Mandarin Library Automation; (OPAC) Mandarin Library Automation
Function: Ref serv available, Res libr
Open Tues-Sat 10-4:15
Restriction: Closed stack, Non-circulating
Friends of the Library Group

L HOLLAND & KNIGHT LLP*, Law Library, 31 W 52nd St, 10019. SAN 311-7987. Tel: 212-513-3200. FAX: 212-385-9010. Web Site: www.hklaw.com. *Head Librn,* Position Currently Open
Subject Interests: Admiralty, Aviation
Partic in Florida Library Information Network
Restriction: Mem only

M HOSPITAL FOR SPECIAL SURGERY*, Kim Barrett Memorial Library, 535 E 70th St, 8th Flr, Rm 8W-837 West, 10021. SAN 311-8126. Tel: 212-606-1000, 212-606-1210. FAX: 212-774-2779. E-mail: medlib@hss.edu. Web Site: www.hss.edu/academic-kimbarrett-library.asp. *Librn,* Rie Goto; Staff 1 (Non-MLS 1)
Founded 1952
Library Holdings: Bk Titles 4,200; Per Subs 112
Subject Interests: Orthopedic surgery, Orthopedics, Rheumatic diseases
Wireless access
Partic in Metropolitan New York Library Council
Restriction: Badge access after hrs, Open to students, fac & staff
Friends of the Library Group

L HUGHES, HUBBARD & REED LIBRARY, Law Library, One Battery Park Plaza, 16th Flr, 10004. SAN 311-8142. Tel: 212-837-6666. FAX: 212-422-4726. E-mail: library@hugheshubbard.com. *Dir, Libr Serv,*

Patricia E Barbone; Tel: 212-837-6594, E-mail: patricia.barbone@hugheshubbard.com; Staff 5 (MLS 4, Non-MLS 1)
Founded 1942
Library Holdings: Electronic Media & Resources 150; Bk Titles 2,000; Per Subs 25
Subject Interests: Corporate securities, Labor, Litigation, Product liability, Securities law, Tax
Automation Activity & Vendor Info: (Cataloging) Cassidy Cataloguing Services, Inc; (Circulation) EOS International; (OPAC) EOS International; (Serials) EOS International
Wireless access
Function: ILL available
Restriction: Not open to pub

S THE HUGUENOT SOCIETY OF AMERICA LIBRARY*, General Society of Mechanics & Tradesmen Bldg, Ste 510, 20 W 44th St, 10036. SAN 327-1935. Tel: 212-755-0592. E-mail: hugsoc@verizon.net. Web Site: www.huguenotsocietyofamerica.org/programs/library. *Exec Secy,* Judith Oringer
Founded 1883
Library Holdings: Bk Vols 3,000
Subject Interests: Genealogy, Manuscripts
Restriction: Open by appt only

C HUNTER COLLEGE LIBRARIES*, Leon & Toby Cooperman Library, East Bldg, 695 Park Ave, 10065. SAN 353-1155. Tel: 212-772-4146. Circulation Tel: 212-772-4166. Reference Tel: 212-772-4187. FAX: 212-772-4142. Web Site: library.hunter.cuny.edu/leon-toby-cooperman-library. *Chief Librn,* Daniel Ortiz Zapata; Tel: 212-772-4161, E-mail: do727@hunter.cuny.edu; *Dep Chief Librn,* Clay Williams; Tel: 212-772-4143, E-mail: clwillia@hunter.cuny.edu; *Head, Access Serv,* David Donabedian; Tel: 212-772-4176, E-mail: ddonabed@hunter.cuny.edu; *Head, Acq,* Linda Dickinson; Tel: 212-772-4168, E-mail: ldickins@hunter.cuny.edu; *Head, Res & Instruction,* Philip Swan; Tel: 212-396-6733, E-mail: pswan@hunter.cuny.edu; *Head, Syst,* Ilan Zelazny; Tel: 212-772-4171, E-mail: izelazny@hunter.cuny.edu; *Head Librn, Art Slide Libr,* Steven Kowalik; Tel: 212-772-5054, E-mail: skowalik@hunter.cuny.edu; *Instrul Design Librn,* Stephanie Margolin; Tel: 212-772-4172, E-mail: smargo@hunter.cuny.edu; *Outreach Librn,* Sarah Laleman Ward; Tel: 212-772-4108, E-mail: sara.ward@hunter.cuny.edu; *Sci Librn,* Mason Brown; Tel: 212-772-4191, E-mail: mbr0010@hunter.cuny.edu; *Ser Librn,* Lisa Finder; Tel: 212-772-4186, E-mail: lfinder@hunter.cuny.edu; *Assoc Librn, Pub Serv,* Danise Hoover; Tel: 212-772-4190, E-mail: dhoover@hunter.cuny.edu; *ILL Mgr,* Gowen Campbell; Tel: 212-772-4192, E-mail: gcampbel@hunter.cuny.edu; *Cat,* Wendy Tan; Tel: 212-772-4173, E-mail: wtan@hunter.cuny.edu; Staff 48 (MLS 26, Non-MLS 22)
Founded 1870. Enrl 21,295; Fac 1,568; Highest Degree: Master
Library Holdings: AV Mats 14,055; e-books 6,240; e-journals 46,131; Electronic Media & Resources 156; Bk Vols 798,148; Per Subs 962; Videos 432
Special Collections: Archives of the Hunter College Alumni Association; Early English Novels (Stonehill Coll); Eileen Cowe Historical Textbooks; Lenox Hill Neighborhood Coll; Women's City Club of NY Coll
Automation Activity & Vendor Info: (Acquisitions) Ex Libris Group; (Cataloging) Ex Libris Group; (Circulation) Ex Libris Group; (Course Reserve) Ex Libris Group; (ILL) OCLC; (OPAC) Ex Libris Group; (Serials) Ex Libris Group
Wireless access
Function: Archival coll, Computers for patron use, Doc delivery serv, E-Reserves, Electronic databases & coll, ILL available, Learning ctr, Magnifiers for reading, Online cat, Online ref, Orientations, Outreach serv, Photocopying/Printing, Prof lending libr, Ref & res, Ref serv available, Res libr, Spoken cassettes & CDs, Spoken cassettes & DVDs, Telephone ref, VHS videos, Wheelchair accessible
Partic in Metropolitan New York Library Council; OCLC Online Computer Library Center, Inc
Restriction: Authorized patrons, Borrowing privileges limited to fac & registered students, Circ privileges for students & alumni only, Open to fac, students & qualified researchers
Friends of the Library Group

Departmental Libraries:

CENTRO - CENTER FOR PUERTO RICAN STUDIES LIBRARY, 2180 Third Ave, Rm 121, 10035, SAN 325-7533. Tel: 212-396-7874. FAX: 212-396-7707. E-mail: centro.library@hunter.cuny.edu. Web Site: centropr.hunter.cuny.edu/library. *Libr Mgr,* Mr Anibal Arocho; Tel: 212-396-7879, E-mail: aa3260@hunter.cuny.edu; *Ref & Flm Librn,* Felix A Rivera; Tel: 212-396-7880, E-mail: xrivera@hunter.cuny.edu; *Sr Archivist,* Pedro Juan Hernandez; Tel: 212-396-7877, E-mail: dhernand@hunter.cuny.edu; *Digital Archivist,* Lindsay Dumas Wittwer; Tel: 212-396-7882, E-mail: ld833@hunter.cuny.edu; Staff 9 (MLS 5, Non-MLS 4)
Founded 1973
Library Holdings: AV Mats 500; Bk Vols 25,000
Special Collections: Archival Holdings on the Puerto Rican Diaspora; Dissertations on Puerto Rican Subjects; Film Coll on Puerto Rican Themes; Microforms on Latino Periodicals in New York; Monographs on Puerto Rican/Latino Studies Subjects; Oral History Coll; Periodicals/Microforms on Puerto Rico; Photographic Coll of the Puerto Rican Migration
Subject Interests: Latino studies, Puerto Rican studies
Function: Art exhibits, Bilingual assistance for Spanish patrons, CD-ROM, Computers for patron use, Electronic databases & coll, Internet access, Online ref, Orientations, Outside serv via phone, mail, e-mail & web, Photocopying/Printing, Ref serv available, Serves people with intellectual disabilities, Telephone ref, VHS videos, Wheelchair accessible
Open Mon-Fri 10-5
Restriction: Non-circulating coll, Non-circulating to the pub, Not a lending libr, Open to pub for ref only, Open to students, fac & staff, Photo ID required for access, Pub ref by request

CM HEALTH PROFESSIONS LIBRARY, Hunter College Brookdale Campus, 425 E 25th St, 10010, SAN 353-118X. Tel: 212-481-5117. FAX: 212-772-5116. Web Site: library.hunter.cuny.edu/health-professions. *Head of Libr,* John Carey; E-mail: john.carey@hunter.cuny.edu; *Instrul & Ref Librn,* John Pell; E-mail: jpell@hunter.cuny.edu; Staff 5 (MLS 3, Non-MLS 2)
Founded 1909. Highest Degree: Doctorate
Library Holdings: Bk Vols 26,000; Per Subs 330
Automation Activity & Vendor Info: (Circulation) Ex Libris Group
Restriction: Open to students, fac & staff

SCHOOLS OF SOCIAL WORK & PUBLIC HEALTH LIBRARY, 2180 Third Ave, 10035, SAN 353-121X. Tel: 212-396-7654. Circulation Tel: 212-396-7655. Reference Tel: 212-396-7656. FAX: 212-396-7683. Web Site: library.hunter.cuny.edu/schools-social-work-public-health. *Head of Libr,* Margaret Bausman; Tel: 212-396-7659, E-mail: mbausman@hunter.cuny.edu; *Soc Work Librn,* Adina Mulliken; Tel: 212-396-7665, E-mail: am2621@hunter.cuny.edu; Staff 4 (MLS 2, Non-MLS 2)
Founded 1969
Library Holdings: Bk Vols 47,386; Per Subs 139

L HUNTON & WILLIAMS LLP*, Law Library, 200 Park Ave, 10166. SAN 371-8433. Tel: 212-309-1000. Interlibrary Loan Service Tel: 212-309-1077. FAX: 212-309-1100. *Librn,* Alina Alvarez-Lenda; Tel: 212-309-1078, E-mail: aalvarez-lenda@hunton.com; *Librn,* Deborah Totaram; Staff 2 (Non-MLS 2)
Library Holdings: Bk Titles 25,000; Per Subs 5,000
Subject Interests: Legal
Automation Activity & Vendor Info: (Acquisitions) Sydney; (Cataloging) Sydney; (Circulation) Sydney; (OPAC) Sydney; (Serials) Sydney
Wireless access
Function: ILL available
Restriction: Co libr

S HYDROMINE INC LIBRARY*, 230 Park Ave, Ste 950, 10169. SAN 329-8469. Tel: 212-953-4400. FAX: 212-953-2266.
Library Holdings: Bk Vols 4,000

S INSURANCE INFORMATION INSTITUTE LIBRARY*, 110 William St, 10038. SAN 324-6272. Tel: 212-346-5500. Web Site: www.iii.org. *Dir, Res,* Maria Sassian
Founded 1960
Library Holdings: Bk Titles 1,500; Per Subs 130
Subject Interests: Casualty ins, Property ins
Automation Activity & Vendor Info: (Acquisitions) Inmagic, Inc.; (Cataloging) Inmagic, Inc.; (Circulation) Inmagic, Inc.; (Course Reserve) Inmagic, Inc.; (ILL) Inmagic, Inc.; (Media Booking) Inmagic, Inc.; (OPAC) Inmagic, Inc.; (Serials) Inmagic, Inc.
Wireless access
Restriction: Open by appt only

SR INTERCHURCH CENTER, Ruth Stafford Peale Library, 475 Riverside Dr, Ste 250, 10115. SAN 311-8266. Tel: 212-870-3804. FAX: 212-870-2440. Web Site: www.interchurch-center.org/library. *Librn,* Tracey Del Duca; E-mail: tdelduca@interchurch-center.org; Staff 2 (MLS 1, Non-MLS 1)
Founded 1978
Library Holdings: Bk Vols 17,000; Per Subs 55
Special Collections: Denominational Yearbooks; Religious Research Projects (H Paul Douglass), micro
Subject Interests: Missions, Nonprofit mgt, Relig, Soc problems
Automation Activity & Vendor Info: (ILL) OCLC; (OPAC) TLC (The Library Corporation)
Function: Res libr
Partic in Metropolitan New York Library Council; NY Area Theol Libr Asn
Restriction: Mem only, Open to others by appt

S INTERNATIONAL CENTER OF PHOTOGRAPHY LIBRARY*, Concourse, 1114 Avenue of the Americas, 10036-7703. SAN 324-1823. Tel: 212-857-0004. FAX: 212-857-0091. E-mail: library@icp.org. Web Site: www.icp.org. *Chief Librn,* Position Currently Open; *Assoc Librn,* Position Currently Open; Staff 5 (MLS 3, Non-MLS 2)
Founded 1977
Library Holdings: AV Mats 200; DVDs 200; Bk Vols 28,000; Per Subs 50; Videos 200
Special Collections: Oral History
Automation Activity & Vendor Info: (Cataloging) OCLC; (OPAC) LibraryWorld, Inc
Wireless access
Function: 24/7 Online cat, Archival coll, Art exhibits, Electronic databases & coll, Internet access, Magazines, Online cat, Photocopying/Printing, Res libr, Scanner
Restriction: Non-circulating, Not a lending libr, Open by appt only, Open to pub by appt only, Visitors must make appt to use bks in the libr
Friends of the Library Group

S ISTITUTO ITALIANO DI CULTURA, BIBLIOTECA, 686 Park Ave, 10065. SAN 311-8347. Tel: 212-879-4242. FAX: 212-861-4018. E-mail: visualarts.iicnewyork@esteri.it. Web Site: www.iicnewyork.esteri.it. *Library Contact,* Barbara Dalfovo; E-mail: barbara.dalfovo@esteri.it
Founded 1959
Library Holdings: Bk Titles 8,000
Subject Interests: Italy
Open Mon-Fri 9-4

L JACKSON LEWIS LLP*, Law Library, 666 Third Ave, 29th Flr, 10017. SAN 372-4247. Tel: 212-545-4000, 212-545-4033. Web Site: www.jacksonlewis.com. *Chief Knowledge Officer,* Catherine M Dillon; E-mail: Catherine.Dillon@jacksonlewis.com
Library Holdings: Bk Vols 10,000
Automation Activity & Vendor Info: (Acquisitions) Inmagic, Inc.; (Cataloging) Inmagic, Inc.
Wireless access

S JAPAN SOCIETY, C V Starr Library, 333 E 47th St, 10017. SAN 311-8355. Tel: 212-715-1273. FAX: 212-715-1279. Web Site: www.japansociety.org/education/language-center. *Dir,* Tomoyo Kamimura; E-mail: tkamimura@japansociety.org; Staff 1 (MLS 1)
Library Holdings: Bk Titles 14,000; Per Subs 116
Subject Interests: Archit, Art, Econ, Hist, Lang arts
Restriction: Authorized patrons, Employees only, Mem only

S JBI INTERNATIONAL*, Jewish Braille Institute of America, 110 E 30th St, 10016. SAN 327-1994. Tel: 212-889-2525. Toll Free Tel: 800-433-1531. FAX: 212-689-3692. E-mail: library@jbilibrary.org. Web Site: www.jbilibrary.org. *Head Librn,* Arlene Arfe; *Librn,* Inna Suholutsky; *Libr Distribution Mgr,* Barry Pelofsky
Founded 1931
Library Holdings: Audiobooks 13,000; Braille Volumes 68,000; Large Print Bks 1,000; Bk Titles 13,000; Spec Interest Per Sub 4; Talking Bks 13,000
Subject Interests: Jewish bks, Jewish per
Publications: Concert, Lecture & Poetry Series - Audio (Monthly); JBI Voice - Audio (Monthly); Jewish Braille Review - Braille (Monthly); The JBI Periodicals Series - Audio (Monthly)
Special Services for the Blind - Audio mat; Bks & mags in Braille, on rec, tape & cassette; Bks on flash-memory cartridges; Braille alphabet card; Braille bks; Children's Braille; Club for the blind; Digital talking bk; Extensive large print coll; Free checkout of audio mat; Home delivery serv; Large print bks; Large print bks & talking machines; Production of talking bks; Rec of textbk mat; Student ref mat taped; Talking bks; Web-Braille
Open Mon-Fri 9-5

S JEWISH BOARD OF FAMILY & CHILDREN SERVICES*, Mary & Louis Robinson Library, 135 W 50th St, 6th Flr, 10020. SAN 327-1978. Tel: 212-582-9100, 888-523-2769. *Library Contact,* Brenda Romback; Staff 1 (MLS 1)
Founded 1968
Library Holdings: Bk Vols 5,000; Per Subs 60
Subject Interests: Mental health
Automation Activity & Vendor Info: (Cataloging) JayWil Software Development, Inc; (Circulation) JayWil Software Development, Inc
Wireless access
Restriction: Staff use only

R JEWISH THEOLOGICAL SEMINARY LIBRARY*, 3080 Broadway, 10027. SAN 311-8398. Tel: 212-678-8844. E-mail: library@jtsa.edu. Web Site: www.jtsa.edu/library. *Librn,* David Kraemer; E-mail: dakraemer@jtsa.edu; Staff 14.5 (MLS 11, Non-MLS 3.5)
Founded 1903. Enrl 450; Fac 30; Highest Degree: Doctorate
Library Holdings: AV Mats 8,000; CDs 150; DVDs 45; e-books 250; e-journals 100; Music Scores 6,000; Bk Vols 400,000; Per Subs 788; Videos 1,250
Special Collections: Bible Coll; Hebrew Incunabula, archives; Hebrew Manuscripts, micro; Liturgical Works; Rabbinics; Rare Books
Subject Interests: Bible, Hebrew lit, Israel, Jewish hist, Judaism, Liturgy, Rabbinics
Automation Activity & Vendor Info: (Acquisitions) Ex Libris Group; (Cataloging) Ex Libris Group; (Circulation) Ex Libris Group; (Course Reserve) Ex Libris Group; (ILL) Ex Libris Group; (OPAC) Ex Libris Group; (Serials) Ex Libris Group
Wireless access
Function: Archival coll, Art exhibits, Audio & video playback equip for onsite use, Distance learning, Doc delivery serv, E-Reserves, Electronic databases & coll, ILL available, Internet access, Mail & tel request accepted, Online cat, Online ref, Photocopying/Printing, Ref & res, Ref serv available, Scanner
Publications: News from the Library
Partic in Metropolitan New York Library Council; OCLC Online Computer Library Center, Inc
Open Mon-Thurs 8:30-8, Sun 10:30-7
Restriction: Photo ID required for access
Friends of the Library Group

C JOHN JAY COLLEGE OF CRIMINAL JUSTICE*, Lloyd George Sealy Library, 899 Tenth Ave, 10019. SAN 311-8401. Tel: 212-237-8000, 212-237-8246. Reference Tel: 212-237-8247. FAX: 212-237-8221. Web Site: www.lib.jjay.cuny.edu. *Chief Librn,* Dr Larry E Sullivan; E-mail: lsullivan@jjay.cuny.edu; *Assoc Librn, Info Syst,* Bonnie R Nelson; E-mail: bnelson@jjay.cuny.edu; *Assoc Librn, Pub Serv,* Dr Bladek Marta; Tel: 212-237-8997, E-mail: mbladek@jjay.cuny.edu; *Assoc Librn, Tech Serv,* Maria Kiriakova; Tel: 212-237-8260, E-mail: mkiriakova@jjay.cuny.edu; *Circ Librn,* Dr Jeffrey Kroessler; Tel: 212-237-8236, E-mail: jkroessler@jjay.cuny.edu; *Electronic Res Librn,* Maureen Richards; Tel: 212-237-8234, E-mail: marichards@jjay.cuny.edu; *Emerging Tech Librn,* Robin Camille Davis; Tel: 212-237-8261, E-mail: robdavis@jjay.cuny.edu; *ILL Librn,* Karen Okamoto; E-mail: kokamoto@jjay.cmy.edu; *Media Librn,* Ellen Sexton; Tel: 212-237-8258, E-mail: esexton@jjay.cuny.edu; *Reserves Librn,* Kathleen Collins; Tel: 212-237-8242, E-mail: kcollins@jjay.cuny.edu; *Ser Librn,* Dolores Grande; Tel: 212-237-8235, E-mail: dgrande@jjay.cuny.edu; *Spec Coll Librn,* Dr Ellen Belcher; Tel: 212-237-8238, E-mail: ebelcher@jjay.cuny.edu. Subject Specialists: *Info syst,* Bonnie R Nelson; Staff 15.7 (MLS 14.4, Non-MLS 1.3)
Founded 1965. Enrl 11,000; Fac 325; Highest Degree: Master
Library Holdings: e-books 42,062; e-journals 26,000; Bk Vols 247,969; Per Subs 14,374
Special Collections: Flora R Schreiber Papers; New York Criminal Court Transcripts & Records 1890-1920; NYC Police Dept Blotters, Manhatten 1920-1933; Police Department Annual Reports; Sing Sing Prison (Warden Lewis E Lawes Papers)
Subject Interests: Criminal justice, Fire serv admin, Forensic psychol, Pub admin, Sci
Automation Activity & Vendor Info: (Acquisitions) Ex Libris Group; (Cataloging) Ex Libris Group; (Circulation) Ex Libris Group; (Course Reserve) Docutek; (ILL) OCLC; (OPAC) Ex Libris Group; (Serials) Ex Libris Group
Wireless access
Publications: Newsletter; Research Guides; Self-Guided Workbooks
Partic in Criminal Justice Info Exchange; OCLC Online Computer Library Center, Inc
Restriction: Limited access for the pub, Open to students, fac, staff & alumni

S JUILLIARD SCHOOL, Lila Acheson Wallace Library, 60 Lincoln Center Plaza, 10023-6588. SAN 311-8436. Tel: 212-799-5000, Ext 265. FAX: 212-769-6421. E-mail: library@juilliard.edu. Web Site: www.juilliard.edu/school/library-and-archives. *VPres, Libr & Info Serv,* Jane Gottlieb; *Archivist, Dir,* Jeni Dahmus; *Dir, Tech Serv,* Alan Klein; Staff 13 (MLS 6, Non-MLS 7)
Founded 1905. Enrl 1,769; Fac 300; Highest Degree: Doctorate
Library Holdings: CDs 14,000; DVDs 8,000; Music Scores 87,000; Bk Titles 27,000; Per Subs 230; Videos 3,000
Special Collections: First & Early Editions of Liszt Piano Works; Juilliard Manuscript Coll, autographs, first eds, sketchbks; Kneisel Hall Archives; Opera Librettos of 19th Century; Opera Piano-Vocal Scores; Peter Jay Sharp Special Colls, bks, concert progs, correspondence, ms, news clippings, papers, photogs, rec, scores
Subject Interests: Dance, Drama, Music
Automation Activity & Vendor Info: (Acquisitions) Innovative Interfaces, Inc; (Cataloging) Innovative Interfaces, Inc; (Circulation) Innovative Interfaces, Inc; (Course Reserve) Innovative Interfaces, Inc; (ILL) Innovative Interfaces, Inc; (Media Booking) Innovative Interfaces, Inc; (OPAC) Innovative Interfaces, Inc; (Serials) Innovative Interfaces, Inc
Wireless access
Publications: Guide to The Juilliard School Archives

Partic in Metropolitan New York Library Council; OCLC Online Computer Library Center, Inc
Open Mon-Thurs 8:30am-9pm, Fri 8:30-7, Sat 9-6, Sun 2-7 (Winter); Mon-Thurs 9-5 (Summer)
Restriction: Open to researchers by request, Open to students, fac & staff
Friends of the Library Group

L KATTEN MUCHIN ROSENMAN LLP*, Law Library, 575 Madison Ave, 10022-2585. SAN 312-0384. Tel: 212-940-8800. FAX: 212-940-8776. Web Site: www.kattenlaw.com. *Ref Librn,* Chris Klobucar; Staff 3 (MLS 3)
Founded 1946
Library Holdings: Bk Vols 50,000; Per Subs 700
Automation Activity & Vendor Info: (Acquisitions) EOS International; (Cataloging) EOS International; (Circulation) EOS International; (ILL) EOS International; (Serials) EOS International
Wireless access
Restriction: Staff use only

L KELLEY DRYE & WARREN LLP*, Law Library, 101 Park Ave, 10178. SAN 327-2052. Tel: 212-808-7800. FAX: 212-808-7897. Web Site: www.kelleydrye.com. *Ref Librn,* David Reith; E-mail: dreith@kelleydrye.com
Automation Activity & Vendor Info: (Cataloging) EOS International; (Circulation) EOS International; (OPAC) EOS International
Wireless access
Restriction: Staff use only

L KIRKLAND & ELLIS LLP*, Law Library, 601 Lexington Ave, 10022. SAN 372-2317. Tel: 212-446-4990. FAX: 212-446-4900. Web Site: www.kirkland.com. *Libr Serv Mgr,* Paulette Toth; E-mail: paulette.Toth@kirkland.com
Automation Activity & Vendor Info: (Cataloging) SirsiDynix; (OPAC) SirsiDynix
Wireless access
Open Mon-Fri 9-7

L KRAMER, LEVIN, NAFTALIS & FRANKEL LLP*, Law Library, 1177 Avenue of the Americas, 10036. SAN 372-4212. Tel: 212-715-9321. FAX: 212-715-8000. E-mail: librarygroup@kramerlevin.com. Web Site: www.kramerlevin.com. *Dir, Knowledge Mgt,* Brian Boyle; E-mail: bboyle@kramerlevin.com; *Ref (Info Servs),* Evelyn Gomez
Library Holdings: Bk Titles 5,000; Bk Vols 15,000; Per Subs 300
Automation Activity & Vendor Info: (Acquisitions) Sydney; (Cataloging) Sydney; (Circulation) Sydney; (Course Reserve) Sydney; (ILL) Sydney; (Media Booking) Sydney; (OPAC) Sydney; (Serials) Sydney
Restriction: Open to staff only

L LATHAM & WATKINS*, Law Library, 885 Third Ave, Ste 1000, 10022. SAN 372-4522. Tel: 212-906-1200. FAX: 212-751-4864. Web Site: www.lw.com. *Libr Supvr,* Adria Hirsch; E-mail: adria.hirsch@lw.com
Library Holdings: Bk Vols 20,000; Per Subs 150
Restriction: Staff use only

S LEAGUE OF AMERICAN ORCHESTRAS*, Knowledge Center, 33 W 60th St, 5th Flr, 10023. SAN 329-2975. Tel: 212-262-5161. FAX: 212-262-5198. Web Site: www.americanorchestras.org. *Knowledge Mgr,* James McCain; E-mail: jmccain@americanorchestras.org
Library Holdings: Bk Titles 300
Special Collections: League Publications; Orchestra Program, bks
Subject Interests: Am orchestras, Govt, Orchestra mgt
Restriction: Mem only

S LEGAL AID SOCIETY, Central Library & Information Center, 199 Water St, 10038. SAN 371-1722. Tel: 212-577-3300. Web Site: legalaidnyc.org. *Librn,* Alex Reznik; E-mail: areznik@legal-aid.org
Library Holdings: Bk Vols 500
Restriction: Staff use only

M LENOX HILL HOSPITAL-NORTHWELL HEALTH, Health Sciences Library, 100 E 77th St, 10075. SAN 311-8614, *Dir, Libr Serv,* William Self; E-mail: wself@northwell.edu; Staff 1 (MLS 1)
Founded 1925
Library Holdings: e-books 6,700; e-journals 16,000; Electronic Media & Resources 20
Subject Interests: Dentistry, Med, Nursing
Wireless access
Function: Health sci info serv
Partic in Brooklyn-Queens-Staten Island-Manhattan-Bronx Health Sciences Librarians; Medical Library Association; Metropolitan New York Library Council; NY & NJ Regional Med Libr
Restriction: Staff use only

S LESBIAN, BISEXUAL, GAY & TRANSGENDER COMMUNITY CENTER*, Pat Parker-Vito Russo Center Library, 208 W 13th St, 10011. Tel: 212-620-7310. E-mail: archive@gaycenter.org, library@gaycenter.org. Web Site: www.gaycenter.org/library. *Librn,* Michael Santangelo; Staff 1 (MLS 1)
Library Holdings: AV Mats 700; Bk Titles 12,396; Bk Vols 20,138; Per Subs 20; Videos 1,595
Subject Interests: Fiction, Film, Gay liberation, Non-fiction
Automation Activity & Vendor Info: (Cataloging) Follett Software; (Circulation) Follett Software; (OPAC) Follett Software
Wireless access
Open Sat & Sun 12-4

C LIM COLLEGE LIBRARY*, 216 E 45th St, 2nd Flr, 10017. SAN 311-855X. Tel: 646-218-4126. Reference Tel: 646-218-7737. Administration Tel: 646-218-4695. FAX: 212-750-3453. E-mail: library@limcollege.edu. Web Site: www.limcollege.edu. *Dir, Libr Serv,* Lou Acierno; *Ref Librn,* Lisa Ryan; *Tech Serv,* Amy Wolfe
Founded 1939
Library Holdings: Bk Vols 19,000; Per Subs 240
Special Collections: Merchandising (B Earl Puckett Fund for Retail Education)
Subject Interests: Advertising, Current affairs, Econ, Fashion buying, Lang arts, Math, Mkt, Psychol, Retailing, Visual merchandising
Automation Activity & Vendor Info: (Cataloging) SirsiDynix; (Circulation) SirsiDynix; (OPAC) SirsiDynix
Open Mon-Thurs 8am-9pm, Fri 8-5

L LINKLATERS*, Law Library, 1290 Avenue of the Americas, 10105. SAN 372-4166. Tel: 212-424-9000. FAX: 212-424-9100. Web Site: www.linklaters.com. *Library Contact,* Becky Cohen; E-mail: becky.cohen@linklaters.com
Library Holdings: Bk Titles 1,000; Bk Vols 10,000; Per Subs 100
Automation Activity & Vendor Info: (Circulation) SirsiDynix
Wireless access
Open Mon-Fri 9:30-5:30

L LOEB & LOEB LLP*, Law Library, 345 Park Ave, 10154. SAN 372-2325. Tel: 212-407-4000, 212-407-4961. FAX: 212-407-4990. Web Site: www.loeb.com. *Librn,* Shireen Kumar; E-mail: skumar@loeb.com
Library Holdings: Bk Titles 10,000; Per Subs 500
Wireless access
Restriction: Not open to pub

C MANHATTAN SCHOOL OF MUSIC*, The Peter Jay Sharp Library, 120 Claremont Ave, 10027. SAN 311-8770. Tel: 917-493-4511. Circulation Tel: 917-493-4512. FAX: 212-749-5471. E-mail: library@lists.msmnyc.edu. Web Site: library.msmnyc.edu, www.msmnyc.edu/campus/libraries. *Dir,* Peter Caleb; E-mail: pcaleb@msmnyc.edu; *Librn/Head, Cat,* Janet Weaver; E-mail: jweaver@msmnyc.edu; *Circ Mgr,* Jose Ruiz; E-mail: jruiz@msmnyc.edu; Staff 8 (MLS 4, Non-MLS 4)
Founded 1925. Enrl 900; Highest Degree: Doctorate
Library Holdings: CDs 2,000; DVDs 3,000; Music Scores 50,000; Bk Vols 180,000; Per Subs 107
Special Collections: Mischa Elman Coll; Nicolas Flagello Coll, scores
Subject Interests: Music
Automation Activity & Vendor Info: (Acquisitions) Innovative Interfaces, Inc
Wireless access
Partic in OCLC Online Computer Library Center, Inc
Open Mon-Thurs (Winter) 9-9, Fri 9-6, Sat 9-5, Sun 2-8; Mon-Thurs (Summer) 9-5
Restriction: In-house use for visitors, Students only

S KRISTINE MANN LIBRARY, C G Jung Ctr of New York, 28 E 39th St, 4th Flr, 10016. SAN 311-6018. Tel: 212-697-7877. E-mail: info@junglibrary.org. Web Site: www.junglibrary.org. *Librn,* Lorna Peachin; Staff 2 (MLS 1, Non-MLS 1)
Founded 1945
Library Holdings: Audiobooks 1,200; CDs 200; DVDs 60; Bk Titles 10,000; Bk Vols 21,000; Per Subs 40
Special Collections: Carl Gustav Jung (Jung Press Archive)
Subject Interests: Alchemy, Analytical psychol, Gender studies, Jungian psychol, Mythology, Occult, Relig, Symbolism, Trauma
Wireless access
Function: Res libr
Restriction: Circ to mem only, In-house use for visitors, Private libr, Sub libr

C MARYMOUNT MANHATTAN COLLEGE*, Thomas J Shanahan Library, 221 E 71st St, 10021. SAN 311-886X. Tel: 212-774-4800. Reference Tel: 212-774-4808. FAX: 212-774-4809. Web Site: www.mmm.edu/offices/library. *Libr Dir,* Brian Rocco; Tel: 212-774-4802, E-mail: brocco@mmm.edu; *Electronic Res Librn,* Jason Herman; Tel: 212-774-4804, E-mail: jherman@mmm.edu; *Circ Mgr,* Jonathan Arevalo;

Tel: 212-517-0815, E-mail: jarevalo@mmm.edu; *Media Ctr Coordr,* Jordan Horsley; Tel: 212-774-4805, E-mail: jhorsley@mmm.edu; *Archivist, Bibliographer,* Mary Brown; Tel: 212-774-4817, E-mail: mbrown1@mmm.edu; *Cataloger,* Teresa Yip; Tel: 212-774-4818, E-mail: typ@mmm.edu; Staff 8 (MLS 4, Non-MLS 4)
Founded 1948. Enrl 1,631; Fac 92; Highest Degree: Bachelor
Library Holdings: Bk Titles 65,000; Bk Vols 80,000; Per Subs 650
Special Collections: William Harris Coll
Subject Interests: Communications, Theatre, Women's studies
Automation Activity & Vendor Info: (Cataloging) LibLime; (Circulation) LibLime; (ILL) LibLime; (OPAC) LibLime; (Serials) LibLime
Wireless access
Publications: Resource Aids & Bulletins
Partic in OCLC Online Computer Library Center, Inc; Westchester Academic Library Directors Organization
Special Services for the Deaf - Bks on deafness & sign lang
Open Mon-Thurs 8:30am-10pm, Fri 8:30-5, Sat & Sun 10-5

S ANDREW W MELLON FOUNDATION, Nathan Marsh Pusey Library, 140 E 62nd St, 10065. SAN 375-7188. Tel: 212-838-8400. FAX: 212-888-4172. Web Site: www.mellon.org. *Libr Dir,* Susanne Pichler; E-mail: scp@mellon.org; *Asst Librn,* Lisa Bonifacic; E-mail: lmb@mellon.org; Staff 3 (MLS 3)
Library Holdings: Bk Titles 7,600; Per Subs 150
Subject Interests: Higher educ, Humanities
Automation Activity & Vendor Info: (Cataloging) Inmagic, Inc.; (OPAC) Inmagic, Inc.; (Serials) Inmagic, Inc.
Restriction: Not open to pub

M MEMORIAL SLOAN-KETTERING CANCER CENTER MEDICAL LIBRARY*, Nathan Cummings Center, Rockefeller Research Laboratories, 430 E 67th St, 10065. (Mail add: 1275 York Ave, 10065), SAN 311-8886. Tel: 212-639-7439. Circulation Tel: 212-639-7439. Interlibrary Loan Service Tel: 212-639-7441. Administration Tel: 212-639-2109. FAX: 212-422-2316. Web Site: library.mskcc.org. *Dir, Libr Serv,* Donna Gibson; E-mail: gibsond@mskcc.org; *Librn,* Whitney Bates-Gomez; Tel: 212-639-7442, E-mail: batesw@mskcc.org; *Librn,* Christine Beardsley; Staff 11 (MLS 11)
Library Holdings: e-books 600; e-journals 2,100; Bk Vols 5,000; Per Subs 150
Special Collections: Memorial Sloan-Kettering Cancer Center Archives
Subject Interests: Oncology
Wireless access
Partic in Metropolitan New York Library Council; OCLC Online Computer Library Center, Inc; OCLC Research Library Partnership
Open Mon-Fri 8:30-7
Restriction: Staff use only, Use of others with permission of librn

L MENDES & MOUNT, LLP*, Law Library, 750 Seventh Ave, 10019-6829. SAN 372-4239. Tel: 212-261-8000, 212-261-8338. FAX: 212-261-8750. Web Site: www.mendes.com. *Librn,* Diane Leo; E-mail: diane.leo@mendes.com; Staff 3 (MLS 1, Non-MLS 2)
Library Holdings: Bk Vols 10,000
Restriction: Co libr

C METROPOLITAN COLLEGE OF NEW YORK LIBRARY*, 60 West St, 7th Flr, 10006. SAN 311-6956. Tel: 212-343-1234, Ext 2001. Interlibrary Loan Service Tel: 212-343-1234, Ext 2008. Reference Tel: 212-343-1234, Ext 2010. FAX: 212-343-7398. E-mail: library@mcny.edu. Web Site: www.mcny.edu/library. *Dir, Libr Serv,* Kate Alder; *Digital Serv Librn, Instruction Librn,* Natalia Sucre; *Tech Serv Librn,* Jonathan Frater; Staff 5 (MLS 5)
Founded 1966. Enrl 1,000; Highest Degree: Master
Library Holdings: Bk Titles 26,000; Bk Vols 32,000; Per Subs 400
Special Collections: Audrey Cohen Archives
Subject Interests: Bus, Mgt, Res mgt
Automation Activity & Vendor Info: (Circulation) SirsiDynix; (Course Reserve) SirsiDynix; (OPAC) SirsiDynix; (Serials) EBSCO Online
Wireless access
Function: For res purposes, ILL available
Publications: Library Matters (Newsletter)
Partic in Metropolitan New York Library Council; OCLC Online Computer Library Center, Inc; Westchester Academic Library Directors Organization
Open Mon-Thurs 9-8, Fri & Sat 9-5
Restriction: Access for corporate affiliates

M METROPOLITAN HOSPITAL CENTER*, Frederick M Dearborn Library, 1901 First Ave @ 97th St, 10029. SAN 353-1694. Tel: 212-423-6055. FAX: 212-423-7961. E-mail: mhclibrary@yahoo.com.
Founded 1906
Library Holdings: Bk Titles 5,000; Bk Vols 8,000; Per Subs 90
Subject Interests: Med, Surgery
Automation Activity & Vendor Info: (Cataloging) Professional Software; (Circulation) Professional Software
Wireless access
Partic in National Network of Libraries of Medicine Region 7
Restriction: Open to pub upon request

THE METROPOLITAN MUSEUM OF ART

S CLOISTERS LIBRARY*, Fort Tryon Park, 10040, SAN 353-1848. Tel: 212-396-5319. FAX: 212-795-3640. E-mail: cloisters.library@metmuseum.org. *Librn,* Michael K Carter; Tel: 212-396-5365, E-mail: michael.carter@metmuseum.org
Founded 1938
Library Holdings: Bk Vols 13,000; Per Subs 50
Special Collections: Archives of The Cloisters; George Grey Barnard Papers; Harry Bober Papers; Sumner McKnight Crosby Papers
Subject Interests: European medieval art, Medieval archit, Middle ages
Automation Activity & Vendor Info: (Cataloging) Innovative Interfaces, Inc; (Circulation) Innovative Interfaces, Inc; (OPAC) Innovative Interfaces, Inc
Partic in OCLC Research Library Partnership
Open Tues-Fri 10-4:30

S ROBERT GOLDWATER LIBRARY*, 1000 Fifth Ave, 10028-0198, SAN 353-1872. Tel: 212-570-3707. FAX: 212-570-3879. E-mail: goldwater.library@metmuseum.org. Web Site: library.metmuseum.org. *Head of Libr,* Ross Day; Staff 3 (MLS 1, Non-MLS 2)
Founded 1982
Library Holdings: Bk Titles 15,000; Bk Vols 20,000; Per Subs 224
Subject Interests: African, Native American, Pacific
Partic in Research Libraries Information Network
Publications: Catalog of The Robert Goldwater Library
Restriction: Non-circulating, Open by appt only, Open to fac, students & qualified researchers, Photo ID required for access

S ROBERT LEHMAN COLLECTION LIBRARY*, 1000 Fifth Ave, 10028, SAN 353-1937. Tel: 212-570-3915. FAX: 212-650-2542. E-mail: lehman.library@metmuseum.org. *Librn,* Meg Black; Staff 2 (MLS 1, Non-MLS 1)
Library Holdings: Bk Vols 18,500
Special Collections: Archives of bk, mss, reproductions, correspondence; Photograph Coll, photos, negatives
Subject Interests: Decorative art, Old master drawings, Renaissance, Western European Arts from the 13th to 20th centuries
Function: Res libr
Restriction: Open by appt only, Open to qualified scholars, Open to researchers by request

S THE IRENE LEWISOHN COSTUME REFERENCE LIBRARY, COSTUME INSTITUTE*, 1000 Fifth Ave, 10028, SAN 353-1961. Tel: 212-396-5233, 212-650-2723. FAX: 212-570-3970. E-mail: thecostumeinstitute@metmuseum.org. Web Site: www.metmuseum.org. *Library Contact,* Julie Le; E-mail: juliele@metmuseum.org; Staff 3 (MLS 1, Non-MLS 2)
Founded 1951
Library Holdings: Bk Titles 20,000; Bk Vols 40,000; Per Subs 75
Special Collections: Mainbocher Archive; Norman Norell Coll, scrap bks
Subject Interests: Fashion, Hist of costume
Automation Activity & Vendor Info: (OPAC) Innovative Interfaces, Inc
Function: Res libr
Partic in Metropolitan New York Library Council; Research Libraries Information Network
Restriction: Non-circulating coll, Open by appt only

S LIBRARY & TEACHER RESOURCE CENTER IN THE URIS CENTER FOR EDUCATION*, 1000 Fifth Ave, 10028-0198. Tel: 212-570-3788. E-mail: education@metmuseum.org. Web Site: www.metmuseum.org. *Assoc Librn,* Naomi Niles; Staff 2 (MLS 2)
Founded 1941
Library Holdings: AV Mats 1,000; Bk Vols 6,000; Per Subs 20
Special Collections: Art & Architecture Coll
Subject Interests: Archaeology, Art educ, Art lit, Fine arts, Illustrators, Metrop Mus of Art, Mythology, Visual arts
Partic in Research Libraries Information Network
Restriction: Open to pub for ref only

S THOMAS J WATSON LIBRARY*, 1000 Fifth Ave, 10028-0198, SAN 353-1813. Tel: 212-650-2225. Circulation Tel: 212-650-2175. Interlibrary Loan Service Tel: 212-396-5221. Administration Tel: 212-570-3933. FAX: 212-570-3847. E-mail: watson.library@metmuseum.org. Web Site: library.metmuseum.org. *Dir, Tech Serv,* Daniel Starr; Tel: 212-650-2582, E-mail: daniel.starr@metmuseum.org; *Chief Librn,* Kenneth Soehner; Tel: 212-570-3934, E-mail: ken.soehner@metmuseum.org; *Conserv Librn,* Mindell Dubansky; Tel: 212-570-3220, E-mail: mindell.dubansky@metmuseum.org; *Syst Librn,* Oleg Kreymer; Tel: 212-650-2438, E-mail: oleg.kreymer@metmuseum.org; *Assoc Mgr, Circ & Coll,* Lisa Harms; Tel: 212-650-2344, E-mail: lisa.harms@metmuseum.org; *Acq,* Ross Day; Tel: 212-650-2949, E-mail: ross.day@metmuseum.org; *Electronic Res,* Deborah Vincelli; Tel: 212-650-2912, E-mail: deborah.vincelli@metmuseum.org; *ILL,* Robyn Fleming; E-mail: robyn.fleming@metmuseum.org; *Reader Serv,* Linda

Seckelson; Tel: 212-570-3759, E-mail: linda.seckelson@metmuseum.org; Staff 42 (MLS 17, Non-MLS 25)
Founded 1880
Library Holdings: e-books 30,000; e-journals 2,000; Bk Vols 600,000; Per Subs 2,500
Special Collections: Auction-Sale Catalogs; Autograph Letters; Ephemera on Individual Artists; Museum History Coll
Subject Interests: Archaeology, Archit
Automation Activity & Vendor Info: (Acquisitions) Innovative Interfaces, Inc; (Cataloging) Innovative Interfaces, Inc; (Circulation) Innovative Interfaces, Inc; (ILL) OCLC ILLiad; (OPAC) Innovative Interfaces, Inc; (Serials) Innovative Interfaces, Inc
Function: Res libr
Partic in OCLC Online Computer Library Center, Inc; OCLC Research Library Partnership
Publications: Library Catalog of the Metropolitan Museum of Art
Open Tues-Fri 10-4:45
Friends of the Library Group

S THE MORGAN LIBRARY & MUSEUM*, 225 Madison Ave, 10016. SAN 311-998X. Tel: 212-685-0008. FAX: 212-481-3484. E-mail: readingroom@themorgan.org. Web Site: www.themorgan.org. *Dir, Res Serv,* V Heidi Hass; *Head, Reader Serv,* Maria Molestina-Kurlat; *Mgr, Coll Serv, Mgr, Libr Syst,* Maria Oldal
Founded 1924
Subject Interests: Drawings, Early children's bks, Manuscripts, Prints
Automation Activity & Vendor Info: (Acquisitions) Ex Libris Group; (Cataloging) Ex Libris Group; (Circulation) Ex Libris Group; (OPAC) Ex Libris Group
Function: Res libr
Publications: Exhibition Catalogues; Newsletter
Partic in Research Libraries Information Network
Restriction: Open by appt only
Friends of the Library Group

M MOUNT SINAI BETH ISRAEL, Seymour J Phillips Health Sciences Library, First Ave and 16th St, 4 Silver, Rm 12, 10003. SAN 311-6417. Tel: 212-420-2855. E-mail: LibraryMSBI@mountsinai.org. Web Site: libguides.mssm.edu/MSBI_Library. *Libr Mgr, Med Librn,* Linda Paulls; Tel: 212-420-3858; Staff 1 (MLS 1)
Founded 1946
Library Holdings: e-books 220,000; e-journals 60,000; Electronic Media & Resources 175
Subject Interests: Alcohol, Allied health sci, Behav sci, Drug, Med, Nursing, Nursing educ, Psychiat, Psychol, Soc sci, Surgery
Wireless access
Partic in Metropolitan New York Library Council
Open Mon-Fri 9-5
Restriction: Pub ref by request, Staff use only

CM MOUNT SINAI SCHOOL OF MEDICINE*, Gustave L & Janet W Levy Library, One Gustave L Levy Pl, 10029. (Mail add: PO Box 1102, 10029-6574), SAN 311-9033. Tel: 212-241-7892. Interlibrary Loan Service Tel: 212-241-7795. FAX: 212-831-2625. Web Site: www.mssm.edu/library. *Libr Dir,* Gali Halevi; E-mail: gali.halevi@mssm.edu; Staff 52 (MLS 17, Non-MLS 35)
Enrl 624; Fac 3,530; Highest Degree: Doctorate
Library Holdings: AV Mats 2,512; e-books 5,938; e-journals 23,979; Bk Vols 36,133; Per Subs 24,152
Special Collections: Biomedical Audiovisual & Computer software
Subject Interests: Archives, Med
Automation Activity & Vendor Info: (Acquisitions) SirsiDynix; (Cataloging) SirsiDynix; (Circulation) SirsiDynix; (Course Reserve) SirsiDynix; (ILL) OCLC ILLiad; (OPAC) SirsiDynix; (Serials) SirsiDynix
Wireless access
Partic in National Network of Libraries of Medicine Region 7; OCLC Online Computer Library Center, Inc
Restriction: Not open to pub

M MOUNT SINAI WEST*, Medical Library, 1000 Tenth Ave, 2nd Flr, 10019. SAN 312-0376. Tel: 212-523-6100. FAX: 212-523-6108. E-mail: MSMW.Library@mountsinai.org. Web Site: libguides.mssm.edu/MSMW. *Libr Mgr,* Luke Clinton; E-mail: luke.clinton@mountsinai.org
Founded 1955
Library Holdings: Bk Titles 1,500; Per Subs 400
Subject Interests: Med, Pediatrics, Surgery
Partic in Metrop Consortium
Restriction: Staff use only

S THE MUSEUM OF MODERN ART*, Library & Archives, 11 W 53th St, 10019. SAN 311-9076. Tel: 212-708-9433. Interlibrary Loan Service Tel: 212-708-9441. FAX: 212-333-1122. E-mail: archives@moma.org, library@moma.org. Web Site: www.moma.org/research-and-learning/library. *Head, Libr Serv,* Jillian Suarez; E-mail: jillian_suarez@moma.org; *Head, Archives,* Michelle Harvey; *Head, Metadata Serv, Head, Syst,* Jonathan Lill; *Chief Archivist,* Michelle Elligott; E-mail: michelle_elligott@moma.org; *Mgr, Archives & Spec Coll,* Megan Govin; E-mail: megan_govin@moma.org; Staff 5 (MLS 4, Non-MLS 1)
Founded 1929
Library Holdings: Bk Titles 300,000; Per Subs 250
Special Collections: Artist Files; Artists' Books; Dada & Surrealism (Eluard-Dausse Coll); Latin American Art; Museum of Modern Art Publications; Political Art Documentation & Distribution (PADD) Archives
Subject Interests: Archit, Archives, Art, Design, Drawing, Film, Mixed media, Painting, Sculpture, Video from 1880 to present
Automation Activity & Vendor Info: (Acquisitions) Innovative Interfaces, Inc - Millennium; (Cataloging) Innovative Interfaces, Inc - Millennium; (Circulation) Innovative Interfaces, Inc - Millennium; (OPAC) Innovative Interfaces, Inc - Millennium; (Serials) Innovative Interfaces, Inc - Millennium
Wireless access
Partic in Metropolitan New York Library Council; New York Art Resources Consortium
Friends of the Library Group

S MUSEUM OF THE CITY OF NEW YORK*, Theatre Collection Library, 1220 Fifth Ave, 10029. SAN 325-7371. Tel: 212-534-1672. FAX: 212-423-0758. E-mail: collections@mcny.org. Information Services E-mail: info@mcny.org. Web Site: www.mcny.org. *Pres & Dir,* Ronay Menschel; *Assoc Curator,* Morgan Stevens-Garmon
Special Collections: New York City Stage Productions & Personalities, clippings, correspondence, costume designs, costumes, doc, drawings, memorabilia, paintings, photog, programs, props, scores, scripts, set models & designs
Wireless access
Restriction: Open by appt only, Open to researchers by request

G NASA GODDARD INSTITUTE FOR SPACE STUDIES LIBRARY*, 2880 Broadway, Rm 710, 10025. SAN 311-9092. Tel: 212-678-5613. FAX: 212-678-5552. Web Site: www.giss.nasa.gov. *Mgr,* Zoe Wai; E-mail: zwai@nasa.gov; Staff 1 (MLS 1)
Founded 1961
Library Holdings: Bk Vols 7,000
Subject Interests: Astronomy, Astrophysics, Climate, Geophysics, Global warming, Math, Meteorology, Physics, Planetary atmospheres, Remote sensing of environ
Automation Activity & Vendor Info: (Acquisitions) SirsiDynix; (Cataloging) SirsiDynix; (Circulation) SirsiDynix; (OPAC) SirsiDynix; (Serials) SirsiDynix
Wireless access
Publications: Booklist
Partic in NASA Library Network; OCLC Online Computer Library Center, Inc
Restriction: Staff use only

S NATIONAL MULTIPLE SCLEROSIS SOCIETY*, Professional Resource Center, 733 Third Ave, 10017. SAN 326-5838. Tel: 212-463-7787. FAX: 212-986-7981. E-mail: info@msnyc.org. Web Site: www.nationalmssociety.org/For-Professionals/Clinical-Care. *Dir,* Rosalind Kalb; Staff 3 (MLS 1, Non-MLS 2)
Library Holdings: Bk Titles 1,018; Bk Vols 1,300; Per Subs 25
Special Collections: Multiple Sclerosis, bks, reprints & pamphlets
Subject Interests: Neurology, Nursing
Wireless access
Publications: Online Compendium of MS Information
Partic in Proquest Dialog
Open Mon-Fri 9-5
Restriction: Non-circulating

S NATIONAL PSYCHOLOGICAL ASSOCIATION FOR PSYCHOANALYSIS, INC*, The Douglas F Maxwell Library, 40 W 13th St, 10011. SAN 311-9254. Tel: 212-924-7440. FAX: 212-989-7543. E-mail: info@npap.org. Web Site: npap.org/library. *Librn,* John Augliera; E-mail: jaugliera89@gmail.com
Founded 1958
Library Holdings: Bk Titles 5,000; Per Subs 25
Wireless access
Restriction: Mem only, Students only

THE NEW SCHOOL

C RAYMOND FOGELMAN LIBRARY*, 55 W 13th St, 10011, SAN 311-9319. Tel: 212-229-5307. Circulation Tel: 212-229-5307, Ext 3056. Interlibrary Loan Service Tel: 212-229-5307, Ext 3152. Reference Tel: 212-229-5307, Ext 3058. Administration Tel: 212-229-5307, Ext 3054. FAX: 212-229-5306. Reference E-mail: reference@newschool.edu. Web Site: library.newschool.edu. *Dir,* John Aubry; *Undergrad Serv Librn,* Brita Servaes; Tel: 212-229-5307, Ext 3163, E-mail:

servaesb@newschool.edu; *Ref & Instrul Serv, Instr Coordr,* Paul Abruzzo; Tel: 212-229-5307, Ext 3055, E-mail: abruzzop@newschool.edu; *Ref Serv,* Carmen Hendershott; Tel: 212-229-5307, Ext 3053, E-mail: hendersh@newschool.edu; Staff 12 (MLS 4, Non-MLS 8)
Founded 1919. Enrl 6,500; Fac 1,100; Highest Degree: Doctorate
Library Holdings: Bk Vols 194,000; Per Subs 220
Automation Activity & Vendor Info: (Acquisitions) Ex Libris Group; (Cataloging) Ex Libris Group; (Circulation) Ex Libris Group; (Course Reserve) Ex Libris Group; (OPAC) Ex Libris Group; (Serials) Ex Libris Group
Function: Audio & video playback equip for onsite use, Computers for patron use, Distance learning, E-Reserves, Electronic databases & coll, For res purposes, Homebound delivery serv, ILL available, Internet access, Orientations, Photocopying/Printing, Telephone ref
Partic in Metropolitan New York Library Council; Partnership for Academic Library Collaborative & Innovation
Open Mon-Thurs 8:30am-10:30pm, Fri 8:30-7:30, Sat 9:30-7:30, Sun 10-8:30
Restriction: In-house use for visitors, Off-site coll in storage - retrieval as requested, Open to others by appt, Open to researchers by request, Open to students, fac, staff & alumni, Photo ID required for access

C ADAM & SOPHIE GIMBEL DESIGN LIBRARY*, Two W 13th St, 2nd Flr, 10011, SAN 311-9890. Tel: 212-229-8914. Circulation Tel: 212-229-8914, Ext 4121. Interlibrary Loan Service Tel: 212-229-8914, Ext 4288. Reference Tel: 212-229-8914, Ext 4286. FAX: 212-229-2806. Web Site: library.newschool.edu/gimbel/. *Dir,* John Aubry; Tel: 212-229-5307; *Ref & Instrul Serv Librn,* Jennifer Yao; Tel: 212-229-8914, Ext 4285, E-mail: yaoj@newschool.edu; Staff 8 (MLS 3, Non-MLS 5)
Founded 1896. Enrl 15,479; Fac 2,220; Highest Degree: Master
Library Holdings: CDs 170; DVDs 200; Bk Titles 52,600; Bk Vols 56,000; Per Subs 222
Special Collections: Fashion Design (Claire McCardell Coll), sketchbks; Parsons Archives
Subject Interests: Archit, Costume, Fashion, Fine arts, Graphic, Indust design, Interior design, Lighting, Textiles design
Automation Activity & Vendor Info: (Acquisitions) Ex Libris Group; (Cataloging) Ex Libris Group; (Circulation) Ex Libris Group; (Course Reserve) Ex Libris Group; (OPAC) Ex Libris Group; (Serials) Ex Libris Group
Function: Archival coll, Art exhibits, Audio & video playback equip for onsite use, Electronic databases & coll, ILL available, Internet access, Online ref, Orientations, Photocopying/Printing, Ref & res, Ref serv available, Telephone ref, VHS videos
Partic in Metropolitan New York Library Council; Research Libraries Information Network
Restriction: Access at librarian's discretion, Open to students, fac & staff

C HARRY SCHERMAN LIBRARY*, 150 W 85th St, 10024-4499, SAN 311-8797. Tel: 212-580-0210, Ext 4803. FAX: 212-580-1738. Web Site: library.newschool.edu. *Dir,* Ed Scarcelle; Tel: 212-580-0210, Ext 4828, E-mail: scarcele@newschool.edu; *Asst Dir,* Arsi Ioannidou; Tel: 212-580-0210, Ext 4827; *Head, Circ,* Gregory Briggler; E-mail: briggleg@newschool.edu; Staff 3.5 (MLS 2, Non-MLS 1.5)
Founded 1954. Enrl 320; Highest Degree: Master
Library Holdings: AV Mats 5,000; CDs 6,500; DVDs 450; Music Scores 31,000; Bk Vols 8,100; Per Subs 74
Special Collections: Konstantin Ivanov Viola Coll; Leopald Mannes Compositions; Salzedo Harp Coll; Sylvia Marlowe Harpsichord Coll
Subject Interests: Classical music
Partic in OCLC Online Computer Library Center, Inc; OCLC Research Library Partnership

S NEW YORK ACADEMY OF ART LIBRARY*, 111 Franklin St, 10013-2911. SAN 375-4421. Tel: 212-966-0300. FAX: 212-966-3217. Web Site: nyaa.edu/graduate-program/library/learning-resources. *Librn,* Holly Frisbee; Tel: 212-966-0300, Ext 964
Founded 1990. Enrl 125; Fac 21; Highest Degree: Master
Library Holdings: Bk Titles 7,000; Per Subs 50
Subject Interests: Art hist, Drawing, Painting, Sculpture
Automation Activity & Vendor Info: (Acquisitions) Book Systems; (Cataloging) Book Systems; (Circulation) Book Systems; (Course Reserve) Book Systems; (ILL) Book Systems; (Media Booking) Book Systems; (OPAC) Book Systems; (Serials) Book Systems
Wireless access
Open Mon-Fri 9-9, Sat & Sun 12-5
Restriction: Non-circulating to the pub, Open to others by appt
Friends of the Library Group

M NEW YORK ACADEMY OF MEDICINE LIBRARY*, 1216 Fifth Ave, 10029. SAN 311-9327. Tel: 212-822-7315. E-mail: library@nyam.org. Web Site: nyam.org/library. *Libr Dir,* Paul Theerman, PhD; Tel: 212-822-7350, E-mail: ptheerman@nyam.org; *Hist Coll Librn,* Arlene Shaner; Tel: 212-822-7313, E-mail: ashaner@nyam.org; *Outreach Librn, Ref Serv,* Carrie Levinson; Tel: 212-822-7292, E-mail: clevinson@nyam.org; *Digital Projects Mgr,* Robin Naughton, PhD; Tel: 212-822-7325, E-mail: rnaughton@nyam.org; *Digital & Tech Serv,* Andrea Byrne; Tel: 212-822-7274, E-mail: abyrne@nyam.org; *Libr Asst,* Walter Linton; Tel: 212-822-7362, E-mail: wlinton@nyam.org; Staff 10 (MLS 8, Non-MLS 2)
Founded 1847
Library Holdings: Bk Vols 550,000; Per Subs 1,000
Special Collections: 16-19th Century Medals (Greenwald Coll), medals; Anatomy & Surgery (Lambert Coll); Cardiology (Levy Coll), bks, mss; Engravings of Medical Men (Ladd Coll), prints; Foods & Cookery (Wilson Coll); Francesco Redi & Contemporaries (Cole Coll); German Psychology & Psychiatry (Harms Coll); Medical Americana By & About J & W Hunter (Beekman Coll); Medical Coll; Medical Economics (Michael Davis Coll), VF; Plague (Neinken Coll), bks, broadsides; Rare Medical Works (Friends of Rare Book Room), bk, ms; Theses-16th-18th Century (Gamble-Cranefield), pamphlets
Subject Interests: AIDS, Epidemiology, Health policy, Med, Pub health
Automation Activity & Vendor Info: (Cataloging) OCLC Connexion; (OPAC) LibLime
Wireless access
Function: Res libr
Publications: Author Catalog of the Library & first supplement; Catalog of Biographies in the Library; History of Medicine Series; Illustration Catalog of the Library; Subject Catalog of the Library & first supplement
Restriction: Open by appt only
Friends of the Library Group

GL NEW YORK CITY LAW DEPARTMENT, Office of Corporation Counsel Law Library, 100 Church St, Rm 6-310, 10007. SAN 311-9394. Tel: 212-788-1609, 212-788-1610. FAX: 212-788-1239. Web Site: www.nyc.gov/html/law. *Dep Librn,* James H Meece; Tel: 212-788-0858; *Sr Librn,* Tamar Raum; Tel: 212-356-2005, E-mail: traum@law.nyc.gov; Staff 3 (MLS 3)
Founded 1856
Library Holdings: Bk Titles 71,600; Per Subs 3,000
Subject Interests: Case law, Legal, Legis hist, State & fed statutes
Function: ILL available
Partic in Metropolitan New York Library Council
Restriction: Not open to pub

CM NEW YORK COLLEGE OF PODIATRIC MEDICINE*, Sidney Druskin Memorial Library, 53 E 124th St, 10035. SAN 311-9416. Tel: 212-410-8020. Circulation Tel: 212-410-8018. Interlibrary Loan Service Tel: 212-410-8142. FAX: 212-876-9426. Web Site: www.nycpm.edu. *Chief Med Librn,* Paul Tremblay; E-mail: ptremblay@nycpm.edu; *Asst Med Librn,* Samantha Walsh; E-mail: swalsh@nycpm.edu; *Asst Librn,* Michael Perlman; E-mail: mperlman@nycpm.edu; Staff 5 (MLS 2, Non-MLS 3)
Founded 1911. Fac 5; Highest Degree: Doctorate
Library Holdings: Bk Titles 1,300; Per Subs 250; Spec Interest Per Sub 250
Subject Interests: Dermatology, Family practice, Orthopedics, Podiatry
Automation Activity & Vendor Info: (Acquisitions) Follett Software; (Circulation) Follett Software; (Media Booking) Follett Software; (OPAC) Follett Software; (Serials) Follett Software
Wireless access
Partic in Greater NE Regional Med Libr Program; Metropolitan New York Library Council
Restriction: Not open to pub

GL NEW YORK COUNTY DISTRICT ATTORNEY'S OFFICE LIBRARY*, One Hogan Pl, 10013. SAN 311-9424. Tel: 212-335-4292. FAX: 212-335-4266. Web Site: www.manhattanda.org. *Dir, Libr Serv,* Mary E Matuszak; E-mail: matuszakm@dany.nyc.gov; Staff 2 (MLS 2)
Library Holdings: Bk Titles 26,970; Per Subs 70
Subject Interests: Criminal law
Restriction: Staff use only

S NEW YORK HISTORICAL SOCIETY MUSEUM & LIBRARY*, Patrick D Klingenstein Library, 170 Central Park W, 10024. SAN 311-9521. Tel: 212-873-3400. FAX: 212-875-1591. TDD: 212-873-7489. Reference E-mail: reference@nyhistory.org. Web Site: www.nyhistory.org/library. *Dir, Sr VPres,* Valerie Paley; *Dir of Libr Operations,* Nina Nazionale; E-mail: nina.nazionale@nyhistory.org; Staff 10 (MLS 8, Non-MLS 2)
Founded 1804
Library Holdings: Bk Titles 350,000
Special Collections: 18th & 19th Century New York City & New York State Newspapers; American Almanacs; American Genealogy; American Indian (Accounts of & Captivities); Among the Manuscript Coll: Horatio Gates, Alexander McDougall, Rufus King, American Fur Company, Livingston Family, American Art Union, American Academy of Fine Arts; Circus in America (Leonidas Westervelt); Civil War Regimental Histories & Muster Rolls; Early American; Early American Trials; Early Travels in America; Imprints; Jenny Lind (Leonidas Westervelt); Maps; Military History & Science (Seventh Regiment Military Library); Military History

(Military Order of the Loyal Legion of the United States, Commandery of the State of New York); Naval & Marine History (Naval History Society); Slavery & the Civil War; Spanish American War (Harper)
Subject Interests: Am art, Hist of North Am continent, Hist of NY City, Hist of US, Naval hist, NY genealogy, State
Automation Activity & Vendor Info: (Cataloging) Ex Libris Group
Wireless access
Publications: Catalogs; Indexes; Special Publications
Partic in OCLC Research Library Partnership; Research Libraries Information Network
Open Tues-Sat 10-4:45
Friends of the Library Group

C NEW YORK INSTITUTE OF TECHNOLOGY*, Manhattan Campus, 1855 Broadway, 10023-7692. SAN 353-2291. Tel: 212-261-1526. Reference Tel: 212-261-1527. FAX: 212-261-1681. Web Site: www.nyit.edu/library/manhattan. *Dir,* Elisabete Ferretti; Tel: 212-261-1525, E-mail: eferrett@nyit.edu; Staff 6 (MLS 6)
Founded 1958
Library Holdings: Bk Vols 43,282; Per Subs 764
Subject Interests: Archit, Art, Computer sci
Automation Activity & Vendor Info: (Acquisitions) SirsiDynix; (Cataloging) SirsiDynix; (Circulation) SirsiDynix; (Course Reserve) SirsiDynix; (ILL) SirsiDynix; (OPAC) SirsiDynix; (Serials) SirsiDynix
Wireless access
Publications: Library News; New Acquisitions
Partic in Basic Health Sciences Library Network; Metropolitan New York Library Council; Westchester Academic Library Directors Organization
Open Mon-Fri 8am-11pm, Sat 10-7, Sun 1-7

L NEW YORK LAW INSTITUTE LIBRARY, 120 Broadway, Rm 932, 10271-0043. SAN 311-9548. Tel: 212-732-8720. FAX: 212-608-5911. E-mail: library@nyli.org. Web Site: www.nyli.org. *Exec Dir,* Lucy Curci-Gonzalez; E-mail: lcurcigonzalez@nyli.org; *Dir, IT, Dir, Mkt,* Ellyssa Valenti Kroski; *Head, Ref,* Karen Oesterle; *Research Librn,* Emily Moog; *Tech Serv Librn,* Eileen Dolan; Staff 7 (MLS 6, Non-MLS 1)
Founded 1828
Library Holdings: Bk Vols 300,000
Special Collections: Appellate Divisions, 1st, 2nd & 3rd Departments; Records & Briefs for New York Court of Appeals; United States Court of Appeals for Second Circuit; United States Supreme Court, fiche
Subject Interests: Colonies, Former possessions
Automation Activity & Vendor Info: (Circulation) EOS International; (OPAC) EOS International; (Serials) EOS International
Wireless access
Function: 24/7 Electronic res, 24/7 Online cat
Publications: Newsletter, blog; Twitter
Partic in OCLC Online Computer Library Center, Inc
Restriction: Access at librarian's discretion, Authorized patrons, Authorized scholars by appt, Mem only

L NEW YORK LAW SCHOOL*, Mendik Library, 185 W Broadway, 10013. SAN 311-9564. Tel: 212-431-2332. Circulation Tel: 212-431-2333. FAX: 212-965-8839. E-mail: reference@nyls.edu. Web Site: www.nyls.edu/library. *Dir,* Camille Broussard; Tel: 212-431-2354, E-mail: cbroussard@nyls.edu; *Assoc Librn,* Bill Mills; Tel: 212-431-2380, E-mail: wmills@nyls.edu
Founded 1891
Library Holdings: Bk Vols 435,000; Per Subs 1,450
Subject Interests: Anglo-Am, Intl law, NY
Wireless access
Publications: Current Acquisitions (Bimonthly); Table of Contents
Partic in Metropolitan New York Library Council; OCLC Online Computer Library Center, Inc; Proquest Dialog
Open Mon-Thurs 9am-11pm, Fri 9am-10pm, Sat & Sun 9-9
Restriction: Mem only

L NEW YORK LEGISLATIVE SERVICE, INC LIBRARY*, 120 Broadway, Ste 920, 10271. SAN 372-4328. Tel: 212-962-2826, 212-962-2827, 212-962-2828. FAX: 212-962-1420. E-mail: nylegal@nyls.org. Web Site: www.nyls.org. *Exec Dir,* Steven Harvey; E-mail: steve@nyls.org; *Co-Executive Dir,* Michael Chung; *Res Spec,* Peter Fung; E-mail: peter@nyls.org; *Executive Asst,* Khrystyna Klymyuk
Founded 1932
Library Holdings: Bk Vols 10,000
Special Collections: Governor's Bill Jackets (1905-present); New York City Local Law Bill Jackets (1954-present); New York State Constitution (Contitutional Convention docs); New York State Legislative Documents
Publications: New York City Legislative (Annual); New York State Legislative (Annual)
Open Mon-Fri 9-5

M NEW YORK ORTHOPAEDIC HOSPITAL-COLUMBIA UNIVERSITY COLLEGE OF PHYSICIANS & SURGEONS*, Russell A Hibbs Memorial Library, 622 W 168th St, PH11-1139, 10032. SAN 370-5536. Tel: 212-305-3294. FAX: 212-305-6193. Web Site: www.columbiaortho.org/departments/russell-hibbs-memorial-library. *Ref Librn,* Anca Meret; E-mail: aom1@cumc.edu; Staff 1 (MLS 1)
Founded 1927
Library Holdings: Bk Titles 4,000; Per Subs 25
Special Collections: Rare Books on Orthopaedics
Subject Interests: Orthopedics
Automation Activity & Vendor Info: (Cataloging) Clio
Wireless access
Restriction: Open to students, fac & staff

M NEW YORK PSYCHOANALYTIC SOCIETY & INSTITUTE*, Abraham A Brill Library, 247 E 82nd St, 10028-2701. SAN 311-9599. Tel: 212-879-6900. FAX: 212-879-0588. E-mail: library@nypsi.org. Web Site: nypsi.org/library-archives. *Libr Dir,* Matthew von Unwerth; *Chair, Archives, Chair, Libr Serv, Curator,* Nellie L Thompson; E-mail: nelliet100@aol.com; *Asst Librn,* Nancy Stout; E-mail: nstout@nypsi.org; *Asst Librn,* Adrian Thomas
Library Holdings: Bk Titles 40,000; Per Subs 55
Special Collections: Art (Arieti Papers); Freud's Writings in all Editions & Languages (Sigmund Freud Coll); History, Literature, Languages & Linguistics Coll; Sociology (Ernst Kris Coll). Oral History
Subject Interests: Behav sci, Humanities, Psychiat, Psychoanalysis, Psychol, Soc sci
Automation Activity & Vendor Info: (Cataloging) Inmagic, Inc.; (Circulation) Inmagic, Inc.; (OPAC) Inmagic, Inc.
Wireless access
Partic in Proquest Dialog
Open Mon 5pm-9pm, Tues-Thurs 1-9, Fri 1-5

P THE NEW YORK PUBLIC LIBRARY - ASTOR, LENOX & TILDEN FOUNDATIONS*, 476 Fifth Ave, (@ 42nd St), 10018. SAN 353-2410. Tel: 212-275-6975. Web Site: www.nypl.org. *Pres,* Dr Anthony W Marx; Tel: 212-930-0736, E-mail: president@nypl.org; *V.P. for Capital Planning & Construction,* Risa Honig; Tel: 212-621-0579, E-mail: risahonig@nypl.org; *VPres, Develop,* Jadrien Steele; Tel: 212-930-0852, E-mail: jadriensteele@nypl.org; *VPres/Gen Counsel,* Michele Coleman Mayes; Tel: 212-642-0115, E-mail: michelemayes@nypl.org; *Chief Digital Officer,* Tony Ageh; Tel: 212-930-0792; *Asst Treasurer, Chief Financial Officer,* Shannon Sharp; Tel: 212-621-0241; *Chief Operating Officer, Treas,* Iris Wienshall; E-mail: irisweinshall@nypl.org; *Actg Chief, Branch Library Officer,* Caryl Matute; Tel: 917-229-9503; *Dir,* Brian Bannon; Tel: 212-621-0587; *Andrew W Mellon Dir of the New York Pub Libr,* William P Kelly; Tel: 212-930-0710; *Dir, Pub Relations, Dir, Mkt,* Angela Montefinise; Tel: 212-592-7506
Founded 1895
Wireless access
Publications: Biblion; NYPL News; Staff News; Various Books
Partic in Metropolitan New York Library Council; New York State Interlibrary Loan Network; OCLC Online Computer Library Center, Inc; OCLC Research Library Partnership; Southeastern New York Library Resources Council; Urban Libraries Council
Open Mon & Thurs-Sat 10-6, Tues & Wed 10-8, Sun 1-5
Friends of the Library Group
Branches: 92
53RD STREET BRANCH, 18 W 53rd St, 10019. Tel: 212-714-8400. Web Site: www.nypl.org/locations/53rd-street. *Managing Librn,* Genoveve Stowell
Function: Wheelchair accessible
Open Mon-Sat 11-6
AGUILAR BRANCH, 174 E 110th St, (Between Lexington & Third Aves), 10029-3212, SAN 353-4065. Tel: 212-534-2930. Web Site: www.nypl.org/locations/aguilar. *Libr Mgr,* Ashley Gonzalez
Library Holdings: Bk Vols 60,830
Function: Wheelchair accessible
Open Mon-Fri 10-6, Sat 10-5
ALLERTON BRANCH, 2740 Barnes Ave, (Between Allerton & Arnow Aves), Bronx, 10467, SAN 353-409X. Tel: 718-881-4240. Web Site: www.nypl.org/locations/allerton. *Libr Mgr,* Manuel Martinez
Library Holdings: Bk Vols 40,847
Function: Wheelchair accessible
Open Mon-Fri 10-6, Sat 10-5
BATTERY PARK CITY LIBRARY, 175 North End Ave, 10282. Tel: 212-790-3499. Web Site: www.nypl.org/locations/battery-park-city. *Libr Mgr,* Anne Barreca
Open Mon & Wed 10-6, Tues & Thurs 11-7, Fri & Sat 10-5
BAYCHESTER BRANCH, 2049 Asch Loop N, (North of Bartow Ave), Bronx, 10475, SAN 353-412X. Tel: 718-379-6700. Web Site: www.nypl.org/locations/baychester. *Libr Mgr,* Position Currently Open
Library Holdings: Bk Vols 59,902
Function: Wheelchair accessible
Special Services for the Blind - Closed circuit TV; Reader equip
Open Mon-Thurs 10-7, Fri 10-6, Sat 10-5

HARRY BELAFONTE 115TH STREET BRANCH, 203 W 115th St, 10026, SAN 353-5681. Tel: 212-666-9393. Web Site: www.nypl.org/locations/115th-street. *Libr Mgr,* Tequila A Davis
Library Holdings: Bk Vols 26,430
Function: Wheelchair accessible
Open Mon-Thurs 11-7, Fri & Sat 10-5

BELMONT BRANCH & ENRICO FERMI CULTURAL CENTER, 610 E 186th St, (@ Hughes Ave), Bronx, 10458, SAN 353-4154. Tel: 718-933-6410. Web Site: www.nypl.org/locations/belmont. *Libr Mgr,* Ignayra Lopez
Library Holdings: Bk Vols 74,680
Subject Interests: Italian
Function: Wheelchair accessible
Open Mon-Fri 10-6, Sat 10-5

BLOOMINGDALE BRANCH, 150 W 100th St, (Between Amsterdam & Columbus Aves), 10025-5196, SAN 353-4189. Tel: 212-222-8030. Web Site: www.nypl.org/locations/bloomingdale. *Libr Mgr,* Yajaira Mejia
Library Holdings: Bk Vols 83,825
Function: Wheelchair accessible

BRONX LIBRARY CENTER, 310 E Kingsbridge Rd, (At Briggs Ave), Bronx, 10458, SAN 353-3522. Tel: 718-579-4244. Web Site: www.nypl.org/locations/bronx-library-center. *Libr Mgr,* Melissa Davis
Library Holdings: Bk Vols 183,681
Function: Wheelchair accessible
Special Services for the Deaf - TTY equip
Special Services for the Blind - Closed circuit TV; Reader equip
Open Mon-Thurs 9-9, Fri & Sat 10-8, Sun 12-6

GEORGE BRUCE BRANCH, 518 W 125th St, 10027, SAN 353-4758. Tel: 212-662-9727. Web Site: www.nypl.org/locations/george-bruce. *Libr Mgr,* Junelle Carter-Bowman
Library Holdings: Bk Vols 51,189
Function: Wheelchair accessible
Open Mon-Thurs 12-7, Fri & Sat 11-6

CARDINAL TERENCE COOKE - CATHEDRAL LIBRARY, 560 Lexington Ave, (@ E 50th St, Lower Level), 10022-6828, SAN 353-4278. Tel: 212-752-3824. Web Site: www.nypl.org/locations/cathedral. *Interim Libr Mgr,* Sabine Desrosier
Library Holdings: Bk Vols 26,328
Function: Wheelchair accessible
Open Mon-Thurs 10-6, Fri 10-5

CASTLE HILL BRANCH, 947 Castle Hill Ave, (@ Bruckner Blvd), Bronx, 10473, SAN 353-4243. Tel: 718-824-3838. Web Site: www.nypl.org/locations/castle-hill. *Libr Mgr,* Position Currently Open
Library Holdings: Bk Vols 40,449
Function: Wheelchair accessible
Open Mon & Tues 10-6, Wed & Thurs 11-6, Fri & Sat 10-5

CHATHAM SQUARE BRANCH, 33 E Broadway, (Near Catherine St), 10002-6804, SAN 353-4367. Tel: 212-964-6598. Web Site: www.nypl.org/locations/chatham-square. *Libr Mgr,* Sean Ferguson
Function: Wheelchair accessible
Open Mon-Thurs 10-8, Fri 10-6, Sat 10-5

CITY ISLAND BRANCH, 320 City Island Ave, (Between Bay & Fordham Sts), Bronx, 10464, SAN 353-4391. Tel: 718-885-1703. Web Site: www.nypl.org/locations/city-island. *Libr Mgr,* Tiffany Mccrae
Library Holdings: Bk Vols 35,000
Function: Wheelchair accessible
Open Mon & Thurs 11-7, Tues & Wed 11-6, Fri & Sat 10-5

CLASON'S POINT BRANCH, 1215 Morrison Ave, (Near Westchester Ave), Bronx, 10472, SAN 353-4421. Tel: 718-842-1235. Web Site: www.nypl.org/locations/clasons-point. *Libr Mgr,* Position Currently Open
Library Holdings: Bk Vols 51,823
Function: Wheelchair accessible
Open Mon-Thurs 10-7, Fri & Sat 10-5

COLUMBUS BRANCH, 742 Tenth Ave, (Between E 50th & 51st Sts), 10019-7019, SAN 353-4480. Tel: 212-586-5098. Web Site: www.nypl.org/locations/columbus. *Libr Mgr,* Leiana Spooner
Library Holdings: Bk Vols 22,639
Function: Wheelchair accessible
Open Mon-Thurs 10-7, Fri & Sat 10-5

COUNTEE CULLEN BRANCH, 104 W 136th St, (Near Lenox Ave), 10030-2695, SAN 353-4510. Tel: 212-491-2070. Web Site: www.nypl.org/locations/countee-cullen. *Libr Mgr,* Nicole Nelson
Library Holdings: Bk Vols 65,092
Function: Wheelchair accessible
Special Services for the Blind - Closed circuit TV; Reader equip
Open Mon-Thurs 11-7, Fri & Sat 10-5

DONGAN HILLS BRANCH, 1617 Richmond Rd, (Between Seaview & Liberty Aves), Staten Island, 10304, SAN 353-4545. Tel: 718-351-1444. Web Site: www.nypl.org/locations/dongan-hills. *Libr Mgr,* Sarah Ross
Library Holdings: Bk Vols 54,507
Function: Wheelchair accessible
Special Services for the Blind - Closed circuit TV; Reader equip
Open Mon-Thurs 11-6, Fri & Sat 10-5

EASTCHESTER BRANCH, 1385 E Gun Hill Rd, (Near Eastchester Rd), Bronx, 10469, SAN 353-457X. Tel: 718-653-3292. Web Site: www.nypl.org/locations/eastchester. *Libr Mgr,* Position Currently Open
Library Holdings: Bk Vols 49,648
Function: Wheelchair accessible
Open Mon-Thurs 10-7, Fri & Sat 10-5

EDENWALD BRANCH, 1255 E 233rd St, (@ DeReimer Ave), Bronx, 10466, SAN 353-460X. Tel: 718-798-3355. Web Site: www.nypl.org/locations/edenwald. *Libr Mgr,* Charity Goh
Library Holdings: Bk Vols 39,673
Function: Wheelchair accessible
Open Mon-Thurs 10-7, Fri 10-6, Sat 10-5

EPIPHANY BRANCH, 228 E 23rd St, (Near Second Ave), 10010-4672, SAN 353-4634. Tel: 212-679-2645. Web Site: www.nypl.org/locations/epiphany. *Libr Mgr,* Omisha Covington-Isidore
Library Holdings: Bk Vols 56,563
Function: Wheelchair accessible
Open Mon & Wed 12-7, Tues & Thurs 10-6, Fri & Sat 10-5

58TH STREET BRANCH, 127 E 58th St, (Between Park & Lexington Aves), 10022-1211, SAN 353-4669. Tel: 212-759-7358. Web Site: www.nypl.org/locations/58th-street. *Libr Mgr,* Donna Murphy; Staff 9 (MLS 2, Non-MLS 7)
Founded 1907. Pop 50,000; Circ 375,000
Jul 2012-Jun 2013 Income $865,000, City $850,000, Locally Generated Income $15,000. Mats Exp $165,000, Books $150,000, AV Equip $10,000, AV Mat $5,000. Sal $446,709 (Prof $446,709)
Library Holdings: Audiobooks 1,000; AV Mats 200; Bks-By-Mail 500; CDs 2,000; DVDs 3,000; Large Print Bks 1,000; Bk Vols 60,145
Special Collections: World Languages; Test materials; Large print
Automation Activity & Vendor Info: (Acquisitions) BiblioCommons
Function: Adult bk club, Adult literacy prog, Art exhibits, Audio & video playback equip for onsite use, Bk club(s), Bk reviews (Group), Bks on CD, Bus archives, CD-ROM, Citizenship assistance, Computer training, Computers for patron use, Digital talking bks, Distance learning, E-Reserves, Electronic databases & coll, Family literacy, Free DVD rentals, Health sci info serv, Home delivery & serv to seniorr ctr & nursing homes, Homebound delivery serv, Homework prog, ILL available, Instruction & testing, Internet access, Large print keyboards, Learning ctr, Literacy & newcomer serv, Magnifiers for reading, Music CDs, Online cat, Outreach serv, OverDrive digital audio bks, Photocopying/Printing, Printer for laptops & handheld devices, Prof lending libr, Prog for adults, Ref & res, Ref serv available, Res libr, Scanner, Senior computer classes, Senior outreach, Serves people with intellectual disabilities, Spanish lang bks, Spoken cassettes & CDs, Spoken cassettes & DVDs, Summer & winter reading prog, Summer reading prog, Tax forms, Telephone ref, Workshops, Writing prog
Special Services for the Deaf - Assisted listening device
Special Services for the Blind - Ref in Braille
Open Mon-Thurs 10-6, Fri & Sat 10-5
Friends of the Library Group

FORT WASHINGTON BRANCH, 535 W 179th St, (Between St Nicholas & Audubon Aves), 10033-5799, SAN 353-4693. Tel: 212-927-3533. Web Site: www.nypl.org/locations/fort-washington. *Libr Mgr,* Kassandre Innocent
Library Holdings: Bk Vols 70,441
Open Mon-Fri 10-6, Sat 10-5

GRAND CENTRAL LIBRARY, 135 E 46th St, 10017. Tel: 212-621-0670. Web Site: www.nypl.org/locations/grand-central. *Libr Mgr,* William Hall
Function: Wheelchair accessible
Open Mon-Thurs 10-8, Fri 10-6, Sat 10-5

GRAND CONCOURSE BRANCH, 155 E 173rd St, (East of Grand Concourse), Bronx, 10457, SAN 353-4782. Tel: 718-583-6611. Web Site: www.nypl.org/locations/grand-concourse. *Libr Mgr,* Position Currently Open
Library Holdings: Bk Vols 52,590
Temporarily closed Jan 2019-June 2020

GREAT KILLS BRANCH, 56 Giffords Lane, (@ Margaret St), Staten Island, 10308, SAN 353-4812. Tel: 718-984-6670. Web Site: www.nypl.org/locations/great-kills. *Libr Mgr,* Annamaria Mason
Library Holdings: Bk Vols 27,243
Function: Wheelchair accessible
Open Mon-Thurs 11-6, Fri & Sat 10-5

HAMILTON FISH PARK BRANCH, 415 E Houston St, 10002-1197, SAN 353-4847. Tel: 212-673-2290. Web Site: www.nypl.org/locations/hamilton-fish-park. *Libr Mgr,* Position Currently Open
Library Holdings: Bk Vols 43,374
Open Mon-Thurs 10-7, Fri & Sat 10-5

HAMILTON GRANGE BRANCH, 503 W 145th St, 10031-5101, SAN 353-4871. Tel: 212-926-2147. Web Site: www.nypl.org/locations/hamilton-grange. *Libr Mgr,* Yolounda Bennett-Reid
Library Holdings: Bk Vols 52,247
Function: Wheelchair accessible
Open Mon-Thurs 10-7, Fri 11-6, Sat 10-5

HARLEM BRANCH, Nine W 124th St, 10027-5699, SAN 353-4901. Tel: 212-348-5620. Web Site: www.nypl.org/locations/harlem. *Interim Libr Mgr,* Charmice Hollenquest
Library Holdings: Bk Vols 42,016
Function: Wheelchair accessible
Open Mon-Thurs 11-7, Fri & Sat 10-5

P ANDREW HEISKELL BRAILLE & TALKING BOOK LIBRARY, 40 W 20th St, (Between Fifth & Sixth Aves), 10011-4211, SAN 353-3913. Tel: 212-206-5400. Web Site: www.nypl.org/locations/heiskell. *Chief Librn,* Jill Rothstein
Automation Activity & Vendor Info: (Cataloging) Keystone Systems, Inc (KLAS); (Circulation) Keystone Systems, Inc (KLAS); (OPAC) Keystone Systems, Inc (KLAS)
Function: Wheelchair accessible
Publications: NewsLion (Newsletter)
Special Services for the Blind - Accessible computers; Braille bks; Braille equip; Closed circuit TV magnifier; Digital talking bk; Digital talking bk machines; Internet workstation with adaptive software; Large print bks; Magnifiers; Newsletter (in large print, Braille or on cassette); Scanner for conversion & translation of mats; Screen enlargement software for people with visual disabilities; Screen reader software
Open Mon, Wed, Fri & Sat 10-5, Tues & Thurs Noon-7
Friends of the Library Group

HIGH BRIDGE BRANCH, 78 W 168th St, (@ Woodycrest Ave), Bronx, 10452, SAN 353-4936. Tel: 718-293-7800. Web Site: www.nypl.org/branch/local/bx/hb.cfm. *Libr Mgr,* Deborah Allman
Library Holdings: Bk Vols 39,521
Function: Wheelchair accessible
Open Mon-Thurs 10-7, Fri 10-6, Sat 10-5

HUDSON PARK BRANCH, 66 Leroy St, (Off Seventh Ave, South), 10014-3929, SAN 353-4960. Tel: 212-243-6876. Web Site: www.nypl.org/locations/hudson-park. *Libr Mgr,* Miranda Murray
Library Holdings: Bk Vols 43,074
Open Mon-Thurs 10-8, Fri & Sat 10-5, Sun 1-5

HUGUENOT PARK BRANCH, 830 Huguenot Ave, (@ Dumgole Rd), Staten Island, 10312, SAN 353-4995. Tel: 718-984-4636. Web Site: www.nypl.org/locations/huguenot-park. *Libr Mgr,* Steven Horvath
Library Holdings: Bk Vols 61,676
Function: Wheelchair accessible
Open Mon-Thurs 10-6, Fri & Sat 10-5

HUNTS POINT BRANCH, 877 Southern Blvd, (@ Tiffany St), Bronx, 10459, SAN 353-5029. Tel: 718-617-0338. Web Site: www.nypl.org/locations/hunts-point. *Libr Mgr,* Position Currently Open
Library Holdings: Bk Vols 74,424
Function: Wheelchair accessible
Open Mon-Fri 10-6, Sat 10-5

INWOOD BRANCH, 4790 Broadway, (Near Dyckman St), 10034-4916, SAN 353-5053. Tel: 212-942-2445. Web Site: www.nypl.org/locations/inwood. *Libr Mgr,* Danita Nichols
Library Holdings: Bk Vols 90,298
Function: Wheelchair accessible
Open Mon-Thurs 10-7, Fri & Sat 10-5, Sun 1-5

JEFFERSON MARKET BRANCH, 425 Avenue of the Americas, 10011-8454, SAN 353-5088. Tel: 212-243-4334. Web Site: www.nypl.org/locations/jefferson-market. *Libr Mgr,* Frank Collerius
Library Holdings: Bk Vols 79,977
Function: Wheelchair accessible
Special Services for the Blind - Closed circuit TV; Reader equip
Open Mon-Thurs 1-8, Fri 1-6, Sat 10-5, Sun 1-5

JEROME PARK BRANCH, 118 Eames Pl, Bronx, 10468, SAN 353-5118. Tel: 718-549-5200. Web Site: www.nypl.org/locations/jerome-park. *Libr Mgr,* Shantay Allbright
Library Holdings: Bk Vols 42,371
Function: Wheelchair accessible
Open Mon-Thurs 10-7, Fri & Sat 10-5

KINGSBRIDGE BRANCH, 291 W 231st St, (@ Corlear Ave), Bronx, 10463, SAN 353-5142. Tel: 718-548-5656. Web Site: www.nypl.org/branch/local/bx/kbr.cfm. *Libr Mgr,* Martha Gonzalez-Buitrago
Library Holdings: Bk Vols 61,939
Function: Wheelchair accessible
Special Services for the Blind - Closed circuit TV; Reader equip
Open Mon-Thurs 10-7, Fri & Sat 10-5

KIPS BAY BRANCH, 446 Third Ave, (@ E 31st St), 10016-6025, SAN 353-5177. Tel: 212-683-2520. Web Site: www.nypl.org/locations/kips-bay. *Libr Mgr,* Kaydene Humphrey
Library Holdings: Bk Vols 50,329
Function: Wheelchair accessible
Open Mon-Fri 10-6, Sat 10-5

MACOMB'S BRIDGE BRANCH, 2650 Adam Clayton Powell Jr Blvd, (Between W 152nd & 153rd Sts), 10039-2004, SAN 353-5207. Tel: 212-281-4900. Web Site: www.nypl.org/locations/macombs-bridge. *Libr Mgr,* Lucile Francois
Library Holdings: Bk Vols 11,772
Function: Wheelchair accessible
Open Mon & Tues 11-7, Wed & Thurs 11-6, Fri & Sat 10-5

MARINERS HARBOR LIBRARY, 206 South Ave, (Between Arlington Pl & Brabant St), Staten Island, 10303. Tel: 212-621-0690. Web Site: www.nypl.org/locations/mariners-harbor. *Libr Mgr,* Ogie Omorogbe-Osagie
Function: Wheelchair accessible
Open Mon-Thurs 11-7, Fri & Sat 10-5

FRANCIS MARTIN BRANCH, 2150 University Ave, (@ 181st St), Bronx, 10453, SAN 353-4723. Tel: 718-295-5287. Web Site: www.nypl.org/locations/francis-martin. *Libr Mgr,* Craig Jacob
Library Holdings: Bk Vols 65,995
Function: Wheelchair accessible
Open Mon-Thurs 11-7, Fri 10-6, Sat 10-5

MELROSE BRANCH, 910 Morris Ave, (@ E 162nd St), Bronx, 10451, SAN 353-5231. Tel: 718-588-0110. Web Site: www.nypl.org/locations/melrose. *Libr Mgr,* Kimberly Jefferson-Stratton
Library Holdings: Bk Vols 48,551
Open Mon-Thurs 10-7, Fri & Sat 10-5, Sun 1-5

MID-MANHATTAN LIBRARY, 476 Fifth Ave, (at 42nd St), 10016-0122, SAN 353-5266. Tel: 212-340-0863. Web Site: www.nypl.org/locations/mid-manhattan-library. *Interim Chief Librn,* Caryl Matute
Library Holdings: Bk Vols 1,554,578
Special Collections: Picture Coll
Function: Wheelchair accessible
Special Services for the Deaf - TTY equip
Special Services for the Blind - Reader equip
Open Mon & Thurs 8-8, Tues & Wed 8am-9pm, Fri 8-6, Sat 10-6, Sun (Sept-June) 10-5

MORNINGSIDE HEIGHTS BRANCH, 2900 Broadway, (@ W 113th St), 10025-7822, SAN 353-4456. Tel: 212-864-2530. Web Site: www.nypl.org/locations/morningside-heights. *Libr Mgr,* Position Currently Open
Library Holdings: Bk Vols 65,255
Function: Wheelchair accessible
Open Mon, Tues & Fri 10-6, Wed & Thurs 10-7, Sat 10-5

MORRIS PARK BRANCH, 985 Morris Park Ave, (Between Radcliff & Colden Aves), Bronx, 10462. Tel: 718-931-0636. Web Site: www.nypl.org/locations/morris-park. *Libr Mgr,* Dawn Holloway
Library Holdings: Bk Vols 25,000
Function: Wheelchair accessible
Open Mon-Thurrs 10-7, Fri & Sat 10-5

MORRISANIA BRANCH, 610 E 169th St, (@ Franklin Ave), Bronx, 10456, SAN 353-5479. Tel: 718-589-9268. Web Site: www.nypl.org/locations/morrisania. *Libr Mgr,* Colbert Nembhard
Library Holdings: Bk Vols 44,026
Function: Wheelchair accessible
Open Mon-Thurs 10-7, Fri & Sat 10-5

MOSHOLU BRANCH, 285 E 205th St, (Near Perry Ave), Bronx, 10467, SAN 353-5509. Tel: 718-882-8239. Web Site: www.nypl.org/locations/mosholu. *Libr Mgr,* Jane Addison-Amoyaw
Library Holdings: Bk Vols 61,560
Function: Wheelchair accessible
Open Mon-Thurs 11-7, Fri & Sat 10-5

MOTT HAVEN BRANCH, 321 E 140th St, (@ Alexander Ave), Bronx, 10454, SAN 353-5533. Tel: 718-665-4878. Web Site: www.nypl.org/locations/mott-haven. *Libr Mgr,* Jeanine Cross
Library Holdings: Bk Vols 60,212
Function: Wheelchair accessible
Open Mon-Thurs 10-7, Fri & Sat 10-5

MUHLENBERG BRANCH, 209 W 23rd St, (Near Seventh Ave), 10011-2379, SAN 353-5568. Tel: 212-924-1585. Web Site: www.nypl.org/locations/muhlenberg. *Libr Mgr,* Lateshe Lee
Library Holdings: Bk Vols 41,815
Function: Wheelchair accessible
Open Mon-Thurs 10-7, Fri 10-6, Sat 10-5

MULBERRY STREET BRANCH, Ten Jersey St, 10012-3332. Tel: 212-966-3424. Web Site: www.nypl.org/locations/mulberry-street. *Libr Mgr,* Rebecca Alberto
Library Holdings: Bk Vols 32,655
Function: Wheelchair accessible
Open Mon & Wed 11-7, Tues & Thurs 10-7, Fri & Sat 10-5

NEW AMSTERDAM BRANCH, Nine Murray St, (Between Broadway and Church St), 10007-2223, SAN 371-3423. Tel: 212-732-8186. Web Site: www.nypl.org/locations/new-amsterdam. *Libr Mgr,* Brian Stokes
Library Holdings: Bk Vols 58,231
Function: Wheelchair accessible
Temporarily closed. Due to reopen January 2020

NEW DORP BRANCH, 309 New Dorp Lane, Staten Island, 10306, SAN 353-5622. Tel: 718-351-2977. Web Site: www.nypl.org/locations/new-dorp. *Libr Mgr,* Colleen Chioffe
Function: Wheelchair accessible
Open Mon-Thurs 10-7, Fri & Sat 10-5

NEW YORK PUBLIC LIBRARY FOR THE PERFORMING ARTS, Dorothy & Lewis B Cullman Ctr, 40 Lincoln Center Plaza, 10023-7498, SAN 353-3824. Tel: 917-275-6975. Web Site: www.nypl.org/locations/lpa. *Dir,* Jacqueline Z Davis
Subject Interests: Classical music, Comedy, Dance, Drama, Exercise rec, Folk, Jazz, Monologues, Performing arts, Plays, Popular music, Sound effects, Theatre, World music
Function: Wheelchair accessible
Open Mon & Thurs 10:30-8, Tues, Wed, Fri & Sat 10:30-6

96TH STREET BRANCH, 112 E 96th St, (Near Lexington Ave), 10128-2597, SAN 353-5657. Tel: 212-289-0908. Web Site: www.nypl.org/locations/96th-street. *Libr Mgr,* Sutana Riley
Library Holdings: Bk Vols 59,156
Function: Wheelchair accessible
Open Mon-Thurs 10-7, Fri & Sat 10-5

125TH STREET BRANCH, 224 E 125th St, (Near Third Ave), 10035-1786, SAN 353-5711. Tel: 212-534-5050. Web Site: www.nypl.org/locations/125th-street. *Libr Mgr,* Velma Morton
Library Holdings: Bk Vols 34,090
Open Mon-Thurs 11-7, Fri & Sat 10-5

OTTENDORFER BRANCH, 135 Second Ave, 10003-8304, SAN 353-5746. Tel: 212-674-0947. Web Site: www.nypl.org/locations/ottendorfer. *Libr Mgr,* Kristin Kuehl
Library Holdings: Bk Vols 40,824
Open Mon-Thurs 11-7, Fri & Sat 10-5

PARKCHESTER BRANCH, 1985 Westchester Ave, (@ Pugsley Ave), Bronx, 10462, SAN 353-5770. Tel: 718-829-7830. Web Site: www.nypl.org/locations/parkchester. *Libr Mgr,* Alison Williams
Library Holdings: Bk Vols 46,562
Function: Wheelchair accessible
Open Mon-Thurs 10-8, Fri & Sat 10-5

PELHAM BAY BRANCH, 3060 Middletown Rd, (North of Crosby Ave), Bronx, 10461, SAN 353-5800. Tel: 718-792-6744. Web Site: www.nypl.org/locations/pelham-bay. *Libr Mgr,* Position Currently Open
Library Holdings: Bk Vols 56,629
Function: Wheelchair accessible
Open Mon-Thurs 10-6, Fri & Sat 10-5

PELHAM PARKWAY - VAN NEST LIBRARY, 2147 Barnes Ave, (Near Pelham Pkwy South), Bronx, 10462, SAN 353-6408. Tel: 718-829-5864. Web Site: www.nypl.org/locations/pelham-parkway-van-nest. *Libr Mgr,* Frances Collado
Library Holdings: Bk Vols 51,512
Function: Wheelchair accessible
Open Mon-Fri 10-6, Sat 10-5

PORT RICHMOND BRANCH, 75 Bennett St, (@ Heberton Ave), Staten Island, 10302, SAN 353-5835. Tel: 718-442-0158. Web Site: www.nypl.org/locations/port-richmond. *Libr Mgr,* Peter Levine
Library Holdings: Bk Vols 38,310
Function: Wheelchair accessible
Open Mon-Thurs 11-6, Fri & Sat 10-5

RICHMONDTOWN BRANCH, 200 Clarke Ave, (@ Amber St), Staten Island, 10306, SAN 377-6891. Tel: 718-668-0413. Web Site: www.nypl.org/locations/richmondtown. *Libr Mgr,* Bridget Salvato
Library Holdings: Bk Vols 65,740
Function: Wheelchair accessible
Open Mon-Thurs 10-6, Fri & Sat 10-5

RIVERDALE BRANCH, 5540 Mosholu Ave, (@ W 256th St), Bronx, 10471, SAN 353-5894. Tel: 718-549-1212. Web Site: www.nypl.org/locations/riverdale. *Libr Mgr,* Rebecca Brown-Barbier
Library Holdings: Bk Vols 46,218
Function: Wheelchair accessible
Open Mon-Thurs 10-6, Fri & Sat 10-5

RIVERSIDE BRANCH, 127 Amsterdam Ave, (@ W 65th St), 10023-6447, SAN 353-5924. Tel: 212-870-1810. Web Site: www.nypl.org/locations/riverside. *Libr Mgr,* Magally Gomila
Library Holdings: Bk Vols 69,248
Function: Wheelchair accessible
Open Mon-Thurs 10-7, Fri & Sat 10-5

ROOSEVELT ISLAND BRANCH, 524 Main St, 10044-0001, SAN 377-6875. Tel: 212-308-6243. Web Site: www.nypl.org/locations/roosevelt-island. *Libr Mgr,* Carlos Chavez
Library Holdings: Bk Vols 25,878
Function: Wheelchair accessible
Open Mon & Wed 10-8, Tues & Thurs 10-6, Fri & Sat 10-5

ST AGNES BRANCH, 444 Amsterdam Ave, (@ 81st St), 10024-5506, SAN 353-5959. Tel: 212-621-0619. Web Site: www.nypl.org/locations/st-agnes. *Libr Mgr,* Jennifer Zarr
Library Holdings: Bk Vols 72,517
Function: Wheelchair accessible
Open Mon, Fri & Sat 10-6, Tues-Thurs 10-7

ST GEORGE LIBRARY CENTER, Five Central Ave, (Near Borough Hall), Staten Island, 10301, SAN 353-4006. Tel: 718-442-8560. Web Site: www.nypl.org/locations/st-george-library-center. *Libr Mgr,* Robert Gibbs
Library Holdings: Bk Vols 85,806
Function: Wheelchair accessible
Special Services for the Blind - Closed circuit TV; Reader equip
Open Mon-Thurs 10-7, Fri & Sat 10-5

SCHOMBURG CENTER FOR RESEARCH IN BLACK CULTURE, 515 Malcolm X Blvd, (135th & Malcolm X Blvd), 10037-1801, SAN 353-3468. Web Site: www.nypl.org/locations/schomburg. *Dir,* Joy Bivins; *Asst to the Dir,* Theresa Martin; E-mail: theresamartin@nypl.org
Founded 1926
Library Holdings: Bk Vols 150,000
Special Collections: African Sculpture & Artifacts; Afro-American Paintings, Prints & Sculpture; Haitian Manuscripts (Kurt Fisher & Eugene Maximilien Coll); Harry A Williamson Library of the Negro in Masonry; Malcolm X Coll; Manuscripts of W E B DuBois, Langston Hughes, Claude McKay, Arthur Schomburg, George & Philippa Schuyler, Robert C Weaver, Clarence Cameron White, Richard Wright, Piri Thomas & Amiri Baraka; Papers of John E Bruce, Civil Rights Congress, International Labor Defense, Carnegie-Myrdal Research Memoranda, Alexander Crummell, Oakley Johnson, National Association of Colored Graduate Nurses, National Negro Congress, Phelps-Stokes Fund, Central Africa Project, William Pickens, Richard Parrish New York Urban League, Universal Negro Improvement Association, Paul Robeson, Hugh Smythe & Robert Weaver; Photographs; Rare Books; Tape & Phonograph Records, incl Interviews & Music
Subject Interests: Africa, African-Am throughout the world, with major emphasis on Afro-Am, Caribbean
Function: Res libr, Wheelchair accessible
Publications: Bibliographies; Exhibition catalogs; Schomburg Center Journal
Open Mon & Thurs-Sat 10-6, Tues & Wed 10-8
Restriction: Non-circulating
Friends of the Library Group

STEPHEN A SCHWARZMAN BUILDING, 476 Fifth Ave, (42nd St & Fifth Ave), 10018. Web Site: www.nypl.org/locations/schwarzman. *Dir,* Matthew Knutzen
Special Collections: English & American Literature (Berg Coll); English Romanticism (Pforzheimer Coll); Manuscripts & Archives Division; Photography Coll; Print Coll; Rare Book Division; Spencer Coll; Tobacco (Arents Coll)
Function: Wheelchair accessible
Open Mon & Thurs-Sat 10-6, Tues & Wed 10-8, Sun 1-5

SCIENCE, INDUSTRY & BUSINESS LIBRARY, 188 Madison Ave, (34th St & Madison Ave), 10016-4314, SAN 371-3415. Web Site: www.nypl.org/locations/sibl. *Assoc Dir,* Anne Lehmann; E-mail: annelehmann@nypl.org
Special Collections: Government Publications (United States, United Nations, European Union, New York State); Patent & Trademark Gazettes (European Patent Office & Patent Cooperation Treaty, United States, British & German Patents). US Document Depository
Subject Interests: Advertising, Astronautics, Astronomy, Automobiles, Banking, Beverages, Chem, Communications, Computer sci, Demography, Earth sci, Econ, Electricity, Electronics, Engr, Finance, Food tech, Indust relations, Labor, Manufacturing, Math, Metallurgy, Mining, Mkt, Navigation, Paper, Physics, Plastics, Railroads, Rubber, Sci hist, Shipbuilding, Small bus, Soc statistics, Tech aspects of transportation, Textiles
Function: Wheelchair accessible
Special Services for the Deaf - TTY equip
Open Mon-Thurs 10-8, Fri & Sat 10-6

SEDGWICK BRANCH, 1701 Martin Luther King Jr Blvd, Bronx, 10453, SAN 353-5983. Tel: 718-731-2074. Web Site: www.nypl.org/locations/sedgwick. *Libr Mgr,* Samuel Ansah
Library Holdings: Bk Vols 36,813
Function: Wheelchair accessible
Open Mon-Fri 10-6, Sat 10-5

SEWARD PARK BRANCH, 192 E Broadway, (@ Jefferson St), 10002-5597, SAN 353-6017. Tel: 212-477-6770. Web Site: www.nypl.org/locations/seward-park. *Libr Mgr,* Lakisha Brown
Library Holdings: Bk Vols 59,049
Function: Wheelchair accessible
Open Mon-Thurs 10-8, Fri & Sat 10-5

67TH STREET BRANCH, 328 E 67th St, (Near First Ave), 10021-6296, SAN 353-6041. Tel: 212-734-1717. Web Site: www.nypl.org/locations/67th-street. *Libr Mgr,* Maggie Barbour
Library Holdings: Bk Vols 23,981
Function: Wheelchair accessible

SOUNDVIEW BRANCH, 660 Soundview Ave, (@ Seward Ave), Bronx, 10473, SAN 353-6076. Tel: 718-589-0880. Web Site: www.nypl.org/locations/soundview. *Libr Mgr,* Tanya Bradley
Library Holdings: Bk Vols 52,479
Function: Wheelchair accessible
Open Mon-Thurs 10-6, Fri & Sat 10-5

SOUTH BEACH BRANCH, 21-25 Robin Rd, (@ Ocean Ave & Father Capodanno Blvd), Staten Island, 10305, SAN 353-6106. Tel: 718-816-5834. Web Site: www.nypl.org/locations/south-beach. *Libr Mgr,* Susan Hansen

Library Holdings: Bk Vols 24,953
Function: Wheelchair accessible
Open Mon-Thurs 11-7, Fri & Sat 10-5
SPUYTEN DUYVIL BRANCH, 650 W 235th St, (@ Independence Ave), Bronx, 10463, SAN 353-6165. Tel: 718-796-1202. Web Site: www.nypl.org/locations/spuyten-duyvil. *Libr Mgr,* Tim Tureski
Library Holdings: Bk Vols 56,596
Function: Wheelchair accessible
Open Mon-Thurs 10-6, Fri & Sat 10-5
STAPLETON BRANCH, 132 Canal St, Staten Island, 10304, SAN 353-619X. Tel: 718-727-0427. Web Site: www.nypl.org/locations/stapleton. *Libr Mgr,* Rosa Haire
Library Holdings: Bk Vols 29,960
Function: Wheelchair accessible
Open Mon-Thurs 11-7, Fri & Sat 10-5
THROG'S NECK BRANCH, 3025 Cross Bronx Expressway Extension, (@ East Tremont Ave), Bronx, 10465, SAN 353-622X. Tel: 718-792-2612. Web Site: www.nypl.org/locations/throgs-neck. *Libr Mgr,* Leida Velazquez
Library Holdings: Bk Vols 43,789
Function: Wheelchair accessible
Open Mon-Thurs 10-6, Fri & Sat 10-5
TODT HILL-WESTERLEIGH BRANCH, 2550 Victory Blvd, (Past Willowbrook Rd), Staten Island, 10314, SAN 353-6254. Tel: 718-494-1642. Web Site: www.nypl.org/locations/todt-hill-westerleigh. *Libr Mgr,* Samantha Bright
Library Holdings: Bk Vols 97,766
Function: Wheelchair accessible
Open Mon-Thurs 10-7, Fri & Sat 10-5, Sun 1-5
TOMPKINS SQUARE BRANCH, 331 E Tenth St, 10009-5099, SAN 353-6289. Tel: 212-228-4747. Web Site: www.nypl.org/locations/tompkins-square. *Libr Mgr,* Corinne Neary
Library Holdings: Bk Vols 54,057
Function: Wheelchair accessible
Open Mon-Thurs 11-7, Fri 10-6, Sat 10-5
TOTTENVILLE BRANCH, 7430 Amboy Rd, Staten Island, 10307, SAN 353-6319. Tel: 718-984-0945. Web Site: www.nypl.org/locations/tottenville. *Libr Mgr,* Position Currently Open
Library Holdings: Bk Vols 31,757
Function: Wheelchair accessible
Open Mon-Thurs 11-6, Fri & Sat 10-5
TREMONT BRANCH, 1866 Washington Ave, (@ E 176th St), Bronx, 10457, SAN 353-6343. Tel: 718-299-5177. Web Site: www.nypl.org/locations/tremont. *Libr Mgr,* Wilson Francis
Library Holdings: Bk Vols 29,837
Open Mon-Fri 10-6, Sat 10-5
VAN CORTLANDT BRANCH, 3882 Cannon Pl, Bronx, 10463, SAN 353-6378. Tel: 718-543-5150. Web Site: www.nypl.org/locations/van-cortlandt. *Libr Mgr,* Peter Pamphile
Library Holdings: Bk Vols 31,997
Function: Wheelchair accessible
Open Mon-Thurs 10-7, Fri & Sat 10-5
WAKEFIELD BRANCH, 4100 Lowerre Pl, Bronx, 10466, SAN 353-6432. Tel: 718-652-4663. Web Site: www.nypl.org/locations/wakefield. *Libr Mgr,* Maribel Lugo
Library Holdings: Bk Vols 47,638
Function: Wheelchair accessible
Open Mon-Thurs 10-7, Fri & Sat 10-5
WASHINGTON HEIGHTS BRANCH, 1000 St Nicholas Ave, (@ W 160th St), 10032-5202, SAN 353-6467. Tel: 212-923-6054. Web Site: www.nypl.org/locations/washington-heights. *Libr Mgr,* Vianela Rivas
Library Holdings: Bk Vols 52,826
Function: Wheelchair accessible
Open Mon-Thurs 10-7, Fri & Sat 10-5
WEBSTER BRANCH, 1465 York Ave, (Near E 78th St), 10021-8895, SAN 353-6491. Tel: 212-288-5049. Web Site: www.nypl.org/locations/webster. *Libr Mgr,* Alexandria Aloenshon
Library Holdings: Bk Vols 41,261
Function: Wheelchair accessible
Open Mon-Thurs 11-7, Fri & Sat 10-5
WEST FARMS BRANCH, 2085 Honeywell Ave, (Between E 179th & 180th Sts), Bronx, 10460, SAN 353-6521. Tel: 718-367-5376. Web Site: www.nypl.org/locations/west-farms. *Libr Mgr,* Tambra Gill
Library Holdings: Bk Vols 43,117
Function: Wheelchair accessible
Open Mon-Thurs 10-7, Fri & Sat 10-5
WEST NEW BRIGHTON BRANCH, 976 Castleton Ave, (@ North Burgher Ave), Staten Island, 10310, SAN 353-6556. Tel: 718-442-1416. Web Site: www.nypl.org/locations/west-new-brighton. *Libr Mgr,* Position Currently Open
Library Holdings: Bk Vols 35,105
Function: Wheelchair accessible
Open Mon-Thurs 11-6, Fri & Sat 10-5
WESTCHESTER SQUARE BRANCH, 2521 Glebe Ave, Bronx, 10461, SAN 353-6580. Tel: 718-863-0436. Web Site: www.nypl.org/locations/westchester-square. *Libr Mgr,* Luz Marin
Library Holdings: Bk Vols 42,721
Open Mon & Wed 11-7, Tues & Thurs 10-6, Fri & Sat 10-5
WOODLAWN HEIGHTS BRANCH, 4355 Katonah Ave, (@ E 239th St), Bronx, 10470, SAN 353-6610. Tel: 718-519-9627. Web Site: www.nypl.org/locations/woodlawn-heights. *Libr Mgr,* Rana Smith
Library Holdings: Bk Vols 26,336
Function: Wheelchair accessible
Open Mon-Thurs 10-7, Fri & Sat 10-5
WOODSTOCK BRANCH, 761 E 160th St, (West of Prospect Ave), Bronx, 10456, SAN 353-6645. Tel: 718-665-6255. Web Site: www.nypl.org/locations/woodstock. *Libr Mgr,* Corey Rodriguez
Library Holdings: Bk Vols 40,000
Function: Wheelchair accessible
Open Mon-Fri 10-6, Sat 10-5
YORKVILLE BRANCH, 222 E 79th St, (Between Second & Third Aves), 10021-1295, SAN 353-667X. Tel: 212-744-5824. Web Site: www.nypl.org/locations/yorkville. *Libr Mgr,* Gregory Huchko
Library Holdings: Bk Vols 57,721
Open Mon & Wed 11-7, Tues & Thurs 10-6, Fri & Sat 10-5
Bookmobiles: 1. Bk vols 1,000

C NEW YORK SCHOOL OF INTERIOR DESIGN LIBRARY*, 170 E 70th St, 10021. SAN 321-0545. Tel: 212-472-1500, Ext 214. Circulation Tel: 212-452-4160. Toll Free Tel: 800-336-9743, Ext 214. FAX: 212-472-8175. E-mail: libraryinfo@nysid.edu. Web Site: library.nysid.edu/library. *Dir,* Billy Kwan; Tel: 212-452-4171, E-mail: bkwan@nysid.edu; *Librn,* Meg Donabedian; Tel: 212-452-4174, E-mail: mdonabedian@nysid.edu; *Archivist, Asst Librn,* Nora Reilly; Tel: 212-452-4169, E-mail: nreilly@nysid.edu; *Asst Librn,* Julie Sandy; E-mail: jsandy@nysid.edu; Staff 2 (MLS 2)
Founded 1924. Enrl 700; Fac 85; Highest Degree: Master
Library Holdings: AV Mats 100; Bk Vols 15,000; Per Subs 104
Special Collections: Architecture & Interiors; Digitized Images of Interiors, architecture and decorative arts; History of Furniture
Subject Interests: Archit, Interior design
Automation Activity & Vendor Info: (Acquisitions) Ex Libris Group; (Cataloging) Ex Libris Group; (Circulation) Ex Libris Group; (Course Reserve) Ex Libris Group; (OPAC) Ex Libris Group; (Serials) Ex Libris Group
Wireless access
Function: Photocopying/Printing
Partic in Metropolitan New York Library Council
Open Mon-Thurs 9-9, Fri 9-5, Sat 10-6
Restriction: Open to fac, students & qualified researchers

S THE NEW YORK SOCIETY LIBRARY, 53 E 79th St, 10075. SAN 311-9602. Tel: 212-288-6900. Interlibrary Loan Service Tel: 212-288-6900, Ext 200. E-mail: reference@nysoclib.org. Web Site: www.nysoclib.org. *Head Librn,* Carolyn Waters; Tel: 212-288-6900, Ext 244, E-mail: cwaters@nysoclib.org; *Asst Head Librn,* Meg Donabedian; Tel: 212-288-6900, Ext 210, E-mail: mdonabedian@nysoclib.org; *Head, Acq,* Steve McGuirl; Tel: 212-288-6900, Ext 247, E-mail: smcguirl@nysoclib.org; *Head, Cat & Spec Coll,* Peri Pignetti; Tel: 212-288-6900, Ext 243, E-mail: ppignetti@nysoclib.org; *Head, Children's Libr,* Randi Levy; Tel: 212-288-6900, Ext 216, E-mail: rlevy@nysoclib.org; *Head, Libr Develop,* James Addona; Tel: 212-288-6900, Ext 207, E-mail: jaddona@nysoclib.org; *Head, Exhibitions,* Harriet Shapiro; Tel: 212-288-6000, Ext 221, E-mail: hshapiro@nysoclib.org; *Spec Coll Librn,* Barbara Bieck; Tel: 212-288-6900, Ext 242, E-mail: bbieck@nysoclib.org; *Conservator,* Christina Amato; Tel: 212-288-6900, Ext 249, E-mail: camato@nysoclib.org; *Events Coord,* Sara Holliday; Tel: 212-288-6900, Ext 222, E-mail: sholliday@nysoclib.org; Staff 33 (MLS 14, Non-MLS 19)
Founded 1754
Library Holdings: Audiobooks 1,200; e-books 5,000; e-journals 5,300; Large Print Bks 790; Bk Vols 320,000; Per Subs 120
Special Collections: Irene Sharaff/Mai-Mai Sze Coll; John Hammond Coll, early gothic fiction & literature; John Winthrop Coll; Lorenzo Da Ponte Coll; Reverend John Sharpe Coll
Subject Interests: Art & archit, Biog, Criticism, Exploration, Fiction, Hist, NY City, Poetry, Travel
Automation Activity & Vendor Info: (Acquisitions) Innovative Interfaces, Inc; (Cataloging) Innovative Interfaces, Inc; (Circulation) Innovative Interfaces, Inc; (ILL) OCLC WorldShare Interlibrary Loan; (OPAC) Innovative Interfaces, Inc; (Serials) Innovative Interfaces, Inc
Wireless access
Publications: Annual Report; Books & People (Newsletter); E-news (Online only); Events (Newsletter); New Book List (Monthly)
Open Mon & Fri 9-5, Tues-Thurs 9-7, Sat & Sun 11-5

GM NEW YORK STATE PSYCHIATRIC INSTITUTE, Research Library, 1051 Riverside Dr, Box 114, 10032. SAN 311-9629. Tel: 646-774-8615. FAX: 646-774-8617. Web Site: nyspi.org/. *Asst Librn,* Alfa J Garcia; E-mail:

agarcia@nyspi.columbia.edu. Subject Specialists: *Bibliog instruction, Internet,* Alfa J Garcia
Founded 1896
Library Holdings: Bk Titles 15,000; Bk Vols 30,000; Per Subs 400
Subject Interests: Neurology, Neuropathology, Psychiat, Psychoanalysis, Psychol
Publications: Acquisition (Newsletter)
Open Mon-Fri 9-5

NEW YORK STATE SUPREME COURT
L FIRST JUDICIAL DISTRICT CIVIL LAW LIBRARY*, 60 Centre St, 10007, SAN 353-6793. Tel: 646-386-3670. FAX: 212-374-8159. *Librn,* Julie Gick; E-mail: jgick@courts.state.ny.us
Library Holdings: Bk Vols 60,000
Special Collections: New York City Codes; New York State Statutes; Records & Briefs NY Court of Appeals & Appellate Divisions, 1984-present, micro
Publications: Newsletter (Quarterly)
Open Mon-Fri 9-5
GL FIRST JUDICIAL DISTRICT CRIMINAL LAW LIBRARY*, 100 Centre St, 17th Flr, 10013, SAN 353-6769. Tel: 646-386-3890, 646-386-3891. FAX: 212-748-7908. E-mail: reflibny@courts.state.ny.us. Web Site: www.nycourts.gov/library/nyc_criminal/. *Sr Law Librn,* Ted Pollack; E-mail: tpollack@courts.state.ny.us; *Spec Asst, Budget & Payment Proc,* Felicia Barratsingh; Tel: 646-386-3889, E-mail: fbarrats@courts.state.ny.us; *Online Serv,* Walter Moy. Subject Specialists: *Law,* Ted Pollack
Library Holdings: Bk Titles 35,000; Bk Vols 109,000
Special Collections: Trial Transcripts for New York State, First JD Supreme Court-Criminal Branch
Subject Interests: Court admin, Criminology, Law
Automation Activity & Vendor Info: (Acquisitions) SirsiDynix; (Cataloging) SirsiDynix; (Circulation) SirsiDynix; (ILL) SirsiDynix; (OPAC) SirsiDynix; (Serials) SirsiDynix
Partic in Metropolitan New York Library Council; OCLC Online Computer Library Center, Inc
Restriction: Open to pub by appt only

NEW YORK TIMES
S PHOTO LIBRARY*, 620 Eighth Ave, 5th Flr, 10018, SAN 353-6882. Tel: 212-556-1642. FAX: 646-428-6366. *Dir,* James J Mones; E-mail: jmones@nytimes.com
Special Collections: Photographic Coll
Restriction: Staff use only
S REFERENCE LIBRARY*, 620 Eighth Ave, 5th Flr, 10018, SAN 353-6912. Tel: 212-556-7428. FAX: 212-556-4448. *Dir, Res,* Barbara Gray; Staff 10 (MLS 8, Non-MLS 2)
Library Holdings: Bk Titles 35,000; Bk Vols 40,000; Per Subs 200
Subject Interests: Biog, Journalism, Politics
Function: Res libr
Restriction: Employees only

C NEW YORK UNIVERSITY, Elmer Holmes Bobst Library, 70 Washington Sq S, 10012-1019. SAN 353-6947. Tel: 212-998-2500. Interlibrary Loan Service Tel: 212-998-2511. Administration Tel: 212-998-2445. FAX: 212-995-4070. Web Site: library.nyu.edu. *Dean, Division of Libraries,* Ms H Austin Booth; E-mail: austin.booth@nyu.edu; *Assoc Dean, Res,* Scott Collard; Tel: 212-992-9240, E-mail: sac11@nyu.edu; *Dir, Scholarly Communications & Info,* April Hathcock; E-mail: ah160@nyu.edu; *Head, Bus & Govt Info Services,* Daniel Hickey; Tel: 212-998-2694, E-mail: dh142@nyu.edu; *Head, Humanities & Soc Sci,* Jill Conte; Tel: 212-998-2622, E-mail: jac437@nyu.edu; *Librn for Journalism, Media Culture & Communications,* Katherine Boss; Tel: 212-998-2666, E-mail: keb5@nyu.edu; Staff 113 (MLS 113)
Founded 1831. Enrl 36,719; Fac 2,380; Highest Degree: Doctorate
Library Holdings: e-journals 50,500; Bk Vols 4,090,010
Special Collections: Alfred C Berol Lewis Carroll Coll, bks, letters, ms, photog; Erich Maria Remarque Library Coll; Rare Judaica & Hebraica; Robert Frost Library Coll; Tamiment Institute-Ben Josephson Library & Robert F Wagner Labor Archives; Toumlilene Monastery (Morocco) Library of North Africana; Wiet Coll of Islamic Materials
Wireless access
Publications: New York Labor Heritage; Progressions, Library Division Newsletter
Partic in Metropolitan New York Library Council; OCLC Research Library Partnership; Partnership for Academic Library Collaborative & Innovation
Friends of the Library Group
Departmental Libraries:
JACK BRAUSE LIBRARY, 11 W 42nd St, Ste 510, 10036-8002, SAN 353-7080. Tel: 212-992-3627. FAX: 212-992-3684. E-mail: midtown.library@nyu.edu. Web Site: guides.nyu.edu/jackbrauselibrary. *Head Librn,* Daniel Hickey; E-mail: dhickey@nyu.edu
Founded 1984
Subject Interests: Real estate
Partic in Research Libraries Information Network
Open Mon-Thurs 1-4
Restriction: Closed stack, In-house use for visitors, Limited access based on advanced application, Non-circulating coll, Open to others by appt, Pub by appt only
STEPHEN CHAN LIBRARY OF FINE ARTS & CONSERVATION CENTER LIBRARY, One E 78th St, 10075, SAN 353-7099. Tel: 212-992-5825. FAX: 212-992-5807. E-mail: ifa.library@nyu.edu. Web Site: library.nyu.edu/locations/institute-of-fine-arts. *Head Librn,* Lori Salmon; Tel: 212-992-5908, E-mail: lls5@nyu.edu; *Supvr,* Daniel Biddle; Tel: 212-992-5854, E-mail: dcb3@nyu.edu; Staff 4 (MLS 3, Non-MLS 1)
Library Holdings: Bk Vols 270,000; Per Subs 400
Subject Interests: Archaeology, Art conserv, Art hist, Conserv
Partic in Research Libraries Information Network
Open Mon-Fri 9-5
COURANT INSTITUTE OF MATHEMATICAL SCIENCES, Warren Weaver Hall, 251 Mercer St, 12th Flr, 10012-1110, SAN 353-7129. Tel: 212-998-3315. FAX: 212-995-4808. E-mail: courantlibrary@nyu.edu. Web Site: cims.nyu.edu/dynamic/resources/library. *Head Librn,* Carol Hutchins; E-mail: hutchins@nyu.edu; *Supvr,* Alex Kennedy-Grant; Tel: 212-998-3312, E-mail: akg1@nyu.edu
Founded 1954. Enrl 2,000
Library Holdings: Bk Vols 66,014; Per Subs 300
Special Collections: Mathematics (Courant, Bohr & Friedricks Reprints)
Subject Interests: Computer sci, Fluid mechanics, Math, Robotics
Open Mon-Thurs 9am-9:30pm, Fri 9-7, Sat 10-6 (Fall-Spring); Mon-Thurs 10-9. Fri 10-6 (Summer)
FALES LIBRARY & SPECIAL COLLECTIONS, 70 Washington Sq S, 10012. Tel: 212-998-2596. FAX: 212-995-3835. E-mail: special.collections@nyu.edu. Web Site: library.nyu.edu/locations/special-collections-center. *Dir,* Charlotte Priddle; Tel: 212-998-2598, E-mail: cp1118@nyu.edu; Staff 3 (MLS 3)
Founded 1957
Library Holdings: AV Mats 90,000; Bk Vols 350,000
Special Collections: American Cookbooks from the 18th Century to the Present (Cecily Brownstone Cookbook Coll); British & American Fiction from 1750 to the Present (Fales Library); Printed & Archival Materials Documenting the Downtown New York Art, Literary, Performance & Music Scene from 1973 to the Present (Downtown Coll)
Subject Interests: Am lit, Art, British lit, Cookery, Experimental writing, Film, Video
Automation Activity & Vendor Info: (Cataloging) Innovative Interfaces, Inc; (OPAC) Innovative Interfaces, Inc
Function: Archival coll, For res purposes, Prog for adults, Res libr
Publications: Fales Library Checklist (Collection catalog)
Restriction: Authorized scholars by appt, Closed stack, Non-circulating coll, Open by appt only, Open to fac, students & qualified researchers, Photo ID required for access
Friends of the Library Group
TAMIMENT LIBRARY/ROBERT F WAGNER LABOR ARCHIVES, Special Collections Ctr, 70 Washington Sq S, 2nd Flr, 10012. Tel: 212-998-2630. E-mail: tamiment.wagner@library.nyu.edu. *Univ Archivist,* Janet Bunde; Tel: 212-998-2642, E-mail: jmb583@nyu.edu; *Curator,* Shannon O'Neil; Tel: 212-998-2436, E-mail: smo224@nyu.edu
Library Holdings: Bk Vols 60,502
Special Collections: Oral History
Subject Interests: Labor, Soc liberalism, Utopianism
Publications: New York Labor Heritage
Restriction: Open by appt only
UNITED NATIONS & INTERNATIONAL DOCUMENTS COLLECTIONS, Elmer Holmes Bobst Library, 70 Washington Sq S, 6th Flr, 10012. Tel: 212-998-2610. FAX: 212-995-4442. Web Site: guides.nyu.edu/internationaldocs. *Librn,* Alicia Estes; E-mail: ae2@nyu.edu
Library Holdings: Bk Vols 4,000; Per Subs 530
Special Collections: UN Document Depository
Partic in Metropolitan New York Library Council
Special Services for the Deaf - Assistive tech
Special Services for the Blind - Assistive/Adapted tech devices, equip & products
Open Mon-Fri 10-5
Friends of the Library Group

CL NEW YORK UNIVERSITY SCHOOL OF LAW, Vanderbilt Hall, 40 Washington Sq S, 10012-1099. SAN 353-7218. Tel: 212-998-6300. Circulation Tel: 212-998-6312. Interlibrary Loan Service Tel: 212-998-6302. Reference Tel: 212-998-6600. Administration Tel: 212-998-6321. FAX: 212-995-3477. E-mail: lawlibrary@nyu.edu. Web Site: www.law.nyu.edu/library. *Interim Libr Dir,* Jay Shuman; Tel: 212-998-6310, E-mail: jay.shuman@nyu.edu; *Head, Res & Ref Serv, Interim Deputy Director,* Annmarie Zell; Tel: 212-992-8863, E-mail: annmarie.zell@nyu.edu; *Asst Libr Dir,* Ruthe Rose; Tel: 212-998-6306, E-mail: ruthe.rose@nyu.edu; *Collection Services Admin,* Coleman Ridge; Tel: 212-998-6584, E-mail: coleman.ridge@nyu.edu; Staff 41 (MLS 14, Non-MLS 27)

Library Holdings: Bk Vols 1,101,672
Automation Activity & Vendor Info: (ILL) OCLC ILLiad
Wireless access
Partic in Research Libraries Information Network
Open Mon-Thurs 8am-11:30pm, Fri 8am-10pm, Sat 9-9, Sun 10am-11:30pm

NYACK COLLEGE LIBRARY*, Eastman Library, Two Washington St, 10004-1008. Tel: 646-378-6100, Ext 7711. *Dir, Libr Serv,* Christy Choi; Tel: 646-378-6142, E-mail: christy.choi@nyack.edu; *Ref & Instruction Librn,* Sunya Notley; Tel: 646-378-6100, Ext 7707, E-mail: Sunya.Notley@nyack.edu; Staff 2 (MLS 2)
Subject Interests: Theol
Wireless access
Open Mon-Thurs 10-9, Fri & Sat 10-5:30

L O'MELVENY & MYERS LLP*, Law Library, Times Square Tower, Seven Times Sq, 10036. SAN 371-6074. FAX: 212-326-2061. Web Site: www.omm.com/locations/new-york. *Br Mgr,* Heide-Marie Bliss; Tel: 212-326-2020, E-mail: hbliss@omm.com; *Tech Serv,* Jill Lanier; Tel: 212-326-2022, E-mail: jlanier@omm.com; Staff 4 (MLS 3, Non-MLS 1)
Library Holdings: Bk Vols 15,000
Subject Interests: Law
Automation Activity & Vendor Info: (Course Reserve) Sydney
Function: ILL available
Restriction: Authorized personnel only

L ORRICK, HERRINGTON & SUTCLIFFE*, Law Library, 51 W 52nd St, 10019-6142. SAN 372-4425. Tel: 212-506-5000. FAX: 212-506-5151. Web Site: www.orrick.com. *Mgr, Res,* Mike Fillinger; E-mail: mfillinger@orrick.com; Staff 5 (MLS 2, Non-MLS 3)
Library Holdings: Bk Vols 15,000
Automation Activity & Vendor Info: (Acquisitions) SydneyPlus; (Cataloging) SydneyPlus; (Circulation) SydneyPlus; (OPAC) SydneyPlus; (Serials) SydneyPlus
Wireless access
Restriction: Staff use only

C PACE UNIVERSITY LIBRARY*, Henry Birnbaum Library, New York Civic Ctr, One Pace Plaza, 10038-1502. SAN 353-7420. Tel: 212-346-1332. Reference Tel: 212-346-1331. FAX: 212-346-1615. Web Site: www.pace.edu/library. *Assoc Univ Librn,* Rey Racelis; Tel: 212-346-1598, E-mail: rracelis@pace.edu; *Asst Dir, Libr Tech,* Milton David Almodovar; E-mail: malmodovar@pace.edu; *Head, Access Serv,* Eloise Flood; E-mail: eflood@pace.edu; *Head, Info Serv & Res,* Greg Murphy; E-mail: gmurphy@pace.edu; *Asst Univ Librn, Tech Serv,* Adele Artola; E-mail: aartola@pace.edu; Staff 9 (MLS 9)
Founded 1934. Highest Degree: Doctorate
Library Holdings: Bk Titles 319,000; Bk Vols 424,000; Per Subs 500
Subject Interests: Acctg, Computer sci, Educ, Finance, Liberal arts, Mkt, Nursing, Real estate, Taxation
Automation Activity & Vendor Info: (Acquisitions) Innovative Interfaces, Inc; (Cataloging) Innovative Interfaces, Inc; (Circulation) Innovative Interfaces, Inc; (Course Reserve) Innovative Interfaces, Inc; (ILL) Innovative Interfaces, Inc; (Media Booking) Innovative Interfaces, Inc; (OPAC) Innovative Interfaces, Inc; (Serials) Innovative Interfaces, Inc
Wireless access
Partic in Metropolitan New York Library Council; OCLC Online Computer Library Center, Inc; Westchester Academic Library Directors Organization
Open Mon-Fri 8am-11pm, Sat 10-8, Sun 12-8

R PARK AVENUE SYNAGOGUE*, 50 E 87th St, 10128. SAN 311-9874. Tel: 212-369-2600, Ext 127. FAX: 212-410-7879. Web Site: pasyn.org/resources/library. *Libr Dir,* Marga Hirsch; Staff 1 (MLS 1)
Founded 1956
Library Holdings: Bk Vols 9,000; Per Subs 10
Special Collections: Judaica Picture Books
Subject Interests: 15th-20th Century, Bible, Childrens' bks, Fiction, Holocaust, Israel, Jewish cookbks, Judaica, Judaica novels, Judaica ref, Juv Judaica
Automation Activity & Vendor Info: (Cataloging) OPALS (Open-source Automated Library System); (Circulation) OPALS (Open-source Automated Library System)
Wireless access
Open Mon-Thurs 12-6, Fri by appointment

L PATTERSON, BELKNAP, WEBB & TYLER LLP LIBRARY*, 1133 Avenue of the Americas, 10036. SAN 311-9904. Tel: 212-336-2000. FAX: 212-336-2222. *Head Librn,* Edward Brandwein; E-mail: ebrandwein@pbwt.com; *Law Librn,* Ernest Alamo; E-mail: ealamo@pbwt.com; Staff 4 (MLS 2, Non-MLS 2)
Library Holdings: e-books 27; Bk Vols 5,000; Per Subs 75
Subject Interests: Bankruptcy, Corporate, Equal rights amendments, Estates, Intellectual property, Libel, Litigation, Product liability, Tax

Automation Activity & Vendor Info: (Cataloging) EOS International; (Circulation) EOS International; (ILL) EOS International; (Serials) EOS International
Wireless access
Restriction: Staff use only

L PAUL, WEISS, RIFKIND, WHARTON & GARRISON LLP LIBRARY*, 1285 Avenue of the Americas, 10019-6064. SAN 311-9912. Tel: 212-373-2401. FAX: 212-373-2268. Web Site: www.paulweiss.com. *Dir, Res Serv,* Theresa O'Leary; E-mail: toleary@paulweiss.com; Staff 19 (MLS 10, Non-MLS 9)
Library Holdings: Bk Vols 80,000
Subject Interests: Law
Wireless access
Partic in Research Libraries Information Network
Open Mon-Fri 8:30-7
Restriction: Staff & customers only

L PILLSBURY WINTHROP SHAW PITTMAN LLP*, Law Library, 31 W 52nd St, 10019-6131. SAN 312-1410. Tel: 212-858-1000. FAX: 212-858-1500. Web Site: www.pillsburylaw.com. *Mgr, Res Serv,* Michael Roth; Staff 5 (MLS 3, Non-MLS 2)
Subject Interests: Law
Wireless access
Restriction: Staff use only

S POLISH INSTITUTE OF ARTS & SCIENCES IN AMERICA, INC*, Alfred Jurzykowski Memorial Library, 208 E 30th St, 10016. SAN 312-004X. Tel: 212-686-4164. FAX: 212-545-1130. E-mail: piasany@verizon.net. Web Site: www.piasa.org/library.html. *Exec Dir,* Bozena Leven; Staff 5 (MLS 3, Non-MLS 2)
Founded 1942
Library Holdings: Bk Titles 24,000; Bk Vols 40,000; Per Subs 500
Special Collections: Jan Lechon Coll; Translators Coll; Urbanski Polish-Latin American Coll; Workshops
Open Tues-Thurs 10-3

S POPULATION COUNCIL LIBRARY*, One Dag Hammarskjold Plaza, 10017. SAN 320-4049. Tel: 212-339-0533. FAX: 212-755-6052. E-mail: library@popcouncil.org. Web Site: www.popcouncil.org. *Librn,* Mary Shu; Staff 2 (MLS 1, Non-MLS 1)
Founded 1953
Library Holdings: Bk Titles 7,000; Bk Vols 18,000; Per Subs 350
Subject Interests: Demography, Develop countries, Develop economics, Family planning
Automation Activity & Vendor Info: (Acquisitions) EOS International; (Cataloging) EOS International; (Circulation) EOS International; (ILL) EOS International; (OPAC) EOS International; (Serials) EOS International
Wireless access
Restriction: Not open to pub

S PRINCETON LIBRARY IN NEW YORK*, 15 W 43rd St, 10036. SAN 312-0104. Tel: 212-596-1250. FAX: 212-596-1399. E-mail: library@princetonclub.com. Web Site: www.princetonclub.com/The_Club/The_Library. *Librn,* Erin Tahaney; Staff 1 (Non-MLS 1)
Founded 1962
Library Holdings: Bk Vols 12,000; Per Subs 70
Special Collections: Princetoniana; Woodrow Wilson Coll
Subject Interests: Histories of NY
Automation Activity & Vendor Info: (OPAC) Mandarin Library Automation
Wireless access
Open Mon-Fri 8-8, Sat & Sun 10-4

S PROJECT FOR PUBLIC SPACES, INC*, Media Library, 419 Lafayette St, 7th Flr, 10003. SAN 370-7415. Tel: 212-620-5660. FAX: 212-620-5660. E-mail: info@pps.org. Web Site: www.pps.org. *Pres,* Fred Kent; *VPres,* Ethan Kent; Staff 1 (MLS 1)
Founded 1975
Library Holdings: Bk Titles 1,000
Restriction: Open by appt only

L PROSKAUER ROSE LLP LIBRARY*, 11 Times Sq, 10036. SAN 312-0139. Tel: 212-969-3000, 212-969-5001. FAX: 212-969-2931. E-mail: library@proskauer.com. Web Site: www.proskauer.com. *Ref Librn,* Megan D'Errico; *Mgr, Knowledge Mgt Serv,* Zara Fernandes; Staff 16 (MLS 7, Non-MLS 9)
Founded 1875
Library Holdings: Bk Titles 40,000; Per Subs 400
Special Collections: Labor Law Coll
Wireless access
Restriction: Open by appt only

L PRYOR, CASHMAN LLP*, Law Library, Seven Times Sq, 10036. SAN 372-4433. Tel: 212-421-4100. FAX: 212-326-0806. E-mail: library@pryorcashman.com. Web Site: www.pryorcashman.com. *Library Contact,* Philip Hoffman
Library Holdings: Bk Vols 10,000; Per Subs 78
Restriction: Not open to pub

S RACQUET & TENNIS CLUB LIBRARY*, 370 Park Ave, 10022-5968. SAN 312-0171. Tel: 212-753-9700. *Head Librn,* Gerard J Belliveau, Jr; *Asst Librn,* Sarah Jacobs; Staff 2 (MLS 2)
Founded 1905
Library Holdings: Bk Titles 21,000; Per Subs 40
Special Collections: Court Tennis (Jeu de Paume Coll); Early American Sports; Lawn Tennis
Subject Interests: Sports
Publications: Annual Report to Members
Friends of the Library Group

S REAL ESTATE BOARD OF NEW YORK*, Seymour B Durst Library, 570 Lexington Ave, 2nd Flr, 10022. SAN 312-0201. Tel: 212-532-3100. FAX: 212-481-0420. Web Site: www.rebny.com. *Library Contact,* Angela Caldwell; E-mail: acaldwell@rebny.com; Staff 3 (Non-MLS 3)
Founded 1896
Library Holdings: Bk Titles 850; Per Subs 100
Wireless access
Restriction: Mem only

S REHABILITATION INTERNATIONAL*, Collection on Disability-Handicap Library, 866 United Nations Plaza, Off 422, 10017. SAN 329-1359. Tel: 212-420-1500. FAX: 212-505-0871. E-mail: info@riglobal.org. Web Site: www.riglobal.org. *Secy Gen,* Teuta Rexhepi
Founded 1922
Library Holdings: Bk Vols 3,500
Subject Interests: Barrier free designs, Childhood disability in developing countries, Develop countries, Disability, Legis, Soc policy, Soc security disability progs, Women
Wireless access
Restriction: Mem only

C THE ROCKEFELLER UNIVERSITY*, Rita & Frits Markus Library & Scientific Commons, Welch Hall, 1230 York Ave, RU Box 203, 10065. Tel: 212-327-8904. Interlibrary Loan Service Tel: 212-327-8916. FAX: 212-327-8802. Interlibrary Loan Service FAX: 212-327-7840. E-mail: libref@rockefeller.edu. Web Site: markuslibrary.rockefeller.edu. *Univ Librn,* Matthew Covey; E-mail: mcovey@rockefeller.edu; *Asst Univ Librn,* Jeanine McSweeney; Tel: 212-327-8980, E-mail: mcsweej@rockefeller.edu; *Exhibits Librn, Spec Coll,* Olga Nilova; Tel: 212-327-8868, E-mail: nilovao@rockefeller.edu; *Mgr, Libr Syst,* Douglas Many; Tel: 212-327-8906, E-mail: many@rockefeller.edu. Subject Specialists: *Biology,* Jeanine McSweeney; *Libr syst & software,* Douglas Many; Staff 6 (MLS 4, Non-MLS 2)
Founded 1906. Enrl 204; Fac 350; Highest Degree: Doctorate
Library Holdings: Bk Titles 53,453; Bk Vols 59,823; Per Subs 576
Special Collections: Science & General Interest Books published between 1787 & 1926
Subject Interests: Biochem, Chem, Human genetics, Immunology, Med sci, Microbiology, Physics, Virology
Automation Activity & Vendor Info: (Acquisitions) Innovative Interfaces, Inc; (Cataloging) Innovative Interfaces, Inc; (Circulation) Innovative Interfaces, Inc; (Course Reserve) Innovative Interfaces, Inc; (OPAC) Innovative Interfaces, Inc; (Serials) Innovative Interfaces, Inc
Wireless access
Function: Res libr
Publications: Brochures
Partic in Cas; Metropolitan New York Library Council; OCLC Research Library Partnership
Restriction: Use of others with permission of librn

S ROMANIAN CULTURAL INSTITUTE*, 200 E 38th St, 10016. SAN 320-2143. Tel: 212-687-0180. FAX: 212-687-0181. E-mail: office@rciusa.info. Web Site: www.rciusa.info. *Dir,* Dorian Branea
Founded 1969
Library Holdings: Bk Titles 22,000; Per Subs 60
Special Collections: Bibliographies (Romanian Topics Coll)
Subject Interests: Romania
Wireless access
Open Mon-Fri 9-6

L ROPES & GRAY LLP LIBRARY*, 1211 Avenue of the Americas, 10036. SAN 371-0467. Tel: 212-596-9000. FAX: 212-596-9090. Web Site: www.ropesgray.com/locations/new-york.aspx. *Sr Res Librn,* Lisa Fricker; E-mail: lisa.fricker@ropesgray.com
Library Holdings: Bk Vols 15,500; Per Subs 78
Automation Activity & Vendor Info: (Cataloging) Inmagic, Inc.; (Circulation) Inmagic, Inc.; (ILL) OCLC; (OPAC) Inmagic, Inc.
Restriction: Not open to pub

S RUSSELL SAGE FOUNDATION LIBRARY*, 112 E 64th St, 10065. SAN 324-1815. Tel: 212-752-8641. FAX: 212-688-2684. E-mail: library@rsage.org. Web Site: www.russellsage.org. *Chief Info Officer,* Claire Gabriel; *Research Librn,* Catherine Winograd; Tel: 212-752-8640; Staff 2 (MLS 2)
Founded 1982
Library Holdings: Bk Vols 1,300; Per Subs 68
Special Collections: Russell Sage Foundation Publications
Automation Activity & Vendor Info: (Cataloging) OCLC; (ILL) OCLC; (OPAC) EOS International
Wireless access
Function: ILL available
Partic in Metropolitan New York Library Council

S SALMAGUNDI CLUB LIBRARY*, 47 Fifth Ave, 10003. SAN 312-0473. Tel: 212-255-7740. E-mail: info@salmagundi.org. Web Site: www.salmagundi.org. *Library Contact,* Barbara Genco; E-mail: BAGencoConsulting@gmail.com
Founded 1899
Library Holdings: Bk Vols 6,500
Subject Interests: Art, Coronations, Costumes, Uniforms
Wireless access
Restriction: Mem only

L SATTERLEE, STEPHENS LLP*, Law Library, 230 Park Ave, 10169. SAN 311-6603. Tel: 212-818-9200. FAX: 212-818-9606. E-mail: info@ssbb.com. Web Site: www.ssbb.com. *Librn,* Dolores Fusik; E-mail: dfusik@ssbb.com
Library Holdings: Bk Vols 13,000; Per Subs 25
Wireless access
Restriction: Staff use only

S SCHOLASTIC INC LIBRARY, 557 Broadway, 10012. SAN 312-0511. Tel: 212-343-6171. Administration Tel: 212-343-6742. FAX: 212-389-3317. E-mail: library@scholastic.com. *Archives Mgr, Librn, Tech Serv,* Deimosa Webber-Bey; E-mail: deimosa@scholastic.com; Staff 4 (MLS 4)
Founded 1929
Library Holdings: Bk Vols 100,000; Per Subs 40
Automation Activity & Vendor Info: (Acquisitions) SirsiDynix; (Cataloging) SirsiDynix; (Circulation) SirsiDynix; (OPAC) SirsiDynix-iBistro
Wireless access
Partic in Metropolitan New York Library Council
Restriction: Staff use only

C SCHOOL OF VISUAL ARTS LIBRARY, SVA Library, 380 Second Ave, 2nd Flr, 10010. SAN 312-052X. Tel: 212-592-2660. FAX: 212-592-2655. E-mail: library@sva.edu. Web Site: sva.edu/students/life-at-sva/campus-spaces/library. *Libr Dir,* Caitlin Kilgallen; Tel: 212-592-2663, E-mail: ckilgallen@sva.edu; *Assoc Libr Dir,* Rebecca Clark; Tel: 212-592-2944, E-mail: rclark4@sva.edu; *Head, Tech Serv,* Zimra Panitz; Tel: 212-592-2662, E-mail: zpanitz@sva.edu; *Digital Serv Librn,* Phoebe Stein; Tel: 212-592-2672, E-mail: pstein2@sva.edu; *Instruction/Periodicals Librn,* David Pemberton; Tel: 212-592-2664, E-mail: dpemberton@sva.edu; *Circ Mgr,* Mark Roussel; Tel: 212-592-2689, E-mail: mroussel@sva.edu; *Archivist,* Beth Kleber; Tel: 212-592-2636, E-mail: bkleber@sva.edu; *Cataloger,* David Shuford; Tel: 212-592-2630, E-mail: dshuford@sva.edu; *Visual Res Curator,* Lorraine Gerety; Tel: 212-592-2667, E-mail: lgerety@sva.edu. Subject Specialists: *Art hist,* Caitlin Kilgallen; *Art hist,* Zimra Panitz; *Poetry,* David Pemberton; *Graphic design, Illustration,* Beth Kleber; *Art hist,* David Shuford; *Art hist,* Lorraine Gerety; Staff 8 (MLS 7, Non-MLS 1)
Founded 1962. Enrl 4,300; Fac 1,050; Highest Degree: Master
Library Holdings: CDs 2,000; DVDs 7,500; e-books 180,000; Electronic Media & Resources 35; Bk Vols 78,000; Per Subs 380
Special Collections: Milton Glaser Design Study Center & Archives; Picture Coll; Reinhold Brown Poster Coll; School of Visual Arts Archives
Subject Interests: Design, Fine arts
Automation Activity & Vendor Info: (Acquisitions) Ex Libris Group; (Cataloging) Ex Libris Group; (Circulation) Ex Libris Group; (Course Reserve) Ex Libris Group; (Discovery) EBSCO Discovery Service; (ILL) OCLC; (OPAC) Ex Libris Group; (Serials) Ex Libris Group
Wireless access
Function: Archival coll, Art exhibits, Audio & video playback equip for onsite use, Computers for patron use, ILL available, Magazines, Movies, Music CDs, Online cat, Orientations, Photocopying/Printing, Ref serv available, Scanner, Study rm
Partic in Association of Independent Colleges of Art & Design; Metropolitan New York Library Council; OCLC Online Computer Library Center, Inc

Open Mon-Fri 10-6
Restriction: Open to students, fac, staff & alumni, Photo ID required for access, Use of others with permission of librn
Departmental Libraries:
SVA LIBRARY WEST, 133/141 W 21st St, Lower Level, 10011. Tel: 212-592-2810. *Librn,* Barbara Calderon; Tel: 212-592-2291, E-mail: bcalderon2@sva.edu
Founded 2018
Open Mon-Fri 10-6

L SCHULTE ROTH & ZABEL LLP*, Law Library, 919 Third Ave, 10022. SAN 372-4573. Tel: 212-756-2000. Interlibrary Loan Service Tel: 212-756-2303. FAX: 212-593-5955. Web Site: www.srz.com. *Dir,* Jeffrey Giles; Tel: 212-756-2304, E-mail: jeffrey.giles@srz.com; *Tech Serv,* Daniel Pappas; Tel: 212-756-2237, E-mail: daniel.pappas@srz.com; Staff 14 (MLS 7, Non-MLS 7)
Founded 1969
Library Holdings: AV Mats 100; Bk Titles 8,392; Per Subs 499
Subject Interests: Corporate law, Human rights, Securities indust
Automation Activity & Vendor Info: (Acquisitions) Sydney; (Cataloging) Sydney; (Circulation) Sydney; (ILL) Sydney; (OPAC) Sydney; (Serials) Sydney
Wireless access
Partic in American Association of Law Libraries; SLA
Restriction: Staff use only

L SEWARD & KISSEL LLP*, Law Library, One Battery Park Plaza, 10004. SAN 325-9471. Tel: 212-574-1200. FAX: 212-480-8421. Web Site: www.sewkis.com. *Libr Serv Mgr,* Benjamin Toby; E-mail: toby@sewkis.com
Library Holdings: Bk Titles 1,200; Bk Vols 18,000; Per Subs 100
Wireless access
Restriction: Staff use only

L SEYFARTH & SHAW NEW YORK LIBRARY*, 620 Eighth Ave, Flr 32, 10018-1405. SAN 327-0211. Tel: 212-218-5500. FAX: 212-218-5526. Web Site: www.seyfarth.com. *Libr Mgr,* Gabrielle Lewis; E-mail: glewis@seyfarth.com
Library Holdings: Bk Vols 10,000; Per Subs 100
Subject Interests: Employment, Labor, Securities, Tax
Wireless access
Restriction: Staff use only

L SHEARMAN & STERLING LLP LIBRARY*, 599 Lexington Ave, 10022-6069. SAN 353-7900. Tel: 212-848-8580. Interlibrary Loan Service Tel: 212-848-5400.
Founded 1873
Library Holdings: Bk Vols 12; Per Subs 70
Subject Interests: Antitrust, Capital markets, Intl, Litigation, Securities, Tax
Automation Activity & Vendor Info: (Cataloging) SydneyPlus
Wireless access
Restriction: Not open to pub

S SHEVCHENKO SCIENTIFIC SOCIETY INC*, Library & Archives, 63 Fourth Ave, 10003. SAN 326-0976. Tel: 212-254-5130. FAX: 212-254-5239. E-mail: library@shevchenko.org. Web Site: www.shevchenko.org. *Bibliographer, Librn,* Sergiy Panko; *Archivist,* Ostap Kin; Staff 3 (MLS 1, Non-MLS 2)
Founded 1952
Library Holdings: Bk Titles 45,000; Videos 400
Special Collections: The Immigration of Ukrainians to North & South America, archives & docs, av rare bks
Subject Interests: Ukrainian civilization, Ukrainian culture, Ukrainian hist, Ukrainian lit
Wireless access
Function: Archival coll, Photocopying/Printing, Res libr
Open Mon-Fri 9-4:30 or by appointment
Restriction: Access at librarian's discretion, Not a lending libr

L SIDLEY, AUSTIN LLP*, Law Library, 787 Seventh Ave, 23rd Flr, 10019. SAN 372-2554. Tel: 212-839-5300. Interlibrary Loan Service Tel: 212-839-5445. FAX: 212-839-5599. Web Site: www.sidley.com. *Libr Dir,* Chris Lange; E-mail: clange@sidley.com; *Ref Librn,* Amy Weiner
Library Holdings: Bk Vols 50,000; Per Subs 250
Restriction: Staff use only

L SIMPSON, THACHER & BARTLETT*, Law Library, 425 Lexington Ave, 10017. SAN 312-0619. Tel: 212-455-2800. FAX: 212-455-2502. Web Site: www.stblaw.com/offices/new-york. *Dir,* Sheila Sterling; Staff 14 (MLS 9, Non-MLS 5)
Founded 1884
Library Holdings: Bk Vols 40,000
Subject Interests: Antitrust, Banking, Corp, Labor, Taxation
Automation Activity & Vendor Info: (Cataloging) SirsiDynix; (OPAC) SirsiDynix; (Serials) SirsiDynix
Wireless access
Partic in OCLC Online Computer Library Center, Inc; Research Libraries Information Network
Restriction: Staff use only

L SKADDEN, ARPS, SLATE, MEAGHER & FLOM LIBRARY*, One Manhattan W, 10036. SAN 312-0627. Tel: 212-735-3000. FAX: 212-735-3244. Web Site: www.skadden.com. *Asst Dir,* Anthony Amabile; E-mail: anthony.amabile@skadden.com; Staff 26 (MLS 8, Non-MLS 18)
Founded 1948
Library Holdings: Bk Vols 75,000
Subject Interests: Law
Restriction: Staff use only

S STACKS RARE COIN COMPANY OF NY*, Technical Information Center Library, 123 W 57th St, 10019-2280. SAN 327-0270. Tel: 212-582-2580. Toll Free Tel: 800-566-2580. FAX: 212-245-5018. E-mail: Info@StacksBowers.com. Web Site: www.stacksbowers.com. *Library Contact,* Position Currently Open
Founded 1858
Library Holdings: Bk Vols 5,200
Subject Interests: Numismatics, Syngraphics
Open Mon-Fri 10-5

CM STATE UNIVERSITY OF NEW YORK, STATE COLLEGE OF OPTOMETRY*, Harold Kohn Vision Science Library, 33 W 42nd St, 10036-8003. SAN 312-0759. Tel: 212-938-5690. Administration Tel: 212-938-5691. FAX: 212-938-5696. Web Site: www.sunyopt.edu/library. *Dir,* Elaine Wells; E-mail: ewells@sunyopt.edu; Staff 5 (MLS 2, Non-MLS 3)
Founded 1971. Enrl 283; Fac 150; Highest Degree: Doctorate
Library Holdings: e-books 1,246; Bk Vols 38,000; Per Subs 483
Special Collections: Learning Disabilities & Optometry
Subject Interests: Ophthalmology, Optics, Optometry, Physiological optics
Automation Activity & Vendor Info: (Cataloging) Ex Libris Group; (Circulation) Ex Libris Group; (ILL) OCLC Online; (OPAC) Ex Libris Group
Wireless access
Publications: Kohn Library Holdings (Index to science materials); Newsletter; Tip Sheets (Reference guide)
Partic in Metropolitan New York Library Council; SUNYConnect
Open Mon-Fri (Fall-Spring) 8am-10pm, Sat 10-8:30, Sun 10-10; Mon-Fri (Summer) 8-8, Sat 10-5, Sun 10-6
Restriction: Circ limited

L STROOCK & STROOCK & LAVAN LIBRARY*, 180 Maiden Lane, 10038. SAN 312-0791. Tel: 212-806-5700. FAX: 212-806-6006. Web Site: www.stroock.com. *Dir, Knowledge Serv, Dir, Res Serv,* Harris Crooks; E-mail: hcrooks@stroock.com
Library Holdings: Bk Vols 20,000; Per Subs 500
Automation Activity & Vendor Info: (Cataloging) EOS International
Restriction: Staff use only

L SULLIVAN & CROMWELL LLP*, Information Resources Center, 125 Broad St, 10004. SAN 312-0805. Tel: 212-558-3780. FAX: 212-558-3346. Web Site: www.sullcrom.com. *Mgr, Ref Serv,* Lucy Redmond; Staff 17 (MLS 13, Non-MLS 4)
Founded 1879
Library Holdings: Bk Titles 24,282; Bk Vols 96,273
Automation Activity & Vendor Info: (Acquisitions) Cuadra Associates, Inc; (Cataloging) Cuadra Associates, Inc; (Circulation) Cuadra Associates, Inc; (ILL) Cuadra Associates, Inc; (OPAC) Cuadra Associates, Inc; (Serials) Cuadra Associates, Inc

GL SUPREME COURT, APPELLATE DIVISION*, First Department Law Library, 27 Madison Ave, 10010. SAN 312-0813. Tel: 212-340-0478. Web Site: www.courts.state.ny.us/courts/ad1. *Librn,* Gene Preudhomme
Founded 1901
Library Holdings: Bk Vols 70,000; Per Subs 50
Wireless access
Restriction: Not open to pub

C TEACHERS COLLEGE, COLUMBIA UNIVERSITY*, The Gottesman Libraries of Teachers College, Columbia University, 525 W 120th St, 10027-6696. SAN 353-0345. Tel: 212-678-3494. Interlibrary Loan Service Tel: 212-678-3495. E-mail: library@tc.columbia.edu. Web Site: edlab.tc.columbia.edu, library.tc.columbia.edu. *Dir,* Dr Gary J Natriello; Tel: 212-678-3087, E-mail: gjn6@columbia.edu; *Dir, Res & Develop,* Hui Soo Chae; Tel: 212-678-3448, E-mail: hsc2001@tc.columbia.edu; *Assoc Dir, Head, Media Design Ctr, Sr Creative Dir, Design Strategy & Delivery,* Dr Brian Hughes; Tel: 212-678-3069, E-mail: bhughes@tc.columbia.edu;

Sr Librn, Allen Foresta; Tel: 212-678-3026, E-mail: foresta@tc.columbia.edu; *Sr Librn,* Jennifer L Govan; Tel: 212-678-3022, E-mail: Govan@tc.columbia.edu; Staff 16 (MLS 6, Non-MLS 10)
Founded 1887. Enrl 5,000; Fac 140; Highest Degree: Doctorate
Library Holdings: AV Mats 5,651; CDs 986; e-journals 17,000; Electronic Media & Resources 4,766; Bk Vols 430,432; Per Subs 789; Videos 3,174
Special Collections: 18th-20th Century K-12 Textbooks, American & Foreign; Annie E Moore Illustrated Children's Books (18th & 19th Century); Art Education (including Children's Artworks in the Arthur W Dow, Edwin Ziegfeld & Israeli Children's Peace Art Colls); Black History Series (Educational Coll); Children's Village Records, ms; Education (Historical Photograph Coll); Education (Rare Books of 15th-19th Century); Educational Software Coll (K-12); Educational Tests & Manuals (TC Guidance Laboratory 1915-1960 & Papers of Edward L Thordike & Will McCall); English Children's Books, 18th & 19th Century (Harvey Darton Coll); International Mathematics Education (David E Smith Coll); National Council of Social Studies Records Coll, ms; National Kindergarten Association Records, ms; Nursing Education (Adelaid Nutting History of Nursing Coll); Papers of Prominent Educators; Teachers College Archives
Subject Interests: Adult educ, Applied health sci, Applied linguistics, Art educ, Audiology, Bilingual educ, Clinical psychol, Communications, Computing, Curric, Early childhood educ, Econ, Educ, Educ admin, Educ psychol, English, Evaluation, Health educ, Higher educ, Hist of educ, Intl educ, Math, Nursing educ, Nutrition, Philos, Psychol, Sci educ, Secondary educ, Soc studies, Sociol, Spanish, Speech-lang pathology
Automation Activity & Vendor Info: (Acquisitions) Innovative Interfaces, Inc; (Cataloging) Innovative Interfaces, Inc; (Circulation) Innovative Interfaces, Inc; (OPAC) Innovative Interfaces, Inc; (Serials) Innovative Interfaces, Inc
Wireless access
Function: For res purposes
Publications: Library Bookmarks; Russia & Other Former Soviet Republics
Partic in Metropolitan New York Library Council; Research Libraries Information Network; Wilsonline
Special Services for the Deaf - Assistive tech; Bks on deafness & sign lang; Spec interest per
Special Services for the Blind - Assistive/Adapted tech devices, equip & products; Braille equip; Compressed speech equip; Magnifiers; Thermoform Brailon duplicator
Open Mon-Thurs 8am-11pm, Fri 8-7, Sat 12-7, Sun Noon-11
Restriction: In-house use for visitors, Open to students, fac & staff, Photo ID required for access, Restricted access
Friends of the Library Group

L TORYS LAW LIBRARY*, 1114 Avenue of the Americas, 23 Flr, 10036. SAN 372-4530. Tel: 212-880-6000. FAX: 212-682-0200. E-mail: info@torys.com. Web Site: www.torys.com. *Librn,* Michael B Hoffman; E-mail: mhoffman@torys.com
Library Holdings: Bk Vols 5,000; Per Subs 50
Wireless access

C TOURO COLLEGE LIBRARIES, 320 W 31st St, 10001. SAN 312-0937. Tel: 212-463-0400, Ext 55321. FAX: 212-627-3696. Web Site: www.touro.edu/library. *Dir of Libr,* Bashe Simon; Tel: 212-463-0400, Ext 55523, E-mail: bashe.simon@touro.edu; *Assoc Dir of Libr,* Michoel Rotenfeld; Tel: 212-463-0400, Ext 55224, E-mail: michoel.rotenfeld@touro.edu; *Info Literacy Librn,* Sara Tabaei; E-mail: sara.tabaei@touro.edu; *Archivist,* Philip R Papas; E-mail: philip.pappas@touro.edu; Staff 43 (MLS 27, Non-MLS 16)
Highest Degree: Doctorate
Library Holdings: AV Mats 87,446; CDs 2,442; DVDs 2,192; e-books 604,073; Bk Vols 142,085; Per Subs 180; Videos 2,192
Subject Interests: Bus, Educ, Health sci, Jewish studies, Psychol
Automation Activity & Vendor Info: (ILL) OCLC; (OPAC) Innovative Interfaces, Inc
Wireless access
Publications: Libguides in 31 Disciplines; Touro College Library Blog
Partic in Long Island Library Resources Council; Metropolitan New York Library Council
Open Mon-Thurs 9-9, Fri 9-2

SR TRINITY CHURCH ARCHIVES*, 120 Broadway, 38th Flr, 10271. SAN 320-4405. Tel: 212-602-9652, 212-602-9687. FAX: 212-602-9641. E-mail: archives@trinitywallstreet.org. Web Site: www.trinitywallstreet.org/about/archives. *Archivist,* Joseph Lapinski; *Asst Archivist,* Sarah Quick; Staff 2 (MLS 2)
Founded 1980
Library Holdings: Bk Titles 500
Subject Interests: Episcopal Church, Theol
Open Mon-Fri 9-5 by appointment only

S TURTLE BAY MUSIC SCHOOL LIBRARY*, 244 E 52nd St, 10022. SAN 370-5234. Tel: 212-753-8811. FAX: 212-752-6228. E-mail: info@tbms.org. Web Site: www.tbms.org. *Head Librn,* Bruce Potterton
Founded 1925
Library Holdings: Music Scores 12,000; Bk Titles 1,500
Special Collections: 19th Century & Early 20th Sheet Music; Out of Print Editions of Music; Walter Trampler Viola Coll, scores featuring notations, fingerings & bowings
Restriction: Open to students, fac & staff

R UNIFICATION THEOLOGICAL SEMINARY LIBRARY*, Four W 43rd St, 10036. Tel: 212-563-6647, Ext 106. FAX: 212-563-6431. Web Site: uts.libguides.com/SeminaryLibrary. *Librn,* Bob Wagner; E-mail: r.wagner@uts.edu
Founded 1975
Library Holdings: AV Mats 350; Bk Titles 60,000; Per Subs 70
Subject Interests: Relig
Wireless access
Open Mon-Wed 11-9:30, Thurs 1-7

S UNION LEAGUE CLUB LIBRARY*, 38 E 37th St, 10016. SAN 312-102X. Tel: 212-685-3800, Ext 226. FAX: 212-545-0130. E-mail: library@UnionLeagueClub.org. Web Site: www.unionleagueclub.org. *Librn,* Steele Hearne; E-mail: shearne@unionleagueclub.org
Founded 1863
Library Holdings: Bk Titles 20,000; Per Subs 38
Subject Interests: Am biog, Civil War
Restriction: Not open to pub

S UNITED HOSPITAL FUND OF NEW YORK, Reference Library, 1411 Broadway, 12th Flr, 10018. SAN 312-1070. Tel: 212-494-0720. FAX: 212-494-0800. Web Site: uhfnyc.org. *Librn,* Will Yates; E-mail: wyates@uhfnyc.org; Staff 1 (MLS 1)
Founded 1941
Library Holdings: Bk Titles 2,000; Per Subs 120
Subject Interests: Healthcare econ, Healthcare mgt
Automation Activity & Vendor Info: (OPAC) LibraryWorld, Inc
Wireless access
Partic in Metropolitan New York Library Council
Restriction: Open by appt only

S UNITED LODGE OF THEOSOPHISTS*, Theosophy Hall Library, 347 E 72nd St, 10021. SAN 312-1089. Tel: 212-535-2230. FAX: 212-628-3430. E-mail: ULTNY@aol.com. Web Site: www.ult.org. *Librn,* Rosemary Jourdan
Founded 1922
Library Holdings: Bk Titles 6,800
Subject Interests: Ancient philos, Ancient psychol, Comparative mythology, Comparative relig, Modern philos, Original writings of H P Blavatsky, Original writings of Wm Q Judge, Parapsychol, Reincarnation res in relig, Reincarnation res in sci, Theosophical hist
Restriction: Open by appt only

S UNITED NATIONS CHILDRENS FUND ARCHIVES*, Three UN Plaza, H-12C UNICEF House, 10017. SAN 374-7557. Tel: 212-326-7064. FAX: 212-303-7989. Web Site: www.unicef.org. *Knowledge Mgr,* Mr Dale
Library Holdings: Bk Vols 25,000; Per Subs 200
Partic in Metropolitan New York Library Council
Open Mon-Fri 9-5 by appointment only
Restriction: Open to researchers by request

S UNITED NATIONS DAG HAMMARSKJOLD LIBRARY*, United Nations Headquarters, Rm L-105, First Ave at 42nd St, 10017. Tel: 212-963-3000. E-mail: library-ny@un.org. *Chief Librn,* Thanos Giannakopoulos; Tel: 212-963-0512, E-mail: thanos.giannakopoulos@un.org
Founded 1946
Library Holdings: Bk Vols 100,000; Per Subs 215
Special Collections: Activities & History of the United Nations; Government Documents of Member States; International Affairs 1918-1945 (Woodrow Wilson Memorial Library); League of Nations Documents; Maps Coll; UN Specialized Agencies Documents; United Nations Documents. Oral History; UN Document Depository; US Document Depository
Subject Interests: Disarmament, Econ, Environ, Intl law, Intl relations, Legis, Nat law, Peace-keeping, Polit sci, Sustainable develop, Women
Automation Activity & Vendor Info: (Acquisitions) SirsiDynix; (Cataloging) SirsiDynix; (Circulation) SirsiDynix; (OPAC) SirsiDynix; (Serials) SirsiDynix
Wireless access
Publications: Indexes to Proceedings of General Assembly, Economic & Social Council, Security Council; United Nations Documents Index
Partic in United Nations System Electronic Information Acquisitions Consortium
Open Mon-Fri 9-5:30

GL UNITED STATES COURT OF INTERNATIONAL TRADE, Court Library, One Federal Plaza, 10278. SAN 312-1151. Tel: 212-264-2816. FAX: 212-264-3242. E-mail: Information_Resources_Manager@cit.uscourts.gov. Web Site: www.cit.uscourts.gov. *Dir,* Daniel Campbell; *Dep Dir,* Taryn Rucinski; Staff 5 (MLS 4, Non-MLS 1)
Library Holdings: Bk Titles 5,000; Bk Vols 50,000; Per Subs 100
Subject Interests: Customs law, Law
Automation Activity & Vendor Info: (OPAC) SirsiDynix-WorkFlows
Publications: United States Court of International Trade Reports: Cases Adjudged in the US Court of International Trade (Annual)
Partic in OCLC Online Computer Library Center, Inc
Restriction: Not open to pub

G UNITED STATES DEPARTMENT OF LABOR*, Bureau of Labor Statistics, 201 Varick St, Rm 808, 10014. SAN 312-1194. Tel: 646-264-3600. FAX: 212-337-2532. E-mail: blsinfony@bls.gov. Web Site: www.bls.gov. *Library Contact,* Bruce Bergman; Staff 4 (Non-MLS 4)
Founded 1949
Library Holdings: Bk Vols 1,700; Per Subs 10
Subject Interests: Consumer prices, Earnings, Econ growth, Employment, Indexes, Occupational outlook, Occupational safety, Producer prices, Productivity, Unemployment, Wages
Restriction: Not open to pub

S UNIVERSITY CLUB LIBRARY, One W 54th St, 10019. SAN 312-1224. Tel: 212-572-3418. FAX: 212-572-3452. E-mail: library@universityclubny.org. Web Site: www.universityclubny.org. *Curator, Dir,* Andrew J Berner; *Assoc Dir,* Scott Overall; Staff 2 (MLS 2)
Founded 1865
Library Holdings: Bk Vols 90,000; Per Subs 125
Special Collections: Civil War Ante-bellum Southern History (New York Southern Society Coll); Fine Printing & Limited Editions Coll; George Cruikshank (H Gregory Thomas Coll); Illustrated Books (Tinker Coll); Publishing History (Whitney Darrow Coll); Rare Book Coll
Subject Interests: 1st World War, 2nd World War, Archit, Art, Biog, Civil War, English lit
Automation Activity & Vendor Info: (Cataloging) EOS International; (Circulation) EOS International; (ILL) OCLC; (OPAC) EOS International
Wireless access
Publications: The Illuminator
Partic in Metropolitan New York Library Council
Open Mon-Fri 9-5
Friends of the Library Group

L WACHTELL, LIPTON, ROSEN & KATZ*, Law Library, 51 W 52nd St, 10019. SAN 372-2422. Tel: 212-403-1521. FAX: 212-403-2000. E-mail: alllibrary@wlrk.com. Web Site: www.wlrk.com. *Dir,* Susan Hesse
Library Holdings: Bk Vols 2,000; Per Subs 400
Subject Interests: Corporate law
Automation Activity & Vendor Info: (Cataloging) Horizon; (Circulation) Horizon; (OPAC) Horizon
Wireless access
Restriction: Staff use only

L WARSHAW BURSTEIN, LLP, Law Library, 575 Lexington Avenue, 7th Flr, 10022. SAN 372-4220. Tel: 212-984-7700. FAX: 212-972-9150. Web Site: www.wbny.com. *Library Contact,* Shari Beckerman; E-mail: sbeckerman@wbny.com; Staff 1 (Non-MLS 1)
Library Holdings: Bk Vols 500
Subject Interests: Corporate law, Estates, Litigation, Mergers, Real estate law, Securities law, Tax, Trusts
Open Mon-Fri 9:30-5:30

L WEIL, GOTSHAL & MANGES LLP*, Research Center, 767 Fifth Ave, 10153. SAN 312-1283. Tel: 212-310-8444. Interlibrary Loan Service Tel: 212-735-4560. FAX: 212-310-8007. E-mail: libts@weil.com. Web Site: www.weil.com. *Assoc Dir, Res & Info Serv,* Raul Lopez; Tel: 212-310-8445, E-mail: Raul.Lopez@weil.com; *Asst Librn, ILL,* Daniela Pugh; E-mail: daniela.pugh@weil.com; *Mgr, Res & Competitive Intelligence,* Philip Barahona; E-mail: philip.barahona@weil.com; *Mgr, Resources & Systems Mgmt,* Meredith Mulligan; E-mail: meredith.mulligan@weil.com; *Res Analyst,* Sadys Espitia; E-mail: sadys.espitia@weil.com; *Res Analyst,* Merill Losick; Tel: 212-310-8213, E-mail: Merill.Losick@weil.com; *Res Analyst,* Daniel McLaughlin; E-mail: daniel.mclaughlin@weil.com; *Syst Analyst,* John Terhorst; E-mail: john.terhorst@weil.com; Staff 9 (MLS 8, Non-MLS 1)
Subject Interests: Law
Automation Activity & Vendor Info: (Acquisitions) Sydney; (Cataloging) Sydney; (Circulation) Sydney; (ILL) Sydney; (OPAC) Sydney; (Serials) Sydney
Wireless access
Function: 24/7 Electronic res, 24/7 Online cat
Publications: SmartSearching
Partic in OCLC Online Computer Library Center, Inc; Research Libraries Information Network
Restriction: Authorized personnel only

L WHITE & CASE LAW LIBRARY*, 1221 Avenue of the Americas, 10020-1095. SAN 353-8419. Tel: 212-819-8200. FAX: 212-354-8113. *Dir,* Kathy Skinner; E-mail: kathy.skinner@whitecase.com
Founded 1901

S WHITNEY MUSEUM OF AMERICAN ART*, Frances Mulhall Achilles Library, 99 Gansevoort St, 10014. SAN 312-1380. Tel: 212-570-3648. E-mail: library@whitney.org. Web Site: www.whitney.org/collection/research/library. *Managing Librn,* Ivy Blackman; Tel: 212-570-3682, E-mail: ivy_blackman@whitney.org; *Archives Mgr,* Tara Hart; Tel: 212-671-5335, E-mail: tara_hart@whitney.org; Staff 4 (MLS 3, Non-MLS 1)
Founded 1931
Library Holdings: Bk Titles 50,000; Per Subs 100
Special Collections: American Art Research Concil Papers; Edward Hopper Research Coll; Museum Archives
Subject Interests: 20th Century art, 21st Century art, Am artists
Automation Activity & Vendor Info: (Acquisitions) Ex Libris Group; (Cataloging) Ex Libris Group; (Circulation) Ex Libris Group; (OPAC) Ex Libris Group; (Serials) Ex Libris Group
Function: Res libr
Restriction: Authorized scholars by appt, Circulates for staff only, Closed stack, Not a lending libr, Open by appt only, Photo ID required for access, Restricted access
Friends of the Library Group

L WILLKIE FARR & GALLAGHER LLP*, Law Library, 787 Seventh Ave, 10019. SAN 312-1399. Tel: 212-728-8700. Interlibrary Loan Service Tel: 212-728-8709. FAX: 212-728-3303. E-mail: library@willkie.com. *Dir, Libr Serv,* Debra Glessner; E-mail: dglessner@willkie.com; *Ref Librn,* Sally Munson; Staff 15 (MLS 8, Non-MLS 7)
Library Holdings: Bk Titles 50,000; Per Subs 200
Subject Interests: Securities law, Taxation
Publications: Bulletin
Partic in Dow Jones News Retrieval; OCLC Online Computer Library Center, Inc; Proquest Dialog

S WINDELS MARX LANE & MITTENDORF, LLP LIBRARY*, 156 W 56th St, 10019. SAN 312-1402. Tel: 212-237-1000. Reference Tel: 212-237-1136. FAX: 212-262-1215. Web Site: www.windelsmarx.com. *Mgr, Libr Serv,* Joel Solomon; E-mail: jsolomon@windelsmarx.com
Library Holdings: Bk Titles 10,000
Subject Interests: Banking law, Corporate law, Litigation
Function: ILL available
Restriction: Staff use only

L WINSTON & STRAWN LIBRARY*, 200 Park Ave, 10166-4193. SAN 312-1356. Tel: 212-294-6700. Interlibrary Loan Service Tel: 212-294-4713. FAX: 212-294-4700. Web Site: www.winston.com. *Research Librn,* Mikhail Koulikov; Staff 5 (MLS 2, Non-MLS 3)
Founded 1993
Library Holdings: Bk Vols 100,000; Per Subs 150
Subject Interests: Law
Automation Activity & Vendor Info: (Cataloging) SirsiDynix-Unicorn; (Circulation) SirsiDynix-Unicorn; (OPAC) SirsiDynix-Unicorn
Wireless access
Partic in Illinois Library & Information Network; Proquest Dialog
Open Mon-Fri 9-5

SR STEPHEN WISE FREE SYNAGOGUE, Rabbi Edward E Klein Memorial Library, 30 W 68th St, 10023. SAN 371-6260. Tel: 212-877-4050, Ext 265. FAX: 212-787-7108. E-mail: library@swfs.org. Web Site: www.swfs.org. *Dir, Ch Serv,* Miriam Kalmar; E-mail: mkalmar@swfs.org
Founded 1985
Library Holdings: AV Mats 100; Bks on Deafness & Sign Lang 30; Bk Vols 3,500; Talking Bks 2,002
Special Collections: Stephen Wise Archives, docs, letters
Subject Interests: Judaica
Automation Activity & Vendor Info: (Cataloging) EOS International; (Circulation) EOS International; (OPAC) EOS International
Wireless access
Open Mon-Fri 8:30-3, Sun 10-1
Friends of the Library Group

M WOLTERS KLUWER/AMERICAN JOURNAL OF NURSING, Sophia F Palmer Library, 28 Liberty St, 43rd Flr, 10005. SAN 311-5887. Tel: 646-674-6601. FAX: 212-886-1206. *Librn,* Joanne Jahr; E-mail: joanne.jahr@wolterskluwer.com. Subject Specialists: *Health sci,* Joanne Jahr; Staff 1 (MLS 1)
Founded 1951

Library Holdings: Bk Vols 500; Per Subs 2
Special Collections: International Nursing Index, 1966-2000
Subject Interests: Nursing, Nursing admin, Nursing educ
Automation Activity & Vendor Info: (Acquisitions) Prenax, Inc; (Serials) Prenax, Inc
Wireless access
Function: Doc delivery serv, Health sci info serv, ILL available, Ref & res
Partic in Brooklyn-Queens-Staten Island-Manhattan-Bronx Health Sciences Librarians; Docline
Restriction: Borrowing requests are handled by ILL, Not open to pub

S XAVIER SOCIETY FOR THE BLIND*, National Catholic Press & Lending Library for the Visually Impaired, 248 W 35th St, Ste 1502, 10001-2505. SAN 328-3577. Tel: 212-473-7800. Toll Free Tel: 800-637-9193. FAX: 212-473-7801. E-mail: info@xaviersocietyfortheblind.org. Web Site: www.xaviersocietyfortheblind.org.
Founded 1900
Library Holdings: Audiobooks 911; Braille Volumes 940; CDs 840; Large Print Bks 1; Bk Titles 1,851; Bk Vols 8,366; Per Subs 11; Talking Bks 77
Subject Interests: Braille, Catholicism, Inspirational, Spirituals
Function: Audiobks on Playaways & MP3, Audiobks via web, Bks on CD, Digital talking bks, ILL available, Magazines, Online cat
Publications: Annual Report; Audio Books (Monthly); Braille Calendars (Annual); Catholic Review (Quarterly); Mass Propers (Monthly); Xavier Review (Quarterly); XSB Lending Library Catalog of Braille (Collection catalog)
Special Services for the Blind - Bks & mags in Braille, on rec, tape & cassette; Bks on CD; Bks on flash-memory cartridges; Braille & cassettes; Braille bks; Braille servs; Children's Braille; Digital talking bk; Free checkout of audio mat; Large print bks; Newsletter (in large print, Braille or on cassette); Production of talking bks; Recorded bks; Talking bks; Transcribing serv; Web-Braille
Open Mon-Fri 8-4
Restriction: Authorized patrons, Clients only, Registered patrons only

S YALE CLUB LIBRARY*, 50 Vanderbilt Ave, 10017. SAN 312-1488. Tel: 212-716-2129. FAX: 212-716-2158. E-mail: library@yaleclubnyc.org. Web Site: www.yaleclubnyc.org/library.
Library Holdings: Bk Vols 45,500
Special Collections: Yale Memorabilia & Publications
Wireless access
Restriction: Mem only

C YESHIVA UNIVERSITY LIBRARIES*, 2520 Amsterdam Ave, 10033. (Mail add: 500 W 185th St, 10033), SAN 353-8508. Tel: 646-592-4107. Interlibrary Loan Service Tel: 646-592-4041. FAX: 212-960-0066. Web Site: library.yu.edu. *Dir, Univ Libr,* Paul Glassman; E-mail: paul.glassman@yu.edu; *Libr Syst Adminr,* J B Holderness; E-mail: jb.holderness@yu.edu; *Head, Digital & Web Serv,* Hao Zeng; E-mail: hao.zeng@yu.edu; *Head, Metadata Serv, Head, Processing Services,* Rebecca Malamud; E-mail: malamud@yu.edu; *Archivist,* Deena Schwimmer; E-mail: dschwimm@yu.edu; *Curator, Spec Coll,* Shulamith Z Berger; E-mail: sberger@yu.edu. Subject Specialists: *Hebraica, Judaica,* Shulamith Z Berger; Staff 84 (MLS 37, Non-MLS 47)
Founded 1897. Highest Degree: Doctorate
Jul 2018-Jun 2019. Mats Exp $2,738,536, Books $229,162, Per/Ser (Incl. Access Fees) $860,580, Manu Arch $15,400, AV Equip $24,500, Electronic Ref Mat (Incl. Access Fees) $1,598,221, Presv $10,673. Sal $2,880,016 (Prof $1,872,010)
Library Holdings: AV Mats 8,690; e-books 175,447; e-journals 35,000; Bk Vols 1,083,079
Special Collections: Manuscripts Coll; Pollack Library-Landowne Bloom Coll; Rare Books Coll; Special Colls & Archives
Subject Interests: Hebraica, Judaica, Soc work
Automation Activity & Vendor Info: (Discovery) EBSCO Discovery Service; (OPAC) Innovative Interfaces, Inc
Wireless access
Publications: Inventories to Collections (Archives guide); Rabbinic Manuscripts: Mendel Gottesman Library (Collection catalog)
Partic in LYRASIS; Metropolitan New York Library Council; Northeast Research Libraries Consortium; OCLC Online Computer Library Center, Inc; Westchester Academic Library Directors Organization
Open Thurs-Sun 9am-1am, Fri 9-4

Departmental Libraries:

ALBERT EINSTEIN COLLEGE OF MEDICINE
See Separate Entry under Albert Einstein College of Medicince, Bronx, NY

CL DR LILLIAN & DR REBECCA CHUTICK LAW LIBRARY, Benjamin N Cardozo School of Law, 55 Fifth Ave, 10003-4301, SAN 353-8567. Tel: 212-790-0223. Circulation Tel: 212-790-0285. Reference Tel: 212-790-0220. FAX: 212-790-0236. Reference E-mail: lawref@yu.edu. Web Site: www.cardozo.yu.edu/library. *Interim Dir,* Ingrid Mattson; E-mail: ingrid.mattson@yu.edu; *Asst Dir, Faculty & Scholarly Servs, Educ Coordr,* Christine Anne George; E-mail: christine.george@yu.edu; *Acq Librn,* Grace Collins; E-mail: grace.collins@yu.edu; *Syst & Emerging Tech Librn,* Richard T Kim; E-mail: richard.kim@yu.edu; *Media Serv Spec,* Christopher Higgins; E-mail: christopher.higgins@yu.edu; *Coll, Head, Access Serv,* Anupama Pal; E-mail: anupama.pal@yu.edu; *Admin Serv,* Valerie Sykes; E-mail: fayesyke@yu.edu; Staff 17 (MLS 5, Non-MLS 12)
Founded 1976. Enrl 1,076; Fac 45; Highest Degree: Doctorate
Library Holdings: Bk Titles 98,751; Bk Vols 530,698; Per Subs 6,407
Special Collections: US Document Depository
Subject Interests: Intellectual property, Israeli law, Law, Lit
Automation Activity & Vendor Info: (Acquisitions) Innovative Interfaces, Inc; (Cataloging) Innovative Interfaces, Inc; (Circulation) Innovative Interfaces, Inc; (OPAC) Innovative Interfaces, Inc; (Serials) Innovative Interfaces, Inc
Function: 24/7 Electronic res, 24/7 Online cat
Partic in LYRASIS; Metropolitan New York Library Council; OCLC Online Computer Library Center, Inc
Publications: Current Contents; Research Guides
Open Mon-Thurs 8am-Midnight, Fri 8-4, Sun 10am-Midnight

CR MENDEL GOTTESMAN LIBRARY OF HEBRAICA-JUDAICA, 2520 Amsterdam Ave, 10033. (Mail add: 500 W 185th St, 10033). Tel: 646-592-4190. FAX: 212-960-0066. *Head Librn,* Tina Weiss; E-mail: tina.weiss@yu.edy; *Coll Develop & Ref Librn,* Zvi Erenyi; E-mail: erenyi@yu.edu; *Ref Librn,* Moshe Schapiro; E-mail: schapiro@yu.edu; Staff 3 (MLS 3)
Founded 1897. Highest Degree: Doctorate
Library Holdings: AV Mats 2,996; e-books 304,779; e-journals 44,616; Microforms 3,046; Bk Vols 293,561; Per Subs 1,069
Special Collections: Hebraica Rare Books & Manuscripts; Sephardic Studies Coll
Subject Interests: Bible, Jewish hist, Jewish lit, Jewish philos, Rabbinics
Automation Activity & Vendor Info: (Acquisitions) Innovative Interfaces, Inc; (Cataloging) Innovative Interfaces, Inc; (Circulation) Innovative Interfaces, Inc; (Course Reserve) Docutek; (OPAC) Innovative Interfaces, Inc; (Serials) Innovative Interfaces, Inc
Partic in Metropolitan New York Library Council; OCLC Online Computer Library Center, Inc; Research Libraries Information Network
Open Mon-Thurs & Sun 9am-1am, Fri 9am-12:30pm, Sat 7pm-1am

POLLACK LIBRARY LANDOWNE BLOOM COLLECTION, Wilf Campus, 2520 Amsterdam Ave, 10033, SAN 353-8656. Tel: 646-592-4045, 646-592-4450. Interlibrary Loan Service Tel: 646-592-4041. FAX: 212-960-0066. *Head Librn,* Sandra E Moore; E-mail: sandy.moore@yu.edu; *Electronic Reserves Librn, Scholarly Communications Librn,* Stephanie Gross; E-mail: gross@yu.edu; *Electronic Res & Ref Librn,* Shulamis Hes; E-mail: shulamis.hes@yu.edu; *Outreach Librn, Pub Serv Librn,* Wendy Kosakoff; E-mail: wendy.kosakoff@yu.edu; *ILL Coordr,* Rebekah Shoemake; E-mail: sarah.shoemake@yu.edu; Staff 4 (MLS 4)
Founded 1938
Library Holdings: AV Mats 1,801; Bk Vols 311,885
Special Collections: US Document Depository
Subject Interests: Soc work
Automation Activity & Vendor Info: (Acquisitions) Innovative Interfaces, Inc; (Circulation) Innovative Interfaces, Inc; (Course Reserve) Innovative Interfaces, Inc; (ILL) OCLC; (OPAC) Innovative Interfaces, Inc; (Serials) Innovative Interfaces, Inc
Partic in Metropolitan New York Library Council; OCLC Online Computer Library Center, Inc
Open Mon-Thurs & Sun 9am-1am, Fri 9am-12:30pm

SIMON WIESENTHAL CENTER LIBRARY & ARCHIVES
See Separate Entry under Simon Wiesenthal Center & Museum of Tolerance, Los Angeles, CA

HEDI STEINBERG LIBRARY, 245 Lexington Ave, 10016, SAN 353-8680. Tel: 646-592-4980. Web Site: library.yu.edu/c.php?g=570456&p=3931654. *Head Librn,* Edith Lubetski; E-mail: lubetski@yu.edu; *Ref & Instruction Librn,* Elinor Grumet; E-mail: grumet@yu.edu; *Ref & Instruction Librn,* Hindishe Lee; E-mail: hlee1@yu.edu; *Res & Instruction Librn,* Rina Krautwirth; E-mail: rina.krautwirth@yu.edu; Staff 4 (MLS 4)
Founded 1954
Library Holdings: AV Mats 2,380; Bk Vols 149,000; Per Subs 558
Subject Interests: Hebraica, Judaica
Partic in Metropolitan New York Library Council
Open Mon-Thurs 8:30am-Midnight, Fri 9-1, Sun Noon-Midnight

S YIVO INSTITUTE FOR JEWISH RESEARCH*, Library & Archives, 15 W 16th St, 10011. SAN 312-1496. Tel: 212-246-6080, Ext 5102. FAX: 212-292-1892. E-mail: libraryinquiries@yivo.cjh.org, yivomail@yivo.cjh.org. Web Site: www.yivo.org. *Dir, Archives,* Dr Stephanie Halpern; E-mail: shalpern@yivo.cjh.org; Staff 15 (MLS 8, Non-MLS 7)
Founded 1925
Library Holdings: Bk Vols 350,000; Per Subs 200

Special Collections: Hebrew Immigrant Aid Society Coll; Jewish Music Coll; Jewish Sheet Music; Manuscript Coll; Milwitzki Coll of Ladino Literature; Nazi Coll; Rabbinics (Vilna Coll); Yiddish Linguistics (Weinreich Library Coll)
Subject Interests: Eastern European Jewish hist, Holocaust, Lit, Yiddish (Lang)
Publications: YIVO Bleter (Yiddish); YIVO News/Yedies (English & Yiddish)
Partic in Asn of Jewish Librs; Metropolitan New York Library Council; Research Libraries Information Network
Restriction: Not a lending libr

NEW YORK MILLS

P NEW YORK MILLS PUBLIC LIBRARY*, 399 Main St, 13417. SAN 312-1577. Tel: 315-736-5391. FAX: 315-736-7566. E-mail: newyorkmills@midyork.org. Web Site: www.midyorklib.org/newyorkmills. *Dir,* Diane Berry
Circ 32,949
Library Holdings: Bk Vols 37,036
Automation Activity & Vendor Info: (Cataloging) SirsiDynix-WorkFlows; (Circulation) SirsiDynix-WorkFlows; (OPAC) SirsiDynix-WorkFlows
Wireless access
Mem of Mid-York Library System
Open Mon-Fri 12-8, Sat 10-2
Friends of the Library Group

NEWARK

P NEWARK PUBLIC LIBRARY*, 121 High St, 14513-1492. SAN 312-1585. Tel: 315-331-4370. FAX: 315-331-0552. E-mail: newcirc@pls-net.org. Web Site: newarklibrary.org. *Dir,* Melissa Correia; E-mail: newarklibrarydirector@owwl.org; *Youth Serv Librn,* Alicia Vazquez
Founded 1897. Pop 15,355; Circ 165,000
Library Holdings: Bk Vols 42,000; Per Subs 57
Special Collections: Local History Coll. State Document Depository
Automation Activity & Vendor Info: (Cataloging) Evergreen; (Circulation) Evergreen
Wireless access
Mem of Pioneer Library System
Partic in OCLC Online Computer Library Center, Inc
Open Mon-Thurs 9:30-8, Fri 9:30-6, Sat 9:30-3
Friends of the Library Group

NEWARK VALLEY

P TAPPAN-SPAULDING MEMORIAL LIBRARY*, Six Rock St, 13811. (Mail add: PO Box 397, 13811-0397), SAN 312-1615. Tel: 607-642-9960. FAX: 607-642-9960. E-mail: tslibrary@stny.rr.com. Web Site: tsmlibrary.org. *Dir,* Stephanie Langer-Liblick
Founded 1908. Pop 5,260; Circ 20,615
Wireless access
Function: Bks on cassette, Bks on CD, Children's prog, Computers for patron use, Electronic databases & coll, Family literacy, Free DVD rentals, Holiday prog, Home delivery & serv to seniorr ctr & nursing homes, Homebound delivery serv, ILL available, Instruction & testing, Internet access, Music CDs, Online cat, Online ref, Outreach serv, OverDrive digital audio bks, Photocopying/Printing, Preschool outreach, Prog for children & young adult, Ref & res, Story hour, Summer reading prog, Tax forms, Teen prog, VHS videos
Mem of Finger Lakes Library System
Open Tues 10-8, Wed 2-8, Thurs 3-8, Sat 9-1
Restriction: Authorized patrons

NEWBURGH

S HISTORICAL SOCIETY OF NEWBURGH BAY & THE HIGHLANDS, Helen Gearn Memorial Library, 189 Montgomery St, 12550. SAN 326-579X. Tel: 845-561-3790. E-mail: historicalsocietynb@gmail.com. Web Site: www.newburghhistoricalsociety.com/helen-gearn-memorial-library.
Founded 1951
Library Holdings: Bk Vols 3,000
Special Collections: Charitible Organizations; Environmental Affairs; Local History Coll, (Newburgh, NY area); Natural Resources
Subject Interests: Art & archit, Civil War, Ethnic groups, Mil, Revolutionary war, Soc sci
Partic in Southeastern New York Library Resources Council
Restriction: Open by appt only

C MOUNT SAINT MARY COLLEGE*, Kaplan Family Library & Learning Center, 330 Powell Ave, 12550-3494. SAN 312-1623. Tel: 845-569-3600. Reference Tel: 845-569-3200. FAX: 845-561-0999. E-mail: library@msmc.edu. Web Site: www.msmc.edu/library. *Dir,* Barbara Petruzzelli; Tel: 845-569-3601, E-mail: Barbara.Petruzzelli@msmc.edu; *Access Serv Librn, Outreach Serv Librn,* Jen Park; Tel: 845-569-3546, E-mail: jen.park@msmc.edu; *Coll Develop Librn,* Vivian Milczarski; Tel: 845-569-3523, E-mail: vivian.milczarski@msmc.edu; *Instrul Serv Librn,* Tiffany Davis; Tel: 845-569-3351, E-mail: tiffany.davis@msmc.edu; *Instrul Serv Librn,* Derek Sanderson; Tel: 845-569-3240, E-mail: derek.sanderson@msmc.edu; *Syst & Cat Serv Librn,* Denise A Garofalo; Tel: 845-569-3519, E-mail: garofalo@msmc.edu; Staff 13 (MLS 7, Non-MLS 6)
Founded 1959. Enrl 2,200; Fac 89; Highest Degree: Master
Library Holdings: Bk Vols 80,000; Per Subs 250
Subject Interests: Grad educ programs, Nursing, Sci
Automation Activity & Vendor Info: (Acquisitions) Innovative Interfaces, Inc; (Cataloging) Innovative Interfaces, Inc; (Circulation) Innovative Interfaces, Inc; (Course Reserve) Innovative Interfaces, Inc; (ILL) Innovative Interfaces, Inc; (OPAC) Innovative Interfaces, Inc; (Serials) Innovative Interfaces, Inc
Wireless access
Publications: Faculty Handbook-Student Handbook
Partic in Southeastern New York Library Resources Council
Open Mon-Thurs 7:30am-Midnight, Fri 7:30-7, Sat 10-6, Sun 1-Midnight

G NEW YORK STATE OFFICE OF PARKS, RECREATION & HISTORIC PRESERVATION*, Washington's Headquarters State Historic Site Library, 84 Liberty St, 12550-5603. (Mail add: PO Box 1783, 12551), SAN 326-5404. Tel: 845-562-1195. FAX: 845-561-1789. Web Site: parks.ny.gov/historic-sites/17/details.aspx. *Mgr,* Elyse Goldberg; E-mail: elyse.goldberg@parks.ny.gov
Founded 1850
Library Holdings: Bk Titles 800; Bk Vols 1,000
Special Collections: George Washington Coll, ms, papers; Revolutionary War Colls, ms; Timothy Pickering Coll, ms
Wireless access
Restriction: Non-circulating to the pub

P NEWBURGH FREE LIBRARY*, 124 Grand St, 12550. SAN 353-880X. Tel: 845-563-3600. Circulation Tel: 845-563-3630. Reference Tel: 845-563-3625, 845-563-3626. FAX: 845-563-3602. E-mail: nflref@rcls.org. Web Site: www.newburghlibrary.org. *Dir,* Mary Lou Carolan; Tel: 845-563-3605, E-mail: ml.carolan@rcls.org; *Head, Adult Serv, Head, Ref Serv,* Beth Zambito; Tel: 845-563-3628, E-mail: bzambito@cls.org; *Head, Circ & Tech Serv,* Jason Thomas; Tel: 845-563-3610, E-mail: jthomas@rcls.org; *Head, Youth Serv,* Lisa Kochik; Tel: 845-563-3616, E-mail: lkochik@rcls.org; *Adult Serv, Doc,* Heather Henricksen-Georghiou; Tel: 845-563-3617, E-mail: hhgeo@rcls.org; Staff 22 (MLS 22)
Founded 1852. Pop 63,410; Circ 309,070
Library Holdings: Bk Titles 220,937; Per Subs 430
Special Collections: Children's Lit Coll; Genealogy, bk, micro. State Document Depository; US Document Depository
Subject Interests: Bibliographies, Local hist, Parenting coll
Automation Activity & Vendor Info: (Cataloging) SirsiDynix
Wireless access
Mem of Ramapo Catskill Library System
Partic in New York Online Virtual Electronic Library
Special Services for the Deaf - Bks on deafness & sign lang; Spec interest per
Open Mon-Thurs 9-9, Fri & Sat 9-5, Sun 1-5 (Sept-June); Mon & Thurs 9-9, Tues & Wed 9-5, Sat 10-3 (July-Aug)
Friends of the Library Group

NEWFANE

P NEWFANE PUBLIC LIBRARY*, 2761 Maple Ave, 14108. SAN 312-164X. Tel: 716-778-9344. FAX: 716-778-9344. E-mail: newfanelibrary@nioga.org. Web Site: newfanelibrary.org. *Dir,* Kristine DeGlopper-Banks; E-mail: kdegl@nioga.org
Founded 1911. Pop 9,833; Circ 42,431
Library Holdings: Audiobooks 425; CDs 287; DVDs 673; Large Print Bks 1,040; Bk Vols 20,165; Per Subs 23; Videos 525
Automation Activity & Vendor Info: (Cataloging) SirsiDynix; (Circulation) SirsiDynix; (OPAC) SirsiDynix
Wireless access
Function: Adult bk club, Art exhibits, Bk club(s), Bks on cassette, Bks on CD, Children's prog, Computers for patron use, Free DVD rentals, Holiday prog, ILL available, Music CDs, Outreach serv, Photocopying/Printing, Story hour, Summer reading prog, Tax forms, Wheelchair accessible
Mem of Nioga Library System
Open Mon, Wed & Fri 10-5, Tues & Thurs 12-8, Sat (Sept-June) 11-2
Friends of the Library Group

NEWFIELD

P NEWFIELD PUBLIC LIBRARY*, 198 Main St, 14867. (Mail add: PO Box 154, 14867-0154), SAN 312-1658. Tel: 607-564-3594. FAX: 607-564-3594. E-mail: newfieldpubliclibrary@yahoo.com. Web Site: www.newfieldpubliclibrary.org. *Libr Dir,* Sue Chaffee
Founded 1882. Circ 13,739

Library Holdings: Bk Titles 8,824; Bk Vols 10,500; Per Subs 35
Automation Activity & Vendor Info: (Circulation) Innovative Interfaces, Inc; (OPAC) Innovative Interfaces, Inc
Wireless access
Mem of Finger Lakes Library System
Open Mon 2-5, Tues-Thurs 10-12 & 2-6:30, Fri & Sat 10-Noon

NEWPORT

P NEWPORT FREE LIBRARY, 7390 S Main St, 13416. SAN 312-1666. Tel: 315-845-8533. Web Site: newportfreelibrary.org. *Dir,* Betty Dodge; E-mail: bdodge@midyork.org
Founded 1923. Pop 3,614; Circ 18,784
Library Holdings: Bk Titles 18,000; Per Subs 23
Subject Interests: Cooking, Educ, Fiction, Hist
Wireless access
Mem of Mid-York Library System
Open Tues & Thurs 10-6, Wed 10-2, Fri 1-6

NIAGARA FALLS

P NIAGARA FALLS PUBLIC LIBRARY*, Earl W Brydges Bldg, 1425 Main St, 14305. SAN 353-8958. Tel: 716-286-4894. Reference Tel: 716-286-4881. E-mail: nfplinfo@nioga.org. Web Site: www.niagarafallspubliclib.org. *Dir,* Sarah Potwin; E-mail: spotwin@nioga.org; Staff 11 (MLS 11)
Founded 1838. Pop 55,593; Circ 340,000
Library Holdings: AV Mats 25,000; Bk Vols 325,000
Special Collections: US Document Depository
Subject Interests: Local hist
Automation Activity & Vendor Info: (Acquisitions) Horizon; (Cataloging) Horizon; (Circulation) Horizon; (Course Reserve) Horizon; (ILL) Horizon; (Media Booking) Horizon; (OPAC) Horizon; (Serials) Horizon
Wireless access
Publications: Newsletter
Mem of Nioga Library System
Open Mon-Wed 9-9, Thurs-Sat 9-5
Friends of the Library Group
Branches: 1
LASALLE BRANCH, 8728 Buffalo Ave, 14304. SAN 353-8982. Tel: 716-283-8309. *Dir,* Sarah Potwin
Open Mon & Tues 10-8, Thurs 10-5, Fri 12-5
Friends of the Library Group

NIAGARA UNIVERSITY

C NIAGARA UNIVERSITY LIBRARY*, Four Varsity Dr, 14109. SAN 312-1712. Tel: 716-286-8000. Circulation Tel: 716-286-8020. Interlibrary Loan Service Tel: 716-286-8012. Reference Tel: 716-286-8022. FAX: 716-286-8030. E-mail: reflib@niagara.edu. Web Site: library.niagara.edu. *Dir of Libr,* David Schoen; Tel: 716-286-8001, E-mail: schoen@niagara.edu; *Head, Acq,* Samantha Gust; Tel: 716-286-8031, E-mail: gust@niagara.edu; *Coordr, Pub Serv,* Jonathan Coe; Tel: 716-286-8005, E-mail: jcoe@niagara.edu; Staff 23 (MLS 11, Non-MLS 12)
Founded 1856. Enrl 3,548; Fac 198; Highest Degree: Master
Library Holdings: Bks on Deafness & Sign Lang 60; e-books 117; Bk Titles 202,402; Bk Vols 232,135; Per Subs 22,000
Special Collections: 15th-17th Century Religious Materials
Automation Activity & Vendor Info: (Cataloging) SirsiDynix; (Circulation) SirsiDynix; (OPAC) SirsiDynix
Wireless access
Partic in Western New York Library Resources Council
Open Mon-Thurs 7:30am-Midnight, Fri 7:30-6, Sat 11-6, Sun 11am-Midnight

NICHOLS

P GEORGE P & SUSAN PLATT CADY LIBRARY*, 42 E River St, 13812. (Mail add: PO Box 70, 13812-0070), SAN 312-1720. Tel: 607-699-3835. FAX: 607-699-3835. Web Site: www.cadylibrary.org. *Dir,* Corinne Moshier; E-mail: director@cadylibrary.org
Founded 1927. Circ 14,500
Library Holdings: Bks on Deafness & Sign Lang 17; Bk Vols 10,000; Per Subs 25
Subject Interests: Health
Automation Activity & Vendor Info: (Cataloging) Innovative Interfaces, Inc; (Circulation) Innovative Interfaces, Inc; (ILL) Innovative Interfaces, Inc
Wireless access
Mem of Finger Lakes Library System
Open Mon 2-8:30, Tues, Wed & Fri 2-5:30, Thurs 2-8, Sat 10-Noon
Friends of the Library Group

NINEVEH

P NINEVEH PUBLIC LIBRARY OF COLESVILLE TOWNSHIP*, 3029 NY State Hwy 7, 13813. (Mail add: PO Box 124, 13813-0124), SAN 312-1739. Tel: 607-693-1858. FAX: 607-693-1858. E-mail: ni.ill@4cls.org. *Coordr,* Dottie Brodrick; Tel: 413-636-6972
Founded 1901. Pop 5,441
Library Holdings: Bk Titles 11,000
Wireless access
Mem of Four County Library System
Open Mon-Thurs 12:30-7:30, Fri & Sat 9-3

NORFOLK

P HEPBURN LIBRARY OF NORFOLK*, One Hepburn St, 13667. (Mail add: PO Box 530, 13667-0530), SAN 312-1747. Tel: 315-384-3052. FAX: 315-384-3841. E-mail: norfolk@northnet.org. Web Site: hepburnlibraryofnorfolk.org. *Librn,* Vicky Brothers; Staff 1 (MLS 1)
Pop 4,258; Circ 13,023
Library Holdings: Bk Vols 12,000; Per Subs 23
Automation Activity & Vendor Info: (Acquisitions) Mandarin Library Automation; (Cataloging) Mandarin Library Automation; (Circulation) Mandarin Library Automation; (Course Reserve) Mandarin Library Automation; (ILL) Mandarin Library Automation; (Media Booking) Mandarin Library Automation; (OPAC) Mandarin Library Automation; (Serials) Mandarin Library Automation
Wireless access
Mem of North Country Library System
Partic in Northern New York Library Network
Open Mon, Thurs & Fri 10-12 & 2-8, Tues & Wed 10-12 & 2-9
Friends of the Library Group

NORTH BABYLON

P NORTH BABYLON PUBLIC LIBRARY, 815 Deer Park Ave, 11703-3812. SAN 312-1755. Tel: 631-669-4020. FAX: 631-669-3432. TDD: 631-669-4140. E-mail: info@northbabylonpl.org. Web Site: www.northbabylonpl.org. *Libr Dir,* Marc David Horowitz; E-mail: horowm@northbabylonpl.org; *Librn III,* Maureen Nicolazzi; E-mail: mnicolaz@northbabylonpl.org; *Ch Serv,* Elizabeth Arena; E-mail: earena@northbabylonpl.org; *Circ,* Kristen C Lane; *Computer Serv,* James Jenkins; E-mail: jenkinsj@northbabylonpl.org; *Tech Serv,* Kristen Weyer; E-mail: Kweyer@northbabylonpl.org; Staff 20 (MLS 20)
Founded 1960. Pop 30,666; Circ 224,915
Library Holdings: Bk Vols 113,739; Per Subs 205
Special Collections: Newsday, 1944-2007, microfilm
Automation Activity & Vendor Info: (Cataloging) Innovative Interfaces, Inc; (Circulation) Innovative Interfaces, Inc; (ILL) Innovative Interfaces, Inc; (OPAC) Innovative Interfaces, Inc; (Serials) Innovative Interfaces, Inc
Wireless access
Function: 24/7 Electronic res, 24/7 Online cat, 3D Printer, Adult bk club, Adult literacy prog, Art exhibits, Bk reviews (Group), Bks on CD, CD-ROM, Children's prog, Computer training, Computers for patron use, E-Reserves, Electronic databases & coll, Free DVD rentals, Health sci info serv, Holiday prog, Home delivery & serv to seniorr ctr & nursing homes, Homebound delivery serv, Homework prog, ILL available, Instruction & testing, Internet access, Life-long learning prog for all ages, Magazines, Magnifiers for reading, Mail & tel request accepted, Mango lang, Meeting rooms, Microfiche/film & reading machines, Movies, Museum passes, Music CDs, Online cat, Online ref, Orientations, Outreach serv, Photocopying/Printing, Preschool reading prog, Prog for adults, Prog for children & young adult, Ref & res, Ref serv available, Scanner, Senior computer classes, Senior outreach, Serves people with intellectual disabilities, Spoken cassettes & DVDs, Story hour, Summer & winter reading prog, Summer reading prog, Tax forms, Teen prog, Telephone ref, Winter reading prog
Publications: News & Notes (Bimonthly)
Mem of Suffolk Cooperative Library System
Special Services for the Blind - Talking bks plus
Open Mon-Fri 9-9, Sat 9-5, Sun (Oct-May) 1-5

NORTH BELLMORE

P NORTH BELLMORE PUBLIC LIBRARY, 1551 Newbridge Rd, 11710. SAN 312-1763. Tel: 516-785-6260. FAX: 516-785-7204. E-mail: info@northbellmorelibrary.org. Web Site: www.northbellmorelibrary.org. *Libr Dir,* Jessica Tymecki; E-mail: jtymecki@northbellmorelibrary.org; Staff 38 (MLS 13, Non-MLS 25)
Founded 1946. Pop 25,856; Circ 199,042
Library Holdings: AV Mats 6,188; Bk Titles 106,772; Bk Vols 112,744; Per Subs 348
Automation Activity & Vendor Info: (Circulation) Innovative Interfaces, Inc; (OPAC) Innovative Interfaces, Inc
Wireless access
Function: 24/7 Electronic res, 24/7 Online cat, Adult bk club, After school storytime, Art exhibits, Audiobks on Playaways & MP3, Bk club(s), Bks

on cassette, Bks on CD, Chess club, Children's prog, Computer training, Computers for patron use, E-Readers, Electronic databases & coll, For res purposes, Free DVD rentals, Govt ref serv, Health sci info serv, Holiday prog, Homebound delivery serv, ILL available, Internet access, Magazines, Magnifiers for reading, Mail & tel request accepted, Meeting rooms, Movies, Museum passes, Music CDs, Notary serv, Online cat, Online ref, Outreach serv, Outside serv via phone, mail, e-mail & web, OverDrive digital audio bks, Photocopying/Printing, Preschool reading prog, Printer for laptops & handheld devices, Prog for adults, Prog for children & young adult, Ref & res, Ref serv available, Scanner, Senior computer classes, Spoken cassettes & CDs, Spoken cassettes & DVDs, Story hour, Study rm, Summer & winter reading prog, Summer reading prog, Tax forms, Teen prog, Telephone ref, Visual arts prog, Wheelchair accessible, Winter reading prog, Workshops, Writing prog
Publications: Inklings (Monthly Newsletter)
Mem of Nassau Library System
Open Mon, Tues & Thurs 9-8, Wed 10:30-8, Fri 9-6, Sat 9-5, Sun 1-5
Friends of the Library Group

NORTH CHATHAM

P NORTH CHATHAM FREE LIBRARY*, PO Box 907, 12132-0907. SAN 312-1771. Tel: 518-766-3211. FAX: 518-766-3211. E-mail: Mail@NorthChathamLibrary.org. Web Site: northchathamlibrary.org. *Interim Dir,* Vicki Wills
Founded 1915. Pop 997; Circ 24,058
Library Holdings: CDs 1,210; DVDs 1,634; e-books 12,568; e-journals 145; Bk Titles 13,575; Per Subs 23
Subject Interests: Local hist
Wireless access
Function: Bk club(s), Bks on CD, Children's prog, Computer training, Computers for patron use, Free DVD rentals, ILL available, Internet access, Online cat, Online ref, Photocopying/Printing, Prog for adults, Ref serv available, Senior computer classes, Story hour, Summer reading prog, Wheelchair accessible
Mem of Mid-Hudson Library System
Open Mon-Thurs 2-8, Fri 2-6, Sat 10-2

NORTH COLLINS

P TOWN OF NORTH COLLINS PUBLIC LIBRARY*, 2095 School St, 14111. (Mail add: PO Box 730, 14111-0730), SAN 312-178X. Tel: 716-337-3211. FAX: 716-337-0647. E-mail: NCO@buffalolib.org. Web Site: www.buffalolib.org/content/library-locations/northcollins. *Mgr,* Jacob Rachwal
Founded 1878. Circ 18,772
Library Holdings: Bk Vols 8,000; Per Subs 102
Special Collections: Local Historical & Geneological Resources
Wireless access
Mem of Buffalo & Erie County Public Library System
Open Mon 10-8, Tues & Wed 2-8, Fri 10-5, Sun (Winter) 1-4
Friends of the Library Group

NORTH CREEK

P TOWN OF JOHNSBURG LIBRARY, 219 Main St, 12853. (Mail add: PO Box 7, 12853-0007). Tel: 518-251-4343. FAX: 518-251-9991. Web Site: directory.sals.edu/library.php?lib=JBG, townofjohnsburglibrary.sals.edu. *Dir,* Kate Erwin; E-mail: jbg-director@sals.edu
Pop 2,395; Circ 25,604
Library Holdings: AV Mats 1,200; Bk Vols 41,352; Per Subs 35; Talking Bks 400
Automation Activity & Vendor Info: (Cataloging) Innovative Interfaces, Inc. - Polaris; (Circulation) Innovative Interfaces, Inc. - Polaris; (OPAC) Innovative Interfaces, Inc. - Polaris
Wireless access
Mem of Southern Adirondack Library System
Open Wed & Fri 11-5, Thurs 11-7, Sat 10-2 (Sept-June); Mon 9-12, Wed & Fri 11-5, Thurs 11-7, Sat 10-2 (July & Aug)
Friends of the Library Group

NORTH MERRICK

P NORTH MERRICK PUBLIC LIBRARY, 1691 Meadowbrook Rd, 11566. SAN 312-1798. Tel: 516-378-7474. FAX: 516-378-0876. Reference E-mail: reference@nmerricklibrary.org. Web Site: www.nmerricklibrary.org. *Libr Dir,* Susan Santa; Tel: 516-378-7474, Ext 10; *Ref Librn,* Jeff Baker; *YA Librn,* Kelly Rechsteiner; E-mail: kellyr@nmerricklibrary.org; *Ch Serv,* Helen Friedman; *Ch Serv,* Janet Wasserman; *Pub Relations,* Linda Vasconi; Staff 8 (MLS 8)
Founded 1965. Pop 12,498; Circ 124,054
Library Holdings: Audiobooks 1,100; AV Mats 2,547; Bks on Deafness & Sign Lang 20; CDs 1,680; DVDs 2,850; e-books 432; e-journals 3,500; Electronic Media & Resources 98; High Interest/Low Vocabulary Bk Vols 36; Large Print Bks 1,050; Music Scores 200; Bk Vols 84,334; Per Subs 218
Subject Interests: Art, Cookery
Automation Activity & Vendor Info: (Cataloging) Innovative Interfaces, Inc; (Circulation) Innovative Interfaces, Inc; (OPAC) Innovative Interfaces, Inc
Wireless access
Publications: Yesterday in the Merricks (Local historical information)
Mem of Nassau Library System
Open Mon-Thurs 10-9, Fri 10-6, Sat 10-5 (9:30-1 Summer), Sun 1-5
Friends of the Library Group

NORTH SALEM

P RUTH KEELER MEMORIAL LIBRARY*, North Salem Free Library, 276 Titicus Rd, 10560-1708. SAN 353-9016. Tel: 914-669-5161. FAX: 914-669-5173. E-mail: keelerlibrary@wlsmail.org. Web Site: www.ruthkeelermemoriallibrary.org. *Dir,* Carolyn Reznick; Staff 9 (MLS 3, Non-MLS 6)
Founded 1932. Pop 5,104; Circ 62,614
Jan 2018-Dec 2018 Income $464,185, State $1,496, City $334,417, Locally Generated Income $128,272. Mats Exp $486,999, Books $11,654, Per/Ser (Incl. Access Fees) $3,512, AV Mat $2,678. Sal $255,677 (Prof $248,718)
Library Holdings: Audiobooks 970; AV Mats 3,804; DVDs 2,692; e-books 31,161; Bk Titles 34,497; Per Subs 45
Special Collections: Helen Ferris Tibbets Children's Books; Hellen Whitman Herbal Coll; Local History
Automation Activity & Vendor Info: (Circulation) SirsiDynix
Wireless access
Function: 24/7 Electronic res, 24/7 Online cat, Activity rm, Adult bk club, Art exhibits, Audiobks via web, Bk club(s), Bks on CD, Children's prog, Computer training, Computers for patron use, Digital talking bks, E-Reserves, Electronic databases & coll, Free DVD rentals, Health sci info serv, Holiday prog, Home delivery & serv to seniorr ctr & nursing homes, Homebound delivery serv, ILL available, Internet access, Museum passes, Online cat, Online ref, OverDrive digital audio bks, Photocopying/Printing, Preschool reading prog, Prog for adults, Prog for children & young adult, Ref serv available, Scanner, Spanish lang bks, Spoken cassettes & DVDs, Story hour, Summer reading prog, Tax forms, Teen prog, Telephone ref, VHS videos, Wheelchair accessible, Workshops, Writing prog
Publications: Balanced Rock (Annual); Email Newsletter (Monthly)
Mem of Westchester Library System
Special Services for the Blind - Bks on CD; Copier with enlargement capabilities; Free checkout of audio mat; Home delivery serv; Large print bks; Recorded bks
Open Mon & Thurs 10-7, Tues, Wed, Fri & Sat 10-5
Restriction: Lending limited to county residents
Friends of the Library Group

NORTH TONAWANDA

P NORTH TONAWANDA PUBLIC LIBRARY*, 505 Meadow Dr, 14120. SAN 312-1836. Tel: 716-693-4132. FAX: 716-693-0719. Reference E-mail: ntw@nioga.org. Web Site: www.ntlibrary.org. *Libr Dir,* Kevin Wall; E-mail: kwall@nioga.org; *Coordr, Circ,* Kathleen Marfione; E-mail: kmarfione@nioga.org; *Coordr, Tech Serv,* Terri Rowe; E-mail: trowe@nioga.org; *Adult Ref,* Anya Puccio; E-mail: apuccio@nioga.org; *Ch Serv,* Rebecca Stutzman; E-mail: rstutzma@nioga.org; Staff 23 (MLS 9, Non-MLS 14)
Founded 1893. Pop 33,262; Circ 464,000
Library Holdings: AV Mats 31,518; CDs 10,499; DVDs 3,230; Bk Titles 146,904; Bk Vols 163,272; Per Subs 268; Videos 7,056
Special Collections: Carousels Coll
Subject Interests: Antiques, Handicraft, Local hist
Automation Activity & Vendor Info: (Cataloging) SirsiDynix; (Circulation) SirsiDynix; (OPAC) SirsiDynix
Wireless access
Publications: North Tonawanda Public Library Log (Newsletter)
Mem of Nioga Library System
Open Mon-Thurs 9:30-9, Fri & Sat 9:30-5
Friends of the Library Group

NORTHPORT

GM DEPARTMENT OF VETERANS AFFAIRS*, Northport Medical Library, Bldg 12, 1st Flr, 79 Middleville Rd, 11768-2290. SAN 312-1852. Tel: 631-261-4400, Ext 2962. *Chief Librn,* Wendy Isser; Tel: 631-261-4400, Ext 2966, E-mail: wendy.isser@va.gov
Library Holdings: Bk Titles 4,000; Per Subs 250
Subject Interests: Allied health, Geriatrics, Hospital admin, Med, Psychiat, Psychol, Surgery
Automation Activity & Vendor Info: (Cataloging) EOS International; (Circulation) EOS International; (OPAC) EOS International; (Serials) EOS International
Publications: Library Line (Quarterly)
Partic in Medical & Scientific Libraries of Long Island
Restriction: Staff & patient use

P NORTHPORT-EAST NORTHPORT PUBLIC LIBRARY, 151 Laurel Ave, 11768. SAN 353-9075. Tel: 631-261-6930. FAX: 631-261-6718. Administration FAX: 631-754-6613. E-mail: library@nenpl.org. Web Site: www.nenpl.org. *Libr Dir,* James Olney; *Asst Libr Dir,* Nancy Morcerf; *Network & Syst Adminr,* Anthony Martocello; *Head, Adult/Teen Serv,* Michelle Rung; *Head, Children's Servx,* Lisa Herskowitz; *Head, Commun Serv,* Janet Naideau; Staff 34 (MLS 34)
Founded 1914. Pop 36,499; Circ 563,466
Library Holdings: Bk Vols 237,110; Per Subs 820
Special Collections: Jack Kerouac Coll; Kerovac-Off the Shelf (Bibliography); Milton E Brasher Portfolio; Rosemary Wells Coll. Oral History
Subject Interests: Archit, Art, Boating
Automation Activity & Vendor Info: (Acquisitions) Innovative Interfaces, Inc - Millennium; (Cataloging) Innovative Interfaces, Inc - Millennium; (Circulation) Innovative Interfaces, Inc - Millennium; (Course Reserve) Innovative Interfaces, Inc - Millennium; (ILL) Innovative Interfaces, Inc - Millennium; (OPAC) Innovative Interfaces, Inc - Millennium; (Serials) Innovative Interfaces, Inc - Millennium
Wireless access
Publications: Bibliographies; Booklists; Living in Northport & East Northport; Special Loan Service to Our Schools; The Library (Newsletter); Welcome (Brochure)
Mem of Suffolk Cooperative Library System
Special Services for the Deaf - Adult & family literacy prog; Assisted listening device; Assistive tech; Bks on deafness & sign lang; Closed caption videos; High interest/low vocabulary bks
Special Services for the Blind - Assistive/Adapted tech devices, equip & products; Audio mat; BiFolkal kits; Bks on cassette; Bks on CD; Closed circuit TV magnifier; Computer with voice synthesizer for visually impaired persons; Copier with enlargement capabilities; Home delivery serv; Info on spec aids & appliances; Internet workstation with adaptive software; Large print bks; Large screen computer & software; Low vision equip; Magnifiers; Networked computers with assistive software; Playaways (bks on MP3); Recorded bks; Screen enlargement software for people with visual disabilities; Screen reader software; Talking bks; Talking bks & player equip; ZoomText magnification & reading software
Open Mon-Fri 9-9, Sat 9-5
Friends of the Library Group
Branches: 1
EAST NORTHPORT PUBLIC, 185 Larkfield Rd, East Northport, 11731, SAN 353-9105. Tel: 631-261-2313. FAX: 631-261-1295. E-mail: netwalk@suffolk.lib.ny.us. *Br Librn,* Candace Reeder
Open Mon-Fri 9-9, Sat 9-5
Friends of the Library Group

S NORTHPORT HISTORICAL SOCIETY, 215 Main St, 11768. (Mail add: PO Box 545, 11768-0545), SAN 372-5677. Tel: 631-757-9859. FAX: 631-757-9398. E-mail: info@northporthistorical.org. Web Site: www.northporthistorical.org. *Colls Mgr, Dep Dir,* Teresa Reid; E-mail: curator@northporthistorical.org; Staff 1 (MLS 1)
Founded 1962
Library Holdings: Bk Titles 350
Special Collections: Northport Area History Coll, doc, photog
Open Tues-Sun 1-4:30

NORTHVILLE

P NORTHVILLE PUBLIC LIBRARY*, 341 S Third St, 12134-4231. (Mail add: PO Box 1259, 12134-1259), SAN 376-3099. Tel: 518-863-6922. FAX: 518-863-6922. E-mail: norlib@mvls.info. Web Site: northvillepubliclibrary.weebly.com. *Libr Dir,* Michael S Burnett; E-mail: mburnett@mvls.info
Founded 1986. Pop 3,047; Circ 39,130
Library Holdings: Bk Vols 16,813; Per Subs 60
Automation Activity & Vendor Info: (Acquisitions) Innovative Interfaces, Inc; (Cataloging) Innovative Interfaces, Inc; (Circulation) Innovative Interfaces, Inc; (OPAC) Innovative Interfaces, Inc; (Serials) Innovative Interfaces, Inc
Wireless access
Mem of Mohawk Valley Library System
Open Mon & Sat 9-12, Tues 9-8, Wed & Thurs 9-4, Fri 9-Noon (9-4 April-Aug)
Friends of the Library Group

NORWICH

M CHENANGO MEMORIAL HOSPITAL*, Medical Library, 179 N Broad St, 13815. SAN 312-1860. Tel: 607-337-4111. FAX: 607-337-4286. Web Site: www.nyuhs.org. *Med Librn,* Wendy Surdoval; E-mail: wendy_surdoval@uhs.org
Founded 1972
Library Holdings: Bk Vols 2,000; Per Subs 230
Subject Interests: Clinical med, Geriatric nursing, Nursing
Partic in National Network of Libraries of Medicine Region 7; OCLC Online Computer Library Center, Inc; South Central Regional Library Council
Open Mon-Fri 8:30-4

P GUERNSEY MEMORIAL LIBRARY*, Three Court St, 13815. SAN 312-1879. Tel: 607-334-4034. FAX: 607-336-3901. E-mail: guernsey@4cls.org. Web Site: guernseymemoriallibrary.org. *Dir,* Connie Dalrymple; E-mail: no.connie@4cls.org; *Ch,* Kim Hazen; E-mail: no.kim@4cls.org; Staff 18 (MLS 2, Non-MLS 16)
Founded 1902. Pop 13,600; Circ 133,000
Library Holdings: AV Mats 3,038; Bk Vols 79,116; Per Subs 109
Subject Interests: Genealogy, Health, Job info, Local hist
Automation Activity & Vendor Info: (Acquisitions) SirsiDynix; (Cataloging) SirsiDynix; (Circulation) SirsiDynix; (ILL) SirsiDynix; (OPAC) SirsiDynix
Wireless access
Publications: Glance at Guernsey (Newsletter)
Mem of Four County Library System
Open Mon-Thurs 9-8:30, Fri 9-6, Sat 9-4, Sun 10-4

GL NEW YORK STATE SUPREME COURT SIXTH DISTRICT LAW LIBRARY*, David L Follett Memorial Library, 13 Eaton Ave, 13815. SAN 312-1887. Tel: 607-334-9463. Web Site: www.nycourts.gov/LIBRARY/6JD/chenango/index.shtml. *Librn,* Laurie Burpoe; E-mail: lburpoe@nycourts.gov
Founded 1902
Library Holdings: Bk Vols 10,000
Automation Activity & Vendor Info: (Cataloging) SirsiDynix
Wireless access
Partic in South Central Regional Library Council
Open Mon-Fri 8:30-4:30

NORWOOD

P NORWOOD PUBLIC LIBRARY*, One Morton St, 13668-1100. SAN 312-1909. Tel: 315-353-6692. FAX: 315-353-4688. E-mail: nowlib@ncls.org. Web Site: www.norwoodnylibrary.org. *Dir,* Amanda Jones
Founded 1912. Circ 21,120
Library Holdings: AV Mats 1,205; Large Print Bks 750; Bk Vols 17,884; Per Subs 60; Talking Bks 230
Automation Activity & Vendor Info: (Cataloging) SirsiDynix; (Circulation) SirsiDynix
Wireless access
Mem of North Country Library System
Open Tues 2-8, Wed 10-4, Thurs 4-8, Fri & Sat 12-4
Friends of the Library Group

NUNDA

P BELL MEMORIAL LIBRARY, 16 East St, 14517. (Mail add: PO Box 725, 14517-0725), SAN 312-1917. Tel: 585-468-2266. Web Site: bellmemoriallibrary.org. *Libr Mgr,* Patricia Galbraith; E-mail: NundaLibraryDirector@owwl.org; Staff 3 (Non-MLS 3)
Founded 1912. Pop 5,119; Circ 22,872
Library Holdings: AV Mats 416; CDs 240; Bk Vols 15,748; Per Subs 33; Videos 885
Automation Activity & Vendor Info: (Cataloging) SirsiDynix; (Circulation) SirsiDynix; (OPAC) SirsiDynix; (Serials) SirsiDynix
Wireless access
Mem of Pioneer Library System
Open Tues-Thurs 12-8, Fri 9-5, Sat 10-1

NYACK

P THE NYACK LIBRARY*, 59 S Broadway, 10960. SAN 312-1933. Tel: 845-358-3370. Circulation Tel: 845-358-3370, Ext 211, 845-358-3370, Ext 216. Reference Tel: 845-358-3370, Ext 214. FAX: 845-358-6429. E-mail: info@nyacklibrary.org. Web Site: www.nyacklibrary.org. *Dir,* Angela Z Strong; Tel: 845-358-3370, Ext 221, E-mail: astrong@nyacklibrary.org; *Head, Circ,* Donna Lightfoot Cooper; Tel: 845-358-3370, Ext 212, E-mail: dcooper@nyacklibrary.org; *Head, Ref Serv,* Tracy Dunstan; Tel: 845-358-3370, Ext 213, E-mail: tdunstan@nyacklibrary.org; *Head, Youth Serv,* Aldona Pilmanis; Tel: 845-358-3370, Ext 231, E-mail: apilmanis@nyacklibrary.org; *Teen Librn,* Kim Naples; Tel: 845-358-3370, Ext 238, E-mail: knaples@nyacklibrary.org; *Bus Mgr,* Sharon Alfano; Tel: 845-358-3370, Ext 233, E-mail: salfano@nyacklibrary.org; Staff 28.5 (MLS 8, Non-MLS 20.5)
Founded 1879. Pop 14,699; Circ 203,876
Jul 2012-Jun 2013 Income $2,736,834, State $19,231, County $3,301, Locally Generated Income $2,714,302. Mats Exp $198,396, Books $104,230, Per/Ser (Incl. Access Fees) $10,000, AV Mat $37,328, Electronic Ref Mat (Incl. Access Fees) $46,838. Sal $1,643,636

Library Holdings: AV Mats 17,861; e-books 4,423; Microforms 1,555; Bk Vols 104,664; Per Subs 209
Special Collections: Local History Coll
Automation Activity & Vendor Info: (Acquisitions) SirsiDynix; (Cataloging) SirsiDynix; (Circulation) SirsiDynix; (OPAC) SirsiDynix
Wireless access
Mem of Ramapo Catskill Library System
Open Mon 11-9, Tues-Thurs 10-9, Fri 10-6, Sat 10-5, Sun 12-5
Friends of the Library Group

OAKFIELD

P HAXTON MEMORIAL LIBRARY, Three N Pearl St, 14125. SAN 312-1976. Tel: 585-948-9900. E-mail: haxmemlib@gmail.com. Web Site: www.haxtonlibrary.org. *Libr Dir,* Kimberly Gibson; E-mail: kgibs@nioga.org
Founded 1963. Pop 3,213; Circ 5,900
Library Holdings: Bk Vols 47,000; Per Subs 60
Wireless access
Mem of Nioga Library System
Open Mon & Wed 9-3, Tues 1-5, Thurs 1-5 & 6:30-8:30, Fri 2-5
Friends of the Library Group

OCEANSIDE

M MOUNT SINAI SOUTH NASSAU, Harbhajan Singh Memorial Medical Library, One Healthy Way, 11572. SAN 312-1992. Tel: 516-632-3452. *Dir,* Claire Joseph; E-mail: claire.joseph@snch.org; Staff 1 (MLS 1)
Founded 1958
Library Holdings: Bk Titles 1,100; Per Subs 120
Subject Interests: Med, Nursing, Surgery
Partic in Long Island Library Resources Council
Restriction: Staff use only

P OCEANSIDE LIBRARY, 30 Davison Ave, 11572-2299. SAN 312-1984. Tel: 516-766-2360. FAX: 516-766-1895. E-mail: ocl@oceansidelibrary.com. Web Site: www.oceansidelibrary.com. *Dir,* Ms Christina Marra; Tel: 516-766-2360, Ext 308, E-mail: cmarra@oceansidelibrary.com; *Asst Dir,* Anthony Iovino; Tel: 516-766-2360, Ext 340, E-mail: aiovino@oceansidelibrary.com
Founded 1938. Pop 36,847; Circ 247,812
Jul 2020-Jun 2021. Mats Exp $293,266, Books $153,655, Per/Ser (Incl. Access Fees) $20,000, AV Mat $65,611, Electronic Ref Mat (Incl. Access Fees) $54,000. Sal $2,383,855 (Prof $1,272,931)
Library Holdings: Audiobooks 1,500; AV Mats 26,050; CDs 10,729; DVDs 13,548; e-books 116,743; Bk Vols 125,066; Per Subs 130
Automation Activity & Vendor Info: (Cataloging) Innovative Interfaces, Inc - Sierra; (Circulation) Innovative Interfaces, Inc - Sierra; (ILL) Innovative Interfaces, Inc - Sierra; (OPAC) Innovative Interfaces, Inc; (Serials) EBSCO Online
Wireless access
Function: 24/7 Electronic res, 24/7 Online cat, Adult bk club, Adult literacy prog, Art exhibits, Art programs, Audiobks via web, Bk club(s), Bks on CD, Children's prog, Computer training, Computers for patron use, E-Readers, E-Reserves, Electronic databases & coll, Family literacy, Free DVD rentals, Games & aids for people with disabilities, Genealogy discussion group, Holiday prog, Homework prog, ILL available, Internet access, Large print keyboards, Life-long learning prog for all ages, Literacy & newcomer serv, Magazines, Magnifiers for reading, Meeting rooms, Movies, Museum passes, Music CDs, Online cat, Online ref, Outside serv via phone, mail, e-mail & web, OverDrive digital audio bks, Photocopying/Printing, Preschool reading prog, Prog for adults, Prog for children & young adult, Ref & res, Ref serv available, Res assist avail, Senior computer classes, Serves people with intellectual disabilities, Spanish lang bks, Story hour, Study rm, Summer & winter reading prog, Summer reading prog, Tax forms, Teen prog, Telephone ref, Visual arts prog, Wheelchair accessible, Winter reading prog, Workshops, Writing prog
Publications: Oceanside Library (Newsletter)
Mem of Nassau Library System
Partic in Long Island Library Resources Council
Special Services for the Deaf - Assistive tech
Special Services for the Blind - Magnifiers; Talking bks; ZoomText magnification & reading software
Open Mon-Fri 9:30-9, Sat 9:30-5, Sun (Sept-June) 12-5
Friends of the Library Group

ODESSA

P DUTTON S PETERSON MEMORIAL LIBRARY, 106 First St, 14869. (Mail add: PO Box 46, 14869-0046), SAN 376-3064. Tel: 607-594-2791. FAX: 607-594-2035. E-mail: petersonlibrary@stls.org. Web Site: duttonpetersonlibrary.org. *Dir,* Karin Thomas; E-mail: thomask2@stls.org
Founded 1986
Library Holdings: AV Mats 950; Bk Titles 9,000; Per Subs 12
Automation Activity & Vendor Info: (Cataloging) SirsiDynix; (Circulation) SirsiDynix; (OPAC) SirsiDynix
Wireless access
Mem of Southern Tier Library System
Open Mon & Wed-Fri 10-6, Tues 2-6
Friends of the Library Group

OGDENSBURG

M CLAXTON-HEPBURN MEDICAL CENTER LIBRARY*, 214 King St, 13669. SAN 312-2018. Tel: 315-393-3600, Ext 5378. FAX: 315-393-8506. Web Site: www.claxtonhepburn.org. *Circuit Librn,* Ellen Darabaner; E-mail: edarabaner@shsny.com
Founded 1958
Library Holdings: Bk Vols 300; Per Subs 10
Partic in Northern New York Library Network
Restriction: Med staff only

S NEW YORK STATE DEPARTMENT OF CORRECTIONAL SERVICES, Ogdensburg Correctional Facility General Library, One Correction Way, 13669-2288. SAN 327-1870. Tel: 315-393-0281, Ext 4600. Web Site: doccs.ny.gov/location/ogdensburg-correctional-facility. *Sr Librn,* Joanne Lafontaine; E-mail: joanne.lafontaine@doccs.ny.gov; Staff 1 (MLS 1)
Founded 1982
Apr 2021-Mar 2022 Income $74,840, State $3,000, Parent Institution $71,840. Mats Exp $5,000. Sal $71,400
Library Holdings: AV Mats 2,500; High Interest/Low Vocabulary Bk Vols 348; Large Print Bks 65; Bk Titles 19,000; Per Subs 13; Talking Bks 1,556
Special Collections: Black Culture History & Spanish Language Coll
Automation Activity & Vendor Info: (Acquisitions) Follett Software; (Cataloging) Follett Software; (Circulation) Follett Software; (OPAC) Follett Software
Mem of North Country Library System
Restriction: Inmate patrons, facility staff & vols direct access. All others through ILL only, Not open to pub

P OGDENSBURG PUBLIC LIBRARY*, 312 Washington St, 13669-1518. SAN 312-2034. Tel: 315-393-4325. FAX: 315-393-4344. E-mail: ogdlib@ncls.org. Web Site: www.ogdensburgpubliclibrary.org, www.ogdlib.org. *Dir,* Penny Kerfien; E-mail: pkerfien@ncls.org; *Adult Serv,* Stephanie Young; E-mail: syoung@ncls.org; *Ch Serv,* Dorian Lenney-Wallace; E-mail: dlenney-wallace@ncls.org; Staff 11 (MLS 3, Non-MLS 8)
Founded 1893. Pop 12,364; Circ 66,407
Jan 2017-Dec 2017 Income $654,129, City $551,222, Locally Generated Income $34,416, Other $68,491. Mats Exp $24,100, Books $6,000, Per/Ser (Incl. Access Fees) $5,800, AV Mat $5,000, Electronic Ref Mat (Incl. Access Fees) $7,300. Sal $288,588 (Prof $125,821)
Library Holdings: Audiobooks 1,281; AV Mats 7,999; e-books 5,927; Bk Vols 67,372; Per Subs 95; Videos 5,474
Special Collections: General Newton Martin Curtis Civil War Coll; Ogdensburg History (Ogdensburg Archives), bks, flm, ms. Municipal Document Depository; Oral History
Subject Interests: Local hist
Automation Activity & Vendor Info: (Circulation) SirsiDynix; (OPAC) SirsiDynix
Wireless access
Function: Archival coll, Art exhibits, Bks on cassette, Bks on CD, Children's prog, Computer training, Computers for patron use, Electronic databases & coll, Free DVD rentals, Home delivery & serv to seniorr ctr & nursing homes, ILL available, Internet access, Mail & tel request accepted, Music CDs, Online cat, Online ref, Photocopying/Printing, Prog for adults, Prog for children & young adult, Ref serv available, Scanner, Senior computer classes, Serves people with intellectual disabilities, Story hour, Summer reading prog, Tax forms, Teen prog, Wheelchair accessible
Publications: Between a Book & a Tech Place (Newsletter)
Mem of North Country Library System
Open Mon, Tues & Thurs 9-8, Fri 9-5, Sat 9-3
Friends of the Library Group

OLD CHATHAM

SR SHAKER MUSEUM & LIBRARY*, Emma B King Library, 88 Shaker Museum Rd, 12136. SAN 312-2069. Tel: 518-794-9100, Ext 211. FAX: 518-794-8621. E-mail: contact@shakerml.org. Web Site: www.shakermuseum.us/administrative-campus-research-library. *Dir, Res Serv,* Jerry Grant; Staff 2 (MLS 1, Non-MLS 1)
Founded 1950
Library Holdings: Bk Titles 2,500
Special Collections: Paper Artifacts, drawings, broadsides, advertising labels, product packages, watercolors; Photograph Coll; Society of Shakers: Their Arts, Crafts, Theology, Philosophy, includes membership rolls, patents, deeds, diaries, account books
Subject Interests: Archit, Art, Furniture, Relig, Shakers, Women

Publications: Making His Mark: The World of Shaker Craftsman Orren Haskins; Noble But Plain: The Shaker Meetinghouse at Mount Lebanon; Shaker Adventure; Shaker Museum & Library Broadside (to members); Shakerism & Feminism: Reflections on Women's Religion & the Early Shakers; The Shaker Museum Guide to Shaker Collections & Libraries
Restriction: Open by appt only

OLD FORGE

P OLD FORGE LIBRARY, 220 Crosby Blvd, 13420. (Mail add: PO Box 128, 13420-0128), SAN 312-2077. Tel: 315-369-6008. FAX: 315-369-2754. E-mail: oldforge@midyork.org. Web Site: www.oldforgelibrary.org. *Libr Dir,* Linda Weal; E-mail: lweal@midyork.org; Staff 5 (Non-MLS 5)
Founded 1914. Pop 1,800; Circ 14,179
Library Holdings: Bk Titles 15,830; Per Subs 8
Subject Interests: Adirondack hist
Wireless access
Function: 24/7 Online cat, Adult bk club, Art exhibits, Art programs, Bk club(s), Bks on CD, CD-ROM, Children's prog, Computers for patron use, E-Readers, Electronic databases & coll, Free DVD rentals, Home delivery & serv to seniorr ctr & nursing homes, ILL available, Internet access, Magazines, Museum passes, Online cat, OverDrive digital audio bks, Printer for laptops & handheld devices, Prog for adults, Prog for children & young adult, Story hour, Study rm, Visual arts prog, Wheelchair accessible, Workshops, Writing prog
Mem of Mid-York Library System
Open Mon & Sat 10-2, Tues-Thurs 10-7, Fri 10-4
Friends of the Library Group

OLD WESTBURY

M NEW YORK INSTITUTE OF TECHNOLOGY*, New York College of Osteopathic Medicine Medical Library, Northern Blvd, 11568-8000. SAN 326-1697. Tel: 516-686-3743. FAX: 516-686-3709. Web Site: nyit.edu/library/medicine. *Chief Librn,* Jeanne Strausman; Tel: 516-686-3779, E-mail: jstrausm@nyit.edu; *Med Librn,* Mahnaz Tehrani; E-mail: mtehrani@nyit.edu; Staff 6 (MLS 3, Non-MLS 3)
Founded 1978
Library Holdings: Bk Vols 10,000; Per Subs 415
Automation Activity & Vendor Info: (Cataloging) SirsiDynix; (Circulation) SirsiDynix; (OPAC) SirsiDynix; (Serials) SirsiDynix
Wireless access
Partic in Medical & Scientific Libraries of Long Island
Open Mon-Fri 8am-9pm, Sat 9am-Midnight, Sun 1pm-Midnight
Restriction: Open to students, fac & staff

C NEW YORK INSTITUTE OF TECHNOLOGY, Research Library at Salten Hall, Northern Blvd, 11568. (Mail add: PO Box 8000, 11568-8000), SAN 329-1774. Tel: 516-686-3790. Reference Tel: 516-686-7657. FAX: 516-686-1320. Web Site: www.nyit.edu/library/salten. *Dir, Pub & Tech Serv,* Rosemary Burgos-Mira; E-mail: rburgosm@nyit.edu; Staff 11 (MLS 11)
Founded 1955. Enrl 6,017; Fac 344; Highest Degree: Doctorate
Library Holdings: Bk Vols 60,305; Per Subs 477
Special Collections: Center for Prejudice Reduction
Subject Interests: Archit, Computer sci, Culinary arts, Educ, Engr
Automation Activity & Vendor Info: (Cataloging) SirsiDynix
Wireless access
Publications: Newsletter
Partic in OCLC Online Computer Library Center, Inc; Westchester Academic Library Directors Organization
Open Mon-Thurs 8-8, Fri 8-5

Departmental Libraries:

ART & ARCHITECTURE LIBRARY, EDUCATION HALL, PO Box 8000, 11568-8000. Tel: 516-686-7422, 516-686-7579. FAX: 516-686-7814. Web Site: www.nyit.edu/library/education_hall. *Librn II,* Vanessa Viola; Tel: 516-686-1269, E-mail: vviola@nyit.edu
Library Holdings: Bk Vols 26,500; Per Subs 215; Spec Interest Per Sub 217
Automation Activity & Vendor Info: (Acquisitions) SirsiDynix
Open Mon-Fri 9-5

C STATE UNIVERSITY OF NEW YORK*, College at Old Westbury Library, 223 Store Hill Rd, 11568. (Mail add: PO Box 229, 11568-0229), SAN 312-2093. Tel: 516-876-3156. Interlibrary Loan Service Tel: 516-876-3152. Web Site: libguides.oldwestbury.edu. *Libr Dir,* Antonia DiGregorio; E-mail: digregorioa@oldwestbury.edu; *Res Sharing Librn,* Chante Hope; Tel: 516-876-2895, E-mail: hopec@oldwestbury.edu; *Syst Librn,* Werner Sbaschnik; Tel: 516-876-3154, E-mail: sbaschnikw@oldwestbury.edu; *Sr Asst Librn, Ref,* Joanne Spadaro; Tel: 516-876-2896, E-mail: spadaroj@oldwestbury.edu. Subject Specialists: *Educ,* Joanne Spadaro; Staff 7 (MLS 7)
Founded 1967. Enrl 4,200; Highest Degree: Master
Special Collections: Slavery Source Material Coll, micro; Underground Press Coll, micro; Women's Studies Coll
Subject Interests: Behav sci, Bus, Educ, Ethnic studies, Feminism, Soc sci
Wireless access
Function: AV serv, Computers for patron use, Electronic databases & coll, ILL available, Internet access, Online cat, Online ref, Orientations, Photocopying/Printing
Publications: Focus Bibliographies; Library Information (Pamphlets); Research Guides; Subject List of Periodicals
Partic in OCLC Online Computer Library Center, Inc; SUNYConnect
Open Mon-Fri 8-5
Restriction: Pub use on premises

OLEAN

P OLEAN PUBLIC LIBRARY, 134 N Second St, 14760. SAN 312-2115. Tel: 716-372-0200. FAX: 716-372-8651. E-mail: info@oleanlibrary.org. Web Site: www.oleanlibrary.org. *Dir,* Michelle LaVoie; E-mail: director@oleanlibrary.org; *Asst Dir, Head, Ref,* Kim Mahar; *Head, Circ, Outreach Serv,* Sheryl Soborowski; Staff 5 (MLS 5)
Founded 1871. Pop 16,818; Circ 149,872
Library Holdings: AV Mats 3,559; Bk Titles 107,118; Per Subs 293
Subject Interests: Agr, Archit, Art, Educ
Automation Activity & Vendor Info: (Circulation) SirsiDynix; (OPAC) SirsiDynix
Wireless access
Mem of Chautauqua-Cattaraugus Library System
Open Mon-Thurs 9-7, Fri 9-6, Sat 10-2
Friends of the Library Group

ONEIDA

S MADISON COUNTY HISTORICAL SOCIETY LIBRARY*, 435 Main St, 13421. SAN 325-0741. Tel: 315-363-4136. E-mail: history@mchs1900.org. Web Site: www.mchs1900.org. *Exec Dir,* Sydney Loftus; E-mail: sydney@mchs1900.org; Staff 2 (Non-MLS 2)
Founded 1900
Library Holdings: Bk Vols 2,000
Special Collections: Gerrit Smith Coll; Marshall Hope Coll
Subject Interests: City of Oneida, Genealogy, Hist, Madison County, NY
Wireless access
Function: Archival coll
Restriction: Open to pub by appt only

P ONEIDA PUBLIC LIBRARY*, 220 Broad St, 13421. SAN 312-2123. Tel: 315-363-3050. FAX: 315-363-4217. E-mail: oneida@midyork.org. Web Site: www.midyorklib.org/oneida. *Dir,* Michele Ryan
Founded 1924. Pop 15,300; Circ 94,738
Library Holdings: Bk Vols 58,000; Per Subs 110
Special Collections: Local History & Genealogy, bks, clippings, Cemetery rec; Madison County History; Oneida Community, bks, newsp; Oneida Indian Nation History
Wireless access
Publications: Life at Oneida Library (Quarterly)
Mem of Mid-York Library System
Partic in OCLC Online Computer Library Center, Inc
Open Mon-Thurs 9-8, Fri 9-5, Sat 10-4
Friends of the Library Group

ONEONTA

C HARTWICK COLLEGE*, Stevens-German Library, One Hartwick Dr, 13820. SAN 312-214X. Tel: 607-431-4441. FAX: 607-431-4457. Reference E-mail: reference@hartwick.edu. Web Site: hartwick.edu/academics/stevens-german-library. *Interim Dir,* David Heyduk; Tel: 607-431-4459, E-mail: heydukd0@hartwick.edu; *Librn,* Mike Friery; Tel: 607-431-4440, E-mail: frieryj@hartwick.edu; *Circ Mgr,* Amy Blechman; Tel: 607-431-4455, E-mail: blechmana@hartwick.edu; *Col Archivist,* Shelly Wallace; Tel: 607-431-4450, E-mail: wallaces@hartwick.edu; *ILL Spec,* Dawn Baker; Tel: 607-431-4454, E-mail: bakerd0@hartwick.edu; Staff 10 (MLS 7, Non-MLS 3)
Founded 1928. Enrl 1,450; Fac 113; Highest Degree: Bachelor
Library Holdings: Bk Vols 315,227; Per Subs 2,300
Special Collections: Judge William Cooper Papers, ms; North American Indians (Yager Coll), bk, micro
Subject Interests: Native North American Indians
Automation Activity & Vendor Info: (Acquisitions) Innovative Interfaces, Inc; (Cataloging) Innovative Interfaces, Inc; (Circulation) Innovative Interfaces, Inc; (Course Reserve) Docutek; (ILL) OCLC ILLiad; (Media Booking) Innovative Interfaces, Inc; (OPAC) Innovative Interfaces, Inc
Wireless access
Function: AV serv, E-Reserves, Electronic databases & coll, ILL available, Photocopying/Printing, Ref serv available, Wheelchair accessible, Workshops
Publications: Stevens-German Library (Newsletter)

Partic in OCLC Online Computer Library Center, Inc; South Central Regional Library Council
Open Mon & Tues 8am-1am, Wed & Thurs 8am-11-pm, Fri 8-6, Sat 12-5, Sun Noon-1am

P HUNTINGTON MEMORIAL LIBRARY*, 62 Chestnut St, 13820-2498. SAN 312-2158. Tel: 607-432-1980. FAX: 607-432-5623. E-mail: huntingtonmemoriallibrary@gmail.com. Web Site: hmloneonta.org. *Dir,* Tina Winstead; *Ad,* Sarah Livingston; *Children's Coordr,* Anne Van Deusen; Staff 3 (MLS 2, Non-MLS 1)
Founded 1893. Pop 25,000; Circ 177,541
Library Holdings: AV Mats 2,795; DVDs 1,067; Large Print Bks 3,000; Bk Vols 79,000; Per Subs 115
Special Collections: DAR Lineage Coll; Railroads (Beach Coll), pictures
Automation Activity & Vendor Info: (Acquisitions) SirsiDynix; (Circulation) SirsiDynix; (ILL) SirsiDynix; (OPAC) SirsiDynix
Wireless access
Mem of Four County Library System
Open Mon-Thurs 9-8, Fri 9-5:30, Sat 9-4
Friends of the Library Group

C SUNY ONEONTA, James M Milne Library, 108 Ravine Pkwy, 13820. SAN 312-2166. Tel: 607-436-3702. Circulation Tel: 607-436-2796. Interlibrary Loan Service Tel: 607-436-2726. Reference Tel: 607-436-2722. FAX: 607-436-3081. E-mail: libref@oneonta.edu. Web Site: suny.oneonta.edu/milne-library. *Libr Dir,* Darren Chase; E-mail: darren.chase@oneonta.edu; *Head, Bibliog & Digital Serv,* Michelle Hendley; Tel: 607-436-3341, E-mail: michelle.hendley@oneonta.edu; *Head, Access Serv,* Brendan Aucoin; Tel: 607-436-4141, E-mail: brendan.aucoin@oneonta.edu; *Head, Ref & Instruction,* Mary Lynn Bensen; Tel: 607-436-2729, E-mail: maryl.bensen@oneonta.edu; *Circ,* Cat Wise; Tel: 607-436-2725, E-mail: cathy.wise@oneonta.edu; Staff 24 (MLS 10, Non-MLS 14)
Founded 1889. Enrl 5,458; Fac 468; Highest Degree: Master
Jul 2020-Jun 2021 Income $2,056,097, State $1,886,907, Other $169,190. Mats Exp $698,743, Books $19,616, Per/Ser (Incl. Access Fees) $250,560, AV Mat $12,159, Electronic Ref Mat (Incl. Access Fees) $416,408
Library Holdings: Audiobooks 149; AV Mats 126,886; Bks on Deafness & Sign Lang 64; CDs 2,180; DVDs 2,437; e-books 471,361; e-journals 104,008; Electronic Media & Resources 1,921; High Interest/Low Vocabulary Bk Vols 17; Large Print Bks 71; Music Scores 5,364; Bk Titles 361,175; Bk Vols 399,552; Per Subs 2,784; Videos 122,202
Special Collections: 19th & Early 20th Century Popular Fiction; Early Textbooks & Early Educational Theory; Faculty Publications Coll; James Fenimore Cooper Coll; John Burroughs & Nature Writing (Cornell-Gladstone-Hanlon-Kaufmann Coll); Lantern Slide Coll; Martha Chambers Memorial Coll; Masters Theses; New York State History Coll; New York State Verse Coll; O'Mara Native American Coll; Private Press Publications; SCC Miscellanies; SUNY Oneonta Archives. State Document Depository; US Document Depository
Subject Interests: Educ, Local hist
Automation Activity & Vendor Info: (Acquisitions) Ex Libris Group; (Cataloging) Ex Libris Group; (Circulation) Ex Libris Group; (ILL) OCLC ILLiad; (OPAC) Ex Libris Group; (Serials) Ex Libris Group
Wireless access
Publications: Milne Library Blog (Current awareness service)
Partic in South Central Regional Library Council; SUNYConnect; Westchester Academic Library Directors Organization
Special Services for the Deaf - Bks on deafness & sign lang
Special Services for the Blind - Scanner for conversion & translation of mats; Screen reader software

ONTARIO

P ONTARIO PUBLIC LIBRARY*, 1850 Ridge Rd, 14519. SAN 312-2174. Tel: 315-524-8381. FAX: 315-524-5838. Web Site: www.ontariopubliclibrary.org. *Dir,* Sandra Hylen; E-mail: OntarioLibraryDirector@owwl.org; Staff 7 (MLS 2, Non-MLS 5)
Founded 1914
Jan 2019-Dec 2019 Income $544,357, State $2,972, City $510,100, Locally Generated Income $19,354, Parent Institution $1,931, Other $10,000
Library Holdings: Audiobooks 1,551; Bks on Deafness & Sign Lang 10; CDs 305; DVDs 3,404; e-books 734; e-journals 25; Large Print Bks 1,179; Bk Vols 25,712; Per Subs 34
Special Collections: Cake Pans
Subject Interests: Local hist
Automation Activity & Vendor Info: (Cataloging) Evergreen; (Circulation) Evergreen; (OPAC) Evergreen
Wireless access
Function: 24/7 Electronic res, 24/7 Online cat, Accelerated reader prog, Adult bk club, Art exhibits, Bk club(s), Bk reviews (Group), Bks on cassette, Bks on CD, Children's prog, Computer training, Computers for patron use, Electronic databases & coll, Free DVD rentals, Genealogy discussion group, Holiday prog, Home delivery & serv to seniorr ctr & nursing homes, Homebound delivery serv, ILL available, Instruction & testing, Jazz prog, Magnifiers for reading, Mail & tel request accepted, Music CDs, Online cat, Online ref, Outreach serv, Outside serv via phone, mail, e-mail & web, OverDrive digital audio bks, Photocopying/Printing, Preschool outreach, Prog for adults, Prog for children & young adult, Ref serv available, Senior computer classes, Story hour, Tax forms, Teen prog, Telephone ref, VHS videos, Wheelchair accessible, Workshops
Mem of Pioneer Library System
Partic in Rochester Regional Library Council
Special Services for the Deaf - Bks on deafness & sign lang
Open Mon-Wed 10-8, Thurs & Fri 10-6
Friends of the Library Group

ORANGEBURG

GM NATHAN S KLINE INSTITUTE FOR PSYCHIATRIC RESEARCH, Health Sciences Library, 140 Old Orangeburg Rd, Bldg 35, 10962. SAN 312-2204. FAX: 845-398-5551. Web Site: nki.hospitalservices.senylrc.org. *Dir,* Stuart Moss; E-mail: moss@nki.rfmh.org; Staff 1 (MLS 1)
Founded 1952
Library Holdings: Bk Titles 10,000; Bk Vols 25,000
Special Collections: Family Resource Center
Subject Interests: Biochem, Mental health, Neuroscience, Psychiat, Psychol, Psychopharmacology
Wireless access
Function: Archival coll, For res purposes, Photocopying/Printing
Partic in National Network of Libraries of Medicine Region 7; OCLC Online Computer Library Center, Inc; Southeastern New York Library Resources Council
Restriction: In-house use for visitors, Pub use on premises

P ORANGEBURG LIBRARY*, 20 S Greenbush Rd, 10962-1311. SAN 312-2190. Tel: 845-359-2244. FAX: 845-359-8692. E-mail: org@rcls.org. Web Site: www.orangeburg-library.org. *Dir,* Michelle Galle-Looram; E-mail: mgalle-looram@rcls.org; Staff 4 (MLS 3, Non-MLS 1)
Founded 1962. Pop 3,388; Circ 111,657. Sal $336,000 (Prof $160,000)
Library Holdings: Audiobooks 2,870; Bks on Deafness & Sign Lang 25; CDs 1,000; DVDs 2,870; e-books 1,350; Electronic Media & Resources 49,896; High Interest/Low Vocabulary Bk Vols 15; Large Print Bks 250; Bk Vols 36,319; Per Subs 100; Talking Bks 1,139; Videos 200
Subject Interests: Mystery
Automation Activity & Vendor Info: (Cataloging) SirsiDynix-WorkFlows; (Circulation) SirsiDynix-WorkFlows; (OPAC) SirsiDynix; (Serials) SirsiDynix
Wireless access
Function: Adult bk club, After school storytime, Art exhibits, CD-ROM, E-Reserves, Electronic databases & coll, Homebound delivery serv, ILL available, Internet access, Magnifiers for reading, Mail & tel request accepted, Music CDs, Photocopying/Printing, Prog for adults, Prog for children & young adult, Ref serv available, Summer reading prog, Tax forms, Telephone ref, VHS videos, Wheelchair accessible, Workshops
Publications: Newsletter (Quarterly)
Mem of Ramapo Catskill Library System
Partic in Southeastern New York Library Resources Council
Special Services for the Deaf - Closed caption videos
Special Services for the Blind - Large print bks
Open Mon-Thurs 10-8, Fri 12-5, Sat 10-3, Sun (Winter) 1-5

ORCHARD PARK

J ERIE COMMUNITY COLLEGE-SOUTH CAMPUS*, Library Resource Center, 4041 Southwestern Blvd, 14127. SAN 353-913X. Tel: 716-851-1772. Interlibrary Loan Service Tel: 716-270-5358. Reference Tel: 716-270-5212. FAX: 716-851-1778. *Col Librn,* Justin Cronise; Tel: 716-851-1775, E-mail: cronisej@ecc.edu; Staff 9 (MLS 5, Non-MLS 4)
Founded 1974. Enrl 4,800; Fac 120; Highest Degree: Associate
Sept 2014-Aug 2015. Mats Exp $73,000, Books $66,000, AV Mat $7,000
Library Holdings: AV Mats 1,910; Bk Titles 57,300; Bk Vols 60,180; Per Subs 188
Automation Activity & Vendor Info: (Cataloging) Ex Libris Group; (OPAC) Ex Libris Group
Wireless access
Publications: LRC News; Periodical Holdings List; Study Guides
Partic in Western New York Library Resources Council
Open Mon-Thurs 7:30am-10pm, Fri 7:30-4, Sat 9-3

P ORCHARD PARK PUBLIC LIBRARY, S-4570 S Buffalo St, 14127. SAN 312-2212. Tel: 716-662-9851. FAX: 716-667-3098. E-mail: opk@buffalolib.org. Web Site: www.buffalolib.org/locations-hours/orchard-park-public-library. *Dir,* Peggy Errington; E-mail: erringtonp@buffalolib.org; *Librn,* Kathleen Mack; E-mail: mackk@buffalolib.org; Staff 3 (MLS 3)
Founded 1935. Pop 27,637; Circ 365,637
Library Holdings: Bk Titles 71,837; Per Subs 286
Automation Activity & Vendor Info: (Cataloging) SirsiDynix; (Circulation) SirsiDynix; (OPAC) SirsiDynix; (Serials) SirsiDynix

Wireless access
Mem of Buffalo & Erie County Public Library System
Open Mon, Tues & Fri 10-6, Tues 9-8, Wed 1-8, Sat 10-5
Friends of the Library Group

ORIENT

S OYSTERPONDS HISTORICAL SOCIETY*, Donald H Boerum Research Library, 1555 Village Lane, 11957. (Mail add: PO Box 70, 11957-0070), SAN 312-2220. Tel: 631-323-2480. E-mail: office@ohsny.org. Web Site: www.oysterpondshistoricalsociety.org. *Archivist, Colls Mgr,* Amy Folk; E-mail: collections@ohsny.org
Founded 1944
Library Holdings: Bk Vols 450
Special Collections: Art (William Steeple Davis Coll), paintings; Local Historical Research (Clarence Ashton Wood Coll); Photography (William Steeple Davis & Vinton Richard Colls), black & white glass plates
Subject Interests: 19th Century, Educ, Genealogy, Local hist, Long Island, Relig
Partic in Asn for Conservation
Restriction: Closed stack, Open by appt only
Friends of the Library Group

ORISKANY

P ORISKANY PUBLIC LIBRARY, 621 Utica St, 13424. (Mail add: PO Box 428, 13424-0428), SAN 312-2239. Tel: 315-736-2532. FAX: 315-736-2532. E-mail: oriskany@midyork.org. Web Site: oriskanylibrary.org. *Mgr,* Kim Macera
Founded 1938. Pop 1,500; Circ 10,900
Library Holdings: Bk Titles 12,664; Per Subs 55
Wireless access
Mem of Mid-York Library System
Open Mon & Wed-Fri 1-6:30, Tues 9-1 & 2:30-6:30
Friends of the Library Group

ORISKANY FALLS

P C W CLARK MEMORIAL LIBRARY*, 160 N Main St, 13425. SAN 312-2247. Tel: 315-821-7850. FAX: 315-821-7850. E-mail: oriskanyfalls@midyork.org. Web Site: www.midyorklib.org/oriskanyfalls. *Dir,* Mike Marris; E-mail: mmarris@midyork.org; *Circ,* Bridget Kilts; *Circ,* Kim Maine
Pop 1,600; Circ 10,000
Library Holdings: Bk Vols 12,000; Per Subs 70
Automation Activity & Vendor Info: (Cataloging) SirsiDynix; (Circulation) SirsiDynix; (OPAC) SirsiDynix; (Serials) SirsiDynix
Wireless access
Mem of Mid-York Library System
Open Mon, Wed & Fri 9:30-5:30, Tues & Thurs 2-8, Sat 9:30-12:30

ORWELL

P COGSWELL FREE PUBLIC LIBRARY*, 1999 County Rte 2, 13426. (Mail add: PO Box 35, 13426-0035), SAN 312-2255. Tel: 315-298-5563. FAX: 315-298-5859. E-mail: orwlib@ncls.org. Web Site: www.cogswellfreelibrary.org. *Dir,* Elizabeth Gondak
Circ 9,926
Library Holdings: Bk Vols 8,075; Per Subs 27
Wireless access
Mem of North Country Library System
Open Tues 12-6, Wed 10-12 & 3-6, Thurs 12-5, Sat 9-1

OSCEOLA

P OSCEOLA PUBLIC LIBRARY*, 2117 N Osceola Rd, 13316-5809. Tel: 315-599-7122. FAX: 315-599-7122. E-mail: osclib@ncls.org. Web Site: www.osceolapublic.org. *Dir,* Leona Chereshnoski
Wireless access
Mem of North Country Library System
Open Tues & Thurs 2-8

OSSINING

S NEW YORK STATE DEPARTMENT OF CORRECTIONAL SERVICES*, Sing Sing Correctional Facility Library, 354 Hunter St, 10562. SAN 327-0718. Tel: 914-941-0108. FAX: 914-941-6583. *Sr Librn,* Position Currently Open
Founded 1840. Pop 1,700
Library Holdings: High Interest/Low Vocabulary Bk Vols 1,475; Microforms 236; Bk Vols 18,545; Per Subs 58
Restriction: Staff & inmates only

S OSSINING HISTORICAL SOCIETY MUSEUM*, 196 Croton Ave, 10562. SAN 323-4525. Tel: 914-941-0001. FAX: 914-941-0001. E-mail: ohsm@optimum.net. Web Site: www.ohsm.org. *Curator,* Norm MacDonald
Founded 1931
Library Holdings: Bk Vols 2,000
Special Collections: Croton Aquaduct; Hudson River Fishing; Local Newspapers (Late 18th Century to Present); Sing Sing Prison. Oral History
Subject Interests: Genealogy, Local hist
Function: Res libr
Publications: A Memorial 1775-1983; A Primer of Ossining History; Ossining in the 1940's; Ossining in the 1950's; Ossining Remembered (Quarterly); Sing Sing Prison Electrecutions 1891-1963; Sparta Cemetery Book 1764; William Dolphin's Civil War Diary
Restriction: Non-circulating, Open by appt only

P OSSINING PUBLIC LIBRARY*, 53 Croton Ave, 10562. SAN 312-2263. Tel: 914-941-2416. Circulation Tel: 914-941-2416, Ext 305. Reference Tel: 914-941-2416, Ext 320. FAX: 914-941-7464. E-mail: oplanswers@wlsmail.org. Web Site: ossininglibrary.org. *Dir,* Karen LaRocca-Fels; E-mail: opldirector@wlsmail.org; *Adult Serv Coordr, Asst Dir,* Molly Robbins; *Ch,* Deborah Fletcher; *Emerging Tech Librn, Media Librn,* Bonnie Katz; *Ref & Coll Develop Librn,* John Hawkins; *Ref & Educ Serv Librn,* Cheryl Cohen; *Teen Librn,* Mallory Harlen; E-mail: mharlen@wlsmail.org; *Children's Serv Coordr,* Marci Dressler; *Prog & Events Coordr,* James Trapasso; Staff 45 (MLS 20, Non-MLS 25)
Founded 1893. Pop 33,273; Circ 420,000
Library Holdings: AV Mats 13,231; e-books 767; Electronic Media & Resources 923; Bk Vols 110,654
Special Collections: Job Info Center
Automation Activity & Vendor Info: (Circulation) SirsiDynix
Wireless access
Function: Adult literacy prog, Art exhibits, AV serv, Bilingual assistance for Spanish patrons, Bk club(s), Bks on cassette, Bks on CD, Children's prog, Computer training, Computers for patron use, Free DVD rentals, Home delivery & serv to seniorr ctr & nursing homes, Homebound delivery serv, ILL available, Museum passes, Music CDs, Online cat, Photocopying/Printing, Preschool outreach, Prog for children & young adult, Ref serv available, Scanner, Senior computer classes, Serves people with intellectual disabilities, Spanish lang bks, Story hour, Summer reading prog, Tax forms, Teen prog, Telephone ref, Wheelchair accessible
Publications: Update (Monthly)
Mem of Westchester Library System
Open Mon & Thurs 9-9, Tues & Fri 10-6, Wed 1-9, Sat 11-5, Sun (Sept-June) 1-5
Friends of the Library Group

OSWEGO

S NEW YORK STATE OFFICE OF PARKS, RECREATION & HISTORIC PRESERVATION*, Fort Ontario State Historic Site Research Library, One E Fourth St, 13126. SAN 326-324X. Tel: 315-343-4711. FAX: 315-343-1430. Web Site: www.fortontario.com. *Mgr,* Paul Lear; E-mail: paul.lear@parks.ny.gov
Library Holdings: Bk Titles 1,500; Per Subs 10
Subject Interests: Archit, Hist
Wireless access
Restriction: Open by appt only
Friends of the Library Group

L OSWEGO COUNTY SUPREME COURT*, Law Library, 25 E Oneida St, 13126. Tel: 315-207-7565. FAX: 315-266-4713. E-mail: 5JDLawLibrary@nycourts.gov. Web Site: ww2.nycourts.gov/library/oswego. *Law Libr Asst,* Anne Thomas
Library Holdings: Bk Vols 10,000
Automation Activity & Vendor Info: (Circulation) Horizon; (OPAC) Horizon
Wireless access
Open Mon-Fri 8:30-4:30

P OSWEGO PUBLIC LIBRARY*, 120 E Second St, 13126. SAN 312-2271. Tel: 315-341-5867. FAX: 315-216-6492. E-mail: oswegopl@northnet.org. Web Site: www.oswegopubliclibrary.org. *Dir,* Carol Ferlito; E-mail: cferlito@ncls.org
Founded 1854. Pop 19,195; Circ 108,980
Library Holdings: Bk Vols 55,000; Per Subs 1,188
Special Collections: Local Cemetery Records; Local Oswego County Historical Society Coll, per
Automation Activity & Vendor Info: (Acquisitions) Follett Software; (Cataloging) Follett Software; (Circulation) Follett Software; (Course Reserve) Follett Software; (ILL) Follett Software; (Media Booking) Follett Software; (OPAC) Follett Software; (Serials) Follett Software
Wireless access
Mem of North Country Library System

Open Mon-Thurs 10-8, Fri 10-5, Sat & Sun 12-5; Mon-Thurs (Summer) 10-8, Fri 10-5, Sat 12-5
Friends of the Library Group

C STATE UNIVERSITY OF NEW YORK AT OSWEGO*, Penfield Library, SUNY Oswego, 7060 State Rte 104, 13126-3514. SAN 312-228X. Tel: 315-312-4232. Circulation Tel: 315-312-2560. Interlibrary Loan Service Tel: 315-312-4546. Reference Tel: 315-312-4267. FAX: 315-312-3194. Web Site: www.oswego.edu/library. *Dir,* Sarah Weisman; Tel: 315-312-3557, E-mail: sarah.weisman@oswego.edu; *Assoc Dir,* Position Currently Open; *Archives & Spec Coll Librn,* Elizabeth Young; Tel: 315-312-3537, E-mail: archives@oswego.edu; *Distance Learning Librn,* Jim Nichols; Tel: 315-312-3549, E-mail: jim.nichols@oswego.edu; *Electronic Res/Ser Librn,* Kathryn Johns-Masten; Tel: 315-312-3553, E-mail: kathryn.johnsmasten@oswego.edu; *First Year Experience Librn,* Michelle Bishop; Tel: 315-312-3564, E-mail: michelle.bishop@oswego.edu; *Learning Tech Librn,* Sharona Ginsberg; Tel: 315-312-3544, E-mail: sharona.ginsberg@oswego.edu; *Online Learning Librn,* Laura Harris; Tel: 315-312-3539, E-mail: laura.harris@oswego.edu; *Webmaster Librn,* Emily Mitchell; Tel: 315-312-3540, E-mail: emily.mitchell@oswego.edu; *Coordr, Access Serv,* Ray Morrison; Tel: 315-312-3567, E-mail: ray.morrison@oswego.edu; *Coordr, Coll Develop & Acq,* Deborah Curry; Tel: 315-312-3545, E-mail: deborah.curry@oswego.edu; *Coordr, Libr Instruction,* Karen Shockey; Tel: 315-312-3566, E-mail: karen.shockey@oswego.edu; *Coordr, Libr Tech,* Natalie Sturr; Tel: 315-312-3565, E-mail: natalie.sturr@oswego.edu; *Coordr, Ref Serv,* Christopher Hebblethwaite; Tel: 315-312-3060, E-mail: chris.hebblethwaite@oswego.edu; *Coordr, Res Serv,* Michael Paxton; Tel: 315-312-3562, E-mail: michael.paxton@oswego.edu; *Ref Serv,* Tim Berge; Tel: 315-312-3010, E-mail: timothy.berge@oswego.edu; Staff 18 (MLS 17, Non-MLS 1)
Founded 1861. Enrl 7,937; Fac 341; Highest Degree: Master
Jul 2015-Jun 2016. Mats Exp $613,539, Books $89,446, Per/Ser (Incl. Access Fees) $216,332, AV Mat $8,390, Electronic Ref Mat (Incl. Access Fees) $299,371
Library Holdings: e-books 145,720; Bk Vols 585,864
Special Collections: College Archives; Local & State History (Safe Haven Coll); Local History (Marshall Family Coll); Presidential Papers (Millard Fillmore Coll). Oral History; State Document Depository; US Document Depository
Subject Interests: Bus admin, Educ, Liberal arts
Automation Activity & Vendor Info: (Acquisitions) Ex Libris Group; (Cataloging) Ex Libris Group; (Circulation) Ex Libris Group; (Course Reserve) Atlas Systems; (Discovery) EBSCO Discovery Service; (ILL) OCLC ILLiad; (OPAC) Ex Libris Group; (Serials) Ex Libris Group
Wireless access
Partic in Northern New York Library Network; OCLC Online Computer Library Center, Inc; SUNYConnect

OTEGO

P HARRIS MEMORIAL LIBRARY*, 334 Main St, 13825. (Mail add: PO Box 470, 13825-0470), SAN 312-2298. Tel: 607-988-6661. FAX: 607-988-6661. E-mail: harrislibrary@yahoo.com. Web Site: harrismemoriallibrary.com. *Dir,* Anne Ohman; Staff 1 (MLS 1)
Founded 1923. Pop 3,000; Circ 13,000
Library Holdings: Bk Titles 10,000; Per Subs 45
Wireless access
Mem of Four County Library System
Open Mon (May-Oct) 3-6, Tues & Thurs 10-12 & 2-5, Wed 1-7, Fri 11-5, Sat 9-12
Friends of the Library Group

OTISVILLE

S OTISVILLE STATE CORRECTIONAL FACILITY LIBRARY*, 57 Janitorium Rd, 10963. (Mail add: PO Box 8, 10963-0008), SAN 327-1811. Tel: 845-386-1490. *Sr Librn,* Karrie Williamson; Staff 1 (MLS 1)
Library Holdings: Bk Titles 7,500; Per Subs 41
Automation Activity & Vendor Info: (Cataloging) Follett Software; (Circulation) Follett Software; (OPAC) Follett Software
Restriction: Staff & inmates only

OVID

P EDITH B FORD MEMORIAL LIBRARY*, 7169 N Main St, 14521. (Mail add: PO Box 410, 14521), SAN 312-2301. Tel: 607-869-3031. FAX: 607-869-3031. E-mail: contact@ovidlibrary.org. Web Site: ovidlibrary.org. *Dir,* Shannon O'Connor; E-mail: shannon@ovidlibrary.org
Founded 1899. Pop 6,627; Circ 20,485
Library Holdings: Audiobooks 150; Bk Vols 34,127; Per Subs 30; Videos 150
Automation Activity & Vendor Info: (Acquisitions) Innovative Interfaces, Inc; (Cataloging) Innovative Interfaces, Inc; (OPAC) Innovative Interfaces, Inc
Wireless access
Mem of Finger Lakes Library System
Open Mon & Fri 9-5, Tues-Thurs 10-8, Sat 10-2

OWEGO

P COBURN FREE LIBRARY*, 275 Main St, 13827. SAN 312-231X. Tel: 607-687-3520. Web Site: coburnfreelibrary.org. *Dir,* Meredith Gallardo; E-mail: director@coburnfreelibrary.org; *Asst Dir,* Mandi Wolcott; Staff 2.5 (Non-MLS 2.5)
Founded 1895
Library Holdings: Bk Vols 30,614; Per Subs 28
Special Collections: Genealogy (Dr Hyde Room)
Wireless access
Mem of Finger Lakes Library System
Open Mon, Wed & Fri 10-5, Tues & Thurs 1-5 & 6:30-8:30, Sat (Sept-June) 1-5
Friends of the Library Group

S TIOGA COUNTY HISTORICAL SOCIETY MUSEUM, Research Library, 110 Front St, 13827. SAN 312-2336. Tel: 607-687-2460. E-mail: museum@tiogahistory.org. Web Site: www.tiogahistory.org. *Exec Dir,* Scott MacDonald; E-mail: director@tiogahistory.org
Founded 1914
Library Holdings: Bk Vols 3,000
Special Collections: Local Newspapers, microfilm
Subject Interests: Genealogy, Hist of NY
Wireless access
Function: Res libr
Open Tues-Sat 10-4
Restriction: Non-circulating

OXFORD

G NEW YORK STATE VETERANS HOME LIBRARY*, 4207 St Hwy 220, 13830. SAN 376-0774. Tel: 607-843-3100. FAX: 607-843-3199. Web Site: apps.health.ny.gov/nysvets/web/oxford/new-york-state-veterans-home-oxford. *Dir,* Heeyoun Cho
Library Holdings: Bk Vols 700
Wireless access
Open Mon-Sun 8-4

P OXFORD MEMORIAL LIBRARY, Eight Fort Hill Park, 13830. (Mail add: PO Box 552, 13830-0552), SAN 312-2344. Tel: 607-843-6146. FAX: 607-843-9157. Web Site: oxfordmemoriallibrary.org. *Dir,* Nancy Wilcox; E-mail: ox.nancy@4cls.org; Staff 5 (Non-MLS 5)
Founded 1900. Pop 5,408; Circ 33,500
Library Holdings: Bk Titles 20,500; Per Subs 44
Automation Activity & Vendor Info: (Acquisitions) SirsiDynix; (Cataloging) SirsiDynix; (Circulation) SirsiDynix
Wireless access
Mem of Four County Library System
Open Mon-Thurs 9:30-8, Fri 9:30-5, Sat 9:30-1

OYSTER BAY

P OYSTER BAY-EAST NORWICH PUBLIC LIBRARY*, 89 E Main St, 11771. SAN 312-2352. Tel: 516-922-1212. FAX: 516-922-6453. Administration FAX: 516-624-8693. Web Site: www.oysterbaylibrary.org. *Libr Dir,* Michele Vaccarelli; E-mail: mvaccarelli@nassaulibrary.org; *Head, Ref Serv,* Stacie Hammond; E-mail: oblibrary@oysterbaylibrary.org; *Ch Serv,* Barbara Grodin; E-mail: kidsread@oysterbaylibrary.org; *Circ,* Elisa Herberich; E-mail: oblcirc@gmail.com; *Tech Serv,* Margaret Wanser; *YA Serv,* Stacie Kaloudis; E-mail: skaloudis@oysterbaylibrary.org; Staff 32 (MLS 10, Non-MLS 22)
Founded 1901. Pop 13,458; Circ 155,000
Library Holdings: Bk Titles 79,603; Per Subs 549; Talking Bks 4,313
Special Collections: Presidential (Theodore Roosevelt Coll)
Subject Interests: Career develop, Local hist
Automation Activity & Vendor Info: (Acquisitions) Innovative Interfaces, Inc; (Cataloging) Innovative Interfaces, Inc; (Circulation) Innovative Interfaces, Inc; (OPAC) Innovative Interfaces, Inc
Wireless access
Function: 24/7 Online cat, Adult bk club, Adult literacy prog, Art exhibits, Audiobks on Playaways & MP3, Audiobks via web, Bk club(s), Bks on CD, Children's prog, Computer training, Computers for patron use, Electronic databases & coll, Free DVD rentals, ILL available, Internet access, Magazines, Meeting rooms, Microfiche/film & reading machines, Movies, Museum passes, Music CDs, Notary serv, Online cat, Orientations, Outside serv via phone, mail, e-mail & web, OverDrive digital audio bks, Photocopying/Printing, Prog for adults, Prog for children & young adult, Ref serv available, Scanner, Story hour, Study rm, Summer reading prog, Tax forms, Teen prog, VHS videos, Wheelchair accessible, Workshops, Writing prog
Publications: Newsletter (Bimonthly)
Mem of Nassau Library System

Special Services for the Deaf - Assistive tech
Special Services for the Blind - Closed circuit TV magnifier
Open Mon, Tues & Thurs 9:30-9, Wed 10-9, Fri 9:30-6, Sat 9-5 (9-1 July-Aug), Sun 1-5
Friends of the Library Group

S OYSTER BAY HISTORICAL SOCIETY LIBRARY*, 20 Summit St, 11771. (Mail add: PO Box 297, 11771-0297), SAN 326-1999. Tel: 516-922-5032. E-mail: obhslibrary@optonline.net. Web Site: www.oysterbayhistorical.org/library.html. *Exec Dir,* Philip Blocklyn; *Colls Mgr,* Melanie Derschowitz; Staff 3 (MLS 1, Non-MLS 2)
Founded 1960
Library Holdings: Bk Titles 1,015; Bk Vols 1,028
Special Collections: Early American Tools & Trades (Reichman Coll); Theodore Roosevelt Coll
Subject Interests: Genealogy, Local hist
Publications: Magazine for Members (Quarterly); The Freeholder (Quarterly history journal)
Open Tues-Fri 10-2, Sat 11-3, Sun 1-4
Restriction: Non-circulating to the pub

S SAGAMORE HILL NATIONAL HISTORIC SITE LIBRARY*, 20 Sagamore Hill Rd, 11771-1899. SAN 324-4393. Tel: 516-922-4788. FAX: 516-922-4792. Web Site: www.nps.gov/sahi. *Chief of Cultural Resources,* Susan Sarna; E-mail: susan_sarna@nps.gov
Library Holdings: Bk Titles 850; Bk Vols 950
Special Collections: Theodore Roosevelt Life & Career
Subject Interests: Nat park area, Sagamore Hill
Function: Res libr
Restriction: Non-circulating, Open by appt only

PAINTED POST

P SOUTHERN TIER LIBRARY SYSTEM*, 9424 Scott Rd, 14870-9598. SAN 352-3861. Tel: 607-962-3141. FAX: 607-962-5356. E-mail: communitylibrarypartner@stls.org. Web Site: www.stls.org. *Exec Dir,* Brian M Hildreth; Tel: 607-962-3141, Ext 207; *Dep Dir,* Margo Gustina; Tel: 607-962-3141, Ext 205, E-mail: gustinam@stls.org; Staff 19 (MLS 4, Non-MLS 15)
Founded 1958. Pop 286,225
Library Holdings: Bk Vols 48,000; Per Subs 15
Subject Interests: NY State county hist
Automation Activity & Vendor Info: (Acquisitions) SirsiDynix; (Cataloging) SirsiDynix; (Circulation) SirsiDynix; (OPAC) SirsiDynix
Wireless access
Member Libraries: Addison Public Library; Andover Free Library; Angelica Free Library; Avoca Free Library; Belfast Public Library; Belmont Literary & Historical Society Free Library; Bolivar Free Library; Chemung County Historical Society, Inc; Chemung County Library District; Cohocton Public Library; Colonial Library; Cuba Circulating Library; David A Howe Public Library; Dormann Library; Dr Sandor & Berthe Benedek Memorial Library; Dundee Library; Dutton S Peterson Memorial Library; E J Cottrell Memorial Library; Elizabeth B Pert Library; Essential Club Free Library; Fred & Harriett Taylor Memorial Library; Friendship Free Library; Genesee Library; Greenwood Reading Center; Hornell Public Library; Howard Public Library; Jasper Free Library; Mabel D Blodgett Memorial Reading Center; Middlesex Reading Center; Modeste Bedient Memorial Library; Montour Falls Memorial Library; Penn Yan Public Library; Prattsburg Free Library; Pulteney Free Library; Rushford Free Library; Scio Memorial Library; Southeast Steuben County Library; Twentieth Century Club Library; Watkins Glen Public Library; Wayland Free Library; Whitesville Public Library; Wide Awake Club Library; Wimodaughsian Free Library
Open Mon-Fri 8-4

PALISADES

P PALISADES FREE LIBRARY, 19 Closter Rd, 10964. SAN 312-2379. Tel: 845-359-0136. FAX: 845-359-6124. E-mail: info@palisadesfreelibrary.org. Web Site: www.palisadeslibrary.org. *Dir,* Maria Gagliardi; E-mail: mgagliardi@palisadesfreelibrary.org; *Head, Circ,* Debbie Firestone; *Head, Ref,* Emily Nevill; Staff 5 (MLS 5)
Founded 1891. Pop 1,282; Circ 21,471
Library Holdings: AV Mats 3,285; Bks on Deafness & Sign Lang 10; Electronic Media & Resources 78,050; Bk Vols 23,956
Special Collections: Local History, bks, microflm, maps
Automation Activity & Vendor Info: (Circulation) SirsiDynix-Symphony; (OPAC) SirsiDynix-Enterprise
Wireless access
Function: 24/7 Electronic res, 24/7 Online cat, Bks on CD, Children's prog, Computer training, Computers for patron use, E-Readers, Electronic databases & coll, Free DVD rentals, Home delivery & serv to seniorr ctr & nursing homes, Homebound delivery serv, ILL available, Internet access, Life-long learning prog for all ages, Magazines, Mail & tel request accepted, Meeting rooms, Museum passes, Notary serv, Online cat, Online ref, Outreach serv, OverDrive digital audio bks, Photocopying/Printing, Preschool outreach, Prog for adults, Prog for children & young adult, Ref & res, Ref serv available, Scanner, Story hour, Summer reading prog, Teen prog, Telephone ref, Wheelchair accessible
Mem of Ramapo Catskill Library System
Open Mon-Thurs 11-9, Fri & Sat 11-5, Sun 1-5

PALMYRA

P PALMYRA COMMUNITY LIBRARY*, 402 E Main St, 14522, SAN 312-2387. Tel: 315-597-5276. FAX: 315-597-1375. Web Site: www.palmyracommunitylibrary.org. *Dir,* Patricia Baynes; E-mail: pbaynes@pls-net.org; Staff 8 (MLS 1, Non-MLS 7)
Founded 1901. Pop 7,652; Circ 55,672
Jan 2020-Dec 2020. Mats Exp $30,379, Books $23,904, Per/Ser (Incl. Access Fees) $1,875, AV Mat $4,600. Sal $176,643 (Prof $57,600)
Library Holdings: Audiobooks 795; DVDs 2,354; e-books 273; Large Print Bks 260; Bk Vols 15,387; Per Subs 51
Special Collections: Local History (Genealogy & Palmyra)
Automation Activity & Vendor Info: (Acquisitions) Baker & Taylor; (Cataloging) Evergreen; (Circulation) Evergreen; (OPAC) Evergreen
Wireless access
Function: 24/7 Online cat, Activity rm, Adult bk club, Adult literacy prog, After school storytime, Archival coll, Art exhibits, Art programs, Audiobks via web, Bks on CD, Children's prog, Computer training, Computers for patron use, E-Readers, Electronic databases & coll, Free DVD rentals, Holiday prog, Home delivery & serv to seniorr ctr & nursing homes, Homebound delivery serv, ILL available, Internet access, Life-long learning prog for all ages, Magazines, Mail & tel request accepted, Mango lang, Meeting rooms, Online cat, OverDrive digital audio bks, Photocopying/Printing, Preschool outreach, Prog for adults, Prog for children & young adult, Ref serv available, Scanner, Story hour, Study rm, Summer reading prog, Tax forms, Teen prog, Telephone ref, Wheelchair accessible
Mem of Pioneer Library System
Special Services for the Deaf - Assisted listening device
Special Services for the Blind - Bks on CD; Home delivery serv; Large print bks; Magnifiers
Open Mon-Thurs 10-8, Fri 10-5, Sat (Sept-June) 10-2
Friends of the Library Group

PARISH

P PARISH PUBLIC LIBRARY, Three Church St, 13131. SAN 312-2395. Tel: 315-625-7130. E-mail: parlib@ncls.org. Web Site: www.parishpubliclibrary.org. *Dir,* Linda McNamara; *Libr Asst,* Dawn Campany
Pop 1,700; Circ 7,071
Library Holdings: Bk Titles 10,500; Per Subs 47
Wireless access
Mem of North Country Library System
Open Mon & Wed 11-5, Tues 3-7, Thurs 5pm-7pm, Sat 10-3
Friends of the Library Group

PATCHOGUE

SR CONGREGATIONAL CHURCH OF PATCHOGUE*, Stuart VanCott Memorial Library & Virginia Crowell Children's Library, 95 E Main St, 11772. SAN 371-9405. Tel: 631-475-1235. FAX: 631-207-9470. E-mail: office@churchonmainstreet.org. Web Site: www.churchonmainstreet.org. *Ch Serv, Librn,* Toni Dean; *Librn,* Shirley Werner; Staff 6 (MLS 1, Non-MLS 5)
Founded 1967
Library Holdings: Bk Titles 4,530; Bk Vols 5,350
Subject Interests: Church hist, Local hist, Relig
Partic in Church & Synagogue Libr Asn
Open Mon-Fri 9-1, Sun 10-12

M LONG ISLAND COMMUNITY HOSPITAL*, Medical Library, 101 Hospital Rd, 11772. SAN 312-2409. Tel: 631-447-3010, 631-654-7100. FAX: 631-447-3012. Web Site: licommunityhospital.org. *Library Contact,* Donna Zubeck; E-mail: dzubeck@licommunityhospital.org
Founded 1975
Library Holdings: e-journals 200; Bk Titles 400
Subject Interests: Allied health, Med, Nursing
Automation Activity & Vendor Info: (Cataloging) Professional Software; (OPAC) Professional Software
Wireless access
Open Mon-Fri 8-5

P PATCHOGUE-MEDFORD LIBRARY*, 54-60 E Main St, 11772. SAN 312-2417. Tel: 631-654-4700. Reference Tel: 631-654-4700, Ext 221. Administration Tel: 631-654-4700, Ext 302. FAX: 631-289-3999. E-mail: info@pmlib.org. Web Site: pmlib.org. *Dir,* Danielle Paisley; E-mail: dpaisley@pmlib.org; *Head, Automation & Tech Serv,* Bruce Silverstein; E-mail: bsilverstein@pmlib.org; *Head, Children's Servx,* Jane Drake;

E-mail: jdrake@pmlib.org; *Head, Circ,* Sharon Roman; *Head of Digital Serv & Tech Serv,* Position Currently Open; *Head, Media Serv, Head, Teen Serv,* Jeri Cohen; E-mail: jcohen@pmlib.org; *Head, Ref,* Jose Hernandez; *Head, Ref,* Jessica Oelther; Staff 28 (MLS 27, Non-MLS 1)
Founded 1900. Pop 52,929; Circ 655,516. Sal $4,378,555
Library Holdings: AV Mats 395; CDs 12,786; DVDs 18,889; High Interest/Low Vocabulary Bk Vols 531; Bk Vols 284,451; Per Subs 36,450
Special Collections: Martial Arts (Maccarrone-Kresge Coll); Opera (Sara Courant Coll)
Subject Interests: Adult educ, Consumer health, Foreign lang, Law, Local genealogies, Local hist, Music
Automation Activity & Vendor Info: (Acquisitions) Innovative Interfaces, Inc; (Cataloging) Innovative Interfaces, Inc; (Circulation) Innovative Interfaces, Inc; (ILL) Innovative Interfaces, Inc; (OPAC) Innovative Interfaces, Inc; (Serials) Innovative Interfaces, Inc
Wireless access
Publications: An Index to Selected Popular Song Books; An Index to the Records-Town of Brookhaven up to 1800; Centennial Research Digest; Classical Music Index; Guide to Senior Citizen Services; Newsletter (Bimonthly); Patchogue-Medford Library Community Directory; Songs in Collections; The Library Story: A Patchogue-Medford Library Centennial Story for Children & Parents; The Maccarrone-Kresge Martial Arts Book Collection
Mem of Suffolk Cooperative Library System
Special Services for the Blind - Closed circuit TV; Magnifiers
Open Mon-Fri 9:30-9, Sat 9:30-5:30, Sun (Oct-May) 1-5
Friends of the Library Group

C SAINT JOSEPH'S COLLEGE*, Callahan Library, 25 Audubon Ave, 11772-2399. SAN 352-2067. Tel: 631-687-2630. Reference Tel: 631-687-2632. FAX: 631-654-3255. E-mail: Callahan@sjcny.edu. Web Site: www.sjcny.edu/libraries. *Executive Dir of Libr,* Elzabeth Pollicino-Murphy; E-mail: epollicinomurphy@sjcny.edu; Staff 13 (MLS 6, Non-MLS 7)
Founded 1972. Enrl 4,368; Fac 370; Highest Degree: Master
Library Holdings: AV Mats 1,540; e-books 1,918; e-journals 399; Microforms 3,755; Bk Vols 118,040; Per Subs 258
Special Collections: Archives; Curriculum Library
Subject Interests: Child study, Liberal arts
Automation Activity & Vendor Info: (Acquisitions) Ex Libris Group; (Cataloging) Ex Libris Group; (Circulation) Ex Libris Group; (Course Reserve) Docutek; (ILL) OCLC; (OPAC) Ex Libris Group; (Serials) Ex Libris Group
Wireless access
Function: Audio & video playback equip for onsite use, Computers for patron use, E-Reserves, Electronic databases & coll, ILL available, Photocopying/Printing, Ref serv available, Wheelchair accessible
Partic in OCLC Online Computer Library Center, Inc; Westchester Academic Library Directors Organization
Special Services for the Blind - ZoomText magnification & reading software
Open Mon-Thurs 7:30am-9pm, Fri 7:30-5, Sat 10-6, Sun 1-7
Restriction: Open to students, fac, staff & alumni, Pub use on premises

PATTERSON

P PATTERSON LIBRARY, 1167 Rte 311, 12563. (Mail add: PO Box 418, 12563-0418), SAN 312-2425. Tel: 845-878-6121. FAX: 845-878-3116. Reference E-mail: reference@pattersonlibrary.org. Web Site: pattersonlibrary.org. *Dir,* Stephanie Harrison; E-mail: director@pattersonlibrary.org; Staff 6 (Non-MLS 6)
Founded 1947. Pop 12,000; Circ 60,738
Jan 2019-Dec 2019 Income (Main Library Only) $960,139, State $3,526, City $922,440, Other $10,496
Library Holdings: Talking Bks 7
Special Collections: Maxwell Weaner Music Book Coll
Automation Activity & Vendor Info: (Circulation) Innovative Interfaces, Inc; (OPAC) Innovative Interfaces, Inc
Wireless access
Function: 24/7 Electronic res, 24/7 Online cat, Activity rm, Adult bk club, After school storytime
Mem of Chautauqua-Cattaraugus Library System; Mid-Hudson Library System
Open Mon-Thurs 10-7, Fri 10-5, Sat 10-2
Friends of the Library Group

SR WATCHTOWER BIBLE SCHOOL OF GILEAD LIBRARY*, 100 Watchtower Dr, 12563-9204. (Mail add: One Kings Dr, Tuxedo Park, 10987), SAN 310-9542. Tel: 718-560-5000. Web Site: www.jw.org. *Librn,* Gene Smalley
Library Holdings: Bk Vols 33,000; Per Subs 25
Subject Interests: Relig matters
Automation Activity & Vendor Info: (Cataloging) Inmagic, Inc.; (Circulation) Inmagic, Inc.; (OPAC) Inmagic, Inc.
Wireless access
Open Mon-Fri 8-5

PAUL SMITHS

C PAUL SMITHS COLLEGE OF ARTS & SCIENCES, Joan Weill Adirondack Library, 7833 New York 30, 12970. SAN 312-2433. Tel: 518-327-6313. E-mail: library@paulsmiths.edu. Web Site: library.paulsmiths.edu. *Cataloging & Electronic Resources Librn, Dir, Libr Serv,* Andrew Kelly; Tel: 518-327-6354, E-mail: akelly@paulsmiths.edu; *Student Success Librn,* MacKenzie Davidson; Tel: 518-327-6904, E-mail: mdavidson@paulsmiths.edu; *Libr Tech,* Cooper Ross; Tel: 518-327-6312
Founded 1946. Highest Degree: Bachelor
Subject Interests: Arboriculture, Culinary arts, Environ studies, Fisheries mgt, Forestry, Hotel mgt, Outdoor recreation, Restaurant mgt, Surveying, Sustainability, Wildlife mgt
Wireless access
Partic in OCLC Online Computer Library Center, Inc
Open Mon-Thurs 7:30am-8pm, Fri 7:30-5, Sat 12-4, Sun 12-8

PAVILION

P HOLLWEDEL MEMORIAL LIBRARY*, Five Woodrow Dr, 14525. (Mail add: PO Box 422, 14525-0422). Tel: 585-584-8843. FAX: 585-584-8801. Web Site: hollwedellibrary.org. *Dir,* Suzanne Schauf; E-mail: sscha@nioga.org
Pop 2,476
Library Holdings: DVDs 723; Large Print Bks 150; Bk Vols 13,000; Per Subs 35; Talking Bks 115; Videos 553
Automation Activity & Vendor Info: (Cataloging) SirsiDynix-WorkFlows; (Circulation) SirsiDynix-WorkFlows; (OPAC) SirsiDynix-WorkFlows; (Serials) SirsiDynix-WorkFlows
Wireless access
Function: ILL available, Photocopying/Printing, Prog for adults, Prog for children & young adult, Serves people with intellectual disabilities, Summer reading prog, Wheelchair accessible
Mem of Nioga Library System
Open Mon & Wed 1-5 & 6-8, Tues & Sat 10-12:30, Fri 1-5
Friends of the Library Group

PAWLING

S AKIN FREE LIBRARY*, 378 Old Quaker Hill Rd, 12564-3411. (Mail add: PO Box 345, 12564-0345), SAN 371-0165. Tel: 845-326-6168. Web Site: www.akinfreelibrary.org. *Exec Dir,* Matthew Hogan; E-mail: director@akinfreelibrary.org; Staff 1 (MLS 1)
Founded 1898
Jun 2018-May 2019. Mats Exp $7,000, Books $500, AV Equip $4,000, Presv $2,500. Sal $43,000
Library Holdings: Bk Vols 7,000
Special Collections: Historical Research, Quakers-Pawling 1740-1800; Quaker Hill Series & Ledgers Coll; Quaker Local history 1730-1740
Wireless access
Open Fri-Sun (April-Oct) 11-5; Sun (Nov-March) 11-4

P PAWLING FREE LIBRARY*, 11 Broad St, 12564. SAN 312-2441. Tel: 845-855-3444. FAX: 845-855-8138. Web Site: www.pawlinglibrary.org. *Libr Dir,* Brian Avery; E-mail: director@pawlinglibrary.org; *Adult Prog Coordr,* Donald Partelow; E-mail: adult@pawlinglibrary.org; *Young Adult Prog Coord,* Phil Prout; E-mail: teen@pawlinglibrary.org; *Ch Serv,* Neena McBaer; E-mail: children@pawlinglibrary.org; *Circ,* Tom Clemmons; E-mail: circ@pawlinglibrary.org; Staff 5 (MLS 1, Non-MLS 4)
Founded 1921. Pop 8,377; Circ 100,000
Library Holdings: Bk Vols 40,000
Wireless access
Function: Adult bk club, After school storytime, Archival coll, Art exhibits, Audio & video playback equip for onsite use, Audiobks via web, Bilingual assistance for Spanish patrons, Bk club(s), Bks on CD, Children's prog, Computer training, Computers for patron use, Electronic databases & coll, Family literacy, Free DVD rentals, Holiday prog, Home delivery & serv to seniorr ctr & nursing homes, Homebound delivery serv, ILL available, Internet access, Life-long learning prog for all ages, Literacy & newcomer serv, Magazines, Mail & tel request accepted, Mango lang, Movies, Museum passes, Music CDs, Online cat, Online ref, Outreach serv, Outside serv via phone, mail, e-mail & web, OverDrive digital audio bks, Photocopying/Printing, Preschool outreach, Preschool reading prog, Prog for adults, Prog for children & young adult, Ref & res, Scanner, Senior computer classes, Senior outreach, Serves people with intellectual disabilities, Spanish lang bks, STEM programs, Story hour, Summer reading prog, Tax forms, Teen prog, Telephone ref, Wheelchair accessible, Workshops, Writing prog
Mem of Mid-Hudson Library System
Special Services for the Deaf - Staff with knowledge of sign lang
Open Mon & Fri 12-5, Tues-Thurs 10-8, Sat 10-4, Sun 12-4
Friends of the Library Group

PEARL RIVER

P PEARL RIVER PUBLIC LIBRARY*, 80 Franklin Ave, 10965. SAN 312-2468. Tel: 845-735-4084. FAX: 845-735-4041. E-mail: circulation@pearlriverlibrary.org. Web Site: www.pearlriverlibrary.org. *Libr Dir,* Eugenia Schatoff; E-mail: eschatoff@pearlriverlibrary.org; Staff 8 (MLS 8)
Founded 1935. Pop 15,300; Circ 203,311
Library Holdings: AV Mats 16,703; Bk Vols 103,584; Per Subs 288
Automation Activity & Vendor Info: (Cataloging) SirsiDynix; (Circulation) SirsiDynix; (OPAC) SirsiDynix
Wireless access
Mem of Ramapo Catskill Library System
Open Mon-Thurs 9-9, Fri 9-7, Sat 10-5, Sun 1-5
Friends of the Library Group

PEEKSKILL

P THE FIELD LIBRARY*, Four Nelson Ave, 10566. SAN 312-2476. Tel: 914-737-1212. FAX: 914-737-3288. Web Site: www.peekskill.org. *Dir,* Jennifer Brown; E-mail: jbrown@wlsmail.org; *Asst Dir,* Robert Boyle; E-mail: rboyle@wlsmail.org; *Head, Children's Servx,* Jody Sitts; E-mail: jsitts@wlsmail.org; *Head, Circ,* Nora Mulligan; E-mail: nmulligan@wlsmail.org; *Ch,* Rachel Mandel; E-mail: rmandel@wlsmail.org; *Ref Librn & Local Hist Spec,* Kim Stucko; E-mail: kstucko@wlsmail.org; *Gallery Curator,* Alicia Morgan; E-mail: amorgan@wlsmail.org; Staff 21 (MLS 6, Non-MLS 15)
Founded 1887. Pop 23,500
Library Holdings: Bk Vols 95,498; Per Subs 135
Special Collections: Lincoln Coll; Local History (Peekskill Historical Coll)
Automation Activity & Vendor Info: (Acquisitions) SirsiDynix; (Cataloging) SirsiDynix; (Circulation) SirsiDynix; (Course Reserve) SirsiDynix; (ILL) SirsiDynix; (Media Booking) SirsiDynix; (OPAC) SirsiDynix; (Serials) SirsiDynix
Wireless access
Function: Adult bk club, Archival coll, Art exhibits, Audiobks via web, Bks on CD, Children's prog, Computer training, Computers for patron use, Digital talking bks, Doc delivery serv, Electronic databases & coll, Free DVD rentals, Homebound delivery serv, ILL available, Microfiche/film & reading machines, Music CDs, Online cat, Photocopying/Printing, Prog for adults, Prog for children & young adult, Ref serv available, Res performed for a fee, Scanner, Senior computer classes, Spoken cassettes & CDs, Summer reading prog, Teen prog, Telephone ref, Wheelchair accessible
Mem of Westchester Library System
Open Mon, Tues & Thurs 9-9, Wed 11-9, Fri 9-5, Sat 10-5, Sun 1-4
Friends of the Library Group

PELHAM

P TOWN OF PELHAM PUBLIC LIBRARY*, 530 Colonial Ave, 10803. SAN 312-1801. Tel: 914-738-1234. FAX: 914-738-0809. E-mail: contactus@pelhamlibrary.org. Web Site: www.pelhamlibrary.org. *Dir,* Patricia Perito
Founded 1915. Pop 11,866; Circ 115,000
Library Holdings: e-books 800; Bk Titles 35,000; Per Subs 70
Special Collections: Mysteries
Automation Activity & Vendor Info: (Acquisitions) SirsiDynix; (Cataloging) SirsiDynix; (Circulation) SirsiDynix; (OPAC) SirsiDynix; (Serials) SirsiDynix
Wireless access
Mem of Westchester Library System
Open Mon & Thurs 1-9, Tues, Wed & Fri 10-5, Sat 10-4
Friends of the Library Group

PENFIELD

P PENFIELD PUBLIC LIBRARY*, 1985 Baird Rd, 14526. SAN 312-2506. Tel: 585-340-8720. FAX: 585-340-8748. Web Site: www3.libraryweb.org/penfield/home.aspx. *Regional Dir,* Patricia Uttaro; E-mail: Patricia.Uttaro@libraryweb.org; *Libr Dir,* Bernadette Brinkman; E-mail: bernadette.brinkman@libraryweb.org; *Ch,* Jennifer Caccavale; *Ch,* Judy Carpenter; *Librn,* Kim Catalanello; *Librn,* Candice Johnson; *Librn,* Margaret O'Neil; *Librn,* Todd Randall; *YA Librn,* Lyla Grills; Staff 57 (MLS 15, Non-MLS 42)
Founded 1942. Pop 36,242
Jan 2018-Dec 2018 Income $1,830,043, City $1,753,286, Locally Generated Income $66,135, Other $10,622. Mats Exp $1,755,029, Books $120,645, Per/Ser (Incl. Access Fees) $18,000, AV Mat $43,768, Electronic Ref Mat (Incl. Access Fees) $25,785. Sal $946,932 (Prof $422,522)
Library Holdings: Audiobooks 18,589; AV Mats 29,776; CDs 5,045; DVDs 13,966; e-books 43,980; Electronic Media & Resources 98,350; Bk Vols 135,044; Per Subs 387
Special Collections: Literacy Coll. US Document Depository
Automation Activity & Vendor Info: (Cataloging) CARL.Solution (TLC); (Circulation) CARL.Solution (TLC); (Discovery) CARL.Solution (TLC); (ILL) OCLC ILLiad; (OPAC) CARL.Solution (TLC)
Wireless access
Function: 24/7 Online cat, Adult bk club, Art exhibits, Art programs, Audio & video playback equip for onsite use, Audiobks on Playaways & MP3, Audiobks via web, AV serv, Bk club(s), Bk reviews (Group), Bks on cassette, Bks on CD, CD-ROM, Children's prog, Citizenship assistance, Computer training, Computers for patron use, Digital talking bks, Distance learning, Doc delivery serv, E-Readers, Electronic databases & coll, Family literacy, Free DVD rentals, Games & aids for people with disabilities, Health sci info serv, Holiday prog, Home delivery & serv to seniorr ctr & nursing homes, ILL available, Internet access, Life-long learning prog for all ages, Literacy & newcomer serv, Magazines, Magnifiers for reading, Mail & tel request accepted, Mango lang, Meeting rooms, Microfiche/film & reading machines, Movies, Museum passes, Music CDs, Notary serv, Online cat, Outreach serv, Outside serv via phone, mail, e-mail & web, OverDrive digital audio bks, Photocopying/Printing, Printer for laptops & handheld devices, Prog for adults, Prog for children & young adult, Ref & res, Ref serv available, Res assist avail, Res libr, Scanner, Senior computer classes, Senior outreach, Serves people with intellectual disabilities, Spoken cassettes & CDs, Spoken cassettes & DVDs, STEM programs, Story hour, Study rm, Summer & winter reading prog, Summer reading prog, Tax forms, Teen prog, Telephone ref, Visual arts prog, Wheelchair accessible, Winter reading prog, Workshops
Mem of Monroe County Library System
Special Services for the Deaf - ADA equip; Assisted listening device; Bks on deafness & sign lang; Closed caption videos; High interest/low vocabulary bks; Staff with knowledge of sign lang
Special Services for the Blind - Accessible computers; Aids for in-house use; Assistive/Adapted tech devices, equip & products; Bks available with recordings; Bks on CD; Braille bks; Copier with enlargement capabilities; Descriptive video serv (DVS); Extensive large print coll; Home delivery serv; Info on spec aids & appliances; Internet workstation with adaptive software; Large print bks; Low vision equip; Magnifiers; Networked computers with assistive software; PC for people with disabilities; Playaways (bks on MP3); Recorded bks; Ref serv; Screen enlargement software for people with visual disabilities; Sound rec
Open Mon-Thurs (Winter) 10-9, Fri 10-6, Sat 10-5, Sun 2-5; Mon-Thurs (Summer) 10-9, Fri 10-6, Sat 10-1
Restriction: Non-resident fee
Friends of the Library Group

PENN YAN

P PENN YAN PUBLIC LIBRARY*, 214 Main St, 14527. SAN 312-2514. Tel: 315-536-6114. FAX: 315-536-0131. Web Site: www.pypl.org. *Dir,* Angela Gonzalez; E-mail: agonzalez@pypl.org; *Youth Serv Librn,* Sarah Crevelling; E-mail: screvelling@pypl.org; *Ad,* Alex Andrasik; E-mail: aandrasik@pypl.org; Staff 15 (MLS 3, Non-MLS 12)
Founded 1895. Pop 15,060; Circ 122,582
Library Holdings: AV Mats 4,038; Bk Titles 51,515; Per Subs 100
Subject Interests: Local hist
Automation Activity & Vendor Info: (Acquisitions) Innovative Interfaces, Inc; (Cataloging) Innovative Interfaces, Inc; (Circulation) Innovative Interfaces, Inc; (OPAC) Innovative Interfaces, Inc
Wireless access
Function: 24/7 Electronic res, 24/7 Online cat, Adult bk club, After school storytime
Mem of Southern Tier Library System
Open Mon-Fri 9-7:30, Sat 9-4
Friends of the Library Group

PERRY

P PERRY PUBLIC LIBRARY*, 70 N Main St, 14530-1299. SAN 312-2522. Tel: 585-237-2243. FAX: 585-237-2008. E-mail: perrylibrarydirector@owwl.org. Web Site: www.perry.pls-net.org. *Libr Dir,* Jessica Pacciotti; E-mail: jpacciotti@pls-net.org; *Youth Serv Librn,* Janet N Rossman; E-mail: jrossman@pls-net.org; Staff 2 (MLS 2)
Founded 1914. Pop 6,214; Circ 45,532
Jan 2013-Dec 2013 Income $195,311, State $4,731, Locally Generated Income $175,000, Parent Institution $416, Other $15,164. Mats Exp $20,651, Books $11,426, Per/Ser (Incl. Access Fees) $1,614, AV Equip $3,802, AV Mat $3,255, Electronic Ref Mat (Incl. Access Fees) $554. Sal $97,581 (Prof $74,810)
Library Holdings: Audiobooks 326; DVDs 670; Electronic Media & Resources 18; Bk Vols 22,431; Per Subs 47
Special Collections: Lemuel M Wiles, Artist (Stowell-Wiles Coll), oil paintings; Local History (Clark Rice Coll), photog; Local History (Henry Page Coll)
Automation Activity & Vendor Info: (Cataloging) Evergreen; (Circulation) Evergreen; (OPAC) Evergreen
Wireless access
Mem of Pioneer Library System

Open Mon-Thurs 11-8, Fri 11-5, Sat 9-1
Friends of the Library Group

PERU

P PERU FREE LIBRARY*, 3024 Rte 22, 12972. (Mail add: PO Box 96, 12972), SAN 312-2530. Tel: 518-643-8618. E-mail: perulib@gmail.com. Web Site: cefls.org/libraries/peru. *Dir,* Rebecca Pace
Circ 14,119
Library Holdings: Bk Vols 16,000; Per Subs 40
Automation Activity & Vendor Info: (Cataloging) Horizon; (Circulation) Horizon; (ILL) Horizon; (OPAC) Horizon; (Serials) Horizon
Wireless access
Mem of Clinton-Essex-Franklin Library System
Open Tues-Thurs 10-7, Fri 10-4, Sat 10-3
Friends of the Library Group

PETERSBURGH

P PETERSBURGH PUBLIC LIBRARY, 69 Main St, 12138. (Mail add: PO Box 250, 12138-0250), SAN 312-2549. Tel: 518-658-2927. FAX: 518-658-2927. E-mail: library@petersburghpubliclibrary.org. Web Site: www.petersburghpubliclibrary.org. *Dir,* Anita S Wilson
Circ 24,000
Library Holdings: Bk Vols 23,601; Per Subs 12
Automation Activity & Vendor Info: (Cataloging) Horizon; (Circulation) Horizon; (OPAC) Horizon
Wireless access
Mem of Upper Hudson Library System
Open Mon, Tues, Thurs & Fri 2-6, Wed 2-7, Sat 9:30-12:30

PHELPS

P PHELPS LIBRARY*, Phelps Library & STEAM Lab Makerspace, Eight Banta St, Ste 200, 14532. SAN 312-2557. Tel: 315-548-3120. FAX: 315-548-5314. Web Site: phelpslibrary.org. *Exec Dir,* Leah Hamilton; E-mail: phelpslibrarydirector@owwl.org; Staff 1 (Non-MLS 1)
Founded 1948. Pop 7,017; Circ 34,000
Library Holdings: Bk Vols 20,000; Per Subs 54
Special Collections: Local History/Genealogy
Automation Activity & Vendor Info: (Cataloging) Evergreen; (Circulation) Evergreen
Wireless access
Function: 3D Printer, Activity rm, Adult bk club, Adult literacy prog, Art exhibits, Audiobks via web, AV serv, BA reader (adult literacy), Bk club(s), Bks on CD, CD-ROM, Chess club, Children's prog, Computer training, Computers for patron use, E-Readers, E-Reserves, Electronic databases & coll, Free DVD rentals, Genealogy discussion group, Holiday prog, Home delivery & serv to seniorr ctr & nursing homes, ILL available, Instruction & testing, Internet access, Life-long learning prog for all ages, Magazines, Mango lang, Meeting rooms, Movies, Music CDs, Online cat, Outreach serv, OverDrive digital audio bks, Photocopying/Printing, Preschool reading prog, Prog for adults, Prog for children & young adult, Ref serv available, Scanner, Story hour, Summer reading prog, Teen prog, Visual arts prog, Wheelchair accessible, Workshops
Mem of Pioneer Library System
Open Mon-Thurs 10-8, Fri 10-5, Sat 10-2
Friends of the Library Group

PHILADELPHIA

P BODMAN MEMORIAL LIBRARY*, Eight Aldrich St, 13673. SAN 312-2565. Tel: 315-642-3323. FAX: 315-642-0617. E-mail: philib@ncls.org. Web Site: www.bodmanmemoriallibrary.org. *Dir,* Tracy Tanner; Staff 1 (Non-MLS 1)
Founded 1917. Pop 1,947; Circ 8,361
Jan 2019-Dec 2019 Income (Main Library Only) $53,300, County $2,900, Locally Generated Income $49,000, Other $1,400. Mats Exp Books $1,550
Automation Activity & Vendor Info: (Cataloging) SirsiDynix; (Circulation) SirsiDynix; (OPAC) SirsiDynix
Wireless access
Function: 24/7 Electronic res, 24/7 Online cat, Adult bk club, Audiobks via web, Bks on CD, Children's prog, Computer training, Computers for patron use, Electronic databases & coll, Free DVD rentals, Home delivery & serv to seniorr ctr & nursing homes, Homebound delivery serv, ILL available, Internet access, Large print keyboards, Life-long learning prog for all ages, Magazines, Mail & tel request accepted, Meeting rooms, Movies, Notary serv, Online cat, Online ref, Outreach serv, OverDrive digital audio bks, Photocopying/Printing, Printer for laptops & handheld devices, Prog for adults, Prog for children & young adult, Ref & res, Ref serv available, Scanner, Senior computer classes, Senior outreach, Serves people with intellectual disabilities, Spanish lang bks, Story hour, Study rm, Summer & winter reading prog, Summer reading prog, Tax forms, Teen prog, Wheelchair accessible
Mem of North Country Library System
Special Services for the Blind - Audio mat; Bks on cassette; Bks on CD; Copier with enlargement capabilities; Free checkout of audio mat; Large print bks
Open Mon, Tues & Thurs 2-7, Wed 9-12, Fri 2-5, Sat 10-Noon
Friends of the Library Group

PHILMONT

P PHILMONT PUBLIC LIBRARY, 101 Main St, 12565. (Mail add: PO Box 816, 12565-0816), SAN 312-2573. Tel: 518-672-5010. FAX: 518-672-4367. E-mail: library@philmont.org. Web Site: philmontlibrary.com. *Dir,* Tobi Farley; Staff 2 (MLS 1, Non-MLS 1)
Founded 1898. Pop 1,500; Circ 21,600
Library Holdings: Bks on Deafness & Sign Lang 10; High Interest/Low Vocabulary Bk Vols 250; Bk Vols 25,000
Special Collections: Main Street Coll
Automation Activity & Vendor Info: (Cataloging) Innovative Interfaces, Inc; (Circulation) Innovative Interfaces, Inc; (OPAC) Innovative Interfaces, Inc
Wireless access
Function: ILL available
Mem of Mid-Hudson Library System
Special Services for the Deaf - TTY equip
Special Services for the Blind - Talking bks
Open Mon & Wed 1-7, Thurs & Sat 10-2, Fri 1-5
Friends of the Library Group

PHOENICIA

P PHOENICIA LIBRARY*, 48 Main St, 12464. (Mail add: PO Box 555, 12464-0555), SAN 312-2581. Tel: 845-688-7811. E-mail: phoenicialibrary@gmail.com. Web Site: phoenicialibrary.org. *Dir,* Liz Potter; E-mail: director@phoenicialibrary.org
Founded 1959. Pop 300; Circ 15,000
Library Holdings: Audiobooks 550; CDs 550; DVDs 1,300; e-books 7,800; Bk Vols 6,500
Special Collections: Jerry Bartlett Angling Coll
Automation Activity & Vendor Info: (Cataloging) Innovative Interfaces, Inc; (Circulation) Innovative Interfaces, Inc; (OPAC) Innovative Interfaces, Inc
Wireless access
Function: 24/7 Electronic res, Adult bk club, Bks on CD, Children's prog, Computer training, Computers for patron use, Digital talking bks, Free DVD rentals, Holiday prog, ILL available, Internet access, Life-long learning prog for all ages, Magazines, Mail & tel request accepted, Mango lang, Movies, Music CDs, Online cat, Outreach serv, OverDrive digital audio bks, Photocopying/Printing, Preschool outreach, Preschool reading prog, Prog for adults, Prog for children & young adult, Senior computer classes, Senior outreach, Story hour, Study rm, Summer reading prog, Wheelchair accessible
Mem of Mid-Hudson Library System
Open Mon & Wed 3-5, Fri 3-6, Sat 12-3
Friends of the Library Group

PHOENIX

P PHOENIX PUBLIC LIBRARY*, 34 Elm St, 13135, SAN 312-259X. Tel: 315-695-4355. FAX: 315-695-4355. E-mail: phelib@ncls.org. Web Site: www.phoenixnylibrary.org. *Dir,* Natalie Curran
Founded 1920. Circ 27,659
Library Holdings: Bk Vols 24,100
Subject Interests: Civil War hist, Job info, Local hist
Wireless access
Mem of North Country Library System
Open Mon & Wed 11-8, Tues, Thurs & Fri 11-5, Sat 10-1

PIERMONT

P DENNIS P MCHUGH PIERMONT PUBLIC LIBRARY*, 25 Flywheel Park W, 10968. SAN 312-2603. Tel: 845-359-4595. E-mail: info@piermontlibrary.org. Web Site: piermontlibrary.org. *Dir,* Kristine Palacios; E-mail: kpalacios@piermontlibrary.org; Staff 4 (MLS 4)
Library Holdings: Bk Vols 15,500
Special Collections: Local History Coll
Wireless access
Mem of Ramapo Catskill Library System
Open Mon, Wed & Fri 10-4, Tues & Thurs 12-7

PIKE

P PIKE LIBRARY, 65 Main St, 14130. (Mail add: PO Box 246, 14130-0246), SAN 312-262X. Tel: 585-493-5900. FAX: 585-493-5900. Web Site: www.pikelibrary.us. *Dir,* Tammy Hopkins; E-mail: PikeLibraryDirector@owwl.org
Circ 7,617
Library Holdings: Bk Vols 12,700; Per Subs 42

Wireless access
Mem of Pioneer Library System
Open Mon 1-7, Wed 10-6, Thurs 5-8, Sat 9-Noon

PINE BUSH

P PINE BUSH AREA LIBRARY*, 223-227 Maple Ave, 12566. SAN 312-2638. Tel: 845-744-3375. FAX: 845-744-3375. E-mail: Pbl@rcls.org. Web Site: pinebushareallibrary.org, www.rcls.org/?q=node/83. *Dir,* Doris Callan
Circ 61,000
Library Holdings: Electronic Media & Resources 2,002; Bk Vols 22,715; Videos 1,275
Automation Activity & Vendor Info: (Cataloging) Horizon; (Circulation) Horizon; (OPAC) Horizon; (Serials) Horizon
Wireless access
Mem of Ramapo Catskill Library System
Open Mon & Wed 9-7, Tues & Thurs 11-7, Fri 9-5, Sat 10-2
Friends of the Library Group

PINE HILL

P MORTON MEMORIAL LIBRARY*, 22 Elm St, 12465. SAN 312-2646. Tel: 845-254-4222. FAX: 845-254-4222. Web Site: pinehilllibrary.org. *Dir,* Gisi Vella; E-mail: pihlibrary@gmail.com
Founded 1903. Pop 308; Circ 5,000
Library Holdings: AV Mats 200; High Interest/Low Vocabulary Bk Vols 20; Bk Vols 9,000
Automation Activity & Vendor Info: (OPAC) Innovative Interfaces, Inc
Wireless access
Special Services for the Blind - Bks on CD; Talking bk & rec for the blind cat; Talking bks
Open Tues & Fri 11-5, Wed & Sat 10-2, Thurs 2-6

PINE PLAINS

P PINE PLAINS FREE LIBRARY*, 7775 S Main St, 12567-5653, (Mail add: PO Box 325, 12567-0325), SAN 312-2654. Tel: 518-398-1927. FAX: 518-398-6085. E-mail: info@pineplainslibrary.org, ppflibrary@gmail.com. Web Site: pineplainslibrary.org. *Dir,* Veronica Stork; E-mail: director@pineplainslibrary.org
Pop 2,287; Circ 10,000
Library Holdings: Bk Vols 10,000; Per Subs 28
Automation Activity & Vendor Info: (Cataloging) Innovative Interfaces, Inc - Millennium; (Circulation) Innovative Interfaces, Inc - Millennium; (OPAC) Innovative Interfaces, Inc - Millennium
Wireless access
Mem of Mid-Hudson Library System
Open Mon, Tues, Thurs & Fri 2-7, Wed 2-9, Sat 9-4
Friends of the Library Group

PITTSFORD

L HARRIS, BEACH PLLC*, Law Library, 99 Garnsey Rd, 14534. SAN 371-5205. Tel: 585-419-8800. FAX: 585-419-8814. Web Site: www.harrisbeach.com. *Dir, Libr & Res Serv,* Marie Calvaruso; E-mail: mcalvaruso@harrisbeach.com; *Mgr, Res Serv,* Cyndi Trembley; E-mail: ctrembley@harrisbeach.com
Automation Activity & Vendor Info: (Cataloging) Inmagic, Inc.; (Circulation) Inmagic, Inc.; (OPAC) Inmagic, Inc.; (Serials) Inmagic, Inc.
Wireless access
Restriction: Staff use only

P PITTSFORD COMMUNITY LIBRARY*, 24 State St, 14534. SAN 353-9164. Tel: 585-248-6275. FAX: 585-248-6259. Web Site: townofpittsford.org/home-library. *Dir,* Amanda Madigan; E-mail: amadigan@townofpittsford.org; *Asst Dir,* Kate Procious; Staff 5 (MLS 5)
Founded 1920. Pop 27,219; Circ 378,604
Library Holdings: Bk Vols 90,920
Automation Activity & Vendor Info: (Circulation) TLC (The Library Corporation); (OPAC) TLC (The Library Corporation)
Wireless access
Mem of Monroe County Library System
Open Mon-Thurs 9-9, Fri 9-6, Sat 10-5, Sun 1-5
Friends of the Library Group

PLAINVIEW

SR CHURCH OF JESUS CHRIST OF LATTER DAY SAINTS*, Family History Center, 160 Washington Ave, 11803. SAN 377-5631. Tel: 516-433-0122. E-mail: NY_Plainview@ldsmail.net. Web Site: www.familysearch.org/wiki/en/Plainview_New_York_Family_History_Center. *Dir,* Roberta Olson
Library Holdings: Bk Vols 500
Open Tues & Fri 10-2, Thurs 10-2 & 7-9:30, Sat 11-3

P PLAINVIEW-OLD BETHPAGE PUBLIC LIBRARY*, 999 Old Country Rd, 11803-4995. SAN 312-2689. Tel: 516-938-0077. FAX: 516-433-4645. Web Site: www.poblib.org. *Dir,* Gretchen Browne; Tel: 516-938-0077, Ext 239, E-mail: gbrowne@poblib.org; Staff 106 (MLS 24, Non-MLS 82)
Founded 1955. Pop 28,676; Circ 454,881
Jul 2012-Jun 2013 Income $6,313,650, State $7,800, Locally Generated Income $6,305,850. Mats Exp $430,000, Books $300,000, Per/Ser (Incl. Access Fees) $22,000, Electronic Ref Mat (Incl. Access Fees) $63,000. Sal $3,437,600 (Prof $1,300,000)
Library Holdings: Audiobooks 2,918; AV Mats 26,455; Bks on Deafness & Sign Lang 60; CDs 3,989; DVDs 9,653; e-books 26,652; Bk Vols 183,605; Per Subs 3,925; Talking Bks 1,217
Special Collections: Career; Career-Job Learning; Consumer Information; Law; LI Jewish Genealogical Society Coll; New & Used Automobiles; Plainview Old Bethpage Coll
Subject Interests: Bus info, Career info, College catalogs, Educ opportunities, Employment, Law, Local hist, Med
Automation Activity & Vendor Info: (Acquisitions) Innovative Interfaces, Inc; (Cataloging) Innovative Interfaces, Inc; (Circulation) Innovative Interfaces, Inc; (Course Reserve) Innovative Interfaces, Inc; (ILL) Innovative Interfaces, Inc; (Media Booking) Innovative Interfaces, Inc; (OPAC) Innovative Interfaces, Inc; (Serials) Innovative Interfaces, Inc
Wireless access
Function: Homebound delivery serv
Publications: Library World (Bimonthly)
Mem of Nassau Library System
Partic in OCLC Online Computer Library Center, Inc; Proquest Dialog
Special Services for the Blind - Home delivery serv; Talking bks
Open Mon-Fri 9-9, Sat 9:30-5:30, Sun 1-9
Friends of the Library Group

PLATTSBURGH

M CHAMPLAIN VALLEY PHYSICIANS HOSPITAL MEDICAL CENTER LIBRARY*, 75 Beekman St, 12901. SAN 312-2700. Tel: 518-562-7325. FAX: 518-562-7129. E-mail: cvphlib@cvph.org. Web Site: www.cvph.org/Wellness-Resources/library. *Med Libn,* Jill Tarabula; E-mail: jtarabula@cvph.org; Staff 2 (MLS 2)
Founded 1930
Library Holdings: Bk Titles 1,000; Per Subs 500
Publications: Library Newsletter (Quarterly)
Partic in Health Sci Libr & Info Consortium; National Network of Libraries of Medicine Region 7; Northern New York Library Network; OCLC Online Computer Library Center, Inc
Open Mon-Fri 8:30-5
Restriction: Open to pub for ref only

J CLINTON COMMUNITY COLLEGE*, LeRoy M Douglas Sr Library, 136 Clinton Point Dr, 12901-5690. SAN 312-2719. Tel: 518-562-4241. Interlibrary Loan Service Tel: 518-562-4249. FAX: 518-562-4116. E-mail: douglas.library@clinton.edu. Web Site: www.clinton.edu/campus-resources/douglas-library. *Ref & Instruction Libn,* Catherine Figlioli; E-mail: catherine.figlioli@clinton.edu; *Syst/Electronic Serv Libn,* Sarah Jennette; E-mail: sarah.jennette@clinton.edu; Staff 7 (MLS 4, Non-MLS 3)
Founded 1969. Enrl 1,686; Fac 145; Highest Degree: Associate
Sept 2012-Aug 2013 Income $95,800. Mats Exp $69,150, Books $25,000, Per/Ser (Incl. Access Fees) $13,500, AV Mat $7,650, Electronic Ref Mat (Incl. Access Fees) $23,000. Sal $269,000 (Prof $215,000)
Library Holdings: Bks on Deafness & Sign Lang 17; CDs 640; DVDs 1,930; e-books 401,712; e-journals 58,693; Electronic Media & Resources 1; Large Print Bks 6; Music Scores 26; Bk Titles 41,512; Bk Vols 41,875; Per Subs 40
Special Collections: Adirondack Coll; Special Coll
Subject Interests: Local hist, Regional hist
Automation Activity & Vendor Info: (Acquisitions) Baker & Taylor; (Cataloging) Ex Libris Group; (Circulation) Ex Libris Group; (Course Reserve) Ex Libris Group; (ILL) OCLC ILLiad; (OPAC) Ex Libris Group; (Serials) Ex Libris Group
Wireless access
Partic in Northern New York Library Network; OCLC Online Computer Library Center, Inc; SUNYConnect; Westchester Academic Library Directors Organization
Open Mon-Thurs 8-7, Fri 8-4

P CLINTON-ESSEX-FRANKLIN LIBRARY SYSTEM*, 33 Oak St, 12901-2810. SAN 312-2727. Tel: 518-563-5190. Toll Free Tel: 800-221-1980. FAX: 518-563-0421. E-mail: info2@cefls.org. Web Site: www.cefls.org. *Dir,* Steve Kenworthy; Tel: 518-563-5190, Ext 111, E-mail: skenworthy@cefls.org; *Head, Automation & Tech Serv,* Betsy Brooks; Tel: 518-563-5190, Ext 135, E-mail: bbrooks@cefls.org; *Librn I,* Anne Jobin-Picard; Tel: 518-563-5190, Ext 114, E-mail: ajobin-picard@cefls.org; Staff 10 (MLS 4, Non-MLS 6)
Founded 1954. Pop 169,661

Library Holdings: Audiobooks 2,286; AV Mats 7,368; CDs 1,834; DVDs 2,074; e-books 1,985; Electronic Media & Resources 20; High Interest/Low Vocabulary Bk Vols 7,281; Large Print Bks 10,045; Bk Titles 54,976; Bk Vols 55,554; Per Subs 6; Talking Bks 1,790; Videos 4,294
Automation Activity & Vendor Info: (Cataloging) SirsiDynix; (Circulation) SirsiDynix; (ILL) OCLC; (OPAC) SirsiDynix
Wireless access
Function: Audiobks via web, AV serv, Bks on cassette, Bks on CD, E-Reserves, Electronic databases & coll, Equip loans & repairs, Home delivery & serv to seniorr ctr & nursing homes, ILL available, Internet access, Jail serv, Mail loans to mem, Online cat, Outreach serv, Photocopying/Printing, Senior outreach, Summer reading prog, Telephone ref, VHS videos, Wheelchair accessible, Workshops
Publications: Trailblazer (Newsletter)
Member Libraries: Akwesasne Cultural Center Library; Altona Reading Center; Au Sable Forks Free Library; Beldon Noble Memorial Library; Black Watch Memorial Library; Champlain Memorial Library; Chateaugay Memorial Library; Chazy Public Library; Dannemora Free Library; Dodge Library; Dodge Memorial Library; E M Cooper Memorial Library; Elizabethtown Library Association; Ellenburg Center Reading Center; Hammond Library of Crown Point NY; Keene Public Library; Keene Valley Library Association; Keeseville Free Library; Lake Placid Public Library; Mooers Free Library; New York State Department of Corrections & Community Supervision; Paine Memorial Free Library; Peru Free Library; Plattsburgh Public Library; Sarah A Munsil Free Library; Saranac Lake Free Library; Schroon Lake Public Library; Sherman Free Library; Tupper Lake Public Library; Wadhams Free Library; Waverly Reading Center; Wead Library; Wells Memorial Library; Westport Library Association
Partic in Northern New York Library Network
Special Services for the Deaf - TDD equip
Special Services for the Blind - Aids for in-house use; BiFolkal kits; Large print bks; Magnifiers; Talking bks & player equip
Open Mon-Fri 8-5 (8-4 Summer)

GL NEW YORK STATE SUPREME COURT FOURTH DISTRICT*, Law Library, Clinton County Office Bldg, 137 Margaret St, 3rd Flr, 12901. SAN 312-2735. Tel: 518-285-8518. E-mail: 4JDLawLibrary@nycourts.gov. Web Site: www.courts.state.ny.us.
Library Holdings: Bk Vols 12,000
Wireless access
Open Mon-Fri 9-5

P PLATTSBURGH PUBLIC LIBRARY*, 19 Oak St, 12901-2810. SAN 312-2743. Tel: 518-563-0921. Circulation Tel: 518-536-7446. FAX: 518-563-7539. E-mail: PPLInfo@cityofplattsburg-ny.gov. Web Site: www.plattsburghlib.org. *Dir,* Anne de la Chapelle; E-mail: delachapellea@cityofplattsburgh-ny.gov; *Librn II,* Sarah Spanburgh; E-mail: spanburgh@cityofplattsburg-ny.gov; *Librn I,* Ben Carman; E-mail: CarmanB@cityofplattsburg-ny.gov; *Librn I,* Colleen Pelletier; E-mail: pelletierc@cityofplattsburg-ny.gov; Staff 4 (MLS 4)
Founded 1894. Pop 19,163; Circ 134,687
Library Holdings: Bk Titles 100,000
Special Collections: Clinton County & Plattsburgh History Coll
Automation Activity & Vendor Info: (Circulation) Horizon
Wireless access
Mem of Clinton-Essex-Franklin Library System
Partic in Northern New York Library Network
Open Mon, Fri & Sat 9-5, Tues-Thurs 9-8
Friends of the Library Group

C STATE UNIVERSITY OF NEW YORK COLLEGE AT PLATTSBURGH*, Benjamin F Feinberg Library, Two Draper Ave, 12901-2697. SAN 312-2751. Tel: 518-564-5180. Circulation Tel: 518-564-5182. Interlibrary Loan Service Tel: 518-564-4427. Reference Tel: 518-564-5190. FAX: 518-564-5100. Reference FAX: 518-564-3059. E-mail: reference@plattsburgh.edu. Web Site: web.plattsburgh.edu/library. *Dean of Libr & Info Serv,* Holly Heller-Ross; E-mail: hellerhb@plattsburgh.edu; *Asst Dean, Libr & Info Serv,* Mark Mastrean; Tel: 518-564-5307, E-mail: mastrems@plattsburgh.edu; *Assoc Librn,* Debra Kimok; Tel: 518-564-5206, E-mail: kimokdm@plattsburgh.edu; *Assoc Librn, Coordr, Coll Develop & Delivery,* Gordon Muir; Tel: 518-564-5304, E-mail: muirgd@plattsburgh.edu; *Assoc Librn,* Michelle Toth; Tel: 518-564-5225, E-mail: tothmm@plattsburgh.edu; *Assoc Librn,* Karen Volkman; Tel: 518-564-5305, E-mail: volkmake@plattsburgh.edu; Staff 22.1 (MLS 11.5, Non-MLS 10.6)
Founded 1889. Fac 469; Highest Degree: Master
Jul 2012-Jun 2013 Income $2,512,825. Mats Exp $677,016, Books $69,504, Per/Ser (Incl. Access Fees) $400,190, AV Mat $8,000, Electronic Ref Mat (Incl. Access Fees) $192,322, Presv $7,000. Sal $1,327,587 (Prof $140,393)
Library Holdings: CDs 944; DVDs 1,288; e-books 114,144; e-journals 5,089; Electronic Media & Resources 102; Microforms 711,342; Bk Titles 226,187; Bk Vols 295,056; Per Subs 5,343; Videos 670
Special Collections: College Archives; North Country History (Adirondack & Lake Champlain Regions; Clinton, Essex & Franklin Counties), bks, ms, maps, newsp, pamphlets, per, photog; Rockwell Kent Coll. Canadian and Provincial; Oral History; State Document Depository; US Document Depository
Subject Interests: Adirondack hist, North Country hist
Automation Activity & Vendor Info: (Acquisitions) Ex Libris Group; (Cataloging) Ex Libris Group; (Circulation) Ex Libris Group; (Course Reserve) Docutek; (ILL) OCLC ILLiad; (OPAC) Ex Libris Group; (Serials) Ex Libris Group
Wireless access
Function: Doc delivery serv
Publications: Access The World
Partic in New York State Interlibrary Loan Network; SUNYConnect
Open Mon-Thurs 7:30am-Midnight, Fri 7:30am-8pm, Sat 11-8, Sun Noon-Midnight

PLEASANT VALLEY

P PLEASANT VALLEY FREE LIBRARY, Three Maggiacomo Lane, 12569. (Mail add: PO Box 633, 12569-0633), SAN 312-276X. Tel: 845-635-8460. FAX: 845-635-9556. E-mail: PVFLibrary@gmail.com. Web Site: pleasantvalleylibrary.org. *Dir,* Daniela L Pulice; E-mail: danielapulice@gmail.com; *Head, Children's Servx,* Julie A Poplees; *Head, Circ,* Valerie Britton; Staff 4 (MLS 1, Non-MLS 3)
Founded 1903. Pop 9,864; Circ 85,000
Jan 2019-Dec 2019 Income $447,500, State $2,500, Locally Generated Income $440,000, Other $5,000. Mats Exp $51,000, Books $32,500, Per/Ser (Incl. Access Fees) $1,500, AV Mat $15,000, Electronic Ref Mat (Incl. Access Fees) $2,000. Sal $160,000 (Prof $80,000)
Library Holdings: AV Mats 500; Bks on Deafness & Sign Lang 15; CDs 2,000; DVDs 10,000; Large Print Bks 2,500; Bk Vols 50,000; Per Subs 20; Talking Bks 1,000
Automation Activity & Vendor Info: (Acquisitions) Innovative Interfaces, Inc; (Cataloging) Innovative Interfaces, Inc; (Circulation) Innovative Interfaces, Inc; (Course Reserve) Innovative Interfaces, Inc; (OPAC) Innovative Interfaces, Inc; (Serials) Innovative Interfaces, Inc
Wireless access
Function: 24/7 Electronic res, 24/7 Online cat, Activity rm, Adult bk club, Art exhibits, Audiobks via web, Bks on CD, Chess club, Children's prog, Computers for patron use, Electronic databases & coll, Free DVD rentals, Health sci info serv, Homebound delivery serv, ILL available, Internet access, Mail & tel request accepted, Mango lang, Meeting rooms, Movies, Museum passes, Music CDs, Notary serv, Online cat, OverDrive digital audio bks, Photocopying/Printing, Preschool reading prog, Prog for adults, Prog for children & young adult, Scanner, Story hour, Study rm, Summer reading prog, Tax forms, Wheelchair accessible
Mem of Mid-Hudson Library System
Open Mon-Thurs 10-8, Fri 12-6, Sat 10-2
Friends of the Library Group

PLEASANTVILLE

P MOUNT PLEASANT PUBLIC LIBRARY*, 350 Bedford Rd, 10570-3099. SAN 353-9253. Tel: 914-769-0548. FAX: 914-769-6149. E-mail: reference@mountpleasantlibrary.org. Web Site: www.mountpleasantlibrary.org. *Dir,* John Fearon; Tel: 914-769-0548, Ext 5, E-mail: director@mountpleasantlibrary.org; *Asst Dir,* Vivian Gufarotti; *Head, Children's Servx,* Susan Chajes; *Head, Circ & Tech Serv,* Matt DiTomasso; Staff 20 (MLS 5, Non-MLS 15)
Founded 1893. Pop 33,323; Circ 392,812
Jan 2013-Dec 2013 Income (Main & Associated Libraries) $2,588,134. Mats Exp $230,460, Books $139,898, Per/Ser (Incl. Access Fees) $10,700, AV Mat $69,066, Electronic Ref Mat (Incl. Access Fees) $10,796. Sal $1,187,035
Library Holdings: Audiobooks 2,750; CDs 4,987; DVDs 8,481; Bk Vols 90,013; Per Subs 150
Special Collections: Jacob Burns Film Center Curated Coll of DVDs; Local History Coll; Pleasantville SEPTA Parenting Coll
Automation Activity & Vendor Info: (Cataloging) SirsiDynix; (Circulation) SirsiDynix; (ILL) SirsiDynix
Wireless access
Publications: Inklings; Newsletter (Quarterly)
Mem of Westchester Library System
Open Mon, Tues & Thurs 10-9, Wed 10-6, Fri & Sat 10-5 (10-2 July-Aug), Sun (Sept-June) 1-5
Friends of the Library Group
Branches: 1
MOUNT PLEASANT BRANCH, 125 Lozza Dr, Valhalla, 10595-1268, SAN 353-9288. Tel: 914-741-0276. FAX: 914-495-3864. *Dir,* John Fearon
Open Mon, Tues & Thurs 10-5, Wed 10-8, Fri & Sat 10-2
Friends of the Library Group

C PACE UNIVERSITY*, Edward & Doris Mortola Library, 861 Bedford Rd, 10570-2799. SAN 353-9318. Tel: 914-773-3380. Reference Tel: 914-773-3381. Web Site: libguides.pace.edu. *Admin Dir, Head, Access Serv,* MacDonald Nadine; Tel: 914-773-3854, E-mail: nmacdonald@pace.edu; *Assoc Univ Librn,* Steven Feyl; Tel: 914-773-3233, E-mail: sfeyl@pace.edu; *Asst Univ Librn,* Medaline Philbert; Tel: 914-773-3945, E-mail: mphilbert@pace.edu; *Asst Univ Librn, Coll Mgt,* Noreen McGuire; Tel: 914-773-3815, E-mail: nmcguire@pace.edu; *Asst Univ Librn, Instrul Serv,* Sarah K Burns-Feyl; Tel: 914-773-3220, E-mail: sburnsfeyl@pace.edu; *Head, Info & Res Serv,* Gillen Rose; Tel: 914-773-3382, E-mail: rgillen@pace.edu; *Cat Librn,* June Pang; Tel: 914-773-3255, E-mail: jpang@pace.edu; *Electronic Res Librn,* Christina Blenke; Tel: 914-773-3222, E-mail: cblenke@pace.edu; *Instrul Serv Librn,* Douglas Heimbigner; Tel: 917-773-3244, E-mail: dheimbigner@pace.edu; *Ref Librn,* Harriet Huang; Tel: 914-773-3240, E-mail: hhuang@pace.edu; *ILL,* Sheila Hu; Tel: 914-773-3853, E-mail: shu@pace.edu; Staff 16 (MLS 10, Non-MLS 6)
Founded 1963. Enrl 3,300; Fac 438; Highest Degree: Doctorate
Library Holdings: AV Mats 13,787; DVDs 1,100; e-books 8,352; e-journals 62,417; Microforms 12,971; Bk Titles 195,502; Bk Vols 194,405; Per Subs 41; Videos 359
Special Collections: Rene Dubos; Saint Joan of Arc
Subject Interests: Computer sci, Educ, Lit, Nursing
Automation Activity & Vendor Info: (Acquisitions) Innovative Interfaces, Inc; (Cataloging) Innovative Interfaces, Inc; (Circulation) Innovative Interfaces, Inc; (Course Reserve) Innovative Interfaces, Inc; (ILL) Innovative Interfaces, Inc; (OPAC) Innovative Interfaces, Inc; (Serials) Innovative Interfaces, Inc
Wireless access
Publications: Information Edge (Newsletter); Printed & Online Bibliographic Handouts
Partic in ConnectNY, Inc; Metropolitan New York Library Council; NELLCO Law Library Consortium, Inc.; OCLC Online Computer Library Center, Inc; Westchester Academic Library Directors Organization
Open Mon-Thurs 8:30am-2am, Fri 8am-11pm, Sat 10-8, Sun 10am-2am

POESTENKILL

P POESTENKILL PUBLIC LIBRARY*, Nine Plank Rd, 12140. (Mail add: PO Box 305, 12140-0305). Tel: 518-283-3721. FAX: 518-283-5618. E-mail: info@poestenkilllibrary.org. Web Site: www.poestenkilllibrary.org. *Dir,* Margie Ann Morris; E-mail: margie@poestenkilllibrary.org
Pop 4,054
Library Holdings: AV Mats 850; Large Print Bks 200; Bk Vols 16,000; Talking Bks 350
Automation Activity & Vendor Info: (Cataloging) SirsiDynix; (Circulation) SirsiDynix; (OPAC) SirsiDynix
Wireless access
Mem of Upper Hudson Library System
Open Mon, Fri & Sat 10-1, Tues-Thurs 1-8:30
Friends of the Library Group

POLAND

P POLAND PUBLIC LIBRARY, 8849 N Main St, 13431. SAN 312-2786. Tel: 315-826-3112. FAX: 315-826-5677. Web Site: poland.midyork.org. *Dir,* Paula Johnson; E-mail: pjohnson@midyork.org
Circ 31,288
Library Holdings: AV Mats 800; Bk Vols 15,000; Per Subs 30
Automation Activity & Vendor Info: (Cataloging) SirsiDynix; (Circulation) SirsiDynix; (OPAC) SirsiDynix
Wireless access
Mem of Mid-York Library System
Open Mon 11:30-5:30, Tues, Thurs & Fri 10-4

POPLAR RIDGE

P HAZARD LIBRARY ASSOCIATION*, 2487 Rte 34 B, 13139. (Mail add: PO Box 3, 13139-0003), SAN 312-2794. Tel: 315-364-7975. FAX: 315-364-6704. E-mail: librarian@hazardlibrary.org. Web Site: www.hazardlibrary.org. *Dir,* Lisa Semenza
Founded 1887. Pop 1,286; Circ 14,776
Library Holdings: Bk Titles 6,542
Special Collections: Quaker Coll
Subject Interests: Local hist
Automation Activity & Vendor Info: (Cataloging) Innovative Interfaces, Inc; (Circulation) Innovative Interfaces, Inc; (OPAC) Innovative Interfaces, Inc
Wireless access
Mem of Finger Lakes Library System
Open Tues 9-12 & 2-8, Thurs 1-8, Sat 9-2
Friends of the Library Group

PORT BYRON

P PORT BYRON LIBRARY, 12 Sponable Dr, 13140. (Mail add: PO Box 520, 13140-0520). Tel: 315-776-5694. FAX: 315-776-5693. Web Site: portbyronlibrary.org. *Dir,* Ben Love; E-mail: director@portbyronlibrary.org; Staff 3 (MLS 1, Non-MLS 2)
Pop 2,446
Library Holdings: AV Mats 140; Bk Titles 15,000
Special Collections: Local History Coll
Automation Activity & Vendor Info: (Cataloging) Innovative Interfaces, Inc. - Polaris; (Circulation) Innovative Interfaces, Inc. - Polaris; (ILL) Innovative Interfaces, Inc. - Polaris; (OPAC) Innovative Interfaces, Inc. - Polaris; (Serials) Innovative Interfaces, Inc. - Polaris
Wireless access
Mem of Finger Lakes Library System
Open Mon & Wed 3-8, Tues & Thurs 10-6, Fri 3-6, Sat 10-2

PORT CHESTER

P PORT CHESTER-RYE BROOK PUBLIC LIBRARY*, One Haseco Ave, 10573. SAN 312-2816. Tel: 914-939-6710. Circulation Tel: 914-939-6710, Ext 101. Reference Tel: 914-939-6710, Ext 103, 914-939-6710, Ext 110. FAX: 914-939-4735. Administration FAX: 914-937-2580. Web Site: www.portchester-ryebrooklibrary.org. *Dir,* Robin Lettieri; Tel: 914-939-6710, Ext 114, E-mail: rlettieri@wlsmail.org; *Asst Dir,* Mayra Fortes; Tel: 914-939-6710, Ext 111; *Ch Serv,* Teresa Cotter; Tel: 914-939-6710, Ext 108; *Ref & Info Serv,* Stacey Harris; *Tech Serv,* Tomasa Rodriguez; Tel: 914-939-6710, Ext 107; Staff 18 (MLS 4.7, Non-MLS 13.3)
Founded 1876. Pop 38,314; Circ 232,739
Jun 2017-May 2018 Income $1,689,979, State $11,119, Locally Generated Income $1,475,323, Other $140,589. Mats Exp $92,196. Sal $541,036 (Prof $328,831)
Library Holdings: Audiobooks 5,061; AV Mats 31,135; DVDs 2,930; Bk Titles 66,156; Per Subs 602
Special Collections: Genealogy, bks & original ms; Job Information Center; Local & County History Coll
Subject Interests: Foreign lang
Automation Activity & Vendor Info: (Acquisitions) Evergreen; (Cataloging) Evergreen; (Circulation) Evergreen; (ILL) Evergreen; (OPAC) Evergreen; (Serials) Evergreen
Wireless access
Function: 24/7 Electronic res, 24/7 Online cat, Activity rm, Adult bk club, Adult literacy prog, After school storytime, Archival coll, AV serv, BA reader (adult literacy), Bilingual assistance for Spanish patrons, Bk club(s), Bks on cassette, Bks on CD, Chess club, Children's prog, Citizenship assistance, Computer training, Computers for patron use, E-Reserves, Electronic databases & coll, Family literacy, For res purposes, Free DVD rentals, Health sci info serv, Holiday prog, Home delivery & serv to seniorr ctr & nursing homes, Homebound delivery serv, Homework prog, ILL available, Internet access, Life-long learning prog for all ages, Literacy & newcomer serv, Mail & tel request accepted, Meeting rooms, Microfiche/film & reading machines, Movies, Museum passes, Online cat, Online info literacy tutorials on the web & in blackboard, Online ref, Orientations, Outreach serv, Outside serv via phone, mail, e-mail & web, OverDrive digital audio bks, Photocopying/Printing, Preschool outreach, Printer for laptops & handheld devices, Prog for adults, Prog for children & young adult, Ref & res, Ref serv available, Senior computer classes, Senior outreach, Serves people with intellectual disabilities, Spanish lang bks, Spoken cassettes & CDs, Spoken cassettes & DVDs, Story hour, Summer & winter reading prog, Summer reading prog, Tax forms, Teen prog, Telephone ref, Wheelchair accessible, Workshops
Mem of Westchester Library System
Special Services for the Blind - Bks on cassette; Bks on CD
Open Mon 9-9, Tues 9-8, Wed-Sat 9-5
Friends of the Library Group

PORT EWEN

P TOWN OF ESOPUS PUBLIC LIBRARY, 128 Canal St, 12466. (Mail add: PO Box 1167, 12466-1167), SAN 312-2832. Tel: 845-338-5580. FAX: 845-338-5583. E-mail: info@esopuslibrary.org. Web Site: www.esopuslibrary.org. *Dir,* Brooke Dittmar; Staff 1 (MLS 1)
Founded 1922. Pop 9,331; Circ 45,000
Library Holdings: Bk Vols 25,000; Per Subs 82
Special Collections: John Burrough Coll
Subject Interests: Art, Cooking, Ecology, Health, Hudson River Valley hist, Local hist
Automation Activity & Vendor Info: (Acquisitions) Innovative Interfaces, Inc; (Cataloging) Innovative Interfaces, Inc; (Circulation) Innovative Interfaces, Inc; (ILL) Innovative Interfaces, Inc; (Media Booking) Innovative Interfaces, Inc; (OPAC) Innovative Interfaces, Inc; (Serials) Innovative Interfaces, Inc
Wireless access
Mem of Mid-Hudson Library System
Special Services for the Deaf - Bks on deafness & sign lang

Special Services for the Blind - Audio mat; Bks available with recordings; Bks on cassette; Bks on CD; Large print bks; Talking bks
Open Mon-Wed & Fri 10-6, Thurs 1-6
Friends of the Library Group

PORT HENRY

P SHERMAN FREE LIBRARY*, 20 Church St, 12974. SAN 312-2840. Tel: 518-546-7461. FAX: 518-546-7461. E-mail: shermanfree@yahoo.com. Web Site: www.porthenrymoriah.com/living-here/about/sherman-free-library. *Libr Dir,* Michele Paquette; *Libr Asst,* Amy Decker
Founded 1887. Pop 4,978; Circ 7,778
Library Holdings: Bk Vols 10,500; Per Subs 10
Subject Interests: Local hist, Mining
Automation Activity & Vendor Info: (Cataloging) Horizon; (Circulation) Horizon; (ILL) Horizon; (OPAC) Horizon; (Serials) Horizon
Wireless access
Mem of Clinton-Essex-Franklin Library System
Open Tues & Thurs 12-7, Wed 12-4, Fri 12-5, Sat 10-2
Friends of the Library Group

PORT JEFFERSON

P PORT JEFFERSON FREE LIBRARY, 100 Thompson St, 11777. SAN 312-2867. Tel: 631-473-0022. Administration Tel: 631-473-0631. FAX: 631-473-2903. Administration FAX: 631-473-8661. E-mail: info@portjefflibrary.org. Web Site: www.portjefflibrary.org. *Libr Dir,* Tom Donlon; *YA Serv,* Erin Schaarschmidt; E-mail: pjteen@gmail.com; Staff 7 (MLS 7)
Founded 1908. Pop 7,705; Circ 278,000
Library Holdings: Audiobooks 4,655; AV Mats 24,669; CDs 4,023; DVDs 7,683; High Interest/Low Vocabulary Bk Vols 350; Large Print Bks 2,957; Bk Vols 147,143; Per Subs 250; Spec Interest Per Sub 17; Videos 7,477
Special Collections: Long Island History
Automation Activity & Vendor Info: (Cataloging) Innovative Interfaces, Inc; (Circulation) Innovative Interfaces, Inc; (ILL) Innovative Interfaces, Inc; (OPAC) Innovative Interfaces, Inc
Wireless access
Publications: The Yeoman (Newsletter)
Mem of Suffolk Cooperative Library System
Special Services for the Blind - Closed circuit TV magnifier; Reader equip; Talking bks
Open Mon-Thurs 9:30-9, Fri & Sat 9:30-5
Friends of the Library Group

PORT JEFFERSON STATION

P COMSEWOGUE PUBLIC LIBRARY*, 170 Terryville Rd, 11776. SAN 312-2883. Tel: 631-928-1212. FAX: 631-928-6307. Administration E-mail: administration@cplib.org. Web Site: www.cplib.org. *Libr Dir,* Debra L Engelhardt; *Children & Teen Librn, Ref Serv,* Audrey Asaro; *Ref Serv, Ad,* Susan Guerin; *Circ,* Elizabeth Washburn; *Network Serv,* Len Frosina; *Tech Serv,* Angela DeRosalia
Founded 1966
Library Holdings: Audiobooks 21,709; AV Mats 44,318; DVDs 22,609; Bk Vols 139,288
Automation Activity & Vendor Info: (Cataloging) Innovative Interfaces, Inc; (Circulation) Innovative Interfaces, Inc; (OPAC) Innovative Interfaces, Inc
Wireless access
Function: 24/7 Electronic res, 24/7 Online cat, Activity rm, Adult bk club, Adult literacy prog, After school storytime, Art exhibits, Audiobks via web, AV serv, Bk club(s), Bks on CD, Children's prog, Citizenship assistance, Computer training, Computers for patron use, Distance learning, E-Readers, E-Reserves, Electronic databases & coll, Equip loans & repairs, Family literacy, Free DVD rentals, Holiday prog, Homebound delivery serv, ILL available, Internet access, Life-long learning prog for all ages, Literacy & newcomer serv, Magazines, Magnifiers for reading, Mail & tel request accepted, Meeting rooms, Microfiche/film & reading machines, Movies, Museum passes, Music CDs, Online cat, Outreach serv, Outside serv via phone, mail, e-mail & web, OverDrive digital audio bks, Photocopying/Printing, Preschool outreach, Preschool reading prog, Printer for laptops & handheld devices, Prog for adults, Prog for children & young adult, Ref & res, Ref serv available, Scanner, Senior computer classes, Serves people with intellectual disabilities, Spanish lang bks, Story hour, Study rm, Summer & winter reading prog, Summer reading prog, Tax forms, Teen prog, Telephone ref, VHS videos, Wheelchair accessible, Workshops, Writing prog
Mem of Suffolk Cooperative Library System
Special Services for the Deaf - ADA equip; Adult & family literacy prog; Assisted listening device; High interest/low vocabulary bks
Special Services for the Blind - Accessible computers; Assistive/Adapted tech devices, equip & products; Bks on CD; Extensive large print coll; Home delivery serv; Large print bks; Low vision equip; Screen enlargement software for people with visual disabilities; Screen reader software; Talking bk serv referral; Talking bks; Talking bks & player equip; Text reader
Open Mon-Thurs 9:30-9, Fri & Sat 9:30-5, Sun (Oct-May) 12-4

PORT JERVIS

S MINISINK VALLEY HISTORICAL SOCIETY RESEARCH ARCHIVES, c/o Port Jervis Free Library, 138 Pike St, 2nd Flr, 12771. SAN 325-4607. Tel: 845-856-2375. E-mail: minisinkvalley@gmail.com. Web Site: www.minisink.org. *Exec Dir,* Nancy Conod; Staff 1 (MLS 1)
Founded 1889
Library Holdings: Bk Titles 30,000; Bk Vols 31,000
Subject Interests: Genealogy, Local hist
Publications: Newsletter (Quarterly)
Restriction: Open by appt only

P PORT JERVIS FREE LIBRARY*, 138 Pike St, 12771. SAN 312-2891. Tel: 845-856-7313, 845-856-9154. FAX: 845-858-8710. E-mail: ptj@rcls.org. Web Site: www.portjervislibrary.org. *Libr Dir,* Beverly Arlequeeuw; Tel: 845-856-7313, Ext 6, E-mail: barlequeeuw@rcls.org; Staff 18 (MLS 1, Non-MLS 17)
Founded 1892. Pop 18,000; Circ 147,646
Library Holdings: Bk Titles 46,155; Per Subs 107; Talking Bks 1,201; Videos 2,210
Special Collections: Local Newspaper (115 years of the Port Jervis Union Gazette), microflm; Stephen Crane Materials; Zane Grey Coll
Automation Activity & Vendor Info: (Circulation) SirsiDynix-WorkFlows
Wireless access
Mem of Ramapo Catskill Library System
Open Mon, Tues & Thurs 10-9, Wed & Fri 10-6, Sat 10-5
Friends of the Library Group

PORT LEYDEN

P PORT LEYDEN COMMUNITY LIBRARY*, 3145 Canal St, 13433. (Mail add: PO Box 97, 13433), SAN 312-2913. Tel: 315-348-6077. FAX: 315-348-4234. E-mail: plylib@ncls.org. Web Site: www.portleydenlibrary.org. *Dir,* Lyn Cyr
Founded 1925. Pop 665; Circ 9,402
Library Holdings: Large Print Bks 463; Bk Titles 8,458; Per Subs 20
Automation Activity & Vendor Info: (Cataloging) SirsiDynix; (Circulation) SirsiDynix; (OPAC) SirsiDynix; (Serials) SirsiDynix
Wireless access
Function: Homebound delivery serv, ILL available, Magnifiers for reading, Photocopying/Printing, Prog for children & young adult, Summer reading prog, Wheelchair accessible
Mem of North Country Library System
Open Mon 9-1 & 6-9, Tues & Fri 1-5, Wed 6-9, Sat 9-Noon

PORT WASHINGTON

P PORT WASHINGTON PUBLIC LIBRARY*, One Library Dr, 11050. SAN 312-2921. Tel: 516-883-4400. Information Services Tel: 516-883-4400, Ext 1300. FAX: 516-883-7927. E-mail: library@pwpl.org. Web Site: www.pwpl.org. *Libr Dir,* Keith Klang; Tel: 516-883-3728, Ext 1101, E-mail: kklang@pwpl.org; *Asst Dir,* James Hutter; Tel: 516-883-3728, Ext 1102; *Head, Adult Serv,* Kate Monsour; Tel: 516-883-3728, Ext 1302, E-mail: monsour@pwpl.org; *Head, Children's Servx,* Rachel Fox; Tel: 516-883-3728, Ext 1602, E-mail: foxr@pwpl.org; *Head, Media Serv,* Jonathan Guildroy; Tel: 516-883-3728, Ext 1800, E-mail: guildroy@pwpl.org; *Head, Res Serv,* Janet West; Tel: 516-883-3728, Ext 1402, E-mail: westj@pwpl.org; Staff 50 (MLS 19, Non-MLS 31)
Founded 1892. Pop 30,666; Circ 428,025
Library Holdings: Bk Vols 163,600; Per Subs 337
Special Collections: Long Island Coll; Nautical Center Coll; Sinclair Lewis. Oral History
Subject Interests: Long Island hist
Automation Activity & Vendor Info: (Circulation) Innovative Interfaces, Inc; (OPAC) Innovative Interfaces, Inc
Wireless access
Publications: Flight of Memory: Long Island's Aeronautical Past; It Looks Like Yesterday to Me: Port Washington's Afro-American Heritage; Particles of the Past: Sandmining on Long Island 1870's-1980's; Port Washington (Arcadia Pub); Workers on the Grand Estates of Long Island 1980's-1940's
Mem of Nassau Library System
Partic in OCLC Online Computer Library Center, Inc
Open Mon, Tues & Sat 10-4, Thurs & Fri 12-6
Friends of the Library Group

PORTVILLE

P PORTVILLE FREE LIBRARY, Two N Main St, 14770. (Mail add: PO Box 768, 14770-0768), SAN 312-293X. Tel: 716-933-8441. FAX: 716-933-8441. Web Site: portvillelibrary.org. *Mgr,* Beth M Marvin; E-mail: manager@portvillelibrary.org

Founded 1902. Pop 3,952; Circ 19,712
Library Holdings: Audiobooks 300; DVDs 700; Large Print Bks 900; Bk Vols 42,530; Per Subs 89
Special Collections: Dusenbury Coll; Portville Newspaper Coll
Subject Interests: Local hist
Wireless access
Mem of Chautauqua-Cattaraugus Library System
Open Mon & Thurs 1-8, Tues 10-5, Fri 9-5, Sat 10-1
Friends of the Library Group

POTSDAM

C CLARKSON UNIVERSITY LIBRARIES, Harriet Call Burnap Memorial Library (Main Library), Andrew S Schuler Educational Resources Ctr, CU Box 5590, Eight Clarkson Ave, 13699-5590. SAN 312-2948. Tel: 315-268-2292. FAX: 315-268-7655. Web Site: sites.clarkson.edu/library. *Dean of Libr,* Michelle L Young; Tel: 315-268-4268, E-mail: myoung@clarkson.edu; *Coll Mgt Librn,* Katherine Moss; Tel: 315-268-4452, E-mail: kmoss@clarkson.edu; *Syst Librn,* Peter J Morris; Tel: 315-268-4459, E-mail: pmorris@clarkson.edu; Staff 7 (MLS 5, Non-MLS 2)
Founded 1896. Enrl 3,588; Fac 199; Highest Degree: Doctorate
Jul 2016-Jun 2017 Income (Main Library Only) $1,168,907. Mats Exp $989,862. Sal $672,492 (Prof $297,470)
Library Holdings: Audiobooks 155; CDs 1,518; DVDs 168; e-books 190,980; e-journals 30,430; Electronic Media & Resources 16; Microforms 261,229; Bk Vols 200,000; Per Subs 15; Videos 232
Special Collections: US Document Depository
Subject Interests: Bus, Engr, Sci
Automation Activity & Vendor Info: (Acquisitions) Innovative Interfaces, Inc; (Cataloging) Innovative Interfaces, Inc; (Circulation) Innovative Interfaces, Inc; (Course Reserve) Innovative Interfaces, Inc; (ILL) OCLC; (OPAC) Innovative Interfaces, Inc; (Serials) Innovative Interfaces, Inc
Wireless access
Partic in Associated Colleges of the Saint Lawrence Valley; Northeast Research Libraries Consortium; Northern New York Library Network; OCLC Online Computer Library Center, Inc; Westchester Academic Library Directors Organization
Special Services for the Blind - Assistive/Adapted tech devices, equip & products; Computer access aids; Copier with enlargement capabilities; Low vision equip; ZoomText magnification & reading software

Departmental Libraries:

CM HEALTH SCIENCES LIBRARY, 59 Main St, 1st Flr, 13699. (Mail add: Eight Clarkson Ave, CU Box 5591, 13699). Tel: 315-268-4464. FAX: 315-268-7655. Web Site: sites.clarkson.edu/library/health-sciences-library-2. *Dir of Libr,* Michelle L Young; Tel: 315-268-4268, E-mail: myoung@clarkson.edu; *Health Sci Librn,* Mary Cabral; E-mail: mcabral@clarkson.edu; Staff 1 (MLS 1)
Founded 1999. Enrl 287; Fac 13; Highest Degree: Doctorate
Library Holdings: Audiobooks 8; CDs 26; DVDs 22; e-books 2,131; e-journals 1,166; Bk Vols 6,400; Per Subs 20; Videos 196
Automation Activity & Vendor Info: (ILL) Innovative Interfaces, Inc
Open Mon-Wed 8-6, Tues-Thurs 8-4:30, Fri 9:30-3:30

P POTSDAM PUBLIC LIBRARY*, Civic Ctr, Ste 1, Two Park St, 13676. SAN 312-2956. Tel: 315-265-7230. FAX: 315-268-0306. E-mail: info@potsdamlibrary.org. Web Site: www.potsdamlibrary.org. *Dir,* Annie Chase; E-mail: achase@potsdamlibrary.org; Staff 16 (MLS 3, Non-MLS 13)
Founded 1896. Pop 14,736; Circ 134,891
Library Holdings: Bk Vols 60,339; Per Subs 70
Special Collections: Adult Literacy; Employment Information & Micro-Enterprize Coll
Subject Interests: Local hist
Automation Activity & Vendor Info: (OPAC) SirsiDynix
Wireless access
Mem of North Country Library System
Partic in Northern New York Library Network
Open Mon-Thurs 9-8, Fri & Sat 9-5, Sun Noon-4
Friends of the Library Group
Bookmobiles: 3

C STATE UNIVERSITY OF NEW YORK COLLEGE AT POTSDAM*, Frederick W Crumb Memorial Library, Lougheed Learning Commons, 44 Pierrepont Ave, 13676-2294. SAN 353-9342. Tel: 315-267-2485. Administration Tel: 315-267-2482. FAX: 315-267-2744. E-mail: libcrumb@potsdam.edu. Web Site: library.potsdam.edu. *Dir, Libr Serv,* Jenica Rogers; Tel: 315-267-3328, E-mail: rogersjp@potsdam.edu; *Assoc Librn,* Carol Franck; Tel: 315-267-3310, E-mail: franckcr@potsdam.edu; *Sr Asst Librn,* Holly Chambers; Tel: 315-267-3312, E-mail: chambehe@potsdam.edu; *Automation Syst Librn, Coll Develop Coordr, Syst,* Marianne Hebert; Tel: 315-267-3308, E-mail: hebertm@potsdam.edu; Staff 11.3 (MLS 9, Non-MLS 2.3)
Founded 1816. Enrl 4,445; Fac 345; Highest Degree: Master
Library Holdings: AV Mats 1,805; Bk Titles 238,473; Per Subs 499
Special Collections: College Archives; St Lawrence Seaway (Bertrand H Snell Papers). State Document Depository; US Document Depository
Subject Interests: Educ
Wireless access
Partic in Associated Colleges of the Saint Lawrence Valley; Northern New York Library Network; SUNYConnect
Special Services for the Blind - Assistive/Adapted tech devices, equip & products
Open Mon-Fri 8-4
Restriction: Open to pub for ref & circ; with some limitations

Departmental Libraries:

JULIA E CRANE MEMORIAL LIBRARY, Crane School of Music, Schuette Hall, 44 Pierrepont Ave, 13676-2294, SAN 353-9377. Tel: 315-267-2451. Web Site: library.potsdam.edu/crane. *Music Librn,* Edward Komara; Tel: 315-267-3227, E-mail: komaraem@potsdam.edu; Staff 3 (MLS 1, Non-MLS 2)
Founded 1927. Enrl 620; Fac 70; Highest Degree: Master
Library Holdings: AV Mats 10,792; Music Scores 19,907; Bk Titles 11,103; Per Subs 45
Subject Interests: Music, Music scores, Sound rec

POUGHKEEPSIE

J DUTCHESS COMMUNITY COLLEGE LIBRARY*, Francis U & Mary F Ritz Library, 53 Pendell Rd, 12601-1595. SAN 312-2964. Tel: 845-431-8630. Circulation Tel: 845-431-8639. Interlibrary Loan Service Tel: 845-431-8636. Reference Tel: 845-431-8634. Web Site: www.sunydutchess.edu/academics/library. *Dir,* Cathy Carl; Tel: 845-431-8635, E-mail: cathy.carl@sunydutchess.edu; *Access Serv,* Bonnie Gallagher; Tel: 845-431-8631, E-mail: bonnie.gallagher@sunydutchess.edu; *ILL,* Christine Craig; E-mail: craig@sunydutchess.edu; Staff 7 (MLS 7)
Founded 1957. Enrl 7,700; Fac 119; Highest Degree: Associate
Library Holdings: Bk Titles 84,066; Bk Vols 90,065; Per Subs 110
Automation Activity & Vendor Info: (Acquisitions) Ex Libris Group; (Cataloging) Ex Libris Group; (Circulation) Ex Libris Group; (Discovery) EBSCO Discovery Service; (ILL) OCLC; (OPAC) Ex Libris Group
Wireless access
Partic in Southeastern New York Library Resources Council; SUNYConnect
Open Mon-Thurs 8am-9pm, Fri 8-5, Sat 11-3, Sun 1-6
Restriction: Circ limited

S DUTCHESS COUNTY GENEALOGICAL SOCIETY LIBRARY*, Family History Ctr, LDS Church, 204 Spackenkill Rd, 12603-5135. (Mail add: PO Box 708, 12602-0708), SAN 370-2316. Tel: 845-462-6909. Web Site: www.dcgs-gen.org. *VPres,* Mary Colbert
Founded 1972
Jul 2013-Jun 2014 Income $700. Mats Exp $500
Library Holdings: Bk Titles 900; Spec Interest Per Sub 6
Subject Interests: Genealogy, Heraldry, Hist
Wireless access
Function: Res libr
Publications: The Dutchess (Quarterly)
Open Tues & Thurs 9-1, Wed 7-9
Restriction: Not a lending libr, Pub use on premises

C MARIST COLLEGE*, James A Cannavino Library, 3399 North Rd, 12601-1387. SAN 312-3014. Tel: 845-575-3199. FAX: 845-575-3150. Web Site: library.marist.edu. *Libr Dir,* Rebecca Albitz; Tel: 845-575-3196, E-mail: rebecca.albitz@marist.edu; *Dir, Archives, Spec Coll,* John Ansley; Tel: 845-575-5217, E-mail: john.ansley@marist.edu; *Digital Serv, Sr Librn,* Kathryn Silberger; Tel: 845-575-3419, E-mail: kathryn.silberger@marist.edu; *Assoc Librn, Bibliog Serv,* Marta Cwik; E-mail: marta.cwik@marist.edu; *Assoc Librn, Mgr, Res Mgt,* Judy Diffenderfer; E-mail: judy.diffenderfer@marist.edu; *Asst Librn, Res Serv,* Nancy Calabrese; E-mail: nancy.calabrese@marist.edu; *Asst Librn, Res Serv,* Elizabeth Clarke; E-mail: elizabeth.clarke@marist.edu; *Asst Librn, Res Serv,* Edgar Santiago; E-mail: edgar.santiago@marist.edu; *Asst Librn, Digital Serv,* Monish Singh. Subject Specialists: *Budgeting,* Judy Diffenderfer; Staff 11 (MLS 10, Non-MLS 1)
Founded 1929. Enrl 5,694; Fac 346; Highest Degree: Master
Library Holdings: AV Mats 3,500; e-books 207,000; e-journals 105,000; Electronic Media & Resources 11,000; Bk Vols 240,500
Special Collections: Hudson River Environmental Society Coll; John Tillman Newscasts; Lowell Thomas Coll; Maristiana; Rick Whitsell R&B Rec Coll
Subject Interests: Hudson Valley Regional studies
Automation Activity & Vendor Info: (Acquisitions) Ex Libris Group; (Cataloging) Ex Libris Group; (Circulation) Ex Libris Group; (Course Reserve) Ex Libris Group; (ILL) OCLC WorldShare Interlibrary Loan; (OPAC) Ex Libris Group
Wireless access
Partic in Southeastern New York Library Resources Council; Westchester Academic Library Directors Organization

S MENTAL HEALTH AMERICA LIBRARY, 253 Mansion St, 2nd Flr, 12601. SAN 312-2980. Tel: 845-473-2500, Ext 1325. Web Site: www.mhadutchess.org/library. *Librn,* Janet Caruso; E-mail: jcaruso@mhadutchess.org; Staff 1 (MLS 1)
Founded 1969
Library Holdings: Bk Titles 3,000; Per Subs 40
Subject Interests: Alcoholism, Child psychiat, Child study, Drug abuse, Psychiat, Psychol, Psychotherapy
Automation Activity & Vendor Info: (Cataloging) Koha
Wireless access
Publications: Accessions List; Audio-Visual Catalog; Brochure
Partic in Southeastern New York Library Resources Council
Open Mon-Fri, 9-5

P MID-HUDSON LIBRARY SYSTEM*, 103 Market St, 12601-4098. SAN 312-3022. Tel: 845-471-6060. FAX: 845-454-5940. Web Site: midhudson.org. *Exec Dir,* Rebekkah Smith Aldrich; Tel: 845-471-6060, Ext 239, E-mail: rsmith@midhudson.org; *Asst Dir,* Laurie Shedrick; Tel: 845-471-6060, Ext 220, E-mail: lshedrick@midhudson.org; Staff 13 (MLS 7, Non-MLS 6)
Founded 1959. Pop 619,578
Automation Activity & Vendor Info: (Circulation) Innovative Interfaces, Inc; (ILL) OCLC WorldShare Interlibrary Loan; (OPAC) Innovative Interfaces, Inc
Wireless access
Publications: Mid-Hudson Library System Bulletin (Weekly)
Member Libraries: Alice Curtis Desmond & Hamilton Fish Library; Amenia Free Library; Beekman Library; Blodgett Memorial Library; Brewster Public Library; Cairo Public Library; Catskill Public Library; Chatham Public Library; Claverack Free Library; Clinton Community Library; Dover Plains Library; East Fishkill Community Library; Elting Memorial Library; Fishkill Correctional Facility Library; Germantown Library; Greenville Public Library; Grinnell Library; Heermance Memorial Library; Highland Public Library; Howland Public Library; Hudson Area Library; Hunter Public Library; Hurley Library; Hyde Park Free Library; Julia L Butterfield Memorial Library; Kent Public Library; Kinderhook Memorial Library; Kingston Library; La Grange Association Library; Livingston Free Library; Mahopac Public Library; Marlboro Free Library; Millbrook Library; Morton Memorial Library & Community House; Mountain Top Library; New Lebanon Library; North Chatham Free Library; NorthEast-Millerton Library; Olive Free Library Association; Patterson Library; Pawling Free Library; Philmont Public Library; Phoenicia Library; Pine Plains Free Library; Plattekill Public Library; Pleasant Valley Free Library; Poughkeepsie Public Library District; Putnam Valley Free Library; Red Hook Public Library; Reed Memorial Library; Roeliff Jansen Community Library Association, Inc; Rosendale Library; Sarah Hull Hallock Free Library; Saugerties Public Library; Staatsburg Library; Stanford Free Library; Starr Library; Stone Ridge Public Library; Tivoli Free Library; Town of Esopus Public Library; Town of Ulster Public Library; Valatie Free Library; West Hurley Public Library; Windham Public Library; Woodstock Public Library District
Partic in Southeastern New York Library Resources Council
Open Mon-Fri 8:30-4:30

GL NEW YORK STATE SUPREME COURT NINTH JUDICIAL DISTRICT*, Dutchess County Supreme Court Law Library, 50 Market St, 2nd Flr, 12601-3203. SAN 312-3030. Tel: 845-431-1859. E-mail: 9JDLawLibrary@nycourts.gov. Web Site: www.nycourts.gov/courts/9jd/dutchess/dutchesslibrary.shtml. *Library Contact,* Karen Boback
Founded 1904
Library Holdings: Bk Titles 15,000
Special Collections: Legal Reference Material
Subject Interests: Law
Wireless access
Open Mon-Fri 9-1 & 2-5

P POUGHKEEPSIE PUBLIC LIBRARY DISTRICT*, Adriance Memorial Library, 93 Market St, 12601. SAN 353-9407. Tel: 845-485-3445. Circulation Tel: 845-485-3445, Ext 3701. Reference Tel: 845-485-3445, Ext 3702. Administration Tel: 845-485-3445, Ext 3306. FAX: 845-485-3789. E-mail: info@poklib.org. Web Site: www.poklib.org. *Libr Dir,* Thomas A Lawrence; E-mail: tlawrence@poklib.org; *Head, Br & Outreach Serv,* Lynn Lucas; Tel: 845-485-3445, Ext 3410, E-mail: llucas@poklib.org; *Head, Ref & Adult Serv,* Deborah Weltsch; E-mail: dweltsch@poklib.org; *Head, Tech Serv,* Chris Morgan; Tel: 845-485-3445, Ext 3357, E-mail: cmorgan@poklib.org; *Head, Youth Serv,* Nicole Guenkel; Tel: 845-485-3445, Ext 3320, E-mail: nguenkel@poklib.org; *Bus Mgr,* Barbara Lynch; E-mail: blynch@poklib.org; *Network Adminr,* Bruce Sullivan; E-mail: bsullivan@poklib.org; Staff 62 (MLS 18, Non-MLS 44)
Founded 1841. Pop 73,500
Library Holdings: Bk Vols 180,000; Per Subs 460
Special Collections: Foundation Center
Subject Interests: Genealogy, Local hist
Automation Activity & Vendor Info: (Acquisitions) Innovative Interfaces, Inc; (Cataloging) Innovative Interfaces, Inc; (Circulation) Innovative Interfaces, Inc; (ILL) Innovative Interfaces, Inc; (OPAC) Innovative Interfaces, Inc
Wireless access
Mem of Mid-Hudson Library System
Open Mon-Thurs 9-9, Fri & Sat 9-5, Sun 2-5
Friends of the Library Group
Branches: 1
BOARDMAN ROAD BRANCH, 141 Boardman Rd, 12603, SAN 353-9466. Tel: 845-485-3445. FAX: 845-454-9308. *Asst Dir,* Lauren Muffs; Tel: 845-485-3445, Ext 3310
Library Holdings: Bk Titles 10,800; Bk Vols 11,100
Open Mon, Wed & Fri 9-8, Tues, Thurs & Sat 9-5

M VASSAR BROTHERS MEDICAL CENTER*, Knowledge Resources Library, 45 Reade Pl, 12601. SAN 312-3049. Tel: 845-437-3121. FAX: 845-437-3002. E-mail: vbmclibrary@health-quest.org. Web Site: vbmc.libguides.com/library. *Librn,* Mary Jo Russell; Staff 2 (MLS 1, Non-MLS 1)
Founded 1951
Library Holdings: e-books 250; e-journals 600; Electronic Media & Resources 24; Bk Titles 75; Per Subs 18
Special Collections: Medical Center Archives
Subject Interests: Cardiology, Internal med, Nursing, Oncology, Pediatrics, Surgery
Automation Activity & Vendor Info: (OPAC) LibLime; (Serials) OVID Technologies
Wireless access
Function: 24/7 Electronic res, Archival coll, Computers for patron use, Electronic databases & coll, Online cat, Ref serv available, Res libr
Partic in National Network of Libraries of Medicine Region 7; Southeastern New York Library Resources Council
Special Services for the Deaf - Assistive tech
Open Mon-Fri 7:30-4
Restriction: Badge access after hrs, Hospital employees & physicians only, Non-circulating coll, Not a lending libr, Open to pub by appt only

C VASSAR COLLEGE LIBRARY*, 124 Raymond Ave, Box 20, 12604. SAN 312-3057. Tel: 845-437-5760. Interlibrary Loan Service Tel: 845-437-5765. FAX: 845-437-5864. E-mail: librarysitemgr@vassar.edu. Web Site: library.vassar.edu. *Dir of Libr,* Andrew Ashton; Tel: 845-437-5787, E-mail: anashton@vassar.edu; *Head, Coll, Head, Discovery Serv,* Debra Bucher; Tel: 845-437-7762, E-mail: debucher@vassar.edu; *Head, Spec Coll,* Ronald Patkus; Tel: 845-437-5798, E-mail: patkus@vassar.edu; *Research Librn, Res Serv,* Gretchen Lieb; Tel: 845-437-5770, E-mail: grlieb@vassar.edu; *Access Serv Librn, Digital Archivist,* Laura Streett; Tel: 845-437-5716, E-mail: lastreett@vassar.edu; Staff 18 (MLS 15, Non-MLS 3)
Founded 1861. Enrl 2,414; Fac 246; Highest Degree: Bachelor
Library Holdings: Bk Vols 890,304
Special Collections: College History & Archives; Early Atlases & Maps; Elizabeth Bishop Papers; Incunabula; John Burroughs Journals; Mark Twain Coll, ms; Mary McCarthy Papers; Robert Owens Coll; Ruth Benedict Papers; Village Press; Women, bks, ms. State Document Depository; US Document Depository
Automation Activity & Vendor Info: (Acquisitions) Innovative Interfaces, Inc; (Cataloging) Innovative Interfaces, Inc; (Circulation) Innovative Interfaces, Inc; (Course Reserve) Docutek; (ILL) Innovative Interfaces, Inc; (Media Booking) Innovative Interfaces, Inc; (OPAC) Innovative Interfaces, Inc; (Serials) Innovative Interfaces, Inc
Wireless access
Partic in Southeastern New York Library Resources Council
Open Mon-Fri 8:30-5
Departmental Libraries:
ART LIBRARY, Taylor Hall, Rm 216, 124 Raymond Ave, 12604-0022, SAN 321-4230. Tel: 845-437-5790. Web Site: library.vassar.edu/art-library. *Librn,* Thomas E Hill; Tel: 845-437-5791, E-mail: thhill@vassar.edu
Founded 1937
Open Mon-Fri 8:30-5
GEORGE SHERMAN DICKINSON MUSIC LIBRARY, 124 Raymond Ave, Box 38, 12604-0038, SAN 320-0507. Tel: 845-437-7492. FAX: 845-437-7335. E-mail: musiclib@vassar.edu. Web Site: library.vassar.edu/musiclibrary/home. *Music Librn,* Sarah Canino; Tel: 845-437-7492, E-mail: sacanino@vassar.edu
Library Holdings: Music Scores 30,000; Bk Vols 20,000
Open Mon-Fri 1-4
Restriction: Open to pub by appt only

POUND RIDGE

P POUND RIDGE LIBRARY*, Hiram Halle Memorial Library, 271 Westchester Ave, 10576-1714. SAN 312-3065. Tel: 914-764-5085. FAX: 914-764-5319. E-mail: info@PoundRidgeLibrary.org. Web Site: www.poundridgelibrary.org. *Dir*, Position Currently Open
Founded 1953. Pop 4,700; Circ 74,484
Library Holdings: Bk Vols 57,152; Per Subs 98
Special Collections: Art; Phonograph Records
Automation Activity & Vendor Info: (Cataloging) SirsiDynix; (Circulation) SirsiDynix; (OPAC) SirsiDynix
Wireless access
Mem of Westchester Library System
Open Tues & Thurs 10-8, Wed, Fri & Sat 10-5 (10-1 July-Sept)

PRATTSBURGH

P PRATTSBURG FREE LIBRARY*, 26 Main St, 14873. SAN 376-6969. Tel: 607-522-3490. FAX: 607-522-3490. Web Site: prattsburgfreelibrary.org. *Dir*, Justin Zeh; E-mail: zehj@stls.org; Staff 1 (Non-MLS 1)
Founded 1981. Pop 2,000; Circ 6,200
Library Holdings: Bk Vols 8,533
Automation Activity & Vendor Info: (Circulation) SirsiDynix; (OPAC) SirsiDynix
Wireless access
Mem of Southern Tier Library System
Open Tues & Thurs 12-8, Wed 10-6, Fri 12-6, Sat 10-2

PROSPECT

P PROSPECT FREE LIBRARY*, 915 Trenton Falls St, 13435. (Mail add: PO Box 177, 13435-0177), SAN 376-3080. Tel: 315-896-2736. FAX: 315-896-4045. E-mail: prospect@midyork.org. Web Site: prospect.midyork.org. *Dir*, Betsy Mack
Pop 300
Library Holdings: Bk Vols 8,000; Per Subs 40
Wireless access
Mem of Mid-York Library System
Special Services for the Blind - Bks on cassette
Open Mon (Winter) 4-7, Tues 2-7, Wed 2-4 & 6-8, Thurs 2-8, Fri 1-3, Sat 10-Noon; Mon (Summer) 4-8, Tues & Thurs 4:30-8, Wed 2-4, Fri 1-3, Sat 10-Noon

PULASKI

P PULASKI PUBLIC LIBRARY, 4917 N Jefferson St, 13142. SAN 312-3073. Tel: 315-298-2717. FAX: 315-298-2717. E-mail: pullib@ncls.org. Web Site: www.pulaskinypubliclibrary.org. *Dir*, Nikole Ives
Circ 22,189
Library Holdings: Bk Vols 22,000; Per Subs 35
Automation Activity & Vendor Info: (Cataloging) SirsiDynix-Unicorn; (Circulation) SirsiDynix-WorkFlows; (OPAC) SirsiDynix-Unicorn
Wireless access
Mem of North Country Library System
Special Services for the Blind - Bks & mags in Braille, on rec, tape & cassette
Open Mon, Wed & Fri 9-5, Tues & Thurs 9-7, Sat 9-1
Friends of the Library Group

PULTENEY

P PULTENEY FREE LIBRARY*, 9226 County Rte 74, 14874. (Mail add: PO Box 215, 14874-0215), SAN 312-3081. Tel: 607-868-3652. FAX: 607-868-3652. Web Site: pulteney.org. *Dir*, Barbara Radigan; E-mail: radiganb@stls.org; *Libr Asst*, Jayne Peastee
Founded 1881. Pop 1,274; Circ 8,760
Library Holdings: Audiobooks 313; DVDs 550; Bk Titles 13,500; Per Subs 13
Automation Activity & Vendor Info: (Circulation) SirsiDynix; (OPAC) SirsiDynix
Wireless access
Mem of Southern Tier Library System
Special Services for the Deaf - Bks on deafness & sign lang; High interest/low vocabulary bks
Special Services for the Blind - Large print bks
Open Tues & Thurs 12-8, Wed 12-6, Sat 9-1

PURCHASE

C MANHATTANVILLE COLLEGE LIBRARY, 2900 Purchase St, 10577. SAN 312-309X. Tel: 914-323-5275. Reference Tel: 914-323-5282. FAX: 914-694-8139. E-mail: library@mville.edu. Web Site: www.mville.edu/academics/library. *Dir*, Jeff Rosedale; Tel: 914-323-5277, E-mail: jeff.rosedale@mville.edu; *Head, Patron Serv*, Albert Neal; Tel: 914-323-3133, E-mail: albert.neal@mville.edu; *Head, Coll Serv*, Catherine Medeot; E-mail: catherine.medeot@mville.edu; *Educ Spec, Librn*, Lynda Hanley; Tel: 914-323-5314, E-mail: lynda.hanley@mville.edu; *Online Serv Librn*, Tim Conley-Abrams; Tel: 914-323-5441, E-mail: timothy.conley-abrams@mville.edu; *Spec Coll Librn*, Lauren Ziarko; Tel: 914-323-5422, E-mail: lauren.ziarko@mville.edu; *Coordr, Info Literacy*, Paula Moskowitz; Tel: 914-323-3159, E-mail: paula.moskowitz@mville.edu. Subject Specialists: *Educ*, Lynda Hanley; *Students with disabilities*, Paula Moskowitz; Staff 9 (MLS 7, Non-MLS 2)
Founded 1841. Fac 102; Highest Degree: Doctorate
Library Holdings: Bk Titles 183,576; Bk Vols 238,700; Per Subs 1,010
Special Collections: Alexander Stephens Letters
Subject Interests: Art, Asian studies, Educ, Music
Automation Activity & Vendor Info: (Acquisitions) OCLC Worldshare Management Services; (Cataloging) OCLC Worldshare Management Services; (Circulation) OCLC Worldshare Management Services; (Course Reserve) Blackboard Inc; (ILL) OCLC ILLiad; (OPAC) OCLC Worldshare Management Services; (Serials) OCLC Worldshare Management Services
Wireless access
Partic in Metropolitan New York Library Council; OCLC Online Computer Library Center, Inc; Westchester Academic Library Directors Organization

P PURCHASE FREE LIBRARY, 3093 Purchase St, 10577. SAN 312-3103. Tel: 914-948-0550. FAX: 914-328-3405. E-mail: pfl@wlsmail.org. Web Site: www.purchasefreelibrary.org. *Dir*, Donna Murray; Staff 5 (MLS 1, Non-MLS 4)
Founded 1928. Pop 3,480; Circ 31,649
Library Holdings: Bk Titles 11,700; Per Subs 32
Subject Interests: Bus mat, Local hist
Automation Activity & Vendor Info: (Acquisitions) SirsiDynix; (Circulation) SirsiDynix; (ILL) SirsiDynix
Wireless access
Mem of Westchester Library System
Open Mon-Fri 9:30-5:30, Sat 9:30-3:30
Friends of the Library Group

C STATE UNIVERSITY OF NEW YORK*, Purchase College Library, 735 Anderson Hill Rd, 10577-1400. SAN 312-3111. Tel: 914-251-6400. Circulation Tel: 914-251-6401. Interlibrary Loan Service Tel: 914-251-6428. Reference Tel: 914-251-6410. Administration Tel: 914-251-6435. FAX: 914-251-6437. Reference E-mail: lib.reference@purchase.edu. Web Site: www.purchase.edu/library. *Libr Dir*, Patrick F Callahan; Tel: 914-251-6436, E-mail: patrick.callahan@purchase.edu; *Dir, Teaching, Learning & Tech Ctr*, Keith Landa; Tel: 914-251-6450, E-mail: keith.landa@purchase.edu; *Head, Instrul Serv*, Rebecca Oling; Tel: 914-251-6417, E-mail: rebecca.oling@purchase.edu; *Head, Ref*, Darcy Gervasio; Tel: 914-251-6423, E-mail: darcy.gervasio@purchase.edu; *Art Librn*, Kimberly Detterbeck; Tel: 914-251-6406, E-mail: kimberly.detterbeck@purchase.edu; *Electronic Res Librn*, Carrie Marten; E-mail: carrie.marten@purchase.edu; *Ref Librn & Stacks Mgr*, Joseph Swatski; Tel: 914-251-6411, E-mail: joseph.swatski@purchase.edu; *Res Sharing Librn*, Timothy Hickey; E-mail: timothy.hickey@purchase.edu. Subject Specialists: *Asian studies, Hist, Journalism*, Patrick F Callahan; *Biology, Instrul tech*, Keith Landa; *Jewish studies, Lit*, Rebecca Oling; *Art hist, Design, Visual arts*, Kimberly Detterbeck; *Philos*, Carrie Marten; *Archives*, Joseph Swatski; Staff 20 (MLS 6.5, Non-MLS 13.5)
Founded 1967. Enrl 4,224; Fac 150; Highest Degree: Master
Jul 2015-Jun 2016. Mats Exp $389,988. Sal $1,901,880
Library Holdings: Bk Vols 235,698
Special Collections: US Document Depository
Subject Interests: Art, Film, Music, Theatre
Automation Activity & Vendor Info: (Cataloging) Ex Libris Group; (Circulation) Ex Libris Group; (Discovery) EBSCO Discovery Service; (ILL) OCLC ILLiad; (OPAC) Ex Libris Group; (Serials) Ex Libris Group
Wireless access
Function: 24/7 Online cat, Art exhibits, Computers for patron use, Electronic databases & coll, ILL available, Internet access, Magazines, Microfiche/film & reading machines, Online cat, Online ref, Photocopying/Printing, Ref serv available, Scanner, Telephone ref, Wheelchair accessible
Partic in Metropolitan New York Library Council; SUNYConnect; Westchester Academic Library Directors Organization
Special Services for the Blind - Assistive/Adapted tech devices, equip & products; Computer with voice synthesizer for visually impaired persons; Low vision equip; Reader equip
Open Mon-Thurs 8am-2am, Fri 8am-10pm, Sat 11-8, Sun 12pm-2am
Restriction: Circ privileges for students & alumni only, Non-circulating of rare bks
Friends of the Library Group

PUTNAM VALLEY

P PUTNAM VALLEY FREE LIBRARY, 30 Oscawana Lake Rd, 10579. SAN 312-312X. Tel: 845-528-3242. FAX: 845-528-3297. E-mail: staff@putnamvalleylibrary.org. Web Site: www.putnamvalleylibrary.org. *Dir,* Dede Farabaugh; E-mail: director@putnamvalleylibrary.org
Founded 1936. Circ 60,060
Library Holdings: AV Mats 4,516; Bk Vols 41,298
Special Collections: Fine Arts (Harry N Abrams Coll)
Automation Activity & Vendor Info: (Cataloging) Innovative Interfaces, Inc - Millennium; (Circulation) Innovative Interfaces, Inc - Millennium; (OPAC) Innovative Interfaces, Inc - Millennium
Wireless access
Mem of Mid-Hudson Library System
Open Mon, Tues, Thurs & Fri 10-5, Wed 2-7, Sat 10-4

QUEENSBURY

J ADIRONDACK COMMUNITY COLLEGE LIBRARY*, Scoville Learning Ctr, 640 Bay Rd, 12804. SAN 311-2462. Tel: 518-743-2260. FAX: 518-745-1442. E-mail: librarian@sunyacc.edu. Web Site: library.sunyacc.edu. *Chair, Dir,* Emily Goodspeed; Tel: 518-743-2200, Ext 2351, E-mail: goodspeede@sunyacc.edu; *Instrul Serv Librn, Ref (Info Servs),* Joyce Miller; Tel: 518-743-2200, Ext 2485, E-mail: millerja@sunyacc.edu; *Ref Librn, Syst Librn,* Teresa Ronning; E-mail: ronningt@sunyacc.edu. Subject Specialists: *Tech,* Emily Goodspeed; *Bus, Sci,* Joyce Miller; *Criminal justice, Law, Soc sci,* Teresa Ronning; Staff 6 (MLS 4, Non-MLS 2)
Founded 1961. Enrl 3,300; Fac 100; Highest Degree: Associate
Library Holdings: DVDs 1,000; e-books 136,000; e-journals 60,000; Bk Titles 46,000; Per Subs 200; Videos 24,000
Special Collections: Local History (Hill Coll)
Subject Interests: Criminal justice, Liberal arts, Nursing
Automation Activity & Vendor Info: (Cataloging) Ex Libris Group; (Circulation) Ex Libris Group; (Course Reserve) Ex Libris Group; (Discovery) Ex Libris Group; (ILL) OCLC WorldShare Interlibrary Loan; (OPAC) Ex Libris Group
Wireless access
Function: 24/7 Online cat, ILL available, Telephone ref
Publications: Subject Pathfinders (Research guide)
Partic in Cap District Libr Coun for Ref & Res Resources; OCLC Online Computer Library Center, Inc; SUNYConnect
Open Mon-Thurs 7:30am-8pm, Fri 8-4,
Restriction: Authorized patrons

QUOGUE

P QUOGUE LIBRARY*, Four Midland St, 11959. (Mail add: PO Box 5036, 11959-5036), SAN 312-3138. Tel: 631-653-4224. FAX: 631-653-6151. E-mail: info@quoguelibrary.org. Web Site: www.quoguelibrary.org. *Dir, Operations,* Susan McKenna; Staff 1 (MLS 1)
Founded 1897. Circ 40,689
Library Holdings: Audiobooks 672; DVDs 2,718; e-books 9,733; Bk Vols 29,795; Per Subs 50
Wireless access
Mem of Suffolk Cooperative Library System
Partic in Partnership of Automated Librs in Suffolk
Special Services for the Blind - Large print bks & talking machines
Open Mon & Sun 12-5, Tues & Thurs 10-8, Wed, Fri & Sat 10-5

RANDOLPH

P RANDOLPH FREE LIBRARY, 26 Jamestown St, 14772. SAN 312-3146. Tel: 716-358-3712. FAX: 716-358-2039. E-mail: randolphfreelibrary@windstream.net. Web Site: www.randolphlibrary.info. *Dir,* Mary Johnson; E-mail: director@randolphlibrary.info; Staff 1 (Non-MLS 1)
Founded 1909. Pop 1,393; Circ 32,719
Library Holdings: Bk Titles 20,350; Bk Vols 22,700; Per Subs 40
Special Collections: Garden Club Coll, bks, pamphlets & per; Local Newspaper 1876-1979, micro. State Document Depository; UN Document Depository; US Document Depository
Subject Interests: Antiques, Local genealogy
Wireless access
Mem of Chautauqua-Cattaraugus Library System
Open Mon, Tues & Thurs 1-9, Wed 6-9, Fri & Sat 10-5

RANSOMVILLE

P RANSOMVILLE FREE LIBRARY*, 3733 Ransomville Rd, 14131. SAN 312-3154. Tel: 716-791-4073. FAX: 716-791-4073. Web Site: www.ransomvillelibrary.org. *Dir,* Phila Ibaugh
Library Holdings: Bk Vols 25,000; Per Subs 75
Wireless access
Mem of Nioga Library System
Open Mon & Wed 2-8, Tues & Thurs 10-8, Sat (Sept-June) 2-5
Friends of the Library Group

RAQUETTE LAKE

P RAQUETTE LAKE FREE LIBRARY, One Dillon Rd, 13436. (Mail add: PO Box 129, 13436-0129), SAN 312-3162. Tel: 315-354-4005. FAX: 315-354-4005. Web Site: raquettelakelibrary.sals.edu. *Dir & Librn,* Carolynn Dufft; E-mail: raq-director@sals.edu
Pop 114; Circ 8,436
Library Holdings: Bk Vols 9,400; Per Subs 50
Special Collections: Adirondack Region
Subject Interests: Adirondack hist
Automation Activity & Vendor Info: (Cataloging) Innovative Interfaces, Inc; (Circulation) Innovative Interfaces, Inc; (OPAC) Innovative Interfaces, Inc; (Serials) Innovative Interfaces, Inc
Wireless access
Publications: Winter Newsletter
Mem of Southern Adirondack Library System
Open Mon & Tues 1-7, Thurs 12-6, Sat 12-3 (Winter); Mon, Tues & Thurs 11-7, Sat 1-7 (Summer)

RAVENA

P RCS COMMUNITY LIBRARY*, 95 Main St, 12143. SAN 312-3170. Tel: 518-756-2053. FAX: 518-756-8595. E-mail: info@rcscommunitylibrary.org. Web Site: www.rcscommunitylibrary.org. *Dir,* Judith Wines; *Principal Librn,* Barbara Goetschius; *Librn,* Bryan Rowzee; *Circ Mgr,* Carol Melewski; Staff 4 (MLS 3, Non-MLS 1)
Founded 1994. Pop 14,505; Circ 56,000
Special Collections: Hudson River Valley Coll
Automation Activity & Vendor Info: (Cataloging) SirsiDynix; (Circulation) SirsiDynix; (ILL) SirsiDynix; (OPAC) SirsiDynix
Wireless access
Publications: Newsletter
Mem of Upper Hudson Library System
Open Mon-Thurs 9-8:30, Fri 9-5, Sat (July-Aug) 10-1
Friends of the Library Group

RAY BROOK

S ADIRONDACK CORRECTIONAL FACILITY LIBRARY*, 196 Ray Brook Rd, 12977. SAN 327-1749. Tel: 518-891-1343. FAX: 518-891-1343. *Sr Librn,* Suzanne Orlando; Staff 1 (MLS 1)
Library Holdings: High Interest/Low Vocabulary Bk Vols 12; Bk Vols 6,000; Per Subs 37
Subject Interests: Spanish lang
Automation Activity & Vendor Info: (Cataloging) Follett Software; (Circulation) Follett Software; (OPAC) Follett Software
Open Mon-Fri 7-3

S RAY BROOK FEDERAL CORRECTIONAL INSTITUTION LIBRARY*, 128 Ray Brook Rd, 12977. (Mail add: PO Box 300, 12977-0300). Tel: 518-897-4000, 518-897-4161. Web Site: www.bop.gov/locations/institutions/rbk. *Educ Spec,* Tom Breeyear; E-mail: tbreeyear@bop.gov
Library Holdings: Bk Vols 6,000
Special Collections: Britannica of the Western World
Wireless access
Restriction: Staff & inmates only

RED CREEK

P RED CREEK FREE LIBRARY, 6817 Main St, 13143. (Mail add: PO Box 360, 13143-0360), SAN 312-3189. Tel: 315-754-6679. FAX: 315-754-6679. Web Site: owwl.org/library/redcreek. *Dir,* Belinda Welcher; E-mail: redcreeklibrarydirector@owwl.org
Pop 5,600; Circ 32,000
Library Holdings: Bk Vols 8,000
Subject Interests: Children's bks, Local hist
Automation Activity & Vendor Info: (Cataloging) SirsiDynix; (Circulation) SirsiDynix; (OPAC) SirsiDynix; (Serials) SirsiDynix
Wireless access
Mem of Pioneer Library System
Open Mon, Wed & Fri 10-4, Tues & Thurs 1-6, Sat 9-1

RED HOOK

P RED HOOK PUBLIC LIBRARY*, 7444 S Broadway, 12571. SAN 312-3197. Tel: 845-758-3241. Web Site: www.redhooklibrary.org. *Libr Dir,* Dawn Jardine; E-mail: director@redhooklibrary.org
Founded 1898. Pop 1,903; Circ 71,366
Library Holdings: Audiobooks 1,090; DVDs 711; e-books 1,576; Bk Titles 15,860
Wireless access

Function: Adult bk club, Audiobks via web, Bk club(s), Bks on cassette, Bks on CD, Children's prog, Computers for patron use, Electronic databases & coll, Free DVD rentals, Homebound delivery serv, ILL available, Internet access, Mail & tel request accepted, Music CDs, Online cat, Outreach serv, Outside serv via phone, mail, e-mail & web, Photocopying/Printing, Prog for adults, Prog for children & young adult, Ref serv available, Spoken cassettes & CDs, Spoken cassettes & DVDs, Story hour, Summer reading prog, Tax forms, Teen prog, VHS videos, Wheelchair accessible, Workshops
Publications: Octagon (Newsletter)
Mem of Mid-Hudson Library System
Special Services for the Deaf - Bks on deafness & sign lang; Staff with knowledge of sign lang
Open Mon-Fri 10-7, Sat 10-4
Friends of the Library Group

REMSEN

P DIDYMUS THOMAS MEMORIAL LIBRARY, 9639 Main St, 13438. (Mail add: PO Box 410, 13438-0410), SAN 312-3200. Tel: 315-831-5651. FAX: 315-831-5651. E-mail: remsen@midyork.org. Web Site: remsenlibrary.org. *Co-Dir,* Sandra DeLand; *Co-Dir,* Lorraine Hefner; E-mail: lhefner@midyork.org
Founded 1899. Pop 531; Circ 9,141
Library Holdings: AV Mats 391; Bk Titles 12,914; Per Subs 37
Automation Activity & Vendor Info: (Cataloging) SirsiDynix; (Circulation) SirsiDynix
Wireless access
Publications: History of Remsen, by Millard Roberts
Mem of Mid-York Library System
Open Mon 1-5, Tues & Thurs 2-6, Wed & Fri 2-5, Sat 10-12

RENSSELAER

P RENSSELAER PUBLIC LIBRARY*, 676 East St, 12144. SAN 312-3227. Tel: 518-462-1193. FAX: 518-462-2819. E-mail: library@rensselaerlibrary.org. Web Site: rensselaerlibrary.org. *Libr Dir,* Jane Chirgwin; Staff 3 (MLS 1, Non-MLS 2)
Founded 1920. Pop 9,047; Circ 20,619
Library Holdings: Bk Vols 20,000; Per Subs 20
Wireless access
Function: Computers for patron use, Free DVD rentals, Music CDs, Online cat, OverDrive digital audio bks, Prog for children & young adult, Tax forms
Mem of Upper Hudson Library System
Partic in OCLC Online Computer Library Center, Inc
Open Mon 12-5, Tues & Fri 10-5, Wed & Thurs 10-8, Sat 10-3
Friends of the Library Group

RENSSELAERVILLE

P RENSSELAERVILLE LIBRARY*, 1459 County Rte 351, 12147. (Mail add: PO Box 188, 12147-0188), SAN 312-3251. Tel: 518-797-3949. FAX: 518-797-5211. E-mail: library@rensselaervillelibrary.org. Web Site: rensselaervillelibrary.org. *Dir & Librn,* Heidimarie Carle; E-mail: director@rensselaervillelibrary.org; *Libr Asst,* Katie Caprio; Staff 5 (MLS 1, Non-MLS 4)
Founded 1896. Pop 2,000; Circ 12,482
Library Holdings: Bk Vols 23,123; Per Subs 44
Automation Activity & Vendor Info: (Circulation) Horizon; (OPAC) Horizon
Wireless access
Mem of Upper Hudson Library System
Open Tues & Wed 10-12 & 4-9, Thurs & Fri 4-9, Sat 9-1
Friends of the Library Group

RHINEBECK

P CLINTON COMMUNITY LIBRARY*, 1215 Centre Rd, 12572. Tel: 845-266-5530. FAX: 845-266-5530. E-mail: Clintonlib1215@gmail.com. Web Site: www.clinton.lib.ny.us. *Dir,* Carol Bancroft; Staff 4 (MLS 1, Non-MLS 3)
Founded 1965
Library Holdings: Bk Titles 12,000; Per Subs 18
Special Collections: Local History, Alice & Martin Provensen (Clinton Coll), Illustrators, Local authors
Automation Activity & Vendor Info: (Cataloging) Innovative Interfaces, Inc; (Circulation) Innovative Interfaces, Inc; (OPAC) Innovative Interfaces, Inc
Wireless access
Function: Digital talking bks, Doc delivery serv, ILL available, Orientations, Photocopying/Printing, Prog for adults, Prog for children & young adult, Ref serv available, Spoken cassettes & CDs, Summer reading prog, VHS videos, Wheelchair accessible
Mem of Mid-Hudson Library System
Open Mon, Tues & Thurs 9-5, Fri 11-7, Sat 9-1

P STARR LIBRARY*, 68 W Market St, 12572. SAN 312-3278. Tel: 845-876-4030. E-mail: starrdirector@me.com. Web Site: starrlibrary.org. *Dir,* Stephen Cook; *Asst Dir, Ch,* Brooke Stevens; Staff 6.5 (MLS 2, Non-MLS 4.5)
Founded 1862. Pop 7,762; Circ 90,000
Library Holdings: Bk Vols 35,000
Special Collections: Franklin D Roosevelt Coll; Large Print Coll; Local History (DAR Coll); Rare Book Coll
Automation Activity & Vendor Info: (Cataloging) Innovative Interfaces, Inc - Millennium; (Circulation) Innovative Interfaces, Inc - Millennium; (OPAC) Innovative Interfaces, Inc - Millennium
Wireless access
Function: 24/7 Electronic res, 24/7 Online cat, Activity rm, Adult bk club, Archival coll, Art exhibits, Audio & video playback equip for onsite use, Audiobks on Playaways & MP3, Audiobks via web, AV serv, Bk club(s), Bks on CD, Butterfly Garden, CD-ROM, Children's prog, Computers for patron use, Electronic databases & coll, For res purposes, Free DVD rentals, Home delivery & serv to seniorr ctr & nursing homes, Homebound delivery serv, ILL available, Internet access, Life-long learning prog for all ages, Magazines, Mail & tel request accepted, Mango lang, Meeting rooms, Microfiche/film & reading machines, Movies, Museum passes, Music CDs, Online cat, Online ref, Outreach serv, OverDrive digital audio bks, Photocopying/Printing, Preschool outreach, Prog for adults, Prog for children & young adult, Ref & res, Ref serv available, Scanner, Senior computer classes, Story hour, Teen prog, Wheelchair accessible, Workshops, Writing prog
Mem of Mid-Hudson Library System
Open Mon & Fri 10-5, Tues-Thurs 10-7, Sat 10-4, Sun 1-4
Friends of the Library Group

RHINECLIFF

P MORTON MEMORIAL LIBRARY & COMMUNITY HOUSE*, 82 Kelly St, 12574. (Mail add: PO Box 157, 12574-0157), SAN 312-3286. Tel: 845-876-2903. FAX: 845-876-1584. Web Site: morton.rhinecliff.lib.ny.us. *Dir,* Sandy Bartlett; E-mail: sandy@mortonrhinecliff.org
Circ 7,643
Library Holdings: Bk Vols 7,600; Per Subs 20
Automation Activity & Vendor Info: (Cataloging) Innovative Interfaces, Inc; (Circulation) Innovative Interfaces, Inc; (OPAC) Innovative Interfaces, Inc
Wireless access
Mem of Mid-Hudson Library System
Open Tues, Wed & Fri 10-6, Thurs 11-7, Sat 10-2
Friends of the Library Group

RICHBURG

P COLONIAL LIBRARY, 160 Main St, 14774. SAN 312-3294. Tel: 585-928-2694. *Dir,* Judy Johnson; E-mail: johnsonj@stls.org
Founded 1913. Pop 1,200
Library Holdings: Bk Titles 19,250; Per Subs 25
Automation Activity & Vendor Info: (Cataloging) SirsiDynix; (Circulation) SirsiDynix; (OPAC) SirsiDynix
Wireless access
Mem of Southern Tier Library System
Open Mon & Thurs 9-5, Tues & Wed 3-7

RICHFIELD SPRINGS

P RICHFIELD SPRINGS PUBLIC LIBRARY*, 102 Main St, 13439. (Mail add: PO Box 1650, 13439-1650), SAN 312-3308. Tel: 315-858-0230. FAX: 315-977-0090. E-mail: rs.ill@4cls.org. Web Site: libraries.4cls.org/richfieldsprings.
Founded 1909. Pop 1,561; Circ 22,362
Library Holdings: Bk Vols 15,000; Per Subs 63
Special Collections: Microfilm Coll of RS Mercury 1867-1972, (incl Summer Daily 1888-1917)
Wireless access
Mem of Four County Library System
Open Mon, Wed & Fri 11-5, Tues 11-8, Sat 10-Noon

RICHVILLE

P RICHVILLE FREE LIBRARY*, 87 Main St, 13681-3102. (Mail add: PO Box 42, 13681-0042), SAN 312-3316. Tel: 315-287-1481. FAX: 315-287-0956. E-mail: riclib@ncls.org. Web Site: www.richvillefreelibrary.org. *Dir,* Lila M Youngs
Founded 1926. Pop 500; Circ 3,500
Library Holdings: DVDs 18; Large Print Bks 124; Bk Vols 5,000; Per Subs 30; Talking Bks 38; Videos 200
Special Collections: Adirondack Mountains; St Lawrence County Topographical Maps
Wireless access

Function: Audio & video playback equip for onsite use, Bks on cassette, Bks on CD, Children's prog, Computer training, Computers for patron use, Free DVD rentals, Genealogy discussion group, Holiday prog, ILL available, Instruction & testing, Literacy & newcomer serv, Online cat, Photocopying/Printing, Prog for children & young adult, Scanner, Summer reading prog, Tax forms, VHS videos, Wheelchair accessible
Mem of North Country Library System
Open Mon & Tues 6pm-8pm, Wed 9-12 & 6-8, Fri 6-9
Friends of the Library Group

RIPLEY

P RIPLEY PUBLIC LIBRARY*, 64 W Main St, 14775. (Mail add: PO Box 808, 14775-0808), SAN 312-3324. Tel: 716-736-3913. FAX: 716-736-3923. E-mail: riplylib@fairpoint.net. *Dir,* Rhonda Thompson; E-mail: director@ripleylibrary.org
Founded 1938. Pop 2,460; Circ 29,600
Library Holdings: Bk Titles 10,430; Bk Vols 10,573; Per Subs 47
Wireless access
Mem of Chautauqua-Cattaraugus Library System
Open Mon & Fri 10-5, Tues & Thurs 10-7:30, Sat 9-2
Friends of the Library Group

RIVERDALE

C MANHATTAN COLLEGE, Mary Alice & Tom O'Malley Library, 4513 Manhattan College Pkwy, 10471. SAN 351-9244. Tel: 718-862-7743. Web Site: lib.manhattan.edu. *Exec Dir,* Dr William H Walters; E-mail: william.walters@manhattan.edu; *Dir, Archives & Spec Coll,* Amy Surak; E-mail: amy.surak@manhattan.edu; *Dir, Instrul Design,* Kimberly Jones Woodruff; E-mail: kim.woodruff@manhattan.edu; *Asst Dir, Access Serv,* Amy Handfield; E-mail: amy.handfield@manhattan.edu; *Asst Dir, Res & Instrul Serv,* Sarah E Sheehan; E-mail: sarah.sheehan@manhattan.edu; *Asst Dir, Tech Serv,* Susanne Markgren; E-mail: susanne.markgren@manhattan.edu; *Res & Instruction Librn,* John C Gormley; E-mail: john.gormley@manhattan.edu; *Res & Instruction Librn,* Bernadette M Lopez-Fitzsimmons; E-mail: bernadette.lopez@manhattan.edu; *Res & Instruction Librn,* Laurin Paradise; E-mail: lparadise01@manhattan.edu; *ILL Mgr, Syst Spec,* Brendon Ford; E-mail: brendon.ford@manhattan.edu; *Asst Archivist,* Position Currently Open; *Instrul Designer,* Dr Blair Goodlin, Jr; E-mail: bgoodlin01@manhattan.edu; Staff 13 (MLS 8, Non-MLS 5)
Founded 1853. Enrl 3,800; Fac 300; Highest Degree: Master
Automation Activity & Vendor Info: (Cataloging) ByWater Solutions; (Circulation) ByWater Solutions; (Course Reserve) ByWater Solutions; (Discovery) EBSCO Discovery Service; (ILL) OCLC; (OPAC) ByWater Solutions; (Serials) OCLC
Wireless access
Partic in Metropolitan New York Library Council; Oberlin Group; OCLC Online Computer Library Center, Inc; Westchester Academic Library Directors Organization
Restriction: Authorized personnel only

RIVERHEAD

P RIVERHEAD FREE LIBRARY, 330 Court St, 11901-2885. SAN 312-3340. Tel: 631-727-3228. FAX: 631-727-4762. E-mail: contact@riverheadlibrary.org. Web Site: www.riverheadlibrary.org. *Dir,* Kerrie McMullen-Smith; *Adult/Info Serv Coordr, Asst Dir,* Stephanie McEvoy; *Family & Youth Serv Coordr,* Lauren Strong; *Coordr, Patron Serv,* Chryso Tsoumpelis; *Network Serv, Syst Coordr,* John Eickwort; *Tech Serv Coordr,* David Troyan; *Adult Programming, Mkt,* Rasheima Alvarado; Staff 60 (MLS 10, Non-MLS 50)
Founded 1896. Pop 32,270; Circ 322,875
Library Holdings: AV Mats 18,318; Bk Vols 165,522; Per Subs 334
Special Collections: Long Island Coll; Tanger Wellness Coll
Automation Activity & Vendor Info: (Cataloging) Innovative Interfaces, Inc; (Circulation) Innovative Interfaces, Inc; (Course Reserve) Innovative Interfaces, Inc; (OPAC) Innovative Interfaces, Inc
Wireless access
Function: Adult bk club, After school storytime, Art exhibits, Audiobks via web, Bk club(s), Bks on cassette, Bks on CD, CD-ROM, Children's prog, Computer training, Computers for patron use, Digital talking bks, E-Reserves, Electronic databases & coll, Free DVD rentals, Health sci info serv, Home delivery & serv to seniorr ctr & nursing homes, Homebound delivery serv, Homework prog, ILL available, Internet access, Magnifiers for reading, Mail & tel request accepted, Music CDs, Notary serv, Online cat, Online ref, OverDrive digital audio bks, Photocopying/Printing, Preschool outreach, Prog for adults, Prog for children & young adult, Ref serv available, Senior computer classes, Summer reading prog, Tax forms, Teen prog, Telephone ref, VHS videos, Wheelchair accessible
Publications: Newsletter
Mem of Suffolk Cooperative Library System
Open Mon-Fri 9-7, Sat 9-5
Friends of the Library Group

J SUFFOLK COUNTY COMMUNITY COLLEGE*, Eastern Campus Library, Montaukett Learning Center, 121 Speonk Riverhead Rd, 11901-3499. SAN 320-8907. Tel: 631-548-2536. Reference Tel: 631-548-2538. Administration Tel: 631-548-2539. FAX: 631-369-2641. E-mail: library@sunysuffolk.edu. Web Site: www.sunysuffolk.edu/explore-academics/library. *Head Librn,* Dana Antonucci-Durgan; Tel: 631-548-2540, E-mail: antonud@sunysuffolk.edu; *Libr Instruction, Ref,* Penny J Bealle; Tel: 631-548-2541, E-mail: beallep@sunysuffolk.edu; *Media Serv, Ref & Instruction,* Susan Wood; Tel: 631-548-2544, E-mail: woods@sunysuffolk.edu; *Ref,* Fabio Montella; Tel: 631-548-2569, E-mail: montelf@sunysuffolk.edu. Subject Specialists: *Biochem, Chemistry, Educ,* Dana Antonucci-Durgan; *Gender studies,* Susan Wood; Staff 12 (MLS 7, Non-MLS 5)
Founded 1977. Enrl 3,937; Fac 85; Highest Degree: Associate
Sept 2012-Aug 2013. Mats Exp $61,900, Books $23,000, Per/Ser (Incl. Access Fees) $30,000, AV Equip $7,000, AV Mat $1,500, Presv $400
Library Holdings: AV Mats 300; High Interest/Low Vocabulary Bk Vols 75; Bk Titles 36,001; Bk Vols 37,542; Per Subs 200
Subject Interests: Culinary, Graphic design
Wireless access
Function: Wheelchair accessible
Partic in Information Delivery Services Project; New York State Interlibrary Loan Network; OCLC-LVIS
Open Mon-Thurs 8am-9:15pm, Fri 8-5, Sat 10:30-4:30

S SUFFOLK COUNTY HISTORICAL SOCIETY LIBRARY, 300 W Main St, 11901-2894. SAN 312-3359. Tel: 631-727-2881, Ext 103. FAX: 631-727-3467. Web Site: www.suffolkcountyhistoricalsociety.org. *Head Librn,* Wendy Polhemus-Annibell; E-mail: librarian@schs-museum.org; Staff 3 (MLS 2, Non-MLS 1)
Founded 1886
Library Holdings: Bk Titles 9,400; Bk Vols 15,400; Per Subs 16
Special Collections: Daughters of the Revolution of 1776 Membership Records; Deeds; Federal & State Censuses, microfilm; Late 19th to early 20th century Long Island(Fullerton Photog Coll); Long Island History Coll; Long Island Photog (Ceylon Anderson Coll); Military Coll; Shipwreck Coll; Towns & Wills Coll
Subject Interests: Agr, Genealogy, General Long Island mat, Specifically Suffolk County events, Specifically Suffolk County people
Wireless access
Publications: Journal of the Suffolk County Historical Society (Annual)
Open Wed-Sat 12:30-4:30 by appointment

ROCHESTER

SR ALDERSGATE UNITED METHODIST CHURCH LIBRARY, 4115 Dewey Ave, 14616. SAN 327-0157. Tel: 585-663-3665. FAX: 585-865-8442. E-mail: info@aumcgreece.org. Web Site: www.aumcgreece.org. *Head Librn,* Jane Salminen
Library Holdings: Bk Vols 3,300

R ASBURY FIRST UNITED METHODIST CHURCH*, Resource Library, 1050 East Ave, 14607. SAN 312-3375. Tel: 585-271-1050. FAX: 585-271-3743. Web Site: www.asburyfirst.org/get-involved/resource-library. *Co-Chair,* Bonnie Kay; *Co-Chair,* Elizabeth Woolever
Founded 1977
Library Holdings: Bk Vols 2,500
Wireless access

P BRIGHTON MEMORIAL LIBRARY*, 2300 Elmwood Ave, 14618. SAN 312-3405. Tel: 585-784-5300. FAX: 585-784-5333. E-mail: brightonlibrary@gmail.com. Web Site: www.brightonlibrary.org. *Exec Dir,* Jennifer Ries-Taggart; *Ad,* Lynne Fretz; *Ch Serv Librn,* Elissa Schaeffer; *Ref Serv Librn,* Matthew Bashore; *Commun Relations Mgr,* Judy Rosenberg; *Mgr, Network Serv, Vols Coordr,* Kory Yerkes; *Circ, Prog Coordr,* Deena Viviani; Staff 12 (MLS 12)
Founded 1953. Pop 35,588; Circ 703,000
Library Holdings: Bk Vols 173,492
Subject Interests: Brighton local hist, Judaica
Automation Activity & Vendor Info: (Acquisitions) TLC (The Library Corporation); (Circulation) TLC (The Library Corporation); (OPAC) TLC (The Library Corporation); (Serials) TLC (The Library Corporation)
Wireless access
Mem of Monroe County Library System
Special Services for the Deaf - TDD equip
Special Services for the Blind - Large print bks; Reader equip; Screen reader software; ZoomText magnification & reading software
Open Mon-Thurs 10-9, Fri 10-6, Sat (Fall-Spring) 10-4, Sun 1-4
Friends of the Library Group

P CHILI PUBLIC LIBRARY*, 3333 Chili Ave, 14624. SAN 311-0478. Tel: 585-889-2200. FAX: 585-889-5819. Web Site: www.chililibrary.org. *Dir,* Jeff Baker; E-mail: jbaker@libraryweb.org; *Youth Serv Mgr,* Cathy Kyle; *Ch Serv,* Jennifer Freese; *Ref (Info Servs),* Richard Gagnier

Founded 1962. Pop 27,000; Circ 350,000
Library Holdings: Bk Titles 84,620; Bk Vols 85,948; Per Subs 198; Videos 4,328
Subject Interests: Local hist
Automation Activity & Vendor Info: (Circulation) TLC (The Library Corporation)
Wireless access
Mem of Monroe County Library System
Open Mon-Thurs 9-9, Fri & Sat 9-5, Sun 1-4
Friends of the Library Group

CR COLGATE ROCHESTER CROZER DIVINITY SCHOOL*, Ambrose Swasey Library, 1100 S Goodman St, 14620-2592. SAN 312-3421. Tel: 585-340-9602. Web Site: www.crcds.edu/the-ambrose-swasey-library-at-crcds. *Dir, Libr Serv,* Marge Nead; Tel: 585-340-9601; *Ref Librn,* Desirae Zingarelli-Sweet; E-mail: dzsweet@crcds.edu
Founded 1817. Enrl 120; Fac 21; Highest Degree: Doctorate
Library Holdings: Bk Vols 40,000; Per Subs 103
Special Collections: Bible Coll; Church History
Subject Interests: Behav sci, Relig studies, Soc sci
Automation Activity & Vendor Info: (Cataloging) Ex Libris Group; (Circulation) Ex Libris Group; (Course Reserve) Ex Libris Group; (ILL) OCLC; (OPAC) Ex Libris Group; (Serials) Ex Libris Group
Wireless access
Partic in Rochester Regional Library Council

P GATES PUBLIC LIBRARY*, 902 Elmgrove Rd, 14624. SAN 353-9881. Tel: 585-247-6446. FAX: 585-426-5733. E-mail: gatesreference@libraryweb.org. Web Site: www.gateslibrary.org. *Libr Dir,* Anna Souannavong; E-mail: anna.souannavong@libraryweb.org; *Ad,* Paula Blackburn; E-mail: pblacku@libraryweb.org; *Ch,* Mary Jo Smith; E-mail: mjsmith@libraryweb.org; *Media Librn,* Melissa McHenry; E-mail: mmchenry@libraryweb.org; *Tech Librn,* Cathy Carstens; E-mail: ccarstens@libraryweb.org; *Teen Librn,* Heidi Jung; E-mail: hjung@libraryweb.org; Staff 45 (MLS 7, Non-MLS 38)
Founded 1960. Pop 29,275; Circ 403,055
Library Holdings: AV Mats 16,867; Bk Vols 126,786; Per Subs 236
Special Collections: Italian Coll, bks
Automation Activity & Vendor Info: (Circulation) TLC (The Library Corporation); (OPAC) TLC (The Library Corporation)
Wireless access
Publications: Gates Business Directory; Gates Human Services Directory
Mem of Monroe County Library System
Special Services for the Deaf - Assistive tech
Open Mon-Thurs 9-9, Fri 9-6, Sat 10-5
Friends of the Library Group

P HENRIETTA PUBLIC LIBRARY, 625 Calkins Rd, 14623. SAN 312-3510. Tel: 585-359-7092. FAX: 585-334-6369. E-mail: hplinfo@libraryweb.org. Web Site: www.hpl.org. *Dir,* Adrienne Pettinelli; E-mail: Adrienne.Pettinelli@libraryweb.org; *Ch,* Laura Lintz; E-mail: laura.lintz@libraryweb.org; *Teen Serv Librn,* Ellen Glena; E-mail: ellen.glena@libraryweb.org; *Adult Serv,* Jen Barth; E-mail: jbarth@libraryweb.org; *AV, Per,* Nancy Maxwell; E-mail: nancy.maxwell@libraryweb.org; Staff 8 (MLS 8)
Founded 1958. Pop 39,000; Circ 375,000
Library Holdings: AV Mats 8,208; e-books 237; Bk Vols 95,067; Per Subs 270
Subject Interests: Local hist
Automation Activity & Vendor Info: (Serials) TLC (The Library Corporation)
Wireless access
Mem of Monroe County Library System
Special Services for the Deaf - Closed caption videos; High interest/low vocabulary bks
Special Services for the Blind - Assistive/Adapted tech devices, equip & products; Bks on cassette; Bks on CD; Closed circuit TV magnifier; Home delivery serv; Large print bks
Open Mon-Thurs 9-9, Fri 9-5, Sat 10-5
Friends of the Library Group

M HIGHLAND HOSPITAL LIBRARY*, John R Williams Health Sciences Library, Highland Hospital, 1000 South Ave, 14620. (Mail add: Box 49, 14620), SAN 312-3529. Tel: 585-341-6761. Web Site: www.urmc.rochester.edu/hh/library. *Librn,* Lorraine Porcello; Tel: 585-341-0378, E-mail: lorraine_porcello@urmc.rochester.edu; Staff 2 (MLS 1, Non-MLS 1)
Founded 1967
Special Collections: Highland Hospital Archives Coll, papers, photog, yearbks & other memorabilia
Subject Interests: Allied health, Consumer health, Family med, Geriatrics, Med, Nursing, Obstetrics & gynecology, Oncology, Orthopedics, Women's health
Automation Activity & Vendor Info: (Acquisitions) Ex Libris Group; (Cataloging) Ex Libris Group; (Circulation) Ex Libris Group; (OPAC) Ex Libris Group; (Serials) Ex Libris Group
Wireless access
Function: Archival coll, Computers for patron use, E-Reserves, Electronic databases & coll, Health sci info serv, ILL available, Internet access, Online cat, Photocopying/Printing, Ref serv available
Partic in Rochester Regional Library Council
Open Tues-Thurs 8:30-Noon, Fri 8:30-4:30
Restriction: Badge access after hrs, Hospital staff & commun, In-house use for visitors, Lending to staff only

P IRONDEQUOIT PUBLIC LIBRARY*, 1290 Titus Ave, 14617. SAN 312-3545. Tel: 585-336-6060. E-mail: irondequoit@libraryweb.org. Web Site: www.irondequoitlibrary.org. *Libr Dir,* Greg Benoit; E-mail: greg.benoit@libraryweb.org; *Asst Dir,* Nora Pelish; E-mail: npelish@libraryweb.org; Staff 9 (MLS 9)
Founded 1947. Pop 52,354; Circ 771,623
Library Holdings: Bk Vols 156,718; Per Subs 250
Automation Activity & Vendor Info: (Cataloging) TLC (The Library Corporation); (Circulation) TLC (The Library Corporation); (OPAC) TLC (The Library Corporation)
Wireless access
Mem of Monroe County Library System
Open Mon-Thurs 10-9, Fri 10-6, Sat 10-5 (10-1 July-Aug), Sun (Sept-June) 1-4
Friends of the Library Group

R JEWISH COMMUNITY CENTER OF GREATER ROCHESTER*, Philip Feinbloom Library, 1200 Edgewood Ave, 14618. SAN 325-6790. Tel: 585-461-2000, Ext 239. FAX: 585-461-0805. Web Site: www.jccrochester.org/about-the-jcc/col/library. *Dir, Educ Prog,* Denise Johnson; E-mail: djohnson@jccrochester.org; Staff 1 (Non-MLS 1)
Founded 1973
Library Holdings: Bk Vols 10,000; Per Subs 20
Special Collections: Dr Saul Moress Peace Coll; Holocaust Coll; Jewish Children Coll; Jewish Genealogy, print microfiche; Jewish Themes, videos, audio cassettes
Subject Interests: Judaica
Wireless access
Open Mon-Fri 12-2
Restriction: Not a lending libr
Friends of the Library Group
Branches:
ISRAEL EMIOT MEMORIAL YIDDISH LIBRARY, 1200 Edgewood Ave, 14618-5408. Tel: 585-461-2000, Ext 607. FAX: 585-461-0805. *Librn,* Anna Gossin
Founded 1981
Library Holdings: Bk Vols 1,500
Subject Interests: Yiddish
Open Mon & Wed 3-5:30, Tues 10-2:30, Thurs 10-12:30

S LANDMARK SOCIETY OF WESTERN NEW YORK, INC*, Wenrich Memorial Library, 133 S Fitzhugh St, 14608-2204. SAN 312-3561. Tel: 585-546-7029. FAX: 585-546-4788. Web Site: landmarksociety.org/resources/john-wenrich-memorial-library. *Coordr,* Cynthia Howk; Tel: 585-546-7029, Ext 24, E-mail: chowk@landmarksociety.org; Staff 2 (MLS 1, Non-MLS 1)
Founded 1970
Library Holdings: Bk Titles 3,500
Special Collections: Information on Local Architecture; Local Architectural Surveys
Subject Interests: Bldg techniques, Hist rehabilitation, Hort, Landscape design, Regional archit
Function: Res libr
Partic in Research Libraries Information Network
Restriction: Non-circulating, Open by appt only

MONROE COMMUNITY COLLEGE
J DAMON CITY CAMPUS LIBRARY*, 228 E Main St, 4th Flr 4-101, 14604. Tel: 585-262-1413. Reference Tel: 585-262-1420. Administration Tel: 585-292-2307. FAX: 585-262-1516. E-mail: dcclibrary@monroecc.edu. Web Site: www.monroecc.edu/go/library. *Managing Librn,* Mary Timmons; E-mail: mtimmons@monroecc.edu; *Instrul Serv Librn,* Michael McCullough; E-mail: mmccullough@monroecc.edu; *Ref Serv,* Stephanie Hranjec; E-mail: shranjec@monroecc.edu; *Ref Serv,* William Johnson; E-mail: wjohnson@monroecc.edu; Staff 4 (MLS 4)
Highest Degree: Associate
Library Holdings: Bk Titles 10,000
Restriction: Open to students, fac & staff, Pub use on premises
J LEROY V GOOD LIBRARY*, 1000 E Henrietta Rd, 14692. (Mail add: PO Box 92810, 14692-8910), SAN 312-3596. Tel: 585-292-2665. Circulation Tel: 585-292-2303. Interlibrary Loan Service Tel:

585-292-2318. Reference Tel: 585-292-2319. Administration Tel: 585-292-2307. Interlibrary Loan Service FAX: 585-292-3823. Administration FAX: 585-292-3859. E-mail: shr_ill@monroecc.edu. Web Site: www.monroecc.edu/go/library. *Dir,* Mark McBride; Tel: 585-292-2321, E-mail: mmcbride17@monroecc.edu; *Asst Dir,* Alice Wilson; Tel: 585-292-2304, E-mail: awilson@monroecc.edu; *Coll Develop Librn,* Richard Squires; Tel: 585-292-2314, E-mail: rsquires@monroecc.edu; *Database Control Librn,* Deborah Mohr; Tel: 585-292-2316, E-mail: dmohr@monroecc.edu; *Database Mgt Librn,* Charlene Rezabek; Tel: 585-292-2330, E-mail: crezabek@monroecc.edu; *Ref Librn/Distance Learning,* Pamela Czaja; Tel: 585-292-2308, E-mail: pczaja@monroecc.edu; *Ref Librn/Spec Coll,* Lori Annesi; Tel: 585-292-2338, E-mail: lannesi@monroecc.edu; Staff 16.5 (MLS 10.5, Non-MLS 6)
Founded 1962. Enrl 37,929; Fac 341; Highest Degree: Associate
Library Holdings: Bk Vols 115,531; Per Subs 435
Special Collections: Historical Genocide, Human Rights Issues & Peace Studies (Holocaust & Human Rights Center)
Automation Activity & Vendor Info: (Cataloging) Ex Libris Group; (Circulation) Ex Libris Group; (Course Reserve) Blackboard Inc; (ILL) OCLC ILLiad; (OPAC) Ex Libris Group; (Serials) Ex Libris Group
Function: Art exhibits, Distance learning, ILL available, Scanner
Partic in OCLC Online Computer Library Center, Inc; Rochester Regional Library Council; SUNYConnect
Publications: Point of Use Guides
Special Services for the Deaf - Bks on deafness & sign lang
Special Services for the Blind - Low vision equip
Open Mon-Thurs 8am-9pm, Fri 8-4

P MONROE COUNTY LIBRARY SYSTEM*, 115 South Ave, 14604. SAN 312-3626. Tel: 585-428-8180. Reference Tel: 585-428-8160. Reference FAX: 585-428-8166. Web Site: libraryweb.org. *Dir,* Patricia Uttaro; E-mail: patricia.uttaro@libraryweb.org; *Assoc Libr Dir,* Adam Traub; E-mail: atraub@libraryweb.org
Founded 1952. Pop 729,308
Special Collections: US Document Depository
Wireless access
Member Libraries: Brighton Memorial Library; Chili Public Library; East Rochester Public Library; Fairport Public Library; Gates Public Library; Greece Public Library; Hamlin Public Library; Henrietta Public Library; Irondequoit Public Library; Mendon Public Library; Newman Riga Library; Ogden Farmers' Library; Parma Public Library; Penfield Public Library; Pittsford Community Library; Rochester Public Library; Rush Public Library; Scottsville Free Library; Seymour Library; Webster Public Library
Partic in Rochester Regional Library Council
Open Mon-Fri 9-5

S MONROE COUNTY SENECA PARK ZOO*, Marion C Barry Memorial Library, 2222 St Paul St, 14621-1097. SAN 329-2819. Tel: 585-753-2508. FAX: 585-753-2540. Web Site: senecaparkzoo.org. *Curator,* David Hamilton; Tel: 585-753-2502, E-mail: dhamilton@monroecounty.gov.
Subject Specialists: *Animals,* David Hamilton
Founded 1980
Library Holdings: Bk Titles 208
Subject Interests: Animals, Biology, Hort, Veterinary med, Zoology
Wireless access
Restriction: Staff use only

C NAZARETH COLLEGE OF ROCHESTER LIBRARY, Lorette Wilmot Library, 4245 East Ave, 14618-3790. SAN 312-3634. Tel: 585-389-2129. FAX: 585-389-2145. Web Site: www2.naz.edu/library. *Libr Dir,* Catherine Doyle; Tel: 585-389-2123, E-mail: cdoyle0@naz.edu; *Head, Cat,* Tara Winner-Swete; Tel: 585-389-2185, E-mail: twinner3@naz.edu; *Head, Circ Serv,* Jody Barker; Tel: 585-389-2160, E-mail: jbarker8@naz.edu; *Head, Instruction & Outreach,* Ilka Datig; Tel: 585-389-2128, E-mail: idatig5@naz.edu; *ILL & Serials Librn,* Christine A Sisak; Tel: 585-389-2184, E-mail: csisak5@naz.edu; *Scholarly Communications Librn,* Jennifer S Burr; Tel: 585-389-2133, E-mail: jburr0@naz.edu; *Syst Librn,* Heather Lagoy; Tel: 585-389-2121, E-mail: hlagoy7@naz.edu; *Makerspace Prog Spec,* R Sidney Pruitt; Tel: 585-389-2362, E-mail: rpruitt7@naz.edu; Staff 9.5 (MLS 7.5, Non-MLS 2)
Founded 1924. Enrl 2,810; Fac 175; Highest Degree: Master
Library Holdings: Bk Titles 235,155; Per Subs 27,149
Special Collections: Thomas Merton Coll
Automation Activity & Vendor Info: (Acquisitions) Ex Libris Group; (Cataloging) Ex Libris Group; (Circulation) Ex Libris Group; (Course Reserve) Ex Libris Group; (Discovery) Ex Libris Group; (ILL) OCLC ILLiad; (OPAC) Ex Libris Group; (Serials) Ex Libris Group
Wireless access
Function: 24/7 Online cat, Art exhibits
Publications: Acquisitions List; Periodicals; Special Collections Brochure; Subject Guides
Partic in Information Delivery Services Project; LYRASIS; Rochester Regional Library Council; Westchester Academic Library Directors Organization
Open Mon-Thurs 7:30-Midnight, Fri 7:30am-8pm, Sat 8:30-8, Sun 10 am-Midnight

GL NEW YORK STATE JUDICIAL DEPARTMENT*, Appellate Division Fourth Department Law Library, M Dolores Denman Courthouse, 50 East Ave, Ste 100, 14604-2214. SAN 312-3642. Tel: 585-530-3250. Interlibrary Loan Service Tel: 585-530-3254. Reference Tel: 585-530-3251. Administration Tel: 585-530-3252. FAX: 585-530-3270. Web Site: nycourts.gov/library/ad4. *Libr Dir,* Betsy Vipperman; E-mail: bvipperm@courts.state.ny.us; *Head, Tech Serv, Principal Law Librn,* Joan Thomas Hoolihan; E-mail: jhooliha@courts.state.ny.us; *Tech Serv/Ref Librn,* Robert Cunningham; E-mail: rcunnin@courts.state.ny.us; Staff 12 (MLS 6, Non-MLS 6)
Founded 1849
Library Holdings: Bk Vols 310,000; Per Subs 650
Special Collections: Pre-1850 Law Books; Regional Directories & Plat Books; Women in the Law
Subject Interests: Admin rules, Appeal papers, Citators, Court rpt, Decisions, Indexes, Monographs, Statutes
Automation Activity & Vendor Info: (Acquisitions) SirsiDynix; (Circulation) SirsiDynix; (ILL) SirsiDynix; (OPAC) SirsiDynix
Wireless access
Partic in Rochester Regional Library Council
Open Mon-Fri 9-5
Restriction: Non-circulating to the pub

C RIT LIBRARIES, Wallace Library, 90 Lomb Memorial Dr, 14623-5604. SAN 354-012X. Circulation Tel: 585-475-2562. Interlibrary Loan Service Tel: 585-475-2560. Reference Tel: 585-475-2563. Administration Tel: 585-475-2550, 585-475-2565. FAX: 585-475-7220. Web Site: library.rit.edu. *Dir,* Marcia S Trauernicht; Tel: 585-475-7292, E-mail: mstwml@rit.edu; *Assoc Dir,* Bonnie Swoger; Tel: 585-475-4693, E-mail: bjstwc@rit.edu; *Mgr, Acq & Ser,* Daniel Trout; Tel: 585-475-7283, E-mail: drttwc@rit.edu; *Research & Instruction Services, Sr Mgr,* Karen Lilequist; Tel: 585-475-2559, E-mail: kllwml@rit.edu; *Sr Mgr, Info Technology,* Eric Blevins; Tel: 585-475-7741, E-mail: ecbtwc@rit.edu; *Mgr, Metadata & Scholarship Services,* Gregory Decker; Tel: 585-475-4085, E-mail: gpdtwc@rit.edu; *Cir & Fac Mgr,* Jason Stryker; Tel: 585-475-5819, E-mail: jpsetc@rit.edu; *Univ Archivist,* Elizabeth Cali; Tel: 585-475-2557, E-mail: encwml@rit.edu; *Curator, Melbert B Cary Graphic Arts Coll,* Steven K Galbraith; Tel: 585-475-3961, E-mail: skgtwc@rit.edu; Staff 42 (MLS 24, Non-MLS 18)
Founded 1829. Enrl 19,718; Fac 1,524; Highest Degree: Doctorate
Library Holdings: Bk Titles 304,363; Bk Vols 316,566; Per Subs 3,217
Special Collections: Deaf Studies Archives; Graphic Design Archives; Melbert B Cary Graphic Arts Coll; RIT Archives
Subject Interests: Bookbinding, Bus, Computer sci, Deaf studies, Design, Engr, Graphic arts, Info tech, Printing
Wireless access
Partic in ConnectNY, Inc; LYRASIS; Northeast Research Libraries Consortium; Pi2; Rochester Regional Library Council
Special Services for the Deaf - Bks on deafness & sign lang; Spec interest per; Staff with knowledge of sign lang; TTY equip
Open Mon-Fri 7:30am-Midnight, Sat 10-8, Sun 11am-Midnight

CR ROBERTS WESLEYAN COLLEGE & NORTHEASTERN SEMINARY*, B Thomas Golisano Library, 2301 Westside Dr, 14624-1997. SAN 312-3693. Tel: 585-594-6949. Interlibrary Loan Service Tel: 585-594-6017. Reference Tel: 585-594-6499. FAX: 585-594-6543. Web Site: www.roberts.edu/library. *Dir, Libr Serv,* Matthew Ballard; Tel: 585-594-6501, E-mail: ballard_matthew@roberts.edu; *Access Serv Librn,* Meredith Ader; Tel: 585-594-6141, E-mail: ader_meredith@roberts.edu; *Res & Instruction Librn,* Chip Wiley; Tel: 585-594-6893, E-mail: wiley_chip@roberts.edu; *Syst Librn,* Matthew Davis; Tel: 585-594-6064, E-mail: davis_matthew@roberts.edu; *Operations Mgr,* Sarah Clay; Tel: 585-594-6816, E-mail: clay_sarah@roberts.edu; Staff 6 (MLS 6)
Enrl 1,703; Fac 259; Highest Degree: Master
Library Holdings: CDs 1,464; DVDs 510; e-books 3,086; e-journals 1,466; Electronic Media & Resources 127; Bk Titles 111,000; Bk Vols 126,000; Per Subs 650; Videos 292
Special Collections: Benjamin Titus Roberts Coll, bks, ms & photog; Free Methodist Church History, bks, per, photog; Roberts Wesleyan College Historical Materials
Subject Interests: Art, Biblical studies, Educ, Mgt, Music, Nursing, Psychol, Soc work, Theol
Automation Activity & Vendor Info: (Acquisitions) Ex Libris Group; (Cataloging) Ex Libris Group; (Circulation) Ex Libris Group; (Course Reserve) Ex Libris Group; (ILL) OCLC; (OPAC) Ex Libris Group; (Serials) Ex Libris Group
Wireless access

Function: Audio & video playback equip for onsite use, Computers for patron use, E-Reserves, Electronic databases & coll, Music CDs, Online cat, Photocopying/Printing, VHS videos, Wheelchair accessible
Partic in Christian Library Consortium; OCLC Online Computer Library Center, Inc; Rochester Regional Library Council; Westchester Academic Library Directors Organization
Special Services for the Blind - Reader equip
Open Mon-Thurs 8am-Midnight, Fri 8-6, Sat 9-7, Sun 2-Midnight

S ROCHESTER CIVIC GARDEN CENTER, INC LIBRARY*, Five Castle Park, 14620. SAN 312-3480. Tel: 716-473-5130. FAX: 716-473-8136. E-mail: rcgclib@frontiernet.net. Web Site: www.rcgc.org/librarys. *Admin Coordr,* Marjorie Focarazzo; Staff 8 (MLS 1, Non-MLS 7)
Founded 1945
Library Holdings: DVDs 4; Bk Titles 4,500; Bk Vols 4,800; Per Subs 23; Spec Interest Per Sub 23; Videos 27
Special Collections: 19th Century Garden, bks, cat
Subject Interests: Garden hist, Hort, Landscaping, Natural crafts, Related facets incl flower arrangements
Automation Activity & Vendor Info: (Cataloging) JayWil Software Development, Inc; (OPAC) JayWil Software Development, Inc
Wireless access
Publications: RCGC Class Catalog (Current awareness service); Upstate Gardeners Journal (Bimonthly)
Partic in Rochester Regional Library Council
Open Tues-Thurs 9-4
Restriction: Non-circulating to the pub, Open to pub for ref only

M ROCHESTER GENERAL HOSPITAL, Werner Medical Library, 1425 Portland Ave, 14621. SAN 312-3723. Tel: 585-922-4743. FAX: 585-544-1504. E-mail: wellness@rochesterregional.org. Web Site: rrhlibraries.org. *Libr Dir,* Elizabeth Mamo; E-mail: elizabeth.mamo@rochesterregional.org; *Librn,* Tami Hartzell; E-mail: tami.hartzell@rochestergeneral.org; *Librn,* Mary McVicar-Keim; E-mail: mary.mcvicarkeim@rochestergeneral.org; Staff 8 (MLS 6, Non-MLS 2)
Founded 1983
Automation Activity & Vendor Info: (Cataloging) CyberTools for Libraries; (Circulation) CyberTools for Libraries; (Discovery) TDNet; (ILL) OCLC WorldShare Interlibrary Loan; (OPAC) CyberTools for Libraries
Wireless access
Partic in OCLC Online Computer Library Center, Inc; Rochester Regional Library Council
Open Mon-Fri 8-5
Friends of the Library Group

S ROCHESTER HISTORICAL SOCIETY LIBRARY, 1100 University Ave, 14607. SAN 312-3731. Tel: 585-623-8285. Web Site: www.rochesterhistory.org. *Archivist/Librn, Registrar,* William Keeler; E-mail: wkeeler@rochesterhistory.org
Library Holdings: Bk Vols 15,000
Special Collections: Rochester & Genesee Valley History Coll, bks, ms, photog; Rochester City Directories; Rochester Historical Society Publications
Function: ILL available
Restriction: Non-circulating to the pub, Open by appt only

S ROCHESTER MUSEUM & SCIENCE CENTER LIBRARY*, Schuyler C Townson Library, 657 East Ave, 14607. SAN 354-0189. Tel: 585-271-4320, Ext 315. FAX: 585-271-0492. Web Site: collections.rmsc.org, www.rmsc.org. *Dir,* Steve Fentress; E-mail: sfentress@rmsc.org; *Archivist, Librn,* Leatrice Kemp; E-mail: lea_kemp@rmsc.org; Staff 1 (MLS 1)
Founded 1917
Library Holdings: AV Mats 50; Bk Titles 30,000; Per Subs 60
Special Collections: 19th Century Periodicals, Almanacs, Posters, Greeting Cards; African American History (Howard W Coles Coll); Domestic Architecture (Barrows, Thomas Boyd & William H Richardson Coll), architectural drawings; Flour Milling Industry (Moseley & Motley Coll), mss; Rochester Button Company, mss; Rochester History; Stone Coll - Glass Plate Negatives
Subject Interests: Anthrop, Antiques, Archaeology, Costume, Local hist, Native Am especially Iroquois, Natural hist
Automation Activity & Vendor Info: (Cataloging) OCLC; (ILL) OCLC
Wireless access
Partic in OCLC Online Computer Library Center, Inc; Rochester Regional Library Council
Open Mon-Sun by appointment only
Restriction: Open to pub for ref only

P ROCHESTER PUBLIC LIBRARY*, 115 South Ave, 14604-1896. SAN 354-0243. Tel: 585-428-7300. FAX: 585-428-8353. TDD: 585-428-8023. Web Site: libraryweb.org, roccitylibrary.org/location/central. *Dir,* Patricia Uttaro; Tel: 585-428-8045, E-mail: Patricia.Uttaro@libraryweb.org; *Asst Dir,* Tolley Reeves; Tel: 585-428-8345, E-mail: Tolley.Reeves@libraryweb.org
Founded 1911. Pop 713,968; Circ 1,779,111
Library Holdings: Bk Titles 950,000; Per Subs 5,620
Special Collections: Black History (Wheatley Branch Coll); Department Coll, film; Local History, bks, photogs, newsp; Reynolds Audio Visual. US Document Depository
Automation Activity & Vendor Info: (Acquisitions) TLC (The Library Corporation); (Cataloging) OCLC; (Circulation) TLC (The Library Corporation); (OPAC) TLC (The Library Corporation); (Serials) TLC (The Library Corporation)
Wireless access
Publications: Directory of Associations in Monroe County; Directory of Clubs in Monroe County; Guide to Grant Markers; Human Services Directory; Neighborhood Associations; Visiting Artists Directory
Mem of Monroe County Library System
Partic in OCLC Online Computer Library Center, Inc
Special Services for the Deaf - Bks on deafness & sign lang; Captioned film dep; Spec interest per; Staff with knowledge of sign lang
Open Mon & Wed 10-8:30, Tues & Fri 10-6, Thurs 11-6, Sat 10-5
Friends of the Library Group
Branches: 10
ARNETT, 310 Arnett Blvd, 14619, SAN 354-0278. Tel: 585-428-8214. *Br Mgr,* Bruce Tehan; E-mail: bruce.tehan@libraryweb.org
Subject Interests: African-Am hist
Open Mon & Wed 11-6, Tues & Thurs 11-7, Fri 11-5, Sat 10-2
CHARLOTTE, 3557 Lake Ave, 14612, SAN 354-0332. Tel: 585-428-8216. *Br Mgr,* Paul Tantillo
Subject Interests: Boating, Local hist
Open Mon-Thurs 11:30-7, Fri 11:30-5:30, Sat 10-2
HIGHLAND, 971 South Ave, 14620, SAN 354-0510. Tel: 585-428-8206. *Br Mgr,* Erin Clarke
Open Mon 1-7, Tues & Thurs 10-6, Wed & Fri 1-6, Sat 10-2
LINCOLN, 851 Joseph Ave, 14621, SAN 354-0421. Tel: 585-428-8210. *Br Mgr,* Jason Gogniat; E-mail: jason.gogniat@libraryweb.org
Subject Interests: African-Am hist, Spanish lang
Open Mon-Wed 10-6, Thurs & Fri 12-6, Sat 12-4
LYELL, 956 Lyell Ave, 14606, SAN 325-4356. Tel: 585-428-8218. *Br Mgr,* Patricia Connor; E-mail: patricia.connor@libraryweb.org
Open Mon 12-8, Tues & Fri 12-6, Sat 10-2
MAPLEWOOD, 1111 Dewey Ave, 14613, SAN 354-0456. Tel: 585-428-8220. *Br Mgr,* Johanna Buran; E-mail: johanna.buran@libraryweb.org
Open Mon-Thurs 11:30-7, Fri 11:30-5:30, Sat 10-2
MONROE, 809 Monroe Ave, 14607, SAN 354-0480. Tel: 585-428-8202. *Supvr,* Mary Clare Scheg; E-mail: Mary.Scheg@libraryweb.org
Open Mon 12-8, Tues 10-6, Wed 12-6, Thurs & Fri 11-6, Sat 10-2
SULLY BRANCH, 530 Webster Ave, 14609. (Mail add: 115 South Ave, 14604). Tel: 585-428-8208. Web Site: roccitylibrary.org/location/sully. *Br Supvr,* Maria Heeks-Heinlein; Tel: 585-428-8290, E-mail: Maria.Heeks-Heinlein@libraryweb.org
Founded 1954
Function: 3D Printer, ILL available, Meeting rooms, Museum passes, Notary serv, Photocopying/Printing, Res assist avail, Scanner
Open Mon & Wed-Fri 11-6, Tues 11-7, Sat 12-4
PHILLIS WHEATLEY COMMUNITY, 33 Dr Samuel McCree Way, 14608, SAN 354-057X. Tel: 585-428-8212. *Br Mgr,* Lori Frankunas; E-mail: lori.frankunas@libraryweb.org
Special Collections: Oral History
Subject Interests: African-Am hist
Open Mon & Wed Noon-7, Tues & Thurs 10-6, Fri Noon-6, Sat 10-2
WINTON, 611 Winton Rd N, 14609, SAN 354-060X. Tel: 585-428-8204. *Br Mgr,* Barbara Nichols; E-mail: barbara.nichols@libraryweb.org
Subject Interests: Russian lang
Open Mon 11-8, Tues-Fri 11-6, Sat 11-2
Bookmobiles: 1

C SAINT JOHN FISHER COLLEGE*, Lavery Library, 3690 East Ave, 14618-3599. SAN 312-2662. Tel: 585-385-8165. Interlibrary Loan Service Tel: 585-385-8106. Reference Tel: 585-385-8141. Administration Tel: 585-385-8164. FAX: 585-385-8445. Web Site: www.sjfc.edu/library. *Dir,* Melissa Jadlos; E-mail: mjadlos@sjfc.edu; *Head, Ref & Ser,* Marianne Simmons; Tel: 585-385-7399, E-mail: msimmons@sjfc.edu; *Acq Librn, Head, Tech Serv,* Kate Ross; Tel: 585-385-8136, E-mail: kross@sjfc.edu; *Access Serv Librn,* Kourtney Blackburn; Tel: 585-385-7340, E-mail: kblackburn@sjfc.edu; *Assessment & Online Prog Librn,* Christina Hillman; Tel: 585-385-8493, E-mail: chillman@sjfc.edu; *Educ Librn,* Stacia Maiorani; Tel: 585-385-8140, E-mail: smaiorani@sjfc.edu; *Instruction & Archives Librn,* Nancy Greco; Tel: 585-385-8139, E-mail: ngreco@sjfc.edu; *Outreach & Spec Coll Librn,* Michelle Price; Tel: 585-899-3743, E-mail: mprice@sjfc.edu; *Syst Librn,* Benjamin Hockenberry; Tel: 585-385-8382, E-mail: bhockenberry@sjfc.edu; *Circ Coordr,* Stacy Celata; E-mail: scelata@sjfc.edu; *ILL Coordr,* Alicia Marrese; E-mail: amarrese@sjfc.edu. Subject Specialists: *Nursing, Pharm, Sci,* Michelle Price; Staff 9 (MLS 9)
Founded 1951. Enrl 3,809; Fac 451; Highest Degree: Doctorate

Library Holdings: AV Mats 7,669; e-books 21,297; Bk Vols 149,111; Per Subs 48,882
Special Collections: Anti-Slavery Newspapers; Frederick Douglass Newspapers; George P Decker Papers; Theodore C. Cazeau Grand Army of the Republic Coll
Subject Interests: Bus, Educ, Liberal arts, Nursing, Pharm
Automation Activity & Vendor Info: (Acquisitions) Ex Libris Group; (Cataloging) Ex Libris Group; (Circulation) Ex Libris Group; (Course Reserve) Ex Libris Group; (ILL) OCLC ILLiad; (OPAC) Ex Libris Group; (Serials) Ex Libris Group
Wireless access
Partic in Information Delivery Services Project; Rochester Regional Library Council
Open Mon-Thurs 7:45am-Midnight, Fri 7:45am-10pm, Sat 8:45am-10pm, Sun 8:45am-Midnight
Restriction: In-house use for visitors, Non-circulating to the pub

S THE STRONG MUSEUM*, Brian Sutton-Smith Library & Archives of Play, One Manhattan Sq, 14607. SAN 312-3790. Tel: 585-263-2700, 585-410-6349. FAX: 585-263-2493. E-mail: library@museumofplay.org. Web Site: www.museumofplay.org/about/library-archives-play. *Librn,* Beth Lathrop; Staff 2 (MLS 1, Non-MLS 1)
Founded 1972
Library Holdings: Bk Titles 160,000
Special Collections: 19th & 20th Century Trade Catalogs; 19th & Early 20th Century Children's; Fore-Edge Paintings Coll; Patent Papers for Dolls & Toys; Winslow Homer Coll
Subject Interests: 19th Century Am domestic life bks inc socio-cultural hist, Decorative art, Early 20th Century Am domestic life bks inc socio-cultural hist
Automation Activity & Vendor Info: (Cataloging) OCLC; (OPAC) EOS International
Wireless access
Partic in Rochester Regional Library Council
Restriction: Open by appt only

R TEMPLE SINAI LIBRARY, 363 Penfield Rd, 14625. SAN 312-3820. Tel: 585-381-6890. FAX: 585-381-4921. E-mail: office@tsinai.org. Web Site: www.tsinai.org/library. *Educ Dir, Library Contact,* Ilan Adar; E-mail: iadar@tsinai.org
Founded 1974
Library Holdings: Bk Titles 5,000
Subject Interests: Judaica
Wireless access
Open Mon-Thurs 9-5, Fri 9-3

L UNDERBERG & KESSLER LAW LIBRARY*, 300 Bausch & Lomb Pl, 14604. SAN 372-252X. Tel: 585-258-2800. FAX: 585-258-2821. Web Site: underbergkessler.com. *Librn,* Jane Snyder; E-mail: jsnyder@underbergkessler.com
Library Holdings: Bk Vols 8,000

M UNITY HOSPITAL MEDICAL LIBRARY*, 1555 Long Pond Rd, 14626. SAN 327-2338. Tel: 585-723-7755. FAX: 585-723-7078. *Dir,* Raymond W Curtin; E-mail: raymond.curtin@rochesterregional.org; *Med Librn,* Steven F Buckley; E-mail: steven.buckley@rochesterregional.org; Staff 1.5 (MLS 1.5)
Founded 1946
Library Holdings: Bk Vols 1,900; Per Subs 140
Automation Activity & Vendor Info: (Cataloging) CyberTools for Libraries; (Circulation) CyberTools for Libraries; (OPAC) CyberTools for Libraries; (Serials) CyberTools for Libraries
Wireless access
Function: Health sci info serv
Partic in OCLC Online Computer Library Center, Inc
Restriction: Open to staff, patients & family mem

C UNIVERSITY OF ROCHESTER*, Rush Rhees Library, River Campus Libraries, 755 Library Rd, 14627-0055. SAN 354-0693. Tel: 585-275-4461. Interlibrary Loan Service Tel: 585-275-4454. FAX: 585-273-5309. Web Site: library.rochester.edu/rhees. *Dean of Libr, Vice Provost, Andrew H & Janet Dayton Neilly,* Mary Ann Mavrinac; E-mail: maryann.mavrinac@rochester.edu; *Assoc Dean,* Jennifer Bowen; E-mail: jbowen@library.rochester.edu; Staff 65 (MLS 33, Non-MLS 32)
Founded 1850. Enrl 10,290; Fac 1,347; Highest Degree: Doctorate
Library Holdings: Bk Vols 3,259,159; Per Subs 44,175
Special Collections: 19th & 20th Century Public Affairs Colls (Papers of William Henry Seward, Thurlow Weed, David Jayne Hill, Susan B Anthony, Rev William C Gannett, Thomas E Dewey, Marion Folsom, Kenneth Keating & Frank Horton); 19th Century Botany & Horticulture Colls (Ellwanger & Barry Nursery Papers & Library, Historian Christopher Lasch Archives, Political Scientist William Riker); American Literature Coll (Washington Irving, Henry James, Mark Twain, William Dean Howells, Edward Everett Hale (filmed bks), William Heyen (filmed bks, historical children's bks, ms & printed works), Christopher Morley, Adelaide Crapsey (ms & printed works), Henry W Clune (ms & printed works), Frederick Exley (ms & printed works), John A Williams (ms & printed works), John Gardner (ms & printed works), Jerre Mangione (ms & printed works), Plutzik Library (ms & printed works), Paul Zimmer Papers); Art & Architecture Colls (Claude Bragdon Papers, Drawings & Printed Works; Dyrer & Dryer Papers); English History & Literature Colls (Eikon Basilike, John Dryden, Restoration Drama, John Ruskin, John Masefield, Benjamin Disraeli, Sean O'Casey, Edward Gorey, 19th & 20th Century Theatre Manuscripts, Robert Southey (ms & printed works), Arnold Bennett); Leonardo da Vinci Coll; Optical Industry Trade Catalogs; Regional History (New York State Settlement, Land Development & Local History, especially Rochester & Monroe County, Native Americans, Early Upstate New York Printing, Manuscript Records of Rochester Benevolent Organizations, Businesses & Industry); Social & Natural Science Colls (Papers of Anthropologist Lewis Henry Morgan & Scientists Herman LeRoy Fairchild, Henry A Ward, Carl E Akeley, Printed Works of Charles Darwin). State Document Depository; US Document Depository
Wireless access
Partic in Association of Research Libraries; Rochester Regional Library Council
Friends of the Library Group

Departmental Libraries:

CHARLOTTE WHITNEY ALLEN LIBRARY, Memorial Art Gallery, 500 University Ave, 14607, SAN 354-0758. Tel: 585-276-8999. FAX: 585-473-6266. E-mail: maglibinfo@mag.rochester.edu. Web Site: mag.rochester.edu/library. *Art Librn,* Lu Harper; Tel: 585-276-8997, E-mail: lharper@mag.rochester.edu; *Libr Asst,* Kathleen Nicastro; Tel: 585-276-8901, E-mail: knicastr@mag.rochester.edu; Staff 1.5 (MLS 1, Non-MLS 0.5)
Founded 1913
Library Holdings: Bk Vols 45,408; Per Subs 60
Special Collections: Fritz Trautmann Coll, scrapbks; MAG Archives; Rochester Art Club Coll, 1880-present, exhibition cats
Subject Interests: Art hist, Museology
Open Wed-Fri 1-5

ART-MUSIC, Rush Rhees Library, 14627, SAN 354-0723. Tel: 585-275-4476. FAX: 585-273-1032. E-mail: artlib@library.rochester.edu. Web Site: www.library.rochester.edu/artmusic. *Head Librn,* Stephanie Frontz; E-mail: sfrontz@library.rochester.edu
Library Holdings: CDs 2,500; Bk Titles 70,000; Per Subs 200
Special Collections: Robert MacCameron Coll, papers & photos, Artists' Books
Subject Interests: Archit, Art hist, Cultural studies, Mus, Sound rec
Friends of the Library Group

CARLSON SCIENCE & ENGINEERING LIBRARY, 160 Trustee Rd, 14627-0236, SAN 327-9138. Tel: 585-275-4488. FAX: 585-273-4656. Web Site: www.library.rochester.edu/carlson. *Dir,* Zahra Kamarei; Tel: 585-275-1763, E-mail: zkamarei@library.rochester.edu; Staff 6 (MLS 6)
Special Collections: USGS Topographic Maps
Subject Interests: Biology, Chem, Computer sci, Engr, Geol, Maps, Math, Statistics
Friends of the Library Group

PHYSICS-OPTICS-ASTRONOMY LIBRARY - RIVER CAMPUS, 374 Bausch & Lomb Hall, 14627-0171, SAN 327-9197. Tel: 585-275-4469. FAX: 585-273-5321. Web Site: www.library.rochester.edu/poalibrary. *Dir,* Zary Kamerei; Staff 1 (MLS 1)
Highest Degree: Doctorate
Special Collections: History of Optics
Subject Interests: Astronomy, Optics, Physics
Friends of the Library Group

ROSSELL HOPE ROBBINS LIBRARY, Rush Rhees Library, Rm 416, 14627, SAN 372-509X. Tel: 585-275-0110. Web Site: www.library.rochester.edu/robbins. *Dir,* Anna Seibach-Larsen; Tel: 585-275-9197, E-mail: annasiebachlarsen@library.rochester.edu; *Supvr,* Katie Papas; E-mail: kpapas@library.rochester.edu
Founded 1987
Library Holdings: Bk Titles 15,000
Special Collections: Medieval Literature (Offprint Coll)
Subject Interests: Medieval English lit, Medieval studies
Restriction: Non-circulating to the pub
Friends of the Library Group

SIBLEY MUSIC LIBRARY, 27 Gibbs St, 14604-2596, SAN 354-0901. Tel: 585-274-1350. Circulation Tel: 585-274-1300. FAX: 585-274-1380. Web Site: www.esm.rochester.edu/sibley. *Assoc Dean,* Daniel Zager; E-mail: dzager@esm.rochester.edu; *Head, Pub Serv,* James Farrington; E-mail: jfarrington@esm.rochester.edu; *Spec Coll & Archives Librn,* David Peter Coppen; E-mail: dcoppen@esm.rochester.edu; Staff 8 (MLS 6, Non-MLS 2)
Founded 1904. Enrl 853; Fac 96; Highest Degree: Doctorate
Library Holdings: AV Mats 105,731; Microforms 14,403; Bk Titles 240,524; Bk Vols 387,752; Per Subs 620
Special Collections: 17th Century Sacred Music (Olschki Coll); Books & Scores (Oscar Sonneck Library); Chamber Music; Folk Music (Krehbiel Coll); Music Biography, Theatre & Librettos (Pougin Coll);

Music Manuscripts (Howard Hanson, Gardner Read, Burrill Philips, Weldon Hart Coll, Karl Weigl & Alec Wilder Colls); Music Publishing (Sengstack Archives); Performers' Coll (Malcolm Frager, Jan DeGaetani & Jacques Gordon Colls)
Subject Interests: Chamber music, Hist of music, Libretti, Music theory, Musical theatre, Opera, Solo lit
Automation Activity & Vendor Info: (Acquisitions) Ex Libris Group; (Cataloging) Ex Libris Group; (Circulation) Ex Libris Group; (OPAC) Ex Libris Group; (Serials) Ex Libris Group
Partic in OCLC Online Computer Library Center, Inc

CM UNIVERSITY OF ROCHESTER MEDICAL CENTER*, Edward G Miner Library, 601 Elmwood Ave, 14642. Tel: 585-275-3361. Administration Tel: 585-275-3363. FAX: 585-756-7762. E-mail: Miner_information@urmc.rochester.edu. Web Site: www.urmc.rochester.edu/libraries/miner. *Dir,* Jennifer Raynor; Tel: 716-275-4869, E-mail: JenniferRaynor@urmc.rochester.edu; *Adminr,* Susan Anderson; Tel: 716-275-3363, E-mail: Susan_Anderson@urmc.rochester.edu. Subject Specialists: *Admin, Finance,* Susan Anderson; Staff 31 (MLS 9, Non-MLS 22)
Library Holdings: e-journals 1,100; Bk Titles 58,000; Bk Vols 240,000; Per Subs 1,200
Subject Interests: Hist of med, Med, Nursing
Automation Activity & Vendor Info: (Acquisitions) Ex Libris Group; (Cataloging) Ex Libris Group; (Circulation) Ex Libris Group; (OPAC) Ex Libris Group; (Serials) Ex Libris Group
Wireless access
Partic in Miraclenet; Northeast Research Libraries Consortium; Rochester Regional Library Council
Open Mon-Thurs (Winter) 7:30am-Midnight, Fri 7:30am-10pm, Sat 10-10, Sun 10am-Midnight; Mon-Thurs (Summer) 7:30am-10pm, Fri 7:30am-8pm, Sat 10-5, Sun Noon-10

Departmental Libraries:

BASIL G BIBBY LIBRARY, Eastman Dental, Rm 208, 625 Elmwood Ave, 14620, SAN 312-3456. Tel: 585-275-5010. FAX: 585-273-1230. Web Site: www.urmc.rochester.edu/libraries/bibby. *Librn,* Lorraine Porcello; E-mail: lorraine_porcello@urmc.rochester.edu; *Libr Asst,* Jaimi Miller; E-mail: Jaimi_miller@urmc.rochester.edu; Staff 2 (MLS 1, Non-MLS 1)
Founded 1947
Library Holdings: Bk Vols 2,100; Per Subs 35
Special Collections: Eastman Dental & Dentistry History Coll, archives
Subject Interests: Dentistry
Automation Activity & Vendor Info: (Course Reserve) Blackboard Inc
Function: Archival coll, Computers for patron use, Electronic databases & coll, For res purposes, Health sci info serv, ILL available, Online cat, Photocopying/Printing
Partic in New York State Interlibrary Loan Network
Publications: Basil G Bibby Library Gazette (Online only)
Open Mon 8-5, Tues 8-4:30, Wed 1:30-5, Thurs 8:30-4:30, Fri 8:30-Noon
Restriction: Badge access after hrs, Hospital staff & commun, In-house use for visitors, Lending to staff only

ROCKVILLE CENTRE

P LAKEVIEW PUBLIC LIBRARY, 1120 Woodfield Rd, 11570. SAN 312-3855. Tel: 516-536-3071. FAX: 516-536-6260. Web Site: www.lakeviewlibrary.org. *Dir,* Camina Raphael-Lubin; E-mail: clubin@nassaulibrary.org; *Librn,* Sean Edwards; *Librn,* Mamta Mehta; E-mail: lklref@nassaulibrary.org; *Ch,* Ivy Reckson; *YA Librn,* Jennifer Dunlop; E-mail: jdunlop@nassaulibrary.org; *Circ,* Jacinta Bowman; *Treas,* Opal Ramdial; Staff 10 (MLS 10)
Founded 1973. Pop 6,500
Library Holdings: Bks on Deafness & Sign Lang 15; CDs 450; DVDs 1,200; e-journals 109; Bk Vols 60,000; Videos 1,127
Special Collections: Black Experience, bks, micro, per
Subject Interests: Foreign lang bks
Automation Activity & Vendor Info: (Cataloging) Innovative Interfaces, Inc; (Circulation) Innovative Interfaces, Inc; (OPAC) Innovative Interfaces, Inc
Wireless access
Publications: Community Directory of Community Organizations; Community Library (Newsletter)
Mem of Nassau Library System
Partic in Long Island Library Resources Council; New York State Interlibrary Loan Network
Open Mon-Thurs 10-6, Fri 9-5, Sat 9-1
Friends of the Library Group

C MOLLOY COLLEGE*, James E Tobin Library, 1000 Hempstead Ave, 11571. (Mail add: PO Box 5002, 11571-5002), SAN 312-3871. Tel: 516-323-3911. Interlibrary Loan Service Tel: 516-323-3914. Reference Tel: 516-323-3912. Administration Tel: 516-323-3926. Toll Free Tel: 888-466-5569. FAX: 516-323-4910. E-mail: molloylibrarian@gmail.com. Web Site: www.molloy.edu/library. *Libr Dir,* Judith Drescher; Tel: 516-323-3925, E-mail: jdrescher@molloy.edu; *Assoc Librn, Head, Instrul Serv,* Bloom Susie; Tel: 516-323-3927, E-mail: sbloom@molloy.edu; *Assoc Librn, Head, Ref Serv,* Nikki Palumbo; Tel: 516-323-3929, E-mail: npalumbo@molloy.edu; *Assoc Librn, Head, Tech Serv,* Tim Hasin; Tel: 516-323-3921, E-mail: thasin@molloy.edu; *Access Serv Librn, Media Librn, Ser Librn,* David Nochimson; Tel: 516-323-3928, E-mail: dnochimson@molloy.edu; *Acq Librn,* Bob Martin; Tel: 516-323-3922; *Digital Commons Curator, Electronic Res Librn,* Tabitha Ochtera; Tel: 516-323-3917, E-mail: tochtera@molloy.edu; *Assoc Librn, Health Sci Librn,* Theresa Rienzo; Tel: 516-323-3930, E-mail: trienzo@molloy.edu; *Instrul & Ref Librn,* Wenhui Chen; Tel: 516-323-3584, E-mail: wchen@molloy.edu. Subject Specialists: *Organizational behavior, Psychol,* Judith Drescher; *Fine arts, Hist, Paralegal studies,* Bloom Susie; *Bus, Educ, Soc work,* Nikki Palumbo; *Computer sci, Math, Modern lang,* Tim Hasin; *Environ sci, Sociol, Theatre arts,* David Nochimson; *Interdisciplinary, Theol,* Bob Martin; *English, New media, Philos,* Tabitha Ochtera; *Allied health, Nursing,* Theresa Rienzo; Staff 27 (MLS 22, Non-MLS 5)
Founded 1955. Enrl 3,420; Fac 350; Highest Degree: Doctorate
Special Collections: Historical Artifacts (Barbara H Hagan School of Nursing Coll)
Automation Activity & Vendor Info: (Acquisitions) Ex Libris Group; (Cataloging) Ex Libris Group; (Circulation) Ex Libris Group; (Course Reserve) Atlas Systems; (Discovery) ProQuest; (ILL) OCLC ILLiad; (OPAC) Ex Libris Group; (Serials) SerialsSolutions
Wireless access
Function: 24/7 Electronic res, 24/7 Online cat, Audio & video playback equip for onsite use, Computers for patron use, Distance learning, E-Reserves, Electronic databases & coll, ILL available, Instruction & testing, Internet access, Literacy & newcomer serv, Magazines, Microfiche/film & reading machines, Online cat, Online info literacy tutorials on the web & in blackboard, Online ref, Outreach serv, Ref serv available, Scanner, Study rm, VHS videos
Partic in Information Delivery Services Project; Long Island Library Resources Council; Westchester Academic Library Directors Organization
Open Mon-Thurs 8am-10pm, Fri 8-8, Sat 10-6, Sun 12-8

P ROCKVILLE CENTRE PUBLIC LIBRARY, 221 N Village Ave, 11570. SAN 312-388X. Tel: 516-766-6257. Circulation Tel: 516-766-6257, Ext 3. Reference Tel: 516-766-6257, Ext 5. Administration Tel: 516-766-6257, Ext 4. FAX: 516-766-6090. E-mail: info@rvcpl.org. Web Site: www.rvclibrary.org. *Libr Dir,* Catherine Overton; E-mail: coverton@rvcpl.org; *Head, Adult Serv,* Ellen Berman; E-mail: eberman@rvcpl.org; *Head, Youth Serv,* Jennifer Marino; E-mail: jmarino@rvcpl.org; Staff 65 (MLS 20, Non-MLS 45)
Founded 1882. Pop 24,747; Circ 307,986
Library Holdings: Large Print Bks 4,379; Bk Vols 179,320; Per Subs 300
Special Collections: Rockville Centre History, bks, pictures, newsp
Subject Interests: Civil War, Educ, Hist
Automation Activity & Vendor Info: (Circulation) Innovative Interfaces, Inc; (OPAC) Innovative Interfaces, Inc
Wireless access
Function: Adult bk club, After school storytime, Art exhibits, E-Reserves, Electronic databases & coll, Homebound delivery serv, ILL available, Large print keyboards, Magnifiers for reading, Online ref, Photocopying/Printing, Prog for adults, Prog for children & young adult, Summer reading prog, Tax forms, Wheelchair accessible, Workshops
Publications: Library Newsletter
Mem of Nassau Library System
Open Mon, Wed & Thurs 9-7, Tues 10-7, Fri 9-6, Sat 9-5, Sun (Sept-June) 1-5
Friends of the Library Group

RODMAN

P RODMAN PUBLIC LIBRARY*, 12509 School St, 13682. (Mail add: PO Box B, 13682-0002), SAN 312-3898. Tel: 315-232-2522. FAX: 315-232-3853. E-mail: rodlib@ncls.org. Web Site: www.rodmanpubliclibrary.org. *Mgr,* Karen Marriott; Staff 1 (Non-MLS 1)
Founded 1922. Pop 1,700; Circ 7,000
Library Holdings: Bk Vols 2,700
Wireless access
Function: 24/7 Electronic res, 24/7 Online cat, Activity rm
Mem of North Country Library System
Partic in Northern New York Library Network
Open Mon 11-5, Wed & Fri 10-5

ROME

P JERVIS PUBLIC LIBRARY ASSOCIATION, INC*, 613 N Washington St, 13440-4296. SAN 312-3901. Tel: 315-336-4570. Web Site: www.jervislibrary.org. *Dir,* Lisa M Matte; *Asst Dir,* Kari Tucker; *Chief Librn, Local Hist/Genealogy & Ref Serv,* Lori Chien; *Chief Librn, Pub Digital Literacy,* Peter Chien; *Sr Librn, Adult Engagement & Outreach,*

Mary Beth Portley; *Ch Serv Librn,* Alanna Blasi; *Teen Serv Librn,* Stephanie Markham. Subject Specialists: *Genealogy, Local hist,* Lori Chien; Staff 8 (MLS 7, Non-MLS 1)
Founded 1894. Pop 33,125; Circ 264,533
Jan 2015-Dec 2015 Income $1,498,160, State $27,000, City $322,903, County $261,482, Locally Generated Income $69,775, Other $817,000. Mats Exp $149,267, Books $109,849, Per/Ser (Incl. Access Fees) $7,200, AV Mat $16,990, Electronic Ref Mat (Incl. Access Fees) $14,428, Presv $800. Sal $759,451
Library Holdings: Audiobooks 5,908; AV Mats 73; Bks on Deafness & Sign Lang 108; CDs 5,908; DVDs 4,610; e-books 772; Electronic Media & Resources 335; Large Print Bks 2,660; Microforms 2,603; Bk Vols 104,658; Per Subs 199; Videos 858
Special Collections: Civil Engineering Canals, Aqueducts, Railroads (John B Jervis Papers), letters, ms, microfilm, bks; Revolutionary War (Bright-Huntington Coll), ms
Automation Activity & Vendor Info: (Acquisitions) SirsiDynix; (Cataloging) SirsiDynix; (Circulation) SirsiDynix; (ILL) SirsiDynix; (OPAC) SirsiDynix; (Serials) SirsiDynix
Wireless access
Function: Adult bk club, Bk club(s), Bks on CD, Children's prog, Computer training, Computers for patron use, Electronic databases & coll, Free DVD rentals, ILL available, Microfiche/film & reading machines, Music CDs, Online cat, OverDrive digital audio bks, Photocopying/Printing, Prog for adults, Prog for children & young adult, Ref & res, Story hour, Summer reading prog, Tax forms, Teen prog, Telephone ref, Wheelchair accessible
Mem of Mid-York Library System
Partic in Central New York Library Resources Council
Special Services for the Deaf - Staff with knowledge of sign lang
Special Services for the Blind - Bks on CD; Large print bks
Open Mon-Thurs 9:30-8:30, Fri 9:30-5:30, Sat 9:30-5
Friends of the Library Group

S MOHAWK CORRECTIONAL FACILITY LIBRARY*, 6514 Rte 26, 13442. (Mail add: PO Box 8450, 13442-8450). Tel: 315-339-5232. Web Site: www.doccs.ny.gov/faclist.html#M. *Sr Librn,* James Kallies
Library Holdings: Per Subs 70
Automation Activity & Vendor Info: (Cataloging) Follett Software; (Circulation) Follett Software
Restriction: Not open to pub

S ROME HISTORICAL SOCIETY*, William E & Elaine Scripture Memorial Library, 200 Church St, 13440. SAN 312-391X. Tel: 315-336-5870. FAX: 315-336-5912. E-mail: info@romehistoricalsociety.org. Web Site: www.romehistoricalsociety.org. *Exec Dir,* Arthur Simmons; Staff 2 (Non-MLS 2)
Founded 1936
Library Holdings: Bk Vols 3,500
Special Collections: Journals, Letters; Maps, Photogs, Newsp; Oral Histories; Rome Turney Radiator Company Records Coll 1905-33. Oral History
Wireless access
Function: Res libr
Open Tues-Fri 9-3, Sat 10-2

A UNITED STATES AIR FORCE, Air Force Research Laboratory-Information Directorate Technical Library, Air Force Research Lab RIOIS, Bldg 3, 525 Brooks Rd, 13441-4505. SAN 352-5031. Tel: 315-330-7600. Reference Tel: 315-330-7607. FAX: 315-330-3314. E-mail: Tech.Library@us.af.mil. Staff 4 (MLS 2, Non-MLS 2)
Founded 1952
Subject Interests: Artificial intelligence, Computer sci, Electronics, Math
Automation Activity & Vendor Info: (Cataloging) OCLC; (Circulation) EOS International; (ILL) OCLC WorldShare Interlibrary Loan; (OPAC) EOS International
Wireless access
Function: Res libr
Restriction: Staff use only

ROOSEVELT

P ROOSEVELT PUBLIC LIBRARY*, 27 W Fulton Ave, 11575. SAN 354-1029. Tel: 516-378-0222. FAX: 516-377-3238. E-mail: rpl@rooseveltlibrary.org. Reference E-mail: reference@rooseveltlibrary.org. Web Site: www.rooseveltlibrary.org. *Dir,* Dr Lambert Shell; E-mail: lshell@rooseveltlibrary.org; *Librn,* Mary E Cardwell; E-mail: mcardwell@rooseveltlibrary.org; *Librn,* Carol Gilliam; E-mail: cgilliam@rooseveltlibrary.org; *Librn,* Stacey Smith-Brown; E-mail: sbrown@rooseveltlibrary.org; Staff 4 (MLS 4)
Founded 1934. Pop 15,564
Library Holdings: Bk Titles 48,000; Bk Vols 60,000
Subject Interests: African-Am studies
Wireless access
Publications: Four Seasons Library News Bulletin
Mem of Nassau Library System
Open Mon, Tues & Thurs 9-8, Wed Noon-8, Fri 9-5, Sat 9-1
Branches: 1
CHILDREN'S ROOM, 27 W Fulton Ave, 11575. Tel: 516-378-0222. FAX: 516-378-1011. *Youth Serv,* Alisa Neumayer
Library Holdings: Bk Titles 12,702; Bk Vols 13,074
Subject Interests: African-Am studies
Open Mon & Wed 12-8, Tues & Thurs 9-8, Fri & Sat 9-5

ROSCOE

P ROSCOE FREE LIBRARY*, 85 Highland Ave, 12776. (Mail add: PO Box 339, 12776-0339), SAN 312-3928. Tel: 607-498-5574. FAX: 607-498-5575. E-mail: jconroy@rcls.org. Web Site: www.rcls.org/ros. *Dir, Historian,* Dr Joyce Conroy
Founded 1920. Pop 2,100; Circ 15,000
Library Holdings: Bk Titles 15,000; Per Subs 23
Special Collections: Local History Coll, newsp on microfilm (1894-1942)
Wireless access
Mem of Ramapo Catskill Library System
Open Mon, Tues & Thurs 10-12 & 1-5, Fri 11-1 & 2-6, Sat 10-2

ROSE

P ROSE FREE LIBRARY*, 4069 Main St, 14542. SAN 312-3936. Tel: 315-587-2335. FAX: 315-587-2335. Web Site: roselibrary.org. *Dir,* Donna J Norris; E-mail: RoseLibraryDirector@owwl.org
Founded 1912. Pop 2,684; Circ 15,325
Library Holdings: Bk Vols 10,635; Per Subs 25
Automation Activity & Vendor Info: (Cataloging) Evergreen; (Circulation) Evergreen; (OPAC) Evergreen; (Serials) Evergreen
Wireless access
Mem of Pioneer Library System
Open Mon & Wed 2-8, Tues & Thurs 10-2, Fri 2-6, Sat (Sept-June) 10-Noon

ROSENDALE

P ROSENDALE LIBRARY*, 264 Main St, 12472. (Mail add: PO Box 482, 12472-0482), SAN 312-3944. Tel: 845-658-9013. FAX: 845-658-3752. E-mail: rosendalelibrary@hvi.net. Web Site: rosendalelibrary.org. *Dir,* Wendy Alexander; Staff 5 (MLS 1, Non-MLS 4)
Founded 1958. Pop 6,352; Circ 35,162
Library Holdings: Bk Titles 22,826
Subject Interests: Local hist
Automation Activity & Vendor Info: (Circulation) Innovative Interfaces, Inc; (ILL) Innovative Interfaces, Inc; (OPAC) Innovative Interfaces, Inc
Wireless access
Function: Art exhibits, AV serv, Bks on cassette, Bks on CD, Children's prog, Citizenship assistance, Computers for patron use, Electronic databases & coll, ILL available, Internet access, Online cat, Photocopying/Printing, Senior computer classes, Story hour, Summer reading prog, Wheelchair accessible
Mem of Mid-Hudson Library System
Open Mon, Tues & Thurs 11-7:30, Wed & Fri 11-5, Sat 10-3
Friends of the Library Group

ROSLYN

P BRYANT LIBRARY, Two Paper Mill Rd, 11576. SAN 312-3952. Tel: 516-621-2240. FAX: 516-621-7211. Administration FAX: 516-621-2542. E-mail: info@bryantlibrary.org. Web Site: www.bryantlibrary.org. *Dir,* Victor Caputo; E-mail: vcaputo@bryantlibrary.org; *Asst Dir,* Deepa Chandra; *Dir, Pub Relations,* Melissa Rubin; E-mail: mrubin@bryantlibrary.org; *Head, Circ,* Kathleen Micucci; E-mail: kmicucci@bryantlibrary.org; *Ad,* Beth Siegel; E-mail: bsiegel@bryantlibrary.org; *AV Serv Librn, Tech Serv,* Lauren Fazio; E-mail: lfazio@bryantlibrary.org; *Ch,* Mary Carole Moore; E-mail: mcmoore@bryantlibrary.org; *Archivist,* Carol Clarke; E-mail: localhistory@bryantlibrary.org
Founded 1878. Pop 18,221; Circ 285,140
Library Holdings: AV Mats 51,141; DVDs 1,481; Electronic Media & Resources 55; Large Print Bks 1,671; Bk Titles 155,027; Bk Vols 164,188; Videos 9,666
Special Collections: Christopher Morley Coll; Local History Coll, photog; Roslyn Architecture Coll; William Cullen Bryant Coll. Oral History
Automation Activity & Vendor Info: (Circulation) Innovative Interfaces, Inc; (OPAC) Innovative Interfaces, Inc
Publications: Pathways to the Past; Regular Newsletter; W C Bryant in Roslyn
Mem of Nassau Library System
Open Mon-Fri 9-7, Sat 9-5
Friends of the Library Group

M SAINT FRANCIS HOSPITAL & HEART CENTER, Medical Library, 100 Port Washington Blvd, 11576. SAN 312-3960. Tel: 516-562-6673. *Librn,* Ellen Rothbaum; E-mail: ellen.rothbaum@chsli.org; Staff 1 (MLS 1)
Founded 1949
Library Holdings: e-books 1,100; e-journals 700
Subject Interests: Cardiology, Cardiovascular
Wireless access
Publications: Newsletter; Periodicals Holding List
Partic in Long Island Library Resources Council; Medical & Scientific Libraries of Long Island; National Network of Libraries of Medicine Region 7
Open Mon-Fri 8-4
Restriction: Access for corporate affiliates

ROUND LAKE

P ROUND LAKE LIBRARY*, 31 Wesley Ave, 12151. (Mail add: PO Box 665, 12151-0665), SAN 312-3987. Tel: 518-899-2285. FAX: 518-899-0006. E-mail: roundlake@sals.edu. Web Site: roundlake.sals.edu. *Dir,* Jennifer Hurd; Staff 8 (MLS 3, Non-MLS 5)
Founded 1897. Pop 15,000; Circ 23,000
Library Holdings: Bk Vols 15,000; Per Subs 20
Special Collections: Centennial Coll; Round Lake Historical Coll; Victoriana Coll
Automation Activity & Vendor Info: (Acquisitions) Innovative Interfaces, Inc; (Cataloging) Innovative Interfaces, Inc; (Circulation) Innovative Interfaces, Inc
Wireless access
Mem of Southern Adirondack Library System
Open Mon-Fri 10-8, Sat 10-3
Friends of the Library Group
Branches: 1
MALTA COMMUNITY CENTER, One Bayberry Dr, Malta, 12020. Tel: 518-682-2495. FAX: 518-682-2492. *Br Mgr,* Jennifer Hurd
Library Holdings: DVDs 250; Bk Vols 5,000; Per Subs 20; Talking Bks 110
Open Mon-Fri 10-8, Sat 9-Noon

ROUSES POINT

P DODGE MEMORIAL LIBRARY, 144 Lake St, 12979. SAN 312-4002. Tel: 518-297-6242. E-mail: library@rousespointny.com. Web Site: www.cefls.org/libraries/rouses-point, www.rousespointny.com/the_village/rouses_point_dodge_memorial_library. *Dir,* Anne Paulson
Founded 1907. Pop 2,377
Library Holdings: Audiobooks 500; DVDs 527; Large Print Bks 1,050; Bk Vols 14,000; Per Subs 19
Automation Activity & Vendor Info: (Cataloging) Horizon; (Circulation) Horizon; (OPAC) Horizon
Wireless access
Function: 24/7 Electronic res, 24/7 Online cat, Adult bk club, Bks on CD, Children's prog, Computers for patron use, E-Reserves, Electronic databases & coll, Free DVD rentals, Holiday prog, Home delivery & serv to seniorr ctr & nursing homes, Homebound delivery serv, ILL available, Internet access, Magazines, Mail & tel request accepted, Meeting rooms, Movies, Museum passes, Online cat, Online info literacy tutorials on the web & in blackboard, Online ref, OverDrive digital audio bks, Photocopying/Printing, Preschool reading prog, Scanner, Story hour, Summer reading prog, Wheelchair accessible
Mem of Clinton-Essex-Franklin Library System
Open Mon, Wed & Fri 10-5, Tues & Thurs 10-6, Sat 10-1
Friends of the Library Group

ROXBURY

S ROXBURY LIBRARY ASSOCIATION, 53742 State Hwy 30, 12474. (Mail add: PO Box 186, 12474-0186), SAN 312-4010. Tel: 607-326-7901. FAX: 607-326-7901. E-mail: frontdesk@roxburylibraryonline.org. Interlibrary Loan Service E-mail: ro.ill@4cls.org. Web Site: www.roxburylibraryonline.com. *Dir,* Dian Seiler; E-mail: dian@roxburylibraryonline.org; Staff 2 (Non-MLS 2)
Founded 1903. Pop 2,509; Circ 4,000
Library Holdings: AV Mats 310; Bk Titles 19,020; Per Subs 32; Talking Bks 62; Videos 298
Special Collections: John Burroughs Coll, bks, pictures; Local History, bks, ledgers, maps. Oral History
Subject Interests: Natural sci
Automation Activity & Vendor Info: (ILL) SirsiDynix-WorkFlows
Wireless access
Function: Adult literacy prog, Archival coll, Art exhibits
Publications: History of the Town of Roxbury
Mem of Four County Library System
Open Mon, Wed, Thurs & Sat 10-2
Restriction: Authorized patrons

RUSH

P RUSH PUBLIC LIBRARY*, 5977 E Henrietta Rd, 14543. SAN 312-4029. Tel: 585-533-1370. FAX: 585-533-1546. Web Site: www.rushlibrary.org. *Dir,* Kirsten Flass; E-mail: kflass@libraryweb.org; Staff 11 (Non-MLS 11)
Founded 1914. Pop 3,604; Circ 30,461
Library Holdings: Bk Vols 19,427; Per Subs 48
Subject Interests: Archit, Art, Craft, Hist
Automation Activity & Vendor Info: (Cataloging) CARL.Solution (TLC); (Circulation) CARL.Solution (TLC); (OPAC) CARL.Solution (TLC); (Serials) CARL.Solution (TLC)
Wireless access
Function: Adult bk club, Bks on CD, Children's prog, Computers for patron use, Free DVD rentals, Homebound delivery serv, ILL available, Museum passes, Music CDs, Online cat, OverDrive digital audio bks, Photocopying/Printing, Preschool outreach, Prog for adults, Prog for children & young adult, Ref & res, Summer reading prog, Tax forms, Teen prog, Telephone ref, Wheelchair accessible, Workshops
Mem of Monroe County Library System
Open Mon, Wed & Fri 1-8, Tues & Thurs 11-8, Sat 10-2
Friends of the Library Group

RUSHFORD

P RUSHFORD FREE LIBRARY, 9012 Main St, 14777-9700. (Mail add: PO Box 8, 14777-0008), SAN 312-4037. Tel: 585-437-2533. FAX: 585-437-9940. Web Site: rushfordfreelibrary.org. *Dir,* Rebecca Cole; E-mail: coleb@stls.org
Circ 8,223
Library Holdings: Bk Vols 16,815
Wireless access
Publications: Newsletter
Mem of Southern Tier Library System
Open Mon & Sat 9-12, Tues & Thurs 1-5 & 6-8, Fri 9-12 & 1-5

RUSHVILLE

P MABEL D BLODGETT MEMORIAL READING CENTER*, 35 S Main St, 14544-9648. SAN 352-3950. Tel: 585-554-3939. Web Site: www.villageofrushville.org/reading_center.php. *Dir,* Dobie Baker; E-mail: bakerd@stls.org; Staff 1 (Non-MLS 1)
Library Holdings: Bk Vols 7,500
Special Collections: Local history
Wireless access
Function: Homebound delivery serv, Prog for children & young adult
Mem of Southern Tier Library System
Open Mon & Wed 3-7, Fri 1-5, Sat 9-1
Friends of the Library Group

RUSSELL

P RUSSELL PUBLIC LIBRARY*, 24 Pestle St, 13684. Tel: 315-347-2115. FAX: 315-347-2229. E-mail: ruslib@ncls.org. Web Site: www.russellny.org/library.html. *Librn,* Brenda Hale
Pop 1,794
Wireless access
Mem of North Country Library System
Open Mon-Thurs 10-6

RYE

P RYE FREE READING ROOM*, 1061 Boston Post Rd, 10580. SAN 312-4053. Tel: 914-967-0480. Circulation Tel: 914-967-0481. Administration Tel: 914-231-3160. Information Services Tel: 914-231-3161. FAX: 914-967-5522. Web Site: www.ryelibrary.org. *Dir,* Chris Shoemaker; E-mail: cshoemaker@ryelibrary.org; *Asst Dir,* Position Currently Open; *Ch,* Lisa Dettling; Tel: 914-231-3162, E-mail: ldettling@ryelibrary.org; *Teen Libra,* Sarah Prosser; E-mail: sprosser@ryelibrary.org; *Bus Mgr,* Mary Beth Lubeck; Tel: 914-231-3164, E-mail: mblubeck@ryelibrary.org
Founded 1884. Pop 15,170; Circ 175,000
Subject Interests: Rye hist
Automation Activity & Vendor Info: (Circulation) Evergreen; (OPAC) Evergreen
Wireless access
Function: Activity rm, Adult bk club, Art exhibits, Art programs, Audiobks on Playaways & MP3, Audiobks via web, Bk club(s), Bks on CD, Children's prog, Computer training, Computers for patron use, Electronic databases & coll, Free DVD rentals, Homebound delivery serv, Homework prog, ILL available, Magazines, Magnifiers for reading, Meeting rooms, Movies, Museum passes, Notary serv, Online cat, OverDrive digital audio bks, Photocopying/Printing, Prog for adults, Prog for children & young adult, Ref serv available, Scanner, Summer reading prog, Telephone ref, Wheelchair accessible
Publications: Annual Report
Mem of Westchester Library System
Open Mon & Fri 9:30-5, Tues, Wed & Thurs 9:30-8, Sat 10-5, Sun Noon-5

S RYE HISTORICAL SOCIETY*, Knapp House Library & Archives, 265 Rye Beach Ave, 10580. (Mail add: One Purchase St, 10580), SAN 312-4061. Tel: 914-967-7588. FAX: 914-967-6253. E-mail: archivist@ryehistoricalsociety.org. Web Site: www.ryehistory.org. *Exec Dir,* Sheri Jordan; E-mail: sheri.jordan@ryehistory.org; *Researcher,* Daniel Marino
Founded 1964
Library Holdings: Bk Titles 920; Bk Vols 1,100
Special Collections: Rye History, photogs, slides (manuscripts 557.25 cu ft). Oral History
Subject Interests: Genealogy, Local hist
Publications: Estates of Grace; Father Burke's Dream to Rescue Children of the Inner City: St Benedict's Home, Rye, NY, 1891-1941; One Hundred Years of Health Care: 1889-1989; Read about Rye 1660-1960; Rye in the Twenties; Silent Companions: Dummy Board Figures of the 17th through 19th Centuries; The Art of Lauren Ford
Open Wed & Thurs 10-3, Sat 11:30-3

SACKETS HARBOR

P HAY MEMORIAL LIBRARY*, 105 S Broad, 13685. (Mail add: PO Box 288, 13685-0288), SAN 312-4088. Tel: 315-646-2228. FAX: 315-646-2228. E-mail: sahlib@ncls.org. Web Site: haymemoriallibrary.org. *Dir,* Katie Male-Riordan; Staff 1 (Non-MLS 1)
Founded 1900. Pop 3,323; Circ 9,505
Library Holdings: Electronic Media & Resources 11; Bk Vols 6,267; Per Subs 32; Talking Bks 527; Videos 487
Automation Activity & Vendor Info: (Circulation) SirsiDynix-WorkFlows; (OPAC) SirsiDynix-WorkFlows
Wireless access
Function: Adult bk club, Bks on cassette, Bks on CD, Children's prog, Computers for patron use, Free DVD rentals, Holiday prog, Homebound delivery serv, ILL available, Online cat, OverDrive digital audio bks, Photocopying/Printing, Prog for adults, Story hour, Summer reading prog, Tax forms, VHS videos, Wheelchair accessible
Mem of North Country Library System
Open Tues-Thurs 1:30-5:30, Sat 10-1
Friends of the Library Group

SAG HARBOR

P JOHN JERMAIN MEMORIAL LIBRARY, 201 Main St, 11963. SAN 312-4096. Tel: 631-725-0049. FAX: 631-725-0597. E-mail: info@johnjermain.org. Web Site: johnjermain.org. *Dir,* Catherine Creedon; Tel: 631-725-0049, Ext 223, E-mail: catherine@johnjermain.org; *Asst Dir,* Wonda Miller; Tel: 631-725-0049, Ext 234, E-mail: wmiller@johnjermain.org; *Head, Children's Dept,* Diana LaMarca; Tel: 631-725-0049, Ext 231, E-mail: dlamarca@johnjermain.org; *Head, Ref,* Susan Mullin; Tel: 631-725-0049, Ext 232, E-mail: suem@johnjermain.org; *Youth Serv Librn,* Jaime Mott; Tel: 631-725-0049, Ext 230, E-mail: jmott@johnjermain.org
Founded 1910. Pop 6,741; Circ 97,859
Library Holdings: Bk Vols 43,172; Per Subs 117
Subject Interests: Whaling
Automation Activity & Vendor Info: (Cataloging) Innovative Interfaces, Inc - Sierra
Wireless access
Mem of Suffolk Cooperative Library System
Open Mon-Wed & Fri 9-6, Thurs 9-9, Sat & Sun 10-4
Friends of the Library Group

SAINT BONAVENTURE

C SAINT BONAVENTURE UNIVERSITY*, Friedsam Memorial Library, 3261 W State Rd, 14778. (Mail add: PO Box AS, 14778), SAN 312-410X. Tel: 716-375-2323. FAX: 716-375-2389. Web Site: www.sbu.edu/academics/library. *Dir, Library & Faculty Resource Ctr,* Ann M Tenglund; Tel: 716-375-2378, E-mail: ateng@sbu.edu; *Adjunct Ref Librn,* Marsia Painter; E-mail: mpainter@sbu.edu; *Adjunct Ref Librn,* Christine Zeitler; E-mail: czeitler@sbu.edu; *Spec Coll Librn,* Paul J Spaeth; Tel: 716-375-2327, E-mail: pspaeth@sbu.edu; *Circ Supvr, Evening Supvr,* Maureen Bernas; Tel: 716-375-2337, E-mail: mbernas@sbu.edu; *Technical Spec,* Tami Attwell; Tel: 716-375-2347, E-mail: tattwell@sbu.edu; *Archivist,* Dennis Frank; Tel: 716-375-2322, E-mail: dfrank@sbu.edu; *Adjunct Archivist,* Amber Cheladyn; E-mail: achelady@sbu.edu; *Govt Doc, Ref & Instruction,* Mary Ellen Ash; Tel: 716-375-2343, E-mail: mash@sbu.edu; *ILL, Ref & Instruction,* Cathy Maldonado; Tel: 716-375-2153, E-mail: cmaldona@sbu.edu; Staff 7.8 (MLS 5.8, Non-MLS 2)
Founded 1858. Enrl 2,100; Fac 155; Highest Degree: Master
Library Holdings: Bk Titles 225,000; Bk Vols 494,088; Per Subs 881
Special Collections: Franciscan Institute; Jim Bishop Coll, ms; Rare Books, incunabula & ms; Robert Lax Coll, ms; Thomas Merton Coll, ms. State Document Depository; US Document Depository
Automation Activity & Vendor Info: (Acquisitions) SirsiDynix; (Cataloging) SirsiDynix; (Circulation) SirsiDynix; (Course Reserve) SirsiDynix; (Discovery) EBSCO Online; (ILL) OCLC WorldShare Interlibrary Loan; (OPAC) SirsiDynix; (Serials) SirsiDynix
Wireless access
Partic in Western New York Library Resources Council
Open Mon-Thurs 8am-1am, Fri 8am-10pm, Sat 10-10, Sun 10am-1am

SAINT JOHNSVILLE

P MARGARET REANEY MEMORIAL LIBRARY*, 19 Kingsbury Ave, 13452. SAN 312-4126. Tel: 518-568-7822. FAX: 518-568-7822. Web Site: margaretreaneylibrary.blogspot.com, www.mvls.info/members/stj. *Dir,* Dawn Lamphere; E-mail: dlamphere@mvls.info
Circ 20,436
Library Holdings: Bk Titles 31,000; Bk Vols 31,200; Per Subs 22
Special Collections: Local Hist Coll, genealogies, newspapers, & hist ref
Automation Activity & Vendor Info: (Circulation) SirsiDynix
Wireless access
Mem of Mohawk Valley Library System
Open Mon 9:30-8:30, Tues, Wed & Fri 9:30-5, Sat 10-Noon

SAINT REGIS FALLS

P WAVERLY READING CENTER*, Main St, 12980. Tel: 518-856-9720. Web Site: cefls.org/libraries/waverly. *Dir,* Christine Egeland; E-mail: adkwoman1@gmail.com
Mem of Clinton-Essex-Franklin Library System
Open Mon 11:30-4:30, Wed 4:30-6:30, Sat 11-2

SALAMANCA

P SALAMANCA PUBLIC LIBRARY*, 155 Wildwood Ave, 14779. SAN 312-4134. Tel: 716-945-1890. FAX: 716-945-2741. Web Site: salamancalibrary.org. *Dir,* Jennifer L Stickles; E-mail: jstickles@salmun.com; Staff 3 (MLS 1, Non-MLS 2)
Founded 1920. Pop 5,895; Circ 66,617
Apr 2012-Mar 2013 Income $287,196, City $277,196, Locally Generated Income $10,000. Mats Exp $23,000, Books $15,000, Per/Ser (Incl. Access Fees) $4,500, AV Mat $3,500. Sal $144,357 (Prof $61,000)
Library Holdings: AV Mats 5,676; Bk Titles 39,410; Bk Vols 42,602; Per Subs 118
Special Collections: Iroquois & Seneca Indians (Iroquoia); Salamanca Historical Coll
Automation Activity & Vendor Info: (Circulation) Follett Software; (OPAC) Follett Software
Wireless access
Mem of Chautauqua-Cattaraugus Library System
Open Mon 9-7, Tues & Thurs 9-9, Wed & Sat 9-1, Fri 9-5:30
Friends of the Library Group

S SENECA NATION LIBRARIES, Allegany Branch, 830 Broad St, 14779. (Mail add: PO Box 231, 14779-0231), SAN 375-166X. Tel: 716-945-3157. FAX: 716-945-9770. E-mail: alleg.library@sni.org. Web Site: senecanationlibrary.wordpress.com. *Dir,* Krista Jacobs; E-mail: krista.jacobs@sni.org; *Libr Supvr,* Anita Jacobs; E-mail: anita.jacobs@sni.org
Founded 1979
Library Holdings: Bk Vols 18,000; Per Subs 374
Special Collections: Native American Materials
Wireless access
Mem of Chautauqua-Cattaraugus Library System
Open Mon-Wed 8-7, Thurs & Fri 8-5, Sat 9-1 (Winter); Mon & Wed-Fri 8-4:30, Tues 8-7 (Summer)
Friends of the Library Group
Branches:
CATTARAUGUS BRANCH, Three Thomas Indian School Dr, Irving, 14081-9505. Tel: 716-532-9449. FAX: 716-532-6115. E-mail: catt.library@sni.org. Web Site: senecanationlibrary.wordpress.com/cattaraugus-branch-about-us. *Supvr,* Karen F John; E-mail: karen.f.john@sni.org; *Libr Tech,* Jasmine Lay; E-mail: jasmine.lay@sni.org
Circ 5,300
Library Holdings: Bk Vols 14,000
Open Mon-Wed 8-7, Thurs & Fri 8:4:30, Sat 9-1 (Winter); Mon, Thurs & Fri 8-4:30, Tues & Wed 8-6 (Summer)

SALEM

P BANCROFT PUBLIC LIBRARY, 181 Main St, 12865. (Mail add: PO Box 478, 12865), SAN 312-4142. Tel: 518-854-7463. FAX: 518-854-7463. Web Site: www.bancroftlibrary.org. *Dir,* Lori Stokem; E-mail: slm-director@sals.edu; Staff 1 (Non-MLS 1)
Pop 9,877; Circ 16,150
Library Holdings: Bk Vols 15,025; Per Subs 17
Automation Activity & Vendor Info: (Acquisitions) Innovative Interfaces, Inc; (Circulation) Innovative Interfaces, Inc; (Media Booking) Innovative

Interfaces, Inc; (OPAC) Innovative Interfaces, Inc; (Serials) Innovative Interfaces, Inc
Wireless access
Mem of Southern Adirondack Library System
Open Mon & Fri 1-6, Tues & Thurs 1-8, Wed 10-6, Sat 10-2
Friends of the Library Group

SALISBURY CENTER

P KIRBY FREE LIBRARY OF SALISBURY CENTER*, 105 Rte 29A, 13454. (Mail add: PO Box 322, 13454-0322), SAN 376-3137. Tel: 315-429-9006. FAX: 315-429-9006. E-mail: salisbury@midyork.org. Web Site: www.midyorklib.org/salisbury. *Dir,* Holly Eckler; *Librn,* Sue Jorrey
Pop 1,954
Library Holdings: Bk Vols 8,000
Special Collections: Christian Coll
Wireless access
Mem of Mid-York Library System
Open Mon 3:30-7:30, Tues & Thurs 10-12 & 1-5, Wed 4-7, Fri 10-Noon

SANBORN

J NIAGARA COUNTY COMMUNITY COLLEGE, Henrietta G Lewis Library, 3111 Saunders Settlement Rd, 14132. SAN 312-4150. Tel: 716-614-6705, 716-614-6780. Circulation Tel: 716-614-6783. Reference Tel: 716-614-6786. FAX: 716-614-6816, 716-614-6828. E-mail: refdesk@niagaracc.suny.edu. Web Site: libguides.niagaracc.suny.edu. *Dir, Tech Serv Librn,* Jenn Linn; Tel: 716-614-6787, E-mail: jlinn@niagaracc.suny.edu; *Pub Serv Librn,* Andy Aquino; E-mail: aaquino@niagaracc.suny.edu; Staff 12 (MLS 6, Non-MLS 6)
Founded 1963. Enrl 5,000; Highest Degree: Associate
Library Holdings: Bk Titles 85,042; Bk Vols 94,921; Per Subs 500
Subject Interests: Archives
Automation Activity & Vendor Info: (Acquisitions) Ex Libris Group; (Circulation) Ex Libris Group; (Course Reserve) Ex Libris Group; (OPAC) Ex Libris Group; (Serials) Ex Libris Group
Wireless access
Publications: Pathfinders; Periodicals in the LLC; What's New
Partic in OCLC Online Computer Library Center, Inc; SUNYConnect; Western New York Library Resources Council
Open Mon-Fri 8-4

P SANBORN-PEKIN FREE LIBRARY*, 5884 West St, 14132. (Mail add: PO Box 176, 14132), SAN 312-4169. Tel: 716-731-9933. FAX: 716-731-9933. Web Site: www.sanbornpekinlibrary.com. *Dir,* Linda Deeks; E-mail: ldeeks@nioga.org
Pop 4,000; Circ 52,966
Library Holdings: Bk Vols 45,000; Per Subs 64
Automation Activity & Vendor Info: (Cataloging) SirsiDynix; (Circulation) SirsiDynix; (OPAC) SirsiDynix; (Serials) SirsiDynix
Wireless access
Mem of Nioga Library System
Open Mon & Wed-Fri 2-8, Tues 2-6, Sat 10-1

SANDY CREEK

P ANNIE PORTER AINSWORTH MEMORIAL LIBRARY, 6064 S Main St, 13145. (Mail add: PO Box 69, 13145-0069), SAN 312-4177. Tel: 315-387-3732. FAX: 315-387-2005. E-mail: scrlib@ncls.org. Web Site: www.ainsworthmemoriallibrary.org. *Libr Dir,* Jessica Godfrey
Founded 1928
Automation Activity & Vendor Info: (Acquisitions) SirsiDynix-WorkFlows; (Cataloging) SirsiDynix-WorkFlows; (Circulation) SirsiDynix-WorkFlows; (ILL) SirsiDynix-WorkFlows; (OPAC) SirsiDynix-WorkFlows; (Serials) SirsiDynix-WorkFlows
Wireless access
Mem of North Country Library System
Open Mon, Tues, Thurs & Fri 10-6, Sat 10-1

SARANAC LAKE

J NORTH COUNTRY COMMUNITY COLLEGE LIBRARIES*, Saranac Lake Campus Library, 23 Santanoni Ave, 12983-2046. (Mail add: PO Box 89, 12983-0089), SAN 312-4185. Tel: 518-891-2915. Web Site: www.nccc.edu/library. *Interim Dir, Libr Serv,* Brian O'Connor; Tel: 518-891-2915, Ext 222, E-mail: boconnor@nccc.edu; *Acq & Cat,* Phil Gallos; Tel: 518-891-2915, Ext 225, E-mail: pgallos@nccc.edu; *ILL & Circ,* Irene Finlayson; Tel: 518-891-2915, Ext 218, E-mail: ifinlayson@nccc.edu; Staff 1 (MLS 1)
Founded 1967. Enrl 1,672; Fac 50; Highest Degree: Associate
Library Holdings: Bks on Deafness & Sign Lang 34; e-books 4,600; e-journals 18,000; Electronic Media & Resources 36; Bk Titles 62,517; Bk Vols 64,451; Per Subs 130; Videos 641
Special Collections: Adirondack History (Adirondack Coll), bks, maps & prints; Nettie Marie Jones Fine Arts Coll. State Document Depository
Subject Interests: Adirondack hist, Criminal justice, Nursing, Radiologic tech
Automation Activity & Vendor Info: (Cataloging) OCLC; (Circulation) Follett Software; (ILL) OCLC; (OPAC) Ex Libris Group
Wireless access
Publications: From the Top of the Hill (Newsletter)
Partic in New York Online Virtual Electronic Library; Northern New York Library Network; OCLC Online Computer Library Center, Inc; SUNYConnect; Westchester Academic Library Directors Organization
Special Services for the Deaf - Accessible learning ctr; Assistive tech; Bks on deafness & sign lang
Special Services for the Blind - Aids for in-house use; Bks on cassette; Bks on CD; Computer with voice synthesizer for visually impaired persons; Copier with enlargement capabilities; Dragon Naturally Speaking software; Magnifiers; Rec; Recorded bks; Screen enlargement software for people with visual disabilities; Sound rec; Talking bk & rec for the blind cat; Talking bks; Talking bks & player equip; Text reader
Open Mon-Thurs 7:30am-8pm, Fri 7:30-4:30, Sun 1-6
Departmental Libraries:
MALONE CAMPUS LIBRARY, 75 William St, Malone, 12953. Tel: 518-483-4550, Ext 224. *Libr Coord,* Kate Wells; E-mail: kwells@nccc.edu
Open Mon-Thurs 8:30-4:30
TICONDEROGA CAMPUS LIBRARY, 11 Hawkeye Trail, Ticonderoga, 12883. Tel: 518-585-4454, Ext 2208. *Campus Librn,* Mary Ann Rockwell; E-mail: marockwell@nccc.edu
Open Mon-Thurs 8:30-4:30

P SARANAC LAKE FREE LIBRARY*, 109 Main St, 12983. SAN 312-4207. Tel: 518-891-4190. FAX: 518-891-5931. E-mail: saranaclakefreelibrary@gmail.com. Web Site: www.slfl.org. *Dir,* Peter Benson; E-mail: slfl.pete@gmail.com
Founded 1907. Circ 66,207
Library Holdings: AV Mats 7,553; Bk Titles 33,232; Bk Vols 36,171
Special Collections: Adirondack History Coll; Mounted Wildlife Museum
Automation Activity & Vendor Info: (Cataloging) SirsiDynix; (Circulation) SirsiDynix; (OPAC) SirsiDynix
Wireless access
Publications: Newsletter
Mem of Clinton-Essex-Franklin Library System
Open Mon-Fri 11-5:30, Sat 11-1
Friends of the Library Group

M TRUDEAU INSTITUTE LIBRARY*, 154 Algonquin Ave, 12983. SAN 312-4215. Tel: 518-891-3080, Ext 152. FAX: 518-891-5126. Web Site: trudeauinstitute.org. *Info Spec,* Kelly Stanyon; E-mail: kstanyon@trudeauinstitute.org; Staff 1 (MLS 1)
Founded 1964
Library Holdings: Bk Vols 15,000; Per Subs 24
Subject Interests: Immunology, Virology
Wireless access
Function: Archival coll, Doc delivery serv, For res purposes, ILL available
Restriction: Open by appt only

SARATOGA SPRINGS

S NATIONAL MUSEUM OF RACING & HALL OF FAME, John A Morris Research Library, 191 Union Ave, 2nd Flr, 12866. SAN 312-4231. Tel: 518-584-0400, Ext 122. FAX: 518-584-4574. E-mail: nmrhistorian@racingmuseum.net. Web Site: www.racingmuseum.org/visit/research-library. *Dir,* Cate Masterson; Tel: 518-584-0400, Ext 100; *Colls Mgr,* Stephanie Luce; Tel: 518-584-0400, Ext 117, E-mail: sluce@racingmuseum.net; *Curator,* Victoria Reisman; Tel: 518-584-0400, Ext 113, E-mail: vreisman@racingmuseum.net; *Historian,* Mike Veitch; E-mail: mveitch@racingmuseum.net; Staff 4 (MLS 2, Non-MLS 2)
Founded 1950
Library Holdings: Bk Titles 2,000; Bk Vols 2,950; Per Subs 10
Subject Interests: Horses, Thoroughbred horse racing
Publications: Horses & Members in the National Racing Hall of Fame; The Race Horses of America 1832-1872
Partic in Capital District Library Council; OCLC Online Computer Library Center, Inc
Restriction: Open by appt only

M SARATOGA HOSPITAL*, Medical Library, 211 Church St, 12866. SAN 328-316X. Tel: 518-583-8301. FAX: 518-580-4285. E-mail: shlibrary@saratogahospital.org. Web Site: vweq.cdlc.scoolaid.net. *Librn,* Donna Winkelman; Staff 0.5 (MLS 0.5)
Library Holdings: Bk Titles 481; Per Subs 60
Wireless access
Partic in Capital District Library Council; National Network of Libraries of Medicine Region 7
Open Mon-Fri 9-4

P SARATOGA SPRINGS PUBLIC LIBRARY*, 49 Henry St, 12866. SAN 312-424X. Tel: 518-584-7860. Reference Tel: 518-584-7860, Ext 304. Information Services Tel: 518-584-7860, Ext 210. FAX: 518-584-7866. Web Site: www.sspl.org. *Libr Dir,* A Issac Pulver; Tel: 518-584-7860, Ext 201, E-mail: ipulver@sals.edu; *Head, Adult Serv,* Jennifer Ogrodowski; Tel: 518-584-7860, Ext 205; *Head, Circ, Head, Tech Serv,* Jennifer Ferriss; Tel: 518-584-7860, Ext 242; *Teen Librn,* Heather Cunningham; Tel: 518-584-7860, Ext 260; Staff 12 (MLS 12)
Founded 1950. Pop 46,000; Circ 630,000
Library Holdings: Bk Titles 85,000; Bk Vols 207,000; Per Subs 400
Special Collections: Balneology; Hydrotherapy; Saratogiana
Wireless access
Publications: Bibliography of Research Materials on Saratoga Springs
Mem of Southern Adirondack Library System
Open Mon-Thurs 9-9, Fri 9-6, Sat 9-5, Sun 12-5
Friends of the Library Group

C SKIDMORE COLLEGE, Lucy Scribner Library, 815 N Broadway, 12866. SAN 312-4266. Tel: 518-580-5502. Interlibrary Loan Service Tel: 518-580-5520. Reference Tel: 518-580-5503. FAX: 518-580-5541. E-mail: illdesk@skidmore.edu. Web Site: lib.skidmore.edu. *Col Librn,* Marta Brunner; Tel: 518-580-5506, E-mail: mbrunner@skidmore.edu; *Acq Librn, Bibliog Serv,* Dung Lam Chen; E-mail: duchen@skidmore.edu; Staff 22.2 (MLS 9.2, Non-MLS 13)
Founded 1911. Enrl 2,468; Fac 169; Highest Degree: Master
Library Holdings: e-journals 70,000; Bk Vols 350,000
Special Collections: College Archives; Edith Wharton Coll; Edna St Vincent Millay Coll; Hebraica-Judaica (Leo Usdan Coll); Late 19th Century Illustrated Books Coll; Max Beerbohm Coll; Saratogiana (Anita P Yates Coll), bks, photogs. State Document Depository; US Document Depository
Subject Interests: Art
Automation Activity & Vendor Info: (Acquisitions) Ex Libris Group; (Cataloging) Ex Libris Group; (Circulation) Ex Libris Group; (ILL) OCLC ILLiad; (OPAC) Ex Libris Group; (Serials) Ex Libris Group
Wireless access
Partic in Capital District Library Council; OCLC Online Computer Library Center, Inc
Friends of the Library Group

P SOUTHERN ADIRONDACK LIBRARY SYSTEM*, 22 Whitney Pl, 12866-4596. SAN 312-4274. Tel: 518-584-7300. FAX: 518-587-5589. Web Site: www.sals.edu. *Dir,* Sara Dallas; Tel: 518-584-7300, Ext 205, E-mail: sdallas@sals.edu; *Pub Serv Consult & Outreach Coordr,* Erica Freudenberger; Tel: 518-584-7300, Ext 211, E-mail: efreudenberger@sals.edu; *Coll Develop,* Jill Ryder; Tel: 518-584-7300, Ext 216, E-mail: jryder@sals.edu; Staff 4 (MLS 4)
Founded 1958. Pop 302,933
Library Holdings: Bk Vols 94,023; Per Subs 25
Automation Activity & Vendor Info: (Acquisitions) Innovative Interfaces, Inc; (Cataloging) Innovative Interfaces, Inc; (Circulation) Innovative Interfaces, Inc; (ILL) Innovative Interfaces, Inc; (OPAC) Innovative Interfaces, Inc; (Serials) Innovative Interfaces, Inc
Wireless access
Publications: Newsletter
Member Libraries: Argyle Free Library; Ballston Spa Public Library; Bancroft Public Library; Bolton Free Library; Caldwell-Lake George Library; Cambridge Public Library; Clifton Park-Halfmoon Public Library; Corinth Free Library; Crandall Public Library; Easton Library; Fort Edward Free Library; Galway Public Library; Great Meadow Correctional Facility Library; Greenwich Free Library; Hadley-Luzerne Public Library; Horicon Free Public Library; Hudson Falls Free Library; Indian Lake Public Library; Long Lake Public Library; Mechanicville District Public Library; Pember Library & Museum of Natural History; Raquette Lake Free Library; Richards Library; Round Lake Library; Saratoga Springs Public Library; Schuylerville Public Library; Stillwater Public Library; Stony Creek Free Library; The Whitehall Free Library; Town of Ballston Community Library; Town of Chester Public Library; Town of Inlet Public Library; Town of Johnsburg Library; Town of Lake Pleasant Public Library; Washington Correctional Facility Library; Waterford Public Library
Partic in Capital District Library Council
Special Services for the Deaf - ADA equip
Open Mon-Fri 8:30-4:30

GL SUPREME COURT LIBRARY AT SARATOGA SPRINGS*, City Hall, 3rd Flr, 474 Broadway, 12866-2297. SAN 312-4282. Tel: 518-451-8777. E-mail: 4JDLawLibrary@nycourts.gov. *Librn,* Vicki Heidelberger
Founded 1866
Library Holdings: Bk Vols 20,000
Special Collections: Directories of Saratoga Springs (1884-present)
Subject Interests: Law
Automation Activity & Vendor Info: (Acquisitions) SirsiDynix-WorkFlows; (Cataloging) SirsiDynix-WorkFlows; (Circulation) SirsiDynix-WorkFlows; (Serials) SirsiDynix-WorkFlows
Wireless access
Open Mon-Fri 8-12 & 1-3:45

SAUGERTIES

P SAUGERTIES PUBLIC LIBRARY*, 91 Washington Ave, 12477. SAN 312-4304. Tel: 845-246-4317. FAX: 845-246-0858. Web Site: saugertiespubliclibrary.org. *Dir,* Katie Scott-Childress; E-mail: director@saugertiespubliclibrary.org; Staff 10 (MLS 3, Non-MLS 7)
Founded 1894. Pop 19,000; Circ 75,282
Library Holdings: AV Mats 3,354; Bk Vols 43,308; Per Subs 82
Special Collections: Local Newspapers Coll, microfilm; New York State, Ulster County & Local History Coll, bks, newsp, pamphlet
Automation Activity & Vendor Info: (Cataloging) Innovative Interfaces, Inc; (Circulation) Innovative Interfaces, Inc; (ILL) Innovative Interfaces, Inc; (OPAC) Innovative Interfaces, Inc
Wireless access
Mem of Mid-Hudson Library System
Open Mon-Thurs 10-8, Fri 10-6, Sat 10-5
Friends of the Library Group

SAVONA

P DR SANDOR & BERTHE BENEDEK MEMORIAL LIBRARY*, 7 McCoy St, 14879. (Mail add: PO Box 475, 14879-0475), SAN 312-4312. Tel: 607-583-4426. FAX: 607-583-4426. E-mail: savona@stls.org. Web Site: benedekmemoriallibrary.org. *Libr Dir,* Candy Wilson; E-mail: wilsonc@stls.org
Pop 860; Circ 17,000
Library Holdings: Bk Titles 11,000; Per Subs 20
Automation Activity & Vendor Info: (Cataloging) SirsiDynix; (Circulation) SirsiDynix; (OPAC) SirsiDynix; (Serials) SirsiDynix
Wireless access
Mem of Southern Tier Library System
Open Mon-Fri 2-7
Friends of the Library Group

SAYVILLE

P SAYVILLE LIBRARY, 88 Greene Ave, 11782. SAN 312-4320. Tel: 631-589-4440. FAX: 631-244-0045. E-mail: connect@sayvillelibrary.org. Web Site: www.sayvillelibrary.org. *Dir,* Jennifer Fowler; E-mail: jennifer@sayvillelibrary.org; *Asst Dir,* Robert Goykin; E-mail: rgoykin@sayvillelibrary.org; *Head, Patron Serv,* Morgan Brett; E-mail: morgan@sayvillelibrary.org; *Head, Adult Serv,* Tim Sicurella; E-mail: tsicurella@sayvillelibrary.org; *Head, Outreach Serv,* Jonathan Pryer; E-mail: jpryer@sayvillelibrary.org; *Head, Teen Serv,* Marianne Ramirez; E-mail: marianne@sayvillelibrary.org; *Head, Youth Serv,* Donna DiBerardino; E-mail: donnad@sayvillelibrary.org; Staff 14 (MLS 14)
Founded 1914. Pop 18,131
Library Holdings: AV Mats 19,808; CDs 3,147; DVDs 2,050; e-journals 16,549; Large Print Bks 2,600; Bk Vols 108,683; Per Subs 255; Talking Bks 3,369; Videos 6,890
Special Collections: Local History Coll; Long Island Coll
Automation Activity & Vendor Info: (Acquisitions) Innovative Interfaces, Inc; (Cataloging) Innovative Interfaces, Inc; (Circulation) Innovative Interfaces, Inc; (Course Reserve) Innovative Interfaces, Inc; (OPAC) Innovative Interfaces, Inc
Wireless access
Mem of Suffolk Cooperative Library System
Open Mon-Thurs 10-9, Fri 10-6, Sat 9:30-5
Friends of the Library Group

SCARSDALE

P SCARSDALE PUBLIC LIBRARY*, 54 Olmsted Rd, 10583. SAN 312-4339. Tel: 914-722-1300. FAX: 914-722-1305. Web Site: www.scarsdalelibrary.org. *Dir,* Elizabeth Bermel; E-mail: ebermel@wlsmail.org; *Adminr, Support Serv,* Roberta Stein-Ham; E-mail: steinham@wlsmail.org; *Head, Children's Servx,* Karen Zielinski; *Ch,* Aisha Bell; *Local Hist Librn,* Daniel Glauber; *Ref Librn,* Barbara Kokot; *Adult Serv Mgr, YA Mgr,* Wendy Archer; Staff 56 (MLS 26, Non-MLS 30)
Founded 1928. Pop 17,823; Circ 409,034
Library Holdings: Audiobooks 7,397; AV Mats 11,965; e-books 4,581; Bk Vols 122,758; Per Subs 300
Subject Interests: Japanese (Lang), Local hist, Newsp items
Automation Activity & Vendor Info: (Acquisitions) SirsiDynix; (Circulation) SirsiDynix; (OPAC) SirsiDynix
Wireless access
Mem of Westchester Library System
Partic in Westlynx
Friends of the Library Group

SCHAGHTICOKE

P ARVILLA E DIVER MEMORIAL LIBRARY*, 136 Main St, 12154. SAN 312-4355. Tel: 518-753-4344. FAX: 518-753-4344. Web Site: diverlibrary.org. *Dir,* Nick Matulis; E-mail: director@diverlibrary.org; Staff 1 (MLS 1)
Founded 1939. Circ 5,708
Library Holdings: Audiobooks 223; DVDs 458; Large Print Bks 22; Bk Vols 7,000; Per Subs 20
Wireless access
Function: After school storytime, Archival coll, Audio & video playback equip for onsite use, Audiobks via web, Bks on cassette, Bks on CD, Children's prog, Computer training, Computers for patron use, Free DVD rentals, Holiday prog, ILL available, Music CDs, OverDrive digital audio bks, Photocopying/Printing, Prog for adults, Prog for children & young adult, Scanner, Summer reading prog, VHS videos, Wheelchair accessible, Workshops
Mem of Upper Hudson Library System
Open Mon 10-6, Tues-Thurs 1-6, Sat 10-1
Friends of the Library Group

SCHENECTADY

S DUDLEY OBSERVATORY LIBRARY*, 15 Nott Terrace Heights, 12308. SAN 354-1509. Tel: 518-382-7890, Ext 239. E-mail: info@dudleyobservatory.org. Web Site: vwd6-cdlc.kari.opalsinfo.net, www.dudleyobservatory.org. *Archivist,* Angela Matyi; Staff 1 (MLS 1)
Founded 1852
Library Holdings: Bk Titles 5,000; Per Subs 15
Special Collections: Archives of Dudley Observatory; Benjamin A Gould Jr Library
Subject Interests: Astronomy, Astrophysics, Hist of astronomy, Space sci
Automation Activity & Vendor Info: (ILL) OCLC
Wireless access
Partic in Capital District Library Council
Restriction: Circ limited, Open by appt only

M ELLIS MEDICINE, Medical-Nursing Library, 1101 Nott St, 12308. SAN 312-4371. Tel: 518-243-4000, 518-243-4381. FAX: 518-243-1429. E-mail: library@ellismedicine.org. Web Site: www.ellismedlibrary.org. *Librn,* Emily Spinner
Founded 1930
Library Holdings: Bk Titles 2,815; Bk Vols 3,150; Per Subs 210
Special Collections: Nursing History
Wireless access
Partic in Cap District Libr Coun for Ref & Res Resources; New York State Interlibrary Loan Network
Restriction: Staff use only

SR FIRST REFORMED CHURCH OF SCHENECTADY, Norman B Johnson Memorial Library, Eight N Church St, 12305-1699. SAN 371-7712. Tel: 518-377-2201. FAX: 518-374-4098. E-mail: 1streformed@gmail.com. Web Site: www.1streformed.com.
Founded 1838
Library Holdings: Bk Titles 7,600
Special Collections: Children's Coll; Christmas Coll
Subject Interests: Art, Hist, Lit, Music, Relig
Special Services for the Deaf - Bks on deafness & sign lang
Open Mon-Fri 8-4

S KNOLLS ATOMIC POWER LABORATORY INC, LIBRARY*, 2401 River Rd, 12309. SAN 371-0998. Tel: 518-395-6000. FAX: 518-395-7761. Web Site: www.knollslab.com. *Mgr,* Barry Van Steele; Staff 5 (MLS 1, Non-MLS 4)
Founded 1946
Library Holdings: Bk Titles 6,729; Bk Vols 18,955; Per Subs 250
Restriction: Not open to pub

P MOHAWK VALLEY LIBRARY SYSTEM*, 858 Duanesburg Rd, 12306. SAN 312-438X. Tel: 518-355-2010. FAX: 518-355-0674. E-mail: mvls@mvls.info. Web Site: www.mvls.info. *Dir,* Eric Trahan; E-mail: etrahan@mvls.info; *Asst Dir, Ch Serv,* Sue Z Rokos; E-mail: srokos@mvls.info; *Mem Serv Librn,* Sharon O'Brien; E-mail: sobrien@mvls.info; *Outreach Serv Librn,* Lois Gordon; E-mail: lgordon@mvls.info; Staff 6.5 (MLS 4, Non-MLS 2.5)
Founded 1959. Pop 293,226
Library Holdings: Bk Vols 56,761
Wireless access
Member Libraries: Amsterdam Free Library; Canajoharie Library; Community Library; Fort Hunter Free Library; Fort Plain Free Library; Frothingham Free Library; Gloversville Public Library; Johnstown Public Library; Margaret Reaney Memorial Library; Middleburgh Library; Northville Public Library; Schenectady County Public Library; Schoharie Free Association Library; Sharon Springs Free Library
Partic in Cap District Libr Coun for Ref & Res Resources
Open Mon-Fri 8:30-4:30
Restriction: Staff use only

GL NEW YORK STATE SUPREME COURT LAW LIBRARY*, JOSEPH F EGAN MEMORIAL SUPREME COURT LAW LIBRARY, Schenectady County Judicial Bldg, 612 State St, 12305. SAN 312-4363. Tel: 518-285-8518. FAX: 518-451-8730. E-mail: 4JDLawLibrary@nycourts.gov. *Sr Law Librn,* Dana Wantuch; Staff 3 (MLS 1, Non-MLS 2)
Library Holdings: Bk Vols 27,650
Automation Activity & Vendor Info: (Acquisitions) SirsiDynix; (Cataloging) SirsiDynix; (Circulation) SirsiDynix; (ILL) SirsiDynix; (OPAC) SirsiDynix; (Serials) SirsiDynix
Wireless access
Open Mon-Fri 9-12 & 1-4:30

J SCHENECTADY COUNTY COMMUNITY COLLEGE*, Begley Library & Instructional Technology Center, 78 Washington Ave, 12305. SAN 312-4428. Tel: 518-381-1235. Reference Tel: 518-381-1242. Administration Tel: 518-381-1240. FAX: 518-381-1252. Web Site: www.sunysccc.edu/library/index.html. *Dir, Libr Serv,* Lynne King; E-mail: kinglo@sunysccc.edu; *Head, Tech Serv,* David Moore; E-mail: mooreds@sunysccc.edu; Staff 7 (MLS 5, Non-MLS 2)
Founded 1968. Enrl 2,901; Highest Degree: Bachelor
Library Holdings: Bks on Deafness & Sign Lang 50; Bk Titles 74,000; Bk Vols 81,000; Per Subs 400
Special Collections: College Memorabilia Coll
Subject Interests: Culinary arts, Fire sci, Hotel tech, Paralegal, Travel & tourism
Automation Activity & Vendor Info: (Cataloging) OCLC Connexion; (Circulation) Ex Libris Group; (ILL) OCLC ILLiad; (OPAC) Ex Libris Group
Wireless access
Publications: A Guide to Begley Library & the Instructional Technology Center
Partic in Cap District Libr Coun for Ref & Res Resources; OCLC Online Computer Library Center, Inc; SUNYConnect
Open Mon-Thurs (Winter) 8am-8:30pm, Fri 8-4:30, Sat 10-2; Mon-Thurs (Summer) 8:30-7, Fri 8:30-1

S SCHENECTADY COUNTY HISTORICAL SOCIETY, Grems-Doolittle Library, 32 Washington Ave, 12305. SAN 321-0030. Tel: 518-374-0263, Ext 3. FAX: 518-688-2825. Web Site: schenectadyhistorical.org/library.
Founded 1905
Library Holdings: Bk Vols 5,000
Special Collections: Archives (Carl Company Coll); Diaries of Harriet Mumford Paige; Personal Papers (Charles P Steinmetz Coll). Oral History
Subject Interests: Genealogy, Local hist
Wireless access
Publications: A History of the Schenectady PATENT; Duanesburg Memorial Census, rev; Images of America: Glennville; Images of America: Rotterdam; The Markers Speak
Open Mon-Fri 9-5, Sat 10-2
Restriction: Non-circulating

P SCHENECTADY COUNTY PUBLIC LIBRARY, 99 Clinton St, 12305-2083. SAN 354-1266. Tel: 518-388-4500. Circulation Tel: 518-388-4538. Interlibrary Loan Service Tel: 518-388-4518. Reference Tel: 518-388-4511. FAX: 518-386-2241. E-mail: scp-ref@mvls.info. Web Site: www.scpl.org. *Dir,* Karen Bradley; *Asst Dir,* Devon Hedges; *Asst Dir, Libr Operations,* Beth DeMidio; *Adult Serv Coordr,* Mary Ann Warner; *Youth Serv Coordr,* Kaela Wallman; Staff 84 (MLS 24, Non-MLS 60)
Founded 1894. Pop 154,727; Circ 1,003,344
Automation Activity & Vendor Info: (Cataloging) Innovative Interfaces, Inc; (Circulation) Innovative Interfaces, Inc; (OPAC) Innovative Interfaces, Inc; (Serials) Innovative Interfaces, Inc
Wireless access
Mem of Mohawk Valley Library System
Partic in Capital District Library Council
Open Mon, Tues, Thurs & Fri 9-5, Wed 9-6, Sat 9-1
Friends of the Library Group
Branches: 7
GLENVILLE BRANCH, 20 Glenridge Rd, Scotia, 12302, SAN 370-9299. Tel: 518-386-2243. FAX: 518-386-2243. *Library Contact,* Janet Quick
Open Mon & Wed 10-5, Thurs 10-6
MONT PLEASANT, 1036 Crane St, 12303, SAN 354-1320. Tel: 518-386-2245. FAX: 518-370-7137. *Library Contact,* Christine Symes
Open Tues & Thurs 10-5
NISKAYUNA BRANCH, 2400 Nott St E, Niskayuna, 12309, SAN 370-128X. Tel: 518-386-2249. *Library Contact,* Dori Trela
Open Mon 10-6, Tues-Fri 10-5
QUAKER STREET, 133 Bull St, Delanson, 12053. (Mail add: PO Box 157, Delanson, 12053-0157), SAN 354-1339. Tel: 518-895-2719. FAX: 518-895-2719. *Library Contact,* Cindy McKeon
Open Wed & Thurs 10-5

ROTTERDAM, 1100 N Westcott Rd, 12306, SAN 354-138X. Tel: 518-356-3440. FAX: 518-356-3467. *Library Contact,* Sheila Woods
Open Mon & Fri 10-5, Tues 10-6

SCOTIA BRANCH, 14 Mohawk Ave, 12302, SAN 354-1355. Tel: 518-386-2247. FAX: 518-366-2247. *Library Contact,* Brenda Rice
Founded 1929
Open Tues & Fri 10-5
Friends of the Library Group

WOODLAWN, Two Sanford St, 12304, SAN 354-141X. Tel: 518-386-2248. FAX: 518-386-2248. *Library Contact,* Devery Gara
Open Mon & Thurs 10-5

C UNION COLLEGE*, Schaffer Library, 807 Union St, 12308. SAN 354-1479. Tel: 518-388-6277. Circulation Tel: 518-388-6280. Interlibrary Loan Service Tel: 518-388-6282. Reference Tel: 518-388-6281. FAX: 518-388-6619, 518-388-6641. Web Site: www.union.edu/schaffer-library. *Col Librn,* Frances J Maloy; Tel: 518-388-6739, E-mail: maloyf@union.edu; *Digital Scholarship Librn, Dir, Pub Serv,* Jennifer N Grayburn; E-mail: grayburj@union.edu; *Head, Access Serv,* Robyn Reed; E-mail: reedr@union.edu; *Govt Doc Librn, Head, Coll Develop,* Raik Zaghloul; E-mail: zaghlour@union.edu; *Spec Coll & Archives Librn,* Andrea Belair; E-mail: belaira@union.edu; *Curator of Art & Exhibitions,* Julie Lohnes; E-mail: lohnesj@union.edu; Staff 28.5 (MLS 14.5, Non-MLS 14)
Founded 1795. Enrl 2,189; Fac 203
Jul 2016-Jun 2017. Mats Exp $1,965,574, Books $391,637, Per/Ser (Incl. Access Fees) $1,498,448, AV Mat $26,654, Electronic Ref Mat (Incl. Access Fees) $31,307, Presv $17,528. Sal $1,371,822 (Prof $950,250)
Library Holdings: AV Mats 11,943; Bk Titles 367,348; Bk Vols 614,490; Per Subs 6,248
Special Collections: 19th Century American Wit & Humor (Bailey Coll); French Civilization to End of 19th Century (John Bigelow Library Coll); Local History (Schenectady Coll); Manuscript Coll; Microscopy (Kellert Coll); Rare Book Coll; Science & Technology (Schenectady Archives of Science & Technology Coll), personal papers of various General Electric Co Scientists; Union College Archives; William J Stillman Coll. US Document Depository
Automation Activity & Vendor Info: (Acquisitions) Innovative Interfaces, Inc; (Cataloging) Innovative Interfaces, Inc; (Circulation) Innovative Interfaces, Inc
Wireless access
Partic in OCLC Online Computer Library Center, Inc
Friends of the Library Group

SCHOHARIE

S THE OLD STONE FORT MUSEUM, Schoharie County Historical Society Library, 145 Fort Rd, 12157. SAN 312-4452. Tel: 518-295-7192. FAX: 518-295-7187. E-mail: office@schohariehistory.net. Web Site: theoldstonefort.org/visit-library. *Mus Dir,* Melinda McTaggart; *Curator,* Daniel J Beams; E-mail: curator@theoldstonefort.org
Founded 1889
Library Holdings: Bk Titles 1,600; Bk Vols 2,000
Special Collections: Area Business Papers; Area Town/County/Village Papers; Civil War Papers; Folklore & Folklife
Subject Interests: Genealogy, Local hist, NY State hist
Wireless access
Publications: Schoharie County Historical Review
Restriction: Not a lending libr, Open by appt only, Open to pub with supv only

P SCHOHARIE FREE ASSOCIATION LIBRARY*, Mary Beatrice Cushing Memorial Library, 103 Knower Ave, 12157. (Mail add: PO Box 519, 12157-0519), SAN 312-4460. Tel: 518-295-7127. FAX: 518-295-7127. E-mail: sholib@midtel.net. Web Site: www.schoharielibrary.org. *Dir,* Catherine Caiazzo
Founded 1916. Pop 1,016; Circ 15,148
Library Holdings: Bk Vols 20,000; Per Subs 44
Automation Activity & Vendor Info: (Cataloging) Innovative Interfaces, Inc; (Circulation) Innovative Interfaces, Inc; (OPAC) Innovative Interfaces, Inc; (Serials) Innovative Interfaces, Inc
Wireless access
Mem of Mohawk Valley Library System
Open Mon & Thurs 1-5 & 6-9, Tues & Fri 10-5, Sat 10-2

SCHROON LAKE

P SCHROON LAKE PUBLIC LIBRARY, 15 Leland Ave, 12870. (Mail add: PO Box 398, 12870-0398), SAN 312-4479. Tel: 518-532-7737, Ext 13. FAX: 518-532-9474. E-mail: library@schroon.net. Web Site: lakelibrary129.wordpress.com. *Dir,* Jane A Bouchard; Staff 2 (Non-MLS 2)
Founded 1979
Library Holdings: Bk Vols 30,000; Per Subs 35
Automation Activity & Vendor Info: (Cataloging) SirsiDynix; (Circulation) SirsiDynix; (OPAC) SirsiDynix; (Serials) SirsiDynix
Wireless access
Mem of Clinton-Essex-Franklin Library System
Open Tues, Wed & Fri 10-4, Thurs 10-6, Sat 10-2
Friends of the Library Group

SCHUYLERVILLE

P SCHUYLERVILLE PUBLIC LIBRARY*, 52 Ferry St, 12871. SAN 312-4487. Tel: 518-695-6641. FAX: 518-695-3619. Web Site: schuylervillelibrary.sals.edu. *Libr Dir,* Caitlin Johnson; E-mail: svl-director@sals.edu; *Ad,* Michelle Isopo; Staff 4 (MLS 1, Non-MLS 3)
Founded 1905. Pop 9,881; Circ 37,340
Library Holdings: AV Mats 703; DVDs 1,425; Large Print Bks 118; Bk Titles 20,853; Per Subs 54; Talking Bks 531
Special Collections: Battle of Saratoga
Automation Activity & Vendor Info: (Cataloging) Innovative Interfaces, Inc; (Circulation) Innovative Interfaces, Inc; (OPAC) Innovative Interfaces, Inc; (Serials) Innovative Interfaces, Inc
Wireless access
Mem of Southern Adirondack Library System
Open Mon-Fri 10-8, Sat 10-2
Friends of the Library Group

SCOTTSVILLE

P SCOTTSVILLE FREE LIBRARY*, 28 Main St, 14546. SAN 312-4509. Tel: 585-889-2023. FAX: 585-889-7938. Web Site: scottsville.libraryweb.org. *Dir,* Elizabeth Andreae; E-mail: Elizabeth.Andreae@libraryweb.org
Founded 1917. Pop 5,149; Circ 60,315
Library Holdings: Bk Vols 42,391; Per Subs 51
Automation Activity & Vendor Info: (Circulation) TLC (The Library Corporation)
Wireless access
Mem of Monroe County Library System
Open Mon, Wed & Thurs 1-8, Tues 10-8, Fri 10-5, Sat 10-1
Friends of the Library Group
Branches: 1
MUMFORD BRANCH, 883 George St, Mumford, 14511. (Mail add: PO Box 89, Mumford, 14511-0089). Tel: 718-538-6124. Web Site: www.rochester.lib.ny.us/scottsville/mumford.html. *Br Mgr,* Kathy Smith
Open Mon, Wed & Fri 2-8, Sat 10-1

SEA CLIFF

P SEA CLIFF VILLAGE LIBRARY, 300 Sea Cliff Ave, 11579. (Mail add: PO Box 280, 11579-0280), SAN 312-4517. Tel: 516-671-4290. FAX: 516-759-6613. E-mail: scinfo@seaclifflibrary.org. Web Site: www.seaclifflibrary.org. *Libr Dir,* Camille Purcell; E-mail: camille@seaclifflibrary.org
Founded 1905. Circ 39,390
Library Holdings: AV Mats 1,998; Bk Titles 24,000; Per Subs 80
Automation Activity & Vendor Info: (Cataloging) Innovative Interfaces, Inc - Sierra; (Circulation) Innovative Interfaces, Inc - Sierra; (OPAC) Innovative Interfaces, Inc - Sierra
Wireless access
Publications: Newsletter
Mem of Nassau Library System
Open Mon 1-4:30, Tues-Fri 10-1 & 2:30-4:30, Sat 10-1:30
Friends of the Library Group

SEAFORD

P SEAFORD PUBLIC LIBRARY*, 2234 Jackson Ave, 11783-2691. SAN 312-4525. Tel: 516-221-1334. FAX: 516-826-8133. E-mail: seafordreference@nassaulibrary.info. Web Site: www.seafordlibrary.org. *Dir,* Frank J McKenna; E-mail: seaforddirector@nassaulibrary.info; Staff 30 (MLS 8, Non-MLS 22)
Founded 1956. Pop 16,687; Circ 162,398
Library Holdings: Bk Vols 83,747
Automation Activity & Vendor Info: (Acquisitions) Innovative Interfaces, Inc - Millennium; (Cataloging) Innovative Interfaces, Inc - Millennium; (Circulation) Innovative Interfaces, Inc - Millennium; (ILL) OCLC FirstSearch; (OPAC) Innovative Interfaces, Inc - Millennium
Wireless access
Publications: Newsletter (Monthly)
Mem of Nassau Library System
Partic in Long Island Library Resources Council
Open Mon-Thurs 10-9, Fri 10-6, Sat 10-5
Friends of the Library Group

SELDEN

J SUFFOLK COUNTY COMMUNITY COLLEGE*, Ammerman Campus Library, 533 College Rd, 11784-2899. SAN 354-1568. Tel: 631-451-4800. Reference Tel: 631-451-4830. Administration Tel: 631-451-4173. FAX:

631-451-4697. Web Site: www.sunysuffolk.edu/explore-academics/library. *Libr Dir,* Susan Lieberthal; E-mail: liebers@sunysuffolk.edu; *Ref Librn,* Jennifer Farquahar; E-mail: farquhj@sunysuffolk.edu; *Circ Librn,* Kathy Hand; E-mail: handk@sunysuffolk.edu; *Coll Develop Librn,* Deborah Provenzano; E-mail: provend@sunysuffolk.edu; *Govt Doc Librn,* Krista Gruber; E-mail: gruberk@sunysuffolk.edu; Staff 7 (MLS 7)
Founded 1960. Enrl 12,700; Fac 300; Highest Degree: Associate
Library Holdings: Bk Titles 100,000; Bk Vols 105,610; Per Subs 500
Special Collections: Long Island Coll
Subject Interests: Allied health, Nursing
Automation Activity & Vendor Info: (Acquisitions) Ex Libris Group; (Cataloging) OCLC Connexion; (Circulation) Ex Libris Group; (OPAC) Ex Libris Group; (Serials) Ex Libris Group
Wireless access
Publications: Centralized Media & Periodicals Catalog; Newsletter; Student Handbook
Partic in SUNYConnect
Open Mon-Thurs 8am-10pm, Fri 8-6, Sat 9-4

SENECA FALLS

CM NEW YORK CHIROPRACTIC COLLEGE LIBRARY*, 2360 State Rte 89, 13148-9460. (Mail add: PO Box 800, 13148-0800), SAN 320-457X. Tel: 315-568-3244. Interlibrary Loan Service Tel: 315-568-3245. FAX: 315-568-3119. E-mail: library@nycc.edu. Web Site: www.nycc.edu/student-resources/library. *Dir,* Bethyn A Boni; E-mail: bboni@nycc.edu; *Media & Digital Res Librn,* Suellen Christopoulos-Nutting; E-mail: snutting@nycc.edu; *Acq, Circ, ILL,* Mary Fiorito; E-mail: mfiorito@nycc.edu; Staff 3 (MLS 3)
Founded 1919. Enrl 763; Fac 47; Highest Degree: Doctorate
Library Holdings: Bk Vols 16,521; Per Subs 407; Spec Interest Per Sub 52
Subject Interests: Acupuncture, Anatomy, Chiropractic & Oriental med, Nutrition, Radiology
Automation Activity & Vendor Info: (Cataloging) SirsiDynix; (Circulation) SirsiDynix; (OPAC) SirsiDynix
Wireless access
Partic in Chiropractic Libr Consortium; South Central Regional Library Council
Open Mon-Thurs 7:45am-10pm, Fri 7:45-5, Sat & Sun 12-10

S SENECA FALLS HISTORICAL SOCIETY LIBRARY*, 55 Cayuga St, 13148. SAN 329-4307. Tel: 315-568-8412. FAX: 315-568-8426. E-mail: sfhs@rochester.rr.com. Web Site: www.sfhistoricalsociety.org. *Exec Dir,* Chris Podzuweit; E-mail: sfhs@rochester.rr.com
Founded 1896
Library Holdings: Bk Titles 1,500; Per Subs 10
Special Collections: Civil War Coll; Women's Rights Coll
Subject Interests: Seneca County hist, Seneca Falls hist, Victorian era
Wireless access
Function: Res libr
Open Mon-Fri 9-4
Restriction: In-house use for visitors

P SENECA FALLS LIBRARY*, 47 Cayuga St, 13148. SAN 312-455X. Tel: 315-568-8265. Circulation Tel: 315-568-8265, Ext 2. FAX: 315-856-8460. Web Site: senecafallslibrary.org. *Dir,* Jenny Burnett; Tel: 315-568-8265, Ext 3, E-mail: director@senecafallslibrary.org; *Circ Mgr,* Suzanne Mathewson; E-mail: smatthewson@senecafallslibrary.org
Founded 1881. Pop 6,861; Circ 38,048
Library Holdings: AV Mats 524; e-books 1,851; Bk Vols 27,047; Per Subs 44; Talking Bks 1,839
Special Collections: DAR Coll; Genealogy Coll
Automation Activity & Vendor Info: (Circulation) Innovative Interfaces, Inc
Wireless access
Mem of Finger Lakes Library System
Open Mon-Fri 10-8, Sat 10-5, Sun (Sept-May) 2-5
Friends of the Library Group

SETAUKET

P EMMA S CLARK MEMORIAL LIBRARY, 120 Main St, 11733-2868. SAN 312-4568. Tel: 631-941-4080. FAX: 631-941-4541. E-mail: askus@emmaclark.org. Web Site: www.emmaclark.org. *Dir,* Ted Gutmann; Tel: 631-941-4080, Ext 112, E-mail: ted@emmaclark.org; *Head, Adult Serv,* Joan Kahnhauser; Tel: 631-941-4080, Ext 116, E-mail: joan@emmaclark.org; *Head, Children's Servx,* Brian Debus; Tel: 631-941-4080, Ext 134, E-mail: brian@emmaclark.org; *Circ Serv,* Aileen Clark; Tel: 631-941-4080, Ext 114, E-mail: aileen@emmaclark.org; *Computer Serv,* Robert Johnson; Tel: 631-941-4080, Ext 132, E-mail: bob@emmaclark.org; *Tech Serv,* Ruth Crane; Tel: 631-941-4080, Ext 122, E-mail: ruth@emmaclark.org; Staff 49 (MLS 15, Non-MLS 34)
Founded 1892. Pop 48,424; Circ 512,000
Jan 2016-Dec 2016 Income $5,192,000. Mats Exp $699,500. Sal $2,774,145 (Prof $1,497,212)
Library Holdings: Bk Vols 196,000; Per Subs 400
Subject Interests: Long Island hist
Automation Activity & Vendor Info: (Cataloging) Innovative Interfaces, Inc - Sierra; (Circulation) Innovative Interfaces, Inc - Sierra; (Discovery) Innovative Interfaces, Inc; (ILL) Innovative Interfaces, Inc - Sierra; (OPAC) Innovative Interfaces, Inc
Wireless access
Function: 24/7 Electronic res, 24/7 Online cat, Activity rm, Adult bk club, Adult literacy prog, After school storytime, Art exhibits, Audiobks on Playaways & MP3, Audiobks via web, Bk club(s), Bks on cassette, Bks on CD, CD-ROM, Children's prog, Computer training, Computers for patron use, Digital talking bks, E-Readers, E-Reserves, Electronic databases & coll, Free DVD rentals, Home delivery & serv to seniorr ctr & nursing homes, Homebound delivery serv, ILL available, Internet access, Life-long learning prog for all ages, Magazines, Magnifiers for reading, Mango lang, Meeting rooms, Microfiche/film & reading machines, Movies, Museum passes, Music CDs, Online cat, Outreach serv, OverDrive digital audio bks, Photocopying/Printing, Prog for adults, Prog for children & young adult, Ref & res, Ref serv available, Scanner, Senior computer classes, Senior outreach, Study rm, Summer & winter reading prog, Summer reading prog, Teen prog, Telephone ref, VHS videos, Wheelchair accessible
Mem of Suffolk Cooperative Library System
Partic in Partnership of Automated Librs in Suffolk
Open Mon-Fri 9:30-9, Sat 9-5, Sun 10-5

SHARON SPRINGS

P SHARON SPRINGS FREE LIBRARY*, 129 Main St, 13459. (Mail add: PO Box 268, 13459-0268), SAN 312-4576. Tel: 518-284-3126. E-mail: shs@mvls.info. Web Site: shslib.blogspot.com. *Libr Dir,* Helen Thomas
Circ 6,010
Library Holdings: Bk Vols 7,000
Automation Activity & Vendor Info: (Cataloging) Innovative Interfaces, Inc; (Circulation) Innovative Interfaces, Inc; (OPAC) Innovative Interfaces, Inc
Wireless access
Mem of Mohawk Valley Library System
Open Mon & Thurs 10-6, Tues, Wed & Fri 3-8, Sat 10-1

SHELTER ISLAND

P SHELTER ISLAND PUBLIC LIBRARY*, 37 N Ferry Rd, 11964. (Mail add: PO Box 2016, 11964-2016), SAN 312-4584. Tel: 631-749-0042. FAX: 631-749-1575. E-mail: info@shelterislandpubliclibrary.org. Web Site: silibrary.org. *Libr Dir,* Terry Z Lucas; E-mail: tlucas@silibrary.org; *Asst Dir,* Laura Dickerson; E-mail: ldickerson@silibrary.org
Founded 1885. Circ 23,565
Wireless access
Mem of Suffolk Cooperative Library System
Open Mon-Fri 9:30-7, Sat 9:30-5
Friends of the Library Group

SHERBURNE

P SHERBURNE PUBLIC LIBRARY*, Two E State St, 13460. (Mail add: PO Box 702, 13460-0702), SAN 312-4592. Tel: 607-674-4242. FAX: 607-674-4242. E-mail: sh.ill@4cls.org. Web Site: sherburnelibraryny.org. *Libr Mgr,* Colleen Law-Tefft
Pop 3,903; Circ 29,384
Library Holdings: Bk Vols 17,000; Per Subs 40
Automation Activity & Vendor Info: (Cataloging) SirsiDynix-WorkFlows; (Circulation) SirsiDynix-WorkFlows; (OPAC) SirsiDynix-WorkFlows; (Serials) SirsiDynix-WorkFlows
Wireless access
Mem of Four County Library System
Open Mon-Wed 1-8, Thurs & Fri 10-5, Sat 10-12

SHERMAN

P MINERVA FREE LIBRARY*, 116 Miller St, 14781. (Mail add: PO Box 588, 14781-0588), SAN 312-4606. Tel: 716-761-6378. FAX: 716-761-6335. E-mail: info@minervalibrary.org. Web Site: www.minervalibrary.org. *Dir,* Shellie Williams
Founded 1907. Pop 1,505; Circ 6,738
Library Holdings: Bk Vols 14,500; Per Subs 15
Automation Activity & Vendor Info: (Cataloging) SirsiDynix; (Circulation) SirsiDynix; (OPAC) SirsiDynix; (Serials) SirsiDynix
Wireless access
Mem of Chautauqua-Cattaraugus Library System
Open Tues 4-8, Thurs 9-4 & 6-8, Fri 9-3, Sat 9-Noon
Friends of the Library Group

SHERRILL

P SHERRILL-KENWOOD FREE LIBRARY*, 543 Sherrill Rd, 13461-1263. SAN 312-4614. Tel: 315-363-5980. FAX: 315-363-4133. E-mail: sherrill@midyork.org. Web Site: www.sherrillkenwoodlibrary.org. *Libr Mgr,* Mary Kay Junglen; Staff 1 (Non-MLS 1)
Founded 1912. Pop 3,583; Circ 36,490. Sal $72,000 (Prof $40,000)
Library Holdings: Audiobooks 622; CDs 40; DVDs 1,375; e-books 26; Electronic Media & Resources 9; Large Print Bks 475; Bk Titles 20,180; Per Subs 102
Automation Activity & Vendor Info: (Circulation) SirsiDynix; (OPAC) SirsiDynix
Wireless access
Function: Adult bk club, Art exhibits, Audiobks via web, Bks on cassette, Bks on CD, Children's prog, Computer training, Computers for patron use, Digital talking bks, E-Reserves, Electronic databases & coll, Family literacy, Free DVD rentals, Holiday prog, ILL available, Internet access, Mail & tel request accepted, Music CDs, Online cat, Online ref, Outside serv via phone, mail, e-mail & web, OverDrive digital audio bks, Photocopying/Printing, Preschool reading prog, Prog for adults, Prog for children & young adult, Ref serv available, Scanner, Senior computer classes, Spoken cassettes & CDs, Story hour, Summer & winter reading prog, Summer reading prog, Tax forms, Teen prog, Telephone ref, VHS videos, Wheelchair accessible, Winter reading prog, Workshops
Mem of Mid-York Library System
Open Mon & Wed 1-8, Tues & Thurs 11-8, Fri 1-6, Sat (Sept-June) 10-2
Friends of the Library Group

SHIRLEY

P MASTICS-MORICHES-SHIRLEY COMMUNITY LIBRARY*, 407 William Floyd Pkwy, 11967. SAN 312-4622. Tel: 631-399-1511. FAX: 631-281-4442. Web Site: www.communitylibrary.org. *Dir,* Kerri Rosalia; E-mail: director@communitylibrary.org; *Asst Dir,* Tara D'Amato; *Head, Adult Serv, Head, Ref,* Josephine Wuthenow; *Head, Bus Serv,* Christopher Nowak; *Head, Children's Servx,* Rachel Wyneken; *Head, Circ Serv,* Anne Marie Hoffman; *Head, Tech Serv,* Lorraine Squires; *Head, Teen Serv,* Kerrilynn Jorgensen; Staff 22 (MLS 22)
Founded 1974. Pop 63,000; Circ 758,971
Library Holdings: AV Mats 116,145; Bk Vols 272,319; Per Subs 27,141
Subject Interests: Italian lang, Local hist, Spanish
Automation Activity & Vendor Info: (Acquisitions) Innovative Interfaces, Inc; (Cataloging) Innovative Interfaces, Inc; (Circulation) Innovative Interfaces, Inc; (ILL) Innovative Interfaces, Inc; (OPAC) Innovative Interfaces, Inc
Wireless access
Publications: Newsletter
Mem of Suffolk Cooperative Library System
Partic in Long Island Library Resources Council
Open Mon-Thurs 9-9, Fri 9-6, Sat 9-5, Sun (Sept-June) 12-4

SHOREHAM

P NORTH SHORE PUBLIC LIBRARY*, 250 Rte 25A, 11786-9677. SAN 320-4960. Tel: 631-929-4488. FAX: 631-929-4551. E-mail: Info@northshorepubliclibrary.org. Web Site: northshorepubliclibrary.org. *Dir,* Laura Hawrey; E-mail: laura@northshorepubliclibrary.org; *Asst Dir, Ref (Info Servs),* Janis Tousey; *Ch Serv,* L Blend; *Ch Serv,* Bernadette Regina; *Circ,* A Caravello; *ILL,* M Clark; *Ser, Tech Serv,* Kathryn Kalin; *YA Serv,* Maura Parsons; Staff 34 (MLS 12, Non-MLS 22)
Founded 1975. Pop 22,933; Circ 287,780
Library Holdings: Bk Titles 97,506; Per Subs 342
Automation Activity & Vendor Info: (Acquisitions) Innovative Interfaces, Inc; (Cataloging) Innovative Interfaces, Inc; (Circulation) Innovative Interfaces, Inc; (OPAC) Innovative Interfaces, Inc; (Serials) Innovative Interfaces, Inc
Wireless access
Mem of Suffolk Cooperative Library System
Open Mon-Fri 9:30-9, Sun 1-5
Friends of the Library Group

SHORTSVILLE

P RED JACKET COMMUNITY LIBRARY*, Seven Lehigh Ave, 14548. (Mail add: PO Box 370, 14548-0370). Tel: 585-289-3559. Web Site: redjacket.owwl.org. *Libr Dir,* Andrea Tillinghast; E-mail: RedJacketLibraryDirector@owwl.org; *Youth Serv Librn,* Christine LaTerra; Staff 5 (MLS 2, Non-MLS 3)
Founded 1998. Pop 6,700
Library Holdings: AV Mats 1,260; Large Print Bks 669; Bk Vols 30,000; Per Subs 13; Talking Bks 487
Automation Activity & Vendor Info: (Cataloging) Evergreen; (Circulation) Mandarin Library Automation; (OPAC) Mandarin Library Automation
Wireless access
Mem of Pioneer Library System
Open Tues & Thurs 12-7, Wed & Fri 10-5, Sat 10-2
Friends of the Library Group

SHRUB OAK

P JOHN C HART MEMORIAL LIBRARY*, 1130 Main St, 10588. SAN 354-1622. Tel: 914-245-5262. FAX: 914-245-2216. Web Site: www.yorktownlibrary.org. *Dir,* Yvonne Cech; E-mail: ycech@wlsmail.org; *ILL, Ref Librn,* Reva Queler; *Circ Supvr,* Margaret Groccia; *Adult Serv,* Ellen Tannenbaum; *Ch Serv,* Marca McClenon; *Circ,* Deborah Sarno; *Tech Serv,* Maria Stolfi; *YA Serv,* Maureen Connelly; Staff 24 (MLS 10, Non-MLS 14)
Founded 1920. Pop 35,000; Circ 490,273
Library Holdings: Bk Vols 109,000
Special Collections: Special Education Jerome Thaler Weather Coll
Automation Activity & Vendor Info: (Acquisitions) Evergreen; (Cataloging) Evergreen; (Circulation) Evergreen; (ILL) OCLC ILLiad; (OPAC) Evergreen
Wireless access
Mem of Westchester Library System
Open Mon-Thurs 9:30-8, Fri & Sat 9:30-5, Sun (Oct-April) 12-4
Friends of the Library Group

SIDNEY

P SIDNEY MEMORIAL PUBLIC LIBRARY*, Eight River St, 13838. SAN 312-4649. Tel: 607-563-1200, 607-563-8021. FAX: 607-563-7675. Web Site: sidneylibrary.org. *Dir,* Beth Paine; E-mail: si.beth@4cls.org
Founded 1887. Pop 8,088
Library Holdings: Bk Vols 57,887; Per Subs 100
Subject Interests: Local hist
Automation Activity & Vendor Info: (Cataloging) SirsiDynix; (Circulation) SirsiDynix; (OPAC) SirsiDynix
Wireless access
Publications: Newsletter
Mem of Four County Library System
Open Mon-Thurs 9-8:30, Fri 9-6, Sat 9:30-4, Sun 1-4
Friends of the Library Group
Branches: 2
MASONVILLE BRANCH, 15565 State Hwy 8, 13838-2721. Tel: 607-265-3330. FAX: 607-265-3330.
Open Tues-Thurs 3:30-7, Fri 1-5, Sat 10-2
SIDNEY CENTER BRANCH, 10599 County Hwy 23, Unadilla, 13849. Tel: 607-369-7500.
Open Mon-Fri 1-5, Tues & Thurs 3:30-8, Wed & Sat 10-2

SILVER CREEK

P ANDERSON-LEE LIBRARY*, 43 Main St, 14136. SAN 312-4657. Tel: 716-934-3468. FAX: 716-934-3037. E-mail: anderson_lee_library@hotmail.com. Web Site: www.andersonleelibrary.org. *Libr Dir,* Tyler Annis; Staff 1 (MLS 1)
Founded 1924. Circ 57,028
Library Holdings: Bk Vols 25,000
Mem of Chautauqua-Cattaraugus Library System
Open Tues & Thurs 10-2
Friends of the Library Group

SILVER SPRINGS

P GAINESVILLE PUBLIC LIBRARY, Ten Church St, 14550. (Mail add: PO Box 321, 14550-0321), SAN 312-4665. Tel: 585-493-2970. FAX: 585-493-2970. Web Site: owwl.org/library/silversprings. *Dir,* Becky Mann; E-mail: silverspringslibrarydirector@owwl.org
Pop 2,288; Circ 12,289
Library Holdings: Bk Vols 12,500; Per Subs 47
Automation Activity & Vendor Info: (Cataloging) SirsiDynix; (Circulation) SirsiDynix; (OPAC) SirsiDynix
Wireless access
Mem of Pioneer Library System
Open Mon & Fri 10-12 & 4-6, Tues & Thurs 10-12 & 4-7, Wed 4-6, Sat (Sept-June) 10-12

SINCLAIRVILLE

P SINCLAIRVILLE FREE LIBRARY, 15 Main St, 14782. (Mail add: PO Box 609, 14782-0609), SAN 312-4673. Tel: 716-962-5885. FAX: 716-962-5885. E-mail: info@sinclairvillelibrary.org. Web Site: www.sinclairvillelibrary.org. *Libr Mgr,* Beth Hadley; *Libr Asst,* Jessica Huling; Staff 1 (Non-MLS 1)
Founded 1870. Pop 665; Circ 17,264
Library Holdings: Bk Vols 12,159; Per Subs 50
Subject Interests: Local hist
Wireless access
Mem of Chautauqua-Cattaraugus Library System
Open Mon 2-7, Wed 9-5, Thurs 2-7, Fri 10-4, Sat 10-1

SKANEATELES

P SKANEATELES LIBRARY ASSOCIATION*, 49 E Genesee St, 13152. SAN 312-4681. Tel: 315-685-5135. E-mail: help@skaneateleslibrary.org. Web Site: skaneateleslibrary.org. *Libr Dir,* Nickie Marquis; E-mail: nmarquis@skaneateleslibrary.org; Staff 1 (MLS 1)
Founded 1878. Circ 75,759
Library Holdings: Large Print Bks 978; Bk Titles 31,417; Bk Vols 32,946; Per Subs 100; Talking Bks 1,643
Special Collections: Barrow Art Gallery (local artist's work late 19th century); Large Print Books Coll; Unabridged Book-on-Tapes
Subject Interests: Art, Arts, Gardening, Local hist
Automation Activity & Vendor Info: (Cataloging) Innovative Interfaces, Inc; (Circulation) Innovative Interfaces, Inc; (OPAC) Innovative Interfaces, Inc
Wireless access
Mem of Onondaga County Public Libraries
Special Services for the Blind - Talking bks
Open Mon-Thurs 9-8, Fri 9-5, Sat 9-4, Sun 12-4

SLOATSBURG

P SLOATSBURG PUBLIC LIBRARY*, One Liberty Rock Rd, 10974-2392. SAN 322-8355. Tel: 845-753-2001. FAX: 845-753-2144. E-mail: sloatsburgpubliclibrary@gmail.com. Web Site: sloatsburglibrary.org. *Libr Dir,* Annmarie McAnany; E-mail: amcanany@rcls.org; Staff 1 (Non-MLS 1)
Founded 1959. Pop 3,124; Circ 49,000
Library Holdings: AV Mats 5,992; Bk Titles 30,209; Bk Vols 31,587; Per Subs 87; Talking Bks 3,154
Subject Interests: Local hist
Automation Activity & Vendor Info: (Circulation) SirsiDynix; (ILL) SirsiDynix; (OPAC) SirsiDynix
Wireless access
Publications: Books & Beyond (Newsletter)
Mem of Ramapo Catskill Library System
Special Services for the Deaf - TTY equip
Open Mon-Thurs 10-9, Fri 10-6, Sat 10-5, Sun 12-5 (Sept-June); Mon-Thurs 10-9, Fri 10-6, Sat 10-5 (July-Aug)
Friends of the Library Group

SMITHTOWN

P SMITHTOWN LIBRARY*, One N Country Rd, 11754. SAN 354-1657. Tel: 631-360-2480. FAX: 631-265-2044. Web Site: www.smithlib.org. *Dir,* Robert Lusak; E-mail: rlusak@smithlib.org; *Asst Libr Dir,* Patricia Thomas; E-mail: pthomson@smithlib.org; Staff 108 (MLS 38, Non-MLS 70)
Founded 1905. Pop 112,762; Circ 895,374
Library Holdings: AV Mats 47,032; Bk Vols 299,153; Per Subs 9,319
Special Collections: Long Island (Richard Handley & Charles E Lawrence Coll), bk, ms, fiche, microflm
Subject Interests: Behav sci, Soc sci
Automation Activity & Vendor Info: (Acquisitions) Innovative Interfaces, Inc; (Cataloging) Innovative Interfaces, Inc; (Circulation) Innovative Interfaces, Inc; (Course Reserve) Innovative Interfaces, Inc; (ILL) Innovative Interfaces, Inc; (OPAC) Innovative Interfaces, Inc; (Serials) Innovative Interfaces, Inc
Wireless access
Function: Adult literacy prog, Govt ref serv, Home delivery & serv to seniorr ctr & nursing homes, Homebound delivery serv, ILL available, Outside serv via phone, mail, e-mail & web, Photocopying/Printing, Prof lending libr, Prog for children & young adult, Ref serv available, Summer reading prog, Telephone ref, Wheelchair accessible
Publications: Inside Your Library (Monthly)
Mem of Suffolk Cooperative Library System
Special Services for the Deaf - ADA equip; Bks on deafness & sign lang; Closed caption videos; Coll on deaf educ; High interest/low vocabulary bks
Special Services for the Blind - Accessible computers; BiFolkal kits; Bks on cassette; Bks on CD; Cassette playback machines; Cassettes; Closed circuit TV magnifier; Copier with enlargement capabilities; Extensive large print coll; Home delivery serv; Internet workstation with adaptive software; Large print bks; Large screen computer & software; PC for people with disabilities; Photo duplicator for making large print; Recorded bks; Ref serv; Screen enlargement software for people with visual disabilities; Talking bk & rec for the blind cat; Talking bk serv referral; Talking bks; Talking bks & player equip; Talking bks from Braille Inst; Talking bks plus; Videos on blindness & physical disabilities; ZoomText magnification & reading software
Open Mon-Thurs 9:30-9, Fri 9:30-6, Sat 9:30-5, Sun 1-5 (Sept-May)
Friends of the Library Group
Branches: 3
COMMACK BRANCH, Three Indian Head Rd, Commack, 11725, SAN 354-1681.
Open Mon-Thurs 9:30-9, Fri 9:30-6, Sat 9:30-5
Friends of the Library Group
KINGS PARK BRANCH, One Church St, Kings Park, 11754, SAN 354-1711.
Open Mon-Thurs 9:30-9, Fri 9:30-6, Sat 9:30-5
Friends of the Library Group
NESCONSET BRANCH, 148 Smithtown Blvd, Nesconset, 11767, SAN 354-1746.
Open Mon-Thurs 9:30-9, Fri 9:30-6, Sat 9:30-5
Friends of the Library Group

SMYRNA

P SMYRNA PUBLIC LIBRARY*, Seven E Main St, 13464. (Mail add: PO Box 202, 13464-0202), SAN 312-472X. Tel: 607-627-6271. FAX: 607-627-6271. E-mail: sm.ill@4cls.org. Web Site: libraries.4cls.org/smyrna. *Dir,* Clara Lantz
Pop 1,418
Library Holdings: Bk Vols 4,500; Per Subs 25
Wireless access
Mem of Four County Library System
Open Mon, Wed, & Fri 10-2, Tues & Thurs 2-6, Sat 10-Noon

SODUS

P SODUS COMMUNITY LIBRARY*, 17 Maple Ave, 14551. SAN 312-4738. Tel: 315-483-9292. FAX: 315-483-9616. E-mail: soduslibrary@owwl.org. Web Site: www.soduslibrary.org. *Mgr,* Carol Garland; Staff 1 (Non-MLS 1)
Founded 1907. Pop 7,686; Circ 60,000
Library Holdings: Bk Vols 31,000; Per Subs 105
Special Collections: Antique Books & Periodicals of Collectibles; Crocks; Glass (Clyde); Jars (Lyons); Jugs
Automation Activity & Vendor Info: (Acquisitions) Baker & Taylor; (Cataloging) Evergreen; (Circulation) Evergreen; (OPAC) Evergreen; (Serials) Evergreen
Wireless access
Function: 24/7 Electronic res, 24/7 Online cat, Adult bk club, Audiobks via web, Bks on CD, Children's prog, Computers for patron use, Electronic databases & coll, Free DVD rentals, ILL available, Internet access, Magazines, Mango lang, Meeting rooms, Online cat, OverDrive digital audio bks, Photocopying/Printing, Preschool reading prog, Printer for laptops & handheld devices, Prog for adults, Prog for children & young adult, Scanner, Story hour, Study rm, Summer reading prog, Tax forms, Teen prog, Wheelchair accessible
Mem of Pioneer Library System
Open Mon-Thurs 10-8, Fri & Sat 10-5, Sun 2-5
Friends of the Library Group

SOLVAY

P SOLVAY PUBLIC LIBRARY*, 615 Woods Rd, 13209-1681. SAN 312-4754. Tel: 315-468-2441. FAX: 315-468-0373. Web Site: solvaylibrary.org. *Dir,* Dan W Golden; E-mail: dgolden@onlib.org; *Ch Serv, Librn,* Dawn Marmor; Staff 15 (MLS 3, Non-MLS 12)
Founded 1903. Pop 6,584; Circ 95,000
Library Holdings: Bk Vols 34,000; Per Subs 75
Special Collections: Local History; Solvay Process Co
Automation Activity & Vendor Info: (Cataloging) Innovative Interfaces, Inc; (Circulation) Innovative Interfaces, Inc; (OPAC) Innovative Interfaces, Inc
Wireless access
Mem of Onondaga County Public Libraries
Open Mon-Wed 9-8, Thurs & Fri 9-5, Sat 10-5 (9-1 Summer), Sun (Oct-May) 1-5
Friends of the Library Group

SOMERS

P SOMERS LIBRARY, Rte 139 & Reis Park, 10589. (Mail add: PO Box 443, 10589), SAN 312-4762. Tel: 914-232-5717. Administration Tel: 914-232-1285. FAX: 914-232-1035. E-mail: somers@wlsmail.org. Web Site: www.somerslibrary.org. *Dir,* Jennifer Daddio; E-mail: somersdirector@wlsmail.org; *Head of Adult & Young Adult Services, Librn,* Tara Ferretti; E-mail: tferretti@wlsmail.org; *Head, Children's Servx, Librn,* Vicki DiSanto; E-mail: vdisanto@wlsmail.org; *Head, Circ,* Edith Felis; E-mail: efelis@wlsmail.org; *Head, Tech Serv,* Corinna Hamann; E-mail: chamann@wlsmail.org; Staff 4 (MLS 4)
Founded 1876. Pop 20,434; Circ 241,583
Library Holdings: CDs 3,943; DVDs 4,841; e-books 1,140; Bk Titles 94,475; Per Subs 113
Subject Interests: Local hist
Automation Activity & Vendor Info: (Cataloging) Evergreen; (Circulation) Evergreen; (ILL) Evergreen; (OPAC) Evergreen
Wireless access
Function: 24/7 Electronic res, 24/7 Online cat, Accelerated reader prog, Activity rm, Adult bk club, After school storytime, Archival coll, Art exhibits, Audiobks via web, Bi-weekly Writer's Group, Bk club(s), Bks on

CD, CD-ROM, Children's prog, Computer training, Computers for patron use, Electronic databases & coll, For res purposes, Free DVD rentals, Genealogy discussion group, Holiday prog, Home delivery & serv to seniorr ctr & nursing homes, Homebound delivery serv, ILL available, Instruction & testing, Internet access, Life-long learning prog for all ages, Magazines, Magnifiers for reading, Mail & tel request accepted, Meeting rooms, Movies, Music CDs, Online cat, Online info literacy tutorials on the web & in blackboard, Online ref, Orientations, Outreach serv, OverDrive digital audio bks, Photocopying/Printing, Preschool outreach, Preschool reading prog, Printer for laptops & handheld devices, Prog for adults, Prog for children & young adult, Ref & res, Ref serv available, Scanner, Senior computer classes, Senior outreach, Spoken cassettes & CDs, Spoken cassettes & DVDs, Story hour, Study rm, Summer & winter reading prog, Summer reading prog, Tax forms, Teen prog, Telephone ref, Visual arts prog, Wheelchair accessible, Workshops, Writing prog
Publications: News from Somers Library (Newsletter)
Mem of Westchester Library System
Open Mon, Wed & Fri 10-5, Tues & Thurs 10-8, Sat 10-3
Friends of the Library Group

SONYEA

S GROVELAND CORRECTIONAL FACILITY LIBRARY, 7000 Sonyea Rd, 14556. (Mail add: PO Box 50, 14556-0050), SAN 327-2354. Tel: 585-658-2871. Web Site: doccs.ny.gov/location/groveland-correctional-facility. *Librn,* Ms Maren Kyle; E-mail: maren.kyle@doccs.ny.gov
Library Holdings: Bk Titles 10,000
Automation Activity & Vendor Info: (Cataloging) Follett Software; (Circulation) Follett Software
Restriction: Not open to pub

SOUTH FALLSBURG

P FALLSBURG LIBRARY INC*, 12 Railroad Plaza, 12779. (Mail add: PO Box 730, 12779-0730). Tel: 845-436-6067. FAX: 845-434-1254. E-mail: fbr@rcls.org. Web Site: fallsburglibrary.org. *Dir,* Kelly Wells; Staff 2 (MLS 1, Non-MLS 1)
Founded 1999. Pop 10,217; Circ 36,000
Library Holdings: AV Mats 3,000; Bk Vols 25,000; Per Subs 40
Automation Activity & Vendor Info: (Acquisitions) Horizon; (Cataloging) Horizon; (Circulation) Horizon; (ILL) Horizon; (OPAC) Horizon
Mem of Ramapo Catskill Library System
Open Mon & Thurs 9:30-5, Tues & Wed 9:30-7, Fri 9:30-4, Sun 9:30-2
Friends of the Library Group

SOUTH NEW BERLIN

P SOUTH NEW BERLIN FREE LIBRARY, 3320 State Hwy 8, 13843. (Mail add: PO Box 9, 13843), SAN 312-4789. Tel: 607-859-2420. E-mail: southnewberlinlibrary@gmail.com. Web Site: libraries.4cls.org/southnewberlin. *Libr Dir,* Robin Avolio; *Librn,* Nancy Dibbell; *Librn,* Michelle Reinhardt
Founded 1921. Pop 633; Circ 4,239
Library Holdings: AV Mats 882; Bk Vols 6,760; Per Subs 21
Wireless access
Mem of Four County Library System
Open Mon-Fri 2-6
Friends of the Library Group

SOUTH SALEM

P LEWISBORO LIBRARY*, 15 Main St, 10590. (Mail add: PO Box 477, 10590-0477), SAN 312-4797. Tel: 914-763-3857, 914-875-9004. E-mail: lewisborolibrary@gmail.com. Web Site: www.lewisborolibrary.org. *Dir,* Cynthia Rubino; E-mail: crubino@wlsmail.org; Staff 12 (MLS 4, Non-MLS 8)
Founded 1798. Pop 12,410; Circ 102,000
Library Holdings: Audiobooks 5,000; DVDs 3,000; e-books 6,000; Electronic Media & Resources 127; Large Print Bks 500; Bk Vols 48,000; Per Subs 70; Talking Bks 4,171
Automation Activity & Vendor Info: (OPAC) SirsiDynix
Wireless access
Function: 24/7 Electronic res, 24/7 Online cat, Adult bk club, Audiobks on Playaways & MP3, Audiobks via web, Bks on CD, Children's prog, Computer training, Computers for patron use, Electronic databases & coll, Free DVD rentals, Homebound delivery serv, ILL available, Internet access, Life-long learning prog for all ages, Magazines, Movies, Museum passes, Online cat, OverDrive digital audio bks, Photocopying/Printing, Printer for laptops & handheld devices, Ref & res, Scanner, Senior computer classes, Story hour, Summer reading prog, Tax forms, Teen prog, Wheelchair accessible, Writing prog
Publications: Newsletter
Mem of Westchester Library System
Special Services for the Blind - Bks on CD; Home delivery serv; Large print bks; Playaways (bks on MP3)
Open Mon-Thurs 10-6, Fri 10-5, Sat 10-1 (June-Aug); Mon-Thurs 10-6, Fri 10-5, Sat 10-4 (Sept-May)
Restriction: Pub by appt only
Friends of the Library Group

SOUTHAMPTON

P ROGERS MEMORIAL LIBRARY, 91 Coopers Farm Rd, 11968. SAN 312-4819. Tel: 631-283-0774. FAX: 631-287-6539. Reference FAX: 631-287-6537. Web Site: www.myrml.org. *Dir,* Liz Burns; Tel: 631-283-0774, Ext 501, E-mail: liz@myrml.org; *Head, Computer Serv,* Raymond Larsen; *Head, Tech Serv, ILL,* Annmarie Davies; *Circ Mgr,* Connie Gaud; *Family Dept Supvr,* Marci Byrne; *Reference Dept Supervisor,* Beth Gates; *Adult Programming,* Yvette Postelle; *YA Serv,* Casey Fehn; Staff 48 (MLS 11, Non-MLS 37)
Founded 1895. Pop 14,500; Circ 135,762
Jan 2021-Dec 2021. Mats Exp $4,852,061, Books $116,622, Per/Ser (Incl. Access Fees) $1,976, AV Mat $28,748, Electronic Ref Mat (Incl. Access Fees) $71. Sal $3,269,866
Library Holdings: Audiobooks 151,341; AV Mats 17,454; e-books 458,456; Electronic Media & Resources 610,777; Per Subs 269
Special Collections: Long Island Coll
Automation Activity & Vendor Info: (Acquisitions) Innovative Interfaces, Inc; (Cataloging) Innovative Interfaces, Inc; (Circulation) Innovative Interfaces, Inc; (OPAC) Innovative Interfaces, Inc; (Serials) Innovative Interfaces, Inc
Wireless access
Function: 24/7 Online cat, 3D Printer, Activity rm, Adult bk club, Adult literacy prog, Archival coll, Art exhibits, Art programs, Audio & video playback equip for onsite use, Audiobks on Playaways & MP3, Audiobks via web, AV serv, BA reader (adult literacy), Bilingual assistance for Spanish patrons, Bk club(s), Bks on CD, Children's prog, Citizenship assistance, Computer training, Computers for patron use, Digital talking bks, E-Readers, E-Reserves, Electronic databases & coll, Equip loans & repairs, Games & aids for people with disabilities, Home delivery & serv to seniorr ctr & nursing homes, Homebound delivery serv, ILL available, Instruction & testing, Internet access, Large print keyboards, Magazines, Magnifiers for reading, Meeting rooms, Microfiche/film & reading machines, Movies, Museum passes, Music CDs, Notary serv, Online cat, Outreach serv, Outside serv via phone, mail, e-mail & web, OverDrive digital audio bks, Passport agency, Photocopying/Printing, Printer for laptops & handheld devices, Prog for adults, Prog for children & young adult, Ref & res, Ref serv available, Res assist avail, Scanner, Spanish lang bks, Summer & winter reading prog, Summer reading prog, Tax forms, Teen prog, Telephone ref, Wheelchair accessible, Winter reading prog, Workshops
Mem of Suffolk Cooperative Library System
Open Mon-Thurs 9:30-8, Fri 10-7, Sat 10-5, Sun 1-5
Friends of the Library Group

SOUTHOLD

P SOUTHOLD FREE LIBRARY*, 53705 Main Rd, 11971. (Mail add: PO Box 697, 11971-0697), SAN 312-4843. Tel: 631-765-2077. FAX: 631-765-2197. E-mail: southoldlibrary@gmail.com. Web Site: southoldlibrary.org. *Dir,* Caroline MacArthur; E-mail: caroline@southoldlibrary.org; Staff 15 (MLS 3, Non-MLS 12)
Founded 1797. Pop 6,000; Circ 93,267
Library Holdings: High Interest/Low Vocabulary Bk Vols 30; Bk Titles 38,598; Per Subs 80
Special Collections: Southold History & Genealogy (Whitaker Coll)
Automation Activity & Vendor Info: (Cataloging) Innovative Interfaces, Inc - Sierra; (Circulation) Innovative Interfaces, Inc - Sierra; (Course Reserve) Innovative Interfaces, Inc - Sierra; (ILL) Innovative Interfaces, Inc - Sierra; (Media Booking) Innovative Interfaces, Inc - Sierra; (OPAC) Innovative Interfaces, Inc - Sierra
Wireless access
Mem of Suffolk Cooperative Library System
Special Services for the Blind - Dep for Braille Inst; Talking bks
Open Mon-Fri 9:30-9, Sat 9:30-5, Sun 1-5
Friends of the Library Group

S SOUTHOLD HISTORICAL SOCIETY MUSEUM LIBRARY*, 54325 Main Rd, 11971. (Mail add: PO Box 1, 11971-0001), SAN 327-2192. Tel: 631-765-5500. FAX: 631-765-8510. E-mail: info@southoldhistorical.org. Web Site: www.southoldhistoricalsociety.org. *Exec Dir,* Deanna Witte-Walker; *Colls Mgr,* Amy Folk
Founded 1965
Library Holdings: Bk Vols 1,500
Subject Interests: Local hist
Wireless access

SPARKILL

C SAINT THOMAS AQUINAS COLLEGE*, Lougheed Library, 125 Rte 340, 10976. SAN 312-4851. Tel: 845-398-4219. Reference Tel: 845-398-4218. Web Site: stac.libguides.com/lougheedlibrary. *Libr Dir,* Virginia Dunnigan; Tel: 845-398-4216, E-mail: vdunniga@stac.edu; *Ref & ILL Librn,* Sharon Skopp; Tel: 845-398-4215, E-mail: sskopp@stac.edu; *Syst & Tech Serv Librn,* Yu-Hung Lin; Tel: 845-398-4222, E-mail: ylin@stac.edu; Staff 10 (MLS 5, Non-MLS 5)
Founded 1952. Enrl 1,608; Highest Degree: Master
Library Holdings: Bk Titles 97,000; Bk Vols 110,000; Per Subs 400
Automation Activity & Vendor Info: (Cataloging) LibLime; (Circulation) LibLime
Wireless access
Function: ILL available
Publications: Library Guide
Partic in Southeastern New York Library Resources Council; Westchester Academic Library Directors Organization
Open Mon-Thurs 8am-11pm, Fri 8-4, Sun 1-7

SPENCER

P SPENCER LIBRARY*, 41 N Main St, 14883-9100. (Mail add: PO Box 305, 14883-0305), SAN 312-486X. Tel: 607-589-4496. FAX: 607-589-4271. E-mail: splibrary@htva.net. Web Site: spencernylibrary.org. *Head Librn,* Elizabeth Helmetsie
Founded 1830. Circ 22,689
Library Holdings: Bk Vols 16,427; Per Subs 10
Special Collections: Spencer Needles Coll, 1888-1977
Automation Activity & Vendor Info: (Acquisitions) Innovative Interfaces, Inc
Wireless access
Mem of Finger Lakes Library System
Open Mon 9-2, Tues-Fri 3-8, Sat 10-2

SPENCERPORT

P OGDEN FARMERS' LIBRARY*, 269 Ogden Center Rd, 14559. SAN 312-4878. Tel: 585-617-6181. FAX: 585-352-3406. E-mail: library@ogdenlibrary.com. Web Site: www.ogdenlibrary.com. *Dir,* John Cohen; E-mail: jcohen@ogdenlibrary.com; *Ad,* Kate Vreeland; E-mail: kvreeland@ogdenlibrary.com; *Ch Serv Librn,* Anne Strang; E-mail: astrang@ogdenlibrary.com; *Genealogy Librn, Teen Serv Librn,* Caitlin Crilly; E-mail: ccrilly@ogdenlibrary.com; Staff 17 (MLS 4, Non-MLS 13)
Founded 1817. Pop 16,912; Circ 179,579
Library Holdings: Bk Vols 63,648; Per Subs 136
Special Collections: Genealogy Coll; Local History Coll
Automation Activity & Vendor Info: (Circulation) TLC (The Library Corporation); (OPAC) TLC (The Library Corporation)
Wireless access
Function: Adult bk club, Archival coll, Art exhibits, Audio & video playback equip for onsite use, Audiobks via web, AV serv, Bk reviews (Group), Bks on cassette, Bks on CD, CD-ROM, Children's prog, Computer training, Computers for patron use, E-Reserves, Electronic databases & coll, Family literacy, Free DVD rentals, Genealogy discussion group, Holiday prog, Home delivery & serv to seniorr ctr & nursing homes, Homebound delivery serv, ILL available, Instruction & testing, Internet access, Magnifiers for reading, Mail & tel request accepted, Music CDs, Notary serv, Online cat, Online info literacy tutorials on the web & in blackboard, Online ref, Outreach serv, Outside serv via phone, mail, e-mail & web, OverDrive digital audio bks, Photocopying/Printing, Preschool outreach, Prog for adults, Prog for children & young adult, Ref & res, Ref serv available, Res libr, Scanner, Senior outreach, Serves people with intellectual disabilities, Spoken cassettes & CDs, Spoken cassettes & DVDs, Story hour, Summer & winter reading prog, Tax forms, Teen prog, Telephone ref, VHS videos, Wheelchair accessible, Workshops
Mem of Monroe County Library System
Open Mon-Thurs 9-9, Fri 9-5
Friends of the Library Group

SPRING VALLEY

P FINKELSTEIN MEMORIAL LIBRARY, 24 Chestnut St, 10977. SAN 312-4886. Tel: 845-352-5700. Circulation Tel: 845-352-5700, Ext 250. Reference E-mail: fmlref@rcls.org. Web Site: finkelsteinlibrary.org. *Libr Dir,* Laura Wolven; Tel: 845-352-5700, Ext 283, E-mail: lmwolven@rcls.org; *Head, Adult Serv,* Judy Joseph; Tel: 845-352-5700, Ext 293, E-mail: jjoseph@rcls.org; *Head, Circ,* Elyse Stoller; Tel: 845-352-5700, Ext 227, E-mail: estoller@rcls.org; *Head, Info Tech,* Robert Rowe; Tel: 845-352-5700, Ext 294, E-mail: rrowe@rcls.org; *Head, Tech Serv & Cat,* Kathleen Preston; Tel: 845-352-5700, Ext 218, E-mail: kpreston@rcls.org; *Head, Youth Serv,* Elizabeth Portillo; Tel: 845-352-5700, Ext 235, E-mail: eportillo@rcls.org; *Ch Serv,* Sue Donohue; Tel: 845-352-5700, Ext 235; Staff 45 (MLS 19, Non-MLS 26)
Founded 1917. Pop 100,000; Circ 700,000
Library Holdings: AV Mats 20,000; Bk Vols 225,000; Per Subs 518; Talking Bks 3,000
Subject Interests: Educ, Foreign lang, Holocaust, Local hist
Automation Activity & Vendor Info: (Cataloging) SirsiDynix; (Circulation) SirsiDynix; (ILL) SirsiDynix; (OPAC) SirsiDynix
Wireless access
Publications: ADLIB (Quarterly Newsletter)
Mem of Ramapo Catskill Library System
Partic in Southeastern New York Library Resources Council
Special Services for the Deaf - Assistive tech; Bks on deafness & sign lang
Special Services for the Blind - Aids for in-house use; Assistive/Adapted tech devices, equip & products; Audio mat; Bks on cassette; Bks on CD; Computer with voice synthesizer for visually impaired persons; Home delivery serv; Large print & cassettes; Talking bks
Open Mon-Thurs 9-9, Fri 9-6, Sat & Sun 1-5
Friends of the Library Group
Bookmobiles: 1

SPRINGFIELD CENTER

S SPRINGFIELD LIBRARY*, 129 County Hwy 29A, 13468. (Mail add: PO Box 142, 13468). Tel: 315-858-5802. FAX: 315-858-5876. E-mail: sp.ill@4cls.org. *Dir,* Position Currently Open
Founded 1999
Jan 2020-Dec 2020 Income $15,750, City $15,000, Locally Generated Income $750
Library Holdings: Audiobooks 52; DVDs 790; Bk Vols 9,872
Wireless access
Mem of Four County Library System
Open Mon 12-4 & 6-8, Wed 9-2, Thurs 2-8, Sat 9-Noon

SPRINGVILLE

P HULBERT PUBLIC LIBRARY OF THE TOWN OF CONCORD*, Concord Public, 18 Chapel St, 14141. SAN 312-4908. Tel: 716-592-7742. FAX: 716-592-0399. E-mail: con@buffalolib.org. Web Site: www.buffalolib.org/locations-hours/concord-public-library, www.townofconcordny.com/hulbert_library.php3. *Dir,* Jennifer Morris; Staff 3 (MLS 1, Non-MLS 2)
Library Holdings: Bk Vols 34,000; Per Subs 52
Wireless access
Mem of Buffalo & Erie County Public Library System
Open Tues, Thurs & Sat 10-3, Wed & Fri 12-7

STAATSBURG

P STAATSBURG LIBRARY*, 70 Old Post Rd, 12580-0397. SAN 312-4916. Tel: 845-889-4683. FAX: 845-889-8414. E-mail: staatslibrary@gmail.com. Web Site: staatsburglibrary.org. *Dir,* Lorraine Rothman
Founded 1894. Pop 3,840; Circ 9,550
Library Holdings: Bk Vols 12,023; Per Subs 21
Automation Activity & Vendor Info: (Cataloging) Innovative Interfaces, Inc - Millennium; (Circulation) Innovative Interfaces, Inc - Millennium; (OPAC) Innovative Interfaces, Inc - Millennium
Wireless access
Mem of Mid-Hudson Library System
Open Mon & Wed 10-12 & 2-8, Thurs 2-5, Fri 2-8, Sat 10-2
Friends of the Library Group

STAMFORD

P STAMFORD VILLAGE LIBRARY*, 117 Main St, 12167. SAN 312-4924. Tel: 607-652-5001. FAX: 607-652-5001. E-mail: st.ill@4cls.org. *Mgr,* Pat Parks; E-mail: st.patricia@4cls.org; *Libr Asst,* Fred Hitchcock; E-mail: st.fred@4cls.org
Founded 1908. Pop 1,286; Circ 18,181
Library Holdings: Bk Vols 22,007; Per Subs 29
Special Collections: Local Historical Papers & Memorabilia
Automation Activity & Vendor Info: (Circulation) SirsiDynix; (OPAC) SirsiDynix
Wireless access
Function: 24/7 Electronic res, 24/7 Online cat, Adult bk club, Adult literacy prog, Archival coll, Audiobks via web, Bks on CD, Children's prog, Computer training, Computers for patron use, Doc delivery serv, Electronic databases & coll, Free DVD rentals, ILL available, Internet access, Magazines, Microfiche/film & reading machines, Movies, Music CDs, Online cat, Outreach serv, OverDrive digital audio bks, Photocopying/Printing, Preschool reading prog, Prog for adults, Prog for children & young adult, Senior outreach, Summer reading prog, VHS videos, Workshops, Writing prog
Mem of Four County Library System
Open Mon 12-5, Wed & Fri 10-5, Tues & Thurs 1-7, Sat 11-2

STANFORDVILLE

P STANFORD FREE LIBRARY, 6035 Rte 82, 12581. SAN 312-4932. Tel: 845-868-1341. FAX: 845-868-7482. E-mail: stanfordlibrary@optonline.net. Web Site: www.stanfordlibrary.org. *Dir,* Christa Cerul
Pop 3,495; Circ 16,601
Library Holdings: Bk Vols 12,000; Per Subs 10
Automation Activity & Vendor Info: (Cataloging) Innovative Interfaces, Inc - Millennium; (Circulation) Innovative Interfaces, Inc - Millennium; (OPAC) Innovative Interfaces, Inc - Millennium; (Serials) Innovative Interfaces, Inc - Millennium
Wireless access
Mem of Mid-Hudson Library System
Open Mon & Wed 9-12 & 2-8, Tues, Thurs & Fri 2-8, Sat 9-2

STATEN ISLAND

C COLLEGE OF STATEN ISLAND LIBRARY*, 2800 Victory Blvd, 10314-6609. SAN 354-1770. Tel: 718-982-4001. Circulation Tel: 718-982-4011. Interlibrary Loan Service Tel: 718-982-4014. Reference Tel: 718-982-4010. FAX: 718-982-4002. E-mail: library@csi.cuny.edu. Web Site: www.library.csi.cuny.edu. *Chief Librn,* Wilma L Jones; E-mail: wilma.jones@csi.cuny.edu; Staff 51 (MLS 19, Non-MLS 32)
Founded 1976. Enrl 12,600; Fac 823; Highest Degree: Doctorate
Library Holdings: AV Mats 7,726; e-books 3,000; e-journals 15,000; Electronic Media & Resources 143; Bk Vols 232,510; Per Subs 8,215
Special Collections: Staten Island Coll
Subject Interests: Computer sci, Educ, Engr, Hist, Media culture, Nursing, Polymer chem
Automation Activity & Vendor Info: (Acquisitions) Ex Libris Group; (Cataloging) Ex Libris Group; (Circulation) Ex Libris Group; (Course Reserve) Ex Libris Group; (ILL) OCLC; (OPAC) Ex Libris Group; (Serials) Ex Libris Group
Wireless access
Function: Archival coll, Art exhibits, Audio & video playback equip for onsite use, AV serv, CD-ROM, Distance learning, Doc delivery serv, Electronic databases & coll, Equip loans & repairs, Health sci info serv, ILL available, Internet access, Online ref, Orientations, Photocopying/Printing, Ref & res, Ref serv available, VHS videos, Wheelchair accessible
Publications: CSI Library (Newsletter)
Partic in Metropolitan New York Library Council; OCLC Online Computer Library Center, Inc
Special Services for the Deaf - Assisted listening device; Assistive tech; Closed caption videos; TDD equip
Special Services for the Blind - Assistive/Adapted tech devices, equip & products; Computer with voice synthesizer for visually impaired persons
Open Mon-Thurs 8am-10pm, Fri 8-8, Sat 8:30-7, Sun 12-7
Restriction: Authorized patrons, Authorized scholars by appt, Borrowing privileges limited to fac & registered students, In-house use for visitors, Non-circulating coll, Photo ID required for access

S JACQUES MARCHAIS MUSEUM OF TIBETAN ART LIBRARY*, 338 Lighthouse Ave, 10306. SAN 312-4959. Tel: 718-987-3500. FAX: 718-351-0402. Web Site: www.tibetanmuseum.org. *Exec Dir,* Meg Ventrudo; E-mail: mventrudo@tibetanmuseum.org
Founded 1945
Library Holdings: Bk Vols 1,200
Subject Interests: Archit, Art, Asia, Ethical philos, Lang arts, Oriental culture, Relig studies, Tibet
Wireless access
Restriction: Authorized scholars by appt

M RICHMOND UNIVERSITY MEDICAL CENTER*, Dimitrios Fournarakis Medical Library, 355 Bard Ave, 10310-1664. SAN 312-4991. Tel: 718-818-3117. FAX: 718-818-4720. E-mail: library@rumcsi.org. *Libr Dir,* Andrea Rudner; E-mail: arudner@rumcsi.org
Founded 1925
Library Holdings: AV Mats 168; CDs 67; e-books 63; e-journals 50; Bk Vols 3,000; Per Subs 160
Subject Interests: Cardiology, Gynecology, Internal med, Nursing, Obstetrics, Pathology, Pediatrics, Psychiat, Radiology, Surgery
Automation Activity & Vendor Info: (Cataloging) Professional Software; (OPAC) Professional Software
Wireless access
Function: ILL available
Partic in Basic Health Sciences Library Network; Brooklyn-Queens-Staten Island-Manhattan-Bronx Health Sciences Librarians; National Network of Libraries of Medicine Region 7
Restriction: Open to staff only

C ST JOHN'S UNIVERSITY, Loretto Memorial Library, Staten Island Campus, 300 Howard Ave, 10301. SAN 312-4983. Tel: 718-390-4457. Interlibrary Loan Service Tel: 718-990-6441. Reference Tel: 718-390-4460. FAX: 718-390-4290. Web Site: www.stjohns.edu/libraries/about-libraries/campus-libraries/loretto-memorial-library-staten-island. *Dir,* Lois Cherepon; Tel: 718-390-4521, E-mail: cherepol@stjohns.edu; *Librn,* Ann Jusino; Tel: 718-390-4359, E-mail: jusinoa@stjohns.edu; Staff 2 (MLS 2)
Founded 1972. Enrl 800; Fac 44; Highest Degree: Master
Library Holdings: e-books 18,547; Bk Titles 100,723; Bk Vols 153,566; Per Subs 15
Subject Interests: Educ
Automation Activity & Vendor Info: (Acquisitions) Koha; (Cataloging) Koha; (Circulation) Koha; (Course Reserve) Koha; (ILL) OCLC ILLiad; (OPAC) Koha; (Serials) Koha
Wireless access
Partic in American Theological Library Association; Metropolitan New York Library Council; OCLC Online Computer Library Center, Inc; Westchester Academic Library Directors Organization
Open Mon-Thurs 8am-9pm, Fri 8-4
Friends of the Library Group

S STATEN ISLAND HISTORICAL SOCIETY LIBRARY*, 441 Clarke Ave, 10306. SAN 312-5025. Tel: 718-351-1611, Ext 299. Web Site: www.historicrichmondtown.org. *Library Contact,* Carlotta DeFillo; E-mail: cdefillo@historicrichmondtown.org
Founded 1933
Library Holdings: Bk Vols 5,000
Special Collections: Staten Island Manuscript Coll (1670 to present), 18th & 19th Century History
Subject Interests: Local hist
Wireless access
Function: Archival coll, Bus archives, Photocopying/Printing, Res libr, Res performed for a fee
Publications: Staten Island Historian
Restriction: Non-circulating, Not a lending libr, Open to pub by appt only

S STATEN ISLAND INSTITUTE OF ARTS & SCIENCES*, Archives & Library, Snug Harbor Cultural Ctr, Bldg H, 1000 Richmond Terrace, 10301. SAN 354-1835. Tel: 718-727-1135. FAX: 718-273-5683. Web Site: www.statenislandmuseum.org. *Archives Mgr,* Gabriella Leone; Tel: 718-483-7122, E-mail: GLeone@StatenIslandMuseum.org; Staff 2 (MLS 1, Non-MLS 1)
Founded 1881
Library Holdings: Bk Vols 17,000
Special Collections: Black Community on Staten Island (Crooke Coll & Gravelle Coll); Britton, Desosway & Gratacap Family (Charles G Hine Coll); Conservation History Coll, bks, clippings, letters; Daguerreotypes (H H Cleaves Coll); Davis, Hollick & Anthon Archives; Environmental Coll; Kreischer Family (Chapin Coll); Leng (Harry B Weiss Coll); Manuscript Coll; Staten Island & Environments Coll, docs, maps, photogs, scrapbks; Staten Island Newspaper (Curtis Coll), maps, photogs, print; Staten Island Newspapers from 1828 to 1945, micro; Steele Family (Mabel Abbott Coll); Women's Suffrage (Delvan Coll)
Subject Interests: Archaeology, City planning, Conserv of mat, Environ, Local Black hist, Museology, Natural sci, Staten Island
Wireless access
Restriction: Open by appt only

M STATEN ISLAND UNIVERSITY HOSPITAL/NORTHWELL HEALTH, Charles N Accettola Medical Library, 475 Seaview Ave, 10305. SAN 312-5033. Tel: 718-226-9545. Interlibrary Loan Service Tel: 718-226-9547. FAX: 718-226-8582. E-mail: siuh_library@northwell.edu. Web Site: professionals.northwell.edu/continuing-professional-education/libraries. *Dir, Med Libr,* Yelena Friedman; E-mail: yfriedman@northwell.edu; *Coordr,* Bridget Scanlon; E-mail: bscanlon@northwell.edu; Staff 2 (MLS 1, Non-MLS 1)
Founded 1938
Library Holdings: e-books 38,000; e-journals 11,600
Wireless access
Partic in Brooklyn-Queens-Staten Island-Manhattan-Bronx Health Sciences Librarians; BSHL; Metropolitan New York Library Council; National Network of Libraries of Medicine Region 7; NY NJ-MLA
Open Mon-Fri 9-5

GL SUPREME COURT LIBRARY*, Richmond Supreme Court Law Library, 25 Hyatt St, Rm 515, 10301-1968. SAN 312-505X. Tel: 718-675-8711. FAX: 718-447-6104. *Law Librn,* Anita Postyn; E-mail: apostyn@nycourts.gov; Staff 1 (MLS 1)
Founded 1920
Library Holdings: Bk Titles 1,600; Bk Vols 66,500; Per Subs 200
Wireless access
Open Mon-Fri 9-1

C WAGNER COLLEGE, Horrmann Library, One Campus Rd, 10301. SAN 312-5076. Tel: 718-390-3401. Reference Tel: 718-390-3402. E-mail: library@wagner.edu. Web Site: www.wagner.edu/library. *Libr Dir,* Denis Schaub; Tel: 718-390-3378, E-mail: dschaub@wagner.edu; *Archivist, Instruction Librn,* Lisa Holland; Tel: 718-420-4219, E-mail:

lisa.holland@wagner.edu; *Ref & Instruction Libn,* Daniel Perkins; Tel: 718-390-3379, E-mail: daniel.perkins@wagner.edu; *Tech Serv & Syst Libn,* Catherine Perkins; Tel: 718-390-3377, E-mail: catherine.perkins@wagner.edu; Staff 14 (MLS 5, Non-MLS 9)
Founded 1889. Enrl 2,280; Fac 206; Highest Degree: Master
Library Holdings: e-journals 11,879; Music Scores 1,000; Bk Titles 150,000; Bk Vols 250,000; Per Subs 548; Talking Bks 136; Videos 2,500
Special Collections: Literature (Edwin Markham Coll), bks & monographs
Subject Interests: Chem, Educ, Nursing
Automation Activity & Vendor Info: (Acquisitions) OCLC CatExpress; (Cataloging) OCLC CatExpress; (Circulation) Ex Libris Group; (Course Reserve) OpenAccess Software, Inc; (ILL) OCLC ILLiad
Wireless access
Publications: College Workstudy Handbook; Faculty Guide; Periodicals Holdings List; Student Guide
Partic in Metropolitan New York Library Council
Special Services for the Blind - Computer with voice synthesizer for visually impaired persons
Restriction: Private libr
Friends of the Library Group

STEPHENTOWN

P STEPHENTOWN MEMORIAL LIBRARY, 472 State Rte 43, 12168. SAN 312-5092. Tel: 518-733-5750. E-mail: director@stephentownlibrary.org. Web Site: www.stephentownlibrary.org. *Libr Dir,* Kim Roppolo
Founded 1946. Pop 2,903; Circ 24,771
Jan 2020-Dec 2020 Income $123,025
Library Holdings: Audiobooks 900; Bks on Deafness & Sign Lang 20; CDs 300; DVDs 2,100; Large Print Bks 200; Bk Titles 14,400; Per Subs 24; Videos 100
Special Collections: Grant Seeking (Foundation Center Coll)
Wireless access
Function: Adult bk club, Art exhibits, Audio & video playback equip for onsite use, Audiobks on Playaways & MP3, Audiobks via web, Bks on cassette, Bks on CD, Children's prog, Computer training, Computers for patron use, Digital talking bks, E-Readers, Electronic databases & coll, Family literacy, Free DVD rentals, Govt ref serv, Health sci info serv, Homebound delivery serv, ILL available, Internet access, Life-long learning prog for all ages, Magazines, Magnifiers for reading, Mango lang, Meeting rooms, Movies, Museum passes, Music CDs, Online cat, Online info literacy tutorials on the web & in blackboard, Online ref, Outreach serv, Outside serv via phone, mail, e-mail & web, OverDrive digital audio bks, Photocopying/Printing, Preschool reading prog, Printer for laptops & handheld devices, Prog for adults, Prog for children & young adult, Ref serv available, Scanner, Senior computer classes, Senior outreach, Serves people with intellectual disabilities, Spanish lang bks, Spoken cassettes & CDs, Spoken cassettes & DVDs, Story hour, Summer reading prog, Tax forms, Teen prog, Telephone ref, VHS videos, Wheelchair accessible
Mem of Upper Hudson Library System
Special Services for the Deaf - Bks on deafness & sign lang
Special Services for the Blind - Bks on cassette; Bks on CD; Braille bks; Cassette playback machines; Cassettes; Children's Braille; Copier with enlargement capabilities; Disability awareness prog; Extensive large print coll; Free checkout of audio mat; Home delivery serv; Large print bks; Low vision equip; Playaways (bks on MP3)
Open Mon-Thurs 12-6, Fri 12-5, Sat 10-2
Friends of the Library Group

STILLWATER

S NATIONAL PARK SERVICE*, Saratoga National Historical Park Archives, 648 Rte 32, 12170. SAN 312-5114. Tel: 518-664-9821, Ext 221. FAX: 518-664-9830. Web Site: www.nps.gov/sara. *Curator,* Christine Valosin; E-mail: Christine_Valosin@nps.gov
Founded 1941
Library Holdings: Bk Titles 1,000
Special Collections: Northern Campaign of 1777
Subject Interests: Am Revolution
Wireless access
Restriction: Open by appt only

P STILLWATER PUBLIC LIBRARY*, 662 Hudson Ave, 12170. (Mail add: PO Box 485, 12170-0485), SAN 312-5122. Tel: 518-664-6255. FAX: 518-664-6826. E-mail: stilib@sals.edu. Web Site: stillwater.sals.edu. *Libr Dir,* Sara Kipp; E-mail: skipp@sals.edu; Staff 1 (MLS 1)
Founded 1949. Pop 7,444; Circ 26,931
Jul 2017-Jun 2018 Income $222,495
Library Holdings: Bk Vols 19,354; Per Subs 10
Wireless access
Function: 24/7 Electronic res, 24/7 Online cat, Adult bk club, After school storytime
Mem of Southern Adirondack Library System
Open Mon-Thurs 10-8, Fri & Sat 10-3
Friends of the Library Group

STOCKTON

P MARY E SEYMOUR MEMORIAL FREE LIBRARY*, 22 N Main St, 14784-0432. (Mail add: PO Box 128, 14784-0128), SAN 354-1959. Tel: 716-595-3323. FAX: 716-595-3323. Web Site: www.stocktonlibraries.org. *Dir,* Hannah Abram; E-mail: director@stocktonlibraries.org
Founded 1899. Pop 2,301; Circ 17,928
Library Holdings: Bk Titles 17,000; Bk Vols 27,895; Per Subs 25
Special Collections: Local History (Town of Stockton), bks, church records, military records
Wireless access
Mem of Chautauqua-Cattaraugus Library System
Special Services for the Blind - Bks on cassette
Open Tues & Thurs 1-7, Fri 1-5, Sat 10-2
Friends of the Library Group
Branches: 1
CASSADAGA BRANCH, 18 Maple Ave, Cassadaga, 14718. (Mail add: PO Box 384, Cassadaga, 14718). Tel: 716-595-3822. FAX: 716-595-3822.
Special Services for the Blind - Bks on cassette
Open Mon & Wed 1-7, Fri 9-Noon, Sat 10-2
Friends of the Library Group

STONE RIDGE

P STONE RIDGE PUBLIC LIBRARY*, 3700 Main St, 12484. (Mail add: PO Box 188, 12484), SAN 312-5130. Tel: 845-687-7023. FAX: 845-687-0094. Web Site: stoneridgelibrary.org. *Libr Dir,* Jody Ford; Tel: 845-687-7023, Ext 104, E-mail: jford@stoneridgelibrary.org; *Prog Mgr,* Diane DeChillo; Tel: 845-687-7023, Ext 108, E-mail: dianedechillo@stoneridgelibrary.org; *Ch Serv,* Julianna Arms; Tel: 845-687-7023, Ext 107, E-mail: julianna@stoneridgelibrary.org; Staff 8 (MLS 2, Non-MLS 6)
Founded 1909. Pop 7,500; Circ 66,718
Library Holdings: Bk Vols 25,000; Per Subs 100
Special Collections: Oral History
Automation Activity & Vendor Info: (Circulation) Innovative Interfaces, Inc; (OPAC) Innovative Interfaces, Inc
Wireless access
Mem of Mid-Hudson Library System
Open Mon 11:30-5:30, Tues-Sat 10-4
Friends of the Library Group

J ULSTER COUNTY COMMUNITY COLLEGE*, Macdonald DeWitt Library, 491 Cottekill Rd, 12484. SAN 312-5149. Tel: 845-687-5213. Interlibrary Loan Service Tel: 845-687-5212. Reference Tel: 845-687-5208. FAX: 845-687-5220. E-mail: askref@sunyulster.edu. Web Site: www.sunyulster.edu/library. *Dir, Libr Serv,* Kari Mack; E-mail: mackk@sunyulster.edu; *Asst Libn, Ref,* Judith Capurso; E-mail: capursoj@sunyulster.edu; *Libr Asst, Ref,* Mari Mastronardo; E-mail: mastronm@sunyulster.edu; *Circ,* Lisa Fabiano; E-mail: fabianol@sunyulster.edu; *Tech Serv,* Louise Boyle; E-mail: boylel@sunyulster.edu; Staff 4 (MLS 4)
Founded 1963
Library Holdings: e-books 92,417; e-journals 47,000; Bk Titles 73,365; Bk Vols 80,767
Subject Interests: Local hist
Automation Activity & Vendor Info: (Cataloging) OCLC Connexion; (Circulation) Ex Libris Group; (ILL) OCLC ILLiad; (OPAC) Ex Libris Group; (Serials) Ex Libris Group
Wireless access
Partic in OCLC Online Computer Library Center, Inc; Southeastern New York Library Resources Council; SUNYConnect
Open Mon-Thurs 8-7, Fri 8-5, Sat & Sun 9-3

STONY BROOK

THE LONG ISLAND MUSEUM OF AMERICAN ART, HISTORY & CARRIAGES

S GERSTENBURG CARRIAGE REFERENCE LIBRARY*, 1200 Rte 25A, 11790-1992, SAN 323-5610. Tel: 631-751-0066, Ext 232. FAX: 631-751-0353. E-mail: mail@longislandmuseum.org. Web Site: www.longislandmuseum.org. *Colls Mgr,* Christa Zaros
Founded 1950
Library Holdings: Bk Titles 5,000
Subject Interests: Accoutrements, Carriage archives, Carriage decoration, Carriage design, Carriage per, Horse drawn transportation, Horses
Restriction: Open by appt only

S KATE STRONG HISTORICAL LIBRARY*, 1200 Rte 25A, 11790, SAN 312-5157. Tel: 631-751-0066. FAX: 631-751-0353. E-mail: mail@longislandmuseum.org. Web Site: www.longislandmuseum.org. *Colls Mgr,* Christa Zaros
Founded 1942
Library Holdings: Bk Titles 4,000

Special Collections: Decoys (Otto Johs Memorial Library)
Subject Interests: 19th Cent trade cat, Am art hist, Costumes, Decoys, Hunting, Local Long Island mat
Restriction: Open by appt only

C STONY BROOK UNIVERSITY*, Frank Melville Jr Memorial Library, W-1502 Melville Library, John S Toll Dr, 11794-3300. SAN 354-2017. Tel: 631-632-7100. Circulation Tel: 631-632-7115. Interlibrary Loan Service Tel: 631-632-7133. Reference Tel: 631-632-7110. FAX: 631-632-7116. Web Site: www.library.stonybrook.edu. *Dean of Libr,* Constantia Constantinou; E-mail: Constantia.Constantinou@stonybrook.edu; Staff 70 (MLS 30, Non-MLS 40)
Founded 1957. Enrl 19,487; Fac 1,900; Highest Degree: Doctorate
Library Holdings: CDs 40,910; e-books 2,500; e-journals 62,000; Electronic Media & Resources 300; Microforms 3,837,093; Bk Vols 1,976,172; Per Subs 35,222; Videos 8,087
Special Collections: 19th Century Children's Books; AIDC (Barcoding Industry) Coll; Current Fine Publishing & Printing (Perishable Press Coll); Environmental Defense Coll; Ezra Pound Coll; Fielding Dawson Coll; Hispanic Literature & Culture (Jorge Carrera Andrade Coll); Jacob K Javits Papers; Jacqueline Newman Chinese Cookbook Coll; Long Island Historical Documents (Pre Revolutionary War - Civil War); Robert Creeley Coll; Robert Payne Coll; William Butler Yeats Papers, microform. State Document Depository; US Document Depository
Subject Interests: Behav sci, Engr, Environ studies, Music, Natural sci, Soc sci
Automation Activity & Vendor Info: (Acquisitions) Ex Libris Group; (Cataloging) Ex Libris Group; (Circulation) Ex Libris Group; (Course Reserve) Ex Libris Group; (ILL) OCLC; (Media Booking) OCLC; (OPAC) Ex Libris Group; (Serials) Ex Libris Group
Wireless access
Publications: Daily Bulletin (Newsletter); Library Connections (Biannually); The Screen Porch
Partic in Association of Research Libraries; Long Island Library Resources Council; OCLC Online Computer Library Center, Inc; OCLC Research Library Partnership; Research Libraries Information Network; SUNYConnect
Special Services for the Deaf - Assistive tech; Staff with knowledge of sign lang
Special Services for the Blind - Assistive/Adapted tech devices, equip & products; Audio mat; Copier with enlargement capabilities; Large print bks; Reader equip
Open Mon-Thurs 8:30am-Midnight, Fri 8:30-8, Sat 10-6, Sun Noon-Midnight
Friends of the Library Group

Departmental Libraries:

CHEMISTRY, Chemistry Bldg, C-299, 11794-3425. Tel: 631-632-7145. FAX: 631-632-9191. *Sci Librn,* Clara Y Tran; E-mail: yuet.tran@stonybrook.edu; Staff 2 (MLS 1, Non-MLS 1)
Open Mon-Fri 8:30-5
Friends of the Library Group

CM HEALTH SCIENCES LIBRARY, HST Level 3, Rm 136, 8034 SUNY Stony Brook, 11794-8034, SAN 354-2165. Tel: 631-444-2512. Web Site: www.library.stonybrook.edu/healthsciences. *Head, Health Sci Libr,* Jamie Saragossi; E-mail: jamie.saragossi@stonybrook.edu; Staff 24 (MLS 5, Non-MLS 19)
Founded 1969. Enrl 2,293; Fac 557; Highest Degree: Doctorate
Library Holdings: e-books 4,200; e-journals 10,000; Bk Vols 280,000; Per Subs 20
Special Collections: History of Medicine, Dentistry & Nursing
Subject Interests: Allied health, Basic health sci, Dentistry, Med, Nursing, Soc welfare
Automation Activity & Vendor Info: (Acquisitions) Ex Libris Group; (Cataloging) Ex Libris Group; (Circulation) Ex Libris Group; (Course Reserve) Ex Libris Group; (OPAC) Ex Libris Group; (Serials) Ex Libris Group
Partic in National Network of Libraries of Medicine Region 7; OCLC Online Computer Library Center, Inc; SUNYConnect
Open Mon-Thurs 8:30am-12:30am, Fri 8am-9pm, Sat 10-7, Sun 1pm-12:30am

MARINE & ATMOSPHERIC SCIENCES INFORMATION CENTER, 165 Challenger Hall, 11794-5000. Tel: 631-632-8679. FAX: 631-632-2364. Web Site: www.somas.stonybrook.edu. *Librn,* Donna Sammis; E-mail: donna.sammis@stonybrook.edu
Open Mon-Fri 9-5

MATHEMATICS-PHYSICS-ASTRONOMY, Physics Bldg C-124, 11794-3855. Tel: 631-632-7145. FAX: 631-632-9192. Web Site: www.physics.sunysb.edu. *Assoc Dir,* Sherry Chang; E-mail: sherry.chang@stonybrook.edu
Open Mon-Thurs 8:30am-10pm, Fri 8:30-5, Sat 2-6, Sun 2-10

MUSIC, Melville Library, Rm W1530, 11794-3333. Tel: 631-632-7097. FAX: 631-632-1741. *Head Librn,* Gisele Ira Schierhorst; E-mail: gisele.schierhorst@stonybrook.edu
Open Mon-Thurs 8:30am-9pm, Fri 8:30-5, Sat 2-6, Sun 2-6

SCIENCE & ENGINEERING LIBRARY, Frank Melville Jr Memorial Library N-1001, 11794-3301. Tel: 631-632-7148. FAX: 631-632-7186. *Library Contact,* Robert Tolliver; E-mail: robert.tolliver@stonybrook.edu

STONY CREEK

P STONY CREEK FREE LIBRARY*, 37 Harrisburg Rd, 12878. (Mail add: PO Box 64, 12878-0064), SAN 312-5165. Tel: 518-696-5911. FAX: 518-696-5911. Web Site: stonycreekfreelibrary.sals.edu. *Dir,* Rebecca Gordon; E-mail: rgordon@sals.edu
Founded 1916. Pop 734; Circ 4,803
Library Holdings: AV Mats 1,058; Bk Vols 8,052
Wireless access
Mem of Southern Adirondack Library System
Open Tues, Thurs & Sat 9-1, Wed 1-5, Fri 3-7

STONY POINT

P ROSE MEMORIAL LIBRARY, 79 E Main St, 10980-1699. SAN 312-5173. Tel: 845-786-2100. FAX: 845-786-6042. E-mail: stp@rcls.org. Web Site: www.rosememoriallibrary.org. *Dir,* Alice Meacham; E-mail: ameacham@rcls.org; *Ad,* Oscar Chrin; *Youth Serv Librn,* Susan Babcock; Staff 3 (MLS 2, Non-MLS 1)
Founded 1950. Pop 15,049; Circ 55,371
Jan 2018-Dec 2018 Income $501,596, State $4,414, City $295,000, Locally Generated Income $200,000, Other $41,882. Mats Exp $570,183, Books $30,753, AV Mat $8,733, Electronic Ref Mat (Incl. Access Fees) $4,314. Sal $350,417 (Prof $124,596)
Library Holdings: Audiobooks 2,375; AV Mats 3,888; CDs 1,024; DVDs 3,483; e-books 20,596; Bk Vols 26,960; Per Subs 78
Subject Interests: Local hist
Automation Activity & Vendor Info: (Cataloging) SirsiDynix; (Circulation) SirsiDynix; (OPAC) SirsiDynix
Wireless access
Function: 24/7 Electronic res, 24/7 Online cat, Adult bk club, Art exhibits, Art programs, Audiobks via web, AV serv, Bk club(s), Bks on CD, Children's prog, Computer training, Computers for patron use, Electronic databases & coll, Free DVD rentals, Holiday prog, Homebound delivery serv, ILL available, Internet access, Large print keyboards, Life-long learning prog for all ages, Magazines, Magnifiers for reading, Mail & tel request accepted, Mail loans to mem, Movies, Museum passes, Music CDs, Notary serv, Online cat, OverDrive digital audio bks, Photocopying/Printing, Preschool outreach, Preschool reading prog, Prog for adults, Prog for children & young adult, Ref & res, Ref serv available, Scanner, Senior outreach, Spanish lang bks, STEM programs, Story hour, Summer reading prog, Tax forms, Teen prog, Telephone ref, Wheelchair accessible
Mem of Ramapo Catskill Library System
Open Mon & Wed 10-7:30, Tues, Thurs & Fri 10-4:30, Sat 10-3:30, Sun 12-3:30
Restriction: Free to mem
Friends of the Library Group

STORMVILLE

S NEW YORK STATE DEPARTMENT OF CORRECTIONAL SERVICES*, Green Haven Correctional Facility Library, 594 Rte 216, 12582. SAN 354-2254. Tel: 845-221-2711, Ext 4562. *Library Contact,* Eileen Pucci; E-mail: eileen.pucci@doccs.ny.gov; Staff 1.5 (MLS 1, Non-MLS 0.5)
Founded 1942
Library Holdings: AV Mats 200; Large Print Bks 30; Bk Vols 7,000; Per Subs 99; Spec Interest Per Sub 30; Talking Bks 50
Special Collections: Black History Coll; Spanish Coll
Subject Interests: Coping skills mat, Occult
Automation Activity & Vendor Info: (Cataloging) Follett Software; (Circulation) Follett Software
Wireless access
Partic in Northern New York Library Network
Special Services for the Blind - Bks on cassette
Restriction: Not open to pub

SUFFERN

J ROCKLAND COMMUNITY COLLEGE LIBRARY, 145 College Rd, 10901. SAN 312-519X. Tel: 845-574-4000. Circulation Tel: 845-574-4408. Interlibrary Loan Service Tel: 845-574-4412. Reference Tel: 845-574-4097. FAX: 845-574-4473. E-mail: library@sunyrockland.edu. Web Site: libguides.sunyrockland.edu/homepage, www.sunyrockland.edu/campus-life/library. *Access Serv Librn,* Sarah Levy; Tel: 845-574-4472, E-mail: slevy@sunyrockland.edu; *Electronic Res Librn,* Clare O'Dowd; Tel: 845-754-4402, E-mail: codowd@sunyrockland.edu; *Tech Serv,* Kim Weston; Tel: 845-574-4407, E-mail: kweston@sunyrockland.edu; Staff 11 (MLS 4, Non-MLS 7)
Founded 1959. Enrl 5,500; Fac 500; Highest Degree: Associate

Sept 2021-Aug 2022 Income $1,000,000. Mats Exp $319,500, Books $36,500, Other Print Mats $18,000, AV Mat $15,000, Electronic Ref Mat (Incl. Access Fees) $250,000. Sal $700,300 (Prof $440,300)
Library Holdings: DVDs 5,200; e-books 305,000; e-journals 251,000; Electronic Media & Resources 120,000; Bk Titles 28,000; Per Subs 97
Automation Activity & Vendor Info: (Acquisitions) Ex Libris Group; (Cataloging) Ex Libris Group; (Circulation) Ex Libris Group; (Course Reserve) Ex Libris Group; (Discovery) Ex Libris Group; (ILL) OCLC Online; (OPAC) Ex Libris Group; (Serials) EBSCO Online
Wireless access
Function: 24/7 Electronic res, 24/7 Online cat, Activity rm, Archival coll, AV serv, Computers for patron use, Doc delivery serv, Electronic databases & coll, Health sci info serv, ILL available, Internet access, Magazines, Meeting rooms, Movies, Online cat, Online ref, Outside serv via phone, mail, e-mail & web, OverDrive digital audio bks, Photocopying/Printing, Printer for laptops & handheld devices, Ref & res, Ref serv available, Scanner, Study rm
Partic in Ex Libris Aleph; OCLC Online Computer Library Center, Inc; Southeastern New York Library Resources Council; SUNYConnect; Westchester Academic Library Directors Organization

S SALVATION ARMY SCHOOL FOR OFFICER TRAINING*, Brengle Library, 201 Lafayette Ave, 10901. SAN 312-5203. Tel: 845-368-7228. FAX: 845-357-6644. Web Site: tsacfotny.salvationarmy.org/ny/library. *Libr Dir,* Robin Rader; E-mail: RRader@use.salvationarmy.org; *Librn, Tech Serv,* Emily Nevill; E-mail: Emily.Nevill@use.salvationarmy.org; *Asst Librn,* Jose Rodriguez-Morell; E-mail: Jose.Rodriguez-Morell@USE.SalvationArmy.Org; Staff 3 (MLS 1, Non-MLS 2)
Founded 1936. Enrl 90
Library Holdings: Bk Titles 22,000; Bk Vols 27,000; Per Subs 225
Special Collections: Salvation Army Publications
Automation Activity & Vendor Info: (Cataloging) CASPR; (Circulation) CASPR; (OPAC) CASPR
Wireless access
Partic in Southeastern New York Library Resources Council
Open Mon-Thurs 8:30-10, Fri & Sat 8:30-4

P SUFFERN FREE LIBRARY*, 210 Lafayette Ave, 10901. SAN 312-5211. Tel: 845-357-1237. FAX: 845-357-3156. E-mail: circ@suffernfreelibrary.org. Web Site: www.suffernfreelibrary.org. *Dir,* Carol Connell-Connor; *Head, Ad Ref Serv,* Amy LaRocca; E-mail: alarocca@rcls.org; *Head, Children's Servx,* Jennifer Smith; E-mail: jknoerze@rcls.org; *Head, Circ Serv,* Nancy Wendt; E-mail: nwendt@rcls.org; *Commun Serv,* Miguelina Molina; E-mail: mmolina@rcls.org; *Teen Serv,* Jennifer Cohen; E-mail: jcohen@rcls.org; Staff 38 (MLS 9, Non-MLS 29)
Founded 1926. Pop 27,426; Circ 518,043
Library Holdings: AV Mats 19,599; DVDs 9,438; Electronic Media & Resources 41,108; Bk Vols 137,639; Per Subs 280
Subject Interests: Local hist
Automation Activity & Vendor Info: (Acquisitions) SirsiDynix; (Cataloging) SirsiDynix
Wireless access
Publications: Newsletter (Bimonthly)
Mem of Ramapo Catskill Library System
Open Mon-Thurs 10-9, Fri & Sat 10-5, Sun 12-5

SYOSSET

SR ORTHODOX CHURCH IN AMERICA, Office of History & Archives, 6850 N Hempstead Tpk, 11791. (Mail add: PO Box 675, 11791-0675), SAN 327-2176. Tel: 516-922-0550, Ext 121. Web Site: oca.org/history-archives. *Archivist,* Alexis Liberovsky; E-mail: alex@oca.org
Library Holdings: Bk Vols 1,000; Per Subs 200
Wireless access
Restriction: Open by appt only

P SYOSSET PUBLIC LIBRARY*, 225 S Oyster Bay Rd, 11791-5897. SAN 312-5254. Tel: 516-921-7161. Reference Tel: 516-921-7161, Ext 217. Administration Tel: 516-921-7151, Ext 213. FAX: 516-921-8771. E-mail: spladministration@syossetlibrary.org. Web Site: www.syossetlibrary.org. *Dir,* Karen Liebman; *Asst Dir,* Pam Martin; *Head, Children's Servx,* Sue Ann Reale; *Syst Adminr,* Megan Kass; Staff 79 (MLS 34, Non-MLS 45)
Founded 1961. Pop 33,716; Circ 237,693
Library Holdings: Bk Vols 247,155; Per Subs 339
Subject Interests: Local hist
Automation Activity & Vendor Info: (Acquisitions) Innovative Interfaces, Inc - Millennium
Wireless access
Publications: Newsletter
Mem of Nassau Library System
Open Mon-Thurs 9-9, Fri 10-6, Sat 9-5, Sun 12-5
Friends of the Library Group

SYRACUSE

L BOND, SCHOENECK & KING, PLLC*, Law Library, One Lincoln Ctr, 13202-1355. SAN 372-2384. Tel: 315-218-8000. FAX: 315-218-8100. Web Site: www.bsk.com. *Dir,* Maureen T Kays; *Law Librn,* Allison Perry; Staff 3 (MLS 2, Non-MLS 1)
Library Holdings: Bk Vols 25,000; Per Subs 100
Partic in Central New York Library Resources Council
Open Mon-Fri 9-5

M CROUSE HEALTH LIBRARY, 736 Irving Ave, 13210. SAN 312-5327. Tel: 315-470-7380. FAX: 315-470-7443. E-mail: library@crouse.org. Web Site: www.crouse.org/library. *Libr Mgr,* Ellen Owens; Staff 1 (MLS 1)
Founded 1916
Special Collections: Nursing Archives
Subject Interests: Healthcare, Med, Nursing
Automation Activity & Vendor Info: (OPAC) LibraryWorld, Inc
Wireless access
Function: 24/7 Electronic res, 24/7 Online cat, Archival coll, Audio & video playback equip for onsite use, Computers for patron use, Doc delivery serv, Electronic databases & coll, Health sci info serv, Mail & tel request accepted, Online cat, Online info literacy tutorials on the web & in blackboard, Online ref, Orientations, Outreach serv, Outside serv via phone, mail, e-mail & web, Photocopying/Printing, Ref & res, Ref serv available, Wheelchair accessible
Partic in Central New York Library Resources Council; National Network of Libraries of Medicine Region 7

S ERIE CANAL MUSEUM RESEARCH LIBRARY*, 318 Erie Blvd E, 13202. SAN 312-5289. Tel: 315-471-0593. FAX: 315-471-7220. E-mail: curator@eriecanalmuseum.org. Web Site: eriecanalmuseum.org. *Curator of Coll,* Ashley Maready; Tel: 315-471-0593, Ext 13
Library Holdings: Bk Titles 500; Bk Vols 5,000; Per Subs 50
Special Collections: Erie Canal (State Engineers & Surveyors), doc
Subject Interests: NY State canal hist
Open Mon-Sat 10-5, Sun 10-3 (10-5 Dec)
Restriction: Non-circulating, Researchers only

S EVERSON MUSEUM OF ART LIBRARY*, Richard V Smith Art Reference Library, 401 Harrison St, 13202. SAN 312-5335. Tel: 315-474-6064, Ext 309. FAX: 315-474-6943. Web Site: www.everson.org. *Curator,* Garth Johnson; E-mail: gjohnson@everson.org
Founded 1896
Library Holdings: Bk Vols 16,400; Per Subs 20
Special Collections: American Ceramics, ms; Archives of Ceramic National Exhibitions, 1932-present
Subject Interests: Am, Ceramics, Exhibition catalogs, Oriental art
Open Mon & Thurs 9-3

P FAIRMOUNT COMMUNITY LIBRARY, 406 Chapel Dr, 13219. SAN 312-5343. Tel: 315-487-8933. FAX: 315-484-9475. E-mail: fclcoordinator@gmail.com. Web Site: fairmountlibrary.org. *Dir,* Brenda Shea; E-mail: bshea@onlib.org
Founded 1957. Pop 5,491; Circ 89,623
Library Holdings: Bk Vols 26,214; Per Subs 40
Subject Interests: Adult fiction
Automation Activity & Vendor Info: (Cataloging) Innovative Interfaces, Inc; (Circulation) Innovative Interfaces, Inc; (OPAC) Innovative Interfaces, Inc
Wireless access
Mem of Onondaga County Public Libraries
Open Mon-Thurs 11-7, Fri 11-5, Sat 11-2

L HANCOCK ESTABROOK, LLP, Law Library, 1800 AXA Tower One, 100 Madison St, 13202. SAN 327-5302. Tel: 315-565-4500. FAX: 315-565-4600. Web Site: www.hancocklaw.com. *Law Librn,* Donna Byrne; Tel: 315-565-4706, Fax: 315-565-4806, E-mail: dbyrne@hancocklaw.com; Staff 2 (MLS 1, Non-MLS 1)
Founded 1889
Library Holdings: Bk Titles 2,128; Per Subs 50
Subject Interests: Employment, Environ, Estates, Health law, Intellectual property, Labor, Real estate, Tax, Trial practice law
Automation Activity & Vendor Info: (Acquisitions) Inmagic, Inc.; (Cataloging) Inmagic, Inc.; (Circulation) Inmagic, Inc.
Function: Doc delivery serv, Ref serv available
Restriction: Private libr

C LE MOYNE COLLEGE, Noreen Reale Falcone Library, 1419 Salt Springs Rd, 13214. SAN 312-536X. Tel: 315-445-4153. Circulation Tel: 315-445-4330. Interlibrary Loan Service Tel: 315-445-4333. Administration Tel: 315-445-4320. FAX: 315-445-4642. Web Site: lemoyne.edu/library. *Libr Dir,* Inga Barnello; Tel: 315-445-4321, E-mail: barnello@lemoyne.edu; *Head, Pub Serv,* Lisa Chaudhuri; Tel:

315-445-4681, E-mail: doylel@lemoyne.edu; *Research Servs Librn*, Phoebe DiSalvo-Harms; Tel: 315-445-4326, E-mail: desalvpa@lemoyne.edu; *Research Servs Librn*, Virginia Young; E-mail: youngvp@lemoyne.edu; *Sci Librn*, Kari Zhe-Heimerman; Tel: 315-445-4627, E-mail: zheheikm@lemoyne.edu; *Syst Librn*, Tom Keays; Tel: 315-445-4322, E-mail: keaysht@lemoyne.edu; *Tech Serv Librn*, I-Chene Tai; Tel: 315-445-4331, E-mail: tai@lemoyne.edu. Subject Specialists: *Bus, Educ*, Lisa Chaudhuri; *Communications, English lit, Film, Humanities, Philos, Relig studies*, Phoebe DiSalvo-Harms; *Health sci, Nursing, Occupational therapy, Physicians assistance studies, Psychol*, Virginia Young; *Computer sci, Info syst, Math*, Tom Keays; *Communications, Music, Theatre*, I-Chene Tai; Staff 11 (MLS 7, Non-MLS 4)
Founded 1946. Fac 323; Highest Degree: Doctorate
Jun 2019-May 2020 Income $1,749,217, State $6,501, Federal $61,789, Locally Generated Income $111,642, Parent Institution $1,569,285
Library Holdings: CDs 992; Music Scores 545
Special Collections: Danny Biasone Syracuse Nationals Coll; Irish Literature (Father William Noon, S J Coll); Jesuitica (Jesuit History); McGrath Music Coll
Subject Interests: Archives, Philos, Relig
Automation Activity & Vendor Info: (Acquisitions) Innovative Interfaces, Inc; (Cataloging) Innovative Interfaces, Inc; (Circulation) Innovative Interfaces, Inc; (Course Reserve) Innovative Interfaces, Inc; (ILL) OCLC WorldShare Interlibrary Loan; (Media Booking) Innovative Interfaces, Inc; (OPAC) Innovative Interfaces, Inc; (Serials) Innovative Interfaces, Inc
Wireless access
Function: Archival coll, Art exhibits, Audio & video playback equip for onsite use, Computers for patron use, Doc delivery serv, E-Reserves, Electronic databases & coll, Health sci info serv, ILL available, Internet access, Magazines, Meeting rooms, Music CDs, Online cat, Online info literacy tutorials on the web & in blackboard, Online ref, Outside serv via phone, mail, e-mail & web, Photocopying/Printing, Printer for laptops & handheld devices, Ref & res, Ref serv available, Res assist avail, Scanner, Telephone ref, Wheelchair accessible
Publications: Bibliography of Le Moyne College Authors (1946-1992)
Partic in Central New York Library Resources Council; OCLC Online Computer Library Center, Inc
Special Services for the Deaf - Accessible learning ctr
Open Mon-Thurs 8am-2am, Fri 8-7, Sat 9-7, Sun 9am-2am
Restriction: Badge access after hrs, Open to pub for ref & circ; with some limitations

L MACKENZIE, HUGHES LLP*, Law Library, Mackenzie Hughes Tower, 440 S Warren St, 13202. (Mail add: PO Box 4967, 13221-4967), SAN 312-5378. Tel: 315-474-7571. FAX: 315-474-6409. E-mail: info@mackenziehughes.com. Web Site: www.mackenziehughes.com. *Libr Admin*, Position Currently Open
Library Holdings: Bk Vols 16,500; Per Subs 110
Subject Interests: Civil litigation, Corporate, Employment law, Estates, Labor law, Real estate, Tax, Worker compensation
Partic in Proquest Dialog
Open Mon-Fri 9-5

S MANUFACTURERS ASSOCIATION OF CENTRAL NEW YORK LIBRARY*, 5788 Widewaters Pkwy, 13214. SAN 312-5386. Tel: 315-474-4201. FAX: 315-474-0524. Web Site: www.macny.org. *Library Contact*, Patty Clark; Tel: 315-474-4201, Ext 10, E-mail: pclark@macny.org
Library Holdings: Bk Vols 2,100; Per Subs 25
Subject Interests: Collective bargaining, Human resources, Unions
Open Mon-Fri 8:30-5

GL NEW YORK STATE UNIFIED COURT SYSTEM, Supreme Court Onondaga Law Library, Onondaga County Courthouse, 401 Montgomery St, 13202. SAN 312-5424. Tel: 315-671-1150. Reference Tel: 315-671-1151. Toll Free Tel: 800-268-7869. FAX: 315-671-1160. E-mail: Onondaga_Law_Library@NYCourts.gov. Web Site: www.nycourts.gov/library/onondaga. *Law Librn*, Ellen R Fuller; E-mail: efuller@nycourts.gov; Staff 4 (MLS 1, Non-MLS 3)
Founded 1849
Library Holdings: Bk Titles 15,556; Bk Vols 165,000; Per Subs 600
Special Collections: Native American Law Materials. State Document Depository
Subject Interests: Extensive NY state, Fed legal mats, Shared fed dep
Wireless access
Restriction: Open by appt only

J ONONDAGA COMMUNITY COLLEGE*, Sidney B Coulter Library, 4585 W Seneca Tpk, 13215-4585. SAN 312-5432. Tel: 315-498-2334. Interlibrary Loan Service Tel: 315-498-2338. FAX: 315-498-7213. E-mail: library@sunyocc.edu. Web Site: library.sunyocc.edu. *Chairperson*, Pauline Lynch Shostack; Tel: 315-498-2708, E-mail: shostacp@sunyocc.edu; *Acq Librn, Cat Librn*, Jeffrey Harr; Tel: 315-498-2144, E-mail: harrj@sunyocc.edu; *Archives Librn, Ref Librn*, Jessamyn Magri; Tel: 315-498-2135, E-mail: j.a.magri@sunyocc.edu; *Circ Librn, Instruction Librn, ILL Librn*, Fantasia Thorne-Ortiz; Tel: 315-498-2337, E-mail: f.a.thorne-ortiz@sunyocc.edu; *Electronic Res Librn, Media Serv, Reserves*, Lisa Hoff; Tel: 315-498-2340, E-mail: l.m.hoff@sunyocc.edu; Staff 8 (MLS 7, Non-MLS 1)
Founded 1962. Enrl 11,886; Fac 1,349; Highest Degree: Associate
Sept 2015-Aug 2016 Income $1,143,248. Mats Exp $176,697, Books $56,960, Per/Ser (Incl. Access Fees) $58,148, Micro $8,241, AV Equip $749, AV Mat $3,215, Electronic Ref Mat (Incl. Access Fees) $39,864, Presv $196. Sal $922,119 (Prof $461,168)
Library Holdings: Audiobooks 126; Bks on Deafness & Sign Lang 75; CDs 3,863; DVDs 3,250; e-books 296,511; e-journals 7; Electronic Media & Resources 7; Microforms 452; Bk Titles 55,969; Bk Vols 77,854; Per Subs 123; Videos 222
Special Collections: Central New York History; Faculty Authors; Local History Coll; Onondaga Community College Archives
Automation Activity & Vendor Info: (Acquisitions) Ex Libris Group; (Cataloging) Ex Libris Group; (Circulation) Ex Libris Group; (Course Reserve) Ex Libris Group; (ILL) OCLC ILLiad; (Media Booking) Ex Libris Group; (OPAC) Ex Libris Group; (Serials) EBSCO Online
Wireless access
Publications: Library Brochure; Periodical Holdings
Partic in Central New York Library Resources Council; OCLC Online Computer Library Center, Inc; SUNYConnect; Westchester Academic Library Directors Organization
Special Services for the Deaf - Bks on deafness & sign lang; Closed caption videos
Special Services for the Blind - Accessible computers; Closed caption display syst; Computer with voice synthesizer for visually impaired persons; Internet workstation with adaptive software; Large screen computer & software; Screen enlargement software for people with visual disabilities; Screen reader software; Sound rec; ZoomText magnification & reading software
Open Mon-Thurs 8am-9pm, Fri 8-4:30, Sun 12-6
Restriction: Circ limited

P ONONDAGA COUNTY PUBLIC LIBRARIES*, Robert P Kinchen Central Library, The Galleries of Syracuse, 447 S Salina St, 13202-2494. SAN 354-2319. Tel: 315-435-1900. Reference E-mail: reference@onlib.org. Web Site: www.onlib.org. *Exec Dir*, Janet Park; E-mail: director@onlib.org; *Communications Dir*, Kathy Coffta Sims; E-mail: kcoffta@onlib.org; *Dir, Info Syst*, Dane A Dell; E-mail: ddell@onlib.org; *Adminr, Libr Operations*, Charles Diede; E-mail: cdiede@onlib.org; *Br Serv Adminr & Initiatives*, Dawn Marmor; E-mail: dmarmor@onlib.org; *Br Mgr*, Rene Battelle; E-mail: rbattelle@onlib.org; Staff 52 (MLS 52)
Founded 1852. Pop 467,026; Circ 1,569,383
Library Holdings: Bk Vols 1,700,000
Special Collections: Foundation Center; Historic Syracuse, microfiche. US Document Depository
Subject Interests: Genealogy, Literacy, Local hist
Automation Activity & Vendor Info: (Cataloging) Innovative Interfaces, Inc; (Circulation) Innovative Interfaces, Inc; (OPAC) Innovative Interfaces, Inc
Wireless access
Member Libraries: Baldwinsville Public Library; Community Library of DeWitt & Jamesville; East Syracuse Free Library; Elbridge Free Library; Fairmount Community Library; Fayetteville Free Library; Jordan Bramley Library; LaFayette Public Library; Liverpool Public Library; Manlius Library; Marcellus Free Library; Maxwell Memorial Library; Minoa Library; Northern Onondaga Public Library; Onondaga Free Library; Salina Library; Skaneateles Library Association; Solvay Public Library; Tully Free Library
Partic in Central New York Library Resources Council; OCLC Online Computer Library Center, Inc
Special Services for the Deaf - TDD equip; TTY equip; Videos & decoder
Special Services for the Blind - Reader equip
Open Mon, Thurs & Fri 8:30-5, Tues & Wed 8:30-7:30, Sat 9-5
Friends of the Library Group
Branches: 10
BEAUCHAMP BRANCH LIBRARY, 2111 S Salina St, 13205, SAN 354-2343. Tel: 315-435-3395. FAX: 315-435-2729. Web Site: www.onlib.org/locations/city-libraries/beauchamp-branch-library. *Br Mgr*, Ossie Edwards; E-mail: oedwards@onlib.org
Open Mon, Wed, Fri & Sat 9-5, Tues & Thurs 9-7:30
BETTS BRANCH LIBRARY, 4862 S Salina St, 13205, SAN 354-2378. Tel: 315-435-1940. FAX: 315-435-1944. Web Site: www.onlib.org/locations/city-libraries/betts-branch-library. *Br Mgr*, Jane Kalkbrenner; E-mail: jkalkbrenner@onlib.org
Open Mon & Wed 9-7:30, Tues, Thurs, Fri & Sat 9-5, Sun 1-5
HAZARD BRANCH LIBRARY, 1620 W Genesee St, 13204, SAN 354-2408. Tel: 315-435-5326. Web Site: www.onlib.org/locations/city-libraries/hazard-branch-library. *Br Mgr*, Carol Johnson; E-mail: cajohns@onlib.org
Open Mon, Wed, Fri & Sat 9-5, Tues & Thurs 9-7:30
Friends of the Library Group

MUNDY BRANCH LIBRARY, 1204 S Geddes St, 13204, SAN 354-2432. Tel: 315-435-3797. FAX: 315-435-8557. Web Site: www.onlib.org/locations/city-libraries/mundy-branch-library. *Br Mgr,* Rebecca Maguire; E-mail: rmaguire@onlib.org
Open Mon, Tues & Thurs-Sat 9-5, Wed 9-7:30
Friends of the Library Group

PAINE BRANCH LIBRARY, 113 Nichols Ave, 13206, SAN 354-2467. Tel: 315-435-5442. FAX: 315-435-3553. Web Site: www.onlib.org/locations/city-libraries/paine-branch-library. *Br Mgr,* Katie Hayduke; E-mail: khayduke@onlib.org
Open Mon & Tues 9-7:30, Wed-Sat 9-5

PETIT BRANCH LIBRARY, 105 Victoria Pl, 13210, SAN 354-2491. Tel: 315-435-3636. FAX: 315-435-2731. Web Site: www.onlib.org/locations/city-libraries/petit-branch-library. *Br Mgr,* Jane Kalkbrenner; E-mail: jkalkbrenner@onlib.org
Open Mon & Thurs 9-7:30, Tues, Wed, Fri & Sat 9-5

SOULE BRANCH LIBRARY, 101 Springfield Rd, 13214, SAN 354-2521. Tel: 315-435-5320. FAX: 315-435-5322. Web Site: www.onlib.org/locations/city-libraries/soule-branch-library. *Br Mgr,* Joanne Teska; E-mail: jteska@onlib.org
Open Mon & Thurs-Sat 9-5, Tues & Wed 9-7:30, Sun 1-5

SOUTHWEST COMMUNITY CENTER, 401 South Ave, 13204, SAN 354-2610. Tel: 315-671-5814. Web Site: www.onlib.org/locations/city-libraries/syracuse-community-connections-library. *Librn,* Dan Smith
Open Mon-Thurs 11-5

SYRACUSE NORTHEAST COMMUNITY CENTER, 716 Hawley Ave, 13203, SAN 354-2580. Tel: 315-472-6343. Web Site: www.onlib.org/locations/city-libraries/syracuse-northeast-community-center. *Librn,* Tatiana Sahm
Open Mon-Fri 10-5

WHITE BRANCH BRANCH LIBRARY, 763 Butternut St, 13208, SAN 354-2556. Tel: 315-435-3519. FAX: 315-435-3367. Web Site: www.onlib.org/locations/city-libraries/white-branch-library. *Br Mgr,* Renate Dunsmore; E-mail: rcdunsmore@onlib.org
Open Mon, Tues, Fri & Sat 9-5, Wed & Thurs 9-7:30

P ONONDAGA FREE LIBRARY*, 4840 W Seneca Tpk, 13215. SAN 312-5440. Tel: 315-492-1727. FAX: 315-492-1323. E-mail: info@oflibrary.org. Web Site: www.oflibrary.org. *Libr Dir,* Susan Morgan; E-mail: smorgan@oflibrary.org; *Adult/YA Serv Librn, Asst Libr Dir,* Alyssa Newton; *Digital Serv Librn, Tech Librn,* Chantal Rotherman; *Youth Serv,* Maggie Gall-Maynard; Staff 4 (MLS 2, Non-MLS 2)
Founded 1961. Pop 26,000; Circ 139,010
Library Holdings: AV Mats 5,086; Bk Vols 31,459; Per Subs 173
Automation Activity & Vendor Info: (Cataloging) Innovative Interfaces, Inc; (Circulation) Innovative Interfaces, Inc
Wireless access
Mem of Onondaga County Public Libraries
Open Mon-Thurs 9-8:30, Fri & Sat 10-5, Sun 1-5
Friends of the Library Group

M SAINT JOSEPH'S HOSPITAL HEALTH CENTER*, College of Nursing & Medical Library, 206 Prospect Ave, 13203. SAN 312-5467. Tel: 315-448-5053, 315-466-5040. FAX: 315-423-6804. Web Site: www.sjhcon.edu/campus-hospital, www.sjhsyr.org. *Mgr,* Antonina Hylen; E-mail: antonina.hylen@sjhsyr.org; *Librn,* Peter Mathe; E-mail: peter.mathe@sjhsyr.org; *Computer Serv,* Matthew Dwyer; E-mail: matthew.dwyer@sjhsyr.org; Staff 4 (MLS 3, Non-MLS 1)
Founded 1948
Library Holdings: DVDs 20; e-books 60; e-journals 500; Bk Vols 4,500; Per Subs 100; Videos 250
Subject Interests: Nursing, Nursing hist
Automation Activity & Vendor Info: (Cataloging) EOS International; (Circulation) EOS International; (OPAC) EOS International
Wireless access
Publications: Accession List (Monthly)
Partic in Central New York Library Resources Council
Open Mon-Fri 8am-9pm, Sat & Sun 12:30-9

C STATE UNIVERSITY OF NEW YORK, COLLEGE OF ENVIRONMENTAL SCIENCE & FORESTRY, F Franklin Moon Library, One Forestry Dr, 13210. SAN 312-5483. Tel: 315-470-6711. FAX: 315-470-4766. Web Site: www.esf.edu/moonlib. *Dir of Libr,* Matthew R Smith; Tel: 315-470-6724; *Archives,* Jane Verostek; Tel: 315-470-6718, E-mail: jmveros@esf.edu; *Circ,* Nan Clark; Tel: 315-470-6726, E-mail: nfclark@esf.ede; *ILL,* Ruth Owens; Tel: 315-470-4780, E-mail: rmowens@esf.edu; Staff 9 (MLS 5, Non-MLS 4)
Founded 1911. Enrl 2,100; Fac 125; Highest Degree: Doctorate
Library Holdings: e-journals 67,956; Electronic Media & Resources 168; Bk Vols 135,258
Subject Interests: Environ studies, Forestry, Landscape archit, Natural res, Outdoor recreation, Paper sci, Plant pathology, Polymer chem
Automation Activity & Vendor Info: (Acquisitions) Ex Libris Group; (Cataloging) Ex Libris Group; (Circulation) Ex Libris Group; (ILL) OCLC ILLiad; (OPAC) Ex Libris Group; (Serials) Ex Libris Group
Wireless access
Publications: Point of Use Guides (Newsletter)
Partic in Central New York Library Resources Council; OCLC Online Computer Library Center, Inc; SUNYConnect
Open Mon-Thurs 8am-10pm, Fri 8-5, Sat 12-6, Sun 2-10
Friends of the Library Group

CM SUNY UPSTATE MEDICAL UNIVERSITY*, Health Sciences Library, 766 Irving Ave, 13210-1602. SAN 312-5475. Tel: 315-464-7091. E-mail: library@upstate.edu. Web Site: library.upstate.edu. *Dir,* Cristina Pope; E-mail: popec@upstate.edu; *Dep Dir,* Wendi Ackerman; Tel: 315-464-8141, E-mail: ackermaw@upstate.edu; *Asst Dir, Customer Serv,* Rebecca Kindon; Tel: 315-464-7193, E-mail: kindonr@upstate.edu; *Digital Content Librn,* Laura Schlueter; Tel: 315-464-7195, E-mail: schlueL@upstate.edu; *Ref Librn,* Christine Kucharski; Tel: 315-464-7199, E-mail: kucharsC@upstate.edu; *Ref Librn,* Amy Slutzky; Tel: 315-464-7104, E-mail: slutzkya@upstate.edu; *Ref Librn,* Virginia Young; Tel: 315-464-7084, E-mail: youngv@upstate.edu; *Info Res Mgr,* Kimberly Nolan; Tel: 315-464-7113, E-mail: nolanki@upstate.edu; *Clinical Libr Coordr,* Olivia Tsistinas; Tel: 315-464-7200, E-mail: TsistiJO@upstate.edu; *Curator,* Cara Howe; Tel: 315-464-4585, E-mail: howec@upstate.edu. Subject Specialists: *Historical Coll,* Cara Howe; Staff 22 (MLS 13, Non-MLS 9)
Founded 1912
Library Holdings: e-books 1,049; e-journals 33,816; Bk Titles 47,725; Bk Vols 210,858; Per Subs 74; Videos 2,138
Special Collections: Geneva Coll; Medicine (Americana Coll); Rare Books Coll; Stephen Smith Coll
Subject Interests: Behav sci, Med, Pre-clinical sci, Soc sci
Automation Activity & Vendor Info: (Circulation) Ex Libris Group; (ILL) Atlas Systems; (OPAC) Ex Libris Group; (Serials) SerialsSolutions
Wireless access
Partic in Central New York Library Resources Council; National Network of Libraries of Medicine Region 7; OCLC Online Computer Library Center, Inc; SUNYConnect

CL SYRACUSE UNIVERSITY COLLEGE OF LAW LIBRARY*, 228 Dineen Hall, 950 Irving Ave, 13244-6070. SAN 354-2793. Tel: 315-443-9560. Circulation Tel: 315-443-9570. Reference Tel: 315-443-9572. FAX: 315-443-9567. E-mail: library@law.syr.edu. Web Site: www.law.syr.edu/law-library. *Law Libr Dir/Law Librn,* Jan Fleckenstein; Tel: 315-443-9571, E-mail: jflecken@law.syr.edu; *Asst Dir, Student Learning,* Christine Demetros; Tel: 315-443-9531, E-mail: cdemetr@law.syr.edu; Staff 12 (MLS 7, Non-MLS 5)
Founded 1899
Library Holdings: Bk Titles 61,782; Bk Vols 238,620; Per Subs 5,660
Special Collections: US Document Depository
Subject Interests: Family law, Intl law, Law mgt, Legal hist, Trial practice
Automation Activity & Vendor Info: (Cataloging) Ex Libris Group; (Circulation) Ex Libris Group; (Course Reserve) Ex Libris Group; (OPAC) Ex Libris Group; (Serials) Ex Libris Group
Wireless access
Publications: Acquisitions Bulletin; Electronic Newsletter; Law Library Guide; Library Update
Partic in OCLC Online Computer Library Center, Inc
Open Mon-Sun 7am-Midnight
Restriction: 24-hr pass syst for students only, Circ limited, In-house use for visitors

C SYRACUSE UNIVERSITY LIBRARIES, E S Bird Library, 222 Waverly Ave, 13244-2010. SAN 354-2645. Tel: 315-443-2573. Interlibrary Loan Service Tel: 315-443-3725. FAX: 315-443-2060. E-mail: libref@syr.edu. Web Site: library.syr.edu. *Dean of Libr, Univ Librn,* David Seaman; Tel: 315-443-5533, E-mail: dseaman@syr.edu; *Assoc Dean, Academic Undergrad Success,* Lisa Moeckel; Tel: 315-443-9790, E-mail: lemoecke@syr.edu; *Assoc Dean, Access & Res Mgt,* Roberta Gwilt; Tel: 315-443-9773, E-mail: rbgwilt@syr.edu; *Assoc Dean, Res,* Scott Warren; Tel: 315-443-8339, E-mail: sawarr01@syr.edu; *Asst Dean, Advan,* Ronald L Thiele; Tel: 315-443-2537, E-mail: rlthiele@syr.edu; *Exec Dir, Operations,* Terriruth Carrier; Tel: 315-443-1187, E-mail: tecarrie@syr.edu; *Budget Dir,* Jennifer Collins; Tel: 315-443-5781, E-mail: jrcollins@syr.edu; *Dir, Info Tech,* Russell Silverstein; Tel: 315-443-4300, E-mail: rusilver@syr.edu; *Director, Strategic Marketing Comms,* Christina Hatem; Tel: 315-443-9788, E-mail: cjhatem@syr.edu; *Spec Coll, Univ Archivist,* Meg Mason; Tel: 315-443-8380, E-mail: mamaso02@syr.edu; Staff 104 (MLS 40, Non-MLS 64)
Founded 1871. Enrl 21,789; Fac 1,546; Highest Degree: Doctorate
Library Holdings: e-books 328,000; e-journals 173,000; Bk Vols 4,500,000; Per Subs 174,654
Special Collections: Albert Schweitzer Papers; Anna Hyatt Huntington Papers; Arna Bontemps Papers; Averill Harriman Gubernatorial Papers; Benjamin Spock Papers; C P Huntington Papers; Cartoonist Coll; Continuing Education Coll; Dorothy Thompson Papers; Earl R Browder Papers; Gerrit & Peter Smith Coll; Grove Press Archive; Leopold Von

Ranke Library; Loyalists in the American Revolutionary War (Spire Coll); Marcel Breuer Coll; Margaret Bourke-White Coll; Mary Walker Papers; Modern American Private Press Books; Morris Lapidus Papers; Novotny Library of Economic History; Oneida Community Coll; Peggy Bacon Papers; Revolution; Rudyard Kipling First Editions; Science Fiction Books & Manuscripts; Shaker Coll; Sol Feinstone Library; Stephen Crane First Editions & Manuscripts; Street & Smith Archive; William Hobart-Royce Balzac Coll; William Safire Coll; William Safire Papers. State Document Depository; US Document Depository
Automation Activity & Vendor Info: (Acquisitions) Ex Libris Group; (Cataloging) Ex Libris Group; (Circulation) Ex Libris Group; (Course Reserve) Ex Libris Group; (ILL) OCLC ILLiad; (OPAC) Ex Libris Group; (Serials) Ex Libris Group
Wireless access
Publications: Library Connection (Newsletter)
Partic in Association of Research Libraries; Central New York Library Resources Council; OCLC Online Computer Library Center, Inc; OCLC Research Library Partnership
Special Services for the Blind - Computer with voice synthesizer for visually impaired persons; Talking bks
Friends of the Library Group
Departmental Libraries:
CARNEGIE LIBRARY, Carnegie Bldg, 130 Sims Dr, 13244. (Mail add: 222 Waverly Ave, 13244-5040). Tel: 315-443-2160. E-mail: carnegie@syr.edu. Web Site: library.syr.edu/departments/carnegie.php. *Librn,* Juan Denzer; Tel: 315-443-5537, E-mail: jpdenzer@syr.edu; *Librn,* Emily Hart; Tel: 315-443-2403, E-mail: ekhart@syr.edu; Staff 7 (MLS 4, Non-MLS 3)
Subject Interests: Biology, Chem, Computer sci, Engr, Health & wellness, Libr & info sci, Math, Mil sci, Naval sci, Nutrition, Photog, Physics, Tech arts
Function: Computers for patron use, E-Reserves, Electronic databases & coll, Online ref, Photocopying/Printing, Ref serv available, Res libr, Telephone ref
Open Mon-Fri 8-5
Restriction: Borrowing privileges limited to fac & registered students, Borrowing requests are handled by ILL, Open to students, fac, staff & alumni, Pub use on premises

TANNERSVILLE

P MOUNTAIN TOP LIBRARY, 6093 Main St, 12485. (Mail add: PO Box 427, 12485-0427), SAN 311-2810. Tel: 518-589-5707. FAX: 518-589-5023. E-mail: tanmttoplib@aol.com. Web Site: mountaintoplibrary.org. *Libr Dir,* Maureen Garcia
Founded 1900. Pop 1,700; Circ 20,591
Library Holdings: AV Mats 1,360; Electronic Media & Resources 21; Large Print Bks 258; Microforms 8; Bk Vols 16,000; Per Subs 170; Talking Bks 210
Special Collections: Postcards
Subject Interests: Local hist
Automation Activity & Vendor Info: (Circulation) Innovative Interfaces, Inc; (Course Reserve) Innovative Interfaces, Inc; (ILL) Innovative Interfaces, Inc; (Media Booking) Innovative Interfaces, Inc; (OPAC) Innovative Interfaces, Inc
Wireless access
Publications: Library Cookbook
Mem of Mid-Hudson Library System
Open Mon-Thurs 10-4, Fri 10-5, Sat 10-2

TAPPAN

P TAPPAN LIBRARY*, 93 Main St, 10983. SAN 312-5548. Tel: 845-359-3877. E-mail: tappanlibrary@tappanlibrary.org. Web Site: www.tappanlibrary.org. *Dir,* Sara Nugent; Staff 2 (MLS 2)
Founded 1956. Pop 6,867
Library Holdings: Bk Vols 48,140
Special Collections: Major John Andre Coll; Sean McCarthy Poetry Coll
Subject Interests: Local hist, Poetry
Automation Activity & Vendor Info: (Circulation) Horizon; (ILL) Horizon; (OPAC) Horizon
Wireless access
Function: Adult literacy prog, ILL available, Magnifiers for reading, Prog for adults, Prog for children & young adult, Ref serv available, Summer reading prog, Telephone ref, Wheelchair accessible
Publications: Newsletter
Mem of Ramapo Catskill Library System
Open Mon-Thurs 10-8, Fri 10-7, Sat & Sun 12-5
Friends of the Library Group

TARRYTOWN

S HISTORIC HUDSON VALLEY LIBRARY*, 639 Bedford Rd, 10591. SAN 312-5599. Tel: 914-366-6901. FAX: 914-631-0089. E-mail: librarian@hudsonvalley.org. Web Site: hudsonvalley.org/resources/library-and-collections. *Librn,* Catalina Hannan; Staff 1.5 (MLS 1.5)
Founded 1951
Library Holdings: Bk Titles 22,000; Bk Vols 25,000; Per Subs 90
Special Collections: Washington Irving Editions; Washington Irving's Personal Library
Subject Interests: 17th Century, 18th Century, 19th Century Hudson River Valley hist, Archit, Decorative art, Slavery
Function: Archival coll, Art exhibits, Bus archives, Microfiche/film & reading machines, Ref serv available, Res libr, Wheelchair accessible
Restriction: Open by appt only

S HISTORICAL SOCIETY SERVING SLEEPY HOLLOW & TARRYTOWN*, Society Library, One Grove St, 10591. SAN 312-5564. Tel: 914-631-8374. E-mail: historyatgrove@aol.com. Web Site: www.thehistoricalsociety.net/research. *Curator, Exec Dir,* Sara Mascia
Founded 1889
Library Holdings: Bk Titles 3,500
Special Collections: Children's Books of Earlier Times & Related History Books for Children; Civil War Memorabilia; Civil War Papers of Capt Charles H Rockwell; Indians (Leslie V Case Coll), artifacts; John Paulding, Isaac Van Wart & David Williams Coll, artifacts, docs; Life Along the Hudson River Valley, art, bks, per, photogs; Local Families & Their History, bks, genealogies, micro, records, VF; Local Newspapers, micro; Local Photographs Coll, 1800s- Present; Local Schools & Churches, art, bks; Local Writers, bks, ms; Major Andre: His Capture & His Captors, bks, pictures; Maps (Tarrytown, North Tarrytown, Pocantico Hills, Westchester County & New York State 1700 - Present); Old Dutch Church History & Burying Ground; Revolutionary War Memorabilia; Ward B Burnett Post GAR Coll, records; World War I & World War II Coll
Subject Interests: Am Revolutionary War, Genealogy, Local hist, Regional newspapers, State
Publications: Postcards of Local Historic Sites & Events; The Capture of Major John Andre, September 23, 1780 (An Excerpt from Westchester County During the American Revolution by Otto Hufeland); The Chronicle
Open Wed, Thurs & Sat 2-4

P WARNER LIBRARY, 121 N Broadway, 10591. SAN 312-5610. Tel: 914-631-7734. FAX: 914-631-2324. Web Site: www.warnerlibrary.org. *Dir,* Position Currently Open; *Sr Librn, Ch Serv,* Patricia Cohn; *Ch,* Barbara Cohen; *Ref Librn,* Lisa Shirley; *Ref Librn,* Cassandra Troini; Staff 21 (MLS 6, Non-MLS 15)
Founded 1929. Pop 20,300; Circ 146,083
Library Holdings: High Interest/Low Vocabulary Bk Vols 300; Bk Vols 88,218; Per Subs 170
Special Collections: Rockwell Kent Coll; Washington Irving Coll, large print
Subject Interests: Literacy, Local hist
Automation Activity & Vendor Info: (Acquisitions) SirsiDynix; (Cataloging) SirsiDynix; (Circulation) SirsiDynix; (OPAC) SirsiDynix; (Serials) SirsiDynix
Wireless access
Function: Adult literacy prog, ILL available, Prog for adults, Prog for children & young adult, Ref serv available, Wheelchair accessible
Publications: Warner Library Newsletter
Mem of Westchester Library System
Open Mon & Thurs 1-9, Tues & Wed 10-6, Fri & Sat 10-5, Sun 1-5
Friends of the Library Group

THERESA

P THERESA FREE LIBRARY*, 301 Main St, 13691. SAN 312-5629. Tel: 315-628-5972. FAX: 315-628-4839. Web Site: www.theresafreelibrary.org. *Dir,* Kristy Perry; E-mail: kperry@ncls.org
Pop 1,853; Circ 12,132
Library Holdings: Bk Vols 7,000
Wireless access
Mem of North Country Library System
Open Tues, Thurs & Fri 12-5 & 7-9, Sat 9-1
Friends of the Library Group

THOUSAND ISLAND PARK

P THOUSAND ISLAND PARK LIBRARY*, 42743 Saint Lawrence Ave, 13692. SAN 312-5637. Tel: 315-482-9098, 315-559-7460. FAX: 315-482-9098. E-mail: tiparklibrary@gmail.com. Web Site: www.tiparklibrary.org. *Dir,* Mary Popovich
Circ 6,247
Library Holdings: Bk Vols 6,750
Wireless access
Mem of North Country Library System
Open Mon-Fri 9-12 & 1-4:30, Sat (June-Sept) 9-12
Friends of the Library Group

TICONDEROGA

P BLACK WATCH MEMORIAL LIBRARY*, 99 Montcalm St, 12883. SAN 312-5645. Tel: 518-585-7380. FAX: 518-585-3209. E-mail: blackwatch@townofticonderoga.org. Web Site: cefls.org/libraries/ticonderoga. *Dir,* Heather Johns
Founded 1906. Pop 5,486; Circ 19,421
Library Holdings: Bk Titles 14,110; Per Subs 32
Special Collections: State Document Depository; UN Document Depository; US Document Depository
Automation Activity & Vendor Info: (Cataloging) SirsiDynix; (Circulation) SirsiDynix; (OPAC) SirsiDynix
Wireless access
Mem of Clinton-Essex-Franklin Library System
Open Tues 10-7, Wed-Fri 10-5, Sat 10-3
Friends of the Library Group

S FORT TICONDEROGA MUSEUM*, Thompson-Pell Research Center, 30 Fort Ti Rd, 12883. (Mail add: PO Box 390, 12883-0390), SAN 312-5653. Tel: 518-585-2821. FAX: 518-585-2210. E-mail: info@fort-ticonderoga.org. Web Site: www.fort-ticonderoga.org. *Curator,* Matthew Keagle; E-mail: mkeagle@fort-ticonderoga.org
Founded 1909
Library Holdings: Bk Vols 13,000; Per Subs 20; Spec Interest Per Sub 20
Special Collections: 18th Century English & American Newspapers & Literary Magazines; 18th Century Military Weapons & Artillery Coll; Archival Coll, diaries, ms, maps, orderly bks & photos; Ella Ferris Pell Coll; Military Manuals, 18th-early 19th Century; Skene Papers; William L Stone Coll
Subject Interests: Colonial, Fr & Indian War, Mil hist 1609-1780, Revolutionary wars in Champlain Valley, Upper Hudson valleys
Wireless access
Publications: Bulletin of the Fort Ticonderoga Museum, Vol 1 (1927 - present)
Restriction: Non-circulating to the pub, Open by appt only

S TICONDEROGA HISTORICAL SOCIETY LIBRARY*, Hancock House, Six Moses Circle, 12883. SAN 325-9668. Tel: 518-585-7868. FAX: 518-585-6367. E-mail: tihistory@bridgepoint1.com. Web Site: www.tihistory.org. *Library Contact,* Diane O'Connor
Founded 1898
Library Holdings: Bk Titles 8,000; Bk Vols 10,000
Special Collections: Account Books; Diaries; Local History Books; Manuscripts; Newspapers; Photos
Wireless access
Publications: Patches & Patterns Extended
Restriction: Non-circulating to the pub, Open by appt only

TIVOLI

P TIVOLI FREE LIBRARY*, 86 Broadway, 12583. (Mail add: PO Box 400, 12583-0400), SAN 312-5661. Tel: 845-757-3771. E-mail: tivolilibrary@gmail.com. Web Site: www.tivolilibrary.org. *Dir,* Michele DelPriore
Founded 1919. Circ 3,536
Library Holdings: Bk Vols 8,000
Automation Activity & Vendor Info: (Circulation) Innovative Interfaces, Inc - Millennium; (OPAC) Innovative Interfaces, Inc - Millennium
Wireless access
Mem of Mid-Hudson Library System
Partic in Association for Rural & Small Libraries
Open Mon & Thurs (Winter) 4-8, Tues & Wed 10-2 & 4-8, Sat 10-2; Mon, Fri (Summer) 2-8, Tues-Thurs 10-8, Sat 10-2

TOMKINS COVE

P TOMKINS COVE PUBLIC LIBRARY*, 419 Liberty Dr N, 10986. SAN 312-567X. Tel: 845-786-3060. FAX: 845-947-5572. Web Site: www.tomkinscovelibrary.org. *Libr Mgr,* Janet Lukas; E-mail: jlukas@rcls.org; Staff 7 (MLS 1, Non-MLS 6)
Founded 1896. Pop 1,800; Circ 12,000
Library Holdings: Bk Vols 22,000; Per Subs 49
Special Collections: Birds & Conservation (Margaret Tomkins Memorial Coll)
Wireless access
Publications: Newsletter (Quarterly)
Mem of Ramapo Catskill Library System
Open Mon-Thurs 1-9, Fri 3-6, Sat 1-4, Sun (Oct-May) 2-5

TONAWANDA

P CITY OF TONAWANDA PUBLIC LIBRARY, 333 Main St, 14150. SAN 312-5696. Tel: 716-693-5043. FAX: 716-693-0825. E-mail: ton@buffalolib.org. Web Site: www.buffalolib.org/locations-hours/city-tonawanda-public-library. *Dir,* John Gaff; Staff 2 (MLS 2)
Pop 16,136; Circ 52,322
Library Holdings: Bk Vols 35,388; Per Subs 75
Automation Activity & Vendor Info: (Cataloging) SirsiDynix; (Circulation) SirsiDynix; (OPAC) SirsiDynix
Wireless access
Mem of Buffalo & Erie County Public Library System
Open Mon & Thurs 9-8, Tues & Fri 9-5, Wed 9-3, Sat 9-2
Friends of the Library Group
Bookmobiles: 1

TROY

P BRUNSWICK COMMUNITY LIBRARY*, 4118 State Hwy 2, 12180-9029. Tel: 518-279-4023. FAX: 518-279-0527. E-mail: library@brunswicklibrary.org. Web Site: www.brunswicklibrary.org. *Libr Dir,* Sara Hopkins; E-mail: director@brunswicklibrary.org; Staff 5 (MLS 2, Non-MLS 3)
Library Holdings: Audiobooks 632; AV Mats 1,461; CDs 121; DVDs 200; Large Print Bks 633; Bk Titles 8,836; Per Subs 55
Automation Activity & Vendor Info: (Acquisitions) SirsiDynix; (Cataloging) SirsiDynix; (Circulation) SirsiDynix; (Course Reserve) SirsiDynix; (ILL) SirsiDynix; (OPAC) SirsiDynix; (Serials) SirsiDynix
Wireless access
Function: 24/7 Electronic res, 24/7 Online cat, Adult bk club, Bk club(s), Bk reviews (Group), Bks on CD, Children's prog, Computer training, Computers for patron use, Digital talking bks, Doc delivery serv, Electronic databases & coll, Free DVD rentals, Holiday prog, Home delivery & serv to seniorr ctr & nursing homes, Homebound delivery serv, ILL available, Internet access, Laminating, Life-long learning prog for all ages, Magazines, Mail & tel request accepted, Mango lang, Meeting rooms, Movies, Museum passes, Music CDs, Online cat, Online info literacy tutorials on the web & in blackboard, Online ref, Outreach serv, Outside serv via phone, mail, e-mail & web, OverDrive digital audio bks, Photocopying/Printing, Preschool outreach, Preschool reading prog, Printer for laptops & handheld devices, Prog for adults, Prog for children & young adult, Ref serv available, Serves people with intellectual disabilities, Spoken cassettes & CDs, Spoken cassettes & DVDs, Study rm, Summer & winter reading prog, Summer reading prog, Tax forms, Teen prog, VHS videos, Writing prog
Mem of Upper Hudson Library System
Open Mon-Sat 10-6
Friends of the Library Group

J HUDSON VALLEY COMMUNITY COLLEGE*, Dwight Marvin Library & Instructional Media Center, 80 Vandenburgh Ave, 12180. SAN 312-5742. Tel: 518-629-7330. Interlibrary Loan Service Tel: 518-629-7387. Reference Tel: 518-629-7337. Information Services Tel: 518-629-7336. FAX: 518-629-7509. Web Site: www.hvcc.edu/lrc. *Dir,* Brenda Hazard; Tel: 518-629-7388, E-mail: b.hazard@hvcc.edu; *Asst Admin,* Patricia Kaiser; Tel: 518-629-7333, E-mail: p.kaiser@hvcc.edu; *Cat & Syst Librn,* Katie Jezik; Tel: 518-629-7395, E-mail: k.jezik@hvcc.edu; *Circ/ILL Librn,* Sue Grayson; Tel: 518-629-7555, E-mail: s.grayson@hvcc.edu; *Ref Librn,* Cynthia Koman; Tel: 518-629-7360, E-mail: c.koman@hvcc.edu; *Ref Librn,* Valerie Waldin; Tel: 518-629-7319, E-mail: v.waldin@hvcc.edu; *Instruction Coordr,* Robert Matthews; Tel: 518-629-7392, E-mail: r.matthews@hvcc.edu; *Coordr, Ref & Electronic Serv,* Anne La Belle; Tel: 518-629-7384, E-mail: a.labelle@hvcc.edu; *Circ,* Tylan Nino; E-mail: t.nino@hvcc.edu; *ILL,* Jennifer Acker; E-mail: j.acker1@hvcc.edu; *Per,* Sherry LaMarche; Tel: 518-629-7322, E-mail: s.lamarche@hvcc.edu; *Tech Asst,* John Staerker; Tel: 518-629-7323, E-mail: j.staerker@hvcc.edu; Staff 10 (MLS 10)
Founded 1953. Enrl 8,808; Fac 310
Library Holdings: AV Mats 5,776; Bk Titles 97,624; Bk Vols 9,213; Per Subs 110
Special Collections: History (Microbook Library Journal of American Civilization Coll), micro; History of Western Civilization (Microbook); Video Encyclopedia of the 20th Century
Subject Interests: Automotive tech, Bus, Child develop, Dental, Engr tech, Liberal arts, Med, Mortuary sci
Wireless access
Publications: Dwight Marvin LRC Guide; Faculty LRC Handbook; From the Library (Acquisitions); Kaleidoscope; Policies & Procedures Manual; Previews (from the Media Center); Student Guide; Worksheets & Bibliographic
Partic in Capital District Library Council; OCLC Online Computer Library Center, Inc; SUNYConnect
Open Mon-Thurs (Winter) 7am-10pm, Fri 7-4:30, Sat 9-4; Mon, Tues & Fri (Summer) 7-4, Wed & Thurs 7am-10pm

GL NEW YORK STATE SUPREME COURT*, Rensselear County Law Library, Court House Annex, 86 Second St, 12180-4098. SAN 312-5769. Tel: 518-285-6183. FAX: 518-274-0590. E-mail: rensselaerlawlibrary@nycourts.gov. Web Site: ww2.nycourts.gov/courts/3jd/law-library.shtml. *Principal Law Librn,* Position Currently Open

Founded 1909
Library Holdings: Bk Titles 1,100; Bk Vols 43,000
Subject Interests: Law, NY State
Automation Activity & Vendor Info: (Acquisitions) SirsiDynix; (Cataloging) SirsiDynix; (Circulation) SirsiDynix; (OPAC) SirsiDynix; (Serials) SirsiDynix
Wireless access
Open Mon-Fri 9-4:45
Restriction: Open to pub for ref only

S RENSSELAER COUNTY HISTORICAL SOCIETY & HART CLUETT MUSEUM, Dean P Taylor Research Library, 57 Second St, 12180. SAN 312-5785. Tel: 518-272-7232. Reference E-mail: research@hartcluett.org. Web Site: www.hartcluett.org/library. *Archivist, Curator,* Stacy P Draper; E-mail: spdraper@hartcluett.org
Founded 1927
Library Holdings: Bk Titles 3,000
Special Collections: Burden Iron Company Papers; Cable Flax Mill Papers; Cluett, Peabody & Co Papers; Congressman Dean P Taylor Papers; Hart Family Papers; Marshall Mills Papers; Organizational Papers (Troy Chromatics, Thursday Morning Club, Troy Day Home, etc); Rensselaer County Families Papers; Samaritan Hospital School of Nursing Papers
Subject Interests: Archit, Archives, Genealogy, Manuscripts, Rensselaer County hist
Wireless access
Publications: Rensselaer County History Research at the RCHS Research Library
Restriction: Non-circulating, Open by appt only

C RENSSELAER LIBRARIES*, Folsom Library, Rensselaer Architecture Library, Greene Bldg 308, 3rd Flr, 110 Eighth St, 12180-3590. SAN 354-2971. Tel: 518-276-8310. Administration Tel: 518-276-8300. FAX: 518-276-2044. Circulation E-mail: circadm@rpi.edu. Web Site: library.rpi.edu. *Dir,* Andrew White; E-mail: whitea9@rpi.edu; *Assoc Dir,* Tracy Allen; E-mail: allent6@rpi.edu; *Assoc Dir,* Liz King; E-mail: kinge3@rpi.edu; *Syst Adminr,* George Biggar; *Tech & Metadata Librn,* Kathryn Dunn; *Inst Archivist, Mgr, Archives & Spec Coll,* John Dojka; E-mail: dojkaj@rpi.edu; *Pub Serv Mgr,* Tanis Kreiger; E-mail: kreigt@rpi.edu; *Mgr, Tech Serv,* Patricia Hults; *Automation Archivist,* Tammy Gobert; Staff 22 (MLS 12, Non-MLS 10)
Founded 1824. Enrl 6,559; Fac 400; Highest Degree: Doctorate
Library Holdings: e-books 69,757; e-journals 19,241; Bk Vols 338,687
Special Collections: Architecture Coll
Subject Interests: Archit, Engr, Experimental media, Hist of sci & tech, Info tech
Automation Activity & Vendor Info: (Acquisitions) Innovative Interfaces, Inc - Millennium; (Cataloging) Innovative Interfaces, Inc - Millennium; (Circulation) Innovative Interfaces, Inc - Millennium; (ILL) OCLC ILLiad; (OPAC) Innovative Interfaces, Inc - Millennium; (Serials) Innovative Interfaces, Inc - Millennium
Wireless access
Function: ILL available, Ref serv available, Wheelchair accessible
Partic in Capital District Library Council; ConnectNY, Inc
Special Services for the Blind - Closed circuit TV magnifier; Reader equip
Open Mon-Thurs 7:30am-10pm, Fri 7:30-5, Sat 8-4, Sun Noon-8
Restriction: Pub use on premises
Friends of the Library Group

C SAGE COLLEGES LIBRARIES*, James Wheelock Clark Library, 65 First St, 12180. SAN 354-303X. Tel: 518-244-2249. Interlibrary Loan Service Tel: 518-244-2320. Reference Tel: 518-244-2431. FAX: 518-244-2400. Reference E-mail: libref@sage.edu. Web Site: library.sage.edu. *Libr Dir,* Lisa Brainard; Tel: 518-244-2430, E-mail: brainl@sage.edu; *Access Serv Librn,* Regina Vertone; Tel: 518-292-1784, E-mail: vertor@sage.edu; *Electronic Res Librn,* Jennifer Anderson; Tel: 518-292-1701, E-mail: anderj6@sage.edu; *Info Literacy Librn,* Amy Pass; Tel: 518-244-3106, E-mail: passa@sage.edu; *Syst Librn,* Christopher White; Tel: 518-244-4521, E-mail: whitec2@sage.edu; *Tech Serv Librn,* Terrance Wasielewski; Tel: 518-224-2435, E-mail: wasiet@sage.edu; *Archivist,* Kelly Grant; Tel: 518-244-2471; Staff 13 (MLS 7, Non-MLS 6)
Founded 1916. Fac 150; Highest Degree: Doctorate
Library Holdings: AV Mats 6,093; e-books 10,000; e-journals 50,000; Microforms 7,100; Bk Titles 134,378; Bk Vols 154,101; Per Subs 284
Special Collections: 20th Century Poetry (Carol Ann Donahue Memorial Coll). State Document Depository
Subject Interests: Allied health, Women's studies
Automation Activity & Vendor Info: (Acquisitions) LibLime Koha; (Cataloging) LibLime Koha; (Circulation) LibLime Koha; (Course Reserve) LibLime Koha; (ILL) OCLC ILLiad; (OPAC) LibLime Koha; (Serials) LibLime Koha
Wireless access
Publications: Newsletter
Partic in Cap District Libr Coun for Ref & Res Resources; OCLC Online Computer Library Center, Inc; Westchester Academic Library Directors Organization

M SAMARITAN HOSPITAL SCHOOL OF NURSING*, Health Sciences Library, 1300 Massachusetts Ave, 12180. SAN 312-5793. Tel: 518-268-5000, 518-268-5035. FAX: 518-268-5806. Web Site: www.sphp.com. *Libr Supvr,* Kathy Kindness; E-mail: kathy.kindness@sphp.com
Founded 1955
Library Holdings: Electronic Media & Resources 4; Bk Titles 500; Per Subs 21
Subject Interests: Med, Nursing
Restriction: Staff use only

P TROY PUBLIC LIBRARY*, 100 Second St, 12180-4005. SAN 354-3064. Tel: 518-274-7071. FAX: 518-271-9154. Reference E-mail: troyref@thetroylibrary.org. Web Site: www.thetroylibrary.org. *Dir,* Paul Hicok; E-mail: hicokp@thetroylibrary.org; Staff 25 (MLS 5, Non-MLS 20)
Founded 1835. Pop 44,169; Circ 278,453
Library Holdings: Bk Titles 89,240; Bk Vols 131,000; Per Subs 412
Special Collections: US Document Depository
Subject Interests: Genealogy, Local hist
Automation Activity & Vendor Info: (Circulation) SirsiDynix
Wireless access
Publications: Annual Report; Friends Newsletter
Mem of Upper Hudson Library System
Open Mon-Thurs 9-8, Fri 9-5, Sat 9-5 (9-1 Summer), Sun (Sept-May) 1-5
Friends of the Library Group
Branches: 1
LANSINGBURGH BRANCH, 27 114th St, 12182, SAN 354-3129. Tel: 518-235-5310. *Dir,* Paul Hicok
Library Holdings: Bk Vols 11,983
Open Mon-Wed 1-7, Thurs & Fri 10-4, Sat 10-4 (10-1 Summer)
Friends of the Library Group

TRUMANSBURG

P ULYSSES PHILOMATHIC LIBRARY, 74 E Main St, 14886. (Mail add: PO Box 655, 14886), SAN 312-5815. Tel: 607-387-5623. FAX: 607-387-3823. E-mail: upl@trumansburglibrary.org. Web Site: www.trumansburglibrary.org. *Libr Dir,* Laura Mielenhausen; E-mail: director@trumansburglibrary.org; *Librn,* Clay Chiment; E-mail: librarian@trumansburglibrary.org; Staff 3 (MLS 1, Non-MLS 2)
Founded 1935. Pop 4,775; Circ 37,374
Jan 2020-Dec 2020 Income $348,386
Library Holdings: AV Mats 228; Electronic Media & Resources 16; Bk Titles 19,400; Per Subs 47; Talking Bks 501
Automation Activity & Vendor Info: (Cataloging) Innovative Interfaces, Inc; (Circulation) Innovative Interfaces, Inc; (OPAC) Innovative Interfaces, Inc
Wireless access
Mem of Finger Lakes Library System
Open Mon, Tues, Thurs & Fri 10-5, Wed 10-7, Sat 10-2
Friends of the Library Group

TUCKAHOE

P TUCKAHOE PUBLIC LIBRARY*, 71 Columbus Ave, 10707. SAN 312-5823. Tel: 914-961-2121. FAX: 914-961-3832. Web Site: www.tuckahoe.com/library. *Dir,* Swadesh Pachnanda; E-mail: spachnan@wlsmail.org; Staff 17 (MLS 6, Non-MLS 11)
Founded 1912. Pop 6,486; Circ 84,960
Library Holdings: Bk Vols 66,000; Per Subs 100
Special Collections: Tuckahoe History (files, newsps on microfilm 1918-1931, pamphlets, photogs)
Automation Activity & Vendor Info: (Cataloging) SirsiDynix; (Circulation) SirsiDynix; (OPAC) SirsiDynix
Wireless access
Publications: Monthly calendar of events; Newsletter
Mem of Westchester Library System
Open Mon & Wed 10:30-8:30, Tues, Thurs & Fri 10:30-5:30, Sat 10-5 (10-1 June-Aug)
Friends of the Library Group

TULLY

P TULLY FREE LIBRARY, 12 State St, 13159. (Mail add: PO Box 250, 13159-0250), SAN 312-5858. Tel: 315-696-8606. FAX: 315-696-8120. E-mail: tullyfree@tullyfreelibrary.org. Web Site: www.tullyfreelibrary.org. *Libr Dir,* Annabeth Hayes; *Ch Serv,* Sonja Shepherd
Founded 1935. Pop 5,968; Circ 30,421
Library Holdings: AV Mats 770; Bks on Deafness & Sign Lang 10; DVDs 1,826; e-books 54,972; Bk Titles 15,186; Per Subs 100; Talking Bks 500
Special Collections: Civil War

Automation Activity & Vendor Info: (Cataloging) Innovative Interfaces, Inc; (Circulation) Innovative Interfaces, Inc; (OPAC) Innovative Interfaces, Inc
Wireless access
Mem of Onondaga County Public Libraries
Open Mon-Thurs 10-7, Fri 10-5, Sat 10-2

TUPPER LAKE

P TUPPER LAKE PUBLIC LIBRARY*, Goff-Nelson Memorial Library, 41 Lake St, 12986. SAN 354-3188. Tel: 518-359-9421. FAX: 518-554-1019. E-mail: goffnelson@gmail.com. *Libr Dir,* Peg Mauer; Staff 7 (MLS 1, Non-MLS 6)
Founded 1932. Pop 6,712; Circ 76,888
Library Holdings: Bk Vols 42,000; Per Subs 150
Special Collections: Adirondack Mountains, NY
Automation Activity & Vendor Info: (Circulation) Horizon; (OPAC) Horizon
Wireless access
Function: 24/7 Online cat, Activity rm, Adult bk club, Archival coll, Audiobks on Playaways & MP3, Audiobks via web, Bi-weekly Writer's Group, Bk club(s), Bks on CD, CD-ROM, Children's prog, Computer training, Computers for patron use, Digital talking bks, E-Readers, E-Reserves, Electronic databases & coll, For res purposes, Free DVD rentals, Games & aids for people with disabilities, Holiday prog, ILL available, Instruction & testing, Internet access, Jail serv, Laminating, Life-long learning prog for all ages, Magazines, Mail & tel request accepted, Mail loans to mem, Makerspace, Meeting rooms, Microfiche/film & reading machines, Movies, Museum passes, Music CDs, Online cat, Online ref, Outside serv via phone, mail, e-mail & web, OverDrive digital audio bks, Photocopying/Printing, Preschool outreach, Preschool reading prog, Printer for laptops & handheld devices, Prof lending libr, Prog for adults, Prog for children & young adult, Ref & res, Ref serv available, Res assist avail, Res libr, Res performed for a fee, Scanner, Senior computer classes, Serves people with intellectual disabilities, Spanish lang bks, Spoken cassettes & CDs, STEM programs, Story hour, Study rm, Summer & winter reading prog, Summer reading prog, Tax forms, Teen prog, VHS videos, Wheelchair accessible, Winter reading prog, Workshops, Writing prog
Mem of Clinton-Essex-Franklin Library System
Open Mon-Wed 9:30-8, Thurs & Fri 9:30-5:30, Sat 10-2
Restriction: Non-resident fee

TURIN

P B ELIZABETH STRONG MEMORIAL LIBRARY*, Turin Library, 6312 E Main St, 13473. (Mail add: PO Box 27, 13473-0027), SAN 312-5866. Tel: 315-348-6433. FAX: 315-348-6433. E-mail: turlib@ncls.org. Web Site: www.turinlibrary.org. *Dir,* Sharon Stewart
Founded 1947. Circ 7,699
Library Holdings: Bk Vols 2,200; Per Subs 50
Wireless access
Mem of North Country Library System
Open Mon 3-6, Wed 1-9, Thurs 7pm-9pm

TUXEDO PARK

P TUXEDO PARK LIBRARY, 227 Rte 17, 10987. (Mail add: PO Box 776, 10987-0776), SAN 312-5882. Tel: 845-351-2207. FAX: 845-351-2213. E-mail: tuxpl@rcls.org. Web Site: www.tuxedoparklibrary.org. *Dir,* Diane Loomis; *Asst Dir,* Cathy Sandak; Staff 11 (MLS 1, Non-MLS 10)
Founded 1901. Pop 3,334; Circ 56,697
Jan 2021-Dec 2021 Income $594,368. Mats Exp $65,025
Library Holdings: AV Mats 7,607; Bk Titles 30,072; Per Subs 129
Special Collections: Tuxedo Park Library Local History Coll, oral hist, photos, doc, & slides
Automation Activity & Vendor Info: (Cataloging) Horizon; (Circulation) Horizon; (OPAC) Horizon
Wireless access
Publications: Newsletter (Quarterly)
Mem of Ramapo Catskill Library System
Open Mon, Tues & Fri 9-5:30, Wed & Thurs 9-9, Sat 10-4, Sun (Sept-Jun) 11-3
Friends of the Library Group

UNADILLA

P UNADILLA PUBLIC LIBRARY*, 193 Main St, 13849. (Mail add: PO Box 632, 13849-0632), SAN 312-5904. Tel: 607-369-3131. FAX: 607-369-4500. E-mail: unadilla@gmail.com. Web Site: libraries.4cls.org/unadilla. *Dir,* Andrea Edwards
Pop 1,489; Circ 6,116
Library Holdings: Bk Vols 12,000; Per Subs 18
Automation Activity & Vendor Info: (OPAC) SirsiDynix-WorkFlows
Wireless access
Mem of Four County Library System
Open Mon & Wed 6pm-8pm, Tues & Thurs 10-12, 1-5 & 6-8, Sat 10-2

UNION SPRINGS

P SPRINGPORT FREE LIBRARY*, 171 Cayuga St, 13160. (Mail add: PO Box 501, 13160), SAN 312-5912. Tel: 315-889-7766. FAX: 315-889-7766. Web Site: springportfreelibrary.org. *Librn,* Carla Piperno-Jones
Pop 2,367; Circ 44,291
Library Holdings: Bk Titles 11,000; Per Subs 24
Automation Activity & Vendor Info: (Cataloging) Innovative Interfaces, Inc; (Circulation) Innovative Interfaces, Inc; (OPAC) Innovative Interfaces, Inc; (Serials) Innovative Interfaces, Inc
Wireless access
Mem of Finger Lakes Library System
Open Mon, Tues & Thurs 2-8, Fri & Sat 10-2

UNIONDALE

P NASSAU LIBRARY SYSTEM*, 900 Jerusalem Ave, 11553-3039. SAN 354-3242. Tel: 516-292-8920. FAX: 516-565-0950. E-mail: nls@nassaulibrary.org. Web Site: www.nassaulibrary.org. *Dir,* Caroline Ashby; E-mail: cashby@nassaulibrary.org; *Asst Dir, Tech Operations,* Robert Drake; E-mail: rdrake@nassaulibary.org; *Bus Mgr,* Jan Heinlein; E-mail: heinlein@nassaulibrary.org; *Mgr, Cat Serv,* Michele Zwierski; E-mail: mzwierski@nassaulibrary.org; *ILL Mgr,* Moira Flynn; E-mail: msflynn@nassaulibrary.org; *Tech Operations Mgr,* James McHugh; E-mail: jmchugh@nassaulibrary.org; *Youth Serv Mgr,* Renee McGrath; E-mail: rmcgrath@nassaulibrary.org; *Outreach Serv Spec,* Nicole Scherer; E-mail: nscherer@nassaulibrary.org; Staff 15 (MLS 11, Non-MLS 4)
Founded 1959. Pop 1,334,544
Automation Activity & Vendor Info: (Acquisitions) Innovative Interfaces, Inc; (Cataloging) Innovative Interfaces, Inc; (Circulation) Innovative Interfaces, Inc; (ILL) OCLC; (OPAC) Innovative Interfaces, Inc
Wireless access
Function: Electronic databases & coll, ILL available, Jail serv, Online cat, Outreach serv, OverDrive digital audio bks
Member Libraries: Baldwin Public Library; Bayville Free Library; Bellmore Memorial Library; Bethpage Public Library; Bryant Library; East Meadow Public Library; East Rockaway Public Library; East Williston Public Library; Elmont Memorial Library; Farmingdale Public Library; Floral Park Public Library; Franklin Square Public Library; Freeport Memorial Library; Garden City Public Library; Glen Cove Public Library; Gold Coast Public Library; Great Neck Library; Hempstead Public Library; Henry Waldinger Memorial Library; Hewlett-Woodmere Public Library; Hicksville Public Library; Hillside Public Library; Island Park Public Library; Island Trees Public Library; Jericho Public Library; Lakeview Public Library; Levittown Public Library; Locust Valley Library; Long Beach Public Library; Lynbrook Public Library; Malverne Public Library; Manhasset Public Library; Massapequa Public Library; Merrick Library; Mineola Memorial Library; North Bellmore Public Library; North Merrick Public Library; Oceanside Library; Oyster Bay-East Norwich Public Library; Peninsula Public Library; Plainedge Public Library; Plainview-Old Bethpage Public Library; Port Washington Public Library; Rockville Centre Public Library; Roosevelt Public Library; Sea Cliff Village Library; Seaford Public Library; Shelter Rock Public Library; Syosset Public Library; Uniondale Public Library; Wantagh Public Library; West Hempstead Public Library; Westbury Memorial Public Library; Williston Park Public Library
Partic in Long Island Library Resources Council
Restriction: Not a lending libr, Not open to pub

L RIVKIN RADLER LLP*, Law Library, West Tower, 926 RXR Plaza, 11556-0926. SAN 372-2368. Tel: 516-357-3453, 516-357-3454, 516-357-3455. FAX: 516-357-3333. *Head Librn,* Aurelia Sanchez; E-mail: Aurelia.Sanchez@rivkin.com; Staff 3 (MLS 3)
Library Holdings: Bk Vols 10,000; Per Subs 50
Restriction: Staff use only

L RUSKIN MOSCOU FALTISCHEK, PC*, Law Library, East Tower, 15th Flr, 1425 RXR Plaza, 11556-0190. SAN 374-4868. Tel: 516-663-6000, 516-663-6525. FAX: 516-663-6725. Web Site: www.rmfpc.com. *Librn,* Paul Nardone; E-mail: pnardone@rmfpc.com
Founded 1968
Library Holdings: Bk Titles 893; Bk Vols 10,000

P UNIONDALE PUBLIC LIBRARY*, 400 Uniondale Ave, 11553. SAN 312-5920. Tel: 516-489-2220. FAX: 516-489-4005. E-mail: aserve@uniondalelibrary.org. Web Site: www.uniondalelibrary.org. *Dir,* Position Currently Open; *Asst Dir,* Marin Martin; E-mail: mmartin@uniondalelibrary.org; *Head, Adult Serv,* Guo Ilgar; Tel: 516-489-2220, Ext 208, E-mail: iguo@uniondalelibrary.org; *Head, Adult Serv,* Irene Winkler; E-mail: iwinkler@uniondalelibrary.org; *Head, Children's Servx,* Michelle Minervini; Tel: 516-489-2220, Ext 215, E-mail: mminervini@uniondalelibrary.org; *Head, Ref, Head, YA,* Syntychia

Kendrick-Samuel; E-mail: skendricksamuel@uniondalelibrary.org; *Circ Serv,* Tricia Smith-Duhaney; Tel: 516-489-2220, Ext 235, E-mail: tsmithduhaney@uniondalelibrary.org
Founded 1954. Pop 25,000; Circ 160,000
Library Holdings: Bk Vols 115,000
Wireless access
Publications: Uniondale Public Library (Newsletter)
Mem of Nassau Library System
Open Mon, Wed & Thurs 9-9, Tues 10-9, Fri 9-6, Sat 10-5 (10-2 Summer), Sun (Oct-June) 1-4
Friends of the Library Group

UPPER JAY

P WELLS MEMORIAL LIBRARY*, 12230 NYS Rte 9N, 12987. (Mail add: PO Box 57, 12987-0057), SAN 312-5939. Tel: 518-946-2644. FAX: 518-946-2644. E-mail: upperjaylibrary@whiteface.net. Web Site: www.wellsmemoriallibrary.com. *Libr Dir,* Karen Rappaport
Founded 1906. Pop 2,506
Library Holdings: AV Mats 1,000; Large Print Bks 200; Bk Vols 12,000; Per Subs 35; Talking Bks 120
Special Collections: Adirondack-NY Coll
Wireless access
Mem of Clinton-Essex-Franklin Library System
Partic in Northern New York Library Network
Open Tues-Thurs 12-5, Sat 11-4

UPPER NYACK

R THE REFORM TEMPLE OF ROCKLAND LIBRARY, (Formerly Reform Temple of Brocham Library), 330 N Highland Ave, 10960. SAN 312-5947. Tel: 845-358-2248. FAX: 845-358-3450. E-mail: info@rtrny.org. Web Site: rtrny.org.
Library Holdings: Bk Titles 1,200; Bk Vols 1,250; Per Subs 14
Wireless access
Open Tues 4:15-8:15, Sun 9-1

UPTON

S BROOKHAVEN NATIONAL LABORATORY*, Information Technology Division, Research Library, Bldg 477, 11973-5000. SAN 312-5955. Tel: 631-344-3483. FAX: 631-344-2090. Web Site: www.bnl.gov/library. *Mgr,* Patricia Garvey; Tel: 631-344-6062, E-mail: pgarvey@bnl.gov; *Tech Serv,* Leah Donley; Tel: 631-344-7469, E-mail: donley@bnl.gov; Staff 5 (MLS 4, Non-MLS 1)
Founded 1947
Library Holdings: e-books 3,900; e-journals 10,600; Bk Titles 31,560; Bk Vols 45,220; Per Subs 465
Subject Interests: Biology, Chem, Energy, Engr, Med, Nuclear sci, Physics
Automation Activity & Vendor Info: (Acquisitions) SirsiDynix; (Cataloging) SirsiDynix
Publications: Newsletter (Monthly)
Partic in Long Island Library Resources Council; OCLC Online Computer Library Center, Inc
Restriction: Open by appt only, Staff use only

UTICA

M FAXTON SAINT LUKE'S HEALTHCARE*, Saint Luke's Campus, 1656 Champlin Ave, 13502. (Mail add: PO Box 479, 13503-0479), SAN 373-6148. Tel: 315-624-6059. FAX: 315-624-6947. Web Site: www.mvhealthsystem.org/mvhs-libraries/st-lukes-campus. *Dir, Libr Serv,* Halyna Liszczynskyj; E-mail: hliszczy@mvhealthsystem.org
Library Holdings: e-books 19; e-journals 120; Bk Titles 810; Per Subs 143
Subject Interests: Cardiology, Long term care, Nursing, Obstetrics, Oncology, Pediatrics
Partic in Central New York Library Resources Council

P MID-YORK LIBRARY SYSTEM*, 1600 Lincoln Ave, 13502. SAN 312-5998. Tel: 315-735-8328. FAX: 315-735-0943. Web Site: www.midyork.org. *Exec Dir,* Wanda Bruchis; E-mail: wbruchis@midyork.org; Staff 7 (MLS 3, Non-MLS 4)
Founded 1960. Pop 369,377
Library Holdings: Bk Vols 85,000; Per Subs 20
Automation Activity & Vendor Info: (Acquisitions) Baker & Taylor; (Cataloging) OCLC Connexion; (Circulation) SirsiDynix; (ILL) OCLC; (OPAC) SirsiDynix-iBistro
Wireless access
Publications: Book Buying Lists; Core Collection Reference Buying Guide; Get Ready Sheet; Headhunters Guide to Genealogical Resources in Central NY; MYLS Reporter; Union List of Periodicals
Member Libraries: Barneveld Free Library; Bridgewater Free Library; C W Clark Memorial Library; Camden Public Library; Canastota Public Library; Cazenovia Public Library; Clayville Library Association; DeRuyter Free Library; Didymus Thomas Memorial Library; Dolgeville-Manheim Public Library; Dunham Public Library; Earlville Free Library; Erwin Library & Institute; Frank J Basloe Library; Frankfort Free Library; Hamilton Public Library; Holland Patent Free Library; Ilion Free Public Library; Jervis Public Library Association, Inc; Jordanville Public Library; Kirby Free Library of Salisbury Center; Kirkland Town Library; Little Falls Public Library; Middleville Free Library; Morrisville Public Library; New Hartford Public Library; New Woodstock Free Library; New York Mills Public Library; Newport Free Library; Old Forge Library; Oneida County Historical Society Library; Oneida Public Library; Oriskany Public Library; Poland Public Library; Prospect Free Library; Sherrill-Kenwood Free Library; Sullivan Free Library; Utica Public Library; Vernon Public Library; Waterville Public Library; Weller Public Library; West Winfield Library; Western Town Library; Westmoreland Reading Center; Woodgate Free Library
Partic in Central New York Library Resources Council; OCLC Online Computer Library Center, Inc
Restriction: Not open to pub

J MOHAWK VALLEY COMMUNITY COLLEGE LIBRARY*, 1101 Sherman Dr, 13501-5394. SAN 312-6005. Tel: 315-792-5408. Interlibrary Loan Service Tel: 315-792-5669. Reference Tel: 315-792-5561. Administration Tel: 315-792-5399. FAX: 315-792-5666. Web Site: www.mvcc.edu/academics/library. *Dir of Libr,* Steven Frisbee; E-mail: sfrisbee@mvcc.edu; *Ref & Instruction Librn,* Colleen Kehoe-Robinson; Tel: 315-731-5737, E-mail: ckehoe-robinson@mvcc.edu; *Cataloger,* Krista Hartman; *Circ,* Anne Ichihana; Tel: 315-731-5735; *Electronic Res, ILL & Ser,* Louise Charbonneau; Tel: 315-731-5793; *ILL,* Sherry Day; Staff 13 (MLS 13)
Founded 1946. Enrl 6,000
Library Holdings: Bk Titles 62,022; Bk Vols 92,000; Per Subs 650
Special Collections: Career Center; Children's Books
Automation Activity & Vendor Info: (Acquisitions) Ex Libris Group; (Cataloging) Ex Libris Group; (Circulation) Ex Libris Group; (Course Reserve) Ex Libris Group; (ILL) OCLC ILLiad; (OPAC) Ex Libris Group; (Serials) Ex Libris Group
Wireless access
Publications: Newsletter
Partic in Central New York Library Resources Council; OCLC Online Computer Library Center, Inc; SUNYConnect
Open Mon-Thurs 8am-9pm, Fri 8-4, Sat 12-5, Sun 1-6
Friends of the Library Group

S MUNSON-WILLIAMS-PROCTOR ARTS INSTITUTE LIBRARY*, Art Reference Library, 310 Genesee St, 13502. SAN 354-3307. Tel: 315-797-0000, Ext 2123. FAX: 315-797-5608. E-mail: library@mwpai.edu. Web Site: www.mwpai.org/view/library. *Libr Serv Dir,* Kathleen Salsbury; Tel: 315-797-0000, Ext 2228, E-mail: ksalsbur@mwpai.edu; Staff 3 (MLS 1, Non-MLS 2)
Founded 1960
Library Holdings: CDs 2,500; DVDs 1,500; Bk Vols 26,000; Per Subs 50; Videos 500
Special Collections: Autographs & Bookplates (Proctor Families Coll); Rare Books (Fountain Elms Coll)
Subject Interests: Art hist, Fine arts
Automation Activity & Vendor Info: (Cataloging) Mandarin Library Automation; (Circulation) Mandarin Library Automation; (Course Reserve) Mandarin Library Automation; (ILL) OCLC WorldShare Interlibrary Loan; (OPAC) Mandarin Library Automation; (Serials) Mandarin Library Automation
Function: Adult bk club, Archival coll, CD-ROM, Electronic databases & coll, Mail & tel request accepted, Photocopying/Printing, Ref & res, Telephone ref, VHS videos
Partic in Central New York Library Resources Council
Open Mon-Thurs 9-9, Fri 9-5, Sat 12-5, Sun 3-8
Restriction: Circ limited, In-house use for visitors, Non-circulating of rare bks

GL NEW YORK SUPREME COURT, Law Library-Oneida County, 235 Elizabeth St, 13501. SAN 312-6013. Tel: 315-266-4570. FAX: 315-798-6470. Web Site: www.nycourts.gov/library/oneida/index.shtml. *Sr Librn,* Paula J Eannace; Staff 4 (MLS 1, Non-MLS 3)
Library Holdings: Bk Titles 250,000; Per Subs 500
Special Collections: Legal Treatises for Practitioners, 18th & 19th Centuries
Subject Interests: Am legal mats, NY legal mats
Wireless access
Partic in OCLC Online Computer Library Center, Inc
Open Mon-Fri 8:30-4:30

S ONEIDA COUNTY HISTORICAL SOCIETY LIBRARY*, 1608 Genesee St, 13502-5425. SAN 325-9684. Tel: 315-735-3642. FAX: 315-735-3642. E-mail: ochs@oneidacountyhistory.org. Web Site: oneidacountyhistory.org. *Exec Dir,* Brian J Howard; *Commun Outreach Coordr,* Rebecca McLain

Founded 1876
Library Holdings: Bk Titles 2,500; Bk Vols 4,000
Special Collections: Journals & Letters, family & business recos
Subject Interests: Genealogy, Indust, Local bus, Oneida County hist
Wireless access
Function: Archival coll, Art exhibits, Computers for patron use, Photocopying/Printing, Ref serv available, Wheelchair accessible
Mem of Mid-York Library System
Open Mon-Fri (June-Sept) 10-4, Tues-Fri (Oct-May) 10-4, Sat 10-2
Restriction: Access for corporate affiliates, Authorized patrons, Fee for pub use, Non-circulating, Not a lending libr

M SAINT ELIZABETH MEDICAL CENTER*, College of Nursing Library, 2215 Genesee St, 13501. SAN 324-539X. Tel: 315-798-8209. Web Site: www.secon.edu. *Dir, Libr Serv,* Halyna Liszczynski; E-mail: hliszczy@mvhealthsystem.org; Staff 1 (MLS 1)
Library Holdings: Bk Titles 5,005; Per Subs 48
Subject Interests: Nursing
Wireless access
Partic in Central New York Library Resources Council
Restriction: Staff use only

C STATE UNIVERSITY OF NEW YORK POLYTECHNIC INSTITUTE, Peter J Cayan Library, 100 Seymour Rd, 13502. (Mail add: PO Box 3050, 13504-3050), SAN 312-6021. Tel: 315-792-7245. Circulation Tel: 315-792-7246. Reference Tel: 315-792-7251. FAX: 315-792-7517. E-mail: library@sunypoly.edu. Web Site: sunypoly.edu/library. *Assoc Librn, Interim Dir,* Rebecca Hewitt; E-mail: hewittr@sunypoly.edu; *Pub Serv Librn,* Sam Nesbitt; E-mail: nesbits@sunypoly.edu; *Services & Resources Supervisor,* Allison Fiegal; E-mail: fiegala@sunypoly.edu; Staff 7 (MLS 6, Non-MLS 1)
Founded 1969. Enrl 2,450; Fac 200; Highest Degree: Master
Library Holdings: e-books 300,000; e-journals 1,600; Bk Vols 158,000; Per Subs 181
Special Collections: State Document Depository; US Document Depository
Subject Interests: Bus, Computer sci, Health, Technologies
Automation Activity & Vendor Info: (Cataloging) Ex Libris Group; (Circulation) Ex Libris Group; (ILL) OCLC ILLiad; (OPAC) Ex Libris Group
Wireless access
Function: E-Reserves, ILL available, Internet access, Online ref, Ref serv available, Telephone ref, Wheelchair accessible
Partic in SUNYConnect; Westchester Academic Library Directors Organization
Open Mon-Thurs 8-4, Fri 8-Noon (Summer); Mon-Thurs 8am-10pm, Fri 8-8, Sun Noon-8
Restriction: Open to pub for ref & circ; with some limitations

C UTICA COLLEGE*, Frank E Gannett Memorial Library, 1600 Burrstone Rd, 13502-4892. SAN 312-603X. Tel: 315-792-3041. Interlibrary Loan Service Tel: 315-792-3262. Information Services Tel: 315-792-3044. FAX: 315-792-3361. E-mail: library@utica.edu. Web Site: www.utica.edu/academic/library/index.cfm. *Dean, Learning & Libr Serv,* James K Teliha; E-mail: jkteliha@utica.edu; *Cat Librn, Coordr, Tech Serv,* Herb LaGoy; Tel: 315-792-3217, E-mail: hllagoy@utica.edu; *Distance Learning Librn,* Lisa Rogers; Tel: 315-792-3342, E-mail: lrogers@utica.edu; *Ref Librn & Coordr of Electronic Res,* Jan Malcheski; Tel: 315-792-3388, E-mail: jamalche@utica.edu; *Ref Librn/Distance Learning,* Katie Spires; E-mail: mkspires@utica.edu; *Ref Librn,* Janis Winn; Tel: 315-792-3351, E-mail: jcwinn@utica.edu; *Coordr, Access Serv,* Christina Huffaker; E-mail: clhuffak@utica.edu; *Tech Serv Technician,* Lynn M Guca; Tel: 315-233-2485, E-mail: lmguca@utica.edu; Staff 11.5 (MLS 5.5, Non-MLS 6)
Founded 1946. Enrl 4,424; Fac 166; Highest Degree: Master
Library Holdings: Bk Vols 180,000; Per Subs 1,400
Special Collections: Fiction-Scene in Upstate New York Since 1929; Walter Edmonds; Welsh Language Imprints of New York State
Automation Activity & Vendor Info: (Cataloging) OCLC; (Circulation) OCLC Worldshare Management Services; (ILL) OCLC ILLiad; (OPAC) OCLC Worldshare Management Services
Wireless access
Partic in Central New York Library Resources Council; OCLC Online Computer Library Center, Inc
Open Mon-Thurs 8am-Midnight, Fri 8am-10pm, Sat 10-8, Sun 11am-Midnight

P UTICA PUBLIC LIBRARY, 303 Genesee St, 13501. SAN 354-348X. Tel: 315-735-2279. FAX: 315-734-1034. Web Site: uticapubliclibrary.org. *Dir,* Christopher Sagaas; E-mail: csagaas@uticapubliclibrary.org; *Asst Dir,* Heidi McManus; E-mail: hmcmanus@uticapubliclibrary.org; *Youth Serv Dir,* Amanda Stewart; *Ch,* Lisa Renz; *Digital Serv, Outreach Librn,* Brie Jow; *Coordr, Prog, Ref (Info Servs),* Gabrielle Kinney; *Info Tech,* Fritz Meeusen; *Ref (Info Servs),* Robert Lalli; *Ref (Info Servs),* Abigail Williams; Staff 9.5 (MLS 6.3, Non-MLS 3.2)
Founded 1893. Pop 62,235; Circ 96,583
Apr 2020-Mar 2021 Income $1,141,459, State $23,000, County $140,000, Locally Generated Income $805,053, Other $173,406. Mats Exp $64,000. Sal $685,000 (Prof $494,937)
Library Holdings: Audiobooks 3,275; AV Mats 9,233; CDs 3,275; DVDs 4,273; e-books 19,548; Microforms 9,000; Bk Vols 64,856; Per Subs 36
Subject Interests: Genealogy, Local hist
Automation Activity & Vendor Info: (Acquisitions) SirsiDynix; (Cataloging) SirsiDynix; (Circulation) SirsiDynix; (ILL) SirsiDynix; (OPAC) SirsiDynix
Wireless access
Function: Adult bk club, Art exhibits, Bks on CD, Chess club, Children's prog, Computer training, Computers for patron use, Electronic databases & coll, Free DVD rentals, ILL available, Internet access, Magazines, Mail & tel request accepted, Mango lang, Microfiche/film & reading machines, Movies, Music CDs, Notary serv, Online cat, Online ref, Orientations, Outreach serv, Outside serv via phone, mail, e-mail & web, OverDrive digital audio bks, Photocopying/Printing, Preschool outreach, Prog for adults, Prog for children & young adult, Ref serv available, Scanner, Senior computer classes, Spanish lang bks, Story hour, Summer reading prog, Tax forms, Teen prog, Telephone ref, Wheelchair accessible, Writing prog
Mem of Mid-York Library System
Open Mon-Fri 9-5

VALATIE

P VALATIE FREE LIBRARY*, 1036 Kinderhook St, 12184. (Mail add: PO Box 336, 12184-0336), SAN 312-6056. Tel: 518-758-9321. FAX: 518-758-6497. E-mail: valatiefreelibrary@gmail.com. Web Site: valatielibrary.net. *Dir,* Elizabeth Powhida
Circ 8,995
Library Holdings: Bk Vols 10,243
Automation Activity & Vendor Info: (Cataloging) Innovative Interfaces, Inc; (Circulation) Innovative Interfaces, Inc; (OPAC) Innovative Interfaces, Inc
Wireless access
Mem of Mid-Hudson Library System
Open Mon 12-7, Tues & Wed 12-6, Thurs 2-7, Fri 10-5, Sat 9-2

VALHALLA

CM NEW YORK MEDICAL COLLEGE*, Health Sciences Library, Basic Science Bldg, 15 Dana Rd, 10595. SAN 312-6064. Tel: 914-594-4200. Interlibrary Loan Service Tel: 914-594-4201. Reference Tel: 914-594-3168, 914-594-4206. Administration Tel: 914-594-4208. FAX: 914-594-3171. Administration FAX: 914-594-4191. E-mail: hsl_nymc@nymc.edu. Web Site: library.nymc.edu. *Dir,* Marie Ascher; Tel: 914-594-4207, E-mail: marie_ascher@nymc.edu; *Head, Access Serv,* Marta Ambroziak; Tel: 914-594-4204, E-mail: marta_ambroziak@nymc.edu; Staff 17 (MLS 9, Non-MLS 8)
Founded 1976. Enrl 1,100; Fac 1,294; Highest Degree: Doctorate
Library Holdings: e-books 13,883; e-journals 15,888; Bk Titles 59,991; Per Subs 15,888
Special Collections: History of Medicine & Homeopathy (Historical Coll); History of Orthopedics (Alfred Haas Coll); Rare Books (J Alexander van Heuven Coll)
Subject Interests: Biomed sci, Health policy, Homeopathy, Med, Pub health
Automation Activity & Vendor Info: (Cataloging) Ex Libris Group; (Circulation) Ex Libris Group; (Course Reserve) Ex Libris Group; (ILL) OCLC ILLiad; (OPAC) Ex Libris Group; (Serials) Ex Libris Group
Wireless access
Function: Archival coll, Doc delivery serv, Res libr
Restriction: Not open to pub
Friends of the Library Group

J SUNY WESTCHESTER COMMUNITY COLLEGE*, Harold L Drimmer Library/Learning Resource Center, 75 Grasslands Rd, 10595. SAN 312-6080. Tel: 914-785-6960. Circulation Tel: 914-785-6965. Circulation FAX: 914-606-6531. Web Site: www.sunywcc.edu/library. *Chair, Electronic Res Librn,* Jessica Tagliaferro; Tel: 914-606-6808, E-mail: jessica.tagliaferro@sunywcc.edu; *Librn,* Karen Vanterpool; E-mail: karen.vanterpool@sunywcc.edu; *Assessment Librn, Virtual Serv Librn,* Joshua Weber; Tel: 914-606-6819, E-mail: joshua.weber@sunywcc.edu; *Coll Develop Librn, Outreach Librn,* Gloria Meisel; Tel: 914-785-6968, E-mail: gloria.meisel@sunywcc.edu; *Circ, ILL, Per,* Mathurin Towanda; Tel: 914-606-8086, E-mail: towanda.mathurin@sunywcc.edu; Staff 27 (MLS 17, Non-MLS 10)
Founded 1946. Enrl 11,981; Fac 157; Highest Degree: Associate
Library Holdings: Bk Titles 105,501; Bk Vols 138,000; Per Subs 362
Special Collections: College & Career Coll; Legal Coll New York State
Automation Activity & Vendor Info: (Circulation) Ex Libris Group; (OPAC) Ex Libris Group; (Serials) Ex Libris Group

Wireless access
Function: Distance learning, ILL available, Ref serv available
Publications: Periodicals List
Partic in Metropolitan New York Library Council; SUNYConnect; Westchester Academic Library Directors Organization
Open Mon-Thurs 8am-9:30pm, Fri 8-5, Sat 9-5, Sun 1-5

VALLEY COTTAGE

P VALLEY COTTAGE FREE LIBRARY, 110 Rte 303, 10989. SAN 312-6102. Tel: 845-268-7700. FAX: 845-268-7760. Reference E-mail: vclref@rcls.org. Web Site: www.valleycottagelibrary.org. *Dir,* Amelia Kalin; Tel: 845-268-7700, Ext 151; *Asst Dir,* Christy Blanchette; Tel: 845-268-7700, Ext 155; *Head, Adult Serv,* Sean Antonucci; Tel: 845-268-7700, Ext 134; *Head, Children's Servx,* Danelle Connolly; Tel: 845-268-7700, Ext 124; *Head, Circ Serv,* Mia Clowes; Tel: 845-268-7700, Ext 113; *Head, Tech Serv,* Ashley Maraffino; Tel: 845-268-7700, Ext 142; *Head, Teen Serv,* Katrina Hohlfeld; Tel: 845-268-7700, Ext 136; *Ch Serv Librn,* Melinda Watkins; Tel: 845-268-7700, Ext 123; Staff 30 (MLS 8, Non-MLS 22)
Founded 1959. Pop 23,805; Circ 201,957
Library Holdings: DVDs 1,000; Bk Titles 68,985; Per Subs 6,140; Talking Bks 3,795; Videos 2,767
Special Collections: Local History Photog Coll
Subject Interests: Art, Local hist
Automation Activity & Vendor Info: (Acquisitions) SirsiDynix; (Cataloging) SirsiDynix; (Circulation) SirsiDynix; (ILL) SirsiDynix; (OPAC) SirsiDynix
Wireless access
Function: BA reader (adult literacy), Homebound delivery serv, ILL available, Outside serv via phone, mail, e-mail & web, Photocopying/Printing, Prog for children & young adult, Ref serv available, Summer reading prog, Wheelchair accessible
Publications: Focus (Newsletter)
Mem of Ramapo Catskill Library System
Open Mon-Thurs 10-6, Fri 10-5, Sat 10-2
Friends of the Library Group

VALLEY FALLS

P VALLEY FALLS FREE LIBRARY, 42 State St, 12185. (Mail add: PO Box 296, 12185-0296), SAN 312-6110. Tel: 518-753-4230. FAX: 518-753-4230. E-mail: circulation@valleyfallslibrary.org. Web Site: www.valleyfallslibrary.org. *Libr Mgr,* Kelly Akin
Founded 1907. Pop 5,000; Circ 7,094
Jan 2021-Dec 2021 Income $17,797
Library Holdings: Bk Vols 9,000; Per Subs 20
Wireless access
Mem of Upper Hudson Library System
Open Tues 9:30-12 & 1-8, Wed 11-6, Thurs & Fri 9:30-12 & 1-6, Sat 9:30-1

VALLEY STREAM

P HENRY WALDINGER MEMORIAL LIBRARY*, Valley Stream Public Library, 60 Verona Pl, 11582. SAN 312-6137. Tel: 516-825-6422. E-mail: hwmlcontact@hotmail.com. Web Site: www.valleystreamlibrary.org. *Libr Dir,* Mamie Eng; E-mail: directorvs@nassaulibrary.org; Staff 7 (MLS 6, Non-MLS 1)
Founded 1932. Pop 43,473; Circ 130,862
Jun 2013-May 2014 Income $1,462,085, State $56,230, City $1,370,509, Locally Generated Income $35,346. Mats Exp $161,523, Books $102,309, AV Mat $7,693, Electronic Ref Mat (Incl. Access Fees) $51,521. Sal $865,793 (Prof $484,566)
Library Holdings: AV Mats 5,416; e-books 34,436; Bk Vols 109,001; Per Subs 166
Special Collections: Oral History
Subject Interests: Valley Stream hist
Automation Activity & Vendor Info: (Cataloging) Innovative Interfaces, Inc; (Circulation) Innovative Interfaces, Inc; (OPAC) Innovative Interfaces, Inc
Wireless access
Function: 24/7 Electronic res, Adult bk club, After school storytime, Art exhibits, Audiobks via web, Bk club(s), Bks on cassette, Bks on CD, Children's prog, Computer training, Computers for patron use, Digital talking bks, Distance learning, E-Reserves, Electronic databases & coll, Family literacy, Free DVD rentals, Homebound delivery serv, ILL available, Internet access, Magazines, Magnifiers for reading, Microfiche/film & reading machines, Movies, Museum passes, Music CDs, Online cat, Online info literacy tutorials on the web & in blackboard, OverDrive digital audio bks, Photocopying/Printing, Preschool outreach, Preschool reading prog, Prog for adults, Prog for children & young adult, Ref serv available, Spanish lang bks, Spoken cassettes & CDs, Spoken cassettes & DVDs, Story hour, Summer & winter reading prog, Summer reading prog, Tax forms, Teen prog, Telephone ref, VHS videos, Wheelchair accessible, Winter reading prog
Mem of Nassau Library System
Open Mon & Wed 10-6, Tues, Thurs & Fri 10-8:30, Sat 10-4, Sun 12-4 (Fall-Winter); Mon, Tues, Thurs & Fri 10-9, Wed 10-5:30, Sat 10-4 (Summer)

VERNON

P VERNON PUBLIC LIBRARY, 4441 Peterboro St, 13476. (Mail add: PO Box 1048, 13476-1048), SAN 312-6145. Tel: 315-829-2463. E-mail: vernon@midyork.org. Web Site: vernonpubliclibrary.org. *Dir,* Robyn Coufal; *Libr Asst,* Sharon Danboise; *Libr Asst,* Jessica Yerdon
Pop 1,300; Circ 32,841
Library Holdings: Bk Vols 8,500; Per Subs 16
Wireless access
Mem of Mid-York Library System
Open Mon, Wed & Fri 1-6, Tues & Thurs 9-1, Sat 9-11

VESTAL

P FOUR COUNTY LIBRARY SYSTEM*, 304 Clubhouse Rd, 13850-3713. SAN 310-866X. Tel: 607-723-8236. FAX: 607-723-1722. E-mail: contactus@4cls.org. Web Site: fcls.ent.sirsi.net. *Exec Dir,* Steven J Bachman; E-mail: sbachman@4cls.org; *Outreach Mgr, Youth Serv Mgr,* Sarah Reid; Tel: 607-723-8236, Ext 350, E-mail: sreid@4cls.org; *Automation Syst Coordr,* Jeff Henry; Tel: 607-723-8236, Ext 310, E-mail: jbhenry@4cls.org; Staff 17 (MLS 5, Non-MLS 12)
Founded 1960. Pop 361,668; Circ 38,153
Library Holdings: Bk Vols 170,044
Automation Activity & Vendor Info: (Acquisitions) SirsiDynix; (Cataloging) SirsiDynix; (Circulation) SirsiDynix; (ILL) SirsiDynix; (OPAC) SirsiDynix
Wireless access
Function: 24/7 Electronic res, 24/7 Online cat, ILL available
Publications: Directory of Member Libraries; Newsletter
Member Libraries: Afton Free Library; Andes Public Library; Bainbridge Free Library; Bovina Public Library; Broome County Public Library; Cannon Free Library; Cherry Valley Memorial Library; Deposit Free Library; Edmeston Free Library; Fairview Public Library; Fenton Free Library; Franklin Free Library; George F Johnson Memorial Library; Gilbertsville Free Library; Guernsey Memorial Library; Harris Memorial Library; Huntington Memorial Library; Kinney Memorial Library; Lisle Free Library; Louise Adelia Read Memorial Library; Mary L Wilcox Memorial Library; Milford Free Library; Moore Memorial Library; New Berlin Library; Nineveh Public Library of Colesville Township; Oxford Memorial Library; Richfield Springs Public Library; Roxbury Library Association; Sherburne Public Library; Sidney Memorial Public Library; Skene Memorial Library; Smyrna Public Library; South New Berlin Free Library; Springfield Library; Stamford Village Library; Unadilla Public Library; Vestal Public Library; Village Library of Cooperstown; Village Library of Morris; William B Ogden Free Library; Worcester-Schenevus Library; Your Home Public Library
Partic in New York State Interlibrary Loan Network
Open Mon-Fri 8-4:30
Bookmobiles: 1

R TEMPLE ISRAEL LIBRARY*, 4737 Deerfield Pl, 13850-3762. SAN 324-0290. Tel: 607-723-7461. *Librn,* Claire Shefftz; Staff 5 (MLS 1, Non-MLS 4)
Founded 1968
Library Holdings: Bk Titles 2,000; Bk Vols 2,600; Talking Bks 50
Subject Interests: Holocaust, Jewish authors, Jewish fiction, Jewish hist, Jewish lit, Jewish-Am hist, Judaica
Restriction: Mem only
Friends of the Library Group

P VESTAL PUBLIC LIBRARY, 320 Vestal Pkwy E, 13850-1632. SAN 312-6153. Tel: 607-754-4243. Circulation Tel: 607-754-4243, Ext 2. Reference Tel: 607-754-4243, Ext 4. FAX: 607-754-7936. E-mail: reference@vestalpubliclibrary.org. Web Site: www.vestalpubliclibrary.org. *Dir,* Paul K Chapman; *Ref Librn,* Jeannette Green; *Ref Librn,* Ian Hauck; *Youth Serv Librn,* Anna Lake; Staff 5 (MLS 5)
Founded 1947. Pop 26,733; Circ 309,799
Jan 2020-Dec 2020 Income $1,131,521. Mats Exp $41,632
Library Holdings: Bk Titles 96,000; Bk Vols 116,412; Per Subs 256
Special Collections: David Ross Locke Book Coll
Automation Activity & Vendor Info: (Circulation) SirsiDynix
Wireless access
Function: Mail loans to mem
Publications: Friends (Newsletter)
Mem of Four County Library System
Open Mon-Thurs 9-8, Fri 9-5, Sat 10-4
Friends of the Library Group

VICTOR

P VICTOR FARMINGTON LIBRARY*, 15 W Main, 14564. SAN 312-6161. Tel: 585-924-2637. FAX: 585-924-1893. Web Site: victorfarmingtonlibrary.org. *Dir,* Tim Niver; E-mail: tniver@pls-net.org; *Commun Serv Librn,* Greta Selin-Love; E-mail: gselin@pls-net.org; *Youth Serv Librn,* Krystina Dippel; E-mail: kdippel@pls-net.org; *Teen Serv Coordr,* Dori Eisenstat; E-mail: deisenstat@pls-net.org; Staff 3 (MLS 3)
Founded 1939. Pop 24,667; Circ 211,902
Library Holdings: Audiobooks 1,952; Bk Vols 46,633; Per Subs 121
Automation Activity & Vendor Info: (Circulation) SirsiDynix; (OPAC) SirsiDynix
Wireless access
Function: 24/7 Electronic res, 24/7 Online cat, Activity rm, Adult bk club, Art exhibits, Bk club(s), Bk reviews (Group), Bks on CD, Children's prog, Computer training, Computers for patron use, Digital talking bks, Electronic databases & coll, Free DVD rentals, Holiday prog, Home delivery & serv to seniorr ctr & nursing homes, Homebound delivery serv, ILL available, Internet access, Laminating, Life-long learning prog for all ages, Magazines, Mango lang, Meeting rooms, Museum passes, Music CDs, Online cat, OverDrive digital audio bks, Photocopying/Printing, Prog for adults, Prog for children & young adult, Scanner, Senior computer classes, STEM programs, Story hour, Study rm, Summer & winter reading prog, Summer reading prog, Teen prog, Workshops
Mem of Pioneer Library System
Open Mon-Thurs 10-8, Fri 10-6, Sat 10-4, Sun 12-4
Friends of the Library Group

VOORHEESVILLE

P VOORHEESVILLE PUBLIC LIBRARY*, 51 School Rd, 12186. SAN 312-617X. Tel: 518-765-2791. FAX: 518-765-3007. Reference E-mail: reference@voorheesvillelibrary.org. Web Site: www.voorheesvillelibrary.org. *Libr Dir,* Sarahl Alter Clark; E-mail: sarah.clark@voorheesvillelibrary.org; *Asst Dir,* Tracey Pause; E-mail: tracey.pause@voorheesvillelibrary.org; *IT Librn,* Andrew Ward; E-mail: andrew.ward@voorpl.org; *Teen Serv Librn,* Debbie Sternklar; E-mail: debbie.sternklar@voorheesvillelibrary.org; *Youth Serv Librn,* Gail Brown; E-mail: gail.brown@voorheesvillelibrary.org; *Automation Serv,* John Love; E-mail: voorheesvilleIT@voorheesvillelibrary.org; *ILL,* Kathleen Tyrrell; E-mail: kathleen.tyrrell@voorheesvillelibrary.org; *Pub Relations,* Lynn Kohler; E-mail: lynn.kohler@voorpl.org; Staff 13 (MLS 6, Non-MLS 7)
Founded 1915. Pop 7,131; Circ 105,681
Library Holdings: Bk Titles 45,968
Subject Interests: Local hist
Automation Activity & Vendor Info: (Cataloging) SirsiDynix; (Circulation) SirsiDynix; (ILL) SirsiDynix; (OPAC) SirsiDynix
Wireless access
Publications: Bookworm (Bimonthly)
Mem of Upper Hudson Library System
Open Mon-Thurs 10-9, Fri 10-6, Sat 10-5, Sun (Sept-May) 1-5
Friends of the Library Group

WADDINGTON

P HEPBURN LIBRARY OF WADDINGTON*, 30 Main St, 13694. (Mail add: PO Box 205, 13694-0205), SAN 312-6188. Tel: 315-388-4454. FAX: 315-388-4050. E-mail: wadlib@ncls.org. Web Site: www.waddingtonlibrary.org. *Dir,* Mrs Duffy Ashley; Staff 2 (Non-MLS 2)
Founded 1919. Pop 2,000
Library Holdings: Bk Vols 10,125; Per Subs 38
Special Collections: New York State Regional Heritage Coll
Automation Activity & Vendor Info: (Cataloging) SirsiDynix; (Circulation) SirsiDynix; (ILL) SirsiDynix; (OPAC) SirsiDynix; (Serials) SirsiDynix
Wireless access
Mem of North Country Library System
Special Services for the Blind - Talking bks
Open Mon 12-6, Tues & Thurs 12-5, Wed 2-8, Fri 9-2, Sat 10-12
Friends of the Library Group

WADHAMS

P WADHAMS FREE LIBRARY*, 763 NYS Rte 22, 12993. SAN 312-6196. Tel: 518-962-8717. E-mail: info@wadhamsfreelibrary.org. Web Site: wadhamsfreelibrary.org. *Librn,* Elizabeth Rapalee; Staff 2 (Non-MLS 2)
Founded 1897. Pop 250
Library Holdings: Bk Vols 5,000; Per Subs 12
Wireless access
Mem of Clinton-Essex-Franklin Library System
Open Tues-Thurs 3-9, Sat 9-12

WALDEN

P JOSEPHINE-LOUISE PUBLIC LIBRARY*, Five Scofield St, 12586. SAN 312-620X. Tel: 845-778-7621. FAX: 845-778-1946. E-mail: wal@rcls.org. Web Site: waldenlibrary.org. *Libr Dir,* Ginny Neidermier; E-mail: neidg@rcls.org
Founded 1904. Pop 5,277; Circ 35,261
Library Holdings: Bk Titles 20,000; Bk Vols 26,428; Per Subs 42
Wireless access
Mem of Ramapo Catskill Library System
Open Mon-Thurs 10-8, Fri 10-6, Sat 10-2
Friends of the Library Group

WALLKILL

P WALLKILL PUBLIC LIBRARY*, Seven Bona Ventura Ave, 12589-4422. (Mail add: PO Box C, 12589-0258), SAN 312-6218. Tel: 845-895-3707. FAX: 845-895-8659. Web Site: wallkillpubliclibrary.org. *Libr Mgr,* Lisa Palmer; E-mail: lpalmer@rcls.org; *Circ Supvr,* Julie Moussot; E-mail: jmoussot@rcls.org
Founded 1906. Circ 29,977
Special Collections: Regional History Coll, rare bks, pamphlets
Wireless access
Mem of Ramapo Catskill Library System
Open Mon & Fri 10-6, Tues, Wed & Thurs 10-8, Sat 10-2

WALTON

P WILLIAM B OGDEN FREE LIBRARY*, 42 Gardiner Pl, 13856. (Mail add: PO Box 298, 13856), SAN 312-6226. Tel: 607-865-5929. FAX: 607-865-6821. E-mail: wboflibrary@gmail.com. Web Site: libraries.4cls.org/walton. *Dir,* Heather Johnson; Staff 1 (MLS 1)
Founded 1809. Pop 3,088; Circ 28,560
Library Holdings: Bk Vols 19,982; Per Subs 70
Special Collections: Local History (Loose Coll)
Automation Activity & Vendor Info: (Cataloging) SirsiDynix-WorkFlows; (Circulation) SirsiDynix-WorkFlows; (OPAC) SirsiDynix-WorkFlows; (Serials) SirsiDynix-WorkFlows
Wireless access
Mem of Four County Library System
Open Tues & Fri 10-5, Wed & Thurs 2-8, Sat 10-2
Friends of the Library Group

WALWORTH

P WALWORTH-SEELY PUBLIC LIBRARY*, 3600 Lorraine Dr, 14568. SAN 312-6234. Tel: 315-986-1511. FAX: 315-986-5917. Web Site: www.walworthlibrary.org. *Dir,* Seth Jacobus; E-mail: walworthlibrarydirector@owwl.org; Staff 11 (MLS 1, Non-MLS 10)
Founded 1960. Pop 8,402; Circ 79,111
Library Holdings: Bk Titles 42,230
Automation Activity & Vendor Info: (Cataloging) SirsiDynix; (Circulation) SirsiDynix; (OPAC) SirsiDynix; (Serials) SirsiDynix
Wireless access
Mem of Pioneer Library System
Open Mon-Thurs 10-8, Fri 10-6, Sat 10-2
Friends of the Library Group

WANTAGH

P WANTAGH PUBLIC LIBRARY*, 3285 Park Ave, 11793. SAN 312-6250. Tel: 516-221-1200. FAX: 516-826-9357. Web Site: www.wantaghlibrary.org. *Dir,* Joanne Morris; Staff 34 (MLS 7, Non-MLS 27)
Founded 1962. Pop 18,610; Circ 160,000
Library Holdings: Bk Titles 104,302; Bk Vols 124,678; Per Subs 388
Subject Interests: Local hist
Automation Activity & Vendor Info: (Circulation) Innovative Interfaces, Inc; (OPAC) Innovative Interfaces, Inc
Wireless access
Publications: News & Notes (Monthly newsletter)
Mem of Nassau Library System
Open Mon, Wed & Thurs 9-9, Tues 10-9, Fri 9-6, Sat 9-5
Friends of the Library Group

WAPPINGERS FALLS

P GRINNELL LIBRARY, 2642 E Main St, 12590. SAN 312-6277. Tel: 845-297-3428. FAX: 845-297-1506. Web Site: grinnell-library.org. *Dir,* Fran Harrison; Tel: 845-297-3428, Ext 806, E-mail: director@grinnell-library.org; *Ref Librn, Youth Serv,* Rachael Jelley; E-mail: rjelley@grinnell-library.org; *Ref Librn,* Brian Sullivan; E-mail: bsullivan@grinnell-library.org; *Youth Services & Children's Programming,* Molly Stevens; E-mail: mstevens@grinnell-library.org
Founded 1867. Pop 27,048; Circ 154,300

Library Holdings: High Interest/Low Vocabulary Bk Vols 100; Bk Vols 39,630; Per Subs 3,100
Special Collections: Civil War (Ferris Coll), bks, pamphlets
Automation Activity & Vendor Info: (Cataloging) Innovative Interfaces, Inc; (Circulation) Innovative Interfaces, Inc; (OPAC) Innovative Interfaces, Inc
Wireless access
Mem of Mid-Hudson Library System
Open Mon-Thurs 9:30-8, Fri 9:30-6, Sat 9:30-5
Friends of the Library Group

WARRENSBURG

P RICHARDS LIBRARY, 36 Elm St, 12885. SAN 312-6293. Tel: 518-623-3011. FAX: 518-623-2426. Web Site: www.therichardslibrary.com. *Dir,* Michael Sullivan; E-mail: war-director@sals.edu
Founded 1901. Pop 5,313; Circ 9,978
Library Holdings: Audiobooks 581; DVDs 1,025; e-books 8,237; Bk Vols 13,245; Per Subs 24
Subject Interests: Local hist
Wireless access
Function: 24/7 Electronic res, 24/7 Online cat, Activity rm, Adult bk club, Archival coll, Computers for patron use
Mem of Southern Adirondack Library System
Open Mon, Wed & Fri 10-6, Tues & Thurs 10-8, Sat 9-Noon

WARSAW

P WARSAW PUBLIC LIBRARY*, 130 N Main St, 14569. SAN 312-6307. Tel: 585-786-5650. FAX: 585-786-8706. Web Site: www.warsawpubliclibrary.org. *Dir,* Lisa Gricius; E-mail: lgricius@pls-net.org
Founded 1870. Pop 5,074; Circ 75,753
Library Holdings: Bk Vols 35,000; Per Subs 35
Special Collections: Film Depot; Job Info Center; Large Print Coll
Automation Activity & Vendor Info: (Cataloging) SirsiDynix; (Circulation) SirsiDynix; (OPAC) SirsiDynix; (Serials) SirsiDynix
Wireless access
Mem of Pioneer Library System
Open Mon & Tues 10-8, Wed & Thurs 1-8, Fri & Sat 1-5
Friends of the Library Group

WARWICK

P ALBERT WISNER PUBLIC LIBRARY*, One McFarland Dr, 10990-3585. SAN 312-6323. Tel: 845-986-1047. FAX: 845-987-1228. Reference E-mail: warref@rcls.org. Web Site: www.albertwisnerlibrary.org. *Libr Dir,* Rosemary Cooper; E-mail: rcooper@rcls.org; *Head, Adult Serv,* Laurie Angle; Staff 5 (MLS 5)
Pop 23,647
Library Holdings: AV Mats 9,544; Bk Vols 50,111; Per Subs 84
Subject Interests: Local hist
Automation Activity & Vendor Info: (OPAC) Horizon
Wireless access
Function: 24/7 Electronic res, 24/7 Online cat, 3D Printer, Accelerated reader prog, Activity rm, Adult bk club, After school storytime
Mem of Ramapo Catskill Library System
Special Services for the Deaf - ADA equip; Captioned film dep
Special Services for the Blind - Accessible computers; Aids for in-house use; Assistive/Adapted tech devices, equip & products
Open Mon-Thurs 9-8, Fri 9-7, Sat 9-5, Sun 12-4
Friends of the Library Group

WASHINGTONVILLE

P MOFFAT LIBRARY OF WASHINGTONVILLE, Six W Main St, 10992. SAN 312-6331. Tel: 845-496-5483. FAX: 845-496-6854. E-mail: moffat@rcls.org. Web Site: moffatlibrary.org. *Dir,* Carol McCrossen; E-mail: cmccrossen@rcls.org; *Head, Children's Servx, Head, Teen Serv,* Emily Kinney; E-mail: ekinney@rcls.org; *Head, Ref & Adult Serv,* Matt Thorenz; E-mail: mthorenz@rcls.org. Subject Specialists: *Local hist,* Matt Thorenz; Staff 23 (MLS 8, Non-MLS 15)
Founded 1887. Pop 24,000; Circ 104,000
Library Holdings: Audiobooks 1,143; AV Mats 129; CDs 2,576; DVDs 3,754; e-books 36,015; Electronic Media & Resources 290; Large Print Bks 653; Bk Titles 30,390; Bk Vols 30,397; Per Subs 95
Special Collections: Local History Coll
Wireless access
Function: 24/7 Electronic res, 24/7 Online cat, Activity rm, Adult bk club, After school storytime, Archival coll, Art programs, Audio & video playback equip for onsite use, Audiobks via web, Bk club(s), Bks on CD, Children's prog, Computer training, Computers for patron use, Digital talking bks, E-Reserves, Electronic databases & coll, For res purposes, Free DVD rentals, Genealogy discussion group, Holiday prog, Home delivery & serv to seniorr ctr & nursing homes, Homebound delivery serv, ILL available, Internet access, Jazz prog, Life-long learning prog for all ages, Magazines, Mail & tel request accepted, Meeting rooms, Movies, Museum passes, Music CDs, Notary serv, Online cat, Online ref, Outreach serv, Outside serv via phone, mail, e-mail & web, OverDrive digital audio bks, Photocopying/Printing, Preschool outreach, Preschool reading prog, Printer for laptops & handheld devices, Prog for adults, Prog for children & young adult, Ref & res, Ref serv available, Res assist avail, Scanner, Spanish lang bks, Spoken cassettes & CDs, STEM programs, Story hour, Summer & winter reading prog, Summer reading prog, Tax forms, Teen prog, Telephone ref, Wheelchair accessible, Winter reading prog, Workshops
Mem of Ramapo Catskill Library System
Open Mon-Thurs 10-8, Fri 10-6, Sat 10-5, Sun 12-5
Friends of the Library Group

WATER MILL

S PARRISH ART MUSEUM LIBRARY*, 270 Montauk Hwy, 11976. SAN 312-4800. Tel: 631-283-2118. FAX: 631-283-7006. E-mail: info@parrishart.org. Web Site: www.parrishart.org. *Dir, Communications,* Susan Galardi
Founded 1955
Library Holdings: Bk Titles 5,000
Special Collections: Aline B Saarinen Library Coll; Moses & Ida Soyer Library Coll; William Merritt Chase Archives Coll
Wireless access
Function: Res libr
Restriction: Open by appt only

WATERFORD

P WATERFORD PUBLIC LIBRARY*, 117 Third St, 12188. SAN 312-6358. Tel: 518-237-0891. FAX: 518-237-2568. E-mail: watpublibrary@gmail.com. Web Site: www.waterfordlibrary.net. *Dir,* Timothy McDonough; E-mail: director@waterfordlibrary.net; *Youth Serv Librn,* Elizabeth Liddington; Staff 5 (MLS 2, Non-MLS 3)
Founded 1895. Pop 6,800; Circ 60,000
Library Holdings: AV Mats 4,532; Bk Vols 21,587; Per Subs 132; Talking Bks 1,340
Automation Activity & Vendor Info: (Acquisitions) Innovative Interfaces, Inc; (Cataloging) Innovative Interfaces, Inc; (Circulation) Innovative Interfaces, Inc; (ILL) Innovative Interfaces, Inc; (OPAC) Innovative Interfaces, Inc
Wireless access
Mem of Southern Adirondack Library System
Open Mon & Thurs 9-7, Tues & Wed 9-6, Fri 9-5, Sat 10-3 (9-1 July & Aug), Sun (Sept-June) 12-4
Friends of the Library Group

WATERLOO

P WATERLOO LIBRARY & HISTORICAL SOCIETY, 31 E Williams St, 13165. SAN 312-6366. Tel: 315-539-3313. FAX: 315-539-7798. E-mail: waterloolib@gmail.com. Web Site: www.wlhs-ny.com. *Libr Mgr,* Brandi Rozelle
Founded 1876. Pop 5,116; Circ 31,998
Library Holdings: Bk Titles 26,449; Per Subs 20
Subject Interests: Genealogy, Local hist
Automation Activity & Vendor Info: (Cataloging) Innovative Interfaces, Inc; (Circulation) Innovative Interfaces, Inc; (OPAC) Innovative Interfaces, Inc
Wireless access
Function: Adult bk club, Bks on CD, Butterfly Garden, Children's prog, Computers for patron use, For res purposes, Holiday prog, ILL available, Internet access, Laminating, Life-long learning prog for all ages, Magazines, Mango lang, Meeting rooms, Movies, Online cat, OverDrive digital audio bks, Photocopying/Printing, Prog for adults, Prog for children & young adult, Ref & res, Ref serv available, Res assist avail, Res performed for a fee, Scanner, Story hour, Study rm, Summer & winter reading prog, Summer reading prog, Tax forms, Teen prog, Wheelchair accessible
Mem of Finger Lakes Library System
Open Mon-Wed 10-7, Thurs & Fri 10-5, Sat 10-1

WATERTOWN

P EAST HOUNSFIELD FREE LIBRARY, 19438 State Rte 3, 13601. SAN 312-6374. Tel: 315-788-0637. FAX: 315-836-3172. E-mail: eholib@ncls.org. Web Site: www.easthounsfieldlibrary.org. *Dir,* Melissa Carroll
Circ 3,879
Library Holdings: Bk Vols 3,892
Wireless access
Mem of North Country Library System
Open Wed 10-6, Sat 10-2

P ROSWELL P FLOWER MEMORIAL LIBRARY, 229 Washington St, 13601-3388. SAN 312-6382. Tel: 315-785-7705. FAX: 315-788-2584. E-mail: watlib@ncls.org. Web Site: www.flowermemoriallibrary.org. *Libr Dir,* Yvonne Reff; Tel: 315-785-7701, E-mail: yreff@ncls.org; *Ch,* Suzie Renzi-Falge; Tel: 315-785-7709, E-mail: srenzi-falge@ncls.org; *Ref Librn,* Ashley Pickett; Tel: 315-785-7714, E-mail: apickett@ncls.org; *Teen Librn,* Brittani LaJuett; E-mail: blajuett@ncls.org; *Ref,* Amanda Tehonica; Tel: 315-785-7715, E-mail: atehonica@ncls.org. Subject Specialists: *Genealogy,* Amanda Tehonica; Staff 12 (MLS 5, Non-MLS 7)
Founded 1904. Pop 26,705; Circ 140,893
Library Holdings: e-journals 28; Electronic Media & Resources 17; Bk Vols 193,616; Per Subs 140; Talking Bks 1,405; Videos 2,800
Subject Interests: Genealogy, Local hist
Automation Activity & Vendor Info: (Circulation) SirsiDynix; (OPAC) SirsiDynix
Wireless access
Function: 24/7 Electronic res, 24/7 Online cat, Adult bk club, Archival coll, Audiobks via web, Bks on CD, Children's prog, Computer training, Computers for patron use, Electronic databases & coll, Free DVD rentals, ILL available, Internet access, Large print keyboards, Magazines, Magnifiers for reading, Meeting rooms, Microfiche/film & reading machines, Movies, Online cat, OverDrive digital audio bks, Photocopying/Printing, Prog for adults, Prog for children & young adult, Ref & res, Ref serv available, Res assist avail, Scanner, Story hour, Summer reading prog, Tax forms, Teen prog, Telephone ref
Mem of North Country Library System
Partic in Northern New York Library Network
Open Mon, Tues & Wed 9-8, Thurs & Fri 12-8, Sat 9-5
Friends of the Library Group

S JEFFERSON COUNTY HISTORICAL SOCIETY LIBRARY*, 228 Washington St, 13601. SAN 325-9765. Tel: 315-782-3491. FAX: 315-782-2913. E-mail: admin@JeffersonCountyHistory.org. Web Site: www.jeffersoncountyhistory.org. *Interim Exec Dir,* Toni Engleman; *Educ Curator,* Melissa Widrick; E-mail: educator@jeffersoncountyhistory.org
Library Holdings: Bk Vols 1,000
Special Collections: City Directories Coll (1830-1985); Nineteenth Century Maps of Jefferson County; Water Turbines Catalogue
Wireless access
Function: Ref serv available, Res libr
Publications: Exhibition Catalogues; JCHS Bulletin; Newsletter
Restriction: Open by appt only

G NEW YORK STATE DEPARTMENT OF CORRECTIONAL SERVICES*, Watertown Correctional Facility Library, 23147 Swan Rd, 13601-9340. SAN 322-8185. Tel: 315-782-7490. FAX: 315-782-7490, Ext 2099. *Librn,* Joan Pellikka; Staff 1 (MLS 1)
Library Holdings: Bk Titles 9,000; Bk Vols 9,500; Per Subs 84
Special Collections: Spanish Language & Culture
Subject Interests: African-Am hist
Automation Activity & Vendor Info: (Cataloging) Follett Software; (Circulation) Follett Software; (OPAC) Follett Software
Wireless access
Function: ILL available
Restriction: Non-circulating, Not open to pub

GL NEW YORK STATE SUPREME COURT*, Jefferson Law Library, 163 Arsenal St, 13601. SAN 312-6404. Tel: 315-785-3064. FAX: 315-266-4547. Web Site: www.nycourts.gov/library/jefferson. *Law Libr Asst,* Catherine A Miller; E-mail: cmiller@nycourts.gov
Founded 1914
Library Holdings: Bk Titles 850; Bk Vols 45,000; Per Subs 34
Wireless access
Open Mon-Fri 8:30-4:30
Restriction: Circ limited

P NORTH COUNTRY LIBRARY SYSTEM*, 22072 County Rte 190, 13601-1066. SAN 312-6412. Tel: 315-782-5540. FAX: 315-782-6883. Web Site: web.ncls.org. *Dir,* Susan Mitchell; E-mail: smitchell@ncls.org; Staff 8 (MLS 5, Non-MLS 3)
Founded 1947. Pop 372,990
Library Holdings: AV Mats 2,585; Bk Vols 239,363; Per Subs 40; Talking Bks 2,403
Automation Activity & Vendor Info: (Cataloging) SirsiDynix; (Circulation) SirsiDynix; (OPAC) SirsiDynix
Wireless access
Publications: Netbrary System Outreach Services (Newsletter); North Country Library News (Newsletter)
Member Libraries: Adams Center Free Library; Adams Free Library; Annie Porter Ainsworth Memorial Library; B Elizabeth Strong Memorial Library; Beaver Falls Library; Belleville Philomathean Free Library; Bodman Memorial Library; Brantingham Greig Reading & Technology Center; Brownville-Glen Park Library; Canton Free Library; Cape Vincent Community Library; Carthage Free Library; Central Square Library; Clifton Community Library; Cogswell Free Public Library; Constableville Village Library; Croghan Free Library; Crosby Public Library; Depauville Free Library; Dexter Free Library; East Hounsfield Free Library; Ellisburg Free Library; Evans Mills Public Library; Fulton Public Library; Hammond Free Library; Hannibal Free Library; Harrisville Free Library; Hawn Memorial Library; Hay Memorial Library; Henderson Free Library; Hepburn Library of Colton; Hepburn Library of Edwards; Hepburn Library of Hermon; Hepburn Library of Lisbon; Hepburn Library of Madrid; Hepburn Library of Norfolk; Hepburn Library of Waddington; Heuvelton Free Library; Hopkinton Town Library; Lowville Free Library; Lyme Free Library; Lyons Falls Library; Macsherry Library; Mannsville Free Library; Massena Public Library; Mexico Public Library; Morristown Public Library; New York State Department of Correctional Services; Norwood Public Library; Ogdensburg Public Library; Orleans Public Library; Osceola Public Library; Oswego Public Library; Parish Public Library; Phoenix Public Library; Port Leyden Community Library; Potsdam Public Library; Pulaski Public Library; Reading Room Association of Gouverneur; Richville Free Library; Rodman Public Library; Roswell P Flower Memorial Library; Russell Public Library; Sally Ploof Hunter Memorial Library; Theresa Free Library; Thousand Island Park Library; Town of Lewis Library; William H Bush Memorial Library; Williamstown Library
Partic in Northern New York Library Network; NY Libr Asn; OCLC Online Computer Library Center, Inc
Special Services for the Deaf - Bks on deafness & sign lang; Closed caption videos
Special Services for the Blind - BiFolkal kits; Bks on cassette; Bks on CD; Home delivery serv; Large print bks; Talking bks
Open Mon-Fri 8-4:30

M SAMARITAN MEDICAL CENTER*, Hunter-Rice Health Sciences Library, 728 Washington St, 13601. SAN 373-6962. Tel: 315-785-4191. FAX: 315-779-5173. Web Site: library.samaritanhealth.com. *Dir, Libr Serv,* Position Currently Open; *Librn,* Ellen Darabaner; E-mail: edarabaner@shsny.com; *Tech Serv,* Michael Chartrand; Staff 5 (MLS 3, Non-MLS 2)
Library Holdings: Bk Titles 1,000; Per Subs 200
Automation Activity & Vendor Info: (Cataloging) LibLime; (Circulation) LibLime
Wireless access
Open Mon-Fri 8-5

J STATE UNIVERSITY OF NEW YORK - JEFFERSON COMMUNITY COLLEGE*, Jefferson Community College Library, 1220 Coffeen St, 13601-1897. SAN 312-6390. Tel: 315-786-2225. Web Site: sunyjefferson.edu/academics/library. *Interim Dir,* John Thomas; E-mail: jthomas@sunnyjeferson.edu; *Info Literacy,* Carleen Huxley; Tel: 315-786-2402, E-mail: chuxley@sunyjefferson.edu; Staff 7 (MLS 3, Non-MLS 4)
Founded 1963. Enrl 2,600; Fac 70; Highest Degree: Associate
Library Holdings: Audiobooks 357; CDs 433; DVDs 2,160; e-journals 7,000; Electronic Media & Resources 102; Bk Vols 36,693; Per Subs 100; Videos 1,000
Subject Interests: Jefferson County local hist
Automation Activity & Vendor Info: (Cataloging) Ex Libris Group; (Circulation) Ex Libris Group; (Course Reserve) Ex Libris Group; (OPAC) Ex Libris Group; (Serials) Ex Libris Group
Wireless access
Publications: Annual Report
Partic in Northern New York Library Network; OCLC Online Computer Library Center, Inc; SUNYConnect; Westchester Academic Library Directors Organization
Special Services for the Deaf - Assistive tech; Bks on deafness & sign lang; Closed caption videos; Deaf publ
Special Services for the Blind - Ref serv; Talking calculator

S WATERTOWN DAILY TIMES LIBRARY*, 260 Washington St, 13601. SAN 322-9106. Tel: 315-782-1000, Ext 2445. FAX: 315-661-2523. E-mail: news@wdt.net. Web Site: www.watertowndailytimes.com, www.wdt.net. *Chief Librn,* Kelly Burdick; E-mail: kburdick@wdt.net; Staff 3 (MLS 1, Non-MLS 2)
Special Collections: Other Northern New York Newspapers, microfilm
Subject Interests: Northern NY hist
Open Tues-Thurs 1-3

WATERVILLE

P WATERVILLE PUBLIC LIBRARY*, 206 White St, 13480. SAN 312-6420. Tel: 315-841-4651. Web Site: www.watervillepl.org. *Dir,* Jeffrey Reynolds; E-mail: jeff@watervillepl.org; *Asst Dir,* Amanda Briggs; E-mail: amanda@watervillepl.org; Staff 1 (MLS 1)
Founded 1874. Pop 5,500; Circ 39,983
Library Holdings: CDs 1,121; Bk Vols 25,835; Per Subs 41; Videos 1,995
Special Collections: Waterville Times (local newspaper) 1855-1990, microfilm

Automation Activity & Vendor Info: (Cataloging) SirsiDynix; (Circulation) SirsiDynix
Wireless access
Mem of Mid-York Library System
Open Mon, Wed & Fri 10-5:30, Tues-Thurs 2-8, Sat 10-2
Friends of the Library Group
Branches: 1
DEANSBORO BRANCH, Marshall Community Ctr, Deansboro, 13328, SAN 329-5680. Tel: 315-841-4888. E-mail: waterville@midyork.org. Web Site: www.uhls.org/watervliet. *Br Mgr,* Margery Wilson
Library Holdings: Bk Vols 5,183; Per Subs 8; Videos 450
Open Mon 5:30-7:30, Tues 2-6, Thurs & Sat 9:30-11:30, Fri 9:30-11:30 & 2-4
Friends of the Library Group

WATERVLIET

P WATERVLIET PUBLIC LIBRARY*, 1501 Broadway, 12189-2895. SAN 312-6455. Tel: 518-274-4471. FAX: 518-271-0667. Web Site: www.watervlietpubliclibrary.org. *Dir,* Kelly Vadney; E-mail: director@watervlietpubliclibrary.org; Staff 2 (MLS 1, Non-MLS 1)
Founded 1953. Pop 10,207; Circ 15,052
Library Holdings: Bk Vols 16,738; Per Subs 15
Special Collections: City Directories (1855 to present)
Automation Activity & Vendor Info: (Circulation) SirsiDynix; (OPAC) SirsiDynix
Wireless access
Mem of Upper Hudson Library System
Open Mon-Thurs 12:30-8, Fri 2-6, Sat 11-3

WATKINS GLEN

P WATKINS GLEN PUBLIC LIBRARY*, 610 S Decatur St, 14891. SAN 312-6463. Tel: 607-535-2346. FAX: 607-535-7338. Web Site: www.watkinsglenlibrary.org. *Dir,* Stephen Salino; E-mail: salinos@stls.org; *Asst Librn,* Kathy Gascon; Staff 2.6 (MLS 0.6, Non-MLS 2)
Founded 1870. Pop 8,579; Circ 51,231
Jul 2014-Jun 2015 Income $178,778. Mats Exp $28,300, Books $22,500, Other Print Mats $2,300, AV Mat $3,500. Sal $89,508
Library Holdings: AV Mats 4,969; Bk Vols 32,984; Per Subs 42
Automation Activity & Vendor Info: (Circulation) SirsiDynix; (ILL) SirsiDynix; (OPAC) SirsiDynix; (Serials) SirsiDynix
Wireless access
Function: Art exhibits, Audio & video playback equip for onsite use, Bk reviews (Group), Bks on cassette, Bks on CD, Children's prog, Computer training, Computers for patron use, Electronic databases & coll, Free DVD rentals, Holiday prog, ILL available, Instruction & testing, Internet access, Mail & tel request accepted, Music CDs, Online cat, Online ref, Photocopying/Printing, Prog for adults, Prog for children & young adult, Scanner, Senior computer classes, Serves people with intellectual disabilities, Spoken cassettes & CDs, Spoken cassettes & DVDs, Story hour, Summer reading prog, Tax forms, Telephone ref, VHS videos, Wheelchair accessible, Writing prog
Mem of Southern Tier Library System
Open Mon-Fri 11-5 & 7-9, Sat 10-2, Sun 2-4
Friends of the Library Group

WAVERLY

P WAVERLY FREE LIBRARY*, 18 Elizabeth St, 14892. SAN 312-6471. Tel: 607-565-9341. FAX: 607-565-3960. E-mail: wavlib14892@yahoo.com. Web Site: waverlyfreelibrary.org. *Dir,* Chris Brewster; Staff 1 (Non-MLS 1)
Founded 1929. Pop 4,607; Circ 30,087
Library Holdings: AV Mats 1,154; CDs 85; DVDs 2,300; Large Print Bks 900; Bk Vols 40,265; Per Subs 40
Special Collections: Local/regional authors
Subject Interests: Civil War, Local hist
Automation Activity & Vendor Info: (Cataloging) Innovative Interfaces, Inc; (Circulation) Innovative Interfaces, Inc; (OPAC) Innovative Interfaces, Inc
Wireless access
Function: Adult bk club, Adult literacy prog, Art exhibits, Audio & video playback equip for onsite use, Audiobks on Playaways & MP3, Audiobks via web, Bk club(s), Bks on CD, Chess club, Children's prog, Computers for patron use, Digital talking bks, Electronic databases & coll, Free DVD rentals, ILL available, Internet access, Magazines, Magnifiers for reading, Makerspace, Mango lang, Meeting rooms, Movies, Music CDs, Online cat, Outreach serv, Photocopying/Printing, Preschool reading prog, Prog for adults, Prog for children & young adult, Ref serv available, Senior computer classes, STEM programs, Story hour, Summer reading prog, Tax forms, Teen prog, Wheelchair accessible
Mem of Finger Lakes Library System
Special Services for the Deaf - Closed caption videos
Special Services for the Blind - Bks on CD
Open Tues & Thurs 10-8, Wed 10-6, Fri & Sat 11-5

WAYLAND

P WAYLAND FREE LIBRARY*, Gunlocke Memorial Library, 101 W Naples St, 14572. SAN 312-648X. Tel: 585-728-5380. FAX: 585-728-5002. Web Site: gunlockelibrary.org. *Dir,* Jen Farr; Staff 1 (MLS 1)
Founded 1913. Pop 5,000; Circ 35,477. Sal $101,174 (Prof $36,720)
Library Holdings: Audiobooks 1,508; Bks on Deafness & Sign Lang 40; CDs 420; DVDs 1,821; e-books 4,336; Electronic Media & Resources 218; High Interest/Low Vocabulary Bk Vols 80; Large Print Bks 1,636; Bk Titles 28,052; Per Subs 87; Videos 348
Special Collections: Children with Developmental Disabilities (Parent Reference Coll); Local Newspapers, Microfilm; Railroad Coll
Subject Interests: Local hist
Automation Activity & Vendor Info: (Cataloging) SirsiDynix; (Circulation) SirsiDynix; (OPAC) SirsiDynix; (Serials) SirsiDynix
Wireless access
Function: Adult bk club, Bks on CD, Children's prog, Computer training, Computers for patron use, Family literacy, Free DVD rentals, ILL available, Large print keyboards, Microfiche/film & reading machines, Music CDs, Online cat, OverDrive digital audio bks, Photocopying/Printing, Preschool outreach, Preschool reading prog, Printer for laptops & handheld devices, Prog for adults, Prog for children & young adult, Scanner, Senior computer classes, Senior outreach, Story hour, Summer reading prog, Tax forms, Wheelchair accessible
Mem of Southern Tier Library System
Partic in New York Online Virtual Electronic Library
Special Services for the Deaf - TTY equip
Special Services for the Blind - Braille bks
Open Mon-Wed 10-7, Thurs & Fri 10-5, Sat (Winter) 10-2

WEBSTER

P WEBSTER PUBLIC LIBRARY, Webster Plaza, 980 Ridge Rd, 14580. SAN 312-6501. Tel: 585-872-7075. E-mail: webster.reference@libraryweb.org. Web Site: www.websterlibrary.org. *Dir,* Terri Bennett; E-mail: tbennett@libraryweb.org; *Ad, Asst Dir,* Doreen Dailey; E-mail: doreen.dailey@libraryweb.org; *Asst Dir, Learning Librn,* Shana Lynott; E-mail: slynott@libraryweb.org; *Ch Serv Librn,* Jason Poole; E-mail: jpoole@libraryweb.org; *Teen Serv Librn,* Colleen Hernandez; E-mail: colleen.hernandez@libraryweb.org; Staff 24 (MLS 7, Non-MLS 17)
Founded 1929. Pop 45,000; Circ 645,314
Library Holdings: Bk Vols 241,795
Automation Activity & Vendor Info: (Circulation) CARL.Solution (TLC); (OPAC) CARL.Solution (TLC)
Wireless access
Mem of Monroe County Library System
Open Mon-Fri 9-6, Sat 11-3
Friends of the Library Group

WEEDSPORT

P WEEDSPORT LIBRARY*, 2795 E Brutus St, 13166. (Mail add: PO Box 2795, 13166-2795), SAN 325-9781. Tel: 315-834-6222. FAX: 315-834-8621. Web Site: www.weedsportlibrary.org. *Dir,* Cheryl Austin; E-mail: director@weedsportlibrary.org; *Asst Dir,* Linda Quinn
Library Holdings: Bk Vols 14,525; Per Subs 15
Special Collections: Local History; References, clips, docs, maps; School Texts & Photographs
Subject Interests: Genealogy, Local govt
Automation Activity & Vendor Info: (Cataloging) Innovative Interfaces, Inc; (Circulation) Innovative Interfaces, Inc; (OPAC) Innovative Interfaces, Inc
Wireless access
Mem of Finger Lakes Library System
Open Mon-Thurs 10-9, Fri 3-7, Sat 10-2
Friends of the Library Group

WELLSVILLE

C ALFRED STATE COLLEGE, SCHOOL OF APPLIED TECHNOLOGY, Wellsville Campus Library, 2530 River Rd, 14895. SAN 351-8132. Tel: 607-587-3115. FAX: 607-587-3120. Web Site: alfredstate.libguides.com. *Librn,* Cindy Flurschutz; E-mail: flurscc1@alfredstate.edu
Library Holdings: Bk Vols 3,300
Subject Interests: Automotive, Bldg, Construction trades, Culinary trades, Electrical, Welding
Wireless access
Open Mon-Fri (Sept-May) 8-4

P DAVID A HOWE PUBLIC LIBRARY, 155 N Main St, 14895. SAN 312-6544. Tel: 585-593-3410. FAX: 585-593-4176. E-mail: wellsville@stls.org. Web Site: www.davidahowelibrary.org. *Dir,* Nicolas Gunning; Staff 1 (MLS 1)
Founded 1894. Pop 5,241; Circ 127,417

Library Holdings: AV Mats 8,111; Bk Vols 102,476; Per Subs 91
Special Collections: Bird's Egg Coll (Charles Munson Coll); Children's Reference Books; Currier & Ives Coll; Indian Artifacts (Avery Mosher Coll); Lincoln Pictures (Coyle Coll). State Document Depository
Automation Activity & Vendor Info: (Circulation) SirsiDynix; (OPAC) SirsiDynix
Wireless access
Mem of Southern Tier Library System
Open Mon-Thurs 10-8, Fri 10-5, Sat 10-2
Friends of the Library Group

P SCIO MEMORIAL LIBRARY*, 3980 Rte 19, 14895. (Mail add: PO Box 77, Scio, 14895), SAN 312-4495. Tel: 585-593-4816. FAX: 585-593-4816. E-mail: sciolibrary@gmail.com. Web Site: sciolibrary.org. *Dir,* Sue Moyer; E-mail: moyers@stls.org; Staff 1 (Non-MLS 1)
Founded 1906. Pop 1,900; Circ 7,500
Library Holdings: Bk Vols 6,100; Per Subs 20
Subject Interests: Civil War, Genealogy, Quilting
Wireless access
Mem of Southern Tier Library System
Open Tues & Thurs 10-5, Wed 1-7
Friends of the Library Group

WEST BABYLON

P WEST BABYLON PUBLIC LIBRARY*, 211 Rte 109, 11704. SAN 324-4873. Tel: 631-669-5445. FAX: 631-669-6539. E-mail: businessoffice@wbpl.us. Web Site: wbab.suffolk.lib.ny.us. *Dir,* Gail Pepa; *Ad, Computer Serv Librn,* Jill Cuba; *Ch Serv Librn,* Ilana Silver; *Children & Teen Librn,* Carisse Bormann; *Ref Serv Librn,* Nicole Haas; Staff 31 (MLS 14, Non-MLS 17)
Founded 1982. Pop 28,271; Circ 323,739
Jul 2016-Jun 2017. Mats Exp $328,340, Books $174,937, Per/Ser (Incl. Access Fees) $12,925, AV Mat $57,722, Electronic Ref Mat (Incl. Access Fees) $82,756
Library Holdings: Audiobooks 8,704; AV Mats 5,841; e-books 5,623; Electronic Media & Resources 5,010; Bk Vols 97,687; Per Subs 227; Videos 3,736
Automation Activity & Vendor Info: (Acquisitions) Innovative Interfaces, Inc - Sierra; (Cataloging) Innovative Interfaces, Inc - Sierra; (Circulation) Innovative Interfaces, Inc - Sierra; (Discovery) Innovative Interfaces, Inc - Sierra; (ILL) Innovative Interfaces, Inc - Sierra; (OPAC) Innovative Interfaces, Inc - Sierra; (Serials) Innovative Interfaces, Inc - Sierra
Wireless access
Function: 24/7 Electronic res, 24/7 Online cat, Activity rm, Adult bk club, Adult literacy prog, After school storytime, Art exhibits, Audiobks via web, Bks on CD, E-Readers, Electronic databases & coll, Museum passes
Publications: Newsletter (Monthly)
Mem of Suffolk Cooperative Library System
Special Services for the Deaf - TTY equip; Videos & decoder
Open Mon-Thurs 10-9, Fri & Sat 10-5, Sun (Oct-May) 1-5
Friends of the Library Group

WEST CHAZY

P DODGE LIBRARY*, Nine Fisk Rd, 12992. (Mail add: PO Box 226, 12992-0226), SAN 312-6560. Tel: 518-493-6131. FAX: 518-493-6131. E-mail: dodge_library@yahoo.com. Web Site: www.dodgelibrary.org. *Dir,* Linda Dupee
Circ 9,097
Library Holdings: Bk Vols 7,500; Per Subs 15
Special Collections: New England, New York, Pennsylvania & New Jersey Genealogy (Nell B Sullivan Memorial Coll)
Subject Interests: Local hist
Automation Activity & Vendor Info: (Cataloging) Horizon; (Circulation) Horizon; (OPAC) Horizon
Wireless access
Mem of Clinton-Essex-Franklin Library System
Open Tues & Thurs 9-6, Sat 9-Noon

WEST HAVERSTRAW

M HELEN HAYES HOSPITAL*, Medical Library, Rte 9 W, 10993. SAN 312-6579. Tel: 845-786-4000, 845-786-4185. Interlibrary Loan Service Tel: 845-786-4188. FAX: 845-786-4692. Web Site: hhh.hospitalservices.senylrc.org. *Chief Operating Officer,* Kathleen Martucci; Tel: 845-786-4201; Staff 2 (MLS 1, Non-MLS 1)
Founded 1960
Library Holdings: Bk Titles 1,500; Per Subs 100
Subject Interests: Arthritis, Hearing, Neurology, Occupational therapy, Orthopedics, Phys therapy, Rehabilitation med, Speech
Wireless access
Partic in Health Info Librs of Westchester; Middle Atlantic Regional Med Libr Prog; Southeastern New York Library Resources Council
Open Mon-Fri 12-4

WEST HEMPSTEAD

P WEST HEMPSTEAD PUBLIC LIBRARY, 500 Hempstead Ave, 11552. SAN 312-6587. Tel: 516-481-6591. FAX: 516-481-2608. Reference E-mail: reference@whplibrary.org. Web Site: www.whplibrary.org. *Dir,* Regina Mascia; E-mail: regina.mascia@whnypl.org; Staff 41 (MLS 13, Non-MLS 28)
Founded 1967. Pop 18,301; Circ 221,732
Jul 2019-Jun 2020 Income $3,822,884. Mats Exp $351,714, Books $168,000, Per/Ser (Incl. Access Fees) $15,000, AV Equip $7,000, AV Mat $97,000, Electronic Ref Mat (Incl. Access Fees) $64,714. Sal $1,659,944 (Prof $841,729)
Library Holdings: Audiobooks 5,713; CDs 5,713; DVDs 14,230; e-books 99,649; Large Print Bks 2,500; Bk Vols 96,288; Per Subs 145
Automation Activity & Vendor Info: (Cataloging) Innovative Interfaces, Inc - Sierra; (Circulation) Innovative Interfaces, Inc - Sierra; (ILL) OCLC FirstSearch; (Media Booking) OCLC FirstSearch; (OPAC) Innovative Interfaces, Inc - Sierra; (Serials) EBSCO Discovery Service
Wireless access
Function: 24/7 Electronic res, 24/7 Online cat, Adult bk club, Adult literacy prog, Art exhibits, Audiobks via web, Bilingual assistance for Spanish patrons, Bks on CD, Children's prog, Citizenship assistance, Computers for patron use, Electronic databases & coll, Family literacy, Free DVD rentals, Genealogy discussion group, Holiday prog, Homework prog, ILL available, Internet access, Large print keyboards, Life-long learning prog for all ages, Magazines, Mail & tel request accepted, Meeting rooms, Movies, Museum passes, Music CDs, Notary serv, Online cat, Online ref, Outreach serv, OverDrive digital audio bks, Photocopying/Printing, Preschool reading prog, Prog for adults, Prog for children & young adult, Ref & res, Ref serv available, Scanner, Senior outreach, Spanish lang bks, Spoken cassettes & CDs, Spoken cassettes & DVDs, STEM programs, Story hour, Study rm, Summer reading prog, Tax forms, Teen prog, Telephone ref, Wheelchair accessible, Workshops
Publications: Newsletter (Quarterly)
Mem of Nassau Library System
Partic in Long Island Library Resources Council; New York State Interlibrary Loan Network
Special Services for the Blind - Large print bks
Restriction: Borrowing requests are handled by ILL, ID required to use computers (Ltd hrs), Non-resident fee
Friends of the Library Group

WEST HURLEY

P WEST HURLEY PUBLIC LIBRARY*, 42 Clover St, 12491. SAN 312-6595. Tel: 845-679-6405. FAX: 845-679-2144. E-mail: mailbox@westhurleylibrary.org. Web Site: westhurleylibrary.org. *Dir,* Kara Lustiber; Staff 1 (MLS 1)
Founded 1989. Pop 3,352; Circ 37,747
Jan 2018-Dec 2018 Income $226,715, State $2,400, Other $224,315. Mats Exp $28,655, Books $17,054, Other Print Mats $665, Electronic Ref Mat (Incl. Access Fees) $10,936. Sal $36,558 (Prof $60,410)
Library Holdings: Audiobooks 1,203; DVDs 1,362; e-books 15,116; Electronic Media & Resources 25; Bk Titles 16,552; Per Subs 19
Subject Interests: Local hist
Automation Activity & Vendor Info: (Cataloging) Innovative Interfaces, Inc; (OPAC) Innovative Interfaces, Inc
Wireless access
Function: Adult bk club, Audio & video playback equip for onsite use, Audiobks on Playaways & MP3, Bk club(s), Bks on CD, Children's prog, Computer training, Computers for patron use, Digital talking bks, Electronic databases & coll, Free DVD rentals, Holiday prog, ILL available, Internet access, Magazines, Mango lang, Meeting rooms, Movies, Museum passes, Online cat, OverDrive digital audio bks, Photocopying/Printing, Preschool reading prog, Prog for adults, Prog for children & young adult, Scanner, Story hour, Summer reading prog, Tax forms, Workshops
Mem of Mid-Hudson Library System
Open Mon & Wed 1-7, Tues & Fri 10-6, Sat 10-3
Friends of the Library Group

WEST ISLIP

M GOOD SAMARITAN HOSPITAL*, Medical Library, 1000 Montauk Hwy, 11795. SAN 312-6609. Tel: 631-376-3380. FAX: 631-376-4166. *Librn,* Joshua Seymour; E-mail: joshua.seymour@chsli.org; Staff 1 (MLS 1)
Founded 1961
Library Holdings: Bk Titles 700; Per Subs 60
Special Collections: Medical Coll, texts & journals
Wireless access
Function: Ref serv available
Partic in Medical & Scientific Libraries of Long Island
Restriction: Staff use only

P WEST ISLIP PUBLIC LIBRARY, Three Higbie Lane, 11795-3999. SAN 312-6617. Tel: 631-661-7080. FAX: 631-661-7137. Administration FAX: 631-661-6573. E-mail: contactus@westisliplibrary.org. Reference E-mail: reference@westisliplibrary.org. Web Site: www.wipublib.org. *Dir,* Andrew Hamm; E-mail: ahamm@westisliplibrary.org; *Head, Adult Serv,* Maureen Heuer; *Head, Children's Servx,* Elizabeth Sullivan; Staff 12 (MLS 12)
Founded 1957. Pop 28,042; Circ 113,956
Library Holdings: Audiobooks 2,284; AV Mats 23,376; CDs 8,122; DVDs 12,317; e-books 415,952; e-journals 160; Electronic Media & Resources 515,610; Large Print Bks 5,670; Bk Titles 155,611; Per Subs 190
Special Collections: Career Center (Grace O'Connor)
Automation Activity & Vendor Info: (Acquisitions) Innovative Interfaces, Inc; (Cataloging) Innovative Interfaces, Inc; (Circulation) Innovative Interfaces, Inc; (Course Reserve) Innovative Interfaces, Inc; (ILL) Innovative Interfaces, Inc; (OPAC) Innovative Interfaces, Inc
Wireless access
Publications: Library Newsletter; The Source
Mem of Suffolk Cooperative Library System
Open Mon-Thurs 10-9, Fri 10-6, Sat 9-5
Friends of the Library Group

WEST LEYDEN

P TOWN OF LEWIS LIBRARY*, 5213 Osceola Rd, 13489. Tel: 315-942-6813. E-mail: wlylib@ncls.org. Web Site: westleydenlibrary.org. *Dir,* Susan Kornatowski
Mem of North Country Library System
Open Tues 10:30-Noon, Thurs 2-4, Thurs 6:30-8

WEST NYACK

P WEST NYACK FREE LIBRARY, 65 Strawtown Rd, 10994. SAN 312-6633. Tel: 845-358-6081. FAX: 845-358-4071. E-mail: administrator@westnyacklibrary.org. Web Site: www.westnyacklibrary.org. *Dir,* Rhonda Rossman; E-mail: director@westnyacklibrary.org; *Head, Circ,* Dina Rosco; E-mail: circulation@westnyacklibrary.org; *Head, Pub Serv,* Myrna Sigal; E-mail: publicservice@westnyacklibrary.org; *Head, Tech Serv,* Carmela Fiore; E-mail: technicalservices@westnyacklibrary.org; *Adult Programs,* Susan Ferber; E-mail: sferber@westnyacklibrary.org; Staff 3.9 (MLS 3.3, Non-MLS 0.6)
Founded 1959. Pop 7,547; Circ 95,597
Library Holdings: AV Mats 9,201; Bk Vols 50,568; Per Subs 155
Automation Activity & Vendor Info: (Cataloging) SirsiDynix-Symphony; (Circulation) SirsiDynix-Symphony; (ILL) SirsiDynix-Symphony; (OPAC) SirsiDynix-Symphony
Wireless access
Publications: Newsletter
Mem of Ramapo Catskill Library System
Partic in Library Association of Rockland County; NY Libr Asn
Open Mon-Thurs 9:30-9, Fri 9:30-5, Sat 10-5, Sun 1-5 (Winter); Mon-Thurs 9:30-9, Fri 9:30-5, Sat 10-4 (Summer)
Friends of the Library Group

WEST POINT

UNITED STATES ARMY

AM USA MEDDAC*, Keller Army Community Hospital, Bldg 900, US Military Academy, 10996-1197, SAN 354-3676. Tel: 845-938-4883. *Librn,* Becky Michaels; E-mail: rebecca.michaels2.civ@mail.mil; Staff 1 (MLS 1)
Library Holdings: e-books 30; e-journals 20; Bk Vols 500; Per Subs 16; Spec Interest Per Sub 16
Special Collections: Sports Medicine Coll
Subject Interests: Sports med
Function: Online cat
Partic in Army Medical Department - Medical Library & Information Network; Federal Library & Information Center Committee; Southeastern New York Library Resources Council
Special Services for the Blind - Web-Braille
Restriction: Mil only
Friends of the Library Group

A WEST POINT POST LIBRARY*, 622 Swift Rd, 10996-1981, SAN 354-3668. Tel: 845-938-2974. FAX: 845-938-3019. *Librn,* Suzanne Moskala
Library Holdings: Bk Titles 33,000; Bk Vols 37,000; Per Subs 65
Subject Interests: Mil hist
Automation Activity & Vendor Info: (Circulation) EOS International
Partic in OCLC Online Computer Library Center, Inc

C UNITED STATES MILITARY ACADEMY LIBRARY*, Jefferson Hall Library & Learning Ctr, 758 Cullum Rd, 10996. SAN 312-6641. Tel: 845-938-8301. Circulation Tel: 845-938-2230. Reference Tel: 845-938-8325. FAX: 845-938-4000. E-mail: library@westpoint.edu. Web Site: westpoint.edu/library. *Assoc Dean, Librn,* Christopher Barth; E-mail: christopher.barth@usma.edu; *Assoc Dir for Finance & Personnel,* Samuel Richards; *Assoc Dir, Coll Serv,* David Stockton; *Assoc Dir, Curricular Engagement,* Dan Pritchard; *Assoc Dir, Spec Coll & Archives,* Suzanne Christoff; *AV Librn,* Michael Arden; *Cat Librn,* Marie Dennett; *Collection Support Librn,* Dawn L Crumpler; *Ref Librn,* Celeste Evans; *Engagement Librn,* Laura Mosher; *Plebe Experience Librn,* Karen Shea; *Syst Librn,* Larry Tietze; *Info Support Coord,* Pam Long; *Curator of Archives,* Alicia Mauldin-Ware; *Curator, Rare Bks,* Elaine McConnell; *Ms Curator,* Susan Lintelmann. Subject Specialists: *Humanities,* Dawn L Crumpler
Founded 1802. Highest Degree: Bachelor
Special Collections: Cadet Textbooks; Chess Coll; Hudson Highlands History; Military Arts & Sciences; Omar N Bradley Papers; Orientalia; Papers & Writings of Academy Graduates; US Army History; West Pointiana. US Document Depository
Automation Activity & Vendor Info: (OPAC) Innovative Interfaces, Inc - Millennium; (Serials) Innovative Interfaces, Inc - Millennium
Wireless access
Publications: Archives & Manuscript Inventory Lists; Friends of the West Point Library Newsletter (Large print newspapers); Library Handbook; New Accessions; Subject Bibliographies
Partic in ConnectNY, Inc; OCLC Online Computer Library Center, Inc; Southeastern New York Library Resources Council
Open Mon-Thurs 7am-11:15pm, Fri 7am-9pm, Sat 10-9, Sun 10am-11:15pm
Restriction: Authorized patrons

WEST SAYVILLE

S LONG ISLAND MARITIME MUSEUM LIBRARY, 86 West Ave, 11796-1908. (Mail add: PO Box 184, 11796-0184), SAN 312-665X. Tel: 631-447-8679, 631-854-4974. FAX: 631-854-4979. E-mail: limm@limaritime.org. Web Site: www.limaritime.org. *Exec Dir,* Terry Lister Blitman; *Librn,* Barbara Forde; E-mail: barbaralimm@gmail.com
Founded 1966
Library Holdings: Bk Titles 3,000
Special Collections: Photograph Coll, copy prints, glass plates, original & copy negatives, original historic prints, slides
Subject Interests: America's Cup races, Boatbuilding, Groundings, Lifesaving, Local captains, Local hist, Local shipwrecks, Racing, Shellfishing, Ship models, Vessels, Wildfowling, Yachting
Wireless access
Restriction: Open by appt only

WEST SENECA

P WEST SENECA PUBLIC LIBRARY*, 1300 Union Rd, 14224. SAN 312-6676. Tel: 716-674-2928. FAX: 716-674-9206. Web Site: www.buffalolib.org/content/library-locations/westseneca. *Dir,* Robert Alessi; E-mail: alessir@buffalolib.org; Staff 3 (MLS 3)
Founded 1935. Circ 332,994
Library Holdings: Bk Vols 65,000
Automation Activity & Vendor Info: (Cataloging) SirsiDynix; (Circulation) SirsiDynix; (OPAC) SirsiDynix
Wireless access
Mem of Buffalo & Erie County Public Library System
Open Mon-Thurs 9-8, Fri 9-5, Sat 10-4
Friends of the Library Group

WEST SHOKAN

P OLIVE FREE LIBRARY ASSOCIATION*, 4033 Rte 28A, 12494. SAN 312-6684. Tel: 845-657-2482. FAX: 845-657-2664. E-mail: helpdesk@olivefreelibrary.org. Web Site: olivefreelibrary.org. *Dir,* Chrissy Lawlor
Founded 1952. Pop 4,000
Library Holdings: Bk Titles 35,000; Per Subs 52
Automation Activity & Vendor Info: (Cataloging) Innovative Interfaces, Inc; (Circulation) Innovative Interfaces, Inc; (ILL) Innovative Interfaces, Inc; (Media Booking) Innovative Interfaces, Inc; (OPAC) Innovative Interfaces, Inc
Wireless access
Mem of Mid-Hudson Library System
Open Mon & Tues 10-8, Wed & Thurs 1-8, Fri 1-5, Sat 10-4

WEST WINFIELD

P WEST WINFIELD LIBRARY*, Bisby Hall, 179 South St, 13491-2826. (Mail add: PO Box 487, 13491-0487), SAN 312-6692. Tel: 315-822-6394. FAX: 315-822-6394. E-mail: westwinfield@midyork.org. Web Site: www.midyorklib.org/westwinfield. *Libr Mgr,* Ruth Rowe
Founded 1895. Pop 871; Circ 25,196
Library Holdings: Bk Vols 22,000; Per Subs 16
Automation Activity & Vendor Info: (Cataloging) SirsiDynix; (Circulation) SirsiDynix; (OPAC) SirsiDynix; (Serials) SirsiDynix
Wireless access
Mem of Mid-York Library System

Open Mon, Tues, Thurs & Fri 12:30-5:30, Wed 10-12 & 6-8, Sat 10-12
Friends of the Library Group

WESTBURY

P WESTBURY MEMORIAL PUBLIC LIBRARY*, 445 Jefferson St, 11590. SAN 354-3870. Tel: 516-333-0176. FAX: 516-333-1752. E-mail: contactus@westburylibrary.org. Web Site: www.westburylibrary.org. *Dir,* Position Currently Open; *Head, Ref,* Camina Raphael-Lubin; E-mail: clubin@westburylibrary.org; Staff 32 (MLS 8, Non-MLS 24)
Founded 1924. Pop 25,488
Library Holdings: Bk Vols 99,500; Per Subs 100
Special Collections: Old English & American Children's Books
Automation Activity & Vendor Info: (Acquisitions) Innovative Interfaces, Inc; (Cataloging) Innovative Interfaces, Inc; (Circulation) Innovative Interfaces, Inc; (Course Reserve) Innovative Interfaces, Inc; (ILL) Innovative Interfaces, Inc; (OPAC) Innovative Interfaces, Inc; (Serials) Innovative Interfaces, Inc
Wireless access
Publications: Bi-Monthly Program Schedules; Newsletters
Mem of Nassau Library System
Open Mon 10-9, Tues-Fri 9-9, Sat 9-5 (9-1 July-Aug), Sun 1-5
Branches: 1
CHILDREN'S LIBRARY, 374 School St, 11590, SAN 354-3900. Tel: 516-333-0176. E-mail: westburykids@westburylibrary.org. Web Site: westburylibrary.org/childrens. *Head, Children's Libr,* Emily Farrell; E-mail: emilyfarrell@westburylibrary.org
Library Holdings: Bk Vols 18,500; Per Subs 17
Special Collections: Old Children's Books
Open Mon 10-8, Tues-Thurs 9-8, Fri 9-5

WESTERLO

P WESTERLO PUBLIC LIBRARY*, 604 State Rte 143, 12193. (Mail add: PO Box 267, 12193), SAN 376-3072. Tel: 518-797-3415. FAX: 518-797-3415. Web Site: www.westerlolibrary.org. *Dir,* Sue A Hoadley; E-mail: director@westerlolibrary.org; Staff 1 (MLS 1)
Founded 1986. Pop 3,361; Circ 17,494
Jan 2019-Dec 2019 Income $83,661, State $1,418, City $79,843, Locally Generated Income $400, Other $2,000. Mats Exp $12,909, Books $6,403, Per/Ser (Incl. Access Fees) $425, AV Mat $5,019, Electronic Ref Mat (Incl. Access Fees) $1,062. Sal $52,172 (Prof $27,500)
Library Holdings: Audiobooks 154; CDs 190; DVDs 2,500; Large Print Bks 51; Bk Titles 7,754; Per Subs 17
Automation Activity & Vendor Info: (Cataloging) Innovative Interfaces, Inc - Sierra; (Circulation) Innovative Interfaces, Inc - Sierra; (OPAC) Innovative Interfaces, Inc - Sierra
Wireless access
Function: 24/7 Electronic res, 24/7 Online cat, Adult bk club, After school storytime, Computers for patron use, ILL available, Internet access, Online cat, Photocopying/Printing, Story hour, Tax forms, Wheelchair accessible
Mem of Upper Hudson Library System
Open Mon 2-6, Tues 2-8, Wed & Sat 9-2, Thurs 3-8, Fri 4-8

WESTERNVILLE

P WESTERN TOWN LIBRARY, 9172 Main St, 13486. (Mail add: PO Box 247, 13486-0247), SAN 312-6730. Tel: 315-827-4118. E-mail: westernville@midyork.org. Web Site: westerntownlibrary.org. *Dir,* Mary Jo Miller
Founded 1921. Pop 1,951
Library Holdings: Bk Titles 10,532; Per Subs 20
Automation Activity & Vendor Info: (Cataloging) SirsiDynix
Wireless access
Mem of Mid-York Library System
Open Tues-Thurs 2-8, Sat 10-Noon

WESTFIELD

S CHAUTAUQUA COUNTY HISTORICAL SOCIETY & MCCLURG MUSEUM LIBRARY*, Moore Park, New York State Rts 394 & 20, 14787. (Mail add: PO Box 7, 14787-0007), SAN 312-6749. Tel: 716-326-2977. E-mail: cchs@mcclurgmuseum.org. Web Site: www.mcclurgmuseum.org/collection/library/library. *Pres,* Cristie Herbst
Founded 1950
Library Holdings: Bk Titles 2,000
Special Collections: Correspondence (Albion Tourgee Coll), micro; Diaries (E T Foote Papers)
Subject Interests: Chautauqua County hist, Genealogy
Publications: History of Chautauqua County, 1938-1978
Open Tues-Sat 10-4
Restriction: Open to pub for ref only

P PATTERSON LIBRARY*, 40 S Portage St, 14787. SAN 312-6757. Tel: 716-326-2154. FAX: 716-326-2554. Web Site: www.pattersonlibrary.info. *Libr Dir,* Thomas S Vitale; E-mail: director@pattersonlib.org; *Admin Librn, Tech Serv/Ref Librn,* Janice Hogenboom; E-mail: operations@pattersonlib.org; *Circ, Senior Clerk,* Joan Brown; E-mail: circulation@pattersonlib.org; *Gallery Curator, Programmer,* Nancy Nixon Ensign; E-mail: curator@pattersonlib.org; *Children's Prog, Makerspace Prog Spec, YA Serv,* Emily Collins; E-mail: childprograms2@pattersonlib.org; *Programmer, YA Serv,* Jack Rosen; E-mail: yaprograms@pattersonlib.org; *Children's Programmer, Programmer,* Amy Stephenson; E-mail: childprograms@pattersonlib.org. Subject Specialists: *Admin,* Thomas S Vitale; *Bus,* Janice Hogenboom; Staff 10 (MLS 2, Non-MLS 8)
Founded 1896. Pop 5,194; Circ 69,694
Jan 2019-Dec 2019 Income $318,000, City $97,000, County $4,972, Other $216,028. Mats Exp $16,000, Books $10,000, Per/Ser (Incl. Access Fees) $1,500, AV Mat $1,800, Electronic Ref Mat (Incl. Access Fees) $2,700. Sal $117,000 (Prof $80,000)
Library Holdings: Bk Vols 38,812; Per Subs 3,063
Special Collections: Genealogy & Local History (Crandall Coll); Mounted Birds; Photographs (Mateer Coll & Sherman Coll); Shell Coll; World War I Posters. Oral History
Subject Interests: Antiques, Collectibles, Cooking, Gardening, Local hist
Automation Activity & Vendor Info: (Cataloging) Koha; (Circulation) Koha; (OPAC) Koha
Wireless access
Function: 24/7 Electronic res, 24/7 Online cat, 3D Printer, Adult bk club, Adult literacy prog, Archival coll, Art exhibits, Art programs, Audiobks on Playaways & MP3, Bi-weekly Writer's Group, Bk club(s), Bks on CD, Children's prog, Citizenship assistance, Computer training, Computers for patron use, Digital talking bks, E-Readers, Electronic databases & coll, Family literacy, For res purposes, Free DVD rentals, Games & aids for people with disabilities, Health sci info serv, Holiday prog, Homework prog, ILL available, Internet access, Life-long learning prog for all ages, Magazines, Makerspace, Mango lang, Meeting rooms, Microfiche/film & reading machines, Movies, Museum passes, Music CDs, Notary serv, Online cat, Outreach serv, OverDrive digital audio bks, Passport agency, Photocopying/Printing, Preschool outreach, Prog for adults, Prog for children & young adult, Ref & res, Ref serv available, Res assist avail, Res libr, Scanner, Senior computer classes, Senior outreach, Serves people with intellectual disabilities, STEM programs, Story hour, Summer reading prog, Tax forms, Teen prog, Visual arts prog, Wheelchair accessible, Words travel prog, Workshops, Writing prog
Publications: Patterson Library; Westfield's Magnificent Legacy by M Poshka
Special Services for the Blind - BiFolkal kits; Bks on CD; Copier with enlargement capabilities; Digital talking bk; Digital talking bk machines; Extensive large print coll; Large print bks; Large print bks & talking machines
Open Mon, Wed, Fri & Sat 9-5, Tues & Thurs 9-8
Friends of the Library Group

WESTHAMPTON BEACH

P WESTHAMPTON FREE LIBRARY, Seven Library Ave, 11978-2697. SAN 312-6773. Tel: 631-288-3335. FAX: 631-288-5715. Web Site: westhamptonlibrary.net. *Libr Dir,* Danielle Waskiewicz; Tel: 631-288-3335, Ext 116, E-mail: danielle@westhamptonlibrary.org; *Asst Dir,* Jay Janoski; Tel: 631-288-3335, Ext 120; *Homebound Serv,* Jan Camarda; Tel: 631-288-3335, Ext 125; *Youth Serv,* Sonja Roese; Tel: 631-288-3335, Ext 166; Staff 7 (MLS 4, Non-MLS 3)
Founded 1897. Pop 9,405; Circ 175,000
Library Holdings: AV Mats 4,728; Bk Vols 43,345; Per Subs 181
Automation Activity & Vendor Info: (Cataloging) PALS; (Circulation) PALS; (OPAC) PALS
Wireless access
Function: ILL available
Publications: Newsletter
Mem of Suffolk Cooperative Library System
Open Mon-Fri 10-7, Sat & Sun 11-4
Friends of the Library Group

WESTMORELAND

P WESTMORELAND READING CENTER*, 50 Station Rd, 13490. (Mail add: PO Box 310, 13490-0310). Tel: 315-853-8001, Ext 5. Web Site: www.midyorklib.org/westmoreland. *Sr Librn,* Riley A McFadden
Library Holdings: AV Mats 900; Bk Titles 1,100; Talking Bks 100
Mem of Mid-York Library System
Open Mon & Fri 2-5, Tues 5-8, Wed 8-12, Thurs 1-4, Sat 9-1

WESTPORT

P WESTPORT LIBRARY ASSOCIATION, Six Harris Lane, 12993. SAN 312-6781. Tel: 518-962-8219. FAX: 518-962-8219. E-mail: library12993@gmail.com. Web Site: www.westportnylibrary.org. *Dir,* Cory Piekarski
Founded 1887. Circ 7,980
Library Holdings: Bk Titles 15,000; Bk Vols 16,000

Automation Activity & Vendor Info: (Cataloging) Horizon; (Circulation) Horizon; (OPAC) Horizon; (Serials) Horizon
Wireless access
Mem of Clinton-Essex-Franklin Library System
Open Tues & Thurs 10-6, Sat 9-1 (Sept-June); Tues, Thurs & Fri 10-6, Sat 9-1 (July-Aug)

WHITE PLAINS

C BERKELEY COLLEGE*, White Plains Campus, 99 Church St, 10601. SAN 378-3979. Tel: 914-694-1122, Ext 3371. Web Site: www.berkeleycollege.edu. *Dir,* Amanda Piekart; E-mail: adp@berkeleycollege.edu; Staff 2 (MLS 2)
Library Holdings: Bk Titles 12,000; Per Subs 100
Subject Interests: Bus, Computers, Fashion, Mkt
Automation Activity & Vendor Info: (Circulation) TLC (The Library Corporation); (OPAC) TLC (The Library Corporation)
Wireless access
Function: AV serv, ILL available
Partic in Metropolitan New York Library Council
Open Mon-Thurs 8am-10pm, Fri 8-4, Sat 9-3:30

L LIBRARY OF THE LEGAL AID SOCIETY OF WESTCHESTER COUNTY*, 150 Grand St, Ste 100, 10601. SAN 312-6838. Tel: 914-286-3400. FAX: 914-682-4112. E-mail: info@laswest.org. Web Site: www.laswest.org. *Dir,* Mina Pease
Founded 1936
Library Holdings: Bk Vols 6,200; Per Subs 12
Subject Interests: Criminology, Matrimonial legal mat
Restriction: Not open to pub

MERCY COLLEGE
See Dobbs Ferry

S NATIONAL ECONOMIC RESEARCH ASSOCIATES, INC*, 360 Hamilton Ave, 10th Flr, 10601. SAN 311-922X. Tel: 914-448-4000. FAX: 914-448-4040. *Assoc Dir, Info Res,* Jennifer Bennett; Tel: 212-345-2993, E-mail: jennifer.bennett@nera.com; *Dir, Info Res & Knowledge Mgt,* Barbara Hirsh; Tel: 914-448-4090, E-mail: barbara.hirsh@nera.com; *Info Res Mgr,* Barbara Eames; Tel: 202-466-9271, E-mail: barbara.eames@nera.com; *Info Res Mgr,* Hanna Shearring; E-mail: hanna.shearring@nera.com; *Mgr, Knowledge Mgt,* Janice Keeler; Tel: 312-573-2813, E-mail: janice.keeler@nera.com; *Sr Assoc,* Andrew Wall; E-mail: andrew.wall@nera.com; *Info Res, Sr Assoc,* Arah Joseph; Tel: 212-345-9068, E-mail: arah.joseph@nera.com; *Sr Assoc, Info Res N Am,* William Chamis; Tel: 212-345-9304, E-mail: william.chamis@nera.com; *Sr Assoc, Info Res N Am,* Julia Specter; Tel: 213-346-3028, E-mail: julia.specter@nera.com; *Assoc, Info Res,* Taj Parmesar; Tel: 914-448-4064, E-mail: taj.parmesar@nera.com; Staff 10 (MLS 9, Non-MLS 1)
Founded 1961
Library Holdings: Bk Titles 9,000; Per Subs 100
Subject Interests: Antitrust, Bus, Econ, Energy economics, Environ, Financial, Intellectual property, Securities, Transfer pricing, Utilities
Automation Activity & Vendor Info: (Cataloging) EOS International; (Circulation) EOS International; (OPAC) EOS International; (Serials) EOS International
Restriction: Employees only

M NEW YORK PRESBYTERIAN HOSPITAL-WEILL CORNELL*, Westchester Division Medical Library, 21 Bloomingdale Rd, 10605. SAN 312-6870. Tel: 914-997-5897. *Dir,* Terrie Wheeler; E-mail: tew2004@med.cornell.edu; *Med Librn,* Stella Sigal; E-mail: srs3002@nyp.org; Staff 1 (MLS 1)
Founded 1823
Library Holdings: Bk Vols 1,000; Per Subs 100
Subject Interests: Clinical psychol, Psychiat, Psychiat nursing
Wireless access
Partic in National Network of Libraries of Medicine Region 7
Open Mon-Fri 9-5

GL NEW YORK STATE SUPREME COURT NINTH JUDICIAL DISTRICT, Westchester County Supreme Court Law Library, Ninth Judicial District, 9th Flr, 111 Dr Martin Luther King Blvd, 10601. SAN 354-3994. Tel: 914-824-5660. E-mail: 9JDLawLibrary@nycourts.gov. *Dir,* Zoya Golban; E-mail: zgolban@nycourts.gov; *Sr Librn,* Ed Murphy; Staff 2 (MLS 2)
Founded 1908
Library Holdings: Bk Vols 300,000; Per Subs 45
Special Collections: Records on Appeal (Second Department & Court of Appeals), micro
Automation Activity & Vendor Info: (Cataloging) SirsiDynix
Wireless access
Open Mon-Fri 9-5
Restriction: Open to pub for ref only

CL PACE UNIVERSITY*, School of Law Library, 78 N Broadway, 10603. SAN 312-6897. Tel: 914-422-4273. Interlibrary Loan Service Tel: 914-422-4137. Reference Tel: 914-422-4208. Administration Tel: 914-422-4249. Web Site: www.law.pace.edu/library. *Actg Dir,* Deborah L Heller; Tel: 914-422-4339, E-mail: dheller2@law.pace.edu; *Head, Coll Serv,* Vicky Gannon; Tel: 914-422-4369, E-mail: vgannon@law.pace.edu; *Ref Librn,* Gail Whittemore; E-mail: gwhittemore@law.pace.edu; *Cataloger,* Helen Choi; Tel: 914-422-4648, E-mail: hchoi@law.pace.edu. Subject Specialists: *Admin law, Environ law,* Deborah L Heller; *Admin law, Land, Law,* Vicky Gannon; *Corporate law, Govt doc,* Gail Whittemore; Staff 9 (MLS 4, Non-MLS 5)
Founded 1976. Enrl 635; Fac 30; Highest Degree: Doctorate
Jul 2020-Jun 2021. Mats Exp $799,576, Books $70,057, Per/Ser (Incl. Access Fees) $410,483, Micro $8,050, AV Mat $1,953, Electronic Ref Mat (Incl. Access Fees) $281,907, Presv $10,508. Sal $1,165,524 (Prof $799,576)
Library Holdings: DVDs 642; Electronic Media & Resources 43,659; Microforms 64,169; Bk Titles 80,942; Bk Vols 140,133; Per Subs 1,315
Special Collections: David Sive Archive; Pace Law School Archives; Papers of the Hon John Carey; Yonkers Archives. US Document Depository
Subject Interests: Energy, Environ law, Intl law
Automation Activity & Vendor Info: (Acquisitions) Innovative Interfaces, Inc; (Cataloging) Innovative Interfaces, Inc; (Circulation) Innovative Interfaces, Inc; (Course Reserve) Innovative Interfaces, Inc; (ILL) OCLC ILLiad; (OPAC) Innovative Interfaces, Inc; (Serials) Innovative Interfaces, Inc
Wireless access
Function: 24/7 Online cat, Archival coll, Electronic databases & coll, Govt ref serv, Internet access, Microfiche/film & reading machines, Online cat, Online ref, Res libr, Wheelchair accessible
Publications: Environmental Notes (Online only); LibGuides (Research guide); Pace Law Library Blog (Online only)
Partic in Metropolitan New York Library Council; OCLC Online Computer Library Center, Inc; Westchester Academic Library Directors Organization
Open Mon-Thurs 8:30-9, Fri 8:30-5, Sat & Sun 9-5
Restriction: Authorized patrons, Borrowing privileges limited to fac & registered students, Borrowing requests are handled by ILL, Fee for pub use, Non-circulating to the pub, Open to students, fac & staff

P WHITE PLAINS PUBLIC LIBRARY*, 100 Martine Ave, 10601. SAN 312-6927. Tel: 914-422-1400. Circulation Tel: 914-422-1490. Reference Tel: 914-422-1480. FAX: 914-422-1462. E-mail: librarian@whiteplainslibrary.org. Web Site: www.whiteplainslibrary.org. *Dir,* Brian Kenney; Tel: 914-422-1406, E-mail: bkenney@whiteplainslibrary.org; *Asst Dir,* Kathleen Degyansky; E-mail: kdegyansky@whiteplainslibrary.org; *Local Hist Librn,* Ben Himmelfarb; *Coll Mgt,* Christiane Deschamps; *Adult Serv,* Tim Baird; *Circ,* Mary Black; *Syst,* John Lollis; *Youth Serv,* Joshua Carlson; Staff 18 (MLS 18)
Founded 1899. Pop 53,000; Circ 600,947
Library Holdings: Bk Vols 309,000; Per Subs 2,300
Special Collections: Children's Literature Research Coll; Folklore/Fairy Tale Coll; Percy Grainger Music Coll; Westchester County/White Plains Local History Coll
Subject Interests: Local hist
Automation Activity & Vendor Info: (Acquisitions) SirsiDynix; (Cataloging) SirsiDynix; (Circulation) SirsiDynix; (Course Reserve) SirsiDynix; (ILL) SirsiDynix; (Media Booking) SirsiDynix; (OPAC) SirsiDynix; (Serials) SirsiDynix
Wireless access
Publications: Annual Report
Mem of Westchester Library System
Special Services for the Deaf - TTY equip
Open Mon-Thurs 10-9, Fri 10-6, Sat 10-5, Sun 1-5
Friends of the Library Group

WHITEHALL

P THE WHITEHALL FREE LIBRARY*, 12 William St, 12887. Tel: 518-499-1366. FAX: 518-499-1366. Web Site: whitehalllibrary.sals.edu. *Actg Dir,* Karen Gordon; E-mail: kgordon@sals.edu
Library Holdings: AV Mats 615; Bk Vols 14,000; Per Subs 15; Talking Bks 365
Automation Activity & Vendor Info: (Cataloging) Innovative Interfaces, Inc; (Circulation) Innovative Interfaces, Inc; (OPAC) Innovative Interfaces, Inc
Wireless access
Mem of Southern Adirondack Library System
Open Mon, Wed & Fri 4-8:30, Tues 4-7, Thurs 1:30-6, Sat 10-2; Tues (Summer) 3:30-8:30, Wed & Fri 3-8:30, Thurs 2-6, Sat 10-3

WHITESBORO

P DUNHAM PUBLIC LIBRARY, 76 Main St, 13492. SAN 312-6943. Tel: 315-736-9734. FAX: 315-736-3265. Web Site: www.whitesborolibrary.org. *Libr Dir,* April R Bliss; E-mail: abliss@midyork.org; *Youth Serv Librn,* Christina Paniccia; E-mail: cpaniccia@midyork.org; *Ref Librn,* Dennis Kininger; E-mail: dkininger@midyork.org; Staff 5 (MLS 3, Non-MLS 2)
Founded 1926. Pop 26,133; Circ 146,841
Oct 2021-Sept 2022 Income $1,162,720, County $30,632, Locally Generated Income $1,125,388, Other $6,700. Mats Exp $799,545, Books $44,812, Electronic Ref Mat (Incl. Access Fees) $10,951. Sal $544,000 (Prof $254,513)
Library Holdings: Audiobooks 3,104; AV Mats 7,061; CDs 4,409; DVDs 6,464; e-books 14,788; Electronic Media & Resources 3,104; Bk Vols 40,728; Per Subs 126
Special Collections: Helen Dunham Coll
Automation Activity & Vendor Info: (Acquisitions) SirsiDynix; (Cataloging) SirsiDynix; (Circulation) SirsiDynix; (OPAC) SirsiDynix
Wireless access
Function: 24/7 Online cat, Activity rm, Adult bk club, Adult literacy prog, ILL available, Prog for adults, Prog for children & young adult, Summer reading prog
Mem of Mid-York Library System
Partic in New York Online Virtual Electronic Library
Open Mon-Thurs 9-8, Fri 9-5, Sat 10-2

WHITESVILLE

P WHITESVILLE PUBLIC LIBRARY*, 500 Main St, 14897-9703. (Mail add: PO Box 158, 14897-0158). Tel: 607-356-3645. FAX: 607-356-3645. E-mail: whitesville@stls.org. Web Site: whitesvillelibrary.org. *Dir,* Karen M Smith; E-mail: smithk@stls.org
Founded 1923
Library Holdings: CDs 50; DVDs 25; Bk Titles 4,500; Per Subs 20; Videos 250
Subject Interests: Local hist
Wireless access
Function: Homebound delivery serv
Mem of Southern Tier Library System
Open Mon & Wed 9-5, Tues & Thurs 2-6, Fri 9-3, Sat 9-2

WHITNEY POINT

P MARY L WILCOX MEMORIAL LIBRARY*, 2630 Main St, 13862. SAN 312-696X. Tel: 607-692-3159. FAX: 607-692-3159. E-mail: wp.ill@4cls.org. Web Site: www.marywilcoxlibrary.com. *Dir,* Stephanie Champney
Founded 1959. Pop 1,008; Circ 25,555
Library Holdings: Bk Vols 15,430; Per Subs 23
Automation Activity & Vendor Info: (Acquisitions) SirsiDynix; (Cataloging) SirsiDynix; (Circulation) SirsiDynix; (Course Reserve) SirsiDynix; (ILL) SirsiDynix; (Media Booking) SirsiDynix; (OPAC) SirsiDynix; (Serials) SirsiDynix
Wireless access
Mem of Four County Library System
Open Mon & Fri 11-5, Tues 11-8, Wed & Thurs 11-6, Sat 11-3
Friends of the Library Group

WILLIAMSON

P WILLIAMSON PUBLIC LIBRARY*, 6380 Rte 21, Ste 1, 14589. SAN 312-6978. Tel: 315-589-2048. FAX: 315-589-5077. E-mail: williamson@pls-net.org. Web Site: williamsonlibrary.org. *Dir,* Kim Iraci; E-mail: WilliamsonLibraryDirector@owwl.org; *Ch Serv,* Michelle Byrne; Staff 11 (MLS 1, Non-MLS 10)
Founded 1911. Pop 6,777; Circ 168,807
Library Holdings: AV Mats 7,098; Bk Titles 30,684; Per Subs 182
Automation Activity & Vendor Info: (Circulation) Evergreen
Wireless access
Function: Home delivery & serv to seniorr ctr & nursing homes, Homebound delivery serv, ILL available, Internet access, Magnifiers for reading, Photocopying/Printing, Prog for adults, Prog for children & young adult, Ref serv available, Summer reading prog, Telephone ref, Wheelchair accessible
Mem of Pioneer Library System
Open Mon-Thurs 9:30-8:30, Fri 9:30-5, Sat 10-2
Friends of the Library Group

WILLIAMSTOWN

P WILLIAMSTOWN LIBRARY, 2877 County Rte 17N, 13493. (Mail add: PO Box 4, 13493). Tel: 315-964-2802. FAX: 315-964-2804. E-mail: wmtlib@ncls.org. Web Site: www.williamstownlibrary.org. *Dir,* Beverly Ripka
Founded 2000
Function: 24/7 Electronic res, 24/7 Online cat, Adult bk club
Mem of North Country Library System
Open Mon 9-12 & 5-8, Tues 2:30-5:30, Wed, Fri & Sat 9-Noon, Thurs 9-12 & 6-8

WILLIAMSVILLE

J ERIE COMMUNITY COLLEGE-NORTH*, R R Dry Memorial Library, 6205 Main St, 14221-7095. SAN 310-9712. Tel: 716-851-1273. E-mail: info@ecc.edu. Web Site: www.ecc.edu/library. *Sr Librn,* Matthew Best; Tel: 716-220-5262, E-mail: bestm@ecc.edu; Staff 13 (MLS 6, Non-MLS 7)
Founded 1946. Enrl 8,900; Fac 278; Highest Degree: Associate
Library Holdings: Bks on Deafness & Sign Lang 50; Bk Vols 78,244; Per Subs 380
Special Collections: College Archives
Subject Interests: Allied health
Automation Activity & Vendor Info: (Acquisitions) Ex Libris Group; (Cataloging) Ex Libris Group; (Circulation) Ex Libris Group; (Course Reserve) Ex Libris Group; (ILL) Ex Libris Group; (Media Booking) Ex Libris Group; (OPAC) Ex Libris Group; (Serials) Ex Libris Group
Wireless access
Function: ILL available
Publications: Faculty Handbook; Library Guidebook; Library Handbook; Workbook in Library Skills
Partic in Western New York Library Resources Council
Special Services for the Deaf - Bks on deafness & sign lang
Open Mon-Thurs 7:30am-10pm, Fri 7:30-4, Sat 9-3

SR TEMPLE BETH TZEDEK*, Klein-Amdur Library, 1641 N Forest Rd, 14221. SAN 327-4632. Tel: 716-838-3232. FAX: 716-835-6154. E-mail: library@btzbuffalo.org, office@btzbuffalo.org. Web Site: btzbuffalo.org/51-klein-amdur. *Librn,* Craig Posmantur; Staff 2 (MLS 1, Non-MLS 1)
Library Holdings: Audiobooks 75; AV Mats 247; Braille Volumes 21; CDs 116; Large Print Bks 22; Music Scores 175; Bk Vols 9,000; Per Subs 13
Wireless access
Function: Audio & video playback equip for onsite use
Open Tues 3:20-6:20, Thurs 12:30-2:30, Sun 9-Noon

WILLISTON PARK

P WILLISTON PARK PUBLIC LIBRARY*, 494 Willis Ave, 11596. SAN 312-6986. Tel: 516-742-1820. FAX: 516-294-5004. Web Site: www.willistonparklibrary.org. *Dir,* Donna McKenna; E-mail: dmckenna@nassaulibrary.org; *Youth Serv Librn,* Emily Willis
Founded 1937. Pop 7,261; Circ 77,206
Library Holdings: Bk Vols 35,000; Per Subs 88
Automation Activity & Vendor Info: (Acquisitions) Innovative Interfaces, Inc - Sierra; (Cataloging) Innovative Interfaces, Inc - Sierra; (Circulation) Innovative Interfaces, Inc - Sierra; (ILL) Innovative Interfaces, Inc - Sierra; (OPAC) Innovative Interfaces, Inc - Sierra
Wireless access
Mem of Nassau Library System
Open Mon 10:30-8:30, Tues, Thurs & Fri 10:30-5:30, Wed 1-8:30, Sat 10-4
Friends of the Library Group

WILLSBORO

P PAINE MEMORIAL FREE LIBRARY, Two Gilliland Ln, 12996. SAN 312-6994. Tel: 518-963-4478. E-mail: painememorialfreelibrary@outlook.com. Web Site: painememorialfreel.wixsite.com/website. *Dir,* Position Currently Open
Pop 1,800; Circ 46,051
Library Holdings: Bk Vols 20,000; Per Subs 40
Automation Activity & Vendor Info: (Acquisitions) SirsiDynix; (Cataloging) SirsiDynix; (Circulation) SirsiDynix; (Course Reserve) SirsiDynix; (ILL) SirsiDynix; (Media Booking) SirsiDynix; (OPAC) SirsiDynix; (Serials) SirsiDynix
Wireless access
Mem of Clinton-Essex-Franklin Library System
Open Mon-Fri 9-5, Sat 10-2

WILMINGTON

P E M COOPER MEMORIAL LIBRARY*, 5751 Rte 86, 12997. (Mail add: PO Box 29, 12997-0029), SAN 376-6896. Tel: 518-946-7701. FAX: 518-946-7701. E-mail: library@wilmingtoncooperlibrary.net. Web Site: www.wilmingtoncooperlibrary.org. *Dir,* Samantha Baer
Library Holdings: Bk Titles 7,000
Automation Activity & Vendor Info: (Cataloging) Horizon; (Circulation) Horizon; (OPAC) Horizon
Wireless access
Mem of Clinton-Essex-Franklin Library System
Open Wed & Thurs 9-12 & 1-5, Fri 9-12 & 1-3, Sat 9-2
Friends of the Library Group

WILSON

P WILSON COMMUNITY LIBRARY, 265 Young St, 14172-9500. (Mail add: PO Box 579, 14172-0579), SAN 312-7001. Tel: 716-751-6070. FAX: 716-751-6526. E-mail: wilsoncommunitylibrary@gmail.com. Web Site: www.wilsoncommunitylibrary.org. *Libr Dir,* Meghan Brauer; E-mail: mbrauer@nioga.org; Staff 2 (Non-MLS 2)
Pop 5,640; Circ 25,754
Library Holdings: Bk Vols 23,000
Automation Activity & Vendor Info: (Circulation) SirsiDynix; (OPAC) SirsiDynix
Wireless access
Function: Art exhibits, CD-ROM, Home delivery & serv to seniorr ctr & nursing homes, ILL available, Internet access, Magnifiers for reading, Music CDs, Photocopying/Printing, Prog for adults, Prog for children & young adult, Ref serv available, Spoken cassettes & CDs, Summer reading prog, VHS videos, Wheelchair accessible
Mem of Nioga Library System
Open Mon, Tues & Thurs 10-8, Wed 2-8, Fri 10-5, Sat 10-1
Friends of the Library Group

WINDHAM

P WINDHAM PUBLIC LIBRARY, Church & Main Sts, 12496. (Mail add: PO Box 158, 12496-0158), SAN 312-701X. Tel: 518-734-4405. FAX: 518-734-4405. E-mail: windhamlib@gmail.com. Web Site: windhamlibrary.org. *Dir,* Candace Begley; Staff 3 (Non-MLS 3)
Founded 1922. Pop 1,660; Circ 30,671
Library Holdings: Bks on Deafness & Sign Lang 10; CDs 168; DVDs 208; Electronic Media & Resources 17,851; Large Print Bks 343; Bk Titles 15,150; Per Subs 60; Videos 887
Wireless access
Publications: TOPS Booklist
Mem of Mid-Hudson Library System
Special Services for the Deaf - Bks on deafness & sign lang; Closed caption videos
Special Services for the Blind - Bks on cassette; Bks on CD; Large print bks
Open Tues, Wed & Fri 10-5, Thurs 10-8, Sat 10-1; Mon-Wed & Fri 10-5, Thurs 10-8, Sat 10-1 (April-Sept)

WINGDALE

P DOVER PLAINS LIBRARY, 1797 Rte 22, 12594-1444. SAN 311-130X. Tel: 845-832-6605. FAX: 845-832-6616. Web Site: doverplainslibrary.org. *Dir,* Donna Perolli; E-mail: director@doverlib.org; Staff 1 (MLS 1)
Founded 1904. Pop 8,600; Circ 37,000
Jan 2022-Dec 2022 Income $285,000. Mats Exp $10,800. Sal $183,000
Library Holdings: Bk Vols 20,000
Wireless access
Function: 24/7 Electronic res, 24/7 Online cat, Accelerated reader prog, Activity rm, Adult bk club, Adult literacy prog, Archival coll, Art exhibits, Audio & video playback equip for onsite use, Audiobks on Playaways & MP3, Audiobks via web, Bk club(s), Bks on cassette, Bks on CD, CD-ROM, Children's prog, Computer training, Computers for patron use, Doc delivery serv, E-Readers, E-Reserves, Electronic databases & coll, Equip loans & repairs, Family literacy, Free DVD rentals, Games & aids for people with disabilities, Holiday prog, Home delivery & serv to seniorr ctr & nursing homes, Homebound delivery serv, ILL available, Instruction & testing, Internet access, Magazines, Magnifiers for reading, Mango lang, Movies, Museum passes, Music CDs, Online cat, Online ref, Outreach serv, OverDrive digital audio bks, Photocopying/Printing, Preschool outreach, Preschool reading prog, Prog for adults, Prog for children & young adult, Ref & res, Ref serv available, Scanner, Senior outreach, Serves people with intellectual disabilities, Spanish lang bks, Story hour, Study rm, Summer & winter reading prog, Summer reading prog, Teen prog, VHS videos, Wheelchair accessible
Mem of Mid-Hudson Library System
Open Mon-Fri 10-8, Sat 10-4
Friends of the Library Group

WOLCOTT

P WOLCOTT CIVIC FREE LIBRARY, 5890 New Hartford St, 14590. SAN 312-7028. Tel: 315-594-2265. Web Site: wolcott.owwl.org. *Libr Mgr,* Dorothy Patt; E-mail: dpatt@pls-net.org
Pop 1,496
Library Holdings: Bk Vols 12,000; Per Subs 32
Automation Activity & Vendor Info: (Cataloging) Evergreen; (Circulation) Evergreen
Wireless access
Mem of Pioneer Library System
Open Mon, Wed & Fri 2-8, Tues & Thurs 11-5, Sat 11-2

WOODBOURNE

S WOODBOURNE CORRECTIONAL FACILITY LIBRARY*, 99 Prison Rd, 12788. (Mail add: PO Box 1000, 12788-1000), SAN 327-1706. Tel: 845-434-7730, Ext 4601. FAX: 845-434-7730. *Librn,* Emma Kent
Library Holdings: Bk Titles 17,000; Per Subs 70
Automation Activity & Vendor Info: (Cataloging) Follett Software; (Circulation) Follett Software; (OPAC) Follett Software; (Serials) Follett Software
Open Mon-Tues & Thurs-Fri 8-11 & 12:45-3, Wed 12:30-3:30 & 6:30-8:25

WOODGATE

P WOODGATE FREE LIBRARY, 11051 Woodgate Dr, 13494. (Mail add: PO Box 52, 13494-0052), SAN 312-7060. Tel: 315-392-4814. FAX: 315-392-4814. E-mail: woodgate@midyork.org. Web Site: www.woodgatelibrary.org. *Dir,* Sandy Pascucci
Founded 1932. Pop 1,535; Circ 2,698
Library Holdings: Bk Vols 8,499
Subject Interests: Adirondack Mountain hist
Wireless access
Mem of Mid-York Library System
Open Mon 3-8, Wed 2-6, Thurs & Sat 9-3
Friends of the Library Group

WOODSTOCK

P WOODSTOCK PUBLIC LIBRARY DISTRICT, Five Library Lane, 12498. SAN 312-7079. Tel: 845-679-2213. FAX: 845-679-7149. E-mail: info@woodstock.org. Web Site: www.woodstock.org. *Libr Dir,* Jessica A Kerr; *Librn I,* Kim Apolant; *Coordr, Ch Serv,* Dawn Meola; Staff 7 (MLS 2, Non-MLS 5)
Founded 1913. Pop 5,884; Circ 77,005
Library Holdings: Bk Vols 50,178
Subject Interests: Archit, Art, Belles lettres, Hist, Music
Automation Activity & Vendor Info: (Acquisitions) Innovative Interfaces, Inc; (Cataloging) Innovative Interfaces, Inc; (Circulation) Innovative Interfaces, Inc; (OPAC) Innovative Interfaces, Inc
Wireless access
Mem of Mid-Hudson Library System
Open Mon, Tues, Thurs & Fri 10-6, Wed 10-7, Sat 10-5
Friends of the Library Group

WORCESTER

P WORCESTER-SCHENEVUS LIBRARY, (Formerly Worcester Free Library), 170 Main St, 12197. (Mail add: PO Box 461, 12197-0461), SAN 312-7087. Tel: 607-397-7309. FAX: 607-435-6981. E-mail: wo.ill@4cls.org. Web Site: worcesterfreelibrary.org. *Dir,* Toni Basso; E-mail: wo.basso@4cls.org; Staff 2 (Non-MLS 2)
Founded 1909. Pop 3,000
Library Holdings: Bk Vols 6,000; Per Subs 15
Wireless access
Function: 24/7 Electronic res, 24/7 Online cat, Adult bk club, After school storytime
Mem of Four County Library System
Open Tues-Thurs 10-6, Fri 12-5, Sat 10-2
Friends of the Library Group

WURTSBORO

P MAMAKATING LIBRARY*, 128 Sullivan St, 12790. (Mail add: PO Box 806, 12790), SAN 370-3576. Tel: 845-888-8004. FAX: 845-888-8008. E-mail: mamcirc@rcls.org. Web Site: www.mamakatinglibrary.org. *Dir,* Peggy Johansen
Library Holdings: Bk Vols 19,000
Open Mon, Wed & Fri 10-5, Tues & Thurs 10-7, Sat 10-4
Friends of the Library Group

WYANDANCH

P WYANDANCH PUBLIC LIBRARY*, 14 S 20th St, 11798. SAN 312-7095. Tel: 631-643-4848. FAX: 631-643-9664. E-mail: wyandanchlib@gmail.com. Web Site: wyan.suffolk.lib.ny.us. *Dir,* Donna Murray
Founded 1974. Pop 11,005
Library Holdings: Bk Titles 58,000; Bk Vols 60,282; Per Subs 96
Wireless access
Mem of Suffolk Cooperative Library System
Open Mon-Thurs 10-9, Fri 10-6, Sat 10-5, Sun 1-5
Friends of the Library Group

WYNANTSKILL

P NORTH GREENBUSH PUBLIC LIBRARY, 141 Main Ave, 12198. SAN 321-0995. Tel: 518-283-0303. FAX: 518-283-0303. E-mail: library@northgreenbushlibrary.org. Web Site: www.northgreenbushlibrary.org. *Librn*, Mary Klimack; Staff 1 (MLS 1)
Founded 1964. Pop 10,304; Circ 63,500
Library Holdings: Bk Titles 55,000; Per Subs 50
Automation Activity & Vendor Info: (Cataloging) Innovative Interfaces, Inc; (Circulation) Innovative Interfaces, Inc; (OPAC) Innovative Interfaces, Inc
Wireless access
Mem of Upper Hudson Library System
Open Mon-Fri 10-7, Sat 10-2
Friends of the Library Group

WYOMING

P WYOMING FREE CIRCULATING LIBRARY, 114 S Academy St, 14591. (Mail add: PO Box 248, 14591-0248), SAN 312-7117. Tel: 585-495-6840. FAX: 585-495-6840. TDD: 800-662-1220. Web Site: wyominglibrary.wordpress.com. *Dir*, Cheryl Ebel-Northup; E-mail: WyomingLibraryDirector@owwl.org
Pop 434; Circ 3,830
Library Holdings: AV Mats 1,277; Electronic Media & Resources 783; Bk Titles 9,586; Per Subs 30
Wireless access
Mem of Pioneer Library System
Open Mon 11-6, Wed 12-7, Thurs 12-5, Sat 10-2 (Sept-June)
Friends of the Library Group

YONKERS

CR SAINT JOSEPH'S SEMINARY*, Corrigan Memorial Library, 201 Seminary Ave, 10704. SAN 312-7184. Tel: 914-968-6200, Ext 8255. FAX: 914-968-8787. Web Site: www.dunwoodie.edu/library-home. *Libr Dir*, Connor Flatz; E-mail: cflatz@corriganlibrary.org; Staff 4 (MLS 2, Non-MLS 2)
Founded 1896. Enrl 75; Fac 33; Highest Degree: Master
Library Holdings: e-journals 30; Microforms 10,750; Bk Vols 103,329; Per Subs 210
Subject Interests: Canon law, Liturgy, Relig studies, Scriptures, Theol
Automation Activity & Vendor Info: (Cataloging) TLC (The Library Corporation); (Circulation) TLC (The Library Corporation); (Discovery) EBSCO Discovery Service; (ILL) OCLC WorldShare Interlibrary Loan; (OPAC) TLC (The Library Corporation); (Serials) EBSCO Discovery Service
Wireless access
Partic in OCLC Online Computer Library Center, Inc
Open Mon, Tues & Thurs 8am-10pm, Wed 8-8, Sat 10-5
Restriction: Open to students

CR SAINT VLADIMIR'S ORTHODOX THEOLOGICAL SEMINARY LIBRARY*, Father Georges Florovsky Library, 575 Scarsdale Rd, 10707-1699. SAN 312-7192. Tel: 914-961-8313. Interlibrary Loan Service Tel: 914-961-8313, Ext 333. FAX: 914-961-4507. E-mail: librarian@svots.edu. Web Site: library.svots.edu. *Librn*, Eleana Silk; E-mail: es@svots.edu
Founded 1938. Enrl 74; Fac 11; Highest Degree: Doctorate
Jul 2014-Jun 2015 Income $157,000. Mats Exp $62,795, Books $26,295, Per/Ser (Incl. Access Fees) $35,000, Micro $500, Presv $1,000. Sal $86,500
Library Holdings: Bk Vols 186,529; Per Subs 357
Special Collections: Byzantine History & Art; Russian History & Culture (incl 19th Century Russian Theological Periodicals); Theology, History & Culture of the Orthodox Church
Subject Interests: Liturgical music, Rec
Automation Activity & Vendor Info: (Cataloging) Koha; (Circulation) Koha; (Course Reserve) Koha; (ILL) OCLC; (OPAC) Koha; (Serials) Koha
Wireless access
Function: Online ref, Ref serv available, Wheelchair accessible
Open Mon-Thurs, 8:30-5 & 6:30-9:30, Fri, 8:30-5
Restriction: Open to pub for ref & circ; with some limitations

S YONKERS HISTORICAL SOCIETY*, Grinton I Will Library, 1500 Central Park Ave, 10710. (Mail add: PO Box 190, 10710-0181), SAN 371-4381. Tel: 914-961-8940. FAX: 914-961-8915. E-mail: yhsociety@aol.com. Web Site: www.ypl.org/yonkers-historical-society, yonkershistoricalsociety.org. *Pres*, Deidre Rylander
Library Holdings: Bk Titles 225
Special Collections: City Directory Coll (1890-1930); Photograph Coll
Wireless access
Publications: The Historian; Yonkers History (Newsletter)
Restriction: Open by appt only

P YONKERS PUBLIC LIBRARY*, One Larkin Ctr, 10701. SAN 354-4230. Tel: 914-337-1500. FAX: 914-376-3004. Web Site: www.ypl.org. *Dir*, Edward Falcone; E-mail: efalcone@ypl.org; *Dep Dir*, Susan Thaler; E-mail: sthaler@ypl.org; *Bus Mgr*, Vivian Presedo; E-mail: vpresedo@ypl.org
Founded 1893. Pop 202,000; Circ 796,150
Jul 2019-Jun 2020 Income (Main & Associated Libraries) $10,000,512, State $56,875, City $9,869,637, Locally Generated Income $74,000. Mats Exp $552,150, Books $430,967, Per/Ser (Incl. Access Fees) $121,183. Sal $7,580,324
Library Holdings: Audiobooks 918; AV Mats 76,741; CDs 33,095; DVDs 42,728; e-books 12,116; Bk Vols 319,526; Per Subs 415
Special Collections: Jewish Interest (Kogan Coll); Theatre & Dramatic Arts (John G Jutkowitz Memorial Coll). US Document Depository
Subject Interests: Agr, Archit, Art, Hist, Indust, Music
Automation Activity & Vendor Info: (Cataloging) Evergreen; (Circulation) Evergreen; (OPAC) Evergreen
Wireless access
Function: 24/7 Online cat, 3D Printer, Activity rm, Adult bk club, Adult literacy prog, After school storytime, Archival coll, Art exhibits, Art programs, Audio & video playback equip for onsite use, Audiobks on Playaways & MP3, Audiobks via web, AV serv, Bilingual assistance for Spanish patrons, Bk club(s), Bks on CD, Children's prog, Computer training, Computers for patron use, Digital talking bks, Electronic databases & coll, Free DVD rentals, Genealogy discussion group, Govt ref serv, Homebound delivery serv, Homework prog, ILL available, Internet access, Life-long learning prog for all ages, Literacy & newcomer serv, Magazines, Magnifiers for reading, Mail & tel request accepted, Mango lang, Meeting rooms, Microfiche/film & reading machines, Movies, Museum passes, Music CDs, Notary serv, Online cat, Online info literacy tutorials on the web & in blackboard, Online ref, Orientations, Outreach serv, Outside serv via phone, mail, e-mail & web, OverDrive digital audio bks, Photocopying/Printing, Preschool outreach, Preschool reading prog, Printer for laptops & handheld devices, Prog for adults, Prog for children & young adult, Ref & res, Ref serv available, Res assist avail, Scanner, Senior computer classes, Spanish lang bks, STEM programs, Story hour, Study rm, Summer & winter reading prog, Summer reading prog, Tax forms, Teen prog, Telephone ref, Wheelchair accessible, Winter reading prog, Workshops
Mem of Westchester Library System
Friends of the Library Group
Branches: 3
CRESTWOOD, 16 Thompson St, 10707, SAN 354-432X. Tel: 914-779-3774. *Br Mgr*, Zahra Baird; E-mail: z@ypl.org; Staff 1.5 (MLS 1.5)
Founded 1926
Function: 24/7 Electronic res, 24/7 Online cat, Bk club(s), Bks on CD, Children's prog, Computer training, Computers for patron use, Electronic databases & coll, Free DVD rentals, Holiday prog, Homework prog, ILL available, Internet access, Magazines, Magnifiers for reading, Mango lang, Movies, Museum passes, Music CDs, Online cat, Online ref, Orientations, OverDrive digital audio bks, Photocopying/Printing, Prog for adults, Prog for children & young adult, Ref serv available, Senior computer classes, Story hour, Tax forms
Open Mon, Wed, Fri & Sat 9-5, Tues & Thurs 10-9, Sun 12-5
Friends of the Library Group
RIVERFRONT LIBRARY, One Larkin Center, 10701, SAN 375-8656. Tel: 914-337-1500. FAX: 914-376-3004. *Br Adminr*, Sandy Amoyaw; Tel: 914-375-7941, E-mail: samoyaw@ypl.org; Staff 33 (MLS 16, Non-MLS 17)
Founded 2002
Function: 24/7 Electronic res, 24/7 Online cat, Activity rm, Adult literacy prog, After school storytime, Archival coll, Art exhibits, Bilingual assistance for Spanish patrons, Bk club(s), Bks on CD, Children's prog, Computer training, Computers for patron use, Electronic databases & coll, Free DVD rentals, Holiday prog, Homebound delivery serv, Homework prog, ILL available, Internet access, Life-long learning prog for all ages, Magazines, Magnifiers for reading, Mail & tel request accepted, Mango lang, Meeting rooms, Microfiche/film & reading machines, Movies, Museum passes, Music CDs, Notary serv, Online cat, Online ref, Orientations, Outreach serv, OverDrive digital audio bks, Photocopying/Printing, Preschool reading prog, Printer for laptops & handheld devices, Prog for adults, Prog for children & young adult, Ref serv available, Scanner, Senior computer classes, Spanish lang bks, Story hour, Study rm, Summer reading prog, Tax forms, Teen prog, Telephone ref, Wheelchair accessible, Workshops
Open Mon-Thurs 9-8, Fri, Sat 9-5, Sun 12-5
Friends of the Library Group
GRINTON I WILL BRANCH, 1500 Central Park Ave, 10710, SAN 354-4389. Tel: 914-337-5963. FAX: 914-337-9114. *Br Adminr*, Christian Zabriskie; Tel: 914-337-5973, E-mail: czabriskie@ypl.org; Staff 39 (MLS 17, Non-MLS 22)
Founded 1962
Subject Interests: Dramatic arts, Fine arts, Music

Function: 24/7 Electronic res, 24/7 Online cat, Activity rm, Adult bk club, After school storytime, Art exhibits, Bk club(s), Bks on CD, Children's prog, Computer training, Computers for patron use, Electronic databases & coll, Free DVD rentals, Holiday prog, Homebound delivery serv, Homework prog, ILL available, Internet access, Life-long learning prog for all ages, Magazines, Magnifiers for reading, Mango lang, Meeting rooms, Microfiche/film & reading machines, Movies, Museum passes, Music CDs, Notary serv, Online cat, OverDrive digital audio bks, Photocopying/Printing, Preschool reading prog, Printer for laptops & handheld devices, Prog for adults, Prog for children & young adult, Ref serv available, Scanner, Senior computer classes, Spanish lang bks, Story hour, Summer reading prog, Tax forms, Teen prog, Wheelchair accessible
Open Mon-Thurs 9-9, Fri & Sat 9-5, Sun 12-5
Friends of the Library Group

YORKTOWN HEIGHTS

S IBM CORP*, Thomas J Watson Research Center Library, 1101 Kitchawan Rd, 10598. SAN 312-7206. Tel: 914-945-1415. E-mail: watlib@us.ibm.com. Web Site: www.research.ibm.com/labs/watson. *Staff Librn,* Kathleen Falcigno; Staff 1 (MLS 1)
Subject Interests: Bus, Chem, Computer sci, Engr, Info tech, Math, Phys sci
Automation Activity & Vendor Info: (Cataloging) Horizon; (Circulation) Horizon; (ILL) OCLC
Wireless access
Restriction: Employees only, Not open to pub

MERCY COLLEGE
See Dobbs Ferry

S PUTNAM NORTHERN WESTCHESTER BOCES*, Professional Library, 200 BOCES Dr, 10598. SAN 371-0181. Tel: 914-248-2392. FAX: 914-248-2419. E-mail: info@pnwboces.org. Web Site: www.pnwboces.org/library. *Coordr,* Joseph Mannozzi; E-mail: jmannozzi@pnwboces.org; *Libr Assoc,* Kathy Friedlander; E-mail: kfriedlander@pnwboces.org; Staff 3 (MLS 1, Non-MLS 2)
Library Holdings: Bk Vols 5,000; Per Subs 115
Automation Activity & Vendor Info: (Cataloging) OPALS (Open-source Automated Library System); (Circulation) OPALS (Open-source Automated Library System)
Wireless access
Open Mon-Thurs 7:30-4, Fri 7:30-3

YOUNGSTOWN

S OLD FORT NIAGARA ASSOCIATION LIBRARY & ARCHIVES, Old Fort Niagara Visitor Ctr, Fort Niagara State Park, 14174. (Mail add: PO Box 169, 14174-0169), SAN 325-9803. Tel: 716-745-7611. FAX: 716-745-9141. Web Site: www.oldfortniagara.org. *Curator & Asst Site Dir,* Jerome P Brubaker; E-mail: jbrubaker@oldfortniagara.org; Staff 1 (MLS 1)
Founded 1927
Library Holdings: Bk Titles 2,650; Bk Vols 3,000
Special Collections: Archaeological Specimens; Historical Objects Coll; Historical Photographic Images; History of Western New York & the Niagara region in general & Fort Niagara (1678-1963), with specific focus on 18th & early 19th centuries; Manuscript Items
Wireless access
Function: Archival coll, Res libr
Publications: Fortress Niagara, Journal of the Old Fort Niagara Association
Restriction: Access at librarian's discretion, Non-circulating, Open by appt only
Friends of the Library Group

P YOUNGSTOWN FREE LIBRARY, 240 Lockport St, 14174. SAN 312-7222. Tel: 716-745-3555. FAX: 716-745-7122. E-mail: yfl@nioga.org. Web Site: youngstownfreelibrary.org. *Libr Dir,* Sonora Miller; E-mail: smiller@nioga.org; Staff 1 (MLS 1)
Founded 1949. Circ 22,787
Jan 2021-Dec 2021. Mats Exp $28,200, Books $16,000, Per/Ser (Incl. Access Fees) $4,000, Other Print Mats $1,500, AV Equip $200, AV Mat $6,500. Sal $73,610 (Prof $45,320)
Library Holdings: DVDs 1,064; e-books 9,461; Bk Vols 23,618; Per Subs 89
Automation Activity & Vendor Info: (Cataloging) SirsiDynix-WorkFlows; (Circulation) SirsiDynix-WorkFlows; (ILL) SirsiDynix-WorkFlows; (OPAC) SirsiDynix-WorkFlows; (Serials) SirsiDynix-WorkFlows
Wireless access
Function: 24/7 Electronic res, 24/7 Online cat, Adult bk club, Art exhibits, Audiobks on Playaways & MP3, Audiobks via web, Bk club(s), Bks on CD, Children's prog, Computer training, Computers for patron use, Digital talking bks, E-Reserves, Electronic databases & coll, For res purposes, Free DVD rentals, Holiday prog, ILL available, Internet access, Life-long learning prog for all ages, Literacy & newcomer serv, Magazines, Magnifiers for reading, Mail & tel request accepted, Meeting rooms, Music CDs, Online cat, Online ref, Outreach serv, Outside serv via phone, mail, e-mail & web, OverDrive digital audio bks, Photocopying/Printing, Preschool outreach, Preschool reading prog, Prog for adults, Prog for children & young adult, Ref & res, Ref serv available, Res assist avail, Scanner, Senior computer classes, Senior outreach, STEM programs, Story hour, Summer reading prog, Tax forms, Telephone ref, Wheelchair accessible, Workshops, Writing prog
Mem of Nioga Library System
Open Mon, Wed & Thurs 1:30-8:30, Tues 9:30-8:30, Fri 10-2, Sat (Sept-May) 10-2
Restriction: Fee for pub use, Free to mem, Non-resident fee
Friends of the Library Group

NORTH CAROLINA

Date of Statistics: FY 2021
Population, 2020 U.S. Census: 10,439,388
Population Served by Public Libraries: 10,580,509
Total Volumes in Public Libraries: 14,869,562
Volumes Per Capita: 1.41
Total Public Library Circulation: 49,290,435
Circulation Per Capita: 4.66
Digital Resources:
Total e-books: 15,552,966
Total audio items (physical & downloadable units): 3,497,240
Total video items (physical & downloadable units): 4,088,459
Total computers for use by the public: 7,345
Total annual wireless sessions: 2,155,279
Income and Expenditures:
Total Public Library Income (including Grants-in-Aid): $277,151,285
Source of Income: 85% local funds; 10% state aid; 1% federal; 4% other
Expenditures Per Capita: $23.54
Grants-in-Aid to Public Libraries:
Federal (LSTA): $1,948,575
State Aid: $14,182,131
Formula for State Aid: One half of appropriation distributed as block grants; one half appropriation distributed as per capita income equalization grants
Number of County or Multi-County (regional libraries): 59 county and 12 regional libraries
Counties Served: 100
Number of Bookmobiles in State: 25
Information provided courtesy of: Susan Forbes, Assistant State Librarian; State Library of North Carolina

AHOSKIE

J ROANOKE-CHOWAN COMMUNITY COLLEGE*, Learning Resources Center, Jernigan Bldg-103, 109 Community College Rd, 27910. SAN 312-7249. Tel: 252-862-1209. FAX: 252-862-1358. E-mail: lrc@roanokechowan.edu. Web Site: libguides.roanokechowan.edu. *Dir, Libr Serv,* Carol Anne Hankinson; Tel: 252-862-1250; Staff 1 (MLS 1)
Founded 1967. Enrl 900; Fac 38; Highest Degree: Associate
Library Holdings: Bk Titles 23,731; Per Subs 38
Automation Activity & Vendor Info: (Acquisitions) SirsiDynix; (Cataloging) SirsiDynix; (Circulation) SirsiDynix; (Course Reserve) SirsiDynix; (ILL) SirsiDynix; (Media Booking) SirsiDynix; (OPAC) SirsiDynix; (Serials) SirsiDynix
Wireless access
Partic in Community Colleges Libraries in North Carolina; NC State ILL Network
Open Mon-Thurs 8-7, Fri 8-5

ALBEMARLE

J STANLY COMMUNITY COLLEGE*, Learning Resources Center, Snyder Bldg, 28001. (Mail add: 141 College Dr, 28001), SAN 354-4621. Tel: 704-991-0259. FAX: 704-991-0112. Web Site: stanly.libguides.com. *Dir, Libr Serv,* Joel Ferdon; Tel: 704-991-0261, E-mail: jferdon0525@stanly.edu; *Librn,* Sharon Faulkner; Tel: 704-991-0337, E-mail: sfaulkner3852@stanly.edu; *Libr Tech,* Gail Perkins; Tel: 704-991-0259, E-mail: gperkins5132@stanly.edu; *Librn,* Janet Ross; Tel: 704-991-0337, E-mail: jross7791@stanly.edu; Staff 4 (MLS 3, Non-MLS 1)
Founded 1972. Enrl 2,000; Highest Degree: Associate
Library Holdings: Bk Titles 20,000; Bk Vols 22,000; Per Subs 185
Subject Interests: Computer lang, Nursing, Respiratory therapy
Automation Activity & Vendor Info: (Cataloging) SirsiDynix; (Circulation) SirsiDynix; (OPAC) SirsiDynix
Wireless access
Special Services for the Deaf - Closed caption videos
Special Services for the Blind - Bks on CD
Open Mon-Thurs 7:30am-8pm, Fri 7:30-3; Mon-Thurs (Summer) 7:30-6

P STANLY COUNTY PUBLIC LIBRARY*, 133 E Main St, 28001. SAN 354-4478. Tel: 704-986-3759. Circulation Tel: 704-986-3755. Administration Tel: 704-986-3765. FAX: 704-983-6713. Web Site: www.stanlycountylibrary.org. *Dir,* Melanie Holles; Tel: 704-986-3766, E-mail: mholles@stanlycountylibrary.org; *Ref (Info Servs),* Joyce Morgan; Staff 27 (MLS 5, Non-MLS 22)
Founded 1927. Pop 60,936; Circ 210,050
Library Holdings: Bk Titles 79,050; Per Subs 50
Subject Interests: Local hist
Automation Activity & Vendor Info: (Cataloging) Innovative Interfaces, Inc; (Circulation) Innovative Interfaces, Inc; (OPAC) Innovative Interfaces, Inc
Wireless access
Open Mon-Thurs 9-8, Fri & Sat 9-5, Sat (Summer) 9-1
Friends of the Library Group
Branches: 4
BADIN BRANCH, 62 Pine St, Badin, 28009, SAN 354-4508. Tel: 704-422-3218. *Br Mgr,* Treva Allmon; Staff 2 (Non-MLS 2)
Open Mon, Wed & Fri 1-5, Tues 10-2, Thurs 3-7
Friends of the Library Group
LOCUST BRANCH, 186 Ray Kennedy Dr, Locust, 28097. (Mail add: PO Box 400, Locust, 28097-0400), SAN 375-2909. Tel: 704-888-0103. *Br Mgr,* Karen Hartsell; Staff 3 (Non-MLS 3)
Open Mon-Thurs 1-7, Fri 1-5, Sat 9-1
Friends of the Library Group
NORWOOD BRANCH, 207 Pee Dee Ave, Norwood, 28128. (Mail add: PO Box 1217, Norwood, 28128-1217), SAN 354-4532. Tel: 704-474-3625. *Br Mgr,* Lisa Davis; Staff 3 (Non-MLS 3)
Open Mon-Thurs 1-7, Fri & Sat 9-1
Friends of the Library Group
OAKBORO BRANCH, 214 S Main St, Oakboro, 28129, SAN 354-4567. Tel: 704-485-4310. *Br Mgr,* Alice Carliff; Staff 2 (Non-MLS 2)
Open Mon 9-1, Wed-Fri 1-5, Tues 3-7
Friends of the Library Group

ANDREWS

P ANDREWS PUBLIC LIBRARY*, 871 Main St, 28901. (Mail add: PO Drawer 700, 28901-0700), SAN 312-7257. Tel: 828-321-5956. FAX: 828-321-3256. E-mail: andrewslibrary28901@gmail.com. Web Site: www.nantahalalibrary.org. *Co-Mgr,* Kelly Bryant; E-mail: kbryant@nantahalalibrary.org; *Co-Mgr,* Jacqueline Hulse; E-mail: jhulse@nantahalalibrary.org; Staff 3 (MLS 1, Non-MLS 2)
Founded 1915. Circ 42,000
Library Holdings: Bk Vols 15,000
Special Collections: African American Books (Purel Miller Coll)
Wireless access
Mem of Nantahala Regional Library
Open Tues & Thurs 10-7, Wed & Fri 10-6, Sat 10-2
Friends of the Library Group

ASHEBORO

J RANDOLPH COMMUNITY COLLEGE LIBRARY*, 629 Industrial Park Ave, 27205-7333. SAN 312-7273. Tel: 336-633-0204. Administration Tel: 336-633-0272. FAX: 336-629-4695. E-mail: library@randolph.edu. Web Site: libguides.randolph.edu. *Dean, Libr Serv,* Debbie S Luck; E-mail: dsluck@randolph.edu; *Electronic Serv Librn,* Jenny Thomas; E-mail: jsthomas@randolph.edu; *Instrul Serv Librn,* Donna Windish; E-mail: dcwindish@randolph.edu; Staff 6 (MLS 3, Non-MLS 3)
Founded 1962. Highest Degree: Associate
Library Holdings: AV Mats 2,000; e-books 44,700; Electronic Media & Resources 73; Bk Titles 24,000; Per Subs 66
Special Collections: Bienenstock Furniture Library (High Point, North Carolina), microfiche

Subject Interests: Archit, Art, Interior design, Nursing, Photog, Pottery, Tech educ, Vocational
Automation Activity & Vendor Info: (Cataloging) SirsiDynix; (Circulation) SirsiDynix; (Course Reserve) SirsiDynix; (ILL) SirsiDynix; (OPAC) SirsiDynix; (Serials) SirsiDynix
Wireless access
Function: Computers for patron use, Internet access, Online cat, Ref & res, Ref serv available, Scanner, Wheelchair accessible
Partic in Community Colleges Libraries in North Carolina
Open Mon-Fri 9-3
Restriction: Open to pub for ref & circ; with some limitations, Open to students, fac & staff

P RANDOLPH COUNTY PUBLIC LIBRARY*, Headquarters, 201 Worth St, 27203. SAN 354-4745. Tel: 336-318-6800. Circulation Tel: 336-318-6801. Reference Tel: 336-318-6803. FAX: 336-318-6823. E-mail: info@randolphlibrary.org. Web Site: www.randolphlibrary.org. *Dir,* Ross Holt; E-mail: rholt@randolphlibrary.org; *Asst Dir,* Niccole Hugg; E-mail: nhuggsuttles@randolphlibrary.org; Staff 43.3 (MLS 10, Non-MLS 33.3)
Founded 1936. Pop 139,399; Circ 547,371
Library Holdings: Audiobooks 5,097; AV Mats 823; CDs 1,487; DVDs 7,749; e-books 3; Large Print Bks 7,119; Bk Vols 424,936; Per Subs 244; Videos 7,106
Special Collections: Microfilm; NC History Coll
Subject Interests: Local hist
Automation Activity & Vendor Info: (Acquisitions) Horizon; (Cataloging) Horizon; (Circulation) Horizon; (OPAC) Horizon
Wireless access
Function: Accelerated reader prog, Adult bk club, After school storytime, Archival coll, Art exhibits, Audiobks via web, Bilingual assistance for Spanish patrons, Bk club(s), Bks on cassette, Bks on CD, CD-ROM, Chess club, Children's prog, Computer training, Computers for patron use, Electronic databases & coll, Free DVD rentals, Genealogy discussion group, Holiday prog, Home delivery & serv to seniorr ctr & nursing homes, Homebound delivery serv, ILL available, Internet access, Large print keyboards, Magnifiers for reading, Mail & tel request accepted, Music CDs, Online cat, Online ref, Orientations, Outreach serv, Outside serv via phone, mail, e-mail & web, Photocopying/Printing, Preschool outreach, Prog for adults, Prog for children & young adult, Ref serv available, Senior computer classes, Senior outreach, Serves people with intellectual disabilities, Spoken cassettes & CDs, Story hour, Summer reading prog, Tax forms, Teen prog, Telephone ref, VHS videos, Wheelchair accessible
Publications: Randolph County Public Library News
Special Services for the Deaf - Bks on deafness & sign lang; High interest/low vocabulary bks
Special Services for the Blind - Assistive/Adapted tech devices, equip & products; Audio mat; Bks on cassette; Bks on CD; Cassettes; Extensive large print coll; Home delivery serv; Large print bks; Low vision equip; Magnifiers; Ref serv; Talking bks; VisualTek equip
Open Mon-Thurs 9-9, Fri 9-6, Sat 9-5
Restriction: Non-circulating of rare bks
Friends of the Library Group

ASHEVILLE

J ASHEVILLE-BUNCOMBE TECHNICAL COMMUNITY COLLEGE*, Don C Locke Library, 340 Victoria Rd, 28801. SAN 312-7281. Tel: 828-398-7301. FAX: 828-251-6074. Web Site: www.abtech.edu/library. *Dir,* Russell Taylor; Tel: 828-398-7307, E-mail: russelltaylor@abtech.edu; *Cat & Tech Serv Librn,* Erica Hennig; Tel: 828-398-7574, E-mail: ericachennig@abtech.edu; *Access Serv & Syst, Librn,* Margaret Higgins; Tel: 828-398-7302, E-mail: margaretahiggins@abtech.edu; Staff 8 (MLS 3, Non-MLS 5)
Founded 1959. Highest Degree: Associate
Library Holdings: Audiobooks 600; DVDs 2,000; Bk Titles 49,000; Per Subs 290; Videos 2,000
Subject Interests: Allied health, Engr tech, Law enforcement
Automation Activity & Vendor Info: (Acquisitions) SirsiDynix; (Cataloging) SirsiDynix; (Circulation) SirsiDynix; (Course Reserve) SirsiDynix; (ILL) OCLC; (OPAC) SirsiDynix; (Serials) EBSCO Online
Wireless access
Partic in NC Dept of Commun Cols
Open Mon-Thurs 7:30am-9pm, Fri 7:30-5; Mon-Thurs (Summer) 8-8, Fri 8-5

P BUNCOMBE COUNTY PUBLIC LIBRARIES*, 67 Haywood St, 28801. SAN 354-5040. Tel: 828-250-4700. Administration Tel: 828-250-4711. FAX: 828-250-4746. TDD: 828-255-5216. E-mail: library@buncombecounty.org. Web Site: www.buncombecounty.org/library. *Dir,* Jim Blanton; E-mail: jim.blanton@buncombecounty.org; *Spec Coll Librn,* Zoe Rhine; *Ch Serv,* Jesse Figuera; *Ref (Info Servs),* Ken Miller; *Tech Serv,* Forest Doyle; Staff 78 (MLS 14, Non-MLS 64)
Founded 1879. Pop 210,550; Circ 1,372,547
Library Holdings: AV Mats 47,235; Bk Vols 495,117; Per Subs 830
Special Collections: Thomas Wolfe Coll
Subject Interests: NC
Automation Activity & Vendor Info: (Acquisitions) SirsiDynix; (Cataloging) SirsiDynix; (Circulation) SirsiDynix; (OPAC) SirsiDynix
Wireless access
Publications: Happenings (Monthly newsletter)
Open Mon-Thurs 10-8, Fri 10-6, Sat 10-5
Friends of the Library Group
Branches: 11
BLACK MOUNTAIN BRANCH, 105 Dougherty St, Black Mountain, 28711, SAN 354-5067. Tel: 828-250-4756. *Br Mgr,* Melisa Presley
Library Holdings: Bk Vols 41,576
Open Mon & Wed-Fri 10-6, Tues 10-8, Sat 10-5
Friends of the Library Group
EAST ASHEVILLE, 902 Tunnel Rd, 28805, SAN 354-5075. Tel: 828-250-4738. *Librn/Mgr,* Alexandra Duncan
Library Holdings: Bk Vols 32,006
Open Tues & Thurs 9-8, Wed & Fri 9-6, Sat 9-5
Friends of the Library Group
ENKA-CANDLER BRANCH, 1404 Sand Hill Rd, Enka, 28715, SAN 377-5941. Tel: 828-250-4758. *Librn,* Leisa Stamey
Library Holdings: Bk Vols 31,682
Open Mon & Wed-Fri 10-6, Tues 10-8, Sat 10-5
Friends of the Library Group
FAIRVIEW BRANCH, One Taylor Rd, Fairview, 28730. Tel: 828-250-6484. *Librn,* Jamie McDowell
Library Holdings: Bk Vols 22,838
Open Mon & Wed-Fri 10-6, Tues 10-8, Sat 10-5
Friends of the Library Group
LEICESTER BRANCH, 1561 Alexander Rd, Leicester, 28748. Tel: 828-250-6480. FAX: 828-683-8874. *Br Mgr,* Susan Gransee
Library Holdings: Bk Vols 16,816
Open Mon & Wed-Fri 10-6, Tues 10-8, Sat 10-5
Friends of the Library Group
NORTH ASHEVILLE, 1030 Merrimon Ave, 28804, SAN 354-5105. Tel: 828-250-4752. *Librn/Mgr,* Julie Niwinski
Library Holdings: Bk Vols 30,064
Open Mon, Wed & Fri 10-6, Tues & Thurs 10-8, Sat 10-5
Friends of the Library Group
OAKLEY/SOUTH ASHEVILLE, 749 Fairview Rd, 28803, SAN 354-513X. Tel: 828-250-4754. *Librn,* Cheryl Middleton
Library Holdings: Bk Vols 25,045
Open Tues & Thurs 9-8, Wed & Fri 9-6, Sat 9-5
Friends of the Library Group
SKYLAND/SOUTH BUNCOMBE, 260 Overlook Rd, 28803, SAN 354-5121. Tel: 828-250-6488. *Librn,* Anna Bloream
Library Holdings: Bk Vols 45,727
Open Mon & Wed-Fri 10-6, Tues 10-8, Sat 10-5
Friends of the Library Group
SWANNANOA BRANCH, 101 W Charleston St, Swannanoa, 28778, SAN 354-5148. Tel: 828-250-6486. FAX: 828-686-5516. E-mail: swannanoa.library@buncombecounty.org. *Librn/Mgr,* Carla Hollar
Library Holdings: Bk Vols 17,596
Open Tues 10-8, Wed-Fri 10-6, Sat 10-2
Friends of the Library Group
WEAVERVILLE BRANCH, 41 N Main St, Weaverville, 28787, SAN 354-5156. Tel: 828-250-6482. *Librn,* Jill Totman
Library Holdings: Bk Vols 38,726
Open Mon & Wed-Fri 10-6, Tues 10-8, Sat 10-5
Friends of the Library Group
WEST ASHEVILLE, 942 Haywood Rd, 28806, SAN 354-5164. Tel: 828-250-4750. *Librn,* Sherry Roane
Library Holdings: Bk Vols 49,682
Open Mon & Wed-Fri 10-6, Tues 10-8, Sat 10-5
Friends of the Library Group

GM DEPARTMENT OF VETERANS AFFAIRS*, Medical Center Library, 1100 Tunnel Rd, 28805. SAN 312-732X. Tel: 828-298-7911, Ext 5358. FAX: 828-299-2500. Web Site: www.asheville.va.gov. *Librn,* Justin Jameson
Library Holdings: Bk Titles 1,500
Subject Interests: Cardiovascular, Gen med, Thoracic surgery
Wireless access
Open Mon-Fri 8-4:30

M MOUNTAIN AREA HEALTH EDUCATION CENTER, Library Science, 121 Hendersonville Rd, 28803. SAN 354-4982. Tel: 828-257-4444. FAX: 828-257-4712. E-mail: library@mahec.net. Web Site: mahec.net/innovation-and-research/library-services. *Dir, Libr Serv,* Joan Colburn; Tel: 828-257-4438, E-mail: joan.colburn@mahec.net; *Librn,* Ellen Justice; Tel: 828-257-4446, E-mail: ellen.justice@mahec.net; *Librn,* Emily Mazure; Tel: 828-257-4441, E-mail: emily.mazure@mahec.net; *Librn,* Elisabeth Wallace; Tel: 828-257-4473, E-mail: elisabeth.wallace@mahec.net; *ILL/Doc Delivery Serv,* Scout Shaw; E-mail: scout.shaw@mahec.net; Staff 5 (MLS 4, Non-MLS 1)
Founded 1972

Subject Interests: Allied health, Cultural diversity, Dentistry, Family practice, Gen med, Gen surgery, Internal med, Nursing, Obstetrics & gynecology, Pharm, Pop health, Psychiat, Pub health
Wireless access
Function: Electronic databases & coll, Ref serv available

G NATIONAL OCEANIC & ATMOSPHERIC ADMINISTRATION*, National Centers for Environmental Information Library, 151 Patton Ave, 28801-5001. SAN 312-729X. Tel: 828-271-4335. FAX: 828-271-4009. Web Site: www.ncdc.noaa.gov. *Librn,* Jewel Ward; E-mail: jewel.ward@noaa.gov; Staff 1 (MLS 1)
Founded 1961
Library Holdings: Bk Vols 3,000; Per Subs 20
Subject Interests: Climatology, Meteorology, Oceanography
Automation Activity & Vendor Info: (Cataloging) SirsiDynix-WorkFlows; (Circulation) SirsiDynix-WorkFlows; (OPAC) SirsiDynix
Partic in NOAA Libraries Network; OCLC Online Computer Library Center, Inc
Restriction: By permission only, Staff use only

S SOUTHERN HIGHLAND CRAFT GUILD*, Robert W Gray Library Collection-Folk Art Center, Blue Ridge Pkwy, Milepost 382, 370 Riceville Rd, 28805. (Mail add: PO Box 9545, 28815-0545), SAN 325-7657. Tel: 828-298-7928. FAX: 828-298-7962. E-mail: library@craftguild.org. Web Site: www.southernhighlandguild.org. *Librn,* Deborah Schillo; Staff 2 (MLS 1, Non-MLS 1)
Founded 1930
Library Holdings: CDs 15; DVDs 55; Bk Vols 20,000; Per Subs 45; Videos 150
Special Collections: Hand Crafts & History of Southern Highlands Region, rare & out-of-print bks; Manuscript Colls of Mountain Craft Persons, 1892-; Southern Highland Craft Guild Archival Records, 1929-
Wireless access
Function: Ref serv available
Open Mon-Sun (Jan-March) 9-5; Mon-Sun (April-Dec) 9-6
Restriction: Non-circulating

C UNIVERSITY OF NORTH CAROLINA AT ASHEVILLE*, D Hiden Ramsey Library, One University Heights, CPO 1500, 28804-8504. SAN 312-7311. Tel: 828-251-6336. Interlibrary Loan Service Tel: 828-251-6436. Administration Tel: 828-251-6729. Interlibrary Loan Service FAX: 828-251-6012. E-mail: libref@unca.edu. Web Site: library.unca.edu. *Interim Univ Librn,* Brandy Bourne; Tel: 828-251-6639, E-mail: bbourne@unca.edu; *Head, Access Serv,* Noel Jones; Tel: 828-251-6249, E-mail: nrjones@unca.edu; *Head, Spec Coll, Univ Archivist,* Gene Hyde; Tel: 828-251-6645, E-mail: ghyde@unsa.edu; *Res Mgt Librn, Tech Serv Librn,* Barbara Svenson; Tel: 828-251-6547, E-mail: bsvenson@unca.edu; Staff 24 (MLS 10, Non-MLS 14)
Founded 1928. Enrl 3,460; Fac 207; Highest Degree: Master
Library Holdings: AV Mats 13,850; CDs 2,670; DVDs 2,871; e-books 24,805; e-journals 43,083; Microforms 860,972; Bk Titles 297,985; Bk Vols 384,383; Per Subs 7,246; Videos 4,398
Special Collections: Harrison Coll of Early American History; Manuscript & Photograph Coll, documents the history of Western North Carolina; Peckham Coll of WWI Narratives; Speculation Land Materials; University Archives. State Document Depository; US Document Depository
Subject Interests: Liberal arts
Automation Activity & Vendor Info: (Acquisitions) Innovative Interfaces, Inc; (Cataloging) Innovative Interfaces, Inc; (Circulation) Innovative Interfaces, Inc; (Course Reserve) Innovative Interfaces, Inc; (OPAC) Innovative Interfaces, Inc; (Serials) Innovative Interfaces, Inc
Wireless access
Publications: Making Sense of Library Research (Research guide)
Partic in LYRASIS; Western North Carolina Library Network
Open Mon-Thurs 8am-Midnight, Fri 8-6, Sat 10-6, Sun 1-Midnight
Friends of the Library Group

AYDEN

P QUINERLY OLSCHNER PUBLIC LIBRARY, 451 Second St, 28513-7179. (Mail add: PO Box 40, 28513-0040), SAN 312-7354. Tel: 252-481-5836. E-mail: library@ayden.com. Web Site: www.ayden.com/departments/customer-service. *Dir,* Rachelle Mondovich
Pop 4,500; Circ 135,040
Library Holdings: Bk Vols 18,000; Per Subs 15
Wireless access
Open Mon-Fri 8:30-1 & 2-5:30

BAKERSVILLE

P MITCHELL COUNTY PUBLIC LIBRARY, 18 N Mitchell Ave, 28705. (Mail add: PO Box 26, 28705-0026), SAN 312-7370. Tel: 828-688-2511. E-mail: mcpl@amyregionallibrary.org. Web Site: www.amyregionallibrary.org/locations/mitchell-county-library-bakersville. *Br Mgr,* Cynthia Burleson; E-mail: cynthia@amyregionallibrary.org; *Assoc Librn,* Melinda H Boyd
Founded 1948. Pop 14,391
Library Holdings: Bk Vols 35,000; Per Subs 39
Special Collections: North Carolina Mineral & Geology Coll
Wireless access
Function: Prog for children & young adult, Summer reading prog
Mem of Avery-Mitchell-Yancey Regional Library System
Open Mon, Wed & Fri 9-5, Tues & Thurs 9-6, Sat 9-12
Friends of the Library Group
Bookmobiles: 1

BANNER ELK

C LEES-MCRAE COLLEGE*, Dottie M Shelton Learning Commons, 191 Main St W, 28604-9238. (Mail add: PO Box 128, 28604-0128), SAN 312-7389. Tel: 828-898-8727. Circulation Tel: 828-898-2419. Administration Tel: 828-898-8770. Toll Free Tel: 800-280-4562. FAX: 828-898-8710. Web Site: lmc.edu/index.htm. *Dir, Libr Serv,* Jessica Bellemer; E-mail: bellemerj@lmc.edu; *Asst Librn,* Christine Mook; Tel: 828-898-8945, E-mail: mookc@lmc.edu; Staff 5 (MLS 2, Non-MLS 3)
Founded 1900. Highest Degree: Bachelor
Library Holdings: Bk Vols 98,000; Per Subs 343
Special Collections: Southern Appalachian Region (A B Stirling Coll)
Publications: Puddingstone Press
Partic in Appalachian College Association; Mountain College Libr Network
Open Mon-Thurs 8am-11pm, Fri 8-5, Sat 1-5, Sun 4-11

BARCO

P CURRITUCK COUNTY PUBLIC LIBRARY*, 4261 Caratoke Hwy, 27917-9707. SAN 312-7966. Tel: 252-453-8345. FAX: 252-453-8717. Web Site: co.currituck.nc.us/library. *Br Head,* Brenda Miller; E-mail: bmiller@earlibrary.org; *Librn,* Laura Salmons; *Ch Serv,* Cheryl Carollo; Staff 5 (MLS 1, Non-MLS 4)
Founded 1948. Pop 19,000; Circ 66,000
Library Holdings: Bk Titles 36,000; Per Subs 100
Special Collections: Family Genealogy Coll. Oral History
Subject Interests: Genealogy
Mem of East Albemarle Regional Library
Open Mon-Fri 9-6, Sat 8:30-5
Branches: 2
COROLLA BRANCH, 1123 Ocean Trail, Corolla, 27927-9998. (Mail add: PO Box 123, Corolla, 27927-0123). Tel: 252-453-0496. FAX: 252-453-6960. *Br Mgr,* Teresa Westerman
Library Holdings: AV Mats 130; Bk Vols 4,200; Per Subs 15; Talking Bks 200
Open Mon-Wed & Fri 9-5, Thurs 10-6
Friends of the Library Group
MOYOCK PUBLIC LIBRARY, 126 Campus Dr, Moyock, 27958. Tel: 252-435-6419. FAX: 252-435-0680. *Mgr,* Ashley Trotter
Open Mon-Wed & Fri 9-5, Thurs 10-6

BAYBORO

P PAMLICO COUNTY PUBLIC LIBRARY*, 603 Main St, 28515. SAN 312-7400. Tel: 252-745-3515. E-mail: pamlicolibrary@hotmail.com. Web Site: www.pamlicolibrary.com. *County Librn,* Katherine Clowers; *Ch,* Fran Benninger; Staff 12 (MLS 2, Non-MLS 10)
Founded 1964. Pop 13,000
Library Holdings: Bks on Deafness & Sign Lang 25; High Interest/Low Vocabulary Bk Vols 275; Bk Titles 23,592; Per Subs 123
Subject Interests: Genealogy, Local hist, Spanish
Automation Activity & Vendor Info: (Circulation) SirsiDynix
Wireless access
Function: Ref serv available
Mem of Craven-Pamlico-Carteret Regional Library System
Partic in Association for Rural & Small Libraries
Special Services for the Blind - Large print bks
Open Mon & Tues Noon-8, Wed & Thurs 9-8, Fri 9-6, Sat 10-2
Friends of the Library Group

BEAUFORT

P CARTERET COUNTY PUBLIC LIBRARY*, 1702 Live Oak St, Ste 100, 28516. SAN 312-7419. Tel: 252-728-2050. FAX: 252-728-1857. E-mail: library@carteretcountylibraries.org. Web Site: carteret.cpclib.org. *Librn,* Susan W Simpson; E-mail: susansimpson@carteretcountylibraries.org
Founded 1939. Pop 57,050; Circ 149,840
Library Holdings: Bk Vols 60,000; Per Subs 112
Subject Interests: County hist, Genealogy
Automation Activity & Vendor Info: (Cataloging) Horizon; (Circulation) Horizon; (OPAC) Horizon
Wireless access
Function: Homebound delivery serv
Mem of Craven-Pamlico-Carteret Regional Library System

Open Mon-Thurs 8:30am-9pm, Fri 8:30-6, Sat 8:30-5
Friends of the Library Group
Branches: 4
BOGUE BANKS, 320 Salter Path Rd, Ste W, Pine Knoll Shores, 28512, SAN 321-9569. Tel: 252-247-4660. FAX: 252-247-2802. *Librn,* Susan W Simpson
Circ 7,325
Library Holdings: Bk Vols 11,447; Per Subs 36
Open Mon-Sat 8:30-5
Friends of the Library Group
DOWN EAST PUBLIC, 702 Hwy 70 E Otway, 28516. Tel: 252-728-1333. FAX: 252-504-2009. Web Site: carteret.cpclib.org/del. *Br Mgr,* Tia Douglass; E-mail: tdouglass@carteretcountylibraries.org
Founded 2011
Open Mon & Fri 9-6, Wed 9-8, Sat 10-2
NEWPORT PUBLIC LIBRARY, 210 Howard Blvd, Newport, 28570. (Mail add: PO Box 727, Newport, 28570), SAN 312-9357. Tel: 252-223-5108. FAX: 252-223-6116. *Librn,* Alice Chavez
Circ 10,621
Library Holdings: Bk Vols 15,000; Per Subs 21
Open Mon-Thurs 9-8, Fri 9-6, Sat 9-4
Friends of the Library Group
WESTERN CARTERET, 230 Taylor Notion Rd, Cape Carteret, 28584, SAN 377-7987. Tel: 252-393-6500. FAX: 252-393-6660. *Librn,* Susan W Simpson
Library Holdings: Bk Vols 9,260
Open Mon, Wed, Fri & Sat 8:30-5, Tues & Thurs 8:30-8
Friends of the Library Group

BELMONT

C BELMONT ABBEY COLLEGE*, Abbot Vincent Taylor Library, 100 Belmont-Mt Holly Rd, 28012. SAN 312-7443. Tel: 704-461-6748. Circulation Tel: 704-461-6737. Interlibrary Loan Service Tel: 704-461-6744. Reference Tel: 704-461-6741. Administration Tel: 704-461-6740. FAX: 704-461-6743. E-mail: libreference@bac.edu. Web Site: www.belmontabbeycollege.edu. *Dir, Libr Serv,* Donald Beagle; E-mail: DonaldBeagle@bac.edu; *Admin Librn, Instrul Librn,* Kristine Robinson; E-mail: kristinerobinson@bac.edu; *Info Fluency Librn, Learning Tech Librn,* Heather Smith; E-mail: heathersmith@bac.edu; *Cat/ILL Librn,* Zachary Housel; E-mail: zacharyhousel@bac.edu; *Digital Librn, Media Librn, Ser Librn,* Megin Vickers; E-mail: meginvickers@bac.edu; *Evening Librn, Ref Spec,* Bradley Baker; E-mail: bradleybaker@bac.edu; *Ref Asst,* Komal Sodha; E-mail: komalsodha@bac.edu; Staff 12 (MLS 6, Non-MLS 6)
Founded 1876. Enrl 1,642; Fac 74
Library Holdings: CDs 600; DVDs 400; e-books 400,000; e-journals 15,000; Bk Titles 150,000; Per Subs 200
Special Collections: Autographed Books; Benedictine Coll; Napoleonic Coll; North & South Carolina Coll, old & rare bks; Valuable Books from 15th-18th Centuries, brought by Monks from Europe
Subject Interests: Hist, Relig studies
Automation Activity & Vendor Info: (Cataloging) OCLC Online; (ILL) OCLC Online
Wireless access
Publications: Friends Newsletter; Library Handbook; Operational Manual of the Library; Periodicals Holdings List
Open Mon-Wed 8am-Midnight, Thurs 8am-10pm, Fri 8-5, Sat 1-5, Sun 1:30pm-Midnight
Friends of the Library Group

BENSON

P MARY DUNCAN PUBLIC LIBRARY, 100 W Main St, 27504. SAN 355-1733. Tel: 919-894-3724. FAX: 919-894-1283. E-mail: library@townofbenson.com. Web Site: mdpl-nc.org/new. *Dir,* Derrick Barefoot; E-mail: dbarefoot@townofbenson.com; Staff 1 (Non-MLS 1)
Pop 3,500; Circ 10,000
Library Holdings: Bk Vols 25,000
Automation Activity & Vendor Info: (Circulation) Innovative Interfaces, Inc; (OPAC) Innovative Interfaces, Inc
Partic in North Carolina Libraries for Virtual Education
Open Mon-Thurs 9-7, Fri 9-5, Sat 9-12

BOILING SPRINGS

C GARDNER-WEBB UNIVERSITY*, John R Dover Memorial Library, 110 S Main St, 28017. (Mail add: PO Box 836, 28017-0836), SAN 312-7508. Tel: 704-406-4290. Circulation Tel: 704-406-4295. Interlibrary Loan Service Tel: 704-406-3050. Reference Tel: 704-406-3925. Toll Free Tel: 800-253-8330. Web Site: gardner-webb.edu/resources/library. *Dean of Libr,* Pam Dennis; Tel: 704-406-4298, E-mail: pdennis@gardner-webb.edu; *Assoc Dean of Libr, Univ Archivist,* Natalie Bishop; Tel: 704-406-3274, E-mail: nebishop@gardner-webb.edu; *Acq Librn,* Katie Harmon; Tel: 704-406-4296, E-mail: kharmon4@gardner-webb.edu; *Digital Scholarship Librn, User Experience Librn,* Holly Mabry; Tel: 704-406-2184, E-mail: hmabry@gardner-webb.edu; *Instruction Librn,* Katie Hartley; Tel: 704-406-4293, E-mail: khartley1@gardner-webb.edu; *Syst Librn,* Daniel Jolley; Tel: 704-406-2109, E-mail: djolley@gardner-webb.edu; *Circ Mgr,* Steve Harrington; Tel: 704-406-2183, E-mail: sharrington@gardner-webb.edu; *Coordr, AV,* Ary Bottoms; Tel: 704-406-4291, E-mail: ibottoms@gardner-webb.edu; *Circ Asst, Per Asst,* Matthew Barger; Tel: 704-406-4311, E-mail: mbarger@gardner-webb.edu; *Cataloger,* Karen Davis; Tel: 704-406-4290, E-mail: kdavis@gardner-webb.edu; *ILL,* Kevin Bridges; E-mail: kdbridges@gardner-webb.edu. Subject Specialists: *Music,* Pam Dennis; *Educ,* Natalie Bishop; *Relig studies,* Katie Harmon; *Communications, World lang,* Holly Mabry; *Counseling, Health sci, Psychol,* Katie Hartley; *Computer sci, Hist,* Daniel Jolley; *Bookbinding, Printing,* Ary Bottoms; Staff 11 (MLS 6, Non-MLS 5)
Founded 1928. Enrl 2,800; Fac 185; Highest Degree: Doctorate
Jul 2019-Jun 2020. Mats Exp $488,250. Sal $430,000
Library Holdings: CDs 1,417; DVDs 3,115; e-books 700,000; e-journals 409,032; Electronic Media & Resources 200; Microforms 201,339; Music Scores 2,525; Bk Titles 700,017; Per Subs 1,214
Special Collections: Baptist Historical Coll; Church Curriculum Laboratory Coll; Elementary, Middle, Secondary Curriculum Lab; Gardner-Webb Publications; Hymnal Coll; Literary Societies and Publications; Thomas Dixon Coll. US Document Depository
Subject Interests: Educ, Relig
Automation Activity & Vendor Info: (Acquisitions) OCLC Worldshare Management Services; (Cataloging) OCLC Worldshare Management Services; (Circulation) OCLC Worldshare Management Services; (Course Reserve) OCLC Worldshare Management Services; (ILL) OCLC; (OPAC) OCLC Worldshare Management Services; (Serials) OCLC Worldshare Management Services
Wireless access
Function: 24/7 Electronic res, 24/7 Online cat, Art exhibits, Audio & video playback equip for onsite use, Computers for patron use, Electronic databases & coll, Govt ref serv, Internet access, Magazines, Microfiche/film & reading machines, Movies, Music CDs, Online cat, Orientations, Ref serv available, Scanner, Spoken cassettes & DVDs, Wheelchair accessible
Partic in Carolinas Theological Library Consortium; LYRASIS; Metrolina Libr Asn; Mountain College Libr Network; NC Libr Asn
Special Services for the Deaf - ADA equip; Am sign lang & deaf culture; Bks on deafness & sign lang; Captioned film dep; Closed caption videos; Coll on deaf educ; Interpreter on staff; Sign lang interpreter upon request for prog; Staff with knowledge of sign lang
Special Services for the Blind - Accessible computers; Assistive/Adapted tech devices, equip & products; Bks & mags in Braille, on rec, tape & cassette; Braille bks; Braille equip; Copier with enlargement capabilities; Dragon Naturally Speaking software; Merlin electronic magnifier reader; Reading & writing aids; Recorded bks; ZoomText magnification & reading software
Open Mon-Thurs 7:30am-Midnight, Fri 7:30-5, Sat 1-5, Sun 3-Midnight (Sept-May)
Friends of the Library Group

BOONE

C APPALACHIAN STATE UNIVERSITY*, Carol Grotnes Belk Library, 218 College St, 28608. (Mail add: PO Box 32026, 28608-2026), SAN 354-5199. Circulation Tel: 828-262-2818. Reference Tel: 828-262-2820. FAX: 828-262-3001. Web Site: www.library.appstate.edu. *Dean of Libr,* Dane Ward; Tel: 828-262-6725, E-mail: warddm1@appstate.edu; *Assoc Dean of Libr,* Ericka Patillo; E-mail: patilloej@appstate.edu
Founded 1903. Enrl 13,500; Fac 34; Highest Degree: Doctorate
Library Holdings: AV Mats 56,703; Electronic Media & Resources 81,220; Bk Titles 576,497; Bk Vols 823,377; Per Subs 5,306
Special Collections: Appalachian Mountains Regional Materials. Oral History; US Document Depository
Subject Interests: Educ
Automation Activity & Vendor Info: (Acquisitions) Innovative Interfaces, Inc; (Cataloging) Innovative Interfaces, Inc; (Circulation) Innovative Interfaces, Inc; (Course Reserve) Innovative Interfaces, Inc; (ILL) Innovative Interfaces, Inc; (Media Booking) Innovative Interfaces, Inc; (OPAC) Innovative Interfaces, Inc; (Serials) Innovative Interfaces, Inc
Publications: Appalnotes (Newsletter)
Partic in Western North Carolina Library Network
Open Mon-Thurs 7:30am-Midnight, Fri 7:30-9, Sat 10-6, Sun 12:30-Midnight
Friends of the Library Group
Departmental Libraries:
WILLIAM LEONARD EURY APPALACHIAN COLLECTION, 218 College St, 28608. (Mail add: ASU Box 32026, 28608). Tel: 828-262-2186. FAX: 828-262-2553. Web Site: www.library.appstate.edu/appcoll/. *Librn, W L Eury Appalachian Coll,* Dr Fred J Hay; E-mail: hayfj@appstate.edu; *Dir, Rec Mgt,* Norma Riddle; E-mail: riddlenm@appstate.edu; *Ref Librn,* Greta Browning; Tel: 828-262-7974, E-mail: browningge@appstate.edu; *Libr Spec,* Dean

Williams; E-mail: willmsda@appstate.edu. Subject Specialists: *African diaspora, Appalachia,* Dr Fred J Hay; Staff 5 (MLS 3, Non-MLS 2)
Founded 1968. Fac 3
Library Holdings: CDs 1,500; DVDs 35; Bk Vols 40,000; Per Subs 200; Videos 1,500
Special Collections: William Leonard Eury Appalachian Coll
Subject Interests: Appalachian studies
Function: For res purposes
Publications: Appalachian Journal (College journal)
Open Mon-Thurs 8am-10pm, Fri 8-5, Sat 10-5, Sun 1-10
Friends of the Library Group

MUSIC LIBRARY, 813 Rivers St, 28608-2097. (Mail add: PO Box 32097, 28608-2097). Tel: 828-262-2388. FAX: 828-265-8642. Web Site: www.library.appstate.edu/music. *Mgr,* Tom Byland; E-mail: bylandtp@appstate.edu; *Music Librn,* Gary Boye; Tel: 828-262-2389, E-mail: boyegr@appstate.edu. Subject Specialists: *Music,* Tom Byland
Open Mon-Thurs 8am-10pm, Fri 8-5, Sat 1-5, Sun 4-10

M NORTHWEST AREA HEALTH EDUCATION CENTER LIBRARY AT BOONE, Watauga Medical Ctr, 336 Deerfield Rd, 28607-5008. (Mail add: PO Box 2600, 28607-2600), SAN 325-7711. Tel: 828-262-4300. FAX: 828-265-5048. Web Site: northwestahec.org/library, www.wakehealth.edu/Northwest-AHEC. *Libr Mgr,* Robin Daniels; E-mail: rdaniels@apprhs.org; Staff 1 (Non-MLS 1)
Library Holdings: Bk Titles 1,100; Per Subs 10
Subject Interests: Allied health, Med, Nursing
Open Mon-Fri 7-5

P WATAUGA COUNTY PUBLIC LIBRARY, 140 Queen St, 28607. SAN 320-8338. Tel: 828-264-8784. FAX: 828-264-1794. Web Site: www.arlibrary.org/watauga. *County Librn,* Monica Caruso; E-mail: mcaruso@arlibrary.org; *Youth Serv Librn,* Judith Winecoff; E-mail: jwinecoff@arlibrary.org; Staff 6 (MLS 1, Non-MLS 5)
Founded 1932. Pop 44,000; Circ 286,303
Library Holdings: Bk Vols 86,000; Per Subs 110
Special Collections: Boone Historical Society Papers
Subject Interests: NC
Automation Activity & Vendor Info: (Cataloging) SirsiDynix; (Circulation) SirsiDynix; (OPAC) SirsiDynix
Wireless access
Mem of Appalachian Regional Library
Special Services for the Deaf - Bks on deafness & sign lang
Special Services for the Blind - Computer with voice synthesizer for visually impaired persons
Open Mon-Thurs 10-6, Fri & Sat 10-4
Friends of the Library Group
Branches: 1
WESTERN WATAUGA, 1085 Old US Hwy 421, Sugar Grove, 28679, SAN 376-8120. Tel: 828-297-5515. FAX: 828-297-7805. Web Site: arlibrary.org/wwatauga-branch/w-watauga-branch. *Br Mgr,* Jackie Cornette; E-mail: jcornette@arlibrary.org; Staff 2 (Non-MLS 2)
Founded 1986
Open Mon & Wed 10-5, Tues-Thurs 10-7
Friends of the Library Group

BOONVILLE

P BOONVILLE COMMUNITY PUBLIC LIBRARY*, 121 W Main St, 27011. (Mail add: PO Box 786, 27011-0786). Tel: 336-367-7737. FAX: 336-367-7767. E-mail: bnv@nwrl.org. Web Site: nwrlibrary.org/boonville. *Br Mgr,* Angie Walker; E-mail: awalker@nwrl.org; Staff 2 (Non-MLS 2)
Founded 1999. Pop 3,372
Library Holdings: Bk Vols 5,000
Automation Activity & Vendor Info: (Acquisitions) SirsiDynix; (Cataloging) SirsiDynix; (Circulation) SirsiDynix
Wireless access
Mem of Northwestern Regional Library
Open Mon & Thurs 9:30-6, Tues, Wed & Fri 9:30-5:30, Sat 10-1
Friends of the Library Group

BREVARD

C BREVARD COLLEGE*, James Addison Jones Library, One Brevard College Dr, 28712-4283. SAN 312-7516. Tel: 828-884-8268. E-mail: library@brevard.edu. Web Site: my.brevard.edu/ICS/Library, www.brevard.edu/library. *Libr Dir,* Marie Jones; Tel: 828-884-8248, E-mail: marie.jones@brevard.edu; *Cat & Acq,* Melodie Farnham; Tel: 828-884-8368, E-mail: melodie.farnham@brevard.edu; *Info Serv Librn,* William Heinz; Tel: 828-884-8135, E-mail: william.heinz@brevard.edu; *Info Serv Librn,* Nancy Williard; Tel: 828-884-8298, E-mail: nancy.williard@brevard.edu; *Tech Asst,* George Stahlberg; E-mail: stahlberg_g@brevard.edu; Staff 4.5 (MLS 3.5, Non-MLS 1)
Founded 1934. Enrl 700; Fac 52; Highest Degree: Bachelor
Library Holdings: AV Mats 4,508; CDs 2,243; DVDs 268; e-books 350,000; e-journals 30,000; Electronic Media & Resources 200; Microforms 3,325; Music Scores 1,497; Bk Titles 45,944; Bk Vols 58,718; Per Subs 120; Videos 1,101
Subject Interests: Art, Ecology, Environ studies, Music, Outdoor wilderness educ, Psychol, Southern lit, Teacher licensure
Automation Activity & Vendor Info: (Acquisitions) TDNet; (Cataloging) OCLC; (Circulation) Innovative Interfaces, Inc; (Course Reserve) Innovative Interfaces, Inc; (ILL) OCLC Online; (OPAC) TDNet; (Serials) EBSCO Online
Wireless access
Function: Computers for patron use, E-Reserves, Electronic databases & coll, ILL available, Online cat, Online ref, Photocopying/Printing, Ref & res, Ref serv available, Scanner, Wheelchair accessible
Partic in Appalachian College Association; Carolina Consortium; LYRASIS; Mid-Atlantic Library Alliance; NC Asn of Independent Cols & Univs; North Carolina Libraries for Virtual Education
Open Mon-Thurs 7:30am-11pm, Sat 10-6, Sun 3:30-11

SR FIRST BAPTIST CHURCH*, Media Center, 94 S Gaston St, 28712. SAN 329-9813. Tel: 828-883-8251. FAX: 828-883-8573. E-mail: info@fbcbrevard.org.
Library Holdings: Bk Vols 3,860; Per Subs 20
Restriction: Mem only

P TRANSYLVANIA COUNTY LIBRARY*, 212 S Gaston St, 28712. SAN 312-7524. Tel: 828-884-3151. FAX: 828-877-4230. E-mail: library@transylvaniacounty.org. Web Site: library.transylvaniacounty.org. *Libr Dir,* Rishara Finsel; E-mail: rishara.finsel@transylvaniacounty.org; *Local Hist Librn,* Marcy Thompson; E-mail: marcy.thompson@transylvaniacounty.org; *Youth Serv Librn,* Laura Gardner; E-mail: laura.gardner@transylvaniacounty.org; *Bus Mgr,* Saronda Morgan; E-mail: saronda.morgan@transylvaniacounty.org; *Adult Serv Coordr,* Lisa Sheffield; E-mail: lisa.sheffield@transylvaniacounty.org; *Bkmobile/Outreach Serv,* Brenda Ivers; E-mail: brenda.ivers@transylvaniacounty.org; Staff 15 (MLS 6, Non-MLS 9)
Founded 1912. Pop 31,091; Circ 352,980
Library Holdings: Bk Vols 109,785
Automation Activity & Vendor Info: (Cataloging) TLC (The Library Corporation); (Circulation) TLC (The Library Corporation); (OPAC) TLC (The Library Corporation)
Wireless access
Publications: Library Herald (Newsletter)
Open Mon & Thurs 9:30-8, Tues, Wed, Fri & Sat 9:30-5:30
Friends of the Library Group
Bookmobiles: 1

BRYSON CITY

P MARIANNA BLACK LIBRARY*, 33 Fryemont St, 28713. SAN 312-7532. Tel: 828-488-3030. FAX: 828-488-9857. Web Site: www.fontanalib.org. *County Librn,* Jeffrey Delfield; E-mail: jdelfield@fontanalib.org; Staff 6 (MLS 1, Non-MLS 5)
Founded 1929. Pop 13,981
Library Holdings: Bk Titles 44,000
Subject Interests: Genealogy
Wireless access
Mem of Fontana Regional Library
Partic in North Carolina Libraries for Virtual Education
Open Mon & Wed 10-5:30, Tues & Thurs 10-7, Fri & Sat 10-4
Friends of the Library Group

P FONTANA REGIONAL LIBRARY*, 33 Fryemont St, 28713. SAN 312-7540. Tel: 828-488-2382. Automation Services Tel: 828-488-6983. FAX: 828-488-2638. E-mail: info@fontanalib.org. Web Site: www.fontanalib.org. *Dir,* Karen Wallace; *Mgr, Info Tech,* John Tyndall; Staff 42 (MLS 8, Non-MLS 34)
Founded 1944. Pop 82,102; Circ 325,996
Library Holdings: Bks on Deafness & Sign Lang 100; CDs 1,773; DVDs 1,474; High Interest/Low Vocabulary Bk Vols 489; Large Print Bks 4,630; Bk Titles 106,183; Bk Vols 167,278; Per Subs 459; Talking Bks 6,025; Videos 7,801
Automation Activity & Vendor Info: (Cataloging) TLC (The Library Corporation); (Circulation) SirsiDynix; (ILL) OCLC; (OPAC) SirsiDynix
Wireless access
Member Libraries: Albert Carlton-Cashiers Community Library; Jackson County Public Library; Macon County Public Library; Marianna Black Library
Open Mon-Fri 8-5
Friends of the Library Group
Bookmobiles: 1

BUIES CREEK

C CAMPBELL UNIVERSITY, Wiggins Memorial Library, 113 Main St, 27506. (Mail add: PO Box 98, 27506-0098), SAN 312-7559. Circulation Tel: 910-893-1462. Reference Tel: 910-893-1467. Toll Free Tel:

800-334-4111, Ext 1462. Reference E-mail: reference@campbell.edu. Web Site: library.campbell.edu. *Dean of Libr,* Sarah Steele; Tel: 910-893-1466, E-mail: steeles@campbell.edu; *Asst Dean of Libr, Head of Research & Instruction Services,* Elizabeth Dobbins; Tel: 910-893-1449, E-mail: dobbinse@campbell.edu; *Head, Access Serv,* Marie Berry; Tel: 910-893-1762, E-mail: berrym@campbell.edu; *Head, Tech Serv & Syst,* Siu-Ki Wong; Tel: 910-893-1469, E-mail: wong@campbell.edu; *Bus Librn,* Daniel Maynard; Tel: 910-893-7930, E-mail: maynard@campbell.edu; *Reference & Electronic Resources Librn,* Steve Bahnaman; Tel: 910-893-1760, E-mail: bahnamans@campbell.edu; *Ref & Instruction Librn,* Brooke Taxakis; Tel: 910-814-5579, E-mail: taxakisb@campbell.edu; *Ref & Print Res Librn,* Ron Epps; Tel: 910-893-1472, E-mail: eppsw@campbell.edu; *Circ Mgr,* Cindy Adams; Tel: 910-814-5563, E-mail: adamsc@campbell.edu; Staff 18 (MLS 10, Non-MLS 8)
Founded 1887. Enrl 4,539; Fac 155; Highest Degree: Doctorate
Library Holdings: AV Mats 8,772; e-books 210,127; e-journals 55,265; Electronic Media & Resources 77,377; Microforms 178,000; Bk Titles 187,655; Bk Vols 229,608; Per Subs 318
Special Collections: US Document Depository
Automation Activity & Vendor Info: (Acquisitions) Ex Libris Group; (Cataloging) Ex Libris Group; (Circulation) Ex Libris Group; (Course Reserve) Ex Libris Group; (ILL) OCLC ILLiad; (OPAC) Ex Libris Group; (Serials) Ex Libris Group
Wireless access
Publications: History of Carrie Rich Memorial; Newsline (Friends Newsletter)
Partic in North Carolina Libraries for Virtual Education; OCLC Online Computer Library Center, Inc
Open Mon-Thurs 7:30am-Midnight, Fri 7:30-6, Sat 11-5, Sun 2-Midnight
Friends of the Library Group

Departmental Libraries:

CL NORMAN ADRIAN WIGGINS SCHOOL OF LAW LIBRARY, 225 Hillsborough St, Ste 203, Raleigh, 27603, SAN 321-7124. Tel: 919-865-5869. FAX: 919-865-5995. E-mail: library@law.campbell.edu. Web Site: law.campbell.edu/learn/campbell-law-library. *Dir, Law Libr,* Olivia L Weeks; Tel: 919-865-5870, E-mail: weekso@campbell.edu; *Assoc Dir, Head, Res Serv,* Caitlin Swift; *Head, Pub Serv, Institutional Archivist,* Kimberly Hocking; *Cat Librn,* Sophia Gregory; *Ref Librn,* Adrienne DeWitt; *Asst Librn, Tech Serv,* Teresa Teague; Staff 7 (MLS 5, Non-MLS 2)
Founded 1976. Enrl 465; Fac 27; Highest Degree: Doctorate
Library Holdings: Bk Titles 21,231; Bk Vols 196,328; Per Subs 2,584
Automation Activity & Vendor Info: (ILL) SirsiDynix
Open Mon-Thurs 7am-Midnight, Fri 7am-9pm, Sat 9-6, Sun 1pm-Midnight
Restriction: Open to pub for ref only

BURGAW

P PENDER COUNTY PUBLIC LIBRARY, 103 S Cowan St, 28425. (Mail add: PO Box 879, 28425-0879), SAN 312-7567. Tel: 910-259-1234. E-mail: infodesk@pendercountync.gov. Web Site: penderpubliclibrary.org. *Dir,* Allen Phillips-Bell; Tel: 910-259-0306, E-mail: abell@pendercountync.gov; *Early Literacy Coordr, Outreach Serv,* Susan Watters; E-mail: swatters@pendercountync.gov; *Circ,* Misty Barnes; Tel: 910-259-6558, E-mail: mbarnes@pendercountync.gov; *Ref (Info Servs), Teen Serv,* Shannon Kidney; E-mail: skidney@pendercountync.gov; *Youth Serv,* Deanna Smith; E-mail: dlsmith@pendercountync.gov. Subject Specialists: *Circ & libr serv,* Misty Barnes; *Children's prog,* Deanna Smith; Staff 12 (MLS 1, Non-MLS 11)
Founded 1942
Library Holdings: e-journals 42; Per Subs 116
Special Collections: Dallas Herrings Carolina Heritage Research Coll(Genealogy/Local History)
Automation Activity & Vendor Info: (Acquisitions) TLC (The Library Corporation); (Cataloging) TLC (The Library Corporation); (Circulation) TLC (The Library Corporation); (ILL) OCLC FirstSearch; (OPAC) TLC (The Library Corporation); (Serials) EBSCO Discovery Service
Wireless access
Function: 24/7 Electronic res, 24/7 Online cat, After school storytime, Archival coll, Audiobks via web, Bilingual assistance for Spanish patrons, Bks on CD, Children's prog, Computers for patron use, Electronic databases & coll, Free DVD rentals, ILL available, Internet access, Magazines, Microfiche/film & reading machines, Museum passes, Online cat, Online ref, Outside serv via phone, mail, e-mail & web, OverDrive digital audio bks, Photocopying/Printing, Preschool outreach, Preschool reading prog, Printer for laptops & handheld devices, Prog for adults, Prog for children & young adult, Ref & res, Ref serv available, Res libr, Scanner, Serves people with intellectual disabilities, Spanish lang bks, Spoken cassettes & DVDs, Story hour, Study rm, Telephone ref, Wheelchair accessible
Partic in LYRASIS; Mid-Atlantic Library Alliance
Open Mon, Wed & Fri 10-6, Tues & Thurs 10-7, Sat 10-2
Friends of the Library Group

Branches: 1
HAMPSTEAD BRANCH, 75 Library Dr, Hampstead, 28443. Tel: 910-270-4603. FAX: 910-270-5015. *Br Mgr,* Karen Burkette
Library Holdings: Bk Vols 90,000; Per Subs 65
Special Collections: North Carolina Coll
Open Mon, Wed & Fri 9-6, Tues & Thurs 10-7, Sat 10-2
Friends of the Library Group

BURLINGTON

S ALAMANCE COUNTY HISTORIC PROPERTIES COMMISSION*, Historic Restoration Resources Library, 215 N Graham Hopedale Rd, 27217. SAN 325-7886. Tel: 336-570-4053. FAX: 336-570-4055. E-mail: planning@alamance-nc.com. *Dir,* Libby Hodges
Library Holdings: Bk Vols 200
Special Collections: Municipal Document Depository
Subject Interests: Genealogy
Open Mon-Fri 8-5

P ALAMANCE COUNTY PUBLIC LIBRARIES*, 342 S Spring St, 27215. SAN 354-5288. Tel: 336-229-3588. FAX: 336-229-3592. Web Site: www.alamancelibraries.org. *Dir,* Susana Goldman; *Assoc Dir, Tech Serv,* Martha Sink; Tel: 336-513-4754, E-mail: msink@alamancelibraries.org; Staff 24 (MLS 10, Non-MLS 14)
Founded 1962. Pop 150,000; Circ 855,115
Jul 2012-Jun 2013 Income (Main & Associated Libraries) $2,571,116, State $240,600, City $10,000, County $2,201,269, Other $119,247. Mats Exp $183,661, Books $109,411, Per/Ser (Incl. Access Fees) $17,750, Micro $1,000, AV Mat $50,000, Electronic Ref Mat (Incl. Access Fees) $5,500. Sal $1,385,773
Library Holdings: Bk Vols 226,842; Per Subs 309
Subject Interests: Local hist
Automation Activity & Vendor Info: (Acquisitions) TLC (The Library Corporation); (Cataloging) TLC (The Library Corporation); (Circulation) TLC (The Library Corporation); (OPAC) TLC (The Library Corporation)
Wireless access
Function: Adult bk club, After school storytime, Art exhibits, Bk club(s), Bks on CD, Children's prog, Computer training, Computers for patron use, E-Reserves, Family literacy, Holiday prog, Homebound delivery serv, ILL available, Microfiche/film & reading machines, Music CDs, Online cat, Photocopying/Printing, Preschool outreach, Preschool reading prog, Prog for adults, Prog for children & young adult, Ref & res, Ref serv available, Scanner, Spanish lang bks, Story hour, Summer reading prog, Tax forms, Teen prog, Telephone ref, Wheelchair accessible
Open Mon-Thurs 9-9, Fri & Sat 9-6, Sun 1-5
Friends of the Library Group

Branches: 4
GRAHAM PUBLIC LIBRARY, 211 S Main St, Graham, 27253, SAN 354-5296. Tel: 336-570-6730. FAX: 336-570-6732. *Br Mgr,* Wendy Kimbro; E-mail: wkimbro@alamancelibraries.org; Staff 6.6 (MLS 1, Non-MLS 5.6)
Pop 12,833
Library Holdings: Bk Titles 47,049; Per Subs 62
Open Mon & Tues 9-8, Wed-Sat 9-6, Sun (Sept-May) 2-5
Friends of the Library Group

MAY MEMORIAL LIBRARY, 342 S Spring St, 27215, SAN 354-5342. Tel: 336-229-3588. FAX: 336-229-3592. *Br Mgr,* Deana Cunningham; E-mail: dcunningham@alamancelibraries.org; *Head, Ref (Info Serv),* Lisa Kobrin; E-mail: lkobrin@alamancelibraries.org; Staff 18 (MLS 7, Non-MLS 11)
Founded 1938. Pop 130,800; Circ 289,514
Library Holdings: Bk Titles 96,065; Per Subs 154
Subject Interests: Genealogy, Local hist
Open Mon-Thurs 9-9, Fri & Sat 9-6, Sun 1-5
Friends of the Library Group

MEBANE PUBLIC LIBRARY, 101 S First St, Mebane, 27302, SAN 354-5318. Tel: 919-563-6431. FAX: 919-563-5098. *Br Mgr,* Katherine Arends; E-mail: karends@alamancelibraries.org; Staff 10.1 (MLS 1, Non-MLS 9.1)
Founded 1936. Pop 7,284; Circ 133,560
Library Holdings: Bk Titles 42,026; Per Subs 71
Open Mon & Tues 9-8, Wed-Sat 9-6, Sun (Sept-May) 2-5
Friends of the Library Group

NORTH PARK, North Park Community Ctr, 849 Sharpe Rd, 27217, SAN 354-5377. Tel: 336-226-7185. FAX: 336-513-5425. *Librn,* Alexis Vivian; Staff 1 (Non-MLS 1)
Library Holdings: Bk Titles 9,123; Per Subs 22
Open Mon-Thurs (Sept-May) 3:30-8; Mon-Fri (June-Aug) 9-5:30

M ALAMANCE REGIONAL MEDICAL CENTER; DIV OF CONE HEALTH*, Medical Library, 1240 Huffman Mill Rd, 27216. SAN 371-2850. Tel: 336-538-7574. FAX: 336-538-7571. *Librn,* Marian Blecker; E-mail: marian.blecker2@conehealth.com
Library Holdings: Bk Vols 500; Per Subs 20

Wireless access
Open Mon-Fri 8-4:30

BURNSVILLE

P AVERY-MITCHELL-YANCEY REGIONAL LIBRARY SYSTEM*, 289 Burnsville School Rd, 28714. (Mail add: PO Drawer 310, 28714-0310), SAN 313-0037. Tel: 828-682-4476. FAX: 828-682-6277. Web Site: www.amyregionallibrary.org. *Regional Dir,* Amber Westfall Briggs; E-mail: director@amyregionallibrary.org; *Ch Serv Librn,* Karen Dobrogosz; E-mail: cya@amyregionallibrary.org; *Outreach Librn,* Sylvia Archer; E-mail: amyrloutreach@gmail.com; *Spec Projects Librn,* James C Byrd; *Bus Mgr,* Mitchell Allen; E-mail: cfo@amyregionallibrary.org; *Cat,* Rella Dale; E-mail: tech@amyregionallibrary.org; Staff 10 (MLS 2, Non-MLS 8)
Founded 1961. Pop 42,979; Circ 256,933
Library Holdings: Audiobooks 1,899; CDs 1,074; Electronic Media & Resources 3,667; Large Print Bks 9,876; Microforms 2,487; Bk Vols 160,786; Per Subs 198; Talking Bks 1,897
Special Collections: Census Records on microfilm; Genealogy Holdings; North Carolina Mineral & Geology; Precious Stones Book Coll
Subject Interests: Local hist, NC hist
Automation Activity & Vendor Info: (Acquisitions) TLC (The Library Corporation); (Cataloging) TLC (The Library Corporation); (Circulation) TLC (The Library Corporation); (OPAC) TLC (The Library Corporation); (Serials) TLC (The Library Corporation)
Wireless access
Function: VHS videos
Member Libraries: Avery County Morrison Public Library; Mitchell County Public Library; Spruce Pine Public Library; Yancey County Public Library
Partic in LYRASIS; OCLC Online Computer Library Center, Inc
Special Services for the Blind - Bks on cassette; Large print bks
Open Mon-Fri 9-5
Restriction: Restricted borrowing privileges
Friends of the Library Group
Bookmobiles: 1. Librn, Sylvia Archer

P YANCEY COUNTY PUBLIC LIBRARY*, 321 School Circle, 28714. (Mail add: PO Box 1659, 28714), SAN 312-7575. Tel: 828-682-2600. FAX: 828-682-3060. E-mail: ycpl@amyregionallibrary.org. Web Site: www.amyregionallibrary.org. *Librn,* Cindy Gibson; Staff 1 (MLS 1)
Founded 1945. Pop 14,955; Circ 84,483
Library Holdings: Bk Vols 40,000
Subject Interests: Genealogy, Local hist
Automation Activity & Vendor Info: (Circulation) TLC (The Library Corporation); (OPAC) TLC (The Library Corporation); (Serials) TLC (The Library Corporation)
Wireless access
Function: Adult bk club, Archival coll, Art exhibits, Audiobks via web, AV serv, Bk club(s), Bks on CD, Children's prog, Computers for patron use, Digital talking bks, Electronic databases & coll, Family literacy, Free DVD rentals, Games & aids for people with disabilities, Home delivery & serv to seniorr ctr & nursing homes, Homebound delivery serv, Internet access, Literacy & newcomer serv, Magnifiers for reading, Mail & tel request accepted, Microfiche/film & reading machines, Music CDs, Online cat, Outreach serv, Outside serv via phone, mail, e-mail & web, Photocopying/Printing, Preschool outreach, Prog for children & young adult, Scanner, Senior outreach, Serves people with intellectual disabilities, Spanish lang bks, Spoken cassettes & CDs, Spoken cassettes & DVDs, Story hour, Summer & winter reading prog, Tax forms, Teen prog, Wheelchair accessible, Writing prog
Mem of Avery-Mitchell-Yancey Regional Library System
Open Mon, Wed & Fri 9-5, Tues & Thurs 9-8, Sat 10-1
Friends of the Library Group

CAMDEN

P CAMDEN COUNTY LIBRARY*, 104 Investors Way, Units CDEF, 27921. (Mail add: PO Box 190, 27921-0190). Tel: 252-331-2543. FAX: 252-331-2196. E-mail: camdenlibrarian@earlibrary.org. Web Site: www.camdencountync.gov/departments/library. *Head Librn,* Kim Perry; *Children's Spec,* Rachel Bryant; *Circ Spec,* Alfreda Gordon
Founded 2013
Automation Activity & Vendor Info: (Cataloging) TLC (The Library Corporation)
Wireless access
Mem of East Albemarle Regional Library
Open Mon-Fri 9-5
Friends of the Library Group

CAMP LEJEUNE

A UNITED STATES MARINE CORPS*, Harriotte B Smith Library, 1401 West Rd, Bldg 1220, 28547-2539. SAN 354-5466. Tel: 910-451-5724. Circulation Tel: 910-451-3026. Reference Tel: 910-451-1979. FAX: 910-451-3808. Web Site: library.usmc-mccs.org, www.mccslejeune-newriver.com/libraries. *Dir,* Judy Bradford; E-mail: bradfordj@usmc-mccs.org; Staff 22 (MLS 3, Non-MLS 19)
Founded 1942
Library Holdings: DVDs 300; Bk Titles 150,000; Per Subs 310; Talking Bks 5,300; Videos 4,000
Special Collections: Military History Coll
Automation Activity & Vendor Info: (Acquisitions) SirsiDynix; (Cataloging) OCLC; (Circulation) SirsiDynix; (ILL) SirsiDynix; (OPAC) SirsiDynix; (Serials) SirsiDynix
Open Mon-Fri 8-7, Sat & Sun 10-6
Restriction: Mil only

AM UNITED STATES NAVY*, Medical Library, Naval Hospital, 100 Brewster Blvd, 28547-2538. SAN 354-5490. Tel: 910-450-4076. FAX: 910-450-3941. Web Site: www.med.navy.mil/sites/nhcl. *Dir, Libr Serv,* JoAnn T Hall; E-mail: joann.hall@med.navy.mil. Subject Specialists: *Med res,* JoAnn T Hall; Staff 1 (MLS 1)
Founded 1942
Library Holdings: Bk Titles 300; Bk Vols 600; Per Subs 15
Subject Interests: Med, Sci
Function: ILL available
Restriction: Staff use only

CARTHAGE

P MOORE COUNTY LIBRARY*, 101 Saunders St, 28327. SAN 312-7591. Tel: 910-947-5335. FAX: 910-947-3660. E-mail: carthagenclibrary@gmail.com. Web Site: srls.libguides.com/c.php?g=812032. *Dir,* Alice Thomas; E-mail: alice.thomas@srls.info; *Libr Serv Supvr,* Martha Blaisdell; Staff 1 (MLS 1)
Founded 1969. Pop 74,769
Library Holdings: Large Print Bks 1,724; Bk Vols 85,816; Per Subs 88; Talking Bks 1,973
Subject Interests: Genealogy, Local hist, Spanish lang mat
Wireless access
Function: ILL available
Mem of Sandhill Regional Library System
Open Mon-Fri 8:30-6, Sat 10-4
Friends of the Library Group
Branches: 4
PAGE MEMORIAL, 100 N Poplar St, Aberdeen, 28315, SAN 376-2874. Tel: 910-944-1200. FAX: 910-944-1200. E-mail: aberdeenlibrary@yahoo.com. *Br Mgr,* Margaret Porterfield
Open Mon-Fri 2-6
PINEBLUFF BRANCH, 305 E Baltimore Ave, Pinebluff, 28373-8903, SAN 312-9454. Tel: 910-281-3004. FAX: 910-281-3004. *Br Mgr,* Patty Underwood; E-mail: patty.underwood@srls.info
Open Mon-Fri 2-6
Friends of the Library Group
ROBBINS BRANCH, 161 E Magnolia Dr, Robbins, 27325. Tel: 910-948-4000. FAX: 910-948-4000. *Br Mgr,* Sue Aklus; E-mail: sueaklus@yahoo.com
Open Tues 10-1 & 2-8, Wed, Thurs & Fri 8-1 & 2-6, Sat 10-2
Friends of the Library Group
VASS BRANCH, 128 Seaboard St, Vass, 28394. Tel: 910-245-2200. FAX: 910-245-2200. *Br Mgr,* Debbie Seal; E-mail: vasslibrarylady.mc@gmail.com
Open Tues 9:30-8, Wed-Fri 8:30-5:30, Sat 8:30-1
Friends of the Library Group
Bookmobiles: 1. Librn, Ann Gibbon. Bk titles 1,600

CARY

R SHEPHERDS THEOLOGICAL SEMINARY LIBRARY*, Paul K Jackson Memorial Library, 6051 Tryon Rd, 27518. Tel: 919-390-1104. Web Site: shepherds.edu/academics/jackson-library. *Dir, Libr Serv,* William Coberly; E-mail: wcoberly@shepherds.edu. Subject Specialists: *Hermeneutics,* William Coberly
Founded 2003. Enrl 75; Fac 12; Highest Degree: Master
Library Holdings: Bk Titles 22,000; Per Subs 15
Automation Activity & Vendor Info: (Cataloging) Book Systems; (Circulation) Book Systems; (Course Reserve) Book Systems; (ILL) OCLC WorldShare Interlibrary Loan; (OPAC) Book Systems
Wireless access
Function: Audio & video playback equip for onsite use, Computers for patron use, Distance learning, Electronic databases & coll, Internet access, Online cat, Orientations, Wheelchair accessible
Partic in Carolinas Theological Library Consortium
Restriction: Authorized patrons

CASHIERS

P ALBERT CARLTON-CASHIERS COMMUNITY LIBRARY*, 249 Frank Allen Rd, 28717. (Mail add: PO Box 2127, 28717-2127), SAN 375-5037. Tel: 828-743-0215. FAX: 828-743-1638. Web Site:

www.fontanalib.org/cashiers. *Br Librn,* Serenity Richards; E-mail: srichards@fontanalib.org; Staff 5 (MLS 1, Non-MLS 4)
Founded 1994. Pop 1,700; Circ 25,000
Library Holdings: AV Mats 300; Bks on Deafness & Sign Lang 15; CDs 50; DVDs 200; Large Print Bks 500; Bk Vols 25,029; Per Subs 59; Talking Bks 1,017
Automation Activity & Vendor Info: (Acquisitions) Baker & Taylor; (Cataloging) Evergreen; (Circulation) Evergreen; (OPAC) Evergreen; (Serials) Evergreen
Wireless access
Function: Story hour, Summer reading prog, Tax forms, Teen prog, Telephone ref, Wheelchair accessible, Workshops
Mem of Fontana Regional Library
Open Tues, Wed & Fri 10-5:30, Thurs 10-7, Sat 10-4
Restriction: Non-circulating of rare bks, Non-resident fee
Friends of the Library Group

CHAPEL HILL

S CAROLINA POPULATION CENTER, CPC Research Communications & Library Services, 123 W Franklin St, 27516. SAN 312-7621. Tel: 919-445-6945. FAX: 919-445-6956. E-mail: cpclib@unc.edu. Web Site: www.cpc.unc.edu/about/services-to-cpc/research-services. *Dir, Libr & Res Serv,* Lori Delaney; Tel: 919-962-6157, E-mail: lori_delaney@unc.edu; Staff 2 (MLS 2)
Founded 1967. Highest Degree: Doctorate
Library Holdings: Bk Titles 6,000; Per Subs 175
Subject Interests: Adolescent sexuality, Demography, Develop countries, Family planning, Human sexual behavior
Automation Activity & Vendor Info: (OPAC) SirsiDynix
Wireless access
Function: Res libr
Publications: In-house documentation for the Internet & other automated services
Partic in Proquest Dialog; SDC Info Servs
Open Mon-Fri 8:30-5

P CHAPEL HILL PUBLIC LIBRARY*, 100 Library Dr, 27514. SAN 312-763X. Tel: 919-968-2777. Circulation Tel: 919-968-2779. Reference Tel: 919-968-2780. FAX: 919-968-2838. E-mail: library@townofchapelhill.org. Web Site: www.chapelhillpubliclibrary.org. *Dir,* Susan Brown; E-mail: sbrown2@townofchapelhill.org; *Asst Dir, Head, Tech Serv,* Meeghan Rosen; Tel: 919-969-2046, E-mail: mrosen@townofchapelhill.org; *Head, Youth Serv,* Karin Michel; *Accounts Coord,* Tim Logue; *Outreach Coordr,* Krystal Black; Staff 8 (MLS 8)
Founded 1958. Pop 54,904; Circ 1,018,000
Automation Activity & Vendor Info: (Cataloging) Innovative Interfaces, Inc; (Circulation) Innovative Interfaces, Inc; (OPAC) Innovative Interfaces, Inc
Wireless access
Open Mon, Thurs & Sat 10-5, Tues 10-7
Friends of the Library Group

C UNIVERSITY OF NORTH CAROLINA AT CHAPEL HILL*, University Libraries - Davis Library, 208 Raleigh St, CB 3916, 27515. SAN 354-5520. Tel: 919-962-1053. Interlibrary Loan Service Tel: 919-962-1326. Reference Tel: 919-962-1151. Administration Tel: 919-962-1301. Circulation FAX: 919-962-0484. Reference FAX: 919-962-5537. Administration FAX: 919-843-8936. Reference E-mail: reference@unc.edu. Web Site: library.unc.edu. *Vice Provost & Univ Librn,* Elaine L Westbrooks; E-mail: elainelw@email.unc.edu; *Assoc Univ Librn, Digital Strat, Assoc Univ Librn, Info Tech,* Tim Shearer; E-mail: tim.sheare@unc.edu; *Asst Univ Librn, Admin Serv, Financial Serv,* Catherine Gerdes; E-mail: cagerdes@email.unc.edu; *Dir, Pub Serv,* Joe Williams; E-mail: joewilliams@unc.edu; *Dir, Res, Instrul Serv,* Jacqueline Solis; E-mail: jsolis@email.unc.edu; *Head, Presv,* Andrew Hart; E-mail: ashart@email.unc.edu; *Conservator, Spec Coll,* Rebecca Smyrl; E-mail: rsmyrl@email.unc.edu; *Govt Info Librn,* Renee Bosman; E-mail: rbosman@email.unc.edu; *Res & Instruction Librn,* Sarah Carrier; E-mail: scarrier@email.unc.edu; *Archivist,* Nick Graham; E-mail: ngraham@email.unc.edu; *Undergrad Libr Instruction,* Dayna Durbin; E-mail: ddurbin@email.unc.edu; Staff 131 (MLS 128, Non-MLS 3)
Founded 1796. Enrl 29,278; Fac 3,221; Highest Degree: Doctorate
Jul 2012-Jun 2013. Mats Exp $41,369,628
Library Holdings: Bk Vols 4,665,658; Per Subs 113,065
Special Collections: North Carolina Coll; Rare Book Coll; Southern Folklife Coll; Southern Historical Coll; University Archives. State Document Depository; UN Document Depository; US Document Depository
Wireless access
Publications: Windows (Newsletter)
Partic in Association of Research Libraries; Association of Southeastern Research Libraries; Carolina Consortium; Center for Research Libraries; LYRASIS; OCLC Online Computer Library Center, Inc; Triangle Research Libraries Network
Open Mon-Thurs 8am-10pm, Fri 8-6, Sat 10-5, Sun 2-10
Friends of the Library Group

Departmental Libraries:

CL KATHRINE R EVERETT LAW LIBRARY, UNC Law Library, 160 Ridge Rd, CB 3385, 27599-3385, SAN 354-5695. Tel: 919-962-1191. Interlibrary Loan Service Tel: 919-962-1196. Reference Tel: 919-962-1194. Administration Tel: 919-962-1322. FAX: 919-962-1193. Reference FAX: 919-843-7810. Reference E-mail: law_reference@unc.edu. Web Site: library.law.unc.edu. *Dir,* Anne Klinefelter; E-mail: klinefel@email.unc.edu; *Dep Dir,* Julie Kimbrough; Tel: 919-962-5118, Fax: 919-962-2294, E-mail: jlkimbro@email.unc.edu; Staff 18 (MLS 11, Non-MLS 7)
Library Holdings: Bk Titles 74,721; Bk Vols 315,325; Per Subs 6,277
Subject Interests: Law
Automation Activity & Vendor Info: (Acquisitions) SirsiDynix; (Cataloging) Innovative Interfaces, Inc; (Media Booking) Innovative Interfaces, Inc
Partic in OCLC Online Computer Library Center, Inc; TRLN

CM HEALTH SCIENCES, 355 S Columbia St, CB 7585, 27599, SAN 354-5857. Tel: 919-962-0800. Administration Tel: 919-966-2111. FAX: 919-966-5592. Web Site: www.hsl.unc.edu. *Assoc Univ Librn, Dir, Health Sci Libr,* Nandita S Mani, PhD; E-mail: nanditam@unc.edu; *Clinical Librn,* Sarah Wright; E-mail: wrightst@email.unc.edu; Staff 65 (MLS 27, Non-MLS 38)
Founded 1952. Highest Degree: Doctorate
Library Holdings: Bk Titles 128,737; Bk Vols 310,978; Per Subs 4,193
Subject Interests: Allied health, Dentistry, Med, Nursing, Pub health, Rare bks
Automation Activity & Vendor Info: (Acquisitions) Innovative Interfaces, Inc; (Cataloging) SirsiDynix; (Circulation) SirsiDynix; (OPAC) SirsiDynix
Partic in LYRASIS; National Network of Libraries of Medicine Region 1; OCLC Online Computer Library Center, Inc
Publications: Annual Report; Brochures; Friends (Newsletter); News & Views (Newsletter)
Open Mon-Thurs 7:30am-Midnight, Fri 7:30-5, Sat Noon-5, Sun Noon-Midnight
Friends of the Library Group

HIGHWAY SAFETY RESEARCH CENTER, Boiling Creek Ctr, Ste 300, 730 Martin Luther King Jr Blvd, 27514. (Mail add: 730 Martin Luther King Jr Blvd, CB 3430, 27599-3430), SAN 312-7656. Tel: 919-962-2202. FAX: 919-962-8710. Web Site: www.hsrc.unc.edu. *Dir,* Randa Radwan; E-mail: radwan@hsrc.unc.edu; *Research Librn,* Ms Chris Gomola; E-mail: gomola@hsrc.unc.edu; Staff 3 (MLS 1, Non-MLS 2)
Founded 1970
Subject Interests: Bicycle safety, Driver behav, Driver educ, Evaluation of hwy safety prog, Licensing, Pedestrian safety, Traffic records
Partic in Eastern Transportation Knowledge Network; OCLC Online Computer Library Center, Inc
Publications: Research Publications of the University of NC Highway Safety Research Center
Open Mon-Fri 8-5
Restriction: Open to pub for ref only

ROBERT B HOUSE UNDERGRADUATE, 203 South Rd, CB 3942, 27514-3942, SAN 354-5555. Tel: 919-962-1355. FAX: 919-962-2697. Web Site: library.unc.edu/house. *Head of Libr,* Suchi Mohanty; E-mail: smohanty@email.unc.edu
Library Holdings: Bk Vols 84,903
Partic in TRLN
Open Mon-Thurs 7:45-Midnight, Fri 7:45-6, Sat 10-5, Sun 2-Midnight

INFORMATION & LIBRARY SCIENCE, 115B Manning Hall, CB 3360, 27599, SAN 354-5709. Tel: 919-962-8361. FAX: 919-962-8071. E-mail: silslibraray@unc.edu. Web Site: library.unc.edu/sils. *Librn,* Rebecca Vargha; E-mail: vargha@ils.unc.edu; Staff 2 (MLS 1, Non-MLS 1)
Founded 1931
Library Holdings: Bk Vols 100,000
Subject Interests: Children's lit, Libr & info sci
Automation Activity & Vendor Info: (Cataloging) Innovative Interfaces, Inc; (OPAC) Innovative Interfaces, Inc
Open Mon-Thurs 7:45am-10pm, Fri 7:45-6, Sun Noon-10

KENAN SCIENCE LIBRARY, G301 Venable Hall, CB 3290, 27599-3290, SAN 354-5644. Tel: 919-962-1188. E-mail: kenan-library@listserv.unc.edu. Web Site: library.unc.edu/science. *Actg Head, Info Serv,* Therese Triumph; E-mail: thtriump@email.unc.edu; *Sci Librn,* David Romito; E-mail: dromito@email.unc.edu
Partic in Proquest Dialog
Open Mon-Thurs 9-5, Fri 9-5

MUSIC, 201 South Rd, CB 3906, 27514-3906, SAN 354-5768. Tel: 919-966-1113. FAX: 919-843-0418. Web Site: www.lib.unc.edu/music. *Head of Libr,* Philip Vandermeer; E-mail: vanderme@email.unc.edu
Library Holdings: AV Mats 43,000; Music Scores 81,000; Bk Vols 54,000
Open Mon-Fri 9-5

SCHOOL OF GOVERNMENT KNAPP LIBRARY, Knapp-Sanders Bldg, CB No 3330, 27599-3330, SAN 354-5687. Tel: 919-962-2760. FAX: 919-966-4762. Web Site: www.sog.unc.edu/library. *Librn,* Alex Hess, III; E-mail: hess@sog.unc.edu; *Asst Librn,* Frank Alford; E-mail: alford@sog.unc.edu
Library Holdings: Bk Vols 16,498
Open Mon-Fri 8-5

JOSEPH CURTIS SLOANE ART LIBRARY, 102 Hanes Art Ctr, CB 3405, 27599-3405, SAN 354-558X. Tel: 919-962-2397. FAX: 919-962-0722. Web Site: www.lib.unc.edu/art. *Head of Libr,* Alice Whiteside; E-mail: awhitesi@email.unc.edu; *Tech Asst,* Joshua Hockensmith; E-mail: hockensm@email.unc.edu
Library Holdings: Bk Vols 100,357
Open Mon-Thurs 9-5

CHARLOTTE

J CENTRAL PIEDMONT COMMUNITY COLLEGE LIBRARY, 1201 Elizabeth Ave, 28235. (Mail add: PO Box 35009, 28235-5009), SAN 312-7680. Tel: 704-330-6885. FAX: 704-330-6887. Web Site: www.cpcc.edu/academics/library. *Dean of Libr,* Gloria Kelley; Tel: 704-330-6441, E-mail: Gloria.Kelley@cpcc.edu; *Dir, Libr Serv,* Jennifer Arnold; Tel: 704-330-6635, E-mail: Jennifer.Arnold@cpcc.edu; *Asst Dir, Instruction & Res Serv Librn,* Garrison Libby; Tel: 704-330-6498, E-mail: garrison.libby@cpcc.edu; *Asst Dir, Pub Serv,* Martin House; Tel: 704-330-6752, E-mail: martin.house@cpcc.edu; *Asst Dir for Res,* Kimberley Balcos; Tel: 704-330-6023, E-mail: kimberley.balcos@cpcc.edu; Staff 32 (MLS 17, Non-MLS 15)
Founded 1963. Highest Degree: Associate
Library Holdings: Bk Vols 100,000; Per Subs 4,350
Automation Activity & Vendor Info: (Acquisitions) Innovative Interfaces, Inc - Sierra; (Cataloging) Innovative Interfaces, Inc - Sierra; (Circulation) Innovative Interfaces, Inc - Sierra; (Course Reserve) Innovative Interfaces, Inc - Sierra; (ILL) OCLC; (OPAC) Innovative Interfaces, Inc - Sierra
Wireless access
Publications: Periodicals Holdings; Search Guides
Partic in Carolina Consortium; North Carolina Libraries for Virtual Education; OCLC Online Computer Library Center, Inc
Special Services for the Deaf - Assistive tech; TTY equip
Special Services for the Blind - Accessible computers
Open Mon-Thurs 7:30-8, Fri 7:30-5

M CHARLOTTE AHEC LIBRARY*, Medical Education Bldg, 1000 Blythe Blvd, 28203-5812. (Mail add: PO Box 32861, 28232), SAN 312-7818. Tel: 704-355-3129. FAX: 704-355-7138. Web Site: www.charlotteahec.org. *Dir,* Alan Williams; E-mail: alan.williams@AtriumHealth.org; *Med Librn,* Brenda Almeyda; E-mail: Brenda.Almeyda@AtriumHealth.org; *Med Librn,* Laura Leach; E-mail: Laura.Leach@AtriumHealth.org; *Project Coordr,* Sarah Kimmel; E-mail: sarah.kimmel@AtriumHealth.org
Founded 1909
Library Holdings: AV Mats 2,000; Bk Titles 6,000; Per Subs 520
Subject Interests: Allied health, Clinical med, Nursing
Automation Activity & Vendor Info: (Cataloging) EOS International; (Circulation) EOS International; (OPAC) EOS International; (Serials) EOS International
Partic in National Network of Libraries of Medicine Region 1; Proquest Dialog
Open Mon-Fri 8-5

P CHARLOTTE MECKLENBURG LIBRARY*, 310 N Tryon St, 28202-2176. SAN 354-6039. Tel: 704-416-0100. Circulation Tel: 704-416-0304. Interlibrary Loan Service Tel: 704-416-0105. Reference Tel: 704-416-0101. Administration Tel: 704-416-0600. FAX: 704-416-0130. Administration FAX: 704-416-0677. Web Site: www.cmlibrary.org. *Chief Exec Officer,* Lenoir C Keesler, Jr; *Chief Innovation Officer,* Seth Ervin; *Adult Serv Coordr,* Chantez Neymoss; *Children's Serv Coordr,* Jesse Isley; *Circ Coordr,* Caitlin Moen; *Commun Partnerships Coordr,* Martha Yesowitch; *Tech Coordr,* Michael Engelbrecht; *Teen Serv Coordr,* Holly Summers-Gil; *Govt Doc, Ser,* Mimi Curlee; *ILL,* LaCreasha McCloud; *Ref (Info Servs),* Michael Wozniak; Staff 457 (MLS 121, Non-MLS 336)
Founded 1903. Pop 1,055,791; Circ 6,307,027
Jul 2016-Jun 2017 Income (Main & Associated Libraries) $39,785,256, State $612,394, City $2,500, Federal $81,682, County $36,440,898, Other $2,647,782
Library Holdings: Bk Vols 900,249
Special Collections: Business Management Coll; Census; Genealogy Coll; Local History Coll; Mecklenburg Research Room. State Document Depository; US Document Depository
Subject Interests: Bus, Children's lit, Hist, Popular culture, Textiles
Automation Activity & Vendor Info: (Acquisitions) SirsiDynix; (Cataloging) SirsiDynix; (Circulation) SirsiDynix; (ILL) SirsiDynix; (OPAC) SirsiDynix; (Serials) SirsiDynix
Wireless access
Function: 24/7 Online cat, Adult bk club, Adult literacy prog, After school storytime, Archival coll, Art exhibits, Audiobks on Playaways & MP3, Audiobks via web, Bilingual assistance for Spanish patrons, Bk club(s), Bk reviews (Group), Bks on CD, Bus archives, Children's prog, Computer training, Computers for patron use, Electronic databases & coll, Games & aids for people with disabilities, Govt ref serv, Holiday prog, Home delivery & serv to seniorr ctr & nursing homes, Homebound delivery serv, Homework prog, ILL available, Internet access, Jail serv, Life-long learning prog for all ages, Magazines, Meeting rooms, Microfiche/film & reading machines, Movies, Music CDs, Online cat, Outreach serv, OverDrive digital audio bks, Photocopying/Printing, Prog for adults, Prog for children & young adult, Ref & res, Ref serv available, Res libr, Senior computer classes, Senior outreach, Spanish lang bks, Study rm, Summer reading prog, Tax forms, Teen prog, Telephone ref, Wheelchair accessible, Workshops, Writing prog
Publications: African-American Album, Vol II (CD-ROM); An African-American Album; CIO; Novello: Ten Years of Great American Writing (Anthology); Plum Thickets & Field Daisies; Trapping Time Between the Branches (Poetry Book)
Partic in LYRASIS; OCLC Online Computer Library Center, Inc
Open Mon-Fri 8-5
Friends of the Library Group
Branches: 19

BEATTIES FORD ROAD BRANCH, 2412 Beatties Ford Rd, 28216, SAN 377-5968. Tel: 704-416-3000. FAX: 704-416-3100. *Libr Mgr,* Hannah Terrell; E-mail: hterrell@cmlibrary.org
Founded 1957
Special Collections: African-American Resource Coll
Open Mon-Thurs 9-8, Fri & Sat 9-5; Sun (Sept-May) 1-5

CORNELIUS BRANCH, 21105 Catawba Ave, Cornelius, 28031, SAN 354-6128. Tel: 704-416-3800. FAX: 704-416-3900. *Libr Mgr,* Position Currently Open
Open Mon-Thurs 9-8, Fri & Sat 9-5; Sun (Sept-May) 1-5

DAVIDSON BRANCH, 119 S Main St, Davidson, 28036, SAN 354-6152. Tel: 704-416-4000. *Branch Lead,* Marie Harris; E-mail: mharris@cmlibrary.org
Founded 1995
Open Mon-Thurs 9-8; Fri & Sat 9-5; Sun 1-5 (Sept-May)

HICKORY GROVE BRANCH, 5935 Hickory Grove Rd, 28215, SAN 328-6940. Tel: 704-416-4400. *Branch Lead,* Debra Sharp; E-mail: dsharp@cmlibrary.org
Founded 1986
Open Mon-Thurs 9-8, Fri & Sat 9-5, Sun (Sept-May) 1-5

IMAGINON: THE JOE & JOAN MARTIN CENTER, 300 E Seventh St, 28202. Tel: 704-416-4600. FAX: 704-416-4700. Web Site: www.imaginon.org. *Branch Lead,* Stephanie Long-Murphy; E-mail: smurphy@cmlibrary.org; *Children's Mgr,* Jenna Marrotta; E-mail: jmarrotta@cmlibrary.org; *Circ Mgr,* Frank Mendoza; E-mail: fmendoza@cmlibrary.org; *Teen Serv,* Holly Summers; E-mail: hsummers@cmlibrary.org
Founded 2005
Special Collections: Children's Book Illustrators Coll; Interactive Exhibits
Subject Interests: Animation, Children's lit, Film, Gaming, Music creation, Scripts, Teen lit
Open Mon-Thurs 9-8; Fri & Sat 9-5; Sun (Sept-May)1-5

INDEPENDENCE REGIONAL, 6000 Conference Dr, 28212, SAN 354-6241. Tel: 704-416-4800. *Branch Lead,* Shawn Krizanik; E-mail: skrizanik@cmlibrary.org
Founded 1996
Open Mon-Thurs 9-8, Fri & Sat 9-5, Sun (Sept-May) 1-5

MATTHEWS BRANCH, 230 Matthews Station St, Matthews, 28105, SAN 354-6276. Tel: 704-416-5000. FAX: 704-416-5100. *Branch Lead,* Cynthia McDonald; E-mail: cmcdonald@cmlibrary.org
Founded 1985
Open Mon-Thurs 9-8, Fri & Sat 9-5, Sun (Sept-May) 1-5

MINT HILL BRANCH, 6840 Matthews-Mint Hill Rd, Mint Hill, 28227, SAN 354-6306. Tel: 704-416-5200. FAX: 704-416-5300. *Branch Lead,* Anne Masters; E-mail: amasters@cmlibrary.org
Founded 1999
Open Mon-Thurs 9-8, Fri & Sat 9-5, Sun (Sept-May) 1-5

MORRISON REGIONAL LIBRARY, 7015 Morrison Blvd, 28211, SAN 354-642X. Tel: 704-416-5400. *Branch Lead,* Position Currently Open
Founded 1991
Open Mon-Thurs 9-8, Fri & Sat 9-5

MOUNTAIN ISLAND BRANCH, 4420 Hoyt Galvin Way, 28214, SAN 354-6365. Tel: 704-416-5600. FAX: 704-416-5710. *Branch Lead,* Mark Engelbrecht; E-mail: mengelbrecht@cmlibrary.org
Founded 2005
Open Mon-Thurs 9-8; Fri & Sat 9-5; Sun 1-5 (Sept-May)

MYERS PARK BRANCH, 1361 Queens Rd, 28207, SAN 354-6454. Tel: 704-416-5800. *Branch Lead,* Harold Escalante; E-mail: hescalante@cmlibrary.org
Founded 1956
Open Mon-Thurs 9-8, Fri & Sat 9-5, Sun (Sept- May) 1-5

NORTH COUNTY REGIONAL, 16500 Holly Crest Lane, Huntersville, 28078, SAN 377-600X. Tel: 704-416-6000. FAX: 704-416-6100.
Founded 1997
Closed for renovation Fall 2019-

PLAZA MIDWOOD BRANCH, 1623 Central Ave, 28205, SAN 354-6187. Tel: 704-416-6200. FAX: 704-416-6300. *Branch Lead,* Catherine Haydon; E-mail: chaydon@cmlibrary.org
Founded 1995
Open Mon-Thurs 9-8, Fri & Sat 9-5, Sun (Sept-May) 1-5

SCALEYBARK BRANCH, 101 Scaleybark Rd, 28209, SAN 325-4275. Tel: 704-416-6400. FAX: 704-416-6500. *Branch Lead,* Beatriz Guevara; E-mail: bguevara@cmlibrary.org
Founded 1985
Open Mon-Thurs 9-8, Fri & Sat 9-5, Sun (Sept-May) 1-5

SOUTH COUNTY REGIONAL, 5801 Rea Rd, 28277, SAN 377-6026. Tel: 704-416-6600. *Branch Lead,* Laura Highfill; E-mail: lhighfill@cmlibrary.org
Founded 1998
Open Mon-Thurs 9-8, Fri & Sat 9-5, Sun (Sept-May) 1-5

STEELE CREEK, 13620 Steele Creek Rd, 28273, SAN 373-7187. Tel: 704-416-6800. FAX: 704-416-6900. *Branch Lead,* Rhonda Pinkney; E-mail: rpinkney@cmlibrary.org
Founded 1994
Open Mon-Thurs 9-8, Fri & Sat 9-5, Sun (Sept-May) 1-5

SUGAR CREEK, 4045 N Tryon St, 28206, SAN 354-6489. Tel: 704-416-7000. FAX: 704-416-7100. *Branch Lead,* Rosalind Moore; E-mail: rmoore@cmlibrary.org
Open Mon-Thurs 9-8, Fri & Sat 9-5, Sun (Sept-May) 1-5

UNIVERSITY CITY REGIONAL, 301 East W T Harris Blvd, 28262, SAN 372-008X. Tel: 704-416-7200. FAX: 704-416-7300. *Branch Lead,* Jonita Edmonds; E-mail: jedmonds@cmlibrary.org
Founded 1999
Open Mon-Thurs 9-8, Fri & Sat 9-5, Sun (Sept-May) 1-5

WEST BOULEVARD BRANCH, 2157 West Blvd, 28208, SAN 322-5003. Tel: 704-416-7400. FAX: 704-416-7500. *Branch Lead,* LaJuan Pringle; E-mail: lpringle@cmlibrary.org
Founded 1996
Open Mon-Thurs 9-8, Fri & Sat 9-5, Sun (Sept-May) 1-5

S CHARLOTTE MUSEUM OF HISTORY, Hezekiah Alexander Homesite - Lassiter Research Library, 3500 Shamrock Dr, 28215. SAN 325-7592. Tel: 704-568-1774. FAX: 704-566-1817. E-mail: info@charlottemuseum.org. Web Site: www.charlottemuseum.org. *Pres & Chief Exec Officer,* Adria Focht
Library Holdings: Bk Titles 3,000; Bk Vols 3,500; Per Subs 10
Special Collections: Alexander Geneology (Hez Alexander)
Wireless access
Restriction: Open by appt only

S DUKE ENERGY CORP*, David Nabow Library, 526 S Church St, NC E01H, 28202. SAN 354-5946. Tel: 704-382-4095. FAX: 704-382-7826. E-mail: corporatelibraryservices@duke-energy.com. Web Site: www.duke-energy.com. *Libr Mgr, Sr Archivist,* Chris Hamrick; Staff 3 (Non-MLS 3)
Founded 1967
Library Holdings: Bk Titles 3,000; Per Subs 40
Subject Interests: Automation, Civil, Electrical, Environ, Humanities, Mechanical, Nuclear engr, Soc sci
Automation Activity & Vendor Info: (Acquisitions) SirsiDynix; (Cataloging) SirsiDynix; (Circulation) SirsiDynix; (OPAC) SirsiDynix; (Serials) SirsiDynix
Wireless access
Function: For res purposes
Restriction: Co libr

C ECPI UNIVERSITY, Charlotte Campus Library, 4800 Airport Center Pkwy, 28208. Tel: 704-399-1010, Ext 66209. FAX: 704-399-9144. Web Site: char.ecpi.net.
Enrl 500; Fac 30; Highest Degree: Associate
Library Holdings: Bk Titles 5,461; Bk Vols 6,109
Subject Interests: Computer sci, Computer tech, Nursing
Automation Activity & Vendor Info: (Cataloging) Follett Software; (Circulation) Follett Software; (OPAC) Follett Software
Open Mon & Tues 8:30-6, Wed & Thurs 8:30-5:30, Fri 8:30-2

C JOHNSON & WALES UNIVERSITY, Charlotte Campus Library, 801 W Trade St, 28202. Tel: 980-598-1611. Administration FAX: 980-598-1606. Web Site: clt.library.jwu.edu. *Dir, Libr Serv,* Jean Moats; Tel: 980-598-1608, E-mail: jean.moats@jwu.edu; *Ref & Instruction Librn,* Valerie Freeman; Tel: 980-598-1609; *Ref Librn,* Mariko Dailey; Tel: 980-598-1603; *Ref Librn,* Laura McShane; Tel: 980-598-1605; *Ref Librn,* Kathryn Oosterhuis; Tel: 980-598-1604; Staff 5 (MLS 5)
Founded 2004
Automation Activity & Vendor Info: (Acquisitions) OCLC Worldshare Management Services; (Cataloging) OCLC Worldshare Management Services; (Circulation) OCLC Worldshare Management Services; (Discovery) OCLC Worldshare Management Services; (ILL) OCLC WorldShare Interlibrary Loan; (OPAC) OCLC Worldshare Management Services; (Serials) OCLC Worldshare Management Services
Wireless access
Open Mon-Wed 8am-10pm, Thurs 8am-9pm, Fri 9-4, Sun 1-8

C JOHNSON C SMITH UNIVERSITY, James B Duke Memorial Library, 100 Beatties Ford Rd, 28216. SAN 312-7753. Tel: 704-371-6731, 704-371-6740. Circulation Tel: 704-371-6745. FAX: 704-378-1191. E-mail: refdesk@jcsu.edu. Web Site: library.jcsu.edu. *Dir, Libr Serv,* Monika Rhue; Tel: 704-371-6730, E-mail: mrhue@jcsu.edu; *Educ Tech Librn,* Keisha Parris; E-mail: kparris@jcsu.edu; *Univ Archivist,* Brandon Lunsford; E-mail: bdlunsford@jcsu.edu; *Cat,* Barbara Carr; E-mail: bcarr@jcsu.edu; *Evening Libr Asst,* Daijai Williams; E-mail: dswilliams@jcsu.edu. Subject Specialists: *Archives, Digitization, Info literacy,* Monika Rhue; Staff 11 (MLS 8, Non-MLS 3)
Founded 1867. Enrl 1,306; Fac 105; Highest Degree: Master
Library Holdings: AV Mats 1,239; e-books 203,000; Electronic Media & Resources 59; Microforms 179,616; Bk Vols 105,500; Per Subs 300
Special Collections: Black Heritage Rare Book Coll; Black Life & Literature (Schomburg Coll), microfilm; Black Presbyterian Coll (Inez Moore Parker Archives); Charlotte REACH 2010; Eva M Clayton Coll. Oral History
Automation Activity & Vendor Info: (Acquisitions) Innovative Interfaces, Inc - Millennium; (Cataloging) OCLC; (Circulation) Innovative Interfaces, Inc - Millennium; (Course Reserve) Innovative Interfaces, Inc - Millennium; (ILL) OCLC; (OPAC) Innovative Interfaces, Inc - Millennium; (Serials) Innovative Interfaces, Inc - Millennium
Wireless access
Function: Archival coll, Art exhibits, Computers for patron use, Distance learning, Doc delivery serv, E-Reserves, Electronic databases & coll, ILL available, Instruction & testing, Internet access, Learning ctr, Online cat, Online info literacy tutorials on the web & in blackboard, Orientations, Photocopying/Printing, Ref serv available, Scanner
Publications: The Informer (Biannually)
Partic in HBCU Library Alliance; LYRASIS; North Carolina Libraries for Virtual Education
Special Services for the Deaf - Accessible learning ctr
Open Mon-Thurs 8am-11pm, Fri 8-5, Sun 2pm-11pm

L K&L GATES LAW LIBRARY*, Hearst Tower, 214 N Tryon St, 47th Flr, 28202. SAN 372-2104. Tel: 704-331-7553. FAX: 704-353-3253. Web Site: www.klgates.com. *Libr Mgr,* Lee Elliott Carnes; E-mail: lee.carnes@klgates.com; *Ref Librn,* Stephanie Dooley; Staff 2 (MLS 2)
Founded 1957
Library Holdings: Bk Titles 4,000; Per Subs 125
Automation Activity & Vendor Info: (Cataloging) SirsiDynix-WorkFlows
Wireless access

R LEVINE-SKLUT JUDAIC LIBRARY, 5007 Providence Rd, Ste 107, 28226. SAN 312-7893. Tel: 704-944-6783. E-mail: library@jewishcharlotte.org. Web Site: jewishcharlotte.org/cje, lsj-hl.mimas.opalsinfo.net. Staff 6 (MLS 2, Non-MLS 4)
Founded 1986
Library Holdings: CDs 50; DVDs 100; Large Print Bks 50; Bk Titles 15,000; Bk Vols 17,000; Per Subs 20; Videos 400
Special Collections: Judaica Coll. Oral History
Automation Activity & Vendor Info: (Cataloging) OPALS (Open-source Automated Library System); (Circulation) OPALS (Open-source Automated Library System)
Wireless access
Open Mon-Thurs 9-4, Fri & Sun 9-1
Restriction: 24-hr pass syst for students only
Friends of the Library Group

S MINT MUSEUM*, J A Jones & Delhom-Gambrell Reference Libraries, 2730 Randolph Rd, 28207. SAN 326-4599. Tel: 704-337-2000, 704-337-2023. FAX: 704-337-2101. E-mail: library@mintmuseum.org. Web Site: mintmuseum.org/library/. *Dir, Libr & Archives,* Joyce Weaver; E-mail: joyce.weaver@mintmuseum.org; *Dir, Engagement & Learning,* Cynthia Moreno; E-mail: cynthia.moreno@mintmuseum.org; *Archivist,* Ellen Show; Tel: 704-337-2092, E-mail: ellen.show@mintmuseum.org; *Cataloger,* Nancy Mosley; E-mail: nancy.mosley@mintmuseum.org; Staff 2.5 (MLS 2.5)
Library Holdings: Bk Vols 25,000; Per Subs 75
Special Collections: Decorative Arts & Ceramics Primary Source Material, 17th-19th Centuries
Subject Interests: Craft, Decorative art, Design, Fashion, Fine arts
Automation Activity & Vendor Info: (Acquisitions) Innovative Interfaces, Inc; (Cataloging) Innovative Interfaces, Inc; (Circulation) Innovative Interfaces, Inc; (OPAC) Innovative Interfaces, Inc; (Serials) Innovative Interfaces, Inc

Wireless access
Function: Archival coll, For res purposes, Internet access, Magazines, Online cat, Photocopying/Printing, Ref & res, Ref serv available, Res assist avail, Res libr, Scanner
Restriction: Circulates for staff only, Non-circulating, Open by appt only

L MOORE & VAN ALLEN PLLC*, Law Library, Bank of America Corporate Ctr, 100 N Tryon, Ste 4700, 28202-4003. SAN 372-235X. Tel: 704-331-1000, 704-331-3746. FAX: 704-339-5946. Web Site: www.mvalaw.com. *Mgr, Knowledge Mgt, Mgr, Res,* Tamara S Acevedo; E-mail: tamaraacevedo@mvalaw.com
Library Holdings: Bk Titles 5,000; Bk Vols 11,000; Per Subs 200
Automation Activity & Vendor Info: (Acquisitions) EOS International; (Cataloging) EOS International; (Circulation) EOS International; (Serials) EOS International

M NOVANT HEALTH PRESBYTERIAN MEDICAL CENTER*, Library Services, 200 Hawthorne Lane, 28204-2528. (Mail add: PO Box 33549, 28233-3549), SAN 312-7869. Tel: 704-384-4258. FAX: 704-384-5058. E-mail: lrc@novanthealth.org. Web Site: www.novanthealth.org. *Med Librn,* Carla Edwards
Library Holdings: Bk Vols 6,500; Per Subs 150
Subject Interests: Med, Nursing
Automation Activity & Vendor Info: (Cataloging) EOS International; (Circulation) EOS International; (OPAC) EOS International; (Serials) EOS International
Wireless access

C QUEENS UNIVERSITY OF CHARLOTTE*, Everett Library, 1900 Selwyn Ave, 28274. SAN 354-6543. Tel: 704-337-2401. FAX: 704-337-2517. Web Site: library.queens.edu. *Libr Dir,* Carolyn Radcliff; Tel: 704-337-2400, E-mail: radcliffc@queens.edu; *Admin Serv Coordr,* Cindy Nicholson; Tel: 704-337-2708, E-mail: nicholsonc@queens.edu; *Instruction Librn, Pub Serv Librn,* Sherrill Shiraz; Tel: 704-337-2470, E-mail: shirazs@queens.edu; *Electronic Res & Syst Librn,* Brian Trippodo; Tel: 704-688-2766, E-mail: trippodob@queens.edu; *Evening Libr Asst,* Nils Reckemeier; Tel: 704-337-7585, E-mail: reckemeiern@queens.edu; Staff 8 (MLS 4, Non-MLS 4)
Founded 1857. Enrl 2,250; Fac 122; Highest Degree: Master
Library Holdings: Bk Titles 35,331; Bk Vols 43,745; Per Subs 101
Special Collections: Oral History
Subject Interests: 18th Century Charlotte, Local hist, Queen's College hist
Automation Activity & Vendor Info: (Acquisitions) Koha; (Cataloging) Koha; (Circulation) Koha; (Course Reserve) Koha; (ILL) OCLC ILLiad; (Media Booking) Koha; (OPAC) Koha; (Serials) Koha
Wireless access
Partic in Charlotte Area Educ Consortium; LYRASIS
Open Mon-Thurs 9-7, Fri 9-5, Sun 6pm-8pm
Friends of the Library Group

R REFORMED THEOLOGICAL SEMINARY LIBRARY*, Charlotte Campus, 2101 Carmel Rd, 28226. Tel: 704-688-4230. FAX: 704-366-9295. E-mail: library.charlotte@rts.edu. Web Site: rts.edu/academics/library. *Libr Dir,* Rev Ken McMullen; Tel: 704-688-4229, E-mail: kmcmullen@rts.edu
Wireless access
Open Mon, Tues & Thurs 8-8, Wed 8-5, Fri 8-4

R UNION PRESBYTERIAN SEMINARY LIBRARY*, Charlotte Campus, 5141 Sharon Rd, 28210. Tel: 980-636-1700. *Dir,* David Mayo; Tel: 980-636-1665, E-mail: dmayo@upsem.edu; *Circ,* Susan Craig; E-mail: scraig@upsem.edu; *Circ,* Kevin Davis; E-mail: kevin.davis@upsem.edu
Open Tues 12-4, Thurs 1-5

C UNIVERSITY OF NORTH CAROLINA AT CHARLOTTE*, J Murrey Atkins Library, 9201 University City Blvd, 28223-0001. SAN 312-7907. Tel: 704-687-0494. Circulation Tel: 704-687-0491. Reference Tel: 704-687-2241. Web Site: library.uncc.edu. *Dean,* Anne Moore; E-mail: amoor168@uncc.edu; *Assoc Dean, Coll Serv,* Michael Winecoff; Tel: 704-687-1126, E-mail: mkwineco@uncc.edu; *Assoc Dean, Pub Serv,* Stephanie Otis; Tel: 704-687-5679, E-mail: sotis@uncc.edu; *Assoc Dean, Spec Coll & Univ Archives,* Dawn Schmitz; Tel: 704-687-1674, E-mail: Dawn.Schmitz@uncc.edu; *Asst Dean, Tech Strategy,* Bob Price; Tel: 704-687-0490, E-mail: Bob.Price@uncc.edu; Staff 32 (MLS 32)
Founded 1946. Highest Degree: Doctorate
Library Holdings: AV Mats 110,870; e-books 24,380; Bk Titles 551,399; Bk Vols 969,680; Per Subs 34,486
Special Collections: 17th & 18th Century English Drama; Contemporary, Social & Political History of Charlotte & Mecklenburg County; NC state & county document. Oral History; UN Document Depository; US Document Depository
Automation Activity & Vendor Info: (Acquisitions) OCLC WorldShare Interlibrary Loan; (Cataloging) OCLC WorldShare Interlibrary Loan; (Circulation) OCLC WorldShare Interlibrary Loan; (Course Reserve) OCLC WorldShare Interlibrary Loan; (ILL) OCLC WorldShare Interlibrary Loan; (Media Booking) OCLC WorldShare Interlibrary Loan; (OPAC) OCLC WorldShare Interlibrary Loan; (Serials) OCLC WorldShare Interlibrary Loan
Wireless access
Publications: Atlis
Partic in OCLC Online Computer Library Center, Inc
Open Mon-Thurs 7:30am-Midnight, Fri 7:30am-8pm, Sat 10-8, Sun 11am-Midnight

CHEROKEE

S MUSEUM OF THE CHEROKEE INDIAN*, Archives, 589 Tsali Blvd, 28719. (Mail add: PO Box 1599, 28719-1599), SAN 325-7630. Tel: 828-497-3481, Ext 301. FAX: 828-497-4985. Web Site: www.cherokeemuseum.org/archives. *Archivist,* Nelda Reid; E-mail: nreid@cherokeemuseum.org
Founded 1948
Library Holdings: Bk Vols 4,000
Restriction: Open by appt only

CHERRY POINT

A UNITED STATES MARINE CORPS*, Air Station Library, Bldg 298, Marine Corps Air Sta, 28533-0009. (Mail add: PSC Box 8009, 28533-8009), SAN 354-6691. Tel: 252-466-3552. FAX: 252-466-5402. Web Site: library.usmc-mccs.org, mccs.ent.sirsi.net/client/cherry_point. *Dir,* Thomas Donaldson; E-mail: donaldsontm@usmc-mccs.org; Staff 10 (MLS 3, Non-MLS 7)
Founded 1942
Library Holdings: AV Mats 4,000; DVDs 5,000; e-books 100,095; Bk Vols 35,350; Per Subs 118
Subject Interests: Mil hist (US), Mil sci
Automation Activity & Vendor Info: (Cataloging) SirsiDynix; (Circulation) SirsiDynix; (ILL) OCLC FirstSearch; (OPAC) SirsiDynix; (Serials) SirsiDynix
Wireless access
Open Mon-Fri 9-7, Sat & Sun 12-5

CLAYTON

P HOCUTT-ELLINGTON MEMORIAL LIBRARY*, 100 S Church St, 27520. SAN 355-1709. Tel: 919-553-5542. FAX: 919-553-1529. Web Site: www.townofclaytonnc.org/library. *Dir,* Joy Garretson; E-mail: jgarretson@townofclaytonnc.org; Staff 6 (MLS 1, Non-MLS 5)
Automation Activity & Vendor Info: (Acquisitions) Innovative Interfaces, Inc
Wireless access
Function: Adult bk club, Bk club(s), Children's prog, Computers for patron use, Online cat, Outreach serv, Photocopying/Printing, Ref serv available, Senior outreach, Story hour, Summer reading prog, Tax forms, Workshops
Open Mon-Wed 10-6, Thurs 1-8, Fri 10-5, Sat 9-12
Friends of the Library Group

CLINTON

P SAMPSON-CLINTON PUBLIC LIBRARY*, J C Holliday Memorial Library, 217 Graham St, 28328. SAN 354-6721. Tel: 910-592-4153. FAX: 910-590-3504. Web Site: www.sampsonnc.com/departments/library_services. *Libr Dir,* Johnnie Pippin; E-mail: jpippin@sampsonnc.com; *Br Mgr,* Stephanie Johnson; E-mail: sbjohnson@sampsonnc.com; *Ch,* Tiffany Savage; E-mail: tsavage@sampsonnc.com; *Info Serv Assoc,* Erin Heath; E-mail: eheath@sampsonnc.com; *Tech Serv,* Liz Murphy; *Libr Asst,* Sheila Lamb; *Libr Asst,* Karen Parham; *Libr Asst,* Position Currently Open; Staff 4 (MLS 1, Non-MLS 3)
Founded 1935
Library Holdings: AV Mats 15; DVDs 141; Large Print Bks 1,261; Bk Vols 46,454; Per Subs 103; Talking Bks 523; Videos 1,554
Special Collections: North Carolina & Local History Coll, bks & microflm
Subject Interests: Local hist
Automation Activity & Vendor Info: (Cataloging) Innovative Interfaces, Inc; (Circulation) Innovative Interfaces, Inc; (ILL) OCLC WorldShare Interlibrary Loan; (OPAC) Innovative Interfaces, Inc
Wireless access
Function: After school storytime, Audiobks via web, AV serv, Bks on CD, Computers for patron use, Digital talking bks, Electronic databases & coll, Free DVD rentals, Home delivery & serv to seniorr ctr & nursing homes, Homebound delivery serv, ILL available, Internet access, Magazines, Microfiche/film & reading machines, Online cat, Outreach serv, OverDrive digital audio bks, Photocopying/Printing, Prog for adults, Prog for children & young adult, Ref serv available, Scanner, Spoken cassettes & CDs, Summer reading prog, Tax forms, VHS videos
Open Mon-Fri 9-6, Sat 11-5
Restriction: Non-circulating coll, Photo ID required for access

Branches: 3
BRYAN MEMORIAL, 302 W Weeksdale St, Newton Grove, 28366, SAN 354-673X. Tel: 910-594-1260. Web Site: www.sampsonnc.com/departments/library_services/bryan_memorial_library.php. *Br Mgr,* Jean Simmons; E-mail: jsimmons@sampsonnc.com; *Libr Asst,* Terry Eads; *Libr Asst,* Position Currently Open
Founded 1983
Library Holdings: AV Mats 8; DVDs 172; Large Print Bks 239; Bk Vols 17,083; Per Subs 21; Talking Bks 160; Videos 977
Function: After school storytime, Audiobks via web, Bks on CD, Computers for patron use, Digital talking bks, Electronic databases & coll, Free DVD rentals, ILL available, Internet access, Magazines, OverDrive digital audio bks, Photocopying/Printing, Summer reading prog, Tax forms
Open Mon, Tues, Thurs & Fri 9-1:30 & 2:30-6
MIRIAM B LAMB MEMORIAL, 144 S Church St, Garland, 28441. (Mail add: PO Box 426, Garland, 28441-0426), SAN 354-6780. Tel: 910-529-2441. Web Site: www.sampsonnc.com/departments/library_services/miriam_lamb_memorial_library.php. *Br Mgr,* Colanda Faison; E-mail: cfaison@sampsonnc.com; *Libr Asst,* Philip Teachey; *Libr Asst,* Brittaney Wrench; Staff 1 (Non-MLS 1)
Founded 1977
Library Holdings: AV Mats 7; DVDs 139; Large Print Bks 186; Bk Vols 7,692; Per Subs 15; Talking Bks 81; Videos 217
Function: After school storytime, Audiobks via web, Bks on CD, Computers for patron use, Digital talking bks, Electronic databases & coll, ILL available, Internet access, Magazines, OverDrive digital audio bks, Photocopying/Printing, Summer reading prog, Tax forms
Open Mon-Wed & Fri 9-12:30 & 1:30-6
ROSEBORO PUBLIC LIBRARY, 300 W Roseboro St, Roseboro, 28382. (Mail add: PO Box 2066, Roseboro, 28382-2066), SAN 354-6810. Tel: 910-525-5436. Web Site: www.sampsonnc.com/departments/library_services/roseboro_public_library.php. *Br Mgr,* Colanda Faison; E-mail: cfaison@sampsonnc.com; *Libr Asst,* Rachel Corbin; *Libr Asst,* Joann Melvin; Staff 1 (Non-MLS 1)
Founded 1939
Function: After school storytime, Audiobks via web, Bks on CD, Computers for patron use, Electronic databases & coll, Free DVD rentals, ILL available, Internet access, Magazines, OverDrive digital audio bks, Photocopying/Printing, Summer reading prog, Tax forms
Open Mon & Wed-Fri 9-1:30 & 2:30-6

J SAMPSON COMMUNITY COLLEGE LIBRARY*, Kitchin Hall, 1801 Sunset Ave, 28328. (Mail add: PO Box 318, 28329-0318), SAN 312-794X. Tel: 910-900-4308. FAX: 910-592-8048. Web Site: www.sampsoncc.edu/resources-services/library-services. *Dir, Libr Serv,* Donna Odum; Tel: 910-900-4038, E-mail: dodum@sampsoncc.edu; Staff 2 (MLS 1, Non-MLS 1)
Founded 1966. Enrl 1,330; Fac 44
Library Holdings: Bk Titles 30,000; Per Subs 250
Automation Activity & Vendor Info: (Acquisitions) SirsiDynix; (Cataloging) SirsiDynix; (Circulation) SirsiDynix
Wireless access
Publications: AV Handbook; LRC Handbook; Manual of Policies & Procedures
Open Mon-Thurs 7:30-7, Fri 7:30-4

CLYDE

J HAYWOOD COMMUNITY COLLEGE*, Learning Resource Center, 185 Freedlander Dr, 28721. SAN 312-7958. Tel: 828-627-4550. FAX: 828-627-4553. E-mail: library@haywood.edu. Web Site: www.haywood.edu. *Dir,* Bill Kinyon; Tel: 828-627-4551, E-mail: wrkinyon@haywood.edu; *Librn, Technology Spec,* Ngaire Smith; Tel: 828-565-4172, E-mail: nsmith@haywood.edu; Staff 2 (MLS 2)
Founded 1967. Enrl 1,600; Fac 59; Highest Degree: Associate
Jul 2012-Jun 2013. Mats Exp $50,000, Books $35,165, Per/Ser (Incl. Access Fees) $13,500, AV Mat $78
Library Holdings: Bk Vols 40,000; Per Subs 160
Special Collections: Folkmoot
Subject Interests: Auto trades, Bldg construction, Bus admin, Cosmetology, Criminal justice, Electrical installation, Fish, Forest mgt, Machinist, Manufacturing engr tech, Med off asst, Nursing educ, Production crafts, Welding
Automation Activity & Vendor Info: (Acquisitions) SirsiDynix; (Cataloging) SirsiDynix; (Circulation) SirsiDynix; (Course Reserve) SirsiDynix; (ILL) SirsiDynix; (Media Booking) SirsiDynix; (OPAC) SirsiDynix; (Serials) SirsiDynix
Wireless access
Function: Prof lending libr
Partic in CCLINK; Community College Libraries in North Carolina; North Carolina Libraries for Virtual Education; OCLC Online Computer Library Center, Inc

COLUMBIA

P TYRRELL COUNTY PUBLIC LIBRARY, 414 Main St, 27925. (Mail add: PO Box 540, 27925-0540), SAN 312-7974. Tel: 252-796-3771. FAX: 252-796-1167. E-mail: tyrrell@pettigrewlibraries.org. Web Site: pettigrewlibraries.libguides.com/PRL/TCL. *Librn,* Jared Jacavone; E-mail: jjacavone@pettigrewlibraries.org; Staff 1 (MLS 1)
Pop 4,000; Circ 37,505
Library Holdings: Bk Vols 27,000; Per Subs 29
Subject Interests: Genealogy, Local hist
Automation Activity & Vendor Info: (Cataloging) TLC (The Library Corporation); (Circulation) TLC (The Library Corporation); (OPAC) TLC (The Library Corporation)
Mem of Pettigrew Regional Library
Open Mon-Fri 10-4

COLUMBUS

P POLK COUNTY PUBLIC LIBRARY*, 1289 W Mills St, 28722. SAN 312-7982. Tel: 828-894-8721. FAX: 828-894-2761. E-mail: pcpl@polklibrary.org. Web Site: polklibrary.org. *Dir,* Marcie Dowling; E-mail: mdowling@polklibrary.org; *Tech Serv Librn,* Wannangwa Dever; E-mail: wdever@polklibrary.org; *Youth Serv Librn,* Jen Pace Dickenson; E-mail: jdickenson@polklibrary.org; *Pub Serv Mgr,* Alan Smith; *Outreach Coordr,* Rita Owens; E-mail: rowens@polklibrary.org; Staff 6 (MLS 1, Non-MLS 5)
Founded 1960. Circ 92,604
Library Holdings: Bk Vols 45,624; Per Subs 190
Subject Interests: Genealogy, Literacy, Local hist
Wireless access
Publications: Friends of the Polk County Library (Newsletter)
Open Mon & Fri 9-6, Tues-Thurs 9-8, Sat 9-4
Friends of the Library Group
Branches: 1
SALUDA BRANCH, 44 W Main St, Saluda, 28773. Tel: 828-749-2117. FAX: 828-749-2118. *Br Mgr,* Bob McCall; *Pub Serv,* Jeff Jenkins
Open Mon-Fri 9-6, Sat 9-1
Friends of the Library Group
Bookmobiles: 1. Outreach Servs Librn, Rita Owens

CONCORD

C BARBER SCOTIA COLLEGE*, Sage Memorial Library, 145 Cabarrus Ave W, 28025. SAN 312-7990. Tel: 704-789-2900. Web Site: www.b-sc.edu. *Pres,* Melvin Douglas; E-mail: president@b-sc.edu; Staff 4 (MLS 2, Non-MLS 2)
Founded 1867. Enrl 700; Fac 60; Highest Degree: Bachelor
Library Holdings: Bk Vols 49,000; Per Subs 102
Subject Interests: African-Am
Automation Activity & Vendor Info: (Circulation) Ex Libris Group
Publications: The Sageline (Newsletter)

M CABARRUS COLLEGE HEALTH SCIENCES LIBRARY*, Atrium Cabarrus Medical Library, 920 Church St N, 28025. SAN 312-8008. Tel: 704-403-1798. FAX: 704-403-1776. Web Site: www.carolinashealthcare.org/education/cabarrus-college-of-health-sciences. *Libr Mgr, Med Librn,* Cassie Dixon; E-mail: cassie.dixon@atriumhealth.org; *Med Librn,* Amy Burns; E-mail: Amy.burns@atriumhealth.org; Staff 2 (MLS 2)
Founded 1966
Library Holdings: Bk Vols 6,300; Per Subs 150
Special Collections: Health Care & Medical Subjects,
Subject Interests: Allied health, Med, Nursing
Function: 24/7 Electronic res, 24/7 Online cat
Open Mon-Thurs 8-4, Fri 8-1

P CABARRUS COUNTY PUBLIC LIBRARY*, 27 Union St N, 28025. SAN 312-8016. Tel: 704-920-2050. FAX: 704-784-3822. E-mail: library@cabarruscounty.us. Web Site: www.cabarruscounty.us/library. *Dir of Libr,* Emery Ortiz, Jr; Tel: 704-920-2063, E-mail: emortiz@cabarruscounty.us; *Br Mgr,* Kyle White; Tel: 704-920-2066, E-mail: kbwhite@cabarruscounty.us; Staff 3 (MLS 3)
Founded 1911. Pop 140,000; Circ 58,000
Library Holdings: AV Mats 8,399; Electronic Media & Resources 11; Large Print Bks 3,000; Bk Vols 260,000; Per Subs 537; Videos 7,122
Special Collections: Concord & Cabarrus County History Coll; Holt Coll, original art
Automation Activity & Vendor Info: (Cataloging) SirsiDynix; (Circulation) SirsiDynix; (ILL) OCLC; (OPAC) SirsiDynix
Wireless access
Publications: Conspectus (Newsletter)
Open Mon-Thurs 9-8, Fri & Sat 10-6
Restriction: Lending limited to county residents
Friends of the Library Group

Branches: 3
HARRISBURG BRANCH, 201 Sims Pkwy, Harrisburg, 28075. Tel: 704-920-2080. FAX: 704-455-2017. Web Site: www.cabarruscounty.us/government/departments/library/harrisburg-library. *Br Mgr,* Davey Beauchamp; Tel: 704-920-2320, E-mail: dcbeauchamp@cabarruscounty.us; Staff 1 (MLS 1)
Open Mon-Thurs 9-8, Fri & Sat 10-6
Friends of the Library Group
KANNAPOLIS BRANCH, 850 Mountain St, Kannapolis, 28081, SAN 325-3813. Tel: 704-920-1180. FAX: 704-938-3512. Web Site: www.cabarruscounty.us/government/departments/library/kannapolis-library. *Br Mgr,* Terry B Prather; Tel: 704-920-2303, E-mail: tbprather@cabarruscounty.us; Staff 7 (MLS 2, Non-MLS 5)
Founded 1986
Special Collections: Local History Coll
Open Mon-Thurs 9-8, Fri & Sat 10-6
Friends of the Library Group
MT PLEASANT BRANCH, 8556 Cook St, Mount Pleasant, 28124, SAN 377-6050. Tel: 704-436-2202. FAX: 704-436-8205. Web Site: www.cabarruscounty.us/government/departments/library/mt-pleasant-library. *Br Mgr,* Jackie Mills; Tel: 704-920-2310, E-mail: jamills@cabarruscounty.us
Founded 1996
Open Mon-Thurs 9-7, Fri & Sat 10-5
Friends of the Library Group
Bookmobiles: 1

COVE CITY

P COVE CITY-CRAVEN COUNTY PUBLIC LIBRARY*, 102 N Main St, 28523. (Mail add: PO Box 399, 28523-0399), SAN 320-4995. Tel: 252-638-6363. FAX: 252-638-4639. Web Site: cpcrl.org/cove-city-craven-county-public-library. *Librn,* Nancy Chase; E-mail: ncchase45@yahoo.com; *Ch Serv,* Barbara Avery
Founded 1979. Pop 600; Circ 8,020
Library Holdings: Bk Titles 7,500; Per Subs 13; Talking Bks 28
Automation Activity & Vendor Info: (Cataloging) Horizon; (Circulation) Horizon; (OPAC) Horizon
Mem of Craven-Pamlico-Carteret Regional Library System
Open Mon-Thurs 2-8, Fri 2-6
Friends of the Library Group

CULLOWHEE

C WESTERN CAROLINA UNIVERSITY*, Hunter Library, 176 Central Dr, 28723. SAN 312-8024. Tel: 828-227-7307. Circulation Tel: 828-227-7485. Reference Tel: 828-227-7465. Toll Free Tel: 866-928-5424. FAX: 828-227-7015. Web Site: www.wcu.edu/hunter-library. *Dean, Libr Serv,* Farzaneh Razzaghi; Tel: 828-227-3406, E-mail: frazzaghi@email.wcu.edu; *Assoc Dean,* Shamella Cromartie; Tel: 828-227-3543, E-mail: scromartie@email.wcu.edu; *Head, Content Org,* Kristin Calvert; Tel: 828-227-3397, E-mail: kcalvert@email.wcu.edu; *Head, Res & Instrul Serv,* Sarah Steiner; Tel: 828-227-3417, E-mail: sksteiner@email.wcu.edu; *Acq Librn,* Whitney Jordan; Tel: 828-227-3729, E-mail: wjordan@email.wcu.edu; *Cataloging & Metadata Librn,* Beth Thompson; Tel: 828-227-3728, E-mail: bthompson@email.wcu.edu; *Coll Develop Librn,* Jessica Zellers; Tel: 828-227-3801, E-mail: jhzellers@email.wcu.edu; *Electronic Res Librn,* Mark Stoffan; Tel: 828-227-3489, E-mail: mstoffan@email.wcu.edu; *Ref Librn/Educ Liaison,* Beth McDonough; Tel: 828-227-3423, E-mail: bmcdono@email.wcu.edu; *Ref Librn/Sci Liaison,* Krista Schmidt; Tel: 828-227-2215, E-mail: schmidt@email.wcu.edu; *Res & Instruction Librn,* Cara Barker; Tel: 828-227-3413, E-mail: cmbarker@email.wcu.edu; *Information Literacy Coord, Res & Instruction Librn,* Heidi Buchanan; Tel: 828-227-3408, E-mail: hbuchanan@email.wcu.edu; *Res & Instruction Librn,* Allison Cruse; Tel: 828-227-3876, E-mail: acruce@email.wcu.edu; *Res & Instruction Librn,* Ann Hallyburton; Tel: 828-227-3418, E-mail: ahallyb@email.wcu.edu; *Syst Librn,* Gillian Ellern; Tel: 828-227-3746, E-mail: ellern@email.wcu.edu; *Ref Spec,* Elizabeth Marcus; Tel: 828-227-3398, E-mail: emarcus@email.wcu.edu. Subject Specialists: *Law,* Sarah Steiner; *Counseling, Educ,* Beth McDonough; *Biology, Chemistry, Physics,* Krista Schmidt; *Art, Music, Psychol,* Cara Barker; *English, Hist, Philos,* Heidi Buchanan; *Bus,* Allison Cruse; *Health sci,* Ann Hallyburton; Staff 50 (MLS 18, Non-MLS 32)
Founded 1922. Enrl 8,665; Fac 433; Highest Degree: Doctorate
Library Holdings: AV Mats 16,818; e-books 454,917; Bk Vols 609,484
Special Collections: Southern Highlands; Spider Coll. State Document Depository; US Document Depository
Subject Interests: Acad support, Appalachia, Cherokee Indians, Maps
Automation Activity & Vendor Info: (Acquisitions) Innovative Interfaces, Inc; (Cataloging) Innovative Interfaces, Inc; (Circulation) Innovative Interfaces, Inc; (Course Reserve) Innovative Interfaces, Inc; (ILL) Innovative Interfaces, Inc; (OPAC) Innovative Interfaces, Inc; (Serials) Innovative Interfaces, Inc
Wireless access
Partic in LYRASIS; Western North Carolina Library Network; WNCLN
Friends of the Library Group

CURRIE

S US NATIONAL PARK SERVICE*, Moores Creek Battlefield Library, 40 Patriots Hall Dr, 28435. SAN 370-310X. Tel: 910-283-5591. FAX: 910-283-5351. Web Site: www.nps.gov/mocr. *Library Contact,* Matthew Woods; E-mail: Matthew.Woods@nps.gov
Library Holdings: Bk Vols 800
Open Mon-Sun 9-5
Restriction: Not a lending libr

DALLAS

J GASTON COLLEGE*, Morris Library & Media Center, 201 Hwy 321 S, 28034-1499. SAN 312-8040. Tel: 704-922-6359. Interlibrary Loan Service Tel: 704-922-6358. Reference Tel: 704-922-6357. Administration Tel: 704-922-6355. FAX: 704-922-2342. Web Site: www.gaston.edu/library. *Dir of Libr,* Dr Harry Cooke; E-mail: cooke.harry@gaston.edu; *ILL, Pub Serv Spec,* Pat Hull; E-mail: hull.patricia@gaston.edu; *ILL, Pub Serv,* Libby Stone; E-mail: stone.libby@gaston.edu; *Libr Tech,* Harriet Dameron; Tel: 704-922-6356, E-mail: dameron.harriet@gaston.edu; *Ref Serv,* Calvin Craig; E-mail: craig.calvin@gaston.edu; *Tech Serv,* Sharon Hedgepeth; Tel: 704-922-6361, E-mail: day-lowe.sharon@gaston.edu; Staff 8 (MLS 4, Non-MLS 4)
Founded 1964. Enrl 5,000; Fac 106; Highest Degree: Associate
Jul 2017-Jun 2018. Mats Exp $67,000. Sal $360,994
Library Holdings: AV Mats 4,528; CDs 450; Bk Titles 44,965; Bk Vols 50,272; Per Subs 192
Special Collections: Civil War Coll
Subject Interests: Local hist
Automation Activity & Vendor Info: (Cataloging) SirsiDynix; (Circulation) SirsiDynix; (ILL) SirsiDynix; (OPAC) SirsiDynix; (Serials) SirsiDynix
Wireless access
Partic in Community Colleges Libraries in North Carolina
Open Mon-Thurs 7:30am-9pm, Fri (Summer) 7:30-4
Departmental Libraries:
HARVEY A JONAS LIBRARY, 511 S Aspen St, Lincolnton, 28092. Tel: 704-748-1050. FAX: 704-748-1068. *Dir of Libr,* Dr Harry Cooke; E-mail: cooke.harry@gaston.edu; *Coordr, Libr Serv,* Position Currently Open; Staff 3 (Non-MLS 3)
Library Holdings: Bk Titles 1,000
Open Mon-Thurs 8am-9pm, Fri 8-4 (8-Noon Summer)
KIMBRELL CAMPUS & TEXTILE CENTER LIBRARY, 7220 Wilkinson Blvd, Belmont, 28012. (Mail add: PO Box 1044, Belmont, 28012). Tel: 704-825-6278. FAX: 704-825-6345. *Coordr, Libr Serv,* Jody Mosteller; E-mail: mosteller.jody@gaston.edu; Staff 2 (Non-MLS 2)

DANBURY

P DANBURY PUBLIC LIBRARY*, 1007 N Main St, 27016. SAN 312-8059. Tel: 336-593-2419. FAX: 336-593-3232. E-mail: dnb@nwrl.org. Web Site: nwrlibrary.org/danbury. *Br Librn,* Lisa Lawless; E-mail: llawless@nwrl.org
Founded 1945
Library Holdings: Large Print Bks 300; Bk Vols 25,000; Per Subs 10
Automation Activity & Vendor Info: (Acquisitions) SirsiDynix; (Cataloging) SirsiDynix; (Circulation) SirsiDynix
Wireless access
Mem of Northwestern Regional Library
Open Mon, Wed & Fri 9-5:30, Tues & Thurs 9-8, Sat 9-1
Bookmobiles: 1. Libr Contact, Jeannie Wall

DAVIDSON

C DAVIDSON COLLEGE*, E H Little Library, 209 Ridge Rd, 28035-0001. (Mail add: PO Box 7200, 28035-7200), SAN 312-8067. Tel: 704-894-2331. Interlibrary Loan Service Tel: 704-894-2159. FAX: 704-894-2625. E-mail: library@davidson.edu. Web Site: www.davidson.edu/library. *Libr Dir,* Lisa Forrest; E-mail: liforrest@davidson.edu; *Access Serv, Asst Dir, Operations,* Denise Sherrill; E-mail: desherrill@davidson.edu; *Asst Dir, Research, Learning & Scholarly Comms,* Sara Swanson; E-mail: saswanson@davidson.edu; *Cat Librn, Syst Librn,* Alexa Torchynowycz; E-mail: altorchynowycz@davidson.edu; *Cat/Metadata Librn,* Kim Sanderson; E-mail: kisanderson@davidson.edu; *Spec Coll Outreach Librn,* Sharon H Byrd; E-mail: shbyrd@davidson.edu; *Music Libr Mgr,* Jon Hill; E-mail: jmhill@davidson.edu; *Col Archivist & Rec Mgt Coordr,* Debbie Lee Landi; E-mail: dilandi@davidson.edu; *ILL Coordr,* Joe Gutekanst; E-mail: jogutekanst@davidson.edu; Staff 11 (MLS 10, Non-MLS 1)
Founded 1837. Enrl 1,668; Fac 162; Highest Degree: Bachelor
Special Collections: Bruce Rogers Coll; Davidsoniana Coll; Mecklenburg Declaration of Independence Coll; Peter S Ney Coll; Robert Burns Coll; W P Cumming Map Coll; Woodrow Wilson Coll. Oral History; US Document Depository

Automation Activity & Vendor Info: (Acquisitions) SirsiDynix; (Cataloging) SirsiDynix; (Circulation) SirsiDynix; (Course Reserve) SirsiDynix; (ILL) OCLC ILLiad; (OPAC) SirsiDynix; (Serials) SirsiDynix
Wireless access
Partic in Carolina Consortium; LYRASIS; North Carolina Libraries for Virtual Education; Oberlin Group
Open Mon-Thurs 8am-1am, Fri & Sat 10-9, Sun 10am-1am

DOBSON

P DOBSON COMMUNITY LIBRARY*, 113 S Crutchfield St, 27017. (Mail add: PO Box 1264, 27017-1264), SAN 312-8091. Tel: 336-386-8208. FAX: 336-386-4086. *Br Librn,* Cindy Brannock; E-mail: cbrannock@nwrl.org; *Asst Librn,* Salina Zagurski
Library Holdings: Large Print Bks 300; Bk Titles 7,500; Bk Vols 8,000; Per Subs 20
Automation Activity & Vendor Info: (Acquisitions) SirsiDynix; (Cataloging) SirsiDynix; (Circulation) SirsiDynix
Wireless access
Mem of Northwestern Regional Library
Open Mon-Fri 9-6, Sat 10-4
Friends of the Library Group

J SURRY COMMUNITY COLLEGE*, Learning Resources Center, R Bldg, 630 S Main St, 27017. Tel: 336-386-3259. Reference Tel: 336-386-3260. Administration Tel: 336-386-3252. FAX: 336-386-3692. E-mail: library@surry.edu. Web Site: library.surry.edu. *Assoc Dean, Learning Res,* Dr David Wright; *Dir, Academic Support, Dir, Res,* Alan Unsworth; Tel: 336-386-3317, E-mail: unswortha@surry.edu; *Ref Librn,* Maria Luisa Saldarriaga-Osorio; Tel: 336-386-3501, E-mail: osoriom@surry.edu; *Archives, Genealogy Serv,* Sebrina Mabe; Tel: 336-386-3459, E-mail: mabesc@surry.edu; Staff 7.1 (MLS 2.5, Non-MLS 4.6)
Founded 1965. Enrl 3,029; Fac 88; Highest Degree: Associate
Library Holdings: AV Mats 3,717; Bk Titles 33,122; Bk Vols 36,580; Per Subs 125
Special Collections: Genealogy & Local History (Surratt Room)
Subject Interests: Enology, Local hist, Viticulture
Partic in Community Colleges Libraries in North Carolina
Open Mon-Thurs 7:30am-9pm, Fri 7:30-2:30

DUBLIN

J BLADEN COMMUNITY COLLEGE LIBRARY*, 7418 NC Hwy 41 W, 28332. (Mail add: PO Box 266, 28332-0266), SAN 312-8105. Tel: 910-879-5641. FAX: 910-879-5642. E-mail: library@bladencc.edu. Web Site: www.bladencc.edu/campus-resources/library. *Dir, Libr Serv,* Sherwin Rice; Tel: 910-879-5646, E-mail: srice@bladencc.edu; Staff 5 (MLS 1, Non-MLS 4)
Founded 1967. Enrl 1,400; Fac 28; Highest Degree: Associate
Library Holdings: AV Mats 1,992; e-books 185; Bk Vols 20,000; Per Subs 120; Talking Bks 400
Automation Activity & Vendor Info: (Cataloging) SirsiDynix; (Circulation) SirsiDynix; (OPAC) SirsiDynix
Wireless access
Open Mon-Thurs 8-8, Fri 8-3 (Fall & Spring); Mon-Thurs 7:30-6 (Summer)

DURHAM

C DUKE UNIVERSITY LIBRARIES*, 411 Chapel Dr, 27708. (Mail add: PO Box 90193, 27708-0193), SAN 354-6845. Tel: 919-660-5800. Circulation Tel: 919-660-5870. Interlibrary Loan Service Tel: 919-660-5890. Reference Tel: 919-660-5880. FAX: 919-660-5923. Circulation FAX: 919-660-5964. Reference FAX: 919-684-2855. E-mail: asklib@duke.edu. Web Site: www.library.duke.edu. *Univ Librn & Vice Provost for Libr Affairs,* Deborah Jakubs, PhD; E-mail: deborah.jakubs@duke.edu; *Assoc Univ Librn,* Naomi Nelson; Tel: 919-668-7886, E-mail: naomi.nelson@duke.edu; *Assoc Univ Librn, Coll & User Serv,* Robert Byrd; Tel: 919-660-5821, E-mail: robert.byrd@duke.edu; *Assoc Univ Librn, Admin,* Ann Elsner; Tel: 919-660-5947, E-mail: ann.elsner@duke.edu; *Assoc Univ Librn, Develop,* Tom Hadzor; Tel: 919-660-5940, E-mail: t.hadzor@duke.edu; *Assoc Univ Librn, Info Tech,* Tim McGeary; *Dir, Communications,* Aaron Welborn; *Dir, Copyright & Scholarly Communication,* David Hansen; Tel: 919-668-4451, E-mail: david.hansen@duke.edu; *Head, Access & Delivery Serv,* Andrea Loigman; Tel: 919-660-5872; *Head, Cat & Metadata Serv,* Rosalyn Raeford; Tel: 919-660-5892, E-mail: ros.raeford@duke.edu; *Head, Coll Develop,* Jeff Kosokoff; Tel: 919-660-7892; *Head, Core Serv, IT,* John Pormann; *Head, Data & Visualization Serv,* Joel Herndon, PhD; Tel: 919-660-5946, E-mail: joel.herndon@duke.edu; *Head, Digital Projects,* Will Sexton; Tel: 919-660-5888; *Head, Digital Scholarship Serv,* Liz Milewicz, PhD; Tel: 919-660-5911; *Head, East Campus Libr,* Kelley Lawton; Tel: 919-660-5990, E-mail: kelley.lawton@duke.edu; *Head, Electronic Res & Ser Mgt,* Beverly Dowdy; Tel: 919-613-5185, E-mail: beverly.dowdy@duke.edu; *Head, Intl & Area Studies,* Kristina Troost, PhD; Tel: 919-660-5844, E-mail: kktroost@duke.edu; *Head, Libr Serv Ctr,* Marvin Tillman; Tel: 919-596-3962, Fax: 919-598-3103, E-mail: marvin.tillman@duke.edu; *Head Music Libr,* Laura Williams; Tel: 919-660-5952, E-mail: laura.williams@duke.edu; *Head, Res & Instrul Serv,* Kim Duckett; *Mgr, Libr Human Res,* Kimberly Burhop; Tel: 919-660-5937, E-mail: kim.burhop@duke.edu; *Univ Archivist,* Valerie Gillispie; Tel: 919-684-8929; *Presv Officer,* Winston Atkins; Tel: 919-660-5843, E-mail: winston.atkins@duke.edu. Subject Specialists: *Manuscripts, Rare bks,* Naomi Nelson; *Data serv, Soc sci, Statistics,* Joel Herndon, PhD; *US hist,* Kelley Lawton; *Japan,* Kristina Troost, PhD; *Music,* Laura Williams; Staff 137 (MLS 80, Non-MLS 57)
Founded 1838. Enrl 14,600; Fac 1,784; Highest Degree: Doctorate
Jul 2012-Jun 2013. Mats Exp $14,162,443. Sal $16,040,842
Library Holdings: AV Mats 147,727; DVDs 16,699; e-books 203,442; e-journals 91,695; Microforms 4,359,354; Bk Vols 6,073,696
Special Collections: African & African Americana Coll; American History Coll; American Literature Coll; Art & Architecture Coll; British & Commonwealth History Coll; Cartography Coll; Classics Coll; Comics & Pulp Culture Coll; Documentary Photography Coll; Drama Coll; English Literature Coll; German Literature & Culture Coll; History of Advertising Coll; History of Economics Coll; History of Science Coll; Iconology Coll; Italian Literature & Culture Coll; Judaica Coll; Latin Americana Coll; Medieval & Renaissance Culture Coll; Music Coll; Religion Coll; Southern Americana Coll; Travel Coll; Women's Studies & History of Feminism Coll. US Document Depository
Automation Activity & Vendor Info: (Acquisitions) Ex Libris Group; (Cataloging) Ex Libris Group; (Circulation) Ex Libris Group
Wireless access
Publications: Duke University Libraries
Partic in Asn of College & Res Libr; Association of Research Libraries; Association of Southeastern Research Libraries; Carolina Consortium; LYRASIS; NELLCO Law Library Consortium, Inc.; OCLC Online Computer Library Center, Inc
Friends of the Library Group

Departmental Libraries:

CR DIVINITY SCHOOL LIBRARY, 407 Chapel Dr, 27708. (Mail add: PO Box 90972, 27708-0972), SAN 354-6969. Tel: 919-660-3453. Circulation Tel: 919-660-3450. FAX: 919-681-7594. Web Site: library.divinity.duke.edu. *Dir,* Beth Sheppard; E-mail: bsheppard@div.duke.edu; *Ref & Pub Serv Librn,* Shanee Murrain; Tel: 919-660-3549, E-mail: smurrian@div.duke.edu; *Circ Mgr,* Melissa Harrel; Tel: 919-660-3449, E-mail: melissa.h@duke.edu; *Asst Mgr, Circ,* Anne Marie Boyd; Tel: 919-660-3546, E-mail: anne.marie.boyd@duke.edu; Staff 5 (MLS 3, Non-MLS 2)
Library Holdings: Bk Vols 370,000; Per Subs 708
Subject Interests: Biblical studies, Methodism
Open Mon-Thurs (Winter) 8am-11pm, Fri 8-5, Sat 10-6, Sun 2-10; Mon-Fri (Summer) 8-5

FORD LIBRARY, 100 Fuqua Dr, 27708. (Mail add: Fuqua School of Business, PO Box 90122, 27708-0122). Tel: 919-660-7870. FAX: 919-660-7950. Web Site: library.fuqua.duke.edu. *Dir,* Meg Trauner; Tel: 919-660-7869, E-mail: mtrauner@duke.edu; *Librn, Research, Planning & Evaluation,* Bethany Costello; E-mail: bethany.koestner@duke.edu; *Syst Librn,* Carlton Brown; Tel: 919-660-7871, E-mail: carlton.brown@duke.edu; *Access Serv,* Amy Brenan; Tel: 919-660-7873, E-mail: amy.brenan@duke.edu; *Cat,* Linda McCormick; Tel: 919-660-8016, E-mail: linda.mccormick@duke.edu; *Pub Serv,* Jane Day; Tel: 919-660-7874, E-mail: jnday@duke.edu; *Ref (Info Servs),* Paula Robinson; Tel: 919-660-7942, E-mail: robinson@duke.edu; Staff 10 (MLS 7, Non-MLS 3)
Founded 1983. Enrl 1,600; Fac 120; Highest Degree: Doctorate
Library Holdings: AV Mats 3,000; Microforms 450,000; Bk Vols 40,000; Per Subs 300
Subject Interests: Bus
Automation Activity & Vendor Info: (OPAC) Ex Libris Group; (Serials) Ex Libris Group
Open Mon-Thurs 7:30am-Midnight, Fri 7:30am-10pm, Sat 10-8, Sun 10-Midnight

CL J MICHAEL GOODSON LAW LIBRARY, 210 Science Dr, 27708. (Mail add: PO Box 90361, 27708-0361), SAN 354-7051. Circulation Tel: 919-613-7128. Interlibrary Loan Service Tel: 919-613-7122. Reference Tel: 919-613-7121. Administration Tel: 919-613-7114. FAX: 919-613-7237. Web Site: www.law.duke.edu/lib. *Sr Assoc Dean for Info Serv,* Richard A Danner; Tel: 919-613-7115, E-mail: danner@law.duke.edu; *Asst Dean, Libr Serv,* Melanie J Dunshee; Tel: 919-613-7119, E-mail: dunshee@law.duke.edu; *Head, Coll Serv,* Karen B Douglas; Tel: 919-613-7116, E-mail: douglas@law.duke.edu; *Head, Ref Serv,* Jennifer L Behrens; Tel: 919-613-7198, E-mail: behrens@law.duke.edu; *Acq Librn,* Shyama Agrawal; Tel: 919-613-7070, E-mail: agrawal@law.duke.edu; *Digital Res Librn,* Sean Chen; Tel: 919-613-7028, E-mail: schen@law.duke.edu; *Foreign & Intl Law Ref Librn,* Kristina J Alayan; Tel: 919-613-7118, E-mail: alayan@law.duke.edu; *Ref Librn,* Jane Bahnson; Tel: 919-613-7113, E-mail: bahnson@law.duke.edu; *Ref Librn,* Kelly Leong; Tel: 919-613-7041, E-mail: leong@law.duke.edu; *Ref Librn,* Marguerite Most;

Tel: 919-613-7120, E-mail: most@law.duke.edu; *Ref Librn,* Laura M Scott; Tel: 919-613-7164, E-mail: scott@law.duke.edu; *Empirical Res Analyst,* Guangya Liu; Tel: 919-613-7178, E-mail: guangya.liu@law.duke.edu; Staff 13 (MLS 12, Non-MLS 1)
Founded 1931. Enrl 730; Highest Degree: Doctorate
Special Collections: US Document Depository
Partic in Legal Information Preservation Alliance; Triangle Research Libraries Network
Restriction: Circ limited

CM MEDICAL CENTER LIBRARY & ARCHIVES, DUMC Box 3702, Ten Searle Dr, 27710-0001, SAN 354-7116. Tel: 919-660-1100. Interlibrary Loan Service Tel: 919-660-1138. Administration Tel: 919-660-1150. FAX: 919-681-7599. Interlibrary Loan Service FAX: 919-660-1188. E-mail: medical-librarian@dm.duke.edu. Web Site: www.mclibrary.duke.edu. *Assoc Dean, Libr Serv,* Patricia Thibodeau; Tel: 919-660-1148, E-mail: patricia.thibodeau@duke.edu; *Dep Dir,* Rick Peterson; E-mail: rick.peterson@duke.edu; *Dir, Archives & Digital Initiatives,* Russell Koonts; Tel: 919-383-2653, E-mail: russell.koonts@duke.edu; *Assoc Dir, Coll Serv,* Emma Cryer; Tel: 919-660-1140, E-mail: emma.cryer@duke.edu; *Assoc Dir, Res & Educ,* Megan Von Isenburg; Tel: 919-660-1131, E-mail: megan.vonisenburg@duke.edu; *Asst Dir, Archival Coll & Serv,* Jolie Braun; E-mail: jolie.braun@duke.edu; *Asst Dir, Admin Serv, Bus Mgr,* Vanessa Sellars; Tel: 919-660-1149, E-mail: vanessa.sellars@duke.edu; *Asst Dir, Communications & Web Content Mgt,* Beverly Murphy; Tel: 919-660-1127, E-mail: beverly.murphy@duke.edu; *Mgr, Access Serv,* Elizabeth Berney; E-mail: elizabeth.berney@duke.edu; *Doc Delivery & ILL Mgr/Access Serv,* Louis Wiethe; Tel: 919-660-1179, E-mail: Louis.Wiethe@duke.edu; Staff 46 (MLS 16, Non-MLS 30)
Founded 1930. Fac 1,800; Highest Degree: Doctorate
Library Holdings: Bk Vols 296,491
Special Collections: Duke Medical Authors. Oral History
Partic in National Network of Libraries of Medicine Region 1; OCLC Online Computer Library Center, Inc; Triangle Research Libraries Network
Publications: Archives (Newsletter); Medical Center Library News (Newsletter)
Open Mon-Fri 7:30am-Midnight, Sat 12-8, Sun Noon-Midnight

PEARSE MEMORIAL LIBRARY-MARINE LAB, Nicholas Sch Environ & Earth Sci Marine Lab, 135 Duke Marine Lab Rd, Beaufort, 28516-9721, SAN 377-0702. Tel: 252-504-7510. FAX: 252-504-7648. E-mail: marlib@duke.edu. *Librn,* David M Talbert; E-mail: talbert@duke.edu
Library Holdings: Bk Vols 25,607
Subject Interests: Biochem, Botany, Coastal resource mgt, Marine biol, Marine biotech, Oceanography
Open Mon-Thurs 7:30-6

PERKINS & BOSTOCK LIBRARIES, 411 Chapel Dr, 27708, SAN 354-690X. Tel: 919-660-5870.
Library Holdings: Bk Vols 191,290
Subject Interests: Botany, Environ, Forestry, Zoology
Open Mon-Fri 8-5

WILLIAM R PERKINS LILLY LIBRARY, 2500 Campus Dr, Campus Box 90725, 27708-0725. Tel: 919-660-5995. FAX: 919-660-5999. E-mail: lilly-requests@duke.edu. Web Site: www.lib.duke.edu/lilly. *Head Librn,* Kelley Lawton; E-mail: kelley.lawton@duke.edu; *Librn,* Lee Sorensen. Subject Specialists: *Art,* Lee Sorensen
Library Holdings: Bk Vols 250,000
Subject Interests: Art hist, Drama, Philos, Visual arts

WILLIAM R PERKINS MUSIC LIBRARY, 113 Mary Duke Biddle Music Bldg, 27708, SAN 354-7175. Tel: 919-660-5950. FAX: 919-684-6556. E-mail: music-requests@duke.edu. Web Site: www.lib.duke.edu/music/. *Music Librn,* Laura Williams; Tel: 919-660-5992, E-mail: laura.williams@duke.edu
Library Holdings: Bk Vols 96,818
Special Collections: African-American Music (William Grant Still Coll); Venetian Music (Berdes Papers); Viennese Music (Weinmann Coll)
Subject Interests: Music
Open Mon-Thurs 8am-10pm, Fri 8-5, Sat 10-5, Sun 2-10 (Winter); Mon-Fri 9-5 (Summer)

DAVID M RUBENSTEIN RARE BOOK & MANUSCRIPT LIBRARY, 316 Perkins Library, 411 Chapel Dr, 27708. (Mail add: PO Box 90185, 27708-0185). Tel: 919-660-5822. Administration Tel: 919-660-5820. FAX: 919-660-5934. Web Site: library.duke.edu/rubenstein. *Dir,* Naomi Nelson; Tel: 919-668-7556, E-mail: naomi.nelson@duke.edu; *Head, Res Serv,* David Pavelich; *Head, Tech Serv,* Sarah Schmidt. Subject Specialists: *Manuscripts, Rare bks,* Naomi Nelson

P DURHAM COUNTY LIBRARY*, Headquarters, 300 N Roxboro St, 27701. (Mail add: PO Box 3809, 27702-3809), SAN 354-7205. Tel: 919-560-0100. Circulation Tel: 919-560-0131. Interlibrary Loan Service Tel: 919-560-0104. Reference Tel: 919-560-0110. Administration Tel: 919-560-0163. Automation Services Tel: 919-560-0189. FAX: 919-560-0137. Reference FAX: 919-560-0106. Web Site: www.durhamcountylibrary.org. *Dir,* Tammy Baggett; Tel: 919-560-0160, E-mail: tbaggett@dconc.gov; *Dep Dir,* Terry B Hill; Tel: 919-560-0164, E-mail: tbhill@dconc.gov; Staff 120.8 (MLS 40, Non-MLS 80.8)
Founded 1897. Circ 1,513,603
Library Holdings: Audiobooks 26,174; AV Mats 17,392; Bk Vols 554,598; Per Subs 1,219
Special Collections: African-American History & Literature Coll, bks, per; Durham Biography & History Coll, including Durham County Library History; Durham Historical Photographs (Archival); North Carolina History & Literature, bks, microfilm, per, newsp, rec, v-tapes, slides, CDs
Automation Activity & Vendor Info: (Cataloging) SirsiDynix; (Circulation) SirsiDynix; (OPAC) SirsiDynix
Wireless access
Publications: Branching Out (Quarterly newsletter); Seasons Readings; The Best of Friends Newsletter; The Grapevine Staff Newsletter (Bimonthly)
Partic in LYRASIS; OCLC Online Computer Library Center, Inc
Special Services for the Deaf - TTY equip
Open Mon-Fri 8:30-5
Friends of the Library Group
Branches: 6

BRAGTOWN, 3200 Dearborn Dr, 27704, SAN 354-723X. Tel: 919-560-0210. Web Site: durhamcountylibrary.org/location/bragtown. *Mgr,* Kathleen Hayes; E-mail: khayes@dconc.gov
Founded 1962
Library Holdings: Bk Vols 5,229; Per Subs 30
Open Mon 2-9, Tues-Fri 10-5
Friends of the Library Group

EAST REGIONAL, 211 Lick Creek Lane, 27703. Tel: 919-560-0203. Reference Tel: 919-560-0213. FAX: 919-598-8673. Web Site: durhamcountylibrary.org/location/east. *Mgr,* Lauren Doll; Tel: 919-560-0128, E-mail: ldoll@dconc.gov
Founded 2006
Open Mon, Tues & Thurs 9-9, Wed 9-6, Fri & Sat 9:30-6, Sun 2-6

NORTH REGIONAL, 221 Milton Rd, 27712, SAN 354-7302. Tel: 919-560-0231. Reference Tel: 919-560-0236. FAX: 919-560-0246. Web Site: durhamcountylibrary.org/location/north. *Mgr,* Stephanie Fennell; Tel: 919-560-0243, E-mail: sfennell@dconc.gov
Founded 2007
Open Mon, Tues & Thurs 9-9, Wed 9-6, Fri & Sat 9:30-6, Sun 2-6

SOUTH REGIONAL, 4505 S Alston Ave, 27713, SAN 354-7329. Tel: 919-560-7409. Web Site: durhamcountylibrary.org/location/south. *Mgr,* Che Anderson; E-mail: tanderson@dconc.gov
Open Mon, Tues & Thurs 9-9, Wed 9-6, Fri & Sat 9:30-6, Sun 2-6

SOUTHWEST, 3605 Shannon Rd, 27707, SAN 354-7264. Tel: 919-560-8590. FAX: 919-560-0542. Web Site: durhamcountylibrary.org/location/southwest. *Interim Mgr,* Ruth Link; E-mail: rlink@dconc.gov
Founded 1992
Library Holdings: Large Print Bks 500; Bk Vols 69,000; Per Subs 120
Subject Interests: Children's videos
Function: Photocopying/Printing
Open Mon, Tues & Thurs 9-9, Wed 9-6, Fri & Sat 9:30-6, Sun 2-6

STANFORD L WARREN BRANCH, 1201 Fayetteville St, 27707, SAN 354-7388. Tel: 919-560-0270. FAX: 919-560-0283. E-mail: slwarren@dclnc.gov. Web Site: durhamcountylibrary.org/location/warren. *Interim Mgr,* Claudia Aleman; Tel: 919-560-0274, E-mail: caleman-toomes@dconc.gov
Founded 1940
Library Holdings: Bk Vols 29,492; Per Subs 40
Special Collections: African-American Cultural History Coll
Open Mon, Tues & Thurs 9-9, Wed 9-6, Fri & Sat 9:30-6
Friends of the Library Group

Bookmobiles: 1. Outreach & Mobile Servs Mgr, Kathi Sippen

J DURHAM TECHNICAL COMMUNITY COLLEGE*, 1637 Lawson St, 27703. (Mail add: PO Box 11307, 27703-0307), SAN 312-8148. Tel: 919-536-7211. FAX: 919-686-3471. E-mail: library@durhamtech.edu. Web Site: www.durhamtech.edu/library.htm. *Dir,* Julie C Humphrey; E-mail: humphreyj@durhamtech.edu; *Pub Serv Librn,* Wendy Ramseur; E-mail: ramseurw@durhamtech.edu; *Ref Librn,* Susan Baker; E-mail: bakers@durhamtech.edu; *Asst Dir, Ref, Asst Dir, Tech Serv,* Julie Humphrey; E-mail: humphrej@durhamtech.edu
Founded 1961. Enrl 1,740
Library Holdings: Bk Vols 44,998; Per Subs 16,569
Subject Interests: Educ, Law, Liberal arts, Med
Automation Activity & Vendor Info: (Circulation) SirsiDynix; (OPAC) SirsiDynix
Wireless access
Publications: Library Handbook; News from the Library; Periodical Holdings
Partic in Carolina Consortium; Community Colleges Libraries in North Carolina; OCLC Online Computer Library Center, Inc
Open Mon-Thurs (Winter) 8am-8:30pm, Fri 8-5, Sat 9-1; Mon-Thurs (Summer) 8-6:30, Fri 8-Noon

Departmental Libraries:
NORTHERN DURHAM CENTER, 2401 Snow Hill Rd, 27712, SAN 377-0524. Tel: 919-536-7240. FAX: 919-686-3519. *Librn,* Santosh Shonek
Open Mon-Thurs 9-6
ORANGE COUNTY CAMPUS, 525 College Park Rd, Hillsborough, 27278. Tel: 919-536-7211. FAX: 919-536-7297. ; Staff 1 (MLS 1)
Open Mon-Thurs 9-6

S FOREST HISTORY SOCIETY LIBRARY*, 701 William Vickers Ave, 27701-3162. SAN 301-5807. Tel: 919-682-9319. FAX: 919-682-2349. Web Site: foresthistory.org/research-explore/archives-library. *Dir, Libr & Archives,* Eben Lehman; E-mail: eben.lehman@foresthistory.org; *Librn,* Jason Howard; E-mail: jason.howard@foresthistory.org; *Historian,* James Lewis; E-mail: james.lewis@foresthistory.org. Subject Specialists: *Environ hist,* Eben Lehman; Staff 2 (MLS 2)
Founded 1946
Library Holdings: AV Mats 500; Bk Vols 9,500; Per Subs 200; Spec Interest Per Sub 100; Videos 250
Special Collections: American Forest Council Archives; American Forestry Association Archives; Interview Coll, tapes & transcripts; National Forest Products Association Archives; Society of American Foresters Archives; United States Forest Service. Oral History
Subject Interests: Conserv, Environ hist, Forestry
Wireless access
Function: Archival coll, ILL available, Internet access, Res libr
Open Mon-Fri 8-5
Restriction: Non-circulating coll

C NORTH CAROLINA CENTRAL UNIVERSITY*, James E Shepard Memorial Library, 1801 Fayetteville St, 27707-3129. (Mail add: PO Box 19436, 27707-0019), SAN 354-7590. Tel: 919-530-7310. Circulation Tel: 919-530-6426. Reference Tel: 919-530-6473. Toll Free Tel: 800-662-7644 (NC only). FAX: 919-530-7612. Web Site: web.nccu.edu/shepardlibrary. *Dir, Libr Serv,* Dr Theodosia Shields; Tel: 919-530-6475, E-mail: tshields@nccu.edu; *Asst Dir, Libr Serv,* Jamillah Scott-Branch; Tel: 919-530-7312, E-mail: jscottbr@nccu.edu; *Head, Access Serv,* Vickie V Spencer; Tel: 919-530-7305, E-mail: vspencer@nccu.edu; *Head, Curric Mat(s) Ctr,* Karen E Grimwood; Tel: 919-530-6383, E-mail: kgrimwood@nccu.edu; *Head, Ser,* Position Currently Open; *Head, Tech Serv,* Position Currently Open; *Info Literacy Librn,* Hafsa Murad; Tel: 919-530-7315, E-mail: hmurad@nccu.edu; *Govt Doc, Res & Instrul Serv Librn,* Eric Morris; Tel: 919-530-6598, E-mail: emorris@nccu.edu; *Syst Librn,* Yan Wang; Tel: 919-530-5240, E-mail: ywang@nccu.edu; Staff 31 (MLS 15, Non-MLS 16)
Founded 1923. Enrl 5,482; Fac 284; Highest Degree: Master
Library Holdings: Bk Titles 450,000; Bk Vols 500,597; Per Subs 1,928
Special Collections: African American (Martin Coll). US Document Depository
Subject Interests: Local hist
Automation Activity & Vendor Info: (Cataloging) SirsiDynix; (Circulation) SirsiDynix
Wireless access
Publications: Annual Reports; SNN: Shepard News Network
Partic in LYRASIS
Open Mon-Thurs 7:30am-2am, Fri 7:30-5, Sat 10-6, Sun 2-2
Friends of the Library Group
Departmental Libraries:
MUSIC, 1801 Fayetteville St, 27707. Tel: 919-530-6220. FAX: 919-530-7979. Web Site: www.nccu.edu/library/music.html. *Librn,* Vernice Faison; E-mail: vfaison@nccu.edu
Library Holdings: Bk Vols 12,000
CL SCHOOL OF LAW LIBRARY, 640 Nelson St, 27707, SAN 354-768X. Tel: 919-530-6333. Circulation Tel: 919-530-5189. Interlibrary Loan Service Tel: 919-530-6608. Reference Tel: 919-530-6715. Administration Tel: 919-530-6244. FAX: 919-530-7926. Web Site: law.nccu.edu/library. *Interim Dir,* Nichelle Perry; Tel: 919-530-5188, E-mail: nperry@nccu.edu; *Access Serv Librn,* Jonathan Beeker; E-mail: jbeeker@nccu.edu; *Sr Ref Librn,* Michelle T Cosby; Tel: 919-530-5241, E-mail: mcosby@nccu.edu; *Cataloger,* Wadad Giles; Tel: 919-530-7177, E-mail: wgiles@nccu.edu; Staff 15 (MLS 7, Non-MLS 8)
Founded 1939. Enrl 362; Highest Degree: Doctorate
Library Holdings: Bk Vols 450,000
Special Collections: Civil Rights (McKissick Coll)
Subject Interests: Civil rights, NC law, Tax
Function: Ref serv available
Partic in OCLC Online Computer Library Center, Inc; Triangle Research Libraries Network
Restriction: Limited access for the pub
SCHOOL OF LIBRARY & INFORMATION SCIENCES, James E Shepard Memorial Library, 3rd Flr, 1801 Fayetteville St, 27707. Tel: 919-530-7323. FAX: 919-530-6402. Web Site: www.nccuslis.org/slislib. *Univ Librn,* Virginia Purefoy Jones; E-mail: vpjones@nccu.edu; *Libr Tech,* Marie Preston; Tel: 919-530-6400, E-mail: mpreston@nccu.edu; Staff 2 (MLS 2)
Founded 1939. Highest Degree: Master
Library Holdings: Bk Vols 46,000
Special Collections: Black Librarian's Coll; William Tucker Coll
Subject Interests: Children's lit, Info sci, Libr sci
Partic in OCLC Online Computer Library Center, Inc
Open Mon-Thurs 8am-10pm, Fri & Sat 8-5, Sun 2-5

S NORTH CAROLINA MUSEUM OF NATURAL SCIENCES*, Brimley Memorial Library, 433 W Murray Ave, 27704-3101. (Mail add: PO Box 15190, 27704-0190), SAN 328-1833. Tel: 919-220-5429. FAX: 919-220-5575. Web Site: naturalsciences.org/research-collections/brimley-library. *Head Librn,* Janet Edgerton; Tel: 919-707-9810, E-mail: janet.edgerton@naturalsciences.org; *Asst Head Librn,* Margaret Cotrufo; Tel: 919-707-9831, E-mail: margaret.cotrufo@naturalsciences.org; Staff 1 (MLS 1)
Founded 1980
Library Holdings: Bk Titles 3,550; Per Subs 11
Open Mon-Fri 9-4

S NORTH CAROLINA SCHOOL OF SCIENCE & MATHEMATICS LIBRARY, Borden Mace Library, Library, Instructional Technologies & Communications, 1219 Broad St, 27705. Tel: 919-416-2916. FAX: 919-416-2890. Automation Services FAX: 919-416-2955. E-mail: library@ncssm.edu. Web Site: www.ncssm.edu/library. *Libr Dir,* Dr Robin Boltz; Tel: 919-416-2914, E-mail: boltz@ncssm.edu; *Librn,* Keith Beisner; E-mail: beisner@ncssm.edu; *Evening Librn,* Evan Miles; E-mail: evan.miles@ncssm.edu; *Archives, Records Librn,* Sharron Johnson; Tel: 919-416-2657, E-mail: sharron.johnson@ncssm.edu; Staff 3 (MLS 3)
Founded 1980. Enrl 680; Fac 2; Highest Degree: Certificate
Library Holdings: Audiobooks 200; AV Mats 500; Bks on Deafness & Sign Lang 5; CDs 300; DVDs 500; e-journals 10,000; Electronic Media & Resources 25; Bk Titles 22,000; Bk Vols 24,000; Videos 300
Automation Activity & Vendor Info: (Acquisitions) Follett Software; (Cataloging) Follett Software; (Circulation) Follett Software; (ILL) OCLC WorldShare Interlibrary Loan; (OPAC) Follett Software; (Serials) EBSCO Online
Function: Archival coll, Art exhibits, Audio & video playback equip for onsite use, Audiobks via web, AV serv, Bk club(s), Bks on cassette, Bks on CD, CD-ROM, Computer training, Computers for patron use, Digital talking bks, E-Reserves, Electronic databases & coll, Equip loans & repairs, Free DVD rentals, ILL available, Instruction & testing, Internet access, Learning ctr, Literacy & newcomer serv, Music CDs, Online cat, Online info literacy tutorials on the web & in blackboard, Online ref, Orientations, Photocopying/Printing, Prof lending libr, Prog for children & young adult, Ref & res, Ref serv available, Res libr, Scanner, Summer reading prog, Teen prog, VHS videos, Workshops
Open Mon-Fri 8am-10pm, Fri 8-5, Sun 5-10
Restriction: Authorized patrons, Borrowing privileges limited to fac & registered students, Borrowing requests are handled by ILL, External users must contact libr, In-house use for visitors, Lending limited to county residents, Limited access for the pub, Mem organizations only, Non-circulating of rare bks, Non-circulating to the pub, Open to fac, students & qualified researchers, Open to pub upon request, Open to researchers by request, Open to students, fac & staff, Open to students, fac, staff & alumni, Photo ID required for access, Pub ref by request, Researchers by appt only, Secured area only open to authorized personnel, Visitors must make appt to use bks in the libr

S ORGANIZATION FOR TROPICAL STUDIES LIBRARY, Duke University, 410 Swift Ave, 27705. (Mail add: PO Box 90630, 27708-0630), SAN 377-5259. Tel: 919-684-5774. FAX: 919-684-5661. E-mail: ots@duke.edu. Web Site: www.ots.ac.cr. *Chief Exec Officer,* Dr Elizabeth Braker; E-mail: ebraker@duke.edu
Founded 1963
Library Holdings: Bk Vols 1,000
Subject Interests: Natural res

M RHINE RESEARCH CENTER*, Institute for Parapsychology, 2741 Campus Walk Ave, Bldg 500, 27705-3707. SAN 322-8851. Tel: 919-309-4600. E-mail: office@rhine.org. Web Site: www.rhine.org. *Librn,* Barbara Ensrud; E-mail: barbara@rhine.org
Founded 1930
Library Holdings: Bk Vols 10,000; Per Subs 70
Special Collections: Foreign language books on parapsychology; J B Rhine & Louisa Rhine Archival Coll, unpublished mss, theses & dissertations
Subject Interests: Parapsychol, Psychol res, Related areas
Restriction: Open by appt only

SR WATTS STREET BAPTIST CHURCH LIBRARY, 800 Watts St, 27701. SAN 328-4433. Tel: 919-688-1366. FAX: 919-688-7255. Web Site: www.wattsstreet.org.
Library Holdings: Bk Titles 1,000
Open Mon-Fri 8:30-5

EAST BEND

P EAST BEND PUBLIC LIBRARY*, 420 Flint Hill Rd, 27018. SAN 376-2882. Tel: 336-699-3890. FAX: 336-699-2359. E-mail: ebn@nwrl.org. Web Site: nwrlibrary.org/eastbend. *Br Librn,* Susan Hutchens; E-mail: shutchens@nwrl.org; *Asst Br Librn,* Margaret Speer; E-mail: mspeer@nwrl.org
Founded 1985
Library Holdings: Bk Vols 15,000; Per Subs 18
Automation Activity & Vendor Info: (Acquisitions) SirsiDynix; (Cataloging) SirsiDynix; (Circulation) SirsiDynix; (Course Reserve) SirsiDynix; (ILL) SirsiDynix; (Media Booking) SirsiDynix; (OPAC) SirsiDynix; (Serials) SirsiDynix
Wireless access
Mem of Northwestern Regional Library
Open Mon 9-7, Tues-Thurs 9-5:30, Fri 9-2, Sat 9-12
Friends of the Library Group

EDEN

P ROCKINGHAM COUNTY PUBLIC LIBRARY*, 527 Boone Rd, 27288. SAN 354-7744. Tel: 336-627-1106. FAX: 336-623-1258. Web Site: www.rcpl.org. *Libr Dir,* Michael Roche; E-mail: mroche@co.rockingham.nc.us; *Supvr, Outreach Serv,* Rachel Fetzer; Tel: 336-627-3729, E-mail: rfetzer@co.rockingham.nc.us; *Ch Serv,* Rachel Holden; E-mail: rshaw@co.rockingham.nc.us; *Extn Serv, Pub Serv,* Calvert Smith; Tel: 336-349-8476, E-mail: csmith@co.rockingham.nc.us; *Ref (Info Servs),* Rebecca Smith; Tel: 336-623-3168, E-mail: rsmith@co.rockingham.nc.us; Staff 33 (MLS 9, Non-MLS 24)
Founded 1934. Pop 91,928; Circ 513,241
Library Holdings: Bk Vols 293,724; Per Subs 624
Subject Interests: African-Am, Bus, Genealogy, State hist
Automation Activity & Vendor Info: (Cataloging) Evergreen; (Circulation) Evergreen
Wireless access
Function: AV serv, Home delivery & serv to seniorr ctr & nursing homes, Homebound delivery serv, ILL available, Internet access, Photocopying/Printing, Prof lending libr, Prog for children & young adult, Ref serv available, Summer reading prog, Telephone ref, Wheelchair accessible
Publications: Genealogy Bibliography; Rockingham County Public Library Patron Brochure; Suggested Reading List for Home Extension Groups (Annual)
Open Mon-Fri 8-5
Friends of the Library Group
Branches: 4
EDEN BRANCH, 598 S Pierce St, 27288, SAN 354-7779. Tel: 336-623-3168. FAX: 336-623-1171. *Br Mgr,* Katherine Seaver; Tel: 336-623-3168, E-mail: kseaver@co.rockingham.nc.us
Function: 24/7 Electronic res, 24/7 Online cat, Activity rm, Adult bk club, Archival coll
Open Mon & Thurs 9-8, Tues, Wed & Fri 9-6, Sat 9-4
Friends of the Library Group
MADISON MAYODAN BRANCH, 140 E Murphy St, Madison, 27025, SAN 354-7809. Tel: 336-548-6553. FAX: 336-548-2010. *Librn/Mgr,* Joan Waynick; *Libr Asst,* Shirley Brim-Jones. Subject Specialists: *Genealogy,* Shirley Brim-Jones
Subject Interests: Genealogy, Local hist
Open Tues 9-6, Thurs 9-8, Sat 9-4
Friends of the Library Group
REIDSVILLE BRANCH, 204 W Morehead St, Reidsville, 27320, SAN 354-7868. Tel: 336-349-8476. FAX: 336-342-4824. *Br Mgr,* Calvert Smith; E-mail: csmith@rcpl.org
Subject Interests: African-Am
Automation Activity & Vendor Info: (OPAC) Innovative Interfaces, Inc
Open Mon & Thurs 9-8, Tues, Wed & Fri 9-6, Sat 9-4
Friends of the Library Group
STONEVILLE BRANCH, 201 E Main St, Stoneville, 27048. (Mail add: PO Box 20, Stoneville, 27048-0020), SAN 354-7892. Tel: 336-573-9040. FAX: 336-573-2774. *Br Supvr,* Julia Johnson; E-mail: jjohnson@rcpl.org; *Librn,* Joan Waynick
Open Mon & Wed 12-5, Tues 1-6, Thurs 1-8, Fri 10-6
Friends of the Library Group
Bookmobiles: 1

EDENTON

P SHEPARD-PRUDEN MEMORIAL LIBRARY*, 106 W Water St, 27932. SAN 312-8199. Tel: 252-482-4112. FAX: 252-482-5451. E-mail: shepard-pruden@pettigrewlibraries.org. Web Site: pettigrewlibraries.libguides.com/PRL/SPML. *Dir,* Judi Bugniazet; E-mail: jbugniazet@pettigrewlibraries.org; *Librn,* Jennifer Finlay; E-mail: jfinlay@pettigrewlibraries.org; Staff 6 (MLS 1, Non-MLS 5)
Founded 1921. Pop 14,368; Circ 48,748
Library Holdings: Bk Titles 24,697; Bk Vols 29,379; Per Subs 69
Subject Interests: Local hist
Wireless access
Mem of Pettigrew Regional Library
Open Mon & Tues 10-7, Wed-Fri 10-5, Sat 10-1
Friends of the Library Group

ELIZABETH CITY

J COLLEGE OF THE ALBEMARLE LIBRARY*, 1208 N Road St, 27906. (Mail add: PO Box 2327, 27906-2327), SAN 354-7922. Tel: 252-335-0821, Ext 2270. FAX: 252-335-0649. Web Site: www.albemarle.edu/student-resources/academic-support/library. *Dir, Libr Serv,* Rodney Wooten; Tel: 252-335-0821, Ext 2268, E-mail: rodney_wooten91@albemarle.edu; *Tech Serv,* Shirley Outlaw; Tel: 252-335-0821, Ext 2271, E-mail: shirley_outlaw@albemarle.edu
Founded 1961
Library Holdings: Bk Titles 28,000; Bk Vols 35,000; Per Subs 232
Subject Interests: North Caroliniana
Wireless access
Partic in North Carolina Information Network; OCLC Online Computer Library Center, Inc
Open Mon-Fri 8-4:30

P EAST ALBEMARLE REGIONAL LIBRARY*, 100 E Colonial Ave, 27909. SAN 312-8202. Tel: 252-335-2511. FAX: 252-335-2386. Web Site: www.youseemore.com/EARL. *Dir,* Jonathan Wark; E-mail: jwark@earlibrary.org; *Head of Br Serv,* Jackie King; E-mail: jking@earlibrary.org; Staff 31 (MLS 4, Non-MLS 27)
Founded 1964. Pop 89,939; Circ 390,995
Library Holdings: Bk Vols 170,000; Per Subs 350
Subject Interests: NC
Automation Activity & Vendor Info: (Cataloging) TLC (The Library Corporation); (Circulation) TLC (The Library Corporation); (OPAC) TLC (The Library Corporation)
Wireless access
Member Libraries: Camden County Library; Currituck County Public Library; Dare County Library; Pasquotank County Library
Open Mon-Fri 8:30-5
Bookmobiles: 1

C ELIZABETH CITY STATE UNIVERSITY, G R Little Library, 1704 Weeksville Rd, 27909. SAN 312-8210. Tel: 252-335-3427. Circulation Tel: 252-335-8513. Administration Tel: 252-335-3586. FAX: 252-335-3446. Web Site: www.ecsu.edu/library. *Dir, Libr Serv,* Dr Juanita Midgette Spence; E-mail: jmidgette@ecsu.edu; *Electronic Res, Librn, Ser,* David Dusto; Tel: 252-335-3432, E-mail: dadusto@ecsu.edu; *Access Serv, Circ, Librn,* Cynthia Horne; E-mail: crhorne@ecsu.edu; *Distance Educ, Info Literacy, Librn,* Position Currently Open; *Music Librn,* Nurhak Tuncer-Bayramli; Tel: 252-335-3632, E-mail: ntuncerbayramli@ecsu.edu; *Acq & Cat, Libr Tech,* Leah Banks; Tel: 252-335-3429, E-mail: lcbanks@ecsu.edu; *Libr Tech, Ser,* Chiquita Mitchell; Tel: 252-335-8519, E-mail: cdmitchell@ecsu.edu; *Tech Serv,* Mary Jordan; Tel: 252-335-8515, E-mail: mrjordan@ecsu.edu; Staff 7 (MLS 5, Non-MLS 2)
Founded 1892. Enrl 1,700; Fac 156; Highest Degree: Master
Jul 2019-Jun 2020. Mats Exp $843,506. Sal $372,501 (Prof $271,330)
Library Holdings: DVDs 1,931; e-books 202,607; e-journals 27,790; Electronic Media & Resources 31,946; Bk Vols 249,897; Per Subs 123
Special Collections: Children's Vintage Coll; State Normal School Coll, 1891-1939; State Teacher's College Coll, 1939-1963; Walter N Ridley Heritage Coll
Automation Activity & Vendor Info: (Acquisitions) SirsiDynix-WorkFlows; (Cataloging) SirsiDynix-WorkFlows; (Circulation) SirsiDynix-WorkFlows; (Course Reserve) SirsiDynix-WorkFlows; (Discovery) ProQuest; (ILL) OCLC WorldShare Interlibrary Loan; (OPAC) SirsiDynix-WorkFlows; (Serials) SirsiDynix-WorkFlows
Wireless access
Function: 24/7 Electronic res, 24/7 Online cat, Archival coll, Electronic databases & coll, For res purposes, ILL available, Instruction & testing, Internet access, Movies, Online cat, Online info literacy tutorials on the web & in blackboard, Online ref, Ref & res, Ref serv available
Partic in Carolina Consortium; Eastern Carolina Libr Network; LYRASIS; NC State Libr Info Network; North Carolina Libraries for Virtual Education; OCLC Online Computer Library Center, Inc
Open Mon-Thurs 8-8, Fri 8-5, Sun 12-8
Restriction: Authorized patrons, Borrowing privileges limited to fac & registered students, Borrowing requests are handled by ILL
Friends of the Library Group

CR MID-ATLANTIC CHRISTIAN UNIVERSITY*, Watson-Griffith Library, 715 N Poindexter St, 27909-4054. SAN 312-8237. Tel: 252-334-2057. Administration Tel: 252-334-2046. FAX: 252-334-2577. Web Site: www.macuniversity.edu. *Dir,* Ken Gunselman; E-mail: ken.gunselman@macuniversity.edu; *Asst Dir,* Alice K Andrews; Tel: 252-334-2027, E-mail: alice.andrews@macuniversity.edu; Staff 3 (MLS 1, Non-MLS 2)

Founded 1948. Enrl 172; Fac 17; Highest Degree: Bachelor
Library Holdings: Bk Vols 35,000; Per Subs 188
Special Collections: Creationism Coll; Deaf Coll; Disciplíana Coll
Subject Interests: Christian educ, Deaf studies, Prof life, Relig
Automation Activity & Vendor Info: (Cataloging) Mandarin Library Automation; (Circulation) Mandarin Library Automation; (OPAC) Mandarin Library Automation
Wireless access
Function: ILL available
Partic in Christian Libr Network; LYRASIS
Open Mon-Thurs 7:30am-8pm, Fri 7:30-5, Sat 12:30-2:30

S NORTH CAROLINA DEPARTMENT OF CORRECTION*, Pasquotank Correctional Institution Library, 527 Commerce Dr, Caller No 5005, 27906. Tel: 252-331-4881. FAX: 252-331-4866. Web Site: www.ncdps.gov/adult-corrections/prisons/prison-facilities/pasquotank-correctional-institution. *Librn,* Ms K Cofield
Library Holdings: Bk Vols 12,000
Automation Activity & Vendor Info: (Cataloging) Brodart; (Circulation) Brodart
Restriction: Not open to pub

P PASQUOTANK COUNTY LIBRARY, 100 E Colonial Ave, 27909. SAN 312-8229. Tel: 252-335-2473. FAX: 252-331-7449. Web Site: pasquotanklibrary.org. *Dir,* Kellen Whitehurst; E-mail: kwhitehurst@earlibrary.org; *Ch Serv,* Rebecca Soule; E-mail: rsoule@earlibrary.org; *Circ, Tech Serv,* Christine Wilson; E-mail: cwilson@earlibrary.org; *Info Serv,* Beatheia Jackson; E-mail: bjackson@earlibrary.org
Founded 1930. Pop 36,732; Circ 131,140
Library Holdings: AV Mats 1,041; Large Print Bks 1,911; Bk Vols 62,000; Per Subs 88; Talking Bks 1,795
Subject Interests: NC hist
Automation Activity & Vendor Info: (Cataloging) TLC (The Library Corporation); (Circulation) TLC (The Library Corporation); (ILL) OCLC; (OPAC) TLC (The Library Corporation)
Wireless access
Mem of East Albemarle Regional Library
Special Services for the Blind - Braille bks; Large print & cassettes; Large screen computer & software; Magnifiers
Open Mon-Fri 8:30-6:30, Sat 9-1
Friends of the Library Group
Bookmobiles: 1. Librn, Monek Adams

ELIZABETHTOWN

P BLADEN COUNTY PUBLIC LIBRARY*, 111 N Cyprus St, 28337. (Mail add: PO Box 1419, 28337-1419), SAN 354-7981. Tel: 910-862-6990. FAX: 910-862-8777. Web Site: bladenco.libguides.com/home. *Dir,* Kelsey Edwards; E-mail: kedwards@bladenco.org; Staff 10 (MLS 1, Non-MLS 9)
Founded 1939. Pop 32,000; Circ 200,591
Library Holdings: Large Print Bks 3,000; Bk Vols 76,413; Per Subs 85; Talking Bks 539
Special Collections: North Carolina Genealogy
Subject Interests: Bladen County genealogy, Local hist, NC genealogy
Automation Activity & Vendor Info: (Cataloging) TLC (The Library Corporation); (Circulation) TLC (The Library Corporation); (OPAC) TLC (The Library Corporation)
Wireless access
Open Mon, Wed & Fri 8:30-6, Tues & Thurs 8:30-8:30, Sat 8:30am-12:30pm
Branches: 2
BRIDGER MEMORIAL, 313 S Main St, Bladenboro, 28320. (Mail add: PO Box 1259, Bladenboro, 28320-1259), SAN 354-8015. Tel: 910-863-4586. *Br Mgr,* Kayla Parker; E-mail: kparker@bladenco.org
Library Holdings: Bk Titles 4,000
Open Mon 9-7, Tues 9-6, Wed-Fri 1-6
CLARKTON PUBLIC, 10413 N College St, Clarkton, 28433. (Mail add: PO Box 665, Clarkton, 28433-0665), SAN 354-804X. Tel: 910-647-3661. *Br Mgr,* Greta Jackson; E-mail: gjackson@bladenco.org
Library Holdings: Bk Vols 5,000
Open Mon 9-6, Tues 9-7, Wed-Fri 1-6
Bookmobiles: 1

ELKIN

P ELKIN PUBLIC LIBRARY*, 111 N Front St, 28621. SAN 312-8245. Tel: 336-835-5586. FAX: 336-835-5008. E-mail: elk@nwrl.org.
Library Holdings: Bk Titles 25,000
Special Collections: Hendren Nature Coll; Lillard History Coll
Mem of Northwestern Regional Library
Friends of the Library Group

P NORTHWESTERN REGIONAL LIBRARY*, 111 N Front St, 2nd Flr, 28621. SAN 312-8253. Tel: 336-835-4894. Administration Tel: 336-835-2609. FAX: 336-835-1356. E-mail: info@nwrl.org. Web Site: www.nwrl.org. *Dir of Libr,* Joan Sherif; Tel: 336-835-4894, Ext 1001, E-mail: jsherif@nwrl.org; *Commun Serv, Program Librn,* Tyler Wilmoth; Tel: 336-835-4894, Ext 1003, E-mail: twilmoth@nwrl.org; *Bus Officer,* Karen Howard; Tel: 336-835-4894, Ext 1002, E-mail: khoward@nwrl.org; *Cataloger,* Sunnie Prevette; Tel: 336-835-4894, Ext 1005, E-mail: sprevette@nwrl.org; *ILL,* Tonya Triplett; Tel: 336-835-4894, Ext 1004, E-mail: ttriplett@nwrl.org; Staff 46 (MLS 4, Non-MLS 42)
Founded 1959. Pop 163,573; Circ 593,828
Library Holdings: DVDs 445; Large Print Bks 18,853; Bk Vols 319,272; Per Subs 225; Talking Bks 17,024; Videos 47,963
Subject Interests: Local hist
Automation Activity & Vendor Info: (Cataloging) SirsiDynix; (Circulation) SirsiDynix; (OPAC) SirsiDynix
Wireless access
Member Libraries: Alleghany County Public Library; Boonville Community Public Library; Charles H Stone Memorial Library; Danbury Public Library; Dobson Community Library; East Bend Public Library; Elkin Public Library; Jonesville Public Library; King Public Library; Lowgap Public Library; Mount Airy Public Library; Walnut Cove Public Library; Yadkin County Public Library
Open Mon-Fri 8-5
Friends of the Library Group
Bookmobiles: 1

ELON

C ELON UNIVERSITY, Carol Grotnes Belk Library, 308 N O'Kelly Ave, 27244-0187. (Mail add: 2550 Campus Box, 27244), SAN 354-8074. Tel: 336-278-6600. Interlibrary Loan Service Tel: 336-278-6580. Administration Tel: 336-278-6579. Information Services Tel: 336-278-6599. Web Site: www.elon.edu/library. *Dean of Libr,* Joan Ruelle; E-mail: jruelle@elon.edu; *Archives Librn,* Randall Bowman; Tel: 336-278-6571, E-mail: rbowman@elon.edu; *Archives Librn,* Libby Coyner; Tel: 336-278-6531, E-mail: lcoyner@elon.edu; *Assessment & User Experience Librn,* Angela Wacker; Tel: 336-278-5015, E-mail: awacker@elon.edu; *Bus Res Librn,* Betty L Garrison; Tel: 336-278-6581, E-mail: bgarrison@elon.edu; *Digital Coll Librn, Syst Librn,* Shaunta Alvarez; Tel: 336-278-6576, E-mail: salvarez@elon.edu; *Electronic Res Librn,* Vicki Siler; Tel: 336-278-6592, E-mail: vsiler@elon.edu; *Outreach & Marketing Librn,* Alison Van Norman; Tel: 336-278-6587, E-mail: avannorman@elon.edu; *Research Librn, Sci Librn,* Jesse Akman; Tel: 336-278-6584, E-mail: jakman2@elon.edu; *Coordr, Instruction & Outreach,* Patrick Rudd; Tel: 336-278-6574, E-mail: prudd@elon.edu; *Coord, Libr Coll,* Shannon Tennant; Tel: 336-278-6585, E-mail: stennant@elon.edu; *Coordr, Libr Res, Coord, Scholarly Services,* Teresa LePors; Tel: 336-278-6577, E-mail: lepors@elon.edu; *Coordr, Spec Coll & Univ Archives,* Chrystal Carpenter; Tel: 226-278-6681, E-mail: ccarpenter8@elon.edu; *ILL, Reserves, Spec,* Lynn Melchor; E-mail: lmelchor@elon.edu; *Evening Library Specialist,* Nikida Jeffreys; E-mail: njeffreys@elon.edu; Staff 15 (MLS 14, Non-MLS 1)
Founded 1889. Enrl 6,991; Fac 439; Highest Degree: Doctorate
Library Holdings: AV Mats 25,857; e-books 196,192; e-journals 59,199; Bk Titles 592,824
Special Collections: Church History Coll (United Church of Christ-Southern Conference Archives), bks, ms, memorabilia; Civil War (McClendon Coll); Elon University Archives; Faculty Publications; North Carolina Authors (Johnson Coll), autographed first editions
Automation Activity & Vendor Info: (Acquisitions) OCLC Worldshare Management Services; (Cataloging) OCLC Worldshare Management Services; (Circulation) OCLC; (Course Reserve) OCLC; (ILL) OCLC; (OPAC) OCLC; (Serials) OCLC
Wireless access
Function: 24/7 Electronic res, 24/7 Online cat, Archival coll, Bks on CD, Computers for patron use, Electronic databases & coll, ILL available, Internet access, Mango lang, Music CDs, Online cat, Outreach serv, Ref serv available, Res assist avail, Spanish lang bks
Partic in Carolina Consortium; LYRASIS; NC Asn of Independent Cols & Univs; OCLC Online Computer Library Center, Inc
Restriction: 24-hr pass syst for students only, In-house use for visitors, Open to fac, students & qualified researchers, Open to pub for ref & circ; with some limitations

ENFIELD

P LILLY PIKE SULLIVAN MUNICIPAL LIBRARY*, 103 SE Railroad St, 27823. SAN 312-8261. Tel: 252-445-5203. FAX: 252-445-4321. E-mail: lillypikesullivanlibrary@gmail.com. Web Site: halifaxnc.libguides.com/hcl. *Br Mgr,* Cheryl S Dickens; *Asst Librn, Children's Prog,* Cynthia Williams
Founded 1938. Pop 3,000; Circ 40,570
Library Holdings: Bk Vols 30,000; Per Subs 20
Special Collections: Commonwealth Microfilms 1908-1995; NC History Coll, AV

Wireless access
Open Mon-Fri 8:30-5, Sat 9-12

FAIRMONT

R FAIRMONT FIRST BAPTIST CHURCH*, Stinceon Ivey Memorial Library, 416 S Main, 28340. SAN 312-8296. Tel: 910-628-0626. FAX: 910-628-0627. E-mail: gabby1653@hotmail.com.
Founded 1956
Library Holdings: Bk Vols 5,000

FARMVILLE

P FARMVILLE PUBLIC LIBRARY, 4276 W Church St, 27828. SAN 312-8318. Tel: 252-753-3355. E-mail: library@farmvillenc.gov. Web Site: www.farmvillelibrary.org. *Libr Dir,* Angie Bates; E-mail: abates@farmvillenc.gov; *Ad,* Connie Widney; E-mail: cwidney@farmvillenc.gov; *Children & Teen Librn,* Heather Harden; E-mail: hharden@farmvillenc.gov; *Libr Tech,* Candis Williams; E-mail: cwilliams@farmvillenc.gov; Staff 4 (MLS 2, Non-MLS 2)
Founded 1930. Pop 4,634; Circ 25,653
Library Holdings: Audiobooks 540; AV Mats 300; e-books 107,790; Large Print Bks 300; Bk Vols 35,000; Per Subs 120; Videos 1,490
Automation Activity & Vendor Info: (Cataloging) Evergreen; (Circulation) Evergreen; (OPAC) Evergreen
Wireless access
Function: After school storytime, Archival coll
Open Mon-Thurs 9-8, Fri 9-6, Sat 9-3
Restriction: Authorized patrons
Friends of the Library Group

FAYETTEVILLE

P CUMBERLAND COUNTY PUBLIC LIBRARY & INFORMATION CENTER*, Headquarters, 300 Maiden Lane, 28301-5032. SAN 354-8139. Tel: 910-483-7727. Reference Tel: 910-483-7727, Ext 1345. Administration Tel: 910-483-7727, Ext 1304. FAX: 910-486-5372. E-mail: library@cumberland.lib.nc.us. Web Site: www.cumberland.lib.nc.us/ccplsite. *Dir,* Cotina Jones; E-mail: cjones@cumberland.lib.nc.us; *Br Head, Mgr,* Birch Barnes; E-mail: bbarnes@cumberland.lib.nc.us; *Div Mgr,* Pamela Kource; E-mail: pkource@cumberland.lib.nc.us; *Mkt & Communications Mgr,* Kellie Tomita; E-mail: ktomita@cumberland.lib.nc.us
Automation Activity & Vendor Info: (Circulation) Evergreen
Wireless access
Function: Home delivery & serv to seniorr ctr & nursing homes, ILL available, Internet access, Photocopying/Printing, Prog for adults, Prog for children & young adult, Ref serv available, Summer reading prog, Telephone ref, Wheelchair accessible
Special Services for the Deaf - Staff with knowledge of sign lang; TTY equip
Open Mon-Thurs 9-9, Fri & Sat 9-6, Sun 2-6
Friends of the Library Group
Branches: 8
BORDEAUX, 3711 Village Dr, 28304-1530, SAN 354-8198. E-mail: bor@cumberland.lib.nc.us. *Br Mgr,* Amanda Dekker; E-mail: adekker@cumberland.lib.nc.us
Founded 1986
Open Mon-Wed 9-9, Thurs-Sat 9-6
CLIFFDALE REGIONAL BRANCH, 6882 Cliffdale Rd, 28314-1936, SAN 371-1374. E-mail: clf@cumberland.lib.nc.us. *Br Mgr,* Jennifer Hatcher; E-mail: jhatcher@cumberland.lib.nc.us
Founded 1991
Open Mon-Thurs 9-9, Fri & Sat 9-6, Sun 2-6

L CUMBERLAND COUNTY COURT LIBRARY, Courthouse, Rm 341, 117 Dick St, 28301, SAN 354-8163. Tel: 910-321-6600. FAX: 910-485-5291. *Br Mgr,* Position Currently Open
Open Mon-Fri 8-1 & 2-5
EAST REGIONAL BRANCH, 4809 Clinton Rd, 28312-8401, SAN 378-150X. E-mail: erl@cumberland.lib.nc.us. *Br Mgr,* Position Currently Open
Founded 1999
Open Mon-Thurs 9-9, Fri & Sat 9-6, Sun 2-6
HOPE MILLS BRANCH, 3411 Golfview Rd, Hope Mills, 28348-2266, SAN 354-8317. E-mail: hpm@cumberland.lib.nc.us. *Br Mgr,* MaryAnne Sommer; E-mail: msommer@cumberland.lib.nc.us
Founded 1992
Open Mon-Wed 9-9, Thurs-Sat 9-6
NORTH REGIONAL, 855 McArthur Rd, 28311-2053, SAN 378-1488. E-mail: nrl@cumberland.lib.nc.us. *Br Mgr,* Mary Campbell; E-mail: mcampbel@cumberland.lib.nc.us
Founded 1998
Function: After school storytime, Computer training, Computers for patron use, Free DVD rentals, Online cat, Photocopying/Printing, Spoken cassettes & CDs, Summer reading prog
Open Mon-Thurs 9-9, Fri & Sat 9-6, Sun 2-6
SPRING LAKE BRANCH, 101 Laketree Blvd, Spring Lake, 28390-3189, SAN 354-8341. E-mail: spl@cumberland.lib.nc.us. *Br Mgr,* Michelle Gross; E-mail: mgross@cumberland.lib.nc.us
Founded 1999
Open Mon-Wed 9-9, Thu-Sat 11-6
WEST BRANCH, 7469 Century Circle, 28306-3141. E-mail: wrl@cumberland.lib.nc.us. *Br Mgr,* Jennifer Hatcher

C FAYETTEVILLE STATE UNIVERSITY*, Charles W Chesnutt Library, 1200 Murchison Rd, 28301-4298. SAN 312-8334. Tel: 910-672-1231. Reference Tel: 910-672-1233. Web Site: libguides.uncfsu.edu/c.php?g=763207, www.uncfsu.edu/library. *Dir, Libr Serv,* Forrest C Foster; E-mail: ffoster1@uncfsu.edu; *Assoc Dir, Coll Develop,* Jan Whitfield; Tel: 910-672-1520, E-mail: jwhitfield@uncfsu.edu; *Head, Pub Serv,* Shamella Cromartie; Tel: 910-672-1750, E-mail: scromart@uncfsu.edu; *Head, Ref & ILL Serv,* Robert Foster; E-mail: rfoster@uncfsu.edu; *Acq Librn,* Jinong Sun; Tel: 910-672-1642, E-mail: jsun@uncfsu.edu; *Cat Librn,* Position Currently Open; *Info Tech, Librn,* Ophelia Chapman; Tel: 910-672-1546, E-mail: ochapma1@uncfsu.edu; Staff 24 (MLS 10, Non-MLS 14)
Founded 1867. Enrl 6,091; Fac 266; Highest Degree: Doctorate
Library Holdings: AV Mats 6,449; CDs 1,115; e-books 224,581; e-journals 46,732; Electronic Media & Resources 52,187; Bk Titles 223,687; Per Subs 314; Videos 4,974
Special Collections: US Govt Doc, Archives. US Document Depository
Subject Interests: African-Am, Ethnic studies
Automation Activity & Vendor Info: (Acquisitions) OCLC Worldshare Management Services; (Cataloging) OCLC Worldshare Management Services; (Circulation) OCLC Worldshare Management Services; (Course Reserve) OCLC Worldshare Management Services; (Discovery) EBSCO Discovery Service; (ILL) OCLC ILLiad; (OPAC) OCLC Worldshare Management Services
Wireless access
Publications: Acquisitions List; Ches-Notes (Newsletter)
Partic in LYRASIS; North Carolina Libraries for Virtual Education
Open Mon-Thurs 7:45am-12am, Fri 7:45am-10pm, Sat 8-5, Sun 2-11; Mon-Thurs (Summer) 7:30am-9pm, Fri 7:30-6, Sat 11-5
Friends of the Library Group

J FAYETTEVILLE TECHNICAL COMMUNITY COLLEGE*, Paul H Thompson Library, 2201 Hull Rd, 28303. SAN 312-8342. Tel: 910-678-8247. Reference Tel: 910-678-0080. FAX: 910-678-8401. E-mail: library@faytechcc.edu. Web Site: www.faytechcc.edu/campus-life/library. *Dir,* Laurence Gavin; Tel: 910-678-8382, E-mail: gavinl@faytechcc.edu; *Access Serv, Pub Serv,* Deborah Foster; Tel: 910-678-8257, E-mail: fosterd@faytechcc.edu; Staff 9 (MLS 3, Non-MLS 6)
Founded 1961. Enrl 8,000; Fac 250; Highest Degree: Associate
Library Holdings: Bk Titles 64,000; Per Subs 100
Subject Interests: Health occupation, Law
Automation Activity & Vendor Info: (Circulation) SirsiDynix; (Serials) SirsiDynix
Wireless access
Function: Telephone ref
Partic in Community Colleges Libraries in North Carolina
Open Mon-Thurs 7:45am-9pm, Fri 7:45-7

C METHODIST UNIVERSITY, Davis Memorial Library, 5400 Ramsey St, 28311. SAN 312-8350. Tel: 910-630-7123. Circulation Tel: 910-630-7645. Administration Tel: 910-630-7587. FAX: 910-630-7119. Reference E-mail: reference@methodist.edu. Web Site: www.methodist.edu/library. *Dir, Libr Serv,* Tracey Sherrod; E-mail: tsherrod@methodist.edu; *Archivist/Librn, Asst Dir,* Arleen Fields; E-mail: afields@methodist.edu; Staff 14 (MLS 5, Non-MLS 9)
Founded 1960. Enrl 2,255; Fac 150; Highest Degree: Master
Library Holdings: AV Mats 13,799; e-books 388,123; e-journals 14,275; Electronic Media & Resources 39,596; Bk Vols 79,523; Per Subs 470
Special Collections: Lafayette Coll
Automation Activity & Vendor Info: (Acquisitions) Ex Libris Group; (Cataloging) Ex Libris Group; (Circulation) Ex Libris Group; (Media Booking) Ex Libris Group; (OPAC) Ex Libris Group; (Serials) Ex Libris Group
Wireless access
Open Mon-Thurs 7am-Midnight, Fri 7-6, Sat 1-5, Sun 3pm-Midnight

M SOUTHERN REGIONAL AREA HEALTH EDUCATION CENTER*, Information Access Center, Library Services, 1601 Owen Dr, 28304. SAN 312-8326. Tel: 910-678-7273. FAX: 910-323-4007. Reference E-mail: reference@sr-ahec.org. Web Site: www.southernregionalahec.org/library-services. *Dir, Libr Serv,* Lisa Kilburn; Tel: 910-678-7222, E-mail: Lisa.Kilburn@sr-ahec.org; Staff 3 (MLS 1, Non-MLS 2)
Founded 1977
Jul 2015-Jun 2016. Mats Exp $62,000
Library Holdings: AV Mats 50; e-books 200; e-journals 5,000; Bk Titles 1,000; Per Subs 5

Subject Interests: Allied health, Consumer health, Family med, Med, Mental health, Nursing, Osteopathic med
Automation Activity & Vendor Info: (Cataloging) LibraryWorld, Inc; (Circulation) LibraryWorld, Inc; (OPAC) LibraryWorld, Inc
Wireless access
Partic in Medical Library Association; Mid-Atlantic Chapter-Med Libr Asn; National Network of Libraries of Medicine Region 1; US National Library of Medicine
Open Mon-Fri 8-5

FLAT ROCK

J BLUE RIDGE COMMUNITY COLLEGE LIBRARY*, Henderson County Campus, 180 W Campus Dr, 28731. SAN 312-8377. Tel: 828-694-1879. Interlibrary Loan Service Tel: 828-694-1685. E-mail: library@blueridge.edu. Web Site: library.blueridge.edu. *Dir,* Alison Norvell; Tel: 828-694-1636, E-mail: a_norvell@blueridge.edu; *Electronic Res Librn,* Dane Secor; Tel: 828-694-1824, E-mail: d_secor@blueridge.edu; *Librn,* Phillip Bergen; Tel: 828-694-1681, E-mail: p_bergen@blueridge.edu; Staff 2.5 (MLS 2.5)
Founded 1969. Fac 55; Highest Degree: Associate
Jul 2013-Jun 2014. Mats Exp $53,869. Sal $161,852
Library Holdings: Bk Vols 43,364
Automation Activity & Vendor Info: (Cataloging) SirsiDynix; (Circulation) SirsiDynix; (Course Reserve) SirsiDynix; (OPAC) SirsiDynix
Wireless access
Function: Bks on cassette, Bks on CD, Computers for patron use, ILL available, Photocopying/Printing, Ref serv available
Partic in NC Dept of Commun Cols
Open Mon-Thurs 8am-9pm, Fri 8-4:30
Restriction: Open to pub for ref & circ; with some limitations, Open to students, fac & staff

Departmental Libraries:

TRANSYLVANIA COUNTY CAMPUS, 45 Oak Park Dr, Brevard, 28712. Tel: 828-883-2520, Ext 1906. *Librn,* Michele Handy; Tel: 828-694-1906, E-mail: m_handy@blueridge.edu
Open Mon-Thurs 8am-9:30pm, Fri 8-4

FOREST CITY

P MOONEYHAM PUBLIC LIBRARY*, 240 E Main St, 28043. SAN 355-1288. Tel: 828-248-5224. FAX: 828-248-5224. Web Site: www.townofforestcity.com/library. *Libr Dir,* Denise Strickland; E-mail: denisestrickland@townofforestcity.com; *Libr Asst,* Lauren Heavner
Library Holdings: AV Mats 200; Bks on Deafness & Sign Lang 10; DVDs 200; Large Print Bks 60; Bk Vols 15,600; Per Subs 15; Talking Bks 100
Wireless access
Open Mon-Fri 8-5

FORT BRAGG

UNITED STATES ARMY

A MARQUAT MEMORIAL LIBRARY*, Bank Hall, Bldg D-3915, 3004 Ardennes St, 28310-9610, SAN 354-8430. Tel: 910-396-5370. FAX: 910-432-7788. *Chief, Libr Serv,* Margaret Harrison; Tel: 910-396-3958; *Sr Librn,* Jane Crabill; Tel: 910-432-8184, E-mail: jane.crabill@us.army.mil; *Acq, Cat,* C Labsan; Tel: 910-432-6503; *ILL,* Eva Murphy; Tel: 910-432-9222, E-mail: eva.murphy@us.army.mil; *Ref (Info Servs),* Nan Kutulas; Tel: 910-432-8920, E-mail: nancy.kutulas@us.army.mil; Staff 5 (MLS 2, Non-MLS 3)
Founded 1952
Library Holdings: Bk Vols 33,000; Per Subs 126
Subject Interests: Area studies, Civil affairs, Geopolitics, Intl relations, Lang, Mil assistance, Polit sci, Psychol operations, Regional studies, Spec forces, Spec operations, Terrorism, Unconventional warfare
Automation Activity & Vendor Info: (Cataloging) TLC (The Library Corporation); (Circulation) TLC (The Library Corporation); (ILL) OCLC; (OPAC) TLC (The Library Corporation)
Partic in OCLC Online Computer Library Center, Inc
Publications: Accession List; Bibliographics (2/yr); Library Guide; Periodicals Holdings List
Open Mon-Fri 9-4:30
Restriction: Circ to mil employees only

A JOHN L THROCKMORTON LIBRARY*, IMSE-BRG-MWR-L Bldg 1-3346, Randolph St, 28310-5000, SAN 354-8406. Tel: 910-396-2665. Circulation Tel: 910-396-1691. Reference Tel: 910-396-3523. FAX: 910-907-2274. Web Site: www.fortbraggmwr.com/library.php. *Chief Librn,* Philip Quinones; *Ref Librn,* Ron Jackson; *Ref Librn,* Bernadette Ross; Staff 13 (MLS 3, Non-MLS 10)
Founded 1941
Library Holdings: Bk Vols 125,000; Per Subs 200
Subject Interests: Current affairs, Hist, Intl relations, Mil sci, Testing
Automation Activity & Vendor Info: (Acquisitions) SirsiDynix; (Cataloging) SirsiDynix; (Circulation) SirsiDynix; (ILL) OCLC; (OPAC) SirsiDynix; (Serials) SirsiDynix
Partic in OCLC Online Computer Library Center, Inc
Publications: Bibliographies
Open Mon-Thurs 9-8, Fri & Sat 10-6

AM WOMACK ARMY MEDICAL CENTER, MEDICAL LIBRARY*, WAMC Stop A, 2817 Reilly Rd, 28310-7301. Tel: 910-907-7323. FAX: 910-907-7449. *Librn,* Jennifer Kuntz
Library Holdings: Bk Vols 3,800; Per Subs 179
Function: ILL available, Photocopying/Printing
Restriction: Not open to pub

FOUR OAKS

P JAMES BRYAN CREECH PUBLIC LIBRARY*, 206 W Hatcher St, 27524. SAN 355-1768. Tel: 919-963-6013. E-mail: jbcplib@yahoo.com. *Librn,* Tonie Collins
Circ 5,047
Library Holdings: AV Mats 536; Large Print Bks 76; Bk Vols 10,110; Talking Bks 115
Wireless access
Open Wed 10-6, Thurs 2-6, Sat 2-5

FRANKLIN

P MACON COUNTY PUBLIC LIBRARY*, 149 Siler Farm Rd, 28734. SAN 312-8385. Tel: 828-524-3600, 828-524-3700. FAX: 828-524-9550. Web Site: www.fontanalib.org/franklin. *Dir,* Karen Wallace; E-mail: kwallace@fontanalib.org; Staff 23 (MLS 2, Non-MLS 21)
Founded 1890. Pop 34,000
Library Holdings: Bk Vols 75,000
Automation Activity & Vendor Info: (Cataloging) Evergreen; (Circulation) Evergreen; (OPAC) Evergreen
Wireless access
Function: Distance learning
Mem of Fontana Regional Library
Open Mon-Thurs 9-6, Fri 10-5, Sat 10-1
Friends of the Library Group

Branches: 2

HUDSON LIBRARY, 554 Main St, Highlands, 28741. (Mail add: PO Box 430, Highlands, 28741-0430), SAN 312-8830. Tel: 828-526-3031. FAX: 828-526-5278. Web Site: www.fontanalib.org/highlands. *Br Librn,* Carlyn Morenus; Staff 5 (MLS 1, Non-MLS 4)
Founded 1884
Library Holdings: Bk Vols 22,367; Per Subs 80; Talking Bks 650; Videos 800
Open Tues-Fri 10-5, Sat 10-4

NANTAHALA COMMUNITY, 128 Nantahala School Rd, Topton, 28781. Tel: 828-321-3020. FAX: 828-321-3020. Web Site: www.fontanalib.org/nantahala. *Br Mgr,* Sharon Crosby
Founded 1986
Library Holdings: AV Mats 100; Bk Vols 800; Per Subs 13; Talking Bks 60
Open Mon-Sat 10-4
Friends of the Library Group

GASTONIA

R FLINT-GROVES BAPTIST CHURCH LIBRARY*, 2017 E Ozark Ave, 28054. SAN 312-8393. Tel: 704-865-4068. FAX: 704-865-8008. Web Site: www.flintgroves.org. *Librn,* Pam Grindstaff; E-mail: phgrindstaff3@gmail.com
Automation Activity & Vendor Info: (Acquisitions) Book Systems; (Cataloging) Book Systems; (Circulation) Book Systems; (OPAC) Book Systems
Wireless access
Open Mon-Fri 8:30-4:30
Friends of the Library Group

P GASTON COUNTY PUBLIC LIBRARY*, 1555 E Garrison Blvd, 28054. SAN 312-8407. Tel: 704-868-2164. FAX: 704-853-0609. Web Site: www.gastonlibrary.org. *Dir,* Laurel Morris; E-mail: laurel.morris@gastongov.com; *Asst Dir,* Paul Ward, Jr; E-mail: paul.ward@gastongov.com; *Br Serv Supvr,* Sarah Miller; *Supvr, Circ,* Andrew Pierce; *Supvr, Coll Develop,* Tanya Jones; *Ref Serv Supvr,* Jane Kaylor; *Supvr, Youth Serv,* Emily Winfrey; *Digital Serv Coordr,* Chad Eller; Staff 23 (MLS 15, Non-MLS 8)
Founded 1904
Automation Activity & Vendor Info: (Acquisitions) Innovative Interfaces, Inc; (Cataloging) Innovative Interfaces, Inc; (Circulation) Innovative Interfaces, Inc; (OPAC) Innovative Interfaces, Inc
Wireless access
Function: 24/7 Electronic res, 24/7 Online cat, 3D Printer, Activity rm, Adult bk club, Art exhibits, Audiobks on Playaways & MP3, Audiobks via web, AV serv, Bilingual assistance for Spanish patrons, Bk club(s), Bks on CD, Children's prog, Citizenship assistance, Computer training, Computers for patron use, Digital talking bks, E-Reserves, Electronic databases & coll, Family literacy, For res purposes, Free DVD rentals, Genealogy discussion

group, Govt ref serv, Health sci info serv, Holiday prog, ILL available, Internet access, Learning ctr, Life-long learning prog for all ages, Literacy & newcomer serv, Magazines, Mail & tel request accepted, Mango lang, Meeting rooms, Microfiche/film & reading machines, Movies, Music CDs, Online cat, Outreach serv, Outside serv via phone, mail, e-mail & web, OverDrive digital audio bks, Photocopying/Printing, Preschool outreach, Preschool reading prog, Prog for adults, Prog for children & young adult, Ref & res, Ref serv available, Res assist avail, Scanner, Senior computer classes, Senior outreach, Serves people with intellectual disabilities, Spanish lang bks, Spoken cassettes & CDs, Spoken cassettes & DVDs, Story hour, Summer reading prog, Tax forms, Teen prog, Telephone ref, Visual arts prog, Wheelchair accessible, Workshops, Writing prog
Open Mon, Tues & Thurs 10-9, Wed & Sat 10-6, Fri 10-2
Friends of the Library Group
Branches: 9
BELMONT BRANCH, 125 Central Ave, Belmont, 28012, SAN 312-7451. Tel: 704-825-5426. FAX: 704-825-5426. *Br Mgr,* Katie Cox
Open Mon, Tues & Fri 10-6, Wed & Sat 10-2, Thurs 12-8
BESSEMER CITY BRANCH, 207 N 12th St, Bessemer City, 28016, SAN 312-7478. Tel: 704-629-3321. FAX: 704-629-3321. *Br Mgr,* Sandra Love-Corum
Function: 3D Printer, Art programs, STEM programs
Open Mon 12-8, Tues, Thurs & Fri 10-6, Wed & Sat 10-2
CHERRYVILLE BRANCH, 605 E Main St, Cherryville, 28021, SAN 312-7923. Tel: 704-435-6767. FAX: 704-435-6767. *Br Mgr,* Traci Pollitt
Open Mon, Thurs & Fri 10-6, Tues 12-8, Wed & Sat 10-2
Friends of the Library Group
DALLAS BRANCH, 105 S Holland St, Dallas, 28034, SAN 312-8032. Tel: 704-922-3621. FAX: 704-922-3621. *Br Mgr,* Chrissie McGovern
Open Mon, Tues & Fri 10-6, Wed & Sat 10-2, Thurs 12-8
Friends of the Library Group
FERGUSON BRANCH, Erwin Ctr, 913 N Pryor St, 28052, SAN 372-5189. Tel: 704-868-8046. FAX: 704-868-8046. *Br Supvr,* Alex Dickman; *Br Supvr,* Kyle Hearns
Open Mon, Tues & Thurs 3-9, Wed 5-9, Fri 1-5, Sat 10-2
Friends of the Library Group
MOUNT HOLLY BRANCH, 245 W Catawba Ave, Mount Holly, 28120, SAN 312-925X. Tel: 704-827-3581. FAX: 704-827-8573. *Br Mgr,* Debra Trogdon-Livingston
Open Mon 12-8, Tues, Thurs & Fri 10-6, Wed & Sat 10-2
Friends of the Library Group
STANLEY BRANCH, 205 N Peterson St, Stanley, 28164, SAN 320-9083. Tel: 704-263-4166. FAX: 704-263-4166. *Br Mgr,* Michelle Osborne
Open Mon, Thurs & Fri 10-6, Tues 12-8, Wed & Sat 10-2
Friends of the Library Group
TECH@LOWELL, 203 McAdenville Rd, Lowell, 28098, SAN 312-908X. Tel: 704-824-1266. FAX: 704-824-1266. *Br Mgr,* Kendall Ramsey
Function: 3D Printer
Open Mon, Wed, Thurs & Fri 10-6, Tues 12-8
Friends of the Library Group
UNION ROAD, 5800 Union Rd, 28056. Tel: 704-852-4073. FAX: 704-852-9631. *Br Mgr,* Rene Crump
Open Mon 12-8, Tues, Thurs & Fri 10-6, Wed & Sat 10-2
Friends of the Library Group

GOLDSBORO

S CHERRY HOSPITAL*, Learning Resource Center Library, 1401 W Ash St, 27530. SAN 325-7827. Tel: 919-731-3200. *Library Contact,* Rayne Caudill
Library Holdings: Bk Vols 3,000; Per Subs 30
Automation Activity & Vendor Info: (Cataloging) Follett Software; (Circulation) Follett Software; (Serials) Follett Software
Partic in Wayne Info Network
Open Mon-Fri 8-12 & 1-5

J WAYNE COMMUNITY COLLEGE*, Dr Clyde A. Erwin, Jr. Library, 3000 Wayne Memorial Dr, 27534. (Mail add: PO Box 8002, 27533-8002), SAN 312-8431. Tel: 919-739-6891. Reference Tel: 919-739-6890. FAX: 919-736-3204. E-mail: wcc-library@waynecc.edu. Web Site: www.waynecc.edu/library. *Dir, Libr Serv,* Dr Ruth Aletha Andrew; E-mail: raandrew@waynecc.edu; Staff 6 (MLS 3, Non-MLS 3)
Founded 1965. Enrl 3,000; Fac 115; Highest Degree: Associate
Library Holdings: DVDs 63; e-books 430,000; e-journals 23,000; Electronic Media & Resources 107; Bk Vols 35,000; Per Subs 10
Special Collections: Wayne Community College Historical Archives
Automation Activity & Vendor Info: (Acquisitions) SirsiDynix-WorkFlows; (Cataloging) SirsiDynix-WorkFlows; (Circulation) SirsiDynix-WorkFlows; (Discovery) EBSCO Discovery Service; (ILL) OCLC WorldShare Interlibrary Loan; (OPAC) SirsiDynix-iLink
Wireless access
Function: Computers for patron use, Distance learning, Electronic databases & coll, ILL available, Online cat, Photocopying/Printing, Ref serv available, Telephone ref
Open Mon-Thurs 7:45am-8pm, Fri 7:45-1

P WAYNE COUNTY PUBLIC LIBRARY*, 1001 E Ash St, 27530. SAN 354-849X. Tel: 919-735-1824. FAX: 919-731-2889. Web Site: www.wcpl.org. *Dir,* Donna Phillips; Tel: 919-735-1880, E-mail: donna.phillips@waynegov.com; *Asst Dir,* Maegen Wilson; Tel: 919-580-4014, E-mail: maegen.wilson@waynegov.com; *Head, Children's Dept,* Anna Snyder; Tel: 919-735-1824, Ext 5104, E-mail: anna.snyder@waynegov.com; *Head, Ref Serv,* Cindy Pendergraph; Tel: 919-735-1824, Ext 5106, E-mail: cindy.pendergraph@waynegov.com; *Head, Tech Serv,* Will Szwagiel; Tel: 919-299-8105, Ext 8010, E-mail: Will.Szwagiel@waynegov.com; Staff 39 (MLS 13, Non-MLS 26)
Founded 1907. Pop 140,000
Library Holdings: Bk Vols 100,000; Per Subs 212
Subject Interests: Genealogy, Local hist
Automation Activity & Vendor Info: (Acquisitions) Innovative Interfaces, Inc; (Cataloging) Innovative Interfaces, Inc; (Circulation) Innovative Interfaces, Inc; (ILL) Innovative Interfaces, Inc; (OPAC) Innovative Interfaces, Inc
Wireless access
Function: 24/7 Electronic res, 24/7 Online cat, Activity rm, Adult bk club, After school storytime, Archival coll, Art exhibits, Art programs, Audiobks on Playaways & MP3, Bk club(s), Bks on CD, Butterfly Garden, Children's prog, Computer training, Computers for patron use, Electronic databases & coll, Family literacy, Holiday prog, Home delivery & serv to seniorr ctr & nursing homes, Homework prog, ILL available, Internet access, Life-long learning prog for all ages, Magazines, Magnifiers for reading, Meeting rooms, Microfiche/film & reading machines, Movies, Online cat, Online ref, Outreach serv, OverDrive digital audio bks, Photocopying/Printing, Preschool outreach, Preschool reading prog, Prog for adults, Prog for children & young adult, Ref & res, Ref serv available, Res assist avail, Senior computer classes, Senior outreach, Specialized serv in classical studies, STEM programs, Study rm, Summer reading prog, Tax forms, Teen prog, Telephone ref, Wheelchair accessible
Publications: Calendar; Friend Reminders; Friends Newsletter
Open Mon-Thurs 9-9, Fri & Sat 9-5:30
Friends of the Library Group
Branches: 3
FREMONT PUBLIC, 202 N Goldsboro St, Fremont, 27830, SAN 354-8554. Tel: 919-705-1893. Web Site: nc-waynecountylibrary.civicplus.com/Directory.aspx?did=6. *Mgr,* Lisa Stevens; E-mail: lisa.stevens@waynegov.com
Open Mon & Thurs 2-6, Tues, Wed & Fri 9-1
PIKEVILLE PUBLIC, 107 W Main St, Pikeville, 27863. (Mail add: PO Box 909, Pikeville, 27863-0909), SAN 354-8589. Tel: 919-705-1892. Web Site: nc-waynecountylibrary.civicplus.com/Directory.aspx?did=7. *Mgr,* Lisa Stevens
Open Mon, Thurs & Sat 9-1, Tues & Wed 2-6
STEELE MEMORIAL, 119 W Main St, Mount Olive, 28365, SAN 354-8643. Tel: 919-299-8105. Web Site: nc-waynecountylibrary.civicplus.com/Directory.aspx?did=8. *Br Mgr,* Melanie Powell; E-mail: melanie.powell@waynegov.com; Staff 1 (MLS 1)
Special Collections: Marion Hargrove Coll, ms
Function: Bilingual assistance for Spanish patrons, Children's prog, Computers for patron use, Free DVD rentals, ILL available, Notary serv, Photocopying/Printing, Story hour, Summer reading prog, Wheelchair accessible
Open Mon, Wed & Fri 9-6, Tues & Thurs 9-8, Sat 10-3
Restriction: Open to pub for ref & circ; with some limitations
Friends of the Library Group

GRAHAM

J ALAMANCE COMMUNITY COLLEGE LIBRARY, Learning Resources Center, 1247 Jimmie Kerr Rd, 27253. (Mail add: PO Box 8000, 27253-8000), SAN 312-8733. Tel: 336-506-4116. FAX: 336-578-5561. E-mail: lrc@alamancecc.edu. Web Site: library.alamancecc.edu/library. *Dir, Learning Res Ctr,* Sara Thynne; E-mail: sara.thynne@alamancecc.edu; *Pub Serv Librn,* Rebekah Scott; Tel: 336-506-4198, E-mail: rebekah.scott@alamancecc.edu
Founded 1960. Enrl 4,300; Fac 250; Highest Degree: Associate
Library Holdings: AV Mats 1,200; Bk Vols 39,000; Per Subs 200
Subject Interests: Applied arts, Econ, Educ, Engr tech, Mechanical occupations
Wireless access
Open Mon-Thurs (Fall-Spring) 7:30am-8pm, Fri 7:30-4, Sat 8-Noon; Mon-Thurs (Summer) 7:30am-8pm, Fri 7:30-Noon

GRANTSBORO

J PAMLICO COMMUNITY COLLEGE*, Library Services & Student Success Center, 5049 Hwy 306 S, 28529. (Mail add: PO Box 185, 28529-0185), SAN 312-8474. Tel: 252-249-1851, Ext 3034. FAX: 252-249-2377. Web Site: pamlicocc.libguides.com/library. *Dir, Libr Serv,* Paul Goodson; E-mail: pgoodson@pamlicocc.edu; *Libr Tech,* Jeremy

Lachman; Tel: 252-249-1851, Ext 3034, E-mail: jlachman@pamlicocc.edu; Staff 2 (MLS 1, Non-MLS 1)
Founded 1963. Enrl 500; Fac 50; Highest Degree: Associate
Library Holdings: Bk Titles 10,000; Per Subs 6,000
Special Collections: Black History Coll. State Document Depository
Subject Interests: African-Am hist, Econ, Ethnic studies, Health, Local hist, Vocational
Automation Activity & Vendor Info: (Acquisitions) SirsiDynix; (Cataloging) SirsiDynix; (Circulation) SirsiDynix; (Course Reserve) SirsiDynix; (ILL) SirsiDynix; (Media Booking) SirsiDynix; (OPAC) SirsiDynix; (Serials) SirsiDynix
Wireless access
Function: 24/7 Electronic res, 24/7 Online cat, Audio & video playback equip for onsite use, Bks on CD, Computer training, Computers for patron use, Distance learning, ILL available, Internet access, Magazines, Online info literacy tutorials on the web & in blackboard, Online ref, Photocopying/Printing, Res assist avail, Study rm
Partic in Community Colleges Libraries in North Carolina; OCLC Online Computer Library Center, Inc
Open Mon-Thurs 7:30-7:30,, Fri 7:30am-1pm

GREENSBORO

C BENNETT COLLEGE*, Thomas F Holgate Library, 900 E Washington St, 27401-3239. SAN 312-8482. Tel: 336-517-2139. Web Site: library.bennett.edu. *Libr Dir,* Joan Williams; Tel: 336-517-2141, E-mail: jwilliams@bennett.edu; *Circ Librn,* Position Currently Open; *Archivist, Curator,* Position Currently Open; Staff 2 (MLS 1, Non-MLS 1)
Founded 1939. Enrl 242; Fac 34; Highest Degree: Bachelor
Library Holdings: AV Mats 2,400; e-books 36,000; Bk Vols 98,000; Per Subs 150
Special Collections: Art (Carnegie Art Coll), bks, repro; Bennett College Archives, bks, clippings, photog; Bennett College History; Black Studies, Women (Afro-American Women's Coll), bks, clippings, photog; Individual Biography (Norris Wright Cuney Papers), clippings, correspondence; Palmer Coll
Subject Interests: African-Am women
Automation Activity & Vendor Info: (Acquisitions) OCLC; (Cataloging) OCLC; (Circulation) OCLC; (Course Reserve) OCLC; (Discovery) OCLC; (ILL) OCLC; (OPAC) OCLC; (Serials) OCLC
Wireless access
Partic in OCLC Online Computer Library Center, Inc
Open Mon-Thurs 8am-10pm, Fri 8-5, Sun 6pm-10pm; Mon-Fri (Summer) 8-5
Friends of the Library Group

S CENTER FOR CREATIVE LEADERSHIP LIBRARY, One Leadership Pl, 27410. SAN 321-0553. Tel: 336-286-4083. FAX: 336-286-4087. E-mail: library@ccl.org. Web Site: www.ccl.org. *Dir, Info Res & Knowledge Mgt,* Kerry Haworth; E-mail: haworthk@ccl.org; *Mgr, Knowledge Mgt,* Samantha Clarke; E-mail: clarkes@ccl.org; *Knowledge Management Analyst,* Emily Crockett; E-mail: crockette@ccl.org. Subject Specialists: *Taxonomy,* Emily Crockett; Staff 4 (MLS 3, Non-MLS 1)
Founded 1970
Library Holdings: Electronic Media & Resources 12; Bk Vols 8,000; Per Subs 150
Subject Interests: Indust/organizational psychol
Partic in LYRASIS
Open Mon-Fri 8-5
Restriction: In-house use for visitors

R CURRIE LIBRARY*, 617 N Elm St, 27401. SAN 312-8547. Tel: 336-373-0445. Circulation Tel: 336-478-4732. FAX: 336-275-9398. Web Site: www.fpcgreensboro.org. *Librn,* Nancy Fuller; Tel: 336-478-4712, E-mail: nfuller@fpcgreensboro.org; Staff 1 (MLS 1)
Founded 1925
Library Holdings: Bk Titles 18,000; Per Subs 21
Subject Interests: Music
Open Mon-Thurs 9:30-3:30, Fri 9:30-Noon, Sun 9am-10:20pm

C ECPI UNIVERSITY, Greensboro Campus Library, 7802 Airport Center Dr, 27409. Tel: 336-665-1400. FAX: 336-664-0801. Web Site: gsbo.ecpi.net.
Enrl 380; Fac 30; Highest Degree: Associate
Library Holdings: Bk Titles 4,400; Bk Vols 5,100; Per Subs 75
Subject Interests: Computer sci, Computer tech, Nursing
Automation Activity & Vendor Info: (Cataloging) Follett Software; (Circulation) Follett Software; (OPAC) Follett Software
Wireless access
Open Mon-Thurs 8am-10:30pm, Fri 8-5

R FIRST BAPTIST CHURCH LIBRARY, 1000 W Friendly Ave, 27401. SAN 312-8539. Tel: 336-274-3286, Ext 229. FAX: 336-274-3288. Web Site: www.fbcgso.org. *Dir, Libr Serv,* Anita Cranford; E-mail: anita@fbcgso.org; Staff 1 (Non-MLS 1)
Founded 1947
Library Holdings: Bk Vols 16,000; Per Subs 20
Subject Interests: Children's lit, Relig
Wireless access

L FOX ROTHSCHILD LLP*, Law Library, 230 N Elm St, 27401. SAN 325-7908. Tel: 336-378-5485. FAX: 336-378-5400. *Res Analyst,* Carolyn Santanella. Subject Specialists: *Knowledge mgt,* Carolyn Santanella; Staff 1 (MLS 1)
Library Holdings: Bk Vols 15,000; Per Subs 125
Restriction: Not open to pub, Staff use only

C GREENSBORO COLLEGE, James Addison Jones Library, 815 W Market St, 27401. SAN 312-8555. Tel: 336-272-7102, Ext 5241. E-mail: library@greensboro.edu. Web Site: www.greensboro.edu/library. *Dir,* William Ritter; Tel: 336-272-7102, Ext 5734, E-mail: will.ritter@greensboro.edu; Staff 5 (MLS 3, Non-MLS 2)
Founded 1838. Enrl 1,000; Fac 103; Highest Degree: Master
Library Holdings: Audiobooks 90; DVDs 300; e-books 177,091; e-journals 21,089; Music Scores 1,221; Bk Titles 254,687; Videos 562
Subject Interests: Music, Spec educ
Wireless access
Publications: Friends of the Greensboro College Newsletter; Guide to the James Addison Jones Library
Partic in LYRASIS
Open Mon-Thurs 7:30am-Midnight, Fri 7:30-5, Sun 2-Midnight (Fall & Spring); Mon-Thurs 8:30-8, Fri 8:30-5 (Summer)
Friends of the Library Group

S GREENSBORO HISTORICAL MUSEUM ARCHIVES LIBRARY*, 130 Summit Ave, 27401-3004. SAN 326-4521. Tel: 336-373-2043. FAX: 336-373-2204. Web Site: greensborohistory.org. *Dir,* Carol Ghiorsi Hart; Tel: 336-373-2306, E-mail: carol.hart@greensboro-nc.gov; *Archivist,* Elise Allison; Tel: 336-373-2976, E-mail: elise.allison@greensboro-nc.gov; *Curator of Coll,* Jon B Zachman; Tel: 336-373-4589, E-mail: jon.zachman@greensboro-nc.gov; Staff 1 (MLS 1)
Founded 1924
Library Holdings: Bk Titles 5,000; Per Subs 12
Special Collections: Dolley Madison Coll, bks, letters, docs; O Henry Coll, bks, newsp clippings
Restriction: Staff use only

P GREENSBORO PUBLIC LIBRARY*, 219 N Church St, 27402. (Mail add: PO Box 3178, 27402-3178), SAN 354-8678. Tel: 336-373-2471. Interlibrary Loan Service Tel: 336-373-2159. Reference Tel: 336-373-2471, Ext 2. Web Site: library.greensboro-nc.gov/home. *Dir,* Brigitte Blanton; E-mail: brigitte.blanton@greensboro-nc.gov; *Mgr,* Stacey Reid; E-mail: stacey.reid@greensboro-nc.gov; *Fac Mgr,* Jim B Young; E-mail: jim.young@greensboro-nc.gov; Staff 32 (MLS 32)
Founded 1902. Pop 395,100; Circ 1,103,180
Library Holdings: Bk Vols 511,858; Per Subs 500
Special Collections: Oral History
Subject Interests: Genealogy, Local hist
Automation Activity & Vendor Info: (Acquisitions) SirsiDynix; (Cataloging) SirsiDynix; (Circulation) SirsiDynix; (Serials) SirsiDynix
Wireless access
Publications: Clubs & Organizations Directory; Globa Greensboro Directory
Special Services for the Deaf - Bks on deafness & sign lang; Captioned film dep; High interest/low vocabulary bks; Spec interest per; Staff with knowledge of sign lang; TTY equip
Open Mon-Thurs 10-7, Fri & Sat 9-6
Branches: 6
BLANCHE S BENJAMIN BRANCH, 1530 Benjamin Pkwy, 27408, SAN 354-8708. Tel: 336-373-7540. Web Site: library.greensboro-nc.gov/locations/benjamin. *Br Mgr,* Court Duvall; E-mail: court.duvall@greensboro-nc.gov
Library Holdings: Bk Vols 54,693
Open Mon-Thurs 10-7, Fri & Sat 9-6
VANCE H CHAVIS LIFELONG LEARNING BRANCH, 900 S Benbow Rd, 27406, SAN 354-8791. Tel: 336-373-5838. Web Site: library.greensboro-nc.gov/locations/vance-chavis. *Br Mgr,* Brandon Britt; Tel: 336-373-5841, E-mail: brandon.britt@greensboro-nc.gov
Library Holdings: Bk Vols 33,000
Open Mon-Thurs 10-7, Fri & Sat 9-6
KATHLEEN CLAY EDWARDS FAMILY BRANCH, 1420 Price Park Rd, 27410, SAN 354-8767. Tel: 336-373-2923. Web Site: library.greensboro-nc.gov/locations/kathleen-clay-edwards-family-branch. *Br Mgr,* Katie Fanstill; E-mail: katie.fanstill@greensboro-nc.gov
Library Holdings: Bk Vols 53,000; Per Subs 70
Open Mon-Thurs 10-7, Fri & Sat 9-6
GLENWOOD COMMUNITY LIBRARY, 1901 W Florida St, 27403, SAN 375-5517. Tel: 336-297-5000. Web Site: library.greensboro-nc.gov/locations/glenwood. *Br Mgr,* Amy Matthews; E-mail: amy.matthews@greensboro-nc.gov

Library Holdings: Bk Vols 32,800
Open Mon-Thurs 10-7, Fri & Sat 9-6
HEMPHILL, 2301 W Vandalia Rd, 27407, SAN 354-8821. Tel: 336-373-2925. Web Site: library.greensboro-nc.gov/locations/hemphill-branch. *Br Mgr,* Julia Hendricks; E-mail: julia.hendricks@greensboro-nc.gov
Library Holdings: Bk Vols 41,771
Open Mon-Thurs 10-7, Fri & Sat 9-6
MCGIRT-HORTON, 2501 Phillips Ave, 27405, SAN 354-8732. Tel: 336-373-5810. Web Site: library.greensboro-nc.gov/locations/mcgirt-horton. *Br Mgr,* Bebe Jallah; E-mail: bebe.jallah@greensboro-nc.gov
Library Holdings: Bk Vols 27,000; Per Subs 35
Open Mon-Thurs 10-7, Fri & Sat 9-6
Bookmobiles: 1

C GUILFORD COLLEGE*, Hege Library, 5800 W Friendly Ave, 27410-4175. SAN 312-8563. Tel: 336-316-2450. Interlibrary Loan Service Tel: 336-316-2439. E-mail: library@guilford.edu. Web Site: library.guilford.edu/friendly.php?s=homepage. *Dir, Learning Tech, Libr Dir,* Suzanne M Bartels; Tel: 336-316-2046, E-mail: bartelssm@guilford.edu; *Access & Info Serv Librn,* Elizabeth J Wade; Tel: 336-316-2368, E-mail: wadeej@guilford.edu; *Experience Design Librn,* Megan M Dickerson; E-mail: dickersonmm@guilford.edu; *Access & Info Serv Assoc,* Martha E Davis; Tel: 336-316-2265, E-mail: mdavis2@guilford.edu; *Digital Pedagogy, Scholarship Technologist,* Tierney Steelberg; Tel: 336-316-2113, E-mail: steelbergtc@guilford.edu; Staff 7 (MLS 5, Non-MLS 2)
Founded 1837. Enrl 1,515; Fac 145; Highest Degree: Bachelor
Jun 2017-May 2018. Mats Exp $342,000, Books $10,000, Per/Ser (Incl. Access Fees) $242,000, AV Mat $10,000, Electronic Ref Mat (Incl. Access Fees) $80,000. Sal $287,756
Library Holdings: AV Mats 1,994; Bks-By-Mail 514; DVDs 1,994; e-books 170,134; e-journals 6,901; Electronic Media & Resources 160,350; Bk Vols 198,457; Per Subs 150
Special Collections: Historical coll; Religious Society of Friends (Quaker)
Subject Interests: Hist, North Caroliniana
Automation Activity & Vendor Info: (Acquisitions) OCLC; (Cataloging) OCLC; (Circulation) OCLC
Wireless access
Partic in OCLC-LVIS
Special Services for the Blind - Reader equip
Open Mon-Thurs (Winter) 8am-Midnight, Fri 8-5, Sat 10-7, Sun Noon-Midnight; Mon-Fri (Summer) 8:30-5
Restriction: Restricted access, Restricted borrowing privileges
Friends of the Library Group
Departmental Libraries:
QUAKER ARCHIVES, Hege Library, 5800 W Friendly Ave, 27410. Tel: 336-316-2450. *Col Archivist/Librn,* Gwendolyn Gosney Erickson; E-mail: gerickso@guilford.edu
Subject Interests: Genealogy, Hist
Open Tues-Fri 9-12 & 2-5
Restriction: Restricted access, Restricted borrowing privileges

S LANDMARK COMMUNICATIONS*, News & Record Library & Archives, 200 E Market St, 27401-2910. (Mail add: PO Box 20848, 27420-0848), SAN 312-858X. Tel: 336-373-7169. Toll Free Tel: 800-553-6880. FAX: 336-373-4437. E-mail: newslibrary@newsbank.com. Web Site: www.greensboro.com. *Librn,* Diane Lamb
Founded 1969
Library Holdings: Bk Titles 1,000; Bk Vols 1,075; Per Subs 25
Wireless access
Restriction: Private libr

MOSES CONE HEALTH SYSTEM
M MOSES H CONE MEMORIAL HOSPITAL LIBRARY*, 1200 N Elm St, 27401, SAN 312-8520. Tel: 336-832-7484. FAX: 336-832-7328. Web Site: www.gahec.org/library. *Dir,* Edward Donnald; Staff 3.5 (MLS 2.5, Non-MLS 1)
Founded 1952
Library Holdings: e-books 70; e-journals 511; Bk Titles 7,071; Per Subs 200
Special Collections: Greensboro Medical History Library; Local History of Medicine
Subject Interests: Life sci, Med
Partic in National Network of Libraries of Medicine Region 1
Publications: Newsletter-Offline
Open Mon-Thurs 8-6, Fri 8-5
Restriction: Circulates for staff only
M WESLEY LONG COMMUNITY HOSPITAL MEDICAL LIBRARY*, 501 N Elam Ave, 27403, SAN 325-3120. Tel: 336-832-1299. FAX: 336-832-0370. Web Site: www.gahec.org/library.
Founded 1978
Library Holdings: Bk Titles 410; Per Subs 10
Subject Interests: Allied health, Healthcare, Med, Nursing
Open Mon-Wed & Fri 8:30-2

M WOMEN'S HOSPITAL OF GREENSBORO LIBRARY*, 801 Green Valley, 27408. Tel: 336-832-6878. FAX: 336-832-6893. Web Site: www.gahec.org/library. *Librn,* Monica Williamson Young
Library Holdings: Bk Vols 700; Per Subs 250
Automation Activity & Vendor Info: (Cataloging) Horizon; (Circulation) Horizon; (OPAC) Horizon
Open Mon-Thurs 8-5

C NORTH CAROLINA AGRICULTURAL & TECHNICAL STATE UNIVERSITY*, F D Bluford Library, 1601 E Market St, 27411-0002. SAN 312-8598. Tel: 336-285-4164. Reference Tel: 336-285-4185. Toll Free Tel: 888-246-1272. E-mail: circ@ncat.edu. Web Site: www.library.ncat.edu. *Dean, Libr Serv,* Vicki Coleman; E-mail: vcoleman@ncat.edu; *Asst Dean,* Forrest Foster; E-mail: ffoster@ncat.edu; *Adminr, Budget & Collections,* Tiffany Russell; E-mail: tbrussell@ncat.edu; *Head, Access Serv, Head Bldg Serv,* Octavious Spruill; E-mail: odspruil@ncat.edu; *Head, Bibliog & Metadata Serv, Head, Discovery Serv,* Iyanna Sims; E-mail: iyanna@ncat.edu; *Head, Engagement & Instructional Servs, Head, Res Serv,* Joanie Chavis; E-mail: jchavis@ncat.edu; *Head, Libr Syst,* Stephen Bollinger; E-mail: spbollin@ncat.edu; *Eng Librn, Spec Projects Librn,* John Teleha; E-mail: teleha@ncat.edu; Staff 49 (MLS 19, Non-MLS 30)
Founded 1892. Enrl 12,900; Fac 650; Highest Degree: Doctorate
Special Collections: Black Studies Coll; University Archives. State Document Depository; US Document Depository
Subject Interests: Agr, Educ, Engr, Nursing
Automation Activity & Vendor Info: (Acquisitions) OCLC Worldshare Management Services; (Cataloging) OCLC Worldshare Management Services; (Circulation) OCLC Worldshare Management Services; (Course Reserve) OCLC Worldshare Management Services; (ILL) OCLC Worldshare Management Services; (Media Booking) OCLC Worldshare Management Services; (OPAC) OCLC Worldshare Management Services; (Serials) OCLC Worldshare Management Services
Wireless access
Function: Archival coll, Audio & video playback equip for onsite use, AV serv, Bk club(s), Computer training, Distance learning, Doc delivery serv, E-Reserves, Electronic databases & coll, For res purposes, ILL available, Mail & tel request accepted, Online info literacy tutorials on the web & in blackboard, Online ref, Orientations, Outside serv via phone, mail, e-mail & web, Photocopying/Printing, Ref & res, Ref serv available, Telephone ref, VHS videos, Workshops
Partic in Carolina Consortium; LYRASIS; North Carolina Libraries for Virtual Education
Special Services for the Deaf - Assistive tech
Special Services for the Blind - Assistive/Adapted tech devices, equip & products
Restriction: Limited access for the pub, Non-circulating coll, Non-circulating of rare bks, Open to pub for ref & circ; with some limitations

C UNIVERSITY LIBRARIES, UNIVERSITY OF NORTH CAROLINA AT GREENSBORO*, Walter Clinton Jackson Library, 320 College Ave, 27412-0001. (Mail add: PO Box 26170, 27402-6170), SAN 312-8628. Circulation Tel: 336-334-5304. Interlibrary Loan Service Tel: 336-334-5849. Reference Tel: 336-334-5419. Administration Tel: 336-334-5880. Automation Services Tel: 336-334-4238. Toll Free Tel: 888-245-0180. FAX: 336-334-5399. Interlibrary Loan Service FAX: 336-334-5097. Web Site: library.uncg.edu. *Dean,* Martin Halbert; E-mail: martin.halbert@uncg.edu; *Assoc Dean, Pub Serv,* Kathy M Crowe; E-mail: kathy_crowe@uncg.edu; *Asst Dean, Admin Serv,* Michael A Crumpton; E-mail: macrumpt@uncg.edu; *Asst Dean, Coll Mgt & Scholarly Communications,* Beth R Bernhardt; Tel: 336-256-1210, E-mail: beth_bernhardt@uncg.edu; *Asst Dean, Info Tech & Electronic Res,* Tim M Bucknall; E-mail: bucknall@uncg.edu; *Asst Dean, Spec Coll & Univ Archivist,* Dr Keith Gorman; E-mail: k_gorman@uncg.edu; *Develop, Exec Dir,* Karlene Jennings; Tel: 336-256-0112, E-mail: knjennin@uncg.edu; *Dir, Mkt & Communications,* Hollie Stevenson-Parrish; E-mail: hdsteven@uncg.edu; *Head, Access Serv,* Cathy Griffith; Tel: 336-334-5492, E-mail: cathy_griffith@uncg.edu; *Head, Presv Serv,* Audrey L Sage; E-mail: audrey_sage@uncg.edu; *Head, Res, Outreach & Instruction,* Amy Harris Houk; Tel: 336-256-0275, E-mail: amy_harris@uncg.edu; *Head, Tech Serv,* Christine M Fischer; E-mail: cmfische@uncg.edu; *ILL Mgr,* Dallas Burkhardt; E-mail: djburkha@uncg.edu; *Univ Archivist,* Erin Lawrimore; E-mail: erlawrim@uncg.edu; Staff 89 (MLS 35, Non-MLS 54)
Founded 1892. Enrl 17,707; Fac 1,005; Highest Degree: Doctorate
Jul 2013-Jun 2014. Mats Exp $4,086,743. Sal $6,418,168 (Prof $2,461,995)
Library Holdings: AV Mats 52,507; DVDs 16,144; e-books 473,878; e-journals 53,284; Microforms 733,462; Bk Vols 2,235,868; Per Subs 1,100
Special Collections: American Trade Bindings; Cello Music & Literature, artifacts, ms, textiles; Children's Authors Coll, bks, ms; Children's Books (Lois Lenski Coll), bks, ms; Creative Writers Coll, bks, ms, photog; Early Dance Book Coll; Early Juvenile Literature Coll; Emily Dickinson Coll; George Herbert Coll, bks, ms; Girls' Series Books; Greensboro & Guilford County Civil Rights Oral History, ms, tapes; Home Economics Pamphlet

Coll; Joseph Bryan Coll, ms; Papermaking; Physical Education Coll, bks, ms; Private Presses & Book Arts; Randall Jarrell Coll, bks, music, tapes; Rare Book Coll; Robbie Emily Dunn Coll of American Detective Fiction; Rupert Brooke Coll; T E Lawrence Coll; University Archives; Way & Williams Coll, artwork, bks, ms; Women Veterans Coll; Women's Studies (Woman's Coll), bks, ms, pamphlets. Oral History; State Document Depository; US Document Depository
Automation Activity & Vendor Info: (Acquisitions) OCLC WorldShare Interlibrary Loan; (Cataloging) OCLC WorldShare Interlibrary Loan; (Circulation) OCLC WorldShare Interlibrary Loan; (Course Reserve) Blackboard Inc; (ILL) OCLC ILLiad; (OPAC) OCLC WorldShare Interlibrary Loan; (Serials) OCLC WorldShare Interlibrary Loan
Wireless access
Function: Archival coll, Art exhibits, Audiobks via web, Bks on cassette, Bks on CD, Computers for patron use, Distance learning, Doc delivery serv, E-Reserves, Electronic databases & coll, Equip loans & repairs, Govt ref serv, Music CDs, Online info literacy tutorials on the web & in blackboard, Online ref, Outside serv via phone, mail, e-mail & web, Photocopying/Printing, Ref serv available, Wheelchair accessible
Publications: Library Columns (Newsletter)
Partic in Association of Southeastern Research Libraries; Carolina Consortium; Coalition for Networked Information; LYRASIS; North Carolina Libraries for Virtual Education; North Carolina Preservation Consortium; OCLC Online Computer Library Center, Inc; Scholarly Publ & Acad Resources Coalition
Special Services for the Deaf - Bks on deafness & sign lang
Open Mon-Thurs 7:30am-9pm, Fri 7:30-6, Sat 11-6, Sun 12-9
Friends of the Library Group

Departmental Libraries:

HAROLD SCHIFFMAN MUSIC LIBRARY, 100 McIver St, 27402. (Mail add: PO Box 26170, 27402-6170). Tel: 336-334-5610, 336-334-5771. FAX: 336-256-0155. Web Site: library.uncg.edu/info/depts/music. *Head Music Libr,* Sarah B Dorsey; E-mail: sarah_dorsey@uncg.edu; *Day Circ Mgr,* Alaina Jones; E-mail: kajones@uncg.edu; *Evening & Weekend Circ Mgr,* Evan O'Neal; E-mail: eeoneal@uncg.edu
Library Holdings: CDs 13,056; DVDs 694; Music Scores 47,366; Bk Vols 23,020; Videos 464
Open Mon-Thurs (Fall-Winter) 7:45am-10pm, Fri 7:45-5, Sat 12-5, Sun 1-10; Mon-Thurs (Summer) 8-7, Fri 8-5

SR WESTMINISTER PRESBYTERIAN CHURCH LIBRARY*, 3906 W Friendly Ave, 27410. SAN 375-1996. Tel: 336-299-3785. FAX: 336-299-5837. E-mail: info@westpreschurch.org. Web Site: www.westpreschurch.org. *Libr Dir,* Butch Sherrill
Library Holdings: Bk Titles 250

GREENVILLE

EAST CAROLINA UNIVERSITY

C J Y JOYNER LIBRARY*, E Fifth St, 27858-4353, SAN 378-4509. Tel: 252-328-6518. Interlibrary Loan Service Tel: 252-328-6068. Reference Tel: 252-328-6677. Administration Tel: 252-328-6514. Toll Free Tel: 866-291-5581. FAX: 252-328-6892. Interlibrary Loan Service FAX: 252-328-6618. Reference FAX: 252-328-2271. Reference E-mail: askref@ecu.edu. Web Site: www.ecu.edu/lib. *Academic Services, Dir,* Janice Steed Lewis; Tel: 252-328-2267, E-mail: lewisja@ecu.edu; *Asst Dir, Scholarly Communications & Coll,* Joseph Thomas; Tel: 252-737-2728, E-mail: thomasw@ecu.edu; *Asst Dir, Pub Serv,* Mark Sanders; Tel: 242-328-2900, E-mail: sandersm@ecu.edu; *Asst Dir, Tech Operations, Discovery Serv,* Amanda McLellan; Tel: 252-328-2780, E-mail: mclellana15@ecu.edu; *Asst Dir, Spec Coll,* John Lawrence; Tel: 252-328-4088, E-mail: lawrencej@ecu.edu; *Asst Dir, Libr Engagement Facilitator,* Heather White; Tel: 252-328-2870, E-mail: whiteh@ecu.edu; Staff 35 (MLS 30, Non-MLS 5)
Founded 1907. Enrl 28,651; Fac 2,074; Highest Degree: Doctorate
Jul 2019-Jun 2020 Income $12,959,333. Mats Exp $4,252,145. Sal $5,428,337 (Prof $3,018,434)
Library Holdings: e-journals 89,776; Electronic Media & Resources 455; Microforms 2,117,313; Music Scores 30,857; Bk Vols 2,430,115
Special Collections: Local History (North Carolina Coll); Regional History (East Carolina Manuscript Coll); Southern Authors (Stuart Wright Coll). Oral History; State Document Depository; US Document Depository
Automation Activity & Vendor Info: (Acquisitions) SirsiDynix; (Cataloging) SirsiDynix; (Circulation) SirsiDynix; (Course Reserve) SirsiDynix; (ILL) OCLC ILLiad; (OPAC) SirsiDynix; (Serials) SerialsSolutions
Function: Art exhibits, Computers for patron use, Distance learning, Doc delivery serv, E-Reserves, Electronic databases & coll, Free DVD rentals, Govt ref serv, ILL available, Music CDs, Online cat, Online info literacy tutorials on the web & in blackboard, Online ref, Orientations, Outreach serv, Photocopying/Printing, Ref & res, Ref serv available, Scanner, Telephone ref, Wheelchair accessible
Partic in Association of Southeastern Research Libraries; Carolina Consortium; LYRASIS; Scholarly Publ & Acad Resources Coalition
Friends of the Library Group

CM WILLIAM E LAUPUS HEALTH SCIENCES LIBRARY*, 500 Health Sciences Dr, 27834, SAN 354-8880. Tel: 252-744-2219. Reference Tel: 252-744-2230. Administration Tel: 252-744-2212. Toll Free Tel: 888-820-0522. FAX: 252-744-2672. Administration FAX: 252-744-2300. Web Site: www.ecu.edu/laupuslibrary. *Interim Dir,* Beth Ketterman; E-mail: kettermane@ecu.edu; *Dir, Eastern AHEC Libr Serv/Head, Outreach Serv,* Jeffrey G Coghill; Tel: 252-744-2066, E-mail: coghillj@ecu.edu; *Asst Dir, Admin,* Teresa D Tripp; Tel: 252-744-3495, E-mail: trippt@ecu.edu; *Asst Dir, User Serv,* Roger G Russell; Tel: 252-744-3215, E-mail: russellr@ecu.edu; *Head, Access Serv & Doc Delivery,* Vicki Daughtridge; Fax: 252-744-3311, E-mail: daughtridgev@ecu.edu; *Spec Projects Librn,* Susan N Simpson; Tel: 252-744-2904, E-mail: simpsons@ecu.edu; *Coordr, Ser,* Janet P Heath; Tel: 252-744-2234, E-mail: heathj@ecu.edu; Staff 15 (MLS 15)
Founded 1969. Highest Degree: Doctorate
Library Holdings: AV Mats 4,428; Bk Titles 33,365; Bk Vols 35,094; Per Subs 346
Special Collections: History of Medicine Special Coll
Subject Interests: Allied health, Med, Nursing
Automation Activity & Vendor Info: (Acquisitions) SirsiDynix
Partic in LYRASIS
Special Services for the Deaf - TDD equip
Open Mon-Thurs 7:30am-Midnight, Fri 7:30am-8pm, Sat 9-8, Sun Noon-10; Mon-Thurs (Summer) 7:30am-10pm, Fri 7:30-5, Sat 9-5, Sun Noon-10
Friends of the Library Group

C MUSIC LIBRARY*, A J Fletcher Music Ctr, Rm A110, 27858, SAN 354-8899. Tel: 252-328-6250. E-mail: musiclibrary@ecu.edu. Web Site: www.ecu.edu/cs-lib/music.cfm. *Head Librn,* David Hursh; Tel: 252-328-1239, E-mail: hurshd@ecu.edu; *Head, Access Serv,* Dorthea Taylor; Tel: 252-328-1242; *Head, Tech Serv,* Judith Barber; Tel: 252-328-1240, E-mail: barberju@ecu.edu; *Asst Music Librn,* Christopher Holden; Tel: 252-328-1241, E-mail: holdenc@ecu.edu; *Evening & Weekend Access Serv Mgr,* Kevin-Andrew Cronin; Tel: 252-328-1238, E-mail: cronink@ecu.edu; Staff 5 (MLS 2, Non-MLS 3)
Founded 1958. Highest Degree: Doctorate
Library Holdings: AV Mats 30,444; Music Scores 43,375; Bk Titles 19,626; Bk Vols 25,248
Function: Audio & video playback equip for onsite use, Computers for patron use, ILL available, Music CDs, Ref serv available, Wheelchair accessible
Open Mon-Thurs 8am-10pm, Fri 8-5, Sat 1-5, Sun 1-10

P SHEPPARD MEMORIAL LIBRARY, 530 S Evans St, 27858. SAN 312-8660. Tel: 252-329-4580. Circulation Tel: 252-329-4579. Reference Tel: 252-329-4376. Administration Tel: 252-329-4586. FAX: 252-329-4587. Web Site: www.sheppardlibrary.org. *Dir,* Greg Needham; Tel: 252-329-4585, E-mail: gneedham@sheppardlibrary.org; *Adult Serv, Head, Tech Serv,* Tammy Fulcher; Tel: 252-329-4254, E-mail: tfulcher@sheppardlibrary.org; *Ch,* Amber Winstead; Fax: 252-329-4878, E-mail: awinstead@sheppardlibrary.org; *Ref Librn, Ser,* Kim Averette; E-mail: kaverette@sheppardlibrary.org; *Bus & Finance Mgr,* Lynn Woolard; E-mail: lwoolard@sheppardlibrary.org; Staff 5 (MLS 3, Non-MLS 2)
Founded 1929. Pop 194,274; Circ 481,611
Library Holdings: CDs 7,453; DVDs 9,182; Electronic Media & Resources 98; Bk Vols 237,000; Per Subs 377; Talking Bks 1,842
Automation Activity & Vendor Info: (Cataloging) TLC (The Library Corporation); (Circulation) TLC (The Library Corporation)
Wireless access
Function: ILL available
Publications: The Bookmark (Newsletter)
Open Mon-Thurs 9-9, Fri & Sat 9-6, Sun 2-5
Friends of the Library Group

Branches: 4

MARGARET LITTLE BLOUNT (BETHEL) LIBRARY, 201 Ives St, Bethel, 27812. (Mail add: PO Box 1170, Bethel, 27812), SAN 373-5370. Tel: 252-825-0782. FAX: 252-825-0782. *Br Coordr,* Mildred Elliott; E-mail: melliott@sheppardlibrary.org
Open Tues-Thurs 1-5
Friends of the Library Group

GEORGE WASHINGTON CARVER LIBRARY, 618 W 14th Ave, 27834, SAN 374-678X. Tel: 252-329-4583. FAX: 252-329-4126. *Br Coordr, Librn,* Mildred Elliott; E-mail: melliott@sheppardlibrary.org
Open Mon-Thurs 9-8, Fri 9-6, Sat 11-3
Friends of the Library Group

EAST, 2000 Cedar Lane, 27858, SAN 374-6798. Tel: 252-329-4582. FAX: 252-329-4127. *Br Mgr,* Kisha Green; E-mail: kgreen@sheppardlibrary.org
Open Mon-Thurs 9-8, Fri 9-6, Sat 11-3
Friends of the Library Group

WINTERVILLE PUBLIC, 2613 Railroad St, Winterville, 28590, SAN 373-5389. Tel: 252-756-1786. FAX: 252-355-0287. *Br Coordr,* Amanda Prokop; E-mail: aprokop@sheppardlibrary.org
Open Mon-Thurs 9-8, Fri 9-6, Sat 1-5
Friends of the Library Group
Bookmobiles: 1

GRIFTON

P GRIFTON PUBLIC LIBRARY, 568 Queen St, 28530. (Mail add: PO Box 579, 28530-0579), SAN 312-8679. Tel: 252-524-0345. FAX: 252-524-5545. E-mail: gplibrary@msn.com. Web Site: gplibrary.wixsite.com/griftonnc. *Librn,* Shirley Mewborn; *Librn,* Emily Beasley; Staff 2 (MLS 2)
Founded 1960. Pop 5,180; Circ 16,853
Library Holdings: Audiobooks 161; DVDs 635; Large Print Bks 456; Bk Titles 16,057
Automation Activity & Vendor Info: (Acquisitions) Follett Software; (Cataloging) Follett Software; (Circulation) Follett Software
Wireless access
Function: Audiobks via web, Children's prog, Computers for patron use, Free DVD rentals, Magazines, Online cat, OverDrive digital audio bks, Photocopying/Printing, Serves people with intellectual disabilities, Summer reading prog, Wheelchair accessible
Open Mon-Thurs 11:30-6:30, Fri 11:30-5:30, Sat 9-1
Restriction: Circ to mem only

HALIFAX

P HALIFAX COUNTY LIBRARY*, 33 S Granville St, 27839. (Mail add: PO Box 97, 27839-0097), SAN 312-8687. Tel: 252-583-3631. FAX: 252-583-8661. Web Site: www.halifaxnc.com/232/Library. *Dir,* Virginia Orvedahl; E-mail: orvedahlg@halifaxnc.com; Staff 11 (MLS 1, Non-MLS 10)
Founded 1941. Pop 55,432
Library Holdings: Bk Vols 65,000; Per Subs 180
Subject Interests: Genealogy, Local hist
Automation Activity & Vendor Info: (Cataloging) Innovative Interfaces, Inc; (Circulation) Innovative Interfaces, Inc; (OPAC) Innovative Interfaces, Inc
Wireless access
Publications: Monthly Newsletter
Open Mon & Wed 8:30-6, Tues, Thurs & Fri 8:30-5, Sat 9-12:30
Friends of the Library Group
Branches: 3
W C JONES JR MEMORIAL, 127 W S Main St, Littleton, 27850. (Mail add: PO Box 455, Littleton, 27850), SAN 328-6983. Tel: 252-586-3608. FAX: 252-586-3495. *Librn,* Sheila Milan
Open Mon-Fri 9-5, Sat 9-12:30
Friends of the Library Group
SCOTLAND NECK MEMORIAL, 1600 Main St, Scotland Neck, 27874-1438. (Mail add: PO Box 126, Scotland Neck, 27874-0126), SAN 371-3679. Tel: 252-826-5578. FAX: 252-826-5037. *Librn,* Martha Leach
Library Holdings: Bk Vols 13,000; Per Subs 25
Subject Interests: Genealogy
Open Mon, Wed & Fri 8:30-5, Tues & Thurs 8:30-7, Sat 9-12
Friends of the Library Group
WELDON MEMORIAL, Six W First St, Weldon, 27890, SAN 328-6967. Tel: 252-536-3837. FAX: 252-536-2477. *Librn,* LaTarsha Thomas
Open Mon-Fri 8:30-5, Sat 9-12:30
Bookmobiles: 1

HAMLET

J RICHMOND COMMUNITY COLLEGE LIBRARY*, J Richard Conder Bldg, 1042 W Hamlet Ave, 28345. (Mail add: PO Box 1189, 28345-1189), SAN 312-8709. Tel: 910-410-1752. FAX: 910-582-7045. Web Site: library.richmondcc.edu. *Libr Tech,* Sarah Anderson; E-mail: smanderson@richmondcc.edu; Staff 4.5 (MLS 3, Non-MLS 1.5)
Founded 1964. Enrl 2,570; Fac 60; Highest Degree: Associate
Jul 2012-Jun 2013. Mats Exp $70,133, Books $33,542, Per/Ser (Incl. Access Fees) $34,500, AV Mat $2,091. Sal $290,164 (Prof $172,020)
Library Holdings: Audiobooks 239; AV Mats 318; Bks on Deafness & Sign Lang 250; DVDs 2,731; Large Print Bks 57; Bk Titles 28,718; Bk Vols 27,842; Per Subs 104; Videos 3,268
Special Collections: Easy Books for Early Childhood Program; North Carolina Coll
Subject Interests: Col transfer, Vocational
Automation Activity & Vendor Info: (Acquisitions) SirsiDynix; (Cataloging) SirsiDynix; (Circulation) SirsiDynix; (Course Reserve) SirsiDynix; (ILL) OCLC Online; (Media Booking) SirsiDynix; (OPAC) SirsiDynix; (Serials) SirsiDynix
Wireless access
Function: Archival coll, Art exhibits, Bks on cassette, Bks on CD, Computers for patron use, Digital talking bks, Distance learning, Doc delivery serv, Electronic databases & coll, Health sci info serv, ILL available, Instruction & testing, Internet access, Magnifiers for reading, Online cat, Online info literacy tutorials on the web & in blackboard, Orientations, Outreach serv, Outside serv via phone, mail, e-mail & web, Photocopying/Printing, Ref serv available, Scanner, Spoken cassettes & DVDs, Telephone ref, VHS videos, Wheelchair accessible, Workshops
Partic in Community Colleges Libraries in North Carolina; North Carolina Libraries for Virtual Education
Special Services for the Blind - Audio mat; Bks on cassette; Bks on CD; Cassette playback machines; Copier with enlargement capabilities; Large print bks; Magnifiers; Ref serv
Open Mon-Thurs 7:30am-9pm, Fri 7:30-2:30
Restriction: ID required to use computers (Ltd hrs), Non-circulating coll, Non-circulating of rare bks, Open to pub for ref & circ; with some limitations, Photo ID required for access, Restricted borrowing privileges, Restricted loan policy

HAVELOCK

P HAVELOCK-CRAVEN COUNTY PUBLIC LIBRARY*, 301 Cunningham Blvd, 28532. Tel: 252-447-7509. FAX: 252-447-7422. Web Site: www.havelocklibrary.org. *Librn,* Margie Garrison; E-mail: mmgarrison@live.com; Staff 1 (Non-MLS 1)
Founded 1974. Pop 21,000; Circ 44,723
Library Holdings: Audiobooks 1,920; AV Mats 2,072; Bk Vols 26,700; Per Subs 45
Wireless access
Function: 24/7 Electronic res, 24/7 Online cat, Accelerated reader prog, Adult bk club, After school storytime, Art exhibits, Audiobks on Playaways & MP3, Audiobks via web, AV serv, Bk club(s), Bks on cassette, Bks on CD, Children's prog, Computers for patron use, Digital talking bks, E-Reserves, Electronic databases & coll, ILL available, Internet access, Laminating, Large print keyboards, Magazines, Magnifiers for reading, Music CDs, Online cat, Photocopying/Printing, Preschool reading prog, Scanner, Spanish lang bks, Spoken cassettes & CDs, Spoken cassettes & DVDs, Story hour, Summer & winter reading prog, Summer reading prog, Tax forms, VHS videos, Wheelchair accessible
Mem of Craven-Pamlico-Carteret Regional Library System
Open Mon-Wed 10-8, Thurs & Fri 10-6, Sat 10-4
Friends of the Library Group

HAYESVILLE

P MOSS MEMORIAL LIBRARY*, 26 Anderson St, 28904. (Mail add: PO Box 900, 28904-0900), SAN 312-8741. Tel: 828-389-8401. FAX: 828-389-3734, Web Site: www.youseemore.com/Nantahala/directory.asp. *Br Librn,* Mary Fonda; E-mail: mfonda@nantahalalibrary.org
Founded 1942
Library Holdings: Large Print Bks 3,000; Bk Vols 35,000; Per Subs 50
Automation Activity & Vendor Info: (Cataloging) TLC (The Library Corporation); (Circulation) TLC (The Library Corporation); (OPAC) TLC (The Library Corporation)
Mem of Nantahala Regional Library
Open Tues 9-8, Wed-Sat 9-5
Friends of the Library Group

HENDERSON

P H LESLIE PERRY MEMORIAL LIBRARY, 205 Breckenridge St, 27536. SAN 354-8910. Tel: 252-438-3316. Circulation Tel: 252-438-3316, Ext 221. Reference Tel: 252-438-3316, Ext 237. FAX: 252-438-3744. Web Site: www.perrylibrary.org. *Dir,* Patti McAnally; E-mail: pmcanally@perrylibrary.org; *Asst Dir,* Christy Bondy; E-mail: cbondy@perrylibrary.org; *Youth Serv Librn,* Amanda Yetter; E-mail: ayetter@perrylibrary.org; Staff 15 (MLS 3, Non-MLS 12)
Founded 1924. Pop 45,300; Circ 56,971
Library Holdings: Audiobooks 2,093; e-books 107,778; Bk Vols 136,224; Per Subs 200; Talking Bks 4,280; Videos 1,525
Subject Interests: Local hist
Automation Activity & Vendor Info: (Acquisitions) TLC (The Library Corporation); (Cataloging) TLC (The Library Corporation); (Circulation) TLC (The Library Corporation); (ILL) OCLC; (OPAC) TLC (The Library Corporation)
Wireless access
Publications: Children's Newsletter; Friends Newsletter
Partic in LYRASIS
Open Mon-Fri 10-6
Friends of the Library Group

J VANCE-GRANVILLE COMMUNITY COLLEGE*, Learning Resources Center, 200 Community College Rd, 27536. (Mail add: PO Box 917, 27536-0917), SAN 312-875X. Tel: 252-738-3279. FAX: 252-738-3372. E-mail: library@vgcc.edu. Web Site: library.vgcc.edu. *Dir,* Elaine Stem; E-mail: steme@vgcc.edu; *Librn,* Jennie Davis; Staff 7 (MLS 4, Non-MLS 3)
Founded 1970. Highest Degree: Associate

Jul 2012-Jun 2013. Mats Exp $153,000, Books $68,000, Per/Ser (Incl. Access Fees) $60,000, AV Mat $25,000
Library Holdings: Bk Titles 38,000; Bk Vols 43,443; Per Subs 250
Subject Interests: Children's bks, Current novels
Automation Activity & Vendor Info: (Cataloging) SirsiDynix; (Circulation) SirsiDynix; (ILL) SirsiDynix; (OPAC) SirsiDynix
Wireless access
Publications: LRC Brochure; Student Handbook
Partic in Community Colleges Libraries in North Carolina; North Carolina Libraries for Virtual Education; OCLC Online Computer Library Center, Inc
Open Mon-Thurs 8-5, Fri 8-3
Departmental Libraries:
FRANKLIN CAMPUS, 8100 NC 56 Hwy, Louisburg, 27549. (Mail add: PO Box 777, Louisburg, 27549-0777). Tel: 919-738-3606. FAX: 919-496-6604.
Library Holdings: Bk Vols 2,000
Open Mon, Tues & Thurs 9-6, Wed 9-5
SOUTH CAMPUS, 1547 S Campus Dr, Creedmoor, 27522-7381. (Mail add: PO Box 39, Creedmoor, 27522-0039). Tel: 252-738-3504. FAX: 919-528-1201. *Librn,* Position Currently Open
Fac 5; Highest Degree: Associate
Library Holdings: Bk Vols 10,000; Per Subs 50
Open Mon-Thurs 8-6, Fri 8-3
WARREN CAMPUS, 210 W Ridgeway St, Warrenton, 27589-1838. (Mail add: PO Box 207, Warrenton, 27589-0207). Tel: 252-738-3686. FAX: 252-257-3612. *Library Contact,* Kim Jackson; Staff 1 (Non-MLS 1)
Library Holdings: Bk Vols 5,000
Open Mon-Thurs 8-5, Fri 8-3

HENDERSONVILLE

SR FRUITLAND BAPTIST BIBLE COLLEGE, Randy Kilby Memorial Library, (Formerly Fruitland Baptist Bible Institute), 1455 Gillaim Rd, 28792. SAN 312-8768. Tel: 828-685-8886, Ext 3. FAX: 828-685-8888. E-mail: library@fruitland.edu. Web Site: www.fruitland.edu/library. *Librn,* Ben Tackett; Staff 2 (MLS 1, Non-MLS 1)
Founded 1949
Library Holdings: Bk Titles 35,000; Per Subs 30
Wireless access
Open Mon 8-5, Tues & Thurs 7am-10pm, Wed 7-4:30, Fri 7am-1pm

P HENDERSON COUNTY PUBLIC LIBRARY*, 301 N Washington St, 28739. SAN 354-897X. Tel: 828-697-4725. Web Site: www.hendersoncountync.gov/library. *Dir,* Trina Rushing; Tel: 828-697-4725, Ext 2334, E-mail: trushing@henderson.lib.nc.us
Founded 1914. Circ 948,000
Wireless access
Open Mon-Thurs 9-8, Fri & Sat 9-5
Friends of the Library Group
Branches: 5
EDNEYVILLE BRANCH, Two Firehouse Rd, 28792, SAN 377-8312. Tel: 828-687-1218. *Br Head,* Cindy Camp-Fisher
Founded 1989
Open Mon & Tues 9-7, Wed & Thurs 9-5, Fri & Sat 10-2
Friends of the Library Group
ETOWAH BRANCH, 101 Brickyard Rd, Etowah, 28729, SAN 354-8988. Tel: 828-891-6577. *Br Head,* Karen Bryant
Founded 1982
Library Holdings: Bk Vols 18,302
Open Mon & Wed 9-7, Tues & Thurs 9-5, Fri & Sat 10-2
Friends of the Library Group
FLETCHER BRANCH, 120 Library Rd, Fletcher, 28732, SAN 354-9003. Tel: 828-687-1218. *Br Head,* Lisa Whitney
Founded 1977
Library Holdings: Bk Vols 15,000
Open Mon & Wed 10-7, Tues & Thurs 10-5, Fri & Sat 10-4
Friends of the Library Group
GREEN RIVER, 50 Green River Rd, Zirconia, 28790, SAN 377-8339. Tel: 828-697-4969. *Br Head,* Ashley Shackle
Founded 1990
Open Mon & Fri 9-5, Tues & Thurs 9-6, Wed & Sat 9-1
Friends of the Library Group
MILLS RIVER LIBRARY, 124 Town Center Dr, Ste 1, Mills River, 28759. Tel: 828-890-1850. *Br Head,* Brittany Wist Smith
Founded 2005
Friends of the Library Group

HERTFORD

P PERQUIMANS COUNTY LIBRARY*, 514 S Church St, 27944. SAN 312-8776. Tel: 252-426-5319. FAX: 252-426-1556. *Librn,* Michele Lawrence; E-mail: mlawrence@pettigrewlibraries.org; Staff 6 (MLS 1, Non-MLS 5)
Founded 1937. Pop 12,000; Circ 46,728
Library Holdings: Audiobooks 1,191; AV Mats 3,680; Bks on Deafness & Sign Lang 10; Braille Volumes 2; CDs 528; DVDs 682; Large Print Bks 2,476; Bk Titles 32,395; Bk Vols 33,814; Per Subs 47; Videos 1,307
Special Collections: CCR&R, games, puzzles & toys for young children
Subject Interests: Genealogy, Local hist
Automation Activity & Vendor Info: (Acquisitions) TLC (The Library Corporation); (Cataloging) TLC (The Library Corporation); (Circulation) TLC (The Library Corporation); (OPAC) TLC (The Library Corporation)
Wireless access
Function: 24/7 Online cat, Audiobks via web, Bks on CD, Children's prog, Computers for patron use, Electronic databases & coll, Free DVD rentals, Home delivery & serv to seniorr ctr & nursing homes, ILL available, Laminating, Magazines, Magnifiers for reading, Music CDs, Online cat, Photocopying/Printing, Preschool outreach, Prog for adults, Prog for children & young adult, Ref serv available, Scanner, Spoken cassettes & CDs, Story hour, Summer reading prog, Tax forms, Telephone ref, Wheelchair accessible
Mem of Pettigrew Regional Library
Open Mon, Tues & Thurs 9:30-7, Wed & Fri 9:30-5, Sat 9:30-Noon
Friends of the Library Group

HICKORY

J CATAWBA VALLEY COMMUNITY COLLEGE LIBRARY*, Cuyler A Dunbar Bldg, 2550 Hwy 70 SE, 28602. SAN 312-8784. Tel: 828-327-7000, Ext 4229. Web Site: www.cvcc.edu/Services/Library. *Dir, Libr Serv,* Staci Wilson; Tel: 828-327-7400, Ext 4525, E-mail: swilson@cvcc.edu; *Ref & Instruction Librn,* Ari Sigal; Tel: 828-327-7000, Ext 4355, E-mail: asigal@cvcc.edu; Staff 1 (MLS 1)
Founded 1960. Enrl 2,049; Fac 180
Library Holdings: Bk Titles 28,000; Bk Vols 30,000; Per Subs 200
Subject Interests: Decoration, Furniture
Automation Activity & Vendor Info: (Acquisitions) Keystone Systems, Inc (KLAS); (Cataloging) Keystone Systems, Inc (KLAS); (Circulation) Keystone Systems, Inc (KLAS)
Wireless access
Publications: Library Information Pamphlet
Partic in Northwest AHEC
Open Mon-Thurs 7:30am-8pm, Fri 7:30-4:30

P HICKORY PUBLIC LIBRARY, Patrick Beaver Memorial Library, 375 Third St NE, 28601. SAN 354-9038. Tel: 828-304-0500. FAX: 828-304-0023. Web Site: www.hickorync.gov/library. *Libr Dir,* Sarah Greene; E-mail: sgreene@hickorync.gov; *Head, Ref & Tech Serv,* Beth Bradshaw; *Youth Serv Librn,* Lisa Neal; *Circ Supvr,* Amy Horn; Staff 7 (MLS 7)
Founded 1922. Pop 40,020; Circ 326,443
Library Holdings: AV Mats 14,874; Bk Vols 112,490; Per Subs 354
Special Collections: Career Enhancement
Subject Interests: Baseball, Genealogy, Learning disabilities, Local hist
Automation Activity & Vendor Info: (Cataloging) TLC (The Library Corporation); (Circulation) TLC (The Library Corporation); (OPAC) TLC (The Library Corporation)
Wireless access
Function: Outreach serv
Publications: Calendar (Monthly)
Special Services for the Blind - Computer with voice synthesizer for visually impaired persons
Open Mon-Thurs 9-9, Fri & Sat 9-5
Friends of the Library Group
Branches: 1
RIDGEVIEW, 706 First St SW, 28602, SAN 354-9062. Tel: 828-345-6037. FAX: 828-267-0485. *Br Mgr,* Hannah Norcutt; Staff 2 (MLS 2)
Circ 5,215
Library Holdings: Bk Vols 7,500
Subject Interests: African-Am
Open Mon-Thurs 9-9, Fri & Sat 9-5
Friends of the Library Group

C LENOIR-RHYNE UNIVERSITY LIBRARIES*, Carl A Rudisill Library, 625 7th Ave NE, 28601. (Mail add: PO Box 7548, 28603-7548), SAN 312-8806. Tel: 828-328-7236. FAX: 828-328-7338. Web Site: library.lr.edu. *Dean, Univ Libr Serv,* Rita Johnson; E-mail: rita.johnson@lr.edu; *Asst Dir, Coll Develop, Instruction & Ref Librn,* Burl McCuiston; E-mail: mccuiston@lr.edu; *Health Sci Librn,* Patrice Hall; E-mail: patrice.hall@lr.edu; *Instruction & Ref Librn,* Dawn Behrend; E-mail: dawn.behrend@lr.edu; *Instruction & Ref Librn,* Michael Munson; E-mail: michael.munson@lr.edu; *Coordr, Instrul Tech,* Jessica O'Brien; E-mail: jessica.obrien@lr.edu; *Admin Coordr, Tech Serv,* Greg Callahan; E-mail: callahang@lr.edu; *Circ, Libr Spec, Mat,* Caryn Sumic; E-mail: caryn.sumic@lr.edu; Staff 9.5 (MLS 6.5, Non-MLS 3)
Founded 1891. Enrl 2,339; Fac 137; Highest Degree: Master
Jun 2017-May 2018. Mats Exp $300,978, Books $16,418, Per/Ser (Incl. Access Fees) $200,900, Other Print Mats $35,000, AV Mat $1,109,

Electronic Ref Mat (Incl. Access Fees) $47,551. Sal $314,040 (Prof $250,040)
Library Holdings: CDs 6,341; DVDs 1,321; e-books 537,443; e-journals 28,271; Bk Vols 121,005; Per Subs 49
Special Collections: Martin Luther Works Coll (Wiemar Edition); Quetzalcoatl Coll
Automation Activity & Vendor Info: (Acquisitions) Innovative Interfaces, Inc; (Cataloging) Innovative Interfaces, Inc; (Circulation) Innovative Interfaces, Inc; (Course Reserve) Innovative Interfaces, Inc; (Discovery) EBSCO Online; (ILL) OCLC WorldShare Interlibrary Loan; (OPAC) Innovative Interfaces, Inc; (Serials) Innovative Interfaces, Inc
Wireless access
Partic in Appalachian College Association; Carolina Consortium; LYRASIS; NC Asn of Independent Cols & Univs; OCLC Online Computer Library Center, Inc
Open Mon-Thurs 8am-Midnight, Fri 8-5, Sat 11-5, Sun 2-Midnight

CM NORTHWEST AREA HEALTH EDUCATION CENTER*, Library Services, Catawba Valley Medical Ctr, 810 Fairgrove Church Rd, 28602. SAN 325-7738. Tel: 828-326-3662, Ext 3482. FAX: 828-326-3484. *Senior Outreach Librn,* Karen Lee Martinez; Tel: 828-326-3482, E-mail: martinez@wakehealth.edu; *Outreach Librn,* Janice Moore; E-mail: jdmoore@wakehealth.edu; Staff 2 (MLS 2)
Library Holdings: Bk Titles 2,200; Bk Vols 2,300
Subject Interests: Allied health, Med, Nursing
Wireless access
Partic in Northwest AHEC Library Information Network
Open Mon-Fri 8-5

HIGH POINT

S BERNICE BIENENSTOCK FURNITURE LIBRARY*, 1009 N Main St, 27262. SAN 325-7967. Tel: 336-883-4011. FAX: 336-883-6579. E-mail: info@furniturelibrary.com. Web Site: www.furniturelibrary.com. *Libr Dir,* Karla Webb
Founded 1970
Library Holdings: Bk Vols 7,000; Per Subs 10
Open Mon-Fri 9-12 & 1-5

P HIGH POINT PUBLIC LIBRARY, 901 N Main St, 27262. (Mail add: PO Box 2530, 27261-2530), SAN 354-9097. Tel: 336-883-3660. Circulation Tel: 336-883-3661. Reference Tel: 336-883-3641. Administration Tel: 336-883-3631. Information Services Tel: 336-883-3693. FAX: 336-883-3636. Web Site: www.highpointnc.gov/2328/Public-Library. *Libr Dir,* Mary M Sizemore; Tel: 336-883-3694, E-mail: mary.sizemore@highpointnc.gov; *Asst Dir,* Lorrie Russell; Tel: 336-883-3644, E-mail: lorrie.russell@highpointnc.gov; *Div Mgr, Children's Serv,* Jim Zola; Tel: 336-883-3668, E-mail: jim.zola@highpointnc.gov; *Div Mgr, Reader Serv,* Nancy Metzner; Tel: 336-883-3650, E-mail: nancy.metzner@highpointnc.gov; *Div Mgr, Res Serv,* Ginny Lewis; Tel: 336-883-3643, E-mail: ginny.lewis@highpointnc.gov; *Div Mgr, Tech Serv,* Kim Coleman; Tel: 336-883-3645, E-mail: kim.coleman@highpointnc.gov; *Mgr, Lending Serv,* Shelly Witcher,; Tel: 336-883-3651, E-mail: shelly.witcher@highpointnc.gov; *Supvr, AV & Media Serv,* Julie Raynor; Tel: 336-883-3093, E-mail: julie.raynor@highpointnc.gov; *Supvr, Computer Serv & Ref (Info Serv),* Mario Ramos; Tel: 336-883-3633, E-mail: mario.ramos@highpointnc.gov; *Syst Adminr,* Jamie Beck; E-mail: jamie.beck@highpointnc.gov; *Genealogy Serv,* Marcellaus Joiner; Tel: 336-883-3637, E-mail: marcellaus.joiner@highpointnc.gov; *ILL, Ref (Info Servs),* Shelley Oglesby; Tel: 336-883-8585, E-mail: shelley.oglesby@highpointnc.gov; *Ref (Info Servs),* John Raynor; Tel: 336-883-3216, E-mail: john.raynor@highpointnc.gov; Staff 17.5 (MLS 17.5)
Founded 1926. Pop 116,065; Circ 820,021
Jul 2021-Jun 2022 Income $5,867,484, State $86,312, City $5,248,072, County $500,000, Locally Generated Income $33,100. Mats Exp $336,712, Books $142,512, Per/Ser (Incl. Access Fees) $327, Micro $3,667, AV Mat $29,381, Electronic Ref Mat (Incl. Access Fees) $107. Sal $3,603,194
Library Holdings: Audiobooks 6,256; AV Mats 329,381; DVDs 23,125; e-books 816,392; Bk Vols 142,512; Per Subs 327
Special Collections: Municipal Document Depository
Subject Interests: Design, Furniture, Genealogy, Local hist, NC
Automation Activity & Vendor Info: (Acquisitions) TLC (The Library Corporation); (Cataloging) TLC (The Library Corporation); (Circulation) TLC (The Library Corporation); (Discovery) Ex Libris Group; (ILL) OCLC WorldShare Interlibrary Loan; (OPAC) TLC (The Library Corporation); (Serials) TLC (The Library Corporation)
Wireless access
Function: 24/7 Electronic res, 24/7 Online cat, Activity rm, Adult bk club, Adult literacy prog, After school storytime, Archival coll, Audiobks on Playaways & MP3, Audiobks via web, AV serv, Bk club(s), Bks on CD, Butterfly Garden, CD-ROM, Children's prog, Computer training, Computers for patron use, Digital talking bks, E-Reserves, Electronic databases & coll, Equip loans & repairs, Free DVD rentals, Games & aids for people with disabilities, Genealogy discussion group, Health sci info serv, Holiday prog, Home delivery & serv to seniorr ctr & nursing homes, Homebound delivery serv, ILL available, Internet access, Large print keyboards, Life-long learning prog for all ages, Magazines, Magnifiers for reading, Mail & tel request accepted, Meeting rooms, Microfiche/film & reading machines, Movies, Online cat, Online info literacy tutorials on the web & in blackboard, Online ref, Outreach serv, Outside serv via phone, mail, e-mail & web, OverDrive digital audio bks, Photocopying/Printing, Preschool outreach, Preschool reading prog, Printer for laptops & handheld devices, Prog for adults, Prog for children & young adult, Ref & res, Ref serv available, Res assist avail, Satellite serv, Senior computer classes, Senior outreach, Serves people with intellectual disabilities, Spanish lang bks, Spoken cassettes & CDs, Spoken cassettes & DVDs, STEM programs, Story hour, Study rm, Summer & winter reading prog, Summer reading prog, Teen prog, Telephone ref, Wheelchair accessible, Winter reading prog
Publications: Library Whispers (Newsletter)
Partic in North Carolina Libraries for Virtual Education
Special Services for the Blind - Assistive/Adapted tech devices, equip & products; Bks on CD; Computer access aids; Extensive large print coll; Large print bks; Magnifiers; PC for people with disabilities
Open Mon-Thurs 9-8, Fri 9-6, Sat 9-6, Sun 1:30-5:30
Restriction: Non-resident fee
Friends of the Library Group
Bookmobiles: 1. Libr Assoc, Kim Wilks

C HIGH POINT UNIVERSITY*, Smith Library, One University Pkwy, 27268. SAN 312-8814. Tel: 336-841-9102. Interlibrary Loan Service Tel: 336-841-9170. Reference Tel: 336-841-9101. Administration Tel: 336-841-9215. FAX: 336-888-5123. Web Site: www.highpoint.edu/library. *Dir,* David L Bryden; Tel: 336-841-9215, E-mail: dbryden@highpoint.edu; *Syst Coordr, Tech Serv,* Alex Frey; Tel: 336-841-9152, E-mail: afrey@highpoint.edu; *Ref Librn,* Jenny Erdmann; Tel: 336-841-9068, E-mail: jerdmann@highpoint.edu; *ILL,* Robert Fitzgerald, Jr; Tel: 336-841-9170, E-mail: rfitzger@highpoint.edu; *Cat, Ser,* Sheri Teleha; Tel: 336-841-4549, E-mail: steleha@highpoint.edu; *Circ Serv,* La-Nita Williams; E-mail: nwilliam@highpoint.edu; *Digital Serv Librn,* Josh Harris; Tel: 336-841-9103, E-mail: media@highpoint.edu; *Acq, Supvr,* Karen Harbin; Tel: 336-841-9100, E-mail: kharbin@highpoint.edu; Staff 10 (MLS 8, Non-MLS 2)
Founded 1924. Enrl 5,100; Fac 350; Highest Degree: Doctorate
Library Holdings: DVDs 10,000; e-books 450,000; Bk Vols 250,000; Per Subs 32,000
Special Collections: Home Furnishings Marketing Coll; Methodist Archives; North Carolina Coll
Subject Interests: Liberal arts
Automation Activity & Vendor Info: (Acquisitions) OCLC; (Cataloging) OCLC
Wireless access
Partic in Carolina Consortium; North Carolina Libraries for Virtual Education; OCLC Online Computer Library Center, Inc
Restriction: Authorized patrons
Friends of the Library Group

HILLSBOROUGH

P ORANGE COUNTY PUBLIC LIBRARY*, 137 W Margaret Lane, 27278. SAN 312-8849. Tel: 919-245-2525. FAX: 919-644-3003. Web Site: www.co.orange.nc.us/156/library. *Dir,* Lucinda Munger; E-mail: lmunger@orangecountync.gov; *Asst Dir,* Andrea Tullos; E-mail: atullos@orangecountync.gov; Staff 14 (MLS 7, Non-MLS 7)
Founded 1912. Pop 118,227; Circ 154,873
Library Holdings: Bk Vols 86,369; Per Subs 420
Subject Interests: Genealogy, Local hist
Automation Activity & Vendor Info: (Cataloging) Innovative Interfaces, Inc; (Circulation) Innovative Interfaces, Inc; (OPAC) Innovative Interfaces, Inc
Wireless access
Open Mon-Thurs 9-8, Fri & Sat 9-6, Sun 12-6
Friends of the Library Group
Branches: 2
CARRBORO BRANCH, McDougle Middle School, 900 Old Fayetteville Rd, Chapel Hill, 27516, SAN 377-7901. Tel: 919-969-3006. FAX: 919-969-3008. *Br Mgr,* Anne Pusey; E-mail: apusey@co.orange.nc.us; *Circ,* Janet Caudle; E-mail: jcaudle@co.orange.nc.us; Staff 6 (MLS 2, Non-MLS 4)
Library Holdings: Bk Vols 19,450; Per Subs 75
Automation Activity & Vendor Info: (Cataloging) ComPanion Corp; (Circulation) ComPanion Corp
Open Mon-Thurs 3:30-8, Sat 10-2, Sun 1-5
Friends of the Library Group
CARRBORO CYBRARY BRANCH, Carrboro Century Ctr, 100 N Greensboro St, Carrboro, 27510. Tel: 919-918-7387. FAX: 919-918-3960. E-mail: cybrary@co.orange.nc.us. *Br Mgr,* Ann Pusey; *Circ Supvr,* Vanessa Soleic; Staff 1.3 (MLS 1.3)
Founded 2004
Library Holdings: Bk Vols 369; Per Subs 23

Function: Adult bk club, Adult literacy prog, Bk club(s), Bks on cassette, Bks on CD, Computer training, Computers for patron use, Digital talking bks, ILL available, Magnifiers for reading, Online cat, Photocopying/Printing, Prog for adults, Ref serv available, Scanner, Spoken cassettes & CDs, Wheelchair accessible
Open Mon-Fri 9-4, Sat 10-2
Friends of the Library Group

HUDSON

J CALDWELL COMMUNITY COLLEGE & TECHNICAL INSTITUTE*, Broyhill Center for Learning Resources, 2855 Hickory Blvd, 28638. SAN 312-9020. Tel: 828-726-2309. FAX: 828-726-2603. Reference E-mail: reference@cccti.edu. Web Site: www.cccti.edu/Library. *Dir,* Alison Beard; Tel: 828-726-2311, E-mail: abeard@cccti.edu; *Librn,* Amber Jacks; Tel: 828-726-2312, E-mail: ajacks@cccti.edu; Staff 8 (MLS 3, Non-MLS 5)
Founded 1966. Highest Degree: Associate
Library Holdings: DVDs 536; Bk Vols 43,285; Per Subs 112; Videos 1,408
Automation Activity & Vendor Info: (Cataloging) SirsiDynix; (Circulation) SirsiDynix; (ILL) OCLC; (OPAC) SirsiDynix
Wireless access
Publications: Audio-visual & book acquisitions lists; Audio-visual catalog
Partic in Community Colleges Libraries in North Carolina; Northwest AHEC; Northwest AHEC Library Information Network
Open Mon-Thurs 7:30am-8pm, Fri 7:30-4

JACKSONVILLE

J COASTAL CAROLINA COMMUNITY COLLEGE*, Learning Resources Center, 444 Western Blvd, 28546. SAN 312-8865. Tel: 910-938-6237. FAX: 910-455-7027. E-mail: AskALibrarian@coastalcarolina.edu. Web Site: coastalcarolina.libguides.com/library. *Dir, Libr Serv,* Sally Goodman; Tel: 910-938-6793, E-mail: goodmans@coastalcarolina.edu; *Subject Liaison Librn,* Lauren Przywara; Tel: 910-938-6239, E-mail: przywaral@coastalcarolina.edu; *Subject Liaison Librn,* Audrey Stewart; Tel: 910-938-6278, E-mail: stewarta@coastalcarolina.edu; *Circ Mgr,* Teresa Ortega; Tel: 910-938-6147, E-mail: ortegat@coastalcarolina.edu; *Acq,* Kerry Brinker; Tel: 910-938-6844, E-mail: brinkerk@coastalcarolina.edu; *ILL,* Marilyn Gresham; Tel: 910-938-6114, E-mail: greshamm@coastalcarolina.edu. Subject Specialists: *Allied health, Nursing,* Sally Goodman; *Fine arts, Humanities,* Lauren Przywara; *Bus, Hist, Tech,* Audrey Stewart; Staff 6 (MLS 3, Non-MLS 3)
Founded 1965. Enrl 1,745; Fac 125; Highest Degree: Associate
Library Holdings: CDs 1,837; DVDs 7,172; Microforms 20,758; Bk Titles 45,000; Per Subs 53
Special Collections: Oral History
Automation Activity & Vendor Info: (Cataloging) SirsiDynix; (Circulation) SirsiDynix; (Course Reserve) SirsiDynix; (ILL) SirsiDynix; (OPAC) SirsiDynix
Wireless access
Partic in Community Colleges Libraries in North Carolina; North Carolina Libraries for Virtual Education; OCLC Online Computer Library Center, Inc
Open Mon-Thurs 7am-9:30pm, Fri 7-5, Sat 9-5

P ONSLOW COUNTY PUBLIC LIBRARY*, 58 Doris Ave E, 28540. SAN 354-9186. Tel: 910-455-7350. Circulation Tel: 910-455-7350, Ext 1412. Administration Tel: 910-455-7350, Ext 1419. FAX: 910-989-5790. E-mail: library@onslowcountync.gov. Web Site: www.onslowcountync.gov/150/Library. *Dir,* Virginia Sharp March; E-mail: virginia_march@onslowcountync.gov; *Ad,* Senatra Spearmon; Tel: 910-455-7350, Ext 1417, E-mail: senatra_spearmon@onslowcountync.gov; *Pub Serv Librn,* Laurel Beckley-Jackson; Tel: 910-455-7350, Ext 1421, E-mail: laurel_jackson@onslowcountync.gov; *Tech Serv Librn,* Deborah Wadleigh; Tel: 910-455-7350, Ext 1415, E-mail: deborah_wadleigh@onslowcountync.gov; Staff 40 (MLS 4, Non-MLS 36)
Founded 1936. Pop 180,000
Library Holdings: AV Mats 3,695; Bks on Deafness & Sign Lang 33; Large Print Bks 2,472; Bk Titles 59,618; Bk Vols 75,026; Per Subs 131; Talking Bks 1,347
Special Collections: Oral History Coll Relating to Building Camp Lejeune Marine Base
Subject Interests: Genealogy, Local hist
Automation Activity & Vendor Info: (Cataloging) Innovative Interfaces, Inc; (Circulation) Innovative Interfaces, Inc; (OPAC) Innovative Interfaces, Inc
Wireless access
Function: 24/7 Electronic res, 24/7 Online cat, Adult bk club, Bks on CD, Children's prog, Computers for patron use, Electronic databases & coll, Family literacy, Free DVD rentals, Genealogy discussion group, Homebound delivery serv, ILL available, Internet access, Magazines, Mango lang, Meeting rooms, Microfiche/film & reading machines, Online cat, OverDrive digital audio bks, Photocopying/Printing, Preschool reading prog, Prog for adults, Prog for children & young adult, Ref & res, Ref serv available, Scanner, Spanish lang bks, STEM programs, Story hour, Study rm, Summer reading prog, Tax forms, Teen prog, Wheelchair accessible
Partic in NCIN; North Carolina Libraries for Virtual Education; OCLC Online Computer Library Center, Inc
Open Mon-Thurs 9-9, Fri & Sat 9-6, Sun 1-5
Friends of the Library Group
Branches: 3
RICHLANDS BRANCH, 299 S Wilmington St, Richlands, 28574, SAN 354-9216. Tel: 910-324-5321. FAX: 910-989-5793. E-mail: lib_rl@onslowcountync.gov. *Br Mgr,* Position Currently Open
Library Holdings: AV Mats 1,644; Large Print Bks 361; Bk Titles 22,182; Bk Vols 23,445; Talking Bks 551
Open Mon-Wed & Fri 9-6, Thurs 10-7, Sat 9-3
Friends of the Library Group
SNEADS FERRY BRANCH, 1330 Hwy 210, Sneads Ferry, 28460, SAN 354-9232. Tel: 910-327-6471. FAX: 910-937-1369. *Br Mgr,* Liza Barrett; Tel: 910-327-6471, Ext 1429, E-mail: liza_barrett@onslowcountync.gov
Library Holdings: AV Mats 1,666; Bks on Deafness & Sign Lang 11; Large Print Bks 225; Bk Titles 19,876; Bk Vols 20,759; Per Subs 33; Talking Bks 493
Open Mon-Wed & Fri 9-6, Thurs 10-7, Sat 9-3
Friends of the Library Group
SWANSBORO BRANCH, 1460 W Corbett Ave, Swansboro, 28584, SAN 354-9240. Tel: 910-326-4888. FAX: 910-989-5792. *Br Mgr,* Tracy Daly; Tel: 910-326-4888, Ext 141, E-mail: tracy_daly@onslowcountync.gov
Library Holdings: AV Mats 1,953; Bks on Deafness & Sign Lang 13; Large Print Bks 643; Bk Titles 21,833; Bk Vols 223,199; Per Subs 29; Talking Bks 641
Open Mon-Wed & Fri 9-6, Thurs 10-7, Sat 9-3
Friends of the Library Group

A UNITED STATES MARINE CORPS*, MCAS New River Library, Bldg AS213-213, Bancroft St, 28545. SAN 354-9275. Tel: 910-449-6715. FAX: 910-449-6957. Web Site: library.usmc-mccs.org. *Dir,* Judy Bradford
Founded 1956
Library Holdings: AV Mats 1,000; Bk Titles 7,000; Per Subs 25
Subject Interests: Alcohol abuse control, Automobile maintenance repair, Drug abuse, Human relations, Juv picture bks, Microcomputer, Mil preparedness, Sports, Vietnam conflict, World War II
Automation Activity & Vendor Info: (Cataloging) SirsiDynix; (Circulation) SirsiDynix; (OPAC) SirsiDynix
Wireless access
Open Mon-Fri 8-5, Sat 10-5

JAMESTOWN

J GUILFORD TECHNICAL COMMUNITY COLLEGE*, Learning Resource Center, 601 E Main St, 27282. (Mail add: PO Box 309, 27282-0309), SAN 354-9305. Tel: 336-334-4822, Ext 50290. Web Site: www.gtcc.edu/library. *Dir, Libr Serv,* Monica Young; Tel: 336-334-4822, Ext 50587, E-mail: mwyoung@gtcc.edu; *Pub Serv Librn,* Ricky Baker; Tel: 336-334-4822, Ext 50519, E-mail: rdbaker2@gtcc.edu; *Ref Serv Librn,* Alisha Webb; Tel: 336-334-4822, Ext 50330, E-mail: amwebb@gtcc.edu; *Tech Serv Librn,* Carol Keck; Tel: 336-334-4822, Ext 50259, E-mail: cakeck@gtcc.edu; Staff 12 (MLS 7, Non-MLS 5)
Founded 1958. Enrl 11,884; Fac 231; Highest Degree: Associate
Library Holdings: AV Mats 7,585; e-books 25,000; Bk Titles 70,120; Bk Vols 84,134; Per Subs 300
Subject Interests: Archit, Automotive tech, Commercial art, Commun col, Dental sci, Engr, Nursing, Paralegal, Surgical tech
Automation Activity & Vendor Info: (Acquisitions) SirsiDynix; (Cataloging) SirsiDynix; (Circulation) SirsiDynix; (Course Reserve) SirsiDynix; (Media Booking) SirsiDynix; (OPAC) SirsiDynix; (Serials) SirsiDynix
Wireless access
Publications: Faculty Guide; Newsletter; Periodicals List; Student-How-To-Bookmarks
Partic in NC Dept of Commun Cols
Open Mon-Fri 9-4
Friends of the Library Group

P JAMESTOWN PUBLIC LIBRARY*, 200 W Main St, 27282. SAN 370-6648. Tel: 336-454-4815. FAX: 336-454-0630. E-mail: info@jamestownpubliclibrary.com. Web Site: jamestownpubliclibrary.com. *Libr Dir,* Jim McGaha; *Librn,* Sue Elder; *Ch,* Carol Reed; *Libr Asst,* Morgan Grove; *Libr Asst,* Sue Rothermel; Staff 5 (MLS 2, Non-MLS 3)
Founded 1988. Pop 12,000; Circ 62,000; Fac 5
Jan 2014-Dec 2014 Income $153,130, City $50,000, County $55,500, Other $37,630. Mats Exp $15,500, Books $14,500, Per/Ser (Incl. Access Fees) $1,000. Sal $80,000
Library Holdings: Audiobooks 351; Bks on Deafness & Sign Lang 12; DVDs 414; High Interest/Low Vocabulary Bk Vols 423; Large Print Bks 449; Bk Titles 16,016; Bk Vols 17,613; Per Subs 54
Automation Activity & Vendor Info: (Acquisitions) Follett Software; (Cataloging) Follett Software; (Circulation) Follett Software

Wireless access
Function: Adult bk club, Archival coll, Art exhibits, Audiobks via web, Bks on CD, Children's prog, Computer training, Computers for patron use, Free DVD rentals, Holiday prog, Instruction & testing, Internet access, Magazines, Movies, Online cat, OverDrive digital audio bks, Photocopying/Printing, Preschool reading prog, Prog for adults, Prog for children & young adult, Scanner, Senior computer classes, Story hour, Study rm, Summer reading prog, Tax forms, Teen prog
Publications: FOL (Newsletter); Library News Article (Newsletter)
Special Services for the Deaf - Closed caption videos
Open Mon-Fri 9-6, Sat 10-1
Restriction: Authorized patrons, Lending limited to county residents
Friends of the Library Group

JONESVILLE

P JONESVILLE PUBLIC LIBRARY*, 560 Winston Rd, 28642. SAN 312-8873. Tel: 336-835-7604. FAX: 336-526-4226. E-mail: jva@nwrl.org. Web Site: nwrlibrary.org/jonesville. *Br Mgr,* Jennifer Rogers; E-mail: jrogers@nwrl.org; Staff 3 (Non-MLS 3)
Founded 1962. Pop 5,000; Circ 68,000
Library Holdings: Bks on Deafness & Sign Lang 10; Bk Titles 20,000
Automation Activity & Vendor Info: (Circulation) SirsiDynix; (OPAC) SirsiDynix
Wireless access
Function: Audio & video playback equip for onsite use, Audiobks via web, AV serv, Bks on CD, Children's prog, Computer training, Computers for patron use, Free DVD rentals, ILL available, Internet access, Magazines, Movies, Notary serv, Outreach serv, Outside serv via phone, mail, e-mail & web, OverDrive digital audio bks, Photocopying/Printing, Preschool outreach, Preschool reading prog, Prog for adults, Prog for children & young adult, Scanner, Senior outreach, Spanish lang bks, Spoken cassettes & CDs, Story hour, Summer reading prog, Tax forms, Teen prog, Telephone ref, VHS videos, Wheelchair accessible
Mem of Northwestern Regional Library
Open Mon, Wed & Fri 8:30-5:30, Tues & Thurs 8:30-7:30, Sat 9-1
Friends of the Library Group

KENANSVILLE

P DUPLIN COUNTY LIBRARY*, Dorothy Wightman Library, 107 Bowden Dr, 28349. (Mail add: PO Box 930, 28349-0930), SAN 312-889X. Tel: 910-296-2117. FAX: 910-296-2172. Web Site: www2.youseemore.com/duplin. *Dir,* Laura Jones; E-mail: laura.jones@duplincountync.com; *Br Supvr,* Shannon Sutton; E-mail: shannon.sutton@duplincountync.com; *Youth Serv Coordr,* Donna Jones; E-mail: djones@duplincountync.com
Founded 1920. Pop 39,995
Library Holdings: Large Print Bks 400; Bk Titles 42,600; Bk Vols 75,000; Per Subs 200
Subject Interests: NC hist
Automation Activity & Vendor Info: (Acquisitions) TLC (The Library Corporation); (Cataloging) TLC (The Library Corporation); (Circulation) TLC (The Library Corporation)
Wireless access
Open Mon-Fri 9-6, Sat 10-2
Branches: 5
FLORENCE GALLIER LIBRARY, 104 W Main St, Magnolia, 28453. (Mail add: PO Box 333, Magnolia, 28453-0333). Tel: 910-289-7056. FAX: 910-289-7056. *Br Librn,* Position Currently Open
Library Holdings: Bk Vols 1,600
Open Mon, Thurs & Fri 2-5:45
EMILY S HILL LIBRARY, 106 Park Circle Dr, Faison, 28341. (Mail add: PO Box 129, Faison, 28341-0129), SAN 376-2912. Tel: 910-267-0601. FAX: 910-267-0601. *Libr Asst,* Mary Scott; E-mail: mary.scott@duplincountync.com
Library Holdings: Bk Titles 45,000; Bk Vols 50,000
Automation Activity & Vendor Info: (Acquisitions) TLC (The Library Corporation); (Cataloging) TLC (The Library Corporation); (Circulation) TLC (The Library Corporation)
Open Mon-Fri 2-5:45
PHILLIP LEFF MEMORIAL LIBRARY, 807 Broad St, Beulaville, 28518. (Mail add: PO Box 721, Beulaville, 28518-0721), SAN 376-2920. Tel: 910-298-4677. FAX: 910-298-4677. *Libr Asst,* Maureen Murphy; E-mail: maureen.murphy@duplincountync.com
Library Holdings: Bk Titles 20,000; Bk Vols 30,000; Per Subs 10
Automation Activity & Vendor Info: (Acquisitions) TLC (The Library Corporation); (Cataloging) TLC (The Library Corporation); (Circulation) TLC (The Library Corporation)
Open Mon, Tues, Thurs & Fri 10-12:30 & 2-5:45
ROSE HILL COMMUNITY MEMORIAL LIBRARY, 113 S Walnut St, Rose Hill, 28458. (Mail add: PO Box 94, Rose Hill, 28458-0094), SAN 320-8311. Tel: 910-289-2490. FAX: 910-289-2186. *Libr Asst,* Bernard Hall; E-mail: bernard.hall@dublincountync.com
Pop 1,500; Circ 11,000
Library Holdings: Bk Vols 7,150
Automation Activity & Vendor Info: (Circulation) TLC (The Library Corporation)
Open Mon-Fri 2-6
WARSAW-KORNEGAY LIBRARY, 117 E College St, Warsaw, 28398, SAN 376-2904. Tel: 910-293-4664. FAX: 910-293-4664. *Libr Asst,* Linda Hewett; E-mail: linda.hewett@duplincountync.com
Library Holdings: Bk Vols 6,000
Open Mon & Fri 9-1 & 2-5:45, Tues & Thurs 2-5:45

J JAMES SPRUNT COMMUNITY COLLEGE*, William H Wiggs Library, Boyette Bldg, 133 James Sprunt Dr, 28349. (Mail add: PO Box 398, 28349), SAN 312-8903. Tel: 910-275-6330. E-mail: jscclibrary@jamessprunt.edu. Web Site: jamessprunt.libguides.com. *Dir, Libr Serv,* Colleen Kehoe-Robinson; Tel: 910-275-6332, E-mail: ckehoe-robinson@jamessprunt.edu; *Librn,* Matthew Vincett; E-mail: mvincett@jamessprunt.edu; Staff 3 (MLS 1, Non-MLS 2)
Founded 1966. Enrl 1,200; Highest Degree: Associate
Library Holdings: Bk Titles 2,500; Per Subs 200
Special Collections: Local History (Duplin County NC))
Wireless access
Function: ILL available, Internet access, Photocopying/Printing, Wheelchair accessible
Partic in Community College Libraries in North Carolina
Open Mon-Thurs (Fall & Spring) 7:30-6:30, Fri 8-Noon; Mon-Thurs (Summer) 7-6:30
Restriction: Open to pub for ref only, Open to students, fac & staff, Pub use on premises

KENLY

P KENLY PUBLIC LIBRARY*, 205 Edgerton St, 27542. SAN 355-1792. Tel: 919-284-4217. Web Site: townofkenly.com/government/departments/library. *Librn,* Erin Walton; E-mail: erin.walton@townofkenly.com; Staff 1 (Non-MLS 1)
Circ 8,731
Library Holdings: Large Print Bks 220; Bk Vols 14,156; Per Subs 27; Talking Bks 44
Wireless access
Open Mon & Wed 9-5:30, Tues & Thurs 9-7, Fri 9-5, Sat 9-12

KING

P KING PUBLIC LIBRARY, 101 Pilot View Dr, 27021. (Mail add: PO Box 629, 27021-0629), SAN 312-8911. Tel: 336-983-3868. FAX: 336-983-0769. E-mail: kin@nwrl.org. Web Site: www.nwrl.org/king. *Librn,* Gretchen Parker; *Asst Librn,* Melody Johnson
Library Holdings: Bk Titles 30,000; Per Subs 35
Automation Activity & Vendor Info: (Acquisitions) Evergreen; (Cataloging) Evergreen; (Circulation) Evergreen; (Course Reserve) Evergreen; (ILL) Evergreen; (Media Booking) Evergreen; (OPAC) Evergreen; (Serials) Evergreen
Mem of Northwestern Regional Library
Open Mon, Tues & Thurs 9-7:30, Wed & Fri 9-5:30, Sat 10-1
Friends of the Library Group

KINGS MOUNTAIN

P MAUNEY MEMORIAL LIBRARY, 100 S Piedmont Ave, 28086. (Mail add: PO Box 429, 28086), SAN 312-892X. Tel: 704-739-2371. FAX: 704-734-4499. E-mail: info@mauneylibrary.org. Web Site: www.mauneylibrary.org/249/mauney-memorial-library. *Libr Mgr,* Christina Martin; E-mail: christina.martin@mauneylibrary.org; Staff 8.1 (MLS 1, Non-MLS 7.1)
Founded 1936. Pop 10,965; Circ 77,681
Library Holdings: Bk Vols 59,623; Per Subs 69
Subject Interests: Local family hist
Automation Activity & Vendor Info: (Acquisitions) SirsiDynix; (Cataloging) SirsiDynix; (Circulation) SirsiDynix; (ILL) OCLC FirstSearch; (OPAC) SirsiDynix
Wireless access
Function: Homebound delivery serv, ILL available, Prog for children & young adult, Summer reading prog, Telephone ref, Wheelchair accessible
Partic in CLEVE-NET; NCIN
Open Mon-Fri 9-5
Friends of the Library Group

KINSTON

C LENOIR COMMUNITY COLLEGE*, Learning Resources Center, 231 Hwy 58 S, 28504-6836. (Mail add: PO Box 188, 28502-0188), SAN 312-8954. Tel: 252-527-6223, Ext 504. FAX: 252-233-6879. Web Site: www.lenoircc.edu/lrc. *Dir,* Richard M Garafolo; E-mail: rmgarafolo48@lenoircc.edu; Staff 3 (MLS 1, Non-MLS 2)
Founded 1964. Enrl 3,200; Fac 184; Highest Degree: Associate
Library Holdings: Bk Titles 30,000; Bk Vols 42,000; Per Subs 25

Special Collections: Local Eastern North Carolina
Subject Interests: Distance learning classroom, Genealogy, Local hist, Writing across the curric
Automation Activity & Vendor Info: (Cataloging) SirsiDynix-WorkFlows; (Circulation) SirsiDynix-WorkFlows; (ILL) OCLC WorldShare Interlibrary Loan; (OPAC) SirsiDynix
Wireless access
Publications: Local History Brochure
Partic in Community College Libraries in North Carolina; Community Colleges Libraries in North Carolina
Special Services for the Deaf - Closed caption videos
Open Mon-Thurs (Winter) 7:45-7:30, Fri 7:45-3; Mon-Thurs (Summer) 7:30-7:30

P NEUSE REGIONAL LIBRARY*, Kinston-Lenoir County Public Library (Headquarters), 510 N Queen St, 28501. SAN 312-8962. Tel: 252-527-7066. Circulation Tel: 252-527-7066, Ext 120. Reference Tel: 252-527-7066, Ext 134. Administration Tel: 252-527-7066, Ext 130. FAX: 252-527-8220. Circulation FAX: 252-527-9235. E-mail: nrl@neuselibrary.org. Web Site: www.neuselibrary.org. *Dir of Libr,* Melanie Morgan; E-mail: mmorgan@neuselibrary.org; *Asst Dir,* Sarah Sever; E-mail: ssever@neuselibrary.org; *Head, Circ,* Shannon Riggs; E-mail: sriggs@neuselibrary.org; *Head, Ref,* Justin Stout; E-mail: jstout@neuselibrary.org; *Head, Youth Serv,* Amber Hargett; E-mail: ahargett@neuselibrary.org; Staff 10 (MLS 4, Non-MLS 6)
Founded 1962. Pop 90,915; Circ 339,864. Sal $889,020 (Prof $678,000)
Library Holdings: AV Mats 6,599; CDs 243; DVDs 12,019; e-books 89; Electronic Media & Resources 71; Large Print Bks 4,109; Bk Vols 197,187; Per Subs 401; Videos 675
Special Collections: Eastern North Carolina Genealogy (Sybil Hyatt Coll); Foreign Language Coll; Henry Pearson Art Coll; Modern Fiction on Cassette and CD; North Carolina - Specialized in Eastern North Carolina; North Carolina Original Art Coll; Piranesi Art Print Coll
Automation Activity & Vendor Info: (Acquisitions) TLC (The Library Corporation); (Cataloging) TLC (The Library Corporation); (Circulation) TLC (The Library Corporation); (OPAC) TLC (The Library Corporation); (Serials) TLC (The Library Corporation)
Wireless access
Function: Adult bk club, After school storytime, Art exhibits, Bks on cassette, Bks on CD, CD-ROM, Children's prog, Computer training, Computers for patron use, Electronic databases & coll, Holiday prog, ILL available, Instruction & testing, Music CDs, Notary serv, Online cat, Orientations, Photocopying/Printing, Prog for adults, Prog for children & young adult, Ref serv available, Spoken cassettes & CDs, Spoken cassettes & DVDs, Story hour, Summer reading prog, Tax forms, Teen prog, Wheelchair accessible, Workshops
Publications: A Trip to the Library; African American Bibliography; Neuse Regional Library Upcoming Events (Monthly); Personnel Policies Manual; School Video Annotated Catalog; Security Guard Manual; Statistical Report (Quarterly)
Open Mon-Thurs 9-9, Fri & Sat 9-6, Sun 2-6
Friends of the Library Group
Branches: 7
COMFORT PUBLIC LIBRARY, 4889 Hwy 41 W, Trenton, 28585, SAN 320-5959. Tel: 910-324-5061. FAX: 910-324-5061. E-mail: comfort@neuselibrary.org. *Br Mgr,* Lorie Watson
Pop 360
Library Holdings: Bk Vols 9,000
Open Tues & Thurs 12-6
GREENE COUNTY PUBLIC LIBRARY, 229-G Kingold Blvd, Snow Hill, 28580, SAN 312-9985. Tel: 252-747-3437. FAX: 252-747-7489. E-mail: greeneco@neuselibrary.org. *Br Mgr,* Donna Edwards
Open Mon-Thurs 9-8, Fri 9-6, Sat 10-3
Friends of the Library Group
LA GRANGE PUBLIC LIBRARY, 119 E Washington St, La Grange, 28551, SAN 312-8989. Tel: 252-566-3722. FAX: 252-566-9768. E-mail: lagrange@neuselibrary.org. *Br Mgr,* Rose Hernandez; E-mail: rburton@neuselibrary.org
Special Collections: Law Books
Open Mon, Wed & Fri 9-6, Tues & Thurs 9-7, Sat 10-3
Friends of the Library Group
MAYSVILLE PUBLIC LIBRARY, 601 Seventh St, Maysville, 28555, SAN 320-5924. Tel: 910-743-3796. FAX: 910-743-3796. E-mail: maysville@neuselibrary.org. *Br Mgr,* Karen Kahlert
Pop 900
Library Holdings: Bk Titles 1,000; Per Subs 24
Open Tues-Fri 1-6, Sat 10-3
PINK HILL PUBLIC LIBRARY, 114 W Broadway St, Pink Hill, 28572, SAN 312-9470. Tel: 252-568-3631. FAX: 252-568-3631. E-mail: pinkhill@neuselibrary.org. *Br Mgr,* Sheree Casias; E-mail: scasias@neuselibrary.org
Open Mon, Wed & Fri 9-6, Tues & Thurs 9-7, Sat 10-3
Friends of the Library Group
POLLOCKSVILLE PUBLIC LIBRARY, 415 Green Hill St, Pollocksville, 28573, SAN 320-5932. Tel: 252-224-5011. FAX: 252-224-5011. E-mail: pollocksville@neuselibrary.org. *Br Mgr,* Rosina Venegas
Library Holdings: Bk Vols 3,800; Per Subs 12
Special Collections: North Carolina Coll
Open Tues-Fri 1-6, Sat 10-3
TRENTON PUBLIC LIBRARY, 204 Lakeview Dr, Trenton, 28585, SAN 320-5940. Tel: 252-448-4261. FAX: 252-448-4261. E-mail: trenton@neuselibrary.org. *Br Mgr,* Megan Mercer
Founded 1974. Pop 1,048
Library Holdings: Bk Vols 5,000; Per Subs 17
Open Tues-Fri 1-6, Sat 10-3

LAURINBURG

C ST ANDREWS UNIVERSITY, DeTamble Library, 1700 Dogwood Mile, 28352. SAN 312-9012. Tel: 910-277-5049. Interlibrary Loan Service Tel: 910-277-5023. Web Site: libguides.sa.edu/detamble. *Libr Dir,* Mary Harvin McDonald; Tel: 910-277-5023, E-mail: mhm@sa.edu; *Libr Res Coordr,* Thomas Waage; Tel: 910-277-5025, E-mail: waagetf@sa.edu; Staff 4 (MLS 1, Non-MLS 3)
Founded 1964. Enrl 500; Fac 35; Highest Degree: Master
Library Holdings: Audiobooks 2,022; AV Mats 474; CDs 10; DVDs 638; e-books 500,000; e-journals 19,584; Electronic Media & Resources 20,806; Microforms 14,960; Bk Vols 88,000; Per Subs 38
Special Collections: Ezra Pound (Hal & Dolores Sieber Coll); Graphic Novel Coll; Special & Rare Book Coll; St Andrews Coll; Theatre (Amos Abrams Coll), bks & memorabilia. US Document Depository
Automation Activity & Vendor Info: (Acquisitions) OCLC; (Cataloging) OCLC; (Circulation) OCLC; (Course Reserve) OCLC; (ILL) OCLC WorldShare Interlibrary Loan; (OPAC) OCLC; (Serials) OCLC
Wireless access
Partic in Carolina Consortium; OCLC Online Computer Library Center, Inc
Open Mon-Thurs 8:30am-10pm, Fri 8:30-5, Sun 4-10

P SCOTLAND COUNTY MEMORIAL LIBRARY*, 312 W Church St, 28352-3720. SAN 354-933X. Tel: 910-276-0563. FAX: 910-276-4032. Web Site: www.scotlandcounty.org/188/Library. *Dir,* Leon L Gyles; E-mail: lgyles@scotlandcounty.org; *Youth Serv Librn,* Denise D Dunn; E-mail: ddunn@scotlandcounty.org; *Circ Coordr,* Louise Williams; E-mail: lwilliams@scotlandcounty.org; *Outreach Coordr,* Annie Clymer; E-mail: aclymer@scotlandcounty.org; *Tech Serv Coordr,* Kendria Finkley; E-mail: kfinkley@scotlandcounty.org; Staff 1 (MLS 1)
Founded 1941. Pop 35,600; Circ 135,119
Library Holdings: Large Print Bks 4,000; Bk Vols 65,000; Per Subs 40; Talking Bks 3,200
Special Collections: Heritage Room (North Carolina Coll)
Automation Activity & Vendor Info: (Acquisitions) TLC (The Library Corporation); (Cataloging) TLC (The Library Corporation); (Circulation) TLC (The Library Corporation); (Course Reserve) TLC (The Library Corporation); (OPAC) TLC (The Library Corporation)
Wireless access
Publications: Annual Report; Brochures
Special Services for the Deaf - Deaf publ
Special Services for the Blind - Audio mat; Bks on CD; Talking bks
Open Mon, Wed & Fri 9:30-6, Tues & Thurs 9:30-7, Sat 9-2
Bookmobiles: 1

LENOIR

P CALDWELL COUNTY PUBLIC LIBRARY*, 120 Hospital Ave, 28645-4454. SAN 312-9039. Tel: 828-757-1270. FAX: 828-757-1413. Information Services FAX: 828-757-1484. E-mail: library@caldwellcountync.org. Web Site: ccpl.libguides.com. *Interim Libr Dir,* Leslie Griffin; E-mail: lgriffin@caldwellcountync.org; *Ref Librn,* Erica Derr; Tel: 828-757-1270, E-mail: ederr@caldwellcountync.org; Staff 19 (MLS 5, Non-MLS 14)
Founded 1930. Pop 77,415; Circ 305,342
Library Holdings: CDs 1,500; DVDs 500; Bk Vols 100,000; Per Subs 399; Talking Bks 3,112; Videos 4,018
Subject Interests: Caldwell county hist
Automation Activity & Vendor Info: (Circulation) Evergreen; (OPAC) Evergreen
Wireless access
Open Mon, Tues & Thurs 9-8, Wed, Fri & Sat 9-5:30
Friends of the Library Group
Branches: 2
GRANITE FALLS PUBLIC, 24 S Main St, Granite Falls, 28630, SAN 312-8466. Tel: 828-396-7703. FAX: 828-396-2723. *Br Librn,* Susan Clark
Library Holdings: CDs 300; DVDs 300; Large Print Bks 1,000; Bk Vols 21,426; Per Subs 92; Talking Bks 300
Open Mon-Wed, Fri & Sat 9-5:30, Thurs 11:30-8
Friends of the Library Group

HUDSON PUBLIC, 530 Central St, Hudson, 28638-1230, SAN 324-5802. Tel: 828-728-4207. FAX: 828-726-1325. *Br Librn,* Susan Clark
Library Holdings: CDs 300; DVDs 300; Large Print Bks 1,000; Bk Vols 20,326; Talking Bks 300; Videos 300
Open Mon & Wed-Fri 9-5:30, Tues 11:30-8
Friends of the Library Group

LEXINGTON

P DAVIDSON COUNTY PUBLIC LIBRARY SYSTEM*, 602 S Main St, 27292. SAN 312-9055. Tel: 336-242-2040. Administration Tel: 336-242-2063. Information Services Tel: 336-242-2005. FAX: 336-248-4122. Administration FAX: 336-249-8161. Web Site: www.co.davidson.nc.us/library. *Libr Dir,* Sheila Killebrew; E-mail: sheila.killebrew@davidsoncountync.gov; *Asst Libr Dir,* Susan Craven; E-mail: susan.craven@davidsoncountync.gov; Staff 44 (MLS 9, Non-MLS 35)
Founded 1928
Library Holdings: Per Subs 101
Special Collections: Literature (Gerald R Johnson & Richard Walser Colls); North Carolina Coll, bks, microfilm. US Document Depository
Subject Interests: Genealogy, Local hist
Automation Activity & Vendor Info: (Acquisitions) Evergreen; (Cataloging) Evergreen; (Circulation) Evergreen; (ILL) OCLC Online; (OPAC) Evergreen; (Serials) EBSCO Online
Wireless access
Function: 24/7 Electronic res, 24/7 Online cat, 3D Printer, Adult bk club, Adult literacy prog, After school storytime, AV serv, Govt ref serv, Homebound delivery serv, ILL available, Internet access, Magnifiers for reading, Online cat, Photocopying/Printing, Prog for adults, Prog for children & young adult, Ref serv available, Summer reading prog, Telephone ref, Wheelchair accessible, Workshops
Special Services for the Deaf - Bks on deafness & sign lang; Closed caption videos; High interest/low vocabulary bks
Special Services for the Blind - Accessible computers; Aids for in-house use; Assistive/Adapted tech devices, equip & products; Bks on CD; Copier with enlargement capabilities; Home delivery serv; Large print bks; Magnifiers; Playaways (bks on MP3)
Open Mon-Fri 8:30-5
Friends of the Library Group
Branches: 4
DENTON PUBLIC, 310 W Salisbury St, Denton, 27239-6944. (Mail add: PO Box 578, Denton, 27239-0578), SAN 312-8075. Tel: 336-859-2215. FAX: 336-859-5006. *Br Mgr,* Susan Craven; E-mail: susan.craven@davidsoncountync.gov; Staff 4 (MLS 1, Non-MLS 3)
Founded 1946
Function: 24/7 Electronic res, 24/7 Online cat, Adult bk club, Online cat
Open Mon & Thurs 9-8, Tues, Wed & Fri 9-5:30, Sat 10-2
NORTH DAVIDSON PUBLIC, 559 Critcher Dr, Welcome, 27374. (Mail add: PO Box 1749, Welcome, 27374-1749), SAN 313-0304. Tel: 336-242-2050. FAX: 336-731-3719. *Br Mgr,* Christina Adams; E-mail: christina.adams@davidsoncountync.gov; Staff 4 (MLS 1, Non-MLS 3)
Founded 1955
Function: 24/7 Electronic res, Adult bk club, Online cat
Open Mon 9:30-8, Tues-Thurs 9:30-7, Fri 9-5:30, Sat 10-2
Friends of the Library Group
THOMASVILLE PUBLIC, 14 Randolph St, Thomasville, 27360-4638, SAN 313-0142. Tel: 336-474-2690. FAX: 336-472-4690. *Asst Dir,* Sarah Hudson; E-mail: sarah.hudson@davidsoncountync.gov; Staff 11 (MLS 2, Non-MLS 9)
Founded 1928
Special Collections: Gerald R Johnson Coll; History of Thomasville; Wint Capel
Function: 24/7 Electronic res, Adult bk club, Online cat
Open Mon-Thurs 9-8, Fri 9-5:30, Sat 9:30-3
Friends of the Library Group
WEST DAVIDSON PUBLIC, 246 Tyro School Rd, 27295-6006. Tel: 336-853-4800. FAX: 336-853-4803. *Br Mgr,* Jan Beck; E-mail: jan.beck@davidsoncountync.gov; Staff 3 (MLS 1, Non-MLS 2)
Founded 2000
Function: 24/7 Electronic res, 24/7 Online cat
Open Mon & Thurs 9-8, Tues & Wed 9-6, Fri 9-5:30, Sat 10-2
Bookmobiles: 1. Tech, Jennifer Ward. Bk titles 5,264

LILLINGTON

P HARNETT COUNTY PUBLIC LIBRARY*, 601 S Main St, 27546-6107. (Mail add: PO Box 1149, 27546-1149), SAN 354-9429. Tel: 910-893-3446. FAX: 910-893-3001. Web Site: harnett.libguides.com/library. *Dir,* Angela McCauley; E-mail: amccauley@harnett.org; *Ch,* Autumn Landers; *Info Syst Librn,* Joanna Cox; *Adult Serv, Ref Librn,* Laura Bright; E-mail: lbright@harnett.org; *Tech Serv Librn,* Kim Sirois; E-mail: ksirois@harnett.org; *Circ Mgr,* Heather Giunta; *Adult Outreach/Prog Coordr,* Ardith Eyring; *Outreach & Children's Serv,* Michelle Wester; Staff 9 (MLS 3, Non-MLS 6)
Founded 1941. Pop 101,737; Circ 337,529
Library Holdings: AV Mats 9,101; High Interest/Low Vocabulary Bk Vols 30; Bk Vols 200,000; Per Subs 412; Talking Bks 5,182
Special Collections: Photo Coll
Subject Interests: Cooking, Local hist
Automation Activity & Vendor Info: (Acquisitions) Infor Library & Information Solutions; (Cataloging) Infor Library & Information Solutions; (Circulation) Infor Library & Information Solutions; (OPAC) Infor Library & Information Solutions; (Serials) Infor Library & Information Solutions
Wireless access
Function: Homebound delivery serv
Partic in North Carolina Libraries for Virtual Education
Open Mon-Thurs 9-8, Fri 9-5, Sat 9-1
Friends of the Library Group
Branches: 5
ANDERSON CREEK PUBLIC, 914 Anderson Creek School Rd, Bunn Level, 28323. Tel: 910-814-4012. FAX: 910-814-0262. E-mail: libstaff@harnett.org. *Dir,* Angela McCauley
Founded 1998
Open Tues & Thurs 4-8, Sat 10-2
Friends of the Library Group
ANGIER PUBLIC, 28 N Raleigh St, Angier, 27501-6073, SAN 354-9453. Tel: 919-639-4413. Web Site: www.angier.org/angier-library. *Br Head,* Amanda Davis; E-mail: abdavis@angier.org
Library Holdings: Bk Vols 21,000
Open Mon, Wed & Fri 9-5, Tues & Thurs 9-6:30
Friends of the Library Group
COATS BRANCH, 29 E Main St, Coats, 27521. (Mail add: PO Box 675, Coats, 27521), SAN 354-9488. Tel: 910-230-1944. E-mail: coatslibrary@harnett.org. Web Site: www.coatsnc.org/library. *Libr Supvr,* Teresa Brown; Staff 1 (Non-MLS 1)
Library Holdings: Bk Vols 5,033
open Mon-Thurs 10-6, Fri 10-3
Friends of the Library Group
DUNN PUBLIC, 110 E Divine St, Dunn, 28334, SAN 312-8113. Tel: 910-892-2899. Administration Tel: 910-892-2560. FAX: 910-892-8385. Web Site: www.dunn-nc.org/library. *Dir,* Michael B Williams; E-mail: mwilliams@dunn-nc.org; *Prog Spec,* Paula Avery; E-mail: pavery@dunn-nc.org; *Prog Spec,* Patsy Baggett; E-mail: pbaggett@dunn-nc.org; *Prog Spec,* Susan James; E-mail: sjames@dunn-nc.org; Staff 4 (MLS 1, Non-MLS 3)
Founded 1921. Pop 24,908; Circ 66,484
Jul 2013-Jun 2014 Income $243,200. Mats Exp $38,500, Books $35,000, Per/Ser (Incl. Access Fees) $3,500. Sal $137,900
Library Holdings: Audiobooks 300; DVDs 800; Large Print Bks 1,650; Bk Vols 25,000; Per Subs 64
Function: Adult bk club, Art exhibits, Bks on CD, Children's prog, Computers for patron use, Free DVD rentals, Online cat, Photocopying/Printing, Preschool reading prog, Printer for laptops & handheld devices, Prog for adults, Prog for children & young adult, Ref serv available, Scanner, Story hour, Summer reading prog, Tax forms, Telephone ref
Open Mon-Wed 9-6, Thurs 11-8, Fri 9-5, Sat 9-1; Tues (Summer) 9-6, Thurs 11-6
Friends of the Library Group
ERWIN PUBLIC, 110 West F St, Erwin, 28339. (Mail add: PO Box 459, Erwin, 28339), SAN 354-9518. Tel: 910-897-5780. FAX: 910-897-4474. Web Site: www.erwin-nc.org/departments-services/library. *Librn,* Jeanne L Serrette; E-mail: jserrette@erwin-nc.org
Founded 1973. Pop 4,697; Circ 59,342
Library Holdings: Bk Vols 8,400; Per Subs 15
Open Mon-Fri 9-5
Friends of the Library Group

LINCOLNTON

P LINCOLN COUNTY PUBLIC LIBRARY*, Charles R Jonas Library, 306 W Main St, 28092. SAN 312-9063. Tel: 704-735-8044. FAX: 704-732-9042. Web Site: www.mylincolnlibrary.org. *Dir,* Jennifer Sackett; E-mail: jsackett@lincolncounty.org; *Mgr, Prog & Outreach,* Phillip Overholtzer; E-mail: poverholtzer@lincolncounty.org; *Br Supvr,* Helena Brittain; E-mail: hbrittain@lincolncounty.org; Staff 16 (MLS 1, Non-MLS 15)
Founded 1925. Pop 78,265; Circ 329,072
Library Holdings: AV Mats 12,337; Bk Vols 121,121
Special Collections: Lincoln County Historical & Genealogical Coll
Automation Activity & Vendor Info: (Circulation) Innovative Interfaces, Inc; (OPAC) Innovative Interfaces, Inc; (Serials) Innovative Interfaces, Inc
Open Mon, Tues & Thurs 9-9, Wed 10-6, Fri & Sat 9-6
Friends of the Library Group
Branches: 2
FLORENCE SOULE SHANKLIN MEMORIAL, 7837 Fairfield Forest Rd, Denver, 28037, SAN 329-5885. Tel: 704-483-3589. FAX: 704-483-8317. *Br Mgr,* Pamela Sweezy; E-mail: psweezy@lincolncounty.org; Staff 4 (MLS 4)

Founded 1980. Circ 113,790
Open Mon 10-8, Tues, Thurs & Fri 9-6, Wed 10-6, Sat 10-2
Friends of the Library Group
WEST LINCOLN, 5545 W Hwy 27, Vale, 28168. Tel: 704-276-9946. FAX: 704-276-1243. *Br Mgr,* Position Currently Open
Founded 2002. Circ 31,421
Function: 24/7 Electronic res, 24/7 Online cat, 3D Printer, Adult bk club, Bk club(s), Bks on CD, Children's prog, Computer training, Computers for patron use, Electronic databases & coll, Free DVD rentals, Holiday prog, ILL available, Internet access, Life-long learning prog for all ages, Mango lang, Movies, Online cat, Preschool reading prog, Prog for adults, Prog for children & young adult, STEM programs, Story hour, Tax forms, Teen prog
Open Mon 10-8, Tues-Fri 10-6, Sat 10-1
Friends of the Library Group
Bookmobiles: 1

LOUISBURG

P FRANKLIN COUNTY LIBRARY*, Louisburg Main Library, 906 N Main St, 27549-2199. SAN 354-9542. Tel: 919-496-2111. Interlibrary Loan Service Tel: 919-496-6764. FAX: 919-496-1339. Web Site: www.franklincountync.us/services/library. *Dir,* Holt Kornegay; E-mail: HKornegay@franklincountync.us; *Ad, Ref Serv Librn,* Scott Mumford; *Tech Serv,* Bill Morrison; *YA Serv, Youth Serv,* Christy Allen; Staff 16 (MLS 2, Non-MLS 14)
Founded 1937. Pop 50,000
Library Holdings: Bk Vols 105,000; Per Subs 183
Wireless access
Function: ILL available, Internet access, Photocopying/Printing, Prog for children & young adult, Ref serv available, Summer reading prog, Wheelchair accessible
Open Mon-Fri 10-7, Sat 10-5
Restriction: Open to pub for ref & circ; with some limitations
Friends of the Library Group
Branches: 3
BUNN BRANCH, 610 Main St, Bunn, 27508, SAN 375-3336. Tel: 919-496-6764. FAX: 919-497-5821. *Br Supvr,* Alyce Kidd
Library Holdings: Bk Vols 5,000; Per Subs 20
Open Mon-Fri 12-7
FRANKLINTON BRANCH, Nine W Mason St, Franklinton, 27525, SAN 354-9577. Tel: 919-494-2736. FAX: 919-494-2466. *Br Supvr,* Alyce Kidd
Library Holdings: Bk Vols 4,000; Per Subs 20
Open Mon-Fri 12-7
YOUNGSVILLE BRANCH, 218 US 1A Hwy S, Youngsville, 27596, SAN 354-9607. Tel: 919-556-1612. FAX: 919-556-9633. *Br Supvr,* Alyce Kidd
Open Mon-Fri 10-7, Sat 1-5
Friends of the Library Group
Bookmobiles: 1

J LOUISBURG COLLEGE*, Cecil W Robbins Library, 501 N Main St, 27549-7704. SAN 312-9071. Tel: 919-497-3269. Administration Tel: 919-497-3217. FAX: 919-496-5444. Web Site: www.louisburg.edu/academics/library. *Dir, Libr Serv,* Kristine M Jones; E-mail: kjones@louisburg.edu; *Instruction Coordr, Ref Librn,* Ilishe Mikos; Tel: 919-497-3349, E-mail: imikos@louisburg.edu; Staff 6 (MLS 3, Non-MLS 3)
Founded 1890. Enrl 690; Fac 40
Library Holdings: Bk Titles 51,000; Per Subs 55
Special Collections: Louisburg College & Town Archives, mixed
Subject Interests: Relig in Am
Automation Activity & Vendor Info: (Cataloging) TLC (The Library Corporation); (Circulation) TLC (The Library Corporation); (Course Reserve) TLC (The Library Corporation); (ILL) TLC (The Library Corporation); (Media Booking) TLC (The Library Corporation); (OPAC) TLC (The Library Corporation)
Wireless access
Partic in North Carolina Libraries for Virtual Education
Open Mon-Thurs 8:30am-11pm, Fri 8:30-4, Sat 1-4, Sun 5pm-9pm

LOWGAP

P LOWGAP PUBLIC LIBRARY*, 9070 W Pine St, 27024. SAN 376-6837. Tel: 336-352-3000. FAX: 336-352-3000. Web Site: nwrl.org/friendly.php?s=LowgapPublicLibrary. *Librn,* Ronda Galyean; E-mail: rondagalyean@gmail.com
Library Holdings: Bk Vols 6,500; Per Subs 50
Automation Activity & Vendor Info: (Cataloging) SirsiDynix; (Circulation) SirsiDynix
Wireless access
Function: Bks on CD, Children's prog, ILL available, Photocopying/Printing
Mem of Northwestern Regional Library
Open Tues & Thurs 2:30-8

LUMBERTON

J ROBESON COMMUNITY COLLEGE*, Anne Moss-Biggs Library, Bldg 4, 5160 Fayetteville Rd, 28360-2158. (Mail add: PO Box 1420, 28359), SAN 312-9098. Tel: 910-272-3700, Ext 3321. FAX: 910-618-5685. E-mail: library@robeson.edu. Web Site: www.robeson.edu/rcclib. *Dir,* Maryellen O'Brien; Tel: 910-272-3324, E-mail: mobrien@robeson.edu; Staff 3 (MLS 3)
Founded 1965. Enrl 2,100; Fac 50
Library Holdings: Bk Titles 18,000; Per Subs 112
Subject Interests: Vocational tech
Automation Activity & Vendor Info: (Acquisitions) SirsiDynix; (Cataloging) SirsiDynix; (Circulation) SirsiDynix; (Course Reserve) SirsiDynix; (ILL) SirsiDynix; (OPAC) SirsiDynix; (Serials) SirsiDynix
Open Mon-Thurs 7:30am-8pm, Fri 7:30-3

P ROBESON COUNTY PUBLIC LIBRARY*, 101 N Chestnut St, 28359. (Mail add: PO Box 988, 28359-0988), SAN 354-9631. Tel: 910-738-4859. FAX: 910-739-8321. E-mail: info@robesoncountylibrary.org. Web Site: robesoncountylibrary.org. *Dir,* Katie Fountain; E-mail: kfountain@robesoncountylibrary.org; *Sr Admin Assoc,* Carmela Williams; E-mail: cwilliams@robesoncountylibrary.org; Staff 19 (MLS 3, Non-MLS 16)
Founded 1967. Pop 130,000; Circ 198,083
Library Holdings: AV Mats 10,429; Bk Titles 92,000; Bk Vols 142,846; Per Subs 129
Special Collections: Genealogy (Biggs Coll, Hodgin Coll, Rhodes Coll); Local History (McLean Coll)
Subject Interests: Indian mats
Automation Activity & Vendor Info: (Cataloging) Innovative Interfaces, Inc; (Circulation) Innovative Interfaces, Inc; (OPAC) Innovative Interfaces, Inc
Wireless access
Open Mon, Wed, Fri & Sat 9-6, Tues & Thurs 9-9
Friends of the Library Group
Branches: 6
DONALD A BONNER PUBLIC LIBRARY, 113 E Main St, Rowland, 28383, SAN 328-6770. Tel: 910-422-3996. *Br Mgr,* Octavia Locklear; E-mail: olocklear@robesoncountylibrary.org; Staff 1 (Non-MLS 1)
Open Mon-Fri 2-6
HECTOR MACLEAN PUBLIC LIBRARY, 106 S Main St, Fairmont, 28340, SAN 354-9682. Tel: 910-628-9331. FAX: 910-628-9331. *Br Mgr,* Audrey McNeese; E-mail: amcneese@robesoncountylibrary.org; Staff 1 (Non-MLS 1)
Library Holdings: Bk Titles 4,000
Open Mon-Fri 1-6
Friends of the Library Group
ANNIE HUBBARD MCEACHERN PUBLIC, 221 W Broad St, Saint Pauls, 28384, SAN 312-9888. Tel: 910-865-4002. FAX: 910-865-4002. *Br Mgr,* Joy Andrews; E-mail: jandrews@robesoncountylibrary.org; Staff 2 (Non-MLS 2)
Pop 2,130; Circ 5,304
Library Holdings: Bk Vols 20,000; Per Subs 25
Open Mon-Thurs 10-12 & 1-6, Fri 10-1
MCMILLAN MEMORIAL LIBRARY, 205 E Second Ave, Red Springs, 28377, SAN 312-9675. Tel: 910-843-4205. *Br Mgr,* Zach Bullard; E-mail: zbullard@robesoncountylibrary.org
Founded 1964. Pop 5,000; Circ 12,000
Library Holdings: Bk Titles 13,000; Per Subs 24
Open Mon-Fri 2-6
GILBERT PATTERSON MEMORIAL, 210 N Florence St, Maxton, 28364, SAN 354-9666. Tel: 910-844-3884. FAX: 910-844-3884. *Br Mgr,* Cynthia Lester; E-mail: clester@robesoncountylibrary.org; Staff 1 (Non-MLS 1)
Library Holdings: Bk Vols 6,500
Open Mon-Fri 11-6
Friends of the Library Group
PEMBROKE PUBLIC, 413 S Blaine St, Pembroke, 28372. (Mail add: PO Box 1295, Pembroke, 28372), SAN 373-1839. Tel: 910-521-1554. FAX: 910-521-1554. *Br Mgr,* Tammy Vincent; E-mail: tvincent@robesoncountylibrary.org; Staff 2 (Non-MLS 2)
Open Mon-Wed & Fri 9-12 & 1-6, Thurs 1-8
Bookmobiles: 1

MANTEO

G CAPE HATTERAS NATIONAL SEASHORE*, Technical Library, 1401 National Park Dr, 27954-9708. SAN 312-911X. Tel: 252-473-2111. FAX: 252-473-2595. Web Site: nps.gov/caha. *Library Contact,* Jami Lanier; Tel: 252-473-2111, Ext 9021, E-mail: Jami_P_Lanier@nps.gov
Founded 1955
Library Holdings: Bk Titles 4,200; Per Subs 10

Special Collections: Cape Hatteras National Seashore; Fort Raleigh NHS; Wright Brothers NMEM. Oral History; US Document Depository
Subject Interests: Hist, Natural hist of NC Outer Banks
Open Mon-Fri 9-4

P DARE COUNTY LIBRARY*, 700 N Hwy 64-264, 27954. (Mail add: PO Box 1000, 27954), SAN 354-9690. Tel: 252-473-2372. FAX: 252-473-6034. Web Site: www.darenc.com/departments/libraries. *Dir,* Jonathan Wark; E-mail: jwark@earlibrary.org; *Mgr,* Veronica Brickhouse; E-mail: vbrickhouse@earlibrary.org; *Ch,* Tammy Batschelet; E-mail: tbatschelet@earlibrary.org; Staff 2 (MLS 2)
Founded 1935. Pop 36,000; Circ 230,000
Library Holdings: Bk Titles 85,000; Per Subs 100
Special Collections: North Carolina & Dare County Maps
Automation Activity & Vendor Info: (Cataloging) TLC (The Library Corporation); (Circulation) TLC (The Library Corporation); (Course Reserve) TLC (The Library Corporation); (ILL) OCLC Connexion; (OPAC) TLC (The Library Corporation)
Wireless access
Mem of East Albemarle Regional Library
Open Mon & Thurs 10-7, Tues, Wed & Fri 10-5:30, Sat 10-4
Branches: 2
HATTERAS BRANCH, PO Box 309, Hatteras, 27943-0309, SAN 354-9720. Tel: 252-986-2385. FAX: 252-986-2952. *Br Mgr,* Helen Hudson
Open Tues, Thurs & Fri 9:30-5:30, Wed 1-7, Sat 9:30-12:30
KILL DEVIL HILLS BRANCH, 400 Mustian St, Kill Devil Hills, 27948, SAN 370-5994. Tel: 252-441-4331. FAX: 252-441-0608. *Br Mgr,* Kathy Lassiter; *Ref Serv,* Naomi Rhodes
Open Mon, Thurs & Fri 9-5:30, Tues & Wed 10-7, Sat 10-4

G NORTH CAROLINA OFFICE OF ARCHIVES & HISTORY, Outer Banks History Center, One Festival Park Blvd, 27954. (Mail add: PO Box 250, 27954-0250), SAN 373-1138. Tel: 252-473-2655. FAX: 252-473-1483. E-mail: obhc@ncdcr.gov. Web Site: archives.ncdcr.gov/researchers/outer-banks-history-center. *Asst Curator, Cataloger, Librn,* Sarah Downing; E-mail: sarah.downing@ncdcr.gov; *Archivist,* Tama Creef; E-mail: tama.creef@ncdcr.gov; *Archivist,* Stuart Parks; E-mail: stuart.parks@ncdcr.gov; Staff 4 (MLS 1, Non-MLS 3)
Founded 1988
Library Holdings: Bk Vols 30,000; Per Subs 75
Special Collections: African American History; Civil War History; Colonial American History; Early Exploration; Lighthouses; Maritime History & Culture; US Life Saving Service, Shipwrecks; Wright Brothers. Oral History
Subject Interests: Civil War, Genealogy, Local hist, Maritime hist, Native Am, Oral hist, Tourism, Weather
Open Mon-Fri 9-5
Restriction: Non-circulating
Friends of the Library Group
Branches:
NORTH CAROLINA MARITIME MUSEUM, CHARLES R MCNEILL MARITIME LIBRARY, 315 Front St, Beaufort, 28516, SAN 374-9894. Tel: 252-504-7740. E-mail: maritime@ncmail.net. *Librn,* Tessa Johnstone; E-mail: tessa.johnstone@ncdcr.gov
Founded 1985
Library Holdings: Bk Titles 4,000; Per Subs 27; Spec Interest Per Sub 26
Subject Interests: Boatbuilding, Maritime hist, Natural hist, NC hist
Function: Res libr
Open Mon-Fri 9-5, Sat 10-5, Sun 1-5
Restriction: Non-circulating

MARION

P MCDOWELL COUNTY PUBLIC LIBRARY, 90 W Court St, 28752. SAN 354-9755. Tel: 828-652-3858. FAX: 828-652-2098. E-mail: mcdowellcountypubliclibrary@yahoo.com. Web Site: www.mcdowellpubliclibrary.org. *Libr Dir,* Marlan Brinkley, Jr; E-mail: librarydirector@mcdowellpubliclibrary.org; Staff 13 (MLS 1, Non-MLS 12)
Founded 1960. Pop 45,000
Library Holdings: Bk Titles 53,000; Bk Vols 109,546; Per Subs 252
Subject Interests: Genealogy, Local hist
Automation Activity & Vendor Info: (Acquisitions) Evergreen; (Cataloging) Evergreen; (Circulation) Evergreen; (OPAC) Evergreen
Wireless access
Open Mon, Wed & Fri 10-5:30, Tues & Thurs 10-7, Sat 11-5
Friends of the Library Group
Branches: 1
MARION DAVIS MEMORIAL BRANCH / OLD FORT LIBRARY, 65 Mitchell St, Old Fort, 28762, SAN 354-978X. Tel: 828-668-7111. FAX: 828-668-4013. *Br Mgr,* Carmen Melinn; E-mail: cmelinn@mcdowellpubliclibrary.org; Staff 2 (Non-MLS 2)
Founded 1960
Open Tues & Thurs 10-7, Wed & Fri 10-5:30, Sat 11-5
Friends of the Library Group

J MCDOWELL TECHNICAL COMMUNITY COLLEGE LIBRARY*, 54 College Dr, 28752-8728. SAN 312-9136. Tel: 828-652-0401. Circulation Tel: 828-652-0604. Administration Tel: 828-652-0697. Web Site: www.mcdowelltech.edu. *Dir, Libr Serv,* Ramona DeAngelus; E-mail: rcdeangelus92@go.mcdowelltech.edu; Staff 3 (MLS 1, Non-MLS 2)
Founded 1964. Enrl 1,200; Fac 49; Highest Degree: Associate
Jul 2012-Jun 2013 Income $225,332. Mats Exp $31,623, Books $16,539, Per/Ser (Incl. Access Fees) $7,603, AV Mat $2,741, Electronic Ref Mat (Incl. Access Fees) $4,740. Sal $142,501 (Prof $66,792)
Library Holdings: AV Mats 8,572; CDs 23; DVDs 187; Bk Vols 28,789; Per Subs 121; Videos 1,011
Automation Activity & Vendor Info: (Cataloging) SirsiDynix; (Circulation) SirsiDynix; (Course Reserve) SirsiDynix; (ILL) SirsiDynix; (OPAC) SirsiDynix
Wireless access
Publications: Handbook (Online only)
Partic in Community Colleges Libraries in North Carolina; OCLC Online Computer Library Center, Inc
Open Mon-Thurs 8-7, Fri 8-1; Mon-Thurs (Summer) 8-7

MARS HILL

C MARS HILL UNIVERSITY, Renfro Library, 147 Bailey St, 28754. (Mail add: PO Box 6704, 28754), SAN 312-9144. Tel: 828-689-1244. Circulation Tel: 828-689-1518. Reference Tel: 828-689-1468. E-mail: library-staff@mhu.edu. Web Site: library.mhu.edu. *Dir, Libr Serv,* Kevin Mulhall; Tel: 828-689-1561, E-mail: kevin_mulhall@mhu.edu; Staff 8.5 (MLS 5, Non-MLS 3.5)
Founded 1856. Enrl 1,300; Fac 88; Highest Degree: Master
Library Holdings: AV Mats 3,990; e-books 277,900; e-journals 21,850; Microforms 178,000; Music Scores 4,628; Bk Vols 90,000; Per Subs 150
Special Collections: Folk Music (Bascom Lamar Lunsford Southern Appalachia Music); Southern Appalachia (Southern Appalachia Photo Archives)
Automation Activity & Vendor Info: (Acquisitions) Innovative Interfaces, Inc - Sierra; (Cataloging) Innovative Interfaces, Inc - Sierra; (Circulation) Innovative Interfaces, Inc - Sierra; (Course Reserve) Innovative Interfaces, Inc - Sierra; (OPAC) Innovative Interfaces, Inc - Sierra; (Serials) Innovative Interfaces, Inc - Sierra
Wireless access
Partic in Appalachian College Association; NC Asn of Independent Cols & Univs
Open Mon-Fri 9-5

MARSHALL

P MADISON COUNTY PUBLIC LIBRARY*, 1335 N Main St, 28753-6901. SAN 354-981X. Tel: 828-649-3741. FAX: 828-649-3504. Web Site: www.madisoncountylibrary.net. *Dir,* Kim Bellofatto; E-mail: kbellofatto@madisoncountync.gov; Staff 8 (MLS 1, Non-MLS 7)
Founded 1955. Pop 19,976; Circ 114,611
Library Holdings: Bk Vols 60,156; Per Subs 63; Talking Bks 3,762
Automation Activity & Vendor Info: (Cataloging) TLC (The Library Corporation); (Circulation) TLC (The Library Corporation); (OPAC) TLC (The Library Corporation)
Wireless access
Function: Homebound delivery serv, ILL available, Photocopying/Printing, Prog for adults, Prog for children & young adult, Spoken cassettes & CDs, Summer reading prog, Wheelchair accessible
Open Mon-Fri 9-6, Sat 9-2
Friends of the Library Group
Branches: 2
HOT SPRINGS BRANCH, 170 Bridge St, Hot Springs, 28743, SAN 354-9879. Tel: 828-622-3584. FAX: 828-622-3584. *Br Mgr,* Peggy Gorforth; E-mail: pgoforth@madisoncountync.gov
Library Holdings: AV Mats 201; CDs 90; DVDs 700; Large Print Bks 125; Bk Vols 5,464; Per Subs 20; Talking Bks 47; Videos 300
Open Mon-Fri 10-6, Sat 10-2
Friends of the Library Group
MARS HILL BRANCH, 25 Library St, Mars Hill, 28754-9783, SAN 354-9909. Tel: 828-689-5183. FAX: 828-689-5183. *Br Mgr,* Shawna Bryce; E-mail: sbryce@madisoncountync.gov
Library Holdings: AV Mats 999; Large Print Bks 1,615; Bk Vols 17,653; Per Subs 32; Talking Bks 290
Open Mon-Fri 9-6, Sat 9-2
Friends of the Library Group

MAURY

S NORTH CAROLINA DEPARTMENT OF CORRECTION*, Eastern Correctional Institution Library, PO Box 215, 28554-0215. Tel: 252-747-8101, Ext 2186. FAX: 252-747-5697. Web Site: www.ncdps.gov/adult-corrections/prisons/prison-facilities/eastern-correctional-institution.

Library Holdings: Bk Vols 8,500
Automation Activity & Vendor Info: (Cataloging) Book Systems
Restriction: Not open to pub

MISENHEIMER

C PFEIFFER UNIVERSITY*, G A Pfeiffer Library, 48380 US Hwy 52 N, 28109. (Mail add: PO Box 930, 28109-0930), SAN 312-9160. Tel: 704-463-3350. Interlibrary Loan Service Tel: 704-463-3353. Web Site: library.pfeiffer.edu. *Libr Dir, Ref & ILL Librn,* Lara B Little; E-mail: lara.little@pfeiffer.edu; *Archives Librn, Syst Adminr,* Jonathan C Hutchinson; Tel: 704-463-3361, E-mail: jonathan.hutchinson@pfeiffer.edu; *Acq, Coll Develop Librn,* Damion Miller; Tel: 704-463-3352, E-mail: damion.miller@pfeiffer.edu; *Coordr, Circ,* Cindy Newport; Tel: 704-463-3363, E-mail: cindy.newport@pfeiffer.edu; *Cat,* Jennifer Cease; Tel: 704-463-3351, E-mail: jennifer.cease@pfeiffer.edu; Staff 5.5 (MLS 4, Non-MLS 1.5)
Founded 1917. Enrl 1,100; Fac 70; Highest Degree: Master
Library Holdings: AV Mats 2,368; e-books 180,000; Electronic Media & Resources 83; Bk Vols 111,000; Per Subs 200
Special Collections: Pfeiffer University Archival Materials
Subject Interests: Am, Educ, English lit, Music, Relig studies
Automation Activity & Vendor Info: (Acquisitions) Innovative Interfaces, Inc; (Cataloging) Innovative Interfaces, Inc; (Circulation) Innovative Interfaces, Inc; (Course Reserve) Innovative Interfaces, Inc; (Discovery) SerialsSolutions; (OPAC) Innovative Interfaces, Inc
Wireless access
Function: 24/7 Electronic res, 24/7 Online cat, Archival coll, Computers for patron use, Distance learning, E-Readers, Electronic databases & coll, ILL available, Internet access, Magazines, Microfiche/film & reading machines, Music CDs, Online cat, Online info literacy tutorials on the web & in blackboard, Online ref, Photocopying/Printing, Ref & res, Telephone ref
Partic in Carolina Consortium; North Carolina Libraries for Virtual Education
Restriction: Limited access for the pub, Non-circulating of rare bks
Friends of the Library Group
Departmental Libraries:
PFEIFFER LIBRARY AT CHARLOTTE, 1515 Mockingbird Lane, Charlotte, 28209, SAN 375-4324. Tel: 704-945-7305. FAX: 704-521-8617. *Dir of Info Support Serv, Charlotte Campus,* Jeri Brentlinger; E-mail: jeri.brentlinger@pfeiffer.edu
Highest Degree: Master
Library Holdings: Bk Vols 2,000; Per Subs 1
Subject Interests: Acctg, Bus admin, Christian educ, Criminal justice, Health admin, Liberal arts, Marriage & family therapy, Organizational mgt
Automation Activity & Vendor Info: (Serials) Innovative Interfaces, Inc
Open Mon-Thurs 12-10
Friends of the Library Group

MOCKSVILLE

P DAVIE COUNTY PUBLIC LIBRARY*, 371 N Main St, 27028-2115. SAN 354-9933. Tel: 336-753-6030. FAX: 336-751-1370. Web Site: www.daviecountync.gov/896/Public-Library. *Dir,* Derrick Wold; E-mail: dwold@daviecountync.gov; Staff 4 (MLS 4)
Founded 1943. Pop 40,970; Circ 147,088
Library Holdings: Audiobooks 3,908; DVDs 1,756; Large Print Bks 5,056; Bk Vols 69,271; Per Subs 116
Subject Interests: Local hist
Automation Activity & Vendor Info: (Cataloging) Evergreen; (Circulation) Evergreen; (OPAC) Evergreen
Wireless access
Publications: History of Davie County; The Historic Architecture of Davie County
Special Services for the Blind - Bks on cassette; Bks on CD; Large print bks; Low vision equip
Open Mon-Thurs 9-8:30, Fri 9-5:30, Sat 9-3, Sun 2-5
Friends of the Library Group
Branches: 1
COOLEEMEE BRANCH, 7796 Hwy 801 S, Cooleemee, 27014. (Mail add: PO Box 25, Cooleemee, 27014-0025). Tel: 336-284-2805. FAX: 336-284-2805. *Librn,* Jane Blue
Automation Activity & Vendor Info: (OPAC) SirsiDynix-iBistro
Open Mon-Fri 10-5

MONROE

P UNION COUNTY PUBLIC LIBRARY*, 316 E Windsor St, 28112. SAN 354-9992. Tel: 704-283-8184. FAX: 704-282-0657. TDD: 704-225-8554. Web Site: www.unioncountync.gov/library. *Libr Dir,* Nina Chaffin; E-mail: nina.chaffin@unioncountync.gov; *Asst Libr Dir,* Lindsey Shuford; E-mail: lindsey.shuford@unioncountync.gov; *Acq, Colls Librn,* Rachel Webb; E-mail: rachel.webb@unioncountync.gov; *Local Hist Librn,* Gypsy Houston; E-mail: gypsy.houston@unioncountync.gov; *Teen/Tech Librnb,* Stephanie Johnson; E-mail: stephanie.johnson@unioncountync.gov; *Circ Mgr,* Lizbeth Olivares; E-mail: lizbeth.olivares@unioncountync.gov; *Juv Serv Coordr,* Shelley Fearn; E-mail: shelley.fearn@unioncountync.gov; *Tech Coordr, Training Coordr,* Stephanie Wiley; E-mail: stephanie.wiley@unioncountync.gov. Subject Specialists: *Genealogy,* Gypsy Houston; Staff 64 (MLS 10, Non-MLS 54)
Founded 1930. Pop 138,928; Circ 646,976
Library Holdings: Audiobooks 6,997; CDs 5,203; DVDs 5,868; e-books 116; Large Print Bks 6,130; Bk Vols 191,640; Per Subs 330; Videos 2,040
Subject Interests: Genealogy, Local hist
Automation Activity & Vendor Info: (Cataloging) TLC (The Library Corporation); (Circulation) TLC (The Library Corporation); (OPAC) TLC (The Library Corporation)
Wireless access
Function: Adult bk club, Bilingual assistance for Spanish patrons, Bks on CD, CD-ROM, Children's prog, Computer training, Computers for patron use, Electronic databases & coll, Family literacy, Free DVD rentals, Music CDs, Online cat, Photocopying/Printing, Prog for adults, Prog for children & young adult, Ref serv available, Scanner, Story hour, Summer reading prog, Tax forms, Wheelchair accessible
Special Services for the Deaf - Bks on deafness & sign lang; High interest/low vocabulary bks; TDD equip; TTY equip
Special Services for the Blind - Assistive/Adapted tech devices, equip & products; Descriptive video serv (DVS); Home delivery serv; Large print bks; Talking bks
Open Mon-Thurs 9-7, Fri 9-6, Sat 1-5, Sun 2-5
Friends of the Library Group
Branches: 3
LOIS MORGAN EDWARDS MEMORIAL, 414 Hasty St, Marshville, 28103, SAN 355-0052. Tel: 704-624-2828. FAX: 704-624-2055.
Automation Activity & Vendor Info: (Acquisitions) TLC (The Library Corporation)
Open Mon & Tues 9-8, Wed & Thurs 9-7, Fri 9-6, Sat 9-5, Sun 2-5
Friends of the Library Group
UNION WEST REGIONAL, 123 Unionville-Indian Trail Rd, Indian Trail, 28079, SAN 355-0028. Tel: 704-821-7475. FAX: 704-821-4279. *Br Mgr,* Betsy Cullen; E-mail: bcullen@union.lib.nc.us
Open Mon & Tues 9-8, Wed & Thurs 9-7, Fri 9-6, Sat 9-5, Sun 2-5
Friends of the Library Group
WAXHAW BRANCH, 509 S Providence St, Waxhaw, 28173, SAN 355-0087. Tel: 704-843-3131. FAX: 704-843-5538. *Br Mgr,* Beth Myles; E-mail: bmyles@union.lib.nc.us
Open Mon & Thurs 9-8, Tues, Wed & Fri 9-6, Sat 9-5
Friends of the Library Group

MONTREAT

C MONTREAT COLLEGE*, L Nelson Bell Library, 310 Gaither Circle, 28757. (Mail add: PO Box 1297, 28757-1297), SAN 312-9187. Tel: 828-669-8012, Ext 3504. FAX: 828-350-2083. E-mail: reference@montreat.edu. Web Site: www.montreat.edu/mymontreat/library. *Dir,* Elizabeth Pearson; Tel: 828-669-8012, Ext 3502, E-mail: epearson@montreat.edu; *Electronic Res Librn,* Nathan King; Tel: 828-669-8012, Ext 3508, E-mail: nking@montreat.edu; *Instrul & Ref Librn,* Dr Phoebe Maa; Tel: 828-669-8012, Ext 3505, E-mail: phoebe.maa@montreat.edu; Staff 4 (MLS 3, Non-MLS 1)
Founded 1898. Enrl 800; Fac 44; Highest Degree: Master
Library Holdings: AV Mats 7,612; CDs 150; DVDs 150; e-books 132,470; Electronic Media & Resources 40; Microforms 117,155; Bk Vols 79,000; Per Subs 26
Special Collections: College Archives; Crosby Adams Music Coll
Subject Interests: Bus, Clinical mental health counseling, Environ educ, Outdoor educ, Psychol, Theol studies
Automation Activity & Vendor Info: (Acquisitions) Innovative Interfaces, Inc; (Cataloging) OCLC Connexion; (Circulation) Innovative Interfaces, Inc - Millennium; (ILL) OCLC WorldShare Interlibrary Loan; (OPAC) Innovative Interfaces, Inc - Millennium
Wireless access
Function: Adult bk club, Photocopying/Printing
Publications: Friends (Newsletter)
Partic in Appalachian College Association; Carolina Consortium; LYRASIS; OCLC Online Computer Library Center, Inc
Open Mon-Thurs (Winter) 8am-Midnight, Fri 8-5, Sat 1-5, Sun 2-11; Mon-Fri (Summer) 8-5
Friends of the Library Group

MOORESVILLE

P MOORESVILLE PUBLIC LIBRARY*, 304 S Main St, 28115. SAN 312-9195. Tel: 704-664-2927. FAX: 704-799-4106. *Dir,* Marian Lytle; E-mail: mlytle@mooresvillenc.gov; *Asst Dir,* Nancy Handy; E-mail: nhandy@ci.mooresville.nc.us; *Head, Circ,* Robin Howard; E-mail: rhoward@ci.mooresville.nc.us; *Head, Digital Serv, Tech Serv,* Chao Huang; E-mail: chuang@ci.mooresville.nc.us; *Youth Serv Librn,* Dara Cain; E-mail: dcain@ci.mooresville.nc.us; Staff 7 (MLS 7)

Founded 1894. Pop 35,156; Circ 500,000
Library Holdings: Audiobooks 6,831; DVDs 11,015; e-books 40,000; Large Print Bks 2,000; Bk Vols 117,477; Per Subs 165
Automation Activity & Vendor Info: (Cataloging) Horizon; (Circulation) Horizon; (Discovery) SirsiDynix; (OPAC) SirsiDynix
Wireless access
Function: 24/7 Electronic res, 24/7 Online cat, Activity rm, Adult bk club, After school storytime, Archival coll, Art exhibits, Audiobks on Playaways & MP3, Audiobks via web, Bk club(s), Bks on CD, Children's prog, Computers for patron use, Electronic databases & coll, ILL available, Internet access, Magazines, Mango lang, Meeting rooms, Online cat, Outreach serv, OverDrive digital audio bks, Photocopying/Printing, Preschool outreach, Printer for laptops & handheld devices, Prog for adults, Prog for children & young adult, Ref serv available, Story hour, Study rm, Summer reading prog, Teen prog
Open Mon-Thurs 9-9, Fri 9-6, Sat 10-3
Friends of the Library Group

MOREHEAD CITY

J CARTERET COMMUNITY COLLEGE LIBRARY*, Michael J Smith Bldg, 201 College Circle, 28557. SAN 312-9209. Tel: 252-222-6213. Reference Tel: 252-222-6247. FAX: 252-222-6219. E-mail: library@carteret.edu. Web Site: carteret.edu/library. *Dir,* Elizabeth Baker; Tel: 252-222-6216, E-mail: bakere@carteret.edu; *Ref Librn/Instrul Serv,* Eva Earles; E-mail: earlese@carteret.edu; Staff 4.5 (MLS 2, Non-MLS 2.5)
Founded 1965. Enrl 1,800; Fac 225; Highest Degree: Associate
Library Holdings: AV Mats 2,002; Bk Titles 18,182; Per Subs 31
Special Collections: Audiovisual; Law Library; Reference
Automation Activity & Vendor Info: (Cataloging) SirsiDynix-WorkFlows; (Circulation) SirsiDynix-WorkFlows; (OPAC) SirsiDynix-WorkFlows
Wireless access
Partic in Community Colleges Libraries in North Carolina
Open Mon-Thurs 8-7, Fri 8-4 (Fall & Spring); Mon-Thurs 8-5 (Summer)

MORGANTON

M BROUGHTON HOSPITAL*, John S McKee Jr Memorial Library, 1000 S Sterling St, 28655. SAN 372-4948. Tel: 828-433-2303. FAX: 828-433-2097. Web Site: www.ncdhhs.gov/divisions/dsohf/broughton-hospital. *Librn,* Karen Gilliam; Tel: 828-433-2111, E-mail: karen.gilliam@dhhs.nc.gov
Library Holdings: Bk Vols 1,100; Per Subs 35
Wireless access

P BURKE COUNTY PUBLIC LIBRARY*, 204 S King St, 28655-3535. SAN 312-9225. Tel: 828-764-9260. FAX: 828-433-1914. E-mail: refdesk@bcpls.org. Web Site: www.bcpls.org. *Dir,* Jim Wilson; Tel: 828-764-9276, E-mail: jwilson@bcpls.org; Staff 18 (MLS 3, Non-MLS 15)
Founded 1924. Pop 89,148; Circ 210,000
Library Holdings: Bk Vols 97,921; Per Subs 210
Special Collections: North Carolina History, bks, micro & VF. Oral History
Subject Interests: Art, Environ studies, Genealogy, Local hist
Wireless access
Publications: Brochure on services
Special Services for the Deaf - TDD equip
Open Mon & Wed 9-8, Tues, Thurs & Fri 9-6, Sat 9-5
Friends of the Library Group
Branches: 2
C B HILDEBRAND PUBLIC, 201 S Center St, Hildebran, 28637. (Mail add: PO Box 643, Hildebran, 28637), SAN 378-1798. Tel: 828-397-3600. FAX: 828-397-3600. *Br Mgr,* Betty Riley
Founded 1997
Open Mon 3-8, Tues-Fri 10-5, Sat 10-2
Friends of the Library Group
VALDESE BRANCH, 213 St Germain Ave SE, Valdese, 28690-2846, SAN 321-9283. Tel: 828-874-2421. FAX: 828-874-1211. *Br Mgr,* Betty Riley; E-mail: briley@bcpls.org
Open Mon & Wed 9-6, Tues & Thurs 9-8, Fri 12-6, Sat 9-5
Friends of the Library Group
Bookmobiles: 1

NORTH CAROLINA DEPARTMENT OF CORRECTION
S FOOTHILLS CORRECTIONAL INSTITUTION LIBRARY*, 5150 Western Ave, 28655. Tel: 828-438-5585. FAX: 828-438-6281. *Librn,* LeeAnn McRary
Library Holdings: Bk Vols 5,500; Per Subs 24
Automation Activity & Vendor Info: (Cataloging) Brodart; (Circulation) Brodart
Open Mon-Fri 8-10:45 & 1-3:45
S WESTERN YOUTH INSTITUTION LIBRARY*, 5155 Western Ave, 28655-9696. (Mail add: PO Box 1439, 28680-1439), SAN 372-5464. Tel: 828-438-6037, Ext 270. FAX: 828-438-6076. *Librn,* Bill Smith
Founded 1971
Library Holdings: Bk Vols 13,000; Per Subs 161
Special Collections: NC DOC Educational Services Video Coll
Automation Activity & Vendor Info: (Cataloging) Follett Software; (Circulation) Follett Software
Special Services for the Deaf - Bks on deafness & sign lang; High interest/low vocabulary bks

J WESTERN PIEDMONT COMMUNITY COLLEGE, Library & Academic Success Center (ASC), Phifer Hall, 1001 Burkemont Ave, 28655. SAN 312-9233. Tel: 828-448-6195. FAX: 828-448-6173. TDD: 828-438-6066. E-mail: library@wpcc.edu. Web Site: www.wpcc.edu/library. *Dean,* Ann Marie McNeely; E-mail: amcneely@wpcc.edu; *Libr Dir,* Nancy L Daniel; Tel: 828-448-3160, E-mail: ndaniel@wpcc.edu; *Circ Mgr,* Ruth Brisson; E-mail: rbrisson@wpcc.edu; Staff 5 (MLS 3, Non-MLS 2)
Founded 1966. Enrl 3,939; Fac 156; Highest Degree: Associate
Library Holdings: AV Mats 6,203; Bks on Deafness & Sign Lang 51; e-books 1,604; Bk Vols 42,105; Per Subs 167
Special Collections: Grace DiSanto Poetry Coll; Mark Twain (Dr Jean C Ervin Coll); Senator Sam J Ervin, Jr, Coll
Automation Activity & Vendor Info: (Cataloging) EOS International; (Circulation) EOS International; (ILL) OCLC; (OPAC) EOS International; (Serials) EOS International
Wireless access
Function: Art exhibits, Distance learning, Electronic databases & coll, ILL available, Wheelchair accessible
Publications: Learning Resources (Annual report); Library & Media Services for Faculty & Staff Handbook; Periodical Holdings (Serials catalog); Videotape Collection Catalog
Partic in Community College Libraries in North Carolina; NC Info Hwy; Northwest AHEC Library Information Network
Special Services for the Deaf - Bks on deafness & sign lang
Open Mon-Thurs 7:30am-8pm, Fri 7:30-5 (Winter); Mon-Thurs 8-7, Fri 8-2 (Summer)

MOUNT AIRY

P MOUNT AIRY PUBLIC LIBRARY*, 145 Rockford St, 27030-4759. SAN 312-9241. Tel: 336-789-5108. FAX: 336-786-5838. E-mail: mta@nwrl.org. Web Site: nwrl.org/friendly.php?s=MtAiryPublicLibrary. *Librn,* Pat Gwyn; E-mail: pgwyn@nwrl.org; *Asst Librn,* Tommie Smith; E-mail: tsmith@nwrl.org; Staff 7 (Non-MLS 7)
Founded 1930
Library Holdings: Bk Vols 57,500; Per Subs 25
Automation Activity & Vendor Info: (Acquisitions) SirsiDynix; (Cataloging) SirsiDynix; (Circulation) SirsiDynix; (OPAC) SirsiDynix-iBistro
Wireless access
Mem of Northwestern Regional Library
Open Mon-Thurs 8:30-8, Fri 8:30-5, Sat 10-1
Friends of the Library Group

MOUNT OLIVE

C UNIVERSITY OF MOUNT OLIVE, Moye Library, 646 James B Hunt Dr, 28365-1699. (Mail add: 634 Henderson St, 28365), SAN 312-9268. Tel: 919-658-7869. Toll Free Tel: 800-653-0854, Ext 1412. FAX: 919-658-8934. E-mail: library@umo.edu. Web Site: www.umo.edu/academics/library. *Dir, Libr Serv,* Pamela R Wood; Tel: 919-658-7753, E-mail: pwood@moc.edu; *Cat & Tech Serv Librn,* Heather Day; Tel: 919-299-4589, E-mail: hday@umo.edu; *Evening/Weekend Supvr,* Beth Rose; Tel: 919-658-4912, E-mail: nrose@umo.edu; *Access Serv,* Wes Warren; E-mail: jwarren@umo.edu; *Curator,* Gary Barefoot; Tel: 919-658-7869, Ext 1416, E-mail: gbarefoot@moc.edu; Staff 5 (MLS 3, Non-MLS 2)
Founded 1951. Enrl 3,700; Highest Degree: Master
Library Holdings: Bks on Deafness & Sign Lang 25; CDs 141; DVDs 161; e-books 11,056; Large Print Bks 17; Music Scores 34; Bk Titles 57,164; Bk Vols 66,375; Per Subs 3,755; Videos 345
Special Collections: Free Will Baptist History, bks, flm, micro, ms, pamphlets, clippings
Automation Activity & Vendor Info: (Cataloging) OCLC; (Circulation) OCLC; (Discovery) OCLC; (ILL) OCLC; (OPAC) OCLC Worldshare Management Services
Function: Electronic databases & coll, ILL available, Internet access, Movies, Online cat, Photocopying/Printing, Scanner, VHS videos
Partic in OCLC Online Computer Library Center, Inc
Open Mon-Thurs 8am-10pm, Fri 8-4, Sun 2-10 (Fall-Spring); Mon-Thurs 8-8, Fri 8-4 (Summer)

MURFREESBORO

C CHOWAN UNIVERSITY*, Whitaker Library, One University Pl, 27855. SAN 312-9276. Tel: 252-398-6212. FAX: 252-398-1301. E-mail: library@chowan.edu. Web Site: libguides.chowan.edu/home. *Univ Librn,* Georgia Williams; Tel: 252-398-6439, E-mail: willig@chowan.edu; *Assoc Dir, Libr Serv, Spec Coll,* Linda Hassell; Tel: 252-398-6586, E-mail:

hassel@chowan.edu; *Instruction Coordr, Ref Librn,* Sarah Bonner; Tel: 252-398-6533, E-mail: bonnes@chowan.edu; *Pub Serv Asst,* Deborah Baugham; Tel: 252-398-6202, E-mail: baughd@chowan.edu; *Pub Serv Asst,* Frances Cole; Tel: 252-398-6592, E-mail: frances@chowan.edu; *Tech Serv Asst,* William Metcalfe; Tel: 252-398-6271, E-mail: metcaw@chowan.edu; Staff 6.5 (MLS 3, Non-MLS 3.5)
Founded 1848. Enrl 1,400; Highest Degree: Master
Special Collections: McDowell Coll of Archives & Antiquities (Chowan & local history); Oscar Creech Baptist Coll; Subject Specific Coll for Educ Students & Music Students Housed in Teacher Resource Center & Daniel Hall Music Media Center
Automation Activity & Vendor Info: (Acquisitions) Innovative Interfaces, Inc; (Cataloging) Innovative Interfaces, Inc; (Circulation) Innovative Interfaces, Inc; (Course Reserve) Innovative Interfaces, Inc; (Discovery) EBSCO Discovery Service; (ILL) Innovative Interfaces, Inc; (OPAC) Innovative Interfaces, Inc; (Serials) Innovative Interfaces, Inc
Wireless access
Open Mon-Thurs 7:45am-11pm, Fri 7:45-4, Sat 10-4, Sun 2-11; Mon-Thurs (Summer) 8-5, Fri 8-4
Restriction: Open to pub for ref & circ; with some limitations
Friends of the Library Group

MURPHY

P MURPHY PUBLIC LIBRARY*, Nine Blumenthal St, 28906. SAN 312-9284. Tel: 828-837-2417. FAX: 828-837-6416. *Librn,* Jeffrey L Murphy; E-mail: jmurphy@nantahalalibrary.org; Staff 6 (MLS 1, Non-MLS 5)
Founded 1919. Circ 161,172
Library Holdings: Bk Vols 24,132; Per Subs 92
Subject Interests: Genealogy
Automation Activity & Vendor Info: (Acquisitions) TLC (The Library Corporation); (Cataloging) TLC (The Library Corporation); (Circulation) TLC (The Library Corporation); (OPAC) TLC (The Library Corporation)
Mem of Nantahala Regional Library
Open Mon-Wed & Fri 9-6, Thurs 9-9, Sat 9-2
Friends of the Library Group

P NANTAHALA REGIONAL LIBRARY*, 11 Blumenthal St, 28906. SAN 312-9292. Tel: 828-837-2025. FAX: 828-837-6416. Web Site: www.youseemore.com/Nantahala. *Dir,* Daphne Simmons; E-mail: dchildres@nantahalalibrary.org
Founded 1942. Pop 41,753; Circ 255,691
Library Holdings: Bk Vols 14,000; Per Subs 250
Special Collections: Cherokee Indian Coll
Wireless access
Function: ILL available, Photocopying/Printing, Prog for children & young adult, Summer reading prog
Member Libraries: Andrews Public Library; Graham County Public Library; Moss Memorial Library; Murphy Public Library
Partic in NC Online Libr Network; North Carolina Libraries for Virtual Education; OCLC Online Computer Library Center, Inc
Open Mon-Fri 8-4:30
Friends of the Library Group
Bookmobiles: 1

J TRI-COUNTY COMMUNITY COLLEGE*, Dr Carl D Dockery Library, 21 Campus Circle, 28906. SAN 312-9306. Tel: 828-835-4218, 828-837-6810. FAX: 828-837-0028. E-mail: library@tricountycc.edu. Web Site: www.tricountycc.edu/learning-resources/library. *Dir, Learning Res,* Rachel McLean; E-mail: rmclean@tricountycc.edu; *Librn,* Katrina Miller; E-mail: kmiller@tricountycc.edu; *Libr Tech,* Deborah Kenyon; E-mail: dkenyon@tricounty.cc.edu; Staff 2 (MLS 2)
Founded 1974. Enrl 1,193; Fac 60; Highest Degree: Associate
Library Holdings: Bk Titles 8,000; Per Subs 169
Automation Activity & Vendor Info: (Cataloging) SirsiDynix-WorkFlows; (Circulation) SirsiDynix; (Course Reserve) SirsiDynix-WorkFlows; (ILL) SirsiDynix-WorkFlows; (OPAC) SirsiDynix-iLink; (Serials) SirsiDynix-WorkFlows
Wireless access
Function: Audio & video playback equip for onsite use, Bks on cassette, Bks on CD, CD-ROM, Computers for patron use, Distance learning, Doc delivery serv, Electronic databases & coll, Internet access, Music CDs, Online cat, Orientations, Photocopying/Printing, Ref & res, Ref serv available, Scanner, Spoken cassettes & CDs, Spoken cassettes & DVDs, VHS videos
Partic in Community Colleges Libraries in North Carolina
Open Mon-Thurs 8-7, Fri 8-Noon
Restriction: Hospital employees & physicians only

NASHVILLE

P NASHVILLE PUBLIC LIBRARY*, Harold D Cooley Library, 114 W Church St, 27856. (Mail add: Drawer 987, 27856). Tel: 252-459-2106. FAX: 252-459-8819. Web Site: www.townofnashville.com/community/town-library. *Libr Dir,* Emily Enderle; E-mail: emily.enderle@townofnashvillenc.gov; Staff 1 (MLS 1)
Founded 1942
Library Holdings: AV Mats 650; Bk Vols 20,000; Per Subs 57; Talking Bks 250
Automation Activity & Vendor Info: (Cataloging) TLC (The Library Corporation); (Circulation) TLC (The Library Corporation); (OPAC) TLC (The Library Corporation)
Wireless access
Open Mon-Fri 9-6, Sat 9-3
Friends of the Library Group

NEW BERN

J CRAVEN COMMUNITY COLLEGE*, R C Godwin Memorial Library, 800 College Ct, 28562. SAN 312-9314. Tel: 252-638-7272. Interlibrary Loan Service Tel: 252-638-6421. E-mail: library@cravencc.edu. Web Site: www.cravencc.edu/library. *Dir, Libr Serv,* Wendy White; E-mail: whitew@cravencc.edu; Staff 2 (MLS 2)
Founded 1966. Enrl 1,150; Fac 75; Highest Degree: Associate
Jan 2017-Dec 2017. Mats Exp $39,973, Books $11,804, Per/Ser (Incl. Access Fees) $5,550, AV Mat $6,111, Electronic Ref Mat (Incl. Access Fees) $16,508. Sal $145,424
Library Holdings: DVDs 1,776; e-books 240,600; e-journals 22,000; Electronic Media & Resources 22,000; Bk Titles 17,065; Bk Vols 18,759; Per Subs 30
Automation Activity & Vendor Info: (Cataloging) SirsiDynix; (Circulation) SirsiDynix; (ILL) SirsiDynix; (OPAC) SirsiDynix
Wireless access
Partic in Community Colleges Libraries in North Carolina
Open Mon-Thurs 7:30am-8pm, Fri 8-2:30

P CRAVEN-PAMLICO-CARTERET REGIONAL LIBRARY SYSTEM*, 400 Johnson St, 28560. SAN 312-9322. Tel: 252-638-7800. FAX: 252-638-7817. Web Site: cpcrl.org. *Interim Dir,* Kat Clowers; E-mail: katherine.clowers@cpcrl.org; Staff 4 (MLS 4)
Founded 1962. Pop 163,753; Circ 598,496
Library Holdings: AV Mats 6,000; Bk Vols 260,000; Per Subs 200
Special Collections: Genealogy East North Carolina; North Carolina Coll
Automation Activity & Vendor Info: (Cataloging) Horizon; (Circulation) Horizon; (ILL) Horizon
Wireless access
Member Libraries: Carteret County Public Library; Cove City-Craven County Public Library; Havelock-Craven County Public Library; New Bern-Craven County Public Library; Pamlico County Public Library; Vanceboro Public Library
Open Mon-Thurs 9-9, Fri & Sat 9-6, Sun (Oct-May) 2-6
Friends of the Library Group
Bookmobiles: 2

P NEW BERN-CRAVEN COUNTY PUBLIC LIBRARY*, 400 Johnson St, 28560-4098. SAN 312-9330. Tel: 252-638-7800. Reference Tel: 252-638-7807. FAX: 252-638-7817. E-mail: librarian@nbccpl.org. Web Site: newbern.cpclib.org. *Head Librn,* Cassandra Hunsucker; *Ref Librn,* Wendy L Rosen; *Spec Coll Librn,* Victor T Jones, Jr; *Circ Supvr,* Joan Robbins; *Youth Serv Supvr,* Pam Jenkins; Staff 4 (MLS 4)
Founded 1906. Pop 27,650; Circ 244,522
Library Holdings: Bk Vols 99,821; Per Subs 223
Special Collections: North Carolina Coll
Automation Activity & Vendor Info: (OPAC) TLC (The Library Corporation)
Wireless access
Function: 24/7 Online cat, Archival coll, Art exhibits, Bk club(s), Bks on CD, Children's prog, Computer training, Computers for patron use, Electronic databases & coll, ILL available, Internet access, Large print keyboards, Magazines, Magnifiers for reading, Mail & tel request accepted, Mango lang, Meeting rooms, Movies, Music CDs, Notary serv, OverDrive digital audio bks, Photocopying/Printing, Preschool reading prog, Prog for adults, Prog for children & young adult, Ref serv available, Story hour, Study rm, Summer reading prog, Tax forms, Telephone ref, Wheelchair accessible, Writing prog
Mem of Craven-Pamlico-Carteret Regional Library System
Special Services for the Deaf - Staff with knowledge of sign lang
Special Services for the Blind - Bks on CD; Large print bks; Magnifiers
Open Mon-Thurs 9-9, Fri & Sat 9-6, Sun (Fall-Spring) 2-6
Friends of the Library Group

S TRYON PALACE*, Gertrude Carraway Research Library, 529 S Front St, 28562-5614. (Mail add: PO Box 1007, 28563-1007), SAN 325-8009. Tel: 252-639-3500, 252-639-3593. FAX: 252-514-4876. E-mail: info@tryonpalace.org. Web Site: www.tryonpalace.org. *Research Historian,* Lindy Cummings; E-mail: lindy.cummings@ncdcr.gov; Staff 1 (Non-MLS 1)
Founded 1959
Library Holdings: Bk Titles 4,750

Subject Interests: Archit, Decorative art, Gardening, Mus studies, NC hist
Automation Activity & Vendor Info: (Cataloging) OCLC Connexion
Function: Microfiche/film & reading machines, Res libr, Wheelchair accessible
Restriction: Circulates for staff only, In-house use for visitors, Non-circulating, Open to pub by appt only

NEWLAND

P AVERY COUNTY MORRISON PUBLIC LIBRARY*, 150 Library Pl, 28657. (Mail add: PO Box 250, 28657), SAN 312-9349. Tel: 828-733-9393. FAX: 828-733-9393. E-mail: acpl@amyregionallibrary.org. Web Site: www.amyregionallibrary.org. *Head Librn,* Phyllis Burroughs; *Asst Librn,* Debbie McLean
Pop 17,946
Library Holdings: Large Print Bks 500; Bk Vols 10,000; Per Subs 30; Talking Bks 300
Special Collections: Robert Morrison Reference Coll
Subject Interests: Genealogy, Local hist
Automation Activity & Vendor Info: (Cataloging) TLC (The Library Corporation); (Circulation) TLC (The Library Corporation)
Wireless access
Mem of Avery-Mitchell-Yancey Regional Library System
Open Mon & Tues 9-8, Wed-Fri 9-5, Sat 10-1
Bookmobiles: 1

NEWTON

P CATAWBA COUNTY LIBRARY*, 115 West C St, 28658. SAN 355-0117. Tel: 828-465-8664. FAX: 828-465-8983. E-mail: mylibrary@catawbacountync.gov. Web Site: www.catawbacountync.gov/library/. *Dir,* Suzanne White; E-mail: Suzanne@catawbacountync.gov; *Asst Dir,* Siobhan Loendorf; Tel: 828-465-8292, E-mail: sloendorf@catawbacountync.gov; Staff 34.8 (MLS 13, Non-MLS 21.8)
Founded 1936. Pop 116,108; Circ 468,898
Library Holdings: Audiobooks 9,527; DVDs 23,073; Bk Vols 153,330; Per Subs 241
Special Collections: State Document Depository
Wireless access
Function: 24/7 Electronic res, 24/7 Online cat, 3D Printer, Accelerated reader prog, Activity rm, Adult bk club, Adult literacy prog, After school storytime, Archival coll, Art exhibits, Art programs, Audiobks via web, Bilingual assistance for Spanish patrons, Bk club(s), Bks on CD, Children's prog, Computer training, Computers for patron use, Digital talking bks, Distance learning, Electronic databases & coll, Family literacy, Free DVD rentals, Games & aids for people with disabilities, Govt ref serv, Health sci info serv, Holiday prog, Homework prog, ILL available, Instruction & testing, Internet access, Jail serv, Large print keyboards, Life-long learning prog for all ages, Magazines, Mail & tel request accepted, Makerspace, Mango lang, Meeting rooms, Microfiche/film & reading machines, Movies, Notary serv, Online cat, Outreach serv, Outside serv via phone, mail, e-mail & web, OverDrive digital audio bks, Photocopying/Printing, Preschool outreach, Preschool reading prog, Printer for laptops & handheld devices, Prog for adults, Prog for children & young adult, Ref & res, Ref serv available, Res assist avail, Scanner, Senior computer classes, Senior outreach, Serves people with intellectual disabilities, Spanish lang bks, Spoken cassettes & CDs, Spoken cassettes & DVDs, STEM programs, Story hour, Study rm, Summer & winter reading prog, Summer reading prog, Teen prog, Telephone ref, Visual arts prog, Wheelchair accessible, Winter reading prog, Workshops, Writing prog
Publications: Library Connections (Newsletter)
Open Mon-Thurs 9-8, Fri & Sat 9-6
Friends of the Library Group
Branches: 6
CLAREMONT BRANCH, 3288 E Main St, Claremont, 28610-1248. Tel: 828-466-6817. *Librn,* Stephanie Abbott
Open Tues-Fri 12-6, Sat 9-2
Friends of the Library Group
CONOVER BRANCH, 403 Conover Station SE, Conover, 28613. Tel: 828-466-5108. FAX: 828-466-5109. *Librn,* Stephanie Abbott
Open Tues 12-8, Wed-Fri 9-6, Sat 9-2
MAIDEN BRANCH, 11 S A Ave, Maiden, 28650, SAN 355-0133. Tel: 828-428-2712. FAX: 828-428-3845.
Open Tues 12-8, Wed-Fri 9-6, Sat 9-2
SAINT STEPHENS BRANCH, 3225 Springs Rd, Hickory, 28601-9700, SAN 329-6490. Tel: 828-466-6821. *Librn,* Debbie Hosford
Open Mon & Tues 12-8, Wed, Thurs & Fri, 9-8, Sat 9-6
SHERRILLS FORD-TERRELL BRANCH, 9154 Sherrills Ford Rd, Terrell, 28682, SAN 355-0141. Tel: 828-466-6827. *Br Serv Mgr,* Jenny Gerami-Markham
Open Mon & Tues 12-8, Wed-Sat 9-6
Friends of the Library Group
SOUTHWEST BRANCH, West Over Plaza, 2944 Hwy 127 S, Hickory, 28602, SAN 376-9283. Tel: 828-466-6818. *Librn,* April Green
Open Mon & Tues 12-8, Wed, Thurs & Fri 9-6, Sat 9-2
Bookmobiles: 1. Librn, Sarah Sherfy. Bk vols 5,774

S HISTORICAL ASSOCIATION OF CATAWBA COUNTY*, History Museum Library & Archives, 30 N College Ave, 28658. (Mail add: PO Box 73, 28658-0073), SAN 312-9365. Tel: 828-465-0383. FAX: 828-465-9813. E-mail: cchamuseum@gmail.com. Web Site: www.catawbahistory.org. *Exec Dir,* Dr Amber Clawson Albert; Tel: 828-465-0383, Ext 303, E-mail: cchadirector@gmail.com; *Librn,* Position Currently Open
Founded 1954
Library Holdings: Bk Titles 4,713; Bk Vols 5,200
Special Collections: 19th Century Law (Shipp Coll) 1750-1885; Civil War (Long Island Coll), family papers; Clapp Family Letters; Col Cilley papers; Decorative Arts (Mrs Eaton Coll), 1920-1930 magazines. Oral History
Subject Interests: Family hist, Regional hist
Wireless access
Friends of the Library Group

NORTH WILKESBORO

P WILKES COUNTY PUBLIC LIBRARY*, 215 Tenth St, 28659. SAN 312-9381. Tel: 336-838-2818. FAX: 336-667-2638. Web Site: www.arlibrary.org/wilkes. *County Librn,* Aimee James; E-mail: ajames@arlibrary.org; *Adult Serv Mgr,* Mary Lynn Tugman; E-mail: mltugman@arlibrary.org; *Circ Mgr,* Laurie Love; E-mail: llove@arlibrary.org; *Tech Serv Mgr,* Nicole R de Bruijn; E-mail: ndebruijn@arlibrary.org; *Youth Serv Mgr,* Elizabeth Lee; E-mail: elee@arlibrary.org; Staff 24 (MLS 4, Non-MLS 20)
Founded 1909. Pop 65,632; Circ 325,807
Library Holdings: CDs 4,931; DVDs 682; Large Print Bks 2,654; Bk Vols 99,254; Per Subs 110; Talking Bks 3,061; Videos 3,649
Special Collections: Spanish Language Coll
Subject Interests: Genealogy, Local hist
Automation Activity & Vendor Info: (Circulation) SirsiDynix
Wireless access
Function: Homebound delivery serv, ILL available, Internet access, Photocopying/Printing, Prog for children & young adult, Ref serv available, Summer reading prog, Telephone ref, Wheelchair accessible
Mem of Appalachian Regional Library
Special Services for the Blind - Computer with voice synthesizer for visually impaired persons
Open Mon-Thurs 9-7, Fri & Sat 9-5
Friends of the Library Group
Branches: 1
TRAPHILL BRANCH, 6938 Traphill Rd, Traphill, 28685. (Mail add: PO Box 113, Traphill, 28685). Tel: 336-957-2534. FAX: 336-957-2534. *Br Mgr,* Ola K Norman; E-mail: onorman@arlibrary.org; Staff 1 (Non-MLS 1)
Library Holdings: AV Mats 926; Bk Vols 8,275
Special Services for the Deaf - Closed caption videos
Special Services for the Blind - Audio mat; Bks on cassette; Bks on CD; Large print bks
Open Tues & Thurs 10-1 & 2-6, Sat 9-4:30
Friends of the Library Group
Bookmobiles: 2. Bkmobile Spec, Wesley Knight

OXFORD

P GRANVILLE COUNTY LIBRARY SYSTEM*, Richard H Thornton Library, 210 Main St, 27565-3321. (Mail add: PO Box 339, 27565), SAN 355-0176. Tel: 919-693-1121. FAX: 919-693-2244. Web Site: www.granville.lib.nc.us. *Dir,* Will Robinson; E-mail: will.robinson@granvillecounty.org; *Adult Serv,* Melanie Baldwin; *Ch Serv,* Amy Carlson; Staff 19 (MLS 3, Non-MLS 16)
Founded 1935. Pop 51,852
Library Holdings: AV Mats 4,905; Bks on Deafness & Sign Lang 43; High Interest/Low Vocabulary Bk Vols 188; Large Print Bks 1,479; Bk Vols 71,716; Per Subs 267; Talking Bks 1,992; Videos 5,593
Special Collections: Granville County History; North Carolina History & Genealogy Coll
Automation Activity & Vendor Info: (Cataloging) SirsiDynix; (Circulation) SirsiDynix; (OPAC) SirsiDynix
Wireless access
Open Mon-Fri 10-12 & 2-4
Friends of the Library Group
Branches: 3
BEREA BRANCH, 1211 Hwy 158, Berea, 27565, SAN 329-6326. Tel: 919-693-1231. FAX: 919-693-1231. *Br Mgr,* Abbe Few; Staff 1 (Non-MLS 1)
Open Tues & Thurs 10-12 & 2-4

SOUTH, 1547 S Campus Dr, Creedmoor, 27522-7381, SAN 355-0230. Tel: 919-528-1752. FAX: 919-528-1752. *Br Mgr,* Zina Hardee
Function: ILL available, Photocopying/Printing, Prog for children & young adult, Summer reading prog, Wheelchair accessible
Open Mon-Fri 10-12 & 2-4

STOVALL BRANCH, 300 Main St, Stovall, 27582, SAN 355-0265. Tel: 919-693-5722. FAX: 919-693-5722. *Br Mgr,* Deborah Bullock; Staff 1 (Non-MLS 1)
Function: Photocopying/Printing, Summer reading prog
Open Mon-Thurs 10-12 & 2-4
Friends of the Library Group

PEMBROKE

C UNIVERSITY OF NORTH CAROLINA AT PEMBROKE*, Mary Livermore Library, One University Dr, 28372. (Mail add: PO Box 1510, 28372-1510), SAN 312-9438. Tel: 910-521-6516. FAX: 910-521-6547. Reference E-mail: library@uncp.edu. Web Site: www.uncp.edu/academics/library. *Dean, Libr Serv,* Jessica Collogan; Tel: 910-521-6365, E-mail: jessica.collogan@uncp.edu; *Dir, Archives, Dir, Spec Coll,* June Power; E-mail: june.power@uncp.edu; *Distance Educ & Outreach Librn,* Michael Alewine; *Dir, Ref Serv, Dir, Instrul Serv,* Robert Arndt; E-mail: robert.arndt@uncp.edu; *Research Librn,* David W Young; E-mail: david.young@uncp.edu; Staff 13 (MLS 13)
Founded 1887. Enrl 6,661; Fac 436; Highest Degree: Master
Library Holdings: AV Mats 8,774; e-books 59,858; Electronic Media & Resources 165; Bk Titles 376,901; Bk Vols 370,900; Per Subs 33,163
Special Collections: Lumbee Indian History Coll. State Document Depository; US Document Depository
Automation Activity & Vendor Info: (Acquisitions) Innovative Interfaces, Inc; (Cataloging) Innovative Interfaces, Inc; (Circulation) Innovative Interfaces, Inc; (Course Reserve) Innovative Interfaces, Inc; (ILL) OCLC; (OPAC) Innovative Interfaces, Inc; (Serials) Innovative Interfaces, Inc
Wireless access
Publications: Informational Handouts; Library Lines (Newsletter)
Partic in LYRASIS; OCLC Online Computer Library Center, Inc
Open Mon-Thurs 7:30am-Midnight, Fri 7:30am-11pm, Sat 9am-11pm, Sun 2-Midnight
Friends of the Library Group

PILOT MOUNTAIN

P CHARLES H STONE MEMORIAL LIBRARY*, 319 W Main St, 27041. (Mail add: PO Box 10, 27041-0010), SAN 312-9446. Tel: 336-368-2370. FAX: 336-368-9587. E-mail: pmt@mwrl.org. Web Site: nwrl.org/friendly.php?s=Pilot. *Librn,* Anna L Nichols; E-mail: annanichols@nwrl.org; *Asst Librn,* Dewey P Sturdivant; E-mail: dsturdivant@nwrl.org
Pop 6,000
Library Holdings: Bk Vols 70,000; Per Subs 75
Automation Activity & Vendor Info: (Acquisitions) SirsiDynix; (Cataloging) SirsiDynix; (Circulation) SirsiDynix; (Course Reserve) SirsiDynix; (ILL) SirsiDynix; (Media Booking) SirsiDynix; (OPAC) SirsiDynix; (Serials) SirsiDynix
Wireless access
Mem of Northwestern Regional Library
Partic in NW Regional Libr Syst
Open Mon 9-8, Tues-Thurs 8:30-5:30, Fri 12-5:30, Sat 9-1

PINEHURST

P GIVEN MEMORIAL LIBRARY & TUFTS ARCHIVES*, 150 Cherokee Rd, 28370. (Mail add: PO Box 159, 28370), SAN 312-9462. Tel: 910-295-6022. FAX: 910-295-9053. E-mail: info@giventufts.com. Web Site: giventufts.org. *Exec Dir,* Audrey Moriorty; E-mail: audrey@giventufts.com
Founded 1963. Pop 8,785; Circ 59,897
Library Holdings: Bk Vols 17,000; Per Subs 110
Special Collections: Local History Coll, 1896-date (Tufts Archives Wing), correspondence, docs, negatives, micro, photogs; Original Donald Ross golf course plans
Subject Interests: Golf
Automation Activity & Vendor Info: (Cataloging) LibraryWorld, Inc; (Circulation) LibraryWorld, Inc; (OPAC) LibraryWorld, Inc; (Serials) LibraryWorld, Inc
Publications: What's New (brochure monthly)
Open Mon-Fri 9:30-5, Sat 9:30-12:30
Friends of the Library Group

J SANDHILLS COMMUNITY COLLEGE*, Katharine L Boyd Library, 3395 Airport Rd, 28374. SAN 312-7605. Tel: 910-695-3819. E-mail: library@sandhills.edu. Web Site: www.sandhills.edu/katharine-boyd-library-sandhills-community-college-6. *Dir, Libr Res,* Carl Danis; E-mail: danisc@sandhills.edu; *Assoc Dean, Learning Res,* Tammy Stewart; Tel: 910-695-3821, E-mail: stewartt@sandhills.edu; *Dir, Student & Public Outreach,* Micky Konold; Tel: 910-695-3817, E-mail: konoldm@sandhills.edu; *Circ Supvr,* Brenda Quick; Tel: 910-695-3969, E-mail: quickb@sandhills.edu; *LRC Supvr,* Judy Hines; Tel: 910-695-3890, E-mail: hinesj@sandhills.edu; *Tech Serv Supvr,* Windie Barnes; Tel: 910-695-3818, E-mail: barnesw@sandhills.edu
Founded 1965. Enrl 4,000; Fac 123
Library Holdings: Bk Titles 78,000; Per Subs 358
Wireless access
Open Mon-Thurs (Fall & Spring) 7:45am-8pm, Fri 7:45-4, Sat 9-1; Mon-Thurs (Summer) 7:45-5, Fri 7:45am-1pm

PITTSBORO

P CHATHAM COUNTY PUBLIC LIBRARIES*, Administrative Office, 197 NC Hwy 87 N, 27312. Tel: 919-545-8081. Web Site: www.chathamnc.org/government/departments-programs/library. *Libr Dir,* Linda Clarke; E-mail: lclarke@chathamlibraries.org; Staff 1 (MLS 1)
Wireless access
Friends of the Library Group
Branches: 3

CHATHAM COMMUNITY LIBRARY, 197 NC Hwy 87 N, 27312, SAN 354-5326. Tel: 919-545-8084. FAX: 919-545-8080. *Br Mgr,* Jennifer Gillis; E-mail: jgillis@chathamlibraries.org; Staff 3 (Non-MLS 3)
Founded 1943
Library Holdings: AV Mats 2,265; CDs 764; DVDs 650; Large Print Bks 325; Bk Vols 40,000; Videos 2,625
Automation Activity & Vendor Info: (Acquisitions) Innovative Interfaces, Inc; (Cataloging) Innovative Interfaces, Inc; (Circulation) Innovative Interfaces, Inc; (ILL) OCLC FirstSearch; (OPAC) Innovative Interfaces, Inc
Open Mon-Thurs 9-8, Fri 9-6, Sat 9-5
Friends of the Library Group

GOLDSTON PUBLIC LIBRARY, 9235 Pittsboro-Goldston Rd, Goldston, 27252-0040. (Mail add: PO Box 40, Goldston, 27252-0040), SAN 354-530X. Tel: 919-898-4522. *Br Mgr,* Sharon Brewer; E-mail: sbrewer@chathamlibraries.org; Staff 1 (Non-MLS 1)
Founded 1952
Library Holdings: AV Mats 100; CDs 125; DVDs 100; Large Print Bks 100; Bk Titles 12,000; Per Subs 30; Videos 450
Open Mon & Wed 10-1 & 2-6, Thurs 10-1 & 2-8, Fri 1-5, Sat 9-1
Friends of the Library Group

WREN MEMORIAL LIBRARY, 500 N Second Ave, Siler City, 27344, SAN 354-5334. Tel: 919-742-2016. FAX: 919-742-5546. *Br Mgr,* Mike Cowell; E-mail: mcowell@chathamlibraries.org; Staff 3 (Non-MLS 3)
Founded 1941. Pop 17,000; Circ 45,000
Library Holdings: AV Mats 2,593; Large Print Bks 350; Bk Titles 37,000; Bk Vols 39,000; Per Subs 55
Automation Activity & Vendor Info: (Acquisitions) Innovative Interfaces, Inc
Partic in North Carolina Libraries for Virtual Education
Open Mon 12-8, Tues-Fri 10-6, Sat 9-5
Bookmobiles: 1. Librn, Edna Johnson

PLYMOUTH

P PETTIGREW REGIONAL LIBRARY*, 201 E Third St, 27962. SAN 355-029X. Tel: 252-793-2875. FAX: 252-793-2818. E-mail: headquarters@pettigrewlibraries.org. Web Site: pettigrewlibraries.libguides.com, www.pettigrewlibraries.org. *Regional Dir,* Judi Bugniazet; E-mail: jbugniazet@pettigrewlibraries.org; *Br Head,* Position Currently Open; Staff 26 (MLS 5, Non-MLS 21)
Founded 1955. Pop 44,184; Circ 187,172
Library Holdings: Audiobooks 5,029; Bk Vols 118,554; Per Subs 196; Videos 5,715
Subject Interests: Local hist
Automation Activity & Vendor Info: (Acquisitions) TLC (The Library Corporation); (Cataloging) TLC (The Library Corporation); (Circulation) TLC (The Library Corporation); (OPAC) TLC (The Library Corporation)
Wireless access
Function: Adult bk club, Adult literacy prog, AV serv, Bks on cassette, Bks on CD, Children's prog, Computers for patron use, E-Reserves, Electronic databases & coll, Free DVD rentals, Holiday prog, Home delivery & serv to seniorr ctr & nursing homes, Homebound delivery serv, ILL available, Music CDs, Notary serv, Online cat, Online ref, Outreach serv, Photocopying/Printing, Prog for adults, Prog for children & young adult, Ref serv available, Scanner, Senior outreach, Spoken cassettes & CDs, Spoken cassettes & DVDs, Story hour, Summer reading prog, Tax forms, Telephone ref, VHS videos, Wheelchair accessible
Member Libraries: Perquimans County Library; Shepard-Pruden Memorial Library; Tyrrell County Public Library; Washington County Library
Open Mon-Fri 8:30-4:30
Friends of the Library Group

P WASHINGTON COUNTY LIBRARY*, 201 E Third St, 27962. SAN 320-4081. Tel: 252-793-2113. FAX: 252-793-2818. E-mail: washington@pettigrewlibraries.org. Web Site: pettigrewlibraries.libguides.com/PRL/WCL, www.pettigrewlibraries.org. *Dir,* Judi Bugniazet; E-mail: jbugniazet@pettigrewlibraries.org; Staff 6 (MLS 1, Non-MLS 5)
Founded 1918. Pop 12,646; Circ 22,828
Library Holdings: Bk Vols 40,000; Per Subs 67
Special Collections: Local History Coll
Automation Activity & Vendor Info: (Acquisitions) TLC (The Library Corporation); (Cataloging) TLC (The Library Corporation); (Circulation) TLC (The Library Corporation); (ILL) TLC (The Library Corporation); (OPAC) TLC (The Library Corporation)
Wireless access
Function: 24/7 Electronic res, 24/7 Online cat, Accelerated reader prog, Activity rm, Adult bk club, Archival coll, Art exhibits, Audiobks via web, AV serv, Bk club(s), Bks on CD, Children's prog, Computer training, Computers for patron use, Digital talking bks, Distance learning, Doc delivery serv, E-Readers, E-Reserves, Electronic databases & coll, For res purposes, Free DVD rentals, Holiday prog, Home delivery & serv to seniorr ctr & nursing homes, Homebound delivery serv, ILL available, Internet access, Laminating, Life-long learning prog for all ages, Magazines, Meeting rooms, Microfiche/film & reading machines, Movies, Notary serv, Online cat, Online info literacy tutorials on the web & in blackboard, Online ref, Outreach serv, Outside serv via phone, mail, e-mail & web, OverDrive digital audio bks, Photocopying/Printing, Preschool outreach, Prog for adults, Prog for children & young adult, Ref & res, Scanner, Senior computer classes, Serves people with intellectual disabilities, Spanish lang bks, Story hour, Study rm, Summer reading prog, Tax forms, Wheelchair accessible
Mem of Pettigrew Regional Library
Open Mon-Thurs 10-7, Fri 10-5:30, Sat 10-1
Friends of the Library Group

POLKTON

J SOUTH PIEDMONT COMMUNITY COLLEGE*, Horne Library, L L Polk Campus, 680 Hwy 74, 28135. (Mail add: PO Box 126, 28135), SAN 354-4710. Tel: 704-272-5389. Administration Tel: 704-272-5300. FAX: 704-272-5384. E-mail: library@spcc.edu. Web Site: www.spcc.edu/libraries. *Interim Libr Dir,* Dana Glauner; E-mail: dglauner@spcc.edu; Staff 7 (MLS 4, Non-MLS 3)
Founded 1967. Enrl 1,893; Highest Degree: Associate
Library Holdings: Bk Titles 18,614; Per Subs 225
Special Collections: Civil War (Linn D Garibaldi Coll), bks, docs, pictures; Historical & Personal Memorabilia (D Garibaldi Coll), bks, docs, pictures; Survey Maps (Frank Clarke Coll)
Subject Interests: Early childhood, Law, Lit, Nursing, Relig, Sociol
Automation Activity & Vendor Info: (Cataloging) SirsiDynix
Wireless access
Partic in Community Colleges Libraries in North Carolina; NC Dept of Commun Cols
Open Mon-Thurs (Fall-Spring) 7:45-5:30, Fri 7:45-3; Mon-Thurs (Summer) 7:30-6

Departmental Libraries:

CARPENTER LIBRARY, Technical Education Bldg, 4209 Old Charlotte Hwy, Monroe, 28110. Tel: 704-290-5851. FAX: 704-290-5880. *Libr Tech,* Marion Sabin
Library Holdings: Bk Vols 25,000
Open Mon-Thurs 8-7:30, Fri 8-3

PRINCETON

P PRINCETON PUBLIC LIBRARY*, 101 Dr Donnie Jones Blvd, 27569. Tel: 919-936-9996. FAX: 919-936-2962. *Librn,* Hope Dougherty
Circ 717
Library Holdings: Large Print Bks 13; Bk Vols 910; Per Subs 69; Talking Bks 67
Wireless access
Partic in North Carolina Libraries for Virtual Education
Open Mon, Tues & Thurs 4-7, Sun 2-5

RAEFORD

P HOKE COUNTY PUBLIC LIBRARY, 334 N Main St, 28376. SAN 312-9500. Tel: 910-875-2502. FAX: 910-875-2207. Web Site: srls.libguides.com/c.php?g=796628, www.hokecounty.net/160/Library. *Dir,* Sheila Brown Evans; E-mail: sheila.evans@srls.info
Founded 1934. Pop 24,939; Circ 14,565
Library Holdings: Bk Titles 38,000; Bk Vols 40,000
Automation Activity & Vendor Info: (Cataloging) TLC (The Library Corporation); (Circulation) TLC (The Library Corporation)
Wireless access
Mem of Sandhill Regional Library System
Open Mon-Fri 8-5
Friends of the Library Group

RALEIGH

C ECPI UNIVERSITY*, Raleigh Campus Library, 4101 Doie Cope Rd, 27613. Tel: 919-571-0057, Ext 68606. FAX: 919-571-0780. Web Site: www.ecpi.edu. *Campus Librn,* Heather Mitchell-Botts; E-mail: hmitchellbotts@ecpi.edu; Staff 3 (MLS 1, Non-MLS 2)
Founded 1990. Highest Degree: Associate
Library Holdings: AV Mats 160; Bk Vols 6,439; Per Subs 108
Automation Activity & Vendor Info: (Cataloging) Follett Software; (Circulation) Follett Software; (OPAC) Follett Software
Function: Photocopying/Printing
Open Mon-Thurs 7:30am-9:30pm, Fri 7:30-3:30

L HUNTON ANDREWS KURTH LLP*, Law Library, One Bank of America Plaza, Ste 1400, 421 Fayetteville St, 27601. SAN 372-2538. Tel: 919-899-3000. FAX: 919-833-6352. Web Site: www.hunton.com. *Library Contact,* Kathy Muth; Staff 2 (MLS 1, Non-MLS 1)
Founded 1980
Library Holdings: Bk Vols 10,000; Per Subs 70
Wireless access
Function: Res libr

C MEREDITH COLLEGE*, Carlyle Campbell Library, 3800 Hillsborough St, 27607-5298. SAN 312-9543. Tel: 919-760-8532. Interlibrary Loan Service Tel: 919-760-8446. Reference Tel: 919-760-8095. FAX: 919-760-2830. E-mail: library@meredith.edu. Web Site: infotogo.meredith.edu. *Dean of Libr,* Laura Davidson; E-mail: davidson@meredith.edu; *Head, Archives, Head, Tech Serv,* Carrie Nichols; E-mail: nicholsc@meredith.edu; *Head, Circ,* Donna Garner; E-mail: garnerd@meredith.edu; *Head, Media Serv,* Brian Thornburg; Tel: 919-760-8457, E-mail: bdthornburg@meredith.edu; *Head, Ref,* Jeff Kincheloe Waller; Tel: 919-760-8382, E-mail: jhwaller@meredith.edu; Staff 8 (MLS 7, Non-MLS 1)
Founded 1899. Enrl 2,168; Fac 130; Highest Degree: Master
Library Holdings: Audiobooks 97; AV Mats 18,990; CDs 2,576; DVDs 2,601; e-books 119,885; e-journals 27,000; Microforms 5,496; Music Scores 8,849; Bk Titles 252,000; Per Subs 2,867; Videos 5,441
Special Collections: Clyde Edgerton Coll
Subject Interests: Educ, Music, Women's studies
Automation Activity & Vendor Info: (Acquisitions) Innovative Interfaces, Inc; (Cataloging) Innovative Interfaces, Inc; (Circulation) Innovative Interfaces, Inc; (Course Reserve) Innovative Interfaces, Inc; (OPAC) Innovative Interfaces, Inc; (Serials) Innovative Interfaces, Inc
Wireless access
Publications: Friends of the Carlyle Campbell Library (Newsletter)
Partic in Carolina Consortium; LYRASIS
Open Mon-Thurs (Fall-Spring) 7:45am-Midnight, Fri 7:45-5, Sat 11-5, Sun 1-Midnight
Friends of the Library Group

G NORTH CAROLINA DEPARTMENT OF LABOR*, Charles H Livengood Jr Memorial Library, 111 Hillsborough St, Rm C510, 27603-1762. (Mail add: 1101 Mail Service Ctr, 27699-1101), SAN 322-7782. Tel: 919-807-2848, 919-807-2850. Toll Free Tel: 800-625-2267. FAX: 919-807-2849. E-mail: dol.library@labor.nc.gov. Web Site: www.labor.nc.gov/safety-and-health/library. *Head Librn,* Nick J Vincelli; Staff 2 (MLS 1, Non-MLS 1)
Founded 1973
Library Holdings: AV Mats 1,000; Bk Vols 8,000; Per Subs 60
Special Collections: Labor Law (Charles H Livengood, Jr Coll), bks, arbitrations
Subject Interests: Labor law, Occupational law, Occupational safety
Automation Activity & Vendor Info: (Circulation) Ex Libris Group; (OPAC) Ex Libris Group
Partic in National Network of Libraries of Medicine Region 1
Open Mon-Fri 8-5

GL NORTH CAROLINA LEGISLATIVE LIBRARY*, 500 Legislative Office Bldg, 300 N Salisbury St, 27603-5925. SAN 321-0863. Tel: 919-733-9390. FAX: 919-715-5460. E-mail: library@ncleg.gov. Web Site: www.ncleg.net/library. *Libr Dir,* Anthony Aycock; E-mail: anthony.aycock@ncleg.gov; *Ref Librn,* Jane W Basnight; *Ref Librn,* Julia B Covington; E-mail: julia.covington@ncleg.net; *Tech Librn & Indexer,* Brian M Peck; E-mail: brian.peck@ncleg.net; *Boards Comn Asst,* Kelsey E Lewis; E-mail: kelsey.lewis@ncleg.net; *Tech Asst,* Russell Miles; E-mail: russell.miles@ncleg.net; Staff 6 (MLS 6)
Founded 1967
Library Holdings: Bk Vols 20,000
Special Collections: Legislation (Committee Notebooks); Legislative Reports; State & County History
Subject Interests: Hist, Law, Legislation
Wireless access
Open Mon-Fri 8-5

G NORTH CAROLINA MUSEUM OF ART*, Art Reference Library, 2110 Blue Ridge Rd, 27607-6494. (Mail add: 4630 Mail Service Ctr, 27699-4630), SAN 312-956X. Tel: 919-664-6770. E-mail: artreferencelibrary@ncartmuseum.org. Web Site: ncartmuseum.org/art/library/. *Head Librn,* Erin Rutherford. Subject Specialists: *Art hist, Fine arts, Literacy,* Erin Rutherford; Staff 1 (MLS 1)
Founded 1956
Library Holdings: Bk Vols 40,000; Per Subs 30
Special Collections: W. R. Valentiner; John Levy Galleries
Subject Interests: Art hist, Fine arts
Automation Activity & Vendor Info: (Cataloging) Evergreen; (ILL) OCLC WorldShare Interlibrary Loan; (OPAC) Evergreen
Wireless access
Function: Ref serv available, Res libr
Partic in OCLC Online Computer Library Center, Inc
Restriction: Circulates for staff only, Non-circulating, Not a lending libr, Open to pub by appt only

P NORTH CAROLINA REGIONAL LIBRARY FOR THE BLIND & PHYSICALLY HANDICAPPED*, 1841 Capital Blvd, 27635. SAN 312-9578. Tel: 919-733-4376. Toll Free Tel: 888-388-2460. FAX: 919-733-6910. TDD: 919-733-1462. E-mail: nclbph@ncdcr.gov. Web Site: statelibrary.ncdcr.gov/lbph. *Dir,* Carl Keehn; E-mail: carl.keehn@ncdcr.gov; *Asst Regional Librn,* Catherine Rubin; E-mail: catherine.rubin@ncdcr.gov; *Coll Mgt Librn,* Joshua Berkov; E-mail: joshua.berkov@ncdcr.gov; *Outreach & Vols Serv Librn,* Gina Powell; E-mail: gina.powell@ncdcr.gov; *Syst & Digital Serv Librn,* Craig Hayward; E-mail: craig.hayward@ncdcr.gov; Staff 25 (MLS 5, Non-MLS 20)
Founded 1958. Pop 12,000; Circ 499,000
Library Holdings: Bk Titles 80,000; Bk Vols 311,000
Subject Interests: NC
Publications: Newsletter, Braille, large type & tape (2 issues annually)
Special Services for the Deaf - TDD equip
Special Services for the Blind - Braille bks; Digital talking bk; Large print bks
Open Mon-Fri 8-5
Friends of the Library Group

S NORTH CAROLINA STATE MUSEUM OF NATURAL SCIENCES*, H H Brimley Memorial Library, 11 W Jones St, 27601-1029. SAN 312-9594. Tel: 919-707-9800. FAX: 919-715-2356. Web Site: naturalsciences.org/research-collections/brimley-library. *Head Librn,* Janet G Edgerton; Tel: 919-707-9810, E-mail: janet.edgerton@naturalsciences.org; *Head Asst Librn,* Margaret Cotrufo; Tel: 919-707-9831, E-mail: margaret.cotrufo@naturalsciences.org; Staff 2 (MLS 1, Non-MLS 1)
Founded 1941
Library Holdings: Bk Titles 10,000; Bk Vols 12,000; Per Subs 80
Subject Interests: Ecology, Environ studies, Natural hist, Paleontology, Sci educ, Systematics, Vertebrate zool
Automation Activity & Vendor Info: (Cataloging) Follett Software; (Circulation) Follett Software
Function: For res purposes
Partic in LYRASIS
Open Mon-Fri 9-4:30

C NORTH CAROLINA STATE UNIVERSITY LIBRARIES*, D H Hill Library, Two Broughton Dr, 27695. (Mail add: NC State University Libraries, Campus Box 7111, 27695-7111), SAN 355-0443. Tel: 919-515-7188. Circulation Tel: 919-515-3364. Interlibrary Loan Service Tel: 919-515-2116. Reference Tel: 919-515-3364. FAX: 919-515-3628. Web Site: www.lib.ncsu.edu. *Dir, Interim Vice Provost,* Gregory Raschke; E-mail: greg_raschke@ncsu.edu; *Dep Dir,* Carolyn Argentati; E-mail: carolyn_argentati@ncsu.edu; *Coll & Scholarly Communications, Interim Assoc Dir,* Eleanor Brown; E-mail: eleanor_brown@ncsu.edu; *Digital Serv, Interim Assoc Dir,* Jill Sexton; E-mail: jksexton@ncsu.edu; *Assoc Dir, Mat Mgt,* David Goldsmith; E-mail: david_goldsmith@ncsu.edu; *Assoc Dir, Learning Spaces,* Patrick Deaton; E-mail: patrick_deaton@ncsu.edu; *Head, Access Serv,* Sydney Thompson; Tel: 919-513-3586; *Head, Acq & Discovery,* Maria Collins; Tel: 919-515-3188, E-mail: maria_collins@ncsu.edu; *Head, Collections & Research Strategy,* Hilary Davis; Tel: 919-513-0654, E-mail: hilary_davis@ncsu.edu; *Head, Digital Libr Initiatives,* Jason Ronallo; Tel: 919-513-3778, E-mail: jason_ronallo@ncsu.edu; *Actg Head, Info Tech,* Emily Lynema; Tel: 919-513-8031; *Actg Head, Res, Spec Coll,* Gwyneth Thayer; Tel: 919-513-3315, E-mail: gathayer@ncsu.edu; *Interim Head, Res & Instrul Serv,* Mira Waller; Tel: 919-585-3855, E-mail: mpark@ncsu.edu; Staff 215 (MLS 111, Non-MLS 104)
Founded 1887. Enrl 33,755; Fac 2,380; Highest Degree: Doctorate
Library Holdings: Bk Vols 5,200,000; Per Subs 100,000
Special Collections: Agricultural Innovation; Animal Welfare & Rights (Tom Regan Coll); Architecture, Landscape Architecture & Design; Entomology (Tippman & Metcalf Coll); History of Computing & Simulation; NCSU History; Plant & Forestry Genetics & Genomics; Textiles; United States Patent Coll; Veterinary Medicine; Zoological Health. State Document Depository; US Document Depository
Subject Interests: Agr, Archit, Entomology, Plant genetics, Textiles, Veterinary med, Zoology
Automation Activity & Vendor Info: (Acquisitions) SirsiDynix; (Cataloging) SirsiDynix; (OPAC) SirsiDynix
Wireless access
Publications: Annual Report; Exhibit Catalogs; Focus Magazine
Partic in Association of Research Libraries; Association of Southeastern Research Libraries; Center for Research Libraries; LYRASIS; Triangle Research Libraries Network
Special Services for the Deaf - Assisted listening device; Assistive tech
Special Services for the Blind - Assistive/Adapted tech devices, equip & products
Friends of the Library Group

Departmental Libraries:

COLLEGE OF EDUCATION MEDIA CENTER, 400 Poe Hall, Campus Box 7801, 27695-7801, SAN 366-0524. Tel: 919-515-3191. FAX: 919-515-7634. *Dir,* Bethany Smith; Tel: 919-513-0545, E-mail: bethany_smith@ncsu.edu; *Asst Dir,* Nathan Stevens; Tel: 919-515-3191, E-mail: nathan_stevens@ncsu.edu; *Librn,* Kerri Brown-Parker; Tel: 919-515-3191, E-mail: kmbrownp@ncsu.edu; Staff 3 (MLS 2, Non-MLS 1)
Library Holdings: Bk Vols 26,500
Special Collections: North Carolina State Adopted Textbooks; Standardized Test Library
Subject Interests: Middle sch, Psychol, Secondary educ
Publications: Information Brochure; Newsletter

JAMES B HUNT JR LIBRARY, 1070 Partners Way, Campus Box 7132, 27606. Administration Tel: 919-515-7110. *Vice Provost & Dir,* Susan Nutter; E-mail: susan_nutter@ncsu.edu; *Dep Dir,* Carolyn Argentati; E-mail: carolyn_argentati@ncsu.edu; Staff 63 (MLS 21, Non-MLS 42)
Founded 2013
Library Holdings: Bk Vols 1,437,450
Friends of the Library Group

WILLIAM RAND KENAN, JR LIBRARY OF VETERINARY MEDICINE, 1060 William Moore Dr, Campus Box 8401, 27607, SAN 355-0516. Tel: 919-513-6218. FAX: 919-513-6400. *Dir,* Kristine Alpi; Tel: 919-513-6219, E-mail: kristine_alpi@ncsu.edu; Staff 3 (MLS 2, Non-MLS 1)
Library Holdings: Bk Vols 41,600
Subject Interests: Biochem, Biology, Med, Veterinary med
Partic in Triangle Research Libraries Network
Publications: Blog; Brochures
Friends of the Library Group

HARRYE B LYONS DESIGN LIBRARY, 209 Brooks Hall, Campus Box 7701, 27695-7701, SAN 355-0532. Tel: 919-515-2207. FAX: 919-515-7330. Web Site: lib.ncsu.edu/design. *Dir,* Karen DeWitt; Tel: 919-513-3860, E-mail: karen_dewitt@ncsu.edu; Staff 4 (MLS 2, Non-MLS 2)
Library Holdings: Bk Vols 43,000
Special Collections: Slide Coll, pamphlet file, product file
Subject Interests: Archit, Art, Graphic, Indust design, Landscape archit, Visual design
Publications: Blog
Friends of the Library Group

NATURAL RESOURCES LIBRARY, Jordan Hall, Rm 1102, 2800 Faucette Dr, Campus Box 7114, 27695-7114, SAN 355-0478. Tel: 919-515-2306. FAX: 919-515-3687. *Dir,* Karen Ciccone; Tel: 919-515-3513, E-mail: karen_ciccone@ncsu.edu; Staff 2 (MLS 1, Non-MLS 1)
Library Holdings: Bk Vols 27,000
Subject Interests: Forestry, Geographic Info Syst, Natural res, Paper sci, Recreation, Tourism mgt, Wood sci
Friends of the Library Group

GL NORTH CAROLINA SUPREME COURT LIBRARY*, 500 Justice Bldg, Two E Morgan St, 27601-1428. SAN 312-9608. Tel: 919-831-5709. FAX: 919-831-5732. E-mail: ncsclib@sc.nccourts.org. Web Site: www.nccourts.gov/courts/supreme-court/supreme-court-library. *Librn,* Thomas Davis; E-mail: tpd@sc.nccourts.org; *Asst Librn, Tech Serv,* Jennifer McLean; Tel: 919-831-5902, E-mail: jlm@sc.nccourts.org; Staff 4 (MLS 3, Non-MLS 1)
Founded 1812
Library Holdings: Bk Vols 160,543; Per Subs 882
Special Collections: US Document Depository
Automation Activity & Vendor Info: (Cataloging) SirsiDynix; (OPAC) SirsiDynix; (Serials) SirsiDynix
Wireless access
Open Mon-Fri 8:30-4:30
Restriction: Non-circulating to the pub

L PARKER, POE, ADAMS & BERNSTEIN, LLP*, Law Library, PNC Plaza, 301 Fayetteville St, Ste 1400, 27601. SAN 372-2546. Tel: 919-828-0564. FAX: 919-834-4564. Web Site: www.parkerpoe.com. *Dir, Libr Serv,* Lisa W Williams; E-mail: lisawilliams@parkerpoe.com
Founded 1990
Library Holdings: Bk Vols 9,000; Per Subs 39
Wireless access
Restriction: Not open to pub

M REX HEALTHCARE LIBRARY*, 4420 Lake Boone Trail, 27607. SAN 312-9624. Tel: 919-784-3032. FAX: 919-784-1670. E-mail: RexLibrary@unchealth.unc.edu. Web Site: www.rexhealth.com. *Managing Librn,* Mrs Deniz Ender; Staff 1 (MLS 1)
Library Holdings: e-books 500; e-journals 200; High Interest/Low Vocabulary Bk Vols 100; Bk Vols 1,500
Subject Interests: Med, Nursing
Automation Activity & Vendor Info: (Acquisitions) EOS International; (Cataloging) EOS International; (Circulation) EOS International; (OPAC) EOS International; (Serials) EOS International
Wireless access
Partic in Mid-Atlantic Chapter-Med Libr Asn
Special Services for the Blind - Talking bks
Restriction: Staff use only

C SAINT AUGUSTINE'S COLLEGE*, The Prezell R Robinson Library, 1315 Oakwood Ave, 27610-2298. SAN 312-9632. Tel: 919-516-4145. FAX: 919-516-4758. Web Site: www.st-aug.edu/prezell-r-robinson-library. *Dir, Libr Serv,* Tiwanna S Nevels; Tel: 919-516-4150, E-mail: tsnevels@st-aug.edu; *Circ Mgr, Doc Delivery,* Frederick Sills; Tel: 919-516-4148, E-mail: fsills@st-aug.edu; Staff 9 (MLS 4, Non-MLS 5)
Founded 1974. Enrl 1,600; Highest Degree: Master
Library Holdings: Bk Vols 100,000; Per Subs 200
Special Collections: Curriculum Materials; James Boyer; Prezell R Robinson Papers (Delany Coll); Saint Agnes Coll. Oral History
Subject Interests: African-Am hist, Econ, Ethnic studies, Music, Soc sci
Wireless access
Publications: Library newsletter
Partic in Coop Raleigh Col; NC Asn of Independent Cols & Univs
Open Mon-Thurs 8-8, Fri 8-5, Sun 1-8
Friends of the Library Group

C SHAW UNIVERSITY*, James E Cheek Learning Resources Center, 118 E South St, 27601. SAN 312-9659. Tel: 919-546-8407. FAX: 919-831-1161. E-mail: thelibrary@shawu.edu. Web Site: www.shawu.edu/Academics/James_Cheek_Learning_Resource_Center.aspx. *Interim Dir, Libr Serv,* Tom Clark; Tel: 919-582-3750, E-mail: tomclark@shawu.edu; *Librn,* Musette McKelvey; Tel: 919-546-8406, E-mail: mmckelvey@shawu.edu; *Circ Librn,* Lizzette Tapp; Tel: 919-582-8438, E-mail: ltapp@shawu.edu; *Libr Spec,* Velma Williams; Tel: 919-582-8438, E-mail: velma.williams@shawu.edu; *Libr Asst,* Michael Allen; Tel: 919-546-8526, E-mail: mallen@shawu.edu; *Libr Asst,* Patricia Powell; Tel: 919-546-8324, E-mail: ppowell@shawu.edu. Subject Specialists: *Divinity,* Musette McKelvey; Staff 10 (MLS 5, Non-MLS 5)
Founded 1865. Enrl 2,300; Fac 120; Highest Degree: Master
Library Holdings: Bk Titles 94,000; Bk Vols 102,000; Per Subs 100
Special Collections: John Wilson Fleming African-American Coll; Mollie Huston Lee African-American Coll; Schomburg Microfilm Coll
Automation Activity & Vendor Info: (Cataloging) SirsiDynix; (Circulation) SirsiDynix; (OPAC) SirsiDynix
Function: Prof lending libr
Publications: Cheek CD & DVD Collection (Film catalog); Circulation Manual (Library handbook); Collection Development Policies Manual (Library handbook); Curriculum Materials Library Manual (Library handbook); Divinity School Library Manual (Library handbook); Library Annual Reports; Reference & Information Literacy Instruction Manual (Reference guide)
Partic in Coop Raleigh Col; NC Asn of Independent Cols & Univs
Special Services for the Deaf - Coll on deaf educ
Open Mon-Thurs 8am-11pm, Fri 8-5, Sat 12-5, Sun 3-11; Mon-Fri (Summer) 8-5

P STATE LIBRARY OF NORTH CAROLINA*, 109 E Jones St, 27601. (Mail add: 4640 Mail Service Ctr, 27699-4600), SAN 355-0389. Tel: 919-814-6780. Reference Tel: 919-807-7450. FAX: 919-733-8748. Reference FAX: 919-733-5679. E-mail: slnc.reference@ncdcr.gov. Web Site: statelibrary.ncdcr.gov. *State Librn,* Timothy G Owens; Tel: 919-814-6784, E-mail: timothy.owens@ncdcr.gov; *Asst State Librn,* Position Currently Open; *Dir, Libr Develop,* Tanya Prokrym; Tel: 919-814-6789, E-mail: tanya.prokrym@ncdcr.gov; Staff 75.5 (MLS 37, Non-MLS 38.5)
Founded 1812
Library Holdings: AV Mats 1,000; Braille Volumes 11,318; Large Print Bks 23,187; Bk Vols 170,229; Per Subs 125; Talking Bks 312,955
Special Collections: State Document Depository; US Document Depository
Subject Interests: Demographics, Genealogy, North Caroliniana, Statistics
Automation Activity & Vendor Info: (Acquisitions) Ex Libris Group; (Cataloging) Ex Libris Group; (Circulation) Ex Libris Group; (ILL) OCLC; (OPAC) Ex Libris Group; (Serials) Ex Libris Group
Wireless access
Publications: Checklist of Official North Carolina State Publications; State Library Update
Partic in Association for Rural & Small Libraries; LYRASIS
Open Mon-Fri 9-5, Sat 9-2
Branches: 1
LIBRARY FOR THE BLIND & PHYSICALLY HANDICAPPED
See Separate Entry under North Carolina Regional Library for the Blind & Physically Handicapped

P WAKE COUNTY PUBLIC LIBRARY SYSTEM*, Library Administration Building, 4020 Carya Dr, 27610-2900. SAN 355-0567. Tel: 919-250-1200. Interlibrary Loan Service Tel: 919-250-1205. Administration Tel: 919-250-1206. Information Services Tel: 910-212-7930. Web Site: www.wakegov.com/libraries. *Libr Dir,* Michael J Wasilick; E-mail: libraryadministration@wakegov.com; *Dep Libr Dir,* Ann M Burlingame; *Coll,* Theresa Lynch; E-mail: theresa.lynch@wakegov.com; *Tech,* Ben McFadden; E-mail: ben.mcfadden@wakegov.com; Staff 212.5 (MLS 105, Non-MLS 107.5)
Founded 1898. Circ 10,998,242
Library Holdings: Bk Vols 1,714,645
Special Collections: African American (Mollie Houston Lee Coll), bks, clippings, fiche; North Carolina History Coll
Automation Activity & Vendor Info: (Acquisitions) SirsiDynix; (Cataloging) OCLC; (Circulation) SirsiDynix; (ILL) OCLC ILLiad; (OPAC) SirsiDynix
Wireless access
Branches: 23
ATHENS DRIVE COMMUNITY LIBRARY, 1420 Athens Dr, 27606, SAN 355-0605. Tel: 919-233-4000. *Libr Mgr,* Lauren Nicholson; E-mail: lauren.nicholson@wakegov.com; Staff 2 (MLS 2)
Open Mon-Thurs 10-8, Fri & Sat 10-6, Sun 1-5
CARY COMMUNITY LIBRARY, 315 Kildaire Farm Rd, Cary, 27511, SAN 355-0656. Tel: 919-460-3350. *Libr Mgr,* Liz Bartlett; E-mail: lbartlett@wakegov.com; Staff 10 (MLS 10)
Open Mon-Thurs 10-8, Fri & Sat 10-6, Sun 1-5
DURALEIGH ROAD COMMUNITY LIBRARY, 5800 Duraleigh Rd, 27612, SAN 372-4123. Tel: 919-881-1344. *Libr Mgr,* Vanessa Marchetti; E-mail: vanessa.marchetti@wakegov.com; Staff 2 (MLS 2)
Open Mon-Thurs 10-8, Fri & Sat 10-6, Sun 1-5
EAST REGIONAL LIBRARY, 946 Steeple Square Ct, Knightdale, 27545, SAN 355-0869. Tel: 919-217-5300. *Libr Mgr,* Brandy Hamilton; E-mail: brandy.hamilton@wakegov.com; Staff 10 (MLS 10)
Founded 1999
Open Mon-Thurs 10-8, Fri & Sat 10-6, Sun 1-5
EXPRESS LIBRARY FAYETTEVILLE STREET, Wake County Off Bldg, 336 Fayetteville St, 27601, SAN 376-9259. Tel: 919-856-6690. *Libr Mgr,* Robert Cauthen; E-mail: robert.cauthen@wakegov.com; Staff 1 (MLS 1)
Open Mon-Fri 10-6
FUQUAY-VARINA COMMUNITY LIBRARY, 271 Bramblehill Dr, Fuquay-Varina, 27526, SAN 355-0710. Tel: 919-557-2788. *Commun Libr Mgr,* Janet West; E-mail: janet.west@wakegov.com; Staff 4 (MLS 4)
Open Mon-Thurs 10-8, Fri & Sat 10-6, Sun 1-5
GREEN ROAD COMMUNITY LIBRARY, 4101 Green Rd, 27604, SAN 376-9267. Tel: 919-790-3200. *Libr Mgr,* Michelle S Hildreth; E-mail: michelle.hildreth@wakegov.com; Staff 3.5 (MLS 3.5)
Founded 1997
Open Mon-Thurs 10-8, Fri & Sat 10-6, Sun 1-5
RICHARD B HARRISON COMMUNITY LIBRARY, 1313 New Bern Ave, 27610, SAN 355-0834. Tel: 919-856-5720. *Libr Mgr,* Beverly Williams; E-mail: beverly.williams@wakegov.com; Staff 3.5 (MLS 3.5)
Special Collections: Mollie H Lee Coll
Open Mon-Thurs 10-8, Fri & Sat 10-6, Sun 1-5
HOLLY SPRINGS COMMUNITY LIBRARY, 300 W Ballentine St, Holly Springs, 27540. Tel: 919-577-1660. *Libr Mgr,* Maryjo George; E-mail: maryjo.george@wakegov.com; Staff 3.5 (MLS 3.5)
Founded 2006
Open Mon-Thurs 10-8, Fri & Sat 10-6, Sun 1-5
LEESVILLE COMMUNITY LIBRARY, 5105 Country Trail, 27613. Tel: 919-571-6661. *Libr Mgr,* Katherine Barr; E-mail: katherine.barr@wakegov.com; Staff 3.5 (MLS 3.5)
Founded 2009
Open Mon-Thurs 10-8, Fri & Sat 10-6, Sun 1-5
MIDDLE CREEK COMMUNITY LIBRARY, 111 Middle Creek Park Ave, Apex, 27539. Tel: 919-890-7400. *Libr Mgr,* Deborah Davis; E-mail: Deborah.Davis@wakegov.com; Staff 3.5 (MLS 3.5)
Founded 2017
Open Mon-Thurs 10-8, Fri & Sat 10-6, Sun 1-5

MORRISVILLE COMMUNITY LIBRARY, 310 Town Hall Dr, Morrisville, 27560. Tel: 919-463-8460. *Libr Mgr,* Helen Yamamoto; E-mail: hyamamoto@wakegov.com
Founded 2020
Open Mon-Thurs 10-8, Fri & Sat 10-6, Sun 1-5

NORTH REGIONAL LIBRARY, 7009 Harps Mill Rd, 27615, SAN 355-0893. Tel: 919-870-4000. *Libr Mgr,* Carol Laing; E-mail: carol.laing@wakegov.com; Staff 10 (MLS 10)
Open Mon-Thurs 10-8, Fri & Sat 10-6, Sun 1-5

NORTHEAST REGIONAL LIBRARY, 14401 Green Elm Lane, 27614. Tel: 919-570-7166. *Libr Mgr,* Connie Harr; E-mail: connie.harr@wakegov.com; Staff 10 (MLS 10)
Founded 2016
Open Mon-Thurs 10-8, Fri & Sat 10-6, Sun 1-5

EVA PERRY REGIONAL LIBRARY, 2100 Shepherd's Vineyard Dr, Apex, 27502, SAN 355-0591. Tel: 919-387-2100. *Libr Mgr,* Carrie Lee; E-mail: carrie.lee@wakegov.com; Staff 10 (MLS 10)
Founded 1996
Open Mon-Thurs 10-8, Fri & Sat 10-6, Sun 1-5

OLIVIA RANEY LOCAL HISTORY LIBRARY, 4016 Carya Dr, 27610, SAN 376-9275. Tel: 919-250-1196. *Libr Mgr,* Yvonne Allen; E-mail: yallen@wakegov.com; Staff 2 (MLS 2)
Founded 1996
Special Collections: Elizabeth Reid Murray Coll
Subject Interests: Genealogy, Local hist
Open Mon-Fri 10-6, Sat 10-2

SOUTHEAST REGIONAL LIBRARY, 908 Seventh Ave, Garner, 27529, SAN 329-6415. Tel: 919-662-2250. *Libr Mgr,* Nicole Lambert; E-mail: nicole.lambert@wakegov.com; Staff 10 (MLS 10)
Founded 1989
Open Mon-Thurs 10-8, Fri & Sat 10-6, Sun 1-5

SOUTHGATE COMMUNITY LIBRARY, 1601-14 Cross Link Rd, 27610, SAN 355-0958. Tel: 919-856-6598. *Libr Mgr,* Avis Jones; E-mail: Avis.Jones@wakegov.com; Staff 2 (MLS 2)
Open Mon-Thurs 10-8, Fri & Sat 10-6, Sun 1-5

VILLAGE REGIONAL LIBRARY, 1930 Clark Ave, 27605, SAN 355-0621. Tel: 919-856-6710. *Libr Mgr,* Robert Lambert; E-mail: robert.lambert@wakegov.com; Staff 10 (MLS 10)
Founded 1974
Open Mon-Thurs 10-8, Fri & Sat 10-6, Sun 1-5

WAKE FOREST COMMUNITY LIBRARY, 400 E Holding Ave, Wake Forest, 27587, SAN 355-0982. Tel: 919-554-8498. *Libr Mgr,* Valerie Pierce; E-mail: valerie.pierce@wakegov.com; Staff 3.5 (MLS 3.5)
Founded 1961
Open Mon-Thurs 10-8, Fri & Sat 10-6, Sun 1-5

WENDELL COMMUNITY LIBRARY, 207 S Hollybrook Rd, Wendell, 27591, SAN 355-1016. Tel: 919-365-2600. *Libr Mgr,* Crystal L Mitchener; E-mail: crystal.mitchener@wakegov.com; Staff 2 (MLS 2)
Founded 1950
Open Mon-Thurs 10-8, Fri & Sat 10-6, Sun 1-5

WEST REGIONAL LIBRARY, 4000 Louis Stephens Dr, Cary, 27519. Tel: 919-463-8500. *Libr Mgr,* Debbie Shreve; E-mail: debra.shreve@wakegov.com; Staff 10 (MLS 10)
Founded 2006
Open Mon-Thurs 10-8, Fri & Sat 10-6, Sun 1-5

ZEBULON COMMUNITY LIBRARY, 1000 Dogwood Ave, Zebulon, 27597, SAN 355-1040. Tel: 919-404-3610. *Libr Mgr,* Amy Mason; E-mail: amy.mason@wakegov.com; Staff 2 (MLS 2)
Founded 1952
Open Mon-Thurs 10-8, Fri & Sat 10-6, Sun 1-5

J WAKE TECHNICAL COMMUNITY COLLEGE*, Bruce I Howell Library, Bldg D, 100 Level, 9101 Fayetteville Rd, 27603-5696. SAN 312-9667. Tel: 919-866-5644. FAX: 919-662-3575. E-mail: SWCLibrary@waketech.edu. Web Site: researchguides.waketech.edu/HowellLibraryServices. *Dean, Libr Serv,* Carenado Davis; E-mail: cdavis19@waketech.edu; *Pub Serv Librn,* Paula Hartman; E-mail: pahartman@waketech.edu; *Tech Serv,* Jim Gray; E-mail: jegray@waketech.edu; Staff 6 (MLS 6)
Founded 1962. Enrl 15,000; Highest Degree: Certificate
Library Holdings: AV Mats 5,254; CDs 750; DVDs 101; Bk Vols 68,902; Per Subs 299
Subject Interests: Arts, Bus, Health sci, Sciences, Vocational tech
Automation Activity & Vendor Info: (Acquisitions) ADLiB; (Cataloging) SirsiDynix; (Circulation) SirsiDynix; (ILL) SirsiDynix; (OPAC) SirsiDynix
Wireless access
Function: Distance learning, Doc delivery serv, Internet access, Photocopying/Printing, Ref serv available, Telephone ref, Wheelchair accessible
Publications: Library Handbook
Partic in Community Colleges Libraries in North Carolina
Special Services for the Deaf - TTY equip
Open Mon-Thurs 7:30am-9pm, Fri 7:30-5

Departmental Libraries:

PERRY HEALTH SCIENCES LIBRARY, Bldg C, Rm 123, 2901 Holston Lane, 27610-2092. Tel: 919-747-0002. E-mail: HSCLibrary@waketech.edu. Web Site: researchguides.waketech.edu/PHSL. *Campus Librn,* Anita Young; E-mail: aryoung@waketech.edu; *Pub Serv Librn,* Brian Clossey; E-mail: bclossey@waketech.edu; *Ref Librn,* Burnette Bell; E-mail: blbell@waketech.edu; Staff 3 (MLS 3)
Library Holdings: AV Mats 1,850; DVDs 350; Bk Vols 9,965; Per Subs 97
Function: Health sci info serv
Open Mon-Thurs 7:30am-9pm, Fri 7:30-5

SCOTT NORTHERN WAKE LIBRARY, 6600 Louisburg Rd, NF 241, 27616. Tel: 919-532-5550. E-mail: wakenorthlibrary@waketech.edu. Web Site: researchguides.waketech.edu/NorthCampus. *Campus Librn,* Savanida Duangudom; Tel: 919-532-5553, E-mail: sduangudom@waketech.edu; *Evening Librn,* Jennifer Mincey; E-mail: jmincey1@waketech.edu; *Pub Serv Librn,* Todd Nuckells; E-mail: tnuckells@waketech.edu; Staff 13.6 (MLS 7.8, Non-MLS 5.8)
Highest Degree: Associate
Library Holdings: e-books 24,000; Bk Titles 90,000; Per Subs 14
Automation Activity & Vendor Info: (Cataloging) SirsiDynix-Unicorn; (Circulation) SirsiDynix-Unicorn
Function: Computers for patron use, E-Reserves, Electronic databases & coll, Internet access, Online cat, Online info literacy tutorials on the web & in blackboard, Online ref, Photocopying/Printing
Open Mon-Thurs 7:30am-9pm, Fri 7:30-5, Sat 9-1
Restriction: 24-hr pass syst for students only, Open to pub for ref & circ; with some limitations, Open to students, fac & staff

WESTERN WAKE LIBRARY, Millpond Village, Ste 200, 3434 Kildaire Farms Rd, Cary, 27518-2277. Tel: 919-335-1029. E-mail: wakewestlibrary@waketech.edu. Web Site: researchguides.waketech.edu/WesternWakeLibrary. *Campus Librn,* Katy Hoffler; E-mail: kshoffler@waketech.edu; Staff 1 (MLS 1)
Founded 2006. Enrl 2,000; Highest Degree: Associate
Library Holdings: Bk Titles 3,000; Bk Vols 3,100
Special Collections: Curriculum Support
Automation Activity & Vendor Info: (Course Reserve) SirsiDynix
Function: Electronic databases & coll, Ref serv available
Publications: Wake Tech Libraries (Library handbook)
Open Mon-Thurs 8-4, Fri 8-1
Restriction: Open to students, fac & staff

C WILLIAM PEACE UNIVERSITY*, Lucy Cooper Finch Library, 15 E Peace St, 27604-1194. SAN 312-9616. Tel: 919-508-2302. Reference Tel: 919-508-2304. FAX: 919-508-2787. E-mail: library@peace.edu. Web Site: www.peace.edu/academics/academic-resources/library. *Dir,* Nathan Hellmers; Tel: 919-508-2303, E-mail: njhellmers@peace.edu; *Librn,* Diane Jensen; Tel: 919-508-2305, E-mail: djensen@peace.edu; *Librn,* Elaine Teague; E-mail: eeteague@peace.edu; *Libr Asst,* Paul King; E-mail: pfking@peace.edu; Staff 4 (MLS 4)
Founded 1856. Enrl 700; Fac 35; Highest Degree: Bachelor
Library Holdings: AV Mats 120; CDs 694; DVDs 327; e-books 100,000; e-journals 140,000; Microforms 525; Music Scores 760; Bk Titles 45,000; Bk Vols 49,000; Per Subs 42,000
Subject Interests: Liberal arts
Automation Activity & Vendor Info: (Acquisitions) Mandarin Library Automation; (Cataloging) Mandarin Library Automation; (Circulation) Mandarin Library Automation; (ILL) OCLC FirstSearch; (OPAC) Mandarin Library Automation
Wireless access
Function: Archival coll, Art exhibits, Audio & video playback equip for onsite use, Computers for patron use, Electronic databases & coll, Equip loans & repairs, Free DVD rentals, ILL available, Internet access, Microfiche/film & reading machines, Online cat, Online ref, Photocopying/Printing, Ref & res, Ref serv available, Scanner
Partic in Coop Raleigh Col
Open Mon-Thurs 7:30am-11pm, Fri 7:30am-8pm, Sat 10-6, Sun 2-11
Restriction: Badge access after hrs, Borrowing privileges limited to fac & registered students, Borrowing requests are handled by ILL, Circ privileges for students & alumni only, Non-circulating to the pub

L WILLIAMS MULLEN LIBRARY*, 301 Fayetteville St, Ste 1700, 27601. (Mail add: PO Box 1000, 27601-1000), SAN 372-2341. Tel: 919-981-4038. FAX: 919-981-4300. Web Site: www.williamsmullen.com/offices/raleigh-nc. *Dir,* Lara Dresser; E-mail: ldresser@williamsmullen.com; Staff 1 (MLS 1)
Library Holdings: Bk Titles 3,000; Bk Vols 12,000; Per Subs 200
Subject Interests: Legal mat
Automation Activity & Vendor Info: (Cataloging) EOS International; (OPAC) EOS International; (Serials) EOS International
Wireless access
Restriction: External users must contact libr, Not open to pub

RESEARCH TRIANGLE PARK

S AMERICAN ASSOCIATION OF TEXTILE CHEMISTS & COLORISTS LIBRARY*, One Davis Dr, 27709. (Mail add: PO Box 12215, 27709-2215), SAN 329-8353. Tel: 919-549-3534. FAX: 919-549-8933. Web Site: www.aatcc.org. *Tech Asst,* Valerie Fogg; E-mail: foggv@aatcc.org
Library Holdings: Bk Vols 2,500; Per Subs 15
Restriction: Not a lending libr, Not open to pub, Open by appt only, Use of others with permission of librn

G ENVIRONMENTAL PROTECTION AGENCY LIBRARY*, 109 Alexander Dr, Rm C261, 27711. (Mail add: MDC267-01, 109 TW Alexander Dr, 27711), SAN 354-7507. Tel: 919-541-2777. FAX: 919-541-1405. E-mail: libraryrpt.reprint@epa.gov. Web Site: www.epa.gov/libraries/research-triangle-park-library-services. *Dir,* Anthony Holderied; E-mail: holderied.anthony@epa.gov; Staff 8.5 (MLS 4, Non-MLS 4.5)
Library Holdings: e-journals 1,000; Microforms 150,000; Bk Titles 6,000; Bk Vols 18,000; Per Subs 400
Special Collections: APTIC File
Subject Interests: Air chem, Air pollution, Engr, Health effects of pollution
Wireless access
Publications: Check It Out (Newsletter)
Partic in Federal Library & Information Network; OCLC Online Computer Library Center, Inc
Open Mon-Fri 9-3

S ISA - THE INTERNATIONAL SOCIETY OF AUTOMATION*, Albert F Sperry Library, 67 TW Alexander Dr, 27709. SAN 315-0763. Tel: 919-549-8411. FAX: 919-549-8288. Web Site: www.isa.org. *Librn/Standards Adminr,* Linda Wolffe; Tel: 910-990-9257
Founded 1950
Library Holdings: CDs 250; Bk Vols 3,600
Special Collections: ISA Archives; Measurement, Process Control Theory & Application; Process Control Engineering, journals & references
Subject Interests: Computer, Control tech, Electronic engr, Instrumentation
Function: Archival coll
Publications: Intech (Monthly); ISA Transactions (Quarterly); Process Control Engineering Reference Books
Restriction: Staff use only

S NATIONAL HUMANITIES CENTER LIBRARY*, Seven Alexander Dr, 27709. (Mail add: PO Box 12256, 27709-2256), SAN 320-9334. Tel: 919-549-0661. FAX: 919-990-8535. E-mail: info@nationalhumanitiescenter.org. Web Site: nationalhumanitiescenter.org/the-library. *Libr Dir,* Brooke Andrade; E-mail: bandrade@nationalhumanitiescenter.org; *Assoc Librn,* Sarah Harris; E-mail: sharris@nationalhumanitiescenter.org; *Asst Librn,* Joe Milillo; E-mail: jmilillo@nationalhumanitiescenter.org; Staff 3 (MLS 2, Non-MLS 1)
Founded 1978
Library Holdings: Bk Titles 2,200; Bk Vols 2,500; Per Subs 20
Special Collections: Robert F & Margaret S Goheen Coll of Fellows' Works
Wireless access
Publications: Library Guide for Users
Partic in LYRASIS; OCLC Online Computer Library Center, Inc

G NATIONAL INSTITUTE OF ENVIRONMENTAL HEALTH SCIENCES LIBRARY*, 111 TW Alexander Dr, Bldg 101, 27709. (Mail add: PO Box 12233, Mail Drop A0-01, 27709), SAN 312-973X. Tel: 984-287-3609. E-mail: library@niehs.nih.gov. Web Site: www.niehs.nih.gov/research/resources/library. *Libr Mgr,* Erin Knight; E-mail: erin.knight2@nih.gov; Staff 5 (MLS 3, Non-MLS 2)
Founded 1967
Library Holdings: e-books 300; e-journals 9,000; Bk Titles 15,000; Bk Vols 20,000; Per Subs 40
Subject Interests: Carcinogenesis, Environ health, Epigenetics, Molecular biol, Toxicology
Automation Activity & Vendor Info: (Cataloging) Innovative Interfaces, Inc - Millennium; (Circulation) Innovative Interfaces, Inc - Millennium; (OPAC) Innovative Interfaces, Inc - Millennium
Wireless access
Function: Res libr
Partic in Coalition for Networked Information; Federal Library & Information Network; National Network of Libraries of Medicine Region 1; OCLC Online Computer Library Center, Inc
Open Mon-Fri 8:30-5

S NORTH CAROLINA BIOTECHNOLOGY CENTER LIFE SCIENCE INTELLIGENCE*, 15 T W Alexander Dr, 27709. (Mail add: PO Box 13547, 27709-3547), SAN 329-1111. Tel: 919-541-9366. Information Services Tel: 919-549-8880. E-mail: research@ncbiotech.org. Web Site: www.ncbiotech.org. *VPres,* Susan Corbett; *Client Serv Librn, Outreach Librn,* Lori Melliere; *Res Analyst,* Jessica Dixon Reece; *Sr Res Analyst,* Sperry Krueger; *Sr Res Analyst,* Karin Shank; Staff 7 (MLS 7)
Founded 1986
Library Holdings: Per Subs 30
Automation Activity & Vendor Info: (Cataloging) Inmagic, Inc.; (OPAC) Inmagic, Inc.
Wireless access
Function: Res libr
Open Mon-Fri 9-4:30
Restriction: Not a lending libr

S RTI INTERNATIONAL*, Library & Information Services, 3040 E Cornwallis Rd, 27709. (Mail add: PO Box 12194, 27709-2194), SAN 312-9756. Tel: 919-541-8787. E-mail: publications@rti.org. Web Site: www.rti.org. *Dir, Libr & Info Serv,* Mariel Christian; Tel: 919-541-6303, E-mail: mchristian@rti.org; *Ref Librn,* Mark E Howell; Tel: 919-541-6364; Staff 6 (MLS 5, Non-MLS 1)
Founded 1958
Subject Interests: Chem, Educ, Energy, Engr, Environ engr, Environ studies, Med
Automation Activity & Vendor Info: (Discovery) EBSCO Discovery Service; (ILL) OCLC

G US ENVIRONMENTAL PROTECTION AGENCY LIBRARY*, 109 T W Alexander Dr, Rm C261, 27711. (Mail add: MD 267-01, 4930 Old Page Rd, Durham, 27703), SAN 312-9748. Tel: 919-541-2777. FAX: 919-541-1405. E-mail: library.rtp@epa.gov. Web Site: www.epa.gov/libraries/research-triangle-park-library-services. *Libr Dir,* Anthony Holderied; E-mail: holderied.anthony@epa.gov; Staff 5 (MLS 4, Non-MLS 1)
Library Holdings: Bk Vols 6,000; Per Subs 3,000
Subject Interests: Air pollution, Toxicology
Wireless access
Open Mon-Fri 9-3
Restriction: Open to authorized patrons

ROANOKE RAPIDS

P ROANOKE RAPIDS PUBLIC LIBRARY, 319 Roanoke Ave, 27870. SAN 312-9764. Tel: 252-533-2890. E-mail: rrpl@roanokerapidsnc.com. Web Site: www.youseemore.com/roanokerapids. *Interim Head Librn,* Jacqueline Moore; Staff 1 (MLS 1)
Founded 1933. Pop 14,738
Library Holdings: Bk Titles 40,000
Automation Activity & Vendor Info: (Cataloging) TLC (The Library Corporation); (Circulation) TLC (The Library Corporation); (OPAC) TLC (The Library Corporation)
Wireless access
Open Mon-Fri 10-3
Friends of the Library Group

ROBBINSVILLE

P GRAHAM COUNTY PUBLIC LIBRARY*, 80 Knight St, 28771. SAN 312-9772. Tel: 828-479-8796. FAX: 828-479-3156. *Br Librn,* Mary Griffin; E-mail: mgriffin@nantahalalibrary.org; Staff 4.5 (MLS 1, Non-MLS 3.5)
Founded 1984. Pop 7,500; Circ 33,000
Library Holdings: CDs 250; DVDs 300; Large Print Bks 1,600; Bk Titles 22,000; Bk Vols 22,500; Per Subs 47; Talking Bks 1,020; Videos 1,580
Automation Activity & Vendor Info: (Circulation) TLC (The Library Corporation)
Wireless access
Function: Bks on cassette, Bks on CD, Children's prog, Computers for patron use, Electronic databases & coll, Free DVD rentals, ILL available, Internet access, Large print keyboards, Mail & tel request accepted, Music CDs, Online cat, Photocopying/Printing, Prog for children & young adult, Scanner, Tax forms, Telephone ref, VHS videos
Mem of Nantahala Regional Library
Open Tues 11-8, Wed-Fri 9-6, Sat 9-1
Friends of the Library Group

ROBERSONVILLE

P ROBERSONVILLE PUBLIC LIBRARY, 119 S Main St, 27871. (Mail add: PO Box 1060, 27871-1060), SAN 312-9780. Tel: 252-508-0342. E-mail: rpl@bhmlib.org. Web Site: bhmlib.org/robersonville. *Libr Mgr,* Gail Cargile; E-mail: gcargile@bhmlib.org
Pop 1,300
Library Holdings: Bk Vols 6,000; Per Subs 20
Wireless access
Partic in North Carolina Libraries for Virtual Education
Open Tues-Fri 10-3
Friends of the Library Group

ROCKINGHAM

P THOMAS H LEATH MEMORIAL LIBRARY*, 412 E Franklin St, 28379-4995. SAN 312-9802. Tel: 910-895-6337. FAX: 910-895-5851. Web Site: srls.libguides.com. *Br Supvr,* Shannon Hearne; E-mail: shannon.hearne@srls.info; Staff 6 (MLS 1, Non-MLS 5)
Founded 1962. Pop 9,171; Circ 44,384
Library Holdings: Audiobooks 949; AV Mats 2,426; Bk Titles 44,249; Per Subs 57; Videos 1,229
Special Collections: Local & State Genealogy Coll
Automation Activity & Vendor Info: (Cataloging) TLC (The Library Corporation); (Circulation) TLC (The Library Corporation); (OPAC) TLC (The Library Corporation)
Wireless access
Function: Bks on CD, Children's prog, Computer training, Computers for patron use, Electronic databases & coll, ILL available, Internet access, Notary serv, Online cat, Online ref, Outreach serv, Photocopying/Printing, Preschool outreach, Prog for adults, Prog for children & young adult, Ref & res, Ref serv available, Senior outreach, Spoken cassettes & CDs, Story hour, Summer reading prog, Tax forms, Teen prog, Telephone ref, VHS videos, Wheelchair accessible, Workshops
Publications: Statistical & Financial Reports
Mem of Sandhill Regional Library System
Special Services for the Deaf - Bks on deafness & sign lang
Special Services for the Blind - Audio mat; Bks on cassette; Bks on CD; Braille & cassettes; Braille bks; Large print & cassettes; Large print bks
Open Mon 9-7, Tues-Thurs 9-6, Fri & Sat 9-5
Friends of the Library Group
Branches: 2
HAMLET PUBLIC, 302 Main St, Hamlet, 28345-3304, SAN 312-8695. Tel: 910-582-3477. FAX: 910-582-3478. Web Site: www.srls.info/richmond/richmondbranches.html. *Mgr,* Patsy Hardee; Staff 3 (Non-MLS 3)
Founded 1922. Pop 6,800; Circ 39,517
Library Holdings: Bk Vols 25,000; Per Subs 50
Subject Interests: Fiction, Local hist
Automation Activity & Vendor Info: (Acquisitions) TLC (The Library Corporation); (Cataloging) TLC (The Library Corporation); (Circulation) TLC (The Library Corporation); (OPAC) TLC (The Library Corporation)
Open Mon-Fri 9:30-6, Sat 9:30-12:30
Friends of the Library Group
KEMP-SUGG MEMORIAL, 279 Second St, Ellerbe, 28338-9001, SAN 320-5002. Tel: 910-652-6130. FAX: 910-652-6130. Web Site: www.srls.info/richmond/richmondbranches.html. *Supvr,* Sami Poore; E-mail: samikemp@yahoo.com; Staff 1 (Non-MLS 1)
Founded 1978. Pop 1,500; Circ 7,983
Library Holdings: Bk Vols 6,254; Per Subs 13
Subject Interests: Artifacts, Local hist
Open Mon, Tues, Thurs & Fri 9-12:30 & 2-5:30, Sat 10-Noon
Friends of the Library Group

P SANDHILL REGIONAL LIBRARY SYSTEM*, 412 E Franklin St, 28379. Tel: 910-997-3388. FAX: 910-997-2516. E-mail: srlslibraries@srls.info. Web Site: srls.libguides.com. *Dir,* Jesse Gibson; E-mail: jesse.gibson@srls.info
Wireless access
Member Libraries: Hampton B Allen Library; Hoke County Public Library; Montgomery County Library; Moore County Library; Thomas H Leath Memorial Library
Open Mon-Fri 8:30-5

ROCKY MOUNT

P BRASWELL MEMORIAL PUBLIC LIBRARY*, 727 N Grace St, 27804-4842. Tel: 252-442-1951. Administration Tel: 252-442-1951, Ext 254. FAX: 252-442-7366. Information Services FAX: 252-442-7180. Web Site: www.braswell-library.org. *Dir,* Catherine Roche; E-mail: croche@braswell-library.org; *Asst Dir,* Gloria Sutton; E-mail: gsutton@braswell-library.org; *Assoc Dir, Support Serv,* Phillip Whitford; E-mail: pwhitford@braswell-library.org; Staff 27 (MLS 7, Non-MLS 20)
Founded 1922. Pop 106,000; Circ 402,000
Library Holdings: Audiobooks 6,187; AV Mats 10,000; e-books 20,899; Microforms 1,069; Bk Vols 122,671; Per Subs 150; Videos 4,492
Special Collections: Parent-Teacher Coll
Subject Interests: African-Am, Civil War, Genealogy
Automation Activity & Vendor Info: (Acquisitions) TLC (The Library Corporation); (Cataloging) TLC (The Library Corporation); (Circulation) TLC (The Library Corporation); (OPAC) TLC (The Library Corporation); (Serials) TLC (The Library Corporation)
Wireless access
Publications: Braswell Memorial Library (Newsletter)
Special Services for the Blind - Audio mat; Bks on cassette; Bks on CD; Large print bks
Open Mon-Thurs 10-8, Fri & Sat 10-6
Friends of the Library Group

J NASH COMMUNITY COLLEGE LIBRARY, 522 N Old Carriage Rd, 27804-9441. (Mail add: PO Box 7488, 27804-0788), SAN 312-9837. Tel: 252-451-8248. Web Site: nashcc.edu/campus-life/student-resources/library. *Assoc Libr Dir,* Robert James; Tel: 252-451-8308, E-mail: rmjames752@nashcc.edu; *Librn,* Jerry Judd; Tel: 252-451-8210, E-mail: gjjudd253@nashcc.edu; *Libr Asst,* Position Currently Open; *Libr Support Spec,* Position Currently Open; Staff 5 (MLS 2, Non-MLS 3)
Founded 1967. Highest Degree: Associate
Special Collections: College Archives; Tim Valentine Coll; Teaching & Learning Coll; Small Business Coll; Early Childhood Coll; Young Adult; Seed Library; Little Free Library
Automation Activity & Vendor Info: (Cataloging) SirsiDynix; (Circulation) SirsiDynix; (OPAC) SirsiDynix
Wireless access
Partic in Community College Libraries in North Carolina
Open Mon-Thurs 8-6, Fri 8-1

C NORTH CAROLINA WESLEYAN COLLEGE*, Elizabeth Braswell Pearsall Library, 3400 N Wesleyan Blvd, 27804. SAN 312-9845. Tel: 252-985-5350. Circulation Tel: 252-985-5231. Interlibrary Loan Service Tel: 252-985-5234. Reference E-mail: reference@ncwc.edu. Web Site: www.ncwc.edu/library. *Dir, Libr Serv,* Dr Esther O Burgess; Tel: 252-985-5134, E-mail: eburgess@ncwc.edu; *Coll Develop Librn,* Rachel McWilliams; Tel: 252-985-5343, E-mail: rmcwilliams@ncwc.edu; *Embedde Librn, Online Serv Librn,* Terrence J Martin; Tel: 252-985-5238, E-mail: tmartin@ncwc.edu; *Emerging Tech Librn, Outreach Librn,* Dwain Teague; Tel: 252-985-5230, E-mail: dteague@ncwc.edu; *Instruction & Assessment Librn,* Vincent Chip Larkin; Tel: 252-985-5233, E-mail: clarkin@ncwc.edu; *Ref Librn,* Elizabeth Winstead; Tel: 252-985-5350, E-mail: ewinstead@ncwc.edu; *Circ Supvr,* Jason Boone; Tel: 252-985-5231, E-mail: sdavenport@ncwc.edu; *Night Supvr,* Linwood James; E-mail: ljames@ncwc.edu; *Tech Serv Assoc,* Grace Wallace; Tel: 252-985-5234, E-mail: gwallace@ncwc.edu. Subject Specialists: *Educ, Foreign lang,* Dr Esther O Burgess; *Mkt, Psychol, Relig,* Rachel McWilliams; *Sociol, Theatre,* Terrence J Martin; *Communication, English, Hist, Polit sci,* Dwain Teague; *Art hist, Computer info syst, English,* Vincent Chip Larkin; Staff 9 (MLS 6, Non-MLS 3)
Founded 1960. Enrl 1,108; Fac 55; Highest Degree: Master
Jun 2019-May 2020 Income $421,500. Mats Exp $421,500
Library Holdings: AV Mats 1,730; DVDs 1,330; Microforms 36,000; Music Scores 8,075; Per Subs 1,670
Special Collections: Black Mountain College Coll, bks & art prints; Music Coll; United Methodist Church & North Caroliniana (Hardee-Rives Coll), rare bks, fine eds. US Document Depository
Automation Activity & Vendor Info: (Acquisitions) TLC (The Library Corporation); (Cataloging) TLC (The Library Corporation); (Circulation) TLC (The Library Corporation); (ILL) OCLC; (OPAC) TLC (The Library Corporation)
Wireless access
Function: 24/7 Electronic res, 24/7 Online cat, 3D Printer, Archival coll, Art exhibits, Audio & video playback equip for onsite use, Audiobks via web, AV serv, Computers for patron use, Distance learning, Doc delivery serv, Electronic databases & coll, Free DVD rentals, ILL available, Internet access, Learning ctr, Meeting rooms, Online cat, Online ref, Orientations, Outreach serv, Photocopying/Printing, Printer for laptops & handheld devices, Ref & res, Ref serv available, Res assist avail, Telephone ref, Workshops
Open Mon-Thurs (Fall & Spring) 7:30am-1am, Fri 7:30-7, Sat 10-5, Sun 1pm-1am ; Mon-Thurs (Summer) 8am-9pm, Fri 8-6

ROXBORO

P PERSON COUNTY PUBLIC LIBRARY*, 319 S Main St, 27573. SAN 312-9861. Tel: 336-597-7881. FAX: 336-597-5081. Web Site: www.personcounty.net/departments-services/departments-i-z/library. *Libr Dir,* Tina Norris; E-mail: tnorris@personcountync.gov; *Asst Dir,* Kate Millard; E-mail: kmillard@personcounty.net; *Ch,* Amanda Weaver; E-mail: aweaver@personcounty.net; *Ref Librn,* Becky Schneider; E-mail: bschneider@personcounty.net; *Outreach Coordr,* Susan Bowen; E-mail: sbowen@personcounty.net; Staff 7 (MLS 1, Non-MLS 6)
Founded 1936. Pop 36,000; Circ 12,000
Library Holdings: Bks on Deafness & Sign Lang 28; Bk Titles 51,161; Per Subs 177
Special Collections: Large Print Books; Local History Coll; North Carolina Room (geneology, local hist)
Automation Activity & Vendor Info: (Acquisitions) Innovative Interfaces, Inc; (Cataloging) Innovative Interfaces, Inc; (Circulation) Innovative Interfaces, Inc; (OPAC) Innovative Interfaces, Inc; (Serials) Innovative Interfaces, Inc
Wireless access
Function: ILL available
Open Mon-Thurs 9-6, Fri 9-5, Sat 10-4
Friends of the Library Group

J PIEDMONT COMMUNITY COLLEGE*, Gordon P Allen Learning Resources Center, 1715 College Dr, 27573. (Mail add: PO Box 1197, 27573-1197), SAN 376-5822. Tel: 336-599-1181, Ext 489. FAX: 336-599-9146. Web Site: www.piedmont.cc.nc.us. *Dean of Libr,* Lionell Parker; E-mail: lionell.parker@piedmontcc.edu; *Circ,* Deborah Brown; *Distance Educ,* Joseph Solomon; Tel: 336-599-1181, Ext 253; *Instr,* Libbie McPhaul-Moore; Tel: 336-599-1181, Ext 445, E-mail: libbie.mcphaul-moore@piedmontcc.edu; *Ref Librn,* Vanessa L Nwanze; Tel: 336-599-1181, Ext 235; *Tech Serv Librn,* Ernest Avery; Tel: 336-599-1181, Ext 231; Staff 3 (MLS 2, Non-MLS 1)
Founded 1970
Library Holdings: Bk Titles 16,906; Bk Vols 18,354; Per Subs 165
Automation Activity & Vendor Info: (Acquisitions) SirsiDynix; (Cataloging) SirsiDynix; (Circulation) SirsiDynix; (ILL) SirsiDynix; (Media Booking) SirsiDynix; (Serials) SirsiDynix
Open Mon-Thurs (Winter) 7:30am-9pm, Fri 7:30-5, Sat 8-3; Mon-Thurs (Summer) 7:30-8, Fri 7:30-12:30
Departmental Libraries:
CASWELL LEARNING RESOURCES CENTER, 331 Piedmont Dr, Yanceyville, 27379. (Mail add: PO Box 1150, Yanceyville, 27379). Tel: 336-694-5707, Ext 231, 336-694-5707, Ext 286. FAX: 336-694-5893. Web Site: www.piedmontcc.edu/lrc. *Dir,* Lionell Parker; Tel: 336-599-1181, Ext 248, E-mail: parkerl@piedmontcc.edu
Open Mon & Wed 7:30-5, Tues & Thurs 7:30-6, Fri (Summer) 7:30-12:30

RUTHERFORDTON

P NORRIS PUBLIC LIBRARY*, 132 N Main, 28139. SAN 355-1318. Tel: 828-287-4981. FAX: 828-287-0660. E-mail: nplibrary@rutherfordton.net. *Librn,* Patricia A Hardin; *Libr Assoc,* Cindy Bowlin; *Libr Assoc,* Vanessa Harbison
Library Holdings: Large Print Bks 600; Bk Vols 44,000; Per Subs 60; Talking Bks 500
Subject Interests: Local hist
Automation Activity & Vendor Info: (Cataloging) TLC (The Library Corporation); (Circulation) TLC (The Library Corporation); (OPAC) TLC (The Library Corporation)
Wireless access
Open Mon, Wed & Thurs 9:30-5:30, Tues 9:30-7, Fri 9:30-5, Sat 9:30-Noon
Friends of the Library Group

SALEMBURG

G NORTH CAROLINA JUSTICE ACADEMY*, Learning Resource Center Library, 200 W College St, 28385. (Mail add: PO Box 99, 28385), SAN 321-0154. Tel: 910-525-4151, Ext 267. FAX: 910-525-4491. Web Site: www.ncja.ncdoj.gov/library. *Libr Supvr,* Michael Cummings; E-mail: mcummings@ncdoj.gov; *Librn,* Eric Barta; Staff 3 (MLS 1, Non-MLS 2)
Founded 1975
Library Holdings: AV Mats 2,300; Bk Vols 23,000; Per Subs 150
Special Collections: Criminal Justice; Law Enforcement Policy & Procedures Manuals
Subject Interests: Law, Law enforcement
Wireless access
Function: ILL available
Publications: Acquisitions List (Monthly); AV catalog (Irregular)
Open Mon-Thurs 8am-9pm, Fri 8-5
Restriction: Open to pub for ref & circ; with some limitations

SALISBURY

C CATAWBA COLLEGE*, Corriher-Linn-Black Library, 2300 W Innes St, 28144-2488. SAN 312-9896. Tel: 704-637-4448. Interlibrary Loan Service Tel: 704-637-4214. Interlibrary Loan Service E-mail: ill@catawba.edu. Web Site: libweb.catawba.edu. *Libr Dir,* Earl Givens, Jr; Tel: 704-637-4212, E-mail: ebgivens15@catawba.edu; *Head, Coll Mgt,* Constance Grant; Tel: 704-637-4228, E-mail: cbgrant@catawba.edu; *Circ Supvr,* Whitney Owens; Tel: 704-637-4239, E-mail: wpmullis@catawba.edu; *ILL Supvr,* Jean Wurster; E-mail: jwurster@catawba.edu; *Tech Serv Assoc,* Mark Wurster; Tel: 704-637-4783, E-mail: mwurster@catawba.edu; *Tech Serv Assoc,* Ray Porter; Tel: 704-637-4215, Fax: rporter@catawba.edu; Staff 11.5 (MLS 5.5, Non-MLS 6)
Founded 1851. Enrl 1,270; Fac 90; Highest Degree: Master
Library Holdings: CDs 185; DVDs 245; Music Scores 444; Bk Titles 126,483; Bk Vols 167,452; Per Subs 594; Videos 1,200
Special Collections: Catawba College Archives; Poetry Council of North Carolina Coll; Wolfe Coll. State Document Depository; US Document Depository
Subject Interests: Environ sci, Intl bus, NC poetry, Teacher educ, Theatre arts
Automation Activity & Vendor Info: (Acquisitions) Ex Libris Group; (Cataloging) Ex Libris Group; (Circulation) Ex Libris Group; (Course Reserve) Ex Libris Group; (OPAC) Ex Libris Group; (Serials) Ex Libris Group
Wireless access
Partic in Asn Col & Res Librs; Charlotte Area Educ Consortium; LYRASIS; Metrolina Libr Asn; NC Libr Asn; North Carolina Libraries for Virtual Education
Open Mon-Thurs (Fall & Spring) 8am-11pm, Fri 8-5, Sat 10-5, Sun 1:30-11; Mon-Thurs (Summer) 8am-9pm, Fri 8-5, Sat 12-5, Sun 2-6
Friends of the Library Group

GM DEPARTMENT OF VETERANS AFFAIRS*, W G Hefner VA Medical Center Library, 1601 Brenner Ave, 28144. SAN 312-9926. Tel: 704-638-9000, Ext 3403. FAX: 704-638-3483. *Chief Librn,* Nancy Martino; E-mail: nancy.martino@va.gov
Founded 1953
Library Holdings: CDs 150; DVDs 78; Bk Vols 800; Per Subs 120
Special Collections: Business/Careers
Subject Interests: Geriatrics, Med, Nursing, Psychiat, Psychol, Surgery
Partic in Northwest AHEC
Restriction: Staff use only

R HOOD THEOLOGICAL SEMINARY LIBRARY, 300 Bldg, 1810 Luthern Synod Dr, 28144. Tel: 704-636-6779. Web Site: hoodseminary.libguides.com/library, www.hoodseminary.edu/academics/information/library. *Dir, Writing Ctr Dir,* Patricia Commander; E-mail: pcommander@hoodseminary.edu; *Libr Asst, Marketing & Communications Coord,* Kelly Bryant; Tel: 704-636-6840, E-mail: kbryant@hoodseminary.edu
Open Mon, Thurs & Sat (Spring-Fall) 8-5, Tues & Wed 8-8, Fri 8am-9pm; Mon-Thurs (Summer) 8-5, Fri 8-5 (8-Noon July)

C LIVINGSTONE COLLEGE, Andrew Carnegie Library, 701 W Monroe St, 28144. SAN 355-1377. Tel: 704-216-6030. Toll Free Tel: 800-835-3435. FAX: 704-216-6798. Web Site: www.livingstone.edu. *Dir,* Laura Johnson; E-mail: ljohnson@livingstone.edu; *Cat Librn,* Kim Allman; Tel: 704-216-6325, E-mail: kallman@livingstone.edu; *Circ Librn,* Gregory Hill; Tel: 704-216-6956, E-mail: ghill@livingstone.edu; *Ref Librn,* Joan Hill; Tel: 704-216-6031, E-mail: jhill@livingstone.edu; Staff 5 (MLS 4, Non-MLS 1)
Founded 1908. Enrl 900; Fac 60; Highest Degree: Bachelor
Library Holdings: Bk Vols 75,000; Spec Interest Per Sub 15
Special Collections: African-American Coll. State Document Depository
Subject Interests: African-Am hist
Automation Activity & Vendor Info: (Acquisitions) OCLC Worldshare Management Services; (Cataloging) OCLC Worldshare Management Services; (Circulation) OCLC Worldshare Management Services; (Course Reserve) OCLC Worldshare Management Services; (Discovery) OCLC Worldshare Management Services; (ILL) OCLC Worldshare Management Services; (OPAC) OCLC Worldshare Management Services; (Serials) EBSCO Online
Wireless access
Function: ILL available
Publications: Newsletter
Partic in NC Asn of Independent Cols & Univs; North Carolina Libraries for Virtual Education
Open Mon-Thurs (Fall & Spring) 8am-10pm, Fri 8-5, Sat 10-5, Sun 3-10; Mon-Fri (Summer) 8-5
Friends of the Library Group

SR NORTH CAROLINA SYNOD OF THE ELCA*, Heilig Resource Center, 1988 Lutheran Synod Dr, 28144. SAN 327-6422. Tel: 704-633-4861. FAX: 704-638-0508. Web Site: www.nclutheran.org/ministries/heilig_center.php. *Dir,* Catherine Fink; Tel: 704-633-4861, Ext 9574, E-mail: cfink@nclutheran.org; *Res Ctr Mgr,* Elizabeth Smith; Tel: 704-633-4861, Ext 9573, E-mail: esmith@nclutheran.org; Staff 2 (Non-MLS 2)
Founded 1955
Library Holdings: AV Mats 6; CDs 150; DVDs 845; Electronic Media & Resources 15; Music Scores 363; Bk Titles 3,720; Spec Interest Per Sub 12; Videos 518
Wireless access
Open Mon-Thurs 8-12 & 1-5, Fri 8-Noon

J ROWAN-CABARRUS COMMUNITY COLLEGE*, RCCC Library, 1333 Jake Alexander Blvd, 28145. (Mail add: PO Box 1595, 28145-1595), SAN 377-788X. Tel: 704-216-3693. Web Site: www.rccc.edu/lrc/. *Interim Dir,* Lisa Shores; E-mail: lisa.shores@rccc.edu; Staff 7 (MLS 3, Non-MLS 4)
Founded 1964. Enrl 2,900; Fac 80; Highest Degree: Associate
Library Holdings: Bk Titles 40,000; Per Subs 425
Subject Interests: Archives, Early childhood, Liberal arts, Med, Small bus
Automation Activity & Vendor Info: (Cataloging) SirsiDynix; (Circulation) SirsiDynix; (OPAC) SirsiDynix
Wireless access
Partic in OCLC Online Computer Library Center, Inc
Open Mon-Thurs 7:45-7, Fri 7:45-2

Departmental Libraries:
NCRC, 399 Biotechnology Lane, Kannapolis, 28081. Tel: 704-216-7141. *Coordr of Libr, Interim Dir,* Lisa Shores; Staff 4 (MLS 2, Non-MLS 2)
Founded 2011. Highest Degree: Associate
Function: 24/7 Electronic res, 24/7 Online cat
SOUTH CAMPUS, 1531 Trinity Church Rd, Concord, 28027-7601. Tel: 704-216-3694. FAX: 704-788-2169. Web Site: www.rowancabarrus.edu/lrc. *Coordr, Libr Sci,* Timothy Hunter; E-mail: timothy.hunter@rccc.edu; Staff 2.5 (MLS 2.5)
Highest Degree: Associate
Library Holdings: Bk Vols 7,000; Per Subs 75
Open Mon-Thurs 7:45am-8pm, Fri 7:45-5, Sat 9-1

P ROWAN PUBLIC LIBRARY*, 201 W Fisher St, 28144-4935. SAN 355-1431. Tel: 704-216-8228, 980-432-8670. Administration Tel: 704-216-8240. Information Services Tel: 704-216-8243. FAX: 704-216-8237. E-mail: info@rowancountync.gov. Web Site: www.rowancountync.gov/307/Library. *Libr Dir,* Melissa Oleen; E-mail: Melissa.oleen@rowancountync.gov; *Librn, Libr Serv Mgr,* Laurie Lydia; E-mail: Laurie.Lydia@rowancountync.gov; *Children's Serv Supvr,* Hope Loman; E-mail: Hope.Loman@rowancountync.gov; *Librn II,* Gretchen Witt; E-mail: gretchen.witt@rowancountync.gov. Subject Specialists: *Genealogy, Local hist,* Gretchen Witt; Staff 47 (MLS 10, Non-MLS 37)
Founded 1911. Pop 133,134; Circ 683,414
Library Holdings: Bk Vols 226,661; Per Subs 386
Special Collections: Oral History
Subject Interests: Genealogy, Local hist
Automation Activity & Vendor Info: (Acquisitions) TLC (The Library Corporation); (Cataloging) TLC (The Library Corporation); (Circulation) TLC (The Library Corporation); (ILL) OCLC Connexion; (OPAC) TLC (The Library Corporation)
Wireless access
Function: After school storytime, AV serv, Electronic databases & coll, Home delivery & serv to seniorr ctr & nursing homes, Homebound delivery serv, ILL available, Internet access, Magnifiers for reading, Mail & tel request accepted, Photocopying/Printing, Preschool outreach, Prog for adults, Prog for children & young adult, Ref serv available, Wheelchair accessible
Publications: News Etc Newsletter (Monthly)
Special Services for the Deaf - TDD equip; TTY equip
Open Mon-Wed 9-9, Thurs 9-6, Fri & Sat 9-5
Friends of the Library Group
Branches: 2
EAST BRANCH, 110 Broad St, Rockwell, 28138. (Mail add: PO Box 550, Rockwell, 28138), SAN 312-9810. *Interim Branch Supervisor,* Brooke Taylor; E-mail: brooke.taylor@rowancountync.gov
Open Mon-Wed 9-8, Thurs & Fri 9-5, Sat 10-1
Friends of the Library Group
SOUTH, 920 Kimball Rd, China Grove, 28023, SAN 355-1466. *Librn,* Paul Birkhead; E-mail: Paul.Birkhead@rowancountync.gov
Open Mon-Wed 9-9, Thurs 9-6, Fri & Sat 9-5
Friends of the Library Group
Bookmobiles: 1

SANFORD

J CENTRAL CAROLINA COMMUNITY COLLEGE LIBRARIES*, 1105 Kelly Dr, 27330. SAN 312-9934. Tel: 919-718-7244. FAX: 919-718-7378. Web Site: www.cccc.edu/library. *Dir, Libr Serv,* Tara Guthrie; Tel: 919-718-7245, E-mail: tguthrie@cccc.edu; *Electronic Serv Librn, Online Learning Librn,* Nora Burmeister; Tel: 919-718-7435, E-mail: nburmeister@cccc.edu; *Pub Serv Librn,* Samantha O'Connor; Tel: 919-718-7340, E-mail: soconnor@cccc.edu; *Lead Libr Asst,* BJ Thompson; Tel: 919-718-7375, E-mail: bthompson@cccc.edu; *Evening Libr Asst,* Jessica Thomas; Tel: 919-718-7244, E-mail: jthom627@cccc.edu; *Circ, Libr Asst,* Peggy Cotten; Tel: 919-718-7244, E-mail: pcotten@cccc.edu; *Acq, Libr Asst,* Crystal Prevatte; Tel: 919-718-7207, E-mail: cprevatte@cccc.edu; Staff 6.5 (MLS 3, Non-MLS 3.5)
Founded 1962. Enrl 5,421; Highest Degree: Associate
Library Holdings: Audiobooks 264; DVDs 2,016; e-books 696; Microforms 6; Bk Titles 17,809; Bk Vols 18,319; Per Subs 54
Special Collections: Best Sellers; Spanish; Young Adult; Graphic Novels; Educational DVDs; Popular DVDs; Audio Books; Early Childhood; Legal Reference.
Automation Activity & Vendor Info: (Cataloging) SirsiDynix; (Circulation) SirsiDynix; (Course Reserve) SirsiDynix; (ILL) OCLC Connexion; (OPAC) SirsiDynix
Wireless access
Publications: Library Newsletter
Partic in Community College Libraries in North Carolina
Open Mon-Thurs 7:30am-8pm, Fri 7:30-3:30
Departmental Libraries:
HARNETT COUNTY CAMPUS, 1075 E Cornelius Harnett Blvd, Lillington, 27546, SAN 378-1259. Tel: 910-814-8843. FAX: 910-814-8894. *Instruction & Outreach Librn,* Grace Sharrar; Tel: 910-814-8814, E-mail: gsharrar@cccc.edu; *Libr Asst,* Barbara Bera; Tel: 910-814-8873, E-mail: bbera@cccc.edu; Staff 2 (MLS 1, Non-MLS 1)
Founded 1991. Highest Degree: Associate
Automation Activity & Vendor Info: (Cataloging) SirsiDynix-WorkFlows; (Circulation) SirsiDynix-WorkFlows; (Course Reserve) SirsiDynix-WorkFlows; (OPAC) SirsiDynix-WorkFlows
Open Mon-Thurs 7:30-7, Fri 7:30-3:30

P LEE COUNTY LIBRARY, Sanford Branch, 107 Hawkins Ave, 27330. SAN 355-1490. Tel: 919-718-4665. FAX: 919-775-1832. Web Site: www.leecountync.gov/library. *Dir, Libr Serv,* Beth List; E-mail: blist@leecountync.gov; *Librn,* Allison Sills; *Outreach Serv Spec, Youth Serv Spec,* Delisa Williams; E-mail: dtwilliams@leecountync.gov; Staff 12 (MLS 2, Non-MLS 10)
Founded 1933. Pop 54,417; Circ 173,964
Library Holdings: Bk Titles 135,000; Per Subs 110
Special Collections: Central North Carolina Historic Newspapers (microfilm)
Automation Activity & Vendor Info: (Cataloging) Evergreen; (Circulation) Evergreen
Wireless access
Function: 24/7 Electronic res, 24/7 Online cat, Activity rm, Adult bk club, Archival coll
Partic in Lee County
Special Services for the Deaf - ADA equip
Special Services for the Blind - Assistive/Adapted tech devices, equip & products; BiFolkal kits
Open Mon-Fri 9-5
Restriction: Authorized patrons
Friends of the Library Group
Branches: 1
BROADWAY BRANCH, 206 S Main St, Broadway, 27505. (Mail add: 107 Hawkins Ave, 27330), SAN 355-1520. Tel: 919-258-6513. *Dir, Libr Serv,* Beth List
Open Mon-Wed 2-6
Friends of the Library Group

SELMA

P SELMA PUBLIC LIBRARY*, 301 N Pollock St, 27576. SAN 355-1857. Tel: 919-965-8613, Ext 7001. FAX: 919-765-4637. Web Site: selma-nc.com/departments/library. *Librn,* Phyllis Brown; E-mail: pbrown@selma-nc.com; Staff 1 (MLS 1)
Circ 23,039
Library Holdings: AV Mats 861; Large Print Bks 1,549; Bk Vols 23,888; Per Subs 23; Talking Bks 453
Wireless access
Open Mon-Wed 9-6, Thurs 9-8, Fri 9-5, Sat 9-Noon

SEYMOUR JOHNSON AFB

A UNITED STATES AIR FORCE, Seymour Johnson Air Force Base Library FL4809, 4FSS/FSDL, 1520 Goodson St, Bldg 3660, 27531. SAN 355-158X. Tel: 919-722-5825. FAX: 919-722-5835. E-mail: libraryweb@us.af.mil. Web Site: accc.ent.sirsi.net/client/en_US/s-johnson. *Dir,* Kim Huskins Webb; Staff 5 (MLS 1, Non-MLS 4)
Founded 1956
Library Holdings: Bk Titles 41,000; Per Subs 50
Subject Interests: Aeronaut, Biog, Educ, Humanities, Mil sci, Polit sci
Automation Activity & Vendor Info: (Acquisitions) SirsiDynix-WorkFlows; (Cataloging) SirsiDynix; (Circulation) SirsiDynix; (ILL) OCLC; (OPAC) SirsiDynix
Wireless access
Partic in OCLC Online Computer Library Center, Inc; Proquest Dialog; Wayne Info Network
Open Mon-Wed & Fri 10-6, Thurs 10-7, Sat 10-5

SHELBY

J CLEVELAND COMMUNITY COLLEGE*, Jim & Patsy Rose Library, 137 S Post Rd, 28152. SAN 312-9950. Tel: 704-669-4024. Interlibrary Loan Service Tel: 704-669-4086. Reference Tel: 704-669-4053. FAX: 704-669-4036. E-mail: library@clevelandcc.edu. Web Site: library.clevelandcc.edu. *Dean, Learning Res,* Barbara McKibbin; Tel: 704-669-4116; *Dir, Libr Serv,* Leslie Queen; E-mail: queenl356@clevelandcc.edu; *Tech Serv Librn,* Emily Von Pfahl; Tel: 704-669-4042, E-mail: vonpfahle@clevelandcc.edu; *AV Coordr,* Roger Perry; Tel: 704-669-4032, E-mail: perryr@clevelandcc.edu; *Libr Serv Coordr,* Victoria Linder; E-mail: linderv@clevelandcc.edu; *Learning Syst Spec,* Cornelius Logan; Tel: 704-669-4129, E-mail: loganc@clevelandcc.edu; Staff 10.3 (MLS 4.5, Non-MLS 5.8)
Founded 1965. Enrl 3,400; Fac 90; Highest Degree: Associate
Library Holdings: Bk Titles 22,951; Bk Vols 27,594; Per Subs 312
Automation Activity & Vendor Info: (Cataloging) SirsiDynix; (Circulation) SirsiDynix; (Course Reserve) SirsiDynix; (Discovery) ProQuest; (ILL) OCLC ILLiad; (OPAC) SirsiDynix; (Serials) SirsiDynix

Wireless access
Open Mon-Thurs 7:30am-9pm, Fri 7:30-2

P CLEVELAND COUNTY LIBRARY SYSTEM*, 104 Howie Dr, 28150. (Mail add: PO Box 1120, 28151-1120), SAN 312-9942. Tel: 704-487-9069. FAX: 704-487-4856. Web Site: ccml.libguides.com. *Dir,* Carol H Wilson; E-mail: cwilson@ccml.org; Staff 20 (MLS 3, Non-MLS 17)
Founded 1909. Pop 86,158; Circ 330,000
Library Holdings: AV Mats 9,058; Bk Vols 140,000; Per Subs 96
Subject Interests: Genealogy, Local hist
Automation Activity & Vendor Info: (Cataloging) SirsiDynix; (Circulation) SirsiDynix
Wireless access
Publications: Libri Amicus (Newsletter)
Open Mon-Thurs 10-8, Fri & Sat 10-2
Friends of the Library Group
Branches: 1
SPANGLER BRANCH LIBRARY, 112 Piedmont Dr, Lawndale, 28090, SAN 370-0127. Tel: 704-538-7005. FAX: 704-538-0801. *Librn,* Deborah Page; E-mail: dpage@ccml.org
Founded 1990
Open Mon-Wed 2-6,Thurs 9-6, Sat 9-1
Friends of the Library Group
Bookmobiles: 1

SMITHFIELD

J JOHNSTON COMMUNITY COLLEGE LIBRARY*, Learning Resource Ctr, Bldg E, 245 College Rd, 27577. (Mail add: PO Box 2350, 27577-2350), SAN 312-9977. Tel: 919-464-2251. FAX: 919-464-2250. E-mail: jcclibraryhelp@johnstoncc.edu. Web Site: johnstoncc.libguides.com/libraryhome1/libraryhome. *Lead Librn,* Jennifer Seagraves; Tel: 919-464-2254; *Pub Serv Librn,* Britney Shawley; Tel: 919-464-2277; *Libr Spec,* April Bass; Tel: 919-464-2259; Staff 5.5 (MLS 3.5, Non-MLS 2)
Founded 1969
Library Holdings: Bk Vols 36,000; Per Subs 350
Special Collections: Children's Coll; Jane Dillard Music Coll; North Carolina Hist & JCC Archives
Automation Activity & Vendor Info: (Cataloging) SirsiDynix; (Circulation) SirsiDynix
Wireless access
Partic in CCLINK
Open Mon-Thurs (Fall & Spring) 7:30am-8pm, Fri 8-3; Mon-Thurs (Summer) 7:30-6
Friends of the Library Group

P PUBLIC LIBRARY OF JOHNSTON COUNTY & SMITHFIELD*, 305 E Market St, 27577-3919. SAN 355-1644. Tel: 919-934-8146. FAX: 919-934-8084. Web Site: www.pljcs.org. *Interim Dir,* Katie Guthrie; E-mail: kguthrie@pljcs.org; *Bus Mgr,* Katie Barbour; E-mail: kbarbour@pljcs.org; Staff 4 (MLS 3, Non-MLS 1)
Founded 1966. Pop 168,878; Circ 464,444
Library Holdings: Audiobooks 13,156; AV Mats 8,562; Bk Titles 206,901; Bk Vols 251,038; Per Subs 75
Subject Interests: Genealogy, Local hist
Automation Activity & Vendor Info: (Acquisitions) Innovative Interfaces, Inc; (Cataloging) Innovative Interfaces, Inc; (Circulation) Innovative Interfaces, Inc; (OPAC) Innovative Interfaces, Inc; (Serials) Innovative Interfaces, Inc
Wireless access
Function: Adult bk club, Art exhibits, Bk club(s), Bks on cassette, Bks on CD, Chess club, Children's prog, Computer training, Computers for patron use, Magnifiers for reading, Music CDs, Online cat, Photocopying/Printing, Preschool outreach, Prog for adults, Prog for children & young adult, Ref & res, Ref serv available, Scanner, Senior computer classes, Story hour, Summer reading prog, Teen prog, Telephone ref, VHS videos
Open Mon & Thurs 9-8, Tues, Wed & Fri 9-5:30, Sat 9-5
Friends of the Library Group
Bookmobiles: 1. Libr Contact, Racquel Aguilera

SOUTHERN PINES

P SOUTHERN PINES PUBLIC LIBRARY*, 170 W Connecticut Ave, 28387-4819. SAN 312-9993. Tel: 910-692-8235. FAX: 910-695-1037. E-mail: lib@southernpines.net. Web Site: www.southernpines.net/399/library. *Dir,* Amanda Brown; E-mail: abrown@sppl.net; Staff 10.3 (MLS 4, Non-MLS 6.3)
Founded 1922. Pop 12,717; Circ 117,667
Library Holdings: AV Mats 9,278; e-books 23,694; Bk Vols 65,752; Per Subs 129
Special Collections: English as a Second Language (ESL); Large Print Coll
Automation Activity & Vendor Info: (Cataloging) TLC (The Library Corporation); (Circulation) TLC (The Library Corporation); (ILL) OCLC; (OPAC) TLC (The Library Corporation)
Wireless access
Publications: Bookends (Newsletter)
Open Mon-Fri 10-5
Friends of the Library Group

SOUTHPORT

P BRUNSWICK COUNTY LIBRARY*, Margaret & James Harper Library, 109 W Moore St, 28461. SAN 355-1881. Tel: 910-457-6237. Web Site: www.brunswickcountync.gov/library. *Dir,* Maurice T Tate; E-mail: maurice.tate@brunswickcountync.gov; *Mgr,* Denise Ballard; E-mail: denise.ballard@brunswickcountync.gov; Staff 1 (MLS 1)
Founded 1912. Pop 75,000; Circ 200,000
Library Holdings: AV Mats 3,600; Bk Vols 100,000
Automation Activity & Vendor Info: (Cataloging) Innovative Interfaces, Inc; (Circulation) Innovative Interfaces, Inc; (OPAC) Innovative Interfaces, Inc
Wireless access
Open Mon-Fri 9-6
Friends of the Library Group
Branches: 4
G V BARBEE SR BRANCH, 8200 E Oak Island Dr, Oak Island, 28465, SAN 375-2925. Tel: 910-278-4283. FAX: 910-278-4049. *Br Mgr,* Susan Angelow
Library Holdings: Large Print Bks 3,000; Bk Vols 20,000; Per Subs 20; Talking Bks 1,000
Open Mon-Fri 9-6, Sat 9-1, Sun 2-6
Friends of the Library Group
HICKMANS CROSSROADS LIBRARY, 1040 Calabash Rd, Calabash, 28467. Tel: 910-575-0173. FAX: 910-575-0176. *Br Mgr,* Christi Iffergan; E-mail: ciffergan@brunsco.net
Founded 2004
Library Holdings: Bk Vols 9,000; Per Subs 30
Open Mon-Fri 9-6
Friends of the Library Group
LELAND BRANCH, 487 Village Rd, Leland, 28451, SAN 355-1911. Tel: 910-371-9442. FAX: 910-371-1856. *Br Mgr,* Lisa Milligan
Library Holdings: Bk Vols 10,000
Open Mon-Fri 9-6, Sat 9-1, Sun 2-6
Friends of the Library Group
ROURK LIBRARY, 5068 Main St, Shallotte, 28459, SAN 355-1946. Tel: 910-754-6578. FAX: 910-754-6874. *Mgr,* Felecia Hardy
Open Mon-Fri 8:30-6, Sat 9-1, Sun 2-6
Friends of the Library Group

SPARTA

P ALLEGHANY COUNTY PUBLIC LIBRARY*, 115 Atwood St, 28675. (Mail add: PO Box 656, 28675-0656), SAN 313-0002. Tel: 336-372-5573. FAX: 336-372-4912. Web Site: www.nwrl.org. *Librn,* Debra Brewer; E-mail: dbrewer@nwrl.org
Pop 10,000
Library Holdings: Bk Vols 40,000; Per Subs 25
Subject Interests: Genealogy, Local hist
Automation Activity & Vendor Info: (Acquisitions) SirsiDynix; (Cataloging) SirsiDynix; (Circulation) SirsiDynix; (Course Reserve) SirsiDynix; (ILL) SirsiDynix; (Media Booking) SirsiDynix; (OPAC) SirsiDynix; (Serials) SirsiDynix
Wireless access
Mem of Northwestern Regional Library
Open Mon & Thurs 8:30-6, Tues, Wed & Fri 8:30-5:30, Sat 8:30-1:30
Friends of the Library Group

SPENCER

P SPENCER PUBLIC LIBRARY*, 300 Fourth St, 28159. (Mail add: PO Box 152, 28159-0152), SAN 313-0010. Tel: 704-636-9072. Web Site: www.ci.spencer.nc.us. *Librn,* Beverly McCraw; E-mail: librarian@ci.spencer.nc.us
Founded 1943. Pop 3,075; Circ 13,497
Library Holdings: Bk Vols 10,500; Per Subs 40
Wireless access
Open Mon-Thurs 2-6, Fri 9-6

SPINDALE

J ISOTHERMAL COMMUNITY COLLEGE LIBRARY*, 286 ICC Loop Rd, 28160. (Mail add: PO Box 804, 28160-0804), SAN 313-0029. Tel: 828-395-1307. E-mail: library@isothermal.edu. Web Site: library.isothermal.edu. *Dir, Libr Serv,* Charles P Wiggins; Tel: 828-395-1306, E-mail: cpwiggins@isothermal.edu; *Evening Librn,* Jennifer Stevens; Tel: 828-395-1525, E-mail: jstevens@isothermal.edu; Staff 4 (MLS 2, Non-MLS 2)

Founded 1965. Enrl 2,987; Highest Degree: Associate
Library Holdings: AV Mats 2,334; Bk Titles 37,704; Bk Vols 42,368; Per Subs 42
Special Collections: Old Tryon Historical Coll
Subject Interests: Genealogy, Local hist
Automation Activity & Vendor Info: (Acquisitions) TLC (The Library Corporation); (Cataloging) TLC (The Library Corporation); (Circulation) TLC (The Library Corporation); (Course Reserve) TLC (The Library Corporation); (ILL) OCLC; (OPAC) TLC (The Library Corporation)
Wireless access
Function: Archival coll, Art exhibits, Audio & video playback equip for onsite use, Computers for patron use, Electronic databases & coll, ILL available, Internet access, Magnifiers for reading, Microfiche/film & reading machines, Online cat, Photocopying/Printing, Wheelchair accessible
Publications: Library Handbook; Periodical Holdings List (Collection catalog)
Partic in CMC Library Consortium; NC Dept of Commun Cols
Special Services for the Blind - Assistive/Adapted tech devices, equip & products; Audio mat; Copier with enlargement capabilities; Magnifiers; Ref serv
Open Mon-Thurs 7:45-7, Fri 7:45-4:30

P RUTHERFORD COUNTY LIBRARY*, 255 Callahan Koon Rd, 28160. SAN 355-1229. Tel: 828-287-6115. FAX: 828-287-6119. Web Site: www.rutherfordcountylibrary.org. *Dir,* April Young; E-mail: april.young@rutherfordcountync.gov; *Ch, YA Librn,* Tamara Edwards; Tel: 828-287-6119; *Circ Librn,* Stephanie Long; Tel: 828-287-6396; *IT Spec, Makerspace Mrg,* Kenneth Odom; Tel: 828-287-6327; *Mkt, Outreach Serv,* Maria Davis; Tel: 828-287-6118; Staff 1 (MLS 1)
Founded 1938. Pop 63,432; Circ 224,561
Library Holdings: AV Mats 9,857; e-books 22,693; Bk Vols 74,229; Per Subs 58; Talking Bks 2,812
Special Collections: North Carolina History & Genealogy Coll
Subject Interests: Genealogy, Rutherford county hist
Automation Activity & Vendor Info: (Cataloging) TLC (The Library Corporation); (Circulation) TLC (The Library Corporation); (ILL) OCLC; (OPAC) TLC (The Library Corporation)
Wireless access
Publications: Booklist; Horn Book; Library Journal
Open Mon, Wed & Fri 9:30-5:30, Thurs 9:30-8, Sat 10-3
Branches: 2
HAYNES BRANCH, 2669 Hwy 221A, Mooresboro, 28114, SAN 355-1253. Tel: 828-288-4039. FAX: 828-287-6419. *Br Mgr,* Erika Woody
Library Holdings: Bk Vols 25,000
Open Mon, Tues, Thurs & Fri 10-6, Wed 10-5, Sat 10-1
MOUNTAINS BRANCH, 150 Bills Creek Rd, Lake Lure, 28746, SAN 377-0249. Tel: 828-287-6392. FAX: 828-287-6418. *Br Librn,* Joy Sharp; Tel: 828-287-6417; *Asst Librn,* Angela Turner; Staff 2 (MLS 1, Non-MLS 1)
Founded 1995
Library Holdings: CDs 1,061; DVDs 2,225; Large Print Bks 341; Bk Titles 21,422; Talking Bks 1,453
Function: Accelerated reader prog, Adult bk club, Audio & video playback equip for onsite use, Audiobks via web, Bks on CD, Children's prog, Computers for patron use, Free DVD rentals, Genealogy discussion group, ILL available, Music CDs, Online cat, OverDrive digital audio bks, Photocopying/Printing, Preschool reading prog, Prog for adults, Prog for children & young adult, Senior outreach, Story hour, Summer reading prog, Tax forms, VHS videos, Wheelchair accessible
Open Mon, Tues, Thurs & Fri 10-6, Wed & Sat 10-3
Friends of the Library Group

P SPINDALE PUBLIC LIBRARY, 131 Tanner St, 28160. SAN 355-1342. Tel: 828-286-3879. FAX: 828-286-8338. Web Site: www.spindalenc.net/home/departments/library. *Librn,* Amy Clayton; E-mail: ataylor@spindalenc.net; *Asst Librn,* Sharon Melton; Staff 2 (Non-MLS 2)
Founded 1926
Library Holdings: Bk Vols 25,000
Wireless access
Open Mon-Fri 8:30-5

SPRING HOPE

S INTERNATIONAL WILD WATERFOWL ASSOCIATION, Lee Ridge Aviaries Reference Library, 1633 Bowden Rd, 27882. (Mail add: PO Box 1251, 27882-1251), SAN 372-6444. Tel: 252-478-5610. *Librn,* Walter Sturgeon
Founded 1975
Library Holdings: Bk Titles 1,500
Special Collections: Natural History, bks, videos & slides
Subject Interests: Arctic, Govt aid & subsidies, Natural hist
Restriction: Open by appt only, Private libr

SPRUCE PINE

J MAYLAND COMMUNITY COLLEGE, Carolyn Munro Wilson Learning Resources Center, 200 Mayland Dr, 28777. (Mail add: PO Box 547, 28777-0547), SAN 373-8698. Tel: 828-766-1211. FAX: 828-765-0728. E-mail: lrc@mayland.edu. Web Site: www.mayland.edu/lrc. *Dean of Learning Resource Ctr, Distance Educ,* Jon Wilmesherr; E-mail: jwilmesherr@mayland.edu; *Tech Serv,* Debra Barnett; E-mail: dbarnett@mayland.edu; Staff 3 (MLS 1, Non-MLS 2)
Founded 1972
Library Holdings: Bk Titles 20,000; Bk Vols 25,000; Per Subs 125
Automation Activity & Vendor Info: (Cataloging) SirsiDynix; (Circulation) SirsiDynix
Wireless access
Partic in Community Colleges Libraries in North Carolina
Open Mon-Thurs 7:30-7, Fri 8-4

P SPRUCE PINE PUBLIC LIBRARY*, 142 Walnut Ave, 28777. SAN 313-0045. Tel: 828-765-4673. E-mail: sppl@amyregionallibrary.org. Web Site: www.amyregionallibrary.org/sprucepine. *Head Librn,* Cathy Silver; *Asst Librn,* Ayla Archer
Founded 1952. Pop 2,333
Library Holdings: Bk Vols 45,000; Per Subs 60
Subject Interests: Genealogy, Local hist
Function: Homebound delivery serv, Prog for children & young adult, Summer reading prog
Mem of Avery-Mitchell-Yancey Regional Library System
Open Mon & Tues 9-8, Wed-Fri 9-5, Sat 10-1
Friends of the Library Group

STATESVILLE

P IREDELL COUNTY PUBLIC LIBRARY*, 201 N Tradd St, 28677. (Mail add: PO Box 1810, 28687-1810), SAN 313-0061. Tel: 704-878-3090. Interlibrary Loan Service Tel: 704-878-5423. Reference Tel: 704-928-2400. Administration Tel: 704-878-3091. FAX: 704-878-5449. Web Site: www.iredell.lib.nc.us/179/Statesville-Main-Library. *Dir,* Juli Moore; Tel: 704-878-3092, E-mail: jmoore@iredell.lib.nc.us; *Ref Librn,* Mardi J Durham; Tel: 704-878-3109, E-mail: mdurham@iredell.lib.nc.us; *Local Hist Librn,* Joel Reese; Tel: 704-878-3093, E-mail: jreese@iredell.lib.nc.us; *Circ Mgr,* Gary Elam; Tel: 704-928-2405, E-mail: gelam@iredell.lib.nc.us; *Youth Serv Mgr,* Carole Dennis; Tel: 704-928-2414, E-mail: cdennis@iredell.lib.nc.us; *IT Spec,* Kyle Broome; Tel: 704-878-3148, E-mail: kbroome@iredell.lib.nc.us; *Prog Spec,* Teng Cha; Tel: 704-878-5448, E-mail: tcha@iredell.lib.nc.us; *Cataloger,* Kimberly Crawford; Tel: 704-878-3147, E-mail: kcrawford@iredell.lib.nc.us; Staff 31 (MLS 7, Non-MLS 24)
Founded 1967. Pop 122,660; Circ 973,305
Library Holdings: Bks on Deafness & Sign Lang 65; Bk Titles 142,000; Bk Vols 186,000; Per Subs 290; Spec Interest Per Sub 43
Subject Interests: Genealogy, Local hist
Automation Activity & Vendor Info: (Cataloging) SirsiDynix
Wireless access
Special Services for the Deaf - TDD equip
Open Mon-Thurs 9-9, Fri & Sat 9-6
Friends of the Library Group
Branches: 1
HARMONY BRANCH, 3393 Harmony Hwy, Harmony, 28634. (Mail add: PO Box 419, Harmony, 28634-0419). Tel: 704-546-7086. FAX: 704-546-7549. *Br Mgr,* Melissa Spivey; E-mail: mspivey@iredell.lib.nc.us
Founded 2003
Library Holdings: Bk Vols 15,000; Per Subs 43
Open Mon, Wed, Fri & Sat 9-6, Tues & Thurs 11-7
Friends of the Library Group
Bookmobiles: 1

J MITCHELL COMMUNITY COLLEGE*, Mildred & J P Huskins Library, 500 W Broad St, 28677. SAN 313-007X. Tel: 704-878-3271. Web Site: mitchellcc.edu/library. *Libr Coord,* Beverly Rufty; Tel: 704-878-3249, E-mail: brufty@mitchellcc.edu; *Librn,* Courtney Wierckz; Tel: 704-878-5423, E-mail: cwierckz@mitchellcc.edu
Founded 1852
Library Holdings: Bk Titles 40,000; Bk Vols 42,000; Per Subs 180
Subject Interests: Criminal justice, Lit, Nursing, Soc sci
Automation Activity & Vendor Info: (Cataloging) Ex Libris Group; (Circulation) Ex Libris Group; (OPAC) Ex Libris Group; (Serials) Ex Libris Group
Wireless access
Function: ILL available, Photocopying/Printing
Partic in Charlotte Area Educ Consortium
Open Mon-Thurs 7:30-7:30, Fri 7:30-2; Mon-Thurs 7:30-6 (7:30-Noon Summer)

SUPPLY

J BRUNSWICK COMMUNITY COLLEGE LIBRARY*, 50 College Rd, 28462. (Mail add: PO Box 30, 28462-0030). Tel: 910-755-7331. Toll Free Tel: 800-754-1050, Ext 331. Web Site: www.brunswickcc.edu/library. *Dir, Learning Res,* Carmen B Ellis; Tel: 910-755-7351, E-mail: Ellisc@brunswickcc.edu; *Librn,* Liza Palmer; E-mail: liza00137@brunswickcc.edu; *Libr Tech,* Delois Hines; Tel: 910-755-8514, E-mail: hinesd@brunswickcc.edu
Founded 1979. Enrl 1,119
Library Holdings: Bk Vols 20,000; Per Subs 80
Special Collections: North Carolina Records Coll, microfilm
Subject Interests: Genealogy, Local hist
Automation Activity & Vendor Info: (Acquisitions) SirsiDynix; (Cataloging) SirsiDynix; (Circulation) SirsiDynix; (Course Reserve) SirsiDynix; (OPAC) SirsiDynix
Wireless access
Open Mon-Thurs 7:30-7:30, Fri 8-3

SWANNANOA

C WARREN WILSON COLLEGE, Pew Learning Center & Ellison Library, 701 Warren Wilson Rd, 28778. (Mail add: Campus Box 6358, PO Box 9000, Asheville, 28815-9000), SAN 313-0088. Tel: 828-771-3061. Circulation Tel: 828-771-3058. FAX: 828-771-7085. Web Site: www.warren-wilson.edu/academics/library. *Libr Dir,* Chris Nugent; E-mail: nugent@warren-wilson.edu; *Coll Mgt Librn, Dir,* Brian J Conlan; E-mail: bconlan@warren-wilson.edu; *Dir, Electronic Res Librn,* David O Bradshaw; Tel: 828-771-3059, E-mail: dobrshaw@warren-wilson.edu; *Digital Librn, Instruction Prog & Info Literacy Librn,* Criss Guy; Tel: 828-771-3062, E-mail: cguy@warren-wilson.edu; *Circ Serv Mgr, ILL,* Teresa Imfeld; Tel: 828-771-3064, E-mail: timfeld@warren-wilson.edu; *Archives,* Position Currently Open. Subject Specialists: *Sound,* David O Bradshaw; Staff 5 (MLS 5)
Founded 1894. Enrl 750; Fac 76; Highest Degree: Master
Library Holdings: AV Mats 3,719; e-books 220,000; e-journals 77,000; Bk Titles 80,000; Per Subs 145; Spec Interest Per Sub 20
Special Collections: Arthur S Link Library of American History; James McClure Clarke Papers
Subject Interests: Appalachian studies, Archives, Environ studies, Local hist, Women studies
Automation Activity & Vendor Info: (Acquisitions) Innovative Interfaces, Inc - Sierra; (Cataloging) Innovative Interfaces, Inc - Sierra; (Circulation) Innovative Interfaces, Inc - Sierra; (Course Reserve) Innovative Interfaces, Inc - Sierra; (ILL) OCLC WorldShare Interlibrary Loan; (OPAC) Innovative Interfaces, Inc - Sierra; (Serials) Innovative Interfaces, Inc - Sierra
Wireless access
Partic in Appalachian College Association; Berks County Library Association; Carolina Consortium; LYRASIS; OCLC Online Computer Library Center, Inc
Open Mon-Thurs 8:30am-10pm, Fri 8:30-5, Sun 1-8

SYLVA

P JACKSON COUNTY PUBLIC LIBRARY, 310 Keener St, 28779-3241. SAN 313-010X. Tel: 828-586-2016. FAX: 828-631-2943. Web Site: www.fontanalib.org/sylva. *County Librn,* Tracy Fitzmaurice; Tel: 828-586-2016, Ext 303, E-mail: tfitzmaurice@fontanalib.org; Staff 20 (MLS 4, Non-MLS 16)
Founded 1928. Pop 40,000; Circ 100,000
Jul 2021-Jun 2022 Income $1,255,000, County $1,200,000, Locally Generated Income $40,000, Other $15,000. Mats Exp $52,040, Books $35,000, Per/Ser (Incl. Access Fees) $3,000, Micro $40, AV Mat $7,000, Electronic Ref Mat (Incl. Access Fees) $7,000. Sal $650,000
Library Holdings: Audiobooks 2,000; CDs 1,500; DVDs 2,500; Large Print Bks 2,200; Microforms 150; Bk Vols 65,000; Per Subs 93; Videos 300
Automation Activity & Vendor Info: (Acquisitions) Baker & Taylor; (Cataloging) Evergreen; (Circulation) Evergreen; (OPAC) Evergreen
Wireless access
Function: 24/7 Electronic res, 24/7 Online cat, 3D Printer, Accelerated reader prog, Activity rm, Adult bk club, Art exhibits, Art programs, Audio & video playback equip for onsite use, Audiobks on Playaways & MP3, Audiobks via web, Bks on CD, Children's prog, Computer training, Computers for patron use, Digital talking bks, Electronic databases & coll, Holiday prog, ILL available, Internet access, Large print keyboards, Life-long learning prog for all ages, Magazines, Magnifiers for reading, Meeting rooms, Microfiche/film & reading machines, Movies, Notary serv, Online cat, OverDrive digital audio bks, Photocopying/Printing, Preschool outreach, Preschool reading prog, Printer for laptops & handheld devices, Prog for adults, Prog for children & young adult, Ref & res, Ref serv available, Scanner, Senior computer classes, Serves people with intellectual disabilities, Spanish lang bks, STEM programs, Story hour, Study rm, Summer & winter reading prog, Summer reading prog, Tax forms, Teen prog, Telephone ref, Wheelchair accessible, Workshops
Publications: Fontana Flyer (Newsletter)
Mem of Fontana Regional Library
Special Services for the Deaf - Assisted listening device
Special Services for the Blind - Accessible computers; Assistive/Adapted tech devices, equip & products; Playaways (bks on MP3)
Open Mon & Wed 9-6, Tues & Thurs 9-8, Fri & Sat 9-5
Restriction: Co libr
Friends of the Library Group

J SOUTHWESTERN COMMUNITY COLLEGE LIBRARY*, 447 College Dr, 28779. SAN 313-0118. Tel: 828-339-4288. Toll Free Tel: 800-447-4091, Ext 4288. FAX: 828-339-4613. Web Site: southwesterncc.edu/library. *Dir,* Tina Adams; E-mail: t_adams@southwesterncc.edu; Staff 3 (MLS 2, Non-MLS 1)
Founded 1964
Library Holdings: Bk Vols 32,000; Per Subs 120
Wireless access
Open Mon-Thurs 8-8, Fri 8-3

TARBORO

J EDGECOMBE COMMUNITY COLLEGE*, Learning Resources Center, 2009 W Wilson St, 27886. SAN 312-9829. Tel: 252-618-6570. FAX: 252-823-6817. Web Site: www.edgecombe.edu/student-portal/library-lrc. *Dir, Libr Serv,* Deborah B Parisher; E-mail: parisherd@edgecombe.edu; Staff 8 (MLS 3, Non-MLS 5)
Founded 1968. Enrl 2,200; Fac 142
Library Holdings: Bk Titles 38,929; Bk Vols 43,687; Per Subs 245
Special Collections: North Carolina County Records & History, bks, micro
Subject Interests: Acctg, Admin off tech, Autobody, Computer prog, Cosmetology, Health info tech, Imaging tech, Indust electrical-electronics tech, Indust maintenance tech, Law enforcement, Manufacturing engr tech, Mechanical drafting tech, Nursing, Radiology, Respiratory care, Soc work, Surgical tech, Teacher associates
Automation Activity & Vendor Info: (Acquisitions) SirsiDynix; (Cataloging) SirsiDynix; (Circulation) SirsiDynix; (Course Reserve) SirsiDynix; (ILL) SirsiDynix; (Media Booking) SirsiDynix; (OPAC) SirsiDynix; (Serials) SirsiDynix
Wireless access
Partic in Carolina Consortium; OCLC Online Computer Library Center, Inc
Open Mon-Thurs 7:30am-8pm, Fri 7:30-4 (Fall-Spring); Mon-Thurs 7:15am-7pm (Summer)

Departmental Libraries:

ROCKY MOUNT CAMPUS, 225 Tarboro St, Rocky Mount, 27801, SAN 373-6210. Tel: 252-823-5166. FAX: 252-985-2212. *Dir, Libr Serv,* Deborah B Parisher; E-mail: parisherd@edgecombe.edu
Open Mon-Thurs (Fall-Spring) 7:30am-9pm, Fri 7:30-4; Mon-Thurs (Summer) 7:15am-7pm

P EDGECOMBE COUNTY MEMORIAL LIBRARY*, 909 Main St, 27886. SAN 313-0126. Tel: 252-823-1141. FAX: 252-823-7699. Web Site: edgecombelibrary.libguides.com/homepage. *Dir,* Roman Leary; E-mail: rleary@edgecombelibrary.org; *Asst Dir,* Sue Howard; E-mail: showard@edgecombelibrary.org; *Adult Serv Coordr, Circ Desk Supvr,* Anna Adams; E-mail: aadams@edgecombelibrary.org; *Children's Coordr,* Crystal Sessoms; E-mail: csessoms@edgecombelibrary.org; *Ref Asst,* Brian Everett; E-mail: beverette@edgecombelibrary.org; *Local Hist/Genealogy, Spec,* Pam Edmondson; E-mail: pedmondson@edgecombelibrary.org; *Outreach Serv, Spec,* Yolanda Thigpen; E-mail: ythigpen@edgecombelibrary.org; Staff 12 (MLS 2, Non-MLS 10)
Founded 1920. Pop 56,000; Circ 126,468
Library Holdings: Large Print Bks 10,000; Bk Vols 101,708; Per Subs 300; Talking Bks 4,000; Videos 178
Special Collections: NC History Coll
Automation Activity & Vendor Info: (Cataloging) TLC (The Library Corporation); (Circulation) TLC (The Library Corporation); (OPAC) TLC (The Library Corporation)
Wireless access
Publications: Newsletter
Partic in NC State Libr Info Network; OCLC Online Computer Library Center, Inc
Open Mon-Thurs 9-9, Fri 9-6, Sat 9-5
Friends of the Library Group

Branches: 1

PINETOPS BRANCH, 201 S First St, Pinetops, 27864. (Mail add: PO Box 688, Pinetops, 27864-0688), SAN 377-0338. Tel: 252-827-4621. FAX: 252-827-0426. *Br Mgr,* Kathy Causway; E-mail: kcausway@edgecombelibrary.org
Library Holdings: Bk Vols 7,200
Open Mon, Wed & Fri 9-6, Tues & Thurs 9-8
Friends of the Library Group

TAYLORSVILLE

P ALEXANDER COUNTY LIBRARY, 77 First Ave SW, 28681. SAN 313-0134. Tel: 828-632-4058. FAX: 828-632-1094. Web Site: www.alexanderlibrary.org. *Dir,* Laura Crooks; E-mail: lcrooks@alexandercountync.gov
Founded 1967. Pop 38,360; Circ 92,250
Library Holdings: Bk Titles 51,450; Per Subs 120
Special Collections: Local History Room
Automation Activity & Vendor Info: (Acquisitions) SirsiDynix; (Cataloging) SirsiDynix; (Circulation) SirsiDynix; (Course Reserve) SirsiDynix; (ILL) SirsiDynix; (Media Booking) SirsiDynix; (OPAC) SirsiDynix; (Serials) SirsiDynix
Wireless access
Open Mon & Thurs 9-7, Tues, Wed & Fri 9-6, Sat 9-3
Friends of the Library Group
Branches: 2
BETHLEHEM, 45 Rink Dam Rd, Hickory, 28601. Tel: 828-495-8753. *Br Mgr,* Glenda Leonard
Open Mon & Wed 9-2, Tues & Thurs 12-7, Fri 12-5
Friends of the Library Group
STONY POINT BRANCH, 431 Ruritan Park Rd, Stony Point, 28678. *Br Mgr,* Zachary Mull
Open Mon & Wed 9-1, Tues & Thurs 3-7

THOMASVILLE

J DAVIDSON COUNTY COMMUNITY COLLEGE*, 297 DCCC Rd, 27360-7385. (Mail add: PO Box 1287, Lexington, 27293-1287), SAN 312-9047. Tel: 336-249-8186. Reference Tel: 336-224-4727. FAX: 336-248-8531. E-mail: library@davidsonccc.edu. Web Site: davidsonccc.edu/academics/library. *Dir, Libr Serv,* Jason Setzer; Tel: 336-249-8186, Ext 6207, E-mail: Jason_Setzer@davidsonccc.edu; Staff 3 (MLS 3)
Founded 1963. Enrl 2,100; Fac 66
Library Holdings: Bk Titles 57,000; Per Subs 236
Wireless access

TROY

J MONTGOMERY COMMUNITY COLLEGE LIBRARY*, 1011 Page St, 27371. SAN 313-0150. Tel: 910-898-9650. Administration Tel: 910-898-9645. FAX: 910-576-2176. Web Site: www.montgomery.edu/library. *Dean, Info Tech & Learning Res,* Stephanie Weishner; E-mail: weishners2525@montgomery.edu
Founded 1967. Highest Degree: Associate
Library Holdings: CDs 140; Bk Vols 18,300; Per Subs 100; Videos 300
Subject Interests: Forestry, Gunsmithing, Pottery, Taxidermy
Automation Activity & Vendor Info: (Cataloging) SirsiDynix; (Circulation) SirsiDynix; (Course Reserve) SirsiDynix; (ILL) SirsiDynix; (OPAC) SirsiDynix
Wireless access
Partic in NC State Ref Libr
Open Mon-Thurs (Winter) 8-7, Fri 8-3; Mon-Thurs (Summer) 8-5, Fri 8-3

P MONTGOMERY COUNTY LIBRARY*, 215 W Main, 27371. SAN 355-2004. Tel: 910-572-1311. FAX: 910-576-5565. *Librn,* David Atkins; E-mail: david.atkins@srls.info; Staff 1965 (MLS 1965)
Pop 26,822; Circ 119,681
Library Holdings: Bk Vols 62,009; Per Subs 200
Special Collections: Bobbin lace making
Subject Interests: Local hist
Automation Activity & Vendor Info: (Acquisitions) TLC (The Library Corporation); (Cataloging) TLC (The Library Corporation); (Circulation) TLC (The Library Corporation); (OPAC) TLC (The Library Corporation)
Wireless access
Function: 24/7 Electronic res, 24/7 Online cat, After school storytime, Bks on CD, Computers for patron use, Digital talking bks, E-Readers, Electronic databases & coll, For res purposes, Holiday prog, ILL available, Internet access, Magazines, Mango lang, Meeting rooms, Microfiche/film & reading machines, OverDrive digital audio bks, Photocopying/Printing, Prog for adults, Prog for children & young adult, Scanner, Story hour, Summer reading prog
Mem of Sandhill Regional Libr Syst; Sandhill Regional Library System
Open Mon-Fri, 9:30-6, Sat 9:30-12:30
Friends of the Library Group
Branches: 4
ALLEN LIBRARY, 307 Page St, Biscoe, 27209-0518, SAN 355-2039. Tel: 910-428-2551. FAX: 910-428-2551. *Br Mgr,* ; Staff 1 (Non-MLS 1)
Circ 28,499
Automation Activity & Vendor Info: (Acquisitions) Baker & Taylor; (Cataloging) TLC (The Library Corporation); (Circulation) TLC (The Library Corporation); (OPAC) TLC (The Library Corporation)
Function: 24/7 Electronic res, 24/7 Online cat, Computers for patron use, Electronic databases & coll, Internet access, Mango lang, Online cat, OverDrive digital audio bks, Photocopying/Printing, Story hour, Summer reading prog
Open Mon, Tues, Thurs & Fri 2-6
Friends of the Library Group
JOHN C CURRIE MEMORIAL LIBRARY CANDOR BRANCH, 138 S School Rd, Candor, 27229, SAN 355-2063. Tel: 910-974-4033. FAX: 910-974-4033. *Br Mgr,* Cathy H Harris; Staff 1 (Non-MLS 1)
Circ 44,657
Automation Activity & Vendor Info: (Acquisitions) Baker & Taylor; (Cataloging) TLC (The Library Corporation); (Circulation) TLC (The Library Corporation); (OPAC) TLC (The Library Corporation)
Open Mon-Fri 2-6
Friends of the Library Group
MOUNT GILEAD BRANCH, 110 W Allenton St, Mount Gilead, 27306, SAN 355-2098. Tel: 910-439-6651. FAX: 910-439-6651. *Br Mgr,* Cindy Brooks; Staff 1 (Non-MLS 1)
Circ 15,262
Automation Activity & Vendor Info: (Acquisitions) TLC (The Library Corporation); (Cataloging) TLC (The Library Corporation); (Circulation) The Library Co-Op, Inc; (OPAC) TLC (The Library Corporation)
Function: 24/7 Electronic res, 24/7 Online cat, Electronic databases & coll, Internet access, Mango lang, Online cat, OverDrive digital audio bks, Photocopying/Printing, Scanner, Summer reading prog
Open Mon, Tues, Thurs & Fri 2-6
Friends of the Library Group
STAR BRANCH, 222 S Main St, Star, 27356, SAN 355-2128. Tel: 910-428-2338. FAX: 910-428-2338. *Br Mgr,* Shannon Doutt Dolgos; Staff 1 (Non-MLS 1)
Circ 28,156
Automation Activity & Vendor Info: (Acquisitions) TLC (The Library Corporation); (Cataloging) TLC (The Library Corporation); (Circulation) TLC (The Library Corporation); (OPAC) The Library Co-Op, Inc
Function: 24/7 Electronic res, 24/7 Online cat, Adult bk club, Audiobks via web, Bks on CD, Computers for patron use, Digital talking bks, ILL available, Mango lang, Online cat, OverDrive digital audio bks, Photocopying/Printing, Preschool reading prog, Prog for adults, Story hour, Summer reading prog
Open Mon, Thurs & Fri 2-6, Tues & Wed 9:30-1:30
Friends of the Library Group

TRYON

S THE LANIER LIBRARY ASSOCIATION*, 72 Chestnut St, 28782. SAN 313-0169. Tel: 828-859-9535. E-mail: thelanierlibrary@gmail.com. Web Site: thelanierlibrary.org. *Libr Dir,* Amber Keeran; Staff 5 (MLS 1, Non-MLS 4)
Founded 1890
Library Holdings: Bk Titles 27,000; Per Subs 63
Special Collections: Sidney Lanier Coll; Tryon Area Authors
Wireless access
Publications: New Book List (Monthly); Newsletter (Monthly)
Open Tues-Thurs 9:30-4:30, Sat 9:30-1, Sun 1-4
Restriction: Mem only

VANCEBORO

P VANCEBORO PUBLIC LIBRARY, 7931 Main St, 28586. (Mail add: PO Box 38, 28586-0038), SAN 313-0177. Tel: 252-244-0571. FAX: 252-244-1335. Web Site: mycprl.org/vanceboro. *Librn,* Julie Cox; E-mail: julie.cox@cpcrl.org
Circ 12,546
Library Holdings: Bk Vols 12,222; Per Subs 10
Wireless access
Mem of Craven-Pamlico-Carteret Regional Library System
Open Mon-Fri 10-6
Friends of the Library Group

WADESBORO

P HAMPTON B ALLEN LIBRARY, 120 S Greene St, 28170. SAN 313-0185. Tel: 704-694-5177. FAX: 704-694-5178. E-mail: circleft@gmail.com. Web Site: srls.libguides.com/c.php?g=811906. *Libr Mgr,* Ms Kit Brewer; E-mail: kit.brewer@srls.info
Founded 1923. Pop 25,000; Circ 44,000
Library Holdings: Bk Titles 52,000; Per Subs 120
Subject Interests: Genealogy, Local hist
Automation Activity & Vendor Info: (Cataloging) TLC (The Library Corporation); (Circulation) TLC (The Library Corporation); (OPAC) TLC (The Library Corporation)
Wireless access
Mem of Sandhill Regional Library System
Partic in OCLC Online Computer Library Center, Inc
Open Mon 9:30-5:30, Tues & Thurs 8:30-6:30, Wed 8:30-Noon, Fri 8:30-5:30, Sat 9-Noon
Friends of the Library Group
Bookmobiles: 1

WAKE FOREST

R SOUTHEASTERN BAPTIST THEOLOGICAL SEMINARY LIBRARY*, 114 N Wingate St, 27587. SAN 313-0193. Tel: 919-761-2251. Circulation Tel: 919-863-8251. Interlibrary Loan Service Tel: 919-761-2323. Reference Tel: 919-761-2258. E-mail: reference@sebts.edu. Web Site: library.sebts.edu. *Dir,* Jason Fowler; Tel: 919-863-2250, E-mail: jfowler@sebts.edu; *Head, Tech Serv,* Donna Wells; Tel: 919-863-2253, E-mail: dwells@sebts.edu; *Archives Mgr, Digital Coll Mgr,* Steve Jones; Tel: 919-863-2220, E-mail: sjones@sebts.edu; *Supvr, Circ,* Michele Shinholser; Tel: 919-863-2256, E-mail: mshinholser@sebts.edu; *Coordr, Acq,* Steve Frary; Tel: 919-863-2330, E-mail: Frary@sebts.edu; *Ref Coordr,* Dougald McLaurin; Tel: 919-863-2204, E-mail: dmclaurin@sebts.edu; *Coordr, Ser,* Jeannie Beck; Tel: 919-863-2325, E-mail: jbeck@sebts.edu; Staff 9 (MLS 4, Non-MLS 5)
Founded 1951. Enrl 1,915; Fac 54; Highest Degree: Doctorate
Library Holdings: e-books 386,000; Bk Titles 156,654; Bk Vols 188,500; Per Subs 782
Special Collections: Baptists (Baptist Documents Coll); Education Curriculum Lab; Lifeway Curriculum
Subject Interests: Baptist hist, Biblical studies, Christianity, Doctrine, Philos, Relig studies, Theol
Automation Activity & Vendor Info: (Acquisitions) SirsiDynix; (Cataloging) SirsiDynix; (Circulation) SirsiDynix; (Course Reserve) SirsiDynix; (OPAC) SirsiDynix; (Serials) SirsiDynix
Function: ILL available
Partic in LYRASIS; OCLC Online Computer Library Center, Inc
Open Mon, Tues & Thurs 7am-10pm, Wed 7-6, Fri 7-4, Sat 10-5

WALLACE

P THELMA DINGUS BRYANT LIBRARY*, 409 W Main St, 28466-2909. SAN 313-0207. Tel: 910-285-3796. FAX: 910-285-8224. E-mail: tdblibrary@townofwallace.com. *Libr Dir,* Sharon Robison; *Ch Serv,* Cara Rothstein; Staff 3 (Non-MLS 3)
Founded 1969. Circ 42,000
Library Holdings: DVDs 65; Large Print Bks 244; Bk Titles 30,300; Per Subs 35; Talking Bks 634; Videos 666
Subject Interests: English (Lang), Spanish
Automation Activity & Vendor Info: (Circulation) Follett Software
Wireless access
Friends of the Library Group

WALNUT COVE

P WALNUT COVE PUBLIC LIBRARY*, 106 W Fifth St, 27052. (Mail add: PO Box 706, 27052-0706), SAN 313-0215. Tel: 336-591-7496. FAX: 336-591-8494. E-mail: wco@nwrl.org. Web Site: nwrl.org/c.php?g=613331&p=4261221. *Br Librn,* Christine Boles; E-mail: cboles@nwrl.org
Founded 1970. Pop 3,500
Library Holdings: Bk Vols 28,000
Special Collections: Danbury Reporter, bd vols; Stokes News, bd vols
Automation Activity & Vendor Info: (Acquisitions) SirsiDynix-WorkFlows; (Cataloging) SirsiDynix; (Circulation) SirsiDynix; (OPAC) SirsiDynix
Wireless access
Mem of Northwestern Regional Library
Open Mon, Wed & Fri 9-5:30, Tues & Thurs 9-8, Sat 9-1
Friends of the Library Group

WARRENTON

P WARREN COUNTY MEMORIAL LIBRARY, 119 South Front St, 27589. SAN 313-0223. Tel: 252-257-4990. FAX: 252-257-4089. Web Site: www.wcmlibrary.org. *Dir,* Cheryl Reddish; Tel: 252-257-4990, Ext 100, E-mail: CherylReddish@warrencountync.gov; *Circ, Soc Media Coordr, Tech,* Tiffany Macklin; E-mail: TiffanyMacklin@warrencountync.gov; *Circ,* Richard Smithey; Tel: 252-257-4990, Ext 201, E-mail: RichardSmithey@warrencountync.gov; *Circ, Ref,* David Spence; Tel: 252-257-4990, Ext 202, E-mail: DavidSpence@warrencountync.gov; *Circ, Tech Serv,* Catha Harrison; E-mail: CathaHarrison@warrencountync.gov; Staff 1 (MLS 1)
Founded 1937. Pop 19,871; Circ 23,044
Library Holdings: CDs 187; DVDs 1,574; e-books 71,510; Large Print Bks 1,396; Bk Vols 31,622; Per Subs 33; Talking Bks 810
Automation Activity & Vendor Info: (Cataloging) Follett Software; (Circulation) Follett Software; (OPAC) Follett Software
Wireless access
Open Mon-Thurs 9-7, Fri 9-5, Sat 10-2
Friends of the Library Group

WASHINGTON

J BEAUFORT COUNTY COMMUNITY COLLEGE*, Learning Resources Center, 5337 US Hwy 264 E, 27889. (Mail add: PO Box 1069, 27889-1069), SAN 313-024X. Tel: 252-940-6282. FAX: 252-946-9575. E-mail: library@beaufortccc.edu. Web Site: beaufortccc.libguides.com/libraryhome. *Dir, Libr Res Ctr,* Paula Hopper; Tel: 252-940-6243, E-mail: paula.hopper@beaufortccc.edu; Staff 5 (MLS 2, Non-MLS 3)
Founded 1968
Library Holdings: Bk Vols 35,000; Per Subs 150
Automation Activity & Vendor Info: (Cataloging) SirsiDynix; (Circulation) SirsiDynix; (OPAC) SirsiDynix
Wireless access
Function: Audio & video playback equip for onsite use, AV serv, Bks on CD, CD-ROM, Computers for patron use, Distance learning, Equip loans & repairs, Free DVD rentals, ILL available, Internet access, Orientations, Outside serv via phone, mail, e-mail & web, Photocopying/Printing, Ref serv available, Scanner, Wheelchair accessible
Partic in Community Colleges Libraries in North Carolina
Open Mon-Thurs 8am-9pm, Fri 8-4

P BEAUFORT, HYDE & MARTIN COUNTY REGIONAL LIBRARY*, Old Court House, 158 N Market St, 27889. SAN 313-0258. Tel: 252-946-6401. FAX: 252-946-0352. Web Site: bhmlib.org. *Dir,* Amanda Corbett; E-mail: acorbett@bhmlib.org; Staff 19 (MLS 3, Non-MLS 16)
Founded 1941. Pop 76,024; Circ 195,802
Library Holdings: Bk Vols 117,000; Per Subs 275
Automation Activity & Vendor Info: (Cataloging) Evergreen; (Circulation) Evergreen; (OPAC) Evergreen
Wireless access
Open Mon-Fri 9-5
Friends of the Library Group
Branches: 7
BATH COMMUNITY, 102 S Harding St, Bath, 27808, SAN 377-6352. Tel: 252-923-6371. FAX: 252-923-0497. Web Site: bhmlib.org/bath. *Br Mgr,* Ann Wiggins
Library Holdings: Bk Vols 5,000; Per Subs 15
Open Mon-Fri 10-6, Sat 9-Noon
Friends of the Library Group
BELHAVEN PUBLIC, 333 E Main St, Belhaven, 27810, SAN 312-7435. Tel: 252-943-2993. FAX: 252-943-2606. Web Site: bhmlib.org/belhaven. *Br Mgr,* Pat Saunders
Library Holdings: Large Print Bks 500; Bk Vols 6,000; Per Subs 20
Open Mon-Fri 9:30-5:30, Sat 9:30-1
Friends of the Library Group
HAZEL W GUILFORD MEMORIAL, 524 E Main St, Aurora, 27806, SAN 377-6417. Tel: 252-322-5046. Web Site: bhmlib.org/aurora. *Br Mgr,* Robina Norman
Library Holdings: Large Print Bks 150; Bk Vols 2,000; Per Subs 20
Open Mon-Wed & Fri 9-5, Thurs 11-7, Sat 9-Noon
Friends of the Library Group
HYDE COUNTY PUBLIC, 33460 US 264, Rm 5, Engelhard, 27824. Tel: 252-925-2222. FAX: 252-926-0311. Web Site: bhmlib.org/engelhard. *Br Mgr,* Gail Blake
Library Holdings: AV Mats 400; Bk Titles 22,000; Bk Vols 25,000; Per Subs 40
Open Mon-Thurs 10-12:30 & 1-5:30, Sat 10-12:30 & 1-4
MARTIN MEMORIAL, 200 N Smithwick St, Williamston, 27892, SAN 377-6433. Tel: 252-792-7476. FAX: 252-792-8964. Web Site: bhmlib.org/mml. *Br Mgr,* Ann Phelps; Staff 5 (MLS 1, Non-MLS 4)
Library Holdings: Audiobooks 100; DVDs 150; Large Print Bks 750; Microforms 200; Bk Vols 40,000; Per Subs 70; Videos 25
Special Collections: Local Genealogy Coll; North Carolina Coll
Function: Accelerated reader prog, Adult bk club, Bks on CD, Children's prog, Computers for patron use, Electronic databases & coll, Free DVD rentals, Holiday prog, ILL available, Online cat, Photocopying/Printing, Preschool outreach, Prog for adults, Prog for children & young adult, Ref & res, Ref serv available, Story hour, Summer reading prog, Tax forms, Teen prog, Wheelchair accessible
Open Mon-Wed & Fri 9:30-5:30, Thurs 9:30-8, Sat 9:30-1, Sun 2-5
Friends of the Library Group
OCRACOKE SCHOOL & COMMUNITY LIBRARY, 225 Back Rd, Ocracoke, 27960, SAN 376-2890. Tel: 252-928-4436. FAX: 252-928-4436. Web Site: www.bhmlib.org/ocracoke. *Br Mgr,* Sundae Horn
Pop 1,000
Library Holdings: Large Print Bks 120; Bk Vols 5,000; Per Subs 25
Special Collections: North Carolina Fiction, Nonfiction & Reference Coll. Municipal Document Depository
Open Mon, Tues, Thurs & Fri 3-7, Wed 3-8, Sat 9-1
Friends of the Library Group

ROBERSONVILLE PUBLIC, 119 S Main St, Robersonville, 27871, SAN 377-6468. Tel: 252-508-0342. FAX: 252-795-3359. Web Site: bhmlib.org/robersonville. *Br Mgr,* Sallie Schauppeet
Library Holdings: Bk Titles 6,000; Bk Vols 16,000
Open Mon-Fri 9-5, Sat 10-1
Friends of the Library Group
Bookmobiles: 2

P GEORGE H & LAURA E BROWN LIBRARY, 122 Van Norden St, 27889. SAN 313-0266. Tel: 252-946-4300. FAX: 252-975-2015. Web Site: washington-nc.libguides.com. *Dir,* Sandra Silvey; E-mail: ssilvey@washingtonnc.gov; *Tech Serv Supvr,* Kim Davenport; Staff 2 (MLS 2)
Founded 1911. Pop 15,510; Circ 80,404
Library Holdings: Bk Vols 41,900; Per Subs 69
Special Collections: Bellamy Papers; Bible Translations Coll; C F Warren Coll; Cemetery Records; County Newspapers Found & Filmed by North Carolina State Archives, dated prior to 1900; Current Local Newspaper, microfilm; Dunstan Papers; E J Warren Coll; Ernest Harding Civil War Coll; Fowle Papers; Gould Marsh Ledger, 1805-11; Havens Ledgers; John Respess Papers, copy; Jonathan Havens Coll; Josiah Fowle Ledger, 1808-47, copy; Local Daughters of the American Revolution Records, copies; Wiswall Papers. Oral History
Subject Interests: Career Information Center, Carolina hist, Civil War, Genealogy
Automation Activity & Vendor Info: (Cataloging) TLC (The Library Corporation); (Circulation) TLC (The Library Corporation)
Wireless access
Partic in North Carolina Information Network; OCLC Online Computer Library Center, Inc
Open Mon-Sat 9-6
Friends of the Library Group

WAYNESVILLE

P HAYWOOD COUNTY PUBLIC LIBRARY*, 678 S Haywood St, 28786. SAN 355-2152. Tel: 828-452-5169. FAX: 828-452-6746. Web Site: www.haywoodlibrary.org. *Dir,* Kathy Vossler; Tel: 828-356-2504, E-mail: kathy.vossler@haywoodcountync.gov; *Asst Dir,* Caroline Roten; Tel: 828-356-2518, E-mail: caroline.roten@haywoodcountync.gov; *Ad,* Kathy Olsen; Tel: 828-356-2507, E-mail: kathleen.olsen@haywoodcountync.gov; *Commun Engagement Librn,* Deanna Lyles; Tel: 828-356-2519, E-mail: deanna.lyles@haywoodcountync.gov; *Youth Serv Librn,* Lisa Hartzell; Tel: 828-356-2511, E-mail: lisa.hartzell@haywoodcountync.gov; Staff 26 (MLS 6, Non-MLS 20)
Founded 1891. Pop 62,317; Circ 465,000
Library Holdings: Bk Vols 14,000; Per Subs 500
Subject Interests: NC genealogy
Automation Activity & Vendor Info: (Acquisitions) Evergreen; (Cataloging) Evergreen; (Circulation) Evergreen; (ILL) Evergreen; (OPAC) Evergreen; (Serials) Evergreen
Wireless access
Function: 24/7 Electronic res, 24/7 Online cat, Activity rm, Adult bk club, Adult literacy prog, Archival coll, Art exhibits, Art programs, Audiobks on Playaways & MP3, Audiobks via web, Bi-weekly Writer's Group, Bk club(s), Bks on CD, Butterfly Garden, Chess club, Children's prog, Computer training, Computers for patron use, Digital talking bks, Electronic databases & coll, Family literacy, For res purposes, Free DVD rentals, Health sci info serv, Holiday prog, Home delivery & serv to seniorr ctr & nursing homes, ILL available, Instruction & testing, Internet access, Life-long learning prog for all ages, Magazines, Mail & tel request accepted, Meeting rooms, Microfiche/film & reading machines, Movies, Music CDs, Online cat, Online info literacy tutorials on the web & in blackboard, Online ref, Outreach serv, OverDrive digital audio bks, Photocopying/Printing, Preschool outreach, Preschool reading prog, Printer for laptops & handheld devices, Prof lending libr, Prog for adults, Prog for children & young adult, Ref & res, Ref serv available, Res assist avail, Scanner, Senior computer classes, Senior outreach, Serves people with intellectual disabilities, Spanish lang bks, STEM programs, Story hour, Study rm, Summer & winter reading prog, Summer reading prog, Tax forms, Teen prog, Telephone ref, Visual arts prog, Wheelchair accessible, Winter reading prog, Workshops, Writing prog
Publications: Paperclips: Haywood County Public Library & Friends (Newsletter)
Open Mon-Wed & Fri 9-6, Thurs 9-7, Sat 9-5
Friends of the Library Group
Branches: 3
CANTON BRANCH, 11 Pennsylvania Ave, Canton, 28716, SAN 355-2187. Tel: 828-648-2924. FAX: 828-648-0377. *Ch, Mgr,* Jennifer Stuart; E-mail: jennifer.stuart@haywoodcountync.gov; *Ch,* Deanna Lyles; E-mail: deanna.lyles@haywoodcountync.gov; Staff 3 (MLS 1, Non-MLS 2)
Library Holdings: Bk Vols 25,000; Per Subs 75
Function: 24/7 Electronic res, 24/7 Online cat, Activity rm, Adult bk club, Art exhibits, Art programs, Audiobks on Playaways & MP3, Audiobks via web, Bk club(s), Bks on CD, Butterfly Garden, Chess club, Children's prog, Computer training, Computers for patron use, Electronic databases & coll, Family literacy, Free DVD rentals, Health sci info serv, Holiday prog, Home delivery & serv to seniorr ctr & nursing homes, ILL available, Internet access, Life-long learning prog for all ages, Mango lang, Meeting rooms, Movies, Music CDs, Online cat, OverDrive digital audio bks, Photocopying/Printing, Preschool outreach, Preschool reading prog, Printer for laptops & handheld devices, Prog for adults, Prog for children & young adult, Ref & res, Ref serv available, Scanner, Senior computer classes, Senior outreach, Serves people with intellectual disabilities, STEM programs, Story hour, Summer reading prog, Tax forms, Teen prog, Wheelchair accessible
Open Mon, Wed & Fri 9-6, Tues & Thurs 9-7, Sun 1:30-5
Friends of the Library Group
FINES CREEK, Fines Creek Community Bldg, 190 Fines Creek Rd, Clyde, 28721. Tel: 828-627-0146. ; Staff 2 (MLS 1, Non-MLS 1)
Library Holdings: Bk Vols 3,654
Open Mon & Wed 9-5
Friends of the Library Group
MAGGIE VALLEY, Town Hall, 3987 Soco Rd, Maggie Valley, 28751. Tel: 828-356-2541. FAX: 828-356-2549.
Founded 2002
Library Holdings: Bk Vols 6,544; Per Subs 15
Open Tues & Thurs 9-5
Friends of the Library Group

WELDON

J HALIFAX COMMUNITY COLLEGE LIBRARY*, 100 College Dr, 27890. (Mail add: PO Drawer 809, 27890-0700), SAN 313-0312. Tel: 252-536-7236. FAX: 252-536-0474. E-mail: lrcerc@halifaxcc.edu. Web Site: halifaxcc.edu/Library. *Dir,* Lynn Allen; Tel: 252-536-7237, E-mail: lallen920@halifaxcc.edu; Staff 6 (MLS 1, Non-MLS 5)
Founded 1968. Enrl 1,721; Fac 12; Highest Degree: Associate
Library Holdings: Bk Titles 30,000; Per Subs 100
Special Collections: News Bank Library 1979-present
Subject Interests: Archit, Art, Dental hygiene, Econ, Govt, Hist, Lit, Nursing, Paralegal
Wireless access
Open Mon-Thurs 8-5, Fri 8-4

WENTWORTH

J ROCKINGHAM COMMUNITY COLLEGE*, Gerald B James Library, 315 Wrenn Memorial Rd, 27375. (Mail add: PO Box 38, 27375-0038), SAN 313-0339. Tel: 336-342-4261, Ext 2247. FAX: 336-342-1203. E-mail: library@rockinghamcc.edu. Web Site: www.rockinghamcc.edu/library. *Archives, Dir, Libr Serv,* Mary Gomez; Tel: 336-342-4261, Ext 2320, E-mail: gomezm@rockinghamcc.edu; *Pub Serv Librn,* Dawn-Michelle Oliver; Tel: 336-342-4261, Ext 2315, E-mail: oliverd@rockinghamcc.edu; *Tech Asst,* Teresa Frohock; Tel: 336-342-4261, Ext 2300, E-mail: frohockt@rockinghamcc.edu; Staff 3 (MLS 2, Non-MLS 1)
Founded 1966. Enrl 2,200; Fac 140; Highest Degree: Associate
Library Holdings: Bk Titles 37,500; Bk Vols 45,500; Per Subs 145
Special Collections: Rockingham County Historical Coll, County hist bks, family/genealogy files, local newsp, maps, micro, oral hist, photog, realia
Subject Interests: Rockingham county
Automation Activity & Vendor Info: (Cataloging) SirsiDynix; (Circulation) SirsiDynix; (OPAC) SirsiDynix
Wireless access
Function: 24/7 Electronic res, 24/7 Online cat, Archival coll, Audio & video playback equip for onsite use, Audiobks via web, Computers for patron use, Digital talking bks, Doc delivery serv, Electronic databases & coll, Free DVD rentals, ILL available, Internet access, Magazines, Magnifiers for reading, Mail & tel request accepted, Mango lang, Microfiche/film & reading machines, Movies, Online cat, Online ref, Orientations, Outside serv via phone, mail, e-mail & web, Photocopying/Printing, Ref & res, Ref serv available, Res assist avail, Scanner, Spanish lang bks, Study rm, Telephone ref, Wheelchair accessible
Partic in Community Colleges Libraries in North Carolina; LYRASIS; OCLC Online Computer Library Center, Inc
Open Mon-Thurs 7:45-6, Fri 7:45-3
Restriction: Lending limited to county residents

WEST JEFFERSON

P APPALACHIAN REGIONAL LIBRARY, 148 Library Dr, 28694. SAN 375-5932. Tel: 336-846-2041. FAX: 336-846-7503. Web Site: www.arlibrary.org. *Dir of Libr,* Jane W Blackburn; E-mail: jblackburn@arlibrary.org; Staff 49.7 (MLS 14.6, Non-MLS 35.1)
Founded 1962. Circ 613,970
Library Holdings: Audiobooks 10,333; AV Mats 21,867; DVDs 11,534; e-books 74,242; Bk Vols 199,383; Per Subs 167; Talking Bks 9,148
Special Collections: Local Histories of Ashe, Watauga & Wilkes Counties
Subject Interests: Genealogy, Local hist

Automation Activity & Vendor Info: (Cataloging) Evergreen; (Circulation) Evergreen; (OPAC) Evergreen
Wireless access
Function: 24/7 Electronic res, 24/7 Online cat, Activity rm, Adult bk club, Adult literacy prog, After school storytime, Archival coll, Art exhibits, Audiobks on Playaways & MP3, Audiobks via web, AV serv, Bk club(s), Bks on CD, Butterfly Garden, Children's prog, Citizenship assistance, Computer training, Computers for patron use, Digital talking bks, E-Readers, Electronic databases & coll, Family literacy, Free DVD rentals, Holiday prog, Home delivery & serv to seniorr ctr & nursing homes, Homebound delivery serv, Homework prog, ILL available, Internet access, Life-long learning prog for all ages, Magazines, Magnifiers for reading, Mail & tel request accepted, Meeting rooms, Microfiche/film & reading machines, Movies, Music CDs, Notary serv, Online cat, Online ref, Outreach serv, Outside serv via phone, mail, e-mail & web, OverDrive digital audio bks, Photocopying/Printing, Preschool outreach, Printer for laptops & handheld devices, Prog for adults, Prog for children & young adult, Ref & res, Ref serv available, Scanner, Senior computer classes, Senior outreach, Serves people with intellectual disabilities, Spanish lang bks, Story hour, Study rm, Summer & winter reading prog, Summer reading prog, Tax forms, Teen prog, Telephone ref, Wheelchair accessible, Workshops, Writing prog
Member Libraries: Ashe County Public Library; Watauga County Public Library; Wilkes County Public Library
Open Mon-Thurs 9-7, Fri & Sat 9-5
Friends of the Library Group

P ASHE COUNTY PUBLIC LIBRARY*, 148 Library Dr, 28694. SAN 320-5010. Tel: 336-846-2041. FAX: 336-846-7503. Web Site: www.arlibrary.org. *County Librn,* Suzanne Moore; E-mail: smoore@arlibrary.org; *Adult Serv,* Laura McPherson; *Youth Serv,* Peggy Bailey; Staff 7 (MLS 4, Non-MLS 3)
Founded 1932. Pop 26,000; Circ 174,978
Library Holdings: AV Mats 6,008; Bk Vols 46,769; Per Subs 90
Special Collections: Business & Career; Local History & Genealogy. Oral History
Automation Activity & Vendor Info: (Cataloging) Evergreen; (Circulation) Evergreen; (OPAC) Evergreen; (Serials) EBSCO Online
Wireless access
Mem of Appalachian Regional Library
Open Mon-Thurs 9-7, Fri & Sat 9-5
Friends of the Library Group
Bookmobiles: 1. Outreach Servs, Elaine Adams

WHITEVILLE

P COLUMBUS COUNTY PUBLIC LIBRARY*, Carolyn T High Memorial Library, 407 N JK Powell Blvd, 28472. SAN 355-2217. Tel: 910-642-3116. Reference Tel: 910-641-3976. FAX: 910-642-3839. Web Site: ccplnc.weebly.com. *Dir, Libr Serv,* Morris D Pridgen, Jr; E-mail: mpridgen@columbusco.org; *Cat, Tech Serv,* Faye King; *Ch Serv,* Lizette Dixon; *Circ,* Annie Bowen; *ILL,* Alice Soles; *Ref Serv,* Ann White; *Ser,* Diane Worley; *Syst Adminr,* Chad Benton; Staff 25 (MLS 1, Non-MLS 24)
Founded 1921. Pop 50,198; Circ 257,350
Library Holdings: AV Mats 3,698; Bk Titles 115,000; Bk Vols 120,000; Per Subs 321
Special Collections: Genealogy & Local History; Local newspapers on microfilm; North Carolina
Subject Interests: Genealogy, Local hist
Automation Activity & Vendor Info: (Circulation) Innovative Interfaces, Inc
Wireless access
Function: Homebound delivery serv
Publications: Columbus County, North Carolina: Recollections & Records
Open Mon-Thurs 9-8, Fri 9-5, Sat 10:30-5
Friends of the Library Group
Branches: 5
CHADBOURN COMMUNITY, 301 N Wilson St, Chadbourn, 28431, SAN 377-8479. Tel: 910-654-3322. FAX: 910-654-4392. E-mail: chadbournecommunitylibrary28431@yahoo.com. Web Site: ccplnc.weebly.com/chadbourn.html. *Br Mgr,* Sheena Milliken
Library Holdings: Bk Vols 2,000; Per Subs 33
Automation Activity & Vendor Info: (Acquisitions) Innovative Interfaces, Inc; (Cataloging) Innovative Interfaces, Inc
Open Mon-Thurs 11-6, Fri 11-5
Friends of the Library Group
EAST COLUMBUS LIBRARY, 103 Church Rd, Riegelwood, 28456, SAN 355-2233. Tel: 910-655-4157. FAX: 910-655-9414. Web Site: ccplnc.weebly.com/riegelwood.html. *Br Mgr,* Robin Creech; E-mail: rcreech@columbusco.org; Staff 2 (Non-MLS 2)
Library Holdings: Large Print Bks 150; Bk Vols 11,000; Per Subs 30
Open Mon-Thurs 11-6, Fri 11-5
Friends of the Library Group
FAIR BLUFF COMMUNITY, 315 Railroad St, Fair Bluff, 28439. (Mail add: PO Box 428, Fair Bluff, 28439-0428), SAN 355-2241. Tel: 910-649-7098. FAX: 910-649-7733. E-mail: fairblufflibrary@gmail.com. Web Site: ccplnc.weebly.com/fair-bluff.html. *Br Mgr,* Teresa Blackwell Fountain; Staff 2 (Non-MLS 2)
Library Holdings: Bk Vols 11,000; Per Subs 40; Talking Bks 32; Videos 126
Open Mon-Thurs 11-6, Fri 11-5
Friends of the Library Group
RUBE MCCRAY MEMORIAL, 301 Flemington Dr, Lake Waccamaw, 28450, SAN 375-2933. Tel: 910-646-4616. FAX: 910-646-4747. Web Site: ccplnc.weebly.com/lake-waccamaw.html. *Br Mgr,* Kim Holmes; Staff 2 (Non-MLS 2)
Library Holdings: AV Mats 200; Large Print Bks 175; Bk Vols 10,000; Per Subs 250
Open Mon-Thurs 11-6, Fri 11-5
Friends of the Library Group
TABOR CITY PUBLIC, 101 E Fifth St, Tabor City, 28463, SAN 355-2276. Tel: 910-653-3774. FAX: 910-653-3788. Web Site: ccplnc.weebly.com/tabor-city.html. *Br Mgr,* Position Currently Open
Library Holdings: Bk Vols 17,118; Per Subs 23
Open Mon-Thurs 11-6, Fri 11-5
Friends of the Library Group
Bookmobiles: 1

J SOUTHEASTERN COMMUNITY COLLEGE*, Williamson Library, 4564 Chadbourne Hwy, 28472. (Mail add: PO Box 151, 28472-0151), SAN 313-0347. Tel: 910-642-7141, Ext 358. FAX: 910-642-4513. Web Site: sccnc.edu/library. *Librn,* Kay Houser; Tel: 910-642-7141, Ext 219, E-mail: kay.houser@sccnc.edu; Staff 6 (MLS 2, Non-MLS 4)
Founded 1965. Enrl 1,600; Fac 80
Library Holdings: Bk Vols 74,000; Per Subs 236
Special Collections: North Carolina Colonial Records 1662-1789; North Carolina Genealogy & History Coll; Official Records of the Union & Confederate Armies; Southeastern North Carolina Records, micro; War of the Rebellion
Wireless access
Publications: Library Handbook
Partic in Community Colleges Libraries in North Carolina; LYRASIS; OCLC Online Computer Library Center, Inc; State of Iowa Libraries Online
Open Mon-Thurs 8-8, Fri 8-3 (8-Noon Summer)

WILKESBORO

J WILKES COMMUNITY COLLEGE*, Learning Resources Center/Pardue Library, 1328 S Collegiate Dr, 2nd Flr, 28697. (Mail add: PO Box 120, 28697-0120), SAN 313-0363. Tel: 336-838-6114. FAX: 336-838-6515. E-mail: wccpardue library@gmail.com. Web Site: www.wilkescc.edu/student-resources/pardue-library. *Dir,* Christy Earp; Tel: 336-838-6117, E-mail: cbearp774@wilkescc.edu; *Libr Asst,* Vickie Cothren; Tel: 336-838-6513, E-mail: vlcothren662@wilkescc.edu; Staff 5 (MLS 3, Non-MLS 2)
Founded 1966
Library Holdings: AV Mats 6,867; Bk Titles 60,000; Per Subs 127
Special Collections: James Larkin Pearson Coll; Wilkes County Coll, bks & tapes. Oral History
Automation Activity & Vendor Info: (Acquisitions) SirsiDynix; (Cataloging) SirsiDynix; (Circulation) SirsiDynix; (OPAC) SirsiDynix
Open Mon-Thurs 8-7, Fri 8-Noon; Mon-Thurs (Summer) 8-6, Fri 8-Noon

WILLIAMSTON

J MARTIN COMMUNITY COLLEGE LIBRARY*, 1161 Kehukee Park Rd, 27892-4425. SAN 313-038X. Tel: 252-789-0238. FAX: 252-792-4425. Web Site: martincc.libguides.com/library. *Libr Dir,* Mary Anne Caudle; E-mail: maryanne.caudle@martincc.edu; Staff 2 (MLS 1, Non-MLS 1)
Founded 1968. Enrl 800; Fac 31; Highest Degree: Associate
Library Holdings: High Interest/Low Vocabulary Bk Vols 150; Large Print Bks 150; Bk Vols 15,500; Per Subs 35; Talking Bks 700; Videos 1,150
Special Collections: Easter Rogerson Mizell Genealogy Coll
Subject Interests: Equine tech
Wireless access
Function: 24/7 Electronic res, 24/7 Online cat, Archival coll, Audiobks via web, Bks on CD, Computers for patron use, Electronic databases & coll, Free DVD rentals, ILL available, Internet access, Magazines, Mango lang, Meeting rooms, Microfiche/film & reading machines, Online cat, Scanner, Study rm, Telephone ref, Wheelchair accessible
Partic in Community Colleges Libraries in North Carolina; NC Dept of Commun Cols

WILMINGTON

J CAPE FEAR COMMUNITY COLLEGE*, Learning Resource Center, 415 N Second St, 28401-3905. (Mail add: 411 N Front St, 28401-3910), SAN 313-0401. Tel: 910-362-7030. Administration Tel: 910-362-7033. FAX:

910-362-7005. Web Site: cfcc.edu/library, libguides.cfcc.edu. *Dean,* Catherine Lee; E-mail: calee51@mail.cfcc.edu; *Asst Dir,* Cathy Burwell; Tel: 910-362-7456, E-mail: cburwell534@mail.cfcc.edu; *Sr Ref Librn,* Kayla Page; Tel: 910-362-7530, E-mail: kdpage904@mail.cfcc.edu; *Pub Serv Librn,* Jacob Deininger; Tel: 910-362-7293, E-mail: jddeininger616@mail.cfcc.edu; Staff 6 (MLS 6)
Founded 1964. Fac 660; Highest Degree: Associate
Library Holdings: AV Mats 7,955; e-books 214,774; Bk Vols 47,795; Per Subs 532
Subject Interests: Local hist, NC hist
Automation Activity & Vendor Info: (Cataloging) OCLC CatExpress; (Circulation) Innovative Interfaces, Inc - Sierra; (ILL) OCLC; (OPAC) Innovative Interfaces, Inc - Sierra
Wireless access
Function: 24/7 Online cat, Electronic databases & coll, Internet access, Magazines, Online ref
Partic in Carolina Consortium; North Carolina Libraries for Virtual Education
Open Mon-Thurs 7:30-7, Fri 7:30-5

P NEW HANOVER COUNTY PUBLIC LIBRARY*, Main Library & Law Library, 201 Chestnut St, 28401. SAN 355-2306. Tel: 910-798-6300. Circulation Tel: 910-798-6302. Interlibrary Loan Service Tel: 910-798-6359. Reference Tel: 910-798-6301. Administration Tel: 910-798-6309. FAX: 910-798-6312. TDD: 910-798-6306. Web Site: libguides.nhcgov.com. *Dir,* Paige Owens; Tel: 910-798-6321, E-mail: powens@nhcgov.com; *Supv Librn,* Margaret Miles; Tel: 910-798-6361, E-mail: mmiles@nhcgov.com; *Supv Librn, Ref,* James Rider; Tel: 910-798-6351, E-mail: jrider@nhcgov.com; *Sr Librn,* Kristyn Saroff; Tel: 910-798-6252, E-mail: ksaroff@nhcgov.com; *Law Librn,* Natasha Francois; E-mail: nfrancois@nhcgov.com; *Local Hist Librn,* Travis Souther; Tel: 910-798-6356, E-mail: tsouther@nhcgov.com; *Ch,* Jamie Schrum; Tel: 910-798-6362, E-mail: jschrum@nhcgov.com; *Children's Serv Coordr,* Susan DeMarco; Tel: 910-798-6353, E-mail: sdemarco@nhcgov.com. Subject Specialists: *Bus, Law,* Natasha Francois; *Archives, Genealogy, Local hist,* Travis Souther; *Ch,* Susan DeMarco; Staff 34 (MLS 19, Non-MLS 15)
Founded 1906. Pop 233,239; Circ 1,663,608
Jul 2020-Jun 2021 Income (Main & Associated Libraries) $5,001,741, State $201,789, County $4,799,952
Special Collections: Civil War Materials; Fales Coll; Historic Wilmington Plaques; New Hanover County & City of Wilmington, North Carolina; North Carolina History; Old New Hanover Genealogical Society Publications
Automation Activity & Vendor Info: (Circulation) TLC (The Library Corporation); (OPAC) TLC (The Library Corporation)
Wireless access
Function: 24/7 Electronic res, 24/7 Online cat, Activity rm, Adult bk club, Archival coll, Audiobks on Playaways & MP3, Audiobks via web, AV serv, Bk club(s), Bks on CD, Children's prog, Computer training, Computers for patron use, Digital talking bks, Distance learning, Electronic databases & coll, Free DVD rentals, Govt ref serv, Home delivery & serv to seniorr ctr & nursing homes, Homebound delivery serv, ILL available, Internet access, Life-long learning prog for all ages, Magazines, Magnifiers for reading, Mail & tel request accepted, Makerspace, Meeting rooms, Microfiche/film & reading machines, Movies, Museum passes, Online cat, Online ref, Outreach serv, Outside serv via phone, mail, e-mail & web, OverDrive digital audio bks, Photocopying/Printing, Preschool outreach, Prog for adults, Prog for children & young adult, Ref serv available, Scanner, Senior outreach, Serves people with intellectual disabilities, Spanish lang bks, STEM programs, Story hour, Study rm, Summer reading prog, Teen prog, Telephone ref, Wheelchair accessible
Open Mon & Tues 9-8, Wed & Thurs 9-6, Fri & Sat 9-5, Sun 1-5
Restriction: Non-circulating of rare bks, Non-resident fee
Friends of the Library Group
Branches: 3
NORTHEAST REGIONAL LIBRARY, 1241 Military Cutoff Rd, 28405, SAN 355-2330. Tel: 910-798-6370. Circulation Tel: 910-798-6372. Reference Tel: 910-798-6371. FAX: 910-256-1238. *Supv Librn,* Leigh Thomas; Tel: 910-798-6327, E-mail: lthomas@nhcgov.com; *Ref Librn,* Kelly Colacchio; Tel: 910-798-6378, E-mail: kcolacchio@nhcgov.com; *Sr Librn,* Pam Penza; Tel: 910-798-6366, E-mail: ppenza@nhcgov.com; *Ch,* Max Nunez; Tel: 910-798-6376, E-mail: mnunez@nhcgov.com. Subject Specialists: *Adult, Youth,* Pam Penza
Library Holdings: Bk Vols 9,828
Open Mon & Tues 9-8, Wed & Thurs 9-6, Fri & Sat 9-5, Sun 1-5
PINE VALLEY, 3802 S College Rd, 28412, SAN 372-8323. Tel: 910-798-6390. FAX: 910-452-6417. *Supv Librn,* Patricia Dew; Tel: 910-798-6328, E-mail: pdew@nhcgov.com; *Sr Librn,* Erin Gathercole; Tel: 910-798-6342, E-mail: egathercole@nhcgov.com; *Librn,* Mary Ellen Nolan; Tel: 910-798-6391, E-mail: mnolan@nhcgov.com; *Ch,* Scooter Hayes; Tel: 910-798-6398, E-mail: shayes@nhcgov.com
Open Mon & Tues 9-8, Wed & Thurs 9-6, Fri & Sat 9-5, Sun 1-5
PLEASURE ISLAND BRANCH, 1401 N Lake Park Blvd, Ste 72, Carolina Beach, 28428, SAN 355-2314. Tel: 910-798-6385. FAX: 910-798-6340. *Supv Librn,* Teresa Bishop; Tel: 910-798-6389, E-mail: tbishop@nhcgov.com
Open Mon-Thurs 9-6, Fri 9-5, Sat 9-1

C WILLIAM MADISON RANDALL LIBRARY, 601 S College Rd, 28403-5616. SAN 313-0428. Tel: 910-962-3000. Circulation Tel: 910-962-3272. Interlibrary Loan Service Tel: 910-962-3273. Reference Tel: 910-962-3760. Administration Tel: 910-962-3270. Toll Free Tel: 866-377-8309. FAX: 910-962-3078. Interlibrary Loan Service FAX: 910-962-3863. Web Site: library.uncw.edu. *Dean of Libr,* Lucy Holman; E-mail: holmanl@uncw.edu; *Info Tech, Sr Assoc Dir,* Laura Wiegand McBrayer; E-mail: mcbrayerl@uncw.edu; *Assoc Dir, Spec Coll Librn,* Dr Nathan Saunders; E-mail: saundersn@uncw.edu; *Assoc Dir, Tech Serv, Coll Mgt,* Susannah Benedetti; E-mail: benedettis@uncw.edu; *Assoc Dir, User Experience,* Nicole Tekulve; E-mail: tekulven@uncw.edu; Staff 55 (MLS 26, Non-MLS 29)
Founded 1947. Enrl 17,000; Highest Degree: Doctorate
Library Holdings: Bk Vols 935,000; Per Subs 62,000; Videos 104,000
Special Collections: Audiovisuals. Oral History; State Document Depository; US Document Depository
Subject Interests: Educ, Hist, Marine biol
Automation Activity & Vendor Info: (Acquisitions) Innovative Interfaces, Inc; (Cataloging) Innovative Interfaces, Inc; (Circulation) Innovative Interfaces, Inc; (Course Reserve) Innovative Interfaces, Inc; (ILL) Innovative Interfaces, Inc; (Media Booking) Innovative Interfaces, Inc; (OPAC) Innovative Interfaces, Inc; (Serials) EBSCO Online
Wireless access
Partic in LYRASIS
Special Services for the Blind - Reader equip

M SOUTH EAST AREA HEALTH EDUCATION CENTER MEDICAL LIBRARY*, Robert M Fales Health Sciences Library, 2131 S 17th St, 28401. (Mail add: PO Box 9025, 28402-9025), SAN 324-6418. Tel: 910-343-2180. Circulation Tel: 910-667-9226. Administration Tel: 910-343-0161. FAX: 910-762-7600. E-mail: library@seahec.net. Web Site: www.seahec.net/library. *Dir,* Robert Shapiro; *Educ & Ref Librn,* Allison Paige Matthews; E-mail: allison.matthews@seahec.net; Staff 3 (MLS 2, Non-MLS 1)
Founded 1971
Library Holdings: AV Mats 500; Bk Titles 3,100; Per Subs 330
Special Collections: Children's Health; Consumer Health; History of Medicine; Pastoral Care
Subject Interests: Allied health, Dental, Med, Nursing, Pharm, Psychol, Rehabilitation
Automation Activity & Vendor Info: (Cataloging) EOS International; (Circulation) EOS International; (OPAC) EOS International; (Serials) EOS International
Wireless access
Function: Audio & video playback equip for onsite use, AV serv, CD-ROM, Computer training, Computers for patron use, Doc delivery serv, Electronic databases & coll, Health sci info serv, ILL available, Internet access, Mail loans to mem, Online cat, Orientations, Outreach serv, Photocopying/Printing, Ref serv available, Spanish lang bks, Telephone ref, VHS videos, Wheelchair accessible
Partic in National Network of Libraries of Medicine Region 1
Open Mon-Fri 8-5
Friends of the Library Group

WILSON

C BARTON COLLEGE*, Hackney Library, 400 Atlantic Christian College Dr NE, 27893. (Mail add: PO Box 5000, 27893-7000), SAN 313-0444. Tel: 252-399-6500. Reference Tel: 252-399-6502. FAX: 252-399-6571. Reference E-mail: reference@barton.edu. Web Site: barton.libguides.com. *Dean of Libr,* Robert Cagna; E-mail: rcagna@barton.edu; *Coll & Access Serv Librn,* Richard Fulling; Tel: 252-399-6504, E-mail: rfulling@barton.edu; *Outreach/Pub Serv Librn,* Ann Dolman; Tel: 252-399-6507, E-mail: adolman@barton.edu; *Tech Librn,* Position Currently Open; *Libr Assoc for Coll & Access Serv,* Norma Williams; Tel: 252-399-6506, E-mail: nwilliam@barton.edu; Staff 5 (MLS 4, Non-MLS 1)
Founded 1902. Enrl 1,050; Fac 80; Highest Degree: Master
Library Holdings: AV Mats 3,581; Bk Vols 192,417; Per Subs 13,437
Special Collections: Barton Archives; Disciplìana Coll; North Carolina History. State Document Depository; US Document Depository
Subject Interests: Deaf educ
Automation Activity & Vendor Info: (Cataloging) TLC (The Library Corporation); (Circulation) TLC (The Library Corporation); (Course Reserve) TLC (The Library Corporation); (Discovery) ProQuest; (ILL) OCLC WorldShare Interlibrary Loan; (OPAC) TLC (The Library Corporation); (Serials) SerialsSolutions
Wireless access
Partic in Carolina Consortium; OCLC Online Computer Library Center, Inc
Open Mon-Thurs 8-Midnight, Fri 8-8, Sat 10-7, Sun 2-Midnight

Restriction: Restricted loan policy
Friends of the Library Group

J WILSON COMMUNITY COLLEGE LIBRARY*, 902 Herring Ave, 27893. (Mail add: PO Box 4305, 27893-4305), SAN 313-0452. Tel: 252-246-1235. FAX: 252-243-7148. E-mail: library_support@wilsoncc.edu. Web Site: www.wilsoncc.edu/student-services/library. *Librn,* Kelly Letourneau; Tel: 252-246-1251, E-mail: kl8748@wilsoncc.edu; Staff 6 (MLS 3, Non-MLS 3)
Founded 1958. Enrl 1,285; Fac 65
Library Holdings: Bk Vols 33,000; Per Subs 420
Automation Activity & Vendor Info: (Cataloging) SirsiDynix; (Circulation) SirsiDynix
Wireless access
Partic in Community Colleges Libraries in North Carolina
Special Services for the Deaf - Bks on deafness & sign lang; High interest/low vocabulary bks
Open Mon-Thurs (Fall & Spring) 8am-8:30pm, Fri 8-3; Mon-Thurs (Summer) 7:30am-8:30pm

P WILSON COUNTY PUBLIC LIBRARY*, 249 Nash St W, 27893-3801. SAN 355-2365. Tel: 252-237-5355. Interlibrary Loan Service Tel: 252-237-5068. Reference Tel: 252-237-5028. Web Site: www1.youseemore.com/wilsoncountypl. *Dir,* Molly Westmoreland; Tel: 252-237-5355, Ext 5024, E-mail: mwestmoreland@wilson-co.com; Staff 32.7 (MLS 8, Non-MLS 24.7)
Founded 1937. Pop 82,020; Circ 305,872
Library Holdings: Audiobooks 2,055; DVDs 4,383; e-books 461; Bk Vols 189,582; Per Subs 189
Special Collections: Genealogy Coll; North Carolina Coll, bks, microfilm
Automation Activity & Vendor Info: (Cataloging) TLC (The Library Corporation); (Circulation) TLC (The Library Corporation); (OPAC) TLC (The Library Corporation)
Wireless access
Publications: Wilson County Public Library: A History
Special Services for the Deaf - Bks on deafness & sign lang; High interest/low vocabulary bks
Open Mon-Wed 9-9, Thurs-Sat 9-6
Friends of the Library Group
Branches: 5
BLACK CREEK BRANCH, 103 Central Ave, Black Creek, 27813, SAN 370-9450. Tel: 252-237-3715. FAX: 252-237-3715. *Br Librn,* Sarah Packard; E-mail: spackard@wilson-co.com; Staff 1 (Non-MLS 1)
Library Holdings: Bk Vols 11,390; Per Subs 14
Open Mon-Fri 10-6
CROCKER-STANTONSBURG BRANCH, 114 S Main St, Stantonsburg, 27883, SAN 355-2519. Tel: 252-238-3758. FAX: 252-238-3758. *Br Librn,* Donna Bullard; E-mail: dbullard@wilson-co.com; Staff 1 (Non-MLS 1)
Library Holdings: Bk Vols 11,776; Per Subs 15
Open Mon-Thurs 1:30-5
EAST WILSON BRANCH, 6000-C Ward Blvd, 27893-6488, SAN 355-239X. Tel: 252-237-2627. FAX: 252-237-2627. *Br Librn,* Brenda Edmondson; E-mail: bedmondson@wilson-co.com; Staff 1 (Non-MLS 1)
Library Holdings: Bk Vols 13,819
Open Mon-Thurs 2-5:30
ELM CITY BRANCH, 114 N Railroad St, Elm City, 27822-0717. (Mail add: PO Box 717, Elm City, 27822-0717), SAN 355-242X. Tel: 252-236-4269. FAX: 252-236-4269. *Br Mgr,* Sue Young; E-mail: syoung@wilson-co.com; Staff 1 (Non-MLS 1)
Library Holdings: Bk Vols 19,101
Open Mon-Fri 10-6
LUCAMA BRANCH, 103 E Spring St, Lucama, 27851, SAN 355-2489. Tel: 252-239-0046. FAX: 252-239-0046. *Br Librn,* Karey Blanchard; E-mail: kblanchard@wilson-co.com; Staff 2 (Non-MLS 2)
Library Holdings: Bk Vols 14,057; Per Subs 15
Open Mon-Fri 10-6

WINGATE

C WINGATE UNIVERSITY*, Ethel K Smith Library, 110 Church ST, 28174. (Mail add: Campus Box 3067-WU, 28174-1202), SAN 990-5693. Tel: 704-233-8089. Reference Tel: 704-233-8097. FAX: 704-233-8254. E-mail: library_info@wingate.edu. Web Site: library.wingate.edu. *Libr Dir,* Amee Huneycutt Odom; E-mail: ameeodom@wingate.edu; *Cat Librn,* Marilyn Brown; E-mail: marbrown@wingate.edu; *Coll Develop Librn,* Richard Pipes; E-mail: rpipes@wingate.edu; *E-Resources Librn,* Debbie Hargett; E-mail: dhargett@wingate.edu; *Ref & Instruction Librn,* Isaac Meadows; E-mail: i.meadows@wingate.edu; *Access Serv Mgr,* Kaitlyn Helms; E-mail: k.helms@wingate.edu; *Evening Fac Mgr,* Aimee Dorso; E-mail: ai.dorso@wingate.edu; *Pub Serv Mgr,* Alison Simpson; E-mail: a.simpson@wingate.edu; *Network & Syst Adminr,* Jimm Wetherbee; E-mail: jimm@wingate.edu; Staff 7.5 (MLS 5, Non-MLS 2.5)
Founded 1896. Enrl 2,695; Fac 187; Highest Degree: Doctorate
Automation Activity & Vendor Info: (Acquisitions) Ex Libris Group; (Cataloging) Ex Libris Group; (Circulation) Ex Libris Group; (Course Reserve) Ex Libris Group; (OPAC) Ex Libris Group
Wireless access
Function: 24/7 Electronic res, Art exhibits, Audio & video playback equip for onsite use, Audiobks via web, Computer training, Computers for patron use, Doc delivery serv, E-Reserves, Electronic databases & coll, For res purposes, Health sci info serv, ILL available, Laminating, Learning ctr, Microfiche/film & reading machines, Movies, Music CDs, Online cat, Online ref, Orientations, Outside serv via phone, mail, e-mail & web, Photocopying/Printing, Ref & res, Ref serv available, Res libr, Satellite serv, Scanner, Telephone ref, VHS videos, Wheelchair accessible, Workshops
Partic in Carolina Consortium; Charlotte Area Educ Consortium; LYRASIS; NC Asn of Independent Cols & Univs; OCLC Online Computer Library Center, Inc
Open Mon-Thurs 7:30am-11pm, Fri 7:30-5, Sat 10-5, Sun 3-11
Restriction: Authorized patrons, Borrowing privileges limited to fac & registered students, Off-site coll in storage - retrieval as requested
Friends of the Library Group

WINSTON-SALEM

P FORSYTH COUNTY PUBLIC LIBRARY*, 660 W Fifth St, 27105. SAN 355-2543. Tel: 336-703-2665. Interlibrary Loan Service Tel: 336-703-3030. Administration Tel: 336-703-3011. Information Services Tel: 336-703-3020. FAX: 336-727-2549. Web Site: www.forsythlibrary.org. *Dir,* Sylvia Sprinkle-Hamlin; E-mail: hamlinss@forsythlibrary.org; *Assoc Dir,* Elizabeth Skinner; Staff 105 (MLS 43, Non-MLS 62)
Founded 1903. Pop 358,137; Circ 1,887,526
Library Holdings: AV Mats 62,121; e-books 5,895; Bk Vols 674,902; Per Subs 700
Special Collections: African American Coll; Foreign Language Coll; Frank Jones Photographic Print Coll; Generation Teen; H Kapp Ogburn Philatelic Coll; Nonprofit Resource Center; North Caroliniana, genealogy; Small Business Center. US Document Depository
Subject Interests: Bus, Children's lit, Humanities
Automation Activity & Vendor Info: (Acquisitions) SirsiDynix; (Cataloging) SirsiDynix; (Circulation) SirsiDynix; (Course Reserve) SirsiDynix; (ILL) SirsiDynix; (Media Booking) SirsiDynix; (OPAC) SirsiDynix; (Serials) SirsiDynix
Wireless access
Publications: Annual Report; Bookshelf (Newsletter); Children's Calendar (Monthly); FirstLine Community Directory (Business & organization papers & directories); Jobseeker's Resource Guide: Your Guide to Surviving Unemployment (Research guide); Monthly Calendar of Events; Periodical Holdings (Serials catalog)
Partic in LYRASIS; OCLC Online Computer Library Center, Inc
Special Services for the Deaf - Assistive tech; Videos & decoder
Special Services for the Blind - Assistive/Adapted tech devices, equip & products; Computer with voice synthesizer for visually impaired persons; Home delivery serv
Open Mon-Wed 9-9, Thurs & Fri 9-6, Sat 9-5, Sun (Sept-May) 1-5
Friends of the Library Group
Branches: 9
CARVER SCHOOL ROAD BRANCH, 4915 Lansing Dr W, 27105, SAN 378-1917. Tel: 336-703-2910. FAX: 336-661-4919. Web Site: www.forsyth.cc/library/Carver/default.aspx. *Br Mgr,* Melisa Williams; E-mail: william2@forsythlibrary.org
Library Holdings: e-books 40; Bk Vols 28,518; Per Subs 104
Open Mon-Wed 10-9, Thurs & Fri 10-6, Sat 10-5
Friends of the Library Group
CLEMMONS BRANCH, 3554 Clemmons Rd, Old Hwy 158, Clemmons, 27012, SAN 355-2578. Tel: 336-703-2920. FAX: 336-712-4452. Web Site: www.forsyth.cc/library/Clemmons/default.aspx. *Br Mgr,* Carolyn Price; E-mail: pricecp@forsythlibrary.org; Staff 5 (MLS 2, Non-MLS 3)
Library Holdings: Bk Vols 43,465; Per Subs 100
Open Mon-Wed 10-9, Thurs & Fri 10-6, Sat 10-5
Friends of the Library Group
KERNERSVILLE BRANCH, 130 E Mountain St, Kernersville, 27284, SAN 355-2632. Tel: 336-703-2930. FAX: 336-993-5216. Web Site: www.forsyth.cc/library/Kernersville/default.aspx. *Br Mgr,* William Durham; E-mail: durhamwe@forsythlibrary.org
Library Holdings: e-books 33; Bk Vols 56,053; Per Subs 102
Open Mon-Wed 10-9, Thurs & Fri 10-6, Sat 10-5
Friends of the Library Group
LEWISVILLE BRANCH, 6490 Shallowford Rd, Lewisville, 27023, SAN 355-2667. Tel: 336-703-2940. FAX: 336-945-9745. Web Site: www.forsyth.cc/library/Lewisville/default.aspx. *Br Mgr,* Candace Brennan; E-mail: brennancm@forsyth.cc
Library Holdings: Bk Vols 31,362; Per Subs 78
Open Mon-Wed 10-9, Thurs & Fri 10-6, Sat 10-5
Friends of the Library Group

MALLOY/JORDON EAST WINSTON HERITAGE CENTER, 1110 E Seventh St, 27101, SAN 355-2608. Tel: 336-703-2950. FAX: 336-727-8498. Web Site: www.forsyth.cc/library/MalloyJordan/default.aspx. *Br Mgr,* Yolanda F Bolden; E-mail: boldenyf@forsythlibrary.org
Library Holdings: Bk Vols 24,966; Per Subs 106
Special Collections: Storytime Kits. Oral History
Subject Interests: African-Am hist, Early childhood
Open Mon-Wed 10-9, Thurs & Fri 10-6, Sat 10-5
Friends of the Library Group

REYNOLDA MANOR, 2839 Fairlawn Dr, 27106, SAN 355-2691. Tel: 336-703-2960. FAX: 336-748-3318. Web Site: www.forsyth.cc/library/Reynolda/default.aspx. *Br Mgr,* Jennifer Boneno; E-mail: barretjs@forsythlibrary.org
Library Holdings: e-books 40; Bk Vols 57,260; Per Subs 100
Open Mon-Wed 10-9, Thurs & Fri 10-6, Sat 10-5
Friends of the Library Group

RURAL HALL BRANCH, 7125 Broad St, Rural Hall, 27045, SAN 355-2721. Tel: 336-703-2970. FAX: 336-969-9401. Web Site: www.forsyth.cc/library/RuralHall/default.aspx. *Br Mgr,* Crystal Holland; E-mail: hollandc@forsyth.cc; Staff 3 (MLS 2, Non-MLS 1)
Library Holdings: Bk Vols 39,490; Per Subs 104
Open Mon-Wed 10-9, Thurs & Fri 10-6, Sat 10-5
Friends of the Library Group

SOUTHSIDE, 3185 Buchanan St, 27127, SAN 355-2756. Tel: 336-703-2980. FAX: 336-771-4724. Web Site: www.forsyth.cc/library/Southside/default.aspx. *Br Mgr,* Riedel Slaughter; E-mail: riedeldr@forsythlibrary.org; Staff 5 (MLS 3, Non-MLS 2)
Library Holdings: Bk Vols 54,647; Per Subs 166
Automation Activity & Vendor Info: (Acquisitions) Evergreen; (Cataloging) Evergreen; (Circulation) Evergreen; (ILL) Brodart; (OPAC) Evergreen; (Serials) Evergreen
Function: Adult bk club, Art exhibits, Bks on CD, Children's prog, Computer training, Computers for patron use, Distance learning, Electronic databases & coll, Free DVD rentals, Holiday prog, Homework prog, ILL available, Instruction & testing, Internet access, Music CDs, Online cat, Online ref, Outreach serv, OverDrive digital audio bks, Photocopying/Printing, Preschool outreach, Preschool reading prog, Prog for adults, Prog for children & young adult, Ref & res, Ref serv available, Senior computer classes, Spanish lang bks, Story hour, Summer & winter reading prog, Summer reading prog, Tax forms, Teen prog, Telephone ref, VHS videos, Wheelchair accessible, Winter reading prog, Workshops
Open Mon-Wed 10-9, Thurs & Fri 10-6, Sat 10-5
Friends of the Library Group

WALKERTOWN BRANCH, 2969 Main St, Walkertown, 27051, SAN 374-4167. Tel: 336-703-2990. FAX: 336-595-9080. Web Site: www.forsyth.cc/library/Walkertown/default.aspx. *Br Mgr,* Natalia Tuchina; E-mail: tuchinnb@forsythlibrary.org
Library Holdings: Bk Vols 33,630; Per Subs 96
Open Mon-Wed 10-9, Thurs & Fri 10-6, Sat 10-5
Friends of the Library Group

Bookmobiles: 1. Bk vols 3,000

J FORSYTH TECHNICAL COMMUNITY COLLEGE LIBRARY*, 2100 Silas Creek Pkwy, 27103. SAN 355-287X. Tel: 336-734-7219. Reference Tel: 336-734-7415. Administration Tel: 336-734-7217. Information Services Tel: 336-734-7218. Web Site: www.forsythtech.edu/student-services/bookstores-library/library. *Dean, Learning Res,* J Randel Candelaria; Tel: 336-734-7216, E-mail: rcandelaria@forsythtech.edu; *Outreach Librn,* Placedia Miller; E-mail: pmiller@forsythtech.edu; *Pub Serv Librn,* Tom Gordon; E-mail: tgordon@forsythtech.edu; *Tech Serv Librn,* Ted Labosky; Tel: 336-734-7508, E-mail: tlabosky@forsythtech.edu; *Circ Asst,* Peggy Crater; E-mail: pcrater@forsythtech.edu; Staff 10 (MLS 4, Non-MLS 6)
Founded 1964. Enrl 7,800; Highest Degree: Associate
Library Holdings: e-books 22,000; Bk Titles 49,000; Per Subs 80
Special Collections: Guy Blynn Holocaust Coll
Subject Interests: Archit, Design, Engr, Health tech, Humanities, Transportation tech
Automation Activity & Vendor Info: (Acquisitions) SirsiDynix; (Cataloging) SirsiDynix; (Circulation) SirsiDynix; (ILL) OCLC Online; (OPAC) Horizon; (Serials) SirsiDynix
Wireless access
Function: 24/7 Electronic res, 24/7 Online cat, Audio & video playback equip for onsite use, Audiobks via web, AV serv, Bks on cassette, Computer training, Computers for patron use, Distance learning, Electronic databases & coll, Equip loans & repairs, ILL available, Instruction & testing, Learning ctr, Magnifiers for reading, Music CDs, Online cat, Online ref, Orientations, Photocopying/Printing, Ref & res, Spoken cassettes & CDs, Telephone ref, VHS videos, Wheelchair accessible, Workshops
Open Mon-Thurs 7:30am-8pm, Fri 7:30-3, Sat (Fall & Spring) 9-12
Restriction: Authorized patrons, Open to pub for ref & circ; with some limitations, Open to students, fac & staff

SR MORAVIAN CHURCH IN AMERICA, SOUTHERN PROVINCE*, Archives & Research Library, 457 S Church St, 27101-5314. SAN 326-341X. Tel: 336-722-1742. FAX: 336-725-4514. E-mail: moravianarchives@mcsp.org. Web Site: moravianarchives.org. *Archivist,* J Eric Elliott; Staff 3 (Non-MLS 3)
Founded 1753
Library Holdings: Bk Titles 2,500; Bk Vols 3,000; Per Subs 50
Function: Res libr
Publications: Annotations (Newsletter)
Open Mon-Fri 9:30-12 & 1:30-4:30
Restriction: Non-circulating to the pub
Friends of the Library Group

S MORAVIAN MUSIC FOUNDATION, Peter Memorial Library, 457 S Church St, 27101, SAN 313-0517. Tel: 336-725-0651. FAX: 336-725-4514. E-mail: info@moravianmusic.org. Web Site: www.moravianmusic.org. *Dir,* Dr Nola Reed Knouse; E-mail: nola@moravianmusic.org
Founded 1961
Library Holdings: AV Mats 800; Bk Titles 6,000; Per Subs 10
Special Collections: Music (Lowens Coll of Musical Americana & Manuscripts of Early American Music), bk, ms
Subject Interests: 18th Century music, 19th Century music, Am music, Hymnology, Moravian music
Publications: Catalogs of Music Collection; Newsletter (Quarterly); Publications
Open Mon-Fri 9:30-12 & 1:30-4:30
Restriction: Open to pub for ref only

M NOVANT HEALTH LIBRARY SERVICES - FORSYTH MEDICAL CENTER*, John C Whitaker Library, 3333 Silas Creek Pkwy, 27103-3090. SAN 355-2810. Tel: 336-718-5995. Web Site: www.novanthealth.org. *Mgr,* Margaret Cobb. Subject Specialists: *Health sci,* Margaret Cobb; Staff 2.5 (MLS 1, Non-MLS 1.5)
Founded 1964
Library Holdings: Audiobooks 76; e-books 1,328; e-journals 49,500; Bk Titles 1,000; Bk Vols 3,000; Per Subs 15
Subject Interests: Allied health, Clinical med, Healthcare admin, Nursing
Automation Activity & Vendor Info: (Cataloging) EOS International; (Circulation) EOS International; (OPAC) EOS International; (Serials) EOS International
Wireless access
Open Mon-Fri 8-4:30
Restriction: Circulates for staff only, In-house use for visitors, Med & health res only, Non-circulating to the pub

S OLD SALEM MUSEUMS & GARDENS, Anne P & Thomas A Gray Library, Frank L Horton Museum Ctr, 924 S Main St, 27101. SAN 325-8084. Tel: 336-721-7300, 336-721-7365. FAX: 336-721-7367. E-mail: library@oldsalem.org. Web Site: www.oldsalem.org/library-archives. *Librn,* Margaret Krause; Staff 1 (MLS 1)
Library Holdings: Bk Vols 23,000; Per Subs 125
Automation Activity & Vendor Info: (Cataloging) LibraryWorld, Inc; (OPAC) LibraryWorld, Inc
Wireless access
Restriction: Open by appt only

CR PIEDMONT INTERNATIONAL UNIVERSITY*, George M Manuel Memorial Library, 420 S Broad St, 27101-5025. SAN 313-055X. Tel: 336-714-7894. FAX: 336-725-5522. E-mail; library@piedmontu.edu. Web Site: www.piedmontu.edu/library. *Libr Dir,* Dr Catherine Chatmon; Tel: 336-714-7953, E-mail: chatmonc@piedmontu.edu; *Asst Libr Dir,* Jason Seymour; Tel: 336-714-7952, E-mail: seymourj@piedmontu.edu; Staff 3 (MLS 2, Non-MLS 1)
Founded 1945. Enrl 290; Fac 41; Highest Degree: Doctorate
Library Holdings: CDs 20; DVDs 66; e-books 977; e-journals 3,808; Electronic Media & Resources 4; Microforms 6,000; Music Scores 300; Bk Titles 48,000; Bk Vols 58,000; Per Subs 225; Videos 601
Subject Interests: Educ, Hist, Music, Relig studies
Automation Activity & Vendor Info: (Acquisitions) JayWil Software Development, Inc; (Cataloging) JayWil Software Development, Inc; (Circulation) JayWil Software Development, Inc; (OPAC) JayWil Software Development, Inc; (Serials) EBSCO Online
Wireless access
Function: Photocopying/Printing
Open Mon, Tues & Thurs 7:30am-9pm, Wed & Fri 7:30-5, Sat 10-2

C SALEM COLLEGE*, Dale H Gramley Library, 626 S Church St, 27101. SAN 313-0576. Tel: 336-721-2649. Interlibrary Loan Service Tel: 336-917-5420. FAX: 336-917-5339. Web Site: library.salem.edu. *Dir of Libr,* Elizabeth Novicki; Tel: 336-917-5417, E-mail: elizabeth.novicki@salem.edu; *Circ Supvr,* Stacie Horrell; Tel: 336-917-5419, E-mail: stacie.horrell@salem.edu
Founded 1772. Enrl 1,019; Fac 90; Highest Degree: Master

Library Holdings: Bk Vols 129,577; Per Subs 5,500
Special Collections: Moravian Church Coll; Salem Academy & College Coll
Subject Interests: Lit, Women's hist
Automation Activity & Vendor Info: (Acquisitions) SirsiDynix; (Cataloging) SirsiDynix; (Circulation) SirsiDynix; (Course Reserve) SirsiDynix; (ILL) SirsiDynix; (OPAC) SirsiDynix; (Serials) SirsiDynix
Wireless access
Partic in LYRASIS; NC-PALS
Open Mon-Thurs 8:30am-11:59pm, Fri 8:30-8, Sat 10-8, Sun 1-11:59
Friends of the Library Group

Departmental Libraries:

LORRAINE F RUDOLPH FINE ARTS CENTER LIBRARY, 500 Salem Rd, 27101. Tel: 336-721-2738. FAX: 336-721-2683. *Assoc Libn,* Donna Rothrock; Tel: 336-917-5475, E-mail: donna.rothrock@salem.edu
Library Holdings: CDs 1,957; DVDs 85; Music Scores 9,335; Bk Titles 785; Videos 339
Open Mon-Thurs 8am-10pm, Fri 8-4:30, Sun 2-10

C UNIVERSITY OF NORTH CAROLINA SCHOOL OF THE ARTS LIBRARY*, 1533 S Main St, 27127. SAN 313-0541. Tel: 336-770-3270. Interlibrary Loan Service Tel: 336-770-3257. Reference Tel: 336-770-1479. FAX: 336-770-3271. Web Site: library.uncsa.edu/home/. *Head, Access Serv & Doc Delivery,* Samantha Sheff; E-mail: sheffs@uncsa.edu; *Cat & Digital Res Librn,* Christia Thomason; *Music Librn,* Leslie Kamtman; *Syst & Web Develop Librn,* Benjamin Morgan; *Bibliog Instr, Ref (Info Servs),* Susan Keely; *Cataloger,* Sylvia Koontz. Subject Specialists: *Music,* Christia Thomason; Staff 16 (MLS 7, Non-MLS 9)
Founded 1965. Enrl 1,100; Fac 152; Highest Degree: Master
Jul 2016-Jun 2017 Income $1,218,361, State $1,218,361. Mats Exp $248,149, Books $40,893, Per/Ser (Incl. Access Fees) $129,314, Other Print Mats $47,542, AV Equip $2,000, AV Mat $15,600, Electronic Ref Mat (Incl. Access Fees) $11,500, Presv $13,000. Sal $648,966 (Prof $598,739)
Library Holdings: CDs 25,000; DVDs 12,446; e-books 185,548; e-journals 22,828; Electronic Media & Resources 136; Microforms 25,000; Music Scores 60,000; Bk Vols 106,000; Per Subs 450; Spec Interest Per Sub 200; Videos 2,000
Special Collections: School Archives; Music Scores; Sound Recordings; Moving Image Materials. Oral History
Subject Interests: Art, Dance, Drama, Film, Music
Automation Activity & Vendor Info: (Acquisitions) Innovative Interfaces, Inc; (Cataloging) Innovative Interfaces, Inc; (Circulation) Innovative Interfaces, Inc; (Course Reserve) Innovative Interfaces, Inc; (Discovery) EBSCO Discovery Service; (ILL) OCLC; (OPAC) Innovative Interfaces, Inc; (Serials) Innovative Interfaces, Inc
Wireless access
Partic in Carolina Consortium; LYRASIS; North Carolina Libraries for Virtual Education; OCLC Online Computer Library Center, Inc
Open Mon-Thurs 8am-Midnight, Fri 8-6, Sat Noon-6, Sun 2-Midnight
Restriction: Open to pub for ref & circ; with some limitations, Open to students, fac & staff

C WAKE FOREST UNIVERSITY*, Z Smith Reynolds Library, PO Box 7777, 27109-7777. SAN 355-3116. Tel: 336-758-4931. Interlibrary Loan Service Tel: 336-758-5006. Reference Tel: 336-758-5475. FAX: 336-758-3694, 336-758-8831. Circulation FAX: 336-758-5605. Web Site: zsr.wfu.edu. *Dean,* Tim Pyatt; Tel: 335-758-5090, E-mail: tpyatt@wfu.edu; *Assoc Dean,* Susan Sharpless Smith; Tel: 336-758-5828, E-mail: smithss@wfu.edu; *Dir, Scholarly Communications, Dir, Digital Initiatives,* Molly Keener; Tel: 336-758-5829, E-mail: keenerm@wfu.edu; *Dir, Access Serv,* Mary Beth Lock; Tel: 336-758-6140, E-mail: lockmb@wfu.edu; *Dir, Archives, Dir, Spec Coll,* Tanya Zanish-Belcher; Tel: 336-758-5755, E-mail: zanisht@wfu.edu; *Dir, Res & Instruction Serv,* Rosalind Tedford; Tel: 336-758-5910, E-mail: tedforrl@wfu.edu; *Dir, Res Serv,* Lauren Corbett; Tel: 336-758-6136, E-mail: corbetle@wfu.edu; *Dir, Technology,* Thomas Dowling; Tel: 336-758-5797, E-mail: dowlintp@wfu.edu; *ILL,* James Harper; Tel: 336-758-5675, E-mail: harperjb@wfu.edu; Staff 61 (MLS 33, Non-MLS 28)
Founded 1834. Enrl 7,837; Fac 1,785; Highest Degree: Doctorate
Library Holdings: e-books 592,077; Bk Vols 1,986,093
Special Collections: Anglo-Irish Literature; Dolman Press Archives; Gertrude Stein Coll; Giuseppe De Santis Film Archives; Harold Hayes Manuscripts; History Books & Printing; Holocaust Coll; Joseph E Smith Music Coll; Mark Twain Coll; Maya Angelou Film & Theatre Coll; North Carolina Baptist History; Ronald Watkins Library & Personal Papers; Selected English & American Authors of the 20th Century; W J Cash Manuscripts; Wayne Oates Manuscripts. State Document Depository; US Document Depository
Automation Activity & Vendor Info: (Acquisitions) Ex Libris Group; (Cataloging) Ex Libris Group; (Circulation) Ex Libris Group; (Course Reserve) Ex Libris Group; (ILL) Ex Libris Group; (OPAC) Ex Libris Group; (Serials) Ex Libris Group
Wireless access
Publications: ZSReads (Newsletter)
Partic in Association of Southeastern Research Libraries; LYRASIS; North Carolina Libraries for Virtual Education

Departmental Libraries:

CM COY C CARPENTER MEDICAL LIBRARY, Medical Center Blvd, 27157-1069, SAN 355-3205. Circulation Tel: 336-716-4414. FAX: 336-716-2186. Web Site: www.wakehealth.edu/library. *Dir,* Parks Welch; Tel: 336-716-2299, E-mail: pwelch@wakehealth.edu; *Pub Serv,* David Stewart; E-mail: dstewart@wakehealth.edu; *Tech Serv,* Molly Barnett; E-mail: mbarnett@wakehealth.edu; Staff 20 (MLS 9, Non-MLS 11)
Founded 1941. Enrl 577; Highest Degree: Doctorate
Library Holdings: AV Mats 1,011; DVDs 112; e-books 3,833; e-journals 6,149; Microforms 1,582; Bk Titles 21,394; Bk Vols 23,871; Per Subs 6,149
Special Collections: Arts in Medicine; History of Medicine & Neurology (Rare Book Coll); Samuel Johnson Coll. Oral History
Subject Interests: Life sci, Med
Automation Activity & Vendor Info: (Acquisitions) Ex Libris Group; (Cataloging) Ex Libris Group; (Circulation) Ex Libris Group; (ILL) OCLC ILLiad; (OPAC) Ex Libris Group; (Serials) SerialsSolutions
Partic in Northwest AHEC; OCLC Online Computer Library Center, Inc
Open Mon-Thurs 7am-Midnight, Fri 7-7, Sat 10-7, Sun 1-Midnight

CL PROFESSIONAL CENTER LIBRARY, Worrell Professional Ctr, 1834 Wake Forest Rd, 27109. (Mail add: PO Box 7206, 27109-7206), SAN 355-3140. Tel: 336-758-4520. Reference Tel: 336-758-4520. FAX: 336-758-4508. Web Site: library.law.wfu.edu/. *Assoc Dean, Info Tech,* Christopher Knott; Tel: 336-758-5927; *Assoc Dir, Student Servs,* Maureen Eggert; *Assoc Dir, Coll Serv,* Alan Keely; *Assoc Dir, Tech,* Sally Irvin; *Ref Librn,* Kate Irwin-Smiler; *Ref Librn,* Liz M Johnson; *Tech Serv Librn,* Jennifer Noga; *Metadata Librn,* Leslie Wakeford; *Circ Supvr,* Angie Hobbs; *Coordr, Acq,* Gina Jarrett; *Ser,* Michael Greene; *Libr Spec,* Holly Swenson; *Libr Spec,* Isbel Cruz-Chaudhry; Staff 13 (MLS 8, Non-MLS 5)
Founded 1894. Fac 69; Highest Degree: Doctorate
Library Holdings: Bk Titles 65,330; Bk Vols 122,214
Special Collections: State Document Depository; US Document Depository
Subject Interests: Law
Automation Activity & Vendor Info: (Acquisitions) Ex Libris Group; (Cataloging) Ex Libris Group; (Circulation) Ex Libris Group; (OPAC) Ex Libris Group; (Serials) Ex Libris Group
Partic in OCLC Online Computer Library Center, Inc
Open Mon-Thurs 8am-11pm, Fri 8am-9pm, Sat 9-9, Sun 10am-11pm

C WINSTON-SALEM STATE UNIVERSITY*, C G O'Kelly Library, 601 Martin Luther King Jr Dr, 27110. (Mail add: 227 O'Kelly Library, 27110), SAN 313-0592. Tel: 336-750-2442. Circulation Tel: 336-750-2449. Interlibrary Loan Service Tel: 336-750-2124. Reference Tel: 336-750-2454. Toll Free Tel: 877-269-8813. FAX: 336-750-2459. E-mail: reference@wssu.edu. Web Site: www.wssu.edu/academics/cg-okelly-library. *Univ Librn,* Thomas Flynn; Tel: 336-750-2426, E-mail: flynnth@wssu.edu; *Head Librn,* Wanda K Brown; Tel: 336-750-2446, E-mail: brownwa@wssu.edu; *Librn,* Ian S Hertz; Tel: 336-750-2532, E-mail: hertzis@wssu.edu; *Librn,* Michael A Frye; Tel: 336-750-8938, E-mail: fryema@wssu.edu; *Tech Serv Librn,* Cynthia Levine; Tel: 336-750-2123, E-mail: levineco@wssu.edu; *Access Serv Coordr,* Forrest C Foster; Tel: 336-750-2843, E-mail: fosterfc@wssu.edu; *Media Coordr,* Jeffrey McGill; Tel: 336-750-2452, E-mail: mcgill@wssu.edu. Subject Specialists: *Computer sci,* Thomas Flynn; *Bus,* Ian S Hertz; *Chem, Life sci,* Michael A Frye; Staff 21 (MLS 13, Non-MLS 8)
Founded 1920. Enrl 5,400; Fac 325; Highest Degree: Doctorate
Jul 2012-Jun 2013 Income $3,487,075, State $3,387,075, Federal $100,000. Mats Exp $3,487,075, Books $175,856, Per/Ser (Incl. Access Fees) $227,174, Micro $126,798, AV Equip $1,104,546, AV Mat $49,821, Electronic Ref Mat (Incl. Access Fees) $866,646. Sal $1,426,980
Library Holdings: AV Mats 2,334; DVDs 5,000; e-books 270,000; e-journals 80,000; Microforms 200; Bk Titles 210,000; Bk Vols 257,005; Per Subs 1,648
Special Collections: Black Studies (Curriculum Materials Center)
Automation Activity & Vendor Info: (Acquisitions) Innovative Interfaces, Inc; (Cataloging) Innovative Interfaces, Inc; (Circulation) Innovative Interfaces, Inc; (Course Reserve) Innovative Interfaces, Inc; (ILL) Innovative Interfaces, Inc; (OPAC) Innovative Interfaces, Inc; (Serials) Innovative Interfaces, Inc
Wireless access
Function: ILL available, Ref serv available
Publications: WSSU Friends of the Library (Newsletter)
Partic in Central North Carolina Library Consortium; OCLC Online Computer Library Center, Inc
Open Mon-Thurs (Fall & Spring) 8am-1am, Fri 8-6, Sat 10-4, Sun Noon-1am; Mon-Thurs (Summer) 8-8, Fri 8-5, Sat 10-2, Sun 2-6
Friends of the Library Group

L WOMBLE, BOND DICKINSON*, Law Library, One W Fourth St, 27101. SAN 372-2333. Tel: 336-721-3600, 336-747-4757. FAX: 336-721-3660. Web Site: www.womblebonddickinson.com. *Library Contact,* Susan Garrison; E-mail: susan.garrison@wbd-us.com
Library Holdings: Bk Vols 20,000; Per Subs 50
Restriction: Staff use only

WINTERVILLE

J PITT COMMUNITY COLLEGE*, Learning Resources Center, Clifton W Everett Bldg, 1986 Pitt Tech Rd, 28590. (Mail add: PO Box 7007, Greenville, 27835-7007), SAN 312-8652. Tel: 252-493-7350. Interlibrary Loan Service Tel: 252-493-7352. Reference Tel: 252-493-7360. Administration Tel: 252-493-7354. FAX: 252-321-4404. E-mail: pittref@email.pittcc.edu. Web Site: www.pittcc.edu/campus-life/library. *Libr Dir,* Leigh Russell; E-mail: lrussell@email-pittcc.edu; *Re/Ser Librn,* Stephanie Bowers; E-mail: sbowers@email.pittcc.edu; *Circ,* Arthur Stevenson; E-mail: astevenson@email.pittcc.edu; Staff 20 (MLS 6, Non-MLS 14)
Founded 1964. Enrl 5,300; Fac 240; Highest Degree: Associate
Library Holdings: Bk Titles 35,000; Bk Vols 45,000; Per Subs 575
Wireless access
Partic in Community Colleges Libraries in North Carolina

WINTON

P ALBEMARLE REGIONAL LIBRARY*, 303 W Tryon St, 27986. (Mail add: PO Box 68, 27986-0068), SAN 313-0606. Tel: 252-358-7832. FAX: 252-358-7868. Web Site: www.arlnc.org. *Dir,* Hugh Davis; E-mail: hdavis@arlnc.org; *Syst Adminr,* Lee Bryant; Tel: 252-358-7864; *Financial Serv,* Larry Joyner; Tel: 252-358-7834; *Tech Serv,* Brenda Jones; Tel: 252-358-7854; Staff 19 (MLS 2, Non-MLS 17)
Founded 1948. Pop 76,200; Circ 148,745
Jul 2012-Jun 2013 Income (Main & Associated Libraries) $1,436,194, State $378,579, City $215,348, Federal $24,795, County $443,795, Locally Generated Income $139,314, Other $234,363. Mats Exp $83,630, Books $49,667, Per/Ser (Incl. Access Fees) $5,573, AV Mat $24,880, Electronic Ref Mat (Incl. Access Fees) $3,510. Sal $746,786 (Prof $68,978)
Library Holdings: AV Mats 24,374; Bks on Deafness & Sign Lang 32; Bk Vols 195,264; Per Subs 319
Special Collections: Care Givers Coll; Grandparents as Parents Coll; Historic Murfreesboro, North Carolina (Paul Ronald Jenkins Photographs Coll); World War II Scrapbook
Subject Interests: Genealogy, Local hist
Automation Activity & Vendor Info: (Acquisitions) Evergreen; (Cataloging) Evergreen; (Circulation) Evergreen; (OPAC) Evergreen
Wireless access
Function: Homebound delivery serv, ILL available, Music CDs, Photocopying/Printing, Prog for children & young adult, Spoken cassettes & CDs, Summer reading prog
Partic in OCLC Online Computer Library Center, Inc
Special Services for the Deaf - Bks on deafness & sign lang; High interest/low vocabulary bks
Special Services for the Blind - Bks on cassette; Bks on CD; Copier with enlargement capabilities; Home delivery serv; Large print bks; Talking bks
Branches: 7
AHOSKIE PUBLIC LIBRARY, 210 E Church St, Ahoskie, 27910, SAN 354-4419. Tel: 252-332-5500. FAX: 252-332-6435. *Br Mgr,* Cindy Henderson; *Asst Librn,* Annette Perry
Library Holdings: Bk Vols 16,000; Per Subs 28
Open Mon-Fri 10-6
BERTIE COUNTY PUBLIC LIBRARY, 111 US Hwy 13/17 Bypass, Windsor, 27983, SAN 313-0460. Tel: 252-794-2244. FAX: 252-794-1546. *Br Mgr,* Nancy B Hughes
Special Collections: Genealogy Coll; Local History Coll
Subject Interests: County hist, World War II
Open Mon 10-8, Tues-Fri 10-6, Sat 10-2
GATES COUNTY PUBLIC LIBRARY, 14 Cypress Creek Dr, Gatesville, 27938-9507. (Mail add: PO Box 27, Gatesville, 27938-0027), SAN 312-8423. Tel: 252-357-0110. FAX: 252-357-1285. *Br Mgr,* Patricia B Familar; Staff 3 (MLS 1, Non-MLS 2)
Open Mon, Tues, Thurs & Fri 10-6, Wed 1-8, Sat 10-2
HERTFORD COUNTY LIBRARY, 303 W Tryon St, 27986. (Mail add: PO Box 68, 27986-0068), SAN 313-0614. Tel: 252-358-7855. FAX: 252-358-0368. *Br Mgr,* Tomeka Roulhac; Staff 1.6 (Non-MLS 1.6)
Founded 1948. Pop 20,000
Subject Interests: Genealogy, Local hist
Open Mon & Wed-Fri 10-6, Tues 10-8, Sat 10-2
SALLIE HARRELL JENKINS MEMORIAL LIBRARY, 302 Broad St, Aulander, 27805. (Mail add: PO Box 189, Aulander, 27805-0189), SAN 312-7338. Tel: 252-345-4461. FAX: 252-345-8000. *Br Mgr,* Ellen Chauvin
Open Mon-Thurs 11-5
NORTHAMPTON MEMORIAL LIBRARY, 207 W Jefferson St, Jackson, 27845. (Mail add: PO Box 427, Jackson, 27845-0427), SAN 312-8857. Tel: 252-534-3571. FAX: 252-534-1017. *Br Mgr,* Pam Brett
Open Mon-Wed & Fri 10-6, Thurs 10-8, Sat 10-2
ELIZABETH SEWELL PARKER MEMORIAL LIBRARY, 213 E Main St, Murfreesboro, 27855. (Mail add: PO Drawer 186, Murfreesboro, 27855-0186), SAN 354-4443. Tel: 252-398-4494. FAX: 252-398-5724. *Br Mgr,* Judy Hachey
Special Collections: Murfreesboro, North Carolina (Paul Ronald Jenkins Photographs)
Open Mon-Fri 10-6

YADKINVILLE

P YADKIN COUNTY PUBLIC LIBRARY*, 233 E Main St, 27055. SAN 313-0622. Tel: 336-679-8792. FAX: 336-679-4625. E-mail: ydk@nwrl.org. Web Site: nwrlibrary.org/yadkin. *Br Librn,* Christy Ellington; *Asst Br Mgr,* Andrea Nichols
Founded 1942. Pop 32,000; Circ 58,000
Library Holdings: Bk Titles 57,000; Bk Vols 58,000; Per Subs 10
Special Collections: Local History Coll. Oral History
Automation Activity & Vendor Info: (Cataloging) SirsiDynix; (Circulation) SirsiDynix; (OPAC) SirsiDynix
Wireless access
Mem of Northwestern Regional Library
Open Mon & Thurs 8:30-6:30, Tues, Wed & Fri 8:30-5:30
Friends of the Library Group

YANCEYVILLE

P GUNN MEMORIAL PUBLIC LIBRARY (CASWELL COUNTY PUBLIC LIBRARY)*, 161 Main St E, 27379. SAN 313-0630. Tel: 336-694-6241. FAX: 336-694-9846. E-mail: gunnpublibrary@gmail.com. Web Site: www.caswellcountync.gov/pview.aspx?id=9385&datid=600. *Dir,* Rhonda Griffin; Tel: 336-694-6241, Ext 1116, E-mail: rgriffin@caswellcountync.gov; Staff 7 (MLS 1, Non-MLS 6)
Founded 1937. Pop 23,248; Circ 66,989
Library Holdings: Bk Vols 43,460; Per Subs 107
Special Collections: Local History/Genealogy Coll
Subject Interests: Genealogy, Local hist
Wireless access
Open Mon-Thurs 9-7, Fri 9-5, Sat 9-1
Friends of the Library Group

NORTH DAKOTA

Date of Statistics: FY 2019
Population, 2020 U.S. Census: 765,309
Population Served by Public Libraries: 684,668
Unserved: 77,394
Total Volumes in Public Libraries: 4,725,029
Volumes Per Capita: 6.2
Total Public Library Circulation: 3,552,881
Circulation Per Capita: 4.66
Digital Resources: 2,440
Total e-books: 1,159,194
Total audio items (physical and downloadable units): 1,233,020
Total video items (physical and downloadable units): 213,828
Total computers for use by the public: 742
Total annual wireless sessions: 2,126,564
Income and Expenditures:
Total Public Library Income (including Grants-in-Aid): $21,486,408
Source of Income: Mainly public funds
Expenditure Per Capita: $28.52
Grants-in-Aid for Public Libraries: $129,288
State Aid: $868,791
Number of Bookmobiles in State: 11
Number of County or Multi-county Libraries: 30
Counties Served: 30
Counties Unserved: 23
Information provided courtesy of: Michele Balliet Unrath, State Data Coordinator; North Dakota State Library

ASHLEY

P ASHLEY PUBLIC LIBRARY, 113 First Ave NW, 58413-7037. (Mail add: PO Box 185, 58413-0185). Tel: 701-288-3510. E-mail: ashpublibrary@hotmail.com. *Librn,* Barbara Nitschke
Founded 1913. Pop 882; Circ 2,185
Library Holdings: AV Mats 52; DVDs 50; Large Print Bks 300; Bk Vols 10,600; Talking Bks 25; Videos 42
Wireless access
Open Wed 9-12 & 1-5
Friends of the Library Group

BEACH

P GOLDEN VALLEY COUNTY LIBRARY*, 54 Central Ave S, 58621. (Mail add: PO Box 579, 58621-0579), SAN 313-0665. Tel: 701-872-4627. E-mail: gvcolibrary@outlook.com. Web Site: www.goldenvalleycounty.org/boards/library. *County Librn,* Joanne Tescher
Founded 1910. Pop 2,108; Circ 21,343
Library Holdings: Bk Vols 19,500; Per Subs 42
Wireless access
Open Tues-Thurs 10-12 & 1-5, Fri 1-5, Sat 9-Noon

BELCOURT

J TURTLE MOUNTAIN COMMUNITY COLLEGE LIBRARY*, PO Box 340, 58316-0340. SAN 313-0673. Tel: 701-477-7862, Ext 2084. FAX: 701-477-7805. Web Site: www.tm.edu/departments/library. *Dir,* Laisee Allery; Tel: 701-477-7812, Ext 2081, E-mail: lallery@tm.edu; *Libr Tech,* Harvey La Rocque; Tel: 701-477-7854, Ext 2082, E-mail: hlarocque@tm.edu; Staff 2 (MLS 1, Non-MLS 1)
Founded 1977. Enrl 911; Fac 44; Highest Degree: Bachelor
Library Holdings: AV Mats 1,462; Bks on Deafness & Sign Lang 11; Large Print Bks 54; Bk Titles 22,535; Bk Vols 31,248; Per Subs 135
Special Collections: Elementary Education Coll; Erdrich Coll; Native Americans (Anishanabe Coll), mats
Subject Interests: Native Am
Automation Activity & Vendor Info: (Acquisitions) Follett Software; (Cataloging) Follett Software; (Circulation) Follett Software; (Course Reserve) Follett Software; (Media Booking) Follett Software; (OPAC) Follett Software
Wireless access
Function: ILL available, Photocopying/Printing, Ref serv available, Telephone ref
Partic in Online Dakota Info Network
Open Mon-Fri 8-6

BEULAH

P BEULAH PUBLIC LIBRARY*, Beulah City Hall, 120 Central Ave N, 58523. SAN 355-4252. Tel: 701-873-2884. FAX: 701-873-2885. E-mail: beulahlibrary@gmail.com. Web Site: beulahndlibrary.com. *Dir,* Jessie Mann
Wireless access
Mem of McLean-Mercer Regional Library
Partic in Central Dakota Library Network
Open Mon-Thurs 9-6, Fri 9-5, Sat (Oct-March) 9-Noon

BISMARCK

C BISMARCK STATE COLLEGE LIBRARY*, 1500 Edwards Ave, 58501. (Mail add: PO Box 5587, 58506-5587), SAN 313-069X. Tel: 701-224-5450. FAX: 701-224-5551. E-mail: bsc.library@bismarckstate.edu. Web Site: bismarckstate.edu/academics/academicresources/Library. *Dir, Libr Serv,* Marlene Anderson; Tel: 701-224-5578, E-mail: marlene.anderson@bismarckstate.edu; *Ref & Instruction Librn,* Sandi Bates; Tel: 701-224-5451, E-mail: Sandi.Bates@bismarckstate.edu; *Tech Serv Librn,* Liz Mason; Tel: 701-224-5551, E-mail: liz.mason@bismarckstate.edu; *Libr Assoc,* Laura Kalvoda; Tel: 701-224-5483, E-mail: laura.kalvoda@bismarckstate.edu; Staff 6 (MLS 3, Non-MLS 3)
Founded 1955. Enrl 3,526; Fac 118; Highest Degree: Bachelor
Jul 2020-Jun 2021 Income $565,685. Sal $240,974
Special Collections: BSC Archives (Institutional history)
Subject Interests: Energy, NDak hist
Automation Activity & Vendor Info: (Cataloging) Ex Libris Group; (Circulation) Ex Libris Group; (Course Reserve) Ex Libris Group; (ILL) Ex Libris Group; (OPAC) Ex Libris Group; (Serials) Ex Libris Group
Wireless access
Function: Art exhibits, Audio & video playback equip for onsite use, Audiobks via web, Bks on cassette, Bks on CD, Computers for patron use, Electronic databases & coll, ILL available, Internet access, Microfiche/film & reading machines, Music CDs, Online cat, Online ref, Orientations, Outside serv via phone, mail, e-mail & web, Photocopying/Printing, Ref serv available, Telephone ref, VHS videos, Wheelchair accessible, Winter reading prog, Workshops
Partic in Online Dakota Info Network
Open Mon-Thurs 7:30am-8pm, Fri 7:30-4, Sun 1-4
Restriction: Restricted pub use

P BISMARCK VETERANS MEMORIAL PUBLIC LIBRARY*, 515 N Fifth St, 58501-4081. SAN 313-0789. Tel: 701-355-1480. Interlibrary Loan Service Tel: 701-355-1487. FAX: 701-221-3729. Web Site: www.bismarcklibrary.org. *Dir,* Christine Kujawa; Tel: 701-355-1482, E-mail: ckujawa@bismarcklibrary.org; *Asst Dir,* Elizabeth Jacobs; Tel: 701-355-1483, E-mail: ejacobs@bismarcklibrary.org; *Head, Children's Dept,* Traci Juhala; Tel: 701-355-1489, E-mail: tjuhala@bismarcklibrary.org; *Adult Programming, Head, ILL,* Sarah Matthews; E-mail: smatthews@bismarcklibrary.org; *Head, Ref,* Kate Waldera; Tel: 701-355-1492, E-mail: kwaldera@bismarcklibrary.org; *Head, Tech Serv,* Lora Rose; Tel: 701-355-1488, E-mail: lrose@bismarcklibrary.org; *Mgr, ILL,* Troy Hamre; E-mail: thamre@bismarcklibrary.org; Staff 16 (MLS 8, Non-MLS 8)
Founded 1917. Pop 90,503; Circ 525,655

Jan 2017-Dec 2017 Income $3,445,978, State $314,896, City $2,479,618, County $248,500, Locally Generated Income $402,964. Mats Exp $394,078, Books $275,882, Micro $2,000, AV Mat $37,196, Electronic Ref Mat (Incl. Access Fees) $78,000, Presv $1,000. Sal $1,820,596
Library Holdings: Audiobooks 9,614; DVDs 9,410; e-books 31,794; Bk Vols 188,420; Per Subs 318
Subject Interests: City hist, NDak hist, Rare bks
Automation Activity & Vendor Info: (Cataloging) SirsiDynix; (Circulation) SirsiDynix; (OPAC) SirsiDynix
Wireless access
Function: 24/7 Electronic res, 24/7 Online cat, 3D Printer, Accelerated reader prog, Activity rm, Adult bk club, Adult literacy prog, Archival coll, Art exhibits, Art programs, Audiobks on Playaways & MP3, Audiobks via web, AV serv, Bk club(s), Bks on CD, Chess club, Children's prog, Computer training, Computers for patron use, Doc delivery serv, E-Readers, Electronic databases & coll, Free DVD rentals, Health sci info serv, Holiday prog, Home delivery & serv to seniorr ctr & nursing homes, ILL available, Internet access, Life-long learning prog for all ages, Magazines, Mango lang, Meeting rooms, Microfiche/film & reading machines, Movies, Music CDs, Notary serv, Online cat, Outreach serv, Outside serv via phone, mail, e-mail & web, OverDrive digital audio bks, Photocopying/Printing, Preschool outreach, Printer for laptops & handheld devices, Prog for adults, Prog for children & young adult, Ref & res, Ref serv available, Res assist avail, Scanner, Senior computer classes, Senior outreach, Spanish lang bks, Story hour, Study rm, Summer & winter reading prog, Summer reading prog, Tax forms, Teen prog, Telephone ref, Wheelchair accessible, Winter reading prog
Partic in Central Dakota Library Network; OCLC Online Computer Library Center, Inc
Open Mon-Thurs 9-9, Fri & Sat 9-6, Sun 1-6
Restriction: Non-circulating of rare bks, Non-resident fee
Friends of the Library Group
Bookmobiles: 1. Librn, Keli Trowbridge

GL NORTH DAKOTA LEGISLATIVE COUNCIL LIBRARY*, 600 E Boulevard Ave, 58505-0660. Tel: 701-328-4900. FAX: 701-328-3615. Web Site: www.legis.nd.gov/legislative-council. *Mgr,* Kylah E Aull; E-mail: kaull@nd.gov
Library Holdings: Bk Vols 20,000; Per Subs 120
Wireless access
Open Mon-Fri 8-5

P NORTH DAKOTA STATE LIBRARY*, Liberty Memorial Bldg, Dept 250, 604 East Blvd Ave, 58505-0800. SAN 313-0746. Tel: 701-328-2492. Circulation Tel: 701-328-4657. Interlibrary Loan Service Tel: 701-328-3252. Reference Tel: 701-328-4622. Toll Free Tel: 800-472-2104. FAX: 701-328-2040. E-mail: statelib@nd.gov. Web Site: www.library.nd.gov. *State Librn,* Mary Soucie; *Admin Serv, Dep Dir,* Cynthia Clairmont-Schmidt; Tel: 701-328-4652, E-mail: cclairmont@nd.gov; *Head, Libr Serv,* Carmen Redding; Tel: 701-328-4676, E-mail: creddinge@nd.gov; *Head, Patron Serv,* Stephanie Baltzer Kom; Tel: 701-328-4021, E-mail: sbkom@nd.gov; *Head, Tech Serv,* Ryan Kroh; E-mail: rkroh@nd.gov; *Digital Initiatives,* Trevor Martinson; Tel: 701-328-4629, E-mail: tmartinson@nd.gov; *Marketing Specialist,* BreAnne Meier; Tel: 701-328-4656, E-mail: bmeier@nd.gov; Staff 12 (MLS 12)
Founded 1907
Jul 2019-Jun 2020 Income $3,856,710, State $2,890,710, Federal $966,000. Mats Exp Books $63,000
Library Holdings: CDs 417; e-books 12,011; Large Print Bks 7,380; Per Subs 315; Videos 1,906
Special Collections: North Dakota Coll; State Documents. State Document Depository; US Document Depository
Automation Activity & Vendor Info: (Acquisitions) Innovative Interfaces, Inc; (Cataloging) Innovative Interfaces, Inc; (Circulation) Innovative Interfaces, Inc; (ILL) Innovative Interfaces, Inc; (OPAC) Innovative Interfaces, Inc; (Serials) Innovative Interfaces, Inc
Wireless access
Function: 24/7 Electronic res, 24/7 Online cat
Publications: Discovery (Newsletter); Library Statistics; NDSL Flickertale (Newsletter); State Library Biennial Report
Partic in Association for Rural & Small Libraries; Minitex; Online Dakota Info Network
Special Services for the Blind - Digital talking bk; Digital talking bk machines

GL NORTH DAKOTA SUPREME COURT*, Law Library, Judicial Wing, 2nd Flr, 600 E Boulevard Ave, Dept 182, 58505-0540. SAN 313-0762. Tel: 701-328-4496. FAX: 701-328-3609. Web Site: www.court.state.nd.us/lawlib/www6.htm. *Librn,* Position Currently Open
Founded 1889
Library Holdings: Bk Vols 72,000
Special Collections: North Dakota Legal Materials
Automation Activity & Vendor Info: (ILL) Ex Libris Group; (OPAC) Ex Libris Group
Wireless access
Partic in Online Dakota Info Network
Open Mon-Fri 8-5

M SANFORD HEALTH*, Sanford Health Sciences Library, 622 Ave A East, 58501. SAN 313-0770. Tel: 701-323-5390, 701-323-5392. FAX: 701-323-6967. E-mail: bsm_ill@sanfordhealth.org. Web Site: www.sanfordhealth.org. *Librn,* Trevor Martison; Staff 3 (MLS 2, Non-MLS 1)
Founded 1927
Library Holdings: Bk Vols 7,000; Per Subs 6
Subject Interests: Clinical med, Nursing
Automation Activity & Vendor Info: (Circulation) Ex Libris Group; (ILL) Ex Libris Group
Wireless access
Function: Archival coll, Doc delivery serv, For res purposes, ILL available, Photocopying/Printing, Ref serv available, Telephone ref
Partic in Online Dakota Info Network
Open Mon-Fri 8-5
Restriction: Circ limited, In-house use for visitors, Private libr

S STATE HISTORICAL SOCIETY OF NORTH DAKOTA, State Archives, North Dakota Heritage Ctr, 612 E Boulevard Ave, 58505-0830. SAN 313-072X. Tel: 701-328-2091. E-mail: archives@nd.gov. Web Site: history.nd.gov/archives. *State Archivist,* Shane Molander; E-mail: smolander@nd.gov; *Dept Head, Ref,* Sarah Walker; *Dept Head, Tech Serv,* Virginia Bjorness; Staff 13 (MLS 3, Non-MLS 10)
Founded 1895
Library Holdings: Microforms 3,000; Bk Titles 40,000; Bk Vols 117,500; Per Subs 50
Special Collections: Oral History; State Document Depository; US Document Depository
Subject Interests: Archaeology, Hist of Northern Great Plains, NDak hist, Presv
Automation Activity & Vendor Info: (Cataloging) OCLC Connexion; (ILL) OCLC WorldShare Interlibrary Loan; (OPAC) Ex Libris Group
Wireless access
Function: Archival coll, ILL available, Internet access, Microfiche/film & reading machines, Online cat, Outside serv via phone, mail, e-mail & web, Photocopying/Printing, Ref serv available, Res performed for a fee, Telephone ref, Wheelchair accessible
Publications: North Dakota History (Quarterly); PlainsTalk (Quarterly)
Partic in Minitex; OCLC Online Computer Library Center, Inc
Restriction: Closed stack, In-house use for visitors, Internal use only, Non-circulating coll, Not a lending libr, Open by appt only

J UNITED TRIBES TECHNICAL COLLEGE LIBRARY*, Jack Barden Center, Lower Level, 3315 University Dr, 58504-7565. Tel: 701-221-1782. FAX: 701-530-0625. Web Site: www.uttc.edu. *Libr Dir,* Charlene Weis; E-mail: cweis@uttc.edu; Staff 1 (MLS 1)
Founded 1969
Library Holdings: Bk Vols 9,000
Special Collections: Native American Coll
Automation Activity & Vendor Info: (Cataloging) SirsiDynix; (Circulation) SirsiDynix; (OPAC) SirsiDynix
Wireless access
Partic in Central Dakota Library Network
Open Mon-Fri 8-4:30

C UNIVERSITY OF MARY*, Welder Library, 7500 University Dr, 58504-9652. SAN 313-0711. Tel: 701-355-8070. E-mail: library@umary.edu. Web Site: www.umary.edu/academics/library. *Dir, Libr Serv, Univ Archivist,* David Gray; E-mail: dpgray@umary.edu; Staff 4 (MLS 4)
Founded 1959. Enrl 3,100; Highest Degree: Doctorate
Library Holdings: AV Mats 3,600; e-books 225,000; e-journals 60,000; Bk Vols 52,000; Per Subs 525
Subject Interests: Educ, Nursing, Theol
Automation Activity & Vendor Info: (Acquisitions) SirsiDynix; (Cataloging) Horizon; (Circulation) Horizon; (OPAC) Horizon
Wireless access
Partic in Central Dakota Library Network; OCLC Online Computer Library Center, Inc
Open Mon-Thurs 7:30am-11:30pm, Fri 7:30-6, Sat Noon-6, Sun 1-11:30; Mon-Fri (Summer) 8-4:30

BOTTINEAU

P BOTTINEAU COUNTY PUBLIC LIBRARY*, 314 W Fifth St, 58318-9600. SAN 375-4537. Tel: 701-228-2967. FAX: 701-228-2171. E-mail: bottineaulibrary@yahoo.com. Web Site: bottineaucountyndlibrary.com. *Dir,* Beth Reitan; Staff 3 (MLS 1, Non-MLS 2)
Founded 1922

Library Holdings: Bk Vols 30,000; Per Subs 30
Automation Activity & Vendor Info: (Circulation) Follett Software; (Serials) Follett Software
Wireless access
Function: ILL available
Partic in Online Dakota Info Network
Open Mon-Wed & Fri 9-5:30, Thurs 9-7:30, Sat 10-2
Bookmobiles: 1

J DAKOTA COLLEGE AT BOTTINEAU LIBRARY*, 105 Simrall Blvd, 58318. SAN 313-0797. Tel: 701-228-5454. FAX: 701-228-5656. Web Site: www.dakotacollege.edu. *Dir,* Hattie Albertson; E-mail: hattie.c.albertson@dakotacollege.edu; *Assoc Librn,* Terri Hauge; E-mail: terri.hauge@dakotacollege.edu
Founded 1907. Enrl 644; Fac 26; Highest Degree: Associate
Library Holdings: Audiobooks 110; AV Mats 1,300; e-books 8,075; Bk Titles 25,325; Bk Vols 27,200; Per Subs 180
Subject Interests: Forestry, Hort, Natural sci, Recreation
Wireless access
Partic in Online Dakota Info Network
Open Mon-Thurs 7:30am-10pm, Fri 7:30-4, Sun 6pm-10pm

BOWMAN

P BOWMAN REGIONAL PUBLIC LIBRARY, 18 E Divide St, 58623. (Mail add: PO Box 179, 58623-0179), SAN 313-0800. Tel: 701-523-3797. E-mail: bowlib@ndsupernet.com. Web Site: www.bowmanlibrary.com. *Dir,* Sarah Snavely; *Librn,* Kaitlin Brooks
Founded 1913. Pop 3,200; Circ 13,800
Library Holdings: Bk Vols 23,000; Per Subs 63
Automation Activity & Vendor Info: (Cataloging) Follett Software; (Circulation) Follett Software; (OPAC) Follett Software
Wireless access
Open Mon-Thurs 10-6, Sun 1-5

CANDO

P CANDO COMMUNITY LIBRARY*, 502 Main St, 58324. (Mail add: PO Box 798, 58324-0798). Tel: 701-968-4549. E-mail: cando.library@yahoo.com. Web Site: www.candond.com. *Librn,* Hazel Krack
Library Holdings: Bk Titles 25,000
Open Tues & Thurs 3-8, Wed & Sat 11-2

CARRINGTON

P CARRINGTON CITY LIBRARY*, 87 Eighth Ave N, 58421. SAN 313-0819. Tel: 701-652-3921. FAX: 701-652-3922. E-mail: cgtnlib@daktel.com. Web Site: carringtonlibrary.org. *Librn,* Lenore Franchuk
Founded 1916. Pop 2,267; Circ 9,982
Library Holdings: Bk Vols 12,718; Per Subs 33; Talking Bks 225; Videos 499
Wireless access
Partic in NDak Network for Knowledge
Open Mon-Thur 10:30-5:30, Sat 10:30-1:30
Friends of the Library Group

CASSELTON

P CASSELTON PUBLIC LIBRARY*, 702 First St N, 58012. (Mail add: PO Box 1090, 58012-1090), SAN 313-0827. Tel: 701-347-4861, Ext 13. FAX: 701-347-4505. E-mail: cassndlibrary@casselton.net. Web Site: casseltonndlibrary.com. *Dir,* Sheila Krueger
Pop 2,200
Library Holdings: CDs 80; DVDs 24; Bk Titles 25,000; Per Subs 4; Spec Interest Per Sub 5; Talking Bks 356; Videos 288
Partic in Online Dakota Info Network
Special Services for the Blind - Audio mat; Bks on cassette; Bks on CD; Home delivery serv; Recorded bks; Talking bk serv referral; Talking bks; Talking bks & player equip; Talking bks from Braille Inst
Open Mon 8:30-7, Tues-Thurs 8:30-4:30, Fri 8:30-1
Friends of the Library Group

CAVALIER

P CAVALIER PUBLIC LIBRARY*, 200 Bjornson Dr, 58220. SAN 313-0835. Tel: 701-265-4746. E-mail: cavlibry@polarcomm.com. Web Site: cavalierndlibrary.com. *Dir,* Rebecca Ratchenski; *Asst Librn,* Anne Heck; Staff 1 (Non-MLS 1)
Founded 1915. Pop 1,300; Circ 20,000
Library Holdings: Audiobooks 249; DVDs 183; Large Print Bks 180; Bk Vols 12,039; Per Subs 35; Videos 582
Automation Activity & Vendor Info: (Acquisitions) Follett Software
Wireless access
Partic in Online Dakota Info Network
Open Mon 12:30-8, Tues-Fri 12:30-6, Sat 12:30-3

COOPERSTOWN

P GRIGGS COUNTY PUBLIC LIBRARY*, 902 Burrell Ave, 58425. (Mail add: PO Box 546, 58425-0546), SAN 313-0843. Tel: 701-797-2214. E-mail: gcplibrary@mlgc.com. Web Site: griggscountypubliclibrary.com. *Dir,* Bonnie Krenz; Staff 2 (Non-MLS 2)
Founded 1944. Pop 1,500; Circ 34,887
Library Holdings: AV Mats 300; Large Print Bks 500; Bk Titles 30,000; Per Subs 52; Talking Bks 300
Special Collections: North Dakota Historical Coll
Automation Activity & Vendor Info: (Cataloging) Follett Software; (Circulation) Follett Software
Open Mon 9-12 & 1-5, Tues-Thurs 9-6, Fri 9-5, Sat 9-1
Bookmobiles: 1. In Charge, Bonnie Krenz. Bk titles 4,000

CROSBY

P DIVIDE COUNTY PUBLIC LIBRARY*, 204 First St NE, 58730. (Mail add: PO Box 90, 58730), SAN 313-0851. Tel: 701-965-6305. E-mail: dcl@nccray.net. Web Site: www.dividecountyndlibrary.com. *Dir,* Traci Lund
Founded 1912. Pop 2,283
Library Holdings: Bks-By-Mail 50; Bks on Deafness & Sign Lang 10; Large Print Bks 200; Bk Vols 38,000; Per Subs 44; Talking Bks 100; Videos 350
Special Collections: Local Geneology Coll. Oral History
Subject Interests: Local hist, State hist
Automation Activity & Vendor Info: (Acquisitions) Follett Software; (ILL) Follett Software
Wireless access
Open Mon-Fri 8:30-5

DEVILS LAKE

P LAKE REGION PUBLIC LIBRARY, 423 Seventh St NE, 58301-2529. SAN 313-086X. Tel: 701-662-2220. FAX: 701-662-2281. E-mail: lakeregionpl@gmail.com. Web Site: devilslakendlibrary.com. *Dir,* Ignacio Mendez; Staff 1 (Non-MLS 1)
Founded 1910. Pop 11,536; Circ 24,065
Jan 2020-Dec 2020 Income $220,200, State $18,300, City $181,406, Other $20,400. Mats Exp $190,500, Books $9,740, Per/Ser (Incl. Access Fees) $3,200, AV Mat $1,500, Electronic Ref Mat (Incl. Access Fees) $3,609. Sal $125,539
Library Holdings: Audiobooks 510; CDs 203; DVDs 544; e-books 8,436; Electronic Media & Resources 56; Large Print Bks 1,423; Microforms 293; Bk Vols 40,000; Per Subs 58; Videos 715
Special Collections: George Johnson Genealogy Coll; Germans-From-Russia Coll; Local History Coll; North Dakota Coll; Special Scandinavian Coll
Subject Interests: Hist, Needlework, Recipes
Automation Activity & Vendor Info: (Acquisitions) Book Systems; (Cataloging) Book Systems; (Circulation) Book Systems; (OPAC) Book Systems
Wireless access
Function: Audiobks via web, Bks on cassette, Bks on CD, Children's prog, Computers for patron use, Digital talking bks, Electronic databases & coll, Free DVD rentals, ILL available, Magazines, Microfiche/film & reading machines, Music CDs, Outreach serv, Photocopying/Printing, Prog for adults, Prog for children & young adult, Scanner, Spoken cassettes & CDs, Spoken cassettes & DVDs, Story hour, Summer reading prog, Tax forms, VHS videos, Wheelchair accessible
Special Services for the Deaf - ADA equip; Closed caption videos
Special Services for the Blind - Bks on cassette; Bks on CD; Cassettes; Copier with enlargement capabilities; Extensive large print coll; Free checkout of audio mat; Large print bks
Open Mon, Wed & Fri 9-6, Tues 10:30-6, Thurs 10:30-7, Sat 10:30-3
Restriction: Non-resident fee

C LAKE REGION STATE COLLEGE, Paul Hoghaug Library, 1801 College Dr N, 58301. SAN 313-0878. Tel: 701-662-1533. Toll Free Tel: 800-443-1313. FAX: 701-662-1570. Web Site: lrsc.edu/admissions-aid/student-life/library-learning-commons. *Librn,* Jolie Johnston; E-mail: jolie.johnston@lrsc.edu; Staff 1 (MLS 1)
Founded 1966. Enrl 1,300; Highest Degree: Associate
Library Holdings: Audiobooks 500; Bks on Deafness & Sign Lang 25; CDs 25; DVDs 500; e-books 18,000; Bk Vols 35,000; Per Subs 100; Videos 400
Special Collections: Irish History & Culture
Automation Activity & Vendor Info: (Acquisitions) Ex Libris Group; (Cataloging) Ex Libris Group; (Circulation) Ex Libris Group; (Course Reserve) Ex Libris Group; (ILL) Ex Libris Group; (Media Booking) Ex Libris Group; (OPAC) Ex Libris Group; (Serials) Ex Libris Group

Wireless access
Open Mon-Thurs 7:45am-10pm, Fri 7:45-4:45, Sat 10-6, Sun Noon-10

S NORTH DAKOTA SCHOOL FOR THE DEAF LIBRARY*, 1401 College Dr N, 58301. SAN 313-0886. Tel: 701-665-4400. FAX: 701-665-4409. Web Site: www.nd.gov/ndsd. *Librn,* Susan Schwab-Kjelland; Tel: 701-665-4433, E-mail: susan.schwabkjelland@k12.nd.us
Library Holdings: Bk Vols 4,000; Per Subs 20
Wireless access
Open Mon-Fri 8-4

DICKINSON

P DICKINSON AREA PUBLIC LIBRARY*, 139 Third St W, 58601. SAN 313-0894. Tel: 701-456-7700. FAX: 701-456-7702. E-mail: Dickinson.Library@dickinsongov.com. Web Site: www.dickinsonlibrary.org. *Dir,* Rita Ennen; *Asst Dir,* Renee Newton; Staff 8.5 (MLS 2, Non-MLS 6.5)
Founded 1908. Pop 28,000; Circ 130,000
Jan 2016-Dec 2016 Income (Main & Associated Libraries) $1,048,922, State $114,755, City $530,313, County $347,242, Locally Generated Income $56,611. Mats Exp $138,940, Books $87,270, Per/Ser (Incl. Access Fees) $6,000, AV Mat $34,625, Electronic Ref Mat (Incl. Access Fees) $11,045. Sal $465,145 (Prof $372,661)
Library Holdings: Audiobooks 2,475; DVDs 6,567; e-books 27,229; Large Print Bks 4,216; Bk Vols 91,856; Per Subs 68; Videos 3,056
Special Collections: Dickinson Press, 1883-present
Automation Activity & Vendor Info: (Acquisitions) Ex Libris Group; (Cataloging) Ex Libris Group; (Circulation) Ex Libris Group; (ILL) Ex Libris Group; (OPAC) Ex Libris Group; (Serials) Ex Libris Group
Wireless access
Publications: Library Skills for Adult Education
Partic in NDak Network for Knowledge; OCLC Online Computer Library Center, Inc; Online Dakota Info Network
Open Mon-Thurs 9-8, Fri 9-6, Sat 9-5
Friends of the Library Group
Branches: 1
BILLINGS COUNTY RESOURCE CENTER, PO Box 307, Medora, 58645-0307. Tel: 701-623-4604. FAX: 701-623-4941. *Dir,* Rita Ennen; *Pub Serv,* Jaylene Kovash
Library Holdings: Bk Vols 15,000
Partic in Online Dakota Info Network
Open Mon-Fri 3:15-5, Mon-Fri (Summer) 9-5
Bookmobiles: 1. Librn, Jaylene Kovash. Bk titles 4,375

C DICKINSON STATE UNIVERSITY*, Stoxen Library, 291 Campus Dr, 58601. SAN 313-0908. Tel: 701-483-2135. FAX: 701-483-2006. E-mail: dsu.stoxenlibrary@dickinsonstate.edu. Web Site: www.dickinsonstate.edu/academics/library/. *Univ Librn,* Monica Struck; Tel: 701-483-2136, E-mail: monica.struck@dickinsonstate.edu; *Head, Libr Operations,* Staci Green; Tel: 701-483-2562, E-mail: staci.green@dickinsonstate.edu; Staff 6 (MLS 3, Non-MLS 3)
Founded 1918. Enrl 1,500; Fac 70; Highest Degree: Bachelor
Jul 2013-Jun 2014. Mats Exp $307,078, Books $77,357, Per/Ser (Incl. Access Fees) $143,943, Micro $684, AV Mat $12,892, Electronic Ref Mat (Incl. Access Fees) $72,202. Sal $267,156 (Prof $156,320)
Library Holdings: AV Mats 7,300; e-books 13,046; Bk Vols 96,000; Per Subs 400
Special Collections: Teddy Roosevelt Coll
Subject Interests: Educ
Automation Activity & Vendor Info: (Acquisitions) Ex Libris Group; (Cataloging) Ex Libris Group; (Circulation) Ex Libris Group; (Course Reserve) Ex Libris Group; (ILL) Ex Libris Group; (OPAC) Ex Libris Group; (Serials) Ex Libris Group
Wireless access
Partic in Online Dakota Info Network
Open Mon-Fri 7:30-4:30 (Summer); Mon-Thurs 7:45am-10pm, Fri 7:45-4:30, Sun 4pm-10pm

DRAKE

P DRAKE PUBLIC LIBRARY, 411 Main St, 58736. Tel: 701-465-3732. FAX: 701-465-3634. *Librn,* Kimberly Brandt; E-mail: kim.brandt@k12.nd.us
Library Holdings: CDs 25; Bk Vols 5,000; Per Subs 10
Wireless access
Partic in Online Dakota Info Network
Open Mon-Fri 8-4

EDGELEY

P SOUTH CENTRAL AREA LIBRARY*, Edgeley Public, 530 Main St, 58433. (Mail add: PO Box 218, 58433-0218), SAN 355-323X. Tel: 701-493-2769. FAX: 701-493-2959. E-mail: library@drtel.net. Web Site: edgeleyndlibrary.com. *Dir,* Lynda Dunn
Founded 1958. Pop 10,075; Circ 88,000
Library Holdings: AV Mats 350; Large Print Bks 5,000; Bk Titles 30,000; Bk Vols 15,000; Per Subs 12; Talking Bks 400
Special Collections: North Dakota Coll
Automation Activity & Vendor Info: (Cataloging) Follett Software; (Circulation) Follett Software; (OPAC) Follett Software
Wireless access
Open Mon-Fri 8-5, Sat 9-1
Bookmobiles: 1

ELGIN

P ELGIN PUBLIC LIBRARY*, 121 Main St N, 58533. Tel: 701-584-2181. E-mail: elginlibrary@westriv.com. Web Site: elginndlibrary.com. *Head Librn,* Arla Roth
Library Holdings: Bk Titles 9,500
Open Mon-Fri 9-5

ELLENDALE

P ELLENDALE PUBLIC LIBRARY, 75 First St S, 58436. (Mail add: PO Box 113, 58436-0113), SAN 313-0916. Tel: 701-349-3852. E-mail: elllibrary@drtel.net. Web Site: ellendalendlibrary.com. *Dir,* Jan Reuter
Circ 18,000
Library Holdings: Bk Vols 25,000; Per Subs 10
Wireless access
Open Tues, Wed & Fri 10-5, Thurs 10-8, Sat 9-Noon
Friends of the Library Group

CR TRINITY BIBLE COLLEGE*, The Graham Library, 50 Sixth Ave S, 58436-7150. SAN 313-0924. Tel: 701-349-5407. Toll Free Tel: 800-523-1603. FAX: 701-349-5443. E-mail: tbclibrary@trinitybiblecollege.edu. Web Site: www.trinitybiblecollege.edu/library. *Dir, Libr Serv,* Phyllis Kuno; E-mail: phylliskuno@trinitybiblecollege.edu; Staff 3 (MLS 2, Non-MLS 1)
Founded 1948. Enrl 250; Fac 25; Highest Degree: Master
Library Holdings: e-books 11,730; Bk Titles 57,604; Bk Vols 89,690; Per Subs 175; Videos 518
Special Collections: College & Denomination Archives; Juvenile Coll; North Dakota History (Graham Coll); Rare Coll
Subject Interests: Biblical studies, Evangelism, Missions, Relig studies, Soc sci
Automation Activity & Vendor Info: (Circulation) Ex Libris Group
Wireless access
Function: 24/7 Online cat, Computers for patron use, Electronic databases & coll, ILL available, Internet access, Laminating, Online cat, Photocopying/Printing, Tax forms
Partic in Minitex; Online Dakota Info Network
Open Mon, Tues & Thurs 8am-10pm, Wed 8-5 & 7-10, Fri 8-5, Sat Noon-5
Restriction: Borrowing requests are handled by ILL, Fee for pub use, In-house use for visitors, Non-circulating of rare bks, Pub use on premises

ENDERLIN

P ENDERLIN MUNICIPAL LIBRARY*, 303 Railway St, 58027. SAN 313-0932. Tel: 701-437-2953. FAX: 701-437-2104. E-mail: enderlinlibrary@mlgc.com. Web Site: enderlinnd.com/library. *Librn,* Myrene Peterson
Founded 1911. Pop 986; Circ 5,895
Library Holdings: Bk Vols 26,000; Per Subs 17
Special Collections: SooLine Railroad Resources
Subject Interests: NDak
Automation Activity & Vendor Info: (Acquisitions) Follett Software; (Circulation) Follett Software; (Course Reserve) Follett Software; (ILL) Follett Software
Wireless access
Open Tues & Thurs 12-7, Wed & Fri 12-6, Sat 9-1
Friends of the Library Group

FARGO

GM DEPARTMENT OF VETERANS AFFAIRS*, Medical Library, 2101 N Elm St, 58102. SAN 313-1041. Tel: 701-239-3755. Toll Free Tel: 800-410-9723, Ext 3658. FAX: 701-239-3775. Web Site: www.fargo.va.gov. *Librn,* Ronald Padot; E-mail: ronald.padot@va.gov
Founded 1930
Library Holdings: e-books 65; Bk Titles 860; Per Subs 50
Subject Interests: Clinical med
Automation Activity & Vendor Info: (Cataloging) Ex Libris Group; (ILL) Ex Libris Group
Partic in Online Dakota Info Network
Open Mon-Fri 7:30-4

P FARGO PUBLIC LIBRARY*, 102 N Third St, 58102. SAN 313-0959. Tel: 701-241-1472. Reference Tel: 701-241-1492. Administration Tel: 701-241-8277. FAX: 701-241-8581. Reference E-mail: askreference@fargolibrary.org. Web Site: fargond.gov/city-government/departments/library. *Dir,* Timothy Dirks; Tel: 701-241-1493, E-mail: tdirks@cityoffargo.com; *Dep Dir,* Beth E Postema; E-mail: bpostema@fargolibrary.org; *Mgr, Br Serv,* Lori West; E-mail: lwest@fargolibrary.org; *Ch Serv,* Amber Emery; E-mail: aemery@fargolibrary.org; Staff 40 (MLS 7, Non-MLS 33)
Founded 1900. Pop 105,549
Library Holdings: Audiobooks 2,944; CDs 7,443; DVDs 10,121; e-books 1,437; Electronic Media & Resources 862; Large Print Bks 7,053; Bk Vols 131,025; Per Subs 410
Special Collections: North Dakota Coll
Automation Activity & Vendor Info: (Acquisitions) Ex Libris Group; (Cataloging) Ex Libris Group; (Circulation) Ex Libris Group; (ILL) OCLC; (OPAC) Ex Libris Group; (Serials) Ex Libris Group
Wireless access
Partic in OCLC Online Computer Library Center, Inc; Online Dakota Info Network
Open Mon & Tues 10-8, Wed & Thurs 10-6, Fri 11-6, Sat 9-6
Friends of the Library Group
Branches: 2
DR JAMES CARLSON BRANCH, 2801 32nd Ave S, 58103. Tel: 701-476-4040. Reference Tel: 701-476-5980. FAX: 701-364-2852. *Br Mgr,* Lori West
Founded 2002
Library Holdings: Audiobooks 1,687; CDs 3,608; DVDs 5,553; Large Print Bks 1,560; Bk Vols 49,683; Per Subs 122
Function: AV serv, ILL available, Ref serv available
Open Mon & Tues 10-8, Wed & Thurs 10-6, Fri 11-6, Sat 9-6
NORTHPORT, 2714 Broadway, 58102. Tel: 701-476-4026. *Br Mgr,* Lori West
Library Holdings: Audiobooks 472; CDs 1,953; DVDs 2,755; Bk Titles 16,262; Per Subs 56
Open Mon & Tues 10-8, Wed & Thurs 10-6, Fri 11-6, Sat 9-6

S MASONIC GRAND LODGE LIBRARY*, 201 14th Ave N, 58102. SAN 313-0975. Tel: 701-235-8321. FAX: 701-235-8323. E-mail: grandlodgend@yahoo.com. Web Site: www.ndmasons.com. *Mgr,* Tracey Pfarr
Founded 1889
Library Holdings: Bk Vols 4,000
Subject Interests: Masonic heritage, Philos lit
Publications: North Dakota Mason
Open Mon-Fri 8-12 & 1-4

C NORTH DAKOTA STATE UNIVERSITY LIBRARIES, 1201 Albrecht Blvd, 58108. (Mail add: PO Box 6050, NDSU Dept 2080, 58108-6050), SAN 355-3329. Tel: 701-231-8888. Reference Tel: 701-231-8886. Administration Tel: 701-231-8753. FAX: 701-231-6128. Web Site: library.ndsu.edu. *Interim Dean of Libr,* Hallie Pritchett; Tel: 701-231-8897, E-mail: hallie.pritchett@ndsu.edu; *Bibliographer, Dir,* Michael M Miller; Tel: 701-231-8416, E-mail: michael.miller@ndsu.edu; *Head, Access Serv,* Catherine Kratochvil; Tel: 701-231-8915, E-mail: catherine.kratochvil@ndsu.edu; *Head, Res & Instruction,* Beth Twomey; Tel: 701-231-8141, E-mail: beth.twomey@ndsu.edu; *Head, Resource Acquisition, Mgmt & Discovery,* Jenny Grasto; Tel: 701-231-6462, E-mail: jenny.grasto@ndsu.edu; *Head, Systems & Digital Strategies,* Amy Reese; Tel: 701-231-7288, E-mail: amy.reese@ndsu.edu; *Resource Acquisition & Mgmt Librn,* Barb Davis; Tel: 701-231-8880, E-mail: barb.davis@ndsu.edu; *Agr Sci Librn,* Nicole Juve; Tel: 701-231-8879, E-mail: nicole.km.juve@ndsu.edu; *Eng Librn,* Steve Jeffery; Tel: 701-231-5912, E-mail: steve.jeffery@ndsu.edu; *Govt Info Librn,* Susanne Caro; Tel: 701-231-8863, E-mail: susanne.caro@ndsu.edu; *Health Sci Librn,* Merete Christianson; Tel: 701-231-7965, E-mail: merete.christianson@ndsu.edu; *Humanities Librn,* Maddison Melquist; Tel: 701-231-8394, E-mail: maddison.melquist@ndsu.edu; *Metadata/Cat Librn,* Tina Gross; Tel: 701-231-9677, E-mail: tina.gross@ndsu.edu; *Sci Librn,* Bob Tolliver; Tel: 701-231-7351, E-mail: robert.tolliver@ndsu.edu; *Soc Sci Librn,* Al Bernardo; Tel: 701-231-6534, E-mail: alfred.bernardo@ndsu.edu; *Proc Archivist,* Matt Tallant; Tel: 701-231-8877, E-mail: matthew.tallant@ndsu.edu; Staff 36 (MLS 14, Non-MLS 22)
Founded 1891. Highest Degree: Doctorate
Special Collections: Bonanza Farming; Fred Hultstrand History in Pictures Coll; Germans from Russia Heritage Coll; North Dakota Biography Index; North Dakota Historical Manuscript; North Dakota Pioneer Reminiscences; Senator Milton R Young Photograph Coll; Shott Coll; University Archives. State Document Depository; US Document Depository
Automation Activity & Vendor Info: (Acquisitions) Ex Libris Group; (Cataloging) Ex Libris Group; (Circulation) Ex Libris Group; (Course Reserve) Ex Libris Group; (ILL) Ex Libris Group; (Media Booking) Ex Libris Group; (OPAC) Ex Libris Group; (Serials) Ex Libris Group
Wireless access
Function: Archival coll, Computers for patron use, Doc delivery serv, E-Reserves, Electronic databases & coll, Free DVD rentals, Govt ref serv, Health sci info serv, ILL available, Internet access, Literacy & newcomer serv, Music CDs, Online cat, Online info literacy tutorials on the web & in blackboard, Online ref, Photocopying/Printing, Ref serv available, Tax forms, Wheelchair accessible
Publications: North Dakota Institute for Regional Studies Guide to Manuscripts & Archives; Researching the Germans from Russia; Visual Images from the Northern Prairies
Special Services for the Deaf - TDD equip
Open Mon-Thurs 7:30am-Midnight, Fri 7:30-5, Sat 11-5, Sun 1-Midnight
Restriction: Authorized personnel only
Departmental Libraries:
BUSINESS LEARNING CENTER, Richard H Barry Hall, Rm 22, 811 Second Ave N, 58102. (Mail add: PO Box 6050, NDSU Dept 2080, 58108-6050). Tel: 701-231-8191. FAX: 701-231-6128. Web Site: library.ndsu.edu/locations/branches/business-learning-center. *Access & Res Serv Librn,* Lisa Eggebraaten; Tel: 701-231-8462, E-mail: lisa.eggbraaten@ndsu.edu; *Libr Assoc,* Abigail Erickson; E-mail: abigail.erickson@ndsu.edu
Open Mon-Thurs 10-6, Fri 10-5
KLAI JUBA WALD ARCHITECTURAL STUDIES LIBRARY, Klai Hall, Rm 310, 711 Second Ave N, 58102. (Mail add: PO Box 6050, NDSU Dept 2080, 58108-6050). Tel: 701-231-8616. FAX: 701-231-6128. Web Site: library.ndsu.edu/locations/branches/klai-juba-wald-architectural-studies-library. *Access & Res Serv Librn,* Lisa Eggebraaten; Tel: 701-231-8462, E-mail: lisa.eggbraaten@ndsu.edu
Subject Interests: Archit, Landscape archit
Open Mon-Fri 8-5
NDSU ARCHIVES/INSTITUTE FOR REGIONAL STUDIES, NDSU West Bldg, Rm 123, 3551 7th Ave N, 58102. (Mail add: PO Box 6050, NDSU Dept, 2080, 58108). Tel: 701-231-8914. E-mail: ndsu.archives@ndsu.edu. Web Site: library.ndsu.edu/ndsuarchives. *Dean,* David Bertolini; Tel: 701-231-8338, E-mail: david.bertolini@ndsu.edu; *Proc Archivist,* Matt Tallant; Tel: 701-231-8877, E-mail: matthew.tallant@ndsu.edu
Founded 1950
Library Holdings: Bk Vols 20,000
Open Mon-Fri 8-4

CM SANFORD HEALTH LIBRARY, Sudro Hall 136, 512 N Seventh St, Bismarck, 58501. (Mail add: PO Box 6050, NDSU Dept 2080, 58108-6050). Tel: 791-224-3835. FAX: 701-231-7606. Web Site: library.ndsu.edu/locations/branches/ndsu-nursing-sanford-health-library. *Health Sci Librn,* Merete Christianson; Tel: 701-231-7965, E-mail: merete.christianson@ndsu.edu; *Libr Assoc,* Linnette Schmidkunz; E-mail: linnette.schmidkunz@ndsu.edu
Subject Interests: Nursing, Pharm
Open Mon-Thurs 7-4, Fri 7-1

M SANFORD VIRTUAL LIBRARY*, 1711 S University Dr, 58103. SAN 355-3442. Tel: 701-234-6000. *Librn,* Kellie Mehlhause; Tel: 701-417-4917, E-mail: kellie.mehlhause@sanfordhealth.org; Staff 2 (MLS 1, Non-MLS 1)
Founded 1955
Subject Interests: Allied health, Med, Nursing
Partic in Docline; FS-Info
Restriction: Not open to pub

FINLEY

P FINLEY PUBLIC LIBRARY*, 302 Broadway, 58230. E-mail: capdakota1@gmail.com, contactus@finleypl.org. Web Site: www.finleypl.org. *Library Contact,* Carolyn Paulsen; E-mail: capwhp@gmail.com
Library Holdings: Bk Titles 7,000
Open Thurs 6:30-8, Fri 2-5

FORMAN

P FORMAN PUBLIC LIBRARY*, 347 Main St, 58032. (Mail add: PO Box 382, 58032-0382), SAN 372-5359. Tel: 701-724-4032. E-mail: frmnplib@drtel.net. Web Site: www.formannd.com/recreation/public-library. *Librn,* Debbie Carton
Founded 1972. Pop 1,000
Library Holdings: Audiobooks 100; AV Mats 150; CDs 100; DVDs 200; Large Print Bks 300; Bk Titles 10,000; Per Subs 12; Talking Bks 40; Videos 200
Wireless access
Open Tues & Thurs 10-5:30
Friends of the Library Group

FORT TOTTEN

S VALERIE MERRICK MEMORIAL LIBRARY*, PO Box 479, 58335-0479. Tel: 701-766-1353. FAX: 701-766-1307. Web Site: www.littlehoop.edu/library.html. *Librn,* Helen Jacobs; E-mail: helen.jacobs@littlehoop.edu

Library Holdings: Bk Titles 17,942; Per Subs 39
Open Mon-Fri 8-4:30

FORT YATES

C SITTING BULL COLLEGE LIBRARY, 9299 Hwy 24, 58538. SAN 313-1068. Tel: 701-854-8008. FAX: 701-854-3403. Web Site: sittingbull.edu/sitting-bull-college/students/library. *Dir,* Jodi Thunder Hawk; E-mail: jodi.thunderhawk@sittingbull.edu; *Asst Librn,* Regan Dunn; E-mail: regan.dunn@sittingbull.edu
Founded 1972. Fac 35
Library Holdings: Bk Titles 17,500; Per Subs 70
Special Collections: College Archives; Sioux Indians Coll; Standing Rock Sioux Tribal Archives. Oral History
Wireless access
Open Mon-Fri 8-4:30

GARRISON

P GARRISON PUBLIC LIBRARY*, 32 S Main St, 58540. (Mail add: PO Box 67, 58540-0067), SAN 355-4287. Tel: 701-463-7336. E-mail: garplib@gmail.com. Web Site: garrisonndlibrary.com. *Librn,* Malynda Kramber
Wireless access
Mem of McLean-Mercer Regional Library
Partic in Central Dakota Library Network
Open Mon 8:30-1 & 2-5, Tues-Thurs 10-1 & 2-6, Fri 9-2

GLEN ULLIN

P GLEN ULLIN PUBLIC LIBRARY*, 114 S Main St, 58631. (Mail add: PO Box 67, 58631-0067). Tel: 701-348-3951. *Library Contact,* Laura Wehri
Pop 865
Library Holdings: Audiobooks 289; AV Mats 247; Bk Vols 6,389; Videos 288
Open Wed 4-6, Fri 1:30-3

GRAFTON

P CARNEGIE REGIONAL LIBRARY*, 630 Griggs Ave, 58237. SAN 355-3531. Tel: 701-352-2754. FAX: 701-352-2757. E-mail: crlmain@polarcomm.com. Web Site: graftonndlibrary.com. *Dir,* Jill Bjerke; Tel: 701-331-9073, E-mail: crldir@polarcomm.com; Staff 8 (MLS 1, Non-MLS 7)
Founded 1972. Pop 22,648
Library Holdings: Bk Titles 75,000; Per Subs 58
Subject Interests: NDak hist
Automation Activity & Vendor Info: (Cataloging) Winnebago Software Co; (Circulation) Follett Software
Wireless access
Open Mon-Fri 10-6, Sat 10-2
Branches: 2
ANETA PUBLIC, 309 Main Ave, Aneta, 58212. (Mail add: PO Box 198, Aneta, 58212). Tel: 701-326-4107. E-mail: anetalib@polarcomm.com. Web Site: anetandlibrary.com. *Librn,* Karen Retzlaff; E-mail: karen.e.retzlaff@sendit.nodak.edu
Founded 1908
Library Holdings: Audiobooks 150; AV Mats 300; DVDs 55; Large Print Bks 250; Bk Vols 15,000; Videos 75
Open Mon-Fri 4-6
MICHIGAN PUBLIC, PO Box 331, Michigan, 58259. Tel: 701-259-2122. *Librn,* Bernice Ferguson
Library Holdings: Bk Vols 400
Open Wed 9-2:30

GRAND FORKS

P GRAND FORKS PUBLIC LIBRARY, Grand Forks City/County Public Library, 2110 Library Circle, 58201-6324. SAN 313-1084. Tel: 701-772-8116. Interlibrary Loan Service Tel: 701-772-8116, Ext 19. Reference Tel: 701-772-8116, Ext 12. Automation Services Tel: 701-772-8116, Ext 15. FAX: 701-772-1379. Reference E-mail: reference@gflibrary.com. Web Site: www.gflibrary.com. *Dir,* Wendy Wendt; E-mail: wendy.wendt@gflibrary.com; *Tech Dir,* David Haney; E-mail: david.haney@gflibrary.com; *Exec Adminr,* Kristen Pearson; Tel: 701-772-8116, Ext 14, E-mail: kristen.pearson@gflibrary.com; *IT Spec,* Bryan King; E-mail: bryan.king@gflibrary.com. Subject Specialists: *Computer,* David Haney; Staff 14 (MLS 7, Non-MLS 7)
Founded 1900. Pop 67,000; Circ 819,000
Jan 2020-Dec 2020 Income $3,008,408, State $158,375, City $1,989,599, County $810,490, Locally Generated Income $6,494, Other $41,430. Mats Exp $2,666,070. Sal $1,316,568
Library Holdings: AV Mats 39,315; Bks-By-Mail 3,000; DVDs 10,000; Bk Titles 327,961; Bk Vols 370,000; Per Subs 349; Talking Bks 6,000; Videos 15,315
Special Collections: Local History (Grand Forks Coll), bks & pictures
Subject Interests: Agr
Automation Activity & Vendor Info: (Cataloging) OCLC; (Circulation) Ex Libris Group; (ILL) Ex Libris Group; (OPAC) Ex Libris Group; (Serials) Ex Libris Group
Wireless access
Function: 24/7 Electronic res, 24/7 Online cat, Adult bk club, Audiobks via web, Bi-weekly Writer's Group, Bk club(s), Bks on CD, Chess club, Children's prog, Computer training, Computers for patron use, Electronic databases & coll, Free DVD rentals, ILL available, Internet access, Magazines, Magnifiers for reading, Mail & tel request accepted, Microfiche/film & reading machines, Movies, Music CDs, Online cat, Outside serv via phone, mail, e-mail & web, OverDrive digital audio bks, Photocopying/Printing, Prog for adults, Prog for children & young adult, Ref serv available, Scanner, Story hour, Summer & winter reading prog, Tax forms, Teen prog, Telephone ref
Publications: Check It Out (Monthly newsletter)
Partic in OCLC Online Computer Library Center, Inc; Online Dakota Info Network
Special Services for the Blind - Bks on cassette; Bks on CD; Large print bks
Open Mon-Thurs 9-9, Fri & Sat 9-5, Sun 1-5
Restriction: Non-resident fee
Friends of the Library Group

S NORTH DAKOTA VISION SERVICES-SCHOOL FOR THE BLIND, Vision Resource Center, 500 Stanford Rd, 58203. Tel: 701-795-2700. Circulation Tel: 701-795-2709. Toll Free Tel: 800-421-1181 (ND only). FAX: 701-795-2727. Web Site: www.ndvisionservices.com. *Librn,* Emily Stenberg Brown; Tel: 701-795-2709, E-mail: estenber@nd.gov; *Vision Resource Ctr Specialist,* Karli Talli; Tel: 701-795-2781, E-mail: ktalley@nd.gov
Founded 1908
Library Holdings: AV Mats 550; Large Print Bks 750; Bk Vols 1,350
Special Collections: Braille; BVI Professional; Dual Sensory; Large Print
Automation Activity & Vendor Info: (Cataloging) OCLC
Wireless access
Publications: Reaching Out (Quarterly newsletter)
Special Services for the Deaf - Bks on deafness & sign lang
Special Services for the Blind - Assistive/Adapted tech devices, equip & products; Bks & mags in Braille, on rec, tape & cassette; Bks on cassette; Bks on CD; Braille alphabet card; Braille bks; Braille Webster's dictionary; Children's Braille; Home delivery serv; Info on spec aids & appliances; Large print bks; Newsletter (in large print, Braille or on cassette); Recorded bks; Ref in Braille; Talking bk serv referral; Textbks & bks about music in Braille & large print; Videos on blindness & physical disabilties
Open Mon-Fri 8-4:30

UNIVERSITY OF NORTH DAKOTA
CM HARLEY E FRENCH LIBRARY OF THE HEALTH SCIENCES*, School of Medicine & Health Sciences, 501 N Columbia Rd, Stop 9002, 58202-9002, SAN 355-368X. Tel: 701-777-3993. Interlibrary Loan Service Tel: 701-777-2606. Reference Tel: 701-777-3994. FAX: 701-777-4790. Web Site: undmedlibrary.org. *Dir,* Lila Pedersen; E-mail: lila.pedersen@med.und.edu; *Asst Dir,* Kelly Thirmodson; Tel: 701-777-4129; *Automation Syst Coordr,* Theresa Norton; Tel: 701-777-2946, E-mail: theresa.norton@med.und.edu; *Cat,* Michael Safratowich; Tel: 701-777-2602, E-mail: michael.safratowich@med.und.edu; *Circ,* Jan Gunderson; *ILL,* Allison Ranisate; E-mail: allison.ranisate@med.und.edu; Staff 11 (MLS 10, Non-MLS 1)
Founded 1950. Enrl 1,500; Fac 156; Highest Degree: Doctorate
Library Holdings: e-books 915; e-journals 12,000; Bk Titles 34,000; Bk Vols 43,000; Per Subs 300
Special Collections: History of Medicine (Dr French Coll); History of Pathology (Dr Barger Coll)
Subject Interests: Med, Nursing, Occupational therapy, Phys therapy
Automation Activity & Vendor Info: (Acquisitions) Ex Libris Group; (Cataloging) Ex Libris Group; (Circulation) Ex Libris Group; (Course Reserve) Ex Libris Group; (ILL) Ex Libris Group; (Media Booking) Ex Libris Group; (OPAC) Ex Libris Group; (Serials) Ex Libris Group
Function: ILL available
Partic in OCLC Online Computer Library Center, Inc
Open Mon-Thurs 7:30am-Midnight, Fri 7:30-6, Sat 10-6, Sun 1-Midnight

CL THORMODSGARD LAW LIBRARY*, 215 Centennial Dr, 58202. (Mail add: PO Box 9004, 58202-9004), SAN 355-371X. Tel: 701-777-2204. Interlibrary Loan Service Tel: 701-777-3538. Reference Tel: 701-777-3354. FAX: 701-777-2217. Web Site: www.law.und.nodak.edu. *Dir,* Rhonda Schwartz; E-mail: schwartz@law.und.edu; *Head, Student Serv,* David Haberman; E-mail: haberman@law.und.edu; *Acq, Head, Tech Serv, Ser,* Kaaren Pupino; E-mail: pupino@law.und.edu; *Head, Fac Serv,* Jan Stone; *Circ Mgr, ILL,* Jane Oakland; E-mail: oakland@law.und.edu; *Cat Librn,* Dorrene Devos; E-mail: devos@law.und.edu; *Syst Adminr,* Carl Warrene; E-mail: warrene@law.und.edu; *User Support Serv Coordr,*

Kasey Hanson; *Computer Support Spec, Web Serv,* Mark Conway; Staff 7 (MLS 5, Non-MLS 2)
Founded 1899. Enrl 224; Highest Degree: Doctorate
Library Holdings: AV Mats 456; e-journals 726; Electronic Media & Resources 10; Bk Titles 33,253; Bk Vols 159,447; Per Subs 2,001; Videos 332
Automation Activity & Vendor Info: (Acquisitions) Ex Libris Group; (Cataloging) Ex Libris Group; (Circulation) Ex Libris Group; (Course Reserve) Ex Libris Group; (ILL) Ex Libris Group; (Media Booking) Ex Libris Group; (OPAC) Ex Libris Group; (Serials) Ex Libris Group
Partic in Mid-America Law Library Consortium; OCLC Online Computer Library Center, Inc
Open Mon-Thurs 7:30am-11pm, Fri 7:30am-9pm, Sat 10-9, Sun 10am-11pm

C UNIVERSITY OF NORTH DAKOTA*, Chester Fritz Library, 3051 University Ave, Stop 9000, 58202-9000. SAN 355-3655. Tel: 701-777-2617. Circulation Tel: 701-777-4644. Interlibrary Loan Service Tel: 701-777-4631. Reference Tel: 701-777-4629. FAX: 701-777-3319. TDD: 701-777-3313. E-mail: library@mail.und.edu. Web Site: www.library.und.edu. *Dean of Libr,* Stephanie Walker; E-mail: stephanie.walker@library.und.edu; *Asst Dir,* Sally Dockter; E-mail: sally.dockter@library.und.edu; *Head, Access & Br Serv,* Naomi Frantes; Tel: 701-777-4648, E-mail: naomi.frantes@library.und.edu; *Head, Spec Coll,* Curt Hanson; Tel: 701-777-4626, E-mail: curt.hanson@library.und.edu; *Head, Syst,* Randy Pederson; Tel: 701-777-4643, E-mail: randy.pederson@library.und.edu; *Head, Tech Serv,* Shelby Harken; Tel: 701-777-4634, E-mail: shelby.harken@library.und.edu; *Mgr, Access Serv,* Stan Johnson; Fax: 701-777-6745, E-mail: stan.johnson@library.und.edu; Staff 21 (MLS 16, Non-MLS 5)
Founded 1883. Enrl 15,250; Fac 821; Highest Degree: Doctorate
Jul 2012-Jun 2013. Mats Exp $2,658,459, Books $288,449, Per/Ser (Incl. Access Fees) $1,867,992, AV Mat $17,860, Electronic Ref Mat (Incl. Access Fees) $467,564, Presv $16,594. Sal $2,017,863 (Prof $1,289,745)
Library Holdings: Audiobooks 319; AV Mats 82,329; Braille Volumes 165; CDs 3,711; DVDs 1,305; e-books 78,083; e-journals 58,087; Electronic Media & Resources 128,524; Large Print Bks 59; Microforms 902,163; Music Scores 24,002; Bk Titles 616,366; Bk Vols 712,030; Per Subs 3,029; Videos 1,382
Special Collections: Great Plains (Fred G Aandahl Coll); North Dakota Ethnic Heritage/Family History; North Dakota History (Orin G Libby Coll), ms; Norwegian Local History. Oral History; State Document Depository; US Document Depository
Subject Interests: Educ, Western hist
Automation Activity & Vendor Info: (Acquisitions) Ex Libris Group; (Cataloging) Ex Libris Group; (Circulation) Ex Libris Group; (Course Reserve) Ex Libris Group; (ILL) Ex Libris Group; (OPAC) Ex Libris Group; (Serials) Ex Libris Group
Wireless access
Publications: Guides to Collections; Lux et Lex
Partic in EPSCoR Science Information Group; Minitex; Online Dakota Info Network
Special Services for the Deaf - TDD equip
Special Services for the Blind - Scanner for conversion & translation of mats
Open Mon-Thurs 7:45am-Midnight, Fri 7:45-4:30, Sat 1-5, Sun 1-Midnight

Departmental Libraries:

ENERGY & ENVIRONMENTAL RESEARCH CENTER LIBRARY, 15 N 23rd St, Stop 9018, 58202-9018, SAN 313-1114. Tel: 701-777-5132. FAX: 701-777-5181. Web Site: library.und.edu/eerc. *Librn,* Rosemary Pleva Flynn; E-mail: rflynn@undeerc.org; Staff 1 (MLS 1)
Library Holdings: CDs 105; Bk Titles 4,429; Bk Vols 18,657; Per Subs 60
Special Collections: US Bureau of Mines Materials; US Department of Energy Reports
Subject Interests: Air quality, Climate change, Coal, Geothermal energy, Mining rec, Natural gas, Oil, Solar energy, Synthetic fuels, Toxic wastes, Water

GORDON ERICKSON MUSIC LIBRARY, Hughes Fine Arts Ctr 170, 3350 Campus Rd, Stop 7125, 58202-7125, SAN 371-3261. Tel: 701-777-2817. FAX: 701-777-3319. Web Site: library.und.edu/music. *Br Mgr,* Felecia Clifton; E-mail: felecia.clifton@library.und.edu; Staff 1 (Non-MLS 1)
Founded 1983. Enrl 170; Fac 30; Highest Degree: Doctorate
Library Holdings: Bks on Deafness & Sign Lang 13; CDs 3,550; DVDs 109; Music Scores 24,002; Bk Titles 33,257; Bk Vols 42,687; Per Subs 38; Videos 387
Special Services for the Deaf - Staff with knowledge of sign lang
Special Services for the Blind - Braille bks
Open Mon-Thurs 9-8, Fri 9-4, Sun 4-8
Restriction: Open to fac, students & qualified researchers

F D HOLLAND JR GEOLOGY LIBRARY, 81 Cornell St, Stop 8358, 58202-8358, SAN 371-327X. Tel: 701-777-3221. Interlibrary Loan Service Tel: 701-777-4631. FAX: 701-777-4449. Web Site: library.und.edu/geology. *Br Mgr,* Darin Buri; Tel: 701-777-2408, E-mail: darin.buri@engr.und.edu; Staff 1 (Non-MLS 1)
Library Holdings: CDs 472; Microforms 13,622; Bk Titles 32,144; Bk Vols 88,227; Per Subs 227
Special Collections: Map Coll. US Document Depository
Subject Interests: Environ geol, Geol engr, Hydrogeology, Mining, Petroleum geol
Open Mon-Thurs (Winter) 8am-9pm, Fri 8-4:30; Mon-Fri (Summer) 8-4:30
Friends of the Library Group

GRAND FORKS AFB

A UNITED STATES AIR FORCE*, Grand Forks Air Force Base Library FL4659, 319 FSS/FSDL, 511 Holzapple St, Bldg 201, 58205. SAN 355-3744. Tel: 701-747-3046. E-mail: gfafblibrary@outlook.com. Web Site: 319fss.com/library.html. *Libr Mgr,* Veronica Holseth; Staff 5.7 (MLS 1.2, Non-MLS 4.5)
Founded 1968
Library Holdings: AV Mats 1,704; e-books 7,100; Electronic Media & Resources 33; Bk Vols 33,000; Per Subs 60; Talking Bks 1,620
Special Collections: Chief of Staff Reading Coll
Automation Activity & Vendor Info: (Cataloging) SirsiDynix; (Circulation) SirsiDynix-WorkFlows; (ILL) OCLC; (OPAC) SirsiDynix-iBistro
Wireless access
Function: Art exhibits, Audio & video playback equip for onsite use, Audiobks via web, Bks on CD, CD-ROM, Children's prog, Citizenship assistance, Computer training, Computers for patron use, Digital talking bks, Distance learning, Doc delivery serv, Electronic databases & coll, Equip loans & repairs, Free DVD rentals, Holiday prog, Homebound delivery serv, ILL available, Instruction & testing, Learning ctr, Mail & tel request accepted, Music CDs, Online cat, Orientations, OverDrive digital audio bks, Photocopying/Printing, Preschool outreach, Prof lending libr, Prog for adults, Prog for children & young adult, Ref & res, Ref serv available, Scanner, Story hour, Summer reading prog, Teen prog, Telephone ref, Wheelchair accessible
Partic in OCLC Online Computer Library Center, Inc
Special Services for the Blind - Bks on CD; Playaways (bks on MP3)
Open Tues-Thurs 10-8, Fri-Sat 12-5

HANKINSON

P HANKINSON PUBLIC LIBRARY, 319 Main Ave S, 58041. (Mail add: PO Box 244, 58041-0244), SAN 313-1130. Tel: 701-242-7929. E-mail: hankinsonlibrary@hotmail.com. Web Site: hankinsonndlibrary.com. *Librn,* Lynnette Scheuring
Founded 1904. Pop 1,038; Circ 4,040
Library Holdings: Bk Vols 11,000; Per Subs 17
Wireless access
Open Tues 8:30-12 & 1-5:30, Wed & Thurs 8:30-12 & 1-5, Fri 8:30-Noon

HARVEY

P HARVEY PUBLIC LIBRARY*, 119 E Tenth St, 58341. SAN 313-1149. Tel: 701-324-2156. FAX: 701-324-2156. E-mail: hpublib@gondtc.com. *Librn,* Hannah Tuenge
Founded 1952. Pop 2,700; Circ 44,000
Library Holdings: Bk Titles 22,000; Per Subs 7
Special Collections: Regional Coll, bks
Automation Activity & Vendor Info: (Cataloging) Follett Software; (Circulation) Follett Software
Wireless access
Open Mon-Fri 10-6, Sat 10-3

HATTON

P HATTON SCHOOL & PUBLIC LIBRARY*, 503 Fourth St, 58240. (Mail add: PO Box 200, 58240-0200). Tel: 701-543-3456. FAX: 701-543-3459. Web Site: www.hattonk12.com/organizations/library. *Librn,* Mary Kleveland; E-mail: mary.kleveland@k12.nd.us
Library Holdings: AV Mats 100; Bk Vols 5,500; Per Subs 40; Talking Bks 600
Open Thurs 7pm-9pm, Sat 2-4

HAZEN

P HAZEN PUBLIC LIBRARY, 203 E Main St, 58545. (Mail add: PO Box 471, 58545-0471), SAN 355-4317. Tel: 701-748-2977. FAX: 701-748-2988. E-mail: hazenlibrary@cdln.info. Web Site: hazenndlibrary.com. *Dir,* Cindy Aaser
Wireless access
Mem of McLean-Mercer Regional Library
Partic in Central Dakota Library Network
Open Mon-Fri 9-6
Friends of the Library Group

HEBRON

P HEBRON PUBLIC LIBRARY, 811 Main Ave, 58638. (Mail add: PO Box R, 58638-0448), SAN 375-5967. Tel: 701-878-4110. E-mail: hebronpubliclibrary@gmail.com. Web Site: www.hebronnd.org. *Libr Dir,* Dawn Perrin-Ramos
Founded 1938. Pop 850; Circ 2,213
Library Holdings: AV Mats 330; Bks-By-Mail 84; Large Print Bks 90; Bk Titles 14,000; Talking Bks 110
Wireless access
Partic in Online Dakota Info Network
Open Mon & Wed 10-4, Tues, Thurs & Fri 12-6

HETTINGER

P ADAMS COUNTY LIBRARY*, 103 N Sixth St, 58639. (Mail add: PO Box 448, 58639-0448), SAN 355-3868. Tel: 701-567-2741. FAX: 701-567-2741. E-mail: adamscountylibrarynd@gmail.com. Web Site: www.adamscountylibrary.com. *Dir,* Kristy LaNae; Staff 4 (Non-MLS 4)
Founded 1961. Pop 2,750; Circ 7,890
Library Holdings: AV Mats 750; Large Print Bks 700; Bk Vols 22,789; Per Subs 21; Talking Bks 204
Subject Interests: Norwegian hist
Automation Activity & Vendor Info: (Cataloging) Follett Software; (Circulation) Follett Software
Function: ILL available
Open Mon-Wed 3-7, Thurs 2-5:30, Fri 3:30-5:30
Friends of the Library Group

HOPE

P HOPE CITY LIBRARY*, PO Box 115, 58046-0115. SAN 313-1157. Tel: 701-945-2796. *Librn,* Carol Elston
Founded 1910
Library Holdings: Bk Vols 4,000
Friends of the Library Group

JAMESTOWN

S ANNE CARLSEN LEARNING CENTER*, 701 Third St NW, 58401-2971. (Mail add: PO Box 8000, 58402). Tel: 701-252-3850. Toll Free Tel: 800-568-5175. FAX: 701-952-5159. Web Site: annecenter.org. *Coordr,* Theresa Hanson; E-mail: theresa.hanson@annecenter.org
Library Holdings: AV Mats 2,000; Bk Vols 10,000; Per Subs 23
Automation Activity & Vendor Info: (Cataloging) Winnebago Software Co; (Circulation) Winnebago Software Co; (OPAC) Winnebago Software Co
Wireless access
Open Mon-Fri 7:30-4:30

P JAMES RIVER VALLEY LIBRARY SYSTEM, Alfred Dickey Public Library, 105 Third St SE, 58401. SAN 313-1165. Tel: 701-252-2990. E-mail: adpl@daktel.com. Web Site: jamesriverlibrary.org. *Libr Dir,* Joseph Rector
Founded 1901
Special Collections: Louis L'Amour Memorial Coll; Tom Matchie Coll
Automation Activity & Vendor Info: (Acquisitions) Book Systems; (Cataloging) Book Systems; (Circulation) Book Systems; (OPAC) Book Systems
Wireless access
Open Mon-Thurs 10-8, Fri 10-6, Sat 11-4
Friends of the Library Group
Branches: 1
STUTSMAN COUNTY LIBRARY, 910 Fifth St SE, 58401, SAN 313-119X. Tel: 701-252-1531. Interlibrary Loan Service E-mail: ill@daktel.com. *Dir,* Joe Rector; *Asst Dir,* Jennifer Senger; Staff 1 (MLS 1)
Founded 1954. Pop 6,381; Circ 44,080
Library Holdings: AV Mats 13,960; High Interest/Low Vocabulary Bk Vols 20; Large Print Bks 2,627; Bk Titles 20,000; Bk Vols 26,273; Per Subs 20; Talking Bks 31
Open Mon 10-5, Tues-Fri 9-5
Friends of the Library Group
Bookmobiles: 1. Librns, Doreen Brophy & Jean Zachrison. Bk vols 3,500

GM NORTH DAKOTA STATE HOSPITAL*, Health Science & Patients Library, 2605 Circle Dr, 58401-6905. SAN 355-3922. Tel: 701-253-3679. FAX: 701-253-3204. Web Site: www.nd.gov/dhs/locations/statehospital. *Librn,* Michael Jan; E-mail: mbjan@nd.gov; Staff 1 (Non-MLS 1)
Founded 1958
Library Holdings: e-books 10,000; Bk Titles 4,500; Bk Vols 5,000; Per Subs 25
Special Collections: North Dakota State Hospital Biennial Reports, 1890 to date; North Dakota State Hospital Newsletter (employee newsletter)
Subject Interests: Activity therapy, Adolescence, Alcoholism, Ch, Counseling, Families of alcoholics, Forensic psychiat, Geriatrics, Psychiat treatment, Psychol, Psychopharmacology, Psychotherapy, Soc work, Vocational rehabilitation
Automation Activity & Vendor Info: (Acquisitions) EBSCO Online; (Cataloging) Ex Libris Group; (Circulation) Ex Libris Group; (ILL) Ex Libris Group; (OPAC) Ex Libris Group; (Serials) EBSCO Online
Wireless access
Publications: PsychINFO
Partic in Midwest Health Sci Libr Network
Open Mon & Wed-Fri 9:30-6, Sun 1-6

G UNITED STATES GEOLOGICAL SURVEY*, Northern Prairie Wildlife Research Center Library, 8711 37th St SE, 58401-9736. SAN 313-1203. Tel: 701-253-5500. FAX: 701-253-5553. Web Site: www.npwrc.usgs.gov/resources. *Library Contact,* Mark Sherfy; Staff 1 (MLS 1)
Founded 1965
Library Holdings: AV Mats 120; Bk Titles 11,000; Per Subs 125
Special Collections: Waterfowl Management (Unpublished Papers of Merrill C Hammond)
Subject Interests: Ecology, Global climate change, Mgt of waterfowl, Plant ecology, Predation, Wetland ecology
Automation Activity & Vendor Info: (Acquisitions) Cuadra Associates, Inc; (Cataloging) Cuadra Associates, Inc; (Circulation) Cuadra Associates, Inc; (OPAC) Cuadra Associates, Inc; (Serials) Cuadra Associates, Inc
Function: Res libr
Partic in OCLC Online Computer Library Center, Inc
Open Mon-Fri 8-4:30

C UNIVERSITY OF JAMESTOWN*, Raugust Library, 6070 College Lane, 58405-0001. SAN 313-1173. Tel: 701-252-3467. Circulation Tel: 701-252-3467, Ext 5530. Interlibrary Loan Service Tel: 701-252-3467, Ext 5441. Reference Tel: 701-252-3467, Ext 5433. FAX: 701-253-4446. Web Site: www.uj.edu/library. *Dir,* Phyllis Ann K Bratton; E-mail: pbratton@uj.edu; *Acq,* Prameela Garre; Tel: 701-252-3467, Ext 5432, E-mail: Prameela.Garre@uj.edu; *Cataloger,* Jasmine Lee; Tel: 701-252-3467, Ext 5431, E-mail: jlee@uj.edu; *Circ, ILL,* Brenda Fischer; E-mail: bfischer@uj.edu; *Ref & Instruction,* Position Currently Open; Staff 5 (MLS 2, Non-MLS 3)
Enrl 1,045; Fac 66; Highest Degree: Doctorate
Library Holdings: AV Mats 6,484; Bks on Deafness & Sign Lang 101; CDs 1,302; DVDs 1,663; e-books 15,565; e-journals 68,000; Music Scores 1,066; Bk Titles 113,364; Bk Vols 247,776; Per Subs 80; Talking Bks 523
Special Collections: Children's materials; Western Americana Coll
Subject Interests: NDak hist, Regional poets
Automation Activity & Vendor Info: (Acquisitions) Ex Libris Group; (Cataloging) Ex Libris Group; (Circulation) Ex Libris Group; (Course Reserve) Ex Libris Group; (ILL) Ex Libris Group; (OPAC) Ex Libris Group
Wireless access
Partic in GMRMLN - Region 3 of NLM Network; Minitex; Online Dakota Info Network
Open Mon-Thurs 8am-Midnight, Fri 8-5, Sat 1-5, Sun 2-Midnight

KILLDEER

P KILLDEER PUBLIC LIBRARY*, 101 High St NW, 58640-0579. (Mail add: PO Box 579, 58640-0579), SAN 355-4015. Tel: 701-764-5877. FAX: 701-764-5648. Web Site: www.killdeer.k12.nd.us/library/. *Librn,* Pamela Boepple; E-mail: pam.boepple@k12.nd.us; Staff 4 (MLS 1, Non-MLS 3)
Pop 815; Circ 3,804
Library Holdings: Per Subs 50; Videos 268
Automation Activity & Vendor Info: (Cataloging) Follett Software; (Circulation) Follett Software; (OPAC) Follett Software
Wireless access
Function: 24/7 Electronic res, 24/7 Online cat, Accelerated reader prog
Open Mon-Fri 8:30-3; Mon & Thurs (Summer) 7pm-9pm, Tues 3-5

KINDRED

P KINDRED PUBLIC LIBRARY*, 330 Elm St, 58051. (Mail add: PO Box 63, 58051-0063). Tel: 701-428-3456. E-mail: kindredpubliclibrary@gmail.com. Web Site: www.kindredpubliclibrary.com. *Dir, Admin Serv,* Georgia Berg; *Dir, Programming,* Linda Otterson
Library Holdings: Bk Vols 9,000
Automation Activity & Vendor Info: (Cataloging) Brodart; (Circulation) Brodart
Wireless access
Open Mon, Fri & Sat 10:30-12:30, Tues-Thurs 3:30-7:30
Friends of the Library Group

LA MOURE

P LA MOURE SCHOOL & PUBLIC LIBRARY*, 105 Sixth Ave SE, 58458. SAN 313-1211. Tel: 701-883-5396. FAX: 701-883-5144. Web Site: www.lamoure.k12.nd.us. *Librn,* Hazel Mattice; E-mail: hazel.mattice@k12.nd.us
Circ 17,671
Library Holdings: Bk Vols 23,000
Automation Activity & Vendor Info: (Cataloging) Follett Software; (Circulation) Follett Software; (OPAC) Follett Software
Open Tues & Wed 3:30-5:30
Friends of the Library Group

LAKOTA

P LAKOTA CITY LIBRARY*, A M Tofthagen Library & Museum, 116 B Ave W, 58344. (Mail add: PO Box 307, 58344-0307). Tel: 701-247-2543. E-mail: LakotaLibrary@polarcomm.com. Web Site: lakotandlibrary.com. *Librn,* Angela Jutila
Founded 1927. Pop 781; Circ 12,379
Library Holdings: Large Print Bks 1,350; Bk Vols 12,915; Per Subs 10; Talking Bks 463; Videos 727
Special Collections: Municipal Document Depository; Oral History
Open Mon & Tues 12-5, Thurs 10-3

LANGDON

P CAVALIER COUNTY LIBRARY, 600 Fifth Ave, 58249. SAN 371-5973. Tel: 701-256-5353. FAX: 701-256-5361. E-mail: cavaliercountylibrary@gmail.com. Web Site: cavaliercountyndlibrary.com. *Dir,* Shannon Nuelle; *Asst Librn,* Linda Economy; Staff 2 (Non-MLS 2)
Founded 1940. Pop 4,800; Circ 26,000
Library Holdings: Bk Titles 27,000; Bk Vols 30,000; Per Subs 20; Talking Bks 640
Wireless access
Open Mon, Tues, Thurs & Fri 10-5, Wed 10-7, Sat 10-3

LARIMORE

P EDNA RALSTON PUBLIC LIBRARY, 116 1/2 Towner Ave, 58251. (Mail add: PO Box 6, 58251-0006), SAN 313-122X. Tel: 701-343-2181. E-mail: ednaralstonlibrary@yahoo.com. Web Site: larimorendlibrary.com. *Librn,* Melissa Lehman
Pop 1,350; Circ 3,100
Library Holdings: Bk Vols 14,000
Open Mon 5pm-7pm, Wed 1-5, Sat 9-Noon

LEEDS

P LEEDS PUBLIC LIBRARY*, 221 Main St W, 58346. Tel: 701-466-2930. E-mail: libleeds@gondtc.com. Web Site: leedsndlibrary.com. *Librn,* Diane Hoffmann
Library Holdings: Bk Titles 4,500; Per Subs 15
Open Mon & Thurs 2-5

LIDGERWOOD

P LIDGERWOOD CITY LIBRARY*, 15 Wiley Ave N, 58053. (Mail add: PO Box 280, 58053-0280), SAN 313-1238. Tel: 701-538-4669. Web Site: www.cityoflidgerwoodnd.com, www.lidgerwoodnd.com/City/HTML/Library.html. *Librn,* Orva Krause
Pop 996; Circ 10,795
Library Holdings: Bk Vols 17,021; Per Subs 29
Wireless access
Open Tues-Sat 2-4:30
Friends of the Library Group

LINTON

P LINTON PUBLIC LIBRARY*, Harry L Petrie Public Library, 101 NE First St, 58552-7123. (Mail add: PO Box 416, 58552-0416), SAN 313-1246. Tel: 701-254-4737. E-mail: hlplib@bektel.com. Web Site: lintonndlibrary.com. *Dir,* Carla Frison
Founded 1937. Pop 7,000; Circ 8,000
Library Holdings: Bk Vols 15,000; Per Subs 17
Special Collections: Local Newspaper Bound Copies 1905-present; North Dakota Coll
Wireless access
Function: ILL available, Ref serv available
Open Mon & Thurs 10-6, Wed & Fri 2-5, Sat (Summer) 11-2

LISBON

P LISBON PUBLIC LIBRARY*, 409 Forest St, 58054. (Mail add: PO Box 569, 58054-0569), SAN 313-1254. Tel: 701-683-5174. FAX: 701-683-5174. E-mail: lisbonpl@nd.gov. Web Site: www.lisbonpubliclibrary.com. *Dir,* Bonnie Mattson
Founded 1911. Pop 2,400; Circ 21,500
Library Holdings: Audiobooks 200; Bk Vols 21,000; Per Subs 35
Wireless access
Open Mon-Fri 11-6

S NORTH DAKOTA VETERANS HOME LIBRARY, 1600 Veterans Dr, 58054. (Mail add: PO Box 673, 58054-0673). Tel: 701-683-6534, 701-683-6548. FAX: 701-683-6550. Web Site: www.ndvh.nd.gov. *Activities Coord,* Courtney Jacobson; E-mail: cjacobson@nd.gov
Library Holdings: Bk Vols 1,000; Per Subs 40
Wireless access
Restriction: Residents only

MADDOCK

P MADDOCK COMMUNITY LIBRARY*, 114 Central Ave, 58348. (Mail add: PO Box 188, 58348-0188). Tel: 701-438-2235. FAX: 701-438-2202. Web Site: maddockndlibrary.com. *Dir,* Priscilla Backstrom; E-mail: madcomlib@gmail.com
Pop 498; Circ 1,590
Library Holdings: Audiobooks 50; Bks on Deafness & Sign Lang 5; Large Print Bks 150; Bk Titles 6,000
Wireless access
Open Mon-Fri 9-5

MANDAN

P MORTON MANDAN PUBLIC LIBRARY*, 609 W Main St, 58554. SAN 313-1262. Tel: 701-667-5365. Toll Free Tel: 800-260-4291. FAX: 701-667-5368. E-mail: library@mortonmandanlibrary.org. Web Site: www.cityofmandan.com/library. *Dir,* Jackie Hawes; E-mail: jhawes@mortonmandanlibrary.org; Staff 11 (MLS 3, Non-MLS 8)
Founded 1904
Library Holdings: Bk Titles 30,000; Per Subs 150
Special Collections: Indians of North America; Large Print Books; Railroads
Subject Interests: Local hist, Railroads
Automation Activity & Vendor Info: (Cataloging) SirsiDynix; (Circulation) SirsiDynix; (OPAC) SirsiDynix
Function: 24/7 Electronic res, 24/7 Online cat, Activity rm, Adult bk club, Art programs, Audiobks via web, AV serv, Bk club(s), Bks on CD, Children's prog, Computers for patron use, Electronic databases & coll, Free DVD rentals, Home delivery & serv to seniorr ctr & nursing homes, Homebound delivery serv, ILL available, Internet access, Magazines, Mail & tel request accepted, Meeting rooms, Movies, Notary serv, Online cat, Outreach serv, OverDrive digital audio bks, Passport agency, Photocopying/Printing, Preschool outreach, Prog for adults, Prog for children & young adult, Scanner, STEM programs, Story hour, Study rm, Summer reading prog, Tax forms, Teen prog, Wheelchair accessible
Partic in Central Dakota Library Network
Open Mon-Thurs 9:30-9, Fri & Sat 9:30-5, Sun 1-5
Friends of the Library Group
Bookmobiles: 1

MAX

P MAX COMMUNITY LIBRARY*, 215 Main St, 58759. SAN 322-6212. Tel: 701-679-2263. E-mail: maxlib@rtc.coop. Web Site: maxndlibrary.com. *Library Contact,* Amy Hauf
Wireless access
Mem of McLean-Mercer Regional Library
Partic in Central Dakota Library Network
Open Mon, Tues & Thurs 9-12 & 1-5

MAYVILLE

P MAYVILLE PUBLIC LIBRARY*, 52 Center Ave N, 58257. SAN 313-1300. Tel: 701-788-3388. *Dir,* Margaret Rice
Founded 1900. Pop 2,000; Circ 13,000
Library Holdings: AV Mats 30; Bk Vols 20,000; Per Subs 10
Special Collections: Norwegian Book Coll
Wireless access
Open Tues, Wed & Fri 12-5, Thurs 12-5 & 6-9
Friends of the Library Group

C MAYVILLE STATE UNIVERSITY*, Byrnes-Quanbeck Library, 330 Third St NE, 58257. SAN 313-1319. Tel: 701-788-4819. Toll Free Tel: 800-437-4104, Ext 34814. FAX: 701-788-4846. Web Site: mayvillestate.edu/student-resources/library. *Dir, Libr Serv,* Kelly Kornkven; Tel: 701-788-4816, E-mail: kelly.kornkven@mayvillestate.edu; *Asst Dir, Tech Serv,* Aubrey Madler; Tel: 701-788-4814, E-mail: aubrey.madler@mayvillestate.edu; *Circ/Acq, ILL,* Shannon Hofer; Tel: 701-788-4815, E-mail: shannon.hofer@mayvillestate.edu. Subject Specialists: *Bus admin,* Shannon Hofer; Staff 2.8 (MLS 1.8, Non-MLS 1)
Founded 1889. Enrl 644; Fac 43; Highest Degree: Bachelor
Library Holdings: Bk Titles 70,000; Per Subs 50

Special Collections: North Dakota Coll; STEM Kits
Automation Activity & Vendor Info: (Cataloging) Ex Libris Group; (Circulation) Ex Libris Group; (Course Reserve) Ex Libris Group; (ILL) Ex Libris Group; (OPAC) Ex Libris Group; (Serials) Ex Libris Group
Wireless access
Partic in OCLC Online Computer Library Center, Inc; Online Dakota Info Network
Open Mon-Thurs 8am-10pm, Fri 8-4:30, Sun 6-10; Mon-Fri (Summer) 7:30-4

MILNOR

P SATRE MEMORIAL LIBRARY*, 528 Fifth St, 58060. (Mail add: PO Box 225, 58060-0225). Tel: 701-427-5295. E-mail: satrelib@drtel.net. Web Site: milnorndlibrary.com. *Librn,* Melissa Lynn Bryant
Founded 1973. Pop 711; Circ 10,404
Library Holdings: AV Mats 483; Large Print Bks 100; Bk Vols 11,000; Talking Bks 18
Special Collections: World War II TimeLife Books
Automation Activity & Vendor Info: (Acquisitions) LibraryWorld, Inc; (Cataloging) LibraryWorld, Inc; (Circulation) LibraryWorld, Inc
Wireless access
Open Mon, Tues, Thurs & Fri 12:30-3:30, Wed 4-6

MINNEWAUKAN

P MINNEWAUKAN PUBLIC LIBRARY*, 170 Main St, 58351. (Mail add: PO Box 261, 58351-0261). Tel: 701-473-5735. FAX: 701-473-5377. Web Site: www.minnewaukan.com/Library.htm. *Librn,* Position Currently Open
Founded 1978
Library Holdings: Bk Vols 12,000
Open Mon & Wed 9-4

MINOT

P MINOT PUBLIC LIBRARY*, 516 Second Ave SW, 58701-3792. SAN 313-1335. Tel: 701-852-1045. FAX: 701-852-2595. Web Site: www.minotlibrary.org. *Dir,* Janet Anderson; E-mail: janet.anderson@minotnd.org; *Tech Coordr,* Mary Wheeler; E-mail: mary.wheeler@minotnd.org; *Info Spec,* Debbie Chappo; Tel: 701-852-0333, E-mail: debbie.chappo@minotnd.org; *Ch Serv,* Randi Monley; Tel: 701-838-0606, E-mail: randi.monley@minotnd.org; *ILL,* Marci Julson; E-mail: marci.julson@minotnd.org; *Ref Serv,* Zhaina Moya; E-mail: zhaina.moya@minotnd.org; Staff 5 (MLS 4, Non-MLS 1)
Founded 1908. Pop 36,567; Circ 301,172
Library Holdings: AV Mats 10,590; e-books 13,500; Large Print Bks 4,050; Bk Vols 134,416; Per Subs 300
Special Collections: Minot Daily News, 1895-present, micro; North Dakota Census, micro & CD
Subject Interests: Genealogy, Literacy
Automation Activity & Vendor Info: (Cataloging) Follett Software; (Circulation) Follett Software; (ILL) OCLC; (OPAC) Follett Software
Wireless access
Function: Homebound delivery serv
Publications: Directory of Clubs & Organizations; Peddler (Newsletter)
Special Services for the Deaf - Videos & decoder
Special Services for the Blind - Talking bks
Open Mon-Thurs 9-9, Fri 9-6, Sat 10-5, Sun (Sept-May) 1-5
Friends of the Library Group

C MINOT STATE UNIVERSITY, Gordon B Olson Library, 500 University Ave W, 58707. SAN 313-1343. Tel: 701-858-3201. Information Services Tel: 701-858-3296. Toll Free Tel: 800-777-0750. FAX: 701-858-3581. E-mail: misu.library.reference@ndus.edu. Web Site: www.minotstateu.edu/library/. *Dir,* Jane LaPlante; Tel: 701-858-3857, E-mail: jane.laplante@minotstateu.edu; *Access Serv Librn,* Jolene Nechiporenko; Tel: 701-858-3868, E-mail: jolene.nechiporenko@minotstateu.edu; *Cataloging & Metadata Librn,* Julia Carter; Tel: 701-858-3859, E-mail: julia.carter@minotstateu.edu; *Ref & Instruction Librn,* Ben Bruton; Tel: 701-858-3013, E-mail: ben.bruton@minotstateu.edu; *Ref & Instruction Librn,* Mara West; Tel: 701-858-3095, E-mail: mara.west@minotstateu.edu; *Access Serv,* Sarah Henderson; Staff 11.5 (MLS 6, Non-MLS 5.5)
Founded 1913. Enrl 3,649; Fac 272; Highest Degree: Master
Special Collections: Dakota Territory & North Dakota History Coll; Indians of the North Central States Coll. State Document Depository; US Document Depository
Subject Interests: Educ, Geol
Automation Activity & Vendor Info: (Acquisitions) Ex Libris Group; (Cataloging) Ex Libris Group; (Circulation) Ex Libris Group; (Course Reserve) Docutek; (ILL) Ex Libris Group; (OPAC) Ex Libris Group; (Serials) Ex Libris Group
Wireless access
Partic in Minitex; OCLC Online Computer Library Center, Inc; Online Dakota Info Network
Open Mon-Thurs 7:30am-10pm, Fri 7:30-4:30, Sat 1-5, Sun 1-9

M TRINITY HEALTH*, Angus L Cameron Medical Library, Health Ctr East, 1st Flr, Ste 103, 20 Burdick Expressway W, 58701. SAN 355-4074. Tel: 701-857-5435. FAX: 701-857-5194. E-mail: cameronlibrary@trinityhealth.org. Web Site: trinityhealth.org/library. *Dir,* Michael Skinner; E-mail: michael.skinner_ext@trinityhealth.org; Staff 1 (MLS 1)
Founded 1928
Library Holdings: Bk Titles 2,000; Per Subs 29
Subject Interests: Clinical med
Automation Activity & Vendor Info: (Cataloging) Ex Libris Group; (Circulation) Ex Libris Group; (OPAC) Ex Libris Group
Wireless access
Partic in Greater Midwest Regional Medical Libr Network
Open Mon-Fri 8-4:30

P WARD COUNTY PUBLIC LIBRARY*, 225 Third Ave SE, 58701-4020. SAN 355-4139. Tel: 701-852-5388. Toll Free Tel: 800-932-8932. FAX: 701-837-4960. E-mail: library@co.ward.nd.us. Web Site: www.co.ward.nd.us/161/library. *Dir,* Kerrianne Boetcher; E-mail: kerrianne.boetcher@wardnd.com; Staff 7 (MLS 1, Non-MLS 6)
Founded 1960. Pop 31,709; Circ 101,000
Library Holdings: AV Mats 1,200; Bks on Deafness & Sign Lang 10; CDs 50; DVDs 50; Large Print Bks 1,000; Bk Vols 52,800; Per Subs 35; Talking Bks 500; Videos 2,500
Automation Activity & Vendor Info: (Cataloging) OCLC; (Circulation) ComPanion Corp; (OPAC) ComPanion Corp
Wireless access
Function: 24/7 Electronic res, 24/7 Online cat, Audiobks via web, Bks on CD, Children's prog, Computers for patron use, Electronic databases & coll, Holiday prog, ILL available, Internet access, Magazines, Meeting rooms, Movies, Music CDs, Online cat, OverDrive digital audio bks, Photocopying/Printing, Prog for adults, Prog for children & young adult, Ref serv available, Story hour, Summer reading prog, Tax forms, Teen prog, Wheelchair accessible
Partic in NDak Network for Knowledge
Open Mon-Fri 8-6:30, Sat 9-2
Branches: 1
KENMARE BRANCH, Five NE Third, Memorial Hall, Kenmare, 58746. (Mail add: PO Box 104, Kenmare, 58746-0104), SAN 355-4163. Tel: 701-385-4090. FAX: 701-385-4090. *Librn,* Pauline Nielsen; Staff 1 (Non-MLS 1)
Founded 1976. Pop 2,500; Circ 30,000
Library Holdings: AV Mats 200; Large Print Bks 300; Bk Vols 6,000
Open Mon, Wed & Thurs 9:30-5
Bookmobiles: 1

MINOT AFB

A UNITED STATES AIR FORCE*, Minot Air Force Base Library FL4528, 156 Missile Ave, Ste 1, 58705-5026. SAN 355-4198. Tel: 701-723-3344, 701-723-4418. FAX: 701-727-9850. E-mail: mafblibrary@gmail.com. Web Site: 5thforcesupport.com/activities/library, accc.ent.sirsi.net/client/en_US/minot. *Dir,* Julie Reiten; Staff 5.6 (MLS 1, Non-MLS 4.6)
Founded 1961
Library Holdings: Bk Vols 30,000; Per Subs 20
Special Collections: Air War College Coll; Defense Logistics Studies Information Exchange (DLSIE); Defense Technical Information Center (DTIC); McNaughton Rental Coll; Video Coll
Subject Interests: Aviation, Mil hist, Space studies
Automation Activity & Vendor Info: (Cataloging) SirsiDynix; (Circulation) SirsiDynix; (OPAC) SirsiDynix
Wireless access
Open Mon-Thurs 10-8, Fri 11-7, Sat 11-6

MOHALL

P MOHALL PUBLIC LIBRARY*, 115 W Main, 58761. (Mail add: PO Box 159, 58761-0159), SAN 313-1378. Tel: 701-756-7242. E-mail: mplibrary@srt.com. Web Site: mohalllndlibrary.com. *Librn,* Brianne Kauffmann
Pop 931; Circ 3,589
Library Holdings: Bk Vols 15,670
Wireless access
Open Mon-Thurs 11-5

MOTT

P MOTT PUBLIC LIBRARY, 203 Third St E, 58646-7525. (Mail add: PO Box 57, 58646-0057), SAN 313-1386. Tel: 701-824-2163. FAX: 701-824-4008. E-mail: mottndlibrary@gmail.com. Web Site: mottndlibrary.com. *Dir,* Selena Merriman
Founded 1912. Pop 1,019; Circ 5,513

Library Holdings: Bk Titles 12,065
Open Mon 10-12 & 3-6, Tues & Thurs 10-12 & 2-4, Wed 3-6

NEW ENGLAND

P NEW ENGLAND PUBLIC LIBRARY*, 726 McKenzie Ave, 58647-7105. (Mail add: PO Box 266, 58647-0266). Tel: 701-579-4223. FAX: 701-579-5147. E-mail: nepl@ndsupernet.com. Web Site: newenglandndlibrary.com. *Dir,* Donna Mae Jirges
Pop 555; Circ 6,649
Library Holdings: Audiobooks 55; CDs 75; Large Print Bks 175; Bk Vols 5,980; Per Subs 25
Open Tues (Winter) 3-6, Wed & Thurs 3-5; Mon & Fri (Summer) 10-Noon, Tues 10-12 & 3-6, Wed & Thurs 3-5

NEW ROCKFORD

P NEW ROCKFORD PUBLIC LIBRARY, Ten Eight St N, 58356. SAN 313-1408. Tel: 701-947-5540. FAX: 701-947-5540. E-mail: nrpubliclibrary@gmail.com. Web Site: newrockfordndlibrary.com. *Librn,* Susie Sharp
Pop 1,400; Circ 4,241
Library Holdings: Bk Vols 15,000
Automation Activity & Vendor Info: (Cataloging) Winnebago Software Co; (Circulation) Winnebago Software Co; (OPAC) Winnebago Software Co
Wireless access
Open Mon 12-6, Tues-Fri 11-6
Friends of the Library Group

NEW TOWN

J FORT BERTHOLD LIBRARY*, 220 Eighth Ave N, 58763. (Mail add: PO Box 788, 58763), SAN 371-7275. Tel: 701-627-4677. FAX: 701-627-4677. Web Site: nhsc.edu/. *Dir,* Amy Solis; Staff 3 (MLS 1, Non-MLS 2)
Founded 1985. Enrl 185; Fac 7
Library Holdings: Bk Titles 16,000; Per Subs 150
Special Collections: Indians of North America
Open Mon-Fri 8-5

P NEW TOWN CITY LIBRARY, 307 S Main St, 58763. Tel: 701-627-4846. FAX: 701-627-4316. E-mail: library@cityofnewtown.net. Web Site: newtownndlibrary.com. *City Librn,* Kim Matthews
Library Holdings: Bk Titles 10,000
Automation Activity & Vendor Info: (Cataloging) Follett Software
Wireless access
Function: Magazines, Photocopying/Printing, Scanner
Open Mon & Wed 10-5, Tues & Thurs 10-7, Fri 10-4, Sat 11-2

NORTHWOOD

P NORTHWOOD CITY LIBRARY*, Northwood Public School, 420 Trojan Rd, 58267. Tel: 701-587-5221. FAX: 701-587-5423. Web Site: sites.google.com/a/northwoodk12.com/npslibrary. *Librn,* Wendy Holkesvig; Tel: 701-587-5221, Ext 130, E-mail: Wendy.Holkesvig@northwoodk12.com
Library Holdings: Bk Vols 10,000; Per Subs 10
Automation Activity & Vendor Info: (Acquisitions) Ex Libris Group; (Cataloging) Ex Libris Group; (Circulation) Ex Libris Group; (ILL) Ex Libris Group; (OPAC) Ex Libris Group; (Serials) Ex Libris Group
Partic in Online Dakota Info Network
Open Mon-Fri 4-7, Sat 1-4
Branches: 1
CITY CENTER LIBRARY, 206 Main St, 58267. Tel: 701-581-9101. E-mail: northwoodndlibrary@gmail.com. Web Site: northwoodndlibrary.org. *Librn,* Wendy Holkesvig; E-mail: Wendy.Holkesvig@northwoodk12.com
Open Mon 10-1 & 5-7, Tues-Sat 10-1

OAKES

P OAKES PUBLIC LIBRARY, 804 Main Ave, 58474. SAN 313-1432. Tel: 701-742-3234, Ext 155. FAX: 701-742-2812. Web Site: www.oakes.k12.nd.us/library. *Librn,* Jeanine Pahl; E-mail: jeanine.pahl@k12.nd.us
Founded 1927. Pop 2,500; Circ 20,000
Jan 2016-Dec 2016 Income $16,549, State $1,856, City $14,593, Locally Generated Income $100. Mats Exp $5,000, Books $3,700, Per/Ser (Incl. Access Fees) $500, Other Print Mats $300, AV Mat $300, Electronic Ref Mat (Incl. Access Fees) $200. Sal $10,500
Library Holdings: Audiobooks 92; AV Mats 200; Bks-By-Mail 12; Bks on Deafness & Sign Lang 6; Braille Volumes 2; CDs 8; DVDs 25; Electronic Media & Resources 2; Large Print Bks 200; Bk Titles 30,181; Per Subs 28; Talking Bks 126; Videos 49
Automation Activity & Vendor Info: (Acquisitions) ComPanion Corp; (Cataloging) ComPanion Corp; (Circulation) ComPanion Corp; (OPAC) Carlyle
Wireless access
Open Mon, Tues & Thurs 1:30-5:30, Wed 1:30-7:30, Fri 1:30-3:30

PARK RIVER

P PARK RIVER PUBLIC LIBRARY, 605 Sixth St W, 58270. (Mail add: PO Box 240, 58270-0240), SAN 313-1440. Tel: 701-284-6116. Web Site: sites.google.com/parkriverk12.com/praslibrary. *City Librn,* Haley Ulland; E-mail: haley.ulland@parkriverk12.com; *Librn,* Rochelle Kovarik; E-mail: rochelle.kovarik@parkriverk12.com; Staff 1 (Non-MLS 1)
Founded 1900. Pop 1,450; Circ 3,500
Library Holdings: AV Mats 855; DVDs 70; Bk Titles 19,000; Bk Vols 23,000; Per Subs 65; Videos 740
Automation Activity & Vendor Info: (Cataloging) ComPanion Corp; (Circulation) ComPanion Corp
Open Mon & Thurs 8-3:30 & 6:30-8:30, Tues, Wed & Fri 8-3:30, Sat 9-1; Mon 6:30pm-8:30pm, Tues 12-4, Thurs 4:30-8:30, Sat 9-1 (Summer)
Friends of the Library Group

PEMBINA

P PEMBINA CITY LIBRARY*, Pembina Public School, 155 S Third St, 58271. SAN 313-1467. Tel: 701-825-6217. E-mail: pembinand.library@gmail.com. Web Site: pembinandlibrary.com. *City Librn,* Marcy Cleem
Pop 700; Circ 5,400
Library Holdings: Audiobooks 70; DVDs 75; Large Print Bks 50; Bk Vols 5,500; Per Subs 30; Videos 100
Subject Interests: State hist
Wireless access
Function: Accelerated reader prog, After school storytime, Computers for patron use, ILL available, Online cat, Story hour, Summer reading prog
Partic in Online Dakota Info Network
Open Mon & Fri 6:30pm-8:30pm, Tues 3:45-6, Thurs 3:30-6, Sat 9-11
Restriction: Borrowing requests are handled by ILL, Open to pub for ref & circ; with some limitations

RICHARDTON

SR ASSUMPTION ABBEY LIBRARY*, 418 Third Ave W, 58652-7100. (Mail add: PO Box A, 58652-0901), SAN 313-1475. Tel: 701-974-3315. FAX: 701-974-3317. Web Site: www.assumptionabbey.com/library.htm. *Librn,* Brother Michael Taffe
Founded 1899
Jul 2016-Jun 2017. Mats Exp $8,098, Books $2,660, Per/Ser (Incl. Access Fees) $3,975, Presv $1,463
Library Holdings: Bk Vols 104,000; Per Subs 58
Subject Interests: Church hist, Germans from Russia, Monastic hist, NDak hist
Automation Activity & Vendor Info: (Cataloging) Book Systems
Function: ILL available, Res libr
Partic in NDak Network for Knowledge
Restriction: Circ limited, In-house use for visitors, Open by appt only, Private libr

RIVERDALE

P MCLEAN-MERCER REGIONAL LIBRARY*, 216 Second St, 58565. (Mail add: PO Box 505, 58565-0505), SAN 355-4228. Tel: 701-654-7652. FAX: 701-654-7526. E-mail: mmrlib@westriv.com. Web Site: riverdalendlibrary.com. *Dir,* Beth Bruestle; *Asst Librn,* Tami Hipp
Founded 1959. Pop 26,316; Circ 106,622
Library Holdings: Bk Vols 30,000
Automation Activity & Vendor Info: (Cataloging) SirsiDynix; (Circulation) SirsiDynix; (Course Reserve) SirsiDynix; (ILL) SirsiDynix; (Media Booking) SirsiDynix; (OPAC) SirsiDynix; (Serials) SirsiDynix
Member Libraries: Beulah Public Library; Garrison Public Library; Hazen Public Library; Max Community Library; Stanton Public Library; Turtle Lake Public Library; Underwood Public Library; Washburn Public Library
Partic in Central Dakota Library Network
Open Mon-Fri 8-12 & 1-5
Bookmobiles: 1. Librn, Dawn Grannis

ROLETTE

P ROLETTE CITY LIBRARY, 208 Main St, 58366. E-mail: rolette.city.library@gmail.com. Web Site: rolettelibrary.librarika.com. *Librn,* Beth Mongeon
Library Holdings: Bk Vols 3,136
Wireless access
Open Thurs 3-5

ROLLA

P ROLLA PUBLIC LIBRARY*, 14 SE First St, 58367. (Mail add: PO Box 1200, 58367-1200), SAN 313-1491. Tel: 701-477-3849. FAX: 701-477-9633. E-mail: rollapubliclibrarynd@gmail.com. Web Site: rollandlibrary.org. *Dir,* Peggy Johnson; E-mail: pjohnson@utma.com; *Asst Dir,* Lois Menard
Library Holdings: Bk Vols 20,000; Per Subs 20; Talking Bks 1,000; Videos 400
Wireless access
Open Mon & Wed 4-7, Tues & Thurs 3:15-7, Sat 11-3

RUGBY

P HEART OF AMERICA LIBRARY, 201 Third St SW, 58368-1793. SAN 313-1505. Tel: 701-776-6223. FAX: 701-776-6897. E-mail: heartofamerica@hotmail.com. Web Site: rugbyndlibrary.com. *Dir,* Kimberly Morgan
Founded 1911. Pop 4,675; Circ 33,609
Library Holdings: AV Mats 690; Electronic Media & Resources 56; Bk Vols 31,000; Per Subs 50; Videos 670
Automation Activity & Vendor Info: (Cataloging) Book Systems; (Circulation) Book Systems; (OPAC) Book Systems
Wireless access
Partic in NDak Network for Knowledge
Open Mon-Thurs 10-6, Fri 10-5, Sat 10-4

STANLEY

P STANLEY PUBLIC LIBRARY*, 116 Main St, 58784-4051. (Mail add: PO Box 249, 58784), SAN 313-1513. Tel: 701-628-2223. E-mail: stanleyndlibrary@gmail.com. Web Site: www.stanleyndlibrary.com. *Libr Dir,* Kelly Kudrna
Pop 1,371; Circ 8,000
Library Holdings: Audiobooks 265; DVDs 1,550; Large Print Bks 150; Bk Vols 12,000
Wireless access
Open Mon & Wed-Fri 12:30-5:30, Tues 1-7
Friends of the Library Group

STANTON

P STANTON PUBLIC LIBRARY*, 600 County 37, 58571. (Mail add: PO Box 130, 58571-0130), SAN 370-9078. Tel: 701-745-3235. E-mail: stpl@westriv.com. Web Site: stantonndlibrary.com. *Librn,* Nancy Miller
Mem of McLean-Mercer Regional Library
Partic in Central Dakota Library Network
Open Mon & Thurs 11-6, Wed 11:30-6:30

STEELE

P KIDDER COUNTY LIBRARY*, 115 W Broadway Ave, 58482. (Mail add: PO Box 227, 58482-0227), SAN 313-1521. Tel: 701-475-2855. E-mail: kcpubliclibrary@bektel.com. *Librn,* Gayle Christenson
Founded 1964. Pop 3,800; Circ 11,860
Library Holdings: Bk Vols 24,500; Per Subs 4
Wireless access
Open Mon-Fri 9-12 & 1-5

STREETER

P STREETER CENTENNIAL LIBRARY*, 235 Florence St, 58483, *Librn,* Janet Patton
Library Holdings: Bk Titles 3,000
Open Tues 4-6

TURTLE LAKE

P TURTLE LAKE PUBLIC LIBRARY*, 107 Eggert St, 58575. (Mail add: PO Box 540, 58575-0540), SAN 355-4341. Tel: 701-448-9170. E-mail: tlpublic@westriv.com. Web Site: turtlelakendlibrary.com. *Librn,* Kelly Voth
Library Holdings: Audiobooks 90; DVDs 198; Bk Vols 8,571; Per Subs 4
Wireless access
Mem of McLean-Mercer Regional Library
Partic in Central Dakota Library Network
Open Mon & Thurs 10-5, Tues 10-6

UNDERWOOD

P UNDERWOOD PUBLIC LIBRARY*, 88 Lincoln Ave, 58576. (Mail add: PO Box 304, 58576-0304), SAN 370-9086. Tel: 701-442-3441. FAX: 701-442-5482. E-mail: underwoodlibrary@westriv.com. Web Site: underwoodndlibrary.com. *Libr Dir,* Harmony Higbie; Staff 1 (Non-MLS 1)
Pop 750
Automation Activity & Vendor Info: (Acquisitions) SirsiDynix
Wireless access
Mem of McLean-Mercer Regional Library
Partic in Central Dakota Library Network
Open Mon & Fri 10-2, Tues & Thurs 3-7, Wed 10-2 & 3-6
Restriction: Pub access for legal res only

VALLEY CITY

P VALLEY CITY BARNES COUNTY PUBLIC LIBRARY*, 410 N Central Ave, 58072-2949. SAN 313-1564. Tel: 701-845-3821. Toll Free Tel: 800-532-8600 (ND only). FAX: 701-845-4884. E-mail: vcbclibrary@outlook.com. Web Site: www.vcbclibrary.org. *Libr Dir,* Steve Hammel; *Adult Serv Coordr,* Angela Vinha; *Youth Serv Coordr,* Melissa Lloyd; Staff 8 (MLS 4, Non-MLS 4)
Founded 1903. Pop 11,075; Circ 35,915
Jan 2017-Dec 2017 Income $298,676, State $23,175, City $129,000, County $135,751, Locally Generated Income $5,000, Other $5,750. Mats Exp $38,000, Books $25,000, Per/Ser (Incl. Access Fees) $2,000, AV Mat $9,500, Electronic Ref Mat (Incl. Access Fees) $1,500. Sal $159,943
Library Holdings: Audiobooks 913; CDs 105; DVDs 2,091; Large Print Bks 4,219; Bk Vols 34,935
Special Collections: North Dakota Coll
Automation Activity & Vendor Info: (Acquisitions) Biblionix/Apollo; (Cataloging) Biblionix/Apollo; (Circulation) Biblionix/Apollo; (OPAC) Biblionix/Apollo; (Serials) Biblionix/Apollo
Wireless access
Function: 24/7 Electronic res, 24/7 Online cat, Accelerated reader prog, Activity rm, Adult bk club, Audiobks via web, Bk club(s), Bks on CD, Children's prog, Computers for patron use, E-Reserves, Electronic databases & coll, Free DVD rentals, Genealogy discussion group, Home delivery & serv to seniorr ctr & nursing homes, Homework prog, ILL available, Instruction & testing, Internet access, Life-long learning prog for all ages, Magazines, Meeting rooms, Movies, Music CDs, Online cat, Outside serv via phone, mail, e-mail & web, OverDrive digital audio bks, Photocopying/Printing, Preschool outreach, Prog for adults, Prog for children & young adult, Ref serv available, Scanner, Senior outreach, Serves people with intellectual disabilities, Story hour, Summer reading prog, Tax forms, Teen prog, Wheelchair accessible, Workshops
Partic in Online Dakota Info Network
Open Mon & Tues 10-7, Wed, Fri & Sat 10-5, Thurs 10-8
Friends of the Library Group

C VALLEY CITY STATE UNIVERSITY LIBRARY*, Allen Memorial Library, 101 College St SW, 58072-4098. SAN 313-1572. Tel: 701-845-7277. Administration Tel: 701-845-7275. Automation Services Tel: 701-845-7278. Toll Free Tel: 800-532-8641, Ext 37276. FAX: 701-845-7437. E-mail: library@vcsu.edu. Web Site: library.vcsu.edu. *Dir, Libr Serv, Distance Educ, Info Literacy,* Donna James; E-mail: donna.james@vcsu.edu; *Electronic Res Librn,* Position Currently Open; *User Serv Librn,* Al Bernardo; E-mail: alfred.bernardo@vcsu.edu; *Syst Spec,* Benjamin Ferguson; E-mail: benjamin.ferguson@vcsu.edu; Staff 4 (MLS 3, Non-MLS 1)
Founded 1890. Enrl 855; Fac 59; Highest Degree: Master
Library Holdings: e-books 35,000; Bk Titles 80,000; Bk Vols 100,000; Per Subs 125
Special Collections: James Ployhar Coll, musical scores; North Dakota Coll; Valley City State University Historical Coll; Woiwode Manuscripts Coll. State Document Depository; US Document Depository
Subject Interests: Educ, Local hist, Music
Automation Activity & Vendor Info: (Acquisitions) Ex Libris Group; (Cataloging) Ex Libris Group; (Circulation) Ex Libris Group; (Course Reserve) Ex Libris Group; (ILL) Ex Libris Group; (OPAC) Ex Libris Group; (Serials) Ex Libris Group
Wireless access
Function: 24/7 Electronic res, Archival coll, Art exhibits, Audio & video playback equip for onsite use, Audiobks via web, Bks on CD, Computers for patron use, Digital talking bks, Distance learning, Doc delivery serv, E-Readers, E-Reserves, Electronic databases & coll, Govt ref serv, ILL available, Instruction & testing, Internet access, Learning ctr, Magazines, Microfiche/film & reading machines, Music CDs, Online cat, Online info literacy tutorials on the web & in blackboard, Online ref, Outside serv via phone, mail, e-mail & web, OverDrive digital audio bks, Photocopying/Printing, Printer for laptops & handheld devices, Ref & res, Ref serv available, Scanner, Study rm, Telephone ref, Wheelchair accessible
Partic in Minitex; OCLC Online Computer Library Center, Inc; Online Dakota Info Network
Open Mon-Thurs 7:45am-11pm, Fri 7:45-4
Restriction: Open to pub for ref & circ; with some limitations, Open to students, fac & staff
Friends of the Library Group

VELVA

P VELVA SCHOOL & PUBLIC LIBRARY*, 101 W Fourth St, 58790-7045. (Mail add: PO Box 179, 58790-0179), SAN 313-1580. Tel: 701-338-2022. FAX: 701-338-2023. Web Site: www.velva.k12.nd.us/library. *Librn,* Jen Kramer; E-mail: jen.kramer@k12.nd.us; Staff 2 (Non-MLS 2)
Founded 1913. Pop 1,300; Circ 26,779
Library Holdings: Bk Titles 18,000; Per Subs 120
Automation Activity & Vendor Info: (OPAC) OVID Technologies

WAHPETON

P LEACH PUBLIC LIBRARY, 417 Second Ave N, 58075. SAN 313-1599. Tel: 701-642-5732. FAX: 701-642-5732. E-mail: leachplib@midconetwork.com. Web Site: www.leachlibrarywahpeton.org. *Ad, Libr Dir,* Melissa Bakken; E-mail: melissa.leachplib@midconetwork.com; *Ch,* Rachel Kercher; E-mail: rachel.leachplib@midconetwork.com
Founded 1924. Pop 9,000; Circ 36,100
Library Holdings: Audiobooks 1,768; Bks on Deafness & Sign Lang 15; DVDs 837; Large Print Bks 600; Bk Vols 30,233; Per Subs 75; Videos 557
Special Collections: Local Paper back to 1890, microfilm
Automation Activity & Vendor Info: (Cataloging) Ex Libris Group; (Circulation) Ex Libris Group; (ILL) Ex Libris Group; (OPAC) Ex Libris Group; (Serials) Ex Libris Group
Wireless access
Partic in Online Dakota Info Network
Open Mon 9-7, Tues-Thurs 9-6, Fri 9-4, Sat (Winter) 9-1
Friends of the Library Group

J NORTH DAKOTA STATE COLLEGE OF SCIENCE*, Mildred Johnson Library, 800 Sixth St N, 58076-0001. SAN 313-1602. Tel: 701-671-2298, 701-671-2618. Administration Tel: 701-671-2385. Toll Free Tel: 800-342-4325. FAX: 701-671-2674. E-mail: NDSCS.Library@ndscs.edu. Web Site: www.ndscs.edu/library. *Libr Dir,* Patricia Caldwell; Tel: 701-671-2612, E-mail: patricia.caldwell@ndscs.edu; *Libr Coord,* Amy Carson; Tel: 701-671-2192, E-mail: amy.carson@ndcs.edu; *Libr Assoc,* Michelle Hart; Tel: 701-671-2620, E-mail: michelle.hart@ndscs.edu; *Libr Assoc,* Marylin Vertin; Tel: 701-671-2168, E-mail: marylin.vertin@ndscs.edu; Staff 4 (MLS 2, Non-MLS 2)
Founded 1903. Enrl 2,100; Fac 135; Highest Degree: Associate
Library Holdings: Audiobooks 500; AV Mats 3,700; e-books 11,842; e-journals 1; Bk Vols 70,000; Per Subs 120
Subject Interests: Automotive, Behav sci, Electronics, Foods mgt, Health sci, Soc sci
Automation Activity & Vendor Info: (Acquisitions) Ex Libris Group; (Cataloging) Ex Libris Group; (Circulation) Ex Libris Group; (Course Reserve) Ex Libris Group; (ILL) OCLC Connexion; (OPAC) Ex Libris Group; (Serials) Ex Libris Group
Wireless access
Function: Adult bk club, CD-ROM, Electronic databases & coll, ILL available, Photocopying/Printing, Telephone ref, VHS videos, Wheelchair accessible
Partic in Minitex; OCLC Online Computer Library Center, Inc; Online Dakota Info Network
Open Mon-Thurs 9-8, Fri 9-Noon, Sun 6pm-9pm
Restriction: In-house use for visitors

WALHALLA

P WALHALLA PUBLIC LIBRARY, 1010 Central Ave, 58282-4015. (Mail add: PO Box 587, 58282-0587), SAN 313-1610. Tel: 701-549-3794. FAX: 701-549-3794. E-mail: wlibrary@utma.com. Web Site: walhallandlibrary.com. *Dir,* Brenda Fletcher
Circ 3,470
Library Holdings: Bk Vols 20,400
Automation Activity & Vendor Info: (Cataloging) Follett Software; (Circulation) Follett Software
Wireless access
Open Mon-Fri 11-5

WASHBURN

P WASHBURN PUBLIC LIBRARY*, 705 Main Ave, 58577. (Mail add: PO Box 637, 58577-0637), SAN 355-4376. Tel: 701-462-8180. E-mail: washlib@westriv.com. Web Site: washburnndlibrary.com. *Librn,* Elizabeth Patterson
Wireless access
Mem of McLean-Mercer Regional Library
Partic in Central Dakota Library Network
Open Mon-Thurs 10-6, Sat 10-1

WATFORD CITY

P MCKENZIE COUNTY PUBLIC LIBRARY, 112 Second Ave NE, 58854. (Mail add: PO Box 990, 58854-0990), SAN 313-1629. Tel: 701-444-3785. FAX: 701-444-3730. E-mail: librarian@co.mckenzie.nd.us. Web Site: www.mckenziecountyndlibrary.com. *Libr Dir,* Stephanie Galeazzo; E-mail: sgaleazzo@co.mckenzie.nd.us; *Asst Dir,* Char Mathisen; Staff 4 (MLS 2, Non-MLS 2)
Founded 1958. Pop 18,000; Circ 24,900
Library Holdings: Audiobooks 550; DVDs 401; Large Print Bks 900; Bk Titles 25,000; Bk Vols 26,185; Per Subs 35
Automation Activity & Vendor Info: (Cataloging) Book Systems; (Circulation) Book Systems; (OPAC) Book Systems; (Serials) Book Systems
Wireless access
Publications: Booklist
Partic in NW Regional Libr Coop
Open Mon, Tues, Thurs & Fri 10-6, Wed 10-8
Friends of the Library Group
Bookmobiles: 1

WEST FARGO

P WEST FARGO PUBLIC LIBRARY, 215 Third Street E, 58078. SAN 313-1637. Tel: 701-515-5200. E-mail: askus@westfargolibrary.org. Web Site: www.westfargolibrary.org/732/Public-Library. *Dir,* Carissa Hansen
Founded 1971
Library Holdings: Audiobooks 3,477; CDs 507; DVDs 4,270; e-books 8,557; Bk Titles 55,080; Per Subs 142
Special Collections: United States (State & Local History)
Automation Activity & Vendor Info: (Cataloging) Ex Libris Group; (Circulation) Ex Libris Group; (OPAC) Ex Libris Group
Wireless access
Open Mon-Thurs 10-9, Fri 10-6, Sat 10-5, Sun (Sept-May) 1-5
Friends of the Library Group
Bookmobiles: 1

WILLISTON

P WILLISTON COMMUNITY LIBRARY*, 1302 Davidson Dr, 58801. SAN 313-1645. Tel: 701-774-8805. FAX: 701-572-1186. E-mail: library@ci.williston.nd.us. Web Site: www.willistonNDlibrary.com. *Libr Dir,* Debbie Slais; Staff 7.5 (Non-MLS 7.5)
Founded 1983. Pop 30,000; Circ 500,000
Jan 2016-Dec 2016 Income (Main Library Only) $622,413, State $18,800, City $252,878, County $247,220, Other $103,515. Mats Exp $80,000, Books $50,000, Per/Ser (Incl. Access Fees) $15,000, AV Mat $15,000. Sal $325,821
Library Holdings: Audiobooks 1,638; AV Mats 350; CDs 1,000; DVDs 1,257; Electronic Media & Resources 156; Large Print Bks 2,917; Microforms 100; Bk Vols 58,969; Per Subs 100; Talking Bks 1,638; Videos 53
Special Collections: American Indian Coll; Genealogy Coll; North Dakota Coll
Automation Activity & Vendor Info: (Cataloging) OCLC Connexion; (Circulation) Book Systems; (ILL) OCLC FirstSearch; (OPAC) Book Systems
Wireless access
Function: 24/7 Online cat, Audiobks on Playaways & MP3, Bks on CD, Children's prog, Computers for patron use, Electronic databases & coll, Free DVD rentals, Home delivery & serv to seniorr ctr & nursing homes, ILL available, Internet access, Magazines, Magnifiers for reading, Meeting rooms, Microfiche/film & reading machines, Movies, Music CDs, Online cat, Outreach serv, OverDrive digital audio bks, Photocopying/Printing, Prog for adults, Prog for children & young adult, Scanner, Spanish lang bks, Story hour, Summer reading prog, Tax forms, Teen prog, Wheelchair accessible
Partic in Association for Rural & Small Libraries
Open Mon-Thurs 9-8, Fri 9-5, Sat 1-5, Sun 2-5
Restriction: Non-resident fee
Friends of the Library Group
Bookmobiles: 1

C WILLISTON STATE COLLEGE*, Learning Commons, 1410 University Ave, 58801. Tel: 701-774-4226. Web Site: www.willistonstate.edu/Current-Students/Learning-Commons.html. *Librn,* Monica Struck; Tel: 701-774-4227, E-mail: monica.struck@willistonstate.edu; Staff 1 (MLS 1)
Founded 1966
Library Holdings: AV Mats 600; e-books 6,500; Bk Vols 13,000
Wireless access
Partic in Online Dakota Info Network
Open Mon 8-5, Tues-Thurs 8-5 & 7-9, Fri 8-4:30, Sun 7pm-9pm

OHIO

Date of Statistics: FY 2019
Population, 2020 U.S. Census: 11,693,217
Population Served: 11,510,799
Total Public Library Circulation: 178,824,499
Total Number of All Library Programs: 306,493
Digital Resources:
Total e-books: 109,424,170
Total audio items (physical & downloadable units): 47,722,228
Total video items (physical & downloadable units): 5,860,392
Total computers for use by the public: 14,254
Total annual wireless sessions: 23,951,713
Income and Expenditures:
Information derived from public sources.

ADA

P ADA PUBLIC LIBRARY, 320 N Main St, 45810-1199. SAN 313-1688. Tel: 419-634-5246. FAX: 419-634-9747. E-mail: adalibrarycirc@gmail.com. Web Site: www.adalibrary.org. *Dir,* Rhett Grant; E-mail: adalibrarydirector@gmail.com; Staff 2 (MLS 1, Non-MLS 1)
Founded 1916. Pop 7,900; Circ 54,100
Library Holdings: Bk Vols 23,100; Per Subs 74
Special Collections: City, County & State History
Automation Activity & Vendor Info: (Cataloging) SirsiDynix-WorkFlows; (Circulation) SirsiDynix-WorkFlows; (OPAC) SirsiDynix-WorkFlows
Wireless access
Function: Adult bk club, After school storytime, Audiobks via web, Bk club(s), Bks on CD, Children's prog, Computer training, Computers for patron use, Digital talking bks, Free DVD rentals, Holiday prog, Microfiche/film & reading machines, Music CDs, Notary serv, Online cat, OverDrive digital audio bks, Photocopying/Printing, Preschool outreach, Preschool reading prog, Prog for adults, Prog for children & young adult, Scanner, Story hour, Summer reading prog, Tax forms, Teen prog, Wheelchair accessible, Writing prog
Partic in Serving Every Ohioan Library Center
Special Services for the Deaf - Bks on deafness & sign lang
Special Services for the Blind - Bks on CD; Large print bks
Open Mon-Thurs 10-8, Fri 10-5, Sat 10-2
Friends of the Library Group

C OHIO NORTHERN UNIVERSITY, Heterick Memorial Library, 525 S Main St, 45810. SAN 355-4406. Tel: 419-772-2181. Reference Tel: 419-772-2185. FAX: 419-772-1927. E-mail: reference@onu.edu. Web Site: www.onu.edu/heterick-memorial-library. *Dir,* Kathleen Baril; Tel: 419-772-2188, E-mail: k-baril@onu.edu; *Cataloging & Knowledge Architect Librn,* Jennifer Donley; Tel: 419-772-2193, E-mail: j-donley.1@onu.edu; *Electronic Res Librn,* Heather Crozier; Tel: 419-772-2182, E-mail: h-crozier@onu.edu; *Instruction & Access Services Librn,* Bethany Spieth; Tel: 419-772-2473, E-mail: b-spieth@onu.edu; *Tech & Syst Librn,* Christopher Deems; Tel: 419-772-2183, E-mail: c-deems@onu.edu; *Archivist,* Matthew Francis; Tel: 419-772-1925, E-mail: m-francis@onu.edu
Founded 1915. Enrl 2,936; Fac 215; Highest Degree: Doctorate
Library Holdings: AV Mats 6,591; e-books 207,422; Bk Vols 208,861; Per Subs 90,191
Special Collections: Ohio Northern University Authors
Automation Activity & Vendor Info: (Acquisitions) Innovative Interfaces, Inc; (Cataloging) Innovative Interfaces, Inc; (Circulation) Innovative Interfaces, Inc; (Course Reserve) Innovative Interfaces, Inc; (OPAC) Innovative Interfaces, Inc
Wireless access
Partic in OCLC Online Computer Library Center, Inc; Ohio Library & Information Network; OhioNET
Open Mon-Thurs 7:30am-Midnight, Fri 7:30-5, Sat 1-5, Sun Noon-Midnight

Departmental Libraries:

CL TAGGART LAW LIBRARY, 525 S Main St, 45810. Tel: 419-772-2250. Circulation Tel: 419-772-2239. Interlibrary Loan Service Tel: 419-772-2255. FAX: 419-772-1875. E-mail: law-reference@onu.edu. Web Site: law.onu.edu/taggart-law-library. *Interim Co-Dir, Tech Serv Librn,* Kaylan Ellis; Tel: 419-772-2254, E-mail: k-ellis@onu.edu; *Interim Co-Dir, Ref Librn,* Dustin Johnston-Green; Tel: 419-772-2255, E-mail: d-green.4@onu.edu; *Sr Libr Asst,* Harli Broge; Tel: 419-772-3058, E-mail: h-broge@onu.edu; Staff 2 (MLS 2)
Founded 1885. Enrl 161
Library Holdings: Bk Titles 68,772; Bk Vols 268,635; Per Subs 5
Special Collections: Anthony J Celebrezze Papers. US Document Depository
Automation Activity & Vendor Info: (Acquisitions) Innovative Interfaces, Inc
Function: Res libr
Partic in Ohio Library & Information Network

AKRON

S AKRON ART MUSEUM*, Martha Stecher Reed Art Reference Library, One S High St, 44308-1801. SAN 313-1696. Tel: 330-376-9185, 330-376-9186, Ext 221. FAX: 330-376-1180. Web Site: www.akronartmuseum.org. *Colls Mgr,* Stephanie Petcavage; Tel: 330-376-9186, Ext 228, E-mail: SPetcavage@AkronArtMuseum.org; Staff 1 (MLS 1)
Library Holdings: Bk Titles 15,000; Per Subs 8
Special Collections: Edwin C Shaw Archives
Subject Interests: Am Impressionism, Contemporary painting, Photog, Sculpture
Restriction: Non-circulating, Open by appt only, Photo ID required for access

L AKRON LAW LIBRARY*, 209 S High St, 4th Flr, 44308-1675. SAN 313-1734. Tel: 330-643-2804. Administration Tel: 330-643-8318. Web Site: akronlawlib.summitoh.net. *Law Libr Dir/Law Librn,* Alan Canfora; Tel: 330-643-8318, E-mail: acanfora@akronlawlib.org; *Asst Dir, Ref Librn,* Amber Barnhart; Tel: 330-643-8317, E-mail: abarnhart@akronlawlib.org; Staff 3 (MLS 2, Non-MLS 1)
Founded 1888
Library Holdings: Bk Titles 51,753; Per Subs 249
Automation Activity & Vendor Info: (Cataloging) LibraryWorld, Inc; (Circulation) LibraryWorld, Inc; (OPAC) LibraryWorld, Inc; (Serials) LibraryWorld, Inc
Wireless access
Function: 24/7 Online cat, Archival coll, Computers for patron use, Electronic databases & coll, Govt ref serv, Internet access, Meeting rooms, Online cat, Photocopying/Printing, Prof lending libr, Ref & res, Ref serv available, Res libr
Open Mon-Fri 8-4:30
Restriction: Circ to mem only, Open to pub for ref only

P AKRON-SUMMIT COUNTY PUBLIC LIBRARY*, 60 S High St, 44326. SAN 355-4465. Tel: 330-643-9000. FAX: 330-643-9160. TDD: 330-643-9005. E-mail: bgdiv@akronlibrary.org. Web Site: www.akronlibrary.org. *Exec Dir,* Pamela Hickson-Stevenson; Tel: 330-643-9100, E-mail: phickson@akronlibrary.org; *Dep Dir,* Barbara White; Tel: 330-643-9102, E-mail: bwhite@akronlibrary.org; *Dir, Human Res,* Lisa Peercy; Tel: 330-643-9104, E-mail: lpeercy@akronlibrary.org; *Dir, Mkt,* Carla Davis; Tel: 330-643-9090, E-mail: cdavis@akronlibrary.org; *Facilities Dir,* Carol Roxbury; Tel: 330-643-9175, E-mail: croxbury@akronlibrary.org; *Neighborhood Serv Mgr,* Pat Manning; Tel: 330-643-9082, E-mail: pmanning@akronlibrary.org; *Fiscal Officer,* Michelle Scarpitti; E-mail: mscarpitti@akronlibrary.org; Staff 309 (MLS 118, Non-MLS 191)

Founded 1874. Pop 384,632; Circ 5,155,296

Library Holdings: AV Mats 275,126; Bk Titles 461,283; Bk Vols 1,640,985; Per Subs 1,838

Special Collections: Lighter-than-Air. State Document Depository; US Document Depository

Subject Interests: Genealogy, Local hist, Patents trademarks, Sci fair projects

Automation Activity & Vendor Info: (Acquisitions) SirsiDynix; (Cataloging) SirsiDynix; (Circulation) SirsiDynix; (OPAC) SirsiDynix; (Serials) SirsiDynix

Wireless access

Function: Govt ref serv, Health sci info serv, ILL available, Prog for adults, Prog for children & young adult, Ref serv available, Summer reading prog

Publications: Shelf Life (Newsletter)

Partic in Northeast Ohio Regional Library System; OCLC Online Computer Library Center, Inc

Special Services for the Deaf - High interest/low vocabulary bks; TTY equip

Special Services for the Blind - Reader equip

Open Mon-Thurs 10-8, Fri 10-6, Sat 10-5, Sun 1-5

Friends of the Library Group

Branches: 18

ELLET BRANCH, 2470 E Market St, 44312, SAN 355-4619. Tel: 330-784-2019. FAX: 330-784-6692. *Br Mgr,* Brian Burch; E-mail: bburch@akronlibrary.org; Staff 3 (MLS 3)

Circ 246,446

Library Holdings: Bk Vols 75,000

Open Mon-Thurs 10-8, Fri 12-6, Sat 10-5

Friends of the Library Group

FAIRLAWN-BATH BRANCH, 3101 Smith Rd, 44333, SAN 355-4708. Tel: 330-666-4888. FAX: 330-666-8741. *Br Mgr,* Jane Scott; E-mail: jscott@akronlibrary.org; Staff 3 (MLS 3)

Circ 283,232

Library Holdings: Bk Vols 56,471

Open Mon-Thurs 10-8, Fri 12-6, Sat 10-5

Friends of the Library Group

FIRESTONE PARK BRANCH, 1486 Aster Ave, 44301-2104, SAN 355-452X. Tel: 330-724-2126. FAX: 330-724-4391. *Br Mgr,* Susan Vandenberg; E-mail: svandenberg@akronlibrary.org; Staff 3 (MLS 3)

Circ 135,905

Library Holdings: Bk Vols 41,729

Open Mon-Thurs 10-8, Fri 12-6, Sat 10-5

Friends of the Library Group

GOODYEAR BRANCH, 60 Goodyear Blvd, 44305-4487, SAN 355-4589. Tel: 330-784-7522. FAX: 330-784-6599. *Br Mgr,* Tonya Gardella; E-mail: tgardella@akronlibrary.org; Staff 3 (MLS 3)

Circ 112,462

Library Holdings: Bk Vols 50,103

Open Mon-Thurs 10-8, Fri 12-6, Sat 10-5

Friends of the Library Group

GREEN BRANCH, 4046 Massillon Rd, Uniontown, 44685-4046, SAN 355-4643. Tel: 330-896-9074. FAX: 330-896-9412. *Br Mgr,* Sherry Swisher; E-mail: sswisher@akronlibrary.org; Staff 3 (MLS 3)

Circ 362,518

Library Holdings: Bk Vols 59,875

Open Mon-Thurs 10-8, Fri 12-6, Sat 10-5

Friends of the Library Group

HIGHLAND SQUARE BRANCH, 807 W Market St, 44303-1010, SAN 355-497X. Tel: 330-376-2927. FAX: 330-376-9025. *Br Mgr,* Fred Baerkircher; E-mail: fbaerkircher@akronlibrary.org; Staff 2 (MLS 2)

Circ 135,644

Library Holdings: Bk Vols 48,106

Open Mon-Thurs 10-8, Fri 12-6, Sat 10-5

Friends of the Library Group

KENMORE BRANCH, 969 Kenmore Blvd, 44314-2302, SAN 355-4678. Tel: 330-745-6126. FAX: 330-745-9947. *Interim Br Mgr,* Brian Burch; E-mail: bburch@akronlibrary.org; Staff 2 (MLS 2)

Circ 169,179

Library Holdings: Bk Vols 53,218

Open Mon-Thurs 10-8, Fri 12-6, Sat 10-5

Friends of the Library Group

MAPLE VALLEY BRANCH, 1187 Copley Rd, 44320-2766, SAN 355-4767. Tel: 330-864-5721. FAX: 330-864-8971. *Br Mgr,* Tonya Wright; E-mail: twright@akronlibrary.org; Staff 3 (MLS 3)

Circ 111,244

Library Holdings: Bk Vols 49,810

Open Mon-Thurs 10-8, Fri 12-6, Sat 10-5

Friends of the Library Group

MOGADORE BRANCH, 144 S Cleveland Ave, Mogadore, 44260, SAN 355-4791. Tel: 330-628-9228. FAX: 330-628-3256. *Br Mgr,* Kimberlie DeBenedictis; E-mail: kdebenedictis@akronlibrary.org; Staff 7 (MLS 3, Non-MLS 4)

Circ 200,509

Library Holdings: Bk Vols 56,529

Special Services for the Blind - Vantage closed circuit TV magnifier

Open Mon-Thurs 10-8, Fri 12-6, Sat 10-5

Friends of the Library Group

NORDONIA HILLS BRANCH, 9458 Olde Eight Rd, Northfield, 44067-1952, SAN 355-4856. Tel: 330-467-8595. FAX: 330-467-4332. *Br Mgr,* Katie Hughes; E-mail: khughes@akronlibrary.org; Staff 3 (MLS 3)

Circ 272,393

Library Holdings: Bk Vols 60,153

Open Mon-Thurs 10-8, Fri 12-6, Sat 10-5

Friends of the Library Group

NORTH HILL BRANCH, 183 E Cuyahoga Falls Ave, 44310-3078, SAN 355-4821. Tel: 330-535-9423. FAX: 330-376-5661. *Br Mgr,* Lisa Antognoli Weiser; E-mail: lweiser@akronlibrary.org; Staff 3 (MLS 3)

Circ 64,339

Open Mon-Thurs 10-8, Fri 12-6, Sat 10-5

Friends of the Library Group

NORTHWEST AKRON BRANCH, 1720 Shatto Ave, 44313, SAN 355-449X. Tel: 330-836-1081. FAX: 330-836-1574. *Br Mgr,* Greg Trask; E-mail: gtrask@akronlibrary.org; Staff 3 (MLS 3)

Circ 343,977

Library Holdings: Bk Vols 59,145

Open Mon-Thurs 10-8, Fri 12-6, Sat 10-5

Friends of the Library Group

NORTON BRANCH, 3930 S Cleveland-Massillon Rd, Norton, 44203-5563, SAN 355-4880. Tel: 330-825-7800. FAX: 330-825-5155. *Br Mgr,* Tori Berger; E-mail: vberger@akronlibrary.org; Staff 3 (MLS 3)

Circ 232,531

Library Holdings: Bk Vols 58,360

Open Mon-Thurs 10-8, Fri 12-6, Sat 10-5

Friends of the Library Group

ODOM BOULEVARD BRANCH, 600 Vernon Odom Blvd, 44307-1828, SAN 355-5003. Tel: 330-434-8726. FAX: 330-434-3750. *Br Mgr,* Theresa Boware; E-mail: tboware@akronlibrary.org; Staff 9 (MLS 2, Non-MLS 7)

Founded 1923. Circ 118,199

Library Holdings: Bk Vols 61,827

Open Mon-Thurs 10-8, Fri 12-6, Sat 10-5

Friends of the Library Group

PORTAGE LAKES BRANCH, 4261 Manchester Rd, 44319-2659, SAN 370-3509. Tel: 330-644-7050. FAX: 330-644-0977. *Br Mgr,* Cheryl Luck; E-mail: cluck@akronlibrary.org; Staff 2 (MLS 2)

Circ 189,524

Library Holdings: Bk Vols 51,177

Open Mon-Thurs 10-8, Fri 12-6, Sat 10-5

Friends of the Library Group

RICHFIELD BRANCH, 3761 S Grant St, Richfield, 44286-9603, SAN 355-4910. Tel: 330-659-4343. FAX: 330-659-6205. *Br Mgr,* Jennifer Stencel; E-mail: jstencel@akronlibrary.org; Staff 3 (MLS 3)

Circ 199,729

Library Holdings: Bk Vols 50,388

Open Mon-Thurs 10-8, Fri 12-6, Sat 10-5

Friends of the Library Group

SPRINGFIELD-LAKEMORE BRANCH, 1500 Canton Rd, Ste 360, 44312. Tel: 330-643-4770. *Br Mgr,* Melani Fragge; E-mail: mfragge@akronlibrary.org

Open Mon & Thurs 12-8, Tues 10-8, Wed & Fri 12-6, Sat 10-5

Friends of the Library Group

TALLMADGE BRANCH, 90 Community Rd, Tallmadge, 44278, SAN 355-4945. Tel: 330-633-4345. FAX: 330-633-6324. *Br Mgr,* Michael Bianchi; E-mail: mbianchi@akronlibrary.org; Staff 3 (MLS 3)

Circ 236,361

Library Holdings: Bk Vols 54,613

Subject Interests: Local hist

Open Mon-Thurs 10-8, Fri 12-6, Sat 10-5

Friends of the Library Group

Bookmobiles: 2

M CLEVELAND CLINIC AKRON GENERAL*, Medical Library, One Akron General Ave, 2nd Flr, Rm 2202, 44307. SAN 313-1726. Tel: 330-344-6242. FAX: 330-344-1834. Web Site: akrongeneral.libguides.com/library. *Librn,* Denise Mullins; Tel: 330-344-1558, E-mail: mullind@ccf.org; Staff 2 (MLS 2)

Library Holdings: Bk Titles 3,000; Per Subs 300
Automation Activity & Vendor Info: (Acquisitions) Innovative Interfaces, Inc; (Cataloging) Innovative Interfaces, Inc; (Circulation) Innovative Interfaces, Inc; (OPAC) Innovative Interfaces, Inc; (Serials) Innovative Interfaces, Inc
Wireless access
Partic in Ohio Library & Information Network
Restriction: Badge access after hrs, Staff use only

M MARY HOWER MEDICAL LIBRARY*, One Perkins Sq, 44308-1062. SAN 329-8566. Tel: 330-543-8250. FAX: 530-543-3158. Web Site: www.akronchildrens.org/pages/Mary-A-Hower-Medical-Library. *Med Librn*, Alyssa Portwood; E-mail: aportwood@chmca.org; Staff 3.8 (MLS 1, Non-MLS 2.8)
Library Holdings: Per Subs 200
Subject Interests: Pediatrics & burn injuries
Function: Res libr
Restriction: Staff use only

M SUMMA HEALTH SYSTEM, Medical Library, 55 Arch St, Ste G-3, 44304. SAN 313-1718. Tel: 330-375-3260. FAX: 330-375-3978. *Syst Librn*, Wendy Hess; E-mail: hessw@summahealth.org; *Ref (Info Servs)*, Charlotte Sievert; E-mail: csievert@summahealth.org; Staff 3 (MLS 3)
Founded 1930
Automation Activity & Vendor Info: (Cataloging) Innovative Interfaces, Inc; (Circulation) Innovative Interfaces, Inc
Wireless access
Partic in Ohio Library & Information Network
Restriction: Authorized personnel only, Not open to pub

C UNIVERSITY OF AKRON LIBRARIES*, Bierce Library, 315 Buchtel Mall, 44325-1701. SAN 355-5127. Tel: 330-972-5355. Circulation Tel: 330-972-7656. Interlibrary Loan Service Tel: 330-972-6275. Administration Tel: 330-972-7488. Reference FAX: 330-972-6059. Web Site: www.uakron.edu/libraries. *Dean of Libr*, Dr Aimee deChambeau; E-mail: daimee@uakron.edu; *Head, Access Serv*, Melanie F Smith; Tel: 330-972-7047, E-mail: melani6@uakron.edu; *Head, Archival Serv*, Victor S Fleischer; Tel: 330-972-6253, E-mail: svfleis@uakron.edu; *Head, Ref*, Jeffrey Franks; Tel: 330-972-6052, E-mail: jfranks@uakron.edu; *Libr Syst Coordr*, Susan DiRenzo Ashby; Tel: 330-972-7240, E-mail: ashby@uakron.edu; Staff 62 (MLS 29, Non-MLS 33)
Founded 1872. Enrl 26,257; Fac 797; Highest Degree: Doctorate
Library Holdings: AV Mats 48,423; Bks on Deafness & Sign Lang 884; CDs 4,022; DVDs 928; e-books 2,789; e-journals 1,655,555; Electronic Media & Resources 263; Microforms 168,381; Music Scores 27,960; Bk Vols 1,259,804; Per Subs 15,266
Special Collections: B-26 Archives; Brozek Coll; Herman Muehlstein Rare Book Coll; Paul Belcher Coll; Propaganda Coll, flm; Sylvia Smith Archives; The Archives of the History of American Psychology & the American History Research Center; The University of Akron Archives. State Document Depository; US Document Depository
Subject Interests: Hist of psychol, Polymer, Polymer chem, Rubber indust
Automation Activity & Vendor Info: (Acquisitions) Innovative Interfaces, Inc; (Cataloging) Innovative Interfaces, Inc; (Circulation) Innovative Interfaces, Inc; (Course Reserve) Docutek; (ILL) OCLC; (Media Booking) Innovative Interfaces, Inc; (OPAC) Innovative Interfaces, Inc; (Serials) Innovative Interfaces, Inc
Wireless access
Partic in Center for Research Libraries; OCLC Online Computer Library Center, Inc; OhioNET
Friends of the Library Group

Departmental Libraries:

CL SCHOOL OF LAW LIBRARY, 150 University Ave, 44325. (Mail add: 302 Buchtel Common, 44325). Tel: 330-972-7330. FAX: 330-972-4948. Web Site: www.uakron.edu/law. *Dir*, Paul Richert; E-mail: richert@uakron.edu; *Dep Law Librn*, Kyle Passmore; E-mail: passmore@uakron.edu; *Circ Supvr*, Tiffanie Nevins
Library Holdings: AV Mats 1,772; Electronic Media & Resources 7,459; Microforms 19,458; Bk Titles 46,195
Partic in Ohio Library & Information Network
Open Mon-Fri 7am-11pm, Sat 9-9, Sun 10am-11pm
Friends of the Library Group

SCIENCE & TECHNOLOGY, Auburn Science Engineering Ctr, No 104, 44325-3907. (Mail add: 244 Sumner St, 44325-3907). Tel: 330-972-8323. Reference Tel: 330-972-7195. Administration Tel: 330-972-8196. FAX: 330-972-7033. E-mail: scilib@uakron.edu. *Head Librn*, Jo Ann Calzonetti; E-mail: jc44@uakron.edu; Staff 7.5 (MLS 4.5, Non-MLS 3)
Enrl 26,000; Fac 4; Highest Degree: Doctorate
Special Collections: Rubber
Function: Wheelchair accessible
Open Mon & Thurs 7:30am-11pm, Fri 7:30-6, Sat 9-6, Sun 1-11
Restriction: Badge access after hrs
Friends of the Library Group

ALEXANDRIA

P ALEXANDRIA PUBLIC LIBRARY, Ten Maple Dr, 43001. (Mail add: PO Box 67, 43001-0067), SAN 313-1815. Tel: 740-924-3561. Automation Services Toll Free Tel: 877-772-6657. FAX: 740-924-3007. Web Site: www.alexandrialibrary.org. *Dir*, Carrie Strong; E-mail: cstrong@alexandria.lib.oh.us
Founded 1935. Pop 7,000; Circ 86,500
Jan 2016-Dec 2016 Income $269,274. Mats Exp $50,051, Books $27,458, Per/Ser (Incl. Access Fees) $1,961, Other Print Mats $9,279, AV Mat $8,068, Electronic Ref Mat (Incl. Access Fees) $3,285. Sal $162,001
Library Holdings: Audiobooks 1,294; AV Mats 4,460; CDs 2,978; DVDs 4,460; e-books 181,600; Large Print Bks 2,440; Bk Titles 41,702; Per Subs 90
Subject Interests: Local hist
Automation Activity & Vendor Info: (Acquisitions) Innovative Interfaces, Inc; (Cataloging) Innovative Interfaces, Inc; (Circulation) Innovative Interfaces, Inc; (Course Reserve) Innovative Interfaces, Inc; (Discovery) Innovative Interfaces, Inc; (OPAC) Innovative Interfaces, Inc; (Serials) Innovative Interfaces, Inc
Wireless access
Function: Accelerated reader prog, Activity rm, Adult bk club, After school storytime, Audiobks via web, Bk club(s), Bks on cassette, Bks on CD, Children's prog, Computer training, Computers for patron use, E-Reserves, Electronic databases & coll, Free DVD rentals, Holiday prog, Internet access, Magazines, Meeting rooms, Movies, Music CDs, Notary serv, Online cat, OverDrive digital audio bks, Photocopying/Printing, Preschool reading prog, Printer for laptops & handheld devices, Prog for adults, Prog for children & young adult, Ref serv available, Scanner, Spoken cassettes & CDs, Spoken cassettes & DVDs, Story hour, Summer reading prog, Tax forms, Teen prog, VHS videos, Wheelchair accessible
Publications: Inside the Alexandria Public Library (Monthly newsletter)
Partic in Central Library Consortium
Special Services for the Deaf - Bks on deafness & sign lang
Special Services for the Blind - Bks on cassette; Bks on CD; Cassettes; Copier with enlargement capabilities; Extensive large print coll; Large print bks
Open Mon, Tues & Thurs 10-8, Wed & Sat 10-4
Friends of the Library Group

ALGER

P ALGER PUBLIC LIBRARY*, 100 W Wagner St, 45812. (Mail add: PO Box 18, 45812-0018), SAN 313-1823. Tel: 419-757-7755. FAX: 419-757-7755. Web Site: www.algerlibrary.org. *Dir*, Kathy Herfurth; E-mail: algerlibrarydirector@gmail.com; Staff 6 (Non-MLS 6)
Founded 1939. Pop 4,200; Circ 11,000
Library Holdings: DVDs 850; Large Print Bks 350; Bk Vols 10,000; Per Subs 1
Automation Activity & Vendor Info: (Acquisitions) SirsiDynix; (Cataloging) SirsiDynix-WorkFlows; (Circulation) SirsiDynix-WorkFlows; (ILL) SirsiDynix; (OPAC) SirsiDynix-WorkFlows; (Serials) SirsiDynix-WorkFlows
Wireless access
Function: After school storytime, Audiobks via web, Bks on CD, Children's prog, Computers for patron use, Free DVD rentals, Internet access, Laminating, Online cat, OverDrive digital audio bks, Photocopying/Printing, Preschool reading prog, Prog for children & young adult, Summer reading prog, Telephone ref
Partic in Serving Every Ohioan Library Center
Open Mon & Wed 10-7, Tues & Thurs 10-6, Fri 10-5, Sat 10-1
Friends of the Library Group

ALLIANCE

P RODMAN PUBLIC LIBRARY*, 215 E Broadway St, 44601-2694. SAN 313-1858. Tel: 330-821-2665. E-mail: rodmaninfo@rodmanlibrary.com. Web Site: www.rodmanlibrary.com. *Dir*, Eric Taggart; E-mail: etaggart@rodmanlibrary.com; *Head, Ref, Head, Teen Serv*, DJ Digianantonio; E-mail: ddigianantonio@rodmanlibrary.com; *Head, Tech Serv, Head, Tech*, Karen Perone; E-mail: kperone@rodmanlibrary.com; *Adult Serv Mgr*, Debbie Mikesell; E-mail: dmikesell@rodmanlibrary.com; Staff 20 (MLS 8, Non-MLS 12)
Founded 1900. Pop 38,827; Circ 429,169
Library Holdings: CDs 3,729; DVDs 1,361; Large Print Bks 6,292; Bk Titles 123,736; Bk Vols 169,123; Per Subs 589; Talking Bks 6,489; Videos 7,932
Special Collections: Original Drawings by Brinton Turkle. Oral History
Automation Activity & Vendor Info: (Acquisitions) Innovative Interfaces, Inc; (Cataloging) Innovative Interfaces, Inc; (Circulation) Innovative Interfaces, Inc; (OPAC) Innovative Interfaces, Inc; (Serials) Innovative Interfaces, Inc
Wireless access
Function: AV serv, Homebound delivery serv, ILL available, Magnifiers for reading, Photocopying/Printing, Prog for children & young adult, Ref serv available, Summer reading prog

Publications: Bibliographies; Genealogies
Partic in Serving Every Ohioan Library Center
Special Services for the Deaf - Bks on deafness & sign lang; Closed caption videos; Coll on deaf educ
Special Services for the Blind - Assistive/Adapted tech devices, equip & products; BiFolkal kits; Bks & mags in Braille, on rec, tape & cassette; Bks on cassette; Bks on CD; Computer with voice synthesizer for visually impaired persons; Copier with enlargement capabilities; Extensive large print coll; Large print bks & talking machines; Large screen computer & software; PC for people with disabilities; Screen enlargement software for people with visual disabilities; Screen reader software; Talking bks & player equip
Open Mon-Wed 9-8:30, Thurs-Sat 9-5:30
Restriction: Residents only
Friends of the Library Group
Branches: 1
BRANCH IN THE MALL, 2500 W State St, 44601, SAN 374-4485. Tel: 330-821-1313. *Br Mgr,* Charlene Duro; Staff 3 (MLS 1, Non-MLS 2)
Founded 1990. Pop 38,525; Circ 95,806
Open Mon & Tues 10-8, Wed & Fri 10-5:30, Sat 10-3:30
Friends of the Library Group
Bookmobiles: 1

C UNIVERSITY OF MOUNT UNION LIBRARY*, 1972 Clark Ave, 44601-3993. SAN 313-184X. Tel: 330-823-3844. Circulation Tel: 330-823-4140. Reference Tel: 330-823-3795. FAX: 330-823-3963. Web Site: www.mountunion.edu/library. *Dir,* Robert Garland; Tel: 330-823-3847, E-mail: garlanrr@mountunion.edu; *Cat,* Cynthia Cirone; Tel: 330-823-6642, E-mail: cironeca@mountunion.edu; *Circ,* Gina Maida; Tel: 330-823-4140, E-mail: maidagm@mountunion.edu; *ILL,* Christine Cochran; Tel: 330-823-6659, E-mail: cochrac@mountunion.edu; Staff 6 (MLS 6)
Founded 1846. Enrl 2,110; Fac 125; Highest Degree: Bachelor
Library Holdings: Bk Vols 185,000; Per Subs 150
Special Collections: Graphic Arts (Shilts Rare Books); Greek & Latin Classics (Charles Sutherin). US Document Depository
Subject Interests: Secondary educ
Automation Activity & Vendor Info: (Acquisitions) Innovative Interfaces, Inc; (Cataloging) Innovative Interfaces, Inc; (Circulation) Innovative Interfaces, Inc; (Course Reserve) Innovative Interfaces, Inc; (ILL) Innovative Interfaces, Inc; (OPAC) Innovative Interfaces, Inc; (Serials) Innovative Interfaces, Inc
Wireless access
Partic in Mideastern Ohio Libr Orgn; OCLC Online Computer Library Center, Inc; Ohio Library & Information Network; Ohio Private Academic Libraries; OhioNET; Proquest Dialog
Open Mon-Thurs 7am-Midnight, Fri 7-5, Sat 9-5, Sun Noon-Midnight

AMHERST

P AMHERST PUBLIC LIBRARY*, 221 Spring St, 44001. SAN 313-1866. Tel: 440-988-4230. FAX: 440-988-4115. Web Site: amherst.lib.oh.us. *Libr Adminr,* Donald Dovala; E-mail: dovalaapl@gmail.com; *Circ Mgr,* Dorene Sweet; *Adult Serv Mgr,* Melanie Presler; *Tech Serv Mgr,* Mary Geer; *Fiscal Officer, Tech Mgr,* Kristin Cioffi; *Youth Serv Mgr,* Nancy Tomek; Staff 12 (MLS 2, Non-MLS 10)
Founded 1906. Pop 22,545; Circ 240,700
Library Holdings: Bk Vols 57,000; Per Subs 142
Automation Activity & Vendor Info: (Cataloging) TLC (The Library Corporation); (Circulation) TLC (The Library Corporation); (OPAC) TLC (The Library Corporation)
Wireless access
Open Mon-Thurs 9-8:30, Fri & Sat 10-5, Sun (Sept-May) 1-5
Friends of the Library Group

ANDOVER

P ANDOVER PUBLIC LIBRARY*, 142 W Main St, 44003-9318. (Mail add: PO Box 1210, 44003-1210), SAN 313-1882. Tel: 440-293-6792. FAX: 440-293-5720. E-mail: info@andoverlibrary.com. Web Site: www.andover.lib.oh.us. *Dir,* Nancy Logan; *Ch,* Elizabeth Paul; *Ref & Ad Serv Librn,* Laura York; *Circ, Fiscal Officer,* Linda Weston; *Cataloger, Circ, Pub Serv,* Cindy Schwenk; *Cataloger,* Denise Stasiak; Staff 7 (MLS 1, Non-MLS 6)
Founded 1934. Pop 7,600; Circ 99,117
Library Holdings: Audiobooks 3,571; AV Mats 1,424; Bks on Deafness & Sign Lang 3; CDs 240; DVDs 349; e-books 783; Electronic Media & Resources 260; Large Print Bks 1,722; Bk Titles 29,726; Per Subs 83; Talking Bks 624; Videos 1,362
Special Collections: Local History Coll
Automation Activity & Vendor Info: (Acquisitions) SirsiDynix; (Cataloging) SirsiDynix; (Circulation) BiblioCommons; (ILL) BiblioCommons; (OPAC) SirsiDynix
Wireless access
Open Mon-Thurs 10-7, Fri 10-6, Sat 10-2
Friends of the Library Group

ARCANUM

P ARCANUM PUBLIC LIBRARY*, 101 W North St, 45304-1185. SAN 313-1890. Tel: 937-692-8484. FAX: 937-692-8916. E-mail: arcanumpubliclibrary@gmail.com. Web Site: www.arcanumpubliclibrary.org. *Dir,* Curtis Schafer; E-mail: cschafer.apl@gmail.com; *Assoc Dir,* Peggy Grim
Founded 1911. Pop 9,000; Circ 68,341
Library Holdings: Bk Vols 54,325; Per Subs 204
Automation Activity & Vendor Info: (Cataloging) Evergreen; (Circulation) Evergreen; (ILL) Evergreen; (OPAC) Evergreen
Wireless access
Partic in Consortium of Ohio Libraries; OhioNET
Special Services for the Deaf - Bks on deafness & sign lang; Closed caption videos; High interest/low vocabulary bks
Special Services for the Blind - Accessible computers; Bks on CD; Extensive large print coll; Home delivery serv; Large print bks; Magnifiers; Playaways (bks on MP3)
Open Mon-Thurs 9-8, Fri 9-5, Sat 9-1

ARCHBOLD

P ARCHBOLD COMMUNITY LIBRARY, 205 Stryker St, 43502-1142. SAN 313-1904. Tel: 419-446-2783. FAX: 419-446-2142. E-mail: circulation@archboldlibrary.org. Web Site: www.archboldlibrary.org. *Dir,* Sonya Huser; E-mail: s.huser@archboldlibrary.org; *Fiscal Officer,* Jennifer Harkey; E-mail: jennifer.h@archboldlibrary.org; *Head, Circ Serv,* Rhonda Kempf; *Ch,* Martie Yunker; E-mail: m.yunker@archboldlibrary.org; *Tech Serv,* Michelle Beck; E-mail: m.beck@archboldlibrary.org; Staff 11 (Non-MLS 11)
Founded 1917. Pop 7,300
Library Holdings: Bk Vols 28,000; Per Subs 110
Subject Interests: Local hist
Automation Activity & Vendor Info: (Cataloging) TLC (The Library Corporation); (Circulation) TLC (The Library Corporation); (OPAC) TLC (The Library Corporation)
Wireless access
Function: 24/7 Electronic res, 24/7 Online cat, Accelerated reader prog, Activity rm, Archival coll, Audio & video playback equip for onsite use, Audiobks on Playaways & MP3, Audiobks via web, AV serv, Bks on CD, CD-ROM, Children's prog, Computer training, Computers for patron use, Electronic databases & coll, For res purposes, Free DVD rentals, Home delivery & serv to seniorr ctr & nursing homes, Homebound delivery serv, ILL available, Instruction & testing, Internet access, Laminating, Magazines, Mail & tel request accepted, Meeting rooms, Microfiche/film & reading machines, Movies, Music CDs, Notary serv, Online cat, Outside serv via phone, mail, e-mail & web, OverDrive digital audio bks, Photocopying/Printing, Printer for laptops & handheld devices, Prog for children & young adult, Ref & res, Ref serv available, Scanner, Senior computer classes, Story hour, Study rm, Summer reading prog, Tax forms, Telephone ref, Wheelchair accessible
Partic in NORWELD
Open Mon, Tues & Thurs 9:30-7:30, Wed & Fri 9:30-5:30, Sat 9:30-1:30
Restriction: In-house use for visitors, Non-circulating, Non-circulating coll, Non-circulating of rare bks
Friends of the Library Group

J NORTHWEST STATE COMMUNITY COLLEGE LIBRARY*, 22600 State Rte 34, 43502-9517. SAN 313-1912. Tel: 419-267-1274. E-mail: library@northweststate.edu. Web Site: northweststate.edu/library. *Libr Dir,* Kristi Rotroff; Tel: 419-267-1271, E-mail: krotroff@northweststate.edu; Staff 1 (MLS 1)
Founded 1969. Enrl 3,000; Fac 137; Highest Degree: Associate
Library Holdings: Bk Titles 20,000; Per Subs 375
Automation Activity & Vendor Info: (Acquisitions) Innovative Interfaces, Inc; (Circulation) Innovative Interfaces, Inc; (Course Reserve) Innovative Interfaces, Inc; (ILL) Innovative Interfaces, Inc; (Media Booking) Innovative Interfaces, Inc; (OPAC) Innovative Interfaces, Inc; (Serials) Innovative Interfaces, Inc
Wireless access
Partic in OCLC Online Computer Library Center, Inc; Ohio Library & Information Network; OhioNET
Open Mon-Thurs (Summer) 8-6, Fri 8-4; Mon & Tues (Fall & Spring) 8-8, Wed & Thurs 8-6, Fri 8-4

ASHLAND

P ASHLAND PUBLIC LIBRARY, 224 Claremont Ave, 44805. SAN 313-1920. Tel: 419-289-8188. FAX: 419-281-8552. Web Site: www.ashland.lib.oh.us. *Dir,* Heather Miller; E-mail: hmiller@ashland.lib.oh.us; *Support Serv Mgr,* Katie Buttrey; E-mail: kbuttrey@ashland.lib.oh.us; *Pub Serv Mgr,* Stella Metcalf; E-mail: smetcalf@ashland.lib.oh.us; *Commun Engagement Mgr,* Lindsay

Brandon-Smith; E-mail: lbrandon-smith@ashland.lib.oh.us; Staff 5 (Non-MLS 5)
Founded 1893. Pop 53,484; Circ 511,753
Library Holdings: Audiobooks 4,146; Braille Volumes 14; CDs 3,087; DVDs 21,406; Large Print Bks 4,612; Bk Vols 65,441; Per Subs 75
Special Collections: Toy Coll; Video Game Coll; Adaptive Toy Coll; Board Game Coll; Canvas Bags
Subject Interests: Genealogy, Local hist
Automation Activity & Vendor Info: (Cataloging) SirsiDynix; (Circulation) SirsiDynix; (OPAC) SirsiDynix
Wireless access
Function: 24/7 Electronic res, 24/7 Online cat, Adult bk club, Art programs, Audiobks on Playaways & MP3, Bk club(s), Bks on CD, Children's prog, Computer training, Computers for patron use, Electronic databases & coll, Family literacy, Free DVD rentals, Games & aids for people with disabilities, Holiday prog, Home delivery & serv to seniorr ctr & nursing homes, Homebound delivery serv, ILL available, Internet access, Life-long learning prog for all ages, Magazines, Microfiche/film & reading machines, Movies, Music CDs, Online cat, Outreach serv, OverDrive digital audio bks, Photocopying/Printing, Preschool outreach, Printer for laptops & handheld devices, Prog for adults, Prog for children & young adult, Ref & res, Ref serv available, Scanner, Senior outreach, Serves people with intellectual disabilities, STEM programs, Story hour, Study rm, Summer reading prog, Tax forms, Teen prog, Wheelchair accessible
Partic in Serving Every Ohioan Library Center
Open Mon-Sat 9-7, Sun 12-4
Friends of the Library Group
Bookmobiles: 1

R ASHLAND THEOLOGICAL SEMINARY, Roger E Darling Memorial Library, 910 Center St, 44805. SAN 313-1939. Tel: 419-289-5169. FAX: 419-289-5969. Web Site: seminary.ashland.edu/services/student-services/library. *Libr Mgr, Theological Libn,* Sarah Thomas; E-mail: sthomas4@ashland.edu; Staff 2 (MLS 2)
Founded 1930. Enrl 250; Highest Degree: Doctorate
Library Holdings: Bk Titles 70,980; Bk Vols 82,212
Special Collections: artifacts; Mary, Queen of Scots (Ronk Coll); Religious Debates (Darling Debate)
Automation Activity & Vendor Info: (Cataloging) Innovative Interfaces, Inc; (Circulation) Innovative Interfaces, Inc; (OPAC) Innovative Interfaces, Inc; (Serials) Innovative Interfaces, Inc
Wireless access
Partic in Ohio Library & Information Network

C ASHLAND UNIVERSITY LIBRARY*, 509 College Ave, 44805-3796. SAN 355-5186. Tel: 419-289-5400. Reference Tel: 419-289-5402. FAX: 419-289-5422. E-mail: library@ashland.edu. Web Site: www.ashland.edu/administration/library. *Interim Dir,* Scott Savage; Tel: 419-289-5410, E-mail: ssavage2@ashland.edu; *Head, Circ & Reserves,* Judi Humphrey; E-mail: jhumphre@ashland.edu; *Head, Instruction Serv,* Diane Schrecker; Tel: 419-289-5402, E-mail: dschreck@ashland.edu; *Instruction & Ref Libn,* Jeffrey Pinkham; Tel: 419-289-5407, E-mail: jpinkham@ashland.edu; *Instruction & Ref Libn,* Anita Slack; Tel: 419-289-5427, E-mail: aslack3@ashland.edu; *Tech Serv Libn,* Chloe Bragg; Tel: 419-289-5409, E-mail: cbragg@ashland.edu; *Univ Archivist,* David Roepke; Tel: 419-289-5433, E-mail: droepke@ashland.edu; Staff 8 (MLS 6, Non-MLS 2)
Founded 1878. Enrl 5,979; Fac 257; Highest Degree: Doctorate
Library Holdings: CDs 2,186; DVDs 618; e-books 249,000; e-journals 114,007; Bk Titles 174,296; Bk Vols 202,533; Per Subs 280
Special Collections: 19th Century English Literature (Andrews Special Books Coll), 1st editions; 19th Century Historical Children's Literature (Lulu Wood Coll), 1st editions; American Studies (Libr of American Civilization), microbk; Bibles. State Document Depository; US Document Depository
Subject Interests: Art, Chem, Criminal justice, Econ, Educ, Geol, Health educ, Human serv home econ, Math, Music, Philos, Physics, Radio-TV, Relig, Speech comm, Theatre, Toxicology
Automation Activity & Vendor Info: (Cataloging) Innovative Interfaces, Inc; (Circulation) Innovative Interfaces, Inc; (OPAC) Innovative Interfaces, Inc
Wireless access
Publications: Friends of Library (Newsletter)
Partic in OCLC Online Computer Library Center, Inc; Ohio Library & Information Network; OhioNET
Open Mon-Thurs 7:45am-11pm, Fri 7:45-5, Sat Noon-4, Sun 1-11
Friends of the Library Group

ASHLEY

P WORNSTAFF MEMORIAL PUBLIC LIBRARY*, 302 E High St, 43003. SAN 313-1947. Tel: 740-747-2085. FAX: 740-747-2085. E-mail: wornstaff@gmail.com. Web Site: www.wornstafflibrary.com. *Dir,* Amee Sword; *Ch,* Megan Johnson; Staff 6 (MLS 1, Non-MLS 5)
Founded 1928. Pop 2,500; Circ 32,434
Library Holdings: AV Mats 3,885; Large Print Bks 1,016; Bk Vols 35,535; Per Subs 105; Talking Bks 367
Subject Interests: Local hist, Mysteries, Old westerns
Automation Activity & Vendor Info: (Cataloging) Evergreen; (Circulation) Evergreen; (OPAC) Evergreen
Wireless access
Function: After school storytime, Art programs, Audiobks via web, AV serv, Bks on CD, Children's prog, Computer training, Computers for patron use, Electronic databases & coll, Free DVD rentals, Holiday prog, Home delivery & serv to seniorr ctr & nursing homes, Homebound delivery serv, ILL available, Internet access, Magazines, Movies, Music CDs, Notary serv, Online cat, Online ref, Outreach serv, OverDrive digital audio bks, Photocopying/Printing, Preschool outreach, Preschool reading prog, Printer for laptops & handheld devices, Prog for adults, Prog for children & young adult, Ref serv available, Scanner, STEM programs, Story hour, Summer reading prog, Tax forms, Teen prog, Telephone ref, Wheelchair accessible, Workshops
Publications: Newsletter (Monthly)
Partic in Consortium of Ohio Libraries; Ohio Public Library Information Network
Open Mon-Fri 10-8, Sat 10-5

ASHTABULA

P ASHTABULA COUNTY DISTRICT LIBRARY*, 4335 Park Ave, 44004. SAN 355-5305. Tel: 440-997-9341. FAX: 440-992-7714. Administration FAX: 440-998-1198. E-mail: AskUs@acdl.info. Web Site: www.acdl.info. *Dep Fiscal Officer, Dir,* Penny Neubauer; Tel: 440-997-9341, Ext 322, E-mail: pneubauer@acdl.info; *Fiscal Officer,* Edward Williams; Tel: 440-997-9343, Ext 322, E-mail: ewilliams@acdl.info; *Mkt/Pub Relations Coordr,* Rebecca Moisio; Tel: 440-997-9343, Ext 333, E-mail: rmoisio@acdl.info; Staff 30.6 (MLS 8.6, Non-MLS 22)
Founded 1813. Circ 303,319
Jan 2019-Dec 2019 Income (Main & Associated Libraries) $2,665,362, State $1,410,300, Locally Generated Income $1,109,729, Other $41,086. Mats Exp $260,136, Books $112,381, Per/Ser (Incl. Access Fees) $13,407, Manu Arch $133, Micro $3,600, AV Mat $55,308, Electronic Ref Mat (Incl. Access Fees) $78,906. Sal $990,601
Library Holdings: AV Mats 17,909; e-books 341,925; Bk Vols 105,354; Per Subs 168
Special Collections: Edith R. Morrison & Mary W. Morrison Genealogy & Archive Room Coll. State Document Depository
Subject Interests: Genealogy, Local hist
Automation Activity & Vendor Info: (Acquisitions) SirsiDynix; (Cataloging) SirsiDynix; (Circulation) SirsiDynix; (ILL) OCLC WorldShare Interlibrary Loan; (OPAC) SirsiDynix
Wireless access
Function: 24/7 Electronic res, 24/7 Online cat, Activity rm, Archival coll, Art exhibits, Art programs, Audio & video playback equip for onsite use, Audiobks via web, AV serv, Bks on CD, Butterfly Garden, Children's prog, Computer training, Computers for patron use, Digital talking bks, E-Readers, E-Reserves, Electronic databases & coll, Free DVD rentals, Genealogy discussion group, Govt ref serv, Health sci info serv, Holiday prog, Home delivery & serv to seniorr ctr & nursing homes, Homebound delivery serv, ILL available, Internet access, Laminating, Learning ctr, Life-long learning prog for all ages, Magazines, Magnifiers for reading, Mail & tel request accepted, Makerspace, Meeting rooms, Microfiche/film & reading machines, Movies, Music CDs, Notary serv, Online cat, Outreach serv, Outside serv via phone, mail, e-mail & web, OverDrive digital audio bks, Photocopying/Printing, Preschool outreach, Preschool reading prog, Printer for laptops & handheld devices, Prog for adults, Prog for children & young adult, Ref & res, Ref serv available, Res assist avail, Res libr, Scanner, Senior outreach, Spanish lang bks, Spoken cassettes & CDs, STEM programs, Story hour, Study rm, Summer reading prog, Tax forms, Teen prog, Telephone ref, Visual arts prog, Wheelchair accessible, Writing prog
Publications: (Your) Library Matters (Quarterly)
Partic in Northeast Ohio Regional Library System; OhioNET; Serving Every Ohioan Library Center
Special Services for the Deaf - Closed caption videos
Special Services for the Blind - Aids for in-house use; Bks on CD; Copier with enlargement capabilities; Extensive large print coll; Home delivery serv; HP Scan Jet with photo-finish software; Large print bks; Lending of low vision aids; Low vision equip; Magnifiers; Merlin electronic magnifier reader; Open bk software on pub access PC; Photo duplicator for making large print; Recorded bks; Ref serv; Talking bks from Braille Inst
Open Mon-Thurs 9-8:30, Fri 9-6, Sat 9-5
Friends of the Library Group
Branches: 1
GENEVA PUBLIC LIBRARY, 860 Sherman St, Geneva, 44041, SAN 355-533X. Tel: 440-466-4521. FAX: 440-466-0162. *Br Mgr,* Ryan Whelpley; E-mail: rwhelpley@acdl.info; Staff 13 (MLS 1, Non-MLS 12)
Founded 1832

Special Collections: Archie Bell Materials; Leander Lyon Coll; Mary Louise Legaza Room; Platt R Spencer Materials
Function: 24/7 Electronic res, 24/7 Online cat, Activity rm, Art programs, Audio & video playback equip for onsite use, Audiobks via web, Bilingual assistance for Spanish patrons, Bks on CD, Children's prog, Computer training, Computers for patron use, Digital talking bks, Electronic databases & coll, Free DVD rentals, Holiday prog, Home delivery & serv to seniorr ctr & nursing homes, Homebound delivery serv, ILL available, Internet access, Laminating, Life-long learning prog for all ages, Magnifiers for reading, Mail & tel request accepted, Meeting rooms, Movies, Music CDs, Notary serv, Online cat, Online info literacy tutorials on the web & in blackboard, Online ref, Outreach serv, Outside serv via phone, mail, e-mail & web, OverDrive digital audio bks, Photocopying/Printing, Preschool outreach, Printer for laptops & handheld devices, Prog for adults, Prog for children & young adult, Ref & res, Ref serv available, Res assist avail, Scanner, Spanish lang bks, STEM programs, Story hour, Summer reading prog, Tax forms, Teen prog, Telephone ref, Visual arts prog, Wheelchair accessible, Workshops
Open Mon-Thurs 9-8:30, Fri 9-6, Sat 9-5
Friends of the Library Group

P HARBOR-TOPKY MEMORIAL LIBRARY*, 1633 Walnut Blvd, 44004. SAN 313-1963. Tel: 440-964-9645. FAX: 440-964-6701. Web Site: www.harbortopky.lib.oh.us. *Dir,* Joseph Zappitello; E-mail: joe.zappitello@harbortopky.lib.oh.us; *Head, Ref & Adult Serv,* Andy Pochatko; E-mail: andy.pochatko@harbortopky.lib.oh.us; *Head, Youth Serv,* Kathy Eames; E-mail: kathy.eames@harbortopky.lib.oh.us; Staff 11 (MLS 3, Non-MLS 8)
Founded 1924. Pop 4,200; Circ 150,009
Library Holdings: AV Mats 7,135; CDs 2,608; Bk Vols 50,364; Per Subs 126
Automation Activity & Vendor Info: (Acquisitions) Horizon; (Cataloging) LibLime; (Circulation) LibLime; (ILL) SirsiDynix; (OPAC) Horizon
Wireless access
Function: Homebound delivery serv, ILL available, Photocopying/Printing, Prog for adults, Prog for children & young adult, Ref serv available, Summer reading prog
Partic in Coun of Ashtabula County Librs; Northeastern Ohio Libr Asn
Open Mon-Thurs 10-8, Fri 10-6
Friends of the Library Group

C KENT STATE UNIVERSITY, Ashtabula Campus Library, 3300 Lake Rd, 44004-2316. SAN 313-1955. Tel: 440-964-4239. FAX: 440-964-4271. E-mail: ksualibrary@kent.edu. Web Site: www.kent.edu/ashtabula/library. *Dir,* Amy Thomas; Tel: 440-964-4237, E-mail: aaiello@kent.edu; Staff 3 (MLS 1, Non-MLS 2)
Founded 1961. Enrl 706; Fac 32
Library Holdings: Bk Vols 55,000; Per Subs 120
Wireless access
Open Mon-Thurs 8-4, Fri 8-1

ATHENS

C OHIO UNIVERSITY LIBRARIES*, Vernon R Alden Library, 30 Park Pl, 45701. SAN 355-5429. Tel: 740-593-2702. Circulation Tel: 740-593-2695. Interlibrary Loan Service Tel: 740-593-2691. Reference Tel: 740-593-2699. FAX: 740-593-2708. Reference FAX: 740-593-0138. Web Site: www.library.ohio.edu. *Dean of Libr,* Scott Seaman; Tel: 740-593-2705, E-mail: seaman@ohio.edu; *Asst Dean for Res Serv,* Kelly Broughton; Tel: 740-593-2709, E-mail: broughtk@ohio.edu; Staff 103.8 (MLS 51.8, Non-MLS 52)
Founded 1804. Enrl 20,461; Fac 1,188; Highest Degree: Doctorate
Library Holdings: AV Mats 86,574; Bk Vols 2,468,497; Per Subs 25,557
Special Collections: Cornelius Ryan World War II Papers; E W Scripps Papers; George Voinovich Papers; Morgan History of Chemistry Coll; Nikolais/Louis Dance Coll; Romantic & Georgian Literature (Edmund Blunden Coll); Southeast Asia Coll. State Document Depository; UN Document Depository; US Document Depository
Automation Activity & Vendor Info: (Acquisitions) Innovative Interfaces, Inc; (Cataloging) Innovative Interfaces, Inc; (Circulation) Innovative Interfaces, Inc; (Course Reserve) Innovative Interfaces, Inc; (ILL) OCLC; (Media Booking) Innovative Interfaces, Inc; (OPAC) Innovative Interfaces, Inc; (Serials) Innovative Interfaces, Inc
Wireless access
Publications: Gatherings
Partic in OCLC Online Computer Library Center, Inc
Special Services for the Deaf - Staff with knowledge of sign lang
Special Services for the Blind - Computer with voice synthesizer for visually impaired persons
Open Mon-Thurs 8am-Midnight, Fri 8am-10pm, Sat 10-7, Sun Noon-Midnight
Friends of the Library Group

Departmental Libraries:
MAHN CENTER FOR ARCHIVES & SPECIAL COLLECTIONS, Vernon R Alden Library, 30 Park Pl, Fifth Flr, 45701-2978. Tel: 740-593-2710. FAX: 740-593-2708. *Rec Mgr, Univ Archivist,* William Kimok; Tel: 740-593-2712, E-mail: kimok@ohio.edu; *Archivist/Librn,* Sara Harrington; E-mail: harrings@ohio.edu; *Spec Coll Librn,* Stacey Lavender; E-mail: lavendes@ohio.edu; Staff 6 (MLS 5, Non-MLS 1)
Founded 1963
Library Holdings: Bk Vols 54,000; Per Subs 115
Subject Interests: Georgian lit, Hist of chem, Journalism, Performing arts, Romantic, World War II
Open Mon-Fri 9-5, Sat 12-4
Friends of the Library Group
MUSIC-DANCE, Robert Gidden Hall, Fifth Flr, 45701-2978. Tel: 740-593-4255. FAX: 740-593-9190. *Libr Spec,* Carla Williams; E-mail: williac3@ohio.edu
Library Holdings: CDs 10,000; Music Scores 30,000; Bk Vols 50,000; Videos 1,500
Special Collections: LP Record Coll; Microfiche/Microfilm
Open Mon-Thurs (Winter) 8am-11pm, Fri 8-6, Sat 12-6, Sun 1-11; Mon-Fri (Summer) 8-5
Friends of the Library Group

ATTICA

P SENECA EAST PUBLIC LIBRARY, 14 N Main St, 44807. (Mail add: PO Box 572, 44807-0572), SAN 313-1971. Tel: 419-426-3825. FAX: 419-426-3701. Web Site: senecaeastlibrary.org. *Dir,* Shannon Featheringil; Tel: 419-426-8205, E-mail: feathesh@senecaeastlibrary.org; Staff 2 (MLS 1, Non-MLS 1)
Founded 1924. Pop 5,200; Circ 63,000
Library Holdings: AV Mats 4,005; Bk Titles 33,044; Per Subs 99
Special Collections: Attica Area Historical Room (Attica Area Museum); Attica Area Local History (Archives)
Automation Activity & Vendor Info: (Acquisitions) SirsiDynix; (Cataloging) SirsiDynix; (Circulation) SirsiDynix; (Course Reserve) SirsiDynix; (ILL) SirsiDynix; (OPAC) SirsiDynix; (Serials) SirsiDynix
Wireless access
Function: Adult bk club, After school storytime, Audio & video playback equip for onsite use, Bk club(s), CD-ROM, Doc delivery serv, Electronic databases & coll, Home delivery & serv to seniorr ctr & nursing homes, ILL available, Internet access, Music CDs, Online ref, Orientations, Outside serv via phone, mail, e-mail & web, Photocopying/Printing, Preschool outreach, Prog for children & young adult, Ref & res, Ref serv available, Spoken cassettes & CDs, Spoken cassettes & DVDs, Summer reading prog, Tax forms, Telephone ref, VHS videos, Workshops
Partic in NORWELD; Serving Every Ohioan Library Center
Open Mon-Thurs 9-8:30, Fri 9-5:30, Sat 9:30-2:30
Friends of the Library Group

AVON LAKE

P AVON LAKE PUBLIC LIBRARY*, 32649 Electric Blvd, 44012. SAN 313-198X. Tel: 440-933-8128. Administration Tel: 440-933-7857. FAX: 440-933-5659. Administration FAX: 440-933-6406. Reference E-mail: refdesk@avonlake.lib.oh.us. Information Services E-mail: info@avonlake.lib.oh.us. Web Site: www.alpl.org. *Dir,* William Rutger; Tel: 440-933-3851, E-mail: wrutger@avonlake.lib.oh.us; *Asst Dir,* Gerald Vogel; E-mail: gvogel@avonlake.lib.oh.us; *Mgr, Ch Serv,* Sybil Wendling; *Tech Mgr,* Nick Kelley; Staff 14 (MLS 7, Non-MLS 7)
Founded 1930. Pop 22,602; Circ 620,000. Sal $1,250,000 (Prof $830,000)
Library Holdings: Audiobooks 5,700; AV Mats 34,000; CDs 9,000; DVDs 19,500; e-books 19,000; Large Print Bks 4,500; Bk Vols 104,000; Per Subs 300
Special Collections: DiscoveryWorks Center; Local History & Genealogy (Avon Lake Coll), bks, doc, flm, newsp, photg, videos. Oral History
Subject Interests: Art, Gardening, Multicultural kits, Pre-sch concept kits, Sci kits
Automation Activity & Vendor Info: (Acquisitions) SirsiDynix; (Cataloging) SirsiDynix; (Circulation) SirsiDynix; (ILL) OCLC FirstSearch; (OPAC) SirsiDynix-iBistro
Wireless access
Function: Art exhibits, Audiobks via web, Bks on cassette, Bks on CD, Children's prog, Computer training, Computers for patron use, Electronic databases & coll, Free DVD rentals, Holiday prog, Home delivery & serv to seniorr ctr & nursing homes, Homebound delivery serv, ILL available, Internet access, Large print keyboards, Magnifiers for reading, Mail & tel request accepted, Music CDs, Notary serv, Online cat, Online ref, Orientations, Outreach serv, Outside serv via phone, mail, e-mail & web, OverDrive digital audio bks, Photocopying/Printing, Prog for adults, Prog for children & young adult, Ref & res, Ref serv available, Scanner, Senior computer classes, Senior outreach, Story hour, Summer reading prog, Tax forms, Teen prog, Telephone ref, Wheelchair accessible
Partic in Northeast Ohio Regional Library System
Special Services for the Deaf - Closed caption videos

Special Services for the Blind - Low vision equip; Playaways (bks on MP3); Recorded bks
Open Mon-Thurs 9-9, Fri & Sat 9-5, Sun (Sept-May) 1-5
Friends of the Library Group

BARBERTON

P BARBERTON PUBLIC LIBRARY*, 602 W Park Ave, 44203-2458. SAN 313-2021. Tel: 330-745-1194. FAX: 330-745-8261. Web Site: www.barbertonlibrary.org. *Dir,* Ann Hutchison; E-mail: ann.hutchison@barbertonlibrary.org; *AV Librn,* Dia Thomas; E-mail: dia.thomas@barbertonlibrary.org; *Ch,* Lisa Gilgenbach; E-mail: lisa.gilgenbach@barbertonlibrary.org; *Ch,* Monica Haney; E-mail: monica.haney@barbertonlibrary.org; *Ch,* Abby Lowe; E-mail: abby.lowe@barbertonlibrary.org; *Ch,* Sarah Massey; E-mail: sarah.massey@barbertonlibrary.org; *Local Hist Librn,* Sarah Hays; E-mail: sarah.hays@barbertonlibrary.org; *Teen Serv Librn,* Sarah Granville; E-mail: sarah.granville@barbertonlibrary.org; *Ref Librn,* Mary Kay Ball; E-mail: marykay.ball@barbertonlibrary.org; *Outreach Librn, Ref Mgr,* Paula Wagner; E-mail: paula.wagner@barbertonlibrary.org; *Ch Mgr,* Alison Huey; E-mail: alison.huey@barbertonlibrary.org; *Customer Serv Mgr,* Melissa Futrell; E-mail: melissa.futrell@barbertonlibrary.org; *Tech Serv Mgr,* Jennifer O'Neill; E-mail: jennifer.oneill@barbertonlibrary.org. Subject Specialists: *Consumer health info,* Mary Kay Ball; Staff 9.1 (MLS 9.1)
Founded 1903. Pop 26,385
Library Holdings: e-books 373,194; Electronic Media & Resources 389,387; Bk Vols 75,025; Per Subs 169; Videos 14,016
Special Collections: Barberton History (William A Johnston Coll)
Automation Activity & Vendor Info: (Cataloging) SirsiDynix; (Circulation) SirsiDynix; (ILL) OCLC; (OPAC) SirsiDynix; (Serials) SirsiDynix
Wireless access
Function: 24/7 Electronic res, 24/7 Online cat, Activity rm, Adult bk club, After school storytime, Archival coll, Audiobks on Playaways & MP3, Audiobks via web, AV serv, Bk club(s), Bks on CD, CD-ROM, Children's prog, Computer training, Computers for patron use, Digital talking bks, E-Reserves, Electronic databases & coll, Family literacy, Free DVD rentals, Genealogy discussion group, Health sci info serv, Holiday prog, Home delivery & serv to seniorr ctr & nursing homes, Homebound delivery serv, ILL available, Internet access, Laminating, Life-long learning prog for all ages, Literacy & newcomer serv, Magazines, Magnifiers for reading, Mail & tel request accepted, Meeting rooms, Microfiche/film & reading machines, Movies, Music CDs, Online cat, Online ref, Orientations, Outreach serv, Outside serv via phone, mail, e-mail & web, OverDrive digital audio bks, Photocopying/Printing, Preschool outreach, Preschool reading prog, Printer for laptops & handheld devices, Prog for adults, Prog for children & young adult, Ref & res, Ref serv available, Scanner, Senior computer classes, Senior outreach, Serves people with intellectual disabilities, Spoken cassettes & CDs, Spoken cassettes & DVDs, STEM programs, Story hour, Study rm, Summer & winter reading prog, Summer reading prog, Tax forms, Teen prog, Telephone ref, VHS videos, Wheelchair accessible, Winter reading prog, Writing prog
Publications: Enchanted Times (Quarterly newsletter)
Partic in CLEVNET
Special Services for the Deaf - Bks on deafness & sign lang; Closed caption videos
Special Services for the Blind - Bks on CD; Copier with enlargement capabilities; Extensive large print coll; Free checkout of audio mat; Home delivery serv; Integrated libr/media serv; Large print bks; Magnifiers; Playaways (bks on MP3); Recorded bks; Talking bks & player equip
Open Mon-Thurs 10-8, Fri 10-6, Sat 10-5, Sun (Sept-May) 1-5
Friends of the Library Group
Branches: 1
COMMUNITY HEALTH LIBRARY, Summa Barberton Hospital, 155 Fifth St NE, 1st Flr, 44203-3398. Tel: 330-615-3105. FAX: 330-615-3103. *Librn,* Mary Kay Ball; E-mail: marykay.ball@barbertonlibrary.org. Subject Specialists: *Consumer health info,* Mary Kay Ball; Staff 1 (MLS 1)
Founded 2000
Open Mon-Fri 10-3

BARNESVILLE

P BARNESVILLE HUTTON MEMORIAL LIBRARY*, 308 E Main St, 43713-1410. SAN 313-2048. Tel: 740-425-1651. FAX: 740-425-3504. Web Site: www.barnesvillelibrary.org. *Libr Dir,* Brandi Little; E-mail: blittle@barnesvillelibrary.org; Staff 2 (Non-MLS 2)
Founded 1924. Pop 12,000; Circ 200,075
Library Holdings: Bk Titles 54,000
Subject Interests: Genealogical
Automation Activity & Vendor Info: (Cataloging) SirsiDynix; (Circulation) SirsiDynix; (OPAC) SirsiDynix
Wireless access
Function: 24/7 Electronic res, 24/7 Online cat, Activity rm, After school storytime, Audiobks via web, Bks on CD, CD-ROM, Children's prog, Computers for patron use, Digital talking bks, Electronic databases & coll, For res purposes, Free DVD rentals, Holiday prog, Home delivery & serv to seniorr ctr & nursing homes, Homebound delivery serv, ILL available, Internet access, Laminating, Magazines, Meeting rooms, Microfiche/film & reading machines, Movies, Music CDs, Online cat, Online ref, OverDrive digital audio bks, Photocopying/Printing, Preschool outreach, Printer for laptops & handheld devices, Prog for adults, Prog for children & young adult, Scanner, Spoken cassettes & CDs, Story hour, Study rm, Summer & winter reading prog, Summer reading prog, Tax forms, Wheelchair accessible
Partic in Serving Every Ohioan Library Center
Open Mon & Thurs 9-8, Tues, Wed & Fri 9-6, Sat 9-5

BATAVIA

GL CLERMONT COUNTY LAW LIBRARY ASSOCIATION*, Clermont County Court House, 270 Main St, 45103. SAN 327-716X. Tel: 513-732-7109. FAX: 513-732-0974. E-mail: cclaw@cclla.org. Web Site: www.clermontlawlibrary.com. *Dir,* Carol A Suhre
Library Holdings: Bk Vols 18,000; Per Subs 88
Automation Activity & Vendor Info: (Cataloging) Sydney; (OPAC) Sydney
Partic in OhioNET
Open Mon-Fri 8:30-4:30
Restriction: Non-circulating to the pub

C UNIVERSITY OF CINCINNATI*, Clermont College Library, 4200 Clermont College Dr, 45103-1785. SAN 355-9149. Tel: 513-732-5233. FAX: 513-732-5237. E-mail: clermontlibrary@uc.edu. Web Site: libraries.uc.edu/libraries/clermont.html. *Libr Dir,* Catie Carlson; E-mail: catie.carlson@uc.edu; *Instruction Librn,* Heather Mitchell-Botts; Tel: 513-732-5271, E-mail: heather.botts@uc.edu; *Pub Serv Mgr,* Natalie Winland; E-mail: natalie.winland@uc.edu; *Tech Serv Mgr,* Penny McGinnis; Tel: 513-732-5206; Staff 4 (MLS 2, Non-MLS 2)
Founded 1972. Enrl 3,000; Fac 170
Library Holdings: AV Mats 1,000; e-books 400,000; e-journals 60,000; Bk Vols 30,000; Per Subs 75
Subject Interests: Career
Wireless access
Function: AV serv, ILL available, Photocopying/Printing, Ref serv available, Wheelchair accessible
Open Mon-Thurs (Winter) 7:30am-8pm, Fri 7:30-4; Mon-Thurs (Summer) 7:30-6:30, Fri 7:30-4
Restriction: Open to pub for ref & circ; with some limitations

BEACHWOOD

R ANSHE CHESED FAIRMOUNT TEMPLE*, Arthur J Lelyveld Center for Jewish Learning, 23737 Fairmount Blvd, 44122-2296. SAN 313-3443. Tel: 216-464-1330, Ext 123. FAX: 216-464-3628. E-mail: mail@fairmounttemple.org. Web Site: www.fairmounttemple.org. *Librn,* Julie Moss; E-mail: jmoss@fairmounttemple.org; Staff 2 (MLS 1, Non-MLS 1)
Library Holdings: CDs 50; DVDs 200; Large Print Bks 50; Bk Titles 18,000; Per Subs 25
Special Collections: Celia Smith Rogovin Children's Library; Jewish Genealogy Society of Cleveland
Subject Interests: Archit, Bible, Feminism, Festivals, Hist, Holidays, Holocaust, Jewish art, Jewish fiction, Jewish philos, Judaica, Theol, Women's studies
Automation Activity & Vendor Info: (Cataloging) Follett Software; (OPAC) Follett Software
Wireless access
Partic in Asn of Jewish Librs

SR SUBURBAN TEMPLE - KOL AMI, Gries Library, 22401 Chagrin Blvd, 44122-5345. SAN 328-3291. Tel: 216-991-0700. FAX: 216-991-0705. E-mail: info@suburbantemple.org. Web Site: www.suburbantemple.org. *Exec Dir, Librn,* Shoshana Nyer; E-mail: snyer@suburbantemple.org
Founded 1954
Library Holdings: Bk Titles 6,000; Bk Vols 6,500; Per Subs 15
Subject Interests: Judaism (religion)
Restriction: Not open to pub

R THE TEMPLE-TIFERETH ISRAEL, Lee & Dolores Hartzmark Library, Jack & Lilyan Mandel Bldg, 26000 Shaker Blvd, 44122. SAN 313-3842. Tel: 216-831-3233. FAX: 216-831-4216. Web Site: www.ttti.org/lee-and-dolores-hartzmark-library. *Archivist/Librn,* Jane Rothstein; Tel: 216-455-1724, E-mail: jrothstein@ttti.org; Staff 1 (MLS 1)
Founded 1896
Library Holdings: Bk Titles 12,000; Per Subs 12
Special Collections: Temple Archives
Subject Interests: Judaica, Local hist
Wireless access

Function: Archival coll, Audio & video playback equip for onsite use, Bk club(s), Bks on CD, Children's prog, Computers for patron use, Holiday prog, Meeting rooms, Music CDs, Prog for adults, Prog for children & young adult
Publications: The Loom & the Cloth
Restriction: Circ to mem only
Friends of the Library Group

BEDFORD

S BEDFORD HISTORICAL SOCIETY LIBRARY*, 30 S Park St, 44146-3635. (Mail add: PO Box 46282, 44146-0282), SAN 328-5057. Tel: 440-232-0796. E-mail: museum@bedfordohiohistory.org. Web Site: www.bedfordohiohistory.org. *Dir,* Elmer Schulz; *Librn,* Paul Pojman; *Archivist, Curator,* Deborah Grubb
Founded 1955
Library Holdings: Bk Titles 12,000
Special Collections: 1876 Centennial Coll; Civil War Coll; Early Aviation; Lincolniana Coll; Local Archives Coll; Photograph Coll; Railroads Coll. Municipal Document Depository; Oral History
Wireless access
Open Mon 6:30-9, Tues & Thurs 10-4

BELLAIRE

P BELLAIRE PUBLIC LIBRARY*, 330 32nd St, 43906. SAN 313-2099. Tel: 740-676-9421. FAX: 740-676-7940. E-mail: bellaire@seolibraries.org. Web Site: www.bellaire.lib.oh.us. *Dir,* Mary Roberts; E-mail: mroberts@seolibraries.org; *Asst Dir,* Mary DeGenova; E-mail: mdegenova@seolibraries.org; Staff 6 (MLS 1, Non-MLS 5)
Founded 1927. Pop 18,000
Library Holdings: AV Mats 3,746; CDs 2,500; Bk Vols 80,000; Per Subs 120
Wireless access
Function: Adult bk club, After school storytime, Art exhibits, Audiobks via web, Bks on cassette, Bks on CD, CD-ROM, Children's prog, Computer training, Computers for patron use, Digital talking bks, E-Reserves, Electronic databases & coll, Equip loans & repairs, Holiday prog, ILL available, Instruction & testing, Internet access, Magnifiers for reading, Microfiche/film & reading machines, Music CDs, Online cat, Online info literacy tutorials on the web & in blackboard, Online ref, Orientations, Outreach serv, OverDrive digital audio bks, Photocopying/Printing, Preschool outreach, Preschool reading prog, Printer for laptops & handheld devices, Prof lending libr, Prog for adults, Prog for children & young adult, Ref & res, Ref serv available, Spoken cassettes & CDs, Spoken cassettes & DVDs, Story hour, Summer & winter reading prog, Summer reading prog, Tax forms, Telephone ref, VHS videos, Wheelchair accessible, Winter reading prog
Partic in Serving Every Ohioan Library Center
Special Services for the Deaf - Captioned film dep
Special Services for the Blind - Recorded bks
Open Mon-Wed 9-7, Thurs 9-6, Fri 9-5, Sat 9-2
Friends of the Library Group

BELLE CENTER

P BELLE CENTER FREE PUBLIC LIBRARY*, 103 S Elizabeth St, 43310. (Mail add: PO Box 336, 43310-9780). Tel: 937-464-3611. FAX: 937-464-3611. E-mail: bellectrlibrary@gmail.com. Web Site: bellecenterlibrary.com. *Dir,* Beth Karshner; *Asst Dir,* Susan Johns; *Librn,* Linda Setty
Pop 2,865
Library Holdings: AV Mats 2,150; Bk Vols 20,415; Per Subs 30
Wireless access
Open Mon-Wed 11-7, Thurs 11-3, Sat 10-2

BELLEFONTAINE

P LOGAN COUNTY LIBRARIES*, 220 N Main St, 43311. SAN 355-5666. Tel: 937-599-4189. FAX: 937-599-5503. E-mail: info@logancountylibraries.org. Web Site: www.logancountylibraries.org. *Exec Dir,* Judith A Goodrich; E-mail: jgoodrich@logancountylibraries.org
Founded 1901. Pop 45,688
Library Holdings: Bk Titles 122,264; Bk Vols 168,864; Per Subs 205
Automation Activity & Vendor Info: (Cataloging) SirsiDynix-iBistro; (Circulation) SirsiDynix; (OPAC) SirsiDynix
Wireless access
Partic in NORWELD; Ohio Public Library Information Network; Serving Every Ohioan Library Center
Special Services for the Blind - Aids for in-house use; Bks on cassette; Bks on CD; Free checkout of audio mat; Home delivery serv; Large print & cassettes; Large print bks; Large print bks & talking machines; Magnifiers; Playaways (bks on MP3)
Open Mon-Thurs (Winter) 9-8, Fri & Sat 9-4; Mon-Thurs (Summer) 9-8, Fri 9-4, Sat 9-2

Branches: 5
DEGRAFF BRANCH, 122 S Main St, DeGraff, 43318, SAN 355-5690. Tel: 937-585-5010. *Librn,* Angela Leatherman; E-mail: aleatherrman@logancountylibraries.org
Library Holdings: Bk Vols 2,900
Open Tues & Thurs 1-4:30, Wed 4-7, Fri 9-12 & 1-4:30
LAKEVIEW BRANCH, 130 N Main St, Lakeview, 43331. (Mail add: PO Box 197, Lakeview, 43331-0197), SAN 355-5755. Tel: 937-842-4144. *Librn,* Elaine Castle; E-mail: ecastle@logancountylibraries.org
Library Holdings: Bk Vols 3,100
Open Mon & Wed 4-7, Tues & Thurs 9:30-12 & 1-5
RUSHSYLVANIA BRANCH, 113 N Sandusky St, Rushsylvania, 43347. (Mail add: PO Box 115, Rushsylvania, 43347-0115), SAN 355-578X. Tel: 937-468-9963. *Librn,* Nikki Johnson; E-mail: njohnson@logancountylibraries.org
Open Mon 3-7, Tues & Thurs 10-12 & 1-6
WEST LIBERTY BRANCH, 117 N Detroit St, West Liberty, 43357. (Mail add: PO Box 702, West Liberty, 43357-0702), SAN 355-581X. Tel: 937-465-3656. *Librn,* Nancy Spragen; E-mail: nspragen@logancountylibraries.org
Library Holdings: Bk Vols 4,850
Open Mon 1-7, Tues & Thurs 9-12 & 1-5:30, Fri 10-12 & 1-4, Sat 9-12
WEST MANSFIELD BRANCH, 127 N Main St, West Mansfield, 43358, SAN 355-5844. Tel: 937-355-0033. *Librn,* Bonnie Brose; E-mail: bbrose@logancountylibraries.org
Automation Activity & Vendor Info: (Cataloging) SirsiDynix; (OPAC) SirsiDynix-iBistro
Open Mon 3-6, Tues & Wed 11:30-4:30, Thurs 11-2

BELLEVUE

P BELLEVUE PUBLIC LIBRARY, 224 E Main St, 44811-1467. SAN 313-2102. Tel: 419-483-4769. FAX: 419-483-0158. Web Site: www.bellevue.lib.oh.us. *Dir,* Patty Marsh; Tel: 419-483-8526, E-mail: patty.marsh@bellevue.lib.oh.us; *Adult Serv Mgr,* Tracy Marr; E-mail: tracy.marr@bellevue.lib.oh.us; *Youth Serv Mgr,* Charlene Tolbert; E-mail: charlene.tolbert@bellevue.lib.oh.us; *Circ Supvr,* Susan Gibson; E-mail: susan.gibson@bellevue.lib.oh.us; *Communications Coordr,* Gary Murray; E-mail: gary.murray@bellevue.lib.ohus; Staff 4 (MLS 4)
Founded 1891. Pop 13,339; Circ 193,968
Library Holdings: Audiobooks 2,238; CDs 3,139; DVDs 4,796; e-books 79,089; Electronic Media & Resources 313; Large Print Bks 1,707; Microforms 306; Bk Vols 62,751; Per Subs 218; Videos 1,001
Special Collections: Genealogy; Local history
Wireless access
Partic in CLEVNET
Open Mon-Thurs 9-8, Fri & Sat 9-5

BELLVILLE

S OHIO GENEALOGICAL SOCIETY*, Samuel D Isaly Library, 611 State Rte 97 W, 44813-8813. SAN 313-5934. Tel: 419-886-1903. FAX: 419-886-0092. E-mail: ogs@ogs.org. Web Site: www.ogs.org. *Dir,* Thomas Stephen Neel; E-mail: tneel@ogs.org; Staff 2 (MLS 2)
Founded 1959
Jan 2019-Dec 2019. Mats Exp $571,876, Books $10,166, Per/Ser (Incl. Access Fees) $557, Manu Arch $1,066, Electronic Ref Mat (Incl. Access Fees) $5,832. Sal $142,459
Library Holdings: Bk Titles 76,514; Bk Vols 80,000; Per Subs 130
Special Collections: County & State Source Material, ms; First Families of Ohio (pre-1820 settler lineage society); Ohio Bible Records File; Society of Civil War Families of Ohio
Subject Interests: Genealogy, Hist
Automation Activity & Vendor Info: (Cataloging) Mandarin Library Automation; (OPAC) Mandarin Library Automation
Wireless access
Function: 24/7 Electronic res, 24/7 Online cat, Archival coll, CD-ROM, Computers for patron use, Electronic databases & coll, For res purposes, Genealogy discussion group, ILL available, Internet access, Magazines, Mail loans to mem, Masonic res mat, Meeting rooms, Microfiche/film & reading machines, Online cat, Online ref, Outside serv via phone, mail, e-mail & web, Photocopying/Printing, Prog for adults, Ref & res, Ref serv available, Res assist avail, Res libr, Scanner, Senior outreach, Telephone ref, Workshops
Publications: Ohio Genealogy News; The OGS Quarterly
Open Tues-Sat 9-5

BEREA

C BALDWIN WALLACE UNIVERSITY*, Ritter Library, 57 E Bagley Rd, 44017. SAN 355-5879. Tel: 440-826-2206. FAX: 440-826-8558. E-mail: libguides.bw.edu/library. Web Site: wwwlib@bw.edu. *Dir,* John DiGennaro; E-mail: jdigenna@bw.edu; *Asst Dir,* Charles P Vesei; E-mail: cvesei@bw.edu; Staff 4 (MLS 4)
Founded 1845. Enrl 3,000; Fac 166; Highest Degree: Master
Library Holdings: Bk Titles 160,000; Bk Vols 200,000; Per Subs 800

Special Collections: Folksongs (Harry E Ridenour Coll); Paul & Josephine Mayer Rare Book Coll; Religion (Methodist Historical Coll) bks, artifacts
Subject Interests: Educ, Hist, Music
Automation Activity & Vendor Info: (Circulation) Innovative Interfaces, Inc; (OPAC) Innovative Interfaces, Inc; (Serials) Innovative Interfaces, Inc
Wireless access
Partic in Libr Coun of Greater Cleveland; Northeast Ohio Regional Library System; OCLC Online Computer Library Center, Inc; OhioNET
Open Mon-Thurs 8:30am-Midnight, Fri 8:30-6, Sat 10-6, Sun 12:30-Midnight
Friends of the Library Group

Departmental Libraries:

JONES MUSIC LIBRARY, 49 Seminary St, 44017. (Mail add: 275 Eastland Rd, 44017), SAN 355-5968. Tel: 440-826-2375. E-mail: jonesml@bw.edu. Web Site: libguides.bw.edu/jones. *Dir,* Paul Cary; E-mail: pcary@bw.edu; *Asst Music Librn,* Timothy Collins; E-mail: tacollin@bw.edu; *Cataloger, Tech Serv,* Timothy Keller; E-mail: tkeller@bw.edu. Subject Specialists: *Music,* Paul Cary; Staff 4 (MLS 2, Non-MLS 2)
Founded 1976. Enrl 4,000; Fac 165; Highest Degree: Master. Sal $121,357 (Prof $62,747)
Library Holdings: AV Mats 15,368; CDs 5,626; DVDs 429; Electronic Media & Resources 100; Music Scores 17,754; Bk Vols 10,692; Per Subs 30
Special Collections: Cleveland Music Therapy Consortium Coll; Mildred Kerschner Music Education Curriculum Center
Subject Interests: Music, Music educ, Music therapy
Automation Activity & Vendor Info: (Cataloging) Innovative Interfaces, Inc; (Course Reserve) Innovative Interfaces, Inc; (ILL) Innovative Interfaces, Inc
Partic in Ohio Private Academic Libraries
Open Mon-Thurs 8:30am-9pm, Fri 8:30-5, Sat 1-4, Sun 2-7
Restriction: Open to pub for ref only

RIEMENSCHNEIDER BACH INSTITUTE, Boesel Musical Arts Bldg, Rm 160, 49 Seminary St, 44017. (Mail add: 275 Eastland Rd, 44017). Tel: 440-826-2044, 440-826-2207. FAX: 440-826-8138. E-mail: bachinst@bw.edu. Web Site: www.bw.edu/libraries/riemenschneider-bach-institute. *Dir,* John DiGennaro; E-mail: jdigenna@bw.edu; *Libr Serv Adminr,* Frank Paino; E-mail: fpaino@bw.edu; Staff 4 (Non-MLS 4)
Founded 1969
Library Holdings: CDs 450; DVDs 6; Music Scores 3,500; Bk Vols 12,643; Per Subs 27
Special Collections: Emmy Martin Coll incl many 1st editions & presentation copies; Hans David's Coll mainly from the Baroque Era; J S Bach & His Contemporaries, bks, ms; Riemenschneider's Bach Coll; Tom Villella's Recording & Book Coll
Subject Interests: 17th Century music, 18th Century music, Albert Riemenschneider, J S Bach, Unpublished papers of Hans T David
Function: Archival coll
Partic in Ohio Library & Information Network; Ohio Private Academic Libraries
Publications: BACH: Journal of the Riemenschneider Bach Institute (Periodical)
Open Mon & Wed 9:30-11:30 & 2-5, Tues & Thurs 9:30-11:30 & 1-3
Restriction: Not a lending libr

BETTSVILLE

P BETTSVILLE PUBLIC LIBRARY*, 233 State St, 44815-9999. (Mail add: PO Box 385, 44815), SAN 313-2110. Tel: 419-986-5198. FAX: 419-986-6012. E-mail: librarylady1971@yahoo.com. *Mgr,* Angela Klaiss
Library Holdings: Bk Vols 26,000
Partic in Ohio Public Library Information Network
Open Mon-Thurs 12-8, Fri 12-6, Sat 10-4

BEXLEY

P BEXLEY PUBLIC LIBRARY*, 2411 E Main St, 43209. SAN 313-4032. Tel: 614-231-9709. Circulation Tel: 614-231-8741. Reference Tel: 614-231-8795. Information Services Tel: 614-231-2793. E-mail: bpladmin@bexleylibrary.org. Web Site: www.bexlib.org. *Libr Dir,* Mr Ben Heckman; Tel: 614-545-6940, E-mail: bheckman@bexleylibrary.org; *Asst Dir,* Kent Daniels; Tel: 614-545-6938, E-mail: kdaniels@bexleylibrary.org; Staff 11 (MLS 5, Non-MLS 6)
Founded 1924. Circ 769,707
Library Holdings: Audiobooks 5,734; AV Mats 31,715; Large Print Bks 5,442; Bk Vols 117,181; Per Subs 173
Special Collections: Bexley Author Coll
Automation Activity & Vendor Info: (Cataloging) Innovative Interfaces, Inc; (Circulation) Innovative Interfaces, Inc; (OPAC) Innovative Interfaces, Inc; (Serials) Innovative Interfaces, Inc
Wireless access
Function: Adult bk club, Bks on CD, CD-ROM, Children's prog, Computers for patron use, Electronic databases & coll, Free DVD rentals, Music CDs, Photocopying/Printing, Story hour, Summer reading prog, Wheelchair accessible
Partic in OCLC Online Computer Library Center, Inc
Open Mon-Thurs 9-9, Fri & Sat 9-6, Sun 1-5
Restriction: Lending limited to county residents
Friends of the Library Group

BLANCHESTER

P BLANCHESTER PUBLIC LIBRARY, 110 N Broadway, 45107-1250. SAN 313-2129. Tel: 937-783-3585. FAX: 937-783-2910. Web Site: www.blanlibrary.org. *Dir,* Chris Owens; E-mail: cowens@blanlibrary.org; Staff 9 (MLS 1, Non-MLS 8)
Founded 1935. Pop 8,920; Circ 96,295
Library Holdings: Audiobooks 2,743; AV Mats 8,004; DVDs 5,261; e-books 307,996; Electronic Media & Resources 394,490; Large Print Bks 783; Bk Vols 54,441; Per Subs 118
Automation Activity & Vendor Info: (Cataloging) Evergreen; (Circulation) Evergreen; (OPAC) Evergreen
Wireless access
Function: 24/7 Electronic res, 24/7 Online cat, Activity rm, Adult bk club, After school storytime, Audiobks via web, Bk club(s), Bks on CD, Butterfly Garden, Children's prog, Computers for patron use, Electronic databases & coll, Free DVD rentals, ILL available, Internet access, Magazines, Meeting rooms, Online cat, OverDrive digital audio bks, Photocopying/Printing, Prog for adults, Prog for children & young adult, Ref serv available, Scanner, Story hour, Study rm, Summer reading prog, Tax forms, Telephone ref, Wheelchair accessible
Partic in Consortium of Ohio Libraries; SouthWest Ohio & Neighboring Libraries
Open Mon-Fri 12-6, Sat 1-4
Friends of the Library Group

BLOOMVILLE

P BLISS MEMORIAL PUBLIC LIBRARY*, 20 S Marion St, 44818-9201. (Mail add: PO Box 39, 44818-0039), SAN 313-2137. Tel: 419-983-4675. FAX: 419-983-4675. Web Site: blisslibrary.org. *Dir,* Elizabeth Fry; *Fiscal Officer,* Sarah Kelbley; Staff 4 (Non-MLS 4)
Founded 1935. Pop 1,799; Circ 24,888
Jan 2013-Dec 2013 Income $121,061. Mats Exp $20,674, Books $11,647, Per/Ser (Incl. Access Fees) $3,623, AV Mat $5,183. Sal $46,221
Library Holdings: Bk Titles 25,569; Per Subs 115
Special Collections: Bloomville Gazette (1928), microfilm
Subject Interests: Seneca County hist
Automation Activity & Vendor Info: (Cataloging) SirsiDynix-WorkFlows; (Circulation) SirsiDynix-WorkFlows; (ILL) SirsiDynix-WorkFlows; (Serials) SirsiDynix-WorkFlows
Wireless access
Function: Bks on cassette, Bks on CD, CD-ROM, Children's prog, Computers for patron use, Free DVD rentals, ILL available, Laminating, Magazines, Microfiche/film & reading machines, Movies, Music CDs, Online cat, OverDrive digital audio bks, Photocopying/Printing, Preschool reading prog, Printer for laptops & handheld devices, Scanner, Story hour, Summer & winter reading prog, Tax forms, VHS videos, Wheelchair accessible
Partic in NORWELD; Serving Every Ohioan Library Center
Open Mon-Wed 11-8, Thurs & Fri 11-5, Sat 9-Noon
Friends of the Library Group

BLUFFTON

P BLUFFTON PUBLIC LIBRARY*, 145 S Main St, 45817. SAN 313-2161. Tel: 419-358-5016. FAX: 419-358-9653. Web Site: www.blufftonpubliclibrary.org. *Dir,* Jessica Hermiller; E-mail: hermiller@blufftonpubliclibrary.org; *Fiscal Officer,* James Weaver; Staff 5 (MLS 1, Non-MLS 4)
Founded 1935. Pop 6,800; Circ 87,000
Library Holdings: AV Mats 2,592; Bks on Deafness & Sign Lang 15; High Interest/Low Vocabulary Bk Vols 159; Large Print Bks 2,021; Bk Vols 32,084; Per Subs 116
Automation Activity & Vendor Info: (Cataloging) SirsiDynix; (Circulation) SirsiDynix; (ILL) SirsiDynix-WorkFlows; (OPAC) SirsiDynix-Unicorn; (Serials) SirsiDynix-WorkFlows
Wireless access
Function: Accelerated reader prog, Adult bk club, Bk club(s), Bks on cassette, Bks on CD, Children's prog, Computers for patron use, Electronic databases & coll, Free DVD rentals, Holiday prog, Home delivery & serv to seniorr ctr & nursing homes, Homebound delivery serv, ILL available, Internet access, Magnifiers for reading, Mail & tel request accepted, Music CDs, Online cat, Online ref, Outreach serv, Photocopying/Printing, Prog for adults, Prog for children & young adult, Ref serv available, Story hour, Summer reading prog, Tax forms, Teen prog, Telephone ref, VHS videos, Wheelchair accessible
Publications: Off the Shelf (Newsletter)
Partic in NORWELD; Serving Every Ohioan Library Center

Special Services for the Blind - BiFolkal kits; Bks on cassette; Bks on CD; Extensive large print coll; Large print bks; Large screen computer & software; Low vision equip; Magnifiers
Open Mon-Thurs 9:30-8, Fri 9:30-5:30, Sat 9:30-2
Friends of the Library Group

CR BLUFFTON UNIVERSITY*, Musselman Library, One University Dr, 45817-2104. SAN 313-2153. Tel: 419-358-3262. Reference Tel: 419-358-3450. FAX: 419-358-3384. Web Site: www.bluffton.edu/library. *Dir,* Mary Jean Johnson; Tel: 419-358-3396, E-mail: johnsonmj@bluffton.edu; *Archives & Spec Coll Librn,* Carrie Phillips; Tel: 419-358-3275, E-mail: phillipsc@bluffton.edu; *Syst Librn,* Kathleen Aufderhaar; Tel: 419-358-3414, E-mail: aufderhaark@bluffton.edu; *Access Serv Coordr, Circ Supvr,* Audra Oglesbee; Tel: 419-358-3271, E-mail: oglesbeea@bluffton.edu; Staff 7 (MLS 4, Non-MLS 3)
Founded 1930. Enrl 1,000; Fac 70; Highest Degree: Master
Library Holdings: Bk Titles 94,451; Bk Vols 156,334; Per Subs 700
Special Collections: Mennonite Historical Libr. US Document Depository
Automation Activity & Vendor Info: (Acquisitions) Innovative Interfaces, Inc; (Cataloging) Innovative Interfaces, Inc; (Circulation) Innovative Interfaces, Inc; (Course Reserve) Innovative Interfaces, Inc; (OPAC) Innovative Interfaces, Inc; (Serials) Innovative Interfaces, Inc
Wireless access
Function: Bus archives
Partic in Ohio Private Academic Libraries; OhioNET
Open Mon-Thurs 8:30am-10pm, Fri 8:30-4, Sat 1-4, Sun 4pm-10pm

BOARDMAN

SR BOARDMAN UNITED METHODIST CHURCH LIBRARY, 6809 Market St, 44512. SAN 372-4859. Tel: 330-758-4527. FAX: 330-758-7348. E-mail: office@boardmanmethodist.org. Web Site: www.boardmanmethodist.org. *Librn,* Mary Lou Henneman
Library Holdings: AV Mats 150; Bk Vols 2,000; Per Subs 10
Automation Activity & Vendor Info: (Cataloging) Book Systems
Wireless access

BOWERSTON

P BOWERSTON PUBLIC LIBRARY*, 200 Main St, 44695. (Mail add: PO Box 205, 44695-0205), SAN 313-217X. Tel: 740-269-8531. FAX: 740-269-8503. E-mail: staff@bowerstonelibrary.org. Web Site: www.bowerstonlibrary.org. *Dir,* Diana Cole; E-mail: dcole@bowerstonlibrary.org; *Fiscal Officer,* Teresa Love; E-mail: tlove@bowerstonlibrary.org; *Librn,* Ruth Albright; *Librn,* Becky Flener; *Librn,* Gerri Toole
Founded 1935. Circ 87,005
Library Holdings: Bk Titles 40,000; Per Subs 100
Subject Interests: Local hist, Ohio, Pottery
Automation Activity & Vendor Info: (Cataloging) Horizon; (Circulation) Horizon; (OPAC) Horizon
Wireless access
Partic in Mideastern Ohio Libr Orgn; Serving Every Ohioan Library Center
Open Mon & Thurs 10-8, Tues & Wed 10-5, Fri 10-2, Sat 9-1

BOWLING GREEN

C BOWLING GREEN STATE UNIVERSITY LIBRARIES*, 204 Wm T Jerome Library, 43403-0170. SAN 355-6026. Circulation Tel: 419-372-2051. Interlibrary Loan Service Tel: 419-372-8726. Reference Tel: 419-372-6943. Administration Tel: 419-372-2856. Information Services Tel: 419-372-8664. Toll Free Tel: 866-542-2478. Circulation FAX: 419-372-0475. Interlibrary Loan Service FAX: 419-372-6877. Administration FAX: 419-372-0188. E-mail: libadmin@bgsu.edu. Web Site: www.bgsu.edu/colleges/library. *Dean,* Sara A Bushong; *Assoc Dean,* Colleen Boff; *Chair, Access Serv,* Andrea Boehme; *Chair, Archival Coll & Br,* Susannah Cleveland; *Chair, Coll & Tech Serv, Coordr, Cat & Acq,* Julie Rabine; *Chair, Libr Teaching & Learning, Coordr of Ref Serv,* Eileen Bosch; *Mgr, Libr Info Tech,* Mark Strang; *Coordr, Electronic Res,* Amy Fry; *Coordr, First Year Experience,* Robert Snyder; *Coordr, Libr Instruction,* Eileen Bosch; *ILL,* Sherri Long; Staff 40 (MLS 20, Non-MLS 20)
Founded 1910. Enrl 19,408; Fac 750; Highest Degree: Doctorate
Jul 2016-Jun 2017. Mats Exp $2,738,938. Sal $3,919,025
Special Collections: Browne Popular Culture Coll; Center for Archival Coll; Curriculum Resource Center; Great Lakes Historical Coll; Music Library & Sound Recordings Archives. State Document Depository; US Document Depository
Automation Activity & Vendor Info: (Acquisitions) Innovative Interfaces, Inc; (Cataloging) Innovative Interfaces, Inc; (Circulation) Innovative Interfaces, Inc; (Course Reserve) Docutek; (ILL) OCLC ILLiad; (OPAC) Innovative Interfaces, Inc; (Serials) Innovative Interfaces, Inc
Wireless access
Partic in Ohio Library & Information Network; Ohio Network of American History Research Centers; OhioNET
Friends of the Library Group

Departmental Libraries:
RAY & PAT BROWNE POPULAR CULTURE LIBRARY, Jerome Library, 4th Flr, 43403. Tel: 419-372-2450. FAX: 419-372-7996. *Head Librn,* Nancy Down; Tel: 419-372-6054, E-mail: ndown@bgsu.edu
Special Collections: Allen & John Saunders Coll; Archives of the Romance Writers of America; E T Ned Guymon Detective Fiction Coll; H James Horovitz Science Fiction Coll; Papers of Noted Fiction Authors such as Ruth Rendell, Joanna Russ, Dorothy Daniels & Marcia Muller
Subject Interests: Comic arts, Comic bks, Leisure, Movies, Popular fiction, Radio, Recreation, Romances, Sci fict
CENTER FOR ARCHIVAL COLLECTIONS, Jerome Library, 5th Flr, 43403. Tel: 419-372-2411. FAX: 419-372-0155. E-mail: archive@bgsu.edu. *Head Univ Archivist,* Michlle Sweetser; E-mail: msweets@bgsu.edu
Founded 1968
Special Collections: Delbert Latta Papers; Lud Ashley Papers; Rare Books (Ray Bradbury Coll); Sam Pollock Labor Coll
Subject Interests: Genealogy, Labor hist, State hist
CURRICULUM RESOURCE CENTER, Jerome Library, 43403-0178. Tel: 419-372-2956. Web Site: www.bgsu.edu/colleges/library/crc. *Head Librn,* Colleen Boff; E-mail: cboff@bgsu.edu
Special Collections: Pre-k through 12 Curriculum Materials
Subject Interests: Educ K-12 curriculum, Juv lit
Friends of the Library Group
MUSIC LIBRARY & SOUND RECORDINGS ARCHIVES, Jerome Library, 3rd Flr, 43403. (Mail add: 1001 E Wooster St, 43403). Tel: 419-372-2307. FAX: 419-372-7996. E-mail: mlsra@bgsu.edu. Web Site: www.bgsu.edu/colleges/library/music. *Head Librn,* Susannah Cleveland; Tel: 419-372-9929, E-mail: clevels@bgsu.edu; Staff 4.5 (MLS 3, Non-MLS 1.5)
Founded 1967. Enrl 19,000; Fac 600; Highest Degree: Doctorate
Library Holdings: CDs 50,000; DVDs 800; Music Scores 65,000; Bk Titles 35,000
Special Collections: New Music Festival; Sound Recordings Archives
Subject Interests: Contemporary music, Popular music, Sound rec hist
Function: Archival coll, Art exhibits, Audio & video playback equip for onsite use, Computers for patron use, Electronic databases & coll, Free DVD rentals, ILL available, Instruction & testing, Internet access, Music CDs, Online cat, Online ref, Orientations, Outside serv via phone, mail, e-mail & web, Photocopying/Printing, Ref & res, Ref serv available, Scanner, VHS videos
Friends of the Library Group

P WOOD COUNTY DISTRICT PUBLIC LIBRARY*, 251 N Main St, 43402-2477. SAN 355-6085. Tel: 419-352-5104. FAX: 419-354-0405. Administration FAX: 419-353-8013. E-mail: woodkids@wcdpl.org. Circulation E-mail: woodcirc@wcdpl.org. Reference E-mail: woodref@wcdpl.org. Web Site: wcdpl.org. *Dir,* Michael Penrod; E-mail: michaelpenrod@wcdpl.org; Staff 41 (MLS 3, Non-MLS 38)
Founded 1875. Pop 60,000; Circ 602,000
Jan 2016-Dec 2016 Income (Main & Associated Libraries) $2,640,205, State $1,407,788, Locally Generated Income $999,959, Other $232,458. Mats Exp $388,198, Books $185,214, Per/Ser (Incl. Access Fees) $8,372, AV Mat $174,420, Electronic Ref Mat (Incl. Access Fees) $20,192. Sal $1,041,581
Library Holdings: Audiobooks 6,589; AV Mats 22,135; CDs 4,332; DVDs 16,764; Large Print Bks 6,653; Bk Vols 147,413; Per Subs 235
Subject Interests: Genealogy, Local hist, Mysteries, Shakespeare
Automation Activity & Vendor Info: (Acquisitions) Baker & Taylor; (Cataloging) SirsiDynix; (Circulation) SirsiDynix; (Discovery) SirsiDynix-Enterprise; (ILL) SirsiDynix; (OPAC) SirsiDynix; (Serials) SirsiDynix
Wireless access
Function: Adult bk club, Archival coll, Audiobks via web, AV serv, Bks on CD, Children's prog, Computer training, Computers for patron use, E-Reserves, Family literacy, Home delivery & serv to seniorr ctr & nursing homes, Homebound delivery serv, Homework prog, ILL available, Internet access, Jail serv, Magnifiers for reading, Notary serv, Online cat, Online ref, Outreach serv, OverDrive digital audio bks, Photocopying/Printing, Preschool outreach, Prog for adults, Prog for children & young adult, Ref serv available, Scanner, Spanish lang bks, Story hour, Summer reading prog, Tax forms, Teen prog, Telephone ref, Wheelchair accessible
Partic in Ohio Public Library Information Network; Serving Every Ohioan Library Center
Special Services for the Blind - Talking bks; Talking bks & player equip
Open Mon-Thurs 9-8:30, Fri 9-6, Sat 9-5, Sun 1-5
Friends of the Library Group
Branches: 1
WALBRIDGE BRANCH, 108 N Main, Walbridge, 43465, SAN 355-614X. Tel: 419-666-9900. FAX: 419-666-8217. *Br Supvr,* Matt Mehling; E-mail: mattmehling@wcdpl.org; Staff 3 (Non-MLS 3)
Founded 1987. Pop 16,000; Circ 41,026
Function: 24/7 Electronic res, 24/7 Online cat, 3D Printer, Activity rm, Adult bk club, Bk club(s), Children's prog, Computer training,

Computers for patron use, Free DVD rentals, Holiday prog, Homework prog, Internet access, Life-long learning prog for all ages, Magazines, Movies, Notary serv, Photocopying/Printing, Preschool outreach, Prog for adults, Prog for children & young adult, Ref & res, Senior outreach, Story hour, Summer & winter reading prog, Summer reading prog, Teen prog
Open Mon-Thurs 10-8, Fri & Sat 10-5
Bookmobiles: 1. Librn, Katherine Lawn. Bk titles 2,532

GL WOOD COUNTY LAW LIBRARY, One Courthouse Sq, 43402. SAN 313-2188. Tel: 419-353-3921. FAX: 419-352-9269. Web Site: www.co.wood.oh.us/lawlibrary. *Law Librn,* Sarah Renda; E-mail: srenda@woodcountyohio.gov; *Asst Law Librn,* Serena Sadowski
Library Holdings: Bk Vols 6,000; Per Subs 40
Open Mon-Fri 8:30-4:30

BRADFORD

P BRADFORD PUBLIC LIBRARY*, 138 E Main St, 45308-1108. SAN 313-2196. Tel: 937-448-2612. FAX: 937-448-2615. E-mail: bradfordpublic@gmail.com. Web Site: www.bradfordpubliclibrary.org. *Dir,* Cherie Roeth; E-mail: ceroeth@gmail.com; *Fiscal Officer,* Dennis Baker; *IT Support,* Scott Besecker; Staff 4 (MLS 1, Non-MLS 3)
Founded 1935. Pop 8,000; Circ 73,041
Library Holdings: AV Mats 2,975; Large Print Bks 300; Bk Vols 34,865; Per Subs 149; Talking Bks 794
Special Collections: Local History Room (Darke & Miami Co Information); Old Newspaper on Microfilm & CD. Oral History
Automation Activity & Vendor Info: (Cataloging) Innovative Interfaces, Inc; (Circulation) Innovative Interfaces, Inc
Wireless access
Function: Audio & video playback equip for onsite use, Bk club(s), Electronic databases & coll, ILL available, Photocopying/Printing, Prog for children & young adult, Summer reading prog, VHS videos, Wheelchair accessible
Partic in Miami Valley Librs; SouthWest Ohio & Neighboring Libraries
Special Services for the Blind - Talking bks
Open Mon 9-7, Tues & Thurs 10-7, Fri 10-5, Sat 10-1

BRISTOLVILLE

P BRISTOL PUBLIC LIBRARY*, 1855 Greenville Rd, 44402-9700. (Mail add: PO Box 220, 44402-0220), SAN 313-2218. Tel: 330-889-3651. FAX: 330-889-9794. Web Site: www.bristol-libraryoh.org. *Dept Head, Adult Serv,* Cheryl French; E-mail: cheryl.french@bristol-libraryoh.org; *Youth Serv Dept Head,* D'Lynn Johnson; E-mail: dlynn.johnson@bristol-libraryoh.org; *Fiscal Officer,* Ida Mansfield; Staff 8 (Non-MLS 8)
Founded 1912. Pop 3,000; Circ 177,710
Automation Activity & Vendor Info: (Acquisitions) SirsiDynix-WorkFlows; (Cataloging) SirsiDynix-WorkFlows; (Circulation) SirsiDynix-WorkFlows; (ILL) SirsiDynix-WorkFlows; (OPAC) SirsiDynix-WorkFlows; (Serials) SirsiDynix-WorkFlows
Wireless access
Function: Adult bk club, Art exhibits, Bks on CD, Children's prog, Computers for patron use, Digital talking bks, Electronic databases & coll, Free DVD rentals, Holiday prog, Laminating, Magazines, Music CDs, Notary serv, Online cat, OverDrive digital audio bks, Photocopying/Printing, Prog for adults, Prog for children & young adult, Ref serv available, Story hour, Summer & winter reading prog, Tax forms, Teen prog
Partic in CLEVNET
Special Services for the Deaf - Bks on deafness & sign lang; Closed caption videos
Special Services for the Blind - Audio mat; Bks on cassette; Bks on CD; Large print bks; Talking bks; Videos on blindness & physical disabilties
Open Mon & Thurs 8-7, Tues, Wed & Fri 8-5
Friends of the Library Group

BRYAN

GL WILLIAMS COUNTY LAW LIBRARY ASSOCIATION*, One Courthouse Sq, 43506. SAN 313-2226. Tel: 419-636-3436. FAX: 419-636-9886. Web Site: www.williamscountyoh.gov. *Court Adminr, Librn,* Kimberly Coller; E-mail: kcoller@wmsco.org
Library Holdings: Bk Vols 8,000; Per Subs 10
Wireless access
Open Mon-Fri 8-4

P WILLIAMS COUNTY PUBLIC LIBRARY*, 107 E High St, 43506-1702. SAN 355-6174. Tel: 419-636-6734. FAX: 419-636-3970. Administration FAX: 419-630-0408. Web Site: www.williamsco.lib.oh.us. *Dir,* Jeffrey A Yahraus; E-mail: jeff@mywcpl.org; *Asst Dir,* Susan K Irwin; *Coordr,* Jane Kelly; *Adult Serv,* Ajay Johnson; E-mail: ajay@mywcpl.org; *Ch Serv,* Vickie Zippay; *Syst Adminr,* Tyson Horton. Subject Specialists: *Local hist,* Jane Kelly; Staff 4 (MLS 3, Non-MLS 1)
Founded 1882. Pop 38,000; Circ 500,000
Library Holdings: Bk Titles 102,000; Bk Vols 120,000; Per Subs 610
Subject Interests: Genealogy, Local hist, Ohio
Automation Activity & Vendor Info: (Cataloging) SirsiDynix; (Circulation) SirsiDynix
Wireless access
Publications: Open Book (Newsletter)
Partic in Serving Every Ohioan Library Center
Open Mon-Thurs (Winter) 9-8, Fri & Sat 9-5; Mon-Thurs (Summer) 9-8, Fri 9-5, Sat 9-1
Friends of the Library Group
Branches: 5
EDGERTON BRANCH, 319 N Michigan Ave, Edgerton, 43517. (Mail add: PO Box 488, Edgerton, 43517-0488), SAN 355-6204. Tel: 419-298-3230. FAX: 419-298-3230. *Br Mgr,* Shanea Herman; E-mail: shanea@mywcpl.org
Founded 1936
Library Holdings: Bk Vols 12,000
Open Mon & Tues 1-7, Wed & Thurs 11-6, Fri 11-5
Friends of the Library Group
EDON BRANCH, 103 N Michigan St, Edon, 43518. (Mail add: PO Box 185, Edon, 43518-0185), SAN 355-6239. Tel: 419-272-2839. FAX: 419-272-2839. *Br Mgr,* Cynthia Jewell; E-mail: cynthia@mywcpl.org
Founded 1936
Library Holdings: Bk Vols 11,000
Open Mon & Wed 10-8, Tues, Thurs & Fri 10-5, Sat 9-1
Friends of the Library Group
PIONEER BRANCH, 106 Baubice St, Pioneer, 43554. (Mail add: PO Box 155, Pioneer, 43554-0155), SAN 355-6263. Tel: 419-737-2833. FAX: 419-737-2833. *Br Mgr,* Rose King; E-mail: rose@mywcpl.org
Founded 1936
Library Holdings: Bk Vols 10,000
Open Mon-Thurs 10-7, Fri 10-4, Sat 10-1
Friends of the Library Group
STRYKER BRANCH, 304 S Defiance St, Stryker, 43557. (Mail add: PO Box 137, Stryker, 43557-0137), SAN 355-6298. Tel: 419-682-5081. FAX: 419-682-5081. *Br Mgr,* Connie Aeschliman; E-mail: connie@mywcpl.org
Founded 1936
Library Holdings: Bk Vols 12,000
Open Mon & Tues 1-7, Wed & Thurs 11-6, Fri 11-5
Friends of the Library Group
WEST UNITY BRANCH, 109 S High St, West Unity, 43570. (Mail add: PO Box 522, West Unity, 43570-0522), SAN 355-6328. Tel: 419-924-5237. FAX: 419-924-5237. *Br Mgr,* Ruth Meyer; E-mail: ruth@mywcpl.org; Staff 1 (MLS 1)
Founded 1936
Library Holdings: Bk Vols 12,000
Open Mon, Wed & Thurs 10-8, Tues & Fri 10-5, Sat 9-1
Friends of the Library Group

BUCYRUS

P BUCYRUS PUBLIC LIBRARY*, 200 E Mansfield St, 44820-2381. SAN 313-2234. Tel: 419-562-7327. FAX: 419-562-7437. Web Site: bucyruslibrary.org. *Dir,* Brenda Crider; Tel: 419-562-7327, Ext 102, E-mail: bcrider@bucyruslibrary.org; *Asst Dir,* Rebecca Wilden; Tel: 419-562-7327, Ext 106, E-mail: rwilden@bucyruslibrary.org; *Ch,* Barbara Scott; Tel: 419-562-7327, Ext 104, E-mail: scottb@bucyruslibrary.org; *YA Librn,* Sherry Seiler; Tel: 419-562-7327, Ext 110, E-mail: sseiler@bucyruslibrary.org; *Circ Supvr,* Susan Keller; Tel: 419-562-7327, Ext 101, E-mail: skeller@bucyruslibrary.org; Staff 4 (MLS 1, Non-MLS 3)
Founded 1906. Pop 26,000; Circ 114,144
Library Holdings: Bk Vols 54,000; Per Subs 125
Subject Interests: Genealogy, Local hist
Automation Activity & Vendor Info: (Cataloging) TLC (The Library Corporation); (Circulation) TLC (The Library Corporation); (OPAC) TLC (The Library Corporation)
Wireless access
Partic in Consortium of Ohio Libraries
Open Mon-Thurs 10-8, Fri 10-6, Sat 10-2
Friends of the Library Group

BURTON

P BURTON PUBLIC LIBRARY*, 14588 W Park St, 44021. (Mail add: PO Box 427, 44021-0427), SAN 313-2242. Tel: 440-834-4466. FAX: 440-834-0128. E-mail: email@burton.lib.oh.us. Web Site: www.burton.lib.oh.us. *Libr Dir,* Kathryn Ringenbach; *Adult Serv Mgr,* Paula Wagner; *Coordr, Circ,* Nancy Carlson; *Tech Serv Coordr,* Rochelle Baker; *Fiscal Officer,* Rebecca Herrick; Staff 10.3 (MLS 2.8, Non-MLS 7.5)
Founded 1910. Pop 10,000; Circ 319,159

Library Holdings: Bk Titles 64,300; Bk Vols 72,005; Per Subs 201
Subject Interests: Amish, Local hist, Ohio hist, Puppets
Automation Activity & Vendor Info: (Acquisitions) SirsiDynix; (Cataloging) SirsiDynix; (Circulation) SirsiDynix; (OPAC) SirsiDynix
Wireless access
Function: Adult bk club, Bks on cassette, Bks on CD, CD-ROM, Children's prog, Computers for patron use, Electronic databases & coll, Home delivery & serv to seniorr ctr & nursing homes, Homebound delivery serv, ILL available, Music CDs, Notary serv, Photocopying/Printing, Prog for adults, Prog for children & young adult, Ref & res, Summer reading prog, Tax forms, Telephone ref, VHS videos, Wheelchair accessible
Publications: Friends (Newsletter)
Partic in CLEVNET; Northeast Ohio Regional Library System
Open Mon-Thurs 9-8, Fri 9-6, Sat 10-4
Friends of the Library Group

S GEAUGA COUNTY HISTORICAL SOCIETY*, Shanower Library, 14653 E Park St, 44021. (Mail add: PO Box 153, 44021-0153), SAN 325-4739. Tel: 440-834-1492. E-mail: info@geaugahistorical.org. Web Site: www.centuryvillagemuseum.org. *Library Contact,* Terri Kwasniewski
Founded 1941
Library Holdings: Bk Titles 2,000
Special Collections: Geauga County, Ohio History, corresp, ms, photog; Hitchcock Family Papers. Oral History
Subject Interests: Genealogy, Local hist
Function: Res libr
Publications: Geauga County Historical Quarterly (Newsletter)
Restriction: Open by appt only

C KENT STATE UNIVERSITY*, Geauga Campus Library, 11411 Claridon-Troy Rd, 44021-9535. SAN 324-4407. Tel: 440-834-3717, 440-834-3722. E-mail: mhricko@kent.edu. Web Site: www.kent.edu/geauga/library. *Libr Dir,* Dr Mary Hricko, PhD; Tel: 440-834-3717, E-mail: mhricko@kent.edu. Subject Specialists: *Assessment, Educ, Quality assurance,* Dr Mary Hricko, PhD; Staff 1 (MLS 1)
Founded 1976. Enrl 1,500; Highest Degree: Bachelor
Library Holdings: Bk Titles 3,000; Per Subs 24
Automation Activity & Vendor Info: (Serials) EBSCO Online
Wireless access
Function: 24/7 Online cat, Activity rm
Partic in Ohio Library & Information Network
Open Mon-Thurs 8-7, Fri 8-5

CADIZ

P PUSKARICH PUBLIC LIBRARY*, 200 E Market St, 43907-1185. SAN 313-2250. Tel: 740-942-2623. FAX: 740-942-8047. Web Site: www.harrison.lib.oh.us. *Dir,* Sandi Thompson; E-mail: sthompson@seolibraries.org; Staff 2 (MLS 1, Non-MLS 1)
Founded 1880. Pop 13,874; Circ 126,168
Library Holdings: Bk Titles 50,537; Bk Vols 50,591; Per Subs 185
Subject Interests: Coal, Genealogy, Local hist
Automation Activity & Vendor Info: (Acquisitions) SirsiDynix; (Cataloging) SirsiDynix; (Circulation) SirsiDynix; (Course Reserve) SirsiDynix; (ILL) SirsiDynix; (OPAC) SirsiDynix
Wireless access
Function: 24/7 Electronic res, 24/7 Online cat, Activity rm, Adult bk club, After school storytime, Archival coll
Partic in Serving Every Ohioan Library Center
Open Mon-Fri 11-6
Branches: 2
CLARK MEMORIAL, 102 W Main St, Freeport, 43973. Tel: 740-658-3855, 740-673-0800. FAX: 740-652-6544. *Br Mgr,* Mary Howes
Library Holdings: Bk Vols 10,000; Per Subs 30
Open Mon, Tues, Thurs & Fri 11-6
SCIO BRANCH, 331 W Main St, Scio, 43988. Tel: 740-945-6811. FAX: 740-945-9515. *Br Mgr,* Kathryn Birney
Library Holdings: Bk Vols 12,000; Per Subs 40; Videos 1,600
Open Mon, Tues, Thurs & Fri 11-6

CALDWELL

P CALDWELL PUBLIC LIBRARY*, 517 Spruce St, 43724. (Mail add: PO Box 230, 43724-0230), SAN 313-2269. Tel: 740-732-4506. FAX: 740-732-4795. Web Site: www.caldwell.lib.oh.us. *Dir,* Belinda West; E-mail: bwest@seolibraries.org; Staff 8 (Non-MLS 8)
Founded 1930. Pop 15,000
Library Holdings: Bk Vols 39,026; Per Subs 162
Subject Interests: Genealogy
Automation Activity & Vendor Info: (Circulation) SirsiDynix; (OPAC) SirsiDynix
Wireless access
Function: 24/7 Electronic res, 24/7 Online cat, Audiobks on Playaways & MP3, Audiobks via web, Bks on cassette, Bks on CD, Children's prog, Computers for patron use, Digital talking bks, Free DVD rentals, ILL available, Instruction & testing, Internet access, Laminating, Magazines, Microfiche/film & reading machines, Movies, Music CDs, Notary serv, Online cat, Photocopying/Printing, Story hour, Summer reading prog, Tax forms, VHS videos, Wheelchair accessible
Partic in Serving Every Ohioan Library Center
Open Mon-Wed 8:30-7, Fri 8:30-5, Sat 8:30-2
Restriction: ID required to use computers (Ltd hrs)
Friends of the Library Group

S STATE OF OHIO DEPARTMENT OF CORRECTIONS, Noble Correctional Institution Library, 15708 McConnelsville Rd, 43724. Tel: 740-732-5188. FAX: 740-732-6478. Web Site: drc.ohio.gov/nci. *Librn,* Julie Hupp; E-mail: julie.hupp@odrc.state.oh.us
Library Holdings: Bk Vols 12,000; Per Subs 40
Automation Activity & Vendor Info: (Cataloging) Autolib Library & Information Management Systems; (Circulation) Autolib Library & Information Management Systems; (ILL) Autolib Library & Information Management Systems; (OPAC) Autolib Library & Information Management Systems
Restriction: Not open to pub

CAMBRIDGE

P GUERNSEY COUNTY DISTRICT PUBLIC LIBRARY*, 800 Steubenville Ave, 43725-2385. SAN 355-6352. Tel: 740-432-5946. FAX: 740-868-1089. Web Site: www.guernseycountylibrary.org. *Dir,* Michael Limer; E-mail: michael@guernseycountylibrary.org; Staff 25 (MLS 2, Non-MLS 23)
Founded 1832. Pop 40,000; Circ 350,000
Library Holdings: Bk Vols 130,162; Per Subs 320
Special Collections: Local History & Genealogy (Finley Coll Room)
Automation Activity & Vendor Info: (Cataloging) SirsiDynix; (Circulation) SirsiDynix; (OPAC) SirsiDynix
Wireless access
Partic in Ohio Public Library Information Network; Serving Every Ohioan Library Center
Open Mon-Fri 9-5:30, Sat 10-2
Friends of the Library Group
Branches: 2
BYESVILLE BRANCH, 100 Glass Ave, Byesville, 43723, SAN 355-6387. Tel: 740-685-2236. FAX: 740-868-1446.
Open Mon-Fri 9-5:30, Sat 10-2
Friends of the Library Group
CROSSROADS, 63500 Byesville Rd, 43725. Tel: 740-432-7536. FAX: 740-868-1038.
Open Mon-Fri 9-5:30, Sat 10-2
Bookmobiles: 1. In Charge, Susie Clark. Bk titles 2,500

L GUERNSEY COUNTY LAW LIBRARY*, Guernsey County Court House, 801 Wheeling Ave, Rm D 301, 43725. SAN 325-4747. Tel: 740-432-9258. Web Site: www.guernseycounty.org. *Librn,* Carla Lenhoff; E-mail: clenhoff@guernseycounty.org
Library Holdings: Bk Titles 15,000
Subject Interests: Fed law, Ohio law
Wireless access
Open Mon-Fri 8:30-12 & 1-4
Restriction: Restricted pub use

CANAL FULTON

P CANAL FULTON PUBLIC LIBRARY*, 154 Market St NE, 44614-1196. SAN 313-2285. Tel: 330-854-4148. FAX: 330-854-9520. E-mail: info@canalfultonlibrary.org. Web Site: www.canalfultonlibrary.org. *Libr Dir,* David Brown; E-mail: david@canalfultonlibrary.org; *Mgr, Children's Dept,* Jennifer Hendricks; E-mail: jennifer@canalfultonlibrary.org; *Circ Mgr,* Janet Deans; E-mail: janet@canalfultonlibrary.org; *Mgr, ILL,* Tracey Hayward; E-mail: tracey@canalfultonlibrary.org; *Ref Mgr,* Cheryl Mullins; E-mail: cheryl@canalfultonlibrary.org; *Tech Mgr,* Phinh Khongphatthana; E-mail: phinh@canalfultonlibrary.org. Subject Specialists: *Tech,* Phinh Khongphatthana; Staff 15 (MLS 4, Non-MLS 11)
Founded 1937. Pop 13,248; Circ 186,686
Jan 2018-Dec 2018 Income $2,013,756, State $553,688, State $553,688, Locally Generated Income $453,190, Locally Generated Income $453,190. Mats Exp $119,451, Books $70,580, Per/Ser (Incl. Access Fees) $7,239, AV Mat $35,632, Electronic Ref Mat (Incl. Access Fees) $6,000. Sal $507,833
Library Holdings: Audiobooks 3,994; AV Mats 516; CDs 2,117; DVDs 7,158; e-books 307,886; Electronic Media & Resources 284; Bk Vols 57,065; Per Subs 3,859
Special Collections: Canal Fulton Local History Coll
Subject Interests: Local hist
Automation Activity & Vendor Info: (Acquisitions) SirsiDynix-WorkFlows; (Cataloging) SirsiDynix-WorkFlows; (Circulation) SirsiDynix-WorkFlows
Wireless access

Function: 24/7 Electronic res, 24/7 Online cat, 3D Printer, Accelerated reader prog, Adult bk club, Archival coll, Audiobks on Playaways & MP3, Audiobks via web, Bk club(s), Bks on CD, Children's prog, Computer training, Computers for patron use, Electronic databases & coll, Equip loans & repairs, Free DVD rentals, Home delivery & serv to seniorr ctr & nursing homes, Homebound delivery serv, ILL available, Internet access, Magazines, Music CDs, Online cat, Online info literacy tutorials on the web & in blackboard, OverDrive digital audio bks, Photocopying/Printing, Preschool outreach, Prog for adults, Prog for children & young adult, Ref & res, Scanner, Serves people with intellectual disabilities, Story hour, Summer & winter reading prog, Summer reading prog, Tax forms, Teen prog, Telephone ref, Wheelchair accessible
Publications: Annual report; Current (Newsletter); Finding Aid for the Local History Collection (Archives guide)
Partic in Serving Every Ohioan Library Center
Special Services for the Deaf - Bks on deafness & sign lang
Special Services for the Blind - Bks on CD; Home delivery serv; Large print bks; Magnifiers; Playaways (bks on MP3); Recorded bks
Open Mon-Thurs 9-8, Fri & Sat 9-6
Restriction: Non-circulating of rare bks
Friends of the Library Group

CANTON

M AULTMAN HOSPITAL*, Health Sciences Library, Aultman Education Ctr, C2-230, 2600 Seventh St SW, 44710-1799. SAN 313-2293. Tel: 330-363-5000. Administration Tel: 330-363-3833. FAX: 330-363-2604. E-mail: Healthsciences.Library@Aultman.com. Web Site: aultman.libguides.com, Library.Aultman.com. *Chief Med Librn,* Krystal K Slivka; E-mail: Krystal.Slivka@aultmancollege.edu; *Acad Librn,* Sarah McGill; Tel: 330-363-3471, E-mail: sarah.mcgill@aultmancollege.edu; *Libr Asst,* Elaine Ott; E-mail: elaine.ott@aultmancollege.edu. Subject Specialists: *Med, Nursing,* Krystal K Slivka; Staff 3 (MLS 2, Non-MLS 1)
Highest Degree: Bachelor
Library Holdings: Bk Titles 4,000; Per Subs 50
Subject Interests: Med, Nursing
Automation Activity & Vendor Info: (Cataloging) Innovative Interfaces, Inc - Millennium; (Circulation) Innovative Interfaces, Inc - Millennium; (Course Reserve) Innovative Interfaces, Inc - Millennium; (OPAC) Innovative Interfaces, Inc - Millennium; (Serials) Innovative Interfaces, Inc - Millennium
Wireless access
Partic in Ohio Library & Information Network
Restriction: Authorized patrons, Authorized personnel only, Badge access after hrs, External users must contact libr, Hospital employees & physicians only, Med staff & students, Open to pub by appt only, Staff use only, Students only, Use of others with permission of librn

CR MALONE UNIVERSITY, Everett L Cattell Library, 2600 Cleveland Ave NW, 44709-3308. SAN 313-234X. Tel: 330-471-8317. Interlibrary Loan Service Tel: 330-471-8319. FAX: 330-471-8655. E-mail: libraryservices@malone.edu. Web Site: www.malone.edu/academics/academic-resources/library. *Acq, Archives, Dir, Libr Serv,* Rebecca Fort; Tel: 330-471-8313, E-mail: rfort@malone.edu; *Cataloger, Electronic Serv, Instruction & Ref Librn,* Kristine Owens; Tel: 330-471-8557, E-mail: kowens@malone.edu; *Circ Supvr, ILL,* Mary-Ann Frischkorn; E-mail: mfrischkorn@malone.edu; *Circ Support,* Kurt Drotleff; Tel: 330-471-8215, E-mail: kdrotleff@malone.edu; Staff 3.4 (MLS 1.8, Non-MLS 1.6)
Founded 1892. Enrl 1,473; Highest Degree: Master
Library Holdings: AV Mats 7,687; e-books 502,662; e-journals 74,606; Electronic Media & Resources 6,945; Microforms 481,969; Music Scores 2,772; Bk Vols 147,665; Per Subs 231
Special Collections: Evangelical Friends Church-Eastern Region Archives; Friends Library (Quakers)
Subject Interests: Soc of Friends
Automation Activity & Vendor Info: (Acquisitions) Innovative Interfaces, Inc; (Cataloging) Innovative Interfaces, Inc; (Circulation) Innovative Interfaces, Inc; (Discovery) EBSCO Discovery Service; (ILL) OCLC WorldShare Interlibrary Loan; (OPAC) Innovative Interfaces, Inc; (Serials) Innovative Interfaces, Inc
Wireless access
Function: 24/7 Electronic res, 24/7 Online cat, ILL available, Internet access, Meeting rooms, Microfiche/film & reading machines, Movies, Music CDs, Online cat, Online info literacy tutorials on the web & in blackboard, Online ref, Orientations, Outside serv via phone, mail, e-mail & web, Photocopying/Printing, Ref & res, Ref serv available, Tax forms, Telephone ref
Partic in Association of Christian Librarians; Ohio Library & Information Network; Ohio Private Academic Libraries; OhioNET
Open Mon-Thurs 8am-11pm, Fri 8-4:30, Sun 5pm-10pm (Winter); Mon-Fri 8-5 (Summer)
Restriction: 24-hr pass syst for students only, Non-circulating of rare bks

S WILLIAM MCKINLEY PRESIDENTIAL LIBRARY & MUSEUM*, Ramsayer Research Library, 800 McKinley Monument Dr NW, 44708. SAN 327-683X. Tel: 330-455-7043. FAX: 330-455-1137. E-mail: library@mckinleymuseum.org. Web Site: mckinleystarkcountyresearch.wordpress.com, www.mckinleymuseum.org. *Archivist,* Mark G Holland; Staff 1 (MLS 1)
Founded 1946
Library Holdings: Bk Vols 10,000
Special Collections: Don Mellett Murder & Trial Records, papers & photos; McKinley Presidential Papers, microfilm; Primary & Secondary Sources Focusing on the Life & Legacy of 25th President William McKinley; Stark County, Ohio History Coll. Oral History
Subject Interests: City hist, State hist
Wireless access
Function: Archival coll, Bus archives, For res purposes, Magnifiers for reading, Photocopying/Printing, Ref serv available, Res libr, Wheelchair accessible
Open Mon-Fri 9-4
Restriction: Access at librarian's discretion, In-house use for visitors, Non-circulating, Not a lending libr, Open to pub with supv only, Open to researchers by request, Open to students, fac & staff

M MERCY MEDICAL CENTER*, Medical Library, 1320 Mercy Dr NW, 44708. SAN 355-6689. Tel: 330-489-1462. FAX: 330-489-1127. E-mail: library@cantonmercy.org. Web Site: www.cantonmercy.org/medical-library. *Med Librn,* Marlene Derrick; E-mail: marlene.derrick@cantonmercy.org; Staff 1 (MLS 1)
Founded 1960
Library Holdings: Bk Titles 1,100; Per Subs 88
Subject Interests: Allied health, Health admin, Med
Publications: Core Reference Collection (Accession list); Journals Listing
Open Mon-Fri 7-3:30

P STARK COUNTY DISTRICT LIBRARY*, Stark Library, 715 Market Ave N, 44702. SAN 355-6441. Tel: 330-452-0665. FAX: 330-452-0403. E-mail: main@starklibrary.org. Web Site: starklibrary.org. *Interim Exec Dir,* Jean McFarren; Tel: 330-458-2706, E-mail: jmcfarren@starklibrary.org; *Human Res Dir, Interim Dir, Pub Serv,* Shanna Springer; Tel: 330-458-2701, E-mail: sspringer@starklibrary.org; *Commun Libr Dir,* Jen Welsh; Tel: 330-458-2743, E-mail: jwelsh@starklibrary.org; *Dir, Commun Serv,* Marianna DiGiacomo; Tel: 330-458-2769, E-mail: mdigiacomo@starklibrary.org; *Dir, Operations,* Josh Harris; Tel: 330-458-2702, E-mail: jharris@starklibrary.org; *Coll, Develop Dir,* Gregory Burlingame; Tel: 330-458-2832, E-mail: gburlingame@starklibrary.org; *Develop Dir,* Paula Mastroianni; Tel: 330-458-2709, E-mail: pmastroianni@starklibrary.org; *Facilities Dir,* Mark Saunders; Tel: 330-458-2685, E-mail: msaunders@starklibrary.org; *Fiscal Officer,* Chris Butler; Tel: 330-458-2690, E-mail: cbutler@starklibrary.org; *IT Dir,* Brad Sayre; Tel: 330-458-3140, E-mail: bsayre@starklibrary.org; *Libr Serv Rep,* Derek Gordon; Tel: 330-458-2712, E-mail: dgordon@starklibrary.org; Staff 165.3 (MLS 54.8, Non-MLS 110.5)
Founded 1884. Pop 240,131; Circ 3,850,000
Jan 2013-Dec 2013 Income (Main & Associated Libraries) $14,203,471, State $6,390,872, Federal $3,720, County $7,225,346, Other $583,533. Mats Exp $1,616,406, Books $793,021, Per/Ser (Incl. Access Fees) $102,793, Other Print Mats $7,880, AV Mat $415,512, Electronic Ref Mat (Incl. Access Fees) $297,200. Sal $6,101,755
Library Holdings: AV Mats 410,546; Bks on Deafness & Sign Lang 202; Braille Volumes 159; CDs 78,516; DVDs 79,425; e-books 100,214; Large Print Bks 26,506; Music Scores 357; Bk Vols 599,293; Per Subs 1,411; Talking Bks 168,151; Videos 86,979
Special Collections: Genealogy, African-American Coll. Oral History; State Document Depository
Subject Interests: Career, Grants
Automation Activity & Vendor Info: (Circulation) Innovative Interfaces, Inc
Wireless access
Function: Adult bk club, After school storytime, AV serv, Bk club(s), Bks on cassette, Bks on CD, Chess club, Children's prog, Computer training, Computers for patron use, Doc delivery serv, Holiday prog, Home delivery & serv to seniorr ctr & nursing homes, Homebound delivery serv, Homework prog, ILL available, Music CDs, Notary serv, Online cat, Online ref, Photocopying/Printing, Prog for adults, Prog for children & young adult, Ref & res, Ref serv available, Senior computer classes, Spoken cassettes & CDs, Story hour, Summer reading prog, Tax forms, Teen prog, Wheelchair accessible, Workshops
Publications: Smart Guide (Newsletter)
Partic in OhioNET
Special Services for the Blind - Bks on CD; Braille bks; Talking bks
Open Mon-Thurs 9-8, Fri 9-6, Sat 9-5, Sun (Sept-May) 1-5
Friends of the Library Group

Branches: 9
DEHOFF MEMORIAL BRANCH, 216 Hartford Ave SE, 44707, SAN 355-6476. Tel: 330-452-9014. FAX: 330-452-8224. E-mail: dehoff@starklibrary.org. *Br Mgr,* Linda Bennett; E-mail: lbennett@starklibrary.org; Staff 5 (MLS 1, Non-MLS 4)
Circ 64,256
Special Collections: Oral History; State Document Depository
Function: Computers for patron use, Photocopying/Printing, Prog for children & young adult, Summer reading prog, Teen prog
Open Mon & Tues 10-8, Wed-Fri 10-6, Sat 10-5
Friends of the Library Group
EAST CANTON BRANCH, 224 N Wood St, East Canton, 44730, SAN 355-6506. Tel: 330-488-1501. FAX: 330-488-2509. E-mail: eastcanton@starklibrary.org. *Br Mgr,* Rebecca Baldwin; E-mail: rbaldwin@starklibrary.org; Staff 3.8 (MLS 1, Non-MLS 2.8)
Circ 85,681
Special Collections: Oral History; State Document Depository
Function: Adult bk club, After school storytime, Children's prog, Computers for patron use, Photocopying/Printing, Prog for adults, Summer reading prog, Teen prog
Open Mon & Tues 9-8, Wed-Fri 9-6, Sat 10-5
JACKSON TOWNSHIP BRANCH, 7186 Fulton Dr NW, 44718, SAN 373-5583. Tel: 330-833-1010. FAX: 330-833-3491. E-mail: jackson@starklibrary.org. *Br Mgr,* Kathy Kibler; E-mail: kkibler@starklibrary.org; Staff 10 (MLS 4, Non-MLS 6)
Circ 301,643
Special Collections: Oral History; State Document Depository
Function: Adult bk club, Children's prog, Computers for patron use, Photocopying/Printing, Prog for adults, Summer reading prog, Teen prog
Open Mon-Thurs 9-8, Fri 9-6, Sat 9-5, Sun (Sept-May) 1-5
Friends of the Library Group
LAKE COMMUNITY BRANCH, 565 Market Ave SW, Uniontown, 44685, SAN 355-6530. Tel: 330-877-9975. FAX: 330-877-7568. E-mail: lake@starklibrary.org. *Br Mgr,* Jennifer Welsh; E-mail: jwelsh@starklibrary.org; Staff 9.5 (MLS 3, Non-MLS 6.5)
Circ 317,744
Special Collections: Oral History; State Document Depository
Function: Adult bk club, Children's prog, Computers for patron use, Photocopying/Printing, Prog for adults, Summer reading prog, Teen prog
Open Mon-Thurs 9-8, Fri 9-6, Sat 9-5
Friends of the Library Group
NORTH BRANCH, 189 25th St NW, 44709, SAN 355-6565. Tel: 330-456-4356. FAX: 330-580-1806. E-mail: north@starklibrary.org. *Br Mgr,* Robyn Guedel; E-mail: rguedel@starklibrary.org; Staff 8.5 (MLS 3, Non-MLS 5.5)
Founded 1960. Circ 330,454
Special Collections: Oral History; State Document Depository
Function: Adult bk club, Children's prog, Computers for patron use, Photocopying/Printing, Prog for adults, Summer reading prog, Teen prog
Open Mon-Thurs 9-8, Fri 9-6, Sat 9-5
Friends of the Library Group
PERRY SIPPO BRANCH, 5710 12th St NW, 44708, SAN 355-659X. Tel: 330-477-8482. FAX: 330-479-0015. E-mail: perry@starklibrary.org. *Br Mgr,* Lisa Szeles; E-mail: lszeles@starklibrary.org; Staff 10 (MLS 3, Non-MLS 7)
Circ 259,599
Special Collections: Oral History; State Document Depository
Function: Adult bk club, Children's prog, Computers for patron use, Photocopying/Printing, Prog for adults, Summer reading prog, Teen prog
Open Mon-Thurs 9-8, Fri 9-6, Sat 9-5, Sun (Sept-May) 1-5
Friends of the Library Group
PLAIN COMMUNITY BRANCH, 1803 Schneider St NE, 44721. Tel: 330-494-3399. FAX: 330-497-0466. E-mail: plain@starklibrary.org. *Br Mgr,* Megan Johnson; E-mail: mjohnson@starklibrary.org; Staff 8.5 (MLS 4, Non-MLS 4.5)
Circ 147,206
Function: Adult bk club, Computers for patron use, Photocopying/Printing, Prog for adults, Prog for children & young adult, Summer reading prog, Teen prog
Open Mon-Thurs (Sept-May) 7:30am-8pm, Fri 7:30-6, Sat 9-5, Sun 1-5; Mon-Thurs (June-Aug) 9-8, Fri 9-6, Sat 9-5
Friends of the Library Group
SANDY VALLEY BRANCH, 9754 Cleveland Ave SE, Magnolia, 44643, SAN 355-662X. Tel: 330-866-3366. FAX: 330-866-9859. E-mail: sandyvalley@starklibrary.org. *Br Mgr,* Lisa Murray; E-mail: lmurray@starklibrary.org; Staff 4.5 (MLS 1, Non-MLS 3.5)
Circ 133,888
Special Collections: Oral History; State Document Depository
Function: Adult bk club, After school storytime, Children's prog, Computers for patron use, Photocopying/Printing, Prog for adults, Summer reading prog, Teen prog
Open Mon & Tues 10-8, Wed-Fri 10-6, Sat 10-5
Friends of the Library Group
MADGE YOUTZ BRANCH, 2921 Mahoning Rd NE, 44705, SAN 355-6654. Tel: 330-452-2618. FAX: 330-580-1807. E-mail: madgeyoutz@starklibrary.org. *Br Mgr,* Kathy Clay; E-mail: kclay@starklibrary.org; Staff 4.5 (MLS 3, Non-MLS 1.5)
Circ 85,992
Special Collections: Oral History; State Document Depository
Function: Adult bk club, Chess club, Children's prog, Computers for patron use, Photocopying/Printing, Prog for adults, Summer reading prog, Teen prog
Open Mon & Tues 10-8, Wed-Fri 10-6, Sat 10-5
Friends of the Library Group
Bookmobiles: 1. Mobile Servs Mgr, Brock Hutchison. Bk vols 97,448

L STARK COUNTY LAW LIBRARY*, 110 Central Plaza S, Ste 401, 44702. SAN 328-5812. Tel: 330-451-7380. FAX: 330-451-7381. E-mail: inform@starkcountyohio.gov. Web Site: www.starkcountyohio.gov/law-library. *Dir,* Kendel Croston; Staff 4 (MLS 2, Non-MLS 2)
Founded 1890
Jan 2019-Dec 2019 Income (Main & Associated Libraries) $569,000, County $174,000, Locally Generated Income $348,000, Other $47,000. Mats Exp $331,000, Books $188,000, Electronic Ref Mat (Incl. Access Fees) $143,000. Sal $111,000
Library Holdings: CDs 185; DVDs 4; e-books 54; Microforms 301,613; Bk Titles 4,100; Bk Vols 24,000; Per Subs 30
Subject Interests: Ohio law
Automation Activity & Vendor Info: (Cataloging) SirsiDynix; (Circulation) SirsiDynix; (OPAC) SirsiDynix; (Serials) SirsiDynix
Wireless access
Function: Electronic databases & coll, Online cat
Publications: Legally Speaking (Newsletter)
Partic in Consortium of Ohio County Law Libraries
Open Mon-Fri 8:30-4:30
Restriction: Circ to mem only
Branches:
MASSILLON BRANCH, Two James Duncan Plaza, Massillon, 44646. (Mail add: 110 Central Plaza S, Ste 401, 44702), SAN 329-3807. Tel: 330-451-7380. FAX: 330-451-7381.
Library Holdings: Bk Titles 107; Bk Vols 2,200
Subject Interests: Ohio law
Restriction: Restricted access

CARDINGTON

P CARDINGTON-LINCOLN PUBLIC LIBRARY*, 128 E Main St, 43315. (Mail add: PO Box 38, 43315-0038), SAN 313-2404. Tel: 419-864-8181. FAX: 419-864-8184. E-mail: yourlibrary@cardlinc.org. Web Site: www.cardingtonlibrary.org. *Dir,* Lisa Murray; E-mail: lmurray@cardlinc.org; *Ad,* Lisa Ebert; E-mail: ebertli@cardlinc.org; *Youth Serv Librn,* Hillary Scholz; E-mail: hscholz@cardlinc.org; Staff 3.8 (MLS 1.1, Non-MLS 2.7)
Founded 1896. Pop 6,516; Circ 36,199
Jan 2016-Dec 2016 Income $250,824, State $231,738, Other $19,086. Mats Exp $40,038, Books $17,290, Per/Ser (Incl. Access Fees) $2,578, Other Print Mats $3,243, AV Mat $6,818, Electronic Ref Mat (Incl. Access Fees) $10,109. Sal $115,565
Library Holdings: Audiobooks 754; CDs 140; DVDs 2,458; e-books 268,789; Electronic Media & Resources 3,189; Large Print Bks 442; Bk Titles 26,720; Per Subs 105
Automation Activity & Vendor Info: (Acquisitions) Baker & Taylor; (Circulation) Evergreen; (ILL) Evergreen; (Media Booking) Evergreen; (OPAC) Evergreen
Wireless access
Function: 24/7 Electronic res, 24/7 Online cat, Activity rm, Adult bk club, Adult literacy prog, Art exhibits, Audiobks on Playaways & MP3, Audiobks via web, AV serv, Bk club(s), Bks on CD, Children's prog, Computer training, Computers for patron use, Digital talking bks, E-Reserves, Electronic databases & coll, Free DVD rentals, Govt ref serv, ILL available, Internet access, Laminating, Learning ctr, Life-long learning prog for all ages, Magazines, Magnifiers for reading, Mail & tel request accepted, Meeting rooms, Music CDs, Online cat, Online info literacy tutorials on the web & in blackboard, Online ref, Orientations, Outreach serv, OverDrive digital audio bks, Photocopying/Printing, Preschool outreach, Preschool reading prog, Printer for laptops & handheld devices, Prog for adults, Prog for children & young adult, Ref serv available, Senior computer classes, Story hour, Summer reading prog, Tax forms, Teen prog, Telephone ref, Wheelchair accessible
Partic in Consortium of Ohio Libraries; Ohio Public Library Information Network; OhioNET
Special Services for the Deaf - Bks on deafness & sign lang
Special Services for the Blind - Bks on CD; Large print bks
Open Mon-Thurs 10:30-7, Sat 10:30-2

CAREY

P DORCAS CAREY PUBLIC LIBRARY*, 236 E Findlay St, 43316-1250. SAN 313-2412. Tel: 419-396-7921. FAX: 419-396-3046. Web Site: www.dorcascarey.org. *Dir,* Laura Toland; E-mail: ltoland@seolibraries.org
Founded 1905. Pop 5,800; Circ 84,328
Library Holdings: Bk Titles 38,000; Per Subs 112
Automation Activity & Vendor Info: (Cataloging) SirsiDynix; (Circulation) SirsiDynix; (OPAC) SirsiDynix
Wireless access
Function: AV serv, Homebound delivery serv, ILL available
Partic in Northwestern Libr District; Serving Every Ohioan Library Center
Open Mon-Thurs 9-8, Fri 9-5, Sat 9-1
Friends of the Library Group

CARROLLTON

P CARROLL COUNTY DISTRICT LIBRARY*, 70 Second St NE, 44615. SAN 355-6743. Tel: 330-627-2613. FAX: 330-627-2523. Web Site: carrolllibrary.org. *Dir,* Ellen Finnicum; E-mail: efinnicum@seolibraries.org
Founded 1935. Pop 28,836; Circ 251,859
Library Holdings: Bk Vols 79,786; Per Subs 200
Subject Interests: Local hist, Sports
Automation Activity & Vendor Info: (Cataloging) SirsiDynix; (Circulation) SirsiDynix; (OPAC) SirsiDynix
Wireless access
Partic in Serving Every Ohioan Library Center
Open Mon-Thurs 9-8, Fri 9-6, Sat 9-4:30
Branches: 1
MALVERN BRANCH, 710 E Porter St, Malvern, 44644, SAN 355-6778. Tel: 330-863-0636. FAX: 330-863-0419. *Dir,* Ellen Finnicum; *Br Mgr,* Amy Matthew; Tel: 330-863-0636, E-mail: amatthew@seolibraries.org
Library Holdings: Bk Vols 55,000; Per Subs 65
Open Mon & Fri 9-6, Tues & Thurs 10-7, Sat 9-1
Bookmobiles: 1

CEDARVILLE

CR CEDARVILLE UNIVERSITY*, Centennial Library, 251 N Main St, 45314-0601. SAN 313-2420. Tel: 937-766-7840. Reference Tel: 937-766-7850. FAX: 937-766-2337. E-mail: library@cedarville.edu. Web Site: www.cedarville.edu/Academic-Schools-and-Departments/Library. *Dean, Libr Serv,* Joshua B Michael; *Dir, Pub Serv,* Kari Siders; *Dir, Coll Serv,* Julie Deardorff; *Digital Commons Dir,* Gregory Martin; *Bus Librn,* Nathanael Davis; *Curric Center Librn,* Sharon Kerestes; *Humanities Librn,* Kirsten Setzkorn; *Info Serv Librn,* Jeffery Gates. Subject Specialists: *STEM,* Nathanael Davis; Staff 20 (MLS 9, Non-MLS 11)
Founded 1895. Enrl 3,961; Fac 260; Highest Degree: Doctorate
Jul 2019-Jun 2020 Income $1,835,727, Locally Generated Income $30,418, Parent Institution $1,805,309. Mats Exp $1,704,144, Books $146,182, Per/Ser (Incl. Access Fees) $515,014, Manu Arch $1,605, AV Mat $5,598, Electronic Ref Mat (Incl. Access Fees) $38,573, Presv $5,566. Sal $840,827 (Prof $467,763)
Library Holdings: AV Mats 12,704; CDs 5,487; DVDs 4,852; e-books 170,003; e-journals 26,872; Electronic Media & Resources 6,016; Microforms 10,644; Bk Titles 153,937; Bk Vols 171,991; Per Subs 571; Videos 158
Special Collections: English Bible Coll; University Archives
Subject Interests: Theol studies
Automation Activity & Vendor Info: (Acquisitions) Innovative Interfaces, Inc; (Cataloging) Innovative Interfaces, Inc; (Circulation) Innovative Interfaces, Inc; (Discovery) EBSCO Discovery Service; (ILL) OCLC; (OPAC) Innovative Interfaces, Inc; (Serials) Innovative Interfaces, Inc
Wireless access
Partic in OCLC Online Computer Library Center, Inc; Ohio Library & Information Network; OhioNET; Southwestern Ohio Council for Higher Education
Special Services for the Blind - Bks on CD; Computer with voice synthesizer for visually impaired persons; Internet workstation with adaptive software; Scanner for conversion & translation of mats
Open Mon-Thurs 7:45am-11:30pm, Fri 7:45-7, Sat 10-7, Sun 3:30-11:30

CELINA

P MERCER COUNTY DISTRICT LIBRARY*, 303 N Main St, 45822. SAN 355-6808. Tel: 419-586-4442. FAX: 419-586-3222. E-mail: contact@mercerlibrary.org. Web Site: mercerlibrary.org. *Dir, Fiscal Officer,* Elizabeth Muether; E-mail: elizabeth@mercerlibrary.org; *Assoc Dir,* Vicki DeBolt; E-mail: vicki@mercerlibrary.org; *Circ Mgr,* Renee Carpenter; E-mail: rcarpenter@mercerlibrary.org; *AV,* Jean Shaw; E-mail: jean@mercerlibrary.org; *Info Tech,* Eric Lochtefeld; E-mail: eric@mercerlibrary.org; Staff 15 (MLS 3, Non-MLS 12)
Founded 1899. Pop 39,000; Circ 240,000
Library Holdings: Bk Vols 98,000; Per Subs 125
Subject Interests: Children's lit
Automation Activity & Vendor Info: (Circulation) SirsiDynix
Wireless access
Partic in Serving Every Ohioan Library Center
Open Mon, Tues, Thurs & Fri 9-6, Wed 9-8, Sat 9-5 (Summer); Mon-Fri 9-8, Sat 9-5 (Winter)
Friends of the Library Group
Branches: 3
MENDON BRANCH, 105 W Market St, Mendon, 45862. (Mail add: PO Box 302, Mendon, 45862-0302), SAN 355-6832. Tel: 419-795-6472. FAX: 614-350-2804. E-mail: mendon@mercerlibrary.org. *Br Mgr,* Leigh Ann Shaffer; E-mail: leighann@mercerlibrary.org
Library Holdings: Bk Vols 5,353
Open Mon & Tues 12-6, Wed 12-8, Thurs 9:30-11 & 12-6, Sat 9-12
Friends of the Library Group
SAINT HENRY GRANVILLE TOWNSHIP, 200 E Main St, Saint Henry, 45883. (Mail add: PO Box 320, Saint Henry, 45883), SAN 355-6867. Tel: 419-678-3128. FAX: 614-350-3440. E-mail: sthenry@mercerlibrary.org. *Br Mgr,* Brandy Staugler; E-mail: brandy@mercerlibrary.org
Library Holdings: Bk Vols 10,721
Open Mon, Tues & Thurs 12-8, Wed 9-5, Sat 9-12
Friends of the Library Group
ZAHN-MARION TOWNSHIP BRANCH, Five E Franklin St, Chickasaw, 45826. (Mail add: PO Box 219, Chickasaw, 45826-0219), SAN 355-6824. Tel: 419-925-4966. FAX: 614-350-2722. E-mail: marion@mercerlibrary.org. *Br Mgr,* Juliana Berning; E-mail: juli@mercerlibrary.org; Staff 5 (Non-MLS 5)
Founded 1982
Library Holdings: Audiobooks 50; CDs 400; DVDs 100; Large Print Bks 100; Bk Titles 11,058; Per Subs 45; Videos 300
Open Mon-Wed 1-8, Thurs 10-12 & 1-8, Sat 9-12
Friends of the Library Group

L MERCER COUNTY LAW LIBRARY*, Court House, Rm 206, 101 N Main St, 45822. SAN 329-8841. Tel: 419-584-2572. FAX: 419-586-4000. E-mail: lawlibrary@mercercountyohio.org. *Librn,* Krista Dickman; Staff 1 (Non-MLS 1)
Library Holdings: Bk Vols 4,000; Per Subs 2
Subject Interests: Law, Tax
Wireless access
Partic in Consortium of Ohio County Law Libraries
Open Tues & Thurs 9-1

C WRIGHT STATE UNIVERSITY*, Lake Campus Library & Technology Center, 182 Andrews Hall, 7600 Lake Campus Dr, 45822. SAN 313-2439. Tel: 419-586-0360. Circulation Tel: 419-586-0333. Toll Free Tel: 800-237-1477. FAX: 419-586-8334. Web Site: lake.wright.edu/campus-life/lake-campus-library-technology-center, www.libraries.wright.edu. *Dir, Libr & Tech,* Jamon Antwain Flowers; Tel: 937-775-8360, E-mail: jamon.flowers@wright.edu; Staff 1 (MLS 1)
Founded 1962. Enrl 763; Fac 17; Highest Degree: Master
Library Holdings: Bk Titles 21,107; Bk Vols 30,000; Per Subs 300
Special Collections: Material on History of the American Frontier
Subject Interests: Bibliog instruction, Mat on hist of the Am frontier, Modern lang
Function: ILL available, Internet access, Photocopying/Printing, Prog for children & young adult, Ref serv available, Summer reading prog, Telephone ref
Partic in Ohio Library & Information Network
Special Services for the Blind - Computer with voice synthesizer for visually impaired persons
Open Mon-Fri 9-5
Restriction: Circ limited
Friends of the Library Group

CENTERBURG

P CENTERBURG PUBLIC LIBRARY, 49 E Main St, 43011. (Mail add: PO Box 609, 43011-0609), SAN 313-2447. Tel: 740-625-6538. FAX: 740-625-7311. E-mail: centerburglibrary.17@gmail.com. Web Site: www.centerburg.lib.oh.us. *Dir,* Tina Michel; *Asst Dir,* Chriss White
Founded 1924. Pop 6,100; Circ 72,200
Library Holdings: Bk Vols 30,000; Per Subs 114
Automation Activity & Vendor Info: (Cataloging) Innovative Interfaces, Inc. - Polaris; (Circulation) Innovative Interfaces, Inc. - Polaris
Wireless access
Open Mon-Thurs 10-6, Fri 10-5, Sat 10-3

CENTERVILLE

P WASHINGTON-CENTERVILLE PUBLIC LIBRARY*, 111 W Spring Valley Rd, 45458. SAN 355-6891. Tel: 937-433-8091. FAX: 937-433-1366. Reference E-mail: libadmin@wcpl.lib.oh.us. Web Site: www.wclibrary.info. *Dir,* D Elizabeth Fultz; Tel: 937-610-4420, E-mail: lfultz@wcpl.lib.oh.us; *Patron Serv Mgr,* Bill Menker; Tel: 937-610-4412, E-mail: bmenker@wcpl.lib.oh.us; *Support Serv Mgr,* Robin Poffenberger; Tel:

937-610-4444, E-mail: rpoffenberger@wcpl.lib.oh.us; Staff 20 (MLS 14, Non-MLS 6)
Founded 1930. Pop 56,607
Jan 2018-Dec 2018 Income (Main & Associated Libraries) $7,817,233, State $2,323,156, Locally Generated Income $5,219,077, Other $275,000. Mats Exp $831,521, Books $517,110, Per/Ser (Incl. Access Fees) $34,095, Other Print Mats $18,249, AV Mat $143,880, Electronic Ref Mat (Incl. Access Fees) $118,187. Sal $3,275,688
Library Holdings: Audiobooks 7,900; AV Mats 51,605; CDs 7,976; DVDs 26,978; e-books 110,470; Electronic Media & Resources 81,140; Large Print Bks 9,782; Bk Titles 202,758; Bk Vols 288,393; Per Subs 422; Spec Interest Per Sub 181
Automation Activity & Vendor Info: (Acquisitions) Innovative Interfaces, Inc - Sierra; (Cataloging) Innovative Interfaces, Inc - Sierra; (Circulation) Innovative Interfaces, Inc - Sierra; (OPAC) Innovative Interfaces, Inc
Wireless access
Function: 24/7 Electronic res, 24/7 Online cat, Activity rm, Adult bk club, Art exhibits, Art programs, Audiobks on Playaways & MP3, Bk club(s), Bks on CD, Children's prog, Computer training, Computers for patron use, Electronic databases & coll, Family literacy, Free DVD rentals, Genealogy discussion group, Holiday prog, Home delivery & serv to seniorr ctr & nursing homes, Homebound delivery serv, ILL available, Internet access, Life-long learning prog for all ages, Magazines, Mail & tel request accepted, Meeting rooms, Movies, Music CDs, Online cat, Online ref, Outreach serv, Outside serv via phone, mail, e-mail & web, OverDrive digital audio bks, Passport agency, Photocopying/Printing, Preschool outreach, Preschool reading prog, Printer for laptops & handheld devices, Prog for adults, Prog for children & young adult, Ref & res, Ref serv available, Res assist avail, Scanner, Senior outreach, Serves people with intellectual disabilities, STEM programs, Story hour, Study rm, Summer reading prog, Tax forms, Teen prog, Telephone ref, Wheelchair accessible
Partic in Ohio Library & Information Network
Open Mon-Thurs 10-9, Fri 10-6, Sat 10-5, Sun (Sept-May) 1-5
Friends of the Library Group
Branches: 1
WOODBOURNE LIBRARY, 6060 Far Hills Ave, 45459-1924, SAN 374-681X. Tel: 937-435-3700. Reference E-mail: wbref@wcpl.lib.oh.us.

CHARDON

L GEAUGA COUNTY LAW LIBRARY RESOURCES BOARD*, 100 Short Court St, Ste BA, 44024. SAN 327-6813. Tel: 440-279-2085, 440-285-2222, Ext 2085. FAX: 440-285-3603. E-mail: gcll@nls.net. Web Site: www.co.geauga.oh.us/Departments/Law-Library. *Dir,* Krystal Ann Thompson; Staff 1 (MLS 1)
Library Holdings: Bk Vols 20,000; Per Subs 100
Wireless access
Open Mon-Fri 8-4:30

P GEAUGA COUNTY PUBLIC LIBRARY*, 12701 Ravenwood Dr, 44024-1336. SAN 355-6956. Tel: 440-286-6811. FAX: 440-286-7419. E-mail: administration.center@geaugalibrary.net. Web Site: www.geaugalibrary.net. *Dir,* Edward Worso; Tel: 440-286-6359, E-mail: eworso@geaugalibrary.net; *Asst Dir,* Kris Carroll; E-mail: kcarroll@geaugalibrary.net; *Head, Tech Serv,* Marlene Pelyhes; Tel: 440-286-6811, Ext 2519, E-mail: mpelyhes@geaugalibrary.net; Staff 106 (MLS 17, Non-MLS 89)
Founded 1963. Pop 84,057; Circ 2,014,026
Special Collections: US Document Depository
Subject Interests: Local genealogy
Automation Activity & Vendor Info: (Acquisitions) SirsiDynix-WorkFlows; (Cataloging) SirsiDynix-WorkFlows; (Circulation) SirsiDynix-WorkFlows; (ILL) OCLC WorldShare Interlibrary Loan; (OPAC) SirsiDynix-Enterprise; (Serials) SirsiDynix-WorkFlows
Wireless access
Function: 24/7 Electronic res, Adult bk club, Online cat
Partic in CLEVNET; Northeast Ohio Regional Library System
Special Services for the Blind - BiFolkal kits; Bks on cassette; Bks on CD; Cassette playback machines; Cassettes; Extensive large print coll; Home delivery serv; Magnifiers
Open Mon-Fri 9-9, Sat 9-5
Friends of the Library Group
Branches: 5
BAINBRIDGE BRANCH, 17222 Snyder Rd, Chagrin Falls, 44023, SAN 355-6980. Tel: 440-543-5611. FAX: 440-543-4734. E-mail: bainbridge.library@geaugalibrary.info. *Mgr,* Kris Carroll; E-mail: kris.carroll@geaugalibrary.info
Open Mon-Thurs 9-9, Fri & Sat 9-5, Sun 1-5
Friends of the Library Group
CHARDON BRANCH, 110 E Park St, 44024, SAN 328-7025. Tel: 440-285-7601. FAX: 440-285-3808. E-mail: chardon.library@geaugalibrary.info. *Mgr,* Judith Smith; E-mail: judi.smith@geaugalibrary.info
Subject Interests: Genealogy, Local hist
Open Mon-Thurs 9-9, Fri & Sat 9-5, Sun 1-5
Friends of the Library Group
GEAUGA WEST BRANCH, 13455 Chillicothe Rd, Chesterland, 44026, SAN 355-7014. Tel: 440-729-4250. FAX: 440-729-7517. E-mail: geauga.west@geaugalibrary.info. *Mgr,* Linda Yanko; E-mail: linda.yanko@geaugalibrary.info
Open Mon-Thurs 9-9, Fri & Sat 9-5, Sun 1-5
Friends of the Library Group
MIDDLEFIELD BRANCH, 16167 E High St, Middlefield, 44062, SAN 355-7049. Tel: 440-632-1961. FAX: 440-632-1407. E-mail: middlefield.library@geaugalibrary.info. Web Site: geaugalibrary.net/newsite/locations/middlefield-library. *Mgr,* Rachael Hartman; E-mail: rachael.hartman@geaugalibrary.info
Open Mon-Fri 9-9, Sat 9-5, Sun (Fall-Spring) 1-5
Friends of the Library Group
THOMPSON BRANCH, 6645 Madison Rd, Thompson, 44086, SAN 328-7041. Tel: 440-298-3831. FAX: 440-298-3921. E-mail: thompson.librarystation@geaugalibrary.info. *Libr Mgr,* Kevin Barton
Open Mon, Tues & Thurs 4-8, Wed 10-8, Sat & Sun 12-4
Friends of the Library Group
Bookmobiles: 3. Mgr, Katy Ferrell

CHESTERVILLE

P SELOVER PUBLIC LIBRARY*, 31 State Rte 95, 43317. (Mail add: PO Box 25, 43317-0025), SAN 313-2455. Tel: 419-768-3431. FAX: 419-768-2249. Web Site: www.selover.lib.oh.us. *Dir,* Suzi Lyle; E-mail: slylespl@gmail.com
Founded 1926. Pop 8,000; Circ 47,896
Library Holdings: Bk Titles 19,460; Per Subs 165
Special Collections: National Geographic Coll
Subject Interests: Local hist
Wireless access
Partic in Consortium of Ohio Libraries
Open Tues-Sat 1-7:30

CHILLICOTHE

P CHILLICOTHE & ROSS COUNTY PUBLIC LIBRARY*, 140 S Paint St, 45601. (Mail add: PO Box 185, 45601-0185), SAN 355-7073. Tel: 740-702-4145. FAX: 740-702-4153. E-mail: crcpl@crcpl.org. Web Site: www.crcpl.org. *Dir,* James Hill; Tel: 740-702-4162, E-mail: jhill@crcpl.org; *Fiscal Officer,* Nanette Clary; E-mail: nclary@crcpl.org; *Br Mgr,* Adrienne D'Souza; E-mail: adsouza@crcpl.org; *Circ Mgr, County Br Mgr,* Teresa Myers; E-mail: tmyers@crcpl.org; *IT Mgr,* Brian Phillips; E-mail: bphillips@crcpl.org; *Pub Relations Mgr,* Debbie Nunziato; E-mail: dnunziato@crcpl.org; *Tech Proc Mgr,* Laura Pinnix; E-mail: lpinnix@crcpl.org; *Spec Serv Mgr,* Mike Jones; E-mail: mjones@crcpl.org; *Team Leader,* Erin Mallow; E-mail: emallow@crcpl.org; *Access Serv, Team Leader,* Julie Retherford; E-mail: jretherford@crcpl.org; Staff 11 (MLS 6, Non-MLS 5)
Founded 1859. Pop 78,064; Circ 571,668. Sal $1,373,907
Library Holdings: AV Mats 17,575; Electronic Media & Resources 29,510; Bk Vols 129,901; Per Subs 116
Special Collections: Burton E Stevenson Coll; Ross County Census Records, 1820-1900, micro
Subject Interests: Genealogy
Automation Activity & Vendor Info: (Acquisitions) SirsiDynix; (Cataloging) SirsiDynix; (Circulation) SirsiDynix; (OPAC) SirsiDynix; (Serials) SirsiDynix
Wireless access
Partic in Serving Every Ohioan Library Center
Special Services for the Blind - Talking bks
Open Mon-Thurs 9-9, Fri & Sat 9-5:30
Friends of the Library Group
Branches: 7
KINGSTON BRANCH, 80 Main St, Kingston, 45644. (Mail add: PO Box 185, 45601), SAN 355-7138. Tel: 740-702-4180. FAX: 740-702-4181. Circ 18,999
Library Holdings: CDs 271; DVDs 218; Large Print Bks 46; Bk Vols 7,585; Videos 107
Open Mon 1-8, Tues-Thurs 1-6, Fri 1-5:30
NORTHSIDE BRANCH, 550 Buckeye St, 45601. (Mail add: PO Box 185, 45601), SAN 377-0206. Tel: 740-702-4100. FAX: 740-702-4117.
Library Holdings: CDs 1,298; DVDs 2,034; Large Print Bks 3,960; Bk Vols 48,649; Videos 536
Open Mon-Thurs 10-9, Fri & Sat 10-5:30, Sun 1-5
PAXTON BRANCH, 113 Dewey St, Bainbridge, 45612. (Mail add: PO Box 185, 45601), SAN 355-7162. Tel: 740-702-4185. FAX: 740-702-4186.
Library Holdings: CDs 234; DVDs 289; Large Print Bks 73; Bk Vols 7,653; Videos 117
Open Mon 1-8, Tues-Thurs 1-6, Fri 1-5:30

RICHMOND DALE BRANCH, 770 Main St, Richmond Dale, 45673. (Mail add: PO Box 185, 45601), SAN 355-7197. Tel: 740-702-4190. FAX: 740-702-4191.
Circ 15,342
Library Holdings: CDs 168; DVDs 272; Large Print Bks 60; Bk Vols 6,333; Videos 78
Open Mon 1-8, Tues-Thurs 1-6, Fri 1-5:30

SOUTH SALEM BRANCH, Buckskin Elementary School, 770 Main St, South Salem, 45681. (Mail add: PO Box 185, 45601), SAN 355-7227. Tel: 937-981-2400. FAX: 937-981-3194.
Circ 18,633
Library Holdings: CDs 199; DVDs 180; Large Print Bks 48; Bk Vols 9,862; Videos 103
Open Mon-Thurs 4-8, Sat 1-5

HOWARD S YOUNG BRANCH, 167 Springfield St, Frankfort, 45628. (Mail add: PO Box 185, 45601), SAN 355-7103. Tel: 740-702-4175. FAX: 740-702-4176.
Circ 18,591
Library Holdings: CDs 171; DVDs 265; Large Print Bks 80; Bk Vols 5,403
Open Mon 1-8, Tues-Thurs 1-6, Fri 1-5:30

P CHILLICOTHE & ROSS COUNTY PUBLIC LIBRARY*, Mt Logan Branch Library, 841 E Main St, 45601. Tel: 740-702-4198.
Open Mon-Thurs 3:30-6:30

S CHILLICOTHE CORRECTIONAL INSTITUTION, 15802 State Rte 104 N, 45601. (Mail add: PO Box 5500, 45601), SAN 325-0156. Tel: 740-774-0103. FAX: 740-774-7082. Web Site: www.drc.ohio.gov/CCI. *Librn II,* Cathy Pummill; E-mail: cathy.pummill@odrc.state.oh.us; Staff 1 (MLS 1)
Library Holdings: Bk Titles 14,000; Bk Vols 15,000; Per Subs 100

GM DEPARTMENT OF VETERANS AFFAIRS*, Health Sciences Library, 17273 State Rte 104, 45601. SAN 313-248X. Tel: 740-773-1141, Ext 7627. FAX: 740-772-7021. Web Site: www.chillicothe.va.gov. *Libr Tech,* Tina M Fore; E-mail: tina.fore@va.gov. Subject Specialists: *Med ref,* Tina M Fore
Library Holdings: Bk Vols 3,000
Subject Interests: Nursing, Psychiat
Automation Activity & Vendor Info: (Cataloging) EOS International; (OPAC) EOS International
Wireless access
Restriction: Mem only, Staff use only

C OHIO UNIVERSITY CHILLICOTHE CAMPUS*, Quinn Library, 101 University Dr, 45601-0629. SAN 313-2471. Tel: 740-774-7201. Administration Tel: 740-774-7203. FAX: 740-774-7268. E-mail: ouc.quinnlibrary@ohio.edu. Web Site: www.ohio.edu/chillicothe/library. *Dir,* Brandi Weaver; E-mail: weaverb1@ohio.edu; *Sr Libr Assoc,* Chris Hicks; E-mail: hicksc@ohio.edu; Staff 2 (MLS 1, Non-MLS 1)
Founded 1974. Enrl 2,000; Fac 70; Highest Degree: Bachelor
Library Holdings: AV Mats 79; Bks on Deafness & Sign Lang 156; Bk Titles 47,766; Bk Vols 56,157; Per Subs 247
Special Collections: Dard Hunter Coll; Religious Tolerance Coll, incl rare bks
Automation Activity & Vendor Info: (Acquisitions) Innovative Interfaces, Inc; (Cataloging) Innovative Interfaces, Inc; (Circulation) Innovative Interfaces, Inc; (Course Reserve) Innovative Interfaces, Inc; (ILL) Innovative Interfaces, Inc; (Media Booking) Innovative Interfaces, Inc; (OPAC) Innovative Interfaces, Inc; (Serials) Innovative Interfaces, Inc
Wireless access
Publications: QuinnEssentials (Newsletter)
Partic in Ohio Library & Information Network; OhioNET
Open Mon-Thurs (Fall & Spring) 8-7:30, Fri 8-5; Mon-Thurs (Summer) 8-6, Fri 8-5
Friends of the Library Group

S US NATIONAL PARK SERVICE*, Hopewell Culture National Historical Park Library, 16062 State Rte 104, 45601. SAN 370-3096. Tel: 740-774-1126. FAX: 740-774-1140. Web Site: www.nps.gov/hocu. *Curator,* Andrew Weiland; E-mail: andrew_weiland@nps.gov
Founded 1992
Library Holdings: Bk Vols 1,000
Special Collections: Hopewell Archeological Conference Papers
Subject Interests: Archaeology
Restriction: Open by appt only

CINCINNATI

R ADATH ISRAEL CONGREGATION*, The Nancy Petricoff Meisel Library, 3201 E Galbraith Rd, 45236. SAN 313-2498. Tel: 513-793-1800. FAX: 513-792-5085. E-mail: info@adath-israel.org. Web Site: www.adath-israel.org. *Head of Libr,* Barbara Bresler; Tel: 517-793-1800, Ext 162, E-mail: barbara@adath-israel.org; *Dir of Educ,* Dara Wood; Tel: 517-793-1800, Ext 104; Staff 1 (Non-MLS 1)
Founded 1927
Library Holdings: DVDs 30; Bk Titles 5,800; Per Subs 12
Special Collections: Cookbooks (Kosher); Dr Seuss (Hebrew version); Talmud (& commentaries)
Subject Interests: Culture, Hebrew lit, Jewish hist, Jewish lit, Yiddish
Wireless access
Function: Adult bk club, Children's prog, Preschool reading prog
Publications: AJL Newsletter; Biblical Archaeology; Commentary Magazine; Eretz Magazine; Haddasah Magazine; Jerusalem Report; Moment Magazine; The Forward
Open Wed 4-6:15, Sun 9-12:30
Friends of the Library Group

SR ATHENAEUM OF OHIO*, Eugene H Maly Memorial Library, 6616 Beechmont Ave, 45230-2091. SAN 321-1177. Tel: 513-233-6136. FAX: 513-231-3254. Circulation E-mail: circ@athenaeum.edu. Web Site: library.athenaeum.edu. *Dir,* Connie Song; E-mail: csong@athenaeum.edu; *Assoc Librn,* Claire Ballinger; E-mail: cballinger@athenaeum.edu; *Ser,* Donna Vanderbosch; E-mail: dvanderbosch@athenaeum.edu; Staff 5 (MLS 2, Non-MLS 3)
Founded 1829. Enrl 250; Fac 26; Highest Degree: Master
Library Holdings: AV Mats 951; Braille Volumes 30; CDs 171; e-books 7,100; Bk Titles 91,111; Bk Vols 114,243; Per Subs 287; Videos 247
Special Collections: American Catholic Church History (Archbishop Purcell Special Coll); Rare Books & Manuscripts; Roman Catholic Liturgy Coll; Unusual Bibles (Rare Book Coll)
Subject Interests: Biblical studies, Canon law, Church hist, Pastoral counseling, Roman Catholic theol
Automation Activity & Vendor Info: (Acquisitions) Innovative Interfaces, Inc; (Cataloging) Innovative Interfaces, Inc; (Circulation) Innovative Interfaces, Inc; (Course Reserve) Innovative Interfaces, Inc; (ILL) OCLC WorldShare Interlibrary Loan; (OPAC) Innovative Interfaces, Inc; (Serials) Innovative Interfaces, Inc
Wireless access
Partic in Ohio Library & Information Network; Ohio Private Academic Libraries; SouthWest Ohio & Neighboring Libraries
Open Mon, Tues & Thurs 8-12 & 1-10, Wed 8-12 & 1-7, Fri 8-12 & 1-5, Sat 9-11 & 1-5, Sun 2-6

M BETHESDA NORTH HOSPITAL*, Medical Library, 10500 Montgomery Rd, 45242-4402. Tel: 513-745-1129. FAX: 513-745-1220. Web Site: trihealth.libguides.com. *Med Librn,* Position Currently Open
Library Holdings: e-journals 227; Bk Vols 3,550
Automation Activity & Vendor Info: (Circulation) EOS International
Wireless access
Open Mon-Fri 8-5

G CENTERS FOR DISEASE CONTROL*, National Institute for Occupational Safety & Health Library, Robert A Taft Laboratories, 1090 Tusculum Ave, MS-R20, 45226. SAN 313-2943. Tel: 513-533-8495. Web Site: www.cdc.gov/library. *Librn,* John Bailey; Staff 3 (MLS 1, Non-MLS 2)
Founded 1971
Library Holdings: e-books 7,000; Bk Titles 10,000; Per Subs 150
Subject Interests: Health res, Occupational safety
Partic in OCLC Online Computer Library Center, Inc
Open Mon-Fri 8-4:30

S CINCINNATI ART MUSEUM*, Mary R Schiff Library & Archives, 953 Eden Park Dr, 45202-1557. SAN 313-2544. Tel: 513-639-2978. Administration Tel: 513-639-2976. FAX: 513-721-0129. E-mail: library@cincyart.org. Web Site: www.cincinnatiartmuseum.org/visit/library-archives. *Head Librn,* Lewandowicz Galina; Staff 4 (MLS 4)
Founded 1882
Library Holdings: DVDs 100; Electronic Media & Resources 8; Microforms 100; Bk Vols 86,500; Per Subs 70
Special Collections: Art In Cincinnati (bks, files, archival materials); Auction Catalogs (Christie's & Sotheby's starting from the 1930s, miscellaneous other); Cincinnati Art Museum Coll (archives, bks, files); Cincinnati Artists Coll (artist files, bks, archival materials)
Subject Interests: Exhibition catalogs, Japanese prints, Rookwood pottery
Automation Activity & Vendor Info: (Cataloging) OCLC Connexion; (ILL) OCLC WorldShare Interlibrary Loan; (OPAC) Innovative Interfaces, Inc
Wireless access
Function: Online cat, Prog for adults, Ref & res
Partic in OCLC Online Computer Library Center, Inc; SouthWest Ohio & Neighboring Libraries
Open Tues-Fri 11-5
Restriction: Non-circulating, Pub use on premises

CINCINNATI CHILDREN'S HOSPITAL

M EDWARD L PRATT LIBRARY*, S9.125 ML 3012, 3333 Burnet Ave, 45229-3039, SAN 313-2528. Tel: 513-636-4230. FAX: 513-559-9669. E-mail: prattlibrary@cchmc.org. Web Site: prattlibrary.cchmc.org, www.cincinnatichildrens.org/research/cincinnati/support/pratt/library-services. *Dir,* Melida Busch; E-mail: Melida.Busch@cchmc.org; *Clinical Librn,* Elaine Dean; E-mail: elaine.dean@cchmc.org; *Research Librn,* Alison Kissling; E-mail: alison.kissling@cchmc.org; *Resource Librn,* Holly Spindler; E-mail: Holly.Spindler@cchmc.org; *Coordr,* Cristen Ross; E-mail: Cristen.Ross@cchmc.org; Staff 6 (MLS 4, Non-MLS 2)
Founded 1931
Library Holdings: e-books 1,217; e-journals 76,945; Bk Titles 330
Subject Interests: Developmental biol, Genetics, Pediatrics, Teratology
Partic in National Network of Libraries of Medicine Region 6; OCLC Online Computer Library Center, Inc
Publications: Studies of the Cincinnati Children's Research Foundation
Restriction: Staff use only

M JACK H RUBINSTEIN LIBRARY*, 3430 Burnet Ave, MOB 2 MLC 3000, 45229, SAN 355-8789. Tel: 513-636-4626. FAX: 513-636-0107. Web Site: www.cincinnatichildrens.org. *Mgr,* Barbara Ann Johnson; E-mail: barbara.johnson@chmcc.org; Staff 1 (MLS 1)
Founded 1957
Library Holdings: Bk Vols 8,000; Videos 300
Special Collections: Bibliotherapy Coll; Developmental Disability Research Library; Parents' Library, bks, pamphlets & videos; Toy Library for Children with Special Needs
Subject Interests: Genetics, Handicapping conditions, Learning disabilities, Mental retardation, Pediatrics, Rehabilitation

CR CINCINNATI CHRISTIAN UNIVERSITY*, G M Elliott Library, 2700 Glenway Ave, 45204-3200. SAN 313-2552. Tel: 513-244-8680. Interlibrary Loan Service Tel: 513-244-8435. Administration Tel: 513-244-8197. E-mail: library@ccuniversity.edu. Web Site: library.ccuniversity.edu. *Dir, Libr Serv,* James Lloyd; E-mail: James.Lloyd@ccuniversity.edu; *Pub Serv Coordr,* Deanna Hansee; E-mail: deanna.hansee@ccuniversity.edu; *Tech Serv Asst,* Laura Brown; Tel: 513-244-8139, E-mail: laura.brown@ccuniversity.edu. Subject Specialists: *Biblical studies, Theol,* James Lloyd; Staff 2 (MLS 1, Non-MLS 1)
Founded 1924. Enrl 776; Fac 30; Highest Degree: Master
Special Collections: Hymnals; Restoration Movement
Subject Interests: Biblical studies, Theol
Automation Activity & Vendor Info: (Acquisitions) Innovative Interfaces, Inc - Sierra; (Cataloging) Innovative Interfaces, Inc - Sierra; (Circulation) Innovative Interfaces, Inc - Sierra; (Course Reserve) Innovative Interfaces, Inc - Sierra; (Discovery) EBSCO Discovery Service; (ILL) OCLC WorldShare Interlibrary Loan; (OPAC) Innovative Interfaces, Inc - Sierra; (Serials) Innovative Interfaces, Inc - Sierra
Wireless access
Partic in Christian Library Consortium; OhioNET
Open Mon & Tues 8am-11pm, Wed 8am-10pm, Thurs 8am-11pm; Fri 8-5, Sat 10-5

C CINCINNATI COLLEGE OF MORTUARY SCIENCE LIBRARY, 645 W North Bend Rd, 45224-1428. SAN 327-6791. Tel: 513-761-2020. Administration Tel: 513-618-1933. Toll Free Tel: 888-377-8433. FAX: 513-761-3333. E-mail: library@ccms.edu. Web Site: www.ccms.edu/about-ccms/library. *Dir, Libr & Info Tech,* Molly Jones; E-mail: mjones@ccms.edu; Staff 1 (MLS 1)
Founded 1882. Enrl 100; Fac 15; Highest Degree: Bachelor
Library Holdings: DVDs 30; Bk Titles 1,500; Per Subs 20
Special Collections: Historical mortuary science texts
Wireless access
Partic in SouthWest Ohio & Neighboring Libraries
Open Mon-Fri 8-4

S CINCINNATI MUSEUM CENTER AT UNION TERMINAL, Cincinnati History Library & Archives, 1301 Western Ave, Ste 2133, 45203. SAN 313-2587. Tel: 513-287-7030. Interlibrary Loan Service Tel: 513-287-7089. Toll Free Tel: 800-733-2077. FAX: 513-287-7095. E-mail: library@cincymuseum.org. Web Site: library.cincymuseum.org. *Dir,* Scott Gampfer; Tel: 513-287-7084, E-mail: sgampfer@cincymuseum.org; *Curator, Photog & Prints, Ref Librn,* Jim DaMico; Tel: 513-287-7094, E-mail: jdamico@cincymuseum.org; *Ref Librn,* Anne B Shepherd; Tel: 513-287-7069, E-mail: ashepherd@cincymuseum.org; *Archives Mgr,* Anne Kling; Tel: 513-287-7066, E-mail: akling@cincymuseum.org; Staff 8 (MLS 3, Non-MLS 5)
Founded 1831
Library Holdings: AV Mats 1,000,000; Bk Vols 100,000; Per Subs 320
Special Collections: Cornelius J Hauck Botanical Coll; Peter G Thomson Northwest Territory Coll; Photograph & Manuscript Colls; William H Harrison Coll
Subject Interests: Metrop Cincinnati, Miami purchase, Ohio, Old Northwest territory
Automation Activity & Vendor Info: (Cataloging) Cuadra Associates, Inc; (OPAC) Cuadra Associates, Inc; (Serials) Cuadra Associates, Inc
Wireless access
Function: 24/7 Electronic res, 24/7 Online cat, Archival coll, Bus archives, Microfiche/film & reading machines, Online cat, Ref serv available, Res libr
Partic in OCLC Online Computer Library Center, Inc; SouthWest Ohio & Neighboring Libraries
Restriction: Open by appt only
Branches:
GEIER SCIENCE LIBRARY, 760 W Fifth St, 45203, SAN 313-2633. Tel: 513-455-7183. E-mail: sciencelibrary@cincymuseum.org. Web Site: library.cincymuseum.org/science/sciencelibrary.htm. *Librn,* Phil Yannarella
Library Holdings: Bk Vols 7,500; Per Subs 80
Special Collections: Archaeology; Herpetology; Ornithology; Paleontology
Subject Interests: Natural hist
Restriction: Non-circulating, Open by appt only

S CINCINNATI PSYCHOANALYTIC INSTITUTE*, Frederic T Kapp Memorial Library, 3001 Highland Ave, 45219. SAN 328-1558. Tel: 513-961-8886. FAX: 513-961-0308. Web Site: www.cps-i.org/library. *Librn,* Mary Kroeger Vuyk; Tel: 513-961-8886, Ext 2, E-mail: mkroegervuyk@3001.us; Staff 1 (Non-MLS 1)
Founded 1981
Library Holdings: Bk Titles 4,400; Per Subs 48
Subject Interests: Psychoanalysis, Psychotherapy
Restriction: Mem only
Friends of the Library Group

J CINCINNATI STATE TECHNICAL & COMMUNITY COLLEGE*, Johnnie Mae Berry Library, 3520 Central Pkwy, Rm 170, 45223-2690. SAN 375-2771. Tel: 513-569-1606. FAX: 513-559-1527. Web Site: www.cincinnatistate.edu/students/library. *Dir,* Cindy C Sefton; Tel: 513-569-1699, E-mail: cindy.sefton@cincinnatistate.edu; *Coll Develop, Instrul Serv Librn, Ref (Info Servs),* Kathleen Pickens; Tel: 513-569-1611, E-mail: kathleen.pickens@cincinnatistate.edu; *Circ Coordr,* Myra Justus; Tel: 513-569-4690, E-mail: myra.justus@cincinnatistate.edu; *Archives, Database Coordr, Tech Serv,* Tracey Stivers; Tel: 513-569-1608, E-mail: tracy.stivers@cincinnatistate.edu; *Acq,* Karen Douglas; Tel: 513-569-1607, E-mail: karen.douglas@cincinnatistate.edu; *Ser,* Thelma Barnes; Tel: 513-569-1610
Highest Degree: Associate
Library Holdings: Bk Vols 26,431; Per Subs 339
Wireless access
Partic in OCLC Online Computer Library Center, Inc; Ohio Library & Information Network; SouthWest Ohio & Neighboring Libraries
Open Mon-Thurs 7:30am-10pm, Fri 7:30-4:30, Sat 10-2

GM DEPARTMENT OF VETERANS AFFAIRS, Medical Center Library, 3200 Vine St, 45220-2213. SAN 313-296X. Tel: 513-475-6315. FAX: 513-475-6454. Web Site: www.cincinnati.va.gov. *Library Contact,* Kristen Young; E-mail: kristen.young9@va.gov; Staff 2 (MLS 2)
Library Holdings: e-journals 125; Bk Titles 1,200; Per Subs 180
Automation Activity & Vendor Info: (OPAC) EOS International
Partic in Cincinnati Area Health Sci Libr Asn
Restriction: Staff use only

L DINSMORE & SHOHL LIBRARY*, 255 E Fifth St, Ste 900, 45202-3172. SAN 313-2668. Tel: 513-977-8486. FAX: 513-977-8141. E-mail: library@dinsmore.com. *Dir, Libr Serv,* Tim Hennies; E-mail: timothy.hennies@dinsmore.com; *Law Librn,* Angela Jansen; E-mail: angela.jansen@dinsmore.com; Staff 5 (MLS 4, Non-MLS 1)
Library Holdings: Bk Vols 24,000
Subject Interests: Law
Automation Activity & Vendor Info: (Acquisitions) EOS International; (Cataloging) EOS International; (Circulation) EOS International; (OPAC) EOS International; (Serials) EOS International
Wireless access
Function: For res purposes
Restriction: Private libr

L FROST BROWN TODD LLC, Law Library, 3300 Great American Tower, 301 E Fourth St, 45202. SAN 372-2147. Tel: 513-651-6982. FAX: 513-651-6981. Web Site: www.frostbrowntodd.com. *Libr Mgr,* Tracie Tiegs; E-mail: ttiegs@fbtlaw.com; Staff 2 (MLS 1, Non-MLS 1)
Wireless access
Restriction: Not open to pub

CR GOD'S BIBLE SCHOOL & COLLEGE LIBRARY*, R G Flexon Memorial Library, 507 Ringgold St, 45202. (Mail add: 1810 Young St, 45202-6838), SAN 313-2722. Tel: 513-763-6657. E-mail: library@gbs.edu. Web Site: www.gbs.edu/libraries. *Dir, Libr Serv,* Stephanie Owens; Tel: 513-721-7944, Ext. 5112, E-mail: shoffpauir@gbs.edu; *ILL Coordr, Tech*

Serv, Sarah McBryant; Tel: 513-721-7944, Ext. 5113, E-mail: smcbryant@gbs.edu; Staff 3 (MLS 1, Non-MLS 2)
Founded 1900. Enrl 300; Fac 26; Highest Degree: Master
Library Holdings: AV Mats 2,200; CDs 449; DVDs 209; Electronic Media & Resources 12; Music Scores 400; Bk Titles 41,257; Bk Vols 45,309; Per Subs 210; Spec Interest Per Sub 150; Talking Bks 30; Videos 1,556
Special Collections: Oral History
Subject Interests: Relig
Automation Activity & Vendor Info: (Circulation) Follett Software; (OPAC) Follett Software; (Serials) Follett Software
Wireless access
Function: Archival coll, Audio & video playback equip for onsite use, Bks on CD, Children's prog, Distance learning, For res purposes, Free DVD rentals, ILL available, Learning ctr, Magnifiers for reading, Mail & tel request accepted, Mail loans to mem, Music CDs, Orientations, Outside serv via phone, mail, e-mail & web, Photocopying/Printing, Prog for children & young adult, Ref serv available, Res libr, Spoken cassettes & CDs, Spoken cassettes & DVDs, Story hour, Telephone ref, VHS videos
Partic in SouthWest Ohio & Neighboring Libraries
Open Mon, Tues & Thurs 8am-9pm, Wed 8am-7pm & 8pm-9pm, Fri 8-7, Sat Noon-5

L HAMILTON COUNTY LAW LIBRARY*, Hamilton County Court House, 1000 Main St, Rm 601, 45202. SAN 313-2595. Tel: 513-946-5300. FAX: 513-946-5264. Reference E-mail: reference@cms.hamilton-co.org. Web Site: lawlibrary.hamiltoncountyohio.gov. *Dir, Law Librn,* Lauren Morrison; E-mail: lmorrison@cms.hamilton-co.org; *Ref Librn,* Amy Kurlansky; E-mail: akurlansky@cms.hamilton-co.org; *Syst Librn,* Julie Koehne; E-mail: jkoehne@cms.hamilton-co.org; *Tech Serv Librn,* Bill Tomeo; E-mail: btomeo@cms.hamilton-co.org; Staff 6.7 (MLS 4.7, Non-MLS 2)
Founded 1834
Special Collections: Rare Legal Treatises; United States Session Laws
Subject Interests: Loose-leaf serv, Reporters treatises, Statutes
Automation Activity & Vendor Info: (Cataloging) SirsiDynix; (Circulation) SirsiDynix; (OPAC) SirsiDynix; (Serials) SirsiDynix
Wireless access
Function: Computers for patron use, Govt ref serv, Internet access, Online cat, Photocopying/Printing, Ref serv available
Partic in OCLC Online Computer Library Center, Inc; OhioNET
Open Mon-Fri 8-4
Restriction: Circ limited, Circ to mem only, In-house use for visitors, Non-circulating of rare bks, Pub access for legal res only, Pub use on premises, Restricted loan policy, Restricted pub use, Vols & interns use only

CR HEBREW UNION COLLEGE-JEWISH INSTITUTE OF RELIGION, Klau Library, 3101 Clifton Ave, 45220-2488. SAN 355-7316. Tel: 513-221-1875. Interlibrary Loan Service Tel: 513-487-3281. Reference Tel: 513-487-3287. Administration Tel: 513-487-3276. Information Services Tel: 513-487-3278. FAX: 513-221-0519. E-mail: klau@huc.edu. Interlibrary Loan Service E-mail: ill.cn@huc.edu. Web Site: huc.edu/research/libraries/cincinnati-klau-library. *Dir of Libr,* Yoram Bitton; Tel: 212-824-2267, E-mail: ybitton@huc.edu; *Deputy Dir of Libraries, Libr Dir,* Laurel S Wolfson; Tel: 513-487-3274, E-mail: lwolfson@huc.edu; *Head, Pub Serv,* Abigail Bacon; Tel: 513-487-3088, E-mail: abacon@huc.edu; *Head, Tech Serv,* Alice Finkelstein; Tel: 513-487-3294, E-mail: afinkelstein@huc.edu; *Rare Book & Manuscript Librn,* Dr Jordan Finkin; Tel: 513-487-3272, E-mail: jfinkin@huc.edu; *Asst Librn,* Joshua Fischer; Tel: 513-487-3283, E-mail: jfischer@huc.edu; *Assistant Judaica Librn,* Chana Wolfson; Tel: 513-487-3284, E-mail: cwolfson@huc.edu; *Computer Spec,* Lisa Ben-Hur; E-mail: lbenhur@huc.edu; Staff 13 (MLS 7, Non-MLS 6)
Founded 1875. Enrl 81; Fac 18; Highest Degree: Doctorate
Library Holdings: e-journals 200; Electronic Media & Resources 200; Microforms 38,000; Bk Vols 560,000; Per Subs 1,200
Special Collections: 16th Century Hebrew Printing Coll; Assyriology Coll; Broadside Coll; Hebrew Manuscripts; Inquisition Coll; Jewish Americana to 1850; Jewish Music Coll; Josephus Coll; Printed Bible Coll; Spinoza Coll; Yiddish Theater Coll
Subject Interests: Ancient & Near Eastern studies, Hebraica, Incunabula, Judaica, Rabbinics
Automation Activity & Vendor Info: (Cataloging) OCLC Worldshare Management Services; (Circulation) OCLC Worldshare Management Services; (Discovery) OCLC Worldshare Management Services; (ILL) OCLC WorldShare Interlibrary Loan; (OPAC) OCLC Worldshare Management Services; (Serials) OCLC Worldshare Management Services
Wireless access
Function: 24/7 Electronic res, 24/7 Online cat, ILL available, Ref serv available
Partic in OCLC Online Computer Library Center, Inc
Open Mon-Thurs 9-6

M JEWISH HOSPITAL*, Health Sciences Library, 4777 E Galbraith Rd, 45236. SAN 355-7340. Tel: 513-686-5173. FAX: 513-686-5418. *Mgr, Libr Serv,* Lisa McCormick; Staff 3 (MLS 1, Non-MLS 2)
Founded 1959
Library Holdings: Bk Titles 2,500; Bk Vols 3,000; Per Subs 180
Special Collections: Leisurely Medical Reading Coll; Medical History Coll
Subject Interests: Internal med, Nursing, Surgery
Automation Activity & Vendor Info: (Cataloging) Marcive, Inc; (OPAC) LibraryWorld, Inc
Partic in Greater Midwest Regional Medical Libr Network; Kentucky Medical Library Association
Restriction: Staff use only

S KATZEN INTERNATIONAL INC LIBRARY*, 2300 Wall St, Ste K, 45212-2789. SAN 375-6475. Tel: 513-351-7500. FAX: 513-351-0810. E-mail: info@katzen.com. Web Site: www.katzen.com. *Pres,* Philip W Madson
Library Holdings: Per Subs 30
Subject Interests: Chem engr, Mechanical engr
Open Mon-Fri 8-5

S LLOYD LIBRARY & MUSEUM*, 917 Plum St, 45202. SAN 313-2781. Tel: 513-721-3707. FAX: 513-721-6575. Web Site: www.lloydlibrary.org. *Exec Dir,* Patricia Van Skaik; E-mail: pvanskaik@lloydlibrary.org; *Cataloger, Rare Bk Librn,* Betsy Kruthoffer; E-mail: betsy@lloydlibrary.org; *Ref Librn, Tech Librn,* Erin Campbell; E-mail: ecampbell@lloydlibrary.org; *Libr Office Mgr, Ref Librn,* Alex Herrlein; E-mail: aherrlein@lloydlibrary.org; Staff 4.8 (MLS 4.3, Non-MLS 0.5)
Founded 1885
Library Holdings: Bk Titles 200,000; Per Subs 250
Special Collections: Botanical Art; Botany with an Emphasis on Morphology & Taxonomy; Eclectic Medicine Coll; Linnean Literature Original Editions; Materia Medica, bks, journals; Mycology, bks, ms; Natural History Coll; Pharmacognosy, History of Pharmacy; Pharmacy (Pharmacopeias & Related Subjects); Plant Chemistry & Floras
Subject Interests: Botany, Hist, Natural hist, Pharm
Wireless access
Function: Archival coll, Art exhibits, Computers for patron use, Doc delivery serv, Internet access, Online cat, Online ref, Orientations, Outreach serv, Outside serv via phone, mail, e-mail & web, Photocopying/Printing, Ref serv available, Res libr, Res performed for a fee, Telephone ref, Wheelchair accessible
Publications: Lloydiana: A Publication of the Friends of the Lloyd Library (Quarterly)
Partic in OCLC Online Computer Library Center, Inc; OhioNET
Open Mon-Fri 9-4
Restriction: Closed stack, Non-circulating
Friends of the Library Group

S MERCANTILE LIBRARY ASSOCIATION*, 414 Walnut St, 45202. SAN 313-3028. Tel: 513-621-0717. Web Site: new.mercantilelibrary.com. *Exec Dir,* John Faherty; E-mail: jfaherty@mercantilelibrary.com; *Librn,* Cedric Rose; E-mail: crose@mercantilelibrary.com; *Lit Prog Mgr, Mkt Mgr,* Amy B Hunter; E-mail: ahunter@mercantilelibrary.com
Founded 1835
Library Holdings: Bk Titles 150,000; Per Subs 80
Wireless access
Open Mon-Fri 9-5:30, Sat 10-3

CR MOUNT SAINT JOSEPH UNIVERSITY*, Archbishop Alter Library, 5701 Delhi Rd, 45233-1671. SAN 313-6299. Tel: 513-244-4216. FAX: 513-244-4355. E-mail: library@msj.edu. Web Site: library.msj.edu. *Dir, Libr Serv,* Scott Lloyd; Tel: 513-244-4347, E-mail: scott.lloyd@msj.edu; *Head, Access Serv,* Josh Zeller; Tel: 513-244-4882, E-mail: joshua.zeller@msj.edu; *Head, Coll Serv, Librn III,* Julie Flanders; Tel: 513-244-4798, E-mail: julie.flanders@msj.edu; *Head, Electronic Res, Librn III,* Cynthia Gregory; Tel: 513-244-4762, E-mail: cynthia.gregory@msj.edu; *Head, Ref & Instruction, Librn I,* Bridget McDermott; Tel: 513-244-4880, E-mail: bridget.dumont@msj.edu; Staff 6 (MLS 5, Non-MLS 1)
Founded 1920. Enrl 1,800; Fac 120; Highest Degree: Doctorate
Jul 2014-Jun 2015. Mats Exp $250,000, Books $29,000, Per/Ser (Incl. Access Fees) $150,000, AV Mat $5,000, Electronic Ref Mat (Incl. Access Fees) $8,000. Sal $320,000 (Prof $253,000)
Library Holdings: AV Mats 800; CDs 640; e-books 55,000; e-journals 10,000; Bk Titles 51,000; Bk Vols 88,000; Per Subs 54
Special Collections: Post 1945 American Poetry (Aaron Levine Coll)
Automation Activity & Vendor Info: (Acquisitions) Innovative Interfaces, Inc; (Cataloging) Innovative Interfaces, Inc; (Circulation) Innovative Interfaces, Inc; (Course Reserve) Docutek; (OPAC) Innovative Interfaces, Inc; (Serials) Innovative Interfaces, Inc
Wireless access
Partic in Ohio Library & Information Network
Open Mon-Thurs 7:30am-Noon, Fri 7:30-5, Sat 10-5, Sun 1-9

R NORTHMINSTER PRESBYTERIAN CHURCH LIBRARY*, 703 Compton Rd, 45231. SAN 328-2910. Tel: 513-931-0243. FAX: 513-931-0260. Web Site: www.northminsterchurch.net. *Dir,* Marianne Lord; E-mail: mlord@nmpchurch.org
Library Holdings: Bk Titles 3,000
Wireless access
Open Mon-Fri 11:30-4:30, Sun 8-1

P PUBLIC LIBRARY OF CINCINNATI & HAMILTON COUNTY*, Cincinnati & Hamilton County Public Library, 800 Vine St, 45202-2009. SAN 355-7588. Tel: 513-369-6900. FAX: 513-369-6993. E-mail: info@cincinnatilibrary.org. Web Site: www.cincinnatilibrary.org. *Dir,* Paula Brehm-Heeger; Tel: 513-369-6941; *Chief Develop Officer,* Staci Dennison; Tel: 513-369-4595; *Chief Financial Officer, Fac Mgr,* Molly DeFosse; Tel: 513-369-6967; *Dir, Human Res,* Kyla Hardin; Tel: 513-369-4407; *Regional Br Operations Mgr,* Katie Greifenkamp; Tel: 513-665-3358; *Regional Br Operations Mgr,* Chris Holt; Tel: 513-369-4417; *Regional Br Operations Mgr,* Kathy Bach; Tel: 513-369-4418; *Regional Br Operations Mgr,* Maria Sferra; Tel: 513-369-4419; *Mkt Mgr,* Chris Rice; Tel: 513-369-7817; *Mat Selection & Acq,* Amy Long; Tel: 513-369-6952; *Fac Mgr,* Jeff Gerrein; Tel: 513-369-4515; *Chief Strategy Officer,* Beth Yoke; Tel: 513-369-4568; *Customer Experience Mgr,* Justyn Rampa; Tel: 513-369-6926; *Chief Tech Officer,* Holbrook Sample; Tel: 513-369-4408; *Mgr, Info Tech,* Bill Lane; Tel: 513-369-6948; *ILS Syst Mgr,* Karen Davis; Tel: 513-369-6980; *Tech Officer,* Ryan Bley; Tel: 513-369-4405; *Chief Operating Officer,* Brett Bonfield; Tel: 513-369-6941. Subject Specialists: *Strategy,* Justyn Rampa; *Logistics,* Holbrook Sample; *Logistics,* Ryan Bley; *Operations,* Brett Bonfield; Staff 838 (MLS 191, Non-MLS 647)
Founded 1853. Pop 802,374; Circ 19,953,082
Jan 2017-Dec 2017 Income (Main & Associated Libraries) $59,848,702, State $38,303,779, County $18,212,917, Locally Generated Income $3,332,006. Mats Exp $9,232,214, Books $3,626,835, Per/Ser (Incl. Access Fees) $351,038, AV Mat $1,322,079, Electronic Ref Mat (Incl. Access Fees) $3,926,249, Presv $6,013. Sal $27,151,706
Library Holdings: AV Mats 872,102; Bk Vols 4,967,657; Per Subs 6,528
Special Collections: US Document Depository
Automation Activity & Vendor Info: (Acquisitions) Innovative Interfaces, Inc; (Circulation) Innovative Interfaces, Inc; (OPAC) Innovative Interfaces, Inc; (Serials) Innovative Interfaces, Inc
Wireless access
Function: 24/7 Electronic res, 24/7 Online cat, 3D Printer, Adult bk club, Adult literacy prog, Art exhibits, Audio & video playback equip for onsite use, Audiobks on Playaways & MP3, Audiobks via web, Bilingual assistance for Spanish patrons, Bk club(s), Bks on cassette, Bks on CD, Children's prog, Citizenship assistance, Computer training, Computers for patron use, Doc delivery serv, E-Reserves, Electronic databases & coll, Govt ref serv, Holiday prog, Home delivery & serv to seniorr ctr & nursing homes, Homebound delivery serv, Homework prog, ILL available, Instruction & testing, Internet access, Learning ctr, Life-long learning prog for all ages, Literacy & newcomer serv, Magazines, Mail & tel request accepted, Makerspace, Mango lang, Meeting rooms, Microfiche/film & reading machines, Movies, Music CDs, Online cat, Online ref, Outreach serv, OverDrive digital audio bks, Passport agency, Photocopying/Printing, Preschool reading prog, Prog for adults, Prog for children & young adult, Scanner, Senior computer classes, Senior outreach, Serves people with intellectual disabilities, Spanish lang bks, STEM programs, Story hour, Study rm, Summer reading prog, Tax forms, Teen prog, Wheelchair accessible, Workshops, Writing prog
Publications: @the Library (Newsletter); eLinks (Newsletter); Links (Newsletter); New For You (Newsletter); Ohioana Author List & Program (Bibliographies)
Partic in OCLC Online Computer Library Center, Inc; OhioNET; SouthWest Ohio & Neighboring Libraries
Special Services for the Deaf - TDD equip
Special Services for the Blind - Aids for in-house use; Assistive/Adapted tech devices, equip & products; Audio mat; BiFolkal kits; Braille bks; Descriptive video serv (DVS); Extensive large print coll; Large print bks; Newsletter (in large print, Braille or on cassette)
Open Mon, Tuse & Wed 9-9,Thurs, Fri & Sat 9-6, Sun 1-5
Friends of the Library Group
Branches: 48
ANDERSON, 7450 State Rd, 45230, SAN 355-7685. Tel: 513-369-6030. FAX: 513-369-4444. *Br Mgr,* Denise Scretchen; E-mail: denise.scretchen@cincinnatilibrary.org
Library Holdings: AV Mats 25,517; Bk Vols 105,471
Open Mon-Thurs 10-9, Fri & Sat 10-6
Friends of the Library Group
AVONDALE, 3566 Reading Rd, 45229, SAN 355-7677. Tel: 513-369-4440. FAX: 513-369-4539. *Br Mgr,* Kaya Burgin; E-mail: kaya.burgin@cincinnatilibrary.org
Library Holdings: AV Mats 15,033; Bk Vols 18,225
Open Mon, Tues & Thurs 12-8, Wed, Fri & Sat 10-6
Friends of the Library Group
BLUE ASH BRANCH, 4911 Cooper Rd, Blue Ash, 45242, SAN 355-8630. Tel: 513-369-6051. FAX: 513-369-4464. *Br Mgr,* Sagoree Chatterjee; E-mail: sagoree.chatterjee@cincinnatilibrary.org
Library Holdings: AV Mats 18,758; Bk Vols 77,009
Open Mon-Thurs 10-9, Fri & Sat 10-6
Friends of the Library Group
BOND HILL, 1740 Langdon Farm Rd at Jordan Crossing, 45237, SAN 355-7707. Tel: 513-369-4445. FAX: 513-369-4532. *Br Mgr,* Melissa Davis; E-mail: melissa.davis@cincinnatilibrary.org
Library Holdings: AV Mats 18,239; Bk Vols 37,460
Open Mon, Tues & Thurs 12-8, Wed, Fri & Sat 10-6
Friends of the Library Group
CHEVIOT, 3711 Robb Ave, 45211, SAN 355-7766. Tel: 513-369-6015. FAX: 513-369-6048. *Br Mgr,* Eric Pennington; E-mail: Eric.Pennington@cincinnatilibrary.org
Library Holdings: AV Mats 12,137; Bk Vols 33,586
Open Mon, Tues & Thurs 12-8, Wed, Fri & Sat 10-6
Friends of the Library Group
CLIFTON, 3400 Brookline Ave, 45220, SAN 355-7790. Tel: 513-369-4447. FAX: 513-369-4448. *Br Mgr,* Lisa Hamrick; E-mail: lisa.hamrick@cincinnatilibrary.org
Library Holdings: AV Mats 9,072; Bk Vols 29,174
Open Mon, Tues & Thurs 12-8, Wed, Fri & Sat 10-6, Sun 1-5
Friends of the Library Group
COLLEGE HILL, 1400 W North Bend Rd, 45224, SAN 355-8339. Tel: 513-369-6036. FAX: 513-369-6043. *Br Mgr,* Ashley Barnhill; E-mail: ashley.barnhill@cincinnatilibrary.org
Library Holdings: AV Mats 14,103; Bk Vols 36,025
Open Mon, Tues & Thurs 12-8, Wed, Fri & Sat 10-6
Friends of the Library Group
CORRYVILLE, 2802 Vine St, 45219, SAN 355-8304. Tel: 513-369-6034. FAX: 513-369-4471. *Br Mgr,* Mari Randolph; E-mail: mari.randolph@cincinnatilibrary.org
Library Holdings: AV Mats 10,620; Bk Vols 26,629
Open Mon, Tues & Thurs 12-8, Wed, Fri & Sat 10-6
Friends of the Library Group
COVEDALE, 4980 Glenway Ave, 45238, SAN 355-8428. Tel: 513-369-4460. FAX: 513-369-4461. *Br Mgr,* Position Currently Open
Library Holdings: AV Mats 22,429; Bk Vols 43,711
Open Mon, Tues & Thurs 12-8, Wed, Fri & Sat 10-6
Friends of the Library Group
DEER PARK, 3970 E Galbraith Rd, 45236, SAN 355-7855. Tel: 513-369-4450. FAX: 513-369-4451. *Br Mgr,* Natalie Fields; E-mail: natalie.fields@cincinnatilibrary.org
Library Holdings: AV Mats 13,890; Bk Vols 40,807
Open Mon, Tues & Thurs 12-8, Wed, Fri & Sat 10-6
Friends of the Library Group
DELHI TOWNSHIP, 5095 Foley Rd, 45238, SAN 355-788X. Tel: 513-369-6019. FAX: 513-369-4453. *Br Mgr,* Casey Titschinger; E-mail: casey.titschinger@cincinnatilibrary.org
Library Holdings: AV Mats 22,053; Bk Vols 76,475
Open Mon-Thurs 10-9, Fri & Sat 10-6
Friends of the Library Group
ELMWOOD PLACE, 6120 Vine St, 45216, SAN 355-791X. Tel: 513-369-4452. FAX: 513-369-4534. *Br Mgr,* Rick Mattson; E-mail: Rick.Mattson@cincinnatilibrary.org
Library Holdings: AV Mats 7,257; Bk Vols 11,365
Open Mon & Tues 12-8, Wed & Thurs 12-6, Fri & Sat 10-6
Friends of the Library Group
FOREST PARK BRANCH, 655 Waycross Rd, Forest Park, 45240, SAN 355-8452. Tel: 513-369-4478. FAX: 513-369-4480. *Br Mgr,* Shaun Davidson; E-mail: shaun.davidson@cincinnatilibrary.org
Library Holdings: AV Mats 13,314; Bk Vols 47,366
Open Mon, Tues & Thurs 12-8, Wed, Fri & Sat 10-6
Friends of the Library Group
GENEALOGY & LOCAL HISTORY, South Bldg, 3rd Flr, 800 Vine St, 45202-2009. Tel: 513-369-6905. FAX: 513-369-3123. *Mgr,* Larry Richmond; E-mail: larry.richmond@cincinnatilibrary.org
Special Collections: A Edward Newton Coll; Artist Illustrated Books, (19th & 20th Century); Bible Coll; Book Arts; Charles Dickens Coll; Christopher Morley Coll; Cincinnati Coll; City Directories; Cruikshank Coll; Discovery & Exploration of America Coll; Edgar Rice Burroughs Coll; English Language Dictionary Coll; Ernest Hemingway Coll; Fleischmann Coll; Frank & Dick Merriwell Coll; Glueck Coll; Hatfield Coll; Huenefeld Coll; Inland River Library; J Richard Abell Coll; John Steinbeck Coll; Kahn Dictionary Coll; Lafeadio Hearn Coll; Langstroth Lithograph Coll; Lazarus Coll; Lewis Coll; Loeb Coll; Map Coll; Mark Twain Coll; Mudge Coll; Nora May Nolan Irish Coll; Ohio Valley Coll; Postcard Coll; Posters; Rockwell Kent Coll; Sackett Coll; School Yearbooks; Sir Winston Churchill Coll; Sports Coll; Trager Memorial Coll; US Census Records, (1790-1930); Veterans History Project Archives; W Somerset Maugham Coll; Walpole Coll; Willa Cather Coll; William Faulkner Coll; William Makepeace Thackeray Coll
Subject Interests: African-Am res, Genealogy, Local hist, River hist
Friends of the Library Group

GREEN TOWNSHIP, 6525 Bridgetown Rd, 45248, SAN 370-0968. Tel: 513-369-6095. FAX: 513-369-4482. *Br Mgr,* Kathy Taylor; E-mail: kathy.taylor@cincinnatilibrary.org
Library Holdings: AV Mats 18,402; Bk Vols 73,205
Open Mon-Thurs 10-9, Fri & Sat 10-6
Friends of the Library Group

GREENHILLS, Eight Enfield St, 45218, SAN 355-7979. Tel: 513-369-4441. FAX: 513-369-4535. *Br Mgr,* Jennifer Weikert; E-mail: jennifer.weikert@cincinnatilibrary.org
Library Holdings: AV Mats 6,448; Bk Vols 18,961
Open Mon & Tues 12-8, Wed & Thurs 12-6, Fri & Sat 10-6
Friends of the Library Group

GROESBECK, 2994 W Galbraith Rd, 45239, SAN 355-8002. Tel: 513-369-4454. FAX: 513-369-4455. *Br Mgr,* Ned Heeger-Brehm; E-mail: ned.heeger-brehm@cincinnatilibrary.org
Library Holdings: AV Mats 32,497; Bk Vols 104,753
Open Mon-Thurs 10-9, Fri & Sat 10-6
Friends of the Library Group

HARRISON BRANCH, 10398 New Haven Rd, Harrison, 45030, SAN 355-8037. Tel: 513-369-4442. FAX: 513-369-4443. *Br Mgr,* Michelle Elliott; E-mail: michelle.elliott@cincinnatilibrary.org
Library Holdings: AV Mats 24,785; Bk Vols 68,086
Open Mon-Thurs 10-9, Fri & Sat 10-6
Friends of the Library Group

HOMEWORK CENTER, North Bldg, 1st Flr, 800 Vine St, 45202. Tel: 513-369-3121. *Mgr,* Keith Armour; E-mail: keith.armour@cincinnatilibrary.org
Friends of the Library Group

HYDE PARK, 2747 Erie Ave, 45208, SAN 355-8061. Tel: 513-369-4456. FAX: 513-369-4458. *Br Mgr,* Blossom Smith; E-mail: blossom.smith@cincinnatilibrary.org
Library Holdings: AV Mats 12,785; Bk Vols 50,298
Open Mon, Tues & Thurs 12-8, Wed, Fri & Sat 10-6
Friends of the Library Group

INFORMATION & REFERENCE, South Bldg, 2nd Flr, 800 Vine St, 45202-2009. Tel: 513-369-6900. *Mgr,* Ben Lathrop; E-mail: ben.lathrop@cincinnatilibrary.org
Special Collections: ANSI Standards Coll; ASTM Standards Coll; Cincinnati Freie Presse 1874-1964; Cincinnati Volksblatt 1846-1918; Cincinnati Volksfreunt 1850-1908; Doane Coll; Dr Martin Luther King Jr Coll; Foundation Center Regional Coll; Grants Resource Center; Kane/Merton Coll; Keller Coll; Langstroth Lithograph Coll; Lenke Coll; Orpheus & Apollo Clubs Choral Coll; Plaut Coll; Roedter Coll; Russel Alger Frager Coll; Sackett Coll; Sackett Coll; Schild-SCORE Coll; Seasongood Coll; Straus Mayer Coll; Striker Coll; Theater, Dance & Music Programs; Theological & Religious Library Coll; Trager Memorial Coll; Trager Memorial Coll; Tragger Coll; Twentieth Century Artists Books; Valerio Coll
Subject Interests: Antiques, Applied sci, Archit, Art, Bronzes, Chem, Computer use in bus, Consumer info, Cookery, Costume hist, Dance, Decorative art, Educ, Employment, Engr, Film, Finance, Govt, Graphics, Hort, Intl relations, Libr sci, Mil sci, Music, Natural hist, Occult, Ornithology, Painting, Philos, Politics, Porcelain, Pottery, Psychol, Pure, Real estate, Recreation, Relig, Sculpture, Sociol, Sports
Friends of the Library Group

LOVELAND BRANCH, 649 Loveland-Madeira Rd, Loveland, 45140, SAN 355-8126. Tel: 513-369-4476. FAX: 513-369-4477. *Br Mgr,* Lesleigh Chumbley; E-mail: lesleigh.chumbley@cincinnatilibrary.org
Library Holdings: AV Mats 15,138; Bk Vols 57,088
Open Mon, Tues & Thurs 12-8, Wed, Fri & Sat 10-6
Friends of the Library Group

MADEIRA BRANCH, 7200 Miami Ave, Madeira, 45243, SAN 355-8150. Tel: 513-369-6028. FAX: 513-369-4501. *Br Mgr,* Kathy Kennedy-Brunner; E-mail: kathy.kennedy-brunner@cincinnatilibrary.org
Library Holdings: AV Mats 20,420; Bk Vols 88,250
Open Mon-Thurs 10-9, Fri & Sat 10-6
Friends of the Library Group

MADISONVILLE, 4830 Whetsel Ave, 45227, SAN 355-8185. Tel: 513-369-6029. FAX: 513-369-4537. *Br Mgr,* Terry Barnum; E-mail: terry.barnum@cincinnatilibrary.org; Staff 4 (MLS 1, Non-MLS 3)
Library Holdings: AV Mats 8,280; Bk Vols 16,023
Open Mon & Tues 12-8, Wed & Thurs 12-6, Fri & Sat 10-6
Friends of the Library Group

MAKERSPACE, North Bldg, 2nd Flr, 800 Vine St, 45202-2009. Tel: 513-369-6900. *Mgr,* Bill Hyden; E-mail: bill.hyden@cincinnatilibrary.org
Friends of the Library Group

MARIEMONT BRANCH, 3810 Pocahontas Ave, Mariemont, 45227, SAN 355-8215. Tel: 513-369-4467. FAX: 513-369-4468. *Br Mgr,* Kelly Hartman; E-mail: kelly.hartman@cincinnatilibrary.org
Library Holdings: AV Mats 10,904; Bk Vols 43,519
Open Mon, Tues & Thurs 12-8, Wed, Fri & Sat 10-6
Friends of the Library Group

MIAMI TOWNSHIP, Eight N Miami Ave, Cleves, 45002, SAN 355-8223. Tel: 513-369-6050. FAX: 513-369-4487. *Br Mgr,* Carrie Bernard; E-mail: carrie.bernard@cincinnatilibrary.org
Library Holdings: AV Mats 9,912; Bk Vols 22,499
Open Mon & Tues 12-8, Wed & Thurs 12-6, Fri & Sat 10-6
Friends of the Library Group

MONFORT HEIGHTS, 3825 W Fork Rd, 45247, SAN 355-872X. Tel: 513-369-4472. FAX: 513-369-4473. *Br Mgr,* Lisa Cappel; E-mail: lisa.cappel@cincinnatilibrary.org
Library Holdings: AV Mats 12,895; Bk Vols 51,479
Open Mon, Tues & Thurs 12-8, Wed, Fri & Sat 10-6, Sun 1-5
Friends of the Library Group

MOUNT HEALTHY, 7608 Hamilton Ave, 45231, SAN 355-824X. Tel: 513-369-4469. FAX: 513-369-4470. *Br Mgr,* Elizabeth Hartlaub; E-mail: elizabeth.hartlaub@cincinnatilibrary.org
Library Holdings: AV Mats 10,068; Bk Vols 24,718
Open Mon, Tues & Thurs 12-8, Wed, Fri & Sat 10-6
Friends of the Library Group

MOUNT WASHINGTON, 2049 Beechmont Ave, 45230, SAN 355-8274. Tel: 513-369-6033. FAX: 513-369-6044. *Br Mgr,* Paul Burch; E-mail: paul.burch@cincinnatilibrary.org
Library Holdings: AV Mats 21,589; Bk Vols 41,863
Open Mon, Tues & Thurs 12-8, Wed, Fri & Sat 10-6
Friends of the Library Group

NORTH CENTRAL, 11109 Hamilton Ave, 45231, SAN 370-0976. Tel: 513-369-6068. FAX: 513-369-4459. *Br Mgr,* Kate Denier; E-mail: kate.denier@cincinnatilibrary.org
Library Holdings: AV Mats 23,593; Bk Vols 68,421
Open Mon-Thurs 10-9, Fri & Sat 10-6, Sun 1-5
Friends of the Library Group

NORTHSIDE, 4219 Hamilton Ave, 45223, SAN 355-7820. Tel: 513-369-4449. FAX: 513-369-4533. *Br Mgr,* Sarah Schellenger; E-mail: sarah.schellenger@cincinnatilibrary.org
Library Holdings: AV Mats 14,606; Bk Vols 25,502
Open Mon & Tues 12-8, Wed & Thurs 12-6, Fri & Sat 10-6
Friends of the Library Group

NORWOOD, 4325 Montgomery Rd, 45212, SAN 355-8363. Tel: 513-369-6037. FAX: 513-369-6039. *Br Mgr,* LeeAnn McNabb; E-mail: leeann.mcnabb@cincinnatilibrary.org
Library Holdings: AV Mats 17,006; Bk Vols 33,636
Open Mon, Tues & Thurs 12-8, Wed, Fri & Sat 10-6
Friends of the Library Group

OAKLEY, 4033 Gilmore Ave, 45209, SAN 355-8398. Tel: 513-369-6038. FAX: 513-369-6055. *Br Mgr,* Chris Oaks; E-mail: chris.oaks@cincinnatilibrary.org
Library Holdings: AV Mats 10,562; Bk Vols 36,332
Open Mon, Tues & Thurs 12-8, Wed, Fri & Sat 10-6
Friends of the Library Group

OUTREACH SERVICES, 800 Vine St, 45202-2009, SAN 355-7596. Tel: 513-369-6963. *Outreach Serv Mgr,* Drew D Pearson; Tel: 513-665-3352, E-mail: drew.pearson@cincinnatilibrary.org
Library Holdings: AV Mats 13,558; Bk Vols 371,878
Special Collections: Dwyer Special Needs Coll; Large Print Coll
Friends of the Library Group

PLEASANT RIDGE, 6233 Montgomery Rd, 45213, SAN 355-8487. Tel: 513-369-4488. FAX: 513-369-4489. *Br Mgr,* Jennifer Korn; E-mail: jennifer.korn@cincinnatilibrary.org
Library Holdings: AV Mats 14,818; Bk Vols 40,368
Open Mon, Tues & Thurs 12-8, Wed, Fri & Sat 10-6
Friends of the Library Group

POPULAR, South Bldg, 1st Flr, 800 Vine St, 45202-2009. Tel: 513-369-6919. *Mgr,* Ella Mulford; E-mail: ella.mulford@cincinnatilibrary.org
Special Collections: Adler Coll; American International Music Fund Tapes; Dr Martin Luther King Jr Coll; Marsh Coll; Meister Coll; Oscar Treadwell Coll
Friends of the Library Group

PRICE HILL, 3215 Warsaw Ave, 45205, SAN 355-8517. Tel: 513-369-4490. FAX: 513-369-4538. *Br Mgr,* Position Currently Open
Library Holdings: AV Mats 19,029; Bk Vols 20,311
Open Mon & Tues 12-8, Wed & Thurs 12-6, Fri & Sat 10-6
Friends of the Library Group

READING BRANCH, 8740 Reading Rd, Reading, 45215, SAN 355-8665. Tel: 513-369-4465. FAX: 513-369-4466. *Br Mgr,* Cate Crusham; E-mail: cate.crusham@cincinnatilibrary.org
Library Holdings: AV Mats 15,462; Bk Vols 30,511
Open Mon, Tues & Thurs 12-8, Wed, Fri & Sat 10-6, Sun 1-5
Friends of the Library Group

SAINT BERNARD, Ten McClelland Ave, 45217, SAN 355-8576. Tel: 513-369-4462. FAX: 513-369-4463. *Br Mgr,* Kate Kraus; E-mail: kate.kraus@cincinnatilibrary.org
Library Holdings: AV Mats 7,900; Bk Vols 19,865
Open Mon, Tues & Thurs 12-8, Wed, Fri & Sat 10-6, Sun 1-5
Friends of the Library Group

SHARONVILLE, 10980 Thornview Dr, 45241, SAN 355-8606. Tel: 513-369-6049. FAX: 513-369-4504. *Br Mgr,* Tina Riehle; E-mail: tina.riehle@cincinnatilibrary.org
Library Holdings: AV Mats 17,257; Bk Vols 66,632
Open Mon-Thurs 10-9, Fri & Sat 10-6, Sun 1-5
Friends of the Library Group

SYMMES TOWNSHIP, 11850 E Enyart Rd, Loveland, 45140, SAN 370-0984. Tel: 513-369-6001. FAX: 513-369-4481. *Br Mgr,* Tara Kressler; E-mail: tara.kressler@cincinnatilibrary.org
Library Holdings: AV Mats 32,409; Bk Vols 132,533
Open Mon-Thurs 10-9, Fri & Sat 10-6
Friends of the Library Group

TECHCENTER, South Bldg, 2nd Flr, 800 Vine St, 45202-2009. FAX: 513-369-3123. *Mgr,* Bill Hyden; E-mail: bill.hyden@cincinnatilibrary.org
Friends of the Library Group

WALNUT HILLS, 2533 Kemper Lane, 45206, SAN 355-869X. Tel: 513-369-6053. FAX: 513-369-4492. *Br Mgr,* Kendall Kidder-Goshorn; E-mail: kendall.kidder-goshorn@cincinnatilibrary.org
Library Holdings: AV Mats 18,823; Bk Vols 23,489
Open Mon, Tues & Thurs 12-8, Wed, Fri & Sat 10-6
Friends of the Library Group

WEST END, 805 Ezzard Charles Dr, 45203, SAN 355-8096. Tel: 513-369-6026. FAX: 513-369-4536. *Br Mgr,* Sondra Presley; E-mail: sondra.presley@cincinnatilibrary.org
Library Holdings: AV Mats 10,378; Bk Vols 14,935
Open Mon & Tues 12-8, Wed & Thurs 12-6, Fri & Sat 10-6
Friends of the Library Group

WESTWOOD, 3345 Epworth Ave, 45211, SAN 355-8754. Tel: 513-369-4474. FAX: 513-369-4475. *Br Mgr,* Travis Castleberry; E-mail: travis.castleberry@cincinnatilibrary.org
Library Holdings: AV Mats 19,845; Bk Vols 43,368
Open Mon, Tues & Thurs 12-8, Wed, Fri & Sat 10-6
Friends of the Library Group

WYOMING BRANCH, 500 Springfield Pike, Wyoming, 45215, SAN 355-7731. Tel: 513-369-6014. FAX: 513-369-6052. *Br Mgr,* Tom Gardner; E-mail: tom.gardner@cincinnatilibrary.org
Library Holdings: AV Mats 14,127; Bk Vols 52,910
Open Mon, Tues & Thurs 12-8, Wed, Fri & Sat 10-6
Friends of the Library Group

YOUTH SERVICES, North Bldg, 1st Flr, 800 Vine St, 45202-2009. Tel: 513-369-6922. *Children's Mgr,* Ted Rice; E-mail: ted.rice@cincinnatilibrary.org
Special Collections: Goldsmith Coll
Friends of the Library Group

R ROCKDALE TEMPLE*, Sidney G Rose Library, 8501 Ridge Rd, 45236. SAN 313-2846. Tel: 513-891-9900. FAX: 513-891-0515. E-mail: library@rockdaletemple.org, shalom@rockdaletemple.org. Web Site: www.rockdaletemple.org. *Vols Librn,* Karen Zanger
Founded 1960
Library Holdings: Bk Vols 5,000; Per Subs 4
Subject Interests: Judaica
Automation Activity & Vendor Info: (Cataloging) Library Concepts
Wireless access
Open Mon-Fri 9:30-4:30
Restriction: Open to pub for ref & circ; with some limitations

R ST JOHN'S WESTMINSTER UNION CHURCH*, John H Holmes Library, 1085 Neeb Rd, 45233. SAN 313-2986. Tel: 513-347-4613. E-mail: info@sjwuc.org. Web Site: www.sjwuc.org. *Librn,* Joan Key
Founded 1960
Library Holdings: Bk Titles 2,000; Bk Vols 5,500; Per Subs 10
Special Collections: Old Bibles
Subject Interests: Bible study, Devotional, Geriatrics, Relig educ

S TAFT MUSEUM OF ART LIBRARY*, 316 Pike St, 45202-4293. SAN 313-2897. Tel: 513-241-0343. FAX: 513-241-2266. E-mail: taftmuseum@taftmuseum.org. Web Site: www.taftmuseum.org. *Assoc Librn,* Tamera Lenz Muente; Tel: 513-352-5136; *Asst Curator,* Ann Glasscock; *Curatorial Asst,* Angela Fuller
Founded 1932
Library Holdings: Bk Vols 3,000
Special Collections: Taft Art Coll Archives
Subject Interests: Archit, Art, Decorative arts of 16th to 19th centuries
Publications: Taft Museum: Collections & Its History (4 vols)
Restriction: Open by appt only

L TAFT, STETTINIUS & HOLLISTER LLP*, Law Library, 425 Walnut St, Ste 1800, 45202-3957. SAN 313-2900. Tel: 513-381-2838. FAX: 513-381-0205. Web Site: www.taftlaw.com/offices/1-cincinnati. *Research Librn,* Melanie Farrell; E-mail: mfarrell@taftlaw.com; Staff 3 (MLS 2, Non-MLS 1)
Library Holdings: Bk Vols 30,000
Restriction: Staff use only

L THOMPSON HINE LLP*, Law Library, 1400 Scripps Ctr, 312 Walnut St, 45202. SAN 372-2112. Tel: 513-352-6528. FAX: 513-241-4771. E-mail: library@thompsonhine.com. Web Site: www.thompsonhine.com. *Assoc Dir, Libr Operations,* Barbara Silbersack; Staff 2 (MLS 2)
Library Holdings: Bk Vols 2,000; Per Subs 100
Automation Activity & Vendor Info: (Cataloging) Horizon; (Circulation) Horizon; (OPAC) Horizon; (Serials) Horizon
Wireless access
Restriction: Not open to pub

M TRIHEALTH, INC*, Good Samaritan Hospital Library, 375 Dixmyth Ave, 45220-2489. SAN 313-2730. Tel: 513-862-2433. FAX: 513-862-4984. E-mail: library@trihealth.com. Web Site: trihealth.libguides.com/home, www.trihealth.com/research-and-education/education/library-services. *Dean, Libr Serv,* Beth Moores; E-mail: beth_moores@trihealth.com; Staff 5 (MLS 1, Non-MLS 4)
Founded 1915
Library Holdings: Bk Titles 9,000; Bk Vols 9,500
Special Collections: History of Nursing
Subject Interests: Biomed, Nursing, Obstetrics, Perinatology, Surgery
Automation Activity & Vendor Info: (Cataloging) EOS International; (Circulation) EOS International; (OPAC) EOS International; (Serials) EOS International
Wireless access
Publications: Library News
Partic in SouthWest Ohio & Neighboring Libraries
Open Mon-Fri 8-5

C UNION INSTITUTE & UNIVERSITY LIBRARY, 2090 Florence Ave, 45206. SAN 362-6466. Tel: 513-487-1487. E-mail: library@myunion.edu. Web Site: library.myunion.edu. *Libr Dir,* Matthew Pappathan; Tel: 513-487-1251, E-mail: matthew.pappathan@myunion.edu; *Electronic Res Librn,* Aura Fluet; Tel: 513-487-1210, E-mail: aura.fluet@myunion.edu; *Ref Librn,* Susan Whitehead; Tel: 513-487-1243, E-mail: susan.whitehead@myunion.edu; Staff 3 (MLS 3)
Founded 1934. Highest Degree: Doctorate
Library Holdings: e-journals 125,000; Electronic Media & Resources 150
Subject Interests: Applied psychol, Creative writing, Holistic studies, Visual arts, Women's studies
Partic in LYRASIS
Open Mon-Fri 9-5
Restriction: Open to students, fac & staff

L US COURT OF APPEALS FOR THE SIXTH CIRCUIT LIBRARY*, 540 Potter Stewart US Courthouse, 100 E Fifth St, 45202-3911. (Mail add: 317 Potter Stewart US Courthouse, 45202), SAN 313-2927. Tel: 513-564-7321. FAX: 513-564-7329. E-mail: CA06-Library@ca6.uscourts.gov. Web Site: www.ca6.uscourts.gov. *Circuit Librn,* Owen G Smith; Tel: 513-564-7324, E-mail: owen_smith@ca6.uscourts.gov; *Cleveland Satellite Librn,* Irene Milan; Tel: 216-357-7275; *Columbus Satellite Librn,* Ellen Smith; Tel: 614-719-3180; *Detroit Satellite Librn,* Elise Keller; Tel: 313-234-5255; *Digital Serv Librn,* Tom Vanderloo; *Grand Rapids Satellite Librn,* Mary Andrews; Tel: 616-456-2068; *Louisville Satellite Librn,* Bonnie Robinson; Tel: 502-625-3850; *Memphis Satellite Librn,* Karen Kalnins; Tel: 901-495-1357; *Toledo Satellite Librn,* Marianne Mussett; *Archivist,* Neil Reed; Staff 27 (MLS 15, Non-MLS 12)
Founded 1895
Library Holdings: Bk Vols 250,000
Special Collections: Primarily Anglo-American Legal Coll
Automation Activity & Vendor Info: (Acquisitions) SirsiDynix; (Cataloging) SirsiDynix; (Serials) SirsiDynix
Publications: Sixth Circuit History (Online only)
Partic in Federal Library & Information Network; OCLC Online Computer Library Center, Inc
Open Mon-Fri 8-5
Restriction: Access at librarian's discretion

CL UNIVERSITY OF CINCINNATI*, Robert S Marx Law Library, 2540 Clifton Ave, 45219. (Mail add: PO Box 210142, 45221-0142), SAN 355-905X. Tel: 513-556-0163. Circulation Tel: 513-556-3016. Administration Tel: 513-556-0159. FAX: 513-556-6265. E-mail: marxlawlib@ucmail.uc.edu. Web Site: law.uc.edu/education/library. *Assoc Dean of Libr, Dir, Law Libr,* Michael Whiteman; E-mail: whitemm@ucmail.uc.edu; *Assoc Dir, Pub & Res Serv,* Susan Boland; Tel: 513-556-4407, E-mail: susan.boland@uc.edu; *Bibliog Serv Librn, Spec Coll Librn,* Akram Sadeghi Pari; Tel: 513-556-0154, E-mail: akram.sadeghipari@uc.edu; *Coll & Access Serv Librn,* Lisa Britt-Wernke; Tel: 513-556-0156, E-mail: lisa.britt@uc.edu; *Electronic Serv/Ref Librn,* Ronald Jones; Tel: 513-556-0158, E-mail: ronald.jones@uc.edu; *Media Serv Spec,* Mike Mimms; Tel: 513-556-0161, E-mail: michael.mimms@uc.edu; *Research & Instruction Services,* Shannon Kemen; Tel: 513-556-6407, E-mail: shannon.kemen@uc.edu; *Libr Assoc,*

Rhonda Wiseman; Tel: 513-556-0165, E-mail: rhonda.wiseman@uc.edu; Staff 11 (MLS 8, Non-MLS 3)
Founded 1833. Enrl 300; Fac 40; Highest Degree: Doctorate
Special Collections: Church & State Coll; Cincinnati Legal History & Reports of Various Courts; Early Ohio Legal Coll, history reports; Human Rights; Land Use & Planning. US Document Depository
Subject Interests: Human rights, Intl law, Law
Automation Activity & Vendor Info: (Acquisitions) Innovative Interfaces, Inc; (Cataloging) Innovative Interfaces, Inc; (Circulation) Innovative Interfaces, Inc; (ILL) OCLC; (OPAC) Innovative Interfaces, Inc; (Serials) Innovative Interfaces, Inc
Wireless access
Function: Electronic databases & coll, ILL available, Internet access, Online cat, Photocopying/Printing, Ref serv available
Partic in Mid-America Law Library Consortium; OCLC Online Computer Library Center, Inc; Ohio Library & Information Network; SouthWest Ohio & Neighboring Libraries
Restriction: 24-hr pass syst for students only

C UNIVERSITY OF CINCINNATI*, Blue Ash College Library, 9555 Plainfield Rd, Muntz 113, 45236. SAN 355-9173. Tel: 513-745-5710. FAX: 513-745-5767. E-mail: ucbalibrary@ucblueash.edu. Web Site: www.libraries.uc.edu/ucba. *Dir,* Heather Maloney; Tel: 513-936-1541, E-mail: heather.maloney@uc.edu; *Ref, Sr Assoc Librn, Web Serv,* Michelle McKinney; Tel: 513-936-1546, E-mail: michelle.mckinney@uc.edu; Staff 7 (MLS 4, Non-MLS 3)
Founded 1967. Enrl 2,000; Fac 100
Library Holdings: Bk Vols 50,000; Per Subs 450
Automation Activity & Vendor Info: (Acquisitions) Innovative Interfaces, Inc
Wireless access
Open Mon-Thurs (Fall/Spring) 7:30am-9pm, Fri 7:30-5, Sat 12-4 ; Mon-Thurs (Summer) 8-6:30, Fri 8-4

C UNIVERSITY OF CINCINNATI LIBRARIES*, Walter C Langsam Library, PO Box 210033, 45221-0033. SAN 355-8843. Tel: 513-556-1515. Circulation Tel: 513-556-1424. Interlibrary Loan Service Tel: 513-556-1461. Reference Tel: 513-556-1867. FAX: 513-556-0325. Web Site: libraries.uc.edu. *Dean & Univ Librn,* Xuemao Wang; E-mail: xuemao.wang@uc.edu; *Assoc Dean, Pub Serv,* Brad Warren; E-mail: warrenbz@uc.edu; *Admin Assoc,* Regina Tassell; E-mail: regina.tassell@uc.edu; Staff 93 (MLS 42, Non-MLS 51)
Founded 1819. Enrl 43,598; Fac 1,166; Highest Degree: Doctorate
Library Holdings: e-books 1,533,274; e-journals 121,649; Bk Vols 4,500,741
Special Collections: 18th Century British Anonymous Poetical Pamphlets (Dobell Coll); 19th & 20th Century Astronomy (Cincinnati Observatory Coll), journals, monographs, recs; 19th & 20th Century German-Americana (Fick Coll); 20th Century English Language Poetry (Elliston Coll); American Labor History (McNamara Coll); Celtic Studies (Knott-Radner Coll); Classical Studies, incl Art, Language, Literature, History, Civilization, Philosophy, Religion, Archaeology, Greek & Latin Paleography (Burnam Classical Library); D H Lawrence Manuscripts & Dorothy Brett Correspondence (D H Lawrence Coll); Dale Warland Singers Coll; History of Chemistry (Oesper Coll); Modern Greek Studies Coll; Urban Studies Coll. US Document Depository
Automation Activity & Vendor Info: (Acquisitions) Innovative Interfaces, Inc; (Cataloging) Innovative Interfaces, Inc; (Circulation) Innovative Interfaces, Inc; (Course Reserve) Docutek; (ILL) OCLC ILLiad
Wireless access
Function: E-Reserves, Equip loans & repairs, Govt ref serv, ILL available, Photocopying/Printing, Wheelchair accessible, Workshops
Publications: Source (Newsletter)
Partic in Asn Col & Res Librs; Association of Research Libraries; Center for Research Libraries; OCLC Research Library Partnership; Ohio Library & Information Network; OhioNET; SouthWest Ohio & Neighboring Libraries
Special Services for the Blind - Assistive/Adapted tech devices, equip & products; Audio mat; Braille equip; Closed circuit TV; Computer with voice synthesizer for visually impaired persons; Copier with enlargement capabilities; Magnifiers
Friends of the Library Group

Departmental Libraries:

ARCHIVES & RARE BOOKS, Blegan Library, 8th Flr, 2602 McMicken Circle, 45221. (Mail add: PO Box 210113, 45221-0113), SAN 323-5734. Tel: 513-556-1959. FAX: 513-556-2113. E-mail: archives@ucmail.uc.edu. Web Site: libraries.uc.edu/arb. *Head of Libr, Univ Archivist,* Kevin Grace; E-mail: kevin.grace@uc.edu; *Ref/Coll Librn,* Suzanne Maggard Reller; Tel: 513-556-7016, E-mail: suzanne.maggard@uc.edu; *Digital Archivist/Rec Mgr,* Eira Tansey; Tel: 513-556-1958, E-mail: eira.tansey@uc.edu
Special Collections: German-Americana Coll; Ohio Network Coll; Rare Book Coll; University Archives; Urban Studies Coll
Open Mon-Fri 8-5

CHEMISTRY-BIOLOGY, 503 Rieveschl, A-3, 45221. (Mail add: PO Box 210151, 45221-0151), SAN 355-8878. Tel: 513-556-1498. FAX: 513-556-1103. Web Site: libraries.uc.edu/chem-bio. *Dir, Science & Engineering Libraries,* Ted Baldwin; Tel: 513-556-4211, E-mail: ted.baldwin@uc.edu
Special Collections: The Oesper History of Chemistry Coll

CLASSICS, 417 Blegen Library, 45221, SAN 355-8908. Tel: 513-556-1315. FAX: 513-556-6244. Web Site: libraries.uc.edu/classics. *Head Librn,* Rebecka Lindau; E-mail: rebecka.lindau@uc.edu
Special Collections: Modern Greek Coll

COLLEGE-CONSERVATORY OF MUSIC, 600 Blegen Library, 45221. (Mail add: PO Box 210152, 45221-0152), SAN 355-8932. Tel: 513-556-1970. FAX: 513-556-3777. Web Site: libraries.uc.edu/ccm. *Head Librn,* Dr Jenny Doctor; E-mail: jenny.doctor@uc.edu; *Asst Music Librn,* Paul Cauthen; Tel: 513-556-1965, E-mail: paul.cauthen@uc.edu
Special Collections: Dale Warland Singers Coll; Everett Helm Coll; Parvin Titus Coll; Thomas Cobbe Coll of Composer Portraits

COLLEGE OF EDUCATION, CRIMINAL JUSTICE & HUMAN SERVICES LIBRARY, 400 Teachers College, 45221. (Mail add: PO Box 210219, 45221-0219), SAN 329-0166. Tel: 513-556-1430. FAX: 513-556-2122. Web Site: libraries.uc.edu/cech. *Head of Libr,* Katie Foran-Mulcahy; Tel: 513-556-1758, E-mail: foranmkn@uc.edu

COLLEGE OF ENGINEERING & APPLIED SCIENCE LIBRARY, 850 Baldwin Hall, 45221. (Mail add: PO Box 210018, 45221-0018), SAN 355-8991. Tel: 513-556-1550. FAX: 513-556-2654. Web Site: libraries.uc.edu/ceas. *Dir, Science & Engineering Libraries,* Ted Baldwin; Tel: 513-556-4211, E-mail: ted.baldwin@uc.edu

DESIGN, ARCHITECTURE ART & PLANNING, 5480 Aronoff Ctr, 45221. (Mail add: PO Box 210016, 45221-0016), SAN 355-8967. Tel: 513-556-1335. FAX: 513-556-3006. Web Site: libraries.uc.edu/daap. *Visual Res Librn,* Elizabeth Meyer; Tel: 513-556-0279, E-mail: elizabeth.meyer@uc.edu; *Circ Supvr,* Sara Mihaly; Tel: 513-556-1321, E-mail: sara.mihaly@uc.edu

GEOLOGY-MATHEMATICS-PHYSICS, 240 Braunstein Hall, 45221. (Mail add: PO Box 210153, 45221-0153), SAN 355-9025. Tel: 513-556-1324. FAX: 513-556-1930. Web Site: libraries.uc.edu/gmp. *Dir, Science & Engineering Libraries,* Ted Baldwin; Tel: 513-556-4211, E-mail: ted.baldwin@uc.edu
Founded 2004

CM DONALD C HARRISON HEALTH SCIENCES LIBRARY, 231 Albert Sabin Way, 45267, SAN 355-9238. Tel: 513-558-0127. FAX: 513-558-2682. Web Site: libraries.uc.edu/hsl. *Dir, IT Serv & Circ,* Birsen Kaya; Tel: 513-558-0345, E-mail: birsen.kaya@uc.edu; *Asst Dir,* Lori Harris; Tel: 513-558-0315, E-mail: lori.harris@uc.edu; *Asst Dir, Research & Informatics,* Kristen Burgess; Tel: 513-558-3071, E-mail: kristen.burgess@uc.edu; *Educ Librn, Res,* Emily Kean; Tel: 513-558-3849, E-mail: emily.kean@uc.edu; *Info Serv Librn,* Edith Starbuck; Tel: 513-558-1433, E-mail: edith.starbuck@uc.edu; *Tech Serv Librn,* Sharon Ann Purtee; Tel: 513-558-1019, E-mail: sharon.purtee@uc.edu; *ILL, Supvr,* Gerald Wagner; Tel: 513-558-8389, E-mail: gerald.wagner@uc.edu; *Info Spec,* Tiffany Grant; Tel: 513-558-9153, E-mail: tiffany.grant@uc.edu
Founded 1974
Subject Interests: Allied health, Basic med sci, Clinical med sci, Healthcare delivery, Hist of med, Non-print instrul mat in med, Nursing, Patient educ, Pharm
Partic in OCLC Online Computer Library Center, Inc; Proquest Dialog
Publications: University of Cincinnati Serials Holdings List

HENRY R WINKLER CENTER FOR THE HISTORY OF THE HEALTH PROFESSIONS, 231 Albert Sabin Way, 45267. Tel: 513-558-5120. FAX: 513-558-2682. E-mail: CHHP@uc.edu. Web Site: www.libraries.uc.edu/winkler-center.html. *Archivist, Curator,* Gino Pasi; Tel: 513-558-5123, E-mail: gino.pasi@uc.edu
Founded 1974
Special Collections: 63 Archives (including Robert A Kehoe & Albert S Sabin Archives); History of Laser Medicine; History of Medicine in West (Daniel Drake, Reuben Dimond Mussey & David A Tucker Colls), bks & ms; Local & State Medical Archives, photog & portraits. Oral History
Restriction: Open by appt only

R WESTWOOD FIRST PRESBYTERIAN CHURCH LIBRARY*, 3011 Harrison Ave, 45211. SAN 313-2994. Tel: 513-661-6846. Web Site: wfpc.org.
Founded 1957
Library Holdings: Bk Titles 4,000; Bk Vols 4,200; Per Subs 16
Special Collections: Anchor Bible Series; Books & Materials on Cincinnati; General (Henderson Coll); Large Print Coll, bks & pers; New Interpreter's Bible Series; Presbyterian Church College Catalogue Coll
Subject Interests: Bible ref, Relig bks
Automation Activity & Vendor Info: (Cataloging) Follett Software; (Circulation) Follett Software
Publications: Adult Education Class (Bibliographies); Church Curriculum Materials Lists; Holiday Bibliographies; Newsletter (Annual)
Special Services for the Blind - Large print bks

R ISAAC M WISE TEMPLE*, Ralph & Julia Cohen Library, 8329 Ridge Rd, 45236. SAN 313-3001. Tel: 513-793-2556, Ext 123. FAX: 513-793-3322. Web Site: wisetemple.org. *Librn,* Andrea Rapp; E-mail: arapp@wisetemple.org. Subject Specialists: *Israel, Jewish holocaust, Judaica,* Andrea Rapp; Staff 1 (MLS 1)
Founded 1931
Library Holdings: Bk Titles 15,000; Bk Vols 20,000; Per Subs 35
Subject Interests: Holocaust, Judaica
Automation Activity & Vendor Info: (Cataloging) Surpass; (Circulation) Surpass; (OPAC) Surpass
Wireless access
Open Mon & Wed 12-5, Tues & Thurs 9-3

CR XAVIER UNIVERSITY*, McDonald Memorial Library, 1535 Musketeer Dr, 45207. (Mail add: 3800 Victory Pkwy, 45207), SAN 313-301X. Tel: 513-745-3881. FAX: 513-745-1932. E-mail: xulib@xavier.edu. Web Site: www.xavier.edu/library. *Dir, Univ Libr,* Ken Gibson; Tel: 513-745-4359, E-mail: gibsonk6@xavier.edu; *Asst Dir, Pub Serv,* Alison Morgan; Tel: 513-745-3931, E-mail: morgan@xavier.edu; *Head, Access Serv,* Anne Davies; Tel: 513-745-4803, E-mail: davies@xavier.edu; *Head, Coll Mgt,* Daphne Miller; Tel: 513-745-1007, E-mail: millerda@xavier.edu; *Head, Coll Serv,* Angela Irvine; Tel: 513-745-4804, E-mail: irvinea2@xavier.edu; *Head, Libr Syst,* Michelle Early; Tel: 513-745-4817, E-mail: early@xavier.edu; *Head, User Experience,* James Green; Tel: 513-745-1940, E-mail: greenj11@xavier.edu; *Historian,* Rev Thomas Kennealy; Tel: 513-745-4822, E-mail: kennealy@xavier.edu; Staff 26 (MLS 13, Non-MLS 13)
Founded 1831. Enrl 6,666; Fac 373; Highest Degree: Doctorate
Library Holdings: AV Mats 6,918; Bks on Deafness & Sign Lang 112; DVDs 4,302; High Interest/Low Vocabulary Bk Vols 52; Per Subs 583; Talking Bks 137
Special Collections: Bibles, Incunabula & Jesuitica; Catholic Boy's Fiction (Francis Finn, SJ, Coll)
Subject Interests: Gen, Philos, Theol
Automation Activity & Vendor Info: (Acquisitions) Innovative Interfaces, Inc; (Cataloging) Innovative Interfaces, Inc; (Circulation) Innovative Interfaces, Inc; (ILL) Innovative Interfaces, Inc; (OPAC) Innovative Interfaces, Inc; (Serials) Innovative Interfaces, Inc
Wireless access
Function: Archival coll, Doc delivery serv, ILL available, Telephone ref
Partic in OCLC Online Computer Library Center, Inc; Ohio Library & Information Network; OhioNET; SouthWest Ohio & Neighboring Libraries
Open Mon-Thurs 7am-1am, Fri 7-7, Sat 8-5, Sun 10am-1am
Friends of the Library Group

CIRCLEVILLE

CR OHIO CHRISTIAN UNIVERSITY*, Melvin & Laura Maxwell Library, 1476 Lancaster Pike, 43113. SAN 313-3036. Tel: 740-477-7747. E-mail: library@ohiochristian.edu. Web Site: my.ohiochristian.edu/maxwell-library. *Dir, Libr Serv,* Paul Roberts; E-mail: proberts@ohiochristian.edu; Staff 2.5 (MLS 1.5, Non-MLS 1)
Founded 1947. Highest Degree: Master
Library Holdings: CDs 669; DVDs 496; Bk Vols 50,042; Per Subs 32
Special Collections: Stout Bible Coll
Subject Interests: Bible, Missions, Theol
Automation Activity & Vendor Info: (Cataloging) Innovative Interfaces, Inc - Sierra; (Circulation) Innovative Interfaces, Inc - Sierra; (Discovery) EBSCO Discovery Service; (ILL) OCLC FirstSearch; (OPAC) Innovative Interfaces, Inc - Sierra
Wireless access
Publications: New Books List
Partic in Ohio Library & Information Network
Open Mon-Thurs 7:30am-10pm, Fri 7:30-5, Sun 6pm-9pm

P PICKAWAY COUNTY DISTRICT PUBLIC LIBRARY*, 1160 N Court St, 43113-1725. SAN 313-3052. Tel: 740-477-1644. FAX: 740-474-2855. Web Site: www.pickawaylib.org. *Dir,* David Fausnaugh; Tel: 740-477-1644, Ext 223, E-mail: director@pickawaylib.org; *Mgr, Info Tech,* David Townsend; Tel: 740-477-1644, Ext 232, E-mail: pclit@pickawaylib.org; *Coord, Coll Develop, Tech Serv,* Shelah Stahr; Tel: 740-477-1644, Ext 222, E-mail: pclacqmgr@pickawaylib.org; *Coordr, Ch Serv,* Sharon Edington; Tel: 740-477-1644, Ext 228, E-mail: youthmgr@pickawaylib.org; *Coordr, Circ,* Mary Stanton; Tel: 740-477-1644, Ext 225, E-mail: circulationmgr@pickawaylib.org; *Ref Coordr,* Sarah Hintz; Tel: 740-477-1644, Ext 227, E-mail: referencemgr@pickawaylib.org; *Outreach Serv, Team Leader,* Kim Davis; Tel: 740-477-1644, Ext 230, E-mail: outreachmgr@pickawaylib.org; Staff 17 (MLS 8, Non-MLS 9)
Founded 1834. Pop 50,325
Library Holdings: Per Subs 168
Automation Activity & Vendor Info: (Acquisitions) SirsiDynix; (Cataloging) SirsiDynix; (Circulation) SirsiDynix; (ILL) SirsiDynix; (OPAC) SirsiDynix; (Serials) SirsiDynix
Wireless access
Partic in Cent Libr Consortium; OCLC Online Computer Library Center, Inc; OhioNET
Open Mon-Thurs 10-8, Fri & Sat 10-6, Sun (Sept-May) 1-5
Friends of the Library Group
Branches: 1
FLOYD E YOUNKIN BRANCH, 51 Long St, Ashville, 43103. Tel: 740-983-8856. Circulation Tel: 740-983-8856, Ext 21. FAX: 740-983-4287. *Br Mgr,* Joy Jewett; Tel: 740-983-8856, Ext 23, E-mail: jjewett@pickawaylib.org
Open Mon-Thurs (Fall & Spring) 9:30-8, Sat 9:30-5, Sun 1-5; Mon (Summer) 9:30-8, Tues-Thurs 9:30-6, Sat 9:30-5
Friends of the Library Group
Bookmobiles: 1. Team Leader, Kim Davis

GL PICKAWAY COUNTY LAW LIBRARY ASSOCIATION*, Pickaway County Law Library Resources Board, 207 S Court St, Pickaway County Courthouse, 43113. SAN 313-3060. Tel: 740-474-8376. FAX: 740-420-5421. Administration E-mail: amalott@pickaway.org. *Dir,* Alice Malott; E-mail: amalott@pickaway.org
Open Mon 9-12

CLEVELAND

L BAKER & HOSTETLER LLP LIBRARY*, Key Tower, 127 Public Sq, Ste 200, 44114-1214. SAN 313-3133. Tel: 216-621-0200, 216-861-7199. FAX: 216-696-0740. Web Site: www.bakerlaw.com. *Librn,* Jamie Klausner; Staff 2 (MLS 2)
Founded 1916. Circ 39,795
Library Holdings: Bk Vols 54,000
Automation Activity & Vendor Info: (Acquisitions) SirsiDynix; (Cataloging) SirsiDynix; (Circulation) SirsiDynix; (Course Reserve) SirsiDynix; (ILL) SirsiDynix; (Media Booking) SirsiDynix; (OPAC) SirsiDynix; (Serials) SirsiDynix
Restriction: Staff use only

C CASE WESTERN RESERVE UNIVERSITY*, Kelvin Smith Library, 11055 Euclid Ave, 44106. (Mail add: 10900 Euclid Ave, 44106-7151), SAN 355-9416. Tel: 216-368-3506. Interlibrary Loan Service Tel: 216-368-3517. Administration Tel: 216-368-2992. FAX: 216-368-6950. E-mail: asksl@case.edu. Web Site: www.case.edu/library. *Vice Provost & Univ Librn,* Arnold Hirshon; E-mail: arnold.hirshon@case.edu; *Assoc Dir, Curator,* Roger Zender; Tel: 216-368-5637, E-mail: rez7@case.edu; *Assoc Dir, Acad Engagement Serv,* Jose Diaz; Tel: 216-368-6508, E-mail: jxd572@case.edu; *Head, Access & Delivery Serv, Team Leader,* Jennine Vlach; Tel: 216-368-0555, E-mail: jav48@case.edu; *Budget Officer, Head, Assessment & Planning, Team Leader,* Gina Midlik; Tel: 216-368-5292, E-mail: gina.midlik@case.edu; *Digital Learning Librn, Head, Digital Scholarship Serv, Team Leader,* Jennifer Green; Tel: 216-368-3756, E-mail: jxg854@case.edu; *Acq & Metadata Serv Team Leader,* Paul Heyde; Tel: 216-368-6599, E-mail: pch36@case.edu; *Mgr, Human Res & Diversity Prog, Team Leader,* Marel Corredor-Hyland; Tel: 216-368-2990, E-mail: mxc277@case.edu; *Res Serv, Team Leader,* Jennifer Starkey; Tel: 216-368-6511, E-mail: jms565@case.edu; *Spec Coll Archivist, Team Leader,* William Claspy; Tel: 216-368-3595, E-mail: wpc@case.edu; Staff 40 (MLS 30, Non-MLS 10)
Highest Degree: Doctorate
Library Holdings: e-books 1,343,028; Bk Titles 3,183,958; Bk Vols 3,219,958
Special Collections: British and American Autographs and Letters; British Literature; Cleveland Play House archive; French Revolution; German Literature & Philology; History of Science & Technology; Natural History; Performance Art Festival archive; Public Housing & Urban Development; Science Fiction; Thoreau; Victorian Illustrated Literature. US Document Depository
Automation Activity & Vendor Info: (Acquisitions) Innovative Interfaces, Inc; (Cataloging) Innovative Interfaces, Inc; (Circulation) Innovative Interfaces, Inc; (OPAC) Innovative Interfaces, Inc; (Serials) Innovative Interfaces, Inc
Wireless access
Partic in LYRASIS; OCLC Online Computer Library Center, Inc; Ohio Library & Information Network; OhioNET
Departmental Libraries:
LILLIAN & MILFORD HARRIS LIBRARY, Jack Joseph & Morton Mandel School of Applied Social Sciences, 11235 Bellflower Rd, 44106-7164, SAN 355-9564. Tel: 216-368-2302. FAX: 216-368-2106. Reference E-mail: harrisref@case.edu. Web Site: msass.case.edu/harrislibrary. *Dir,* Samantha C Skutnik; Tel: 216-368-2283, E-mail: samantha.skutnik@case.edu; *Ref & Instrul Serv Librn,* Kristen J Kirchgesler; E-mail: kristen1@case.edu; *Tech Serv Librn,* June Hund; E-mail: june.hund@case.edu; *Access Serv, Circ Serv,* Lena Ford; E-mail: lena.ford@case.edu; Staff 5 (MLS 3, Non-MLS 2)
Founded 1916. Enrl 600; Fac 30; Highest Degree: Doctorate
Library Holdings: AV Mats 979; Bk Vols 40,421; Per Subs 267
Subject Interests: Soc work

Automation Activity & Vendor Info: (Acquisitions) Innovative Interfaces, Inc - Millennium; (Cataloging) Innovative Interfaces, Inc - Millennium; (Circulation) Innovative Interfaces, Inc - Millennium; (Course Reserve) Innovative Interfaces, Inc - Millennium; (ILL) OCLC ILLiad; (OPAC) Innovative Interfaces, Inc - Millennium; (Serials) Innovative Interfaces, Inc - Millennium
Special Services for the Blind - Accessible computers; Assistive/Adapted tech devices, equip & products; Magnifiers
Open Mon-Thurs 8-7, Fri 8-5, Sat & Sun 11-5

CL SCHOOL OF LAW LIBRARY, 11075 East Blvd, 44106-7148, SAN 355-9599. Tel: 216-368-2792. Interlibrary Loan Service Tel: 216-368-8862. Reference Tel: 216-368-5206. FAX: 216-368-1002. Web Site: law.cwru.edu. *Dir, Law Libr,* C Andrew Plumb-Larrick; E-mail: cap95@case.edu; *Assoc Dir for Operations,* Robert Myers; Tel: 216-368-8656, E-mail: rrm8@case.edu; *Head, Cat,* Deborah Dennison; Tel: 216-368-6040, E-mail: dsd2@case.edu; *Head, Circ,* Donna Ertin; Tel: 216-368-8510, E-mail: dme@case.edu; *Head, Ref,* Andy Dorchak; Tel: 216-368-2842, E-mail: axd10@case.edu; *Access Serv,* Lisa Peters; Tel: 216-368-2793, E-mail: lkp@case.edu; *Electronic Res,* Megan Allen; Tel: 216-368-5223, E-mail: mja5@case.edu; *Electronic Res,* Judy Kaul; Tel: 216-368-8570, E-mail: jak4@case.edu; *Govt Doc,* Petite Sarajean; Tel: 216-368-6356, E-mail: sjw3@case.edu; *Ref (Info Servs),* Cheryl Cheatham; Tel: 216-368-1611, E-mail: csc4@case.edu; Staff 25 (MLS 11, Non-MLS 14)
Founded 1893. Enrl 747; Fac 54; Highest Degree: Doctorate
Library Holdings: Bk Titles 96,000; Bk Vols 297,786; Per Subs 9,962
Special Collections: Anglo-American Common Law; Audiovisual Coll; Government Documents Coll; Legal Clinic; Microforms Coll; Rare Book Coll
Subject Interests: Comparative law, Computers, Foreign, Law, Med
Automation Activity & Vendor Info: (Acquisitions) Innovative Interfaces, Inc; (Cataloging) Innovative Interfaces, Inc; (Circulation) Innovative Interfaces, Inc; (Course Reserve) Innovative Interfaces, Inc; (OPAC) Innovative Interfaces, Inc; (Serials) Innovative Interfaces, Inc
Partic in Lexis, OCLC Online Computer Libr Ctr, Inc; Mid-America Law Library Consortium; Worldcat
Publications: Acquisitions List; Computer Lab Manual, 2nd ed; Guide to Periodicals; Research Guides & Pathfinder Series
Open Mon-Thurs 7:30am-Midnight, Fri 7:30am-10pm, Sat 8:30-8, Sun Noon-Midnight

S CLEVELAND BOTANICAL GARDEN*, Eleanor Squire Library, 11030 East Blvd, 44106. SAN 313-3486. Tel: 216-707-2812. Web Site: www.cbgarden.org. *Head Librn,* Gary Esmonde; Staff 2 (MLS 1, Non-MLS 1)
Founded 1930
Library Holdings: Bk Titles 10,000; Per Subs 30
Special Collections: Botany (Warren H Corning Coll); Flowering Plant Index of Illustration & Information
Subject Interests: Garden hist, Gardening, Hort, Landscape design
Wireless access
Function: Res libr
Partic in OCLC Online Computer Library Center, Inc
Open Tues-Sat 9-5, Sun 12-5
Restriction: Circ limited
Friends of the Library Group

M CLEVELAND CLINIC LIBRARY SERVICES*, Floyd D Loop Alumni Library, 9500 Euclid Ave, NA30, 44195-5243. SAN 313-3184. Tel: 216-444-5697. FAX: 216-444-0271. E-mail: library@ccf.org. Web Site: clevelandclinic.org/library. *Dir,* Michelle Kraft; Tel: 216-445-7338, E-mail: kraftm@ccf.org; Staff 11 (MLS 11)
Subject Interests: Clinical med, Med res
Automation Activity & Vendor Info: (Acquisitions) Innovative Interfaces, Inc
Wireless access
Partic in Med Libr Asn of NE Ohio; National Network of Libraries of Medicine Region 6; Ohio Library & Information Network
Open Mon-Fri 7:30-6:30, Sat 8:30-4:30

CM CLEVELAND HEALTH SCIENCES LIBRARY*, Health Education Campus Library, Allen Memorial Medical Library, 11000 Euclid Ave, 44106-7130. SAN 355-9351. Tel: 216-368-4540. Interlibrary Loan Service Tel: 216-368-6424. Reference Tel: 216-368-3218. FAX: 216-368-3008. Reference E-mail: chslref@case.edu. Web Site: case.edu/chslibrary/. *Dir,* Jessica E DeCaro; Tel: 216-368-3219, E-mail: jessica.decaro@case.edu; *Head, Electronic Res,* Shannon Butcheck; Tel: 216-368-3644, E-mail: shannon.butcheck@case.edu; *Coll Develop Librn, Rare Bks,* Thomas Hayes; Tel: 216-368-3642, E-mail: twh7@case.edu; *User Serv Librn,* Vivian McCallum; Tel: 216-368-1396, E-mail: vxm54@case.edu; *Circ Mgr,* Chris Dolwick; Tel: 216-368-6422, E-mail: crd@case.edu; Staff 6 (MLS 6)
Founded 1965
Special Collections: Cole Coll of Venereals; Darwin Coll; Freud Coll; History of Medicine Dittrick Museum of Medical History, all media, archival mat; Marshall Herbal Coll
Subject Interests: Biology, Dentistry, Med, Nursing, Nutrition
Automation Activity & Vendor Info: (Acquisitions) Innovative Interfaces, Inc; (Cataloging) Innovative Interfaces, Inc; (Circulation) Innovative Interfaces, Inc; (Course Reserve) Innovative Interfaces, Inc; (ILL) OCLC ILLiad; (OPAC) Innovative Interfaces, Inc; (Serials) Innovative Interfaces, Inc
Wireless access
Publications: Cleveland Medical Library Association (Newsletter)
Partic in National Network of Libraries of Medicine Region 6; OCLC Online Computer Library Center, Inc; Ohio Library & Information Network; OhioNET
Open Mon-Thurs (Winter) 8am-Midnight, Fri 8-7, Sat 9-5, Sun 1-9; Mon-Thurs (Summer) 8am-9pm, Fri 8-7, Sat 9-5

Departmental Libraries:

ALLEN MEMORIAL MEDICAL LIBRARY, 11000 Euclid Ave, 44106-7130, SAN 355-9386. Tel: 216-368-3643. Circulation Tel: 216-368-3641. Web Site: case.edu/chsl/library/allen.html. *Coll Develop Librn, Engagement Librn,* Thomas Hayes; Tel: 216-368-3642, E-mail: thomas.hayes@case.edu; *Archives Mgr, Colls Mgr,* Jennifer Nieves; Tel: 216-368-3648, E-mail: jennifer.nieves@case.edu; Staff 1 (MLS 1)
Open Mon-Fri 8:30-7, Sat 9-5

DITTRICK MEDICAL HISTORY CENTER, 11000 Euclid Ave, 44106-7130. Tel: 216-368-3648. FAX: 216-368-0165. E-mail: curator@case.edu. Web Site: artsci.case.edu/dittrick/museum/contact-us. *Chief Curator,* Amanda Mahoney; Tel: 216-368-6391; Staff 2 (Non-MLS 2)
Open Mon, Tues, Thurs & Fri 9-4:30, Wed 9-7, Sat 10-2
Friends of the Library Group

C CLEVELAND INSTITUTE OF ART*, Jessica Gund Memorial Library, 11610 Euclid Ave, 44106. SAN 313-3214. Tel: 216-421-7440. Administration Tel: 216-421-7442. FAX: 216-421-7439. E-mail: library@cia.edu. Web Site: www.cia.edu/library. *Libr Dir,* Laura M Ponikvar; E-mail: lponikvar@cia.edu; *Asst Dir, Tech Serv Librn,* Dana M Bjorklund; Tel: 216-421-7446, E-mail: dbjorklund@cia.edu; Staff 7 (MLS 4, Non-MLS 3)
Founded 1882. Enrl 500; Fac 70; Highest Degree: Bachelor
Library Holdings: AV Mats 133,000; CDs 184; DVDs 221; Electronic Media & Resources 15; Bk Vols 45,403; Per Subs 140; Videos 460
Special Collections: Books Made by Artists Coll
Subject Interests: Artists bks, Contemporary intl art, Craft, Design, Modern art, Photog
Automation Activity & Vendor Info: (Cataloging) Innovative Interfaces, Inc; (Circulation) Innovative Interfaces, Inc; (Course Reserve) Innovative Interfaces, Inc; (OPAC) Innovative Interfaces, Inc
Wireless access
Partic in OCLC Online Computer Library Center, Inc

S CLEVELAND INSTITUTE OF MUSIC*, Robinson Music Library, 11021 East Blvd, 44106-1776. SAN 313-3222. Tel: 216-795-3114. FAX: 216-791-3063. Web Site: www.cim.edu/aboutcim/library. *Libr Dir,* Dr Kevin McLaughlin; Tel: 216-795-3181, E-mail: kevin.mclaughlin@cim.edu; *Metadata Librn, Metadata Serv,* Anne Lockard; Tel: 216-791-5000, Ext 215, E-mail: anne.lockard@cim.edu; *Sr Res Serv Librn,* Denise Green; Tel: 216-791-5000, Ext 699, E-mail: denise.green@cim.edu; Staff 7 (MLS 5, Non-MLS 2)
Founded 1922. Highest Degree: Doctorate
Library Holdings: AV Mats 28,609; Music Scores 42,902; Bk Vols 10,726; Per Subs 110
Special Collections: Audio Visual
Subject Interests: Music
Automation Activity & Vendor Info: (Cataloging) OCLC; (OPAC) Innovative Interfaces, Inc
Wireless access
Partic in OhioNET
Open Mon-Thurs 8am-9pm, Fri 8-5, Sat 9-9, Sun 12-8
Restriction: Private libr

L CLEVELAND LAW LIBRARY, One W Lakeside Ave, 4th Flr, 44113-1078. SAN 313-3230. Tel: 216-861-5070. FAX: 216-861-1606. E-mail: lawlib@clelaw.lib.oh.us. Web Site: clevelandlawlibrary.org. *Chief Admin Officer, Librn,* Kathleen M Dugan; *Librn, Network Serv,* Eric Hess; E-mail: ehess@clelaw.lib.oh.us; *Ref & Circ Librn,* Ashley Sprankle; E-mail: ashley.sprankle@clelaw.lib.oh.us; *Tech Serv Librn,* Terri Faulhaber; E-mail: tfaulhaber@clelaw.lib.oh.us; Staff 5 (MLS 3, Non-MLS 2)
Founded 1869
Library Holdings: Bk Vols 110,000; Per Subs 90
Special Collections: Ohio Records & Briefs
Subject Interests: Law
Automation Activity & Vendor Info: (Acquisitions) SirsiDynix; (Cataloging) SirsiDynix; (Circulation) SirsiDynix; (ILL) OCLC; (OPAC) SirsiDynix; (Serials) SirsiDynix
Wireless access
Publications: Research Guide Series; FAQ's; Ohio Legal Periodical Index

Partic in CLEVNET; OCLC Online Computer Library Center, Inc; Ohio Law Library Consortium
Open Mon-Fri 8:30-5
Restriction: Mem only

S CLEVELAND METROPARKS ZOO LIBRARY*, 3900 Wildlife Way, 44109. SAN 327-7631. Tel: 216-635-3333. FAX: 216-661-3312. E-mail: zoolibrary@clevelandmetroparks.com. Web Site: www.clevelandmetroparks.com/zoo/learn/educational-programs/educational-opportunities/zoo-library. *Librn,* Rochelle LeMaster; E-mail: rll@clevelandmetroparks.com; Staff 1 (MLS 1)
Founded 1992
Library Holdings: Bk Vols 11,000; Per Subs 150
Subject Interests: Conserv, Educ, Zoology
Automation Activity & Vendor Info: (Cataloging) LibraryWorld, Inc
Function: Res libr
Restriction: Non-circulating, Open to others by appt, Staff use only

S CLEVELAND MUSEUM OF ART*, Ingalls Library, 11150 East Blvd, 44106-1797. SAN 313-3257. Tel: 216-707-2530. Administration Tel: 216-707-2538. FAX: 216-421-0921. Web Site: library.clevelandart.org, www.clevelandart.org/research/library. *Dir,* Heather Saunders; E-mail: HSaunders@clevelandart.org; *Dir, Archives,* Leslie Cade; E-mail: lcade@clevelandart.org; *Head, Access Serv,* Matthew Gengler; E-mail: mgengler@clevelandart.org; *Cat Librn,* Chloe Bragg; E-mail: CBragg@clevelandart.org; *Ser & Electronic Res Librn,* Jason Schafer; E-mail: JSchafer@clevelandart.org; *Digital Archivist, Syst Librn,* Susan Hernandez; E-mail: SHernandez@clevelandart.org; Staff 22 (MLS 7, Non-MLS 15)
Founded 1916
Library Holdings: AV Mats 862,000; e-journals 2,247; Electronic Media & Resources 101; Bk Titles 346,755; Bk Vols 500,000; Per Subs 1,120
Special Collections: American Committee on South Asian Art Coll; Arndt-Brunn Greek & Roman Portraits Coll; Asian Art Photographic Distribution, photog; Bartsch Coll; Biblioteca Berenson Archive, photog; Christie's Coll, micro; Cicognara Fiche; Courtauld Institute of Art: The Witt Library, The Conway Library; Decimal Index to Art of the Low Countries (DIAL), photog; Foto Marburg; National Palace Museum; Victoria & Albert Museum
Subject Interests: Art, Asian art, Decorative art
Automation Activity & Vendor Info: (Acquisitions) Ex Libris Group; (Cataloging) Ex Libris Group; (Circulation) Ex Libris Group; (ILL) OCLC WorldShare Interlibrary Loan; (OPAC) Ex Libris Group; (Serials) Ex Libris Group
Wireless access
Function: Res libr
Partic in Northeast Ohio Regional Library System; OCLC Online Computer Library Center, Inc; OCLC Research Library Partnership; OhioNET
Open Tues-Fri 10-4:50
Restriction: Non-circulating
Friends of the Library Group

S CLEVELAND MUSEUM OF NATURAL HISTORY*, Harold T Clark Library, One Wade Oval Dr, University Circle, 44106-1767. SAN 313-3265. Tel: 216-231-4600, Ext 3222. FAX: 216-231-5919. Web Site: www.cmnh.org/discover/library. *Librn,* Joe Tait; E-mail: jtait@cmnh.org; Staff 1 (MLS 1)
Founded 1922
Library Holdings: Bk Vols 60,000; Per Subs 650
Special Collections: Rare Book Coll
Subject Interests: Anthrop, Archaeology, Astronomy, Botany, Ecology, Geol, Mineralogy, Natural hist, Paleontology, Zoology
Wireless access
Open Tues-Sat 9-5 by appointment
Restriction: Circulates for staff only, Open to pub for ref only

P CLEVELAND PUBLIC LIBRARY*, 325 Superior Ave, 44114-1271. SAN 355-9688. Tel: 216-623-2800. Circulation Tel: 216-623-2872. Administration Tel: 216-623-2827. Administration FAX: 216-623-7015. E-mail: information@cpl.org. Web Site: cpl.org. *Exec Dir, CEO,* Felton Thomas, Jr; E-mail: Felton.Thomas@cpl.org; *Dir,* John Skrtic; Tel: 216-623-2878, E-mail: John.Skrtic@cpl.org; *Dir, Br,* Harriette Parks; Tel: 216-623-7652, E-mail: Harriette.Parks@cpl.org; *Dir, Tech Serv,* Sandy Jelar Elwell; Tel: 216-623-2817, E-mail: sandy.jelar@cpl.org; *Chief Knowledge Officer,* Timothy R Diamond; Tel: 216-623-2832, E-mail: Timothy.Diamond@cpl.org; *Chief Operating Officer,* Jeremiah Swetel; E-mail: Jeremiah.Swetel@cpl.org; Staff 157 (MLS 157)
Founded 1869. Pop 400,787; Circ 4,915,642
Library Holdings: Audiobooks 33,398; CDs 173,795; DVDs 184,333; e-books 50,687; Microforms 4,596,870; Music Scores 18,000; Bk Vols 3,337,617; Per Subs 11,827
Special Collections: Baseball History Coll; Cleveland Theatre History Coll; Cookbook Coll; Dog Coll; Historical Photograph Coll; History of Architecture, drawings, photos, plans; History of Business (Corporate Annual Reports); History of Children's Literature Coll; Industrial Standards; John G White Chess & Checkers Coll; John G White Folklore Coll; Local History & Genealogy Coll; Map Coll; Music Coll, performance parts, sheet music; Rare Books; Visual & Modern Arts (Lockwood Thompson Coll). State Document Depository; UN Document Depository; US Document Depository
Automation Activity & Vendor Info: (Acquisitions) SirsiDynix; (Cataloging) SirsiDynix; (Circulation) SirsiDynix; (ILL) SirsiDynix; (OPAC) BiblioCommons; (Serials) SirsiDynix
Wireless access
Function: 24/7 Electronic res, 24/7 Online cat, 3D Printer, Activity rm, Adult bk club, Archival coll, Art exhibits, Art programs, Audiobks on Playaways & MP3, Audiobks via web, Bilingual assistance for Spanish patrons, Bk club(s), Bks on cassette, Bks on CD, Bus archives, Butterfly Garden, Chess club, Children's prog, Computer training, Computers for patron use, Electronic databases & coll, For res purposes, Govt ref serv, Holiday prog, Home delivery & serv to seniorr ctr & nursing homes, Homebound delivery serv, Homework prog, ILL available, Internet access, Life-long learning prog for all ages, Magazines, Mail & tel request accepted, Makerspace, Meeting rooms, Microfiche/film & reading machines, Movies, Museum passes, Music CDs, Online cat, Outreach serv, Outside serv via phone, mail, e-mail & web, OverDrive digital audio bks, Photocopying/Printing, Preschool outreach, Printer for laptops & handheld devices, Prog for adults, Prog for children & young adult, Ref & res, Res assist avail, Res libr, Scanner, Senior computer classes, Senior outreach, Spanish lang bks, STEM programs, Story hour, Summer reading prog, Tax forms, Teen prog, Telephone ref, Wheelchair accessible, Writing prog
Partic in CLEVNET; OCLC Online Computer Library Center, Inc; OhioNET
Special Services for the Deaf - Bks on deafness & sign lang
Special Services for the Blind - Accessible computers; Assistive/Adapted tech devices, equip & products; Digital talking bk; Digital talking bk machines
Open Mon-Sat 10-6
Friends of the Library Group
Branches: 28
ADDISON, 6901 Superior Ave, 44103, SAN 370-9345. Tel: 216-623-6906. FAX: 216-623-6909. E-mail: Addison.Branch@cpl.org. *Br Mgr,* Tonya Briggs
Circ 183,093
Open Mon, Tues & Thurs 10-7, Wed, Fri & Sat 10-6
BROOKLYN, 3706 Pearl Rd, 44109, SAN 356-0287. Tel: 216-623-6920. FAX: 216-623-6970. E-mail: Brooklyn.Branch@cpl.org. *Actg Br Mgr,* Ron Roberts
Circ 108,922
Open Mon, Tues & Thurs 10-7, Wed, Fri & Sat 10-6
CARNEGIE WEST, 1900 Fulton Rd, 44113, SAN 356-0317. Tel: 216-623-6927. FAX: 216-623-6929. E-mail: Carnegie.West.Branch@cpl.org. *Br Mgr,* Angela Guinther
Circ 164,735
Open Mon, Tues & Thurs 10-7, Wed, Fri & Sat 10-6
COLLINWOOD, 856 E 152nd St, 44110, SAN 356-0376. Tel: 216-623-6934. FAX: 216-623-6936. E-mail: Collinwood.Branch@cpl.org. *Br Mgr,* Caroline Peak
Circ 126,298
Open Mon, Tues & Thurs 10-7, Wed, Fri & Sat 10-6
EAST 131ST STREET, 3830 E 131st St, 44120, SAN 356-0430. Tel: 216-623-6941. FAX: 216-623-6978. E-mail: E131.Branch@cpl.org. *Actg Br Mgr,* Marina Marquez
Circ 70,499
Open Mon, Tues & Thurs 10-7, Wed, Fri & Sat 10-6
EASTMAN, 11602 Lorain Ave, 44111, SAN 356-049X. Tel: 216-623-6955. FAX: 216-623-6957. E-mail: Eastman.Branch@cpl.org. *Br Mgr,* Kenneth Knape
Circ 233,862
Open Mon, Tues & Thurs 10-7, Wed, Fri & Sat 10-6
FLEET, 7224 Broadway Ave, 44105, SAN 356-052X. Tel: 216-623-6962. FAX: 216-623-6964. E-mail: Fleet.Branch@cpl.org. *Br Mgr,* Pasha Moncrief Robinson
Circ 161,990
Open Mon, Tues & Thurs 10-7, Wed, Fri & Sat 10-6
FULTON, 3545 Fulton Rd, 44109, SAN 356-0538. Tel: 216-623-6969. FAX: 216-623-6972. E-mail: Fulton.Branch@cpl.org. *Actg Br Mgr,* Steve Capuozzo
Circ 148,064
Open Mon, Tues & Thurs 10-7, Wed, Fri & Sat 10-6
GARDEN VALLEY, 7201 Kinsman Rd, Ste 101, 44104, SAN 356-0554. Tel: 216-623-6976. FAX: 216-623-7186. E-mail: Garden.Valley.Branch@cpl.org. *Br Mgr,* Maria Estrella
Circ 57,095
Open Mon, Tues & Thurs 10-7, Wed, Fri & Sat 10-6

GLENVILLE, 11900 St Clair Ave, 44108, SAN 356-0589. Tel: 216-623-6983. FAX: 216-623-6985. E-mail: Glenville.Branch@cpl.org. *Br Mgr,* Sharon Jefferson
Circ 106,841
Open Mon, Tues & Thurs 10-7, Wed, Fri & Sat 10-6
HARVARD-LEE, 16918 Harvard Ave, 44128, SAN 356-0619. Tel: 216-623-6990. FAX: 216-623-6992. E-mail: Harvard.Lee.Branch@cpl.org. *Actg Br Mgr,* Kristen Schmidt
Circ 122,398
Open Mon, Tues & Thurs 10-7, Wed, Fri & Sat 10-6
HOUGH, 1566 Crawford Rd, 44106, SAN 325-3368. Tel: 216-623-6997. FAX: 216-623-6999. E-mail: Hough.Branch@cpl.org. *Br Mgr,* Lexy Kmiecik
Circ 79,029
Open Mon, Tues & Thurs 10-7, Wed, Fri & Sat 10-6
LANGSTON HUGHES, 10200 Superior Ave, 44106, SAN 377-8029. Tel: 216-623-6975. FAX: 216-623-6974. E-mail: Langston.Hughes.Branch@cpl.org. *Br Mgr,* William Bradford
Circ 94,860
Open Mon, Tues & Thurs 10-7, Wed, Fri & Sat 10-6
JEFFERSON, 850 Jefferson Ave, 44113, SAN 356-0643. Tel: 216-623-7004. FAX: 216-623-7007. E-mail: Jefferson.Branch@cpl.org. *Br Mgr,* Jaime DeClet
Circ 125,293
Open Mon, Tues & Thurs 10-7, Wed, Fri & Sat 10-6
MARTIN LUTHER KING JR, 1962 Stokes Blvd, 44106, SAN 356-0678. Tel: 216-623-7018. FAX: 216-623-7020. E-mail: Martin.Luther.King.Branch@cpl.org. *Actg Br Mgr,* Shanell Jones
Circ 108,668
Open Mon, Tues & Thurs 10-7, Wed, Fri & Sat 10-6
LORAIN, 8216 Lorain Ave, 44102, SAN 356-0708. Tel: 216-623-7011. FAX: 216-623-7014. E-mail: Lorain.Branch@cpl.org. *Br Mgr,* Crystal Tancak
Circ 150,565
Open Mon, Tues, & Thurs 10-7, Wed, Fri & Sat 10-6
MEMORIAL-NOTTINGHAM, 17109 Lake Shore Blvd, 44110, SAN 356-0732. Tel: 216-623-7039. FAX: 216-623-7042. E-mail: Memorial.Nottingham.Branch@cpl.org. *Br Mgr,* Magnolia Peters
Circ 210,316
Open Mon, Tues & Thurs 10-7, Wed, Fri & Sat 10-6
MOUNT PLEASANT, 14000 Kinsman Rd, 44120, SAN 356-0791. Tel: 216-623-7032. FAX: 216-623-7035. E-mail: Mt.Pleasant.Branch@cpl.org. *Br Mgr,* Lori Scurka
Circ 87,799
Open Mon, Tues & Thurs 10-7, Wed, Fri & Sat 10-6
P OHIO LIBRARY FOR THE BLIND & PHYSICALLY DISABLED, 17121 Lake Shore Blvd, 44110-4006, SAN 313-3303. Tel: 216-623-2911. Toll Free Tel: 800-362-1262 (Ohio). FAX: 216-623-7036. E-mail: olbpd@cpl.org. *Mgr,* William Reed; E-mail: William.Reed@cpl.org
Founded 1931. Circ 691,237
Special Collections: Talking Books, Braille Books & Musical Scores, Print Braille Books, Described DVDs & Blu-Rays, Described Video Cassettes, Playaways
Publications: Bibliographies; Catalogs of Locally Produced Cassettes & Braille; Juvenile Patrons Newsletter (Quarterly); Ohioana; Patrons Newsletter (Quarterly)
Special Services for the Blind - Digital talking bk; Home delivery serv; Internet workstation with adaptive software; Local mags & bks recorded; Low vision equip; Magnifiers; Micro-computer access & training; PC for people with disabilities; Playaways (bks on MP3); Recorded bks; Scanner for conversion & translation of mats; Screen enlargement software for people with visual disabilities; Screen reader software; Spanish Braille mags & bks; Web-Braille; ZoomText magnification & reading software
Open Mon-Fri 9-5
RICE, 11535 Shaker Blvd, 44120, SAN 356-0856. Tel: 216-623-7046. FAX: 216-623-7049. E-mail: Rice.Branch@cpl.org. *Br Mgr,* Amiya Hutson
Circ 162,701
Open Mon, Tues & Thurs 10-7, Wed, Fri & Sat 10-6
ROCKPORT, 4421 W 140th St, 44135, SAN 356-0880. Tel: 216-623-7053. FAX: 216-623-7055. E-mail: Rockport.Branch@cpl.org. *Br Mgr,* Forrest Lykins
Circ 283,241
Open Mon, Tues & Thurs 10-7, Wed, Fri & Sat 10-6
SOUTH, 3096 Scranton Rd, 44113, SAN 356-0910. Tel: 216-623-7060. FAX: 216-623-7063. E-mail: South.Branch@cpl.org. *Br Mgr,* Jaime Declet
Circ 118,840
Open Mon,Tues & Thurs 10-7, Wed, Fri & Sat 10-6
SOUTH BROOKLYN, 4303 Pearl Rd, 44109, SAN 356-0945. Tel: 216-623-7067. FAX: 216-623-7069. E-mail: South.Brooklyn.Branch@cpl.org. *Br Mgr,* Luigi Russo
Circ 266,329
Open Mon, Tues & Thurs 10-7, Wed, Fri & Sat 10-6
STERLING, 2200 E 30th St, 44115, SAN 356-097X. Tel: 216-623-7074. FAX: 216-623-7072. E-mail: Sterling.Branch@cpl.org. *Br Mgr,* Monica Rudzinski
Circ 75,907
Open Mon, Tues & Thurs 10-7, Wed, Fri & Sat 10-6
UNION, 3463 E 93rd St, 44104, SAN 356-1062. Tel: 216-623-7088. FAX: 216-623-7082. E-mail: Union.Branch@cpl.org. *Br Mgr,* Marcie Williams
Circ 85,174
Open Mon,Tues & Thurs 10-7, Wed, Fri & Sat 10-6
WALZ, 7910 Detroit Ave, 44102, SAN 356-1097. Tel: 216-623-7095. FAX: 216-623-7099. E-mail: Walz.Branch@cpl.org. *Br Mgr,* Kathleen Lefkowitz
Circ 217,726
Open Mon, Tues & Thurs 10-7, Wed, Fri & Sat 10-6
WEST PARK, 3805 W 157th St, 44111, SAN 356-1127. Tel: 216-623-7102. FAX: 216-623-7104. E-mail: West.Park.Branch@cpl.org. *Br Mgr,* Michael Dalby
Circ 309,415
Open Mon, Tues & Thurs 10-7, Wed, Fri & Sat 10-6
WOODLAND, 5806 Woodland Ave, 44104, SAN 356-1186. Tel: 216-623-7109. FAX: 216-623-7113. E-mail: Woodland.Branch@cpl.org. *Br Mgr,* Maria Estrella
Circ 126,053
Open Mon, Tues & Thurs 10-7, Wed, Fri & Sat 10-6

CLEVELAND STATE UNIVERSITY
CL CLEVELAND-MARSHALL LAW LIBRARY*, Cleveland-Marshall College of Law, 1801 Euclid Ave, 44115-2223, SAN 356-1240. Tel: 216-687-2250. Circulation Tel: 216-687-2251. Reference Tel: 216-687-6877. FAX: 216-687-6881. Web Site: www.law.csuohio.edu/lawlibrary. *Assoc Prof of Law, Dir,* Lauren M Collins; Tel: 216-687-3547, E-mail: l.m.collins36@csuohio.edu; *Dir, Technology,* Dan Thomas; Tel: 216-523-7372; *Assoc Dir,* Jan R Babbit; Tel: 216-687-6913, E-mail: j.babbit@csuohio.edu; *Access & Fac Serv Librn,* Amy Burchfield; Tel: 216-687-6885, E-mail: amy.burchfield@law.csuohio.edu; *Digital Content Serv/Ref Librn,* Jacquelyn McCloud; Tel: 216-523-7364, E-mail: jacquelyn.mccloud@law.csuohio.edu; *Educ Prog Librn,* Laura Ray; Tel: 216-687-6880, E-mail: laura.ray@law.csuohio.edu; *Electronic Serv Librn,* Sue Altmeyer; Tel: 216-687-4894, E-mail: sue.altmeyer@law.csuohio.edu; Staff 22 (MLS 9, Non-MLS 13)
Founded 1897. Enrl 752; Fac 43; Highest Degree: Doctorate
Library Holdings: Bk Titles 172,599; Bk Vols 538,239
Special Collections: Briefs & Records of Ohio Supreme Court, microform; Briefs & Records of US Supreme Court, microform; CIS Index & US Legislative Hist microfiche
Automation Activity & Vendor Info: (Acquisitions) Innovative Interfaces, Inc; (Cataloging) Innovative Interfaces, Inc; (Circulation) Innovative Interfaces, Inc; (Course Reserve) Innovative Interfaces, Inc; (ILL) Clio; (OPAC) Innovative Interfaces, Inc; (Serials) Innovative Interfaces, Inc
Partic in OCLC Online Computer Library Center, Inc; Ohio Library & Information Network
Open Mon-Thurs 8am-11pm, Fri 8am-9pm, Sat 8-8, Sun 10-10
C MICHAEL SCHWARTZ LIBRARY*, Rhodes Tower, Ste 501, 2121 Euclid Ave, 44115-2214, SAN 356-1216. Tel: 216-687-2475. Circulation Tel: 216-687-2478. Interlibrary Loan Service Tel: 216-687-2445. Reference Tel: 216-687-5300. Automation Services Tel: 216-687-6956. FAX: 216-687-9380. Interlibrary Loan Service FAX: 216-687-2383. Reference FAX: 216-687-2403. Web Site: library.csuohio.edu. *Dir,* Dr Glenda A Thornton; E-mail: g.thornton@csuohio.edu; *Asst Dir, Admin & Syst,* David Lodwick; E-mail: d.lodwick@csuohio.edu; *Asst Dir, Discovery Support Services,* Barbara Strauss; Tel: 216-687-2362, E-mail: b.strauss@csuohio.edu; *Asst Dir, Pub Serv,* Kathyanne Dobda; Tel: 216-875-9738, E-mail: k.dobda@csuohio.edu; *Head, Coll Mgt,* Carol Zsulya; Tel: 216-523-7373, E-mail: c.zsulya@csuohio.edu; *Cat Librn,* Yuezeng Shen Yang; Tel: 216-687-5274, E-mail: y.s.yang@csuohio.edu; *Digital Initiatives Librn,* Marsha Miles; Tel: 216-687-2369, E-mail: m.a.miles24@csuohio.edu; *First Year Experience Librn,* Ann Marie Smeraldi; Tel: 216-687-5020, E-mail: a.smeraldi@csuohio.edu; *Librn,* Diane Kolosionek; Tel: 216-802-3358, E-mail: d.kolosionek44@csuohio.edu; *Librn,* Gail Marredeth; Tel: 216-687-2291, E-mail: g.marredeth@csuohio.edu; *Librn,* Fran Mentch; Tel: 216-687-2365, E-mail: f.mentch@csuohio.edu; *Librn,* Theresa Nawalaniec; Tel: 216-687-3504, E-mail: t.nawalaniec@csuohio.edu; *Performing Arts & Humanities Librn,* Mandi Goodsett; E-mail: a.goodsett@csuohio.edu; *Spec Coll Librn,* William Barrow; Tel: 216-687-6998, E-mail: w.barrow@csuohio.edu; *Coordr, Fac & Admin Serv,* Bob Cieslik; Tel: 216-687-2256, E-mail: r.cieslik@csuohio.edu.
Subject Specialists: *Middle Eastern studies, Music, Urban agr,* Barbara Strauss; *Educ,* Kathyanne Dobda; *Bus, Communication, Econ,* Carol Zsulya; *Contemporary poetry, English lang, Lit,* Ann Marie Smeraldi; *Educ, Polit sci, Urban,* Diane Kolosionek; *Biog, Environ studies, Nursing,* Gail Marredeth; *Biomed, Health sci, Nursing,* Fran Mentch;

Engr, Sciences, Theresa Nawalaniec; *Dance, Local hist, Theatre,* William Barrow; Staff 23 (MLS 15, Non-MLS 8)
Founded 1928. Enrl 12,957; Fac 564; Highest Degree: Doctorate
Library Holdings: AV Mats 134,118; e-books 30,579; e-journals 43,072; Microforms 730,210; Music Scores 13,906; Bk Titles 516,463; Bk Vols 1,083,843; Per Subs 10,944
Special Collections: Black History (Walker Coll); Bridge Engineering (Watson Bridge Coll); Cleveland Memory; Cleveland Press Coll; Cleveland Union Terminal Coll; French-American/Great Lakes Industrial History Coll; Hazel Hutchison Collister Contemporary Poetry Coll; Marquis de Lafayette Microfilm Coll. US Document Depository
Automation Activity & Vendor Info: (ILL) Innovative Interfaces, Inc
Partic in OCLC Online Computer Library Center, Inc; OhioNET
Special Services for the Deaf - Assisted listening device
Special Services for the Blind - Assistive/Adapted tech devices, equip & products
Open Mon-Thurs 7:30am-10pm, Fri 7:30-6, Sat 8-5, Sun 2-10
Friends of the Library Group

CUYAHOGA COMMUNITY COLLEGE

J EASTERN CAMPUS LIBRARY*, 4250 Richmond Rd, Highland Hills, 44122-6195, SAN 320-9202. Tel: 216-987-2085. Information Services Tel: 216-987-2088. FAX: 216-987-2054. Web Site: www.tri-c.edu/library. *Dir,* Terry Hancox; Tel: 216-987-2087, E-mail: terry.hancox@tri-c.edu; *Libr*n, Anna Lauer; Tel: 216-987-2091, E-mail: anna.lauer@tri-c.edu; *Librn,* John Rasel; Tel: 216-987-2321, E-mail: John.Rasel@tri-c.edu; Staff 4 (MLS 3, Non-MLS 1)
Founded 1971. Enrl 6,168; Fac 110; Highest Degree: Associate
Library Holdings: Bk Titles 38,000; Bk Vols 40,100; Per Subs 200
Automation Activity & Vendor Info: (Acquisitions) Innovative Interfaces, Inc; (Cataloging) Innovative Interfaces, Inc; (Circulation) Innovative Interfaces, Inc; (Course Reserve) Innovative Interfaces, Inc; (ILL) Innovative Interfaces, Inc; (OPAC) Innovative Interfaces, Inc; (Serials) Innovative Interfaces, Inc
Partic in Northeast Ohio Regional Library System; OCLC Online Computer Library Center, Inc; OhioNET
Open Mon-Thurs 8-8, Fri & Sat 9am-2pm

J LIBRARY TECHNICAL SERVICES*, 2900 Community College Ave, MRC507, 44115-3123, SAN 322-5747. Tel: 216-987-3383. FAX: 216-987-4404. E-mail: tpd-acquisitions@tri-c.edu. *Supvr,* Constance Clemons; *Supvr,* Laquodra Simmons; Staff 4 (MLS 1, Non-MLS 3)
Automation Activity & Vendor Info: (Acquisitions) Innovative Interfaces, Inc; (Cataloging) Innovative Interfaces, Inc; (Circulation) Innovative Interfaces, Inc; (OPAC) Innovative Interfaces, Inc; (Serials) Innovative Interfaces, Inc
Partic in OCLC Online Computer Library Center, Inc; Ohio Library & Information Network
Open Mon-Fri 8:30-5

J METROPOLITAN CAMPUS LIBRARY*, 2900 Community College Ave, 44115, SAN 356-1275. Tel: 216-987-4296. FAX: 216-987-4404. *Asst Dean,* Tonya Briggs; E-mail: tonya.briggs@tri-c.edu; *Asst Prof, Librn,* Daniel Overfield; E-mail: Daniel.Overfield@tri-c.edu; Staff 13 (MLS 4, Non-MLS 9)
Founded 1968. Enrl 4,194; Fac 205
Library Holdings: Bk Titles 49,877; Bk Vols 53,883; Per Subs 391
Automation Activity & Vendor Info: (Acquisitions) Innovative Interfaces, Inc; (Cataloging) Innovative Interfaces, Inc; (Circulation) Innovative Interfaces, Inc; (Course Reserve) Innovative Interfaces, Inc; (ILL) Innovative Interfaces, Inc; (OPAC) Innovative Interfaces, Inc; (Serials) Innovative Interfaces, Inc
Open Mon-Thurs 8am-10pm, Fri 8-5, Sat 8:30-4

J WESTERN CAMPUS LIBRARY*, 11000 Pleasant Valley Rd, Parma, 44130-5199, SAN 320-9210. Tel: 216-987-5416. FAX: 216-987-5050. *Asst Dean,* Michael Collura; E-mail: michael.collura@tri-c.edu; *Asst Prof, Librn,* Paula DuPerow; E-mail: paula.duperow@tri-c.edu; Staff 13 (MLS 4, Non-MLS 9)
Founded 1966. Enrl 5,049
Library Holdings: Bk Titles 55,372; Bk Vols 62,570; Per Subs 377
Automation Activity & Vendor Info: (Acquisitions) Innovative Interfaces, Inc; (Cataloging) Innovative Interfaces, Inc; (Circulation) Innovative Interfaces, Inc; (Course Reserve) Innovative Interfaces, Inc; (ILL) Innovative Interfaces, Inc; (OPAC) Innovative Interfaces, Inc; (Serials) Innovative Interfaces, Inc
Partic in OCLC Online Computer Library Center, Inc
Open Mon-Thurs 8am-10pm, Fri 8-5, Sat 8:30-4

G CUYAHOGA COUNTY ARCHIVES LIBRARY, 3951 Perkins Ave, 44114. SAN 313-3362. Tel: 216-443-7250. FAX: 216-443-3636. E-mail: archive@cuyahogacounty.us. Web Site: publicworks.cuyahogacounty.us/en-US/Archives.aspx. *Archivist,* Dr Judith G Cetina, PhD
Founded 1975
Library Holdings: Bk Titles 2,150
Subject Interests: Cleveland, Cuyahoga County, Genealogy
Open Mon, Wed & Fri 8:30-3

S DUNHAM TAVERN MUSEUM LIBRARY*, 6709 Euclid Ave, 44103. SAN 321-0871. Tel: 216-431-1060. E-mail: dunhamtavern@sbcglobal.net. Web Site: www.dunhamtavern.org. *Library Contact,* Dori Shimelonis
Founded 1954
Library Holdings: Bk Titles 750
Subject Interests: Antiques, Cleveland hist, Ohio
Open Wed & Sun 1-4

M FAIRVIEW HOSPITAL, Medical Library, 18101 Lorain Ave, 44111. SAN 356-2115. Tel: 216-476-7117. FAX: 216-476-7803. E-mail: fhmedlibrary@ccf.org. Web Site: my.clevelandclinic.org/locations/fairview-hospital. *Med Librn,* Irene Szentkiralyi; Staff 1 (MLS 1)
Library Holdings: Bk Vols 1,600; Per Subs 120
Subject Interests: Med, Nursing, Surgery
Automation Activity & Vendor Info: (Cataloging) Innovative Interfaces, Inc - Sierra; (Circulation) Innovative Interfaces, Inc - Sierra
Wireless access
Partic in MLANO; National Network of Libraries of Medicine Region 6
Restriction: Staff use only

S FEDERAL RESERVE BANK OF CLEVELAND, Research Library, 1455 E Sixth St, 44114. SAN 313-3451. Reference Tel: 216-579-2050. FAX: 216-579-3172. E-mail: 4d.Library@clev.frb.org. Web Site: www.clevelandfed.org. *Libr Mgr,* Diane Mogren; Staff 4 (MLS 4)
Founded 1918
Subject Interests: Banking, Econ, Finance, Reserve syst
Publications: Fed in Print (Online only)
Partic in OCLC Online Computer Library Center, Inc
Restriction: Not open to pub

G FEDERAL TRADE COMMISSION*, Cleveland Regional Office, 1111 Superior Ave, Ste 200, 44114. SAN 313-346X. Tel: 216-263-3455. FAX: 216-263-3426. Web Site: www.ftc.gov. *Regional Dir,* Jon Miller Steiger; Tel: 216-263-3442
Library Holdings: Bk Vols 2,500; Per Subs 15
Restriction: Staff use only

L HAHN, LOESER & PARKS*, Law Library, 200 Public Sq, Ste 2800, 44114. SAN 372-2139. Tel: 216-621-0150. FAX: 216-241-2824. Web Site: www.hahnlaw.com. *Librn,* Beth Langton; E-mail: blangton@hahnlaw.com
Library Holdings: Bk Vols 3,000; Per Subs 40
Wireless access
Restriction: Not open to pub

L JONES DAY*, Law Library, 901 Lakeside Ave, 44114. SAN 313-3575. Tel: 216-586-3939. *Assoc Dir, Libr Operations,* Jo Ann Fisher; *Research Servs Librn,* Rachel Kusmik; *Libr Serv Mgr,* Suzanne Young; Staff 4 (MLS 3, Non-MLS 1)
Library Holdings: Bk Vols 2,500; Per Subs 50
Subject Interests: Corporate law, Law, Taxation
Wireless access
Restriction: Staff use only

L MCDONALD HOPKINS, LLC*, Law Library, 600 Superior Ave E, Ste 2100, 44114. SAN 372-2279. Tel: 216-348-5400. FAX: 216-348-5474. *Librn,* Mike Melillo; E-mail: mmelillo@mcdonaldhopkins.com; Staff 1 (Non-MLS 1)
Library Holdings: Bk Vols 10,000; Per Subs 100
Automation Activity & Vendor Info: (Serials) TLC (The Library Corporation)
Wireless access
Restriction: Open to staff only

M METROHEALTH MEDICAL CENTER*, Harold H Brittingham Memorial Library, 2500 MetroHealth Dr, 44101-1998. SAN 313-3249. Tel: 216-778-5623. E-mail: library@metrohealth.org. Web Site: www.metrohealth.org. *Chief Librn,* Laura A Frater; E-mail: lfrater@metrohealth.org; Staff 6 (MLS 2, Non-MLS 4)
Founded 1937
Library Holdings: Bk Vols 4,000; Per Subs 100
Special Collections: Arthritis & Rheumatism (Stecher Coll); Heritage Recognition Coll; Highland View Hospital Library Coll. Oral History
Subject Interests: Med, Nursing
Automation Activity & Vendor Info: (Cataloging) SydneyPlus; (Circulation) SydneyPlus; (OPAC) SydneyPlus
Wireless access
Partic in Med Libr Asn of NE Ohio; National Network of Libraries of Medicine Region 6

G NASA*, John H Glenn Research Center at Lewis Field, 21000 Brookpark Rd, MS142-3, 44135. SAN 313-3664. Circulation Tel: 216-433-5761. Interlibrary Loan Service Tel: 216-433-8305. FAX: 216-433-8139. Web Site: www.nasa.gov/centers/glenn/home. *Chief Librn,* Kate Dunlap; *Supv Librn,* Jaime Scibelli; *Sci Librn,* Robin Pertz; *Doc Delivery,* Janis Dick; *ILL,* Marcia Stegenga; Staff 6 (MLS 4, Non-MLS 2)
Founded 1941. Pop 5,000
Library Holdings: Bk Titles 25,000; Bk Vols 80,500; Per Subs 300
Special Collections: NACA Documents
Subject Interests: Aeronaut, Engr, Power, Propulsion, Space communications mat, Space sci, Space shuttles, Space sta, Structures
Automation Activity & Vendor Info: (Cataloging) SirsiDynix; (Circulation) SirsiDynix; (ILL) OCLC; (OPAC) SirsiDynix; (Serials) SirsiDynix
Wireless access
Function: Res libr
Partic in NASA Library Network; Nat Res Libr Alliance
Restriction: Staff use only

S ROMANIAN ETHNIC ARTS MUSEUM LIBRARY*, 3256 Warren Rd, 44111. SAN 321-0561. Tel: 216-941-5550. FAX: 216-941-3068. E-mail: st.mary.cathedral@sbcglobal.net. Web Site: www.smroc.org/culture.php. *Library Contact,* Fr Remus Grama; Staff 1 (MLS 1)
Founded 1928
Library Holdings: Bk Titles 5,500
Subject Interests: Culture, Romanian art
Restriction: Open by appt only

S ST ANDREW'S ABBEY, Slovak Institute & Library, 10510 Buckeye Rd, 44104. SAN 328-3674. Tel: 216-721-5300, Ext 294. FAX: 216-791-8268. E-mail: slovakinstitute@standrewabbey.org. Web Site: slovakinstitute.com, standrewabbey.org/slovak-institute. *Dir,* Milan Kobulsky
Founded 1952
Library Holdings: Bk Vols 11,000; Per Subs 200
Function: Archival coll
Open Tues-Thurs 10-3

S SHERWIN-WILLIAMS AUTOMOTIVE FINISHES CORP LIBRARY*, 4440 Warrensville Center Rd, 44128. SAN 375-9644. Tel: 216-332-8427. *Librn,* Beth Maher Rinz; E-mail: elizabeth.m.rinz@sherwin.com. Subject Specialists: *Chem,* Beth Maher Rinz; Staff 1 (MLS 1)
Library Holdings: Bk Titles 6,000; Per Subs 50
Automation Activity & Vendor Info: (Cataloging) EOS International; (Circulation) EOS International; (OPAC) EOS International; (Serials) EOS International
Restriction: Staff use only

L THOMPSON, HINE LLP*, Law Library, 3900 Key Ctr, 127 Public Sq, 44114-1291. SAN 372-2295. Tel: 216-566-5651. E-mail: library@thompsonhine.com. Web Site: www.thompsonhine.com. *Librn,* Christine Stouffer
Library Holdings: Bk Vols 30,000; Per Subs 150
Restriction: Not open to pub

L TUCKER ELLIS LLP*, Law Library, 950 Main Ave, Ste 1100, 44113-7213. SAN 313-3125. Tel: 216-592-5000. FAX: 216-592-5009. *Law Librn,* Ellen Smith; *Libr Asst,* Joseph Lara; Staff 2 (MLS 1, Non-MLS 1)
Library Holdings: Bk Vols 20,000
Restriction: Private libr

S UKRAINIAN MUSEUM-ARCHIVES INC*, 1202 Kenilworth Ave, 44113. SAN 323-5270. Tel: 216-781-4329. E-mail: staff@umacleveland.org. Web Site: www.umacleveland.org. *Exec Dir,* Taras Szmagala; *Curator,* Aniza Kraus; E-mail: aniza@umacleveland.org. Subject Specialists: *Ethnography, Ukrainian traditional mat culture,* Aniza Kraus
Founded 1952
Library Holdings: Bk Vols 35,000; Per Subs 40
Special Collections: Taras Shevchenko, Ukrainian Revolution, Ukrainian Religion Periodical Coll outside of Ukraine, 1900-present
Wireless access
Open Tues-Sat 10-3

S UNITED STATES BOOK EXCHANGE LIBRARY*, 2969 W 25th St, 44113. SAN 370-6370. Tel: 216-241-6960. FAX: 216-241-6966. E-mail: usbe@usbe.com. Web Site: usbe.com. *Pres,* John T Zubal; *Librn,* Thomas A Zubal; *Circ,* Jean Marie Vovos; *Coll Develop,* Robert Farkas; *ILL, Per,* Marilyn Zubal; Staff 9 (MLS 3, Non-MLS 6)
Founded 1948
Library Holdings: Bk Titles 10,000
Publications: USBE: For Members Only
Partic in OCLC Online Computer Library Center, Inc

L WALTER & HAVERFIELD LLP*, Law Library, The Tower at Erieview, Ste 3500, 1301 E Ninth St, 44114-1821. SAN 325-5387. Tel: 216-781-1212. FAX: 216-575-0911. E-mail: info@walterhav.com. Web Site: www.walterhav.com. *Libr Coord,* Patricia Coles; E-mail: pcoles@walterhav.com; Staff 2 (MLS 1, Non-MLS 1)
Founded 1932
Subject Interests: Bus, Labor
Wireless access
Restriction: Not open to pub

S WESTERN RESERVE HISTORICAL SOCIETY RESEARCH LIBRARY*, 10825 East Blvd, 44106-1777. SAN 313-3915. Tel: 216-721-5722. Reference Tel: 216-721-5722, Ext 1509. FAX: 216-721-0891. Reference E-mail: reference@wrhs.org. Web Site: www.wrhs.org. *Mgr, Archives & Spec Coll,* Margaret Roulett; Tel: 216-721-5722, Ext 1519, E-mail: mroulett@wrhs.org; Staff 5.5 (MLS 3, Non-MLS 2.5)
Founded 1867
Library Holdings: Bk Titles 238,000
Special Collections: Automobile Marque Files; Presidential Campaign Memorabilia; Sports History Coll; Wallace H Cathcart Shaker Coll; William Palmer Civil War Coll. Oral History
Subject Interests: Abolitionism, African-Am, Am genealogy, Family hist, Irish hist, Italian, Jewish hist, Local hist, Philanthropy, Relig hist, Slavery, Sports
Automation Activity & Vendor Info: (Cataloging) Cuadra Associates, Inc; (OPAC) Cuadra Associates, Inc
Wireless access
Function: 24/7 Online cat, Archival coll, Art exhibits, Bus archives, Computers for patron use, Electronic databases & coll, For res purposes, Genealogy discussion group, Holiday prog, Internet access, Life-long learning prog for all ages, Masonic res mat, Meeting rooms, Microfiche/film & reading machines, Online cat, Photocopying/Printing, Prog for adults, Ref & res, Ref serv available, Res libr, Res performed for a fee, Scanner, Study rm, Wheelchair accessible, Workshops
Partic in OCLC Online Computer Library Center, Inc
Open Thurs-Sat 10-5
Restriction: Closed stack, Non-circulating, Off-site coll in storage - retrieval as requested
Friends of the Library Group

L WESTON HURD, LLP*, Law Library, The Tower at Erieview, Ste 1900, 1301 E Ninth St, 44114-1862. SAN 371-9057. Tel: 216-241-6602, Ext 3383. Toll Free Tel: 800-336-4952. FAX: 216-621-8369. Web Site: www.westonhurd.com. *Mkt Mgr,* Maria Murphy; E-mail: mmurphy@westonhurd.com
Special Collections: Employment Law; Insurance Law; Products Liability Law; Tax Law
Wireless access
Restriction: Staff use only

CLEVELAND HEIGHTS

P CLEVELAND HEIGHTS-UNIVERSITY HEIGHTS PUBLIC LIBRARY*, Lee Road Branch, 2345 Lee Rd, 44118-3493. SAN 356-2387. Tel: 216-932-3600. FAX: 216-932-0932. TDD: 216-321-0739. Web Site: heightslibrary.org. *Dir,* Nancy S Levin; Tel: 216-932-3600, Ext 1240, E-mail: nlevin@heightslibrary.org; *Dep Dir,* Kim DeNero-Ackroyd; E-mail: kackroyd@heightslibrary.org; Staff 108.7 (MLS 27.4, Non-MLS 81.3)
Founded 1916. Pop 61,194; Circ 1,816,766
Library Holdings: Audiobooks 58,368; AV Mats 24,597; Bks on Deafness & Sign Lang 1,000; e-books 15,944; Electronic Media & Resources 223; Bk Vols 284,276; Per Subs 1,033; Talking Bks 5,174; Videos 26,875
Special Collections: Parenting Coll
Automation Activity & Vendor Info: (Cataloging) SirsiDynix; (Circulation) SirsiDynix; (OPAC) SirsiDynix
Wireless access
Function: Adult bk club, Adult literacy prog, After school storytime, Art exhibits, Audiobks via web, AV serv, Bk club(s), Bk reviews (Group), Bks on cassette, Bks on CD, Children's prog, Computer training, Computers for patron use, Doc delivery serv, E-Reserves, Electronic databases & coll, Free DVD rentals, Games & aids for people with disabilities, Homebound delivery serv, ILL available, Instruction & testing, Internet access, Large print keyboards, Mail & tel request accepted, Music CDs, Online cat, Online ref, Outreach serv, OverDrive digital audio bks, Photocopying/Printing, Preschool outreach, Prog for adults, Prog for children & young adult, Ref serv available, Scanner, Senior computer classes, Senior outreach, Spoken cassettes & CDs, Spoken cassettes & DVDs, Story hour, Summer reading prog, Tax forms, Teen prog, Telephone ref, VHS videos, Wheelchair accessible, Workshops
Publications: Check Us Out; CH-UH Organizations; CH-UH Quick Information; Potamus Press; YAZine
Partic in CLEVNET; Northeast Ohio Regional Library System
Special Services for the Deaf - High interest/low vocabulary bks; TTY equip

Open Mon-Fri 9-9, Sat 9-5:30, Sun 1-5
Friends of the Library Group
Branches: 3
COVENTRY VILLAGE BRANCH, 1925 Coventry Rd, 44118-2001, SAN 356-2417. Tel: 216-321-3400. Circulation Tel: 216-321-3600, Ext 610. Reference Tel: 216-321-3600, Ext 600. FAX: 216-321-0739. TDD: 216-321-0739. *Br Mgr,* Patricia Gray; Tel: 216-932-3600, Ext 620, E-mail: pgray@heightslibrary.org
Library Holdings: Bks on Deafness & Sign Lang 1,000; Bk Vols 32,808
Open Mon, Tues & Thurs 12-8:30, Wed, Fri & Sat 9-5:30, Sun 1-5
Friends of the Library Group
NOBLE NEIGHBORHOOD BRANCH, 2800 Noble Rd, 44121-2208, SAN 356-2441. Tel: 216-291-5665. FAX: 216-291-1798. *Br Mgr,* Constance Dickerson; Tel: 216-932-3600, Ext 721, E-mail: cdickers@heightslibrary.org
Library Holdings: Bk Vols 41,275
Open Mon, Tues & Thurs 1-9, Wed, Fri & Sat 9-5:30
Friends of the Library Group
UNIVERSITY HEIGHTS BRANCH, 13866 Cedar Rd, University Heights, 44118-3201, SAN 356-2476. Tel: 216-321-4700. FAX: 216-321-3049. *Br Mgr,* Aurora Martinez; E-mail: amartine@heightslibrary.org
Library Holdings: Bk Vols 42,370
Open Mon, Tues & Thurs 12:30-9, Wed, Fri & Sat 9-5:30, Sun 1-5
Friends of the Library Group

M CLEVELAND PSYCHOANALYTIC CENTER LIBRARY*, 2460 Fairmount Blvd, Ste 312, 44106. SAN 324-6922. Tel: 216-229-5959. FAX: 216-229-7321. Web Site: psychoanalysiscleveland.org. *Librn,* Amy M Crognale; Tel: 216-229-5959, Ext 102, E-mail: librarian@psychoanalysiscleveland.org; Staff 2 (MLS 1, Non-MLS 1)
Founded 1962
Library Holdings: DVDs 2; Bk Titles 2,500; Per Subs 20; Videos 1
Special Collections: Manuscript Coll; Sigmund Freud (Complete Psychological Works)
Subject Interests: Child analysis, Psychoanalysis
Open Mon-Fri 8-4:30

CLYDE

P CLYDE PUBLIC LIBRARY, 222 W Buckeye St, 43410. SAN 313-394X. Tel: 419-547-7174. FAX: 419-547-0480. E-mail: help.desk@clyde.lib.oh.us. Web Site: clydelibrary.org. *Dir,* Beth Leibengood; E-mail: beth.leibengood@clyde.lib.oh.us; *Ad,* Angela Herrera; *Ch,* Deborah Meyer; Staff 3 (MLS 1, Non-MLS 2)
Founded 1903. Pop 8,100; Circ 115,300
Library Holdings: AV Mats 5,203; CDs 560; DVDs 2,838; Large Print Bks 603; Bk Titles 36,000; Bk Vols 39,000; Per Subs 111; Videos 37
Special Collections: Clyde Coll; Maj Gen James B McPherson Coll; Roger Young Coll; Sherwood Anderson Coll
Automation Activity & Vendor Info: (Circulation) SirsiDynix-Enterprise
Wireless access
Function: Adult bk club, Adult literacy prog, After school storytime, Archival coll, Art exhibits, Audiobks via web, AV serv, Bk club(s), Bks on cassette, Bks on CD, CD-ROM, Children's prog, Computer training, Computers for patron use, Digital talking bks, Electronic databases & coll, Free DVD rentals, Games & aids for people with disabilities, Holiday prog, Home delivery & serv to seniorr ctr & nursing homes, Homebound delivery serv, ILL available, Internet access, Literacy & newcomer serv, Magnifiers for reading, Mail & tel request accepted, Music CDs, Online cat, Online ref, Outreach serv, OverDrive digital audio bks, Photocopying/Printing, Preschool outreach, Prog for adults, Prog for children & young adult, Ref & res, Ref serv available, Scanner, Senior outreach, Spoken cassettes & CDs, Story hour, Summer reading prog, Tax forms, Teen prog, Telephone ref, Wheelchair accessible
Partic in CLEVNET; NORWELD
Special Services for the Deaf - Bks on deafness & sign lang
Special Services for the Blind - Aids for in-house use; Audio mat; BiFolkal kits; Bks on cassette; Bks on CD; Cassettes; Home delivery serv; Large print & cassettes; Large print bks; Large print bks & talking machines; Playaways (bks on MP3); Recorded bks; Talking bk & rec for the blind cat; Talking bks; Talking bks & player equip
Open Mon-Thurs 9-8:30, Fri 9-5, Sat 9-1
Friends of the Library Group

COLDWATER

P COLDWATER PUBLIC LIBRARY*, 305 W Main St, 45828. SAN 313-3958. Tel: 419-678-2431. FAX: 419-678-8516. Web Site: www.coldwaterpubliclibrary.org. *Dir,* Jane Bruggeman; E-mail: Bruggemanja@coldwaterpubliclibrary.org
Founded 1936
Special Collections: Census, microfilm; Local Newspaper, microfilm
Automation Activity & Vendor Info: (Circulation) SirsiDynix; (ILL) SirsiDynix; (OPAC) SirsiDynix
Wireless access
Partic in NORWELD
Open Mon-Thurs 9-7, Fri 9-5, Sat 9-12:30

COLUMBIANA

P COLUMBIANA PUBLIC LIBRARY, 332 N Middle St, 44408. SAN 313-3966. Tel: 330-482-5509. FAX: 330-482-9669. E-mail: cpl@columbiana.lib.oh.us. Web Site: www.columbiana.lib.oh.us. *Dir, Fiscal Officer,* Carol Cobbs; E-mail: ccobbs@columbiana.lib.oh.us; *Ad,* Kathryn Clewell; E-mail: kclewell@columbiana.lib.oh.us; *YA Librn,* Amy Geary; E-mail: gearyam@columbiana.lib.oh.us; *Youth Serv Mgr,* Carrie Radman; E-mail: radmanca@columbiana.lib.oh.us; *Tech Coordr,* Katelyn Salmen; E-mail: khouck@columbiana.lib.oh.us; Staff 18 (MLS 5, Non-MLS 13)
Founded 1934. Pop 7,857; Circ 152,434
Jan 2020-Dec 2020 Income $936,474, State $865,008, Federal $33,777, Locally Generated Income $37,689. Mats Exp $134,955, Books $53,325, Per/Ser (Incl. Access Fees) $6,268, AV Mat $22,004
Library Holdings: Audiobooks 4,823; CDs 2,282; DVDs 7,962; Bk Vols 59,915; Per Subs 129
Automation Activity & Vendor Info: (Cataloging) Innovative Interfaces, Inc. - Polaris; (Circulation) Innovative Interfaces, Inc. - Polaris; (OPAC) Innovative Interfaces, Inc. - Polaris
Wireless access
Open Mon-Sat 9-8
Friends of the Library Group

COLUMBUS

S THE AMERICAN SOCIETY FOR NONDESTRUCTIVE TESTING LIBRARY & ARCHIVE, 1711 Arlingate Lane, 43228. (Mail add: PO Box 28518, 43228-0518), SAN 372-7963. Tel: 614-274-6003. Toll Free Tel: 800-222-2768. FAX: 614-274-6899. Web Site: www.asnt.org. *Library Contact,* Cara Markland; E-mail: cmarkland@asnt.org
Founded 1990
Library Holdings: Bk Titles 2,000; Per Subs 100
Function: Doc delivery serv, Photocopying/Printing

L BAILEY CAVALIERI LLC*, Law Library, One Columbus, Ten W Broad St, Ste 2100, 43215. SAN 372-2058. Tel: 614-221-3155. FAX: 614-221-0479. E-mail: info@baileycav.com. Web Site: baileycav.com. *Librn,* Brenda Barnett
Library Holdings: Bk Vols 15,000; Per Subs 45
Restriction: Staff use only

L BAKER & HOSTETLER LIBRARY*, 200 Civic Center Dr, Ste 2100, 43215-4138. SAN 329-0603. Tel: 614-228-1541, Ext 2670. FAX: 614-462-2616. Web Site: www.bakerlaw.com/columbus. *Librn,* Karen Hoyt; Staff 2 (MLS 1, Non-MLS 1)
Library Holdings: Bk Vols 15,000; Per Subs 95
Subject Interests: Legal mat
Automation Activity & Vendor Info: (OPAC) SirsiDynix
Partic in OhioNET
Restriction: Staff use only

C BYRD POLAR RESEARCH CENTER*, Goldthwait Polar Library, 176 Scott Hall, 1090 Carmack Rd, 43210-1002. SAN 313-4202. Tel: 614-292-6715. FAX: 614-292-4697. E-mail: gpl@bpcrc.osu.edu. Web Site: byrd.osu.edu/groups/goldthwait-polar-library. *Librn,* Allie Thomas; E-mail: thomas.2689@osu.edu; Staff 3 (MLS 1, Non-MLS 2)
Founded 1969
Library Holdings: Bk Titles 8,000; Bk Vols 12,000; Per Subs 215
Special Collections: Reprint Coll
Subject Interests: Climatology, Geol, Geomorphology, Glaciology, Global change, Meteorology, Polar regions
Function: Res libr
Partic in Ohio Library & Information Network
Friends of the Library Group

C CAPITAL UNIVERSITY, Blackmore Library, One College & Main, 43209. SAN 356-2565. Tel: 614-236-6614. Reference Tel: 614-236-6351. FAX: 614-236-6490. Circulation E-mail: circdesk@capital.edu. Reference E-mail: refdesk@capital.edu. Web Site: www.capital.edu/library. *Head Librarian, Library Services,* Matthew Cook; *Head Librn, Tech Serv,* Zaineb Bayahy; *Student Success Librn,* Shaunda Vasudev; *Circ Mgr,* Scott Bates; *Tech Serv Asst,* Meghan Crawford; Staff 5 (MLS 3, Non-MLS 2)
Founded 1876. Enrl 3,384; Fac 158; Highest Degree: Master
Library Holdings: AV Mats 10,454; CDs 3,043; DVDs 3,324; e-books 171,873; e-journals 80,050; Electronic Media & Resources 49,902; Microforms 2,032; Music Scores 6,262; Bk Titles 104,318; Bk Vols 115,913; Per Subs 427
Special Collections: Juvenile Literature (Lois Lenski Coll), bk & ms; University Archives. US Document Depository
Subject Interests: Art, Educ, Music, Relig studies

Automation Activity & Vendor Info: (Acquisitions) Innovative Interfaces, Inc; (Cataloging) Innovative Interfaces, Inc; (Circulation) Innovative Interfaces, Inc; (OPAC) Innovative Interfaces, Inc; (Serials) Innovative Interfaces, Inc
Wireless access
Partic in Ohio Libr Coun; OhioNET
Open Mon-Thurs 8am-10pm, Fri 8-5, Sat & Sun 1-5

Departmental Libraries:

CL LAW SCHOOL LIBRARY, 303 E Broad St, 43215, SAN 356-259X. Tel: 614-236-6464. Web Site: www.law.capital.edu. *Libr Dir,* Jennifer L Wondracek; Tel: 614-236-6448, E-mail: jwondracek@law.capital.edu; *Head, Pub Serv, Ref Librn,* Michael Bird; Tel: 614-236-6463, E-mail: mbird5@law.capital.edu; *Head, Tech Serv,* Phyllis Post; Tel: 614-236-6483, E-mail: ppost@law.capital.edu; *Ref Librn,* Daniel Baker-Jones; Tel: 614-236-6539, E-mail: dbakerjones@law.capital.edu; Staff 5 (MLS 4, Non-MLS 1)
Founded 1903. Enrl 526; Fac 24; Highest Degree: Doctorate
Function: Electronic databases & coll, ILL available, Online cat, Photocopying/Printing, Ref & res, Ref serv available, Telephone ref, Wheelchair accessible
Partic in OCLC Online Computer Library Center, Inc; Ohio Library & Information Network
Restriction: Authorized patrons, Borrowing privileges limited to fac & registered students, Not open to pub, Open to students, fac, staff & alumni

C COLUMBUS COLLEGE OF ART & DESIGN, Packard Library, 60 Cleveland Ave, 43215. SAN 313-4091. Tel: 614-222-3273. FAX: 614-222-6193. E-mail: library@ccad.edu. Web Site: ccad.libguides.com/website. *Chief Info Officer,* Matt Gardzina; E-mail: mgarzina@ccad.edu; *Instruction Librn,* Christine Mannix; E-mail: cmannix@ccad.edu; *Cataloging & Instruction Librn,* Dai Newman; E-mail: dnewman@ccad.edu; *Archivist,* Brenda Foster; E-mail: bfoster@ccad.edu; Staff 7 (MLS 4, Non-MLS 3)
Founded 1931. Enrl 1,068; Fac 67; Highest Degree: Master
Library Holdings: DVDs 1,800; Bk Vols 54,000; Per Subs 250
Subject Interests: Art & archit
Automation Activity & Vendor Info: (Acquisitions) Innovative Interfaces, Inc; (Cataloging) Innovative Interfaces, Inc; (Circulation) Innovative Interfaces, Inc; (Course Reserve) Innovative Interfaces, Inc; (Discovery) EBSCO Discovery Service; (OPAC) Innovative Interfaces, Inc; (Serials) Innovative Interfaces, Inc
Wireless access
Partic in Ohio Library & Information Network; Ohio Private Academic Libraries
Open Mon-Thurs 8-8, Fri 8-5, Sun 1-5

P COLUMBUS METROPOLITAN LIBRARY*, Main Library, 96 S Grant Ave, 43215-4702. SAN 356-3790. Tel: 614-645-2275. FAX: 614-849-1157. Web Site: www.columbuslibrary.org. *Chief Exec Officer,* Patrick Losinski; E-mail: plosinski@columbuslibrary.org; *Chief Admin Officer,* Charlie Hansen; E-mail: chansen@columbuslibrary.org; *Chief Cust Experience Officer,* Alison Circle; E-mail: acircle@columbuslibrary.org; Staff 800 (MLS 100, Non-MLS 700)
Founded 1872. Pop 850,548; Circ 17,100,000
Jan 2014-Dec 2014 Income (Main & Associated Libraries) $72,976,479. Mats Exp $6,953,017. Sal $37,103,582
Library Holdings: Bk Vols 1,995,564; Per Subs 5,515
Special Collections: Black Heritage Coll; ESOL; Local History (Columbus & Ohio), bks, micro, VF. State Document Depository; US Document Depository
Wireless access
Publications: Check It Out (Quarterly)
Partic in Central Library Consortium; OCLC Online Computer Library Center, Inc
Special Services for the Deaf - Bks on deafness & sign lang; High interest/low vocabulary bks; Spec interest per; Staff with knowledge of sign lang; TDD equip; TTY equip
Open Mon-Thurs 9-9, Fri & Sat 9-6, Sun 1-5
Friends of the Library Group

Branches: 22

BARNETT BRANCH, 3434 E Livingston Ave, 43227, SAN 356-4215. FAX: 614-479-4339. *Mgr,* Tiffani Carter; Staff 7 (MLS 5, Non-MLS 2)
Founded 1963. Circ 234,540
Library Holdings: Bk Vols 90,000
Special Services for the Deaf - TDD equip
Open Mon-Thurs 9-8, Fri & Sat 9-6, Sun 1-5
Friends of the Library Group

CANAL WINCHESTER BRANCH, 115 Franklin St, Canal Winchester, 43110. *Mgr,* Matt Craft
Open Mon-Thurs 12-7, Fri & Sat 12-6
Friends of the Library Group

DRIVING PARK BRANCH, 1422 E Livingston Ave, 43205, SAN 356-3944. FAX: 614-479-4379. *Mgr,* Cheryl Evans
Circ 71,081
Library Holdings: Bk Vols 29,000
Special Services for the Deaf - TDD equip
Open Mon-Thurs 9-8, Fri & Sat 9-6, Sun 1-5
Friends of the Library Group

DUBLIN BRANCH, 75 N High St, Dublin, 43017, SAN 356-3979. FAX: 614-479-4179. *Mgr,* Joe Yersavich
Circ 1,558,342
Library Holdings: Bk Vols 140,000
Special Services for the Deaf - TDD equip
Open Mon-Thurs 9-9, Fri & Sat 9-6, Sun 1-5
Friends of the Library Group

FRANKLINTON BRANCH, 1061 W Town St, 43222, SAN 356-4002. FAX: 614-479-4419. *Mgr,* Steve Pullen
Founded 1995. Circ 124,123
Special Collections: Local History Books & Clippings
Function: Electronic databases & coll, Photocopying/Printing, Prog for adults, Prog for children & young adult, Ref serv available, Summer reading prog, Tax forms, Wheelchair accessible
Special Services for the Deaf - TDD equip
Open Mon-Thurs 9-8, Fri & Sat 9-6, Sun 1-5
Friends of the Library Group

GAHANNA BRANCH, 310 Granville St, Gahanna, 43230, SAN 356-4037. FAX: 614-479-4279. *Mgr,* Nate Oiver
Founded 1969. Circ 1,174,913
Library Holdings: Bk Vols 143,103
Function: Res libr
Special Services for the Deaf - TDD equip
Open Mon-Thurs 9-9, Fri & Sat 9-6, Sun 1-5
Friends of the Library Group

HILLIARD BRANCH, 4500 Hickory Chase Way, Hilliard, 43026, SAN 356-4061. FAX: 614-479-4149. *Mgr,* Robin Nesbitt
Circ 1,591,721
Library Holdings: Bk Vols 170,000
Special Services for the Deaf - TDD equip
Open Mon-Thurs 9-9, Fri & Sat 9-6, Sun 1-5
Friends of the Library Group

HILLTOP BRANCH, 511 S Hague Ave, 43204, SAN 356-4126. FAX: 614-479-4439. *Mgr,* John Tetzloff
Circ 519,700
Library Holdings: Bk Vols 119,719
Special Services for the Deaf - TDD equip
Open Mon-Thurs 9-9, Fri & Sat 9-6, Sun 1-5
Friends of the Library Group

KARL ROAD BRANCH, 1467 Karl Rd, 43229, SAN 356-424X. FAX: 614-479-4259. *Mgr,* Keith Hanson
Founded 1988. Circ 720,080
Library Holdings: Bk Vols 170,000
Special Services for the Deaf - TDD equip
Open Mon-Thurs 9-9, Fri & Sat 9-6, Sun 1-5
Friends of the Library Group

MARTIN LUTHER KING BRANCH, 1467 E Long St, 43203, SAN 356-4150. FAX: 614-479-4219. *Mgr,* Keisha Gibbs
Founded 1953. Circ 127,794
Library Holdings: Bk Vols 30,000
Special Services for the Deaf - TDD equip
Open Mon-Thurs 9-8, Fri & Sat 9-6, Sun 1-5
Friends of the Library Group

LINDEN BRANCH, 2223 Cleveland Ave, 43211, SAN 356-4185. FAX: 614-479-4239. *Mgr,* Laura Johnson
Founded 1928. Circ 135,494
Library Holdings: Bk Vols 52,050
Special Services for the Deaf - TDD equip
Open Mon-Thurs 9-8, Fri & Sat 9-6, Sun 1-5
Friends of the Library Group

MARION-FRANKLIN BRANCH, 2740 Lockbourne Rd, 43207. *Mgr,* Matt Craft
Open Mon-Thurs 12-7, Fri & Sat 12-6
Friends of the Library Group

NEW ALBANY BRANCH, 200 Market St, New Albany, 43054, SAN 378-0333. FAX: 614-479-4549. *Mgr,* Benjamin Reid
Founded 2003. Circ 880,868
Library Holdings: Bk Vols 120,000
Special Services for the Deaf - TDD equip
Open Mon-Thurs 9-9, Fri & Sat 9-6, Sun 1-5
Friends of the Library Group

NORTHERN LIGHTS BRANCH, 4093 Cleveland Ave, 43224, SAN 356-4274. FAX: 614-479-4249. *Mgr,* Andrea Villanueva
Founded 1956. Circ 326,299
Library Holdings: Bk Vols 72,926
Open Mon-Thurs 9-8, Fri & Sat 9-6, Sun 1-5
Friends of the Library Group

NORTHSIDE BRANCH, 1423 N High St, 43201, SAN 356-4304. FAX: 614-479-4119. *Mgr,* Adam Hochstetter
Founded 1940. Circ 357,420
Library Holdings: Bk Vols 48,000

Special Services for the Deaf - TDD equip
Open Mon-Thurs 9-8, Fri & Sat 9-6, Sun 1-5
Friends of the Library Group
PARSONS BRANCH, 1113 Parsons Ave, 43206, SAN 356-4339. FAX: 614-479-4319. *Mgr,* Anne Heidrich
Founded 1956. Circ 164,471
Library Holdings: Bk Vols 37,000
Special Services for the Deaf - TDD equip
Open Mon-Thurs 9-8, Fri & Sat 9-6, Sun 1-5
Friends of the Library Group
REYNOLDSBURG BRANCH, 1402 Brice Rd, Reynoldsburg, 43068, SAN 356-4363. FAX: 614-479-4349. *Mgr,* Dave Dennison
Founded 1980. Circ 1,157,804
Library Holdings: Bk Vols 170,000
Special Services for the Deaf - TDD equip
Open Mon-Thurs 9-9, Fri & Sat 9-6, Sun 1-5
Friends of the Library Group
SHEPARD BRANCH, 850 N Nelson Rd, 43219, SAN 356-4398. FAX: 614-479-4229. *Mgr,* Anne Jubera
Founded 1939. Pop 112,501
Library Holdings: Bk Vols 33,000
Special Services for the Deaf - TDD equip
Open Mon-Thurs 9-8, Fri & Sat 9-6, Sun 1-5
Friends of the Library Group
SOUTH HIGH BRANCH, 3540 S High St, 43207, SAN 356-4428. FAX: 614-479-4369. *Mgr,* Summer Sherman
Founded 1971. Circ 274,358
Library Holdings: Bk Vols 84,000
Special Services for the Deaf - TDD equip
Open Mon-Thurs 9-8, Fri & Sat 9-6, Sun 1-5
Friends of the Library Group
SOUTHEAST, 3980 S Hamilton Rd, Groveport, 43125, SAN 370-9418. FAX: 614-479-4359. *Mgr,* Cindy Cawley
Founded 1991. Circ 853,097
Library Holdings: Bk Vols 112,346
Function: Photocopying/Printing, Prog for children & young adult, Summer reading prog, Tax forms, Wheelchair accessible
Special Services for the Deaf - TDD equip
Open Mon-Thurs 9-9, Fri & Sat 9-6, Sun 1-5
Friends of the Library Group
WHETSTONE BRANCH, 3909 N High St, 43214, SAN 326-7938. FAX: 614-479-4159. *Mgr,* Jennifer Hess
Founded 1997. Circ 1,408,640
Library Holdings: Bk Vols 170,000
Special Services for the Deaf - TDD equip
Open Mon-Thurs 9-9, Fri & Sat 9-6, Sun 1-5
Friends of the Library Group
WHITEHALL BRANCH, 4445 E Broad St, 43213, SAN 356-4452. FAX: 614-479-4329. *Mgr,* Kacy Cox
Founded 1950. Circ 317,757
Library Holdings: Bk Vols 63,000
Special Services for the Deaf - TDD equip
Open Mon-Thurs 9-9, Fri & Sat 9-6, Sun 1-5
Friends of the Library Group
Bookmobiles: 2

J COLUMBUS STATE COMMUNITY COLLEGE LIBRARY*, 550 E Spring St, 43215. SAN 313-4121. Tel: 614-287-2465. Reference Tel: 614-287-2460. Toll Free Tel: 800-621-6407. FAX: 614-287-2457. E-mail: information@cscc.edu. Web Site: library.cscc.edu/home, www.cscc.edu/library. *Dir of Libr,* Bruce Massis; Tel: 614-287-5484, Fax: 614-287-6029, E-mail: bmassis@cscc.edu; *Asst Dir,* Tracy Kemp; Tel: 614-287-5879, E-mail: tkemp@cscc.edu; *Supvr, Multimedia Support Ctr/Circ,* Vanessa Langhurst; Tel: 614-287-2267, E-mail: vlanghur@cscc.edu; *Ref Supvr,* Brianne Miller; Tel: 614-287-5380, E-mail: bmille10@cscc.edu; *Acq, Metadata Serv,* Robin Buser; Tel: 614-287-2469, E-mail: rbuser@cscc.edu. Subject Specialists: *Admin, Mgt,* Bruce Massis; *Admin, Mgt,* Tracy Kemp; Staff 35 (MLS 23, Non-MLS 12)
Founded 1965. Enrl 28,000; Fac 283; Highest Degree: Associate
Jul 2017-Jun 2018 Income Parent Institution $1,884,378. Mats Exp $241,649, Books $141,319, Per/Ser (Incl. Access Fees) $55,121, Electronic Ref Mat (Incl. Access Fees) $45,209. Sal $1,147,910 (Prof $1,147,910)
Library Holdings: Audiobooks 185; Bks-By-Mail 1,791; DVDs 1,337; e-books 80,759; e-journals 52,921; Electronic Media & Resources 4,134; Microforms 49; Bk Titles 32,991; Bk Vols 40,153; Per Subs 286; Videos 2,779
Subject Interests: Automotive, Construction, Criminal justice, Dental hygiene, Dietetics, Fire sci, Landscaping, Nursing, Paralegal studies, Radiography, Respiratory care, Surgical tech
Automation Activity & Vendor Info: (Acquisitions) Innovative Interfaces, Inc - Sierra; (Cataloging) Innovative Interfaces, Inc - Sierra; (Circulation) Innovative Interfaces, Inc - Sierra; (Course Reserve) Innovative Interfaces, Inc - Sierra; (ILL) OCLC WorldShare Interlibrary Loan; (OPAC) Innovative Interfaces, Inc - Sierra; (Serials) Innovative Interfaces, Inc - Sierra
Wireless access
Function: Ref serv available
Partic in Ohio Library & Information Network; OhioNET
Special Services for the Blind - Accessible computers
Open Mon-Thurs 7:30am-10pm, Fri 7:30-6, Sat 9-4

C FRANKLIN UNIVERSITY LIBRARY*, Phillips Hall, 1st Flr, 303 S Grant Ave, 43215. (Mail add: 201 S Grant Ave, 43215), SAN 313-4164. Tel: 614-341-6252, 614-947-6550. Toll Free Tel: 866-341-6252. FAX: 614-461-0957. E-mail: library@franklin.edu. Web Site: www.franklin.edu/library. *Dir,* Alyssa Darden; Tel: 614-947-6685, E-mail: alyssa.darden@franklin.edu; *Acq Librn,* Marc Jaffy; Tel: 614-947-6561, E-mail: marc.jaffy@franklin.edu; *Librn,* Karen Caputo; Tel: 614-947-6604, E-mail: karen.caputo@franklin.edu; *Pub Serv Librn, Outreach,* Christopher Casey; Tel: 614-947-6565, E-mail: christopher.casey@franklin.edu; *Librn,* Karen Caputo; Tel: 614-947-6604, E-mail: karen.caputo@franklin.edu; *Syst Librn,* Kristi Lobrano; Tel: 614-947-6223, E-mail: kristi.lobrano@franklin.edu; *Access Serv Mgr,* Hannah Goodrick; Tel: 614-947-6568, E-mail: hannah.goodrick@franklin.edu; Staff 15 (MLS 7, Non-MLS 8)
Founded 1966. Enrl 6,100; Highest Degree: Master
Library Holdings: Bk Titles 12,200; Bk Vols 15,200; Per Subs 350
Subject Interests: Bus
Automation Activity & Vendor Info: (Acquisitions) Innovative Interfaces, Inc; (Cataloging) Innovative Interfaces, Inc; (Circulation) Innovative Interfaces, Inc; (Course Reserve) Innovative Interfaces, Inc; (ILL) OCLC Online; (OPAC) Innovative Interfaces, Inc; (Serials) Innovative Interfaces, Inc
Wireless access
Partic in Ohio Library & Information Network; OhioNET
Open Mon-Thurs 8am-10pm, Fri 8-5, Sat 9-5, Sun 1-5

P GRANDVIEW HEIGHTS PUBLIC LIBRARY*, 1685 W First Ave, 43212. SAN 313-4172. Tel: 614-486-2951. FAX: 614-481-7021. Web Site: www.ghpl.org. *Dir,* Ryan McDonnell; E-mail: rmcdonnell@ghpl.org; *Dir, Support Serv,* Denise Shedloski; *Dir, Patron Serv,* Eileen McNeil; *Teen Librn,* Jennifer Lawson; *Circ Serv Mgr,* Anne Richards; *Tech Coordr,* Nate Nguyen; *Fiscal Officer,* Terri McKeown; Staff 32 (MLS 6, Non-MLS 26)
Founded 1924. Pop 7,000; Circ 772,000
Library Holdings: CDs 10,000; DVDs 13,000; e-books 38,000; Bk Vols 129,000; Per Subs 120
Subject Interests: Archit, Art, Behav sci, Bus info, Computer, Cookery, Relig studies, Soc sci
Automation Activity & Vendor Info: (Acquisitions) Innovative Interfaces, Inc; (Cataloging) Innovative Interfaces, Inc; (Circulation) Innovative Interfaces, Inc; (ILL) Innovative Interfaces, Inc; (OPAC) Innovative Interfaces, Inc; (Serials) Innovative Interfaces, Inc
Wireless access
Partic in Cent Libr Consortium
Open Mon-Thurs 10-8:30, Fri 10-6, Sat 10-5, Sun 1-5

L JONES DAY*, Law Library, 325 John H McConnell Blvd, Ste 600, 43215-2673. (Mail add: PO Box 165017, 43216-5017). Tel: 614-469-3939. FAX: 614-461-4198. Web Site: www.jonesday.com. *Libr Serv Mgr,* Nancy S Seymour; *Research Librn,* Morris Jackson
Restriction: Not open to pub, Private libr

L KEGLER BROWN HILL + RITTER*, Law Library, 65 E State St, Ste 1800, 43215. SAN 372-1949. Tel: 614-255-5502. FAX: 614-464-2634. *Dir, Libr Serv,* Keith S Knopf; E-mail: kknopf@keglerbrown.com; Staff 1 (MLS 1)
Library Holdings: DVDs 2; e-books 16; e-journals 6; Bk Titles 500; Bk Vols 6,000; Per Subs 25; Videos 20
Automation Activity & Vendor Info: (Cataloging) TLC (The Library Corporation); (Serials) TLC (The Library Corporation)
Wireless access
Restriction: Access at librarian's discretion, By permission only, Employee & client use only, Not open to pub

M MOUNT CARMEL*, Health Sciences Library, Center for Learning & Education, 127 S Davis Ave, 3rd-4th Flrs, 43222. SAN 313-4229. Tel: 614-234-5214. FAX: 614-234-1257. E-mail: library@mchs.com. Web Site: library.mchs.com. *Regional Libr Serv Dir,* Stevo Roksandic; Tel: 614-234-1644, E-mail: sroksandic@mchs.com; *Lead Librn,* Noreen Mulcahy; Tel: 614-234-5337, E-mail: nmulcahy@mchs.com; Staff 7 (MLS 5, Non-MLS 2)
Founded 1964
Library Holdings: Bk Vols 10,000; Per Subs 500
Subject Interests: Allied health, Med, Nursing
Automation Activity & Vendor Info: (Acquisitions) Innovative Interfaces, Inc; (Cataloging) Innovative Interfaces, Inc; (OPAC) Innovative Interfaces, Inc
Wireless access

Partic in GMR; Medical Library Association; Michigan Health Sciences Libraries Association; Ohio Library & Information Network; Ohio Private Academic Libraries; OhioNET
Open Mon-Thurs 8am-9pm, Fri 8-5, Sat 8:30-12:30; Mon-Fri (Summer) 8-5

S NATIONWIDE LIBRARY*, One Nationwide Plaza 1-01-409, 43215. SAN 313-4237. Tel: 614-249-2255. FAX: 614-249-2218. E-mail: library@nationwide.com. *Libr Services Analyst,* Jack Miller; *Libr Serv Mgr,* Steve Hausfeld; *Librn,* John W Holtzclaw; *Librn,* Karen Hoyt; *Librn,* David Schneider; Staff 6 (MLS 3, Non-MLS 3)
Founded 1935
Library Holdings: Bk Vols 10,000; Per Subs 150
Subject Interests: Ins
Automation Activity & Vendor Info: (Cataloging) SirsiDynix; (Circulation) SirsiDynix; (OPAC) SirsiDynix; (Serials) SirsiDynix
Partic in OhioNET
Restriction: Restricted access

GL OHIO ATTORNEY GENERAL*, Law Library, 30 E Broad St, 15th Flr, 43215. SAN 313-4245. Tel: 614-466-2465. Toll Free FAX: 866-478-7866. *Dir, Libr Serv,* Carol Ottolenghi; Staff 3 (MLS 3)
Founded 1846
Library Holdings: Bk Vols 5,000
Subject Interests: Cases, Law statutes
Wireless access
Partic in Ohio Library & Information Network
Restriction: Staff use only

G OHIO BUREAU OF WORKER'S COMPENSATION, Division of Safety & Hygiene Library, 30 W Spring St, third Flr, 43215-2256. SAN 356-2891. Tel: 614-466-7388. Toll Free Tel: 800-644-6292. FAX: 614-644-9634. E-mail: library@bwc.state.oh.us. Web Site: info.bwc.ohio.gov/wps/portal/gov/bwc. *Libr Adminr,* Sharon Roney; Tel: 614-466-0580, E-mail: sharon.roney@bwc.state.oh.us; *Ref Librn,* Andrew Hart; E-mail: andrew.hart@bwc.state.oh.us; *Video Librn,* Amie Klein; E-mail: amelia.klein@bwc.state.oh.us; Staff 3 (MLS 3)
Founded 1974
Library Holdings: Bk Vols 5,000; Per Subs 180; Videos 800
Subject Interests: Accident prevention, Indust hygiene, Indust toxicology, Noise control, Occupational med, Occupational rehab, Occupational safety
Function: Free DVD rentals, Govt ref serv, ILL available, Online cat, Outside serv via phone, mail, e-mail & web, Ref & res, Ref serv available, Res libr
Partic in Ohio Library & Information Network
Open Mon-Fri 8-5

C OHIO DOMINICAN UNIVERSITY LIBRARY*, 1216 Sunbury Rd, 43219. SAN 356-2808. Tel: 614-251-4752. Interlibrary Loan Service Tel: 614-251-4637. Reference Tel: 614-251-4754. Toll Free Tel: 888-681-8044. FAX: 614-252-2650. E-mail: library@ohiodominican.edu. Web Site: www.ohiodominican.edu/library. *Head Librn,* Michelle Sarff; E-mail: sarffm@ohiodominican.edu; *Head, Access Serv,* Timothy Sandusky; E-mail: sanduskt@ohiodominican.edu; *Head, Ref & Instruction,* Christina Bonner; E-mail: bonnerc@ohiodominican.edu; *Coll Serv Librn,* Jim Layden; E-mail: jlaydenj3@ohiodominican.edu; Staff 10 (MLS 6, Non-MLS 4)
Founded 1924. Enrl 2,700; Highest Degree: Master
Special Collections: Anne O'Hara McCormick Coll; Catholic Diocese of Columbus Newspaper Coll; Mary Teeter Zimmerman Coll
Subject Interests: Bus, Educ, Health, Humanities, Philos, Theol
Automation Activity & Vendor Info: (Acquisitions) Innovative Interfaces, Inc; (Cataloging) Innovative Interfaces, Inc; (Circulation) Innovative Interfaces, Inc; (Course Reserve) Innovative Interfaces, Inc; (ILL) OCLC; (OPAC) Innovative Interfaces, Inc; (Serials) Innovative Interfaces, Inc
Wireless access
Partic in OCLC Online Computer Library Center, Inc; OhioNET

M OHIO HEALTH-RIVERSIDE METHODIST HOSPITAL*, D J Vincent Medical Library, 3535 Olentangy River Rd, 43214-3998. SAN 313-4407. Tel: 614-566-5230. FAX: 614-544-6967. E-mail: medlib@ohiohealth.com. *Dir,* Stacy Gall; Staff 5 (MLS 3, Non-MLS 2)
Founded 1946
Library Holdings: Bk Titles 5,000; Per Subs 1,000
Automation Activity & Vendor Info: (Cataloging) EOS International; (Circulation) EOS International; (OPAC) EOS International; (Serials) EOS International
Wireless access
Function: For res purposes, ILL available, Internet access, Photocopying/Printing, Ref serv available, Res libr
Partic in OCLC Online Computer Library Center, Inc; OhioNET
Restriction: Hospital employees & physicians only

S OHIO HISTORY CONNECTION*, Archives-Library, 800 E 17th Ave, 43211. SAN 313-4296. Tel: 614-297-2510. FAX: 614-297-2546. Reference E-mail: reference@ohiohistory.org. Web Site: www.ohiohistory.org/learn/archives-library. *Dir, Mus & Libr Serv,* Megan Wood; Tel: 614-297-2576, E-mail: mwood@ohiohistory.org
Founded 1885
Library Holdings: Bk Titles 140,000; Bk Vols 144,043
Special Collections: Ohio Memory (images from Ohio libraries); State Archives of Ohio. Oral History; State Document Depository
Subject Interests: Archaeology, Genealogy, Natural hist, Ohio hist
Automation Activity & Vendor Info: (Cataloging) Cuadra Associates, Inc; (ILL) OCLC FirstSearch; (OPAC) Cuadra Associates, Inc; (Serials) Cuadra Associates, Inc
Wireless access
Partic in OCLC Online Computer Library Center, Inc; Ohio Network of American History Research Centers; OhioNET
Open Wed-Sat 10-5
Restriction: Non-circulating to the pub

G OHIO LEGISLATIVE SERVICE COMMISSION LIBRARY*, 77 S High St, 9th Flr, 43215-6136. SAN 313-4326. Tel: 614-466-5312. FAX: 614-644-1721. *Adminr,* Debbie Tavenner; Tel: 614-466-2241, E-mail: debbie.tavenner@lsc.ohio.gov; *Asst Librn,* Kelly Pickett; Tel: 614-466-2242, E-mail: kelly.pickett@lsc.ohio.gov; Staff 3 (MLS 2, Non-MLS 1)
Founded 1953
Library Holdings: Bk Titles 16,000
Special Collections: Bulletins of the Ohio General Assembly; Journals of the Ohio House & Senate; Laws of Ohio
Subject Interests: Legis mat, Ohio legal mat
Automation Activity & Vendor Info: (Cataloging) Inmagic, Inc.
Wireless access
Restriction: Open to others by appt, Open to staff only, Restricted access

S OHIO SCHOOL FOR THE DEAF LIBRARY*, 500 Morse Rd, 43214. SAN 373-1073. Tel: 614-728-1414. Administration Tel: 614-728-4030. FAX: 614-728-4060. Web Site: www.ohioschoolforthedeaf.org/ourdepartments/library.aspx. *Librn,* Nancy Boone; E-mail: boone@osd.oh.gov; *Libr Asst,* Tatum Cook; E-mail: cookta@osd.oh.gov; Staff 2 (MLS 1, Non-MLS 1)
Library Holdings: Bk Vols 10,000; Per Subs 45
Special Collections: Deafness Coll, bks, videos, CDs; Ohio Chronicle 1868-1999
Special Services for the Deaf - TDD equip
Restriction: Open by appt only

THE OHIO STATE UNIVERSITY LIBRARIES

C AGRICULTURAL TECHNICAL INSTITUTE LIBRARY*, Halterman Hall, 1328 Dover Rd, Wooster, 44691-4000, SAN 313-8143. Tel: 330-287-1294. Toll Free Tel: 800-647-8283 (Ohio only). FAX: 330-287-1333. E-mail: atilibrary@osu.edu. Web Site: library.osu.edu. *Libr Dir,* Kathy Yoder; *Ref Librn,* Abagail Burky; E-mail: burkey.48@osu.edu; *Mgr, Tech Serv,* Kristen Purdy; Tel: 330-287-1225, E-mail: purdy.23@osu.edu; Staff 3 (MLS 2, Non-MLS 1)
Founded 1972. Enrl 704; Fac 44
Library Holdings: Bk Vols 6,700; Per Subs 205
Special Collections: ATI Historical Archives (Through Ohio State Knowledge Bank)
Subject Interests: Agr, Animal sci, Cattle production, Construction, Dairy production, Engr, Environ sci, Floral design, Golf course mgt, Hort
Automation Activity & Vendor Info: (Acquisitions) Innovative Interfaces, Inc; (Cataloging) Innovative Interfaces, Inc; (Circulation) Innovative Interfaces, Inc; (Course Reserve) Innovative Interfaces, Inc; (ILL) Innovative Interfaces, Inc; (OPAC) Innovative Interfaces, Inc; (Serials) Innovative Interfaces, Inc
Open Mon-Thurs 8-8, Fri 8-5

C ARCHIVES*, 2700 Kenny Rd, 43210, SAN 326-6869. Tel: 614-292-2409. FAX: 614-688-4150. Web Site: library.osu.edu/sites/archives/index.php. *Archivist,* Tamar Chute; Tel: 614-292-3271, E-mail: chute.6@osu.edu; *Archivist,* Laura Kissel; Tel: 614-688-8173, E-mail: kissel.4@osu.edu; *Ref (Info Servs),* Bertha Ihnat; Tel: 614-292-2409, E-mail: ihnat.1@osu.edu; Staff 6 (MLS 5, Non-MLS 1)
Founded 1965. Enrl 48,000; Fac 2,800; Highest Degree: Doctorate
Special Collections: Papers of Admiral Richard E Byrd; Papers of Sir Hubert Wilkins; Records of Dr Frederick A Cook Society; Senator John Glenn Archives. Oral History
Function: Archival coll
Partic in OCLC Online Computer Library Center, Inc
Open Mon-Fri 9-12 & 1-4:30
Restriction: Non-circulating
Friends of the Library Group

C BIOLOGICAL SCIENCES & PHARMACY*, 102 Riffe Bldg, 496 W 12th Ave, 43210-1214, SAN 356-3049. Tel: 614-292-1744. FAX: 614-688-3123. Web Site: library.osu.edu/sites/biosci. *Head of Libr,*

Natalie Kupferberg; E-mail: kupferberg.1@osu.edu; *Head, Sci Libr,* Bruce A Leach; E-mail: leach.5@osu.edu; Staff 6 (MLS 2, Non-MLS 4)
Founded 1994
Library Holdings: Bk Vols 120,000; Per Subs 1,300
Subject Interests: Biochem, Biophysics, Botany, Chem, Entomology, Genetics, Med chem, Microbiology, Pharmaceutics, Pharmacology, Zoology
Function: Res libr
Partic in OCLC Online Computer Library Center, Inc

C LOUIS BROMFIELD LIBRARY - MANSFIELD CAMPUS*, 1660 University Dr, Mansfield, 44906-1599, SAN 313-5950. Tel: 419-755-4324. Circulation Tel: 419-755-4331. Interlibrary Loan Service Tel: 419-755-4398. Reference Tel: 419-755-4326. FAX: 419-755-4327. *Libr Operations Mgr,* Kay Foltz; Tel: 419-755-4013, E-mail: foltz.2@osu.edu; Staff 5 (MLS 2, Non-MLS 3)
Founded 1966. Enrl 1,640; Fac 90; Highest Degree: Master
Library Holdings: CDs 100; Bk Vols 50,000; Per Subs 300; Talking Bks 50; Videos 2,000
Function: ILL available, Ref serv available, Telephone ref, Wheelchair accessible
Partic in Ohio Library & Information Network
Restriction: Open to pub for ref & circ; with some limitations

C FINE ARTS*, Wexner Ctr for the Arts, 1871 N High St, 43210, SAN 356-3251. Tel: 614-292-6184. FAX: 614-292-4573. Web Site: library.osu.edu/sites/finearts. *Libr Mgr,* Gretchen Donelson; E-mail: donelson.9@osu.edu; *Circ,* Clint Tomlinson; E-mail: tomlinson.42@osu.edu; *Ref (Info Servs),* Leta Hendricks; E-mail: hendricks.3@osu.edu; Staff 3 (MLS 1, Non-MLS 2)
Library Holdings: Bk Vols 140,000; Per Subs 400
Subject Interests: Art, Art educ, Design, Hist of art
Function: Res libr
Publications: New Acquisitions List (Quarterly)
Open Mon-Thurs 8am-10pm, Fri 8-6, Sat 12-6, Sun 2-10
Restriction: Circ limited

C FOOD, AGRICULTURAL & ENVIRONMENTAL SCIENCES*, 045 Agriculture Administration Bldg, 2120 Fyffe Rd, 43210-1066, SAN 356-3014. Tel: 614-292-6125. Reference Tel: 614-292-9563. FAX: 614-292-0590. *Librn,* Florian Diekmann, PhD; E-mail: diekmann.4@osu.edu; *Librn,* Jessica R Page; Tel: 614-688-8474, E-mail: page.84@osu.edu; *Circ Supvr,* Anutosh Datta. Subject Specialists: *Agr sci, Environ sci, Food sci,* Florian Diekmann, PhD; *Environ sci, Food sci, Veterinary med,* Jessica R Page; Staff 2 (MLS 1, Non-MLS 1)
Founded 1956. Highest Degree: Doctorate
Library Holdings: Bk Vols 89,304; Per Subs 1,138
Subject Interests: Agr econ, Agr environ, Agronomy, Animal sci, Crop sci, Food sci, Forestry, Hort, Natural res, Plant pathology, Rural sociol
Automation Activity & Vendor Info: (Acquisitions) Innovative Interfaces, Inc; (Cataloging) OCLC; (Circulation) Innovative Interfaces, Inc; (Course Reserve) Innovative Interfaces, Inc; (ILL) OCLC ILLiad; (OPAC) Innovative Interfaces, Inc; (Serials) Innovative Interfaces, Inc
Partic in Council of Independent Colleges; OCLC Online Computer Library Center, Inc
Special Services for the Blind - Assistive/Adapted tech devices, equip & products
Open Mon-Wed 8-8, Thurs & Fri 8-5, Sun 4-8
Restriction: In-house use for visitors, Open to students, fac & staff
Friends of the Library Group

CM PHILIP B HARDYMON MEDICAL LIBRARY*, 1492 E Broad St, 43205, SAN 324-5888. Tel: 614-257-3248. FAX: 614-257-3904. *Librn,* Rebecca Mehling
Founded 1956
Library Holdings: Bk Titles 4,000
Subject Interests: Med
Partic in Greater Midwest Regional Medical Libr Network
Open Mon-Fri 7:30-4

C HILANDAR RESEARCH LIBRARY & RESEARCH CENTER FOR MEDIEVAL SLAVIC STUDIES*, 119 Thompson Library, 1858 Neil Avenue Mall, 43210, SAN 326-9353. Tel: 614-292-0634. FAX: 614-292-8417. E-mail: hilandar@osu.edu. Web Site: rcmss.osu.edu. *Curator,* Dr Predrag Matejic; E-mail: matejic.1@osu.edu; *Assoc Curator,* Mary-Allen Johnson. Subject Specialists: *Medieval Slavic studies,* Dr Predrag Matejic; *Slavic linguistics,* Mary-Allen Johnson; Staff 2 (MLS 2)
Founded 1978. Fac 2
Library Holdings: Microforms 4,000; Bk Vols 8,000; Per Subs 10
Special Collections: Early Cyrillic Coll, bks, microfilm; Hilandar Monastery (Mt Athos, Greece), mss, microfilm
Subject Interests: Medieval Slavic studies
Function: Res libr
Publications: Cyrillic Manuscript Heritage (Newsletter)
Open Mon-Fri 9-5
Restriction: Non-circulating
Friends of the Library Group

C BILLY IRELAND CARTOON LIBRARY & MUSEUM*, 27 W 17th Ave Mall, 43210-1393, SAN 326-6656. Tel: 614-292-0538. FAX: 614-292-9101. E-mail: cartoons@osu.edu. Web Site: cartoons.osu.edu. *Curator,* Jenny E Robb; Staff 4 (MLS 2, Non-MLS 2)
Founded 1977
Library Holdings: Bk Vols 50,000
Special Collections: Original American Cartoon Art & Related Published Works
Function: Res libr
Partic in Consortium of Popular Culture Collections in the Midwest
Open Mon-Fri 9-5
Restriction: Non-circulating
Friends of the Library Group

C JEROME LAWRENCE & ROBERT E LEE THEATRE RESEARCH INSTITUTE*, 1430 Lincoln Tower, 1800 Cannon Dr, 43210-1230, SAN 327-8913. Tel: 614-292-6614. FAX: 614-688-8417. Web Site: library.osu.edu/sites/tri. *Dir,* Carol Pitts Diedrichs; *Ref Librn,* Orville Martin; E-mail: martin.369@osu.edu; *Curator,* Nena Couch; E-mail: couch.1@osu.edu; *Assoc Curator,* Beth Kattelman; E-mail: kattelman.1@osu.edu; *Asst Curator,* Kathleen Kopp; E-mail: kopp.1@osu.edu. Subject Specialists: *18th Century culture, Dance, Performing arts,* Nena Couch; Staff 3.5 (MLS 3, Non-MLS 0.5)
Founded 1951. Highest Degree: Doctorate
Library Holdings: Bk Vols 5,000
Special Collections: Company Organization Archives: Alpha Psi Omega, American Playwrights Theatre, American Theatre Critics Association, Best Plays, Black Theatre Network, Columbus Symphony Orchestra, Contemporary American Theatre Company, Cupola, Curtiss Show Print (Nyle Stateler), Dalcroze School of Music (Hilda Schuster), Dalcroze Society of America, East Lynne Company, Ensemble Theatre of Cincinnati, Gallery Players, Grandparents Living Theatre, Harmount Company, Hartman Theatre, Horse Cave Theatre, International Al Jolson Society, Los Angeles Theatre Center, Lancton Lucier Vaudeville, Players Theatre, Washington Theatre, Windsor Indoor Chautauqua; Czech Theatre: Jarka Burian Papers; Designs by Helen Anyzova, Jan Dusek, Marie Frankova, Josef Jelinek, Jaroslav Malina, Petr Matasek, Marta Roskopfova, Jan Sladek, Katerina Stefkova, Zuzana Stefunkova, Frantisek Troster, Ladislav Vychodil, Jana Zborilova; Designs, Artwork & Photographs Colls: Boris Anisfeld, Armbruster Scenic Studio, William Barclay, Alexandre Benois, Daphne Dare, Raoul Pene Du Bois, Alexandra Exter, Robert Fletcher, Peter Flinsch, French Theatre Prints, Ella Gerber, Mordecai Gorelik, George Hall, Russell Hastings, David Hays, Edith Head, Al Hirschfeld, Donald Horton, Norris Houghton, Ray Lee Jackson, Toni-Leslie James, Robert Edmond Jones, Gerald Kahan, Simon Lissim, Mircea Marosin, Gordon Micunis, Jo Mielziner, Tanya Moiseiwitsch, Motley, Sam Norkin, Dennis Parker, William Pitkin, Helene Pons, Sanford Roth, Tom Skelton, Robert Slusser Dance Photographs, Leandro Soto, Paul Stiga, Tony Straiges, Sophie Vielle, Sylvia Westerman; Personal Papers: Doris Cole Abrahams, Hollis Alpert, Isabel Bigley Barnett, Mary Bishop, Robert Breen, Jarka Burian, Lucien Bonheur, Sam Coit, John Colman, Paul Denis, Nelson Eddy & Jeanette MacDonald, Tom Eyen, Paulette Goddard/Burgess Meredith, Jed Harris, Eileen Heckart, Mary Henderson, Norris Houghton, Nancy Kelly, Madge Kendal, William F Kilmer Vaudeville, Sidney Kingsley, Ted Lange, Jerome Lawrence & Robert E Lee, Katherine Locke, Sam Locke, Charles H McCaghy Coll of Exotic Dance from Burlesque to Clubs, Bebe Miller, Don Nigro, Ethel Outland, Oysher Family, John Patrick, Robert Post, Peter Rankin, Louis Robin, Randy Skinner, Irwin Spector, Meridee Stein, Twyla Tharp, Robert A Wachsman, Clifton Webb, Ella Richey Wells, Earl Wilson, Luke Yankee; Script Colls: As the World Turns, Dramatists Play Service, International Centre for Women Playwrights, Playwrights, Samuel French; Theatre Critics: American Theatre Critics Association, Alice T Carter, Tish Dace, Marianne Evett, Bill Fark, Michael Grossberg, Henry Hewes, Holly Hill, Jeffrey Eric Jenkins, Larry Ledford, Elizabeth Maupin, E B Radcliffe, Jean Reed, Maxine Rose, Cathern Stadem, Caldwell Titcomb, Gerald Weales; Vertical Files: Artists, Japanese Theatre, Music & Opera, Dance Company, Production, Theatre Companies. Oral History
Subject Interests: Costume design, Lighting, Performing arts, Regional theatre, Theatrical dance
Function: Archival coll
Partic in Consortium of Popular Culture Collections in the Midwest
Restriction: Non-circulating
Friends of the Library Group

C LIMA CAMPUS LIBRARY*, 4240 Campus Dr, Lima, 45804, SAN 313-5721. Tel: 419-995-8401. Interlibrary Loan Service Tel: 419-995-8336. Reference Tel: 419-995-8326. FAX: 419-995-8138. E-mail: lima-library@osu.edu. Web Site: www.lima.ohio-state.edu/library/index.php. *Dir, Libr Serv,* Tina Schneider; E-mail: schneider.290@osu.edu; *Circ Supvr,* Kathy Stedke; Tel: 419-995-8361, E-mail: stedke.1@osu.edu; *Ref Librn/Instrul Serv,* Calvin Cleary
Founded 1966. Enrl 4,100; Fac 199; Highest Degree: Master
Library Holdings: Bk Vols 80,000; Per Subs 517

Publications: Library Handbook for Faculty; Student Assistants Handbook; User Instruction Sheets
Open Mon-Thurs (Winter) 8-8, Fri 8-5, Sat 10-2; Mon, Thurs & Fri (Summer) 8-5, Tues & Wed 8-7

C MARION CAMPUS LIBRARY*, 1469 Mount Vernon Ave, Marion, 43302, SAN 313-6027. Tel: 740-725-6254. Administration Tel: 740-725-6231. FAX: 740-725-6309. E-mail: marionlibrary@osu.edu. Web Site: marionlibrary.osu.edu. *Dir,* Betsy L Blankenship; E-mail: blankenship.5@osu.edu; *Circ, Tech Serv,* Patricia Wood; Tel: 740-725-6335, E-mail: wood.360@osu.edu; Staff 3 (MLS 2, Non-MLS 1)
Founded 1957. Enrl 3,757; Fac 130
Library Holdings: AV Mats 2,785; CDs 307; DVDs 144; e-books 467,034; e-journals 118,713; Microforms 3,498; Bk Vols 52,599; Per Subs 160; Videos 1,293
Special Collections: Richard Myers Music Coll (Sheet Music); Warren G Harding - Norman Thomas Research Coll
Subject Interests: Children's lit, Educ, Lit, Nursing, Psychol
Automation Activity & Vendor Info: (Acquisitions) Innovative Interfaces, Inc; (Cataloging) Innovative Interfaces, Inc; (Circulation) Innovative Interfaces, Inc; (Course Reserve) Innovative Interfaces, Inc; (ILL) OCLC ILLiad; (Media Booking) Innovative Interfaces, Inc; (OPAC) Innovative Interfaces, Inc; (Serials) Innovative Interfaces, Inc
Open Mon-Thurs 8am-9pm, Fri 8-5

CL MICHAEL E MORITZ LAW LIBRARY*, 55 W 12th Ave, 43210-1391, SAN 313-4350. Tel: 614-292-6691. Circulation Tel: 614-292-3987. Reference Tel: 614-292-9463. FAX: 614-292-3202. Reference E-mail: lawlibref@osu.edu. Web Site: www.moritzlaw.osu.edu/library/. *Asst Dir, Tech Serv, Interim Dir,* Mary Hamburger; Tel: 614-292-9466, E-mail: hamburger.11@osu.edu; *Asst Dir, Pub Serv,* Matt Cooper; *Circ Mgr,* Kaylie Vermillion; E-mail: vermillion.41@osu.edu; Staff 17 (MLS 7, Non-MLS 10)
Founded 1891. Enrl 727; Fac 49; Highest Degree: Doctorate
Library Holdings: Bk Titles 175,681; Bk Vols 789,615; Per Subs 7,192
Special Collections: Ohio Legal Materials
Subject Interests: Dispute resolution
Function: ILL available
Partic in Big Ten Academic Alliance; Center for Research Libraries; OCLC Online Computer Library Center, Inc; OhioNET
Open Mon-Thurs (Winter) 7:15am-Midnight, Fri 7:15-9, Sat 9-9, Sun 10am-Midnight; Mon-Thurs (Summer) 7:15am-11pm, Fri 7:15-6, Sat 9-5, Sun 12-6

CM GRANT MORROW III MD LIBRARY AT NATIONWIDE CHILDREN'S HOSPITAL*, 700 Children's Dr, Rm ED-244, 43205, SAN 356-3707. Tel: 614-722-3200. FAX: 614-722-3205. Web Site: library.osu.edu/sites/chi. *Dir,* Linda DeMuro; Tel: 614-722-3203, E-mail: linda.demuro@nationwidechildrens.org; Staff 4 (MLS 2, Non-MLS 2)
Founded 1953
Library Holdings: Bk Titles 10,000; Bk Vols 25,000; Per Subs 225
Special Collections: Consumer Health in Pediatrics
Subject Interests: Pediatrics
Automation Activity & Vendor Info: (Circulation) Innovative Interfaces, Inc; (OPAC) Innovative Interfaces, Inc
Partic in Association of Research Libraries; OSU Librs
Open Mon-Thurs 8:30-7, Fri 8:30-5

C MUSIC & DANCE*, 166 Sullivant Hall, 1813 N High St, 43210-1307, SAN 356-3499. Tel: 614-292-2319. Reference Tel: 614-688-0163. Administration Tel: 614-688-0106. FAX: 614-247-6794. Web Site: library.osu.edu/sites/music. *Head of Libr,* Alan Green; Staff 6 (MLS 2, Non-MLS 4)
Founded 1949
Library Holdings: CDs 28,000; Bk Vols 140,000; Per Subs 615; Videos 3,441
Special Collections: American Popular Songs; Dance V-tapes; Medieval Chant microfilm; Nordic Music Archive; Renaissance Music microfilm
Subject Interests: Dance, Hist, Music educ, Music indust, Performance, Therapy, World music
Partic in OCLC Online Computer Library Center, Inc
Publications: Newsletter
Open Mon-Thurs (Winter) 8-8, Fri 8-6, Sat 12-6, Sun 2-8; Mon-Fri (Summer) 10-5

C NEWARK CAMPUS LIBRARY*, Warner Library & Student Ctr, 1179 University Dr, Newark, 43055-1797, SAN 313-6442. Tel: 740-366-9307. Interlibrary Loan Service Tel: 740-364-9501. Reference Tel: 740-366-9308. Administration Tel: 740-364-9513. FAX: 740-366-9264. E-mail: askus@osu.edu. Web Site: www.cotc.edu/library, www.newark.osu.edu/library. *Dir,* Susan Scott; E-mail: scott.37@osu.edu; *Ref Librn,* Katie Blocksidge; E-mail: blocksidge.3@osu.edu; *Evening Circ Supvr,* Mrs Shawn Brookbank; Tel: 740-366-9183, E-mail: brookbank.14@osu.edu; *Weekend Supvr,* Mrs Jesse Higel; *Archivist, Ref (Info Servs),* John Crissinger; E-mail: crissinger.5@osu.edu; *Circ, ILL, Reserves,* Tauni Graham; E-mail: graham.151@osu.edu; Staff 6 (MLS 4, Non-MLS 2)
Founded 1957. Enrl 6,900; Fac 350; Highest Degree: Master
Library Holdings: Bk Vols 47,000; Per Subs 250; Videos 2,000
Special Collections: Newark Earthworks
Subject Interests: Native Am
Open Mon-Thurs (Winter) 8am-10pm, Fri 8-5, Sat 10-4, Sun 1-5; Mon-Thurs (Summer) 7:30am-9pm, Fri 7:30-5, Sat 10-4

C ORTON MEMORIAL LIBRARY OF GEOLOGY*, 180 Orton Hall, 155 S Oval Mall, 43210, SAN 356-3316. Tel: 614-292-2428. Web Site: library.osu.edu/about/locations/geology-library. *Libr Mgr,* Patti Dittoe; Tel: 614-292-6549, E-mail: dittoe.1@osu.edu; Staff 2 (MLS 1, Non-MLS 1)
Founded 1923
Library Holdings: Bk Vols 111,000; Per Subs 651
Subject Interests: Geol, Mineralogy, Paleontology, Polar studies
Automation Activity & Vendor Info: (OPAC) Innovative Interfaces, Inc
Partic in OCLC Online Computer Library Center, Inc
Open Mon-Thurs 8-8, Fri 8-5, Sun 2-6

CM JOHN A PRIOR HEALTH SCIENCES LIBRARY*, 376 W Tenth Ave, 43210-1240, SAN 356-3677. Tel: 614-292-4861. Reference Tel: 614-292-4869. FAX: 614-292-1920. E-mail: hslinfo@osumc.edu. Web Site: library.med.ohio-state.edu. *Dir,* Pamela S Bradigan; Tel: 614-292-4866, E-mail: bradigan.1@osu.edu; *Asst Dir,* Lynda J Hartel; Tel: 614-292-4892, E-mail: hartel.642@osu.edu; *Curator,* Judith A Wiener; Tel: 614-292-9273, Fax: 614-292-9919, E-mail: wiener3@osu.edu; *Info Tech,* Eric H Schnell; Tel: 614-292-4870, E-mail: schnell.9@osu.edu; Staff 40 (MLS 10, Non-MLS 30)
Founded 1849. Enrl 3,462; Fac 791
Library Holdings: AV Mats 1,905; e-books 953; Bk Vols 215,686; Per Subs 19,106
Special Collections: US Document Depository
Subject Interests: Allied med professions, Cancer, Dentistry, Med, Nursing, Optometry
Automation Activity & Vendor Info: (Cataloging) OCLC; (OPAC) Innovative Interfaces, Inc
Publications: Health Science Library Service Bulletin (Monthly); Health Sciences Library List of Serials
Open Mon-Thurs 7:30am-11:45pm, Fri 7:30am-7:45pm, Sat 10-5:45
Friends of the Library Group

C SCIENCE & ENGINEERING*, 175 W 18th Ave, 43210, SAN 373-5923. Tel: 614-292-0211. Interlibrary Loan Service Tel: 614-292-6211. Reference Tel: 614-292-3022. FAX: 614-292-3062. Interlibrary Loan Service FAX: 614-292-3061. Web Site: library.osu.edu/sites/sel. ; Staff 5 (MLS 5)
Library Holdings: Bk Vols 370,283; Per Subs 2,600
Special Collections: US Document Depository
Subject Interests: Archit, Astronomy, Chem, Computer, Engr genetic sci, Info serv, Landscape archit, Math, Physics, Statistics
Partic in OCLC Online Computer Library Center, Inc

C WILLIAM OXLEY THOMPSON LIBRARY*, 1858 Neil Ave Mall, 43210-1286, SAN 356-2921. Tel: 614-292-6785. FAX: 614-292-7859. Web Site: library.osu.edu. *Dir,* Carol Diedrichs; Tel: 614-292-2365, Fax: 614-292-2443, E-mail: diedrichs.1@osu.edu; *Assoc Dir, Coll & Tech Serv,* Karla Strieb; *Assoc Dir, Info Tech,* Beth Warner; *Assoc Dir, Res & Educ,* Alison Armstrong; Staff 166 (MLS 68, Non-MLS 98)
Founded 1873. Enrl 56,867; Fac 2,930; Highest Degree: Doctorate
Library Holdings: e-books 526,075; Bk Titles 4,921,972; Bk Vols 7,117,102
Special Collections: 19th Century Paperback Coll; Admiral Richard E Byrd Papers; American Association of Editorial Cartoonist Archives; American Fiction 18th Century through Contemporary (William Charvat Coll); American Playwrights' Theatre Records; American Sheet Music (ABC & Fanny Arms Colls); Arion Press Coll; Armbruster Scenic Design; Australiana; Authors Coll (Nelson Algren, W H Auden, Samuel Beckett, Robert Breen, William S Burroughs, Frederick Busch, Milton Caniff, Raymond Carver, Miguel de Cervantes, Hart Crane, Emily Dickinson, Will Eisner, T S Eliot, John Gardner, Nathaniel Hawthorne, Ernest Hemingway, Chester Hines, Eileen Heckart, T J Holmes, Jerome Lawrence & Robert E Lee, Richard Lewis, Jack London, Ralph D Mershon, Anais Nin, Jessica Mitford, James Purdy, Jesse Stuart, Twyla Tharp, Dylan Thomas, James Thurber, F L Utley, William T Vollman, Edith Wharton, Jon Whitcom); Book Plate Literature; Conjunctions Literary Journal Archive; Daguerrotypes & Ambrotypes (Floyd & Marion Rinhart Coll); Dance Notation Coll; Emanuel Rudolph Children's Science Coll; English Drama Coll; European Econ Community; Film Scripts; Little Magazines; Mather Bibliography (T J Holmes Papers); Medieval Slavic Manuscripts; Northprint Press German; Ohio News Photographers Association Archives; Oriole Press Coll; Peter D Franklin Cookbook Coll; Philip Sills Coll, film posters & stills; Reformation History Coll; Renaissance to 18th Century Coll; Science Fiction Paperbacks & Magazines; Secondary School Curricula (W W Charters Papers); Stanley J Kahrl 17th Century Drama Coll; UFO Coll. State Document Depository; UN Document Depository; US Document Depository
Automation Activity & Vendor Info: (Acquisitions) Innovative Interfaces, Inc - Millennium; (Cataloging) Innovative Interfaces, Inc - Millennium; (Circulation) Innovative Interfaces, Inc - Millennium; (ILL)

OCLC ILLiad; (OPAC) Innovative Interfaces, Inc - Millennium; (Serials) Innovative Interfaces, Inc - Millennium
Function: Archival coll, Art exhibits, Audio & video playback equip for onsite use, Computers for patron use, Distance learning, Doc delivery serv, E-Reserves, Electronic databases & coll, ILL available, Microfiche/film & reading machines, Online cat, Online ref, Photocopying/Printing, Ref & res, Res libr, Telephone ref
Partic in Association of Research Libraries; OCLC Online Computer Library Center, Inc; OCLC Research Library Partnership
Open Mon-Thurs 7:30am-Midnight, Fri 7:30am-10pm, Sat 8am-10pm, Sun 11am-Midnight
Friends of the Library Group

CM VETERINARY MEDICINE*, 225 Veterinary Medicine Academic Bldg, 1900 Coffey Rd, 43210, SAN 356-3618. Tel: 614-292-6107. FAX: 614-292-7476. Web Site: library.osu.edu/sites/vetmed. *Veterinary Med Librn,* Jessica Page; E-mail: page.84@osu.edu; *Circ Supvr,* David Sharp; E-mail: sharp.20@osu.edu; Staff 3 (MLS 1, Non-MLS 2)
Library Holdings: Bk Vols 40,000; Per Subs 630
Automation Activity & Vendor Info: (ILL) OVID Technologies
Partic in OCLC Online Computer Library Center, Inc
Open Mon-Thurs 8am-10pm, Fri 8-6, Sat 10-6, Sun 12-9

S OHIOANA LIBRARY*, 274 E First Ave, Ste 300, 43201. SAN 313-413X. Tel: 614-466-3831. FAX: 614-728-6974. E-mail: ohioana@ohioana.org. Web Site: www.ohioana.org. *Dir,* David Weaver; *Librn,* Courtney Brown; Staff 4 (MLS 1, Non-MLS 3)
Founded 1929
Library Holdings: Bk Titles 43,500; Bk Vols 46,000
Special Collections: Books written by Ohioans or about Ohio & Ohioans; Dawn Powell Coll; George Randolph Chester Coll; James Thurber Coll; Louis Bromfield Coll; Martha Finley Coll; Mildred Wirt Benson Coll; R L Stine Coll; Rollo W Brown Coll; Sherwood Anderson Coll; W D Howells Coll; Women's History in Ohio; Zane Gray Coll
Subject Interests: Bks by Ohioans or about Ohio, Music by Ohio composers, Rare bks, Scrapbks of biog info
Automation Activity & Vendor Info: (OPAC) Innovative Interfaces, Inc
Publications: Educational Resource List; Ohioana Quarterly; Ohioana-Ohio Literary Map
Partic in Ohio Library & Information Network; OhioNET
Open Mon-Fri 8:30-4:30
Restriction: In-house use for visitors, Not a lending libr

M OHIOHEALTH GRANT MEDICAL CENTER, Medical Library, 340 E Town St, Ste 7-200, 7th flr, 43215. (Mail add: 111 S Grant St, Grant Medical Center, 43215), SAN 313-4180. Tel: 614-566-9467, 614-566-9468. *Dir, Libr Serv,* Stacy Gall; Tel: 614-566-5230, E-mail: Stacy.Gall@ohiohealth.com; *Librn,* Lyndsey Schaeffer; E-mail: Lyndsey.Schaeffer@ohiohealth.com; *Asst Librn, Libr Tech,* John Newman; E-mail: john.newman@ohiohealth.com. Subject Specialists: *Med educ, Med ref,* Lyndsey Schaeffer; *Law, Librarianship, Med,* John Newman; Staff 7 (MLS 4, Non-MLS 3)
Founded 1960
Subject Interests: Allied health, Med, Nursing
Automation Activity & Vendor Info: (Cataloging) EOS International; (Circulation) EOS International; (ILL) OCLC; (OPAC) EOS International
Wireless access
Partic in National Network of Libraries of Medicine Region 6
Restriction: Hospital employees & physicians only, Med staff & students, Not open to pub

SR PONTIFICAL COLLEGE JOSEPHINUM*, A T Wehrle Memorial Library, 7625 N High St, 43235-1498. SAN 313-8178. Tel: 614-985-2295. FAX: 614-885-2307. E-mail: libreqs@pcj.edu. Web Site: libguides.pcj.edu/pcjlibrary. *Libr Dir,* Peter G Veracka; E-mail: pveracka@pcj.edu; *Asst Librn,* Beverly S Lane; E-mail: bslane@pcj.edu; *Libr Assoc,* Michelle Brown; E-mail: mbrown@pcj.edu; Staff 3 (MLS 2, Non-MLS 1)
Founded 1888. Enrl 155; Fac 24; Highest Degree: Master
Library Holdings: AV Mats 2,618; e-journals 33,835; Microforms 1,897; Per Subs 204
Subject Interests: Philos, Relig studies, Theol
Automation Activity & Vendor Info: (Acquisitions) Innovative Interfaces, Inc; (Cataloging) Innovative Interfaces, Inc; (Circulation) Innovative Interfaces, Inc; (Course Reserve) Innovative Interfaces, Inc; (ILL) Innovative Interfaces, Inc; (Media Booking) Innovative Interfaces, Inc; (OPAC) Innovative Interfaces, Inc; (Serials) Innovative Interfaces, Inc
Wireless access
Partic in OCLC Online Computer Library Center, Inc; Ohio Library & Information Network; Ohio Private Academic Libraries; OhioNET

L PORTER, WRIGHT, MORRIS & ARTHUR, LLP*, Law Library, Huntington Ctr, 41 S High St, 43215-6194. SAN 326-1727. Administration Tel: 614-227-2090. FAX: 614-227-2100. Web Site: www.porterwright.com. *Dir, Libr Serv,* Susan M Schaefgen; E-mail: sschaefgen@porterwright.com; *Ref Librn,* Robert Oszakiewski; E-mail: roszakiewski@porterwright.com; Staff 4 (MLS 2, Non-MLS 2)
Founded 1846
Automation Activity & Vendor Info: (Acquisitions) Softlink America; (Cataloging) Softlink America; (Circulation) Softlink America; (OPAC) Softlink America; (Serials) Softlink America
Restriction: Not open to pub

L SQUIRE PATTON BOGGS*, Law Library, 2000 Huntington Ctr, 41 S High St, 43215. SAN 323-8539. Tel: 614-365-2700. FAX: 614-365-2499. *Librn,* Patricia Christian; Staff 2 (MLS 2)
Library Holdings: Bk Titles 1,200; Bk Vols 13,000; Per Subs 50

P STATE LIBRARY OF OHIO*, 274 E First Ave, Ste 100, 43201. SAN 356-4487. Tel: 614-644-7061. Circulation Tel: 614-644-6950. Interlibrary Loan Service Tel: 614-644-6956. Reference Tel: 614-644-7051. Toll Free Tel: 800-686-1532 (Ohio only). FAX: 614-466-3584. Reference FAX: 614-644-7004. E-mail: refhelp@library.ohio.gov. Web Site: www.library.ohio.gov. *State Librn,* Wendy Knapp; E-mail: wknapp@library.ohio.gov; *Assoc State Librn, Libr Develop,* Evan Struble; Tel: 614-644-6914, E-mail: estruble@library.ohio.gov; *Assoc State Librn, Libr Serv,* Ann M Watson; Tel: 614-728-4988, E-mail: awatson@library.ohio.gov; *Head, Fiscal Serv,* Jamie Pardee; Tel: 614-644-6879, E-mail: jpardee@library.ohio.gov; Staff 38 (MLS 14, Non-MLS 24)
Founded 1817
Jul 2017-Jun 2018 Income $21,807,930, State $5,295,114, Federal $5,350,000, Other $11,162,816. Mats Exp $1,913,446, Books $125,436, Electronic Ref Mat (Incl. Access Fees) $1,788,010. Sal $5,501,110
Library Holdings: Bks on Deafness & Sign Lang 984; e-books 95,031; Microforms 231,500; Bk Titles 1,220,470; Per Subs 116
Special Collections: Rare Books Coll. State Document Depository; US Document Depository
Subject Interests: Admin, Behav sci, Econ, Educ, Soc sci
Automation Activity & Vendor Info: (Acquisitions) Innovative Interfaces, Inc; (Cataloging) Innovative Interfaces, Inc; (Circulation) Innovative Interfaces, Inc; (Discovery) EBSCO Discovery Service; (ILL) OCLC; (OPAC) Innovative Interfaces, Inc; (Serials) Innovative Interfaces, Inc
Wireless access
Function: 24/7 Electronic res, 24/7 Online cat, Archival coll, Computers for patron use, Digital talking bks, Electronic databases & coll, For res purposes, Govt ref serv, ILL available, Internet access, Magazines, Meeting rooms, Microfiche/film & reading machines, Online cat, OverDrive digital audio bks, Photocopying/Printing, Res libr, Wheelchair accessible
Publications: Directory of Ohio Libraries; State Library News; Statistics Categorized by Income; Statistics of Ohio Libraries
Partic in Ohio Library & Information Network; Ohio Public Library Information Network
Special Services for the Blind - Talking bks
Open Mon-Fri 8-5

GL SUPREME COURT OF OHIO*, Law Library, 65 S Front St, 11th Flr, 43215-3431. SAN 313-4431. Tel: 614-387-9680. FAX: 614-387-9689. E-mail: libref@sc.ohio.gov. Web Site: www.supremecourtofohio.gov/legalresources/lawlibrary. *Dir,* Ken Kozlowski; E-mail: ken.kozlowski@sc.ohio.gov; *Ref Librn,* Michelle Graff; Tel: 614-387-9692, E-mail: michelle.graff@sc.ohio.gov; *Tech Serv Librn,* Anna Gault; Tel: 614-387-9654, E-mail: anna.gault@sc.ohio.gov; *Pub Serv Mgr,* Erin Waltz; Tel: 614-387-9668, E-mail: erin.waltz@sc.ohio.gov; *Tech Serv Mgr,* Marlys Bradshaw; Tel: 614-387-9661, E-mail: marlys.bradshaw@sc.ohio.gov; Staff 8.5 (MLS 5, Non-MLS 3.5)
Founded 1860
Library Holdings: Bk Vols 400,000; Per Subs 1,740
Special Collections: Ohio & US Legal Treatises, Cases & Statutes
Wireless access
Function: 24/7 Online cat
Publications: The Supreme Court of Ohio Law Library Handbook
Partic in OCLC Online Computer Library Center, Inc; OhioNET
Open Mon-Fri 8-5
Restriction: Open to pub for ref & circ; with some limitations

S TIFERETH ISRAEL*, Minnie Cobey Memorial Library, 1354 E Broad St, 43205. SAN 313-4083. Tel: 614-253-8523, Ext 112. FAX: 614-253-8323. Web Site: www.tiferethisrael.org/library.html. *Librn,* Helen Chronister; E-mail: hchronister@tiferethisrael.org
Founded 1950
Library Holdings: Bk Titles 4,500; Bk Vols 5,000; Per Subs 30
Special Collections: Talmud (Babylonian Talmud Coll)
Subject Interests: Bible, Judaism, Prayer bks, Relig studies, Talmud
Wireless access
Open Tues & Thurs Noon-5, Wed 11:30-2:30

R TRINITY LUTHERAN SEMINARY AT CAPITAL UNIVERSITY, Hamma Library, 2199 E Main St, 43205. SAN 313-4466. Tel: 614-236-6857. E-mail: tlslibrary@capital.edu. Web Site:

libguides.capital.edu/Hamma. *Head Librn,* Elli Cucksey; Tel: 614-236-6853, E-mail: ecucksey@capital.edu; Staff 1 (MLS 1)
Founded 1830. Enrl 100; Fac 20; Highest Degree: Master
Library Holdings: Bk Vols 131,358; Per Subs 185
Special Collections: Ecola Christian Music Coll; New Testament studies (Lenski Memorial Coll); Simmons Gospel Music Coll; The Dr Donald L Huber Rare Book Room
Subject Interests: Theol
Automation Activity & Vendor Info: (Acquisitions) Innovative Interfaces, Inc - Sierra; (Cataloging) Innovative Interfaces, Inc - Sierra; (Circulation) Innovative Interfaces, Inc - Sierra; (Course Reserve) Innovative Interfaces, Inc - Sierra; (Discovery) EBSCO Discovery Service; (ILL) OCLC; (OPAC) Innovative Interfaces, Inc - Sierra; (Serials) Innovative Interfaces, Inc - Sierra
Wireless access
Partic in OCLC Online Computer Library Center, Inc; Ohio Library & Information Network; OhioNET

TWIN VALLEY BEHAVIORAL HEALTHCARE

M FORENSIC PATIENTS' LIBRARY*, 2200 W Broad St, 43223, SAN 320-3565. Tel: 614-752-0333, Ext 5451. FAX: 614-752-0385. *Library Contact,* Liz Smith
Library Holdings: Bk Vols 5,500; Per Subs 21
Subject Interests: Med, Psychiat

M MARLIN R WEDEMEYER STAFF LIBRARY*, 2200 W Broad St, 43223, SAN 313-4067. Tel: 614-752-0333, Ext 5454. FAX: 614-752-0385.
Library Holdings: Bk Titles 3,366; Per Subs 80
Subject Interests: Med, Psychiat

P UPPER ARLINGTON PUBLIC LIBRARY*, 2800 Tremont Rd, 43221. SAN 357-282X. Tel: 614-486-9621. Reference Tel: 614-486-3342. Administration Tel: 614-486-0900. FAX: 614-486-4530. Web Site: www.ualibrary.org. *Dir,* Beth Hatch; E-mail: director@ualibrary.org; *Asst Dir,* Kate Porter; E-mail: kporter@ualibrary.org; *Dir, Support Serv,* Gregory Ramage; E-mail: gramage@ualibrary.org; *Adult Serv Mgr,* Vita Marinello; E-mail: vmarinello@ualibrary.org; *Circ Mgr,* Annette Heffernan; E-mail: aheffernan@ualibrary.org; *Fac Mgr,* Steve Benson; E-mail: sbenson@ualibrary.org; *Human Res Mgr,* Julie Whitt; E-mail: jwhitt@ualibrary.org; *Mkt & Commun Relations Mgr,* Christine Minx; E-mail: cminx@ualibrary.org; *Media Serv Mgr,* ; *Ref Mgr,* ; *Tech Serv Mgr,* Jennifer Christensen; E-mail: jchristensen@ualibrary.org; *Youth Serv Mgr,* Tracie Steele; E-mail: tsteele@ualibrary.org; Staff 17.7 (MLS 15.8, Non-MLS 1.9)
Founded 1967. Pop 34,150; Circ 1,920,119
Jan 2017-Dec 2017 Income (Main & Associated Libraries) $6,028,046. Mats Exp $750,887. Sal $3,097,430
Special Collections: School Reading; UA Archives (Digital Coll); Upper Arlington High School Digital Yearbooks; Upper Arlington Hist & Authors Coll
Subject Interests: Foreign lang
Automation Activity & Vendor Info: (Acquisitions) Innovative Interfaces, Inc; (Cataloging) Innovative Interfaces, Inc; (Circulation) Innovative Interfaces, Inc; (OPAC) Innovative Interfaces, Inc; (Serials) Innovative Interfaces, Inc
Wireless access
Function: 24/7 Electronic res, 24/7 Online cat, Adult bk club, Art exhibits, Audiobks on Playaways & MP3, Bks on CD, Children's prog, Computer training, Computers for patron use, Electronic databases & coll, Free DVD rentals, Holiday prog, Home delivery & serv to seniorr ctr & nursing homes, Homebound delivery serv, Internet access, Life-long learning prog for all ages, Magazines, Meeting rooms, Microfiche/film & reading machines, Music CDs, Online cat, OverDrive digital audio bks, Passport agency, Photocopying/Printing, Printer for laptops & handheld devices, Prog for adults, Prog for children & young adult, Ref serv available, Scanner, Story hour, Summer reading prog, Tax forms, Wheelchair accessible
Partic in Central Library Consortium
Open Mon-Thurs 10-9, Fri 10-6, Sat 10-5, Sun 1-5
Friends of the Library Group
Branches: 2
LANE ROAD BRANCH, 1945 Lane Rd, Upper Arlington, 43220, SAN 357-2854. Tel: 614-459-0273. FAX: 614-459-3437. *Br Mgr,* Pam Cole; E-mail: pcole@ualibrary.org; *Ch Serv,* Sue Emrick; E-mail: semrick@ualibrary.org
Open Mon-Thurs 10-9, Fri 10-6, Sat 10-5, Sun 1-5
Friends of the Library Group
MILLER PARK BRANCH, 1901 Arlington Ave, Upper Arlington, 43212, SAN 357-2889. Tel: 614-488-5710. FAX: 614-487-2032. *Br Mgr,* Kate Albers; E-mail: kalbers@ualibrary.org; *Ch Serv,* Sarah Manley; E-mail: smanley@ualibrary.org
Open Mon-Thurs 10-9, Fri 10-6, Sat 10-5, Sun 1-5
Friends of the Library Group

CONNEAUT

P CONNEAUT PUBLIC LIBRARY*, 304 Buffalo St, 44030-2658. SAN 356-4630. Tel: 440-593-1608. FAX: 440-593-4470. Web Site: www.conneaut.lib.oh.us. *Exec Dir,* Kathy Zappitello; E-mail: Kathy.Zappitello@conneaut.lib.oh.us; *Asst Dir,* Cindy Prather; E-mail: Cindy.Prather@conneaut.lib.oh.us; *Youth Serv,* Stephanie Gildone; E-mail: Stephanie.Gildone@conneaut.lib.oh.us
Founded 1908. Pop 17,000
Library Holdings: AV Mats 17,686; Bk Vols 52,513; Per Subs 127
Special Collections: Large Print Coll; Local History Coll, newspapers 1835-1982, micro; Media, audios; New Grove Directory of Music & Musicians Coll; Old Radio Shows Coll, cassettes; Young Adult Coll
Subject Interests: Local hist, Local newsp, Music, Self help
Automation Activity & Vendor Info: (Cataloging) LibLime; (Circulation) LibLime; (OPAC) LibLime
Wireless access
Publications: Annual Report; Brochure of Services
Partic in Northeast Ohio Regional Library System
Special Services for the Deaf - TDD equip
Special Services for the Blind - Audio mat; Bks on CD; Cassettes; Computer with voice synthesizer for visually impaired persons; Copier with enlargement capabilities; Home delivery serv; Large print bks; Magnifiers; Reading & writing aids
Open Mon-Fri 10-7, Sat 9-1
Friends of the Library Group

COSHOCTON

P COSHOCTON PUBLIC LIBRARY, 655 Main St, 43812-1697. SAN 323-679X. Tel: 740-622-0956. FAX: 740-622-4331. E-mail: info@coshoctonlibrary.org. Web Site: www.coshoctonlibrary.org. *Dir,* Jennifer M Austin; E-mail: jaustin@coshoctonlibrary.org; *Ref Librn,* Mike Ontko; E-mail: montko@coshoctonlibrary.org; *Br Mgr,* Andrea Schweitzer Smith; E-mail: aschweitzer@coshoctonlibrary.org; *Fiscal Officer,* Kim Eick; *Adult Serv Mgr,* Megan Baughman; E-mail: mbaughman@coshoctonlibrary.org; *Youth Serv Mgr,* Deborah Crowdy; E-mail: dcrowdy@coshoctonlibrary.org; *Adult Serv Coordr,* Robbie Kehl; E-mail: rkekl@coshoctonlibrary.org; *Pub Relations Coordr,* Jennifer Williams; E-mail: jwilliams@coshoctonlibrary.org; Staff 18.9 (MLS 3, Non-MLS 15.9)
Founded 1904. Pop 36,901; Circ 375,175
Library Holdings: e-books 99,491; Bk Vols 116,490; Per Subs 193
Special Collections: State Document Depository
Subject Interests: Genealogy, Local hist
Automation Activity & Vendor Info: (Acquisitions) SirsiDynix; (Cataloging) SirsiDynix; (Circulation) SirsiDynix; (OPAC) SirsiDynix
Wireless access
Publications: Library Connections (Newsletter)
Partic in Northeast Ohio Regional Library System; Serving Every Ohioan Library Center
Special Services for the Deaf - Bks on deafness & sign lang; High interest/low vocabulary bks
Special Services for the Blind - Talking bks
Open Mon-Wed 9-8, Thurs & Fri 9:30-6, Sat 9:30-5
Friends of the Library Group
Branches: 1
WEST LAFAYETTE BRANCH, 601 E Main St, West Lafayette, 43845, SAN 323-6811. Tel: 740-545-6672. FAX: 740-545-6418. E-mail: wlbranch@coshoctonlibrary.org. Web Site: www.coshoctonpl.org/west-lafayette/index.php. *Br Mgr,* Andrea Schweitzer
Circ 62,163
Library Holdings: Bk Vols 13,000
Partic in State Libr of Ohio
Open Mon-Wed 10-7, Thurs & Fri 10-5, Sat 10-3
Friends of the Library Group
Bookmobiles: 1. Mgr, Kris Ringwalt. Bk titles 3,000

COVINGTON

P J R CLARKE PUBLIC LIBRARY, 102 E Spring St, 45318. SAN 313-4512. Tel: 937-473-2226. FAX: 937-473-8118. E-mail: info@jrclarkelibrary.org. Web Site: www.jrclarkelibrary.org. *Dir,* Cherie Roeth; Staff 9 (Non-MLS 9)
Founded 1917. Pop 5,124; Circ 174,350
Library Holdings: AV Mats 2,476; Large Print Bks 633; Bk Vols 59,738; Per Subs 131; Talking Bks 698
Special Collections: J R Clarke Family Coll; Obituary Index
Subject Interests: Civil War, Hist
Automation Activity & Vendor Info: (Acquisitions) Follett Software; (Cataloging) Follett Software; (Circulation) Follett Software
Wireless access
Publications: Newsletter (Monthly)
Partic in Consortium of Ohio Libraries; Miami Valley Librs

Open Mon & Wed 9-7, Tues, Thurs & Fri 9-5, Sat 9-1
Friends of the Library Group

CRESTLINE

P CRESTLINE PUBLIC LIBRARY*, 324 N Thoman St, 44827-1410. SAN 313-4520. Tel: 419-683-3909. FAX: 419-683-3022. Web Site: crestlinepubliclibrary.org. *Librn,* Cheryl Swihart; *Ch Serv,* Lynn Altftadt; Staff 6 (MLS 6)
Founded 1925. Pop 8,400; Circ 110,148
Library Holdings: Bk Vols 68,636; Per Subs 215
Special Collections: Books on Cassette; County Census Records; County Court Records; County Death Records, micro; Filmed Periodicals; Historical Picture Coll; Large Print Books; Ohio Local Newspaper, 113 years, micro; Read-Alongs; Videos
Subject Interests: Railroad printed mat
Automation Activity & Vendor Info: (Cataloging) TLC (The Library Corporation); (Circulation) TLC (The Library Corporation); (OPAC) TLC (The Library Corporation)
Wireless access
Special Services for the Deaf - Captioned film dep; High interest/low vocabulary bks
Special Services for the Blind - Bks on cassette; Large print bks
Open Mon 9-9, Tues-Thurs 9-8, Fri 9-5, Sat 9-1

CUYAHOGA FALLS

P CUYAHOGA FALLS LIBRARY*, Taylor Memorial Association, 2015 Third St, 44221-3294. SAN 313-4563. Tel: 330-928-2117. Circulation Tel: 330-928-2117, Ext 2001. FAX: 330-928-2535. E-mail: mail@cuyahogafallslibrary.org. Web Site: cuyahogafallslibrary.org. *Dir,* Valerie Kocin; E-mail: vkocin@cuyahogafallslibrary.org; *Ch Serv,* Joyce Bigam; E-mail: joyceb@cuyahogafallslibrary.org; Staff 43 (MLS 6, Non-MLS 37)
Founded 1911. Pop 44,832; Circ 772,326
Library Holdings: AV Mats 24,835; Bk Vols 146,620; Per Subs 363
Subject Interests: Local hist
Automation Activity & Vendor Info: (Circulation) Innovative Interfaces, Inc; (ILL) OCLC; (OPAC) Innovative Interfaces, Inc
Wireless access
Publications: Newsletter (Monthly)
Special Services for the Deaf - TDD equip
Open Mon-Thurs 9-9, Fri 9-6, Sat 9-5, Sun 12-5
Friends of the Library Group

DAYTON

M DAYTON CHILDREN'S HOSPITAL, Medical Library, One Children's Plaza, 45404-1815. SAN 313-4571. Tel: 937-641-3307. Interlibrary Loan Service Tel: 937-641-5072. Web Site: www.childrensdayton.org. *Med Librn, Research Librn,* Luzviminda Sinha; E-mail: sinhal@childrensdayton.org. Subject Specialists: *Pediatrics,* Luzviminda Sinha; Staff 1 (MLS 1)
Founded 1967
Library Holdings: Bk Vols 1,720; Per Subs 180
Wireless access
Function: 24/7 Electronic res, 24/7 Online cat
Restriction: Badge access after hrs, Not open to pub
Friends of the Library Group

P DAYTON METRO LIBRARY*, 215 E Third St, 45402. SAN 356-4754. Tel: 937-463-2665. Circulation Tel: 937-496-8905. Reference Tel: 937-496-8910. FAX: 937-496-4300. Web Site: www.daytonmetrolibrary.org. *Exec Dir,* Timothy Kambitsch; E-mail: tkambitsch@daytonmetrolibrary.org; *Br Mgr,* Kimber Fox; *Outreach Serv Mgr,* Kim Bautz; Tel: 937-496-8956; Staff 545 (MLS 76, Non-MLS 469)
Founded 1847. Pop 458,677; Circ 644,768
Library Holdings: Bk Vols 2,206,735; Per Subs 919
Special Collections: Local History (Dayton Room). State Document Depository; US Document Depository
Automation Activity & Vendor Info: (Acquisitions) Innovative Interfaces, Inc; (Cataloging) Innovative Interfaces, Inc; (Circulation) Innovative Interfaces, Inc; (OPAC) Innovative Interfaces, Inc
Wireless access
Special Services for the Deaf - High interest/low vocabulary bks; TTY equip
Open Mon, Tues & Thurs 9:30-8:30, Wed, Fri & Sat 9:30-6, Sun 1-5
Friends of the Library Group
Branches: 18
BELMONT, 1041 Watervliet Ave, 45420, SAN 356-4789. Tel: 937-496-8920. *Br Mgr,* Mark Roma
Library Holdings: Bk Vols 36,853
Open Mon, Tues & Thurs 9:30-8:30, Wed, Fri & Sat 9:30-6
Friends of the Library Group
BROOKVILLE BRANCH, 120 Blue Pride Dr, Brookville, 45309. Tel: 937-496-8922. FAX: 937-496-4322. *Br Mgr,* Elaine Lindstrom
Open Mon, Tues & Thurs 9:30-8:30, Wed, Fri & Sat 9:30-6
Friends of the Library Group
BURKHARDT, 4680 Burkhardt Ave, 45431, SAN 356-4843. Tel: 937-496-8924. FAX: 937-496-4324. *Br Mgr,* Francesca Hary
Open Mon, Tues & Thurs 9:30-8:30, Wed, Fri & Sat 9:30-6
Friends of the Library Group
ELECTRA C DOREN BRANCH, 701 Troy St, 45404, SAN 356-4908. Tel: 937-496-8928. FAX: 937-496-4328. *Br Mgr,* Jonathan Cline
Founded 1927
Open Mon, Tues & Thurs 9:30-8:30, Wed, Fri & Sat 9:30-6
Friends of the Library Group
EAST, 2008 Wyoming St, 45410, SAN 356-4932. Tel: 937-496-8930. FAX: 937-496-4330. *Br Mgr,* Position Currently Open
Open Mon, Tues & Thurs 9:30-8:30, Wed, Fri & Sat 9:30-6
Friends of the Library Group
HUBER HEIGHTS, 6160 Chambersburg Rd, 45424, SAN 356-4991. Tel: 937-496-8934. FAX: 937-496-4334. *Br Mgr,* Carol Mitchell
Open Mon, Tues & Thurs 9:30-8:30, Wed, Fri & Sat 9:30-6
Friends of the Library Group
KETTERING-MORAINE, 3496 Far Hills Ave, Kettering, 45429, SAN 356-5025. Tel: 937-496-8938. FAX: 937-496-4338. *Br Mgr,* Teresa Huntley
Open Mon, Tues & Thurs 9:30-8:30, Wed, Fri & Sat 9:30-6
Friends of the Library Group
MADDEN HILLS, 2542 Germantown St, 45408, SAN 356-505X. Tel: 937-496-8942. FAX: 937-496-4342. *Br Mgr,* Winnie Johnson
Open Mon, Tues & Thurs 9:30-8:30, Wed, Fri & Sat 9:30-6
Friends of the Library Group
MIAMI TOWNSHIP, 2718 Lyons Rd, Miamisburg, 45342. Tel: 937-496-8944. FAX: 937-496-4344. *Br Mgr,* Cheryl C Wirtley
Open Mon, Tues & Thurs 9:30-8:30, Wed, Fri & Sat 9:30-6
Friends of the Library Group
MIAMISBURG BRANCH, 545 E Linden Ave, Miamisburg, 45342, SAN 356-5084. Tel: 937-496-8946. FAX: 937-496-4346. *Br Mgr,* David Hicks
Open Mon, Tues & Thurs 9:30-8:30, Wed, Fri & Sat 9:30-6
Friends of the Library Group
NEW LEBANON BRANCH, 715 W Main St, New Lebanon, 45345, SAN 356-5114. Tel: 937-496-8948. *Br Mgr,* Carol Macmann
Open Mon, Tues & Thurs 9:30-8:30, Wed, Fri & Sat 9:30-6
Friends of the Library Group
NORTHMONT, 333 W National Rd, Englewood, 45322, SAN 356-5149. Tel: 937-496-8950. *Br Mgr,* Shari Bowers
Open Mon, Tues & Thurs 9:30-8:30, Wed, Fri & Sat 9:30-6
Friends of the Library Group
NORTHWEST BRANCH, 2410 Philadelphia Dr, 45406. *Br Mgr,* Sharon Taste
Open Mon, Tues & Thurs 9:30-8:30, Wed, Fri & Sat 9:30-6
Friends of the Library Group
TROTWOOD BRANCH, 651 E Main St, Trotwood, 45426, SAN 356-5203. Tel: 937-496-8958. FAX: 937-496-4358. *Br Mgr,* Caitlin Wissler
Open Mon, Tues & Thurs 9:30-8:30, Wed, Fri & Sat 9:30-6
Friends of the Library Group
VANDALIA BRANCH, 330 S Dixie Dr, Vandalia, 45377, SAN 356-5238. Tel: 937-496-8960. FAX: 937-496-4360. *Br Mgr,* Suzanne Sandridge
Open Mon, Tues & Thurs 9:30-8:30, Wed, Fri & Sat 9:30-6
Friends of the Library Group
WEST CARROLLTON BRANCH, 300 E Central Ave, West Carrollton, 45449, SAN 356-5262. Tel: 937-496-8962. FAX: 937-496-4362. *Br Mgr,* Karen Findlay; Staff 3 (MLS 2, Non-MLS 1)
Open Mon, Tues & Thurs 9:30-8:30, Wed, Fri & Sat 9:30-6
Friends of the Library Group
WESTWOOD, 3207 Hoover Ave, 45407, SAN 356-5297. Tel: 937-496-8964. FAX: 937-496-4364. *Br Mgr,* Winnie Johnson
Open Mon, Tues & Thurs 9:30-8:30, Wed, Fri & Sat 9:30-6
Friends of the Library Group
WILMINGTON-STROOP, 3980 Wilmington Pike, 45429. Tel: 937-496-8966. FAX: 937-496-4366. *Br Mgr,* Mike Hensel; Staff 4 (MLS 4)
Founded 1976. Circ 550,000
Open Mon, Tues & Thurs 9:30-8:30, Wed, Fri & Sat 9:30-6
Friends of the Library Group
Bookmobiles: 1

S KETTERING FOUNDATION LIBRARY*, 200 Commons Rd, 45459. SAN 374-9320. Tel: 937-434-7300. Toll Free Tel: 800-221-3657. FAX: 937-439-9837. Web Site: www.kettering.org/library. *Libr Mgr,* Collette McDonough; E-mail: cmcdonough@kettering.org; Staff 2 (MLS 1, Non-MLS 1)
Library Holdings: Bk Vols 3,500; Per Subs 60
Special Collections: Abstracts Coll, staff-written abstracts, articles
Subject Interests: Democracy
Function: ILL available

Partic in OCLC Online Computer Library Center, Inc
Restriction: Not open to pub, Staff use only

L MONTGOMERY COUNTY LAW LIBRARY*, 505 Montgomery County Courts Bldg, 41 N Perry St, 45402. (Mail add: PO Box 972, 45422-2490), SAN 372-1981. Tel: 937-225-4496. FAX: 937-225-5056. Web Site: www.mcohio.org/government/county_agencies/law_library. *Law Librn,* Brenda Williams; E-mail: williamsb@mcohio.org
Library Holdings: Bk Vols 141,260; Per Subs 4,214
Open Mon-Fri 8:30-5

SR NORTH AMERICAN CENTER FOR MARIANIST STUDIES LIBRARY, Chaminade Ctr, 4435 E Patterson Rd, 45430-1083. Tel: 937-429-2521. Web Site: nacms.org. *Librn,* Brother Andrew J Kosmowski; E-mail: kosmowskia1@udayton.edu; *Librn,* Teresa Trimboli; E-mail: trimbotz@udayton.edu; Staff 2 (MLS 2)
Founded 1986
Library Holdings: Bk Titles 4,223; Bk Vols 8,869
Special Collections: Marianist history & spirituality
Automation Activity & Vendor Info: (Cataloging) MITINET, Inc; (OPAC) ComPanion Corp
Wireless access
Open Tues-Fri 9-5
Restriction: Non-circulating, Open to pub for ref only

M PREMIER HEALTH, MIAMI VALLEY HOSPITAL, Library & Knowledge Services, One Wyoming St, 45409. SAN 313-4687. Tel: 937-208-2612. FAX: 937-208-2569. Web Site: premierhealth.com/healthcare-professionals/physician-connect/research-and-trials/medical-libraries. *Mgr,* Leslie Lindsey; Tel: 937-208-2617, E-mail: lalindsey@premierhealth.com; *Assoc Librn,* Janet Petty; Tel: 937-208-2624, E-mail: jlpetty@premierhealth.com; Staff 5 (MLS 2, Non-MLS 3)
Founded 1926
Library Holdings: Bk Titles 10,000; Bk Vols 42,000; Per Subs 500
Subject Interests: Hospital admin, Med, Nursing, Nutrition
Automation Activity & Vendor Info: (Serials) Innovative Interfaces, Inc
Partic in National Network of Libraries of Medicine Region 6; Ohio Library & Information Network
Restriction: Staff use only

J SINCLAIR COMMUNITY COLLEGE LIBRARY*, 444 W Third St, 45402-1460. SAN 313-475X. Tel: 937-512-3007. Reference Tel: 937-512-3004. Toll Free Tel: 800-315-3000. FAX: 937-512-4564. E-mail: ask@sinclair.libanswers.com. Web Site: www.sinclair.edu/services/academic/library. *Dir,* Debra Oswald; E-mail: debra.oswald@sinclair.edu; *Librn,* Austin Pevler; Tel: 937-512-3925, E-mail: austin.pevler@sinclair.edu; *Tech Serv & Syst Librn,* Andrea Christman; Tel: 937-512-4513, E-mail: andrea.christman@sinclair.edu; *Ref (Info Servs),* Lajmar Anderson; Tel: 937-512-3003, E-mail: lajmar.anderson@sinclair.edu; *Ref (Info Servs),* Sonya Kirkwood; Tel: 937-512-3005, E-mail: sonya.kirkwood@sinclair.edu; *Ref (Info Servs),* Julie McDaniel; Tel: 937-512-2107, E-mail: julie.mcdaniel@sinclair.edu; *Ref (Info Servs),* Andrew J Walsh; Tel: 937-512-2852, E-mail: andrew.walsh662@sinclair.edu. Subject Specialists: *English, Lang,* Debra Oswald; *Bus, Info tech, Paralegal,* Austin Pevler; *Liberal arts, Soc sci,* Lajmar Anderson; *Health sci, Life sci,* Sonya Kirkwood; *STEM,* Andrew J Walsh; Staff 7 (MLS 7)
Founded 1887. Enrl 23,241; Fac 1,129; Highest Degree: Associate
Library Holdings: Bk Vols 147,613; Per Subs 509
Subject Interests: Computer sci, Early childhood educ, Multicultural studies, Ohio law, Prof develop, Quality in higher educ
Automation Activity & Vendor Info: (Acquisitions) Innovative Interfaces, Inc; (Circulation) Innovative Interfaces, Inc
Partic in Ohio Library & Information Network; OhioNET; Southwestern Ohio Council for Higher Education
Special Services for the Deaf - Bks on deafness & sign lang
Open Mon-Thurs (Winter) 7:30am-9:30pm, Fri 7:30-5, Sat 9-4; Mon-Thurs (Summer) 7:30am-9:30pm, Fri 7:30-4:30

R TEMPLE ISRAEL*, Rabbi Louis Witt Memorial Library, 130 Riverside Dr, 45405. SAN 313-4792. Tel: 937-496-0050. Toll Free Tel: 888-777-0490. Web Site: tidayton.org/library. *Exec Dir,* Suzanne Shaw; E-mail: suzanne@tidayton.org
Library Holdings: Bk Vols 7,000
Subject Interests: Judaica

L THOMPSON HINE LLP*, Law Library, Discovery Place, 10050 Innovation Dr, Ste 400, 45342-4934. SAN 328-3690. Tel: 937-443-6600. FAX: 937-443-6635. E-mail: library@thompsonhine.com. Web Site: www.thompsonhine.com. *Librn,* Janie Hack; Tel: 937-443-6823, E-mail: janie.hack@thompsonhine.com
Founded 1911
Library Holdings: Bk Vols 35,000; Per Subs 216

R UNITED THEOLOGICAL SEMINARY*, O'Brien Library, 4501 Denlinger Rd, 45426. SAN 313-4806. Tel: 937-529-2201, Ext 3400. E-mail: obrienlibrary@united.edu. Web Site: united.edu/obrien-library. *Dir,* Sarah D Brooks Blair; E-mail: sblair@united.edu; *Asst Dir,* Ken Cochrane; E-mail: kscochrane@united.edu; *Acq & Coll,* Lesia Harvey; E-mail: lesiah@united.edu; *Circ Coordr,* Caryn Dalton; E-mail: cdalton@united.edu; *ILL, Per,* Brillie Scott; E-mail: brscott@united.edu; Staff 3 (MLS 3)
Founded 1871
Library Holdings: Bk Vols 144,000; Per Subs 500
Special Collections: Edmund S Lorenz Hymnal Coll; Evangelical Church Coll; Evangelical United Brethren Church Coll; J Allan Ranck Coll of Friendship Press; United Brethren in Christ Church Coll; United Methodist Church Coll; Waldensian-Methodist Coll. Oral History
Partic in OCLC Online Computer Library Center, Inc; OhioNET

C UNIVERSITY OF DAYTON LIBRARIES, Roesch Library, 300 College Park Dr, 45469. SAN 356-5416. Tel: 937-229-4221. Circulation Tel: 937-229-4270. Interlibrary Loan Service Tel: 937-229-4527. Reference Tel: 937-229-4234. Administration Tel: 937-229-4265. Automation Services Tel: 937-229-3551. FAX: 937-229-4215. Reference E-mail: library@udayton.edu. Web Site: www.udayton.edu/libraries. *Dean, Univ Libr,* Kathleen Webb; E-mail: kwebb1@udayton.edu; *Assoc Dean, Engagement & Operations,* Ione T Damasco; Tel: 937-229-4238, E-mail: idamasco1@udayton.edu; *Director, Collections, Strategies & Services,* Tina Beis; E-mail: cbeis1@udayton.edu; *Dir, Educ & Info Delivery,* Hector Escobar; Tel: 937-229-5141, E-mail: hescobar1@udayton.edu; *Dir, Info Syst & Digital Access,* Ben Daigle; E-mail: bdaigle1@udayton.edu; *Coordr, Access Serv,* Amanda Black; Tel: 937-229-5408, E-mail: ablack2@udayton.edu; *Coordr, Instruction & Ref,* Heidi Gauder; Tel: 937-229-4259, E-mail: hgauder1@udayton.edu; *Univ Archivist & Coordr of Spec Coll,* Kristina Schulz; Tel: 937-229-4256, E-mail: kschulz1@udayton.edu; Staff 45 (MLS 19, Non-MLS 26)
Founded 1850. Enrl 12,028; Fac 639; Highest Degree: Doctorate
Special Collections: Charles W Whalen Jr Congressional Papers; Erma Bombeck Papers; Marian Library; Si Burick & Miriam Joseph Baseball Colls; US Catholic Coll. US Document Depository
Subject Interests: Catholicism, Educ, Theol
Automation Activity & Vendor Info: (Acquisitions) Innovative Interfaces, Inc; (Cataloging) Innovative Interfaces, Inc; (Circulation) Innovative Interfaces, Inc; (Discovery) EBSCO Discovery Service; (ILL) OCLC ILLiad; (OPAC) Innovative Interfaces, Inc; (Serials) Innovative Interfaces, Inc
Wireless access
Partic in Center for Research Libraries; LYRASIS; Ohio Library & Information Network; OhioNET; Southwestern Ohio Council for Higher Education

Departmental Libraries:

CR MARIAN LIBRARY, 300 College Park Dr, 45469-1390, SAN 313-4814. Tel: 937-229-4214. FAX: 937-229-4258. E-mail: marianlibrary@udayton.edu. Web Site: udayton.edu/marianlibrary. *Dir,* Sarah B Cahalan; Tel: 937-229-4203; Staff 12 (MLS 4, Non-MLS 8)
Founded 1943
Partic in Ohio Library & Information Network
Publications: Marian Library (Newsletter)
Open Mon-Fri 8:30-4:30
Friends of the Library Group

CL UNIVERSITY OF DAYTON SCHOOL OF LAW*, Zimmerman Law Library, 300 College Park, 45469-2772. SAN 356-5440. Tel: 937-229-2314. Information Services Tel: 937-229-4810. FAX: 937-229-2555. E-mail: library@udayton.edu. Web Site: udayton.edu/law/library. *Dir,* Susan N Elliott; E-mail: elliott@udayton.edu; *Asst Dir, Pub Serv,* Maureen H Anderson; *Ref Librn,* Paul D Venard; Staff 5 (MLS 4, Non-MLS 1)
Founded 1974. Enrl 424; Fac 34; Highest Degree: Doctorate
Library Holdings: Bk Vols 337,943; Per Subs 4,278
Automation Activity & Vendor Info: (Acquisitions) Innovative Interfaces, Inc; (Cataloging) Innovative Interfaces, Inc; (Circulation) Innovative Interfaces, Inc; (Serials) Innovative Interfaces, Inc
Wireless access
Publications: Aquisitions Update
Partic in Ohio Library & Information Network; Southwestern Ohio Council for Higher Education
Open Mon-Thurs 8am-11pm, Fri 8-8, Sat 10-8, Sun Noon-10
Restriction: Circ limited, Restricted pub use

C WRIGHT STATE UNIVERSITY LIBRARIES*, 126 Dunbar Library, 3640 Colonel Glenn Hwy, 45435-0001. SAN 356-553X. Tel: 937-775-2525. Administration Tel: 937-775-2380. FAX: 937-775-2356. Web Site: www.libraries.wright.edu. *Univ Librn,* Sheila Shellabarger; Tel: 937-775-2685, E-mail: sheila.shellabarger@wright.edu; *Assoc Univ Librn, Coll & Serv,* Karen Wilhoit; Tel: 937-775-3039, E-mail: karen.wilhoit@wright.edu; *Assoc Univ Librn, Pub Serv,* Sue Polanka; Tel:

937-775-3142, E-mail: sue.polanka@wright.edu; *Head, Digital Libr Serv,* Jane Wildermuth; Tel: 937-775-3927, E-mail: jane.wildermuth@wright.edu; *Head, Spec Coll & Archives,* Dawne Dewey; Tel: 937-775-2011, E-mail: dawne.dewey@wright.edu; *Head, Tech Serv,* Marty Jenkins; Tel: 937-775-4983, E-mail: martin.jenkins@wright.edu; *Educ Serv Librn, Med Librn,* Bette Sydelko; Tel: 937-775-3840, E-mail: bette.sydelko@wright.edu; Staff 40.2 (MLS 23.5, Non-MLS 16.7)
Founded 1967. Enrl 16,952; Fac 831; Highest Degree: Doctorate
Library Holdings: e-journals 6,500; Bk Titles 573,914; Bk Vols 870,792; Per Subs 4,320
Special Collections: Aerospace Medical Association Archives; Aerospace Medicine & Human Factors Engineering (Ross A McFarland Coll); Andrews S Iddings Papers; Anthropometry (HTE Hertzburg Coll); Aviation Crash Research (Howard Hashbrook Coll); Children's Literature, including Books Illustrated by Arthur Rackham; Cincinnati Coll (Dayton Ballet Co, Overholser Civil War Diary, Glenn Curtiss Photographs, Springfield Urban League Records, Clayton Bruckner Papers, Early Local Records from Auglaize, Champaign, Clark, Darke, Greene & Mercer Counties); Dayton Urban League Papers; Early Aviation Coll; Glenn Thompson Papers; Governor James M Cox Papers; History of Medicine; Local & Regional History Coll, includes Miami Valley Genealogical Society Library; Miami Conservancy District Papers; Miami Valley Area & Early Aviation Photograph Coll; Miami, Montgomery, Logan, Preble & Shelby Counties; O S Kelly Company Papers; Paul Laurence Dunbar Coll; Space & Life Sciences (William Rhornton Coll); Unpublished Manuscripts Coll: Wright Brothers Papers, Governor James M Cox Papers, Dayton Urban League Papers; Wright Brothers Papers
Subject Interests: Biochem, Cardiology, Med, Microbiology, Nursing, Physiology
Automation Activity & Vendor Info: (Acquisitions) Innovative Interfaces, Inc; (Cataloging) Innovative Interfaces, Inc; (Circulation) Innovative Interfaces, Inc; (Course Reserve) Docutek; (ILL) OCLC ILLiad; (Media Booking) Innovative Interfaces, Inc; (OPAC) Innovative Interfaces, Inc; (Serials) Innovative Interfaces, Inc
Wireless access
Publications: Access; Diaries: 1857-1917 by Bishop Milton Wright; Guide to Local Government Records & Newspapers at WSU; Guide to Manuscripts
Partic in OCLC Online Computer Library Center, Inc; Ohio Library & Information Network; OhioNET
Friends of the Library Group

DEFIANCE

C DEFIANCE COLLEGE*, Pilgrim Library, 201 College Pl, 43512-1667. SAN 313-4849. Tel: 419-783-2481. FAX: 419-783-2594. E-mail: library@defiance.edu. Web Site: library.defiance.edu. *Asst Dean, Libr & Acad Support Serv,* Lisa Crumit-Hancock; Tel: 419-783-2332, E-mail: lcrumithancock@defiance.edu; *Archives Coordr, Lead Librn, Metadata Coordr,* Barbara Sedlock; Tel: 419-783-2487, E-mail: bsedlock@defiance.edu; *AV Coordr, Media Coordr,* Matt Slawinski; Tel: 419-783-2615, E-mail: mslawinski@defiance.edu; *Coordr, Circ,* Collette Knight; Tel: 419-783-2482, E-mail: knightc@defiance.edu; Staff 5 (MLS 4, Non-MLS 1)
Enrl 861; Fac 57; Highest Degree: Master
Library Holdings: AV Mats 2,826; Bk Vols 107,454; Per Subs 375
Special Collections: American History (Indian Wars of Northwest Ohio, 1785-1815), bk & micro
Function: ILL available, Ref serv available, Telephone ref
Partic in NOLC; Ohio Library & Information Network; Ohio Private Academic Libraries; OhioNET
Open Mon-Thurs 8am-Midnight, Fri 8-4:30, Sat 9-5, Sun 3pm-Midnight
Restriction: Open to pub for ref & circ; with some limitations, Open to students, fac & staff

P DEFIANCE PUBLIC LIBRARY*, 320 Fort St, 43512-2186. SAN 356-5653. Tel: 419-782-1456. FAX: 419-782-6235. Web Site: www.defiancelibrary.org. *Dir,* Cara Potter; E-mail: cpotter@defiancelibrary.org; Staff 3 (MLS 3)
Founded 1895. Pop 39,825
Jan 2015-Dec 2015. Mats Exp $1,697,363, Books $110,251, AV Mat $38,976. Sal $191,628
Library Holdings: AV Mats 6,298; DVDs 8,236; e-books 196,468; Bk Vols 33,643; Per Subs 117
Special Collections: Ohioana; Slocum
Subject Interests: Local hist
Automation Activity & Vendor Info: (Cataloging) SirsiDynix; (Circulation) SirsiDynix; (OPAC) SirsiDynix
Wireless access
Function: Activity rm, Adult bk club, Audiobks on Playaways & MP3, Audiobks via web, AV serv, Bk club(s), Bks on cassette, Bks on CD, Children's prog, Computer training, Computers for patron use, Digital talking bks, E-Reserves, Electronic databases & coll, Equip loans & repairs, Free DVD rentals, ILL available, Internet access, Laminating, Magazines, Magnifiers for reading, Microfiche/film & reading machines, Movies, Music CDs, Online cat, Online info literacy tutorials on the web & in blackboard, Online ref, Outreach serv, Photocopying/Printing, Preschool outreach, Printer for laptops & handheld devices, Prog for adults, Prog for children & young adult, Ref & res, Ref serv available, Res performed for a fee, Serves people with intellectual disabilities, Spoken cassettes & CDs, Spoken cassettes & DVDs, Story hour, Summer & winter reading prog, Summer reading prog, Tax forms, Teen prog, Telephone ref, Wheelchair accessible, Winter reading prog
Partic in NORWELD; Ohio Public Library Information Network; Serving Every Ohioan Library Center
Open Mon-Thurs 9-8, Fri 9-6, Sat 10-2
Friends of the Library Group
Branches: 2
JOHNSON MEMORIAL, 116 W High St, Hicksville, 43526, SAN 356-5688. Tel: 419-542-6200. FAX: 419-542-1015. *Br Mgr,* Angela Powell; E-mail: apowell@defiancelibrary.org
Open Mon & Tues 12-8, Wed 10-8, Fri 12-6, Sat 10-1
Friends of the Library Group
SHERWOOD BRANCH, 117 N Harrison St, Sherwood, 43556. (Mail add: PO Box 4586, Sherwood, 43556-0586), SAN 374-7190. Tel: 419-899-4343. FAX: 419-899-4343. *Br Mgr,* Kathy Holtsberry; E-mail: kholtsberry@defiancelibrary.org
Open Mon & Wed 12-8, Tues & Thurs 9-6, Fri & Sat 9-12
Friends of the Library Group

DELAWARE

P DELAWARE COUNTY DISTRICT LIBRARY*, 84 E Winter St, 43015. SAN 313-4857. Tel: 740-362-3861. Administration Tel: 740-363-7277. FAX: 740-369-0196. Administration FAX: 740-362-0391. E-mail: askus@delawarelibrary.org. Web Site: www.delawarelibrary.org. *Dir,* George Needham; E-mail: gneedham@delawarelibrary.org; *Dep Dir,* Molly Meyers LaBadie; *Adult Serv Mgr,* Joseph O'Rourke; *Communications Mgr,* Nicole Fowles; *Outreach Serv Mgr,* Robbie Apt; *Youth Serv Mgr,* Kelly Cochran; *Circ Supvr,* Pam Taylor; *Tech Serv,* Kyle Halstead; *Human Res Mgr,* Amanda Sheterom; Staff 10 (MLS 8, Non-MLS 2)
Founded 1906. Pop 125,797
Library Holdings: Per Subs 299
Special Collections: Harness Racing Coll
Subject Interests: Local hist
Automation Activity & Vendor Info: (Cataloging) OCLC; (Circulation) Innovative Interfaces, Inc; (ILL) OCLC; (OPAC) Innovative Interfaces, Inc
Wireless access
Function: 24/7 Electronic res, 24/7 Online cat, 3D Printer, Adult bk club, After school storytime, Archival coll, Art exhibits, Audio & video playback equip for onsite use, Audiobks on Playaways & MP3, Audiobks via web, AV serv, Bk club(s), Bk reviews (Group), Bks on CD, Children's prog, Computer training, Computers for patron use, Digital talking bks, E-Reserves, Electronic databases & coll, Free DVD rentals, Genealogy discussion group, Govt ref serv, Holiday prog, Home delivery & serv to seniorr ctr & nursing homes, Homebound delivery serv, ILL available, Internet access, Jail serv, Large print keyboards, Life-long learning prog for all ages, Literacy & newcomer serv, Magazines, Magnifiers for reading, Mail & tel request accepted, Makerspace, Meeting rooms, Microfiche/film & reading machines, Movies, Notary serv, Online cat, Online ref, Orientations, Outreach serv, Outside serv via phone, mail, e-mail & web, OverDrive digital audio bks, Photocopying/Printing, Preschool outreach, Preschool reading prog, Printer for laptops & handheld devices, Prog for adults, Prog for children & young adult, Ref serv available, Res assist avail, Scanner, Senior computer classes, Senior outreach, Spoken cassettes & CDs, Spoken cassettes & DVDs, STEM programs, Story hour, Study rm, Summer reading prog, Tax forms, Teen prog, Telephone ref, Visual arts prog, Wheelchair accessible, Winter reading prog, Writing prog
Partic in Central Library Consortium; Southeast Regional Library System
Open Mon-Thurs 9-9, Fri 9-6, Sat 9-5, Sun 12-5
Friends of the Library Group
Branches: 3
ORANGE BRANCH, 7171 Gooding Blvd, 43015. Tel: 740-549-2665. *Br Mgr,* Sara Kennedy; E-mail: skennedy@delawarelibrary.org
Founded 2011
Function: 24/7 Electronic res, Activity rm, Adult bk club, Adult literacy prog, After school storytime, Art exhibits, Audio & video playback equip for onsite use, Audiobks on Playaways & MP3, Audiobks via web, AV serv, Bk club(s), Bks on CD, Children's prog, Computer training, Computers for patron use, Digital talking bks, Electronic databases & coll, Free DVD rentals, Holiday prog, ILL available, Instruction & testing, Internet access, Life-long learning prog for all ages, Magazines, Meeting rooms, Movies, Notary serv, Online cat, Orientations, OverDrive digital audio bks, Photocopying/Printing, Preschool outreach, Preschool reading prog, Printer for laptops & handheld devices, Prog for adults, Prog for children & young adult, Senior computer classes, Senior outreach, Spoken cassettes & CDs, Spoken cassettes & DVDs, Story hour, Study rm, Summer reading prog, Tax forms, Teen prog, Visual arts prog, Wheelchair accessible, Writing prog
Friends of the Library Group

OSTRANDER BRANCH, 75 N Fourth St, Ostrander, 43061. (Mail add: PO Box 6, Ostrander, 43061), SAN 372-5618. Tel: 740-666-1410. FAX: 740-666-1437. *Br Mgr,* Harla Lawson
Open Tues-Thurs 10-8, Fri & Sat 10-4
Friends of the Library Group
POWELL BRANCH, 460 S Liberty Rd, Powell, 43065, SAN 373-2908. Tel: 614-888-9160. FAX: 614-888-7358. *Br Mgr,* Amanda Henning
Open Mon-Thurs 9-9, Fri 9-6, Sat 9-5, Sun 12-5
Friends of the Library Group
Bookmobiles: 1. Outreach Servs Mgr, Robbie Apt. Bk titles 5,000

GL DELAWARE COUNTY LAW LIBRARY*, 20 W Central Ave, 43015. SAN 327-3806. Tel: 740-833-2545. FAX: 740-833-2548. Web Site: www.co.delaware.oh.us/index.php/law-library. *Chief Admin,* Juli D Jones; E-mail: JDJones@co.delaware.oh.us; Staff 1 (Non-MLS 1)
Library Holdings: Bk Vols 6,000
Function: Computers for patron use, Photocopying/Printing
Partic in Ohio Regional Asn of Law Librs
Open Mon-Fri 10-12 & 1-4
Restriction: Open to pub for ref only

CR METHODIST THEOLOGICAL SCHOOL*, Dickhaut Library, 3081 Columbus Pike, 43015. SAN 313-4873. Tel: 740-363-1146. Circulation Tel: 740-362-3450. FAX: 740-362-3456. E-mail: library@mtso.edu. Web Site: libguides.mtso.edu/library. *Dir,* Paul Burnam; Tel: 740-362-3435, E-mail: pburnam@mtso.edu; *Asst Librn, Ref (Info Servs),* David Powell; Tel: 740-362-3438, E-mail: dpowell@mtso.edu; *Pub Serv Asst,* Beth Bringman; Tel: 740-362-3439, E-mail: bbringman@mtso.edu. Subject Specialists: *Church hist, Church leadership, Counseling,* Paul Burnam; *Biblical studies, Theol,* David Powell; Staff 3 (MLS 2, Non-MLS 1)
Founded 1960. Enrl 115; Fac 18; Highest Degree: Doctorate
Jul 2015-Jun 2016. Mats Exp $65,750, Books $30,000, Per/Ser (Incl. Access Fees) $15,000, AV Equip $150, AV Mat $500, Electronic Ref Mat (Incl. Access Fees) $20,000. Sal $175,570 (Prof $143,067)
Library Holdings: AV Mats 4,310; Microforms 1,862; Bk Titles 135,690; Per Subs 142
Special Collections: Denominational Coll of the United Methodist Church & its Predecessor Bodies, bks & micro
Subject Interests: Biblical studies, Church hist, Theol
Automation Activity & Vendor Info: (Acquisitions) Innovative Interfaces, Inc; (Cataloging) Innovative Interfaces, Inc; (Circulation) Innovative Interfaces, Inc; (Course Reserve) Innovative Interfaces, Inc; (ILL) OCLC; (OPAC) Innovative Interfaces, Inc; (Serials) Innovative Interfaces, Inc
Wireless access
Function: Art exhibits, Audio & video playback equip for onsite use, Audiobks via web, AV serv, Computers for patron use, Doc delivery serv, E-Reserves, Electronic databases & coll, ILL available, Internet access, Music CDs, Online cat, Online ref, Orientations, Outside serv via phone, mail, e-mail & web, Photocopying/Printing, Ref & res, Ref serv available, Scanner, Telephone ref, VHS videos, Wheelchair accessible
Partic in OCLC Online Computer Library Center, Inc; Ohio Library & Information Network; Ohio Private Academic Libraries; OhioNET; Theological Consortium of Greater Columbus
Restriction: Circ limited, External users must contact libr, In-house use for visitors, Non-circulating of rare bks, Non-resident fee, Open to students, fac & staff, Open to students, fac, staff & alumni, Pub use on premises, Restricted borrowing privileges, Restricted loan policy

C OHIO WESLEYAN UNIVERSITY, L A Beeghly Library, 43 Rowland Ave, 43015-2370. SAN 313-4881. Tel: 740-368-3225. Reference Tel: 740-368-3242. FAX: 740-368-3222. E-mail: libraries@owu.edu. Web Site: library.owu.edu. *Dir of Libr,* Dee Peterson; Tel: 740-368-3240, E-mail: dmpeters@owu.edu; *Curator, Digital Initiatives Librn,* Eugene Rutigliano; Tel: 740-368-3233, E-mail: earutigl@owu.edu; *Pub Serv Librn,* Holly Birk; Tel: 740-368-3207, E-mail: hebirk@owu.edu; *Pub Serv Librn,* Calvin Cleary; Tel: 740-368-3237, E-mail: cjcleary@owu.edu; *Spec Coll Librn,* Stacey Chaney-Blankenship; Tel: 740-368-3288, E-mail: sbchaney@owu.edu; Staff 8 (MLS 7.3, Non-MLS 0.7)
Founded 1842. Enrl 1,800; Fac 163; Highest Degree: Bachelor
Library Holdings: Bk Vols 500,000
Special Collections: Archive of Ohio United Methodism; Browning (Gunsaulus Coll); James Joyce (Staples Coll); Schubert (20th Century Imprints Coll); Walt Whitman (Bayley Coll). US Document Depository
Wireless access
Partic in Five Colleges of Ohio; Oberlin Group; OCLC Online Computer Library Center, Inc; Ohio Library & Information Network; OhioNET

DELPHOS

P DELPHOS PUBLIC LIBRARY*, 309 W Second St, 45833-1695. SAN 313-489X. Tel: 419-695-4015. FAX: 419-695-4025. Web Site: www.delphos.lib.oh.us. *Dir,* Kelly Rist; E-mail: krist@seolibraries.org; *Youth Serv Librn,* Rachel Strahm; E-mail: rstrahm@seolibraries.org; Staff 6 (MLS 2, Non-MLS 4)
Founded 1912. Pop 12,000; Circ 258,597
Library Holdings: Bk Vols 82,567; Per Subs 230
Special Collections: Delphos Newspapers, 1872-2014
Subject Interests: Local hist
Automation Activity & Vendor Info: (Cataloging) SirsiDynix-WorkFlows; (Circulation) SirsiDynix-WorkFlows; (OPAC) SirsiDynix; (Serials) SirsiDynix-WorkFlows
Wireless access
Partic in NORWELD; Ohio Public Library Information Network; Serving Every Ohioan Library Center
Open Mon-Fri 10-6, Sat 10-Noon

DELTA

P DELTA PUBLIC LIBRARY*, 402 Main St, 43515-1304. SAN 313-4903. Tel: 419-822-3110. FAX: 419-822-5310. Web Site: deltapubliclibrary.org. *Dir,* Candy Baird
Founded 1911. Pop 7,000; Circ 79,840
Library Holdings: Bk Titles 53,000; Per Subs 180
Automation Activity & Vendor Info: (Cataloging) Follett Software; (Circulation) Follett Software; (OPAC) Follett Software
Wireless access
Partic in NW Ohio Libr District
Open Mon-Wed 9:30-7:30, Thurs 10-5:30, Fri 9:30-5:30, Sat 10-2
Friends of the Library Group

DESHLER

P PATRICK HENRY SCHOOL DISTRICT PUBLIC LIBRARY*, Deshler Edwin Wood Memorial Library, 208 N East Ave, 43516. SAN 356-5718. Tel: 419-278-3616. FAX: 419-278-3616. Web Site: phlibraries.org. *Dir,* Lori Tietje; E-mail: director@phlibraries.org; *Br Mgr,* Debra Wensink; *Mgr, Ch Serv,* Tamara Johnson; *Libr Asst,* Lauri Phillips
Founded 1924. Pop 5,000
Library Holdings: Bk Vols 22,027; Per Subs 150
Special Collections: Genealogy, bks, flm; Ohio & Local History, bks, fs, slides
Wireless access
Partic in Serving Every Ohioan Library Center
Open Mon 8:30-5, Tues-Thurs 8:30-7, Fri 8:30-4, Sat 8:30-Noon
Branches: 2
HAMLER BRANCH, 230 Randolph St, Hamler, 43524, SAN 356-5742. Tel: 419-274-3821. FAX: 419-274-3821. *Br Mgr,* Ramona Malinowski
Founded 1941
Library Holdings: Bk Vols 13,760
Open Mon Noon-5, Tues & Thurs 9-2, Wed Noon-8, Fri Noon-6, Sat 10-2
Friends of the Library Group
MALINTA BRANCH, 204 N Henry St, Malinta, 43535, SAN 356-5777. Tel: 419-256-7223. FAX: 419-256-7223. *Br Mgr,* Gwenn Maas
Founded 1964
Library Holdings: Bk Vols 18,147
Open Thurs (Winter) 8-3; Tues & Thurs (Summer) 9-2

DOVER

P DOVER PUBLIC LIBRARY, 525 N Walnut St, 44622. SAN 313-4911. Tel: 330-343-6123. FAX: 330-343-2087. Web Site: www.doverlibrary.org. *Dir,* Jim Gill; E-mail: director@doverlibrary.org; *Fiscal Officer,* Jamie Rieger; *Adult Serv Mgr,* Paula Fawcett; *Outreach Serv Mgr, Teen Serv Mgr,* Liz Strauss; *Tech Serv Mgr,* Wendy Contini; *Tech Mgr,* Jen Miller; *Youth Serv Mgr,* Claire Kandle
Founded 1923. Pop 20,000; Circ 226,778
Library Holdings: Bk Vols 93,000; Per Subs 320
Automation Activity & Vendor Info: (Cataloging) Innovative Interfaces, Inc; (Circulation) Innovative Interfaces, Inc; (OPAC) Innovative Interfaces, Inc
Wireless access
Partic in Mideastern Ohio Libr Orgn
Open Mon-Thurs 9-6, Fri & Sat 9-5
Friends of the Library Group

DUBLIN

S OCLC LIBRARY, ARCHIVE & MUSEUM, 6565 Kilgour Pl, 43017. Circulation Tel: 614-761-5095. Administration Tel: 614-761-5217. Automation Services Tel: 614-764-4300. FAX: 614-718-7592. *Archivist, Libr Mgr,* Kemberly AM Lang; E-mail: langk@oclc.org; *Archive Spec, Sr Librn,* Terry Butterworth; E-mail: butterwt@oclc.org; Staff 2 (MLS 2)
Founded 1977
Library Holdings: Audiobooks 60; CDs 71; DVDs 220; e-books 52,642; e-journals 20,839; Microforms 26; Bk Titles 6,809; Bk Vols 7,088; Per Subs 23
Special Collections: Historic Dewey Decimal Coll; Library Network Newsletters; OCLC Archives; OCLC Museum; State Library & State Library Association Newsletters

Subject Interests: Info sci, Libr sci
Automation Activity & Vendor Info: (Acquisitions) OCLC Worldshare Management Services; (Cataloging) OCLC Worldshare Management Services; (Circulation) OCLC Worldshare Management Services; (Discovery) OCLC; (ILL) OCLC WorldShare Interlibrary Loan; (OPAC) OCLC Worldshare Management Services
Wireless access
Open Mon-Fri 8-5

DUNKIRK

P HARDIN NORTHERN PUBLIC LIBRARY*, 153 N Main St, 45836-1064. (Mail add: PO Box 114, 45836-0114), SAN 313-4938. Tel: 419-759-3558. FAX: 419-759-3558. E-mail: hardinnorthernpl@gmail.com. Web Site: hardinnorthernpl.org. *Librn,* Rebecca Coker
Library Holdings: Bk Vols 10,000; Per Subs 60
Automation Activity & Vendor Info: (Cataloging) SirsiDynix; (Circulation) SirsiDynix; (OPAC) SirsiDynix
Partic in NORWELD; Serving Every Ohioan Library Center
Open Mon, Tues & Thurs 1-8, Wed 10-5, Fri 12-5, Sat 9-Noon

EAST CLEVELAND

P EAST CLEVELAND PUBLIC LIBRARY*, 14101 Euclid Ave, 44112-3891. SAN 356-5807. Tel: 216-541-4128. FAX: 216-541-1790. Web Site: eastclevelandpubliclibrary.org. *Dir,* Carlos Latimer; E-mail: carlos.latimer@ecpl.lib.oh.us; *Ch,* Pamela Henderson; E-mail: phenderson@ecpl.lib.oh.us; *IT Mgr, Network Serv,* Theresa Flood; E-mail: theresa.flood@ecpl.lib.oh.us; Staff 33 (MLS 7, Non-MLS 26)
Founded 1916. Pop 37,000; Circ 211,743
Library Holdings: Bk Vols 210,000; Per Subs 200
Special Collections: Black Heritage Coll; Holograph Letters of the Presidents from George Washington to James E Carter; Illustrated Children's Book (W H Quinby Coll). State Document Depository
Subject Interests: African-Am lit, Behav sci, Soc sci
Automation Activity & Vendor Info: (Acquisitions) SirsiDynix; (Cataloging) SirsiDynix; (Circulation) SirsiDynix; (Course Reserve) SirsiDynix; (ILL) SirsiDynix; (Media Booking) SirsiDynix; (OPAC) SirsiDynix; (Serials) SirsiDynix
Publications: Annual Report; Black Heritage Bibliography
Partic in Northeast Ohio Regional Library System
Open Mon-Thurs 10-7, Fri & Sat 10-6
Friends of the Library Group

EAST LIVERPOOL

P CARNEGIE PUBLIC LIBRARY*, 219 E Fourth St, 43920-3143. SAN 313-4946. Tel: 330-385-2048. Circulation Tel: 330-385-2048, Ext 100. Reference Tel: 330-385-2048, Ext 102. FAX: 330-385-7600. E-mail: carnegie@seolibraries.org. Web Site: www.carnegie.lib.oh.us. *Dir,* Melissa A W Percic; E-mail: mpercic@seolibraries.org; *Asst Dir, Fiscal Officer,* Mary Deem; Tel: 330-385-2048, Ext 103, E-mail: mdeem@seolibraries.org; *Circ,* Jackie Hicks; *Tech Serv & Automation,* Tom Marlatt; Tel: 330-385-2048, Ext 108, E-mail: tmarlatt@seolibraries.org; *Youth Serv,* Kim Blevins; Tel: 330-385-2048, Ext 101; Staff 8 (MLS 3, Non-MLS 5)
Founded 1900. Pop 11,062; Circ 100,000
Library Holdings: Bk Vols 70,652; Per Subs 104
Special Collections: State Document Depository
Subject Interests: Local hist
Automation Activity & Vendor Info: (Cataloging) SirsiDynix-WorkFlows; (Circulation) SirsiDynix-WorkFlows; (Discovery) SirsiDynix; (ILL) SirsiDynix-WorkFlows; (OPAC) SirsiDynix-Enterprise; (Serials) SirsiDynix-WorkFlows
Wireless access
Function: Activity rm, Adult bk club, Audiobks via web, Bks on cassette, Bks on CD, Children's prog, Computers for patron use, E-Reserves, Electronic databases & coll, Free DVD rentals, Home delivery & serv to seniorr ctr & nursing homes, Homebound delivery serv, ILL available, Internet access, Magazines, Meeting rooms, Microfiche/film & reading machines, Movies, Online cat, OverDrive digital audio bks, Photocopying/Printing, Preschool reading prog, Prog for adults, Prog for children & young adult, Ref serv available, Spoken cassettes & CDs, Story hour, Summer & winter reading prog, Summer reading prog, Tax forms, VHS videos, Wheelchair accessible
Partic in Serving Every Ohioan Library Center
Open Mon & Thurs 9-7, Tues & Wed 9-5, Fri & Sat 9-1
Restriction: Non-resident fee

C KENT STATE UNIVERSITY*, Blair Memorial Library, 400 E Fourth St, Rm 216, 43920-5769. SAN 313-4954. Tel: 330-382-7401, 330-382-7421. FAX: 330-382-7561. Web Site: www.kent.edu/columbiana/libraries. *Sr Libr Assoc,* Wendy Adkins; E-mail: wjadkins@kent.edu
Founded 1968. Enrl 798; Fac 35; Highest Degree: Bachelor
Library Holdings: Bk Vols 31,320; Per Subs 44
Wireless access
Open Mon-Thurs 8-6, Fri 8-1

EAST PALESTINE

P EAST PALESTINE MEMORIAL PUBLIC LIBRARY*, 309 N Market St, 44413. SAN 313-4962. Tel: 330-426-3778. FAX: 330-426-4950. E-mail: eplibmail@yahoo.com. Web Site: www.east-palestine.lib.oh.us. *Dir,* Tamra Hess; *Asst Dir, Youth Serv Librn,* Noreen McBride; Staff 6 (MLS 2, Non-MLS 4)
Founded 1920. Pop 4,721; Circ 83,860
Jan 2017-Dec 2017 Income $413,088, State $395,744, Locally Generated Income $17,344. Mats Exp $54,784. Sal $188,258
Subject Interests: Local hist
Automation Activity & Vendor Info: (Cataloging) Innovative Interfaces, Inc; (Circulation) Innovative Interfaces, Inc; (OPAC) Innovative Interfaces, Inc
Wireless access
Function: 24/7 Electronic res, 24/7 Online cat, Adult bk club, After school storytime, Audiobks via web, Bk club(s), Bks on CD, Children's prog, Computer training, Computers for patron use, Free DVD rentals, Home delivery & serv to seniorr ctr & nursing homes, Homebound delivery serv, ILL available, Internet access, Laminating, Magazines, Magnifiers for reading, Museum passes, Music CDs, Online cat, OverDrive digital audio bks, Photocopying/Printing, Preschool reading prog, Prog for adults, Prog for children & young adult, Ref serv available, Scanner, Senior computer classes, Story hour, Summer reading prog, Tax forms, Teen prog, Telephone ref, Wheelchair accessible
Partic in Northeast Ohio Regional Library System
Open Mon-Thurs 9-8, Fri & Sat 9-5
Restriction: Non-resident fee
Friends of the Library Group

EASTLAKE

P WILLOUGHBY-EASTLAKE PUBLIC LIBRARY*, Administrative Offices, 35150 Lakeshore Blvd, 44095. SAN 357-3214. Tel: 440-943-2203. FAX: 440-918-1309. E-mail: wepl.contact@welibrary.info. Web Site: we247.org. *Dir,* Rick Werner; E-mail: rick.werner@welibrary.info; *Dep Dir,* Eric Linderman; E-mail: eric.linderman@welibrary.info; *Fiscal Officer,* Vicki Simmons; E-mail: vicki.simmons@welibrary.info; Staff 38 (MLS 14, Non-MLS 24)
Founded 1827. Pop 67,023; Circ 789,490
Library Holdings: Bk Vols 215,048; Per Subs 477
Special Collections: Willoughby Historical Society & News/Herald, micro
Automation Activity & Vendor Info: (Acquisitions) SirsiDynix; (Cataloging) SirsiDynix; (Circulation) SirsiDynix; (OPAC) SirsiDynix; (Serials) SirsiDynix
Wireless access
Partic in Cleveland Integrated Automated Libr Regional Network; Northeast Ohio Regional Library System
Open Mon-Thurs 9-9, Fri & Sat 9-5, Sun (Oct-April) 1-5
Friends of the Library Group
Branches: 4
EASTLAKE BRANCH, 36706 Lake Shore Blvd, 44095, SAN 357-3249. Tel: 440-942-7880. FAX: 440-942-4095. *Br Mgr,* Amy Senning; E-mail: amy.senning@welibrary.info
Founded 1956. Circ 243,125
Library Holdings: High Interest/Low Vocabulary Bk Vols 36
Open Mon-Thurs 9-9, Fri & Sat 9-5, Sun (Oct-April) 1-5
Friends of the Library Group
WILLOUGHBY BRANCH, 30 Public Sq, Willoughby, 44094, SAN 357-3273. Tel: 440-942-3200. FAX: 440-942-4312. *Br Mgr,* Deborah Mullen; E-mail: deborah.mullen@welibrary.info
Founded 1909. Circ 277,109
Library Holdings: High Interest/Low Vocabulary Bk Vols 90
Special Collections: Microfilm Coll; News-Herald Coll; Willoughby Historical Society Coll
Open Mon-Thurs 9-9, Fri & Sat 9-5, Sun (Oct-April) 1-5
Friends of the Library Group
WILLOUGHBY HILLS BRANCH, 35400 Chardon Rd, Willoughby Hills, 44094. Tel: 440-942-3362. FAX: 440-942-3780. *Br Mgr,* Holly Ferkol; E-mail: holly.ferkol@welibrary.info
Founded 1985
Open Mon-Thurs 11-8, Sat 11-5
Friends of the Library Group
WILLOWICK BRANCH, 263 E 305th St, Willowick, 44095, SAN 357-3303. Tel: 440-943-4151. FAX: 440-530-3991. *Br Mgr,* Mollie Burns; E-mail: mollie.burns@welibrary.info
Founded 1924. Circ 269,265
Library Holdings: High Interest/Low Vocabulary Bk Vols 56
Open Mon-Thurs 9-9, Fri & Sat 9-5, Sun (Oct-April) 1-5
Friends of the Library Group

EATON

P PREBLE COUNTY DISTRICT LIBRARY*, 450 S Barron St, 45320-2402. SAN 356-5890. Tel: 937-456-4250. FAX: 937-456-6092. E-mail: pcdl@preblelibrary.org. Web Site: preblelibrary.org. *Dir,* Lauren Robinson; E-mail: laurenr@preblelibrary.org; *Network Adminr,* Doug Montgomery; *Outreach Serv Libm,* Danita Cook; *Syst Librn,* Jen Murphy; *Cat,* Diane Knaff; *Ch Serv,* Sarah Tozier; Tel: 937-456-4331; Staff 39 (MLS 6, Non-MLS 33)
Founded 1959. Pop 39,605; Circ 269,953
Library Holdings: Bk Titles 150,000; Bk Vols 174,000; Per Subs 980
Special Collections: ASL Coll
Subject Interests: Genealogy, Local hist
Automation Activity & Vendor Info: (Cataloging) SirsiDynix; (Circulation) SirsiDynix; (OPAC) SirsiDynix
Wireless access
Publications: Library Ink (Newsletter)
Partic in Miami Valley Librs; Ohio Public Library Information Network; OhioNET; Serving Every Ohioan Library Center; SouthWest Ohio & Neighboring Libraries
Special Services for the Deaf - Bks on deafness & sign lang; Closed caption videos; Coll on deaf educ; Deaf publ; Described encaptioned media prog; High interest/low vocabulary bks; Interpreter on staff; Sign lang interpreter upon request for prog; Sorenson video relay syst; Staff with knowledge of sign lang
Special Services for the Blind - Accessible computers; Assistive/Adapted tech devices, equip & products; Audio mat; BiFolkal kits; Bks & mags in Braille, on rec, tape & cassette; Bks on CD; Braille & cassettes; Braille alphabet card; Braille bks; Children's Braille; Dep for Braille Inst; Descriptive video serv (DVS); Disability awareness prog; Extensive large print coll; Home delivery serv; Large print & cassettes; Large print bks; Large print bks & talking machines; Large type calculator; Lending of low vision aids; Magnifiers; Reader equip; Ref serv; Sound rec; Soundproof reading booth; Talking bk & rec for the blind cat; Talking bk serv referral; Talking bks & player equip; Talking machines
Friends of the Library Group
Branches: 9
BROOKE-GOULD MEMORIAL, 301 N Barron St, 45320-1705, SAN 356-5955. Tel: 937-456-4331. FAX: 937-456-4774. TDD: 937-456-6804. *Br Mgr,* Carly Wall
Founded 1815
Library Holdings: AV Mats 10,000; Bks on Deafness & Sign Lang 200; Braille Volumes 50; Bk Titles 140,000; Per Subs 307; Videos 14,000
Special Services for the Deaf - Interpreter on staff
Open Mon-Thurs 9-8, Fri & Sat 9-5
CAMDEN, 104 S Main St, 45311, SAN 356-5920. Tel: 937-452-3142. FAX: 937-452-7365. *Librn,* Toni Keesler
Founded 1837
Special Collections: Eleanor I Jones Archives
Open Mon, Wed & Thurs 12-8, Tues 2-8, Fri & Sat 10-2
Friends of the Library Group
ELDORADO BRANCH, 150 N Main St, 45321. (Mail add: PO Box 244, Eldorado, 45321-0244), SAN 356-598X. Tel: 937-273-4933. FAX: 937-273-5673. *Librn,* Angie Ballard
Open Tues & Thurs 12-6, Sat 1-4
LIBRARY ADMINISTRATION & RESOURCE CENTER, 450 S Barron St, 45320-2402. Tel: 937-456-4520. *Dir,* Lauren Robinson
Special Collections: Preble County Historical Society & Preble County Genealogical Society Genealogy
Subject Interests: Local hist
Publications: Library Ink (Monthly newsletter)
Open Mon-Fri 8-5
Friends of the Library Group
NEW PARIS BRANCH, 115 N Washington St, New Paris, 45347, SAN 356-6013. Tel: 937-437-7242. FAX: 937-437-0772. *Librn,* Lisa Stall
Founded 1902
Open Mon-Wed 2-8, Fri 10-4, Sat 10-2
Friends of the Library Group
PREBLE COUNTY ROOM, 450 S Barron St, 45320-2402. Tel: 937-456-4250. E-mail: pcroom@preblelibrary.org. *Supvr,* Marlene Ressler
Special Collections: Genealogical & Historian Resources
Open Mon-Fri 8-5
WEST ALEXANDRIA BRANCH, 16 N Main St, West Alexandria, 45381, SAN 356-6048. Tel: 937-533-4095. FAX: 937-533-4119. *Br Librn,* Michelle Laughlin
Founded 1896
Special Collections: West Alexandria Archives
Open Mon & Wed 12-7, Tues 1-7, Fri 12-4, Sat 10-2
Friends of the Library Group
WEST ELKTON BRANCH, Town Hall, 135 N Main St, West Elkton, 45070, SAN 328-7068. Tel: 937-787-4873. FAX: 937-787-3153. *Librn,* Anna Garey
Founded 1935
Open Mon, Wed & Thurs 1-6
Friends of the Library Group
WEST MANCHESTER BRANCH, 212 S High St, West Manchester, 45382. (Mail add: PO Box 138, West Manchester, 45382-0138), SAN 371-3032. Tel: 937-678-8503. FAX: 937-678-4030. *Br Librn,* Angie Ballard
Founded 1961
Open Mon & Wed 12-6, Sat 9:30-12:30
Friends of the Library Group

ELMORE

P HARRIS-ELMORE PUBLIC LIBRARY, 328 Toledo St, 43416. (Mail add: PO Box 45, 43416-0045), SAN 356-6072. Tel: 419-862-2482. FAX: 419-862-2123. E-mail: elmorelibrary@gmail.com. Web Site: harriselmorelibrary.org. *Dir,* Jennifer Fording; E-mail: director@harriselmorelibrary.org; Staff 19 (MLS 2, Non-MLS 17)
Founded 1947. Pop 15,000; Circ 124,663
Library Holdings: Bk Vols 40,000; Per Subs 75
Special Collections: Local History
Subject Interests: Genealogy
Automation Activity & Vendor Info: (Cataloging) SirsiDynix; (Circulation) SirsiDynix
Wireless access
Function: Accelerated reader prog, Adult bk club, Archival coll, Audiobks via web, Bks on cassette, Bks on CD, Children's prog, Computers for patron use, E-Reserves, Electronic databases & coll, Free DVD rentals, Holiday prog, Home delivery & serv to seniorr ctr & nursing homes, ILL available, Internet access, Magnifiers for reading, Music CDs, Notary serv, Online cat, Online ref, Outside serv via phone, mail, e-mail & web, OverDrive digital audio bks, Photocopying/Printing, Preschool outreach, Prog for adults, Prog for children & young adult, Spoken cassettes & CDs, Spoken cassettes & DVDs, Tax forms, Teen prog, Telephone ref, VHS videos, Wheelchair accessible
Partic in NORWELD; Serving Every Ohioan Library Center
Open Mon, Wed & Fri 10-5, Tues & Thurs 10-6, Sat 10-2
Branches: 1
GENOA BRANCH, 602 West St, Genoa, 43430, SAN 356-6102. Tel: 419-855-3380. FAX: 419-855-7012. *Br Mgr,* Ariel Gresh; E-mail: genoamanager@harriselmorelibrary.org; Staff 8 (MLS 1, Non-MLS 7)
Library Holdings: Bk Vols 35,000; Per Subs 60
Function: AV serv, Home delivery & serv to seniorr ctr & nursing homes, Homebound delivery serv, ILL available, Prog for adults, Prog for children & young adult, Ref serv available, Summer reading prog, Telephone ref, Wheelchair accessible
Open Mon, Wed & Fri 10-5, Tues & Thurs 10-6, Sat 10-2
Friends of the Library Group

ELYRIA

P ELYRIA PUBLIC LIBRARY SYSTEM*, 320 Washington Ave, 44035-5199. SAN 313-4997. Tel: 440-323-5747. Reference Tel: 440-322-0461. Administration Tel: 440-322-0175. FAX: 440-323-5788. Administration FAX: 440-323-1078. TDD: 440-323-1322. E-mail: epl@elyrialibrary.org. Web Site: www.elyrialibrary.org. *Dir,* Lyn Crouse; E-mail: lyn.crouse@elyrialibrary.org; *Dep Dir,* Kathleen E Runser; Tel: 440-322-0174, E-mail: kathleen.runser@elyrialibrary.org
Founded 1870. Pop 63,650; Circ 1,117,432
Special Collections: Local History (Ely Papers)
Automation Activity & Vendor Info: (Cataloging) SirsiDynix; (Circulation) SirsiDynix; (OPAC) SirsiDynix
Wireless access
Publications: The Next Chapter (Newsletter)
Partic in CLEVNET; Northeast Ohio Regional Library System
Friends of the Library Group
Branches: 3
KEYSTONE-LAGRANGE BRANCH, 133 E Commerce Dr, LaGrange, 44050. Tel: 440-322-0119. FAX: 440-355-8082. *Mgr,* Debby Krejsa
Friends of the Library Group
SOUTH BRANCH, 340 15th St, 44035. Tel: 440-323-7519. FAX: 440-323-7518. *Mgr,* Michelle Ryan
WEST RIVER, 1194 West River Rd N, 44035. Tel: 440-324-2270. FAX: 440-324-4766.

S LORAIN COUNTY HISTORICAL SOCIETY*, Gerald Hicks Memorial Library, 284 Washington Ave, 44035. SAN 327-3822. Tel: 440-322-3341. FAX: 440-322-2817. E-mail: library@lchs.org. Web Site: sites.google.com/site/loraincountyhistoricalsociety/library. *Exec Dir,* Kerri Broome; *Librn,* Donna McGuire; *Archivist,* Eric Greenly; Staff 2 (MLS 2)
Library Holdings: Bk Vols 3,500
Wireless access
Open Tues & Fri 10-4
Restriction: Access at librarian's discretion, Closed stack, Non-circulating to the pub, Not a lending libr

GL LORAIN COUNTY LAW LIBRARY*, 226 Middle Ave, 44035. SAN 313-5012. Tel: 440-329-5567. FAX: 440-322-1724. Web Site: www.lorainlawlib.org. *Libr Dir,* Mary Kovacs; E-mail: mkovacs@lorainlawlib.org; Staff 2 (MLS 1, Non-MLS 1)
Founded 1889
Library Holdings: Bk Titles 18,000; Per Subs 25
Subject Interests: Law
Wireless access
Open Mon-Fri 8:30-4:30
Restriction: Mem only

M UNIVERSITY HOSPITAL ELYRIA MEDICAL CENTER*, Dr Joseph M Strong Memorial Library, 630 E River St, 44035. SAN 313-4989. Tel: 404-827-5569. *Librn,* Adora Glorioso; E-mail: adora.glorioso@uhhospitals.org; Staff 1 (MLS 1)
Founded 1927
Library Holdings: Bk Vols 1,500
Subject Interests: Hospital admin, Med, Nursing, Nutrition, Pub health
Automation Activity & Vendor Info: (Acquisitions) LibraryWorld, Inc; (Cataloging) LibraryWorld, Inc; (Circulation) LibraryWorld, Inc
Function: For res purposes, ILL available, Res libr
Restriction: Lending to staff only

EUCLID

P EUCLID PUBLIC LIBRARY*, 631 E 222nd St, 44123-2091. SAN 356-6137. Tel: 216-261-5300. FAX: 216-261-0575. Web Site: www.euclidlibrary.org. *Dir,* Kacie Armstrong; Tel: 216-261-5300, Ext 101, E-mail: karmstrong@euclidlibrary.org; *Adult Serv Mgr,* Karla Bowman; Tel: 216-261-5300, Ext 301, E-mail: kbowman@euclidlibrary.org; *Circ Mgr,* Cheryl Burley; Tel: 216-261-5300, Ext 501, E-mail: cburley@euclidlibrary.org; *Tech Mgr,* Matthew Augustine; Tel: 216-261-5300, Ext 601, E-mail: maugustine@euclidlibrary.org; Staff 98 (MLS 16, Non-MLS 82)
Founded 1935. Pop 52,717; Circ 1,236,314
Library Holdings: AV Mats 57,586; Bk Vols 279,392; Per Subs 472
Special Collections: Oral History
Automation Activity & Vendor Info: (Cataloging) SirsiDynix; (Circulation) SirsiDynix; (OPAC) SirsiDynix
Wireless access
Function: ILL available
Publications: Library Lines (Newsletter)
Partic in CLEVNET; Northeast Ohio Regional Library System
Open Mon-Thurs 10-9, Fri 10-5, Sat 9-5, Sun (Oct-May) 1-5
Friends of the Library Group

FAIRFIELD

SR HOME MISSIONERS OF AMERICA*, Glenmary Novitiate Library, 4119 Glenmary Trace, 45014. (Mail add: PO Box 465618, Cincinnati, 45246-5618), SAN 328-5723. Tel: 513-874-8900. FAX: 513-874-1690. Web Site: www.glenmary.org. *Archivist,* Lucy Putnam; Tel: 513-881-7439, E-mail: lputnam@glenmary.org
Library Holdings: Bk Vols 900
Restriction: Open by appt only

FAIRPORT HARBOR

P FAIRPORT HARBOR PUBLIC LIBRARY*, 335 Vine St, 44077-5799. SAN 313-5020. Tel: 440-354-8191. Administration Tel: 440-354-8191, Ext 6521. FAX: 440-354-6059. E-mail: director@fairport.lib.oh.us. Web Site: www.fairportlibrary.com. *Dir,* Kara Cervelli; E-mail: kara.cervelli@fairport.lib.oh.us; *Ad,* Cathy Norman; E-mail: cathy.norman@fairport.lib.oh.us; *Computer Librn,* Vance Todd; E-mail: vance.todd@fairport.lib.oh.us; *Cat, Tech Serv,* Carrie Todd; Tel: 440-354-8191, Ext 6523, E-mail: carrie.todd@fairport.lib.oh.us; *Youth Serv,* Gianna Conti; Tel: 440-354-8191, Ext 6524, E-mail: gianna.conti@fairport.lib.oh.us; Staff 7 (MLS 1, Non-MLS 6)
Founded 1922. Pop 3,180; Circ 83,000
Subject Interests: Finnish (Lang), Hungarian (Lang), Local hist
Automation Activity & Vendor Info: (Cataloging) SirsiDynix; (Circulation) SirsiDynix; (ILL) SirsiDynix
Wireless access
Function: 24/7 Electronic res, 24/7 Online cat, Activity rm, Adult bk club, After school storytime, Archival coll, Art exhibits, Art programs, Audiobks via web, AV serv, Bk club(s), Bks on CD, Children's prog, Computer training, Computers for patron use, Digital talking bks, Distance learning, E-Reserves, Electronic databases & coll, Equip loans & repairs, Family literacy, For res purposes, Free DVD rentals, Holiday prog, Home delivery & serv to seniorr ctr & nursing homes, Homebound delivery serv, ILL available, Internet access, Life-long learning prog for all ages, Magazines, Magnifiers for reading, Mail & tel request accepted, Meeting rooms, Movies, Music CDs, Notary serv, Online cat, Online ref, Outreach serv, OverDrive digital audio bks, Photocopying/Printing, Preschool outreach, Prog for adults, Prog for children & young adult, Ref & res, Ref serv available, Res assist avail, Res libr, Scanner, Senior computer classes, Senior outreach, Serves people with intellectual disabilities, Spanish lang bks, Story hour, Summer reading prog, Tax forms, Teen prog, Telephone ref, Visual arts prog, Wheelchair accessible, Writing prog
Partic in Association for Rural & Small Libraries; CLEVNET; Northeast Ohio Regional Library System
Open Mon-Thurs 9-8, Fri 9-5, Sat 12-5
Friends of the Library Group

FAYETTE

P NORMAL MEMORIAL LIBRARY*, Fayette Library, 301 N Eagle St, 43521. (Mail add: PO Box 100, 43521-0100), SAN 313-5039. Tel: 419-237-2115. FAX: 419-237-2002. E-mail: normallibrary@live.com. Web Site: fayette-nml.org. *Dir,* Sally Canfield; *Ch Serv,* Denise Jensen; *Tech Serv,* Susan Stuckey
Founded 1929. Pop 2,500; Circ 31,608
Library Holdings: Bk Vols 22,500; Per Subs 100
Automation Activity & Vendor Info: (Cataloging) SirsiDynix; (Circulation) SirsiDynix; (OPAC) SirsiDynix
Wireless access
Partic in Serving Every Ohioan Library Center
Open Mon & Wed 10-8, Tues 10-5, Thurs & Fri 1-5, Sat 10-1

FINDLAY

S BLACK HERITAGE LIBRARY & MULTICULTURAL CENTER*, 817 Harmon St, 45840. Tel: 419-423-4954. Web Site: blackheritagecenter.org. *Exec Dir,* Nina Sherard-Parker
Founded 1982
Library Holdings: AV Mats 500; Bk Vols 3,500
Subject Interests: African-Am art, African-Am culture, African-Am hist, Multicultural art, hist & culture
Open Mon-Thurs 4-6, Fri 3-5, Sat 10-2 & by appointment
Friends of the Library Group

P FINDLAY-HANCOCK COUNTY DISTRICT PUBLIC LIBRARY*, 206 Broadway, 45840-3382. SAN 356-6226. Tel: 419-422-1712. FAX: 419-422-0638. Web Site: www.findlaylibrary.org. *Dir,* Sarah Clevidence; E-mail: clevidsa@findlaylibrary.org; *Children's Mgr,* Brittany Lutes; *Tech Serv Mgr,* Sharon Mason; Staff 73 (MLS 6, Non-MLS 67)
Founded 1888. Pop 73,824; Circ 804,668
Library Holdings: Bk Vols 176,405; Per Subs 306
Special Collections: Foreign Language DVDs; Genealogy Coll; Local History Coll
Automation Activity & Vendor Info: (Cataloging) SirsiDynix; (Circulation) SirsiDynix; (OPAC) SirsiDynix
Wireless access
Function: Adult bk club, After school storytime, Audiobks via web, AV serv, Bk club(s), Bks on CD, CD-ROM, Chess club, Computer training, Computers for patron use, Digital talking bks, E-Reserves, Electronic databases & coll, Family literacy, Free DVD rentals, Home delivery & serv to seniorr ctr & nursing homes, ILL available, Internet access, Jail serv, Magnifiers for reading, Music CDs, Online cat, Outreach serv, OverDrive digital audio bks, Photocopying/Printing, Prog for adults, Prog for children & young adult, Ref & res, Ref serv available, Senior computer classes, Spoken cassettes & CDs, Spoken cassettes & DVDs, Story hour, Summer reading prog, Tax forms, Teen prog, Telephone ref, VHS videos, Wheelchair accessible
Publications: Book Ends (Newsletter)
Partic in Serving Every Ohioan Library Center
Open Mon-Thurs 9:30-8:30, Fri & Sat 9:30-5, Sun 1-5
Friends of the Library Group

L HANCOCK COUNTY LAW LIBRARY ASSOCIATION*, 300 S Main St, 4th Flr, 45840. SAN 313-5055. Tel: 419-424-7077. FAX: 419-424-7832. E-mail: hancocklawlib@co.hancock.oh.us. *Chief Admin, Law Librn,* Sandra J Stoll; Staff 1 (Non-MLS 1)
Founded 1903
Library Holdings: Bk Vols 24,500
Wireless access
Open Mon-Fri 8:30-4:30
Restriction: Non-circulating

C THE UNIVERSITY OF FINDLAY*, Shafer Library, 1000 N Main St, 45840-3695. SAN 313-5047. Tel: 419-434-4627. E-mail: library@findlay.edu. Web Site: www.findlay.edu/offices/academic/shafer-library. *Univ Librn & Col Librn for Bus,* Andrew Whitis; Tel: 419-434-5735, E-mail: whitis@findlay.edu; *Col Librn for Educ,* Margaret Hirschy; Tel: 419-434-4260, E-mail: hirschym@findlay.edu; *Col Librn for Health Professions, Pharm & Sci,* Rebecca Quintus; Tel: 419-434-4549, E-mail: quintus@findlay.edu; *Electronic Res Librn,* Drew Balduff; Tel: 419-434-5880, E-mail: balduff@findlay.edu; *Access Serv Coordr,* Pam Carles; Tel: 419-434-4612, E-mail: carlesp@findlay.edu; Staff 7 (MLS 4, Non-MLS 3)

Founded 1882. Enrl 4,186; Fac 225; Highest Degree: Doctorate
Special Collections: State Document Depository; US Document Depository
Automation Activity & Vendor Info: (Acquisitions) Innovative Interfaces, Inc - Sierra; (Cataloging) Innovative Interfaces, Inc - Sierra; (Circulation) Innovative Interfaces, Inc - Sierra; (OPAC) Innovative Interfaces, Inc - Sierra; (Serials) Innovative Interfaces, Inc - Sierra
Wireless access
Partic in OCLC Online Computer Library Center, Inc; OhioNET

FOREST

P FOREST-JACKSON PUBLIC LIBRARY, 102 W Lima St, 45843-1128. SAN 313-508X. Tel: 419-273-2400. FAX: 419-273-8007. Web Site: forestlibrary.org. *Dir,* Karen Moore; E-mail: forestlibrarydirector@gmail.com; Staff 6 (Non-MLS 6)
Founded 1936. Pop 5,700; Circ 51,742
Library Holdings: Bk Vols 12,244
Automation Activity & Vendor Info: (Cataloging) SirsiDynix; (Circulation) SirsiDynix; (OPAC) SirsiDynix
Wireless access
Function: 24/7 Online cat, Accelerated reader prog, Activity rm, Adult bk club, After school storytime, Archival coll, Audiobks via web, Bk club(s), Bks on CD, Children's prog, Computer training, Computers for patron use, Electronic databases & coll, Free DVD rentals, ILL available, Internet access, Magazines, Meeting rooms, Movies, Music CDs, Online cat, Online ref, Outreach serv, Photocopying/Printing, Preschool outreach, Prog for adults, Prog for children & young adult, Scanner, Story hour, Summer reading prog, Tax forms
Partic in Serving Every Ohioan Library Center
Open Mon-Thurs 10-8, Fri 10-5, Sat 10-1
Friends of the Library Group

FORT RECOVERY

P FORT RECOVERY PUBLIC LIBRARY*, 113 N Wayne St, 45846. (Mail add: PO Box 309, 45846-0309), SAN 313-5098. Tel: 419-375-2869. FAX: 419-375-2525. Web Site: www.fortrecoverylibrary.org. *Dir,* Linda Nietfeld; E-mail: lnietfeld@seolibraries.org; Staff 5 (Non-MLS 5)
Founded 1928. Circ 55,246
Library Holdings: Bk Vols 53,625; Per Subs 71
Automation Activity & Vendor Info: (Cataloging) SirsiDynix-WorkFlows; (Circulation) SirsiDynix-WorkFlows; (OPAC) SirsiDynix-WorkFlows
Wireless access
Partic in Serving Every Ohioan Library Center
Open Mon & Wed 10-5:30, Tues 10-7, Fri 9-5:30, Sat 9-1
Friends of the Library Group

FOSTORIA

P KAUBISCH MEMORIAL PUBLIC LIBRARY*, 205 Perry St, 44830-2265. SAN 313-5101. Tel: 419-435-2813. FAX: 419-435-5350. Web Site: www.fostoria.lib.oh.us. *Dir,* Scott Scherf; E-mail: sscherf@seolibraries.org; *Head, Tech Serv,* Kelli Foster; *Head, Youth Serv,* Tara Bahnsen; *Fiscal Officer,* Diana Ziegman-Nye; Staff 7 (MLS 1, Non-MLS 6)
Founded 1892. Pop 25,000; Circ 178,410
Library Holdings: Bk Vols 84,748; Per Subs 189
Wireless access
Partic in Serving Every Ohioan Library Center
Special Services for the Blind - Audio mat; Bks available with recordings; Bks on CD; Large print bks; Talking bks & player equip
Open Mon-Thurs 9-8, Fri 9-5, Sat 9-2
Friends of the Library Group

FRANKLIN

P FRANKLIN-SPRINGBORO PUBLIC LIBRARY, 44 E Fourth St, 45005. SAN 313-511X. Tel: 937-746-2665. FAX: 937-746-2847. E-mail: fspl@fspl.org. Web Site: www.franklin.lib.oh.us. *Libr Dir,* Martha M Bush; E-mail: bushma@fspl.org; *Libr Mgr,* Susan Horner; *Asst Dir,* Vicky Sweeney; Staff 17 (MLS 5, Non-MLS 12)
Founded 1923. Pop 55,770; Circ 458,171
Library Holdings: AV Mats 1,328; CDs 1,674; DVDs 2,495; Large Print Bks 3,382; Bk Vols 150,535; Per Subs 381; Talking Bks 5,375; Videos 7,432
Automation Activity & Vendor Info: (Acquisitions) Innovative Interfaces, Inc; (Cataloging) Innovative Interfaces, Inc; (Circulation) Innovative Interfaces, Inc; (OPAC) Innovative Interfaces, Inc
Wireless access
Function: Audio & video playback equip for onsite use, Audiobks via web, Bk club(s), Bks on cassette, Bks on CD, Children's prog, Computers for patron use, Electronic databases & coll, Home delivery & serv to seniorr ctr & nursing homes, ILL available, Music CDs, Notary serv, Online cat, Photocopying/Printing, Preschool outreach, Summer reading prog, Tax forms, Wheelchair accessible
Partic in Miami Valley Librs; SouthWest Ohio & Neighboring Libraries
Special Services for the Deaf - Sorenson video relay syst
Special Services for the Blind - Assistive/Adapted tech devices, equip & products; Bks on cassette; Bks on CD; Home delivery serv; Large print bks; Low vision equip; Talking bks
Open Mon-Fri 10-6, Sat 12-4
Friends of the Library Group
Branches: 1
SPRINGBORO BRANCH, 125 Park Lane, Springboro, 45066, SAN 370-5765. Tel: 937-748-3200. FAX: 937-748-4831. *Br Mgr,* Gwen Motley; Staff 11 (MLS 1, Non-MLS 10)
Founded 1990
Open Mon-Fri 10-6, Sat 12-4
Friends of the Library Group

FREMONT

P BIRCHARD PUBLIC LIBRARY OF SANDUSKY COUNTY*, 423 Croghan St, 43420. SAN 356-6315. Tel: 419-334-7101. FAX: 419-334-4788. Web Site: www.birchard.lib.oh.us. *Libr Dir,* Pam Hoesman; E-mail: pam.hoesman@birchard.lib.oh.us; *Network Adminr,* Calista Hall; *Operations & Bus Mgr,* Carrie Sidell; *Adult & Tech Serv Coordr,* Grady Brecheisen; *Outreach Coordr, Youth Serv Coordr,* Ellen Buehrer; *YA Serv,* Elizabeth Thompson; Staff 9.5 (MLS 3, Non-MLS 6.5)
Founded 1873. Pop 48,087
Library Holdings: Bk Vols 154,660
Subject Interests: Pres Rutherford B Hayes, War of 1812
Automation Activity & Vendor Info: (Acquisitions) SirsiDynix; (Cataloging) SirsiDynix; (Circulation) SirsiDynix; (ILL) SirsiDynix; (OPAC) SirsiDynix; (Serials) SirsiDynix
Wireless access
Function: 24/7 Electronic res, 24/7 Online cat, Adult bk club, Archival coll, Audiobks on Playaways & MP3, Audiobks via web, AV serv, Bk club(s), Bks on CD, Children's prog, Computer training, Computers for patron use, Digital talking bks, Distance learning, E-Reserves, Electronic databases & coll, Family literacy, Free DVD rentals, Home delivery & serv to seniorr ctr & nursing homes, Homebound delivery serv, ILL available, Internet access, Magazines, Magnifiers for reading, Meeting rooms, Microfiche/film & reading machines, Movies, Music CDs, Notary serv, Online cat, Photocopying/Printing, Preschool reading prog, Spanish lang bks, Summer reading prog, Tax forms, Wheelchair accessible
Partic in CLEVNET
Open Mon-Thurs 9-8:30, Fri 9-5:30, Sat 9-5, Sun 1-5
Friends of the Library Group
Branches: 3
GIBSONBURG BRANCH, 100 N Webster St, Gibsonburg, 43431, SAN 356-634X. Tel: 419-637-2173. *Br Supvr,* Carol Montgomery
Circ 44,889
Open Mon & Wed 12-8, Tues 9-5:30, Thurs 12-5:30, Fri 12-4, Sat 10-3
GREEN SPRINGS MEMORIAL, 217 N Broadway, Green Springs, 44836, SAN 356-6374. Tel: 419-639-2014. *Br Supvr,* Zeferina Anguiano
Circ 21,834
Open Mon & Wed 12-8, Tues 9-5:30, Thurs 12-5:30, Fri 12-4, Sat 10-3
WOODVILLE BRANCH, 101 E Main, Woodville, 43469, SAN 356-6404. Tel: 419-849-2744. *Br Supvr,* Rene Dix
Circ 36,525
Open Mon & Wed 12-8, Tues 9-5:30, Thurs 12-5:30, Fri 12-4, Sat 10-3
Friends of the Library Group

S RUTHERFORD B HAYES PRESIDENTIAL LIBRARY & MUSEUMS, Spiegel Grove, 43420-2796. SAN 313-5128. Tel: 419-332-2081. FAX: 419-332-4952. E-mail: hayeslib@rbhayes.org. Web Site: www.rbhayes.org. *Exec Dir,* Christie Weininger; E-mail: cweininger@rbhayes.org; *Head Librn,* John Ransom; E-mail: jransom@rbhayes.org; *Libr Tech,* Sharon Barnett; E-mail: sbarnett@rbhayes.org; *Libr Tech,* Pat Breno; E-mail: pbreno@rbhayes.org; Staff 4 (MLS 3, Non-MLS 1)
Founded 1911
Library Holdings: Bk Vols 75,000; Per Subs 100
Special Collections: Abraham Lincoln Coll; Benson J Lossing Coll, ms; David Ross Locke Coll, ms; History of the United States, 19th-20th Century (Rutherford B Hayes Personal Library); Nineteenth Century Cookbooks; Rutherford B Hayes Family Coll, ms; Sandusky River Valley & the Great Lakes Coll; Thomas Nast Coll, ms; William & Mary B Claflin Coll, ms; William Dean Howells Coll, ms; William M Evarts Coll, ms
Subject Interests: Croquet, Econ hist (1865-1917), Genealogy, Gilded Age US (1865-1917), Local hist, Ohio, Presidents, Reconstruction in the South, US political soc
Automation Activity & Vendor Info: (OPAC) OCLC Connexion
Wireless access
Function: ILL available
Publications: The Statesman (Newsletter)
Partic in Ohio Library & Information Network
Open Mon, Tues & Thurs-Sat 9-5
Restriction: Non-circulating to the pub

GL SANDUSKY COUNTY LAW LIBRARY*, 100 N Park Ave, No 106, 43420. SAN 327-3849. Tel: 419-334-6165. FAX: 419-334-6156. Web Site: www.sandusky-county.com/index.php?page=law-library. *Law Librn,* Cyndi Zienta; E-mail: Zienta_cyndi@co.sandusky.oh.us
Open Mon-Fri 8-4:30

J TERRA STATE COMMUNITY COLLEGE LIBRARY*, General Technologies Bldg, B301, 2830 Napoleon Rd, 43420-9670. SAN 313-5136. Tel: 419-559-2318. E-mail: library@terra.edu. Web Site: www.terra.edu/degrees_programs/library. *Librn, Mgr,* Amy Kreilick; Tel: 419-559-2121, E-mail: akreilick01@terra.edu; Staff 3.5 (MLS 1, Non-MLS 2.5)
Founded 1971. Enrl 2,603; Fac 263; Highest Degree: Associate
Library Holdings: CDs 908; DVDs 450; Bk Titles 30,802; Per Subs 71
Automation Activity & Vendor Info: (Acquisitions) Innovative Interfaces, Inc - Millennium; (Cataloging) Innovative Interfaces, Inc - Millennium; (Circulation) Innovative Interfaces, Inc - Millennium; (Course Reserve) Innovative Interfaces, Inc - Millennium; (ILL) Innovative Interfaces, Inc - Millennium; (OPAC) Innovative Interfaces, Inc - Millennium; (Serials) Innovative Interfaces, Inc - Millennium
Wireless access
Function: Archival coll, Bks on CD, Computers for patron use, Electronic databases & coll, ILL available, Music CDs, Online cat, Photocopying/Printing, Ref & res, Scanner, Wheelchair accessible
Partic in Ohio Library & Information Network
Open Mon-Thurs 8-5, Fri 8-4
Restriction: Authorized patrons, In-house use for visitors, Open to authorized patrons, Open to students, fac, staff & alumni

GALION

P GALION PUBLIC LIBRARY*, 123 N Market St, 44833. SAN 313-5144. Tel: 419-468-3203. FAX: 419-468-7298. E-mail: galion@galionlibrary.org. Web Site: www.galion.lib.oh.us, www.galionlibrary.org. *Dir,* Mike Kirk; E-mail: mkirk@galion.library.org; Staff 14 (MLS 3, Non-MLS 11)
Founded 1901. Pop 12,000; Circ 230,244
Library Holdings: Audiobooks 2,617; AV Mats 13,621; CDs 2,462; DVDs 4,503; Electronic Media & Resources 2; Large Print Bks 3,016; Bk Vols 86,871; Per Subs 102
Special Collections: Local & Ohio History (Ohio Room)
Automation Activity & Vendor Info: (Cataloging) Innovative Interfaces, Inc; (Circulation) Innovative Interfaces, Inc; (OPAC) Innovative Interfaces, Inc
Wireless access
Function: 24/7 Online cat, Archival coll, Art programs, Audiobks on Playaways & MP3, Audiobks via web, AV serv, Bks on CD, Children's prog, Computers for patron use, Digital talking bks, Distance learning, Doc delivery serv, Equip loans & repairs, Free DVD rentals, Holiday prog, Home delivery & serv to seniorr ctr & nursing homes, Homebound delivery serv, ILL available, Instruction & testing, Internet access, Laminating, Large print keyboards, Life-long learning prog for all ages, Magazines, Mail & tel request accepted, Meeting rooms, Microfiche/film & reading machines, Movies, Music CDs, Online cat, Outreach serv, OverDrive digital audio bks, Photocopying/Printing, Preschool outreach, Printer for laptops & handheld devices, Prog for adults, Prog for children & young adult, Ref serv available, Res assist avail, Res performed for a fee, Scanner, Serves people with intellectual disabilities, Spanish lang bks, Spoken cassettes & CDs, STEM programs, Story hour, Summer & winter reading prog, Summer reading prog, Tax forms, Teen prog, Telephone ref, Wheelchair accessible, Winter reading prog, Workshops, Writing prog
Partic in Consortium of Ohio Libraries
Open Mon-Thurs 9-8:30, Fri 9-6, Sat 9-5
Restriction: Borrowing requests are handled by ILL, Circ limited, ID required to use computers (Ltd hrs), In-house use for visitors, Non-circulating of rare bks, Pub use on premises
Friends of the Library Group

GALLIPOLIS

P GALLIA COUNTY DISTRICT LIBRARY*, Dr Samuel L Bossard Memorial Library, Seven Spruce St, 45631. SAN 313-5152. Tel: 740-446-7323. Administration Tel: 740-446-7323, Ext 235. FAX: 740-446-1701. E-mail: library@bossardlibrary.org. Web Site: bossardlibrary.org. *Dir,* Deborah Saunders; E-mail: DSaunders@bossardlibrary.org; *Ref Librn,* Randall Fulks; *Circ Mgr,* Susan Randolph; *Mobile Serv Mgr,* Jack Mowery; *Youth Serv Prog Coordr,* Rachael Barker; *Dep Fiscal Officer,* Kimberely Trout; Staff 1 (MLS 1)
Founded 1899. Pop 32,000; Circ 196,006
Special Collections: Depression Era Fiction (O O McIntyre Coll); Genealogy, local & surrounding counties. Municipal Document Depository
Subject Interests: Genealogy, Local hist
Automation Activity & Vendor Info: (Acquisitions) Innovative Interfaces, Inc; (Cataloging) Innovative Interfaces, Inc; (Circulation) Innovative Interfaces, Inc; (OPAC) Innovative Interfaces, Inc; (Serials) Innovative Interfaces, Inc
Wireless access
Function: 24/7 Electronic res, 24/7 Online cat, Activity rm, Adult bk club, AV serv, Bk club(s), Bks on CD, Children's prog, Computer training, Computers for patron use, Electronic databases & coll, Holiday prog, Home delivery & serv to seniorr ctr & nursing homes, Homebound delivery serv, ILL available, Internet access, Magazines, Meeting rooms, Movies, Music CDs, Online cat, Outreach serv, OverDrive digital audio bks, Photocopying/Printing, Preschool outreach, Preschool reading prog, Prog for adults, Prog for children & young adult, Ref serv available, Senior computer classes, Senior outreach, Story hour, Summer & winter reading prog, Summer reading prog, Tax forms, Teen prog, Wheelchair accessible, Winter reading prog, Workshops, Writing prog
Partic in Southeast Regional Library System
Special Services for the Deaf - Assistive tech
Open Mon-Fri 9am-8pm, Sat 9-5, Sun 1-5

GAMBIER

C KENYON COLLEGE LIBRARY & INFORMATION SERVICES*, Olin Library & Gordon Keith Chalmers Memorial Library, Olin & Chalmers Libraries, 103 College Dr, 43022. SAN 313-5187. Reference Tel: 740-427-5691. Administration Tel: 740-427-5187. Web Site: lbis.kenyon.edu. *VPres, Libr & Info Serv,* Ronald Griggs; Tel: 740-427-5632, E-mail: griggs@kenyon.edu; *Assoc VPres, Libr Dir,* Amy E Badertscher; Tel: 740-427-5605, E-mail: badertschera@kenyon.edu; *Dir, Coll Serv,* Chris Hudson; E-mail: hudsonc@kenyon.edu; *Dir, Res & Instruction Serv,* Julia Warga; E-mail: glynnj@kenyon.edu; *Assoc Dir, Access Serv,* Joan Nielson; E-mail: nielsonj@kenyon.edu; Staff 18 (MLS 12, Non-MLS 6)
Founded 1824. Enrl 1,700; Fac 190; Highest Degree: Bachelor
Library Holdings: Bk Vols 420,385; Per Subs 8,185
Special Collections: Kenyon College Archives; Kenyon Review Archives; Letters of Charles Pettit McIlvane; Letters of Philander Chase; Typography Coll; William Butler Yeats Publications (Riker Coll). Oral History; US Document Depository
Wireless access
Function: Accelerated reader prog
Partic in Five Colleges of Ohio; Ohio Library & Information Network; OhioNET
Restriction: Hospital employees & physicians only

GARRETTSVILLE

P PORTAGE COUNTY DISTRICT LIBRARY*, Administration Library, 10482 South St, 44231. SAN 356-6854. Tel: 330-527-5082. Toll Free Tel: 800-500-5179. FAX: 330-527-4370. Web Site: www.portagecounty.lib.oh.us. *Dir,* Jon Harris; Tel: 330-527-5082, Ext 219, E-mail: jharris@portagelibrary.org; *Asst Dir, Coll Develop Mgr,* Corrine Alldridge; Tel: 330-527-5082, Ext 229, E-mail: calldridge@portagelibrary.org
Founded 1935. Pop 85,000
Library Holdings: Bk Vols 259,361; Per Subs 530
Automation Activity & Vendor Info: (Acquisitions) Innovative Interfaces, Inc; (Cataloging) Innovative Interfaces, Inc; (Circulation) Innovative Interfaces, Inc; (ILL) Innovative Interfaces, Inc; (OPAC) Innovative Interfaces, Inc; (Serials) Innovative Interfaces, Inc
Wireless access
Partic in Northeast Ohio Regional Library System
Open Mon-Fri 9-5
Friends of the Library Group
Branches: 5
AURORA MEMORIAL, 115 E Pioneer Trail, Aurora, 44202-9349, SAN 356-6889. Tel: 330-562-6502. FAX: 330-562-2084. *Mgr,* Cathy Morgan; E-mail: cmorgan@portagelibrary.org
Founded 1966
Library Holdings: Bk Vols 76,000
Open Mon-Wed 10-8, Fri 10-6, Sat 9-5
Friends of the Library Group
GARRETTSVILLE BRANCH, 10482 South St, 44231. Tel: 330-527-4378. Toll Free Tel: 800-500-6504. FAX: 330-527-4370. *Mgr,* Mary Lu Rosier; E-mail: mrosier@portagelibrary.org
Founded 1936
Library Holdings: Bk Vols 65,000
Open Mon-Wed 10-8, Fri 10-6, Sat 9-5
Friends of the Library Group
RANDOLPH BRANCH, 1639 State Rte 44, Randolph, 44265. (Mail add: PO Box 368, Randolph, 44265-0368), SAN 356-6927. Tel: 330-325-7003. FAX: 330-325-7740. *Mgr,* Andrew Fearn; E-mail: afearn@portagelibrary.org
Founded 1981
Library Holdings: Bk Vols 22,699
Open Mon & Tues 2-7, Wed, Fri & Sat 10-3
Friends of the Library Group

STREETSBORO BRANCH, 8990 Kirby Lane, Streetsboro, 44241-1723, SAN 356-6943. Tel: 330-626-4458. FAX: 330-626-1737. *Mgr,* Andrew Fearn; E-mail: afearn@portagelibrary.org
Founded 1976
Library Holdings: Bk Vols 42,179
Open Mon & Tues 11-7, Wed & Fri 10-6, Sat 9-5
Friends of the Library Group

WINDHAM BRANCH, 9005 Wilverne Dr, Windham, 44288, SAN 356-6978. Tel: 330-326-3145. FAX: 330-326-2490. *Mgr,* Mary Lu Rosier; E-mail: mrosier@portagelibrary.org
Founded 1945
Library Holdings: Bk Vols 22,985
Open Mon & Fri 10-4, Tues & Thurs 12-6:30
Friends of the Library Group

Bookmobiles: 2

GERMANTOWN

P GERMANTOWN PUBLIC LIBRARY*, 51 N Plum St, 45327. SAN 313-5209. Tel: 937-855-4001. FAX: 937-855-6098. E-mail: info@gtownlibrary.net. Web Site: www.germantown.lib.oh.us. *Dir,* Joe Knueven; *Asst Dir,* Gillian Izor; *Youth Serv Coordr,* Kelsey McCoy; Staff 3 (MLS 2, Non-MLS 1)
Founded 1888. Pop 11,500; Circ 216,012
Library Holdings: Bk Titles 94,993; Per Subs 79
Special Collections: Local History (Germantown Historical Coll), bks, pamphlets
Automation Activity & Vendor Info: (Cataloging) Evergreen; (Circulation) Evergreen; (ILL) OCLC FirstSearch; (OPAC) Evergreen
Wireless access
Function: After school storytime, AV serv, CD-ROM, Computer training, Digital talking bks, E-Reserves, Home delivery & serv to seniorr ctr & nursing homes, Homebound delivery serv, Homework prog, ILL available, Mail & tel request accepted, Music CDs, Outside serv via phone, mail, e-mail & web, Photocopying/Printing, Preschool outreach, Prog for adults, Prog for children & young adult, Ref & res, Spoken cassettes & CDs, Summer reading prog, Tax forms, Telephone ref, VHS videos, Wheelchair accessible
Partic in Miami Valley Librs; Ohio Public Library Information Network
Open Mon-Thurs 10-8, Fri & Sat 10-3
Friends of the Library Group

GIRARD

P GIRARD FREE LIBRARY*, 105 E Prospect St, 44420. SAN 313-5217. Tel: 330-545-2508. Circulation Tel: 330-545-2508, Ext 102. Reference Tel: 330-545-2508, Ext 104. Administration Tel: 330-545-2508, Ext 303. FAX: 330-545-8213. Web Site: www.girardfreelibrary.org. *Dir,* RoseAnn Lubert; E-mail: lubertr@girardfreelibrary.org; *Asst Dir,* Colleen Keller; Staff 15 (MLS 2, Non-MLS 13)
Founded 1919. Pop 11,000; Circ 133,491
Library Holdings: AV Mats 7,578; Bk Vols 67,706; Per Subs 120
Special Collections: World War II Coll
Subject Interests: Biographies, Cooking, Hist, Lit, Music, Soc issues
Automation Activity & Vendor Info: (Cataloging) SirsiDynix; (Circulation) SirsiDynix; (OPAC) SirsiDynix
Wireless access
Function: Adult bk club, Electronic databases & coll, Homebound delivery serv, ILL available, Internet access, Music CDs, Online ref, Photocopying/Printing, Preschool outreach, Prog for children & young adult, Spoken cassettes & CDs, Summer reading prog, Tax forms, VHS videos, Wheelchair accessible
Partic in Northeast Ohio Regional Library System
Open Mon-Thurs 9-8, Fri 9-5, Sat 10-4
Friends of the Library Group

GNADENHUTTEN

P GNADENHUTTEN PUBLIC LIBRARY*, 160 N Walnut St, 44629. (Mail add: PO Box 216, 44629-0216), SAN 313-5225. Tel: 740-254-9224. FAX: 740-254-9841. E-mail: gnadenhuttenpl@gmail.com. Web Site: www.gnadenlibrary.org. *Dir,* Linda Hren; *Youth Serv,* April King; Staff 5 (Non-MLS 5)
Founded 1936. Pop 5,082
Library Holdings: Audiobooks 300; AV Mats 1,100,700; DVDs 900; Large Print Bks 650; Bk Titles 26,480; Per Subs 72
Subject Interests: Early Ohio hist, Indians, Moravian missions
Automation Activity & Vendor Info: (Cataloging) SirsiDynix-WorkFlows; (Circulation) SirsiDynix-WorkFlows; (OPAC) SirsiDynix-Enterprise
Wireless access
Function: 24/7 Electronic res, Computers for patron use, Electronic databases & coll, Holiday prog, ILL available, Internet access, Life-long learning prog for all ages, Movies, Online cat, Prog for children & young adult, STEM programs, Story hour, Summer reading prog, Tax forms, Teen prog, Wheelchair accessible
Partic in Serving Every Ohioan Library Center
Open Mon-Thurs 9-7, Fri 9-5, Sat 9-1
Restriction: In-house use for visitors

GRAFTON

P GRAFTON - MIDVIEW PUBLIC LIBRARY*, 983 Main St, 44044-1492. SAN 313-5233. Tel: 440-926-3317. FAX: 440-926-3000. Web Site: www.gmplibrary.org. *Dir,* Adele Infante; E-mail: ainfante@gmplibrary.org; Staff 12 (MLS 7, Non-MLS 5)
Founded 1944. Pop 24,487; Circ 187,797
Jan 2017-Dec 2017 Income $1,210,310, State $605,192, Locally Generated Income $577,683, Other $27,435. Mats Exp $135,053. Sal $575,849 (Prof $66,788)
Library Holdings: Audiobooks 4,726; AV Mats 7,827; Bks on Deafness & Sign Lang 28; DVDs 4,081; e-books 220,767; Electronic Media & Resources 78; Large Print Bks 1,253; Bk Titles 38,140; Per Subs 84; Videos 2
Special Collections: Automotive Repair Manuals Coll; Local Author Coll; Local History Coll
Automation Activity & Vendor Info: (Cataloging) TLC (The Library Corporation); (Circulation) TLC (The Library Corporation); (OPAC) TLC (The Library Corporation)
Wireless access
Function: 24/7 Electronic res, 24/7 Online cat, Activity rm, Adult bk club, After school storytime, Bks on cassette, Bks on CD, Children's prog, Computer training, Computers for patron use, E-Reserves, Electronic databases & coll, Family literacy, Free DVD rentals, Homework prog, ILL available, Music CDs, Online cat, Online ref, Outreach serv, Photocopying/Printing, Preschool outreach, Prog for adults, Prog for children & young adult, Ref serv available, Scanner, Senior computer classes, Story hour, Summer reading prog, Tax forms, Teen prog, Telephone ref, VHS videos, Wheelchair accessible
Partic in Northeast Ohio Regional Library System; Ohio Public Library Information Network
Open Mon, Tues, Thurs 9:30-8, Fri 9:30-6, Wed & Sat 9:30-5; Sun (Sept-May) 1-5
Friends of the Library Group

GRANVILLE

C DENISON UNIVERSITY LIBRARIES, William Howard Doane Library, Seeley G Mudd Learning Center, Douthit Hall, 400 West Loop, 43023. (Mail add: 100 W College St, 43023), SAN 313-5241. Tel: 740-587-6235. Interlibrary Loan Service Tel: 740-587-6431. Reference Tel: 740-587-6682. Administration Tel: 740-587-6225. FAX: 740-587-6285. Reference E-mail: reference@denison.edu. Web Site: denison.edu/campus/library. *Dir of Libr,* BethAnn Zambella; Tel: 740-587-6215, E-mail: zambellab@denison.edu; *Dep Dir,* Debra Andreadis; Tel: 740-587-6512, Fax: 740-587-5653, E-mail: andreadisd@denison.edu; *Asst Dir, Coll & Scholarly Res,* Earl Griffith; Tel: 740-587-6619, E-mail: griffith@denison.edu; *Discovery Librn,* Sarah Schaff; Tel: 740-587-6470, E-mail: schaffs@denison.edu; *Electronic Res Librn, Scholarly Communications Librn,* Yuimi Hlasten; Tel: 740-587-5354, E-mail: hlasteny@denison.edu; *Fine Arts Liaison Librn,* Stephanie Kays; Tel: 740-587-6688, E-mail: kayss@denison.edu; *Humanities Liaison Librn,* Amy Elliott; Tel: 740-587-8651, E-mail: elliottm@denison.edu; *Natural Sci Liaison Librn,* Yiming Guo; Tel: 740-587-5714, E-mail: guoy@denison.edu; *Soc Sci Liaison Librn,* Lisa Morrison; Tel: 740-587-6389, E-mail: morrisonl@denison.edu; *Spec Coll Librn, Univ Archivist,* Sasha Griffin; Tel: 740-587-6399, E-mail: griffins@denison.edu; Staff 23 (MLS 10, Non-MLS 13)
Founded 1831. Enrl 2,300; Fac 235; Highest Degree: Bachelor
Jul 2020-Jun 2021. Mats Exp $1,498,187. Sal $1,362,220
Library Holdings: e-books 1,977,358; e-journals 174,377; Electronic Media & Resources 617; Bk Titles 424,704; Bk Vols 484,520; Per Subs 1,351
Special Collections: US Document Depository
Automation Activity & Vendor Info: (Acquisitions) Innovative Interfaces, Inc; (Cataloging) Innovative Interfaces, Inc; (Circulation) Innovative Interfaces, Inc; (Discovery) ProQuest; (ILL) OCLC Tipasa; (OPAC) Innovative Interfaces, Inc; (Serials) EBSCO Online
Wireless access
Function: 24/7 Online cat, Archival coll, Art exhibits, Audio & video playback equip for onsite use, Audiobks via web, AV serv, CD-ROM, Computers for patron use, Doc delivery serv, E-Reserves, Electronic databases & coll, Equip loans & repairs, Free DVD rentals, ILL available, Internet access, Learning ctr, Microfiche/film & reading machines, Music CDs, Online cat, Online info literacy tutorials on the web & in blackboard, Online ref, Orientations, Photocopying/Printing, Ref serv available, Telephone ref, VHS videos
Partic in Five Colleges of Ohio; OCLC Online Computer Library Center, Inc; Ohio Library & Information Network; OhioNET
Open Mon-Thurs 8:30am-2am, Fri 8:30am-Midnight, Sat 10:30am-Midnight, Sun 10:30am-2am
Restriction: Open to students, fac & staff, Use of others with permission of librn

P GRANVILLE PUBLIC LIBRARY*, 217 E Broadway, 43023-1398. SAN 313-525X. Tel: 740-587-0196. FAX: 740-587-0197. Web Site: www.granvillelibrary.org. *Libr Dir,* Anita Carroll; E-mail: acarroll@granvillelibrary.org; *Ch,* Betsy Wernert; E-mail: bwernert@granvillelibrary.org; *Commun Engagement Librn,* Julia Walden; E-mail: jwalden@granvillelibrary.org; *Pub Serv Librn,* Emily Shellhouse; E-mail: eshellhouse@granvillelibrary.org; *Fiscal Officer,* Carol Gissinger; *Tech Serv,* Sarah Baker; E-mail: sbaker@granvillelibrary.org; Staff 11.5 (MLS 3, Non-MLS 8.5)
Founded 1912. Pop 12,939; Circ 295,634
Library Holdings: AV Mats 5,305; Bk Titles 65,323; Per Subs 150
Automation Activity & Vendor Info: (Cataloging) SirsiDynix; (Circulation) SirsiDynix; (ILL) OCLC WorldShare Interlibrary Loan; (OPAC) SirsiDynix
Wireless access
Open Mon-Thurs 9-9, Fri & Sat 9-6
Friends of the Library Group

GRATIS

P MARION LAWRENCE MEMORIAL LIBRARY*, 15 E Franklin St, 45330. Tel: 937-787-3502. FAX: 937-787-3502. E-mail: gratlib@gmail.com. *Dir,* Penny Johnston; *Librn,* JoAnn Harris
Circ 5,101
Library Holdings: Bk Vols 14,426; Per Subs 58
Automation Activity & Vendor Info: (Cataloging) SirsiDynix; (Circulation) SirsiDynix; (OPAC) SirsiDynix
Partic in Miami Valley Librs; Serving Every Ohioan Library Center
Open Mon & Thurs 2-8, Tues & Wed 1-5, Sat 10-1

GREENVILLE

GL GREENVILLE LAW LIBRARY ASSOCIATION, Darke County Law Library, 124 W Fifth St, 45331. SAN 327-3865. Tel: 937-547-9741. FAX: 937-547-9743. E-mail: darkelawlibrary@gmail.com. *Librn,* Melinda Guerra; Staff 1 (Non-MLS 1)
Founded 1875
Library Holdings: Bk Vols 8,500
Open Mon 8am-11am, Fri 9-Noon
Restriction: Non-circulating to the pub

P GREENVILLE PUBLIC LIBRARY*, 520 Sycamore St, 45331-1438. SAN 313-5284. Tel: 937-548-3915. FAX: 937-548-3837. Web Site: www.greenville-publiclibrary.org. *Dir,* John L Vehre, Jr; E-mail: john@greenville-publiclibrary.org; *Asst Dir,* Susi Halley; *Circ Supvr,* Julie Kennett; *Ref Supvr,* Deb Cameron; Staff 3 (MLS 1, Non-MLS 2)
Founded 1889. Pop 25,000; Circ 268,000
Library Holdings: Bk Vols 100,000; Per Subs 211
Special Collections: Annie Oakley Coll; Genealogy of Darke County Coll; Saint Clair Coll; Sheet Music Coll; Signed Limited Editions Coll. State Document Depository
Automation Activity & Vendor Info: (Cataloging) Innovative Interfaces, Inc; (Circulation) Innovative Interfaces, Inc; (OPAC) Innovative Interfaces, Inc
Wireless access
Function: AV serv, Games & aids for people with disabilities, Home delivery & serv to seniorr ctr & nursing homes, Homebound delivery serv, ILL available, Internet access, Magnifiers for reading, Photocopying/Printing, Prog for children & young adult, Summer reading prog
Special Services for the Deaf - TTY equip
Special Services for the Blind - Magnifiers; Production of talking bks
Open Mon-Thurs 9-8, Fri 9-6, Sat 9-4
Friends of the Library Group
Bookmobiles: 1

GROVE CITY

P SOUTHWEST PUBLIC LIBRARIES*, SPL Admin, 3359 Broadway, 43123. SAN 356-6439. Tel: 614-875-6716. Web Site: www.swpl.org. *Dir,* Mark M Shaw; E-mail: mshaw@swpl.org; *Asst Dir,* Bethanne Johnson; E-mail: bjohnson@swpl.org; *Head, Tech Serv,* Patrick Crossen; E-mail: pcrossen@swpl.org; *Ad, Ref Serv Librn,* Emma Trudeau; E-mail: etrudeau@swpl.org; *Circ Serv Librn,* Katie Geddes; E-mail: kpuckett@swpl.org; *Youth Serv Librn,* Lore Lehr; E-mail: llehr@swpl.org; Staff 15 (MLS 11, Non-MLS 4)
Founded 1891. Pop 120,900; Circ 1,200,000
Library Holdings: Bk Vols 267,000; Per Subs 380
Special Collections: Local History Coll. Oral History
Wireless access
Publications: Happenings (Newsletter); The Update
Partic in Discovery Place Librs; OCLC Online Computer Library Center, Inc; Ohio Public Library Information Network; OhioNET
Open Mon-Thurs 9:30-9, Fri & Sat 9:30-6, Sun 1-5
Friends of the Library Group
Branches: 1
WESTLAND AREA LIBRARY, 4740 W Broad St, Columbus, 43228, SAN 356-6498. Tel: 614-878-1301. FAX: 614-878-3454. *Libr Mgr,* Michele Lowe; *Ad,* John Kazalia; *Circ Serv Librn,* Denise Southworth; *Youth Serv Librn,* Mary Allen
Friends of the Library Group

HAMILTON

L JOHN F HOLCOMB BUTLER COUNTY LAW LIBRARY, Ten Journal Sq, Ste 200, 45011. SAN 313-5292. Tel: 513-887-3455. FAX: 513-887-3696. Web Site: www.bclawlib.org. *Adminr,* Kristy Wells; E-mail: Wellskm@butlercountyohio.org; Staff 1 (MLS 1)
Founded 1889
Library Holdings: Bk Vols 40,000; Per Subs 150
Automation Activity & Vendor Info: (Cataloging) EOS International; (Circulation) EOS International; (OPAC) EOS International; (Serials) EOS International
Publications: Bibliographies; Newsletter (Bimonthly); User's Guide
Partic in OhioNET
Open Mon-Fri 8:30-4:30

P LANE PUBLIC LIBRARIES*, 300 N Third St, 45011-1629. SAN 356-6587. Tel: 513-894-7156. Administration Tel: 513-894-0113. FAX: 513-894-2718. E-mail: comments@lanepl.org. Web Site: www.lanepl.org. *Dir,* Joseph Greenward; E-mail: j.greenward@lanepl.org; *Libr Mgr,* Carol Bowling; E-mail: c.bowling@lanepl.org; Staff 13.8 (MLS 13.8)
Founded 1866. Pop 185,142; Circ 2,364,966
Library Holdings: CDs 3,234; DVDs 49,552; e-books 1,919; Bk Vols 505,816; Per Subs 643; Videos 4,135
Special Collections: George Cummins Local History Room; Smith Library of Regional History
Automation Activity & Vendor Info: (Acquisitions) SirsiDynix; (Cataloging) SirsiDynix; (Circulation) SirsiDynix; (OPAC) SirsiDynix
Wireless access
Function: Adult bk club, Bk club(s), Bk reviews (Group), Bks on cassette, Bks on CD, CD-ROM, Children's prog, Computer training, Computers for patron use, Digital talking bks, E-Reserves, Electronic databases & coll, Free DVD rentals, Holiday prog, ILL available, Internet access, Jazz prog, Music CDs, Online cat, Online ref, Photocopying/Printing, Prog for adults, Prog for children & young adult, Ref serv available, Senior computer classes, Spoken cassettes & CDs, Spoken cassettes & DVDs, Story hour, Summer reading prog, Tax forms, Teen prog, Telephone ref, VHS videos, Wheelchair accessible
Partic in OCLC Online Computer Library Center, Inc; OhioNET
Open Mon-Thurs 9-8, Fri & Sat 9-6
Friends of the Library Group
Branches: 2
FAIRFIELD LANE LIBRARY, 1485 Corydale Dr, Fairfield, 45014, SAN 356-6641. Tel: 513-858-3238. FAX: 513-858-3298. *Br Mgr,* Valerie Simmons; E-mail: v.simmons@lanepl.org; Staff 3.7 (MLS 2.8, Non-MLS 0.9)
Circ 1,255,531
Open Mon-Thurs 9-8, Fri & Sat 9-6
Friends of the Library Group
SMITH LIBRARY OF REGIONAL HISTORY
See Separate Entry in Oxford, Ohio
Bookmobiles: 1. Serv Mgr, Fran Meyer

HARRISON

S AMERICAN WATCHMAKERS-CLOCKMAKERS INSTITUTE LIBRARY*, 701 Enterprise Dr, 45030-1696. SAN 324-573X. Tel: 513-367-9800. Toll Free Tel: 866-367-2924. FAX: 513-367-1414. E-mail: awci@awci.com, memserv@awci.com. Web Site: www.awci.com/library. *Educ Dir,* Jason Champion; E-mail: jason@awci.com; *Mem Serv Librn,* Maureen Seals
Founded 1960
Library Holdings: Bk Titles 3,000; Bk Vols 3,500; Per Subs 6
Subject Interests: Clock historical, Hist of time, Jewelry, Repair, Watch
Wireless access
Publications: AWI Library Index; Horological Times
Restriction: Mem only, Open by appt only

HIGHLAND HILLS

S GLOBAL ISSUES RESOURCE CENTER LIBRARY*, Bldg ESS-3100, Cuyahoga Community College, East Student Services, 4250 Richmond Rd, 44122. SAN 323-4274. Tel: 216-987-0595. *Dir,* Scott Trimmer; E-mail: Scott.Trimmer@tri-c.edu; Staff 2 (MLS 2)
Library Holdings: Bk Titles 887
Special Collections: Conflict Resolution; Curricula; Energy; Environment; Global Education
Wireless access

Publications: Audio-Visual Catalog; Bibliographies On Energy Issues, Enviromental Concerns & Global Education; Games & Simulations Catalog; Resources to Teach About Conflict Resolution
Partic in Northeast Ohio Regional Library System; Ohio Library & Information Network

HILLSBORO

P HIGHLAND COUNTY DISTRICT LIBRARY*, Ten Willettsville Pike, 45133. SAN 356-6730. Tel: 937-393-3114. FAX: 937-250-7551. E-mail: hillsboro@highlandco.org. Web Site: www.highlandco.org. *Dir,* Suzanne Roberts; E-mail: director@highlandco.org; *Asst Dir,* Joanna Sullivan; Staff 23 (MLS 3, Non-MLS 20)
Founded 1898. Pop 42,833; Circ 672,197
Library Holdings: AV Mats 16,808; Bk Vols 158,215; Per Subs 371
Special Collections: State Document Depository
Subject Interests: Genealogy, Investment, Local hist
Automation Activity & Vendor Info: (Cataloging) SirsiDynix; (Circulation) SirsiDynix
Wireless access
Function: ILL available
Partic in Serving Every Ohioan Library Center
Special Services for the Blind - Bks on cassette; Bks on CD; Large print bks
Open Mon-Thurs 10-8, Fri & Sat 10-5
Branches: 4
GREENFIELD BRANCH, 1125 Jefferson St, Greenfield, 45123, SAN 356-6765. Tel: 937-981-3772. FAX: 937-250-7552. E-mail: greenfield@highlandco.org. Web Site: www.highlandco.org/content/greenfield. *Br Mgr,* Spencer McNeil
Open Mon-Thurs 10-7, Fri 10-5, Sat 10-3
LEESBURG BRANCH, 240 E Main St, Leesburg, 45135, SAN 356-679X. Tel: 937-780-7295. FAX: 937-250-7553. E-mail: leesburg@highlandco.org. Web Site: www.highlandco.org/content/leesburg. *Br Mgr,* Melinda McGee
Pop 4,000
Open Mon & Thurs 10-7, Tues, Wed & Fri 10-5, Sat 10-3
LYNCHBURG BRANCH, 102 S Main St, Lynchburg, 45142, SAN 356-682X. Tel: 937-364-2511. FAX: 937-250-7554. E-mail: lynchburg@highlandco.org. Web Site: www.highlandco.org/content/lynchburg. *Br Mgr,* Elaine Williams
Open Mon & Thurs 10-7, Tues, Wed & Fri 10-5, Sat 10-3
ROCKY FORK BRANCH, 11125 North Shore Dr, 45133. Tel: 937-661-6866. FAX: 937-519-1180. E-mail: rockyfork@highlandco.org. *Br Mgr,* Kathy Chaney
Open Mon, Tues & Thurs 10-6, Fri 10-5, Sat 10-1

GL HIGHLAND COUNTY LAW LIBRARY*, Courthouse, 105 N High St, 45133. SAN 327-3903. Tel: 937-393-4863. FAX: 937-393-6878. E-mail: highlandcoll@yahoo.com. *Librn,* Michelle Vanzant-Salyer; Staff 1 (Non-MLS 1)
Library Holdings: Bk Vols 8,000; Per Subs 25
Subject Interests: Civil law, Criminal law, Domestic law
Partic in Ohio Asn of Regional Law Libr
Open Mon-Fri 9-3
Restriction: Open to pub with supv only

J SOUTHERN STATE COMMUNITY COLLEGE LIBRARY, 100 Hobart Dr, 45133-9487. (Mail add: 1270 US Rte 62 NW, Washington Court House, 43160), SAN 325-3260. Tel: 740-333-5115, Ext 5510, 937-393-3431, Ext 3680. Toll Free Tel: 800-628-7722, Ext 3680 (Ohio only). FAX: 740-333-4622. E-mail: library@sscc.edu. Web Site: library.sscc.edu. *Interim Dir, Libr Serv,* Dr Jessica Wise; Tel: 740-333-5115, Ext 5510, E-mail: jwise@sscc.edu; *Libr Serv Coordr,* ReBecca Griffith; Tel: 937-393-3431, Ext 3681, E-mail: rgriffith@sscc.edu; Staff 2 (Non-MLS 2)
Founded 1985. Enrl 1,500; Fac 48; Highest Degree: Associate
Library Holdings: AV Mats 995; e-books 5,904; Bk Titles 40,856; Bk Vols 42,512; Per Subs 214
Special Collections: Appalachia
Automation Activity & Vendor Info: (Acquisitions) Innovative Interfaces, Inc; (Cataloging) OCLC; (Circulation) Innovative Interfaces, Inc; (Course Reserve) Innovative Interfaces, Inc; (ILL) OCLC; (OPAC) Innovative Interfaces, Inc; (Serials) Innovative Interfaces, Inc
Wireless access
Function: Art exhibits, Audio & video playback equip for onsite use, AV serv, Computers for patron use, Distance learning, Doc delivery serv, E-Readers, For res purposes, Health sci info serv, ILL available, Instruction & testing, Internet access, Large print keyboards, Magazines, Magnifiers for reading, Online cat, Online ref, Photocopying/Printing, Printer for laptops & handheld devices, Prog for children & young adult, Ref serv available, Scanner, Telephone ref, Wheelchair accessible
Partic in Ohio Library & Information Network; OhioNET; SouthWest Ohio & Neighboring Libraries; Southwestern Ohio Council for Higher Education
Special Services for the Deaf - Sorenson video relay syst
Restriction: ID required to use computers (Ltd hrs), Photo ID required for access

HIRAM

C HIRAM COLLEGE LIBRARY*, 11694 Hayden St, 44234. (Mail add: PO Box 67, 44234-0067), SAN 313-5330. Tel: 330-569-5489. Interlibrary Loan Service Tel: 330-569-5359. Administration Tel: 330-569-5353. FAX: 330-569-5491. E-mail: library@hiram.edu. Web Site: library.hiram.edu. *Dir,* Janet Vogel; E-mail: vogelj@hiram.edu; *Syst/Electronic Res Librn,* Chris Schmidt; Tel: 330-569-5363, E-mail: schmidtcj@hiram.edu; *Doc, Ref (Info Servs),* Jeffery Wanser; Tel: 330-569-5358, E-mail: wanserjc@hiram.edu; *ILL,* Terri Foy; E-mail: foytm@hiram.edu; Staff 5 (MLS 3, Non-MLS 2)
Founded 1900. Enrl 950; Fac 81; Highest Degree: Master
Jul 2015-Jun 2016. Mats Exp $271,040, Books $26,212, Per/Ser (Incl. Access Fees) $191,595, AV Mat $2,573, Electronic Ref Mat (Incl. Access Fees) $59,660. Sal $278,981 (Prof $203,857)
Library Holdings: CDs 20,669; DVDs 1,856; e-books 144,662; e-journals 10,214; Bk Vols 180,596; Per Subs 130; Videos 3,688
Special Collections: Education (Burke Aaron Hinsdale Coll, Textbooks 1773 to present & E B Wakefield Coll), corresp, ms; History (James A Garfield Coll & Henry Family Papers), corresp, ms; Literature (Nicholas Vachel Lindsay Coll & Juvenile Literature Coll 1828 to present), bks, corresp, ms, per. State Document Depository; US Document Depository
Subject Interests: Biology, Humanities
Automation Activity & Vendor Info: (Acquisitions) Innovative Interfaces, Inc; (Cataloging) Innovative Interfaces, Inc; (Circulation) Innovative Interfaces, Inc; (Discovery) EBSCO Discovery Service; (OPAC) Innovative Interfaces, Inc; (Serials) Innovative Interfaces, Inc
Wireless access
Function: ILL available, Photocopying/Printing, Ref serv available, Telephone ref
Publications: The Flyleaf (Newsletter)
Partic in Ohio Library & Information Network; OhioNET
Open Mon-Thurs 8am-11pm, Fri 8-6, Sat 9-5, Sun 1-11
Restriction: Circ limited, Non-circulating to the pub
Friends of the Library Group

HOLGATE

P HOLGATE COMMUNITY LIBRARY, 204 Railway Ave, 43527. SAN 313-5349. Tel: 419-264-7965. FAX: 419-264-1261. Web Site: holgatecommunitylibrary.com. *Dir,* Lynn Swary; E-mail: lynn71254@yahoo.com
Founded 1922. Pop 2,500; Circ 19,458
Library Holdings: Bk Titles 28,400; Per Subs 170
Automation Activity & Vendor Info: (Cataloging) SirsiDynix-Enterprise; (Circulation) SirsiDynix-Enterprise; (OPAC) SirsiDynix-Enterprise
Wireless access
Partic in NORWELD; Serving Every Ohioan Library Center
Open Mon & Tues 11-7, Wed & Fri 11-5, Thurs & Sat 9-Noon

HOMER

P HOMER PUBLIC LIBRARY*, 385 South St NW, 43027. (Mail add: PO Box 49, 43027-0049), SAN 313-5357. Tel: 740-892-2020. FAX: 740-892-2036. E-mail: homer@seolibraries.org. Web Site: www.homer.lib.oh.us. *Dir,* Amie Hatfield; E-mail: ahatfield@seolibraries.org; *Fiscal Officer,* Chet Geiger; Staff 3 (Non-MLS 3)
Founded 1895. Circ 36,600
Library Holdings: AV Mats 3,100; Bk Titles 30,000; Bk Vols 35,000; Per Subs 115
Special Collections: Antique Tractors; Homer History; Victoria Claflin Woodhull
Subject Interests: Agr
Automation Activity & Vendor Info: (Circulation) Follett Software; (OPAC) Follett Software
Wireless access
Partic in Serving Every Ohioan Library Center
Open Mon, Tues & Thurs 10-8, Wed 10-6, Fri 10-4, Sat 10-Noon

HUBBARD

P HUBBARD PUBLIC LIBRARY, 436 W Liberty St, 44425. SAN 313-5365. Tel: 330-534-3512. Web Site: www.beyond-books.org. *Dir,* Lorena Hegedus; E-mail: lorena@beyond-books.org; *Tech Adminr,* Molly Auchter; E-mail: molly@beyond-books.org; *Adult Serv Supvr,* Nathan Dempsey; E-mail: nate@beyond-books.org; *Circ Supvr, Tech Serv,* Charlene Helsel-Kather; E-mail: charlene@beyond-books.org; *Youth Serv,* Mary Anne Russo; E-mail: maryanne@beyond-books.org; Staff 6 (MLS 5, Non-MLS 1)
Founded 1937. Pop 13,552; Circ 261,309
Subject Interests: Local hist

Automation Activity & Vendor Info: (Cataloging) SirsiDynix-WorkFlows; (Circulation) SirsiDynix-WorkFlows; (Discovery) SirsiDynix-Enterprise; (OPAC) SirsiDynix-Enterprise
Wireless access
Function: 24/7 Electronic res, 24/7 Online cat, 3D Printer, Accelerated reader prog, Activity rm, Adult bk club, After school storytime, Audio & video playback equip for onsite use, Audiobks on Playaways & MP3, Audiobks via web, AV serv, Bk club(s), Bks on CD, Children's prog, Computer training, Computers for patron use, Digital talking bks, E-Readers, E-Reserves, Electronic databases & coll, Family literacy, Free DVD rentals, Govt ref serv, Health sci info serv, Holiday prog, Home delivery & serv to seniorr ctr & nursing homes, Homebound delivery serv, ILL available, Internet access, Jail serv, Life-long learning prog for all ages, Magazines, Mail & tel request accepted, Makerspace, Meeting rooms, Microfiche/film & reading machines, Movies, Museum passes, Music CDs, Notary serv, Online cat, Online ref, Outreach serv, Outside serv via phone, mail, e-mail & web, OverDrive digital audio bks, Photocopying/Printing, Preschool outreach, Printer for laptops & handheld devices, Prof lending libr, Prog for adults, Prog for children & young adult, Ref & res, Ref serv available, Res assist avail, Scanner, Senior outreach, STEM programs, Story hour, Study rm, Summer & winter reading prog, Summer reading prog, Tax forms, Teen prog, Telephone ref, Wheelchair accessible
Partic in CLEVNET
Special Services for the Deaf - TTY equip
Open Mon-Thurs 9-8, Fri & Sat 9-5
Friends of the Library Group

HUDSON

P HUDSON LIBRARY & HISTORICAL SOCIETY, 96 Library St, 44236-5122. SAN 313-5373. Tel: 330-653-6658. Administration Tel: 230-653-6658, Ext 1014. FAX: 330-650-3373. E-mail: AskUs@hudson.lib.oh.us. Web Site: www.hudsonlibrary.org. *Exec Dir,* E Leslie Polott; E-mail: Leslie.Polott@hudson.lib.oh.us; *Head, Adult Serv,* Polly Reynolds; *Head, Circ,* Marcy Shipley; *Head, Tech Serv,* Gretchen Myers; *Head, Youth Serv,* Laura Lehner; Staff 18 (MLS 13, Non-MLS 5)
Founded 1910. Pop 22,300; Circ 711,987
Library Holdings: Bk Titles 130,262; Per Subs 700
Special Collections: John Brown, Abolitionist Leader (Clarence S Gee), bks, holographs, pictures, clippings
Subject Interests: Genealogy
Automation Activity & Vendor Info: (Acquisitions) SirsiDynix; (Cataloging) SirsiDynix; (Circulation) SirsiDynix; (OPAC) SirsiDynix
Wireless access
Function: Archival coll, Art exhibits, CD-ROM, Homebound delivery serv, ILL available, Internet access, Music CDs, Photocopying/Printing, Prog for adults, Prog for children & young adult, Ref serv available, Summer reading prog, VHS videos, Wheelchair accessible
Publications: Books to Bytes (Newsletter)
Partic in CLEVNET; Northeast Ohio Regional Library System
Open Mon-Thurs 9-8, Fri & Sat 9-5
Friends of the Library Group

HURON

C BOWLING GREEN STATE UNIVERSITY*, Firelands College Library, One University Dr, 2nd Flr, 44839-9791. SAN 313-5381. Tel: 419-372-0739. FAX: 419-433-9696. Web Site: www.firelands.bgsu.edu/library. *Libr Dir,* Leo Mallias; Tel: 419-372-0681, E-mail: lmallia@bgsu.edu; *Libr Assoc,* Ms Clitha Mason; Tel: 419-372-0652, E-mail: clitham@bgsu.edu; Staff 5 (MLS 2, Non-MLS 3)
Founded 1968. Enrl 2,055; Fac 49; Highest Degree: Bachelor
Library Holdings: AV Mats 1,475; Bks on Deafness & Sign Lang 10; DVDs 13; Bk Titles 31,175; Bk Vols 40,000; Per Subs 249; Videos 734
Special Collections: Holocaust Teaching Resource Coll. State Document Depository
Subject Interests: Firelands of the Conn Western Reserve
Automation Activity & Vendor Info: (Cataloging) OCLC; (Circulation) Innovative Interfaces, Inc; (Course Reserve) Innovative Interfaces, Inc; (ILL) OCLC; (OPAC) Innovative Interfaces, Inc; (Serials) Innovative Interfaces, Inc
Wireless access
Function: Archival coll, Audio & video playback equip for onsite use, Computers for patron use, Doc delivery serv, E-Reserves, Electronic databases & coll, ILL available, Instruction & testing, Internet access, Online ref, Photocopying/Printing, Ref & res, Ref serv available, VHS videos
Publications: Firelands College Library Newsletter
Partic in Ohio Library & Information Network; OhioNET
Open Mon-Wed (Winter) 8am-7:30pm, Thurs & Fri 8-5; Mon-Fri (Summer) 8-5

P HURON PUBLIC LIBRARY*, 333 Williams St, 44839. SAN 313-539X. Tel: 419-433-5009. FAX: 419-433-7228. E-mail: huron@huronlibrary.org. Web Site: www.huronlibrary.org. *Dir,* Vikki Morrow-Ritchie; E-mail: vikki.morrow-ritchie@huronlibrary.org; *Head, Customer Serv, Head, Tech Serv,* Shelby Tillinghast; E-mail: shelby.tillinghast@huronlibrary.org; *Head, Pub Serv,* Holly Lynn; E-mail: holly.lynn@huronlibrary.org; *Head, Youth Serv,* Melissa Harrington; E-mail: melissa.harrington@huronlibrary.org; Staff 13 (MLS 3, Non-MLS 10)
Founded 1933. Pop 10,551; Circ 189,127
Wireless access
Function: 24/7 Electronic res, Accelerated reader prog, Activity rm, Adult bk club, Art exhibits, Audiobks via web, Bk club(s), Bks on CD, Chess club, Children's prog, Computer training, Computers for patron use, Digital talking bks, Electronic databases & coll, Free DVD rentals, Home delivery & serv to seniorr ctr & nursing homes, ILL available, Instruction & testing, Internet access, Jazz prog, Magazines, Magnifiers for reading, Music CDs, Notary serv, Online cat, OverDrive digital audio bks, Passport agency, Photocopying/Printing, Preschool outreach, Preschool reading prog, Prog for adults, Prog for children & young adult, Scanner, Story hour, Study rm, Summer reading prog, Tax forms, Teen prog, Telephone ref, Wheelchair accessible
Partic in CLEVNET
Special Services for the Deaf - TTY equip
Special Services for the Blind - Bks & mags in Braille, on rec, tape & cassette; Cassette playback machines
Open Mon-Thurs 9-8:30, Fri & Sat 9-5, Sun 1-5
Friends of the Library Group

INDEPENDENCE

CM KENT STATE UNIVERSITY COLLEGE OF PODIATRIC MEDICINE*, Morton & Norma Seidman & Dr Harvey & Sharon Kaplan Library & Media Center, 6000 Rockside Woods Blvd, 44131. SAN 313-3710. Tel: 216-916-7505. Web Site: www.kent.edu/cpm/library. *Dir, Libr Serv,* Donna Perzeski; Tel: 216-916-7506, E-mail: dperzesk@kent.edu
Enrl 300; Fac 25; Highest Degree: Doctorate
Wireless access
Open Mon-Fri 7am-10pm, Sat & Sun 9am-10pm

IRONTON

P BRIGGS LAWRENCE COUNTY PUBLIC LIBRARY*, Ironton Library, 321 S Fourth St, 45638. SAN 313-5446. Tel: 740-532-1124. FAX: 740-532-4948. Web Site: www.briggslibrary.com. *Exec Dir,* Joseph Jenkins; E-mail: jjenkins@briggslibrary.org; *Ch,* Jan Gullet; *Adult Serv,* Lori Shafer; Staff 44 (MLS 3, Non-MLS 41)
Founded 1881. Pop 61,834
Subject Interests: Genealogy, Local hist
Automation Activity & Vendor Info: (Cataloging) TLC (The Library Corporation); (Circulation) TLC (The Library Corporation); (OPAC) TLC (The Library Corporation)
Wireless access
Function: 24/7 Electronic res, 24/7 Online cat, Activity rm, Adult bk club, Art exhibits, Art programs, Audiobks via web, AV serv, Bk club(s), Bks on CD, Children's prog, Computer training, Computers for patron use, Electronic databases & coll, Free DVD rentals, Genealogy discussion group, Home delivery & serv to seniorr ctr & nursing homes, Homebound delivery serv, ILL available, Internet access, Magazines, Magnifiers for reading, Meeting rooms, Microfiche/film & reading machines, Movies, Music CDs, Online cat, Outreach serv, OverDrive digital audio bks, Photocopying/Printing, Preschool reading prog, Prog for adults, Prog for children & young adult, Ref serv available, Story hour, Summer reading prog, Tax forms, Teen prog, Visual arts prog, Wheelchair accessible
Partic in Ohio Public Library Information Network
Special Services for the Blind - Lending of low vision aids; Talking bks & player equip
Open Mon-Thurs 10-8, Fri & Sat 10-5
Friends of the Library Group
Branches: 4
CHESAPEAKE BRANCH, 11054 County Rd 1, Cheseapeake, 45619. Tel: 740-867-3390. FAX: 740-867-4881. *Br Mgr,* Tami Jones; E-mail: tjones@briggslibrary.org; Staff 2 (MLS 2)
Pop 60,000; Circ 66,000
Library Holdings: CDs 1,200; Bk Titles 20,000; Per Subs 30
Open Mon, Wed & Thurs 10-5:30, Tues 10-7:30, Fri & Sat 10-5
PROCTORSVILLE BRANCH, 410 Elizabeth St, Proctorville, 45669. Tel: 740-886-6697. FAX: 740-886-7175. Web Site: www.briggslibrary.org. *Librn,* Betty James; E-mail: bettyjames@briggslibrary.org
Founded 1990
Open Mon, Tues & Wed 10-5:30, Thurs 10-7:30, Fri & Sat 10-5
Friends of the Library Group
SOUTHERN, 317 Solida Rd, South Point, 45680. Tel: 740-377-2288. FAX: 740-377-9298. E-mail: aut@briggslibrary.org. *Br Mgr,* Alda Wagner; E-mail: awagner@briggslibrary.org
Open Mon 10-7:30, Tues-Thurs 10-5:30, Fri & Sat 10-5
Friends of the Library Group

SYMMES VALLEY BRANCH, 14778 State Rte 141, Willow Wood, 45696. Tel: 740-643-2086. FAX: 740-643-2086. *Br Mgr,* Becky Vissing; E-mail: bvissing@briggslibrary.org
Open Mon-Thurs (Winter) 3-8, Sat 10-3; Mon & Tues (Summer) 10-5:30, Wed, Thurs & Fri 10-3

L LAWRENCE COUNTY LAW LIBRARY ASSOCIATION*, Lawrence County Courthouse, 4th Flr Annex, 111 S Fourth St, 45638-1586. SAN 313-5454. Tel: 740-533-0582. FAX: 740-533-1084. E-mail: lawco.ohiolib@gmail.com. *Librn,* Sharon K Bradshaw
Founded 1911
Library Holdings: Bk Titles 15,000
Wireless access
Restriction: Not open to pub

C OHIO UNIVERSITY*, Southern Campus Library, Collins Ctr, 2nd Flr, 1804 Liberty Ave, 45638. SAN 313-5462. Tel: 740-533-4622. FAX: 740-533-4631. E-mail: ouslibrary@ohio.edu. Web Site: www.ohio.edu/southern/library. *Librn,* Mary J Stout; E-mail: stout@ohio.edu; Staff 4 (MLS 1, Non-MLS 3)
Founded 1956. Enrl 1,903; Highest Degree: Master
Library Holdings: Bk Vols 25,000; Per Subs 200
Special Collections: Catherine Toothman Coll; David E Carter Coll
Automation Activity & Vendor Info: (Acquisitions) Innovative Interfaces, Inc; (Cataloging) Innovative Interfaces, Inc; (Circulation) Innovative Interfaces, Inc; (OPAC) Innovative Interfaces, Inc; (Serials) Innovative Interfaces, Inc
Wireless access
Partic in OCLC Online Computer Library Center, Inc; OhioNET
Special Services for the Blind - ZoomText magnification & reading software
Open Mon-Thurs 8-6, Fri 8-5

JACKSON

P JACKSON CITY LIBRARY, 21 Broadway St, 45640-1695. SAN 313-5470. Tel: 740-286-4111. FAX: 740-286-2615. E-mail: jackson@jacksoncitylibrary.org. Web Site: www.jacksoncitylibrary.org. *Dir,* Roger Donaldson; E-mail: rdonaldson@jacksoncitylibrary.org; *Youth Serv,* Sharon Leali; Staff 1 (MLS 1)
Founded 1901. Pop 27,181; Circ 73,210
Library Holdings: Bk Vols 45,000; Per Subs 135
Special Collections: Appalachian Children's Books; Jackson County History & Genealogy
Subject Interests: Appalachian children's books, Genealogy, Jackson County hist
Wireless access
Open Mon-Thurs 9-6, Fri 10-5, Sat 10-2

L JACKSON COUNTY LAW LIBRARY*, 226 E Main St, 45640-1764. (Mail add: PO Box 882, 45640-0882). Tel: 740-286-5460. FAX: 740-288-2161. *Librn,* Joseph Kirby; E-mail: joe@colekirbylaw.com
Open Mon-Fri 8-4

JEFFERSON

L ASHTABULA COUNTY LAW LIBRARY*, County Courthouse, 25 W Jefferson St, 44047. SAN 372-1957. Tel: 440-576-3690. FAX: 440-576-1506. Web Site: courts.co.ashtabula.oh.us/law_library.htm. *Dir & Librn,* Shara H Parkomaki; E-mail: shparkomaki@ashtabulacounty.us; Staff 40 (Non-MLS 40)
Automation Activity & Vendor Info: (Cataloging) LibraryWorld, Inc
Wireless access
Open Mon-Fri 8-4:30
Restriction: Non-circulating

P HENDERSON MEMORIAL PUBLIC LIBRARY ASSOCIATION*, 54 E Jefferson St, 44047-1198. SAN 313-5489. Tel: 440-576-3761. FAX: 440-576-8402. Web Site: www.henderson.lib.oh.us. *Dir,* Beverly Follin; E-mail: bev.follin@hmpl.info; Staff 5 (MLS 2, Non-MLS 3)
Founded 1883. Pop 5,500; Circ 168,622
Library Holdings: Bk Vols 55,000
Automation Activity & Vendor Info: (Cataloging) SirsiDynix-WorkFlows; (Circulation) SirsiDynix-WorkFlows; (OPAC) SirsiDynix
Wireless access
Function: 24/7 Electronic res, 24/7 Online cat, Activity rm, Adult bk club, Art exhibits, Audiobks via web, AV serv, Bk club(s), Bks on CD, Chess club, Children's prog, Computer training, Computers for patron use, Electronic databases & coll, Free DVD rentals, Holiday prog, Home delivery & serv to seniorr ctr & nursing homes, Homebound delivery serv, Internet access, Laminating, Life-long learning prog for all ages, Magazines, Meeting rooms, Movies, Music CDs, Notary serv, Online cat, Online info literacy tutorials on the web & in blackboard, Online ref, Outreach serv, OverDrive digital audio bks, Photocopying/Printing, Preschool outreach, Printer for laptops & handheld devices, Prog for adults, Prog for children & young adult, Ref & res, Ref serv available, Scanner, Senior computer classes, Senior outreach, Story hour, Summer & winter reading prog, Summer reading prog, Tax forms, Teen prog, Telephone ref, Writing prog
Partic in CLEVNET; Northeast Ohio Regional Library System
Open Mon-Thurs 9-8, Fri & Sat 9-5, Sun 1-5

KENT

P KENT FREE LIBRARY*, 312 W Main, 44240-2493. SAN 313-5497. Tel: 330-673-4414. FAX: 330-673-0226. E-mail: kflinfo@kentfreelibrary.org. Web Site: www.kentfreelibrary.org. *Dir,* Stacey Richardson; E-mail: stacey.richardson@kentfreelibrary.org; *Commun Serv, Spec Serv Mgr,* Kristen Pool; E-mail: kristen.pool@kentfreelibrary.org; Staff 10 (MLS 10)
Founded 1892. Pop 33,704
Library Holdings: AV Mats 15,976; Bk Titles 160,686; Per Subs 363
Automation Activity & Vendor Info: (Acquisitions) Innovative Interfaces, Inc; (Cataloging) Innovative Interfaces, Inc; (Circulation) Innovative Interfaces, Inc; (OPAC) Innovative Interfaces, Inc; (Serials) Innovative Interfaces, Inc
Wireless access
Partic in Northeast Ohio Regional Library System; Portage Library Consortium
Open Mon-Thurs 9-9, Fri 9-6, Sat 9-5, Sun 1-5
Friends of the Library Group

C KENT STATE UNIVERSITY LIBRARIES, Risman Plaza, 1125 Risman Dr, 44242. (Mail add: PO Box 5190, 44242-0001), SAN 356-7001. Tel: 330-672-2962. Circulation Tel: 330-672-7905. Interlibrary Loan Service Tel: 330-672-2670. Reference Tel: 330-672-3150. FAX: 330-672-4811. Interlibrary Loan Service FAX: 330-672-2265. Reference FAX: 330-672-3964. E-mail: library@kent.edu. Web Site: library.kent.edu. *Dean,* Kenneth Burhanna; E-mail: kburhanna@kent.edu; *Assoc Dean,* Kara L Robinson; Tel: 330-672-1664, E-mail: krobinso@kent.edu; *Interim Asst Dean, Libr Dir,* Rob Kairis; Tel: 330-244-3326, E-mail: rkairis@kent.edu; *Asst Dean for Tech, Collections & Branch Libraries,* Mike Collura; Tel: 330-672-0499, E-mail: mcollura@kent.edu; *Head, Cat,* Margaret Maurer; Tel: 330-672-1702, E-mail: mbmaurer@kent.edu; *Head, Copyright & Scholarly Communication,* Cynthia Kristof; Tel: 330-672-1641, E-mail: ckristof@kent.edu; *Head, Project Mgmt,* Melissa Spohn; Tel: 330-672-1682, E-mail: mspohn@kent.edu; *Director, Circulation Services,* Kelly L Shook; Tel: 330-672-1648, E-mail: kshook2@kent.edu; *Spec Coll Librn,* Anita Clary; Tel: 330-672-2751, E-mail: aclary@kent.edu; *Acting University Archivist, Head, Spec Coll & Archives,* Cara Gilgenbach; Tel: 330-672-1677, E-mail: cgilgenb@kent.edu; *Copyright & Interlibrary Loan Associate,* Tony Snyder; Tel: 330-672-1634, E-mail: tsnyder5@kent.edu; Staff 84 (MLS 36, Non-MLS 48)
Founded 1913. Enrl 35,000; Fac 735; Highest Degree: Doctorate
Library Holdings: e-books 900,000; e-journals 120,000; Bk Vols 2,853,965; Per Subs 60,015
Special Collections: 19th & 20th Century American Literature Coll; Borowitz True Crime Coll; Contemporary American Poetry - especially James Broughton, Robert Duncan, Robert Frost, W C Williams; History of Books & Printing; Local Historical Archives Coll; May 4 Coll; Open Theater; Queen Marie of Rumania Coll; University Archives Coll. State Document Depository; UN Document Depository; US Document Depository
Automation Activity & Vendor Info: (Acquisitions) Innovative Interfaces, Inc; (Cataloging) Innovative Interfaces, Inc; (Circulation) Innovative Interfaces, Inc; (Course Reserve) Docutek; (ILL) OCLC; (Media Booking) Innovative Interfaces, Inc; (OPAC) Innovative Interfaces, Inc; (Serials) Innovative Interfaces, Inc
Wireless access
Function: Res libr
Publications: Footnotes
Partic in Association of Research Libraries; Center for Research Libraries; OCLC Online Computer Library Center, Inc; Ohio Library & Information Network
Restriction: 24-hr pass syst for students only
Friends of the Library Group

Departmental Libraries:

FASHION, Rockwell Hall, Rm 131, 515 Hilltop Dr, 44242, SAN 377-6344. Tel: 330-672-9500. FAX: 330-672-9578. E-mail: fashionlibrary@kent.edu. Web Site: library.kent.edu/fashion-library. *Head Librn,* Edith Serkownek; Tel: 330-672-9502, E-mail: eserkown@kent.edu; *Adjunct Librn,* Bryan Kvet; E-mail: bkvet@kent.edu; Staff 1.5 (MLS 1.5)

MAP, McGilvrey Hall, Rm 410, 325 S Lincoln St, 44242. (Mail add: PO Box 5190, 44242-5190), SAN 356-701X. Tel: 330-672-2017. E-mail: maplibrary@kent.edu. Web Site: library.kent.edu/map-library. *Head of Libr,* Michael Hawkins; Tel: 330-672-1663, E-mail: mhawki11@kent.edu
Library Holdings: Bk Titles 500; Bk Vols 3,000
Special Collections: California AAA Map Coll (Depository); GeoDEX AGS (Milwaukee); Sanborn Insurance Map & Atlas Coll
Subject Interests: Climate, Geog, Geol, Soils, Topography, Urban geog

JOSEPH F MORBITO ARCHITECTURE LIBRARY, 132 S Lincoln St, Rm 110E, 44242. (Mail add: PO Box 5190, 44242-5190), SAN 328-7572. Tel: 330-672-2876. E-mail: archlibrary@kent.edu. Web Site: library.kent.edu/architecture-library. *Head, Archit Libr,* Nick Fagan; Tel: 330-672-1637, E-mail: ngfagan@kent.edu; Staff 2 (MLS 1, Non-MLS 1)
Founded 1987. Enrl 550; Highest Degree: Master
Library Holdings: AV Mats 300; CDs 50; DVDs 25; Bk Vols 14,000; Per Subs 87
Special Collections: HABS & HAER Documentation, micro, print; HABS & HAER, print, micro; Historic Urban Plans & Views; Sanborn Fire Insurance Maps (online)
Subject Interests: Archit, Archit hist, Architects & firms, Architectural styles, Bldg types, Drawing & model making, Historic presv, Landscape archit, Mat & methods, Prof practice, Site planning, Structures, Sustainable architecture, Urban planning
Open Mon-Fri 9-5

PERFORMING ARTS, D-004 Center for Performing Arts, 1325 Theatre Dr, 44242. (Mail add: PO Box 5190, 44242), SAN 356-7052. Tel: 330-672-2004. FAX: 330-672-4482. E-mail: performingartslibrary@kent.edu. Web Site: library.kent.edu/performing-arts-library. *Head Librn,* Joe Clark; Tel: 330-672-1667, E-mail: jclark88@kent.edu; *Adjunct Librn,* Troy Cherrington; Tel: 330-672-2134, E-mail: tcherrin@kent.edu; Staff 3 (MLS 2, Non-MLS 1)
Enrl 400; Fac 40; Highest Degree: Doctorate
Library Holdings: CDs 5,000; DVDs 200; Music Scores 50,000; Bk Vols 90,000; Per Subs 150; Videos 600
Special Collections: Choralist Coll
Function: AV serv, Electronic databases & coll, Music CDs, Ref & res, VHS videos
Restriction: Open to students, fac & staff

KENTON

P MARY LOU JOHNSON HARDIN COUNTY DISTRICT LIBRARY, 325 E Columbus St, 43326-1546. SAN 313-5500. Tel: 419-673-2278. FAX: 419-674-4321. Web Site: mljlibrary.org. *Dir,* Samuel Norris; E-mail: snorris@mljlibrary.org; *Cat,* Marilyn Holland; Staff 14 (Non-MLS 14)
Founded 1853. Pop 34,000; Circ 174,000
Library Holdings: Audiobooks 4,418; AV Mats 7,927; Bk Vols 68,075; Per Subs 89
Special Collections: Playaways
Subject Interests: Genealogy
Automation Activity & Vendor Info: (Acquisitions) Innovative Interfaces, Inc; (Cataloging) Innovative Interfaces, Inc; (Circulation) Innovative Interfaces, Inc; (OPAC) Innovative Interfaces, Inc
Wireless access
Function: 24/7 Electronic res, 24/7 Online cat, 3D Printer, Accelerated reader prog, Activity rm, Adult bk club, After school storytime, Archival coll, Audiobks via web, Bilingual assistance for Spanish patrons, Bk club(s), Bks on CD, CD-ROM, Children's prog, Computer training, Computers for patron use, Digital talking bks, E-Readers, E-Reserves, Electronic databases & coll, For res purposes, Free DVD rentals, Holiday prog, Home delivery & serv to seniorr ctr & nursing homes, Homebound delivery serv, Homework prog, ILL available, Internet access, Laminating, Life-long learning prog for all ages, Magazines, Magnifiers for reading, Mail & tel request accepted, Meeting rooms, Microfiche/film & reading machines, Movies, Music CDs, Notary serv, Online cat, Outreach serv, OverDrive digital audio bks, Photocopying/Printing, Preschool outreach, Preschool reading prog, Printer for laptops & handheld devices, Prog for adults, Prog for children & young adult, Ref & res, Ref serv available, Res assist avail, Res performed for a fee, Scanner, Senior computer classes, Senior outreach, Serves people with intellectual disabilities, Spanish lang bks, STEM programs, Story hour, Study rm, Summer reading prog, Tax forms, Teen prog, Wheelchair accessible
Partic in NORWELD; Ohio Libr Coun; OhioNET; State Libr of Ohio
Special Services for the Deaf - Assisted listening device
Special Services for the Blind - Accessible computers; Assistive/Adapted tech devices, equip & products; BiFolkal kits; Bks available with recordings; Bks on CD; Copier with enlargement capabilities; Low vision equip; Talking bk serv referral
Open Mon-Thurs 9-8, Fri & Sat 9-5

KETTERING

CM KETTERING COLLEGE*, Learning Commons, 3737 Southern Blvd, 45429-1299. SAN 356-7060. Tel: 937-395-8053. FAX: 937-395-8861. Web Site: www.kc.edu/library. *Cat, Interim Dir,* Pamela Stevens; Tel: 937-395-8053, Ext 4, E-mail: pamela.stevens@kc.edu; *Ref Librn,* Kathy Salgado; Tel: 937-395-8053, Ext 6; *Circ,* Stella Freeman; Tel: 937-395-8053, Ext 3; Staff 3 (MLS 2, Non-MLS 1)
Founded 1967. Enrl 725; Fac 79; Highest Degree: Doctorate
Jan 2019-Dec 2019. Mats Exp $171,100, Books $47,500, Per/Ser (Incl. Access Fees) $73,600, AV Mat $50,000
Library Holdings: Audiobooks 193; AV Mats 4,568; e-books 966; e-journals 160; Bk Titles 24,341; Bk Vols 25,853; Per Subs 211
Subject Interests: Allied health, Nursing, Seventh Day Adventists
Automation Activity & Vendor Info: (Cataloging) Innovative Interfaces, Inc; (Circulation) Innovative Interfaces, Inc; (Discovery) EBSCO Discovery Service; (ILL) OCLC; (OPAC) Innovative Interfaces, Inc; (Serials) Innovative Interfaces, Inc
Wireless access
Partic in Ohio Library & Information Network; OhioNET; Southwestern Ohio Council for Higher Education
Open Mon-Thurs 8am-9pm, Fri 8-2:30
Friends of the Library Group

KINGSVILLE

P KINGSVILLE PUBLIC LIBRARY*, 6006 Academy St, 44048. (Mail add: PO Box 57, 44048-0057), SAN 313-5535. Tel: 440-224-0239. FAX: 440-224-0029. Web Site: www.kingsville.lib.oh.us. *Dir,* Mariana Branch; E-mail: mariana.branch@kingsvillelibrary.org
Founded 1886. Circ 114,214
Library Holdings: Audiobooks 1,355; DVDs 2,307; Bk Vols 46,530; Per Subs 148; Videos 300
Special Collections: Local Estate Memoriabilia; Local History
Subject Interests: Circulating per, Current best sellers, Hobbies
Wireless access
Function: Homebound delivery serv, Prog for children & young adult, Wheelchair accessible
Partic in Independently Cooperating Ashtabula Network; Ohio Libr Coun
Special Services for the Deaf - TDD equip
Open Mon-Thurs 9-7, Fri 9-6, Sat 9-4
Friends of the Library Group

KINSMAN

P KINSMAN FREE PUBLIC LIBRARY*, 6420 Church St, 44428-9702. (Mail add: PO Box 166, 44428-0166), SAN 313-5543. Tel: 330-876-2461. FAX: 330-876-3335. Reference E-mail: Reference@kinsmanlibrary.org. Web Site: www.kinsmanlibrary.org. *Dir,* Kimberly Danielle Garrett; Tel: 330-876-2461, E-mail: kimg@kinsmanlibrary.org; Staff 6 (MLS 1, Non-MLS 5)
Founded 1885. Pop 6,496; Circ 152,379
Special Collections: Clarence Darrow Coll; Dr Ernest L Scott Coll
Wireless access
Function: 24/7 Electronic res, 24/7 Online cat, Activity rm, Adult bk club
Partic in CLEVNET
Open Mon, Wed & Fri 9-5, Tues & Thurs 11-7, Sat 9-1
Friends of the Library Group

KIRTLAND

S HERB SOCIETY OF AMERICA LIBRARY*, 9019 Kirtland Chardon Rd, 44094. SAN 329-4978. Tel: 440-256-0514. FAX: 440-256-0541. E-mail: library@herbsociety.org. Web Site: www.herbsociety.org/hsa-learn/hsa-library. Staff 1 (Non-MLS 1)
Founded 1944
Library Holdings: Bk Vols 3,800; Per Subs 24; Videos 30
Special Collections: Rare Herbals
Subject Interests: Ethnobotany, Folklore, Herbs, Hort
Function: Online cat, Ref serv available
Special Services for the Blind - Braille bks
Open Mon-Thurs 9-3
Restriction: Circ to mem only, In-house use for visitors, Non-circulating of rare bks
Friends of the Library Group

S HOLDEN ARBORETUM*, Warren H Corning Library, 9550 Sperry Rd, 44094. SAN 313-6116. Tel: 440-946-4400, Ext 225. FAX: 440-256-5836. E-mail: holden@holdenarb.org. Web Site: www.holdenarb.org. *Interim Librn,* Catherine Wells; E-mail: cwells@holdenarb.org; Staff 2 (MLS 2)
Founded 1963
Library Holdings: Bk Titles 8,000; Bk Vols 9,000; Per Subs 60
Special Collections: Warren H Corning Horticulture Classics, 1200 vols
Subject Interests: Botany, Environ studies, Hort, Natural hist, Natural sci
Automation Activity & Vendor Info: (Cataloging) EOS International; (Circulation) EOS International; (OPAC) EOS International; (Serials) EOS International
Publications: Arbor Day Resources (List of materials available for use at the Corning Library); Native Woody Plant Resources (List of materials for use at the Corning Library)
Partic in Northeast Ohio Regional Library System
Open Tues-Sat 10-5

P KIRTLAND PUBLIC LIBRARY*, 9267 Chillicothe Rd, 44094. SAN 313-5551. Tel: 440-256-7323. FAX: 440-256-1372. Reference E-mail: kirtland.library@kirtland.lib.oh.us. Web Site: www.kirtland.lib.oh.us. *Dir,*

Jane R Carle; E-mail: jcarle@kirtland.lib.oh.us; *Ref Serv, Ad,* Gina Barkett; E-mail: gbarkett@kirtland.lib.oh.us; Staff 10 (MLS 3, Non-MLS 7)
Founded 1936. Pop 7,600; Circ 207,879
Library Holdings: AV Mats 5,177; Large Print Bks 2,130; Bk Titles 65,597; Per Subs 265; Talking Bks 2,343
Subject Interests: Local hist
Automation Activity & Vendor Info: (Circulation) SirsiDynix
Function: Wheelchair accessible
Partic in CLEVNET; Northeast Ohio Regional Library System
Open Mon-Thurs 9-9, Fri 9-6, Sat 9-5, Sun 12-4
Friends of the Library Group

J LAKELAND COMMUNITY COLLEGE LIBRARY*, Bldg C, Rm 3051, 7700 Clocktower Dr, 44094-5198. SAN 313-6132. Tel: 440-525-7069. Circulation Tel: 440-525-7424. Reference Tel: 440-525-7425. FAX: 440-525-7602. E-mail: lakelandlibrary@lakelandcc.edu. Web Site: lakelandcc.edu/library. *Chairperson, Ref (Info Servs),* Michelle Rossman; E-mail: mrossman@lakelandcc.edu; Staff 10 (MLS 3, Non-MLS 7)
Founded 1967. Enrl 4,300
Library Holdings: Bk Titles 46,000; Bk Vols 57,000; Per Subs 600
Automation Activity & Vendor Info: (Acquisitions) Innovative Interfaces, Inc; (Cataloging) Innovative Interfaces, Inc; (Circulation) Innovative Interfaces, Inc; (Course Reserve) Innovative Interfaces, Inc; (Media Booking) Innovative Interfaces, Inc; (OPAC) Innovative Interfaces, Inc; (Serials) Innovative Interfaces, Inc
Wireless access
Partic in East Central Illinois Consortium; Northeast Ohio Regional Library System; Ohio Library & Information Network
Open Mon-Thurs (Summer) 8-8, Fri 8-Noon; Mon-Thurs (Winter) 8am-9pm, Fri 9-5, Sat 9-1

LAKEWOOD

S LAKEWOOD HISTORICAL SOCIETY LIBRARY*, 14710 Lake Ave, 44107. SAN 329-9546. Tel: 216-221-7343. E-mail: museum@lakewoodhistory.org. Web Site: lakewoodhistory.org. *Exec Dir,* Gregory Palumbo; E-mail: director@lakewoodhistory.org; *Curator,* Jessamyn Yenni; E-mail: curator@lakewoodhistory.org
Library Holdings: Bk Vols 200
Subject Interests: Lakewood, Rockport Township
Publications: Lakewood: The First Hundred Years
Restriction: Open by appt only

P LAKEWOOD PUBLIC LIBRARY, 15425 Detroit Ave, 44107. SAN 356-7125. Tel: 216-226-8275. Web Site: www.lakewoodpubliclibrary.org. *Dir,* James Crawford; E-mail: jcrawford@lkwdpl.org
Founded 1916. Pop 56,646
Wireless access
Open Mon-Thurs 9-9, Fri & Sat 9-6
Friends of the Library Group
Branches: 1
MADISON, 13427 Madison Ave, 44107, SAN 356-715X. Tel: 216-228-7428. *Br Mgr,* Judy Grzybowski
Open Mon-Sat 9-6
Friends of the Library Group

LANCASTER

P FAIRFIELD COUNTY DISTRICT LIBRARY*, 219 N Broad St, 43130-3098. SAN 356-7184. Tel: 740-653-2745. FAX: 740-653-4199. Web Site: www.fcdlibrary.org. *Libr Dir,* Becky Schaade; E-mail: bschaade@fcdlibrary.org; *Coord, Ad Serv,* Lea Carrigan; E-mail: lcarrigan@fcdlibrary.org; *Coordr, Circ & Customer Serv,* Samantha Betts; E-mail: sbetts@fcdlibrary.org; *Coordr, Info Tech & Tech Serv,* Ruchie Rice; E-mail: rrice@fcdlibrary.org; *Fiscal Officer,* Alyssa England; E-mail: aengland@fcdlibrary.org; Staff 60 (MLS 10, Non-MLS 50)
Founded 1878. Pop 97,138; Circ 1,019,248
Jan 2015-Dec 2015 Income (Main & Associated Libraries) $3,673,938, State $2,475,401, Federal $19,097, Locally Generated Income $1,081,248, Other $98,192. Mats Exp $420,266, Books $220,127, Per/Ser (Incl. Access Fees) $19,718, AV Equip $41,960, AV Mat $117,659, Electronic Ref Mat (Incl. Access Fees) $20,802. Sal $1,626,390
Library Holdings: Audiobooks 13,000; CDs 13,000; DVDs 41,664; e-books 165,594; Bk Vols 211,175; Per Subs 308
Special Collections: History of Fairfield County & Lancaster
Automation Activity & Vendor Info: (Acquisitions) Innovative Interfaces, Inc; (Cataloging) Innovative Interfaces, Inc; (Circulation) Innovative Interfaces, Inc; (ILL) OCLC; (OPAC) Innovative Interfaces, Inc; (Serials) Innovative Interfaces, Inc
Wireless access
Function: 24/7 Electronic res, 24/7 Online cat, Accelerated reader prog, Activity rm, Adult bk club, Adult literacy prog, After school storytime, Archival coll, Art exhibits, Audiobks via web, Bk club(s), Bks on CD, CD-ROM, Children's prog, Computer training, Computers for patron use, Digital talking bks, E-Reserves, Electronic databases & coll, Free DVD rentals, Holiday prog, Home delivery & serv to seniorr ctr & nursing homes, Homebound delivery serv, ILL available, Internet access, Large print keyboards, Magazines, Magnifiers for reading, Mail & tel request accepted, Mango lang, Meeting rooms, Microfiche/film & reading machines, Music CDs, Online cat, Online info literacy tutorials on the web & in blackboard, Online ref, Orientations, Outreach serv, OverDrive digital audio bks, Photocopying/Printing, Preschool outreach, Preschool reading prog, Prog for adults, Prog for children & young adult, Ref & res, Ref serv available, Scanner, Senior computer classes, Senior outreach, Story hour, Study rm, Summer & winter reading prog, Summer reading prog, Tax forms, Teen prog, Telephone ref, Wheelchair accessible, Winter reading prog
Publications: Keywords (Quarterly)
Partic in Central Library Consortium
Special Services for the Deaf - ADA equip; Bks on deafness & sign lang
Special Services for the Blind - Bks on CD; Copier with enlargement capabilities; Extensive large print coll; Low vision equip; Playaways (bks on MP3)
Open Mon, Tues & Thurs 10-8, Wed & Sat 10-5, Fri 12-5, Sun 1-5
Restriction: Circ limited
Friends of the Library Group
Branches: 4
BALTIMORE BRANCH / GRILEY MEMORIAL, 205 E Market St, Baltimore, 43105, SAN 356-7214. Tel: 740-862-8505. *Br Mgr,* Debbie Fields; E-mail: dfields@fcdlibrary.org; Staff 4 (MLS 1, Non-MLS 3)
Circ 80,590
Function: 24/7 Electronic res, 24/7 Online cat, Activity rm, After school storytime, Audiobks via web, Bks on CD, Children's prog, Computers for patron use, Digital talking bks, E-Reserves, Electronic databases & coll, Free DVD rentals, Holiday prog, Homebound delivery serv, ILL available, Internet access, Magazines, Mail & tel request accepted, Mango lang, Meeting rooms, Music CDs, Online cat, OverDrive digital audio bks, Photocopying/Printing, Preschool reading prog, Prog for children & young adult, Ref serv available, Spoken cassettes & CDs, Story hour, Summer & winter reading prog, Tax forms, Telephone ref, Wheelchair accessible, Winter reading prog
Open Mon, Tues & Thurs 10-7, Wed & Fri 10-5, Sun 1-5
Restriction: Circ limited
Friends of the Library Group
BREMEN RUSHCREEK MEMORIAL BRANCH, 200 School St, Bremen, 43107, SAN 356-7249. Tel: 740-569-7246. *Br Mgr,* Debbie Fields; E-mail: dfields@fcdlibrary.org; Staff 5 (MLS 1, Non-MLS 4)
Automation Activity & Vendor Info: (Circulation) Innovative Interfaces, Inc; (OPAC) Innovative Interfaces, Inc
Function: 24/7 Electronic res, 24/7 Online cat, Activity rm, After school storytime, Bks on CD, Children's prog, Computer training, Computers for patron use, Digital talking bks, E-Reserves, Electronic databases & coll, Family literacy, Free DVD rentals, Holiday prog, Homebound delivery serv, ILL available, Internet access, Magazines, Mango lang, Music CDs, Online cat, Outreach serv, OverDrive digital audio bks, Photocopying/Printing, Preschool reading prog, Prog for children & young adult, Ref serv available, Senior computer classes, Story hour, Summer & winter reading prog, Summer reading prog, Tax forms, Telephone ref, Wheelchair accessible, Winter reading prog
Open Tues-Thurs 10-7, Fri 10-5, Sat 10-2
Friends of the Library Group
JOHNS MEMORIAL BRANCH, 116 E High St, Amanda, 43102. (Mail add: PO Box 279, Amanda, 43102-0279), SAN 329-2258. Tel: 740-969-2785. *Br Mgr,* Debbie Fields; E-mail: dfields@fcdlibrary.org; Staff 3 (MLS 1, Non-MLS 2)
Automation Activity & Vendor Info: (Acquisitions) Innovative Interfaces, Inc; (Circulation) Innovative Interfaces, Inc; (OPAC) Innovative Interfaces, Inc
Function: 24/7 Electronic res, 24/7 Online cat, After school storytime, Bks on CD, CD-ROM, Children's prog, Computer training, Computers for patron use, Digital talking bks, E-Reserves, Electronic databases & coll, Free DVD rentals, Holiday prog, Home delivery & serv to seniorr ctr & nursing homes, ILL available, Internet access, Magazines, Mango lang, Music CDs, Online cat, Outreach serv, OverDrive digital audio bks, Photocopying/Printing, Preschool reading prog, Prog for children & young adult, Ref serv available, Senior computer classes, Story hour, Summer & winter reading prog, Summer reading prog, Tax forms, Wheelchair accessible, Winter reading prog
Open Mon, Tues & Thurs 10-7, Wed 10-5, Sat 10-2
Friends of the Library Group
NORTHWEST BRANCH, 2855 Helena Dr NW, Carroll, 43112. Tel: 740-756-4391. *Br Mgr,* Shannon Smith; E-mail: ssmith@fcdlibrary.org; *Mgr, Tech Serv,* Allison Moore; E-mail: amoore@fcdlibrary.org; Staff 8 (MLS 2, Non-MLS 6)
Circ 51,165
Automation Activity & Vendor Info: (Cataloging) Innovative Interfaces, Inc; (Circulation) Innovative Interfaces, Inc; (OPAC) Innovative Interfaces, Inc
Function: 24/7 Electronic res, 24/7 Online cat, Activity rm, Bks on CD, Children's prog, Computer training, Computers for patron use, Digital

talking bks, E-Reserves, Electronic databases & coll, Family literacy, Free DVD rentals, Holiday prog, Homebound delivery serv, ILL available, Internet access, Learning ctr, Magazines, Mango lang, Music CDs, Online cat, Outreach serv, OverDrive digital audio bks, Photocopying/Printing, Preschool outreach, Preschool reading prog, Prog for children & young adult, Ref serv available, Senior computer classes, Story hour, Study rm, Summer & winter reading prog, Summer reading prog, Tax forms, Wheelchair accessible, Winter reading prog
Open Tues, Wed & Thurs 10-7, Fri 10-5, Sat 10-2, Sun 1-5
Friends of the Library Group

C OHIO UNIVERSITY-LANCASTER LIBRARY*, Hannah V McCauley Library, 1570 Granville Pike, 43130-1097. SAN 313-5608. Tel: 740-681-3350. Web Site: www.ohio.edu/lancaster/library. *Dir, Libr Serv,* Judy Carey Nevin; Tel: 740-681-3351, E-mail: careynev@ohio.edu; *Ref Librn,* Julia Robinson; Tel: 740-681-3348, E-mail: robinsj1@ohio.edu; Staff 4 (MLS 3, Non-MLS 1)
Founded 1956. Enrl 2,300; Fac 150; Highest Degree: Master
Library Holdings: AV Mats 1,000; Bks on Deafness & Sign Lang 322; e-books 2,000; Bk Titles 55,000; Per Subs 267; Talking Bks 20
Special Collections: Charles Goslin Coll; Herbert M Turner Pioneer Coll
Automation Activity & Vendor Info: (Cataloging) OCLC; (Circulation) Innovative Interfaces, Inc; (Course Reserve) Innovative Interfaces, Inc; (OPAC) Innovative Interfaces, Inc; (Serials) Innovative Interfaces, Inc
Wireless access
Function: Art exhibits, AV serv, Computers for patron use, Doc delivery serv, E-Reserves, Equip loans & repairs, Free DVD rentals, ILL available, Instruction & testing, Learning ctr, Online cat, Photocopying/Printing, Ref serv available, Scanner, Wheelchair accessible
Partic in OCLC Online Computer Library Center, Inc; Ohio Library & Information Network; OhioNET
Open Mon-Thurs (Fall-Spring) 8-7, Fri 8-5; Mon-Fri (Summer) 8-5
Friends of the Library Group

LEAVITTSBURG

S STATE OF OHIO DEPARTMENT OF CORRECTIONS*, Trumbull Correctional Institution Library, 5701 Burnette Rd, 44430. (Mail add: PO Box 901, 44430-0901). Tel: 330-898-0820, Ext 7408. FAX: 330-898-2011. *Librn,* Diane Filkorn; E-mail: diane.filkorn@odrc.state.oh.us
Library Holdings: Bk Vols 10,344; Per Subs 66
Restriction: Not open to pub

LEBANON

S LEBANON CORRECTIONAL INSTITUTION LIBRARY*, 3791 State Rd 63, 45036. (Mail add: PO Box 56, 45036), SAN 313-5624. Tel: 513-932-1211. FAX: 513-932-5803. *Librn,* Billy Bailey; Staff 1 (MLS 1)
Founded 1961
Library Holdings: Bk Vols 12,000
Subject Interests: Law

P LEBANON PUBLIC LIBRARY*, 101 S Broadway, 45036. SAN 313-5632. Tel: 513-932-2665. FAX: 513-932-7323. Web Site: www.lebanonlibrary.org. *Dir,* Julie K Sanvidge; *Ch,* Connie LaVallee; *Tech Ctr Supvr,* Robb White; *Acq,* Dylan Posa; E-mail: dylanposa@lebanonlibrary.org; *Ch Serv,* Marissa M Redenbaugh; *Circ,* Barb S Leitschuh
Founded 1904. Pop 41,000; Circ 432,000
Library Holdings: Bk Vols 153,000; Per Subs 70
Wireless access
Function: 24/7 Electronic res, 24/7 Online cat, Adult bk club, Adult literacy prog, Audiobks on Playaways & MP3, Audiobks via web, Bk club(s), Bks on CD, Children's prog, Computer training, Computers for patron use, E-Reserves, Electronic databases & coll, Home delivery & serv to seniorr ctr & nursing homes, Homebound delivery serv, ILL available, Online cat, Photocopying/Printing, Preschool outreach, Prog for adults, Ref serv available, Story hour, Summer reading prog, Tax forms, Teen prog, Telephone ref
Open Mon-Thurs 10-8, Fri & Sat 9-5, Sun (Oct-April) 1-4

S WARREN COUNTY HISTORICAL SOCIETY, Research Library, 105 S Broadway, 45036. SAN 327-7283. Tel: 513-932-1817. FAX: 513-932-8560. E-mail: wchs@wchsmuseum.org. Web Site: www.wchsmuseum.org. *Exec Dir,* Dr Michael L Coyan; *Educ Dir, Historian,* John J Zimkus
Founded 1945
Library Holdings: Bk Titles 10,000; Per Subs 20
Special Collections: Genealogical & History of Warren County & Southwest Ohio in General; Marcus Mote Coll; Russel Wright Coll; Shaker Coll
Open Tues-Fri 9-4, Sat 10-5

GL WARREN COUNTY LAW LIBRARY ASSOCIATION, 500 Justice Dr, 45036. SAN 313-5640. Tel: 513-695-1309. FAX: 513-695-2947. Web Site: www.warrenbar.org/member.htm. *Exec Secy,* Lisa M Cook; E-mail: cooklm@co.warren.oh.us
Library Holdings: Bk Vols 5,600
Special Collections: Ohio Law
Wireless access
Open Mon & Tues 1-4:30

LEETONIA

P LEETONIA COMMUNITY PUBLIC LIBRARY*, 181 Walnut St, 44431. SAN 313-5659. Tel: 330-427-6635. FAX: 330-427-2378. E-mail: leetonialibrary@gmail.com. Web Site: www.leetonialibrary.org. *Dir,* Christopher Simmons; E-mail: cs.leetonialibrary@gmail.com; Staff 2 (MLS 2)
Founded 1935. Pop 2,400; Circ 51,376
Jan 2015-Dec 2015 Income $235,924. Mats Exp $15,840, Books $11,994, Per/Ser (Incl. Access Fees) $1,846, AV Mat $2,000. Sal $141,404
Library Holdings: Bk Vols 41,009; Per Subs 42
Wireless access
Function: 24/7 Electronic res, 24/7 Online cat, Activity rm, Adult bk club, Adult literacy prog, After school storytime, Archival coll, Bi-weekly Writer's Group, Bk club(s), Bks on CD, Children's prog, Computer training, Computers for patron use, E-Readers, E-Reserves, Electronic databases & coll, Free DVD rentals, Holiday prog, Homebound delivery serv, ILL available, Instruction & testing, Internet access, Laminating, Magazines, Mail & tel request accepted, Microfiche/film & reading machines, Movies, Music CDs, Notary serv, Online cat, OverDrive digital audio bks, Photocopying/Printing, Preschool outreach, Preschool reading prog, Prog for adults, Prog for children & young adult, Ref serv available, Scanner, Senior computer classes, Story hour, Study rm, Summer & winter reading prog, Tax forms, Teen prog, Telephone ref, Workshops
Partic in Serving Every Ohioan Library Center
Open Mon, Tues & Thurs 9:30-7, Wed, Fri & Sat 9:30-4
Friends of the Library Group

LEWISBURG

P BROWN MEMORIAL LIBRARY, 101 S Commerce St, 45338. (Mail add: PO Box 640, 45338-0640), SAN 313-5667. Tel: 937-962-2377. FAX: 937-962-1010. Web Site: brownmemorial.lib.oh.us. *Dir,* Mary Ellen Lakes; E-mail: mlakes@seolibraries.org; Staff 5 (Non-MLS 5)
Founded 1935. Pop 1,790; Circ 51,209
Library Holdings: Bks on Deafness & Sign Lang 10; Large Print Bks 370; Bk Vols 24,000; Per Subs 35; Talking Bks 530
Automation Activity & Vendor Info: (Circulation) SirsiDynix-Enterprise; (OPAC) SirsiDynix-Enterprise
Wireless access
Partic in Miami Valley Librs; Serving Every Ohioan Library Center
Open Mon-Thurs 10-8, Sat 10-3

LIBERTY CENTER

P LIBERTY CENTER PUBLIC LIBRARY*, 124 East St, 43532. (Mail add: PO Box 66, 43532), SAN 313-5675. Tel: 419-533-5721. FAX: 419-533-4849. Web Site: www.libertycenterlibrary.org. *Dir,* Arla Marie Fry; E-mail: afry@libertycenterlibrary.org; Staff 6 (Non-MLS 6)
Founded 1929. Pop 5,647; Circ 35,937
Automation Activity & Vendor Info: (Cataloging) SirsiDynix; (Circulation) SirsiDynix; (ILL) SirsiDynix; (OPAC) SirsiDynix
Wireless access
Function: 24/7 Electronic res, 24/7 Online cat, Activity rm, Adult bk club, After school storytime, Audiobks via web, Bk club(s), Bks on CD, Children's prog, Computers for patron use, Free DVD rentals, Internet access, Laminating, Magazines, Meeting rooms, Movies, Online cat, OverDrive digital audio bks, Preschool outreach, Prog for adults, Scanner, Study rm, Summer reading prog, Teen prog, Wheelchair accessible
Partic in NORWELD; Serving Every Ohioan Library Center
Open Mon, Tues & Thurs 10-8, Wed & Fri 10-5, Sat 9-3
Friends of the Library Group

LIMA

S ALLEN COUNTY HISTORICAL SOCIETY*, Elizabeth M MacDonell Memorial Library, 620 W Market St, 45801. SAN 313-5683. Tel: 419-222-9426. FAX: 419-222-0649. E-mail: acmuseum@wcoil.com. Web Site: www.allencountymuseum.org/ACM2/Library.html. *Dir,* Amy Craft; E-mail: acraft@wcoil.com; *Curator of Archives, Curator of Ms, Librn,* Anna B Selfridge; E-mail: aselfridge@wcoil.com; Staff 1 (MLS 1)
Founded 1908
Library Holdings: Bk Titles 10,000; Per Subs 45
Special Collections: History of Ohio, Local History & Genealogy, archives, bks, clippings, micro, ms, photo; Labor, Railroad & Interurban History (John H Keller Railroad & Lima Locomotive Works Coll)
Automation Activity & Vendor Info: (Cataloging) EOS International

Function: Archival coll, Bus archives, For res purposes, ILL available, Photocopying/Printing, Ref & res
Publications: Allen County Historical Society Newsletter; The Allen County Reporter
Open Tues-Fri 1-5, Sat 1-4
Restriction: Non-circulating, Not a lending libr, Open to pub for ref only, Pub use on premises

S ALLEN-OAKWOOD CORRECTIONAL FACILITY LIBRARY*, 2338 N West St, 45801. SAN 313-5713. Tel: 419-225-8000. FAX: 419-224-5828. *Librn,* Denise Carter
Library Holdings: Audiobooks 55; AV Mats 715; CDs 12; DVDs 47; Large Print Bks 50; Bk Titles 4,000; Per Subs 12; Videos 700
Subject Interests: Music, Video
Special Services for the Blind - Bks on cassette
Restriction: Not open to pub

G ALLEN OAKWOOD CORRECTIONAL INSTITUTION LIBRARY*, 2338 N West St, 45801. (Mail add: PO Box 4501, 45802), SAN 323-8237. Tel: 419-224-8000. *Librn,* Denise Carter
Founded 1987
Library Holdings: Bks on Deafness & Sign Lang 4; DVDs 21; High Interest/Low Vocabulary Bk Vols 196; Large Print Bks 163; Bk Titles 14,168; Bk Vols 15,432; Per Subs 73; Videos 848
Special Collections: Afro-American Coll; Law Library; Native American Coll; Re-Entry Coll; Spanish Coll
Automation Activity & Vendor Info: (Acquisitions) Mandarin Library Automation; (Cataloging) Mandarin Library Automation; (Circulation) Mandarin Library Automation; (OPAC) Mandarin Library Automation
Special Services for the Blind - Bks on cassette; Bks on CD
Restriction: Non-circulating to the pub, Staff & inmates only

P LIMA PUBLIC LIBRARY*, 650 W Market St, 45801. SAN 356-7303. Tel: 419-228-5113. FAX: 419-224-2669. Web Site: www.limalibrary.com. *Dir,* Gary Fraser; E-mail: fraser@limalibrary.com; *Head of Br Serv, Head, Youth Serv,* Debbie Buettner; E-mail: buettnerd@limalibrary.com; Staff 48 (MLS 15, Non-MLS 33)
Founded 1884. Pop 89,689; Circ 847,557
Library Holdings: AV Mats 56,385; CDs 15,000; DVDs 17,463; e-books 8,334; Large Print Bks 12,474; Bk Vols 344,288; Per Subs 634; Talking Bks 6,774; Videos 896
Special Collections: Art-Architecture Coll; Jewish Culture; Judaic Materials (Dorfmann Coll). State Document Depository; US Document Depository
Subject Interests: Bibliographies
Automation Activity & Vendor Info: (Acquisitions) TLC (The Library Corporation); (Cataloging) TLC (The Library Corporation); (Circulation) TLC (The Library Corporation)
Wireless access
Function: Computers for patron use, E-Reserves, Electronic databases & coll, Home delivery & serv to seniorr ctr & nursing homes, Homebound delivery serv, ILL available, Internet access, Jail serv, Magnifiers for reading, Mail & tel request accepted, Music CDs, Online cat, Online ref, Outreach serv, Outside serv via phone, mail, e-mail & web, OverDrive digital audio bks, Photocopying/Printing, Preschool outreach, Prog for adults, Prog for children & young adult, Ref & res, Ref serv available, Res performed for a fee, Senior computer classes, Spoken cassettes & DVDs, Story hour, Summer reading prog, Tax forms, Teen prog, Telephone ref, VHS videos, Wheelchair accessible
Partic in OCLC Online Computer Library Center, Inc
Special Services for the Blind - Talking bks
Open Mon, Tues & Thurs 9-8, Wed, Fri & Sat 9-5
Friends of the Library Group
Branches: 4
CAIRO BRANCH, 108 Everrett Dr, Cairo, 45820. (Mail add: PO Box 216, Cairo, 45820-0216), SAN 356-7338. Tel: 419-641-7744. FAX: 419-641-6274. *Libr Assoc,* Kim Sciranka; E-mail: scirankak@limalibrary.com; Staff 2 (Non-MLS 2)
Library Holdings: Bk Vols 11,078
Open Mon & Tues 12-8, Thurs 10-6, Fri & Sat 9-1
Friends of the Library Group
ELIDA BRANCH, 500 E Kiracofe Ave, Elida, 45807, SAN 356-7362. Tel: 419-339-6097. FAX: 419-339-6554. *Libr Assoc,* Sue Wildermuth; E-mail: wildermuths@limalibrary.com
Library Holdings: Bk Vols 13,235
Open Mon & Tue 12-8, Thurs 10-6, Fri & Sat 9-1
Friends of the Library Group
LAFAYETTE BRANCH, 225 E Sugar St, Lafayette, 45854, SAN 356-7427. Tel: 419-649-6482. FAX: 419-649-9488. *Libr Assoc,* Marcille Coates; E-mail: coatesm@limalibrary.com
Library Holdings: Bk Vols 11,612
Open Mon & Thurs 1:30-4:30 & 5:30-8, Tues 5:30-8
Friends of the Library Group
SPENCERVILLE BRANCH, 2489 Wisher Dr, Spencerville, 45887, SAN 356-7451. Tel: 419-647-4307. FAX: 419-647-6393. *Libr Assoc,* Vija Lee; E-mail: leev@limalibrary.com; Staff 2 (MLS 1, Non-MLS 1)
Library Holdings: Bk Vols 19,884
Open Mon & Tues 12-8, Thurs 10-6, Fri & Sat 9-1
Friends of the Library Group

M ST RITA'S MEDICAL CENTER*, Norman Browning Medical Library, 730 W Market St, 3rd Flr, 45801-4667. SAN 313-573X. Tel: 419-996-5842. FAX: 419-996-5166. Web Site: www.mercy.com/lima/patients-and-visitors/norman-browning-medical-library. *Coordr,* Kathy Herold; E-mail: kaherold@mercy.com
Founded 1948
Library Holdings: Bk Titles 450; Bk Vols 1,041; Per Subs 64
Subject Interests: Med
Wireless access
Partic in Medical Library Association; Ohio Health Sciences Library Association; Regional Med Libr - Region 3
Open Mon-Fri 8-4

LISBON

L COLUMBIANA COUNTY LAW LIBRARY*, 32 N Park Ave, 44432. SAN 327-7267. Tel: 330-420-3662. FAX: 330-424-7902. E-mail: lcolumbianalaw@neo.rr.com. Web Site: www.columbianacountylawlibrary.org. *Librn,* Ron Vest; E-mail: rvestccll@neo.rr.com
Library Holdings: Bk Vols 15,000
Wireless access
Restriction: Not open to pub

P LEPPER PUBLIC LIBRARY, 303 E Lincoln Way, 44432-1400. SAN 313-5748. Tel: 330-424-3117. FAX: 330-424-7343. Web Site: www.lepperlibrary.org. *Dir,* Marcy Kaiser; E-mail: marcy@lepperlibrary.org; Staff 4 (MLS 2, Non-MLS 2)
Founded 1897. Pop 58,000
Library Holdings: Audiobooks 3,147; CDs 42; DVDs 5,127; e-books 830,393; Electronic Media & Resources 562,441; Large Print Bks 1,142; Microforms 532; Bk Vols 36,576; Per Subs 54
Subject Interests: Local hist
Automation Activity & Vendor Info: (Cataloging) Innovative Interfaces, Inc; (Circulation) Innovative Interfaces, Inc; (ILL) Innovative Interfaces, Inc; (OPAC) Innovative Interfaces, Inc
Wireless access
Function: 24/7 Electronic res, 24/7 Online cat, After school storytime, Archival coll, Art exhibits, Art programs, Audiobks via web, AV serv, Bk club(s), Bks on CD, Children's prog, Computer training, Computers for patron use, Distance learning, E-Reserves, Electronic databases & coll, Free DVD rentals, Holiday prog, Homebound delivery serv, ILL available, Internet access, Laminating, Magazines, Mail & tel request accepted, Makerspace, Meeting rooms, Microfiche/film & reading machines, Movies, Museum passes, Notary serv, Online cat, Outside serv via phone, mail, e-mail & web, OverDrive digital audio bks, Photocopying/Printing, Preschool outreach, Preschool reading prog, Prog for adults, Prog for children & young adult, Ref & res, Ref serv available, Scanner, Senior computer classes, STEM programs, Story hour, Summer & winter reading prog, Summer reading prog, Tax forms, Teen prog, Telephone ref, Wheelchair accessible, Winter reading prog, Writing prog
Partic in Northeast Ohio Regional Library System; Ohio Public Library Information Network
Open Mon & Thurs 9-8, Tues & Wed 9-6, Fri & Sat 9-5

LITHOPOLIS

P THE WAGNALLS MEMORIAL LIBRARY*, 150 E Columbus St, 43136. (Mail add: PO Box 217, 43136-0217), SAN 313-5756. Tel: 614-837-4765. FAX: 614-837-0781. Web Site: www.wagnalls.org. *Dir,* Tami Morehart; E-mail: tmore@wagnalls.org; Staff 12 (MLS 3, Non-MLS 9)
Founded 1925. Pop 1,074
Special Collections: Letters (O Henry to Mabel Wagnalls Jones Coll); Paintings (John Ward Dunsmore Coll); Paintings (Norman Rockwell Coll); Poetry Hand Written & Framed (Edwin Markham Coll)
Automation Activity & Vendor Info: (Acquisitions) Innovative Interfaces, Inc; (Cataloging) Innovative Interfaces, Inc; (Circulation) Innovative Interfaces, Inc; (Serials) Innovative Interfaces, Inc
Wireless access
Function: 24/7 Electronic res, 24/7 Online cat, Accelerated reader prog, Activity rm, Adult bk club, Audiobks on Playaways & MP3, Audiobks via web, Bk club(s), Bks on CD, Children's prog, Computer training, Computers for patron use, E-Reserves, Electronic databases & coll, Free DVD rentals, Holiday prog, ILL available, Internet access, Magazines, Meeting rooms, Music CDs, Online cat, Online ref, OverDrive digital audio bks, Photocopying/Printing, Preschool reading prog, Prog for adults, Prog for children & young adult, Senior computer classes, Story hour,

Summer reading prog, Tax forms, Teen prog, Wheelchair accessible, Writing prog
Partic in Cent Libr Consortium
Open Mon-Thurs 10-8, Sat 10-2
Restriction: Non-circulating of rare bks
Friends of the Library Group

LOGAN

P LOGAN-HOCKING COUNTY DISTRICT LIBRARY*, 230 E Main St, 43138. SAN 313-5764. Tel: 740-385-2348. FAX: 740-385-9093. Web Site: www.hocking.lib.oh.us. *Libr Dir,* Mary Leffler; E-mail: director.loganhockinglibrary@gmail.com; Staff 12 (MLS 1, Non-MLS 11)
Founded 1948. Pop 29,000; Circ 287,575
Library Holdings: Bk Titles 115,590; Per Subs 265
Special Collections: Ohio History & Literature
Automation Activity & Vendor Info: (Acquisitions) Follett Software; (Cataloging) Follett Software; (Circulation) Follett Software; (OPAC) Follett Software; (Serials) Follett Software
Partic in Ohio Public Library Information Network
Open Mon-Thurs 9-8, Fri & Sat 9-5, Sun 1-5
Branches: 1
LAURELVILLE BRANCH, 16240 Maple St, Laurelville, 43135. (Mail add: PO Box 396, Laurelville, 43135-0396). Tel: 740-332-4700. FAX: 740-332-1379. *Librn,* Andrew Harold
Library Holdings: Bk Titles 2,000; Per Subs 70
Open Mon & Tues 9-7, Wed-Fri 9-5, Sat 9-3, Sun 1-5

LONDON

P LONDON PUBLIC LIBRARY, 20 E First St, 43140. SAN 313-5772. Tel: 740-852-9543. FAX: 740-852-3691. Web Site: mylondonlibrary.org. *Dir,* Bryan Howard; E-mail: bhoward@mylondonlibrary.org; *Coordr, Outreach Serv,* Andy Scaggs; E-mail: ascaggs@mylondonlibrary.org; *Youth Serv Coordr,* Mary Anne Wood; E-mail: mwood@mylondonlibrary.org; *Fiscal Officer,* Rebecca Stickel; E-mail: rstickel@mylondonlibrary.org; Staff 14 (MLS 2, Non-MLS 12)
Founded 1905. Pop 1,600; Circ 124,470
Jan 2019-Dec 2019 Income $1,117,849, State $557,587, City $480,620, Other $79,500. Mats Exp $1,269,326, Books $162,000, Per/Ser (Incl. Access Fees) $88,300, Other Print Mats $54,169, Electronic Ref Mat (Incl. Access Fees) $19,590. Sal $577,690
Library Holdings: Bks on Deafness & Sign Lang 15; High Interest/Low Vocabulary Bk Vols 25; Bk Titles 38,104; Bk Vols 40,600; Per Subs 106
Automation Activity & Vendor Info: (Cataloging) Innovative Interfaces, Inc; (Circulation) Innovative Interfaces, Inc
Wireless access
Partic in Miami Valley Librs
Open Mon-Thurs 9-8, Fri 10-6, Sat 10-5
Friends of the Library Group

GL MADISON COUNTY LAW LIBRARY*, One N Main, Rm 205, 43140-1068. SAN 313-5780. Tel: 740-852-9515. FAX: 740-852-7144. Web Site: www.co.madison.oh.us. *Librn,* Yvette Wilson; E-mail: ywilson@co.madison.oh.us
Founded 1903
Library Holdings: Bk Titles 20,000
Subject Interests: Fed, Ohio law, Statutes, Texts, Treatises
Open Mon-Fri 8-4

S STATE OF OHIO DEPARTMENT OF CORRECTIONS*, London Correctional Institute Library, 1580 State Rte 56 SW, 43140. (Mail add: PO Box 69, 43140-0069), SAN 313-5799. Tel: 740-852-2454. FAX: 740-852-1591. *Librn,* Position Currently Open; Staff 9 (MLS 1, Non-MLS 8)
Founded 1970
Library Holdings: High Interest/Low Vocabulary Bk Vols 900; Bk Titles 16,000; Bk Vols 17,000; Per Subs 45; Spec Interest Per Sub 20
Subject Interests: Westerns
Automation Activity & Vendor Info: (Acquisitions) EOS International; (Cataloging) EOS International; (Circulation) EOS International

LORAIN

P LORAIN PUBLIC LIBRARY SYSTEM*, 351 Sixth St, 44052. SAN 356-7486. Tel: 440-244-1192. Administration FAX: 440-244-4888. Web Site: www.lorainpubliclibrary.org. *Dir,* Anastasia Diamond-Ortiz; *Asst Dir,* Cheryl Grizzell; E-mail: cgrizzell@lpls.info; Staff 25 (MLS 14, Non-MLS 11)
Founded 1901. Pop 135,275; Circ 2,076,434
Library Holdings: AV Mats 185,890; Bk Titles 483,366; Per Subs 1,216
Special Collections: Hageman & Toni Morrison Coll
Subject Interests: Ethnic studies, Genealogy, Hist, Spanish (Lang)
Automation Activity & Vendor Info: (Cataloging) SirsiDynix; (Circulation) SirsiDynix; (OPAC) SirsiDynix
Wireless access
Function: Accelerated reader prog, Adult literacy prog, Audio & video playback equip for onsite use, Audiobks via web, Bilingual assistance for Spanish patrons, Bks on CD, CD-ROM, Children's prog, Computer training, Computers for patron use, Distance learning, Electronic databases & coll, Holiday prog, Homebound delivery serv, Homework prog, ILL available, Instruction & testing, Internet access, Music CDs, Online cat, Online ref, Outreach serv, OverDrive digital audio bks, Photocopying/Printing, Printer for laptops & handheld devices, Prog for adults, Prog for children & young adult, Ref serv available, Spanish lang bks, Summer & winter reading prog, Summer reading prog, Tax forms, Teen prog, Telephone ref, VHS videos, Wheelchair accessible, Winter reading prog
Partic in CLEVNET; Northeast Ohio Regional Library System; OhioNET
Open Mon-Thurs 9-8:30, Fri & Sat 9-6, Sun (Winter) 1-4
Friends of the Library Group
Branches: 5
AVON BRANCH, 37485 Harvest Dr, Avon, 44011-2812, SAN 356-7516. Tel: 440-934-4743. FAX: 440-934-4165. *Br Mgr,* Donna Kelly; E-mail: dkelly@lpls.info; Staff 5 (MLS 1, Non-MLS 4)
Founded 1956. Pop 21,193; Circ 233,971
Library Holdings: AV Mats 14,987; Bk Titles 42,388; Per Subs 155
Open Mon, Tues & Thurs 10-8:30, Wed 12-8:30, Fri 10-6, Sat 10-5
Friends of the Library Group
COLUMBIA BRANCH, 13824 W River Rd N, Columbia Station, 44028, SAN 356-7540. Tel: 440-236-8751. FAX: 440-236-8956. *Br Mgr,* John Guscott; E-mail: jguscott@lpls.info; Staff 4 (MLS 1, Non-MLS 3)
Founded 1955. Pop 7,538; Circ 96,035
Library Holdings: AV Mats 6,594; Bk Titles 24,723; Per Subs 112
Open Mon, Wed & Thurs 12-8, Tues 10-8, Fri 12-6, Sat 10-2
Friends of the Library Group
DOMONKAS BRANCH, 4125 E Lake Rd, Sheffield Lake, 44054, SAN 356-7605. Tel: 440-949-7410. FAX: 440-949-7741. *Br Mgr,* Anne Godec; E-mail: agodec@lpls.info; Staff 5 (MLS 1, Non-MLS 4)
Founded 1964. Pop 13,123; Circ 156,050
Library Holdings: AV Mats 13,459; Bk Titles 40,340; Per Subs 86
Open Mon, Tues & Thurs 10-8:30, Wed 12-8:30, Fri 2-6, Sat 10-5
Friends of the Library Group
NORTH RIDGEVILLE BRANCH, 35700 Bainbridge Rd, North Ridgeville, 44039. Tel: 440-327-8326. *Br Mgr,* Jennifer Winkler; Staff 9 (MLS 3, Non-MLS 6)
Founded 1958. Pop 29,470; Circ 588,058
Library Holdings: AV Mats 30,563; Bk Titles 82,974; Per Subs 272
Open Mon, Tues & Thurs 10-8:30, Wed 12-8:30, Fri & Sat 10-6, Sun (Winter) 1-5
Friends of the Library Group
SOUTH LORAIN, 2121 Homewood Dr, 44055, SAN 356-763X. Tel: 440-277-5672. FAX: 440-277-5727. *Br Mgr,* Ally Morgan; Staff 3 (MLS 1, Non-MLS 2)
Founded 1907. Pop 21,608; Circ 154,581
Library Holdings: AV Mats 20,376; Bk Titles 39,196; Per Subs 128
Automation Activity & Vendor Info: (Cataloging) SirsiDynix; (Circulation) SirsiDynix
Open Mon, Tues & Thurs 11-8, Wed 12-8, Fri 2-6, Sat 11-5
Friends of the Library Group
Bookmobiles: 1. Outreach Servs Supvr, Frances Johnson

LOUDONVILLE

P LOUDONVILLE PUBLIC LIBRARY*, 122 E Main St, 44842. SAN 313-5829. Tel: 419-994-5531. FAX: 419-994-4321. E-mail: info@loudonvillelibrary.org. Web Site: www.loudonvillelibrary.org. *Dir,* Position Currently Open; *Adult Serv, Ref,* Joy Zemrock; E-mail: zemrocjo@loudonvillelibrary.org; Staff 6 (MLS 2, Non-MLS 4)
Founded 1905. Pop 10,000; Circ 200,374
Library Holdings: Audiobooks 936; CDs 1,746; DVDs 1,196; Large Print Bks 2,007; Bk Vols 49,158; Per Subs 130; Videos 236
Special Collections: Genealogy & Local History Coll; Parent Teacher Coll
Automation Activity & Vendor Info: (Cataloging) OCLC; (Circulation) SirsiDynix
Wireless access
Function: Accelerated reader prog, Adult bk club, After school storytime, Archival coll, Audiobks via web, AV serv, Bk club(s), Children's prog, Computer training, Computers for patron use, Digital talking bks, E-Reserves, Electronic databases & coll, Family literacy, Free DVD rentals, Holiday prog, Home delivery & serv to seniorr ctr & nursing homes, Homebound delivery serv, ILL available, Internet access, Magnifiers for reading, Mail & tel request accepted, Music CDs, Online cat, Online ref, Outreach serv, Outside serv via phone, mail, e-mail & web, OverDrive digital audio bks, Photocopying/Printing, Preschool outreach, Prog for adults, Prog for children & young adult, Ref & res, Ref serv available, Scanner, Senior computer classes, Senior outreach, Spoken cassettes & CDs, Spoken cassettes & DVDs, Story hour, Summer reading prog, Tax forms, Teen prog, Telephone ref, VHS videos, Wheelchair accessible
Partic in Serving Every Ohioan Library Center

Open Mon, Tues & Thurs 10-8, Wed & Fri 10-6, Sat 10-4
Friends of the Library Group

LOUISVILLE

P LOUISVILLE PUBLIC LIBRARY*, 700 Lincoln Ave, 44641-1474. SAN 313-5837. Tel: 330-875-1696. FAX: 330-875-3530. E-mail: public.relations@louisvillelibrary.org. Web Site: www.louisvillelibrary.org. *Dir,* Jason Buydos; E-mail: jason.buydos@louisvillelibrary.org; *Adult & Teen Serv Mgr,* Deb Long; E-mail: deborah.long@louisvillelibrary.org; *Mgr, Ch Serv,* Rebecca DiFrancesco; E-mail: becky.difrancesco@louisvillelibrary.org; *Circ Mgr,* Darla Evans; E-mail: darla.evans@louisvillelibrary.org; Staff 4 (MLS 4)
Founded 1935. Pop 13,000
Library Holdings: Bk Vols 120,000; Per Subs 225
Subject Interests: Constitution, Local hist
Automation Activity & Vendor Info: (Acquisitions) Innovative Interfaces, Inc
Wireless access
Partic in Mideastern Ohio Libr Orgn; Serving Every Ohioan Library Center
Open Mon-Thurs 10-8, Fri & Sat 10-5, Sat (Summer 10-2), Sun 1-5
Friends of the Library Group

MADISON

P MADISON PUBLIC LIBRARY*, 6111 Middle Ridge Rd, 44057-2818. SAN 313-587X. Tel: 440-428-2189. FAX: 440-428-7402. E-mail: info@madison-library.info. Web Site: www.madison-library.info. *Libr Dir,* Dee Culbertson; E-mail: dee.culbertson@madison-library.info; Staff 7 (MLS 3, Non-MLS 4)
Founded 1915. Pop 19,000; Circ 475,000
Library Holdings: AV Mats 26,054; CDs 6,809; DVDs 19,500; e-books 373,194; Large Print Bks 7,540; Bk Vols 77,483; Per Subs 279
Subject Interests: Genealogy, Local hist
Automation Activity & Vendor Info: (Acquisitions) SirsiDynix; (Cataloging) SirsiDynix; (Circulation) SirsiDynix; (OPAC) BiblioCommons
Wireless access
Function: 24/7 Electronic res, 24/7 Online cat, 3D Printer, Activity rm, Adult bk club, Art exhibits, Art programs, Audiobks via web, Bk club(s), Bks on CD, Children's prog, Computer training, Computers for patron use, Digital talking bks, Distance learning, E-Readers, E-Reserves, Electronic databases & coll, Family literacy, Free DVD rentals, Govt ref serv, Home delivery & serv to seniorr ctr & nursing homes, Homebound delivery serv, ILL available, Internet access, Laminating, Life-long learning prog for all ages, Magazines, Mail & tel request accepted, Makerspace, Meeting rooms, Music CDs, Notary serv, Online cat, Outreach serv, OverDrive digital audio bks, Passport agency, Photocopying/Printing, Preschool outreach, Preschool reading prog, Printer for laptops & handheld devices, Prog for adults, Prog for children & young adult, Ref serv available, Scanner, Senior computer classes, Senior outreach, STEM programs, Study rm, Summer reading prog, Tax forms, Teen prog, Telephone ref, Wheelchair accessible
Publications: Dear Friends (Newsletter)
Partic in CLEVNET
Special Services for the Blind - Talking bks
Open Mon-Fri 9-8, Sat 9-5
Friends of the Library Group

MANSFIELD

R FIRST CONGREGATIONAL CHURCH LIBRARY*, 640 Millsboro Rd, 44903. SAN 313-5888. Tel: 419-756-3046. FAX: 419-756-5834. Web Site: www.mansfieldfcc.com. *Library Contact,* Deana Vail; E-mail: dee@mansfieldfcc.com
Library Holdings: Bk Vols 2,500
Open Mon-Fri 9-4:30

S KINGWOOD CENTER LIBRARY*, 50 N Trimble Rd, 44906. SAN 313-590X. Tel: 419-522-0211, Ext 108. E-mail: info@kingwoodcenter.org. Web Site: www.kingwoodcenter.org/education/library. *Dir,* Chuck Gleaves; Tel: 419-522-0211, Ext 104, E-mail: cgleaves@kingwoodcenter.org
Founded 1953
Library Holdings: AV Mats 50; Bk Titles 8,500; Per Subs 100
Subject Interests: Hort
Restriction: Mem only, Open by appt only, Researchers by appt only
Friends of the Library Group

R MANSFIELD 1ST EPC LIBRARY*, 399 S Trimble Rd, 44906. SAN 313-5896. Tel: 419-756-7066. E-mail: office@mansfield1st.com. *Library Contact,* Corey Slater
Founded 1960
Library Holdings: Bk Titles 3,500
Special Collections: Old Bibles Coll
Open Mon-Thurs 9-4

P MANSFIELD-RICHLAND COUNTY PUBLIC LIBRARY*, 43 W Third St, 44902-1295. SAN 356-7788. Tel: 419-521-3100. Circulation Tel: 419-521-3140. Reference Tel: 419-521-3110. FAX: 419-525-4750. TDD: 419-521-3113. Web Site: www.mrcpl.org. *Dir,* Chris May; E-mail: cmay@mrcpl.org; *Dep Dir,* Mary Frankenfield; Tel: 419-521-3127; *Dep Fiscal Officer,* Mary Dwyer; Tel: 419-521-3125; *Youth Serv Coordr,* Katie Gatten; Tel: 419-521-3148; *Coll Res Mgr,* Molly Ernst; Tel: 419-521-3133; *Human Res Mgr,* Paula Nehrkorn; Tel: 419-521-3147; *Communications Coordr,* Jessica Ney; Tel: 419-521-3101, E-mail: communications@mrcpl.org; *Coord, Ad Serv, Coordr, AV,* Megan Anderson; Tel: 419-521-3121; *IT Coordr,* Peter Moore; Tel: 419-521-3105, Fax: 419-521-3126, E-mail: automation@mrcpl.org
Founded 1887. Pop 125,000; Circ 1,700,000
Library Holdings: AV Mats 53,000; CDs 36,000; Bk Titles 248,360; Bk Vols 516,231; Talking Bks 12,000; Videos 221,000
Special Collections: Personal Library of Senator John Sherman
Subject Interests: Adult literacy, Found, Genealogy, Grants, Local hist
Automation Activity & Vendor Info: (Acquisitions) SirsiDynix; (Cataloging) SirsiDynix; (Circulation) SirsiDynix; (OPAC) SirsiDynix
Function: ILL available
Publications: News From the Mansfield/Richland County Public Library (Newsletter)
Partic in Ohio Library & Information Network
Special Services for the Deaf - TDD equip
Friends of the Library Group
Branches: 8
BELLVILLE BRANCH, 97 Bell St, Bellville, 44813, SAN 356-7818. Tel: 419-886-3811. FAX: 419-886-3791. *Br Mgr,* Josh Andra
Founded 1920. Pop 1,568; Circ 127,959
Library Holdings: Bk Vols 14,000
Function: ILL available
Open Mon-Thurs 9-8, Fri & Sat 9-5
Friends of the Library Group
BUTLER BRANCH, 21 Elm St, Butler, 44822, SAN 356-7842. Tel: 419-883-2220. FAX: 419-883-2220. *Br Mgr,* Natasha Waltz
Library Holdings: Bk Vols 11,997
Open Mon-Thurs 10-8, Fri 10-5, Sat 9-3
Friends of the Library Group
CRESTVIEW BRANCH, 1575 State Rte 96 E, Ashland, 44805-9262. Tel: 419-895-0010. FAX: 419-895-0010. *Br Mgr,* Elizabeth Donaldson
Library Holdings: Bk Vols 6,825
Open Mon, Tues & Thurs 10-8, Wed & Fri 10-5, Sat 9-3
LEXINGTON BRANCH, 25 Lutz Ave, Lexington, 44904, SAN 356-7877. Tel: 419-884-2500. FAX: 419-884-3695. *Br Mgr,* Danica Perry
Library Holdings: Bk Vols 39,958
Open Mon-Thurs 9-8, Fri & Sat 9-5
Friends of the Library Group
LUCAS BRANCH, 34 W Main St, Lucas, 44843, SAN 370-9213. Tel: 419-892-2576. FAX: 419-892-2576. *Br Mgr,* Position Currently Open
Library Holdings: Bk Vols 15,371
Open Mon, Tues & Thurs 11-8, Wed & Fri 11-5, Sat 9-3
Friends of the Library Group
MADISON BRANCH, 1395 Grace St, 44905, SAN 376-1541. Tel: 419-589-7050. FAX: 419-589-7108. *Br Mgr,* Kinsey Landin
Library Holdings: Bk Vols 27,996
Open Mon-Thurs 9-8, Fri & Sat 9-5
Friends of the Library Group
ONTARIO BRANCH, 2221 Village Mall Dr, 44906, SAN 328-9842. Tel: 419-529-4912. FAX: 419-529-3693. *Br Mgr,* Matt Bachelder
Library Holdings: Bk Vols 35,134
Open Mon-Thurs 9-8, Fri & Sat 9-5
Friends of the Library Group
PLYMOUTH BRANCH, 29 W Broadway, Plymouth, 44865, SAN 356-7907. Tel: 419-687-5655. FAX: 419-687-5655. *Br Mgr,* Ellen Kollie
Library Holdings: Bk Vols 26,505
Open Mon-Thurs 10-8, Fri 10-5, Sat 9-3
Friends of the Library Group

GL RICHLAND COUNTY LAW LIBRARY RESOURCES BOARD*, Richland County Law Library, 50 Park Ave E, Flr L2, 44902. SAN 313-5969. Tel: 419-774-5595. FAX: 419-524-9979. E-mail: rclawlibrary@richlandcourtsoh.us. Web Site: richlandcourtsoh.us/lawlibrary.php. *Law Librn,* Traycee Davis
Library Holdings: Bk Titles 19,000; Per Subs 15
Wireless access
Restriction: Authorized patrons, Co libr, Limited access for the pub, Open to pub for ref only, Open to pub with supv only, Open to qualified scholars, Pub access for legal res only, Restricted borrowing privileges

S STATE OF OHIO DEPARTMENT OF CORRECTIONS, Mansfield Correctional Institution Library, 1150 N Main St, 44903. (Mail add: PO Box 788, 44901-0788), SAN 313-5942. Tel: 419-526-2595. Web Site: drc.ohio.gov/manci. *Librn,* McKalee Weidner; Staff 1 (MLS 1)
Library Holdings: Bk Vols 8,500

Subject Interests: Criminal law
Partic in State Libr of Ohio

MARIETTA

C MARIETTA COLLEGE*, Legacy Library, 215 Fifth St, 45750. SAN 313-5977. Tel: 740-376-4757. FAX: 740-376-4843. E-mail: library@marietta.edu. Web Site: library.marietta.edu. *Dir,* Dr Douglas Anderson; E-mail: nda001@marietta.edu; *Head, Tech Serv & Syst,* Angela Burdiss; Tel: 740-376-4537, E-mail: burdissa@marietta.edu; *Ref & Access Serv Librn,* J Peter Thayer; Tel: 740-376-4361, E-mail: thayerp@marietta.edu; *Ref & Instruction Librn,* Joseph Straw; Tel: 740-376-4541, E-mail: js001@marietta.edu; *Spec Coll Librn,* Katy Scullin; Tel: 740-376-4464, E-mail: ks006@marietta.edu. Subject Specialists: *Fine arts, Performing arts,* Dr Douglas Anderson; *Sci,* Angela Burdiss; *Soc sci,* J Peter Thayer; *Educ, Humanities,* Joseph Straw; Staff 10 (MLS 5, Non-MLS 5)
Founded 1835. Enrl 1,254; Fac 117; Highest Degree: Master
Library Holdings: AV Mats 10,885; e-books 171,853; e-journals 16,076; Bk Vols 166,070
Special Collections: 16th-19th Century Rare Book Coll; Americana (Stimson Coll), bks; Local History (Fischer Coll & Hoag Coll), photos; Northwest Territory & Early Ohio (Ohio Company of Associates Coll & General Rufus Putnam Papers Coll), docs, ms; Notable Personnages (Slack Coll), autographs & docs; Ohio History & Scientific Coll (Hildreth Coll), bks & ms. State Document Depository; US Document Depository
Automation Activity & Vendor Info: (Acquisitions) Innovative Interfaces, Inc - Sierra; (Cataloging) Innovative Interfaces, Inc - Sierra; (Circulation) Innovative Interfaces, Inc - Sierra; (Course Reserve) Innovative Interfaces, Inc - Sierra; (ILL) Clio; (OPAC) Innovative Interfaces, Inc - Sierra; (Serials) Innovative Interfaces, Inc - Sierra
Wireless access
Partic in Ohio Library & Information Network; OhioNET
Open Mon-Thurs 8am-Midnight, Fri 8-6, Sat Noon-4, Sun Noon-Midnight

M MARIETTA MEMORIAL HOSPITAL*, Medical Library, 401 Matthew St, 45750-1699. SAN 373-8329. Tel: 740-374-1455. FAX: 740-374-4959. *Med Librn,* Angela Tucker; E-mail: atucker@mhsystem.org; Staff 1 (MLS 1)
Library Holdings: Bk Vols 1,800; Per Subs 175
Subject Interests: Hospital admin, Med, Nursing
Wireless access
Partic in National Network of Libraries of Medicine Region 6
Restriction: Staff use only

S OHIO HISTORICAL SOCIETY*, Campus Martius Museum Library, 601 Second St, 45750-2122. SAN 313-5985. Tel: 740-373-3750. Toll Free Tel: 800-860-0145. FAX: 740-373-3680. E-mail: info@campusmartiusmuseum.org. Web Site: mariettamuseums.org/campus-martius. *Dir,* Le Ann Hendershot; E-mail: lhendershot@campusmartiusmuseum.org
Founded 1885
Library Holdings: Bk Titles 500
Subject Interests: Area genealogy prior to 1830, Early Northwest Territory, Ohio, River mat, Wash County
Function: For res purposes
Open Mon-Fri (Nov-Feb) 9:30-5; Wed-Sat (March-Oct) 9:30-5, Sun 12-5

GL WASHINGTON COUNTY LAW LIBRARY, 205 Putnam St, 45750-3017. SAN 370-3223. Tel: 740-373-6623, Ext 214. FAX: 740-373-2085. E-mail: washcolaw@sbcglobal.net. Web Site: www.washingtongov.org/index.aspx?NID=148. *Law Librn,* Terry Mullins
Library Holdings: Bk Vols 15,050
Special Collections: Ohio Law Cases 1800's Through Current
Open Mon & Wed 8-12 & 1-4, Fri 8-Noon
Restriction: Open to pub for ref only

P WASHINGTON COUNTY PUBLIC LIBRARY*, 615 Fifth St, 45750-1973. SAN 356-7966. Tel: 740-373-1057. Reference Tel: 740-373-1057, Ext 208. Administration Tel: 740-373-1057, Ext 223. Reference FAX: 740-373-2860. Administration FAX: 740-376-2171. Web Site: www.wcplib.info. *Dir,* Justin Mayo; E-mail: j.mayo@wcplib.info; *Outreach Serv Mgr,* Andrea Ralston; *Youth Serv Mgr,* Julie Stacy; Staff 68 (MLS 2, Non-MLS 66)
Founded 1829. Pop 62,500; Circ 705,000
Library Holdings: Bk Vols 217,500; Per Subs 245
Special Collections: Local History & Genealogy Coll
Automation Activity & Vendor Info: (Cataloging) SirsiDynix; (Circulation) SirsiDynix; (OPAC) Horizon
Wireless access
Partic in Solo
Open Mon, Tues & Thurs 9-8, Wed & Fri 9-6, Sat 10-4
Friends of the Library Group
Branches: 5
BARLOW BRANCH, 8370 State Rte 339, Barlow, 45712. (Mail add: PO Box 175, Barlow, 45712-0175), SAN 378-1216. Tel: 740-678-0103. FAX: 740-678-0046. *Br Mgr,* Anna Henry; E-mail: a.henry@wcplib.info; Staff 9 (Non-MLS 9)
Founded 1998. Circ 75,253
Open Mon-Thurs 9-8, Fri 9-6, Sat 10-4
Friends of the Library Group
BELPRE BRANCH, 2012 Washington Blvd, Belpre, 45714, SAN 356-7990. Tel: 740-423-8381. FAX: 740-423-8305. *Br Mgr,* Tam Wamer; E-mail: t.wamer@wcplib.info
Circ 111,478
Open Mon-Wed 9-8, Thurs & Fri 9-6, Sat 9-4
Friends of the Library Group
BEVERLY LIBRARY, MacIntosh St, Beverly, 45715. (Mail add: PO Box 728, Beverly, 45715-0728), SAN 356-8024. Tel: 740-984-4060. FAX: 740-984-2083. *Br Mgr,* Susan Chipps; E-mail: s.chipps@wcplib.info
Open Mon-Wed 10-8, Thurs & Fri 10-5, Sat 10-3
Friends of the Library Group
LOCAL HISTORY & GENEALOGY, 418 Washington St, 45750. Tel: 740-376-2172. FAX: 740-376-2175. E-mail: genealogy@wcplib.lib.oh.us.
Library Holdings: Bk Vols 4,000
Automation Activity & Vendor Info: (Cataloging) Horizon; (Circulation) Horizon
Open Mon, Tues & Thurs 10-7, Fri 10-5, Sat 10-4
NEW MATAMORAS BRANCH, 100 Merchant St, New Matamoras, 45767. (Mail add: PO Box 279, New Matamoras, 45767-0279), SAN 356-8059. Tel: 740-865-3386. FAX: 740-865-2054. *Br Mgr,* Kelly Brady; E-mail: k.brady@wcplib.info
Founded 1936. Circ 29,471
Open Mon-Wed 9-7, Fri 9-6, Sat 9-4
Friends of the Library Group
Bookmobiles: 1

J WASHINGTON STATE COMMUNITY COLLEGE*, Carson K Miller Library, 710 Colegate Dr, 45750. SAN 322-6948. Tel: 740-568-1914. E-mail: refdesk@wscc.edu. Web Site: www.wscc.edu/current/library. *Dir, Libr Serv,* Jeff Graffius; Tel: 740-374-8716, Ext 3108, E-mail: jgraffius@wscc.edu; *Asst Librn,* Doug Unsold; E-mail: dunsold1@wscc.edu; Staff 7 (MLS 1, Non-MLS 6)
Founded 1990. Enrl 2,209; Fac 174; Highest Degree: Associate
Library Holdings: AV Mats 700; Bk Titles 18,659; Bk Vols 20,245
Subject Interests: Allied health, Computer tech, Nursing
Automation Activity & Vendor Info: (Cataloging) Innovative Interfaces, Inc; (Circulation) Innovative Interfaces, Inc; (Course Reserve) Innovative Interfaces, Inc; (ILL) Innovative Interfaces, Inc; (OPAC) Innovative Interfaces, Inc; (Serials) Innovative Interfaces, Inc
Wireless access
Partic in Ohio Library & Information Network; OhioNET

MARION

S MARION CORRECTIONAL INSTITUTION LIBRARY*, 940 Marion-Williamsport Rd, 43301. (Mail add: PO Box 57, 43301-0057), SAN 313-6000. Tel: 740-382-5781. *Librn,* Mr King
Founded 1957
Library Holdings: Bk Titles 22,000; Per Subs 50
Special Collections: Law Library Coll
Automation Activity & Vendor Info: (Cataloging) Mandarin Library Automation; (Circulation) Mandarin Library Automation; (OPAC) Mandarin Library Automation
Function: ILL available, Ref serv available
Partic in State Libr of Ohio
Restriction: Internal circ only

GL MARION COUNTY OHIO LAW LIBRARY*, 258 W Center St, 43302. SAN 313-6019. Tel: 740-223-4170. FAX: 740-223-4179. E-mail: lawlib@ohio.net. Web Site: www.marionlawlibrary.org. *Librn,* Heather Ebert
Library Holdings: Bk Vols 17,000
Wireless access
Open Mon-Fri 8:30-11 & 12-4:30

P MARION PUBLIC LIBRARY*, 445 E Church St, 43302-4290. SAN 356-8083. Tel: 740-387-0992. Web Site: www.marionlibrary.org. *Exec Dir, Fiscal Officer,* Gary Branson; E-mail: director@marionlibrary.org; *Head, Exten Serv,* David Hepp; *Head, Patron Serv,* Gary Butler; *Head, Tech Serv,* Amy Deuble; *Head, Youth Serv,* Whittney Mahle; *Communications Mgr,* Diane Watson; Staff 30 (MLS 7, Non-MLS 23)
Founded 1886. Pop 66,501; Circ 371,488
Jan 2017-Dec 2017 Income (Main & Associated Libraries) $2,145,690, State $2,034,315, Federal $7,588, Locally Generated Income $103,787. Mats Exp $198,894, Books $136,134, Per/Ser (Incl. Access Fees) $9,780, Other Print Mats $5,984, AV Mat $39,204, Electronic Ref Mat (Incl. Access Fees) $7,792. Sal $1,051,235 (Prof $540,096)

Library Holdings: Audiobooks 5,459; DVDs 16,290; e-books 124,603; Bk Titles 274,194; Bk Vols 316,720; Per Subs 107
Special Collections: Marion Local History. State Document Depository; US Document Depository
Automation Activity & Vendor Info: (Acquisitions) Innovative Interfaces, Inc; (Cataloging) Innovative Interfaces, Inc; (Circulation) Innovative Interfaces, Inc; (OPAC) Innovative Interfaces, Inc; (Serials) Innovative Interfaces, Inc
Wireless access
Function: 24/7 Online cat, Audiobks on Playaways & MP3, Audiobks via web, AV serv, Bks on CD, Children's prog, Computers for patron use, Electronic databases & coll, Free DVD rentals, Govt ref serv, Home delivery & serv to seniorr ctr & nursing homes, Homebound delivery serv, ILL available, Internet access, Magazines, Meeting rooms, Microfiche/film & reading machines, Online cat, OverDrive digital audio bks, Photocopying/Printing, Prog for adults, Prog for children & young adult, Story hour, Study rm, Summer reading prog, Tax forms, Wheelchair accessible
Open Mon-Thurs 9-8, Fri & Sat 9-4, Sun 1-4
Friends of the Library Group
Branches: 3
CALEDONIA BRANCH, 112 E Marion St, Caledonia, 43314. (Mail add: 445 E Church St, 43302), SAN 356-8113. Tel: 419-845-3666. *Head, Exten Serv,* David Hepp
Founded 1938. Circ 4,474
Library Holdings: Bk Vols 5,210
Open Mon & Thurs 2-6
Friends of the Library Group
HENKLE-HOLLIDAY MEMORIAL, 86 S High, La Rue, 43332. (Mail add: 445 E Church St, 43302), SAN 356-8148. Tel: 740-499-3066. *Head, Exten Serv,* David Hepp
Founded 1936. Circ 6,664
Library Holdings: Bk Vols 5,979
Open Mon & Thurs 2-6
Friends of the Library Group
PROSPECT BRANCH, 116 N Main, Prospect, 43342. (Mail add: 445 E Church St, 43302), SAN 356-8172. Tel: 740-494-2684. *Head, Exten Serv,* David Hepp
Founded 1937. Circ 2,274
Library Holdings: Bk Vols 4,811
Open Mon & Thurs 2-6
Friends of the Library Group

MARTINS FERRY

P BELMONT COUNTY DISTRICT LIBRARY*, Martins Ferry Public Library, 20 James Wright Pl, 43935. SAN 356-8202. Tel: 740-633-0314. FAX: 740-633-6242. Web Site: www.bcdlibrary.org. *Dir,* Anthony Orsini; E-mail: aorsini@bcdlibrary.org; *Ad,* Ellen Kollie; E-mail: ekollie@bcdlibrary.org; *Youth Serv Librn,* Anessa Keifer; E-mail: akeifer@bcdlibrary.org; Staff 20 (MLS 3, Non-MLS 17)
Founded 1927. Pop 37,000; Circ 422,000
Library Holdings: AV Mats 7,700; High Interest/Low Vocabulary Bk Vols 22; Bk Titles 200,000; Bk Vols 211,377; Per Subs 220; Videos 13,000
Special Collections: James Wright Poetry Coll
Automation Activity & Vendor Info: (Acquisitions) SirsiDynix-WorkFlows; (Cataloging) SirsiDynix-WorkFlows; (Circulation) SirsiDynix-WorkFlows; (OPAC) SirsiDynix-WorkFlows
Wireless access
Function: 24/7 Electronic res, Activity rm, Adult bk club, After school storytime, Archival coll, Art exhibits, Audiobks on Playaways & MP3, Audiobks via web, Bk club(s), Bks on CD, CD-ROM, Children's prog, Computer training, Computers for patron use, Digital talking bks, Electronic databases & coll, Family literacy, Free DVD rentals, Holiday prog, Home delivery & serv to seniorr ctr & nursing homes, Homebound delivery serv, ILL available, Internet access, Laminating, Life-long learning prog for all ages, Literacy & newcomer serv, Magazines, Meeting rooms, Microfiche/film & reading machines, Movies, Music CDs, Notary serv, Online cat, Online info literacy tutorials on the web & in blackboard, Online ref, OverDrive digital audio bks, Photocopying/Printing, Preschool outreach, Prog for adults, Prog for children & young adult, Ref & res, Ref serv available, Senior computer classes, Senior outreach, Spoken cassettes & CDs, Story hour, Study rm, Summer reading prog, Tax forms, Teen prog, Telephone ref, Wheelchair accessible
Partic in Serving Every Ohioan Library Center
Open Mon-Thurs 9-8, Fri 9-6, Sat 10-5
Restriction: Borrowing requests are handled by ILL
Friends of the Library Group
Branches: 5
BETHESDA BRANCH, 112 N Main St, Bethesda, 43719, SAN 356-8237. Tel: 740-484-4532. FAX: 740-484-4732. *Br Mgr,* Karen Davis; E-mail: kdavis@bcdlibrary.org; Staff 3 (Non-MLS 3)
Library Holdings: Bk Vols 5,149
Open Mon & Wed 12-7, Fri 12-4, Sat 10-Noon
Friends of the Library Group
BRIDGEPORT BRANCH, 661 Main St, Bridgeport, 43912, SAN 356-8261. Tel: 740-635-2563. FAX: 740-635-6974. *Br Mgr,* Cammie Hanson; E-mail: chanson@bcdlibrary.org; Staff 3 (Non-MLS 3)
Library Holdings: Bk Vols 10,000
Open Mon & Tues 11-6, Thurs & Fri 11-4
POWHATAN POINT BRANCH, 339 N State Rte 7, Powhatan Point, 43942, SAN 356-8350. Tel: 740-795-4624. FAX: 740-795-4624. *Br Mgr,* Jane Stratton; E-mail: jstratton@bcdlibrary.org; Staff 2 (Non-MLS 2)
Library Holdings: Bk Vols 3,000
Open Mon & Wed 12-7, Fri 12-4, Sat 11-1
VICTORIA READ FLUSHING BRANCH, 300 High St, Flushing, 43977. (Mail add: PO Box 214, Flushing, 43977-0214), SAN 356-8296. Tel: 740-968-3891. FAX: 740-968-0648. *Br Mgr,* Ferda Shari; E-mail: sferda@bcdlibrary.org; Staff 3 (Non-MLS 3)
Library Holdings: Bk Vols 10,000
Open Mon & Wed 12-7, Fri 12-4, Sat 11-2
Friends of the Library Group
SHADYSIDE BRANCH, 4300 Central Ave, Shadyside, 43947, SAN 356-8385. Tel: 740-676-0506. FAX: 740-676-0123. *Br Mgr,* Lisa Millhouse; E-mail: lmillhouse@bcdlibrary.org; Staff 4 (MLS 1, Non-MLS 3)
Library Holdings: Bk Vols 21,838
Open Mon-Wed 11-7, Fri 9-5, Sat 11-3
Friends of the Library Group

MARYSVILLE

P MARYSVILLE PUBLIC LIBRARY*, 231 S Plum St, 43040-1596. SAN 356-8415. Tel: 937-642-1876. FAX: 937-642-3457. Web Site: marysvillelib.org. *Dir,* Nieca Nowels; Tel: 937-642-1876, Ext 33, E-mail: nnowels@marysvillelib.org; *Asst Dir,* Kate McCartney; Tel: 937-642-1876, Ext 34, E-mail: kmccartney@marysvillelib.org; *Fiscal Officer,* Mike Schmenk; Tel: 937-642-1876, Ext 30, E-mail: mschmenk@marysvillelib.org; *Adult Serv Mgr, Info Serv Mgr,* Lauren Lemmon; Tel: 937-642-1876, Ext 32, E-mail: llemmon@marysvillelib.org; *Youth Serv Mgr,* Christiana Congelio; Tel: 937-642-1876, Ext 25, E-mail: ccongelio@marysvillelib.org; Staff 5 (MLS 5)
Pop 30,912; Circ 600,000
Subject Interests: Genealogy
Automation Activity & Vendor Info: (Acquisitions) Baker & Taylor; (Cataloging) Innovative Interfaces, Inc; (Circulation) Innovative Interfaces, Inc; (OPAC) Innovative Interfaces, Inc
Wireless access
Partic in Cent Libr Consortium
Open Mon-Thurs 9-8, Fri 9-6, Sat 9-5, Sun 1-5
Friends of the Library Group
Branches: 1
RAYMOND BRANCH, 21698 Main St, Raymond, 43067. (Mail add: 231 S Plum St, 43040), SAN 356-844X. Tel: 937-246-4795. FAX: 937-246-2347. *Dir,* Nieca Nowels; *Asst Dir,* Kate McCartney; Tel: 937-642-1876, Ext 34, E-mail: kmccartney@marysvillelib.org; *Patron Serv Mgr,* Renee Martin; Tel: 937-642-1876, Ext 26, E-mail: rmartin@marysvillelib.org
Open Tues & Wed 11-7, Thurs 9-5, Fri 11-5, Sat 10-2
Friends of the Library Group

S OHIO REFORMATORY FOR WOMEN LIBRARY*, 1479 Collins Ave, 43040-8808. SAN 313-6035. Tel: 937-642-1065, Ext 2064. FAX: 937-645-3835. *Librn,* Ms McLoughlin; Staff 1 (MLS 1)
Founded 1959
Library Holdings: Large Print Bks 150; Bk Vols 7,000; Per Subs 50
Automation Activity & Vendor Info: (Cataloging) Mandarin Library Automation; (Circulation) Mandarin Library Automation
Restriction: Not open to pub

MASON

P MASON PUBLIC LIBRARY*, 200 Reading Rd, 45040. SAN 313-6051. Tel: 513-398-2711. FAX: 513-398-9342. E-mail: masonpl@masonpl.org, masonplcir@masonpl.org. Web Site: masonpl.org. *Dir,* Sarah B Brown
Founded 1978. Pop 56,000; Circ 280,000
Library Holdings: Bk Titles 131,000; Per Subs 260
Special Collections: Mason History Coll
Wireless access
Publications: News & Views; Pulse Journal
Open Mon-Thurs 10-8, Fri & Sat 9-5, Sun (Oct-May) 1-5
Friends of the Library Group

MASSILLON

P MASSILLON PUBLIC LIBRARY*, 208 Lincoln Way E, 44646-8416. SAN 356-8474. Tel: 330-832-9831. Interlibrary Loan Service Tel: 330-832-9831, Ext 311. Reference Tel: 330-832-9831, Ext 312. Administration Tel: 330-832-9831, Ext 314. FAX: 330-830-2182. Reference E-mail: mpl.ref@gmail.com. Web Site: www.massillonlibrary.org. *Dir,* Sherie L Brown; E-mail:

brownsh@massillonlibrary.org; *ILS Llbrn, Mgr, Tech Serv,* Karen Sykeny; Tel: 330-832-9831, Ext 318, E-mail: sykenyka@massillonlibrary.org; *Mgr, Ch Serv,* Laura Klein; Tel: 330-832-9831, Ext 319, E-mail: kleinla@massillonlibrary.org; *Mgr, Outreach Serv,* Anne Juhasz; Tel: 330-832-9831, Ext 329, E-mail: juhaszan@massillonlibrary.org; *Adult Serv Mgr,* Jessica Watkins; Tel: 330-832-9831, Ext 307, E-mail: watkinje@massillonlibrary.org; *Circ Serv Mgr,* Cynthia Rudy; Tel: 330-832-9831, Ext 332, E-mail: rudycy@massillonlibrary.org; *Fiscal Officer,* Amie Lynn; *YA Spec,* Susan Baker; E-mail: bakersu@massillonlibrary.org; Staff 54 (MLS 3, Non-MLS 51)
Founded 1897. Pop 30,447; Circ 1,001,434
Special Collections: Early Ohio & Quaker History (Rotch-Wales Coll), mss; Lillian Gish Coll, letters, bks, films, videos, clippings
Subject Interests: Cooking, Gardening
Automation Activity & Vendor Info: (Acquisitions) Innovative Interfaces, Inc - Sierra; (Cataloging) Innovative Interfaces, Inc - Sierra; (Circulation) Innovative Interfaces, Inc - Sierra; (OPAC) Innovative Interfaces, Inc - Sierra
Wireless access
Function: AV serv, Bk club(s), Electronic databases & coll, Genealogy discussion group, Homebound delivery serv, ILL available, Photocopying/Printing, Prog for adults, Prog for children & young adult, Ref serv available, Senior computer classes, Spoken cassettes & CDs, Spoken cassettes & DVDs, Summer reading prog, Tax forms, Wheelchair accessible
Publications: Newsletter (Monthly)
Partic in Northeast Ohio Regional Library System; Ohio Public Library Information Network; OhioNET
Open Mon-Wed 10-8, Thurs 10-6, Fri & Sat 10-5
Friends of the Library Group
Branches: 2
BARRY ASKREN MEMORIAL BRANCH, 1200 Market St NE, Navarre, 44662, SAN 356-8539. Tel: 330-879-2113. FAX: 330-879-5574. *Mgr,* Angel Vaugh; E-mail: vaughnan@massillonlibrary.org
Open Mon-Fri 9-5, Wed 9-8, Sat 9-2
PAM S BELLONI BRANCH, 12000 Navarre Rd SW, Brewster, 44662-9486, SAN 356-8504. Tel: 330-767-9939. FAX: 330-767-0192. *Mgr,* Patty McGrath; E-mail: mcgratpa@massillonlibrary.org
Library Holdings: Bk Vols 12,645
Open Mon & Wed-Fri 8:30-4, Tues 8:30-7

MAUMEE

M SAINT LUKE'S HOSPITAL*, Dr R A Hendricks Memorial Library, 5901 Monclova Rd, 43537-1855. Tel: 419-893-5917. *Med Staff Spec,* Cam Thomas; E-mail: camille.thomas@stlukeshospital.com
Library Holdings: Bk Vols 500

R SAINT PAUL'S EPISCOPAL CHURCH LIBRARY*, 310 Elizabeth St, 43537. SAN 313-6078. Tel: 419-893-3381. E-mail: office@stpaulsmaumee.org. Web Site: www.stpaulsmaumee.org. *Librn,* Jane Baessler; Staff 2 (MLS 2)
Founded 1958
Library Holdings: AV Mats 130; Bk Titles 1,790; Bk Vols 1,800
Subject Interests: Anglicana, Church, Relig
Open Mon-Fri 9-4

J STAUTZENBERGER COLLEGE LIBRARY*, 1796 Indian Wood Circle, 43537. Tel: 419-866-0261. Web Site: www.sctoday.edu. *Librn, Res Serv Spec,* Lori Van Liere; E-mail: lori.vanliere@sctoday.edu
Founded 1926. Enrl 750; Highest Degree: Associate
Library Holdings: CDs 2; Bk Titles 558; Per Subs 24; Spec Interest Per Sub 22; Videos 15
Subject Interests: Bus tech, Health & wellness, Info tech, Legal tech, Med tech, Real estate, Veterinary tech
Wireless access
Restriction: Access at librarian's discretion, Circ limited, In-house use for visitors, Not open to pub, Open to students, fac & staff

MAYFIELD HEIGHTS

M HILLCREST HOSPITAL, Medical Library, 6780 Mayfield Rd, 44124. Tel: 440-312-3250. FAX: 440-312-4799. Web Site: ccflib.stacksdiscovery.com. *Med Librn,* Mary Miles; E-mail: mmiles@ccf.org; Staff 1 (MLS 1)
Founded 1974
Automation Activity & Vendor Info: (Cataloging) Innovative Interfaces, Inc - Sierra; (Circulation) Innovative Interfaces, Inc - Sierra; (ILL) Innovative Interfaces, Inc - Sierra; (OPAC) Innovative Interfaces, Inc - Sierra; (Serials) EBSCO Online
Wireless access
Function: Audiobks via web, Computer training, Doc delivery serv, Electronic databases & coll, For res purposes, ILL available, Internet access, Online cat, Photocopying/Printing, Ref serv available, Study rm
Partic in MLANO; Ohio Health Sciences Library Association
Open Mon-Fri 8-4:30
Restriction: Badge access after hrs, Borrowing requests are handled by ILL, Hospital employees & physicians only, In-house use for visitors, Internal circ only

MCARTHUR

P HERBERT WESCOAT MEMORIAL LIBRARY*, 120 N Market St, 45651-1218. SAN 313-5845. Tel: 740-596-5691. FAX: 740-596-2477. Web Site: www.vintoncountypublic.lib.oh.us. *Dir,* Diana Johnston; E-mail: diana.librarygal@outlook.com; *Ch,* Kathi Steele
Founded 1934
Library Holdings: Bk Vols 50,000; Per Subs 171
Subject Interests: Vinton County hist
Wireless access
Open Mon-Fri 9:30-6, Sat 8:30-12:30
Friends of the Library Group
Bookmobiles: 1

MCCOMB

P MCCOMB PUBLIC LIBRARY*, 113 S Todd St, 45858. (Mail add: PO Box 637, 45858-0637), SAN 313-5853. Tel: 419-293-2425. FAX: 419-293-2748. Web Site: mccombpl.org. *Dir,* Jane Schaffner; E-mail: jschaffner@mccombpl.org; *Asst Dir, Head, Circ,* Laurie Bales; E-mail: lbales@mccombpl.org; *Ch,* Annette Schroeder; E-mail: aschroeder@mccombpl.org
Founded 1935. Circ 80,000
Library Holdings: Bk Vols 45,769; Per Subs 95
Special Collections: Art Coll, prints; Civil War (Andrews Raiders), displays
Subject Interests: Local hist
Automation Activity & Vendor Info: (Cataloging) Innovative Interfaces, Inc; (Circulation) Innovative Interfaces, Inc; (OPAC) Innovative Interfaces, Inc
Wireless access
Partic in NORWELD; Serving Every Ohioan Library Center
Open Mon-Wed 10-8, Thurs & Fri 10-5, Sat 10-3
Friends of the Library Group

MCCONNELSVILLE

P KATE LOVE SIMPSON MORGAN COUNTY LIBRARY, 358 E Main St, 43756. SAN 313-5861. Tel: 740-962-2533. FAX: 740-962-3316. E-mail: katelove@seolibraries.org. Web Site: www.morgan.lib.oh.us. *Dir,* Tara Sidwell; E-mail: tsidwell@seolibraries.org; Staff 14 (MLS 1, Non-MLS 13)
Founded 1920. Pop 14,897; Circ 132,254
Library Holdings: AV Mats 5,359; Bks on Deafness & Sign Lang 13; Large Print Bks 2,273; Bk Vols 60,890; Per Subs 77
Subject Interests: Genealogy, Local hist
Automation Activity & Vendor Info: (Cataloging) SirsiDynix; (Circulation) SirsiDynix; (ILL) SirsiDynix; (OPAC) SirsiDynix
Wireless access
Function: Home delivery & serv to seniorr ctr & nursing homes, Homebound delivery serv, ILL available, Prog for children & young adult, Summer reading prog, Telephone ref, Wheelchair accessible
Partic in Serving Every Ohioan Library Center
Open Mon, Wed & Fri 9-4, Tues & Thurs 11-6, Sat 9-1
Friends of the Library Group
Branches: 1
CHESTERHILL BRANCH, 7520 Marion St, Chesterhill, 43728. Tel: 740-554-7104. FAX: 740-554-7253. *Br Mgr,* Cheryl Kirkbright; Staff 2 (Non-MLS 2)
Founded 1936
Library Holdings: Bk Vols 11,000
Function: ILL available, Prog for children & young adult, Summer reading prog, Telephone ref, Wheelchair accessible
Open Mon & Fri 10-4, Tues & Wed 12-6, Sat 9-1
Bookmobiles: 1

MECHANICSBURG

P MECHANICSBURG PUBLIC LIBRARY, 60 S Main St, 43044. SAN 313-6108. Tel: 937-834-2004. FAX: 937-834-3396. E-mail: mpl@mechanicsburgohlibrary.org. Web Site: mechanicsburg.lib.oh.us. *Dir,* Rebecca Wilden; E-mail: rfw@mechanicsburgohlibrary.org; Staff 5 (MLS 2, Non-MLS 3)
Founded 1935
Jan 2019-Dec 2019 Income $385,498, State $284,702, Locally Generated Income $89,262, Other $11,534. Mats Exp $57,158, Books $23,783, Per/Ser (Incl. Access Fees) $3,275, AV Mat $4,724, Electronic Ref Mat (Incl. Access Fees) $25,376. Sal $217,205
Library Holdings: Audiobooks 84,141; CDs 361; DVDs 2,894; e-books 290,638; Electronic Media & Resources 65; Large Print Bks 1,300; Bk Titles 25,898; Per Subs 60; Videos 3,613
Subject Interests: Family hist, Local hist

Automation Activity & Vendor Info: (Cataloging) SirsiDynix-WorkFlows; (Circulation) SirsiDynix-WorkFlows; (OPAC) SirsiDynix-Enterprise; (Serials) SirsiDynix-WorkFlows
Wireless access
Function: 24/7 Electronic res, 24/7 Online cat, Activity rm, Adult bk club, Archival coll, Art exhibits, Art programs, Audiobks on Playaways & MP3, Audiobks via web, AV serv, Bk club(s), Bks on CD, Children's prog, Computer training, Computers for patron use, Electronic databases & coll, For res purposes, Free DVD rentals, Govt ref serv, Health sci info serv, Holiday prog, Homebound delivery serv, Homework prog, ILL available, Instruction & testing, Internet access, Laminating, Large print keyboards, Life-long learning prog for all ages, Magazines, Magnifiers for reading, Mail & tel request accepted, Meeting rooms, Movies, Music CDs, Notary serv, Online cat, Outreach serv, Outside serv via phone, mail, e-mail & web, OverDrive digital audio bks, Photocopying/Printing, Preschool outreach, Preschool reading prog, Printer for laptops & handheld devices, Prog for adults, Prog for children & young adult, Ref & res, Ref serv available, Res assist avail, Scanner, Senior outreach, Serves people with intellectual disabilities, STEM programs, Story hour, Study rm, Summer & winter reading prog, Summer reading prog, Tax forms, Teen prog, Telephone ref, Visual arts prog, Wheelchair accessible, Winter reading prog
Publications: Email Newsletter (Monthly)
Partic in Ohio Public Library Information Network
Special Services for the Deaf - Closed caption videos; High interest/low vocabulary bks
Special Services for the Blind - Bks on CD; Home delivery serv; Large print bks; Magnifiers; Playaways (bks on MP3)
Open Mon-Fri 10-7, Sat 10-2

MEDINA

P MEDINA COUNTY DISTRICT LIBRARY*, 210 S Broadway, 44256. SAN 356-8598. Tel: 330-725-0588. Administration Tel: 330-722-6235. FAX: 330-725-2053. TDD: 330-722-6120. Web Site: www.medina.lib.oh.us. *Dir,* Julianne Bedel; E-mail: bedel@mcdl.info; *Asst Dir,* Suzie Muniak; E-mail: muniak@mcdl.info; *Br Mgr,* Christine Gramm; *Coll Res Mgr,* Ms Chri Weaver-Pieh; E-mail: weaver-pieh@mcdl.info; *Tech Serv Mgr,* Sue Schuld; E-mail: schuld@mcdl.info; Staff 170 (MLS 20, Non-MLS 150)
Founded 1905. Pop 130,500; Circ 2,219,488
Library Holdings: Bk Titles 142,547; Bk Vols 575,853; Per Subs 1,289
Subject Interests: Genealogy, Local hist
Automation Activity & Vendor Info: (Circulation) Ex Libris Group
Wireless access
Function: Archival coll
Publications: Library Live (Newsletter)
Partic in CLEVE-NET
Open Mon-Thurs 9-8:30, Fri 9-6, Sat 9-5, Sun (Sept-May) 1-5
Friends of the Library Group
Branches: 5
BRUNSWICK COMMUNITY, 3649 Center Rd, Brunswick, 44212-0430, SAN 356-8628. Tel: 330-273-4150. FAX: 330-225-0310. *Mgr,* Connie Sureck
Open Mon-Thurs 9-8:30, Fri 9-6, Sat 9-5, Sun (Sept-May) 1-5
Friends of the Library Group
BUCKEYE LIBRARY, 6625 Wolff Rd, 44256-6211. Tel: 330-725-4415. FAX: 330-723-6148. *Mgr,* Laura Kettering
Open Mon-Thurs 10-8, Fri & Sat 10-4
Friends of the Library Group
HIGHLAND LIBRARY, 4160 Ridge Rd, 44256-8618. Tel: 330-239-2674, 330-278-4271. FAX: 330-239-1378. *Mgr,* Eric Lucius
Open Mon-Thurs 10-8, Fri & Sat 10-4
Friends of the Library Group
LODI LIBRARY, 635 Wooster St, Lodi, 44254-1311, SAN 356-8687. Tel: 330-948-1885. FAX: 330-948-2410. *Mgr,* Ms Jamie Stilla
Library Holdings: Bk Vols 25,534
Open Mon-Thurs 10-8, Fri & Sat 10-4
Friends of the Library Group
SEVILLE LIBRARY, 45 Center St, Seville, 44273, SAN 356-8717. Tel: 330-769-2852. FAX: 330-769-1774. *Mgr,* Katie Graefnitz
Library Holdings: Bk Vols 22,121
Open Mon-Thurs 10-8, Fri & Sat 10-4
Friends of the Library Group
Bookmobiles: 1. Mgr, Ann Plazek

L MEDINA COUNTY LAW LIBRARY ASSOCIATION, 93 Public Sq, 44256. SAN 320-2232. Tel: 330-725-9744. *Law Libr Asst,* Gina Hotchkiss; E-mail: ghotchkiss@medinaco.org; Staff 2 (Non-MLS 2)
Founded 1899
Restriction: Not open to pub

MENTOR

P MENTOR PUBLIC LIBRARY*, 8215 Mentor Ave, 44060. SAN 356-8741. Tel: 440-255-8811. FAX: 440-578-2622. Web Site: www.mentorpl.org. *Exec Dir,* Cheryl Kuonen; *Dep Dir, Human Res Mgr,* Jen Grill; *Fiscal Officer,* Colleen Snyder; *Adult Info Serv Mgr,* Amy Senning; *Mgr, Ch Serv,* Kim Sidorick; *Circ Mgr,* Judy Schulz; *Commun Engagement Mgr,* Jason Lea; *IT Mgr,* Ed Mikolic; Staff 55 (MLS 10, Non-MLS 45)
Founded 1819. Pop 65,461; Circ 837,685
Library Holdings: AV Mats 24,178; CDs 17,044; DVDs 14,843; e-books 65; Electronic Media & Resources 685; Bk Vols 247,256; Per Subs 346
Automation Activity & Vendor Info: (Acquisitions) Innovative Interfaces, Inc; (Cataloging) Innovative Interfaces, Inc; (Circulation) Innovative Interfaces, Inc; (OPAC) Innovative Interfaces, Inc
Wireless access
Function: Accelerated reader prog, Adult bk club, After school storytime, Art exhibits, Audiobks via web, AV serv, Bk club(s), Bk reviews (Group), Bks on cassette, Bks on CD, CD-ROM, Children's prog, Computer training, Computers for patron use, Digital talking bks, Electronic databases & coll, Free DVD rentals, Holiday prog, Home delivery & serv to seniorr ctr & nursing homes, Homebound delivery serv, ILL available, Instruction & testing, Internet access, Jail serv, Jazz prog, Magnifiers for reading, Mail & tel request accepted, Music CDs, Notary serv, Online cat, Online ref, Outreach serv, Outside serv via phone, mail, e-mail & web, OverDrive digital audio bks, Photocopying/Printing, Preschool outreach, Prof lending libr, Prog for adults, Prog for children & young adult, Ref & res, Ref serv available, Scanner, Senior computer classes, Senior outreach, Serves people with intellectual disabilities, Spoken cassettes & CDs, Spoken cassettes & DVDs, Story hour, Summer reading prog, Tax forms, Teen prog, Telephone ref, VHS videos, Wheelchair accessible, Writing prog
Publications: Cover to Cover (Monthly newsletter)
Partic in Northeast Ohio Regional Library System; Ohio Libr Coun; Ohio Public Library Information Network; OhioNET
Special Services for the Deaf - Bks on deafness & sign lang; Closed caption videos; Staff with knowledge of sign lang
Special Services for the Blind - Assistive/Adapted tech devices, equip & products; Audio mat; Closed circuit TV magnifier; Large print & cassettes; Large print bks; Large print bks & talking machines; Magnifiers; Recorded bks; Ref serv; Talking bk & rec for the blind cat; Talking bk serv referral; Talking bks
Open Mon-Thurs 9-9, Fri & Sat 9-5, Sun 11-5
Friends of the Library Group
Branches: 2
HEADLANDS, 4669 Corduroy Rd, 44060, SAN 356-8776. Tel: 440-257-2000. *Br Mgr,* Josh Sebrasky
Founded 1964
Open Mon & Wed 1-9, Tues & Thurs-Sat 9-5
MENTOR-ON-THE-LAKE, 5642 Andrews Rd, 44060, SAN 356-8806. Tel: 440-257-2512. FAX: 440-257-6886. *Br Mgr,* Mary Detling
Founded 1998
Open Mon & Wed 1-9, Tues & Thurs-Sat 9-5

METAMORA

P EVERGREEN COMMUNITY LIBRARY*, 253 Maple St, 43540. (Mail add: PO Box E, 43540), SAN 313-6175. Tel: 419-644-2771. FAX: 419-644-5778. Web Site: www.evergreencommunitylibrary.org. *Dir,* Jane Dominique; E-mail: jdominique@evergreencommunitylibrary.org; *Ch,* Martie Yunker; E-mail: myunker@evergreencommunitylibrary.org; *YA Librn,* Debbie Henricks; E-mail: debhenricks@gmail.com
Founded 1927. Pop 7,000; Circ 72,943
Library Holdings: Bk Vols 37,000; Per Subs 130
Automation Activity & Vendor Info: (Cataloging) Innovative Interfaces, Inc; (Circulation) Innovative Interfaces, Inc; (OPAC) Innovative Interfaces, Inc
Wireless access
Partic in Association for Rural & Small Libraries; Northwestern Libr District
Open Mon 12-8, Tues & Thurs 10-6, Wed 10-8, Fri 12-5, Sat 10-2

MIDDLEBURG HEIGHTS

R MIDDLEBURG HEIGHTS COMMUNITY CHURCH LIBRARY*, United Church of Christ, 7165 Big Creek Pkwy, 44130. SAN 313-6205. Tel: 440-842-7743. Web Site: www.mhcucc.org. *Librn,* Lois Reinke
Library Holdings: Bk Titles 1,068
Subject Interests: Family, Relig
Restriction: Mem only

MIDDLETOWN

P MIDPOINTE LIBRARY SYSTEM*, 125 S Broad St, 45044. SAN 356-889X. Tel: 513-424-1251. Administration Tel: 513-424-0659. FAX: 513-424-6585. Web Site: www.midpointelibrary.org. *Dir,* Travis Bautz; E-mail: tbautz@midpointelibrary.org; *Fiscal Officer,* Deborah Preston;

E-mail: dpreston@midpointelibrary.org; *Mgr, Human Res,* Katherine A Stengel; E-mail: kstengel@midpointelibrary.org; Staff 83 (MLS 16.5, Non-MLS 66.5)
Founded 1911. Pop 180,783; Circ 2,125,964
Library Holdings: Audiobooks 48,514; AV Mats 33,377; e-books 142,248; Bk Vols 299,905; Per Subs 820
Special Collections: George C Crout Local History Coll
Subject Interests: Genealogy, Ohioana
Wireless access
Partic in Ohio Library & Information Network
Special Services for the Blind - Talking bks
Open Mon-Thurs 9-9, Fri 9-7, Sat 9-5, Sun 11-5
Friends of the Library Group
Branches: 4
LIBERTY TOWNSHIP BRANCH, 7100 Foundry Row, Ste S-234, Liberty Township, 45069. Tel: 513-318-1580. *Br Mgr,* Allison Knight
Open Tues-Sat 10-7, Sun 1-5
MONROE BRANCH, One Tennesse Ave, Monroe, 45050. Tel: 513-360-6224. *Br Mgr,* Kim Mullally; E-mail: kmullally@midpointelibrary.org
Open Mon-Fri 10-7, Sat 10-5
TRENTON BRANCH, 200 Edgewood Dr, Trenton, 45067, SAN 356-892X. Tel: 513-988-9050. FAX: 513-988-5059. *Br Mgr,* Amy Young; Tel: 513-988-9930, E-mail: ayoung@midpointelibrary.org
Founded 1974
Library Holdings: AV Mats 5,120; Bk Vols 15,578; Per Subs 107
Open Mon-Thurs 9-9, Fri 9-7, Sat 9-5, Sun 1-5
Friends of the Library Group
WEST CHESTER BRANCH, 9363 Centre Pointe Dr, West Chester, 45069, SAN 356-8954. Tel: 513-777-3131. FAX: 513-777-8452. *Br Mgr,* Steven Mayhugh; Tel: 513-777-3717, E-mail: smayhugh@middletownlibrary.org
Library Holdings: AV Mats 31,381; Bk Vols 101,481; Per Subs 404
Open Mon-Thurs 9-9, Fri 9-7, Sat 9-5, Sun 1-5
Friends of the Library Group

MILAN

P MILAN-BERLIN LIBRARY DISTRICT*, 19 E Church St, 44846. (Mail add: PO Box 1550, 44846-1550), SAN 356-8989. Tel: 419-499-4117. Administration Tel: 419-499-4696. FAX: 419-499-4697. Web Site: www.milan-berlin.lib.oh.us. *Dir,* James Tolbert; E-mail: james.tolbert@milan-berlin.lib.oh.us; Staff 1 (MLS 1)
Founded 1877. Pop 9,462; Circ 222,807
Library Holdings: AV Mats 12,666; Bk Vols 79,061; Per Subs 130
Special Collections: Barbour Coll; Birth & Death Records; Census Index; Family Genealogies; Immigration Records; Local History (Edison Coll); Local newspaper; Passenger Lists. Oral History
Subject Interests: Genealogy, Local hist
Automation Activity & Vendor Info: (Cataloging) SirsiDynix; (Circulation) SirsiDynix; (ILL) SirsiDynix; (OPAC) SirsiDynix
Wireless access
Partic in Northeast Ohio Regional Library System
Open Mon-Thurs 9:30-7:30, Fri & Sat 9:30-5
Branches: 1
BERLIN PUBLIC LIBRARY, Four E Main St, Berlin Heights, 44814-9602. (Mail add: PO Box 139, Berlin Heights, 44814-0139), SAN 356-9012. Tel: 419-588-2250. FAX: 419-588-0025. *Br Mgr,* Joanne Chaffee
Open Mon-Thurs 9:30-7:30, Fri & Sat 9:30-5

MILFORD

P CLERMONT COUNTY PUBLIC LIBRARY*, Administration Office, 5920 Buckwheat Rd, 45150. SAN 355-5542. Tel: 513-732-2736. Web Site: www.clermontlibrary.org. *Dir,* Chris Wick; E-mail: cwick@clermontlibrary.org; *Asst Dir,* Leslie Jacobs; E-mail: ljacobs@clermontlibrary.org; Staff 182 (MLS 19, Non-MLS 163)
Founded 1955. Pop 195,385; Circ 1,689,696
Library Holdings: Audiobooks 26,723; CDs 26,485; DVDs 49,924; e-books 212; Electronic Media & Resources 52; Large Print Bks 24,990; Microforms 246; Bk Vols 448,708; Per Subs 1,084; Videos 9,098
Special Collections: Oral History; State Document Depository
Subject Interests: Genealogy, Local hist
Automation Activity & Vendor Info: (Acquisitions) Innovative Interfaces, Inc; (Cataloging) Innovative Interfaces, Inc; (Circulation) Innovative Interfaces, Inc; (Course Reserve) Innovative Interfaces, Inc; (ILL) Innovative Interfaces, Inc; (OPAC) Innovative Interfaces, Inc; (Serials) Innovative Interfaces, Inc
Wireless access
Function: Adult bk club, Audiobks via web, Bks on cassette, Bks on CD, Children's prog, Computer training, Computers for patron use, Electronic databases & coll, Family literacy, Free DVD rentals, Genealogy discussion group, Holiday prog, ILL available, Large print keyboards, Magnifiers for reading, Music CDs, Notary serv, Online cat, Online ref, Outreach serv, OverDrive digital audio bks, Photocopying/Printing, Preschool outreach, Prog for adults, Prog for children & young adult, Ref serv available, Senior outreach, Spoken cassettes & CDs, Spoken cassettes & DVDs, Story hour, Summer reading prog, Tax forms, Teen prog, Telephone ref, Wheelchair accessible
Partic in Ohio Public Library Information Network; SouthWest Ohio & Neighboring Libraries
Open Mon-Fri 8-4:30
Friends of the Library Group
Branches: 10
AMELIA BRANCH, 58 Maple St, Amelia, 45102, SAN 329-594X. Tel: 513-752-5580. FAX: 513-752-5266. *Br Mgr,* Beth Lammrish; E-mail: blammrish@clermontlibrary.org
Open Mon & Tues 12-8, Wed & Thurs 10-6, Fri & Sat 9-5
BATAVIA-DORIS WOOD BRANCH, 180 S Third St, Batavia, 45103-2806, SAN 355-5550. Tel: 513-732-2128. FAX: 513-732-2498. *Br Mgr,* Chris Rich; E-mail: crich@clermontlibrary.org
Open Mon & Tues 12-8, Wed & Thurs 10-6, Fri & Sat 9-5
BETHEL BRANCH, 611 W Plane St, Bethel, 45106-1302, SAN 355-5577. Tel: 513-734-2619. FAX: 513-734-1321. *Br Mgr,* Allison Lehman; E-mail: alehman@clermontlibrary.org; *Br Supvr,* Patty Szuszkiewicz; E-mail: pszuszkiewicz@clermontlibrary.org
Open Mon & Tues 12-8, Wed & Thurs 10-6, Fri & Sat 9-5
FELICITY BRANCH, 209 Prather Rd, Felicity, 45120, SAN 374-4299. Tel: 513-876-4134. FAX: 513-876-3619. *Br Supvr,* Amy Vogel; E-mail: avogel@clermontlibrary.org
Open Mon & Tues 12-8, Wed & Thurs 10-6, Fri & Sat 9-5
GOSHEN BRANCH, 6678 State Rte 132, Goshen, 45122, SAN 323-777X. Tel: 513-722-1221. FAX: 513-722-2158. *Br Mgr,* Lisa Breithaupt; E-mail: lbreithaupt@clermontlibrary.org
Open Mon & Tues 12-8, Wed & Thurs 10-6, Fri & Sat 9-5
MIAMI TOWNSHIP BRANCH, 5920 Buckwheat Rd, 45150, SAN 355-5607. Tel: 513-248-0700. FAX: 513-248-4579. *Br Mgr,* Laurie Henry; E-mail: lhenry@clermontlibrary.org
Open Mon & Tues 12-8, Wed & Thurs 10-6, Fri & Sat 9-5
NEW RICHMOND BRANCH, 103 River Valley Blvd, New Richmond, 45157, SAN 355-5615. Tel: 513-553-0570. FAX: 513-553-0574. *Br Mgr,* Amy Buskey; E-mail: abuskey@clermontlibrary.org
Open Mon & Tues 12-8, Wed & Thurs 10-6, Fri & Sat 9-5
OWENSVILLE BRANCH, 2548 US Rte 50, Owensville, 45160. (Mail add: PO Box 875, Owensville, 45160-0875), SAN 377-7197. Tel: 513-732-6084. FAX: 513-732-9168. *Br Mgr,* Chris Rich; E-mail: crich@clermontlibrary.org
Open Mon & Tues 12-8, Wed & Thurs 10-6, Fri & Sat 9-5
UNION TOWNSHIP, 4450 Glen Este-Withamsville Rd, Cincinnati, 45245, SAN 355-5631. Tel: 513-528-1744. FAX: 513-528-0539. *Br Mgr,* Garria Blundell; E-mail: gblundell@clermontlibrary.org
Open Mon & Tues 12-8, Wed & Thurs 10-6, Fri & Sat 9-5
WILLIAMSBURG BRANCH, 594 Main St, Williamsburg, 45176, SAN 329-5966. Tel: 513-724-1070. FAX: 513-724-5549. *Br Mgr,* Emily Wichman; E-mail: ewichman@clermontlibrary.org
Open Mon & Tues 12-8, Wed & Thurs 10-6, Fri & Sat 9-5

MILLERSBURG

P HOLMES COUNTY DISTRICT PUBLIC LIBRARY*, 3102 Glen Dr, 44654. SAN 356-9047. Tel: 330-674-5972. Circulation Tel: 330-674-5972, Ext 200. Reference Tel: 330-674-5972, Ext 203. FAX: 330-674-1938. E-mail: holmeslibrary@holmeslib.org. Web Site: www.holmeslibrary.org. *Dir,* Paula Cicconetti; Tel: 330-674-5972, Ext 202, E-mail: pcicconetti@holmeslib.org; Staff 35 (MLS 5, Non-MLS 30)
Founded 1928. Pop 40,000; Circ 459,837
Library Holdings: Bk Titles 74,500; Bk Vols 145,000; Per Subs 128
Special Collections: Amish & Mennonite Genealogies Coll
Automation Activity & Vendor Info: (Cataloging) SirsiDynix; (Circulation) SirsiDynix; (ILL) SirsiDynix; (OPAC) SirsiDynix
Wireless access
Publications: History of Holmes County
Partic in Serving Every Ohioan Library Center
Open Mon, Tues & Thurs 10-8, Wed, Fri & Sat 10-5
Friends of the Library Group
Branches: 2
KILLBUCK BRANCH, 160 W Front St, Killbuck, 44637. (Mail add: PO Box 99, Killbuck, 44637-0099), SAN 356-9136. Tel: 330-276-0882. FAX: 330-276-0882. *Librn,* Sharon Hoxworth
Circ 8,000
Open Mon & Wed 10-5, Tues & Thurs 1-7, Sat 10-2
WALNUT CREEK BRANCH, 4877 Olde Pump St, Walnut Creek, 44687. (Mail add: 3102 Glen Dr, 44654), SAN 356-9195. Tel: 330-893-3464. FAX: 330-893-8464. *Br Mgr,* Kimberli Hiller
Circ 18,000
Open Mon & Wed 10-4, Tues & Thurs 2-8, Sat 10-4
Bookmobiles: 2

L HOLMES COUNTY LAW LIBRARY*, Courthouse, Ste 204, One E Jackson St, 44654. SAN 327-3911. Tel: 330-763-2956. E-mail: lawlibrary@co.holmes.oh.us. *Librn,* Pamela Maxfield-Ontko
Partic in Ohio Law Library Consortium
Open Mon & Thurs 8:30-11:30

MINERAL CITY

P MINERAL CITY NICOLE DONANT LIBRARY*, 8503 N High St, 44656. (Mail add: PO Box 326, 44656). Tel: 330-859-9100. E-mail: mcndlmail@gmail.com. *Dir,* Marlene Roadpouch
Founded 2006
Library Holdings: Bk Titles 6,000
Wireless access
Friends of the Library Group

MINERVA

P MINERVA PUBLIC LIBRARY, 677 Lynnwood Dr, 44657-1200. SAN 313-6256. Tel: 330-868-4101. FAX: 330-868-4267. Web Site: www.minervalibrary.info. *Exec Dir,* Tom Dillie; E-mail: minervadirector@gmail.com; *Fiscal Officer,* Christina Davies; E-mail: mplfiscalofficer@gmail.com; *Youth Serv Mgr,* Kathy Heller; E-mail: minervalibraryyouth@gmail.com; Staff 4 (MLS 3, Non-MLS 1)
Founded 1913. Pop 12,289; Circ 212,338
Jan 2015-Dec 2015 Income $730,512, State $701,445, Locally Generated Income $29,067. Mats Exp $60,927, Books $31,988, Per/Ser (Incl. Access Fees) $7,382, Other Print Mats $240, AV Mat $21,306. Sal $296,085 (Prof $140,672)
Library Holdings: Audiobooks 3,276; CDs 3,096; DVDs 12,172; e-books 725,000; Large Print Bks 2,451; Microforms 80; Bk Vols 86,095; Per Subs 157
Subject Interests: Circus, Clowns, Local genealogy, Local hist
Automation Activity & Vendor Info: (Cataloging) SirsiDynix-WorkFlows; (Circulation) SirsiDynix-WorkFlows; (OPAC) SirsiDynix
Wireless access
Function: 24/7 Electronic res, 24/7 Online cat, Activity rm, Adult bk club, Art exhibits, Audiobks via web, Bk club(s), Bks on CD, Children's prog, Computer training, Computers for patron use, Digital talking bks, Electronic databases & coll, Free DVD rentals, ILL available, Internet access, Magazines, Magnifiers for reading, Mail & tel request accepted, Mango lang, Meeting rooms, Microfiche/film & reading machines, Movies, Music CDs, Online cat, OverDrive digital audio bks, Photocopying/Printing, Preschool outreach, Prog for adults, Prog for children & young adult, Ref serv available, Scanner, Story hour, Study rm, Summer & winter reading prog, Summer reading prog, Tax forms, Teen prog, Telephone ref, Wheelchair accessible, Winter reading prog
Partic in Serving Every Ohioan Library Center
Open Mon & Thurs 10-8, Tues, Wed & Friday 10-5, Sat 10-2

MONROEVILLE

P MONROEVILLE PUBLIC LIBRARY*, 34 Monroe St, 44847. (Mail add: PO Box 276, 44847-0276), SAN 313-6264. Tel: 419-465-2035. FAX: 419-465-2812. Web Site: monroevillepl.org. *Dir,* Vikki Morrow-Ritchie; E-mail: vmorrow@monroevillepl.org
Pop 2,000; Circ 46,000
Library Holdings: Bk Vols 21,000; Per Subs 32
Automation Activity & Vendor Info: (Cataloging) SirsiDynix; (Circulation) SirsiDynix; (OPAC) SirsiDynix
Wireless access
Partic in NORWELD; Serving Every Ohioan Library Center
Open Mon, Wed & Fri 10-5, Tues & Thurs 10-7, Sat 10-1
Friends of the Library Group

MONTGOMERY

SR MONTGOMERY PRESBYTERIAN CHURCH LIBRARY, 9994 Zig Zag Rd, 45242. SAN 328-414X. Tel: 513-891-8670. E-mail: mpc.office@mpchurch.net. Web Site: mpchurch.net.
Library Holdings: Bk Vols 2,250
Special Collections: Audiovisual Materials; Children's bks
Subject Interests: Relig
Open Mon-Thurs 9:30-4:30

MONTPELIER

P MONTPELIER PUBLIC LIBRARY*, 216 E Main St, 43543-1199. SAN 356-925X. Tel: 419-485-3287. FAX: 419-485-5671. Web Site: montpelierpubliclibrary.oplin.org. *Dir,* Angie Humphrey; E-mail: ahumphrey@seolibraries.org; Staff 8 (Non-MLS 8)
Founded 1927. Pop 38,000; Circ 67,066
Library Holdings: Bk Vols 60,150; Per Subs 70
Automation Activity & Vendor Info: (Cataloging) SirsiDynix; (Circulation) SirsiDynix
Wireless access
Partic in NORWELD; Serving Every Ohioan Library Center
Open Mon & Thurs 9-8, Tues, Wed & Fri 9-5, Sat 10-1

MORROW

P SALEM TOWNSHIP PUBLIC LIBRARY*, 535 W Pike St, 45152. SAN 313-6272. Tel: 513-899-2588. FAX: 513-899-9420. E-mail: salemtwppl@salem-township.lib.oh.us. Web Site: www.salem-township.lib.oh.us. *Dir,* Jerri A Short; E-mail: shortje@salem-township.lib.oh.us
Founded 1884. Pop 30,822; Circ 211,559
Library Holdings: DVDs 1,146; Bk Titles 74,525; Bk Vols 85,106; Per Subs 226; Talking Bks 14,601; Videos 5,825
Automation Activity & Vendor Info: (Circulation) Innovative Interfaces, Inc; (OPAC) Innovative Interfaces, Inc
Wireless access
Function: ILL available
Open Mon & Tues 10-8, Wed & Thurs 10-6, Fri 10-5, Sat (Winter) 10-2

MOUNT GILEAD

P MOUNT GILEAD PUBLIC LIBRARY*, 41 E High St, 43338-1429. SAN 313-6280. Tel: 419-947-5866. FAX: 419-947-9252. E-mail: staff@mglibrary.org. Web Site: www.mt-gilead.lib.oh.us. *Dir,* Mike Kirk; E-mail: mike@mglibrary.org
Founded 1908
Library Holdings: Bk Vols 27,098; Per Subs 104
Automation Activity & Vendor Info: (Cataloging) Follett Software; (Circulation) Follett Software; (OPAC) Follett Software
Wireless access
Partic in Consortium of Ohio Libraries
Open Mon-Thurs 10:30-7, Fri & Sat 10:30-5
Friends of the Library Group

MOUNT ORAB

P BROWN COUNTY PUBLIC LIBRARY*, 613 S High St, 45154. (Mail add: PO Box 527, 45154-0527). Tel: 937-444-0181. FAX: 937-444-6502. E-mail: bcpl.bcplinfo@gmail.com. Web Site: www.browncountypubliclibrary.org. *Exec Dir,* Lynn A Harden; E-mail: bcpl.bookly@gmail.com; *Asst Dir,* Heather Patten; E-mail: bcpl.pattenhe@gmail.com; Staff 2 (MLS 2)
Founded 1920. Pop 32,500
Library Holdings: Bk Vols 103,050; Per Subs 380
Special Collections: State Document Depository
Automation Activity & Vendor Info: (Cataloging) SirsiDynix; (Circulation) SirsiDynix; (ILL) SirsiDynix; (OPAC) SirsiDynix
Wireless access
Function: 24/7 Electronic res, 24/7 Online cat, Accelerated reader prog, Activity rm, Adult bk club, Audio & video playback equip for onsite use, Audiobks on Playaways & MP3, Audiobks via web, Bk club(s), Bks on cassette, Bks on CD, CD-ROM, Children's prog, Computer training, Computers for patron use, Digital talking bks, Distance learning, Electronic databases & coll, Equip loans & repairs, Family literacy, Free DVD rentals, Holiday prog, Home delivery & serv to seniorr ctr & nursing homes, Homebound delivery serv, Homework prog, ILL available, Internet access, Magazines, Magnifiers for reading, Mail & tel request accepted, Meeting rooms, Microfiche/film & reading machines, Movies, Music CDs, Online cat, Orientations, Outside serv via phone, mail, e-mail & web, OverDrive digital audio bks, Photocopying/Printing, Preschool outreach, Preschool reading prog, Prog for adults, Prog for children & young adult, Ref & res, Ref serv available, Scanner, Senior computer classes, Senior outreach, Spoken cassettes & CDs, Spoken cassettes & DVDs, Story hour, Summer & winter reading prog, Summer reading prog, Tax forms, Teen prog, Telephone ref, VHS videos, Wheelchair accessible, Winter reading prog, Workshops
Friends of the Library Group
Branches: 4
FAYETTEVILLE-PERRY BRANCH, 406 N East St, Fayetteville, 45118. Tel: 513-274-2665. FAX: 513-274-2738. E-mail: fayettevilleperrylibrary@gmail.com. *Mgr,* Amber Becraft-Johnan; E-mail: bcpl.abecraftjohnan@gmail.com
Founded 1999
Friends of the Library Group
MT ORAB BRANCH, 613 S High St, 45154. Tel: 937-444-1414. FAX: 937-444-6502. E-mail: bcplmto@gmail.com. *Mgr,* Heather Patten; E-mail: bcpl.pattenhe@gmail.com; Staff 1 (MLS 1)
Founded 1998
Open Mon, Tues & Thurs 9-8, Fri & Sat 9-4
Friends of the Library Group
SARDINIA BRANCH, 13309 Purdy Rd, Sardinia, 45171. Tel: 937-446-1565. FAX: 937-445-1506. E-mail: sardinialibrary@gmail.com. *Mgr,* Ginny Bridges; E-mail: bcpl.bridgegi@gmail.com
Founded 1999
Open Mon & Tues 11-6, Wed & Thurs 11-7, Fri & Sat 11-4
Friends of the Library Group

MARY P SHELTON BRANCH, 200 W Grant Ave, Georgetown, 45121. Tel: 937-378-3197. FAX: 937-378-4296. E-mail: marysheltonlibrary@gmail.com. *Mgr,* Tonya Hensley; E-mail: bcpl.hensleto@gmail.com
Founded 1920
Open Mon & Tues 10-8, Wed & Thurs 10-7, Fri & Sat 10-4
Friends of the Library Group

MOUNT STERLING

P MOUNT STERLING PUBLIC LIBRARY*, 60 W Columbus St, 43143. SAN 313-6302. Tel: 740-869-2430. FAX: 740-869-3617. E-mail: sterlinglibrary60@yahoo.com. Web Site: www.mtsterlingpubliclibrary.org. *Dir,* Christopher Siscoe; *Asst Dir,* Sharon Morgan; *Fiscal Officer,* Abbie Riley; Staff 12 (Non-MLS 12)
Founded 1913. Pop 10,995; Circ 40,568
Library Holdings: Bks on Deafness & Sign Lang 30; Bk Vols 35,000; Per Subs 40
Automation Activity & Vendor Info: (Acquisitions) SirsiDynix; (Cataloging) SirsiDynix; (Circulation) SirsiDynix; (Course Reserve) SirsiDynix; (OPAC) SirsiDynix
Wireless access
Partic in Ohio Public Library Information Network; Serving Every Ohioan Library Center
Open Mon & Wed 10-5, Tues & Thurs 12-7, Fri & Sat 10-2
Friends of the Library Group

MOUNT VERNON

M KNOX COMMUNITY HOSPITAL*, Medical Library, 1330 Coshocton Rd, 43050. SAN 327-5612. Tel: 740-393-9000. FAX: 740-399-3113. *Lead Doc Imaging/Application Spec,* Todd Williams; E-mail: todd.williams@knoxcommhosp.org
Library Holdings: Bk Vols 1,215; Per Subs 15

C MOUNT VERNON NAZARENE UNIVERSITY*, Thorne Library & Learning Resource Center, 800 Martinsburg Rd, 43050-9500. SAN 313-6310. Tel: 740-397-9000, Ext 4240. FAX: 740-397-8847. Web Site: library.mvnu.edu. *Libr Dir,* Tim Radcliffe; E-mail: tradcliffe@mvnu.edu; *Asst Dir, Student Serv Librn,* Gayle Riedel; E-mail: gayle.riedel@mvnu.edu; Staff 2 (MLS 2)
Founded 1968. Enrl 2,205; Fac 256; Highest Degree: Master
Library Holdings: AV Mats 3,419; CDs 861; DVDs 420; e-books 806; Microforms 23; Bk Titles 100,952; Bk Vols 164,235; Videos 673
Special Collections: Church of the Nazarene, Doctrine, History & Missions
Automation Activity & Vendor Info: (Acquisitions) Innovative Interfaces, Inc - Sierra; (Cataloging) Innovative Interfaces, Inc - Sierra; (Circulation) Innovative Interfaces, Inc - Sierra; (Course Reserve) Innovative Interfaces, Inc - Sierra; (Discovery) EBSCO Discovery Service; (ILL) OCLC; (Media Booking) Innovative Interfaces, Inc - Sierra; (OPAC) Innovative Interfaces, Inc - Sierra; (Serials) Innovative Interfaces, Inc - Sierra
Wireless access
Partic in Ohio Library & Information Network; OhioNET

P PUBLIC LIBRARY OF MOUNT VERNON & KNOX COUNTY*, 201 N Mulberry St, 43050-2413. SAN 356-9314. Tel: 740-392-2665. Reference Tel: 740-392-2665, Ext 230. FAX: 740-397-3866. E-mail: library@knox.net. Web Site: www.knox.net. *Dir,* John K Chidester; E-mail: jchidest@knox.net; *Asst Dir,* Cassandra Peters; *Circ,* Teresa Goeppinger; *Tech Serv,* Carol Patterson; *YA Serv,* Morgan Newton; Staff 18 (MLS 4, Non-MLS 14)
Founded 1888
Library Holdings: Bk Vols 166,395; Per Subs 651
Automation Activity & Vendor Info: (Acquisitions) Innovative Interfaces, Inc; (Cataloging) Innovative Interfaces, Inc; (Circulation) Innovative Interfaces, Inc; (Course Reserve) Innovative Interfaces, Inc; (ILL) Innovative Interfaces, Inc; (Media Booking) Innovative Interfaces, Inc; (OPAC) Innovative Interfaces, Inc; (Serials) Innovative Interfaces, Inc
Wireless access
Function: 24/7 Online cat, Activity rm, Adult bk club, After school storytime, Archival coll, Audiobks on Playaways & MP3, Audiobks via web, AV serv, Bk club(s), Bks on CD, Children's prog, Computer training, Computers for patron use, Digital talking bks, E-Readers, Electronic databases & coll, Free DVD rentals, Games & aids for people with disabilities, Holiday prog, Home delivery & serv to seniorr ctr & nursing homes, Homebound delivery serv, ILL available, Internet access, Jail serv, Magazines, Magnifiers for reading, Makerspace, Mango lang, Meeting rooms, Microfiche/film & reading machines, Movies, Music CDs, Notary serv, Online cat, Online ref, Outreach serv, Outside serv via phone, mail, e-mail & web, OverDrive digital audio bks, Photocopying/Printing, Preschool outreach, Preschool reading prog, Prog for adults, Prog for children & young adult, Ref & res, Ref serv available, Res assist avail, Satellite serv, Senior computer classes, Senior outreach, Serves people with intellectual disabilities, Spanish lang bks, Spoken cassettes & CDs, Spoken cassettes & DVDs, STEM programs, Story hour, Summer & winter reading prog, Summer reading prog, Tax forms, Teen prog, Wheelchair accessible, Winter reading prog, Workshops, Writing prog
Open Mon-Thurs 9-8, Fri & Sat 9-5, Sun 1-5
Friends of the Library Group
Branches: 3
DANVILLE PUBLIC, 512 S Market St, Danville, 43014-9609, SAN 356-9349. Tel: 740-599-2665. FAX: 740-599-2665. *Mgr,* Elizabeth Carpenter; Staff 1 (Non-MLS 1)
Library Holdings: Bk Vols 21,000
Open Mon & Tues 1-8, Wed-Fri 10-5, Sat 1-5
Friends of the Library Group
FREDERICKTOWN COMMUNITY, One Burgett Dr, Fredericktown, 43019, SAN 356-9373. Tel: 740-694-2665. FAX: 740-694-3106. *Br Mgr,* Janelle Cothren; Staff 1 (Non-MLS 1)
Library Holdings: Bk Vols 42,500
Open Mon-Thurs 10-8, Fri & Sat 10-5
Friends of the Library Group
GAMBIER PUBLIC, 115 Meadow Lane, Gambier, 43022. (Mail add: PO Box 1984, Gambier, 43022), SAN 370-0194. Tel: 740-427-2665. FAX: 740-427-2665. *Librn,* Elizabeth Carpenter; Staff 1 (Non-MLS 1)
Library Holdings: Bk Vols 15,480
Open Mon & Thurs-Sat 10-12:30 & 1:30-5, Tues & Wed 11-8
Friends of the Library Group

MOUNT VICTORY

P RIDGEMONT PUBLIC LIBRARY*, 124 E Taylor St, 43340. (Mail add: PO Box 318, 43340-0318), SAN 356-9403. Tel: 937-354-4445. FAX: 937-354-4445. Web Site: www.ridgemont.lib.oh.us. *Dir,* Beccy Ramsey; E-mail: bramsey@rrohio.com; *Ch Serv,* Kate Hanson
Circ 22,396
Library Holdings: Bk Vols 17,000; Per Subs 19
Wireless access
Partic in NORWELD; Serving Every Ohioan Library Center
Open Mon, Tues & Thurs 10-6, Sat 10-1
Branches: 1
RIDGEWAY BRANCH, 109 Main St, Ridgeway, 43345. (Mail add: PO Box 2, Ridgeway, 43345-0002), SAN 356-9438. Tel: 937-363-3066. FAX: 937-363-3066. *Librn,* Molly Gallo

NAPOLEON

L HENRY COUNTY LAW LIBRARY*, 609 N Perry St, 43545. SAN 327-6570. Tel: 419-599-1936. FAX: 419-592-4451. *Library Contact,* John Donovan; E-mail: jonh@bgp.nu
Library Holdings: Bk Titles 5,000

P NAPOLEON PUBLIC LIBRARY*, 310 W Clinton St, 43545. SAN 356-9462. Tel: 419-592-2531. FAX: 419-599-1472. Reference E-mail: napoleonpubliclibrary@gmail.com. Web Site: www.napoleon.lib.oh.us. *Dir,* Betsy K Eggers; E-mail: beggers@seolibraries.org; *Fiscal Officer,* Laurie Norden; *Outreach Librn,* Barb George; *Adult Serv,* Su Jones; *Ch Serv,* Lori Brownson; Staff 14.8 (MLS 2, Non-MLS 12.8)
Founded 1906. Pop 28,000; Circ 135,875
Library Holdings: AV Mats 10,690; Bk Vols 145,140; Per Subs 252; Videos 1,153
Special Collections: County Papers from 1852, microfilm
Automation Activity & Vendor Info: (Cataloging) Innovative Interfaces, Inc; (Circulation) Innovative Interfaces, Inc; (ILL) Innovative Interfaces, Inc; (OPAC) Innovative Interfaces, Inc
Wireless access
Partic in NORWELD; Serving Every Ohioan Library Center
Open Mon & Thurs 9:30-8:30, Tues, Wed & Fri 9:30-5:30, Sat 9:30-1
Branches: 2
FLORIDA PUBLIC, 671 County Rd 17D, 43545-9215, SAN 356-9470. Tel: 419-762-5876. FAX: 419-762-5645. *Br Head,* Paula Steele
Function: Accelerated reader prog, Art exhibits, Audiobks via web, Children's prog, Computers for patron use, Electronic databases & coll, ILL available, OverDrive digital audio bks, Photocopying/Printing, Preschool reading prog, Story hour, Tax forms
Open Mon-Wed 1-5:30, Thurs 2-6:30
MCCLURE COMMUNITY, 110 Cross St, McClure, 43534-0035, SAN 356-9497. Tel: 419-748-8922. FAX: 419-748-8917. *Br Head,* Barbara Dawson
Function: Accelerated reader prog, Computers for patron use, ILL available, Photocopying/Printing, Preschool reading prog, Tax forms
Open Mon, Tues & Wed 1-5:30, Thurs 2-6:30

NELSONVILLE

P ATHENS COUNTY PUBLIC LIBRARIES*, 95 W Washington, 45764-1177. SAN 356-9527. Tel: 740-753-2118. FAX: 740-753-3543. E-mail: nelpl@athenscounty.lib.oh.us. Web Site: www.myacpl.org. *Dir,* Nicholas Tepe; E-mail: ntepe@myacpl.org; *Asst Libr Dir,* Lindsay Place; E-mail: lplace@myacpl.org; *Outreach Serv Mgr,* Laura O'Neil; E-mail:

loneil@myacpl.org; *Access Serv Coordr,* Heather McElfresh; E-mail: hmcelfresh@myacpl.org; *Youth Serv Coordr,* Taryn Lentes; Tel: 740-592-4272, E-mail: tlentes@myacpl.org; *Communications Officer,* Becca Lachman; E-mail: blachman@myacpl.org; *Fiscal Officer,* Hannah King; E-mail: hking@myacpl.org; *Web Developer,* Owen Leonard; E-mail: oleonard@myacpl.org; Staff 11 (MLS 8, Non-MLS 3)
Founded 1935. Pop 61,000; Circ 563,000
Library Holdings: Bk Vols 60,000; Per Subs 189
Automation Activity & Vendor Info: (Cataloging) Koha; (Circulation) Koha; (OPAC) Koha; (Serials) Koha
Wireless access
Function: Activity rm, Adult bk club, After school storytime, Archival coll, Art exhibits, Audiobks on Playaways & MP3, Audiobks via web, AV serv, Bi-weekly Writer's Group, Bk club(s), Bks on CD, Chess club, Children's prog, Computer training, Computers for patron use, E-Reserves, Electronic databases & coll, Holiday prog, ILL available, Internet access, Jail serv, Laminating, Life-long learning prog for all ages, Magazines, Magnifiers for reading, Meeting rooms, Movies, Music CDs, Online cat, Outreach serv, OverDrive digital audio bks, Photocopying/Printing, Preschool outreach, Prog for adults, Prog for children & young adult, Ref serv available, Scanner, Senior computer classes, Serves people with intellectual disabilities, Story hour, Summer reading prog, Tax forms, Teen prog, Wheelchair accessible, Workshops
Partic in Southeast Regional Library System
Open Mon 10-7, Tues-Thurs 10-6, Fri 10-5, Sat 9-1
Branches: 6
ATHENS PUBLIC LIBRARY, 30 Home St, Athens, 45701, SAN 356-9551. Tel: 740-592-4272. FAX: 740-594-4204. *Br Mgr,* Julie Standish; E-mail: jstandish@myacpl.org
Library Holdings: Bk Vols 133,000
Open Mon-Thurs 9-8, Fri & Sat 9-5
Friends of the Library Group
CHAUNCEY PUBLIC, 29 Converse St, Chauncey, 45719. (Mail add: PO Box 3777, Chauncey, 45719), SAN 356-9586. Tel: 740-797-2512. FAX: 740-797-2512. *Br Mgr,* Lee Branner
Library Holdings: Bk Vols 7,000
Open Mon-Fri 10-6, Sat 9-1
COOLVILLE PUBLIC, 26401 Main St, Coolville, 45723-9059. (Mail add: PO Box 109, Coolville, 45723-0109), SAN 376-8503. Tel: 740-667-3354. FAX: 740-667-3354. *Br Mgr,* Roxanne Rupe; E-mail: rrupe@myacpl.org
Library Holdings: Bk Vols 11,000
Open Mon-Fri 10-6
GLOUSTER PUBLIC, 20 Toledo St, Glouster, 45732, SAN 356-9616. Tel: 740-767-3670. FAX: 740-767-3670. *Br Mgr,* Karen M Guffey; E-mail: kguffey@myacpl.org; *Ch,* Deb Couch
Library Holdings: Bk Vols 21,000
Open Mon-Thurs 10-6, Fri 9-5, Sat 9-1
THE PLAINS PUBLIC, 14 S Plains Rd, The Plains, 45780, SAN 375-6009. Tel: 740-797-4579. FAX: 740-797-4579. *Br Mgr,* Ken Robinson
Library Holdings: Bk Vols 35,000
Open Mon-Fri 10-6, Sat 9-1
WELLS PUBLIC LIBRARY, 5200 Washington Rd, Albany, 45710, SAN 376-8511. Tel: 740-698-3059. FAX: 740-698-3059. *Br Mgr,* Mary VanDoren; E-mail: mvandoren@myacpl.org
Library Holdings: Bk Vols 14,000
Open Mon 10-7, Tues-Thurs 10-6, Fri 10-5, Sat 9-1

J HOCKING COLLEGE LIBRARY*, Davidson Hall, First Flr, 3301 Hocking Pkwy, 45764. SAN 313-6337. Tel: 740-753-6332. Reference Tel: 740-753-6334. E-mail: library@hocking.edu. Web Site: libguides.hocking.edu, www.hocking.edu/library. *Dir,* Jeff Graffius; Tel: 740-753-6338, E-mail: graffiusj@hocking.edu; Staff 4 (MLS 3, Non-MLS 1)
Founded 1968. Enrl 5,330; Fac 200; Highest Degree: Associate
Library Holdings: AV Mats 5,000; Bk Titles 17,500; Bk Vols 18,000; Per Subs 236
Subject Interests: Culinary arts, Forestry, Natural res, Nursing, Police sci
Automation Activity & Vendor Info: (Cataloging) Innovative Interfaces, Inc; (Circulation) Innovative Interfaces, Inc; (ILL) Innovative Interfaces, Inc; (OPAC) Innovative Interfaces, Inc; (Serials) Innovative Interfaces, Inc
Wireless access
Function: ILL available, Internet access, Online cat, Online ref, Photocopying/Printing, Ref & res, Ref serv available, Res libr, Scanner, VHS videos, Wheelchair accessible
Partic in Ohio Library & Information Network
Open Mon-Thurs (Winter) 7am-10pm, Fri 7-4, Sun Noon-5; Mon-Fri (Summer) 8-4

S HOCKING CORRECTIONAL FACILITY LIBRARY*, 16759 Snake Hollow Rd, 45764-9658. (Mail add: PO Box 59, 45764-0059), SAN 322-8134. Tel: 740-753-1917. FAX: 740-753-4277. *Librn,* Daniel Okoro; E-mail: daniel.okoro@odrc.state.oh.us; Staff 1 (MLS 1)
Founded 1983
Library Holdings: Large Print Bks 1,500; Bk Titles 16,000; Per Subs 84; Spec Interest Per Sub 36; Talking Bks 250
Special Collections: Ohio Criminal Law
Special Services for the Deaf - High interest/low vocabulary bks
Special Services for the Blind - Bks on cassette; Large print bks

NEW CARLISLE

P NEW CARLISLE PUBLIC LIBRARY*, 111 E Lake Ave, 45344-1418. SAN 313-6345. Tel: 937-845-3601. FAX: 937-845-0908. Web Site: www.new-carlisle.lib.oh.us. *Libr Dir,* Beth Freeman; E-mail: bfreeman@seolibraries.org; *Ch,* Maggie Bollar; *Circ Mgr,* Beverly Sparks; E-mail: bsparks@seolibraries.org; Staff 16 (MLS 2, Non-MLS 14)
Founded 1933. Pop 20,000; Circ 194,108
Library Holdings: Bk Titles 63,522; Per Subs 185
Automation Activity & Vendor Info: (Acquisitions) Horizon; (Cataloging) Horizon; (Circulation) Horizon; (ILL) Horizon; (Media Booking) Horizon; (OPAC) Horizon; (Serials) Horizon
Wireless access
Partic in Serving Every Ohioan Library Center
Open Tues 10-8, Wed, Fri & Sat 10-6, Thurs 12-8
Friends of the Library Group

NEW CONCORD

CR MUSKINGUM UNIVERSITY*, Roberta A Smith University Library, Ten College Dr, 43762. SAN 313-6353. Tel: 740-826-8152. FAX: 740-826-8404. E-mail: library@muskingum.edu. Web Site: www.muskingum.edu/library. *Libr Dir,* Nainsi Houston, PhD; Tel: 740-826-8260, E-mail: nhouston@muskingum.edu; *Ref & Instruction Librn,* Nicole Arnold; Tel: 740-826-8154, E-mail: nicoler@muskingum.edu; *Ref & Instruction Librn,* Linda Hatfield; Tel: 740-826-8017, E-mail: lhatfield@muskingum.edu; *Ref & Instruction Librn,* Alaine Kay; Tel: 740-826-8157, E-mail: akay@muskingum.edu; *Libr Serv Mgr,* Josh Springer; Tel: 740-826-8156, E-mail: springer@muskingum.edu; Staff 5 (MLS 4, Non-MLS 1)
Founded 1837. Enrl 2,300; Fac 105; Highest Degree: Master
Jul 2014-Jun 2015. Mats Exp $183,900, Books $43,600, Per/Ser (Incl. Access Fees) $15,000, Micro $10,000, AV Mat $10,000, Electronic Ref Mat (Incl. Access Fees) $105,000, Presv $300
Library Holdings: CDs 893; DVDs 531; e-books 25,000; e-journals 12,000; Bk Titles 137,000; Bk Vols 209,000; Per Subs 310; Videos 2,004
Special Collections: Archives Coll. State Document Depository; US Document Depository
Automation Activity & Vendor Info: (Acquisitions) Innovative Interfaces, Inc; (Cataloging) Innovative Interfaces, Inc; (Circulation) Innovative Interfaces, Inc; (Course Reserve) Innovative Interfaces, Inc; (Discovery) EBSCO Discovery Service; (ILL) OCLC FirstSearch; (OPAC) Innovative Interfaces, Inc; (Serials) Innovative Interfaces, Inc
Wireless access
Function: Computers for patron use, Distance learning, Doc delivery serv, E-Readers, E-Reserves, Electronic databases & coll, Free DVD rentals, ILL available, Instruction & testing, Internet access, Laminating, Magazines, Microfiche/film & reading machines, Movies, Music CDs, Online cat, Online info literacy tutorials on the web & in blackboard, Online ref, Orientations, Outside serv via phone, mail, e-mail & web, Photocopying/Printing, Prof lending libr, Prog for adults, Ref & res, Ref serv available, Scanner, Study rm, Wheelchair accessible, Workshops
Partic in Ohio Library & Information Network; Ohio Private Academic Libraries
Open Mon-Thurs 8am-11pm, Fri 8-8, Sat 10-5, Sun 1-11
Restriction: Open to pub for ref & circ; with some limitations

NEW LEXINGTON

P PERRY COUNTY DISTRICT LIBRARY*, 117 S Jackson St, 43764-1382. SAN 356-9640. Tel: 740-342-4194. FAX: 740-342-4204. Web Site: www.pcdl.org. *Dir,* Melissa Marolt; E-mail: mmarolt@pcdl.org; Staff 3 (MLS 3)
Founded 1935. Pop 35,040; Circ 392,461
Library Holdings: Bk Titles 58,300; Bk Vols 137,262; Per Subs 198
Subject Interests: Genealogy, Local hist
Automation Activity & Vendor Info: (Acquisitions) Anacortes Software Inc; (Cataloging) SirsiDynix; (Circulation) SirsiDynix
Wireless access
Partic in Serving Every Ohioan Library Center
Open Mon-Thurs 10-8, Fri 10-5, Sat 10-3
Branches: 5
CORNING BRANCH, 113 11th Hill St, Corning, 43730. (Mail add: PO Box 395, Corning, 43730-0395), SAN 356-9675. Tel: 740-347-4763. FAX: 740-347-9219. E-mail: corning@pcdl.org. *Br Mgr,* Peggy Pingle
Open Mon & Wed 10-1 & 2-6, Fri 10-1 & 2-5
CROOKSVILLE BRANCH, 111 E Main St, Crooksville, 43731, SAN 356-9705. Tel: 740-982-4821. FAX: 740-982-3133. E-mail: crooksville@pcdl.org. *Br Mgr,* Angela Donaldson
Open Mon & Wed 10-7, Fri 10-5, Sat 10-1

JUNCTION CITY BRANCH, 108 W Main St, Junction City, 43748. (Mail add: PO Box 157, Junction City, 43748), SAN 356-973X. Tel: 740-987-7646. FAX: 740-987-2238. E-mail: junctioncity@pcdl.org. *Br Mgr,* Paula Cotterman
Open Mon & Wed 10-7, Fri 10-5, Sat 10-1
Friends of the Library Group
SOMERSET BRANCH, 103 Public Sq, Somerset, 43783. (Mail add: PO Box 277, Somerset, 43783-0277), SAN 356-9799. Tel: 740-743-1161. FAX: 740-743-9139. E-mail: somerset@pcdl.org. *Br Mgr,* Deborah Boley
Open Mon-Wed 10-7, Fri 10-5, Sat 10-2
Friends of the Library Group
THORNVILLE BRANCH, 99 E Columbus St, Thornville, 43076. (Mail add: PO Box 292, Thornville, 43782-0013), SAN 356-9829. Tel: 740-246-5133. FAX: 740-246-3994. E-mail: thornville@pcdl.org. *Br Mgr,* Sharon Chaffin
Open Mon-Wed 10-7, Fri 10-5, Sat 10-2

NEW LONDON

P NEW LONDON PUBLIC LIBRARY, 67 S Main St, 44851-1137. SAN 313-6361. Tel: 419-929-3981. FAX: 419-929-0007. E-mail: nlpl@seolibraries.org. Web Site: www.newlondonpubliclibrary.org. *Dir,* Anne Lowery; E-mail: ALowery@seolibraries.org; Staff 11 (MLS 1, Non-MLS 10)
Founded 1916. Pop 6,560
Jan 2020-Dec 2020 Income $370,447, State $213,513, Locally Generated Income $126,700, Other $30,234. Mats Exp $33,352, Books $21,990, Per/Ser (Incl. Access Fees) $1,937, Micro $177, AV Mat $9,248. Sal $154,562 (Prof $47,084)
Library Holdings: DVDs 5,294; e-books 269,585; Bk Titles 25,606; Per Subs 33
Subject Interests: Genealogy, Local hist
Automation Activity & Vendor Info: (Cataloging) SirsiDynix-WorkFlows; (Circulation) SirsiDynix-WorkFlows; (OPAC) SirsiDynix-Enterprise
Wireless access
Function: 24/7 Electronic res, 24/7 Online cat, Activity rm, Adult bk club, Audiobks on Playaways & MP3, Audiobks via web, Bk club(s), Bks on CD, Children's prog, Computers for patron use, Electronic databases & coll, Equip loans & repairs, Free DVD rentals, Holiday prog, ILL available, Internet access, Laminating, Life-long learning prog for all ages, Magazines, Mail & tel request accepted, Microfiche/film & reading machines, Movies, Music CDs, Online cat, OverDrive digital audio bks, Photocopying/Printing, Preschool outreach, Prog for adults, Prog for children & young adult, Ref & res, Scanner, Senior outreach, Story hour, Summer & winter reading prog, Summer reading prog, Tax forms, Teen prog, VHS videos, Wheelchair accessible, Winter reading prog
Partic in Serving Every Ohioan Library Center
Open Mon, Wed & Fri 10-5, Tues & Thurs 10-8, Sat 9-1
Restriction: Access at librarian's discretion
Friends of the Library Group

NEW MADISON

P NEW MADISON PUBLIC LIBRARY*, 142 S Main St, 45346. (Mail add: PO Box 32, 45346-0032), SAN 313-637X. Tel: 937-996-1741. FAX: 937-996-1473. E-mail: info@newmadisonpubliclibrary.org. Web Site: www.newmadisonpubliclibrary.org. *Dir,* Brenda Miller; E-mail: brenda@newmadisonpubliclibrary.org; Staff 9 (Non-MLS 9)
Founded 1934
Library Holdings: Bk Vols 47,000; Per Subs 200
Subject Interests: Local hist
Automation Activity & Vendor Info: (Cataloging) SirsiDynix; (Circulation) SirsiDynix; (OPAC) SirsiDynix
Wireless access
Function: 24/7 Electronic res, 24/7 Online cat, Activity rm, Adult bk club, Adult literacy prog, Archival coll, Audiobks on Playaways & MP3, Audiobks via web, Bk club(s), Bks on CD, Butterfly Garden, Children's prog, Computers for patron use, E-Reserves, Electronic databases & coll, Family literacy, Free DVD rentals, Holiday prog, Homebound delivery serv, ILL available, Internet access, Life-long learning prog for all ages, Magazines, Mail & tel request accepted, Makerspace, Meeting rooms, Movies, Music CDs, Online cat, Online ref, Outreach serv, Outside serv via phone, mail, e-mail & web, OverDrive digital audio bks, Photocopying/Printing, Preschool outreach, Preschool reading prog, Printer for laptops & handheld devices, Prog for adults, Prog for children & young adult, Ref & res, Res assist avail, Scanner, Serves people with intellectual disabilities, Spanish lang bks, STEM programs, Story hour, Summer & winter reading prog, Summer reading prog, Tax forms, Teen prog, Wheelchair accessible, Winter reading prog
Partic in Serving Every Ohioan Library Center
Open Mon & Tues 9-8, Wed-Fri 9-6, Sat 9-1
Friends of the Library Group

NEW PHILADELPHIA

C KENT STATE UNIVERSITY*, Tuscarawas Campus Library, 330 University Dr NE, 44663-9452. SAN 313-6388. Tel: 330-308-7471. FAX: 330-308-7553. Web Site: www.kent.edu/tusc/library. *Dir,* Cherie Bronkar; Tel: 330-308-7456, E-mail: cbronkar@kent.edu; *Sr Libr Assoc,* Tammie Beaber; E-mail: tbeaber@kent.edu
Founded 1968. Enrl 817
Library Holdings: Bk Titles 45,000; Bk Vols 58,000; Per Subs 250
Special Collections: Moravian Coll; Ohio Authors Coll; Olmstead Local History Coll
Subject Interests: Local hist, Nursing
Wireless access
Open Mon-Thurs 8am-9pm, Fri 8-5

L TUSCARAWAS COUNTY LAW LIBRARY ASSOCIATION*, 125 E High Ave, 44663. SAN 313-640X. Tel: 330-365-3224. Web Site: www.co.tuscarawas.oh.us/lawlibrary.htm. *Librn,* Kathy Moreland; E-mail: moreland@co.tuscarawas.oh.us
Founded 1865
Library Holdings: Bk Titles 30,000; Per Subs 10; Videos 10
Open Mon-Fri 8-12 & 1-4:30

P TUSCARAWAS COUNTY PUBLIC LIBRARY*, 121 Fair Ave NW, 44663-2600. SAN 356-9853. Tel: 330-364-4474. FAX: 330-364-8217. Web Site: www.tusclibrary.org. *Dir,* Michelle Ramsell; E-mail: mramsell@tusclibrary.org; *Asst Dir,* Brian Herzog; E-mail: bherzog@tusclibrary.org; *Mgr, Ad Serv,* Robyn Guedel; E-mail: rguedel@tusclibrary.org; *Mgr, Ch Serv,* Linda Uhler; E-mail: luhler@tusclibrary.org; *Mgr, Info Tech,* Richard Wiltrout; E-mail: rwiltrout@tusclibrary.org; Staff 5 (MLS 4, Non-MLS 1)
Founded 1905. Pop 54,415; Circ 682,729
Library Holdings: AV Mats 23,717; CDs 7,695; DVDs 4,698; Bk Vols 117,043; Per Subs 372; Videos 5,454
Automation Activity & Vendor Info: (Acquisitions) Horizon; (Cataloging) Horizon; (Circulation) Horizon; (Course Reserve) Horizon; (ILL) Horizon; (Media Booking) Horizon; (OPAC) Horizon
Wireless access
Function: Telephone ref
Partic in Serving Every Ohioan Library Center
Special Services for the Deaf - Staff with knowledge of sign lang; TDD equip
Open Mon-Thurs 9-8:30, Fri 10-6, Sat 9-5
Friends of the Library Group
Branches: 4
BOLIVAR BRANCH, 455 W Water St, Bolivar, 44612-9224. (Mail add: PO Box 588, Bolivar, 44612-0588), SAN 356-9888. Tel: 330-874-2720. *Br Mgr,* Christina Stump; E-mail: cstump@tusclibrary.org
Library Holdings: CDs 821; DVDs 462; Bk Titles 17,744; Per Subs 45; Talking Bks 305; Videos 682
Open Mon & Fri 10-5m Tues 10-8, Thurs 1-8, Sat 10-2
Friends of the Library Group
EMMA HUBER MEMORIAL LIBRARY, 356 Fifth St SW, Strasburg, 44680, SAN 356-9918. Tel: 330-878-5711. *Br Mgr,* Emily Crilley; E-mail: ecrilley@tusclibrary.org
Library Holdings: CDs 655; DVDs 430; Bk Vols 8,920; Per Subs 25; Talking Bks 278; Videos 379
Open Tues 10-5, Wed 10-8, Thurs 1-8, Fri 1-6
Friends of the Library Group
SUGARCREEK BRANCH, 120 S Broadway, Sugarcreek, 44681. (Mail add: PO Box 309, Sugarcreek, 44681-0309), SAN 356-9942. Tel: 330-852-2813. *Br Mgr,* Christine Pierpoint; E-mail: cpierpoint@tusclibrary.org
Library Holdings: CDs 597; DVDs 476; Bk Vols 12,719; Per Subs 49; Talking Bks 164; Videos 954
Open Mon & Wed 10-5, Tues 10-8, Fri 1-8, Sat 10-2
Friends of the Library Group
TUSCARAWAS BRANCH, 209 S Main St, Tuscarawas, 44682. (Mail add: PO Box 337, Tuscarawas, 44682-0337), SAN 356-9977. Tel: 740-922-2748. *Br Mgr,* Tabitha Johnson; E-mail: tjohnson@tusclibrary.org
Library Holdings: CDs 595; DVDs 449; Bk Vols 7,867; Per Subs 27; Talking Bks 23; Videos 413
Friends of the Library Group
Bookmobiles: 1. Supvr, Lacy Bartley

NEW STRAITSVILLE

P NEW STRAITSVILLE PUBLIC LIBRARY*, 102 E Main St, 43766. (Mail add: PO Box 8, 43766-0008), SAN 313-6418. Tel: 740-394-2717. FAX: 740-394-2817. Web Site: www.new-straitsville.lib.oh.us. *Head Librn,* Linda Kemper; E-mail: nsplkemperl@gmail.com; *Asst Librn,* Patty Spencer
Founded 1916. Circ 29,019
Library Holdings: Bk Vols 18,000; Per Subs 35

Automation Activity & Vendor Info: (Cataloging) ComPanion Corp; (Circulation) ComPanion Corp; (OPAC) ComPanion Corp
Wireless access
Open Mon-Thurs 2-7

NEWARK

S THE DAWES ARBORETUM LIBRARY, 7770 Jacksontown Rd SE, 43056. SAN 325-2760. Tel: 740-323-2355. Toll Free Tel: 800-443-2937. FAX: 740-323-4058. E-mail: information@dawesarb.org. Web Site: www.dawesarb.org. *Exec Dir,* Luke Messinger
Founded 1970
Library Holdings: Bk Titles 3,000
Special Collections: 19th and 20th Century History
Subject Interests: Art, Gardening, Juv, Landscaping, Politics, Travel, Wildlife
Restriction: Non-circulating, Not open to pub

S HEISEY COLLECTORS OF AMERICA, INC*, Louise Ream Library, 169 W Church St, 43055. SAN 324-4555. Tel: 740-345-2932. FAX: 740-345-9638. Web Site: www.heiseymuseum.org. *Curator, Dir,* Jack Burriss; Tel: 740-345-2932, Ext 4, E-mail: curator@heiseymuseum.org; Staff 8 (MLS 1, Non-MLS 7)
Founded 1974
Library Holdings: Bk Titles 600; Per Subs 50
Special Collections: Heisey Company Correspondence & Information
Subject Interests: A H Heisey & Co, Am glass
Publications: Heisey News (Monthly)
Open Tues-Sat 10-4, Sun 1-4
Restriction: Non-circulating

P LICKING COUNTY LIBRARY*, 101 W Main St, 43055-5054. SAN 357-0002. Tel: 740-349-5500. FAX: 740-349-5535. Web Site: www.lickingcountylibrary.org. *Dir,* Babette Wofter; Tel: 740-349-5503, E-mail: bwofter@lickingcountylibrary.org; *Fiscal Officer,* Sandra Lodge; Tel: 740-349-5505, E-mail: slodge@lickingcountylibrary.org; *Commun Engagement Mgr,* Laura Appleman; Tel: 740-349-5523, E-mail: lappleman@lickingcountylibrary.org; *Extended Serv, Mgr,* Julia Walden; Tel: 740-349-5507, E-mail: jwalden@lickingcountylibrary.org; *Human Res Mgr,* Tracey Wolfle; Tel: 740-349-5501, E-mail: twolfle@lickingcountylibrary.org; *Mat Mgr, Supvr,* Shirley Smith; Tel: 740-349-5530, E-mail: ssmith@lickingcountylibrary.org; *Pub Serv Mgr,* Mary Harmon; Tel: 740-349-5521, E-mail: mharman@lickingcountylibrary.org; *Support Serv Mgr,* Deb Holman; Tel: 740-349-5504, E-mail: dholman@lickingcountylibrary.org; *Circ Supvr,* Ada Myers; Tel: 740-349-5531, E-mail: amyers@lickingcountylibrary.org; *Adult Serv Coordr,* Gretchen Persohn; Tel: 740-349-5524, E-mail: gpersohn@lickingcountylibrary.org; *Youth Serv Coordr,* Marisa Glaviano; Tel: 740-349-5551, E-mail: mglaviano@lickingcountylibrary.org; Staff 16 (MLS 11, Non-MLS 5)
Founded 1908. Pop 121,246; Circ 1,420,407
Library Holdings: Audiobooks 21,584; e-books 307,886; Bk Titles 276,891; Per Subs 205; Videos 54,629
Special Collections: State Document Depository
Subject Interests: Local hist
Automation Activity & Vendor Info: (Acquisitions) SirsiDynix; (Cataloging) OCLC; (Circulation) SirsiDynix; (OPAC) SirsiDynix-WorkFlows
Wireless access
Function: 24/7 Electronic res, 24/7 Online cat, Adult bk club, After school storytime, Archival coll, Art exhibits, Audio & video playback equip for onsite use, Audiobks on Playaways & MP3, Audiobks via web, AV serv, Bk club(s), Bks on CD, Butterfly Garden, Children's prog, Computer training, Computers for patron use, Digital talking bks, E-Readers, Electronic databases & coll, Free DVD rentals, Holiday prog, Home delivery & serv to seniorr ctr & nursing homes, Homebound delivery serv, ILL available, Internet access, Jail serv, Magazines, Magnifiers for reading, Makerspace, Mango lang, Meeting rooms, Microfiche/film & reading machines, Movies, Museum passes, Music CDs, Notary serv, Online cat, Online info literacy tutorials on the web & in blackboard, Online ref, Orientations, Outreach serv, OverDrive digital audio bks, Photocopying/Printing, Preschool reading prog, Printer for laptops & handheld devices, Prog for adults, Prog for children & young adult, Ref & res, Ref serv available, Res assist avail, Scanner, Senior computer classes, Senior outreach, Serves people with intellectual disabilities, Spanish lang bks, Story hour, Study rm, Summer & winter reading prog, Summer reading prog, Tax forms, Teen prog, Wheelchair accessible, Winter reading prog, Workshops
Partic in Serving Every Ohioan Library Center
Special Services for the Blind - Bks on CD; Digital talking bk machines; Large print bks; Playaways (bks on MP3); Recorded bks; Talking bks; Talking bks & player equip
Open Mon-Thurs 9-8, Fri 9-5:30, Sat 9-5
Friends of the Library Group

Branches: 5
MARY E BABCOCK BRANCH, 320 N Main St, Johnstown, 43031, SAN 357-0061. Tel: 740-967-2982. FAX: 740-967-0729. *Br Mgr,* Julie McElhaney; E-mail: jmcelhaney@lickingcountylibrary.org; Staff 1 (MLS 1)
Function: 24/7 Electronic res, 24/7 Online cat, Adult bk club, After school storytime, Audiobks via web, AV serv, Bk club(s), Bks on CD, Children's prog, Computer training, Computers for patron use, E-Readers, Electronic databases & coll, Free DVD rentals, Magazines, Mango lang, Meeting rooms, Movies, Museum passes, Music CDs, Online cat, Photocopying/Printing, Prog for adults, Prog for children & young adult, Scanner, STEM programs, Story hour, Study rm, Summer & winter reading prog, Summer reading prog, Tax forms, Teen prog, Wheelchair accessible
Open Mon-Thurs 10-7, Fri & Sat 10-3
Friends of the Library Group
BUCKEYE LAKE BRANCH, King's Plaza, 4455 Walnut Rd, Rte 79, Buckeye Lake, 43008. Tel: 740-928-0472. FAX: 740-928-0486. *Br Supvr,* Emily Hankinson; E-mail: ahankinson@lickingcountylibrary.org; Staff 1 (MLS 1)
Function: 24/7 Electronic res, 24/7 Online cat, Adult bk club, After school storytime, Bk club(s), Bks on CD, Children's prog, Computer training, Computers for patron use, E-Readers, Electronic databases & coll, Free DVD rentals, Holiday prog, ILL available, Internet access, Magazines, Mango lang, Meeting rooms, Movies, Museum passes, Music CDs, Online cat, OverDrive digital audio bks, Photocopying/Printing, Printer for laptops & handheld devices, Prog for adults, Prog for children & young adult, Scanner, Senior computer classes, STEM programs, Story hour, Study rm, Summer & winter reading prog, Summer reading prog, Tax forms, Teen prog, Wheelchair accessible
Open Mon-Thurs 10-7, Fri 10-5, Sat 10-3
Friends of the Library Group
HEBRON BRANCH, 934 W Main St, Hebron, 43025, SAN 357-0037. Tel: 740-928-3923. FAX: 740-928-9437. *Br Supvr,* Deirdre McIntyre; E-mail: dmcintyre@lickingcountylibrary.org; Staff 1 (MLS 1)
Circ 41,778
Function: 24/7 Electronic res, 24/7 Online cat, Adult bk club, After school storytime, Bk club(s), Bks on cassette, Bks on CD, Butterfly Garden, Children's prog, Computer training, Computers for patron use, E-Readers, Electronic databases & coll, Free DVD rentals, Holiday prog, ILL available, Internet access, Magazines, Mango lang, Movies, Museum passes, Music CDs, Online cat, OverDrive digital audio bks, Photocopying/Printing, Printer for laptops & handheld devices, Prog for adults, Prog for children & young adult, Scanner, Senior computer classes, Story hour, Summer & winter reading prog, Summer reading prog, Tax forms, Teen prog, Wheelchair accessible
Open Mon-Thurs 10-7, Fri 10-5, Sat 10-3
Friends of the Library Group
HERVEY MEMORIAL, 15 N Main, Utica, 43080. (Mail add: PO Box 512, Utica, 43080-0512), SAN 357-0126. Tel: 740-892-2400. FAX: 740-892-2400. *Br Supvr,* Jennifer Mitchell; E-mail: jmitchell@lickingcountylibrary.org; Staff 1 (Non-MLS 1)
Function: 24/7 Electronic res, 24/7 Online cat, Bk club(s), Bks on CD, Children's prog, Computer training, Computers for patron use, E-Readers, Electronic databases & coll, Free DVD rentals, Holiday prog, ILL available, Internet access, Magazines, Mango lang, Movies, Museum passes, Music CDs, Online cat, OverDrive digital audio bks, Photocopying/Printing, Prog for adults, Prog for children & young adult, Scanner, Senior computer classes, Story hour, Summer & winter reading prog, Summer reading prog, Tax forms, Teen prog
Open Mon-Thurs 10-7, Fri & Sat 10-3
Friends of the Library Group
EMERSON R MILLER BRANCH, 990 W Main St, 43055, SAN 357-0096. Tel: 740-344-2155. FAX: 740-344-4271. *Br Supvr,* Bobbi Galvin; E-mail: bgalvin@lickingcountylibrary.org; Staff 1 (MLS 1)
Circ 114,539
Function: 24/7 Electronic res, 24/7 Online cat, Adult bk club, After school storytime, Audiobks on Playaways & MP3, Audiobks via web, Bk club(s), Bks on CD, Children's prog, Computer training, Computers for patron use, E-Readers, Electronic databases & coll, Free DVD rentals, Holiday prog, ILL available, Internet access, Magazines, Mango lang, Meeting rooms, Movies, Museum passes, Music CDs, Online cat, OverDrive digital audio bks, Photocopying/Printing, Printer for laptops & handheld devices, Prog for adults, Prog for children & young adult, Ref serv available, Scanner, Senior computer classes, Serves people with intellectual disabilities, Story hour, Study rm, Summer reading prog, Tax forms, Teen prog, Telephone ref, Wheelchair accessible
Open Mon-Thurs 10-8, Fri 10-5, Sat 10-3
Friends of the Library Group
Bookmobiles: 1. Supvr, Rhonda Adams. Bk titles 4,700

NEWCOMERSTOWN

P NEWCOMERSTOWN PUBLIC LIBRARY*, 123 E Main St, 43832. SAN 313-6450. Tel: 740-498-8228. FAX: 740-498-8221. Web Site: nctlib.org. *Dir,* Mr Cody Addy; E-mail: caddy@nctlib.org; Staff 3 (MLS 1, Non-MLS 2)
Founded 1935. Pop 6,819; Circ 62,000
Library Holdings: Bk Vols 35,000; Per Subs 79
Wireless access
Partic in Serving Every Ohioan Library Center
Open Mon-Fri 10-6, Sat 10-1
Friends of the Library Group

NEWTON FALLS

P NEWTON FALLS PUBLIC LIBRARY*, 204 S Canal St, 44444-1694. SAN 313-6469. Tel: 330-872-1282. FAX: 330-872-9153. Web Site: www.newtonfalls.org. *Dir,* Kerry Reed; E-mail: KerryReed@newtonfalls.org; Staff 7 (MLS 5, Non-MLS 2)
Founded 1930. Pop 9,611; Circ 223,898
Subject Interests: Local hist
Automation Activity & Vendor Info: (Cataloging) TLC (The Library Corporation); (Circulation) TLC (The Library Corporation); (OPAC) TLC (The Library Corporation); (Serials) TLC (The Library Corporation)
Wireless access
Function: Prog for children & young adult, Ref serv available, Senior computer classes, Spoken cassettes & CDs, Spoken cassettes & DVDs, Summer reading prog, Tax forms, Telephone ref, VHS videos, Wheelchair accessible, Workshops
Partic in Northeast Ohio Regional Library System
Open Mon-Thurs 9-8, Fri & Sat 9-5
Friends of the Library Group

NILES

P MCKINLEY MEMORIAL LIBRARY, 40 N Main St, 44446-5082. SAN 313-6477. Tel: 330-652-1704. FAX: 330-652-5788. E-mail: mckinley@mcklib.org. Web Site: www.mckinley.lib.oh.us. *Dir,* Michelle M Alleman; Tel: 330-652-1704, Ext 5, E-mail: malleman@mcklib.org; Staff 20 (MLS 6, Non-MLS 14)
Founded 1908. Pop 19,500; Circ 290,000
Library Holdings: AV Mats 8,000; CDs 1,200; DVDs 3,300; Large Print Bks 2,400; Bk Vols 72,000; Per Subs 120; Talking Bks 2,200; Videos 700
Special Collections: President William McKinley Coll, bk, micro & mus artifacts
Automation Activity & Vendor Info: (Acquisitions) SirsiDynix; (Cataloging) SirsiDynix-Enterprise; (Circulation) SirsiDynix-Enterprise
Wireless access
Function: 24/7 Electronic res, 24/7 Online cat, Activity rm, Adult bk club, After school storytime, Archival coll, Audiobks on Playaways & MP3, Audiobks via web, AV serv, Bk club(s), Bks on CD, Children's prog, Computer training, Computers for patron use, E-Reserves, Electronic databases & coll, Family literacy, Free DVD rentals, Holiday prog, Home delivery & serv to seniorr ctr & nursing homes, Homebound delivery serv, Internet access, Magazines, Mail & tel request accepted, Movies, Music CDs, Online cat, Photocopying/Printing, Preschool outreach, Preschool reading prog, Printer for laptops & handheld devices, Prog for adults, Prog for children & young adult, Ref & res, Ref serv available, Res libr, Scanner, Story hour, Summer reading prog, Teen prog, Telephone ref
Partic in CLEVNET
Open Mon, Wed & Thurs 9-5,Tues 9-7, Fri & Sat 11-3
Friends of the Library Group

NORTH BALTIMORE

P NORTH BALTIMORE PUBLIC LIBRARY*, 230 N Main St, 45872-1125. SAN 313-6493. Tel: 419-257-3621. FAX: 419-257-3859. Web Site: nbpubliclibrary.org. *Dir,* Holly Emahiser Ryder; *Asst Dir,* Cheryl Heilman; *Fiscal Officer,* Cheryl Halter; Staff 13 (MLS 1, Non-MLS 12)
Founded 1919. Pop 4,283; Circ 114,172
Library Holdings: AV Mats 4,780; Bk Vols 57,152; Per Subs 100
Special Collections: Film, Television & Theater
Automation Activity & Vendor Info: (Cataloging) SirsiDynix; (Circulation) SirsiDynix; (ILL) SirsiDynix
Wireless access
Function: Adult bk club, After school storytime, CD-ROM, ILL available, Music CDs, Photocopying/Printing, Prog for adults, Prog for children & young adult, Ref serv available, Summer reading prog, Tax forms, Telephone ref, VHS videos, Wheelchair accessible
Partic in NORWELD
Open Mon-Thurs 9-8, Fri 9-5, Sat 9-1
Friends of the Library Group

NORTH CANTON

C KENT STATE UNIVERSITY, Stark Campus Library, 6000 Frank Ave NW, 44720-7548. SAN 313-2331. Tel: 330-244-3330, 330-499-9600. FAX: 330-494-6212. E-mail: starklibrary@listserv.kent.edu. Web Site: www.kent.edu/stark/library. *Libr Dir,* Rob Kairis; Tel: 330-244-3326, E-mail: rkairis@kent.edu; *Online Learning Librn,* Melissa Bauer; Tel: 330-244-3320, E-mail: mbauer10@kent.edu; *Ref & Instruction Librn,* Theodore Guedel; Tel: 330-244-3322, E-mail: tguedel@kent.edu; *Cat,* Mary Birtalan; Tel: 330-244-3323, E-mail: mbirtalan@kent.edu; *Ser,* Brenna Schweizer; Tel: 330-244-3248, E-mail: bschweiz@kent.edu; Staff 3 (MLS 3)
Founded 1967. Enrl 5,000; Pop 5,000; Circ 5,000; Fac 130; Highest Degree: Master
Jul 2020-Jun 2021 Income $125,000. Mats Exp $27,986, Books $401, Per/Ser (Incl. Access Fees) $19,371, Electronic Ref Mat (Incl. Access Fees) $7,895, Presv $319. Sal $298,396 (Prof $200,326)
Library Holdings: Audiobooks 41; AV Mats 4,374; CDs 634; DVDs 2,013; Microforms 637; Music Scores 619; Bk Titles 50,414; Bk Vols 80,414; Per Subs 133; Videos 3,740
Automation Activity & Vendor Info: (Cataloging) Innovative Interfaces, Inc - Millennium; (Circulation) Innovative Interfaces, Inc - Millennium; (Course Reserve) Innovative Interfaces, Inc - Millennium; (Discovery) EBSCO Discovery Service; (ILL) Innovative Interfaces, Inc - Millennium; (Media Booking) Innovative Interfaces, Inc - Millennium; (OPAC) Innovative Interfaces, Inc - Millennium; (Serials) Innovative Interfaces, Inc - Millennium
Wireless access
Function: 24/7 Electronic res, 24/7 Online cat, 3D Printer, Adult bk club, Archival coll, Art exhibits, Audio & video playback equip for onsite use, Bk club(s), Bks on CD, CD-ROM, Computers for patron use, Distance learning, Electronic databases & coll, Equip loans & repairs, For res purposes, Free DVD rentals, ILL available, Internet access, Magazines, Meeting rooms, Microfiche/film & reading machines, Movies, Music CDs, Online cat, Online info literacy tutorials on the web & in blackboard, Online ref, Orientations, Outside serv via phone, mail, e-mail & web, Photocopying/Printing, Ref & res, Ref serv available, Res libr, Scanner, Study rm, VHS videos, Wheelchair accessible
Partic in Ohio Library & Information Network
Special Services for the Deaf - ADA equip
Open Mon-Thurs 7:30am-10pm, Fri 8-5, Sat 9-2

P NORTH CANTON PUBLIC LIBRARY, 185 N Main St, 44720-2595. SAN 357-0150. Tel: 330-499-4712. FAX: 330-499-3452. Web Site: ncantonlibrary.com. *Dir,* Andrea Legg; Tel: 330-499-4712, Ext 315, E-mail: alegg@northcantonlibrary.org; *Head, Children's Dept,* Jamie Macris; E-mail: jmacris@northcantonlibrary.org; *Commun Relations Mgr,* Christina Weyrick; E-mail: cweyrick@northcantonlibrary.org; *Patron Serv Mgr,* Nancy Myers; E-mail: nmyers@northcantonlibrary.org; *Fiscal Officer,* Kelly Boggs; E-mail: kboggs@northcantonlibrary.org; *Dep Fiscal Officer,* Stephanie Shaffer; E-mail: sshaffer@northcantonlibrary.org; Staff 18 (MLS 5, Non-MLS 13)
Founded 1926. Pop 29,575; Circ 966,255
Library Holdings: Audiobooks 7,278; CDs 8,350; DVDs 21,609; e-books 183,874; Electronic Media & Resources 1,170; Bk Vols 111,631
Subject Interests: Art
Automation Activity & Vendor Info: (Acquisitions) Innovative Interfaces, Inc; (Cataloging) Innovative Interfaces, Inc; (Circulation) Innovative Interfaces, Inc; (OPAC) Innovative Interfaces, Inc
Wireless access
Function: 24/7 Electronic res, 24/7 Online cat, Activity rm, Adult bk club, Art exhibits, Art programs, Audiobks on Playaways & MP3, Audiobks via web, AV serv, Bk club(s), Bks on CD, Children's prog, Computer training, Computers for patron use, Digital talking bks, Electronic databases & coll, Equip loans & repairs, Family literacy, Free DVD rentals, Games & aids for people with disabilities, Health sci info serv, Holiday prog, Home delivery & serv to seniorr ctr & nursing homes, Homebound delivery serv, Homework prog, ILL available, Instruction & testing, Internet access, Life-long learning prog for all ages, Literacy & newcomer serv, Magazines, Mail & tel request accepted, Meeting rooms, Movies, Music CDs, Notary serv, Online cat, Online info literacy tutorials on the web & in blackboard, Online ref, Outreach serv, Outside serv via phone, mail, e-mail & web, OverDrive digital audio bks, Photocopying/Printing, Preschool outreach, Prog for adults, Prog for children & young adult, Ref & res, Ref serv available, Res assist avail, Senior outreach, Serves people with intellectual disabilities, Spanish lang bks, STEM programs, Story hour, Study rm, Summer & winter reading prog, Summer reading prog, Tax forms, Teen prog, Telephone ref, Visual arts prog, Wheelchair accessible, Winter reading prog, Workshops, Writing prog
Publications: On The Shelf (Newsletter)
Special Services for the Deaf - ADA equip; Closed caption videos; Sign lang interpreter upon request for prog
Special Services for the Blind - Playaways (bks on MP3)
Open Mon-Thurs 10-8, Fri 10-6, Sat 9-5
Friends of the Library Group

S TIMKEN CO*, Research Library, 4500 Mt Pleasant Rd NW, WHQ-05, 44720. SAN 313-2382. Tel: 234-262-2049. FAX: 234-262-2282. *Managing Librn,* Patricia Cromi; E-mail: patricia.cromi@timken.com; Staff 1 (MLS 1)
Founded 1966
Library Holdings: Bk Titles 9,000; Per Subs 50
Subject Interests: Engr res, Ferrous metallurgical res
Partic in OhioNET

SR UNITED CHURCH OF CHRIST, Zion United Church of Christ Memorial Library, 415 S Main St, 44720-3027. SAN 328-1426. Tel: 330-499-8191. E-mail: zionucc@gmail.com.
Founded 1964
Library Holdings: AV Mats 31; Bk Titles 3,907
Special Collections: Adult & Children's Books; Religious & Selected Secular Books
Wireless access
Function: Adult literacy prog, Bk reviews (Group), Prog for children & young adult, Ref serv available
Partic in Church & Synagogue Libr Asn
Restriction: Staff & mem only

C WALSH UNIVERSITY*, Brother Edmond Drouin Library, 2020 E Maple St, 44720-3336. SAN 313-2390. Tel: 330-490-7185. Interlibrary Loan Service Tel: 330-490-7501. Reference Tel: 330-244-4942. Automation Services Tel: 330-490-7186. Toll Free Tel: 888-627-1826. FAX: 330-490-7270. E-mail: library@walsh.edu. Web Site: www.walsh.edu/library. *Dir, Libr Serv,* LuAnn Boris; E-mail: lboris@walsh.edu; *Archival Serv Librn,* Katie Hutchison; Tel: 330-244-4968, E-mail: khutchison@walsh.edu; *Instrul Librn,* Stephanie Henderson; Tel: 330-490-7187, E-mail: shenderson@walsh.edu; *Pub Serv Librn,* Alyssa Mitchell; Tel: 330-490-7501, E-mail: amitchell@walsh.edu. Subject Specialists: *Communication, Computer sci, Educ, Hist, Juv lit,* Katie Hutchison; *Biology, Chemistry, Exercise sci, Health sci, Life sci, Psychol,* Stephanie Henderson; *Anthrop, Bus, Ethics, Foreign affairs, Foreign lang, Geog, Govt, Law, Linguistics, Math, Mus studies, Philos, Statistics, Writing,* Alyssa Mitchell; Staff 8 (MLS 4, Non-MLS 4)
Founded 1960. Enrl 2,710; Fac 133; Highest Degree: Doctorate
Jul 2016-Jun 2017
Library Holdings: AV Mats 4,434; e-books 226,183; e-journals 174,704; Electronic Media & Resources 19,501; Per Subs 200
Automation Activity & Vendor Info: (Acquisitions) Innovative Interfaces, Inc - Sierra; (Cataloging) Innovative Interfaces, Inc - Sierra; (Circulation) Innovative Interfaces, Inc - Sierra; (Course Reserve) Innovative Interfaces, Inc - Sierra; (Discovery) EBSCO Discovery Service; (ILL) OCLC WorldShare Interlibrary Loan; (OPAC) Innovative Interfaces, Inc - Sierra; (Serials) Innovative Interfaces, Inc - Sierra
Wireless access
Function: 24/7 Electronic res, 24/7 Online cat, Archival coll, Computers for patron use, Electronic databases & coll, ILL available, Internet access, Music CDs, Online cat, Ref serv available, Spoken cassettes & CDs
Publications: New Items List (Acquisition list)
Partic in OCLC Online Computer Library Center, Inc; Ohio Library & Information Network; Ohio Private Academic Libraries; OhioNET
Open Mon-Thurs 7:45am-11pm, Fri 7:45-5, Sat Noon-5, Sun 1-10; Mon-Thurs (Summer) 8-7, Fri 8-4, Sat 12-5
Restriction: Authorized patrons, Borrowing privileges limited to fac & registered students, Borrowing requests are handled by ILL, Fee for pub use, In-house use for visitors, Open to fac, students & qualified researchers

NORTH ELYRIA

J LORAIN COUNTY COMMUNITY COLLEGE*, Barbara & Mike Bass Library/Community Resource Center, 1005 Abbe Rd N, 44035-1691. SAN 313-5004. Tel: 440-366-4026. Interlibrary Loan Service Tel: 440-366-7336. Reference Tel: 440-366-4106. Administration Tel: 440-366-7289. Toll Free Tel: 800-995-5222, Ext 7289. FAX: 440-366-4127. E-mail: ask@lorainccc.libanswers.com. Web Site: www.lorainccc.edu/library. *Dean of Library & eLearning,* Karla Aleman; E-mail: kaleman@lorainccc.edu; *Ref Librn,* Rita Blanford; Tel: 440-366-7279, E-mail: rblanfor@lorainccc.edu; *Ref Librn,* Helen DeBalzo Green; Tel: 440-366-7282, E-mail: hdebalzo@lorainccc.edu; *Ref Librn,* Bethany Miller; E-mail: bmiller2@lorainccc.edu; *Instrul Serv/Ref Librn,* Christine Sheetz; Tel: 440-366-7288, E-mail: csheetz@lorainccc.edu; *Circ Supvr,* Kathy Hodkey; Tel: 440-366-7286, E-mail: khodkey@lorainccc.edu; Staff 16 (MLS 4, Non-MLS 12)
Founded 1964. Enrl 10,000; Fac 263; Highest Degree: Associate
Library Holdings: CDs 300; Bk Titles 93,000; Bk Vols 111,000; Per Subs 610
Automation Activity & Vendor Info: (Acquisitions) Innovative Interfaces, Inc; (Cataloging) Innovative Interfaces, Inc; (Circulation) Innovative Interfaces, Inc; (ILL) Innovative Interfaces, Inc; (OPAC) Innovative Interfaces, Inc
Wireless access
Partic in Ohio Library & Information Network; OhioNET
Special Services for the Deaf - Assistive tech
Special Services for the Blind - Accessible computers
Open Mon-Thurs 9am-7pm, Fri 9-4:30, Sat 10-3

NORWALK

R FIRST PRESBYTERIAN CHURCH LIBRARY*, 21 Firelands Blvd, 44857. SAN 313-6531. Tel: 419-668-1923. FAX: 419-663-5115. Web Site: www.firstpresbyterian.net/library. *Dir,* Kathleen Wheeler; E-mail: kwheeler@firstpresbyterian.net
Founded 1948
Library Holdings: Bk Titles 3,900; Per Subs 10
Special Collections: Archival Coll, Weekly Bulletin & Monthly Newsletter (1950-1992 complete, 1921-1949 incomplete)
Subject Interests: Biog, Children's educ, Family life, Fiction, Health, Personal problems, Relig related
Publications: Bulletins (Weekly); Newsletter (Monthly)
Open Mon-Fri 9-5, Sun 8-Noon

GL HURON COUNTY LAW LIBRARY*, Court House, 1st Flr, Two E Main St, 44857. SAN 313-654X. Tel: 419-351-4244. FAX: 419-663-5026. Web Site: www.huroncountybar.org/content/law-library. *Librn,* Michael L Clark; E-mail: mikeclarklaw@gmail.com
Library Holdings: Bk Vols 13,000
Wireless access
Open Mon-Fri 8:30-4:30

P NORWALK PUBLIC LIBRARY*, 46 W Main St, 44857. SAN 313-6558. Tel: 419-668-6063. FAX: 419-663-2190. E-mail: norwalk@norwalk.lib.oh.us. Web Site: www.norwalk.lib.oh.us. *Dir,* Stacey Church; E-mail: stacey.church@norwalk.lib.oh.us; Staff 2 (MLS 2)
Founded 1861. Pop 54,000; Circ 181,277
Library Holdings: Bk Titles 85,000; Per Subs 210
Special Collections: Huron County History & Genealogy; Local Newspapers, micro
Wireless access
Partic in NORWELD
Open Mon & Wed 9:30-8:30, Tues & Thurs 10:30-6, Fri & Sat 9:30-5
Friends of the Library Group

OAK HARBOR

P OAK HARBOR PUBLIC LIBRARY*, 147 W Main St, 43449-1344. SAN 313-6566. Tel: 419-898-7001. FAX: 419-898-0747. E-mail: ohpl@seolibraries.org. Web Site: oakharborpubliclibrary.org. *Dir,* Lina Hall; E-mail: lhall@seolibraries.org; Staff 5.6 (MLS 1.6, Non-MLS 4)
Founded 1908. Pop 10,300; Circ 108,196
Library Holdings: AV Mats 6,180; e-books 35; Large Print Bks 758; Bk Vols 40,008; Per Subs 132
Automation Activity & Vendor Info: (Cataloging) SirsiDynix; (Circulation) SirsiDynix; (ILL) SirsiDynix; (OPAC) SirsiDynix
Wireless access
Partic in NORWELD; Ohio Public Library Information Network; Serving Every Ohioan Library Center
Open Mon-Thurs 9:30-8, Fri 9:30-5, Sat 9:30-3, Sun (Summer) 1-4
Friends of the Library Group

OAK HILL

P OAK HILL PUBLIC LIBRARY, 226 South Front St, 45656. Tel: 740-682-6457. FAX: 740-682-3522. Web Site: www.youseemore.com/oakhill. *Dir,* Peggy Johnson; E-mail: peggyjohnson45656@gmail.com; *Ch,* Patches Martin; *Fiscal Officer,* Beth Lloyd
Founded 1956
Library Holdings: Bk Vols 46,058
Wireless access
Open Mon-Fri 10-6, Sat 10-2

OAKWOOD

P WRIGHT MEMORIAL PUBLIC LIBRARY, 1776 Far Hills Ave, 45419-2598. SAN 313-4830. Tel: 937-294-7171. Administration Tel: 937-294-8572. FAX: 937-294-8578. Web Site: www.wrightlibrary.org. *Dir,* Kristi J Hale; E-mail: hale@wrightlibrary.org; *Fiscal Officer,* Mary Hopton; E-mail: fiscalofficer@wrightlibrary.org; *Libr Operations Coordr,* Brian Potts; E-mail: potts@wrightlibrary.org; *Youth Serv Coordr,* Jacqui Taylor; *Ref Serv,* Elizabeth Schmidt; E-mail: schmidt@wrightlibrary.org; *Tech Serv,* Robyn Case; E-mail: case@wrightlibrary.org; Staff 14.5 (MLS 9.5, Non-MLS 5)
Founded 1913. Pop 9,120; Circ 429,594
Library Holdings: Bk Vols 148,000
Automation Activity & Vendor Info: (Acquisitions) Innovative Interfaces, Inc. - Polaris; (Cataloging) Innovative Interfaces, Inc. - Polaris; (Circulation) Innovative Interfaces, Inc. - Polaris; (OPAC) Innovative Interfaces, Inc

Wireless access
Function: 24/7 Electronic res, 24/7 Online cat, Accelerated reader prog, Activity rm, Adult bk club, Audiobks on Playaways & MP3, Audiobks via web, AV serv, Bi-weekly Writer's Group, Bk club(s), Bks on CD, Children's prog, Computer training, Computers for patron use, E-Readers, Electronic databases & coll, Equip loans & repairs, Family literacy, Free DVD rentals, Genealogy discussion group, Home delivery & serv to seniorr ctr & nursing homes, Homebound delivery serv, ILL available, Instruction & testing, Internet access, Life-long learning prog for all ages, Magazines, Mail & tel request accepted, Meeting rooms, Microfiche/film & reading machines, Movies, Museum passes, Music CDs, Notary serv, Online cat, Online info literacy tutorials on the web & in blackboard, Online ref, Orientations, Outreach serv, Outside serv via phone, mail, e-mail & web, OverDrive digital audio bks, Passport agency, Photocopying/Printing, Preschool outreach, Preschool reading prog, Printer for laptops & handheld devices, Prog for adults, Prog for children & young adult, Ref serv available, Scanner, Senior computer classes, Serves people with intellectual disabilities, STEM programs, Story hour, Study rm, Summer & winter reading prog, Summer reading prog, Tax forms, Teen prog, Telephone ref, Wheelchair accessible, Winter reading prog, Writing prog
Partic in Ohio Library & Information Network; Ohio OPLIN GOSIP Network; OhioNET
Open Mon-Fri 10-9, Sat 10-5, Sun 1-5

OBERLIN

C OBERLIN COLLEGE LIBRARY*, 148 W College St, 44074. SAN 357-0215. Tel: 440-775-8285. FAX: 440-775-6586. E-mail: reference@oberlin.edu. Web Site: www2.oberlin.edu/library. *Dir of Libr,* Alexia Hundson-Ward; Tel: 440-775-5024, E-mail: alexia.hudson-ward@oberlin.edu; *Asst Dir, Pub Serv, Head, Pub Serv,* Allison Gallaher; Tel: 440-775-5019, E-mail: allison.gallaher@oberlin.edu; *Head, Coll & Acq,* Jessica Grim; Tel: 440-775-5035, E-mail: jessica.grim@oberlin.edu; *Head, Discovery Serv, Head, Metadata Serv,* Selina Wang; Tel: 440-775-5113, E-mail: selina.wang@oberlin.edu; *Media Res & Reserves Mgr,* Michael Palazzolo; Tel: 440-775-5036, E-mail: michael.palazzolo@oberlin.edu; *ILL Supvr,* Diane Lee; Tel: 440-775-5039, E-mail: diane.lee@oberlin.edu; Staff 21.5 (MLS 19, Non-MLS 2.5)
Founded 1833. Enrl 2,853; Fac 327; Highest Degree: Master
Jul 2016-Jun 2017 Income (Main & Associated Libraries) $7,590,366. Mats Exp $7,253,062, Books $819,134, Per/Ser (Incl. Access Fees) $1,598,088. Sal $3,180,613 (Prof $1,457,099)
Library Holdings: AV Mats 162,577; Music Scores 142,909; Bk Vols 1,533,043; Per Subs 188,472
Special Collections: Aldous Huxley (Robert H Jackson Coll); American Communist Party Pamphlets; American Dime Novels; Anti-Slavery Coll; Archive of the Seal Press, 1976-2001; Book Arts Coll; Civil War Popular Song Lyrics; Early Printed Books; Edwin Arlington Robinson Coll; History of the Book; Illuminated Manuscripts; Jack Schaefer Coll; Japanese Artist Books (Mary Ainsworth Coll); Oberliniana Coll; Orrin W June War of 1812 Coll; Sheet Music Coll; Spanish Drama Coll; The 19th Century Spanish Romantic Novel; Thorton Wilder Coll; Upton Sinclair Coll; Violin Society of America (H K Goodkind Coll), violin construction. US Document Depository
Automation Activity & Vendor Info: (Acquisitions) Innovative Interfaces, Inc; (Cataloging) Innovative Interfaces, Inc; (Circulation) Innovative Interfaces, Inc; (Course Reserve) Blackboard Inc; (Discovery) ProQuest; (ILL) OCLC; (OPAC) Innovative Interfaces, Inc; (Serials) Innovative Interfaces, Inc
Wireless access
Function: 24/7 Electronic res, 24/7 Online cat, Archival coll, Audio & video playback equip for onsite use, AV serv, Computers for patron use, Doc delivery serv, E-Reserves, Electronic databases & coll, Govt ref serv, ILL available, Internet access, Magazines, Mail & tel request accepted, Meeting rooms, Microfiche/film & reading machines, Music CDs, Online cat, Online ref, Orientations, Outreach serv, Outside serv via phone, mail, e-mail & web, Photocopying/Printing, Ref & res, Ref serv available, Res assist avail, Res libr, Scanner, Study rm, Tax forms, Telephone ref, VHS videos, Wheelchair accessible
Publications: Library Perspectives (External newsletter)
Partic in Five Colleges of Ohio; Oberlin Group; Ohio Library & Information Network; OhioNET
Special Services for the Deaf - Assistive tech
Special Services for the Blind - Closed circuit TV; Dragon Naturally Speaking software; Large screen computer & software; ZoomText magnification & reading software
Open Mon-Thurs 8am-2am, Fri 8am-10pm, Sat 10-10, Sun 10am-2am
Restriction: Open to pub for ref & circ; with some limitations
Friends of the Library Group
Departmental Libraries:
CONSERVATORY LIBRARY, Oberlin Conservatory of Music, 77 W College St, 44074-1588, SAN 357-0274. Tel: 440-775-8280. Circulation Tel: 440-775-8288. Reference Tel: 440-775-5129. E-mail: con.ref@oberlin.edu. Web Site: www2.oberlin.edu/library/cons. *Head of Libr,* Deborah Campana; Tel: 440-775-5128, E-mail: Deborah.Campana@oberlin.edu; *Pub Serv Libr,* Kathleen Abromeit; Tel: 440-775-5131, E-mail: kathleen.abromeit@oberlin.edu; *Coordr, Circ,* Greg Solow; Tel: 440-775-5136, E-mail: greg.solow@oberlin.edu; Staff 11 (MLS 4, Non-MLS 7)
Founded 1865
Library Holdings: AV Mats 137,718; Bk Vols 209,602
Open Mon-Thurs 8-5:30 & 7-11, Fri 8-5:30 & 7-9, Sat 12-5:30, Sun 1-5:30 & 7-11
SCIENCE LIBRARY, Science Ctr N174, 119 Woodland St, 44074-1083, SAN 357-0304. Tel: 440-775-8310. E-mail: science.library@oberlin.edu. Web Site: www2.oberlin.edu/library/science. *Head, Sci Libr, Sci Librn,* Alison Scott Ricker; Tel: 440-775-5146, E-mail: aricker@oberlin.edu; Staff 2 (MLS 1, Non-MLS 1)
Founded 1965
Library Holdings: Bk Vols 93,454
Function: ILL available
Open Mon-Thurs 8:30am-Midnight, Fri 8:30-5:30, Sat 12:30-5:30, Sun 12:30-Midnight
CLARENCE WARD ART LIBRARY, Allen Art Bldg, 83 N Main St, 44074-1193, SAN 357-024X. Tel: 440-775-8635. FAX: 440-775-5145. E-mail: art.library@oberlin.edu. Web Site: www2.oberlin.edu/library/art. *Head of Libr,* Barbara Prior; E-mail: barbara.prior@oberlin.edu; Staff 2 (MLS 1, Non-MLS 1)
Library Holdings: Bk Vols 112,606
Open Mon-Thurs 8:30am-11pm, Fri 8:30-5:30, Sat 12:30-5:30, Sun 12:30-11

P OBERLIN PUBLIC LIBRARY, 65 S Main St, 44074-1626. SAN 313-6604. Tel: 440-775-4790. FAX: 440-774-2880. E-mail: oberlinpubliclibrary@yahoo.com. Web Site: www.oberlinlibrary.org. *Dir,* Darren McDonough; Staff 3 (MLS 3)
Founded 1947. Pop 18,831; Circ 281,860
Library Holdings: Bk Titles 130,000; Bk Vols 151,000; Per Subs 235
Subject Interests: Children's lit, Folklore, Ohio
Automation Activity & Vendor Info: (Acquisitions) TLC (The Library Corporation); (Cataloging) TLC (The Library Corporation); (Circulation) TLC (The Library Corporation); (OPAC) TLC (The Library Corporation)
Open Mon-Thurs 10-8:30, Fri & Sat 10-6, Sun 1-5
Friends of the Library Group

ORIENT

S CORRECTIONAL RECEPTION CENTER LIBRARY*, 11271 State Rte 762, 43146. Tel: 614-877-2441. *Librn,* Alice Jamez; E-mail: Alice.Jamez@odrc.state.oh.us; Staff 1 (MLS 1)
Founded 1987
Automation Activity & Vendor Info: (Acquisitions) Mandarin Library Automation; (Cataloging) Mandarin Library Automation; (Circulation) Mandarin Library Automation; (Course Reserve) Mandarin Library Automation; (ILL) Mandarin Library Automation
Function: Audio & video playback equip for onsite use, AV serv, Bk club(s), ILL available, Internet access, Magazines, Mail loans to mem, Movies, Music CDs, Online cat, Orientations, Photocopying/Printing, Prof lending libr, Prog for adults, Prog for children & young adult, Ref serv available, Serves people with intellectual disabilities, Spanish lang bks, Specialized serv in classical studies, VHS videos, Workshops

S PICKAWAY CORRECTIONAL INSTITUTION LIBRARY*, 11781 State Rte 762, 43146. (Mail add: PO Box 209, 43146-0209), SAN 371-6031. Tel: 614-877-4362. FAX: 614-877-0735. *Librn,* Nnacho Igwe; Staff 1 (MLS 1)
Library Holdings: High Interest/Low Vocabulary Bk Vols 100; Large Print Bks 50; Bk Titles 25,000; Per Subs 86; Talking Bks 30

ORRVILLE

P ORRVILLE PUBLIC LIBRARY*, 230 N Main St, 44667. SAN 313-6620. Tel: 330-683-1065. FAX: 330-683-1984. E-mail: orrville.library@orrville.lib.oh.us. Web Site: www.orrville.lib.oh.us. *Dir,* Daphne Silchuk-Ashcraft; E-mail: opldirector@orrville.lib.oh.us; Staff 4 (MLS 4)
Founded 1925. Pop 11,314; Circ 513,136
Library Holdings: Audiobooks 20,570; AV Mats 42,678; Bks on Deafness & Sign Lang 47; CDs 6,875; DVDs 4,671; e-books 17,896; Large Print Bks 518; Bk Vols 60,030; Per Subs 165; Talking Bks 20,570; Videos 6,314
Subject Interests: Railroads
Automation Activity & Vendor Info: (Acquisitions) SirsiDynix; (Cataloging) SirsiDynix; (Circulation) SirsiDynix
Wireless access
Function: Adult literacy prog, After school storytime, Art exhibits, Audiobks via web, Bks on cassette, Bks on CD, Children's prog, Computer training, Computers for patron use, Digital talking bks, Doc delivery serv, E-Reserves, Electronic databases & coll, Free DVD rentals, Holiday prog, Home delivery & serv to seniorr ctr & nursing homes, Homebound delivery serv, ILL available, Internet access, Large print keyboards,

Magnifiers for reading, Mail & tel request accepted, Music CDs, Online cat, Online ref, Orientations, Outreach serv, Outside serv via phone, mail, e-mail & web, OverDrive digital audio bks, Photocopying/Printing, Preschool outreach, Prog for adults, Prog for children & young adult, Ref & res, Ref serv available, Scanner, Senior computer classes, Senior outreach, Serves people with intellectual disabilities, Spoken cassettes & CDs, Spoken cassettes & DVDs, Story hour, Summer reading prog, Tax forms, Teen prog, Telephone ref, VHS videos, Visual arts prog, Wheelchair accessible, Workshops
Partic in CLEVNET; Northeast Ohio Regional Library System
Special Services for the Deaf - TDD equip; TTY equip
Special Services for the Blind - Accessible computers; Aids for in-house use; Assistive/Adapted tech devices, equip & products; Audio mat; BiFolkal kits; Bks on cassette; Bks on CD; Cassettes; Digital talking bk; Disability awareness prog; Home delivery serv; Internet workstation with adaptive software; Large print bks; Large screen computer & software; Low vision equip; Magnifiers; PC for people with disabilities; Playaways (bks on MP3); Recorded bks; Scanner for conversion & translation of mats; Sound rec; Soundproof reading booth; Talking bk serv referral; Videos on blindness & physical disabilties
Open Mon, Tues & Thurs 9-8, Wed & Fri 9-6, Sat 10-3
Friends of the Library Group

C UNIVERSITY OF AKRON LIBRARIES, Wayne College Library, 1901 Smucker Rd, 44667. SAN 313-6639. Tel: 330-972-8789. Administration Tel: 330-972-8951. FAX: 330-683-1381. E-mail: waynelibrary@uakron.edu. Web Site: wayne.uakron.edu/library. *Libr Dir,* Maureen Lerch; E-mail: mlerch@uakron.edu; Staff 2.3 (MLS 1, Non-MLS 1.3)
Founded 1972. Enrl 1,300; Fac 3; Highest Degree: Bachelor
Library Holdings: AV Mats 1,700; Bk Vols 18,781; Per Subs 12
Automation Activity & Vendor Info: (Acquisitions) Innovative Interfaces, Inc
Wireless access
Partic in Ohio Library & Information Network

ORWELL

P GRAND VALLEY PUBLIC LIBRARY, One N School St, 44076. (Mail add: PO Box 188, 44076-0188), SAN 313-6647. Tel: 440-437-6545. FAX: 440-437-1017. Web Site: www.grandvalleypubliclibrary.org. *Dir,* Cheryl Selby; E-mail: cselby@seolibraries.org; *Asst Dir, Outreach Serv,* Daniel Tanner; E-mail: dtanner@seolibraries.org; *Head, Circ,* Vinnie Utz; E-mail: vutz@seolibraries.org. Subject Specialists: *Home,* Daniel Tanner
Founded 1903. Pop 10,229; Circ 70,421
Library Holdings: AV Mats 5,241; DVDs 2,118; e-books 1,900; Electronic Media & Resources 307; Bk Vols 41,485; Per Subs 64; Videos 3,123
Automation Activity & Vendor Info: (Cataloging) SirsiDynix-Enterprise; (Circulation) SirsiDynix-Enterprise; (OPAC) SirsiDynix-Enterprise
Wireless access
Function: 24/7 Electronic res, 24/7 Online cat, Accelerated reader prog, Adult bk club, After school storytime, Archival coll, Audiobks via web, AV serv, Bk club(s), Bks on CD, CD-ROM, Children's prog, Computer training, Computers for patron use, E-Readers, Electronic databases & coll, Free DVD rentals, Holiday prog, Home delivery & serv to seniorr ctr & nursing homes, Homebound delivery serv, ILL available, Internet access, Laminating, Magazines, Mail & tel request accepted, Movies, Music CDs, Online cat, Online ref, OverDrive digital audio bks, Photocopying/Printing, Preschool outreach, Preschool reading prog, Printer for laptops & handheld devices, Prof lending libr, Prog for adults, Prog for children & young adult, Ref & res, Ref serv available, Scanner, Senior computer classes, Senior outreach, Story hour, Summer & winter reading prog, Summer reading prog, Tax forms, Teen prog, Wheelchair accessible, Winter reading prog
Partic in Northeast Ohio Regional Library System; Serving Every Ohioan Library Center
Open Mon-Thurs 9-7, Fri 9-5
Friends of the Library Group

OTTAWA

P PUTNAM COUNTY DISTRICT LIBRARY*, The Educational Service Ctr, 136 Putnam Pkwy, 45875-1471. SAN 357-0339. Tel: 419-523-3747. FAX: 419-523-6477. Web Site: www.mypcdl.org. *Dir,* Kelly Ward; E-mail: kward@seolibraries.org; *Local Hist Libn,* Ruth Wilhelm; E-mail: rwilhelm@seolibraries.org; *Ref (Info Servs),* Pat Meyer; E-mail: pmeyer@seolibraries.org; *Youth Serv,* Valerie Laukhuf; E-mail: vlaukhuf@seolibraries.org
Founded 1924. Circ 282,505
Library Holdings: Bk Vols 163,583; Per Subs 329
Wireless access
Partic in NORWELD; Serving Every Ohioan Library Center
Open Mon-Thurs 9-8, Fri 9-5, Sat 9-Noon
Friends of the Library Group

Branches: 7
COLUMBUS GROVE BRANCH, 317 N Main St, Columbus Grove, 45830, SAN 357-0363. Tel: 419-659-2355.
Founded 1936
Open Mon 2-8, Tues & Thurs 9-6, Sat 9-3
Friends of the Library Group
CONTINENTAL BRANCH, 301 S Sixth St, Continental, 45831, SAN 357-0371. Tel: 419-596-3727.
Open Mon & Wed 10-7, Tues 9-5, Thurs & Fri 10-5, Sat 9-12
FORT JENNINGS BRANCH, 655 N Water St, Fort Jennings, 45844-0218, SAN 328-7807. Tel: 419-286-2351.
Founded 1986
Open Tues 9-6, Thurs 2-8, Sat 9-3
Friends of the Library Group
KALIDA BRANCH, 301 N Third St, Kalida, 45853. (Mail add: PO Box 270, Kalida, 45853), SAN 357-038X. Tel: 419-532-2129.
Founded 1973
Open Mon 9-6:30, Wed 9-5, Sat 9-Noon
Friends of the Library Group
LEIPSIC MEMORIAL, 305 W Main St, Leipsic, 45856, SAN 357-0398. Tel: 419-943-2604.
Founded 1979
Library Holdings: Bk Vols 8,400; Per Subs 30
Open Tues 2-8, Wed & Thurs 9-6, Sat 9-5
Friends of the Library Group
OTTOVILLE-MONTEREY BRANCH, 150 Park Dr, Ottoville, 45876. (Mail add: PO Box 517, Ottoville, 45876-0517), SAN 357-0428. Tel: 419-453-2111.
Founded 1962. Circ 28,000
Library Holdings: Bk Titles 10,000; Per Subs 22
Open Mon 2-8, Wed 9-6, Sat 9-3
Friends of the Library Group
PANDORA-RILEY BRANCH, 118 E Main St, Pandora, 45877. (Mail add: PO Box 478, Pandora, 45877), SAN 328-8544. Tel: 419-384-3232.
Founded 1939
Open Mon 2-8, Tues & Wed 9-6, Sat 9-3
Friends of the Library Group
Bookmobiles: 1

OXFORD

C MIAMI UNIVERSITY LIBRARIES*, King Library, 151 S Campus Ave, 45056. SAN 357-0452. Tel: 513-529-4141. Circulation Tel: 513-529-2433. Interlibrary Loan Service Tel: 513-529-6147. FAX: 513-529-3110. Interlibrary Loan Service FAX: 513-529-1682. Web Site: www.lib.miamioh.edu. *Dean & Univ Librn,* Jerome Conley; Tel: 513-529-3934, E-mail: conleyj@miamioh.edu; *Assoc Dean,* Aaron Shrimplin; Tel: 513-529-6823, E-mail: aaron.shrimpin@miamioh.edu; *Asst Dean,* Belinda Barr; Tel: 513-529-7096, E-mail: barrb@miamioh.edu; *Asst Dean,* John Millard; Tel: 513-529-6789, E-mail: millarj@miamioh.edu; *Dir, Libr Tech,* Stan Brown; Tel: 513-529-2351, E-mail: brownsj1@miamioh.edu; *Head of Instruction,* Kevin Messner; Tel: 513-529-7204, E-mail: krmessner@miamioh.edu; *Head, Spec Coll & Archives,* William Modrow; Tel: 513-529-2024, E-mail: modrowwm@miamioh.edu; *Coordr, Access Serv,* Rob Withers; Tel: 513-529-6148, E-mail: witherre@miamioh.edu; Staff 48 (MLS 39, Non-MLS 9)
Founded 1809. Enrl 17,035; Fac 843; Highest Degree: Doctorate
Library Holdings: e-books 625,641; e-journals 31,531; Bk Titles 2,607,746; Bk Vols 2,779,539; Per Subs 1,135
Special Collections: 19th Century Gift Books; 19th Century Trade Cards; Clyde N, Bowden Postcard Coll; Cradle of Coaches (Sports); Early 20th Century Postcards; Early Printed Books; Freedom Summer; Imperial & Revolutionary Russia; James T Farrell; John H James Family Papers; King Coll of Early Juvenile Books & Periodicals; Kuchler Vegetation Maps; Louise Bogan Library; McGuffey Readers & other 19th Century Schoolbooks; Miami University Archives; Native American Women Playwrights Archive; Native Americans/Myaamia (Miami); Northwest Territory and Ohio Regional History; Railroads/Transportation; Rodolfo Usigli Archive; Samual Fulton Covington Coll and Family Papers; Shakespeare First Four Folios; US Civil War/Jefferson Davis & Confederacy; W H McGuffey Family Papers; Western College Memorial Archives; William Dean Howells; World Vegetation Maps. State Document Depository; UN Document Depository; US Document Depository
Automation Activity & Vendor Info: (Acquisitions) Innovative Interfaces, Inc; (Cataloging) Innovative Interfaces, Inc; (Circulation) Innovative Interfaces, Inc; (Course Reserve) Innovative Interfaces, Inc; (ILL) OCLC ILLiad; (OPAC) Innovative Interfaces, Inc; (Serials) Innovative Interfaces, Inc
Wireless access
Partic in Center for Research Libraries; Coalition for Networked Information; Ohio Library & Information Network; OhioNET

Departmental Libraries:

AMOS MUSIC LIBRARY, Center for the Performing Arts, 45056. (Mail add: 151 S Campus Ave, 45056), SAN 357-0517. Tel: 513-529-2299. FAX: 513-529-1378. *Music Librn,* Barry Zaslow; E-mail: zaslowbj@miamioh.edu; Staff 1 (MLS 1)
Subject Interests: Music, Music educ, Musical theatre, Musicology

BUSINESS, ENGINEERING, SCIENCE, & TECHNOLOGY LIBRARY, Laws Hall, 551 E High St, 45056. (Mail add: 151 S Campus Ave, 45056), SAN 357-0541. Tel: 513-529-6886. FAX: 513-529-1736. Web Site: www.lib.miamioh.edu/system/best-library. *Bus Librn,* Susan Hurst; Tel: 513-529-7204, E-mail: hursts@miamioh.edu; *Computing & Engineering Librn,* Matthew Benzing; E-mail: matt.benzing@miamioh.edu; Staff 5 (MLS 5)
Founded 1978
Special Collections: Kuchler Vegetation Maps
Subject Interests: Bus, Computer sci, Engr, Life sci, Phys sci, Psychol

GARDNER-HARVEY LIBRARY, 4200 N University Blvd, Middletown, 45042-3497, SAN 313-6221. Tel: 513-727-3222. Web Site: www.mid.miamioh.edu/library. *Dir,* John Burke; Tel: 513-727-3293, E-mail: burkejj@miamioh.edu; *Pub Serv Librn,* Jessica Long; E-mail: longjh@miamioh.edu; *Libr Assoc,* Jennifer Hicks; E-mail: hicksjl2@miamioh.edu; Staff 5 (MLS 3, Non-MLS 2)
Founded 1966. Enrl 2,600; Fac 100; Highest Degree: Bachelor
Jul 2013-Jun 2014 Income $520,993. Mats Exp $128,000, Books $65,000, Per/Ser (Incl. Access Fees) $7,000, Other Print Mats $10,000, Electronic Ref Mat (Incl. Access Fees) $46,000
Library Holdings: AV Mats 4,500; e-books 49,115; Bk Vols 24,000; Per Subs 50
Special Collections: Instructional Materials (IMC Coll), bks & AV
Automation Activity & Vendor Info: (Discovery) EBSCO Discovery Service
Function: Adult bk club, Computers for patron use, Electronic databases & coll, Equip loans & repairs, Free DVD rentals, ILL available, Mango lang, Online cat, Online info literacy tutorials on the web & in blackboard, Online ref, Photocopying/Printing, Ref serv available, Scanner, Wheelchair accessible
Partic in Ohio Library & Information Network
Special Services for the Blind - Assistive/Adapted tech devices, equip & products
Open Mon-Thurs (Summer) 8-6, Fri 8-5; Mon-Thurs (Fall) 8-8, Fri 8-5

WALTER HAVIGHURST SPECIAL COLLECTIONS & UNIVERSITY ARCHIVES, 321 King Library, Western College Memorial Archives, 45056. (Mail add: 151 S Campus Ave, 45056). Tel: 513-529-6720. E-mail: Archives@MiamiOH.edu, SpeColl@MiamiOH.edu. Web Site: spec.lib.miamioh.edu/home. *Univ Archivist,* Jacqueline Johnson; E-mail: johnsoj@MiamiOH.edu; Staff 1 (MLS 1)
Open Mon-Fri 8-5

RENTSCHLER LIBRARY, 1601 University Blvd, Hamilton, 45011, SAN 313-5322. Tel: 513-785-3235. FAX: 513-785-3231. Web Site: www.ham.miamioh.edu/library. *Dir,* Krista McDonald; E-mail: mcdonak@miamioh.edu; *Asst Dir,* Mark L Shores; E-mail: shoresml@miamioh.edu; *Ref Serv,* Polly Whitaker; E-mail: whitakpj@miamioh.edu; Staff 6 (MLS 4, Non-MLS 2)
Founded 1968. Fac 38; Highest Degree: Bachelor
Library Holdings: Bk Vols 71,275; Per Subs 356
Automation Activity & Vendor Info: (OPAC) Innovative Interfaces, Inc
Partic in OCLC Online Computer Library Center, Inc; Ohio Library & Information Network

SOUTHWEST OHIO REGIONAL DEPOSITORY, 4200 N University Blvd, Middletown, 45042-3458. Tel: 513-727-3474. FAX: 513-727-3478. E-mail: sword@miamioh.edu. *Mgr,* Pam Lipscomb; E-mail: lipscope@Miamioh.edu; Staff 1 (Non-MLS 1)
Library Holdings: Bk Vols 2,450,207

WERTZ ART & ARCHITECTURE LIBRARY, Alumni Hall, 45056. (Mail add: 151 S Campus Ave, 45056), SAN 357-0487. Tel: 513-529-6638. FAX: 513-529-4159. *Art Librn, Humanities Librn,* Stefanie Hilles; Tel: 513-529-6650, E-mail: hilless@miamioh.edu; Staff 1 (MLS 1)
Subject Interests: Archit, Art, Art educ, Interior design
Friends of the Library Group

P SMITH LIBRARY OF REGIONAL HISTORY*, 441 S Locust St, 45056. SAN 329-8027. Tel: 513-523-3035. FAX: 513-523-6661. E-mail: sml@lanepl.org. Web Site: www.lanepl.org/smith. *Mgr,* Brad Spurlock; E-mail: b.spurlock@lanepl.org; Staff 2 (MLS 1, Non-MLS 1)
Founded 1981
Library Holdings: CDs 31; DVDs 40; Microforms 431; Bk Titles 3,927; Bk Vols 4,029; Per Subs 26; Videos 43
Special Collections: Archives of Businesses, Churches, Schools, Cemeteries, Clubs, Organizations; Butler County Birth, Death & Marriage Records, Wills, Deeds on microfilm; Clyde Bowden Digital Postcard Coll; Manuscripts (Diaries, Letters); Newspapers; Photographs; Southwestern Ohio Bluegrass Music Heritage. Municipal Document Depository; Oral History
Subject Interests: Hist, Ohio
Automation Activity & Vendor Info: (ILL) OCLC
Wireless access
Function: 24/7 Electronic res, 24/7 Online cat, Archival coll, Res libr
Publications: Burial Grounds of Oxford (Local historical information); Celebrating the Oxford, Ohio Bicentennial, 1810-2010: Local History Articles (Local historical information); Commemorating the Ohio Bicentennial, 1803-2003: Butler County History Articles (Local historical information); Oxford & Miami University During World War II (Local historical information); To Dwell with Fond Reflection: Families Who Lived in the McGuffey House (Local historical information); Walking Tours of Oxford's Historic Districts (Local historical information)
Open Mon & Wed-Fri 10-12 & 1-5, Tues 10-12 & 1-8, Sat 10-1
Restriction: Non-circulating coll
Friends of the Library Group

PAINESVILLE

S LAKE COUNTY HISTORICAL SOCIETY*, P K Smith Research Library, 415 Riverside Dr, 44077. SAN 313-6124. Tel: 440-639-2945. FAX: 440-639-2947. E-mail: collections@lakehistory.org, research@lakehistory.org. Web Site: www.lakehistory.org. *Colls Mgr,* Lynn Vandevort; E-mail: lvandevort@lakehistory.org
Founded 1938
Library Holdings: Bk Vols 3,500
Subject Interests: Antiques, Garfield family, Genealogy, Local hist
Function: Res libr
Publications: Here is Lake County, Ohio (1964); Lake County Historical Society (Quarterly)
Restriction: Open by appt only

C LAKE ERIE COLLEGE*, James F Lincoln Library, 391 W Washington St, 44077-3309. SAN 313-6663. Tel: 440-375-7400. Administration Tel: 440-375-7405. Web Site: www.lec.edu/library. *Dir,* Jeanna Purses; E-mail: jpurses@lec.edu; *Cat, ILL,* Lori Greuber; Tel: 440-375-7402; Staff 2 (MLS 1, Non-MLS 1)
Founded 1859. Enrl 1,042; Fac 105; Highest Degree: Master
Library Holdings: AV Mats 1,821; e-books 108,846; Electronic Media & Resources 85,632; Bk Titles 40,635; Bk Vols 42,843
Special Collections: College Archives
Subject Interests: Equestrian studies
Automation Activity & Vendor Info: (Cataloging) Innovative Interfaces, Inc - Sierra; (Circulation) Innovative Interfaces, Inc - Sierra; (Course Reserve) Innovative Interfaces, Inc - Sierra; (Discovery) EBSCO Discovery Service; (ILL) OCLC ILLiad; (OPAC) Innovative Interfaces, Inc - Sierra
Wireless access
Function: Archival coll, Computers for patron use, Electronic databases & coll, ILL available, Photocopying/Printing, Ref serv available, Telephone ref
Partic in OhioNET

P MORLEY LIBRARY*, 184 Phelps St, 44077-3926. SAN 357-0665. Tel: 440-352-3383. FAX: 440-352-2653. Reference E-mail: reference@morleylibrary.org. Web Site: www.morleylibrary.org. *Dir,* Aurora Martinez; E-mail: amartinez@morleylibrary.org; *Teen Librn,* Jennifer Webster; E-mail: jwebster@morleylibrary.org; *Ch Mgr,* Barbara Bailey; E-mail: bbailey@morleylibrary.org; *Circ Serv Mgr,* Talma Wilkinson; E-mail: twilkinson@morleylibrary.org; *Ref Serv Mgr,* Charley Voelker; E-mail: cvoelker@morleylibrary.org; *Tech Serv Mgr,* Teri Blakemore; E-mail: tblakemore@morleylibrary.org; *Database Coordr,* Louise Kloss; E-mail: lkloss@morleylibrary.org; *Ref Serv, Ad,* Carl Engel; E-mail: ctengel@morleylibrary.org. Subject Specialists: *Local hist,* Carl Engel; Staff 39.1 (MLS 10, Non-MLS 29.1)
Founded 1899. Pop 52,404; Circ 552,076
Jan 2013-Dec 2013 Income $2,493,538, State $1,290,641, Locally Generated Income $1,116,380, Other $86,517. Mats Exp $394,125, Books $218,329, Per/Ser (Incl. Access Fees) $31,425, Other Print Mats $347, AV Mat $81,330, Electronic Ref Mat (Incl. Access Fees) $62,694. Sal $1,214,642
Library Holdings: Audiobooks 12,457; AV Mats 955; DVDs 19,126; e-books 3,037; Bk Titles 154,550; Per Subs 330
Special Collections: Foundation Center Resource Center; Obituary Files, 1822 to Present
Subject Interests: Genealogy, Local hist
Automation Activity & Vendor Info: (Acquisitions) TLC (The Library Corporation); (Cataloging) TLC (The Library Corporation); (Circulation) TLC (The Library Corporation); (OPAC) TLC (The Library Corporation)
Wireless access
Function: Ref serv available
Partic in Northeast Ohio Regional Library System
Open Mon-Thurs 9-9, Fri 9-6, Sat 9-5, Sun (Oct-April) 1-5
Friends of the Library Group

PARMA

P CUYAHOGA COUNTY PUBLIC LIBRARY*, 2111 Snow Rd, 44134-2728. SAN 356-1305. Tel: 216-398-1800. Circulation Tel: 216-749-9485. Toll Free Tel: 800-749-5560. FAX: 216-398-1748. E-mail: cuyahogacountypubliclibrary@cuyahoga.lib.oh.us. Web Site: www.cuyahogalibrary.org. *Exec Dir,* Tracy Strobel; Tel: 216-749-9419, E-mail: tstrobel@cuyogalibrary.org; *Dir, Literacy & Learning,* Pam Jankowski; *Dir, Communications & External Relations,* Hallie Rich; *Human Res Dir,* George Sample; *IT Dir,* James Haprian; *Fiscal Officer, Operations Dir,* Scott Morgan; *Dir, Tech Serv,* Daniel Barden; Staff 570 (MLS 121, Non-MLS 449)

Founded 1922. Pop 616,527; Circ 19,586,929

Jan 2015-Dec 2015. Mats Exp $9,023,564. Sal $27,833,068

Library Holdings: Audiobooks 100,506; Braille Volumes 180; CDs 177,875; DVDs 488,647; e-books 374,814; Large Print Bks 63,006; Microforms 611; Bk Vols 1,456,540; Per Subs 5,143

Special Collections: State Document Depository

Automation Activity & Vendor Info: (Acquisitions) Innovative Interfaces, Inc; (Cataloging) Innovative Interfaces, Inc; (Circulation) Innovative Interfaces, Inc; (OPAC) Innovative Interfaces, Inc; (Serials) Innovative Interfaces, Inc

Wireless access

Partic in OCLC Online Computer Library Center, Inc; OhioNET

Special Services for the Deaf - TTY equip

Open Mon-Fri 8-5

Friends of the Library Group

Branches: 28

BAY VILLAGE BRANCH, 502 Cahoon Rd, Bay Village, 44140-2179, SAN 356-133X. Tel: 440-871-6392. FAX: 440-871-5320. *Br Mgr,* Jessica Breslin

Open Mon-Thurs 9-9, Fri & Sat 9-5:30, Sun 1-5

Friends of the Library Group

BEACHWOOD BRANCH, 25501 Shaker Blvd, Beachwood, 44122-2306, SAN 356-1356. Tel: 216-831-6868. FAX: 216-831-0412. *Br Mgr,* Aimee Lurie

Special Collections: Holocaust Coll

Open Mon-Thurs 9-9, Fri & Sat 9-5:30, Sun 1-5

Friends of the Library Group

BEREA BRANCH, Seven Berea Commons, Berea, 44017-2524, SAN 356-1399. Tel: 440-234-5475. FAX: 440-234-2932. *Br Mgr,* Cathy Schultis

Open Mon-Thurs 9-9, Fri & Sat 9-5:30, Sun 1-5

Friends of the Library Group

BRECKSVILLE BRANCH, 9089 Brecksville Rd, Brecksville, 44141-2313, SAN 356-1429. Tel: 440-526-1102. FAX: 440-526-8793. *Br Mgr,* Melanie Rapp-Weiss

Open Mon-Thurs 9-9, Fri & Sat 9-5:30, Sun 1-5

Friends of the Library Group

BROOK PARK BRANCH, 6155 Engle Rd, Brook Park, 44142-2105, SAN 356-1453. Tel: 216-267-5250. FAX: 216-267-3776. *Br Mgr,* Nick Cronin

Open Mon-Thurs 9-9, Fri & Sat 9-5:30, Sun 1-5

Friends of the Library Group

BROOKLYN BRANCH, 4480 Ridge Rd, Brooklyn, 44144-3353, SAN 356-1488. Tel: 216-398-4600. FAX: 216-398-1545. *Br Mgr,* Ron Block

Open Mon-Thurs 9-9, Fri & Sat 9-5:30, Sun 1-5

Friends of the Library Group

CHAGRIN FALLS BRANCH, 100 E Orange St, Chagrin Falls, 44022-2735, SAN 356-1518. Tel: 440-247-3556. FAX: 440-247-0179. *Br Mgr,* Katherine Malmquist

Open Mon-Thurs 9-9, Fri & Sat 9-5:30, Sun 1-5

Friends of the Library Group

FAIRVIEW PARK BRANCH, 21255 Lorain Rd, Fairview Park, 44126-2120, SAN 356-1542. Tel: 440-333-4700. FAX: 440-333-0697. *Br Mgr,* Jesse Sanders

Special Collections: State Document Depository

Special Services for the Deaf - TTY equip

Open Mon-Thurs 9-9, Fri & Sat 9-5:30, Sun 1-5

Friends of the Library Group

GARFIELD HEIGHTS BRANCH, 5409 Turney Rd, Garfield Heights, 44125-3203, SAN 356-1577. Tel: 216-475-8178. FAX: 216-475-1015. *Br Mgr,* Lane Edwards

Open Mon-Thurs 9-9, Fri & Sat 9-5:30, Sun 1-5

Friends of the Library Group

GATES MILLS BRANCH, 1491 Chagrin River Rd, Gates Mills, 44040-9703, SAN 356-1607. Tel: 440-423-4808. FAX: 440-423-1363. *Br Mgr,* Katherine Malmquist

Open Mon-Thurs 9-9, Fri & Sat 9-5:30, Sun 1-5

Friends of the Library Group

INDEPENDENCE BRANCH, 6361 Selig Dr, Independence, 44131-4926, SAN 356-1631. Tel: 216-447-0160. FAX: 216-447-1371. *Br Mgr,* Melanie Rapp-Weiss

Open Mon-Thurs 9-9, Fri & Sat 9-5:30, Sun 1-5

Friends of the Library Group

MAPLE HEIGHTS BRANCH, 5225 Library Lane, Maple Heights, 44137-1242, SAN 356-1690. Tel: 216-475-5000. FAX: 216-587-7284. *Br Mgr,* Steven Haynie

Open Mon-Thurs 9-9, Fri & Sat 9-5:30, Sun 1-5

Friends of the Library Group

MAYFIELD BRANCH, 500 SOM Ctr Rd, Mayfield Village, 44143-2103, SAN 356-1720. Tel: 440-473-0350. FAX: 440-473-0774. *Br Mgr,* William Rubin

Open Mon-Thurs 9-9, Fri & Sat 9-5:30, Sun 1-5

Friends of the Library Group

METROHEALTH MEDICAL CENTER BRANCH, 2500 MetroHealth Dr, Cleveland, 44109. Tel: 216-778-7670. *Br Mgr,* Jesse Sanders

Open Mon-Fri 9-5:30

MIDDLEBURG HEIGHTS BRANCH, 16699 Bagley Rd, Middleburg Heights, 44130, SAN 356-1755. Tel: 440-234-3600. FAX: 440-234-0849. *Br Mgr,* Holly Camino

Open Mon-Thurs 9-9, Fri & Sat 9-5:30, Sun 1-5

Friends of the Library Group

NORTH OLMSTED BRANCH, 27403 Lorain Rd, North Olmsted, 44070-4037, SAN 356-178X. Tel: 440-777-6211. FAX: 440-777-4312. *Br Mgr,* Andrew Harant

Open Mon-Thurs 9-9, Fri & Sat 9-5:30, Sun 1-5

Friends of the Library Group

NORTH ROYALTON BRANCH, 5071 Wallings Rd, North Royalton, 44133-5120, SAN 356-181X. Tel: 440-237-3800. FAX: 440-237-6149. *Br Mgr,* Jeanne Cilenti

Open Mon-Thurs 9-9, Fri & Sat 9-5:30, Sun 1-5

Friends of the Library Group

OLMSTED FALLS BRANCH, 8100 Mapleway Dr, Olmsted Falls, 44138, SAN 356-1844. Tel: 440-235-1150. FAX: 440-235-0954. *Br Mgr,* Andrew Harant

Open Mon-Thurs 9-9, Fri & Sat 9-5, Sun 1-5

Friends of the Library Group

ORANGE BRANCH, 31975 Chagrin Blvd, Pepper Pike, 44124-5916, SAN 356-1879. Tel: 216-831-4282. FAX: 216-831-0714. *Br Mgr,* Anthony Furino

Open Mon-Thurs 9-9, Fri & Sat 9-5:30, Sun 1-5

Friends of the Library Group

PARMA BRANCH, 6996 Powers Blvd, 44129-6602, SAN 356-1933. Tel: 440-885-5362. FAX: 440-884-2263. *Br Mgr,* Kathleen Sullivan

Open Mon-Thurs 9-9, Fri & Sat 9-5:30, Sun 1-5

Friends of the Library Group

PARMA HEIGHTS BRANCH, 6206 Pearl Rd, Parma Heights, 44130-3045, SAN 356-1909. Tel: 440-884-2313. FAX: 440-884-2713. *Br Mgr,* Nick Cronin

Open Mon-Thurs 9-9, Fri & Sat 9-5:30, Sun 1-5

Friends of the Library Group

PARMA-SNOW BRANCH, 2121 Snow Rd, 44134-2728, SAN 356-1968. Tel: 216-661-4240. FAX: 216-661-1019. *Br Mgr,* Stacey Boycik

Open Mon-Thurs 9-9, Fri & Sat 9-5:30, Sun 1-5

Friends of the Library Group

RICHMOND HEIGHTS BRANCH, 5235 Wilson Mills Rd, Richmond Heights, 44143-3016, SAN 329-6075. Tel: 440-449-2666. FAX: 440-473-3264. *Br Mgr,* William Rubin

Open Mon-Thurs 9-9, Fri & Sat 9-5:30, Sun 1-5

Friends of the Library Group

SOLON BRANCH, 34125 Portz Pkwy, Solon, 44139-6803, SAN 356-1992. Tel: 440-248-8777. FAX: 440-248-5369. *Br Mgr,* Julie Liedtke

Open Mon-Thurs 9-9, Fri & Sat 9-5:30, Sun 1-5

Friends of the Library Group

SOUTH EUCLID-LYNDHURST BRANCH, 1876 S Green Rd, South Euclid, 44121-4018, SAN 356-2026. Tel: 216-382-4880. FAX: 216-382-4584. *Br Mgr,* Brijin Boddy

Open Mon-Thurs 9-9, Fri & Sat 9-5:30, Sun 1-5

Friends of the Library Group

SOUTHEAST BRANCH, 70 Columbus Rd, Bedford, 44146-2836, SAN 356-1364. Tel: 440-439-4997. FAX: 440-439-5846. *Br Mgr,* Vicki Adams-Cook

Open Mon-Thurs 9-9, Fri & Sat 9-5:30, Sun 1-5

Friends of the Library Group

STRONGSVILLE BRANCH, 18700 Westwood Dr, Strongsville, 44136-3431, SAN 356-2050. Tel: 440-238-5530. FAX: 440-572-8685. *Br Mgr,* Donna Meyers

Open Mon-Thurs 9-9, Fri & Sat 9-5:30, Sun 1-5

Friends of the Library Group

WARRENSVILLE HEIGHTS BRANCH, 4415 Northfield Rd, Warrensville Heights, 44128-4603, SAN 356-2085. Tel: 216-464-5280. FAX: 216-464-6475. *Br Mgr,* Ali Boyd

Open Mon-Thurs 9-9, Fri & Sat 9-5:30, Sun 1-5

PATASKALA

P PATASKALA PUBLIC LIBRARY*, 101 S Vine St, 43062. SAN 313-6698. Tel: 740-927-9986. FAX: 740-964-6204. Web Site: pataskalalibrary.org. *Dir/Fiscal Officer,* Jeffrey Rothweiler; E-mail:

jeffrothweiler@pataskalalibrary.org; *Asst Dir,* Mary Kruse; E-mail: mkruse@pataskalalibrary.org; *Network Adminr,* Scott Kammeyer; E-mail: skammeyer@pataskalalibrary.org; *Ch,* Laura Scarberry; E-mail: lscarberry@pataskalalibrary.org; Staff 3 (MLS 2, Non-MLS 1)
Founded 1937. Pop 12,000; Circ 254,000
Library Holdings: AV Mats 9,000; Bk Vols 66,000; Per Subs 53
Special Collections: Accords Coll
Wireless access
Partic in Central Library Consortium
Open Mon-Thurs 12-6, Fri & Sat 10-2
Friends of the Library Group

PAULDING

P PAULDING COUNTY CARNEGIE LIBRARY*, 205 S Main St, 45879-1492. SAN 313-6701. Tel: 419-399-2032. FAX: 419-399-2114. Web Site: www.pauldingcountylibrary.org. *Dir,* Susan Pieper; E-mail: spieper@pauldingcountylibrary.org; *Head, Tech Serv,* Teresa Reel; *Head, Youth Serv,* Susan Deatrick; E-mail: susand@pauldingcountylibrary.org; Staff 19 (MLS 1, Non-MLS 18)
Founded 1916. Pop 19,432; Circ 205,527
Special Collections: Civil War Interest; High School Yearbooks (County High Schools); Local History & Genealogy; Paulding County Newspapers (1859-present), micro and digitized; Paulding County Obituary Card File; Rare Books; World War II Interest
Subject Interests: County genealogy, Local hist
Automation Activity & Vendor Info: (Acquisitions) Innovative Interfaces, Inc; (Circulation) Innovative Interfaces, Inc; (OPAC) Innovative Interfaces, Inc
Wireless access
Function: 24/7 Electronic res, 24/7 Online cat, Activity rm, Adult bk club, After school storytime, Archival coll, Audio & video playback equip for onsite use, Audiobks on Playaways & MP3, Audiobks via web, AV serv, Bk club(s), Bks on CD, CD-ROM, Children's prog, Computer training, Computers for patron use, Digital talking bks, Electronic databases & coll, Family literacy, Free DVD rentals, Genealogy discussion group, Govt ref serv, Health sci info serv, Holiday prog, Home delivery & serv to seniorr ctr & nursing homes, Homework prog, ILL available, Instruction & testing, Internet access, Laminating, Learning ctr, Life-long learning prog for all ages, Magazines, Mail & tel request accepted, Meeting rooms, Microfiche/film & reading machines, Movies, Music CDs, Notary serv, Online cat, Online info literacy tutorials on the web & in blackboard, Online ref, Orientations, Outreach serv, OverDrive digital audio bks, Photocopying/Printing, Preschool outreach, Preschool reading prog, Prof lending libr, Prog for adults, Prog for children & young adult, Ref & res, Ref serv available, Scanner, Senior computer classes, Serves people with intellectual disabilities, Story hour, Summer & winter reading prog, Summer reading prog, Teen prog, Telephone ref, Visual arts prog, Wheelchair accessible, Winter reading prog
Partic in Ohio Public Library Information Network
Special Services for the Blind - Audio mat; Bks on cassette; Bks on CD; Large print bks; Playaways (bks on MP3); Talking bk & rec for the blind cat
Open Mon-Thurs 9-8, Fri 9-6, Sat 9-1
Restriction: Non-circulating coll, Non-circulating of rare bks, Non-circulating to the pub, Non-resident fee
Friends of the Library Group
Branches: 3
ANTWERP BRANCH, 205 N Madison St, Antwerp, 45813-8411. (Mail add: PO Box 1027, Antwerp, 45813-1027). Tel: 419-258-2855. FAX: 419-258-2855. *Br Mgr,* Sara Molitor Newman; E-mail: saran@pauldingcountylibrary.org
Founded 1991
Open Mon & Tues 12-7:30, Wed-Fri 10-5, Sat 9-1
Friends of the Library Group
COOPER COMMUNITY, 206 N First St, Oakwood, 45873. (Mail add: PO Box 348, Oakwood, 45873-0348). Tel: 419-594-3337. FAX: 419-594-3337. *Br Mgr,* Sarah Finnegan; E-mail: sfinnegan@pauldingcountylibrary.org
Founded 2000
Open Mon & Tues 12-7:30, Wed-Fri 10-5, Sat 9-1
Friends of the Library Group
PAYNE BRANCH, 101 N Main St, Payne, 45880. (Mail add: PO Box 210, Payne, 45880-0210). Tel: 419-263-3333. FAX: 419-263-3333. *Br Mgr,* Suzi Yenser; E-mail: syenser@pauldingcountylibrary.org
Founded 1996
Open Mon & Tues 12-7:30, Wed-Fri 10-5, Sat 9-1
Friends of the Library Group
Bookmobiles: 1. Mgr, Kathy Heffley

PEEBLES

P ADAMS COUNTY PUBLIC LIBRARY*, Peebles Public Library, 157 High St, 45660. SAN 356-7753. Tel: 937-587-2085. FAX: 937-587-5043. Web Site: adamscolibrary.org. *Exec Dir,* Nicholas Slone; E-mail: sloneni@adamscolibrary.org; *Libr Asst, Pub Serv,* Beverly Kiser
Wireless access
Partic in Serving Every Ohioan Library Center
Open Mon & Thurs 11-5, Tues & Wed 1-7, Fri 1-5
Friends of the Library Group
Branches: 3
MANCHESTER PUBLIC LIBRARY, 401 Pike St, Manchester, 45144, SAN 356-7729. Tel: 937-549-3359. FAX: 937-549-4219. *Libr Asst, Pub Serv,* Peggy McCartney
Open Mon & Thurs 11-5, Tues & Wed 1-7, Fri 1-5
Friends of the Library Group
NORTH ADAMS PUBLIC LIBRARY, 2469 Moores Rd, Seaman, 45679. Tel: 937-386-2556. FAX: 937-386-2974. *Libr Asst, Pub Serv,* Josh Brown
Open Mon & Thurs 1-7, Tues & Wed 11-5, Fri 1-5
Friends of the Library Group
WEST UNION PUBLIC LIBRARY, 212 E Sparks St, West Union, 45693, SAN 376-9631. Tel: 937-544-2591. FAX: 937-544-2092. *Libr Asst, Pub Serv,* Tara Dryden
Open Mon & Thurs 1-7, Tues & Wed 11-5, Fri 1-5
Friends of the Library Group

PEMBERVILLE

P PEMBERVILLE PUBLIC LIBRARY*, 375 E Front St, 43450. (Mail add: PO Box 809, 43450-0809), SAN 357-072X. Tel: 419-287-4012. Web Site: www.pembervillelibrary.org. *Dir,* Susan Titkemeier; E-mail: SLang@seolibraries.org; *Ch Serv,* Laurel Rakas; Staff 5 (MLS 2, Non-MLS 3)
Founded 1937. Pop 9,000; Circ 98,000
Library Holdings: High Interest/Low Vocabulary Bk Vols 50; Bk Titles 55,000; Per Subs 145
Subject Interests: Local hist
Automation Activity & Vendor Info: (Cataloging) SirsiDynix; (Circulation) SirsiDynix; (Course Reserve) SirsiDynix; (ILL) SirsiDynix; (OPAC) SirsiDynix; (Serials) SirsiDynix
Function: Doc delivery serv, ILL available, Photocopying/Printing, Ref serv available, Telephone ref
Partic in Northwestern Libr District; Serving Every Ohioan Library Center
Open Mon-Thurs 9-8, Fri 9-2, Sat 10-3
Friends of the Library Group
Branches: 2
LUCKEY BRANCH, 228 Main St, Luckey, 43443. (Mail add: PO Box 190, Luckey, 43443), SAN 377-824. FAX: 419-801-4053. *Dir,* Susan Titkemeier; Tel: 419-287-4012, E-mail: slang@seolibraries.org
Open Mon-Thurs 3:30-7:30, Fri 2-5, Sat 10-Noon
Friends of the Library Group
STONY RIDGE BRANCH, 5805 Fremont Pike, Stony Ridge, 43463, SAN 357-0754. Tel: 419-837-5948. FAX: 419-714-7061. *Br Coordr,* Laura King; E-mail: liblady1@yahoo.com
Library Holdings: Bk Vols 23,000
Open Mon & Tues 12-8, Wed 9-5, Thurs 12-5, Sat 10-12
Friends of the Library Group

PENINSULA

S PENINSULA LIBRARY & HISTORICAL SOCIETY, 6105 Riverview Rd, 44264. (Mail add: PO Box 236, 44264-0236), SAN 313-671X. Tel: 330-467-7323, 330-657-2291. FAX: 330-657-2311. E-mail: info@peninsulalibrary.org. Web Site: www.peninsulalibrary.org. *Dir,* Randy Bergdorf; E-mail: rbergdorf@peninsulalibrary.org; *Ad,* Anne M Matusz; Staff 13 (MLS 3, Non-MLS 10)
Founded 1943. Pop 553,371
Library Holdings: Bk Vols 40,000; Per Subs 105
Special Collections: Local History Coll
Automation Activity & Vendor Info: (Cataloging) SirsiDynix; (Circulation) SirsiDynix; (OPAC) SirsiDynix
Wireless access
Function: Archival coll, ILL available, Internet access, Photocopying/Printing, Prog for adults, Prog for children & young adult, Ref serv available, Summer reading prog, Telephone ref, Wheelchair accessible
Publications: Bi-monthly Newsletter
Open Mon-Thurs 9-8, Fri & Sat 9-5
Friends of the Library Group
Branches:
CUYAHOGA VALLEY HISTORICAL MUSEUM, 1775 Main St, 2nd Flr, 44264. (Mail add: PO Box 236, 44264-0236). Tel: 330-657-2892. *Dir,* Randy Bergdorf
Library Holdings: Bk Titles 40,000; Per Subs 105
Automation Activity & Vendor Info: (Acquisitions) SirsiDynix

Open Wed & Fri 12-4
Friends of the Library Group

PEPPER PIKE

R PARK SYNAGOGUE*, Leonard Senkfor Library, 27500 Shaker Blvd, 44124. SAN 370-7083. Tel: 216-371-2244, Ext 223, 216-831-5363, Ext 223. FAX: 216-321-0639. Web Site: www.parksynagogue.org. *Librn,* Julie Moss; E-mail: jmoss@parksyn.org; Staff 1 (MLS 1)
Subject Interests: Judaica, Juv
Partic in Asn of Jewish Librs
Friends of the Library Group

R TEMPLE ON THE HEIGHTS*, Jack Jacobson Memorial Library, 27501 Fairmount Blvd, 44124. SAN 313-3931. Tel: 216-831-6555. FAX: 216-831-4599. Web Site: www.bnaijeshurun.org/learn-with-us-libraries. *Librn,* Dr R Raphael Simon; E-mail: ralphsimon@bnaijeshurun.org; Staff 2 (MLS 1, Non-MLS 1)
Founded 1928
Library Holdings: Bk Vols 9,000

C URSULINE COLLEGE*, Ralph M Besse Library, 2550 Lander Rd, 44124-4398. SAN 313-3885. Tel: 440-449-4202. Web Site: www.ursuline.edu/library. *Dir,* Suzanna Schroeder-Green; E-mail: sschroeder@ursuline.edu; *Asst Dir,* Kathy Fisher; E-mail: kfisher@ursuline.edu; *Archivist, Ref & Instruction Librn,* Mara Shatat; E-mail: Mara.shatat@ursuline.edu; *Tech Serv Librn,* Tabitha Barr; E-mail: Tabitha.barr@Ursuline.edu; *Acq,* Helen Tramte; E-mail: htramte@ursuline.edu; Staff 12 (MLS 6, Non-MLS 6)
Founded 1871. Enrl 1,175; Fac 74; Highest Degree: Doctorate
Jul 2013-Jun 2014 Income $733,996. Mats Exp $254,779, Books $43,000, Per/Ser (Incl. Access Fees) $53,850, AV Mat $14,500, Electronic Ref Mat (Incl. Access Fees) $25,000, Presv $800. Sal $485,141
Library Holdings: AV Mats 8,617; e-books 110,963; e-journals 49,163; Electronic Media & Resources 22,626; Microforms 4,675; Bk Titles 94,422; Bk Vols 108,928; Per Subs 46
Subject Interests: Art therapy, Nursing
Automation Activity & Vendor Info: (Acquisitions) Innovative Interfaces, Inc; (Cataloging) Innovative Interfaces, Inc; (Circulation) Innovative Interfaces, Inc; (OPAC) Innovative Interfaces, Inc; (Serials) Innovative Interfaces, Inc
Wireless access
Partic in OCLC Online Computer Library Center, Inc; Ohio Library & Information Network; Ohio Private Academic Libraries; OhioNET
Open Mon-Thurs 7:30am-11pm, Fri 7:30-7, Sat 10-7, Sun 1-11
Friends of the Library Group

PERRY

P PERRY PUBLIC LIBRARY, 3753 Main St, 44081-9501. SAN 313-6728. Tel: 440-259-3300. FAX: 440-259-3977. E-mail: askus@perry.lib.oh.us. Web Site: www.perrypubliclibrary.org. *Dir,* Emily Skunda; E-mail: emily.skunda@perry.lib.oh.us; *Dept Head, Ref,* Sharon Detering; E-mail: sdetering@perry.lib.oh.us; *Dept Head, Tech Serv,* Kari Betchik; E-mail: kbetchik@perry.lib.oh.us; *Circ Supvr,* Linda Moats; E-mail: lmoats@perry.lib.oh.us; *Ch Serv,* Kara Cervelli; *ILL,* Annie Rohde; E-mail: annie.rohde@perry.lib.oh.us; *Ref Serv,* Siobhan McCann; Staff 6 (MLS 4, Non-MLS 2)
Founded 1929. Pop 9,001; Circ 195,285
Jan 2019-Dec 2019 Income $1,012,806, State $376,330, Locally Generated Income $570,500, Parent Institution $49,996, Other $15,980. Mats Exp $125,100. Sal $651,400
Library Holdings: Audiobooks 7,052; e-books 245,700; Bk Titles 50,000; Per Subs 162; Videos 8,177
Automation Activity & Vendor Info: (Cataloging) SirsiDynix-Enterprise; (Circulation) SirsiDynix-Enterprise; (ILL) SirsiDynix-Enterprise; (OPAC) SirsiDynix-Enterprise
Wireless access
Function: Adult bk club, Audiobks via web, Bk club(s), Bks on CD, CD-ROM, Chess club, Children's prog, Computer training, Computers for patron use, Electronic databases & coll, Free DVD rentals, Homebound delivery serv, ILL available, Magnifiers for reading, Music CDs, Online cat, OverDrive digital audio bks, Photocopying/Printing, Prog for adults, Prog for children & young adult, Story hour, Summer reading prog, Tax forms, Teen prog, Wheelchair accessible
Partic in CLEVNET; Northeastern Ohio Libr Asn
Open Mon-Fri 9-6, Sat 11-4
Friends of the Library Group

PERRYSBURG

J OWENS COMMUNITY COLLEGE LIBRARY*, 30335 Oregon Rd, 43551. (Mail add: PO Box 10000, Toledo, 43699-1947), SAN 313-6736. Tel: 567-661-7015. FAX: 567-661-7021. E-mail: libhelp@owens.edu. Web Site: www.owens.edu/library. *Dir, Libr Serv,* Jane A Berger; Tel: 567-661-7459, E-mail: jane_berger2@owens.edu; *Acq Librn,* Michael Aked; Tel: 567-661-7031, E-mail: michael_aked@owens.edu; *Ser Librn,* Paul L Weaver; Tel: 567-661-7234, E-mail: paul_weaver2@owens.edu; *Tech Librn,* Monica Mason; E-mail: monica_mason2@owens.edu; *Tech Serv Librn,* Alyssa Moskwa; E-mail: alyssa_moskwa@owens.edu; *Access Serv Supvr,* Jennifer Blum; Tel: 567-661-7016, E-mail: jennifer_blum@owens.edu; Staff 6 (MLS 5, Non-MLS 1)
Founded 1966. Enrl 22,000; Fac 1,400; Highest Degree: Associate
Library Holdings: Bk Titles 38,600; Bk Vols 49,800; Per Subs 400
Automation Activity & Vendor Info: (Acquisitions) Innovative Interfaces, Inc; (Cataloging) Innovative Interfaces, Inc; (Circulation) Innovative Interfaces, Inc; (Course Reserve) Docutek; (ILL) Innovative Interfaces, Inc; (Media Booking) Innovative Interfaces, Inc; (OPAC) Innovative Interfaces, Inc; (Serials) Innovative Interfaces, Inc
Wireless access
Partic in OCLC Online Computer Library Center, Inc; Ohio Library & Information Network; OhioNET
Special Services for the Blind - Assistive/Adapted tech devices, equip & products
Restriction: Open to pub for ref & circ; with some limitations, Open to students, fac & staff, Photo ID required for access

P WAY PUBLIC LIBRARY*, 101 E Indiana Ave, 43551. SAN 313-6744. Tel: 419-874-3135. FAX: 419-874-6129. Web Site: www.waylibrary.info/. *Dir,* Janel Haas; Tel: 419-874-3135, Ext 102, E-mail: Janel.haas@waylibrary.info; *Head, Tech Serv,* Linda Rutz; Tel: 419-874-3135, Ext 114, E-mail: Linda.Rutz@waylibrary.info; *Hist Coll Librn,* Richard Baranowski; Tel: 419-874-3135, Ext 110, E-mail: Richard.Baranowski@waylibrary.info; *Pub Serv Coordr,* Lynn Fleure; Tel: 419-874-3135, Ext 111, E-mail: Lynn.Fleure@waylibrary.info; *Youth Serv Coordr,* Melissa Tallis; Tel: 419-874-3135,Ext 109, E-mail: melisa.tallis@waylibrary.info; *Graphic & Visual Design Spec,* Rose Mills; Tel: 419-874-3135, Ext 108, E-mail: Rose.Mills@waylibrary.info; *Syst Adminr,* Travis McAfee; Tel: 419-874-3135, Ext 103, E-mail: Travis.McAfee@waylibrary.info; Staff 12 (MLS 6, Non-MLS 6)
Founded 1881. Pop 25,000
Library Holdings: Bk Vols 101,156; Per Subs 222
Special Collections: Perrysburg Local History Coll
Automation Activity & Vendor Info: (OPAC) Horizon
Wireless access
Partic in NORWELD; Serving Every Ohioan Library Center
Open Mon-Thurs 9-8:30, Fri 9-6:30, Sat 9-5:30, Sun 1-5
Friends of the Library Group

PICKERINGTON

P PICKERINGTON PUBLIC LIBRARY*, 201 Opportunity Way, 43147-1296. SAN 313-6752. Tel: 614-837-4104. Circulation Tel: 614-837-4104, Ext 232. Reference Tel: 614-837-4104, Ext 233. FAX: 614-837-8425. Web Site: pickeringtonlibrary.org/. *Dir,* Tony Howard; Tel: 614-837-4101, Ext 222, E-mail: thoward@pickeringtonlibrary.org; *Asst Dir,* Kenton Daniels; Tel: 614-837-4101, Ext 226; *Adult Serv Mgr,* Donna Matturri; Tel: 614-837-4101, Ext 241, E-mail: dmatturri@pickeringtonlibrary.org; *Youth Serv,* Cathy Burden; Tel: 614-837-4101, Ext 230, E-mail: cburden@pickeringtonlibrary.org; Staff 6 (MLS 3, Non-MLS 3)
Founded 1915. Pop 34,000; Circ 366,727
Library Holdings: AV Mats 21,271; Bk Vols 103,143; Per Subs 296
Automation Activity & Vendor Info: (Acquisitions) SirsiDynix; (Cataloging) SirsiDynix; (Circulation) SirsiDynix; (OPAC) SirsiDynix; (Serials) SirsiDynix
Wireless access
Publications: Monthly Newsletter
Partic in Cent Libr Consortium
Open Mon-Thurs 9-8, Fri & Sat 9-6, Sun 1-5
Friends of the Library Group

PIQUA

J EDISON STATE COMMUNITY COLLEGE LIBRARY, 1973 Edison Dr, 45356. SAN 313-6779. Tel: 937-778-7950. FAX: 937-778-7958. E-mail: library@edisonohio.edu. Web Site: www.edisonohio.edu/library. *Libr Dir,* Lisa Hoops; Tel: 937-778-7955; *Librn,* Nicole Dunn; E-mail: ndunn2@edisonohio.edu; Staff 4 (MLS 2, Non-MLS 2)
Founded 1973. Enrl 3,000; Highest Degree: Associate
Library Holdings: AV Mats 2,019; Bk Vols 23,324; Per Subs 38; Videos 1,108
Subject Interests: Early childhood educ, Nursing
Automation Activity & Vendor Info: (Cataloging) Innovative Interfaces, Inc; (Circulation) Innovative Interfaces, Inc; (Course Reserve) Innovative Interfaces, Inc; (Media Booking) Innovative Interfaces, Inc; (OPAC) Innovative Interfaces, Inc; (Serials) Innovative Interfaces, Inc
Wireless access
Function: 24/7 Electronic res, 24/7 Online cat

Partic in Ohio Library & Information Network; Southwestern Ohio Council for Higher Education
Open Mon-Thurs 8:30-7, Fri 8-4

P PIQUA PUBLIC LIBRARY*, 116 W High St, 45356. SAN 313-6787. Tel: 937-773-6753. FAX: 937-773-5981. E-mail: referencedept@piqualibrary.org. Web Site: www.youseemore.com/piqua. *Dir,* James C Oda; E-mail: joda@piqualibrary.org; *Senior Coord,* Nancy Spillane; Staff 3 (MLS 3)
Founded 1890. Pop 25,000; Circ 260,926
Library Holdings: Bk Vols 136,000; Per Subs 165
Special Collections: Oral History
Subject Interests: Local hist
Automation Activity & Vendor Info: (Cataloging) Brodart; (Circulation) Brodart; (OPAC) Brodart
Partic in Miami Valley Librs
Open Mon-Thurs 10-8:30, Fri & Sat 10-5:30
Friends of the Library Group

PLAIN CITY

P PLAIN CITY PUBLIC LIBRARY*, 305 W Main St, 43064-1148. SAN 313-6795. Tel: 614-873-4912. Circulation Tel: 614-873-4912, Ext 121. Reference Tel: 614-873-4912, Ext 130. FAX: 614-873-8364. Web Site: plaincitylib.org. *Dir,* Chris Long; Tel: 614-873-4912, Ext 123, E-mail: clong@plaincitylib.org; *Circ Mgr,* Malinda Millington; Tel: 614-873-4912, Ext 126, E-mail: mmillington@plaincitylib.org; *Ref,* Jane Isaacs; E-mail: jisaacs@plaincitylib.org; *Youth Serv,* Amanda Warner; Tel: 614-873-4912, Ext 131, E-mail: awarner@plaincitylib.org; Staff 19 (MLS 3, Non-MLS 16)
Founded 1944. Circ 142,672
Library Holdings: Bk Titles 54,896; Per Subs 114
Subject Interests: Genealogy, Local hist
Wireless access
Partic in Cent Libr Consortium
Open Mon-Thurs 10-9, Fri & Sat 10-6
Friends of the Library Group

POMEROY

P MEIGS COUNTY DISTRICT PUBLIC LIBRARY*, 216 W Main St, 45769. SAN 357-0789. Tel: 740-992-5813. FAX: 740-992-6140. E-mail: contact@meigslibrary.org. Web Site: www.meigslibrary.org. *Dir,* Kristi Eblin; E-mail: keblin@meigslibrary.org; *Asst Dir,* Chelsea Poole; *Coordr, Ch Serv,* Emily Sanders; Staff 4 (Non-MLS 4)
Founded 1881. Pop 23,641; Circ 140,062
Library Holdings: Bk Vols 110,000; Per Subs 300
Automation Activity & Vendor Info: (Cataloging) TLC (The Library Corporation); (Circulation) TLC (The Library Corporation); (OPAC) TLC (The Library Corporation)
Wireless access
Special Services for the Deaf - High interest/low vocabulary bks
Open Mon-Fri 9-8, Sat 9-5, Sun 1-5
Friends of the Library Group
Branches: 3
EASTERN, 38850 State Rte 7, Reedsville, 45772, SAN 378-1232. Tel: 740-985-3747. FAX: 740-985-3746.
Open Mon-Sat 10-6
Friends of the Library Group
MIDDLEPORT BRANCH, 178 S Third St, Middleport, 45760, SAN 357-0819. Tel: 740-992-5713. FAX: 740-992-4207.
Open Mon-Sat 10-6
Friends of the Library Group
RACINE BRANCH, 210 Tyree Blvd, Racine, 45771, SAN 377-8290. Tel: 740-949-8200. FAX: 740-949-8300.
Open Mon-Sat 10-6
Friends of the Library Group

PORT CLINTON

P IDA RUPP PUBLIC LIBRARY, Port Clinton Public Library, 310 Madison St, 43452. SAN 313-6817. Tel: 419-732-3212. Administration Tel: 419-732-3221. FAX: 419-734-9867. E-mail: idarupp@seolibraries.org. Web Site: www.idarupp.org. *Dir,* Lindsay Faust; E-mail: lfaust@seolibraries.org; *Asst Dir,* Courtney McGrath; Staff 19 (MLS 4, Non-MLS 15)
Founded 1908. Pop 20,000; Circ 293,827
Library Holdings: Audiobooks 4,000; DVDs 4,200; e-books 8,930; Bk Titles 80,800
Special Collections: Bataan Memorial Coll; Genealogy & Local History Coll; Ohioana & Rare Book Coll; Patricia A Snider Great Lakes Coll
Automation Activity & Vendor Info: (Cataloging) SirsiDynix; (Circulation) SirsiDynix; (OPAC) SirsiDynix
Wireless access
Function: 24/7 Electronic res, Activity rm, Adult bk club, Audiobks on Playaways & MP3, Audiobks via web, AV serv, Bk club(s), Bks on CD, Children's prog, Computer training, Computers for patron use, E-Reserves, Electronic databases & coll, Free DVD rentals, Home delivery & serv to seniorr ctr & nursing homes, ILL available, Internet access, Magazines, Magnifiers for reading, Meeting rooms, Microfiche/film & reading machines, Movies, Music CDs, Notary serv, Online cat, Online info literacy tutorials on the web & in blackboard, Online ref, OverDrive digital audio bks, Photocopying/Printing, Preschool outreach, Preschool reading prog, Printer for laptops & handheld devices, Prog for adults, Prog for children & young adult, Ref serv available, Scanner, Senior outreach, Story hour, Study rm, Summer & winter reading prog, Teen prog, Telephone ref
Partic in Ohio Public Library Information Network; Serving Every Ohioan Library Center
Open Mon-Wed, Fri & Sat 10-5, Thurs 1-8
Friends of the Library Group
Branches: 2
ERIE ISLANDS LIBRARY, 281 Concord Ave, Put-In-Bay, 43456, SAN 328-0101. Tel: 419-285-4004. FAX: 419-285-4004. *Br Mgr,* Karen Wilhelm; E-mail: kwilhelm@seolibraries.org; Staff 4 (Non-MLS 4)
Library Holdings: Bk Titles 7,000
Open Mon, Wed, Fri & Sat 10-2, Tues & Thurs 3-7
Friends of the Library Group
MARBLEHEAD PENINSULA BRANCH, 710 W Main St, Marblehead, 43440. Tel: 419-798-0477. FAX: 419-798-0479. *Br Mgr,* Erin Sandvick
Function: Computers for patron use, ILL available, Notary serv, Photocopying/Printing, Scanner
Open Mon, Wed, Fri & Sat 10-2, Tues & Thurs 3-7

PORTSMOUTH

P PORTSMOUTH PUBLIC LIBRARY*, 1220 Gallia St, 45662-4185. SAN 357-0843. Tel: 740-354-5688. FAX: 740-353-3483. TDD: 740-354-6039. Web Site: www.yourppl.org. *Dir,* Paige Williams; Tel: 740-353-5990, E-mail: pwilliams@yourppl.org; Staff 53 (MLS 6, Non-MLS 47)
Founded 1831
Library Holdings: Bk Titles 102,787; Bk Vols 213,680; Per Subs 390
Special Collections: Northwest Territories Coll
Subject Interests: Local hist
Automation Activity & Vendor Info: (Acquisitions) TLC (The Library Corporation); (Cataloging) TLC (The Library Corporation); (Circulation) TLC (The Library Corporation); (ILL) TLC (The Library Corporation); (OPAC) TLC (The Library Corporation); (Serials) TLC (The Library Corporation)
Wireless access
Function: 24/7 Electronic res, Activity rm, Adult bk club, Archival coll, Art exhibits, Bk club(s), Bks on CD, Children's prog, Computer training, Computers for patron use, Electronic databases & coll, Free DVD rentals, Home delivery & serv to seniorr ctr & nursing homes, Homebound delivery serv, ILL available, Internet access, Magazines, Meeting rooms, Music CDs, Notary serv, Online cat, OverDrive digital audio bks, Photocopying/Printing, Preschool outreach, Preschool reading prog, Prog for children & young adult, Ref serv available, Story hour, Summer reading prog, Tax forms, Teen prog, Wheelchair accessible
Open Mon-Thurs 9-8, Fri & Sat 9-5
Branches: 4
VERNAL G RIFFE BRANCH, 3850 Rhodes Ave, New Boston, 45662, SAN 357-0878. Tel: 740-456-4412. FAX: 740-456-4047. *Br Mgr,* Jessica Kamer; Staff 4 (Non-MLS 4)
Founded 1941
Open Mon 10-8, Wed, Thurs & Fri 10-6, Sat 10-5
W GORDON RYAN BRANCH, 103 Lucasville-Minford Rd, Lucasville, 45648-0744, SAN 370-9027. Tel: 740-259-6119. FAX: 740-259-3168. *Br Mgr,* Gwen Suter; Staff 4 (Non-MLS 4)
Founded 1990
Open Mon 10-8, Tues, Wed & Fri 10-6, Sat 10-5
SOUTH WEBSTER BRANCH, 496 Webster St, South Webster, 45682, SAN 326-8462. Tel: 740-778-2122. FAX: 740-778-3436. *Br Mgr,* Lacy Stevenson; Staff 4 (Non-MLS 4)
Founded 1984
Open Tues 10-8, Wed, Thurs & Fri 10-6, Sat 10-5
WHEELERSBURG BRANCH, 10745 Old Gallia Pike, Wheelersburg, 45694, SAN 357-0894. Tel: 740-574-6116. FAX: 740-574-8280. *Br Mgr,* Barbara Biggs; Staff 4 (Non-MLS 4)
Founded 1965
Open Mon, Thurs & Fri 10-6, Tues 10-8, Sat 10-5
Bookmobiles: 1

L SCIOTO COUNTY LAW LIBRARY*, Scioto County Court House, 3rd Flr, 602 Seventh St, 45662. SAN 313-6825. Tel: 740-355-8259. FAX: 740-353-9480. E-mail: librarian@sciotolawlibrary.com. Web Site: sciotolawlibrary.org. *Librn,* Sandra Blevins
Library Holdings: Bk Vols 25,100
Wireless access
Restriction: External users must contact libr

C SHAWNEE STATE UNIVERSITY*, Clark Memorial Library, 940 Second St, 45662-4344. SAN 357-0967. Tel: 740-351-3323. Circulation Tel: 740-351-3519. Interlibrary Loan Service Tel: 740-351-3353. Reference Tel: 740-351-3321. Administration Tel: 740-351-3267. FAX: 740-351-3432. E-mail: ssulibrary@shawnee.edu. Web Site: www.shawnee.edu/off/cml/index.html. *Dean of Libr,* Janet Stewart; E-mail: jstewart@shawnee.edu; *Ref & Instruction Librn,* Marla Beebe; Tel: 740-351-3461, E-mail: mbeebe@shawnee.edu; *Tech Serv Librn,* Suzanne Johnson Varney; Tel: 740-351-3410, E-mail: svarney@shawnee.edu; *Access Serv, Outreach Serv,* Zachary Lewis; Tel: 740-351-3492, E-mail: zlewis@shawnee.edu. Subject Specialists: *Sci, Teacher educ,* Marla Beebe; *English, Humanities,* Zachary Lewis; Staff 11 (MLS 4, Non-MLS 7)
Founded 1967. Enrl 3,500; Fac 327; Highest Degree: Master
Library Holdings: Audiobooks 324; AV Mats 23,036; Bks on Deafness & Sign Lang 96; CDs 1,544; DVDs 802; e-books 56,938; e-journals 64,465; Electronic Media & Resources 309,662; Large Print Bks 39; Microforms 264,999; Music Scores 402; Bk Titles 186,367; Per Subs 218; Videos 4,428
Special Collections: Albert Parry Coll; Bob Wilson Coll; Jessie Stuart Coll; Louis A Brennan Coll; Southern Ohio Valley Writers; Vernal G Riffe Memorabilia. US Document Depository
Automation Activity & Vendor Info: (Acquisitions) Innovative Interfaces, Inc - Sierra; (Cataloging) Innovative Interfaces, Inc - Sierra; (Circulation) Innovative Interfaces, Inc - Sierra; (Course Reserve) Innovative Interfaces, Inc - Sierra; (ILL) OCLC Online; (OPAC) Innovative Interfaces, Inc - Sierra; (Serials) Innovative Interfaces, Inc - Sierra
Wireless access
Partic in Ohio Library & Information Network; OhioNET
Special Services for the Deaf - ADA equip; Closed caption videos; Sign lang interpreter upon request for prog
Special Services for the Blind - Daisy reader; Low vision equip; Magnifiers; Rec; Sound rec; Text reader
Open Mon-Thurs(Fall & Spring) 7:30am-11pm, Fri 7:30-5, Sat 8:30-4:30, Sun Noon-Midnight; Mon-Thurs (Summer) 8am-9pm, Fri 8-5, Sun 1-6

RAVENNA

S PORTAGE COUNTY HISTORICAL SOCIETY MUSEUM & LIBRARY*, 6549 N Chestnut St, 44266. SAN 326-4106. Tel: 330-296-3523. E-mail: pchsohio@neo.rr.com. Web Site: www.portagecountyhistoricalsociety.org/library.html. *Pres,* Wayne Enders; *Librn,* Barb Petroski; Staff 9 (Non-MLS 9)
Founded 1951
Library Holdings: Bk Vols 1,000
Special Collections: Frederick J Loudin Coll
Subject Interests: Genealogy, Hist, Local hist
Function: Archival coll, Photocopying/Printing, Res libr
Publications: Newsletter (Quarterly)
Open Thurs & Sat 2-5
Restriction: Not a lending libr, Open to pub with supv only

L PORTAGE COUNTY LAW LIBRARY*, 241 S Chestnut St, 44266. SAN 372-2023. Tel: 330-297-3661. E-mail: portagecountylawlibrary@neo.rr.com. Web Site: www.portagecountylawlibrary.com. *Librn,* Alessandra Reckner
Founded 1896
Library Holdings: Bk Titles 12,000; Per Subs 20
Function: Bilingual assistance for Spanish patrons
Open Mon-Fri 8-4

P REED MEMORIAL LIBRARY*, 167 E Main St, 44266-3197. SAN 313-6833. Tel: 330-296-2827. Circulation Tel: 330-296-2827, Ext 400. Reference Tel: 330-296-2827, Ext 200. Administration Tel: 330-296-2827, Ext 103. FAX: 330-296-3780. Web Site: www.reed.lib.oh.us. *Dir,* Brian C Hare; Tel: 330-296-2827, Ext 101, E-mail: bhare@reedlibrary.org; *Head, Children's Servx,* Angela Young; Tel: 330-296-2827, Ext 301, E-mail: ayoung@reedlibrary.org; *Head, Circ,* Karen Ross; Tel: 330-296-2827, Ext 401, E-mail: kross@reedlibrary.org; *Head, Ref,* Darlene McKenzie; Tel: 330-296-2827, Ext 201, E-mail: dmckenzie@reedlibrary.org; *Head, Tech Serv,* Cindy Wenger; Tel: 330-296-2827, Ext 501, E-mail: cwenger@reedlibrary.org; Staff 7 (MLS 7)
Founded 1915. Pop 21,030; Circ 171,172
Library Holdings: AV Mats 10,064; CDs 2,289; DVDs 997; Bk Titles 91,000; Bk Vols 94,241; Per Subs 206; Videos 3,621
Special Collections: Local Paper Film from early 1800-present; Ravenna & Mantua Ohio Glass Coll
Subject Interests: Local hist
Automation Activity & Vendor Info: (Acquisitions) Innovative Interfaces, Inc; (Cataloging) Innovative Interfaces, Inc; (Circulation) Innovative Interfaces, Inc; (OPAC) Innovative Interfaces, Inc; (Serials) Innovative Interfaces, Inc
Wireless access
Function: Adult bk club, Chess club, Computer training, Electronic databases & coll, Homebound delivery serv, ILL available, Magnifiers for reading, Mail & tel request accepted, Photocopying/Printing, Prog for adults, Prog for children & young adult, Ref serv available, Spoken cassettes & CDs, Summer reading prog, Tax forms, Telephone ref, VHS videos, Wheelchair accessible
Publications: Reed the News (Newsletter)
Partic in Portage Library Consortium
Special Services for the Blind - Reader equip; Talking bks & player equip; Videos on blindness & physical disabilties
Open Mon-Thurs 9-9, Fri 9-6, Sat 9-5, Sun 1-5
Friends of the Library Group

RICHWOOD

P RICHWOOD NORTH UNION PUBLIC LIBRARY*, Four E Ottawa St, 43344-1296. SAN 313-6841. Tel: 740-943-3054. FAX: 740-943-9211. Web Site: www.richwoodlibrary.org. *Dir,* Audrey Deel; E-mail: audreydeel@richwoodlibrary.org
Founded 1882. Pop 2,200; Circ 44,000
Library Holdings: Bk Titles 72,000; Bk Vols 73,500; Per Subs 149
Special Collections: Oral History
Partic in Serving Every Ohioan Library Center
Open Mon-Thurs 11-7, Fri 9-6, Sat 9-2

RIO GRANDE

C UNIVERSITY OF RIO GRANDE*, Jeanette Albiez Davis Library, 218 N College Ave, 45674. SAN 313-685X. Tel: 740-245-7005. Interlibrary Loan Service Tel: 740-245-7398. Reference Tel: 740-245-7344. Toll Free Tel: 800-282-7201. FAX: 740-245-7096. E-mail: refdesk@rio.edu. Web Site: www.rio.edu/library. *Dir,* Amy Wilson; Tel: 740-245-7382, E-mail: awilson@rio.edu; *Metadata Librn, Syst Librn,* Kayla Fleming; E-mail: kfleming@rio.edu; *Ref Librn,* Timothy M Snow; E-mail: tsnow@rio.edu; Staff 5 (MLS 4, Non-MLS 1)
Founded 1876. Enrl 1,986; Fac 90; Highest Degree: Master
Library Holdings: AV Mats 2,412; Microforms 446,409; Bk Vols 94,197; Per Subs 230
Special Collections: US Document Depository
Automation Activity & Vendor Info: (Acquisitions) Innovative Interfaces, Inc
Function: Art exhibits, Computers for patron use, Distance learning, Electronic databases & coll, Govt ref serv, ILL available, Online cat, Online info literacy tutorials on the web & in blackboard, Photocopying/Printing, Ref serv available, Telephone ref, Wheelchair accessible
Publications: Ex Libris Et Al (Newsletter); Instructional Material (Reference guide); LibGuides (Online only); Pathfinders (Reference guide); Student Newspaper Column (Newsletter)
Partic in Ohio Library & Information Network; OhioNET
Open Mon-Thurs 8am-10pm, Fri 8-5, Sat 1-5, Sun 5-9
Restriction: Circ limited, In-house use for visitors, Open to pub for ref & circ; with some limitations, Open to students, fac & staff, Pub use on premises
Friends of the Library Group

RIPLEY

P UNION TOWNSHIP PUBLIC LIBRARY*, 27 Main St, 45167-1231. SAN 313-6868. Tel: 937-392-4871. FAX: 937-392-1631. E-mail: info@ripleylibrary.com. Web Site: www.ripleylibrary.com. *Dir,* Alison J Gibson; E-mail: gibsonal@ripleylibrary.com
Founded 1915. Pop 34,966; Circ 155,000
Library Holdings: Bk Vols 45,000; Per Subs 195
Special Collections: Local History, Ripley, Ohio
Automation Activity & Vendor Info: (Acquisitions) SirsiDynix; (Cataloging) SirsiDynix; (Circulation) SirsiDynix; (Serials) SirsiDynix
Wireless access
Function: Bks on cassette, Bks on CD, Children's prog, Computer training, Computers for patron use, Electronic databases & coll, Free DVD rentals, Holiday prog, Home delivery & serv to seniorr ctr & nursing homes, ILL available, Internet access, Music CDs, Online cat, Online ref, Photocopying/Printing, Prog for children & young adult, Ref & res, Spoken cassettes & CDs, Story hour, Summer reading prog, Tax forms, VHS videos, Wheelchair accessible
Partic in Serving Every Ohioan Library Center
Open Mon-Thurs 10-8, Fri 10-6, Sat 10-4
Friends of the Library Group
Branches: 2
ABERDEEN BRANCH LIBRARY, 1730 US Rte 52, Aberdeen, 45101-9302. Tel: 937-795-2534. FAX: 937-795-2681. *Dir,* Alison Gibson; Tel: 937-392-4871
Automation Activity & Vendor Info: (Cataloging) SirsiDynix; (Circulation) SirsiDynix; (ILL) SirsiDynix; (Serials) SirsiDynix
Open Mon, Wed & Fri 12-6, Tues & Thurs 12-8, Sat 10-2
Friends of the Library Group
RUSSELLVILLE BRANCH LIBRARY, 280 W Main St, Russellville, 45168-8730. Tel: 937-377-2700. FAX: 937-377-1302. *Dir,* Gibson Alison
Library Holdings: Bk Vols 6,500; Per Subs 39

Automation Activity & Vendor Info: (Cataloging) SirsiDynix; (Circulation) SirsiDynix; (ILL) SirsiDynix; (Serials) SirsiDynix
Open Mon & Wed 12-8, Tues & Thurs 10-6, Fri 12-4, Sat 10-2
Friends of the Library Group

ROCK CREEK

P ROCK CREEK PUBLIC LIBRARY*, 2988 High St, 44084-9703. SAN 313-6876. Tel: 440-563-3340. FAX: 440-563-9566. E-mail: rockcreeklib@rockcreekpl.org. Web Site: rockcreekpl.org. *Dir,* Janice Despenes; E-mail: despenesj@gmail.com; Staff 5 (Non-MLS 5)
Founded 1937. Pop 3,500; Circ 75,006
Library Holdings: Bks on Deafness & Sign Lang 30; Bk Titles 28,000; Per Subs 99
Special Collections: Ruth E Smik Art Coll
Automation Activity & Vendor Info: (Cataloging) SirsiDynix
Wireless access
Function: Telephone ref
Partic in Coun of Ashtabula County Librs; Northeast Ohio Regional Library System
Open Mon-Thurs 9-7, Fri 9-6, Sat 9-1
Friends of the Library Group

ROCKFORD

P ROCKFORD CARNEGIE LIBRARY*, 162 S Main St, 45882-9260. (Mail add: PO Box 330, 45882-0330), SAN 313-6884. Tel: 419-363-2630. FAX: 419-363-3723. Web Site: www.rcpubliclibrary.org. *Libr Dir,* Shelley Muhlenkamp; E-mail: sm@rcpubliclibrary.org; Staff 2 (Non-MLS 2)
Founded 1902. Pop 3,400; Circ 39,092
Jan 2017-Dec 2017 Income $206,500, State $145,000, Locally Generated Income $60,000, Other $1,500. Mats Exp $33,475, Books $24,800, Per/Ser (Incl. Access Fees) $2,500, AV Mat $6,175. Sal $98,000 (Prof $40,000)
Library Holdings: Audiobooks 451; DVDs 1,850; e-books 220,767; Large Print Bks 1,243; Bk Titles 19,495; Bk Vols 20,000; Per Subs 51
Automation Activity & Vendor Info: (Cataloging) SirsiDynix; (Circulation) SirsiDynix; (OPAC) SirsiDynix
Wireless access
Function: 24/7 Electronic res, 24/7 Online cat, Accelerated reader prog, Activity rm, Art exhibits, Bks on cassette, Bks on CD, Children's prog, Computer training, Computers for patron use, Free DVD rentals, Home delivery & serv to seniorr ctr & nursing homes, Homebound delivery serv, ILL available, Internet access, Laminating, Magazines, Meeting rooms, Online cat, Orientations, OverDrive digital audio bks, Photocopying/Printing, Preschool outreach, Preschool reading prog, Prog for children & young adult, Ref & res, Story hour, Study rm, Summer reading prog, Wheelchair accessible
Partic in NORWELD; Serving Every Ohioan Library Center
Open Mon-Thurs 10-8, Fri 10-5:30, Sat 10-2
Friends of the Library Group

ROCKY RIVER

P ROCKY RIVER PUBLIC LIBRARY*, 1600 Hampton Rd, 44116-2699. SAN 313-6892. Tel: 440-333-7610. FAX: 440-333-4184. Web Site: rrpl.org. *Dir,* Jamie L Mason; Tel: 440-895-3716, E-mail: j.mason@rrpl.org; *Dep Dir,* Trent Ross; Tel: 440-895-3727, E-mail: t.ross@rrpl.org; *Adult Serv Mgr,* Dori Olivos; Tel: 440-895-3753, E-mail: d.olivos@rrpl.org; *Ch Mgr,* Charlotte Blasier; Tel: 440-895-3736, E-mail: c.blasier@rrpl.org; *Circ Mgr,* Bridget Russ; Tel: 440-895-3739, E-mail: b.russ@rrpl.org; *Support Serv Mgr,* Peter Matera; Tel: 440-895-3749, E-mail: p.matera@rrpl.org; *Tech Mgr,* Jim Lack; Tel: 440-895-3765, E-mail: j.lack@rrpl.org; Staff 15 (MLS 15)
Founded 1928. Pop 20,582; Circ 878,261
Library Holdings: Bk Vols 130,824
Special Collections: Cowan Pottery Museum
Subject Interests: Rocky River city hist
Automation Activity & Vendor Info: (Circulation) SirsiDynix-DRA
Wireless access
Function: Art exhibits, Children's prog, Computer training, Electronic databases & coll, Homebound delivery serv, ILL available, OverDrive digital audio bks, Prog for adults
Publications: Between the Covers (Bimonthly); Cowan Pottery (Journal); Inside View (Newsletter)
Partic in Northeast Ohio Regional Library System
Open Mon-Thurs 9-9, Fri & Sat 9-6, Sun (Sept-May) 1-5
Friends of the Library Group

ROOTSTOWN

CM NORTHEAST OHIO MEDICAL UNIVERSITY, NEOMED Library, (Formerly Ocasek Oliver Medical Library), 4209 State Rte 44, 44272. (Mail add: PO Box 95, 44272-0095), SAN 313-6914. Tel: 330-325-6600. Reference Tel: 330-325-6604. FAX: 330-325-0522. E-mail: library@neomed.edu. Web Site: www.neomed.edu/library. *Exec Dir,* Terri Robinson; E-mail: trobinson@neomed.edu; *Electronic Res Librn,* Dani Hollar; Tel: 330-325-6601, E-mail: dhollar@neomed.edu; *Ref Librn,* Simon Robins; Tel: 330-325-6378, E-mail: srobins@neomed.edu; Staff 7 (MLS 4, Non-MLS 3)
Founded 1974. Enrl 421; Fac 72; Highest Degree: Doctorate
Library Holdings: Bk Vols 122,569; Per Subs 2,693
Subject Interests: Life sci, Med
Wireless access
Publications: Medical Periodicals in Northeastern Ohio
Partic in Northeast Ohio Regional Library System; Ohio Library & Information Network
Open Mon-Thurs 8am-8pm, Fri 8-5, Sat & Sun Noon-5

ROSSFORD

P ROSSFORD PUBLIC LIBRARY*, 720 Dixie Hwy, 43460-1289. SAN 313-6922. Tel: 419-666-0924. FAX: 419-666-1989. Web Site: www.rossfordlibrary.org. *Dir,* Jeannine Wilbarger; E-mail: jeannine.wilbarger@rossfordlibrary.org; *Asst Dir, Pub Relations Coordr,* Kristine Goldsmith; *Ch,* Jacky Farkas; *Ref Librn,* Lauren Kuhr; *Info Tech, YA Librn,* Matt Harbauer; *Circ Supvr,* Joy Creutz; Staff 4 (MLS 4)
Founded 1936. Pop 13,445; Circ 245,667
Library Holdings: e-books 52; Bk Vols 65,332; Per Subs 174
Subject Interests: Local hist
Automation Activity & Vendor Info: (Circulation) SirsiDynix; (OPAC) SirsiDynix
Wireless access
Partic in NORWELD; SE Ohio Regional Librs; Serving Every Ohioan Library Center
Open Mon-Thurs 9-8, Fri & Sat 9-5, Sun 1-5
Friends of the Library Group

SABINA

P SABINA PUBLIC LIBRARY*, 11 E Elm St, 45169-1330. SAN 313-6930. Tel: 937-584-2319. FAX: 937-584-2751. Web Site: sabinalibrary.com. *Dir,* Peggy Dunn; E-mail: pdunn@sabinalibrary.com; *Asst Dir,* Victoria Olds
Founded 1937. Circ 32,809
Library Holdings: Bk Vols 32,288; Per Subs 90
Wireless access
Partic in Southwestern Ohio Rural Librs
Open Mon, Tues & Thurs 10-7, Fri 10-6, Sat 10-1
Branches: 1
NEW VIENNA LIBRARY, 97 Main St, New Vienna, 45159. Tel: 937-987-4200. *Br Mgr,* Pat Herring-Curtis
Open Mon, Tues & Thurs 12-6, Fri 11-5

SAINT CLAIRSVILLE

J BELMONT COLLEGE*, Library, 68094 Hammond Rd, Rm 1076, 43950-9735. SAN 313-6957. Tel: 740-699-3835. Interlibrary Loan Service Tel: 740-699-3828. Toll Free Tel: 800-423-1188 (OH only). E-mail: refdesk@belmontcollege.edu. Web Site: www.belmontcollege.edu/current-students/student-resources/library. *Coordr, Learning Commons,* Lisa Baker; E-mail: lbaker@belmontcollege.edu; *Libr Spec,* Kimberly Frakowski; Tel: 740-699-3953, E-mail: kfrakowski@belmontcollege.edu
Founded 1971. Highest Degree: Associate
Library Holdings: AV Mats 2,114; Bk Titles 11,112; Bk Vols 12,600; Per Subs 341
Subject Interests: Allied health, Info tech, Nursing
Automation Activity & Vendor Info: (Acquisitions) Innovative Interfaces, Inc; (Cataloging) Innovative Interfaces, Inc; (Circulation) Innovative Interfaces, Inc; (Course Reserve) Innovative Interfaces, Inc; (ILL) OCLC Connexion; (OPAC) Innovative Interfaces, Inc; (Serials) Innovative Interfaces, Inc
Wireless access
Function: 24/7 Online cat, Archival coll, Audio & video playback equip for onsite use, AV serv, Bks on CD, Computers for patron use, Distance learning, Doc delivery serv, Electronic databases & coll, For res purposes, Free DVD rentals, Homework prog, ILL available, Internet access, Learning ctr, Magazines, Magnifiers for reading, Mail & tel request accepted, Mail loans to mem, Online cat, Orientations, Photocopying/Printing, Study rm, Tax forms, Telephone ref, VHS videos, Wheelchair accessible, Workshops
Partic in OCLC Online Computer Library Center, Inc; Ohio Library & Information Network; OhioNET
Open Mon-Thurs 8-6:30, Fri 8-4:30

L BELMONT COUNTY LAW LIBRARY*, Court House, 101 W Main St, 43950. SAN 313-6949. Tel: 740-695-2121, Ext 1053. FAX: 740-695-4968. E-mail: bclawlibrary@gmail.com. *Librn,* Richard Melanko
Library Holdings: Bk Vols 25,000
Open Mon-Fri 8:30-4:30

C OHIO UNIVERSITY*, Eastern Campus, Shannon Hall, 1st Flr, 45425 National Rd, 43950-9724. SAN 313-6965. Tel: 740-695-1720, 740-699-2519. Toll Free Tel: 800-648-3331, Ext 2519. FAX: 740-695-7075. Web Site: www.ohio.edu/eastern/library. *Head Librn,* Donna Capezzuto; Tel: 740-699-2344, E-mail: capezzut@ohio.edu; *Circ, Sr Libr Assoc,* Brad Cecil; Tel: 740-699-2332, E-mail: cecil@ohio.edu; Staff 3 (MLS 2, Non-MLS 1)
Founded 1957. Enrl 900; Highest Degree: Bachelor
Library Holdings: AV Mats 68,000; CDs 65; DVDs 64; Bk Titles 48,135; Bk Vols 72,869; Per Subs 774; Videos 500
Special Collections: Contemporary American Poetry
Subject Interests: Educ, Nursing
Automation Activity & Vendor Info: (Cataloging) Innovative Interfaces, Inc; (Circulation) Innovative Interfaces, Inc; (Course Reserve) Innovative Interfaces, Inc; (ILL) Innovative Interfaces, Inc; (OPAC) Innovative Interfaces, Inc; (Serials) Innovative Interfaces, Inc
Wireless access
Function: Computers for patron use, E-Reserves, Electronic databases & coll, ILL available, Instruction & testing, Internet access, Online cat, Online ref, Orientations, Photocopying/Printing, Ref serv available, Spoken cassettes & CDs, Spoken cassettes & DVDs, VHS videos, Wheelchair accessible
Partic in OCLC Online Computer Library Center, Inc; Ohio Library & Information Network
Special Services for the Blind - Assistive/Adapted tech devices, equip & products
Open Mon-Thurs 8am-8:30pm, Fri 8-4:30; Mon-Fri (Summer) 8-4:30
Restriction: Open to fac, students & qualified researchers, Open to pub for ref & circ; with some limitations

P SAINT CLAIRSVILLE PUBLIC LIBRARY*, 108 W Main St, 43950-1225. SAN 313-6973. Tel: 740-695-2062. FAX: 740-695-6420. Web Site: stclibrary.org. *Libr Dir,* Doug Walsh; E-mail: dwalsh@stclibrary.org; Staff 1 (Non-MLS 1)
Founded 1941. Pop 6,114; Circ 153,144
Library Holdings: Bk Vols 56,523; Per Subs 161
Subject Interests: Genealogy, Local hist
Automation Activity & Vendor Info: (Acquisitions) SirsiDynix; (Cataloging) SirsiDynix; (Circulation) SirsiDynix; (ILL) SirsiDynix; (OPAC) SirsiDynix
Wireless access
Partic in SE Ohio Regional Librs; Serving Every Ohioan Library Center
Open Mon-Wed 10-8, Thurs & Fri 10-6, Sat 10-2
Friends of the Library Group

SAINT MARTIN

J CHATFIELD COLLEGE LIBRARY*, 20918 State Rte 251, 45118. SAN 313-6981. Tel: 513-875-3344. FAX: 513-875-3912. Web Site: chatfield.edu/academics/library. *Mgr, Libr Serv,* Emilia Knisley; E-mail: emilia.knisley@chatfield.edu
Founded 1860. Enrl 350
Library Holdings: Bk Titles 24,000; Per Subs 25
Subject Interests: Appalachian studies, Children's lit, Fiber arts, Local hist
Automation Activity & Vendor Info: (Cataloging) SirsiDynix; (Circulation) SirsiDynix; (OPAC) SirsiDynix
Wireless access
Partic in Serving Every Ohioan Library Center

SAINT MARYS

P ST MARYS COMMUNITY PUBLIC LIBRARY*, 140 S Chestnut St, 45885. SAN 313-699X. Tel: 419-394-7471. FAX: 419-394-7291. E-mail: stmaryshelp@seolibraries.org. Web Site: smcpl.org. *Dir,* Ms Morgan Paul; *Coord, Ad Serv,* Beth Keuneke; Staff 3 (MLS 2, Non-MLS 1)
Founded 1921. Pop 13,269; Circ 134,049
Library Holdings: CDs 4,737; DVDs 4,470; Bk Vols 67,227; Per Subs 161
Special Collections: Jim Tully Coll
Subject Interests: Local hist
Automation Activity & Vendor Info: (Cataloging) SirsiDynix; (Circulation) SirsiDynix; (OPAC) SirsiDynix
Wireless access
Partic in Association for Rural & Small Libraries; NORWELD; SE Ohio Regional Librs; Serving Every Ohioan Library Center
Open Mon-Thurs 10-7, Fri 10-5, Sat 10-2
Friends of the Library Group

SAINT PARIS

P SAINT PARIS PUBLIC LIBRARY*, 127 E Main St, 43072. (Mail add: PO Box 740, 43072-0740), SAN 313-7007. Tel: 937-663-4349. FAX: 937-663-0297. Web Site: stparispubliclibrary.org. *Dir,* Nicole Rush; E-mail: director@stparislibrary.org; *Circ Supvr,* Jo Ozimek; E-mail: ozimekjo@stparislibrary.org; Staff 11 (Non-MLS 11)
Founded 1936. Pop 10,000; Circ 106,000
Library Holdings: Bks on Deafness & Sign Lang 31; Bk Titles 32,000; Bk Vols 37,000; Per Subs 105
Special Collections: AB Graham Coll
Subject Interests: Genealogy
Open Mon-Thurs 9-8, Fri 9-5, Sat 9-1
Friends of the Library Group

SALEM

CR ALLEGHENY WESLEYAN COLLEGE LIBRARY*, 2161 Woodsdale Rd, 44460. SAN 313-7015. Tel: 330-337-6403, Ext 302. E-mail: library@awc.edu. Web Site: awc.edu/library. *Libr Supvr,* Hannah Montgomery; *Librn,* Crystal Whitham; Staff 2 (MLS 1, Non-MLS 1)
Founded 1973. Enrl 57; Fac 8; Highest Degree: Bachelor
Library Holdings: Bk Vols 27,000; Per Subs 84
Automation Activity & Vendor Info: (Cataloging) Follett Software; (Circulation) Follett Software; (Course Reserve) Follett Software; (OPAC) Follett Software
Wireless access
Open Mon-Fri 8-5 & 6:30-10, Sat 10-5

C KENT STATE UNIVERSITY*, Salem Campus Library, 2491 State Rte 45-S, 44460-9412. SAN 313-704X. Tel: 330-337-4213. FAX: 330-337-4144. Web Site: www.kent.edu/columbiana/libraries. *Sr Libr Assoc,* Maegan Richards; Tel: 330-337-4211, E-mail: mrichar4@kent.edu; Staff 1 (MLS 1)
Founded 1962. Fac 140
Library Holdings: AV Mats 886; Bk Vols 22,475; Per Subs 98
Automation Activity & Vendor Info: (Cataloging) Innovative Interfaces, Inc; (Circulation) Innovative Interfaces, Inc; (ILL) Innovative Interfaces, Inc; (Media Booking) Innovative Interfaces, Inc; (OPAC) Innovative Interfaces, Inc
Wireless access
Special Services for the Deaf - Video relay services
Open Mon-Thurs 8am-8:30pm, Fri 8-5; Mon-Thurs (Summer) 8-5, Fri 8-2

P SALEM PUBLIC LIBRARY*, 821 E State St, 44460-2298. SAN 313-7058. Tel: 330-332-0042. FAX: 330-332-4488. E-mail: library@salem.lib.oh.us. Web Site: www.salem.lib.oh.us. *Dir,* Bradley K Stephens; E-mail: brads@salem.lib.oh.us; Staff 18 (MLS 5, Non-MLS 13)
Founded 1895. Pop 17,049; Circ 342,864
Library Holdings: AV Mats 13,080; CDs 2,422; DVDs 1,197; Bk Vols 74,678; Per Subs 225; Talking Bks 3,056; Videos 6,405
Special Collections: Columbiana County & Salem History; Quaker History & Biography
Subject Interests: Anti-slavery
Automation Activity & Vendor Info: (Cataloging) Innovative Interfaces, Inc; (Circulation) Innovative Interfaces, Inc; (OPAC) Innovative Interfaces, Inc
Wireless access
Open Mon-Thurs 9-8:30, Fri & Sat 9-6, Sun (Sept-May) 1-5

SANDUSKY

GL SANDUSKY BAY LAW LIBRARY ASSOCIATION, INC*, 247 Columbus Ave, 44870. SAN 313-7066. Tel: 419-626-4823. FAX: 419-626-4826. *Librn,* Kelly Del Vecchio; E-mail: sblla@aol.com
Library Holdings: Bk Vols 14,450; Per Subs 20
Open Mon-Fri 8-4

P SANDUSKY LIBRARY*, 114 W Adams St, 44870. SAN 357-1025. Tel: 419-625-3834. FAX: 419-625-4574. E-mail: comments@sanduskylib.org. Web Site: www.sanduskylib.org. *Exec Dir,* Molly Carver; E-mail: mcarver@sanduskylib.org; *Asst Dir,* Terri Estel; *Ref (Info Servs),* Dennis McMullen; Staff 37 (MLS 7, Non-MLS 30)
Founded 1895. Pop 52,000
Library Holdings: Bk Vols 207,692; Per Subs 320
Special Collections: Johnson's Island; Local History Archives
Automation Activity & Vendor Info: (Cataloging) SirsiDynix; (Circulation) SirsiDynix; (OPAC) SirsiDynix
Wireless access
Function: 24/7 Electronic res, 24/7 Online cat, Adult bk club, Adult literacy prog
Publications: A View of Sandusky; From the Widow's Walk, Vol I & II
Partic in CLEVNET; Ohio Public Library Information Network
Open Mon-Wed 10-8, Thurs-Sat 10-5
Branches: 2
FOLLETT HOUSE MUSEUM, 404 Wayne St, 44870. *Serv Mgr,* Jeremy Angstadt; Tel: 419-625-3834, E-mail: jangstadt@sanduskylib.org
KELLEYS ISLAND BRANCH, 528 Division St, Kelleys Island, 43438. Tel: 419-746-9575.
Library Holdings: Bk Titles 6,000
Open Mon 5-7, Thurs 2:30-4:30, Sat 11-1

SARDIS

P DALLY MEMORIAL LIBRARY, 37252 Mound St, 43946. (Mail add: PO Box 37, 43946-0037). Tel: 740-483-1288. FAX: 740-483-2311. E-mail: dallylibrary@sbcglobal.net. Web Site: www.dallylibrary.org. *Libr Dir,* Jill A Dennis; Staff 1 (Non-MLS 1)
Founded 2003
Library Holdings: AV Mats 300; Bk Vols 6,000; Per Subs 50
Special Collections: Local History Coll
Automation Activity & Vendor Info: (Cataloging) SirsiDynix; (Circulation) SirsiDynix; (OPAC) SirsiDynix
Wireless access
Function: 24/7 Online cat, Computer training, ILL available, Photocopying/Printing, Prog for children & young adult, Ref & res, Summer reading prog, Tax forms, Telephone ref, VHS videos, Wheelchair accessible
Partic in SE Ohio Automation Consortium; Serving Every Ohioan Library Center
Open Tues-Fri 10-5, Sat 10-2
Friends of the Library Group

SHAKER HEIGHTS

P SHAKER HEIGHTS PUBLIC LIBRARY, 16500 Van Aken Blvd, 44120. SAN 357-1084. Tel: 216-991-2030. Administration Tel: 216-991-5951. FAX: 216-367-3022. Web Site: www.shakerlibrary.org. *Dir,* Amy Switzer; E-mail: director@shakerlibrary.org; *Dep Dir,* Maureen Brodar; E-mail: deputy.director@shakerlibrary.org; *Head, Adult Serv,* Cindy Maxey; E-mail: cindy.maxey@shakerlibrary.org; *Tech Serv Mgr,* Loraine Lamont; E-mail: loraine.lamont@shakerlibrary.org; Staff 71.3 (MLS 20, Non-MLS 51.3)
Founded 1937. Pop 33,963; Circ 1,330,555
Jan 2015-Dec 2015 Income (Main & Associated Libraries) $4,717,355, State $1,499,997, Locally Generated Income $2,648,734, Other $568,624. Mats Exp $609,744, Books $298,354, Per/Ser (Incl. Access Fees) $32,512, Other Print Mats $59,855, AV Mat $219,023. Sal $2,435,427
Library Holdings: AV Mats 25,461; DVDs 31,832; e-books 215,490; Electronic Media & Resources 364,480; Bk Vols 181,042; Per Subs 554
Special Collections: Black Studies; Shaker Heights History, Coll & Archives
Automation Activity & Vendor Info: (Acquisitions) SirsiDynix; (Circulation) SirsiDynix
Wireless access
Publications: Shaker Magazine (Bimonthly)
Partic in CLEVNET; Northeast Ohio Regional Library System
Special Services for the Blind - Computer with voice synthesizer for visually impaired persons
Open Mon-Thurs 11-7, Fri & Sat 9:30-5:30
Friends of the Library Group
Branches: 1
BERTRAM WOODS BRANCH, 20600 Fayette Rd, 44122, SAN 357-1114. Tel: 216-991-2421. FAX: 216-991-3124. *Br Mgr,* Lynne Miller; E-mail: lynne.miller@shakerlibrary.org
Founded 1960
Library Holdings: AV Mats 24,891; Bk Vols 69,253
Open Mon-Thurs 11-7, Fri & Sat 9:30-5:30
Friends of the Library Group

SHAUCK

P PERRY COOK MEMORIAL PUBLIC LIBRARY*, 7406 County Rd 242, 43349. (Mail add: PO Box 214, 43349-0214). Tel: 419-362-7181. FAX: 419-362-1518. Web Site: www.perrycooklibrary.org. *Dir,* Patricia Dollisch; E-mail: patriciad@perrycooklibrary.org
Library Holdings: Bk Titles 25,000; Per Subs 75
Wireless access
Partic in Serving Every Ohioan Library Center
Open Mon-Thurs (Sept-May) 10-8, Fri 10-4, Sat 10-2; Mon-Thurs (Jun-Aug) 10-8, Fri 10-4

SHELBY

P MARVIN MEMORIAL LIBRARY*, 29 W Whitney Ave, 44875-1252. SAN 313-7112. Tel: 419-347-5576. FAX: 419-347-7285. Web Site: marvinlibrary.org. *Dir,* Kathleen Webb; E-mail: kwebb@marvinlibrary.org; *Ch Serv,* Jami Williams; Staff 2 (MLS 1, Non-MLS 1)
Founded 1897. Pop 14,000; Circ 91,632
Library Holdings: AV Mats 7,345; Bk Vols 64,950; Per Subs 103
Subject Interests: Genealogy, Local hist
Automation Activity & Vendor Info: (Acquisitions) Evergreen; (Cataloging) Evergreen; (Circulation) Evergreen; (ILL) Evergreen; (OPAC) Evergreen
Wireless access
Function: 24/7 Electronic res, 24/7 Online cat, Accelerated reader prog, Activity rm, Adult bk club, After school storytime, Archival coll, Art programs, Audiobks via web, AV serv, Bk club(s), Bks on CD, Children's prog, Computer training, Computers for patron use, Doc delivery serv, Electronic databases & coll, Free DVD rentals, Holiday prog, Home delivery & serv to seniorr ctr & nursing homes, Homebound delivery serv, Homework prog, ILL available, Internet access, Laminating, Life-long learning prog for all ages, Magazines, Magnifiers for reading, Mail & tel request accepted, Meeting rooms, Microfiche/film & reading machines, Movies, Music CDs, Online cat, Online info literacy tutorials on the web & in blackboard, Outreach serv, OverDrive digital audio bks, Photocopying/Printing, Preschool outreach, Preschool reading prog, Printer for laptops & handheld devices, Prog for adults, Prog for children & young adult, Scanner, Senior computer classes, Story hour, Study rm, Summer & winter reading prog, Summer reading prog, Tax forms, Teen prog, Wheelchair accessible, Winter reading prog
Partic in Consortium of Ohio Libraries
Open Mon-Thurs 9-8, Fri 9-5, Sat 9-2
Friends of the Library Group

SIDNEY

P SHELBY COUNTY LIBRARIES*, 230 E North St, 45365-2785. SAN 357-1149. Tel: 937-492-8354. Interlibrary Loan Service Tel: 937-492-6851. FAX: 937-492-9229. Web Site: www.shelbyco.lib.oh.us. *Dir,* Suzanne Cline; Tel: 937-492-8354, Ext 102, E-mail: clinesu@sclmail.org; *Tech Coordr,* Rebecca Heilers; Tel: 937-492-8354, Ext 119, E-mail: rheilers@sclmail.org; *Circ, Pub Serv, Ref Serv,* Mark Kister; *ILL,* Ada Bumgarner; *Pub Relations,* Peggy Naseman; *Youth Serv,* Rikki Unterbrink; Staff 36 (MLS 4, Non-MLS 32)
Founded 1869. Pop 48,183; Circ 494,279
Library Holdings: AV Mats 19,535; CDs 3,699; DVDs 7,574; Large Print Bks 4,927; Bk Titles 161,380; Bk Vols 168,816; Per Subs 234; Talking Bks 3,573; Videos 13,433
Automation Activity & Vendor Info: (Cataloging) TLC (The Library Corporation); (Circulation) TLC (The Library Corporation); (ILL) OCLC Online; (OPAC) TLC (The Library Corporation)
Wireless access
Partic in Miami Valley Librs; NORWELD; OCLC Online Computer Library Center, Inc; Ohio Libr Coun; OhioNET
Open Mon-Thur 9-8, Fri 9-6, Sat 11-4
Branches: 5
ANNA COMMUNITY, 304 N Second St, Anna, 45302. (Mail add: PO Box 380, Anna, 45302), SAN 357-1173. Tel: 937-394-2761. FAX: 937-394-2761. *Br Coordr,* Sheila Strunk
Library Holdings: AV Mats 1,518; DVDs 982; Large Print Bks 667; Bk Titles 16,253; Per Subs 13; Talking Bks 350; Videos 312
Special Collections: Lois Lenski Coll
Open Mon & Wed 2-7, Fri 9-6, Sat 9-Noon
Friends of the Library Group
JACKSON CENTER MEMORIAL, 205 S Linden St, Jackson Center, 45334. (Mail add: PO Box 581, Jackson Center, 45334), SAN 357-1262. Tel: 937-596-5300. FAX: 937-596-5300. *Br Coordr,* Cheryl South
Library Holdings: AV Mats 550; DVDs 458; Large Print Bks 114; Bk Titles 14,546; Per Subs 19; Talking Bks 65
Open Mon & Wed 2-7, Fri 9-6, Sat 9-Noon
Friends of the Library Group
RUSSIA BRANCH, 200 Raider St, Russia, 45363. (Mail add: PO Box 445, Russia, 45363-0445), SAN 372-5219. Tel: 937-526-4300. FAX: 937-526-4300. *Br Coordr,* Julie Philipot
Library Holdings: AV Mats 555; DVDs 525; Large Print Bks 12; Bk Titles 11,133; Per Subs 20; Talking Bks 47
Open Mon & Wed 2-7, Fri 9-6, Sat 9-Noon
Friends of the Library Group
PHILIP SHEETS FAMILY BOTKINS BRANCH, 109 E Lynn St, Botkins, 45306. (Mail add: PO Box 524, Botkins, 45306), SAN 357-1203. Tel: 937-693-6671. FAX: 937-693-6671. *Br Coordr,* Jane Vehorn
Library Holdings: AV Mats 604; Large Print Bks 103; Bk Titles 16,134; Per Subs 19; Talking Bks 108
Open Mon & Wed 2-7, Fri 9-6, Sat 9-Noon
Friends of the Library Group
AJ WISE - FORT LORAMIE BRANCH LIBRARY, 300 E Park St, Fort Loramie, 45845. (Mail add: PO Box 342, Fort Loramie, 45845), SAN 357-1238. Tel: 937-295-3155. FAX: 937-295-3155. *Br Coordr,* Rebecca Heilers
Library Holdings: AV Mats 631; DVDs 451; Large Print Bks 138; Bk Titles 14,647; Per Subs 21; Talking Bks 91
Open Mon & Wed 2-7, Fri 9-6, Sat 9-Noon
Friends of the Library Group

SOUTH EUCLID

C NOTRE DAME COLLEGE, Clara Fritzsche Library, 4545 College Rd, 44121. SAN 313-3699. Tel: 216-373-5267. Web Site: www.notredamecollege.edu/resources-and-services/clara-fritzsche-library. *Dir,* Karen Zoller; Tel: 216-373-5266, E-mail: kzoller@ndc.edu; *Tech Serv/Circ Librn,* Joseph Glass; Tel: 216-373-5360, E-mail: jglass@ndc.edu; Staff 2 (MLS 2)
Founded 1922. Enrl 1,612; Fac 185; Highest Degree: Master

Jul 2020-Jun 2021. Mats Exp $250,483, Per/Ser (Incl. Access Fees) $61,864, Electronic Ref Mat (Incl. Access Fees) $2,610, Presv $77. Sal $105,706 (Prof $100,682)
Library Holdings: AV Mats 54; Bks on Deafness & Sign Lang 131; CDs 9; DVDs 175; e-books 167,088; e-journals 53,076; Electronic Media & Resources 4,808; Bk Titles 40,555; Bk Vols 47,417; Per Subs 12; Videos 475
Special Collections: Eastern Church Resource Center; Tolerance Resource Center (Holocaust, Diversity & Antibias Resources)
Subject Interests: Bus, Educ, Lit, Nursing, Theol
Automation Activity & Vendor Info: (Cataloging) Innovative Interfaces, Inc; (Circulation) Innovative Interfaces, Inc; (ILL) OCLC WorldShare Interlibrary Loan; (OPAC) Innovative Interfaces, Inc
Wireless access
Partic in Ohio Library & Information Network
Open Mon-Thurs 8:30-8, Fri 8:30-6

SPRINGFIELD

S CLARK COUNTY HISTORICAL SOCIETY*, Fisher Family Archives & Library, 117 S Fountain Ave, 45502-1207. SAN 320-2240. Tel: 937-324-0657. Reference Tel: 937-324-0657, Ext 234. FAX: 937-324-1992. *Dir of Coll,* Virginia Weygandt; E-mail: Vweygandt@heritagecenter.us; *Curator, Archives & Libr,* Natalie Fritz; E-mail: Nataliemfritz3@gmail.com; *Sr Curator,* Kasey Eichensehr; E-mail: keichensehr@heritagecenter.us; Staff 3 (Non-MLS 3)
Founded 1897
Library Holdings: Bk Titles 2,000; Bk Vols 3,000
Special Collections: Periodicals (Crowell-Collier Publishing Company Coll), mags
Subject Interests: County genealogy, County Probate court rec, Early Clark County hist, Manufacturing & commercial rec, Newsps
Wireless access
Open Wed-Fri 10-5, Sat 10-3
Restriction: Non-circulating

P CLARK COUNTY PUBLIC LIBRARY*, 201 S Fountain Ave, 45506. (Mail add: PO Box 1080, 45501-1080), SAN 357-1297. Circulation Tel: 937-328-6901. Reference Tel: 937-328-6903. FAX: 937-328-6908. Web Site: www.ccplohio.org. *Dir,* Bill Martino; Tel: 937-323-9751, E-mail: bmartino@ccplohio.org; Staff 18 (MLS 12, Non-MLS 6)
Founded 1872. Pop 140,000; Circ 1,014,667
Special Collections: Children's Literature (Lois Lenski Coll), bks, ms
Automation Activity & Vendor Info: (Acquisitions) Innovative Interfaces, Inc; (Cataloging) Innovative Interfaces, Inc; (Circulation) Innovative Interfaces, Inc; (OPAC) Innovative Interfaces, Inc; (Serials) Innovative Interfaces, Inc
Wireless access
Function: Adult bk club, Bks on CD, Children's prog, Computer training, Computers for patron use, Digital talking bks, Free DVD rentals, Homebound delivery serv, ILL available, Internet access, Magazines, Meeting rooms, Microfiche/film & reading machines, Music CDs, Online cat, OverDrive digital audio bks, Photocopying/Printing, Preschool outreach, Preschool reading prog, Prog for adults, Prog for children & young adult, Ref & res, Serves people with intellectual disabilities, Spoken cassettes & CDs, Story hour, Summer reading prog, Tax forms, Teen prog, Telephone ref, Wheelchair accessible
Partic in Miami Valley Librs
Special Services for the Deaf - High interest/low vocabulary bks; Spec interest per
Special Services for the Blind - Talking bks
Open Mon-Thur 9-7:30, Fri 9-4:30, Sat 10-4:30, Sun 1-4:30
Friends of the Library Group
Branches: 4
ENON BRANCH, 209 E Main St, Enon, 45323, SAN 357-1351. Tel: 937-864-2502. *Br Mgr,* Terri Bowman; E-mail: tbowman@ccplohio.org
Open Mon-Thurs 10-7:30, Fri & Sat 10-4:30
Friends of the Library Group
HOUSTON, 5 W Jamestown St, South Charleston, 45368, SAN 357-1327. Tel: 937-462-8047. *Br Mgr,* Tammy Harshbarger; E-mail: tharshba@ccplohio.org
Open Mon-Thurs 10-7:30, Fri & Sat 10-4:30
Friends of the Library Group
PARK BRANCH, 1119 Bechtle Ave, 45504, SAN 357-1386. Tel: 937-322-2498. *Br Mgr,* Jonathan Knight; E-mail: jknight@ccplohio.org
Open Mon-Thur 10-7:30, Fri & Sat 10-4:30
Friends of the Library Group
SOUTHERN VILLAGE, 1123 Sunset Ave, 45505, SAN 357-1416. Tel: 937-322-2226. *Br Mgr,* Michael Lagano; E-mail: mlagano@ccplohio.org
Open Mon-Thur 10-7:30, Fri & Sat 10-4:30
Friends of the Library Group
Bookmobiles: 1

J CLARK STATE COMMUNITY COLLEGE LIBRARY*, 570 E Leffel Lane, 45505. (Mail add: PO Box 570, 45501-0570), SAN 313-7163. Tel: 937-328-6022. E-mail: library@clarkstate.edu. Web Site: clarkstate.edu/student-life/library, lib.clarkstate.edu. *Dir, Libr Serv,* Dr Sterling Coleman; Tel: 937-328-6023, E-mail: colemans@clarkstate.edu; *Ref Librn,* Judy Johnson; E-mail: johnsonj@clarkstate.edu; *Ref Librn,* Amy Korpieski; E-mail: korpieskia@clarkstate.edu; *Archivist, Circ Spec,* Jason Wearly; Tel: 937-328-6022, E-mail: wearlyj@clarkstate.edu; *Ref Spec,* Angela Henry; Tel: 937-328-6016, E-mail: henrya@clarkstate.edu; Staff 5 (MLS 4, Non-MLS 1)
Founded 1966. Enrl 3,194; Fac 81; Highest Degree: Associate
Library Holdings: Audiobooks 500; CDs 2,500; DVDs 1,000; e-books 50,000; e-journals 12,000; Electronic Media & Resources 3,000; Bk Vols 25,000
Automation Activity & Vendor Info: (Cataloging) Innovative Interfaces, Inc; (Circulation) Innovative Interfaces, Inc - Sierra; (Course Reserve) Innovative Interfaces, Inc; (OPAC) Innovative Interfaces, Inc - Sierra; (Serials) Innovative Interfaces, Inc - Sierra
Wireless access
Function: Archival coll, Bks on CD, Computers for patron use, Electronic databases & coll, ILL available, Internet access, Magazines, Online cat, Online ref, Orientations, Photocopying/Printing, Ref serv available, Scanner, Telephone ref, Workshops
Partic in Ohio Library & Information Network; Southwestern Ohio Council for Higher Education
Open Mon-Thurs 8-8, Fri 8-5, Sat 10-2 (Fall-Spring); Mon-Thurs 8-7, Fri 8-5 (Summer)
Restriction: Limited access for the pub

S SPRINGFIELD MUSEUM OF ART LIBRARY*, 107 Cliff Park Rd, 45504. (Mail add: PO Box 34, 45501-0034), SAN 313-7201. Tel: 937-325-4673. E-mail: smoa@springfieldart.net. Web Site: www.springfieldart.net. *Exec Dir,* Ann Fortescue; E-mail: afortescue@springfieldart.net
Founded 1946
Library Holdings: Bk Titles 1,500; Per Subs 1
Special Collections: Photography (Alex Bahnsen Coll)
Open Wed-Sat 9-5, Sun 12:30-4:30
Restriction: Non-circulating

C WITTENBERG UNIVERSITY*, Thomas Library, 801 Woodlawn Ave, 45504. (Mail add: PO Box 7207, 45501-7207), SAN 357-1440. Tel: 937-327-7018. Circulation Tel: 937-327-7512. Reference Tel: 937-327-7511. FAX: 937-327-6139. Web Site: www.wittenberg.edu/lib. *Ref Librn,* Kristen Peters; Tel: 937-327-7533, E-mail: petersk@wittenberg.edu; *Head, Tech Serv,* Suzanne Smailes; Tel: 937-327-7020, E-mail: ssmailes@wittenberg.edu; *Ref Librn,* Alisa Mizikar; Tel: 937-327-7515, E-mail: amizikar@wittenberg.edu; Staff 6 (MLS 3, Non-MLS 3)
Founded 1845. Enrl 1,792; Fac 142; Highest Degree: Master. Sal $810,958 (Prof $408,958)
Library Holdings: AV Mats 26,380; CDs 3,692; DVDs 1,382; e-books 68,552; e-journals 9,334; Microforms 82,850; Bk Titles 400,446; Bk Vols 503,058; Per Subs 14,555; Videos 2,024
Special Collections: Dos Passos Entomological Library; Hymn Book Coll; Japan (Matsumoto Coll); Martin Luther Reformation
Subject Interests: Computer aided design, Music
Automation Activity & Vendor Info: (Acquisitions) Innovative Interfaces, Inc; (Cataloging) Innovative Interfaces, Inc; (Circulation) Innovative Interfaces, Inc; (Course Reserve) Docutek; (Discovery) EBSCO Discovery Service; (OPAC) Innovative Interfaces, Inc; (Serials) Innovative Interfaces, Inc
Wireless access
Partic in OCLC Online Computer Library Center, Inc; Ohio Library & Information Network; Ohio Private Academic Libraries; OhioNET; Southwestern Ohio Council for Higher Education
Open Mon-Thurs (Fall & Winter) 8am-Midnight, Fri 8am-9pm, Sat 10-9, Sun Noon-Midnight; Mon-Fri (Summer) 8-4:30

STEUBENVILLE

J EASTERN GATEWAY COMMUNITY COLLEGE LIBRARY*, Jefferson County Campus Library, 4000 Sunset Blvd, 43952-3598. SAN 313-7252. Tel: 740-264-5591, Ext 1653. FAX: 740-264-1338. E-mail: libhelp@egcc.edu. Web Site: library.egcc.edu. *Dir, Libr Serv,* Lois Rekowski; E-mail: lrekowski@egcc.edu; Staff 3 (MLS 1, Non-MLS 2)
Founded 1969. Enrl 1,100; Fac 36; Highest Degree: Associate
Library Holdings: Bk Titles 12,925; Bk Vols 14,090; Per Subs 80
Automation Activity & Vendor Info: (Cataloging) Innovative Interfaces, Inc; (Circulation) Innovative Interfaces, Inc; (Course Reserve) Innovative Interfaces, Inc; (ILL) Innovative Interfaces, Inc; (Media Booking) Innovative Interfaces, Inc; (OPAC) Innovative Interfaces, Inc; (Serials) Innovative Interfaces, Inc
Wireless access
Partic in Ohio Library & Information Network
Open Mon-Thurs 8-6, Fri 8-5

C FRANCISCAN UNIVERSITY OF STEUBENVILLE*, St. John Paul II Library, 1235 University Blvd, 43952-1763. SAN 313-7236. Tel: 740-283-6366. E-mail: library@franciscan.edu. Web Site: library.franciscan.edu. *Dir,* Amy Leoni; E-mail: aleoni@franciscan.edu; *Cat Librn,* Jack Wu; E-mail: jwu@franciscan.edu; *Ref (Info Servs),* Kathleen Donohue; E-mail: kdonohue@franciscan.edu; Staff 7 (MLS 5, Non-MLS 2)
Founded 1946. Enrl 2,488; Highest Degree: Master
Library Holdings: Bk Vols 201,000; Per Subs 728
Subject Interests: Catholic orthodoxy, Counseling, Educ, Franciscans, Liberal arts, Mulloy, Phenomenology, Psychol, Theol
Automation Activity & Vendor Info: (Cataloging) OCLC; (Circulation) Innovative Interfaces, Inc; (OPAC) Innovative Interfaces, Inc; (Serials) Innovative Interfaces, Inc
Wireless access
Partic in OCLC Online Computer Library Center, Inc; Ohio Library & Information Network; Ohio Private Academic Libraries; OhioNET
Open Mon-Thurs 8:30am-11pm, Fri 8:30am-9pm, Sat 9-9, Sun 1pm-11pm

GL JEFFERSON COUNTY LAW LIBRARY*, 301 Market St, 3rd Flr, 43952. SAN 313-7244. Tel: 740-283-8553. FAX: 740-283-8629. E-mail: law_library@jeffcch.com. Web Site: jeffersoncountyoh.com/law-library. *Law Librn,* Ardis J Stein
Library Holdings: Bk Vols 20,000; Per Subs 30
Open Mon-Fri 8:30-12 & 1-4:30

P PUBLIC LIBRARY OF STEUBENVILLE & JEFFERSON COUNTY*, 407 S Fourth St, 43952-2942. SAN 357-153X. Tel: 740-282-9782. FAX: 740-282-2919. Administration FAX: 740-282-0615. Web Site: www.steubenville.lib.oh.us. *Dir,* Michael Gray; E-mail: mgray@seolibraries.org; *Asst Dir,* Position Currently Open; *Archivist,* Erika Grubbs; Tel: 740-264-6166, E-mail: egrubbs@seolibraries.org; *Pub Serv,* Jennifer Cesta; E-mail: jcesta@seolibraries.org; Staff 66 (MLS 4, Non-MLS 62)
Founded 1899. Pop 69,709
Jan 2017-Dec 2017 Income (Main & Associated Libraries) $3,990,825, State $2,429,833, County $1,505,925, Locally Generated Income $89,300. Mats Exp $3,900,800, Books $230,000, Per/Ser (Incl. Access Fees) $17,000, AV Mat $75,000, Electronic Ref Mat (Incl. Access Fees) $96,500. Sal $2,482,000
Library Holdings: Audiobooks 12,861; CDs 8,568; DVDs 21,739; e-books 269,585; Large Print Bks 9,661; Microforms 1,005; Bk Titles 140,657; Bk Vols 189,956; Per Subs 70
Special Collections: Electronic Local History (Digital Shoebox); Steubenville & Jefferson County. State Document Depository; US Document Depository
Subject Interests: Local genealogy, Local hist
Automation Activity & Vendor Info: (Cataloging) SirsiDynix; (Circulation) SirsiDynix; (OPAC) SirsiDynix
Wireless access
Function: Adult bk club, Audiobks on Playaways & MP3, AV serv, Bk club(s), Bks on CD, Children's prog, Computer training, Computers for patron use, Digital talking bks, E-Readers, E-Reserves, Electronic databases & coll, Free DVD rentals, Home delivery & serv to seniorr ctr & nursing homes, Homebound delivery serv, ILL available, Internet access, Laminating, Magazines, Mail & tel request accepted, Meeting rooms, Notary serv, Online cat, Online ref, Photocopying/Printing, Printer for laptops & handheld devices, Prog for adults, Prog for children & young adult, Ref serv available, Senior outreach, Story hour, Study rm, Tax forms, Telephone ref, Wheelchair accessible
Publications: PLSJ Library News (Newsletter)
Partic in Serving Every Ohioan Library Center
Open Mon-Thurs 9-8, Fri & Sat 9-5
Branches: 6
ADENA BRANCH, 167 Hanna Ave, Adena, 43901-7953. (Mail add: 407 S Fourth St, 43952-2942), SAN 357-1548. Tel: 740-546-3782. FAX: 740-546-3382. *Librn,* Betsy Ford
Open Mon, Tues & Thurs 11-7, Fri & Sat 11-5
BRILLIANT BRANCH, 103 Steuben St, Brilliant, 43913, SAN 357-1564. Tel: 740-598-4028. FAX: 740-598-4456. *Librn,* Karen Merritt
Open Mon-Fri 11-7
DILLONVALE-MT PLEASANT BRANCH, 192 Cole St, Dillonvale, 43917, SAN 357-1599. Tel: 740-769-2090. FAX: 740-769-2771. *Librn,* Sandy Scott
Open Mon, Tues & Thurs 11-7, Fri & Sat 11-5
SCHIAPPA BRANCH, 4141 Mall Dr, 43952, SAN 328-7920. Tel: 740-264-6166. FAX: 740-264-7397. *Librn,* Betsy Ford
Subject Interests: Genealogy, Local hist, Ohio
Open Mon-Fri 9-9, Sat 9-5, Sun 1-5
TILTONSVILLE BRANCH, 702 Walden Ave, Tiltonsville, 43963, SAN 357-1688. Tel: 740-859-5163. FAX: 740-859-0603. *Librn,* Merritt Karen
Open Mon, Tues & Thurs 11-7, Fri & Sat 11-5
TORONTO BRANCH, 607 Daniels St, Toronto, 43964, SAN 357-1718. Tel: 740-537-1262. FAX: 740-537-5447. *Librn,* Bridget Dougherty
Open Mon-Thurs 10-8, Fri & Sat 10-5
Bookmobiles: 1

STOW

P STOW-MUNROE FALLS PUBLIC LIBRARY*, 3512 Darrow Rd, 44224. SAN 313-7279. Tel: 330-688-3295. Administration FAX: 330-688-0448. Web Site: www.smfpl.org. *Dir,* Douglas H Dotterer; E-mail: ddotterer@smfpl.org; *Head, Children's Servx,* Lydia Gamble; *Head, Circ,* Alisha Greenawalt-Johnson; *Head, Ref Serv,* Amy Garrett; *Head, Syst Admin,* Jorge DeCardenas; *Pub Relations & Mkt Mgr,* Ann Malthaner; *Fiscal Officer,* Linda Sutherland; Staff 40.1 (MLS 13.8, Non-MLS 26.3)
Founded 1924. Pop 37,890; Circ 794,364
Library Holdings: Audiobooks 19,095; CDs 11,526; DVDs 18,297; e-books 31,922; Electronic Media & Resources 170; Bk Titles 99,210; Per Subs 168
Subject Interests: Local hist archives
Automation Activity & Vendor Info: (Acquisitions) LibLime; (Cataloging) OCLC; (Circulation) LibLime; (ILL) OCLC WorldShare Interlibrary Loan
Wireless access
Partic in Northeast Ohio Regional Library System; OCLC Online Computer Library Center, Inc
Open Mon-Thurs 9-9, Fri 9-6, Sat 9-5, Sun 1-5
Friends of the Library Group

STRONGSVILLE

S GARDENVIEW HORTICULTURAL PARK LIBRARY*, 16711 Pearl Rd, 44136-6048. SAN 321-0146. Tel: 440-238-6653. E-mail: gardenviewhp@gmail.com. Web Site: sites.google.com/site/gvhpark, www.gardenviewhp.org. *Chmn,* Joseph P Tooman
Founded 1949
Library Holdings: Bk Titles 5,000
Subject Interests: Animals, Birds, Gardening, Self sufficiency, Travel
Function: Ref serv available

SUNBURY

P COMMUNITY LIBRARY*, 44 Burrer Dr, 43074. SAN 313-7295. Tel: 740-965-3901. FAX: 740-965-1258. E-mail: ask@yourcl.org. Web Site: www.yourcl.org. *Dir/Fiscal Officer,* Chauncey G Montgomery; E-mail: chauncey@yourcl.org; Staff 2 (MLS 2)
Founded 1944
Library Holdings: AV Mats 10,000; Bk Titles 90,000; Per Subs 250
Subject Interests: Genealogy, Local hist
Automation Activity & Vendor Info: (Acquisitions) TLC (The Library Corporation); (Cataloging) TLC (The Library Corporation); (Circulation) TLC (The Library Corporation); (ILL) Fretwell-Downing; (OPAC) TLC (The Library Corporation)
Wireless access
Function: Adult bk club, Archival coll, Audio & video playback equip for onsite use, AV serv, Bk club(s), Bks on CD, Chess club, Children's prog, Computer training, Computers for patron use, E-Reserves, Electronic databases & coll, Equip loans & repairs, Family literacy, Free DVD rentals, Govt ref serv, Health sci info serv, Holiday prog, Home delivery & serv to seniorr ctr & nursing homes, Homebound delivery serv, ILL available, Instruction & testing, Internet access, Magnifiers for reading, Mail & tel request accepted, Music CDs, Notary serv, Online cat, Online ref, Outside serv via phone, mail, e-mail & web, Photocopying/Printing, Preschool outreach, Prog for adults, Prog for children & young adult, Ref serv available, Scanner, Senior computer classes, Senior outreach, Spoken cassettes & CDs, Summer reading prog, Tax forms, Teen prog, Telephone ref, VHS videos, Wheelchair accessible, Workshops
Partic in CALICO; Consortium of Ohio Libraries
Open Mon-Thurs 9-8, Fri & Sat 9-5
Restriction: Authorized patrons
Friends of the Library Group

SWANTON

P SWANTON LOCAL SCHOOL DISTRICT PUBLIC LIBRARY*, 305 Chestnut St, 43558. SAN 313-7309. Tel: 419-826-2760. FAX: 419-826-1020. E-mail: swantonpl@gmail.com. Web Site: swantonpubliclibrary.org. *Dir,* Adam Walter; E-mail: awalter.spl@gmail.com; *Fiscal Officer,* Douglas Deacon; E-mail: ddeacon.spl@gmail.com; *Head, Adult Serv,* Anna Burwell; E-mail: aburwell.spl@gmail.com; *Head, Tech Serv,* Jason Dehm; E-mail: jdehm.spl@gmail.com; *Head, Youth Serv,* Leanna Chappell; E-mail: lchappell.spl@gmail.com; *Tech Serv, Youth Serv Librn,* Staci Treece; E-mail: streece.spl@gmail.com; Staff 10 (MLS 2, Non-MLS 8)
Founded 1936. Pop 14,700
Library Holdings: Bk Titles 37,750; Per Subs 150
Wireless access
Function: ILL available
Partic in NORWELD
Open Mon-Thurs 10-8:30, Fri & Sat 10-5:30, Sun (Oct-April) 1-5
Friends of the Library Group

SYCAMORE

P MOHAWK COMMUNITY LIBRARY*, 200 S Sycamore Ave, 44882. SAN 313-7317. Tel: 419-927-2407. FAX: 419-927-2958. Web Site: www.mohawkcl.org. *Dir,* Susan Runion; E-mail: susan.runion@mohawkcl.org
Pop 6,603; Circ 109,936
Library Holdings: Bk Vols 20,000; Per Subs 69
Wireless access
Partic in NORWELD; Serving Every Ohioan Library Center
Open Mon-Fri 9-8, Sat 9-2

SYLVANIA

CR LOURDES UNIVERSITY*, Duns Scotus Library, 6832 Convent Blvd, 43560. SAN 313-7325. Tel: 419-824-3761. FAX: 419-824-3511. E-mail: lourdeslibrary@lourdes.edu. Web Site: www.lourdes.edu. *Dir, Libr Serv,* Sister Sandra Rutkowski; Tel: 419-824-3762, E-mail: srutkowski@lourdes.edu; Staff 4 (MLS 3, Non-MLS 1)
Founded 1916. Enrl 1,200; Fac 160; Highest Degree: Master
Library Holdings: AV Mats 1,571; Bk Vols 70,000; Per Subs 448
Special Collections: Franciscan Order
Subject Interests: Art, Rare bks
Automation Activity & Vendor Info: (Cataloging) Innovative Interfaces, Inc; (Circulation) Innovative Interfaces, Inc; (OPAC) Innovative Interfaces, Inc; (Serials) Innovative Interfaces, Inc
Partic in Ohio Library & Information Network; Ohio Private Academic Libraries
Open Mon-Thurs 8:30am-9pm, Fri 8:30-2, Sat 9-4
Restriction: Authorized patrons

R TEMPLE - CONGREGATION SHOMER EMUNIM LIBRARY*, 6453 Sylvania Ave, 43560-3999. SAN 313-7341. Tel: 419-885-3341. FAX: 419-882-2778. Web Site: www.templese.com. *Librn,* Alice Applebaum; Staff 2 (MLS 1, Non-MLS 1)
Founded 1875
Library Holdings: Bk Titles 5,000; Per Subs 10
Special Collections: Art (Gertner Memorial Book Shelf)
Subject Interests: Judaica, Related mat
Automation Activity & Vendor Info: (Cataloging) JayWil Software Development, Inc
Function: Res libr
Open Mon, Tues, Thurs & Fri 9-4:30, Wed 4-6, Sun 9:30-12

TALLMADGE

S TALLMADGE HISTORICAL SOCIETY LIBRARY*, 12 Tallmadge Circle, 44278. (Mail add: PO Box 25, 44278). Tel: 330-630-9760. E-mail: TallmadgeHistory@gmail.com. Web Site: tallmadge-ohio.org, www.tallmadgehistory.com. *Pres,* Christopher Grimm
Founded 1858
Library Holdings: Bk Titles 300
Special Collections: Four handwritten Civil War Diaries of Charles H Sackett (1861, 1862, 1864 & 1869); The Bronson Papers Coll (10 large handwritten volumes of local history & family geneaology of Tallmadge from approx 1820 to his death in 1886)
Friends of the Library Group

TIFFIN

C HEIDELBERG UNIVERSITY*, Beeghly Library, Ten Greenfield St, 44883-2420. SAN 313-735X. Tel: 419-448-2104. Interlibrary Loan Service Tel: 419-448-2108. Reference Tel: 419-448-2246. FAX: 419-448-2578. E-mail: library@heidelberg.edu. Web Site: www.heidelberg.edu/academics/resources-and-support/beeghly-library. *Dir,* Laurie Repp; Tel: 419-448-2106, E-mail: lrepp@heidelberg.edu; *Univ Archivist,* H Robert Berg; Tel: 419-448-2087, E-mail: rberg@heidelberg.edu; Staff 3 (MLS 2.5, Non-MLS 0.5)
Founded 1850. Enrl 1,300; Fac 92; Highest Degree: Master
Library Holdings: e-books 125,000; Bk Titles 120,963; Bk Vols 150,471; Per Subs 392
Special Collections: Correspondence (Besse Coll). US Document Depository
Automation Activity & Vendor Info: (Acquisitions) Innovative Interfaces, Inc; (Cataloging) OCLC Connexion; (Circulation) Innovative Interfaces, Inc; (Course Reserve) Innovative Interfaces, Inc; (ILL) OCLC FirstSearch; (OPAC) Innovative Interfaces, Inc; (Serials) Innovative Interfaces, Inc
Wireless access
Partic in OCLC Online Computer Library Center, Inc; Ohio Library & Information Network; Ohio Private Academic Libraries; OhioNET
Open Mon-Thurs 7:45am-11pm, Fri 7:45-5, Sat 9-1, Sun 1-11; Mon-Thurs (Summer) 9-5, Fri 9-4
Restriction: Open to pub for ref & circ; with some limitations, Open to students, fac, staff & alumni
Friends of the Library Group

L SENECA COUNTY LAW LIBRARY*, Seneca County Courthouse Annex, 71 S Washington St, Ste 1205, 44883. SAN 372-2015. Tel: 419-447-8126. *Law Librn,* Susan Hering Howard; E-mail: senctylawlibrary@gmail.com
Library Holdings: Bk Vols 17,000; Per Subs 20
Wireless access

P TIFFIN-SENECA PUBLIC LIBRARY, 77 Jefferson St, 44883. SAN 313-7368. Tel: 419-447-3751. FAX: 419-447-3045. E-mail: tiffinlibrary@tiffinsenecalibrary.org. Web Site: www.tiffinsenecalibrary.org. *Libr Dir,* Matthew Ross; E-mail: rossma@tiffinsenecalibrary.org; *Fiscal Officer,* Celeste Baker; E-mail: bakerce@tiffinsenecalibrary.org; *Adult Programming, Mgr,* Trinity Lescallett; E-mail: lescaltr@tiffinsenecalibrary.org; *Commun Relations Mgr,* Kayleigh Tschanen-Feasel; E-mail: tschanka@tiffinsenecalibrary.org; *Computer Serv Mgr,* Christopher Brose; E-mail: brosech@tiffinsenecalibrary.org; *Outreach Mgr,* Beth Gottfried; E-mail: gottfrbe@tiffinsenecalibrary.org; *Pub Serv Mgr,* Mandi Gruss; E-mail: grussma@tiffinsenecalibrary.org; *Tech Serv Mgr,* Jo Anne Schiefer; E-mail: schiefjo@tiffinsenecalibrary.org; *Youth Serv Mgr,* Ashley Meece; E-mail: meeceas@tiffinsenecalibrary.org; Staff 14 (MLS 7, Non-MLS 7)
Founded 1880. Pop 31,283; Circ 425,715
Library Holdings: AV Mats 20,463; Bks on Deafness & Sign Lang 36; High Interest/Low Vocabulary Bk Vols 728; Bk Titles 96,886; Per Subs 313
Special Collections: Sign Language Coll
Subject Interests: Glass, Local hist, Seneca County genealogy
Wireless access
Publications: Dimensions (Newsletter)
Partic in NORWELD; Serving Every Ohioan Library Center
Special Services for the Deaf - Captioned film dep
Special Services for the Blind - Talking bks
Open Mon-Thurs 9:30-8:30, Fri & Sat 9:30-5:30
Friends of the Library Group

C TIFFIN UNIVERSITY*, Pfeiffer Library, 139 Miami St, 44883-2162. SAN 313-7376. Tel: 419-448-3435. Reference Tel: 419-448-3436. Automation Services Tel: 419-448-3326. FAX: 419-443-5013. E-mail: library@tiffin.edu. Web Site: www.tiffin.edu/library. *Dir,* Catherine Carlson; E-mail: carlsonc@tiffin.edu; Staff 2 (MLS 2)
Founded 1956. Enrl 1,650; Highest Degree: Master
May 2012-Apr 2013 Income $351,510. Mats Exp $205,790, Books $45,619, Per/Ser (Incl. Access Fees) $61,283, Electronic Ref Mat (Incl. Access Fees) $98,888. Sal $145,720 (Prof $102,252)
Library Holdings: Electronic Media & Resources 70,166; Bk Titles 111,714; Per Subs 125; Videos 145
Subject Interests: Criminal justice, Forensic psychol
Automation Activity & Vendor Info: (Acquisitions) Innovative Interfaces, Inc; (Cataloging) Innovative Interfaces, Inc; (Circulation) Innovative Interfaces, Inc; (Course Reserve) Innovative Interfaces, Inc; (Discovery) EBSCO Discovery Service; (OPAC) Innovative Interfaces, Inc; (Serials) Innovative Interfaces, Inc
Wireless access
Partic in Ohio Library & Information Network; Ohio Private Academic Libraries
Open Mon-Thurs 7:45am-Midnight, Fri 7:45-5, Sat 12-4, Sun 6pm-Midnight

TIPP CITY

P TIPP CITY PUBLIC LIBRARY*, 11 E Main St, 45371. SAN 313-7384. Tel: 937-667-3826. FAX: 937-667-7968. Web Site: www.tippcitylibrary.org. *Dir,* Lisa Santucci; E-mail: director@tippcitylibrary.org; *Ad,* Drew Wichterman; *Teen Librn,* Angela Campbell; *Youth Serv Librn,* Heidi Martin; *IT Mgr,* Ian Mahaffy; Staff 22 (MLS 4, Non-MLS 18)
Founded 1923. Pop 17,000; Circ 215,000
Library Holdings: Audiobooks 2,500; CDs 2,278; DVDs 4,888; Bk Vols 60,000; Per Subs 68
Automation Activity & Vendor Info: (Circulation) SirsiDynix; (OPAC) SirsiDynix
Wireless access
Function: 24/7 Electronic res, 24/7 Online cat, Activity rm, Adult bk club, Art exhibits, Audiobks on Playaways & MP3, Audiobks via web, Bk club(s), Bks on CD, Digital talking bks, Electronic databases & coll, Free DVD rentals, Holiday prog, Home delivery & serv to seniorr ctr & nursing homes, Homebound delivery serv, ILL available, Internet access, Laminating, Magazines, Magnifiers for reading, Makerspace, Meeting rooms, Movies, Music CDs, Notary serv, Online cat, OverDrive digital audio bks, Photocopying/Printing, Preschool outreach, Printer for laptops & handheld devices, Prog for adults, Prog for children & young adult, Ref & res, Scanner, Serves people with intellectual disabilities, STEM programs, Story hour, Summer reading prog, Tax forms, Teen prog
Partic in Miami Valley Librs; Serving Every Ohioan Library Center
Open Mon-Thurs 10-8:30, Fri 10-6, Sat 9-5
Friends of the Library Group

TOLEDO

R EPWORTH UNITED METHODIST CHURCH LIBRARY*, 4855 W Central Ave, 43615. SAN 313-7430. Tel: 419-531-4236. FAX: 419-531-7487. Web Site: www.epworth.com.
Founded 1960
Library Holdings: Bk Titles 2,550
Automation Activity & Vendor Info: (Cataloging) Book Systems
Open Mon-Fri 9-5, Sun 8-12

L LUCAS COUNTY LAW LIBRARY*, Lucas County Family Court Ctr, 905 Jackson St, 43604-5512. SAN 313-7570. Tel: 419-213-4747. FAX: 419-213-4287. Web Site: www.toledolawlibrary.org.
Founded 1870
Library Holdings: Bk Vols 76,000; Per Subs 300
Automation Activity & Vendor Info: (Acquisitions) Mandarin Library Automation; (Cataloging) Mandarin Library Automation; (Circulation) Mandarin Library Automation; (OPAC) Mandarin Library Automation
Wireless access
Partic in Consortium of Ohio County Law Libraries
Open Mon-Fri 8:30-4:30

L MARSHALL & MELHORN*, Law Library, Four SeaGate, 8th Flr, 43604. SAN 313-7473. Tel: 419-249-7100. FAX: 419-249-7151. *Librn,* Barbara Avery
Founded 1895
Library Holdings: Bk Vols 14,230; Per Subs 26
Subject Interests: Civil, Corporate practice, Intellectual property, Labor law, Litigation, Probate, State, Tax

CR MERCY COLLEGE OF OHIO LIBRARY*, 2221 Madison Ave, 43604. SAN 320-4146. Tel: 419-251-1700. FAX: 419-251-1730. E-mail: library@mercycollege.edu. Web Site: mercycollege.edu/my-mercy/library. *Libr Dir,* Rebecca Daniels; Tel: 419-251-1821, E-mail: rebecca.daniels@mercycollege.edu; *Librn,* Sharon Rienerth; Tel: 419-251-1327, E-mail: sharon.rienerth@mercycollege.edu. Subject Specialists: *Healthcare,* Rebecca Daniels; Staff 4 (MLS 2, Non-MLS 2)
Founded 1996. Enrl 1,300; Fac 120; Highest Degree: Master
Subject Interests: Allied health, Biology, Nursing, Radiology, Relig
Wireless access
Function: Computers for patron use, Photocopying/Printing
Partic in Ohio Private Academic Libraries; OhioNET
Restriction: Not open to pub

M NORTHCOAST BEHAVIORAL HEALTHCARE LIBRARY*, Toledo Campus Library, 930 S Detroit Ave, 43614-2701. SAN 313-7589. Tel: 419-381-1881. FAX: 419-389-1967. *Library Contact,* Amanda Villegas; Staff 1 (Non-MLS 1)
Founded 1937
Library Holdings: Bk Titles 100; Bk Vols 5,000
Subject Interests: Biographies, Educ, Fiction, Psychiat, Psychol, Self help

M PROMEDICA TOLEDO HOSPITAL*, Health Science Library, 2142 N Cove Blvd, 43606. SAN 313-7562. Tel: 419-291-4404. FAX: 419-479-6953. E-mail: ProMedicaLibrary@ProMedica.org. Web Site: promedica.libguides.com. *Libr Tech,* Judy Sendelbach; E-mail: judy.sendelbach@promedica.org
Library Holdings: Bk Titles 3,600; Per Subs 460
Subject Interests: Med, Nursing
Automation Activity & Vendor Info: (ILL) OCLC

S STATE OF OHIO DEPARTMENT OF CORRECTIONS, Toledo Correctional Institution Library, 2001 E Central Ave, 43608. Tel: 419-726-7977, Ext 62247. FAX: 419-726-2456. Web Site: drc.ohio.gov/toci. *Librn,* Stacy Betts; E-mail: stacy.betts@odrc.state.oh.us
Library Holdings: Bk Vols 15,500; Per Subs 63
Automation Activity & Vendor Info: (Cataloging) EOS International; (Circulation) EOS International; (OPAC) EOS International

S TOLEDO BLADE-LIBRARY*, 541 N Superior St, 43660. SAN 313-7546. Tel: 419-724-6185. Toll Free Tel: 800-245-3317. Web Site: www.toledoblade.com. *Librn,* Jordie W Henry; E-mail: jhenry@theblade.com
Founded 1835
Special Collections: Electronic Library; Newspaper Clippings
Restriction: Not open to pub

P TOLEDO-LUCAS COUNTY PUBLIC LIBRARY*, 325 Michigan St, 43604. SAN 357-2013. Tel: 419-259-5200. Circulation Tel: 419-259-5202. Administration Tel: 419-259-5256. FAX: 419-255-1334. Web Site: www.toledolibrary.org. *Dir, Fiscal Officer,* Jason Kucsma; E-mail: jason.kucsma@toledolibrary.org; *Dir, Pub Serv,* Cathy Bartel; E-mail: cathy.bartel@toledolibrary.org; *Mgr, Main Libr,* Meg Delaney; Tel: 419-259-5333, E-mail: meg.delaney@toledolibrary.org; *Mgr, Pub Serv,* Andrea Francis; E-mail: andrea.francis@toledolibrary.org; *Mobile Serv Mgr,* Franco Vitella; E-mail: franco.vitella@toledolibrary.org; Staff 376 (MLS 92, Non-MLS 284)
Founded 1838. Pop 441,815; Circ 5,379,516
Jan 2020-Dec 2020. Mats Exp $4,682,414, Books $1,894,791, Per/Ser (Incl. Access Fees) $181,814, Other Print Mats $22,242, AV Mat $1,130,592, Electronic Ref Mat (Incl. Access Fees) $1,452,975. Sal $15,336,367
Library Holdings: AV Mats 355,842; CDs 118,284; e-books 41,665; Electronic Media & Resources 23,620; Bk Vols 1,876,176; Per Subs 3,413; Videos 172,417
Special Collections: State Document Depository; UN Document Depository; US Document Depository
Subject Interests: Careers, Commun info, Genealogy, Glass technology, Govt proc, Grantsmanship
Automation Activity & Vendor Info: (Acquisitions) Innovative Interfaces, Inc; (Cataloging) Innovative Interfaces, Inc; (Circulation) Innovative Interfaces, Inc; (ILL) OCLC; (OPAC) Innovative Interfaces, Inc; (Serials) Innovative Interfaces, Inc
Wireless access
Open Mon-Thurs 9:30-7:30, Fri & Sat 9:30-6
Friends of the Library Group
Branches: 19
BIRMINGHAM, 203 Paine Ave, 43605, SAN 357-2048. Tel: 419-259-5210. FAX: 419-691-8242. *Br Mgr,* Julie McCann; E-mail: julie.mccann@toledolibrary.org
Founded 1920
Library Holdings: Bk Vols 31,951
Open Mon & Tues 9:30-7:30, Wed-Fri 9:30-6
Friends of the Library Group
HEATHERDOWNS, 3265 Glanzman Rd, 43614, SAN 357-2072. Tel: 419-259-5270. FAX: 419-382-3231. *Br Mgr,* Judy Jones; E-mail: judy.jones@toledolibrary.org
Founded 1968
Library Holdings: Bk Vols 147,040
Open Mon-Thurs 9:30-7:30, Fri & Sat 9:30-6
Friends of the Library Group
HOLLAND, 1032 S McCord Rd, Holland, 43528, SAN 326-8268, Tel: 419-259-5240. FAX: 419-865-6706. *Actg Br Mgr,* Hannah Grohowski; E-mail: hannah.grohowski@toledolibrary.org
Founded 1984
Library Holdings: Bk Vols 126,381
Open Mon-Thurs 9:30-7:30, Fri & Sat 9:30-6
Friends of the Library Group
KENT, 3101 Collingwood Blvd, 43610, SAN 357-2102. Tel: 419-259-5340. FAX: 419-243-6536. *Br Mgr,* Susan Skitowski; E-mail: susan.skitowski@toledolibrary.org
Founded 1915
Library Holdings: Bk Vols 67,627
Open Mon & Tues 9:30-7:30, Wed-Sat 9:30-6
Friends of the Library Group
KING ROAD, 3900 King Rd, 43617. Tel: 419-259-5380. *Br Mgr,* Julie Bursten; E-mail: julie.bursten@toledolibrary.org
Open Mon-Thurs 9:30-7:30, Fri & Sat 9:30-6
LAGRANGE, 3422 Lagrange St, 43608, SAN 357-2137. Tel: 419-259-5280. FAX: 419-242-3052. *Br Mgr,* Katie Midgley; E-mail: katie.midgley@toledolibrary.org
Founded 1934
Library Holdings: Bk Vols 39,419
Open Mon & Tues 9:30-7:30, Wed-Sat 9:30-6
Friends of the Library Group
LOCKE, 703 Miami St, 43605, SAN 357-2161. Tel: 419-259-5310. FAX: 419-691-3237. *Actg Br Mgr,* Joseph Cowley; E-mail: joseph.cowley@toledolibrary.org
Founded 1917
Library Holdings: Bk Vols 58,763
Open Mon & Tues 9-9, Wed-Fri 9-5:30
Friends of the Library Group
MAUMEE, 501 River Rd, Maumee, 43537, SAN 357-2196. Tel: 419-259-5360. FAX: 419-259-5203. *Br Mgr,* Allison Fiscus; E-mail: allison.fiscus@toledolibrary.org; Staff 5 (MLS 5)
Founded 1918. Pop 15,000
Library Holdings: DVDs 2,000; Large Print Bks 500; Bk Vols 118,453; Per Subs 200; Talking Bks 500; Videos 3,000
Automation Activity & Vendor Info: (Acquisitions) Innovative Interfaces, Inc; (Cataloging) Innovative Interfaces, Inc; (Circulation) Innovative Interfaces, Inc; (OPAC) Innovative Interfaces, Inc; (Serials) Innovative Interfaces, Inc
Open Mon-Wed 9:30-7:30, Thurs-Sat 9:30-6
Friends of the Library Group
MOTT, 1010 Dorr St, 43607, SAN 357-2226. Tel: 419-259-5230. FAX: 419-255-4237. *Br Mgr,* Kim Penn; E-mail: kim.penn@toledolibrary.org
Founded 1918
Library Holdings: Bk Vols 63,676

Open Mon & Tues 9:30-7:30, Wed-Sat 9:30-6
Friends of the Library Group
OREGON, 3340 Dustin Rd, Oregon, 43616, SAN 357-2250. Tel: 419-259-5250. FAX: 419-691-3341. *Br Mgr,* Lisa Green; E-mail: lisa.green@toledolibrary.org
Founded 1965
Library Holdings: Bk Vols 109,915
Open Mon-Thurs 9:30-7:30, Fri & Sat 9:30-6
Friends of the Library Group
POINT PLACE, 2727 117th St, 43611, SAN 357-2285. Tel: 419-259-5390. FAX: 419-729-5363. *Br Mgr,* Jessica Luce; E-mail: jessica.luce@toledolibrary.org
Founded 1926
Library Holdings: Bk Vols 83,872
Open Mon & Tues 9:30-7:30, Wed-Fri 9:30-6
Friends of the Library Group
REYNOLDS CORNERS, 4833 Dorr St, 43615, SAN 357-2315. Tel: 419-259-5320. *Br Mgr,* Linda Kerul; E-mail: linda.kerul@toledolibrary.org
Founded 1958
Library Holdings: Bk Vols 110,184
Open Mon & Tues 9:30-7:30, Wed-Sat 9:30-6
Friends of the Library Group
SANGER, 3030 W Central Ave, 43606, SAN 357-234X. Tel: 419-259-5370. FAX: 419-536-9573. *Br Mgr,* Faith Hairston; E-mail: faith.hairston@toledolibrary.org
Founded 1953
Library Holdings: Bk Vols 130,607
Open Mon-Thurs 9:30-7:30, Fri & Sat 9:30-6
Friends of the Library Group
SOUTH, 1736 Broadway St, 43609, SAN 357-2374. Tel: 419-259-5395. FAX: 419-243-4217. *Br Mgr,* Celeste Felix Taylor; E-mail: celeste.taylor@toledolibrary.org
Founded 1918
Library Holdings: Bk Vols 39,985
Open Mon & Tues 9:30-7:30, Wed-Fri 9:30-6
Friends of the Library Group
SYLVANIA, 6749 Monroe St, Sylvania, 43560, SAN 357-2439. Tel: 419-882-2089. FAX: 419-882-8993. *Br Mgr,* Benjamin Malczewski; E-mail: benjamin.malczewski@toledolibrary.org
Founded 1927
Library Holdings: Bk Vols 146,627
Open Mon-Thurs 9:30-7:30, Fri & Sat 9:30-6
Friends of the Library Group
TOLEDO HEIGHTS, 423 Shasta Dr, 43609, SAN 357-2463. Tel: 419-259-5220. FAX: 419-385-9297. *Actg Br Mgr,* Ryan Rigaux; E-mail: ryan.rigaux@toledolibrary.org
Founded 1935
Library Holdings: Bk Vols 52,182
Open Mon & Tues 9-9, Wed-Fri 9-5:30
Friends of the Library Group
WASHINGTON, 5560 Harvest Lane, 43623, SAN 357-2498. Tel: 419-259-5330. FAX: 419-472-4991. *Actg Br Mgr,* Angela Bronson; E-mail: angela.bronson@toledolibrary.org
Founded 1928
Library Holdings: Bk Vols 124,789
Open Mon-Thurs 9:30-7:30, Fri & Sat 9:30-6
Friends of the Library Group
WATERVILLE, 800 Michigan Ave, Waterville, 43566, SAN 357-2528. Tel: 419-878-3055. FAX: 419-878-4688. *Br Mgr,* William Harbauer; E-mail: william.harbauer@toledolibrary.org; Staff 7 (MLS 3.5, Non-MLS 3.5)
Founded 1964
Library Holdings: Bk Vols 76,000
Open Mon & Tues 9:30-7:30, Wed-Sat 9:30-6
Friends of the Library Group
WEST TOLEDO, 1320 Sylvania Ave, 43612, SAN 357-2552. Tel: 419-259-5290. FAX: 419-476-0892. *Br Mgr,* Nicole Naylor; E-mail: nicole.naylor@toledolibrary.org; Staff 16 (MLS 4, Non-MLS 12)
Founded 1930
Library Holdings: Bk Vols 114,402
Open Mon-Thurs 9:30-7:30, Fri & Sat 9:30-6
Friends of the Library Group
Bookmobiles: 1

S TOLEDO MUSEUM OF ART REFERENCE LIBRARY*, 2445 Monroe St, 43620. (Mail add: PO Box 1013, 43697-1013), SAN 313-7597. Tel: 419-255-8000. Circulation Tel: 419-254-5770. Administration Tel: 419-254-5771, Ext 7386. FAX: 419-254-5776. E-mail: library@toledomuseum.org. Web Site: www.toledomuseum.org/education/reference-library. *Head Librn,* Alison L Huftalen; E-mail: ahuftalen@toledomuseum.org; *Archivist,* Julie McMaster; Staff 3 (MLS 1, Non-MLS 2)
Founded 1901
Library Holdings: Bk Vols 90,000; Per Subs 100
Special Collections: Norman L Sandfield Library of Netsuke and Asian Art
Subject Interests: Hist of art, Mus studies, Studio art
Automation Activity & Vendor Info: (Acquisitions) Spydus; (Cataloging) Spydus; (Circulation) Spydus; (OPAC) Spydus; (Serials) Spydus
Wireless access
Function: 24/7 Online cat, Adult bk club, Archival coll, Art exhibits, Bk club(s), Computers for patron use, Electronic databases & coll, Free DVD rentals, Internet access, Magazines, Online cat, Outside serv via phone, mail, e-mail & web, Photocopying/Printing, Prog for adults, Ref & res, Ref serv available, Res assist avail, Res libr, Scanner
Open Mon-Thurs (Winter) 10-8, Fri & Sat 12-4; Mon-Thurs (Summer) 10-5, Fri & Sat 12-4
Restriction: Circ limited, Non-circulating of rare bks, Open to students, fac & staff, Restricted borrowing privileges
Friends of the Library Group

S TOLEDO ZOOLOGICAL SOCIETY*, Zoo Library, 2700 Broadway St, 43609. (Mail add: PO Box 140130, 43614-0130), SAN 328-0039. Tel: 419-385-5721, Ext 2043. FAX: 419-389-8670. Web Site: www.toledozoo.org. *Librn,* Deborah Aked; E-mail: deborah.aked@toledozoo.org
Founded 1937
Library Holdings: Bk Titles 2,000; Per Subs 112
Subject Interests: Conserv, Ecology, Zoology
Wireless access
Restriction: Open to others by appt, Staff use only

C UNIVERSITY OF TOLEDO*, William S Carlson Library, 2975 W Centennial Dr, 43606-3396. (Mail add: Mail Stop 509, 2801 W Bancroft St, 43606-3390), SAN 357-2587. Tel: 419-530-2324. Circulation Tel: 419-530-2323. FAX: 419-530-2726. Web Site: www.utoledo.edu/library. *Dean, Univ Libr,* Beau Case; Tel: 419-530-4286, E-mail: beau.case@utoledo.edu; *Assoc Dean,* Thomas Atwood; Tel: 419-530-2833, E-mail: thomas.atwood@utoledo.edu; *Dir, Coll Serv,* Sheryl Stevens; Tel: 419-530-7981, E-mail: sheryl.stevens@utoledo.edu; *Dir, Health Sci Libr,* Jolene M Miller; Tel: 419-383-4959, E-mail: jolene.miller@utoledo.edu; *Dir, Instruction & Ref,* Julia Martin; Tel: 419-530-2492, E-mail: julia.martin@utoledo.edu; *Dir, Operations,* David Remaklus; Tel: 419-530-4030, E-mail: david.remaklus@utoledo.edu; Staff 45 (MLS 19, Non-MLS 26)
Founded 1872. Highest Degree: Doctorate
Special Collections: Afro-American Literature Since the Harlem Renaissance; American Women's Social History, 1840-1920; Broadside Press Coll; Department of Energy; Etheridge Knight Coll; Eudora Welty; Ezra Pound; Foy D Kohler Coll; Gift Books & Annuals; Glass Manufacturing; Henry David Thoreau Coll; Imagist Poets; Jean Gould Coll; Leigh Hunt; Richard Gosser Coll; Scott & Helen Nearing; Southern Authors; Stock Market; T S Eliot; University of Toledo Archives Coll; William Dean Howells; William Faulkner & others. US Document Depository
Subject Interests: Educ, Engr, Humanities, Intl relations, Pharm, Psychol, Sci
Wireless access
Partic in Ohio Library & Information Network
Open Mon-Thurs 7:30am-1am, Fri 7:30-6, Sat 11-6, Sun 11am-1am
Departmental Libraries:
CL LAVALLEY LAW LIBRARY, Mail Stop 508, 2801 W Bancroft St, 43606-3390, SAN 357-2617. Tel: 419-530-2733. FAX: 419-530-5121. Web Site: www.utoledo.edu/law/library/index.html. *Asst Dean, Assoc Prof,* Rick Goheen; *Sr Electronic/Media Serv Librn,* Ryan Overdorf; *Sr Legal Ref Librn,* Marianne Mussett; *Sr Legal Res Librn,* Robert Jacoby; *Acq,* Claudia Dansby; Staff 5 (MLS 5)
Enrl 317; Fac 28; Highest Degree: Doctorate
Special Collections: US Document Depository

CM UNIVERSITY OF TOLEDO*, Mulford Health Science Library, Mulford Library Bldg, 4th Flr, 3025 Library Circle, 43614-8000. (Mail add: Health Science Campus, Mail Stop 1061, 3025 Library Circle, 43610-8000), SAN 357-1807. Tel: 419-383-4225. Interlibrary Loan Service Tel: 419-530-2576. Reference Tel: 419-383-4218. Administration Tel: 419-383-4959. FAX: 419-383-6146. Reference E-mail: mulfordreference@utoledo.edu. Web Site: www.utoledo.edu/library/mulford. *Dir,* Jolene Miller; E-mail: jolene.miller@utoledo.edu; *Health Sci Librn,* Gerald Natal; E-mail: gerald.natal@utoledo.edu; *Nursing Librn,* Jodi Jameson; E-mail: jodi.jameson@utoledo.edu; Staff 4.2 (MLS 4.2)
Founded 1964. Highest Degree: Doctorate
Library Holdings: Bk Titles 38,272; Bk Vols 154,385; Per Subs 2,376
Subject Interests: Allied health, Med, Nursing
Automation Activity & Vendor Info: (Acquisitions) Innovative Interfaces, Inc; (Cataloging) Innovative Interfaces, Inc; (Circulation) Innovative Interfaces, Inc; (Course Reserve) Innovative Interfaces, Inc; (OPAC) Innovative Interfaces, Inc; (Serials) Innovative Interfaces, Inc
Wireless access
Function: Health sci info serv

Partic in Ohio Library & Information Network; OhioNET
Open Mon-Thurs 7:30am-Midnight, Fri 7:30am-9pm, Sat 9-9, Sun 9am-Midnight

TROY

S HOBART INSTITUTE OF WELDING TECHNOLOGY*, John H Blankenbuehler Memorial Library, 400 Trade Sq E, 45373-2400. SAN 313-7600. Tel: 937-332-5603. Toll Free Tel: 800-332-9448, Ext 5603. FAX: 937-332-5220. E-mail: hiwt@welding.org. Web Site: www.welding.org. *Career Dev, Mkt Mgr,* Melinda Jeffery; E-mail: melinda.jeffery@welding.org. Subject Specialists: *Metallurgy, Welding,* Melinda Jeffery; Staff 1 (Non-MLS 1)
Founded 1964
Library Holdings: Bk Vols 5,000; Per Subs 100
Subject Interests: Chem, Metallurgy, Quality assurance, Radiography, Thermal spraying, Welding
Automation Activity & Vendor Info: (Cataloging) EOS International
Wireless access
Publications: The World of Welding (Newsletter)

L MIAMI COUNTY LAW LIBRARY, 201 W Main St, 3rd Flr, 45373. SAN 313-7619. Tel: 937-440-5994. Web Site: www.co.miami.oh.us/164/Law-Library. *Librn,* Holly Johnson; E-mail: hjohnson@miamicountyohio.gov
Library Holdings: Bk Vols 11,000; Per Subs 10
Open Mon-Thurs 9-11:30 & 12:30-3:30

P TROY-MIAMI COUNTY PUBLIC LIBRARY*, 419 W Main St, 45373. SAN 357-2706. Tel: 937-339-0502. FAX: 937-335-4880. E-mail: info@tmcpl.org. Web Site: www.troypubliclibrary.org. *Dir,* Rachelle Miller; E-mail: rmiller@tmcpl.org; *Adult Serv Mgr,* Bill Schlimme; *Outreach Mgr,* Sarah Simon; *Pub Serv Mgr,* DeMarcus Moody; *Youth Serv Mgr,* Nancy Hargrove; Staff 6 (MLS 2, Non-MLS 4)
Founded 1896. Pop 45,997; Circ 675,974
Library Holdings: Audiobooks 8,257; DVDs 15,403; e-books 74,610; Bk Vols 136,811; Per Subs 108
Special Collections: Local history
Automation Activity & Vendor Info: (Circulation) Innovative Interfaces, Inc; (OPAC) Innovative Interfaces, Inc
Wireless access
Function: 24/7 Electronic res, 24/7 Online cat, Accelerated reader prog, Activity rm, Adult bk club, Archival coll, AV serv, Bk club(s), Bks on CD, Chess club, Children's prog, Computers for patron use, Digital talking bks, E-Reserves, Electronic databases & coll, Family literacy, Free DVD rentals, Holiday prog, Home delivery & serv to seniorr ctr & nursing homes, Homebound delivery serv, ILL available, Internet access, Life-long learning prog for all ages, Magazines, Magnifiers for reading, Mail & tel request accepted, Mango lang, Meeting rooms, Microfiche/film & reading machines, Movies, Music CDs, Online cat, Online ref, Outreach serv, Outside serv via phone, mail, e-mail & web, OverDrive digital audio bks, Photocopying/Printing, Preschool outreach, Preschool reading prog, Printer for laptops & handheld devices, Prog for adults, Prog for children & young adult, Ref serv available, Res assist avail, Senior outreach, Serves people with intellectual disabilities, Spanish lang bks, Story hour, Study rm, Summer & winter reading prog, Summer reading prog, Tax forms, Teen prog, Telephone ref, Wheelchair accessible, Winter reading prog, Workshops
Special Services for the Deaf - Assisted listening device; Bks on deafness & sign lang; High interest/low vocabulary bks
Special Services for the Blind - Low vision equip
Open Mon-Thurs 9-8, Fri 9-6, Sat 9-5, Sun 1-5
Friends of the Library Group
Branches: 2
LOCAL HISTORY LIBRARY, 100 W Main St, 45373. Tel: 937-339-4082. *Archivist, Br Mgr,* Patrick Kennedy; E-mail: pkennedy@TMCPL.ORG; Staff 3 (Non-MLS 3)
Subject Interests: Genealogy, Local hist
Function: For res purposes, Mail & tel request accepted, Ref & res, Ref serv available, Res libr, Scanner, Wheelchair accessible
Restriction: Closed stack, Non-circulating
OAKES-BEITMAN MEMORIAL, 12 N Main St, Pleasant Hill, 45359-0811, SAN 357-2730. Tel: 937-676-2731. FAX: 937-676-2731. *Br Mgr,* Andria Wise; Staff 1 (Non-MLS 1)
Circ 57,604
Library Holdings: Bk Vols 17,000; Per Subs 50
Automation Activity & Vendor Info: (Circulation) Innovative Interfaces, Inc; (OPAC) Innovative Interfaces, Inc
Function: 24/7 Electronic res, 24/7 Online cat, Accelerated reader prog, Activity rm, Adult bk club, After school storytime, Audiobks via web, Bk club(s), Bks on CD, Children's prog, Computers for patron use, E-Reserves, Electronic databases & coll, Family literacy, Free DVD rentals, Holiday prog, ILL available, Life-long learning prog for all ages, Magazines, Mango lang, Meeting rooms, Movies, Music CDs, Online cat, Online ref, Photocopying/Printing, Preschool outreach, Preschool reading prog, Printer for laptops & handheld devices, Prog for adults, Prog for children & young adult, Ref serv available, Story hour, Study rm, Summer & winter reading prog, Summer reading prog, Tax forms, Teen prog, Telephone ref, Wheelchair accessible, Winter reading prog, Workshops
Open Mon & Wed 12-8, Tues & Thurs 10-8, Fri 12-5, Sat 10-3
Friends of the Library Group
Bookmobiles: 1

M UPPER VALLEY MEDICAL CENTER*, Health Sciences Library, 3130 N County Rd 25A, 45373. Tel: 937-440-4594. FAX: 937-440-4591. Web Site: www.uvmc.com/portal.aspx?id=67212. *Librn,* Mary J Sutton; E-mail: msutton@uvmc.com
Library Holdings: Bk Vols 500
Wireless access
Open Mon-Fri 8-3:30

TWINSBURG

P TWINSBURG PUBLIC LIBRARY, 10050 Ravenna Rd, 44087. SAN 313-7627. Tel: 330-425-4268. FAX: 330-425-3622. E-mail: librarian@twinsburglibrary.org. Web Site: www.twinsburglibrary.org. *Dir,* Laura Leonard; Tel: 330-425-4268, Ext 5, E-mail: leonardla@twinsburglibrary.org; Staff 12 (MLS 12)
Founded 1910. Circ 793,261
Jan 2020-Dec 2020 Income $3,448,822. Mats Exp $462,655. Sal $1,278,839
Library Holdings: AV Mats 14,753; e-books 716,101; Bk Vols 105,886; Per Subs 419; Videos 27,885
Subject Interests: Twinsburg hist
Automation Activity & Vendor Info: (Cataloging) SirsiDynix; (Circulation) SirsiDynix; (OPAC) SirsiDynix; (Serials) SirsiDynix
Wireless access
Function: Adult bk club, Adult literacy prog, Audio & video playback equip for onsite use, Audiobks via web, AV serv, Bk club(s), Bk reviews (Group), Bks on cassette, Bks on CD, CD-ROM, Children's prog, Computer training, Computers for patron use, Digital talking bks, E-Reserves, Electronic databases & coll, Free DVD rentals, Home delivery & serv to seniorr ctr & nursing homes, Homebound delivery serv, Homework prog, ILL available, Internet access, Magnifiers for reading, Mail & tel request accepted, Music CDs, Notary serv, Online cat, Online ref, Outside serv via phone, mail, e-mail & web, OverDrive digital audio bks, Photocopying/Printing, Preschool outreach, Prog for adults, Prog for children & young adult, Ref & res, Senior computer classes
Publications: A Librarian Told Me So Blog (Online only); Bestsellers (Online only); Booking for a Look (Online only); Calendar of Events (Bimonthly); Taste of Twinsburg Blog (Online only); The ABC Book Reviews Blog & Podcast (Online only); TPL Online Newsletter (Online only); Twinsburg Library News Blog (Online only)
Partic in CLEVNET; Northeast Ohio Regional Library System; Ohio Public Library Information Network
Special Services for the Deaf - Am sign lang & deaf culture; Closed caption videos; TTY equip
Special Services for the Blind - Audio mat; Bks on cassette; Bks on CD; Descriptive video serv (DVS); Large print bks; Low vision equip; ZoomText magnification & reading software
Open Mon-Thurs 9:30-8, Fri & Sat 10-6
Friends of the Library Group

UHRICHSVILLE

P CLAYMONT PUBLIC LIBRARY, 215 E Third St, 44683. SAN 357-2765. Tel: 740-922-3626. FAX: 740-922-3500. Web Site: www.claymontlibrary.org. *Dir,* Donna Moody; E-mail: dmoody@seolibraries.org; Staff 2 (MLS 1, Non-MLS 1)
Founded 1934. Pop 12,000; Circ 199,000
Library Holdings: Bk Vols 40,000; Per Subs 104
Special Collections: Clay History Coll; Railroad Coll
Automation Activity & Vendor Info: (Cataloging) SirsiDynix; (Circulation) SirsiDynix; (ILL) SirsiDynix; (OPAC) SirsiDynix
Wireless access
Partic in SE Ohio Regional Librs; Serving Every Ohioan Library Center
Open Mon, Tues, Thurs & Fri 10-6, Sat 10-4
Friends of the Library Group
Branches: 1
DENNISON BRANCH, 15 N Fourth St, Dennison, 44621, SAN 357-279X. Tel: 740-922-5851. FAX: 740-922-6391. *Br Mgr,* Lois Brown; E-mail: brownlo@oplin.org; Staff 2 (MLS 1, Non-MLS 1)
Library Holdings: Bk Vols 23,938; Per Subs 45
Open Mon, Wed & Fri 10-4, Tues & Thurs 2-8
Friends of the Library Group

UNIVERSITY HEIGHTS

C JOHN CARROLL UNIVERSITY*, Grasselli Library & Breen Learning Center, One John Carroll Blvd, 44118. SAN 313-7635. Tel: 216-397-4233. Administration Tel: 216-397-4231. FAX: 216-397-4256. Web Site: lib.jcu.edu. *Dir,* Michelle Millet; Tel: 216-397-3053, E-mail: mmillet@jcu.edu; *Head, Coll, Head, Digital Projects, Head, Res Mgt,* Ruth Connell; Tel: 216-397-1635, E-mail: connell@jcu.edu; Staff 14 (MLS 10, Non-MLS 4)
Founded 1886. Enrl 3,696; Fac 477; Highest Degree: Master
Library Holdings: AV Mats 8,597; e-books 19,416; e-journals 7,485; Microforms 693,759; Bk Vols 761,832; Per Subs 887
Special Collections: Far East (Daniel A Hill Far Eastern Coll); G K Chesterton (John R Bayer Chesterton Coll), bks, micro. State Document Depository; US Document Depository
Subject Interests: Educ, Relig, Theol
Automation Activity & Vendor Info: (Acquisitions) Innovative Interfaces, Inc; (Cataloging) Innovative Interfaces, Inc; (Circulation) Innovative Interfaces, Inc; (Course Reserve) Docutek; (ILL) OCLC ILLiad; (OPAC) Innovative Interfaces, Inc; (Serials) Innovative Interfaces, Inc
Wireless access
Function: Computers for patron use, Magnifiers for reading, Online cat, Online ref, Orientations, Photocopying/Printing, Ref & res, Ref serv available, Scanner, Telephone ref, Workshops
Publications: Library Notes (Newsletter)
Partic in Ohio Library & Information Network; OhioNET
Open Mon-Thurs 8am-2am, Fri 8-8, Sat 10-10, Sun 11am-2am; Mon-Fri (Summer) 8-6
Friends of the Library Group

UPPER SANDUSKY

P UPPER SANDUSKY COMMUNITY LIBRARY, 301 N Sandusky Ave, 43351-1139. SAN 313-7643. Tel: 419-294-1345. FAX: 419-294-4499. Web Site: www.usclibrary.org. *Dir,* Kathleen Whitt; E-mail: kwhitt@seolibraries.org; *Dep Fiscal Officer, Tech Coordr,* Patricia Davidson; E-mail: pdavidson@seolibraries.org; *Homebound Serv,* Holly Higgins; E-mail: hhiggins@seolibraries.org; *Coordr, Youth Serv,* Jill Stansbery; E-mail: jstansbery@seolibraries.org; *Soc Media Coordr,* Krystal Smalley; E-mail: ksmalley@seolibraries.org; Staff 4.5 (MLS 1, Non-MLS 3.5)
Founded 1912. Pop 11,542; Circ 154,405
Jan 2015-Dec 2015 Income $588,526, State $251,139, Locally Generated Income $306,436, Other $30,951
Subject Interests: Genealogy, Local hist
Automation Activity & Vendor Info: (Cataloging) SirsiDynix-WorkFlows; (Circulation) SirsiDynix-WorkFlows; (OPAC) SirsiDynix; (Serials) SirsiDynix-WorkFlows
Wireless access
Function: 24/7 Online cat, Adult bk club, Audio & video playback equip for onsite use, Audiobks on Playaways & MP3, Audiobks via web, AV serv, Bks on CD, Children's prog, Computer training, Computers for patron use, Electronic databases & coll, Free DVD rentals, Home delivery & serv to seniorr ctr & nursing homes, Homebound delivery serv, ILL available, Internet access, Laminating, Magazines, Magnifiers for reading, Mail & tel request accepted, Meeting rooms, Microfiche/film & reading machines, Movies, Notary serv, Online cat, Outreach serv, OverDrive digital audio bks, Photocopying/Printing, Preschool outreach, Preschool reading prog, Printer for laptops & handheld devices, Prog for adults, Prog for children & young adult, Ref serv available, Scanner, Senior outreach, Serves people with intellectual disabilities, Spanish lang bks, Story hour, Summer reading prog, Tax forms, Teen prog, Telephone ref, Wheelchair accessible
Partic in NORWELD; Serving Every Ohioan Library Center
Open Mon-Thurs 9-8:30, Fri 9-6, Sat 9-1
Friends of the Library Group

URBANA

P CHAMPAIGN COUNTY LIBRARY*, 1060 Scioto St, 43078. SAN 313-7651. Tel: 937-653-3811. FAX: 937-653-5679. E-mail: reference@champaigncountylibrary.org. Web Site: www.champaigncountylibrary.org. *Dir,* Ty Henderson; E-mail: thenderson@champaigncountylibrary.org; Staff 22 (MLS 1, Non-MLS 21)
Founded 1890. Pop 25,965; Circ 271,000
Library Holdings: CDs 6,047; DVDs 9,464; e-books 799,285; Electronic Media & Resources 17,658; Bk Vols 106,410; Per Subs 135
Automation Activity & Vendor Info: (Acquisitions) TLC (The Library Corporation); (Cataloging) TLC (The Library Corporation); (Circulation) TLC (The Library Corporation); (OPAC) TLC (The Library Corporation); (Serials) TLC (The Library Corporation)
Wireless access
Function: 24/7 Electronic res, 24/7 Online cat, 3D Printer, Adult bk club, Archival coll, Audiobks on Playaways & MP3, Audiobks via web, AV serv, Bk club(s), Bks on CD, Children's prog, Computer training, Computers for patron use, E-Readers, Electronic databases & coll, Free DVD rentals, Home delivery & serv to seniorr ctr & nursing homes, Homebound delivery serv, ILL available, Internet access, Laminating, Life-long learning prog for all ages, Magazines, Magnifiers for reading, Makerspace, Mango lang, Meeting rooms, Microfiche/film & reading machines, Movies, Music CDs, Online cat, Online ref, Outreach serv, OverDrive digital audio bks, Photocopying/Printing, Preschool outreach, Preschool reading prog, Prog for adults, Prog for children & young adult, Ref serv available, Scanner, Senior outreach, Serves people with intellectual disabilities, Spanish lang bks, STEM programs, Story hour, Study rm, Summer & winter reading prog, Summer reading prog, Tax forms, Teen prog, Telephone ref, Wheelchair accessible, Winter reading prog
Partic in Miami Valley Librs
Special Services for the Blind - Talking bks
Open Mon-Thurs 9-8, Fri & Sat 9-5
Friends of the Library Group

VAN WERT

P BRUMBACK LIBRARY*, 215 W Main St, 45891-1695. SAN 313-7678. Tel: 419-238-2168. FAX: 419-238-3180. E-mail: brumback@brumbacklib.com. Web Site: www.brumbacklib.com. *Dir,* John J Carr; Staff 15 (MLS 2, Non-MLS 13)
Founded 1901. Pop 29,800; Circ 789,350
Jan 2013-Dec 2013 Income (Main & Associated Libraries) $1,070,905. Mats Exp $147,596. Sal $509,507
Library Holdings: Audiobooks 7,438; Bks on Deafness & Sign Lang 127; Braille Volumes 45; CDs 3,544; DVDs 7,815; e-books 142,248; High Interest/Low Vocabulary Bk Vols 392; Large Print Bks 7,000; Microforms 814; Bk Titles 218,971; Bk Vols 235,143; Per Subs 229; Talking Bks 7,438; Videos 3,268
Special Collections: Local History Coll Rare Books; Van Wert Newspapers, 1855 to present on microfilm
Subject Interests: Bks on CD, Children's bks, Genealogy, Local hist, Popular works
Automation Activity & Vendor Info: (Acquisitions) SirsiDynix; (Cataloging) SirsiDynix; (Circulation) SirsiDynix; (OPAC) SirsiDynix; (Serials) SirsiDynix
Wireless access
Function: Wheelchair accessible
Publications: Chapter & Verse Book Review; Chapter Notes (Newsletter)
Partic in NORWELD; Ohio Public Library Information Network
Special Services for the Blind - Accessible computers; BiFolkal kits; Bks available with recordings; Bks on cassette; Bks on CD
Open Mon-Thurs 9-7:30, Fri 9:30-5, Sat 9:30-3:30
Branches: 5
CONVOY BRANCH, 116 E Tully St, Convoy, 45832. (Mail add: PO Box 607, Convoy, 45832-0607), SAN 377-8886. Tel: 419-749-4000. *Librn,* Cindy Money; Staff 1 (Non-MLS 1)
Library Holdings: Bk Vols 38,427; Per Subs 57
Open Mon-Wed 9-12:30 & 1-5:30, Thurs 11-4:30 & 5:30-8, Sat 9-Noon
ROBERT & IOLA KOCH - OHIO CITY BRANCH, 101 Carmean St, Ohio City, 45874, SAN 377-8924. Tel: 419-965-2918. *Librn,* Tressa Ringwald; Staff 1 (Non-MLS 1)
Library Holdings: Bk Vols 29,819; Per Subs 33
Open Mon & Sat 9-Noon, Tues 9-2, Wed 1-5:30, Thurs 5:30-8
MIDDLE POINT BRANCH, 102 Railroad St, Middle Point, 45863. (Mail add: PO Box 295, Middle Point, 45863-0295), SAN 377-8908. Tel: 419-968-2553. E-mail: mpbranch@bright.net. *Librn,* Tressa Ringwald; Staff 1 (Non-MLS 1)
Library Holdings: Bk Vols 27,363; Per Subs 41
Open Mon 1-5:30, Tues 3-8, Wed 9-Noon, Thurs 11:30-4:30, Sat 2-4
WILLSHIRE BRANCH, 323 State St, Willshire, 45898, SAN 377-8940. Tel: 419-495-4138. *Br Mgr,* Rose Mowery; Staff 1 (Non-MLS 1)
Library Holdings: Bk Vols 29,311; Per Subs 30
Open Mon 5-8, Tues 11-3, Wed 1-5:30, Thurs 2:30-4:30, Sat 9-11:30
WREN BRANCH, 103 State Rte 49, Wren, 45899, SAN 377-8967. Tel: 419-495-4174. *Br Mgr,* Rose Mowery; Staff 1 (Non-MLS 1)
Library Holdings: Bk Vols 25,500; Per Subs 31
Open Mon 11-4, Tues 4-8, Wed 9:30-12, Thurs Noon-2, Sat 12:30-5

GL VAN WERT COUNTY LAW LIBRARY ASSOCIATION*, Court House, 3rd Flr, 121 Main St, 45891. SAN 313-7686. Tel: 419-238-6935. FAX: 419-238-2874. E-mail: admiistrator@vwcommonpleas.org. *Librn,* Lagina Enyart
Library Holdings: Bk Vols 17,900
Publications: First Reporter Series in Ultra Fiche; Second Federal Reporter & Supplement
Open Mon-Fri 8-4

VERMILION

P RITTER PUBLIC LIBRARY*, 5680 Liberty Ave, 44089. SAN 313-7708. Tel: 440-967-3798. FAX: 440-967-5482. E-mail: info@ritter.lib.oh.us. Web Site: ritterpubliclibrary.org. *Dir,* Holly Lynn; E-mail: holly.lynn@ritter.lib.oh.us; *Adult Serv,* Amy L Trotter; E-mail:

amy.trotter@ritter.lib.oh.us; *Youth Serv,* Elizabeth Donaldson; E-mail: elizabeth.donaldson@ritter.lib.oh.us; Staff 3 (MLS 3)
Founded 1912. Pop 14,844; Circ 309,608
Library Holdings: CDs 5,455; DVDs 6,456; e-books 22,807; Microforms 74; Bk Vols 56,146; Per Subs 2,097
Wireless access
Function: Adult bk club, Archival coll, Audio & video playback equip for onsite use, Bk club(s), Bks on cassette, Bks on CD, Children's prog, Computer training, Computers for patron use, Digital talking bks, E-Reserves, Electronic databases & coll, Equip loans & repairs, Free DVD rentals, Home delivery & serv to seniorr ctr & nursing homes, Homebound delivery serv, ILL available, Internet access, Mail & tel request accepted, Music CDs, Notary serv, Online cat, Online ref, Outreach serv, Outside serv via phone, mail, e-mail & web, OverDrive digital audio bks, Photocopying/Printing, Preschool outreach, Prog for adults, Prog for children & young adult, Ref & res, Ref serv available, Senior computer classes, Spoken cassettes & CDs, Story hour, Summer reading prog, Tax forms, Teen prog, Telephone ref, VHS videos, Wheelchair accessible
Partic in Ohio Libr Coun
Open Mon-Thurs 9:30-8:30, Fri & Sat 9:30-5:30, Sun 1-5
Restriction: Circ limited, Circ to mem only
Friends of the Library Group

VERSAILLES

P WORCH MEMORIAL PUBLIC LIBRARY*, 790 S Center St, 45380. (Mail add: PO Box 336, 45380-0336), SAN 313-7724. Tel: 937-526-3416. FAX: 937-526-3990. Web Site: www.worch.lib.oh.us. *Dir,* Meme Marlow; E-mail: meme@worch.lib.oh.us
Founded 1937. Pop 6,000; Circ 115,000
Library Holdings: Bk Titles 40,000; Per Subs 190
Subject Interests: Area genealogy, Family, Local genealogy
Automation Activity & Vendor Info: (Cataloging) Evergreen
Wireless access
Partic in Consortium of Ohio Libraries
Open Mon-Thurs 9-8, Sat 9-2
Friends of the Library Group

WADSWORTH

P ELLA M EVERHARD PUBLIC LIBRARY*, Wadsworth Public Library, 132 Broad St, 44281-1897. SAN 378-4495. Tel: 330-334-5761. Reference Tel: 330-335-1294. Administration Tel: 330-335-1299. Automation Services Tel: 330-335-2600. FAX: 330-334-6605. Web Site: www.wadsworthlibrary.com. *Dir,* Daniel Slife; E-mail: director@wadsworthlibrary.com; *Dep Dir, Mgr, Ch Serv,* Nicole Moore; Tel: 330-335-1295; *Coll Develop Librn,* Abby Hindulak; E-mail: abby.hindulak@wadsworthlibrary.com; *Mgr, Ad Serv, Multimedia,* Donald Harmon; Tel: 330-335-8253; *Automation Mgr, Circ Mgr,* Susan Brown; Tel: 330-335-2607; *Bus Mgr, Fiscal Officer,* Patty Moutes; Tel: 330-335-1297; *Fac Mgr, Syst Mgr,* Tim Laino; Tel: 330-335-2600; Staff 11 (MLS 11)
Founded 1922. Pop 27,000; Circ 910,000
Library Holdings: AV Mats 23,628; Bk Vols 156,851; Per Subs 339
Subject Interests: Artwork, Lab kits, Local hist
Automation Activity & Vendor Info: (Acquisitions) Innovative Interfaces, Inc; (Cataloging) Innovative Interfaces, Inc; (Circulation) Innovative Interfaces, Inc; (ILL) Innovative Interfaces, Inc; (OPAC) Innovative Interfaces, Inc; (Serials) Innovative Interfaces, Inc
Wireless access
Function: Home delivery & serv to seniorr ctr & nursing homes, Homebound delivery serv, ILL available, Large print keyboards, Magnifiers for reading, Prog for adults, Prog for children & young adult, Summer reading prog, Wheelchair accessible
Publications: Ellagram (Newsletter)
Special Services for the Deaf - ADA equip; Assistive tech; Closed caption videos
Special Services for the Blind - Audio mat; Bks on cassette; Bks on CD; Cassette playback machines; Cassettes; Computer with voice synthesizer for visually impaired persons; Home delivery serv; Large print & cassettes; Large print bks; Large screen computer & software; Magnifiers; Scanner for conversion & translation of mats; Talking bks; Videos on blindness & physical disabilties
Open Mon-Thurs 9-9, Fri & Sat 9-6
Friends of the Library Group
Bookmobiles: 2

WAPAKONETA

GL AUGLAIZE COUNTY LAW LIBRARY*, County Courthouse, 201 Willipie St, Ste 207, 45895. SAN 313-7767. Tel: 419-739-6749. E-mail: lawlibrary@auglaizecounty.org. Web Site: www2.auglaizecounty.org/departments/law-library. *Librn,* Lucy Merges
Founded 1898
Library Holdings: Bk Vols 10,000
Wireless access
Open Wed 12-3

P AUGLAIZE COUNTY LIBRARIES*, 203 S Perry St, 45895-1999. SAN 357-2919. Tel: 419-738-2921. FAX: 419-738-5168. Web Site: www.auglaizelibraries.org. *Dir,* Beth Steiner; E-mail: bsteiner@auglaizelibraries.org; *Libr Serv Mgr,* Kristine Spyker; E-mail: kspyker@auglaizelibraries.org; Staff 15 (MLS 2, Non-MLS 13)
Founded 1925. Pop 33,458; Circ 304,932
Library Holdings: Audiobooks 1,982; CDs 963; DVDs 4,909; e-books 7,402; Large Print Bks 3,571; Bk Vols 155,311; Per Subs 311; Videos 693
Subject Interests: Dudley Nichols, Genealogy, Neil Armstrong, Ohio hist
Automation Activity & Vendor Info: (Acquisitions) Innovative Interfaces, Inc; (Cataloging) Innovative Interfaces, Inc; (Circulation) Innovative Interfaces, Inc; (OPAC) Innovative Interfaces, Inc; (Serials) Innovative Interfaces, Inc
Wireless access
Function: Adult bk club, Computers for patron use, Prog for children & young adult, Summer reading prog
Open Mon & Thurs Noon-8, Tues & Wed 10-6, Fri & Sat 10-2
Friends of the Library Group
Branches: 5
CRIDERSVILLE PUBLIC LIBRARY, 116 W Main St, Cridersville, 45895, SAN 357-2927. Tel: 419-645-5447. FAX: 419-645-6019. *Br Supvr,* Melissa Luthman; E-mail: mluthman@auglaizelibraries.org; Staff 2 (Non-MLS 2)
Open Mon 11-6:30, Wed 3-6:30, Sat 10-Noon
Friends of the Library Group
NEW BREMEN PUBLIC LIBRARY, 45 S Washington St, New Bremen, 45869, SAN 357-2935. Tel: 419-629-2158. FAX: 419-629-1351. *Br Supvr,* Shelli Parker; Staff 2 (Non-MLS 2)
Open Mon & Tues 12-7, Thurs 10-2, Sat 10-12
Friends of the Library Group
NEW KNOXVILLE COMMUNITY LIBRARY, 304 S Main St, New Knoxville, 45871, SAN 357-2943. Tel: 419-753-2724. FAX: 419-753-2594. *Br Supvr,* Michelle Parker; Staff 1 (Non-MLS 1)
Open Mon 12-7, Thurs 3-7, Sat 10-12
Friends of the Library Group
FRANCIS J STALLO MEMORIAL LIBRARY, 196 E Fourth St, Minster, 45865, SAN 357-2978. Tel: 419-628-2925. FAX: 419-628-4556. *Br Supvr,* Becky Prenger; Staff 4 (Non-MLS 4)
Open Mon & Tues 10-7, Wed 3-7, Fri & Sat 10-12
Friends of the Library Group
EDWARD R & MINNIE D WHITE MEMORIAL LIBRARY, 108 E Wapakoneta St, Waynesfield, 45896, SAN 357-3001. Tel: 419-568-5851. FAX: 419-568-2368. *Br Supvr,* Pamela Kennon; Staff 2 (Non-MLS 2)
Partic in NORWELD
Open Mon & Thurs 12-6, Tues 10-4, Sat 10-12
Friends of the Library Group
Bookmobiles: 1. Outreach Servs, Linda Huber

WARREN

C KENT STATE UNIVERSITY*, Trumbull Campus, Gelbke Library, 4314 Mahoning Ave NW, 44483-1998. Tel: 330-675-8865, 330-847-0571. FAX: 330-675-8825. Web Site: www.kent.edu/trumbull/library. *Sr Libr Asst,* Andrew Budny; E-mail: abudny@kent.edu; Staff 5 (MLS 2, Non-MLS 3)
Founded 1970. Enrl 2,000; Fac 60; Highest Degree: Bachelor
Library Holdings: Bk Titles 55,000; Bk Vols 75,000; Per Subs 235; Videos 450
Special Collections: Holocaust Coll; Ohio Reference Coll; Science Fiction Coll
Wireless access
Open Mon-Thurs (Winter) 8-8, Fri 8-4:30; Mon-Thurs (Summer) 8-5:30, Fri 8-4:30

M STEWARD HEALTH CARE*, Trumbull Regional Medical Center Library, 1350 E Market St, 44482. Tel: 330-675-5704, 330-884-3476. FAX: 330-675-5720. *Librn,* Dan Dunlany; E-mail: dpd@neomed.edu
Library Holdings: e-journals 100; Bk Vols 1,600
Automation Activity & Vendor Info: (Circulation) Innovative Interfaces, Inc; (OPAC) Innovative Interfaces, Inc; (Serials) Innovative Interfaces, Inc
Wireless access
Friends of the Library Group

L TRUMBULL COUNTY LAW LIBRARY*, 120 High St NW, 44481. SAN 372-199X. Tel: 330-675-2525. FAX: 330-675-2527. Web Site: lawlibrary.co.trumbull.oh.us. *Library Contact,* Tara Treharn Keating; E-mail: catrehar@co.trumbull.oh.us; Staff 3 (MLS 1, Non-MLS 2)
Library Holdings: Bk Vols 32,000; Per Subs 56
Wireless access
Open Mon-Fri 8:30-4:30

P WARREN-TRUMBULL COUNTY PUBLIC LIBRARY*, 444 Mahoning Ave NW, 44483. SAN 313-7813. Tel: 330-399-8807. Reference Tel: 330-399-8807, Ext 200. Administration Tel: 330-399-8807, Ext 124. FAX: 330-395-3988. TDD: 330-393-0784. Web Site: www.wtcpl.org. *Dir,* James Wilkins; E-mail: wilkinsj@wtcpl.org; *Asst Dir,* Jan Vaughn; E-mail: vaughnj@wtcpl.org; *Pub Relations Mgr,* Cheryl Bush; *Tech Serv,* Lucretia Wiley; *Youth Serv,* Lori Faust; Staff 34 (MLS 18, Non-MLS 16)
Founded 1890. Pop 160,721; Circ 1,193,268
Library Holdings: CDs 36,779; Bk Vols 415,972; Per Subs 602; Videos 20,117
Subject Interests: Local hist, Ohio
Automation Activity & Vendor Info: (Acquisitions) Innovative Interfaces, Inc; (Cataloging) Innovative Interfaces, Inc; (Circulation) Innovative Interfaces, Inc; (ILL) Innovative Interfaces, Inc; (OPAC) Innovative Interfaces, Inc; (Serials) Innovative Interfaces, Inc
Wireless access
Function: Computers for patron use, Internet access, Magnifiers for reading, Mail & tel request accepted, Mail loans to mem, Masonic res mat, Music CDs, Online cat, Online ref, Prog for adults, Prog for children & young adult, Ref serv available, Story hour, Summer reading prog, Tax forms, Teen prog, VHS videos, Wheelchair accessible
Publications: By the Book (Newsletter)
Partic in Northeast Ohio Regional Library System; OhioNET
Special Services for the Blind - Talking bks
Open Mon & Thurs 10-8, Tues & Wed 10-6, Fri 9-6, Sat 9-5
Friends of the Library Group
Branches: 5
BROOKFIELD BRANCH, 7032 Grove St, Brookfield, 44403, SAN 324-251X. Tel: 330-448-8134. *Br Mgr,* Nancy Gaut
Founded 1982. Circ 80,986
Library Holdings: Bk Vols 23,055
Open Mon-Thurs 9-8, Fri 9-5:30, Sat 9-5
Friends of the Library Group
CORTLAND BRANCH, 578 Lakeview Dr, Cortland, 44410, SAN 324-2528. Tel: 330-638-6335. *Br Mgr,* Karen Murphy
Founded 1977. Circ 101,558
Library Holdings: Bk Vols 25,946
Open Tues & Fri 10-6, Wed & Thurs 12-8, Sat 9-5
Friends of the Library Group
HOWLAND BRANCH, 9095 E Market St, 44484, SAN 370-9000. Tel: 330-856-2011. *Br Mgr,* Diane Thomas
Founded 1990. Circ 173,990
Library Holdings: Bk Vols 35,390
Open Tues & Wed 12-8, Thurs & Fri 10-6, Sat 9-5
Friends of the Library Group
LIBERTY, 415 Churchill-Hubbard Rd, Youngstown, 44505, SAN 377-9971. Tel: 330-759-2589. *Br Mgr,* Claire Hoffman
Founded 1998. Circ 110,137
Library Holdings: Bk Vols 15,159
Open Tues & Thurs 12-8, Wed & Fri 10-6, Sat 9-5
Friends of the Library Group
LORDSTOWN BRANCH, 1471 Salt Springs Rd, 44481, SAN 325-3384. Tel: 330-824-2094. *Br Mgr,* Vera Riffle
Founded 1985. Circ 29,322
Library Holdings: Bk Vols 15,159
Open Mon 12-4 & 4:30-8, Tues-Fri 10-1 & 1:30-6
Friends of the Library Group
Bookmobiles: 1

WARRENSVILLE HEIGHTS

M SOUTH POINTE HOSPITAL LIBRARY*, 20000 Harvard Rd, 44122. SAN 325-1918. Tel: 216-491-7455. FAX: 216-491-7560. E-mail: librarysp@ccf.org. Web Site: my.clevelandclinic.libguides.com/southpointe. *Med Librn,* Mary Pat Harnegie; E-mail: harnegm@ccf.org; *Libr Asst,* Lachelle Bell; E-mail: lbell@ccf.org; Staff 1.5 (MLS 0.5, Non-MLS 1)
Founded 1978
Library Holdings: Bk Titles 5,000; Per Subs 200
Subject Interests: Osteopathic med
Automation Activity & Vendor Info: (Circulation) Follett Software
Partic in Greater Midwest Regional Medical Libr Network; Med Libr Asn of NE Ohio; Northeast Ohio Regional Library System

WASHINGTON COURT HOUSE

P CARNEGIE PUBLIC LIBRARY, 127 S North St, 43160. SAN 313-7848. Tel: 740-335-2540. FAX: 740-335-2928. E-mail: cplwcho@gmail.com. Web Site: www.cplwcho.org. *Dir,* Sarah Nichols; E-mail: snichols@seolibraries.org; *Head, Children's Servx,* Anne Quinn; *Coordr, Tech Support,* Maria Wilburn; Staff 3 (MLS 3)
Founded 1891. Pop 28,500; Circ 214,400
Library Holdings: Bk Vols 69,461; Per Subs 98
Special Collections: Genealogy & Local History Coll
Automation Activity & Vendor Info: (Acquisitions) SirsiDynix; (Circulation) SirsiDynix; (ILL) SirsiDynix; (OPAC) SirsiDynix
Wireless access
Partic in Serving Every Ohioan Library Center
Open Mon-Fri 10-6, Sat 10-2
Branches: 1
JEFFERSONVILLE BRANCH, Eight S Main St, Jeffersonville, 43128-1063. Tel: 740-426-9292. FAX: 740-426-9284. *Br Mgr,* Susan Davis
Founded 1985. Pop 1,400; Circ 27,000
Library Holdings: Bk Titles 5,000; Per Subs 12
Open Mon-Thurs 10-6

GL FAYETTE COUNTY LAW LIBRARY, 110 E Court St, 43160-1355. SAN 313-783X. Tel: 740-335-3608. FAX: 740-335-3608. Web Site: www.fayette-co-oh.com/government/fayette_county_law_library/index.php. *Law Librn,* Mimi Garringer; E-mail: mimi.garringer@fayette-co-oh.com
Library Holdings: Bk Titles 14,000
Special Collections: Ohio Laws
Subject Interests: Bankruptcy, Fed reports, Tax
Open Tues-Thurs 2-4

WAUSEON

L FULTON COUNTY ASSOCIATION*, Law Library, Court House, 210 S Fulton, 43567. SAN 327-7208. Tel: 419-337-9260. FAX: 419-337-9293. *Librn,* Sue Behnfeldt; E-mail: sbehnfeldt@fultoncountyoh.com
Restriction: Not open to pub

P WAUSEON PUBLIC LIBRARY, 117 E Elm St, 43567. SAN 313-7856. Tel: 419-335-6626. FAX: 419-335-0642. Web Site: www.wauseonlibrary.org. *Dir,* Maricela DeLeon; E-mail: mdeleon@seolibraries.org; Staff 2 (Non-MLS 2)
Founded 1875. Pop 10,638
Library Holdings: AV Mats 3,387; Bk Titles 46,403; Per Subs 38
Special Collections: Local History Coll
Automation Activity & Vendor Info: (Cataloging) SirsiDynix; (Circulation) SirsiDynix
Wireless access
Function: 24/7 Online cat, Accelerated reader prog, Adult bk club, AV serv, Bilingual assistance for Spanish patrons, Bks on CD, Chess club, Children's prog, Computer training, Computers for patron use, Free DVD rentals, Holiday prog, Home delivery & serv to seniorr ctr & nursing homes, Homebound delivery serv, ILL available, Internet access, Magazines, Mail & tel request accepted, Meeting rooms, Microfiche/film & reading machines, Music CDs, Online cat, OverDrive digital audio bks, Photocopying/Printing, Preschool outreach, Preschool reading prog, Prog for adults, Prog for children & young adult, Scanner, Senior outreach, Story hour, Summer reading prog, Tax forms, Teen prog, Wheelchair accessible
Publications: Annual Report
Partic in NW Ohio Libr District; Ohio Public Library Information Network; Serving Every Ohioan Library Center
Special Services for the Blind - Large print bks; Talking bks
Open Mon-Fri 10-6

WAVERLY

P GARNET A WILSON PUBLIC LIBRARY OF PIKE COUNTY*, 207 N Market St, 45690-1176. SAN 313-7864. Tel: 740-947-4921. FAX: 740-947-2918. Web Site: www.pikecountylibrary.org. *Dir,* Thomas S Adkins; E-mail: tadkins@seolibraries.org; *Automation Syst Coordr,* Daniel R Moore; E-mail: dmoore@seolibraries.org; *Outreach Serv,* Jennifer Wright; E-mail: jwright@seolibraries.org; Staff 30 (MLS 1, Non-MLS 29)
Founded 1939. Pop 27,988; Circ 222,623
Library Holdings: Bk Vols 89,005; Per Subs 248
Special Collections: Pike County Local History/Genealogy Room
Automation Activity & Vendor Info: (Cataloging) TLC (The Library Corporation); (Circulation) TLC (The Library Corporation); (OPAC) TLC (The Library Corporation)
Wireless access
Partic in Serving Every Ohioan Library Center
Special Services for the Blind - Talking bks
Open Mon-Thurs 9-8, Fri 9-6, Sat 9-5
Branches: 2
EASTERN BRANCH, 310 E Third St, Beaver, 45613. Tel: 740-226-4408. FAX: 740-226-4408. *Dir,* Thomas S Adkins; Staff 4 (MLS 1, Non-MLS 3)
Founded 2000
Open Mon 10-6, Tues 10-8, Wed-Fri 12-6, Sat 11-4
PIKETON BRANCH, 200 E Second St, Piketon, 45661-8047. (Mail add: PO Box 762, Piketon, 45661-0762), SAN 376-7914. Tel: 740-289-3064. FAX: 740-289-3064. ; Staff 4 (MLS 1, Non-MLS 3)
Founded 1997
Open Mon, Tues & Fri 12-6, Wed 10-6, Thurs 10-8, Sat 11-4

WAYNE

P WAYNE PUBLIC LIBRARY*, 137 E Main St, 43466. SAN 357-3036. Tel: 419-288-2708. FAX: 419-288-3766. Web Site: waynepl.org. *Dir,* Teresa Barnhart; E-mail: tbarnhart@waynepl.org; Staff 5 (MLS 1, Non-MLS 4)
Founded 1945. Pop 8,800; Circ 89,417
Library Holdings: Bk Vols 37,297; Per Subs 135
Wireless access
Partic in Serving Every Ohioan Library Center
Open Mon-Thurs 10-6, Fri & Sat 10-Noon

WAYNESVILLE

P MARY L COOK PUBLIC LIBRARY, 381 Old Stage Rd, 45068. SAN 313-7872. Tel: 513-897-4826. FAX: 513-897-9215. Web Site: mlcook.lib.oh.us. *Dir,* Kelly Maloney; E-mail: maloneke@marylcook.com
Founded 1917. Pop 19,000; Circ 189,300
Library Holdings: AV Mats 5,700; Bk Vols 70,800
Special Collections: Early Quaker Theology; Ohio & Local History
Subject Interests: Genealogy
Automation Activity & Vendor Info: (Cataloging) Innovative Interfaces, Inc
Wireless access
Function: Adult literacy prog, Archival coll, AV serv, For res purposes, Home delivery & serv to seniorr ctr & nursing homes, Homebound delivery serv, ILL available, Large print keyboards, Magnifiers for reading, Photocopying/Printing, Prog for children & young adult, Ref serv available, Summer reading prog, Wheelchair accessible
Publications: Newsletter (Quarterly)
Partic in Miami Valley Librs
Open Mon-Thurs 10-7, Fri 10-5, Sat 9-2
Friends of the Library Group

WELLINGTON

P HERRICK MEMORIAL LIBRARY*, 101 Willard Memorial Sq, 44090-1342. SAN 313-7880. Tel: 440-647-2120. FAX: 440-647-2103. Web Site: www.herrickliboh.org. *Dir,* Janet L Hollingsworth; E-mail: hollinja@herrickliboh.org; *Adult Serv,* Lynne Welch; E-mail: Welchly@herrickliboh.org; *Ch Serv,* Janet Frye; E-mail: fryeja@herrickliboh.org; Staff 10 (MLS 2, Non-MLS 8)
Founded 1904. Pop 9,541; Circ 95,000
Library Holdings: Bk Vols 57,042; Per Subs 168
Special Collections: Wellington Historic Photo Coll. Oral History
Subject Interests: Local hist
Automation Activity & Vendor Info: (Cataloging) OPALS (Open-source Automated Library System); (Circulation) OPALS (Open-source Automated Library System); (OPAC) OPALS (Open-source Automated Library System)
Wireless access
Function: Accelerated reader prog, Archival coll
Open Mon-Thurs 10-8, Fri & Sat 9-5, Sun (Oct-April) 1-5
Friends of the Library Group

WELLSTON

P SYLVESTER MEMORIAL WELLSTON PUBLIC LIBRARY*, 135 E Second St, 45692. SAN 313-7899. Tel: 740-384-6660. FAX: 740-384-5001. E-mail: wellstonlibrary@gmail.com. Web Site: www1.youseemore.com/sylvester. *Dir,* Karen A Yablonsky; *Head Cataloger,* Debbie Lewis; *Head, Circ,* Connie Dickerson; *Ch,* Meghan Carpenter; Staff 1 (Non-MLS 1)
Pop 10,000
Library Holdings: Bk Titles 35,000; Bk Vols 40,000
Wireless access
Open Mon-Wed 10-6, Thurs & Fri 10-5, Sat 10-2
Restriction: Access for corporate affiliates

WELLSVILLE

P WELLSVILLE CARNEGIE PUBLIC LIBRARY, 115 Ninth St, 43968-1431. SAN 313-7902. Tel: 330-532-1526. FAX: 330-532-3127. Web Site: www.wellsville.lib.oh.us. *Dir,* Tracee Murphy; E-mail: murphytr@wellsville.lib.oh.us; *Youth Serv Mgr,* Rachel Freed; E-mail: freedra@wellsville.lib.oh.us; Staff 6 (MLS 1, Non-MLS 5)
Founded 1908. Pop 5,000; Circ 62,000
Library Holdings: AV Mats 820; Bk Vols 50,000; Per Subs 85
Special Collections: Early History of Columbiana County
Automation Activity & Vendor Info: (Cataloging) Innovative Interfaces, Inc; (Circulation) Innovative Interfaces, Inc; (OPAC) Innovative Interfaces, Inc
Wireless access
Function: Adult bk club, Bks on cassette, Bks on CD, Children's prog, Computers for patron use, ILL available, Notary serv, Photocopying/Printing, Prog for children & young adult, Summer reading prog, Wheelchair accessible
Partic in Northeast Ohio Regional Library System
Special Services for the Blind - Bks on cassette; Bks on CD; Talking bks & player equip
Open Mon & Thurs 10-8, Tues, Wed, Fri & Sat 10-6
Friends of the Library Group

WEST JEFFERSON

P HURT-BATTELLE MEMORIAL LIBRARY OF WEST JEFFERSON*, 270 Lily Chapel Rd, 43162-1202. SAN 313-7910. Tel: 614-879-8448. FAX: 614-879-8668. Web Site: www.hbmlibrary.org. *Dir,* Tara McClaskie; E-mail: tmcclaskie@hbmlibrary.org
Founded 1913. Pop 7,500; Circ 81,888
Library Holdings: Bk Vols 44,000; Per Subs 25
Subject Interests: Cookbks, Craft, Med
Automation Activity & Vendor Info: (Cataloging) Follett Software; (Circulation) Follett Software
Wireless access
Function: 24/7 Online cat, 3D Printer, Bks on CD, Chess club, Children's prog, Computer training, Computers for patron use, Electronic databases & coll, Free DVD rentals, Holiday prog, Homebound delivery serv, ILL available, Internet access, Laminating, Large print keyboards, Magazines, Magnifiers for reading, Meeting rooms, Movies, Online cat, Online ref, Outreach serv, OverDrive digital audio bks, Photocopying/Printing, Preschool reading prog, Printer for laptops & handheld devices, Prog for adults, Prog for children & young adult, Ref & res, Scanner, STEM programs, Story hour, Study rm, Summer reading prog, Teen prog, Wheelchair accessible
Partic in Serving Every Ohioan Library Center
Open Mon-Fri 9-8, Sat 10-2
Friends of the Library Group

WEST MILTON

P MILTON-UNION PUBLIC LIBRARY*, 560 S Main St, 45383. SAN 313-7929. Tel: 937-698-5515. FAX: 937-698-3774. Web Site: www.mupubliclibrary.org. *Dir,* Ken Enright Miller; E-mail: kenrightmiller@seolibraries.org; *Pub Relations Mgr,* Staci West; E-mail: swest@seolibraries.org; *Website Mgr,* Erika Bowser; E-mail: ebowser@seolibraries.org; *Libr Office Coord,* Tiana McKay; E-mail: tmckay@seolibraries.org; *Genealogy/Local Hist Spec,* Ruth Dafoe; E-mail: rdafoe@seolibraries.org; *IT Spec,* Dori Mort; E-mail: dmort@seolibraries.org; *Adult Serv,* Kimberly Brubaker; E-mail: kbrubaker@seolibraries.org; *Ch Serv,* Wendy Heisey; E-mail: wheisey@seolibraries.org; *Teen Serv,* Tina Ward; E-mail: cward@seolibraries.org. Subject Specialists: *Inspirational lit, Inspirational reading,* Staci West; *Adult fiction, Adult prog,* Kimberly Brubaker; Staff 8 (Non-MLS 8)
Founded 1937. Pop 10,000
Subject Interests: Local hist
Automation Activity & Vendor Info: (Cataloging) SirsiDynix-WorkFlows; (Circulation) SirsiDynix-WorkFlows; (OPAC) Horizon
Wireless access
Function: 24/7 Electronic res, 24/7 Online cat, Accelerated reader prog, Activity rm, Adult bk club, Audiobks on Playaways & MP3, Audiobks via web, AV serv, Bk club(s), Bks on CD, Children's prog, Computer training, Computers for patron use, Digital talking bks, E-Readers, Electronic databases & coll, Free DVD rentals, Holiday prog, Home delivery & serv to seniorr ctr & nursing homes, Homebound delivery serv, ILL available, Internet access, Large print keyboards, Magazines, Mail & tel request accepted, Mango lang, Microfiche/film & reading machines, Movies, Museum passes, Music CDs, Online cat, Outreach serv, OverDrive digital audio bks, Photocopying/Printing, Preschool outreach, Printer for laptops & handheld devices, Prog for adults, Prog for children & young adult, Ref & res, Ref serv available, Scanner, Spanish lang bks, Story hour, Study rm, Summer & winter reading prog, Summer reading prog, Tax forms, Teen prog, Telephone ref, Wheelchair accessible
Partic in Ohio Public Library Information Network; Serving Every Ohioan Library Center
Special Services for the Blind - Audio mat; Bks on CD; Home delivery serv; Large print bks; Playaways (bks on MP3)
Open Mon-Thurs 10-8, Fri & Sat 9-5
Friends of the Library Group

WESTERVILLE

C HONDROS COLLEGE OF NURSING LIBRARY*, 4140 Executive Pkwy, 43081-3855. SAN 374-7832. Tel: 513-644-6020. Toll Free Tel: 855-906-8773, Ext 6020. E-mail: library@hondros.edu. Web Site: www.nursing.hondros.edu. *Librn,* Beth Smith; E-mail: bsmith@hondros.edu; Staff 1 (MLS 1)
Enrl 2,000; Highest Degree: Bachelor
Subject Interests: Gen educ, Nursing
Wireless access
Function: 24/7 Electronic res

Open Mon-Fri 8-5
Restriction: Authorized patrons

S NATIONAL GROUND WATER ASSOCIATION*, Ground Water Information Center, 601 Dempsey Rd, 43081-8978. SAN 327-392X. Tel: 614-898-7791. Toll Free Tel: 800-551-7379. Administration FAX: 614-898-7786. Web Site: www.ngwa.org. *Dir,* Thad Plumley; E-mail: tplumley@ngwa.org; Staff 2 (MLS 1, Non-MLS 1)
Library Holdings: Bk Vols 24,000; Per Subs 100
Subject Interests: Groundwater protection
Restriction: Mem only, Non-circulating, Not a lending libr

C OTTERBEIN UNIVERSITY*, Courtright Memorial Library, 138 W Main St, 43081. (Mail add: One S Grove St, 43081), SAN 313-7937. Tel: 614-823-1215. Interlibrary Loan Service Tel: 614-823-3072. Reference Tel: 614-823-1984. FAX: 614-823-1921. E-mail: library@otterbein.edu. Web Site: library.otterbein.edu, www.otterbein.edu/resources/library/library.htm. *Dir,* Tiffany Lipstreu; Tel: 614-823-1414, E-mail: tlipstreu@otterbein.edu; *Assessment Librn, Spec Projects Librn,* Kristin Cole; Tel: 614-823-1026; *Digital Initiatives Librn,* Sarah Whybrew; Tel: 614-823-1939, E-mail: swhybrew@otterbein.edu; *Electronic Access Librn,* Allen Reichert; Tel: 614-823-1164, E-mail: preichert@otterbein.edu; *Info Literacy Librn,* Rares Piloiu; Tel: 614-823-1314, E-mail: rpiloiu@otterbein.edu; *Pub Serv Librn,* Jessica Crossfield McIntosh; Tel: 614-823-1366, E-mail: JCrossfieldMcIntosh@otterbein.edu; *Syst Librn,* Jane Wu; Tel: 614-823-1027, E-mail: jwu@otterbein.edu; *Circ Supvr,* Rebecca Gale; Tel: 614-823-1799, E-mail: rgale@otterbein.edu; *Circ Supvr,* Rebecca Raeske-Grinch; E-mail: rraeske-grinch@otterbein.edu; *Tech Serv Coordr,* Elizabeth Zeitz; Tel: 614-823-1938, E-mail: ezeitz@otterbein.edu; *Archivist,* Stephen Grinch; Tel: 614-823-1761, E-mail: sgrinch@otterbein.edu; *Libr Asst,* Position Currently Open; Staff 13 (MLS 7, Non-MLS 6)
Founded 1847. Highest Degree: Doctorate
Special Collections: Americana (J Burr & Jessie M Hughes Memorial); Classics (Marshall B & Mary M Fanning Fund); Ethnics & Political Science (Lewis E Myers Memorial); Humanities (NEH Fund); Science (Elvin & Ruth Warrick Fund)
Automation Activity & Vendor Info: (Acquisitions) Innovative Interfaces, Inc; (Cataloging) Innovative Interfaces, Inc; (Circulation) Innovative Interfaces, Inc; (Course Reserve) Innovative Interfaces, Inc; (Discovery) EBSCO Discovery Service; (ILL) Innovative Interfaces, Inc; (OPAC) Innovative Interfaces, Inc; (Serials) Innovative Interfaces, Inc
Wireless access
Partic in Ohio Library & Information Network; Ohio Private Academic Libraries
Open Mon-Thurs 7:45am-2am, Fri 7:45-6, Sat 12-6, Sun Noon-2am
Friends of the Library Group

P WESTERVILLE PUBLIC LIBRARY, 126 S State St, 43081. SAN 313-7945. Tel: 614-882-7277. Circulation Tel: 614-882-7277, Ext 5. Toll Free Tel: 800-816-0662. FAX: 614-882-4160. Web Site: www.westervillelibrary.org. *Exec Dir,* Erin W Francoeur; E-mail: efrancoeur@westervillelibrary.org; *Asst Dir,* Kristin Michel; E-mail: kmichel@westervillelibrary.org; *Mgr, Outreach Serv,* Julie Kerns; E-mail: jkerns@westervillelibrary.org; *Mgr, Youth Serv,* Robin Gibson; E-mail: rgibson@westervillelibrary.org
Founded 1930. Pop 85,093; Circ 1,622,721
Library Holdings: Bk Vols 283,108; Per Subs 526
Special Collections: Temperance Coll
Subject Interests: Local hist
Automation Activity & Vendor Info: (Acquisitions) Innovative Interfaces, Inc - Millennium; (Cataloging) Innovative Interfaces, Inc; (Circulation) Innovative Interfaces, Inc - Millennium; (ILL) Innovative Interfaces, Inc - Millennium; (Media Booking) Innovative Interfaces, Inc - Millennium; (OPAC) Innovative Interfaces, Inc - Millennium; (Serials) Innovative Interfaces, Inc - Millennium
Wireless access
Publications: Between the Pages (Newsletter)
Partic in OCLC Online Computer Library Center, Inc; Ohio Library & Information Network; Ohio Public Library Information Network; OhioNET
Special Services for the Deaf - Bks on deafness & sign lang; Captioned film dep; Spec interest per; Videos & decoder
Open Mon-Sat 9-6
Friends of the Library Group
Branches: 1
ANTI SALOON LEAGUE MUSEUM & LOCAL HISTORY RESOURCE CENTER, 126 S State St, 43081, SAN 371-3466. Tel: 614-882-7277, Ext 5010. FAX: 614-882-5369. E-mail: localhistory@westervillelibrary.org. *Mgr,* Nina Thomas; E-mail: nthomas@westervillelibrary.org
Open Mon-Fri 9-6, Sat 9-1 & 2-6
Friends of the Library Group

WESTLAKE

M SAINT JOHN WEST SHORE HOSPITAL*, Jack Brill Medical Library, 29000 Center Ridge Rd, 44145. SAN 313-2064. Tel: 440-827-5569. FAX: 440-827-5573. Web Site: www.uhhospitals.org/stjohn. *Med Librn,* Adora Glorioso; Staff 1 (MLS 1)
Library Holdings: Bk Titles 1,100; Per Subs 50
Special Collections: Osteopathic

P WESTLAKE PORTER PUBLIC LIBRARY*, 27333 Center Ridge Rd, 44145-3925. SAN 313-7953. Tel: 440-871-2600. FAX: 440-871-6969. Web Site: www.westlakelibrary.org. *Dir,* Andrew Mangels; E-mail: andrew.mangels@westlakelibrary.org; *Asst Dir,* CJ Lynce; E-mail: cj.lynce@westlakelibrary.org
Founded 1884. Pop 33,000; Circ 1,323,226
Library Holdings: AV Mats 66,618; CDs 18,443; DVDs 14,494; Large Print Bks 7,325; Bk Vols 176,842; Per Subs 520; Talking Bks 10,522; Videos 18,448
Special Collections: Oral History
Subject Interests: Bus, Genealogy, Local hist
Automation Activity & Vendor Info: (Cataloging) OCLC; (Circulation) SirsiDynix; (ILL) OCLC
Wireless access
Partic in Northeast Ohio Regional Library System; OCLC Online Computer Library Center, Inc; OhioNET
Open Mon-Thurs 9-9, Fri & Sat 9-5, Sun 1-5
Friends of the Library Group

WESTON

P WESTON PUBLIC LIBRARY*, 13153 Main St, 43569. (Mail add: PO Box 345, 43569), SAN 313-7961. Tel: 419-669-3415. FAX: 419-669-3216. Web Site: westonpl.org. *Dir,* Shelen A Stevens; E-mail: sstevens@westonpl.org
Founded 1942. Pop 24,000; Circ 88,989
Library Holdings: Bk Vols 72,000; Per Subs 180
Subject Interests: Local hist
Automation Activity & Vendor Info: (Circulation) SirsiDynix
Wireless access
Publications: Weston Advocate (Monthly)
Partic in NORWELD; Serving Every Ohioan Library Center
Open Mon 10-7, Tues & Wed 12-7, Thurs & Fri 10-4
Friends of the Library Group
Branches: 1
GRAND RAPIDS BRANCH, 17620 Bridge St, Grand Rapids, 43522. (Mail add: PO Box 245, Grand Rapids, 43522), SAN 320-0981. Tel: 419-832-5231. FAX: 419-832-8104. *Mgr,* Darla Froman
Founded 1978
Open Mon-Wed 10-8, Thurs & Fri 10-5, Sat 10-3
Friends of the Library Group

WICKLIFFE

R SAINT MARY SEMINARY*, Bruening-Marotta Library, 28700 Euclid Ave, 44092. SAN 313-380X. Tel: 440-943-7665. FAX: 440-585-3528. Web Site: www.stmarysem.edu/library. *Librn,* Dr Alan K Rome; E-mail: akrome@dioceseofcleveland.org; Staff 1 (MLS 1)
Founded 1848. Enrl 90; Fac 15
Library Holdings: Bk Vols 80,000; Per Subs 240; Videos 1,000
Special Collections: Theology (Horstmann Coll)
Subject Interests: Canon law, Church hist, Ecumenism, Liturgy, Pastoral care, Scripture, Spirituality, Theol
Partic in Northeast Ohio Regional Library System
Open Mon-Thurs 8am-10pm, Fri 8-5, Sat 9-5, Sun 1-9

CR TELSHE YESHIVA COLLEGE*, Rabbi A N Schwartz Library, 28400 Euclid Ave, 44092. SAN 370-4203. Tel: 440-943-5300. FAX: 440-943-5303. E-mail: info@telsheyeshiva.edu.
Library Holdings: AV Mats 2,000; Bk Titles 20,000; Per Subs 10

P WICKLIFFE PUBLIC LIBRARY*, 1713 Lincoln Rd, 44092. SAN 313-8003. Tel: 440-944-6010. FAX: 440-944-7264. Circulation E-mail: circstaff.desk@wickliffe.lib.oh.us. Reference E-mail: ref.desk@wickliffe.lib.oh.us. Web Site: wickliffepl.org. *Dir,* Robin Bartley; *Fiscal Officer,* Richard A Zalecky; Staff 11 (MLS 6, Non-MLS 5)
Founded 1934. Pop 12,753; Circ 450,070
Library Holdings: Audiobooks 7,013; CDs 7,013; DVDs 10,958; e-books 11,647; e-journals 4; Electronic Media & Resources 293; High Interest/Low Vocabulary Bk Vols 667; Large Print Bks 3,460; Bk Titles 89,055; Bk Vols 104,159; Per Subs 318; Talking Bks 12,691
Subject Interests: Auto repair, Local hist
Automation Activity & Vendor Info: (Cataloging) SirsiDynix; (Circulation) SirsiDynix; (ILL) SirsiDynix; (OPAC) SirsiDynix
Wireless access

Function: 24/7 Electronic res, 24/7 Online cat, Adult bk club, After school storytime
Publications: Your Wickliffe Connection (Quarterly newsletter)
Partic in CLEVNET; Northeast Ohio Regional Library System
Special Services for the Deaf - Bks on deafness & sign lang; TTY equip
Special Services for the Blind - Aids for in-house use; Audio mat; Bks on cassette; Bks on CD; Large print bks; Magnifiers; Reader equip
Open Mon-Thurs 9-9, Fri 9-6, Sat 9-5, Sun (Nov-May) 1-5
Friends of the Library Group

WILBERFORCE

C CENTRAL STATE UNIVERSITY, Hallie Q Brown Memorial Library, 1400 Brush Row Rd, 45384. (Mail add: PO Box 1004, 45384), SAN 313-8011. Tel: 937-376-6106. Reference Tel: 937-376-6454. Toll Free Tel: 800-388-2781. FAX: 937-376-6132. Web Site: www.centralstate.edu/academics/support/library. *Dir,* Carolin Sterling; Tel: 937-376-6396, E-mail: csterling@centralstate.edu; *Media Spec,* A Carolyn Sanders; Tel: 937-376-6213, E-mail: csanders@centralstate.edu; *Archivist,* Sheila Darrow; Tel: 937-376-6521, E-mail: sdarrow@centralstate.edu; Staff 12 (MLS 6, Non-MLS 6)
Founded 1948. Enrl 2,022; Fac 131; Highest Degree: Master
Library Holdings: e-books 100,000; e-journals 64,000; Bk Vols 300,000; Per Subs 71
Special Collections: African Coll; Black Coll
Automation Activity & Vendor Info: (Acquisitions) Innovative Interfaces, Inc; (Cataloging) Innovative Interfaces, Inc; (Circulation) Innovative Interfaces, Inc; (Course Reserve) Innovative Interfaces, Inc; (ILL) Innovative Interfaces, Inc; (OPAC) Innovative Interfaces, Inc; (Serials) Innovative Interfaces, Inc
Wireless access
Publications: Index to Periodical Articles by & about Blacks; Primary Sources in African American History
Partic in Dayton-Miami Valley Consortium; OCLC Online Computer Library Center, Inc
Open Mon-Thurs 7:45am-10pm, Fri 7:45-5, Sat 1-5, Sun 1-10
Friends of the Library Group

R PAYNE THEOLOGICAL SEMINARY, Reverdy C Ransom Memorial Library, 1230 Wilberforce-Clifton Rd, 45384. (Mail add: PO Box 474, 45384-0474), SAN 313-802X. Tel: 937-971-2853. Toll Free Tel: 888-816-8933. FAX: 937-376-2888. E-mail: library@payneseminary.edu. Web Site: payneseminary.edu/library. *Cataloger,* Lynn Ayers; E-mail: layers@payneseminary.edu; Staff 1 (MLS 1)
Founded 1956. Enrl 95; Fac 9; Highest Degree: Master
Library Holdings: Bk Vols 25,000; Per Subs 67
Special Collections: African American Coll
Subject Interests: Biblical studies, Church hist, Doctrinal theol, Ethics, Ethnic studies, Judaica, Philos
Wireless access
Partic in Statewide California Electronic Library Consortium
Open Mon-Fri 9-5

C WILBERFORCE UNIVERSITY, Rembert E Stokes Library & Information Commons, 1055 N Bickett Rd, 45384-5801. (Mail add: PO Box 1001-1003, 45384-1003), SAN 313-8038. Tel: 937-502-3955. E-mail: library@wilberforce.edu. Web Site: wilberforce.edu/academic-affairs/the-rembert-e-stokes-library-and-information-commons. *Dir,* Stephenie Rostron; E-mail: srostron@wilberforce.edu; Staff 2 (MLS 1, Non-MLS 1)
Founded 1856. Enrl 755; Fac 51; Highest Degree: Bachelor
Library Holdings: CDs 100; DVDs 50; e-books 12,000; e-journals 500; Bk Vols 70,000; Per Subs 500; Videos 200
Special Collections: Afro-American History (Arnett-Coppin & Payne), scrapbks, newsp clippings, handbills & some correspondence; History of African Methodist Episcopal Church; Joseph Lewis Oral History Coll. Oral History
Automation Activity & Vendor Info: (Cataloging) OCLC; (Circulation) OCLC; (Course Reserve) OCLC; (OPAC) OCLC
Wireless access
Partic in OCLC Online Computer Library Center, Inc; Ohio Library & Information Network; Ohio Private Academic Libraries
Open Mon-Fri 9-5

WILLARD

P HURON COUNTY COMMUNITY LIBRARY*, Willard Memorial Library, Six W Emerald St, 44890. SAN 357-3095. Tel: 419-933-8564. Administration Tel: 419-933-2544. FAX: 419-933-4783. TDD: 800-750-0750. Web Site: www.huroncolib.org. *Dir,* Laura Lee Wilson; E-mail: director@huroncolib.org; *Fiscal Officer,* Joshua Figley; E-mail: fiscaloffice@huroncolib.org; *Library Services, Staff Coordr,* Jen Farrell; E-mail: jfarrell@huroncolib.org; Staff 16 (MLS 2, Non-MLS 14)
Founded 1921. Pop 27,957; Circ 180,505
Jan 2019-Dec 2019. Mats Exp $165,050. Sal $657,500
Library Holdings: AV Mats 16,389; Bk Vols 60,929; Per Subs 62
Special Collections: Grant Coll; Local History Coll (Huron County); Ohio History Coll; Railroad Books
Automation Activity & Vendor Info: (Cataloging) SirsiDynix; (Circulation) SirsiDynix; (ILL) SirsiDynix; (Media Booking) SirsiDynix; (OPAC) SirsiDynix; (Serials) SirsiDynix
Wireless access
Function: 24/7 Electronic res, 24/7 Online cat, Activity rm, Adult bk club, After school storytime, Archival coll, Audiobks via web, AV serv, Bilingual assistance for Spanish patrons, Bk club(s), Bks on CD, Children's prog, Computer training, Computers for patron use, Digital talking bks, E-Readers, E-Reserves, Electronic databases & coll, Games & aids for people with disabilities, Govt ref serv, Holiday prog, Home delivery & serv to seniorr ctr & nursing homes, Homebound delivery serv, ILL available, Internet access, Laminating, Life-long learning prog for all ages, Magazines, Mail & tel request accepted, Meeting rooms, Movies, Music CDs, Notary serv, Online cat, OverDrive digital audio bks, Photocopying/Printing, Preschool outreach, Preschool reading prog, Prog for adults, Prog for children & young adult, Ref serv available, Scanner, Senior outreach, Serves people with intellectual disabilities, Spanish lang bks, STEM programs, Story hour, Study rm, Summer & winter reading prog, Tax forms, Teen prog, Wheelchair accessible
Partic in NORWELD; Serving Every Ohioan Library Center
Special Services for the Deaf - Assisted listening device; Bks on deafness & sign lang; Closed caption videos
Special Services for the Blind - Aids for in-house use; Bks available with recordings; Bks on CD; Copier with enlargement capabilities; Internet workstation with adaptive software; Large print bks; Large screen computer & software; Magnifiers; Recorded bks; Screen enlargement software for people with visual disabilities; Talking bk serv referral
Friends of the Library Group
Branches: 3

GREENWICH PUBLIC LIBRARY, Four New St, Greenwich, 44837, SAN 357-3125. Tel: 419-752-7331. FAX: 419-752-6801. Web Site: huroncolib.org/greenwich-public-library. *Br Mgr,* Christine Mills; E-mail: cmills@huroncolib.org; Staff 5 (Non-MLS 5)
Function: 24/7 Electronic res, 24/7 Online cat, Adult bk club, Audiobks via web, AV serv, Bk club(s), Bks on CD, Children's prog, Computers for patron use, Electronic databases & coll, Holiday prog, Homebound delivery serv, ILL available, Internet access, Laminating, Life-long learning prog for all ages, Magazines, Mail & tel request accepted, Music CDs, Online cat, OverDrive digital audio bks, Photocopying/Printing, Preschool outreach, Prog for adults, Prog for children & young adult, Ref & res, Scanner, STEM programs, Story hour, Summer reading prog, Tax forms, Teen prog, Telephone ref, Wheelchair accessible
Open Mon 10-7, Tues-Fri 10-5
Friends of the Library Group

NORTH FAIRFIELD PUBLIC LIBRARY, Five E Main St, North Fairfield, 44855. (Mail add: PO Box 175, North Fairfield, 44855), SAN 357-315X. Tel: 419-744-2285. FAX: 419-744-2115. Web Site: huroncolib.org/north-fairfield-public-library. *Br Mgr,* Christine Mills; E-mail: cmills@huroncolib.org; Staff 4 (Non-MLS 4)
Function: 24/7 Electronic res, 24/7 Online cat, Adult bk club, Bks on CD, Children's prog, Computers for patron use, Holiday prog, Homebound delivery serv, ILL available, Internet access, Magazines, Mail & tel request accepted, Movies, Notary serv, Online cat, Online ref, OverDrive digital audio bks, Photocopying/Printing, Preschool outreach, Prog for children & young adult, Ref & res, Scanner, Story hour, Summer reading prog, Tax forms, Teen prog, Telephone ref, Wheelchair accessible

WAKEMAN COMMUNITY LIBRARY, 33 Pleasant St, Wakeman, 44889, SAN 357-3184. Tel: 440-839-2976. FAX: 440-839-2560. Web Site: huroncolib.org/wakeman-community-library. *Br Mgr,* Victoria Vogel; Staff 5 (MLS 1, Non-MLS 4)
Founded 1951
Function: Activity rm, Adult bk club, After school storytime, Audiobks via web, AV serv, Bk club(s), Bks on cassette, Children's prog, Computer training, Computers for patron use, Electronic databases & coll, Holiday prog, Homebound delivery serv, ILL available, Internet access, Laminating, Magazines, Meeting rooms, Movies, Music CDs, Notary serv, Online cat, Online ref, Outreach serv, Photocopying/Printing, Preschool outreach, Prog for adults, Prog for children & young adult, Ref & res, Story hour, Summer reading prog, Tax forms, Teen prog, Telephone ref, Wheelchair accessible
Friends of the Library Group

WILMINGTON

GL CLINTON COUNTY LAW LIBRARY, Clinton County Courthouse, 3rd Flr, 46 S South St, 45177. SAN 313-8062. Tel: 937-382-2428. FAX: 937-382-7632. Web Site: co.clinton.oh.us/departments/LawLibrary. *Law Librn,* Martha Worstine; E-mail: Worstine.Martha@clintoncountyohio.us
Founded 1905
Library Holdings: Bk Vols 25,000

Wireless access
Open Tues-Thurs 9-12 & 1-4

C WILMINGTON COLLEGE, Sheppard Arthur Watson Library, 120 College St, 45177. (Mail add: Pyle Center 1227, 1870 Quaker Way, 45177-2473), SAN 313-8070. Tel: 937-481-2345. Toll Free Tel: 800-341-9318. E-mail: library@wilmington.edu. Web Site: libguides.wilmington.edu/watsonlibrary. *Dir,* Lucinda Chandler; E-mail: lucinda_chandler@wilmington.edu; *Head, Ref (Info Serv),* Elizabeth House; Tel: 937-481-2441, E-mail: elizabeth_house@wilmington.edu; *Cataloger, Librn,* Lee Bowman; Tel: 937-481-2394; *Mgr, Tech Serv,* Kathy Hatfield; Tel: 937-481-2398, E-mail: kathernh@wilmington.edu; *Circ Coordr,* Kim Bowman; E-mail: kim.bowman@wilmington.edu. Subject Specialists: *Quaker res,* Elizabeth House; *Archives,* Lee Bowman; Staff 5 (MLS 3, Non-MLS 2)
Founded 1870. Enrl 1,350; Fac 76; Highest Degree: Master
Library Holdings: e-books 445,622; e-journals 96,519; Electronic Media & Resources 7,469; Bk Titles 74,179; Per Subs 100; Videos 2,552
Special Collections: College Archives; Peace Resources Center-Hiroshima & Nagasaki Memorial Coll; Quakers-Quakerism Coll, bks, ms, per
Automation Activity & Vendor Info: (Acquisitions) Innovative Interfaces, Inc; (Cataloging) Innovative Interfaces, Inc; (Circulation) Innovative Interfaces, Inc; (Course Reserve) Innovative Interfaces, Inc; (Discovery) EBSCO Discovery Service; (ILL) OCLC; (OPAC) Innovative Interfaces, Inc; (Serials) Innovative Interfaces, Inc
Wireless access
Function: Archival coll, Doc delivery serv, Electronic databases & coll, ILL available, Internet access, Magazines, Mail & tel request accepted, Microfiche/film & reading machines, Online cat, Online info literacy tutorials on the web & in blackboard, Orientations, Photocopying/Printing, Printer for laptops & handheld devices, Ref serv available, Scanner, Telephone ref, Wheelchair accessible
Partic in OCLC Online Computer Library Center, Inc; Ohio Library & Information Network; Ohio Private Academic Libraries; OhioNET; Southwestern Ohio Council for Higher Education
Special Services for the Blind - Scanner for conversion & translation of mats
Open Mon-Thurs 8am-10pm, Fri 8-5, Sun 6pm-10pm; Mon-Thurs 8-5 (Summer)
Restriction: Access at librarian's discretion, Authorized patrons, Authorized personnel only, Authorized scholars by appt, Circ to mem only, Non-circulating of rare bks, Off-site coll in storage - retrieval as requested, Open to researchers by request, Open to students, fac, staff & alumni, Private libr, Registered patrons only, Researchers by appt only

P WILMINGTON PUBLIC LIBRARY OF CLINTON COUNTY, 268 N South St, 45177-1696. SAN 313-8089. Tel: 937-382-2417. FAX: 937-382-1692. Web Site: www.wilmington.lib.oh.us. *Dir,* Joe Knueven; Staff 4 (MLS 2, Non-MLS 2)
Founded 1899. Pop 42,000; Circ 170,061
Library Holdings: Audiobooks 1,476; AV Mats 8,669; Bks on Deafness & Sign Lang 37; CDs 1,341; DVDs 3,994; Large Print Bks 1,422; Bk Vols 46,886; Per Subs 40; Videos 1,858
Special Collections: Ohio Coll; Wilmington News-Journal
Subject Interests: Genealogy, Ohio
Automation Activity & Vendor Info: (Cataloging) Follett Software; (Circulation) Follett Software; (OPAC) Follett Software
Wireless access
Partic in Consortium of Ohio Libraries
Open Mon-Thurs 10-6, Fri 10-4, Sat 10-2
Friends of the Library Group
Branches: 1
CLINTON-MASSIE BRANCH, 2556 Lebanon Rd, Clarksville, 45113. Tel: 937-289-1079. *Br Mgr,* Kat McKay
Founded 2004
Open Mon-Thurs 1-6

WOODSFIELD

P MONROE COUNTY DISTRICT LIBRARY, 96 Home Ave, 43793. SAN 313-8100. Tel: 740-472-1954. FAX: 740-472-1110. Web Site: www.monroecounty.lib.oh.us. *Dir,* Kathy South; E-mail: ksouth@seolibraries.org
Founded 1939. Pop 14,700; Circ 200,000
Jan 2019-Dec 2019 Income $520,144. Mats Exp $83,371
Library Holdings: AV Mats 2,514; DVDs 500; Bk Vols 70,000; Per Subs 140; Talking Bks 1,100; Videos 2,014
Automation Activity & Vendor Info: (Acquisitions) SirsiDynix; (Cataloging) SirsiDynix; (Circulation) SirsiDynix; (OPAC) SirsiDynix; (Serials) EBSCO Online
Wireless access
Partic in Serving Every Ohioan Library Center
Open Mon, Tues, Thurs & Fri 10-5, Wed 10-7, Sat 10-2

WOOSTER

C THE COLLEGE OF WOOSTER LIBRARIES*, 1140 Beall Ave, 44691-2364. SAN 313-8119. Tel: 330-263-2442. Circulation Tel: 330-263-2137. Interlibrary Loan Service Tel: 330-263-2136. Reference Tel: 330-263-2096. Administration Tel: 330-263-2152. FAX: 330-263-2253. Web Site: wooster.edu/academics/libraries. *Interim Librn,* Zachary Sharrow; E-mail: zsharrow@wooster.edu; *Head, Access Serv,* Michael Buttrey; E-mail: mbuttrey@wooster.edu; *Discovery Serv Librn, Head, Coll Mgt,* Mark Gooch; Tel: 330-263-2522, E-mail: mgooch@wooster.edu; *Digital Scholarship Librn, Head, Core Serv, IT,* Jacob Heil; Tel: 330-263-2204, E-mail: jheil@wooster.edu; *Librn,* Annie Dempsey; Tel: 330-263-2154, E-mail: adempsey@wooster.edu; *Institutional Repository/Digital Coll Librn,* Jennifer Yandle; Tel: 330-263-2130, E-mail: jyandle@wooster.edu; *Res & Info Serv Librn,* Elys Kettling Law; Tel: 330-263-2443, E-mail: ekettling@wooster.edu; *Sci Librn,* Zachary Sharrow; *Spec Coll Librn,* Denise Monbarren; Tel: 330-263-2527, E-mail: dmonbarren@wooster.edu; *Admin Coordr,* Upi Gunawan; *Digital Coll Curator,* Catie Heil; Tel: 330-263-2225, E-mail: cheil@wooster.edu; *Access Services Assoc, Evening Supvr, Sci,* Alena Michal; Tel: 330-263-2275, E-mail: amichal@wooster.edu; *Acq Assoc,* Erin Christine; Tel: 330-263-2467; *Cataloging Assoc,* Kathleen Garvey; Tel: 330-263-2093, E-mail: kgarvey@wooster.edu; *Collection Mgmt Assoc,* Amy Sexton; Tel: 330-263-2107, E-mail: asexton@wooster.edu; *ILL Assoc,* Dottie Sines; E-mail: dsines@wooster.edu; *Access Serv,* Position Currently Open; Staff 17 (MLS 8, Non-MLS 9)
Founded 1866. Enrl 1,826; Fac 140; Highest Degree: Bachelor
Library Holdings: AV Mats 23,761; Bk Titles 525,192; Bk Vols 622,273; Per Subs 1,195
Special Collections: 17th Century British Studies (Wallace Notestein Coll); American Politics (Paul O Peters Coll); Drama & Theatre (Gregg D Wolfe Memorial Library of the Theatre). US Document Depository
Automation Activity & Vendor Info: (Acquisitions) Innovative Interfaces, Inc; (Cataloging) Innovative Interfaces, Inc; (Circulation) Innovative Interfaces, Inc; (Course Reserve) Innovative Interfaces, Inc; (ILL) Innovative Interfaces, Inc; (Media Booking) Innovative Interfaces, Inc; (OPAC) Innovative Interfaces, Inc; (Serials) Innovative Interfaces, Inc
Wireless access
Function: Res libr
Partic in Five Colleges of Ohio; Oberlin Group; OCLC Online Computer Library Center, Inc; Ohio Library & Information Network; OhioNET
Special Services for the Blind - Assistive/Adapted tech devices, equip & products
Open Mon-Thurs 8am-Midnight, Fri 8-7, Sat 10-7, Sun Noon-Midnight (Fall); Mon-Fri 8-5
Restriction: Open to pub for ref & circ; with some limitations

S OHIO AGRICULTURAL RESEARCH & DEVELOPMENT CENTER LIBRARY*, 1680 Madison Ave, 44691-4096. SAN 313-8135. Tel: 330-263-3773. FAX: 330-263-3689. E-mail: library_oardc@osu.edu. Web Site: osu.libguides.com/oardclibrary. *Librn,* Gwen Short; E-mail: short.67@osu.edu; *Assoc Librn,* Laura Applegate; Tel: 330-202-3580, E-mail: applegate.87@osu.edu; Staff 2 (MLS 1, Non-MLS 1)
Founded 1892
Library Holdings: Bk Vols 69,742; Per Subs 250
Subject Interests: Sci related to agr
Automation Activity & Vendor Info: (Acquisitions) Innovative Interfaces, Inc; (Cataloging) OCLC; (Circulation) Innovative Interfaces, Inc; (ILL) OCLC ILLiad; (OPAC) Innovative Interfaces, Inc; (Serials) Innovative Interfaces, Inc
Wireless access
Partic in Council of Independent Colleges; OCLC Online Computer Library Center, Inc; Ohio Library & Information Network; OhioNET
Open Mon-Fri 8-5

GL WAYNE COUNTY LAW LIBRARY*, Wayne County Courthouse, 107 W Liberty St, 44691-4850. SAN 313-816X. Tel: 330-287-7721. E-mail: lawlib@sssnet.com. Web Site: www.waynelawlibrary.org. *Librn,* William B Weiss
Founded 1903
Library Holdings: Bk Vols 9,000
Wireless access
Partic in Consortium of Ohio County Law Libraries
Open Mon-Fri 9-1

P WAYNE COUNTY PUBLIC LIBRARY*, 220 W Liberty St, 44691. (Mail add: PO Box 1349, 44691-7086), SAN 357-3338. Tel: 330-262-0916. Circulation Tel: 330-804-4659. Reference Tel: 330-804-4666. FAX: 330-804-4745. Interlibrary Loan Service FAX: 330-804-4745. Reference FAX: 330-804-4747. Administration FAX: 330-262-2905. E-mail: wooster@wcpl.info. Web Site: wcpl.info. *Dir,* Jennifer Shatzer; Tel: 330-262-0986, E-mail: jshatzer@wcpl.info; *Asst Dir,* Susan Roberts; Tel: 330-262-4087, E-mail: sroberts@wcpl.info; *Br Coordr,* Rita Lowe; Tel: 330-804-4698, E-mail: rlowe@wcpl.info; *Fiscal Officer,* Katherine Long;

Tel: 330-804-4680, E-mail: klong@wcpl.info; *Human Res,* Susan Buchwalter; Tel: 330-804-4683, E-mail: sbuchwalter@wcpl.info; Staff 76 (MLS 18.5, Non-MLS 57.5)
Founded 1897. Pop 103,658; Circ 2,033,725
Jan 2018-Dec 2018 Income (Main & Associated Libraries) $5,714,281, State $3,067,776, County $2,032,757, Locally Generated Income $268,052, Other $323,285. Mats Exp $706,355, Books $405,117, Per/Ser (Incl. Access Fees) $108,805, Other Print Mats $1,618, AV Mat $147,910, Electronic Ref Mat (Incl. Access Fees) $42,908. Sal $2,223,064
Library Holdings: CDs 23,727; DVDs 37,348; e-books 286,038; Electronic Media & Resources 92,325; Bk Vols 312,339; Per Subs 719
Subject Interests: Genealogy, Local hist
Automation Activity & Vendor Info: (Acquisitions) SirsiDynix; (Cataloging) SirsiDynix; (Circulation) SirsiDynix; (ILL) SirsiDynix; (OPAC) SirsiDynix; (Serials) SirsiDynix
Wireless access
Function: 24/7 Electronic res, 24/7 Online cat, Art exhibits, Audiobks via web, Bk club(s), Bks on cassette, Bks on CD, CD-ROM, Children's prog, Computer training, Computers for patron use, Digital talking bks, Distance learning, E-Reserves, Electronic databases & coll, Family literacy, Free DVD rentals, Games & aids for people with disabilities, Holiday prog, Home delivery & serv to seniorr ctr & nursing homes, Homebound delivery serv, ILL available, Internet access, Magazines, Magnifiers for reading, Mail & tel request accepted, Meeting rooms, Movies, Music CDs, Online cat, Online ref, Outreach serv, Outside serv via phone, mail, e-mail & web, OverDrive digital audio bks, Photocopying/Printing, Preschool outreach, Preschool reading prog, Prog for adults, Prog for children & young adult, Ref & res, Ref serv available, Res assist avail, Senior computer classes, Senior outreach, Spoken cassettes & CDs, Spoken cassettes & DVDs, STEM programs, Story hour, Study rm, Summer reading prog, Tax forms, Teen prog, Wheelchair accessible, Workshops
Partic in CLEVNET
Special Services for the Deaf - Assistive tech; Bks on deafness & sign lang; Closed caption videos; Described encaptioned media prog; High interest/low vocabulary bks
Special Services for the Blind - Assistive/Adapted tech devices, equip & products; Audio mat; Bks available with recordings; Bks on cassette; Bks on CD; Cassette playback machines; Cassettes; Computer access aids; Descriptive video serv (DVS); Digital talking bk; Extensive large print coll; Home delivery serv; Internet workstation with adaptive software; Large print & cassettes; Large print bks; Large print bks & talking machines; Large screen computer & software; Low vision equip; Magnifiers; Recorded bks; Screen reader software; Sound rec; Talking bk serv referral; Talking bks & player equip; ZoomText magnification & reading software
Open Mon, Tues & Thurs 9:30-8:30, Wed & Fri 9:30-6, Sat 9:30-3
Friends of the Library Group
Branches: 6
CRESTON BRANCH, 116 S Main St, Creston, 44217. (Mail add: PO Box 396, Creston, 44217-0396), SAN 357-3397. Tel: 330-804-4732. FAX: 330-804-4703. E-mail: creston@wcpl.info. *Br Mgr,* Amy Anderson; E-mail: aanderson@wcpl.info
Subject Interests: Local hist
Open Mon, Tues & Thurs 10-8, Wed & Fri 10-5, Sat 10-2
Friends of the Library Group
DALTON BRANCH, 127 S Church St, Dalton, 44618. (Mail add: PO Box 597, Dalton, 44618-0597), SAN 323-8342. Tel: 330-828-8486. FAX: 330-828-0255. E-mail: dalton@wcpl.info. *Br Mgr,* Teresa Jager; E-mail: tjager@wcpl.info
Founded 1989
Partic in CLEVNET
Open Mon, Tues & Thurs 10-8, Wed & Fri 10-5, Sat 10-2
Friends of the Library Group
DOYLESTOWN BRANCH, 169 N Portage St, Doylestown, 44230, SAN 357-3427. Tel: 330-804-4689. E-mail: doylestown@wcpl.info. *Br Mgr,* Beth Brawley; E-mail: bbrawley@wcpl.info
Open Mon, Tues & Thurs 10-8, Wed & Fri 10-5, Sat 10-2
Friends of the Library Group
RITTMAN BRANCH, 49 W Ohio Ave, Rittman, 44270, SAN 357-3451. Tel: 330-925-2761. FAX: 330-925-6217. E-mail: rittman@wcpl.info. *Br Mgr,* Pam Schemrich; E-mail: pschemrich@wcpl.info
Open Mon, Tues & Thurs 10-8, Wed & Fri 10-5, Sat 10-5
Friends of the Library Group
SHREVE BRANCH, 189 W McConkey St, Shreve, 44676. (Mail add: PO Box 612, Shreve, 44676-0612), SAN 357-3362. Tel: 330-567-2219. FAX: 330-567-2791. E-mail: shreve@wcpl.info. *Br Mgr,* Nancy Fortune; E-mail: nfortune@wcpl.info
Subject Interests: Local hist
Open Mon, Tues & Thurs 10-8, Wed & Fri 10-5, Sat 10-2
Friends of the Library Group
WEST SALEM BRANCH, 99 E Buckeye St, West Salem, 44287. Tel: 330-804-4712. E-mail: westsalem@wcpl.info. *Br Supvr,* Debbie Starcher; Fax: 419-853-4572, E-mail: dstarcher@wcpl.info
Open Tues 10-8, Wed 1-5, Thurs 12-8, Sat 10-2
Friends of the Library Group
Bookmobiles: 2. Mgr, Trisha Durieux

WORTHINGTON

S WORTHINGTON HISTORICAL SOCIETY LIBRARY, 50 W New England Ave, 43085. SAN 327-5639. Tel: 614-885-1247. E-mail: info@worthingtonhistory.org. Web Site: www.worthingtonhistory.org. *Pres,* Jutta Catharine Pegues; *Coll Curator,* Sue Whitaker
Founded 1955
Library Holdings: Bk Vols 5,500
Special Collections: Manuscript Colls
Subject Interests: Archives, Interior design, Local hist
Restriction: Open by appt only

P WORTHINGTON LIBRARIES*, Old Worthington Library, 820 High St, 43085. SAN 313-8186. Tel: 614-807-2626. Administration Tel: 614-807-2600. FAX: 614-807-2642. Web Site: www.worthingtonlibraries.org. *Dir,* Chuck Gibson; Tel: 614-807-2601, E-mail: cgibson@worthingtonlibraries.org; *Dep Dir,* Monica Baughman; Tel: 614-807-2602, E-mail: mbaughman@worthingtonlibraries.org; *Dir, Commun Engagement,* Lisa Fuller; Tel: 614-807-2604, E-mail: lfuller@worthingtonlibraries.org; *Chief Fiscal Officer,* Sam Kraly; Tel: 614-807-2609, E-mail: skraly@worthingtonlibraries.org; *Libr Mgr,* Debbie Hogan; Tel: 614-807-2622, E-mail: dhogan@worthingtonlibraries.org; *Tech Serv Mgr,* Anne Reilly; Tel: 614-807-2631, E-mail: areilly@worthingtonlibraries.org; Staff 99 (MLS 28, Non-MLS 71)
Founded 1925. Pop 73,586; Circ 3,556,803
Library Holdings: Bk Vols 410,843
Special Collections: Worthington History Coll. US Document Depository
Subject Interests: Local authors
Wireless access
Publications: A Page Turner (Newsletter)
Partic in Central Library Consortium
Open Mon-Thurs 9-9, Fri & Sat 9-6, Sun 1-5
Friends of the Library Group
Branches: 2
NORTHWEST LIBRARY, 2280 Hard Rd, Columbus, 43235. FAX: 614-807-2659. *Libr Mgr,* Jeff Regensburger; Tel: 614-807-2652, E-mail: jregensb@worthingtonlibraries.org; *Circ Mgr,* Jessi Tisdale; Tel: 614-807-2655, E-mail: jtisdale@worthingtonlibraries.org
Open Mon-Thurs 9-9, Fri & Sat 9-6, Sun 1-5
WORTHINGTON PARK LIBRARY, 1389 Worthington Centre Dr, 43085. FAX: 614-807-2676. *Libr Mgr,* Amy Brown; Tel: 614-807-2624, E-mail: abrown@worthingtonlibraries.org; *Circ Mgr,* Erin Wilson; Tel: 614-807-2674, E-mail: ewilson@worthingtonlibraries.org
Open Mon-Thurs 9-9, Fri & Sat 9-6, Sun 1-5

WRIGHT-PATTERSON AFB

UNITED STATES AIR FORCE
A AIR FORCE RESEARCH LABORATORY, WRIGHT RESEARCH SITE*, Det 1 AFRL/WSC, Bldg 642, Rm 1300, 2950 Hobson Way, 45433-7765, SAN 357-3605. Tel: 937-255-5511. Interlibrary Loan Service Tel: 937-255-5511, Ext 4262. Reference Tel: 937-255-5511, Ext 4238. FAX: 937-656-7746. E-mail: afrl.wsc.library@wpafb.af.mil. Web Site: www.afrl.af.mil/wrslibrary. *Dir,* Annette Sheppard; Tel: 937-255-5511, Ext 4205; *Ref (Info Servs),* Carol Reed; Tel: 937-255-5511, Ext 4271; Staff 11 (MLS 5, Non-MLS 6)
Founded 1919
Library Holdings: Bk Vols 84,000; Per Subs 170
Special Collections: Lahm-Chandler Coll of Aeronautica
Subject Interests: Aeronautical res, Aerospace med, Avionics, Co-applications to aeronaut, Computer sci, Engr, Flight dynamics, Mat, Propulsion
Function: ILL available

A THE D'AZZO RESEARCH LIBRARY*, AFIT/ENWL, 2950 Hobson Way, Bldg 642, 45433-7765, SAN 357-3664. Tel: 937-255-6565, Ext 4207. Circulation Tel: 937-255-3005. Interlibrary Loan Service Tel: 937-255-6565, Ext 4227. FAX: 937-656-7746. Web Site: www.afit.edu/library. *Dir,* Laurene E Zaporozhetz; Tel: 937-255-6565, Ext 4216, E-mail: laurene.zaporozhetz@afit.edu; Staff 15 (MLS 9, Non-MLS 6)
Founded 1946
Oct 2012-Sept 2013 Income $2,455,545. Mats Exp $1,248,246, Books $25,333, Per/Ser (Incl. Access Fees) $1,219,043, Micro $452, AV Mat $204
Library Holdings: CDs 149; DVDs 1,462; e-journals 213; Microforms 1,225,783; Bk Vols 138,808; Per Subs 574
Special Collections: Air Force Institute of Technology Theses & Dissertations
Subject Interests: Astronautics, Computers, Engr, Math, Mil logistics
Partic in OCLC Online Computer Library Center, Inc; Southwestern Ohio Council for Higher Education
Open Mon-Thurs 8-6, Fri 8-5

A NATIONAL AIR & SPACE INTELLIGENCE CENTER RESEARCH CENTER*, 4180 Watson Way, 45433-5648, SAN 357-363X. Tel: 937-257-3531. FAX: 937-257-0122. *Chief, Acq & Res Flight,* Thomas

Rohmiller; E-mail: thomas.rohmiller@wpafb.af.mil; *Ref (Info Servs),* Joseph Burke; E-mail: joseph.burke@wpafb.af.mil; Staff 15 (MLS 9, Non-MLS 6)
Automation Activity & Vendor Info: (Cataloging) EOS International; (Circulation) EOS International; (ILL) OCLC; (OPAC) EOS International

A WRIGHT-PATTERSON AIR FORCE BASE LIBRARY FL2300*, 88 MSG/SVMG, Bldg 1226, 5435 Hemlock St, 45433-5420, SAN 357-3575. Tel: 937-257-4340, 937-257-4815. FAX: 937-656-1776. Web Site: www.88thservices.com/library.htm. *Chief Librn,* Nathaniel Laubner; *Sr Libr Tech,* Deborah Thomas; *Ref Librn,* Amanda Lindsay; Staff 8 (MLS 2, Non-MLS 6)
Founded 1942
Library Holdings: AV Mats 4,600; Bk Titles 36,000; Per Subs 500
Special Collections: Air War Coll; Chief of Staff of the Air Force Reading List; Total Quality Management Coll
Subject Interests: Mil hist
Automation Activity & Vendor Info: (Acquisitions) SirsiDynix; (Cataloging) SirsiDynix; (Circulation) SirsiDynix; (OPAC) SirsiDynix
Function: AV serv, ILL available, Photocopying/Printing, Prog for children & young adult, Summer reading prog
Open Tues-Thurs 10-9, Fri 10-6, Sat 10-5, Sun 11-6
Restriction: Access for corporate affiliates

AM UNITED STATES AIR FORCE SCHOOL OF AEROSPACE MEDICINE*, Franzello AeroMedical Library, USAFSAM/EDM, 2510 Fifth St, Bldg 840 E100, 45433. SAN 330-1893. Tel: 937-938-3592. Circulation Tel: 937-938-2860. E-mail: SAMFranAeroMedLib@us.af.mil. *Lead Librn,* Kristen Young; Staff 6 (MLS 4, Non-MLS 2)
Founded 1913
Library Holdings: e-books 712; Microforms 4,256; Bk Titles 29,503; Spec Interest Per Sub 50
Special Collections: Archives relating to Medicine and Aerospace
Subject Interests: Aerospace med
Automation Activity & Vendor Info: (Acquisitions) SirsiDynix; (Cataloging) SirsiDynix; (Circulation) SirsiDynix; (Course Reserve) SirsiDynix; (Discovery) EBSCO Discovery Service; (ILL) OCLC; (OPAC) SirsiDynix; (Serials) SirsiDynix
Wireless access
Partic in Docline; Federal Library & Information Network
Open Mon-Thurs 7-5, Fri 7-4:30

G UNITED STATES DEPARTMENT OF DEFENSE, Defense Institute of Security Cooperation Studies Library, 2475 K St, Rm 315, Bldg 52, 45433-7641. SAN 357-3516. Tel: 937-255-5567. FAX: 937-255-8258. *Dir,* Patricia A White; Tel: 937-713-3259, E-mail: patricia.a.white248.civ@mail.mil; *Acq, ILL,* Maggie Williams; Tel: 937-713-3258; Staff 3 (MLS 1, Non-MLS 2)
Founded 1977
Library Holdings: DVDs 150; Bk Vols 14,000; Per Subs 221; Videos 750
Special Collections: Human Rights; Regional Studies; Security Assistance
Subject Interests: Polit sci
Function: 24/7 Online cat, Govt ref serv, ILL available, Ref serv available, Telephone ref
Partic in OCLC Online Computer Library Center, Inc
Open Mon-Fri 7-5

XENIA

GL GREENE COUNTY LAW LIBRARY, Court House, 3rd Flr, 45 N Detroit St, 45385. SAN 313-8194. Tel: 937-562-5115. FAX: 937-562-5116. Web Site: www.co.greene.oh.us/index.aspx?NID=411. *Librn,* Nancy Hedges; E-mail: nhedges@co.greene.oh.us; *Asst Librn,* Brenda Davis
Library Holdings: Bk Vols 12,000; Per Subs 25
Wireless access
Open Mon-Fri 8-4
Restriction: Open to pub for ref only

P GREENE COUNTY PUBLIC LIBRARY*, 76 E Market St, 45385-3100. (Mail add: PO Box 520, 45385-0520), SAN 357-3729. Tel: 937-352-4000. FAX: 937-372-4673. Web Site: www.greenelibrary.info. *Dir,* Karl Colon; E-mail: kcolon@gcpl.lib.oh.us; *Asst Dir, Mgr,* Brenda Charney; Staff 10 (MLS 6, Non-MLS 4)
Founded 1878. Pop 157,000; Circ 2,279,973
Library Holdings: AV Mats 83,771; Large Print Bks 7,696; Bk Titles 220,100; Bk Vols 547,729; Per Subs 635
Subject Interests: Local hist
Automation Activity & Vendor Info: (Acquisitions) Innovative Interfaces, Inc - Millennium; (Cataloging) Innovative Interfaces, Inc - Millennium; (Circulation) Innovative Interfaces, Inc - Millennium; (ILL) Innovative Interfaces, Inc - Millennium; (OPAC) Innovative Interfaces, Inc; (Serials) Innovative Interfaces, Inc - Millennium
Wireless access
Partic in Miami Valley Librs; OCLC Online Computer Library Center, Inc; Ohio Public Library Information Network; OhioNET; SouthWest Ohio & Neighboring Libraries
Special Services for the Blind - Bks available with recordings; Bks on cassette; Bks on CD; Computer with voice synthesizer for visually impaired persons; Descriptive video serv (DVS); Home delivery serv; Talking bks
Open Mon-Thurs 9-9, Fri & Sat 9-6, Sun (Sept-May) 1-5
Friends of the Library Group
Branches: 7
BEAVERCREEK COMMUNITY LIBRARY, 3618 Dayton-Xenia Rd, Beavercreek, 45432-2884, SAN 357-3753. Tel: 937-352-4001. FAX: 937-426-0481. Web Site: greenelibrary.info/locations/b. *Head Librn,* Nancy Madden; E-mail: nmadden@gcpl.lib.oh.us
Library Holdings: AV Mats 18,982; Bk Vols 136,367
Open Mon-Thurs 10-8, Fri 10-5, Sat 10-6
Friends of the Library Group
CEDARVILLE COMMUNITY LIBRARY, 20 S Miller St, Cedarville, 45314-8556. (Mail add: PO Box 26, Cedarville, 45314-0026), SAN 357-3818. Tel: 937-352-4006. FAX: 937-766-2847. Web Site: greenelibrary.info/locations/c. *Head Librn,* Eden Allison; E-mail: eallison@gcpl.lib.oh.us
Library Holdings: AV Mats 7,910; Bk Vols 27,817
Open Mon-Thurs 10-8, Fri 10-6, Sat 10-5
Friends of the Library Group
FAIRBORN COMMUNITY LIBRARY, One E Main St, Fairborn, 45324-4798, SAN 357-3842. Tel: 937-878-9383. FAX: 937-878-0374. Web Site: greenelibrary.info/locations/f. *Head Librn,* Ann Cooper; E-mail: acooper@gcpl.lib.oh.us
Library Holdings: AV Mats 13,610; Bk Vols 103,277
Open Mon-Thurs 10-9, Fri 10-6, Sat 10-5
Friends of the Library Group
JAMESTOWN COMMUNITY LIBRARY, 86 Seaman Dr, Jamestown, 45335, SAN 357-3877. Tel: 937-352-4005. FAX: 937-675-6605. Web Site: greenelibrary.info/locations/j. *Head Librn,* Paul Gregor; E-mail: pgregor@gcpl.lib.oh.us
Library Holdings: AV Mats 7,662; Bk Vols 32,055
Open Mon-Thurs 10-8, Fri 10-6, Sat 10-5
Friends of the Library Group
WINTERS-BELLBROOK COMMUNITY LIBRARY, 57 W Franklin St, Bellbrook, 45305-1904, SAN 357-3788. Tel: 937-352-4004. FAX: 937-848-3074. Web Site: greenelibrary.info/locations/w. *Head Librn,* Susan Jeffery; E-mail: sjeffery@gcpl.lib.oh.us; Staff 3.5 (MLS 2, Non-MLS 1.5)
Founded 1906
Library Holdings: AV Mats 6,276; Bk Vols 33,887
Open Mon-Thurs 10-8, Fri 10-6, Sat 10-5
Friends of the Library Group
XENIA COMMUNITY LIBRARY, 76 E Market St, 45385-0520. Tel: 937-352-4000. FAX: 937-376-5523. Web Site: greenelibrary.info/locations/x. *Head Librn,* Melissa Fasanella; E-mail: mfasanella@gcpl.lib.oh.us
Library Holdings: AV Mats 19,820; Bk Vols 138,659
Open Mon-Thurs 10-8, Fri 10-6, Sat 10-5
Friends of the Library Group
YELLOW SPRINGS COMMUNITY LIBRARY, 415 Xenia Ave, Yellow Springs, 45387-1837, SAN 357-3931. Tel: 937-352-4003. FAX: 937-767-2044. Web Site: greenelibrary.info/locations/y. *Head Librn,* Connie Collett; E-mail: ccollett@gcpl.lib.oh.us
Library Holdings: AV Mats 9,511; Bk Vols 48,122
Open Mon-Thurs 10-8, Fri 10-6, Sat 10-5
Friends of the Library Group
Bookmobiles: 1. Coordr, Kay Webster. Bk titles 6,792

YELLOW SPRINGS

C ANTIOCH COLLEGE*, Olive Kettering Memorial Library, One Morgan Pl, 45387-1694. SAN 313-8216. Tel: 937-769-1240. FAX: 937-769-1239. E-mail: ac-library@antiochcollege.edu. Web Site: antiochcollege.libguides.com. *Dir,* Kevin Mulhall; Tel: 937-319-0104, E-mail: kmulhall@antiochcollege.org; *Col Archivist,* Scott Sanders; Tel: 973-319-0111, E-mail: ssanders@antiochcollege.org; *Tech Asst,* Sandy Coulter; E-mail: scoulter@antiochcollege.edu; Staff 5 (MLS 2, Non-MLS 3)
Founded 1852. Enrl 110; Fac 13; Highest Degree: Bachelor. Sal $293,424 (Prof $158,826)
Library Holdings: AV Mats 6,651; Bks on Deafness & Sign Lang 20; e-books 17,536; Bk Titles 194,203; Bk Vols 295,169; Per Subs 403
Special Collections: Antioch hist; Arthur Morgan Coll, doc, files; Horace Mann (Robert Straker Coll), bks, doc. Oral History
Automation Activity & Vendor Info: (Acquisitions) Innovative Interfaces, Inc; (Cataloging) Innovative Interfaces, Inc; (Circulation) Innovative Interfaces, Inc; (Course Reserve) Innovative Interfaces, Inc; (ILL) Innovative Interfaces, Inc; (Media Booking) Innovative Interfaces, Inc; (OPAC) Innovative Interfaces, Inc; (Serials) Innovative Interfaces, Inc
Wireless access

Partic in OCLC Online Computer Library Center, Inc; Ohio Library & Information Network; Ohio Private Academic Libraries; OhioNET; Southwestern Ohio Council for Higher Education
Open Mon-Wed 8:30-8, Thurs 8:30am-9pm, Fri 8:30-5, Sun 1-5

YOUNGSTOWN

S BUTLER INSTITUTE OF AMERICAN ART, Hopper Research Library, 524 Wick Ave, 44502. SAN 313-8259. Tel: 330-743-1711. FAX: 330-743-9567. E-mail: library@butlerart.com. Web Site: www.butlerart.com. *Libr & Archives Mgr,* Jean Shreffler; Tel: 330-743-1711, Ext 1312; Staff 2 (Non-MLS 2)
Founded 1986
Library Holdings: Bk Titles 5,900; Bk Vols 6,000
Special Collections: American Colonial to Contemporary Art, oils, watercolors, drawings, original prints; Sculpture & Ceramics
Subject Interests: Am art, Artists
Restriction: Mem only, Non-circulating to the pub, Open by appt only

GL MAHONING COUNTY LAW LIBRARY*, Courthouse 4th Flr, 120 Market St, 44503-1752. SAN 313-8267. Tel: 330-740-2295. Circulation Tel: 330-740-2295, Ext 7780. Reference Tel: 330-740-2295, Ext 7782. FAX: 330-744-1406. Web Site: www.mahoningcountyoh.gov/861/Law-Library. *Librn,* Susan McGrew; E-mail: smcgrew@mahoningcountyoh.gov; *Circ,* Patti Burkard; E-mail: pburkard@mahoningcountyoh.gov; Staff 2 (MLS 1, Non-MLS 1)
Founded 1906
Library Holdings: Bk Vols 25,000; Per Subs 140
Special Collections: Ohio Legal Journals
Subject Interests: Mahoning County legal mat, Ohio, Penn law, Selected city ordinances
Automation Activity & Vendor Info: (Cataloging) LibraryWorld, Inc; (Circulation) LibraryWorld, Inc; (OPAC) LibraryWorld, Inc; (Serials) LibraryWorld, Inc
Wireless access
Function: 24/7 Online cat, Electronic databases & coll, Internet access, Notary serv, Online cat, Ref & res, Ref serv available, Res assist avail, Res libr, Scanner, Wheelchair accessible
Open Mon-Fri 8-4:15
Restriction: By permission only, Circ limited, Circ to mem only, Pub access for legal res only, Pub use on premises

M MERCY HEALTH SAINT ELIZABETH HEALTH CENTER*, Medical Library, 1044 Belmont Ave, 44501-1790. SAN 357-4504. Tel: 330-480-3039. *Dir, Med Libr,* Dr Kimbroe Carter; E-mail: kjcarter@mercy.com; *Librn,* Lori Gawdyda; Tel: 330-480-3589, Fax: 330-480-7977, E-mail: lori_gawdyda@mercy.com; Staff 2 (MLS 1, Non-MLS 1)
Founded 1911
Library Holdings: Bk Titles 2,500; Per Subs 66
Subject Interests: Med, Surgery
Wireless access
Open Mon-Fri 7:30-4

P PUBLIC LIBRARY OF YOUNGSTOWN & MAHONING COUNTY*, 305 Wick Ave, 44503. SAN 357-3966. Tel: 330-744-8636. FAX: 330-744-3355. Administration FAX: 330-744-2258. TDD: 330-744-7211. Web Site: www.libraryvisit.org. *Exec Dir,* Aimee Fifarek; E-mail: afifarek@libraryvisit.org; *Dep Dir,* Deborah McCullough; E-mail: dmccullough@libraryvisit.org; *Chief Fiscal Officer,* Mark Mrofchak; E-mail: mmrofchak@libraryvisit.org; *Communications & Pub Relations Dir,* Janet S Loew; E-mail: jloew@libraryvisit.org; *Develop Dir,* Deborah Liptak; E-mail: dliptak@libraryvisit.org; *Facilities Dir,* Dave Foster; E-mail: dfoster@libraryvisit.org; *Human Res Dir,* Gina Sherock; E-mail: gsherock@libraryvisit.org; *Dir, Staff Develop,* Diane Vicarel; E-mail: dvicarel@libraryvisit.org; *Tech Dir,* Tom Casey; E-mail: tcasey@libraryvisit.org; *Dir, Youth Serv, Programming,* Erin Phemester
Founded 1880. Pop 237,270
Library Holdings: Bk Vols 221,071
Special Collections: US Document Depository
Subject Interests: Genealogy
Automation Activity & Vendor Info: (Acquisitions) Innovative Interfaces, Inc; (Cataloging) Innovative Interfaces, Inc; (Circulation) Innovative Interfaces, Inc; (OPAC) Innovative Interfaces, Inc
Wireless access
Publications: It's Happening This Month
Partic in OCLC Online Computer Library Center, Inc; OhioNET
Open Mon-Thurs 9-9, Fri & Sat 9-5:30
Friends of the Library Group
Branches: 14
AUSTINTOWN, 600 S Raccoon Rd, 44515, SAN 357-3990. Web Site: www.libraryvisit.org/locations-hours/austintown-library.
Library Holdings: Bk Vols 92,892
Open Mon-Thurs 9-9, Fri & Sat 9-5:30, Sun (Sept-May) 1-5
Friends of the Library Group
BOARDMAN, 7680 Glenwood Ave, 44512, SAN 357-4024. Web Site: www.libraryvisit.org/locations-hours/boardman-branch-library.
Library Holdings: Bk Vols 80,352
Open Mon-Thurs 9-9, Fri & Sat 9-5:30, Sun (Sept-May) 1-5
Friends of the Library Group
BROWNLEE WOODS LIBRARY, 4010 Sheridan Rd, 44514, SAN 357-4059. Web Site: www.libraryvisit.org/locations-hours/brownlee-woods-library.
Library Holdings: Bk Vols 27,571
Open Mon-Wed, Fri & Sat 10-6
CAMPBELL EXPRESS BRANCH, 280 Sixth St, Campbell, 44405, SAN 357-4083. Web Site: www.libraryvisit.org/locations-hours/campbell-library.
Library Holdings: Bk Vols 22,158
Open Mon-Thurs 10-6
CANFIELD BRANCH, 43 W Main St, Canfield, 44406, SAN 357-4113. Web Site: www.libraryvisit.org/locations-hours/canfield-library.
Library Holdings: Bk Vols 49,744
Open Mon-Thurs 9-9; Fri & Sat 9-5:30; Sun (Sept-May) 1-5
Friends of the Library Group
EAST LIBRARY, 430 Early Rd, 44505, SAN 357-4148. Web Site: www.libraryvisit.org/locations-hours/east-library.
Library Holdings: Bk Vols 22,035
Open Mon-Wed 10-8, Thurs & Sat 10-6
GREENFORD BRANCH, 7441 W South Range Rd, Greenford, 44422, SAN 369-7835. Web Site: www.libraryvisit.org/locations-hours/greenford-library.
Library Holdings: Bk Vols 7,537
Open Tues-Thurs 10-6
MICHAEL KUSALABA BRANCH LIBRARY, 2815 Mahoning Ave, 44509, SAN 357-4350. Web Site: www.libraryvisit.org/locations-hours/michael-kusalaba-library.
Library Holdings: Bk Vols 40,300
Open Mon-Thurs 10-8, Fri & Sat 10-6
Friends of the Library Group
NEWPORT, 3730 Market St, 44507, SAN 357-4415. Web Site: www.libraryvisit.org/locations-hours/newport-library.
Library Holdings: Bk Vols 30,445
Open Mon-Thurs 10-8, Fri & Sat 10-6, Sun (Sept-May) 1-5
Friends of the Library Group
POLAND BRANCH, 311 S Main St, Poland, 44514, SAN 357-4326. Web Site: www.libraryvisit.org/locations-hours/poland-library.
Library Holdings: Bk Vols 70,250
Open Mon-Thurs 9-9, Fri & Sat 9-5:30, Sun (Sept-May) 1-5
Friends of the Library Group
SEBRING BRANCH, 195 W Ohio Ave, Sebring, 44672, SAN 357-4385. Web Site: www.libraryvisit.org/locations-hours/sebring-library.
Library Holdings: Bk Vols 25,120
Open Mon-Thurs & Sat 9-5:30
SPRINGFIELD BRANCH, 10418 Main St, New Middletown, 44442, SAN 369-7851. Web Site: www.libraryvisit.org/locations-hours/springfield-library.
Library Holdings: Bk Vols 16,088
Open Mon-Thurs & Sat 10-6
STRUTHERS, 95 Poland Ave, 44471, SAN 357-444X. Web Site: www.libraryvisit.org/locations-hours/struthers-library.
Library Holdings: Bk Vols 30,917
Open Tues-Sat 10-6
TRI-LAKES BRANCH, 13820 Mahoning Ave, North Jackson, 44451. Web Site: www.libraryvisit.org/locations-hours/tri-lakes-library.
Library Holdings: Bk Vols 17,260
Open Mon, Wed, Thurs & Sat 10-6, Tues 10-8
Bookmobiles: 1

C YOUNGSTOWN STATE UNIVERSITY, William F Maag Jr Library, One University Plaza, 44555-0001. SAN 313-8291. Tel: 330-941-3675. Circulation Tel: 330-941-3678. Interlibrary Loan Service Tel: 330-941-1721. Reference Tel: 330-941-3686. FAX: 330-941-3734. Web Site: www.maag.ysu.edu. *Co-Dir, Head, Research & Academic Support,* Christine Adams; Tel: 330-941-3681, E-mail: cmadams02@ysu.edu; *Co-Dir, Head, Library Services & Ops,* Ana Torres; Tel: 330-941-1717, E-mail: amtorres02@ysu.edu; *Acq Librn,* John Popadak; Tel: 330-941-3679, E-mail: jepopadak@ysu.edu; *Cat Librn,* Kevin Whitfield; Tel: 330-941-2922, E-mail: kjwhitfield@ysu.edu; *Curric Res Ctr Librn,* Alyssa Annico; Tel: 330-941-2511, E-mail: ajannico@ysu.edu; *Info Literacy,* Rebecca K Moore; Tel: 330-941-1720, E-mail: rkmoore@ysu.edu; Staff 38 (MLS 17, Non-MLS 21)
Founded 1931. Enrl 15,194; Highest Degree: Doctorate
Library Holdings: Bk Titles 656,990; Bk Vols 792,673; Per Subs 1,344
Special Collections: Early Americana. Oral History; US Document Depository
Subject Interests: Bus, Educ, Mgt, Sci tech
Automation Activity & Vendor Info: (Acquisitions) Innovative Interfaces, Inc; (Cataloging) Innovative Interfaces, Inc; (Circulation) Innovative Interfaces, Inc; (Course Reserve) Innovative Interfaces, Inc; (ILL)

Innovative Interfaces, Inc; (OPAC) Innovative Interfaces, Inc; (Serials) Innovative Interfaces, Inc
Wireless access
Function: ILL available, Res libr
Partic in NE Ohio Major Acad & Res Librs; Northeast Ohio Regional Library System; OCLC Online Computer Library Center, Inc; Ohio Library & Information Network; OhioNET
Open Mon-Thurs 7:30am-10pm, Fri 7:30-5, Sat 9-5, Sun 1-9 (Fall & Spring); Mon-Thurs 7:30am-9pm, Fri 7:30-5, Sat 9-5 (Summer)
Friends of the Library Group

ZANESFIELD

S DR EARL S SLOAN LIBRARY, 2817 Sandusky St, 43360. (Mail add: PO Box 116, 43360-0116), SAN 374-5759. Tel: 937-592-8343. FAX: 937-592-6474. E-mail: sloan.library@gmail.com. Web Site: sloanlibraryoh.org.
Founded 1913. Pop 197
Library Holdings: Audiobooks 240; DVDs 275; Large Print Bks 90; Bk Titles 7,500; Per Subs 20; Spec Interest Per Sub 3; Videos 30
Special Collections: Local Newpaper Mad River Blade Originals 1874-1876; Original County Historical Society coll; T & OC Train Depot Photos of Logan County
Wireless access
Function: 24/7 Online cat, Audio & video playback equip for onsite use, Bks on CD, Bus archives, Children's prog, Computers for patron use, Doc delivery serv, For res purposes, Holiday prog, Instruction & testing, Internet access, Magazines, Magnifiers for reading, Meeting rooms, Movies, Photocopying/Printing, Prog for children & young adult, Ref & res, Res assist avail, Res performed for a fee, Senior outreach, Summer & winter reading prog
Partic in Ohio Public Library Information Network
Open Mon, Tues & Thurs 1-7, Wed 10-5, Sat 10-2
Restriction: Non-circulating of rare bks, Restricted borrowing privileges

ZANESVILLE

S MUSKINGUM COUNTY GENEALOGICAL SOCIETY LIBRARY*, Muskingum County Chapter OGS Library, c/o John McIntire Public Library, 220 N Fifth St, Second Flr, 43701-3508. (Mail add: PO Box 2427, 43702-2427), SAN 313-8321. Tel: 740-453-0391, Ext 139. FAX: 740-455-6357. E-mail: genealogy@muskingumlibrary.org, publicity@mccogs.org. Web Site: muskingumlibrary.org/research/genealogy-library-2, www.mccogs.org. *Librn,* Brooke Anderson
Founded 1975
Library Holdings: Bk Titles 5,000; Per Subs 12
Special Collections: Early Muskingum County Newspapers, micro; Family Histories; Genealogical Society Newsletters; History (Professor Kline Coll), rpts; Marriage & Cemetary Records; Muskingum County & Surrounding Counties Genealogical Materials; Muskingum County History & Genealogy; Norris Schneider Coll, ms; Passenger & Immigration Lists Indexes, Naturalizations, Local Probate Court Records on microfilm, Maps, Atlases, Ancestor Chart File; United States Wars
Publications: books on county marriages, cemeteries, county courthouse dockets; The Muskingum Quarterly (Newsletter)
Open Mon-Fri 10-5, Sat 10-1

GL MUSKINGUM COUNTY LAW LIBRARY, 22 N Fifth St, 43701. SAN 313-833X. Tel: 740-455-7154. FAX: 740-588-4362. E-mail: lawlib@muskingumcounty.org. *Law Librn,* Sharon Ball
Library Holdings: Bk Titles 6,000

P MUSKINGUM COUNTY LIBRARY SYSTEM*, John McIntire Library, 220 N Fifth St, 43701-3587. SAN 357-4563. Tel: 740-453-0391. FAX: 740-455-6937. Web Site: www.muskingumlibrary.org. *Dir,* Jennifer Spillman; Tel: 740-453-0391, Ext 129, E-mail: jspillman@muskingumlibrary.org; *Asst Dir,* Stephanie Freas; E-mail: stephanie@muskingumlibrary.org; *Dir, Commun Relations, Mkt,* Sean Fennell; Tel: 740-453-0391, Ext 121, E-mail: seanf@muskingumlibrary.org; *IT Dir,* Joe Dusenbery; Tel: 740-453-0391, Ext 152, E-mail: joe@muskingumlibrary.org; *Mgr, Human Res,* Lynn Mercer; Tel: 740-453-0391, Ext 133, E-mail: lynnm@muskingumlibrary.org; *Fiscal Officer,* Stacey Russell; Tel: 740-453-0391, Ext 130, E-mail: stacey@muskingumlibrary.org; Staff 8 (MLS 8)
Founded 1903. Pop 85,579; Circ 833,805
Library Holdings: Audiobooks 8,498; AV Mats 2,530; CDs 9,287; DVDs 19,478; Bk Vols 259,915; Per Subs 185; Videos 1,338
Special Collections: Business & Industry; History (Ohio Coll); Zanesville & Muskingum County History
Automation Activity & Vendor Info: (Acquisitions) TLC (The Library Corporation); (Cataloging) TLC (The Library Corporation); (Circulation) TLC (The Library Corporation)
Wireless access
Publications: Newsletter
Partic in OhioNET
Friends of the Library Group
Branches: 5
DRESDEN BRANCH, 816 Main St, Dresden, 43821, SAN 357-4598. Tel: 740-754-1003. *Br Mgr,* Tracy Tom
Circ 70,082
Friends of the Library Group
DUNCAN FALLS-PHILO BRANCH, 222 Main St, Duncan Falls, 43734. (Mail add: PO Box 472, Duncan Falls, 43734), SAN 373-8515. Tel: 740-674-7100. *Br Mgr,* Kathy Kirkbride
Circ 49,273
Friends of the Library Group
NEW CONCORD BRANCH, 77 W Main St, New Concord, 43762, SAN 357-4652. Tel: 740-826-4184. *Br Mgr,* Carmaline Sturtz
Circ 72,358
Friends of the Library Group
ROSEVILLE BRANCH, 41 N Main, Roseville, 43777, SAN 357-4687. Tel: 740-697-0237. *Br Mgr,* Juanita Kinney
Circ 39,266
SOUTH BRANCH, 2530 Maysville Pike, South Zanesville, 43701, SAN 357-4717. Tel: 740-454-1511. *Br Mgr,* Leandra Leffel
Circ 73,603
Friends of the Library Group

C OHIO UNIVERSITY-ZANESVILLE/ZANE STATE COLLEGE, Zanesville Campus Library, Herrold Hall, 1425 Newark Rd, 43701. SAN 313-8348. Tel: 740-588-1404. FAX: 740-453-0706. Web Site: ohio.edu/library/about/regional-campus-libraries/zanesville. *Mgr, Libr Serv,* Janelle Hubble; Tel: 740-588-1408, E-mail: hubble@ohio.edu; *Libr Support Spec,* Tracey Humphrey; Tel: 740-588-1405, E-mail: humphret@ohio.edu; Staff 3 (MLS 1, Non-MLS 2)
Enrl 2,000; Fac 245; Highest Degree: Bachelor
Library Holdings: Bk Titles 62,000; Per Subs 18,000
Special Collections: Muskingum County History (Zanesville Heritage Coll); Zanesville Pottery (Axline Coll)
Subject Interests: Appalachia, Local hist, Pottery
Automation Activity & Vendor Info: (Cataloging) Innovative Interfaces, Inc; (Circulation) Innovative Interfaces, Inc; (Course Reserve) Innovative Interfaces, Inc; (ILL) Inmagic, Inc.; (OPAC) Innovative Interfaces, Inc; (Serials) Innovative Interfaces, Inc
Wireless access
Function: Art exhibits, Doc delivery serv, ILL available, Internet access, Magnifiers for reading, Orientations, Ref serv available, Summer reading prog, Telephone ref, VHS videos, Wheelchair accessible
Partic in OCLC Online Computer Library Center, Inc; Ohio Library & Information Network
Special Services for the Deaf - TTY equip
Open Mon-Thurs 8-8, Fri 8-3, Sat (Fall & Spring) 9-1
Restriction: Authorized patrons
Friends of the Library Group

S ZANESVILLE MUSEUM OF ART*, Longaberger Art Research Library, 620 Military Rd, 43701. SAN 313-8356. Tel: 740-452-0741. FAX: 740-452-0797. *Dir,* Laine Snyder; E-mail: laine@zanesvilleart.org
Founded 1936
Library Holdings: AV Mats 45; DVDs 20; Bk Titles 2,100
Subject Interests: Art hist, Fine arts
Wireless access
Function: Internet access
Open Wed, Thurs & Fri 12-4
Restriction: Open to pub for ref only

OKLAHOMA

Date of Statistics: FY 2021
Population, 2020 U.S. Census: 3,959,353
Population Served by Public Libraries: 3,262,957
Total Volumes in Public Libraries: 5,785,401
Volumes Per Capita: 1.46
Total Public Library Circulation: 23,417,016
Circulation Per Capita Served: 5.91
Digital Resources:
Total e-books: 8,153,198
Total audio items (physical & downloadable units): 3,736,247
Total video items (physical & downloadable units): 946,320
Total computers for use by the public: 3,126
Total annual wireless sessions: 2,754,187
Income and Expenditures:
Total Public Library Operating Expenditures: $123,568,269
Expenditures Per Capita: $31.21
Expenditures Per Capita Served: $37.87
Grants-in-Aid to Libraries: $1,635,278
Federal (LSTA): $675,545 (direct grants)
Total LSTA: $2,398,470
State Aid: $1,489,276
Number of County or Systems Libraries: 6 multi-county; 2 city-county; 5 county
Counties Served: 30 counties served by eight library systems with 102 outlets; 5 counties served by five county libraries with 6 outlets; 42 counties served by 107 city libraries
Number of Bookmobiles in State: 4
Information provided courtesy of: Cathy Van Hoy, Public Library Consultant.

ADA

P ADA PUBLIC LIBRARY*, 124 S Rennie, 74820. SAN 313-8364. Tel: 580-436-8125. FAX: 580-436-0534. E-mail: staff@ada.lib.ok.us. Web Site: www.ada.lib.ok.us. *Dir,* Jolene Poore; E-mail: jpoore@ada.lib.ok.us; *Cat,* Lisa Smith; E-mail: lsmith@ada.lib.ok.us; *Ch Serv,* Debbie Whelchel; E-mail: dlwhelchel@ada.lib.ok.us; *Circ,* Betty Blansett; E-mail: bblansett@ada.lib.ok.us; *ILL,* Gary Colbert; E-mail: gcolbert@ada.lib.ok.us
Founded 1936. Pop 15,820; Circ 140,000
Library Holdings: DVDs 12,000; Bk Vols 75,000; Per Subs 20
Automation Activity & Vendor Info: (Acquisitions) Book Systems; (Cataloging) Book Systems; (Circulation) Book Systems
Wireless access
Open Mon-Fri 8-7, Sat 9-1
Friends of the Library Group

C EAST CENTRAL UNIVERSITY*, Linscheid Library, 1100 E 14th St, 74820. SAN 357-4741. Tel: 580-559-5376. Reference Tel: 580-559-5371. FAX: 580-559-5469. E-mail: refdesk@ecok.edu. Web Site: library.ecok.edu. *Libr Dir,* Dana Belcher; Tel: 580-559-5564, E-mail: dbelcher@ecok.edu; *Media Serv Librn,* Patrick Baumann; Tel: 580-559-5373, E-mail: pbaumann@ecok.edu; *Pub Serv Librn,* Marla Lobley; Tel: 580-559-5308, E-mail: mlobley@ecok.edu; *Coll Serv Librn,* Casey Lowry; Tel: 580-559-5842, E-mail: clowry@ecok.edu; *Instrul Serv Librn,* Calantha Tillotson; Tel: 580-559-5370, E-mail: ctillotsn@ecok.edu; *Tech Serv Librn,* Megan Hasler; Tel: 580-559-5229, E-mail: mhasler@ecok.edu; Staff 13 (MLS 6, Non-MLS 7)
Founded 1909. Enrl 3,100; Fac 186; Highest Degree: Master
Library Holdings: AV Mats 7,865; e-journals 11,569; Bk Titles 127,376; Bk Vols 176,491; Per Subs 702
Automation Activity & Vendor Info: (Acquisitions) Innovative Interfaces, Inc; (Cataloging) Innovative Interfaces, Inc; (Circulation) Innovative Interfaces, Inc; (Course Reserve) Innovative Interfaces, Inc; (ILL) Innovative Interfaces, Inc; (OPAC) Innovative Interfaces, Inc; (Serials) Innovative Interfaces, Inc
Wireless access
Open Mon-Thurs 8am-10pm, Fri 8-5, Sun 2-8

ALLEN

P ALLEN PUBLIC LIBRARY*, 214 E Broadway, 74825. (Mail add: PO Box 343, 74825-0343), SAN 377-2020. Tel: 580-857-2933. Web Site: allen.okpls.org. *Dir,* Paula Nelson; E-mail: director@allen.lib.ok.us
Library Holdings: Bk Titles 7,000; Per Subs 12
Automation Activity & Vendor Info: (Circulation) Follett Software
Wireless access
Open Mon-Thurs 12-6, Fri 11-5

ALTUS

P ALTUS PUBLIC LIBRARY*, 421 N Hudson, 73521. SAN 313-8380. Tel: 580-477-2890. FAX: 580-477-3626. E-mail: spls@spls.lib.ok.us. Web Site: www.spls.lib.ok.us. *Exec Dir,* Katherine Hale; E-mail: khale@spls.lib.ok.us; *Br Mgr,* Bailee Hutchison; E-mail: bhutchison@spls.lib.ok.us
Founded 1936. Pop 23,000
Library Holdings: Bk Vols 60,000; Per Subs 75
Automation Activity & Vendor Info: (Cataloging) SirsiDynix; (Circulation) SirsiDynix
Mem of Southern Prairie Library System
Open Mon, Fri & Sat 10-6, Tues-Thurs 10-9
Friends of the Library Group

S OKLAHOMA HISTORICAL SOCIETY-MUSEUM OF THE WESTERN PRAIRIE*, Bernice Ford-Price Memorial Reference Library, 1100 Memorial Dr, 73521. SAN 327-9227. Tel: 580-482-1044. FAX: 580-482-0128. E-mail: muswestpr@okhistory.org. Web Site: www.okhistory.org. *Dir, Res,* Chad Williams; E-mail: chadw@okhistory.org; *Dep Dir, Res,* Laura Martin; E-mail: lmartin@okhistory.org; Staff 1 (Non-MLS 1)
Founded 1973
Library Holdings: Bk Titles 1,899
Special Collections: Southwest Oklahoma Coll. Oral History
Subject Interests: Archival, Local hist, Local oral hist
Function: For res purposes
Restriction: Non-circulating to the pub, Open by appt only

P SOUTHERN PRAIRIE LIBRARY SYSTEM*, 421 N Hudson, 73521. (Mail add: PO Box 1141, 73522), SAN 313-8399. Tel: 580-477-2890. Toll Free Tel: 888-302-9053. FAX: 580-477-3626. E-mail: spls@spls.lib.ok.us. Web Site: www.spls.lib.ok.us. *Dir,* Katherine Hale; E-mail: khale@spls.lib.ok.us; Staff 8 (MLS 2, Non-MLS 6)
Founded 1973. Pop 28,439; Circ 67,901
Library Holdings: AV Mats 1,051; Bk Titles 50,003; Bk Vols 52,003; Per Subs 76
Special Collections: English as a Second Language Coll; Literacy Coll
Subject Interests: African-Am heritage, Alternate sources of energy, Genealogy, Hispanic-Am heritage
Automation Activity & Vendor Info: (Acquisitions) SirsiDynix; (Cataloging) SirsiDynix; (Circulation) SirsiDynix; (ILL) OCLC; (OPAC) SirsiDynix-WorkFlows
Wireless access
Member Libraries: Altus Public Library; Hollis Public Library
Partic in Association for Rural & Small Libraries; OCLC Online Computer Library Center, Inc; OLTN
Special Services for the Blind - Accessible computers; Aids for in-house use; Bks on CD; Copier with enlargement capabilities; Extensive large print coll; Large print bks; Lending of low vision aids; Magnifiers; Screen enlargement software for people with visual disabilities
Open Mon, Fri & Sat 10-6, Tues-Thurs 10-9
Friends of the Library Group

J WESTERN OKLAHOMA STATE COLLEGE*, Learning Resources Center, 2801 N Main St, 73521. SAN 313-8402. Tel: 580-477-7770. FAX: 580-477-7777. E-mail: lrc@wosc.edu. Web Site: wosc.edu/library. *Dir,* Suzanne Rooker; Tel: 580-477-7944, E-mail: suzanne.rooker@wosc.edu; *Tech Asst,* Joanne Huff; Tel: 580-477-7948, E-mail: joanne.huff@wosc.edu; Staff 2 (MLS 1, Non-MLS 1)
Founded 1926. Enrl 1,420; Fac 100; Highest Degree: Associate
Library Holdings: AV Mats 2,368; Bks on Deafness & Sign Lang 15; e-books 763; Bk Vols 38,859; Per Subs 35
Automation Activity & Vendor Info: (Cataloging) Auto-Graphics, Inc; (Circulation) Auto-Graphics, Inc; (Course Reserve) Auto-Graphics, Inc; (ILL) OCLC Connexion; (OPAC) Auto-Graphics, Inc
Wireless access
Open Mon-Thurs 7:30am-9pm, Fri 7:30-5

ALTUS AIR FORCE BASE

A UNITED STATES AIR FORCE*, Altus Air Force Base Library FL4419, 97 FSS/FSDL, 109 E Ave, Bldg 65, 73523-5134. Tel: 580-481-6302. FAX: 580-482-0469. Web Site: altusfss.com/library. *Libr Dir,* Chad Harding
Founded 1953
Library Holdings: Bk Vols 25,000; Per Subs 53
Subject Interests: Aeronaut, Polit sci
Automation Activity & Vendor Info: (Cataloging) OCLC Connexion; (Circulation) SirsiDynix-Unicorn; (ILL) OCLC WorldShare Interlibrary Loan
Wireless access
Partic in OCLC Online Computer Library Center, Inc
Restriction: Not open to pub

ALVA

P ALVA PUBLIC LIBRARY*, 504 Seventh St, 73717. Tel: 580-327-1833. FAX: 580-327-5329. E-mail: alvalibrary@alva.lib.ok.us. Web Site: www.alvaok.org/vnews/display.v/SEC/Alva%20Public%20Library. *Dir, Res,* Sandra Ott; E-mail: SandraH@alvaok.org; *Ad,* Mandi Schoenhals; E-mail: mandis@alva.lib.ok.us; Staff 2 (MLS 2)
Pop 5,000; Circ 63,447
Library Holdings: AV Mats 1,548; Bk Vols 49,546; Per Subs 121; Talking Bks 679
Special Collections: Daughters of the American Revolution (DAR) Coll
Subject Interests: Genealogy, Okla
Automation Activity & Vendor Info: (Cataloging) OCLC; (Circulation) Biblionix; (ILL) OCLC; (Serials) DEMCO
Wireless access
Open Mon 9-8, Tues-Fri 9-5:30, Sat 9-1
Friends of the Library Group

C NORTHWESTERN OKLAHOMA STATE UNIVERSITY*, J W Martin Library, 709 Oklahoma Blvd, 73717. SAN 357-4830. Tel: 580-327-8574. FAX: 580-327-8501. E-mail: nwlibraries@nwosu.edu. Web Site: www.nwosu.edu/library. *Dir, Libr Serv,* Shannon Leaper; E-mail: seleaper@nwosu.edu; Staff 11 (MLS 4, Non-MLS 7)
Founded 1897. Enrl 2,000; Fac 75; Highest Degree: Master
Library Holdings: Bk Vols 159,000; Per Subs 1,405
Special Collections: Indian Artifacts; William J Mellor Coll, bks, paintings, sculpture, stereoptican slides, cylinder records & player. US Document Depository
Subject Interests: Agr, Behav sci, Educ, Libr sci, Soc sci
Wireless access
Function: Govt ref serv, ILL available
Restriction: Restricted pub use

ANADARKO

P ANADARKO COMMUNITY LIBRARY*, 215 W Broadway, 73005. SAN 313-8429. Tel: 405-247-7351. Toll Free Tel: 888-607-1747. FAX: 405-247-2024. E-mail: library@cityofanadarko.org. Web Site: www.anadarkopl.okpls.org. *Libr Dir,* Janis Kindred; E-mail: jkindred@cityofanadarko.org
Founded 1912. Pop 8,200; Circ 45,638
Library Holdings: Bk Vols 33,000; Per Subs 80
Special Collections: Oklahoma History
Subject Interests: Art, Native Am, Native Am hist, Okla
Automation Activity & Vendor Info: (Circulation) Follett Software
Wireless access
Open Mon-Thurs 9-6, Fri 9-5, Sat 9-Noon
Friends of the Library Group

ANTLERS

P ANTLERS PUBLIC LIBRARY*, 104 SE Second St, 74523-4000. SAN 313-8437. Tel: 580-298-5649. FAX: 580-298-3567. E-mail: antlerslibrary@antlers.lib.ok.us. Web Site: www.antlerslibrary.okpls.org. *Libr Dir,* Patti Lehman; *Asst Librn,* Kathie O'Keefe; Staff 2 (Non-MLS 2)
Founded 1959. Pop 2,989; Circ 12,262
Library Holdings: Bk Vols 14,000
Automation Activity & Vendor Info: (Cataloging) Follett Software; (Circulation) Follett Software; (OPAC) Follett Software
Wireless access
Function: Audio & video playback equip for onsite use, ILL available, Magnifiers for reading, Photocopying/Printing, Preschool outreach, Prog for children & young adult, Spoken cassettes & CDs, Summer reading prog, VHS videos, Wheelchair accessible
Open Tues & Thurs 10-6, Wed 9-5, Fri 10-5, Sat 9-Noon

ARDMORE

P ARDMORE PUBLIC LIBRARY*, 320 E St NW, 73401. SAN 313-8445. Tel: 580-223-8290. Circulation Tel: 580-223-9524. FAX: 580-221-3240. Web Site: www.ardmorelibrary.org. *Dir,* Daniel Gibbs; E-mail: dgibbs@ardmorelibrary.org; *Ad,* Amber Carter; E-mail: acarter@ardmorelibrary.org; *Literacy Librn, Outreach Librn,* Elizabeth Gaylor; *Pub Serv Librn,* Lorena L Smith; E-mail: lsmith@ardmorelibrary.org; *Tech Serv Librn,* Lynnette Haggerty; E-mail: lhaggerty@ardmorelibrary.org; *Youth Serv Librn,* Angela Armstrong; Staff 6 (MLS 4, Non-MLS 2)
Founded 1906
Library Holdings: Audiobooks 4,947; DVDs 4,970; Electronic Media & Resources 9; Bk Vols 75,913; Per Subs 153
Special Collections: Eliza Cruce Hall Doll Museum Coll, bks, dolls, slides; McGalliard Local History Coll, clippings, photog, publs
Automation Activity & Vendor Info: (Acquisitions) Innovative Interfaces, Inc; (Cataloging) Innovative Interfaces, Inc; (Circulation) Innovative Interfaces, Inc; (ILL) OCLC; (OPAC) SirsiDynix; (Serials) Innovative Interfaces, Inc
Wireless access
Function: 24/7 Electronic res, 24/7 Online cat, Adult bk club, Adult literacy prog, Archival coll, Audio & video playback equip for onsite use, Audiobks via web, Bilingual assistance for Spanish patrons, Bks on CD, Children's prog, Citizenship assistance, Computer training, Computers for patron use, Digital talking bks, Electronic databases & coll, For res purposes, Free DVD rentals, ILL available, Internet access, Meeting rooms, Movies, Music CDs, Notary serv, Online cat, OverDrive digital audio bks, Photocopying/Printing, Prog for children & young adult, Ref serv available, Scanner, Serves people with intellectual disabilities, Spanish lang bks, Story hour, Study rm, Summer reading prog, Tax forms, Teen prog, Wheelchair accessible
Open Mon-Thurs 9-8, Fri 9-5, Sat & Sun 1-5
Friends of the Library Group

S SAMUEL ROBERTS NOBLE FOUNDATION, INC, Noble Foundation Library, 2510 Sam Noble Pkwy, 73401. SAN 313-8453. Tel: 580-224-6264. FAX: 580-224-6265. E-mail: library@noble.org. Web Site: www.noble.org.
Founded 1951
Library Holdings: e-journals 12,000; Bk Titles 34,100; Per Subs 430
Special Collections: Plant Specimen Identity Coll & Archives. Oral History
Subject Interests: Agr, Chem, Forage, Plant biol
Automation Activity & Vendor Info: (Acquisitions) Ex Libris Group; (Cataloging) Ex Libris Group; (Circulation) Ex Libris Group; (Course Reserve) Ex Libris Group; (ILL) Ex Libris Group; (Media Booking) Ex Libris Group; (OPAC) Ex Libris Group; (Serials) Ex Libris Group
Wireless access
Function: Archival coll, Electronic databases & coll
Publications: Library Guide
Restriction: Co libr

P SOUTHERN OKLAHOMA LIBRARY SYSTEM*, Champion Public Library/Headquarters, 601 Railway Express St, 73401. SAN 357-4954. Tel: 580-223-3164. FAX: 580-223-3280. E-mail: ardmore@southernoklibrarysystem.org. Reference E-mail: reference@southernoklibrarysystem.org. Web Site: www.southernoklibrarysystem.org. *Exec Dir,* Lynn McIntosh; E-mail: lmcintosh@southernoklibrarysystem.org; *Adult Serv, Head, Ref,* Pam Bean; E-mail: pbean@southernoklibrarysystem.org; *Bus Mgr,* Dawnah Iliff; *Circ Coordr,* Rudy Ellis; E-mail: rellis@southernoklibrarysystem.org; *Br Coordr,* Alyson Hayes; E-mail: ahayes@southernoklibrarysystem.org; *Mkt Coordr, Pub Info,* Gail Currier; E-mail: gcurrier@southernoklibrarysystem.org; *ILL Serv,* Vanneshia Crane; E-mail: vcrane@southernoklibrarysystem.org; *Tech Serv,* David Moran; E-mail: dmoran@southernoklibrarysystem.org; *Youth Serv,* Stephanie Way; E-mail: sway@southernoklibrarysystem.org; Staff 14 (MLS 3, Non-MLS 11)
Founded 1960. Pop 97,024; Circ 997,378
Jul 2017-Jun 2018 Income (Main & Associated Libraries) $1,821,098, State $72,002, County $1,703,979, Other $45,117. Mats Exp $99,651, Books $54,003, Per/Ser (Incl. Access Fees) $8,423, Micro $620, AV Mat $12,021, Electronic Ref Mat (Incl. Access Fees) $24,584. Sal $900,973

Library Holdings: Audiobooks 3,587; DVDs 12,888; e-books 37,593; Electronic Media & Resources 48; Bk Titles 67,957; Bk Vols 131,424; Per Subs 177
Subject Interests: Art, Civilized tribes, Okla hist, Texoma
Automation Activity & Vendor Info: (Cataloging) TLC (The Library Corporation); (Circulation) TLC (The Library Corporation)
Wireless access
Function: 24/7 Electronic res, 24/7 Online cat, Activity rm, Adult bk club, Audiobks on Playaways & MP3, Audiobks via web, Bk club(s), Bks on CD, Children's prog, Computer training, Computers for patron use, Distance learning, Electronic databases & coll, Free DVD rentals, Games & aids for people with disabilities, Homework prog, ILL available, Internet access, Magazines, Meeting rooms, Microfiche/film & reading machines, Movies, Music CDs, Online cat, Online ref, Outreach serv, OverDrive digital audio bks, Photocopying/Printing, Prog for adults, Prog for children & young adult, Ref & res, Ref serv available, Story hour, Summer reading prog, Tax forms, Teen prog, Telephone ref, Wheelchair accessible, Writing prog
Open Mon-Thurs 8:30-7:30, Fri 8:30-5, Sat 10-2
Friends of the Library Group

Branches: 7

ATOKA COUNTY LIBRARY, 279 East A St, Atoka, 74525, SAN 357-4989. Tel: 580-889-3555. FAX: 580-889-8860. E-mail: atoka@southernoklibrarysystem.org. Web Site: www.southernoklibrarysystem.org/atoka-county-library. *Br Mgr,* JoAnn Mixon; Staff 1 (MLS 1)
Open Mon-Thurs 11:30-5:30, Fri 11:30-2:30, Sat 10-1
Friends of the Library Group

DAVIS PUBLIC LIBRARY, 209 E Benton Ave, Davis, 73030, SAN 357-5047. Tel: 580-369-2468. FAX: 580-369-3290. E-mail: davis@southernoklibrarysystem.org. Web Site: www.southernoklibrarysystem.org/davis-public-library. *Br Mgr,* Jonathan Edwards; Staff 1 (Non-MLS 1)
Open Mon-Thurs 11:30-5:30, Fri 11:30-2:30, Sat 10-1
Friends of the Library Group

HEALDTON COMMUNITY LIBRARY, 554 S Fourth St, Healdton, 73438, SAN 357-5071. Tel: 580-229-0590. FAX: 580-229-0654. E-mail: healdton@southernoklibrarysystem.org. Web Site: www.southernoklibrarysystem.org/healdton-community-library. *Br Mgr,* Lori Ratliff; Staff 1 (Non-MLS 1)
Open Mon-Thurs 11:30-5:30, Fri 11:30-2:30, Sat 10-1
Friends of the Library Group

JOHNSTON COUNTY LIBRARY, 116 W Main St, Tishomingo, 73460, SAN 357-5160. Tel: 580-371-3006. FAX: 580-371-0042. E-mail: tishomingo@southernoklibrarysystem.org. Web Site: www.southernoklibrarysystem.org/johnston-county-library. *Br Mgr,* Michael Henthorn; Staff 1 (Non-MLS 1)
Open Mon-Thurs 11:30-5:30, Fri 11:30-2:30, Sat 10-1
Friends of the Library Group

LOVE COUNTY LIBRARY, 500 S Hwy 77, Marietta, 73448, SAN 357-5101. Tel: 580-276-3783. FAX: 580-276-1483. E-mail: marietta@southernoklibrarysystem.org. Web Site: www.southernoklibrarysystem.org/love-county-library. *Br Mgr,* Niki Powell; Staff 1 (Non-MLS 1)
Open Mon-Thurs 11:30-5:30, Fri 11:30-2:30, Sat 10-1
Friends of the Library Group

MARY E PARKER MEMORIAL LIBRARY, 500 W Broadway, Sulphur, 73086, SAN 357-5136. Tel: 580-622-5807. FAX: 580-622-6395. E-mail: sulphur@southernoklibrarysystem.org. Web Site: www.southernoklibrarysystem.org/parker-memorial-library. *Br Mgr,* Ginger Britt; Staff 1 (Non-MLS 1)
Open Mon-Thurs 11:30-5:30, Fri 11:30-2:30, Sat 10-1
Friends of the Library Group

WILSON PUBLIC LIBRARY, 1087 US Hwy 70A, Wilson, 73463, SAN 357-5195. Tel: 580-668-2486. FAX: 580-668-9280. E-mail: wilson@southernoklibrarysystem.org. Web Site: www.southernoklibrarysystem.org/wilson-public-library. *Br Mgr,* Stephanie Ferguson; Staff 1 (Non-MLS 1)
Open Mon & Wed 1-6, Thurs 12-5
Friends of the Library Group

C UNIVERSITY CENTER OF SOUTHERN OKLAHOMA LIBRARY, 2901 Mt Washington Rd, 73401. SAN 375-426X. Tel: 580-319-0340. *Libr Dir,* Terri Greer; E-mail: tgreer@ucso.osrhe.edu
Founded 1983. Enrl 1,300; Highest Degree: Master
Library Holdings: e-books 16,000; Bk Titles 14,000; Bk Vols 18,000; Per Subs 130
Automation Activity & Vendor Info: (Cataloging) SirsiDynix; (Circulation) SirsiDynix; (Course Reserve) SirsiDynix; (ILL) OCLC; (OPAC) SirsiDynix; (Serials) SirsiDynix
Wireless access
Function: AV serv, ILL available, Res libr
Open Mon-Thurs 8-5, Fri 8-4

ARKOMA

P ARKOMA PUBLIC LIBRARY, 1101 Main St, 74901. (Mail add: PO Box 446, 74901-0446), SAN 376-5946. Tel: 918-875-3971. Toll Free FAX: 866-596-4379. E-mail: arkoma@seolibraries.com. Web Site: seolibraries.com/about/hours-locations/arkoma. *Dir,* Angie King
Library Holdings: Bk Vols 10,000
Automation Activity & Vendor Info: (Circulation) SirsiDynix
Wireless access
Mem of Southeast Oklahoma Library System (SEOLS)
Open Mon 9-1, Tues-Thurs 9-6, Fri 9-5

ATOKA

S OKLAHOMA DEPARTMENT OF CORRECTIONS, Howard McLeod Correctional Center Library, 19603 E Whippoorwill Ln, 74525-5560. Tel: 580-889-6651. FAX: 580-889-5561. Web Site: oklahoma.gov/doc/facilities/state-institutions/howard-mcleod-correctional-center. *Supvr,* Chelsea Catlett; E-mail: chelsea.catlett@doc.ok.gov
Library Holdings: Bk Vols 7,000
Open Tues-Thurs 9-6, Fri 8-5, Sat 8-4

BARNSDALL

P BARNSDALL PUBLIC LIBRARY-ETHEL BRIGGS MEMORIAL LIBRARY*, 410 S Fifth St, 74002. (Mail add: PO Box 706, 74002-0706), SAN 313-8461. Tel: 918-847-2118. FAX: 918-847-2118. E-mail: barnsdalllibrary@yahoo.com. Web Site: www.ethelbriggs.lib.ok.us. *Librn,* Cecilia Hibdon; E-mail: chibdonlibrary@yahoo.com
Founded 1931. Pop 1,400; Circ 8,065
Library Holdings: Bk Titles 12,204
Subject Interests: Hist, Music
Wireless access
Open Mon-Fri 2-6

BARTLESVILLE

P BARTLESVILLE PUBLIC LIBRARY*, 600 S Johnstone, 74003. SAN 313-847X. Tel: 918-338-4161. Reference Tel: 918-338-4169. Administration Tel: 918-338-4163. Information Services Tel: 918-338-4168. FAX: 918-338-4185. E-mail: bpl@cityofbartlesville.org. Web Site: www.bartlesville.lib.ok.us. *Libr Dir,* Shellie McGill; E-mail: mrmcgill@cityofbartlesville.org; Staff 19 (MLS 3, Non-MLS 16)
Founded 1913. Pop 50,706; Circ 419,904
Jul 2014-Jun 2015 Income $1,304,151, State $19,752, City $1,131,298, Federal $17,500, Locally Generated Income $125,601, Other $10,000. Mats Exp $133,531, Books $79,348, Per/Ser (Incl. Access Fees) $6,470, Micro $2,030, AV Mat $16,844, Electronic Ref Mat (Incl. Access Fees) $28,839. Sal $856,582
Library Holdings: Audiobooks 3,030; AV Mats 8,420; e-books 31,997; Bk Titles 106,100; Per Subs 94
Special Collections: Genealogy Coll; Local Historical Museum; Local History Coll; Oklahoma History Coll. State Document Depository
Subject Interests: Native American, Okla tribes
Automation Activity & Vendor Info: (Acquisitions) Innovative Interfaces, Inc; (Cataloging) Innovative Interfaces, Inc; (Circulation) Innovative Interfaces, Inc; (Course Reserve) Innovative Interfaces, Inc; (ILL) Innovative Interfaces, Inc
Wireless access
Function: Adult bk club, Archival coll, Art exhibits, Audio & video playback equip for onsite use, Audiobks via web, BA reader (adult literacy), Bk club(s), Bk reviews (Group), Bks on CD, Children's prog, Citizenship assistance, Computer training, Computers for patron use, Digital talking bks, Electronic databases & coll, Family literacy, Free DVD rentals, Genealogy discussion group, Homebound delivery serv, ILL available, Instruction & testing, Internet access, Literacy & newcomer serv, Magnifiers for reading, Music CDs, Online cat, Online info literacy tutorials on the web & in blackboard, Online ref, Outreach serv, Outside serv via phone, mail, e-mail & web, Photocopying/Printing, Preschool outreach, Prog for adults, Prog for children & young adult, Ref & res, Ref serv available, Senior computer classes, Story hour, Summer reading prog, Tax forms, Teen prog, Telephone ref, Wheelchair accessible
Publications: The Bartlesville Bookmark (Newsletter)
Special Services for the Deaf - TDD equip
Open Mon-Thurs 9-9, Fri & Sat 9-5:30, Sun (Sept-May) 1:30-5:30
Restriction: Borrowing requests are handled by ILL
Friends of the Library Group

C OKLAHOMA WESLEYAN UNIVERSITY LIBRARY*, Janice & Charles Drake Library, 2201 Silver Lake Rd, 74006. SAN 313-8488. Tel: 918-335-6298. Interlibrary Loan Service Tel: 918-335-6286. FAX: 918-335-6220. E-mail: elib@okwu.edu. Web Site: www.okwu.edu/library. *Off-Campus Librn,* Stephanie Leupp; E-mail: sleupp@okwu.edu; *Pub Serv Librn,* Cheryl Salerno; E-mail: csalerno@okwu.edu; Staff 3 (MLS 2, Non-MLS 1)
Founded 1958. Enrl 969; Fac 55; Highest Degree: Master

Library Holdings: e-books 14,800; Bk Titles 77,378; Bk Vols 93,580; Per Subs 182
Special Collections: Holiness Coll; Josh McDowell Legacy Coll
Automation Activity & Vendor Info: (Cataloging) Auto-Graphics, Inc; (Circulation) Auto-Graphics, Inc; (ILL) Auto-Graphics, Inc; (OPAC) Auto-Graphics, Inc
Wireless access
Function: Outside serv via phone, mail, e-mail & web
Partic in Association of Christian Librarians
Open Mon-Thurs 7:30am-Midnight, Fri 7:30-5, Sat 11-5, Sun 2pm-Midnight
Restriction: Access at librarian's discretion

S PHILLIPS 66 RESEARCH LIBRARY*, 190 PLB PRC, 74003-6670. SAN 357-5314. Tel: 918-977-5875. Web Site: www.phillips66.com. *Dir,* Laura Allen-Ward; E-mail: Laura.Allen-Ward@p66.com; Staff 5 (MLS 3, Non-MLS 2)
Founded 1947
Library Holdings: e-books 2,000; e-journals 200; Bk Vols 60,000; Per Subs 100; Videos 100
Subject Interests: Chem, Physics, Plastics, Polymer sci
Automation Activity & Vendor Info: (Cataloging) EOS International; (Circulation) EOS International; (Discovery) EBSCO Discovery Service; (OPAC) EOS International; (Serials) EOS International
Wireless access
Function: Doc delivery serv, Electronic databases & coll, For res purposes, Internet access, Online cat, Orientations, Ref & res, Ref serv available, Res libr
Partic in Amigos Library Services, Inc; OCLC Online Computer Library Center, Inc
Restriction: Access for corporate affiliates, Authorized patrons, Authorized personnel only, By permission only, Co libr, Employees & their associates, Employees only, Not open to pub

S WOOLAROC MUSEUM LIBRARY*, 1925 Woolaroc Ranch Rd, 74003. (Mail add: PO Box 1647, 74005), SAN 370-4149. Tel: 918-336-0307. Toll Free Tel: 888-966-5276. FAX: 918-336-0084. E-mail: woolarocmail@woolaroc.org. Web Site: www.woolaroc.org. *Curator,* Linda Stone; Tel: 918-336-0307, Ext 32
Founded 1929
Subject Interests: Anthrop, Ethnology, Firearms, Native Am, Oil, Ranching, Western art, Zoology
Open Wed-Sun 10-5; Tues-Sun (Summer) 10-5
Restriction: Lending to staff only, Open to others by appt

BEAVER

P BEAVER COUNTY PIONEER LIBRARY*, 201 Douglas St, 73932. (Mail add: PO Box 579, 73932-0579), SAN 313-850X. Tel: 580-625-3076. Toll Free Tel: 866-516-1528. FAX: 580-625-3076. E-mail: beavercountylibrary@gmx.com. Web Site: www.beaverpl.okpls.org. *Librn,* Denise Janko
Circ 8,675
Library Holdings: Bk Titles 16,550; Per Subs 10
Automation Activity & Vendor Info: (Circulation) Follett Software
Wireless access
Open Mon-Thurs 10-6, Sat 9-Noon
Friends of the Library Group

BETHANY

C SOUTHERN NAZARENE UNIVERSITY*, R T Williams Learning Resources Center, 4115 N College, 73008. SAN 313-8518. Tel: 405-491-6351. FAX: 405-491-6355. E-mail: LRCreference@snu.edu. Web Site: www.snu.edu/library. *Libr Dir,* Katie King; Tel: 405-491-6351, Ext 6543, E-mail: kking@snu.edu; *Ref Librn,* Joshua Achipa; E-mail: jachipa@snu.edu; Staff 3 (MLS 3)
Founded 1920. Enrl 1,900; Fac 75; Highest Degree: Master
Library Holdings: Bk Titles 80,000; Bk Vols 103,000; Per Subs 200
Special Collections: Hymnological Coll; Ross Hayslip Bible Coll; Signatures (John E Moore Letter Coll)
Subject Interests: Educ, Nursing, Relig, Sciences
Automation Activity & Vendor Info: (Circulation) Follett Software; (OPAC) Follett Software
Wireless access
Partic in OCLC Online Computer Library Center, Inc
Open Mon-Thurs (Spring & Fall) 7:45-Midnight, Fri 7:45-5, Sat 11-5, Sun 7:30pm-Midnight; Mon-Thurs (Summer & Winter) 8-6, Fri 8-5, Sat Noon-5

CR SOUTHWESTERN CHRISTIAN UNIVERSITY LIBRARY*, Springer Learning Center, C H Springer Bldg, 7210 NW 39th Expressway, 73008. (Mail add: PO Box 340, 73008-0340), SAN 313-9654. Tel: 405-789-7661, Ext 2221. FAX: 405-495-0078. E-mail: library@swcu.edu. Web Site: swcu.libguides.com/home. *Libr Dir,* Michael Lowder; E-mail: michael.lowder@swcu.edu; Staff 1 (MLS 1)
Founded 1946. Enrl 500; Highest Degree: Master
Library Holdings: AV Mats 145; CDs 25; DVDs 120; Bk Titles 28,000; Bk Vols 30,000
Special Collections: Pentecostal Resource Coll
Automation Activity & Vendor Info: (Cataloging) Mandarin Library Automation; (Circulation) Mandarin Library Automation; (OPAC) Mandarin Library Automation
Wireless access
Open Mon-Thurs (Fall & Winter) 8:30am-10pm, Fri 8:30-5; Mon, Wed & Thurs (Summer) 8:30-5, Tues 8:30-6

BINGER

P BINGER PUBLIC LIBRARY*, 217 W Main, 73009. (Mail add: PO Box 202, 73009). Tel: 405-656-2621. *Dir,* Judy Hill
Founded 1976. Pop 660
Library Holdings: AV Mats 210; DVDs 21; Bk Vols 6,700; Per Subs 10; Talking Bks 107; Videos 12
Function: Photocopying/Printing
Open Mon & Thurs 11-4

BLACKWELL

P BLACKWELL PUBLIC LIBRARY*, 123 W Padon, 74631-2805. SAN 313-8534. Tel: 580-363-1809. FAX: 580-363-7214. E-mail: librarydirector@blackwellok.org. *Dir, Pub Libr Serv,* Position Currently Open; *Asst Librn, Ch,* Stacy Diaz-Cortez; E-mail: sdiaz@blackwellok.org; Staff 1 (Non-MLS 1)
Founded 1903. Pop 7,500; Circ 117,807
Library Holdings: Bk Titles 34,000; Bk Vols 36,250; Per Subs 79
Subject Interests: Genealogy
Automation Activity & Vendor Info: (Acquisitions) Biblionix/Apollo; (Cataloging) Biblionix/Apollo; (Circulation) Biblionix/Apollo
Wireless access
Open Mon-Fri 10-6, Sat 10-2
Friends of the Library Group

BOISE CITY

P SOUTAR MEMORIAL LIBRARY*, Four S Ellis Ave, 73933. (Mail add: PO Box 1088, 73933-1088), SAN 313-8542. Tel: 580-544-2715. FAX: 580-544-2705. E-mail: soutarlib@yahoo.com. Web Site: soutarlibrary.okpls.org. *Librn,* Alma Fay Twyman
Founded 1958. Pop 2,475; Circ 11,376
Library Holdings: Bk Vols 15,000
Automation Activity & Vendor Info: (Cataloging) Biblionix/Apollo; (Circulation) Biblionix/Apollo
Wireless access
Open Tues & Thurs 11:30-6, Wed 9-12 & 1-6, Fri 12-6, Sat 9-12
Friends of the Library Group

BOLEY

S JOHN H LILLEY CORRECTIONAL CENTER, Leisure Library, 407971 Hwy 62E, 74829. SAN 371-7070. Tel: 918-667-3381. FAX: 918-667-3959. *Principal,* Dr Ricky Martin; E-mail: ricky.martin@doc.ok.gov
Library Holdings: Bk Vols 5,000; Per Subs 10
Restriction: Not open to pub

BRISTOW

P BRISTOW PUBLIC LIBRARY*, Montfort & Allie B Jones Memorial Library, 111 W Seventh Ave, 74010-2401. SAN 313-8550. Tel: 918-367-6562. FAX: 918-367-1156. E-mail: joneslibrarybristow@gmail.com. Web Site: www.bristowlibrary.okpls.org. *Dir,* Heather Hutto; E-mail: librarydirectorbristow@gmail.com
Pop 4,062; Circ 68,000
Library Holdings: Bk Titles 30,000; Per Subs 65
Special Collections: Henson Room - Olympic memorabila/olympic medals/wrestling bks, art, etc
Subject Interests: Okla
Automation Activity & Vendor Info: (Circulation) Follett Software
Open Tues-Fri 9-6, Sat 9-1

BROKEN BOW

P BROKEN BOW PUBLIC LIBRARY, 404 N Broadway St, 74728. SAN 313-8569. Toll Free Tel: 866-218-6582. Toll Free FAX: 866-305-4588. E-mail: brokenbow@seolibraries.com. Web Site: www.seolibraries.com/about/hours-locations/broken-bow. *Br Mgr,* Tanya Schaefer
Founded 1920. Pop 20,000; Circ 110,000
Library Holdings: Bk Titles 33,000; Per Subs 75

Automation Activity & Vendor Info: (Acquisitions) SirsiDynix; (Cataloging) SirsiDynix; (Circulation) SirsiDynix
Wireless access
Function: Adult bk club, Art exhibits, Audio & video playback equip for onsite use, Bi-weekly Writer's Group, CD-ROM, Electronic databases & coll, Games & aids for people with disabilities, Home delivery & serv to seniorr ctr & nursing homes, Homebound delivery serv, ILL available, Internet access, Music CDs, Online info literacy tutorials on the web & in blackboard, Online ref, Photocopying/Printing, Preschool outreach, Prog for children & young adult, Ref & res, Spoken cassettes & CDs, Spoken cassettes & DVDs, Summer reading prog, Tax forms, Telephone ref, VHS videos, Wheelchair accessible, Workshops
Mem of Southeast Oklahoma Library System (SEOLS)
Open Mon-Thurs 9-6, Fri 9-5, Sat 9-2
Friends of the Library Group

BUFFALO

P BUFFALO PUBLIC LIBRARY*, 11 E Turner, 73834. (Mail add: PO Box 439, 73834-0265). Tel: 580-735-2995. FAX: 580-735-6157. E-mail: bufpublibrary@buffalo.lib.ok.us. Web Site: www.buffalo.lib.ok.us. *Dir,* Kathy Summars
Pop 1,160; Circ 2,210
Library Holdings: AV Mats 554; Bk Vols 8,039; Talking Bks 147
Automation Activity & Vendor Info: (Cataloging) Follett Software; (Circulation) Follett Software; (OPAC) Follett Software
Wireless access
Open Mon, Thurs & Fri 2:30-6, Tues 2-5, Wed 9-12 & 2-5

CARMEN

P CARMEN PUBLIC LIBRARY, 112 N Sixth St, 73726. (Mail add: PO Box 98, 73726-0098). Tel: 580-987-2301. FAX: 580-987-2303. E-mail: town_of_carmen@yahoo.com. Web Site: carmen.okpls.org. *Dir,* Jessica Tidwell
Pop 389; Circ 5,000
Library Holdings: AV Mats 40; Bk Vols 6,000; Talking Bks 12
Automation Activity & Vendor Info: (Cataloging) Follett Software; (Circulation) Follett Software
Wireless access
Open Mon-Thurs 12:30-5:30

CARNEGIE

P CARNEGIE PUBLIC LIBRARY, Six E Main St, 73015. SAN 313-8577. Tel: 580-654-1980. E-mail: carnlibr@carnegienet.net. Web Site: townofcarnegie.com/library. *Dir,* Barbara Cotten
Founded 1953. Pop 1,598; Circ 6,922
Library Holdings: Bk Vols 12,845
Subject Interests: Genealogy, Hist, Relig studies
Partic in Okla Telecommunications Interlibr Syst
Open Mon-Thurs 1-6, Fri 11-4

CATOOSA

P CATOOSA PUBLIC LIBRARY*, 105 E Oak, 74015. (Mail add: PO Box 489, 74015-0489). Tel: 918-266-1684. FAX: 918-266-1685. Web Site: catoosapubliclibrary.com. *Libr Dir,* Carol Anderson; E-mail: canderson@catoosapubliclibrary.com
Pop 5,449; Circ 16,002
Library Holdings: AV Mats 537; Large Print Bks 100; Bk Vols 14,000; Per Subs 50; Talking Bks 542
Subject Interests: Spanish
Automation Activity & Vendor Info: (Cataloging) Follett Software; (Circulation) Follett Software; (ILL) OCLC ILLiad; (OPAC) Follett Software
Open Mon 1-5, Tues-Thurs 9-7, Fri 9-3, Sat 10-2
Friends of the Library Group

CHANDLER

P CHANDLER PUBLIC LIBRARY*, 1021 Manvel Ave, 74834. SAN 329-7101. Tel: 405-258-3204. FAX: 405-258-3205. Web Site: www.chandlerlibrary.okpls.org. *Chief Librn,* Carmen Harkins; E-mail: charkins@chandlerok.com; *Asst Librn,* Sandra Helm; E-mail: shelm@chandlerok.com; Staff 2 (MLS 1, Non-MLS 1)
Founded 1987. Pop 3,219; Circ 9,704
Jul 2017-Jun 2018 Income $120,696. Mats Exp $82,729. Sal $65,119
Library Holdings: CDs 170; DVDs 165; Large Print Bks 245; Bk Titles 13,000
Automation Activity & Vendor Info: (Circulation) Book Systems
Wireless access
Function: 24/7 Electronic res, 24/7 Online cat, Accelerated reader prog
Open Mon-Fri 9-6, Sat 9-12
Friends of the Library Group

CHECOTAH

P JIM LUCAS CHECOTAH PUBLIC LIBRARY*, 626 W Gentry, 74426-2218. SAN 313-8593. Tel: 918-473-6715. FAX: 918-473-6603. E-mail: checotahpl@eols.org. Web Site: eols.org/library-location/jim-lucas-checotah-public-library. *Br Mgr,* Kathy Smith; E-mail: ksmith@eols.org
Founded 1971
Library Holdings: Bk Vols 30,000; Per Subs 40
Subject Interests: Genealogy, Literacy, Local hist
Automation Activity & Vendor Info: (Circulation) SirsiDynix
Wireless access
Mem of Eastern Oklahoma Library System
Open Mon-Fri 8-6, Sat 9-1
Friends of the Library Group

CHELSEA

P CHELSEA PUBLIC LIBRARY*, 618 Pine St, 74016-0064. SAN 313-8607. Tel: 918-789-3364. FAX: 918-789-4219. E-mail: chelseapubliclibrary@yahoo.com. *Libr Dir,* Darla J Cole
Pop 2,500
Library Holdings: Bk Vols 5,400; Per Subs 10
Automation Activity & Vendor Info: (Circulation) Follett Software
Wireless access
Open Tues 9-7, Wed-Fri 9-5, Sat 9-12

CHEROKEE

P CHEROKEE-CITY-COUNTY PUBLIC LIBRARY*, 123 S Grand Ave, 73728. SAN 313-8615. Tel: 580-596-2366. FAX: 580-596-2968. E-mail: cherlb_2000@yahoo.com. Web Site: www.cherokee.okpls.org. *Dir,* Seneca West; Staff 1 (Non-MLS 1)
Founded 1907. Pop 6,000
Library Holdings: Bk Vols 15,000
Subject Interests: Agr, Genealogy, Relig studies
Automation Activity & Vendor Info: (Cataloging) Follett Software; (Circulation) Follett Software; (ILL) Follett Software
Wireless access
Open Mon-Thurs 10-6, Fri 10-5, Sat 9-Noon
Friends of the Library Group

CHICKASHA

P CHICKASHA PUBLIC LIBRARY*, 527 W Iowa Ave, 73018. SAN 313-8623. Tel: 405-222-6075. FAX: 405-222-6072. Web Site: chickashapl.okpls.org. *Dir,* Lillie Huckaby; E-mail: lillie.huckaby@chickasha.org; *ILL,* Sandra Robertson; E-mail: sandra.robertson@chickasha.org; *Youth Serv,* Courtney Mayall; E-mail: courtney.mayall@chickasha.org; *Libr Asst,* Michelle Skinner; E-mail: michelle.skinner@chickasha.org; Staff 6 (MLS 2, Non-MLS 4)
Founded 1905. Pop 16,358
Library Holdings: AV Mats 2,758; Bk Titles 50,882; Bk Vols 52,170; Per Subs 93
Automation Activity & Vendor Info: (Acquisitions) Auto-Graphics, Inc; (Cataloging) Auto-Graphics, Inc; (Circulation) Auto-Graphics, Inc; (OPAC) Auto-Graphics, Inc
Wireless access
Function: 24/7 Electronic res, 24/7 Online cat, Accelerated reader prog, Adult bk club, Bk club(s), Bks on CD, Children's prog, Computers for patron use, Electronic databases & coll, Free DVD rentals, Homebound delivery serv, ILL available, Internet access, Magazines, Magnifiers for reading, Mail & tel request accepted, Meeting rooms, Notary serv, Online cat, OverDrive digital audio bks, Photocopying/Printing, Prog for adults, Prog for children & young adult, Scanner, Story hour, Summer reading prog, Tax forms, Teen prog, Wheelchair accessible
Open Mon-Thurs 9:30-7, Fri 9:30-6, Sat 10-2
Friends of the Library Group

C UNIVERSITY OF SCIENCE & ARTS OF OKLAHOMA*, Nash Library, 1901 S 17th St, 73018. (Mail add: 1727 W Alabama Ave, 73018), SAN 313-8631. Tel: 405-574-1343. FAX: 405-574-1220. E-mail: nashlibrary@usao.edu. Web Site: library.usao.edu. *Libr Asst I,* Rhonda Mayo; Tel: 405-574-1263, E-mail: rmayo@usao.edu; *Interim Dir,* Nicole McMonagle; Tel: 405-574-1341, E-mail: nmcmonagle@usao.edu; Staff 4 (MLS 3, Non-MLS 1)
Founded 1908. Enrl 920; Fac 59; Highest Degree: Bachelor
Jul 2017-Jun 2018 Income State $105,000. Mats Exp $88,000, Per/Ser (Incl. Access Fees) $4,000, Manu Arch $1,000, AV Mat $2,000, Electronic Ref Mat (Incl. Access Fees) $80,000, Presv $1,000. Sal $55,000 (Prof $90,000)
Library Holdings: Bks on Deafness & Sign Lang 300; e-books 50; Bk Titles 65,000; Bk Vols 70,000; Per Subs 30
Special Collections: Oklahoma & Southwestern US History (Anna Lewis Coll); Oklahoma College for Women Archives; Te Ata Coll

Automation Activity & Vendor Info: (Cataloging) Koha; (Circulation) Koha; (Discovery) EBSCO Discovery Service; (ILL) OCLC WorldShare Interlibrary Loan; (OPAC) Koha
Wireless access
Partic in Amigos Library Services, Inc; OCLC Online Computer Library Center, Inc
Special Services for the Deaf - Bks on deafness & sign lang; Coll on deaf educ; Spec interest per

CLAREMORE

S J M DAVIS ARMS & HISTORICAL MUSEUM*, Research Library, 330 N JM Davis Blvd, 74017. (Mail add: PO Box 966, 74018), SAN 327-6309. Tel: 918-341-5707. FAX: 918-341-5771. Web Site: www.thegunmuseum.com. *Dir,* Wayne McCombs; E-mail: director@thegunmuseum.com
Founded 1970
Library Holdings: Bk Titles 3,500
Subject Interests: Firearms
Function: Ref serv available
Open Tues-Sat 10-5
Restriction: Not a lending libr

C ROGERS STATE UNIVERSITY LIBRARY*, Stratton Taylor Library, 1701 W Will Rogers Blvd, 74017-3252. SAN 313-864X. Tel: 918-343-7716. Administration Tel: 918-343-7715. FAX: 918-343-7897. E-mail: library@rsu.edu. Web Site: www.rsu.edu/library. *Dir,* Alan Lawless; E-mail: alawless@rsu.edu; *Assoc Dir,* Kaitlin Crotty; Tel: 918-343-7717, E-mail: kcrotty@rsu.edu; *Electronic Res & Syst Librn,* Cecily Tubbs; Tel: 918-343-7719, E-mail: ctubbs@rsu.edu; *Coll Develop Librn,* Michelle Owens; Tel: 918-343-7720, E-mail: mowens@rsu.edu; *Distance Learning Librn, First Year Experience Librn,* Ashley Bean; Tel: 918-343-7786, E-mail: abean@rsu.edu. Subject Specialists: *Assessment, Graphic design, Info literacy,* Kaitlin Crotty; *Govt doc,* Cecily Tubbs; Staff 5 (MLS 5)
Founded 1909. Highest Degree: Master
Jul 2020-Jun 2021 Income $818,924. Mats Exp $300,000. Sal $325,217 (Prof $238,539)
Library Holdings: CDs 1,434; DVDs 2,211; e-books 423,501; Bk Vols 78,260
Automation Activity & Vendor Info: (Acquisitions) SirsiDynix; (Cataloging) SirsiDynix; (Circulation) SirsiDynix; (Course Reserve) SirsiDynix; (Discovery) ProQuest; (ILL) OCLC WorldShare Interlibrary Loan; (OPAC) SirsiDynix; (Serials) SirsiDynix
Wireless access
Function: Archival coll, Audio & video playback equip for onsite use, AV serv, Bks on CD, Computers for patron use, Digital talking bks, Doc delivery serv, Electronic databases & coll, Equip loans & repairs, Free DVD rentals, Govt ref serv, ILL available, Music CDs, Online cat, Online ref, Orientations, Photocopying/Printing, Ref & res, Ref serv available, Spoken cassettes & CDs, Spoken cassettes & DVDs, Telephone ref, VHS videos, Wheelchair accessible
Open Mon-Thurs 7:30am-10pm, Fri 7:30-6, Sat 12-8:30, Sun 1:30-10

P WILL ROGERS LIBRARY*, 1515 N Florence Ave, 74017. SAN 313-8658. Tel: 918-341-1564. FAX: 918-342-0362. Web Site: www.claremorecity.com/168/Library. *Dir,* Sherry Beach; E-mail: sbeach@claremorecity.com; *Asst Dir,* Leslie Rogers; Staff 6 (MLS 1, Non-MLS 5)
Founded 1936
Library Holdings: Bk Titles 55,000; Per Subs 42
Special Collections: Oklahoma & Indian History Coll
Subject Interests: Okla newsp from before statehood to present day
Automation Activity & Vendor Info: (Acquisitions) TLC (The Library Corporation); (Cataloging) TLC (The Library Corporation); (Circulation) TLC (The Library Corporation)
Wireless access
Open Mon & Tues 9:30-8, Wed & Thurs 9:30-6, Fri & Sat 9:30-5
Friends of the Library Group

S WILL ROGERS MEMORIAL MUSEUM LIBRARY, 1720 W Will Rogers Blvd, 74017. (Mail add: PO Box 157, 74018-0157), SAN 320-2259. Tel: 918-341-0719. Circulation Tel: 918-343-8118. FAX: 918-343-8119. E-mail: wrinfo@willrogers.com. Web Site: www.willrogers.com. *Curator of Coll,* Jennifer Holt; Tel: 918-343-8124, E-mail: jholt@willrogers.com; Staff 3 (MLS 3)
Library Holdings: CDs 123; DVDs 26; Bk Vols 2,750; Videos 76
Special Collections: Oral History
Subject Interests: Aviation, Cherokee Indians, Civil War, Film, Genealogy, Local hist, Politics, State hist, Vaudeville, Will Rogers
Function: Res performed for a fee
Publications: Will Rogers, genealogy (bibliographies)
Restriction: Open by appt only

CLEVELAND

P JAY C BYERS MEMORIAL LIBRARY*, 215 E Wichita Ave, 74020. Tel: 918-358-2676. FAX: 918-358-5606. E-mail: info@jcbyerslibrary.org. Web Site: jcbyerslibrary.okpls.org. *Libr Dir,* Michelle Miller; E-mail: mmiller@jcbyers.lib.ok.us; *Libr Asst,* Debby Luthy; E-mail: dluthy@jcbyers.lib.ok.us; *Libr Asst,* Dawn Miears; E-mail: dmiears@jcbyers.lib.ok.us
Founded 1936. Pop 3,282; Circ 38,609
Library Holdings: AV Mats 30; Bk Vols 13,000; Per Subs 20; Talking Bks 60
Automation Activity & Vendor Info: (Cataloging) Book Systems; (Circulation) Book Systems
Wireless access
Function: Bk club(s), Home delivery & serv to seniorr ctr & nursing homes, Homebound delivery serv, ILL available, Prog for children & young adult, Summer reading prog, VHS videos, Wheelchair accessible
Open Mon-Fri 9:30-6, Sat 10-2
Friends of the Library Group

CLINTON

P WESTERN PLAINS LIBRARY SYSTEM*, 501 S 28th St, 73601-3996. SAN 313-8666. Tel: 580-323-0974. FAX: 580-323-1190. Web Site: www.wplibs.com. *Exec Dir,* Tim Miller; E-mail: tim.miller@wplibs.com; Staff 23 (MLS 3, Non-MLS 20)
Founded 1966. Pop 45,000; Circ 201,000
Special Collections: State Document Depository
Automation Activity & Vendor Info: (Acquisitions) TLC (The Library Corporation); (Cataloging) TLC (The Library Corporation); (Circulation) TLC (The Library Corporation); (ILL) OCLC; (OPAC) TLC (The Library Corporation)
Wireless access
Function: ILL available, Internet access, Prog for children & young adult, Summer reading prog
Partic in Amigos Library Services, Inc; OLTN
Special Services for the Blind - Talking bks
Open Mon 8-5, Tues-Thurs 9-7, Fri 9-5
Restriction: Non-circulating coll
Friends of the Library Group
Branches: 7
CLINTON PUBLIC LIBRARY, 721 Frisco Ave, 73601-3320, SAN 376-5938. Tel: 580-323-2165. FAX: 580-323-7884. E-mail: clinton.public@wplibs.com. *Br Mgr,* Kathy Atchley; Staff 3 (Non-MLS 3)
Founded 1968. Pop 8,833; Circ 44,160
Library Holdings: Bks on Deafness & Sign Lang 50; Bk Vols 75,000; Per Subs 50
Special Collections: State Document Depository
Function: AV serv
Open Mon-Thurs 9-7, Fri & Sat 9-5, Sun 1-5
Restriction: Access for corporate affiliates
Friends of the Library Group
CORDELL PUBLIC LIBRARY, 208 S College, Cordell, 73632-5210, SAN 376-5954. Tel: 580-832-3530. FAX: 580-832-3530. E-mail: cordell.public@wplibs.com. *Libr Mgr,* Rhonda Schmidt
Library Holdings: Bk Titles 50,000; Per Subs 12
Open Mon-Thurs 9-6, Fri & Sat 9-5
Friends of the Library Group
HAZEL CROSS LIBRARY, 111 W Broadway, Thomas, 73669, SAN 376-6004. Tel: 580-661-3532. FAX: 580-661-3532. E-mail: hazel.cross@wplibs.com. *Libr Mgr,* Tonya Baldwin
Library Holdings: Bk Titles 5,000; Bk Vols 5,100; Per Subs 10
Open Mon-Thurs 10-6, Fri 10-5, Sat 9-1
SEILING PUBLIC LIBRARY, 209 N Main St, Seiling, 73663, SAN 376-5997. Tel: 580-922-4259. FAX: 580-922-4259. E-mail: seiling.public@wplibs.com. *Libr Mgr,* Wanda Moldrup
Library Holdings: Bk Titles 13,000; Bk Vols 13,400; Per Subs 14
Open Mon-Thurs 10-6, Fri 10-5, Sat 9-1
SENTINEL PUBLIC LIBRARY, 210 E Main St, Sentinel, 73664, SAN 376-5989. Tel: 580-393-2244. E-mail: sentinel.public@wplibs.com. *Libr Mgr,* Nicole Huntzinger; Staff 1 (Non-MLS 1)
Library Holdings: Bk Titles 3,000
Open Tues & Wed 10-6, Fri 10-5
MINNIE R SLIEF MEMORIAL LIBRARY, 201 S Cearlock St, Cheyenne, 73628, SAN 376-5962. Tel: 580-497-3777. E-mail: minnier.slief@wplibs.com. *Libr Mgr,* Laura Garcia; Staff 1 (Non-MLS 1)
Founded 1968
Library Holdings: DVDs 67; Bk Vols 9,000; Per Subs 15; Videos 365
Open Mon-Thurs 10-5:30, Fri 10-5, Sat 9-1
WEATHERFORD PUBLIC LIBRARY, 219 E Frankin, Weatherford, 73096-5134, SAN 325-1330. Tel: 580-772-3591. FAX: 580-772-3591. E-mail: weatherford.public@wplibs.com. *Librn,* Position Currently Open
Founded 1969. Pop 12,000; Circ 42,000
Library Holdings: Bk Vols 63,000; Per Subs 40

Open Mon-Thurs 9-7, Fri & Sat 9-5, Sun 1-5
Friends of the Library Group
Bookmobiles: 1. Mgr, Cammy Huterson

COALGATE

P COAL COUNTY PUBLIC LIBRARY*, 115 W Ohio St, 74538. SAN 376-6446. Tel: 580-927-3103. Toll Free FAX: 866-328-0175. E-mail: coalgate@seolibraries.com. Web Site: www.seolibraries.com/about/hours-locations/coal. *Br Mgr,* Dario Bellettini; E-mail: dario.bellettini@seolibraries.com
Library Holdings: Bk Titles 25,000; Per Subs 17
Automation Activity & Vendor Info: (Circulation) SirsiDynix
Wireless access
Mem of Southeast Oklahoma Library System (SEOLS)
Open Mon-Fri 10-6, Sat 10-3

COWETA

P COWETA PUBLIC LIBRARY*, 120 E Sycamore St, 74429. (Mail add: PO Box 850, 74429-0850). Tel: 918-486-6532. FAX: 918-486-3497. Web Site: www.cityofcoweta-ok.gov/169/Public-Library. *Dir,* Julia Stephens; E-mail: jstephens@cityofcoweta-ok.gov
Pop 9,569; Circ 60,778
Library Holdings: Audiobooks 385; DVDs 823; Large Print Bks 1,029; Bk Titles 23,294; Bk Vols 25,270
Automation Activity & Vendor Info: (Acquisitions) Book Systems; (Cataloging) Book Systems; (Circulation) Book Systems; (ILL) OCLC WorldShare Interlibrary Loan; (OPAC) Book Systems
Wireless access
Function: 24/7 Electronic res, 24/7 Online cat, Art programs, Bks on CD, ILL available, Laminating, Magazines, Prog for adults, Prog for children & young adult, Scanner, Summer reading prog, Tax forms
Open Mon, Tues & Thurs 10-8, Wed 10-6, Fri 10-5, Sat 10-2
Friends of the Library Group

COYLE

SR ST FRANCIS OF THE WOODS*, Cimarron Heights Library, 11414 W Hwy 33, 73027. (Mail add: PO Box 400, 73027-0400), SAN 326-7016. Tel: 405-466-3774. FAX: 405-466-3722. Web Site: www.stfrancisofthewoods.org/library. *Dir,* Brad Wilson; E-mail: director@stfrancisofthewoods.org
Founded 1982
Library Holdings: Bk Titles 19,000; Bk Vols 23,000
Special Collections: C G Jung Writings Coll, bks, journals; Francis of Assisi (St Francis Coll)
Subject Interests: Relig
Publications: Newsletter for St Francis of the Woods (Quarterly)
Open Mon-Fri 9-5

CRESCENT

P JAMES LOWE LOG CABIN LIBRARY, (Formerly Crescent Community Library), 403 E Monroe St, 73028. (Mail add: PO Box 759, 73028-0759). Tel: 405-310-8200, Ext 6. Web Site: cityofcrescent.com/log-cabin-library. *Dir,* Kayla Kinney; E-mail: kkinney@cityofcrescent.com
Pop 1,281; Circ 4,708
Library Holdings: AV Mats 30; Bk Vols 8,000; Per Subs 19; Talking Bks 100
Subject Interests: Mil hist
Automation Activity & Vendor Info: (Cataloging) Follett Software; (Circulation) Follett Software; (OPAC) Follett Software
Wireless access
Open Mon & Wed 10-2, Tues & Thurs 10-6, Fri 11-2

CUSHING

P CUSHING PUBLIC LIBRARY*, 215 N Steele Ave, 74023-3319. (Mail add: PO Box 551, 74023-0551), SAN 313-8674. Tel: 918-225-4188. FAX: 918-225-6201. E-mail: cushingpubliclibrary.org@gmail.com. Web Site: cushinglibrary.okpls.org. *Dir,* La Dawn Connor; *Asst Librn,* Roselee Maynard
Founded 1939. Pop 7,500; Circ 56,760
Library Holdings: Bk Vols 65,000; Per Subs 82
Special Collections: Genealogy (Cushing Family), bks, flm, micro; Law (Payne County Law Books); Local History
Subject Interests: Law
Automation Activity & Vendor Info: (Circulation) Innovative Interfaces, Inc
Wireless access
Open Mon-Thurs 9-8, Fri & Sat 9-6

DEWEY

P HERBERT F TYLER MEMORIAL LIBRARY*, 821 N Shawnee, 74029. SAN 313-8682. Tel: 918-534-2106. E-mail: deweylibrary@cityofdewey.com. *Dir,* Jordan Mayer
Founded 1941. Pop 4,000; Circ 16,012
Library Holdings: AV Mats 800; Large Print Bks 1,000; Bk Vols 15,000; Per Subs 32
Automation Activity & Vendor Info: (Cataloging) Follett Software; (Circulation) Follett Software
Open Mon-Fri 8:30-5:30, Sat 10-1
Friends of the Library Group

DRUMRIGHT

P DRUMRIGHT PUBLIC LIBRARY*, 104 E Broadway, 74030. SAN 313-8690. Tel: 918-352-2228. FAX: 918-352-9261. *Libr Dir,* Brenda L Grisham; E-mail: blgrisham@drumright.lib.ok.us
Circ 4,152
Library Holdings: Bk Vols 30,000; Per Subs 15
Automation Activity & Vendor Info: (Cataloging) Follett Software; (Circulation) Follett Software
Open Mon 11-8, Tues, Wed, Fri & Sat 11-4, Thurs 2-8

DUNCAN

P DUNCAN PUBLIC LIBRARY, 2211 N Hwy 81, 73533. SAN 313-8704. Tel: 580-255-0636. FAX: 580-255-6136. Web Site: www.youseemore.com/duncan. *Dir,* Amy Ryker; E-mail: amy.ryker@duncanok.gov; *Head, Circ, Head, Per,* Terrie Renfro; E-mail: terrie.renfro@duncanok.gov; *Cat,* Lynn Thacker; E-mail: lynn.thacker@duncanok.gov; *Children's & Youth Serv,* Darbie LaFontain; E-mail: darbie.lafontain@duncanok.gov; *ILL, Programming,* Jessica Allmon; E-mail: jessica.allmon@duncanok.gov; Staff 11 (MLS 1, Non-MLS 10)
Founded 1921. Pop 23,007; Circ 140,030
Library Holdings: Bk Titles 60,000; Per Subs 140
Subject Interests: Genealogy
Automation Activity & Vendor Info: (Circulation) TLC (The Library Corporation)
Wireless access
Partic in Okla Telecommunications Interlibr Syst
Open Mon, Tues & Thurs 9:30-7, Wed & Fri 9:30-6, Sat 9:30-1:30
Friends of the Library Group

DURANT

P DONALD W REYNOLDS COMMUNITY CENTER & LIBRARY*, 1515 W Main St, 74701. SAN 313-8739. Tel: 580-924-3486, 580-931-0231. Toll Free FAX: 844-995-3486. Web Site: www.donaldwreynolds.okpls.org. *Libr Dir,* Robbee Tonubbee; E-mail: rtonubbee@durant.org; *Literacy Coordr, Prog Dir,* Ashley Nunley; *Asst Librn,* Gina Brown; E-mail: ginab@durant.org; *Ch, Circ Serv,* Jami Ellis; *Adminr,* Angie Mullen; *Cat, Tech Serv,* Joy Cornelison; *Circ Serv,* Creston Brown; *Circ Serv,* Jennifer Simpkins
Founded 1926. Pop 12,000; Circ 20,000
Library Holdings: Bk Titles 55,000; Bk Vols 66,514; Per Subs 25
Automation Activity & Vendor Info: (Acquisitions) TLC (The Library Corporation); (Cataloging) TLC (The Library Corporation); (Circulation) TLC (The Library Corporation); (ILL) OCLC; (OPAC) TLC (The Library Corporation)
Wireless access
Function: ILL available
Open Mon-Thurs 9-8, Fri & Sat 9-5
Friends of the Library Group

C SOUTHEASTERN OKLAHOMA STATE UNIVERSITY*, Henry G Bennett Memorial Library, 425 W University, 74701-0609. Tel: 580-745-2702. Circulation Tel: 580-745-2932. Interlibrary Loan Service Tel: 580-745-2931. Reference Tel: 580-745-2935. Administration Tel: 580-745-3172. FAX: 580-745-7463. Web Site: www.se.edu/library. *Electronic Ser Librn, Libr Dir,* Sandra Thomas; E-mail: sthomas@se.edu; *Acq & Coll Develop Librn,* DeAnn Prince; *Govt Doc Librn,* Brandon Burnette; Tel: 580-745-2795, E-mail: bburnette@se.edu; *Circ Supvr, ILL, Ref & Instruction,* Greg Dawson; Tel: 580-745-2934, E-mail: gdawson@se.edu; Staff 9 (MLS 4, Non-MLS 5)
Founded 1913. Enrl 4,075; Highest Degree: Master
Library Holdings: CDs 5,082; e-books 8,000; Microforms 513,852; Bk Titles 109,100; Bk Vols 191,240; Per Subs 981; Videos 2,566
Special Collections: Brigance Coll; Curriculum Materials; Juvenile Literature Coll; Native American Coll; OJ Harvey Coll; Shakespeare Coll. State Document Depository; US Document Depository
Subject Interests: Educ, Hist, Lit
Automation Activity & Vendor Info: (Acquisitions) SirsiDynix; (Cataloging) SirsiDynix; (Circulation) SirsiDynix; (Course Reserve)

SirsiDynix; (Discovery) EBSCO Discovery Service; (ILL) SirsiDynix; (OPAC) SirsiDynix; (Serials) SirsiDynix
Wireless access
Partic in OCLC Online Computer Library Center, Inc
Open Mon-Thurs (Spring & Fall) 7:30am-10pm, Fri 7:30-5:30, Sat 1-5, Sun 3-10; Mon-Thurs (Summer) 8-8, Sun 3-8
Restriction: 24-hr pass syst for students only

EDMOND

CR OKLAHOMA CHRISTIAN UNIVERSITY*, Beam Library, 2501 E Memorial Rd, 73013. (Mail add: PO Box 11000, Oklahoma City, 73136-1100), SAN 313-945X. Tel: 405-425-5312. Interlibrary Loan Service Tel: 405-425-5324. Reference Tel: 405-425-5322. Administration Tel: 405-425-5320. FAX: 405-425-5313. Web Site: library.oc.edu. *Libr Dir,* Tamie Lyn Willis; E-mail: tamie.willis@oc.edu; *Archivist, Head, Tech Serv,* Jennifer Compton; Tel: 405-425-5314, E-mail: jennifer.compton@oc.edu; *Electronic Res & Ref Librn,* Dara Tinius; Tel: 405-425-5315, E-mail: dara.tinius@oc.edu; *Instrul Librn, Theological Librn,* Chris Rosser; Tel: 405-425-5323, E-mail: chris.rosser@oc.edu; *Acq Mgr,* Kimberly Cannon; Tel: 405-425-5319, E-mail: kimberly.cannon@oc.edu; *Circ Mgr,* Position Currently Open; *ILL Mgr,* Connie Maple; E-mail: connie.maple@oc.edu; *Tech Serv Asst,* Michelle Sheldon; Tel: 405-425-5311, E-mail: michelle.sheldon@oc.edu. Subject Specialists: *Theol,* Chris Rosser; Staff 7.5 (MLS 4, Non-MLS 3.5)
Founded 1950. Enrl 2,200; Fac 100; Highest Degree: Master
Special Collections: Rare Books Coll; Restoration History Coll (A coll of materials from the Stone-Campbell Movement & by Church of Christ authors)
Automation Activity & Vendor Info: (Acquisitions) SirsiDynix; (Cataloging) SirsiDynix; (Circulation) SirsiDynix; (Course Reserve) SirsiDynix; (Discovery) EBSCO Discovery Service; (ILL) OCLC; (OPAC) SirsiDynix; (Serials) SirsiDynix
Wireless access
Partic in Amigos Library Services, Inc; Asn of Christian Librs; Christian Col Libr; Oklahoma Council of Academic Libr Directors
Special Services for the Blind - Assistive/Adapted tech devices, equip & products
Open Mon, Tues & Thurs 7:30am-11pm, Wed 7:30-5 & 9-11, Fri 7:30-5, Sat 12-5, Sun 1:30-11

C UNIVERSITY OF CENTRAL OKLAHOMA*, Max Chambers Library, 100 N University Dr, 73034. (Mail add: PO Box 192, 73034-0192), SAN 313-8747. Tel: 405-974-3361. Interlibrary Loan Service Tel: 405-974-2876. Reference Tel: 405-974-2878. FAX: 405-974-3806, 405-974-3874. E-mail: library@uco.edu. Web Site: library.uco.edu. *Exec Dir,* Habib Tabatabai; Tel: 405-974-2865, E-mail: htabatabai@uco.edu; *Dir, Access Serv, Dir, Operations,* Carolyn Mahin; Tel: 405-974-2595, E-mail: cmahin@uco.edu; *Dir, Archives & Spec Coll, Dir, Libr Develop,* Nicole Willard; Tel: 405-974-2882, E-mail: nwillard@uco.edu; *Dir, Learning Res, User Experience Librn,* Deborah Thompson; Tel: 405-974-2880, E-mail: dthompson@uco.edu; *Data Mgt, Dir, Technology,* Beth Jones; Tel: 405-974-2883, E-mail: ejones42@uco.edu. Subject Specialists: *Bus,* Carolyn Mahin; Staff 20 (MLS 18, Non-MLS 2)
Founded 1890. Enrl 12,020; Fac 572; Highest Degree: Master
Library Holdings: Bk Titles 612,720; Bk Vols 960,412; Per Subs 2,147
Special Collections: Alice Ayler Orphan Train Coll, V-tapes; Bill Burchardt Coll; Dale McConathy Coll; Don Betz Coll; John George Coll; Oklahoma Townsite Coll; World War II (Sidney Bray Coll). Oral History; State Document Depository; US Document Depository
Automation Activity & Vendor Info: (Acquisitions) Ex Libris Group; (Cataloging) Ex Libris Group; (Circulation) Ex Libris Group; (Course Reserve) Ex Libris Group; (ILL) OCLC ILLiad; (OPAC) Ex Libris Group; (Serials) Ex Libris Group
Wireless access
Function: Art exhibits, Audio & video playback equip for onsite use, Bks on CD, CD-ROM, Computers for patron use, Distance learning, Doc delivery serv, E-Reserves, Electronic databases & coll, Govt ref serv, Internet access, Microfiche/film & reading machines, Music CDs, Online cat, Online info literacy tutorials on the web & in blackboard, Online ref, Photocopying/Printing, Printer for laptops & handheld devices, Ref & res, Ref serv available, Scanner, Spoken cassettes & CDs, Spoken cassettes & DVDs, Telephone ref, VHS videos, Wheelchair accessible
Partic in Amigos Library Services, Inc; Onenet
Open Mon-Thurs 7:30am-2am, Fri 7:30-6, Sat 10-6, Sun Noon-2am
Restriction: In-house use for visitors
Friends of the Library Group

EL RENO

S BUREAU OF PRISONS*, Federal Correctional Institution Library, 4205 OK-66, 73036. SAN 313-8755. Tel: 405-262-4875. FAX: 405-262-6266. *Librn,* Brandon Bowers
Founded 1960
Library Holdings: Bk Vols 5,000; Per Subs 17
Restriction: Not open to pub

S CANADIAN COUNTY HISTORICAL MUSEUM LIBRARY*, 300 S Grand Ave, 73036. SAN 327-571X. Tel: 405-262-5121. E-mail: info@canadiancountymuseum.com. Web Site: canadiancountymuseum.com. *Curator,* Pat Reuter
Library Holdings: Bk Vols 300
Special Collections: Indian Artifacts, Rock Island Railroad Effects, domestic, church & farming implements
Subject Interests: Local hist
Open Wed-Sat 10-4, Sun 1-4

P EL RENO CARNEGIE LIBRARY*, 215 E Wade St, 73036-2753. SAN 313-8763. Tel: 405-262-2409. FAX: 405-422-2136. E-mail: library@elrenolibrary.org. Web Site: elrenolibrary.okpls.org. *Libr Dir,* Kiley Ingram; E-mail: kingram@cityofelreno.com; *Asst Dir, Circ Tech,* Teresa Carey; E-mail: tcarey@elrenolibrary.org
Pop 15,000
Library Holdings: Bk Vols 31,700; Per Subs 149
Special Collections: Edna May Armold Archives
Automation Activity & Vendor Info: (Circulation) Biblionix
Wireless access
Open Mon-Thurs 9-7, Fri 9-5, Sat 9-1
Friends of the Library Group

J REDLANDS COMMUNITY COLLEGE*, A R Harrison Learning Resources Center, 1300 S Country Club Rd, 73036. SAN 313-8771. Tel: 405-422-1254. FAX: 405-422-1200. E-mail: library@redlandscc.edu. Web Site: library.redlandscc.edu. *Dir,* Position Currently Open; Staff 4 (MLS 1, Non-MLS 3)
Founded 1965. Fac 44; Highest Degree: Associate
Library Holdings: Audiobooks 150; AV Mats 1,200; CDs 20; DVDs 500; e-books 40,000; Bk Titles 12,390; Bk Vols 20,184; Per Subs 100; Videos 390
Automation Activity & Vendor Info: (Cataloging) OCLC WorldShare Interlibrary Loan; (Circulation) TLC (The Library Corporation); (ILL) OCLC WorldShare Interlibrary Loan; (OPAC) TLC (The Library Corporation)
Wireless access
Function: Distance learning, For res purposes, ILL available, Photocopying/Printing, Ref serv available, Telephone ref, Wheelchair accessible
Partic in Amigos Library Services, Inc; Oklahoma Council of Academic Libr Directors
Open Mon-Thurs 8-8, Fri 8-5, Sat 10-2

S UNITED STATES CAVALRY ASSOCIATION, United States Cavalry Memorial Research Library, 3220 N Jesse Reno St, 73036. Tel: 405-422-6330. E-mail: info@uscavalryassociation.org. Web Site: www.uscavalryassociation.org. *Librn,* Samuel R Young
Founded 1999
Library Holdings: Bk Vols 4,000; Per Subs 20
Special Collections: Cavalry Biography, biographical data files; Hiram Tuttle Papers (US Army Officer, Member of US Olympic Equestrian Team 1932 & 1936)
Subject Interests: Archives, Equine/equestrian, Manuscripts
Open Mon-Fri 8-4

ELGIN

P ELGIN COMMUNITY LIBRARY, 108 Thoma Dr, 73538. (Mail add: PO Box 310, 73538-0310). Tel: 580-492-6650. FAX: 580-454-6650. E-mail: elginoklibrary@gmail.com. Web Site: www.elginlibrary.org. *Dir,* Leslie Durham
Founded 1985. Pop 3,500
Library Holdings: Audiobooks 126; DVDs 1,675; Bk Vols 12,520
Wireless access
Function: 24/7 Online cat, 3D Printer, Adult bk club, After school storytime
Open Tues-Fri 9-6, Sat 9-1
Friends of the Library Group

ELK CITY

P ELK CITY CARNEGIE LIBRARY*, 221 W Broadway, 73644. SAN 313-878X. Tel: 580-225-0136. E-mail: library@elkcity.com. *Dir,* DeAun Ivester; E-mail: ivesterd@elkcity.com; *Ch Serv,* Donna McNaught; E-mail: mcnaughtd@elkcity.com; Staff 2 (Non-MLS 2)
Founded 1912. Pop 16,000; Circ 76,000
Library Holdings: Bk Vols 47,000; Per Subs 35
Special Collections: Local obit files; Southwest Literature. Oral History
Automation Activity & Vendor Info: (Circulation) Follett Software
Function: 24/7 Electronic res, 24/7 Online cat, 3D Printer, Activity rm, Adult bk club, Audiobks via web, AV serv, Computers for patron use, Free

DVD rentals, Holiday prog, ILL available, Scanner, Spanish lang bks, Story hour
Open Mon, Wed & Fri 10-6, Tues & Thurs 10-9, Sat 10-2
Friends of the Library Group

ENID

P PUBLIC LIBRARY OF ENID & GARFIELD COUNTY, 120 W Maine, 73701-5606. Tel: 580-234-6313. FAX: 580-249-9280. E-mail: publiclibrary@enid.org. Web Site: enid.okpls.org. *Interim Dir,* Erin Crawford; *Dep Dir,* Ms Theri Ray; *Ref Serv,* Sarah Cariker; Staff 19 (MLS 2, Non-MLS 17)
Founded 1899. Pop 63,700; Circ 160,540
Library Holdings: Audiobooks 1,762; Bk Titles 74,230; Bk Vols 80,845; Per Subs 160; Videos 1,608
Special Collections: Oklahoma Books & Authors (Marquis James Coll). US Document Depository
Automation Activity & Vendor Info: (Acquisitions) Follett Software; (Cataloging) Follett Software; (Circulation) Follett Software; (OPAC) Follett Software
Wireless access
Function: Adult literacy prog, Bks on CD, Computers for patron use, Electronic databases & coll, Free DVD rentals, Govt ref serv, ILL available, Online cat, Photocopying/Printing, Ref serv available, Summer reading prog, Tax forms, Wheelchair accessible
Open Mon-Thurs 9-7, Fri & Sat 9-6
Friends of the Library Group

ERICK

P ERICK PUBLIC LIBRARY*, 200 S Sheb Wooley, 73645. (Mail add: PO Box 385, 73645-0385). Tel: 580-526-3425. E-mail: ericklibrary@dobsonteleco.com. *Librn,* Kelley Brianne Greer
Pop 1,100
Library Holdings: AV Mats 350; Bk Vols 11,000; Per Subs 17; Talking Bks 179
Wireless access
Open Mon 2-7, Wed & Fri 12-5

EUFAULA

P EUFAULA MEMORIAL LIBRARY*, 301 S First St, 74432-3201. SAN 313-8801. Tel: 918-689-2291. Toll Free Tel: 888-291-8148. FAX: 918-689-4124. E-mail: eufaulapl@eols.org. Web Site: eols.org/library-location/eufaula-memorial-library. *Br Mgr,* Brittany Moore; E-mail: bmoore@eols.org
Founded 1971
Library Holdings: Bk Titles 28,937; Per Subs 30
Subject Interests: Video
Automation Activity & Vendor Info: (Circulation) SirsiDynix
Wireless access
Mem of Eastern Oklahoma Library System
Open Mon-Thurs 9-6, Fri 9-5, Sat 9-1
Friends of the Library Group

FAIRFAX

P FAIRFAX PUBLIC LIBRARY, 158 E Elm, 74637. SAN 313-881X. Tel: 918-642-5535. FAX: 918-642-3350. E-mail: library@fairfax.lib.ok.us. Web Site: www.fairfax.lib.ok.us. *Dir,* Marcy Sterling; *Librn,* Howardean Rhoads
Founded 1922. Pop 1,300
Library Holdings: Bk Vols 13,000
Special Collections: Area History
Wireless access
Function: 24/7 Electronic res, 24/7 Online cat, Bks on CD, Children's prog, Free DVD rentals, ILL available, Internet access, Online cat, OverDrive digital audio bks, Photocopying/Printing, Scanner
Open Tues-Thurs 1-6

FAIRVIEW

P FAIRVIEW CITY LIBRARY, 115 S Sixth Ave, 73737-2141. (Mail add: PO Box 419, 73737-0419), SAN 313-8828. Tel: 580-227-2190. FAX: 580-227-2187. E-mail: fairviewlibrary@yahoo.com, librarian@fairviewok.org. Web Site: fairviewoklibrary.org. *Dir,* Tamara Cornelsen; E-mail: fairviewlibrary@yahoo.com; *Ch,* Crystal Jackson; E-mail: librarian3@fairviewok.org; Staff 3 (Non-MLS 3)
Founded 1909. Pop 2,618; Circ 15,907
Special Collections: Oklahoma Heritage Coll
Subject Interests: Genealogy
Automation Activity & Vendor Info: (Circulation) Follett Software
Wireless access
Function: 24/7 Online cat, Adult bk club, Bk club(s), Bks on CD, Children's prog, Computer training, Computers for patron use, Electronic databases & coll, Free DVD rentals, Govt ref serv, Holiday prog, Home delivery & serv to seniorr ctr & nursing homes, ILL available, Internet access, Laminating, Large print keyboards, Magazines, Meeting rooms, Movies, Online cat, OverDrive digital audio bks, Preschool reading prog, Printer for laptops & handheld devices, Prog for adults, Prog for children & young adult, Scanner, Senior computer classes, Serves people with intellectual disabilities, Story hour, Study rm, Summer reading prog, Wheelchair accessible
Open Mon-Fri 8:30-6, Sat 9-Noon
Friends of the Library Group

FORT GIBSON

P Q B BOYDSTUN LIBRARY*, 201 E South Ave, 74434. (Mail add: PO Box 700, 74434-0700), SAN 313-8836. Tel: 918-478-3587. Toll Free Tel: 888-291-8151. FAX: 918-478-4599. E-mail: fortgibsonpl@eols.org. Web Site: eols.org/library-location/q-b-boydstun-library. *Br Mgr,* Rhonda Lee; E-mail: rlee@eols.org
Founded 1978
Library Holdings: Large Print Bks 1,500; Bk Vols 22,000; Per Subs 25; Talking Bks 1,000
Subject Interests: Mysteries, Popular, Romances, Western
Automation Activity & Vendor Info: (Cataloging) SirsiDynix; (Circulation) SirsiDynix
Wireless access
Mem of Eastern Oklahoma Library System
Open Mon-Fri 9-6, Sat 9-2

FORT SILL

UNITED STATES ARMY

A NYE LIBRARY*, 1640 Randolph Rd, 73503-9022, SAN 357-5462. Tel: 580-442-2048, 580-442-3806. FAX: 580-442-7346. Administration FAX: 580-442-7347. E-mail: nye.lib@us.army.mil. Web Site: www.sillmwr.com/recreation-leisure/nye-library. *Librn,* Joan Auwen; E-mail: joan.e.auwen.naf@mail.mil; Staff 10 (MLS 1, Non-MLS 9)
Founded 1953
Library Holdings: Audiobooks 2,004; AV Mats 604; CDs 1,057; DVDs 7,003; Large Print Bks 483; Bk Titles 73,028; Bk Vols 79,378; Per Subs 77
Special Collections: Books for College Libraries, microfiche; College Catalogs, microfiche; Webster University Deposit Coll
Subject Interests: Adult educ, Consumer educ, Family life, Home, Mil sci
Automation Activity & Vendor Info: (Cataloging) Innovative Interfaces, Inc - Millennium; (Circulation) Innovative Interfaces, Inc - Millennium
Function: Adult bk club, Art exhibits, Audio & video playback equip for onsite use, Audiobks via web, Bks on CD, Children's prog, Computer training, Computers for patron use, Digital talking bks, Electronic databases & coll, Free DVD rentals, Holiday prog, Internet access, Microfiche/film & reading machines, Music CDs, Online cat, Online ref, Orientations, OverDrive digital audio bks, Photocopying/Printing, Prog for adults, Prog for children & young adult, Spanish lang bks, Story hour, Summer reading prog, Teen prog, Wheelchair accessible, Workshops
Partic in OCLC Online Computer Library Center, Inc
Publications: The Tattler (Monthly newsletter)
Special Services for the Deaf - Bks on deafness & sign lang; Closed caption videos
Special Services for the Blind - Bks on CD; Copier with enlargement capabilities; Free checkout of audio mat; Large print bks; Playaways (bks on MP3); Recorded bks
Open Mon-Thurs 10-8, Fri-Sun 10-5
Restriction: Authorized patrons, Mil, family mem, retirees, Civil Serv personnel NAF only

A MORRIS J SWETT TECHNICAL LIBRARY*, Snow Hall 16, Bldg 730, 73503-5100, SAN 357-5438. Tel: 580-442-4525. FAX: 580-442-7300. *Librn,* Jo Ann Knight; E-mail: jo.ann.knight@us.army.mil; *Tech Serv,* Cora Daebler; *Tech Serv,* Daniel Heintzman; Staff 3 (MLS 1, Non-MLS 2)
Founded 1911
Library Holdings: Bk Vols 79,000; Per Subs 65
Special Collections: In-House Indexes; Janes Series; Military Periodical Analytical Index File, VF; Rare Books Coll; Special Bibliographies; Subject Headings to the Library Coll; U Military Science Classification System; Unit Histories-Field Artillery, bk, microfilm, fiche
Subject Interests: Ammunition, Ballistics, Field artillery, Mil hist, Mil sci, Missiles, Ordnance, Weapon systs, Weapons
Partic in OCLC Online Computer Library Center, Inc
Open Mon-Fri 7-5

FREDERICK

P FREDERICK PUBLIC LIBRARY*, 200 E Grand, 73542. SAN 313-8844. Tel: 580-335-3601. FAX: 580-335-3601. E-mail: library@frederickok.org. *Dir,* Dena Northcutt; Staff 3 (MLS 1, Non-MLS 2)
Founded 1915. Circ 16,384
Library Holdings: Bk Vols 15,000; Per Subs 36

Automation Activity & Vendor Info: (Cataloging) Biblionix/Apollo; (Circulation) Biblionix/Apollo; (ILL) OCLC ILLiad
Wireless access
Open Mon-Thurs 10:30-6, Fri 10:30-4:30, Sat 9-12
Friends of the Library Group

GEARY

P GEARY PUBLIC LIBRARY*, 106 W Main St, 73040. (Mail add: PO Box 216, 73040-0216), SAN 313-8852. Tel: 405-884-2372. FAX: 405-884-2372. E-mail: library@cityofgeary.com. *Dir,* Lois Margerum; Staff 1 (Non-MLS 1)
Founded 1933. Pop 1,200; Circ 14,000
Library Holdings: Bk Titles 10,000; Per Subs 10
Wireless access
Function: Workshops
Open Tues & Wed 10-5:30, Fri 10-6

GOODWELL

C OKLAHOMA PANHANDLE STATE UNIVERSITY*, Marvin E McKee Library, 409 W Sewell, 73939. (Mail add: PO Box 370, 73939-0370), SAN 313-8860. Tel: 580-349-1540. Toll Free Tel: 800-664-6778. FAX: 580-349-1541. E-mail: mckeelib@opsu.edu. Web Site: www.opsu.edu/McKeeLibrary. *Libr Dir,* Alton Tony Hardman; Tel: 580-349-1542, E-mail: tony.hardman@opsu.edu; *Access Serv Librn,* Katy Levings; Tel: 580-349-1547, E-mail: katy.levings@opsu.edu; *Archives & Spec Coll Librn, Cat Librn, Tech Serv Librn,* Bonnie Maille; Tel: 580-349-1546, E-mail: bonnie.maille@opsu.edu; *Acq Asst,* Dawn Lloyd; Tel: 580-349-1548, E-mail: dlloyd@opsu.edu; Staff 4 (MLS 2, Non-MLS 2)
Founded 1909. Enrl 1,367; Fac 65; Highest Degree: Bachelor
Library Holdings: Audiobooks 874; AV Mats 1,629; Bks on Deafness & Sign Lang 20; CDs 115; DVDs 642; e-books 34,616; e-journals 26,000; Electronic Media & Resources 106; High Interest/Low Vocabulary Bk Vols 200; Large Print Bks 25; Music Scores 2,572; Bk Titles 10,558; Bk Vols 116,652; Per Subs 53
Special Collections: Elementary Education (McKee Library Youth Coll); Howsley Poetry & Shakespeare Coll; K-12 Education (McKee Library Textbook Review Center); McKee Library Archive Coll, bks, ephemera, per; State Public Schools (McKee Library Curriculum Coll). State Document Depository
Automation Activity & Vendor Info: (Acquisitions) Ex Libris Group; (Cataloging) Ex Libris Group; (Circulation) Ex Libris Group; (Course Reserve) Ex Libris Group; (ILL) OCLC WorldShare Interlibrary Loan; (OPAC) Ex Libris Group; (Serials) Ex Libris Group
Wireless access
Function: 24/7 Electronic res, 24/7 Online cat, Adult literacy prog, Archival coll, Audio & video playback equip for onsite use, CD-ROM, Computers for patron use, Doc delivery serv, E-Reserves, Electronic databases & coll, ILL available, Internet access, Music CDs, Online info literacy tutorials on the web & in blackboard, Outside serv via phone, mail, e-mail & web, Photocopying/Printing, Ref & res, Ref serv available, Res libr, Spoken cassettes & CDs, Spoken cassettes & DVDs, VHS videos, Wheelchair accessible
Partic in Amigos Library Services, Inc; Oklahoma Council of Academic Libr Directors
Special Services for the Blind - ZoomText magnification & reading software
Open Mon-Thurs 8am-10pm, Fri 8-4:30, Sun 1-10
Restriction: Borrowing privileges limited to fac & registered students

GRANDFIELD

P GRANDFIELD PUBLIC LIBRARY, 101 W Second St, 73546-9449. (Mail add: PO Box 725, 73546-0725), SAN 313-8879. Tel: 580-479-5598. FAX: 580-479-5534. E-mail: grandpl@hotmail.com. *Librn,* Cathy Haney
Founded 1944. Pop 1,200; Circ 1,809
Library Holdings: Bk Titles 9,006; Bk Vols 10,092; Per Subs 3
Wireless access
Open Tues & Wed 2-6, Thurs-Sat 9-1
Friends of the Library Group

GRANITE

S OKLAHOMA STATE REFORMATORY LIBRARY*, 1700 E First St, 73547. (Mail add: PO Box 514, 73547-0514), SAN 313-8887. Tel: 580-480-3700. FAX: 580-480-3989. *Librn,* John Slater; E-mail: john.slater@doc.state.ok.us; Staff 1 (MLS 1)
Pop 1,000
Library Holdings: Bk Vols 12,000; Per Subs 50

GROVE

P GROVE PUBLIC LIBRARY*, 1140 NEO Loop, 74344-8602. SAN 313-8895. Tel: 918-786-2945. Toll Free Tel: 888-291-8150. FAX: 918-786-5233. E-mail: grovepl@eols.org. Web Site: eols.org/library-location/grove-public-library. *Br Mgr,* Brenda Newnam; E-mail: bnewnam@eols.org
Founded 1963. Pop 20,000
Library Holdings: Bk Vols 31,000; Per Subs 38
Subject Interests: Genealogy
Automation Activity & Vendor Info: (Circulation) SirsiDynix
Wireless access
Mem of Eastern Oklahoma Library System
Open Mon, Wed & Fri 8:30-5, Tues & Thurs 8:30-7, Sat 8-12

GUTHRIE

P GUTHRIE PUBLIC LIBRARY*, 201 N Division, 73044-3201. SAN 313-8909. Tel: 405-282-0050. FAX: 405-282-2804. Web Site: guthrie.okpls.org/. *Dir, Libr Serv,* Suzette Chang; E-mail: schang@cityofguthrie.com; *Asst Dir,* Candy Ford; E-mail: cford@cityofguthrie.com; Staff 7 (MLS 1, Non-MLS 6)
Founded 1903. Pop 40,000; Circ 78,000
Library Holdings: Audiobooks 1,040; AV Mats 5,031; Bks on Deafness & Sign Lang 18; CDs 416; DVDs 3,575; e-books 30,000; e-journals 200; Large Print Bks 1,696; Bk Vols 26,569; Per Subs 25
Special Collections: Oklahoma History (Helen Holmes Coll)
Automation Activity & Vendor Info: (Cataloging) Biblionix/Apollo; (Circulation) Biblionix/Apollo; (ILL) OCLC WorldShare Interlibrary Loan; (OPAC) Biblionix/Apollo
Wireless access
Function: 24/7 Electronic res, 24/7 Online cat, Activity rm, Adult bk club, After school storytime, Audiobks on Playaways & MP3, Audiobks via web, Bk club(s), Bks on CD, Children's prog, Computers for patron use, Digital talking bks, E-Reserves, Electronic databases & coll, Family literacy, Free DVD rentals, Holiday prog, ILL available, Internet access, Laminating, Life-long learning prog for all ages, Magazines, Magnifiers for reading, Mango lang, Meeting rooms, Movies, Music CDs, Notary serv, Online cat, Online ref, Outside serv via phone, mail, e-mail & web, OverDrive digital audio bks, Photocopying/Printing, Preschool reading prog, Prog for adults, Prog for children & young adult, Ref & res, Ref serv available, Senior outreach, Serves people with intellectual disabilities, Story hour, Study rm, Summer & winter reading prog, Summer reading prog, Tax forms, Teen prog, Wheelchair accessible
Open Mon, Wed & Fri 9-6, Tues & Thurs 9-8, Sat 9-1
Restriction: Non-resident fee
Friends of the Library Group

GUYMON

P GUYMON PUBLIC LIBRARY & ARTS CENTER*, 1718 N Oklahoma St, 73942. SAN 313-8917. Tel: 580-338-7330. FAX: 580-338-2659. E-mail: guymonpublib@guymon.lib.ok.us. Web Site: guymon.okpls.org. *Dir,* Rachel Sides; E-mail: rsides@guymon.lib.ok.us; Staff 6 (Non-MLS 6)
Founded 2013. Pop 12,000; Circ 39,557
Library Holdings: Bk Vols 30,000; Per Subs 45
Automation Activity & Vendor Info: (Acquisitions) Baker & Taylor; (Cataloging) Biblionix/Apollo; (Circulation) Biblionix/Apollo; (ILL) OCLC WorldShare Interlibrary Loan
Wireless access
Function: 24/7 Electronic res, Adult literacy prog, After school storytime, Archival coll, Art exhibits, Audiobks via web, Bilingual assistance for Spanish patrons, Bks on CD, Children's prog, Citizenship assistance, Computers for patron use, E-Readers, Electronic databases & coll, Free DVD rentals, Genealogy discussion group, Home delivery & serv to seniorr ctr & nursing homes, ILL available, Magazines, Mango lang, Movies, Online cat, OverDrive digital audio bks, Photocopying/Printing, Preschool reading prog, Prog for adults, Prog for children & young adult, Scanner, Spanish lang bks, Spoken cassettes & CDs, Story hour, Summer reading prog, Telephone ref, Wheelchair accessible
Open Mon-Thurs 9:30-7, Fri 9:30-5, Sat 9:30-2
Friends of the Library Group

HARTSHORNE

P HARTSHORNE PUBLIC LIBRARY*, 720 Pennsylvania Ave, 74547. SAN 376-592X. Tel: 918-297-2113. FAX: 866-935-9736. E-mail: hartshorne@seolibraries.com. Web Site: cityofhartshorne.com/library, www.seolibraries.com/about/hours-locations/hartshorne. *Asst Br Mgr,* Cindy Bedford; E-mail: cindy.bedford@seolibraries.com
Library Holdings: Bk Vols 5,000; Per Subs 20
Automation Activity & Vendor Info: (Circulation) SirsiDynix
Wireless access
Mem of Southeast Oklahoma Library System (SEOLS)
Open Tues & Thurs 8-7, Wed & Fri 8-6, Sat 10-3

HASKELL

P RIEGER MEMORIAL LIBRARY*, 116 N Broadway, 74436. (Mail add: PO Box 429, 74436-0429), SAN 313-8925. Tel: 918-482-3614. Toll Free Tel: 888-482-3614. FAX: 918-482-3266. E-mail: haskellpl@eols.org. Web Site: eols.org/library-location/rieger-memorial-library. *Br Mgr,* Holly Hughes; E-mail: hhughes@eols.org
Founded 1971
Library Holdings: Bk Vols 13,000; Per Subs 48
Automation Activity & Vendor Info: (Cataloging) SirsiDynix; (Circulation) SirsiDynix
Wireless access
Mem of Eastern Oklahoma Library System
Open Mon, Wed & Fri 12-5, Tues 10-6, Thurs 10-5, Sat 10-1

HEAVENER

P HEAVENER PUBLIC LIBRARY*, 203 E Ave C, 74937. (Mail add: PO Box 246, 74937-0246), SAN 313-8933. Tel: 918-653-2870. E-mail: heavener@seolibraries.com. Web Site: www.seolibraries.com/about/hours-locations/heavener. *Br Mgr,* Rachel Morton; E-mail: rachel.morton@seolibraries.com
Pop 2,566; Circ 27,917
Library Holdings: Bk Vols 23,000; Per Subs 25
Automation Activity & Vendor Info: (Circulation) SirsiDynix
Mem of Southeast Oklahoma Library System (SEOLS)
Open Tues-Fri 9-6, Sat 9-2
Friends of the Library Group

HELENA

S CRABTREE CORRECTIONAL CENTER*, Law Library, 216 N Murray St, 73741-1017. (Mail add: Rte 1, Box 8, 73741-9606). Tel: 580-852-3221. Web Site: doc.ok.gov/james-crabtree-correctional-center. *Library Contact,* Position Currently Open
Library Holdings: Bk Vols 100
Restriction: Not open to pub

HENNESSEY

P HENNESSEY PUBLIC LIBRARY, 525 S Main, 73742. SAN 313-8941. Tel: 405-853-2073. FAX: 405-853-6500. E-mail: info@hennessey.lib.ok.us. Web Site: hennesseypl.okpls.org. *Dir,* Lyndsey Kopsa; *Children & Youth Serv Librn,* Jennie Moreno; Staff 1 (Non-MLS 1)
Founded 1938. Pop 2,100; Circ 14,388
Jul 2015-Jun 2016 Income (Main Library Only) $187,369, City $129,689, Locally Generated Income $57,680. Mats Exp $25,430, Books $22,192, Per/Ser (Incl. Access Fees) $923, Micro $55, AV Mat $760, Electronic Ref Mat (Incl. Access Fees) $1,500. Sal $74,761
Library Holdings: Audiobooks 1,191; AV Mats 2,712; Bks on Deafness & Sign Lang 10; Braille Volumes 10; CDs 601; DVDs 1,374; Bk Vols 26,977; Per Subs 23
Special Collections: AFI 100 Best Films; Hennessey Clipper from 1890; Hennessey Heritage Coll; National Geographic, complete, leather bound; Ortman Film Memorial
Automation Activity & Vendor Info: (Circulation) Biblionix
Wireless access
Function: 24/7 Electronic res, 24/7 Online cat, Accelerated reader prog, Archival coll, ILL available
Open Mon-Fri 9-6
Friends of the Library Group

HENRYETTA

P HENRYETTA PUBLIC LIBRARY, 518 W Main St, 74437. SAN 313-895X. Tel: 918-652-7377. FAX: 918-652-2796. E-mail: hplib@henryettalibrary.org. Web Site: www.henryettalibrary.org. *Libr Dir,* Joann Hott; *Asst Librn,* Kathy Crosby
Founded 1910. Pop 6,096; Circ 17,450
Library Holdings: Audiobooks 108; CDs 150; DVDs 60; Large Print Bks 350; Bk Titles 20,000; Bk Vols 25,000; Per Subs 74; Videos 85
Automation Activity & Vendor Info: (Cataloging) Book Systems
Wireless access
Function: CD-ROM, Children's prog, Computers for patron use, Free DVD rentals, Home delivery & serv to seniorr ctr & nursing homes, Homebound delivery serv, ILL available, Magnifiers for reading, Music CDs, Photocopying/Printing, Story hour, Summer reading prog, Tax forms, Wheelchair accessible
Partic in Okla Libr Technology Network
Open Mon-Fri 10-6, Sat 10-1
Friends of the Library Group

HINTON

P HINTON PUBLIC LIBRARY*, 123 E Main St, 73047. (Mail add: PO Box 34, 73047-0034). Tel: 405-542-6167. E-mail: library@hintonok.com. Web Site: www.hintonok.com/community/library.php. *Dir,* Taylor Meriwether
Pop 2,175; Circ 13,639
Library Holdings: AV Mats 700; Large Print Bks 200; Bk Vols 8,700; Talking Bks 120
Automation Activity & Vendor Info: (Cataloging) Follett Software; (Circulation) Follett Software; (OPAC) Follett Software
Wireless access
Open Mon 10-7, Tues-Fri 10-5, Sat 9-Noon

HOBART

P HOBART PUBLIC LIBRARY, 200 S Main St, 73651. SAN 313-8968. Tel: 580-726-2535. FAX: 580-726-3600. E-mail: hobartpl@hobart.lib.ok.us. Web Site: www.hobartlibrary.okpls.org. *Dir,* Brandy Tointigh; Staff 2 (Non-MLS 2)
Founded 1912. Circ 39,609
Library Holdings: Audiobooks 481; AV Mats 1,487; CDs 411; DVDs 979; Large Print Bks 2,508; Bk Titles 32,028; Per Subs 20; Videos 566
Automation Activity & Vendor Info: (Acquisitions) Book Systems; (Cataloging) Book Systems; (Circulation) Book Systems; (ILL) OCLC WorldShare Interlibrary Loan; (OPAC) Book Systems
Wireless access
Function: 24/7 Online cat, Accelerated reader prog, Bks on CD, Children's prog, Computers for patron use, Free DVD rentals, Genealogy discussion group, Home delivery & serv to seniorr ctr & nursing homes, Homebound delivery serv, Internet access, Magazines, Meeting rooms, Online cat, OverDrive digital audio bks, Photocopying/Printing, Printer for laptops & handheld devices, Prog for adults, Ref serv available, Scanner, Spanish lang bks, Summer reading prog
Open Mon-Fri 9-6, Sat 9-Noon
Friends of the Library Group

HODGEN

S JIM E HAMILTON CORRECTIONAL CENTER*, Leisure Library, 53468 Mineral Springs Rd, 74939-3064. SAN 371-7704. Tel: 918-653-7831, Ext 386. FAX: 918-653-3814. *Library Contact,* Tanja Aguilar; E-mail: tanja.aguilar@doc.ok.gov
Founded 1970
Library Holdings: High Interest/Low Vocabulary Bk Vols 50; Bk Titles 7,480; Per Subs 61; Talking Bks 34
Automation Activity & Vendor Info: (ILL) OCLC ILLiad
Open Mon-Fri 11-7

HOLDENVILLE

P GRACE M PICKENS PUBLIC LIBRARY*, 209 E Ninth St, 74848. SAN 313-8976. Tel: 405-379-3245. Toll Free Tel: 888-567-4719. FAX: 405-379-5725. E-mail: library@cityofholdenville.net. Web Site: www.holdenvillepl.okpls.org. *Dir,* Kim McNaughton
Founded 1902. Pop 5,181; Circ 26,912
Library Holdings: Bk Vols 24,000
Automation Activity & Vendor Info: (Acquisitions) Follett Software; (Cataloging) Follett Software; (Circulation) Follett Software
Special Services for the Blind - Bks on cassette
Open Mon-Fri 8-5
Friends of the Library Group

HOLLIS

P HOLLIS PUBLIC LIBRARY, W Broadway & Second St, 73550. (Mail add: PO Box 73, 73550-0073), SAN 313-8984. Tel: 580-688-2744. Toll Free Tel: 888-554-5358. FAX: 580-688-9736. E-mail: hpl@spls.lib.ok.us. Web Site: www.spls.lib.ok.us/hollis. *Libr Mgr,* Chelsea Leigh; E-mail: cleigh@spls.lib.ok.us
Founded 1973. Pop 3,500; Circ 9,991
Library Holdings: Bk Vols 15,000; Per Subs 15
Automation Activity & Vendor Info: (Circulation) SirsiDynix
Mem of Southern Prairie Library System
Open Tues 12-7, Wed & Thurs 10-5, Fri 9-2, Sat 9-1

HOMINY

S DICK CONNER CORRECTIONAL CENTER LEISURE LIBRARY*, 129 Conner Rd, 74035. SAN 324-0126. Tel: 918-594-1300, Ext 3312. FAX: 918-594-1324. *Librn,* Kathy Graham
Founded 1979
Library Holdings: Bk Titles 8,000; Per Subs 35
Partic in Okla Telecommunications Interlibr Syst
Restriction: Not open to pub

P HOMINY PUBLIC LIBRARY*, 121 W Main, 74035. SAN 313-8992. Tel: 918-885-4486. FAX: 918-885-2837. E-mail: hominy.library@gmail.com. Web Site: www.hominy.lib.ok.us. *Dir,* Jimmie Ratliff; E-mail: jimmieratliff@cityofhominy.com; Staff 3 (MLS 1, Non-MLS 2)
Founded 1925. Pop 2,274; Circ 12,500
Library Holdings: Bk Vols 10,000
Automation Activity & Vendor Info: (Cataloging) Brodart; (Circulation) Brodart
Open Mon, Wed & Fri 9-5, Tues & Thurs 9-6, Sat 9-Noon

HOOKER

P OLIVE WARNER MEMORIAL LIBRARY*, 111 S Broadway, 73945. (Mail add: PO Box 576, 73945), SAN 313-900X. Tel: 580-652-2835. Toll Free Tel: 800-651-0975. FAX: 580-652-2831. E-mail: OWL73945@yahoo.com. Web Site: www.owl.okpls.org. *Dir,* Carolyn Blackwelder
Founded 1916. Pop 1,778; Circ 5,992
Library Holdings: AV Mats 210; Bk Vols 16,758; Per Subs 12
Special Collections: Hooker Advance Microfilm, 1907-present
Automation Activity & Vendor Info: (Circulation) Follett Software
Wireless access
Publications: Hooker History, Vol I-III
Open Mon 7pm-9pm, Tues & Thurs 11-6, Sat 2-5
Friends of the Library Group

HUGO

P CHOCTAW COUNTY PUBLIC LIBRARY*, Donald W Reynolds Library & Learning Center, 703 E Jackson St, 74743. SAN 313-9018. Tel: 580-326-5591. FAX: 866-259-6548. E-mail: hugo@seolibraries.com. Web Site: www.seolibraries.com/about/hours-locations/choctaw. *Br Mgr,* Bessi Black; E-mail: bessi.black@seolibraries.com; *Asst Librn,* Lisa Heady; *Asst Librn,* Karen C Hart; E-mail: Karen.hart@oklibrary.net; *Asst Ch,* Toni Love; E-mail: toni.love@oklibrary.net
Founded 1920. Pop 15,403
Library Holdings: Audiobooks 750; AV Mats 4; Bks-By-Mail 30,000; Bks on Deafness & Sign Lang 5; Braille Volumes 1; DVDs 600; e-books 250; High Interest/Low Vocabulary Bk Vols 40; Large Print Bks 650; Music Scores 7; Bk Vols 28,770; Per Subs 60; Talking Bks 20
Special Collections: Circus Coll, bks, mags, posters
Automation Activity & Vendor Info: (Circulation) SirsiDynix; (ILL) SirsiDynix; (OPAC) SirsiDynix
Wireless access
Function: 24/7 Electronic res, 24/7 Online cat, Accelerated reader prog, Adult bk club, Adult literacy prog, Archival coll, Art exhibits
Mem of Southeast Oklahoma Library System (SEOLS)
Partic in OCLC Online Computer Library Center, Inc
Open Mon, Tues & Thurs 9-7, Wed & Fri 9-6, Sat 9-2
Friends of the Library Group

HULBERT

P HULBERT COMMUNITY LIBRARY*, 201 N Broadway, 74441. (Mail add: PO Box 148, 74441-0148). Tel: 918-772-3383. Toll Free Tel: 888-291-8149. FAX: 918-772-3310. E-mail: hulbertpl@eols.org. Web Site: eols.org/library-location/hulbert-community-public-library. *Br Mgr,* Cherokee Lowe; E-mail: clowe@eols.org; *Asst Br Mgr,* Pamela Davis
Circ 951
Library Holdings: Bk Vols 14,314; Per Subs 10
Automation Activity & Vendor Info: (Cataloging) SirsiDynix; (Circulation) SirsiDynix; (OPAC) SirsiDynix
Wireless access
Mem of Eastern Oklahoma Library System
Open Mon, Wed, Fri & Sat 9-2, Tues & Thurs 2-7
Friends of the Library Group

IDABEL

P IDABEL PUBLIC LIBRARY*, 103 E Main St, 74745. (Mail add: PO Box 778, 74745-0778), SAN 313-9026. Tel: 580-286-6406. E-mail: idabel@seolibraries.com. Web Site: www.seolibraries.com/about/hours-locations/idabel. *Br Mgr,* Linda Potts; E-mail: linda.potts@seolibraries.com; *Asst Librn,* Julie Woods
Pop 5,946
Library Holdings: Bk Vols 40,000; Per Subs 40
Automation Activity & Vendor Info: (Acquisitions) SirsiDynix; (Cataloging) SirsiDynix; (Circulation) SirsiDynix; (Course Reserve) SirsiDynix; (ILL) SirsiDynix; (Media Booking) SirsiDynix
Wireless access
Mem of Southeast Oklahoma Library System (SEOLS)
Open Mon-Thurs 9-7, Fri 9-5, Sat 9-3
Friends of the Library Group

INOLA

P INOLA PUBLIC LIBRARY*, 15 North Broadway, 74036. (Mail add: PO Box 1237, 74036-1237). Tel: 918-543-8862. Administration Tel: 918-543-3177. FAX: 918-543-3999. E-mail: inolalibrary@yahoo.com. Web Site: inola.okpls.org. *Dir,* Monica M Clark; E-mail: ipldirector@yahoo.com; *Asst Librn,* Marguerite Allen; Staff 2 (Non-MLS 2)
Founded 1967. Pop 80,757
Special Collections: Indian Cultural Coll
Subject Interests: Indians
Automation Activity & Vendor Info: (Acquisitions) Book Systems; (Cataloging) Book Systems; (Circulation) Book Systems; (ILL) OCLC ILLiad; (OPAC) Book Systems
Wireless access
Function: Home delivery & serv to seniorr ctr & nursing homes, ILL available, Photocopying/Printing, Spoken cassettes & CDs, Summer reading prog, Tax forms, VHS videos, Wheelchair accessible
Open Mon, Wed & Fri 10-4:30, Tues & Thurs 12-7
Restriction: In-house use for visitors, Lending libr only via mail, Lending limited to county residents, Open to pub for ref & circ; with some limitations

JAY

P DELAWARE COUNTY LIBRARY*, 429 S Ninth St, 74346. (Mail add: PO Box 387, 74346-0387), SAN 313-9034. Tel: 918-253-8521. FAX: 918-253-8726. E-mail: jaypl@eols.org. Web Site: eols.org/library-location/delaware-county-library. *Mgr,* Shelly Cook; E-mail: scook@eols.org; *Ch,* Kelly Daugherty; Staff 6 (MLS 1, Non-MLS 5)
Founded 1970. Pop 3,492; Circ 37,379
Library Holdings: AV Mats 3,015; Bks on Deafness & Sign Lang 49; DVDs 358; Large Print Bks 619; Bk Vols 24,734; Per Subs 25; Videos 1,047
Automation Activity & Vendor Info: (Circulation) SirsiDynix
Wireless access
Function: 24/7 Electronic res, 24/7 Online cat, Activity rm, Audiobks on Playaways & MP3, Bks on CD, Children's prog, Computer training, Computers for patron use, Distance learning, Electronic databases & coll, Free DVD rentals, Home delivery & serv to seniorr ctr & nursing homes, ILL available, Internet access, Laminating, Large print keyboards, Life-long learning prog for all ages, Magazines, Mail & tel request accepted, Mango lang, Meeting rooms, Movies, Notary serv, Online cat, Outreach serv, OverDrive digital audio bks, Photocopying/Printing, Preschool outreach, Preschool reading prog, Prog for adults, Prog for children & young adult, Scanner, Serves people with intellectual disabilities, Spoken cassettes & CDs, Summer reading prog, Tax forms, Wheelchair accessible
Mem of Eastern Oklahoma Library System
Open Mon, Wed & Fri 9-6, Tues & Thurs 9-8, Sat 9-1
Restriction: Authorized patrons, Circ to mem only, In-house use for visitors, Lending limited to county residents, Mem only, Non-resident fee
Friends of the Library Group

KANSAS

P KANSAS PUBLIC LIBRARY*, 200 W Tulsa Ave, 74347. (Mail add: PO Box 397, 74347-0397). Tel: 918-868-5257. FAX: 918-868-2350. E-mail: kansaspl@eols.org. Web Site: eols.org/library-location/kansas-public-library. *Mgr,* Cherokee Lowe; E-mail: clowe@eols.org
Library Holdings: Bk Vols 6,000; Per Subs 20
Automation Activity & Vendor Info: (Cataloging) SirsiDynix; (Circulation) SirsiDynix; (OPAC) SirsiDynix
Wireless access
Mem of Eastern Oklahoma Library System
Open Mon, Tues & Thurs 1-7, Wed 1-6, Fri & Sat 9-2
Friends of the Library Group

KAW CITY

P KAW CITY PUBLIC LIBRARY*, 900 Morgan Sq E, 74641. (Mail add: PO Box 30, 74641-0030), SAN 321-9917. Tel: 580-269-1317. FAX: 580-269-2957. E-mail: kawcitylibrary@yahoo.com. *Librn,* Position Currently Open
Founded 1902. Pop 371; Circ 954
Library Holdings: Large Print Bks 80; Bk Vols 3,300
Subject Interests: Indian, Local hist
Wireless access
Function: Bk club(s), Bks on cassette, Bks on CD, CD-ROM, Children's prog, Computer training, Computers for patron use, Family literacy, Games & aids for people with disabilities, ILL available, Music CDs, Notary serv, Online cat, Photocopying/Printing, Prog for children & young adult, Scanner, Spoken cassettes & CDs, Summer reading prog, Teen prog, VHS videos, Wheelchair accessible, Workshops
Special Services for the Blind - Audio mat; Bks & mags in Braille, on rec, tape & cassette; Bks available with recordings; Bks on cassette; Bks on

CD; Cassette playback machines; Cassettes; Free checkout of audio mat; Large print bks; Volunteer serv
Open Mon-Fri 8-4:30

KELLYVILLE

P KELLYVILLE PUBLIC LIBRARY, 230 E Buffalo, 74039. (Mail add: PO Box 1170, 74039-1170). Tel: 918-247-3740. FAX: 918-322-1759. E-mail: kellyvillelibrary@gmail.com. Web Site: kellyville.biblionix.com. *Libr Dir,* Jacqueline Case
Pop 906; Circ 10,833
Library Holdings: AV Mats 200; Bk Vols 13,000; Talking Bks 51
Automation Activity & Vendor Info: (Cataloging) Biblionix/Apollo; (Circulation) Biblionix/Apollo; (OPAC) Biblionix/Apollo
Wireless access
Open Mon-Thurs Noon-6, Fri 8-4
Friends of the Library Group

KINGFISHER

P KINGFISHER MEMORIAL LIBRARY*, 505 W Will Rogers Dr, 73750. SAN 313-9042. Tel: 405-375-3384. Toll Free Tel: 888-995-9795. FAX: 405-375-3306. E-mail: librarian@kingfisher.lib.ok.us. Web Site: kingfisher.booksys.net/opac/kml/#menuHome, www.kingfisher.org/kingfisher-living/library. *Dir,* Mike Tautkus; *Ch,* Stacy Themer; Staff 5 (Non-MLS 5)
Founded 1905. Pop 8,351; Circ 51,960
Library Holdings: Bk Vols 42,000; Per Subs 75
Special Collections: Civil War Coll; Kingfisher Coll; Okla Coll
Automation Activity & Vendor Info: (Cataloging) Follett Software; (Circulation) Follett Software
Open Mon-Thurs 9-7, Fri 9-5, Sat 9-1
Friends of the Library Group

KONAWA

P KENNEDY LIBRARY OF KONAWA*, 701 W South St, 74849. Tel: 580-925-3662. FAX: 580-925-3882. Web Site: www.konawa.k12.ok.us/115611_2. *Library Contact,* Michelle Yott
Pop 1,479; Circ 18,318
Library Holdings: AV Mats 598; Bk Vols 15,000; Per Subs 25; Talking Bks 30
Subject Interests: Genealogy
Automation Activity & Vendor Info: (Cataloging) ComPanion Corp; (Circulation) ComPanion Corp; (OPAC) ComPanion Corp
Open Mon & Wed-Fri 8-3:30, Tues 8-7
Friends of the Library Group

LANGLEY

P LANGLEY PUBLIC LIBRARY*, 325 W Osage, 74350. (Mail add: PO Box 655, 74350-0655). Tel: 918-782-4461. FAX: 918-782-1056. E-mail: langleypl@gmail.com. Web Site: langleypl.okpls.org. *Dir,* Jeanie Norman
Pop 671; Circ 12,910
Library Holdings: AV Mats 250; Bk Vols 9,950; Talking Bks 500
Automation Activity & Vendor Info: (Cataloging) Follett Software; (Circulation) Follett Software
Open Mon 1-7, Tues 9-12 & 1-5
Friends of the Library Group

LANGSTON

C LANGSTON UNIVERSITY, G Lamar Harrison Library, 701 Sammy Davis Jr Dr, 73050. (Mail add: PO Box 1500, 73050-1500), SAN 313-9050. Tel: 405-466-3292. FAX: 405-466-3459. Web Site: www.langston.edu/library. *Dean of Libr,* Dr Lynne Simpson; Tel: 405-466-3294, E-mail: lynne.simpson@langston.edu; *University College Servs Librn,* Elender Shirley; Tel: 405-466-2968, E-mail: elender.shirley@langston.edu; *Head, Tech Serv,* Caitlin Corbett; Tel: 405-466-3412, E-mail: caitlin.corbett@langston.edu; *Libr Assoc,* Jada Burris; E-mail: jsburris@langston.edu; *Libr Assoc,* Misty Ellerby; E-mail: mbellerby@langston.edu; *Libr Assoc,* Patrick Franks; E-mail: pefranks@langston.edu; *Libr Assoc,* Sarah Reid; E-mail: sareid@langston.edu; *Public Access Coord,* Kim Cobb; Tel: 405-466-3603, E-mail: kimcobb@langston.edu; *Syst Analyst,* Clarence Harkins; E-mail: charkins@langston.edu. Subject Specialists: *African studies, Educ, Health sci,* Dr Lynne Simpson; *African studies, African-Am studies,* Elender Shirley
Founded 1949. Enrl 2,172; Fac 69; Highest Degree: Doctorate
Library Holdings: Bk Vols 60,000; Per Subs 972
Special Collections: Black Studies (M B Tolson Black Heritage Center), multimedia. US Document Depository
Subject Interests: Allied health, Multi-cultural, Urban
Wireless access
Publications: The G Lamar Harrison Library Handbook
Open Mon-Thurs 8am-10pm, Fri 8-5, Sun 2-10

LAWTON

C CAMERON UNIVERSITY LIBRARY*, 2800 W Gore Blvd, 73505-6377. SAN 313-9069. Circulation Tel: 580-581-2956. Interlibrary Loan Service Tel: 580-581-2382. Reference Tel: 580-581-2957. FAX: 580-581-2970. E-mail: library@cameron.edu. Web Site: www.cameron.edu/library. *Interim Asst Dir,* Barbara Pickthon; Tel: 580-581-2855, E-mail: barbarap@cameron.edu; *Head, Access Serv,* Wensheng Wang; Tel: 580-581-6710, E-mail: wwang@cameron.edu; *Cat Librn,* Cathy Blackman; Tel: 580-581-2917, E-mail: cathyb@cameron.edu; *Electronic Res & Syst Librn,* Jana Gowen; Tel: 580-581-5915, E-mail: jgowan@cameron.edu; *Instruction & Assessment Librn,* James Scholz; Tel: 580-581-5916, E-mail: jscholz@cameron.edu; Staff 12 (MLS 5, Non-MLS 7)
Founded 1908. Enrl 4,355; Fac 149; Highest Degree: Master
Library Holdings: e-books 265,566; Music Scores 4,522; Bk Titles 155,124; Bk Vols 241,674; Per Subs 94
Subject Interests: Agr, Behav sci, Educ, Media, Soc sci
Automation Activity & Vendor Info: (Acquisitions) Innovative Interfaces, Inc; (Cataloging) Innovative Interfaces, Inc; (Circulation) Innovative Interfaces, Inc; (OPAC) Innovative Interfaces, Inc; (Serials) Innovative Interfaces, Inc
Wireless access
Open Mon-Thurs 7:30am-Midnight, Fri 7:30-6, Sat 10-6, Sun 1-10

P LAWTON PUBLIC LIBRARY*, 110 SW Fourth St, 73501-4034. SAN 357-5497. Tel: 580-581-3450. FAX: 580-248-0243. Web Site: www.lawtonok.gov/departments/library. *Dir,* Kristin Herr; E-mail: kherr@lawtonok.gov; *Head, Ref,* Jim Maroon; E-mail: jmaroon@lawtonok.gov; *Head, Tech Serv,* Denise Flusche; E-mail: dflusche@lawtonok.gov
Founded 1904. Pop 108,144; Circ 259,215
Library Holdings: Bk Vols 120,513; Per Subs 327
Special Collections: Oklahoma (Voices of Oklahoma); Southwest Oklahoma Genealogical Research Coll. Municipal Document Depository; State Document Depository
Automation Activity & Vendor Info: (Cataloging) Biblionix/Apollo; (Circulation) Biblionix/Apollo
Wireless access
Partic in Okla Telecommunications Interlibr Syst
Open Mon, Tues & Wed 9-8, Thurs, Fri & Sat 9-6
Friends of the Library Group
Branches: 1
BRANCH LIBRARY, 1304 NW Kingswood, 73505-4076, SAN 357-5527. Tel: 580-581-3457.
Library Holdings: Bk Vols 4,200
Open Tues & Thurs Noon-5 , Sat 10-3
Friends of the Library Group

S MUSEUM OF THE GREAT PLAINS*, Library & Archives, 601 NW Ferris Ave, 73507. SAN 313-9077. Tel: 580-581-3460. FAX: 580-581-3458. Web Site: www.discovermgp.org/library-archives. *Curator,* Deborah Baroff; E-mail: deb.b@discovermgp.org
Founded 1960
Library Holdings: Bk Titles 30,000
Special Collections: Business of Early Lawton (Harry Buckingham Coll), archives; Extensive Hist of Transportation Coll with wagon & carriage manufacturers' catalogs & trade magazines (1869-1926); Manuscript Coll; Plains Indians Photograph Coll; Politics & Law of Early Lawton (Charles Black Coll & L M Gensman Coll), archives; Settlement of Southwestern Oklahoma, agr & hardware cat; Show Business 1900-1940 (Mildred Chrisman Coll), archives; State Politics in 1960s (Fred Harris Coll), archives; Wedel Coll
Subject Interests: Agr, Anthrop, Archaeology, Ecology, Hist of trans-Mississippi West, Settlement on southern plains
Publications: Great Plains Journal; MGP Record (Newsletter)
Restriction: Non-circulating to the pub, Open by appt only

LINDSAY

P LINDSAY COMMUNITY LIBRARY*, 112 W Choctaw, 73052. Tel: 405-756-3449. FAX: 405-756-2268. E-mail: citylibrary@ci.lindsay.ok.us. Web Site: www.cityoflindsay.com/library. *Dir,* Brenda Norrell
Pop 2,889; Circ 15,289
Library Holdings: Bk Vols 15,600; Talking Bks 400
Automation Activity & Vendor Info: (Cataloging) Follett Software; (Circulation) Follett Software; (OPAC) Follett Software
Wireless access
Open Mon-Wed & Fri 9-4, Thurs 11-7, Sat 9-Noon

LOCUST GROVE

P LOCUST GROVE PUBLIC LIBRARY*, 715 E Main St, 74352. (Mail add: PO Box 697, 74352-0697). Tel: 918-479-6585. FAX: 918-479-6582. E-mail: locustgrovelibrary@gmail.com. Web Site:

www.locustgrovelibrary.okpls.org. *Dir,* Marea Breedlove; Staff 2 (Non-MLS 2)
Founded 1993. Pop 1,405; Circ 8,283
Library Holdings: AV Mats 265; Bk Vols 9,685
Special Collections: Louis L'Amour Coll
Automation Activity & Vendor Info: (Cataloging) Book Systems; (Circulation) Book Systems; (OPAC) Book Systems
Wireless access
Function: 24/7 Electronic res, 24/7 Online cat, Archival coll, Bks on CD, Children's prog, Computers for patron use, For res purposes, Free DVD rentals, ILL available, Internet access, Laminating, Magazines, Mail & tel request accepted, Online cat, Photocopying/Printing, Story hour, Wheelchair accessible
Open Tues 12-7, Wed-Fri 9-5
Friends of the Library Group

MADILL

P MADILL CITY COUNTY LIBRARY, 500 W Overton St, 73446. SAN 313-9107. Tel: 580-795-2749. FAX: 580-316-3370. E-mail: madlib@texomaonline.com. Web Site: mccl.okpls.org. *Dir,* Shirley A Harkins; E-mail: madlib@texomaonline.com; *Asst Librn, Pub Relations,* Vera J Anderson; *Asst Librn,* Dawn White
Founded 1915. Pop 15,000
Library Holdings: Bk Vols 25,000
Automation Activity & Vendor Info: (Acquisitions) Book Systems; (Circulation) Book Systems; (ILL) OCLC WorldShare Interlibrary Loan; (OPAC) EBSCO Online
Wireless access
Function: 24/7 Online cat, Bks on CD, Children's prog, Computers for patron use, Electronic databases & coll, Free DVD rentals, ILL available, Internet access, Magazines, Microfiche/film & reading machines, Online cat, Printer for laptops & handheld devices, Scanner, Spanish lang bks, Summer reading prog, Tax forms, Wheelchair accessible
Open Mon, Tues, Thurs & Fri 9:30-6:30, Wed 9:30-7, Sat 9-1:30
Restriction: ID required to use computers (Ltd hrs), In-house use for visitors, Lending limited to county residents
Friends of the Library Group

MANGUM

P MARGARET CARDER PUBLIC LIBRARY, 201 W Lincoln Ave, 73554. SAN 313-9115. Tel: 580-782-3185. Toll Free Tel: 888-212-8531. FAX: 580-782-5308. E-mail: mangumlibrary@gmail.com. Web Site: cityofmangum.com/library. *Dir,* Martha Young
Founded 1922. Pop 3,000; Circ 12,500
Library Holdings: Bk Titles 13,000; Per Subs 20
Automation Activity & Vendor Info: (Circulation) Follett Software
Wireless access
Open Mon, Wed & Fri 10-5, Tues & Thurs 10-6, Sat 9-Noon
Friends of the Library Group

MANNFORD

P MANNFORD PUBLIC LIBRARY, 101 Green Valley Park Rd, 74044. (Mail add: PO Box 193, 74044-0193). Tel: 918-865-2665. FAX: 918-865-3429. E-mail: mpl@cimtel.net. *Dir,* Colleen Branson; E-mail: cbranson@mannford.lib.ok.us; Staff 3 (Non-MLS 3)
Founded 1981. Pop 3,076; Circ 24,630
Library Holdings: Audiobooks 5; AV Mats 1,000; CDs 179; DVDs 976; Electronic Media & Resources 1,288; Large Print Bks 1,188; Bk Vols 24,630; Per Subs 4
Special Collections: Local area newspapers (hard copies); Mannford High School Yearbooks
Automation Activity & Vendor Info: (Cataloging) Book Systems; (Circulation) Book Systems; (ILL) OCLC FirstSearch; (OPAC) Book Systems
Wireless access
Function: 24/7 Online cat, Adult bk club, Bks on CD, Children's prog, Computer training, Computers for patron use, E-Reserves, Free DVD rentals, Holiday prog, ILL available, Internet access, Laminating, Magazines, Meeting rooms, Movies, Music CDs, Online cat, OverDrive digital audio bks, Photocopying/Printing, Prog for children & young adult, Scanner, Story hour, Summer reading prog, Tax forms, Teen prog, Telephone ref, Wheelchair accessible
Open Mon & Tues 10-6, Wed-Fri 10-5, Sat 9-12

MARLOW

P GARLAND SMITH PUBLIC LIBRARY, 702 W. Main, 73055. SAN 313-9123. Tel: 580-658-5354. FAX: 580-658-9110. E-mail: love2read73055@gmail.com. Web Site: www.garlandsmithpubliclibrary.okpls.org. *Dir,* Tina Bennett; E-mail: tinabennett@gs.lib.ok.us; *Tech Librn,* Patty Ellsworth; *Asst Librn,* Ann Russell; Staff 2 (Non-MLS 2)
Founded 1938. Pop 4,700; Circ 21,200
Library Holdings: Bk Vols 15,600; Per Subs 25
Automation Activity & Vendor Info: (Circulation) Biblionix
Wireless access
Open Mon, Wed & Fri 12-5, Tues & Thurs 9-7, Sat 9-1
Friends of the Library Group

MAYSVILLE

P ELLIOTT LASATER MAYSVILLE PUBLIC LIBRARY*, 506 Williams St, 73057. (Mail add: PO Box 599, 73057-0599), SAN 313-9719. Tel: 405-867-4748. FAX: 405-867-4749. E-mail: maysvillepl@gmail.com. Web Site: maysvillelibrary.okpls.org. *Librn,* Janet Dinwiddie
Founded 1963. Pop 1,500
Library Holdings: Bk Titles 31,000; Bk Vols 31,500
Automation Activity & Vendor Info: (Circulation) Follett Software
Wireless access
Open Mon-Thurs 8-5:30, Fri 8-Noon

MCALESTER

S JACKIE BRANNON CORRECTIONAL CENTER LIBRARY, 900 N West St, 74501. (Mail add: PO Box 1999, 74502-1999). Tel: 918-421-3349. Web Site: oklahoma.gov/doc/facilities/state-institutions/jackie-brannon-correctional-center. *Principal,* Dean Wood; Tel: 918-421-3350, E-mail: dean.wood@doc.state.ok.us; *Librn,* Ramona Allen
Library Holdings: Bk Vols 8,500; Per Subs 15
Automation Activity & Vendor Info: (Cataloging) Follett Software; (Circulation) Follett Software; (OPAC) Follett Software
Restriction: Not open to pub

P MCALESTER PUBLIC LIBRARY*, 401 N Second St, 74501. SAN 313-9093. Tel: 918-426-0930. Toll Free FAX: 888-384-2964. E-mail: mcalester@seolibraries.com. Web Site: www.seolibraries.com/about/hours-locations/mcalester. *Br Mgr,* Ellen Barlow; E-mail: ellen.barlow@seolibraries.com
Pop 40,524; Circ 122,805
Library Holdings: Bk Vols 70,000; Per Subs 115
Special Collections: Local Newspaper Coll, dating back to 1890's. State Document Depository
Automation Activity & Vendor Info: (Circulation) SirsiDynix
Wireless access
Publications: Book List
Mem of Southeast Oklahoma Library System (SEOLS)
Open Mon-Thurs 9-7, Fri 9-6, Sat 9-5, Sun 1-5
Friends of the Library Group

P SOUTHEAST OKLAHOMA LIBRARY SYSTEM (SEOLS), (Formerly Southeastern Public Library System of Oklahoma), 401 N Second St, 74501. SAN 313-9085. Tel: 918-426-0456. Toll Free Tel: 800-562-9520. FAX: 866-596-8188. Web Site: seolibraries.com. *Exec Dir,* Michael Hull; E-mail: michael.hull@seolibraries.com; *ILL,* Christopher Elliott; E-mail: christopher.elliott@seolibraries.com; *Tech Serv,* Miranda Wisor; E-mail: miranda.wisor@seolibraries.com; Staff 77 (MLS 2, Non-MLS 75)
Founded 1967. Pop 171,994; Circ 770,994
Jul 2021-Jun 2022 Income $5,275,918, State $114,211, County $4,216,249, Locally Generated Income $87,561, Other $469,779. Mats Exp $645,858. Sal $2,826,493
Library Holdings: CDs 27,688; DVDs 34,314; e-books 3,515; Microforms 1,994; Bk Vols 401,700; Per Subs 436
Special Collections: All County Newspapers on Microfilm. State Document Depository
Automation Activity & Vendor Info: (Acquisitions) SirsiDynix; (Cataloging) SirsiDynix; (Circulation) SirsiDynix; (OPAC) SirsiDynix; (Serials) SirsiDynix
Wireless access
Member Libraries: Arkoma Public Library; Broken Bow Public Library; Choctaw County Public Library; Coal County Public Library; Hartshorne Public Library; Heavener Public Library; Idabel Public Library; Latimer County Public Library; Mattie Terry Public Library; McAlester Public Library; Patrick Lynch Public Library; Spiro Public Library; Stigler Public Library; Talihina Public Library; Wister Public Library
Friends of the Library Group

A UNITED STATES ARMY*, John L Byrd Jr Technical Library for Explosives Safety, Bldg 35, One C Tree Rd, 74501. SAN 375-0671. Tel: 918-420-8787. FAX: 918-420-8473. *Librn,* Blossom M Hampton; Staff 3 (MLS 2, Non-MLS 1)
Founded 1984
Library Holdings: Bk Titles 4,500; Bk Vols 27,117; Per Subs 16
Special Collections: Accident Reports; Archives Search Reports; Site Plans & Maps; World War II Ordinance Minutes
Automation Activity & Vendor Info: (OPAC) SirsiDynix
Restriction: Non-circulating, Not open to pub

MEDFORD

P MEDFORD PUBLIC LIBRARY, 123 S Main St, 73759. SAN 313-9131. Tel: 580-395-2342. FAX: 580-395-2342. E-mail: medfordpubliclibrary@gmail.com. Web Site: www.grantcountyok.com/medford_library.html. *Dir,* Charlene Moss; Staff 3 (Non-MLS 3)
Founded 1933. Pop 1,000; Circ 4,100
Library Holdings: Bk Titles 6,000; Bk Vols 11,700; Per Subs 15
Special Collections: Oklahoma Geneaology & History Coll
Automation Activity & Vendor Info: (Circulation) Follett Software
Wireless access
Function: Bks on cassette, Bks on CD, Children's prog, Computers for patron use, Internet access, Large print keyboards, Online cat, Online ref, Orientations, Photocopying/Printing, Ref & res, Story hour, Summer reading prog
Open Mon-Fri 10:30-5:30; Mon-Fri 8:30-3:30 (Summer)
Restriction: Non-circulating of rare bks

MIAMI

R FIRST BAPTIST CHURCH*, Library-Media Center, 24 A St SW, 74354. (Mail add: PO Box 1030, 74355-1030), SAN 313-914X. Tel: 918-542-1691. FAX: 918-542-1753. E-mail: fbcmiamioffice@gmail.com. Web Site: www.firstbaptistmiami.church. *Dir,* Ruth Ann Farris; Staff 8 (MLS 2, Non-MLS 6)
Library Holdings: AV Mats 380; Bk Titles 5,400
Subject Interests: Christian life, Growth, Missions
Restriction: Mem only

P MIAMI PUBLIC LIBRARY, 200 N Main St, 74354. SAN 313-9158. Tel: 918-541-2292. FAX: 918-542-9363. Web Site: miamipl.okpls.org. *Dir,* Marcia Johnson; E-mail: mjohnson@miamiokla.net; *Asst Libr Dir,* Callie Cortner; *Ch,* Judy Beauchamp; Staff 9 (MLS 1, Non-MLS 8)
Founded 1920. Pop 13,565; Circ 107,800
Library Holdings: AV Mats 5,010; Bk Titles 50,400; Bk Vols 52,700; Per Subs 118
Special Collections: Miami NewsRecord: 1901 to present, microfilm; Tar Creek Superfund Site Documents
Subject Interests: Genealogy, Indian hist, Okla
Automation Activity & Vendor Info: (Cataloging) Biblionix; (Circulation) Biblionix; (OPAC) Biblionix
Wireless access
Open Mon, Wed & Thurs 9-8, Tues & Fri 9-5, Sat 9-1
Friends of the Library Group

J NORTHEASTERN OKLAHOMA A&M COLLEGE*, Dayle Creech Library, 200 I St NE, 74354. SAN 313-9166. Tel: 918-540-6381. Web Site: www.neo.edu/library. *Libr Coord,* Leslie Hayes; E-mail: leslie.hayes@neo.edu; Staff 3 (MLS 1, Non-MLS 2)
Founded 1925. Enrl 2,286; Fac 123
Library Holdings: Bk Titles 90,000; Per Subs 150
Special Collections: NEO Archive
Partic in Okla Telecommunications Interlibr Syst
Open Mon-Thurs 8-8, Fri 8-4, Sun 2-6

MIDWEST CITY

J ROSE STATE COLLEGE*, Learning Resources Center, 6420 SE 15th St, 73110. SAN 313-9174. Tel: 405-733-7370. Reference Tel: 405-733-7543. E-mail: refdesk@rose.edu. Web Site: www.rose.edu/lrc. *Dir, Libr Serv,* Melissa Huffman; Tel: 405-733-7538, E-mail: mhuffman@rose.edu; *Coordr, Tech Serv, Libr Syst Coordr,* Mary Kirk; Tel: 405-736-0268, E-mail: mkirk@rose.edu; Staff 10 (MLS 6, Non-MLS 4)
Founded 1970. Enrl 5,200; Highest Degree: Associate
Library Holdings: Bk Vols 109,000; Per Subs 425
Special Collections: History of College (Rose State College Colls)
Subject Interests: Hist, Law, Lit
Automation Activity & Vendor Info: (Acquisitions) Ex Libris Group; (Cataloging) Ex Libris Group; (Circulation) Ex Libris Group; (Course Reserve) Ex Libris Group; (ILL) OCLC; (OPAC) Ex Libris Group; (Serials) EBSCO Online
Wireless access
Function: AV serv, ILL available, Photocopying/Printing, Ref serv available, Telephone ref
Partic in OCLC Online Computer Library Center, Inc
Special Services for the Deaf - Assistive tech; Sorenson video relay syst; TDD equip
Special Services for the Blind - Assistive/Adapted tech devices, equip & products; Magnifiers; Videos on blindness & physical disabilties; ZoomText magnification & reading software
Open Mon-Thurs 7:30am-9pm, Fri 7:30-5, Sun 1-8
Restriction: Open to pub for ref & circ; with some limitations
Friends of the Library Group

MOORE

C RANDALL UNIVERSITY*, Geri Ann Hull Learning Resource Center, 3701 S I-35, 73160. (Mail add: PO Box 7208, 73153-1208), SAN 313-9182. Tel: 405-912-9025. Administration Tel: 405-912-9024. FAX: 405-912-9050. Web Site: www.library.ru.edu. *Dir, Libr Serv,* Nancy Draper; E-mail: ndraper@ru.edu; Staff 1 (MLS 1)
Founded 1968. Enrl 320; Fac 50; Highest Degree: Master
Library Holdings: Bk Titles 22,000; Bk Vols 26,000; Per Subs 232
Special Collections: Free Will Baptist Historical Coll
Automation Activity & Vendor Info: (Cataloging) TLC (The Library Corporation); (Circulation) TLC (The Library Corporation); (OPAC) TLC (The Library Corporation)
Wireless access
Function: 24/7 Online cat
Restriction: Non-circulating to the pub

MOUNDS

P JULIA CROWDER MCCLELLAN MEMORIAL LIBRARY, Mounds Public Library, 15 W 14th St, 74047. (Mail add: PO Box 310, 74047-0310). Tel: 918-827-3949. FAX: 918-827-6010. E-mail: moundspubliclibrary@gmail.com. Web Site: mounds.lib.ok.us/index.html. *Dir,* Lucille Abbot; Staff 1 (MLS 1)
Pop 5,000; Circ 14,000
Library Holdings: Audiobooks 300; AV Mats 500; DVDs 200; Large Print Bks 30; Bk Titles 14,000; Talking Bks 200
Special Collections: Local Yearbooks & History Coll, 1971-2002
Automation Activity & Vendor Info: (Acquisitions) Biblionix; (Cataloging) Biblionix; (Circulation) Biblionix; (Course Reserve) Biblionix
Wireless access
Function: After school storytime, Bks on cassette, Bks on CD, Children's prog, Computer training, Computers for patron use, Electronic databases & coll, Notary serv, Photocopying/Printing, Wheelchair accessible
Open Mon-Thurs 9:30-1 & 2-6
Friends of the Library Group

MOUNTAIN VIEW

P ADDIE DAVIS MEMORIAL LIBRARY, 301 N Fourth St, 73062. (Mail add: PO Box 567, 73062-0567), SAN 372-6614. Tel: 580-347-2397. FAX: 580-347-2397. E-mail: mtnviewlibrary@live.com. *Librn,* Sandra Lightfoot
Founded 1983. Pop 848; Circ 3,089
Library Holdings: Bk Titles 7,500; Bk Vols 8,468; Per Subs 15
Automation Activity & Vendor Info: (Cataloging) Biblionix
Open Mon, Wed & Fri 1-6

MULDROW

P MULDROW PUBLIC LIBRARY, 711 W Shanntel Smith Blvd, 74948. (Mail add: PO Box 449, 74948-0449), SAN 313-9190. Tel: 918-427-6703. Toll Free Tel: 888-291-8153. FAX: 918-427-7315. E-mail: muldrowpl@eols.org. Web Site: www.eols.org/library-location/muldrow-public-library. *Dir,* Bethia Owens; E-mail: bowens@eols.org
Founded 1979
Library Holdings: Bk Vols 11,000; Per Subs 15
Subject Interests: Local hist
Automation Activity & Vendor Info: (Cataloging) SirsiDynix; (Circulation) SirsiDynix
Wireless access
Publications: Willison Library Bulletin
Mem of Eastern Oklahoma Library System
Open Mon & Wed 12-5, Tues, Thurs & Fri 9-6, Sat 9-Noon
Friends of the Library Group

MUSKOGEE

J BACONE COLLEGE*, Merritt D Betts American Indian Research Library, 2299 Old Bacone Rd, 74403. SAN 313-9204. Tel: 918-685-0814. FAX: 918-781-7376. Web Site: www.bacone.edu/academics/merritt-d-betts-library. *Librn,* David McMillan; E-mail: mcmilland@bacone.edu; Staff 1 (MLS 1)
Founded 1880. Enrl 900; Fac 40
Library Holdings: Bk Vols 42,000
Subject Interests: Behav sci, Local hist, Native Am studies, Nursing, Soc sci
Wireless access
Open Mon-Thurs 8-5 & 6-10, Fri 8-5

P EASTERN OKLAHOMA LIBRARY SYSTEM, 14 E Shawnee, 74403-1001. SAN 313-9212. Tel: 918-683-2846. FAX: 918-683-0436. Web Site: www.eols.org. *Exec Dir,* Mary J Moroney; Tel: 918-683-2846, Ext 239, E-mail: mmoroney@eols.org; Staff 116 (MLS 16, Non-MLS 100)
Founded 1973. Pop 243,022; Circ 700,000

Jul 2019-Jun 2020 Income $5,808,343, State $92,205, City $16,740, Federal $8,000, County $5,435,854, Locally Generated Income $3,000, Other $252,544. Mats Exp $928,768, Books $328,889, Per/Ser (Incl. Access Fees) $26,239, Other Print Mats $3,512, Micro $675, AV Mat $441,521, Electronic Ref Mat (Incl. Access Fees) $127,932. Sal $2,618,108
Library Holdings: Audiobooks 1,800; AV Mats 442; CDs 15,601; DVDs 44,565; e-books 205,475; Electronic Media & Resources 3,242; Bk Vols 326,507; Per Subs 300
Special Collections: Local History (Essa Gladney Coll), Tahlequah Branch; Native Americans & Early Oklahoma History (Grant Foreman Coll), Muskogee Branch
Subject Interests: Early hist Indian Territory, Genealogy
Automation Activity & Vendor Info: (Acquisitions) Horizon; (Cataloging) Horizon; (Circulation) Horizon; (ILL) OCLC; (OPAC) Horizon
Wireless access
Function: 24/7 Electronic res, 24/7 Online cat, 3D Printer, Adult bk club, Adult literacy prog, After school storytime, Archival coll, Audiobks on Playaways & MP3, Audiobks via web, Bk club(s), Bks on CD, CD-ROM, Children's prog, Citizenship assistance, Computer training, Computers for patron use, Digital talking bks, E-Readers, Electronic databases & coll, Family literacy, Free DVD rentals, Genealogy discussion group, Holiday prog, ILL available, Internet access, Laminating, Life-long learning prog for all ages, Literacy & newcomer serv, Magazines, Mail & tel request accepted, Mango lang, Meeting rooms, Microfiche/film & reading machines, Movies, Notary serv, Online cat, Online ref, Outreach serv, Outside serv via phone, mail, e-mail & web, OverDrive digital audio bks, Photocopying/Printing, Preschool outreach, Preschool reading prog, Prog for adults, Prog for children & young adult, Ref & res, Ref serv available, Scanner, Senior computer classes, Story hour, Study rm, Summer & winter reading prog, Summer reading prog, Tax forms, Teen prog, Telephone ref, Wheelchair accessible
Member Libraries: Delaware County Library; Eufaula Memorial Library; Grove Public Library; Hulbert Community Library; Jim Lucas Checotah Public Library; John F Henderson Public Library; Kansas Public Library; Muldrow Public Library; Muskogee Public Library; Q B Boydstun Library; Rieger Memorial Library; Stanley Tubbs Memorial Library; Stilwell Public Library; Tahlequah Public Library; Warner Public Library
Friends of the Library Group

S EASTERN OKLAHOMA VA HEALTHCARE SYSTEM*, Health Sciences Library, 1011 Honor Heights Dr, 74401. SAN 313-9263. Tel: 918-577-3000, Ext 4082. FAX: 918-577-3752. Web Site: www.muskogee.va.gov. *Librn,* Amy Vandewalker; Tel: 918-577-4082, E-mail: amy.vandewalker@va.gov; Staff 1 (MLS 1)
Founded 1946
Library Holdings: Bk Vols 6,847
Special Collections: Persian Gulf War Coll; Vietnam Veterans Coll
Subject Interests: Allied health fields, Med, Nursing
Publications: Journal Holdings
Open Mon-Fri 8-4:30

L MUSKOGEE LAW LIBRARY ASSOCIATION*, Muskogee County Court House, 220 State St, 74401. SAN 313-9239. Tel: 918-682-7873. E-mail: muskogeelawlibrary@yahoo.com. *Law Librn,* Chris James; Tel: 918-348-1415
Library Holdings: Bk Vols 10,000
Open Mon-Fri 8-4:30

P MUSKOGEE PUBLIC LIBRARY*, 801 W Okmulgee, 74401. SAN 313-9247. Tel: 918-682-6657. FAX: 918-682-9466. E-mail: muskogeepl@eodls.org. Web Site: www.eodls.org/muskogee. *Mgr,* Rene Myers; Staff 4 (MLS 2, Non-MLS 2)
Founded 1909. Pop 199,225
Library Holdings: Bk Vols 247,015; Per Subs 625
Special Collections: Local Hist (Grant Foreman Room)
Automation Activity & Vendor Info: (Acquisitions) SirsiDynix; (Cataloging) SirsiDynix; (Circulation) SirsiDynix; (Course Reserve) SirsiDynix; (ILL) SirsiDynix; (Media Booking) SirsiDynix; (OPAC) SirsiDynix; (Serials) SirsiDynix
Mem of Eastern Oklahoma Library System
Open Mon, Tues & Thurs 9-9, Wed & Fri 9-6, Sat 9-5:30
Friends of the Library Group

MUSTANG

P MUSTANG PUBLIC LIBRARY*, 1201 N Mustang Rd, 73064. (Mail add: 1501 N Mustang Rd, 73064). Tel: 405-376-2226. FAX: 405-376-9925. Web Site: www.mustanglibrary.org. *Dir,* Julie Slupe; E-mail: jslupe@cityofmustang.org; *Youth Serv Librn,* Nichole Valencia; E-mail: nvalencia@cityofmustang.org; *Circ Mgr,* Tyler Worsham; E-mail: tworsham@cityofmustang.org; Staff 3 (MLS 1, Non-MLS 2)
Pop 45,000; Circ 213,580
Jul 2013-Jun 2014 Income $415,762, State $16,524, City $399,238. Mats Exp $55,120, Books $32,550, Per/Ser (Incl. Access Fees) $2,600, AV Mat $9,745, Electronic Ref Mat (Incl. Access Fees) $10,225. Sal $253,031
Library Holdings: Audiobooks 2,230; DVDs 4,344; e-books 23,062; e-journals 234; Electronic Media & Resources 40; Large Print Bks 1,000; Bk Titles 48,999; Bk Vols 57,700; Per Subs 301
Automation Activity & Vendor Info: (Acquisitions) TLC (The Library Corporation); (Cataloging) TLC (The Library Corporation); (Circulation) TLC (The Library Corporation); (ILL) OCLC; (OPAC) TLC (The Library Corporation)
Wireless access
Function: 24/7 Electronic res, Audiobks via web, Bks on CD, CD-ROM, Children's prog, Computers for patron use, Free DVD rentals, Holiday prog, Life-long learning prog for all ages, Mango lang, Movies, Music CDs, Online cat, OverDrive digital audio bks, Photocopying/Printing, Preschool outreach, Preschool reading prog, Prog for adults, Prog for children & young adult, Ref serv available, Story hour, Study rm, Summer reading prog, Tax forms, Teen prog, Wheelchair accessible
Open Mon, Wed & Thurs 9-8, Tues 9-9, Fri & Sat 9-5:30
Friends of the Library Group

NEWKIRK

P NEWKIRK PUBLIC LIBRARY*, 116 N Maple Ave, 74647-4011. SAN 313-9271. Tel: 580-362-3934. FAX: 580-362-1028. E-mail: newkirkpublib@gmail.com. Web Site: www.newkirkpl.okpls.org. *Dir,* Marcina Overman; Staff 1 (Non-MLS 1)
Founded 1910. Pop 2,271
Library Holdings: Audiobooks 308; Large Print Bks 1,037; Bk Titles 16,979; Per Subs 52; Videos 3,672
Automation Activity & Vendor Info: (Cataloging) Biblionix/Apollo; (Circulation) Biblionix/Apollo
Wireless access
Function: ILL available, Prog for children & young adult
Open Mon-Thurs 10-6, Fri 10-5, Sat 1-4
Restriction: Circ to mil employees only
Friends of the Library Group

NORMAN

M GRIFFIN MEMORIAL HOSPITAL, Professional Medical Research Library, Bldg 54 205, 900 E Main St, 73071. (Mail add: PO Box 151, 73071), SAN 313-928X. Tel: 405-573-6602. FAX: 405-573-6684. *Prog Coordr,* Pam Melton; E-mail: pam.melton@odmhsas.org; Staff 1 (Non-MLS 1)
Library Holdings: Bk Vols 2,000; Per Subs 50
Special Collections: Old Psychiatry Book Archive
Subject Interests: Psychiat
Wireless access
Function: Archival coll, For res purposes, ILL available, Ref serv available, Res libr, Telephone ref
Publications: Nothing but Psychiatry (Research books & journal)
Restriction: Med staff only

S NATIONAL WEATHER CENTER LIBRARY*, 120 David L Boren Blvd, Ste 4300, 73072-7303. SAN 313-9298. Tel: 405-325-1171. FAX: 405-325-1130. E-mail: nwclibrary@ou.edu. Web Site: www.ou.edu/nwc/library. *Librn,* Claire Curry; E-mail: cmcurry@ou.edu; *Librn,* Amanda Schilling; E-mail: amanda.schilling@ou.edu. Subject Specialists: *Geog,* Claire Curry; *Meteorology,* Amanda Schilling; Staff 1 (MLS 1)
Founded 1973
Jul 2015-Jun 2016 Income $137,400. Mats Exp $160,000, Books $8,000, Per/Ser (Incl. Access Fees) $45,000. Sal Prof $60,000
Library Holdings: DVDs 40; Bk Vols 5,000; Per Subs 35; Videos 25
Subject Interests: Atmospheric physics, Computer prog, Meteorology, Severe storms dynamics, Storm hazards to aircraft, Tornado studies
Wireless access
Function: Computers for patron use, Electronic databases & coll, Govt ref serv, ILL available, Online cat, Orientations, Photocopying/Printing, Ref & res, Res libr, Scanner, Workshops
Partic in NOAA Libraries Network
Restriction: Authorized patrons, Open to fac, students & qualified researchers

P PIONEER LIBRARY SYSTEM*, Norman Public Library Headquarters, 300 Norman Ctr Ct, 73072. SAN 357-5616. Tel: 405-801-4500. FAX: 405-801-4516. E-mail: mc@pioneerlibrarysystem.org. Web Site: pioneerlibrarysystem.org. *Exec Dir,* Lisa Wells; Tel: 405-801-4511, E-mail: lwells@pioneerlibrarysystem.org; *Assoc Dir, Tech,* Andy Peters; Tel: 405-801-4560, E-mail: apeters@pioneerlibrarysystem.org; *Finance Mgr,* Doug Buck; Tel: 405-801-4505, E-mail: dbuck@pioneerlibrarysystem.org; *Colls Mgr,* Jennifer Marshall; *Human Res, Spec,* Elissa Fox; Staff 68 (MLS 48, Non-MLS 20)
Founded 1957. Pop 363,796; Circ 2,878,855

Jul 2012-Jun 2013 Income $14,087,627. Mats Exp $1,980,843. Sal $7,074,368
Library Holdings: Bk Titles 207,978; Bk Vols 768,408
Special Collections: Oklahoma Coll
Automation Activity & Vendor Info: (Acquisitions) Brodart; (Cataloging) SirsiDynix; (Circulation) SirsiDynix; (ILL) OCLC
Wireless access
Publications: My Library (Newsletter); Pioneer Library System Annual Report
Open Mon-Fri 8-5
Friends of the Library Group

Branches: 12

BLANCHARD PUBLIC, 205 NE Tenth St, Blanchard, 73010. (Mail add: PO Box 614, Blanchard, 73010), SAN 357-5640. Tel: 405-485-2275. FAX: 405-485-9452. *Br Mgr,* Becky Pauls; E-mail: bpauls@pioneerlibrarysystem.org
Pop 7,600; Circ 119,582
Library Holdings: Bk Titles 22,208; Bk Vols 24,240
Open Mon-Thurs 9-7, Fri 9-6, Sat 9-5, Sun 1-5
Friends of the Library Group

MCLOUD PUBLIC, 133 N Main, McLoud, 74851, SAN 370-9019. Tel: 405-788-4132. FAX: 405-964-5389. *Br Mgr,* Wanda Haynes; E-mail: whaynes@pioneerlibrarysystem.org
Pop 4,050; Circ 46,962
Library Holdings: Bk Titles 13,828; Bk Vols 14,954
Open Mon-Thurs 10-7, Fri 10-6, Sat 10-1, Sun 1-5
Friends of the Library Group

MOORE PUBLIC, 225 S Howard, Moore, 73160, SAN 357-5675. Tel: 405-793-5100. FAX: 405-793-8755. *Br Mgr,* Chris Manna; E-mail: cmanna@pioneerlibrarysystem.org
Pop 56,315; Circ 764,111
Library Holdings: Bk Titles 134,371; Bk Vols 184,859
Open Mon-Thurs 9-9, Fri 9-8, Sat 9-5, Sun 1-6
Friends of the Library Group

NEWCASTLE PUBLIC, 705 NW Tenth St, Newcastle, 73065. (Mail add: PO Box 780, Newcastle, 73065-0780), SAN 357-5691. Tel: 405-387-5076. FAX: 405-387-5204. *Br Mgr,* Phil Clark; E-mail: philc@pioneerlibrarysystem.org
Pop 7,847; Circ 83,685
Library Holdings: Bk Titles 26,248; Bk Vols 28,315
Open Mon-Thurs 9-7, Fri 9-6, Sat 9-5, Sun 1-5
Friends of the Library Group

NOBLE PUBLIC, 204 N Fifth St, Noble, 73068. (Mail add: PO Box 2120, Noble, 73068), SAN 328-7238. Tel: 405-872-5713. FAX: 405-872-8329. *Br Mgr,* Cathy Adams; E-mail: cadams@pioneerlibrarysystem.org
Pop 6,624; Circ 92,414
Library Holdings: Bk Titles 27,961; Bk Vols 32,167
Open Mon-Thurs 9-7, Fri 9-6, Sat 9-5, Sun 1-5
Friends of the Library Group

NORMAN PUBLIC LIBRARY CENTRAL, 225 N Webster, 73069, SAN 357-5705. Tel: 405-701-2600. FAX: 405-701-2608. *Assoc Dir, Br Mgr,* Caroline Dulworth; E-mail: caroline@pioneerlibrarysystem.org
Pop 113,273; Circ 1,062,842
Library Holdings: Bk Titles 167,244; Bk Vols 251,700
Open Mon-Thurs 9-9, Fri 9-8, Sat 9-5, Sun 1-6
Friends of the Library Group

NORMAN PUBLIC LIBRARY EAST, 3051 Alameda St, 73071. Tel: 405-217-0770. FAX: 405-217-3453. Web Site: pioneerlibrarysystem.org/hometowns/norman-east. *Br Mgr,* Kelly Sitzman; E-mail: ksitzman@pioneerlibrarysystem.org
Founded 2018
Open Mon-Thurs 9-9, Fri 9-8, Sat 9-5, Sun 1-6
Friends of the Library Group

NORMAN PUBLIC LIBRARY WEST, 300 Norman Ctr Court, 73069. Tel: 405-701-2644. FAX: 405-701-2648. *Br Mgr,* Mike Pierson; Tel: 405-701-2645, Ext 588, E-mail: mpierson@pioneerlibrarysystem.org
Circ 119,413
Library Holdings: Bk Titles 18,194; Bk Vols 19,135
Open Mon-Thurs 9-9, Fri & Sat 9-8, Sun 1-6

PURCELL PUBLIC, 919 N Ninth, Purcell, 73080, SAN 357-573X. Tel: 405-527-5546. FAX: 405-527-7140. *Br Mgr,* Rebekah Lynam; E-mail: rlynam@pioneerlybrarysystem.org
Pop 6,006; Circ 96,854
Library Holdings: Bk Titles 37,818; Bk Vols 42,419
Open Mon-Thurs 9-7, Fri 9-6, Sat 9-5, Sun 1-5
Friends of the Library Group

SHAWNEE PUBLIC, 101 N Philadelphia, Shawnee, 74801, SAN 357-5764. Tel: 405-275-6353. FAX: 405-273-0590. *Br Mgr, Regional Coordr,* Peggy Cook; E-mail: peggy@pioneerlibrarysystem.org
Pop 30,212; Circ 287,035
Library Holdings: Bk Titles 73,607; Bk Vols 86,644
Open Mon-Thurs 9-9, Fri 9-6, Sat 9-5, Sun 1-5
Friends of the Library Group

SOUTHWEST OKLAHOMA CITY PUBLIC LIBRARY, 2201 SW 134th St, Oklahoma City, 73170. Tel: 405-979-2200. FAX: 405-692-6394. *Br Mgr, Regional Coordr,* Ashley Welke; E-mail: awelke@pioneerlibrarysystem.org
Circ 121,643
Library Holdings: Bk Titles 57,523; Bk Vols 62,329
Open Mon-Thurs 9-9, Fri 9-8, Sat 9-5, Sun 1-6
Friends of the Library Group

TECUMSEH PUBLIC, 114 N Broadway, Tecumseh, 74873, SAN 357-5799. Tel: 405-598-5955. FAX: 405-598-5416. *Br Mgr,* Beth Lyle; E-mail: bethlyle@pioneerlibrarysystem.org
Pop 6,537; Circ 64,543
Library Holdings: Bk Titles 20,258; Bk Vols 21,823
Open Mon-Thurs 10-7, Fri 10-6, Sat 10-1, Sun 1-5
Friends of the Library Group

C UNIVERSITY OF OKLAHOMA LIBRARIES*, Bizzell Memorial Library (Main), 401 W Brooks St, 73019. SAN 357-5829. Tel: 405-325-3341. FAX: 405-325-7550. Web Site: libraries.ou.edu. *Interim Dean of Libr,* Carl Grant; E-mail: carl.grant@ou.edu; *Assoc Dean of Finance, Adm & Human Resources,* Rhonda Cannon; E-mail: rhondacannon@ou.edu; *Assoc Dean, Spec Coll,* Bridget Burke; E-mail: bridget.burke@ou.edu; *Assoc Dean, Scholarly Communications & Access, Assoc Dean, Scholarly Res,* Karen Rupp-Serrano; E-mail: krs@ou.edu; *Develop, Digital Innovations Librn, Sr Dir,* Twila Camp; E-mail: tcamp@ou.edu; *Pub Serv, Sr Dir, Strategic Initiatives Librn,* Sarah Robbins; E-mail: srobbins@ou.edu; *Communications Coordr,* Chelsea Julian; E-mail: libpr@ou.edu
Founded 1895. Highest Degree: Doctorate
Special Collections: Bass Business History Coll; Chinese Literature Translation Archive; History of Science Coll; John & Mary Nichols Rare Books Collection: English, European & American Lit 15th century-present; Western History Coll; William Bennett Bizzell Bible Coll. State Document Depository; UN Document Depository; US Document Depository
Automation Activity & Vendor Info: (Circulation) SirsiDynix
Wireless access
Partic in Amigos Library Services, Inc; Association of Research Libraries; Center for Research Libraries; Coalition for Networked Information; Greater Western Library Alliance; Oklahoma Library Technology Network
Open Mon-Thurs 7:30am-2am, Fri & Sat 9am-9pm, Sun Noon-2am
Friends of the Library Group

Departmental Libraries:

ARCHITECTURE, Architecture Library, LLG8, 830 Van Vleet Oval, 73019, SAN 357-5853. Tel: 405-325-5521. FAX: 405-325-6637. *Librn,* Matt Stock
Open Mon-Fri 8-5

ENGINEERING, Engineering Library, 222FH, 865 Asp Ave, 73019, SAN 357-5977. Tel: 405-325-2941. FAX: 405-325-0345. *Eng Librn,* James Bierman
Library closed for renovation

FINE ARTS, 500 W Boyd St, 73019, SAN 357-5888. Tel: 405-325-4243. FAX: 405-325-4243. *Librn,* Matt Stock
Special Collections: Bixler Files (clippings on theater, film & dance)
Subject Interests: Art, Arts mgt, Dance, Music
Open Mon-Fri 8-5

CL DONALD E PRAY LAW LIBRARY, 300 Timberdell Rd, 73019, SAN 357-606X. Tel: 405-325-4311. FAX: 405-325-6282. Web Site: www.law.ou.edu/library. *Dir,* Darin K Fox; *Assoc Dir,* Joel Wegemer; *Tech Serv Librn,* Marilyn Nicely; E-mail: mnicely@ou.edu. Subject Specialists: *Legal res,* Darin K Fox; Staff 14 (MLS 7, Non-MLS 7)
Founded 1909. Enrl 520; Fac 35; Highest Degree: Doctorate
Library Holdings: Bk Vols 207,475; Per Subs 4,371
Special Collections: Native Peoples Law. US Document Depository
Partic in Mid-America Law Library Consortium; OCLC Online Computer Library Center, Inc
Publications: DataBase Spotlights; Law Library Guide (Reference guide); Law Library Newsletter (Annual); New Books & DataBase List

WESTERN HISTORY COLLECTION, Western History Collection, 452 MH, 630 Parrington Oval, 73019, SAN 357-5861. Tel: 405-325-3641. FAX: 405-325-6069. *Curator, Western Hist Coll,* Marshall Todd Fuller; Tel: 405-325-3678, E-mail: tfuller@ou.edu; *Assoc Curator,* Lina Ortega; E-mail: lortega@ou.edu
Library Holdings: Bk Vols 70,838
Special Collections: Abraham Lincoln & the Civil War (Henry B Bass Coll); Congressional Papers (48 Congressmen); History of Kansas & Surrounding States, North American Indians, Cattle Trade, Mining (Alan W Farley Coll); Indian Music Tapes; Indian Nation Papers; Indian-Pioneer Papers; North American Indians & Indian Art (Fred P Schonwald Coll); Oral History of Oklahoma Indian Tribes (Doris Duke Coll); Political Speeches (Helen Gahagan Douglas Coll); Western Americana (Edward Everett Dale Coll). Oral History
Open Mon-Fri 8-8, Sat 9-1
Friends of the Library Group

YOUNGBLOOD ENERGY (GEOLOGY) LIBRARY, Youngblood Energy Library, R220, 100 E Boyd, 73019, SAN 357-6000. Tel: 405-325-6451. FAX: 405-325-6451. *Interim Librn,* James Bierman
Open Mon-Fri 8-5

NOWATA

P NOWATA CITY-COUNTY LIBRARY, 224 S Pine St, 74048. SAN 324-0002. Tel: 918-273-3363. FAX: 918-273-1818. E-mail: helpdesk@nowataok.gov. Web Site: nowataok.gov/nowata-city-county-library. *Librn,* Marilyn Biggerstaff; E-mail: mbiggernccl@gmail.com; Staff 2 (MLS 2)
Founded 1966. Pop 10,500; Circ 16,484
Library Holdings: Bk Titles 23,080; Per Subs 30
Automation Activity & Vendor Info: (Cataloging) Follett Software; (Circulation) Follett Software
Wireless access

OKEENE

P OKEENE PUBLIC LIBRARY*, 215 N Main, 73763. (Mail add: PO Box 706, 73763-0706), SAN 313-9328. Tel: 580-822-3306. FAX: 580-822-3309. E-mail: reading@okeene.lib.ok.us. Web Site: www.okeene.okpls.org. *Dir,* Lee Ann Barnes; *Res,* Deborah Nayor/Farhar; Staff 2 (MLS 1, Non-MLS 1)
Founded 1934. Pop 1,500; Circ 2,000
Library Holdings: Bk Vols 6,000
Automation Activity & Vendor Info: (Cataloging) Book Systems; (Circulation) Book Systems; (OPAC) Book Systems
Wireless access
Open Mon-Thurs 2-5:30, Fri 2-5

OKEMAH

P OKEMAH PUBLIC LIBRARY*, 301 S Second St, 74859. Tel: 918-623-1915. FAX: 918-623-0489. Web Site: www.okemah.okpls.org. *Dir,* Teresa M Labbe; E-mail: tlabbeopl@yahoo.com; Staff 1 (MLS 1)
Pop 3,128
Library Holdings: Bk Vols 27,000
Automation Activity & Vendor Info: (Cataloging) Biblionix; (Circulation) Biblionix
Wireless access
Open Mon-Thurs 10:30-6, Fri 10:30-5:30, Sat 11-2
Friends of the Library Group

OKLAHOMA CITY

R EMANUEL SYNAGOGUE*, William Davis Memorial Library, 900 NW 47th St, 73118. SAN 313-9387. Tel: 405-528-2113. FAX: 405-528-2121. Web Site: www.emanuelokc.org.
Library Holdings: Bk Vols 3,000; Per Subs 6
Subject Interests: Hebrew, Judaica
Partic in Metronet
Under renovation until Summer 2020-
Restriction: Not open to pub

FEDERAL AVIATION ADMINISTRATION

S CIVIL AEROSPACE MEDICAL INSTITUTE LIBRARY*, 6500 S MacArthur, AAM-400a, 73169, SAN 357-6213. Tel: 405-954-4398. FAX: 405-954-4379. Web Site: www.faa.gov. *Librn,* Roni Anderson; E-mail: roni.anderson@faa.gov; Staff 2 (MLS 2)
Library Holdings: Bk Vols 6,000; Per Subs 200
Subject Interests: Aerospace med, Aviation psychol, Human factors
Automation Activity & Vendor Info: (Cataloging) EOS International; (ILL) OCLC; (OPAC) EOS International; (Serials) EOS International
Partic in OCLC Online Computer Library Center, Inc
Open Mon-Fri 7:30-5

S MIKE MONRONEY AERONAUTICAL CENTER LIBRARY*, Academy Bldg 14, Rm 114, 6500 S MacArthur Blvd, 73169. (Mail add: AMA-23A, PO Box 25082, 73125-0082), SAN 357-6183. Tel: 405-954-2665. FAX: 405-954-4742. Web Site: www.academy.faa.gov/library. *Librn,* Elaine Regier; Staff 1 (MLS 1)
Founded 1962
Library Holdings: Bk Titles 23,000; Bk Vols 30,000; Per Subs 40; Spec Interest Per Sub 25; Videos 93
Special Collections: FAA Orders; FAA Research Reports
Subject Interests: Aviation, Educ, Electronics, Mgt
Automation Activity & Vendor Info: (Cataloging) OCLC; (ILL) OCLC; (OPAC) CyberTools for Libraries
Function: ILL available, Ref serv available
Partic in OCLC Online Computer Library Center, Inc
Restriction: By permission only

M INTEGRIS SOUTHWEST MEDICAL CENTER*, Scott Hendren Medical Library, 4401 S Western Ave, 73109. SAN 371-5507. Tel: 405-636-7437. FAX: 405-636-7660. Web Site: integrisok.com/locations/hospital/integris-southwest-medical-center. *Librn,* Sonya Palmer; E-mail: sonya.palmer@integrisok.com
Founded 1966
Library Holdings: Bk Titles 2,100; Per Subs 100
Subject Interests: Clinical med
Wireless access
Open Mon-Fri 8-4:30

L MCAFEE & TAFT*, Law Library, Two Leadership Sq, 10th Flr, 211 N Robinson Ave, 73102-7103. SAN 326-5900. Tel: 405-235-9621. FAX: 405-235-0439. Web Site: www.mcafeetaft.com. *Libr Adminr,* Mike Davis; E-mail: mike.davis@mcafeetaft.com; Staff 1 (MLS 1)
Founded 1952
Library Holdings: Bk Vols 14,000; Per Subs 35
Subject Interests: Aviation, Banking, Bankruptcy, Corporate securities, Employee benefits, Environ, Intellectual property, Litigation, Real estate, Tax
Wireless access
Restriction: Staff use only

P METROPOLITAN LIBRARY SYSTEM IN OKLAHOMA COUNTY*, 300 Park Ave, 73102. SAN 357-6302. Tel: 405-606-3825. Administration Tel: 405-606-3725. FAX: 405-606-3722. Web Site: www.metrolibrary.org. *Exec Dir,* Julie Ballou; E-mail: director@metrolibrary.org; *Dep Exec Dir, Pub Serv,* Chris Kennedy; *Dep Exec Dir, Tech,* Anne Fischer
Founded 1965. Pop 766,215; Circ 6,018,467
Jul 2014-Jun 2015 Income (Main & Associated Libraries) $34,146,139, State $281,497, Federal $4,730, County $32,534,402, Other $1,325,510. Mats Exp $5,052,276, Books $2,185,978, Per/Ser (Incl. Access Fees) $179,376, AV Mat $1,322,489, Electronic Ref Mat (Incl. Access Fees) $1,364,433. Sal $16,479,387
Library Holdings: AV Mats 266,375; CDs 87,916; DVDs 101,229; e-books 80,142; Bk Titles 283,482; Bk Vols 1,172,964; Per Subs 2,172
Special Collections: Black History Coll; Holocaust Resource Coll; Oklahoma Coll. US Document Depository
Automation Activity & Vendor Info: (Circulation) TLC (The Library Corporation); (OPAC) TLC (The Library Corporation)
Wireless access
Publications: Info Magazine (Monthly)
Partic in OCLC Online Computer Library Center, Inc; Oklahoma Library Technology Network
Friends of the Library Group
Branches: 20

ALMONTE LIBRARY, 2914 SW 59th St, 73119-6402. E-mail: almonte@metrolibrary.org. *Mgr, Libr Operations,* Brandon Beckham
Pop 37,992; Circ 135,531
Library Holdings: AV Mats 9,089; CDs 3,564; DVDs 4,447; Bk Titles 30,992; Bk Vols 35,160; Per Subs 122
Open Mon-Thurs 9-9, Fri 9-6, Sat 9-5, Sun 1-6

BELLE ISLE LIBRARY, 5501 N Villa Ave, 73112-7164, SAN 357-6361. E-mail: belleisle@metrolibrary.org. *Mgr, Libr Operations,* Lindsey Bryan
Pop 77,642; Circ 322,771
Library Holdings: AV Mats 20,926; CDs 5,356; DVDs 9,275; Bk Titles 95,013; Bk Vols 101,078; Per Subs 140
Open Mon-Thurs 9-9, Fri 9-6, Sat 9-5, Sun 1-6

BETHANY LIBRARY, 7941 NW 23rd, Bethany, 73008. (Mail add: 3510 N Mueller Ave, Bethany, 73008-3971). E-mail: bethany@metrolibrary.org. *Mgr, Libr Operations,* Erin Bedford
Pop 36,163; Circ 254,472
Library Holdings: AV Mats 15,193; CDs 4,244; DVDs 5,276; Bk Titles 59,336; Bk Vols 63,121; Per Subs 97
Open Mon-Thurs 9-9, Fri 9-6, Sat 9-5, Sun 1-6

CAPITOL HILL LIBRARY, 327 SW 27th St, 73109, SAN 357-6426. E-mail: capitolhill@metrolibrary.org. *Mgr, Libr Operations,* Position Currently Open
Pop 32,824; Circ 97,022
Library Holdings: AV Mats 10,296; CDs 2,519; DVDs 3,383; Bk Titles 35,106; Bk Vols 37,347; Per Subs 135
Open Mon-Thurs 9-9, Fri 9-6, Sat 9-5, Sun 1-6

CHOCTAW LIBRARY, 2525 Muzzy St, Choctaw, 73020-8717, SAN 357-6663. E-mail: choctaw@metrolibrary.org. *Mgr, Libr Operations,* Christopher Stofel
Pop 19,303; Circ 145,850
Library Holdings: AV Mats 14,437; CDs 4,968; DVDs 6,442; Bk Titles 38,171; Bk Vols 42,619; Per Subs 109
Open Mon-Thurs 9-9, Fri 9-6, Sat 9-5, Sun 1-6

DEL CITY LIBRARY, 4509 SE 15th St, Del City, 73115-3098, SAN 357-6450. E-mail: delcity@metrolibrary.org. *Mgr, Libr Operations,* Angel Suhrstedt
Pop 41,903; Circ 147,888
Library Holdings: AV Mats 13,542; CDs 3,881; DVDs 5,302; Bk Titles 49,310; Bk Vols 52,458; Per Subs 69
Open Mon-Thurs 9-9, Fri 9-6, Sat 9-5, Sun 1-6

EDMOND LIBRARY, Ten S Blvd, Edmond, 73034-3798, SAN 357-6515. E-mail: edmond@metrolibrary.org. *Mgr, Libr Operations,* Ashley Welke
Pop 86,292; Circ 808,304
Library Holdings: AV Mats 31,164; CDs 10,477; DVDs 10,957; Bk Titles 123,553; Bk Vols 131,439; Per Subs 195
Open Mon-Thurs 9-9, Fri 9-6, Sat 9-5, Sun 1-6

RALPH ELLISON LIBRARY, 2000 NE 23rd St, 73111-3402, SAN 357-6485. E-mail: ralphellison@metrolibrary.org. *Mgr, Libr Operations,* Kimberly Francisco
Pop 28,800; Circ 93,450
Library Holdings: AV Mats 12,423; CDs 3,815; DVDs 3,697; Bk Titles 43,157; Bk Vols 45,911; Per Subs 91
Open Mon-Thurs 9-9, Fri 9-6, Sat 9-5, Sun 1-6
Friends of the Library Group

HARRAH LIBRARY, 1930 N Church Ave, Harrah, 73045. (Mail add: PO Box 893, Harrah, 73045), SAN 327-9960. E-mail: harrah@metrolibrary.org. *Mgr, Libr Operations,* Christopher Stofel
Pop 6,035; Circ 40,612
Library Holdings: AV Mats 3,144; CDs 1,389; DVDs 1,028; Bk Titles 13,383; Bk Vols 13,451; Per Subs 45
Open Mon & Wed-Fri 9-6, Tues 9-8, Sat 9-5

JONES LIBRARY, 9295 Willa Way, Jones, 73049, SAN 374-7387. E-mail: jones@metrolibrary.org. *Mgr, Libr Operations,* Paula Joseph-Johnson
Pop 4,722; Circ 10,201
Library Holdings: AV Mats 1,369; CDs 464; DVDs 529; Bk Titles 4,145
Open Mon & Wed-Fri 9-6, Tues 9-8, Sat 9-5

LUTHER LIBRARY, 310 NE Third St, Luther, 73054-9999, SAN 374-7395. E-mail: luther@metrolibrary.org. *Mgr, Libr Operations,* Paula Joseph-Johnson
Pop 3,984; Circ 30,836
Library Holdings: AV Mats 2,715; CDs 968; DVDs 1,072; Bk Titles 7,736; Per Subs 14
Open Mon & Wed-Fri 9-6, Tues 9-8, Sat 9-5

MIDWEST CITY LIBRARY, 8143 E Reno Ave, Midwest City, 73110-3999, SAN 357-654X. E-mail: midwestcity@metrolibrary.org. *Mgr, Libr Operations,* Randy Wayland
Pop 43,720; Circ 341,577
Library Holdings: AV Mats 22,968; CDs 7,140; DVDs 8,842; Bk Titles 84,907; Bk Vols 90,327; Per Subs 156
Open Mon-Thurs 9-9, Fri 9-6, Sat 9-5, Sun 1-6

NICOMA PARK LIBRARY, 2240 Overholser Dr, Nicoma Park, 73066. (Mail add: PO Box 756, Nicoma Park, 73066-0756), SAN 357-6698. E-mail: nicomapark@metrolibrary.org. *Mgr, Libr Operations,* Paula Joseph-Johnson
Pop 11,300; Circ 16,435
Library Holdings: AV Mats 1,682; CDs 629; DVDs 527; Bk Titles 5,500; Per Subs 33
Open Tues-Thurs 9:30-5:30, Fri & Sat 9-5

RONALD J NORICK DOWNTOWN LIBRARY, 300 Park Ave, 73102-3600, SAN 357-6337. E-mail: downtown@metrolibrary.org. *Mgr, Libr Operations,* Courtney Taddonio
Pop 67,604; Circ 151,803
Library Holdings: AV Mats 21,867; CDs 8,840; DVDs 7,021; Bk Titles 138,096; Bk Vols 143,850; Per Subs 360
Special Collections: Genealogy Coll; Holocaust Resource Coll (Preserving the memory & teaching the lessons of the Holocaust); Oklahoma Coll (Materials by Oklahomans or about Oklahoma). US Document Depository
Open Mon-Thurs 9-9, Fri 9-6, Sat 9-5, Sun 1-6

NORTHWEST LIBRARY, 5600 NW 122nd St, 73142-4204. E-mail: northwest@metrolibrary.org. *Mgr, Libr Operations,* Mark Schuster
Pop 72,963; Circ 568,734
Library Holdings: AV Mats 27,036; CDs 10,007; DVDs 11,510; Bk Titles 140,448; Bk Vols 149,412; Per Subs 251
Open Mon-Thurs 9-9, Fri 9-6, Sat 9-5, Sun 1-6

OUTREACH-BOOK CENTERS & BOOKS BY MAIL, 300 NE 50th St, 73105-1838. E-mail: outreach@metrolibrary.org.
Circ 248,080
Library Holdings: AV Mats 3,779; CDs 1,834; DVDs 1,906; Bk Vols 30,779

SOUTHERN OAKS LIBRARY, 6900 S Walker Ave, 73139-7203, SAN 357-6574. E-mail: southernoaks@metrolibrary.org. *Mgr, Libr Operations,* Todd Podzemny
Pop 55,568; Circ 277,791
Library Holdings: AV Mats 24,738; CDs 8,122; DVDs 8,221; Bk Titles 102,510; Bk Vols 109,053; Per Subs 129
Open Mon-Thurs 9-9, Fri 9-6, Sat 9-5, Sun 1-6

THE VILLAGE LIBRARY, 10307 N Pennsylvania Ave, The Village, 73120-4110, SAN 357-6604. E-mail: village@metrolibrary.org. *Mgr, Libr Operations,* Jason Wiggins
Pop 45,302; Circ 256,582
Library Holdings: AV Mats 17,744; CDs 5,757; DVDs 6,177; Bk Titles 66,183; Bk Vols 70,408; Per Subs 132
Open Mon-Thurs 9-9, Fri 9-6, Sat 9-5, Sun 1-6
Friends of the Library Group

WARR ACRES LIBRARY, 5901 NW 63rd St, Warr Acres, 73132-7502, SAN 357-6639. E-mail: warracres@metrolibrary.org. *Mgr, Libr Operations,* Laura Warren
Pop 44,710; Circ 233,444
Library Holdings: AV Mats 14,131; CDs 3,313; DVDs 4,995; Bk Titles 59,972; Bk Vols 63,800; Per Subs 67
Open Mon-Thurs 9-9, Fri 9-6, Sat 9-5, Sun 1-6

WRIGHT EXTENSION LIBRARY, 2101 Exchange Ave, 73108-2625, SAN 357-6728. E-mail: wright@metrolibrary.org. *Mgr, Libr Operations,* Courtney Taddonio
Pop 15,291; Circ 6,455
Library Holdings: AV Mats 1,911; CDs 629; DVDs 622; Bk Titles 6,149; Per Subs 27
Open Tues-Thurs 9:30-5:30, Fri & Sat 9-5

CR MID-AMERICA CHRISTIAN UNIVERSITY*, Charles Ewing Brown Library, 3500 SW 119th St, 73170-9797. SAN 316-4438. Tel: 405-691-3800. Circulation Tel: 405-691-3800, Ext 174. Interlibrary Loan Service Tel: 405-691-3800, Ext 168. FAX: 405-692-3165. E-mail: library@macu.edu. Web Site: www.macu.edu/academics/library. *Co-Dir,* Michael Foote; Tel: 405-692-3291, E-mail: mfoote@macu.edu; *Co-Dir,* Elissa Patadal; Tel: 405-692-3168, E-mail: epatadal@macu.edu; Staff 5 (MLS 2, Non-MLS 3)
Founded 1953. Enrl 650; Fac 20; Highest Degree: Bachelor
Library Holdings: Bk Titles 48,000; Per Subs 250; Spec Interest Per Sub 20
Special Collections: Archives of Church of God (Charles Ewing Brown Coll); Wesleyan Holiness Theology (Kenneth E Jones Coll)
Subject Interests: Behav sci, Biblical studies, Bus (non-profit), Christian, Church ministries, English, Sacred music, Teacher educ
Partic in Onenet
Open Mon-Thurs 7:30am-11pm, Fri 7:30-5, Sat 11-4, Sun 5pm-11pm

S NATIONAL COWBOY & WESTERN HERITAGE MUSEUM*, Donald C & Elizabeth M Dickinson Research Center, 1700 NE 63rd St, 73111. SAN 327-5655. Tel: 405-478-2250, Ext 290. FAX: 405-478-6421. Web Site: www.nationalcowboymuseum.org/research. *Curator of Archives, Dir,* Kimberly Roblin; E-mail: kroblin@nationalcowboymuseum.org; *Digital Archivist,* Holly Hasenfratz; E-mail: hhasenfratz@nationalcowboymuseum.org; *Digital Archivist, Ms Archivist,* Kera Newby; Tel: 405 478 2250, E-mail: knewby@nationalcowboymuseum.org; *Libr Tech,* Karen Spilman; Tel: 405-478-2250, Ext 290, E-mail: kspilman@nationalcowboymuseum.org; Staff 4 (MLS 3, Non-MLS 1)
Founded 1997
Library Holdings: AV Mats 3,480; CDs 357; DVDs 254; Electronic Media & Resources 1,139; Bk Titles 44,655; Per Subs 64; Videos 3,500
Special Collections: Arthur & Shifra Silberman Native American Painting Reference Library Research Files; Blucher Custom Boot Company Coll of Fitting; Contemporary Western Artists' Personal Papers, including Bettina Steinke & Tom Lovell; James E & Laura G Fraser Studio Coll; Joe De Yong Personal Papers; On-Line Image Archive; Photographic Archives (primarily Rodeo); Robert E Cunningham Coll, glass negatives; Saddlery Catalogs (Ron Bledsoe Coll); Western Americana (Glenn D Shirley Coll), Dime novels, movie posters, res files. Oral History
Subject Interests: Conserv, Cowboys, Firearms, Hist of the Am West, Hunting, Native Am art, Native American, Photog, Ranching, Western, Western art
Automation Activity & Vendor Info: (Cataloging) Auto-Graphics, Inc; (Circulation) Auto-Graphics, Inc; (OPAC) Auto-Graphics, Inc
Wireless access
Restriction: Open by appt only

S THE NINETY-NINES, INC*, Museum of Women Pilots Library, 4300 Amelia Earhart Rd, 73159-0040. SAN 371-2303. Tel: 405-685-7969. FAX: 405-685-7985. E-mail: museum@ninety-nines.org. Web Site: www.ninety-nines.org. *Adminr,* Laura Ohrenberg; E-mail: HQ@ninety-nines.org
Founded 1975
Library Holdings: Bk Vols 850
Special Collections: Amelia Earhart, Louis Thaden, Matilde Moisant, Grace Harris, Hazel Jones, Lucile Wright, Jerri Cobb, Edna Gardner Whyte & Jackie Cochran Colls; Jessie Woods Photo Coll
Restriction: Private libr

J OKLAHOMA CITY COMMUNITY COLLEGE*, Keith Leftwich Memorial Library, 7777 S May Ave, 73159. SAN 313-9646. Tel: 405-682-7564. Interlibrary Loan Service Tel: 405-682-1611, Ext 7668. Reference Tel: 405-682-1611, Ext 7251. Administration Tel: 405-682-1611, Ext 7699. FAX: 405-682-7585. E-mail: library@occc.edu. Web Site: libguides.occc.edu. *Dir, Libr Serv,* Ann Raia; Tel: 405-682-1611, Ext 7468, E-mail: ann.f.raia@occc.edu; *Cataloger/Ref Librn,* MaryGrace Berkowitz; Tel: 405-682-1611, Ext 7229, E-mail: mberkowitz@occc.edu; *Circ Librn,*

Johnny Hill; Tel: 405-682-1611, Ext 7315, E-mail: johnny.c.hill@occc.edu; *Ref & Instruction Librn,* Katie King; Tel: 405-682-1611, Ext 7643, E-mail: kathryn.m.king@occc.edu; *Syst Librn,* Dana Tuley-Williams; Tel: 405-682-1611, Ext 7390, E-mail: dtuley@occc.edu; Staff 7 (MLS 4.5, Non-MLS 2.5)
Founded 1972. Enrl 14,300; Fac 140; Highest Degree: Associate
Library Holdings: e-books 10,000; Bk Vols 120,000; Per Subs 700
Subject Interests: Humanities, Nursing, Soc sci
Automation Activity & Vendor Info: (Acquisitions) SirsiDynix; (Cataloging) SirsiDynix; (Circulation) SirsiDynix; (Course Reserve) SirsiDynix; (ILL) OCLC; (OPAC) SirsiDynix; (Serials) SirsiDynix
Wireless access
Open Mon-Thurs 7:30am-9pm, Fri 7:30-5, Sat 9-3

S OKLAHOMA CITY MUSEUM OF ART*, Library-Resource Center, 415 Couch Dr, 73102. SAN 373-109X. Tel: 405-236-3100. FAX: 405-236-3122. E-mail: info@okcmoa.com. Web Site: www.okcmoa.com. *Curator,* Roja Najafi
Library Holdings: Bk Vols 6,000
Wireless access
Open Tues-Fri 1-5
Restriction: Non-circulating

C OKLAHOMA CITY UNIVERSITY*, Dulaney-Browne Library, 2501 N Blackwelder, 73106. SAN 357-6752. Tel: 405-208-5068. Interlibrary Loan Service Tel: 405-208-5874. Administration Tel: 405-208-5072. Web Site: www.okcu.edu/library. *Dir,* Victoria Swinney, PhD; E-mail: vswinney@okcu.edu; *Access Serv Librn,* Kristen Burkholder, PhD; E-mail: kburkholder@okcu.edu; *Monographs Librn,* Robert Dorman, PhD; E-mail: rdorman@okcu.edu; *Music Librn,* Bonnie Elizabeth Fleming, PhD; E-mail: befleming@okcu.edu; *Archivist, Spec Coll Librn,* Christina Wolf; E-mail: cwolf@okcu.edu; *Theol & Ref LIbrn,* Lee Webb; E-mail: lwebb@okcu.edu; *ILL Spec,* Carissa Maben; E-mail: ckmaben@okcu.edu; Staff 6 (MLS 6)
Founded 1904. Enrl 3,000; Fac 186; Highest Degree: Doctorate
Jul 2019-Jun 2020 Income $1,026,635. Mats Exp $237,811, Books $65,367, Per/Ser (Incl. Access Fees) $171,029, Presv $1,415. Sal $582,759 (Prof $350,695)
Library Holdings: Audiobooks 294; CDs 8,359; e-journals 67,879; Music Scores 13,301; Bk Titles 172,980; Bk Vols 226,698; Videos 9,239
Special Collections: Methodist History Coll; Oklahoma History (George H Shirk History Center Coll)
Automation Activity & Vendor Info: (Acquisitions) OCLC Worldshare Management Services; (Cataloging) OCLC Worldshare Management Services; (Circulation) OCLC Worldshare Management Services; (Course Reserve) OCLC Worldshare Management Services; (Discovery) OCLC Worldshare Management Services; (ILL) OCLC WorldShare Interlibrary Loan; (OPAC) OCLC Worldshare Management Services
Wireless access
Function: Archival coll, Computers for patron use, Distance learning, Doc delivery serv, E-Reserves, Electronic databases & coll, Govt ref serv, ILL available, Internet access, Music CDs, Online cat, Online info literacy tutorials on the web & in blackboard, Online ref, Orientations, Photocopying/Printing, Prof lending libr, Ref serv available, Scanner, Tax forms, Telephone ref, VHS videos, Wheelchair accessible
Partic in Mid-America Law Library Consortium; OCLC Online Computer Library Center, Inc; Oklahoma Council of Academic Libr Directors
Open Mon-Thurs 7:30am-10pm, Fri 7:30-7, Sat 10-7, Sun 1-10
Restriction: Open to pub for ref & circ; with some limitations

Departmental Libraries:

CL SCHOOL OF LAW LIBRARY, 2501 N Blackwelder, 73106, SAN 357-6787. Tel: 405-208-5271. FAX: 405-208-5172. *Dir,* Lee Peoples; Tel: 405-208-6030, E-mail: lpeoples@okcu.edu; *Assoc Law Libr Dir,* Jennifer Prilliman; *Asst Dir, Tech Serv,* Nancy A Cowden; *Head, Access Serv,* Jenny Watson; *Head, Ref,* Tim Gatton; *ILL Librn,* Natalie Vaughn; *Syst Librn,* Kathryn Broad; Staff 7 (MLS 7)
Founded 1922. Enrl 620
Library Holdings: Bk Titles 96,875; Bk Vols 317,000
Partic in LexisNexis; OCLC Online Computer Library Center, Inc
Open Mon-Fri 7:30am-11pm, Sat 9am-11pm, Sun 1-11

S OKLAHOMA CITY ZOO*, Zoological Library, 2101 NE 50th, 73111. SAN 321-1894. Tel: 405-425-0277. FAX: 405-425-0243. Web Site: www.okczoo.org. *Librn,* Position Currently Open
Founded 1970
Library Holdings: Bk Titles 5,000; Per Subs 40
Automation Activity & Vendor Info: (Circulation) Follett Software
Wireless access
Open Mon-Sat 8-5

GL OKLAHOMA COUNTY LAW LIBRARY*, 321 Park Ave, Rm 247, 73102-3695. SAN 313-9484. Tel: 405-713-1353. FAX: 405-713-1852. E-mail: lawlibrary@oklahomacounty.org. Web Site: www.oklahomacounty.org. *Dir,* Venita L Hoover; E-mail: venhoo@oklahomacounty.org; Staff 1 (MLS 1)
Library Holdings: Bk Vols 47,000; Per Subs 25
Wireless access
Open Mon-Fri 8:30-5

G OKLAHOMA DEPARTMENT OF HUMAN SERVICES, Records Management Section, 200 E Hill St, 73105. SAN 313-9506. Tel: 405-521-2502. FAX: 405-521-0789. *Rec Mgt Adminr,* Mary Gail Foster; E-mail: mary.foster@okdhs.org; Staff 5 (MLS 1, Non-MLS 4)
Founded 1966
Special Collections: DHS Archives; History of Oklahoma Department of Human Services
Wireless access
Publications: Departmental Publications, Reports & Flyers
Restriction: Non-circulating coll

P OKLAHOMA DEPARTMENT OF LIBRARIES*, 200 NE 18th St, 73105. SAN 313-9514. Tel: 405-521-2502. Reference Tel: 405-522-3505. Toll Free Tel: 800-522-8116. FAX: 405-525-7804. Web Site: libraries.ok.gov. *Dir,* Susan McVey; Tel: 405-522-3172, E-mail: susan.mcvey@libraries.ok.gov; *Dep Dir,* Vicki Sullivan; E-mail: vicki.sullivan@libraries.ok.gov; *Head, Libr Develop,* Vicki Mohr; Tel: 405-522-3293, E-mail: vicki.mohr@libraries.ok.gov; *US Govt Doc Librn,* Position Currently Open; *Mgr, Libr Serv,* Christine Chen; *LSTA Coordr,* Judy Tirey; E-mail: judy.tirey@libraries.ok.gov; *Pub Info Officer,* Bill Young; E-mail: bill.young@libraries.ok.gov; *Archivist,* Jan Davis; *Cat, Pub Serv, Ref/Tech Serv,* Position Currently Open. Subject Specialists: *Law, Legis ref,* Christine Chen; Staff 23 (MLS 16, Non-MLS 7)
Founded 1893
Library Holdings: e-books 575; Bk Vols 270,000; Per Subs 1,604
Special Collections: Oklahoma Coll; State Government Archives. State Document Depository; US Document Depository
Subject Interests: Law
Automation Activity & Vendor Info: (Acquisitions) OCLC Worldshare Management Services; (Cataloging) OCLC; (Circulation) OCLC Worldshare Management Services; (ILL) OCLC WorldShare Interlibrary Loan; (OPAC) OCLC Worldshare Management Services; (Serials) OCLC Worldshare Management Services
Wireless access
Function: 24/7 Online cat, Archival coll, Govt ref serv, ILL available, Internet access, Photocopying/Printing, Ref serv available, Workshops
Publications: Oklahoma Agencies, Boards & Commissions (Annual); Oklahoma Almanac (Reference guide)
Open Mon-Fri 8-5
Restriction: Authorized patrons, Circ limited, Non-circulating to the pub, Open to pub for ref only, Pub use on premises

S OKLAHOMA HISTORICAL SOCIETY*, John & Eleanor Kilpatrick Research Center, Oklahoma History Ctr, 800 Nazih Zuhdi Dr, 73105. SAN 357-6825. Tel: 405-522-5225. FAX: 405-522-0644. E-mail: research@okhistory.org. Web Site: www.okhistory.org. *Dir,* Chad A Williams; Tel: 405-522-5207, E-mail: chadw@okhistory.org; *Dep Dir,* Laura Martin; Tel: 402-522-5225, E-mail: lmartin@okhistory.org; *Tech Serv Librn,* Patricia Jones; Tel: 405-522-4025, E-mail: pjones@okhistory.org; Staff 7 (MLS 3, Non-MLS 4)
Founded 1893
Library Holdings: CDs 1,000; Microforms 33,000; Bk Titles 8,500; Bk Vols 86,000; Per Subs 80
Special Collections: Alice Robertson Papers; Barde Coll; David L Payne Papers; Emmett Starr's Manuscripts; Frederic B Severs Papers; Grant Foreman Papers; Indian-Pioneer History; Oklahoma Photograph Coll; Robert L Williams Papers; Whipple Coll, bks, ms, photogs. Oral History
Subject Interests: 65 Indian tribes of Okla, Hist of Okla
Automation Activity & Vendor Info: (Cataloging) Cuadra Associates, Inc; (OPAC) Cuadra Associates, Inc
Wireless access
Function: Archival coll, Homebound delivery serv, Ref serv available, Res libr
Publications: Chronicles of Oklahoma (Quarterly)
Open Tues-Sat 10-4:45
Restriction: Not a lending libr, Open to dept staff only, Open to pub for ref only
Friends of the Library Group

P OKLAHOMA LIBRARY FOR THE BLIND & PHYSICALLY HANDICAPPED*, 300 NE 18th St, 73105. SAN 313-9549. Tel: 405-521-3514. Toll Free Tel: 800-523-0288. FAX: 405-521-4582. TDD: 405-521-4672. E-mail: olbph@okdrs.gov. Web Site: www.olbph.org. *Libr Dir,* Kevin Treese; E-mail: ktreese@okdrs.gov; *Librn,* Erin Byrne; E-mail: ebyrne@okdrs.gov; *Librn,* Andrew Shockley; E-mail: ashockley@okdrs.gov; *Librn,* Sammie Willis; E-mail: swillis@okdrs.gov
Founded 1933
Special Collections: Oklahoma History & Oklahoma Authors
Automation Activity & Vendor Info: (Cataloging) Keystone Systems, Inc (KLAS); (Circulation) Keystone Systems, Inc (KLAS); (OPAC) Keystone Systems, Inc (KLAS); (Serials) Keystone Systems, Inc (KLAS)

Wireless access
Function: 24/7 Electronic res, 24/7 Online cat, Audiobks via web, Digital talking bks, Mail loans to mem, Wheelchair accessible
Publications: Bright Future (Quarterly)
Special Services for the Deaf - TDD equip
Special Servs for the Blind - Braille servs; Digital talking bk; Digital talking bk machines; Newsletter (in large print, Braille or on cassette); Newsline for the Blind; Newsp reading serv; Production of talking bks; Recorded bks; Talking bks; Talking bks & player equip
Open Mon-Fri 8-5
Restriction: Registered patrons only
Friends of the Library Group

J OKLAHOMA STATE UNIVERSITY-OKLAHOMA CITY LIBRARY*, 900 N Portland, 73107. SAN 313-9581. Tel: 405-945-3251. FAX: 405-945-3289. E-mail: okc.reference@okstate.edu. Web Site: www.osuokc.edu/library. *Dir, Libr Serv,* Elaine Regier; Tel: 405-945-9104, E-mail: elaine.regier@okstate.edu; Staff 4 (MLS 2, Non-MLS 2)
Founded 1961. Enrl 4,000; Fac 58; Highest Degree: Associate
Library Holdings: Bks on Deafness & Sign Lang 400; Bk Titles 15,000; Bk Vols 15,373; Per Subs 330
Subject Interests: Fire, Hort, Nursing, Police
Automation Activity & Vendor Info: (Cataloging) Ex Libris Group; (Circulation) Ex Libris Group; (Course Reserve) Ex Libris Group; (OPAC) Ex Libris Group; (Serials) Ex Libris Group
Wireless access
Partic in OCLC Online Computer Library Center, Inc
Open Mon-Thurs 8-5:45

L PHILLIPS MURRAH*, Law Library, Corporate Tower, 13th Flr, 101 N Robinson Ave, 73102. SAN 372-2120. Tel: 405-235-4100. FAX: 405-235-4133. Web Site: phillipsmurrah.com. *Librn,* Maribeth Mills; E-mail: mdmills@phillipsmurrah.com
Restriction: Staff use only

M SAINT ANTHONY HOSPITAL*, O'Donoghue Medical Library, 1000 N Lee St, 73102-1080. (Mail add: PO Box 205, 73101-0205), SAN 313-9611. Tel: 405-272-6284. FAX: 405-272-7075.
Founded 1950
Library Holdings: Bk Vols 2,500; Per Subs 178
Subject Interests: Cardiology, Dentistry, Neurology, Nursing, Orthopedics, Psychiat
Partic in S Cent Regional Med Libr Program
Open Mon-Fri 7:30-4

S TRONOX LLC*, Technical Center Library, 3301 NW 150th St, 73134. (Mail add: PO Box 268859, 73126-8859), SAN 357-6272. Tel: 405-775-5000. FAX: 405-775-5027. *Libr Serv Supvr,* Sandy Harris
Founded 1964
Library Holdings: Bk Vols 13,000; Per Subs 50
Special Collections: Patent-Chemicals Coll, flm, microcard & paper; Rare Earth Coll, articles & rpt
Subject Interests: Chem, Chem tech
Wireless access
Restriction: Staff use only

GL US COURTS LIBRARY - TENTH CIRCUIT COURT OF APPEALS*, 2305 US Courthouse, 200 NW Fourth St, 73102. SAN 374-6038. Tel: 405-609-5460. FAX: 405-609-5461. Web Site: www.okwd.uscourts.gov. *Tech Serv,* Sheila Camp; Tel: 405-609-5463; Staff 2 (MLS 1, Non-MLS 1)
Founded 1990
Library Holdings: Bk Titles 2,000; Bk Vols 42,000; Per Subs 450
Special Collections: Oral History
Subject Interests: Law
Restriction: Open to pub for ref only

CM UNIVERSITY OF OKLAHOMA HEALTH SCIENCES CENTER*, Robert M Bird Health Sciences Library, 1105 N Stonewall Ave, 73117-1220. (Mail add: PO Box 26901, 73126-0901), SAN 357-6876. Tel: 405-271-2285. Circulation Tel: 405-271-2285, Ext 48701. Interlibrary Loan Service Tel: 405-271-2285, Ext 48753. Reference Tel: 405-271-2285, Ext 48752. Administration Tel: 405-271-2285, Ext 48755. FAX: 405-271-3297. Web Site: library.ouhsc.edu. *Dir,* Joy Summers-Ables; Fax: 405-271-6186, E-mail: joy-summers-ables@ouhsc.edu; *Bibliographer,* Shari Clifton; Tel: 405-271-2285, Ext 48752, E-mail: shari-clifton@ouhsc.edu; *Cat,* Jack Wagner; Tel: 405-271-2285, Ext 48758, E-mail: jack-wagner@ouhsc.edu; *Circ,* Phill Jo; Tel: 405-271-2285, Ext 48751, E-mail: phill-jo@ouhsc.edu; *Ser,* Position Currently Open; Staff 31 (MLS 8, Non-MLS 23)
Founded 1928. Enrl 3,166; Fac 1,238; Highest Degree: Doctorate
Jul 2017-Jun 2018 Income $4,644,833. Mats Exp $3,565,747, Books $98,217, Per/Ser (Incl. Access Fees) $2,315,625, Electronic Ref Mat (Incl. Access Fees) $581,532. Sal $1,155,080 (Prof $660,900)
Library Holdings: AV Mats 6,539; Bk Titles 147,170; Bk Vols 131,390; Per Subs 8,695
Special Collections: American Indian Health Coll; Medical History Coll; Rare Books
Subject Interests: Allied health, Biomed sci, Dentistry, Med, Nursing, Pharm, Pub health
Automation Activity & Vendor Info: (Cataloging) Ex Libris Group; (Circulation) Ex Libris Group; (OPAC) Ex Libris Group; (Serials) Ex Libris Group
Wireless access
Partic in National Network of Libraries of Medicine Region 3; OCLC Online Computer Library Center, Inc; Oklahoma Health Sciences Library Association; South Central Academic Medical Libraries Consortium
Open Mon-Thurs 7am-Midnight, Fri 7am-10pm, Sat 8am-9pm, Sun 10am-Midnight
Friends of the Library Group

OKMULGEE

J OKLAHOMA STATE UNIVERSITY*, Institute of Technology Library, 1801 E Fourth, 74447-0088. SAN 313-9697. Tel: 918-293-5080. Reference Tel: 918-293-5078. FAX: 918-293-4628. Web Site: www.osuit.edu/academics/library. *Dir,* Jenny Duncan; Tel: 918-293-5488, E-mail: jenny.duncan@okstate.edu; Staff 3 (MLS 2, Non-MLS 1)
Founded 1946. Enrl 2,039; Fac 118; Highest Degree: Bachelor
Library Holdings: Bk Vols 8,572; Per Subs 350
Subject Interests: Vocational tech
Wireless access
Open Mon-Thurs 7am-8pm, Fri 7-4:30, Sun 2-6

P OKMULGEE PUBLIC LIBRARY*, 218 S Okmulgee Ave, 74447. SAN 313-9700. Tel: 918-756-1448. FAX: 918-758-1148. E-mail: library@okmcity.net. Web Site: www.okmulgeeonline.com/SecondaryPages/Library. *Dir,* Kristin Cunningham; *Ch,* Jessica Brown; E-mail: jbrown@okmcity.net; *Genealogy Serv,* Traci Barber; Staff 7 (MLS 1, Non-MLS 6)
Founded 1907. Pop 17,906; Circ 139,306
Library Holdings: Audiobooks 1,973; Bk Vols 60,000; Per Subs 150; Videos 2,697
Subject Interests: Creek Indians
Automation Activity & Vendor Info: (Cataloging) Book Systems; (Circulation) Book Systems; (OPAC) Book Systems
Wireless access
Publications: Index to Okmulge Daily Times Obituaries 1950-
Open Mon & Thurs 8-8, Tue & Wed 8-6, Fri 8-5, Sat 8-12
Friends of the Library Group

PAULS VALLEY

P NORA SPARKS WARREN LIBRARY, 210 N Willow St, 73075. Tel: 405-238-5188. FAX: 405-331-5599. Web Site: paulsvalley.okpls.org. *Dir,* Shari Kendall; E-mail: skendall@cityofpaulsvalley.com; *Librn,* Rhonda Slayden; *Librn,* Lisa Webster; Staff 3 (Non-MLS 3)
Founded 1951. Pop 6,256
Automation Activity & Vendor Info: (Cataloging) Biblionix; (Circulation) Biblionix; (ILL) OCLC
Wireless access
Function: 24/7 Online cat, Adult bk club, Bks on CD, Children's prog, Citizenship assistance, Computer training, Computers for patron use, E-Readers, Electronic databases & coll, Free DVD rentals, ILL available, Internet access, Magazines, Mail & tel request accepted, Meeting rooms, Microfiche/film & reading machines, Online cat, OverDrive digital audio bks, Photocopying/Printing, Scanner, Senior computer classes, Story hour, Summer reading prog
Open Mon-Thurs 9-6, Fri 9-5, Sat 9-Noon
Friends of the Library Group

PAWHUSKA

P PAWHUSKA PUBLIC LIBRARY*, 1801 Lynn Ave, 74056. SAN 313-9735. Tel: 918-287-3989. FAX: 918-287-3989. E-mail: pawhuskalibrary@gmail.com. Web Site: www.pawhuska.org/departments#library. *Dir,* Yvonne Rose; E-mail: yrose@pawhuska.lib.ok.us; Staff 1 (Non-MLS 1)
Founded 1924. Pop 3,590; Circ 58,887
Library Holdings: Bk Titles 40,000; Per Subs 75
Special Collections: Audio Cassettes & Videos; Genealogy Coll; Newspapers, microfilm; Osage Indian Coll; United States Census, microfilm
Automation Activity & Vendor Info: (Circulation) Follett Software
Publications: Library Brochure
Open Mon-Wed & Fri 10-6, Thurs 1-6, Sat 10-4

PAWNEE

P PAWNEE PUBLIC LIBRARY*, 653 Illinois St, 74058. SAN 313-9743. Tel: 918-762-2138. FAX: 918-762-2101. Web Site: www.pawneepubliclibrary.net. *Librn,* Kathy McKinnis; E-mail: kathy@pawneepubliclibrary.net
Founded 1936. Pop 2,443; Circ 5,671
Library Holdings: Bk Titles 7,200; Per Subs 12
Automation Activity & Vendor Info: (Circulation) Follett Software
Wireless access
Special Services for the Blind - Talking bks
Open Mon-Fri 10-6, Sat 10-2
Friends of the Library Group

PERKINS

P THOMAS-WILHITE MEMORIAL LIBRARY*, 101 E Thomas, 74059. (Mail add: PO Box 519, 74059-0519), SAN 313-9751. Tel: 405-547-5185. FAX: 405-547-1040. E-mail: perkinslibrary@cityofperkins.net. Web Site: cityofperkins.net/library. *Dir,* Alison Bloyd; E-mail: abloyd@cityofperkins.net; *Circ/Cat Librn,* Jennifer Decker; Staff 2 (MLS 2)
Founded 1954. Pop 4,000; Circ 24,000
Library Holdings: Bk Titles 12,852; Bk Vols 13,281
Automation Activity & Vendor Info: (Acquisitions) Biblionix/Apollo; (Cataloging) Biblionix/Apollo; (Circulation) Biblionix/Apollo; (OPAC) Biblionix/Apollo; (Serials) EBSCO Online
Wireless access
Open Mon-Thurs 10-6, Fri 10-5, Sat 10-1
Friends of the Library Group

PERRY

P PERRY CARNEGIE LIBRARY*, 302 N Seventh St, 73077. SAN 313-976X. Tel: 580-336-4721. FAX: 580-336-5497. E-mail: staff@perry.lib.ok.us. *Libr Dir,* Pamela Rigg; E-mail: director@perry.lib.ok.us; *Ch Serv,* Catherine Carmack; Tel: 580-336-7300; Staff 1 (MLS 1)
Founded 1909. Pop 11,000; Circ 38,800
Library Holdings: Bk Titles 26,503; Bk Vols 29,000; Per Subs 69; Talking Bks 546; Videos 1,604
Automation Activity & Vendor Info: (Cataloging) Follett Software; (Circulation) Biblionix/Apollo
Function: Activity rm, Audiobks via web, Bks on CD, Computers for patron use, Free DVD rentals, Magazines, Meeting rooms, Online cat, Preschool reading prog, Prog for adults, Prog for children & young adult, Story hour, Summer reading prog, Wheelchair accessible
Open Mon-Thurs 9-6, Fri 9-5, Sat 9-Noon
Friends of the Library Group

PONCA CITY

P PONCA CITY LIBRARY*, 515 E Grand Ave, 74601. SAN 313-9786. Tel: 580-767-0345. Circulation Tel: 580-767-0350. E-mail: library@poncacityok.gov. Web Site: www.poncacityok.gov/155/Library. *Dir,* Holly LaBossiere
Founded 1904. Pop 26,000; Circ 289,855
Library Holdings: Bk Vols 75,000; Per Subs 264
Special Collections: Oriental & 20th Century Western Paintings (Matzene Art Coll)
Subject Interests: Genealogy
Automation Activity & Vendor Info: (Acquisitions) SirsiDynix; (Cataloging) SirsiDynix; (Circulation) SirsiDynix; (ILL) OCLC; (OPAC) SirsiDynix
Wireless access
Partic in OCLC Online Computer Library Center, Inc; OLTN
Open Mon-Thurs 9-9, Fri 9-6, Sat 9-5, Sun (Sept-May) 2-5
Friends of the Library Group

POND CREEK

P POND CREEK CITY LIBRARY*, 105 S Second St, 73766. (Mail add: PO Box 6, 73766-0006), SAN 323-4711. Tel: 580-532-6319. FAX: 580-532-4913. E-mail: cityofpondcreeklibrary@yahoo.com. Web Site: www.pondcreekok.com/library. *Librn,* Billie Lloyd
Founded 1934. Pop 1,050
Library Holdings: Bk Titles 8,875; Bk Vols 10,000; Per Subs 14; Talking Bks 146; Videos 285
Special Services for the Deaf - Bks on deafness & sign lang; High interest/low vocabulary bks
Open Tues-Fri 8:30-12 & 1-4:30

POTEAU

J CARL ALBERT STATE COLLEGE*, Joe E White Library, 1507 S McKenna, 74953. SAN 313-9808. Tel: 918-647-1311. FAX: 918-647-1314. Web Site: www.carlalbert.edu/student-services/library. *Dir of Libr,* Terri Carroll; E-mail: tcarroll@carlalbert.edu; *Ref & Circ Librn,* Tonya Sutton; E-mail: tsutton@carlalbert.edu
Founded 1934. Enrl 2,300; Fac 75
Library Holdings: e-books 10,000; Bk Vols 25,000; Per Subs 100
Automation Activity & Vendor Info: (Cataloging) SirsiDynix; (Circulation) SirsiDynix; (Course Reserve) SirsiDynix; (OPAC) SirsiDynix
Wireless access
Partic in OCLC Online Computer Library Center, Inc
Open Mon-Thurs 8am-6:30pm, Fri 8-4

P PATRICK LYNCH PUBLIC LIBRARY*, 206 S McKenna St, 74953. SAN 313-9794. Tel: 918-647-4444. FAX: 918-647-8910. E-mail: poteau@seolibraries.com. Web Site: www.seolibraries.com/about/hours-locations/patrick-lynch. *Br Mgr,* Leslie Langley; E-mail: leslie.langley@seolibraries.com; *Ch Serv,* Carole Gill; *Circ,* Nancie Anne Gordon; *ILL,* Mona Goodrich
Founded 1929. Pop 19,000; Circ 120,244
Library Holdings: Audiobooks 593; e-books 3,000; Bk Vols 54,000; Per Subs 45
Subject Interests: Genealogy, Literacy
Automation Activity & Vendor Info: (Circulation) SirsiDynix
Wireless access
Mem of Southeast Oklahoma Library System (SEOLS)
Open Mon-Fri 9-7, Sat 9-5
Friends of the Library Group

PRAGUE

P HAYNIE PUBLIC LIBRARY*, 1619 W Main St, 74864. SAN 313-9824. Tel: 405-567-4013. *Libr Dir,* Debbie Clonts; E-mail: debbie.clonts@haynielibrary.com
Circ 16,675
Library Holdings: Bk Vols 16,000
Wireless access
Open Tues-Fri 8:30-5:30, Sat 8-Noon
Friends of the Library Group

PRYOR

P PRYOR PUBLIC LIBRARY*, 505 E Graham, 74361. SAN 313-9832. Tel: 918-825-0777. FAX: 918-825-0856. Web Site: www.pryor.okpls.org. *Libr Dir,* Cari Rerat; E-mail: rerat@pryorlibrary.org; *Acq Librn, Circ,* Marie Reist; *Admin Librn,* Jacinda Ramsey; *Youth Serv Librn,* Amanda Gardner
Founded 1939. Pop 32,000; Circ 103,063
Library Holdings: Bk Titles 30,000; Per Subs 100
Special Collections: Autographs of United States Presidents (Harrison Coll), letters; Civil War Coll; Genealogy Coll
Subject Interests: Hist
Automation Activity & Vendor Info: (Cataloging) Follett Software; (Circulation) Follett Software
Wireless access
Open Mon-Thurs 1-9, Tues, Wed & Fri 9-5, Sat 9-Noon
Friends of the Library Group

RINGLING

P GLEASON MEMORIAL LIBRARY, 101 E Main St, 73456. SAN 377-5666. Tel: 580-662-2925. FAX: 580-662-2525. E-mail: gleasonmemorial@att.net. Web Site: ringling.okpls.org. *Dir,* Renee Yocum
Founded 1994
Library Holdings: Bk Titles 6,000
Function: 24/7 Online cat, Bks on CD, Children's prog, Computer training, Computers for patron use, Electronic databases & coll, Free DVD rentals, Govt ref serv, Health sci info serv, Homebound delivery serv, ILL available, Internet access, Mail & tel request accepted, Online cat, Outreach serv, Outside serv via phone, mail, e-mail & web, OverDrive digital audio bks, Photocopying/Printing, Preschool outreach, Preschool reading prog, Printer for laptops & handheld devices, Prog for adults, Prog for children & young adult, Ref & res, Ref serv available, Story hour, Summer reading prog, Telephone ref
Open Mon & Fri 9-1, Tues-Thurs 1-6
Friends of the Library Group

RUSH SPRINGS

P GLOVER SPENCER MEMORIAL LIBRARY*, 100 S Sixth St, Corner SE Sixth & Blakely Ave, 73082. (Mail add: PO Box 576, 73082-0576), SAN 313-9840. Tel: 580-476-2108. FAX: 580-476-2129. Web Site: www.glover.lib.ok.us. *Dir,* Tom Gashlin; E-mail: director@glover.lib.ok.us
Pop 1,500; Circ 7,440
Library Holdings: AV Mats 1,000; Bk Vols 11,000

Automation Activity & Vendor Info: (Circulation) Follett Software
Open Mon & Wed-Fri Noon-5, Tues Noon-7, Sat 9-Noon
Friends of the Library Group

SALLISAW

P STANLEY TUBBS MEMORIAL LIBRARY*, 101 E Cherokee St, 74955-4621. SAN 313-9859. Tel: 918-775-4481. Toll Free Tel: 888-291-8154 (in 918 area code only). FAX: 918-775-4129. Web Site: www.eodls.org/sallisaw. *Br Mgr,* Bethia Owens; Staff 5 (Non-MLS 5)
Founded 1967. Pop 8,000
Library Holdings: Bk Vols 34,000
Automation Activity & Vendor Info: (Acquisitions) SirsiDynix; (Cataloging) SirsiDynix; (Circulation) SirsiDynix
Wireless access
Mem of Eastern Oklahoma Library System
Open Mon & Thurs 9-8, Tues, Wed & Fri 9-6, Sat 9-1

SAPULPA

P BARTLETT-CARNEGIE SAPULPA PUBLIC LIBRARY*, 27 W Dewey, 74066. SAN 313-9875. Tel: 918-224-5624. FAX: 918-224-3546. E-mail: SapulpaLibrary@CityOfSapulpa.net. Web Site: www.cityofsapulpa.net/269/Sapulpa-Public-Library. *Dir,* Martha Stalker; Tel: 918-248-5978; *Asst Librn,* Karen Skaggs; E-mail: KSkaggs@cityofsapulpa.net; *Ch,* Kristin Haddock; E-mail: KHaddock@cityofsapulpa.net; *Circ Librn,* Rhonda Jones; E-mail: RJones@cityofsapulpa.net; *Genealogy Librn,* Mickey Allcock; E-mail: MAllcock@cityofsapulpa.net; *Genealogy Librn,* Cathy Mattix;; Tel: 918-248-5979, E-mail: CMattix@cityofsapulpa.net; *ILL,* Susan Johnson; E-mail: sjohnson@cityofsapulpa.net; *Per Librn,* Karen Marler; E-mail: KMarler@cityofsapulpa.net; Staff 8 (MLS 3, Non-MLS 5)
Founded 1917. Pop 20,250
Library Holdings: Bk Vols 58,000; Per Subs 86
Special Collections: Euchee/Yuchi Indian Tribe Coll; Indians of North America Coll; Oklahoma Coll; Sylvia Welch Genealogical Library Coll, bks, micro
Automation Activity & Vendor Info: (Cataloging) Innovative Interfaces, Inc; (Circulation) Innovative Interfaces, Inc; (OPAC) Innovative Interfaces, Inc
Wireless access
Function: 24/7 Electronic res, 24/7 Online cat, Accelerated reader prog, Activity rm, Adult literacy prog, Archival coll, Bks on CD, Children's prog, Computer training, Computers for patron use, Electronic databases & coll, For res purposes, Genealogy discussion group, Homebound delivery serv, ILL available, Internet access, Life-long learning prog for all ages, Magazines, Mango lang, Meeting rooms, Microfiche/film & reading machines, Movies, Music CDs, Online cat, Scanner, Spanish lang bks, Story hour, Teen prog, VHS videos, Wheelchair accessible
Partic in OLTN
Open Mon & Thurs 9-6, Tues & Wed 9-8, Fri 9-5, Sat 10-2
Restriction: Borrowing requests are handled by ILL
Friends of the Library Group

SAYRE

P SAYRE PUBLIC LIBRARY*, 113 E Poplar, 73662. SAN 329-8043. Tel: 580-928-2641. FAX: 580-928-1189. E-mail: sayrepl1@sayre.lib.ok.us. Web Site: www.sayre.lib.ok.us. *Dir,* Sue Warnke
Founded 1921. Pop 2,881; Circ 7,500
Library Holdings: Bk Titles 7,500; Bk Vols 9,000
Special Collections: Genealogical Research, 1900-; Local Newspapers for Sayre Journal & Sayre Record, 1901-; Sayre Record, microfilm
Automation Activity & Vendor Info: (Cataloging) Follett Software; (Circulation) Follett Software; (OPAC) Follett Software
Function: ILL available
Open Tues 10-5, Wed & Fri 10:30-5, Thurs 12-7, Sat 9-Noon
Friends of the Library Group

SEMINOLE

P SEMINOLE PUBLIC LIBRARY*, 424 N Main, 74868. SAN 313-9905. Tel: 405-382-4221. FAX: 405-382-0050. Web Site: seminole.okpls.org, www.seminole-oklahoma.net/library.html. *Dir,* Jeanette Kennedy; E-mail: jkennedy@seiminole-oklahoma.net
Founded 1929. Pop 17,071; Circ 45,516
Library Holdings: Bk Vols 30,000; Per Subs 65
Special Collections: Large Print Coll
Subject Interests: Native Am - Seminole Tribe
Automation Activity & Vendor Info: (Cataloging) Follett Software; (Circulation) Follett Software
Wireless access
Function: ILL available, Photocopying/Printing, Ref serv available
Partic in Okla Telecommunications Interlibr Syst
Open Mon-Wed 7:30-6, Thurs 7:30-7, Fri 7:30-5, Sat 8:30am-12:30pm
Friends of the Library Group

J SEMINOLE STATE COLLEGE*, David L Boren Library, Junction Hwy 9 & David L Boren Blvd, 74818. (Mail add: PO Box 351, 74818-0351), SAN 313-9891. Tel: 405-382-9950, Ext 243. FAX: 405-382-9511. Web Site: www.sscok.edu/BorenLibrary/LibraryPg.html. *Dir,* Carol Parker; E-mail: c.parker@sscok.edu
Founded 1970. Enrl 2,000; Fac 41
Library Holdings: Bk Titles 31,000; Per Subs 301
Special Collections: Library of American Civilization (American History Coll), ultrafiche
Wireless access
Open Mon & Thurs 8-8, Tues, Wed & Fri 8-4

SHATTUCK

P SHATTUCK PUBLIC LIBRARY*, 101 S Main St, 73858. (Mail add: PO Box 129, 73858-0129), SAN 320-5037. Tel: 580-938-5104. FAX: 580-938-5104. E-mail: shattpl@pldi.net. *Libr Dir,* Lois Fessler
Circ 4,837
Library Holdings: Bk Vols 9,118; Per Subs 15
Special Collections: History (Northwest Oklahoman Coll), newsps
Subject Interests: Ellis County hist
Automation Activity & Vendor Info: (Circulation) Book Systems
Partic in Okla Telecommunications Interlibr Syst
Open Mon & Thurs 10-6, Tues & Wed 10-5
Friends of the Library Group

SHAWNEE

CR OKLAHOMA BAPTIST UNIVERSITY*, Mabee Learning Center, 500 W University, OBU Box 61309, 74804-2504. SAN 313-9913. Tel: 405-585-4500. Circulation Tel: 405-585-4800. Interlibrary Loan Service Tel: 405-585-4519. Administration Tel: 405-585-4522. Web Site: okbu.libguides.com. *Dir, Libr Serv,* Julie Rankin; E-mail: julie.rankin@okbu.edu; Staff 10 (MLS 5, Non-MLS 5)
Founded 1911. Enrl 1,468; Fac 105; Highest Degree: Master
Library Holdings: Bk Vols 225,000; Per Subs 450
Special Collections: Baptist History Center; BB McKinney Hymn Coll, bks, ms. US Document Depository
Subject Interests: Archives, Relig
Automation Activity & Vendor Info: (Acquisitions) SirsiDynix; (Cataloging) SirsiDynix; (Circulation) SirsiDynix; (ILL) OCLC Online; (OPAC) SirsiDynix; (Serials) EBSCO Online
Wireless access
Function: Archival coll, AV serv, Govt ref serv, ILL available, Outside serv via phone, mail, e-mail & web, Photocopying/Printing, Ref serv available, Res libr, Telephone ref, Wheelchair accessible
Partic in OCLC Online Computer Library Center, Inc
Open Mon-Thurs 7:30am-11pm, Fri 7:30-5, Sat 1-9, Sun 3-11
Restriction: Open to students, fac & staff

SPIRO

P SPIRO PUBLIC LIBRARY*, 208 S Main St, 74959. SAN 313-993X. Tel: 918-962-3461. Toll Free FAX: 866-599-1478. E-mail: spiro@seolibraries.com. Web Site: www.seolibraries.com/about/hours-locations/spiro. *Br Mgr,* Shannon Elder; E-mail: shannon.elder@seolibraries.com; *Librn,* Glenda Stokes; *Asst Librn,* Dava Hanna
Pop 2,057; Circ 6,485
Library Holdings: Bk Vols 15,000
Automation Activity & Vendor Info: (Cataloging) SirsiDynix; (Circulation) SirsiDynix
Wireless access
Mem of Southeast Oklahoma Library System (SEOLS)
Open Tues-Fri 9-6, Sat 9-2
Friends of the Library Group

STIGLER

P STIGLER PUBLIC LIBRARY, 410 NE Sixth St, 74462. SAN 313-9948. Toll Free Tel: 866-240-6884. Toll Free FAX: 866-696-7978. E-mail: stigler@seolibraries.com. Web Site: www.seolibraries.com/about/hours-locations/stigler. *Mgr,* Tracy Allred
Founded 1968. Pop 2,650
Library Holdings: Bk Titles 22,000; Per Subs 32
Automation Activity & Vendor Info: (Circulation) SirsiDynix
Wireless access
Mem of Southeast Oklahoma Library System (SEOLS)
Open Mon-Fri 9-6, Sat 9-2

STILLWATER

S NATIONAL WRESTLING HALL OF FAME LIBRARY & MUSEUM*, 405 W Hall of Fame Ave, 74075. SAN 313-9972. Tel: 405-377-5243. FAX: 405-377-5244. E-mail: info@nwhof.org. Web Site: nwhof.org. *Exec Dir,* Lee Roy Smith; E-mail: lsmith@nwhof.org; Staff 3 (MLS 3)

Founded 1976
Library Holdings: Bk Titles 112; Bk Vols 170
Subject Interests: Wrestling
Open Mon-Fri 9-4:30, Sat 10-2

C OKLAHOMA STATE UNIVERSITY LIBRARIES*, Athletic Ave, 216, 74078. SAN 357-6965. Administration Tel: 405-744-6321. FAX: 405-744-9775. E-mail: libraryhelp@okstate.edu. Web Site: www.library.okstate.edu. *Dean of Libr,* Sheila Grant Johnson; E-mail: sheila.johnson@okstate.edu; *Assoc Dean, Libr Operations,* Robin Leech; Tel: 405-744-9780, E-mail: robin.leech@okstate.edu; *Assoc Dean, Spec Coll,* Mary Larson; Tel: 405-744-6588, E-mail: mary.larson@okstate.edu; *Dir, Libr Syst,* Rod K McAbee; Tel: 405-744-5955; *Dir of Libr Grad & Res Serv,* Victor Baeza; Tel: 405-744-1241, E-mail: victor.baeza@okstate.edu; *Head, Access Serv,* Dr Johnny Johnson; E-mail: johnny.johnson@okstate.edu; *Head, Cat,* Co-Ming Chan; E-mail: co_ming.chan@okstate.edu; *Head, Humanities & Soc Sci,* Steve Locy; E-mail: steven.locy@okstate.edu; *Archit Librn,* Susan Bobo; Tel: 405-744-6034, E-mail: susan.bobo@okstate.edu; *Veterinary Med Librn,* Liz Amos; Tel: 405-744-6655; *Admin Serv,* Karen A Neurohr; Tel: 405-744-2376, E-mail: karen.neurohr@okstate.edu; Staff 106 (MLS 41, Non-MLS 65)
Founded 1894. Enrl 20,956; Fac 893; Highest Degree: Doctorate
Special Collections: Architecture, bks & per; Curriculum Guides & Text Books (Curriculum Materials Library); Oklahoma Governors & Politicians (Papers of Gov Henry S Johnston & Gov Henry Bellmon, Senate Papers of Henry Bellmon); OSU History & Publications, bks, ms; Papers of Angie Debo; Soil Conservation, Water Resources & Agriculture (Oklahoma), bks, ms; US Patent & Trademark Depository Library; Veterinary Medicine, bks & per; Women's Archives, per & ms. Oral History; State Document Depository; US Document Depository
Subject Interests: Agr, Biochem, Botany, Chem, Econ, Educ, Engr, Geol, Hist of the Am West, Math, Physics
Automation Activity & Vendor Info: (Acquisitions) Ex Libris Group; (Cataloging) Ex Libris Group; (Circulation) Ex Libris Group; (Course Reserve) Ex Libris Group; (ILL) OCLC ILLiad; (OPAC) Ex Libris Group; (Serials) Ex Libris Group
Wireless access
Publications: Perspectives (External newsletter)
Partic in Association of Research Libraries; Greater Western Library Alliance; Okla Libr Technology Network; Okla Res & Commun Librs Consortium
Friends of the Library Group

Departmental Libraries:

ARCHITECTURE, School of Architecture Bldg, Rm 160, 74078, SAN 357-699X. Tel: 405-744-6047. *Librn,* Susan Bobo; Staff 1 (MLS 1)

CM WILLIAM E BROCK MEMORIAL LIBRARY AT OSU CENTER FOR VETERINARY HEALTH SCIENCES, 102 McElroy Hall, 74078, SAN 357-7023. Tel: 405-744-6655. FAX: 405-744-5609. E-mail: lib-vet@okstate.edu. *Head Librn,* Lynne Simpson; Tel: 405-744-2135, E-mail: lynne.simpson@okstate.edu; Staff 2 (MLS 1, Non-MLS 1)

DIGITAL LIBRARY SERVICES, Edmon Low Library, Rm 215A, 74078. Tel: 405-744-9161. *Head, Digital Initiatives,* Nicole Sump-Crethar; Tel: 405-744-9109, E-mail: sumpcre@okstate.edu; Staff 4 (MLS 3, Non-MLS 1)

DOCUMENTS DEPARTMENT, Edmon Low Library, 5th Flr, 74078, SAN 374-4205. Tel: 405-744-6546. *Head Librn,* Suzanne Reinman; Tel: 405-744-9788, E-mail: suzanne.reinman@okstate.edu; Staff 10 (MLS 4, Non-MLS 6)
Special Collections: UN Document Depository; US Document Depository
Subject Interests: Patent, Trademarks
Open Mon-Fri 8-5

HUMANITIES & SOCIAL SCIENCES DIVISION, Edmon Low Library, 3rd Flr, 74078-1071, SAN 327-9014. *Head Librn,* Steve Locy; Tel: 405-744-3272, E-mail: steven.locy@okstate.edu; Staff 7 (MLS 6, Non-MLS 1)

SCIENCE & ENGINEERING DIVISION, Edmon Low Library, 3rd Flr, 74078-1071, SAN 327-8999. *Head Librn,* Victor Baeza; Tel: 405-744-1241, E-mail: victor.baeza@okstate.edu; Staff 5 (MLS 5)

SPECIAL COLLECTIONS & UNIVERSITY ARCHIVES, Library 204, 74078. Tel: 405-744-6311. *Head, Spec Coll & Archives,* David C Peters; Tel: 405-744-6597, E-mail: david.peters@okstate.edu; Staff 5 (MLS 2, Non-MLS 3)
Special Collections: Oral History
Function: Archival coll, Photocopying/Printing
Restriction: Registered patrons only

MARY L WILLIAMS CURRICULUM MATERIALS LIBRARY, 001 Willard Hall, 74078, SAN 373-8841. Web Site: www.library.okstate.edu/education-and-teaching-library. *Librn,* Shannon Bowman; Tel: 405-744-9776, E-mail: shannon.bowman@okstate.edu; *Librn,* Rebecca Weber; Tel: 405-744-9769, E-mail: rebecca.weber@okstate.edu; Staff 2 (MLS 1, Non-MLS 1)
Special Collections: Della Thomas Alice in Wonderland Coll, bks, artifacts; Historical Children's Literature
Open Mon-Fri 8-5

P STILLWATER PUBLIC LIBRARY*, 1107 S Duck St, 74074. SAN 313-9964. Tel: 405-372-3633. Interlibrary Loan Service Tel: 405-372-3633, Ext 8119. Reference Tel: 405-372-3633, Ext 8106. Administration Tel: 405-372-3633, Ext 8100. FAX: 405-624-0552. Web Site: library.stillwater.org. *Dir,* Lynda Reynolds; Tel: 405-372-3633, Ext 8101; *Ch,* Elizabeth Murray; Tel: 405-372-3633, Ext 8116, E-mail: emurray@stillwater.org; *Circ Mgr,* Andrea Kane; Tel: 405-372-3633, Ext 8114, E-mail: akane@stillwater.org; *Adult Serv,* Stacy DeLano; Tel: 405-372-3633, Ext 8124, E-mail: sdelano@stillwater.org; *Tech Serv,* Bea LeValley; Tel: 405-372-3633, Ext 8121, E-mail: blevalley@stillwater.org; Staff 12 (MLS 5, Non-MLS 7)
Founded 1923. Pop 80,850; Circ 373,257
Jul 2016-Jun 2017 Income (Main Library Only) $1,386,093, State $23,337, City $1,301,285, Federal $4,000, Other $57,471. Mats Exp $147,869, Books $74,604, Per/Ser (Incl. Access Fees) $2,224, Other Print Mats $196, Micro $345, AV Mat $6,729, Electronic Ref Mat (Incl. Access Fees) $63,771. Sal $863,074
Library Holdings: AV Mats 11,080; e-books 38,576; Bk Vols 81,054; Per Subs 78
Special Collections: Genealogy Coll; Local Govt Coll; Stillwater Coll. Municipal Document Depository
Automation Activity & Vendor Info: (Cataloging) SirsiDynix; (Circulation) SirsiDynix; (ILL) SirsiDynix; (OPAC) SirsiDynix
Wireless access
Function: 24/7 Electronic res, 24/7 Online cat, Accelerated reader prog, Adult bk club, After school storytime, Archival coll, Art exhibits, Audio & video playback equip for onsite use, Bk club(s), Bks on CD, Children's prog, Computer training, Computers for patron use, Electronic databases & coll, Free DVD rentals, Genealogy discussion group, Govt ref serv, Home delivery & serv to seniorr ctr & nursing homes, Homebound delivery serv, ILL available, Internet access, Life-long learning prog for all ages, Magazines, Magnifiers for reading, Mail & tel request accepted, Meeting rooms, Microfiche/film & reading machines, Movies, Music CDs, Notary serv, Online cat, Online ref, Outreach serv, Outside serv via phone, mail, e-mail & web, OverDrive digital audio bks, Photocopying/Printing, Preschool outreach, Preschool reading prog, Printer for laptops & handheld devices, Prog for adults, Prog for children & young adult, Ref serv available, Scanner, Senior computer classes, Senior outreach, Serves people with intellectual disabilities, Spanish lang bks, Spoken cassettes & CDs, Spoken cassettes & DVDs, Story hour, Study rm, Summer & winter reading prog, Summer reading prog, Tax forms, Teen prog, Telephone ref, VHS videos, Wheelchair accessible, Winter reading prog, Workshops
Special Services for the Deaf - Assisted listening device; Bks on deafness & sign lang; Closed caption videos; High interest/low vocabulary bks; Sign lang interpreter upon request for prog
Special Services for the Blind - Accessible computers; Assistive/Adapted tech devices, equip & products; Audio mat; Bks on cassette; Bks on CD; Braille bks; Children's Braille; Copier with enlargement capabilities; Extensive large print coll; Home delivery serv; Internet workstation with adaptive software; Large print bks; Low vision equip; Magnifiers; Micro-computer access & training; Reading & writing aids; Screen enlargement software for people with visual disabilities; Screen reader software; Talking bks; ZoomText magnification & reading software
Open Mon-Thurs 9-9, Fri & Sat 9-6, Sun 1-5
Friends of the Library Group

STILWELL

P STILWELL PUBLIC LIBRARY*, Five N Sixth St, 74960. SAN 313-9980. Tel: 918-696-7512. Toll Free Tel: 888-378-8947. FAX: 918-696-4007. E-mail: stilwellpl@eols.org. Web Site: eols.org/library-location/stilwell-public-library. *Br Mgr,* Kathleen Connelly-Brown; E-mail: kconnelly-brown@eols.org
Founded 1972
Library Holdings: Bk Vols 16,000; Per Subs 10
Automation Activity & Vendor Info: (Circulation) Horizon; (ILL) Horizon
Wireless access
Mem of Eastern Oklahoma Library System
Open Mon-Fri 9-6, Sat 9-1
Friends of the Library Group

STRATFORD

P CHANDLER-WATTS MEMORIAL LIBRARY, 340 N Oak, 74872. (Mail add: PO Box 696, 74872-0696). Tel: 580-759-2684. FAX: 580-759-3121. Web Site: cwlibrary.okpls.org. *Dir,* Teresia Harrison; E-mail: tharrison@stratford.k12.ok.us
Pop 1,474; Circ 19,843
Library Holdings: AV Mats 400; CDs 38; DVDs 200; Bk Vols 19,200; Per Subs 10; Talking Bks 100

Automation Activity & Vendor Info: (Cataloging) Follett Software; (Circulation) Follett Software
Open Mon 8-4, Tues-Fri 8-6
Friends of the Library Group

STROUD

P SAC & FOX NATIONAL PUBLIC LIBRARY & ARCHIVES*, 920883 S Hwy 99, 74079-5178. SAN 374-6690. Tel: 918-968-3526. FAX: 918-968-4837. Web Site: sacandfox.biblionix.com. *Libr Dir,* Kathy J Platt; E-mail: kathy.platt@sacandfoxnation-nsn.gov; *Hist Researcher,* Catherine Joy Walker; E-mail: Cathrine.Walker@sacandfoxnation-nsn.gov; Staff 3 (Non-MLS 3)
Founded 1987. Pop 34,000; Circ 2,273
Library Holdings: Audiobooks 93; Bks on Deafness & Sign Lang 8; CDs 70; DVDs 1,945; Large Print Bks 68; Music Scores 1; Bk Titles 7,352; Per Subs 15; Talking Bks 13
Special Collections: Jim Thorpe Coll, lang tapes, restricted bks, treaties; Sac & Fox Archives, newsp, oral hist, photos. Oral History
Automation Activity & Vendor Info: (Cataloging) Biblionix; (Circulation) Biblionix
Wireless access
Function: Archival coll, Art exhibits, Audio & video playback equip for onsite use, CD-ROM, Children's prog, Computers for patron use, Digital talking bks, E-Readers, Free DVD rentals, Genealogy discussion group, ILL available, Internet access, Jail serv, Magazines, Mail & tel request accepted, Meeting rooms, Movies, Music CDs, Online cat, OverDrive digital audio bks, Printer for laptops & handheld devices, Prog for children & young adult, Ref & res, Tax forms
Open Mon-Fri 8-6

P STROUD PUBLIC LIBRARY*, 301 W Seventh St, 74079. (Mail add: PO Box 599, 74079-0599), SAN 313-9999. Tel: 918-968-2567. FAX: 918-968-4700. E-mail: library@cityofstroud.com. Web Site: www.cityofstroud.com/library. *Librn,* Marsha Morgan
Founded 1936. Pop 3,000; Circ 15,000
Library Holdings: Bk Vols 12,000
Special Collections: Oral History
Automation Activity & Vendor Info: (Circulation) Follett Software
Open Mon & Tues 9-1 & 2-6, Wed-Fri 9-1 & 2-5, Sat 9-Noon
Friends of the Library Group

SULPHUR

S NATIONAL PARK SERVICE*, Travertine Nature Center Library, Chickasaw National Recreation Area, 901 W First St, 73086. SAN 314-0008. Tel: 580-622-7234. FAX: 580-622-6931. Web Site: www.nps.gov/chic. *Chief of Interpretation,* Ron Parker; Tel: 580-622-7231, E-mail: Ron_Parker@nps.gov
Founded 1969
Library Holdings: Bk Vols 1,800; Per Subs 30
Subject Interests: Biology, Botany, Ecology, Geol, Native Am
Open Mon-Sun 9-4:30
Restriction: Ref only

S OKLAHOMA SCHOOL FOR THE DEAF*, Galloway-Clerc Library, 1100 E Oklahoma St, 73086. SAN 314-0016. Tel: 580-622-4974. FAX: 580-622-4959. Web Site: www.osd.k12.ok.us. *Librn,* Lesa Price; E-mail: lprice@osd.k12.ok.us; Staff 1 (MLS 1)
Founded 1898
Library Holdings: Bks on Deafness & Sign Lang 466; Bk Titles 9,407; Bk Vols 9,459; Per Subs 53; Videos 180
Automation Activity & Vendor Info: (Cataloging) Follett Software; (Circulation) Follett Software; (OPAC) Follett Software
Function: Wheelchair accessible
Special Services for the Deaf - Bks on deafness & sign lang; Deaf publ; Sorenson video relay syst; Staff with knowledge of sign lang; TTY equip

TAFT

OKLAHOMA DEPARTMENT OF CORRECTIONS
S JESS DUNN LEISURE LIBRARY*, 601 S 124th St W, 74463. (Mail add: PO Box 316, 74463-0316), SAN 324-4334. Tel: 918-682-7841, Ext 6544. FAX: 918-687-3431. *Head Librn,* Judy Foy; Staff 1 (MLS 1)
Library Holdings: Bk Vols 10,000; Per Subs 10
Function: For res purposes, Orientations
Restriction: Staff & inmates only

S DR EDDIE WARRIOR LEISURE LIBRARY*, 400 N Oak St, 74463. (Mail add: PO Box 315, 74463-0315), SAN 371-5329. Tel: 918-683-8365. FAX: 918-683-1586. *Librn,* Stephany Kash; Staff 1 (MLS 1)
Founded 1989
Library Holdings: Bk Vols 7,600
Special Services for the Deaf - High interest/low vocabulary bks; Spec interest per

TAHLEQUAH

C NORTHEASTERN STATE UNIVERSITY*, John Vaughan Library, 711 N Grand Ave, 74464-2333. SAN 314-2333. Tel: 918-456-5511, Ext 3200. Circulation Tel: 918-456-5511, Ext 3235. Reference Tel: 918-456-5511, Ext 3240. FAX: 918-458-2197. E-mail: library@nsuok.edu. Web Site: library.nsuok.edu. *Exec Dir,* Position Currently Open; *Dir, Libr Syst,* Darren Tobey; E-mail: tobey@nsuok.edu; *Head, Access Serv,* Aaron Pope; E-mail: popea@nsuok.edu; *Head, Res & Instrul Serv,* Brandon Oberg; E-mail: oberg@nsuok.edu; *Head, Tech Serv,* James Dodd; E-mail: dodd04@nsuok.edu; *Coll Spec,* Ashley Stoddard; E-mail: stoddard@nsuok.edu; *Univ Archivist,* Brenda Kay Bradford; E-mail: cochra07@nsuok.edu. Subject Specialists: *Historical Coll, Spec coll,* Ashley Stoddard; Staff 21 (MLS 10, Non-MLS 11)
Founded 1909. Enrl 8,833; Fac 340; Highest Degree: Doctorate
Library Holdings: e-books 75,241; e-journals 13,941; Bk Titles 324,379; Bk Vols 415,275; Per Subs 5,685
Special Collections: Native American History Coll. State Document Depository; US Document Depository
Automation Activity & Vendor Info: (Acquisitions) OCLC Worldshare Management Services; (Cataloging) OCLC Worldshare Management Services; (Circulation) OCLC Worldshare Management Services; (Course Reserve) OCLC Worldshare Management Services; (ILL) OCLC Tipasa; (OPAC) OCLC Worldshare Management Services; (Serials) OCLC Worldshare Management Services
Wireless access
Partic in Amigos Library Services, Inc; Grateful Med; OCLC Online Computer Library Center, Inc; Okla Libr Technology Network; WebDocs
Special Services for the Deaf - ADA equip
Special Services for the Blind - Assistive/Adapted tech devices, equip & products
Open Mon-Thurs 7:30am-Midnight, Fri 7:30-5, Sat 11-5, Sun 2-Midnight

Departmental Libraries:

BROKEN ARROW CAMPUS LIBRARY, 3100 E New Orleans St, Broken Arrow, 74014. Tel: 918-449-6459. Administration Tel: 918-449-6452. FAX: 918-449-6454. Web Site: library.nsuok.edu/nsuba/index.html. *Dir,* Dr Pamela Louderback; Tel: 918-449-6453, E-mail: louderba@nsuok.edu; *Instruction Librn,* Tom Rink; Tel: 918-449-6457, E-mail: rink@nsuok.edu; *Instruction Librn,* Karl Siewert; Tel: 918-449-6449, E-mail: siewert@nsuok.edu; *Syst Librn,* Brandon Martin; E-mail: martin70@nsuok.edu; *Tech Serv Librn,* Garnet Nowell; E-mail: nowell@nsuok.edu; Staff 6 (MLS 5, Non-MLS 1)
Founded 2001. Enrl 3,300; Fac 60; Highest Degree: Master
Library Holdings: e-books 35,000; e-journals 11,000; Bk Titles 11,000; Bk Vols 17,000; Per Subs 138
Partic in Grateful Med; OCLC Online Computer Library Center, Inc; Oklahoma Council of Academic Libr Directors; OLTN
Special Services for the Deaf - Assisted listening device
Special Services for the Blind - Assistive/Adapted tech devices, equip & products
Open Mon-Thurs 8:30am-9pm, Fri & Sat 8:30-5

P TAHLEQUAH PUBLIC LIBRARY, 120 S College Ave, 74464. SAN 376-6438. Tel: 918-456-2581. Toll Free Tel: 888-291-8149. FAX: 918-458-0590. E-mail: tahlequahpl@eols.org. Web Site: eols.org/library-location/tahlequah-public-library. *Br Mgr,* Robin Mooney; E-mail: rmooney@eols.org
Library Holdings: Bk Vols 50,000; Per Subs 20
Automation Activity & Vendor Info: (Cataloging) Horizon; (Circulation) Horizon
Wireless access
Mem of Eastern Oklahoma Library System
Open Mon-Thurs 9-8, Fri 9-6, Sat 9-5:30
Friends of the Library Group

TALIHINA

P TALIHINA PUBLIC LIBRARY*, 900 Second St, 74571. SAN 314-0059. Tel: 918-567-2002. FAX: 918-567-2921. E-mail: talihina@seolibraries.com. Web Site: www.seolibraries.com/about/hours-locations/talihina. *Asst Br Mgr,* Ruth McClard
Founded 1969
Library Holdings: Bk Vols 22,000; Per Subs 20
Special Collections: Oklahoma Coll
Automation Activity & Vendor Info: (Circulation) SirsiDynix
Wireless access
Function: Children's prog, Free DVD rentals, Genealogy discussion group, ILL available, Internet access, Music CDs, Photocopying/Printing, Prog for adults, Prog for children & young adult, Scanner, Teen prog, VHS videos
Mem of Southeast Oklahoma Library System (SEOLS)
Open Tues-Fri 10-6, Sat 10-4
Friends of the Library Group

TECUMSEH

S CENTRAL OKLAHOMA JUVENILE CENTER LIBRARY*, 700 S Ninth St, 74873. Tel: 405-598-4146. FAX: 405-598-4158. Web Site: www.ok.gov/oja/Residential_Treatment_Centers/Central_OK_Juvenile_Center.
Library Holdings: Bk Vols 9,000; Per Subs 30
Restriction: Not open to pub

TEXHOMA

P TEXHOMA PUBLIC LIBRARY*, Main St, 73949. SAN 314-0067. Tel: 580-423-7150. Web Site: harringtonlc.org/texhomapublic. *Librn,* Carol Coble
Founded 1926. Pop 1,200; Circ 4,708
Library Holdings: Bk Vols 16,000
Partic in Harrington Library Consortium
Open Mon, Wed & Fri 3-6, Tues & Thurs 3-8, Sat 8-Noon

TINKER AFB

A UNITED STATES AIR FORCE*, Tinker Air Force Base Library, 72nd FSS/FSDL, Bldg 5702, 6120 Arnold St, 73145-8101. SAN 357-7058. Tel: 405-734-2626. FAX: 405-734-9511. Web Site: tinkerliving.com/Library, www.tinker.af.mil/Links/Tinker-Living/Library. *Librn,* Peter Nardin
Founded 1943
Library Holdings: Bk Vols 10,500
Special Collections: Total Quality Management
Subject Interests: Aeronaut engr, Recreational
Wireless access
Partic in OCLC Online Computer Library Center, Inc
Open Tues-Thurs 10-6, Fri 10-5, Sat 9-5

TISHOMINGO

J MURRAY STATE COLLEGE LIBRARY*, Learning Resource Center, One Murray Campus St, Ste LS 101, 73460. SAN 314-0075. Tel: 580-387-7310. Interlibrary Loan Service Tel: 580-371-2371, Ext 209. Administration Tel: 580-387-7301. FAX: 580-371-9844. E-mail: askMSClibrary@mscok.edu. Web Site: www.mscok.edu/current-students/library. *Libr Dir,* Stephen Finlay; E-mail: sfinlay@mscok.edu; Staff 3 (MLS 1, Non-MLS 2)
Founded 1930. Enrl 1,958; Fac 43; Highest Degree: Associate
Library Holdings: Audiobooks 131; CDs 14; DVDs 636; e-books 162; Bk Titles 14,375; Bk Vols 15,313; Per Subs 4
Automation Activity & Vendor Info: (Cataloging) TLC (The Library Corporation); (Circulation) TLC (The Library Corporation); (Course Reserve) TLC (The Library Corporation); (OPAC) TLC (The Library Corporation)
Wireless access
Publications: Library Handbook; Student Worker's Handbook
Partic in OCLC Online Computer Library Center, Inc
Open Mon-Thurs 7:30am-8:30pm, Fri 7:30-4:30, Sun 4:30pm-8:30pm

TONKAWA

J NORTHERN OKLAHOMA COLLEGE*, Vineyard Library, 1220 E Grand Ave, 74653-4022. (Mail add: PO Box 310, 74653-0310), SAN 314-0083. Tel: 580-628-6250. FAX: 580-628-6209. Web Site: www.noc.edu/library2. *Dir, Libr Serv,* Benjamin Hainline; E-mail: ben.hainline@noc.edu; *Library Services,* Jean Gilbert; E-mail: jean.gilbert@noc.edu; Staff 6 (MLS 2, Non-MLS 4)
Founded 1901. Enrl 1,600; Fac 65; Highest Degree: Associate
Library Holdings: Bk Titles 41,000; Per Subs 227
Special Collections: Oklahoma Coll. Oral History
Subject Interests: Native Am hist
Automation Activity & Vendor Info: (Acquisitions) Ex Libris Group; (Cataloging) Ex Libris Group; (Circulation) Ex Libris Group; (OPAC) Ex Libris Group
Function: Res libr
Open Mon-Thurs 7:30am-9pm, Fri 7:30-5

P TONKAWA PUBLIC LIBRARY, 216 N Seventh St, 74653. SAN 314-0091. Tel: 580-628-3366. FAX: 580-628-3688. E-mail: tonkawalibrary@yahoo.com. Web Site: tonkawalibrary.okpls.org. *Dir,* Megan Hill
Founded 1922. Pop 3,127; Circ 15,700
Library Holdings: Bk Titles 21,000; Per Subs 36
Special Collections: Oklahoma Coll
Automation Activity & Vendor Info: (Circulation) Biblionix
Wireless access
Open Mon & Tues 10-6, Wed-Fri 9-5, Sat 10-1
Friends of the Library Group

TULSA

M ASCENSION SAINT JOHN MEDICAL CENTER*, Health Sciences Library, 1923 S Utica Ave, 74104. SAN 314-0261. Tel: 918-744-2970. FAX: 918-744-3209. E-mail: library@sjmc.org. *Librn,* Position Currently Open
Founded 1946
Library Holdings: Bk Vols 12,000; Per Subs 135
Subject Interests: Behav sci, Catholic bio-ethics, Educ, Med, Nursing, Soc sci
Open Mon-Fri 8-4:30

R FIRST UNITED METHODIST CHURCH*, Broadhurst Library, 1115 S Boulder, 74119-2492. SAN 314-0121. Tel: 918-587-9481, Ext 152. FAX: 918-584-5228. Web Site: www.fumctulsa.org. *Library Contact,* Lory Ferrin; E-mail: loryferrin@fumctulsa.org; Staff 12 (Non-MLS 12)
Founded 1940
Library Holdings: Bk Titles 15,263; Per Subs 20
Special Collections: Children's Library; Famous Christian Art Reproductions; John Charles Wesley Coll; Methodist Rare Book Coll
Subject Interests: Christian life, Educ
Wireless access
Open Mon-Thurs 10-3, Sun 9-12:30
Friends of the Library Group

L GABLE & GOTWALS, INC*, Law Library, 1100 Oneok Plaza, 100 W Fifth St, 74103. SAN 372-2236. Tel: 918-595-4800. FAX: 918-595-4990. Web Site: www.gablelaw.com. *Adminr,* Patti Flynn; Tel: 918-595-4938, E-mail: pflynn@gablelaw.com; Staff 4 (MLS 2, Non-MLS 2)
Founded 1944
Library Holdings: Bk Vols 10,000; Per Subs 100

S THOMAS GILCREASE INSTITUTE OF AMERICAN HISTORY & ART LIBRARY, Helmerich Center for American Research, 1400 Gilcrease Museum Rd, 74127. SAN 314-0148. Tel: 918-596-2700. Toll Free Tel: 888-655-2278. FAX: 918-596-2770. Web Site: www.gilcrease.org/helmerich-center/using-the-library. *Librn,* Renee Harvey; Tel: 918-631-6441, E-mail: renee-harvey@utulsa.edu; *Sr Curator,* Laura Fry; Tel: 918-596-2745, E-mail: laura-fry@utulsa.edu; Staff 2 (MLS 1, Non-MLS 1)
Founded 1942
Library Holdings: Bk Titles 42,204; Per Subs 25
Special Collections: Manuscripts
Subject Interests: Native Am hist, Western hist
Automation Activity & Vendor Info: (Cataloging) Innovative Interfaces, Inc
Restriction: Open by appt only

CM OKLAHOMA STATE UNIVERSITY - CENTER FOR HEALTH SCIENCES*, Medical Library, 1111 W 17th St, 74107-1898. SAN 314-0156. Tel: 918-561-8449. Interlibrary Loan Service Tel: 918-561-8448. Reference Tel: 918-561-1119. FAX: 918-561-8412. Web Site: health.okstate.edu/library. *Dir, Med Libr,* Jon Goodell; Tel: 918-562-8451, E-mail: jon.goodell@okstate.edu; *Assessment Librn, User Experience Librn,* Scott Murray; Tel: 918-561-8221, E-mail: scott.murray@okstate.edu; *Events & Outreach, Librn, Res,* Linda London; Tel: 918-561-8466, E-mail: linda.london@okstate.edu; *Electronic Res Librn,* Lou Ann Thompson; Tel: 918-561-8457, E-mail: louann.thompson@okstate.edu; Staff 3 (MLS 3)
Founded 1974. Enrl 380; Highest Degree: Doctorate
Library Holdings: AV Mats 4,142; e-books 170; e-journals 11,498; Bk Titles 28,077; Bk Vols 57,979; Per Subs 356; Videos 687
Special Collections: Anatomical Models & Realia; Case Histories for Massachusetts General Hospital; College Archives; National Library of Medicine Literature Searches; Osteopathic Literature
Subject Interests: Med
Automation Activity & Vendor Info: (Acquisitions) Ex Libris Group; (Cataloging) Ex Libris Group; (Circulation) Ex Libris Group; (Course Reserve) Ex Libris Group; (OPAC) Ex Libris Group; (Serials) Ex Libris Group
Wireless access
Partic in National Network of Libraries of Medicine Region 3; SCAMeL
Open Mon 6am-Midnight, Tues-Fri 7am-Midnight, Sat & Sun 9am-Midnight
Restriction: Open to pub for ref only

C OKLAHOMA STATE UNIVERSITY - TULSA LIBRARY*, 700 N Greenwood Ave, 74106-0702. SAN 326-8993. Tel: 918-594-8130. Reference Tel: 918-594-8137. FAX: 918-594-8145. Web Site: www.osu-tulsa.okstate.edu/library. *Libr Dir,* Lynn Wallace; Tel: 918-594-8451, E-mail: lynn.wallace@okstate.edu; *Curric Mat Librn, Ref Librn,* Robert David Bell; Tel: 918-594-8136, E-mail: rd.bell@okstate.edu; *Instruction Librn, Ref Librn,* Thomas Thorisch; Tel: 918-594-8146, E-mail: tom.thorisch@okstate.edu; *Outreach Librn,* Emrys Moreau; Tel: 918-594-8453, E-mail: emrys.moreau@okstate.edu; *Coordr, Pub Serv,*

Dona Davidson; Tel: 918-594-8139, E-mail: dona.davidson@okstate.edu; *Archivist, Coll,* Milissa Burkart; Tel: 918-594-8132, E-mail: milissa.burkart@okstate.edu. Subject Specialists: *Engr, Sci,* Robert David Bell; Staff 7 (MLS 7)
Founded 1999. Enrl 2,700; Fac 63; Highest Degree: Doctorate
Library Holdings: Audiobooks 24; AV Mats 2,897; Bks on Deafness & Sign Lang 260; CDs 1,272; DVDs 615; e-books 83,000; Electronic Media & Resources 150; Bk Vols 145,597; Per Subs 67,241; Videos 2,236
Special Collections: Center for Poets & Writers Manuscript Coll; Cyrus Stevens Avery Papers; Eric Coll (from 1980); Michael Wallis Manuscript Coll; Michael Wallis Route 66 Archive; Tulsa Race Riot of 1921
Subject Interests: Computer sci, Educ, Engr, Psychol
Automation Activity & Vendor Info: (Acquisitions) Ex Libris Group; (Cataloging) Ex Libris Group; (Circulation) Ex Libris Group; (Course Reserve) Ex Libris Group; (ILL) OCLC ILLiad; (OPAC) Ex Libris Group; (Serials) Ex Libris Group
Wireless access
Partic in OCLC Online Computer Library Center, Inc; Oklahoma Council of Academic Libr Directors
Special Services for the Deaf - Accessible learning ctr; Bks on deafness & sign lang
Special Services for the Blind - ZoomText magnification & reading software
Open Mon-Thurs 9am-9:45pm, Fri & Sat 9-4:45, Sun 1-8:45
Restriction: Open to pub for ref & circ; with some limitations

C ORAL ROBERTS UNIVERSITY LIBRARY*, John D Messick Learning Resources Center, 7777 S Lewis Ave, 74171. SAN 314-0199. Tel: 918-495-6723. Circulation Tel: 918-495-6391. Reference Tel: 918-495-6887. FAX: 918-495-6893. Interlibrary Loan Service FAX: 918-495-7428. Web Site: www.oru.edu/library. *Dean, Learning Res,* Mark E Roberts, PhD; E-mail: mroberts@oru.edu; *Asst Dir,* Jane Malcolm; Tel: 918-495-7495, E-mail: jmalcolm@oru.edu; *Dir, Archives, Dir, Holy Spirit Res Ctr,* Daniel Isgrigg, PhD; Tel: 918-495-6899, E-mail: disgrigg@oru.edu; *Acq, Head, Cat, Libr Syst Adminr,* Dana Higeons; Tel: 918-495-6885, E-mail: dhigeons@oru.edu; *Head, Access Serv, Webmaster,* Dr Angela Sample; Tel: 918-495-6895, E-mail: asample@oru.edu; *Actg Librn, Digital Scholarship Librn, Research Librn,* Thad R Horner; Tel: 918-495-6889, E-mail: thorner@oru.edu; *Instruction Librn, Ref Librn,* Myra Bloom; Tel: 918-495-7174, E-mail: mbloom@oru.edu; *Advanced Library Generalist, Electronic Res Mgr,* Daniel Eller; Tel: 918-495-7168, E-mail: deller@oru.edu; *Archives, Rec Mgr,* Roger Rydin; Tel: 918-495-6750, E-mail: rrydin@oru.edu; *Supvr, Access Serv,* Carolyn Prescott; E-mail: cprescott@oru.edu; *Cat Spec,* Position Currently Open; *Cat Asst,* Jennifer Horton; Tel: 918-495-6881, E-mail: jehorton@oru.edu; *Archives Asst, Ref, Res,* Hope Smashey; E-mail: hsmashey@oru.edu. Subject Specialists: *New Testament,* Mark E Roberts, PhD; *Bus,* Jane Malcolm; *Theol,* Daniel Isgrigg, PhD; *Educ, Info literacy,* Dr Angela Sample; *Theol,* Thad R Horner; Staff 11 (MLS 6, Non-MLS 5)
Founded 1963. Enrl 4,160; Fac 260; Highest Degree: Doctorate
May 2019-Apr 2020. Mats Exp $380,604, Books $25,200, Per/Ser (Incl. Access Fees) $42,577, Other Print Mats $575, AV Mat $433, Electronic Ref Mat (Incl. Access Fees) $309,248, Presv $2,571. Sal $923,700 (Prof $724,814)
Library Holdings: Audiobooks 1,830; AV Mats 14,480; CDs 1,936; DVDs 2,071; e-books 212,181; Microforms 50,246; Music Scores 5,713; Bk Titles 226,973; Bk Vols 259,622; Videos 2,618
Special Collections: Brad Young Coll; Curriculum Media Center; Elmar Camillo Dos Santos Coll; Holy Spirit Research Center; Howard Ervin Coll; Jewish Theological Seminary Coll; Music Listening Room; Oral Roberts University Archives; William Sanford LaSor Coll
Subject Interests: Biblical studies, Missions, Pentecostalism, Theol
Automation Activity & Vendor Info: (Acquisitions) Innovative Interfaces, Inc - Sierra; (Cataloging) Innovative Interfaces, Inc - Sierra; (Circulation) Innovative Interfaces, Inc - Sierra; (Course Reserve) Innovative Interfaces, Inc - Sierra; (Discovery) EBSCO Discovery Service; (ILL) OCLC; (OPAC) Innovative Interfaces, Inc - Sierra; (Serials) Innovative Interfaces, Inc - Sierra
Wireless access
Partic in Christian Library Consortium; OCLC Online Computer Library Center, Inc; Oklahoma Health Sciences Library Association; Westchester Academic Library Directors Organization
Restriction: Open to pub upon request, Open to students, fac, staff & alumni

Departmental Libraries:

HOLY SPIRIT RESEARCH CENTER, 7777 S Lewis Ave, 74171. Tel: 918-495-6391. E-mail: hsrc@oru.edu. Web Site: oru.libguides.com/HSRC. *Dir, Holy Spirit Res Ctr,* Daniel Isgrigg; Tel: 918-495-6899, E-mail: disgrigg@oru.edu; *Archivist,* Roger Rydin; Tel: 918-495-6750; Staff 1 (Non-MLS 1)
Fac 1
Library Holdings: AV Mats 9,313; CDs 66; DVDs 115; Microforms 37; Music Scores 51; Bk Vols 13,051; Per Subs 25; Videos 822
Special Collections: Howard M Ervin Coll
Subject Interests: Charismatic, Divine healing, Pentecostal, Pneumatology
Open Mon-Fri 12:30-4:20

S PALOMINO HORSE BREEDERS OF AMERICA LIBRARY*, 15253 E Skelly Dr, 74116. SAN 326-4130. Tel: 918-438-1234. FAX: 918-438-1232. E-mail: yellahrses@palominohba.com. Web Site: www.palominohba.com. *Librn,* Terri Green; E-mail: tgreen@palominohba.com
Founded 1941
Library Holdings: Bk Vols 500; Per Subs 175
Open Mon-Thurs 8:30-4:30, Fri 8:30-12:30

S PHILBROOK MUSEUM OF ART*, H A & Mary K Chapman Library, 2727 S Rockford Rd, 74114-4104. (Mail add: PO Box 52510, 74152-0510), SAN 314-0210. Tel: 918-748-5306. FAX: 918-748-5303. E-mail: library@philbrook.org. Web Site: philbrook.org. *Librn & Archivist,* Thomas Elton Young; Staff 1 (MLS 1)
Founded 1940
Library Holdings: Bk Vols 26,000; Per Subs 70
Special Collections: American Indian (Roberta C Lawson Library); Eugene B. Adkins Library & Archive; Native American Artists Coll, VF; Nettie Wheeler Coll; Oklahoma Artists Coll, VF; Tulsa Art Association Coll; Waite Phillips Coll
Subject Interests: Fine arts, Visual arts
Automation Activity & Vendor Info: (Cataloging) Follett Software; (Circulation) Follett Software; (OPAC) Follett Software
Function: Archival coll, ILL available, Ref serv available, Telephone ref
Partic in OCLC Online Computer Library Center, Inc
Open Mon-Tues 10-12 & 1-5, Wed-Fri 10-12
Restriction: Circulates for staff only

CR PHILLIPS THEOLOGICAL SEMINARY LIBRARY, 901 N Mingo Rd, 74116. SAN 357-5403. Tel: 918-270-6437. Administration Tel: 918-270-6459. FAX: 918-270-6490. E-mail: ptslibrary@ptstulsa.edu. Web Site: www.ptstulsa.edu. *Dean of the Library & Research Servs,* Sandy Shapoval; E-mail: sandy.shapoval@ptstulsa.edu; *Asst Dean, Instruction Librn,* Katherine Casey; Tel: 918-270-6432, E-mail: katherine.casey@ptstulsa.edu; *Access Serv Librn, Reserves Librn,* Avery Welden; Tel: 918-270-6427, E-mail: avery.welden@ptstulsa.edu; *Archives Librn, Presv,* Position Currently Open; *Cat Librn,* Lucy Franklin; Tel: 918-270-6430, E-mail: lucy.franklin@ptstulsa.edu; Staff 5.3 (MLS 5, Non-MLS 0.3)
Founded 1950. Enrl 166; Fac 15; Highest Degree: Doctorate
Subject Interests: Relig, Theol
Automation Activity & Vendor Info: (Acquisitions) Ex Libris Group; (Cataloging) Ex Libris Group; (Circulation) Ex Libris Group; (Course Reserve) Ex Libris Group; (ILL) OCLC WorldShare Interlibrary Loan; (OPAC) Ex Libris Group; (Serials) EBSCO Online
Wireless access
Partic in OCLC Online Computer Library Center, Inc

C SPARTAN COLLEGE OF AERONAUTICS & TECHNOLOGY LIBRARY*, 8820 E Pine St, 74115. Tel: 918-831-8604. FAX: 918-831-5245. Web Site: www.spartan.edu. *Dir,* Melody Walden; Tel: 918-831-8605, E-mail: melody.walden@spartan.edu
Library Holdings: Bk Vols 13,000
Automation Activity & Vendor Info: (Acquisitions) Follett Software; (Cataloging) Follett Software; (Circulation) Follett Software; (OPAC) Follett Software
Wireless access
Open Mon-Thurs 6:30am-9:30pm, Fri 6:30am-5pm

P TULSA CITY-COUNTY LIBRARY*, Administrative Offices, 400 Civic Ctr, 74103. SAN 357-735X. Tel: 918-549-7323. Interlibrary Loan Service Tel: 918-549-7395. FAX: 918-549-7376. E-mail: askus@tulsalibrary.org. Web Site: www.tulsalibrary.org. *Chief Exec Officer, Dir,* Kimberly Johnson; E-mail: kim.johnson@tulsalibrary.org; *Chief Financial Officer,* Gail Morris; Staff 289 (MLS 67, Non-MLS 222)
Founded 1961
Jul 2012-Jun 2013 Income $28,343,478. Mats Exp $3,792,641, Books $1,979,894, Per/Ser (Incl. Access Fees) $626,174, AV Mat $462,475, Electronic Ref Mat (Incl. Access Fees) $295,808. Sal $17,037,031
Library Holdings: Bk Titles 1,691,103
Special Collections: A J Levorsen Geology Coll, bks, maps; Land Office Survey Map Coll; Shakespeare Coll. State Document Depository; US Document Depository
Subject Interests: African-Am hist, Indust
Automation Activity & Vendor Info: (Acquisitions) Innovative Interfaces, Inc; (Cataloging) Innovative Interfaces, Inc; (Circulation) Innovative Interfaces, Inc; (ILL) Innovative Interfaces, Inc; (OPAC) Innovative Interfaces, Inc
Wireless access
Publications: Annual Report; Open Book (Quarterly)
Partic in Okla Libr Technology Network; SDC Search Serv

Special Services for the Deaf - High interest/low vocabulary bks; TDD equip
Special Services for the Blind - Home delivery serv
Open Mon-Thurs 9-9, Fri 9-6, Sat 9-5, Sun 1-5
Friends of the Library Group
Branches: 26
BIXBY BRANCH, 20 E Breckinridge, Bixby, 74008, SAN 357-7449. *Br Mgr,* Melissa Smith; Staff 2 (MLS 1, Non-MLS 1)
Library Holdings: Bk Vols 35,485
Open Mon, Wed & Fri 10-6, Tues & Thurs 12-8, Sat 10-5
BROKEN ARROW BRANCH, 300 W Broadway Ave, Broken Arrow, 74012, SAN 357-7473. *Br Mgr,* Marie Welden
Library Holdings: Bk Vols 61,372
Open Mon-Thurs 10-8, Fri 10-6, Sat 10-5
BROOKSIDE, 1207 E 45th Pl, 74105, SAN 357-7503. *Br Mgr,* Kelly Bayles; Staff 5 (MLS 2, Non-MLS 3)
Library Holdings: Bk Vols 45,493
Open Mon-Thurs 10-8, Fri 10-6, Sat 10-5
CENTRAL LIBRARY, 400 Civic Ctr, 74103, SAN 357-7414. *Br Mgr,* Buddy Ingalls
Library Holdings: Bk Vols 539,000
Open Mon-Thurs 9-9, Fri 9-6, Sat 9-5, Sun 1-5
COLLINSVILLE BRANCH, 1223 Main, Collinsville, 74021, SAN 357-7538. *Br Mgr,* Rhonda Weldon; Staff 2 (MLS 1, Non-MLS 1)
Library Holdings: Bk Vols 30,957
Open Mon, Wed & Fri 10-6, Tues & Thurs 12-8, Sat 10-5
GENEALOGY CENTER, Hardesty Regional Library, 8316 E 93rd St, 74133. Tel: 918-549-7691. E-mail: genaskus@tulsalibrary.org. *Mgr,* Kathy Huber
Library Holdings: CDs 300; Bk Vols 9,295
Special Collections: All Census Records for Oklahoma; Passenger & Immigration Lists Index; Roster of Confederate Soldiers; Roster of the Union Soldiers; The DAR Lineage Book; The Final Rolls of the Five Civilized Tribes; The New England Historical & Genealogical Register; The War of the Rebellion; Tulsa City Funeral Home Records; Tulsa County Cemetery Records
Subject Interests: Genealogy
Open Mon-Thurs 9-9, Fri 9-6, Sat 9-5, Sun 1-5
GLENPOOL BRANCH, 730 E 141st St, Glenpool, 74033. (Mail add: PO Box 580, 74101), SAN 326-7954. *Br Mgr,* Jesse Weitenhagen
Library Holdings: Bk Vols 32,117
Open Mon, Wed & Fri 10-6, Tues & Thurs 12-8, Sat 10-5
NATHAN HALE LIBRARY, 6038 E 23rd St, 74114, SAN 357-7627. *Br Mgr,* Sara Martinez; Staff 4 (MLS 1, Non-MLS 3)
Library Holdings: Bk Vols 39,000
Open Mon-Fri 10-6, Sat 10-5
HARDESTY REGIONAL LIBRARY, 8316 E 93rd St, 74133, SAN 357-7937. *Br Mgr,* Emily Archibald
Library Holdings: Bk Vols 163,504
Open Mon-Thurs 9-9, Fri 9-6, Sat 9-5, Sun 1-5
PEGGY V HELMERICH LIBRARY, 5131 E 91st St, 74137, SAN 371-4942. *Br Mgr,* Mike Weibel; Staff 7 (MLS 1, Non-MLS 6)
Library Holdings: Bk Vols 66,512
Open Mon-Thurs 10-8, Fri & Sat 10-5
JENKS BRANCH, 523 West B St, Jenks, 74037, SAN 357-7651. *Br Mgr,* Cheryl Newman; Staff 2 (MLS 1, Non-MLS 1)
Library Holdings: Bk Vols 35,812
Open Mon, Wed & Fri 10-6, Tues & Thurs 10-8, Sat 10-5
HERMAN & KATE KAISER LIBRARY, 5202 S Hudson Ave, Ste B, 74135. *Br Mgr,* Jason Patteson; Staff 4 (MLS 3, Non-MLS 1)
Founded 2008
Library Holdings: Bk Vols 58,689
Function: Computers for patron use, Free DVD rentals, ILL available, Music CDs, Online cat, Preschool outreach, Preschool reading prog, Prog for children & young adult, Spanish lang bks, Story hour, Summer & winter reading prog, Tax forms, Teen prog, Telephone ref, Wheelchair accessible
Open Mon-Thurs 10-8, Fri 10-6, Sat 10-5
KENDALL-WHITTIER BRANCH, 21 S Lewis St, 74104, SAN 357-7562. *Br Mgr,* David Nofire
Library Holdings: Bk Vols 34,624
Open Mon-Fri 10-6, Sat 10-5
JUDY Z KISHNER LIBRARY, 10150 N Cincinnati Ave E, 74073, SAN 357-7953. *Br Mgr,* David Morris; Staff 2 (MLS 1, Non-MLS 1)
Library Holdings: Bk Vols 18,680
Open Mon, Wed & Fri 10-6, Tues & Thurs 12-8, Sat 10-5
MARTIN REGIONAL LIBRARY, 2601 S Garnett Rd, 74129, SAN 357-7686. *Br Mgr,* Rebecca Howard; Staff 12 (MLS 4, Non-MLS 8)
Library Holdings: Bk Vols 110,016
Open Mon-Thurs 9-9, Fri 9-6, Sat 9-5, Sun 1-5
MAXWELL PARK, 1313 N Canton Ave, 74115, SAN 328-7947. *Br Mgr,* Chamong Siong; Staff 4 (MLS 1, Non-MLS 3)
Library Holdings: Bk Vols 35,788
Open Mon-Fri 10-6, Sat 10-5
OUTREACH SERVICES, 2901 S Harvard, Ste A, 74114. Tel: 918-549-7481. *Mgr,* Tracy Scott; Staff 7 (MLS 1, Non-MLS 6)
Founded 1970
Library Holdings: Bk Vols 23,751
Special Collections: Blindness & Other Handicaps Reference Material
OWASSO BRANCH, 103 W Broadway, Owasso, 74055, SAN 357-7775. *Br Mgr,* Jennifer McQuade; Staff 4 (MLS 1, Non-MLS 3)
Library Holdings: Bk Vols 52,432
Open Mon-Thurs 10-8, Fri 10-6, Sat 10-5
CHARLES PAGE BRANCH, 551 E Fourth St, Sand Springs, 74063, SAN 357-7805. *Br Mgr,* Mark Carlson; Staff 2 (MLS 1, Non-MLS 1)
Library Holdings: Bk Vols 29,352
Open Mon, Wed & Fri 10-6, Tues & Thurs 10-8, Sat 10-5
PRATT, 3219 S 113th West Ave, Sand Springs, 74063, SAN 357-783X. *Br Mgr,* Chris Lair; Staff 3 (MLS 1, Non-MLS 2)
Library Holdings: Bk Vols 46,619
Open Mon, Wed & Fri 10-6, Tues & Thurs 10-8, Sat 10-5
RUDISILL REGIONAL LIBRARY, 1520 N Hartford, 74106, SAN 357-7740. *Br Mgr,* Keith Jemison; Staff 6 (MLS 1, Non-MLS 5)
Library Holdings: Bk Vols 71,156
Open Mon-Thurs 9-9, Fri & Sat 9-5, Sun 1-5
SCHUSTERMAN-BENSON LIBRARY, 3333 E 32nd Pl, 74135, SAN 357-7597. *Br Mgr,* Brad Thomas; Staff 7 (MLS 2, Non-MLS 5)
Founded 1955
Library Holdings: Bk Vols 47,561
Open Mon-Thurs 10-8, Fri & Sat 10-5
SKIATOOK BRANCH, 316 E Rogers Blvd, Skiatook, 74070, SAN 357-7929. *Br Mgr,* Michelle Beckes
Library Holdings: Bk Vols 28,963
Open Mon, Wed & Fri 10-6, Tues & Thurs 12-8, Sat 10-5
SOUTH BROKEN ARROW, 3600 S Chestnut, Broken Arrow, 74011, SAN 374-7093. *Br Mgr,* Kelli McDowell; Staff 5 (MLS 2, Non-MLS 3)
Library Holdings: Bk Vols 36,692
Open Mon-Thurs 10-8, Fri & Sat 10-5
SUBURBAN ACRES, 4606 N Garrison Ave, 74126, SAN 357-7988. *Br Mgr,* Sherrie Wallace
Library Holdings: Bk Vols 23,556
Open Mon-Fri 10-6, Sat 10-5
ZARROW REGIONAL LIBRARY, 2224 W 51st, 74107, SAN 357-8003. *Br Mgr,* Ellen Cummings; Staff 5 (MLS 1, Non-MLS 4)
Library Holdings: Bk Vols 58,172
Open Mon-Thurs 9-9, Fri & Sat 9-5, Sun 1-5
Bookmobiles: 1

TULSA COMMUNITY COLLEGE LIBRARIES
J METRO CAMPUS*, 909 S Boston Ave, 74119-2011, SAN 357-8046. Tel: 918-595-7172. Reference Tel: 918-595-7296. FAX: 918-595-7179. E-mail: mlibrarian@tulsacc.edu. Web Site: lrc.tulsacc.edu. *Dean,* Paula Settoon; Tel: 918-595-7461, E-mail: paula.settoon@tulsacc.edu; *Sr Cat Librn,* Cary Isley; Tel: 918-595-7177, E-mail: cisley@tulsacc.edu; *Ref Librn,* Adam Brennan; Tel: 918-595-7330, E-mail: abrennan@tulsacc.edu; *Syst Librn,* Robert Holzmann; Tel: 918-595-7173, E-mail: bholzmann@tulsacc.edu; *Supvr,* Casey Ashe; Tel: 918-595-7285, E-mail: cashe@tulsacc.edu; *Acq,* Mary Kent; Tel: 918-595-7175, E-mail: mkent@tulsacc.edu
Founded 1970. Highest Degree: Associate
Library Holdings: DVDs 301; Bk Vols 38,775; Per Subs 242; Videos 1,501
Subject Interests: Allied health, Computer sci, Foreign lang, Nursing, Paralegal
Function: Electronic databases & coll, Photocopying/Printing
Open Mon-Thurs 7:30am-9:30pm, Fri 7:30-5, Sat 9-1
J NORTHEAST CAMPUS*, 3727 E Apache St, 74115-3151, SAN 357-8070. Tel: 918-595-7501. Interlibrary Loan Service Tel: 918-595-7493. Reference Tel: 918-595-7555. Administration Tel: 918-595-7568. Web Site: library.tulsacc.edu. *Dir,* Emily Tichenor; E-mail: emily.tichenor@tulsacc.edu; *Ref & Instruction Librn,* Gisele A McDaniel; Tel: 918-595-7502, E-mail: gisele.mcdaniel@tulsacc.edu; Staff 7 (MLS 4, Non-MLS 3)
Founded 1978. Enrl 4,088; Fac 61; Highest Degree: Associate
Library Holdings: Audiobooks 100; Bks on Deafness & Sign Lang 200; DVDs 291; Bk Titles 29,122; Per Subs 152; Videos 1,301
Subject Interests: Engr, Hort, Human serv, Humanities, Technologies
Function: Electronic databases & coll, Photocopying/Printing
Open Mon-Thurs 7:30am-9pm, Fri 7:30-6, Sat 8:30am-12:30pm
J SOUTHEAST CAMPUS*, 10300 E 81st St, 74133-4513, SAN 357-8089. Tel: 918-595-7703. Administration Tel: 918-595-7701. FAX: 918-595-7706. *Libr Mgr,* Stephanie Ingold; Tel: 918-595-7730, E-mail: stephanie.ingold@tulsacc.edu; *Ref & Instruction Librn,* Suzanne Haynes; Tel: 918-595-7704, E-mail: shaynes@tulsacc.edu; *Ref & Instruction Librn,* Amy Norman; Tel: 918-595-7702, E-mail: anorman@tulsacc.edu; Staff 5 (MLS 3, Non-MLS 2)
Founded 1984. Enrl 6,385; Fac 82; Highest Degree: Associate
Library Holdings: DVDs 402; Bk Titles 29,355; Per Subs 150; Videos 2,142

Subject Interests: Math, Performing arts
Automation Activity & Vendor Info: (Circulation) Ex Libris Group
Function: Electronic databases & coll, Photocopying/Printing
Partic in Tulsa Area Libr Coop
Open Mon-Fri 7:30am-9:30pm, Sat 8:30-12:30

WEST CAMPUS LIBRARY*, 7505 W 41st St, 74107-8633, SAN 376-9542. Tel: 918-595-8010. Administration Tel: 918-595-8011. FAX: 918-595-8016. Web Site: www.tulsacc.edu/. *Libr Mgr,* Amanda Kuhns; E-mail: amanda.kuhns@tulsacc.edu; *Ref & Instruction Librn,* Megan Donald; Staff 4 (MLS 2, Non-MLS 2)
Founded 1995. Enrl 2,700; Fac 35; Highest Degree: Associate
Library Holdings: CDs 41; Bk Titles 9,034; Per Subs 61; Videos 1,000
Subject Interests: Bus, Early childhood develop, Hospitality, Veterinary tech
Function: Electronic databases & coll, Photocopying/Printing
Open Mon-Thurs 7:30am-9:30pm, Fri 7:30-5, Sat 8:30-12:30

L TULSA COUNTY LAW LIBRARY*, Courthouse, 2nd Flr, 500 S Denver Ave, 74103. SAN 314-027X. Tel: 918-596-5404. FAX: 918-596-4509. E-mail: lawlibrary@tulsacounty.org. Web Site: www.Tulsacounty.org/Tulsacounty/dynamic.aspx?id=738. *Exec Dir,* Joyce M Pacenza; Staff 2 (MLS 1, Non-MLS 1)
Founded 1949
Library Holdings: Bk Titles 900; Bk Vols 30,000
Wireless access
Open Mon-Fri 8:30-5

TULSA WORLD*, Library Department, 315 S Boulder Ave, 74103-3401. (Mail add: PO Box 1770, 74102-1770), SAN 314-0288. Tel: 918-732-8182. FAX: 918-581-8425. Web Site: www.tulsaworld.com. *Librn,* Jason Collington; E-mail: Jason.Collington@tulsaworld.com
Founded 1941
Library Holdings: Bk Vols 1,000
Special Collections: The Tulsa Tribune; Tulsa World
Partic in LexisNexis

L UNITED STATES DISTRICT COURT, Northern District of Oklahoma Library, Page Belcher Federal Bldg, 4th Flr, 333 W Fourth St, 74103. SAN 372-2163. Tel: 918-699-4744. FAX: 918-699-4743. Web Site: www.oknd.uscourts.gov. *Libr Tech,* Ashley Searcy; E-mail: ashley_searcy@ca10.uscourts.gov; Staff 1 (Non-MLS 1)
Library Holdings: Bk Titles 150; Bk Vols 5,000; Per Subs 10
Wireless access
Restriction: Not open to pub, Staff use only

UNIVERSITY OF OKLAHOMA*, Schusterman Library, Schusterman Ctr, 4502 E 41st St, 74135. SAN 321-9771. Tel: 918-660-3220. Interlibrary Loan Service Tel: 918-660-3225. FAX: 918-660-3215. Web Site: library.tulsa.ou.edu. *Dir,* Stewart Brower; Tel: 918-660-3222, E-mail: stewart-brower@ouhsc.edu; *Assoc Dir,* Katie Prentice; Tel: 918-660-3216, E-mail: katherine-prentice@ouhsc.edu; *Ref & Instruction Librn,* Alyssa Migdalski; Tel: 918-660-3224, E-mail: alyssa-migdalski@ouhsc.edu; *Tech Serv Librn,* Toni Hoberecht; Tel: 918-660-3231, E-mail: toni-hoberecht@ouhsc.edu; Staff 13 (MLS 3, Non-MLS 10)
Founded 1976. Enrl 1,800; Highest Degree: Doctorate
Library Holdings: AV Mats 600; Bk Vols 55,000; Per Subs 675
Subject Interests: Allied health, Med, Nursing, Pharmacology, Pub health, Soc work
Automation Activity & Vendor Info: (Cataloging) SirsiDynix; (Circulation) SirsiDynix; (Course Reserve) Docutek; (ILL) OCLC ILLiad; (OPAC) SirsiDynix; (Serials) SirsiDynix
Wireless access
Function: Audio & video playback equip for onsite use, CD-ROM, Computer training, Distance learning, E-Reserves, Electronic databases & coll, Health sci info serv, ILL available, Instruction & testing, Internet access, Online cat, Online info literacy tutorials on the web & in blackboard, Online ref, Photocopying/Printing, Ref & res, Ref serv available, Telephone ref, Workshops
Partic in SCAMeL
Open Wed-Fri 7:30-6
Restriction: Circ limited, Limited access for the pub, Open to students, fac & staff

UNIVERSITY OF TULSA LIBRARIES*, McFarlin Library, 2933 E Sixth St, 74104-3123. SAN 357-8135. Tel: 918-631-2873. Reference Tel: 918-631-2880. FAX: 918-631-3791. Web Site: utulsa.edu/mcfarlin-Library, utulsa.libguides.com/library_homepage. *Dean of Libr,* Adrian W Alexander; *Dir,* Francine Fisk; Tel: 918-631-2495, Fax: 918-631-2150, E-mail: francine-fisk@utulsa.edu; *Acq,* Steve Nobles; Tel: 918-631-2869, E-mail: sjn@utulsa.edu; *Ref (Info Servs),* Ann Blakely; Tel: 918-631-3061, E-mail: ann-blakely@utulsa.edu; Staff 37 (MLS 14, Non-MLS 23)
Founded 1894. Enrl 4,171; Highest Degree: Doctorate
Library Holdings: e-books 1,000,000; e-journals 113,000; Bk Titles 537,580; Bk Vols 900,000; Per Subs 2,258
Special Collections: American Indian Law & History (Robertson-Shleppey-Milam Coll); Modernist Literature including libraries of Edmond Wilson & Cyril Connelly; Papers of Jean Rhys, Anna Kavan, Stevie Smith, Rebecca West, Richard Ellmann, Richard Murphy, V S Naipaul, publisher Andre Deutsch & others; Strong holdings of James Joyce, Robert Graves, D H Lawrence & others. State Document Depository; US Document Depository
Subject Interests: Am, British, Earth sci, Irish lit, Liberal arts, Modern hist, Modernist, Petroleum
Automation Activity & Vendor Info: (Acquisitions) Innovative Interfaces, Inc; (Cataloging) Innovative Interfaces, Inc; (Circulation) Innovative Interfaces, Inc; (Course Reserve) Innovative Interfaces, Inc; (ILL) Innovative Interfaces, Inc; (OPAC) Innovative Interfaces, Inc; (Serials) Innovative Interfaces, Inc
Wireless access
Partic in Mid-America Law Library Consortium; OCLC Online Computer Library Center, Inc; OCLC-LVIS
Open Mon-Thurs 7:30am-Midnight, Fri 7:30-6, Sat 12-8, Sun 1-Midnight

Departmental Libraries:

CL MABEE LEGAL INFORMATION CENTER, 3120 E Fourth Pl, 74104-3189, SAN 357-8194. Tel: 918-631-2404. Reference Tel: 918-631-2460. Administration Tel: 918-631-2459. FAX: 918-631-3556. Web Site: law.utulsa.edu/mabee-legal-info-center. *Dir,* Melanie Nelson; E-mail: melanie-nelson@utulsa.edu; *Coll Develop, Law Librn,* Daniel Bell; E-mail: daniel-bell@utulsa.edu; Staff 17 (MLS 9, Non-MLS 8)
Founded 1923. Enrl 624; Fac 56; Highest Degree: Doctorate
Library Holdings: Bk Titles 181,591; Bk Vols 375,359; Per Subs 3,253
Special Collections: Bernard Schwartz Archives; College of Law History Archives. US Document Depository
Subject Interests: Energy, Environ, Native Am
Partic in OCLC Online Computer Library Center, Inc
Publications: Library Guide
Open Mon-Thurs 7:30am-11pm, Fri Noon-8, Sat 9-8, Sun Noon-11
Restriction: Mem only

VALLIANT

P MATTIE TERRY PUBLIC LIBRARY*, 311 N Johnson, 74764. (Mail add: PO Box 630, 74764-0630). Tel: 866-258-6157. FAX: 866-276-2649. E-mail: valliant@seolibraries.com. Web Site: www.seolibraries.com/about/hours-locations/mattie-terry. *Br Mgr,* Jessica Brents; E-mail: jessica.brents@seolibraries.com
Founded 1998
Library Holdings: Bk Vols 14,409; Per Subs 10
Special Collections: Arts & Crafts Coll; Oklahoma Coll
Automation Activity & Vendor Info: (Cataloging) SirsiDynix; (Circulation) SirsiDynix; (OPAC) SirsiDynix
Wireless access
Mem of Southeast Oklahoma Library System (SEOLS)
Open Tues & Thurs 10-6, Wed & Fri 10-5, Sat 10-3

VANCE AFB

A UNITED STATES AIR FORCE, Vance Air Force Base Library, 71 FTW/ASRCC-CSSL, 446 McAffrey Ave, Bldg 314, Ste 24, 73705-5710. SAN 357-8259. Tel: 580-213-7368. FAX: 580-213-7589. Web Site: www.youseemore.com/vanceafb. *Librn,* Catherine Reed-Benge; E-mail: catherine.reed-benge.ctr@us.af.mil; Staff 3 (MLS 1, Non-MLS 2)
Founded 1941
Library Holdings: Bk Vols 20,000; Per Subs 50
Subject Interests: Aviation, Flying
Wireless access
Open Mon, Tues & Thurs 10-6, Wed 10:30-6:30, Fri & Sat 1-5

VINITA

P VINITA PUBLIC LIBRARY*, 215 W Illinois Ave, 74301. Tel: 918-256-2115. FAX: 918-256-2309. E-mail: library@cityofvinita.com. Web Site: vinitapl.okpls.org. *Dir,* Susan Walters; E-mail: director@cityofvinita.com; *Asst Dir,* Charla Sageser
Founded 1923. Pop 6,472
Library Holdings: AV Mats 400; Bk Vols 29,500; Talking Bks 500
Special Collections: Cherokee Nation Genealogy & History Coll; Will Rogers Coll
Automation Activity & Vendor Info: (Cataloging) Follett Software; (Circulation) Follett Software
Wireless access
Open Mon-Wed & Fri 11-6, Thurs 11-7, Sat 11-3

WAGONER

P WAGONER CITY PUBLIC LIBRARY*, 302 N Main St, 74467-3834. SAN 314-0318. Tel: 918-485-2126. FAX: 918-485-0179. *Libr Dir,* Barnett Janie; E-mail: librarydirector@wagonerok.org; *Children's Coordr,* Heather Cameron; *ILL Coordr,* Lori McGlothlin; *Circ Tech,* Donna Mensing; *Circ Tech,* Mallory Naugle

Founded 1912. Pop 7,700; Circ 45,012
Library Holdings: Large Print Bks 592; Bk Vols 20,000; Per Subs 21
Automation Activity & Vendor Info: (Cataloging) Follett Software; (Circulation) Follett Software; (ILL) Follett Software; (OPAC) Follett Software
Open Mon-Thurs 9-6, Fri 9-5, Sat 10-2
Friends of the Library Group

WALTERS

P WALTERS PUBLIC LIBRARY*, 202 N Broadway St, 73572-1226. (Mail add: PO Box 485, 73572-0485), SAN 314-0326. Tel: 580-875-2006. FAX: 580-875-2023. E-mail: walterspublib@gmail.com. *Librn,* Gina Suson; Staff 2 (Non-MLS 2)
Founded 1922. Pop 6,198; Circ 30,400
Library Holdings: Audiobooks 157; AV Mats 278; CDs 15; DVDs 112; Large Print Bks 120; Per Subs 5; Videos 275
Special Collections: Oklahoma Section
Subject Interests: Genealogy
Automation Activity & Vendor Info: (Cataloging) Book Systems; (Circulation) Book Systems; (Course Reserve) Book Systems; (ILL) Book Systems
Wireless access
Open Mon-Fri 11-5:30, Sat 10-1

WARNER

J CONNORS STATE COLLEGE*, Carl O Westbrook Library Learning Center, 700 College Rd, 74469-9700. SAN 314-0334. Tel: 918-463-6210. Administration Tel: 918-463-6269. Web Site: connorsstate.edu. *Dir, Libr Serv,* Ona Britton-Spears; E-mail: ona.britton-spears@connorsstate.edu; *Libr Tech,* Becky Warner Rayborn; E-mail: becky.rayborn@connorsstate.edu; Staff 4 (MLS 2, Non-MLS 2)
Founded 1909. Enrl 2,200; Highest Degree: Associate
Library Holdings: Bk Vols 24,695; Per Subs 57
Subject Interests: Native American
Automation Activity & Vendor Info: (Acquisitions) Ex Libris Group; (Cataloging) OCLC Online; (Circulation) Ex Libris Group; (Course Reserve) Ex Libris Group; (ILL) OCLC Online; (OPAC) Ex Libris Group
Wireless access
Function: 24/7 Electronic res, 24/7 Online cat, Adult bk club, Art exhibits, Audiobks via web, AV serv, Bk club(s), Bks on CD, Computers for patron use, Distance learning, E-Reserves, Electronic databases & coll, Free DVD rentals, Health sci info serv, ILL available, Instruction & testing, Internet access, Jail serv, Laminating, Magazines, Magnifiers for reading, Mail & tel request accepted, Movies, Online cat, Online info literacy tutorials on the web & in blackboard, Orientations, Outreach serv, OverDrive digital audio bks, Photocopying/Printing, Printer for laptops & handheld devices, Prog for adults, Ref & res, Res libr, Scanner, Study rm, Telephone ref, VHS videos, Wheelchair accessible, Workshops
Special Services for the Blind - Accessible computers; Aids for in-house use; Assistive/Adapted tech devices, equip & products; Bks on CD
Open Mon & Tues 8am-8:30pm, Wed & Thurs 8-6, Fri 8-4
Restriction: Borrowing privileges limited to fac & registered students, In-house use for visitors, Open to students, fac & staff, Open to students, fac, staff & alumni, Photo ID required for access

Departmental Libraries:

MUSKOGEE PORT CAMPUS LIBRARY, 2501 N 41st St E, Muskogee, 74403. Tel: 918-684-5408. E-mail: csclibrary@connorsstate.edu. *Dir, Libr Serv,* Ona Britton-Spears; Tel: 918-463-6269, E-mail: ona.britton-spears@connorsstate.edu
Automation Activity & Vendor Info: (Cataloging) Ex Libris Group; (OPAC) Ex Libris Group
Open Mon-Thurs (Fall & Spring) 8am-9pm, Fri 8-3:30

P WARNER PUBLIC LIBRARY, 207 Eighth St, 74469. (Mail add: PO Box 120, 74469-0120), SAN 376-5970. Tel: 918-463-2363. Toll Free Tel: 888-234-0606. FAX: 918-463-2711. E-mail: warnerpl@eols.org. Web Site: eols.org/library-location/warner-public-library. *Br Mgr,* Holly Hughes
Founded 1981
Library Holdings: DVDs 1,700; Bk Vols 18,000; Videos 700
Automation Activity & Vendor Info: (Circulation) SirsiDynix
Wireless access
Mem of Eastern Oklahoma Library System
Open Mon & Wed 1-6, Tues & Thurs 9-7, Fri 1-5, Sat 9-1
Friends of the Library Group

WATONGA

P WATONGA PUBLIC LIBRARY*, 301 N Prouty, 73772. SAN 314-0342. Tel: 580-623-7748. FAX: 580-623-7747. E-mail: bookwoman@watonga.lib.ok.us. Web Site: www.watongapl.okpls.org. *Dir,* Terri Crawford; *Asst Dir,* Sharon Barnes; E-mail: sbarnes@watonga.lib.ok.us; Staff 4 (MLS 2, Non-MLS 2)
Founded 1906. Pop 5,000; Circ 38,313
Library Holdings: Bk Titles 28,000; Bk Vols 32,000; Per Subs 34
Special Collections: Local History (Blaine County Coll), bks & interview tapes
Subject Interests: Local genealogy, Local hist
Automation Activity & Vendor Info: (Circulation) Follett Software
Wireless access
Publications: Books in Print; Publishers Weekly; Subject Guide to Books in Print
Partic in Okla Telecommunications Interlibr Syst
Open Mon-Fri 10-5:30, Sat 10-1
Friends of the Library Group

WAURIKA

P WAURIKA PUBLIC LIBRARY*, 203 S Meridian St, 73573. SAN 314-0350. Tel: 580-228-3274. FAX: 580-228-2907. E-mail: waurikapubliclibrary@gmail.com. Web Site: waurika.okpls.org. *Libr Dir,* Darren Biby
Circ 17,938
Library Holdings: Bk Vols 10,048
Open Mon, Wed, Thurs & Fri 10-5, Tues 10-7
Friends of the Library Group

WAYNOKA

P WAYNOKA PUBLIC LIBRARY, 1659 Cecil St, 73860. SAN 314-0369. Tel: 580-824-6181. FAX: 580-824-0282. E-mail: waynokalibrary@hotmail.com. *Dir,* Jo Ann Bellmon
Pop 1,370; Circ 5,404
Library Holdings: Bk Vols 5,000
Automation Activity & Vendor Info: (Circulation) Follett Software
Wireless access
Open Mon-Fri 1:30-5:30

WEATHERFORD

C SOUTHWESTERN OKLAHOMA STATE UNIVERSITY*, Al Harris Library, 100 Campus Dr, 73096-3002. SAN 357-8283. Tel: 580-774-7023. Interlibrary Loan Service Tel: 580-774-7026. Reference Tel: 580-774-7082. Information Services Tel: 580-774-3730. FAX: 580-774-3112. Web Site: library.swosu.edu. *Dir of Libr,* Jason Dupree; Tel: 580-774-7081, E-mail: jason.dupree@swosu.edu; *Electronic Res & Per Librn,* Position Currently Open; *Instrul Serv Librn,* Frederic Murray; Tel: 580-774-7113, E-mail: frederic.murray@swosu.edu; *Ref & Digitization Librn,* Phillip Fitzsimmons; Tel: 580-774-3030, E-mail: phillip.fitzsimmons@swosu.edu; *Syst & Web Mgt Librn,* Jonathan Woltz; Tel: 580-774-7074, E-mail: jonathan.woltz@swosu.edu; *Tech Serv Librn,* Linda Pye; Tel: 580-774-7021, E-mail: linda.pye@swosu.edu; *Circ Serv Coordr,* Jennifer Macaulay; E-mail: jennifer.macaulay@swosu.edu; *Acq Tech,* Casady Church; Tel: 580-774-3737, E-mail: casady.church@swosu.edu; *Digitization Tech,* Ben Dressler; Tel: 580-774-7024, E-mail: benjamin.dressler@swosu.edu; *Media Tech, Syst Tech,* Doug Reichmann; Tel: 580-774-7069, E-mail: doug.reichmann@swosu.edu; *Res Sharing Tech,* Ashlee Merritt; E-mail: ashlee.merritt@swosu.edu; *Ser Tech,* Barbara Roddam; Tel: 580-774-7022, E-mail: barbara.roddam@swosu.edu; *Tech Serv Technician,* Janet Black; Tel: 580-774-3089, E-mail: janet.black@swosu.edu; Staff 14 (MLS 6, Non-MLS 8)
Founded 1902. Enrl 4,153; Fac 207; Highest Degree: Doctorate
Library Holdings: AV Mats 2,500; e-books 495,000; e-journals 112,500; Electronic Media & Resources 13,500,000; Bk Vols 296,000; Per Subs 800; Spec Interest Per Sub 108
Special Collections: SWOSU Digital Commons; Thomas P. Stafford Coll. State Document Depository; US Document Depository
Subject Interests: Educ, Humanities, Sciences
Automation Activity & Vendor Info: (Acquisitions) OCLC Worldshare Management Services; (Cataloging) OCLC Worldshare Management Services; (Circulation) OCLC Worldshare Management Services; (Course Reserve) OCLC Worldshare Management Services; (Discovery) OCLC Worldshare Management Services; (ILL) OCLC WorldShare Interlibrary Loan; (Serials) OCLC Worldshare Management Services
Wireless access
Function: 24/7 Electronic res, 24/7 Online cat, Archival coll, Audio & video playback equip for onsite use, AV serv, Computers for patron use, Doc delivery serv, E-Reserves, Electronic databases & coll, Equip loans & repairs, Govt ref serv, ILL available, Instruction & testing, Internet access, Magazines, Magnifiers for reading, Mail & tel request accepted, Meeting rooms, Microfiche/film & reading machines, Movies, Online cat, Online ref, Outreach serv, Photocopying/Printing, Printer for laptops & handheld devices, Ref serv available, Scanner, Spoken cassettes & CDs, Study rm, Telephone ref, Wheelchair accessible, Writing prog
Partic in Amigos Library Services, Inc; Oklahoma Council of Academic Libr Directors
Special Services for the Deaf - ADA equip
Open Mon-Thurs 7:30am-11pm, Fri 7:30-5, Sat 12-5, Sun 3-11

Restriction: Authorized patrons, Authorized scholars by appt, In-house use for visitors, Non-circulating coll, Non-circulating of rare bks, Open to fac, students & qualified researchers, Open to students, fac, staff & alumni, Pub use on premises

Departmental Libraries:

O H MCMAHAN LIBRARY, 409 E Mississippi St, Sayre, 73662. Tel: 580-928-5533, Ext 2185. FAX: 580-928-5533, Ext 2135. *Librn,* April Miller; E-mail: april.miller@swosu.edu; Staff 1 (MLS 1)
Founded 1971. Fac 10; Highest Degree: Associate
Library Holdings: Bk Titles 6,500; Per Subs 50
Automation Activity & Vendor Info: (Acquisitions) OCLC Worldshare Management Services; (Cataloging) OCLC Worldshare Management Services; (Circulation) OCLC Worldshare Management Services; (Course Reserve) OCLC Worldshare Management Services; (Discovery) OCLC Worldshare Management Services; (ILL) OCLC WorldShare Interlibrary Loan; (Serials) OCLC Worldshare Management Services
Function: 24/7 Electronic res, 24/7 Online cat, Computers for patron use, Electronic databases & coll, ILL available, Instruction & testing, Internet access, Magazines, Mail & tel request accepted, Outreach serv, Photocopying/Printing, Ref serv available, Telephone ref, Writing prog
Open Mon-Fri 9-5
Restriction: Authorized patrons, In-house use for visitors, Open to students, Open to students, fac, staff & alumni, Pub use on premises

WESTVILLE

P JOHN F HENDERSON PUBLIC LIBRARY*, 1152 N Williams Ave, 74965. (Mail add: PO Box 580, 74965-0580), SAN 314-0377. Tel: 918-723-5002. Toll Free Tel: 888-291-8147. FAX: 918-723-3400. E-mail: westvillepl@eols.org. Web Site: eols.org/library-location/john-f-henderson-public-library. *Mgr,* Stephanie Freedle
Founded 1969. Pop 1,049
Library Holdings: Bk Vols 17,693; Per Subs 20
Automation Activity & Vendor Info: (Circulation) SirsiDynix
Wireless access
Mem of Eastern Oklahoma Library System
Open Mon-Thurs 9-6, Fri 9-2, Sat 9-Noon

WETUMKA

P WETUMKA PUBLIC LIBRARY*, 202 N Main, 74883. SAN 324-0347. Tel: 405-452-3785. FAX: 405-452-5825. *Librn,* Joan Hill; E-mail: joanhill29@gmail.com
Pop 1,451
Library Holdings: DVDs 400; Bk Titles 10,000; Bk Vols 17,547; Videos 483
Wireless access
Open Mon & Tues 2-6, Wed-Fri 1-5

WEWOKA

S SEMINOLE NATION MUSEUM LIBRARY*, 524 S Wewoka Ave, 74884. (Mail add: PO Box 1532, 74884-1532), SAN 375-6718. Tel: 405-257-5580. FAX: 405-257-5580. Web Site: www.seminolenationmuseum.org. *Pres,* Dr Steve Walker; *Exec Dir,* Richard Ellwanger; E-mail: director@seminolenationmuseum.org
Founded 1974
Library Holdings: Bk Titles 2,000
Subject Interests: African-Am hist, Cultural hist
Open Mon-Sat 10-5
Restriction: In-house use for visitors

P WEWOKA PUBLIC LIBRARY*, 118 W Fifth St, 74884. SAN 314-0385. Tel: 405-257-3225. E-mail: librarian@cityofwewoka.com. *Librn,* Carolyn Trimble; *Asst Librn,* Dorothy McNally
Founded 1928
Library Holdings: Bk Vols 15,000
Wireless access
Open Mon-Fri 9:30-5:30, Sat 9-Noon

WILBURTON

C EASTERN OKLAHOMA STATE COLLEGE*, Library Media Center, Bill H Hill Library Bldg, 2nd & 3rd Flrs, 1301 W Main St, 74578. SAN 314-0393. Tel: 918-465-1875. FAX: 918-465-0112. Web Site: www.eosc.edu/library. *Dir, Libr & Media Serv,* Maria Martinez; Tel: 918-465-1711, E-mail: mmartinez@eosc.edu; Staff 3 (MLS 1, Non-MLS 2)
Founded 1909. Enrl 1,800; Fac 48
Wireless access
Function: Photocopying/Printing

LATIMER COUNTY PUBLIC LIBRARY*, 301 W Ada Ave, 74578. SAN 314-0407. Tel: 918-465-3751. FAX: 866-991-0480. E-mail: wilburton@seolibraries.com. Web Site: www.seolibraries.com/about/hours-locations/latimer. *Br Mgr,* Shawna L White-Busby; E-mail: shawna.busby@seolibraries.com; *Asst Librn,* Margetta Pate
Pop 3,000
Library Holdings: Bk Vols 11,000
Automation Activity & Vendor Info: (Cataloging) SirsiDynix; (Circulation) SirsiDynix; (Serials) EBSCO Online
Wireless access
Mem of Southeast Oklahoma Library System (SEOLS)
Open Mon 9-6, Tues, Wed & Thurs 10-6, Fri 10-5, Sat 10-3
Friends of the Library Group

WISTER

P WISTER PUBLIC LIBRARY*, 211 Plum St, 74966. SAN 314-0415. Toll Free Tel: 866-261-3592. Toll Free FAX: 866-437-4311. E-mail: wister@seolibraries.com. Web Site: www.seolibraries.com/about/hours-locations/wister. *Br Mgr,* Sheila Reid; E-mail: sheila.reid@seolibraries.com; *Ch Serv,* Sheila Pickering Reid; Staff 2 (Non-MLS 2)
Pop 1,200; Circ 13,000
Library Holdings: Bk Titles 10,500; Per Subs 15
Automation Activity & Vendor Info: (Circulation) SirsiDynix
Function: ILL available
Mem of Southeast Oklahoma Library System (SEOLS)
Open Tues-Thurs 9-6, Fri 9-5, Sat 9-2

WOODWARD

P WOODWARD PUBLIC LIBRARY*, 1500 W Main St, 73801. SAN 314-0423. Tel: 580-254-8544. FAX: 580-254-8546. Web Site: woodwardlibrary.okpls.org. *Dir,* Connie Terry; E-mail: cterry@woodward.lib.ok.us; *Adult Serv,* Paula Odell; Staff 6 (Non-MLS 6)
Founded 1899. Pop 12,340; Circ 75,448
Library Holdings: Audiobooks 1,803; DVDs 2,745; e-books 23,437; e-journals 243; Bk Titles 29,182; Per Subs 57
Special Collections: Genealogy; Oklahoma History Coll, bks, pamphlets
Subject Interests: Genealogy, Literacy
Automation Activity & Vendor Info: (Cataloging) Auto-Graphics, Inc; (Circulation) Auto-Graphics, Inc; (OPAC) Auto-Graphics, Inc
Wireless access
Special Services for the Blind - Bks on cassette
Open Mon-Thurs 9-7, Fri 9-Noon, Sat 9-4
Friends of the Library Group

WYNNEWOOD

P WYNNEWOOD PUBLIC LIBRARY*, 108 N Dean A McGee Ave, 73098. Tel: 405-665-2512. FAX: 405-665-4619. E-mail: wynnelib@wynnewood.lib.ok.us. Web Site: wynnewood.okpls.org. *Dir,* Meg Williams; Staff 1 (Non-MLS 1)
Pop 2,400
Library Holdings: AV Mats 400; Bk Vols 15,000; Talking Bks 300
Special Collections: Local & Native American Genealogy Coll; Roster of Union & Confederate Soldiers
Automation Activity & Vendor Info: (Acquisitions) Follett Software; (Cataloging) Follett Software; (Circulation) Follett Software; (OPAC) Follett Software
Wireless access
Open Mon-Fri 9-6
Friends of the Library Group

YALE

P YALE PUBLIC LIBRARY*, 213 N Main, 74085. SAN 314-0431. Tel: 918-387-2135. FAX: 918-387-2616. E-mail: yalelibrary@yaleok.org. Web Site: yale.okpls.org, yaleok.org/page/home/library. *Dir,* Nancy L Griffin; E-mail: ngriffin@yaleok.org; *Asst Librn,* Miranda Brown; Staff 2 (Non-MLS 2)
Founded 1919. Pop 1,392; Circ 24,429
Library Holdings: Audiobooks 267; AV Mats 1,575; CDs 38; DVDs 675; Large Print Bks 220; Bk Vols 22,715; Per Subs 24
Automation Activity & Vendor Info: (Acquisitions) Follett Software; (Cataloging) Follett Software; (ILL) CLSI; (OPAC) Follett Software
Wireless access
Function: ILL available
Partic in OLTN
Open Mon, Tues & Thurs 10-5:30, Wed 10-6:30, Fri 1-5
Friends of the Library Group

YUKON

P MABEL C FRY PUBLIC LIBRARY, 1200 Lakeshore Dr, 73099. SAN 314-044X. Tel: 405-354-8232. FAX: 405-350-7928. Web Site: www.cityofyukonok.gov/city-departments/mabel-c-fry-public-library. *Librn,*

Sara Schieman; E-mail: sschieman@yukonok.gov; *Asst Librn*, Shawna Deeds; E-mail: sdeeds@yukonok.gov; Staff 7 (MLS 4, Non-MLS 3)
Founded 1905. Circ 147,543
Library Holdings: Bk Vols 40,000
Automation Activity & Vendor Info: (Cataloging) Biblionix/Apollo; (Circulation) Biblionix/Apollo; (OPAC) Biblionix/Apollo
Wireless access
Function: 24/7 Electronic res, 24/7 Online cat, Activity rm, Adult bk club
Open Mon-Thurs 9-9, Fri & Sat 9-5
Friends of the Library Group

OREGON

Date of Statistics: FY 2020-2021
Population, 2020 U.S. Census: 4,241,507
Population Served by Public Libraries: 3,973,309
Unserved: 268,198
Total Volumes in Public Libraries: 13,018,875. Note: this number does not contain duplicates of downloadable materials purchased by statewide consortium.
Volumes Per Capita of Population Served: 3.28
Total Public Library Circulation: 13,844,506
Circulation Per Capita of Population Served: 3.48
Digital Resources:
Total e-books: 4,365,545
Total audio items (physical and downloadable units): 2,369,883
Total video items (physical and downloadable units): 1,871,407
Total computers for use by the public: 2,789
Total annual wireless sessions: 4,493,303
Income and Expenditures:
Total Public Library Expenditures: $273,980,085
Expenditures Per Capita of Population Served: $68.96
Grants-in-Aid to Public Libraries (this is total state funded aid): $1,125,671
LSTA Federal Funds Received by State Library: $2,401,036
Grants to Public Libraries from Federal Sources (LSTA): $554,933 (This also includes CARES Act funds administered via the LSTA program. It does not include federal funds that subsidize statewide database licensing support. Subsidies included with state library share.)
State Library's Share from Federal Sources (LSTA): $1,465,103
Number of County Libraries: 7
Counties Served: 36. Note: not all areas of each county are served by a public library.
Number of Bookmobiles in State: 5
Information provided courtesy of: Ross Fuqua, Digital Projects Consultant; State Library of Oregon.

ADAMS

P ADAMS PUBLIC LIBRARY*, 190 Main St, 97810. (Mail add: PO Box 20, 97810-0020), SAN 328-9079. Tel: 541-566-3038. FAX: 541-566-2077. E-mail: library@cityofadamsoregon.com. Web Site: www.cityofadamsoregon.com. *Libr Dir,* Jennifer Davison
Pop 401
Library Holdings: Large Print Bks 200; Bk Vols 5,000; Per Subs 12
Automation Activity & Vendor Info: (Acquisitions) Evergreen
Wireless access
Mem of Umatilla County Special Library District
Open Mon-Thurs 1-6
Friends of the Library Group

AGNESS

P AGNESS COMMUNITY LIBRARY*, 3905 Cougar Lane, 97406. (Mail add: PO Box 33, 97406-0033), SAN 314-0458. Tel: 541-247-6323. FAX: 541-247-6323. E-mail: agnesscommunitylibrary@gmail.com. Web Site: www.galepages.com/s9185356/home. *Dir,* Jhanna Stutzman-Fry; Staff 4 (Non-MLS 4)
Founded 1943. Pop 220; Circ 5,921
Library Holdings: Bk Vols 12,000; Per Subs 30
Subject Interests: Local Native Am
Automation Activity & Vendor Info: (Cataloging) TLC (The Library Corporation)
Open Mon & Thurs 10-5

ALBANY

P ALBANY PUBLIC LIBRARY*, 2450 14th Ave SE, 97322. SAN 357-8348. Tel: 541-917-7580. Circulation Tel: 541-917-7581. Interlibrary Loan Service Tel: 541-917-7582. FAX: 541-917-7586. E-mail: AskAlbany@cityofalbany.net. Web Site: library.cityofalbany.net. *Dir,* Eric Ikenouye; *Asst Dir,* Amanda Bressler; E-mail: amanda.bressler@cityofalbany.net; *Adult Serv,* Elizabeth Sonstegaard; Tel: 541-917-0014, E-mail: elizabeth.sonstegaard@cityofalbany.net; *Circ Serv,* Mardi Hochstetler; E-mail: mardi.hochstetler@cityofalbany.net; *Youth Serv,* April Spisak; Tel: 541-917-0015, E-mail: april.spisak@cityofalbany.net; Staff 11 (MLS 7, Non-MLS 4)
Founded 1907. Pop 45,560; Circ 576,723
Library Holdings: AV Mats 10,792; Bk Vols 132,633; Per Subs 270
Special Collections: Oregon History Coll
Automation Activity & Vendor Info: (Acquisitions) SirsiDynix; (Cataloging) SirsiDynix; (Circulation) SirsiDynix; (OPAC) SirsiDynix
Wireless access
Partic in Linn Libraries Consortium; OCLC Online Computer Library Center, Inc
Open Mon-Wed 10-8, Thurs & Fri 10-6, Sat 10-5
Friends of the Library Group

Branches: 1
DOWNTOWN CARNEGIE, 302 Ferry St SW, 97321-2216, SAN 357-8372. Tel: 541-917-7585. Circulation Tel: 541-917-7588. Administration Tel: 541-917-7584. *Br Mgr,* Jason Darling; E-mail: jason.darling@cityofalbany.net; Staff 2 (MLS 1, Non-MLS 1)
Founded 1913
Library Holdings: Bk Vols 24,000
Subject Interests: Historic home renovation
Open Mon-Fri 10-6
Friends of the Library Group

J LINN-BENTON COMMUNITY COLLEGE LIBRARY*, 6500 SW Pacific Blvd, 97321-3799. SAN 314-0466. Tel: 541-917-4638. Reference Tel: 541-917-4645. FAX: 541-917-4659. Reference E-mail: libref@linnbenton.edu. Web Site: www.linnbenton.edu/library. *Dept Chair, Librn,* Richenda Hawkins; Tel: 541-917-4641, E-mail: hawkinr@linnbenton.edu; *Circ,* Cheryl Carlson; Tel: 541-917-4678, E-mail: carlsoc@linnbenton.edu; Staff 2 (MLS 2)
Founded 1969. Enrl 6,042; Fac 160
Library Holdings: AV Mats 6,997; e-books 2,318; Electronic Media & Resources 250; Bk Titles 42,480; Bk Vols 48,000; Per Subs 169
Subject Interests: Linn-Benton County hist, Nursing, Vocational tech mat
Automation Activity & Vendor Info: (Cataloging) SirsiDynix; (Circulation) SirsiDynix; (ILL) OCLC; (OPAC) SirsiDynix
Partic in Linn Libraries Consortium; OCLC Online Computer Library Center, Inc; Valley Link
Open Mon-Thurs 7:30am-9pm, Fri 7:30-5

G UNITED STATES DEPARTMENT OF ENERGY*, NETL-Albany Library, 1450 Queen Ave SW, 97321-2198. SAN 314-0490. Tel: 541-967-5864. FAX: 541-967-5936. *Libr Tech,* Nellie McKay; E-mail: nellie.mckay@netl.doe.gov; Staff 1 (Non-MLS 1)
Founded 1943
Library Holdings: e-journals 1,500; Bk Titles 10,000; Bk Vols 15,000
Subject Interests: Chem, Energy, Mat sci, Metallurgy, Mineralogy, Physics
Automation Activity & Vendor Info: (Cataloging) EOS International; (Circulation) EOS International; (ILL) OCLC; (OPAC) EOS International; (Serials) EOS International
Function: ILL available, Online cat, Res libr
Partic in OCLC Online Computer Library Center, Inc
Restriction: Open to pub for ref only, Open to pub with supv only, Photo ID required for access

AMITY

P AMITY PUBLIC LIBRARY, 307 Trade St, 97101. (Mail add: PO Box 470, 97101-0470), SAN 376-3315. Tel: 503-835-8181. Web Site: cityofamityoregon.org/library. *Dir,* Anne Jenkins; E-mail: anne.jenkins@ccrls.org
Library Holdings: Bk Vols 15,000
Automation Activity & Vendor Info: (Acquisitions) SirsiDynix; (Cataloging) SirsiDynix; (OPAC) SirsiDynix

Partic in Chemeketa Cooperative Regional Library Service
Open Mon & Wed 12-1, Tues & Thurs 1-5, Sat 10-2
Friends of the Library Group

ARLINGTON

P ARLINGTON PUBLIC LIBRARY, City Hall, 500 W First St, 97812. (Mail add: PO Box 339, 97812-0339), SAN 357-8704. Tel: 541-454-2444. FAX: 541-705-2575. E-mail: arlingtonpubliclibraryor97812@gmail.com. Web Site: arlington.ploud.net. *Librn,* Mary Mitchell
Pop 818; Circ 2,900
Library Holdings: Bk Vols 10,000
Automation Activity & Vendor Info: (Cataloging) Evergreen; (Circulation) Evergreen; (OPAC) Evergreen
Wireless access
Partic in Sage Library System of Eastern Oregon
Open Mon, Tues & Thurs 10-4, Wed 1-5, Fri 10-2
Friends of the Library Group

ASHLAND

C SOUTHERN OREGON UNIVERSITY, Lenn & Dixie Hannon Library, 1250 Siskiyou Blvd, 97520. SAN 314-0504. Tel: 541-552-6860. Interlibrary Loan Service Tel: 541-552-6823. Reference Tel: 541-552-6442. FAX: 541-552-6429. Web Site: hanlib.sou.edu. *Interim Univ Librn,* Dale Vidmar; E-mail: vidmar@sou.edu; *Dept Chair, Research Servs Librn,* Melissa Anderson; Tel: 541-552-6820, E-mail: andersm18@sou.edu; *Cat/Metadata Librn, Coll,* Kate Cleland-Sipfle; Tel: 541-552-6839, E-mail: clelandk@sou.edu; *Coll Develop Librn,* Emily Miller-Francisco; Tel: 541-552-6819, E-mail: millere@sou.edu; *Discovery Librn, Website Mgr,* Tom Dodson; Tel: 541-552-6836, E-mail: dodsont@sou.edu; *Access Serv, Govt Info Librn,* Holly Gabriel; Tel: 541-552-6595, E-mail: gabrielh@sou.edu. Subject Specialists: *Adventure, Communication, Educ, Film studies, Leadership, Video production,* Dale Vidmar; *Bus, Econ, English,* Melissa Anderson; *Anthrop, Environ studies, Foreign lang, Hist, Intl studies, Lit, Music, Native Am studies, Sociol,* Kate Cleland-Sipfle; *Criminal justice, Criminology, Gender, Philos, Psychol, Sexuality, Women's studies,* Emily Miller-Francisco; *Art, Art hist, Creative writing, Theatre arts,* Tom Dodson; *Chemistry, Health, Nursing, Phys educ, Polit sci,* Holly Gabriel; Staff 21 (MLS 9, Non-MLS 12)
Founded 1926. Enrl 5,772; Fac 278; Highest Degree: Master
Library Holdings: Bk Titles 241,000; Bk Vols 310,000; Per Subs 2,028
Special Collections: Oregon State Documents; Shakespeare-Renaissance (Bailey). State Document Depository; US Document Depository
Subject Interests: Ecology, Educ, Local hist, Shakespeare studies
Automation Activity & Vendor Info: (Acquisitions) Ex Libris Group; (Cataloging) Ex Libris Group; (Circulation) Ex Libris Group; (Course Reserve) Ex Libris Group; (OPAC) Ex Libris Group; (Serials) Ex Libris Group
Wireless access
Partic in OCLC Online Computer Library Center, Inc; Orbis Cascade Alliance
Open Mon-Thurs 8am-11pm, Fri 8-5, Sat 11-5, Sun 1-11
Friends of the Library Group

ASTORIA

P ASTORIA PUBLIC LIBRARY, 450 Tenth St, 97103. SAN 314-0512. Tel: 503-325-7323. Web Site: astorialibrary.org. *Dir,* Jimmy Pearson; E-mail: jpearson@astoria.or.us; Staff 11 (MLS 2, Non-MLS 9)
Founded 1892. Pop 9,660
Library Holdings: Bk Vols 53,000; Per Subs 30
Automation Activity & Vendor Info: (Cataloging) TLC (The Library Corporation); (Circulation) TLC (The Library Corporation); (OPAC) TLC (The Library Corporation)
Wireless access
Function: 24/7 Electronic res, 24/7 Online cat, Archival coll, Bks on CD, Free DVD rentals, Magazines, Meeting rooms, Microfiche/film & reading machines, Museum passes, Music CDs, Photocopying/Printing, Prog for adults, Prog for children & young adult, Ref & res, Scanner, Tax forms, Teen prog
Friends of the Library Group

J CLATSOP COMMUNITY COLLEGE-LEARNING RESOURCE CENTER, Dora Badollet Library, 1680 Lexington, 97103. SAN 314-0520. Tel: 503-338-2462. FAX: 503-338-2387. Circulation E-mail: libcirc@clatsop.edu. Web Site: www.clatsopcc.edu/library. *Libr Dir,* Dan McClure; Tel: 503-388-2460, E-mail: dmcclure@clatsopcc.edu; Staff 4 (MLS 1, Non-MLS 3)
Founded 1962. Enrl 1,352; Fac 40; Highest Degree: Associate
Library Holdings: High Interest/Low Vocabulary Bk Vols 225; Bk Vols 35,000; Per Subs 670
Subject Interests: Marine tech, Regional hist
Automation Activity & Vendor Info: (Acquisitions) Ex Libris Group; (Cataloging) Ex Libris Group; (Circulation) Ex Libris Group; (Course Reserve) Ex Libris Group; (OPAC) Ex Libris Group; (Serials) Ex Libris Group
Wireless access
Function: Ref serv available
Partic in Chinook Library Network; OCLC Online Computer Library Center, Inc
Open Mon-Thurs 8-6, Fri 8-5, Sun 12-5 (Fall & Spring); Mon-Thurs 8-8 (Summer)
Restriction: Restricted access

S COLUMBIA RIVER MARITIME MUSEUM, Ted M Natt Research Library, 1792 Marine Dr, 97103. SAN 314-0539. Tel: 503-325-2323. FAX: 503-325-2331. E-mail: library@crmm.org. Web Site: www.crmm.org. *Librn,* Marcy Dunning; *Curator,* Jeffrey Smith; E-mail: smith@crmm.org
Founded 1962
Library Holdings: Bk Titles 12,000; Per Subs 194
Special Collections: Maritime Photo Archive; Vessel Plans Coll
Subject Interests: Folklore, Maritime hist
Wireless access
Publications: Quarterdeck (Newsletter)
Restriction: Non-circulating to the pub, Open by appt only

ATHENA

P ATHENA PUBLIC LIBRARY*, 418 E Main St, 97813. (Mail add: PO Box 450, 97813-0450), SAN 358-0474. Tel: 541-566-2470. FAX: 541-566-2470. E-mail: athenalibrary@cityofathena.com. Web Site: athenalibrary.weebly.com. *Libr Dir,* Carrie Bremer; Staff 1 (Non-MLS 1)
Founded 1914. Pop 1,799
Jul 2017-Jun 2018 Income $84,332. Mats Exp $6,654, Books $5,849, Per/Ser (Incl. Access Fees) $305, AV Mat $500. Sal $42,000
Library Holdings: Audiobooks 24,000; CDs 600; DVDs 15; e-books 42,100; Electronic Media & Resources 24; Bk Titles 12,000; Per Subs 20; Videos 800
Automation Activity & Vendor Info: (Acquisitions) Evergreen; (Cataloging) Evergreen; (Circulation) Evergreen; (ILL) Evergreen; (OPAC) Evergreen
Wireless access
Mem of Umatilla County Special Library District
Open Mon 1-7, Tues 7:30-1:30, Wed 12-5, Thurs 7:30-10:30 & 1-5
Friends of the Library Group

BAKER CITY

P BAKER COUNTY PUBLIC LIBRARY*, 2400 Resort St, 97814-2798. SAN 357-8437. Tel: 541-523-6419. Toll Free Tel: 866-297-1239. FAX: 541-523-9088. E-mail: info@bakerlib.org. Web Site: www.bakerlib.org. *Libr Dir,* Perry Stokes; E-mail: director@bakerlib.org; Staff 13.4 (MLS 1, Non-MLS 12.4)
Founded 1906. Pop 16,750; Circ 153,607
Library Holdings: DVDs 2,317; e-books 2,557; Large Print Bks 3,285; Music Scores 73; Bk Vols 117,363; Per Subs 349; Talking Bks 3,401; Videos 4,261
Special Collections: Baker County Coll; Oregon History Coll
Automation Activity & Vendor Info: (Cataloging) Innovative Interfaces, Inc; (Circulation) Innovative Interfaces, Inc; (OPAC) Innovative Interfaces, Inc
Wireless access
Function: Audio & video playback equip for onsite use, Audiobks via web, Bks on cassette, Bks on CD, CD-ROM, Children's prog, Computer training, Computers for patron use, ILL available, Internet access, Jail serv, Magnifiers for reading, Music CDs, Online cat, Online ref, Outside serv via phone, mail, e-mail & web, OverDrive digital audio bks, Photocopying/Printing, Prog for adults, Prog for children & young adult, Scanner, Spoken cassettes & CDs, Summer reading prog, Tax forms, VHS videos, Wheelchair accessible
Partic in Libraries of Eastern Oregon; Sage Library System of Eastern Oregon
Special Services for the Deaf - Bks on deafness & sign lang; Closed caption videos
Special Services for the Blind - Bks on cassette; Bks on CD; Magnifiers
Open Mon-Thurs 9-7, Fri 9-6, Sat 10-4, Sun 12-4
Restriction: Lending limited to county residents, Non-circulating of rare bks
Friends of the Library Group
Branches: 5
HAINES BRANCH, 818 Cole St, Haines, 97833, SAN 357-8461. Tel: 541-856-3309. E-mail: haines@bakerlib.org.
Founded 1961. Pop 590
HALFWAY BRANCH, 260 Gover Lane, Halfway, 97834. (Mail add: PO Box 922, Halfway, 97834-0922), SAN 357-8496. Tel: 541-742-5279. E-mail: halfway@bakerlib.org.
Pop 550
Open Wed 2-5, Thurs 4-7, Fri 9-12 & 1-4, Sat 9-12
Friends of the Library Group

HUNTINGTON BRANCH, 55 E Jefferson, Huntington, 97907. (Mail add: PO Box 130, Huntington, 97907), SAN 357-8526. Tel: 541-869-2440. E-mail: huntington@bakerlib.org.
Open Mon & Tues 2-5, Wed 4-7, Fri 10-5, Sat 10-1
Friends of the Library Group
RICHLAND BRANCH, 42008 Moody Rd, Richland, 97870, SAN 357-8550. Tel: 541-893-6088. E-mail: richland@bakerlib.org.
Open Mon & Wed 1-5, Tues 8-12, Sat 9-12
Friends of the Library Group
SUMPTER BRANCH, Sumpter Museum Bldg, 245 S Mill St, Sumpter, 97877. (Mail add: PO Box 67, Sumpter, 97877). Tel: 541-894-2253. E-mail: sumpter@bakerlib.org.
Open Wed 3-6, Thurs-Sat 11-3
Friends of the Library Group
Bookmobiles: 1. Bk vols 2,300

BANDON

P BANDON PUBLIC LIBRARY*, 1204 11th St SW, 97411. SAN 314-0563. Tel: 541-347-3221. FAX: 541-347-9363. Web Site: www.cityofbandon.org/general/page/library. *Libr Dir,* Rosalyn McGarva; E-mail: rmcgarva@cclsd.org; *Asst Dir,* Sara Michael; *Ch,* Julie Tipton; Staff 10 (MLS 1, Non-MLS 9)
Pop 4,000; Circ 159,651
Library Holdings: Bk Vols 63,046; Per Subs 93
Automation Activity & Vendor Info: (Cataloging) Innovative Interfaces, Inc; (Circulation) Innovative Interfaces, Inc; (ILL) Innovative Interfaces, Inc; (OPAC) Innovative Interfaces, Inc
Wireless access
Function: 24/7 Electronic res, 24/7 Online cat, Accelerated reader prog, Activity rm, Adult bk club, After school storytime, Art exhibits, Audiobks on Playaways & MP3, Bk club(s), Bks on CD, Children's prog, Computer training, Distance learning, E-Readers, Free DVD rentals, Govt ref serv, Holiday prog, Home delivery & serv to seniorr ctr & nursing homes, ILL available, Instruction & testing, Internet access, Life-long learning prog for all ages, Magazines, Magnifiers for reading, Mail & tel request accepted, Mango lang, Meeting rooms, Movies, Music CDs, Outreach serv, OverDrive digital audio bks, Passport agency, Photocopying/Printing, Preschool outreach, Preschool reading prog, Prog for adults, Prog for children & young adult, Senior computer classes, Spanish lang bks, Spoken cassettes & CDs, Story hour, Summer & winter reading prog, Summer reading prog, Tax forms, Teen prog, VHS videos, Wheelchair accessible, Winter reading prog, Workshops, Writing prog
Publications: Friends (Newsletter)
Mem of Coos County Library Service District
Open Tues-Thurs 10-7, Fri & Sat 10-5
Friends of the Library Group

BANKS

P BANKS PUBLIC LIBRARY*, 42461 NW Market St, 97106. SAN 314-0571. Tel: 503-324-1382. FAX: 503-324-9132. Web Site: www.wccls.org/libraries/banks. *Libr Dir,* Denise Holmes; E-mail: deniseh@wccls.org
Founded 1976
Library Holdings: Bk Vols 20,893; Per Subs 64; Talking Bks 1,394; Videos 1,075
Automation Activity & Vendor Info: (Cataloging) Innovative Interfaces, Inc; (Circulation) Innovative Interfaces, Inc; (OPAC) Innovative Interfaces, Inc
Wireless access
Partic in Washington County Cooperative Library Services
Open Mon, Fri & Sat 10-5, Tues-Thurs 11-7
Friends of the Library Group

BEAVERTON

P BEAVERTON CITY LIBRARY*, 12375 SW Fifth St, 97005-2883. SAN 314-058X. Tel: 503-644-2197. FAX: 503-526-2636. E-mail: librarymail@beavertonoregon.gov. Web Site: www.beavertonlibrary.org. *Libr Dir,* Glenn Ferdman; E-mail: gferdman@beavertonoregon.gov; *Ad,* Linda Fallon; E-mail: lfallon@beavertonoregon.gov; *Circ Mgr,* Melissa Little; E-mail: mlittle@beavertonoregon.gov; *Youth Serv Mgr,* Victoria Campbell; E-mail: vcampbell@beavertonoregon.gov; Staff 85 (MLS 17, Non-MLS 68)
Founded 1938. Pop 136,000; Circ 2,700,000
Special Collections: Local History Coll; World Languages Coll
Automation Activity & Vendor Info: (Acquisitions) Innovative Interfaces, Inc; (Cataloging) Innovative Interfaces, Inc; (Circulation) Innovative Interfaces, Inc; (ILL) OCLC; (OPAC) Innovative Interfaces, Inc; (Serials) Innovative Interfaces, Inc
Wireless access
Function: Audiobks via web, Bks on CD, Children's prog, Computer training, Computers for patron use, Digital talking bks, E-Reserves, Electronic databases & coll, Family literacy, Free DVD rentals, Health sci info serv, Homework prog, ILL available, Magnifiers for reading, Mail & tel request accepted, Music CDs, Online cat, Photocopying/Printing, Prog for adults, Prog for children & young adult, Ref & res, Ref serv available, Spoken cassettes & CDs, Story hour, Summer reading prog, Tax forms, Teen prog, Telephone ref, Wheelchair accessible
Partic in Washington County Cooperative Library Services
Special Services for the Deaf - Assisted listening device; Bks on deafness & sign lang; Closed caption videos; TDD equip
Special Services for the Blind - Assistive/Adapted tech devices, equip & products; Bks on cassette; Bks on CD; Computer with voice synthesizer for visually impaired persons; Large print bks; Magnifiers; Scanner for conversion & translation of mats; Screen enlargement software for people with visual disabilities
Open Mon-Wed 10-8, Thurs-Sat 10-6, Sun 12-6
Friends of the Library Group

CM OREGON NATIONAL PRIMATE RESEARCH CENTER*, McDonald Library, 505 NW 185th Ave, 97006. SAN 314-061X. Tel: 503-690-5309. FAX: 503-690-5243. E-mail: onprclib@ohsu.edu. Web Site: www.ohsu.edu/xd/education/library/about/onprc-isabel-mcdonald-library.cfm. *Research Librn,* Denise Urbanski; E-mail: urbanskd@ohsu.edu. Subject Specialists: *Primatology,* Denise Urbanski; Staff 1 (Non-MLS 1)
Founded 1961
Library Holdings: Bk Titles 3,900; Bk Vols 14,765; Per Subs 81
Special Collections: Primatology Coll
Subject Interests: Biomed lit, Primates
Automation Activity & Vendor Info: (Circulation) Innovative Interfaces, Inc; (ILL) OCLC ILLiad; (OPAC) Innovative Interfaces, Inc; (Serials) Innovative Interfaces, Inc
Wireless access
Function: For res purposes
Partic in Washington County Libr Network
Restriction: Open to pub by appt only

C PIONEER PACIFIC COLLEGE LIBRARY*, 4145 SW Watson Ave, Ste 300, 97005. Tel: 503-682-1862. Web Site: www.pioneerpacific.edu. *Libr Dir,* Patricia Love; E-mail: patricia.love@pioneerpacific.edu; Staff 3 (MLS 1, Non-MLS 2)
Enrl 1,200
Library Holdings: e-books 21,000; Bk Titles 3,000
Wireless access
Open Mon-Thurs 7:30am-10:30pm

BEND

J CENTRAL OREGON COMMUNITY COLLEGE BARBER LIBRARY*, 2600 NW College Way, 97703. SAN 314-0636. Tel: 541-383-7560. Interlibrary Loan Service Tel: 541-383-7561. Reference Tel: 541-383-7567. FAX: 541-383-7406. E-mail: refdesk@cocc.edu. Web Site: cocc.edu/library. *Libr Dir,* Tina Hovekamp; E-mail: thovekamp@cocc.edu; *Acq Librn, Colls Librn,* Catherine Finney; Tel: 541-383-7559; *Discovery Serv Librn, ILS LIbrn,* Tamara Marnell; *Instruction & Outreach Librn,* Kirsten Hostetler; Staff 4.5 (MLS 4.5)
Founded 1950. Enrl 5,742; Fac 155; Highest Degree: Associate
Library Holdings: AV Mats 1,962; Bks on Deafness & Sign Lang 93; e-books 7,262; Bk Titles 65,285; Per Subs 236
Special Collections: Harold Wynne (Papers related to Rajnesshpuram); Records of the Oregon Superintendency of Indian Affairs 1848-1873; USDA Farm Service Agency (National Forest Service Aerial Photograph Coll). US Document Depository
Subject Interests: Native Am
Automation Activity & Vendor Info: (Acquisitions) Innovative Interfaces, Inc; (Cataloging) Ex Libris Group; (Circulation) Ex Libris Group; (Course Reserve) Ex Libris Group; (ILL) OCLC; (Media Booking) Ex Libris Group; (OPAC) Ex Libris Group; (Serials) Ex Libris Group
Wireless access
Function: Outside serv via phone, mail, e-mail & web
Partic in Orbis Cascade Alliance
Open Mon-Thurs 8am-9pm, Fri 8-5, Sat & Sun 12-6
Restriction: Authorized patrons

P DESCHUTES PUBLIC LIBRARY DISTRICT*, 507 NW Wall St, 97703. SAN 357-8585. Tel: 541-312-1020. FAX: 541-389-2982. Web Site: www.deschuteslibrary.org. *Dir,* Todd Dunkelberg; Tel: 541-312-1021, E-mail: toddd@deschuteslibrary.org; *Asst Dir, Operational Serv,* Lynne Mildenstein; Tel: 541-312-1028, E-mail: lynnem@deschuteslibrary.org; *Mgr, Info Tech,* Mark Hovey; Tel: 541-312-1043, E-mail: markh@deschuteslibrary.org; *Adult Serv Mgr,* Sara Thompson; Tel: 541-312-1038, E-mail: sarat@deschuteslibrary.org; *Human Res Mgr,* Jennifer Palmer; Tel: 541-312-1024, E-mail: jennp@deschuteslibrary.org; *Tech Serv Mgr,* Emily O'Neal; Tel: 541-617-7061, E-mail: emilyo@deschuteslibrary.org; Staff 97.8 (MLS 12.8, Non-MLS 85)
Founded 1920. Pop 202,000; Circ 2,000,000
Jul 2019-Jun 2020 Income (Main & Associated Libraries) $14,553,979, State $63,294, Locally Generated Income $13,913,365, Other $646,527.

Mats Exp $1,969,961, Other Print Mats $133,530, Electronic Ref Mat (Incl. Access Fees) $1,215,144. Sal $5,545,935
Library Holdings: Audiobooks 12,146; CDs 9,072; DVDs 27,053; e-books 474,812; e-journals 53; Electronic Media & Resources 63,394; Large Print Bks 6,376; Microforms 124; Bk Vols 300,552; Per Subs 500
Automation Activity & Vendor Info: (Acquisitions) Innovative Interfaces, Inc; (Cataloging) Innovative Interfaces, Inc; (Circulation) Innovative Interfaces, Inc; (Discovery) BiblioCommons; (ILL) OCLC; (OPAC) BiblioCommons
Wireless access
Function: 24/7 Electronic res, 24/7 Online cat, Adult bk club, Audiobks via web, Bk club(s), Bk reviews (Group), Bks on CD, Children's prog, Citizenship assistance, Computer training, Computers for patron use, Digital talking bks, Doc delivery serv, Electronic databases & coll, Equip loans & repairs, For res purposes, Free DVD rentals, Holiday prog, Home delivery & serv to seniorr ctr & nursing homes, Homebound delivery serv, Homework prog, ILL available, Instruction & testing, Internet access, Jail serv, Life-long learning prog for all ages, Literacy & newcomer serv, Magazines, Mail & tel request accepted, Mango lang, Meeting rooms, Microfiche/film & reading machines, Movies, Museum passes, Music CDs, Online cat, Online info literacy tutorials on the web & in blackboard, Online ref, Outreach serv, Outside serv via phone, mail, e-mail & web, OverDrive digital audio bks, Photocopying/Printing, Preschool outreach, Preschool reading prog, Printer for laptops & handheld devices, Prog for adults, Prog for children & young adult, Ref & res, Ref serv available, Res assist avail, Scanner, Senior computer classes, Senior outreach, Serves people with intellectual disabilities, Spanish lang bks, Story hour, Study rm, Summer reading prog, Tax forms, Teen prog, Telephone ref, Wheelchair accessible, Workshops, Writing prog
Special Services for the Deaf - Closed caption videos; Sign lang interpreter upon request for prog; Staff with knowledge of sign lang
Special Services for the Blind - Accessible computers; Bks available with recordings; Bks on CD; Computer with voice synthesizer for visually impaired persons; Copier with enlargement capabilities; Extensive large print coll; Free checkout of audio mat; Home delivery serv; Large print bks; Recorded bks; Talking bks
Open Mon-Fri 9-7

Branches: 6

BEND BRANCH, 601 NW Wall St, 97703, SAN 376-9402. Tel: 541-617-7044. Reference Tel: 541-617-7080. E-mail: downtownbendinfo@deschuteslibrary.org. *Supvr,* Esther Clinton; Tel: 541-312-1052, E-mail: estherc@deschuteslibrary.org; *Supvr,* Laurie Sacher; Tel: 541-312-7052, E-mail: lauries@deschuteslibrary.org
Pop 70,328; Circ 1,009,376
Library Holdings: Bk Titles 172,526; Bk Vols 216,007; Per Subs 274
Open Mon-Fri 10-6, Sat 12-5
Friends of the Library Group

EAST BEND BRANCH, 62080 Dean Swift Rd, 97701. Tel: 541-330-3760. FAX: 541-389-9882. E-mail: eastbendinfo@deschuteslibrary.org. *Commun Librn,* Chandra vanEijnsbergen; Tel: 841-330-6764, E-mail: chandrav@deschutespubliclibrary.org; *Supvr,* Barbara Baker; Tel: 541-330-3761, E-mail: barbarab@deschuteslibrary.org
Open Tues, Wed & Fri 9-6, Thurs 9-8, Sat 9-5

LA PINE BRANCH, 16425 First St, La Pine, 97739. (Mail add: PO Box 40, La Pine, 97739-0040), SAN 325-3236. Tel: 541-312-1090. FAX: 541-536-0752. E-mail: lapineinfo@deschuteslibrary.org. *Commun Librn,* Roxanne Renteria; Tel: 541-312-1091, E-mail: roxanne4@deschuteslibrary.org; *Supvr,* Cathy Zgraggen; Tel: 541-312-1094, E-mail: cathyz@deschuteslibrary.org
Founded 2000. Pop 8,602; Circ 121,124
Library Holdings: Bk Titles 35,229; Bk Vols 36,892; Per Subs 75
Open Tues-Fri 10-6, Sat 10-5
Friends of the Library Group

REDMOND BRANCH, 827 Deschutes Ave, Redmond, 97756, SAN 357-8615. Tel: 541-312-1050. FAX: 541-548-6358. E-mail: redmondinfo@deschuteslibrary.org. *Commun Librn,* Josie Hanneman; Tel: 541-312-1088, E-mail: josieh@deschuteslibrary.org; *Supvr,* Graham Fox; Tel: 541-312-1059, E-mail: grahamf@deschuteslibrary.org
Founded 1917. Pop 21,109; Circ 441,698
Library Holdings: Bk Titles 80,676; Bk Vols 86,313; Per Subs 133
Open Mon & Wed-Fri 10-6, Tues 10-8, Sat 10-5
Friends of the Library Group

SISTERS BRANCH, 110 N Cedar St, Sisters, 97759. (Mail add: PO Box 1209, Sisters, 97759), SAN 357-864X. Tel: 541-312-1070. FAX: 541-549-9620. E-mail: sistersinfo@deschuteslibrary.org. *Commun Librn,* Paige Bentley-Flannery; Tel: 541-617-7078, E-mail: paigeb@deschuteslibrary.org; *Supvr,* Zoe Schumacher; Tel: 541-617-1076, E-mail: zoeanns@deschuteslibrary.org
Founded 1939. Pop 1,430; Circ 101,952
Library Holdings: Bk Titles 25,229; Bk Vols 26,517; Per Subs 72
Open Tues-Fri 10-6, Sat 10-5
Friends of the Library Group

SUNRIVER AREA BRANCH, 56855 Venture Lane, Sunriver, 97707, SAN 377-6700. Tel: 541-312-1080. FAX: 541-593-9286. E-mail: sunriverinfo@deschuteslibrary.org. *Commun Librn,* Roxanne Renteria; *Supvr,* Heidi Powers; Tel: 541-312-1085, E-mail: heidip@deschuteslibrary.org
Founded 1998. Pop 1,700; Circ 96,677
Library Holdings: Bk Titles 29,081; Bk Vols 30,291; Per Subs 86
Open Tues-Fri 10-6, Sat 10-5
Friends of the Library Group

C OREGON STATE UNIVERSITY*, Cascades Campus Library, Tykeson Hall 202, 1500 SW Chandler Ave, 97702. Tel: 541-322-2079. E-mail: library@osucascades.edu. Web Site: library.oregonstate.edu/cascades. *Libr Dir,* Faye Chadwell
Automation Activity & Vendor Info: (Acquisitions) Innovative Interfaces, Inc; (Cataloging) Innovative Interfaces, Inc; (Circulation) Innovative Interfaces, Inc; (OPAC) Innovative Interfaces, Inc; (Serials) Innovative Interfaces, Inc
Wireless access
Open Mon-Thurs 8-7, Fri 8-5

S SCIENTISTS CENTER FOR ANIMAL WELFARE LIBRARY, 2660 NE Hwy 20, Ste 610-115, 97701. SAN 372-7262. Tel: 301-345-3500. E-mail: info@scaw.com. Web Site: www.scaw.com. *Exec Dir,* Linda Tockey
Founded 1978
Library Holdings: Bk Vols 1,000
Publications: SCAW (Newsletter)
Restriction: Mem only

BLUE RIVER

P FRANCES O'BRIEN MEMORIAL LIBRARY*, 51790 McKenzie St, 97413. (Mail add: PO Box 291, 97413-0291). Tel: 541-822-3249. Web Site: www.lanelibrary.org/home/libraries-of-lane-county. *Library Contact,* Susan Savage
Founded 1929
Library Holdings: Bk Vols 40,000
Open Mon-Sat 10-4:30

BOARDMAN

P OREGON TRAIL LIBRARY DISTRICT*, Boardman Library, 200 Main St, 97818. (Mail add: PO Box 849, 97818). Tel: 541-481-2665. FAX: 541-481-2668. E-mail: otldbdmn5@centurylink.net. Web Site: oregontrail.ploud.net/our-locations-and-hours/boardman-library. *Dir,* Kathy Street; E-mail: otlddirector@centurylink.net
Automation Activity & Vendor Info: (Cataloging) Innovative Interfaces, Inc - Millennium; (Circulation) Innovative Interfaces, Inc - Millennium; (ILL) Innovative Interfaces, Inc - Millennium; (OPAC) Innovative Interfaces, Inc - Millennium
Partic in Sage Library System of Eastern Oregon
Open Tues & Wed 10-2 & 3-8, Thurs & Fri 12-5, Sat 10-2
Friends of the Library Group

Branches: 2

HEPPNER BRANCH, 444 North Main St, Heppner, 97836. (Mail add: PO Box 325, Heppner, 97836). Tel: 541-676-9964. Administration Tel: 541-481-3365. FAX: 541-676-5900.
Partic in Sage Library System of Eastern Oregon
Open Tues & Wed 11-8, Thurs Noon-5, Fri 10-5, Sat 11-3
Friends of the Library Group

IRRIGON BRANCH, Irrigon, 97844. Tel: 541-481-2665.
Open Tues & Thurs 10:30-4
Friends of the Library Group

BROOKINGS

P CHETCO COMMUNITY PUBLIC LIBRARY*, 405 Alder St, 97415. SAN 314-0644. Tel: 541-469-7738. FAX: 541-469-6746. E-mail: chetcolibrary@gmail.com. Web Site: www.chetcolibrary.org. *Dir,* Julie Rutherford
Founded 1947. Pop 12,909; Circ 164,770
Library Holdings: Large Print Bks 3,230; Bk Titles 48,961; Bk Vols 51,126; Per Subs 118; Talking Bks 2,644; Videos 1,612
Subject Interests: NW hist
Automation Activity & Vendor Info: (Cataloging) SirsiDynix; (Circulation) SirsiDynix; (OPAC) SirsiDynix
Wireless access
Partic in Ore Libr Asn
Open Mon, Fri & Sat 10-6, Tues-Thurs 10-7
Friends of the Library Group

BROWNSVILLE

P BROWNSVILLE COMMUNITY LIBRARY*, 146 Spaulding Way, 97327. (Mail add: PO Box 68, 97327-0068), SAN 314-0652. Tel: 541-466-5454. E-mail: library@ci.brownsville.or.us. Web Site: www.brownsvillecommunitylibrary.org. *Dir,* Sherri Lemhouse; Staff 12 (Non-MLS 12)
Founded 1911. Pop 1,500; Circ 19,000

Library Holdings: Large Print Bks 350; Bk Vols 18,500; Per Subs 15; Talking Bks 300
Special Collections: Linn County Cemetaries; Oregon Trail Coll
Subject Interests: Genealogy, NW hist
Automation Activity & Vendor Info: (Cataloging) Follett Software; (Circulation) Follett Software
Wireless access
Open Tues, Wed & Fri 10-5, Thurs 1-7, Sat 10-2
Friends of the Library Group

BURNS

P HARNEY COUNTY LIBRARY*, 80 West D St, 97720. SAN 314-0679. Tel: 541-573-6670. FAX: 541-573-1571. Web Site: www.harneycountylibrary.org. *Libr Dir,* Cheryl Hancock; E-mail: cheryl@harneycountylibrary.org; Staff 2.5 (MLS 1, Non-MLS 1.5)
Founded 1903. Pop 7,000; Circ 38,482
Library Holdings: AV Mats 4,800; Bk Vols 25,000; Per Subs 70
Special Collections: Western History Room. Oral History
Automation Activity & Vendor Info: (Cataloging) Evergreen; (Circulation) Evergreen; (OPAC) Evergreen
Wireless access
Function: Bks on cassette, Bks on CD, Children's prog, Computers for patron use, Electronic databases & coll, Free DVD rentals, ILL available, Mail & tel request accepted, Music CDs, Online cat, OverDrive digital audio bks, Photocopying/Printing, Prog for adults, Prog for children & young adult, Story hour, Summer reading prog, Wheelchair accessible
Partic in Sage Library System of Eastern Oregon
Open Mon & Tues 10:30-7, Wed 12-7, Thurs & Fri 10:30-6, Sat 12-4

CANBY

P CANBY PUBLIC LIBRARY*, 220 NE Second Ave, 97013-3732. SAN 314-0687. Tel: 503-266-3394. Administration Tel: 503-266-4021, Ext 230. FAX: 503-266-1709. E-mail: canbyinfo@lincc.org. Web Site: canbylibrary.org. *Libr Dir,* Danny Smith; E-mail: smithd@canbyoregon.gov; *Ch,* Peggy Wickwire; E-mail: pwickwire@lincc.org; *Pub Relations,* Hanna Hofer; E-mail: hoferh@ci.canby.or.us
Pop 22,000; Circ 300,000
Library Holdings: Bk Vols 60,000; Per Subs 70
Special Collections: Emma Wakefield Coll (materials on herbs)
Subject Interests: Children's bks, Christianity, Computer, Herbs, Ore
Automation Activity & Vendor Info: (Cataloging) SirsiDynix; (Circulation) SirsiDynix; (OPAC) SirsiDynix
Wireless access
Open Mon-Thurs 10-8, Fri & Sat 10-5
Friends of the Library Group

CANNON BEACH

P CANNON BEACH LIBRARY, 131 N Hemlock, 97110. (Mail add: PO Box 486, 97110-0486). Tel: 503-436-1391. E-mail: info@cannonbeachlibrary.org. Web Site: cannonbeachlibrary.org. *Libr Mgr,* Jennifer Dixon
Founded 1927
Library Holdings: Bk Vols 13,000
Special Collections: Haystack Rock Coll; Northwest Coll
Wireless access
Open Mon, Wed, Fri & Sat 12-4
Friends of the Library Group

CHARLESTON

C UNIVERSITY OF OREGON*, Loyd & Dorothy Rippey Library, Institute of Marine Biology, 63466 Boat Basin Dr, 97420. (Mail add: PO Box 5389, 97420). Tel: 541-888-2581, Ext 219. Reference E-mail: oimbref@uoregon.edu. Web Site: library.uoregon.edu/scilib/oimb. *Libr Tech II,* Clara Piazzola
Library Holdings: Bk Vols 6,000; Per Subs 60
Wireless access
Restriction: Open by appt only

CLACKAMAS

M KAISER PERMANENTE NORTHWEST REGIONAL LIBRARIES*, KPLibraries NW, Kaiser Sunnyside Medical Ctr, 10180 SE Sunnyside Rd - Health Sciences Library, 97015. Tel: 503-571-4293. Interlibrary Loan Service Tel: 503-571-4165. FAX: 503-571-4291. *Regional Mgr,* Jennifer McBride; E-mail: jennifer.a.mcbride@kp.org; Staff 3 (MLS 2, Non-MLS 1)
Founded 1975
Library Holdings: Bk Titles 1,000; Per Subs 225
Special Collections: Consumer Health Coll
Subject Interests: Med, Nursing
Automation Activity & Vendor Info: (OPAC) Innovative Interfaces, Inc
Wireless access
Function: 24/7 Electronic res
Open Mon-Fri 7:30-5
Restriction: Badge access after hrs, In-house use for visitors, Open to pub for ref & circ; with some limitations, Open to staff, patients & family mem

CLATSKANIE

P CLATSKANIE LIBRARY DISTRICT*, 11 Lillich St, 97016. (Mail add: PO Box 577, 97016-0577), SAN 314-0695. Tel: 503-728-3732. E-mail: clpublic@clatskanie.com. Web Site: www.clatskanielibrary.org. *Dir,* Elizabeth A Kruse; Staff 1 (Non-MLS 1)
Pop 3,190; Circ 23,801
Library Holdings: Bk Vols 23,801; Per Subs 38
Subject Interests: Columbia County hist
Automation Activity & Vendor Info: (Cataloging) SirsiDynix; (Circulation) SirsiDynix; (ILL) OCLC
Wireless access
Open Mon-Wed 10-7, Thurs-Sat 10-5:30; Sat (Summer) 10-3
Friends of the Library Group

CONDON

P GILLIAM COUNTY PUBLIC LIBRARY*, 134 S Main St, 97823. (Mail add: PO Box 34, 97823-0034), SAN 357-8674. Tel: 541-384-6052. FAX: 541-384-6052. Web Site: www.co.gilliam.or.us/government/library. *Libr Dir,* Mary Reser; E-mail: mary.reser@co.gilliam.or.us; *Youth Serv Coordr,* Deanna Campbell; E-mail: deanna.campbell@co.gilliam.or.us; Staff 1 (Non-MLS 1)
Circ 7,176
Library Holdings: Audiobooks 167; DVDs 197; Bk Vols 7,716; Per Subs 2
Automation Activity & Vendor Info: (Cataloging) Evergreen; (Circulation) Evergreen; (ILL) Evergreen; (OPAC) Evergreen; (Serials) Evergreen
Wireless access
Function: 24/7 Electronic res, Audiobks via web, Bks on cassette, Bks on CD, Children's prog, Computers for patron use, Digital talking bks, Free DVD rentals, Home delivery & serv to seniorr ctr & nursing homes, Homebound delivery serv, ILL available, Instruction & testing, Internet access, Mail & tel request accepted, Movies, Museum passes, Online cat, OverDrive digital audio bks, Prog for adults, Prog for children & young adult, Spoken cassettes & CDs, Story hour, Summer reading prog, Tax forms, Wheelchair accessible
Open Mon-Fri 11-5

COOS BAY

P COOS BAY PUBLIC LIBRARY*, 525 Anderson Ave, 97420-1678. SAN 314-0717. Tel: 541-269-1101. FAX: 541-269-7567. E-mail: bayref@cclsd.org. Web Site: www.coosbaylibrary.org. *Dir,* Sami Pierson; E-mail: spierson@cclsd.org; Staff 6 (MLS 3, Non-MLS 3)
Founded 1910. Pop 24,164; Circ 343,485
Library Holdings: AV Mats 15,463; Bk Vols 117,749; Per Subs 254
Special Collections: Oregon History (Helene Stack Bower Oregon Coll). Oral History
Automation Activity & Vendor Info: (Cataloging) Innovative Interfaces, Inc; (Circulation) Innovative Interfaces, Inc; (OPAC) Innovative Interfaces, Inc; (Serials) Innovative Interfaces, Inc
Wireless access
Mem of Coos County Library Service District
Open Mon-Thurs 10-7, Fri & Sat 12-6
Friends of the Library Group

P COOS COUNTY LIBRARY SERVICE DISTRICT*, 525 Anderson Ave, 97420. SAN 322-4279. Tel: 541-269-1101. Reference E-mail: eso@coastlinelibrarynetwork.org. Web Site: www.cooslibraries.org. *Dir,* Stacey Nix
Founded 1980
Member Libraries: Bandon Public Library; Coos Bay Public Library; Coquille Public Library; Dora Public Library; Hazel M Lewis Library; Lakeside Public Library; Myrtle Point Library; North Bend Public Library
Open Mon-Fri 8-5

J SOUTHWESTERN OREGON COMMUNITY COLLEGE LIBRARY*, 1988 Newmark Ave, 97420. SAN 314-0725. Tel: 541-888-7431. Circulation Tel: 541-888-7270. FAX: 541-888-7605. Web Site: www.socc.edu/library. *Info Serv & Instrul Librn,* Noelle Ebert; E-mail: noelle.ebert@socc.edu; *Circ, Libr Tech,* Suzan Villers; Tel: 541-888-7429, E-mail: suzan.villers@socc.edu; *Libr Tech, Tech Serv,* Dawn Jones; Tel: 541-888-7262, E-mail: djones@socc.edu; Staff 2 (MLS 2)
Founded 1962. Highest Degree: Associate
Library Holdings: Bks on Deafness & Sign Lang 40; Bk Titles 35,220; Bk Vols 39,626; Per Subs 219
Automation Activity & Vendor Info: (Cataloging) Innovative Interfaces, Inc; (Circulation) Innovative Interfaces, Inc; (Course Reserve) Innovative Interfaces, Inc; (ILL) OCLC; (OPAC) Innovative Interfaces, Inc

Wireless access
Partic in Coastline; OCLC Online Computer Library Center, Inc
Open Mon-Fri 8:30-5

COQUILLE

P COQUILLE PUBLIC LIBRARY*, 105 N Birch St, 97423-1299. SAN 314-0733. Tel: 541-396-2166. FAX: 541-396-2174. Web Site: www.cityofcoquille.org/comm_services/library.php. *Libr Dir,* Anne Conner; E-mail: aconner@cityofcoquille.org; Staff 2 (MLS 1, Non-MLS 1)
Pop 6,500; Circ 88,201
Library Holdings: Bk Titles 35,082; Per Subs 96
Automation Activity & Vendor Info: (Cataloging) Innovative Interfaces, Inc; (Circulation) Innovative Interfaces, Inc; (OPAC) Innovative Interfaces, Inc
Wireless access
Mem of Coos County Library Service District
Open Mon-Thurs 10-6, Fri 10-5, Sat 12-5
Friends of the Library Group

CORNELIUS

P CORNELIUS PUBLIC LIBRARY*, 1370 N Adair St, 97113. SAN 314-075X. Tel: 503-357-4093. FAX: 503-357-7775. E-mail: cornelius@wccls.org. Web Site: www.ci.cornelius.or.us/library. *Libr Dir,* Karen Hill; E-mail: karenh@wccls.org; Staff 4 (MLS 1, Non-MLS 3)
Founded 1913. Pop 13,718; Circ 92,253
Library Holdings: Bk Vols 21,230; Per Subs 49
Special Collections: Educational CD-ROMs
Subject Interests: Spanish
Automation Activity & Vendor Info: (Cataloging) Innovative Interfaces, Inc; (Circulation) Innovative Interfaces, Inc; (OPAC) Innovative Interfaces, Inc
Wireless access
Function: 24/7 Electronic res, Bilingual assistance for Spanish patrons, Bks on CD, Children's prog, Computers for patron use, E-Readers, Electronic databases & coll, Equip loans & repairs, Free DVD rentals, Homebound delivery serv, ILL available, Internet access, Magazines, Mango lang, Museum passes, Online cat, Online info literacy tutorials on the web & in blackboard, Online ref, Outreach serv, OverDrive digital audio bks, Photocopying/Printing, Preschool reading prog, Prog for adults, Prog for children & young adult, Scanner, Spanish lang bks, Spoken cassettes & CDs, Spoken cassettes & DVDs, Story hour, Summer reading prog, Workshops
Partic in Washington County Cooperative Library Services
Open Mon-Fri 10-7, Sat 10-5, Sun 12-5
Friends of the Library Group

CORVALLIS

L BENTON COUNTY LAW LIBRARY*, 559 NW Monroe Ave, 97330. (Mail add: Sunset Bldg, 4077 SW Research Way, 97333), SAN 373-6652. Tel: 541-766-6673. FAX: 541-766-6893. *Librn,* Martha A Jenkins; E-mail: martha.a.jenkins@co.benton.or.us; Staff 1 (MLS 1)
Jul 2018-Jun 2019. Mats Exp $26,000
Library Holdings: Bk Titles 255; Bk Vols 5,797
Function: Res libr
Restriction: Pub use on premises

P CORVALLIS-BENTON COUNTY PUBLIC LIBRARY*, 645 NW Monroe Ave, 97330. SAN 357-8739. Tel: 541-766-6926. Reference Tel: 541-766-6793. Administration Tel: 541-766-6928. Reference FAX: 541-766-6726. Administration FAX: 541-766-6915. TDD: 541-766-6988. Web Site: cbcpubliclibrary.net. *Libr Dir,* Ashlee Chavez; E-mail: ashlee.chavez@corvallisoregon.gov; *Dep Dir, Pub Serv,* Andrew Cherbas; E-mail: andrew.cherbas@corvallisoregon.gov; Staff 46 (MLS 19, Non-MLS 27)
Founded 1899. Pop 84,000; Circ 1,594,973
Library Holdings: Bk Titles 221,092; Bk Vols 370,055; Per Subs 1,072
Automation Activity & Vendor Info: (Cataloging) TLC (The Library Corporation); (Circulation) TLC (The Library Corporation); (OPAC) TLC (The Library Corporation)
Wireless access
Function: Adult bk club
Friends of the Library Group
Branches: 3
ALSEA COMMUNITY LIBRARY, 19192 Alsea Hwy, Alsea, 97324, SAN 357-8798. Tel: 541-487-5061. FAX: 541-487-5061. *Librn,* Mary Rounds
Open Mon, Wed & Sat 10-4:30, Tues & Thurs 2-8
Friends of the Library Group
MONROE COMMUNITY LAW LIBRARY, 668 Commercial St, Monroe, 97456, SAN 314-1284. Tel: 541-847-5174. FAX: 541-847-5174. *Br Mgr,* Lori Pelkey; E-mail: lori.pelkey@ci.corvallis.or.us
Open Mon 1:30-4:30, Tues & Thurs 10-4:30, Wed 3-8, Sat 10-3
Friends of the Library Group
PHILOMATH COMMUNITY LIBRARY, 1050 Applegate St, Philomath, 97370. (Mail add: PO Box 400, Philomath, 97370-0569), SAN 325-3953. Tel: 541-929-3016. FAX: 541-929-5934. *Asst Dir,* Teresa Landers; Tel: 541-766-6995, E-mail: teresa.landers@ci.corvallis.or.us
Open Mon & Thurs-Sat 10-5, Tues & Wed 10-8
Friends of the Library Group
Bookmobiles: 1

M GOOD SAMARITAN REGIONAL MEDICAL CENTER*, Murray Memorial Library, 3600 NW Samaritan Dr, 97330. SAN 371-8557. Tel: 541-768-6200. Administration Tel: 541-768-4899. FAX: 541-768-5087. E-mail: samlib5@gmail.com. Information Services E-mail: info@samlib.com. Web Site: www.samlib.com. *Mgr, Libr Serv,* Kenneth H Willer; E-mail: kwiller@samhealth.org; *Librn,* Position Currently Open; Staff 2 (MLS 2)
Founded 1976
Library Holdings: e-books 850; e-journals 1,000; Bk Titles 1,100; Per Subs 110
Subject Interests: Med
Automation Activity & Vendor Info: (OPAC) LibraryWorld, Inc
Wireless access
Function: Health sci info serv
Partic in Medical Library Association; National Network of Libraries of Medicine Region 5
Open Mon-Fri 8:30-5
Restriction: Open to pub for ref & circ; with some limitations

C OREGON STATE UNIVERSITY LIBRARIES*, The Valley Library, 121 The Valley Library, 97331-4501. SAN 314-0792. Tel: 541-737-3331. Circulation Tel: 541-737-7254. Interlibrary Loan Service Tel: 541-737-4488. Reference Tel: 541-737-7295. Administration Tel: 541-737-4633. FAX: 541-737-3453. Circulation FAX: 541-737-1328. Reference FAX: 541-737-8224. E-mail: library.web@oregonstate.edu. Web Site: library.oregonstate.edu. *Interim Univ Librn,* Anne-Marie Deitering; E-mail: anne-marie.deitering@oregonstate.edu; *Assoc Univ Librn, Res & Scholarly Communication,* Position Currently Open; *Assoc Univ Librn, Learning Services,* Position Currently Open; *Acq, Dir, Res Sharing,* Kerri Goergen-Doll; Tel: 541-737-7256, E-mail: kerri.goergen-doll@oregonstate.edu; *Head, Emerging Tech & Serv,* Margaret Mellinger; Tel: 541-737-9642, E-mail: margaret.mellinger@oregonstate.edu; *Head, Library Experience & Access,* Beth Filar-Williams; Tel: 541-737-2156, E-mail: beth.filar-williams@oregonstate.edu; *Head Teaching & Engagement,* Jane Nichols; Tel: 541-737-7269, E-mail: jane.nichols@oregonstate.edu; Staff 99 (MLS 34, Non-MLS 65)
Founded 1887. Enrl 31,904; Fac 44; Highest Degree: Doctorate
Jul 2020-Jun 2021. Mats Exp $15,738,619. Sal $5,303,214
Special Collections: Ava Helen & Linus Pauling Coll; Northwest Coll. US Document Depository
Subject Interests: Agr, Environ studies, Forestry, Natural sci, Oceanography
Automation Activity & Vendor Info: (Acquisitions) Ex Libris Group; (Cataloging) Ex Libris Group; (Circulation) Ex Libris Group; (Course Reserve) Ex Libris Group; (ILL) OCLC; (OPAC) Ex Libris Group; (Serials) Ex Libris Group
Wireless access
Function: Archival coll, Doc delivery serv, ILL available, Internet access, Photocopying/Printing, Ref serv available, Res libr
Publications: Library Messenger (Newsletter)
Partic in Greater Western Library Alliance; Orbis Cascade Alliance
Restriction: Open to pub for ref & circ; with some limitations
Departmental Libraries:
SPECIAL COLLECTIONS & ARCHIVES RESEARCH CENTER, 121 The Valley Library, 5th Flr, 97331. Tel: 541-737-2075. FAX: 541-737-8674. E-mail: scarc@oregonstate.edu. Web Site: scarc.library.oregonstate.edu. *Dir, Archives & Spec Coll,* Larry A Landis; Tel: 541-737-0540, E-mail: larry.landis@oregonstate.edu; *Hist of Sci Librn/Curator,* Anne Bahde; E-mail: anne.bahde@oregonstate.edu; *Multicultural Librn,* Natalia Fernandez; Tel: 541-737-3653, E-mail: natalia.fernandez@oregonstate.edu; *Univ Archivist,* Elizabeth A Nielsen; Tel: 541-737-0543, E-mail: elizabeth.nielsen@oregonstate.edu; *Archivist,* Tiah K Edmunson-Morton; Tel: 541-737-7387, E-mail: tiah.edmunson-morton@oregonstate.edu; *Archivist,* Karl R McCreary; Tel: 541-737-0539, E-mail: karl.mccreary@oregonstate.edu; *Info Tech,* Ryan Wick; E-mail: ryan.wick@oregonstate.edu; *Coordr, Pub Serv,* Trevor Sandgathe; E-mail: trevor.sandgathe@oregonstate.edu; *Sr Res Asst,* Chris Petersen; Tel: 541-737-2810, E-mail: chris.petersen@oregonstate.edu
Open Mon-Fri 9-5

G US ENVIRONMENTAL PROTECTION AGENCY, Pacific Ecological Systems Divison (PESD) Library, 200 SW 35th St, 97333. SAN 314-0768. Tel: 541-754-4355. FAX: 541-754-4799. *Librn,* Paul Chasse; E-mail: chasse.paul@epa.gov; Staff 1 (MLS 1)
Founded 1966

Library Holdings: Bk Titles 7,000; Bk Vols 8,000; Per Subs 30
Subject Interests: Environ monitoring & assessment, Global climate change, Habitat res, Modeling wildlife populations, Monitoring freshwater ecosystems, Pesticide res
Automation Activity & Vendor Info: (Cataloging) OCLC; (ILL) OCLC
Function: For res purposes, ILL available, Mail & tel request accepted
Partic in EPA National Libr Network
Restriction: Borrowing requests are handled by ILL, Circulates for staff only, Staff use, pub by appt, Visitors must make appt to use bks in the libr

COTTAGE GROVE

P COTTAGE GROVE PUBLIC LIBRARY*, 700 E Gibbs Ave, 97424. SAN 314-0806. Tel: 541-942-3828. E-mail: library@cottagegrove.org. Web Site: www.cottagegrove.org/library. *Head Librn,* Natasha Chitow; Staff 4 (MLS 1, Non-MLS 3)
Founded 2000. Pop 9,010; Circ 86,997
Library Holdings: Bk Titles 42,098; Per Subs 51; Talking Bks 1,483; Videos 2,030
Special Collections: Oregon Coll
Automation Activity & Vendor Info: (Cataloging) SirsiDynix; (Circulation) SirsiDynix; (OPAC) SirsiDynix
Wireless access
Open Mon & Tues 10-7:45, Wed-Sat 10-5:45
Friends of the Library Group

COVE

S COVE LIBRARY*, 606 Main St, 97824. (Mail add: 1005 Haefer Lane, 97824-8723). Tel: 541-568-4758, 541-568-5001. Web Site: coveoregon.org/cove-library.
Founded 1903
Library Holdings: Audiobooks 80; Bks-By-Mail 3; Bks on Deafness & Sign Lang 3; CDs 40; DVDs 60; High Interest/Low Vocabulary Bk Vols 43; Large Print Bks 32; Bk Titles 3,700; Talking Bks 76; Videos 161
Special Collections: Oregon History Coll. Municipal Document Depository; Oral History; State Document Depository; US Document Depository
Automation Activity & Vendor Info: (Acquisitions) A-G Canada Ltd
Wireless access
Partic in Sage Library System of Eastern Oregon
Special Services for the Deaf - Bks on deafness & sign lang
Special Services for the Blind - Assistive/Adapted tech devices, equip & products; Talking bks
Open Tues & Thurs 10-5

CRESWELL

P LANE LIBRARY DISTRICT, Creswell Library, 64 W Oregon Ave, 97426. (Mail add: PO Box 366, 97426-0366). Tel: 541-895-3053. FAX: 541-895-3507. Web Site: www.creswell-library.org. *Dir,* Su Liudahl; E-mail: director.su@creswell-library.org; Staff 3 (MLS 2, Non-MLS 1)
Founded 2004. Pop 8,000; Circ 48,000
Library Holdings: Bk Vols 32,000; Per Subs 40
Automation Activity & Vendor Info: (Acquisitions) SirsiDynix-Enterprise; (Cataloging) SirsiDynix; (Circulation) SirsiDynix-Enterprise; (ILL) SirsiDynix-Enterprise; (OPAC) SirsiDynix-Enterprise
Wireless access
Function: Adult bk club, Art exhibits, Audiobks via web, Bilingual assistance for Spanish patrons, Bks on cassette, Bks on CD, Children's prog, Computers for patron use, Electronic databases & coll, Free DVD rentals, Genealogy discussion group, Holiday prog, Home delivery & serv to seniorr ctr & nursing homes, Homebound delivery serv, ILL available, Mail & tel request accepted, Music CDs, Online cat, OverDrive digital audio bks, Photocopying/Printing, Preschool outreach, Prog for adults, Prog for children & young adult, Ref serv available, Story hour, Summer reading prog, Tax forms, Teen prog, VHS videos, Wheelchair accessible
Special Services for the Blind - Audio mat; Bks on cassette; Bks on CD; Large print bks; Large type calculator
Open Mon & Fri 12-6, Tues-Thurs 10-7, Sat 10-1
Restriction: Borrowing requests are handled by ILL
Friends of the Library Group

DALLAS

P DALLAS PUBLIC LIBRARY*, 950 Main St, 97338. SAN 314-0822. Tel: 503-623-2633. FAX: 503-623-7357. E-mail: dalref@ccrls.org. Web Site: www.ci.dallas.or.us/102/library. *Libr Mgr,* Mark Greenhalgh-Johnson; Staff 7 (MLS 1, Non-MLS 6)
Founded 1905. Pop 18,500; Circ 189,500
Library Holdings: Bk Titles 68,000; Per Subs 135
Subject Interests: Ore hist
Automation Activity & Vendor Info: (Cataloging) Innovative Interfaces, Inc - Millennium; (Circulation) Innovative Interfaces, Inc - Millennium; (OPAC) Innovative Interfaces, Inc - Millennium
Wireless access
Partic in Chemeketa Cooperative Regional Library Service
Open Mon-Wed 10-7, Thurs & Fri 10-5, Sat 10-3
Friends of the Library Group

DAYTON

P MARY GILKEY CITY LIBRARY*, 416 Ferry St, 97114-9774. (Mail add: PO Box 339, 97114-0339), SAN 329-7586. Tel: 503-864-2221. FAX: 503-864-2956. *Librn,* Cyndi Park; E-mail: cpark@ci.dayton.or.us; Staff 1 (MLS 1)
Founded 1923. Pop 2,495
Library Holdings: Bk Vols 12,000; Per Subs 10
Automation Activity & Vendor Info: (Cataloging) SirsiDynix; (Circulation) SirsiDynix; (OPAC) SirsiDynix
Function: 24/7 Online cat, Bks on CD, Computers for patron use, E-Reserves, Free DVD rentals, Magazines, Movies, Online cat
Partic in Chemeketa Cooperative Regional Library Service
Open Mon-Fri 9-5

DEXTER

S CASCADE FOOTHILLS LIBRARY*, 39095 Dexter Rd, 97431. (Mail add: PO Box 12, 97431-0012). Tel: 541-937-2625. E-mail: cfllib@epud.net. *Board Pres,* Cathy Leonardo; Tel: 541-744-1289; *Dir,* Position Currently Open
Library Holdings: Audiobooks 200; CDs 50; DVDs 100; Large Print Bks 200; Bk Vols 8,000; Videos 60
Wireless access
Function: CD-ROM, Home delivery & serv to seniorr ctr & nursing homes, Homebound delivery serv, Homework prog, Prog for adults, Prog for children & young adult, Spoken cassettes & CDs, Spoken cassettes & DVDs, Summer reading prog, VHS videos, Wheelchair accessible, Workshops
Open Mon 2-6, Wed 1-6, Thurs 10-4, Fri 10-1
Restriction: Private libr
Friends of the Library Group

ECHO

P ECHO PUBLIC LIBRARY, 20 S Bonanza St, 97826. (Mail add: PO Box 9, 97826-0009), SAN 358-0539. Tel: 541-376-6038. FAX: 541-376-6040. E-mail: echopubliclibrary@gmail.com. Web Site: echo-oregon.com/library. *Dir,* Dave Slaght; E-mail: dave@echo-oregon.com; *Librn,* Anna Lemmon; E-mail: echopubliclibrary@gmail.com
Library Holdings: Audiobooks 120; Bk Vols 12,000; Per Subs 20; Videos 1,100
Wireless access
Mem of Umatilla County Special Library District
Open Mon-Fri 9-5

ELGIN

P ELGIN PUBLIC LIBRARY*, 1699 Division St, 97827. SAN 314-0830. Tel: 541-437-2860. FAX: 541-437-0997. E-mail: publiclibrary@cityofelginor.org. Web Site: cityofelginor.org/city-library. *Libr Dir,* Michele Timmons; E-mail: mtimmons@cityofelginor.org; Staff 1 (Non-MLS 1)
Founded 1911. Pop 2,600
Library Holdings: Audiobooks 1,081; DVDs 785; Bk Vols 16,565
Special Collections: Northwest
Wireless access
Function: Computers for patron use, Homebound delivery serv, ILL available, Magnifiers for reading, Mail & tel request accepted, Music CDs, Prog for children & young adult, Spoken cassettes & CDs, Summer reading prog, Tax forms, VHS videos, Wheelchair accessible
Open Mon, Tues & Fri 1-6, Wed 2-8, Thurs 10-6

ENTERPRISE

P ENTERPRISE PUBLIC LIBRARY*, 101 NE First St, 97828-1173. SAN 314-0849. Tel: 541-426-3906. E-mail: enterpl@eoni.com. Web Site: www.enterpriseoregon.org/index.php/services/public-library. *City Librn,* Denine Rautenstrauch
Founded 1911. Pop 3,199; Circ 20,000
Library Holdings: Bk Vols 17,000; Per Subs 57
Automation Activity & Vendor Info: (Cataloging) Follett Software; (Circulation) Follett Software
Wireless access
Open Mon-Fri 10-6, Sat 10-3

P WALLOWA COUNTY LIBRARY*, 207 NW Logan, 97828. SAN 314-0857. Tel: 541-426-3969. FAX: 541-426-3969. Interlibrary Loan Service E-mail: wclib@eoni.com. Web Site: co.wallowa.or.us/community-services/library. *Dir,* Susan Polumsky; Staff 1 (Non-MLS 1)

Founded 1964. Pop 3,140; Circ 6,633
Library Holdings: Bks on Deafness & Sign Lang 22; Bk Vols 21,000
Subject Interests: Local hist, Nez Perce Indians, Ore hist, Pac NW hist
Restriction: Pub access by telephone only
Branches: 2
IMNAHA BRANCH, Imnaha Hwy, Imnaha, 97842. Tel: 541-577-2308. E-mail: imnahalib@gmail.com. *Br Mgr,* Keith Kirts
Library Holdings: Bk Vols 2,000
Open Mon 12-4, Sat 10-2
TROY BRANCH, 66247 Redmond Grade, 97828. Tel: 541-828-7788. FAX: 541-828-7748. *Br Mgr,* Jane Curry
Library Holdings: AV Mats 1,500; Bk Vols 1,800
Open Sat 9-5
Bookmobiles: 2

ESTACADA

P ESTACADA PUBLIC LIBRARY, 825 NW Wade St, 97023. SAN 314-0865. Tel: 503-630-8273. E-mail: eslibrary@lincc.org. Web Site: www.cityofestacada.org/library. *Libr Dir,* Michele Kinnamon; E-mail: michelek@lincc.org; *Ad,* Leslie Pearson; E-mail: lpearson@lincc.org; *Youth Serv Librn,* Deborah VanDetta; E-mail: dvandetta@lincc.org; *Circ Mgr,* Sarah Hibbert; E-mail: shibbert@lincc.org; Staff 6.5 (MLS 1.5, Non-MLS 5)
Founded 1904. Pop 18,500; Circ 290,750
Library Holdings: AV Mats 16,384; CDs 5,838; DVDs 3,285; Large Print Bks 734; Bk Vols 65,000; Per Subs 223; Talking Bks 2,538; Videos 3,552
Special Collections: Estacada History
Automation Activity & Vendor Info: (Acquisitions) SirsiDynix; (Cataloging) SirsiDynix; (Circulation) SirsiDynix; (ILL) OCLC; (OPAC) SirsiDynix
Wireless access
Function: Audiobks via web, Bks on cassette, Bks on CD, Children's prog, Computers for patron use, Electronic databases & coll, Free DVD rentals, ILL available, Internet access, Magnifiers for reading, Mail & tel request accepted, Museum passes, Music CDs, Online cat, Online ref, Outside serv via phone, mail, e-mail & web, OverDrive digital audio bks, Photocopying/Printing, Prog for children & young adult, Ref & res, Ref serv available, Summer reading prog, Tax forms, Teen prog, Telephone ref, VHS videos
Partic in Library Information Network of Clackamas County
Open Mon, Tue, Thurs & Fri 11-5, Wed 11-7, Sat 11-3
Friends of the Library Group

EUGENE

P EUGENE PUBLIC LIBRARY*, Downtown Library, 100 W Tenth Ave, 97401. SAN 314-0881. Tel: 541-682-5450. FAX: 541-682-5898. E-mail: LibraryAskUs@ci.eugene.or.us. Web Site: www.eugene-or.gov/library. *Libr Dir,* Will O'Hearn; Tel: 541-682-5363, E-mail: wohearn@eugene-or.gov; *Adult Serv Mgr,* Erin Finot; *Br Serv Mgr,* Angie Bray; *Circ Mgr,* Maresa Kirk; *Computer Serv Mgr,* Shawn Grant; *Customer Experience Mgr,* LaVena Nohrenberg; *Finance Mgr,* Darry Beal; *Tech Serv Mgr,* Kristynn Johnson; *Youth Serv Mgr,* Kristen Thorp; *Spec Projects,* Nancy Horner; Staff 99.2 (MLS 18.4, Non-MLS 80.8)
Founded 1904. Pop 156,295; Circ 3,000,000. Sal $7,387,935
Library Holdings: AV Mats 89,066; e-books 30,444; Electronic Media & Resources 20,552; Bk Titles 401,616; Per Subs 398
Special Collections: State Document Depository
Automation Activity & Vendor Info: (Acquisitions) Innovative Interfaces, Inc; (Cataloging) Innovative Interfaces, Inc; (Circulation) Innovative Interfaces, Inc; (OPAC) Innovative Interfaces, Inc
Wireless access
Special Services for the Deaf - ADA equip; Assisted listening device; Assistive tech; Coll on deaf educ; Sign lang interpreter upon request for prog; Staff with knowledge of sign lang; Video relay services
Special Services for the Blind - Accessible computers; Assistive/Adapted tech devices, equip & products; Bks on CD; Braille equip; Braille paper; Digital talking bk; Extensive large print coll; Home delivery serv; Internet workstation with adaptive software; Large screen computer & software; Large type calculator; Low vision equip; Magnifiers; Multimedia ref serv (large print, Braille using CD-ROM tech); Networked computers with assistive software; PC for people with disabilities; Rental typewriters & computers; Screen enlargement software for people with visual disabilities; Screen reader software; Text reader; ZoomText magnification & reading software
Open Mon-Thurs 10-8, Fri-Sun 10-6
Friends of the Library Group
Branches: 2
BETHEL BRANCH, 1990 Echo Hollow Rd, 97402-7004. *Br Mgr,* Angela Bray; Staff 6.4 (MLS 0.5, Non-MLS 5.9)
Founded 2000
Special Services for the Deaf - ADA equip; Assistive tech; Bks on deafness & sign lang; Sign lang interpreter upon request for prog
Special Services for the Blind - ABE/GED & braille classes for the visually impaired; Assistive/Adapted tech devices, equip & products; Bks on CD; Digital talking bk; Internet workstation with adaptive software; Large print bks; Screen enlargement software for people with visual disabilities; ZoomText magnification & reading software
Open Tues-Thurs 2-6, Fri & Sat 11-6
SHELDON BRANCH, 1566 Coburg Rd, 97401-4802. *Br Mgr,* Angela Bray; Staff 6.3 (MLS 0.5, Non-MLS 5.8)
Founded 2000
Special Services for the Deaf - ADA equip; Assistive tech; Bks on deafness & sign lang; Sign lang interpreter upon request for prog
Special Services for the Blind - Assistive/Adapted tech devices, equip & products; Bks on CD; Digital talking bk; Internet workstation with adaptive software; Large print bks; Screen enlargement software for people with visual disabilities; ZoomText magnification & reading software
Open Tues-Thurs 2-6, Fri & Sat 11-6

C GUTENBERG COLLEGE*, McKenzie Study Center, 1883 University St, 97403. Tel: 541-683-5141. E-mail: office@gutenberg.edu. Web Site: msc.gutenberg.edu. *Supvr,* Ron Julian
Founded 1979
Library Holdings: Bk Vols 2,600
Open Mon-Fri 8:30am-Midnight

J LANE COMMUNITY COLLEGE LIBRARY*, Library-Center Bldg, 4000 E 30th Ave, 97405-0640. SAN 314-0903. Tel: 541-463-5220. Circulation Tel: 541-463-5273. Interlibrary Loan Service Tel: 541-463-3168. Reference Tel: 541-463-5355. Administration Tel: 541-463-5770. FAX: 541-463-4150. E-mail: library@lanecc.edu. Web Site: library.lanecc.edu. *Dean of Libr,* Ian Coronado; E-mail: coronadoi@lanecc.edu; *Ref Serv,* Claire Dannenbaum; Tel: 541-463-5357, E-mail: dannenbaumc@lanecc.edu; *Ref Serv,* David Doctor; Tel: 541-463-5278, E-mail: doctord@lanecc.edu; *Ref Serv,* Jen Ferro; Tel: 541-463-5825, E-mail: ferroj@lanecc.edu; *Ref Serv,* Meggie Wright; Tel: 541-463-5867, E-mail: wrightm@lanecc.edu
Founded 1964. Enrl 26,176; Fac 508; Highest Degree: Associate
Special Collections: English as a Second Language
Automation Activity & Vendor Info: (Acquisitions) Ex Libris Group; (Cataloging) Ex Libris Group; (Circulation) Ex Libris Group; (Course Reserve) Ex Libris Group; (OPAC) Ex Libris Group; (Serials) Ex Libris Group
Wireless access
Function: ILL available, Photocopying/Printing, Ref serv available, Wheelchair accessible
Partic in OCLC Online Computer Library Center, Inc; Orbis Cascade Alliance
Special Services for the Deaf - Bks on deafness & sign lang; Closed caption videos
Special Services for the Blind - Closed circuit TV; Computer with voice synthesizer for visually impaired persons
Open Mon-Thurs 8-6, Fri 8-5
Restriction: In-house use for visitors

GL LANE COUNTY LAW LIBRARY*, Lane County Public Service Bldg, 125 E Eighth Ave, 97401. SAN 314-0911. Tel: 541-682-4337. FAX: 541-682-4315. E-mail: lclawlib@lanecountyor.gov. Web Site: www.lanecountyor.gov/lawlibrary.
Founded 1948
Library Holdings: Bk Vols 19,200; Per Subs 10
Special Collections: Oregon Law
Automation Activity & Vendor Info: (Cataloging) LibraryWorld, Inc
Wireless access
Open Mon-Fri 8-12 & 1-5

CR NEW HOPE CHRISTIAN COLLEGE*, Flint Memorial Library, 2155 Bailey Hill Rd, 97405. SAN 314-0873. Tel: 541-485-1780, Ext 3309. FAX: 541-343-5801. E-mail: library@newhope.edu. Web Site: www.newhope.edu/library. *Libr Mgr,* Uilani Cordeiro; Staff 1 (MLS 1)
Founded 1925. Enrl 200; Fac 18; Highest Degree: Bachelor
Special Collections: Flint Coll
Automation Activity & Vendor Info: (Cataloging) EOS International; (Circulation) EOS International; (Course Reserve) EOS International; (ILL) OCLC WorldShare Interlibrary Loan; (OPAC) EOS International
Wireless access
Open Mon-Thurs 8:30am-10pm, Fri 8:30-5, Sat 2-8, Sun 6pm-10pm

CR NORTHWEST CHRISTIAN UNIVERSITY*, Edward P Kellenberger Library, 1188 Kincade, 97401. (Mail add: 828 E 11th Ave, 97401), SAN 314-0938. Tel: 541-684-7235. Circulation Tel: 541-684-7233. Interlibrary Loan Service Tel: 541-684-7234. Reference Tel: 541-684-7278. Toll Free Tel: 877-463-6622. FAX: 541-684-7307. E-mail: librarian@nwcu.edu. Web Site: www.nwcu.edu/academics/library. *Dir,* Steve Silver; Tel: 541-684-7237, E-mail: ssilver@nwcu.edu; *Ref & Instruction Librn,* Scott Gallagher-Starr; E-mail: sgallagherstarr@nwcu.edu; *Supvr, Circ, Supvr, ILL* Karen Head; E-mail: khead@nwcu.edu; *Tech Serv Supvr,* Lindsey Quigley;

Tel: 541-684-7246, E-mail: lquigley@nwcu.edu; Staff 4 (MLS 2, Non-MLS 2)
Founded 1895. Enrl 623; Fac 53; Highest Degree: Master
Library Holdings: AV Mats 11,147; Bk Vols 74,000; Per Subs 109
Special Collections: Christian Church History (Disciples of Christ, Discipliana); Museum Coll of African, Asian & Northwest Pioneer Artifacts Archives; Museum Coll of English Bible (Bushnell Coll), rare bks & Bibles; William E. Paul English Bible Coll
Subject Interests: Biblical studies, Bus & mgt, Counseling, Teacher educ
Automation Activity & Vendor Info: (Acquisitions) Ex Libris Group; (Cataloging) Ex Libris Group; (Circulation) Ex Libris Group; (Course Reserve) Ex Libris Group; (ILL) OCLC; (OPAC) Ex Libris Group; (Serials) Ex Libris Group
Wireless access
Partic in Council for Christian Colleges & Universities; Northwest Association of Private Colleges & Universities; OCLC Online Computer Library Center, Inc; Online Private Academic Library Link
Open Mon-Thurs 8am-10pm, Fri 8-5, Sun 3-8
Friends of the Library Group

S OREGON RESEARCH INSTITUTE LIBRARY*, 1776 Millrace Dr, 97403. SAN 325-8122. Tel: 541-484-2123. FAX: 541-484-1108. Web Site: www.ori.org. *Librn,* Megan Juenemann; E-mail: meganj@ori.org; Staff 2 (MLS 2)
Library Holdings: Bk Vols 5,000; Per Subs 85
Subject Interests: Adolescence, Behav sci, Chronic disease, Eating disorders, Psychol, Substance abuse, Tobacco cessation
Automation Activity & Vendor Info: (Cataloging) Inmagic, Inc.; (Circulation) Inmagic, Inc.; (OPAC) Inmagic, Inc.; (Serials) Inmagic, Inc.
Wireless access
Partic in OCLC Online Computer Library Center, Inc
Restriction: Open to staff only

C UNIVERSITY OF OREGON LIBRARIES*, Knight Library, 1501 Kincaid St, 97403-1299. SAN 357-8976. Tel: 541-346-3053. Circulation Tel: 541-346-3065. Interlibrary Loan Service Tel: 541-346-3055. Reference Tel: 541-346-1818. FAX: 541-346-3485. E-mail: libref@uoregon.edu. Web Site: www.libweb.uoregon.edu. *Interim Dean of Libr,* Mark Watson; E-mail: mrwatson@uoregon.edu; *Asst Dean,* Susan Breakenridge; E-mail: sjb1@uoregon.edu; *Interim Assoc Dean,* Ann Miller; *Head, Access Serv,* David Ketchum; Staff 74 (MLS 52, Non-MLS 22)
Founded 1883. Enrl 21,507; Fac 1,209; Highest Degree: Doctorate
Library Holdings: e-books 291,531; e-journals 70,866; Microforms 4,198,103; Bk Titles 1,932,872; Bk Vols 3,138,936; Per Subs 46,879
Special Collections: American History (The American West), ms; American Missions & Missionaries, ms; Children's Literature, Book & Magazine Illustrations, bks, ms; East Asian Literature & Art; Esperanto; Politics (20th Century American Politics, particularly Conservatism), ms; Zeppelins. Canadian and Provincial; State Document Depository; UN Document Depository; US Document Depository
Subject Interests: Archit, Art, Law, Math, Music, Sci
Automation Activity & Vendor Info: (Acquisitions) Innovative Interfaces, Inc; (Cataloging) Innovative Interfaces, Inc; (Circulation) Innovative Interfaces, Inc; (Course Reserve) Innovative Interfaces, Inc; (ILL) OCLC ILLiad; (Media Booking) Innovative Interfaces, Inc; (OPAC) OCLC WorldShare Interlibrary Loan; (Serials) Innovative Interfaces, Inc
Wireless access
Partic in Association of Research Libraries; Center for Research Libraries; Coun of Libr Info Resources; Greater Western Library Alliance; OCLC Online Computer Library Center, Inc; Orbis Cascade Alliance; Pacific Rim Digital Library Alliance
Open Mon-Thurs 8am-Midnight, Fri 8-7, Sat 11-7, Sun 11am-Midnight

Departmental Libraries:

DESIGN LIBRARY, 200 Lawrence Hall, 1190 Franklin Blvd, 97403-1299, SAN 357-900X. Tel: 541-346-3637. FAX: 541-346-2205. E-mail: designlibrary@uoregon.edu. Web Site: library.uoregon.edu/design. *Interim Assoc Dean, Libr Serv, Res Serv,* Nancy Cunningham; E-mail: nancyc@uoregon.edu; *Head Librn,* Andrew Wang; E-mail: awang2@uoregon.edu; Staff 3 (MLS 3)
Founded 1915
Library Holdings: Bk Vols 52,000
Open Mon-Thurs 8-8, Fri 8-5, Sat 1-5, Sun 12-8

CL JOHN E JAQUA LAW LIBRARY, William W Knight Law Ctr, 2nd Flr, 1515 Agate St, 97403. (Mail add: 1221 University of Oregon, 97403-1221), SAN 357-9093. Tel: 541-346-1654, 541-346-3088. FAX: 541-346-1669. E-mail: lawcirc@uoregon.edu. Web Site: library.uoregon.edu/law. *Dir,* Mary Ann Hyatt; Tel: 541-346-3097, E-mail: mahyatt@uoregon.edu; *Libr Mgr,* Hana Chan; Tel: 541-346-8271, E-mail: hchan2@uoregon.edu; *Ref Librn,* Jaye Barlous; Tel: 541-346-1901, E-mail: barlous@uoregon.edu; *Ref Librn,* Angus Nesbit; Tel: 541-346-1673, E-mail: anesbit@law.uoregon.edu; *Ref Librn,* Kelly Reynolds; Tel: 541-346-1567, E-mail: kellycr@oregon.edu; *Ref Librn,* Ilona Tsutsui; Tel: 541-346-1657, E-mail: itsutsui@uoregon.edu; *Evening Coordr,* Ben Farrell; Tel: 541-346-1658, E-mail: bfarrell@uoregon.edu; *Ser Spec,* Elena Chertok; Tel: 541-346-1659, E-mail: echertok@uoregon.edu; *Acq Tech,* Lisa Levitt; Tel: 541-346-3802, E-mail: llevitt@uoregon.edu; *Metadata Serv Tech,* Diane Haas; Tel: 541-346-1656, E-mail: dkhaas@uoregon.edu; Staff 12 (MLS 6, Non-MLS 6)
Founded 1893
Library Holdings: e-books 32,533; e-journals 1,950; Bk Vols 206,065; Per Subs 2,264
Open Mon-Thurs (Winter) 7:30am-Midnight, Fri 7:30am-9pm, Sat 9-9, Sun 9am-Midnight; Mon-Thurs (Summer) 8am-9pm, Fri 8-5, Sat & Sun Noon-9

MATHEMATICS, 218 Fenton Hall, 97403. (Mail add: 1299 University of Oregon, 97403), SAN 357-9131. Tel: 541-346-3023. FAX: 541-346-3012. E-mail: mathlib@uoregon.edu. Web Site: www.libweb.uoregon.edu/scilib/mathlib. *Head of Libr,* Lara Nesselroad; Tel: 541-346-2664, E-mail: lnessel@uoregon.edu; *Ref Librn, Sci Librn,* Ann Zeidman-Karpinski; Tel: 541-346-2663, E-mail: annie@uoregon.edu
Founded 1980. Highest Degree: Doctorate
Library Holdings: Bk Vols 26,000; Per Subs 350
Open Mon-Thurs 11-7, Fri 11-4, Sun Noon-5

ALLAN PRICE SCIENCE COMMONS & RESEARCH LIBRARY, Onyx Bridge, Lower Level, 1344 Franklin Blvd, 97403, SAN 357-9158. Tel: 541-346-3075. Information Services Tel: 541-346-2661. FAX: 541-346-3012. E-mail: scidel@uoregon.edu. Web Site: library.uoregon.edu/price-science-commons-research-library. *Dir, Br,* Nancy Cunningham; Tel: 541-346-1876, E-mail: nancyc@uoregon.edu; *Librn,* Ann Zeidman-Karpinski; Tel: 541-346-2663, E-mail: annie@uoregon.edu; *Ref Librn,* Dean Walton; Tel: 541-346-2871, E-mail: dpwalton@uoregon.edu. Subject Specialists: *Computer sci, Environ studies, Math,* Ann Zeidman-Karpinski; *Biology, Molecular biol, Neuroscience,* Dean Walton; Staff 8 (MLS 4, Non-MLS 4)
Founded 1968. Highest Degree: Doctorate
Library Holdings: Bk Vols 175,000; Per Subs 2,500
Open Mon-Thurs 8am-10pm, Fri 8-6, Sat Noon-6, Sun 11-10

FAIRVIEW

S HYSTER-YALE MATERIALS HANDLING INC*, CBDC Technical Support Resource Center, 4000 NE Blue Lake Rd, 97025. SAN 314-1594. Tel: 503-721-6324. FAX: 503-721-1364. Web Site: www.hyster-yale.com. *Library Contact, Tech Support,* Becky McWrightman. Subject Specialists: *Engr,* Becky McWrightman
Founded 1961
Library Holdings: Bk Titles 16,000; Bk Vols 20,000; Per Subs 60
Subject Interests: Construction safety, Domestic societies, Engr design for mat handling equip, Foreign societies, Indust safety
Restriction: Not open to pub

FLORENCE

P SIUSLAW PUBLIC LIBRARY DISTRICT, 1460 Ninth St, 97439. SAN 314-0954. Tel: 541-997-3132. Circulation Tel: 541-997-3132, Ext 201, 541-997-3132, Ext 203. Reference Tel: 541-997-3132, Ext 205. Administration Tel: 541-997-3132, Ext 211. Automation Services Tel: 541-997-3132, Ext 208. FAX: 541-997-6473. E-mail: ref@siuslawlibrary.org. Web Site: www.siuslawlibrary.info. *Libr Dir,* Meg C Spencer; E-mail: meg@siuslawlibrary.org; *Asst Libr Dir, Ch Serv,* Gayle Waiss; *Circ,* Lynda Green; *Ref Serv, Ad,* Kevin Mittge; Staff 5 (MLS 3, Non-MLS 2)
Founded 1985. Pop 17,146; Circ 202,526. Sal $377,180 (Prof $180,996)
Library Holdings: AV Mats 12,595; e-books 30,174; High Interest/Low Vocabulary Bk Vols 600; Bk Vols 84,721; Per Subs 334
Special Collections: Newspapers published in Florence, 1891 to date, micro; Oregon Past & Present Coll; Reference Library of Frank Herbert. Oral History
Automation Activity & Vendor Info: (Cataloging) OCLC; (Circulation) SirsiDynix-WorkFlows; (ILL) SirsiDynix-WorkFlows; (OPAC) SirsiDynix-iBistro
Wireless access
Function: Art exhibits, Audiobks via web, AV serv, Bk club(s), Bks on cassette, Bks on CD, Computer training, Computers for patron use, Digital talking bks, Electronic databases & coll, Free DVD rentals, Genealogy discussion group, Home delivery & serv to seniorr ctr & nursing homes, Homebound delivery serv, ILL available, Internet access, Large print keyboards, Magnifiers for reading, Mail & tel request accepted, Music CDs, Online ref, Outreach serv, OverDrive digital audio bks, Photocopying/Printing, Preschool outreach, Prog for adults, Prog for children & young adult, Ref & res, Ref serv available, Spoken cassettes & CDs, Spoken cassettes & DVDs, Story hour, Summer reading prog, Tax forms, Telephone ref, VHS videos, Wheelchair accessible
Publications: The Bookmark (Newsletter)
Open Mon & Thurs-Sat 10-6, Tues & Wed 10-8, Sun 1-5
Friends of the Library Group

Branches: 1
MAPLETON BRANCH, 88148 Riverview Ave, Mapleton, 97453. (Mail add: 1460 Ninth St, 97439). Tel: 541-268-4033. E-mail: mapleton@siuslawlibrary.org. *Br Mgr,* Kevin K Mittge; Staff 1 (Non-MLS 1)
Library Holdings: Bk Titles 3,000; Per Subs 12
Automation Activity & Vendor Info: (Acquisitions) SirsiDynix
Open Tues-Sat 12-5

FOREST GROVE

P FOREST GROVE CITY LIBRARY*, 2114 Pacific Ave, 97116. SAN 314-0962. Tel: 503-992-3247. Reference Tel: 503-992-3337. FAX: 503-992-3333. E-mail: fgl-reference@wccls.org. Web Site: www.forestgrove-or.gov/library, www.wccls.org/libraries/forestgrove. *Dir,* Colleen Winters; Tel: 503-992-3246; Staff 12 (MLS 4, Non-MLS 8)
Founded 1909. Pop 22,500; Circ 292,198
Library Holdings: AV Mats 13,520; Bk Vols 87,788; Per Subs 212
Special Collections: Large Print Coll; Spanish Language Coll
Automation Activity & Vendor Info: (Acquisitions) Innovative Interfaces, Inc; (Cataloging) Innovative Interfaces, Inc; (Circulation) Innovative Interfaces, Inc; (OPAC) Innovative Interfaces, Inc
Wireless access
Partic in Washington County Cooperative Library Services
Open Mon-Wed 10-8, Thurs-Sat 10-5
Friends of the Library Group

C PACIFIC UNIVERSITY LIBRARY*, 2043 College Way, 97116. SAN 357-9182. Tel: 503-352-1400. Interlibrary Loan Service Tel: 503-352-1413. Reference Tel: 503-352-1418. Administration Tel: 503-352-1402. FAX: 503-352-1416. Reference E-mail: reference@pacificu.edu. Web Site: www.pacificu.edu/library. *Dir, Univ Librn,* Isaac Gilman; Tel: 503-352-1401, E-mail: gilmani@pacificu.edu; *Dir, Educ Tech & Curricular Innovation,* Al Weiss; Tel: 503-352-1417, E-mail: alweiss@pacificu.edu; *Archives & Spec Coll Librn,* Eva Guggemos; Tel: 503-352-1415, E-mail: guggemos@pacificu.edu; *Health Sci Librn,* Nancy Henderson; Tel: 503-352-7208, Fax: 503-352-7230, E-mail: henderson@pacificu.edu; *Libr Syst & Applications Librn,* Maria McShane; Tel: 503-352-1404, E-mail: maria.mcshane@pacificu.edu; *Res & Instrul Serv Librn,* Lynda R Irons; Tel: 503-352-1409, E-mail: lrirons@pacificu.edu; *Scholarly Communications & Res Serv Librn,* Johanna Meetz; Tel: 503-352-1488, E-mail: jmeetz@pacificu.edu; *Coll Mgt Serv,* Rachel Arkoosh; Tel: 503-352-1411, E-mail: rachel.arkoosh@pacificu.edu. Subject Specialists: *Archives, Soc sci,* Eva Guggemos; *Health sci,* Nancy Henderson; *Humanities, Natural sci,* Lynda R Irons; Staff 20 (MLS 8, Non-MLS 12)
Founded 1849. Enrl 3,810; Fac 457; Highest Degree: Doctorate
Jul 2015-Jun 2016. Mats Exp $1,182,109. Sal $1,210,494
Library Holdings: e-books 286,556; e-journals 83,378; Bk Titles 160,873; Bk Vols 244,070; Per Subs 1,828
Special Collections: Oregon Hist. US Document Depository
Subject Interests: Arts & Sci, Health sci
Automation Activity & Vendor Info: (Acquisitions) Ex Libris Group; (Cataloging) Ex Libris Group; (Circulation) Ex Libris Group; (Course Reserve) Ex Libris Group; (Discovery) Ex Libris Group; (Serials) Ex Libris Group
Wireless access
Partic in OCLC Online Computer Library Center, Inc; Orbis Cascade Alliance
Open Mon-Thurs 7:30am-Midnight, Fri 7:30am-10pm, Sat 10-10, Sun 10am-Midnight

FOSSIL

P FOSSIL PUBLIC LIBRARY*, Fossil City Library, 401 Main St, 97830. (Mail add: PO Box 467, 97830-0487). Tel: 541-763-2046. FAX: 541-763-2124. E-mail: libraryfossil46@gmail.com. *Libr Dir,* Cathy Goldsmith
Library Holdings: AV Mats 228; Bk Titles 4,500
Open Tues-Thurs 1-4

GASTON

P GASTON COMMUNITY LIBRARY*, 116 Front St, 97119. (Mail add: PO Box 129, 97119-0129). Tel: 503-985-3464. FAX: 503-985-1014. *Librn,* Position Currently Open
Library Holdings: Audiobooks 81; AV Mats 20; CDs 80; DVDs 256; Large Print Bks 518; Bk Vols 16,743; Per Subs 5; Spec Interest Per Sub 1; Talking Bks 55; Videos 524
Automation Activity & Vendor Info: (Acquisitions) JayWil Software Development, Inc; (Cataloging) JayWil Software Development, Inc; (Circulation) JayWil Software Development, Inc
Wireless access
Open Tues & Thurs 2-6, Sat 11-1

GLADSTONE

P GLADSTONE PUBLIC LIBRARY*, 135 E Dartmouth St, 97027-2435. SAN 314-0970. Tel: 503-656-2411. FAX: 503-655-2438. Reference E-mail: gladstonepubliclibrary@gmail.com. Web Site: www.gladstonepubliclibrary.org. *Dir,* Mitzi Olson
Pop 17,859; Circ 178,150
Library Holdings: Bk Titles 46,000; Bk Vols 55,000; Per Subs 120
Automation Activity & Vendor Info: (Cataloging) SirsiDynix; (Circulation) SirsiDynix; (OPAC) SirsiDynix
Wireless access
Partic in Library Information Network of Clackamas County
Open Mon-Thurs 10-8, Fri & Sat 11-5:30, Sun 1-5
Friends of the Library Group

GOLD BEACH

P CURRY PUBLIC LIBRARY*, 94341 Third St, 97444. SAN 314-0989. Tel: 541-247-7246. FAX: 541-247-4411. E-mail: currylibrary@cplib.net. Web Site: www.currypubliclibrary.org. *Libr Dir,* Jeremy Skinner; E-mail: jeremy@cplib.net; *Cat Librn,* Jordan Popoff; E-mail: jordan@cplib.net; *Ch,* Alta Denton; E-mail: alta@cplib.net
Founded 1955. Pop 4,949; Circ 53,868
Library Holdings: Bk Vols 30,000; Per Subs 100
Automation Activity & Vendor Info: (Cataloging) TLC (The Library Corporation); (Circulation) TLC (The Library Corporation); (OPAC) TLC (The Library Corporation)
Wireless access
Open Mon-Thurs 10-7, Fri & Sat 10-5, Sun 12-4
Friends of the Library Group

GRANTS PASS

P JOSEPHINE COMMUNITY LIBRARY DISTRICT*, 200 NW C St, 97526-2094. (Mail add: PO Box 1684, 97528). SAN 357-9247. Tel: 541-476-0571. FAX: 541-479-0685. E-mail: info@josephinelibrary.org. Web Site: www.josephinelibrary.org. *Exec Dir,* Kate Lasky; Staff 13 (MLS 3, Non-MLS 10)
Founded 1913. Pop 81,026; Circ 295,476
Library Holdings: Audiobooks 8,000; AV Mats 5,160; CDs 1,000; DVDs 4,400; e-books 25,000; Electronic Media & Resources 24; Large Print Bks 2,200; Bk Vols 145,800; Per Subs 157; Videos 4,200
Subject Interests: Genealogy, Ore hist
Automation Activity & Vendor Info: (Cataloging) Innovative Interfaces, Inc; (Circulation) Innovative Interfaces, Inc; (OPAC) Innovative Interfaces, Inc
Wireless access
Function: Bks on CD, Children's prog, Computers for patron use, E-Reserves, Electronic databases & coll, Free DVD rentals, ILL available, Life-long learning prog for all ages, Magazines, Music CDs, Online cat, OverDrive digital audio bks, Photocopying/Printing, Prog for children & young adult, Ref serv available, Spoken cassettes & DVDs, Story hour, Summer reading prog, Teen prog, VHS videos, Wheelchair accessible, Writing prog
Publications: News of the Grants Pass, Illinois Valley, Williams & Wolf Creek libraries (Newsletter)
Open Tues & Thurs 2-7, Wed & Fri 11-4, Sat Noon-4
Restriction: ID required to use computers (Ltd hrs)
Friends of the Library Group
Branches: 3
ILLINOIS VALLEY, 209 W Palmer St, Cave Junction, 97523. SAN 357-9271. Tel: 541-592-4778. Web Site: josephinelibrary.org/branches/illinois-valley. *Br Mgr,* Roberta Lee; E-mail: rlee@josephinelibrary.org
Library Holdings: Bk Vols 25,000
Open Wed 11-6, Thurs-Sat 11-5
Friends of the Library Group
WILLIAMS BRANCH, 20695 Williams Hwy, Williams, 97544. SAN 357-9301. Tel: 541-846-7020. Web Site: josephinelibrary.org/branchs/williams. *Br Mgr,* Ellie Avis; E-mail: eavis@josephinelibrary.org
Library Holdings: Bk Vols 7,000
Open Tues, Wed & Sat 1-6, Fri 11-4
Friends of the Library Group
WOLF CREEK BRANCH, 102 Ruth Ave, Wolf Creek, 97497. SAN 357-9336. Tel: 541-866-2606. Web Site: josephinelibrary.org/branches/wolf-creek. *Br Mgr,* Paige Gissel; E-mail: pgissel@josephinelibrary.org
Library Holdings: Bk Vols 7,000
Open Wed & Sat 1-6, Fri 11-4
Friends of the Library Group

S JOSEPHINE COUNTY HISTORICAL SOCIETY*, Research Library, 512 SW Fifth St, 97526. SAN 326-1891. Tel: 541-479-7827. Web Site: jocohistorical.org/research.php. *Exec Dir,* Position Currently Open
Founded 1960

Library Holdings: Bk Vols 945
Special Collections: Josephine County (Amos Voorhies Coll), photog
Subject Interests: Local hist
Function: Res libr
Publications: The Oldtimer (Newsletter)
Open Tues-Fri 10-4
Restriction: Not a lending libr

L JOSEPHINE COUNTY LAW LIBRARY*, Justice Bldg, 2nd Flr, 500 NW Sixth St, 97526. SAN 325-8343. Tel: 541-474-5488. FAX: 541-474-5223. Web Site: www.co.josephine.or.us/Page.asp?NavID=2081. *Law Librn,* Beecher Ellison; E-mail: bellison@co.josephine.or.us
Library Holdings: Bk Vols 15,000
Open Mon-Fri 8-12 & 1-5

J ROGUE COMMUNITY COLLEGE*, Redwood Campus Library, Wiseman Ctr, 3345 Redwood Hwy, 97527. SAN 314-0997. Tel: 541-956-7152. FAX: 541-471-3588. Web Site: go.roguecc.edu/department/rcc-libraries. *Dept Chair,* Robert Felthousen; E-mail: RFelthousen@roguecc.edu; *Head, Ref Serv,* Felishia Jenkins; Tel: 541-956-7131, E-mail: FJenkins@Roguecc.edu; *Head, Tech Serv,* Juan Rivera; Tel: 541-956-7148, E-mail: JRivera@Roguecc.edu; *Circ Serv Coordr,* Cessa Vichi; Tel: 541-956-7035, E-mail: CVichi@Roguecc.edu; Staff 7 (MLS 2, Non-MLS 5)
Founded 1971. Enrl 1,400; Fac 70
Library Holdings: Bk Titles 33,600; Per Subs 350
Special Collections: Oregon Outdoors
Subject Interests: Allied health, Nursing, Small bus
Automation Activity & Vendor Info: (Cataloging) Innovative Interfaces, Inc; (Circulation) Innovative Interfaces, Inc; (OPAC) Innovative Interfaces, Inc
Wireless access
Partic in OCLC Online Computer Library Center, Inc
Open Mon-Thurs 8-7, Fri 8-5
Friends of the Library Group
Departmental Libraries:
RIVERSIDE CAMPUS LIBRARY, 205 S Central, Medford, 97501. Tel: 541-245-7512. FAX: 541-774-1046. *Head Librn,* Tom Miller; E-mail: tmiller@roguecc.edu
Library Holdings: Bk Vols 55,000
Open Mon-Thurs 8-8, Fri 8-5, Sat 12-4
TABLE ROCK CAMPUS LIBRARY, 7800 Pacific Ave, White City, 97503. Tel: 541-245-7820. FAX: 541-245-7975. *Circ,* Bonnie Conard
Library Holdings: Bk Vols 900; Per Subs 13
Automation Activity & Vendor Info: (Course Reserve) Innovative Interfaces, Inc
Open Mon & Thurs 9-4, Tues & Wed 9-5

GRESHAM

J MT HOOD COMMUNITY COLLEGE LIBRARIES*, Gresham Campus, 26000 SE Stark St, 97030. SAN 314-1004. Tel: 503-491-7161. Reference Tel: 503-491-7516. FAX: 503-491-7389. Reference E-mail: reference@mhcc.edu. Web Site: www.mhcc.edu/library. *Dean of Libr,* Megan Dugan; Tel: 503-491-7652, E-mail: megan.dugan@mhcc.edu; *Fac Librn,* Sergio Lopez; Tel: 503-491-7694, E-mail: sergio.lopez@mhcc.edu; *Fac Librn,* Mark Peterson; Tel: 503-491-7693, E-mail: mark.peterson@mhcc.edu; *Fac Librn,* Lori Wamsley; Tel: 503-491-7150, E-mail: lori.wamsley@mhcc.edu; *Tech Serv Coordr,* Heather White; Tel: 503-491-7106, E-mail: heather.white@mhcc.edu; *Libr Tech Spec,* Matt Anderson; Tel: 503-491-7671, E-mail: matthew.anderson@mhcc.edu; Staff 6 (MLS 4, Non-MLS 2)
Founded 1965. Highest Degree: Associate
Library Holdings: AV Mats 3,760; e-books 1,824; Bk Titles 65,000; Per Subs 437
Automation Activity & Vendor Info: (Acquisitions) Innovative Interfaces, Inc; (Cataloging) Innovative Interfaces, Inc; (Circulation) Innovative Interfaces, Inc; (Course Reserve) Innovative Interfaces, Inc; (Media Booking) Innovative Interfaces, Inc; (OPAC) Innovative Interfaces, Inc; (Serials) Innovative Interfaces, Inc
Wireless access
Partic in Orbis Cascade Alliance
Open Mon-Thurs 7:30am-8pm, Fri 7:30-5, Sat 11-5
Departmental Libraries:
MAYWOOD CAMPUS, Community Skills Ctr, 10100 NE Prescott, Portland, 97220. Tel: 503-491-6122. *Tech Serv Coordr,* Heather White; E-mail: heather.white@mhcc.edu
Open Mon & Tues 10-7, Wed & Thurs 10-4, Sat 10-2

HARRISBURG

HARRISBURG PUBLIC LIBRARY*, 354 Smith St, 97446. (Mail add: PO Box 378, 97446). Tel: 541-995-6949. Web Site: www.ci.harrisburg.or.us/library. *Librn,* Cheryl Spangler; E-mail: cspangler@ci.harrisburg.or.us
Library Holdings: Bk Titles 6,500
Automation Activity & Vendor Info: (Acquisitions) Follett Software; (Cataloging) Follett Software; (OPAC) Follett Software
Wireless access
Open Mon 3-8, Tues-Thurs 12:30-5, Fri & Sat 10-2:30
Friends of the Library Group

HELIX

P HELIX PUBLIC LIBRARY*, 119 Columbia St, 97835. (Mail add: PO Box 324, 97835-0324), SAN 358-0504. Tel: 541-457-6130. E-mail: helixlibrary@helixtel.com. Web Site: helixlibrary.weebly.com. *Dir,* Annette Kubishta; Staff 1 (Non-MLS 1)
Founded 1906. Pop 270
Mem of Umatilla County Special Library District
Open Mon, Tues & Thurs 10-12 & 1-6
Friends of the Library Group

HERMISTON

P HERMISTON PUBLIC LIBRARY*, 235 E Gladys Ave, 97838. SAN 358-0563. Tel: 541-567-2882. FAX: 541-667-5055. E-mail: library@hermiston.or.us. Web Site: www.hermistonlibrary.us. *Dir,* Mark Rose; E-mail: mrose@hermiston.or.us; *Asst Dir,* Heidi Florenzen; *Pub Serv,* Kelly Martinez; *Tech Serv,* Leeann Baldwin; Staff 8.5 (MLS 1, Non-MLS 7.5)
Founded 1916. Pop 25,752; Circ 92,134
Automation Activity & Vendor Info: (Cataloging) Evergreen; (Circulation) Evergreen; (OPAC) Evergreen
Wireless access
Function: 24/7 Electronic res, 24/7 Online cat, Adult bk club, Art exhibits, Bilingual assistance for Spanish patrons, Bk club(s), Children's prog, Computers for patron use, Homebound delivery serv, ILL available, Internet access, Meeting rooms, Microfiche/film & reading machines, Online cat, OverDrive digital audio bks, Photocopying/Printing, Prog for adults, Prog for children & young adult, Ref serv available, Scanner, Story hour, Summer reading prog, Teen prog, Telephone ref, Wheelchair accessible, Writing prog
Partic in Sage Library System of Eastern Oregon
Special Services for the Blind - Bks on CD; Copier with enlargement capabilities; Large print bks; Talking bk serv referral
Open Mon-Thurs 10-8, Fri & Sat 10-5
Friends of the Library Group

HILLSBORO

P HILLSBORO PUBLIC LIBRARY*, Brookwood Library, 2850 NE Brookwood Pkwy, 97124. SAN 314-1837. Tel: 503-615-6500. FAX: 503-615-6601. TDD: 503-648-9181. E-mail: libraryfeedback@ci.hillsboro.or.us. Web Site: www.hillsboro-oregon.gov/library, www.wccls.org/libraries/hillsborobrookwood. *Libr Dir,* Stephanie Chase; Tel: 503-615-6609, E-mail: stephanie.chase@hillsboro-oregon.gov; *Asst Dir,* Karen Muller; Tel: 503-615-2480, E-mail: karen.muller@hillsboro-oregon.gov; *Circ Mgr,* Linda Osuna; Tel: 503-615-6610, E-mail: linda.osuna@hillsboro-oregon.gov; *Reader Serv Mgr,* Carol Reich; Tel: 503-615-6514
Founded 1914. Pop 133,000; Circ 2,829,680
Jul 2012-Jun 2013 Income (Main & Associated Libraries) $7,435,002, State $13,268, City $2,855,712, County $4,255,421, Locally Generated Income $310,601. Mats Exp $721,303, Books $435,218, Per/Ser (Incl. Access Fees) $32,472, AV Mat $252,113, Electronic Ref Mat (Incl. Access Fees) $1,500. Sal $3,532,267
Library Holdings: AV Mats 55,960; CDs 19,069; DVDs 38,014; Bk Vols 250,850; Per Subs 488
Automation Activity & Vendor Info: (Acquisitions) Innovative Interfaces, Inc; (Cataloging) Innovative Interfaces, Inc; (Circulation) Innovative Interfaces, Inc; (ILL) Innovative Interfaces, Inc; (OPAC) Innovative Interfaces, Inc
Wireless access
Special Services for the Deaf - TDD equip
Special Services for the Blind - Accessible computers; Assistive/Adapted tech devices, equip & products
Open Mon-Thurs 10-8, Fri-Sun 10-6
Friends of the Library Group
Branches: 1
SHUTE PARK BRANCH LIBRARY, 775 SE Tenth Ave, 97123, SAN 314-1020. FAX: 503-615-6501. Web Site: www.wccls.org/libraries/hillsboroshutepark. *Dir,* Stephanie Chase
Special Collections: Spanish Language Coll
Open Mon-Thurs 10-8, Fri-Sun 10-6
Friends of the Library Group

TUALITY HEALTHCARE
M HEALTH SCIENCES LIBRARY*, 335 SE Eighth Ave, 97123, SAN 326-3401. Tel: 503-681-1121. FAX: 503-681-1729. E-mail: tuality.library@tuality.org. *Librn,* Judith Hayes; E-mail:

judith.hayes@tuality.org; *Libr Tech,* Meredith I Solomon; E-mail: meredith.solomon@tuality.org; Staff 1 (Non-MLS 1)
Library Holdings: Bk Titles 750; Bk Vols 800; Per Subs 140
Subject Interests: Clinical med, Hospital admin, Nursing
Partic in Washington County Cooperative Library Services
Open Mon-Fri 9-5
Restriction: Open to others by appt, Staff use only

M TUALITY HEALTH INFORMATION RESOURCE CENTER*, 334 SE Eighth Ave, 97123-4201, SAN 371-3563. Tel: 503-681-1702. FAX: 503-681-1932. E-mail: tuality.library@tuality.org. Web Site: www.wccls.org. *Libr Serv Mgr,* Judith Hayes. Subject Specialists: *Consumer health, Med,* Judith Hayes; Staff 1.3 (MLS 1, Non-MLS 0.3)
Founded 1988
Oct 2012-Sept 2013 Income $70,000. Mats Exp $70,000
Library Holdings: Audiobooks 2; AV Mats 800; Bks on Deafness & Sign Lang 10; CDs 5; DVDs 250; e-books 1,700; e-journals 2,400; Electronic Media & Resources 10; Large Print Bks 5; Bk Titles 900; Per Subs 5
Special Collections: Model/Poster Coll
Subject Interests: Consumer health
Automation Activity & Vendor Info: (Cataloging) Innovative Interfaces, Inc; (Circulation) Innovative Interfaces, Inc; (OPAC) Innovative Interfaces, Inc
Function: Computers for patron use, Doc delivery serv, Electronic databases & coll, Free DVD rentals, Health sci info serv, ILL available, Internet access, Mail & tel request accepted, Ref serv available, Spanish lang bks, Telephone ref
Partic in National Network of Libraries of Medicine Region 5
Open Mon, Tues & Thurs 11-3, Wed & Fri 1-5
Restriction: Open to pub for ref & circ; with some limitations

GL WASHINGTON COUNTY LAW LIBRARY*, 111 NE Lincoln St, 97124. SAN 314-1039. Tel: 503-846-8880. FAX: 503-846-3515. E-mail: lawlibrary@co.washington.or.us. Web Site: www.co.washington.or.us/lawlibrary. *Law Librn,* Lee Van Duzer; Staff 2 (MLS 2)
Founded 1926
Library Holdings: Bk Vols 17,000
Subject Interests: Legal res, Ore
Automation Activity & Vendor Info: (Cataloging) LibraryWorld, Inc
Wireless access
Open Mon-Fri 8-5

INDEPENDENCE

P INDEPENDENCE PUBLIC LIBRARY, 175 Monmouth St, 97351. SAN 314-1047. Tel: 503-838-1811. FAX: 503-838-4486. E-mail: library@ci.independence.or.us. Web Site: www.ci.independence.or.us/library. *Librn,* Jolene Hall; Staff 2 (MLS 1, Non-MLS 1)
Founded 1912. Pop 7,200; Circ 77,500
Library Holdings: AV Mats 5,958; Bk Vols 32,408; Per Subs 57
Special Collections: Local History Coll; Oregon History Coll; Spanish Language Coll
Automation Activity & Vendor Info: (Acquisitions) Innovative Interfaces, Inc; (Cataloging) Innovative Interfaces, Inc; (Circulation) Innovative Interfaces, Inc; (OPAC) Innovative Interfaces, Inc
Wireless access
Function: Audiobks via web, AV serv, Bilingual assistance for Spanish patrons, Bks on cassette, Bks on CD, CD-ROM, Children's prog, Computers for patron use, Homebound delivery serv, ILL available, Music CDs, Online cat, Photocopying/Printing, Prog for adults, Prog for children & young adult, Spoken cassettes & CDs, Spoken cassettes & DVDs, Summer reading prog, Tax forms, Teen prog, Telephone ref, VHS videos, Wheelchair accessible
Partic in Chemeketa Cooperative Regional Library Service
Open Mon & Thurs 10-7, Tues, Wed & Fri 1-7, Sat 10-5
Friends of the Library Group

JEFFERSON

P JEFFERSON PUBLIC LIBRARY, 150 N Second St, Ste B, 97352. (Mail add: PO Box 1068, 97352-1068), SAN 376-3323. Tel: 541-327-3826. E-mail: jeffpl@ccrls.org. Web Site: jeffersonpubliclibrary.org. *Dir,* Amy Isted; E-mail: amy.isted@ccrls.org
Founded 1938. Pop 2,500; Circ 12,854
Library Holdings: Bk Vols 18,000; Per Subs 10
Subject Interests: State hist
Automation Activity & Vendor Info: (Cataloging) Innovative Interfaces, Inc; (Circulation) Innovative Interfaces, Inc; (OPAC) Innovative Interfaces, Inc
Wireless access
Partic in Chemeketa Cooperative Regional Library Service
Open Tues-Thurs 10-6, Sat 10-4
Friends of the Library Group

JOHN DAY

P GRANT COUNTY LIBRARY, 507 S Canyon Blvd, 97845-1050. SAN 314-1055. Tel: 541-575-1992. E-mail: grant047@ortelco.net. Web Site: www.grantcountylibrary.net. *Dir,* Vicki Waters
Pop 8,250; Circ 60,567
Library Holdings: AV Mats 1,000; Bk Vols 80,000; Per Subs 5; Videos 450
Wireless access
Partic in Sage Library System of Eastern Oregon
Open Mon & Wed 1-5, Tues 10-12 & 1-7, Thurs 1-7

JOSEPH

P JOSEPH PUBLIC LIBRARY*, 201 N Main, 97846. (Mail add: PO Box 15, 97846-0015), SAN 314-1063. Tel: 541-432-0141. FAX: 541-432-3832. E-mail: joseph97846@hotmail.com. Web Site: www.josephoregon.org/index.php/city-services/library. *Librn,* Eric Shoudel
Founded 1912. Pop 1,890; Circ 11,069
Library Holdings: AV Mats 800; Bk Vols 12,000; Per Subs 30
Special Collections: Wallowa County History
Automation Activity & Vendor Info: (Cataloging) Evergreen; (Circulation) Evergreen; (OPAC) Evergreen
Wireless access
Open Tues-Sat 12-4
Friends of the Library Group

JUNCTION CITY

P JUNCTION CITY PUBLIC LIBRARY*, 726 Greenwood St, 97448-1628. (Mail add: PO Box 280, 97448-0280), SAN 314-1071. Tel: 541-998-8942. Web Site: junctioncity.ploud.net, www.junctioncity.com/library.html. *Libr Coord,* Freda Darling; E-mail: FDarling@ci.junction-city.or.us
Founded 1924. Pop 5,000; Circ 35,712
Library Holdings: High Interest/Low Vocabulary Bk Vols 50; Large Print Bks 200; Bk Vols 25,000; Per Subs 30
Special Collections: Scandinavian Coll
Automation Activity & Vendor Info: (Cataloging) SirsiDynix; (Circulation) SirsiDynix; (OPAC) SirsiDynix
Publications: JCPL: A Plan for Service
Open Mon & Tues 12-7, Wed & Thurs 12-6, Sat 10-3
Friends of the Library Group

KLAMATH FALLS

J KLAMATH COMMUNITY COLLEGE*, Learning Resource Center, 7390 S Sixth St, 97603. Tel: 541-880-2206. E-mail: kcclrc@klamathcc.edu. Web Site: www.klamathcc.edu. *Learning Res Ctr Dir,* Rick Ball; *Librn,* Marsha Richmond; Staff 2 (MLS 2)
Founded 1996. Enrl 723; Fac 49; Highest Degree: Associate
Library Holdings: Audiobooks 90; Bks on Deafness & Sign Lang 6; CDs 108; DVDs 267; Bk Titles 5,125; Bk Vols 5,602; Per Subs 83; Videos 1,182
Automation Activity & Vendor Info: (Acquisitions) Evergreen; (Cataloging) Evergreen; (Circulation) Evergreen
Wireless access
Partic in Sage Library System of Eastern Oregon
Open Mon-Thurs 8-6, Fri 8-4:30, Sat 10-2

P KLAMATH COUNTY LIBRARY SERVICES DISTRICT*, 126 S Third St, 97601-6394. SAN 357-9484. Tel: 541-882-8894. Reference Tel: 541-882-8894, Ext 18. FAX: 541-882-6166. TDD: 541-885-7183. Web Site: klamathlibrary.org. *Libr Dir,* Nathalie Johnston; Tel: 541-882-8894, Ext 26, E-mail: njohnston@klamathlibrary.org; Staff 50 (MLS 3, Non-MLS 47)
Founded 1913. Pop 67,000; Circ 567,689
Library Holdings: AV Mats 12,808; CDs 11,026; DVDs 11,402; e-books 12,295; Microforms 1,785; Bk Titles 137,961; Bk Vols 185,930; Per Subs 286; Videos 4,510
Subject Interests: Genealogy, Ore
Automation Activity & Vendor Info: (Acquisitions) Innovative Interfaces, Inc; (Cataloging) Innovative Interfaces, Inc; (Circulation) Innovative Interfaces, Inc; (ILL) OCLC ILLiad; (OPAC) Innovative Interfaces, Inc; (Serials) EBSCO Online
Wireless access
Function: 24/7 Electronic res, 24/7 Online cat, Activity rm, Adult bk club, After school storytime, Art exhibits, Audiobks on Playaways & MP3, Audiobks via web, Bk club(s), Bks on CD, Children's prog, Computer training, Computers for patron use, E-Readers, Electronic databases & coll, Equip loans & repairs, Free DVD rentals, Genealogy discussion group, Home delivery & serv to seniorr ctr & nursing homes, Homebound delivery serv, ILL available, Internet access, Jail serv, Magazines, Magnifiers for reading, Makerspace, Mango lang, Meeting rooms, Microfiche/film & reading machines, Music CDs, Online cat, Online ref, Outreach serv, OverDrive digital audio bks, Preschool outreach, Printer for

laptops & handheld devices, Prog for adults, Prog for children & young adult, Ref & res, Ref serv available, Scanner, Senior outreach, Spanish lang bks, Spoken cassettes & CDs, Spoken cassettes & DVDs, STEM programs, Story hour, Study rm, Summer & winter reading prog, Summer reading prog, Tax forms, Teen prog, Telephone ref, Winter reading prog
Special Services for the Deaf - Bks on deafness & sign lang; Closed caption videos; TDD equip
Special Services for the Blind - Bks available with recordings; Bks on cassette; Bks on CD; Talking bks & player equip
Open Mon, Fri & Sat 10-5, Tues & Thurs 10-8, Wed 1-8, Sun 1-5
Restriction: Non-circulating of rare bks
Friends of the Library Group
Branches: 12
BLY BRANCH, Gearhart School, 61100 Metler St, Bly, 97622. (Mail add: PO Box 366, Bly, 97622-0366), SAN 377-7677. Tel: 541-353-2299. FAX: 541-353-2299. E-mail: blystaff@klamathlibrary.org. Web Site: klamathlibrary.org/bly-branch.
Circ 8,263
Library Holdings: CDs 137; DVDs 458; Large Print Bks 180; Bk Titles 3,105; Per Subs 7; Videos 232
Open Tues-Thurs 9-11 & 12-4
BONANZA BRANCH, 31703 Hwy 70, Bonanza, 97623. (Mail add: PO Box 218, Bonanza, 97623-0218), SAN 357-9549. Tel: 541-545-6944. FAX: 541-545-6944. E-mail: bonanzastaff@klamathlibrary.org. Web Site: klamathlibrary.org/bonanza-branch.
Library Holdings: CDs 176; DVDs 363; Large Print Bks 341; Bk Titles 7,109; Per Subs 8; Videos 132
Open Tues & Thurs 10-6, Wed 10-3, Sat 11-3, Sun 12-4
CHEMULT BRANCH, 120 Damon St, Chemult, 97731. (Mail add: PO Box 155, Chemult, 97731-0155), SAN 377-7693. Tel: 541-365-2412. FAX: 541-365-2412. E-mail: chemultstaff@klamathlibrary.org. Web Site: klamathlibrary.org/chemult-branch.
Circ 1,884
Library Holdings: CDs 176; DVDs 363; Large Print Bks 139; Bk Titles 3,240; Per Subs 6; Videos 156
Open Thurs & Fri 10:30-5, Sat 2-5
CHILOQUIN BRANCH, 140 S First Ave, Chiloquin, 97624. (Mail add: PO Box 666, Chiloquin, 97624-0666), SAN 357-9573. Tel: 541-783-3315. FAX: 541-783-3315. E-mail: chiloquinstaff@klamathlibrary.org. Web Site: klamathlibrary.org/chiloquin-branch.
Circ 17,381
Library Holdings: CDs 247; DVDs 587; Large Print Bks 368; Bk Titles 9,690; Per Subs 8; Videos 517
Open Mon & Sat 10-2, Tues-Thurs 10-6, Fri 1-5
Friends of the Library Group

L LOYD DELAP LAW LIBRARY, 126 S Third St, 97601-6388, SAN 357-9662. Tel: 541-882-8894, Ext 30. FAX: 541-885-3624. E-mail: lawlibrary@klamathlibrary.org. Web Site: klamathlibrary.org/loyd-de-lap-law-library.
Founded 1929
Library Holdings: Bk Vols 2,500
Open Mon, Thurs & Fri 10-2, Tues 10-6, Wed 1-6
GILCHRIST BRANCH, 138306 Michigan Ave, Gilchrist, 97737. (Mail add: PO Box 633, Gilchrist, 97737-0633), SAN 378-1461. Tel: 541-433-2186. FAX: 541-433-2186. E-mail: gilchriststaff@klamathlibrary.org. Web Site: klamathlibrary.org/gilchrist-branch.
Circ 1,422
Library Holdings: CDs 142; DVDs 9; Large Print Bks 135; Bk Titles 5,027; Per Subs 6; Videos 169
Open Tues & Sat 10-12:30 & 1-5, Wed 10-2
KENO BRANCH, 15555 Hwy 66, Unit 1, Keno, 97627. (Mail add: PO Box 283, Keno, 97627-0283). Tel: 541-273-0750. FAX: 541-273-0750. E-mail: kenostaff@klamathlibrary.org. Web Site: klamathlibrary.org/keno-branch.
Circ 6,553
Library Holdings: AV Mats 244; CDs 168; DVDs 281; Large Print Bks 179; Bk Titles 4,312; Per Subs 6; Videos 106
Open Tues & Wed 12:30-4:30, Thurs 10-4:30, Sat 10-2
MALIN BRANCH, 2307 Front St, Malin, 97632. (Mail add: PO Box 525, Malin, 97632-0525), SAN 357-9697. Tel: 541-723-5210. FAX: 541-723-5930. E-mail: malinstaff@klamathlibrary.org. Web Site: klamathlibrary.org/malin-branch.
Circ 5,731
Library Holdings: CDs 130; DVDs 220; Large Print Bks 252; Bk Titles 5,188; Per Subs 7; Videos 103
Open Tues & Thurs 9-12 & 1-5:30, Wed 1-5:30, Sat 9-12
Friends of the Library Group
MERRILL BRANCH, 365 W Front St, Merrill, 97633, SAN 377-7715. Tel: 541-798-5393. FAX: 541-798-5393. E-mail: merrillstaff@klamathlibrary.org. Web Site: klamathlibrary.org/merrill-branch.
Circ 6,547
Library Holdings: CDs 138; DVDs 230; Large Print Bks 182; Bk Titles 4,135; Per Subs 6; Videos 111
Open Mon, Wed & Fri 9-12 & 1-5:30, Sat 1-5:30
Friends of the Library Group
SENIOR CENTER BRANCH, 2045 Arthur St, 97603. Tel: 541-205-8220. Web Site: www.klamathlibrary.org/senior-center-branch.
Open Mon & Fri 9:30-1, Thurs 1:30-4
SOUTH SUBURBAN BRANCH, 3625 Summers Lane, 97603. Tel: 541-273-3679. E-mail: ssubstaff@klamathlibrary.org. Web Site: klamathlibrary.org/south-suburban-branch.
Circ 24,862
Library Holdings: CDs 380; DVDs 425; Large Print Bks 299; Bk Titles 7,018; Per Subs 7; Videos 425
Open Mon-Fri 9:30-6, Sat 9:30-5
SPRAGUE RIVER BRANCH, 23402 Sprague River Rd, Sprague River, 97639-8602. (Mail add: PO Box 29, Sprague River, 97639-0029), SAN 377-7731. Tel: 541-533-2769. E-mail: spragueriverstaff@klamathlibrary.org. Web Site: klamathlibrary.org/sprague-river-branch.
Circ 14,654
Library Holdings: CDs 134; DVDs 367; Large Print Bks 145; Bk Titles 4,433; Per Subs 6; Videos 214
Open Tues-Thurs & Fri 10:30-4
Friends of the Library Group

S KLAMATH COUNTY MUSEUM & BALDWIN HOTEL MUSEUM*, Research Library, 1451 Main St, 97601. SAN 314-108X. Tel: 541-883-4208. Web Site: museum.klamathcounty.org. *Mgr,* Todd Kepple; E-mail: tkepple@klamathcounty.org; *Curator,* Niles Reynolds; E-mail: nreynolds@klamathcounty.org
Founded 1960
Library Holdings: Bk Titles 10,000
Special Collections: Early Photographs (Floyd), negatives-prints; Photo Glass Plates (Baldwin), negatives-prints; Photographs, Modoc Indian War & Logging & Lumbering (Ogle), negatives-prints, bks, doc & micro
Subject Interests: Hist, Natural sci, Pre-hist, Wildlife of area
Function: Res libr
Publications: Research Papers
Restriction: Open by appt only

C OREGON INSTITUTE OF TECHNOLOGY LIBRARY*, 3201 Campus Dr, 97601-8801. SAN 314-1098. Tel: 541-885-1772. FAX: 541-885-1777. E-mail: libtech@oit.edu. Web Site: www.oit.edu/libraries. *Univ Librn,* John Schoppert; Tel: 541-885-1783, E-mail: John.Schoppert@oit.edu; *Librn,* Dawn Lowe-Wincentsen; Tel: 503-821-1258, E-mail: dawn.lowewincentsen@oit.edu; *Info Syst Librn,* Karen Kunz; Tel: 541-885-1769, E-mail: karen.kunz@oit.edu; *Instruction Librn,* Aja Bettencourt-McCarthy; *Instrul Serv Librn,* Alla Powers; Tel: 541-885-1774, E-mail: alla.powers@oit.edu; *Tech Serv Librn,* Iris Goodwin; Tel: 541-885-1965, E-mail: iris.godwin@oit.edu; *Mgr, Access Serv,* Jan A Abeita; *Acq/Cat Tech, Govt Doc,* Deniece Davis; *Cat Tech, Govt Doc, ILL,* Chris Haupt; Tel: 541-885-1099, E-mail: christine.haupt@oit.edu; *Operating Syst/Network Analyst,* Joe Hurlbut; *Ser Tech,* Hsiu-Ling Lin. Subject Specialists: *Distance educ, Mechanical engr,* Dawn Lowe-Wincentsen; *Civil engr, Computer engr,* Karen Kunz; *Communications, Mgt,* Aja Bettencourt-McCarthy; *Humanities, Soc sci,* Alla Powers; *Health sci,* Iris Goodwin; Staff 12 (MLS 6, Non-MLS 6)
Founded 1950. Enrl 2,900; Fac 218; Highest Degree: Master
Library Holdings: Bk Titles 91,528; Bk Vols 155,560; Per Subs 2,110
Special Collections: Shaw Historical Library Coll; Western History (Klamath Basin Coll). State Document Depository; US Document Depository
Subject Interests: Computer sci, Engr tech, Hist of sci & tech, Med
Automation Activity & Vendor Info: (Acquisitions) Ex Libris Group; (Cataloging) Ex Libris Group; (Circulation) Ex Libris Group; (Course Reserve) Ex Libris Group; (ILL) Clio; (OPAC) Ex Libris Group; (Serials) Ex Libris Group
Wireless access
Function: Audio & video playback equip for onsite use, Computers for patron use, E-Reserves, Electronic databases & coll, Online cat, Photocopying/Printing, Ref serv available, Scanner, Telephone ref
Publications: Journal of the Shaw Historical Library (Local historical information)
Partic in OCLC Online Computer Library Center, Inc; Orbis Cascade Alliance
Restriction: Borrowing privileges limited to fac & registered students, Non-circulating coll, Non-circulating of rare bks, Open to pub for ref & circ; with some limitations

LA GRANDE

C EASTERN OREGON UNIVERSITY*, Pierce Library, One University Blvd, 97850. SAN 314-1101. Tel: 541-962-3579. Circulation Tel: 541-962-3864. Interlibrary Loan Service Tel: 541-962-3735. Reference Tel: 541-962-3780. FAX: 541-962-3335. Web Site: pierce.eou.edu. *Dir,* Karen

Clay; Tel: 541-962-3792, E-mail: kclay@eou.edu; *Acq & Coll,* Sally Mielke; Tel: 541-962-3865, E-mail: smielke@eou.edu; *Head, Tech Serv,* Sara Rowland; Tel: 541-962-3546, E-mail: srowland@eou.edu; *Circ,* Joy McAndie; Tel: 541-962-3671, E-mail: jmcandie@eou.edu; *Ref & Instruction,* Theresa Gillis; Tel: 541-962-3605, E-mail: tgillis@eou.edu; *Syst,* Jeremiah Kellogg; Tel: 541-962-3017, E-mail: jkellog@eou.edu; Staff 13 (MLS 4, Non-MLS 9)
Founded 1929. Enrl 2,334; Fac 125; Highest Degree: Master
Library Holdings: Bk Titles 115,809; Bk Vols 156,402; Per Subs 854
Special Collections: Native American Literature; Oregon, bks & doc. US Document Depository
Subject Interests: Genealogy, Local hist
Automation Activity & Vendor Info: (Acquisitions) Innovative Interfaces, Inc; (Cataloging) Innovative Interfaces, Inc; (Circulation) Innovative Interfaces, Inc; (OPAC) Innovative Interfaces, Inc; (Serials) Innovative Interfaces, Inc
Wireless access
Publications: Newsletter
Partic in Orbis Cascade Alliance
Open Mon-Thurs 7:30am-11pm, Fri 7:30-5, Sat 11-7, Sun 2-11
Friends of the Library Group

P F MAXINE & THOMAS W COOK MEMORIAL LIBRARY*, 2006 Fourth St, 97850-2496. SAN 314-111X. Tel: 541-962-1339. E-mail: libdirector@cookmemoriallibrary.org. Web Site: www.CookMemorialLibrary.org. *Libr Dir,* Kip Roberson; E-mail: kroberson@cookmemoriallibrary.org; Staff 5 (MLS 1, Non-MLS 4)
Founded 1912. Pop 13,200; Circ 147,229
Jul 2019-Jun 2020 Income $692,674, State $5,314, City $614,315, County $40,000. Mats Exp $69,302, Books $42,660, Per/Ser (Incl. Access Fees) $7,545, AV Mat $12,000, Electronic Ref Mat (Incl. Access Fees) $6,919. Sal $174,921 (Prof $84,000)
Library Holdings: Audiobooks 2,601; DVDs 1,735; e-books 60,360; Electronic Media & Resources 24; Large Print Bks 2,112; Bk Vols 49,096; Per Subs 100
Special Collections: Oregon History Coll
Automation Activity & Vendor Info: (Cataloging) Evergreen; (Circulation) Evergreen; (Discovery) Evergreen; (ILL) Evergreen; (OPAC) Evergreen; (Serials) Evergreen
Wireless access
Function: 24/7 Electronic res, 24/7 Online cat, 3D Printer, Activity rm, Adult bk club, Adult literacy prog, Archival coll, Art exhibits, Art programs, Audiobks on Playaways & MP3, Audiobks via web, Bk club(s), Bks on CD, Children's prog, Computers for patron use, Digital talking bks, Doc delivery serv, E-Readers, Electronic databases & coll, Equip loans & repairs, Family literacy, Free DVD rentals, Holiday prog, Home delivery & serv to seniorr ctr & nursing homes, Homebound delivery serv, Homework prog, ILL available, Internet access, Large print keyboards, Life-long learning prog for all ages, Magazines, Magnifiers for reading, Meeting rooms, Movies, Museum passes, Notary serv, Online cat, Online ref, Outreach serv, Outside serv via phone, mail, e-mail & web, OverDrive digital audio bks, Photocopying/Printing, Preschool outreach, Preschool reading prog, Printer for laptops & handheld devices, Prof lending libr, Prog for adults, Prog for children & young adult, Ref serv available, Scanner, Senior outreach, Spanish lang bks, Story hour, Study rm, Summer reading prog, Teen prog, Telephone ref, Visual arts prog, Wheelchair accessible, Workshops, Writing prog
Publications: Wowbrary (Online only)
Partic in Sage Library System of Eastern Oregon

LAKE OSWEGO

P LAKE OSWEGO PUBLIC LIBRARY*, 706 Fourth St, 97034-2399. SAN 314-1128. Tel: 503-636-7628. Reference Tel: 503-675-2540. Administration Tel: 503-697-6583. FAX: 503-635-4171. Web Site: www.ci.oswego.or.us/library. *Libr Dir,* Melissa Kelly; E-mail: kelly@lakeoswego.city; *Head, Ref, Mgr, Tech Serv,* Jane Carr; Tel: 503-534-5665, E-mail: jcarr@ci.oswego.or.us; *Circ Mgr,* Melissa Kelly; Tel: 503-675-3996, E-mail: kelly@ci.oswego.or.us; *Youth Serv Mgr,* Andrea Milano; Tel: 503-675-2539, E-mail: amilano@ci.oswego.or.us; Staff 23 (MLS 9, Non-MLS 14)
Founded 1930. Pop 42,167; Circ 1,054,030
Library Holdings: AV Mats 40,855; Bk Vols 155,805; Per Subs 286
Special Collections: Northwest Coll, bks & files. Oral History
Subject Interests: Art, Compact discs, Genealogy, Graphic novels, Pacific Northwest
Automation Activity & Vendor Info: (Acquisitions) SirsiDynix; (Cataloging) SirsiDynix; (Circulation) SirsiDynix; (ILL) OCLC
Wireless access
Partic in Library Information Network of Clackamas County; OCLC Online Computer Library Center, Inc
Open Mon-Thurs 10-9, Fri & Sat 10-6, Sun 1-6
Friends of the Library Group

LAKESIDE

P LAKESIDE PUBLIC LIBRARY*, 915 N Lake Rd, 97449. (Mail add: PO Box R, 97449-0811), SAN 329-7608. Tel: 541-759-4432. FAX: 541-759-4752. Web Site: www.cooslibraries.org/. *Libr Dir,* Cheryl Young; E-mail: cyoung@coastlinelibrarynetwork.org; Staff 3 (Non-MLS 3)
Founded 1987. Pop 2,044; Circ 22,758
Library Holdings: Bk Titles 26,724; Per Subs 32
Automation Activity & Vendor Info: (Acquisitions) Innovative Interfaces, Inc; (Cataloging) Innovative Interfaces, Inc; (OPAC) Innovative Interfaces, Inc
Wireless access
Function: 24/7 Electronic res, 24/7 Online cat, After school storytime, Bks on CD, Children's prog, Computers for patron use, Electronic databases & coll, Free DVD rentals, Homework prog, ILL available, Magazines, Music CDs, Online cat, OverDrive digital audio bks, Photocopying/Printing, Prog for children & young adult, Scanner, Spoken cassettes & CDs, Wheelchair accessible
Mem of Coos County Library Service District
Open Mon-Fri 10-4, Wed 10-6, Sat 10-2
Restriction: Authorized patrons
Friends of the Library Group

LAKEVIEW

P LAKE COUNTY LIBRARY DISTRICT*, 26 S G St, 97630. SAN 357-9786. Tel: 541-947-6019. E-mail: info@lakecountylibrary.org. Web Site: www.lakecountylibrary.org. *Dir,* Amy Hutchinson; E-mail: amyh@lakecountylibrary.org; Staff 4.3 (MLS 1, Non-MLS 3.3)
Founded 1948. Pop 7,500; Circ 55,039
Library Holdings: AV Mats 5,011; e-journals 1; Electronic Media & Resources 26; Bk Titles 47,655; Per Subs 63
Special Collections: Oregon Coll
Subject Interests: Agr, Americana
Automation Activity & Vendor Info: (Cataloging) Evergreen; (Circulation) Evergreen; (ILL) Evergreen; (OPAC) Evergreen
Wireless access
Function: Computers for patron use, Electronic databases & coll, ILL available, Magnifiers for reading, Music CDs, Online ref, Photocopying/Printing, Prog for adults, Prog for children & young adult, Ref & res, Summer reading prog, Tax forms, Telephone ref, VHS videos
Partic in Libraries of Eastern Oregon
Special Services for the Deaf - Bks on deafness & sign lang
Special Services for the Blind - Audio mat; Bks on cassette; Bks on CD; Copier with enlargement capabilities; Home delivery serv; Large print bks; Magnifiers
Open Mon & Wed-Fri 8:30-6, Tues 8:30am-9pm, Sat 12-4
Restriction: Lending limited to county residents
Branches: 3
CHRISTMAS VALLEY BRANCH, Christmas Tree Lane, Christmas Valley, 97641. (Mail add: PO Box 87, Christmas Valley, 97641), SAN 357-9794. Tel: 541-576-2336. FAX: 541-576-2336.
Open Tues & Thurs 10-6, Sat 10-2
Friends of the Library Group
PAISELY BRANCH, 513 Mill St, Paisley, 97636. (Mail add: PO Box 99, Paisley, 97636), SAN 357-9816. Tel: 541-943-3911. FAX: 541-943-3911.
Library Holdings: Bk Titles 6,500
Open Tues & Wed 10-6
Friends of the Library Group
SILVER LAKE BRANCH, Hwy 31, Silver Lake, 97638. (Mail add: PO Box 87, Silver Lake, 97638), SAN 357-9840. Tel: 541-576-2146. FAX: 541-576-2146. *Librn,* Rosa Villigrana
Library Holdings: Bk Titles 3,046
Open Mon 10-6

LANGLOIS

P LANGLOIS PUBLIC LIBRARY, 48234 Hwy 101, 97450. (Mail add: PO Box 277, 97450-0277), SAN 314-1144. Tel: 541-348-2066. FAX: 541-348-2066. E-mail: langloislibrary@gmail.com. Web Site: langloispubliclibrary.org. *Dir,* Cynthia Hovind; Staff 2 (MLS 1, Non-MLS 1)
Founded 1955. Pop 740; Circ 12,400
Library Holdings: Bk Vols 14,090; Per Subs 45
Special Collections: Oregon Coll
Wireless access
Function: Adult bk club, Art exhibits, Audiobks via web, Bks on cassette, Bks on CD, Children's prog, Computers for patron use, Electronic databases & coll, Free DVD rentals, ILL available, Instruction & testing, Mail & tel request accepted, Music CDs, Online cat, OverDrive digital audio bks, Photocopying/Printing, Prog for adults, Ref serv available, Scanner, Story hour, Summer reading prog
Partic in Coastline
Open Tues & Fri 11-4:30, Wed & Thurs 11-6:30, Sat 12-4
Friends of the Library Group

LEBANON

P LEBANON PUBLIC LIBRARY*, 55 Academy St, 97355-3320. SAN 314-1152. Tel: 541-258-4926. E-mail: libraryinfo@ci.lebanon.or.us. Web Site: www.lebanonpubliclibrary.com. *Libr Dir,* Carol Dinges; Tel: 541-258-4232, E-mail: LibraryDirector@ci.lebanon.or.us; Staff 9 (Non-MLS 9)
Founded 1910. Pop 16,000
Jul 2015-Jun 2016 Income $634,418, State $2,368, City $581,417, Locally Generated Income $50,633. Mats Exp $56,903, Books $32,411, Per/Ser (Incl. Access Fees) $6,955, Micro $150, AV Mat $9,176, Electronic Ref Mat (Incl. Access Fees) $8,211. Sal $341,141
Library Holdings: Audiobooks 2,848; Bks-By-Mail 293; Braille Volumes 2; Electronic Media & Resources 22; High Interest/Low Vocabulary Bk Vols 400; Large Print Bks 1,000; Microforms 223; Bk Vols 44,867; Per Subs 74; Videos 3,457
Special Collections: Genealogy (End of the Trail Research Coll)
Automation Activity & Vendor Info: (Acquisitions) Evergreen; (Cataloging) Evergreen; (Circulation) Evergreen; (ILL) OCLC FirstSearch; (OPAC) Evergreen
Wireless access
Function: 24/7 Electronic res, 24/7 Online cat, Audiobks via web, Bks on CD, Children's prog, Computers for patron use, Digital talking bks, Distance learning, E-Reserves, Electronic databases & coll, Free DVD rentals, Health sci info serv, ILL available, Internet access, Large print keyboards, Life-long learning prog for all ages, Magazines, Meeting rooms, Microfiche/film & reading machines, Music CDs, Online cat, Online info literacy tutorials on the web & in blackboard, Online ref, OverDrive digital audio bks, Photocopying/Printing, Preschool outreach, Printer for laptops & handheld devices, Prog for adults, Prog for children & young adult, Ref & res, Ref serv available, Res performed for a fee, Spoken cassettes & CDs, Story hour, Study rm, Summer reading prog, Tax forms, Teen prog, Telephone ref, Wheelchair accessible
Partic in Linn Libraries Consortium
Open Mon & Tues 10-6, Wed 10-7, Thurs & Fri 10-5, Sat 10-2
Restriction: Circ to mem only, Non-resident fee
Friends of the Library Group

LINCOLN CITY

P DRIFTWOOD PUBLIC LIBRARY, 801 SW Hwy 101, Ste 201, 97367-2720. SAN 314-1160. Tel: 541-996-2277. E-mail: librarian@lincolncity.org. Web Site: www.driftwoodlib.org. *Libr Dir,* Kirsten Brodbeck-Kenney; E-mail: kbrodbeck-kenney@lincolncity.org; *Ref Librn,* Matthew Baiocchi; E-mail: mbaiocchi@lincolncity.org; *Circ Supvr,* Ken Hobson; E-mail: kenh@lincolncity.org; *Outreach Coordr,* Star Khan; E-mail: skhan@lincolncity.org; *Children's Prog,* Teena Nelson; E-mail: tnelson@lincolncity.org; Staff 12 (MLS 2, Non-MLS 10)
Founded 1965. Pop 12,465; Circ 115,147
Library Holdings: AV Mats 14,225; High Interest/Low Vocabulary Bk Vols 127; Large Print Bks 4,514; Bk Titles 86,000; Per Subs 110; Spec Interest Per Sub 50; Talking Bks 2,677
Subject Interests: Pacific Northwest
Automation Activity & Vendor Info: (Cataloging) OCLC; (Circulation) Innovative Interfaces, Inc; (OPAC) Innovative Interfaces, Inc
Wireless access
Function: 24/7 Electronic res, 24/7 Online cat, Activity rm, Adult bk club, Art programs, Audio & video playback equip for onsite use, Audiobks via web, Bilingual assistance for Spanish patrons, Bk club(s), Bks on CD, Children's prog, Computer training, Computers for patron use, Digital talking bks, Electronic databases & coll, Free DVD rentals, Holiday prog, Home delivery & serv to seniorr ctr & nursing homes, Homebound delivery serv, ILL available, Internet access, Life-long learning prog for all ages, Magazines, Magnifiers for reading, Meeting rooms, Movies, Music CDs, Notary serv, Online cat, Online ref, Outreach serv, Outside serv via phone, mail, e-mail & web, OverDrive digital audio bks, Photocopying/Printing, Preschool outreach, Preschool reading prog, Prog for adults, Prog for children & young adult, Ref & res, Ref serv available, Scanner, Senior computer classes, Senior outreach, Serves people with intellectual disabilities, Spanish lang bks, STEM programs, Story hour, Summer reading prog, Tax forms, Teen prog, Telephone ref, Visual arts prog, Wheelchair accessible, Workshops, Writing prog
Special Services for the Blind - Closed circuit TV
Open Mon-Wed 10-8, Thurs-Sat 10-6, Sun 1-5
Friends of the Library Group

LYONS

P LYONS PUBLIC LIBRARY, 279 Eighth St, 97358-2122. (Mail add: 448 Cedar St, 97358-2124), SAN 376-3293. Tel: 503-859-2366. E-mail: lyonspl@ccrls.org. Web Site: lyons.ccrls.org. *Librn,* Brenda Harris; *Asst Librn,* Stella Cruson
Pop 1,200; Circ 17,369
Library Holdings: AV Mats 2,000; Bks on Deafness & Sign Lang 20; CDs 200; High Interest/Low Vocabulary Bk Vols 100; Large Print Bks 250; Bk Vols 23,232; Per Subs 35; Talking Bks 290; Videos 1,000
Subject Interests: Vietnam
Automation Activity & Vendor Info: (Cataloging) SirsiDynix; (Circulation) SirsiDynix
Wireless access
Function: ILL available, Photocopying/Printing, Ref serv available
Special Services for the Deaf - Staff with knowledge of sign lang
Open Tues & Wed 11:30-5, Thurs 1-6:30, Fri 1-5, Sat 10-3:30
Restriction: Mem only
Friends of the Library Group

MADRAS

P JEFFERSON COUNTY LIBRARY DISTRICT*, 241 SE Seventh St, 97741. SAN 314-1209. Tel: 541-475-3351. FAX: 541-475-7434. E-mail: library@jcld.org. Web Site: www.jcld.org. *Libr Dir,* Jane Ellen Innes; E-mail: je@jcld.org; *Adult Serv Spec,* Position Currently Open; *Cat/ILL Spec,* Jackie May; E-mail: jackie@jcld.org; *Spanish Serv Spec,* Yirah Marrero; E-mail: yirah@jcld.org; *Youth Serv Spec,* Laura Jones; E-mail: laura@jckd.org; *Youth Serv Spec,* Star Todd; E-mail: star@jcld.org. Subject Specialists: *Ore hist,* Jackie May; *Spanish,* Yirah Marrero; Staff 11 (MLS 1, Non-MLS 10)
Founded 1916
Special Collections: Oregon Coll
Automation Activity & Vendor Info: (Cataloging) Innovative Interfaces, Inc; (Circulation) Innovative Interfaces, Inc; (OPAC) Innovative Interfaces, Inc
Wireless access
Function: 24/7 Online cat, Adult bk club, Bilingual assistance for Spanish patrons, Bk club(s), Bks on CD, Children's prog, Computers for patron use, Electronic databases & coll, Free DVD rentals, Holiday prog, Homebound delivery serv, ILL available, Internet access, Magazines, Mail & tel request accepted, Meeting rooms, Movies, Museum passes, Music CDs, Online cat, Outreach serv, Photocopying/Printing, Preschool outreach, Prog for adults, Prog for children & young adult, Ref serv available, Senior outreach, Spanish lang bks, Story hour, Summer reading prog, Tax forms, Teen prog, Telephone ref, VHS videos, Wheelchair accessible
Open Mon-Thurs 9-7, Fri-Sat 11-4
Friends of the Library Group

MCMINNVILLE

C LINFIELD COLLEGE*, Jereld R Nicholson Library, 900 SE Baker St, 97128. SAN 314-1187. Tel: 503-883-2261. Reference Tel: 503-883-2518. FAX: 503-883-2566. Circulation E-mail: library-circulation@linfield.edu. Interlibrary Loan Service E-mail: ill@linfield.edu. Web Site: www.linfield.edu/linfield-libraries.html. *Libr Dir,* Susan Barnes Whyte; Tel: 503-883-2517, E-mail: swhyte@linfield.edu; *Archives, Dir, Info Res,* Rich Schmidt; Tel: 508-883-2734, E-mail: rschmidt@linfield.edu; *Coll, Mgt Librn,* Kathleen Spring; Tel: 503-883-2263, E-mail: kspring@linfield.edu; *Syst Librn,* Barbara Valentine; Tel: 503-883-2573, E-mail: bvalen@linfield.edu; Staff 17 (MLS 7, Non-MLS 10)
Founded 1849. Enrl 2,159; Fac 162; Highest Degree: Bachelor
Library Holdings: Bk Vols 191,233; Per Subs 991
Special Collections: Baptist Pioneer History Coll; Oregon Wine History. US Document Depository
Subject Interests: Canadiana, Environ studies, Gender studies, Pac NW hist
Automation Activity & Vendor Info: (Acquisitions) Ex Libris Group; (Cataloging) Ex Libris Group; (Circulation) Ex Libris Group; (Serials) Ex Libris Group
Wireless access
Partic in OCLC Online Computer Library Center, Inc; Orbis Cascade Alliance
Open Mon-Thurs 7:30am-12am, Fri 7:30-6, Sat 10-4, Sun Noon-Midnight; Mon-Fri (Summer) 8-4:30

Departmental Libraries:

PORTLAND CAMPUS, 2255 NW Northrup, Portland, 97210. (Mail add: 1015 NW 22nd Ave, Portland, 97210), SAN 370-4793. Tel: 503-413-7335. Interlibrary Loan Service Tel: 503-413-7448. Administration Tel: 503-413-7820. FAX: 503-413-8016. *Dir,* Patrice O'Donovan; E-mail: odonovan@linfield.edu; *Head, Coll & Access Serv,* Kent Cline; E-mail: kcline@linfield.edu; *Coll & Access Serv Librn,* Karen Lippert; E-mail: klippert@linfield.edu
Library Holdings: Bk Vols 8,002; Per Subs 143
Subject Interests: Nursing
Open Mon-Thurs 8am-9pm, Fri 8-5, Sat 11-5, Sun 3-9

P MCMINNVILLE PUBLIC LIBRARY*, 225 NW Adams St, 97128. SAN 314-1195. Tel: 503-435-5562. Circulation Tel: 503-435-5561. Reference Tel: 503-435-5568. Administration Tel: 503-435-5550. E-mail: libref@mcminnvilleoregon.gov. Web Site: www.mcminnvilleoregon.gov/library. *Libr Dir,* Jenny Berg; E-mail: jenny.berg@mcminnvilleoregon.gov; *Librn III/Ref,* Ms Courtney Terry; E-mail: courtney.terry@mcminnvilleoregon.gov; *Libr Serv Mgr,* Wendy Whitesitt; E-mail: wendy.whitesitt@mcminnvilleoregon.gov; *Ch Serv,*

Kimbre Chapman; Tel: 503-435-5559, E-mail: kimbre.chapman@mcminnvilleoregon.gov; Staff 8.5 (MLS 4.5, Non-MLS 4)
Founded 1912. Pop 50,029; Circ 352,211
Library Holdings: Audiobooks 4,609; DVDs 5,467; e-books 25,761; Bk Titles 78,750; Per Subs 113
Automation Activity & Vendor Info: (Acquisitions) Innovative Interfaces, Inc; (Cataloging) Innovative Interfaces, Inc; (Circulation) Innovative Interfaces, Inc; (OPAC) Innovative Interfaces, Inc; (Serials) Innovative Interfaces, Inc
Wireless access
Function: Adult bk club, Audiobks via web, Bilingual assistance for Spanish patrons, Bk club(s), Bks on CD, Children's prog, Computer training, Computers for patron use, Digital talking bks, Electronic databases & coll, Free DVD rentals, Home delivery & serv to seniorr ctr & nursing homes, Homebound delivery serv, ILL available, Internet access, Magnifiers for reading, Mail & tel request accepted, Music CDs, Online cat, Online ref, Outreach serv, Outside serv via phone, mail, e-mail & web, OverDrive digital audio bks, Photocopying/Printing, Preschool outreach, Preschool reading prog, Prog for children & young adult, Ref serv available, Scanner, Senior computer classes, Spanish lang bks, Spoken cassettes & CDs, Spoken cassettes & DVDs, Story hour, Summer reading prog, Tax forms, Teen prog, Telephone ref, Wheelchair accessible
Publications: Friends of the Library News
Partic in Chemeketa Cooperative Regional Library Service
Open Tues-Thurs 10-8, Fri 10-5, Sat & Sun 1-5
Friends of the Library Group
Bookmobiles: 1

MEDFORD

L JACKSON COUNTY LAW LIBRARY*, Justice Bldg, Basement, 100 S Oakdale Ave, 97501. SAN 325-8149. Tel: 541-774-6437. FAX: 541-774-6767. E-mail: carriecd@jacksoncounty.org. Web Site: jacksoncountyor.org/Departments/Law-Library.
Library Holdings: Bk Vols 15,000; Per Subs 10
Function: For res purposes
Open Tues, Wed & Thurs 9-1:30
Restriction: Internal use only, Not a lending libr, Pub access for legal res only

P JACKSON COUNTY LIBRARY SERVICES*, 205 S Central Ave, 97501-2730. SAN 357-9875. Tel: 541-774-8679. FAX: 541-774-6748. E-mail: infolib@jcls.org. Web Site: jcls.org. *Libr Dir,* Kari May; E-mail: kmay@jcls.org; *Asst Dir, Support Serv,* Carey Hunt; E-mail: chunt@jcls.org; *Mkt Coordr,* Ryan Bradley; Staff 18 (MLS 10, Non-MLS 8)
Founded 1908. Pop 192,992; Circ 35,000,000
Library Holdings: Bk Vols 567,118; Per Subs 1,560
Special Collections: Oregon Coll; Werner Sheet Music Coll. State Document Depository
Automation Activity & Vendor Info: (Cataloging) Innovative Interfaces, Inc; (Circulation) Innovative Interfaces, Inc
Wireless access
Open Mon-Fri 8-5
Friends of the Library Group
Branches: 15
APPLEGATE BRANCH, 18484 N Applegate Rd, Applegate, 97530. (Mail add: PO Box 3308, Applegate, 97530-3308), SAN 358-0261. Tel: 541-846-7346. FAX: 541-846-7346. *Br Mgr,* Christine Grubb
Open Tues & Fri 2-6, Wed & Sat 10-2
Friends of the Library Group
ASHLAND BRANCH, 410 Siskiyou Blvd, Ashland, 97520-2136, SAN 357-9905. Tel: 541-774-6980. Reference FAX: 541-774-6996. E-mail: ashlib@jcls.org. *Br Mgr,* Kristin Anderson
Special Collections: Shakespeare
Open Mon 10-8, Tues & Wed 10-6, Thurs & Sat Noon-5, Sun Noon-4
Friends of the Library Group
BUTTE FALLS BRANCH, 626 Fir Ave, Butte Falls, 97522. (Mail add: PO Box 138, Butte Falls, 97522-0138), SAN 357-993X. Tel: 541-865-3511. FAX: 541-865-3511. *Br Mgr,* LeeAnn Pierce; Staff 1 (Non-MLS 1)
Open Tues 10-3, Thurs 12-5
Friends of the Library Group
CENTRAL POINT BRANCH, 116 S Third St, Central Point, 97502, SAN 357-9964. Tel: 541-664-3228. *Br Mgr,* Leigh Blair
Open Tues-Fri 10-6, Sat 12-4
Friends of the Library Group
EAGLE POINT BRANCH, 239 W Main St, Eagle Point, 97524. (Mail add: PO Box 459, Eagle Point, 97524-0459), SAN 357-9999. Tel: 541-826-3313. FAX: 541-826-3313. *Br Mgr,* Charlene Prinsen
Open Tues, Wed & Fri 10-4, Thurs 12-6, Sat 12-4
Friends of the Library Group
GOLD HILL BRANCH, 202 Dardanelles St, Gold Hill, 97525-0136. (Mail add: PO Box 258, Gold Hill, 97525-0258), SAN 358-0024. Tel: 541-855-1994. FAX: 541-855-1994. *Br Mgr,* Lorna Hilke; Staff 2 (Non-MLS 2)
Open Mon 10-4, Wed 2-6, Fri 1-5, Sat 12-4
Friends of the Library Group
JACKSONVILLE BRANCH, 340 West C St, Jacksonville, 97530. (Mail add: PO Box 490, Jacksonville, 97530-0490), SAN 358-0059. Tel: 541-899-1665. FAX: 541-899-1665. *Br Mgr,* Laurel Prchal; Staff 2 (Non-MLS 2)
Open Mon & Wed 10-5, Thurs 12-6, Sat 10-2
Friends of the Library Group
MEDFORD BRANCH, 205 S Central Ave, 97501. Tel: 541-774-8689. E-mail: medref@jcls.org. *Br Mgr,* Terra Mcleod
Open Mon-Wed 10-7, Fri & Sun 12-4, Sat 11-4
Friends of the Library Group
PHOENIX BRANCH, 510 W First St, Phoenix, 97535. (Mail add: PO Box 277, Phoenix, 97535-0277), SAN 358-0083. Tel: 541-535-7090. FAX: 541-535-7090. *Br Mgr,* Jody Flemming; Staff 2 (Non-MLS 2)
Open Tues & Thurs 11-5, Wed 1-7, Sat 12-4
Friends of the Library Group
PROSPECT BRANCH, 150 Mill Creek Dr, Prospect, 97536. (Mail add: PO Box 39, Prospect, 97536-0039), SAN 358-0113. Tel: 541-560-3668. FAX: 541-560-3668. *Br Mgr,* LeeAnn Pierce; Staff 1 (Non-MLS 1)
Open Wed & Sat 10-2
Friends of the Library Group
ROGUE RIVER BRANCH, 412 E Main St, Rogue River, 97537. (Mail add: PO Box 1075, Rogue River, 97537-1075), SAN 358-0148. Tel: 541-864-8850. FAX: 541-864-8871. *Br Mgr,* Position Currently Open
Open Mon, Tues & Fri 10-4, Thurs 1-7, Sat 10-2
Friends of the Library Group
RUCH BRANCH, 7919 Hwy 238, Ruch, 97530-9728, SAN 329-6628. Tel: 541-899-7438. *Br Mgr,* Thalia Truesdell
Open Tues 10-5, Thurs 1-7, Sat 11-4
Friends of the Library Group
SHADY COVE BRANCH, 22477 Hwy 62, Shady Cove, 97539-9718, SAN 358-0172. Tel: 541-878-2270. FAX: 541-878-2270. *Br Mgr,* Marion Mensing
Open Tues 12-6, Wed 2-7, Fri 10-5
Friends of the Library Group
TALENT BRANCH, 101 Home St, Talent, 97540. (Mail add: PO Box 597, Talent, 97540-0597), SAN 358-0202. Tel: 541-535-4163. FAX: 541-535-4163. *Br Mgr,* Patrick Mathewes
Open Tues 10-6, Wed & Thurs 12-7, Fri & Sat 10-5
Friends of the Library Group
WHITE CITY BRANCH, 3143 Ave C, White City, 97503-1443, SAN 358-0237. Tel: 541-864-8880. FAX: 541-864-8889. *Br Mgr,* Jo Ann Crosby
Open Mon 11-6, Tues 10-2, Thurs 12-5, Sat 10-4
Friends of the Library Group

MILL CITY

P MILL CITY LIBRARY*, 250 SW Second Ave, 97360. Tel: 503-897-6149. *Library Contact,* Susann Heller-Tuers
Library Holdings: AV Mats 300; Bk Vols 10,000; Per Subs 35; Talking Bks 25
Open Tues-Fri 10-Noon & 1:30-3:30
Friends of the Library Group

MILTON-FREEWATER

P MILTON-FREEWATER PUBLIC LIBRARY*, Eight SW Eighth Ave, 97862. SAN 358-0598. Tel: 541-938-8247. Interlibrary Loan Service Tel: 541-938-8239. Administration Tel: 541-938-8246. FAX: 541-938-8254. Web Site: www.mfcity.com/library. *Libr Dir,* Erin Wells; E-mail: erin.wells@milton-freewater-or.gov; *Ch Serv,* Lili Schmidt; Tel: 541-938-8248, E-mail: lili.schmidt@milton-freewater-or.gov; *ILL,* Sandy Nelson; E-mail: sandy.nelson@milton-freewater-or.gov; Staff 1 (MLS 1)
Founded 1913. Pop 12,000; Circ 50,583
Jul 2013-Jun 2014 Income $333,819, State $1,088, City $128,140, Locally Generated Income $15,401, Other $189,190. Mats Exp $25,000. Sal $178,654
Library Holdings: AV Mats 2,624; Electronic Media & Resources 26; Bk Vols 43,000; Per Subs 54; Videos 1,078
Subject Interests: Genealogy, Local hist
Automation Activity & Vendor Info: (Cataloging) Evergreen; (Circulation) Evergreen; (ILL) Evergreen; (OPAC) Evergreen
Wireless access
Function: Archival coll, Art exhibits, Audiobks via web, Bks on cassette, Bks on CD, Children's prog, Computers for patron use, E-Reserves, Electronic databases & coll, Free DVD rentals, ILL available, Internet access, Magnifiers for reading, Mail & tel request accepted, Microfiche/film & reading machines, Music CDs, Online cat, OverDrive digital audio bks, Photocopying/Printing, Preschool outreach, Preschool reading prog, Prog

for adults, Prog for children & young adult, Spanish lang bks, Spoken cassettes & CDs, Spoken cassettes & DVDs, Story hour, Summer reading prog, Tax forms, VHS videos, Wheelchair accessible
Mem of Umatilla County Special Library District
Partic in Libraries of Eastern Oregon; Sage Library System of Eastern Oregon
Special Services for the Deaf - Bks on deafness & sign lang
Special Services for the Blind - Audio mat; Bks on cassette; Bks on CD; Home delivery serv; Large print bks; Talking bks
Open Mon-Wed 11-7, Thurs & Fri 10-6, Sat 10-2
Restriction: Non-resident fee, Open to pub for ref & circ; with some limitations
Friends of the Library Group

MILWAUKIE

LEDDING LIBRARY OF MILWAUKIE, 10660 SE 21st Ave, 97222. SAN 314-1241. Tel: 503-786-7580. Reference Tel: 503-786-7546. Administration Tel: 503-786-7584. E-mail: ledding@milwaukieoregon.gov. Web Site: www.milwaukieoregon.gov/library. *Dir,* Katie Newell; E-mail: newellk@milwaukieoregon.gov; *Ch Serv,* Jana Hoffman; Tel: 503-786-7585, E-mail: hoffmanj@milwaukieoregon.gov; *Circ,* Kim Olson; Tel: 503-786-7582, E-mail: olsonk@milwaukieoregon.gov; *Ref Serv,* Robert Lanxon; E-mail: lanxonr@milwaukieoregon.gov; Staff 7.5 (MLS 6.5, Non-MLS 1)
Founded 1934
Library Holdings: Bk Vols 88,749; Per Subs 210; Videos 12,010
Subject Interests: Local hist, Northwest
Automation Activity & Vendor Info: (Acquisitions) SirsiDynix; (Cataloging) SirsiDynix; (Circulation) SirsiDynix; (OPAC) SirsiDynix
Wireless access
Function: 24/7 Electronic res, 24/7 Online cat, Adult bk club, After school storytime, Audiobks via web, Bilingual assistance for Spanish patrons, Bk club(s), Bks on CD, CD-ROM, Children's prog, Citizenship assistance, Computers for patron use, E-Readers, E-Reserves, Electronic databases & coll, Equip loans & repairs, Free DVD rentals, Games & aids for people with disabilities, Holiday prog, Homebound delivery serv, ILL available, Internet access, Magazines, Magnifiers for reading, Mail & tel request accepted, Microfiche/film & reading machines, Movies, Museum passes, Music CDs, Online cat, Online info literacy tutorials on the web & in blackboard, Online ref, Outreach serv, Outside serv via phone, mail, e-mail & web, OverDrive digital audio bks, Photocopying/Printing, Preschool outreach, Preschool reading prog, Printer for laptops & handheld devices, Prog for adults, Prog for children & young adult, Ref & res, Ref serv available, Res assist avail, Scanner, Serves people with intellectual disabilities, Spanish lang bks, STEM programs, Story hour, Study rm, Summer reading prog, Tax forms, Teen prog, Telephone ref, Wheelchair accessible, Writing prog
Partic in Library Information Network of Clackamas County
Open Mon-Thurs 9-8, Fri & Sat 10-6, Sun 12-6
Friends of the Library Group

MOLALLA

MOLALLA PUBLIC LIBRARY, 201 E Fifth St, 97038. (Mail add: PO Box 1289, 97038-1289), SAN 314-125X. Tel: 503-829-2593. Reference E-mail: moref@lincc.org. Web Site: www.cityofmolalla.com/library. *Libr Dir,* Diana Hadley; E-mail: dhadley@lincc.org; Staff 5 (MLS 3, Non-MLS 2)
Founded 1900. Circ 115,000
Library Holdings: Bk Vols 35,365; Per Subs 212
Automation Activity & Vendor Info: (Cataloging) SirsiDynix; (Circulation) SirsiDynix; (OPAC) SirsiDynix
Wireless access
Function: 24/7 Electronic res, 24/7 Online cat, Audiobks via web, Bilingual assistance for Spanish patrons, Bks on CD, Children's prog, Computer training, Computers for patron use, Electronic databases & coll, Free DVD rentals, Holiday prog, Home delivery & serv to seniorr ctr & nursing homes, Homebound delivery serv, ILL available, Internet access, Large print keyboards, Magazines, Mail & tel request accepted, Movies, Museum passes, Music CDs, Online cat, Online info literacy tutorials on the web & in blackboard, Outreach serv, OverDrive digital audio bks, Photocopying/Printing, Preschool outreach, Preschool reading prog, Prog for adults, Prog for children & young adult, Senior outreach, Spanish lang bks, STEM programs, Story hours, Summer & winter reading prog, Summer reading prog, Tax forms, Teen prog, Wheelchair accessible, Winter reading prog
Partic in Library Information Network of Clackamas County
Open Mon-Wed 11-7, Thurs & Fri 11-6, Sat & Sun 12-5
Friends of the Library Group

MONMOUTH

MONMOUTH PUBLIC LIBRARY*, 168 S Ecols St, 97361. (Mail add: PO Box 10, 97361-0010), SAN 314-1268. Tel: 503-838-1932. Web Site: www.ci.monmouth.or.us/library. *Libr Dir,* Krist Obrist; E-mail: kobrist@ci.monmouth.or.us; *Librn II,* Howard Feltmann; E-mail: hfeltmann@ci.monmouth.or.us; *Youth Serv Librn,* Carrie Kasperick; E-mail: ckasperick@ci.monmouth.or.us; Staff 9 (MLS 3, Non-MLS 6)
Founded 1934. Pop 17,125; Circ 155,000
Library Holdings: High Interest/Low Vocabulary Bk Vols 100; Bk Vols 66,652; Per Subs 174
Automation Activity & Vendor Info: (Cataloging) SirsiDynix-WorkFlows; (Circulation) SirsiDynix-WorkFlows; (OPAC) SirsiDynix-Enterprise
Wireless access
Partic in Chemeketa Cooperative Regional Library Service
Open Tues-Thurs 10-8, Fri 10-6, Sat 10-5
Friends of the Library Group

WESTERN OREGON UNIVERSITY
C WAYNE & LYNN HAMERSLY LIBRARY*, 345 N Monmouth Ave, 97361-1396, SAN 314-1276. Tel: 503-838-8418. Circulation Tel: 503-838-8902. Reference Tel: 503-838-8899. Administration Tel: 503-838-8240. FAX: 503-838-8399. Interlibrary Loan Service FAX: 503-838-8645. E-mail: refdesk@wou.edu. Web Site: www.wou.edu/library. *Dean of Libr,* Dr Allen McKiel; Tel: 503-838-8886, E-mail: mckiela@wou.edu; *Adjunct Instruction,* Tracy Scharn; Tel: 503-838-8892, E-mail: scharnt@wou.edu; *Archives & Exhibits,* Erin Passehl; Tel: 503-838-8893, E-mail: passehl@wou.edu; *Coll Develop, Tech Serv,* Camila Gabaldon Winningham; Tel: 503-838-8653, E-mail: gabaldonc@wou.edu; *Instruction & Outreach,* Robert Monge; Tel: 803-838-8887, E-mail: monger@wou.edu; *Libr Instruction,* Shirley Lincicum; Tel: 503-838-8890, E-mail: lincics@wou.edu; *Pub Serv,* Janeanne Rockwell-Kincannon; Tel: 503-838-9493, E-mail: kincanj@wou.edu. Subject Specialists: *Computer sci, Health,* Camila Gabaldon Winningham; *English,* Robert Monge; *Creative arts, Hist,* Shirley Lincicum; *Gender studies, Humanities,* Janeanne Rockwell-Kincannon; Staff 17.3 (MLS 6, Non-MLS 11.3)
Founded 1856. Enrl 5,500; Highest Degree: Master
Library Holdings: AV Mats 9,984; e-books 3,149; e-journals 2,600; Bk Titles 187,340; Bk Vols 236,684; Per Subs 798
Special Collections: Archival Materials & Special Coll Relating to University History & Former Governor Robert W Straub; State Adopted Textbooks. State Document Depository; US Document Depository
Automation Activity & Vendor Info: (Acquisitions) Innovative Interfaces, Inc; (Cataloging) Innovative Interfaces, Inc; (Circulation) Innovative Interfaces, Inc; (ILL) Innovative Interfaces, Inc; (OPAC) Innovative Interfaces, Inc; (Serials) Innovative Interfaces, Inc
Partic in OCLC Online Computer Library Center, Inc; Orbis Cascade Alliance
Publications: Hamersly Library Guide (Library handbook)
Special Services for the Deaf - TTY equip

C JENSEN ARCTIC MUSEUM-WESTERN RESEARCH LIBRARY*, 590 W Church St, 97361, SAN 329-1952. Tel: 503-838-8468. FAX: 503-838-8289. E-mail: arctic@wou.edu. Web Site: www.wou.edu/president/advancement/jensen/index.php. *Curator,* Roben Jack Larrison
Founded 1985
Library Holdings: Bk Titles 1,400
Subject Interests: Arctic, Native Am
Publications: Paglan (Newsletter)
Open Wed-Sat 10-4

MOSIER

P MOSIER VALLEY LIBRARY*, 203 Third St, 97040. (Mail add: PO Box 525, 97040-0525). Tel: 541-478-3495. Web Site: www.mosiercommunity.com/services/mosier-valley-library. *Co-Dir,* Joan Hudson; *Co-Dir,* Glenna McCargar
Pop 2,000
Library Holdings: Bk Vols 3,500
Wireless access
Open Mon 1-3 & 5-7, Wed 10-12 & 1-3, Thurs 2-5, Sat 10-Noon
Friends of the Library Group

MOUNT ANGEL

P MOUNT ANGEL PUBLIC LIBRARY*, 290 E Charles St, 97362. (Mail add: PO Box 870, 97362-0870), SAN 314-1306. Tel: 503-845-6401. FAX: 503-845-6261. E-mail: library.mountangel@ccrls.org. Web Site: mountangel.ccrls.org. *Libr Dir,* Jackie A Mills; E-mail: jackie.mills@ccrls.org; *Asst Librn,* Marilyn Clouser; E-mail: marilyn@ccrls.org
Founded 1946. Pop 3,700; Circ 34,711
Library Holdings: AV Mats 2,081; Bk Vols 30,413; Per Subs 58
Wireless access
Function: After school storytime
Partic in Chemeketa Cooperative Regional Library Service
Open Tues 11-6, Wed-Fri 11-5, Sat 11-3
Friends of the Library Group

MYRTLE POINT

P DORA PUBLIC LIBRARY, 56125 Goldbrick Rd, 97458. SAN 376-7256. Tel: 541-572-6009. Interlibrary Loan Service Tel: 541-888-7260. E-mail: dorapublic@gmail.com. Web Site: dorapubliclibrary.org. *Dir,* Betty H Vaughn; Staff 2 (Non-MLS 2)
Founded 1976. Pop 950
Library Holdings: Bk Vols 11,326; Per Subs 35; Talking Bks 470; Videos 1,344
Automation Activity & Vendor Info: (Cataloging) Koha; (Circulation) Koha; (OPAC) Koha
Wireless access
Function: ILL available
Mem of Coos County Library Service District
Partic in Coastline
Open Mon & Wed 1-7, Tues & Thurs 5:30pm-8pm, Fri 1-6, Sat 10-2
Friends of the Library Group

P MYRTLE POINT LIBRARY*, Flora M Laird Memorial Library, 435 Fifth St, 97458-1113. SAN 314-1314. Tel: 541-572-2591. FAX: 541-572-5168. E-mail: myrtlepointlibrary@gmail.com. Web Site: www.ci.myrtlepoint.or.us/general/page/public-library. *Libr Dir,* Barbara Caffey; E-mail: bcaffey@coastlinelibrarynetwork.org
Founded 1925. Pop 4,308; Circ 53,827
Library Holdings: Bk Vols 35,306; Per Subs 77
Automation Activity & Vendor Info: (Cataloging) Innovative Interfaces, Inc; (Circulation) Innovative Interfaces, Inc; (OPAC) Innovative Interfaces, Inc
Wireless access
Mem of Coos County Library Service District
Open Mon-Wed 10-8, Thurs-Sat 12-5

NEWBERG

C GEORGE FOX UNIVERSITY*, Murdock Learning Resource Center, 416 N Meridian St, 97132. SAN 314-1322. Tel: 503-554-2410. Interlibrary Loan Service Tel: 503-554-2423. Reference Tel: 503-554-2419. FAX: 503-554-3599. E-mail: researchhelp@georgefox.edu. Web Site: www.georgefox.edu/library. *Dean of Libr,* Ryan Ingersoll; Tel: 503-554-2411, E-mail: ringersoll@georgefox.edu; *Res & Instruction Librn,* Rob Bohall; Tel: 503-554-2416, E-mail: rbohall@georgefox.edu; *Tech Serv & Syst Librn,* Alexander Rolfe; Tel: 503-554-2414, E-mail: arolfe@georgefox.edu; *ILL Coordr,* Laurie Lieggi; E-mail: llieggi@georgefox.edu
Founded 1891. Enrl 3,485; Highest Degree: Doctorate. Sal $596,001 (Prof $277,189)
Library Holdings: AV Mats 5,649; CDs 524; DVDs 2,003; e-books 148,608; e-journals 56,042; Bk Titles 293,000; Bk Vols 357,000; Videos 1,515
Special Collections: Herbert Hoover Coll, bks, pamphlets, per, photog; Peace Coll, bks, per; Society of Friends (Quaker Coll), bks, pamphlets, per, photog
Automation Activity & Vendor Info: (Acquisitions) Innovative Interfaces, Inc; (Cataloging) Innovative Interfaces, Inc; (Circulation) Innovative Interfaces, Inc; (Course Reserve) Innovative Interfaces, Inc; (OPAC) Innovative Interfaces, Inc; (Serials) Innovative Interfaces, Inc
Wireless access
Partic in OCLC Online Computer Library Center, Inc; Orbis Cascade Alliance
Open Mon-Thurs 7:30am-Midnight, Fri 7:30-5, Sat 9-6, Sun 2-10

Departmental Libraries:

PORTLAND CENTER LIBRARY, Hampton Plaza, 12753 SW 68th Ave, Portland, 97223, SAN 314-1934. Tel: 503-554-6130. Interlibrary Loan Service Tel: 503-554-6132. Reference Tel: 503-554-6136. FAX: 503-554-6134. *Librn,* Charlie Kamilos; Tel: 503-554-6131, E-mail: ckamilos@georgefox.edu; *E-Learning & Ref Librn,* Robin Ashford
Highest Degree: Doctorate
Library Holdings: AV Mats 2,533; CDs 11; DVDs 300; e-journals 28,950; Bk Titles 49,687; Bk Vols 57,612; Per Subs 293; Videos 303
Subject Interests: Counseling, Theol

P NEWBERG PUBLIC LIBRARY*, 503 E Hancock St, 97132. SAN 314-1330. Tel: 503-538-7323. FAX: 503-538-9720. E-mail: nplibrary@newbergoregon.gov. Web Site: www.newbergoregon.gov/library. *Libr Dir,* Will Worthey; Tel: 503-537-1256, E-mail: will.worthey@newbergoregon.gov; *Asst Dir, Ch Mgr,* Korie Buerkle; E-mail: korie.buerkle@newbergoregon.gov; *Ch Mgr,* Mary Lynn Thomas; E-mail: mary.thomas@newbergoregon.gov; *Adult Serv, Vols Serv Coordr,* Denise Reilly; E-mail: denise.reilly@newbergoregon.gov; *YA Serv,* K'lyn Hann; E-mail: klyn.hann@newbergoregon.gov; Staff 13 (MLS 2, Non-MLS 11)
Founded 1912. Pop 22,000; Circ 288,555
Library Holdings: AV Mats 3,500; Bks on Deafness & Sign Lang 10; High Interest/Low Vocabulary Bk Vols 100; Large Print Bks 828; Bk Titles 64,000; Bk Vols 70,000; Per Subs 268; Talking Bks 2,500
Special Collections: Municipal Document Depository
Automation Activity & Vendor Info: (Acquisitions) Innovative Interfaces, Inc; (Cataloging) Innovative Interfaces, Inc; (Circulation) Innovative Interfaces, Inc; (OPAC) Innovative Interfaces, Inc
Wireless access
Function: Audio & video playback equip for onsite use, Home delivery & serv to seniorr ctr & nursing homes, ILL available, Internet access, Photocopying/Printing, Prog for adults, Prog for children & young adult, Ref serv available, Spoken cassettes & CDs, Summer reading prog, Telephone ref, VHS videos, Wheelchair accessible
Partic in Chemeketa Cooperative Regional Library Service
Open Tues-Thurs 10-8, Fri 12-5, Sat 10-5
Friends of the Library Group

NEWPORT

P LINCOLN COUNTY LIBRARY DISTRICT*, 1247 NW Grove St, Ste 2, 97365. (Mail add: PO Box 2027, 97365-0144). Tel: 541-265-3066. FAX: 541-265-3066. E-mail: lcld@lincolncolibrarydist.org. *Dir,* MaryKay Dahlgreen; *Cat,* Jane Cothron; E-mail: jcothron@lincolncolibrarydist.org; Staff 2 (MLS 2)
Founded 1988. Pop 23,835
Jul 2016-Jun 2017 Income $1,503,225, State $3,874, County $1,223,592, Other $91,818. Mats Exp $26,089, Books $3,640, Per/Ser (Incl. Access Fees) $682, AV Mat $648, Electronic Ref Mat (Incl. Access Fees) $5,579. Sal $240,116 (Prof $151,647)
Library Holdings: CDs 627; DVDs 2,364; e-books 22,293; Bk Vols 19,227; Per Subs 35
Special Collections: Native American Coll
Automation Activity & Vendor Info: (Acquisitions) ByWater Solutions; (Cataloging) OCLC CatExpress; (Circulation) ByWater Solutions; (Course Reserve) ByWater Solutions; (ILL) OCLC FirstSearch; (OPAC) ByWater Solutions; (Serials) ByWater Solutions
Wireless access
Function: Doc delivery serv, ILL available, Prof lending libr
Partic in Association for Rural & Small Libraries; Chinook Library Network
Open Mon-Fri 8:30-6:30
Restriction: Prof mat only
Friends of the Library Group

P NEWPORT PUBLIC LIBRARY*, 35 NW Nye St, 97365-3714. SAN 314-1349. Tel: 541-265-2153. TDD: 800-735-2900. Web Site: newportoregon.gov/dept/lib. *Libr Dir,* Ted J Smith; E-mail: t.smith@newportlibrary.org; *Ref Librn, Supv Librn,* Sheryl Eldridge; *Supv Librn, Youth Serv Librn,* Linda Annable; *Supv Librn,* Stacy Johns; *Supv Librn,* Alice MacGougan; Staff 12 (MLS 5, Non-MLS 7)
Founded 1945. Pop 17,500; Circ 287,214
Library Holdings: Bk Vols 71,688
Automation Activity & Vendor Info: (Cataloging) Innovative Interfaces, Inc - Sierra; (Circulation) Innovative Interfaces, Inc - Sierra; (ILL) OCLC; (OPAC) Innovative Interfaces, Inc
Wireless access
Function: After school storytime, Audiobks via web, AV serv, Bilingual assistance for Spanish patrons, Bk club(s), Bks on CD, Children's prog, Computer training, Computers for patron use, Digital talking bks, Electronic databases & coll, Free DVD rentals, Holiday prog, Home delivery & serv to seniorr ctr & nursing homes, Homebound delivery serv, ILL available, Internet access, Magnifiers for reading, Mail & tel request accepted, Music CDs, Online cat, Online ref, OverDrive digital audio bks, Photocopying/Printing, Preschool outreach, Prog for adults, Prog for children & young adult, Ref serv available, Summer reading prog, Tax forms, Teen prog, Telephone ref, VHS videos, Wheelchair accessible
Special Services for the Deaf - Bks on deafness & sign lang
Special Services for the Blind - Assistive/Adapted tech devices, equip & products; VisualTek equip
Open Mon-Wed 10-9, Thurs-Sat 10-6, Sun 12-5
Friends of the Library Group

J OREGON COAST COMMUNITY COLLEGE LIBRARY*, 400 SE College Way, 97366. SAN 374-5945. Tel: 541-867-8526. FAX: 541-265-3820. E-mail: occill@occc.cc.or.us. Web Site: oregoncoastcc.org/library-and-media-services. *Libr Serv Mgr,* Darci L Adolf; Tel: 541-867-8526, E-mail: dadolf@occc.cc.or.us; Staff 2 (MLS 2)
Founded 1993. Enrl 474; Fac 35; Highest Degree: Associate
Library Holdings: e-books 1,800; Bk Vols 8,132; Per Subs 50; Videos 1,500
Automation Activity & Vendor Info: (Cataloging) SirsiDynix; (Circulation) SirsiDynix; (OPAC) SirsiDynix
Wireless access
Partic in Chinook Library Network
Open Mon-Thurs 9-6, Fri 8-5

S OREGON COAST HISTORY CENTER*, Research Library, Burrows House, 545 SW Ninth St, 97365. SAN 370-548X. Tel: 541-265-7509. FAX: 541-265-3992. Web Site: www.oregoncoasthistory.org/research-library. *Curator,* Jeff Syrop; Staff 1 (Non-MLS 1)
Founded 1961
Library Holdings: Bk Titles 600
Special Collections: Lincoln County History, bks, docs, photos; Siletz Tribal History, docs, maps, photos, artifacts
Function: Res libr
Restriction: Open to pub by appt only

C OREGON STATE UNIVERSITY, Marilyn Potts Guin Library, 2030 SE Marine Science Dr, 97365. SAN 321-5342. Tel: 541-867-0249. E-mail: hmsc.library@oregonstate.edu. Web Site: guin.library.oregonstate.edu. *Librn,* Mary Markland; Tel: 541-867-0108, E-mail: mary.markland@oregonstate.edu; Staff 3 (MLS 1, Non-MLS 2)
Founded 1967
Library Holdings: Bk Titles 20,000; Bk Vols 35,000; Per Subs 310
Subject Interests: Aquaculture, Marine fisheries, Marine mammals, Marine sci
Automation Activity & Vendor Info: (Acquisitions) Ex Libris Group; (Cataloging) Ex Libris Group; (Circulation) Ex Libris Group; (Course Reserve) Ex Libris Group; (Discovery) Ex Libris Group; (ILL) Ex Libris Group; (Media Booking) Ex Libris Group; (OPAC) Ex Libris Group; (Serials) Ex Libris Group
Wireless access
Function: Res libr
Partic in OCLC Online Computer Library Center, Inc
Open Mon-Fri 8-5
Friends of the Library Group

NORTH BEND

G BUREAU OF LAND MANAGEMENT*, Coos Bay District Office Library, 1300 Airport Lane, 97459. SAN 314-0709. Tel: 541-756-0100. FAX: 541-751-4303. E-mail: BLM_OR_CB_Mail@blm.gov. Web Site: www.blm.gov. *Admin Officer,* Cheri Murdock; E-mail: cmurdock@blm.gov
Library Holdings: Bk Vols 2,500
Restriction: Not open to pub

P NORTH BEND PUBLIC LIBRARY, 1800 Sherman Ave, 97459. SAN 314-1357. Tel: 541-756-0400. FAX: 541-756-1073. Web Site: northbendoregon.us/library. *Dir,* Haley Lagasse; E-mail: hlagasse@northbendlibrary.org; *Asst Dir,* Teresa Lucas; E-mail: tlucas@northbendlibrary.org; Staff 4 (MLS 4)
Founded 1914. Pop 16,091; Circ 242,168
Library Holdings: Bk Titles 88,230; Bk Vols 112,000; Per Subs 214
Special Collections: City; Oregoniana (Oregon Coll), bks, clippings, pamphlets. Oral History
Wireless access
Mem of Coos County Library Service District
Partic in Coastline
Open Mon-Fri 10-6, Sat 10-1
Friends of the Library Group

NORTH POWDER

P NORTH POWDER LIBRARY, 290 E St, 97867. (Mail add: PO Box 309, 97867-0309). Tel: 541-898-2175. FAX: 541-898-2175. E-mail: npcitylibrary1@gmail.com. *Dir,* Maggie Guthrie
Pop 680; Circ 1,200
Library Holdings: Audiobooks 110; Bk Titles 4,000; Videos 450
Automation Activity & Vendor Info: (Cataloging) Evergreen
Wireless access
Partic in Sage Library System of Eastern Oregon
Open Mon 1-7, Fri 9-3, Sat 10-2

NYSSA

P NYSSA PUBLIC LIBRARY*, 319 Main St, 97913-3845. Tel: 541-372-2978. E-mail: nyssalibrary@nyssacity.org. Web Site: www.nyssacity.org/nyssa-library.html. *Librn,* JoElle Rau; *Asst Librn, Cat,* Jenny Simpson
Pop 6,227
Library Holdings: Bk Vols 24,000; Per Subs 30
Automation Activity & Vendor Info: (Acquisitions) Evergreen; (Cataloging) Evergreen; (Circulation) Evergreen; (Course Reserve) Evergreen; (ILL) Evergreen; (OPAC) Evergreen; (Serials) Evergreen
Wireless access
Open Tues & Thurs 11-7, Wed & Fri 1-5, Sat 11-4
Friends of the Library Group

OAK GROVE

P CLACKAMAS COUNTY LIBRARY, Oak Lodge Public Library, 16201 SE McLoughlin Blvd, 97267. SAN 314-139X. Tel: 503-655-8543. E-mail: oaklodge@lincc.org. Web Site: www.clackamas.us/lib. *Dir,* Mitzi Olson; Staff 1.8 (MLS 0.9, Non-MLS 0.9)
Founded 1938. Pop 84,411; Circ 937,898
Library Holdings: AV Mats 27,354; e-books 2,557; Bk Titles 141,879; Per Subs 276
Automation Activity & Vendor Info: (Acquisitions) SirsiDynix; (Cataloging) SirsiDynix; (Circulation) SirsiDynix; (OPAC) SirsiDynix
Wireless access
Partic in Library Information Network of Clackamas County
Open Mon, Fri, & Sat 10-6, Tues-Thurs Noon-8, Sun Noon-6
Friends of the Library Group
Branches: 1
GLADSTONE PUBLIC LIBRARY, 135 E Dartmouth St, Gladstone, 97027. Tel: 503-655-8540. E-mail: gladstone@lincc.org. *Dir,* Mitzi Olson
Open Mon, Fri & Sat 10-6, Tues & Thurs 12-8, Wed 10-8, Sun 11-6

OAKRIDGE

P OAKRIDGE PUBLIC LIBRARY*, 48326 E First St, 97463. (Mail add: PO Box 1410, 97463-1410), SAN 314-1365. Tel: 541-782-2258. FAX: 541-782-1081. E-mail: oakridgelibrary@ci.oakridge.or.us. Web Site: www.ci.oakridge.or.us. *Coordr,* Georgeanne Samuelson; Staff 1 (Non-MLS 1)
Founded 1950. Pop 3,200; Circ 11,000
Library Holdings: Bk Vols 18,000; Per Subs 30
Automation Activity & Vendor Info: (Cataloging) SirsiDynix; (Circulation) SirsiDynix
Wireless access
Open Mon, Wed & Fri 1-5, Tues & Thurs 9-5, Sat 10-2

ONTARIO

P ONTARIO COMMUNITY LIBRARY*, 388 SW Second Ave, 97914. SAN 358-0350. Tel: 541-889-6371. FAX: 541-889-4279. Web Site: www.ontariocommunitylibrary.org. *Dir,* Darlyne Johnson; E-mail: ontariolibrarydirector@gmail.com; Staff 10 (MLS 1, Non-MLS 9)
Founded 1909. Pop 32,065; Circ 190,085
Library Holdings: Bk Titles 100,847; Per Subs 88
Special Collections: Oregon & Idaho Coll. State Document Depository
Subject Interests: Literacy
Automation Activity & Vendor Info: (Cataloging) Evergreen; (Circulation) Evergreen; (ILL) Evergreen; (OPAC) Evergreen
Wireless access
Function: Prof lending libr, Ref serv available
Open Mon & Wed 10-8, Tues, Thurs & Fri 10-5, Sat 10-4
Friends of the Library Group
Bookmobiles: 1. Librn, Tonya Ito

J TREASURE VALLEY COMMUNITY COLLEGE LIBRARY*, 650 College Blvd, 97914-3423. Tel: 541-881-5929. FAX: 541-881-2724. E-mail: library@tvcc.cc. Web Site: www.tvcc.cc/library. *Libr Dir,* Tara Dominick; E-mail: tdominick@tvcc.cc; Staff 4 (Non-MLS 4)
Founded 1963. Enrl 3,200; Highest Degree: Associate. Sal $225,000
Library Holdings: Audiobooks 250; CDs 100; DVDs 900; e-books 5,000; e-journals 8; Bk Titles 38,000; Bk Vols 42,000; Per Subs 80; Spec Interest Per Sub 40
Special Collections: Japanese American Oral History Project, videos. Oral History
Automation Activity & Vendor Info: (Acquisitions) Evergreen; (Cataloging) Evergreen; (Circulation) Evergreen; (ILL) OCLC FirstSearch; (OPAC) Evergreen; (Serials) Evergreen
Wireless access
Function: Archival coll, Audio & video playback equip for onsite use, Bks on CD, Computers for patron use, Digital talking bks, Distance learning, Electronic databases & coll, Free DVD rentals, ILL available, Instruction & testing, Internet access, Music CDs, Online cat, Online ref, Orientations, Ref & res, Ref serv available, Spoken cassettes & CDs, Wheelchair accessible
Partic in Sage Library System of Eastern Oregon
Special Services for the Deaf - ADA equip
Open Mon-Thurs 7am-9pm, Fri 8-5, Sun 1-9

OREGON CITY

J CLACKAMAS COMMUNITY COLLEGE LIBRARY, 19600 Molalla Ave, 97045. SAN 314-1381. Tel: 503-594-6323. Reference Tel: 503-594-6042. Web Site: libguides.clackamas.edu/home, www.clackamas.edu. *Dept Chair, Librn,* Ms SD DeWaay; Tel: 503-594-6330, E-mail: sd.dewaay@clackamas.edu; *Librn,* Jane Littlefield; Tel: 503-594-3474, E-mail: jane.littlefield@clackamas.edu; *Librn,* Sarah Nolan; Tel: 503-594-3316, E-mail: sarahn@clackamas.edu; *Libr Serv Coordr,* Derek

Cloo; Tel: 503-594-3491, E-mail: derek.cloo@clackamas.edu; Staff 5 (MLS 3, Non-MLS 2)
Founded 1967. Enrl 6,400; Fac 130; Highest Degree: Associate
Library Holdings: Bk Vols 52,600; Per Subs 300
Special Collections: Oregon Coll
Automation Activity & Vendor Info: (Acquisitions) Ex Libris Group; (Cataloging) Ex Libris Group; (Circulation) Ex Libris Group; (Course Reserve) Ex Libris Group; (Discovery) Ex Libris Group; (ILL) Ex Libris Group; (OPAC) Ex Libris Group; (Serials) Ex Libris Group
Wireless access
Function: Electronic databases & coll, Free DVD rentals, ILL available, Internet access, Large print keyboards, Learning ctr, Magazines, Online cat, Online info literacy tutorials on the web & in blackboard, Online ref, Outside serv via phone, mail, e-mail & web, Photocopying/Printing, Ref & res, Res libr, Scanner, Spanish lang bks, Study rm, Telephone ref
Partic in Orbis Cascade Alliance
Open Mon-Thurs 8-8, Fri 8-5, Sat 11-3
Restriction: 24-hr pass syst for students only, Access at librarian's discretion

P OREGON CITY PUBLIC LIBRARY*, 606 John Adams St, 97045. SAN 314-1403. Tel: 503-657-8269. Web Site: www.orcity.org/library. *Libr Dir,* Maureen Cole; E-mail: mcole@orcity.org; *Ad,* Gina Bacon; E-mail: gbacon@orcity.org; *Youth Serv Librn,* Barratt Miller; E-mail: bmiller@orcity.org; *Operations Mgr,* Denise Butcher; E-mail: dbutcher@orcity.org; *Tech Serv,* Betty Joe Armstrong; E-mail: barmstrong@orcity.org
Founded 1909. Pop 58,000; Circ 535,000
Jul 2018-Jun 2019 Income $8,400, State $8,400. Mats Exp $79,843, Books $49,200, Per/Ser (Incl. Access Fees) $4,465, AV Mat $26,178. Sal $358,324
Library Holdings: AV Mats 13,227; Bk Vols 99,558; Per Subs 208
Special Collections: Oregon History (The Oregon Coll), bk, micro
Subject Interests: Genealogy, Local hist, Ore
Automation Activity & Vendor Info: (Acquisitions) SirsiDynix; (Cataloging) SirsiDynix; (Circulation) SirsiDynix; (OPAC) SirsiDynix
Wireless access
Function: 24/7 Electronic res, 24/7 Online cat, Activity rm, Adult bk club, Art exhibits, Audiobks on Playaways & MP3, Audiobks via web, AV serv, Bi-weekly Writer's Group, Bk club(s), Bks on CD, Butterfly Garden, Children's prog, Computer training, Computers for patron use, Digital talking bks, Electronic databases & coll, Free DVD rentals, Genealogy discussion group, Holiday prog, Home delivery & serv to seniorr ctr & nursing homes, ILL available, Internet access, Large print keyboards, Life-long learning prog for all ages, Magazines, Magnifiers for reading, Meeting rooms, Microfiche/film & reading machines, Movies, Museum passes, Music CDs, Online cat, OverDrive digital audio bks, Photocopying/Printing, Printer for laptops & handheld devices, Prog for adults, Prog for children & young adult, Ref serv available, Scanner, Spanish lang bks, Story hour, Study rm, Summer reading prog, Tax forms, Teen prog, Telephone ref, Wheelchair accessible, Workshops, Writing prog
Partic in Library Information Network of Clackamas County
Open Mon-Wed 10-7, Thurs-Sat 10-6, Sun Noon-5
Restriction: Non-circulating of rare bks
Friends of the Library Group

M PROVIDENCE WILLAMETTE FALLS MEDICAL CENTER*, Health Sciences Library, 1500 Division St, 97045. SAN 375-0647. Tel: 503-650-6757. FAX: 503-650-6836. E-mail: ORPWFWillametteLibrary@providence.org. Web Site: oregon.providence.org/location-directory/p/providence-willamette-falls-medical-center. *Dir, Libr Serv,* Heather Martin; E-mail: librarian@providence.org
Library Holdings: Bk Vols 800; Per Subs 450
Subject Interests: Consumer health
Open Mon-Thurs 8-1

PENDLETON

J BLUE MOUNTAIN COMMUNITY COLLEGE LIBRARY*, 2411 NW Carden Ave, 97801. (Mail add: PO Box 100, 97801), SAN 314-1411. Tel: 541-278-5915. Administration Tel: 541-278-5916. Automation Services Tel: 541-276-1470. FAX: 541-276-6119. E-mail: library@bluecc.edu. Web Site: www.bluecc.edu/academics/library. *Dir, Libr & Media Serv,* Brittany Young; E-mail: byoung@bluecc.edu; *Cat, Electronic Res Librn,* Heather Estrada; Tel: 541-278-5913, E-mail: hestrada@bluecc.edu; *Libr Support Serv Asst,* Ashlei Emmons; E-mail: AEmmons@bluecc.edu; *Libr Support Serv Asst,* Kaiden Roba; E-mail: kroba@bluecc.edu; *Tech Serv Asst,* Adam Sims; Tel: 541-278-5912, E-mail: asims@bluecc.edu; Staff 4 (MLS 2, Non-MLS 2)
Founded 1963. Enrl 2,108; Fac 79
Library Holdings: AV Mats 3,518; Bk Titles 34,821; Bk Vols 36,972; Per Subs 367
Special Collections: State Document Depository; US Document Depository
Automation Activity & Vendor Info: (Cataloging) OCLC; (Circulation) Innovative Interfaces, Inc; (Course Reserve) Innovative Interfaces, Inc; (ILL) OCLC; (OPAC) Innovative Interfaces, Inc
Wireless access
Function: AV serv, Res libr
Partic in Sage Library System of Eastern Oregon
Open Mon-Thurs 7:30-6, Fri 7:30-4, Sun 1-5

P PENDLETON PUBLIC LIBRARY, 502 SW Dorion Ave, 97801-1698. SAN 358-0601. Tel: 541-966-0380. FAX: 541-966-0382. Web Site: pendleton.or.us/library. *Libr Dir,* Jennifer Costley; E-mail: jennifer.costley@ci.pendleton.or.us; *Youth Serv Librn,* Briana White; E-mail: briana.white@ci.pendleton.or.us; Staff 7 (MLS 2, Non-MLS 5)
Founded 1987. Pop 23,391; Circ 122,000
Library Holdings: AV Mats 7,685; CDs 317; DVDs 241; Electronic Media & Resources 22; High Interest/Low Vocabulary Bk Vols 221; Large Print Bks 1,954; Bk Titles 60,000; Per Subs 140; Talking Bks 5,175; Videos 2,269
Special Collections: Northeast Oregon; Pacific Northwest; Rodeo & Western Literature
Automation Activity & Vendor Info: (Cataloging) Evergreen; (Circulation) Evergreen; (OPAC) Evergreen
Wireless access
Mem of Umatilla County Special Library District
Partic in Sage Library System of Eastern Oregon
Open Mon-Thurs 10-7, Fri & Sat 10-5
Friends of the Library Group

P UMATILLA COUNTY SPECIAL LIBRARY DISTRICT, 425 S Main St, 97801. (Mail add: PO Box 1689, 97801). Tel: 541-276-6449. Web Site: ucsld.org. *District Dir,* Erin McCusker; E-mail: director@ucsld.org; *Literacy Prog Mgr,* Monica Hoffman; Tel: 541-612-2052, E-mail: takeoff@ucsld.org; *Tech Serv Mgr,* Dea Nowell; Tel: 541-966-0917, E-mail: dea@ucsld.org; Staff 3 (MLS 1, Non-MLS 2)
Pop 62,720
Function: Electronic databases & coll, Family literacy, Outreach serv
Member Libraries: Adams Public Library; Athena Public Library; Echo Public Library; Helix Public Library; Milton-Freewater Public Library; Pendleton Public Library; Pilot Rock Public Library; Stanfield Public Library; Ukiah Public Library; Umatilla Public Library; Weston Public Library

PILOT ROCK

P PILOT ROCK PUBLIC LIBRARY*, 144 N Alder Pl, 97868. (Mail add: PO Box 520, 97868-0520), SAN 358-0628. Tel: 541-443-3285. FAX: 541-443-2253. E-mail: pilotrockpl@centurytel.net. Web Site: pilotrockpubliclibrary.weebly.com. *Dir,* Susan Price
Library Holdings: Bk Titles 6,000; Per Subs 30
Mem of Umatilla County Special Library District
Partic in Sage Library System of Eastern Oregon
Open Mon-Thurs 11-6, Fri 10-5

PORT ORFORD

P PORT ORFORD PUBLIC LIBRARY DISTRICT, 1421 Oregon St, 97465. (Mail add: PO Box 130, 97465), SAN 314-1446. Tel: 541-332-5622. E-mail: polibrary2012@gmail.com. Web Site: www.polibrary.org. *Dir,* Denise Willms; Staff 3 (Non-MLS 3)
Pop 3,232; Circ 25,539
Library Holdings: Bk Titles 22,986; Bk Vols 23,331; Per Subs 50
Automation Activity & Vendor Info: (Acquisitions) Koha; (Cataloging) Koha; (OPAC) Koha
Wireless access
Function: 24/7 Electronic res, 24/7 Online cat, Activity rm, Adult bk club, Adult literacy prog, After school storytime, Archival coll, Art exhibits, Art programs, Audiobks on Playaways & MP3, Audiobks via web, AV serv, Bk club(s), Bks on CD, Chess club, Children's prog, Computer training, Computers for patron use, Digital talking bks, Distance learning, E-Readers, Electronic databases & coll, Equip loans & repairs, Family literacy, Free DVD rentals, Holiday prog, Home delivery & serv to seniorr ctr & nursing homes, Homebound delivery serv, Homework prog, ILL available, Instruction & testing, Internet access, Laminating, Large print keyboards, Life-long learning prog for all ages, Magazines, Magnifiers for reading, Mango lang, Meeting rooms, Movies, Museum passes, Music CDs, Online cat, Online info literacy tutorials on the web & in blackboard, Online ref, Outreach serv, OverDrive digital audio bks, Photocopying/Printing, Preschool outreach, Prog for adults, Prog for children & young adult, Ref & res, Ref serv available, Scanner, Senior computer classes, Senior outreach, Story hour, Study rm, Summer & winter reading prog, Summer reading prog, Tax forms, Teen prog, Telephone ref, Wheelchair accessible, Winter reading prog, Workshops
Partic in Coastline
Open Tues-Fri 11-5, Sat 11-3

Restriction: Non-resident fee
Friends of the Library Group

PORTLAND

L ATER & WYNNE, LLP*, Law Library, Lovejoy Bldg, Ste 900, 1331 NW Lovejoy St, 97209-3280. SAN 372-2201. Tel: 503-226-1191. FAX: 503-226-0079. E-mail: library@aterwynne.com. Web Site: www.aterwynne.com.
Library Holdings: Bk Vols 20,000; Per Subs 50
Open Mon-Fri 8:30-5

G BONNEVILLE POWER ADMINISTRATION LIBRARY & VISITOR CENTER*, 905 NE 11th Ave, 97232. (Mail add: PO Box 3621, 97208-3621), SAN 314-1853. Reference Tel: 503-230-7323. FAX: 503-230-5911. E-mail: library@bpa.gov. *Libr Team Lead,* Bill Zimmerman; Staff 5 (MLS 2, Non-MLS 3)
Founded 1938
Library Holdings: Bk Titles 35,000; Bk Vols 50,000; Per Subs 200
Special Collections: BPA Coll. US Document Depository
Subject Interests: Computer sci, Electrical engr, Fish, Utilities industry, Wildlife
Automation Activity & Vendor Info: (Cataloging) SirsiDynix; (Circulation) SirsiDynix; (ILL) OCLC; (OPAC) SirsiDynix; (Serials) EBSCO Online
Wireless access
Function: 24/7 Online cat, Bks on CD, CD-ROM, Electronic databases & coll, Govt ref serv, Magazines, Notary serv, Online cat, Photocopying/Printing, Ref & res, Telephone ref
Publications: Book lists; Brochure; Pathfinders
Open Mon-Fri 8:30-4:30
Restriction: Badge access after hrs

L BULLIVANT, HOUSER & BAILEY, Law Library, One SW Columbia St, Ste 800, 97204. SAN 372-221X. Tel: 503-228-6351. FAX: 503-295-0915. Web Site: www.bullivant.com. *Libr Mgr,* Maranda Cadungug; Tel: 503-499-4435, E-mail: maranda.cadungug@bullivant.com
Founded 1938
Library Holdings: Bk Vols 5,000; Per Subs 40
Wireless access
Open Mon-Fri 7:30-5

P CEDAR MILL COMMUNITY LIBRARY*, 12505 NW Cornell Rd, Ste 13, 97229. SAN 314-1470. Tel: 503-644-0043. Interlibrary Loan Service Tel: 503-644-0043, Ext 133. Reference Tel: 503-644-0043, Ext 114. Administration Tel: 503-644-0043, Ext 110. FAX: 503-644-3964. E-mail: askuscml@wccls.org. Web Site: library.cedarmill.org. *Exec Dir,* Peter Leonard; E-mail: peterl@wccls.org; *Adult Serv Mgr,* Lynne Erlandson; E-mail: lynee@wccls.org; *Circ Mgr,* Shannon Caster; E-mail: shannonc@wccls.org; *Tech Serv Mgr,* Lori Van Deman; E-mail: loriv@wccls.org; *Youth Serv Mgr,* Nancy Spaulding; E-mail: nancys@wccls.org; Staff 18 (MLS 17, Non-MLS 1)
Founded 1974. Pop 73,110; Circ 2,636,200
Jul 2013-Jun 2014 Income (Main & Associated Libraries) $4,085,391, County $3,395,391, Locally Generated Income $690,000. Mats Exp $377,000, Books $224,000, Per/Ser (Incl. Access Fees) $20,000, AV Equip $500, AV Mat $112,000, Electronic Ref Mat (Incl. Access Fees) $21,000. Sal $2,925,375
Library Holdings: AV Mats 41,939; Bk Vols 205,764; Per Subs 420
Special Collections: Oregon & Pacific Northwest, bks, per; Parent-Teacher Res Coll
Automation Activity & Vendor Info: (Acquisitions) Innovative Interfaces, Inc; (Cataloging) Innovative Interfaces, Inc; (Circulation) Innovative Interfaces, Inc; (OPAC) Innovative Interfaces, Inc
Wireless access
Function: Adult bk club, Archival coll, Audiobks via web, AV serv, Bilingual assistance for Spanish patrons, Bk club(s), Bks on CD, Children's prog, Computer training, Computers for patron use, Digital talking bks, Electronic databases & coll, Free DVD rentals, ILL available, Magnifiers for reading, Mail & tel request accepted, Museum passes, Music CDs, Online cat, Outreach serv, OverDrive digital audio bks, Photocopying/Printing, Preschool outreach, Preschool reading prog, Prog for adults, Prog for children & young adult, Ref serv available, Senior computer classes, Senior outreach, Summer reading prog, Teen prog, Telephone ref, Wheelchair accessible, Workshops
Publications: Library News (Newsletter)
Partic in Washington County Cooperative Library Services
Open Mon-Fri 10-8, Sat 10-5, Sun 12-5
Friends of the Library Group
Branches: 1
BETHANY BRANCH, 15325 NW Central Dr, Ste J-8, 97229. Tel: 503-617-7323. Web Site: library.cedarmill.org/bethany. *Br Mgr,* Marianne Coalson; E-mail: mariannec@wccls.org; Staff 9.2 (MLS 1.4, Non-MLS 7.8)
Founded 2007
Library Holdings: Audiobooks 1,806; CDs 2,732; DVDs 5,632; Electronic Media & Resources 483; Large Print Bks 244; Bk Vols 44,423; Per Subs 49
Open Mon-Fri 10-8, Sat 10-5, Sun 12-5
Friends of the Library Group

P GARDEN HOME COMMUNITY LIBRARY*, 7475 SW Oleson Rd, 97223. SAN 991-3114. Tel: 503-245-9932. Web Site: www.gardenhomelibrary.org. *Dir,* Molly Carlisle
Library Holdings: Bk Titles 18,000; Per Subs 35
Automation Activity & Vendor Info: (Cataloging) Innovative Interfaces, Inc; (Circulation) Innovative Interfaces, Inc; (OPAC) Innovative Interfaces, Inc
Wireless access
Partic in Washington County Cooperative Library Services
Open Mon-Thurs 9-8, Fri 9-6, Sat 9-3, Sun 11-3

S GENEALOGICAL FORUM OF OREGON LIBRARY*, GFO Library, 2505 SE 11th Ave, Ste B-18, 97202. SAN 321-5377. Tel: 503-963-1932. E-mail: library@gfo.org. Web Site: www.gfo.ind.opalsinfo.net/bin/home, www.gfo.org.
Founded 1946
Library Holdings: Braille Volumes 1; CDs 260; DVDs 9; e-books 2; e-journals 4; Electronic Media & Resources 258; Microforms 6,357; Bk Titles 23,208; Bk Vols 27,873; Spec Interest Per Sub 1,658
Special Collections: Manuscripts; Multnomah County Marriages 1855-1923
Subject Interests: Genealogy, Hist
Automation Activity & Vendor Info: (Cataloging) OPALS (Open-source Automated Library System)
Wireless access
Function: 24/7 Online cat, Archival coll, Audio & video playback equip for onsite use, Computers for patron use, Electronic databases & coll, Genealogy discussion group, Internet access, Masonic res mat, Microfiche/film & reading machines, Online cat, Orientations, Outreach serv, Photocopying/Printing, Printer for laptops & handheld devices, Prog for adults, Ref & res, Ref serv available, Res assist avail, Res libr, Res performed for a fee, Scanner, Spoken cassettes & CDs, Workshops, Writing prog
Publications: The Bulletin of the Genealogical Forum of Oregon Inc (Quarterly); The Forum Insider (Newsletter)
Open Mon, Tues & Thurs 9:30-5, Wed 9:30-8, Fri & Sat 9:30-3, Sun 12-5
Restriction: Fee for pub use, Free to mem, Non-circulating, Not a lending libr

M KAISER PERMANENTE*, Center for Health Research, 3800 N Interstate Ave, 97227-1098. SAN 374-5899. Tel: 503-335-6744. E-mail: library@kpchr.org. Web Site: research.kpchr.org. *Libr Serv Mgr,* Todd L Hannon; Staff 1 (MLS 1)
Library Holdings: Bk Titles 9,000; Per Subs 150
Restriction: Open by appt only

L LANE POWELL PC*, Law Library, 601 SW Second Ave, Ste 2100, 97204. SAN 371-6023. Tel: 503-778-2100. FAX: 503-778-2200. Web Site: www.lanepowell.com. *Librn,* Emily Lundeen; E-mail: lundeene@lanepowell.com; Staff 2 (MLS 2)
Founded 1889
Library Holdings: Bk Vols 10,000; Per Subs 100
Automation Activity & Vendor Info: (Cataloging) Inmagic, Inc.; (Serials) Inmagic, Inc.
Wireless access
Partic in OCLC Online Computer Library Center, Inc
Restriction: Private libr

M LEGACY EMANUEL HOSPITAL & HEALTH CENTER LIBRARY*, 2801 N Gantenbein Ave, 97227. SAN 314-1519. Tel: 503-413-2558. FAX: 503-413-2544. E-mail: lhslibrary@lhs.org. Web Site: www.legacyhealth.org/library. *Libr Mgr,* Position Currently Open; *Ref Serv,* Cindy Ramzy; E-mail: cramzy@lhs.org
Founded 1949
Library Holdings: Bk Titles 2,200; Bk Vols 2,700; Per Subs 200
Subject Interests: Emergency med, Pediatrics, Surgery, Trauma med
Function: Res libr
Partic in National Network of Libraries of Medicine Region 5
Open Mon-Fri 8-4:30

LEWIS & CLARK COLLEGE
CL PAUL L BOLEY LAW LIBRARY*, Lewis & Clark Law School, 10015 SW Terwilliger Blvd, 97219, SAN 358-0830. Tel: 503-768-6776. Reference Tel: 503-768-6688. FAX: 503-768-6760. E-mail: lawlib@lclark.edu. Web Site: lawlib.lclark.edu. *Dir,* Peter S Nycum; *Assoc Dir,* Tami Gierloff; *Head, Ref,* Seneca Gray; *Head, Tech Serv,* Kathy Faust; *Electronic Res,* Rob Truman; *Reader Serv,* Lynn Williams; Staff 9 (MLS 7, Non-MLS 2)

Founded 1884. Enrl 720; Fac 40; Highest Degree: Doctorate
Library Holdings: Bk Vols 213,961; Per Subs 4,840
Special Collections: Crime Victim Coll; Milton S Pearl Environmental Law Library; Patent Law Coll; Samuel S Johnson Public Land Law Review Commission Coll. State Document Depository; US Document Depository
Subject Interests: Am law, Antitrust, Environ studies, Intellectual property, Taxation
Automation Activity & Vendor Info: (Acquisitions) Innovative Interfaces, Inc; (Cataloging) Innovative Interfaces, Inc; (Circulation) Innovative Interfaces, Inc; (Course Reserve) Innovative Interfaces, Inc; (ILL) OCLC WorldShare Interlibrary Loan; (Media Booking) Innovative Interfaces, Inc; (OPAC) Innovative Interfaces, Inc; (Serials) Innovative Interfaces, Inc
Function: ILL available, Ref serv available
Partic in OCLC Online Computer Library Center, Inc
Publications: Handbook (Annual); Subject Bibliographies
Open Mon-Thurs 7am-Midnight, Fri 7am-10pm, Sat & Sun 9am-Midnight

C AUBREY R WATZEK LIBRARY*, 0615 SW Palatine Hill Rd, 97219-7899, SAN 358-0806. Tel: 503-768-7274. Circulation Tel: 503-768-7270. Interlibrary Loan Service Tel: 503-768-7280. Reference Tel: 503-768-7285. Administration Tel: 503-768-7275. FAX: 503-768-7282. Web Site: library.lclark.edu. *Interim Dir,* Mark Dahl; Tel: 503-768-7339, E-mail: dahl@lclark.edu; *Assoc Dir,* Elaine Heras; Tel: 503-768-7277; *Acq & Coll Develop Librn,* Jim Bunnelle; E-mail: bunnelle@lclark.edu; *Cat Librn,* Laura Ayling Tucker; E-mail: ayling@lclark.edu; *Fac Outreach Librn,* Dan Kelley; E-mail: dkelley@lclark.edu; *Ref Librn,* Betty Ann Smith; E-mail: smithb@lclark.edu; *Mgr, Access Serv,* Rick Peterson; Staff 13 (MLS 11, Non-MLS 2)
Founded 1867. Enrl 2,466; Fac 163; Highest Degree: Master
Library Holdings: Bk Vols 290,000
Special Collections: Lewis & Clark Expedition Coll. US Document Depository
Subject Interests: Gender studies, Pac NW hist
Automation Activity & Vendor Info: (Acquisitions) Innovative Interfaces, Inc; (Cataloging) Innovative Interfaces, Inc; (Circulation) Innovative Interfaces, Inc; (OPAC) Innovative Interfaces, Inc; (Serials) Innovative Interfaces, Inc
Partic in OCLC Online Computer Library Center, Inc; Orbis Cascade Alliance
Friends of the Library Group

S MAZAMAS LIBRARY & ARCHIVES*, 527 SE 43rd Ave, 97215. SAN 325-8165. Tel: 503-227-2345, Ext 2. FAX: 503-227-0862. E-mail: library@mazamas.org. Web Site: www.mazamas.org/library. *Historical Colls Mgr, Librn,* Mathew Brock; E-mail: mathewbrock@mazamas.org; Staff 1 (MLS 1)
Founded 1915
Library Holdings: Bk Vols 8,000; Per Subs 36
Subject Interests: Mountaineering
Function: Photocopying/Printing
Restriction: Mem only
Friends of the Library Group

L MILLER NASH GRAHAM & DUNN LLP LIBRARY*, 3400 US Bancorp Tower, 111 SW Fifth Ave, 97204-3699. SAN 314-1624. Tel: 503-224-5858. Toll Free Tel: 877-220-5858. FAX: 503-224-0155. *Dir, Libr Serv,* Elise Brickner-Schulz; Tel: 503-205-2427, E-mail: elise.brickner-schulz@millernash.com; *Ref Librn,* Douglas Hull; E-mail: hull@millernash.com; Staff 5 (MLS 3, Non-MLS 2)
Founded 1873
Library Holdings: Bk Titles 8,000; Bk Vols 20,000; Per Subs 400
Subject Interests: Law

P MULTNOMAH COUNTY LIBRARY*, Administrative Offices, 919 NE 19th Ave, Ste 250, 97232. (Mail add: 205 E Russell St, 97212), SAN 358-0865. Tel: 503-988-5123. Web Site: multcolib.org. *Dir of Libr,* Ms Vailey Oehlke; E-mail: vaileyo@multcolib.org; *Dep Dir,* Terrilyn Chun; E-mail: terrilyn@multcolib.org; *Communications Dir,* Shawn Cunningham; E-mail: shawnc@multco.us; *Mkt Dir,* Jeremy Graybill; E-mail: jeremyg@multcolib.org; *Dir, Operations,* Donald Allgeier; E-mail: donalda@multcolib.org; *Dir, Programming,* Katie O'Dell; E-mail: kodell@multcolib.org; *Spec Project Dir,* Cindy Gibbon; E-mail: cindyg@multcolib.org; *Human Res Mgr,* Johnette Easter; E-mail: johnette@multcolib.org; Staff 536 (MLS 84, Non-MLS 452)
Founded 1864. Pop 777,490; Circ 18,500,000
Library Holdings: Per Subs 600
Special Collections: John Wilson Room; McCormack Coll, bks, rec; Oregon Coll; Roses (Thomas Newton Cook Rose Library & Jesse A Currey Memorial Rose Coll). State Document Depository; US Document Depository
Automation Activity & Vendor Info: (Circulation) Innovative Interfaces, Inc
Wireless access
Partic in OCLC Online Computer Library Center, Inc
Open Mon-Fri 8-5
Friends of the Library Group
Branches: 19
ALBINA, 3605 NE 15th Ave, 97212, SAN 358-089X. Web Site: multcolib.org/library-location/albina. *Library Contact,* Lisa White
Founded 1906
Open Mon & Tues 12-8, Wed-Sat 10-6, Sun 12-5
Friends of the Library Group
BELMONT, 1038 SE Cesar E Chavez Blvd, 97214, SAN 358-092X. Web Site: multcolib.org/library-location/belmont. *Library Contact,* Matthew Yake
Founded 1924
Open Mon, Fri & Sat 10-6, Tues 10-8, Wed & Thurs 12-8, Sun 10-5
Friends of the Library Group
CAPITOL HILL, 10723 SW Capitol Hwy, 97219, SAN 358-0954. Web Site: multcolib.org/library-location/capitol-hill. *Library Contact,* Patti Vincent
Founded 1972
Open Mon & Tues 12-8, Wed-Sat 10-6, Sun 12-5
Friends of the Library Group
CENTRAL LIBRARY, 801 SW Tenth Ave, 97205. Web Site: multcolib.org/library-location/central. *Libr Dir,* Angela Weyrens
Founded 1913
Open Mon 10-8, Tues & Wed Noon-8, Thurs-Sat 10-6, Sun 10-5
Friends of the Library Group
FAIRVIEW-COLUMBIA BRANCH, 1520 NE Village St, Fairview, 97024. Web Site: multcolib.org/library-location/fairview-columbia. *Library Contact,* Kylie Park
Founded 2001
Open Mon & Tues Noon-8, Wed-Sat 10-6, Sun Noon-5
Friends of the Library Group
GREGORY HEIGHTS, 7921 NE Sandy Blvd, 97213, SAN 358-0989. Web Site: multcolib.org/library-location/gregory-heights. *Library Contact,* May Dea
Founded 1938
Open Mon & Tues Noon-8, Wed-Sat 10-6, Sun Noon-5
Friends of the Library Group
GRESHAM BRANCH, 385 NW Miller Ave, Gresham, 97030, SAN 358-1012. Web Site: multcolib.org/library-location/gresham. *Library Contact,* Bryan Fearn
Founded 1913
Open Mon, Fri & Sat 10-6, Tues 10-8, Wed & Thurs Noon-8, Sun 10-5
Friends of the Library Group
HILLSDALE, 1525 SW Sunset Blvd, 97239, SAN 358-1349. Web Site: multcolib.org/library-location/hillsdale. *Library Contact,* Jay Hadley
Founded 1921
Open Mon, Fri & Sat 10-6, Tues 10-8, Wed & Thurs Noon-8, Sun 10-5
Friends of the Library Group
HOLGATE, 7905 SE Holgate Blvd, 97206, SAN 358-1047. Web Site: multcolib.org/library-location/holgate. *Library Contact,* Silvana Santana Gabriell
Founded 1914
Open Mon & Tues Noon-8, Wed-Sat 10-6, Sun Noon-5
Friends of the Library Group
HOLLYWOOD, 4040 NE Tillamook St, 97212, SAN 358-1071. Web Site: multcolib.org/library-location/hollywood. *Library Contact,* Martha Flotten
Founded 1917
Open Mon, Fri & Sat 10-6, Tues 10-8, Wed & Thurs Noon-8, Sun 10-5
Friends of the Library Group
KENTON, 8226 N Denver Ave, 97217. Web Site: multcolib.org/library-location/kenton. *Library Contact,* David Miles
Founded 2010
Open Mon & Tues Noon-8, Wed-Sat 10-6, Sun Noon-5
Friends of the Library Group
MIDLAND, 805 SE 122nd Ave, 97233, SAN 358-1160. Web Site: multcolib.org/library-location/midland. *Library Contact,* Darrel Mally
Founded 1958
Open Mon, Fri & Sat 10-6, Tues 10-8, Wed & Thurs Noon-8, Sun 10-5
Friends of the Library Group
NORTH PORTLAND, 512 N Killingsworth St, 97217, SAN 358-1225. Web Site: multcolib.org/library-location/north-portland. *Library Contact,* Kirby McCurtis
Founded 1909
Special Collections: Black Resource Coll
Open Mon & Tues Noon-8, Wed-Sat 10-6, Sun Noon-5
Friends of the Library Group
NORTHWEST, 2300 NW Thurman St, 97210. Web Site: multcolib.org/library-location/northwest. *Library Contact,* Kim Anderson
Founded 2001
Open Mon & Tues Noon-8, Wed-Sat 10-6, Sun Noon-5
Friends of the Library Group

ROCKWOOD, 17917 SE Stark St, 97233, SAN 358-125X. Web Site: multcolib.org/library-location/rockwood. *Library Contact,* David Lee
Founded 1963
Open Mon & Tues Noon-8, Wed-Sat 10-6, Sun Noon-5
Friends of the Library Group

ST JOHNS, 7510 N Charleston Ave, 97203, SAN 358-1284. Web Site: multcolib.org/library-location/st-johns. *Library Contact,* Susie Woodward
Founded 1913
Open Mon & Tues Noon-8, Wed-Sat 10-6, Sun Noon-5
Friends of the Library Group

SELLWOOD-MORELAND, 7860 SE 13th Ave, 97202, SAN 358-1314. Web Site: multcolib.org/library-location/sellwood-moreland. *Library Contact,* Sarah Mead
Founded 1905
Open Mon & Tues Noon-8, Wed-Sat 10-6, Sun Noon-5
Friends of the Library Group

TROUTDALE, 2451 SW Cherry Park Rd, Troutdale, 97060. Web Site: multcolib.org/library-location/troutdale. *Library Contact,* Sarah Oliver
Founded 2010
Open Mon & Tues Noon-8, Wed-Sat 10-6, Sun Noon-5
Friends of the Library Group

WOODSTOCK, 6008 SE 49th Ave, 97206, SAN 358-1373. Web Site: multcolib.org/library-location/woodstock. *Library Contact,* David Lee
Founded 2000
Open Mon & Tues Noon-8, Wed-Sat 10-6, Sun Noon-5
Friends of the Library Group

L MULTNOMAH LAW LIBRARY*, County Courthouse, 4th Flr, 1021 SW Fourth Ave, 97204. SAN 314-1632. Tel: 503-988-3394. E-mail: librarian@multlawlib.org. Web Site: multlawlib.org. *Dir,* Martha Renick; *Law Librn,* Jacquelyn Jurkins
Founded 1890
Library Holdings: Bk Vols 216,500
Wireless access

CR MULTNOMAH UNIVERSITY*, John & Mary Mitchell Library, 8435 NE Glisan St, 97220-5898. SAN 314-1640. Tel: 503-251-5322. Circulation Tel: 503-251-5321. Reference Tel: 503-251-5317. FAX: 503-254-1268. E-mail: library@multnomah.edu. Web Site: www.multnomah.edu/resources/library. *Dir,* Dr Philip M Johnson; Tel: 503-251-5323, E-mail: pjohnson@multnomah.edu; *Head, Pub Serv,* Pam Middleton; E-mail: pamm@multnomah.edu; *Ref Librn,* Suzanne Smith; E-mail: ssmith@multnomah.edu; *Tech Serv,* Susan Spirz; Tel: 503-251-5316, E-mail: sspirz@multnomah.edu; Staff 4 (MLS 2, Non-MLS 2)
Founded 1936. Enrl 828; Fac 40; Highest Degree: Doctorate
Library Holdings: e-books 11,325; Bk Titles 64,000; Bk Vols 77,489; Per Subs 402
Special Collections: Bible Coll
Subject Interests: Biblical studies, Christian educ, Church hist, Practical theol, Theol
Automation Activity & Vendor Info: (Acquisitions) Ex Libris Group; (Cataloging) Ex Libris Group; (Circulation) Ex Libris Group; (Course Reserve) Ex Libris Group; (ILL) OCLC; (Media Booking) Ex Libris Group; (OPAC) Ex Libris Group; (Serials) Ex Libris Group
Wireless access
Partic in OCLC Online Computer Library Center, Inc; Online Private Academic Library Link
Open Mon-Thurs 7:45am-11pm, Fri 7:45-7, Sat 11-6, Sun 3-11

CM NATIONAL UNIVERSITY OF NATURAL MEDICINE LIBRARY*, 49 S Porter St, 97201. SAN 314-1659. Tel: 503-552-1542. FAX: 503-552-1547. E-mail: library@nunm.edu. Web Site: library.nunm.edu. *Univ Librn,* Noelle Stello; E-mail: nstello@nunm.edu; *Assoc Librn,* Christina King; E-mail: cking@nunm.edu
Founded 1956. Enrl 450; Fac 45; Highest Degree: Doctorate
Library Holdings: AV Mats 1,600; Bk Titles 19,000; Per Subs 160
Special Collections: Homeopathic Coll, journals; Naturopathic Coll, journals, rare bks
Subject Interests: Acupuncture, Botanical med, Homeopathy, Naturopathic med, Nutrition, Phys therapy
Automation Activity & Vendor Info: (Cataloging) Ex Libris Group; (Circulation) Ex Libris Group; (OPAC) Ex Libris Group; (Serials) Ex Libris Group
Wireless access
Open Mon-Thurs 7-7, Fri 7-6, Sat 9-5 (Fall-Spring); Mon-Thurs 7-7, Fri 7-5, Sat 9-5 (Summer)

C OREGON COLLEGE OF ART & CRAFT LIBRARY*, 8245 SW Barnes Rd, 97225. SAN 314-1683. Tel: 503-297-5544. FAX: 503-297-9651. E-mail: library@ocac.edu. Web Site: library.ocac.edu. *Dir,* Elsa Loftis; E-mail: eloftis@ocac.edu; Staff 1 (MLS 1)
Highest Degree: Master
Library Holdings: Bk Vols 12,000; Per Subs 90
Subject Interests: Craft hist, Design
Wireless access
Partic in Washington County Cooperative Library Services
Open Mon-Fri 9-5

CM OREGON COLLEGE OF ORIENTAL MEDICINE LIBRARY*, 75 NW Couch St, 97209. SAN 375-4952. Tel: 503-253-3443, Ext 132. Web Site: library.ocom.edu. *Dir, Libr Serv,* Candise Branum; Tel: 503-253-3443, Ext 134, E-mail: cbranum@ocom.edu; *Syst Librn,* Veronica Vichit-Vadakan; Tel: 503-253-3443, Ext 133, E-mail: vvv@ocom.edu; Staff 3 (MLS 3)
Founded 1991. Enrl 230; Fac 15; Highest Degree: Master
Library Holdings: AV Mats 720; Bk Titles 2,000; Bk Vols 2,500; Per Subs 40
Subject Interests: Acupuncture
Automation Activity & Vendor Info: (Cataloging) Inmagic, Inc.; (OPAC) Inmagic, Inc.
Wireless access
Open Mon-Thurs 7:45-7, Fri 7:45-6, Sat 11-3; Mon-Fri (Summer) 7:46-6

CM OREGON HEALTH & SCIENCE UNIVERSITY LIBRARY*, 3181 SW Sam Jackson Park Rd, MC LIB, 97239-3098. (Mail add: PO Box 573, 97207-0573), SAN 358-1551. Tel: 503-494-3460. FAX: 503-494-3227. E-mail: library@ohsu.libanswers.com. Web Site: www.ohsu.edu/xd/education/library/. *Libr Dir, Univ Librn,* Chris Shaffer; Tel: 503-367-4693, E-mail: shafferc@ohsu.edu; *Head, Archives, Head, Historical Coll,* Maija Anderson; Tel: 503-418-2287, E-mail: andermai@ohsu.edu; *Acq Librn, Electronic Res Librn,* Kristina DeShazo; Tel: 503-494-1637, E-mail: deshazok@ohsu.edu; *Ref Librn,* Andrew Hamilton; *Syst Librn, Web Develop Librn,* Laura Zeigen; *Mgr, Ser,* Kathleen Stewart; *Web Serv Mgr,* Shannon Carr; Staff 34 (MLS 13.5, Non-MLS 20.5)
Founded 1919. Enrl 2,586; Fac 2,142; Highest Degree: Doctorate
Library Holdings: Bk Titles 66,929; Bk Vols 221,001; Per Subs 2,429
Special Collections: Historical Photograph Coll; History of Dentistry Coll; History of Medicine Coll; Manuscripts & Archives; Medical Museum, artifacts; OHSU Oral History Project; Oregon Memorial Library for Bereaved Parents; Pacific Northwest & OHSU Publications (PNW Archives)
Automation Activity & Vendor Info: (Acquisitions) Innovative Interfaces, Inc; (Cataloging) Innovative Interfaces, Inc; (Circulation) Innovative Interfaces, Inc; (Course Reserve) Innovative Interfaces, Inc; (ILL) OCLC ILLiad; (Media Booking) Innovative Interfaces, Inc; (OPAC) Innovative Interfaces, Inc; (Serials) Innovative Interfaces, Inc
Wireless access
Function: Prof lending libr
Partic in National Network of Libraries of Medicine Region 5; OCLC Online Computer Library Center, Inc; Orbis Cascade Alliance
Open Mon-Fri 8-6

S OREGON HISTORICAL SOCIETY*, Research Library, 1200 SW Park Ave, 97205. SAN 314-1675. Tel: 503-306-5240. Reference E-mail: libreference@ohs.org. Web Site: www.ohs.org. *Libr Dir,* Shawna Gandy; Tel: 503-306-5265, E-mail: shawna.gandy@ohs.org; Staff 21 (MLS 14, Non-MLS 7)
Founded 1898
Special Collections: Extensive archival coll including Manuscripts, Photographs, Sound Recordings, Film
Subject Interests: Ore, Pac NW hist
Automation Activity & Vendor Info: (Cataloging) OCLC Connexion; (OPAC) SirsiDynix
Wireless access
Function: Res libr
Partic in OCLC Online Computer Library Center, Inc
Open Tues 1-5, Wed-Sat 10-5
Restriction: Closed stack, Non-circulating, Off-site coll in storage - retrieval as requested

S OREGON ZOO ANIMAL MANAGEMENT LIBRARY*, 4001 SW Canyon Rd, 97221. SAN 325-8262. Tel: 503-226-1561. Web Site: www.oregonzoo.org. *Conserv Librn, Res,* Karen Lewis
Library Holdings: Bk Titles 1,152
Subject Interests: Biology, Conserv, Natural hist
Automation Activity & Vendor Info: (Cataloging) Follett Software
Restriction: Open by appt only

C PACIFIC NORTHWEST COLLEGE OF ART, Albert Solheim Library, 511 NW Broadway, 97209. Tel: 503-821-8966. E-mail: ill@pnca.edu. Web Site: library.pnca.edu. *Dir, Libr Serv,* Serenity Ibsen; E-mail: sribsen@pnca.edu; Staff 5 (MLS 2, Non-MLS 3)
Founded 2001. Enrl 500; Highest Degree: Master
Library Holdings: DVDs 3,600; Electronic Media & Resources 99,000; Bk Vols 35,000; Per Subs 100; Videos 800
Special Collections: Oral History
Automation Activity & Vendor Info: (Acquisitions) CompPanion Corp; (Cataloging) ComPanion Corp; (Circulation) ComPanion Corp; (Course

Reserve) ComPanion Corp; (ILL) OCLC FirstSearch; (OPAC) ComPanion Corp; (Serials) ComPanion Corp
Wireless access
Function: Archival coll, Art exhibits, Audio & video playback equip for onsite use, CD-ROM, ILL available, Internet access, Online cat, Orientations, Photocopying/Printing, Ref serv available, Study rm, Telephone ref, VHS videos
Open Mon-Fri 9-5:30
Restriction: Borrowing privileges limited to fac & registered students, Circ limited, Fee for pub use, Limited access for the pub, Open to students, fac, staff & alumni, Pub use on premises

S PORTLAND ART MUSEUM*, Anne & James F Crumpacker Family Library, Mark Bldg, 2nd Flr, 1219 SW Park Ave, 97205. SAN 314-1756. Tel: 503-276-4215. E-mail: library@pam.org. Web Site: portlandartmuseum.org/learn/crumpacker-family-library. *Librn & Archivist,* Position Currently Open
Founded 1892
Library Holdings: Bk Titles 3,500; Per Subs 60
Special Collections: Arts of the Pacific Northwest Coast Indians; Auction Catalogs; Contemporary Art; English Silver; Japanese Prints; Northwest Artists File
Subject Interests: Art hist
Wireless access
Restriction: Open by appt only

J PORTLAND COMMUNITY COLLEGE LIBRARY*, 12000 SW 49th Ave, 97219. (Mail add: PO Box 19000, 97280), SAN 358-1403. Circulation Tel: 971-722-4935. Reference Tel: 971-722-4500. Administration Tel: 971-722-4497. Automation Services Tel: 971-722-4678. FAX: 971-722-8397. Administration FAX: 971-722-8398. TDD: 503-978-5269. Web Site: www.pcc.edu/library. *Dean,* Michelle Bagley; E-mail: michelle.bagley@pcc.edu; Staff 20 (MLS 20)
Founded 1964
Wireless access
Partic in Orbis Cascade Alliance
Open Mon-Fri 7:30-9
Friends of the Library Group

C PORTLAND STATE UNIVERSITY LIBRARY*, 1875 SW Park Ave, 97201-3220. (Mail add: PO Box 1151, 97207-1151), SAN 314-1772. Tel: 503-725-5874. Interlibrary Loan Service Tel: 503-725-3879. Administration Tel: 503-725-4616. FAX: 503-725-4524. Web Site: library.pdx.edu. *Dean, Univ Libr,* Marilyn Moody; *Asst Univ Librn,* Tom Bielavitz; *Asst Univ Librn,* Michael Bowman; *Head, Cataloging & E-Access,* Tom Larsen; *Head, Digital Initiatives,* Karen Bjork; *Head, Spec Coll, Univ Archivist,* Cristine Paschild; *Coll Develop & Mgt Librn,* Jill Emery; *Res & Instruction Librn,* Carly Lamphere; E-mail: lamphere@pdx.edu; *Mgr, Libr Tech,* Nathan Mealey; *Mgr, Access Serv,* Molly Gunderson; *Ref Serv Mgr,* Art Hendricks; *Mgr, Res Serv, Research & Instruction Services,* Sarah Beasley
Founded 1946. Enrl 28,000; Highest Degree: Doctorate
Special Collections: US Document Depository
Wireless access
Partic in Orbis Cascade Alliance

GM PORTLAND VA MEDICAL CENTER LIBRARY*, 3710 SW US Veterans Hospital Rd, P6LIB, 97239-2964. (Mail add: PO Box 1034, 97207-1034), SAN 314-1888. Tel: 503-220-8262, Ext 55955. Interlibrary Loan Service Tel: 503-220-8262, Ext 55039. FAX: 503-721-7816. E-mail: portland.library@med.va.gov. *Chief, Libr Serv,* Sola Whitehead; E-mail: sola.whitehead@va.gov; *Consumer Health Librn,* Kaye Martin; E-mail: kaye.martin@va.gov; Staff 2 (MLS 2)
Library Holdings: AV Mats 1,190; Bk Titles 9,096; Per Subs 191
Subject Interests: Geriatrics, Liver transplant, Med, Nursing, Patient health info, Post-traumatic stress, Psychol
Partic in National Network of Libraries of Medicine Region 5; OCLC Online Computer Library Center, Inc
Restriction: Hospital staff & commun

M PROVIDENCE SAINT VINCENT HOSPITAL & MEDICAL CENTER*, Health Sciences Library, 9205 SW Barnes Rd, 97225. SAN 314-1810. Tel: 503-216-2257. FAX: 503-216-6085. *Dir,* Heather Martin; E-mail: heather.martin@providence.org
Library Holdings: Bk Titles 4,000; Bk Vols 5,000; Per Subs 570
Subject Interests: Cancer, Cardiology, Hospital admin, Internal med, Nursing
Wireless access
Partic in Ore Health Info Network
Restriction: Not open to pub

C REED COLLEGE*, Eric V Hauser Memorial Library, 3203 SE Woodstock Blvd, 97202-8199. SAN 314-1802. Tel: 503-777-7702. Interlibrary Loan Service Tel: 503-777-7750. Reference Tel: 503-777-7554. Administration Tel: 503-777-7780. FAX: 503-777-7786. Web Site: www.library.reed.edu. *Col Librn,* Dena Hutto; Tel: 503-777-7572, E-mail: dhutto@reed.edu; *Head, Access Serv,* James Holmes; *Head, Coll Serv,* Erin Gallagher; *Dir, Res Serv,* Annie Downey; *Data Serv Librn,* David Isaak; *Digital Assets Librn,* Angie Beiriger; *Performing Arts Librn,* Erin Conor; *Spec Coll & Archives Librn,* Gay Walker; *Cat & Metadata,* Abigail Bibee; *Circ,* Mark McDaniel; *Sci,* Linda Maddux; *Visual Res,* Sarah Bavier; *Soc Sci Librn, User Experience Librn,* Joe Marquez; Staff 24.3 (MLS 10, Non-MLS 14.3)
Founded 1911. Enrl 1,427; Fac 137; Highest Degree: Master
Jul 2012-Jun 2013 Income $5,383,770. Mats Exp $2,999,859, Books $604,980, Per/Ser (Incl. Access Fees) $2,027,901, AV Equip $32,779, AV Mat $58,113, Electronic Ref Mat (Incl. Access Fees) $200,022, Presv $16,617. Sal $1,270,466 (Prof $751,460)
Library Holdings: AV Mats 33,673; Bk Titles 1,221,867
Special Collections: US Document Depository
Automation Activity & Vendor Info: (Acquisitions) Ex Libris Group; (Cataloging) Ex Libris Group; (Circulation) Ex Libris Group; (Discovery) Ex Libris Group; (ILL) OCLC ILLiad; (OPAC) Ex Libris Group; (Serials) Ex Libris Group
Wireless access
Partic in Northwest Association of Private Colleges & Universities; OCLC Online Computer Library Center, Inc; Orbis Cascade Alliance
Restriction: Restricted borrowing privileges

L STOEL RIVES LLP*, Law Library, 760 SW Ninth Ave, Ste 3000, 97205. SAN 314-1500. Tel: 503-294-9576. FAX: 503-220-2480. Web Site: www.stoel.com. *Libr Mgr,* Shannon Marich; E-mail: shannon.marich@stoel.com; Staff 10 (MLS 3, Non-MLS 7)
Founded 1906
Library Holdings: Bk Vols 30,000
Automation Activity & Vendor Info: (Cataloging) Inmagic, Inc.
Partic in Proquest Dialog
Restriction: Staff use only

L TONKON TORP LLP*, Law Library, 888 SW Fifth Ave, Ste 1600, 97204. SAN 372-2244. Tel: 503-221-1440. FAX: 503-274-8779. Web Site: tonkon.com. *Coordr,* John McIntyre; E-mail: john.mcintyre@tonkon.com
Founded 1974
Library Holdings: Bk Vols 10,000; Per Subs 50
Automation Activity & Vendor Info: (Cataloging) Inmagic, Inc.
Restriction: Staff use only

A UNITED STATES ARMY CORPS OF ENGINEERS*, Portland District Technical Library, US Army Corps of Engineers, Portland District Library, 333 SW First Ave, 97204. (Mail add: PO Box 2946, 97208-2946), SAN 358-1527. Tel: 503-808-5140. FAX: 503-808-5142. E-mail: cenwp.library@usace.army.mil. Web Site: www.nwp.usace.army.mil/library. *District Librn,* Jennifer Muller; E-mail: jennifer.s.muller@usace.army.mil; Staff 2.5 (MLS 1.5, Non-MLS 1)
Founded 1938
Library Holdings: Bk Titles 15,125; Bk Vols 24,153; Per Subs 40
Special Collections: Portland District Reports
Subject Interests: Civil engr, Cultural res, Dredging, Environ engr, Water resources planning
Automation Activity & Vendor Info: (Cataloging) EOS International; (Circulation) EOS International; (ILL) OCLC FirstSearch; (OPAC) EOS International; (Serials) EOS International
Restriction: Open by appt only, Restricted access

GL UNITED STATES COURTS FOR THE NINTH CIRCUIT LIBRARY*, Mark O Hatfield US Courthouse, 1000 SW Third Ave, 7A40, 97204. SAN 321-3862. Tel: 503-326-8140. FAX: 503-326-8144. *Br Librn,* Julia Sathler; E-mail: Julia_Sathler@LB9.uscourts.gov; Staff 3 (MLS 3)
Library Holdings: Bk Titles 850; Bk Vols 18,000; Per Subs 50
Automation Activity & Vendor Info: (Cataloging) SirsiDynix; (OPAC) SirsiDynix
Closed for renovations 2018-2019 due to reopen May 2019
Restriction: In-house use for visitors, Lending to staff only, Non-circulating to the pub, Open to others by appt, Restricted pub use, Secured area only open to authorized personnel

GL UNITED STATES COURTS FOR THE NINTH CIRCUIT LIBRARY*, 1000 SW Third Ave, 7A40, 97204. Tel: 503-326-8140. *Br Librn,* Julia Sathler; E-mail: julia_sathler@LB9.uscourts.gov; *Asst Librn,* Rebecca Sherman; E-mail: rebecca_sherman@LB9.uscourts.gov; Staff 2 (MLS 2)
Library Holdings: Bk Vols 30,000
Restriction: Circ to mem only

C UNIVERSITY OF PORTLAND*, Clark Library, 5000 N Willamette Blvd, 97203-5743. SAN 314-1861. Tel: 503-943-7111. Interlibrary Loan Service Tel: 503-943-7526. Reference Tel: 503-943-7788. Toll Free Tel: 800-841-8261. FAX: 503-943-7491. E-mail: library@up.edu. Web Site: library.up.edu. *Dean of Libr,* Xan Arch; E-mail: arch@up.edu; *Head, Coll Serv,* Susan E Hinken; E-mail: hinken@up.edu; *Coll Tech Librn,* Bonnie

Parks; E-mail: parks@up.edu; *Ref & Instruction Librn,* Stephanie Michel; E-mail: michel@up.edu; *Ref & Instruction Librn,* Heidi Senior; E-mail: senior@up.edu; *Ref & Instruction Librn,* Diane Sotak; E-mail: sotak@up.edu; Staff 7 (MLS 7)
Founded 1901. Enrl 3,357; Fac 277; Highest Degree: Doctorate
Library Holdings: Bk Titles 190,000; Bk Vols 360,000; Per Subs 1,600
Subject Interests: Catholic theol, Philos
Wireless access
Partic in Northwest Association of Private Colleges & Universities; OCLC Online Computer Library Center, Inc; Orbis Cascade Alliance
Open Mon-Thurs 7am-2am, Fri 7am-9pm, Sat 10-9, Sun 10am-2am

CM UNIVERSITY OF WESTERN STATES LIBRARY*, 8000 NE Tillamook St, 97213. SAN 314-1942. Tel: 503-251-5752. Interlibrary Loan Service Tel: 503-847-2596. Administration Tel: 503-251-5757. FAX: 503-251-5759. E-mail: librarian@uws.edu. Web Site: www.uws.edu/community/library. *Univ Librn,* Stephanie Debner; E-mail: sdebner@uws.edu; *Head, Pub Serv,* Kim Olson-Charles; E-mail: kolson@uws.edu; *Metadata Librn, Syst Librn,* Katie Lockwood; E-mail: klockwood@uws.edu; *Access Serv Asst,* Malia Cumming; E-mail: mcumming@uws.edu; *Libr Asst, ILL,* Karen Kriberney; E-mail: kkriberney@uws.edu; Staff 5 (MLS 3, Non-MLS 2)
Founded 1904. Highest Degree: Doctorate
Library Holdings: CDs 750; DVDs 2,000; e-books 4,300; e-journals 14,000; Electronic Media & Resources 2,500; Bk Titles 9,000; Bk Vols 13,500; Per Subs 300
Special Collections: Massage
Subject Interests: Anatomy, Chiropractic, Exercise & sports sci, Manual therapy, Nutrition
Automation Activity & Vendor Info: (Cataloging) OCLC; (Circulation) Ex Libris Group; (ILL) OCLC; (OPAC) Ex Libris Group; (Serials) EBSCO Online
Wireless access
Publications: Index to Chiropractic Literature (Index to periodicals)
Partic in Medical Library Association; OCLC Online Computer Library Center, Inc
Restriction: Open to fac, students & qualified researchers, Open to pub for ref only

CR WARNER PACIFIC UNIVERSITY*, Otto F Linn Library, 2219 SE 68th Ave, 97215. SAN 314-190X. Tel: 503-517-1102. Reference Tel: 503-517-1033. Web Site: library.warnerpacific.edu. *Dir, Libr Serv,* Lishi Kwasitsu, PhD; E-mail: lkwasitsu@warnerpacific.edu; *Circ Mgr,* Jeff Barnhardt; Tel: 503-517-1037, E-mail: jbarnhardt@warnerpacific.edu; Staff 4 (MLS 2, Non-MLS 2)
Founded 1937. Enrl 970; Highest Degree: Master
Library Holdings: Bk Titles 47,621; Bk Vols 59,251; Per Subs 315
Special Collections: Church of God Archives
Automation Activity & Vendor Info: (Acquisitions) Innovative Interfaces, Inc; (Cataloging) Innovative Interfaces, Inc; (Circulation) Innovative Interfaces, Inc; (Course Reserve) Innovative Interfaces, Inc; (ILL) OCLC FirstSearch; (Serials) Innovative Interfaces, Inc
Wireless access
Function: ILL available
Partic in Northwest Association of Private Colleges & Universities; Orbis Cascade Alliance
Open Mon-Thurs 8am-10pm, Fri 8-5, Sun 12-8
Restriction: Open to fac, students & qualified researchers

S WASHINGTON COUNTY MUSEUM LIBRARY*, 17677 NW Springville Rd, 97229. (Mail add: Washington County Museum, 3300 NW 185th Ave, Ste 260, 97229), SAN 329-2460. Tel: 503-645-5353. FAX: 503-645-5650. E-mail: librarian@washingtoncountymuseum.org. Information Services E-mail: info@washingtoncountymuseum.org. Web Site: www.washingtoncountymuseum.org. Staff 4 (Non-MLS 4)
Founded 1956
Library Holdings: Bk Vols 650
Special Collections: Photograph Coll. Municipal Document Depository; Oral History
Subject Interests: Hist, Presv
Publications: This Far-Off Sunset Land
Restriction: Non-circulating to the pub, Not a lending libr, Open by appt only

P WEST SLOPE COMMUNITY LIBRARY*, 3678 SW 78th Ave, 97225-9019. SAN 324-248X. Tel: 503-292-6416. Administration Tel: 503-297-1428. E-mail: westslopelibrary@gmail.com. Web Site: www.wccls.org/libraries/westslope. *Libr Mgr,* Veronica Eden; E-mail: veronicae@wccls.org; Staff 8.2 (MLS 3, Non-MLS 5.2)
Founded 1950. Pop 11,000; Circ 280,000
Jul 2018-Jun 2019 Income $679,500, State $2,000, County $675,000, Locally Generated Income $2,500. Mats Exp $80,000, Books $55,000, Per/Ser (Incl. Access Fees) $4,000, AV Mat $21,000
Library Holdings: CDs 4,675; DVDs 10,781; e-books 76,771; Electronic Media & Resources 130; Bk Vols 37,755; Per Subs 100
Automation Activity & Vendor Info: (Circulation) Innovative Interfaces, Inc
Wireless access
Function: 24/7 Electronic res, 24/7 Online cat
Partic in Washington County Cooperative Library Services
Open Mon-Thurs 9:30-8, Fri & Sat 9:30-4
Friends of the Library Group

R WESTERN SEMINARY*, Cline-Tunnell Library, 5511 SE Hawthorne Blvd, 97215-3367. SAN 314-1926. Tel: 503-517-1840. Toll Free Tel: 877-517-1800. FAX: 503-517-1801. Web Site: www.westernseminary.edu/students/library. *Dir, Libr & Info Serv,* Matthew Thiesen; Tel: 503-517-1841, E-mail: mthiesen@westernseminary.edu; *Info Serv Librn,* Andy Lofthus; Tel: 503-517-1842, E-mail: alofthus@westernseminary.edu; *Access Serv Coordr,* Position Currently Open; Staff 3 (MLS 2, Non-MLS 1)
Founded 1927. Enrl 830; Fac 97; Highest Degree: Doctorate
Library Holdings: AV Mats 74; Bks on Deafness & Sign Lang 50; CDs 428; DVDs 69; Bk Vols 45,000; Per Subs 30; Videos 74
Special Collections: Pacific Northwest Baptist History Coll
Automation Activity & Vendor Info: (Acquisitions) Ex Libris Group; (Cataloging) Ex Libris Group; (Circulation) Ex Libris Group; (Discovery) Ex Libris Group; (ILL) Ex Libris Group; (OPAC) Ex Libris Group
Wireless access
Partic in OCLC Online Computer Library Center, Inc; Online Private Academic Library Link
Special Services for the Deaf - Bks on deafness & sign lang
Open Mon 8-6, Tues-Thurs 8-5, Fri 8-4, Sat 10-2

POWERS

P HAZEL M LEWIS LIBRARY*, 511 Third Ave, 97466. (Mail add: PO Box 559, 97466-0559), SAN 314-1969. Tel: 541-439-5311. FAX: 541-439-5311. E-mail: hazelmlewis@yahoo.com. *Dir,* Joanie Bedwell; *Ch,* Phyllis Pearce; Staff 2 (Non-MLS 2)
Founded 1935. Pop 680; Circ 26,101
Library Holdings: Bk Vols 25,385; Per Subs 44
Subject Interests: Hist
Automation Activity & Vendor Info: (Cataloging) Innovative Interfaces, Inc; (Circulation) Innovative Interfaces, Inc; (OPAC) Innovative Interfaces, Inc
Wireless access
Function: ILL available
Mem of Coos County Library Service District
Open Mon & Wed 10-6, Tues & Thurs 10-12 & 4-8, Fri & Sat 10-4

PRINEVILLE

P CROOK COUNTY LIBRARY*, 175 NW Meadow Lakes Dr, 97754. SAN 920-7287. Tel: 541-447-7978. FAX: 541-447-1308. E-mail: library@crooklib.org. Web Site: www.crooklib.org. *Interim Dir,* Cindy York; E-mail: cyork@crooklib.org; *Asst Dir,* Jane Scheppke; Tel: 541-447-7978, Ext 303, E-mail: jscheppke@crooklib.org; *Youth Serv,* Mary Ryan; Staff 11 (MLS 2, Non-MLS 9)
Founded 1931. Pop 22,566; Circ 150,032
Jul 2012-Jun 2013 Income $561,555, State $6,406, County $555,149. Mats Exp $71,300
Library Holdings: AV Mats 19,746; DVDs 6,785; e-books 12,295; Bk Titles 47,664; Per Subs 141
Automation Activity & Vendor Info: (Acquisitions) Innovative Interfaces, Inc; (Cataloging) Innovative Interfaces, Inc; (Circulation) Innovative Interfaces, Inc; (ILL) OCLC; (OPAC) Innovative Interfaces, Inc; (Serials) Innovative Interfaces, Inc
Wireless access
Function: Audiobks via web, Bks on CD, Children's prog, Computers for patron use, Electronic databases & coll, Family literacy, Free DVD rentals, ILL available, Magnifiers for reading, Mail & tel request accepted, Music CDs, Online cat, Outreach serv, OverDrive digital audio bks, Photocopying/Printing, Preschool reading prog, Printer for laptops & handheld devices, Prog for adults, Prog for children & young adult, Ref serv available, Spanish lang bks, Story hour, Summer reading prog, Tax forms, Teen prog, Telephone ref, Wheelchair accessible
Open Mon-Wed 9-8, Thurs & Fri 9-6, Sat 10-4
Restriction: Authorized patrons
Friends of the Library Group
Bookmobiles: 1. Bkmobile Coordr, Amber Smith. Bk vols 900

RAINIER

P RAINIER CITY LIBRARY*, 106 B St W, 97048. (Mail add: PO Box 100, 97048-0100), SAN 314-1993. Tel: 503-556-7301, Ext 207. FAX: 503-556-3200. E-mail: rainier_library@yahoo.com. Web Site: rainiercitylibrary.com. *Librn,* Colette Nordstrom; E-mail: colette_nordstrom@rsd.k12.or.us
Pop 1,800; Circ 9,000

Library Holdings: Audiobooks 300; DVDs 650; Large Print Bks 125; Bk Vols 12,000
Special Collections: Rainier History Coll
Wireless access
Open Tues & Sat 10-5, Wed 12-7, Thurs 10-7, Fri 12-5

ROSEBURG

L DOUGLAS COUNTY LAW LIBRARY*, Justice Bldg, Rm 305, 1036 SE Douglas Ave, 97470. SAN 372-2252. Tel: 541-440-4341. E-mail: dclawlib@co.douglas.or.us. Web Site: www.co.douglas.or.us/LawLib. *Librn,* Diana L Hadley
Jul 2012-Jun 2013 Income $93,000. Mats Exp $60,000, Books $40,000, Electronic Ref Mat (Incl. Access Fees) $20,000. Sal $33,000
Library Holdings: Electronic Media & Resources 25; Bk Vols 10,000; Per Subs 10
Subject Interests: Legal mat
Wireless access
Function: For res purposes, Govt ref serv, Photocopying/Printing, Ref & res, Ref serv available, Res libr
Open Mon, Tues & Thurs 10-12 & 1-3, Wed 9-Noon
Restriction: Non-circulating, Open to pub for ref only, Pub access for legal res only

S DOUGLAS COUNTY MUSEUM, Lavola Bakken Research Library, 123 Museum Dr, 97471. SAN 314-2019. Tel: 541-957-7007. FAX: 541-957-7017. E-mail: museum@co.douglas.or.us. Web Site: www.umpquavalleymuseums.org/museums/douglas-county-museum. *Research Librn,* Karen Bratton
Founded 1969
Library Holdings: Bk Vols 2,800
Special Collections: Herbarium Coll of Douglas County; History of Douglas County Coll, ledgers, scrapbooks, county records, unpublished articles, letters, diaries, ms, census & cemetery records, genealogies. Oral History
Subject Interests: Agr, Dougla develop, Douglas county hist, Logging mills, Marine hist, Mining, Natural hist, Railroads, Saw mills, Umpqua Indians
Open Tues-Sat 10-5

J UMPQUA COMMUNITY COLLEGE LIBRARY*, 1140 Umpqua College Rd, 97470. (Mail add: PO Box 967, 97470), SAN 314-2035. Tel: 541-440-4640. Interlibrary Loan Service Tel: 541-677-3245. Reference Tel: 541-677-3244. Toll Free Tel: 800-820-5161. FAX: 541-440-4637. TDD: 541-440-4626. Web Site: www.umpqua.edu/library/. *Dir, Libr Serv,* Mireille Kotoklo; Tel: 541-440-4636, E-mail: mireille.kotoklo@umpqua.edu; *Libr Spec,* Kristen Moser; Tel: 541-440-7682, E-mail: kristen.moser@umpqua.edu; *Circ,* Susan Leek; E-mail: susan.leek@umpqua.edu; *Ref (Info Servs),* Katherine Cunnion; Tel: 541-440-7681, E-mail: katherine.cunnion@umpqua.edu; Staff 8 (MLS 2, Non-MLS 6)
Founded 1964. Enrl 3,000; Fac 69; Highest Degree: Associate
Library Holdings: Bk Vols 50,000; Per Subs 188
Special Collections: Fire Science; Grant
Automation Activity & Vendor Info: (Cataloging) SirsiDynix; (Circulation) SirsiDynix; (Course Reserve) SirsiDynix; (ILL) SirsiDynix; (OPAC) SirsiDynix
Wireless access
Function: ILL available
Publications: Oregon Regional Union List of Serials
Partic in OCLC Online Computer Library Center, Inc
Open Mon-Thurs 7:30am-9pm

SAINT BENEDICT

C MOUNT ANGEL ABBEY LIBRARY*, One Abbey Dr, 97373. SAN 314-2051. Tel: 503-845-3303. Interlibrary Loan Service Tel: 503-845-3317. Web Site: www.mountangelabbey.org/abbey-library. *Libr Dir,* Dr Brian Morin; E-mail: brian.morin@mtangel.edu; *ILL,* Sandi Ritchey; E-mail: sandi.ritchey@mtangel.edu; *Ref,* Brian Morin; E-mail: brian.morin@mtangel.edu; Staff 4 (MLS 2, Non-MLS 2)
Founded 1882. Enrl 230; Fac 40; Highest Degree: Master
Library Holdings: Bk Vols 230,000; Per Subs 380
Special Collections: Civil War; McKuen Philosophy Coll; Patristic & Latin Christian Studies
Subject Interests: Humanities, Philos, Theol
Automation Activity & Vendor Info: (Acquisitions) Ex Libris Group; (Cataloging) Ex Libris Group; (Circulation) Ex Libris Group; (Course Reserve) Ex Libris Group; (OPAC) Ex Libris Group; (Serials) Ex Libris Group
Wireless access
Partic in OCLC Online Computer Library Center, Inc; Online Private Academic Library Link
Open Mon-Thurs (Winter) 8:30-5 & 6:30-9:30, Fri 8:30-5, Sat 10-4; Mon-Fri (Summer) 9-4, Sat 10-3
Friends of the Library Group

SAINT HELENS

P SAINT HELENS PUBLIC LIBRARY*, 375 S 18th St, Ste A, 97051-2022. SAN 314-206X. Tel: 503-397-4544. FAX: 503-366-3020. E-mail: shpl@ci.st-helens.or.us. Web Site: www.ci.st-helens.or.us/library. *Dir,* Margaret Jeffries; E-mail: margaretj@ci.st-helens.or.us; Staff 5.5 (MLS 3, Non-MLS 2.5)
Founded 1914. Pop 12,075; Circ 125,000
Library Holdings: AV Mats 4,400; CDs 837; DVDs 455; Large Print Bks 907; Bk Titles 35,514; Bk Vols 38,609; Per Subs 100; Talking Bks 1,900; Videos 2,500
Special Collections: Municipal Document Depository
Automation Activity & Vendor Info: (Cataloging) TLC (The Library Corporation); (Circulation) TLC (The Library Corporation); (ILL) OCLC; (OPAC) TLC (The Library Corporation)
Wireless access
Function: Art exhibits, CD-ROM, Digital talking bks, Electronic databases & coll, ILL available, Magnifiers for reading, Music CDs, Orientations, Photocopying/Printing, Preschool outreach, Prog for adults, Prog for children & young adult, Summer reading prog, VHS videos
Open Mon-Thurs 10-7, Fri 10-5, Sat 10-2
Friends of the Library Group

SALEM

J CHEMEKETA COMMUNITY COLLEGE LIBRARY*, Bldg 9, 2nd Flr, 4000 Lancaster Dr NE, 97305-1500. (Mail add: PO Box 14007, 97309-7070), SAN 314-2094. Tel: 503-399-5043. Reference Tel: 503-399-5231. FAX: 503-399-5214. Reference E-mail: reference@chemeketa.edu. Web Site: library.chemeketa.edu, libraryguides.chemeketa.edu. *Dean of Libr,* Natalie Beach; Tel: 503-399-5105, E-mail: natalie.beach@chemeketa.edu; Staff 19.3 (MLS 6.8, Non-MLS 12.5)
Founded 1962. Enrl 11,802; Fac 5; Highest Degree: Associate
Library Holdings: e-books 111,000; Bk Vols 65,000
Automation Activity & Vendor Info: (Acquisitions) Ex Libris Group; (Cataloging) Ex Libris Group; (Circulation) Ex Libris Group; (Course Reserve) Ex Libris Group; (ILL) OCLC WorldShare Interlibrary Loan; (OPAC) Ex Libris Group; (Serials) Ex Libris Group
Wireless access
Function: Audio & video playback equip for onsite use, Computers for patron use, Doc delivery serv, E-Reserves, Electronic databases & coll, ILL available, Magnifiers for reading, Online cat, Online ref, Photocopying/Printing, Wheelchair accessible
Partic in Chemeketa Cooperative Regional Library Service; OCLC Online Computer Library Center, Inc; Orbis Cascade Alliance; Valley Link

CR CORBAN UNIVERSITY LIBRARY*, 5000 Deer Park Dr SE, 97317-9392. SAN 314-2221. Tel: 503-375-7016. FAX: 503-375-7196. Web Site: www.corban.edu/library. *Univ Librn,* Garrett Trott; E-mail: gtrott@corban.edu; Staff 2 (MLS 2)
Founded 1935. Enrl 1,100; Fac 55; Highest Degree: Doctorate
Library Holdings: AV Mats 5,237; e-books 8,326; Microforms 7,508; Bk Vols 80,000; Per Subs 575
Special Collections: Prewitt-Allen Archaeology Museum
Subject Interests: Bible, Missions, Theol
Automation Activity & Vendor Info: (Acquisitions) Ex Libris Group; (Cataloging) Ex Libris Group; (Circulation) Ex Libris Group; (Course Reserve) Ex Libris Group; (OPAC) Ex Libris Group; (Serials) Ex Libris Group
Wireless access
Partic in Northwest Association of Private Colleges & Universities; Online Private Academic Library Link

R FIRST BAPTIST CHURCH*, Curry Memorial Library, 395 Marion St NE, 97301. SAN 314-2116. Tel: 503-364-2285. FAX: 503-391-9272. E-mail: fbc@fbcsalem.org. Web Site: www.fbcsalem.org. *Librn,* Arlene Cummings
Library Holdings: CDs 200; DVDs 200; Bk Vols 6,000
Subject Interests: Biblical studies, Christian fiction, Christian living
Open Mon-Thurs & Sun 9-Noon

L MARION COUNTY LAW LIBRARY*, Marion County Courthouse, 100 High St NE, Basement B181, 97301. (Mail add: PO Box 14500, 97309), SAN 372-2155. Tel: 503-588-5090. FAX: 503-373-4386. E-mail: lawlibrary@co.marion.or.us. Web Site: www.co.marion.or.us/LC/LawLibrary. *Librn,* Martha Renick
Library Holdings: Bk Vols 10,000; Per Subs 50
Partic in Midwest Collaborative for Library Services
Open Mon-Fri 8:30-5

G OREGON DEPARTMENT OF TRANSPORTATION LIBRARY, Mill Creek Bldg, 555 13th St NE, 97301. SAN 358-1977. Tel: 503-986-3280. FAX: 503-986-4025. E-mail: library@odot.state.or.us. Web Site: www.oregon.gov/ODOT/About/Pages/Library.aspx. *Librn,* Laura Wilt; E-mail: laura.e.wilt@odot.state.or.us; Staff 1 (MLS 1)
Founded 1937
Library Holdings: Bk Titles 19,000; Bk Vols 20,000; Per Subs 50
Special Collections: Safety costumes; Transportation Safety, v-tapes
Subject Interests: Aeronaut, Engr, Environ, Motor vehicles, Planning, Soils, Transit, Transportation
Automation Activity & Vendor Info: (Cataloging) EOS International; (OPAC) EOS International
Wireless access
Open Mon-Thurs 7-4:30, Fri 7-11

S OREGON SCHOOL FOR THE DEAF LIBRARY*, 999 Locust St NE, 97301-0954. SAN 314-2140. Tel: 503-378-3825. Web Site: www.osd.k12.or.us. *Librn,* Peggy Breen; E-mail: peggy.breen@osd.k12.or.us
Founded 1870
Library Holdings: Bk Vols 14,500; Per Subs 30
Wireless access
Restriction: Not open to pub

S OREGON STATE CORRECTIONAL INSTITUTION LIBRARY*, 3405 Deer Park Dr SE, 97310-3985. SAN 314-2159. Tel: 503-373-7523. FAX: 503-378-8919. *Librn,* Pam McKinney; Staff 1 (MLS 1)
Founded 1959
Library Holdings: Bk Vols 40,289
Restriction: Not open to pub, Staff & inmates only

P OREGON STATE LIBRARY TALKING BOOK & BRAILLE SERVICES*, 250 Winter St NE, 97301. SAN 314-2124. Tel: 503-378-5391. Toll Free Tel: 800-452-0292. FAX: 503-373-7439. E-mail: talkingbooks.info@state.or.us. Web Site: www.oregon.gov/osl/tbabs. *Prog Mgr,* Elke Bruton; Tel: 503-378-5455, E-mail: elke.bruton@state.or.us
Founded 1932
Library Holdings: Bk Titles 60,000; Bk Vols 158,126
Subject Interests: Ore
Automation Activity & Vendor Info: (Circulation) Keystone Systems, Inc (KLAS); (OPAC) Keystone Systems, Inc (KLAS)
Wireless access
Publications: Talking Book & Braille News (Quarterly)
Special Services for the Deaf - TDD equip
Special Services for the Blind - Descriptive video serv (DVS)
Open Mon-Fri 9-12 & 1-4

S OREGON STATE PENITENTIARY LIBRARY*, OSP Maximum, 2605 State St, 97310. SAN 358-2124. Tel: 503-378-2081. *Librn,* Melissa Davidson; E-mail: melissa.a.davidson@doc.state.or.us
Founded 1953
Library Holdings: Bk Vols 10,000
Special Collections: Indian History Coll
Subject Interests: Agr, Archit, Art, Hort, Philos
Special Services for the Deaf - High interest/low vocabulary bks; Spec interest per
Restriction: Not open to pub, Staff & inmates only
Branches:
COFFEE CREEK CORRECTIONAL FACILITY, 24499 SW Grahams Ferry Rd, Wilsonville, 97070. Tel: 503-570-6783. FAX: 503-570-6786. *Librn,* Angela Wheeler
Library Holdings: Bk Vols 8,500
Restriction: Staff & inmates only
OSP MINIMUM, 2809 State St, 97310, SAN 358-2272. Tel: 503-378-2081. *Librn,* M Davidson
Library Holdings: Bk Titles 8,000
Special Collections: Legal Materials
Restriction: Staff & inmates only

M SALEM HEALTH COMMUNITY HEALTH EDUCATION CENTER, Pierce Resource Center & Staff Library, Salem Hospital, 665 Winter St SE, 97301. (Mail add: PO Box 14001, 97309-5014), SAN 321-5474. Tel: 503-814-2432. Toll Free Tel: 866-977-2432 (Ore only). FAX: 503-814-1599. E-mail: library@salemhealth.org. Web Site: salemhealth.org/community-health-education-center. *Librn,* Paul Howard; Staff 1 (MLS 1)
Founded 1972
Library Holdings: Bk Titles 4,000; Per Subs 10
Subject Interests: Med
Automation Activity & Vendor Info: (Acquisitions) EOS International; (Cataloging) EOS International; (Circulation) EOS International; (ILL) OCLC; (Serials) EOS International
Wireless access
Function: Computers for patron use, Doc delivery serv, Electronic databases & coll, Internet access, Photocopying/Printing, Res libr
Partic in OCLC Online Computer Library Center, Inc
Open Mon-Fri 8-5

P SALEM PUBLIC LIBRARY, 585 Liberty St SE, 97301. (Mail add: PO Box 14810, 97309), SAN 358-2396. Tel: 503-588-6315. Administration Tel: 503-588-6071. E-mail: library@cityofsalem.net. Web Site: cityofsalem.net/library. *City Librn,* Sarah Strahl; E-mail: sstrahl@cityofsalem.net; *Dep City Librn,* Kimberley Carroll; Tel: 503-588-6064, E-mail: kcarroll@cityofsalem.net; *Adult Serv Mgr,* Christopher Rumbaugh; Tel: 503-588-6449, E-mail: crumbaugh@cityofsalem.net; *Youth Serv Mgr,* Karen Fischer; Tel: 503-588-6039, E-mail: kfischer@cityofsalem.net; *Circ Supvr,* Karen Kinzie; Tel: 503-588-6090, E-mail: kkinzie@cityofsalem.net; Staff 78 (MLS 13, Non-MLS 65)
Founded 1904. Pop 140,000; Circ 1,338,355
Library Holdings: AV Mats 22,233; Bk Titles 228,312; Bk Vols 485,152; Per Subs 839
Special Collections: Oregon History Coll; Original Art; Salem Historic Photos Coll
Subject Interests: Local hist
Automation Activity & Vendor Info: (Cataloging) Innovative Interfaces, Inc; (Circulation) Innovative Interfaces, Inc; (ILL) OCLC; (OPAC) Innovative Interfaces, Inc
Wireless access
Function: ILL available, Photocopying/Printing, Ref serv available
Publications: Online Newsletter; Salem Public Library (Newsletter)
Open Tues-Thurs 10-9, Fri & Sat 10-6, Sun (Sept-May) 1-5
Friends of the Library Group
Branches: 1
WEST SALEM, 395 Glen Creek Rd NW, 97304, SAN 358-2426. Tel: 503-588-6301. *Libr Mgr,* Karen Fischer
Circ 132,144
Library Holdings: Bk Vols 35,000; Per Subs 45
Automation Activity & Vendor Info: (Acquisitions) Innovative Interfaces, Inc; (Serials) Innovative Interfaces, Inc
Open Mon, Tues, Thurs & Fri 2-6
Friends of the Library Group

S SANTIAM CORRECTIONAL INSTITUTION LIBRARY*, 4005 Aumsville Hwy SE, 97317. Tel: 503-378-3024. Web Site: www.oregon.gov/doc/ops/prison/pages/sci.aspx. *Librn,* Shawn Jenne; E-mail: shawn.m.jenne@doc.state.or.us
Library Holdings: Bk Vols 2,000
Restriction: Not open to pub

P STATE LIBRARY OF OREGON*, 250 Winter St NE, 97301-3950. SAN 358-206X. Tel: 503-378-4243. Reference Tel: 503-378-8800. FAX: 503-585-8059. E-mail: library.help@state.or.us. Web Site: www.oregon.gov/library. *State Librn,* Jennifer Patterson; Tel: 503-378-4367, E-mail: jennifer.patterson@state.or.us; *Ref Librn,* Natalie Brant; Tel: 503-378-5007, E-mail: natalie.brant@state.or.us; *Prog Mgr,* Caren Agata; Tel: 503-378-5030, E-mail: caren.agata@state.or.us; Staff 39.3 (MLS 14, Non-MLS 25.3)
Founded 1905. Pop 2,742,750; Circ 121,079
Library Holdings: AV Mats 2,566; Large Print Bks 315; Bk Titles 63,260; Bk Vols 63,276; Per Subs 301; Talking Bks 127,353
Special Collections: Family History (Genealogy Coll), bks, micro; Grants & Funding, Patent, US Census; Oregon History (Oregoniana); State & Federal Government, bks, doc. State Document Depository; US Document Depository
Subject Interests: Agr, Forestry, Govt
Automation Activity & Vendor Info: (Circulation) Innovative Interfaces, Inc; (OPAC) Innovative Interfaces, Inc
Wireless access
Publications: Letter to Libraries Online
Partic in Association for Rural & Small Libraries; OCLC Online Computer Library Center, Inc
Special Services for the Blind - Braille bks; Talking bks
Open Mon-Fri 8-5

GL STATE OF OREGON LAW LIBRARY*, Supreme Court Bldg, 1163 State St, 97301. SAN 314-2205. Tel: 503-986-5640. E-mail: state.law.library@ojd.state.or.us. Web Site: soll.libguides.com. *State Law Librn,* Cathryn Bowie; E-mail: cathryn.e.bowie@ojd.state.or.us; *Ref Librn,* Lewis Zimmerman; E-mail: lewis.c.zimmerman@ojd.state.or.us; *Tech Serv Librn,* Carin Yaborcik; E-mail: carin.m.yaborcik@ojd.state.or.us; Staff 4 (MLS 3, Non-MLS 1)
Founded 1848
Library Holdings: Bk Titles 12,000; Bk Vols 100,000; Per Subs 200
Automation Activity & Vendor Info: (Acquisitions) EOS International; (Circulation) EOS International; (OPAC) EOS International; (Serials) EOS International
Wireless access

Function: Res libr
Open Mon-Fri 8-5

C WILLAMETTE UNIVERSITY, Mark O Hatfield Library, 900 State St, 97301. SAN 358-2450. Tel: 503-370-6018. Interlibrary Loan Service Tel: 503-370-6267. Reference Tel: 503-370-6560. Administration Tel: 503-370-6312. FAX: 503-370-6141. E-mail: library@willamette.edu. Web Site: library.willamette.edu. *Univ Librn,* Craig Milberg; Tel: 503-370-6561, E-mail: cmilberg@willamette.edu; *Assoc Univ Librarian for Access & Technical Services,* Carol Drost; Tel: 503-370-6715, E-mail: cdrost@willamette.edu; *Assoc Univ Librarian for Collections, Teaching & Research,* Joni R Roberts; Tel: 503-370-6741, E-mail: jroberts@willamette.edu; *Assoc Univ Librn, Syst,* Michael Spalti; Tel: 503-370-6356, E-mail: mspalti@willamette.edu; *Access Serv Librn,* Charity Braceros-Simon; Tel: 503-370-6673, E-mail: cbracerossimon@willamette.edu; *Management & Economics Librn,* Gary Klein; Tel: 503-370-6743, E-mail: gklein@willamette.edu; *Humanities & Fine Arts Librarian,* Doreen Simonsen; Tel: 503-375-5343, E-mail: dsimonse@willamette.edu; *Ref & Instruction Librn,* Shaleigh Westphall; Tel: 503-821-8966, E-mail: snwestphall@willamette.edu; *Sci Librn,* John Repplinger; Tel: 503-370-6525, E-mail: jrepplin@willamette.edu; *Syst Librn,* Bill Kelm; Tel: 503-375-5332, E-mail: bkelm@willamette.edu; *Monographs & Acq Mgr,* Elizabeth Butterfield; Tel: 503-370-6267, E-mail: ebutterf@willamette.edu; *Periodicals/Documents Manager,* Erica Miller; Tel: 503-370-6739, E-mail: emiller@willamette.edu; *Univ Archivist,* Susan Irwin; Tel: 503-370-6764, E-mail: smirwin@willamette.edu. Subject Specialists: *Children's lit, Fiction, Govt doc,* Carol Drost; *Anthrop, Northwest, Sociol,* Joni R Roberts; *Bus, Psychol, Pub policy,* Gary Klein; *Art hist, Music, Theatre,* Doreen Simonsen; *Biology, Chem, Computer sci,* John Repplinger; Staff 18 (MLS 12, Non-MLS 6)
Founded 1842. Fac 279; Highest Degree: Master
Jun 2012-May 2013 Income $1,907,511. Mats Exp $759,272. Sal $830,086 (Prof $692,728)
Library Holdings: AV Mats 11,596; e-books 4,785; Music Scores 6,636; Bk Titles 220,527; Bk Vols 244,734; Per Subs 2,485
Special Collections: Mark O Hatfield Archives; University Archives. US Document Depository
Subject Interests: Pacific Northwest
Automation Activity & Vendor Info: (Acquisitions) Innovative Interfaces, Inc; (Cataloging) Innovative Interfaces, Inc; (Circulation) Innovative Interfaces, Inc; (OPAC) Innovative Interfaces, Inc; (Serials) Innovative Interfaces, Inc
Wireless access
Partic in OCLC Online Computer Library Center, Inc; Orbis Cascade Alliance
Open Mon-Thurs 8am-Midnight, Fri 8am-9pm, Sat 10-6, Sun 10am-Midnight (Winter); Mon-Fri 8-4:30 (Summer)
Friends of the Library Group

Departmental Libraries:

CL J W LONG LAW LIBRARY, 245 Winter St SE, 97301, SAN 358-2485. Tel: 503-370-6386. Circulation Tel: 503-370-5300. Reference Tel: 503-375-5330. FAX: 503-375-5426. E-mail: lawlib-info@willamette.edu. Web Site: www.willamette.edu/law/longlib. *Dir,* Ann Kitchel; Tel: 503-375-5345, E-mail: akitchel@willamette.edu; *Ref & Instrul Serv Librn,* Mary Rumsey; Tel: 503-375-5324, E-mail: mrumsey@willamette.edu; *Access Serv Mgr,* Galin Brown; Tel: 503-375-5421, E-mail: gbrown@willamette.edu; *Cat Spec,* Samantha Foster; Tel: 503-375-5329, E-mail: sfoster@willamette.edu; Staff 9.7 (MLS 3, Non-MLS 6.7)
Founded 1883. Enrl 400; Fac 30; Highest Degree: Doctorate
Library Holdings: Bk Titles 39,880; Bk Vols 300,000; Per Subs 1,200
Special Collections: US Document Depository
Automation Activity & Vendor Info: (Acquisitions) Ex Libris Group; (Cataloging) Ex Libris Group; (Circulation) Ex Libris Group; (Course Reserve) Ex Libris Group; (ILL) OCLC ILLiad; (OPAC) Ex Libris Group
Function: Outside serv via phone, mail, e-mail & web, Ref serv available
Partic in NELLCO Law Library Consortium, Inc.; OCLC Online Computer Library Center, Inc
Open Mon-Fri 7:30-7 (9-5 Summer)
Restriction: 24-hr pass syst for students only, Open to students, fac, staff & alumni, Pub access for legal res only

SANDY

P SANDY PUBLIC LIBRARY, 38980 Proctor Blvd, 97055-8040. SAN 314-223X. Tel: 503-668-5537. FAX: 503-668-3153. Reference E-mail: saref@lincc.lib.or.us. Web Site: www.cityofsandy.com/library. *Dir,* Sarah McIntyre; Tel: 503-489-2168, E-mail: smcintyre@ci.sandy.or.us; *Ch,* Monica Smith; E-mail: msmith@ci.sandy.or.us; *Ref Librn,* Maureen Houck; E-mail: mhouck@ci.sandy.or.us; *Teen Librn,* Rebecca Hanset; E-mail: rhanset@ci.sandy.or.us. Subject Specialists: *Early literacy,* Monica Smith; Staff 12.7 (MLS 4, Non-MLS 8.7)
Founded 1934. Pop 30,123; Circ 439,362
Automation Activity & Vendor Info: (Cataloging) SirsiDynix-WorkFlows; (Circulation) SirsiDynix-WorkFlows; (OPAC) SirsiDynix-Enterprise; (Serials) SirsiDynix-WorkFlows
Wireless access
Function: 24/7 Electronic res, 24/7 Online cat, Activity rm, Adult bk club, Adult literacy prog, Art exhibits, Audiobks via web, Bilingual assistance for Spanish patrons, Bk club(s), Bks on CD, Children's prog, Computer training, Computers for patron use, Digital talking bks, Electronic databases & coll, For res purposes, Free DVD rentals, ILL available, Internet access, Life-long learning prog for all ages, Magazines, Mail & tel request accepted, Meeting rooms, Museum passes, Music CDs, Notary serv, Online cat, Online ref, OverDrive digital audio bks, Photocopying/Printing, Prog for adults, Prog for children & young adult, Ref serv available, Scanner, Serves people with intellectual disabilities, Spanish lang bks, Story hour, Study rm, Summer reading prog, Tax forms, Teen prog, Telephone ref, Wheelchair accessible
Partic in Library Information Network of Clackamas County
Open Mon & Tues 10-7, Wed, Thurs & Fri 10-6, Sat & Sun 12-5
Restriction: Free to mem, Non-resident fee
Friends of the Library Group

SCAPPOOSE

P SCAPPOOSE PUBLIC LIBRARY, 52469 SE Second St, 97056. (Mail add: PO Box 400, 97056-0400), SAN 314-2248. Tel: 503-543-7123. FAX: 503-543-7161. E-mail: scappl@scappooselibrary.org. Web Site: scappooselibrary.org. *Dir,* Jeff Weiss; E-mail: jweiss@scappooselibrary.org; *Ref Tech,* Elisa Mann; *Youth Serv,* Wendi Andrews; Staff 3.5 (MLS 1.7, Non-MLS 1.8)
Founded 1929. Pop 14,000; Circ 71,000
Library Holdings: AV Mats 4,212; Bks on Deafness & Sign Lang 10; CDs 91; DVDs 201; e-books 131,000; e-journals 1; Electronic Media & Resources 9; Large Print Bks 828; Bk Vols 35,000; Per Subs 106; Videos 2,238
Subject Interests: Northwest
Automation Activity & Vendor Info: (Cataloging) TLC (The Library Corporation)
Wireless access
Function: 24/7 Electronic res, 24/7 Online cat, Activity rm, Adult bk club, After school storytime, Bks on CD, Children's prog, Computer training, Computers for patron use, Electronic databases & coll, Free DVD rentals, Holiday prog, ILL available, Instruction & testing, Internet access, Magazines, Magnifiers for reading, Mail & tel request accepted, Meeting rooms, Music CDs, Online cat, Outside serv via phone, mail, e-mail & web, OverDrive digital audio bks, Photocopying/Printing, Printer for laptops & handheld devices, Prog for adults, Prog for children & young adult, Spanish lang bks, Spoken cassettes & CDs, Spoken cassettes & DVDs, Story hour, Summer reading prog, Tax forms, Teen prog, Telephone ref, Wheelchair accessible, Workshops
Open Mon & Fri 10-6, Tues-Thurs 10-8, Sat 10-4
Friends of the Library Group

SCIO

P SCIO PUBLIC LIBRARY*, Town Hall, 38957 NW First Ave, 97374. (Mail add: PO Box 37, 97374-0037), SAN 329-3262. Tel: 503-394-3342. FAX: 503-394-2340. E-mail: slibrary@smt-net.com. Web Site: ci.scio.or.us/library.htm. *Librn,* LaVonne Murray; E-mail: ci.scio.l.murray@smt-net.com
Founded 1940. Pop 2,000
Library Holdings: Bks on Deafness & Sign Lang 10; Bk Vols 12,852
Partic in Linn Libraries Consortium
Open Mon, Wed & Thurs 9-5, Tues 9-7, Fri 9-Noon
Friends of the Library Group

SEASIDE

P SEASIDE PUBLIC LIBRARY*, 1131 Broadway, 97138. SAN 314-2256. Tel: 503-738-6742. FAX: 503-738-6742. E-mail: seasidepl@gmail.com. Web Site: seasidelibrary.org. *Dir,* Esther Moberg
Founded 1935
Library Holdings: Bk Vols 32,000; Per Subs 68
Wireless access
Open Tues-Thurs 9-8, Fri & Sat 9-5, Sun 1-5
Friends of the Library Group

SHERIDAN

P SHERIDAN PUBLIC LIBRARY*, 142 NW Yamhill St, 97378. (Mail add: PO Box 248, 97378-0248), SAN 314-2264. Tel: 503-843-3420. FAX: 503-843-2561. Web Site: www.cityofsheridanor.com/library. *Dir,* Penny Toepel
Pop 2,260; Circ 12,852
Library Holdings: AV Mats 3,000; Bk Vols 25,000; Per Subs 35; Talking Bks 500

Automation Activity & Vendor Info: (Cataloging) Innovative Interfaces, Inc; (Circulation) Innovative Interfaces, Inc
Partic in Chemeketa Cooperative Regional Library Service
Open Tues-Fri 10-7, Sat 10-3
Friends of the Library Group

SHERWOOD

P SHERWOOD PUBLIC LIBRARY, 22560 SW Pine St, 97140-9019. SAN 314-2272. Tel: 503-625-6688. Administration Tel: 503-625-4272. FAX: 503-625-4254. E-mail: askusspl@wccls.org. Web Site: www.sherwoodoregon.gov/library. *Libr Mgr,* Adrienne Doman Calkins; E-mail: domancalkinsa@sherwoodoregon.gov; Staff 10.8 (MLS 6.3, Non-MLS 4.5)
Founded 1935. Pop 22,000; Circ 366,769
Jul 2021-Jun 2022 Income $1,512,945, State $3,259, City $453,768, County $953,243, Locally Generated Income $102,675
Library Holdings: AV Mats 10,800; Bk Vols 36,041; Per Subs 173
Automation Activity & Vendor Info: (Acquisitions) Innovative Interfaces, Inc; (Cataloging) Innovative Interfaces, Inc; (Circulation) Innovative Interfaces, Inc; (OPAC) Innovative Interfaces, Inc
Wireless access
Function: 24/7 Electronic res, 24/7 Online cat, 3D Printer, Adult bk club, Art exhibits, Art programs, Audio & video playback equip for onsite use, Audiobks on Playaways & MP3, Audiobks via web, AV serv, Bilingual assistance for Spanish patrons, Bk club(s), Bks on CD, CD-ROM, Children's prog, Citizenship assistance, Computer training, Computers for patron use, Digital talking bks, Distance learning, Doc delivery serv, Electronic databases & coll, Equip loans & repairs, Family literacy, Free DVD rentals, Games & aids for people with disabilities, Genealogy discussion group, Govt ref serv, Health sci info serv, Holiday prog, Homebound delivery serv, Homework prog, ILL available, Instruction & testing, Internet access, Large print keyboards, Life-long learning prog for all ages, Magazines, Magnifiers for reading, Mail & tel request accepted, Mango lang, Movies, Museum passes, Music CDs, Online cat, Online info literacy tutorials on the web & in blackboard, Online ref, Orientations, Outreach serv, Outside serv via phone, mail, e-mail & web, OverDrive digital audio bks, Photocopying/Printing, Preschool outreach, Preschool reading prog, Printer for laptops & handheld devices, Prof lending libr, Prog for adults, Prog for children & young adult, Ref & res, Ref serv available, Res assist avail, Scanner, Senior outreach, Serves people with intellectual disabilities, Spanish lang bks, STEM programs, Story hour, Summer & winter reading prog, Summer reading prog, Tax forms, Teen prog, Telephone ref, Visual arts prog, Wheelchair accessible, Winter reading prog, Workshops, Writing prog
Partic in Washington County Cooperative Library Services
Open Mon-Thurs 10-8, Fri & Sat 10-6, Sun 1-5
Friends of the Library Group

SILETZ

P SILETZ PUBLIC LIBRARY*, 255 S Gaither St, 97380. (Mail add: PO Box 130, 97380-0130), SAN 376-7248. Tel: 541-444-2855. FAX: 541-444-2855. E-mail: siletz@lincolncolibrarydist.org, siletz@siletzlibrary.org. Web Site: www.facebook.com/SiletzPublicLibrary. *Head Librn,* Carol Rasmussen-Schramm; Staff 3 (Non-MLS 3)
Founded 1954. Pop 3,000
Library Holdings: Bk Titles 15,000; Per Subs 15
Automation Activity & Vendor Info: (Acquisitions) SirsiDynix; (Cataloging) SirsiDynix; (Circulation) SirsiDynix; (Course Reserve) SirsiDynix; (ILL) SirsiDynix; (Media Booking) SirsiDynix; (OPAC) SirsiDynix; (Serials) SirsiDynix
Wireless access
Function: 24/7 Electronic res, 24/7 Online cat, Audiobks on Playaways & MP3, Audiobks via web, Bks on CD, Children's prog, Citizenship assistance, Computers for patron use, Electronic databases & coll, Free DVD rentals, Holiday prog, ILL available, Internet access, Life-long learning prog for all ages, Magazines, Mango lang, Meeting rooms, Movies, Music CDs, Notary serv, Online cat, Online ref, OverDrive digital audio bks, Photocopying/Printing, Prog for adults, Prog for children & young adult, Ref serv available, Scanner, Story hour, Summer reading prog, Tax forms, Teen prog, VHS videos
Partic in Chinook Library Network
Open Wed, Fri & Sat 10-6, Thurs 10-8
Friends of the Library Group

SILVERTON

SILVER FALLS LIBRARY DISTRICT, 410 S Water St, 97381. SAN 314-2280. Tel: 503-873-5173. Reference Tel: 503-873-8796. FAX: 503-873-6227. Web Site: www.silverfallslibrary.org. *Dir,* Christy Davis; *Ad,* Spring Quick; E-mail: squick@ccrls.org; *Youth Serv Librn,* Dena Chaffin; E-mail: dena.chaffin@ccrls.org; *Circ,* Tina Kenney; E-mail: tina.kenney@ccrls.org; Staff 12 (MLS 3, Non-MLS 9)
Founded 1911. Pop 29,913; Circ 196,605
Library Holdings: Bk Vols 69,229; Per Subs 148; Talking Bks 2,897; Videos 4,762
Automation Activity & Vendor Info: (Cataloging) Innovative Interfaces, Inc; (Circulation) Innovative Interfaces, Inc; (OPAC) Innovative Interfaces, Inc
Wireless access
Function: Adult bk club, Art exhibits, Audiobks via web, Bi-weekly Writer's Group, Bks on cassette, Bks on CD, Children's prog, Computers for patron use, Electronic databases & coll, Free DVD rentals, Genealogy discussion group, Homebound delivery serv, ILL available, Internet access, Music CDs, Online cat, OverDrive digital audio bks, Photocopying/Printing, Prog for adults, Prog for children & young adult, Ref serv available, Summer reading prog, Tax forms, VHS videos, Wheelchair accessible
Partic in Chemeketa Cooperative Regional Library Service
Open Tues-Thurs 10-8, Fri 10-6, Sat 10-4, Sun (Sept-May) 1-5
Friends of the Library Group

SPRINGFIELD

M SACRED HEART MEDICAL CENTER AT RIVERBEND*, Library Services, 3333 RiverBend Dr, 2nd Flr S, 97477. (Mail add: PO Box 10905, Eugene, 97440-2905), SAN 314-0946. Tel: 541-222-2280. E-mail: LibrarySHMC@peacehealth.org. Web Site: www.peacehealth.org. *Med Librn,* Ms Bonne Starks; E-mail: bstarks@peacehealth.org; Staff 5 (MLS 3, Non-MLS 2)
Founded 1971
Library Holdings: Bk Vols 8,000; Per Subs 450
Special Collections: Archives (School of Nursing, 1942-70), print, tapes & transcription; Nurse Dolls in Uniform
Subject Interests: Computers in health care, Med, Mgt develop, Nursing
Automation Activity & Vendor Info: (Acquisitions) EOS International; (Cataloging) EOS International; (Circulation) EOS International; (OPAC) EOS International
Wireless access
Function: Doc delivery serv, ILL available, Photocopying/Printing, Ref serv available
Open Mon 12-4, Tues-Thurs 7:30-4

P SPRINGFIELD PUBLIC LIBRARY*, 225 Fifth St, 97477-4697. SAN 314-2299. Tel: 541-726-3766. FAX: 541-726-3747. E-mail: library@ci.springfield.or.us. Web Site: wheremindsgrow.org. *Dir,* Emily David; E-mail: edavid@springfield-or.gov; *Libr Mgr,* Carrie Schindele-Cupples; E-mail: scupples@springfield-or.gov; Staff 7 (MLS 5, Non-MLS 2)
Founded 1908. Pop 55,000; Circ 345,000
Library Holdings: AV Mats 9,249; Electronic Media & Resources 26; Bk Vols 142,300; Per Subs 122
Special Collections: Mystery & Detective Fiction Coll (1920 to present)
Automation Activity & Vendor Info: (Acquisitions) SirsiDynix; (Cataloging) SirsiDynix; (Circulation) SirsiDynix; (OPAC) SirsiDynix; (Serials) SirsiDynix
Wireless access
Partic in OCLC Online Computer Library Center, Inc
Open Mon & Tues 10-8, Wed-Sat 10-6
Friends of the Library Group

STANFIELD

P STANFIELD PUBLIC LIBRARY*, 180 W Coe Ave, 97875. (Mail add: PO Box 489, 97875-0489), SAN 358-0652. Tel: 541-449-1254. FAX: 541-449-3264. E-mail: library@cityofstanfield.com. Web Site: www.stanfieldpubliclibrary.com. *Libr Dir,* Cecili Longhorn; E-mail: librarydirector@cityofstanfield.com; *Libr Asst,* Debbie Baros; Staff 2 (Non-MLS 2)
Founded 1914. Pop 2,900; Circ 6,900
Library Holdings: AV Mats 520; Large Print Bks 40; Bk Titles 7,445; Talking Bks 120
Special Collections: NE Oregon History Coll
Subject Interests: Diabetes, Local hist
Wireless access
Mem of Umatilla County Special Library District
Partic in Sage Library System of Eastern Oregon
Open Mon-Thurs 10-6, Fri 10-2

STAYTON

P STAYTON PUBLIC LIBRARY, 515 N First Ave, 97383-1703. SAN 314-2302. Tel: 503-769-3313. FAX: 503-769-3218. E-mail: staytonpl@ccrls.org. Web Site: www.staytonoregon.gov/page/library_home. *Dir,* Janna Moser; *Youth Serv Librn,* Jennifer Gaetan; Staff 1 (MLS 1)
Founded 1938. Pop 11,000; Circ 237,000
Jul 2012-Jun 2013 Income $427,568, City $260,200, County $80,250, Locally Generated Income $27,500, Other $25,000. Mats Exp $44,200, Books $31,500, Per/Ser (Incl. Access Fees) $3,200, AV Equip $3,000, AV Mat $6,500. Sal $247,534 (Prof $62,412)

Library Holdings: Audiobooks 4,356; DVDs 4,478; Bk Vols 49,230; Per Subs 69; Videos 4,478
Automation Activity & Vendor Info: (Acquisitions) Innovative Interfaces, Inc; (Cataloging) Innovative Interfaces, Inc; (Circulation) Innovative Interfaces, Inc; (ILL) Innovative Interfaces, Inc; (OPAC) Innovative Interfaces, Inc
Wireless access
Function: Art exhibits, Audiobks via web, Bk club(s), Bks on cassette, Bks on CD, Children's prog, Computer training, Computers for patron use, Digital talking bks, E-Reserves, Electronic databases & coll, Family literacy, Free DVD rentals, ILL available, Internet access, Mail & tel request accepted, Microfiche/film & reading machines, Music CDs, Notary serv, Online cat, Online info literacy tutorials on the web & in blackboard, Online ref, Outreach serv, Outside serv via phone, mail, e-mail & web, OverDrive digital audio bks, Photocopying/Printing, Preschool outreach, Preschool reading prog, Prog for adults, Prog for children & young adult, Ref & res, Ref serv available, Spoken cassettes & CDs, Spoken cassettes & DVDs, Story hour, Summer reading prog, Tax forms, Teen prog, Telephone ref, Wheelchair accessible
Partic in Chemeketa Cooperative Regional Library Service
Open Mon-Thurs 10-7, Fri 10-5:30, Sat 10-4
Friends of the Library Group

SWEET HOME

P SWEET HOME PUBLIC LIBRARY, 1101 13th Ave, 97386. SAN 314-2310. Tel: 541-367-5007. FAX: 541-367-3754. Web Site: www.sweethomeor.gov/library. *Libr Dir,* Megan Dazey; E-mail: mdazey@sweethomeor.gov; Staff 4 (MLS 1, Non-MLS 3)
Founded 1942. Pop 9,800; Circ 48,461
Library Holdings: Bk Vols 35,000; Per Subs 25
Subject Interests: Northwest, Western fiction
Wireless access
Function: 24/7 Electronic res, 24/7 Online cat, Adult literacy prog, Bks on CD, Children's prog, Computers for patron use, Digital talking bks, Electronic databases & coll, Free DVD rentals, Internet access, Magazines, Mail & tel request accepted, Movies, Music CDs, Online cat, OverDrive digital audio bks, Preschool reading prog, Prog for children & young adult, Res assist avail, Scanner, Summer reading prog, Tax forms, Teen prog, Telephone ref
Partic in Linn Libraries Consortium
Open Tues 10-6, Wed & Thurs Noon-6, Fri & Sat Noon-4
Friends of the Library Group

THE DALLES

J COLUMBIA GORGE COMMUNITY COLLEGE LIBRARY, 400 E Scenic Dr, 97058. SAN 375-3395. Tel: 541-506-6081. Administration Tel: 541-506-6080. FAX: 541-506-6082. E-mail: library@cgcc.edu. Web Site: www.cgcc.edu/library. *Dean, Library & Learning Commons,* Dylan McManus; E-mail: DMcManus@cgcc.edu; *Digital Access & Public Servs Librn,* Tori Stanek; E-mail: tstanek@cgcc.edu
Founded 1995. Enrl 1,010; Highest Degree: Associate
Library Holdings: Bks on Deafness & Sign Lang 62; CDs 550; DVDs 284; e-books 47,000; Bk Titles 19,500; Per Subs 98; Videos 800
Automation Activity & Vendor Info: (Cataloging) Evergreen; (Circulation) Evergreen; (Course Reserve) Evergreen; (ILL) OCLC; (OPAC) Evergreen
Wireless access
Function: Audio & video playback equip for onsite use, Bks on CD, Computers for patron use, Distance learning, Electronic databases & coll, Equip loans & repairs, ILL available, Literacy & newcomer serv, Music CDs, Online cat, Photocopying/Printing, Ref serv available, Scanner, VHS videos, Wheelchair accessible
Partic in Sage Library System of Eastern Oregon
Open Mon-Thurs 8-6, Fri 8-Noon

M MCMC/CELILO CANCER CENTER*, Planetree Health Resource Center, 1800 E 19th St, 97058. SAN 377-628X. Tel: 541-296-7585. FAX: 541-296-7610. Web Site: www.mcmc.net/our-services/cancer-care.
Founded 1992
Library Holdings: Bk Vols 2,000
Subject Interests: Consumer health info, Med info
Wireless access
Function: Doc delivery serv, Health sci info serv, ILL available, Internet access, Photocopying/Printing, Ref serv available, Wheelchair accessible
Partic in Sage Library System of Eastern Oregon
Open Mon-Fri 8-4

P WASCO COUNTY LIBRARY DISTRICT*, The Dalles Public Library, 722 Court St, 97058. SAN 357-8852. Tel: 541-296-2815. E-mail: thedallespubliclibrary@gmail.com. Web Site: www.wascocountylibrary.com. *Dir, Libr Serv,* Jeff Wavrunek; E-mail: jwavrunek@ci.the-dalles.or.us; *Asst Dir,* Dylan McManus; Staff 6 (MLS 1, Non-MLS 5)
Founded 1909. Pop 21,285; Circ 109,966
Library Holdings: AV Mats 2,116; Bk Vols 65,441; Per Subs 114; Talking Bks 2,326
Subject Interests: Ore hist
Automation Activity & Vendor Info: (Acquisitions) SirsiDynix; (Cataloging) SirsiDynix; (Circulation) SirsiDynix; (OPAC) SirsiDynix
Wireless access
Partic in Sage Library System of Eastern Oregon
Open Mon-Thurs 10-8:30, Fri & Sat 10-6
Friends of the Library Group
Branches: 2
DUFUR SCHOOL-COMMUNITY LIBRARY, 802 NE Fifth St, Dufur, 97021-3034. Tel: 541-467-2509, 541-467-2588. FAX: 541-467-2589. Web Site: www.dufur.k12.or.us. *Librn,* Sarah Tierney; E-mail: sarah.tierney@dufur.k12.or.us
Pop 1,887
Library Holdings: Bk Vols 21,000
Open Mon & Wed (Winter) 8-4, Tues & Thurs 8-4 & 6-8, Fri 8-3:30; Tues & Thurs (Summer) 10-2 & 6-8
SOUTHERN WASCO COUNTY PUBLIC LIBRARY, 410 Deschutes Ave, Maupin, 97037. (Mail add: PO Box 328, Maupin, 97037-0328). Tel: 541-395-2208. FAX: 541-395-2208. E-mail: southernwascolibrary@gmail.com. Web Site: www.geocities.com/maupinlibrary. *Libr Dir,* Valerie D Stephenson; Staff 1 (Non-MLS 1)
Pop 2,555; Fac 2
Library Holdings: AV Mats 1,425; Large Print Bks 200; Bk Titles 6,950; Per Subs 12
Special Collections: Ivan Donaldson Botanical Coll; Local Newspapers, circa 1914-1930
Subject Interests: Genealogy, Local hist
Function: 24/7 Electronic res, 24/7 Online cat, Archival coll, Art exhibits, Audiobks via web, Bks on CD, Children's prog, Free DVD rentals, Holiday prog, ILL available, Internet access, Magazines, Music CDs, Online cat, OverDrive digital audio bks, Preschool outreach, Preschool reading prog, Prog for children & young adult, Ref serv available, Summer reading prog, Teen prog
Open Tues-Thurs 1-6, Fri 11-4

TIGARD

P TIGARD PUBLIC LIBRARY*, 13500 SW Hall Blvd, 97223-8111. SAN 314-2329. Tel: 503-684-6537. Reference Tel: 503-718-2517. FAX: 503-598-7515, 503-718-2797. TDD: 503-644-2197. Web Site: www.tigard-or.gov/library.php. *Libr Dir,* Halsted Bernard; Tel: 503-684-6537, Ext 2501, E-mail: halstedb@tigard-or.gov; *Circ Mgr,* Brent Husher; Tel: 503-684-6537, Ext 2509, E-mail: brenth@tigard-or.gov; *Reader Serv Mgr,* Amber Bell; Tel: 503-684-6537, Ext 2812, E-mail: amber@tigard-or.gov; *Tech Serv Mgr,* Teresa Ferguson; Tel: 503-684-6537, Ext 2505, E-mail: teresaf@tigard-or.gov; *Supvr, Acq,* Meagan Gibson; Tel: 503-684-6537, Ext 2513, E-mail: meagang@tigard-or.gov; *Supvr, Ad Serv,* Annie Sprague; Tel: 503-684-6537, Ext 2649, E-mail: annies@tigard-or.gov; *Supvr, Circ,* Sandra Hughes; Tel: 503-684-6537, Ext 2515, E-mail: sandra@tigard-or.gov; *Supvr, Circ,* Jaime Hutchison; Tel: 503-684-6537, Ext 2510, E-mail: jaimeh@tigard-or.gov; *Supvr, Youth Serv,* Kari Kunst; Tel: 503-684-6537, Ext 2503, E-mail: kari@tigard-or.gov; *Communications Coordr, Outreach Coordr,* Jeanne Peloquin; Tel: 503-684-6537, Ext 2508, E-mail: JeanneP@tigard-or.gov; *Vols Serv Coordr,* Katie Nelson; Tel: 503-684-6537, Ext 2516, E-mail: katien@tigard-or.gov; Staff 38.8 (MLS 15.2, Non-MLS 23.6)
Founded 1963. Pop 67,278; Circ 1,481,715
Library Holdings: Audiobooks 865; AV Mats 3,317; CDs 1,182; DVDs 5,570; Large Print Bks 362; Bk Titles 30,857; Per Subs 256
Automation Activity & Vendor Info: (Acquisitions) Innovative Interfaces, Inc; (Cataloging) Innovative Interfaces, Inc; (Circulation) Innovative Interfaces, Inc; (ILL) Innovative Interfaces, Inc; (OPAC) Innovative Interfaces, Inc
Wireless access
Partic in Washington County Cooperative Library Services
Special Services for the Deaf - Assistive tech; Bks on deafness & sign lang; Closed caption videos; TDD equip
Special Services for the Blind - Bks on cassette; Bks on CD; Computer with voice synthesizer for visually impaired persons; Descriptive video serv (DVS); Home delivery serv; Internet workstation with adaptive software; Large print bks; PC for people with disabilities; Volunteer serv
Open Mon-Fri 10-8, Sat-Sun 10-6
Friends of the Library Group

TILLAMOOK

J TILLAMOOK BAY COMMUNITY COLLEGE LIBRARY*, 4301 Third St, 97141. Tel: 503-842-8222, Ext 1720. FAX: 503-842-2214. Web Site: tillamookbaycc.edu/library/. *Col Librn, Libr Dir,* Masyn Phoenix; Tel: 503-842-8222, Ext 1710, E-mail: masynphoenix@tillamookbaycc.edu
Fac 7; Highest Degree: Associate

Library Holdings: AV Mats 200; Bk Vols 1,500; Per Subs 12
Automation Activity & Vendor Info: (Cataloging) SirsiDynix; (Circulation) SirsiDynix; (OPAC) SirsiDynix
Wireless access
Partic in Chinook Library Network
Open Mon-Thurs 9-7, Fri 9-4:30

P TILLAMOOK COUNTY LIBRARY*, 1716 Third St, 97141. SAN 358-2515. Tel: 503-842-4792. Web Site: tillabook.org. *Dir,* Sara Charlton; E-mail: charlton@co.tillamook.or.us; *Mgr, Br,* Bill Landeau; *Mgr, Main Libr,* Sarah Beeler; Staff 27 (MLS 7, Non-MLS 20)
Founded 1907. Pop 25,000; Circ 352,290
Jul 2012-Jun 2013 Income (Main & Associated Libraries) $4,670,000. Mats Exp $836,500, Books $90,000, AV Mat $21,000. Sal $1,113,500
Library Holdings: Bk Vols 179,150; Per Subs 424
Special Collections: Local History (Oregon). State Document Depository
Automation Activity & Vendor Info: (Cataloging) Innovative Interfaces, Inc - Millennium; (Circulation) Innovative Interfaces, Inc - Millennium; (OPAC) Innovative Interfaces, Inc - Millennium
Wireless access
Partic in OCLC Online Computer Library Center, Inc
Open Mon-Thurs 9-9, Fri & Sat 9-5:30
Friends of the Library Group
Branches: 5
BAY CITY, 5525 B St, Bay City, 97107, SAN 358-254X. Tel: 503-377-0231. Web Site: tillabook.org/Locations-Hours/Bay-City.
Open Tues-Fri 12-5, Sat 10-3
Friends of the Library Group
GARIBALDI BRANCH, City Hall, 107 Sixth St, Garibaldi, 97118, SAN 358-2574. Tel: 503-322-2100. FAX: 503-322-2100. Web Site: tillabook.org/Locations-Hours/Garibaldi.
Open Mon-Fri 12-5, Sat 10-3
Friends of the Library Group
NORTH COUNTY - MANZANITA, 571 Laneda Ave, Manzanita, 97130, SAN 358-2604. Tel: 503-368-6665. FAX: 503-368-6665. Web Site: tillabook.org/Locations-Hours/North-Tillamook-County.
Open Mon, Wed & Fri 12-5, Tues & Thurs 12-8, Sat 10-3
Friends of the Library Group
ROCKAWAY BEACH BRANCH, 120 N Coral, Rockaway Beach, 97136. Tel: 503-355-2665. FAX: 503-355-2665. Web Site: tillabook.org/Locations-Hours/Rockaway-Beach.
Open Mon-Fri 12-5, Sat 10-3
Friends of the Library Group
SOUTH COUNTY, 6200 Camp St, Pacific City, 97135, SAN 358-2639. Tel: 503-965-6163. FAX: 503-965-6163. Web Site: tillabook.org/Locations-Hours/South-Tillamook-County.
Open Mon, Thurs & Fri 12-5, Tues & Wed 12-8, Sat 10-3
Friends of the Library Group
Bookmobiles: 1

S TILLAMOOK COUNTY PIONEER MUSEUM, Research Library, 2106 Second St, 97141. SAN 375-510X. Tel: 503-842-4553. Web Site: www.tcpm.org. *Dir of Mus,* Gary Albright; E-mail: director@tcpm.org; *Researcher,* Ruby Fry-Matson; E-mail: ruby@tcpm.org
Library Holdings: Bk Titles 4,000
Special Collections: Oral History
Wireless access
Function: ILL available, Telephone ref
Restriction: Non-circulating to the pub, Not a lending libr, Open by appt only, Open to pub with supv only

TOLEDO

P TOLEDO PUBLIC LIBRARY*, 173 NW Seventh St, 97391. SAN 314-2337. Tel: 541-336-3132. Web Site: www.cityoftoledo.org/library. *Dir,* Deborah Trusty; E-mail: librarydirector@cityoftoledo.org; *Asst Dir,* Harrison Baker; *Ch,* Denyse Marsh; E-mail: childrens@cityoftoledo.org; *Cat, Tech Serv,* Andrea Haller; Staff 3.4 (Non-MLS 3.4)
Founded 1916. Pop 5,965; Circ 70,884
Library Holdings: Bk Vols 35,000; Per Subs 70
Special Collections: Yaquina Genealogical Society; Yaquina Pacific Railroad Historical Society
Subject Interests: Genealogy, Railroad hist
Automation Activity & Vendor Info: (Cataloging) OCLC; (Circulation) ByWater Solutions; (ILL) OCLC; (OPAC) ByWater Solutions
Wireless access
Partic in Chinook Library Network
Open Mon-Fri 10-6, Sat 10-5

TUALATIN

P TUALATIN PUBLIC LIBRARY, 18878 SW Martinazzi Ave, 97062. SAN 314-2345. Tel: 503-691-3074. Reference Tel: 503-691-3072. FAX: 503-692-3512. E-mail: librarymail@tualatin.gov. Web Site: www.tualatinoregon.gov/library. *Libr Dir,* Jerianne Thompson; Tel: 503-691-3063, E-mail: jthompson@tualatin.gov; Staff 15 (MLS 6, Non-MLS 9)
Founded 1977. Pop 7,700; Circ 230,752
Library Holdings: e-books 48,700; Bk Vols 70,400; Per Subs 180
Automation Activity & Vendor Info: (Cataloging) Innovative Interfaces, Inc; (Circulation) Innovative Interfaces, Inc; (OPAC) Innovative Interfaces, Inc
Wireless access
Partic in Washington County Cooperative Library Services
Open Mon-Sat 10-6
Friends of the Library Group

UKIAH

P UKIAH PUBLIC LIBRARY, 201 Hill St, 97880. (Mail add: PO Box 218, 97880-0218), SAN 376-3285. Tel: 541-427-3735. FAX: 541-427-3730. Web Site: ukiahlibrary.weebly.com. *Librn,* Audrey Dufrey; E-mail: audrey.durfey@ukiah.k12.or.us
Library Holdings: Audiobooks 250; CDs 150; DVDs 425; High Interest/Low Vocabulary Bk Vols 25; Large Print Bks 85; Bk Titles 11,125; Videos 350
Wireless access
Mem of Umatilla County Special Library District
Open Mon-Wed 10-3, Thurs 10-5
Friends of the Library Group

UMATILLA

S TWO RIVERS CORRECTIONAL INSTITUTE LIBRARY*, 82911 Beach Access Rd, 97882. Tel: 541-922-2177. Web Site: www.oregon.gov/doc/ops/prison/pages/trci.aspx. *Coordr, Librn,* Ronda Davis; *Librn,* Stephanie Martin
Library Holdings: Bk Vols 12,000
Restriction: Not open to pub

P UMATILLA PUBLIC LIBRARY, 700 Sixth St, 97882-9507. (Mail add: PO Box 820, 97882-0820), SAN 358-0687. Tel: 541-922-5704. FAX: 541-922-5708. E-mail: library@umatilla-city.org. Web Site: www.umatilla-city.org/library. *Libr Asst,* Kellie Lamoreaux; *Libr Asst,* Susie Sotelo
Library Holdings: Bk Vols 21,604; Per Subs 12
Automation Activity & Vendor Info: (Cataloging) Innovative Interfaces, Inc; (Circulation) Innovative Interfaces, Inc; (OPAC) Innovative Interfaces, Inc
Wireless access
Mem of Umatilla County Special Library District
Open Mon-Thur 10-6, Fri 9-5, Sat 10-2

UNION

P UNION CARNEGIE PUBLIC LIBRARY*, 1825 N Main St, 97883. (Mail add: PO Box 928, 97883-0928), SAN 314-2353. Tel: 541-562-5811. FAX: 541-562-2028. E-mail: library@cityofunion.com. Web Site: cityofunion.com/directory/city-library. *Dir,* Louise Shelden
Founded 1913. Pop 1,200; Circ 168,364
Library Holdings: Bk Vols 15,000
Subject Interests: Alternate energy res
Wireless access
Function: ILL available
Open Mon 10-6, Tues 10-5:30, Wed 4-8, Thurs 1-6, Fri 9-3:30
Friends of the Library Group

VALE

P EMMA HUMPHREY LIBRARY, 150 A St E, 97918-1345. Tel: 541-473-3902. E-mail: valecitylibrary@gmail.com. Web Site: cityofvale.com/government/departments/emma-humphrey-library. *Librn,* Heather Kesey; Staff 1 (Non-MLS 1)
Library Holdings: Bk Titles 17,800; Per Subs 15
Automation Activity & Vendor Info: (Cataloging) Evergreen; (Circulation) Evergreen; (OPAC) Evergreen
Wireless access
Open Tues-Fri 1-5, Sat 1-4

VENETA

P FERN RIDGE PUBLIC LIBRARY*, 88026 Territorial Rd, 97487. (Mail add: PO Box 397, 97487-0397), SAN 314-2361. Tel: 541-935-7512. FAX: 541-935-8013. E-mail: staff@fernridgelibrary.org. Web Site: www.fernridgelibrary.org. *Dir,* Colin Rea; E-mail: crea@fernridgelibrary.org; Staff 5 (Non-MLS 5)
Founded 1966. Pop 12,000; Circ 124,000
Library Holdings: Bk Titles 43,657; Per Subs 75
Automation Activity & Vendor Info: (Cataloging) SirsiDynix; (Circulation) SirsiDynix; (OPAC) SirsiDynix
Wireless access

Publications: Friends of the Library (Newsletter)
Open Tues-Thurs 10-8, Fri 10-6, Sat 10-5
Friends of the Library Group

VERNONIA

P VERNONIA PUBLIC LIBRARY*, 701 Weed Ave, 97064-1102. SAN 314-237X. Tel: 503-429-1818. FAX: 503-429-0729. E-mail: library@vernonia-or.gov. Web Site: www.vernonia-or.gov/departments/library. *Dir,* Shannon Romtvedt; E-mail: shannonr@vernonia-or.gov; *Libr Asst,* Brandi Fennell
Founded 1925. Pop 1,750; Circ 9,633
Library Holdings: Bk Vols 20,000; Per Subs 30
Automation Activity & Vendor Info: (Cataloging) Follett Software; (Circulation) Follett Software
Wireless access
Open Mon, Wed & Fri 10-5, Tues & Thurs 12-7
Friends of the Library Group

WALDPORT

P WALDPORT PUBLIC LIBRARY*, 460 Hemlock St, 97394. (Mail add: PO Box 1357, 97394-1357), SAN 314-2388. Tel: 541-563-5880. FAX: 541-563-6237. E-mail: waldportlibrary@waldport.org. Web Site: www.waldport.org/Departments/library.php, www.waldportlibrary.org. *Libr Dir,* Sue Bennett; E-mail: sbennett@waldportlibrary.org; Staff 2 (Non-MLS 2)
Founded 1919. Pop 4,900; Circ 68,238
Library Holdings: AV Mats 1,936; Electronic Media & Resources 27; Bk Titles 21,000; Per Subs 41
Automation Activity & Vendor Info: (Cataloging) SirsiDynix; (Circulation) SirsiDynix; (OPAC) SirsiDynix
Wireless access
Open Mon & Thurs 10-7, Tues, Wed & Fri 10-5, Sat 10-4
Friends of the Library Group

WALLOWA

P WALLOWA PUBLIC LIBRARY*, 201 N Main, 97885. (Mail add: PO Box 486, 97885-0486). Tel: 541-886-4265. E-mail: wallowapubliclibrary@gmail.com. Web Site: wallowapubliclibrary.org. *Interim Dir,* Kristen Tompeck
Library Holdings: Bk Titles 10,000
Open Mon, Tues & Fri 1-5, Wed 10-2, Thurs 2-6

WARRENTON

P WARRENTON COMMUNITY LIBRARY*, 160 S Main Ave, 97146. (Mail add: PO Box 250, 97146-0250). Tel: 503-861-8156. Administration Tel: 503-861-2233. Web Site: www.ci.warrenton.or.us/library. *Mgr,* Nettie-Lee Calog; E-mail: nlcwcl@yahoo.com
Founded 1991. Pop 4,230
Library Holdings: Bk Titles 13,000; Per Subs 10
Open Mon, Tues, Thurs & Fri 1-5, Wed 1-7, Sat 10-2
Friends of the Library Group

WASCO

P WASCO CITY/COMMUNITY LIBRARY*, Wasco School Events Ctr, 903 Barnett St, 97065. (Mail add: PO Box 202, 97065-0202). Tel: 541-442-8505. Web Site: www.wascooregon.com/id27.html. *Dir,* Danee Rankin
Library Holdings: Bk Vols 7,000
Special Collections: Biographies; Children's Coll; Non-Fiction & Fiction; Oregon History & Authors; US Presidents Coll
Wireless access
Open Mon & Wed 9-12:15 & 1-5:30, Tues & Thurs 9-12:15 & 1-7:30, Fri 9-2
Friends of the Library Group

WELCHES

P HOODLAND LIBRARY, 24525 E Welches Rd, 97067. (Mail add: PO Box 298, 97067). Tel: 503-622-3460. Web Site: www.ci.sandy.or.us/library. *Libr Dir,* Sarah McIntyre; E-mail: smcintyre@ci.sandy.or.us; Staff 3 (MLS 0.5, Non-MLS 2.5)
Pop 5,274
Automation Activity & Vendor Info: (Cataloging) SirsiDynix-WorkFlows; (Circulation) SirsiDynix-WorkFlows; (OPAC) SirsiDynix; (Serials) SirsiDynix-WorkFlows
Wireless access
Partic in Library Information Network of Clackamas County
Open Mon 10-4, Tues 1-7, Wed, Thurs & Fri 12-6, Sat 12-5
Friends of the Library Group

WEST LINN

P WEST LINN PUBLIC LIBRARY*, 1595 Burns St, 97068. SAN 314-240X. Tel: 503-656-7853. Information Services Tel: 503-656-7853, Ext 6. FAX: 503-656-2746. E-mail: wlref@lincc.org. Web Site: westlinnoregon.gov/library. *Dir,* Doug Erickson; Tel: 503-742-6165, E-mail: derickson@westlinnoregon.gov
Founded 1939
Library Holdings: AV Mats 19,486; Bk Vols 82,481; Per Subs 285
Automation Activity & Vendor Info: (Cataloging) SirsiDynix; (Circulation) SirsiDynix; (OPAC) SirsiDynix
Wireless access
Publications: Newsletter
Partic in Library Information Network of Clackamas County
Open Mon-Wed 10-8, Thurs & Fri 10-6, Sat & Sun 12-5

WESTFIR

P WESTFIR CITY LIBRARY, 47441 Westoak Rd, 97492. (Mail add: PO Box 296, 97492-0296). Tel: 541-782-3733. FAX: 541-782-3983. E-mail: westfircity@questoffice.net. *Dir,* Dennis Kronwall
Library Holdings: Bk Titles 9,500
Open Mon, Wed & Fri 9-2

WESTON

P WESTON PUBLIC LIBRARY*, 108 E Main St, 97886. (Mail add: PO Box 550, 97886), SAN 358-0717. Tel: 541-566-2378. FAX: 541-566-2378. E-mail: wcolibrary@cityofwestonoregon.com. Web Site: www.westonpubliclibrary.com. *Librn,* Kathleen Schmidtgall
Library Holdings: Bk Titles 9,000; Per Subs 50
Mem of Umatilla County Special Library District
Open Mon, Wed & Fri 8-12 & 1-5, Tues & Thurs 1:30-7
Friends of the Library Group

WILLAMINA

P WILLAMINA PUBLIC LIBRARY, 382 NE C St, 97396. (Mail add: PO Box 273, 97396-0273), SAN 376-3307. Tel: 503-876-6182. FAX: 503-876-1121. Web Site: willamina.ccrls.org. *Dir,* Sarah Frost; E-mail: frosts@ci.willamina.or.us; *Youth Serv Librn,* Richard Guscott; *Asst Librn,* Karla Johnson
Pop 2,800; Circ 15,100
Library Holdings: AV Mats 2,000; Large Print Bks 300; Bk Titles 28,744; Bk Vols 29,618; Per Subs 6; Talking Bks 510
Automation Activity & Vendor Info: (Acquisitions) SirsiDynix; (Cataloging) SirsiDynix; (Circulation) SirsiDynix
Wireless access
Partic in Chemeketa Cooperative Regional Library Service
Open Mon-Thurs 11-5

WILSONVILLE

P WILSONVILLE PUBLIC LIBRARY*, 8200 SW Wilsonville Rd, 97070. SAN 329-9287. Tel: 503-682-2744. FAX: 503-682-8685. Web Site: www.wilsonvillelibrary.org. *Dir,* Patrick Duke; Tel: 503-570-1590, E-mail: duke@wilsonvillelibrary.org; *Mgr, Libr Operations,* Shasta Barnes; Tel: 503-570-1597, E-mail: barnes@wilsonvillelibrary.org; *Ad,* Greg Martin; Tel: 503-570-1595, E-mail: martin@wilsonvillelibrary.org; *Youth Serv Librn,* Jo Caisse; Tel: 503-570-1592, E-mail: jcaisse@wilsonvillelibrary.org; Staff 15 (MLS 5, Non-MLS 10)
Founded 1982. Pop 25,000; Circ 498,000
Library Holdings: AV Mats 20,516; Large Print Bks 3,318; Bk Vols 82,995; Per Subs 181
Special Collections: Japanese Language Children's Books; Local History & Oregon Genealogy (Heritage Coll)
Subject Interests: Genealogy, Japan, Pacific Northwest
Automation Activity & Vendor Info: (Acquisitions) SirsiDynix; (Cataloging) SirsiDynix; (Circulation) SirsiDynix; (OPAC) SirsiDynix; (Serials) SirsiDynix
Wireless access
Function: Adult bk club, Audio & video playback equip for onsite use, Audiobks via web, Bk club(s), Bks on cassette, Bks on CD, CD-ROM, Children's prog, Computer training, Computers for patron use, Digital talking bks, Electronic databases & coll, Home delivery & serv to seniorr ctr & nursing homes, Homebound delivery serv, ILL available, Instruction & testing, Internet access, Music CDs, Notary serv, Online cat, Online ref, OverDrive digital audio bks, Photocopying/Printing, Prog for adults, Prog for children & young adult, Ref serv available, Senior computer classes, Story hour, Summer reading prog, Tax forms, Teen prog, Telephone ref, VHS videos, Wheelchair accessible, Workshops, Writing prog
Open Mon-Thurs 10-8, Fri-Sat 10-6, Sun 1-6
Friends of the Library Group

WOODBURN

P WOODBURN PUBLIC LIBRARY*, 280 Garfield St, 97071. SAN 314-2442. Tel: 503-982-5252. Circulation Tel: 503-982-5262. FAX: 503-982-5258. E-mail: library@ci.woodburn.or.us, woodburn@ccrls.org. Web Site: www.woodburn-or.gov/?=congent/woodburn-public-library. *City Librn,* John Hunter; Tel: 503-982-5259, E-mail: john.hunter@ci.woodburn.or.us; Staff 9.8 (MLS 3.8, Non-MLS 6)
Founded 1914. Pop 25,000; Circ 158,719
Library Holdings: Bk Vols 55,000; Per Subs 50
Special Collections: Language (Russian & Spanish Coll)
Automation Activity & Vendor Info: (Acquisitions) Innovative Interfaces, Inc; (Cataloging) Innovative Interfaces, Inc; (Circulation) Innovative Interfaces, Inc; (ILL) Innovative Interfaces, Inc; (OPAC) Innovative Interfaces, Inc; (Serials) EBSCO Online
Wireless access
Partic in Chemeketa Cooperative Regional Library Service
Open Mon-Thurs 10-7, Fri 10-5, Sat & Sun 1-5
Friends of the Library Group

YACHATS

P YACHATS PUBLIC LIBRARY*, 560 W Seventh St, 97498. (Mail add: PO Box 817, 97498-0817), SAN 314-2450. Tel: 541-547-3741. FAX: 541-547-3741. E-mail: yachatspl@actionnet.net. *Dir,* Janet Hickam
Pop 695; Circ 4,580
Library Holdings: Bk Vols 15,000; Per Subs 14
Automation Activity & Vendor Info: (Cataloging) Library Concepts
Wireless access
Open Mon-Fri 12-4, Sat 10-4
Friends of the Library Group

PENNSYLVANIA

Date of Statistics: FY 2015
Population, 2020 U.S. Census: 12,783,254
Population Served by Public Libraries: 12,408,832
Unserved: 293,574
Total Volumes in Public Libraries: 30,401,726
Volumes Per Capita: 2.45
Total Public Circulation: 64,534,566
Circulation Per Capita: 5.2 (population served)
Income and Expenditures:
Total Public Library Income: $355,295,844
Sources of Income:
Public Funds: $236,995,786
State Funds: $56,374,567
Federal: $1,699,275
Private Funds (including gifts): $60,226,216
Total Operating Expenditures: $352,133,828
Total Capital Expenditures: $16,976,306
Operating Expenditures Per Capita: $28 (population served)
Grants-in-Aid to Public Libraries:
Federal (Library Services & Technology Act 2014-2015): $5,416,459
State Aid (2014-2015): $53,507,000
Apportionment: To be eligible for state aid, the local financial effort of a library or library system must be at least $5 per capita unless the library serves an economically distressed municipality
Number of County or Multi-County (Regional) Libraries: 54
Counties Served: 67
Number of Bookmobiles in State: 22

ABINGTON

M ABINGTON MEMORIAL HOSPITAL*, Wilmer Memorial Medical Library, 1200 York Rd, 19001. SAN 314-2469. Tel: 215-481-2096. E-mail: WilmerLibrary@Jefferson.edu. Web Site: www.amh.org. *Librn,* Daphne Hyatt; E-mail: daphne.hyatt@jefferson.edu
Founded 1914
Library Holdings: Bk Titles 5,196; Bk Vols 5,300; Per Subs 450
Subject Interests: Dentistry, Med, Nursing, Surgery
Partic in Basic Health Sciences Library Network; NY Regional Med Libr
Open Mon-Fri 7am-7pm
Restriction: Badge access after hrs

R ABINGTON PRESBYTERIAN CHURCH LIBRARY*, 1082 Old York Rd, 19001-4593. SAN 314-2477. Tel: 215-887-4530. FAX: 215-887-5988. Web Site: www.apcusa.org. *Librn,* Position Currently Open
Founded 1956
Library Holdings: Bk Vols 6,046
Subject Interests: Environ studies, Local Presbyterian Church hist, Mostly non-fiction
Open Mon-Fri 8:30-4:30

P ABINGTON TOWNSHIP PUBLIC LIBRARY, Abington Free Library, 1030 Old York Rd, 19001-4594. SAN 358-2663. Tel: 215-885-5180. Circulation Tel: 215-885-5180, Ext 110. Reference Tel: 215-885-5180, Ext 113. FAX: 215-885-9242. Web Site: abingtonfreelibrary.org. *Exec Dir,* Elizabeth A Fitzgerald; Tel: 215-885-5180, Ext 114; *Fiscal Mgr,* Dimitra A Seiler; Tel: 215-885-5180, Ext 117, E-mail: dseiler@mclinc.org; *Ch Serv,* Carolyn DuBois; Tel: 215-885-5180, Ext 129; *Ref (Info Servs),* Mimi Satterthwaite; Staff 8.9 (MLS 8.9)
Founded 1966. Pop 57,853; Circ 486,262
Jan 2020-Dec 2020 Income (Main & Associated Libraries) $2,319,324, State $202,695, City $2,082,432, Locally Generated Income $34,197. Mats Exp $218,808, Books $71,887, Per/Ser (Incl. Access Fees) $16,833, AV Mat $18,562, Electronic Ref Mat (Incl. Access Fees) $47,439. Sal $1,336,482 (Prof $41,000)
Library Holdings: Audiobooks 6,839; AV Mats 27,463; DVDs 16,074; e-books 31,308; Electronic Media & Resources 119; Bk Titles 129,108; Per Subs 210
Automation Activity & Vendor Info: (Acquisitions) Innovative Interfaces, Inc. - Polaris; (Cataloging) OCLC; (Circulation) Innovative Interfaces, Inc. - Polaris; (OPAC) Innovative Interfaces, Inc. - Polaris; (Serials) Innovative Interfaces, Inc. - Polaris
Wireless access
Function: 24/7 Electronic res, 24/7 Online cat, Adult literacy prog
Partic in Montgomery County Library & Information Network Consortium
Open Mon-Thurs 9:30-9, Fri & Sat 9:30-5, Sun 1-5
Friends of the Library Group
Branches: 1
ROSLYN BRANCH, 2412 Avondale Ave, Roslyn, 19001-4203, SAN 358-2698. Tel: 215-886-9818. FAX: 215-886-9818. *Librn,* Margaret Mitchell; E-mail: mmitchell@mclinc.org
Library Holdings: Bk Vols 20,529; Per Subs 27
Open Mon 11-9, Tues, Thurs & Fri 11-6, Sat 11-2
Friends of the Library Group

R OLD YORK ROAD TEMPLE BETH AM LIBRARY*, 971 Old York Rd, 19001. SAN 314-2493. Tel: 215-886-8000. FAX: 215-886-8320. Web Site: www.oyrtbetham.org/education/library. *Librn,* Karen Schwartz
Founded 1964
Library Holdings: AV Mats 187; Bk Titles 5,000; Talking Bks 49
Subject Interests: Judaica, Relig studies
Wireless access
Open Tues 4-9, Sun 9:30-Noon
Restriction: Non-circulating

C PENNSYLVANIA STATE UNIVERSITY*, Abington College Library, 1600 Woodland Rd, 19001. SAN 314-2507. Tel: 215-881-7424. Interlibrary Loan Service Tel: 215-881-7428. Reference Tel: 215-881-7462. FAX: 215-881-7423. E-mail: UL-ABINGTON@lists.psu.edu. Web Site: libraries.psu.edu/abington. *Head Librn,* Dolores R Fidishun; Tel: 215-881-7425, E-mail: dxf19@psu.edu; *Ref Librn,* Paul Smith; E-mail: pms20@psu.edu; *Ref & Instruction Librn,* Binh P Le; Tel: 215-881-7426, E-mail: bpl1@psu.edu; *Ref & Instruction Librn,* Christina E Riehman-Murphy; Tel: 215-881-7911, E-mail: cer20@psu.edu; Staff 6 (MLS 2, Non-MLS 4)
Founded 1950. Enrl 2,493; Fac 90; Highest Degree: Master
Library Holdings: Bk Titles 63,483; Bk Vols 68,950; Per Subs 163; Talking Bks 139; Videos 751
Wireless access
Function: Audio & video playback equip for onsite use, Photocopying/Printing
Partic in Califa; OCLC Online Computer Library Center, Inc; Research Libraries Information Network; San Francisco Bay Area Library & Information Network
Open Mon-Thurs 7:30am-9pm, Fri 7:30-5, Sat 10-2, Sun 1-5

ADAMSTOWN

P ADAMSTOWN AREA LIBRARY*, 3000 N Reading Rd, Rte 272, 19501. (Mail add: PO Box 356, 19501-0356). Tel: 717-484-4200. FAX: 717-484-0738. Web Site: adamstownarealibrary.org. *Dir,* Kathy Thren; E-mail: kthren@adamstown.lib.pa.us; *Youth Serv Coordr,* Jess Zook; Tel: 717-484-4200, E-mail: jzook@adamstown.lib.pa.us; Staff 11 (MLS 2, Non-MLS 9)
Founded 1945. Pop 30,439; Circ 190,000
Library Holdings: Bks on Deafness & Sign Lang 21; Large Print Bks 500; Bk Titles 25,266; Per Subs 35; Talking Bks 1,700; Videos 5,400
Special Collections: Antiques & Collectibles

Automation Activity & Vendor Info: (Cataloging) Innovative Interfaces, Inc; (Circulation) Innovative Interfaces, Inc; (OPAC) Innovative Interfaces, Inc
Wireless access
Function: 24/7 Electronic res, Adult bk club, ILL available
Mem of Library System of Lancaster County
Open Mon-Thurs 9:30-8, Fri 9:30-5; Sat (Summer) 9:30-4:30
Friends of the Library Group

ALBION

P ALBION AREA PUBLIC LIBRARY*, 111 E Pearl St, 16401-1202. SAN 314-2523. Tel: 814-756-5400. FAX: 814-756-5400. E-mail: albion@albionarealibrary.org. Web Site: albionarealibrary.org. *Dir,* Erin Tate; *Asst Librn,* Cheyenne Paris
Pop 1,607; Circ 25,783
Library Holdings: Bk Vols 15,000; Per Subs 24
Automation Activity & Vendor Info: (Cataloging) Infor Library & Information Solutions; (Circulation) Infor Library & Information Solutions
Wireless access
Open Mon & Wed 9-7, Sat 9-3
Friends of the Library Group

S STATE CORRECTIONAL INSTITUTION*, Albion Library, 10745 Rte 18, 16475-0001. Tel: 814-756-5778. FAX: 814-756-9735. Web Site: www.cor.pa.gov/Facilities/StatePrisons/Pages/Albion.aspx. *Librn,* Ms Robin Niberg
Library Holdings: Bk Vols 25,000; Per Subs 75
Automation Activity & Vendor Info: (Cataloging) Follett Software; (Circulation) Follett Software; (OPAC) Follett Software
Partic in Health Sciences Libraries Consortium

ALEXANDRIA

P MEMORIAL PUBLIC LIBRARY OF THE BOROUGH OF ALEXANDRIA*, 313 Main St, 16611. SAN 314-254X. Tel: 814-669-4313. E-mail: alexandriapalibrary@gmail.com. *Librn,* Jill McDonald; Staff 3 (MLS 1, Non-MLS 2)
Founded 1899. Pop 3,465; Circ 12,445
Library Holdings: Audiobooks 586; CDs 173; DVDs 310; Large Print Bks 108; Bk Vols 17,000; Per Subs 12; Talking Bks 90; Videos 179
Special Collections: Oral History
Wireless access
Open Mon & Thurs 10:30-5 & 6:30-8, Tues & Fri 9-5, Sat 9-Noon
Friends of the Library Group

ALIQUIPPA

P BEAVER COUNTY LIBRARY SYSTEM*, 109 Pleasant Dr, Ste 101, 15001. SAN 314-2558. Tel: 724-378-6227. FAX: 724-857-1109. Web Site: www.beaverlibraries.org. *Dir,* Jodi Oliver; E-mail: joliver@beaverlibraries.org; *Tech Coordr,* Mark Stevenson
Pop 169,000
Library Holdings: Bk Vols 309,325; Per Subs 50
Special Collections: Record Album Coll
Automation Activity & Vendor Info: (Cataloging) Innovative Interfaces, Inc; (Circulation) Innovative Interfaces, Inc; (OPAC) Innovative Interfaces, Inc
Wireless access
Function: 24/7 Electronic res, 24/7 Online cat, Accelerated reader prog, Activity rm, Adult bk club, Adult literacy prog, After school storytime, Audiobks via web, AV serv, Bk club(s), Bks on CD, Children's prog, Computer training, Computers for patron use, Distance learning, Electronic databases & coll, Free DVD rentals, Holiday prog, Homework prog, ILL available, Internet access, Learning ctr, Life-long learning prog for all ages, Magazines, Magnifiers for reading, Mail & tel request accepted, Meeting rooms, Microfiche/film & reading machines, Movies, Music CDs, Online cat, Online info literacy tutorials on the web & in blackboard, Online ref, Outreach serv, OverDrive digital audio bks, Photocopying/Printing, Preschool outreach, Preschool reading prog, Prog for adults, Prog for children & young adult, Senior computer classes, Spanish lang bks, Story hour, Study rm, Summer & winter reading prog, Summer reading prog, Tax forms, Teen prog, Telephone ref, Winter reading prog, Writing prog
Publications: Newsletter (Quarterly); Resources for Program Planning
Member Libraries: B F Jones Memorial Library; Baden Memorial Library; Beaver Area Memorial Library; Beaver County Law Library; Carnegie Free Library; Chippewa Branch Library; Community College of Beaver County Library; Laughlin Memorial Library; Monaca Public Library; New Brighton Public Library; Rochester Public Library
Partic in OCLC Online Computer Library Center, Inc; Pittsburgh Regional Libr Consortium
Open Mon-Fri 8:30-4:30
Friends of the Library Group

P B F JONES MEMORIAL LIBRARY*, 663 Franklin Ave, 15001-3736. SAN 314-2566. Tel: 724-375-2900. FAX: 724-375-3274. Web Site: www.beaverlibraries.org/aliquippa.asp. *Libr Dir,* Ann Andrews; E-mail: aandrews@beaverlibraries.org; Staff 3 (MLS 2, Non-MLS 1)
Founded 1921. Pop 30,000; Circ 90,000
Library Holdings: Bk Vols 66,000; Per Subs 130
Special Collections: LPDR for Nuclear Reg Com for Beaver Valley I & II Power Stations; PA Airhelp Resource Center
Automation Activity & Vendor Info: (Cataloging) Innovative Interfaces, Inc; (Circulation) Innovative Interfaces, Inc; (ILL) OCLC; (OPAC) Innovative Interfaces, Inc
Wireless access
Function: 24/7 Electronic res, Adult bk club, Archival coll, Bk club(s), Bks on CD, Chess club, Children's prog, Computer training, Computers for patron use, Digital talking bks, E-Reserves, Electronic databases & coll, Free DVD rentals, ILL available, Laminating, Magazines, Magnifiers for reading, Microfiche/film & reading machines, Movies, Online cat, Outreach serv, OverDrive digital audio bks, Photocopying/Printing, Preschool outreach, Prof lending libr, Prog for adults, Prog for children & young adult, Ref & res, Ref serv available, Scanner, Senior computer classes, Summer reading prog, Tax forms, Teen prog, Telephone ref, Wheelchair accessible
Mem of Beaver County Library System
Partic in Interlibrary Delivery Service of Pennsylvania; OCLC Online Computer Library Center, Inc
Special Services for the Deaf - Accessible learning ctr; Adult & family literacy prog; Am sign lang & deaf culture; Bks on deafness & sign lang
Special Services for the Blind - Audio mat
Open Mon-Wed 9-7:30, Thurs-Sat 9-5
Friends of the Library Group

ALLENTOWN

P ALLENTOWN PUBLIC LIBRARY, 1210 Hamilton St, 18102. SAN 358-2728. Tel: 610-820-2400. Circulation Tel: 610-820-2400, Ext 5. Reference Tel: 610-820-2400, Ext 2. FAX: 610-820-0640. E-mail: aplref@allentownpl.org. Web Site: www.allentownpl.org. *Dir,* Renee Haines; E-mail: hainesr@allentownpl.org; *Acq,* Benjamin Bertalan; *Cat,* Faith McKoy; *Circ,* Anna Barbounis; *ILL,* Nancy Horwath; *Ref,* Kelly Parise; Staff 12 (MLS 12)
Founded 1912. Pop 133,271; Circ 800,400
Library Holdings: Bk Titles 211,100; Per Subs 400
Special Collections: State Document Depository
Subject Interests: Local hist
Automation Activity & Vendor Info: (Acquisitions) SirsiDynix; (Cataloging) SirsiDynix; (Circulation) SirsiDynix; (Course Reserve) SirsiDynix; (ILL) SirsiDynix; (Media Booking) SirsiDynix; (OPAC) SirsiDynix; (Serials) SirsiDynix
Wireless access
Partic in OCLC Online Computer Library Center, Inc
Open Mon & Tues 12-8, Wed-Fri 9-5, Sat 10-2
Friends of the Library Group

C CEDAR CREST COLLEGE*, Cressman Library, 100 College Dr, 18104-6196. SAN 314-2620. Tel: 610-606-4666, Ext 3387. Interlibrary Loan Service Tel: 610-606-3543. Information Services Tel: 610-606-3536. FAX: 610-740-3769. Web Site: library.cedarcrest.edu. *Libr Dir,* MaryBeth Freeh; E-mail: mafreeh@cedarcrest.edu; *Electronic Res, Info & Instrul Serv Librn,* Sheri Schneider; *Tech Serv Librn,* Scott Parkinson; *Lending Serv Coordr,* Kyle Suzanne Crimi; *Media Serv,* Judy Titus; *Ref,* James Gilbert; *Ref Asst,* Nicolas Galante; *Ref Asst,* Nicole Rivera. Subject Specialists: *English,* Nicolas Galante; Staff 4.5 (MLS 3, Non-MLS 1.5)
Founded 1867. Enrl 1,320; Fac 90; Highest Degree: Master
Special Collections: American Poetry, bks, journals; Social Work, bks, journals; Women in the United States, bks, journals
Subject Interests: Women studies
Automation Activity & Vendor Info: (Acquisitions) OCLC Worldshare Management Services; (Cataloging) OCLC Worldshare Management Services; (Circulation) OCLC Worldshare Management Services; (Course Reserve) OCLC Worldshare Management Services; (OPAC) OCLC Worldshare Management Services; (Serials) OCLC Worldshare Management Services
Wireless access
Function: Archival coll, Art exhibits, Audio & video playback equip for onsite use
Publications: Library Services Information Leaflets
Partic in Lehigh Valley Association of Independent Colleges; LYRASIS; OCLC Online Computer Library Center, Inc; Proquest Dialog
Open Mon-Thurs (Winter) 8am-11pm, Fri 8-5, Sat 9am-10pm, Sun Noon-11; Mon & Tues (Summer) 9am-11pm, Wed & Thurs 9-7, Fri 9-5, Sat & Sun Noon-5

M GOOD SHEPHERD REHABILITATION LIBRARY*, 850 S Fifth St, 18103. SAN 374-8626. Tel: 610-776-3100. FAX: 610-776-8336. Web Site: www.goodshepherdrehab.org. *Librn,* Emily Lyter; Tel: 610-776-3220, E-mail: ELyter@gsrh.org
Library Holdings: Bk Titles 536; Bk Vols 600; Per Subs 51
Subject Interests: Med, Pub health
Partic in Basic Health Sciences Library Network
Restriction: Employees & their associates

S LEHIGH COUNTY HISTORICAL SOCIETY*, Scott Andrew Trexler II Memorial Library, Lehigh Valley Heritage Museum, 432 W Walnut St, 18102-5428. SAN 314-2655. Tel: 610-435-1074. FAX: 610-435-9812. Web Site: www.lchs.museum/Library.htm. *Exec Dir,* Joseph Garrera; Tel: 610-435-1074, Ext 19, E-mail: j_garrera@lehighvalleyheritagemuseum.org; *Dir, Libr & Archives,* Jill Youngken; Tel: 610-435-1074, Ext 13, E-mail: j_youngken@lehighvalleyheritagemuseum.org; Staff 2 (MLS 1, Non-MLS 1)
Founded 1906
Library Holdings: Bk Titles 12,000; Per Subs 20
Special Collections: Allentown Imprints; City Directories; Early German Newspapers; Local Church Records; Manuscript Coll; Photograph Coll
Subject Interests: Lehigh County
Wireless access
Open Tues-Fri 10-4, Sat (May-Aug) 10-4

GL LEHIGH COUNTY LAW LIBRARY*, County Court House, 455 W Hamilton St, 18101-1614. SAN 314-2663. Tel: 610-782-3385. Web Site: www.lccpa.org. *Dir,* Lorelei A Broskey; Staff 4 (MLS 1, Non-MLS 3)
Founded 1869
Library Holdings: Bk Titles 2,500; Bk Vols 21,074; Per Subs 35
Special Collections: Ordinances Coll; Pennsylvania Law, Local Municipal & Legislative History
Open Mon-Fri 8-4:30

M LEHIGH VALLEY HOSPITAL*, Medical Library, 1200 Cedar Crest Blvd, 18105. (Mail add: PO Box 689, 18105-1556), SAN 371-5426. Tel: 610-402-8410. E-mail: libraryservices@lvhn.org. Web Site: www.lvhn.org. *Dir,* Linda Schwartz; E-mail: linda_m.schwartz@lvhn.org
Founded 1974
Library Holdings: Bk Vols 2,800; Per Subs 350
Automation Activity & Vendor Info: (Cataloging) CyberTools for Libraries; (Circulation) CyberTools for Libraries
Wireless access
Function: Photocopying/Printing
Open Mon-Fri 8:30-5:30
Restriction: Open to pub for ref only
Branches:
MUHLENBERG MEDICAL LIBRARY, 2545 Schoenersville Rd, Bethlehem, 18017, SAN 327-0904. Tel: 484-884-2237. FAX: 484-861-0711.
Library Holdings: Bk Vols 750; Per Subs 70
Open Mon-Fri 8:30-5:30
Restriction: Open to pub for ref only

C MUHLENBERG COLLEGE*, Trexler Library, 2400 Chew St, 18104-5586. SAN 314-2671. Tel: 484-664-3500. Interlibrary Loan Service Tel: 484-664-3510. Reference Tel: 484-664-3600. Administration Tel: 484-664-3551. FAX: 484-664-3511. E-mail: library@muhlenberg.edu. Web Site: trexler.muhlenberg.edu. *Dir,* Tina Hertel; Tel: 484-664-3550, E-mail: tinahertel@muhlenberg.edu; *Head, Coll Res Mgt,* Penny Lochner; Tel: 484-664-3561, E-mail: pennylochner@muhlenberg.edu; *Head, Pub Outreach & Info Literacy Serv, Ref Serv Librn,* Rachel Hamelers; Tel: 484-664-3601, E-mail: rachelhamelers@muhlenberg.edu; *Assessment Librn, Info Literacy,* Jennifer Jarson; Tel: 484-664-3552, E-mail: jenniferjarson@muhlenberg.edu; *Cat/Metadata Librn,* Thomas Christie; Tel: 484-664-3575, E-mail: thomaschristie@muhlenberg.edu; *Digital Librn, Libr Tech,* Brittany Robertson; Tel: 484-664-3520, E-mail: brittanyrobertson@muhlenberg.edu; *Outreach & Scholarly Communication Librn,* Kelly Cannon; Tel: 484-664-3602, E-mail: kellycannon@muhlenberg.edu; *Spec Coll & Archives Librn,* Susan Falciani; Tel: 484-664-3694, E-mail: susanfalciani@muhlenberg.edu; *Acq & Budget Mgr,* Karen A Gruber; Tel: 484-664-3570, E-mail: karengruber@muhlenberg.edu; *Mgr, ILL,* Kristin Brodt; E-mail: kristinbrodt@muhlenberg.edu. Subject Specialists: *Electronic,* Penny Lochner; *Sciences,* Rachel Hamelers; *Soc sci,* Jennifer Jarson; *Tech, Web design,* Brittany Robertson; *Bus, Humanities,* Kelly Cannon; Staff 16.5 (MLS 8, Non-MLS 8.5)
Founded 1867. Enrl 2,490; Fac 302; Highest Degree: Bachelor
Library Holdings: Audiobooks 457; Bks on Deafness & Sign Lang 70; CDs 2,993; DVDs 6,710; e-books 330,645; e-journals 33,525; Electronic Media & Resources 83,238; Microforms 139,914; Music Scores 30,639; Bk Titles 1,167,374; Bk Vols 201,992; Talking Bks 1,207; Videos 16,128
Special Collections: Abram Samuels Sheet Music Coll; Muhlenberg Family mss; Pennsylvania German Coll; Rare Book Coll; Ray R Brennan Map Coll. Oral History; US Document Depository
Subject Interests: European hist, German lit
Automation Activity & Vendor Info: (Acquisitions) Innovative Interfaces, Inc; (Cataloging) Innovative Interfaces, Inc; (Circulation) Innovative Interfaces, Inc; (Course Reserve) Innovative Interfaces, Inc; (ILL) Innovative Interfaces, Inc; (Media Booking) Innovative Interfaces, Inc; (OPAC) Innovative Interfaces, Inc; (Serials) Innovative Interfaces, Inc
Wireless access
Function: Archival coll, Art exhibits, Audio & video playback equip for onsite use, Bk club(s), Bks on CD, Computer training, Computers for patron use, E-Reserves, Electronic databases & coll, Govt ref serv, ILL available, Instruction & testing, Internet access, Meeting rooms, Music CDs, Online cat, Online info literacy tutorials on the web & in blackboard, Online ref, Outreach serv, Photocopying/Printing, Prog for adults, Ref serv available, Study rm, Tax forms, Telephone ref, VHS videos, Wheelchair accessible
Partic in Partnership for Academic Library Collaborative & Innovation
Special Services for the Deaf - Bks on deafness & sign lang; Closed caption videos
Special Services for the Blind - Assistive/Adapted tech devices, equip & products; Computer with voice synthesizer for visually impaired persons; Reader equip; ZoomText magnification & reading software
Open Mon-Thurs (Fall & Spring) 8am-1am, Fri 8am-10pm, Sat 10-7, Sun 11am-1am; Mon-Thurs (Summer) 9am-10pm, Fri 9-5, Sat & Sun 12-5

P PARKLAND COMMUNITY LIBRARY*, 4422 Walbert Ave, 18104. SAN 314-5646. Tel: 610-398-1361. Circulation Tel: 610-398-1333. Reference E-mail: info@parklandlibrary.org. Web Site: parklandlibrary.org, *Exec Dir,* Debbie Jack; E-mail: jackd@parklandlibrary.org; *Head, Youth Serv,* Jaclyn Hoimes; E-mail: hoimesj@parklandlibrary.org; Staff 23 (MLS 7, Non-MLS 16)
Founded 1973. Pop 54,000; Circ 250,730
Library Holdings: Audiobooks 2,619; AV Mats 8,336; Bks on Deafness & Sign Lang 57; CDs 1,413; DVDs 4,259; e-books 1,502; Electronic Media & Resources 20; Large Print Bks 1,559; Bk Titles 75,000; Per Subs 118
Special Collections: Local History Coll; Penna-German Society Publications
Automation Activity & Vendor Info: (Acquisitions) TLC (The Library Corporation); (Cataloging) TLC (The Library Corporation); (Circulation) TLC (The Library Corporation); (ILL) TLC (The Library Corporation); (OPAC) TLC (The Library Corporation)
Wireless access
Function: Adult bk club, Computer training, Computers for patron use, Electronic databases & coll, Free DVD rentals, Home delivery & serv to seniorr ctr & nursing homes, Homebound delivery serv, ILL available, Internet access, Magnifiers for reading, Music CDs, Online cat, Online ref, OverDrive digital audio bks, Photocopying/Printing, Prof lending libr, Prog for adults, Prog for children & young adult, Ref serv available, Spoken cassettes & CDs, Summer reading prog, Telephone ref, VHS videos, Wheelchair accessible, Workshops
Publications: Friends of the Library Information Paper (FLIP); Newsletter
Special Services for the Blind - Audio mat; Bks on cassette; Bks on CD; Large print bks; Talking bks
Open Mon-Fri 9-12 & 3-6, Sat 9-12
Friends of the Library Group

M SACRED HEART HOSPITAL*, Medical Library, 421 Chew St, 18102. SAN 314-268X. Tel: 610-776-4500. FAX: 610-606-4422. Web Site: www.shh.org.
Founded 1949
Library Holdings: Bk Vols 6,668; Per Subs 128
Subject Interests: Dental, Diagnostic radiology, Family practice, Ophthalmology, Otolaryngology
Partic in National Network of Libraries of Medicine Region 1
Restriction: Staff use only

M ST LUKE'S HOSPITAL-ALLENTOWN CAMPUS*, Learning Resource Center, 1736 Hamilton St, 18103. SAN 322-8266. Tel: 610-770-8355. FAX: 610-770-8736. Web Site: www.slhn.org/research/about-us/library-services/locations. *Dir, Libr Serv,* Maria Collette; Fax: 610-954-4651; *Librn,* Vanessa Reis-Bradley; E-mail: reisbrv@slhn.org; Staff 3 (MLS 2, Non-MLS 1)
Library Holdings: Bk Vols 2,000; Per Subs 75
Function: Archival coll, ILL available, Photocopying/Printing
Partic in Basic Health Sciences Library Network
Open Mon-Fri 9-1
Restriction: Open to others by appt, Open to pub for ref only

ALLISON PARK

P HAMPTON COMMUNITY LIBRARY*, 3101 McCully Rd, 15101. Tel: 412-684-1098. FAX: 412-684-1097. E-mail: hampton@einetwork.net. Web Site: www.hamptoncommunitylibrary.org. *Dir,* Suzanna Krispli
Founded 1990. Pop 17,526
Library Holdings: Bk Vols 40,000; Per Subs 50

Subject Interests: Early children's bks
Automation Activity & Vendor Info: (Acquisitions) Innovative Interfaces, Inc; (Cataloging) Innovative Interfaces, Inc; (Circulation) Innovative Interfaces, Inc; (ILL) Innovative Interfaces, Inc; (OPAC) Innovative Interfaces, Inc
Wireless access
Mem of Allegheny County Library Association (ACLA)
Open Tues-Thurs 9:30-8, Fri 9:30-5, Sat 9-4
Friends of the Library Group

ALTOONA

P ALTOONA AREA PUBLIC LIBRARY*, 1600 Fifth Ave, 16602-3693. SAN 358-2817. Tel: 814-946-0417. Circulation Tel: 814-946-0417, Ext 125. Interlibrary Loan Service Tel: 814-946-0417, Ext 126. Reference Tel: 814-946-0417, Ext 131. Administration Tel: 814-946-0417, Ext 120. FAX: 814-946-3230. Web Site: www.altoonalibrary.org. *Exec Dir,* Jennifer Knisely; Tel: 814-946-0417, Ext 122, E-mail: director@altoonalibrary.org; *Asst Dir,* Kathy Benzel; E-mail: kathybenz@altoonalibrary.org; *Libr Consult,* Amy Horell; Tel: 814-946-0417, Ext 134, E-mail: dlc@altoonalibrary.org; Staff 25.6 (MLS 6, Non-MLS 19.6)
Founded 1927. Pop 62,348; Circ 225,543
Library Holdings: AV Mats 21,772; CDs 1,805; Bk Vols 135,314; Per Subs 220; Talking Bks 4,978; Videos 2,002
Special Collections: Local History (Pennsylvania Room); Railroad Photographs. State Document Depository; US Document Depository
Subject Interests: Adult literacy, Railroad hist
Automation Activity & Vendor Info: (Cataloging) Evergreen; (Circulation) Evergreen; (OPAC) Evergreen
Wireless access
Function: Homebound delivery serv, Large print keyboards, Magnifiers for reading, Outside serv via phone, mail, e-mail & web, Photocopying/Printing, Prof lending libr, Prog for children & young adult, Ref serv available, Serves people with intellectual disabilities, Summer reading prog, Telephone ref, Wheelchair accessible
Mem of Blair County Library System
Partic in Interlibrary Delivery Service of Pennsylvania; OCLC Online Computer Library Center, Inc
Special Services for the Deaf - TTY equip
Open Mon & Thurs 8:30-8, Tues, Wed & Fri 8:30-5, Sat 9-4
Friends of the Library Group

P BLAIR COUNTY LIBRARY SYSTEM*, 1600 Fifth Ave, 16601. SAN 314-2744. Tel: 814-946-0417, Ext 132. FAX: 814-946-3230. E-mail: bcl@blaircountylibraries.org. Web Site: www.blaircountylibraries.org. *County Coordr,* Catherine Martin; Staff 1 (MLS 1)
Pop 129,026
Automation Activity & Vendor Info: (Cataloging) Evergreen; (Circulation) Evergreen; (ILL) OCLC; (OPAC) Evergreen
Member Libraries: Altoona Area Public Library; Bellwood-Antis Public Library; Claysburg Area Public Library; Hollidaysburg Area Public Library; Martinsburg Community Library; Roaring Spring Community Library; Tyrone-Snyder Public Library; Williamsburg Public Library
Open Mon-Fri 8:30-5

GM DEPARTMENT OF VETERANS AFFAIRS*, James E Van Zandt Medical Center Library, 2907 Pleasant Valley Blvd, 2nd Flr, 16602-4305. SAN 314-2760. Tel: 814-943-8164, Ext 7156. FAX: 814-940-7895. Web Site: www.altoona.va.gov/services/Library.asp.
Founded 1950
Library Holdings: AV Mats 414; Bk Titles 2,524; Per Subs 129
Special Collections: Medical Journal Coll, microfilm
Subject Interests: Med, Patient educ
Restriction: Staff & patient use, Staff use only

C PENNSYLVANIA STATE ALTOONA*, Robert E Eiche Library, 3000 Ivyside Park, 16601-3760. SAN 314-2752. Tel: 814-949-5255. Circulation Tel: 814-949-5256. Interlibrary Loan Service Tel: 814-949-5519. Reference Tel: 814-949-5253. FAX: 814-949-5520. E-mail: UL-ALTOONA@list.psu.edu. Web Site: libraries.psu.edu/altoona. *Head Librn,* Bonnie Imler; E-mail: bbi1@psu.edu; *Ref Librn,* Lori Lysiak; E-mail: lal29@psu.edu; Staff 6 (MLS 3, Non-MLS 3)
Founded 1939. Enrl 3,485; Fac 105
Library Holdings: Bk Vols 90,000
Special Collections: Drama & The Dance (Cutler Coll); Drama on Records (Buzzard Coll); Lincoln Coll (Klevan Coll)
Wireless access
Partic in OCLC Online Computer Library Center, Inc; Research Libraries Information Network
Open Mon-Thurs (Winter) 8am-11pm, Fri 8-5, Sat 12-5, Sun 3-11; Mon-Fri (Summer) 8-5

AMBLER

S LTK ENGINEERING SERVICES*, Hank Raudenbush Library, 100 W Butler Ave, 19002. Tel: 215-641-8833. Administration Tel: 215-542-0700. FAX: 215-542-7676. *Librn,* Sabina D Tannenbaum; E-mail: stannenbaum@ltk.com; Staff 1 (MLS 1)
Founded 1974
Library Holdings: Bk Titles 5,500; Per Subs 100
Special Collections: Rail Transit in United States, Canada, Australia
Automation Activity & Vendor Info: (Cataloging) EOS International; (Circulation) EOS International; (OPAC) EOS International
Wireless access
Open Mon-Fri 8-5 by appointment only

TEMPLE UNIVERSITY LIBRARIES
See Philadelphia

AMBRIDGE

P LAUGHLIN MEMORIAL LIBRARY*, 99 Eleventh St, 15003-2305. SAN 314-2795. Tel: 724-266-3857. FAX: 724-266-5670. Web Site: www.beaverlibraries.org/ambridge.asp. *Dir,* Julie Mulcahy; E-mail: jmulcahy@beaverlibraries.org; Staff 2 (MLS 1, Non-MLS 1)
Founded 1929. Pop 13,298; Circ 49,755. Sal $110,000 (Prof $35,000)
Library Holdings: AV Mats 930; CDs 50; DVDs 200; Large Print Bks 200; Bk Titles 24,000; Per Subs 50; Talking Bks 200; Videos 100
Special Collections: Local History (Pennsylvania), bks, maps, slides; Music Coll, cassettes, rec, tapes
Subject Interests: Econ, Hist, Music
Automation Activity & Vendor Info: (Course Reserve) Innovative Interfaces, Inc; (Serials) Innovative Interfaces, Inc
Wireless access
Function: Adult literacy prog, Archival coll, BA reader (adult literacy), Games & aids for people with disabilities, ILL available, Internet access, Magnifiers for reading, Outside serv via phone, mail, e-mail & web, Photocopying/Printing, Prof lending libr, Prog for adults, Prog for children & young adult, Ref serv available, Spoken cassettes & CDs, Summer reading prog, VHS videos, Wheelchair accessible
Mem of Beaver County Library System
Special Services for the Deaf - TTY equip
Open Mon-Thurs 10-7, Fri 10-4, Sat 9-4

S PENNSYLVANIA HISTORICAL & MUSEUM COMMISSION*, Old Economy Village Historical Site Museum, Archives & Library, 270 16th St, 15003. SAN 314-2809. Tel: 724-266-4500. FAX: 724-266-7506. Web Site: www.oldeconomyvillage.org. *Curator,* Sarah Buffington; Tel: 724-266-4500, Ext 111, E-mail: sbuffingto@pa.gov; Staff 1 (Non-MLS 1)
Founded 1805
Library Holdings: Bk Titles 6,180; Bk Vols 6,591; Per Subs 27
Special Collections: Harmony Society (1805-1905), music, papers
Subject Interests: 19th Century indust, German lit, Music, Relig
Wireless access
Open Mon-Fri 9-12 & 1-5
Friends of the Library Group

R TRINITY EPISCOPAL SCHOOL FOR MINISTRY LIBRARY*, 311 11th St, 15003. SAN 371-6937. Tel: 724-266-3838. Circulation Tel: 724-385-8046. FAX: 724-266-4617. E-mail: library@tsm.edu. Web Site: www.tsm.edu/library. *Libr Dir,* Susanah Hanson; E-mail: shanson@tsm.edu; Staff 2 (MLS 2)
Founded 1975. Enrl 105; Fac 22; Highest Degree: Doctorate
Library Holdings: Bk Vols 85,000; Per Subs 390
Subject Interests: Biblical studies, Theol
Automation Activity & Vendor Info: (Cataloging) TLC (The Library Corporation); (Circulation) TLC (The Library Corporation); (OPAC) TLC (The Library Corporation); (Serials) TLC (The Library Corporation)
Wireless access
Partic in Pittsburgh Regional Libr Consortium
Open Mon-Thurs 9-9, Fri & Sat 9-5

ANNVILLE

P ANNVILLE FREE LIBRARY, 216 E Main St, 17003-1599. SAN 314-2825. Tel: 717-867-1802. FAX: 717-867-5754. Web Site: annville.lclibs.org. *Dir,* Dee L Neff; E-mail: dln@lclibs.org; Staff 7 (MLS 1, Non-MLS 6)
Founded 1941. Pop 12,891
Wireless access
Function: ILL available
Mem of Lebanon County Library System
Open Mon-Thurs 10-8, Fri & Sat 10-5 (10-2 Summer)
Friends of the Library Group

C LEBANON VALLEY COLLEGE*, Vernon & Doris Bishop Library, 101 N College Ave, 17003-1400. SAN 314-2833. Tel: 717-867-6977. Interlibrary Loan Service Tel: 717-867-6974. Reference Tel: 717-867-6972. Administration Tel: 717-867-6985. FAX: 717-867-6979. Web Site: www.lvc.edu/library. *Interim Dir,* Maureen Bentz; E-mail: bentz@lvc.edu; *Instruction & Ref Librn,* Donna Lynn Miller; E-mail: miller@lvc.edu; *Libr Tech,* Becky Chanas; E-mail: chanas@lvc.edu; *Tech Serv,* Julia L Harvey; Tel: 717-867-6971, E-mail: harvey@lvc.edu; Staff 9 (MLS 5, Non-MLS 4)
Founded 1867. Enrl 1,731; Fac 100; Highest Degree: Doctorate
Jul 2012-Jun 2013 Income $1,318,974. Mats Exp $746,739, Books $153,912, Per/Ser (Incl. Access Fees) $329,631, Micro $1,326, AV Mat $9,508, Electronic Ref Mat (Incl. Access Fees) $250,055, Presv $2,307. Sal $440,773 (Prof $312,737)
Library Holdings: AV Mats 18,996; CDs 8,427; DVDs 8,368; e-books 139,523; e-journals 48,822; Microforms 7,509; Music Scores 8,104; Bk Titles 154,749; Bk Vols 171,158; Per Subs 4,777; Videos 1,295
Special Collections: Early Iron Industry (C B Montgomery Coll); Pennsylvania German (Hiram Herr Shenk Coll)
Subject Interests: Behav sci, Music, Soc sci
Automation Activity & Vendor Info: (Acquisitions) SirsiDynix; (Cataloging) SirsiDynix; (Circulation) SirsiDynix; (Course Reserve) Blackboard Inc; (ILL) OCLC ILLiad; (OPAC) SirsiDynix; (Serials) SirsiDynix
Wireless access
Partic in Associated College Libraries of Central Pennsylvania; Keystone Library Network; LYRASIS; OCLC Online Computer Library Center, Inc; Partnership for Academic Library Collaborative & Innovation
Open Mon-Thurs 7:30am-Midnight, Fri 7:30am-9pm, Sat 10-7, Sun Noon-Midnight

P PALMYRA PUBLIC LIBRARY, 50 Landings Dr, Ste B, 17003. (Mail add: PO Box 114, Palmyra, 17078), SAN 314-8424. Tel: 717-838-1347. FAX: 717-838-1236. Web Site: palmyra.lclibs.org. *Exec Dir,* Chelsea Weibley; E-mail: cweibley@lclibs.org; *Ch Serv,* Amy Shaffer-Duong; E-mail: missamy@lclibs.org; Staff 10 (MLS 2, Non-MLS 8)
Founded 1954. Pop 22,379; Circ 175,000
Automation Activity & Vendor Info: (Cataloging) Innovative Interfaces, Inc; (Circulation) Innovative Interfaces, Inc
Wireless access
Function: Activity rm, Adult bk club, After school storytime, Archival coll, Audiobks via web, Bks on CD, Children's prog, Computer training, Computers for patron use, Digital talking bks, Free DVD rentals, Home delivery & serv to seniorr ctr & nursing homes, Homework prog, ILL available, Instruction & testing, Life-long learning prog for all ages, Magazines, Movies, Music CDs, Online cat, OverDrive digital audio bks, Photocopying/Printing, Preschool reading prog, Senior computer classes, Summer & winter reading prog, Tax forms, Teen prog, Wheelchair accessible
Mem of Lebanon County Library System
Open Mon & Tues 1-7, Wed & Fri 10-4, Sat 10-2 (9:30-12:30 July & Aug)
Restriction: Non-resident fee
Friends of the Library Group

APOLLO

P APOLLO MEMORIAL LIBRARY*, 219 N Pennsylvania Ave, 15613. SAN 314-2841. Tel: 724-478-4214. FAX: 724-478-1693. E-mail: apollolibrary@hotmail.com. Web Site: www.armstronglibraries.org/apollo. *Libr Dir,* Krista Mason
Founded 1908. Pop 3,699; Circ 28,000
Library Holdings: Bk Vols 30,000; Per Subs 108
Subject Interests: Genealogy, Local hist
Wireless access
Publications: Newsletter (Quarterly)
Open Tues-Thurs 11-7, Fri & Sat 9-4

ARDMORE

P ARDMORE FREE LIBRARY*, 108 Ardmore Ave, 19003-1399. SAN 314-2868. Tel: 610-642-5187. FAX: 610-649-2618. E-mail: ardmorelibrary@lmls.org. Web Site: www.lmls.org/locations-hours/ardmore-library. *Head Librn,* Jane Quin; E-mail: jquin@lmls.org; *Ch Serv,* Dawnita Brown; Staff 2.8 (MLS 1, Non-MLS 1.8)
Founded 1899. Pop 58,000; Circ 109,066
Library Holdings: AV Mats 5,794; Bk Titles 36,000; Per Subs 62
Subject Interests: African-Am studies
Automation Activity & Vendor Info: (Acquisitions) Innovative Interfaces, Inc; (Cataloging) Innovative Interfaces, Inc; (Circulation) Innovative Interfaces, Inc; (OPAC) Innovative Interfaces, Inc
Wireless access
Function: Adult bk club, Adult literacy prog, Bks on cassette, Bks on CD, Children's prog, Computers for patron use, E-Reserves, Electronic databases & coll, Free DVD rentals, Holiday prog, ILL available, Music CDs, Photocopying/Printing, Prog for adults, Prog for children & young adult, Ref serv available, Story hour, Summer reading prog, Tax forms, Wheelchair accessible
Mem of Lower Merion Library System
Partic in Montgomery County Library & Information Network Consortium
Open Mon, Tues & Thurs 10-8, Wed 1-8, Fri & Sat 10-5

R FIRST PRESBYTERIAN CHURCH, William Faulds Memorial Library, Five W Montgomery Ave, 19003-1599. SAN 314-2876. Tel: 610-642-6650. Administration E-mail: admin@ardmorepres.org. Web Site: www.ardmorepres.org.
Founded 1962
Library Holdings: Bk Titles 1,000
Subject Interests: Behav sci, Relig studies, Soc sci
Wireless access
Open Mon-Fri 9-3

P LOWER MERION LIBRARY SYSTEM*, 75 E Lancaster Ave, 19003. SAN 314-3589. Tel: 610-645-6110. FAX: 610-645-4768. E-mail: info@lmls.org. Web Site: www.lmls.org. *Dir of Libr,* David Belanger; E-mail: dbelanger@lmls.org; Staff 61 (MLS 20, Non-MLS 41)
Founded 1935. Pop 60,000; Circ 1,000,000
Library Holdings: Bk Titles 215,694; Bk Vols 424,931; Per Subs 350
Subject Interests: Archit, Art, Hort, Local hist, Music
Wireless access
Function: 24/7 Electronic res, 24/7 Online cat, Adult bk club, Adult literacy prog, Art exhibits, Audiobks on Playaways & MP3, Audiobks via web, Bk club(s), Bks on CD, Bus archives, Children's prog, Computers for patron use, Electronic databases & coll, Free DVD rentals, Health sci info serv, Holiday prog, ILL available, Internet access, Magazines, Mango lang, Meeting rooms, Microfiche/film & reading machines, Movies, Museum passes, Music CDs, Online cat, OverDrive digital audio bks, Photocopying/Printing, Preschool reading prog, Prog for adults, Prog for children & young adult, Ref & res, Ref serv available, Story hour, Study rm, Summer reading prog, Tax forms, Teen prog, Telephone ref, Wheelchair accessible
Member Libraries: Ardmore Free Library; Bala Cynwyd Memorial Library; Belmont Hills Public Library; Gladwyne Free Library; Ludington Public Library; Penn Wynne Library

ASHLAND

P ASHLAND PUBLIC LIBRARY*, 1229 Centre St, 17921-1207. SAN 314-2884. Tel: 570-875-3175. FAX: 570-875-2699. Web Site: www.ashlandpubliclibrary.org. *Libr Dir,* Margaret Schachte; E-mail: margaret16@ashlandlibrary.net
Founded 1939. Pop 5,857; Circ 18,006
Library Holdings: Audiobooks 100; DVDs 1,450; e-books 1,417; Bk Vols 20,000; Per Subs 36
Automation Activity & Vendor Info: (Cataloging) Follett Software; (Circulation) Follett Software; (OPAC) Follett Software
Wireless access
Function: 24/7 Electronic res, 24/7 Online cat, Adult bk club, Audio & video playback equip for onsite use, Audiobks via web, AV serv, Bk club(s), Bks on CD, Children's prog, Computers for patron use, Digital talking bks, E-Readers, E-Reserves, Electronic databases & coll, For res purposes, Free DVD rentals, Govt ref serv, Health sci info serv, ILL available, Internet access, Laminating, Life-long learning prog for all ages, Magazines, Magnifiers for reading, Mail & tel request accepted, Movies, Online cat, Online info literacy tutorials on the web & in blackboard, Online ref, Outside serv via phone, mail, e-mail & web, Photocopying/Printing, Preschool outreach, Preschool reading prog, Printer for laptops & handheld devices, Prog for adults, Prog for children & young adult, Ref & res, Ref serv available, Scanner, STEM programs, Story hour, Summer & winter reading prog, Summer reading prog, Telephone ref, Wheelchair accessible
Open Mon, Tues & Thurs 9-6, Fri 9-5, Sat 8-1

ASTON

P ASTON PUBLIC LIBRARY, 3270 Concord Rd, 19014. SAN 320-8494. Tel: 610-494-5877. FAX: 610-494-1314. Web Site: www.astonlibrary.org. *Dir,* Stephen Sarazin; E-mail: director@astonlibrary.org; Staff 7 (MLS 1, Non-MLS 6)
Founded 1977. Pop 16,592; Circ 97,116
Library Holdings: Bk Vols 35,000; Per Subs 45
Automation Activity & Vendor Info: (Cataloging) Innovative Interfaces, Inc; (Circulation) Innovative Interfaces, Inc; (OPAC) Innovative Interfaces, Inc
Wireless access
Function: 24/7 Electronic res, 24/7 Online cat, Adult bk club, Bk club(s), Children's prog, Computers for patron use, ILL available, Internet access, Magazines, Mango lang, Music CDs, Online cat, OverDrive digital audio bks, Photocopying/Printing, Prog for children & young adult, Spoken

cassettes & CDs, Story hour, Summer reading prog, Tax forms, Wheelchair accessible
Mem of Delaware County Libraries
Open Mon-Fri 11-4
Friends of the Library Group

CR NEUMANN UNIVERSITY LIBRARY*, One Neumann Dr, 19014-1298. SAN 325-2841. Tel: 610-558-5545. Interlibrary Loan Service Tel: 610-361-5216. FAX: 610-459-1370. E-mail: library@neumann.edu. Web Site: www.neumann.edu/academics/library.asp. *Dir,* Tiffany McGregor; Tel: 610-361-2487, E-mail: mcgregot@neumann.edu; *Acq Librn,* Gerald Swiacki; Tel: 610-361-5416, E-mail: SWIACKIG@neumann.edu; *Ref Librn,* Guillermo A Gomez; Tel: 610-558-5557, E-mail: gomezg@neumann.edu; *Information Literacy Coord, Ref Librn,* Maureen Williams; Tel: 610-558-5541, E-mail: williamm@neumann.edu; *Circ Coordr,* Tara Convery; Tel: 610-361-2565, E-mail: converyt@neumann.edu; *Archives,* Sister Marie Therese Carr; Tel: 610-361-5206, E-mail: CARRM@neumann.edu; *ILL, Reserves,* Barbara Selletti; E-mail: sellettb@neumann.edu; *Tech Serv,* Jessica Zappasodi; Tel: 610-555-5543, E-mail: zappasoj@neumann.edu; Staff 9 (MLS 4, Non-MLS 5)
Founded 1965. Enrl 2,800; Fac 200; Highest Degree: Doctorate
Library Holdings: AV Mats 3,000; CDs 300; e-books 2,000; Bk Titles 78,000; Bk Vols 90,000; Per Subs 400; Videos 3,000
Special Collections: Betty Neuman Archives; Curriculum; Franciscan Coll
Subject Interests: Nursing, Pastoral counseling
Automation Activity & Vendor Info: (Acquisitions) EOS International; (Cataloging) SirsiDynix; (Circulation) SirsiDynix; (Course Reserve) Docutek; (ILL) OCLC Online; (OPAC) SirsiDynix; (Serials) SirsiDynix
Wireless access
Partic in LYRASIS; OCLC Online Computer Library Center, Inc; Southeastern Pa Consortium for Higher Educ; Tri-State College Library Cooperative

ATGLEN

P ATGLEN PUBLIC LIBRARY*, 413 Valley Ave, 19310-1402. SAN 314-2906. Tel: 610-593-6848. FAX: 610-593-6848. Web Site: www.ccls.org/158/Atglen-Public-Library. *Dir,* Robbyn Kehoe; E-mail: rkehoe@ccls.org; Staff 2 (Non-MLS 2)
Pop 1,217; Circ 20,186
Library Holdings: Audiobooks 530; AV Mats 1,014; Bk Vols 11,333; Per Subs 33
Wireless access
Function: Adult bk club, Bk club(s), Children's prog, Computers for patron use, Free DVD rentals, Photocopying/Printing, Prog for adults, Prog for children & young adult, Story hour, Summer reading prog, Writing prog
Mem of Chester County Library System
Open Mon-Wed & Fri 10-6, Thurs 10-8, Sat 9-4

ATHENS

P SPALDING MEMORIAL LIBRARY, 724 S Main St, 18810-1010. SAN 314-2914. Tel: 570-888-7117. FAX: 570-882-9202. Web Site: www.spaldinglibrary.org. *Dir,* Tiffany Robbins-Gigee; E-mail: director@spaldinglibrary.org; *Asst Dir,* Meaghann CampBell; *Youth Serv Librn,* Jessica White; Staff 5 (Non-MLS 5)
Founded 1897. Pop 8,795; Circ 34,334
Library Holdings: Bk Vols 30,081; Per Subs 45
Subject Interests: County hist for genealogy, State hist for genealogy
Automation Activity & Vendor Info: (Cataloging) Biblionix; (Circulation) Biblionix
Wireless access
Mem of Bradford County Library System
Open Mon-Thurs 12-8, Fri 9-3, Sat 9-4
Friends of the Library Group

AVALON

P AVALON PUBLIC LIBRARY*, 317 S Home Ave, 15202. SAN 314-2922. Tel: 412-761-2288. FAX: 412-761-7745. E-mail: avalon@einetwork.net. Web Site: avalonlibrary.org. *Dir,* Rania S Sullivan; E-mail: sullivanr@einetwork.net; Staff 4 (MLS 1, Non-MLS 3)
Founded 1940. Pop 4,705; Circ 49,343
Automation Activity & Vendor Info: (Cataloging) Innovative Interfaces, Inc - Millennium; (Circulation) Innovative Interfaces, Inc - Millennium
Wireless access
Function: Adult bk club, After school storytime, Bi-weekly Writer's Group, Bks on CD, Children's prog, Computers for patron use, E-Reserves, Electronic databases & coll, Free DVD rentals, ILL available, Magazines, Magnifiers for reading, Mango lang, Movies, Music CDs, Online cat, OverDrive digital audio bks, Photocopying/Printing, Prog for adults, Prog for children & young adult, Senior computer classes, Story hour, Summer reading prog, Tax forms, Teen prog, Wheelchair accessible
Mem of Allegheny County Library Association (ACLA)
Partic in eiNetwork
Special Services for the Blind - Bks on cassette; Bks on CD; Large print bks
Open Mon & Wed 10-6, Tues & Thurs 12-8, Fri 10-5, Sat 9-4
Friends of the Library Group

AVELLA

P AVELLA AREA PUBLIC LIBRARY*, 11 School Ct, 15312. SAN 376-5725. Tel: 724-587-5688. FAX: 724-587-3432. E-mail: avellalibrary15312@gmail.com. Web Site: www.washlibs.org/avella. *Dir,* Melissa Ansell; E-mail: melissa_ansell@yahoo.com; Staff 3 (MLS 1, Non-MLS 2)
Library Holdings: AV Mats 1,169; Large Print Bks 78; Bk Titles 10,111; Bk Vols 10,841; Per Subs 16; Talking Bks 233; Videos 708
Mem of Washington County Library System
Open Mon-Thurs 10-5, Sat 9-4

AVONMORE

P AVONMORE PUBLIC LIBRARY*, 437 Westmoreland Ave, 15618. (Mail add: PO Box 554, 15618), SAN 314-2930. Tel: 724-697-4415. FAX: 724-697-1322. *Librn,* Daryl McIntosh; Staff 2 (Non-MLS 2)
Pop 3,271; Circ 9,110
Library Holdings: Bk Titles 6,184; Bk Vols 6,415; Per Subs 19; Videos 248
Mem of Westmoreland County Federated Library System
Open Tues & Wed 1-4, Thurs 1-5

BADEN

P BADEN MEMORIAL LIBRARY*, 385 State St, 15005-1946. SAN 314-2949. Tel: 724-869-3960. FAX: 724-242-0681. *Dir,* Jennifer Woolstrum; E-mail: jwoolstrum@beaverlibraries.org; Staff 3 (MLS 1, Non-MLS 2)
Founded 1941. Pop 5,331; Circ 29,116
Library Holdings: Bk Titles 26,840; Bk Vols 27,390; Per Subs 48; Talking Bks 315; Videos 387
Automation Activity & Vendor Info: (Acquisitions) Innovative Interfaces, Inc; (Cataloging) Innovative Interfaces, Inc; (Circulation) Innovative Interfaces, Inc; (Course Reserve) Innovative Interfaces, Inc; (ILL) Innovative Interfaces, Inc; (OPAC) Innovative Interfaces, Inc; (Serials) Innovative Interfaces, Inc
Wireless access
Mem of Beaver County Library System
Open Mon-Thurs & Sat 10-2

BALA CYNWYD

P BALA CYNWYD MEMORIAL LIBRARY, 131 Old Lancaster Rd, 19004-3037. SAN 314-2957. Tel: 610-664-1196. FAX: 610-664-5534. E-mail: balacynwydlibrary@lmls.org. Web Site: www.lmls.org. *Head Librn,* Jean Knapp; E-mail: jknapp@lmls.org; *Head, Circ,* J W Law; E-mail: jlaw@lmls.org; *Head, Ref,* Maria Lerman; E-mail: mlerman@lmls.org; *Ch,* Jane France; E-mail: jfrance@lmls.org
Founded 1915. Pop 14,538; Circ 191,241
Library Holdings: Bk Vols 122,449; Per Subs 90
Special Collections: Music Coll
Subject Interests: Judaica, Music
Automation Activity & Vendor Info: (Acquisitions) Innovative Interfaces, Inc; (Cataloging) Innovative Interfaces, Inc; (Circulation) Innovative Interfaces, Inc; (Course Reserve) Innovative Interfaces, Inc; (OPAC) Innovative Interfaces, Inc
Wireless access
Mem of Lower Merion Library System
Partic in Montgomery County Library & Information Network Consortium
Open Mon-Thurs 10-9, Fri & Sat 10-5, Sun 12-5

P BELMONT HILLS PUBLIC LIBRARY, 120 Mary Watersford Rd, 19004. SAN 314-2965. Tel: 610-664-8427. Web Site: www.lmls.org/locations-hours/belmont-hills-library. *Head Librn,* Elizabeth Barrie; E-mail: ebarrie@lmls.org; Staff 3 (MLS 1, Non-MLS 2)
Founded 1935. Pop 9,812; Circ 63,510
Library Holdings: AV Mats 1,040; Large Print Bks 114; Bk Titles 24,610; Bk Vols 26,080; Per Subs 73; Videos 359
Wireless access
Mem of Lower Merion Library System
Partic in Montgomery County Library & Information Network Consortium
Open Mon, Wed & Thurs 10-6, Tues 10-7, Fri 2-6, Sat 10-2

BANGOR

P BANGOR PUBLIC LIBRARY*, 39 S Main St, 18013-2690. SAN 314-2981. Tel: 610-588-4136. FAX: 610-588-1931. E-mail: info@bangorlibrary.org. Web Site: www.bangorlibrary.org. *Libr Dir,* Kathleen Lynch; E-mail: director@bangorlibrary.org; Staff 1 (Non-MLS 1)

Founded 1922. Pop 18,745; Circ 32,091
Jul 2017-Jun 2018 Income $135,000, State $26,000, City $8,000, Locally Generated Income $101,000
Library Holdings: Bk Vols 32,000; Per Subs 25
Special Collections: Local Newspaper, flm
Subject Interests: Local hist
Wireless access
Publications: Footnotes (Quarterly)
Special Services for the Blind - Bks & mags in Braille, on rec, tape & cassette
Open Mon & Wed 1-8, Tues & Thurs 10-8, Fri 1-5, Sat 10-4
Friends of the Library Group

BEAVER

P BEAVER AREA MEMORIAL LIBRARY*, 100 College Ave, 15009-2794. SAN 314-3015. Tel: 724-775-1132. FAX: 724-775-6982. *Dir,* Diane Wakefield; E-mail: dwakefield@beaverlibraries.org; *Asst Librn,* Mary Jane Ulmer; *Ch Serv,* Jen Cribbs; Staff 3 (MLS 3)
Founded 1948. Pop 18,833; Circ 176,495
Jan 2017-Dec 2017 Income $462,187, State $64,711, County $17,321, Locally Generated Income $91,421. Mats Exp $404,542, Books $51,526, Per/Ser (Incl. Access Fees) $2,914, AV Mat $12,146, Electronic Ref Mat (Incl. Access Fees) $500, Presv $3,002. Sal $240,455
Library Holdings: Audiobooks 6,103; AV Mats 9,183; DVDs 3,079; Bk Vols 55,320; Per Subs 89
Automation Activity & Vendor Info: (Cataloging) Innovative Interfaces, Inc; (Circulation) Innovative Interfaces, Inc; (OPAC) Innovative Interfaces, Inc
Wireless access
Function: 24/7 Electronic res, 24/7 Online cat, Activity rm, Adult bk club
Mem of Beaver County Library System
Open Mon-Thurs 9:30-8, Fri & Sat 9:30-5
Friends of the Library Group

GL BEAVER COUNTY LAW LIBRARY, Court House, 810 Third St, 15009. SAN 314-3023. Tel: 724-770-4659. FAX: 724-728-4133. Web Site: www.beavercountypa.gov/Depts/Courts/LawLib/Pages/default.aspx. *Librn,* Kate Weidner; E-mail: kweidner@beavercountypa.gov; Staff 1 (MLS 1)
Founded 1950
Jan 2015-Dec 2015. Mats Exp $125,000
Library Holdings: Bk Titles 900; Bk Vols 25,000; Per Subs 20
Special Collections: Local court opinions & ordinances
Subject Interests: Penn legal practice
Automation Activity & Vendor Info: (Cataloging) Evolve; (Circulation) Evolve; (OPAC) Evolve
Wireless access
Function: Computers for patron use, Doc delivery serv, Govt ref serv, ILL available, Internet access, Online ref, Res libr, Wheelchair accessible
Mem of Beaver County Library System
Open Mon-Fri 8:30-12 & 1-4:30
Restriction: Access at librarian's discretion, Authorized patrons, Badge access after hrs, Circ limited

BEAVER FALLS

P CARNEGIE FREE LIBRARY, 1301 Seventh Ave, 15010-4219. SAN 314-304X. Tel: 724-846-4340. FAX: 724-846-0370. Web Site: www.beaverlibraries.org/beaverfalls.asp. *Dir,* Rachel Crisci; E-mail: rcrisci@beaverlibraries.org; Staff 1 (MLS 1)
Founded 1902. Pop 17,142; Circ 50,000
Library Holdings: Bk Vols 49,300; Per Subs 204
Special Collections: Beaver Falls Historical Museum
Subject Interests: Genealogy, Penn
Automation Activity & Vendor Info: (Circulation) Innovative Interfaces, Inc; (OPAC) Innovative Interfaces, Inc
Wireless access
Mem of Beaver County Library System
Open Mon-Thurs & Sat 10-5

P CHIPPEWA BRANCH LIBRARY*, 2811 Darlington Rd, 15010. Tel: 724-847-1450. FAX: 724-847-1449. Web Site: beaverlibraries.org/chippewa.asp. *Dir,* Heather Metheny; E-mail: hmetheny@beaverlibraries.org
Library Holdings: Bk Vols 3,000
Automation Activity & Vendor Info: (Circulation) Innovative Interfaces, Inc
Wireless access
Mem of Beaver County Library System
Open Mon & Wed 11-4, Tues 11-8, Thurs 1-8, Sat 10-2

GENEVA COLLEGE*, McCartney Library, 3200 College Ave, 15010-3599. SAN 358-2930. Tel: 724-847-6563. Interlibrary Loan Service Tel: 724-847-6764. Reference Tel: 724-847-6740. Administration Tel: 724-847-6690. Automation Services Tel: 724-847-6637. FAX: 724-847-6687. Web Site: geneva.edu/library. *Dir,* Steven P Kenneally; E-mail: spkennea@geneva.edu; *Acq/Ser Librn,* Kimberly Kaufman; *Cat Librn,* Kathryn Floyd; Tel: 724-847-6688, E-mail: kefloyd@geneva.edu; *Ref & Instruction Librn,* Jennifer Joseph; E-mail: jljoseph@geneva.edu; *Libr Tech,* Abbigail Stauber; E-mail: acgregg@geneva.edu; *Archivist,* Kae Hirschy Kirkwood; Tel: 724-847-6694, E-mail: kkirkwoo@geneva.edu; *Circ,* Sarah McCraly; Tel: 724-847-6563, E-mail: srmccral1@geneva.edu; Staff 16 (MLS 6, Non-MLS 10)
Founded 1931. Enrl 2,100; Fac 131; Highest Degree: Master
Library Holdings: AV Mats 13,767; CDs 1,806; e-journals 25; Electronic Media & Resources 223,044; Bk Titles 173,029; Per Subs 857; Videos 2,380
Special Collections: Early American Imprints, microcard, microfiche; Geneva Author Shelf, bks published by Geneva College alumni, faculty, administration & students; Library of American Civilization, microfiche; Personal Library & Papers of Dr Clarence Macartney (Macartney Coll); Reformed Presbyterian Church (Covenanter Coll); Shaw Shoemaker Coll, microfiche
Automation Activity & Vendor Info: (Acquisitions) Ex Libris Group; (Cataloging) Ex Libris Group; (Circulation) Ex Libris Group; (Course Reserve) Ex Libris Group; (ILL) OCLC; (Media Booking) Ex Libris Group; (OPAC) Ex Libris Group; (Serials) Ex Libris Group
Wireless access
Function: Archival coll, Audio & video playback equip for onsite use, AV serv, Distance learning, ILL available, Internet access, Photocopying/Printing, Ref serv available, Satellite serv, Telephone ref
Publications: Miscellaneous Guides; Miscellaneous Pathfinders
Partic in Keystone Library Network; LYRASIS; OCLC Online Computer Library Center, Inc
Open Mon-Thurs 8am-Midnight, Fri 8-8, Sat 10-5:30
Restriction: Access for corporate affiliates, Authorized scholars by appt, Open to fac, students & qualified researchers, Open to pub with supv only, Open to students, Open to students, fac & staff, Photo ID required for access, Restricted borrowing privileges

BEAVERDALE

P BEAVERDALE PUBLIC LIBRARY, 506 Jefferson Ave, 15921. (Mail add: PO Box 606, 15921-0606), SAN 314-3058. Tel: 814-487-7742. FAX: 814-487-4886. E-mail: beaverdale@cclsys.org. Web Site: www.cclsys.org/beaverdale. *Dir,* Lorrie Smith; E-mail: smithl@cclsys.org
Founded 1965
Special Collections: Beaverdale Coll, photog & memorabilia, newsp articles & yearbks
Subject Interests: Hist
Wireless access
Function: Photocopying/Printing, Prog for children & young adult
Mem of Cambria County Library System & District Center
Open Mon-Wed & Fri 9-12 & 4-7, Thurs 3-7, Sat 9-12 & 12:30-4:30

BEDFORD

P BEDFORD COUNTY LIBRARY*, 240 S Wood St, 15522. SAN 314-3066. Tel: 814-623-5010. FAX: 814-623-2676. Web Site: bedfordcountylibrary.com. *Dir,* Matt Godissart; E-mail: godissartm@bedfordcountylibrary.com; *Asst Dir, Children's Librn,* Rebecca Claar; E-mail: claarb@bedfordcountylibrary.com; *Cataloger, Computer Tech,* Teresa McGinnes; E-mail: mcginnest@bedfordcountylibrary.com. Subject Specialists: *Children's lit,* Rebecca Claar; Staff 8 (MLS 1, Non-MLS 7)
Founded 1944. Pop 29,419; Circ 67,360
Library Holdings: Audiobooks 916; DVDs 1,000; Bk Vols 39,000; Per Subs 26
Automation Activity & Vendor Info: (Acquisitions) Baker & Taylor; (Cataloging) Follett Software; (Circulation) Follett Software; (OPAC) Follett Software
Wireless access
Mem of Bedford County Library System
Open Mon-Fri 9-7, Sat 9-2
Bookmobiles: 1. In Charge, Lorna Pokryfke. Bk vols 3,000

P BEDFORD COUNTY LIBRARY SYSTEM*, 240 S Wood St, 15522. Tel: 814-623-5010. FAX: 814-623-2676. Web Site: bedfordcountylibrary.com. *Libr Dir,* Matt Godissart; E-mail: godissartm@bedfordcountylibrary.com
Wireless access
Member Libraries: Bedford County Library; Everett Free Library; Hyndman Londonderry Public Library; Pioneer Historical Society of Bedford County Inc; Saxton Community Library

S PIONEER HISTORICAL SOCIETY OF BEDFORD COUNTY INC*, Bedford County Historical Society & Pioneer Library, 6441 Lincoln Hwy, 15522. SAN 374-4930. Tel: 814-623-2011. FAX: 814-623-2011. E-mail: bedfordhistory@embarqmail.com. Web Site: www.bedfordpahistory.com. *Exec Dir,* Gillian Leach; Staff 2 (Non-MLS 2)
Subject Interests: Bedford County, County records, Genealogy, Local hist

Wireless access
Publications: The Pioneer Magazine (Quarterly)
Mem of Bedford County Library System
Open Mon-Fri 9-7, Sat 9-2

BELLE VERNON

P BELLE VERNON PUBLIC LIBRARY*, 505 Speer St, 15012-1540. SAN 314-3074. Tel: 724-929-6642. FAX: 724-929-4197. E-mail: bvlibrary@comcast.net. Web Site: www.bellevernonlibrary.org. *Dir,* Elina Filander; Staff 3 (Non-MLS 3)
Founded 1937. Circ 9,514
Library Holdings: Bk Vols 20,500; Per Subs 20
Automation Activity & Vendor Info: (Cataloging) Follett Software; (Circulation) Follett Software; (OPAC) Follett Software
Function: 24/7 Online cat, Adult bk club
Mem of Westmoreland County Federated Library System
Open Mon-Thurs 10-7:30, Sat 9-4 (9-1 Summer)

P ROSTRAVER PUBLIC LIBRARY*, 700 Plaza Dr, 15012. SAN 370-7466. Tel: 724-379-5511. FAX: 724-379-6090. E-mail: r.library@comcast.net. Web Site: www.rostraverlibrary.org. *Dir,* Naomi Cross; *Coordr, Programming,* Kelly Yoskosky
Founded 1958. Pop 12,000
Library Holdings: Bk Titles 20,000; Per Subs 25
Subject Interests: Local hist
Wireless access
Mem of Westmoreland County Federated Library System
Open Mon, Tues, Thurs & Fri 10-2, Wed 2-6
Friends of the Library Group

BELLEFONTE

S AMERICAN PHILATELIC RESEARCH LIBRARY*, 100 Match Factory Pl, 16823. SAN 315-243X. Tel: 814-933-3803. FAX: 814-933-6128. E-mail: aprl@stamps.org. Web Site: stamps.org/About-the-Library. *Libr Dir,* Tara Murray; *Librn,* Scott Tiffney; Tel: 814-933-3803, Ext 246; Staff 4 (MLS 3, Non-MLS 1)
Founded 1968
Library Holdings: Bk Titles 23,000; Per Subs 375
Special Collections: American First Day Cover Society Archives; Daniel Hines Air Mail Coll; Piper File; Richard B Graham Papers; Thomas J Alexander Papers; United States Stamp Files; W Wallace Cleland Papers
Subject Interests: Philately, Postal hist
Automation Activity & Vendor Info: (Cataloging) Inmagic, Inc.
Wireless access
Publications: Philatelic Literature Review (Quarterly)
Open Mon-Fri 8-4:30

GL CENTRE COUNTY LAW LIBRARY*, Courthouse, 3rd Flr, 102 Allegheny St, 16823. SAN 314-3082. Tel: 814-355-6754. FAX: 814-355-6707.
Library Holdings: Bk Vols 20,000; Per Subs 15
Open Mon-Fri 8:30-5

P CENTRE COUNTY LIBRARY & HISTORICAL MUSEUM*, 200 N Allegheny St, 16823-1601. SAN 358-3058. Tel: 814-355-1516. FAX: 814-355-2700. Interlibrary Loan Service FAX: 814-355-0334. Web Site: www.centrecountylibrary.org. *Exec Dir,* Denise Sticha; E-mail: dsticha@centrecountylibrary.org; *Asst Dir, Br Coordr,* Frannie Shue; E-mail: fshue@centrecountylibrary.org; *Dir, Pub Serv,* Tracy Carey; *Adminr,* Robin Zirkle; E-mail: rzirkle@centrecountylibrary.org; *Youth Serv Librn,* Laura Sarge Miller; E-mail: lsarge@centrecountylibrary.org; Staff 16 (MLS 5, Non-MLS 11)
Founded 1938. Pop 58,709; Circ 337,675
Library Holdings: Bk Titles 159,962; Bk Vols 199,553; Per Subs 256
Special Collections: County Documents; Genealogy (Spangler Coll). Oral History
Subject Interests: Hist
Automation Activity & Vendor Info: (Acquisitions) SirsiDynix; (Cataloging) SirsiDynix; (Circulation) SirsiDynix; (OPAC) SirsiDynix
Wireless access
Partic in Interlibrary Delivery Service of Pennsylvania; OCLC Online Computer Library Center, Inc
Special Services for the Deaf - Accessible learning ctr
Open Mon & Wed 10-7, Tues & Thurs 12-7, Fri 10-4, Sat 10-3
Friends of the Library Group
Branches: 2
CENTRE HALL AREA BRANCH, 109 W Beryl St, Centre Hall, 16828. (Mail add: PO Box 492, Centre Hall, 16828-0492). Tel: 814-364-2580. FAX: 814-364-2598. *Br Mgr,* Kathleen Edwards; Staff 2 (Non-MLS 2)
Library Holdings: Bk Titles 13,684; Bk Vols 15,011; Per Subs 37
Open Mon, Wed & Fri 10-3, Tues & Thurs 1-6, Sat 11-2

HOLT MEMORIAL, 17 N Front St, Philipsburg, 16866, SAN 358-3112. Tel: 814-342-1987. FAX: 814-342-0530. *Librn,* Theresa Hutton; Staff 2 (MLS 1, Non-MLS 1)
Library Holdings: Bk Titles 21,290; Bk Vols 22,417; Per Subs 39
Open Mon & Thurs 2-7, Tues, Wed & Fri 11-4, Sat 10-1
Bookmobiles: 1. Dir, Lisa Erickson. Bk vols 3,000

S STATE CORRECTIONAL INSTITUTION*, Rockview Library, Rte 26, Rockview Pl, 16823. (Mail add: Box A, 16823). Tel: 814-355-4874. Web Site: www.cor.pa.gov/Facilities/StatePrisons/Pages/Rockview.aspx. *Principal,* Mr Eby
Library Holdings: Bk Vols 14,000; Per Subs 50
Restriction: Not open to pub

BELLEVUE

P ANDREW BAYNE MEMORIAL LIBRARY, 34 N Balph Ave, 15202-3297. SAN 314-3104. Tel: 412-766-7447. FAX: 412-766-3620. E-mail: baynelibrary@einetwork.net. Web Site: www.baynelibrary.org. *Libr Dir,* Ellen Goodman; E-mail: goodmane@einetwork.net; Staff 7 (MLS 1, Non-MLS 6)
Founded 1927. Pop 8,300; Circ 37,300
Library Holdings: AV Mats 2,400; DVDs 1,000; Bk Vols 14,000; Per Subs 30; Talking Bks 2,300; Videos 1,600
Wireless access
Mem of Allegheny County Library Association (ACLA)
Open Mon, Tues & Thurs 10-5, Wed 10-7, Sat 10-2
Friends of the Library Group

BELLWOOD

P BELLWOOD-ANTIS PUBLIC LIBRARY, 526 Main St, 16617-1910. SAN 314-3112. Tel: 814-742-8234. FAX: 814-742-8235. *Co-Dir,* Hazel A Bilka; E-mail: hab@blwd.k12.pa.us; *Co-Dir,* Jessica Ford Cameron; E-mail: JFC@blwd.k12.pa.us; *Webmaster,* Mike Lingenfelter
Founded 1965. Circ 50,675
Library Holdings: Bk Vols 36,783; Per Subs 75
Automation Activity & Vendor Info: (Cataloging) Follett Software; (Circulation) Follett Software; (OPAC) Follett Software
Wireless access
Mem of Blair County Library System
Open Mon-Thurs 1-8, Sat 9-4

BENTLEYVILLE

P BENTLEYVILLE PUBLIC LIBRARY*, 931 Main St, 15314-1119. SAN 314-3120. Tel: 724-239-5122. FAX: 724-239-5196. E-mail: bentpublib@gmail.com. Web Site: www.washlibs.org/bentleyville. *Dir,* Charlotte Carpenter
Founded 1941. Pop 9,843; Circ 38,000
Library Holdings: Audiobooks 268; DVDs 800; Large Print Bks 797; Bk Titles 24,725; Per Subs 18
Automation Activity & Vendor Info: (Circulation) Follett Software
Wireless access
Function: ILL available
Mem of Washington County Library System
Open Mon & Tues 10-4, Wed & Thurs 12-6, Fri & Sat 10-3
Friends of the Library Group

BERNVILLE

P BERNVILLE AREA COMMUNITY LIBRARY*, 6721 Bernville Rd, 19506. (Mail add: PO Box 580, 19506-0580). Tel: 610-488-1302. FAX: 610-488-1979. E-mail: baclstaff@berks.lib.pa.us. Web Site: www.berks.lib.pa.us/bernvilleacl. *Dir,* Alicea Rodig
Founded 1994. Pop 4,652
Library Holdings: Bk Vols 13,000; Per Subs 20
Automation Activity & Vendor Info: (Cataloging) SirsiDynix; (Circulation) SirsiDynix
Wireless access
Function: Audio & video playback equip for onsite use, CD-ROM, Digital talking bks, Homebound delivery serv, ILL available, Internet access, Orientations, Photocopying/Printing, Prog for adults, Prog for children & young adult, Ref serv available, Serves people with intellectual disabilities, Spoken cassettes & CDs, Summer reading prog, Telephone ref, VHS videos, Wheelchair accessible
Mem of Berks County Public Libraries
Special Services for the Deaf - Bks on deafness & sign lang; Closed caption videos; High interest/low vocabulary bks
Special Services for the Blind - Assistive/Adapted tech devices, equip & products; Audio mat; Bks on cassette; Bks on CD; Computer with voice synthesizer for visually impaired persons; Home delivery serv; Talking bks
Open Mon-Thurs 11-7, Sat 10-2, Sun 2-5

BERWICK

P MCBRIDE MEMORIAL LIBRARY*, 500 N Market St, 18603. SAN 314-3139. Tel: 570-752-2241. FAX: 570-752-8893. Web Site: www.mcbridelibrary.org. *Dir,* Nadine Kramarz; E-mail: dls@mcbridelibrary.org; *Libr Office Mgr,* Gorman Maureen; E-mail: maureeng@mcbridelibrary.org; Staff 11 (MLS 2, Non-MLS 9)
Founded 1916. Pop 17,325; Circ 58,302
Library Holdings: CDs 190; DVDs 700; Bk Titles 40,000; Per Subs 60; Talking Bks 468; Videos 200
Special Collections: Landmark Audio Book Leasing; McNaughton Book Leasing, large print
Subject Interests: Penn hist
Wireless access
Function: 24/7 Electronic res, 24/7 Online cat, Adult bk club, Bk club(s), Bks on CD, Butterfly Garden, Children's prog, Computer training, Computers for patron use, E-Reserves, Electronic databases & coll, Family literacy, Free DVD rentals, Genealogy discussion group, Home delivery & serv to seniorr ctr & nursing homes, Homebound delivery serv, ILL available, Meeting rooms, Online cat, Outreach serv, Photocopying/Printing, Preschool outreach, Preschool reading prog, Prog for adults, Prog for children & young adult, Scanner, Senior computer classes, Summer reading prog, Tax forms, Teen prog
Open Mon & Tues 10-8, Wed 10-6, Thurs & Fri 12-6, Sat 10-2
Friends of the Library Group

BERWYN

P EASTTOWN LIBRARY & INFORMATION CENTER, 720 First Ave, 19312-1769. SAN 314-3147. Tel: 610-644-0138. FAX: 610-251-9739. Web Site: www.easttownlibrary.org. *Dir,* Alan Silverman; E-mail: asilverman@ccls.org; *Asst Dir, Head, Ref,* Audrey Young; E-mail: ayoung@ccls.org; *Head, Circ,* Scott McDonnell; E-mail: smcdonnell@ccls.org; *Head, Tech Serv,* Marcia Fall; E-mail: mfall@ccls.org; *Head, Youth Serv,* Angela Brown; E-mail: abrown@ccls.org; Staff 8 (MLS 6, Non-MLS 2)
Founded 1905. Pop 10,613; Circ 308,423
Jan 2020-Dec 2020 Income $1,036,076, State $72,899, City $700,000, County $70,399, Locally Generated Income $192,778. Mats Exp $161,584, Books $53,176, Per/Ser (Incl. Access Fees) $4,372, AV Mat $9,954, Electronic Ref Mat (Incl. Access Fees) $94,082. Sal $576,975 (Prof $291,435)
Library Holdings: Audiobooks 1,784; CDs 1,057; DVDs 3,023; e-books 39,987; e-journals 111; Electronic Media & Resources 21; Large Print Bks 1,490; Bk Vols 51,266; Per Subs 53
Special Collections: Local History Coll
Automation Activity & Vendor Info: (Acquisitions) Innovative Interfaces, Inc; (Cataloging) Innovative Interfaces, Inc; (Circulation) Innovative Interfaces, Inc; (ILL) Innovative Interfaces, Inc; (OPAC) Innovative Interfaces, Inc; (Serials) Innovative Interfaces, Inc
Wireless access
Function: 24/7 Electronic res, 24/7 Online cat, Adult bk club, Adult literacy prog, Art exhibits, Art programs, Audiobks on Playaways & MP3, Audiobks via web, Bk club(s), Bks on CD, Children's prog, Computer training, Computers for patron use, Digital talking bks, Electronic databases & coll, Family literacy, Free DVD rentals, Genealogy discussion group, Health sci info serv, Homebound delivery serv, ILL available, Internet access, Life-long learning prog for all ages, Literacy & newcomer serv, Magazines, Magnifiers for reading, Mango lang, Meeting rooms, Movies, Museum passes, Music CDs, Notary serv, Online cat, OverDrive digital audio bks, Passport agency, Photocopying/Printing, Preschool outreach, Preschool reading prog, Prog for adults, Prog for children & young adult, Ref serv available, Scanner, STEM programs, Story hour, Study rm, Summer reading prog, Tax forms, Teen prog, Telephone ref, Wheelchair accessible
Publications: Easttown Library Newsletter (Online only)
Mem of Chester County Library System
Special Services for the Blind - Bks on CD; Large print bks; Magnifiers
Open Mon-Thurs 9:30-9, Fri 9:30-6, Sat 10-5, Sun 1:30-5
Friends of the Library Group

BESSEMER

P FRANK D CAMPBELL MEMORIAL LIBRARY*, 17 S Main St, 16112-2535. SAN 314-3155. Tel: 724-667-7939. FAX: 724-667-0898. Web Site: fdclibrary.org. *Dir,* Kari McKenna; Staff 1 (Non-MLS 1)
Founded 1920. Pop 8,334; Circ 14,000
Jan 2016-Dec 2016 Income $71,000, State $25,000, City $1,000, County $25,000, Locally Generated Income $20,000
Library Holdings: AV Mats 660; Bks on Deafness & Sign Lang 4; Braille Volumes 2; CDs 160; DVDs 196; e-books 2,112; Large Print Bks 330; Bk Titles 14,700; Bk Vols 14,800; Per Subs 25; Videos 415
Wireless access
Function: 24/7 Electronic res, 24/7 Online cat, Activity rm, Adult bk club, Audiobks on Playaways & MP3, Audiobks via web, Bk club(s), Bks on CD, Children's prog, Computer training, Computers for patron use, Doc delivery serv, Electronic databases & coll, Equip loans & repairs, Family literacy, Free DVD rentals, Holiday prog, Home delivery & serv to seniorr ctr & nursing homes, Homebound delivery serv, ILL available, Internet access, Laminating, Life-long learning prog for all ages, Literacy & newcomer serv, Magazines, Magnifiers for reading, Mail & tel request accepted, Mail loans to mem, Mango lang, Movies, Online cat, Online ref, OverDrive digital audio bks, Photocopying/Printing, Preschool outreach, Preschool reading prog, Prog for adults, Prog for children & young adult, Ref serv available, Scanner, Senior computer classes, Serves people with intellectual disabilities, Story hour, Summer reading prog, Tax forms, Teen prog, Workshops
Mem of Lawrence County Federated Library System
Open Mon-Thurs 11-7, Fri & Sat 9-4
Restriction: Authorized patrons, Circ to mem only, Free to mem, Non-resident fee
Friends of the Library Group

BETHANY

P BETHANY PUBLIC LIBRARY*, Eight Court St, 18431-9516. SAN 314-6227. Tel: 570-253-4349. E-mail: bethany@waynelibraries.org. Web Site: www.waynelibraries.org/bethany.html. *Dir,* Kate Baxter; E-mail: kbaxter@waynelibraries.org; Staff 3 (Non-MLS 3)
Founded 1936. Pop 1,180; Circ 4,000
Library Holdings: DVDs 100; Large Print Bks 75; Bk Titles 6,200; Per Subs 25
Automation Activity & Vendor Info: (Cataloging) TLC (The Library Corporation); (Circulation) TLC (The Library Corporation)
Function: Archival coll, Audio & video playback equip for onsite use, BA reader (adult literacy), ILL available, Internet access, Photocopying/Printing, Prog for adults, Prog for children & young adult, Summer reading prog, Telephone ref, Workshops
Open Wed-Sat Noon-5
Friends of the Library Group

BETHEL

P BETHEL-TULPEHOCKEN PUBLIC LIBRARY*, 8601 Lancaster Ave, 19507. SAN 314-3163. Tel: 717-933-4060. FAX: 717-674-5989. E-mail: bethelpl@berks.lib.pa.us, sbestaff@hotmail.com. Web Site: www.berkslibraries.org/branch/bethel-tulpehocken. *Dir,* Kaitlin Lehman
Founded 1963. Pop 7,456; Circ 120,000
Library Holdings: Bk Titles 15,000; Per Subs 60
Subject Interests: Behav sci, Educ, Environ studies, Local hist, Soc sci
Automation Activity & Vendor Info: (Cataloging) Innovative Interfaces, Inc; (Circulation) Innovative Interfaces, Inc; (OPAC) Innovative Interfaces, Inc
Wireless access
Mem of Berks County Public Libraries
Open Mon & Thurs 10-8, Tues & Sat 10-2, Fri 10-6, Sun 12-3

BETHEL PARK

P BETHEL PARK PUBLIC LIBRARY*, 5100 W Library Ave, 15102. SAN 314-3171. Tel: 412-835-2207. FAX: 412-835-9360. E-mail: bethelpark@einetwork.net. Web Site: www.bethelparklibrary.org. *Dir,* Christine McIntosh; E-mail: mcintoshc@einetwork.net; Staff 41 (MLS 11, Non-MLS 30)
Founded 1955. Pop 33,724; Circ 346,000
Library Holdings: Bk Titles 97,300; Bk Vols 101,425; Per Subs 123
Special Collections: Municipal Document Depository; US Document Depository
Subject Interests: Adult, Aging, Bus serv, Career, Employment, Investment serv, Literacy, Local hist, Parenting res, Pre-sch daycare, Teacher res ctr
Automation Activity & Vendor Info: (Acquisitions) Innovative Interfaces, Inc; (Cataloging) Innovative Interfaces, Inc; (Circulation) Innovative Interfaces, Inc; (Course Reserve) Innovative Interfaces, Inc; (ILL) Innovative Interfaces, Inc; (OPAC) Innovative Interfaces, Inc; (Serials) Innovative Interfaces, Inc
Wireless access
Function: Adult literacy prog, AV serv, Bus archives, Govt ref serv, Home delivery & serv to seniorr ctr & nursing homes, Homebound delivery serv, ILL available, Internet access, Photocopying/Printing, Prog for adults, Prog for children & young adult, Ref serv available, Summer reading prog, Telephone ref, Wheelchair accessible
Mem of Allegheny County Library Association (ACLA)
Special Services for the Blind - Reader equip
Open Mon-Thurs 9-9, Fri & Sat 9-5, Sun (Winter) 1-5

R CHRIST UNITED METHODIST CHURCH LIBRARY*, 44 Highland Rd, 15102. SAN 314-318X. Tel: 412-835-6621. FAX: 412-835-9130. E-mail: mail@christumc.net. Web Site: christumc.net. *Library Contact,* Mrs Kit Murphy; Staff 1 (Non-MLS 1)
Founded 1960

Library Holdings: Bk Titles 3,741; Bk Vols 3,910; Per Subs 14
Open Mon-Fri 10-3

BETHLEHEM

P BETHLEHEM AREA PUBLIC LIBRARY, 11 W Church St, 18018. SAN 358-3147. Tel: 610-867-3761. Circulation Tel: 610-867-3761, Ext 203. Interlibrary Loan Service Tel: 610-867-3761, Ext 233. Reference Tel: 610-867-3761, Ext 224. FAX: 610-867-2767. E-mail: info@bapl.org. Web Site: www.bapl.org. *Exec Dir,* Josh Berk; Tel: 610-867-3761, Ext 215, E-mail: jberk@bapl.org; *Asst Dir,* Erin Poore; Tel: 610-867-3761, Ext 256, E-mail: epoore@bapl.org; *Head, Acq, Syst & Tech,* Dan Solove; Tel: 610-867-3761, Ext 216, E-mail: dsolove@bapl.org; *Head, Adult Serv,* Matthew Rothfuss; Tel: 610-867-3761, Ext 212; *Head, Youth Serv,* Edana Hoy; Tel: 610-867-3761, Ext 218; *ILL,* Valerie Mann; Tel: 610-867-3761, Ext 233, E-mail: vmann@bapl.org; Staff 33 (MLS 8, Non-MLS 25)
Founded 1901. Pop 118,458; Circ 792,435
Subject Interests: Local hist, Spanish
Automation Activity & Vendor Info: (Cataloging) Innovative Interfaces, Inc - Millennium; (Circulation) Innovative Interfaces, Inc - Millennium; (OPAC) Innovative Interfaces, Inc - Millennium; (Serials) Innovative Interfaces, Inc - Millennium
Wireless access
Open Mon-Wed 9-8, Thurs & Fri 9-6, Sat 10-5
Friends of the Library Group
Branches: 1
SOUTH SIDE, 400 Webster St, 18015, SAN 358-3171. Tel: 610-867-7852. FAX: 610-867-9821. *Br Mgr,* Brenda Grow; E-mail: bgrow@bapl.org; Staff 4 (MLS 1, Non-MLS 3)
Subject Interests: Literacy, Spanish
Open Mon-Thurs 11-6
Friends of the Library Group
Bookmobiles: 1. Librn, Michael Henninger

S HISTORIC BETHLEHEM PARTNERSHIP LIBRARY*, 459 Old York Rd, 18018-5802. (Mail add: 74 W Broad St, Ste 310, 18018-5830), SAN 327-0947. Tel: 610-882-0450. E-mail: info@historicbethlehem.org. Web Site: historicbethlehem.org. *Dir of Coll,* Lindsey Jancay; Tel: 610-882-0450, Ext 63, E-mail: ljancay@historicbethlehem.org
Library Holdings: Bk Vols 3,000
Subject Interests: Decorative art, Local hist
Restriction: Non-circulating, Open by appt only

C LEHIGH UNIVERSITY, Fairchild-Martindale Library, Eight A E Packer Ave, 18015. SAN 358-3295. Tel: 610-758-4357. E-mail: inlts@lehigh.edu. Web Site: library.lehigh.edu. *Vice Provost for Libr & Tech Serv,* Gregory Reihman; Tel: 610-758-6840, E-mail: grr3@lehigh.edu; *Dir, Admin Serv,* Jesse Pearson; Tel: 610-758-3825, E-mail: jwp219@lehigh.edu; *Cat/Metadata Librn,* Lisa McColl; Tel: 610-758-2639, E-mail: lim213@lehigh.edu; *Resource Acquisitions Manager,* Daniel Huang; Tel: 610-758-3035, E-mail: dlh4@lehigh.edu; Staff 26 (MLS 18, Non-MLS 8)
Founded 1865. Enrl 5,600; Fac 410; Highest Degree: Doctorate
Library Holdings: Bk Titles 770,440; Bk Vols 1,145,980; Per Subs 12,000
Special Collections: Bayer Galleria of Rare Books; Lehigh University Archives. State Document Depository; US Document Depository
Automation Activity & Vendor Info: (Acquisitions) SirsiDynix; (Cataloging) OCLC; (Circulation) SirsiDynix; (ILL) OCLC; (Media Booking) SirsiDynix; (OPAC) SirsiDynix
Wireless access
Publications: LTS Connection (Newsletter); Special Collections Flyer
Partic in Interlibrary Delivery Service of Pennsylvania; Lehigh Valley Association of Independent Colleges; OCLC Online Computer Library Center, Inc; Pa Academic Librs Connection Coun; Partnership for Academic Library Collaborative & Innovation
Special Services for the Blind - Reader equip
Open Mon-Thurs 7:45am-2am, Fri 7:45am-Midnight, Sat 9am-Midnight, Sun 9am-2am
Friends of the Library Group
Departmental Libraries:
LINDERMAN LIBRARY, 30 Library Dr, 18015, SAN 358-3325. Tel: 610-758-4506 (Special Collections). FAX: 610-758-6091. E-mail: inspc@lehigh.edu. *Libr Coord,* Kathleen Dugan; Tel: 610-758-4925, E-mail: kpk4@lehigh.edu
Founded 1878. Enrl 6,800; Highest Degree: Doctorate
Special Collections: History of Technology Coll. US Document Depository
Subject Interests: Engr, Hist, Humanities, Sci, Tech
Automation Activity & Vendor Info: (Acquisitions) SirsiDynix-WorkFlows; (Cataloging) SirsiDynix-WorkFlows; (Circulation) SirsiDynix-WorkFlows; (Serials) SirsiDynix-Unicorn
Function: Archival coll
Partic in Philadelphia Area Consortium of Special Collections Libraries
Open Mon-Thurs 7:45am-2am, Fri 7:45am-10pm, Sat 9am-10pm, Sun 9am-2am
Friends of the Library Group

R MORAVIAN ARCHIVES, 41 W Locust St, 18018-2757. SAN 314-321X. Tel: 610-866-3255. E-mail: info@moravianchurcharchives.org. Web Site: www.moravianchurcharchives.org. *Archivist,* Dr Paul M Peucker; *Asst Archivist,* Thomas McCullough; *Proc Archivist,* Kaitlin Trainor; Staff 4 (MLS 3, Non-MLS 1)
Founded 1751
Library Holdings: Bk Vols 20,000; Per Subs 12
Special Collections: Bethlehem Gemeinbibliothek, Library of the Early Moravian Community of Bethlehem; History of Unitas Fratrum (Malin Library)
Subject Interests: Moravian Church hist
Wireless access
Open Mon-Fri 8-4:30
Restriction: In-house use for visitors, Not a lending libr
Friends of the Library Group

C MORAVIAN COLLEGE & MORAVIAN THEOLOGICAL SEMINARY*, Reeves Library, 1200 Main St, 18018. SAN 314-3228. Tel: 610-861-1541. Circulation Tel: 610-861-1544. Interlibrary Loan Service Tel: 610-861-1545. Reference Tel: 610-861-1543. Administration Tel: 610-861-1540. FAX: 610-861-1577. E-mail: libref@moravian.edu. Web Site: www.moravian.edu/reeves. *Dir,* Janet Ohles; E-mail: ohlesj@moravian.edu; *Tech Serv Asst,* Vincent Condello; Tel: 610-861-1679, E-mail: condellov@moravian.edu; Staff 12 (MLS 6, Non-MLS 6)
Founded 1742. Highest Degree: Master
Library Holdings: CDs 1,975; DVDs 536; e-books 150,000; e-journals 14,378; Music Scores 13,350; Bk Vols 220,000; Per Subs 1,037; Videos 2,467
Special Collections: History & Development of the Moravian Church (Groenfeldt Moravian Coll); Rare Books Coll
Subject Interests: Liberal arts, Relig, Theol
Automation Activity & Vendor Info: (Acquisitions) Innovative Interfaces, Inc; (Cataloging) Innovative Interfaces, Inc; (Circulation) Innovative Interfaces, Inc; (Course Reserve) Innovative Interfaces, Inc; (ILL) OCLC Connexion; (OPAC) Innovative Interfaces, Inc; (Serials) Innovative Interfaces, Inc
Wireless access
Function: Archival coll, ILL available, Internet access, Photocopying/Printing, Ref serv available, VHS videos, Wheelchair accessible
Partic in Lehigh Valley Association of Independent Colleges; OCLC Online Computer Library Center, Inc; Partnership for Academic Library Collaborative & Innovation; Southeastern Pennsylvania Theological Library Association
Open Mon-Thurs 8am-Midnight, Fri 8am-9pm, Sat 10-9, Sun Noon-Midnight
Restriction: Restricted borrowing privileges
Friends of the Library Group

J NORTHAMPTON COMMUNITY COLLEGE*, Paul & Harriett Mack Library, College Ctr, 3835 Green Pond Rd, 18020-7599. SAN 314-3236. Tel: 610-861-3360. Reference Tel: 610-861-5359. Administration Tel: 610-861-5358. FAX: 610-861-5373. Web Site: www.northampton.edu/library.htm. *Dir, Libr Serv,* Sandra Sander; E-mail: ssander@northampton.edu; *Asst Dir, Libr Serv,* Samantha Simmonds; E-mail: ssimmonds@northampton.edu; *Acq Librn,* Evonne Loomis; E-mail: eloomis@northampton.edu; *Cat Librn,* Anne Bittner; E-mail: abittner@northampton.edu; *Info Serv Librn,* Courtney Eger; E-mail: ceger@northampton.edu; *Info Serv Librn,* Diane Hahn; E-mail: dhahn@northampton.edu; *Info Serv Librn,* Margaret Murray; E-mail: mmurray@northampton.edu; *Info Serv Librn,* Position Currently Open; Staff 6.5 (MLS 6, Non-MLS 0.5)
Founded 1967. Enrl 13,000; Fac 1,200; Highest Degree: Associate
Library Holdings: Audiobooks 275; CDs 261; DVDs 2,572; e-books 18,599; Electronic Media & Resources 56; Bk Titles 58,050; Bk Vols 67,497; Per Subs 201
Special Collections: College Archives; Dornish Coll of Children's Materials; Foundations & Grants
Automation Activity & Vendor Info: (Acquisitions) SirsiDynix-WorkFlows; (Cataloging) SirsiDynix-WorkFlows; (Circulation) SirsiDynix-WorkFlows; (Discovery) EBSCO Discovery Service; (ILL) OCLC; (OPAC) SirsiDynix-WorkFlows; (Serials) SirsiDynix-WorkFlows
Wireless access
Partic in LYRASIS
Open Mon-Thurs 7:30am-10pm, Fri 7:30-5, Sat 8:30-4:30, Sun 1-8
Departmental Libraries:
ESSA BANK & TRUST FOUNDATION LIBRARY, Keystone Hall, 2411 Rte 715, Tannersville, 18372. Tel: 570-369-1810. *Asst Dir, Libr Serv,* Samantha Simmonds; E-mail: ssimmonds@northampton.edu; *Info Serv Librn,* Leigh Barnes; E-mail: lbarnes@northampton.edu; *Info Serv Librn,* Cassandra Nieves; E-mail: cnieves@northampton.edu; Staff 2.5 (MLS 2.5)
Open Mon-Thurs 7:45am-9pm, Fri 7:45-5, Sat 9-4:30

M ST LUKE'S UNIVERSITY HOSPITAL & HEALTH NETWORK*, W L Estes Jr Memorial Library, 801 Ostrum St, 18015. SAN 358-335X. Tel: 484-526-4650. Interlibrary Loan Service Tel: 484-526-4652. FAX: 484-526-3366. E-mail: estes.library@slhn.org. Web Site: www.slhn.org/hospitals-locations/library-services. *Librn,* Diane Frantz; Tel: 610-954-3407, E-mail: frantzd@slhn.org; *ILL,* Jane Tafaro; E-mail: Jane.Tafaro@sluhn.org; Staff 2.5 (MLS 1.5, Non-MLS 1)
Founded 1947
Library Holdings: e-books 5; e-journals 100; Bk Titles 8,300; Bk Vols 9,500; Per Subs 300; Videos 250
Special Collections: Nursing (Historical Coll)
Subject Interests: Allied health, Med, Nursing, Surgery
Automation Activity & Vendor Info: (Cataloging) LibraryWorld, Inc; (Circulation) LibraryWorld, Inc; (OPAC) LibraryWorld, Inc
Wireless access
Partic in Greater NE Regional Med Libr Program; National Network of Libraries of Medicine Region 1
Open Mon, Thurs & Fri 8-4:30, Tues & Wed 8-8

S URBAN RESEARCH & DEVELOPMENT CORP LIBRARY*, 81 Highland Ave, Ste 120, 18017. SAN 314-3244. Tel: 610-865-0701. FAX: 610-868-7613. E-mail: urdc@urdc.com. Web Site: www.urdc.com. *Librn,* Charlie Schmehl
Founded 1968
Library Holdings: Bk Titles 3,500; Per Subs 25
Subject Interests: Archit, Art, Econ, Engr, Geog, Graphic design, Landscape archit, Regional planning, Soc sci, Urban planning
Restriction: Non-circulating to the pub

BIRDSBORO

P BOONE AREA LIBRARY*, 129 N Mill St, 19508-2340. Tel: 610-582-5666. FAX: 610-582-6826. E-mail: boone@berks.lib.pa.us. Web Site: boonearealibrary.com. *Interim Dir,* Eileen Simms; *Asst Librn,* Lisa Strouse; *Children's/Teen Coordr,* Lynn Gibson; Staff 1 (MLS 1)
Founded 1963. Pop 21,249
Library Holdings: Bk Vols 26,341; Per Subs 65
Automation Activity & Vendor Info: (Cataloging) SirsiDynix; (Circulation) SirsiDynix; (OPAC) SirsiDynix
Wireless access
Function: Activity rm, Adult bk club, Audiobks via web, Bk club(s), Bks on CD, Children's prog, Computer training, Computers for patron use, E-Reserves, Electronic databases & coll, Free DVD rentals, ILL available, Instruction & testing, Internet access, Magazines, Mail & tel request accepted, Movies, Museum passes, Music CDs, Online cat, Online ref, Outside serv via phone, mail, e-mail & web, OverDrive digital audio bks, Photocopying/Printing, Preschool outreach, Preschool reading prog, Prog for adults, Prog for children & young adult, Ref serv available, Scanner, Summer reading prog, Tax forms, Telephone ref, Wheelchair accessible
Mem of Berks County Public Libraries
Open Mon 10-8, Tues & Thurs 1-8, Wed, Fri & Sat 9-4

BLACK LICK

P BURRELL TOWNSHIP LIBRARY*, 190 Park Dr, 15716. (Mail add: PO Box 424, 15716), SAN 324-3702. Tel: 724-248-7122. FAX: 724-248-1803. E-mail: burrelltownshiplibrary@gmail.com. Web Site: www.burrelltownshiplibrary.org. *Libr Dir,* Jen Van Hannak
Founded 1977. Pop 3,669
Library Holdings: DVDs 1,290; Bk Titles 15,000; Per Subs 29
Wireless access
Open Mon 4-8, Tues 10-5, Wed 1-6, Thurs 12-8, Fri 10-4, Sat 9-3

BLAIN

P COMMUNITY LIBRARY OF WESTERN PERRY COUNTY, 104 E Main St, 17006. (Mail add: PO Box 56, 17006-0056). Tel: 717-536-3761. FAX: 717-536-3761. E-mail: blainelibrary@centurylink.net. Web Site: pecoinfo.org/library-hours/western-perry. *Dir,* Lois Parker; Staff 1 (Non-MLS 1)
Pop 3,148; Circ 13,000
Library Holdings: Bk Titles 10,000; Bk Vols 12,000; Per Subs 10
Wireless access
Open Tues, Thurs & Fri 2-7, Wed 8-2, Sat 9-1

BLAIRSVILLE

P BLAIRSVILLE PUBLIC LIBRARY*, 113 N Walnut St, 15717-1348. SAN 314-3260. Tel: 724-459-6077. FAX: 724-459-6097. E-mail: blpub@comcast.net. Web Site: blairsvillepubliclibrary.org. *Dir,* Carol Kuhns
Pop 3,412; Circ 36,743
Library Holdings: Bk Vols 34,567; Per Subs 52
Automation Activity & Vendor Info: (Cataloging) Follett Software; (Circulation) Follett Software; (OPAC) Follett Software
Wireless access
Open Mon & Thurs 1:30-8:30, Tues & Fri 1:30-5, Wed & Sat 10-5

BLOOMSBURG

P BLOOMSBURG PUBLIC LIBRARY*, 225 Market St, 17815-1726. SAN 314-3287. Tel: 570-784-0883. E-mail: bloompl@epix.net. Web Site: www.bloomsburgpl.org. *Dir,* Lydia Kegler, PhD; E-mail: LydiaBloomPL@gmail.com; *Asst Dir,* Sue Prokop; *Children's & Youth Serv, Librn,* Angela Musselman-Leister; E-mail: AngieBloomPL@gmail.com; Staff 4 (MLS 2, Non-MLS 2)
Founded 1889
Library Holdings: Bk Titles 42,000; Per Subs 70
Special Collections: Genealogy Coll
Automation Activity & Vendor Info: (Cataloging) Book Systems; (Circulation) Book Systems; (Discovery) Book Systems; (Media Booking) Book Systems; (OPAC) Book Systems
Wireless access
Function: 24/7 Electronic res, 24/7 Online cat, Activity rm, Audiobks via web, Children's prog, Computers for patron use, E-Reserves, Electronic databases & coll, Family literacy, Free DVD rentals, Holiday prog, ILL available, Internet access, Magazines, Magnifiers for reading, Meeting rooms, Movies, Music CDs, Online cat, OverDrive digital audio bks, Photocopying/Printing, Preschool reading prog, Printer for laptops & handheld devices, Prog for adults, Prog for children & young adult, STEM programs, Story hour, Study rm, Summer & winter reading prog, Summer reading prog, Tax forms, Teen prog, Wheelchair accessible
Open Mon, Tues & Thurs 9-8, Wed & Fri 9-5, Sat 8-Noon
Friends of the Library Group

C BLOOMSBURG UNIVERSITY OF PENNSYLVANIA, Harvey A Andruss Library, 400 E Second St, 17815-1301. SAN 314-3295. Tel: 570-389-4205. Circulation Tel: 570-389-4205. Interlibrary Loan Service Tel: 570-389-4218. Reference Tel: 570-389-4204. FAX: 570-389-5066. Interlibrary Loan Service FAX: 570-389-3895. Web Site: guides.library.bloomu.edu/HarveyAndrussLibrary. *Dir, Libr Serv,* Charlotte Droll; Tel: 570-389-4207, E-mail: cdroll@bloomu.edu; *Archivist & Spec Coll Librn, Historian, Research Librn,* Robert A Dunkelberger; *Research Librn,* Michael J Coffta; *Database Coordr, Research Librn,* Linda Neyer; *Research Librn,* Kathryn Yelinek; *Coordr, Cat,* Marilou Z Hinchcliff; *Research Librn, Education,* Courtney Paddick; Tel: 570-389-4656, E-mail: cpaddick@bloomu.edu. Subject Specialists: *Bus,* Michael J Coffta; *Health sci, Sci,* Linda Neyer; *Govt doc,* Kathryn Yelinek; *Criminal justice, Soc work, Sociol,* Courtney Paddick; Staff 15 (MLS 7, Non-MLS 8)
Founded 1839. Enrl 8,683; Fac 520; Highest Degree: Doctorate
Special Collections: Art Exhibit Catalogs; Bloomsburg University Archives; Covered Bridges Newbery & Caldecott Awards (Elinor R Keefer Coll). State Document Depository; US Document Depository
Subject Interests: Children's lit
Automation Activity & Vendor Info: (Acquisitions) Ex Libris Group; (Cataloging) Ex Libris Group; (Circulation) Ex Libris Group; (Course Reserve) Ex Libris Group; (ILL) OCLC ILLiad; (Media Booking) Ex Libris Group; (OPAC) Ex Libris Group; (Serials) Ex Libris Group
Wireless access
Partic in Interlibrary Delivery Service of Pennsylvania; Keystone Library Network; LYRASIS; OCLC Online Computer Library Center, Inc; Pa Academic Librs Connection Coun; Partnership for Academic Library Collaborative & Innovation
Open Mon-Thurs 7:30am-Midnight, Fri 7:30-4:30, Sat 9-5, Sun Noon-Midnight
Friends of the Library Group

S COLUMBIA COUNTY HISTORICAL & GENEALOGICAL SOCIETY LIBRARY*, 225 Market St, 17815. (Mail add: PO Box 360, 17815-0360), SAN 314-3309. Tel: 570-784-1600. E-mail: research@colcohist-gensoc.org. Web Site: colcohist-gensoc.org. *Exec Dir,* Carol Woolridge
Founded 1914
Library Holdings: Bk Titles 2,000
Special Collections: microfilm,photos
Subject Interests: Columbia County, Genealogy, Local hist
Wireless access
Function: Wheelchair accessible
Publications: Historical Leaflets; Monographs; The Columbian
Open Tues & Fri 9-3, Thurs 1-7:30, Sat 9-11:30
Restriction: Non-circulating to the pub

P COLUMBIA COUNTY TRAVELING LIBRARY*, 702 Sawmill Rd, Ste 101, 17815. SAN 320-8125. Tel: 570-387-8782. E-mail: info@cctlibrary.org. Web Site: www.cctlibrary.org. *Libr Dir,* Ammon Young; E-mail: ammon@cctlibrary.org; *Asst Dir,* Kara Walsh; E-mail: kara@cctlibrary.org; Staff 1.8 (MLS 1, Non-MLS 0.8)
Founded 1941. Pop 30,000
Jan 2018-Dec 2018 Income $146,000, State $22,919, County $70,052, Locally Generated Income $32,029, Other $21,000. Mats Exp $26,500,

Books $24,500, Per/Ser (Incl. Access Fees) $500, AV Mat $1,500. Sal $82,520 (Prof $60,000)
Library Holdings: Audiobooks 835; DVDs 683; Large Print Bks 2,463; Bk Vols 24,080; Per Subs 10
Automation Activity & Vendor Info: (Cataloging) Book Systems; (Circulation) Book Systems; (OPAC) Book Systems
Wireless access
Function: 24/7 Electronic res, 24/7 Online cat, Audiobks via web, Bks on CD, Children's prog, Computers for patron use, Electronic databases & coll, Health sci info serv, Home delivery & serv to seniorr ctr & nursing homes, ILL available, Internet access, Magnifiers for reading, Mail & tel request accepted, Movies, Online cat, Online ref, Outreach serv, Outside serv via phone, mail, e-mail & web, OverDrive digital audio bks, Photocopying/Printing, Preschool outreach, Preschool reading prog, Printer for laptops & handheld devices, Prog for children & young adult, Ref serv available, Scanner, Senior outreach, Serves people with intellectual disabilities, STEM programs, Story hour, Summer reading prog, Telephone ref, Wheelchair accessible
Special Services for the Blind - Assistive/Adapted tech devices, equip & products; Bks available with recordings; Copier with enlargement capabilities; Free checkout of audio mat; Large print bks; Magnifiers
Open Mon-Fri 9-3
Friends of the Library Group
Bookmobiles: 1. Bk vols 3,000

BLOSSBURG

P BLOSSBURG MEMORIAL LIBRARY*, 307 Main St, 16912. SAN 314-3317. Tel: 570-638-2197. FAX: 570-638-2197. E-mail: blosslib@epix.net. Web Site: blossml.edublogs.org. *Dir,* Elisabeth Miranda; Staff 2 (Non-MLS 2)
Founded 1946. Pop 3,899; Circ 11,977
Library Holdings: Audiobooks 379; AV Mats 855; CDs 54; DVDs 577; Large Print Bks 445; Bk Vols 13,149; Per Subs 43; Videos 278
Automation Activity & Vendor Info: (Cataloging) AmLib Library Management System; (Circulation) AmLib Library Management System; (OPAC) AmLib Library Management System
Wireless access
Function: Adult bk club, CD-ROM, Children's prog, Computer training, Computers for patron use, Electronic databases & coll, Free DVD rentals, Holiday prog, ILL available, Online cat, Online ref, Photocopying/Printing, Preschool outreach, Prog for adults, Prog for children & young adult, Ref serv available, Senior outreach, Story hour, Summer reading prog, VHS videos
Mem of Potter-Tioga Library System
Open Mon-Thurs 12-7, Fri 12-5, Sat 9-Noon
Friends of the Library Group

BLUE BELL

J MONTGOMERY COUNTY COMMUNITY COLLEGE*, The Brendlinger Library, 340 DeKalb Pike, 19422-0796. SAN 314-3333. Tel: 215-641-6300, 215-641-6596. FAX: 215-619-7182. E-mail: libraries@mc3.edu. Reference E-mail: refdesk@mc3.edu. Web Site: www.mc3.edu/library. *Dean, Libr & Acad Support,* Jenifer Baldwin
Founded 1966. Enrl 11,000
Special Collections: College Archives. US Document Depository
Automation Activity & Vendor Info: (Acquisitions) SirsiDynix-WorkFlows; (Cataloging) SirsiDynix-WorkFlows; (Circulation) SirsiDynix-WorkFlows; (Course Reserve) SirsiDynix-WorkFlows; (Discovery) EBSCO Discovery Service; (ILL) OCLC ILLiad; (Media Booking) SirsiDynix-WorkFlows; (OPAC) SirsiDynix-Enterprise; (Serials) SirsiDynix-WorkFlows
Wireless access
Function: Archival coll, Art exhibits, Audio & video playback equip for onsite use
Partic in OCLC Online Computer Library Center, Inc; Tri-State College Library Cooperative

R REFORMED EPISCOPAL SEMINARY*, Fred C Kuehner Memorial Library, 826 Second Ave, 19422. SAN 314-9919. Tel: 610-292-9852. FAX: 610-292-9853. Web Site: www.reseminary.edu/modules/tinycontent/index.php?id=60. *Libr Dir,* Rev Jonathan S Riches; E-mail: jonathan.riches@reseminary.edu
Founded 1887
Library Holdings: Bk Vols 23,000
Subject Interests: British Church hist, Liturgy, Puritans, Reformed Episcopal Church
Wireless access
Partic in Southeastern Pennsylvania Theological Library Association
Open Mon-Thurs 8-4

P WISSAHICKON VALLEY PUBLIC LIBRARY*, 650 Skippack Pike, 19422. SAN 358-2906. Tel: 215-643-1320. Circulation Tel: 215-643-1320, Ext 10. Reference Tel: 215-643-1320, Ext 19. FAX: 215-643-6611. E-mail: library@wvpl.org. Web Site: www.wvpl.org. *Dir,* Anne Frank; Tel: 215-643-1320, Ext 11, E-mail: afrank@wvpl.org; Staff 40 (MLS 6, Non-MLS 34)
Founded 1934. Pop 36,697; Circ 398,000
Library Holdings: Audiobooks 5,974; DVDs 8,884; e-books 28,723; Bk Titles 99,201; Bk Vols 114,059; Per Subs 232
Automation Activity & Vendor Info: (Cataloging) Innovative Interfaces, Inc; (Circulation) Innovative Interfaces, Inc; (OPAC) Innovative Interfaces, Inc
Wireless access
Function: ILL available
Partic in Montgomery County Library & Information Network Consortium
Open Mon-Thurs 10-9, Fri & Sat 10-5, Sun 1-4
Friends of the Library Group
Branches: 1
AMBLER BRANCH, 209 Race St, Ambler, 19002, SAN 358-2876. Tel: 215-646-1072. Reference E-mail: reference@wvpl.org. *Dir,* Anne Hall; E-mail: ahall@wvpl.org; Staff 1 (MLS 1)
Founded 1923. Pop 36,697; Circ 54,640
Library Holdings: Bk Titles 36,402; Per Subs 35
Subject Interests: Art, Educ, Natural sci
Publications: Annual Report
Open Mon-Thurs 10-9, Fri & Sat 10-5
Friends of the Library Group

BLUE RIDGE SUMMIT

P BLUE RIDGE SUMMIT FREE LIBRARY*, 13676 Monterey Lane, 17214. (Mail add: PO Box 34, 17214-0034), SAN 314-335X. Tel: 717-794-2240. FAX: 717-794-5929. *Br Mgr,* Megan Warner; E-mail: mwarner@fclspa.org; Staff 2 (Non-MLS 2)
Founded 1922. Pop 9,000
Library Holdings: Bk Vols 10,000; Per Subs 6
Automation Activity & Vendor Info: (Cataloging) Evolve; (Circulation) Evolve
Wireless access
Mem of Franklin County Library System
Open Mon-Thurs 3-8, Sat 10-2

BOYERTOWN

P BOYERTOWN COMMUNITY LIBRARY*, 24 N Reading Ave, 19512. SAN 376-5741. Tel: 610-369-0496. FAX: 610-369-0542. E-mail: boyertowncl@berks.lib.pa.us. Web Site: www.berkslibraries.org/branch/boyertown. *Libr Dir,* Susan Lopez; *Head, Circ,* Sue Elphick; *Asst Circ Mgr,* Debra Focht; *Youth Serv Coordr,* Lisa Rand; Staff 9 (MLS 1, Non-MLS 8)
Founded 1989. Pop 32,060; Circ 215,220. Sal $124,535 (Prof $28,210)
Library Holdings: Audiobooks 2,284; CDs 781; DVDs 3,271; e-books 4,734; Electronic Media & Resources 20; Electronic Media & Resources 20; Bk Vols 33,688; Per Subs 78
Automation Activity & Vendor Info: (Circulation) Horizon; (OPAC) Horizon
Wireless access
Function: Adult bk club, After school storytime, Audiobks via web, Bk club(s), Bks on CD, Children's prog, Computers for patron use, Electronic databases & coll, Free DVD rentals, ILL available, Internet access, Museum passes, Music CDs, Online cat, OverDrive digital audio bks, Passport agency, Photocopying/Printing, Prog for adults, Prog for children & young adult, Spoken cassettes & CDs, Spoken cassettes & DVDs, Story hour, Summer reading prog, Tax forms, Teen prog, Telephone ref, VHS videos, Wheelchair accessible, Writing prog
Mem of Berks County Public Libraries
Open Mon-Wed 10-8, Thurs-Sat 10-5
Friends of the Library Group

BRADDOCK

P BRADDOCK CARNEGIE LIBRARY*, 419 Library St, 15104-1609. Tel: 412-351-5356. FAX: 412-351-6810. Web Site: braddockcarnegielibrary.org. *Exec Dir,* Vicki Vargo; E-mail: vicki@thebcla.org; Staff 2 (MLS 2)
Pop 18,307; Circ 46,810
Library Holdings: Bk Titles 31,261; Bk Vols 32,690; Per Subs 58; Talking Bks 538; Videos 1,170
Automation Activity & Vendor Info: (Cataloging) Innovative Interfaces, Inc; (Circulation) Innovative Interfaces, Inc; (OPAC) Innovative Interfaces, Inc
Wireless access
Mem of Allegheny County Library Association (ACLA)
Open Mon & Fri 10-5, Tues-Thurs 11-8, Sat 9-4

BRADFORD

P BRADFORD AREA PUBLIC LIBRARY*, 67 W Washington St, 16701-1234. SAN 314-3392. Tel: 814-362-6527. FAX: 814-362-4168. E-mail: admin@bradfordlibrary.org. Web Site: www.bradfordlibrary.org.

Exec Dir, Lacey Love; E-mail: director@bradfordlibrary.org; Staff 6 (Non-MLS 6)
Founded 1901. Pop 21,772; Circ 54,159
Library Holdings: AV Mats 3,043; CDs 1,285; Large Print Bks 3,915; Bk Titles 55,258; Per Subs 54; Talking Bks 1,216; Videos 1,041
Special Collections: Local Authors Coll; Local Newspaper (1878-present), micro
Automation Activity & Vendor Info: (Cataloging) Follett Software; (Circulation) Follett Software; (ILL) Follett Software; (OPAC) Follett Software
Wireless access
Open Mon & Wed 10-7, Tues & Thurs-Sat 10-5
Friends of the Library Group

M BRADFORD REGIONAL MEDICAL CENTER*, Huff Memorial Library, 116 Interstate Pkwy, 16701. (Mail add: PO Box 218, 16701-0218), SAN 324-640X. Tel: 814-368-4143. Web Site: www.brmc.com. *Educ Coordr,* Lynette Carll; Staff 1 (Non-MLS 1)
Library Holdings: Bk Titles 1,126; Bk Vols 1,291; Per Subs 47
Restriction: Staff use only

C UNIVERSITY OF PITTSBURGH AT BRADFORD, T Edward & Tullah Hanley Library, 300 Campus Dr, 16701. SAN 314-3406. Tel: 814-362-7610. Reference Tel: 814-362-7615. FAX: 814-362-7688. Web Site: www.library.pitt.edu/bradford. *Head Librn,* Marc Ross; Tel: 814-362-4452, E-mail: marcross@pitt.edu; *Diversity Serv Librn,* Jenelle Johnson; Tel: 814-362-7618, E-mail: jme26@pitt.edu; *Instrul Serv Librn,* Catherine Baldwin; Tel: 814-362-7613, E-mail: cab137@pitt.edu; *Ref & Instruction Librn,* Kimberly Bailey; Tel: 814-362-7621, E-mail: hanold@pitt.edu; *Libr Spec,* Mary Kafferlin; Tel: 814-362-7616, E-mail: mak360@pitt.edu; *Libr Spec,* Katherine Nussbaum; Tel: 814-362-7619, E-mail: ken47@pitt.edu; Staff 7 (MLS 3, Non-MLS 4)
Founded 1963. Enrl 1,500; Fac 141; Highest Degree: Bachelor
Library Holdings: AV Mats 4,646; CDs 688; DVDs 1,542; Microforms 14,125; Bk Vols 95,000; Per Subs 100; Videos 2,000
Special Collections: Fesenmyer Scrap Books; Forres Stewart Photos; Lowenthal Coll; Pennsylvania Civilian Conservation Corps Material
Wireless access
Function: Ref serv available
Publications: Hanley Happenings (Newsletter)
Partic in OCLC Online Computer Library Center, Inc
Open Mon-Thurs 8am-9pm, Fri 8-5, Sun 2-9
Restriction: Open to pub for ref & circ; with some limitations, Restricted access
Friends of the Library Group

BRIDGEVILLE

P BRIDGEVILLE PUBLIC LIBRARY*, 505 McMillen St, 15017. SAN 314-3414. Tel: 412-221-3737. FAX: 412-220-8124. E-mail: bridgeville@einetwork.net. Web Site: bridgevillelibrary.org. *Dir,* Ben Hornfeck; E-mail: hornfeckb2@einetwork.net; Staff 2 (MLS 1.5, Non-MLS 0.5)
Founded 1962. Pop 5,341; Circ 65,177
Library Holdings: Bk Titles 18,878
Automation Activity & Vendor Info: (Cataloging) Innovative Interfaces, Inc; (Circulation) Innovative Interfaces, Inc
Wireless access
Mem of Allegheny County Library Association (ACLA)
Partic in Electronic Info Network
Open Mon-Thurs 10-8, Fri & Sat 10-5
Friends of the Library Group

BRISTOL

P MARGARET R GRUNDY MEMORIAL LIBRARY, 680 Radcliffe St, 19007-5199. SAN 314-3422. Tel: 215-788-7891. FAX: 215-788-4976. Web Site: www.grundylibrary.org. *Libr Adminr,* Dana Barber; E-mail: barberd@grundylibrary.org; *Commun Serv Mgr,* Gretchen Stallone; E-mail: stalloneg@grundylibrary.org; Staff 17 (MLS 5, Non-MLS 12)
Founded 1966. Pop 9,598; Circ 111,598
Library Holdings: AV Mats 1,082; Large Print Bks 192; Bk Titles 71,911; Bk Vols 74,681; Per Subs 121; Talking Bks 91; Videos 310
Special Collections: Bucks County Census 1790-1910, microfilm; Bucks County Courier Times 1911-Present, microfilm
Subject Interests: Local hist
Automation Activity & Vendor Info: (Acquisitions) SirsiDynix; (Circulation) SirsiDynix; (OPAC) SirsiDynix
Wireless access
Mem of Bucks County Free Library
Closed for renovations 2021-

J PENNCO TECH LIBRARY*, 3815 Otter St, 19007. SAN 314-3430. Tel: 215-785-0111. Toll Free Tel: 877-593-3718. Web Site: www.penncotech.edu. *Librn,* Position Currently Open
Founded 1973. Enrl 400; Fac 45; Highest Degree: Associate
Library Holdings: Bk Titles 2,450; Bk Vols 3,000; Per Subs 33
Special Collections: Automotive Technology; Medical Secretary; Pharmacy Technician
Open Mon, Wed & Thurs 8-4 & 6:30-8:30, Tues & Fri 8-4
Restriction: Open to students, fac & staff

BROCKWAY

P MENGLE MEMORIAL LIBRARY*, 324 Main St, 15824-0324. SAN 314-3457. Tel: 814-265-8245. FAX: 814-265-1125. E-mail: mengle@cust.usachoice.net. Web Site: menglelibrary.org. *Dir,* Darlene Marshall; Staff 2 (MLS 2)
Founded 1965. Pop 7,900; Circ 39,000
Library Holdings: Bk Titles 35,000; Per Subs 85
Automation Activity & Vendor Info: (Acquisitions) AmLib Library Management System
Wireless access
Function: Adult bk club, Bks on cassette, Bks on CD, Chess club, Children's prog, Computer training, Computers for patron use, E-Reserves, Family literacy, Free DVD rentals, ILL available, Music CDs, Outreach serv, OverDrive digital audio bks, Photocopying/Printing, Preschool reading prog, Prog for adults, Prog for children & young adult, Story hour, Summer reading prog, Tax forms, Teen prog, VHS videos
Mem of Oil Creek District Library Center
Partic in Jefferson County Library System
Open Mon-Thurs 10-7, Fri 10-5, Sat 10-5 (10-2 Summer)
Friends of the Library Group

BRODHEADSVILLE

P WESTERN POCONO COMMUNITY LIBRARY, 131 Pilgrim Way, 18322. SAN 320-2313. Tel: 570-992-7934. FAX: 570-992-7915. E-mail: wpcl@ptd.net. Web Site: www.westernpoconocommunitylibrary.org. *Libr Dir,* Patti Weiss; Staff 10.6 (MLS 1, Non-MLS 9.6)
Founded 1974. Pop 29,053
Library Holdings: Audiobooks 6,712; Bks on Deafness & Sign Lang 10; CDs 2,878; DVDs 2,707; e-books 1,142; Electronic Media & Resources 32; Large Print Bks 3,109; Bk Titles 72,394; Talking Bks 6,712; Videos 2,707
Special Collections: Monroe County History
Automation Activity & Vendor Info: (Cataloging) Innovative Interfaces, Inc - Sierra; (Circulation) Innovative Interfaces, Inc - Sierra; (ILL) Innovative Interfaces, Inc; (OPAC) Innovative Interfaces, Inc - Sierra
Wireless access
Function: 24/7 Electronic res, 24/7 Online cat, Adult bk club, Adult literacy prog, Art exhibits, Audiobooks on Playaways & MP3, Audiobks via web, Bk club(s), Bks on CD, Children's prog, Citizenship assistance, Computer training, Computers for patron use, Electronic databases & coll, Free DVD rentals, Home delivery & serv to seniorr ctr & nursing homes, Homebound delivery serv, ILL available, Internet access, Life-long learning prog for all ages, Literacy & newcomer serv, Magazines, Magnifiers for reading, Mail & tel request accepted, Meeting rooms, Microfiche/film & reading machines, Museum passes, Music CDs, Online cat, Online ref, Outreach serv, Outside serv via phone, mail, e-mail & web, OverDrive digital audio bks, Photocopying/Printing, Preschool outreach, Prog for adults, Prog for children & young adult, Ref & res, Ref serv available, Senior computer classes, Senior outreach, Serves people with intellectual disabilities, Spoken cassettes & CDs, Spoken cassettes & DVDs, STEM programs, Story hour, Summer reading prog, Tax forms, Teen prog, Telephone ref, Wheelchair accessible, Workshops
Open Mon, Wed & Thurs 9-8, Tues & Fri 9-5, Sat 9-4
Restriction: Non-resident fee

BROOKVILLE

P REBECCA M ARTHURS MEMORIAL LIBRARY*, 223 Valley St, 15825-0223. SAN 314-3465. Tel: 814-849-5512. FAX: 814-849-6211. Web Site: www.rmalib.org. *Dir,* Janine Strohm; E-mail: rmalibdirector@gmail.com; Staff 2 (MLS 1, Non-MLS 1)
Founded 1958. Pop 11,758; Circ 65,938
Library Holdings: Bk Vols 34,717; Per Subs 70; Talking Bks 1,517; Videos 3,750
Subject Interests: Local hist
Automation Activity & Vendor Info: (Cataloging) Evolve; (Circulation) Evolve; (OPAC) Evolve
Wireless access
Function: 24/7 Electronic res, 24/7 Online cat, Adult bk club, After school storytime, Audiobks on Playaways & MP3, Bks on CD, Children's prog, Computers for patron use, E-Readers, Electronic databases & coll, Free DVD rentals, Holiday prog, ILL available, Internet access, Laminating, Life-long learning prog for all ages, Magazines, Meeting rooms, Online cat, Outreach serv, OverDrive digital audio bks, Photocopying/Printing,

Preschool outreach, Prog for adults, Prog for children & young adult, Ref serv available, Scanner, Serves people with intellectual disabilities, STEM programs, Story hour, Summer & winter reading prog, Summer reading prog, Tax forms, Teen prog, Telephone ref, Wheelchair accessible
Mem of Oil Creek District Library Center
Open Tues 9-7, Wed & Thurs 9:30-7, Fri 9-6, Sat 12-4, Sun 1-4
Friends of the Library Group

BROOMALL

R BETH EL NER TAMID LIBRARY, 715 Paxon Hollow Rd, 19008-9998. SAN 314-3473. Tel: 610-356-8700. FAX: 610-356-8700. E-mail: office@cbent.org. Web Site: cbent.org. *Exec Dir,* Larry Marrow
Founded 1959
Library Holdings: Bk Titles 2,791; Bk Vols 2,990; Per Subs 10
Subject Interests: Jewish hist, Judaica
Wireless access
Restriction: Open by appt only

SR CHURCH OF JESUS CHRIST OF LATTER-DAY SAINTS-PHILADELPHIA, Stake Family History Center, 721 Paxon Hollow Rd, 19008. SAN 375-2402. Tel: 610-356-8507. E-mail: broomallfhc@gmail.com. Web Site: www.familysearch.org/wiki/en/Valley_Forge_Pennsylvania_Family_History_Center. *Dir,* Shelli Nye; Staff 1 (Non-MLS 1)
Library Holdings: Bk Vols 500
Special Collections: Philadelphia Coll. Oral History; US Document Depository
Subject Interests: Genealogy
Open Wed 9:30-3

P MARPLE PUBLIC LIBRARY*, 2599 Sproul Rd, 19008-2399. SAN 314-3481. Tel: 610-356-1510. FAX: 610-356-3589. E-mail: marple@delcolibraries.org. Web Site: www.marplelibrary.org. *Dir,* LaTanya Burno; *Head, Adult Serv,* Bridgette Crockett; *Head, Tech Serv,* Antoinette Stabinski; *Ch Serv,* Andrea Mandel; Staff 5 (MLS 5)
Founded 1951. Pop 23,642
Library Holdings: Bk Titles 90,000; Bk Vols 92,000; Per Subs 90
Automation Activity & Vendor Info: (Circulation) Innovative Interfaces, Inc
Wireless access
Mem of Delaware County Libraries
Open Mon-Thurs 10-9, Fri 10-6, Sat 10-5, Sun 1-5
Friends of the Library Group

R TEMPLE SHOLOM IN BROOMALL LIBRARY*, 55 N Church Lane, 19008. SAN 314-349X. Tel: 610-356-5165. FAX: 610-356-6713. E-mail: library@temple-sholom.org. Web Site: www.temple-sholom.org/library. *Librn,* Mary Ann Gould
Library Holdings: Bk Vols 2,500; Per Subs 50
Special Collections: Judaica Coll
Publications: Jerusalem Post; Jewish Exponent; Reform Judaism Inside

BROWNSVILLE

P BROWNSVILLE FREE PUBLIC LIBRARY, 100 Seneca St, 15417-1974. SAN 314-3511. Tel: 724-785-7272. FAX: 724-785-6087. E-mail: brpublib@gmail.com. Web Site: www.bfpl.org. *Dir,* Lori Barron; Staff 3 (MLS 1, Non-MLS 2)
Founded 1927
Library Holdings: DVDs 600; Bk Vols 17,000; Per Subs 20; Talking Bks 109; Videos 62
Automation Activity & Vendor Info: (Cataloging) Follett Software; (OPAC) Follett Software
Wireless access
Open Mon-Fri 10-3

BRYN ATHYN

C BRYN ATHYN COLLEGE*, Swedenborg Library, 2945 College Dr, 19009. SAN 314-352X. Tel: 267-502-2524. Interlibrary Loan Service Tel: 267-502-6030. FAX: 267-502-2637. Web Site: brynathyn.edu/library. *Dir,* Carol Traveny; Tel: 267-502-2531, E-mail: Carol.Traveny@brynathyn.edu; Staff 6 (MLS 4, Non-MLS 2)
Founded 1877. Enrl 286; Fac 33; Highest Degree: Master
Library Holdings: e-journals 7,422; Microforms 1,617; Bk Titles 211,135; Bk Vols 243,869; Per Subs 152
Special Collections: Religion (Swedenborgiana); Scientific Books (Published in 16th, 17th & 18th Centuries)
Subject Interests: Behav sci, Educ, Hist, Natural sci, Relig studies, Soc sci
Automation Activity & Vendor Info: (Cataloging) SirsiDynix; (Circulation) SirsiDynix; (OPAC) SirsiDynix; (Serials) SirsiDynix
Wireless access
Publications: Bi-Lines (Newsletter)
Partic in Health Sci Libr Info Consortium; LYRASIS; OCLC Online Computer Library Center, Inc; Tri-State College Library Cooperative
Open Mon-Thurs 7:30am-10pm, Fri 7:30-5, Sat 10-2, Sun 5pm-10pm
Friends of the Library Group

BRYN MAWR

C AMERICAN COLLEGE*, Vane B Lucas Memorial Library, 270 S Bryn Mawr Ave, 19010-2196. SAN 314-3538. Tel: 610-526-1337. FAX: 610-526-1310. E-mail: library@theamericancollege.edu. Web Site: www.theamericancollege.edu/resources/vane-b-lucas-memorial-library. *Dir,* John H Whitham; Staff 1 (MLS 1)
Founded 1927. Enrl 25,000; Fac 21; Highest Degree: Doctorate
Special Collections: Insurance (Solomon S Huebner Coll), bks, papers & flm; Insurance History Coll. Oral History
Subject Interests: Ins (finance), Taxation
Automation Activity & Vendor Info: (Discovery) EBSCO Discovery Service
Wireless access

C BRYN MAWR COLLEGE*, Mariam Coffin Canaday Library, 101 N Merion Ave, 19010-2899. SAN 314-3546. Circulation Tel: 610-526-5276. Interlibrary Loan Service Tel: 610-526-5278. Reference Tel: 610-526-5279. Administration Tel: 610-526-5271. FAX: 610-526-7480. E-mail: library@brynmawr.edu. Web Site: www.brynmawr.edu/library. *Chief Info Officer, Dir of Libr,* Gina Siesing; E-mail: gsiesing@brynmawr.edu; *Assoc Chief Info Officer,* Florence D Goff; Tel: 610-526-5275, E-mail: fgoff@brynmawr.edu; *Dir, Libr Coll, Head, Spec Coll,* Eric Pumroy; Tel: 610-526-5272, E-mail: epumroy@brynmawr.edu; *Dir, Planning & Communication,* Melissa Kramer; Tel: 610-527-5287, E-mail: mkramer@brynmawr.edu; *Head, Res Support & Educ Tech,* David Consiglio; Tel: 610-526-6534, E-mail: dconsiglio@brynmawr.edu; *Coordr, Info Access & Delivery,* Berry Chamness; Tel: 610-526-5295, E-mail: bchamness@brynmawr.edu; Staff 25 (MLS 18, Non-MLS 7)
Founded 1885. Enrl 1,478; Fac 126; Highest Degree: Doctorate
Library Holdings: Electronic Media & Resources 5,240; Bk Titles 891,443; Per Subs 1,712
Special Collections: Books about Books; College Archives; English & Dutch History Coll; Fine & Graphic Arts Coll; History of & Writing by Women; History of Religion Coll; History of Science Coll; Natural History Coll; Press Books; Theater & Performing Arts Coll; Travel & Exploration Coll; Twentieth Century Lithography Coll; Urban History Coll (New York, London, Paris)
Automation Activity & Vendor Info: (Acquisitions) Innovative Interfaces, Inc; (Cataloging) Innovative Interfaces, Inc; (Circulation) Innovative Interfaces, Inc; (OPAC) Innovative Interfaces, Inc; (Serials) Innovative Interfaces, Inc
Publications: Bryn Mawr Library Card Catalog (Annual); Mirabile Dictu (Periodical)
Partic in OCLC Research Library Partnership; Partnership for Academic Library Collaborative & Innovation; Philadelphia Area Consortium of Special Collections Libraries
Open Mon-Thurs 8am-Midnight, Fri 8am-10pm, Sat 10-10, Sun 10am-Midnight
Friends of the Library Group

Departmental Libraries:

RHYS CARPENTER LIBRARY FOR ART, ARCHAEOLOGY & CITIES, 101 N Merion Ave, 19104-2899. Circulation Tel: 610-526-7912. FAX: 610-526-7975. *Head of Libr,* Camilla MacKay; Tel: 610-526-7910, E-mail: cmackay@brynmawr.edu
Open Mon-Thurs 8am-Midnight, Fri 8-8, Sat 10-7, Sun 12-Midnight

LOIS & REGINALD COLLIER SCIENCE LIBRARY, 101 N Merion Ave, 19104-2899. Tel: 610-526-5118. Circulation Tel: 610-526-7463. FAX: 610-526-7464. *Head of Libr,* Terri Freedman; E-mail: tfreedma@brynmawr.edu
Open Mon-Thurs 8am-Midnight, Fri 8am-10pm, Sat 10-10, Sun 10-Midnight
Friends of the Library Group

M BRYN MAWR HOSPITAL LIBRARY*, Joseph N Pew Jr Medical Library, 130 S Bryn Mawr Ave, 19010. SAN 314-3554. Tel: 484-337-3160. FAX: 484-337-3156. E-mail: bmhlibrary@mlhs.org. *Med Librn,* Joan Wolff; E-mail: wolffj@mlhs.org; Staff 1 (MLS 1)
Founded 1893
Special Collections: Medical Antique Instrument Coll
Automation Activity & Vendor Info: (Cataloging) Innovative Interfaces, Inc; (Serials) Innovative Interfaces, Inc
Wireless access
Partic in Basic Health Sciences Library Network; DEVIC
Open Mon-Fri 9-5
Restriction: Authorized personnel only, Circulates for staff only, In-house use for visitors

R BRYN MAWR PRESBYTERIAN CHURCH*, Converse Library, 625 Montgomery Ave, 19010-3599. SAN 314-3562. Tel: 610-525-2821. Web Site: www.bmpc.org. *Educ Serv,* Carol Schmidt; *Librn,* Kat MacMurray; E-mail: KatRMac2@gmail.com; Staff 7 (MLS 1, Non-MLS 6)
Founded 1878
Library Holdings: Audiobooks 15; AV Mats 100; CDs 10; DVDs 50; Large Print Bks 25; Bk Vols 2,000; Per Subs 13; Videos 100
Subject Interests: Presbyterian Church, Soc issues, Spirituality, Theol
Automation Activity & Vendor Info: (Acquisitions) ResourceMATE; (Cataloging) Marcive, Inc
Wireless access
Publications: Conversations (Annual report)
Open Mon-Sat 9-5, Sun 8-1

J HARCUM COLLEGE*, Charles H Trout Library, 750 Montgomery Ave, 19010-3476. SAN 314-3570. Tel: 610-526-6085. Reference Tel: 610-526-6084. Administration Tel: 610-526-6062. FAX: 610-526-6086. E-mail: library@harcum.edu. Web Site: harcum.libguides.com/troutlibrary. *Libr Dir,* Katie McGowan; Tel: 610-526-6062, E-mail: cmcgowan@harcum.edu; *Evening/Weekend Librn,* William Fanshel; Tel: 610-229-9311, E-mail: wfanshel@harcum.edu; *Ref Librn,* Alice Pakhtigian; E-mail: apakhtigian@harcum.edu; *Tech Serv Librn,* Roxanne Sutton; Tel: 610-526-6022, E-mail: rsutton@harcum.edu; *Coordr, Media Serv,* Daniel Hodas; Tel: 610-526-6167, E-mail: dhodas@harcum.edu; Staff 5 (MLS 4, Non-MLS 1)
Founded 1915. Enrl 1,500; Fac 80; Highest Degree: Associate
Library Holdings: DVDs 500; Bk Titles 20,000; Per Subs 50
Subject Interests: Allied health, Dental assisting, Mkt, Nursing, Phys therapy
Automation Activity & Vendor Info: (Acquisitions) ByWater Solutions; (Cataloging) ByWater Solutions; (Circulation) ByWater Solutions; (Course Reserve) ByWater Solutions; (ILL) OCLC; (OPAC) ByWater Solutions; (Serials) ByWater Solutions
Wireless access
Function: 24/7 Electronic res, 24/7 Online cat
Partic in LYRASIS; OCLC Online Computer Library Center, Inc; Tri-State College Library Cooperative

P LUDINGTON PUBLIC LIBRARY*, Five S Bryn Mawr Ave, 19010-3471. SAN 314-3597. Tel: 610-525-1776. FAX: 610-525-1783. Web Site: www.lmls.org/locations-hours/ludington-library. *Head Librn,* Robyn Langston; E-mail: rlangston@lmls.org; *Head, Circ,* Jennifer Wark; *Head, Ref,* Marcia Bass; E-mail: mbass@lmls.org; *Coordr, Youth Serv,* Darlene Davis; Staff 6 (MLS 6)
Founded 1916. Pop 13,000; Circ 641,574
Library Holdings: Bk Vols 150,000; Per Subs 300
Subject Interests: Archit, Art, Hort
Automation Activity & Vendor Info: (Acquisitions) Innovative Interfaces, Inc; (Cataloging) Innovative Interfaces, Inc; (Circulation) Innovative Interfaces, Inc; (OPAC) Innovative Interfaces, Inc
Wireless access
Function: Audiobks via web, Bks on CD, Children's prog, Computer training, Computers for patron use, Homebound delivery serv, ILL available, Music CDs, Online cat, Online ref, OverDrive digital audio bks, Photocopying/Printing, Prog for adults, Prog for children & young adult, Ref serv available, Story hour, Summer reading prog, Tax forms, Telephone ref, Wheelchair accessible
Publications: Main Line; Union List of Periodicals & Newspapers
Mem of Lower Merion Library System
Partic in Montgomery County Library & Information Network Consortium
Open Mon-Thurs 9-9, Fri 9-6, Sat 9-5, Sun (Winter) 12-5
Friends of the Library Group

BURGETTSTOWN

P BURGETTSTOWN COMMUNITY LIBRARY, Two Kerr St, 15021-1127. SAN 314-3600. Tel: 724-947-9780. FAX: 724-947-5116. E-mail: librarian@burglibrary.org. Web Site: www.burglibrary.org. *Libr Dir,* Kristin Frazier; E-mail: kfrazier@burglibrary.org; Staff 1.5 (Non-MLS 1.5)
Founded 1946. Pop 10,500
Library Holdings: Audiobooks 100; DVDs 20; Large Print Bks 200; Bk Vols 18,900; Per Subs 10; Videos 200
Automation Activity & Vendor Info: (Cataloging) Follett Software; (Circulation) Follett Software
Wireless access
Function: 24/7 Electronic res, 24/7 Online cat, Adult bk club, Audiobks on Playaways & MP3, Audiobks via web, Bk club(s), Bks on CD, Children's prog, Computers for patron use, Free DVD rentals, ILL available, Magazines, Museum passes, Notary serv, Photocopying/Printing, Prog for adults, Prog for children & young adult, Scanner, Story hour, Summer reading prog, Tax forms, Wheelchair accessible
Mem of Washington County Library System
Open Mon & Tues 9-5, Wed & Thurs 9-8, Fri 9-Noon, Sat 9-4
Friends of the Library Group

BUTLER

P BUTLER AREA PUBLIC LIBRARY*, 218 N McKean St, 16001. SAN 314-3643. Tel: 724-287-1715. FAX: 724-285-5090. TDD: 724-287-1718. E-mail: baplreference@bcfls.org. Web Site: www.butlerlibrary.info. *Exec Dir,* Lori Hinderliter; E-mail: lhinderliter@bcfls.org; *Asst Dir,* Peter Bess; E-mail: pbess@bcfls.org; Staff 9 (MLS 4, Non-MLS 5)
Founded 1894. Pop 31,005; Circ 348,068
Library Holdings: Bk Vols 100,748; Per Subs 140
Special Collections: Genealogy
Automation Activity & Vendor Info: (Acquisitions) TLC (The Library Corporation); (Cataloging) TLC (The Library Corporation); (Circulation) TLC (The Library Corporation); (OPAC) TLC (The Library Corporation)
Wireless access
Publications: Annual Report; Newsletter
Mem of Butler County Federated Library System
Partic in LYRASIS; OCLC Online Computer Library Center, Inc
Special Services for the Deaf - Assistive tech; Bks on deafness & sign lang; TDD equip; TTY equip
Special Services for the Blind - Bks on CD; Home delivery serv; Large print bks; Playaways (bks on MP3); Volunteer serv
Open Mon-Thurs 8-8, Fri 8-5, Sat 8-4
Friends of the Library Group

J BUTLER COUNTY COMMUNITY COLLEGE*, Butler County Community College Library, 107 College Dr, 16002. (Mail add: PO Box 1203, 16003-1203), SAN 314-3619. Tel: 724-284-8511. E-mail: library@bc3.edu. Web Site: bc3.edu/services/library/index.html. *Dean, Libr Serv,* Stephen Joseph; *Ref & Instruction Librn,* Jean Shumway; *Circ & Tech Serv Librn,* Martin Miller; Staff 3 (MLS 3)
Founded 1966. Enrl 2,500; Fac 64
Library Holdings: e-journals 109; Bk Titles 35,000; Bk Vols 40,000; Per Subs 94
Subject Interests: Allied health, Lit, Soc issues
Automation Activity & Vendor Info: (Cataloging) Innovative Interfaces, Inc - Millennium; (Circulation) Innovative Interfaces, Inc - Millennium; (Course Reserve) Innovative Interfaces, Inc - Millennium; (ILL) OCLC WorldShare Interlibrary Loan; (OPAC) Innovative Interfaces, Inc - Millennium; (Serials) Innovative Interfaces, Inc - Millennium
Wireless access
Publications: Acquisitions List (Annual report); Bibliographies; Library Instruction on Video; Newsletter (Biennial); Periodicals List (Annual report); Student Handbook
Partic in OCLC Online Computer Library Center, Inc
Open Mon-Thurs 7:30am-9pm, Fri 7:30-4

P BUTLER COUNTY FEDERATED LIBRARY SYSTEM*, 218 N McKean St, 16001. Tel: 724-283-1880. FAX: 724-285-5090. Web Site: www.bcfls.org. *Adminr,* Lori Hinderliter; E-mail: lhinderliter@bcfls.org; Staff 8 (MLS 1, Non-MLS 7)
Founded 1987
Library Holdings: Bk Vols 28,269; Per Subs 30
Automation Activity & Vendor Info: (Cataloging) TLC (The Library Corporation); (Circulation) TLC (The Library Corporation); (OPAC) TLC (The Library Corporation)
Wireless access
Member Libraries: Butler Area Public Library; Chicora Community Library; Cranberry Public Library; Evans City Public Library; Mars Area Public Library; North Trails Public Library; Prospect Community Library; Slippery Rock Community Library; South Butler Community Library; Zelienople Area Public Library
Special Services for the Deaf - TTY equip
Friends of the Library Group
Bookmobiles: 1

GL BUTLER COUNTY LAW LIBRARY*, Courthouse, 124 W Diamond St, Rm 303, 16001. SAN 314-3627. Tel: 724-284-5206. FAX: 724-284-5210. E-mail: law.library@co.butler.pa.us. Web Site: www.co.butler.pa.us/law-library. *Law Librn,* Christine Lorenz
Library Holdings: Bk Titles 20,000; Per Subs 60
Subject Interests: Law, Penn
Open Mon-Fri 8:30-4:30
Restriction: Open to pub for ref only

GM DEPARTMENT OF VETERANS AFFAIRS*, Medical Center Library, 353 N Duffy Rd, 16001. SAN 314-366X. Tel: 724-287-4781. Toll Free Tel: 800-362-8262. E-mail: library529@va.gov. Web Site: www.butler.va.gov. *Education Analyst,* Nancy Reesman; Tel: 878-271-6924, E-mail: nancy.reesman@va.gov; Staff 2 (Non-MLS 2)
Founded 1946
Library Holdings: Bk Titles 1,327; Per Subs 131
Subject Interests: Geriatrics, Med, Nursing, Psychol, Soc work
Partic in Veterans Affairs Library Network
Restriction: Pub use on premises, Staff use only

CALIFORNIA

P CALIFORNIA AREA PUBLIC LIBRARY*, 100 Wood St, 15419. SAN 314-3678. Tel: 724-938-2907. FAX: 724-938-9119. Web Site: calpublib.org. *Dir & Librn,* Claudia L Bennett; E-mail: Director@calpublib.org
Founded 1934
Library Holdings: Audiobooks 65; AV Mats 415; Bks on Deafness & Sign Lang 7; Braille Volumes 2; DVDs 182; Large Print Bks 200; Bk Titles 14,500; Bk Vols 20,000; Per Subs 15; Spec Interest Per Sub 1; Videos 415
Special Collections: Local Hist Coll; Railroads Coll
Automation Activity & Vendor Info: (Acquisitions) Brodart; (Cataloging) Innovative Interfaces, Inc; (Circulation) Innovative Interfaces, Inc; (OPAC) Innovative Interfaces, Inc
Wireless access
Function: 24/7 Electronic res, 24/7 Online cat, ILL available
Publications: California Journal (Newsletter)
Mem of Washington County Library System
Partic in National Network of Libraries of Medicine Region 1; WAGGIN
Open Mon & Wed 10-5, Tues & Thurs 10-7, Fri 10-4, Sat 9-4

C CALIFORNIA UNIVERSITY OF PENNSYLVANIA*, Louis L Manderino Library, 250 University Ave, 15419-1394. SAN 314-3686. Tel: 724-938-4091. Interlibrary Loan Service Tel: 724-938-4049. Reference Tel: 724-938-4094. Administration Tel: 724-938-4096. Automation Services Tel: 724-938-5772. FAX: 724-938-5901. Administration FAX: 724-938-4088. Reference E-mail: reference@calu.edu. Web Site: www.library.calu.edu. *Dean, Libr Serv,* Douglas A Hoover; E-mail: hoover@calu.edu; *Chairperson, Electronic Res Librn, Webmaster,* Loring Prest; Tel: 724-938-5769, E-mail: prest@calu.edu; *Pub Serv, Syst Adminr,* Carol Jones; E-mail: jones@calu.edu; *Govt Doc/Distance Learning Librn,* William Denny; Tel: 724-938-4451, E-mail: denny_w@calu.edu; *Info Literacy/Instrul Tech Librn,* Ryan Sittler; Tel: 724-938-4923, E-mail: sittler@calu.edu; *Res & Electronic Coll Librn,* William Meloy; Tel: 724-938-4067, E-mail: meloy@calu.edu; *Res & Instruction Librn,* Monica Ruane Rogers; E-mail: ruane@calu.edu; *Tech Serv Librn,* Julia F McGinnis; Tel: 724-938-5472, Fax: 724-938-4490, E-mail: mcginnis@calu.edu; *Coordr, Circ,* Daniel Zyglowicz; Tel: 724-938-4092, E-mail: zyglowicz@calu.edu; *ILL,* Diane Greenlief; Tel: 724-938-5539, E-mail: Greenlief@calu.edu; Staff 17 (MLS 8, Non-MLS 9)
Founded 1852. Enrl 8,243; Fac 253; Highest Degree: Doctorate
Library Holdings: Bk Vols 389,566; Per Subs 9,314
Special Collections: State Document Depository; US Document Depository
Automation Activity & Vendor Info: (Acquisitions) Ex Libris Group; (Cataloging) Ex Libris Group; (Circulation) Ex Libris Group; (Course Reserve) Docutek; (ILL) Ex Libris Group; (OPAC) Ex Libris Group; (Serials) Ex Libris Group
Wireless access
Partic in Interlibrary Delivery Service of Pennsylvania; Keystone Library Network; LYRASIS; Partnership for Academic Library Collaborative & Innovation
Open Mon-Thurs 7:30am-11pm, Fri 7:30-5, Sat & Sun 12-8

CAMBRIDGE SPRINGS

P CAMBRIDGE SPRINGS PUBLIC LIBRARY*, 158 McClellan St, 16403-1018. SAN 314-3716. Tel: 814-398-2123. FAX: 814-398-2123. E-mail: cspl@ccfls.org. Web Site: cambridge.ccfls.org. *Dir,* Amanda Scott
Founded 1928. Pop 6,805; Circ 25,388
Library Holdings: AV Mats 608; Bks on Deafness & Sign Lang 25; Large Print Bks 155; Bk Titles 20,000; Bk Vols 21,669; Per Subs 80; Talking Bks 290
Automation Activity & Vendor Info: (Cataloging) Follett Software; (Circulation) Follett Software; (OPAC) Follett Software
Wireless access
Mem of Crawford County Federated Library System
Open Mon 12-8, Tues & Thurs 10-8, Wed & Fri 12-5, Sat 10-5

CAMP HILL

P CLEVE J FREDRICKSEN LIBRARY*, 100 N 19th St, 17011-3900. SAN 314-3732. Tel: 717-761-3900. FAX: 717-761-5493. E-mail: fredricksen@cumberlandcountylibraries.org. Web Site: www.cumberlandcountylibraries.org/FRE. *Dir,* Bonnie Goble; Tel: 717-761-3900, Ext 227, E-mail: bgoble@ccpa.net; *Asst Dir, Develop Dir,* Pamela Rhoads; Tel: 717-761-3900, Ext 244, E-mail: prhoads@ccpa.net; Staff 6 (MLS 6)
Founded 1957. Pop 74,064; Circ 404,089
Library Holdings: Bk Vols 99,796
Automation Activity & Vendor Info: (Acquisitions) SirsiDynix; (Cataloging) SirsiDynix; (Circulation) SirsiDynix; (OPAC) SirsiDynix
Wireless access
Mem of Cumberland County Library System
Open Mon, Tues, Thurs & Fri 9-9, Wed 9-6, Sat & Sun 1-5
Friends of the Library Group
Branches: 1
EAST PENNSBORO, 98 S Enola Dr, Enola, 17025, SAN 376-5695. Tel: 717-732-4274. FAX: 717-732-6478. E-mail: eastpennsboro@ccpa.net. Web Site: www.eastpennsborobranch.org. *Libr Dir,* Bonnie Goble
Pop 26,305; Circ 54,933
Library Holdings: Bk Vols 13,601
Open Mon, Tues & Thurs 10-8, Wed 10-5, Fri 12-5
Friends of the Library Group

M GEISINGER HOLY SPIRIT HOSPITAL, Health Sciences Library, 503 N 21st St, 17011. SAN 325-0164. Tel: 717-763-2664. FAX: 717-763-2136. E-mail: easbury@pennstatehealth.psu.edu. *Librn,* Edie Asbury; E-mail: easbury@pennstatehealth.psu.edu; Staff 1 (MLS 1)
Library Holdings: e-books 2,257; e-journals 6,771; Bk Vols 2,500; Per Subs 21
Subject Interests: Consumer health, Med, Mental health
Automation Activity & Vendor Info: (Cataloging) Softlink America; (Circulation) Softlink America; (OPAC) Softlink America
Wireless access
Function: Computers for patron use, Doc delivery serv, Health sci info serv, ILL available, Internet access, Mail & tel request accepted, Microfiche/film & reading machines, Online cat, Photocopying/Printing, Ref serv available, Telephone ref
Partic in Central Pennsylvania Health Sciences Library Association
Open Mon-Fri 7-6
Restriction: Badge access after hrs, Hospital staff & commun

CANONSBURG

P FRANK SARRIS PUBLIC LIBRARY*, 36 N Jefferson Ave, 15317. SAN 314-3740. Tel: 724-745-1308. FAX: 724-745-4958. E-mail: info@franksarrislibrary.org. Web Site: www.franksarrislibrary.org. *Libr Dir,* Peggy Tseng; E-mail: ptseng@franksarrislibrary.org; *Asst Dir,* Beth Kairush; E-mail: bkairush@franksarrislibrary.org; Staff 11 (MLS 1, Non-MLS 10)
Founded 1879
Library Holdings: Bk Titles 70,000; Per Subs 64
Special Collections: Canonsburg Notes, micro; Federal Census; History of Western Pennsylvania (Johnson Memorial Coll)
Automation Activity & Vendor Info: (Cataloging) AmLib Library Management System; (Circulation) AmLib Library Management System; (OPAC) AmLib Library Management System
Wireless access
Function: Accelerated reader prog, Adult bk club, Archival coll, Bk club(s), Bks on CD, Children's prog, Computers for patron use, E-Reserves, Electronic databases & coll, Free DVD rentals, ILL available, Online cat, Photocopying/Printing, Preschool outreach, Prog for children & young adult, Ref serv available, Story hour, Summer & winter reading prog, Tax forms, Teen prog, Telephone ref, VHS videos, Wheelchair accessible
Mem of Washington County Library System
Partic in Washington County Cooperative Library Services
Special Services for the Blind - ZoomText magnification & reading software
Open Mon-Thurs 10-8, Fri & Sat 10-5
Friends of the Library Group

CANTON

P GREEN FREE LIBRARY*, 38 N Center St, 17724-1304. SAN 314-3767. Tel: 570-673-5744. FAX: 570-673-5005. E-mail: greenfre@frontiernet.net. Web Site: greenfl.edublogs.org. *Dir,* Cathy J Golder
Pop 6,449; Circ 16,460
Library Holdings: Bk Vols 24,000; Per Subs 25
Automation Activity & Vendor Info: (Cataloging) Follett Software; (Circulation) Follett Software
Wireless access
Mem of Bradford County Library System
Open Mon & Thurs 9-1:30 & 2-7, Tues & Fri 8:30-5:30, Sat 9-2, Sun 6pm-8pm
Friends of the Library Group

CARBONDALE

P CARBONDALE PUBLIC LIBRARY*, Five N Main St, 18407. SAN 314-3775. Tel: 570-282-4281. FAX: 570-282-7031. Web Site: lclshome.org/b/carbondale-public-library. *Libr Dir,* Maura Rottmund; E-mail: mrottmund@albright.org; *Youth Serv Librn,* Leigh-Ann Puchalski; E-mail: lguiliani@albright.org
Founded 1874. Pop 12,808; Circ 26,169
Library Holdings: Bk Vols 22,936; Per Subs 65
Automation Activity & Vendor Info: (Acquisitions) SirsiDynix; (Cataloging) SirsiDynix; (Circulation) SirsiDynix; (ILL) SirsiDynix; (OPAC) SirsiDynix

Wireless access
Function: Adult bk club, Chess club, ILL available, Internet access, Magnifiers for reading, Music CDs, Outside serv via phone, mail, e-mail & web, Photocopying/Printing, Prog for adults, Prog for children & young adult, Ref & res, Ref serv available, Spoken cassettes & CDs, Spoken cassettes & DVDs, Summer reading prog, Telephone ref, VHS videos, Wheelchair accessible
Mem of Lackawanna County Library System
Open Mon-Thurs 10-8, Fri & Sat 10-5
Friends of the Library Group

CARLISLE

P BOSLER MEMORIAL LIBRARY, 158 W High St, 17013-2988. SAN 314-3791. Tel: 717-243-4642. FAX: 717-243-8281. E-mail: bosler@cumberlandcountylibraries.org. Web Site: www.cumberlandcountylibraries.org/BOS. *Exec Dir,* Jeffrey D Swope; E-mail: jswope@ccps.net; *Asst Dir,* Tiffany Wivell; E-mail: twivell@ccps.net; Staff 4.6 (MLS 2.8, Non-MLS 1.8)
Founded 1900. Pop 60,700; Circ 265,057
Jan 2020-Dec 2020 Income $1,421,593. Mats Exp $1,421,593
Library Holdings: AV Mats 13,529; e-books 20,568; Electronic Media & Resources 117; Bk Vols 135,413; Per Subs 102
Subject Interests: Local hist
Automation Activity & Vendor Info: (Circulation) Innovative Interfaces, Inc
Wireless access
Function: 24/7 Electronic res, 24/7 Online cat, Activity rm, Adult bk club, Art exhibits, Art programs, Audiobks via web, Bk club(s), Bks on CD, Children's prog, Computer training, Computers for patron use, Digital talking bks, E-Reserves, Electronic databases & coll, Equip loans & repairs, Free DVD rentals, Holiday prog, Home delivery & serv to seniorr ctr & nursing homes, Homebound delivery serv, Homework prog, ILL available, Internet access, Jail serv, Life-long learning prog for all ages, Magazines, Mail & tel request accepted, Meeting rooms, Movies, Museum passes, Music CDs, Online cat, Outreach serv, OverDrive digital audio bks, Photocopying/Printing, Preschool outreach, Preschool reading prog, Prog for adults, Prog for children & young adult, Ref & res, Ref serv available, Scanner, STEM programs, Story hour, Study rm, Summer reading prog, Tax forms, Teen prog, Telephone ref, Visual arts prog, Wheelchair accessible, Workshops, Writing prog
Mem of Cumberland County Library System
Open Mon-Fri 10-9, Sat 10-5, Sun 1-5
Friends of the Library Group

S CUMBERLAND COUNTY HISTORICAL SOCIETY*, Hamilton Library, 21 N Pitt St, 17013-2945. SAN 314-3805. Tel: 717-249-7610. FAX: 717-258-9332. E-mail: info@historicalsociety.com. Web Site: www.historicalsociety.com. *Dir, Libr & Archives,* Cara Holtry; E-mail: ccurtis@historicalsociety.com; Staff 7 (MLS 3, Non-MLS 4)
Founded 1874
Library Holdings: Per Subs 20
Special Collections: A A Line, J N; Carlisle; Carlisle Indian School Coll; Cartography (John V Miller, M D Coll), maps; Choate & Carlisle Indian School, photog; Cumberland County; Cumberland County Firms Business Records, bd; Genealogy, VF; Index to Cumberland County Church & Cemetery Records; Jim Bradley Photograph Coll; John S Steckbeck Coll; Judge James Hamilton Coll, papers, bks & ms; Newspapers, 1749-present & Carlisle Indian School Publications, 1880-1917, bd & micro; Papers of Robert Whitehill, Sylvester B Sadler, Jeremiah Zeamer & others, ms
Subject Interests: Architects, Genealogy, Local hist, Property
Wireless access
Function: Archival coll, Children's prog, For res purposes, Microfiche/film & reading machines, Prog for adults, Prog for children & young adult, Ref & res, Res assist avail, Res libr, Res performed for a fee
Publications: Annual Journal; Monographs
Restriction: Closed stack, Fee for pub use, Free to mem, Non-circulating, Non-circulating of rare bks, Not a lending libr

L CUMBERLAND COUNTY LAW LIBRARY*, Bosler Library, 158 W High St, 17013. SAN 327-098X. Tel: 717-243-4642. FAX: 717-240-6462. E-mail: bosler@cumberlandcountylibraries.org. Web Site: www.cumberlandcountylibraries.org/BOS. *Exec Dir,* Jeff Swope; Staff 1 (Non-MLS 1)
Library Holdings: Electronic Media & Resources 54; Bk Titles 150
Wireless access
Open Mon-Fri 10-9, Sat 10-5, Sun 1-5

CUMBERLAND COUNTY LIBRARY SYSTEM*, 1601 Ritner Hwy, 17013. SAN 314-3813. Tel: 717-240-6175. Web Site: cumberlandcountylibraries.org. *Exec Dir,* Carolyn Blatchley; E-mail: cblatchley@cumberlandcountylibraries.org; *Adult Serv & Outreach Coordr,* Carol Linderman-Justice; Tel: 717-240-7771, E-mail: clindermanjustice@cumberlandcountylibraries.org; *Coordr, Info Tech,* Barbara Leach; Tel: 717-240-7735, E-mail: bleach@cumberlandcountylibraries.org; *Tech Serv Coordr,* Sharon Scott; Tel: 717-240-7872, E-mail: sscott@cumberlandcountylibraries.org; Staff 5 (MLS 5)
Founded 1961. Pop 244,731
Library Holdings: Bk Titles 7,992; Per Subs 26
Automation Activity & Vendor Info: (Acquisitions) Horizon; (Cataloging) Horizon; (Circulation) Horizon; (OPAC) Horizon; (Serials) Horizon
Wireless access
Member Libraries: Amelia S Givin Free Library; Bosler Memorial Library; Cleve J Fredricksen Library; John Graham Public Library; Joseph T Simpson Public Library; New Cumberland Public Library; Shippensburg Public Library
Partic in Capital Area Library District
Open Mon-Fri 8-4:30

C DICKINSON COLLEGE*, Waidner-Spahr Library, 28 N College St, 17013-2311. (Mail add: PO Box 1773, 17013-2896), SAN 314-3821. Tel: 717-245-1397. FAX: 717-245-1439. E-mail: circ@dickinson.edu. Web Site: www.dickinson.edu/library. *Dir, Libr Serv,* Eleanor Mitchell; Tel: 717-245-1864, E-mail: mitchele@dickinson.edu; *Assoc Dir, Access Serv,* Maureen O'Brien Dermott; *Assoc Dir, Info Literacy & Res Serv,* Christine Bombaro; *Assoc Dir, Libr Res & Admin,* Theresa Arndt; E-mail: arndtt@dickinson.edu; *Spec Coll Librn,* Malinda Triller-Doran; *Tech Serv Librn,* Kirk Doran; *Col Archivist,* James Gerencser; Staff 27 (MLS 8, Non-MLS 19)
Founded 1784. Enrl 2,300; Fac 227; Highest Degree: Bachelor
Library Holdings: Bk Titles 388,000; Bk Vols 479,000; Per Subs 12,500
Special Collections: Carl Sandburg Coll, bks, letters, ms; Eli Slifer Coll, letters; Isaac Norris Coll; Jacobs Asian Coll; James Buchanan Coll, letters, ms; John Drinkwater Coll, bks, letters, ms; John F Kennedy Coll, artifacts, bks, per; Joseph Priestly Coll, bks, ms; Marianne Moore Coll, bks, letters; Martin Native American Coll; Moncure Conway Coll, letters. US Document Depository
Subject Interests: E European hist, Russian hist, Russian lit
Automation Activity & Vendor Info: (Acquisitions) SirsiDynix; (Cataloging) SirsiDynix; (Circulation) SirsiDynix; (Course Reserve) SirsiDynix; (ILL) OCLC; (OPAC) SirsiDynix; (Serials) SirsiDynix
Wireless access
Publications: John & Mary's Journal; Manuscript Collections of Dickinson College; Spahr Library Notes
Partic in Associated College Libraries of Central Pennsylvania; Central Pennsylvania Consortium; LYRASIS; Oberlin Group; Partnership for Academic Library Collaborative & Innovation; Westchester Academic Library Directors Organization
Open Mon-Thurs 8am-2am, Fri 8am-10pm, Sat 10-10, Sun 10am-2am
Friends of the Library Group

A UNITED STATES ARMY HERITAGE & EDUCATION CENTER*, 950 Soldiers Dr OR 122, Forbes Ave, 17013-5021. SAN 321-3684. Tel: 717-245-3972. Interlibrary Loan Service Tel: 717-245-3130. Reference Tel: 717-245-3949. FAX: 717-245-3067. E-mail: usarmy.carlisle.awc.mbx.ahec-ves@mail.mil. Web Site: ahec.armywarcollege.edu/. Staff 88 (MLS 13, Non-MLS 75)
Founded 1951. Enrl 1,200; Fac 120; Highest Degree: Master
Library Holdings: Bk Vols 480,000; Per Subs 1,000
Special Collections: Army Doctrinal Publications; Army Heritage Museum Artifacts; Army Unit Histories; Personal Manuscript Coll, paper & photog; Rare Books. Oral History
Subject Interests: Land warfare, US Army hist
Wireless access
Function: Art exhibits, Computers for patron use, Photocopying/Printing, Wheelchair accessible
Open Mon-Sat 10-5
Restriction: Circ limited, Closed stack, Open to pub for ref & circ; with some limitations, Restricted borrowing privileges

CARMICHAELS

P FLENNIKEN PUBLIC LIBRARY, 102 E George St, 15320-1202. SAN 314-3856. Tel: 724-966-5263. FAX: 724-966-9511. Web Site: www.flenniken.org. *Exec Dir,* Nicole Mesich Mitchell; E-mail: director@flenniken.org; Staff 3 (MLS 1, Non-MLS 2)
Founded 1946. Pop 12,356; Circ 40,000
Jan 2020-Dec 2020 Income $206,481, State $56,631, County $39,535, Locally Generated Income $30,350, Other $79,965. Mats Exp $25,076, Books $17,955, AV Mat $4,652, Electronic Ref Mat (Incl. Access Fees) $2,469. Sal $91,644 (Prof $36,500)
Library Holdings: Audiobooks 1,384; AV Mats 2,399; Braille Volumes 4; Bk Vols 32,273; Per Subs 37; Talking Bks 1,000
Subject Interests: Coal, Fiction, Local hist, Women
Automation Activity & Vendor Info: (Cataloging) Innovative Interfaces, Inc; (Circulation) Innovative Interfaces, Inc; (ILL) Innovative Interfaces, Inc; (OPAC) Innovative Interfaces, Inc; (Serials) Innovative Interfaces, Inc

Wireless access
Function: 24/7 Electronic res, 24/7 Online cat, 3D Printer, Activity rm, Adult bk club, Archival coll, Art programs, Audiobks on Playaways & MP3, AV serv, Bk club(s), Bks on CD, Butterfly Garden, Children's prog, Computer training, Computers for patron use, E-Readers, Electronic databases & coll, Free DVD rentals, Homework prog, ILL available, Internet access, Laminating, Magazines, Makerspace, Movies, Online cat, Outreach serv, Outside serv via phone, mail, e-mail & web, OverDrive digital audio bks, Photocopying/Printing, Preschool outreach, Preschool reading prog, Printer for laptops & handheld devices, Prog for adults, Prog for children & young adult, Ref serv available, Scanner, Senior computer classes, Senior outreach, STEM programs, Story hour, Summer & winter reading prog, Tax forms, Teen prog, Telephone ref, VHS videos, Wheelchair accessible
Mem of Greene County Library System
Open Mon & Wed 10-6, Tues & Thurs 10-8, Fri & Sat 10-5
Friends of the Library Group

CARNEGIE

P ANDREW CARNEGIE FREE LIBRARY & MUSIC HALL*, 300 Beechwood Ave, 15106-2699. SAN 314-3864. Tel: 412-276-3456. FAX: 412-276-9472. Web Site: www.carnegiecarnegie.org. *Exec Dir,* Maggie Forbes; *Libr Dir,* Mary Menk; Tel: 412-276-3456, Ext 12, E-mail: menkm2@einetwork.net
Founded 1899. Pop 7,972; Circ 69,208
Library Holdings: Bk Vols 22,871; Per Subs 36
Special Collections: Civil War Memorabilia Coll; Local Newspapers, back to Jan 7, 1872
Wireless access
Function: 24/7 Electronic res, 24/7 Online cat, Audiobks on Playaways & MP3, Bk club(s), Bks on CD, Children's prog, Computer training, Computers for patron use, Electronic databases & coll, Free DVD rentals, Holiday prog, ILL available, Internet access, Life-long learning prog for all ages, Magazines, Mango lang, Meeting rooms, Microfiche/film & reading machines, Movies, Museum passes, Music CDs, Online cat, Outreach serv, OverDrive digital audio bks, Photocopying/Printing, Preschool outreach, Preschool reading prog, Prog for adults, Prog for children & young adult, Ref & res, Scanner, Senior outreach, Serves people with intellectual disabilities, STEM programs, Story hour, Summer & winter reading prog, Summer reading prog, Tax forms, Teen prog, Telephone ref, Wheelchair accessible
Mem of Allegheny County Library Association (ACLA)
Open Mon 2-8, Tues-Thurs 10-7, Fri 10-5, Sat 9-5

CARROLLTOWN

P CARROLLTOWN PUBLIC LIBRARY*, 140 E Carroll St, 15722. (Mail add: PO Box 316, 15722-0316), SAN 314-3880. Tel: 814-344-6300. FAX: 814-344-6355. E-mail: carrolltown@cclsys.org. Web Site: www.cclsys.org/carrolltown. *Libr Dir,* Nancy Lechene
Pop 853; Circ 17,000
Library Holdings: Bk Vols 8,100; Per Subs 15
Automation Activity & Vendor Info: (Cataloging) Follett Software; (Circulation) Follett Software
Wireless access
Mem of Cambria County Library System & District Center
Open Tues-Thurs (Summer) 8-4, Fri 8-3, Sat 8-Noon; Tues (Winter) 9:30-5, Wed 9-4:30, Thurs 9-4, Fri 9-3, Sat 8-3

CASTLE SHANNON

P COMMUNITY LIBRARY OF CASTLE SHANNON*, 3677 Myrtle Ave, 15234-2198. SAN 314-3899. Tel: 412-563-4552. FAX: 412-563-8228. Web Site: castleshannonlibrary.org. *Dir,* Heather Myrah; E-mail: myrahh@einetwork.net; Staff 13 (MLS 4, Non-MLS 9)
Founded 1953. Pop 8,556; Circ 76,674
Library Holdings: AV Mats 5,792; CDs 68; Large Print Bks 342; Bk Vols 42,733; Per Subs 221; Talking Bks 2,311; Videos 3,481
Automation Activity & Vendor Info: (Cataloging) Innovative Interfaces, Inc; (Circulation) Innovative Interfaces, Inc; (OPAC) Innovative Interfaces, Inc
Mem of Allegheny County Library Association (ACLA)
Open Mon & Wed 1-9, Tues & Thurs 10-9, Fri 1-5, Sat 10-5, Sun (Sept-May) 1-5
Friends of the Library Group

CATASAUQUA

P PUBLIC LIBRARY OF CATASAUQUA, Third & Bridge Sts, 18032-2510. (Mail add: PO Box 127, 18032-0127), SAN 314-3902. Tel: 610-264-4151. FAX: 610-264-4593. E-mail: catasauquapl@cliu.org. Web Site: www.catasauquapl.org. *Dir,* Kathleen Morris; Staff 4 (MLS 1, Non-MLS 3)
Founded 1923. Pop 10,800; Circ 37,000
Library Holdings: AV Mats 840; Bk Titles 18,304; Per Subs 49; Videos 410
Subject Interests: Local hist
Wireless access
Partic in Lehigh Carbon Library Cooperative
Open Mon, Wed & Thurs 2-7:30, Tues 10-6, Sat 10-2
Friends of the Library Group

CENTER VALLEY

C DESALES UNIVERSITY*, Trexler Library, 2755 Station Ave, 18034. SAN 314-3910. Tel: 610-282-1100, Ext 1266. FAX: 610-282-2342. E-mail: reference@desales.edu. Web Site: www.desales.edu/home/academics/trexler-library. *Libr Dir,* Debbie Malone; Tel: 610-282-1100, Ext 1253, E-mail: debbie.malone@desales.edu; *Syst Librn,* Amy Manns; E-mail: amy.manns@desales.edu; *Tech Serv Librn,* Scott Parkinson; E-mail: scott.parkinson@desales.edu; *Circ Supvr,* Gloria Biser; E-mail: gloria.biser@desales.edu; *Pub Serv,* Michele Mrazik; E-mail: michele.mrazik@desales.edu; *Pub Serv,* Loretta Ulincy; E-mail: loretta.ulincy@desales.edu; Staff 7 (MLS 6, Non-MLS 1)
Founded 1965. Enrl 3,700; Fac 102; Highest Degree: Doctorate
Library Holdings: DVDs 1,377; e-books 130,000; e-journals 8,000; Music Scores 587; Bk Titles 115,676; Bk Vols 147,270; Per Subs 272; Videos 11,530
Special Collections: American Theatre (John Y Kohl Coll), bks & pamphlets; St Francis De Sales Coll; St Thomas More Coll; Theatre Criticism (Walter Kerr Coll)
Subject Interests: Nursing, Philos, Roman Catholic relig
Automation Activity & Vendor Info: (Acquisitions) Innovative Interfaces, Inc; (Cataloging) Innovative Interfaces, Inc; (Circulation) Innovative Interfaces, Inc; (Media Booking) Innovative Interfaces, Inc; (OPAC) Innovative Interfaces, Inc; (Serials) Innovative Interfaces, Inc
Wireless access
Publications: Newsletter
Partic in Lehigh Valley Association of Independent Colleges; LYRASIS; OCLC Online Computer Library Center, Inc; Partnership for Academic Library Collaborative & Innovation
Open Mon-Thurs 7:30am-1am, Fri 7:30am-9pm, Sat 9-5, Sun Noon-1am
Restriction: Access for corporate affiliates

C PENNSYLVANIA STATE LEHIGH VALLEY LIBRARY, 2809 E Saucon Valley Rd, 18034-8447. SAN 314-5174. Tel: 610-285-5027. FAX: 610-285-5158. E-mail: ul-lehigh-val@list.psu.edu. Web Site: libraries.psu.edu/lehighvalley. *Head Librn,* Jennifer Jarson; Tel: 610-285-5119, E-mail: jmj12@psu.edu; *Ref & Instruction Librn,* Elizabeth Nelson; Tel: 610-285-5028, E-mail: ezn80@psu.edu; *Info Res & Serv Support Spec,* Kathleen Romig; Tel: 610-285-5151, E-mail: kjr3@psu.edu; *Info Res & Serv Support Spec,* Susan Stumpf; Tel: 610-285-5027, E-mail: sms490@psu.edu; Staff 3 (MLS 1, Non-MLS 2)
Founded 1912. Enrl 624; Fac 20
Library Holdings: Audiobooks 175,511; e-books 2,669,546; Microforms 770,130; Music Scores 98,484; Bk Titles 2,838,024; Per Subs 172; Videos 43,877
Automation Activity & Vendor Info: (Circulation) SirsiDynix; (OPAC) SirsiDynix
Wireless access
Partic in OCLC Online Computer Library Center, Inc; Research Libraries Information Network
Open Mon-Thurs 8-8, Fri 8-4, Sat 10-3 (Winter); Mon-Fri 10-2 (Summer)

P SOUTHERN LEHIGH PUBLIC LIBRARY*, 3200 Preston Lane, 18034. SAN 314-4283. Tel: 610-282-8825. FAX: 610-282-8828. E-mail: staff@solehipl.org. Web Site: www.solehipl.org. *Libr Dir,* Lynnette Saeger
Founded 1963
Automation Activity & Vendor Info: (Cataloging) TLC (The Library Corporation); (Circulation) TLC (The Library Corporation); (OPAC) TLC (The Library Corporation); (Serials) TLC (The Library Corporation)
Wireless access
Function: 24/7 Electronic res, 24/7 Online cat, Activity rm, Adult bk club
Partic in Lehigh Carbon Library Cooperative
Open Mon, Tues & Thurs 10-9, Wed, Fri & Sat 10-5
Friends of the Library Group

CHADDS FORD

S BRANDYWINE CONSERVANCY, INC*, Brandywine River Museum Library, One Hoffman's Mill Rd, 19317. (Mail add: PO Box 141, 19317-0141), SAN 314-3929. Tel: 610-388-2700. FAX: 610-388-1197. E-mail: museum@brandywine.org. Web Site: www.brandywine.org. *Curator,* Audrey Lewis
Founded 1971
Library Holdings: Bk Titles 3,622; Bk Vols 5,171; Per Subs 22
Special Collections: American Illustration; N C Wyeth Coll, prints, posters, proofs, calendars; Stanley Arthurs (Blanche Swayne Coll), scrapbks

Subject Interests: Am art, Andrew Wyeth, Howard Pyle, James Wyeth, Local artists, N C Wyeth
Restriction: Open by appt only, Open to pub for ref only

CHAMBERSBURG

P COYLE FREE LIBRARY, 102 N Main St, 17201. SAN 314-3945. Tel: 717-263-1054. Web Site: fclspa.org/locations/coyle-free-library. *Co-Dir,* Sarah Applegate; E-mail: sapplegate@fclspa.org; *Co-Dir,* Denice Bigham; E-mail: dbigham@fclspa.org
Founded 1924. Pop 26,811; Circ 169,290
Library Holdings: AV Mats 4,161; Large Print Bks 2,701; Bk Titles 70,000; Per Subs 175; Talking Bks 2,099
Special Collections: State Document Depository
Subject Interests: Genealogy, Local hist, Spanish
Automation Activity & Vendor Info: (Acquisitions) Evolve; (Cataloging) Evolve; (Circulation) Evolve; (OPAC) Evolve; (Serials) Evolve
Wireless access
Mem of Franklin County Library System
Special Services for the Blind - Talking bks
Open Mon, Wed & Fri 9-6, Tues & Thurs 12-8, Sat 9-2
Friends of the Library Group

S FRANKLIN COUNTY HISTORICAL SOCIETY - KITTOCHTINNY LIBRARY*, 175 E King St, 17201. SAN 374-9231. Tel: 717-264-1667. FAX: 717-264-1451. E-mail: history@pa.net. Web Site: www.franklinhistorical.org. *Exec Dir,* Ann Hull; Staff 1 (Non-MLS 1)
Library Holdings: Bk Titles 26,810; Bk Vols 28,000; Per Subs 21
Subject Interests: Genealogy, Local hist
Open Tues (May-Oct) 10-8, Wed-Sat 10-4; Tues (Nov-April) 5-8, Thurs-Sat 10-4
Restriction: Free to mem

GL FRANKLIN COUNTY LAW LIBRARY ASSOCIATION*, Franklin County Law Library, 100 Lincoln Way E, Ste E, 17201. SAN 314-3953. Tel: 717-267-2071. FAX: 717-264-1992. E-mail: lawlibrary@franklinbar.org. Web Site: www.franklinbar.org. *Exec Dir,* Amelia Ambrose
Library Holdings: Bk Vols 1,000
Open Mon-Fri 8:30-4:30

P FRANKLIN COUNTY LIBRARY SYSTEM*, 101 Ragged Edge Rd S, 17202. SAN 314-3937. Tel: 717-709-0282. FAX: 717-263-2248. E-mail: library@fclspa.org. Web Site: www.fclspa.org. *Exec Dir,* Bernice Crouse; E-mail: bdcrouse@fclspa.org; *Ref (Info Servs),* Moriah Miller; Staff 13 (MLS 8, Non-MLS 5)
Founded 1998. Pop 121,825; Circ 492,052
Library Holdings: AV Mats 13,952; CDs 302; Bk Titles 133,842; Bk Vols 267,684; Per Subs 360; Videos 791
Special Collections: Family Place; Spanish Coll
Subject Interests: Genealogy, Local hist
Automation Activity & Vendor Info: (Cataloging) OCLC; (Circulation) AmLib Library Management System; (ILL) OCLC; (OPAC) AmLib Library Management System
Wireless access
Member Libraries: Alexander Hamilton Memorial Free Library; Blue Ridge Summit Free Library; Coyle Free Library; Fort Loudon Community Library; Grove Family Library; Lilian S Besore Memorial Library; Saint Thomas Library
Partic in Health Sciences Libraries Consortium; OCLC Online Computer Library Center, Inc
Special Services for the Blind - Assistive/Adapted tech devices, equip & products; Descriptive video serv (DVS)
Open Mon-Fri 8:30-3:30
Bookmobiles: 1. Librn, Laura Bailie. Bk titles 6,582

P GROVE FAMILY LIBRARY, 101 Ragged Edge Rd S, 17202. SAN 314-3961. Tel: 717-264-9663. FAX: 717-264-6055. *Dir,* Joan Peiffer; E-mail: jpeiffer@fclspa.org; Staff 3 (MLS 1, Non-MLS 2)
Founded 1948. Pop 25,384
Library Holdings: Bk Vols 61,759
Special Collections: Family Place
Subject Interests: Local hist, Needlework
Automation Activity & Vendor Info: (Circulation) Evolve; (OPAC) Evolve
Wireless access
Function: 24/7 Electronic res, 24/7 Online cat, Activity rm, Adult bk club, Adult literacy prog, Art exhibits, Art programs, Bi-weekly Writer's Group, Bk club(s), Bk reviews (Group), Bks on CD, Children's prog, Computer training, Computers for patron use, E-Reserves, Electronic databases & coll, Family literacy, Free DVD rentals, Govt ref serv, Health sci info serv, Home delivery & serv to seniorr ctr & nursing homes, ILL available, Instruction & testing, Internet access, Large print keyboards, Learning ctr, Life-long learning prog for all ages, Literacy & newcomer serv, Magazines, Mail & tel request accepted, Mail loans to mem, Mango lang, Meeting rooms, Movies, Music CDs, Online cat, Online info literacy tutorials on the web & in blackboard, Online ref, Orientations, Outreach serv, OverDrive digital audio bks, Photocopying/Printing, Preschool outreach, Preschool reading prog, Printer for laptops & handheld devices, Prof lending libr, Prog for adults, Prog for children & young adult, Ref & res, Ref serv available, Res assist avail, Scanner, Senior computer classes, Senior outreach, Serves people with intellectual disabilities, Spanish lang bks, Story hour, Study rm, Summer & winter reading prog, Summer reading prog, Tax forms, Teen prog, Telephone ref, Wheelchair accessible, Winter reading prog, Workshops, Writing prog
Mem of Franklin County Library System
Partic in Health Sciences Libraries Consortium
Open Mon & Thurs 9-4, Tues 12-8, Fri & Sat 9-1
Friends of the Library Group

C WILSON COLLEGE*, John Stewart Memorial Library, 1015 Philadelphia Ave, 17201-1285. SAN 314-397X. Tel: 717-264-4141. Circulation Tel: 717-262-2008. Web Site: library.wilson.edu. *Assoc VPres, Libr Info Tech,* Jose Dieudonne; E-mail: jose.dieudonne@wilson.edu; *Instrul Design Librn, Tech Librn,* James D'Annibale; E-mail: james.dannibale@wilson.edu; *Ref & Instruction Librn,* Kelly Spiese; E-mail: kspiese@wilson.edu; *Coll Mgt,* Shanna Hollich; E-mail: shanna.hollich@wilson.edu; *Circ Tech,* Maleah Friedline; E-mail: maleah.friedline@wilson.edu; Staff 3 (MLS 3)
Founded 1869. Enrl 776; Fac 77; Highest Degree: Master
Library Holdings: Bk Vols 175,372; Per Subs 312
Subject Interests: Art, Local hist, Veterinary med, Women's studies
Automation Activity & Vendor Info: (Acquisitions) LibLime; (Cataloging) LibLime; (Circulation) LibLime; (Course Reserve) LibLime; (ILL) OCLC; (OPAC) LibLime; (Serials) LibLime
Wireless access
Partic in Associated College Libraries of Central Pennsylvania; LYRASIS; OCLC Online Computer Library Center, Inc
Open Mon-Thurs 7:45am-11pm, Fri 7:45-5, Sat 9-5, Sun 1-11

CHARLEROI

P CHARLEROI AREA PUBLIC LIBRARY, 638 Fallowfield Ave, 15022-1996. SAN 314-3988. Tel: 724-483-8282. FAX: 724-483-3478. E-mail: charlibrary@comcast.net. Web Site: www.washlibs.org/tener. *Dir,* Antoinette Zbyl
Founded 1941. Pop 13,175; Circ 16,000
Library Holdings: DVDs 525; Bk Vols 23,746; Per Subs 35; Talking Bks 1,100; Videos 750
Function: Home delivery & serv to seniorr ctr & nursing homes, Homebound delivery serv, ILL available, Prog for adults, Prog for children & young adult, Summer reading prog, VHS videos
Mem of Washington County Library System
Open Mon-Wed 10:30-4:30, Thurs 2:30-6:30, Fri 10:30-4
Friends of the Library Group

CHESTER

P J LEWIS CROZER LIBRARY, 620 Engle St, 19013-2199. SAN 314-4011. Tel: 610-494-3454. FAX: 610-494-8954. E-mail: crozerlibrary@delcolibraries.org. Web Site: www.crozerlibrary.org. *Dir,* Mark Winston; E-mail: crdirector@delcolibraries.org; *Asst Dir,* Joann Simone; Staff 2 (MLS 2)
Founded 1894. Pop 36,854
Library Holdings: AV Mats 1,500; Large Print Bks 175; Bk Titles 18,100; Bk Vols 52,000; Per Subs 90; Talking Bks 250
Subject Interests: African-Am hist, Chester City hist, Del County hist
Automation Activity & Vendor Info: (Cataloging) Innovative Interfaces, Inc; (Circulation) Innovative Interfaces, Inc; (ILL) Innovative Interfaces, Inc
Mem of Delaware County Libraries
Open Tues-Thurs 9-8, Fri & Sat 9-4, Sat (Summer) 9-1
Friends of the Library Group

S DELAWARE COUNTY HISTORICAL SOCIETY*, Research Library, Museum & Archives, 408 Avenue of the States, 19013. SAN 314-402X. Tel: 610-872-0502. Administration Tel: 610-359-0832. FAX: 610-872-0503. Administration FAX: 610-359-0839. Web Site: www.padelcohistory.org. *Asst Curator, Libr Coord,* Margaret F Johnson; E-mail: mfdjohnson@gmail.com; Staff 1 (Non-MLS 1)
Founded 1895
Library Holdings: Bk Titles 7,280; Bk Vols 8,100; Per Subs 19
Special Collections: Atlases & Maps; Borough Township Files, articles, booklets, news clippings, photos; Chester & Upland Borough Birth Records; Chester County Tax Records, 1715-1800, microfilm; Chester F Baker Notebooks; Church Records; Genealogy Coll, bks, ms; Local Historical Places & People (Dr Anna Broomall Notebook Coll), info, news clippings, photos; New Jersey Archives; Newspaper Coll, microfilm; Pennsylvania Archives; Pennsylvania Cemetery Records, Obituaries & Funeral Records; Pennsylvania Census Information; Pennsylvania Colonial

Records; Pennsylvania Magazine of History & Biography, 1877 to date; Photograph Coll. Oral History
Subject Interests: Genealogy, Hist of Delaware county, Maps
Wireless access
Function: Res libr
Publications: The Bulletin (Newsletter)
Open Wed & Fri 9-4, Thurs 1-6:30, Sat 9-2

C WIDENER UNIVERSITY*, Wolfgram Memorial Library, One University Pl, 19013. SAN 358-3503. Tel: 610-499-4067. Interlibrary Loan Service Tel: 610-499-4070. FAX: 610-499-4588. Web Site: www.widener.edu/about/campus-community-resources/wolfgram-memorial-library. *Libr Dir,* Deb Morley; Tel: 610-499-4087, E-mail: dgmorley@widener.edu; *Res & Instruction Librn,* Susan Tsiouris; Tel: 610-499-4069, E-mail: sctsiouris@widener.edu; *Head, Archives,* Jill Borin; E-mail: jmborin@widener.edu; *Head, Res & Instrul Serv,* Molly Wolf; Tel: 610-499-4075, E-mail: mmwolf@widener.edu; Staff 12 (MLS 12)
Founded 1821. Enrl 5,042; Fac 273; Highest Degree: Doctorate
Library Holdings: Bk Titles 157,631; Bk Vols 403,889; Per Subs 2,256
Special Collections: Lindsay Law; Wolfgram Coll (English & American Literature)
Subject Interests: Bus mgt, Clinical psychol, Educ, Engr, Hotel mgt, Humanities, Nursing, Phys therapy, Soc work
Wireless access
Publications: AV Catalog; Faculty Handbook; User Guides; WolfGRAM (Newsletter)
Partic in Interlibrary Delivery Service of Pennsylvania; LYRASIS; NELLCO Law Library Consortium, Inc.; OCLC Online Computer Library Center, Inc; Partnership for Academic Library Collaborative & Innovation; Tri-State College Library Cooperative
Open Mon-Thurs (Winter) 7:30am-11:30pm, Fri 7:30am-8pm, Sat 9-5, Sun Noon-11:30; Mon-Thurs (Summer) 8-8, Fri 9-5, Sat 11-3, Sun 1-5

CHESTER SPRINGS

P CHESTER SPRINGS LIBRARY*, 1709 Art School Rd, 19425-1402. SAN 320-8508. Tel: 610-827-9212. FAX: 610-827-1148. E-mail: cslibrary@ccls.org. Web Site: chesterspringslibrary.org. *Dir,* Nancy Niggel; E-mail: nniggel@ccls.org; Staff 6 (MLS 1, Non-MLS 5)
Founded 1978. Pop 4,024; Circ 31,931
Library Holdings: Audiobooks 1,314; DVDs 1,745; Bk Vols 14,090; Per Subs 26
Subject Interests: Local hist
Automation Activity & Vendor Info: (Acquisitions) Innovative Interfaces, Inc; (Cataloging) Innovative Interfaces, Inc; (Circulation) Innovative Interfaces, Inc; (OPAC) Innovative Interfaces, Inc; (Serials) Innovative Interfaces, Inc
Wireless access
Function: 24/7 Electronic res, 24/7 Online cat, Art programs, Bks on CD, Children's prog, Computers for patron use, Electronic databases & coll, ILL available, Internet access, Magazines, Mango lang, Movies, Music CDs, Online cat, OverDrive digital audio bks, Photocopying/Printing, Preschool outreach, Prog for adults, Prog for children & young adult, Ref serv available, Scanner, STEM programs, Summer reading prog, Teen prog, VHS videos, Wheelchair accessible
Mem of Chester County Library System
Open Mon-Fri 10-6, Sat 10-4, Sun 12-4
Friends of the Library Group

CHEYNEY

C CHEYNEY UNIVERSITY*, Leslie Pinckney Hill Library, 1837 University Circle, 19319. (Mail add: PO Box 200, 19319-0200), SAN 314-4062. Tel: 610-399-2203. FAX: 610-399-2491. Web Site: cheyney.edu/academics/library. *Dir,* Position Currently Open; *Univ Archivist,* F Keith Bingham; *Info Syst Librn,* Beth Jo Mullaney, PhD; E-mail: bmullaney@cheyney.edu; *Circ,* Mary Hutchman; Tel: 610-399-2245, E-mail: mhutchman@cheyney.edu; *Govt Doc, Pub Serv,* Abdul Aden; E-mail: aaden@cheyney.edu; *Tech Serv,* Lily Qi; E-mail: lqi@cheyney.edu; Staff 5 (MLS 4, Non-MLS 1)
Founded 1853. Enrl 746; Fac 107; Highest Degree: Master
Library Holdings: Bk Titles 198,641; Bk Vols 228,421; Per Subs 1,126; Videos 1,279
Special Collections: Afro-American studies; Ethnic Coll; University Archives. State Document Depository; US Document Depository
Automation Activity & Vendor Info: (Cataloging) Ex Libris Group; (Circulation) Ex Libris Group; (ILL) OCLC; (OPAC) Ex Libris Group
Wireless access
Publications: Annual Report; Newsletter; Student & Faculty Handbooks
Partic in Keystone Library Network; OCLC Online Computer Library Center, Inc
Open Mon-Fri 8:30-5

CHRISTIANA

P MOORES MEMORIAL LIBRARY*, Nine W Slokom Ave, 17509-1202. SAN 314-4070. Tel: 610-593-6683. E-mail: chrlib@christianalibrary.org. Web Site: www.christianalibrary.org. *Libr Dir,* Trish Vandenbosch; Staff 5 (Non-MLS 5)
Founded 1881. Pop 4,563; Circ 60,000
Library Holdings: AV Mats 400; Bks on Deafness & Sign Lang 25; DVDs 800; High Interest/Low Vocabulary Bk Vols 50; Large Print Bks 200; Bk Titles 13,000; Per Subs 32; Talking Bks 50; Videos 150
Special Collections: Christiana Riot of 1851 - Prelude to Civil War. State Document Depository
Subject Interests: Local hist
Wireless access
Function: 24/7 Online cat, Activity rm, Adult bk club, Archival coll, Audiobks on Playaways & MP3, Audiobks via web, Bks on CD, Children's prog, Electronic databases & coll, Homework prog, ILL available, Internet access, Learning ctr, Magazines, Meeting rooms, Museum passes, Music CDs, Online cat, Online ref, OverDrive digital audio bks, Photocopying/Printing, Prog for adults, Prog for children & young adult, Scanner, Spoken cassettes & CDs, Story hour, Summer reading prog, Tax forms
Mem of Library System of Lancaster County
Open Mon, Wed & Fri 10-4, Tues & Thurs 1-7, Sat 10-5
Friends of the Library Group

CLAIRTON

P CLAIRTON PUBLIC LIBRARY, 616 Miller Ave, 15025-1497. SAN 358-3538. Tel: 412-233-7966. FAX: 412-233-2536. Web Site: www.clairtonlibrary.org. *Dir,* Emma J Anderson; E-mail: andersone@einetwork.net; Staff 1 (MLS 1)
Founded 1920. Pop 6,700; Circ 35,000
Library Holdings: Bk Vols 35,600; Per Subs 65
Automation Activity & Vendor Info: (Cataloging) Innovative Interfaces, Inc; (Circulation) Innovative Interfaces, Inc; (OPAC) Innovative Interfaces, Inc
Wireless access
Mem of Allegheny County Library Association (ACLA)
Open Mon-Sat 9-4
Friends of the Library Group

CLARION

S CLARION COUNTY HISTORICAL SOCIETY*, Fulton Library & Archives, 18 Grant St, 16214. (Mail add: 17 S Fifth Ave, 16214), SAN 326-2871. Tel: 814-226-4450. FAX: 814-226-7106. E-mail: clarionhistory@comcast.net. Web Site: www.clarioncountyhistoricalsociety.org. *Exec Dir,* Mary Lea Lucas. Subject Specialists: *Genealogy, Local hist,* Mary Lea Lucas; Staff 1 (Non-MLS 1)
Founded 1955
Library Holdings: Bk Titles 2,500; Per Subs 20
Special Collections: Birth & Delayed Birth Certificates; Bound Local Newspaper Books, 1894-1970; Civil War Regimentals; Clarion County Documents & Photographs; County Cemetery Records; Death Certificates; Family Histories; Genealogy, bks & ms; Native American Coll; Obituaries; Western Pennsylvania & County History. Oral History
Subject Interests: County hist, Genealogy
Function: Archival coll, Genealogy discussion group, Photocopying/Printing, Wheelchair accessible, Workshops
Publications: Iron County Chronicle (Newsletter)
Partic in OCLC via Clarion District Libr Asn
Open Tues-Thurs 10-4
Restriction: Not a lending libr, Open evenings by appt

P CLARION FREE LIBRARY, 644 Main St, 16214. SAN 314-4119. Tel: 814-226-7172. FAX: 814-226-6750. E-mail: director@clarionfreelibrary.org. Web Site: clarionfreelibrary.org. *Libr Dir,* Ian Snyder; E-mail: isnyder@clarionfreelibrary.org; *Ch Serv,* Jean Smith; E-mail: jsmith@clarionfreelibrary.org; *ILL,* Vickie Hughes; E-mail: vhughes@clarionfreelibrary.org; Staff 6 (MLS 1, Non-MLS 5)
Founded 1914. Pop 21,254; Circ 121,215
Library Holdings: AV Mats 2,160; Bks on Deafness & Sign Lang 25; High Interest/Low Vocabulary Bk Vols 400; Large Print Bks 1,486; Bk Titles 45,453; Bk Vols 47,753; Per Subs 76; Talking Bks 930
Special Collections: Census 1790 to 1920, microfiche; Clarion News & Leader-Vindicator, 1868-present, newsp on micro
Subject Interests: Local hist
Automation Activity & Vendor Info: (Cataloging) TLC (The Library Corporation); (Circulation) TLC (The Library Corporation); (OPAC) TLC (The Library Corporation)
Wireless access
Function: AV serv, ILL available, Photocopying/Printing, Prof lending libr, Prog for children & young adult, Summer reading prog, Telephone ref, Wheelchair accessible

Mem of Oil Creek District Library Center
Open Mon-Thurs 9-8, Fri 9-5, Sat 8:30-3:30
Friends of the Library Group

C CLARION UNIVERSITY OF PENNSYLVANIA*, Rena M Carlson Library, 840 Wood St, 16214. SAN 358-3597. Tel: 814-393-2343. Circulation Tel: 814-393-2301. Interlibrary Loan Service Tel: 814-393-2481. Reference Tel: 814-393-1841. Interlibrary Loan Service FAX: 814-393-1862. E-mail: libsupport@clarion.edu. Web Site: www.clarion.edu/libraries. *Dean,* Dr Terry S Latour; Tel: 814-393-1931, E-mail: tlatour@clarion.edu; *Database Mgt/Bibliog Access & Control Librn,* Pat Johner; Tel: 814-393-2749, E-mail: pjohner@clarion.edu; *Ref Librn/Info Literacy Coordr,* Mary Buchanan; Tel: 814-393-1811, E-mail: mbuchanan@clarion.edu; *Archivist, Ref Librn,* Corene Glotfelty; Tel: 814-393-1805, E-mail: cglotfelty@clarion.edu; *Coll Develop Coordr, Ref Librn,* Basil D Martin; Tel: 814-393-2303, E-mail: bmartin@clarion.edu; *Ser Librn,* Rachel Newbury; Tel: 814-393-2746, E-mail: tnewbury@clarion.edu; *Virtual Learning & Outreach Librn,* Tonya Otto; Tel: 814-393-2329, E-mail: totto@clarion.edu; *Circ, Libr Tech, Reserves,* Melissa Pierce; Tel: 814-393-2304, E-mail: mpierce@clarion.edu; *ILL, Libr Tech,* Ginger McGiffin; E-mail: gmcgiffin@clarion.edu; Staff 17 (MLS 7, Non-MLS 10)
Founded 1867. Enrl 4,703; Highest Degree: Master
Library Holdings: AV Mats 7,012; e-books 348,037; e-journals 57,405; Electronic Media & Resources 64,542; Microforms 1,504,931; Bk Titles 291,873; Bk Vols 444,818
Special Collections: Harvey Center for Study of Oil Heritage. State Document Depository
Subject Interests: British Commonwealth
Automation Activity & Vendor Info: (Acquisitions) Ex Libris Group; (Cataloging) Ex Libris Group; (Circulation) Ex Libris Group; (Discovery) EBSCO Discovery Service; (ILL) OCLC ILLiad; (OPAC) Ex Libris Group; (Serials) Ex Libris Group
Wireless access
Function: Archival coll, ILL available, Photocopying/Printing
Publications: The United Kingdom of Great Britain & Ireland: An Annotated Bibliography of Documentary Sources in Carlson Library
Partic in Interlibrary Delivery Service of Pennsylvania; Keystone Library Network; LYRASIS; Partnership for Academic Library Collaborative & Innovation
Special Services for the Blind - Computer with voice synthesizer for visually impaired persons; Magnifiers
Open Mon-Thurs 7:45am-Midnight, Fri 7:45-5, Sat 9-5, Sun 1-Midnight

CLARKS SUMMIT

P ABINGTON COMMUNITY LIBRARY, 1200 W Grove St, 18411-9501. SAN 314-4127. Tel: 570-587-3440. Web Site: lclshome.org/b/abington-community-library. *Exec Dir,* Sandy Longo; E-mail: slongo@albright.org; Staff 2 (MLS 2)
Founded 1960. Pop 30,686; Circ 260,019
Library Holdings: Bk Vols 70,000; Per Subs 100
Special Collections: Classical Sheet Music Coll. Oral History
Automation Activity & Vendor Info: (Cataloging) Evergreen; (Circulation) Evergreen; (ILL) OCLC; (OPAC) Evergreen
Wireless access
Function: 24/7 Electronic res, 24/7 Online cat, 3D Printer, Activity rm, Adult bk club, Adult literacy prog, After school storytime, Art exhibits, Art programs, Audio & video playback equip for onsite use, Audiobks on Playaways & MP3, Audiobks via web, Bk club(s), Bks on CD, Children's prog, Computer training, Computers for patron use, Digital talking bks, Electronic databases & coll, Family literacy, For res purposes, Free DVD rentals, Health sci info serv, Holiday prog, ILL available, Internet access, Life-long learning prog for all ages, Magazines, Movies, Music CDs, Online cat, Online ref, Outreach serv, OverDrive digital audio bks, Photocopying/Printing, Preschool outreach, Preschool reading prog, Printer for laptops & handheld devices, Prof lending libr, Prog for adults, Prog for children & young adult, Ref & res, Ref serv available, Res assist avail, Senior computer classes, STEM programs, Story hour, Study rm, Summer & winter reading prog, Summer reading prog, Tax forms, Teen prog, Telephone ref, Visual arts prog, Wheelchair accessible, Winter reading prog, Workshops, Writing prog
Mem of Lackawanna County Library System
Friends of the Library Group

CR CLARKS SUMMIT UNIVERSITY*, Murphy Memorial Library, 538 Venard Rd, 18411-1250. SAN 358-3627. Tel: 570-585-9285. E-mail: library@clarkssummitu.edu. Web Site: www.clarkssummitu.edu/library. *Libr Dir,* Sharon Gardoski; Staff 1 (MLS 1)
Founded 1932. Enrl 750; Highest Degree: Doctorate
Library Holdings: AV Mats 14,000; e-journals 10,777; Per Subs 90
Subject Interests: Biblical studies, Christian educ, Church hist, Church ministries, Church music, Counseling, Theol
Automation Activity & Vendor Info: (Cataloging) OCLC; (Circulation) OCLC; (OPAC) OCLC
Wireless access
Open Mon-Thurs 8am-10pm, Fri 8-5, Sat & Sun 2-10

CLAYSBURG

P CLAYSBURG AREA PUBLIC LIBRARY, 957 Bedford St, 16625. (Mail add: PO Box 189, 16625-0189), SAN 314-4135. Tel: 814-239-2782. FAX: 814-239-8647. E-mail: info@claysburglibrary.org. Web Site: claysburglibrary.org. *Libr Dir,* Jane Knisely; E-mail: cklibraryknisely@gmail.com; *Asst Librn,* Pam Musselman; Staff 2 (Non-MLS 2)
Founded 1965. Pop 6,950; Circ 21,000
Library Holdings: Bks on Deafness & Sign Lang 12; Braille Volumes 1; CDs 210; DVDs 400; Large Print Bks 280; Bk Titles 23,142; Bk Vols 25,000; Per Subs 69; Talking Bks 448; Videos 290
Wireless access
Mem of Blair County Library System
Open Mon & Thurs 9-7, Tues & Wed 9-5, Sat 9-1
Friends of the Library Group

CLEARFIELD

L CLEARFIELD COUNTY LAW LIBRARY*, Courthouse, 2nd Flr, Ste 228, 230 E Market St, 16830. SAN 327-1102. Tel: 814-765-2641, Ext 2096. FAX: 814-765-7649. *Librn,* Carol Mease; Staff 1 (Non-MLS 1)
Library Holdings: Bk Titles 11,421; Bk Vols 13,559; Per Subs 71
Subject Interests: Penn law
Open Mon-Fri 8:30-4
Friends of the Library Group

P JOSEPH & ELIZABETH SHAW PUBLIC LIBRARY*, One S Front St, 16830. SAN 314-4143. Tel: 814-765-3271. FAX: 814-765-6316. Web Site: www.shawlibrary.org. *Dir,* Jayme Stonbraker; E-mail: jstonbraker@shawlibrary.org; Staff 8 (MLS 2, Non-MLS 6)
Founded 1940. Pop 16,930; Circ 41,784
Library Holdings: Audiobooks 299; DVDs 392; Bk Titles 31,600; Per Subs 30
Special Collections: Art (Thomas Murray Chase Coll); Pennsylvania & Clearfield County PA History Coll
Subject Interests: Genealogy, Local hist
Automation Activity & Vendor Info: (Cataloging) Evergreen; (Circulation) Evergreen; (OPAC) Evergreen
Wireless access
Function: 24/7 Electronic res, 24/7 Online cat, Adult bk club, Art exhibits, Bks on CD, Chess club, Children's prog, Electronic databases & coll, Holiday prog, ILL available, Internet access, Magazines, Meeting rooms, Movies, Online cat, OverDrive digital audio bks, Photocopying/Printing, Prog for adults, Prog for children & young adult, Scanner, STEM programs, Story hour, Summer reading prog, Tax forms, Teen prog, Wheelchair accessible
Partic in Cent Pa District
Open Mon, Wed & Sat 10-5, Tues & Thurs 10-9, Fri 12-5
Friends of the Library Group

COALPORT

P GLENDALE AREA PUBLIC LIBRARY INC*, Community Bldg, 961 Forest St, 16627. Tel: 814-672-4378. E-mail: gapli814@gmail.com. *Dir,* Nancy Washell; Fax: 814-672-5973; Staff 1 (Non-MLS 1)
Founded 1979
Library Holdings: Bk Titles 10,640; Bk Vols 11,031; Per Subs 12
Subject Interests: Local hist
Wireless access
Open Mon-Wed 10-4, Thurs 12-8, Sun 1-4
Friends of the Library Group

COATESVILLE

P COATESVILLE AREA PUBLIC LIBRARY, 501 E Lincoln Hwy, 19320-3413. SAN 314-4151. Tel: 610-384-4115. FAX: 610-384-7551. Web Site: coatesvilleareapubliclibrary.org. *Dir,* Penny Kearns Williams; E-mail: pwilliams@ccls.org; Staff 1 (MLS 1)
Founded 1936. Pop 53,400
Special Collections: Local Oral History
Subject Interests: Local hist
Automation Activity & Vendor Info: (Cataloging) Innovative Interfaces, Inc; (Circulation) Innovative Interfaces, Inc; (ILL) Innovative Interfaces, Inc; (OPAC) Innovative Interfaces, Inc
Wireless access
Function: 24/7 Electronic res, 24/7 Online cat, Activity rm, Adult bk club, Bilingual assistance for Spanish patrons, Bk club(s), Bks on CD, Children's prog, Computers for patron use, Electronic databases & coll, Holiday prog, Home delivery & serv to seniorr ctr & nursing homes, ILL available, Internet access, Life-long learning prog for all ages, Magazines, Mango lang, Meeting rooms, Museum passes, Music CDs, Online cat, Online ref, Outreach serv, Outside serv via phone, mail, e-mail & web, OverDrive

digital audio bks, Photocopying/Printing, Preschool outreach, Preschool reading prog, Prog for adults, Prog for children & young adult, Ref & res, Ref serv available, Scanner, Spanish lang bks, STEM programs, Study rm, Summer & winter reading prog, Summer reading prog, Tax forms, Teen prog, Telephone ref, Wheelchair accessible, Winter reading prog, Workshops
Publications: Annual Report
Mem of Chester County Library System
Open Mon & Thurs 10-8, Tues & Wed 10-6, Fri 10-5, Sat 9-4 (10-2 July-Aug)
Restriction: Authorized patrons

GM DEPARTMENT OF VETERANS AFFAIRS LIBRARY*, 1400 Black Horse Hill Rd, 19320-2040. SAN 314-4178. Tel: 610-384-7711 Ext, 3912. FAX: 610-383-0245. Web Site: www.coatesville.va.gov. *Chief Librn,* Julia Cononica; Tel: 610-384-7711, Ext 6119, E-mail: Julia.canonica@va.gov; Staff 1 (MLS 1)
Founded 1931
Library Holdings: Bk Titles 13,680; Bk Vols 14,390; Per Subs 392
Subject Interests: Neurology, Patient health educ, Psychiat
Partic in National Network of Libraries of Medicine Region 1
Restriction: Staff use only

COCHRANTON

P COCHRANTON AREA PUBLIC LIBRARY*, 107 W Pine St, 16314. (Mail add: PO Box 296, 16314), SAN 314-4186. Tel: 814-425-3996. FAX: 814-425-3996. E-mail: capl@ccfls.org. Web Site: cochranton.ccfls.org. *Dir,* Nadena Kramer
Founded 1969. Pop 5,390; Circ 12,411
Library Holdings: Bk Vols 10,000; Per Subs 10
Automation Activity & Vendor Info: (Cataloging) Koha; (Circulation) Koha
Wireless access
Mem of Crawford County Federated Library System
Open Mon & Wed 2-7, Tues & Thurs 9-5, Fri 9-3, Sat 9-4

COLLEGEVILLE

C URSINUS COLLEGE LIBRARY, Myrin Library, 601 E Main St, 19426. (Mail add: PO Box 1000, 19426-1000), SAN 314-4194. Tel: 610-409-3607. FAX: 610-409-3791. E-mail: library@ursinus.edu. Web Site: www.ursinus.edu/library. *Chief Info Officer,* Gene Spencer; Tel: 610-409-3064, E-mail: gspencer@ursinus.edu; *Dir of Research, Teaching & Learning Servs,* Diane Skorina; Tel: 610-409-3022, E-mail: dskorina@ursinus.edu; *Mgr, Libr Operations,* Maureen Damiano; Staff 10 (MLS 6, Non-MLS 4)
Founded 1870. Enrl 1,570; Fac 100; Highest Degree: Bachelor
Library Holdings: Bk Vols 420,000; Per Subs 1,200
Special Collections: College Archives (Ursinusiana Coll); Linda Grace Hoyer Updike Literary Papers; The Pennsylvania Folklife Society Coll. State Document Depository; US Document Depository
Subject Interests: Behav sci, Hist, Natural sci, Penn German, Recreation studies, Soc sci, Women's studies
Automation Activity & Vendor Info: (Acquisitions) OCLC Worldshare Management Services; (Cataloging) OCLC Worldshare Management Services; (Circulation) OCLC Worldshare Management Services; (ILL) OCLC WorldShare Interlibrary Loan; (OPAC) OCLC Worldshare Management Services
Wireless access
Publications: Myrin Library News
Partic in Interlibrary Delivery Service of Pennsylvania; LYRASIS; Partnership for Academic Library Collaborative & Innovation; Tri-State College Library Cooperative
Open Mon-Thurs 8am-2am, Fri 8am-9pm, Sat 9-9, Sun 10am-2am (Fall & Spring); Mon-Thurs 8-7, Fri 8-4:30 (Summer)
Friends of the Library Group

COLLINGDALE

P COLLINGDALE PUBLIC LIBRARY*, 823 MacDade Blvd, 19023-1422. SAN 314-4208. Tel: 610-583-2214. FAX: 610-583-0172. E-mail: collingdale@delcolibraries.org. Web Site: www.delcolibraries.org/collingdale-public-library. *Head Librn,* Stacie Lacava
Founded 1937. Pop 9,100; Circ 16,463
Library Holdings: Bk Vols 14,300; Per Subs 15
Wireless access
Mem of Delaware County Libraries
Open Mon-Thurs 12-6, Fri 12-4, Sat 9-1

COLUMBIA

P COLUMBIA PUBLIC LIBRARY*, 24 S Sixth St, 17512-1599. SAN 314-4224. Tel: 717-684-2255. FAX: 717-684-3003. Web Site: columbiapubliclibrary.org. *Adminr,* Lisa Greybill; E-mail: lgreybill@columbia.lib.pa.us; Staff 1 (Non-MLS 1)
Pop 10,311; Circ 36,910
Library Holdings: Bk Titles 26,817; Bk Vols 27,410; Per Subs 58; Talking Bks 416; Videos 722
Special Collections: Lloyd Mifflin Works
Subject Interests: Civil War, Local art, Local hist
Automation Activity & Vendor Info: (Serials) EBSCO Online
Wireless access
Publications: Newsletter (Monthly)
Mem of Library System of Lancaster County
Open Mon-Thurs 10-8, Fri 10-5, Sat 8-Noon

S NATIONAL WATCH & CLOCK MUSEUM, Library & Research Center, 514 Poplar St, 17512-2124. SAN 321-0251. Tel: 717-684-8261. FAX: 717-684-0142. E-mail: research@nawcc.org. Web Site: www.nawcc.org/research. *Curator, Libr Supvr,* James Campbell; E-mail: jcampbell@nawcc.org; *Archivist,* Ben Errickson; Tel: 717-684-8261, Ext 214, E-mail: berrickson@nawcc.org
Founded 1965
Library Holdings: Bk Vols 34,000; Per Subs 50
Special Collections: Hamilton Watch Co Records & Publications; Seth Thomas Ledgers & Publications
Wireless access
Open Wed-Sat 10-4 (Dec-March); Tues-Thurs 10-5, Fri & Sat 10-4 (April-Nov)
Restriction: Open to pub for ref only

CONNEAUT LAKE

P MARGARET SHONTZ MEMORIAL LIBRARY*, Conneaut Lake Public Library, 145 Second St, 16316. (Mail add: PO Box 5117, 16316), SAN 320-5053. Tel: 814-382-6666. FAX: 814-382-6666. E-mail: shontzpl@ccfls.org. Web Site: shontz.ccfls.org. *Dir,* Amber Pouliot; E-mail: amber.pouliot@ccfls.org
Founded 1971. Pop 4,190
Library Holdings: Bk Titles 16,000; Per Subs 26
Automation Activity & Vendor Info: (Circulation) Follett Software
Wireless access
Mem of Crawford County Federated Library System
Open Mon, Wed & Fri 11-6, Tues & Thurs 11-5

CONNEAUTVILLE

P STONE MEMORIAL LIBRARY*, 1101 Main St, 16406. (Mail add: PO Box 281, 16406-0281), SAN 314-4240. Tel: 814-587-2142. FAX: 814-587-2142. E-mail: stone@ccfls.org. Web Site: stone.ccfls.org. *Librn,* Pam Clark
Founded 1903. Pop 2,086; Circ 19,681
Library Holdings: Bk Titles 20,000; Per Subs 41
Wireless access
Mem of Crawford County Federated Library System
Open Mon & Fri 1-6, Tues & Thurs 9-6, Sat 9-1

CONNELLSVILLE

P CARNEGIE FREE LIBRARY, 299 S Pittsburgh St, 15425. SAN 314-4259. Tel: 724-628-1380. FAX: 724-628-5636. E-mail: carnegie@carnegiefreelib.org. Web Site: www.carnegiefreelib.org. *Dir, Librn,* Sharon Martino; E-mail: sharon@carnegiefreelib.org; Staff 7 (MLS 1, Non-MLS 6)
Founded 1903. Pop 34,835; Circ 45,000
Library Holdings: Audiobooks 380; DVDs 150; Bk Titles 42,265; Per Subs 108; Videos 159
Special Collections: Local & Fayette County History (Pennsylvania Coll)
Automation Activity & Vendor Info: (Cataloging) Follett Software; (Circulation) Follett Software; (OPAC) Follett Software
Wireless access
Publications: Newsletter
Open Mon 10-7, Tues-Thurs 10-6, Fri & Sat 10-5
Friends of the Library Group

COOPERSTOWN

P COOPERSTOWN PUBLIC LIBRARY*, 182 N Main St, 16317. (Mail add: PO Box 264, 16317-0264), SAN 371-5442. Tel: 814-374-4605. FAX: 814-374-4606. Web Site: www.cooperstownlibrary.org. *Br Mgr,* Amanda Barker; E-mail: cplbranchmanager@oilregionlibraries.org; Staff 1 (Non-MLS 1)
Founded 1987. Pop 4,153
Jan 2016-Dec 2016 Income (Main Library Only) $38,432, State $7,478, Locally Generated Income $15,200, Other $15,755. Mats Exp $5,000,

Books $3,500, Per/Ser (Incl. Access Fees) $1,500. Sal $11,962 (Prof $10,942)
Library Holdings: Bks on Deafness & Sign Lang 22; CDs 866; DVDs 449; e-books 1,407; Large Print Bks 100; Bk Titles 13,447; Per Subs 30
Automation Activity & Vendor Info: (Cataloging) TLC (The Library Corporation); (Circulation) TLC (The Library Corporation); (ILL) TLC (The Library Corporation); (OPAC) TLC (The Library Corporation)
Wireless access
Function: 24/7 Electronic res, 24/7 Online cat, Activity rm, Adult bk club, Bks on CD, Children's prog, Citizenship assistance, E-Readers, Holiday prog, Internet access, Magazines, Meeting rooms, Movies, Music CDs, Online cat, Online ref, OverDrive digital audio bks, Prog for adults, Prog for children & young adult, Summer reading prog
Mem of Oil Creek District Library Center
Open Mon & Thurs 1-8, Tues & Fri 9-5

COPLAY

P COPLAY PUBLIC LIBRARY, 49 S Fifth St, 18037-1306. SAN 314-4291. Tel: 610-262-7351. FAX: 610-262-4937. E-mail: coplaypl@gmail.com, coplaypubliclibrary@gmail.com. Web Site: www.coplaypubliclibrary.org. *Libr Dir,* Veronica Laroche; Staff 6 (MLS 2, Non-MLS 4)
Founded 1962. Pop 3,192; Circ 10,000
Library Holdings: Large Print Bks 78; Bk Titles 15,000; Per Subs 30; Talking Bks 490; Videos 1,424
Wireless access
Function: 24/7 Electronic res, 24/7 Online cat, Adult bk club, Audiobks via web, Bks on CD, Children's prog, Computers for patron use, E-Reserves, Electronic databases & coll, Free DVD rentals, Holiday prog, ILL available, Internet access, Life-long learning prog for all ages, Magazines, Mail & tel request accepted, Movies, Online cat, OverDrive digital audio bks, Photocopying/Printing, Preschool reading prog, Prog for adults, Prog for children & young adult, Ref serv available, Scanner, Story hour, Summer & winter reading prog, Summer reading prog, Teen prog, Winter reading prog
Partic in Lehigh Carbon Library Cooperative
Open Mon-Thurs 10-7, Fri & Sat 10-5 (Fall-Spring); Mon-Wed 11-7, Fri 10-5, Sat 10-2 (Summer)

CORAOPOLIS

P CORAOPOLIS MEMORIAL LIBRARY*, 601 School St, 15108-1196. SAN 314-4305. Tel: 412-264-3502. FAX: 412-269-8982. E-mail: coraopolis@einetwork.net. Web Site: coraopolislibrary.org. *Dir,* Jessica Watson; Staff 6 (MLS 1, Non-MLS 5)
Founded 1937. Pop 6,131; Circ 19,300
Library Holdings: AV Mats 3,000; Bks on Deafness & Sign Lang 25; Large Print Bks 300; Bk Vols 28,800; Per Subs 44
Special Collections: Story Coll
Subject Interests: Genealogy, Penn
Automation Activity & Vendor Info: (Cataloging) Innovative Interfaces, Inc; (Circulation) Innovative Interfaces, Inc
Wireless access
Mem of Allegheny County Library Association (ACLA)
Partic in Electronic Info Network
Open Mon-Thurs 10-8, Fri & Sat 10-5

CORRY

P CORRY PUBLIC LIBRARY*, 117 W Washington St, 16407. SAN 314-4321. Tel: 814-664-4404, 814-664-7611. FAX: 814-663-0742. Web Site: corrylibrary.org. *Libr Dir,* Randalee Gross; *Ch Serv,* Tracy Blair; Staff 7.7 (MLS 1, Non-MLS 6.7)
Founded 1900. Pop 12,270; Circ 97,415
Library Holdings: Audiobooks 1,890; AV Mats 2,035; Bk Vols 69,911; Per Subs 108; Spec Interest Per Sub 98
Special Collections: Local Newspaper (Corry Journal, 1902-present), micro
Subject Interests: Genealogy, Penn hist
Automation Activity & Vendor Info: (Acquisitions) SirsiDynix-WorkFlows; (Cataloging) SirsiDynix-WorkFlows; (Circulation) SirsiDynix-WorkFlows; (ILL) SirsiDynix-WorkFlows; (OPAC) SirsiDynix-iBistro; (Serials) SirsiDynix-WorkFlows
Wireless access
Function: Adult bk club, Art exhibits, Bk club(s), Bks on cassette, Bks on CD, CD-ROM, Children's prog, Computers for patron use, Electronic databases & coll, Free DVD rentals, Genealogy discussion group, ILL available, Instruction & testing, Internet access, Mail & tel request accepted, Music CDs, Online cat, Outreach serv, OverDrive digital audio bks, Photocopying/Printing, Preschool outreach, Prog for adults, Prog for children & young adult, Ref serv available, Res performed for a fee, Story hour, Summer reading prog, Tax forms, Telephone ref, VHS videos, Wheelchair accessible
Partic in Share NW Consortium
Open Mon, Tues & Thurs 10-8, Wed 1-8, Fri 10-6, Sat 10-2, Sun 1-4
Friends of the Library Group

COUDERSPORT

P COUDERSPORT PUBLIC LIBRARY, 502 Park Ave, 16915-1672. SAN 314-433X. Tel: 814-274-9382. FAX: 814-274-9137. E-mail: coudersportlibrary@gmail.com. Web Site: www.coudersportlibrary.org. *Dir,* Teri McDowell
Founded 1850. Pop 3,000; Circ 32,100
Library Holdings: Bk Titles 24,350; Bk Vols 27,300; Per Subs 100
Wireless access
Mem of Potter-Tioga Library System
Open Mon, Tues & Thurs 10-6, Fri 10-5, Sat 9-1

CRANBERRY TOWNSHIP

P CRANBERRY PUBLIC LIBRARY*, Municipal Ctr, 2525 Rochester Rd, Ste 300, 16066-6423. SAN 314-7339. Tel: 724-776-9100. FAX: 724-776-2490. E-mail: cranberry@bcfls.org. Web Site: www.cranberrytownship.org. *Dir,* Leslie Pallotta; Tel: 724-776-9100, Ext 1125; *Ad,* Jaci Defelice; Tel: 724-776-9100, Ext 1126; *Tech Serv Libm,* Rebecca Bess; Tel: 724-776-9100, Ext 1147; *Teen Serv Librn,* Janae Smith; Tel: 724-776-9100, Ext 1124, E-mail: jsmith@bcfls.org; *Youth Serv Librn,* Annemarie Lamperski; E-mail: alamperski@bcfls.org; Staff 4 (MLS 2, Non-MLS 2)
Founded 1974. Pop 28,098; Circ 294,366
Jan 2017-Dec 2017 Income $613,000. Mats Exp $64,687. Sal $346,600
Library Holdings: Bk Vols 89,335; Per Subs 86
Automation Activity & Vendor Info: (Cataloging) TLC (The Library Corporation); (Circulation) TLC (The Library Corporation); (OPAC) TLC (The Library Corporation)
Wireless access
Function: 24/7 Electronic res, 24/7 Online cat, Activity rm, Adult bk club, Audiobks via web, AV serv, Bk club(s), Bks on CD, Children's prog, Computer training, Computers for patron use, E-Readers, Electronic databases & coll, Free DVD rentals, Holiday prog, ILL available, Internet access, Life-long learning prog for all ages, Magazines, Magnifiers for reading, Mango lang, Meeting rooms, Microfiche/film & reading machines, Movies, Music CDs, Online cat, OverDrive digital audio bks, Photocopying/Printing, Prog for adults, Prog for children & young adult, Ref serv available, Scanner, Serves people with intellectual disabilities, Study rm, Summer reading prog, Tax forms, Teen prog, Telephone ref, Wheelchair accessible
Mem of Butler County Federated Library System
Partic in Midwest Libr Consortium
Special Services for the Deaf - Closed caption videos; High interest/low vocabulary bks
Special Services for the Blind - Accessible computers; Bks on CD; Braille bks; Children's Braille; Large print bks
Open Mon-Thurs 10-8, Fri 10-5, Sat 10-4, Sun 1-4
Restriction: In-house use for visitors
Friends of the Library Group

CRESCO

P BARRETT PARADISE FRIENDLY LIBRARY*, 6500 Rte 191, 18326. SAN 314-7894. Tel: 570-595-7171. FAX: 570-595-7879. E-mail: brfpubli@ptd.net. Web Site: www.barrettlibrary.org. *Libr Dir,* Mary Ann Lewis; Staff 1 (Non-MLS 1)
Founded 1909. Pop 6,551; Circ 100,000
Library Holdings: Bk Titles 21,000; Per Subs 250
Automation Activity & Vendor Info: (Cataloging) Innovative Interfaces, Inc - Millennium; (Circulation) Innovative Interfaces, Inc - Millennium; (OPAC) Innovative Interfaces, Inc - Millennium
Wireless access
Function: Adult bk club, Audiobks via web, Bk club(s), Bks on cassette, Bks on CD, Children's prog, Computer training, Computers for patron use, Electronic databases & coll, Family literacy, Free DVD rentals, Genealogy discussion group, ILL available, Internet access, Photocopying/Printing, Preschool outreach, Prog for adults, Prog for children & young adult, Ref serv available, Senior computer classes, Spoken cassettes & CDs, Spoken cassettes & DVDs, Story hour, Summer reading prog, Tax forms, Teen prog, Wheelchair accessible
Open Mon-Thurs 10-8, Fri & Sat 10-5
Friends of the Library Group

CRESSON

P CRESSON PUBLIC LIBRARY, 231 Laurel Ave, 16630-1118. SAN 314-4356. Tel: 814-886-2619. FAX: 814-886-9564. E-mail: cresson@cclsys.org, cressonpubliclibrary@yahoo.com. Web Site: www.cclsys.org/cresson. *Dir,* Courtney Sable
Founded 1927. Pop 4,923; Circ 18,904
Library Holdings: Bk Vols 11,041; Per Subs 13
Automation Activity & Vendor Info: (Cataloging) Evergreen; (Circulation) Evergreen; (OPAC) Evergreen
Wireless access

Mem of Cambria County Library System & District Center
Open Mon & Wed 11-7, Tues 11-5, Thurs 1-7, Sat 8-3

C MOUNT ALOYSIUS COLLEGE LIBRARY*, 7373 Admiral Peary Hwy, 16630-1999. SAN 314-4364. Tel: 814-886-6445. FAX: 814-886-5767. Web Site: www.mtaloy.edu/academics/library. *Librn,* Maggie Lykens; E-mail: mlykens@mtaloy.edu; *Ref Librn,* Robert Stere; E-mail: rstere@mtaloy.edu; *Educ Tech Spec,* Lauren Coakley; Tel: 814-886-6541, E-mail: lcoakley@mtaloy.edu; Staff 5 (MLS 2, Non-MLS 3)
Founded 1939. Enrl 1,100; Fac 55; Highest Degree: Master
Library Holdings: Bk Vols 75,000; Per Subs 50
Special Collections: Ecumenical Studies Coll
Subject Interests: Law
Automation Activity & Vendor Info: (Cataloging) SirsiDynix; (Circulation) SirsiDynix; (OPAC) SirsiDynix
Wireless access
Partic in OCLC Online Computer Library Center, Inc
Open Mon-Thurs 8am-10:30pm, Fri 8-5, Sun 2-10:30

CURWENSVILLE

P CLEARFIELD COUNTY PUBLIC LIBRARY, 601 Beech St, 16833. SAN 358-3716. Tel: 814-236-0589. FAX: 814-236-3620. E-mail: staff@clearfieldcountylibrary.org. Web Site: www.clearfieldcountylibrary.org. *Dir,* Kayla Clark; E-mail: kclark@clearfieldcountylibrary.org
Founded 1940. Pop 46,046; Circ 141,741
Library Holdings: Bk Vols 52,000
Special Collections: Oral History of Curwensville
Automation Activity & Vendor Info: (Cataloging) TLC (The Library Corporation); (OPAC) TLC (The Library Corporation)
Wireless access
Partic in Cent Pa District
Open Mon-Fri 9-5
Branches: 1
CURWENSVILLE PUBLIC BRANCH LIBRARY, 601 Beech St, 16833. Tel: 814-236-0355. *Br Mgr,* Lois Francisco; E-mail: lfrancisco@clearfieldcountylibrary.org
Pop 4,853
Library Holdings: Bk Vols 28,000
Open Mon & Wed 9-8, Tues, Thurs & Fri 9-5, Sat 9-4
Friends of the Library Group
Bookmobiles: 1. Bk vols 3,900

DALLAS

P BACK MOUNTAIN MEMORIAL LIBRARY*, 96 Huntsville Rd, 18612. SAN 314-4372. Tel: 570-675-1182. FAX: 570-674-5863. E-mail: bkmtlb@epix.net. Web Site: backmountainlibrary.org. *Dir,* Martha Butler; Staff 1 (MLS 1)
Founded 1945. Pop 34,824; Circ 106,468
Library Holdings: CDs 202; DVDs 103; Large Print Bks 1,008; Bk Vols 76,000; Per Subs 145; Talking Bks 982; Videos 800
Automation Activity & Vendor Info: (Cataloging) Innovative Interfaces, Inc; (Circulation) Innovative Interfaces, Inc; (ILL) Innovative Interfaces, Inc; (OPAC) Innovative Interfaces, Inc
Wireless access
Mem of Luzerne County Library System
Open Mon-Thurs 9:30-6, Fri 9:30-5, Sat 9:30-4
Friends of the Library Group

C MISERICORDIA UNIVERSITY, Mary Kintz Bevevino Library, 301 Lake St, 18612-1098. SAN 314-4380. Tel: 570-674-6231. Administration Tel: 570-674-6225. FAX: 570-674-6342. Reference E-mail: reference@misericordia.edu. Web Site: misericordia.edu/library. *Dir, Libr Serv,* Jennifer Luksa; E-mail: jluksa@misericordia.edu; *Access Serv Mgr,* Colleen Newhart; Tel: 570-674-3036, E-mail: cnewhart@misericordia.edu; *Archivist,* Maureen Cech; Tel: 570-674-6420, E-mail: mcech@misericordia.edu; Staff 10 (MLS 4, Non-MLS 6)
Founded 1924
Special Collections: Center for Nursing History of Northeastern Pennsylvania; Childrens's Literature; Comics & Graphic Novels; Sister Mary Carmel McGarigle Archives
Automation Activity & Vendor Info: (Acquisitions) SirsiDynix; (Cataloging) SirsiDynix; (Circulation) SirsiDynix; (Course Reserve) SirsiDynix; (ILL) OCLC Tipasa; (OPAC) SirsiDynix; (Serials) SirsiDynix
Wireless access
Publications: Book Marks: The Library Newsletter
Partic in LYRASIS; Partnership for Academic Library Collaborative & Innovation
Open Mon-Thurs 8am-Midnight, Fri 8-5, Sat 10-5, Sun 11am-Midnight
Friends of the Library Group

DALTON

P DALTON COMMUNITY LIBRARY*, 113 E Main St, 18414. (Mail add: PO Box 86, 18414-0086), SAN 314-4399. Tel: 570-563-2014. FAX: 570-563-2512. Web Site: www.lclshome.org/b/dalton-community-library. *Dir,* Shu Qiu; *Asst Dir,* Susan Scandres; E-mail: sscondras@albright.org; Staff 1 (MLS 1)
Founded 1948
Library Holdings: Bk Vols 20,000; Per Subs 40
Special Collections: Local History
Subject Interests: Lackawana County hist
Automation Activity & Vendor Info: (Acquisitions) SirsiDynix; (Cataloging) SirsiDynix; (Circulation) SirsiDynix; (Course Reserve) SirsiDynix; (ILL) SirsiDynix; (Media Booking) SirsiDynix; (OPAC) SirsiDynix; (Serials) SirsiDynix
Wireless access
Mem of Lackawanna County Library System
Open Mon & Tues 10-8, Thurs-Sat 10-5
Friends of the Library Group
Bookmobiles: 1

DANVILLE

P THOMAS BEAVER FREE LIBRARY*, 317 Ferry St, 17821-1939. (Mail add: PO Box 177, 17821-0177), SAN 314-4410. Tel: 570-275-4180. FAX: 570-275-8480. Web Site: www.tbflibrary.org. *Dir,* Kathleen McQuiston; E-mail: tbfldirector@ptd.net; *Head, Cat,* Joette Shalongo; *Ch Serv, Pub Serv, YA Serv,* Beth Lynn; Staff 7 (MLS 1, Non-MLS 6)
Founded 1886. Pop 21,286
Library Holdings: Bks on Deafness & Sign Lang 15; Bk Vols 33,027; Per Subs 108
Automation Activity & Vendor Info: (Cataloging) EOS International; (Circulation) EOS International; (OPAC) EOS International
Open Mon 1-8, Tues 10:30-5, Wed 11-5, Thurs 10:30-8, Fri 12-5, Sat 11-3
Friends of the Library Group

M GEISINGER HEALTH SYSTEM*, Health Sciences Library, 100 N Academy Ave, 17822-2101. SAN 358-383X. Tel: 570-271-6463. FAX: 570-271-5738. E-mail: hsl@geisinger.edu. *Dir,* Patricia Ulmer; Tel: 570-214-7343, E-mail: paulmer@geisinger.edu; Staff 8 (MLS 4, Non-MLS 4)
Founded 1927
Library Holdings: AV Mats 925; e-books 78; e-journals 511; Electronic Media & Resources 35; Bk Titles 5,004; Per Subs 511
Special Collections: Geisinger Archives
Subject Interests: Allied health, Hist of med, Med, Med speciaities
Automation Activity & Vendor Info: (Cataloging) OCLC; (ILL) OCLC; (OPAC) Softlink America; (Serials) Infotrieve
Publications: Audiovisual Listing; Guide to Use & Services - Health Sciences Library; Library Bulletin; Periodical Holdings List
Partic in LYRASIS; National Network of Libraries of Medicine Region 1; Proquest Dialog
Open Mon-Fri 7-5
Restriction: Badge access after hrs
Friends of the Library Group

DARBY

P DARBY FREE LIBRARY*, 1001 Main St, 19023-0169. (Mail add: PO Box 164, 19023-0164), SAN 314-4429. Tel: 610-586-7310. FAX: 610-586-2781. E-mail: darby@delco.lib.pa.us. Web Site: darbylibrary.org. *Dir,* Susan Borders; Staff 4 (Non-MLS 4)
Founded 1743. Pop 10,299; Circ 11,127
Library Holdings: Bk Vols 16,260; Per Subs 38
Subject Interests: Darby hist
Wireless access
Function: 24/7 Electronic res, 24/7 Online cat, After school storytime, Children's prog, Computers for patron use, ILL available, Internet access, Preschool outreach, Preschool reading prog, Prog for adults, Prog for children & young adult, Story hour, Summer & winter reading prog, Summer reading prog
Mem of Delaware County Libraries
Open Mon, Wed, Fri & Sat 10-5, Tues & Thurs 10-7

M MERCY FITZGERALD HOSPITAL*, Health Sciences Library, 1500 Lansdowne Ave, MS No 0127, 19023-1200. SAN 314-4437. Tel: 610-237-4150. FAX: 610-237-4830. Web Site: www.trinityhealthma.org. *Mgr, Libr Serv,* Ellen Abramowitz; Staff 1 (MLS 1)
Founded 1933
Jul 2015-Jun 2016. Mats Exp $85,000, Books $3,000, Per/Ser (Incl. Access Fees) $61,000
Library Holdings: CDs 100; DVDs 5; e-journals 850; Bk Titles 500; Videos 10
Subject Interests: Med, Nursing, Surgery
Wireless access

Partic in Basic Health Sciences Library Network; Health Sciences Libraries Consortium
Open Tues-Fri 9-3:30

DAWSON

P BROWNFIELD COMMUNITY LIBRARY*, 291 Banning Rd, 15428. Tel: 724-529-2930. *Library Contact,* Loretta Williams
Library Holdings: Bk Vols 14,000; Per Subs 13
Open Tues 5:30pm-7:30pm, Wed 11am-1pm

DELMONT

P DELMONT PUBLIC LIBRARY*, 77 Greensburg St, 15626. SAN 314-4445. Tel: 724-468-5329. FAX: 724-468-5329. E-mail: delmlib@comcast.net. Web Site: delmontlibrary.org. *Dir,* Denni Grassel; Staff 2 (Non-MLS 2)
Founded 1931. Pop 3,401; Circ 39,000
Library Holdings: Bk Titles 16,400; Per Subs 24
Special Collections: Desert Storm War Coll; War on Drugs
Automation Activity & Vendor Info: (Acquisitions) Follett Software; (Cataloging) Follett Software; (Circulation) Follett Software; (Course Reserve) Follett Software; (OPAC) Follett Software
Wireless access
Function: Adult bk club, After school storytime, Art exhibits, Bk club(s), Bks on cassette, Bks on CD, CD-ROM, Children's prog, Computer training, Computers for patron use, Digital talking bks, E-Reserves, Electronic databases & coll, Free DVD rentals, ILL available, Internet access, Magnifiers for reading, Mail & tel request accepted, Music CDs, Online cat, Outreach serv, Photocopying/Printing, Prog for adults, Prog for children & young adult, Senior computer classes, Serves people with intellectual disabilities, Spoken cassettes & CDs, Spoken cassettes & DVDs, Story hour, Summer reading prog, Tax forms, Teen prog, VHS videos, Wheelchair accessible, Workshops, Writing prog
Mem of Westmoreland County Federated Library System
Open Mon-Thurs 10-7, Sat 9-4
Friends of the Library Group

DILLSBURG

P DILLSBURG AREA PUBLIC LIBRARY*, 204 Mumper Lane, 17019. SAN 314-4453. Tel: 717-432-5613. FAX: 717-432-7641. Web Site: www.yorklibraries.org/dillsburg. *Dir,* Keith Greenawalt; E-mail: kgreenawalt@yorklibraries.org; Staff 7 (MLS 2, Non-MLS 5)
Founded 1953. Pop 21,073; Circ 65,293
Library Holdings: Large Print Bks 210; Bk Vols 33,581; Per Subs 10
Automation Activity & Vendor Info: (Circulation) Innovative Interfaces, Inc - Millennium
Wireless access
Mem of York County Library System
Open Mon-Thurs 10-8, Fri 10-3, Sat 10-5 (10-3 Summer)
Friends of the Library Group

DINGMANS FERRY

P DELAWARE TOWNSHIP LIBRARY ASSOCIATION*, Akenac Park, Rte 739, 106 Connors Way, 18328. Tel: 570-828-2781. Web Site: www.delawaretownshippa.gov. *Dir,* Barbara Braden; Staff 1 (Non-MLS 1)
Library Holdings: Bk Titles 3,280; Bk Vols 3,410; Per Subs 16
Open Mon, Wed & Fri 12-3

DONORA

P DONORA PUBLIC LIBRARY, 510 Meldon Ave, 15033-1333. SAN 314-4461. Tel: 724-379-7940. FAX: 724-379-8809. E-mail: librarian@donoralibrary.com. Web Site: www.donoralibrary.com. *Libr Dir,* Mark G Bizzell Boyer; *Library Contact,* Judy Thomas; *Librn,* Johanna Rubino; E-mail: jrubino@donoralibrary.com; *Librn,* Kenneth Bizzell Boyer; E-mail: kboyer@donoralibrary.com; *Librn,* Nona Galayda; E-mail: ngalayda@donoralibrary.com. Subject Specialists: *Genealogy,* Johanna Rubino; *Cataloging,* Kenneth Bizzell Boyer; Staff 2 (MLS 1, Non-MLS 1)
Founded 1930. Pop 11,739; Circ 16,783
Library Holdings: Bks on Deafness & Sign Lang 12; Bk Titles 27,000; Bk Vols 29,000; Per Subs 83
Automation Activity & Vendor Info: (Cataloging) Follett Software; (Circulation) Follett Software; (OPAC) Follett Software
Wireless access
Mem of Washington County Library System
Open Mon-Thurs 11-7, Fri 11-5, Sat 10-5
Friends of the Library Group

DOUGLASSVILLE

S STV INC LIBRARY SERVICES, 205 W Welsh Dr, 19518. SAN 315-1352. Tel: 610-385-8200, 610-385-8280. *Librn,* Carol Leh; E-mail: carol.leh@stvinc.com; Staff 1 (MLS 1)
Subject Interests: Archit, Engr
Restriction: Co libr, Employees only

DOWNINGTOWN

P DOWNINGTOWN LIBRARY CO, 122 Wallace Ave, 19335. SAN 314-447X. Tel: 610-269-2741. Web Site: downingtownlibrary.org. *Dir,* Elizabeth Hess; E-mail: ehess@ccls.org; Staff 2 (MLS 1, Non-MLS 1)
Founded 1876. Pop 27,613; Circ 55,618
Library Holdings: Bk Titles 23,817; Bk Vols 25,490; Per Subs 61; Talking Bks 374; Videos 610
Special Collections: Oral History
Subject Interests: Local hist
Automation Activity & Vendor Info: (Cataloging) Innovative Interfaces, Inc; (Circulation) Innovative Interfaces, Inc; (OPAC) Innovative Interfaces, Inc
Mem of Chester County Library System
Open Mon-Thurs 9:30-8, Fri 9-5, Sat 9-4 (9-1 July-Aug)
Friends of the Library Group

DOYLESTOWN

P BUCKS COUNTY FREE LIBRARY*, Headquarters, 150 S Pine St, 18901-4932. SAN 358-3899. Tel: 215-348-0332. Web Site: buckslib.org. *Chief Exec Officer,* Martina Kominiarek; Tel: 215-348-0332, Ext 1101, E-mail: ceo@buckslib.org; *Mgr, Pub Relations & Mkt,* Regina Fried; *Asst Libr Mgr,* Yoonmee Hampson; Staff 37 (MLS 37)
Founded 1956. Pop 464,092; Circ 2,249,396
Library Holdings: AV Mats 85,933; Bk Titles 769,357; Bk Vols 925,144; Per Subs 1,013
Special Collections: The Woods Handicapped & Gifted Coll. State Document Depository; US Document Depository
Subject Interests: Foreign fiction
Automation Activity & Vendor Info: (Acquisitions) SirsiDynix; (Cataloging) SirsiDynix; (Circulation) SirsiDynix; (ILL) OCLC FirstSearch; (OPAC) SirsiDynix
Wireless access
Publications: Directory of Libraries in Bucks County; One Calendar - Programs & Events
Member Libraries: Fallsington Library; Free Library of New Hope & Solebury; Free Library of Northampton Township; Margaret R Grundy Memorial Library; Morrisville Free Library Association; Pipersville Free Library; Riegelsville Public Library; Southampton Free Library; Township Library of Lower Southampton; Village Library of Wrightstown; Warminster Township Free Library
Special Services for the Blind - Assistive/Adapted tech devices, equip & products
Open Mon-Thurs 9-9, Fri 9-6, Sat 9-5, Sun 1-5
Friends of the Library Group
Branches: 7
BENSALEM BRANCH, 3700 Hulmeville Rd, Bensalem, 19020-4491, SAN 358-3929. Tel: 215-638-2030. E-mail: hellobn@buckslib.org. *Libr Mgr,* Nicole Lynch; E-mail: lynchn@buckslib.org
Pop 58,434; Circ 278,655
Library Holdings: AV Mats 11,677; Bk Vols 110,212; Per Subs 89
Function: Passport agency
Open Mon-Thurs 9-9, Fri 10-6, Sat 9-5
LEVITTOWN BRANCH, 7311 New Falls Rd, Levittown, 19055-1006, SAN 358-3988. Tel: 215-949-2324. E-mail: hellolv@buckslib.org. *Libr Mgr,* Steve Lorenz; E-mail: lorenzs@buckslib.org
Pop 102,340; Circ 493,930
Library Holdings: AV Mats 19,771; Bk Vols 168,569; Per Subs 130
Open Mon-Thurs 9-8, Fri 10-6, Sat 9-5
LIBRARY CENTER AT DOYLESTOWN, 150 S Pine St, 18901-4932, SAN 358-3953. Tel: 215-348-9081. FAX: 215-348-9489. E-mail: hellody@buckslib.org. *Libr Mgr,* Margarita Hossaini-Vadeh; E-mail: hossaini-vadehm@buckslib.org
Pop 100,977; Circ 1,018,713
Library Holdings: AV Mats 27,816; Bk Vols 191,922; Per Subs 130
Special Collections: US Document Depository
Function: Homebound delivery serv
Open Mon-Thurs 9-9, Fri 9-6, Sat 9-5, Sun 1-5
Friends of the Library Group
JAMES A MICHENER BRANCH, 401 W Mill St, Quakertown, 18951-1248, SAN 358-4011. Tel: 215-536-3306. E-mail: helloqt@buckslib.org. *Libr Mgr,* Beth Anderson; E-mail: andersonb@buckslib.org
Pop 42,082; Circ 289,101
Library Holdings: AV Mats 8,449; Bk Vols 95,123; Per Subs 105
Open Mon-Thurs 10-9, Fri 10-6, Sat 9-5
Friends of the Library Group

PENNWOOD, 301 S Pine St, Langhorne, 19047-2887, SAN 358-4046. Tel: 215-757-2510. E-mail: hellola@buckslib.org. *Libr Mgr,* Judy Benfield; E-mail: benfieldj@buckslib.org
Pop 70,880; Circ 204,627
Library Holdings: AV Mats 20,228; Bk Vols 72,596; Per Subs 84
Special Collections: Handicapped & Gifted Individual (The Wood Coll) Special Services for the Deaf - TTY equip
Open Mon-Thurs 9-8, Fri & Sat 9-5

SAMUEL PIERCE BRANCH, 491 Arthur Ave, Perkasie, 18944-1033, SAN 358-4070. Tel: 215-257-9718. E-mail: hellopk@buckslib.org. *Libr Mgr,* Wayne Lahr; E-mail: lahrw@buckslib.org
Pop 47,020; Circ 269,870
Library Holdings: AV Mats 10,977; Bk Vols 70,324; Per Subs 90
Open Mon-Thurs 9-8, Fri 10-6, Sat 9-5

YARDLEY-MAKEFIELD BRANCH, 1080 Edgewood Rd, Yardley, 19067-1648, SAN 358-4100. Tel: 215-493-9020. E-mail: helloya@buckslib.org. *Libr Mgr,* Patricia Hartman; E-mail: hartmanp@buckslib.org
Pop 42,359; Circ 415,662
Library Holdings: Bk Vols 77,182
Open Mon-Thurs 9-9, Fri 10-6, Sat 9-5
Friends of the Library Group

S BUCKS COUNTY HISTORICAL SOCIETY, Mercer Museum Research Library, 84 S Pine St, 18901-4999. SAN 314-4496. Tel: 215-345-0210, Ext 141. FAX: 215-230-0823. E-mail: mmlib@mercermuseum.org. Web Site: www.mercermuseum.org. *Libr & Archives Mgr,* Annie Halliday; Tel: 215-345-0210, Ext 126, E-mail: ahalliday@mercermuseum.org; *Asst Libr Mgr,* Alexandra DeAngelis; Tel: 215-345-0210, Ext 141, E-mail: adeangelis@mercermuseum.org; Staff 4 (MLS 2, Non-MLS 2)
Founded 1880
Library Holdings: Bk Vols 18,000
Special Collections: A. Oscar Martin architectural drawing coll; Bucks County Historical Society visual image coll; Henry Chapman Mercer coll
Subject Interests: Antiques, Arts & crafts, Genealogy, Local hist, Property, Tools, Trades
Automation Activity & Vendor Info: (Cataloging) Sydney Enterprise; (OPAC) Sydney Enterprise
Wireless access
Function: 24/7 Online cat, Archival coll, Computers for patron use, Doc delivery serv, For res purposes, Internet access, Mail & tel request accepted, Microfiche/film & reading machines, Online cat, Photocopying/Printing, Prog for adults, Ref & res, Ref serv available, Res assist avail, Res libr, Res performed for a fee, Scanner, Telephone ref, Wheelchair accessible
Open Tues & Wed 1-5, Thurs-Sat 10-5
Restriction: Free to mem, Non-circulating, Not a lending libr, Restricted pub use

GL BUCKS COUNTY LAW LIBRARY*, Bucks County Administration Bldg, 55 E Court St, 2nd Flr, 18901. SAN 314-450X. Tel: 215-343-6024. FAX: 215-348-6759. Web Site: www.buckscounty.org/courts/lawlibrary. *Dir,* Barbara Morris; Tel: 215-348-6081; Staff 3 (MLS 2, Non-MLS 1)
Library Holdings: Bk Titles 33,690; Bk Vols 35,190; Per Subs 100
Special Collections: Case Law; Court Rules; Dictionaries; Digests; Federal Statutes; Form Books; Law Encyclopedias; Law-Related Periodicals; National Reporter & System; State Statutes (PA,NJ,NY,DE,FL,MD); Treaties
Subject Interests: Penn law
Automation Activity & Vendor Info: (Cataloging) SirsiDynix; (Circulation) SirsiDynix; (OPAC) SirsiDynix
Open Mon-Fri 8:30-5

C DELAWARE VALLEY UNIVERSITY, Joseph Krauskopf Memorial Library, 700 E Butler Ave, 18901-2699. SAN 314-4534. Circulation Tel: 215-489-2953. Interlibrary Loan Service Tel: 215-489-4957. FAX: 215-230-2967. Web Site: library.delval.edu/library. *Libr Dir,* Peter Kupersmith; E-mail: peter.kupersmith@delval.edu; *Access Serv Librn,* Claire Drolet; E-mail: Claire.Drolet@delval.edu; *Instrul Serv Librn,* Karen Sheldon; Tel: 215-489-4968, E-mail: karen.sheldon@delval.edu; *Cataloger,* Marian Schad; Tel: 215-489-2385; *Grad & Distance Educ,* Elise Georgulis; Tel: 215-489-2386, E-mail: elise.georgulis@delval.edu; Staff 5 (MLS 5)
Founded 1896. Enrl 2,000; Fac 97; Highest Degree: Doctorate
Library Holdings: Bk Vols 50,000; Per Subs 250
Special Collections: Joseph Krauskopf Coll
Subject Interests: Animal sci, Plant sci
Automation Activity & Vendor Info: (Cataloging) TLC (The Library Corporation); (Circulation) TLC (The Library Corporation); (Course Reserve) TLC (The Library Corporation); (OPAC) TLC (The Library Corporation)
Wireless access
Partic in LYRASIS; OCLC Online Computer Library Center, Inc
Open Mon-Thurs 8am-11pm, Fri 8-5:30, Sat 9:30-5:30, Sun 1-11 (Winter); Mon-Thurs 8:30-6:30, Fri 8:30-12, Sat 10-4 (Summer)

DRESHER

R TEMPLE SINAI*, The Martin Josephs Library, 1401 N Limekiln Pike, 19025. SAN 315-0119. Tel: 215-643-6510, Ext 100. FAX: 215-643-9441. Web Site: www.tsinai.com. *Educ Dir,* Shira Weissbach; E-mail: sweissbach@tsinai.com
Library Holdings: Bk Vols 7,500
Subject Interests: Judaica
Wireless access
Open Tues 12-6, Wed 12-5, Sun 9:30-12:30
Friends of the Library Group

DU BOIS

P DUBOIS PUBLIC LIBRARY*, 31 S Brady St, 15801. SAN 314-4577. Tel: 814-371-5930. FAX: 814-371-2282. Web Site: www.duboispubliclibrary.org. *Dir,* Rebecca J McTavish; E-mail: rmctavish@duboispubliclibrary.org; Staff 5 (MLS 1, Non-MLS 4)
Founded 1920. Pop 19,600; Circ 96,000
Jan 2013-Dec 2013 Income $237,580, State $60,380, City $134,000, Locally Generated Income $43,200. Mats Exp $27,600, Books $22,250, Per/Ser (Incl. Access Fees) $1,600, AV Mat $3,250, Electronic Ref Mat (Incl. Access Fees) $500. Sal $176,550
Library Holdings: Audiobooks 800; AV Mats 2,800; CDs 550; DVDs 1,150; Large Print Bks 2,466; Bk Vols 43,250; Per Subs 25; Videos 150
Special Collections: Pennsylvania Room (History & Geneaology). Oral History
Automation Activity & Vendor Info: (Cataloging) AmLib Library Management System; (Circulation) AmLib Library Management System; (OPAC) AmLib Library Management System
Wireless access
Function: Audiobks via web, Bks on CD, Children's prog, Computers for patron use, Electronic databases & coll, Family literacy, Holiday prog, Home delivery & serv to seniorr ctr & nursing homes, Homebound delivery serv, ILL available, Magnifiers for reading, Microfiche/film & reading machines, Museum passes, Music CDs, Online cat, OverDrive digital audio bks, Photocopying/Printing, Preschool outreach, Preschool reading prog, Prog for adults, Prog for children & young adult, Ref serv available, Story hour, Summer reading prog, Tax forms, Teen prog
Open Mon, Tues & Thurs 9-8, Wed & Fri 9-5, Sat 9-4
Restriction: 24-hr pass syst for students only
Friends of the Library Group

C PENNSYLVANIA STATE UNIVERSITY*, DuBois Campus Library, College Pl, 113 Hiller Bldg, 15801. SAN 314-4585. Tel: 814-375-4756. FAX: 814-375-4784. Web Site: libraries.psu.edu/dubois. *Interim Head Librn,* Bonnie Imler; E-mail: bbi1@psu.edu; Staff 3 (MLS 1, Non-MLS 2)
Founded 1935. Enrl 920; Fac 50
Library Holdings: Bk Vols 43,000; Per Subs 125
Special Collections: Wildlife Technology (Paul A Handwerk & David D Wanless Coll)
Automation Activity & Vendor Info: (Acquisitions) SirsiDynix; (Cataloging) SirsiDynix; (Circulation) SirsiDynix; (Course Reserve) SirsiDynix; (ILL) OCLC; (OPAC) SirsiDynix; (Serials) SirsiDynix
Wireless access
Partic in OCLC Online Computer Library Center, Inc; Research Libraries Information Network
Open Mon-Thurs 8-7, Fri 8-4:30

DUNBAR

P DUNBAR COMMUNITY LIBRARY, 60 Connellsville St, 15431. (Mail add: PO Box 306, 15431). Tel: 724-277-4775. E-mail: circdesk@dunbarcl.org. *Librn,* Roxanne Younkin
Library Holdings: DVDs 400; Large Print Bks 50; Bk Vols 22,000; Per Subs 5
Wireless access
Function: Accelerated reader prog, Children's prog, Computer training, Computers for patron use, Homework prog, ILL available, Photocopying/Printing, Story hour, Summer reading prog, Tax forms, Teen prog, Wheelchair accessible
Open Tues 12-3, Wed & Fri 10:30-5, Thurs 10-1

DUSHORE

P SULLIVAN COUNTY LIBRARY*, 206 Center St, 18614. (Mail add: PO Box 309, 18614-0309), SAN 314-4615. Tel: 570-928-9352. E-mail: sullcopl@ptd.net. Web Site: sullivancountylibrary.org. *Dir,* Alan Miller; Staff 2.5 (MLS 1, Non-MLS 1.5)
Founded 1947. Pop 6,556; Circ 35,500
Library Holdings: Bk Vols 16,847; Per Subs 60
Subject Interests: Local hist
Wireless access
Open Tues & Wed 10-6, Thurs 12-7, Fri 10-5, Sat 9-4

EAGLEVILLE

P LOWER PROVIDENCE COMMUNITY LIBRARY*, 50 Parklane Dr, 19403-1171. SAN 375-3115. Tel: 610-666-6640. FAX: 610-666-5109. Web Site: www.lowerprovidencelibrary.org. *Libr Dir,* Marija Skoog; E-mail: mlskoog@mclinc.org; *Head, Children's & Teen Serv,* Sandrah Moles; E-mail: SMoles@mclinc.org; *Head, Circ,* Kathleen Sharkey; E-mail: KSharkey@mclinc.org; *Head, Support Serv,* Jill Kozol; E-mail: JKozol@mclinc.org; *Cat & Coll Mgt Librn,* Emily Rabson; E-mail: ERabson@mclinc.org; *Ref & Ad Serv Librn,* Barbara Loewengart; E-mail: BLoewengart@mclinc.org; Staff 4 (MLS 3, Non-MLS 1)
Founded 1985. Pop 25,400; Circ 223,000
Automation Activity & Vendor Info: (Cataloging) Innovative Interfaces, Inc; (Circulation) Innovative Interfaces, Inc; (OPAC) Innovative Interfaces, Inc
Wireless access
Function: 24/7 Electronic res, 24/7 Online cat, Activity rm, Adult bk club, Adult literacy prog, Audio & video playback equip for onsite use, Audiobks on Playaways & MP3, Audiobks via web, AV serv, Bk club(s), Bks on CD, CD-ROM, Children's prog, Computer training, Computers for patron use, Digital talking bks, Distance learning, E-Readers, E-Reserves, Electronic databases & coll, Family literacy, Holiday prog, ILL available, Internet access, Life-long learning prog for all ages, Literacy & newcomer serv, Magazines, Mail & tel request accepted, Meeting rooms, Movies, Museum passes, Music CDs, Online cat, Online info literacy tutorials on the web & in blackboard, Online ref, Outreach serv, Outside serv via phone, mail, e-mail & web, OverDrive digital audio bks, Photocopying/Printing, Preschool outreach, Preschool reading prog, Prog for adults, Prog for children & young adult, Ref & res, Ref serv available, Scanner, Serves people with intellectual disabilities, Spoken cassettes & CDs, Spoken cassettes & DVDs, Story hour, Study rm, Summer reading prog, Tax forms, Teen prog, Telephone ref, Visual arts prog, Wheelchair accessible, Winter reading prog, Writing prog
Partic in Montgomery County Library & Information Network Consortium
Special Services for the Deaf - Bks on deafness & sign lang
Open Mon-Thurs (Winter) 10-8:30, Fri & Sat 10-5, Sun 1-5; Mon-Thurs (Summer) 10-8:30, Fri 10-5, Sat 10-2
Friends of the Library Group

EAST STROUDSBURG

C EAST STROUDSBURG UNIVERSITY*, Kemp Library, 200 Prospect Ave, 18301-2999. SAN 314-4666. Tel: 570-422-3465. Circulation Tel: 570-422-3126. Reference Tel: 570-422-3594. FAX: 570-422-3151. Web Site: www4.esu.edu/library. *Dean, Libr Serv,* Dr Jingfeng Xia; Tel: 570-422-3152, E-mail: jxia@esu.edu; *Archivist & Spec Coll Librn,* Elizabeth Scott; Tel: 570-422-3584, E-mail: escott8@esu.edu; *Discovery Librn, Electronic Res Librn,* Allyson A Wind; Tel: 570-422-3597, E-mail: awind@esu.edu; *Ref & Instruction Librn,* Michelle Donlin; Tel: 570-422-3150, E-mail: mdonlin@esu.edu; Staff 22 (MLS 10, Non-MLS 12)
Founded 1893. Enrl 6,272; Fac 283; Highest Degree: Master
Library Holdings: AV Mats 12,367; Bk Vols 459,839; Per Subs 1,100
Special Collections: State Document Depository; US Document Depository
Automation Activity & Vendor Info: (Cataloging) Ex Libris Group; (Circulation) Ex Libris Group; (Course Reserve) Docutek; (OPAC) Ex Libris Group; (Serials) Ex Libris Group
Wireless access
Partic in Keystone Library Network; LYRASIS; Northeastern Pennsylvania Library Network; Partnership for Academic Library Collaborative & Innovation
Special Services for the Deaf - Assistive tech
Special Services for the Blind - Assistive/Adapted tech devices, equip & products
Open Mon-Thurs (Fall-Spring) 7:30am-Midnight, Fri 7:30-6, Sat 10-6, Sun 10am-Midnight; Mon-Thurs (Summer) 9-9, Fri 9-5, Sat 10-6, Sun 1-9

EASTON

P EASTON AREA PUBLIC LIBRARY & DISTRICT CENTER*, 515 Church St, 18042-3587. SAN 314-4682. Tel: 610-258-2917. Web Site: www.eastonpl.org. *Dir,* Jennifer Long; Tel: 610-258-2917, Ext 310, E-mail: director@eastonpl.org; *Head, Ref,* Erin Morrow; E-mail: erinm@eastonpl.org; *Coordr, Computer Serv,* Georgia Weber; *Youth Serv Coordr,* Allie Outhouse; Staff 6 (MLS 6)
Founded 1811. Pop 59,000; Circ 400,000
Library Holdings: Bk Vols 187,668; Per Subs 416
Special Collections: Genealogy & Local History, Pennsylvania, Eastern Ohio & Western New Jersey (Henry F Marx Local History Room)
Subject Interests: Hist, Literary criticism
Automation Activity & Vendor Info: (Acquisitions) Evergreen; (Cataloging) Evergreen; (Circulation) Evergreen; (OPAC) Evergreen; (Serials) Evergreen
Wireless access
Publications: Exlibris (Newsletter)
Open Mon-Thurs 9-9, Fri 9-6, Sat 9-5
Friends of the Library Group
Branches: 1
PALMER BRANCH LIBRARY, One Weller Pl, 18045, SAN 320-054X. Tel: 610-258-7492. *Br Mgr,* Katie Cardell; E-mail: katiec@eastonpl.org
Library Holdings: Bk Vols 15,380; Per Subs 38
Open Mon, Fri & Sat 9-5, Tues-Thurs 11-7
Friends of the Library Group

C LAFAYETTE COLLEGE*, David Bishop Skillman Library, 710 Sullivan Rd, 18042-1797. SAN 358-4194. Tel: 610-330-5151. Interlibrary Loan Service Tel: 610-330-5157. Reference Tel: 610-330-5155. FAX: 610-252-0370. Web Site: library.lafayette.edu. *Dean of Libr,* Anne Houston; Tel: 610-330-5147, E-mail: houstana@lafayette.edu; *Dir, Archives & Spec Coll,* Diane Shaw; Tel: 610-330-5401, E-mail: shawd@lafayette.edu; *Dir, Outreach & Access Services,* Kylie Bailin; Tel: 610-330-5154, E-mail: bailink@lafayette.edu; *Dir, Res & Instruction Serv,* Terese Heidenwolf; Tel: 610-330-5153, E-mail: heidenwt@lafayette.edu; Staff 20 (MLS 12, Non-MLS 8)
Founded 1826. Enrl 2,250; Fac 184; Highest Degree: Bachelor
Library Holdings: Bk Titles 494,000; Bk Vols 510,000; Per Subs 8,767; Videos 3,000
Special Collections: American Friends of Lafayette; Conahay Tinsman & Fox Angling Coll; Howard Chandler Christy Coll; Jay Parini Coll; Marquis de LaFayette Coll; Robt & Helen Meyner Coll; Stephen Crane Coll; Wm E Simon Coll
Automation Activity & Vendor Info: (Acquisitions) Innovative Interfaces, Inc; (Cataloging) Innovative Interfaces, Inc; (Circulation) Innovative Interfaces, Inc; (Course Reserve) Innovative Interfaces, Inc; (ILL) Innovative Interfaces, Inc; (Media Booking) Innovative Interfaces, Inc; (OPAC) Innovative Interfaces, Inc; (Serials) Innovative Interfaces, Inc
Wireless access
Publications: Bytes & Books
Partic in Interlibrary Delivery Service of Pennsylvania; Lehigh Valley Association of Independent Colleges; Partnership for Academic Library Collaborative & Innovation
Open Mon-Thurs 7:30am-1am, Fri 7:30am-10pm, Sat 10-10, Sun 10am-1am
Friends of the Library Group
Departmental Libraries:
CL KIRBY LIBRARY OF GOVERNMENT & LAW, Kirby Hall of Civil Rights, 716 Sullivan Rd, 18042-1797, SAN 358-4224. Tel: 610-330-5399. FAX: 610-330-5397. *Librn,* Ana Ramirez-Luhrs; Tel: 610-330-5398, E-mail: luhrsa@lafayette.edu; *Tech Librn,* Keith Faust; Tel: 610-330-3117, E-mail: faustk@lafayette.edu; Staff 8 (MLS 1, Non-MLS 7)
Founded 1930
Library Holdings: Bk Titles 29,690; Bk Vols 31,410; Per Subs 126
Subject Interests: Civil rights, Intl relations, Polit sci
Open Mon-Thurs 7:30am-10pm, Fri 7:30-5, Sat 11-5, Sun 1-11

P MARY MEUSER MEMORIAL LIBRARY*, 1803 Northampton St, 18042-3183. SAN 314-4690. Tel: 610-258-3040. E-mail: meuserlib@rcn.com. Web Site: www.meuserlib.org. *Dir,* Daniel L Redington; *Adult Serv,* Wende Fazio; E-mail: meuserlib.adult@rcn.com; *Ch Serv,* Natasha Stanton; E-mail: meuserlib.juv@rcn.com; Staff 3 (Non-MLS 3)
Founded 1962. Pop 15,000; Circ 5,500
Library Holdings: Bk Vols 49,000; Per Subs 80
Subject Interests: Art, Poetry
Automation Activity & Vendor Info: (Acquisitions) Brodart; (Cataloging) Evolve; (Circulation) Evolve; (OPAC) Evolve
Wireless access
Open Tues-Thurs 9:45-8, Fri 9:45-5, Sat 9-4 (9-1 Summer)
Friends of the Library Group

S NORTHAMPTON COUNTY HISTORICAL & GENEALOGICAL SOCIETY*, Jane S Moyer Library & NCHGS Archives, Sigal Museum, 342 Northampton St, 18042. SAN 314-4712. Tel: 610-253-1222. FAX: 610-253-4701. E-mail: library@northamptonctymuseum.org. Web Site: www.northamptonctymuseum.org. *Exec Dir,* Carey Birgel
Founded 1906
Library Holdings: Bk Titles 9,000; Bk Vols 11,000
Special Collections: Deed Coll; Family Photo Coll; Genealogical File Coll; Manuscript Coll; Merchants' Ledgers; Picture Coll; Postal Card Coll. Oral History
Subject Interests: County hist of Penn, Genealogy, Hist rec, Northampton County
Wireless access
Function: Res libr
Publications: Tales from the Grapevine (Newsletter)
Open Wed-Fri 10-2:30 or by appointment
Restriction: Open to pub for ref only

GL NORTHAMPTON COUNTY LAW LIBRARY, 669 Washington St, 18042-7411. SAN 314-4704. Tel: 610-829-6751. FAX: 610-559-6750. Web Site: www.nccpa.org. *Law Librn,* Lisa Mann; E-mail: lmann@northamptoncounty.org
Founded 1860
Library Holdings: Bk Titles 23,399
Special Collections: Typical Coll for Pa County Law Libr
Open Mon-Fri 8:30-4:30

EBENSBURG

GL CAMBRIA COUNTY FREE LAW LIBRARY*, Courthouse, S Center St, 15931. SAN 314-4739. Tel: 814-472-1501. Toll Free Tel: 800-540-2525, Ext 1501. FAX: 814-472-8393. Web Site: www.cambriacountypa.gov. *Law Librn,* Lynne Dougherty; Staff 2 (MLS 1, Non-MLS 1)
Founded 1920
Library Holdings: Bk Vols 2,500
Subject Interests: Penn law
Open Mon-Fri 9-4

S CAMBRIA COUNTY HISTORICAL SOCIETY LIBRARY*, 615 N Center St, 15931. (Mail add: PO Box 278, 15931-0278), SAN 314-4747. Tel: 814-472-6674. Web Site: www.cambriacountyhistorical.com. *Curator,* Allie Buck; E-mail: awbuck@verizon.net
Founded 1925
Library Holdings: Bk Titles 2,400; Bk Vols 3,100
Subject Interests: Genealogy of families within Cambria County, Hist of Cambria county, Indust, Penn soc & relig life of citizens
Publications: Heritage (Newsletter)
Open Tues-Fri 10-4, Sat 9-1

P EBENSBURG CAMBRIA PUBLIC LIBRARY*, 225 W Highland Ave, 15931-1507. SAN 314-4755. Tel: 814-472-7957. FAX: 814-472-2037. E-mail: ebenpl@yahoo.com. Web Site: www.cclib.lib.pa.us/ebensburg. *Dir,* Mary Makin
Founded 1923. Pop 4,818; Circ 28,900
Library Holdings: Audiobooks 1,400; DVDs 665; e-books 1,547; Bk Titles 24,673; Per Subs 42
Special Collections: Local History Coll
Automation Activity & Vendor Info: (Cataloging) Innovative Interfaces, Inc; (Circulation) Innovative Interfaces, Inc; (OPAC) Innovative Interfaces, Inc
Wireless access
Mem of Cambria County Library System & District Center
Open Mon, Tues & Thurs 1-8, Fri 10-5, Sun 11-6

EDGEWOOD

P C C MELLOR MEMORIAL LIBRARY*, Edgewood Library, One Pennwood Ave, 15218-1627. SAN 315-0844. Tel: 412-731-0909. FAX: 412-731-8969. Web Site: ccmellorlibrary.org/hours-location-contact/ccm-edgewood/. *Libr Dir,* Erin Pierce; E-mail: piercee@einetwork.net; *Asst to the Dir,* Megan Zagorski; E-mail: zagorskim@einetwork.net; Staff 7 (MLS 2, Non-MLS 5)
Founded 1918. Pop 22,623; Circ 108,143
Library Holdings: Large Print Bks 210; Bk Titles 42,819; Bk Vols 44,141; Per Subs 88; Talking Bks 1,291; Videos 1,014
Automation Activity & Vendor Info: (Cataloging) Innovative Interfaces, Inc; (Circulation) Innovative Interfaces, Inc; (OPAC) Innovative Interfaces, Inc
Wireless access
Mem of Allegheny County Library Association (ACLA)
Open Mon-Thurs 10-8, Fri 10-5, Sat 9-4
Friends of the Library Group

EDINBORO

C EDINBORO UNIVERSITY OF PENNSYLVANIA*, Baron-Forness Library, 200 Tartan Dr, 16444. SAN 358-4259. Tel: 814-732-2773. FAX: 814-732-2883. Web Site: www.edinboro.edu/directory/offices-services/library. *Chairperson,* David Obringer; E-mail: obringer@edinboro.edu; *Dir, Univ Libr,* Anthony McMullen; E-mail: amcmullen@edinboro.edu; *Librn,* Dr Monty McAdoo; E-mail: mmcadoo@edinboro.edu; *Soc Media Librn,* Patrick Mundt; Tel: 814-732-1704, E-mail: pmundt@edinboro.edu; *Circ Supvr,* Judy Wilson; E-mail: wilsonj@edinboro.edu; *Bibliog Instr,* John Widner; E-mail: widner@edinboro.edu; *ILL,* Judy Rauenswinter; E-mail: rauenswinter@edinboro.edu; Staff 22 (MLS 10, Non-MLS 12)
Founded 1857. Enrl 7,080; Fac 380; Highest Degree: Master
Library Holdings: AV Mats 10,111; CDs 1,550; DVDs 1,126; e-books 20,720; e-journals 35,738; Microforms 688,352; Bk Titles 309,638; Bk Vols 482,442; Per Subs 844; Videos 2,965
Special Collections: Art Coll; Southeast Asia Coll. State Document Depository
Subject Interests: Educ
Automation Activity & Vendor Info: (Acquisitions) Ex Libris Group; (Cataloging) Ex Libris Group; (Circulation) Ex Libris Group; (Course Reserve) Docutek; (ILL) OCLC; (OPAC) Ex Libris Group; (Serials) Ex Libris Group
Wireless access
Publications: Faculty Guide; Student Guide
Partic in Keystone Library Network; Northwest Interlibrary Cooperative of Pennsylvania; Partnership for Academic Library Collaborative & Innovation
Special Services for the Blind - Large screen computer & software; Reader equip
Open Mon-Thurs 8am-Midnight, Fri 8-6, Sat 9-5, Sun 1:30-10
Friends of the Library Group

ELIZABETHTOWN

C ELIZABETHTOWN COLLEGE, The High Library, One Alpha Dr, 17022-2227. SAN 314-4771. Tel: 717-361-1222. Interlibrary Loan Service Tel: 717-361-1451. Reference Tel: 717-361-1461. Web Site: www.etown.edu/library. *Col Librn, Libr Dir,* Sarah Penniman; Tel: 717-361-1428, E-mail: pennimans@etown.edu; *Coll Develop Librn,* Thomas Zaharevich; Tel: 717-361-1452, E-mail: zaharevicht@etown.edu; *Instruction & Outreach Librn,* Joshua Cohen; Tel: 717-361-1453, E-mail: cohenjp@etown.edu; *Instruction & Scholarly Communications Librn,* Jennifer Strain; Tel: 717-361-1480, E-mail: strainj@etown.edu; *Syst Librn,* Susan Krall; Tel: 717-361-1457, E-mail: kralls@etown.edu; *Archivist,* Rachel Grove Rohrbaugh; Tel: 717-361-1506, E-mail: grover@etown.edu; *Circ Asst,* Clarissa Grunwald; E-mail: grunwaldc@etown.edu; Staff 7 (MLS 6, Non-MLS 1)
Founded 1899. Enrl 1,650; Fac 125; Highest Degree: Master
Library Holdings: CDs 1,677; DVDs 2,578; Music Scores 4,713; Bk Titles 115,074
Special Collections: Church of the Brethren Records; Hess Archives & Special Coll
Subject Interests: Anabaptist & Pietist Studies, Col hist
Automation Activity & Vendor Info: (Acquisitions) Ex Libris Group; (Cataloging) Ex Libris Group; (Circulation) Ex Libris Group; (Course Reserve) Ex Libris Group; (Discovery) Ex Libris Group; (ILL) OCLC ILLiad; (OPAC) Ex Libris Group; (Serials) Ex Libris Group
Wireless access
Partic in Associated College Libraries of Central Pennsylvania; Keystone Library Network; LYRASIS; OCLC Online Computer Library Center, Inc; Partnership for Academic Library Collaborative & Innovation; Westchester Academic Library Directors Organization
Friends of the Library Group

P ELIZABETHTOWN PUBLIC LIBRARY*, Ten S Market St, 17022-2307. SAN 314-478X. Tel: 717-367-7467. FAX: 717-367-6022. E-mail: information@etownpubliclibrary.org. Web Site: www.etownpubliclibrary.org. *Chief Exec Officer,* Deborah Drury; Staff 14 (MLS 3, Non-MLS 11)
Founded 1925. Pop 37,950; Circ 280,000
Library Holdings: AV Mats 1,000; Bks on Deafness & Sign Lang 75; Large Print Bks 750; Bk Titles 42,000; Bk Vols 45,000; Per Subs 80; Talking Bks 150
Special Collections: Braille & Vision Impaired; Business; Community Development; Deaf & Hard of Hearing; Parenting
Automation Activity & Vendor Info: (Cataloging) Innovative Interfaces, Inc; (Circulation) Innovative Interfaces, Inc; (OPAC) Inlex
Wireless access
Function: 24/7 Electronic res, 24/7 Online cat, Adult bk club, After school storytime, Audio & video playback equip for onsite use, AV serv, Bus archives, CD-ROM, Distance learning, Games & aids for people with disabilities, ILL available, Internet access, Large print keyboards, Magnifiers for reading, Music CDs, Photocopying/Printing, Prof lending libr, Prog for adults, Prog for children & young adult, Ref serv available, Spoken cassettes & CDs, Summer reading prog, Telephone ref, VHS videos, Wheelchair accessible, Workshops
Mem of Library System of Lancaster County
Special Services for the Deaf - Bks on deafness & sign lang; Deaf publ; Staff with knowledge of sign lang
Special Services for the Blind - Bks & mags in Braille, on rec, tape & cassette; Bks available with recordings; Bks on cassette; Bks on CD; Braille bks; Cassettes; Large print bks; Magnifiers; PC for people with disabilities
Open Mon Noon-8, Tues & Thurs 9-8, Fri 9-1, Sat 9-4 (9-1 Summer)
Friends of the Library Group

ELKINS PARK

CM PENNSYLVANIA COLLEGE OF OPTOMETRY AT SALUS UNIVERSITY*, Gerard Cottet Library, 8360 Old York Rd, 19027. SAN 314-9625. Tel: 215-780-1260. FAX: 215-780-1263. E-mail: lrc@salus.edu. Web Site: www.salus.edu/Academics/Gerard-Cottet-Library.aspx. *Libr Serv Dir,* Marietta Dooley; E-mail: mdooley@salus.edu; *Librn,* Elyssa Mulcahy;

Tel: 215-780-1262, E-mail: emulcahy@salus.edu; *Libr Tech,* Alison Wilk; Tel: 215-780-1261, E-mail: awilk@salus.edu; Staff 4 (MLS 2, Non-MLS 2)
Founded 1919. Enrl 585; Fac 31
Library Holdings: Bk Titles 24,610; Bk Vols 25,818; Per Subs 316
Special Collections: Antique Eyewear & Ophthalmic Instruments; Old Visual Science Books
Subject Interests: Audiology, Blindness, Clinical med, Low vision, Ocular anatomy, Ocular pharmacology, Ophthalmology, Optometry, Rehabilitation optics, Vision res, Visually impaired
Automation Activity & Vendor Info: (Cataloging) Mandarin Library Automation; (Circulation) Mandarin Library Automation; (OPAC) Mandarin Library Automation
Wireless access
Publications: Infovision (Newsletter); Ocular Bibliographies
Partic in Basic Health Sciences Library Network; Health Sci Libr Info Consortium; National Network of Libraries of Medicine Region 1; Regional Med Libr Network
Open Mon-Fri 8am-11:45pm, Sat & Sun 10am-11:45pm

R REFORM CONGREGATION KENESETH ISRAEL, Meyers Library, 8339 Old York Rd, 19027. SAN 314-4836. Tel: 215-887-8700. FAX: 215-887-1070. Web Site: www.kenesethisrael.org. *Dir, Libr Serv,* Linda Roth; Tel: 215-887-8700, Ext 417, E-mail: Library@kenesethisrael.org; Staff 3 (MLS 1, Non-MLS 2)
Library Holdings: Bk Titles 10,000; Bk Vols 4,000; Per Subs 30
Subject Interests: Judaica
Wireless access
Open Tues & Wed 9:30-3:30, Thurs 10-1, Sun 9:30-Noon

ELKLAND

P ELKLAND AREA COMMUNITY LIBRARY*, 110 E Parkway Ave, 16920-1311. SAN 314-4844. Tel: 814-258-7576. FAX: 814-258-7414. E-mail: eacl@epix.net. Web Site: elklandlibrary.com. *Librn,* LeAnn W Hoaglin
Pop 3,927; Circ 12,599
Library Holdings: Bk Vols 14,000; Per Subs 45
Special Collections: Elkland Journal Coll, bd copies & microfilm
Wireless access
Mem of Potter-Tioga Library System
Open Mon & Tues 1-8, Wed & Fri 8-4, Thurs 12-8, Sat 8-3

ELLWOOD CITY

P ELLWOOD CITY AREA PUBLIC LIBRARY*, 415 Lawrence Ave, 16117-1944. SAN 314-4852. Tel: 724-758-6458. FAX: 724-758-0115. E-mail: Ellwood_Library@lawrencecountylibrary.org. Web Site: www.ellwoodcitylibrary.com. *Dir,* Veronica Pacella; Staff 5 (Non-MLS 5)
Founded 1914. Pop 18,146
Library Holdings: Bk Vols 48,138; Per Subs 75
Mem of Lawrence County Federated Library System
Open Mon-Thurs 10-8, Fri 10-4, Sat 9-4
Friends of the Library Group

ELVERSON

S US DEPARTMENT OF INTERIOR, NATIONAL PARK SERVICE*, Hopewell Furnace National Historic Site Resource Center, Two Mark Bird Lane, 19520. Tel: 610-582-8773, Ext 240. FAX: 610-582-2768. E-mail: hofu_superintendent@nps.gov. Web Site: www.nps.gov/hofu. *Library Contact,* Position Currently Open; Staff 1 (Non-MLS 1)
Founded 1938
Library Holdings: Bk Vols 1,200; Videos 20
Special Collections: Hopewell Furnace Charcoal Iron Industry Coll, microfiche & microfilm; Hopewell Furnace Reports; Old & Rare Books on the History of Iron Making. Oral History
Subject Interests: Hist
Restriction: Not open to pub, Open by appt only, Open to researchers by request

ELYSBURG

P RALPHO TOWNSHIP PUBLIC LIBRARY*, 206 S Market St, 17824. (Mail add: PO Box 315, 17824-0315), SAN 314-4860. Tel: 570-672-9449. E-mail: ralpholib@hotmail.com. Web Site: www2.iu29.org/ralpl. *Dir,* Dean Wade Slusser; Staff 1 (MLS 1)
Founded 1974. Pop 3,131; Circ 14,058
Library Holdings: Bk Vols 21,000; Per Subs 42
Wireless access
Open Mon, Tues & Thurs 1-7, Wed & Fri 11-5
Friends of the Library Group

EMMAUS

P EMMAUS PUBLIC LIBRARY*, 11 E Main St, 18049. SAN 314-4879. Tel: 610-965-9284. E-mail: emmauspl@cliu.org. Web Site: www.emmauspl.org. *Libr Dir,* Maryellen Kanarr; E-mail: epldirector@cliu.org; *Ad,* Lauri Miller; *Tech Serv Librn,* Mary Van Duzer; *Youth Serv Librn,* Susan Monroe; *Circ Mgr/ILL,* Angie Devers; *Libr Office Mgr,* Gayle Hall; Staff 9 (MLS 4, Non-MLS 5)
Founded 1940. Pop 21,000; Circ 100,000
Library Holdings: Bk Vols 90,000; Per Subs 60
Special Collections: Shelter House Coll
Subject Interests: Local hist
Automation Activity & Vendor Info: (Acquisitions) Evergreen; (Cataloging) Evergreen; (Circulation) Evergreen; (Course Reserve) Evergreen; (ILL) Evergreen; (Media Booking) Evergreen; (OPAC) Evergreen; (Serials) Evergreen
Wireless access
Function: 24/7 Electronic res, 24/7 Online cat, Adult bk club, After school storytime, Archival coll, Audiobks on Playaways & MP3, Audiobks via web, AV serv, Bi-weekly Writer's Group, Bk club(s), Bks on CD, Children's prog, Computers for patron use, Digital talking bks, E-Reserves, Electronic databases & coll, Free DVD rentals, Genealogy discussion group, Homebound delivery serv, ILL available, Internet access, Magazines, Meeting rooms, Microfiche/film & reading machines, Movies, Music CDs, Online cat, OverDrive digital audio bks, Photocopying/Printing, Preschool reading prog, Prog for adults, Prog for children & young adult, Ref & res, Ref serv available, Scanner, Senior outreach, Spanish lang bks, STEM programs, Story hour, Study rm, Summer reading prog, Tax forms, Teen prog, Telephone ref, Wheelchair accessible
Partic in Lehigh Carbon Library Cooperative
Open Mon-Thurs 10-9, Sat 10-5
Restriction: Open to pub for ref & circ; with some limitations
Friends of the Library Group

EMPORIUM

P CAMERON COUNTY PUBLIC LIBRARY*, Barbara Moscato Brown Memorial Library, 27 W Fourth St, 15834. SAN 358-4526. Tel: 814-486-8011. FAX: 814-486-3725. Web Site: www.barbaramoscatobrownmemoriallibrary.org. *Libr Dir,* Yelena Kisler; E-mail: brocampl@zitomedia.net; *ILL, Librn,* Sue Ramarge; Staff 4 (MLS 1, Non-MLS 3)
Founded 1940. Pop 5,974
Library Holdings: Large Print Bks 450; Bk Vols 30,300; Per Subs 74
Subject Interests: Penn hist
Automation Activity & Vendor Info: (Cataloging) Evolve; (Circulation) Evolve; (OPAC) Evolve
Wireless access
Open Mon, Tues, Thurs & Fri (Winter) 11-7, Wed & Sat 9-1; Mon, Tues, Thurs & Fri (Summer) 11-6, Wed & Sat 9-1
Friends of the Library Group

EPHRATA

P EPHRATA PUBLIC LIBRARY*, 550 S Reading Rd, 17522. SAN 314-4887. Tel: 717-738-9291. FAX: 717-721-3003. Web Site: www.ephratapubliclibrary.org. *Dir,* Penny Talbert; E-mail: ptalbert@ephratapubliclibrary.org; *Asst Dir,* Abby Balmer; E-mail: abalmer@ephratapubliclibrary.org; Staff 22 (MLS 3, Non-MLS 19)
Founded 1962. Pop 32,796; Circ 560,994
Library Holdings: Bk Vols 106,000; Per Subs 76
Automation Activity & Vendor Info: (Cataloging) Innovative Interfaces, Inc; (Circulation) Innovative Interfaces, Inc; (OPAC) Innovative Interfaces, Inc
Wireless access
Function: 24/7 Electronic res, 24/7 Online cat, Activity rm, Adult bk club, Adult literacy prog, After school storytime, Art exhibits, Art programs, Audiobks on Playaways & MP3, Audiobks via web, Bi-weekly Writer's Group, Bilingual assistance for Spanish patrons, Bk club(s), Bks on CD, Children's prog, Computer training, Computers for patron use, E-Reserves, Electronic databases & coll, Equip loans & repairs, Family literacy, Free DVD rentals, Games & aids for people with disabilities, Genealogy discussion group, Govt ref serv, Health sci info serv, Holiday prog, Home delivery & serv to seniorr ctr & nursing homes, Homebound delivery serv, Homework prog, ILL available, Instruction & testing, Internet access, Life-long learning prog for all ages, Literacy & newcomer serv, Magazines, Mango lang, Meeting rooms, Movies, Museum passes, Music CDs, Notary serv, Online cat, Outreach serv, OverDrive digital audio bks, Passport agency, Photocopying/Printing, Preschool outreach, Preschool reading prog, Prog for adults, Prog for children & young adult, Ref & res, Ref serv available, Satellite serv, Scanner, Senior computer classes, Senior outreach, Serves people with intellectual disabilities, Spanish lang bks, STEM programs, Story hour, Summer & winter reading prog, Summer reading prog, Tax forms, Teen prog, Telephone ref, Visual arts prog, Wheelchair accessible, Winter reading prog, Workshops, Writing prog
Mem of Library System of Lancaster County

Open Mon-Thurs 10-8, Sat 9-1
Friends of the Library Group

S THE HISTORICAL SOCIETY OF THE COCALICO VALLEY LIBRARY, 237 W Main St, 17522. (Mail add: PO Box 193, 17522), SAN 326-5331. Tel: 717-733-1616. E-mail: hscv@cocalicovalleyhs.org. Web Site: www.cocalicovalleyhs.org/museum-library. *Librn,* Cynthia Marquet; Staff 1 (MLS 1)
Founded 1957
Library Holdings: Bk Titles 1,750; Bk Vols 2,075
Special Collections: Ephrata Cloister Imprints (Walter Moyer Coll); Historical Photographs
Subject Interests: Local genealogy, Local hist
Wireless access
Publications: Annual Journal
Open Mon, Wed & Thurs 9:30-6, Sat 8:30-5
Restriction: Non-circulating to the pub

ERDENHEIM

J ANTONELLI INSTITUTE*, Graphic Design & Photography Library, 300 Montgomery Ave, 19038. SAN 372-6967. Tel: 215-836-2222. FAX: 215-836-2794. E-mail: library@antonelli.edu. Web Site: www.antonelli.edu. *Pres,* John Hayden; Tel: 215-948-9222, E-mail: john.hayden@antonelli.edu; *Dir of Educ,* Tricia Fleming; Tel: 215-948-9223, E-mail: tricia.fleming@antonelli.edu
Founded 1938. Enrl 171; Fac 17
Library Holdings: Bk Titles 1,145; Per Subs 42
Open Mon-Thurs 8am-12pm, Fri 8-6

ERIE

SR ANSHE HESED TEMPLE LIBRARY*, 5401 Old Zuck Rd, 16506. SAN 328-6363. Tel: 814-454-2426. FAX: 814-454-2427.
Library Holdings: Bk Vols 4,000
Special Collections: Congregational Archives
Wireless access
Restriction: Congregants only

GM DEPARTMENT OF VETERANS AFFAIRS MEDICAL CENTER*, Medical Library, 135 E 38th St, 16504-1559. SAN 314-5050. Tel: 814-860-2442 (Direct to Library), 814-868-8661. FAX: 814-860-2469. *Librn,* Karla Kaufman; E-mail: karla.kaufman@va.gov; Staff 2 (MLS 1, Non-MLS 1)
Founded 1951
Library Holdings: Bk Vols 35,000; Per Subs 125
Subject Interests: Nursing, Primary health care
Wireless access
Partic in National Network of Libraries of Medicine Region 1; NICOP
Open Mon 8:5:30, Tues-Thurs 7-4:30, Sat 8-4:30

S ERIE COUNTY HISTORICAL SOCIETY*, Library & Archives, Erie County History Ctr, 419 State St, 16501. SAN 324-7619. Tel: 814-454-1813, Ext 26. Reference Tel: 814-454-1813, Ext 28. FAX: 814-454-6890. Web Site: eriehistory.com. *Dir, Libr & Archives,* Annita Andrick; E-mail: aandrick@eriecountyhistory.org; Staff 1.8 (MLS 1, Non-MLS 0.8)
Founded 1903
Library Holdings: Bk Vols 5,800; Per Subs 20
Special Collections: Oral History
Subject Interests: Civil War, Local hist, Penn hist
Function: Workshops
Publications: Ethnic Erie Archives Series (Local historical information); Journal of Erie Studies (Biannually)
Partic in Northwest Interlibrary Cooperative of Pennsylvania; OCLC Online Computer Library Center, Inc
Open Tues-Sat 11-4
Restriction: Staff & prof res

GL ERIE COUNTY LAW LIBRARY, Court House, Rm 01, 140 W Sixth St, 16501. SAN 314-4933. Tel: 814-451-6319. FAX: 814-451-6320. *Librn,* Max C Peaster; E-mail: mpeaster@eriecountypa.gov; Staff 1 (MLS 1)
Founded 1876
Library Holdings: Bk Vols 10,000; Per Subs 10
Subject Interests: Law
Open Mon-Fri 8-4:30

P ERIE COUNTY PUBLIC LIBRARY*, Raymond M Blasco MD Memorial Library, 160 E Front St, 16507. SAN 358-4585. Tel: 814-451-6900. Circulation Tel: 814-451-6929. Interlibrary Loan Service Tel: 814-451-6922. Reference Tel: 814-451-6927. Administration Tel: 814-451-6952. Automation Services Tel: 814-451-6923, 814-451-6925. FAX: 814-451-6907. Administration FAX: 814-451-6969. TDD: 814-451-6931. Reference E-mail: reference@erielibrary.org. Web Site: erielibrary.org. *Dir,* Erin Wincek; Tel: 814-451-6914, E-mail: ewincek@eriecountypa.gov; *Asst Dir,* Sheryl Thomas; Tel: 814-451-6911, E-mail: sthomas@eriecountypa.gov; *Adult Serv Mgr,* Andrew Miller; Tel: 814-451-6932, E-mail: amiller@eriecountypa.gov; *Bus Off Mgr,* Deana Cooper; Tel: 814-451-6980, E-mail: dcooper@eriecountypa.gov; *Circ Mgr,* Correy Connelly; Tel: 814-451-6908, E-mail: cconnelly@eriecountypa.gov; *Outreach Serv Mgr,* Chanel Cook; Tel: 814-451-6959, E-mail: ccook@eriecountypa.gov; *Mgr, Tech Serv,* Anitra Gates; Tel: 814-451-6919, E-mail: agates@eriecountygov.org; *Youth Serv Mgr,* Shane Donaldson; Tel: 814-451-6928, E-mail: sdonaldson@eriecountypa.gov; Staff 21.5 (MLS 16, Non-MLS 5.5)
Founded 1895. Pop 245,275; Circ 1,560,203
Jan 2017-Dec 2017 Income (Main & Associated Libraries) $5,926,600, State $1,882,993, Federal $75,489, County $3,696,344, Locally Generated Income $271,774. Mats Exp $610,209, Books $373,481, Per/Ser (Incl. Access Fees) $22,689, Micro $882, AV Mat $96,700, Electronic Ref Mat (Incl. Access Fees) $111,457, Presv $5,000. Sal $4,188,147 (Prof $32,370)
Library Holdings: Audiobooks 29,448; AV Mats 27,881; DVDs 18,452; e-books 325; Bk Vols 433,943; Per Subs 269; Videos 21,723
Special Collections: Genealogy (Western Pennsylvania). State Document Depository; US Document Depository
Automation Activity & Vendor Info: (Acquisitions) SirsiDynix-WorkFlows; (Cataloging) SirsiDynix-WorkFlows; (Circulation) SirsiDynix-WorkFlows; (OPAC) SirsiDynix-iBistro
Wireless access
Partic in LYRASIS
Open Mon-Thurs 9-8:30, Fri & Sat 9-5, Sun 1-5
Friends of the Library Group
Branches: 4
EDINBORO BRANCH, 413 W Plum St, Edinboro, 16412-2508, SAN 358-4615. Tel: 814-451-7081. *Br Coordr,* Mary Rennie; Tel: 814-451-6910, E-mail: mrennie@erielibrary.org
IROQUOIS AVENUE, 4212 Iroquois Ave, 16511-2198, SAN 358-4674. Tel: 814-451-7082. FAX: 814-451-7092. *Br Mgr,* Kaitlyn Labrozzi; E-mail: klabrozzi@eriecountypa.gov; *Br Coordr,* Mary Rennie; Tel: 814-451-6910, Fax: 814-451-6969, E-mail: mrennie@erielibrary.org
Open Mon-Thurs 10-8, Fri & Sat 10-5
LINCOLN COMMUNITY CENTER, 1255 Manchester Rd, 16505-2614, SAN 358-4763. Tel: 814-451-7085. FAX: 814-451-7095. *Br Coordr,* Mary Rennie; Tel: 814-451-6910, Fax: 814-451-6969, E-mail: mrennie@erielibrary.org
MILLCREEK, 2088 Interchange Rd, Ste 280, 16565-0601, SAN 358-4739. Tel: 814-451-7084. FAX: 814-451-7094. *Br Mgr,* John Euliano; E-mail: jeuliano@eriecountypa.gov; *Br Coordr,* Mary Rennie; Tel: 814-451-6910, Fax: 814-451-6969, E-mail: mrennie@erielibrary.org
Bookmobiles: 1

R FIRST PRESBYTERIAN CHURCH OF THE COVENANT*, Brittain Library, 250 W Seventh St, 16501. SAN 314-4909. Tel: 814-456-4243. FAX: 814-454-3350. *Librn,* Jean Ann Tauber
Founded 1954
Library Holdings: Large Print Bks 100; Bk Vols 7,000; Per Subs 12; Videos 50
Function: Summer reading prog, Wheelchair accessible
Restriction: Restricted access, Restricted borrowing privileges

C GANNON UNIVERSITY*, Nash Library, 619 Sassafras St, 16541. SAN 314-4968. Tel: 814-871-7557. Interlibrary Loan Service Tel: 814-871-5529. FAX: 814-871-5666. E-mail: library@gannon.edu. Web Site: library.gannon.edu. *Dir,* Ken Brundage; E-mail: brundage001@gannon.edu; *Librn,* Lawrence Maxted; E-mail: maxted001@gannon.edu; *Outreach Librn,* Emmett Lombard; E-mail: lombard002@gannon.edu; *Syst Librn,* Betsy Garloch; E-mail: garloch001@gannon.edu; *Archives, Tech Serv,* Lori Grossholz; E-mail: grosshol001@gannon.edu; *ILL,* Mary Beth Earll; E-mail: earll001@gannon.edu; *Ref & Instruction,* Deborah West; E-mail: west001@gannon.edu; Staff 18 (MLS 9, Non-MLS 9)
Founded 1925. Enrl 3,408; Fac 201; Highest Degree: Doctorate. Sal $726,013
Library Holdings: AV Mats 2,853; e-journals 46,118; Bk Vols 265,863; Per Subs 152
Automation Activity & Vendor Info: (Acquisitions) SirsiDynix-WorkFlows; (Cataloging) SirsiDynix-WorkFlows; (Circulation) SirsiDynix-WorkFlows; (ILL) OCLC ILLiad; (OPAC) SirsiDynix; (Serials) SirsiDynix-WorkFlows
Wireless access
Partic in LYRASIS; Partnership for Academic Library Collaborative & Innovation
Open Mon-Thurs 7:30am-Midnight, Fri 7:30am-8pm, Sat 10-10, Sun 10am-Midnight

CM LAKE ERIE COLLEGE OF OSTEOPATHIC MEDICINE*, Learning Resource Center, 1858 W Grandview Blvd, 16509. Tel: 814-866-8451. E-mail: library@lecom.edu. Web Site: lecom.edu/about-lecom/visit-lecom/lecom-learning-resource-center,

www.lecom.edu. *Dir, Learning Res, Dir, Technology,* Daniel Welch; E-mail: dwelch@lecom.edu; Staff 5 (MLS 3, Non-MLS 2)
Founded 1993. Highest Degree: Doctorate
Library Holdings: e-journals 800; Bk Vols 8,500; Per Subs 200
Subject Interests: Osteopathic med
Automation Activity & Vendor Info: (Cataloging) EOS International; (Circulation) EOS International; (OPAC) EOS International; (Serials) EOS International
Wireless access
Partic in LYRASIS
Open Mon-Fri 7am-11pm, Sat & Sun 8am-11pm
Restriction: Open to students, fac & staff

C MERCYHURST UNIVERSITY*, Hammermill Library - Main Campus, 501 E 38th St, 16546. SAN 314-5018. Tel: 814-824-2234. Interlibrary Loan Service Tel: 814-824-3988. Administration Tel: 814-824-2232. FAX: 814-824-2219. Web Site: library.mercyhurst.edu. *Dir, Univ Libr & Distance Learning,* Darci Jones; Tel: 814-824-2237, E-mail: djones@mercyhurst.edu; *Tech Serv Adminr,* Ashley Lambert; Tel: 814-824-2236, E-mail: alambert@mercyhurst.edu; *Pub Serv Librn,* Angela Okey; Tel: 814-824-3068, E-mail: aokey@mercyhurst.edu; *Res & Ref Librn,* Karen Niemla; Tel: 814-824-3871, E-mail: kniemla@mercyhurst.edu; *Acq,* Lynn Falk; E-mail: lfalk@mercyhurst.edu; Staff 8 (MLS 4, Non-MLS 4)
Founded 1926. Highest Degree: Master
Special Collections: Ethnic History Concentrating on Northwest Pennsylvania, bks
Automation Activity & Vendor Info: (Acquisitions) ByWater Solutions; (Cataloging) ByWater Solutions; (Circulation) ByWater Solutions; (Course Reserve) ByWater Solutions; (Discovery) EBSCO Discovery Service; (ILL) ByWater Solutions; (OPAC) ByWater Solutions; (Serials) ByWater Solutions
Wireless access
Partic in Interlibrary Delivery Service of Pennsylvania; LYRASIS; Northwest Interlibrary Cooperative of Pennsylvania; OCLC Online Computer Library Center, Inc; Partnership for Academic Library Collaborative & Innovation
Open Mon-Thurs 7:30am-Midnight, Fri 7:30am-9pm, Sat 9-6, Sun Noon-Midnight
Departmental Libraries:
RIDGE LIBRARY - NORTH EAST CAMPUS, 16 W Division St, North East, 16428, SAN 378-4460. Tel: 814-725-6324. FAX: 814-725-6112. *Dir,* Penny Wise; Tel: 814-725-6326, E-mail: pwise@mercyhurst.edu; Staff 4 (MLS 2, Non-MLS 2)
Enrl 700; Highest Degree: Associate
Library Holdings: Bk Vols 6,933; Per Subs 58
Open Mon-Thurs 7:45am-9pm, Fri 7:45-4, Sat 10-3:30, Sun 3:30-9

C PENN STATE BEHREND*, John M Lilley Library, 4951 College Dr, 16563-4115. SAN 314-5026. Tel: 814-898-6106. FAX: 814-898-6350. E-mail: behrendlibrary@psu.edu. Web Site: libraries.psu.edu/erie. *Head Librn,* Matthew P Ciszek; *Ref & Instruction Librn,* Stephanie Diaz; *Ref & Instruction Librn,* Angela Davis; *Ref & Instruction Librn,* Russell Hall; *Ref & Instruction Librn,* Jane Ingold; *Circ Supvr, Info Res,* Lisa Moyer; *Acq, Info Res & Serv Support Spec,* Melissa Osborn; *Info Res & Serv Support Spec, ILL,* Sarah Koczan. Subject Specialists: *Archives,* Jane Ingold; Staff 9.5 (MLS 5, Non-MLS 4.5)
Founded 1948. Enrl 5,000; Fac 250; Highest Degree: Master
Library Holdings: Bk Vols 133,000; Per Subs 575; Videos 2,500
Special Collections: Behrend Family Coll; Hammermill Paper Company Coll
Wireless access
Open Mon-Thurs 7:45am-Midnight, Fri 7:45am-8pm, Sat Noon-8, Sun Noon-Midnight

M UPMC HAMOT*, Library Services, 201 State St, 16550. SAN 314-4984. Tel: 814-877-3628. FAX: 814-877-6188. Web Site: www.hsls.pitt.edu, www.upmc.com. *Mgr,* Diane Voelker; E-mail: voelkerdr@upmc.edu; Staff 1 (Non-MLS 1)
Founded 1964
Library Holdings: e-books 35; e-journals 124; Bk Titles 1,500; Bk Vols 2,186; Per Subs 100
Subject Interests: Emergency med, Gen surgery, Hospital admin, Internal med, Neurology, Orthopedics, Trauma med
Automation Activity & Vendor Info: (Cataloging) Follett Software; (Circulation) OVID Technologies; (ILL) OCLC FirstSearch
Wireless access
Publications: Columns In-house
Partic in NICOP
Open Mon-Fri 7-3:30

ESSINGTON

TINICUM MEMORIAL PUBLIC LIBRARY*, 620 Seneca St, 19029. SAN 314-5085. Tel: 610-521-9344. FAX: 610-521-3463. E-mail: tinicum@delcolibraries.org. Web Site: tinicumlibrary.org, www.delcolibraries.org/tinicum-memorial-public-library. *Dir,* Linda West; E-mail: tidirector@delcolibraries.org
Pop 4,906; Circ 31,379
Library Holdings: Bk Vols 18,203; Per Subs 30
Wireless access
Mem of Delaware County Libraries
Open Mon, Wed & Thurs 9:30-8, Fri 9:30-4, Sat 9-4

EVANS CITY

P EVANS CITY PUBLIC LIBRARY*, 204 S Jackson St, 16033-1138. SAN 314-5093. Tel: 724-538-8695. FAX: 724-538-5630. E-mail: evanscity@bcfls.org. Web Site: www.evanscitylibrary.org. *Ch Serv Librn, Libr Dir,* Michelina Stickney
Founded 1932. Pop 4,836; Circ 10,000
Library Holdings: Bk Titles 17,000; Per Subs 30
Automation Activity & Vendor Info: (Cataloging) TLC (The Library Corporation); (Circulation) TLC (The Library Corporation); (OPAC) TLC (The Library Corporation)
Mem of Butler County Federated Library System
Open Mon-Thurs 10-6, Sat 9-4

EVERETT

C ALLEGANY COLLEGE OF MARYLAND LIBRARY, Bedford County Campus, 18 N River Lane, 15537. Tel: 814-652-9528. FAX: 814-652-9775. E-mail: libraryhelp@allegany.edu. Web Site: www.allegany.edu/bedford-county-campus/bedford-county-campus-library.html. *Dir, Learning Commons,* Julie Rando; E-mail: jrando@allegany.edu; *Coordr, Libr Serv,* Teresa Wilmes; E-mail: twilmes@allegany.edu
Library Holdings: Bk Titles 48,880; Bk Vols 56,359; Per Subs 440
Automation Activity & Vendor Info: (Acquisitions) Infor Library & Information Solutions; (Cataloging) Infor Library & Information Solutions; (Circulation) Infor Library & Information Solutions; (Course Reserve) Infor Library & Information Solutions; (ILL) Infor Library & Information Solutions; (Media Booking) Infor Library & Information Solutions; (OPAC) Infor Library & Information Solutions; (Serials) Infor Library & Information Solutions
Wireless access
Partic in Maryland Community College Library Consortium; Maryland Interlibrary Loan Organization

P EVERETT FREE LIBRARY*, 137 E Main St, 15537-1259. SAN 314-5115. Tel: 814-652-5922. FAX: 814-652-5425. E-mail: books@everettlibrary.org. Web Site: www.everettlibrary.org. *Dir,* Judy Hillegas; *Ref (Info Servs),* Susan Myers; Staff 2.3 (MLS 0.3, Non-MLS 2)
Founded 1923. Pop 12,903; Circ 47,396
Library Holdings: Bks on Deafness & Sign Lang 27; Bk Titles 41,000; Per Subs 15
Special Collections: Bedford County History; Everett Bicentennial Records Coll; Genealogy; Pennsylvania History
Subject Interests: Local census data
Automation Activity & Vendor Info: (Cataloging) Evergreen; (Circulation) Evergreen; (OPAC) Evergreen
Wireless access
Function: 24/7 Electronic res, 24/7 Online cat, Activity rm, ILL available
Publications: Directory of Pennsylvania Libraries
Mem of Bedford County Library System
Open Mon & Thurs 11-6, Tues 1-8, Wed 10-5, Fri 9-7, Sat 9-4
Restriction: Authorized patrons

EXTON

P CHESTER COUNTY LIBRARY & DISTRICT CENTER*, 450 Exton Square Pkwy, 19341-2496. Interlibrary Loan Service Tel: 610-280-2625. Reference Tel: 610-280-2620. E-mail: cclinfo@ccls.org. Web Site: chescolibraries.org. *Dir,* Marguerite Dube; E-mail: mdube@ccls.org; *Head, Youth Serv,* Jeamme Clancy; *Tech Serv Mgr,* Jenna Persick; *Circ Supvr,* Barbara Bailey; *Multimedia,* Stephanie Sharon
Founded 1962
Mem of Chester County Library System
Open Mon-Thurs 9-9, Fri 9-6, Sat 9:30-5, Sun 1-5
Branches: 1
HENRIETTA HANKIN BRANCH, 215 Windgate Dr, Chester Springs, 19425. Tel: 610-321-1700. E-mail: hhinfo@ccls.org. *Br Mgr,* Beverly Lawler; E-mail: blawler@ccls.org
Open Mon-Thurs 9:30-8, Fri 9:30-6, Sat 9:30-5, Sun 1-5

P CHESTER COUNTY LIBRARY SYSTEM*, 450 Exton Square Pkwy, 19341. SAN 315-3312. Tel: 610-280-2600. FAX: 610-280-2688. Web Site: www.ccls.org. *Exec Dir,* Joseph L Sherwood; E-mail: jsherwood@ccls.org; Staff 75 (MLS 19, Non-MLS 56)
Founded 1928. Pop 412,170
Library Holdings: Bk Vols 282,907; Per Subs 1,117

Special Collections: Adult Reading Large Type Coll; AGR (Adult Graded Reading); Chester County Coll; Chester's Reading Large Type Coll; Children's Reading Large Type Coll; Computer Software Coll; Literacy Coll; Local Newspaper Coll; State & Local Government Rare Books Coll; Work Place Job & Career Information Coll
Automation Activity & Vendor Info: (Acquisitions) Innovative Interfaces, Inc; (Cataloging) Innovative Interfaces, Inc; (Circulation) Innovative Interfaces, Inc; (ILL) Innovative Interfaces, Inc; (OPAC) Innovative Interfaces, Inc; (Serials) Innovative Interfaces, Inc
Wireless access
Publications: Chester County Library Business News; Chester County Library System (Newsletter)
Member Libraries: Atglen Public Library; Avon Grove Library; Chester County Library & District Center; Chester Springs Library; Coatesville Area Public Library; Downingtown Library Co; Easttown Library & Information Center; Honey Brook Community Library; Kennett Library; Malvern Public Library; Oxford Public Library; Parkesburg Free Library; Phoenixville Public Library; Spring City Free Public Library; Tredyffrin Public Library; West Chester Public Library
Partic in Interlibrary Delivery Service of Pennsylvania; OCLC Online Computer Library Center, Inc
Friends of the Library Group

FACTORYVILLE

P FACTORYVILLE PUBLIC LIBRARY, 163 College Ave, 18419. SAN 314-5131. Tel: 570-945-3788. E-mail: fvillelibrary@gmail.com. Web Site: www.facebook.com/factoryville-public-library-187322357969956. *Dir,* Georgianna Fields
Pop 1,500; Circ 4,715
Library Holdings: Bk Vols 6,300
Open Thurs 10-1, Sat 10-Noon

FALLSINGTON

P FALLSINGTON LIBRARY*, 139 Yardley Ave, 19054-1118. SAN 314-514X. Tel: 215-295-4449. E-mail: alertFA@buckslib.org. Web Site: www.buckslib.org/locations. *Dir,* Charlene Randeiro; Staff 2 (Non-MLS 2)
Founded 1800. Pop 35,891; Circ 43,512
Library Holdings: AV Mats 590; Large Print Bks 72; Bk Titles 23,910; Bk Vols 25,611; Per Subs 49; Talking Bks 72; Videos 161
Special Collections: Bucks County; History Coll; Pennsylvania State History Coll; Society of Friends Coll
Automation Activity & Vendor Info: (Cataloging) SirsiDynix; (Circulation) SirsiDynix; (OPAC) SirsiDynix
Mem of Bucks County Free Library
Open Mon, Tues & Thurs 2-8, Wed 11-5, Fri 2-5, Sat 10-3

FARMINGTON

S NATIONAL PARK SERVICE, DEPARTMENT OF INTERIOR*, Fort Necessity National Battlefield Research Library, One Washington Pkwy, 15437. SAN 323-8644. Tel: 724-329-5512. FAX: 724-329-8682. Web Site: www.nps.gov/fone. *Curator,* Brynn Bender; Tel: 814-893-6537
Founded 1979
Library Holdings: Bk Vols 3,000
Special Collections: French & Indian War/National Road
Restriction: Open by appt only

FARRELL

P CLSV STEY-NEVANT LIBRARY*, 1000 Roemer Blvd, 16121-1899. Tel: 724-983-2714. FAX: 724-983-2714. E-mail: steynevant@clsv.net. Web Site: www.steynevantlibrary.com. *Libr Dir,* Robin Pundzak; E-mail: Rpundzak@clsv.net; *Br Mgr,* Abby Kutz; *Children's Prog Coordr,* Samantha Eicher; Staff 4 (Non-MLS 4)
Founded 1931. Pop 4,808; Circ 1,807
Library Holdings: Bk Vols 29,257; Per Subs 228
Special Collections: Black Studies Coll
Automation Activity & Vendor Info: (Cataloging) Evolve; (Circulation) Evolve; (OPAC) Evolve
Wireless access
Open Mon-Thurs 11-7
Friends of the Library Group

FEASTERVILLE

P TOWNSHIP LIBRARY OF LOWER SOUTHAMPTON, 1983 Bridgetown Pike, 19053-4493. SAN 314-5166. Tel: 215-355-1183. FAX: 215-364-5735. E-mail: hellofe@buckslib.org. Web Site: www.lowersouthamptonlibrary.org. *Libr Dir,* Dennis Stranz; E-mail: stranzd@buckslib.org; Staff 2 (MLS 2)
Founded 1956. Pop 17,000; Circ 127,948
Library Holdings: Audiobooks 3,679; DVDs 4,995; e-books 7,000; Bk Vols 69,900; Per Subs 77
Automation Activity & Vendor Info: (Circulation) SirsiDynix; (OPAC) SirsiDynix
Wireless access
Mem of Bucks County Free Library
Open Mon-Thurs 10-8, Sat 9-4
Friends of the Library Group

FLEETWOOD

P FLEETWOOD AREA PUBLIC LIBRARY, 110 W Arch St, Ste 209, 19522-1301. SAN 376-5857. Tel: 610-944-0146. FAX: 610-944-9064. E-mail: fleetwoodapl@berks.lib.pa.us. Web Site: www.berkslibraries.org/fleetwood. *Libr Dir,* Carin Mileshosky; *Youth Serv Coordr,* Stacy Laucks; E-mail: fleetwoodkids0146@gmail.com; Staff 7 (MLS 1, Non-MLS 6)
Founded 1990. Pop 19,000
Library Holdings: Bk Titles 20,000; Per Subs 23
Automation Activity & Vendor Info: (Cataloging) SirsiDynix; (Circulation) Innovative Interfaces, Inc; (OPAC) Innovative Interfaces, Inc
Wireless access
Mem of Berks County Public Libraries
Open Mon-Thurs 10-8, Fri 10-2, Sat 9-4
Friends of the Library Group

FOLCROFT

P BOROUGH OF FOLCROFT PUBLIC LIBRARY*, 1725 Delmar Dr, 19032-2002. SAN 314-5182. Tel: 610-586-1690. FAX: 610-586-2179. E-mail: folcroft@delcolibraries.org. Web Site: www.folcroftlibrary.org. *Libr Dir,* Lisa Fortwangler; E-mail: fodirector@delcolibraries.org; *Ch,* Violet Jolly; Tel: 610-586-2720, E-mail: Focsd@delcolibraries.org; Staff 2 (MLS 1, Non-MLS 1)
Founded 1975. Pop 6,606; Circ 13,479
Library Holdings: Bk Titles 14,390; Bk Vols 15,871; Per Subs 32; Talking Bks 91; Videos 203
Wireless access
Mem of Delaware County Libraries
Open Mon-Wed & Fri 12-5, Thurs 9-5, Sat 9-4

FOLSOM

P RIDLEY TOWNSHIP PUBLIC LIBRARY*, 100 E MacDade Blvd, 19033-2592. SAN 314-5190. Tel: 610-583-0593. FAX: 610-583-9505. E-mail: info@ridleylibrary.org, reference@ridleylibrary.org. Web Site: ridleylibrary.org. *Libr Dir,* Donna Murray; *Asst Dir, Head, Info Serv,* Mary Tobin; *Ch Serv,* Lauren Longbottom; *ILL,* Karen Sacco; *Pub Serv,* Kathleen Ferguson; Staff 25 (MLS 5, Non-MLS 20)
Founded 1957. Pop 30,791; Circ 200,000
Library Holdings: AV Mats 5,459; Bk Vols 73,559; Per Subs 199
Automation Activity & Vendor Info: (Acquisitions) Innovative Interfaces, Inc; (Cataloging) Innovative Interfaces, Inc; (Circulation) Innovative Interfaces, Inc; (Course Reserve) Innovative Interfaces, Inc; (ILL) Innovative Interfaces, Inc; (Media Booking) Innovative Interfaces, Inc; (OPAC) Innovative Interfaces, Inc; (Serials) Innovative Interfaces, Inc
Wireless access
Function: 24/7 Electronic res, Activity rm, Adult bk club, After school storytime, Art exhibits, Audiobks via web, AV serv, Bilingual assistance for Spanish patrons, Bk club(s), Bks on CD, Bus archives, Children's prog, Computer training, Computers for patron use, E-Readers, Electronic databases & coll, Games & aids for people with disabilities, Holiday prog, Homework prog, ILL available, Instruction & testing, Internet access, Jazz prog, Life-long learning prog for all ages, Magazines, Magnifiers for reading, Mango lang, Microfiche/film & reading machines, Movies, Music CDs, Online cat, Online ref, OverDrive digital audio bks, Photocopying/Printing, Preschool outreach, Preschool reading prog, Prog for adults, Prog for children & young adult, Ref serv available, Spoken cassettes & CDs, Story hour, Summer & winter reading prog, Summer reading prog, Tax forms, Teen prog, Telephone ref, VHS videos, Wheelchair accessible, Winter reading prog, Workshops
Publications: Annual report
Mem of Delaware County Libraries
Open Mon-Wed 10-8, Thurs & Fri 10-5, Sat 12-4, Sun 1-4:30
Friends of the Library Group

FORD CITY

P FORD CITY PUBLIC LIBRARY*, 1136 Fourth Ave, 16226-1202. SAN 314-5204. Tel: 724-763-3591. FAX: 724-763-2705. E-mail: fordcity@armstronglibraries.org. Web Site: www.armstronglibraries.org/ford-city. *Dir,* Anita Bowser; E-mail: anita.bowser@armstronglibraries.org; Staff 2.5 (Non-MLS 2.5)
Founded 1945. Pop 3,410; Circ 23,131
Library Holdings: Bk Titles 33,029; Per Subs 58
Special Collections: 75th Anniversary Book of Ford City (Ford City History Coll); Ancestry (Claypool Family in America, Jack Family & Schall/Shaull Family Coll), pamphlets; Apollo People Coll; Armstrong County of Pennsylvania (J H Beers Coll, 1914); Bethel Evangelical Lutheran Church Cemetery Listing 1979; Bethel Township 1878-1978

Centennial; Decendants of Jacob Nunamaker & Katherine (Zell) Nunamaker Coll; Dulany-Furlong & Kindred Families Coll; Easley-Rooker Family History Coll, 2nd draft; Elderton Plumcreek Area-Through the Years; Ford City Centennial 1887-1987; History of Armstrong County (R W Smith Coll, 1883); History of Manorville, pamphlets; History of Slate Lich Presbyterian Church Coll, pamphlets; Lives & Letters From Kiester House; Michael A Sheely Family Coll; The Anderson Family History Coll; The Family of Samuel Wysalin America Coll; Thomas Graham Benner Family Coll
Automation Activity & Vendor Info: (Cataloging) Follett Software; (Circulation) Follett Software; (OPAC) Follett Software
Wireless access
Open Tues-Thurs 10-8, Fri 10-6, Sat 8-3

FORT WASHINGTON

P UPPER DUBLIN PUBLIC LIBRARY*, 805 Loch Alsh Ave, 19034. SAN 358-4135. Tel: 215-628-8744. E-mail: upperdublinlibrary@mclinc.org. Web Site: www.upperdublinlibrary.org. *Dir,* Cherilyn Fiory; *Asst Dir,* Lauren Smyth; *Circ Mgr,* Judy Fraser; *Ch Serv,* Jennifer Sivers; *Mkt & Communications Spec,* India Frazier; *Ref Serv,* Kay Klocko; *Tech Serv,* Kathy Brannon; *Teen Serv,* Molly Kane; Staff 13.5 (MLS 5.4, Non-MLS 8.1)
Founded 1932. Pop 25,878; Circ 249,090
Library Holdings: AV Mats 10,903; Bk Vols 106,772; Per Subs 125
Automation Activity & Vendor Info: (Acquisitions) Innovative Interfaces, Inc; (Cataloging) Innovative Interfaces, Inc; (Circulation) Innovative Interfaces, Inc; (OPAC) Innovative Interfaces, Inc
Wireless access
Function: Adult bk club, Audiobks via web, AV serv, Bk club(s), Bks on cassette, Bks on CD, Children's prog, Computer training, Computers for patron use, Digital talking bks, Free DVD rentals, Holiday prog, ILL available, Instruction & testing, Mail & tel request accepted, Music CDs, Online cat, Outreach serv, Outside serv via phone, mail, e-mail & web, OverDrive digital audio bks, Photocopying/Printing, Preschool outreach, Prog for adults, Prog for children & young adult, Ref serv available, Senior computer classes, Spoken cassettes & CDs, Spoken cassettes & DVDs, Story hour, Summer reading prog, Tax forms, Teen prog, Telephone ref, VHS videos, Wheelchair accessible, Workshops
Partic in Montgomery County Library & Information Network Consortium
Open Mon-Thurs 9:30-9, Fri & Sat 9:30-5, Sun 12-5
Friends of the Library Group

FOXBURG

P FOXBURG FREE LIBRARY, 31 Main St, 16036. (Mail add: PO Box 304, 16036-0304), SAN 314-5255. Tel: 724-659-3431. FAX: 724-659-3214. E-mail: foxburgfreelibrary@gmail.com. Web Site: foxburglibrary.org. *Dir,* LaTrobe Edward Barnitz; Staff 1.5 (MLS 0.5, Non-MLS 1)
Founded 1910. Pop 5,516; Circ 11,346
Library Holdings: Bk Vols 16,479; Per Subs 11
Automation Activity & Vendor Info: (Cataloging) Follett Software
Wireless access
Mem of Oil Creek District Library Center
Open Mon & Tues 12-7, Wed-Sat 10-5

FRACKVILLE

P FRACKVILLE FREE PUBLIC LIBRARY*, 56 N Lehigh Ave, 17931-1424. SAN 314-5263. Tel: 570-874-3382. FAX: 570-874-3382. E-mail: webmaster@frackvillelibrary.com. Web Site: www.frackvillelibrary.com. *Libr Dir,* Kathy Van Gieson; E-mail: kathyvangieson@frackvillelibrary.com; Staff 1 (Non-MLS 1)
Founded 1939. Pop 9,348; Circ 10,293
Library Holdings: Bk Titles 19,124; Per Subs 41; Talking Bks 128; Videos 145
Subject Interests: Local hist
Automation Activity & Vendor Info: (Acquisitions) Follett Software; (Cataloging) SirsiDynix; (Circulation) Follett Software
Wireless access
Function: After school storytime, Bks on CD, Children's prog, Computers for patron use, ILL available, Internet access, Magazines, Magnifiers for reading, Photocopying/Printing, Prog for children & young adult, Ref serv available, Scanner, Spoken cassettes & CDs, Summer reading prog, Telephone ref, Wheelchair accessible
Partic in OCLC Online Computer Library Center, Inc
Open Mon-Thurs 11-7, Fri 11-5, Sat 9-4

S STATE CORRECTIONAL INSTITUTION*, Frackville Library, 1111 Altamont Blvd, 17931. Tel: 570-874-4516. Web Site: www.cor.pa.gov/Facilities/StatePrisons/Pages/Frackville.aspx. *Librn,* Goodson Gomonda; E-mail: ggomonda@pa.gov
Founded 1987
Library Holdings: Bk Vols 15,000
Automation Activity & Vendor Info: (Circulation) Follett Software
Restriction: Not open to pub

FRANKLIN

P FRANKLIN PUBLIC LIBRARY*, 421 12th St, 16323-0421. SAN 314-5271. Tel: 814-432-5062. FAX: 814-432-8998. E-mail: franklinpl@franklinlibrary.org. Web Site: www.franklinlibrary.org. *Br Mgr,* Zoe Oakes; *Children's Coordr,* Lynn Lauderdale; *Young Adult Serv Coordr,* Kathleen Shay; *ILL,* Stephen Snyder; Staff 8 (MLS 1, Non-MLS 7)
Founded 1894. Pop 21,577; Circ 80,034
Library Holdings: AV Mats 2,734; CDs 327; DVDs 97; Large Print Bks 1,355; Bk Titles 43,278; Per Subs 105; Talking Bks 1,229; Videos 1,315
Special Collections: Pennsylvania & Venango County History Coll
Automation Activity & Vendor Info: (Acquisitions) Follett Software; (Cataloging) Follett Software; (Circulation) Follett Software; (OPAC) Follett Software
Wireless access
Function: Activity rm, Adult bk club, Adult literacy prog, Bk club(s), Bks on CD, Children's prog, Computers for patron use, Electronic databases & coll, Free DVD rentals, Home delivery & serv to seniorr ctr & nursing homes, ILL available, Magazines, Mail & tel request accepted, Microfiche/film & reading machines, Movies, Music CDs, Online cat, Outreach serv, OverDrive digital audio bks, Photocopying/Printing, Preschool outreach, Prog for adults, Senior outreach, Story hour, Summer reading prog, Tax forms, Teen prog, VHS videos, Wheelchair accessible
Mem of Oil Creek District Library Center
Open Mon & Fri 10-6, Wed & Thurs 10-8, Sat 10-5
Restriction: Non-resident fee
Friends of the Library Group

GL VENANGO COUNTY LAW LIBRARY*, Venango County Court House, 1168 Liberty St, 16323. (Mail add: PO Box 831, 16323-0831), SAN 324-1173. Tel: 814-432-9612. FAX: 814-432-3149. Web Site: www.co.venango.pa.us. *Law Librn,* Sandra L Baker; E-mail: sbaker@co.venango.pa.us
Library Holdings: Bk Titles 10,000
Subject Interests: Law cases from 25 reporter systs
Wireless access
Open Mon-Fri 8:30-4:30

FREDERICKSBURG

P MATTHEWS PUBLIC LIBRARY, 102 W Main St, 17026. Tel: 717-865-5523. FAX: 717-865-5523. Web Site: matthews.lclibs.org. *Libr Dir,* Sheila Redcay; E-mail: redcay@lclibs.org; Staff 7 (MLS 2, Non-MLS 5)
Founded 1982. Circ 65,000
Library Holdings: Bks on Deafness & Sign Lang 10; Bk Vols 30,000; Per Subs 25
Automation Activity & Vendor Info: (Cataloging) Innovative Interfaces, Inc; (Circulation) Innovative Interfaces, Inc; (OPAC) Innovative Interfaces, Inc
Wireless access
Function: 24/7 Electronic res, 24/7 Online cat, Activity rm, Adult bk club, Bks on CD, Children's prog, Genealogy discussion group, Holiday prog, Home delivery & serv to seniorr ctr & nursing homes, Homebound delivery serv, ILL available, Internet access, Magazines, Meeting rooms, Music CDs, Online cat, Outreach serv, Photocopying/Printing, Preschool outreach, Printer for laptops & handheld devices, Prog for adults, Prog for children & young adult, Ref & res, Ref serv available, STEM programs, Story hour, Study rm, Summer & winter reading prog, Teen prog, Telephone ref, Wheelchair accessible, Winter reading prog, Workshops
Mem of Lebanon County Library System
Open Mon-Thurs 9-8, Fri 9-5, Sat 9-4

FREDERICKTOWN

P FREDERICKTOWN AREA PUBLIC LIBRARY, 38 Water St, 15333. (Mail add: PO Box 625, 15333-0625), SAN 376-575X. Tel: 724-377-0017. FAX: 724-377-2924. E-mail: fredpl@atlanticbbn.net. Web Site: www.washlibs.org/fredericktown. *Actg Dir,* Theda Diethorn
Library Holdings: Bk Titles 10,551; Per Subs 20
Wireless access
Function: Audiobks via web, For res purposes, ILL available, Photocopying/Printing, Prog for children & young adult, Summer reading prog
Mem of Washington County Library System
Open Mon & Wed 11-7, Fri 11-4, Sat 10-3

FREEPORT

P FREEPORT AREA LIBRARY*, 428 Market St, 16229-1122. SAN 314-5301. Tel: 724-295-3616. FAX: 724-295-3616. E-mail: fala@salsgiver.com. Web Site: freeportlibrary.org. *Librn,* Nancy R Hagins; *Asst Librn,* Michele Ciani

Founded 1937. Pop 9,856; Circ 19,234
Library Holdings: Audiobooks 432; Bks on Deafness & Sign Lang 15; Braille Volumes 11; DVDs 1,300; High Interest/Low Vocabulary Bk Vols 375; Large Print Bks 2,094; Microforms 27; Bk Titles 34,772; Bk Vols 36,991; Per Subs 21; Talking Bks 519; Videos 667
Subject Interests: Local genealogy
Wireless access
Function: Adult bk club
Open Mon & Tues 10-6, Wed 10-7, Thurs & Fri 12-5, Sat 10-3
Friends of the Library Group

GALETON

P GALETON PUBLIC LIBRARY, Five Park Ln, 16922. SAN 314-531X. Tel: 814-435-2321. FAX: 814-435-2321. E-mail: gplibr@ptd.net. Web Site: galetonpubliclibrary.org. *Librn,* Darlene Jackson; *Librn,* Kay Sutton
Founded 1907. Pop 2,131; Circ 6,025
Library Holdings: Bk Vols 10,000; Per Subs 21
Subject Interests: Local hist
Mem of Potter-Tioga Library System
Open Mon-Sat 11-4

GALLITZIN

P GALLITZIN PUBLIC LIBRARY*, DeGol Plaza, Ste 30, 411 Convent St, 16641-1244. SAN 314-5328. Tel: 814-886-4041. FAX: 814-886-2125. E-mail: gallitzinpublib@yahoo.com. Web Site: www.cclsys.org/gallitzin. *Dir,* Helen Saylor; *Librn,* Rachel Cain; *Librn,* Michelle Mentzer
Founded 1957. Pop 2,003; Circ 28,000
Library Holdings: Audiobooks 100; Bk Titles 14,633; Per Subs 40
Automation Activity & Vendor Info: (Cataloging) Evergreen; (Circulation) Evergreen; (OPAC) Evergreen
Mem of Cambria County Library System & District Center
Open Mon & Wed 9-5, Tues 1-7, Thurs 9-7, Sat 9-4

GENESEE

P GENESEE AREA LIBRARY, 301 Main St, 16923-8805. (Mail add: PO Box 135, 16923-0135), SAN 376-7272. Tel: 814-228-3328. E-mail: library@geneseelibrary.com. Web Site: www.geneseelibrary.com. *Libr Dir,* Erica Moses; Staff 2 (Non-MLS 2)
Founded 1985. Pop 799; Circ 7,500
Library Holdings: Bk Vols 7,000; Per Subs 16
Wireless access
Function: Accelerated reader prog, Adult bk club, Bks on CD, Children's prog, Computer training, Computers for patron use, ILL available, Internet access, Magazines, Movies, Online cat, Photocopying/Printing, Printer for laptops & handheld devices, Prog for adults, Prog for children & young adult, Senior computer classes, Wheelchair accessible
Mem of Potter-Tioga Library System
Open Tues 11-6, Wed 12-7, Fri 10-6, Sat 9-2
Restriction: Borrowing requests are handled by ILL, ID required to use computers (Ltd hrs), Open to pub for ref & circ; with some limitations, Registered patrons only, Use of others with permission of librn

GETTYSBURG

S ADAMS COUNTY HISTORICAL SOCIETY LIBRARY*, Lutheran Theological Seminary Campus, 368 Springs Ave, 17325. (Mail add: PO Box 4325, 17325-4325), SAN 314-5336. Tel: 717-334-4723. FAX: 717-334-0722. E-mail: info@achs-pa.org. Web Site: www.achs-pa.org. *Exec Dir,* Andrew I Dalton; E-mail: director@achs-pa.org
Founded 1940
Library Holdings: Bk Titles 2,000; Per Subs 10
Special Collections: The Battle of Gettysburg Research Center
Subject Interests: Adams County hist
Publications: Adams County History; Newsletter (Annual)

L ADAMS COUNTY LAW LIBRARY*, Court House, 117 Baltimore St, 17325. SAN 327-1080. Tel: 717-337-9812. Web Site: www.adamscounty.us/Dept/LawLibrary. *Law Librn,* Dr B Bohleke; E-mail: bbohleke@adamscounty.us
Library Holdings: Bk Vols 50,000; Per Subs 10
Wireless access
Open Mon-Fri 8-4:30
Restriction: Non-circulating

P ADAMS COUNTY LIBRARY SYSTEM*, Central Library, 140 Baltimore St, 17325-2311. SAN 358-4887. Tel: 717-334-5716. FAX: 717-334-7992. E-mail: adams@adamslibrary.org. Web Site: www.adamslibrary.org. *Exec Dir,* Laura Goss; *Asst Dir,* Brandt Ensor; Staff 36 (MLS 6, Non-MLS 30)
Founded 1945. Pop 104,000
Library Holdings: Bk Vols 141,155; Per Subs 125
Automation Activity & Vendor Info: (Acquisitions) Evergreen; (Cataloging) Evergreen; (Circulation) Evergreen; (OPAC) Evergreen
Wireless access
Function: 24/7 Electronic res, 24/7 Online cat, Activity rm, Adult bk club, Audiobks via web, Bk club(s), Bks on CD, Children's prog, Computer training, Computers for patron use, E-Reserves, Electronic databases & coll, For res purposes, Free DVD rentals, Home delivery & serv to seniorr ctr & nursing homes, Homebound delivery serv, ILL available, Internet access, Life-long learning prog for all ages, Magazines, Mail & tel request accepted, Mail loans to mem, Mango lang, Meeting rooms, Movies, Music CDs, Online cat, Online info literacy tutorials on the web & in blackboard, Outreach serv, Outside serv via phone, mail, e-mail & web, Photocopying/Printing, Preschool outreach, Prog for adults, Prog for children & young adult, Ref & res, Ref serv available, Res libr, Satellite serv, Scanner, Senior outreach, Spanish lang bks, Spoken cassettes & CDs, Spoken cassettes & DVDs, STEM programs, Story hour, Study rm, Summer & winter reading prog, Summer reading prog, Tax forms, Teen prog, Telephone ref, Wheelchair accessible, Winter reading prog
Open Mon-Thurs 9-8:30, Fri & Sat 9-5, Sun 1-5
Friends of the Library Group
Branches: 5
JEAN BARNETT TRONE MEMORIAL LIBRARY OF EAST BERLIN, 105 Locust St, East Berlin, 17316. (Mail add: PO Box 1014, East Berlin, 17316-1014), SAN 321-6640. Tel: 717-259-9000. FAX: 717-259-7651. E-mail: eblib@adamslibrary.org. Web Site: www.adamslibrary.org/about/locations/trone-memorial-library. *Br Mgr,* Jessica Laganosky; E-mail: jessical@adamslibrary.org; Staff 6 (MLS 1, Non-MLS 5)
Founded 1975
Function: 24/7 Electronic res, 24/7 Online cat, Adult bk club, Audiobks via web, Bk club(s), Bks on CD, Children's prog, Computers for patron use, Electronic databases & coll, Free DVD rentals, ILL available, Internet access, Life-long learning prog for all ages, Magazines, Mango lang, Meeting rooms, Movies, Online cat, Online info literacy tutorials on the web & in blackboard, Outreach serv, Photocopying/Printing, Preschool outreach, Prog for adults, Prog for children & young adult, Scanner, Spoken cassettes & CDs, Spoken cassettes & DVDs, STEM programs, Story hour, Study rm, Summer & winter reading prog, Tax forms, Teen prog, Telephone ref
Open Mon & Wed 10-6, Tues & Thurs 12-8, Fri & Sat 9-4
CARROLL VALLEY BRANCH, 5685 Fairfield Rd, Carroll Valley, 17320. Tel: 717-642-6009. FAX: 717-642-6430. Web Site: www.adamslibrary.org/about/locations/carroll-valley. *Br Mgr,* Sherrie DeMartino
Open Mon & Thurs 2-8, Tues, Wed & Fri 11-5, Sat 10-4
HARBAUGH-THOMAS LIBRARY, 50 W York St, Biglerville, 17307. (Mail add: PO Box 277, Biglerville, 17307-0277). Tel: 717-677-6257. FAX: 717-677-6357. Web Site: www.adamslibrary.org/about/locations/harbaugh-thomas. *Br Mgr,* Barbara Buckley; E-mail: barbarab@adamslibrary.org; Staff 4 (Non-MLS 4)
Library Holdings: Bk Vols 20,000
Function: 24/7 Electronic res, 24/7 Online cat, Activity rm, Adult bk club, Audiobks via web, Bk club(s), Bks on CD, Children's prog, Computers for patron use, E-Reserves, Electronic databases & coll, Free DVD rentals, ILL available, Internet access, Life-long learning prog for all ages, Magazines, Mail & tel request accepted, Mango lang, Meeting rooms, Movies, Online cat, Online info literacy tutorials on the web & in blackboard, Photocopying/Printing, Preschool outreach, Prog for adults, Prog for children & young adult, Scanner, Spanish lang bks, Spoken cassettes & CDs, Spoken cassettes & DVDs, STEM programs, Story hour, Study rm, Summer & winter reading prog, Tax forms, Teen prog
Open Mon 12-6, Tues & Thurs 12-8, Wed & Fri 10-6, Sat 9-5
LITTLESTOWN LIBRARY, 232 N Queen St, Littlestown, 17340. Tel: 717-359-0446. FAX: 717-359-1359. Web Site: www.adamslibrary.org/about/locations/littlestown. *Br Mgr,* Jessica Shelleman; E-mail: jessicas@adamslibrary.org; Staff 2 (Non-MLS 2)
Founded 1997
Function: 24/7 Electronic res, 24/7 Online cat, Adult bk club, Audiobks via web, Bk club(s), Bks on CD, Children's prog, Computers for patron use, E-Reserves, Electronic databases & coll, Free DVD rentals, ILL available, Internet access, Life-long learning prog for all ages, Magazines, Mango lang, Meeting rooms, Movies, Online cat, Online info literacy tutorials on the web & in blackboard, Photocopying/Printing, Preschool outreach, Preschool reading prog, Prog for adults, Prog for children & young adult, Scanner, Spoken cassettes & CDs, Spoken cassettes & DVDs, STEM programs, Story hour, Study rm, Summer & winter reading prog, Tax forms, Teen prog
Open Tues & Thurs 2-8, Wed & Fri 12-6, Sat 10-4
Friends of the Library Group
NEW OXFORD AREA LIBRARY, 122 N Peters St, New Oxford, 17350-1229, SAN 324-5764. Tel: 717-624-2182. FAX: 717-624-1358. Web Site: www.adamslibrary.org/about/locations/new-oxford-area. *Br Mgr,* Emily Holland; E-mail: emilyh@adamslibrary.org; Staff 2 (MLS 1, Non-MLS 1)
Founded 1983. Pop 3,162; Circ 14,189
Library Holdings: Bk Vols 10,000; Per Subs 18

Function: 24/7 Electronic res, 24/7 Online cat, Adult bk club, Audiobks via web, Bk club(s), Bks on CD, Children's prog, Computers for patron use, E-Reserves, Electronic databases & coll, Free DVD rentals, ILL available, Internet access, Life-long learning prog for all ages, Magazines, Mango lang, Movies, Online cat, Online info literacy tutorials on the web & in blackboard, Photocopying/Printing, Preschool outreach, Prog for adults, Prog for children & young adult, Scanner, Spoken cassettes & CDs, Spoken cassettes & DVDs, STEM programs, Story hour, Summer & winter reading prog, Tax forms, Telephone ref, Wheelchair accessible
Open Mon & Thurs 2-8, Tues, Wed & Fri 11-5, Sat 10-4
Friends of the Library Group

C GETTYSBURG COLLEGE, Musselman Library, 300 N Washington St, 17325. SAN 314-5344. Tel: 717-337-6604. Circulation Tel: 717-337-7024. Interlibrary Loan Service Tel: 717-337-7016. Reference Tel: 717-337-6600. FAX: 717-337-7001. Web Site: www.gettysburg.edu/musselman-library. *Dean of Libr,* Robin Wagner; Tel: 717-337-6768, E-mail: rowagner@gettysburg.edu; *Asst Dean, Dir, Scholarly Communications,* Janelle Wertzberger; Tel: 717-337-7010, E-mail: jwertzbe@gettysburg.edu; *Asst Dean, Dir, Commun & Tech Serv,* Jeremy Garskof; Tel: 717-337-6892, E-mail: jgarskof@gettysburg.edu; *Dir, Spec Coll & Archives,* Carolyn Sautter; Tel: 717-337-7002, E-mail: csautter@gettysburg.edu; *Dir, Res & Instruction Serv,* Kerri Odess-Harnish; Tel: 717-337-7018, E-mail: kodessha@gettysburg.edu; *Dir, User Serv,* John Dettinger; Tel: 717-337-6893, E-mail: jdetting@gettysburg.edu; *Syst Librn,* Robert Miessler; Tel: 717-337-7020, E-mail: rmiessle@gettysburg.edu; *Col Archivist,* Amy Lucadamo; Tel: 717-337-7006, E-mail: alucadam@gettysburg.edu; Staff 17 (MLS 15, Non-MLS 2)
Founded 1832. Enrl 2,500; Fac 200; Highest Degree: Bachelor
Library Holdings: Bk Vols 349,466; Per Subs 2,600
Special Collections: Rare books, manuscripts, maps, art works, photos, artifacts; Special Coll & College Archives
Subject Interests: Asian art, Civil War, Col hist, Historic maps, Oral hist, World War I, WWII
Automation Activity & Vendor Info: (Acquisitions) Ex Libris Group; (Cataloging) Ex Libris Group; (Circulation) Ex Libris Group; (Course Reserve) Ex Libris Group; (Discovery) Ex Libris Group; (ILL) OCLC ILLiad; (OPAC) Ex Libris Group; (Serials) Ex Libris Group
Wireless access
Publications: Friends of Musselman Library (Newsletter)
Partic in Associated College Libraries of Central Pennsylvania; Central Pennsylvania Consortium; LYRASIS; Partnership for Academic Library Collaborative & Innovation
Friends of the Library Group

S GETTYSBURG NATIONAL MILITARY PARK LIBRARY*, 1195 Baltimore Pike, Ste 100, 17325. SAN 314-5352. Tel: 717-338-4424. FAX: 717-334-1997. Web Site: www.nps.gov/gett. *Historian,* Christopher Gwinn; E-mail: Christopher_Gwinn@nps.gov; Staff 1 (Non-MLS 1)
Founded 1895
Library Holdings: AV Mats 24; CDs 48; DVDs 12; Bk Titles 5,155; Bk Vols 7,700; Per Subs 10; Spec Interest Per Sub 2; Videos 143
Special Collections: Al Gambone Coll (Civil War, Personalities); Gregory Coco Coll (Civil War Personal Accounts); Harry Pfanz Research Coll (Civil War- Gettysburg); Personnel, Battle of Gettysburg, photos
Subject Interests: Battle of Gettysburg, Campaign, Cycloramas, Eisenhower at Gettysburg, Gettysburg National Cemetery, Lincoln's Gettysburg Address
Function: Res libr
Restriction: Circulates for staff only, In-house use for visitors, Open to pub by appt only, Open to researchers by request

J HACC CENTRAL PENNSYLVANIA'S COMMUNITY COLLEGE*, Gettysburg Campus Library, 731 Old Harrisburg Rd, 17325. Tel: 717-339-3577. Interlibrary Loan Service Tel: 717-780-2623. FAX: 717-337-2329. E-mail: gbglib@hacc.edu. Web Site: libguides.hacc.edu/home/gettysburg. *Librn,* Kathleen Heidecker; E-mail: kbheidec@hacc.edu; Staff 4.3 (MLS 2.3, Non-MLS 2)
Founded 1999. Enrl 2,375; Fac 116; Highest Degree: Associate
Library Holdings: AV Mats 436; e-books 1,773; Bk Titles 8,424; Bk Vols 8,821; Per Subs 76
Automation Activity & Vendor Info: (Acquisitions) SirsiDynix; (Cataloging) SirsiDynix; (Circulation) SirsiDynix; (Course Reserve) Docutek; (ILL) SirsiDynix; (Media Booking) SirsiDynix; (OPAC) SirsiDynix; (Serials) SirsiDynix
Wireless access
Partic in Associated College Libraries of Central Pennsylvania
Open Mon-Thurs (Fall & Spring) 7:30-8, Fri 7:30-4:30; Mon-Fri (Summer) 8-4:30
Restriction: In-house use for visitors, Non-circulating to the pub

UNITED LUTHERAN SEMINARY*, A R Wentz Library, 66 Seminary Ridge, 17325. (Mail add: 61 Seminary Ridge, 17325), SAN 314-5360. Tel: 717-338-3014. E-mail: library@uls.edu. Web Site: library.uls.edu. *Archivist, Libr Dir,* Evan Boyd; Tel: 215-248-6330, E-mail: eboyd@uls.edu; *Archivist, Cataloger,* Sheila Joy; Tel: 717-339-1317, E-mail: sjoy@uls.edu; *Pub Serv Asst,* Cody Swisher; E-mail: cswisher@uls.edu; Staff 3 (MLS 2, Non-MLS 1)
Founded 1826. Enrl 234; Fac 23; Highest Degree: Doctorate
Jul 2017-Jun 2018. Mats Exp $119,765, Per/Ser (Incl. Access Fees) $24,500, Manu Arch $2,600, Electronic Ref Mat (Incl. Access Fees) $31,000, Presv $5,606. Sal $202,500
Library Holdings: Bk Vols 178,000; Per Subs 450
Special Collections: Lutheran Church History in America
Subject Interests: Biblical studies, Church hist, Church-related subjects, Lutheran Church, Pastoral studies, Philos, Preaching, Stewardship, Theol, Worship
Automation Activity & Vendor Info: (Acquisitions) Ex Libris Group; (Cataloging) Ex Libris Group; (Circulation) Ex Libris Group; (Course Reserve) Ex Libris Group; (ILL) OCLC; (OPAC) Ex Libris Group; (Serials) Ex Libris Group
Wireless access
Function: Outside serv via phone, mail, e-mail & web
Partic in Southeastern Pennsylvania Theological Library Association; Washington Theological Consortium
Open Mon-Thurs 8-6, Fri 8-4:30
Restriction: Borrowing privileges limited to fac & registered students, Circ privileges for students & alumni only, Circ to mem only, In-house use for visitors, Non-circulating of rare bks, Off-site coll in storage - retrieval as requested

GIBSONIA

P NORTHERN TIER REGIONAL LIBRARY*, 4015 Dickey Rd, 15044-9713. SAN 314-5379. Tel: 724-449-2665. Reference Tel: 724-449-2665, Ext 25. FAX: 724-443-6755. E-mail: northerntier@einetwork.net. Web Site: northerntierlibrary.org. *Dir,* Diane C Illis; E-mail: illisd@einetwork.net; Staff 6 (MLS 4, Non-MLS 2)
Founded 1954. Pop 22,597; Circ 246,496
Library Holdings: Bk Vols 64,655; Per Subs 87
Automation Activity & Vendor Info: (Cataloging) Innovative Interfaces, Inc; (Circulation) Innovative Interfaces, Inc; (OPAC) Innovative Interfaces, Inc
Wireless access
Function: 24/7 Electronic res, 24/7 Online cat, Activity rm, Adult bk club, Adult literacy prog, Audiobks via web, Bks on CD, Children's prog, Computer training, Computers for patron use, Digital talking bks, Electronic databases & coll, ILL available, Music CDs, Online cat, Photocopying/Printing, Prog for adults, Prog for children & young adult, Ref serv available, Summer reading prog, Tax forms, Telephone ref, Wheelchair accessible
Publications: The Library Link (Monthly)
Mem of Allegheny County Library Association (ACLA)
Partic in Electronic Info Network
Open Mon-Thurs 10-8, Fri 10-5, Sat 9-4
Friends of the Library Group
Branches: 1
PINE CENTER, 700 Warrendale Rd, 15044. Tel: 724-625-5655. *Dir,* Diane C Illis
Library Holdings: Large Print Bks 27; Bk Titles 4,190; Bk Vols 4,360; Per Subs 55
Function: Audiobks via web, Bks on CD, Computers for patron use, ILL available, Internet access, OverDrive digital audio bks, Telephone ref
Open Mon-Thurs 2:30-5:30

GIRARD

P RICE AVENUE COMMUNITY PUBLIC LIBRARY*, 705 Rice Ave, 16417. SAN 314-5387. Tel: 814-774-8286. E-mail: racpl@riceavenuelibrary.org. Web Site: catalog.erielibrary.org/polaris/default.aspx?ctx=18.1033.0.0.5. *Dir,* Ronda Nicholes; Staff 3 (MLS 1, Non-MLS 2)
Founded 1999. Pop 6,500; Circ 31,000
Library Holdings: Bk Vols 16,000; Per Subs 35
Wireless access
Open Mon & Wed 2-7, Tues 9-7, Fri 11-4, Sat 9-3
Friends of the Library Group

GLADWYNE

R BETH DAVID REFORM CONGREGATION*, Jewel K Markowitz Library, 1130 Vaughan Lane, 19035. SAN 314-8661. Tel: 610-896-7485. FAX: 610-642-5406. E-mail: office@bdavid.org. Web Site: www.bdavid.org.
Founded 1947
Library Holdings: Bk Vols 4,500
Special Collections: Judaica for Children
Subject Interests: Judaica

P GLADWYNE FREE LIBRARY*, 362 Righters Mill Rd, 19035-1587. SAN 314-5395. Tel: 610-642-3957. FAX: 610-642-3985. Web Site: www.lmls.org/locations-hours/gladwyne-library. *Librn,* Carolyn G Conti; E-mail: cconti@lmls.org; *Ch Serv,* Alicemarie Collins; Staff 9 (MLS 1, Non-MLS 8)
Founded 1931. Pop 5,720; Circ 101,942
Library Holdings: Bk Vols 44,569; Per Subs 105
Special Collections: Cookbooks; Pennsylvania History Coll
Wireless access
Mem of Lower Merion Library System
Partic in Montgomery County Library & Information Network Consortium
Open Mon-Thurs 10-8, Fri & Sat 10-5
Friends of the Library Group

GLEN MILLS

P RACHEL KOHL COMMUNITY LIBRARY, 687 Smithbridge Rd, 19342. SAN 376-3129. Tel: 610-358-3445. FAX: 610-558-0693. E-mail: rkreference@delcolibraries.org. Web Site: www.kohllibrary.org. *Dir,* Susan Sternberg; E-mail: rkdirector@delcolibraries.org; Staff 11 (MLS 3, Non-MLS 8)
Founded 1979
Automation Activity & Vendor Info: (Cataloging) Innovative Interfaces, Inc; (Circulation) Innovative Interfaces, Inc
Wireless access
Function: 24/7 Electronic res, 24/7 Online cat, 3D Printer, Activity rm, Adult bk club, After school storytime, Audiobks on Playaways & MP3, Audiobks via web, Bk club(s), Bks on CD, Chess club, Children's prog, Computer training, Computers for patron use, E-Reserves, Electronic databases & coll, Free DVD rentals, Home delivery & serv to seniorr ctr & nursing homes, Homebound delivery serv, ILL available, Internet access, Life-long learning prog for all ages, Magazines, Mail & tel request accepted, Mango lang, Meeting rooms, Movies, Museum passes, Music CDs, Online cat, Online info literacy tutorials on the web & in blackboard, Online ref, Outreach serv, OverDrive digital audio bks, Photocopying/Printing, Preschool outreach, Printer for laptops & handheld devices, Prog for adults, Prog for children & young adult, Ref & res, Ref serv available, Res assist avail, Spanish lang bks, Spoken cassettes & CDs, Spoken cassettes & DVDs, STEM programs, Summer reading prog, Tax forms, Teen prog, Telephone ref, Wheelchair accessible, Workshops
Mem of Delaware County Libraries
Partic in Am Pub Libr Asn; Pennsylvania Library Association
Open Mon-Thurs 10-8, Fri & Sat 10-5, Sun (Winter) 1-5
Friends of the Library Group

GLEN ROCK

P ARTHUR HUFNAGEL PUBLIC LIBRARY OF GLEN ROCK*, 32 Main St, 17327. SAN 314-5433. Tel: 717-235-1127. FAX: 717-235-0330. E-mail: hufnagellibrary@yorklibraries.org. Web Site: www.yorklibraries.org/glen-rock-hufnagel. *Dir,* Angela Orwig
Founded 1936. Pop 5,455
Special Collections: Pamphlet Coll
Subject Interests: Local hist
Mem of York County Library System
Open Mon-Thurs 10-7, Sat 10-3
Friends of the Library Group

GLENOLDEN

P GLENOLDEN LIBRARY, 211 S Llanwellyn Ave, 19036. SAN 314-545X. Tel: 610-583-1010. FAX: 610-583-7610. E-mail: glenolden@delcolibraries.org. Web Site: www.glenoldenlibrary.org. *Dir,* Cynthia Long; E-mail: gldirector@delcolibraries.org; *Ch,* Susan Torrie
Founded 1894. Pop 7,633; Circ 17,116
Library Holdings: Bk Titles 16,500; Per Subs 50
Automation Activity & Vendor Info: (Cataloging) Innovative Interfaces, Inc; (Circulation) Innovative Interfaces, Inc
Mem of Delaware County Libraries
Open Mon & Wed 10-7, Tues & Thurs 1-8, Fri 9-4, Sat 9-4 (10-2 Summer)

GLENSHAW

P GLENSHAW PUBLIC LIBRARY, 1504 Butler Plank Rd, 15116-2397. SAN 314-5468. Tel: 412-487-2121. E-mail: glenshawlibrary@gmail.com. Web Site: glenshawpubliclibrary.org. *Dir,* Sandy F Russell
Founded 1895. Circ 7,334
Library Holdings: Bk Titles 12,704; Talking Bks 111
Open Tues 5pm-7pm, Sat 10-2

P SHALER NORTH HILLS LIBRARY*, 1822 Mount Royal Blvd, 15116. SAN 314-5476. Tel: 412-486-0211. FAX: 412-486-8286. E-mail: shaler@einetwork.net. Web Site: www.shalerlibrary.org. *Dir,* Sharon McRae; E-mail: mcraes@einetwork.net; *Adult Serv Mgr,* Beth Lawry; *Youth Serv Coordr,* Ingrid Kalchthaler; *Early Literacy Specialist, Outreach Specialist,* Rebekah Allessandria
Founded 1942. Pop 28,757; Circ 443,000
Library Holdings: AV Mats 10,460; Bk Titles 98,268; Per Subs 216
Automation Activity & Vendor Info: (Cataloging) Innovative Interfaces, Inc; (Circulation) Innovative Interfaces, Inc; (OPAC) Innovative Interfaces, Inc; (Serials) Innovative Interfaces, Inc
Wireless access
Mem of Allegheny County Library Association (ACLA)
Partic in Electronic Info Network
Special Services for the Blind - Assistive/Adapted tech devices, equip & products
Open Mon, Wed & Fri 10-4, Tues & Thurs 1-7, Sat 10-2
Friends of the Library Group

GLENSIDE

C ARCADIA UNIVERSITY*, Bette E Landman Library, 450 S Easton Rd, 19038. SAN 314-5484. Tel: 215-572-2975. Reference Tel: 215-572-2138. Reference E-mail: reference@arcadia.edu. Web Site: www.arcadia.edu/library. *Interim Assoc Dean,* Adam Hess; Tel: 215-572-2842, E-mail: hessa@arcadia.edu; *Access Serv Mgr, Outreach Librn,* Michelle Reale; Tel: 215-572-2139, E-mail: realem@arcadia.edu; *Ref & Instruction Librn, Scholarly Communications Librn,* Larissa Gordon; Tel: 215-572-2136, E-mail: gordonl@arcadia.edu; *Sci Librn,* Calvin Wang; Tel: 215-572-4097, E-mail: wangc@arcadia.edu; *Information Literacy Coord,* Melissa Correll; Tel: 215-572-8528, E-mail: correllm@arcadia.edu; Staff 10 (MLS 4, Non-MLS 6)
Founded 1963. Enrl 3,200; Fac 289; Highest Degree: Doctorate
Library Holdings: AV Mats 3,396; e-books 300; e-journals 7,000; Bk Titles 99,415; Bk Vols 144,232; Per Subs 832
Automation Activity & Vendor Info: (Acquisitions) SirsiDynix; (Cataloging) SirsiDynix; (Circulation) SirsiDynix; (Course Reserve) SirsiDynix; (OPAC) SirsiDynix; (Serials) SirsiDynix
Wireless access
Partic in Interlibrary Delivery Service of Pennsylvania; LYRASIS; OCLC Online Computer Library Center, Inc; Partnership for Academic Library Collaborative & Innovation; Southeastern Pa Consortium for Higher Educ; Tri State Col Libr Coop
Open Mon-Thurs (Fall) 8am-Midnight, Fri 8-5, Sat 10-10, Sun 1pm-Midnight
Friends of the Library Group

P CHELTENHAM TOWNSHIP LIBRARY SYSTEM*, 215 S Keswick Ave, 19038-4420. SAN 314-5506. Tel: 215-885-0457. FAX: 215-885-1239. Web Site: www.cheltenhamlibraries.org. *Dir,* Lisa McClure; E-mail: lmcclure@mclinc.org; Staff 43 (MLS 8, Non-MLS 35)
Founded 1966. Pop 36,875; Circ 296,162
Library Holdings: AV Mats 10,249; Bk Vols 124,191; Per Subs 466
Subject Interests: African-Am hist, Art, Bus ref, Educ software, Handicrafts, Local hist, Multicultural mat
Automation Activity & Vendor Info: (Cataloging) Innovative Interfaces, Inc; (Circulation) Innovative Interfaces, Inc; (OPAC) Innovative Interfaces, Inc
Wireless access
Partic in Montgomery County Library & Information Network Consortium
Open Mon-Fri 9-5
Branches: 4
EAST CHELTENHAM FREE LIBRARY, Rowland Community Ctr, 400 Myrtle Ave, Cheltenham, 19012-2038, SAN 314-3996. Tel: 215-379-2077. FAX: 215-379-1275. E-mail: eastcheltenham@mclinc.org. *Head Librn,* Angela Lane; Staff 8 (MLS 1, Non-MLS 7)
Founded 1957. Pop 7,906; Circ 34,077
Library Holdings: AV Mats 2,056; Bk Vols 29,008; Per Subs 75
Subject Interests: Handicrafts, Multicultural mat
Open Mon 10-9, Tues 10-6, Wed 1-9, Thurs & Fri 1-6, Sat 10-4
Friends of the Library Group
ELKINS PARK FREE LIBRARY, 563 E Church Rd, Elkins Park, 19027-2499, SAN 314-481X. Tel: 215-635-5000. FAX: 215-635-5844. E-mail: elkinspark@mclinc.org. *Head Librn,* John Pappas; Staff 14 (MLS 3, Non-MLS 11)
Founded 1958. Pop 20,995; Circ 186,565
Library Holdings: AV Mats 9,570; Bk Vols 58,522; Per Subs 110
Subject Interests: Popular mat
Automation Activity & Vendor Info: (Acquisitions) Baker & Taylor
Open Mon & Wed 10-9, Tues, Thurs & Fri 10-6, Sat 10-4, Sun 1-4
Friends of the Library Group
GLENSIDE FREE LIBRARY, 215 S Keswick Ave, 19038-4420, SAN 314-5514. Tel: 215-885-0455. FAX: 215-885-1019. E-mail: glenside@mclinc.org. *Head Librn,* Mary Kay Moran; Staff 14 (MLS 4, Non-MLS 10)
Founded 1928. Pop 13,210; Circ 101,849
Library Holdings: AV Mats 15,000; Bk Vols 33,000; Per Subs 110

Automation Activity & Vendor Info: (Cataloging) Innovative Interfaces, Inc; (Circulation) Innovative Interfaces, Inc; (OPAC) Innovative Interfaces, Inc
Open Mon, Wed & Fri 10-6, Tues & Thurs 10-9, Sat 10-4, Sun 1-4
Friends of the Library Group

LAMOTT FREE LIBRARY, 7420 Sycamore Ave, LaMott, 19027-1005, SAN 320-1732. Tel: 215-635-4419. FAX: 215-635-4419. E-mail: lamott@mclinc.org. *Head Librn,* Carolyn Turner-Harris; Staff 3 (Non-MLS 3)
Founded 1966. Pop 1,590; Circ 8,255
Library Holdings: AV Mats 601; Bk Vols 4,954; Per Subs 51
Subject Interests: African-Am hist
Automation Activity & Vendor Info: (Cataloging) Innovative Interfaces, Inc; (Circulation) Innovative Interfaces, Inc; (OPAC) Innovative Interfaces, Inc
Open Mon & Wed 3-8:30, Tues 2-6, Thurs 10-6, Fri 3-6, Sat 12-4
Friends of the Library Group

S CHILD CUSTODY RESEARCH LIBRARY, Child Custody Evaluations Library, PO Box 202, 19038-0202. SAN 326-6184. Tel: 215-576-0177. *Dir,* Dr Ken Lewis; E-mail: DrKenLewis@hotmail.com
Founded 1980
Library Holdings: Bk Titles 800; Per Subs 40
Restriction: Open by appt only, Open to researchers by request

CR WESTMINSTER THEOLOGICAL SEMINARY*, Montgomery Library, 2960 W Church Rd, 19038. (Mail add: PO Box 27009, 19118-7009), SAN 315-0267. Tel: 215-572-3821. Reference Tel: 215-935-3880. E-mail: library@wts.edu. Web Site: students.wts.edu/library. *Dir,* Sandy Finlayson; Tel: 215-572-3823, E-mail: sfinlayson@wts.edu; *Archives & Spec Coll Librn,* Robert McInnes; Tel: 215-572-3856, E-mail: rmcinnes@wts.edu; *Asst Librn,* Steve McKinzie; E-mail: smckinzie@wts.edu; *Tech Serv & Syst Librn,* Donna Campbell; Tel: 215-935-3872, E-mail: dcampbell@wts.edu; *Circ & ILL Mgr,* Donna Roof; Tel: 215-572-3822, E-mail: droof@wts.edu; Staff 5 (MLS 4, Non-MLS 1)
Founded 1929. Enrl 450; Fac 13; Highest Degree: Doctorate
Library Holdings: Bk Vols 133,063; Per Subs 695
Special Collections: Bible Texts & Versions; Early Reformed Theology
Subject Interests: Biblical studies, Reformation, Systematic theol
Automation Activity & Vendor Info: (Acquisitions) Innovative Interfaces, Inc; (Cataloging) Innovative Interfaces, Inc; (Circulation) Innovative Interfaces, Inc; (Course Reserve) Innovative Interfaces, Inc; (ILL) OCLC; (OPAC) Innovative Interfaces, Inc
Wireless access
Partic in OCLC Online Computer Library Center, Inc; Southeastern Pennsylvania Theological Library Association
Restriction: Open to fac, students & qualified researchers

GREENCASTLE

P LILIAN S BESORE MEMORIAL LIBRARY*, 305 E Baltimore St, 17225. SAN 314-5530. Tel: 717-597-7920. FAX: 717-597-5320. Web Site: www.fclspa.org/locations/lilian-s-besore-memorial-library. *Dir,* Kiely Fisher; E-mail: kfisher@fclspa.org; Staff 1 (MLS 1)
Founded 1963. Pop 16,226; Circ 49,931
Library Holdings: Bk Vols 38,528; Per Subs 57
Special Collections: Local History
Automation Activity & Vendor Info: (Circulation) AmLib Library Management System; (OPAC) AmLib Library Management System
Wireless access
Mem of Franklin County Library System
Partic in Health Sciences Libraries Consortium
Open Mon & Thurs 1-6, Tues & Fri 9-2
Friends of the Library Group

GREENSBURG

M EXCELA HEALTH WESTMORELAND HOSPITAL*, Health Sciences Library, 532 W Pittsburgh St, 15601-2282. SAN 358-500X. Tel: 724-537-1275. FAX: 724-537-1890. Web Site: www.excelahealth.org. *Mgr, Libr Serv,* Position Currently Open
Founded 1952
Special Collections: Hospital archives
Wireless access
Open Mon-Fri 9:30-6
Restriction: Restricted pub use, Staff use only

GREENSBURG HEMPFIELD AREA LIBRARY*, 237 S Pennsylvania Ave, 15601-3086. SAN 314-5557. Tel: 724-837-5620. Reference Tel: 724-837-8441. FAX: 724-836-0160. Web Site: www.ghal.org. *Dir,* Jamie Falo; E-mail: jamie.falo@wlnonline.org; *Head, Children's Servx,* Jessica Kiefer; E-mail: jessica.kiefer@wlnonline.org; Staff 6 (MLS 3, Non-MLS 3)
Founded 1936. Pop 79,181; Circ 150,000
Library Holdings: AV Mats 3,716; Large Print Bks 190; Bk Titles 67,431; Bk Vols 82,911; Per Subs 149; Talking Bks 1,511; Videos 580
Special Collections: Pennsylvania Room (Pa History & Geneology)
Subject Interests: Genealogy
Automation Activity & Vendor Info: (Cataloging) Innovative Interfaces, Inc; (Circulation) Innovative Interfaces, Inc; (OPAC) Innovative Interfaces, Inc
Wireless access
Mem of Westmoreland County Federated Library System
Open Mon-Thurs 10-7:50, Sat 10-4:50
Branches: 1
YOUNGWOOD BRANCH, 17 S Sixth St, Youngwood, 15697-1623, SAN 320-8540. Tel: 724-925-9350. Web Site: www.ghal.org/youngwood-area-public-library/about.
Founded 1954. Pop 3,749; Circ 11,272
Library Holdings: Large Print Bks 372; Bk Vols 14,396; Per Subs 24; Talking Bks 552
Automation Activity & Vendor Info: (Cataloging) Innovative Interfaces, Inc; (Circulation) Innovative Interfaces, Inc
Partic in Share Westmoreland Consortium
Open Mon & Thurs 10-7:30, Tues & Fri 10-5

CR SETON HILL UNIVERSITY*, Reeves Memorial Library, One Seton Hill Dr, 15601. SAN 314-5565. Tel: 724-838-4291. Interlibrary Loan Service Tel: 724-830-1584. Administration Tel: 724-838-4270. E-mail: reeves@setonhill.edu. Web Site: setonhill.libguides.com/library. *Dir,* Dr David H Stanley; Tel: 724-838-4270, E-mail: stanley@setonhill.edu; *Cat & Acq,* Mr Adam Pellman; Tel: 724-838-2438, E-mail: pellman@setonhill.edu; *Pub Serv Librn,* Mrs Kelly Clever; Tel: 724-830-1174, E-mail: clever@setonhill.edu; *Per,* Mrs Judith Koveleskie; Tel: 724-838-7828, E-mail: kovelesk@setonhill.edu; *Libr Tech,* Mrs Helene Ciarochi; Tel: 724-830-1091, E-mail: ciarochi@setonhill.edu; *Circ Asst,* Mrs Michelle Frye; Tel: 724-830-1584, E-mail: mfrye@setonhill.edu; Staff 6 (MLS 4, Non-MLS 2)
Founded 1918. Enrl 2,000; Fac 100; Highest Degree: Master
Jul 2015-Jun 2016. Mats Exp $175,417, Books $6,000, Per/Ser (Incl. Access Fees) $34,223, Electronic Ref Mat (Incl. Access Fees) $134,500, Presv $694
Library Holdings: AV Mats 6,665; CDs 970; DVDs 1,406; e-books 88,320; Bk Vols 70,000; Per Subs 192; Videos 2,490
Subject Interests: Entrepreneurship, Fine arts, Holocaust
Automation Activity & Vendor Info: (Acquisitions) Innovative Interfaces, Inc; (Cataloging) Innovative Interfaces, Inc; (Circulation) Innovative Interfaces, Inc; (Course Reserve) Innovative Interfaces, Inc; (ILL) OCLC WorldShare Interlibrary Loan; (OPAC) Innovative Interfaces, Inc; (Serials) Innovative Interfaces, Inc
Wireless access
Partic in LYRASIS; Share Westmoreland Consortium; Westmoreland Acad Librs Consortium
Open Mon-Thurs 8am-11:50pm, Fri 8-4:50, Sat 9-4:50, Sun 1-11:50

C UNIVERSITY OF PITTSBURGH AT GREENSBURG*, Millstein Library, 150 Finoli Dr, 15601-5804. SAN 314-5573. Tel: 724-836-9687. FAX: 724-836-7043. Web Site: www.library.pitt.edu/greensburg. *Dir,* Eve Wider; Tel: 724-836-9688, E-mail: ewider@pitt.edu; *Pub Serv Librn,* Renee Kiner; Tel: 724-836-7914, E-mail: rak137@pitt.edu; *Ref & Pub Serv Librn,* Kelly Safin; Tel: 724-836-7961, E-mail: kab309@pitt.edu; Staff 7 (MLS 3, Non-MLS 4)
Founded 1963. Enrl 1,753; Fac 94; Highest Degree: Bachelor. Sal $368,617
Library Holdings: Audiobooks 162; CDs 660; DVDs 1,674; Microforms 9,744; Music Scores 143; Bk Vols 74,623; Per Subs 72; Videos 2,025
Special Collections: UPG Archives. Oral History
Subject Interests: Hist, Info sci, Lit
Automation Activity & Vendor Info: (Acquisitions) Ex Libris Group; (Cataloging) Ex Libris Group; (Circulation) Ex Libris Group; (Course Reserve) Ex Libris Group; (ILL) Ex Libris Group; (OPAC) Ex Libris Group; (Serials) Ex Libris Group
Wireless access
Partic in LYRASIS; OCLC Online Computer Library Center, Inc; Westmoreland Acad Librs Consortium
Special Services for the Blind - Assistive/Adapted tech devices, equip & products; Computer with voice synthesizer for visually impaired persons; Reader equip
Open Mon-Thurs 8:30am-11pm, Fri 8:30-5, Sat 10-6, Sun 3-11
Friends of the Library Group

P WESTMORELAND COUNTY FEDERATED LIBRARY SYSTEM*, Westmoreland Library Network, 226 Donohoe Rd, Ste 202, 15601. Tel: 724-420-5638. Toll Free Tel: 866-923-5772. FAX: 724-420-5741. E-mail: info@wlnonline.org. Web Site: wlnonline.org. *Exec Dir,* Cesare Muccari; E-mail: cesare.muccari@wlnonline.org; Staff 3 (MLS 2, Non-MLS 1)
Founded 1995. Pop 367,000; Circ 2,100,000
Library Holdings: Audiobooks 18,360; AV Mats 67,770; Bks on Deafness & Sign Lang 200; Braille Volumes 40; CDs 7,300; DVDs 36,270; e-books 6,500; Music Scores 20; Bk Titles 420,400; Bk Vols 740,000; Videos 5,800

Wireless access
Function: 24/7 Electronic res, Adult bk club, Adult literacy prog, Bks on CD, Computers for patron use, Digital talking bks, Free DVD rentals, Holiday prog, ILL available, Internet access, Life-long learning prog for all ages, Magazines, Movies, Music CDs, Online cat, OverDrive digital audio bks, Photocopying/Printing, Prog for adults, Prog for children & young adult, Senior computer classes, Spoken cassettes & CDs, Story hour, Study rm, Summer reading prog, VHS videos
Member Libraries: Adams Memorial Library; Avonmore Public Library; Belle Vernon Public Library; Delmont Public Library; Greensburg Hempfield Area Library; Jeannette Public Library; Ligonier Valley Library; Manor Public Library; Monessen Public Library; Mount Pleasant Free Public Library; Murrysville Community Library; New Alexandria Public Library; New Florence Community Library; Norwin Public Library; Penn Area Library; Peoples Library; Rostraver Public Library; Scottdale Public Library; Sewickley Township Public Library; Smithton Public Library; Trafford Community Public Library; Vandergrift Public Library Association; West Newton Public Library
Open Mon-Fri 9-5

S WESTMORELAND COUNTY HISTORICAL SOCIETY*, Calvin E Pollins Memorial Library, 809 Forbes Trail Rd, 15601. SAN 326-3940. Tel: 724-836-1800, Ext 100. FAX: 724-532-1938. E-mail: library@westmorelandhistory.org. Web Site: www.westmorelandhistory.org. *Libr Coord,* Anita Zanke
Library Holdings: Bk Vols 4,200
Special Collections: Archival Coll; Genealogy Coll
Subject Interests: Genealogy, Local hist
Wireless access
Publications: Westmoreland Chronicle (Newsletter); Westmoreland History Magazine
Open Wed-Sat 10:30-4:30 by appt
Restriction: Not a lending libr

L WESTMORELAND COUNTY LAW LIBRARY*, Two N Main St, Ste 202, 15601. SAN 314-5549. Tel: 724-830-3266. Web Site: www.co.westmoreland.pa.us. *Librn,* Betty Ward; E-mail: eward@co.westmoreland.pa.us
Library Holdings: Bk Vols 24,000; Per Subs 35
Subject Interests: Legal mat
Open Mon, Tues, Thurs & Fri 8:30-4, Wed 8:30-7:30

GREENVILLE

P GREENVILLE AREA PUBLIC LIBRARY*, 330 Main St, 16125-2615. SAN 314-5603. Tel: 724-588-5490. FAX: 724-588-5481. E-mail: director@greenvillelibrary.net. *Dir,* Jeanne Ball; *Ch,* Amy Noble; *Circ Mgr,* Stephanie King; *Cat,* Amanda Graul; Staff 5.1 (MLS 2.3, Non-MLS 2.8)
Founded 1921. Pop 10,631; Circ 41,350
Jan 2015-Dec 2015 Income $269,891. Mats Exp $31,246, Electronic Ref Mat (Incl. Access Fees) $2,000. Sal $114,994
Library Holdings: AV Mats 1,553; DVDs 620; e-books 1,846; Large Print Bks 1,042; Bk Vols 40,898; Per Subs 50
Automation Activity & Vendor Info: (Cataloging) Follett Software; (Circulation) Follett Software; (OPAC) Follett Software
Wireless access
Function: 24/7 Electronic res, 24/7 Online cat, 3D Printer, Activity rm, Adult bk club, Art programs, Audiobks on Playaways & MP3, Audiobks via web, Bk club(s), Bks on CD, Children's prog, Computers for patron use, E-Readers, Electronic databases & coll, Free DVD rentals, ILL available, Internet access, Magazines, Mail & tel request accepted, Mango lang, Microfiche/film & reading machines, Movies, Online cat, OverDrive digital audio bks, Photocopying/Printing, Prog for adults, Prog for children & young adult, Ref & res, Scanner, Spoken cassettes & CDs, STEM programs, Story hour, Summer reading prog, Tax forms, Teen prog, Telephone ref, Wheelchair accessible
Open Tues-Thurs 9:30-8, Fri & Sat 9:30-4:30
Restriction: Authorized patrons
Friends of the Library Group

C THIEL COLLEGE, Langenheim Memorial Library, 75 College Ave, 16125-2183. SAN 314-5611. Tel: 724-589-2124. Interlibrary Loan Service Tel: 724-589-2121. Reference Tel: 724-589-2119. FAX: 724-589-2122. Web Site: www.thiel.edu/library. *Libr Dir,* Tressa A Snyder; Tel: 724-589-2119, E-mail: tsnyder@thiel.edu; *Cat & Ref Librn,* Allen S Morrill; Tel: 724-589-2205, E-mail: amorrill@thiel.edu; *Doc Librn,* Deborah Ross; Tel: 724-589-2127, E-mail: dross@thiel.edu; *Circ Mgr,* Richard Walcott; Tel: 724-589-2118, E-mail: rwalcott@thiel.edu; *Educ Serv Coordr,* Jennifer Lippert; E-mail: jlippert@thiel.edu; *Archivist,* John R Hauser; E-mail: jhauser@thiel.edu; Staff 7 (MLS 5, Non-MLS 2)
Founded 1866. Enrl 1,200; Fac 65; Highest Degree: Bachelor
Library Holdings: CDs 477; DVDs 38; e-books 4,177; e-journals 124; Electronic Media & Resources 31; Bk Titles 148,556; Bk Vols 186,643; Per Subs 460
Special Collections: State Document Depository; US Document Depository
Automation Activity & Vendor Info: (Acquisitions) MultiLIS; (Cataloging) OCLC Connexion; (Circulation) MultiLIS; (Course Reserve) MultiLIS; (ILL) OCLC; (OPAC) MultiLIS; (Serials) MultiLIS
Wireless access
Function: Govt ref serv, ILL available, Ref serv available
Partic in LYRASIS; OCLC Online Computer Library Center, Inc
Open Mon-Thurs 8am-11pm, Fri 8-5, Sun 4-11
Restriction: Limited access for the pub

GROVE CITY

S GEORGE JUNIOR REPUBLIC LIBRARY, 233 George Junior Rd, 16127. (Mail add: PO Box 1058, 16127-5058). Tel: 724-458-9330, Ext 2552. Web Site: gjr.org. *Librn,* Michelle Hemmerlin; E-mail: michelle.hemmerlin@gcasdk12.org
Library Holdings: Bk Vols 20,000
Automation Activity & Vendor Info: (Cataloging) Follett Software; (Circulation) Follett Software; (OPAC) Follett Software
Restriction: Not open to pub

C GROVE CITY COLLEGE*, Henry Buhl Library, 300 Campus Dr, 16127-2198. SAN 314-562X. Tel: 724-458-2047. FAX: 724-458-2181. Web Site: www.gcc.edu/Home/Experience-the-Grove/Facilities/Buhl-Library. *Coll Develop, Dir,* Barbra Munnell; Tel: 724-458-3824, E-mail: bmmunnell@gcc.edu; *Asst Dir, Ref/Bibliog Instruction Librn,* Kim Marks; Tel: 724-450-1532, E-mail: ksmarks@gcc.edu; *Ref/Outreach Librn,* Megan Babal; Tel: 724-264-1007, E-mail: mebabal@gcc.edu; *Acq,* Jill Forsythe; *Bibliog Instr, Ref (Info Servs),* Amy C Cavanaugh; Tel: 724-458-2148, E-mail: accavanaugh@gcc.edu; *Cataloger,* Gretchen Maxiener; Tel: 724-450-4038, E-mail: maxienergl@gcc.edu; *Ser,* Joyce M Kebert; Tel: 724-458-3821, E-mail: jmkebert@gcc.edu; *Tech Serv,* Janet Elder; Tel: 724-458-3823, E-mail: jlelder@gcc.edu; *Tech Serv,* Conni L Shaw; Tel: 724-458-3842, E-mail: clshaw@gcc.edu; Staff 9 (MLS 6, Non-MLS 3)
Founded 1900. Enrl 2,455; Fac 120; Highest Degree: Bachelor
Library Holdings: Audiobooks 450; e-books 322,450; e-journals 46,482; Microforms 4,000; Bk Vols 138,000
Special Collections: Ludwig von Mises Papers, letters, ms & pamphlets
Subject Interests: Am, Behav sci, British, English, European hist, Soc sci
Automation Activity & Vendor Info: (Cataloging) TLC (The Library Corporation); (Circulation) TLC (The Library Corporation); (Discovery) EBSCO Discovery Service; (OPAC) TLC (The Library Corporation)
Wireless access
Partic in LYRASIS

P GROVE CITY COMMUNITY LIBRARY*, 125 W Main St, 16127-1569. SAN 314-5638. Tel: 724-458-7320. FAX: 724-458-7332. E-mail: gccl@grovecitypalibrary.org. Web Site: www.grovecitypalibrary.org. *Interim Dir,* Stacy LJ Hook; E-mail: director@grovecitypalibrary.org; *Children's & Teen Serv Coordr,* Heather Baker; *Cataloger, Technology Spec,* Wendy Riggi; *Circ, ILL,* Matthew Brazell; E-mail: interlibraryloan@grovecitypalibrary.org; Staff 7 (MLS 2, Non-MLS 5)
Founded 1958. Pop 15,000; Circ 48,073
Library Holdings: Bk Vols 31,858; Per Subs 60
Automation Activity & Vendor Info: (Cataloging) Follett Software; (Circulation) Follett Software; (OPAC) Follett Software
Wireless access
Function: 24/7 Electronic res, Accelerated reader prog, Activity rm, Adult bk club, Art exhibits, Audiobks via web, Bk club(s), Bks on CD, CD-ROM, Chess club, Children's prog, Computer training, Computers for patron use, E-Readers, E-Reserves, Electronic databases & coll, Equip loans & repairs, Holiday prog, Home delivery & serv to seniorr ctr & nursing homes, Homebound delivery serv, ILL available, Instruction & testing, Internet access, Life-long learning prog for all ages, Magazines, Magnifiers for reading, Mail & tel request accepted, Movies, Music CDs, Online cat, Outreach serv, Outside serv via phone, mail, e-mail & web, OverDrive digital audio bks, Photocopying/Printing, Preschool outreach, Preschool reading prog, Prog for adults, Prog for children & young adult, Ref & res, Ref serv available, Scanner, Senior computer classes, Story hour, Summer reading prog, Tax forms, Teen prog, Telephone ref, Visual arts prog, Wheelchair accessible, Workshops
Open Mon & Fri 10-8, Tues-Thurs 10-5, Sat 8-3
Friends of the Library Group

GWYNEDD VALLEY

C GWYNEDD MERCY UNIVERSITY*, Keiss Library, 1325 Sumneytown Pike, 19437. (Mail add: PO Box 901, 19437-0901), SAN 314-5654. Tel: 215-646-7300, Ext 21474. Interlibrary Loan Service Tel: 215-646-7300, Ext 21497. Reference Tel: 215-646-7300, Ext 21484. Administration Tel: 215-646-7300, Ext 21496. FAX: 215-641-5596. E-mail: Library@gmercyu.edu. Web Site: www.gmercyu.edu/library. *Libr Dir,* Jingfeng Xia; E-mail: xia.j@gmercyu.edu; *Asst Dir & Syst Librn,* Nancy McGarvey; Tel: 215-646-7300, Ext 21493, E-mail: mcgarvey.n@gmc.edu;

Instrul Serv/Ref Librn, Heather Burychka; Tel: 215-646-7300, Ext 21494, E-mail: burychka.h@gmc.edu; *Coordr, Circ,* Peggy Lopuzanski; Tel: 215-646-7300, Ext 21492, E-mail: lopuzanski.m@gmc.edu; *Acq, ILL,* Pat Smith; E-mail: smith.p@gmercyu.edu; *AV, Circ,* Eileen Wood; Tel: 215-646-7300, Ext 21498, E-mail: wood.e@gmercyu.edu; *Cat, Ref Serv,* Sarah Meade; Tel: 215-646-7300, Ext 21495, E-mail: meade.s@gmercyu.edu; Staff 12 (MLS 7, Non-MLS 5)
Founded 1948. Enrl 2,475; Fac 85; Highest Degree: Doctorate
Library Holdings: AV Mats 10,552; e-books 14,350; e-journals 32,368; Microforms 14,974; Bk Titles 79,153; Bk Vols 86,674; Per Subs 173
Special Collections: Institute for New Orleans History & Culture
Subject Interests: Ireland
Automation Activity & Vendor Info: (Cataloging) SirsiDynix; (Circulation) SirsiDynix; (Course Reserve) SirsiDynix; (ILL) OCLC WorldShare Interlibrary Loan; (OPAC) SirsiDynix; (Serials) SirsiDynix
Wireless access
Function: Bks on CD, Movies, Music CDs, Online cat, Photocopying/Printing, Scanner
Partic in OCLC Online Computer Library Center, Inc; Southeastern Pa Consortium for Higher Educ; Tri-State College Library Cooperative
Open Mon-Thurs 8:30am-10pm, Fri 8:30-4:30, Sat 10-5, Sun 11-6

HAMBURG

P HAMBURG PUBLIC LIBRARY, 35 N Third St, 19526-1502. SAN 314-5670. Tel: 610-562-2843. FAX: 610-562-8136. E-mail: hamburgpl@berks.lib.pa.us. Web Site: berkslibraries.org/branch/hamburg. *Dir,* Chelsea Williams; *Ch,* Becky Hartman; Staff 3 (MLS 1, Non-MLS 2)
Founded 1903. Pop 13,190; Circ 39,197
Library Holdings: Audiobooks 800; AV Mats 1,000; CDs 450; Large Print Bks 1,000; Bk Vols 17,000; Per Subs 80; Talking Bks 600
Special Collections: Hamburg Items 1902-Present, microfilm
Wireless access
Open Mon, Wed & Fri 10-5, Tues 10-8, Thurs 12-8, Sat (Sept-June) 9-4

HANOVER

P GUTHRIE MEMORIAL LIBRARY*, Two Library Pl, 17331. SAN 314-5697. Tel: 717-632-5183. FAX: 717-632-7565. E-mail: gulibrary@yorklibraries.org. Web Site: www.yorklibraries.org/hanover-guthrie. *Exec Dir,* Lisa Kane; E-mail: lkane@yorklibraries.org; *Ch Mgr,* Kelly Horner; Staff 15 (MLS 2, Non-MLS 13)
Founded 1911. Pop 40,711; Circ 406,026
Library Holdings: Bk Vols 99,685; Per Subs 157
Special Collections: Pennsylvania Room
Subject Interests: Genealogy, Local hist, Penn
Automation Activity & Vendor Info: (Circulation) Innovative Interfaces, Inc
Wireless access
Publications: Weekly Newspaper Column
Mem of York County Library System
Special Services for the Deaf - TDD equip
Open Mon-Thurs 10-8, Fri & Sat 10-5
Friends of the Library Group

HARLEYSVILLE

S MENNONITE HISTORIANS OF EASTERN PENNSYLVANIA*, Mennonite Historical Library & Archives, 565 Yoder Rd, 19438-1020. SAN 326-3444. Tel: 215-256-3020. FAX: 215-256-3023. E-mail: info@mhep.org. Web Site: www.mhep.org. *Colls Mgr,* Joel D Alderfer; E-mail: alderferj@mhep.org; *Archivist,* Forrest L Moyer; E-mail: moyerf@mhep.org; Staff 1 (Non-MLS 1)
Founded 1967
Library Holdings: Bk Titles 6,910; Bk Vols 8,384; Per Subs 125
Special Collections: Franconia Mennonite Mission Board Coll, 1917-1971; J C Clemens Coll; Jacob B Mensch Coll; Jacob Fretz Coll; John E Lapp Coll; Local History (Robert C Bucher Coll); Mennonite Church History (Towamencin Mennonite Coll); Salford Mennonite Church Coll, 1718-2000
Subject Interests: Archives, Genealogy, Local biog, Mennonite hist, Montgomery counties, Peace studies, Penn German studies, Theol
Function: Res libr
Publications: MHEP (Newsletter)
Open Tues-Fri 10-5, Sat 10-2
Restriction: Non-circulating to the pub

HARRISBURG

COMMONWEALTH COURT LIBRARY*, 601 Commonwealth Ave, Ste 2300, 17120. SAN 314-5719. Tel: 717-255-1621. FAX: 717-255-1784. Web Site: www.pacourts.us/courts/commonwealth-court. *Librn,* Pam Shoop
Founded 1970
Library Holdings: Bk Titles 500; Bk Vols 20,000
Wireless access
Restriction: Not open to pub

GL DAUPHIN COUNTY LAW LIBRARY*, Dauphin County Courthouse, 4th Flr, 101 Market St, 17101. SAN 314-5735. Tel: 717-780-6605. FAX: 717-780-6481. Web Site: www.dauphincounty.org/government/Court-Departments/Offices-and-Departments/Pages/Law-Library.aspx. *Law Librn,* Laura Motter; E-mail: lmotter@dauphinc.org; Staff 1 (Non-MLS 1)
Founded 1865
Library Holdings: Bk Vols 36,500; Per Subs 9
Open Mon-Fri 8-1
Restriction: Circ limited

P DAUPHIN COUNTY LIBRARY SYSTEM*, 101 Walnut St, 17101. SAN 358-5034. Tel: 717-234-4961. FAX: 717-234-7479. Web Site: www.dcls.org. *Exec Dir,* Karen Cullings; E-mail: Exec-Dir@DCLS.org; *Community Engagement Officer,* Dominic DiFrancesco; E-mail: ComRelDir@DCLS.org; Staff 35 (MLS 21, Non-MLS 14)
Founded 1889. Pop 221,283; Circ 1,114,970
Library Holdings: AV Mats 60,503; CDs 26,228; Large Print Bks 6,504; Per Subs 532; Talking Bks 14,992; Videos 17,715
Special Collections: Grants Info; Job/Career Ctr
Subject Interests: Local hist, Penn
Automation Activity & Vendor Info: (Acquisitions) SirsiDynix; (Cataloging) SirsiDynix; (Circulation) SirsiDynix; (ILL) OCLC; (OPAC) SirsiDynix
Wireless access
Publications: Connect Newsletter (Quarterly); Information Place (Quarterly); Passport (Bimonthly)
Open Mon-Fri 10-5
Friends of the Library Group
Branches: 8
WILLIAM H & MARION C ALEXANDER FAMILY LIBRARY, 200 W Second St, Hummelstown, 17036, SAN 314-6278. Tel: 717-566-0949. FAX: 717-566-7178. E-mail: WebMailAFL@dcls.org. *Br Librn,* Jamie Hansell; Tel: 717-566-0949, Ext 201, E-mail: jhansell@dcls.org; Staff 2 (MLS 2)
Circ 102,340
Library Holdings: AV Mats 6,603; CDs 2,713; Large Print Bks 827; Per Subs 74; Talking Bks 1,467; Videos 2,138
Open Mon-Thurs 10-8, Fri 10-6, Sat 10-3
Friends of the Library Group
EAST SHORE AREA LIBRARY, 4501 Ethel St, 17109, SAN 358-5093. Tel: 717-652-9380. FAX: 717-545-3584. Interlibrary Loan Service FAX: 717-652-5012. E-mail: WebMailESA@dcls.org. *Adminr,* Marjorie McKensie; Tel: 717-652-9380, Ext 1015; Staff 11 (MLS 8, Non-MLS 3)
Circ 608,774
Library Holdings: AV Mats 18,346; CDs 7,921; Large Print Bks 2,525; Per Subs 158; Talking Bks 5,325; Videos 4,637
Open Mon-Thurs 10-9, Fri-Sun 10-5
Friends of the Library Group
ELIZABETHVILLE AREA LIBRARY, 80 N Market St, Elizabethville, 17023, SAN 358-5123. Tel: 717-362-9825. Circulation Tel: 717-362-9825, Ext 1590. FAX: 717-362-8119. E-mail: WebMailEV@dcls.org. *Br Librn,* Michael Kattner; Tel: 717-362-9825, Ext 1802, E-mail: mkattner@dcls.org; Staff 2 (MLS 1, Non-MLS 1)
Circ 104,253
Library Holdings: AV Mats 7,307; CDs 2,958; Large Print Bks 463; Per Subs 58; Talking Bks 1,465; Videos 2,722
Open Tues & Thurs 10-8, Wed 10-5, Fri 10-7, Sat 10-3
Friends of the Library Group
JOHNSON MEMORIAL LIBRARY, 799 E Center St, Millersburg, 17061, SAN 314-7622. Tel: 717-692-2658. FAX: 717-692-5003. E-mail: WebMailJOH@dcls.org. *Br Librn,* Lisa Howald; Tel: 717-692-2658, Ext 1603, E-mail: lhowald@dcls.org; Staff 1 (Non-MLS 1)
Founded 1931. Circ 44,138
Library Holdings: AV Mats 3,892; CDs 1,907; Large Print Bks 337; Per Subs 40; Talking Bks 1,072; Videos 863
Open Mon-Thurs 3:30-7:30, Sat 10-2; Tues-Thurs (Summer) 10-7:30
KLINE LIBRARY, 530 S 29th St, 17104, SAN 358-5212. Tel: 717-234-3934. FAX: 717-234-7713. E-mail: WebMailKL@dcls.org. *Libr Mgr,* Albert Municino; Staff 2 (MLS 1, Non-MLS 1)
Circ 83,264
Library Holdings: AV Mats 8,377; CDs 3,274; Large Print Bks 764; Per Subs 52; Talking Bks 1,762; Videos 3,046
Open Tues-Thurs 10-8, Fri 10-6, Sat 10-5
Friends of the Library Group
MCCORMICK RIVERFRONT LIBRARY, 101 Walnut St, 17101, SAN 358-5069. Tel: 717-234-4976. FAX: 717-234-7479. E-mail: WebMailMRL@dcls.org. *Br Librn,* Albert Municino; Tel: 717-234-4976, Ext 1115, E-mail: amunicino@dcls.org; Staff 2 (MLS 1, Non-MLS 1)
Circ 60,084
Library Holdings: AV Mats 6,469; CDs 3,347; Large Print Bks 554; Per Subs 48; Talking Bks 1,130; Videos 1,896
Open Mon & Wed 9-5, Tues & Thurs 11-7, Fri 10-5, Sat 10-2
Friends of the Library Group

NORTHERN DAUPHIN LIBRARY, 683 Main St, Lykens, 17048, SAN 358-5247. Tel: 717-453-9315. FAX: 717-453-9524. E-mail: WebMailND@dcls.org. *Br Librn,* Michael Kattner; Tel: 717-523-0340, Ext 1802, E-mail: mkattner@dcls.org; Staff 2 (MLS 1, Non-MLS 1)
Circ 57,221
Library Holdings: AV Mats 4,101; CDs 1,756; Large Print Bks 535; Per Subs 44; Talking Bks 1,074; Videos 1,163
Open Mon 10-8, Tues-Thurs 1-8, Fri 10-5, Sat 10-2
Friends of the Library Group

MADELINE L OLEWINE MEMORIAL LIBRARY, 2410 N Third St, 17110, SAN 358-5158. Tel: 717-232-7286. FAX: 717-232-9707. E-mail: WebMailMOM@dcls.org. *Br Librn,* Celia Hartz; Tel: 717-232-7286, Ext 1308, E-mail: chartz@dcls.org; Staff 1 (Non-MLS 1)
Circ 54,896
Library Holdings: AV Mats 5,408; CDs 2,352; Large Print Bks 499; Per Subs 43; Talking Bks 1,697; Videos 1,250
Open Mon 10-8, Tues & Wed 10-7, Thurs 10-6, Fri 12-5, Sat 10-2

J HARRISBURG AREA COMMUNITY COLLEGE*, McCormick Library, One HACC Dr, 17110-2999. SAN 314-5778. Tel: 717-780-2460. Reference Tel: 717-780-2624. Web Site: libguides.hacc.edu/home/harrisburg. *Dir,* Elise Jackson; Tel: 717-780-2466, E-mail: ejackson@hacc.edu; *Ref & Instruction Librn,* Kathleen Conley; Tel: 717-780-1186, E-mail: ksconley@hacc.edu; *Circ, Libr Spec,* Edyta Lonon; Tel: 717-780-1772, E-mail: eklonon@hacc.edu; *Libr Tech,* Borany Kanal-Scott; Tel: 717-780-1795, E-mail: brkanals@hacc.edu; Staff 11.5 (MLS 7, Non-MLS 4.5)
Founded 1964. Enrl 7,659; Fac 205; Highest Degree: Associate. Sal $715,188 (Prof $507,569)
Library Holdings: AV Mats 5,361; e-books 47; Bk Vols 86,656; Per Subs 375
Special Collections: Cooper Law Library
Automation Activity & Vendor Info: (Circulation) SirsiDynix; (Course Reserve) SirsiDynix; (Media Booking) SirsiDynix; (OPAC) SirsiDynix; (Serials) SirsiDynix
Wireless access
Partic in Interlibrary Delivery Service of Pennsylvania
Open Mon-Thurs 7:30am-9pm, Fri 7:30-4:30, Sat 10-6, Sun 1-6; Mon-Thurs (Summer) 7:30am-9pm

C HARRISBURG UNIVERSITY OF SCIENCE & TECHNOLOGY*, Learning Commons, 326 Market St, 17101. Tel: 717-901-5188. E-mail: library@harrisburgu.edu. Web Site: library.harrisburgu.edu. *Univ Librn,* David Runyon; Staff 1 (MLS 1)
Highest Degree: Master
Subject Interests: Games, Sci, Tech
Automation Activity & Vendor Info: (Cataloging) Ex Libris Group; (Circulation) Ex Libris Group; (OPAC) Ex Libris Group
Wireless access
Function: CD-ROM, Electronic databases & coll, Online cat, Photocopying/Printing, Ref serv available
Partic in Associated College Libraries of Central Pennsylvania; Keystone Library Network; LYRASIS; Partnership for Academic Library Collaborative & Innovation
Restriction: Access at librarian's discretion, Borrowing privileges limited to fac & registered students, External users must contact libr, Open to students, fac & staff, Secured area only open to authorized personnel, Use of others with permission of librn

S HISTORICAL SOCIETY OF DAUPHIN COUNTY LIBRARY, Marion C & William H Alexander Library, 219 S Front St, 17104-1619. SAN 326-4270. Tel: 717-233-3462. FAX: 717-233-6059. E-mail: library@dauphincountyhistory.org, office@dauphincountyhistory.org. Web Site: dauphincountyhistory.org. *Librn,* Ken Frew; Staff 1 (Non-MLS 1)
Founded 1869
Library Holdings: Bk Titles 5,335; Per Subs 16
Special Collections: Dauphin County History Coll, archives, genealogy, ms, photos, objects
Function: Res libr
Open Tues-Fri 1-4
Restriction: Free to mem, Non-circulating, Non-circulating coll, Non-circulating of rare bks, Non-circulating to the pub, Not a lending libr

L MCNESS, WALLACE & NURICK LLC*, Information Center, 100 Pine St, 17108. (Mail add: PO Box 1166, 17108-1166), SAN 326-9361. Tel: 717-232-8000. FAX: 717-237-5300. Web Site: www.mcneeslaw.com. *Dir,* Kate Pettegrew; Tel: 717-237-5315, E-mail: kpettegrew@mcneeslaw.com; Staff 3 (MLS 2, Non-MLS 1)
Library Holdings: Bk Vols 15,000; Per Subs 200
Automation Activity & Vendor Info: (Acquisitions) SIMA, Inc; (Cataloging) SIMA, Inc; (Circulation) SIMA, Inc; (OPAC) SIMA, Inc; (Serials) SIMA, Inc
Open Mon-Fri 8-5:30

G PENNSYLVANIA DEPARTMENT OF TRANSPORTATION, Library & Research Center, Commonwealth Keystone Bldg, 6th Flr, 400 North St, 17120-0041. (Mail add: PO Box 3555, 17105-3555). Tel: 717-783-2446. FAX: 717-783-9152. E-mail: penndot_library@state.pa.us.
Founded 1979
Library Holdings: Bk Titles 21,719; Bk Vols 23,452; Per Subs 250
Special Collections: Transportation Research Board Series
Subject Interests: Bus, Engr, Transportation
Automation Activity & Vendor Info: (Circulation) EOS International; (Serials) EOS International
Restriction: Open by appt only, Open to pub for ref only

G PENNSYLVANIA JOINT STATE GOVERNMENT COMMISSION LIBRARY*, 108 Finance Bldg, Rm G-16, 17120. SAN 314-5921. Tel: 717-787-6851. FAX: 717-787-7020. *Librn,* Yelena Khanzhina; Tel: 717-787-6851, E-mail: ykhanzhina@legis.state.pa.us; Staff 1 (Non-MLS 1)
Library Holdings: Bk Titles 3,500; Per Subs 75
Subject Interests: Educ, Finance, Govt, Legis ref mat from other states, Penn statutes
Automation Activity & Vendor Info: (OPAC) Ex Libris Group; (Serials) Ex Libris Group
Wireless access
Restriction: Non-circulating to the pub

GL PENNSYLVANIA LEGISLATIVE REFERENCE BUREAU LIBRARY*, Main Capitol Bldg, Rm 641, 17120-0033. SAN 314-5956. Tel: 717-787-4828. FAX: 717-783-2396. E-mail: LRBRightToKnow@palrb.net. Web Site: www.palrb.net/right-to-know.html. *Law Librn,* Suellen Wolfe; Staff 1 (Non-MLS 1)
Founded 1909
Library Holdings: Bk Vols 12,000; Per Subs 25
Subject Interests: Law, Penn legislature
Function: For res purposes
Open Mon-Fri 8:45-4:45
Restriction: Not a lending libr

GL PENNSYLVANIA OFFICE OF ATTORNEY GENERAL*, Law Library, 1525 Strawberry Sq, 17120. SAN 314-5891. Tel: 717-787-3176. FAX: 717-772-4526. *Librn,* Stephanie Bodene; Staff 3 (MLS 1, Non-MLS 2)
Founded 1873
Library Holdings: Bk Vols 26,500
Restriction: Staff use only

G PENNSYLVANIA PUBLIC UTILITY COMMISSION LIBRARY*, Commonwealth Keystone Bldg, 400 North St, 17120-0079. (Mail add: PO Box 3265, 17105-3265), SAN 324-6078. Tel: 717-783-1740. FAX: 717-783-3458. Web Site: www.puc.pa.gov. *Librn,* Laura Griffin; Tel: 727-772-4597, E-mail: laurgriffi@pa.gov; Staff 1 (Non-MLS 1)
Founded 1977
Subject Interests: Econ, Energy, Engr, Law, Pub utilities
Restriction: Not open to pub

M PINNACLEHEALTH LIBRARY SERVICES*, Community General Osteopathic Hospital Library, 4300 Londonderry Rd, 17103. (Mail add: PO Box 3000, 17105-3000), SAN 314-5727. Tel: 717-657-7247. FAX: 717-657-7248. E-mail: libraries@pinnaclehealth.org. Web Site: www.pinnaclehealth.org. *Librn,* Helen L Houpt; E-mail: hhoupt@pinnaclehealth.org; Staff 1 (MLS 1)
Founded 1977
Library Holdings: e-books 157; e-journals 2,085; Bk Vols 721; Per Subs 8; Videos 10
Subject Interests: Allied health, Hospital admin, Med, Nursing
Automation Activity & Vendor Info: (Acquisitions) EOS International; (Cataloging) EOS International; (Circulation) EOS International; (OPAC) EOS International; (Serials) EOS International
Wireless access
Function: Doc delivery serv, Electronic databases & coll, Internet access, Photocopying/Printing
Partic in Central Pennsylvania Health Sciences Library Association; National Network of Libraries of Medicine Region 1
Restriction: Badge access after hrs, Hospital employees & physicians only

G SENATE LIBRARY OF PENNSYLVANIA, Main Capitol Bldg, Rm 157, 17120-0030. SAN 314-5999. Tel: 717-787-6120. FAX: 717-772-2366. E-mail: senlib@os.pasen.gov. Web Site: www.pasen.gov. *Librn,* Alexandra Barbush; E-mail: abarbush@os.pasen.gov
Library Holdings: Bk Vols 10,000; Per Subs 15
Special Collections: Histories of Legislation for Senate & House of Representatives of Pennsylvania; Legislative Journals for Senate and House of Representatives of Pennsylvania; Transcripts of Hearings for Senate & House of Representatives of Pennsylvania
Open Mon-Fri 8-5

P STATE LIBRARY OF PENNSYLVANIA*, Keystone Bldg Plaza Level, 400 North St, 17120. SAN 314-6022. Tel: 717-787-5968. Circulation Tel: 717-787-3169. Interlibrary Loan Service Tel: 717-787-4130. Reference Tel: 717-783-5950. FAX: 717-772-3265. Circulation E-mail: ra-circulation@pa.gov. Reference E-mail: ra-reflib@pa.gov. Web Site: statelibrary.pa.gov. *Commissioner of Libraries, Deputy Secretary,* Glenn Miller; Tel: 717-787-2646, E-mail: glennmille@pa.gov; *Dir,* Sarah Greene; E-mail: sarahgreene@pa.gov; *Regional Dep Librn, Supvr, Pub Serv,* Kathleen Hale; Tel: 717-787-2327, E-mail: kahale@pa.gov; *Cat Librn, Digital Librn,* William T Fee; Tel: 717-783-7014, E-mail: wfee@pa.gov; *Rare Bk Librn,* Position Currently Open. Subject Specialists: *Digitization,* William T Fee; Staff 33 (MLS 21, Non-MLS 12)
Founded 1745
Jul 2013-Jun 2014 Income $9,344,249. Mats Exp $716,129. Sal $2,939,199
Library Holdings: Audiobooks 5; AV Mats 365; CDs 6,647; DVDs 1,714; e-books 30,351; e-journals 48,532; Electronic Media & Resources 78,807; Microforms 726,444; Bk Titles 1,258,216; Bk Vols 1,709,599; Per Subs 455; Videos 347
Special Collections: Central Pennsylvania Genealogy Coll; Jansen Manuscript Letters Coll; Jansen-Shirk Bookplate Coll; Pennsylvania Colonial Assembly Coll; Pennsylvania Comics; Pennsylvania Imprints, 1689-1865; Pennsylvania Newspapers-Historic & Current. State Document Depository; US Document Depository
Subject Interests: Hist, Law, Penn
Automation Activity & Vendor Info: (Acquisitions) Ex Libris Group; (Cataloging) Ex Libris Group; (Circulation) Ex Libris Group; (ILL) OCLC Online; (OPAC) Ex Libris Group; (Serials) Ex Libris Group
Wireless access
Function: 24/7 Electronic res, Art exhibits, Computers for patron use, Electronic databases & coll, Govt ref serv, ILL available, Magnifiers for reading, Mail & tel request accepted, Microfiche/film & reading machines, Online cat, Online ref, Orientations, Photocopying/Printing, Ref serv available, Scanner, Wheelchair accessible
Publications: Checklist of Official Pennsylvania Publications; Directory-Pennsylvania Libraries; First 100 Years of Pennsylvania Imprints; Revised Classification Scheme for Pennsylvania State Publications
Partic in Associated College Libraries of Central Pennsylvania; Interlibrary Delivery Service of Pennsylvania; Keystone Library Network; LYRASIS; Partnership for Academic Library Collaborative & Innovation; Philadelphia Area Consortium of Special Collections Libraries
Special Services for the Deaf - ADA equip
Special Services for the Blind - Accessible computers; Large screen computer & software; Magnifiers; Screen reader software
Closed for renovations 2019- 2021 or later
Restriction: Circ limited, Non-circulating of rare bks

M UPMC PINNACLE - HARRISBURG*, Hospital Library, Brady Bldg, 1st flr, 205 S Front St, 17101-2099. SAN 314-5786. Tel: 717-782-5533. E-mail: libraries@pinnaclehealth.org. *Library Services, Syst Mgr,* Laurie J Schwing; E-mail: lschwing@pinnaclehealth.org; *Doc Delivery, Librn,* Elizabeth Morgan; Tel: 717-782-5511, E-mail: emorgan@pinnaclehealth.org; *Librn, Tech Serv,* Helen Houpt; Tel: 717-657-7247, Fax: 717-657-7248, E-mail: hhoupt@pinnaclehealth.org. Subject Specialists: *Mgt, Mobile res,* Laurie J Schwing; *Nursing res,* Elizabeth Morgan; *Health literacy,* Helen Houpt; Staff 1.7 (MLS 1.7)
Founded 1936
Library Holdings: Audiobooks 1; CDs 9; DVDs 80; e-books 157; e-journals 2,085; Bk Titles 963; Per Subs 128
Special Collections: Archives of PinnacleHealth System; History of Medicine Coll
Subject Interests: Allied health, Clinical med, Consumer health, Hospital admin, Nursing
Automation Activity & Vendor Info: (Cataloging) EOS International; (Circulation) EOS International; (OPAC) EOS International; (Serials) EOS International
Wireless access
Partic in Central Pennsylvania Health Sciences Library Association; National Network of Libraries of Medicine Region 1; OCLC Online Computer Library Center, Inc
Restriction: Authorized personnel only, Badge access after hrs, Hospital employees & physicians only

HARRISON CITY

P PENN AREA LIBRARY*, 2001 Municipal Court, 15636. (Mail add: PO Box 499, 15636-0499), SAN 359-5897. Tel: 724-744-4414. FAX: 724-744-0226. E-mail: library@pennlib.org. Web Site: www.pennlib.org. *Dir,* Jessica Beichoer; E-mail: jbeichoer@pennlib.org; *Bus Mgr,* Donna Orange; E-mail: dorange@pennlib.org; *Children's Serv Coordr,* Patricia Cappeta; E-mail: pcappeta@pennlib.org; *Circ Serv Coordr,* Dawn Corall; E-mail: dcorrall@pennlib.org; Staff 4 (MLS 1, Non-MLS 3)
Founded 1970. Pop 20,480; Circ 110,869
Automation Activity & Vendor Info: (Acquisitions) Innovative Interfaces, Inc; (Cataloging) Innovative Interfaces, Inc; (Circulation) Innovative Interfaces, Inc; (Course Reserve) Innovative Interfaces, Inc; (ILL) Innovative Interfaces, Inc; (Media Booking) Innovative Interfaces, Inc; (OPAC) Innovative Interfaces, Inc; (Serials) Innovative Interfaces, Inc
Wireless access
Function: Adult bk club, Bks on CD, Children's prog, Computers for patron use, Electronic databases & coll, Free DVD rentals, ILL available, Internet access, Magazines, Online cat, OverDrive digital audio bks, Photocopying/Printing, Prog for adults, Scanner, Study rm, Summer reading prog, Wheelchair accessible, Winter reading prog
Mem of Westmoreland County Federated Library System
Open Mon-Thurs 9-8, Fri & Sat 9-5
Friends of the Library Group

HASTINGS

P HASTINGS PUBLIC LIBRARY*, 312 Beaver St, 16646. (Mail add: PO Box 515, 16646-0515), SAN 314-6065. Tel: 814-247-8231. FAX: 814-247-8871. E-mail: hastings@cclsys.org. Web Site: www.cclsys.org/hastings. *Dir,* Bernadette Dillon; *Asst Librn,* Audrey Bonneau
Pop 2,846; Circ 13,510
Library Holdings: AV Mats 400; Large Print Bks 500; Bk Titles 14,115; Per Subs 45; Talking Bks 150
Automation Activity & Vendor Info: (Cataloging) Follett Software; (Circulation) Follett Software
Wireless access
Function: Home delivery & serv to seniorr ctr & nursing homes, Homebound delivery serv, ILL available, Internet access, Photocopying/Printing, Prog for children & young adult, Summer reading prog, Wheelchair accessible
Mem of Cambria County Library System & District Center
Open Mon-Thurs 12-6, Fri 1-5, Sat 9-4
Friends of the Library Group

HATBORO

R HATBORO BAPTIST CHURCH LIBRARY, 32 N York Rd, 19040. SAN 314-6073. Tel: 215-675-8400. E-mail: hatborobaptist@gmail.com. Web Site: www.hatborobaptistchurch.com. *Librn,* Karen Shubick; Staff 1 (Non-MLS 1)
Founded 1950
Library Holdings: CDs 30; DVDs 56; Bk Titles 2,494; Videos 3
Subject Interests: Christian living, Devotionals, Missions, Relig, Sermons
Open Mon-Wed 9-1, Sun 9:30-1

P UNION LIBRARY COMPANY OF HATBOROUGH, 243 S York Rd, 19040. SAN 323-5475. Tel: 215-672-1420. E-mail: staff@hatborolibrary.org. Web Site: hatborolibrary.org. *Libr Dir,* Michael Celec; E-mail: Director@HatboroLibrary.org; Staff 4 (MLS 1, Non-MLS 3)
Founded 1755. Pop 7,380; Circ 39,000
Library Holdings: Bk Titles 22,000; Per Subs 41
Special Collections: American Civil War Coll; American Revolution; Colonial Subscription Library, circa 1770; Pennsylvania History Coll
Automation Activity & Vendor Info: (Cataloging) Biblionix/Apollo; (Circulation) Biblionix/Apollo; (Discovery) Biblionix; (OPAC) Biblionix/Apollo
Wireless access
Function: 24/7 Electronic res, 24/7 Online cat, Adult bk club, Audiobks on Playaways & MP3, Audiobks via web, Bk club(s), Bks on CD, Children's prog, Computers for patron use, Electronic databases & coll, Free DVD rentals, Holiday prog, ILL available, Internet access, Magazines, Mail & tel request accepted, Mango lang, Movies, Museum passes, Music CDs, Online cat, Online ref, OverDrive digital audio bks, Photocopying/Printing, Preschool reading prog, Prog for adults, Prog for children & young adult, Ref & res, Res assist avail, Scanner, Story hour, Summer & winter reading prog, Summer reading prog, Tax forms
Open Mon-Thurs 10-8, Fri & Sat 10-5

HAVERFORD

C HAVERFORD COLLEGE*, James P Magill Library, 370 Lancaster Ave, 19041-1392. SAN 358-5514. Tel: 610-896-1175. Reference Tel: 610-896-1356. FAX: 610-896-1102. E-mail: library@haverford.edu. Web Site: www.haverford.edu/library. *Librn of the Col,* Terry Snyder; Tel: 610-896-1272, E-mail: tsnyder@haverford.edu; *Assoc Librn, Coordr, Coll Mgt & Metadata Serv,* Norm Medeiros; Tel: 610-896-1173, E-mail: nmedeiro@haverford.edu; *Head, Acq & Ser,* Mike Persick; Tel: 610-896-2971, E-mail: mpersick@haverford.edu; *Curator of Rare Bks & Ms, Head, Spec Coll,* Sarah Horowitz; Tel: 610-896-2948, E-mail: shorowitz@haverford.edu; *Head, Metadata Serv, Visual Res Librn,* Julie Coy; Tel: 610-896-1273, E-mail: jcoy@haverford.edu; *Electronic Res Librn,* Johanna Riordan; Tel: 610-896-1168, E-mail: jriordan@haverford.edu; *Lead Res & Instruction Librn,* Margaret Schaus; Tel: 610-896-1166, E-mail: mschaus@haverford.edu; *Music Librn, User Experience Coord,* Adam Crandell; Tel: 610-896-1169, E-mail: acrandell@haverford.edu; *Res & Instruction Librn,* Anna-Alexandra Fodde-Reguer; Tel: 610-896-1170, E-mail: afodderegu@haverford.edu; *Res*

& Instruction Librn, Semyon Khokhlov; Tel: 610-896-2976, E-mail: skhokhlov@haverford.edu; *Sci Librn,* Carol Howe; Tel: 610-896-1416, E-mail: chowe@haverford.edu; *Circ Serv, Coordr, Bldg Mgt,* Dawn Heckert; Tel: 610-896-1163, E-mail: dheckert@haverford.edu; *Coordr, Digital Scholarship & Serv,* Mike Zarafonetis; Tel: 610-896-4226, E-mail: mzarafon@haverford.edu; *Col Archivist, Rec Mgr,* Krista Oldham; Tel: 610-896-1284, E-mail: koldham@haverford.edu; *Libr Spec III,* Rob Haley; Tel: 610-896-1171, E-mail: rhaley@haverford.edu; *Conservator,* William Bumbarger; Tel: 610-896-1165, E-mail: bbumbarg@haverford.edu; *Curator of Quaker Coll,* Mary Crauderueff; Tel: 610-896-1158, E-mail: mcrauder@haverford.edu; Staff 19 (MLS 17, Non-MLS 2)
Founded 1833. Enrl 1,205; Fac 118; Highest Degree: Bachelor
Jul 2013-Jun 2014. Mats Exp $1,583,000, Books $353,000, Per/Ser (Incl. Access Fees) $1,230,000
Special Collections: Christopher Morley Coll; Cricket Coll; Elizabethan Studies (Philips Coll); Maxfield Parrish Coll; Mysticism (Jones Coll); Near Eastern Manuscripts (Harris Coll); Photography Coll; Quakerism: Friends Tracts of 17th Century (Jenks Coll), archives, doc, journals, maps, meeting minutes, ms, papers, pictures, rec; Roberts Manuscripts Coll; Rufus Jones Writings (Tobias Coll)
Automation Activity & Vendor Info: (Acquisitions) Innovative Interfaces, Inc; (Cataloging) Innovative Interfaces, Inc; (Circulation) Innovative Interfaces, Inc; (Course Reserve) Innovative Interfaces, Inc; (ILL) Innovative Interfaces, Inc; (OPAC) Innovative Interfaces, Inc; (Serials) Innovative Interfaces, Inc
Wireless access
Publications: Connections (Newsletter); Feminae: Medieval Women & Gender Index
Partic in Five Colleges, Inc; LYRASIS; OCLC Online Computer Library Center, Inc; OCLC Research Library Partnership; Partnership for Academic Library Collaborative & Innovation; Philadelphia Area Consortium of Special Collections Libraries

Departmental Libraries:

ASTRONOMY, Observatory, 370 W Lancaster Ave, 19041. Tel: 610-896-1145, 610-896-1291. FAX: 610-896-1102. *Sci,* Carol Howe; Tel: 610-896-1416; Staff 1 (MLS 1)
Subject Interests: Astronomy
Open Mon-Fri 9-5

UNION MUSIC, Union Bldg, 370 W Lancaster Ave, 19041. Tel: 610-896-1005. FAX: 610-896-1102. *Librn,* Adam Crandell; Tel: 610-896-1169, E-mail: acrandel@haverford.edu; Staff 1 (MLS 1)
Open Mon-Thurs 9am-11pm, Fri 9-5, Sat 1-5, Sun 1-11

WHITE SCIENCE, 370 W Lancaster Ave, 19041. Tel: 610-896-1291. FAX: 610-896-1102. *Sci,* Carol Howe; Tel: 610-896-1416; Staff 1 (MLS 1)
Open Mon-Thurs 8am-2am, Fri 8am-9pm, Sat 10-9, Sun 10am-2am

HAVERTOWN

P HAVERFORD TOWNSHIP FREE LIBRARY, 1601 Darby Rd, 19083-3798. SAN 314-6111. Tel: 610-446-3082. Reference Tel: 610-446-3082, Ext 201. FAX: 610-853-3090. E-mail: library@haverfordlibrary.org. Reference E-mail: reference@haverfordlibrary.org. Web Site: www.haverfordlibrary.org. *Dir,* Sukrit D Goswami; Tel: 610-446-3082, Ext 500, E-mail: director@haverfordlibrary.org; *Bus Mgr,* Donna Reeves; Tel: 610-446-3082, Ext 512, E-mail: reeves@haverfordlibrary.org; Staff 6 (MLS 5, Non-MLS 1)
Founded 1934. Pop 48,498; Circ 333,989
Jan 2015-Dec 2015 Income (Main Library Only) $1,446,282, State $153,341, City $1,120,905, County $7,050, Locally Generated Income $141,758, Other $23,228. Mats Exp $144,595
Library Holdings: AV Mats 5,000; Bk Titles 115,000; Per Subs 100
Automation Activity & Vendor Info: (Acquisitions) Innovative Interfaces, Inc - Millennium; (Cataloging) Innovative Interfaces, Inc - Millennium; (Circulation) Innovative Interfaces, Inc - Millennium; (ILL) Innovative Interfaces, Inc - Millennium; (OPAC) Innovative Interfaces, Inc - Millennium; (Serials) Innovative Interfaces, Inc - Millennium
Wireless access
Function: 24/7 Electronic res, 24/7 Online cat, Activity rm, Adult bk club, After school storytime, Archival coll, Audiobks on Playaways & MP3, Audiobks via web, AV serv, Bk club(s), Bk reviews (Group), Bks on CD, CD-ROM, Chess club, Children's prog, Computer training, Computers for patron use, Digital talking bks, Doc delivery serv, E-Readers, E-Reserves, Electronic databases & coll, Equip loans & repairs, Holiday prog, Home delivery & serv to seniorr ctr & nursing homes, Homebound delivery serv, Homework prog, ILL available, Internet access, Jazz prog, Life-long learning prog for all ages, Magazines, Magnifiers for reading, Mail & tel request accepted, Mango lang, Meeting rooms, Movies, Museum passes, Music CDs, Online cat, Online ref, Outreach serv, OverDrive digital audio bks, Photocopying/Printing, Preschool outreach, Preschool reading prog, Prog for adults, Prog for children & young adult, Ref & res, Ref serv available, Scanner, Senior computer classes, Senior outreach, Spanish lang bks, Story hour, Study rm, Summer & winter reading prog, Summer reading prog, Tax forms, Teen prog, Telephone ref, Wheelchair accessible, Winter reading prog, Workshops, Writing prog
Mem of Delaware County Libraries
Open Mon-Wed 10-9, Thurs 10-6, Fri & Sat 10-5
Friends of the Library Group

HAWLEY

P HAWLEY LIBRARY*, 103 Main Ave, 18428-1325. SAN 314-6138. Tel: 570-226-4620. FAX: 570-226-8233. Reference E-mail: hawleyref@waynelibraries.org. Web Site: hawleypubliclibrary.weebly.com, www.waynelibraries.org/hawley. *Exec Dir,* Amy Keane
Founded 1961. Circ 28,000
Library Holdings: Bk Vols 34,000; Per Subs 75
Special Collections: Large Print Books Coll; Memorial Art Coll (von Hake)
Wireless access
Open Tues & Thurs 10-4, Wed & Fri 10-2, Sat 10-1

HAZLETON

P HAZLETON AREA PUBLIC LIBRARY*, 55 N Church St, 18201-5893. SAN 358-5603. Tel: 570-454-2961. FAX: 570-454-0630. Web Site: www.hazletonlibrary.org. *Exec Dir,* Michele Kushmeder; E-mail: mkushmeder@hazletonlibrary.org; *Head, Circ Serv, Head, Tech Serv,* Jane Dougherty; *Head, ILL,* Kathy Ward; *Head, Ref,* Jeffrey Wagner; *Head, Youth Serv,* Mary Jordan; Staff 18 (MLS 2, Non-MLS 16)
Founded 1907. Pop 73,057; Circ 221,591
Library Holdings: CDs 109; Large Print Bks 352; Bk Titles 151,116; Bk Vols 157,819; Per Subs 471; Talking Bks 1,496; Videos 2,296
Special Collections: Hazleton-Mining History (Local History Coll), photog, maps, bks; Pennsylvania History
Automation Activity & Vendor Info: (Cataloging) SirsiDynix-WorkFlows; (Circulation) SirsiDynix; (OPAC) SirsiDynix
Wireless access
Mem of Luzerne County Library System
Open Mon-Thurs 9-8, Fri 9-5, Sat 9-4

Branches: 4

FREELAND BRANCH, 515 Front St, Freeland, 18224, SAN 358-5662. Tel: 570-636-2125. *Librn,* Colleen Tatar; Staff 3 (MLS 1, Non-MLS 2)
Library Holdings: AV Mats 1,142; Large Print Bks 66; Bk Titles 42,811; Bk Vols 44,112; Per Subs 63; Talking Bks 88; Videos 381
Open Mon & Wed (Winter) 1-5 & 6-9, Tues, Thurs & Sat 10-12 & 1-5, Fri 1-5; Mon & Wed (Summer) 1-5 & 6-8, Tues & Thurs 9-12 & 1-5, Fri 12-4

MCADOO, SOUTHSIDE BRANCH, 15 Kelayres Rd, McAdoo, 18237, SAN 358-5697. Tel: 570-929-1120. *Librn,* Sue Piacenti; Staff 2 (MLS 1, Non-MLS 1)
Library Holdings: AV Mats 508; Bk Titles 16,830; Bk Vols 18,510; Per Subs 51; Talking Bks 53; Videos 171
Open Mon-Wed (Winter) 3-8; Mon-Thurs (Summer) 10-3

NUREMBERG BRANCH, Mahanoy St, Nuremberg, 18241. (Mail add: PO Box 36, Nuremberg, 18241-0036), SAN 358-5727. Tel: 570-384-4101. *Librn,* Alice Lisefski; Staff 2 (MLS 1, Non-MLS 1)
Library Holdings: AV Mats 752; Bk Titles 18,751; Bk Vols 19,991; Per Subs 61; Talking Bks 81; Videos 192
Open Mon & Tues (Winter) 10-12 & 1-5, Wed 4-8, Fri 1-5; Mon & Tues (Summer) 10-12 & 1-5, Wed 4-8, Fri 12-4

VALLEY, 211 Main St, Conyngham, 18219, SAN 358-5638. Tel: 570-788-1339. *Librn,* Pat Walser; Staff 3 (MLS 1, Non-MLS 2)
Library Holdings: AV Mats 825; Bk Titles 18,911; Bk Vols 19,902; Per Subs 51; Talking Bks 102; Videos 191
Open Mon & Wed (Winter) 1-5 & 6-9, Tues, Thurs & Sat 10-12 & 1-5, Fri 1-5; Mon & Wed (Summer) 1-5 & 6-8, Tues & Thurs 9-12 & 1-5, Fri 12-4

M LEHIGH VALLEY HOSPITAL-HAZLETON*, Medical Library, 700 E Broad St, 18201. SAN 328-0136. Tel: 570-501-4800. FAX: 570-501-4840. Web Site: www.lvhn.org. *Librn,* Sharon Hrabina
Library Holdings: AV Mats 500; Bk Titles 1,545; Per Subs 266
Subject Interests: Allied health, Consumer health, Med, Nursing
Automation Activity & Vendor Info: (Cataloging) Professional Software
Partic in Basic Health Sciences Library Network; Health Information Library Network of Northeastern Pennsylvania; Northeastern Pennsylvania Library Network
Open Mon-Fri 12:30-4

HEGINS

P TRI-VALLEY FREE PUBLIC LIBRARY*, 633 E Main St, 17938-9303. SAN 320-8427. Tel: 570-682-8922. E-mail: trvpl@epix.net. Web Site: www.trivalleypubliclibrary.weebly.com. *Libr Dir,* Kelly Huss
Founded 1978. Pop 3,600
Library Holdings: Bks on Deafness & Sign Lang 12; Bk Titles 19,385; Bk Vols 21,000; Per Subs 20
Wireless access

Function: Bks on cassette, Bks on CD, Children's prog, Computers for patron use, Free DVD rentals, ILL available, Internet access, Magazines, Online cat, Photocopying/Printing, Summer reading prog, Tax forms, VHS videos, Wheelchair accessible
Open Mon, Wed & Fri 9-12 & 1-5, Tues & Thurs 1-5 & 6-8, Sat 9-1
Restriction: Circ to mem only
Friends of the Library Group

HELLERTOWN

P HELLERTOWN AREA LIBRARY, 409 Constitution Ave, 18055-1928. Tel: 610-838-8381. FAX: 610-838-8466. Web Site: www.hellertownlibrary.org. *Dir,* Noelle Kramer; E-mail: director@hellertownlibrary.org
Library Holdings: Bk Vols 30,000; Per Subs 38
Automation Activity & Vendor Info: (Cataloging) Follett Software; (Circulation) Follett Software; (OPAC) Follett Software
Wireless access
Function: 24/7 Online cat, Activity rm, Adult bk club, Audio & video playback equip for onsite use, Audiobks via web, Bk club(s), Bks on CD, Children's prog, Computers for patron use, Electronic databases & coll, Family literacy, Free DVD rentals, ILL available, Internet access, Life-long learning prog for all ages, Magazines, Meeting rooms, Movies, Music CDs, Online cat, Preschool reading prog, Printer for laptops & handheld devices, Prog for adults, Prog for children & young adult, Scanner, Senior outreach, Study rm, Summer & winter reading prog, Summer reading prog, Tax forms, Teen prog, Wheelchair accessible, Winter reading prog
Open Mon & Wed 10-8, Tues & Thurs 10-6, Fri 9:30-4, Sat 9-4, Sat (Summer) 9-1
Friends of the Library Group

HERMINIE

P SEWICKLEY TOWNSHIP PUBLIC LIBRARY, 201 Highland Ave, 15637. SAN 314-6162. Tel: 724-446-9940. FAX: 724-446-9940. E-mail: sewickley@wlnonline.org. Web Site: www.sewickleytownshippubliclibrary.org. *Libr Dir,* Mandy L Luchs; E-mail: mandy.luchs@wlnonline.org; Staff 1 (MLS 1)
Founded 1952. Pop 6,250; Circ 17,785
Library Holdings: Audiobooks 700; DVDs 1,900; e-books 13,000; Bk Titles 20,200; Per Subs 30
Wireless access
Function: 24/7 Electronic res, 24/7 Online cat, Activity rm, Adult bk club, Bk club(s), Bks on CD, Chess club, Children's prog, Computers for patron use, Electronic databases & coll, Free DVD rentals, Holiday prog, ILL available, Internet access, Laminating, Magazines, Mail & tel request accepted, Makerspace, Meeting rooms, OverDrive digital audio bks, Photocopying/Printing, Preschool outreach, Preschool reading prog, Prog for adults, Prog for children & young adult, Ref serv available, Scanner, STEM programs, Story hour, Summer reading prog, Tax forms, Teen prog, Telephone ref, Wheelchair accessible, Writing prog
Mem of Westmoreland County Federated Library System
Open Mon & Wed 10-7, Tues & Thurs 4-7, Fri 10-5, Sat 9-4
Friends of the Library Group

HERMITAGE

S MERCER COUNTY REGIONAL PLANNING COMMISSION LIBRARY*, 2491 Highland Rd, 16148. SAN 329-8825. Tel: 724-981-2412. FAX: 724-981-7677. E-mail: mail@mcrpc.com. Web Site: www.mcrpc.com. *Exec Dir,* Daniel Gracenin; E-mail: dgracenin@mcrpc.com
Library Holdings: Bk Vols 400
Wireless access

HERSHEY

P HERSHEY PUBLIC LIBRARY*, 701 Cocoa Ave, 17033. SAN 314-6170. Tel: 717-533-6555. FAX: 717-534-1666. E-mail: library@derrytownship.org. Web Site: hersheylibrary.org. *Dir,* Laura O'Grady; Tel: 717-533-6555, Ext 3715, E-mail: lauraogrady@derrytownship.org; *Acq Librn,* Krista Hughes; E-mail: Kristahughes@derrytownship.org; *Ch,* Rita Hunt Smith; E-mail: ritahuntsmith@derrytownship.org; *Ref Librn,* Donna Small; E-mail: donnasmall@derrytownship.org; *Coordr, Circ,* Chris Gawron; E-mail: chrisgawron@derrytownship.org; *Educ Coordr,* Julie Brnik; E-mail: jebrnik@derrytownship.org; *Electronic Res Coordr,* Jeff Cothren; E-mail: jeffc@derrytownship.org; *ILL,* Denise Phillips; E-mail: denisephillips@derrytownship.org; Staff 23 (MLS 7, Non-MLS 16)
Founded 1913. Pop 21,273; Circ 406,000
Library Holdings: Bk Vols 77,930; Per Subs 176
Special Collections: Chocolate, Pennsylvania Coll
Automation Activity & Vendor Info: (Circulation) Innovative Interfaces, Inc; (OPAC) Innovative Interfaces, Inc
Wireless access
Partic in Community Libraries Information Consortium; LYRASIS; OCLC Online Computer Library Center, Inc
Open Mon-Thurs (Winter) 9:30-8, Fri & Sat 9:30-5, Sun 1-5; Mon-Thurs (Summer) 9:30-8, Fri 9:30-5, Sat 9:30-3, Sun 1-5
Friends of the Library Group

CM PENNSYLVANIA STATE UNIVERSITY, COLLEGE OF MEDICINE*, George T Harrell Health Sciences Library, Penn State Hershey, 500 University Dr, 17033. SAN 314-6189. Tel: 717-531-8626. Interlibrary Loan Service Tel: 717-531-8633. Reference Tel: 717-531-8634. Information Services Tel: 717-531-8011. FAX: 717-531-8636. Web Site: www.med.psu.edu/library. *Libr Dir,* Kelly Thormodson; Tel: 717-531-8631, E-mail: kthormodson@pennstatehealth.psu.edu; *Assoc Dir,* Ben Hoover; Tel: 717-531-0003, Ext 285325, E-mail: bhoover@pennstatehealth.psu.edu; *Educ Librn, Instruction Librn,* Nancy Adams; Tel: 717-531-8989, E-mail: nadams@pennstatehealth.psu.edu; *ILL Librn,* Esther Dell; E-mail: eyd1@psu.edu; *Biomedical Info & Emerging Technologies,* Robyn Reed; Tel: 717-531-6137, E-mail: rreed4@pennstatehealth.psu.edu; *Coll Access & Support Serv,* Marie Cirelli; Tel: 717-531-8640, E-mail: mcirelli@pennstatehealth.psu.edu. Subject Specialists: *Computer tech,* Robyn Reed; Staff 7 (MLS 7)
Founded 1965. Enrl 660; Fac 643; Highest Degree: Doctorate. Sal $767,561 (Prof $483,240)
Library Holdings: e-journals 12,170; Bk Titles 17,201; Per Subs 12,177
Subject Interests: Bio engr, Biomed sci, Humanities, Med, Med educ, Nursing
Automation Activity & Vendor Info: (Acquisitions) SirsiDynix-WorkFlows; (Cataloging) SirsiDynix-WorkFlows; (Circulation) SirsiDynix-WorkFlows; (OPAC) SirsiDynix
Wireless access
Partic in Association of Academic Health Sciences Libraries; Greater NE Regional Med Libr Program; National Network of Libraries of Medicine Region 1; OCLC Online Computer Library Center, Inc
Special Services for the Deaf - Assistive tech
Open Mon-Fri 8am-Midnight, Sat & Sun 8am-10pm
Restriction: Open to students, fac & staff

HOLLIDAYSBURG

GL BLAIR COUNTY LAW LIBRARY*, Blair County Courthouse, Rm 3-C, 423 Allegheny St, 16648. SAN 314-6197. Tel: 814-693-3090. Web Site: www.blairco.org/Dept/LawLibrary. *Librn,* Lucy Wolf; Staff 1 (Non-MLS 1)
Founded 1900
Library Holdings: Bk Vols 8,000; Per Subs 20
Special Collections: Law Reviews/Law Journals Coll (From various counties in Pennsylvania, dating back to 1800s), bks
Open Mon-Fri 8-4

P HOLLIDAYSBURG AREA PUBLIC LIBRARY, One Furnace Rd, 16648-1051. SAN 314-6200. Tel: 814-695-5961. FAX: 814-695-6824. Web Site: hollidaysburglibrary.org. *Dir,* Janet Marie Eldred; E-mail: janet@halibrary.org; *Libr Serv Mgr,* Crystal Sue Crissman; E-mail: crystal@halibrary.org; *Children & Teens Program Coord,* Pennie Cadwallader; E-mail: pennie@halibrary.org; *Tech Serv,* Kim Eckard; E-mail: kim@halibrary.org; Staff 2 (MLS 1, Non-MLS 1)
Founded 1943. Pop 24,291; Circ 72,000
Library Holdings: AV Mats 1,762; DVDs 50; Bk Titles 41,632; Bk Vols 42,000; Per Subs 82; Talking Bks 1,162
Subject Interests: Penn
Automation Activity & Vendor Info: (Cataloging) Evergreen; (Circulation) Evergreen; (OPAC) Evergreen
Wireless access
Function: 24/7 Electronic res, 24/7 Online cat, Activity rm, Adult bk club
Mem of Blair County Library System
Open Mon-Thurs 10-8, Fri & Sat 9:30-5, Sun 1-5
Friends of the Library Group

HONESDALE

P WAYNE COUNTY PUBLIC LIBRARY*, 1406 Main St, 18431. SAN 314-6235. Tel: 570-253-1220. FAX: 570-253-1240. Web Site: waynelibraries.org. *Dir,* Ms Tracy Schwarz; E-mail: tschwarz@waynelibraries.org; Staff 2 (MLS 2)
Pop 24,500; Circ 104,000
Library Holdings: AV Mats 3,000; Bks on Deafness & Sign Lang 12; Large Print Bks 3,000; Bk Titles 28,000; Per Subs 95
Automation Activity & Vendor Info: (Cataloging) TLC (The Library Corporation); (Circulation) TLC (The Library Corporation); (OPAC) TLC (The Library Corporation)
Open Mon, Thurs & Fri 10-6, Tues & Wed 10-7, Sat 10-3
Friends of the Library Group

HONEY BROOK

P HONEY BROOK COMMUNITY LIBRARY*, 687 Compass Rd, 19344. SAN 314-6243. Tel: 610-273-3303. FAX: 610-273-9382. Web Site: www.honeybrooklibrary.org. *Dir,* Jennifer Spade; E-mail: jspade@ccls.org; Staff 5 (MLS 1, Non-MLS 4)
Founded 1963
Library Holdings: AV Mats 3,036; Bks on Deafness & Sign Lang 18; CDs 99; DVDs 34; Large Print Bks 415; Bk Titles 24,085; Per Subs 39; Talking Bks 702; Videos 2,201
Special Collections: Home Schooling Coll
Subject Interests: Local hist
Automation Activity & Vendor Info: (Cataloging) Innovative Interfaces, Inc; (Circulation) Innovative Interfaces, Inc; (ILL) Innovative Interfaces, Inc; (OPAC) Innovative Interfaces, Inc
Wireless access
Function: 24/7 Electronic res, 24/7 Online cat, Adult bk club, Audiobks on Playaways & MP3, Audiobks via web, Bk club(s), Bks on CD, Children's prog, Electronic databases & coll, ILL available, Internet access, Magazines, Mango lang, Movies, Music CDs, Online cat, Photocopying/Printing, Preschool reading prog, Prog for adults, Prog for children & young adult, Scanner, STEM programs, Story hour, Summer reading prog, Tax forms, Teen prog, Wheelchair accessible
Mem of Chester County Library System
Open Mon & Wed 11-6, Tues & Thurs 11-8, Fri 11-5, Sat 10-5
Friends of the Library Group

HORSHAM

P HORSHAM TOWNSHIP LIBRARY, 435 Babylon Rd, 19044-1224. (Mail add: PO Box 736, 19044-0736), SAN 378-4525. Tel: 215-443-2609. FAX: 215-443-2697. Web Site: www.horshamlibrary.org. *Libr Dir,* Regina Vesely; E-mail: rvesely@mclinc.org; *Ch,* Ellyn Benner; Tel: 215-443-2609, Ext 206, E-mail: ebenner@mclinc.org; *Tech Serv Librn,* Frances Penner; Tel: 215-443-2609, Ext 211, E-mail: fpenner@mclinc.org; *Circ Supvr,* Stephanie McKenna; Tel: 215-443-2609, Ext 207, E-mail: smckenna@mclinc.org; Staff 5 (MLS 4, Non-MLS 1)
Founded 2004. Pop 26,147; Circ 313,859
Jan 2014-Dec 2014 Income $1,147,219, State $72,939, City $1,021,659, Locally Generated Income $52,621. Mats Exp $141,285, Books $82,166, Per/Ser (Incl. Access Fees) $9,511, AV Mat $18,232, Electronic Ref Mat (Incl. Access Fees) $31,376. Sal $402,147 (Prof $235,366)
Library Holdings: Audiobooks 3,150; CDs 2,141; DVDs 5,869; e-books 886; e-journals 110; Bk Vols 97,183; Per Subs 133
Special Collections: Environmental Remediation (Willow Grove Naval Air Station Administrative Records), print & PDF doc
Automation Activity & Vendor Info: (Acquisitions) Innovative Interfaces, Inc; (Cataloging) Innovative Interfaces, Inc; (Circulation) Innovative Interfaces, Inc; (OPAC) Innovative Interfaces, Inc; (Serials) Innovative Interfaces, Inc
Wireless access
Function: Adult bk club, Art exhibits, Audiobks via web, Bk club(s), Bks on CD, Children's prog, Computers for patron use, Electronic databases & coll, Free DVD rentals, ILL available, Magnifiers for reading, Mango lang, Museum passes, Music CDs, Online cat, OverDrive digital audio bks, Photocopying/Printing, Prog for adults, Prog for children & young adult, Story hour, Summer reading prog, Tax forms, Teen prog, Wheelchair accessible
Partic in Montgomery County Library & Information Network Consortium
Open Mon 12-9, Tues-Thurs 10-9, Fri & Sat 10-5
Friends of the Library Group

HOUSTON

P CHARTIERS-HOUSTON COMMUNITY LIBRARY*, 730 W Grant St, 15342. SAN 314-6251. Tel: 724-745-4300. FAX: 724-745-4233. E-mail: chclbusiness@gmail.com. Web Site: washlibs.org/chartiers-houston. *Libr Mgr,* Laura Swanson; Staff 4 (MLS 1, Non-MLS 3)
Founded 1960. Pop 9,500; Circ 24,822
Library Holdings: Bk Vols 37,717; Per Subs 30
Automation Activity & Vendor Info: (Acquisitions) Follett Software; (Cataloging) Follett Software; (Circulation) Follett Software
Wireless access
Function: Bks on cassette, Bks on CD, Children's prog, Computers for patron use, Electronic databases & coll, Free DVD rentals, Genealogy discussion group, Holiday prog, ILL available, Internet access, Online ref, Photocopying/Printing, Preschool outreach, Prog for adults, Prog for children & young adult, Spoken cassettes & CDs, Spoken cassettes & DVDs, Summer reading prog, Tax forms, VHS videos, Wheelchair accessible
Publications: On & Off the Shelf
Mem of Washington County Library System
Open Mon-Thurs 11:30-7, Fri & Sat 11:30-4
Friends of the Library Group

HOUTZDALE

S STATE CORRECTIONAL INSTITUTION*, Houtzdale Library, 209 Institution Dr, 16698. (Mail add: PO Box 1000, 16698-1000). Tel: 814-378-1000, Ext 1556. FAX: 814-378-1030. Web Site: www.cor.pa.gov/Facilities/StatePrisons/pages/houtzdale.aspx. *Librn,* Mr Brodie Urban
Library Holdings: Per Subs 75
Automation Activity & Vendor Info: (Cataloging) Follett Software; (Circulation) Follett Software
Restriction: Not open to pub

HUGHESVILLE

P HUGHESVILLE AREA PUBLIC LIBRARY*, 146 S Fifth St, 17737. SAN 314-626X. Tel: 570-584-3762. FAX: 570-584-2689. E-mail: hapl@jvbrown.edu. Web Site: www.hughesvillelibrary.org. *Dir,* Kathy Butler; E-mail: kbutler@jvbrown.edu; Staff 4 (MLS 1, Non-MLS 3)
Founded 1941. Pop 5,000; Circ 28,000
Library Holdings: Bk Vols 22,000; Per Subs 32
Automation Activity & Vendor Info: (Circulation) SirsiDynix
Wireless access
Mem of Lycoming County Library System
Open Mon, Tues & Thurs 9:45-8, Fri 9:45-5, Sat 10-5
Friends of the Library Group

HUNLOCK CREEK

S STATE CORRECTIONAL INSTITUTION*, Retreat Library, 660 State Rte 11, 18621. Tel: 570-735-8754. FAX: 570-740-2406. Web Site: www.cor.pa.gov/Facilities/StatePrisons/pages/retreat.aspx. *Asst Librn,* Matthew Jurnak; E-mail: mjurnak@pa.gov
Library Holdings: Bk Vols 9,000; Per Subs 40
Automation Activity & Vendor Info: (Cataloging) Follett Software; (Circulation) Follett Software
Restriction: Not open to pub

HUNTINGDON

P HUNTINGDON COUNTY LIBRARY, 330 Penn St, 16652-1487. SAN 358-5816. Tel: 814-643-0200. FAX: 814-643-0132. E-mail: library@huntingdonlibrary.org. Web Site: www.huntingdonlibrary.org. *Exec Dir,* Lisa Erickson; E-mail: lerickson@huntingdonlibrary.org; Staff 1 (MLS 1)
Founded 1935. Pop 45,600
Library Holdings: DVDs 150; Large Print Bks 2,000; Bk Titles 56,000; Bk Vols 74,437; Per Subs 95; Videos 1,000
Special Collections: State & Local History (Pennsylvania Room)
Automation Activity & Vendor Info: (Cataloging) Follett Software; (Circulation) Follett Software; (OPAC) Follett Software
Wireless access
Open Mon-Thurs 10-7, Fri & Sat 10-5
Friends of the Library Group
Bookmobiles: 1

C JUNIATA COLLEGE*, Beeghly Library, 1700 Moore St, 16652-2119. SAN 314-6286. Tel: 814-641-3450. FAX: 814-641-3435. Web Site: www.juniata.edu/academics/library. *Dean of Libr,* Lisa McDaniels; Tel: 816-641-3458, E-mail: mcdanil@juniata.edu; *Assoc Dir, Head, Coll,* John Mumford; Tel: 814-641-3451, E-mail: mumford@juniata.edu; *Assoc Dir, Head, Libr Syst & Tech,* Julie Woodling; Tel: 814-641-3454, E-mail: woodling@juniata.edu; *Instruction & Outreach Librn,* Jacob Gordon; Tel: 814-641-5323, E-mail: gordonj@juniata.edu; *Coordr, Acq,* Beth Yocum; Tel: 814-641-3455, E-mail: yocum@juniata.edu; *Curator, Rare Bks, Hist Doc Conservator,* Hedda Durnbaugh; Tel: 814-641-3484, E-mail: durnbaughh@juniata.edu; Staff 8.5 (MLS 4, Non-MLS 4.5)
Founded 1876. Enrl 1,450; Fac 90; Highest Degree: Bachelor
Library Holdings: Bk Titles 140,000; Bk Vols 200,000; Per Subs 1,000
Special Collections: Church of the Brethren (College Archives), bks, ms; Early Pennsylvania German Imprints (Abraham Harley Cassel Coll), bks & pamphlets; Pennsylvania Folklore (Henry W Shoemaker Coll); Snow Hill Coll
Automation Activity & Vendor Info: (Acquisitions) SirsiDynix; (Cataloging) SirsiDynix; (Circulation) SirsiDynix; (Course Reserve) SirsiDynix; (ILL) SirsiDynix; (Media Booking) SirsiDynix; (OPAC) SirsiDynix; (Serials) SirsiDynix
Wireless access
Partic in Associated College Libraries of Central Pennsylvania; LYRASIS; OCLC Online Computer Library Center, Inc; Partnership for Academic Library Collaborative & Innovation; Proquest Dialog
Friends of the Library Group

S STATE CORRECTIONAL INSTITUTION*, Smithfield Library, 1120 Pike St, 16652. (Mail add: PO Box 999, 16652-0999). Tel: 814-643-6520. FAX: 814-506-1022. Web Site: www.cor.pa.gov/Facilities/StatePrisons/pages/smithfield.aspx. *Librn,* Renee

Lubert; E-mail: rlubert@pa.gov; *Libr Asst,* Brittany Claycomb; E-mail: bclaycomb@pa.gov
Library Holdings: Bk Vols 19,000; Per Subs 58
Restriction: Not open to pub

HUNTINGDON VALLEY

P HUNTINGDON VALLEY LIBRARY*, 625 Red Lion Rd, 19006. SAN 314-6294. Tel: 215-947-5138. FAX: 215-938-5894. E-mail: hvl.circ@gmail.com. Web Site: www.hvlibrary.org. *Actg Dir,* Pam Dull; E-mail: hvldirector@mclinc.org; Staff 8 (MLS 2, Non-MLS 6)
Founded 1953. Pop 13,000
Library Holdings: Bk Vols 90,000; Per Subs 115
Automation Activity & Vendor Info: (Cataloging) Innovative Interfaces, Inc; (Circulation) Innovative Interfaces, Inc; (ILL) Innovative Interfaces, Inc; (OPAC) Innovative Interfaces, Inc
Wireless access
Function: Adult literacy prog, Audio & video playback equip for onsite use, AV serv, Health sci info serv, Homebound delivery serv, ILL available, Internet access, Photocopying/Printing, Prog for adults, Prog for children & young adult, Ref serv available, Summer reading prog, Telephone ref, Wheelchair accessible, Workshops
Publications: Huntingdon Valley Library (Newsletter)
Partic in Montgomery County Library & Information Network Consortium
Special Services for the Deaf - Bks on deafness & sign lang
Special Services for the Blind - Audio mat; Bks on cassette; Bks on CD; Large print bks; Reader equip; Ref serv; Talking bks; Videos on blindness & physical disabilties
Open Mon-Thurs 10-9, Fri & Sat 10-5, Sun 1-5
Friends of the Library Group

HYNDMAN

P HYNDMAN LONDONDERRY PUBLIC LIBRARY*, 161 Clarence St, 15545. (Mail add: PO Box 733, 15545-0733), SAN 376-5733. Tel: 814-842-3782. FAX: 814-842-3737. E-mail: info@hyndmanlibrary.org. Web Site: www.hyndmanlibrary.org. *Libr Mgr,* Shane Lynn; *Asst Librn,* Polly Groves; Staff 2 (Non-MLS 2)
Founded 1991. Pop 2,902; Circ 4,278
Library Holdings: DVDs 75; Bk Titles 13,084; Bk Vols 13,575; Per Subs 10
Automation Activity & Vendor Info: (Cataloging) Follett Software
Wireless access
Function: CD-ROM, E-Reserves, ILL available, Photocopying/Printing, Spoken cassettes & CDs, Spoken cassettes & DVDs, Summer reading prog, Tax forms, VHS videos, Wheelchair accessible
Mem of Bedford County Library System
Partic in Pennsylvania Library Association
Open Mon-Thurs 1-7, Fri 1-5, Sat 9-5

IMMACULATA

C IMMACULATA UNIVERSITY*, Gabriele Library, 1145 King Rd, 19345-0705. SAN 314-6308. Tel: 484-323-3839. Reference Tel: 484-323-3829. Web Site: library.immaculata.edu. *Dir,* Jeff Rollison; E-mail: jrollison@immaculata.edu; *Syst Adminr,* Lori Monk; E-mail: lmonk@immaculata.edu; *Cat/Ser Librn,* Patty Wilson; E-mail: pwilson@immaculata.edu; *ILL, Ref Librn,* Sister Alice Schaebler; E-mail: aschaebler@immaculata.edu; *Archivist,* Sister Ann Marie Burton; E-mail: aburton@immaculata.edu; Staff 17 (MLS 5, Non-MLS 12)
Founded 1920. Enrl 1,599; Fac 88; Highest Degree: Doctorate
Library Holdings: Bk Titles 138,416; Bk Vols 141,910; Per Subs 755; Videos 504
Special Collections: Dietetics; Spanish American & Chicano Literature Coll
Automation Activity & Vendor Info: (Acquisitions) SirsiDynix; (Cataloging) SirsiDynix; (Circulation) SirsiDynix; (Course Reserve) SirsiDynix; (OPAC) SirsiDynix; (Serials) Sydney
Wireless access
Function: Res libr
Publications: The Gabriele Herald (Newsletter)
Partic in OCLC Online Computer Library Center, Inc; Southeastern Pa Consortium for Higher Educ; Tri-State College Library Cooperative
Open Mon-Thurs 8:30am-11pm, Fri 8:30-5, Sat 10-5, Sun Noon-11
Restriction: In-house use for visitors

R SISTERS, SERVANTS OF THE IMMACULATE HEART OF MARY ARCHIVES*, Villa Maria House of Studies, 1140 King Rd, 19345. (Mail add: PO Box 200, 19345-0200), SAN 375-6408. Tel: 610-647-2160. Reference Tel: 610-647-2160, Ext 522. FAX: 610-889-4874. *Library Contact,* Sister Elaine de Chantal Brookes; E-mail: vmhs1845@gmail.com
Library Holdings: Bk Titles 1,000
Wireless access

INDIANA

S HISTORICAL & GENEALOGICAL SOCIETY OF INDIANA COUNTY*, Frances Strong Helman Library, 621 Wayne Ave, 15701-3072. SAN 326-9302. Tel: 724-463-9600. FAX: 724-463-9899. E-mail: ichistoricalsociety@gmail.com. Web Site: www.rootsweb.com/~paicgs. *Exec Dir,* Jonathan Bogert; *Curator,* Clerissa Connelly
Founded 1939
Library Holdings: Bk Titles 5,000; Bk Vols 8,000; Spec Interest Per Sub 200
Special Collections: Cecil Smith Coll, bks ms; Frances Strong Helman Coll, bks, ms
Subject Interests: Antiques, Genealogy, Local hist, Penn hist, State hist
Automation Activity & Vendor Info: (Acquisitions) EOS International; (Cataloging) EOS International; (OPAC) EOS International; (Serials) EOS International
Publications: Newsletter (Monthly)
Open Tues-Fri 9-4
Restriction: In-house use for visitors, Non-circulating coll

GL INDIANA COUNTY LAW LIBRARY*, County Courthouse, 1st Flr, 825 Philadelphia St, 15701. SAN 314-6316. Tel: 724-465-3956. FAX: 724-465-3152. *Library Contact,* Justina Onuscheck; Tel: 724-465-3961; Staff 1 (Non-MLS 1)
Library Holdings: Bk Titles 15,612; Bk Vols 17,080; Per Subs 135
Open Mon-Fri 8:30-12 & 1-4
Restriction: Non-circulating to the pub

P INDIANA FREE LIBRARY, INC*, 845 Philadelphia St, 15701-3907. SAN 320-8516. Tel: 724-465-8841. FAX: 724-465-9902. Web Site: www.indianafreelibrary.org. *Dir,* Kate Geiger; E-mail: publib.kate@gmail.com; *Circ Librn,* John Swanson; *ILL Librn,* Valetta Shuppe; *Ch Serv,* Joanne Mast; *Youth Serv,* Lauri Steffy; Staff 12 (MLS 7, Non-MLS 5)
Founded 1934. Pop 32,924; Circ 139,684
Library Holdings: Bk Vols 75,000; Per Subs 105
Automation Activity & Vendor Info: (Acquisitions) Book Systems; (Cataloging) Book Systems; (Circulation) Book Systems; (OPAC) Book Systems; (Serials) Book Systems
Wireless access
Function: 24/7 Electronic res, 24/7 Online cat, Activity rm, Adult bk club, Adult literacy prog, Audiobks via web, AV serv, Bk club(s), Bks on CD, CD-ROM, Children's prog, Computer training, Computers for patron use, Distance learning, E-Readers, E-Reserves, Electronic databases & coll, Family literacy, Free DVD rentals, Genealogy discussion group, Govt ref serv, ILL available, Instruction & testing, Internet access, Large print keyboards, Life-long learning prog for all ages, Literacy & newcomer serv, Magazines, Magnifiers for reading, Mail & tel request accepted, Meeting rooms, Movies, Music CDs, Online cat, Online info literacy tutorials on the web & in blackboard, Online ref, Orientations, Outreach serv, OverDrive digital audio bks, Photocopying/Printing, Preschool outreach, Preschool reading prog, Printer for laptops & handheld devices, Prog for adults, Prog for children & young adult, Ref & res, Ref serv available, Res assist avail, Scanner, Senior computer classes, Senior outreach, Serves people with intellectual disabilities, Spoken cassettes & CDs, Spoken cassettes & DVDs, STEM programs, Story hour, Study rm, Summer & winter reading prog, Summer reading prog, Tax forms, Teen prog, Telephone ref, Wheelchair accessible, Winter reading prog, Workshops, Writing prog
Special Services for the Blind - Bks on CD; Copier with enlargement capabilities; Large print bks; Large screen computer & software; Magnifiers; Scanner for conversion & translation of mats; Screen enlargement software for people with visual disabilities
Open Mon & Wed 10-9, Tues & Thurs 10-6, Fri 12-5, Sat 10-5
Restriction: Non-resident fee, Residents only
Friends of the Library Group

C INDIANA UNIVERSITY OF PENNSYLVANIA*, Stapleton Library, 431 S 11th St, Rm 203, 15705-1096. SAN 358-5905. Tel: 724-357-2330. Circulation Tel: 724-357-2340. Reference Tel: 724-357-3006. FAX: 724-357-4891. Web Site: www.iup.edu/library. *Dean of Libr,* Dr Erik Nordberg; E-mail: erik.nordberg@iup.edu; *Asst Dean of Libr, Assessment & Develop,* Beth Kilmarx; E-mail: bkilmarx@iup.edu; *Asst Dean of Libr, Syst & Tech,* D Edward Zimmerman; E-mail: edzimmer@iup.edu; *Acq/Ser Librn,* Jin Ping; E-mail: jinpang@iup.edu; *Coll Develop/E-Res Librn,* Emily Szitas; E-mail: eszitas@iup.edu; *Govt Info/Ref Librn,* Theresa R McDevitt; E-mail: mcdevitt@iup.edu; *Ref Librn,* Sandra L Janicki; E-mail: cspslj@iup.edu; Staff 36 (MLS 15, Non-MLS 21)
Founded 1875. Enrl 13,020; Fac 763; Highest Degree: Doctorate
Library Holdings: AV Mats 50,000; Bk Titles 582,453; Bk Vols 800,000; Per Subs 16,000
Special Collections: Charles Darwin Coll; Herman Melville Coll; James Abbott McNeill Whistler Coll; John Greenleaf Whittier Coll; Nathaniel Hawthorne Coll; Norman Mailer Coll; Regional Coal & Steel Labor & Industrial Archives. State Document Depository; US Document Depository
Subject Interests: Educ, Liberal arts

Automation Activity & Vendor Info: (Acquisitions) Ex Libris Group; (Cataloging) Ex Libris Group; (Circulation) Ex Libris Group; (Course Reserve) Docutek; (ILL) OCLC; (Media Booking) Ex Libris Group; (OPAC) Ex Libris Group; (Serials) Ex Libris Group
Wireless access
Publications: Monumentae: A Union List of Music Monuments in Pennsylvania Chapter, Music Library Assn
Partic in Center for Research Libraries; Keystone Library Network; Partnership for Academic Library Collaborative & Innovation
Open Mon-Thurs 7:45am-12:45am, Fri 7:45-7, Sat 11-5
Friends of the Library Group

Departmental Libraries:

NORTHPOINTE REGIONAL CAMPUS LIBRARY, Academic Bldg, 167 Northpointe Blvd, Freeport, 16229, SAN 314-6634. Tel: 724-294-3300. FAX: 724-294-3307. *Libr Supvr,* William Daugherty; E-mail: william.daugherty@iup.edu; *Librn,* Portia Diaz; E-mail: portia@iup.edu; Staff 4 (MLS 1, Non-MLS 3)
Founded 1962. Enrl 180; Fac 23; Highest Degree: Master
Library Holdings: e-books 16,020; e-journals 14,858; Bk Vols 5,000; Per Subs 10; Videos 231

HAROLD S ORENDORFF LIBRARY, 101 Cogswell Hall, 422 S 11th St, 15705-1071, SAN 358-5921. Tel: 724-357-2892. Circulation Tel: 724-357-3058. FAX: 724-357-4891. Web Site: www.lib.iup.edu/depts/musiclib/music.html. *Librn,* Dr Carl Rahkonen; Tel: 724-357-5644, E-mail: rahkonen@iup.edu; *Tech Serv,* Terice McFerron; Staff 2 (MLS 1, Non-MLS 1)
Founded 1969
Library Holdings: Bk Titles 43,610; Bk Vols 45,811; Per Subs 56; Videos 391
Automation Activity & Vendor Info: (Cataloging) Ex Libris Group; (Circulation) Ex Libris Group
Open Mon, Wed & Thurs 8-8, Tues 8am-10pm, Sun 8-4:30

PUNXSUTAWNEY CAMPUS LIBRARY, 1012 Winslow St, Punxsutawney, 15767, SAN 315-1425. Tel: 814-938-4870. FAX: 814-938-5900. *Tech Serv,* Carol Asamoah; E-mail: carasam@iup.edu
Founded 1962. Enrl 250
Library Holdings: Bk Titles 18,000; Bk Vols 19,842; Per Subs 82; Videos 742
Automation Activity & Vendor Info: (Acquisitions) Ex Libris Group; (Cataloging) Ex Libris Group; (Circulation) Ex Libris Group; (OPAC) Ex Libris Group; (Serials) Ex Libris Group
Partic in OCLC Online Computer Library Center, Inc
Open Mon-Thurs 8am-10:30pm, Fri 8-4, Sat 10-5, Sun 6pm-10:30pm

S STATE CORRECTIONAL INSTITUTION*, Pine Grove Library, 189 Fyock Rd, 15701. Tel: 724-465-9630. FAX: 724-464-5135. Web Site: www.cor.pa.gov/Facilities/StatePrisons/Pages/Pine-Grove.aspx. *Dir, Libr Serv,* Benjamin Weaver; E-mail: benweaver@pa.gov; Staff 2 (MLS 1, Non-MLS 1)
Library Holdings: DVDs 484; Bk Titles 7,827; Bk Vols 9,114; Per Subs 80
Automation Activity & Vendor Info: (Cataloging) Follett Software; (Circulation) Follett Software
Restriction: Not open to pub

INTERCOURSE

P PEQUEA VALLEY PUBLIC LIBRARY*, 31 Center St, 17534. (Mail add: PO Box 617, 17534-0617). Tel: 717-768-3160. Web Site: pvpl.org. *Dir,* Catherine O'Sullivan; E-mail: cosullivan@pvpl.org
Founded 1975. Pop 19,588
Library Holdings: AV Mats 1,172; Bk Vols 16,793; Per Subs 92; Videos 505
Automation Activity & Vendor Info: (Cataloging) Innovative Interfaces, Inc; (Circulation) Innovative Interfaces, Inc; (OPAC) Innovative Interfaces, Inc
Wireless access
Mem of Library System of Lancaster County
Open Mon-Thurs 11-7, Fri 11-5, Sat 8-3

Branches: 1

SALISBURY TOWNSHIP BRANCH LIBRARY, The Family Center of Gap, 835 Houston Run Dr, Ste 220, Gap, 17527. Tel: 717-442-3304. FAX: 717-442-3305. *Br Mgr,* Lisa High; E-mail: lhigh@pvpl.org
Open Mon-Fri 9-8

IRWIN

P NORWIN PUBLIC LIBRARY*, 100 Caruthers Ln, 15642. SAN 358-5964. Tel: 724-863-4700. Circulation Tel: 724-863-4700, Ext 103. Interlibrary Loan Service Tel: 724-863-4700, Ext 104. FAX: 724-863-6195. Web Site: norwinpubliclibrary.net. *Dir,* Falk Diana; E-mail: dfalk@norwinpubliclibrary.net; *Ref Serv,* Bill Mausteller; Staff 4 (MLS 3, Non-MLS 1)
Founded 1937. Pop 40,363; Circ 117,291
Library Holdings: Bk Vols 61,000; Per Subs 55
Special Collections: Standard-Observer (local newspaper)
Publications: Online Serials Database Full Text
Mem of Westmoreland County Federated Library System
Open Mon-Thurs 10-8, Fri & Sat 10-5, Sun 1-5
Friends of the Library Group

JEANNETTE

P JEANNETTE PUBLIC LIBRARY*, 500 Magee Ave, 15644-3416. SAN 314-6359. Tel: 724-523-5702. FAX: 724-523-2357. E-mail: jeannettepl@hotmail.com. Web Site: www.jeannettepubliclibrary.com. *Dir,* Hope Sehring; Staff 6 (MLS 1, Non-MLS 5)
Founded 1932. Pop 14,384; Circ 30,013
Jan 2015-Dec 2015 Income $147,986, State $40,509, City $15,000, County $4,131, Locally Generated Income $53,705, Parent Institution $32,341, Other $2,300. Mats Exp $14,723, Books $7,366, Per/Ser (Incl. Access Fees) $2,020, Micro $100, AV Equip $1,686, AV Mat $3,491, Electronic Ref Mat (Incl. Access Fees) $60. Sal $66,000 (Prof $27,000)
Library Holdings: Audiobooks 486; AV Mats 3,720; Bks on Deafness & Sign Lang 27; CDs 804; DVDs 1,614; Electronic Media & Resources 3; High Interest/Low Vocabulary Bk Vols 25; Large Print Bks 487; Bk Titles 53,355; Bk Vols 54,702; Per Subs 95; Videos 846
Special Collections: Jeannette Coll, artifacts, historic doc
Subject Interests: Glass industry, Local hist
Automation Activity & Vendor Info: (Acquisitions) Innovative Interfaces, Inc; (Cataloging) Innovative Interfaces, Inc; (Circulation) Innovative Interfaces, Inc; (Course Reserve) Innovative Interfaces, Inc; (ILL) Innovative Interfaces, Inc; (OPAC) Innovative Interfaces, Inc
Wireless access
Function: Children's prog, E-Reserves, Photocopying/Printing
Mem of Westmoreland County Federated Library System
Partic in Health Sciences Libraries Consortium; Share Westmoreland Consortium
Special Services for the Deaf - Bks on deafness & sign lang
Special Services for the Blind - Bks on CD
Open Mon-Fri 12-7, Sat 10-5
Friends of the Library Group

JEFFERSON HILLS

P JEFFERSON HILLS PUBLIC LIBRARY*, 925 Old Clairton Rd, 15025. SAN 314-4097. Tel: 412-655-7741. FAX: 412-655-4003. E-mail: jeffersonhills@einetwork.net. Web Site: www.jeffersonhillslibrary.org. *Dir,* Jan Reschenthaler; E-mail: reschenthalerj@einetwork.net; Staff 11 (MLS 1, Non-MLS 10)
Founded 1959. Pop 10,619
Library Holdings: Bk Vols 43,023; Per Subs 50
Automation Activity & Vendor Info: (Circulation) Innovative Interfaces, Inc
Wireless access
Mem of Allegheny County Library Association (ACLA)
Open Mon-Thurs 10-8:30, Sat 10-3, Sun (Winter) 1-4
Friends of the Library Group

JENKINTOWN

S GRA INC LIBRARY*, 115 West Ave, Ste 201, 19046. SAN 314-6383. Tel: 215-884-7500. FAX: 215-884-1385. E-mail: gra@gra-inc.com, library@gra-inc.com. Web Site: gra-inc.com. *Ref Librn,* Gail Kostinko; E-mail: gailk@gra-inc.com; Staff 1 (MLS 1)
Founded 1975
Library Holdings: Bk Titles 8,500; Per Subs 115
Special Collections: US Airline Annual Reports
Subject Interests: Aviation, Econ analysis, Regulatory analysis, Transportation
Automation Activity & Vendor Info: (Cataloging) Inmagic, Inc.
Restriction: Pub ref by request, Staff use only

P JENKINTOWN LIBRARY*, 460 York Rd, 19046. SAN 314-6405. Tel: 215-884-0593. FAX: 215-884-2243. E-mail: jenkstaff@mclinc.org. Web Site: www.jenkintownlibrary.org. *Libr Dir,* Rosalind Lubeck; E-mail: rlubeck@mclinc.org; *ILL,* Linda Diner; Staff 8 (MLS 1, Non-MLS 7)
Founded 1803. Pop 4,422; Circ 65,000
Automation Activity & Vendor Info: (Acquisitions) Innovative Interfaces, Inc; (Cataloging) Innovative Interfaces, Inc; (Circulation) Innovative Interfaces, Inc; (ILL) Innovative Interfaces, Inc; (OPAC) Innovative Interfaces, Inc; (Serials) Innovative Interfaces, Inc
Wireless access
Function: Bk club(s), Bks on CD, Children's prog, Computers for patron use, Free DVD rentals, Holiday prog, ILL available, Internet access, Magazines, Meeting rooms, Museum passes, Music CDs, Online cat, OverDrive digital audio bks, Passport agency, Photocopying/Printing, Preschool reading prog, Prog for adults, Prog for children & young adult, Ref & res, Story hour, Summer & winter reading prog, Tax forms, Teen prog, Wheelchair accessible

Partic in Montgomery County Library & Information Network Consortium
Open Mon-Thurs 10-9, Fri & Sat 10-5

J MANOR COLLEGE*, Basileiad Library, 700 Fox Chase Rd, 19046-3399. SAN 314-6413. Tel: 215-885-5752. Circulation Tel: 215-885-5752. Reference Tel: 215-885-5752. FAX: 215-576-6564. E-mail: library@manor.edu. Web Site: library.manor.edu. *Dir, Libr Serv,* Donna Guerin; E-mail: dguerin@manor.edu; *Librn,* Andrew Pollak; Tel: 215-885-5752, E-mail: apollak@manor.edu; Staff 3 (MLS 2, Non-MLS 1)
Founded 1947. Enrl 700; Highest Degree: Associate
Library Holdings: AV Mats 203; DVDs 155; e-books 1,500; Bk Vols 30,000; Per Subs 9
Special Collections: Catholic Studies Coll; Civil War Coll; Ukrainian Coll
Automation Activity & Vendor Info: (Acquisitions) ByWater Solutions; (Cataloging) ByWater Solutions; (Circulation) ByWater Solutions; (Course Reserve) ByWater Solutions; (OPAC) ByWater Solutions; (Serials) EBSCO Online
Wireless access
Function: 24/7 Electronic res, 24/7 Online cat, Archival coll, Computers for patron use, Electronic databases & coll, For res purposes, Free DVD rentals, Internet access, Learning ctr, Online cat, Online ref, Photocopying/Printing, Ref & res, Ref serv available, Scanner, Study rm
Partic in Tri-State College Library Cooperative
Open Mon-Thurs 8-9, Fri 8-5, Sat 10-2
Restriction: In-house use for visitors, Non-circulating of rare bks

JERSEY SHORE

P JERSEY SHORE PUBLIC LIBRARY*, 110 Oliver St, 17740. SAN 314-6421. Tel: 570-398-9891. FAX: 570-398-9897. E-mail: jspl@jvbrown.edu. Web Site: www.jerseyshorepubliclibrary.org. *Dir,* Charlene Brungard; Staff 6 (MLS 1, Non-MLS 5)
Founded 1950. Pop 6,115
Library Holdings: Bk Vols 13,634; Per Subs 30
Wireless access
Mem of Lycoming County Library System
Open Mon & Fri 9-5, Tues-Thurs 9-8, Sat 9-4
Friends of the Library Group

JIM THORPE

GL CARBON COUNTY LAW LIBRARY*, Carbon County Courthouse, Four Broadway, 2nd Flr, 18229. (Mail add: PO Box 207, 18229-0207), SAN 314-643X. Tel: 570-325-3111. FAX: 570-325-9449. Web Site: www.carboncourts.com. *Asst Admin,* Kelly Hamm; E-mail: khamm@carboncourts.com
Open Mon-Fri 8:30-4:30

P DIMMICK MEMORIAL LIBRARY*, 54 Broadway, 18229-2022. SAN 314-6448. Tel: 570-325-2131. FAX: 570-325-9339. E-mail: dimmickmemoriallibrary@gmail.com. Web Site: www.dimmicklibrary.org. *Interim Dir,* Kara Edmonds; Staff 4 (MLS 1, Non-MLS 3)
Founded 1889. Pop 14,000; Circ 23,182
Library Holdings: Bks on Deafness & Sign Lang 15; Large Print Bks 22; Bk Titles 20,000; Bk Vols 22,000; Per Subs 60; Talking Bks 436
Special Collections: Census Coll, 1780-, microfilm; Firemen Materials; Local Genealogies; Local History Books; Local Newspapers, microfilm
Subject Interests: Census, Genealogy, Local hist, Mining, Railroads
Automation Activity & Vendor Info: (Cataloging) TLC (The Library Corporation); (Circulation) TLC (The Library Corporation); (OPAC) TLC (The Library Corporation)
Wireless access
Function: ILL available, Mail & tel request accepted, Photocopying/Printing, Prog for children & young adult, Ref serv available, Summer reading prog, Telephone ref
Partic in Lehigh Carbon Library Cooperative
Open Mon, Tues & Fri 9-5, Wed & Thurs 9-7, Sat 9-4
Friends of the Library Group

JOHNSONBURG

P JOHNSONBURG PUBLIC LIBRARY*, 520 Market St, 15845. SAN 314-6456. Tel: 814-965-4110. FAX: 814-965-3320. E-mail: jburglib@windstream.net. Web Site: www.johnsonburglibrary.org. *Dir,* Melinda Lewis; Staff 1 (Non-MLS 1)
Founded 1939. Pop 3,003; Circ 22,000
Library Holdings: AV Mats 600; Bks on Deafness & Sign Lang 10; Large Print Bks 130; Bk Vols 18,000; Per Subs 51; Talking Bks 250
Subject Interests: Genealogy, Local hist, Penn hist
Automation Activity & Vendor Info: (Cataloging) Follett Software; (Circulation) Follett Software; (OPAC) Follett Software
Wireless access
Open Mon & Fri 11-5, Tues, Wed & Thurs 11-7, Sat 10-2

JOHNSTOWN

P CAMBRIA COUNTY LIBRARY SYSTEM & DISTRICT CENTER*, 248 Main St, 15901. SAN 358-6022. Tel: 814-536-5131. FAX: 814-536-6905. Interlibrary Loan Service FAX: 814-535-4140. E-mail: campub@cclsys.org. Reference E-mail: reference@cclsys.org. Web Site: www.cclsys.org. *Libr Dir,* Ashley Flynn; E-mail: flynna@cclsys.org; *Head, Children's Servx,* Leah Johncola; E-mail: johncolal@cclsys.org; *Head, Circ,* Nicole Lenz; E-mail: lenza@cclsys.org; *Head, Ref,* Esther Vorhauer; E-mail: vorhauere@cclsys.org; *Network Adminr,* Joel E Koss; E-mail: koss@cclsys.org; Staff 7 (MLS 7)
Founded 1870. Pop 111,715; Circ 161,745
Library Holdings: AV Mats 4,332; Bk Vols 146,304; Per Subs 176; Talking Bks 2,633
Special Collections: State Document Depository; US Document Depository
Automation Activity & Vendor Info: (Cataloging) Innovative Interfaces, Inc; (Circulation) Innovative Interfaces, Inc; (OPAC) Innovative Interfaces, Inc
Wireless access
Member Libraries: Beaverdale Public Library; Carrolltown Public Library; Cresson Public Library; Ebensburg Cambria Public Library; Gallitzin Public Library; Hastings Public Library; Highland Community Library; Lilly-Washington Public Library; Mary S Biesecker Public Library; Nanty Glo Public Library; Northern Cambria Public Library; Patton Public Library; Portage Public Library; South Fork Public Library
Partic in OCLC Online Computer Library Center, Inc
Open Mon & Tues 8-8, Wed & Thurs 8-7, Fri & Sat 9-4
Friends of the Library Group

M CONEMAUGH MEMORIAL MEDICAL CENTER*, Health Sciences Library, 1086 Franklin St, 15905. SAN 314-6472. Tel: 814-534-9413. Circulation Tel: 814-534-9411. FAX: 814-534-3244. Web Site: www.conemaugh.org. *Med Librn,* Ms Kris Kalina; E-mail: kkalina@conemaugh.org; Staff 2 (MLS 1, Non-MLS 1)
Automation Activity & Vendor Info: (Cataloging) Marcive, Inc; (Circulation) Follett Software; (OPAC) Follett Software
Wireless access
Partic in Central Pennsylvania Health Sciences Library Association; Medical Library Association
Open Mon-Fri 6:30-4

R FIRST LUTHERAN CHURCH*, Walden M Holl Parish Library, 415 Vine St, 15901. SAN 314-6480. Tel: 814-536-7521. FAX: 814-536-0855. E-mail: firstlutheran@wpia.net. *Librn,* Carol S Massingill; Staff 2 (MLS 1, Non-MLS 1)
Founded 1954
Library Holdings: Bk Vols 5,032; Per Subs 2
Open Mon-Fri 9-3, Sun 9-12

P HIGHLAND COMMUNITY LIBRARY*, 330 Schoolhouse Rd, 15904-2924. SAN 314-6499. Tel: 814-266-5610. FAX: 814-262-0130. E-mail: highland@cclsys.org. Web Site: www.cclsys.org/highland. *Dir,* Ashlee B Kiel
Founded 1962. Pop 15,153; Circ 67,862
Library Holdings: Bk Titles 30,000; Per Subs 75
Automation Activity & Vendor Info: (Cataloging) Evergreen
Wireless access
Mem of Cambria County Library System & District Center
Open Mon 10-6, Fri & Sat 9-4; Sat (Summer 9-1)
Friends of the Library Group

J PENNSYLVANIA HIGHLANDS COMMUNITY COLLEGE LIBRARY*, 101 Community College Way, 15904. SAN 375-4413. Tel: 814-262-6458. FAX: 814-269-9744. E-mail: library@pennhighlands.edu. Web Site: www.pennhighlandslibrary.org. *Dean, Learning Res,* Dr Barbara A Zaborowski; Tel: 814-262-6425, E-mail: bzabor@pennhighlands.edu; *Info Literacy & eLearning Librn,* Alexander Kirby; Tel: 814-262-6484, E-mail: akirby@pennhighlands.edu. Subject Specialists: *Hist,* Alexander Kirby; Staff 2 (MLS 2)
Founded 1994. Enrl 1,565; Fac 22; Highest Degree: Associate
Jul 2015-Jun 2016. Mats Exp $115,900, Books $29,900, Per/Ser (Incl. Access Fees) $6,000, Electronic Ref Mat (Incl. Access Fees) $80,000. Sal $154,000 (Prof $122,000)
Library Holdings: Bk Titles 13,312; Bk Vols 14,022; Per Subs 15
Special Collections: Greater Johnstown Genealogy Coll
Automation Activity & Vendor Info: (Acquisitions) Follett Software; (Cataloging) Follett Software; (Circulation) Follett Software; (ILL) OCLC FirstSearch; (OPAC) Follett Software
Wireless access
Partic in Health Sciences Libraries Consortium; Pennsylvania Community College Library Consortium
Open Mon-Thurs 8am-9pm, Fri 8-4, Sat 10-4

C UNIVERSITY OF PITTSBURGH, JOHNSTOWN CAMPUS*, Owen Library, 450 Schoolhouse Rd, 15904. SAN 314-6537. Tel: 814-269-7300. Interlibrary Loan Service Tel: 814-269-7292. Reference Tel: 814-269-7295. FAX: 814-269-7286. Web Site: www.library.pitt.edu/johnstown. *Head Librn,* Peter Egler; Tel: 814-269-7288, E-mail: pegler@pitt.edu; *Pub Serv Librn,* April Kelley; Tel: 814-269-7290, E-mail: akelley@pitt.edu; *Instrul Serv, Pub Serv Librn,* David Kupas; Tel: 814-269-1983, E-mail: dmk24@pitt.edu; *Acq & Gifts, Ref Librn,* James Langan; Tel: 814-769-7298, E-mail: jlangan@pitt.edu; Staff 9 (MLS 5, Non-MLS 4)
Founded 1927. Enrl 3,134; Fac 136; Highest Degree: Bachelor
Library Holdings: AV Mats 656; Bk Vols 151,322; Per Subs 360
Automation Activity & Vendor Info: (Acquisitions) Ex Libris Group; (Cataloging) Ex Libris Group; (Circulation) Ex Libris Group; (Course Reserve) Ex Libris Group; (ILL) Ex Libris Group; (Media Booking) Ex Libris Group; (OPAC) Ex Libris Group; (Serials) Ex Libris Group
Wireless access
Partic in OCLC Online Computer Library Center, Inc; Pittcat
Open Mon-Thurs (Sept-May) 8am-10:30pm, Fri 8-5, Sat 10-6, Sun 2-10; Mon-Thurs (June-Aug) 8-6, Fri 8-5

KANE

P FRIENDS MEMORIAL PUBLIC LIBRARY, 230 Chase St, 16735. SAN 358-612X. Tel: 814-837-7010. FAX: 814-837-7010. E-mail: friendslibrarykanepa@gmail.com. Web Site: www.friendslibrary.org. *Dir,* Patty Kunicki
Library Holdings: Bk Vols 14,000; Per Subs 40
Automation Activity & Vendor Info: (Circulation) Follett Software
Wireless access
Open Tues-Thurs 11-6, Sat 9-3

KENNETT SQUARE

P KENNETT LIBRARY*, 216 E State St, 19348-3112. (Mail add: PO Box 730, 19348-0730), SAN 314-6553. Tel: 610-444-2702. Interlibrary Loan Service Tel: 610-444-2988. FAX: 610-444-1752. Web Site: www.kennettlibrary.org. *Libr Dir,* Megan Walters; E-mail: mwalters@ccls.org; *ILL,* Debbie Kellar; Staff 8 (MLS 2, Non-MLS 6)
Founded 1895. Pop 24,611
Library Holdings: AV Mats 4,394; CDs 278; Large Print Bks 235; Bk Titles 46,955; Bk Vols 51,444; Per Subs 161; Talking Bks 992; Videos 490
Special Collections: Antiques (Harlan R Cole Coll); Literature (Bayard Taylor Coll); Local History (Chester County)
Subject Interests: Antiques, Archit, Art, Environ studies, Hist, Hort
Automation Activity & Vendor Info: (Cataloging) Innovative Interfaces, Inc; (Circulation) Innovative Interfaces, Inc
Wireless access
Function: 24/7 Electronic res, 24/7 Online cat, Adult bk club, Adult literacy prog, Audiobks on Playaways & MP3, Audiobks via web, Bilingual assistance for Spanish patrons, Bk club(s), Bks on CD, Children's prog, Citizenship assistance, Computers for patron use, Electronic databases & coll, For res purposes, ILL available, Internet access, Magazines, Mango lang, Meeting rooms, Movies, Online cat, Outreach serv, OverDrive digital audio bks, Photocopying/Printing, Preschool reading prog, Prog for adults, Prog for children & young adult, Ref & res, Ref serv available, Scanner, Spanish lang bks, Story hour, Summer reading prog, Tax forms, Teen prog, Writing prog
Publications: Views a-Foot
Mem of Chester County Library System
Open Mon-Thurs 9-8, Fri 9-5, Sat 9-4

S LONGWOOD GARDENS LIBRARY*, 1001 Longwood Rd, 19348-1805. SAN 314-6545. Tel: 610-388-1000, Ext 5241, 610-388-5440. Interlibrary Loan Service Tel: 610-388-5261, 610-388-5331. E-mail: library@longwoodgardens.org. Web Site: longwoodgardens.org/education/library-archives. *Librn,* David Sleasman; E-mail: dsleasman@longwoodgardens.org; Staff 3 (MLS 1, Non-MLS 2)
Founded 1953
Library Holdings: Bk Vols 25,000; Per Subs 350; Videos 300
Special Collections: Rare Books
Subject Interests: Botany, Hort, Landscape archit
Automation Activity & Vendor Info: (Acquisitions) EOS International; (Cataloging) EOS International; (Circulation) EOS International; (Course Reserve) EOS International; (ILL) OCLC FirstSearch; (OPAC) EOS International; (Serials) EOS International
Wireless access
Function: ILL available, Photocopying/Printing
Partic in Council on Botanical & Horticultural Libraries, Inc; LYRASIS
Open Mon-Fri 8-5
Restriction: Circulates for staff only, Co libr, In-house use for visitors, Lending libr only via mail, Open to pub for ref only

KING OF PRUSSIA

S NEISWANDER LIBRARY OF HOMEOPATHY*, 1006 W 8th Ave, Ste B, 19406. Tel: 800-456-7818, Ext 2251. *Libr Supvr,* Beth Monaco; E-mail: beth@txoptions.com; *Cat, Ref Serv,* Carly Sewell; Tel: 610-283-7567, E-mail: csewell@neiswanderlibrary.org; *Libr Consult,* Annabel Grote
Founded 2016
Library Holdings: Bk Titles 4,500
Special Collections: 19th Century Homeopathic Books, Archival Materials, Homeopathic ephemera
Subject Interests: Hist, Homeopathy
Wireless access
Function: Archival coll, For res purposes, Ref & res, Res assist avail, Res libr
Open Mon-Fri 9-4
Restriction: Access at librarian's discretion, Authorized patrons, Authorized scholars by appt, Limited access for the pub, Non-circulating of rare bks, Non-circulating to the pub, Not a lending libr, Open to pub with supv only

G UNITED STATES NATIONAL PARK SERVICE*, Horace Wilcox Memorial Library at Valley Forge National Historical Park, 151 Library Lane, 19406. (Mail add: Valley Forge National Historical Park, 1400 N Outer Line Dr, 19406-1000), SAN 375-2011. Tel: 610-296-2593. Administration Tel: 610-783-1034. Administration FAX: 610-783-1060. Web Site: www.nps.gov/vafo. *Archivist,* Dona M McDermott; E-mail: dona_mcdermott@nps.gov. Subject Specialists: *Am Revolution,* Dona M McDermott; Staff 1 (Non-MLS 1)
Library Holdings: Bk Vols 8,700; Per Subs 25
Subject Interests: Am Revolution
Function: For res purposes
Restriction: Open by appt only, Ref only to non-staff

P UPPER MERION TOWNSHIP LIBRARY*, 175 W Valley Forge Rd, 19406-2399. SAN 314-6596. Tel: 610-265-4805. FAX: 610-265-3398. E-mail: uppermeriontownshiplibrary@gmail.com. Web Site: www.umtownship.org/departments/library. *Libr Dir,* Laura Arnhold; E-mail: larnhold@mclinc.org; Staff 18 (MLS 6, Non-MLS 12)
Founded 1963. Pop 28,000; Circ 189,000
Library Holdings: Bk Vols 100,000; Per Subs 180
Special Collections: Oral History
Automation Activity & Vendor Info: (Circulation) Innovative Interfaces, Inc; (OPAC) Innovative Interfaces, Inc
Wireless access
Publications: eNewsletter (Online only)
Partic in Montgomery County Library & Information Network Consortium
Open Mon-Thurs (Sept-June) 9-9, Fri 9-5, Sat 10-5, Sun 1-4:30

KINGSTON

L HOURIGAN, KLUGER & QUINN*, Law Library, 600 Third Ave, 18704-5815. SAN 372-1833. Tel: 570-287-3000. Toll Free Tel: 800-760-1529. FAX: 570-287-8005. E-mail: hkq@hkqlaw.com. Web Site: www.hkqpc.com. *Library Contact,* Susan Greenfield; E-mail: sgreenfield@hkqpc.com
Library Holdings: Bk Vols 9,000; Per Subs 50
Restriction: Staff use only

P HOYT LIBRARY*, 284 Wyoming Ave, 18704. SAN 314-660X. Tel: 570-287-2013. FAX: 570-283-2081. E-mail: hoytlib@ptd.net. Web Site: hoytlibrary.org. *Exec Dir,* Melissa A Werner; E-mail: mwerner@luzernelibraries.org; Staff 1 (MLS 1)
Founded 1928. Pop 33,309; Circ 121,661
Library Holdings: Audiobooks 3,659; DVDs 1,691; Bk Vols 62,451; Per Subs 144
Special Collections: Early Americana (William Brewster Coll), bks, maps; Holocaust (Reuben Levy Coll); Jewish History (Levison Coll)
Wireless access
Mem of Luzerne County Library System
Open Mon & Thurs 1-8, Tues, Wed & Fri 9-5, Sat 9-4
Friends of the Library Group

R WYOMING SEMINARY*, Kirby Library, Stettler Learning Resouces Ctr, 2nd Flr, 201 N Sprague Ave, 18704-3593. SAN 314-6626. Tel: 570-270-2168. Web Site: www.semkirbylibrary.org, www.wyomingseminary.org/academics/upper-school-academics/kirby-library. *Dir of Libr,* Ivy Miller; E-mail: imiller@wyomingseminary.org; *Asst Librn,* Brennan Twardoski; Tel: 570-270-2169, E-mail: btwardowski@wyomingseminary.org
Library Holdings: Bk Vols 13,000; Per Subs 15
Automation Activity & Vendor Info: (Acquisitions) Follett Software; (Cataloging) Follett Software; (Circulation) Follett Software; (Course Reserve) Follett Software; (ILL) Follett Software; (OPAC) Follett Software
Wireless access

Function: ILL available
Restriction: Not open to pub

KITTANNING

P KITTANNING PUBLIC LIBRARY*, 280 N Jefferson, 16201. SAN 314-6642. Tel: 724-543-1383. FAX: 724-543-1621. E-mail: kittanninglibrary@hotmail.com. Web Site: www.armstronglibraries.org/kittanning.php. *Dir,* Beth Milanak; E-mail: beth.milanak@armstronglibraries.org; Staff 1 (MLS 1)
Founded 1923. Pop 5,432; Circ 63,750
Library Holdings: AV Mats 175; High Interest/Low Vocabulary Bk Vols 30; Large Print Bks 1,000; Bk Titles 30,000; Per Subs 75; Talking Bks 600
Special Collections: County Histories Coll (including Allegheny, Armstrong, Butler, Clarion, Clearfield, Indiana, Jefferson, Washington & Westmoreland); Family Histories Coll (including Adams, Anderson, Barrackman, Bowser, Booth, Boyer, Claypool, Corbett, Hawk, Lookabaugh, McCullough, Marshall, Minteer, Oblinger, Ralston, Schall, Shellhamer & Wolfe); Kittanning & Armstrong County Notebooks Coll; Newspaper Coll (Armstrong Democrat 1828-1841 & Kittanning Gazette 1825-1833)
Partic in Midwest Libr Consortium
Special Services for the Blind - BiFolkal kits
Open Mon-Wed 11-7, Thurs & Fri 10-5, Sat 9-4
Friends of the Library Group

KNOX

P KNOX PUBLIC LIBRARY*, 305 N Main St, 16232. (Mail add: PO Box 510, 16232-0510), SAN 314-6650. Tel: 814-797-1054. FAX: 814-797-0258. E-mail: knoxpl@usachoice.net. Web Site: www.youseemore.com/KnoxPL. *Dir,* Roxanne J Miller; *Asst Dir,* Brenda Beikert; *Ch,* Erin Lloyd; Staff 3 (Non-MLS 3)
Founded 1935. Pop 7,615
Automation Activity & Vendor Info: (Cataloging) TLC (The Library Corporation); (Circulation) TLC (The Library Corporation); (OPAC) TLC (The Library Corporation)
Wireless access
Function: 24/7 Online cat, Adult bk club, Audiobks via web, Bk club(s), Bks on CD, Children's prog, Computer training, Computers for patron use, Free DVD rentals, ILL available, Internet access, Laminating, Magazines, Magnifiers for reading, Mail & tel request accepted, Movies, Online cat, Online ref, OverDrive digital audio bks, Photocopying/Printing, Preschool reading prog, Prog for children & young adult, Ref serv available, Scanner, Story hour, Summer reading prog, Tax forms, Telephone ref, Wheelchair accessible
Mem of Oil Creek District Library Center
Partic in Health Sciences Libraries Consortium
Special Services for the Blind - Bks on CD; Large print bks; Magnifiers; Merlin electronic magnifier reader
Open Mon, Tues & Thurs 9:30-8, Fri 9:30-4, Sat 9:30-4:30
Restriction: Non-resident fee

KNOXVILLE

P KNOXVILLE PUBLIC LIBRARY*, 112 E Main St, 16928. (Mail add: PO Box 277, 16928-0277), SAN 314-6669. Tel: 814-326-4448. E-mail: kpblibrary@gmail.com. Web Site: www.knoxvillepubliclibrary.com. *Libr Dir,* Sherrie Vitulli; *Asst Librn,* Duffy Laurens; *Asst Librn,* Position Currently Open
Founded 1921. Pop 1,668; Circ 7,649
Library Holdings: AV Mats 790; Bk Vols 11,570; Per Subs 36
Subject Interests: Genealogy, State hist
Wireless access
Mem of Potter-Tioga Library System
Open Mon 9-8:30, Wed & Fri 9-6:30, Sat 9-5

P POTTER-TIOGA LIBRARY SYSTEM*, 106 E Main St, 16928-9745. SAN 314-7290. Tel: 814-274-7422. FAX: 814-274-7422. E-mail: ptls16928@gmail.com. Web Site: www.pottertiogalibrary.org. *Libr Syst Adminr,* Leslie A Wishard
Founded 1975. Pop 60,343; Circ 226,801
Library Holdings: Bk Vols 197,202; Per Subs 413
Member Libraries: Blossburg Memorial Library; Coudersport Public Library; Elkland Area Community Library; Galeton Public Library; Genesee Area Library; Green Free Library; Knoxville Public Library; Mansfield Free Public Library; Oswayo Valley Memorial Library; Ulysses Library Association; Westfield Public Library
Open Mon-Fri 9-5

KUTZTOWN

P KUTZTOWN COMMUNITY LIBRARY*, 70 Bieber Alley, 19530-1113. SAN 314-6677. Tel: 610-683-5820. FAX: 610-683-8155. E-mail: kutztownpl@berks.lib.pa.us. Web Site: www.kutztownlibrary.org. *Dir,* Janet Yost; *Youth Serv Librn,* Taylor Kutz; E-mail: skuchild@berks.lib.pa.us; Staff 1 (MLS 1)
Founded 1949. Pop 17,121; Circ 106,423
Library Holdings: DVDs 4,772; Bk Titles 22,358; Per Subs 18
Subject Interests: City hist, County hist, Quilting, Quilts
Wireless access
Function: 24/7 Electronic res, 24/7 Online cat, Adult bk club, Art exhibits, Audiobks via web, Bk club(s), Bks on CD, Children's prog, Computer training, Computers for patron use, E-Readers, Free DVD rentals, Holiday prog, ILL available, Internet access, Magazines, Movies, Museum passes, Music CDs, Online cat, Passport agency, Photocopying/Printing, Preschool outreach, Preschool reading prog, Printer for laptops & handheld devices, Prog for adults, Prog for children & young adult, Scanner, Story hour, Summer reading prog, Tax forms, Wheelchair accessible
Mem of Berks County Public Libraries
Friends of the Library Group

C KUTZTOWN UNIVERSITY*, Rohrbach Library, 15200 Kutztown Rd, Bldg 5, 19530. SAN 314-6685. Tel: 610-683-4480. Interlibrary Loan Service Tel: 610-683-4745. Reference Tel: 610-683-4165. FAX: 610-683-4747. Web Site: library.kutztown.edu. *Dir, Libr Serv,* Martha Stevenson; E-mail: stevenson@kutztown.edu; *Emerging Tech Librn,* R Bruce Jensen; E-mail: rjensen@kutztown.edu; *Ref Librn,* Sylvia Pham; E-mail: spham@kutztown.edu; *Syst Coordr,* Bruce Gottschall; E-mail: gottscha@kutztown.edu; *Archives, Digital Projects,* Susan Czerny; E-mail: czerny@kutztown.edu; *Curric Mats Ctr,* Karen Wanamaker; E-mail: kwanamak@kutztown.edu; *Electronic Res, Per,* Bob Flatley; E-mail: flatley@kutztown.edu; *Info Literacy,* Krista Prock; E-mail: prock@kutztown.edu; *Metadata Serv, Tech Serv,* Michael Weber; E-mail: weber@kutztown.edu; *Ref (Info Servs),* Ruth Perkins; E-mail: perkins@kutztown.edu; *Tech Serv,* Lynette Breininger; E-mail: breining@kutztown.edu; Staff 25 (MLS 11, Non-MLS 14)
Founded 1866. Enrl 10,200; Fac 401; Highest Degree: Master
Library Holdings: Bks on Deafness & Sign Lang 112; CDs 181; e-journals 80,000; Large Print Bks 388; Bk Vols 517,000; Per Subs 795
Special Collections: Library Science Coll, bks & per; Pennsylvania Coll, bks, per & micro
Subject Interests: Art, Educ, Hist
Automation Activity & Vendor Info: (Acquisitions) Ex Libris Group; (Cataloging) Ex Libris Group; (Circulation) Ex Libris Group; (Course Reserve) Docutek; (ILL) OCLC ILLiad; (OPAC) Ex Libris Group; (Serials) Ex Libris Group
Wireless access
Publications: Rohrbach Library Newsletter
Partic in Associated College Libraries of Central Pennsylvania; Interlibrary Delivery Service of Pennsylvania; Keystone Library Network; Partnership for Academic Library Collaborative & Innovation
Special Services for the Deaf - TTY equip
Special Services for the Blind - Reader equip
Open Mon-Thurs 7:45-Midnight, Fri 7:45-5, Sat 9-5, Sun 2-Midnight

S PENNSYLVANIA GERMAN CULTURAL HERITAGE CENTER*, Heritage Center Library, 22 Luckenbill Rd, 19530. SAN 326-1050. Tel: 610-683-1589. E-mail: pagermanlibrary@kutztown.edu. Web Site: www.kutztown.edu/hcl. *Dir,* Patrick Donmoyer; E-mail: donmoyer@kutztown.edu; *Librn,* Lucy Kern
Founded 1998
Library Holdings: Bk Titles 7,500
Special Collections: Pennsylvania German Society Publications; Yoder Coll
Subject Interests: Folklore, Genealogy, Local hist
Function: Res libr
Open Mon-Fri 10-12 & 1-4

LA PLUME

C KEYSTONE COLLEGE*, Miller Library, One College Green, 18440-0200. SAN 314-6707. Tel: 570-945-8332. Circulation Tel: 570-945-8335. Interlibrary Loan Service Tel: 570-945-3333. FAX: 570-945-8969. E-mail: millerlibrary@keystone.edu. Web Site: web.keystone.edu/library. *Assoc Dean,* Mari Flynn; E-mail: mari.flynn@keystone.edu; *Dir,* Frank J Ohotnicky; E-mail: frank.ohotnicky@keystone.edu; *Access & Ser Librn,* Paula Yunko; E-mail: paula.yunko@keystone.edu; *Res & Instrul Serv Librn,* Ann Parrick; E-mail: ann.parrick@keystone.edu; Staff 11 (MLS 1, Non-MLS 10)
Founded 1934. Enrl 1,660; Fac 250; Highest Degree: Bachelor
Library Holdings: Bk Vols 42,400; Per Subs 283
Special Collections: Local History (Christy Mathewson Coll)
Automation Activity & Vendor Info: (Acquisitions) TLC (The Library Corporation); (Cataloging) OCLC Online; (Circulation) TLC (The Library Corporation); (OPAC) TLC (The Library Corporation)
Wireless access
Publications: Library Guides
Partic in Northeastern Pennsylvania Library Network; OCLC Online Computer Library Center, Inc
Open Mon-Thurs 7:30am-10pm, Fri 7:30-5, Sat 12-5

LACEYVILLE

P LACEYVILLE PUBLIC LIBRARY*, W Main St, 18623. (Mail add: PO Box 68, 18623-0068), SAN 314-6715. Tel: 570-869-1958. *Librn,* Position Currently Open
Circ 5,751
Library Holdings: Bk Vols 8,000; Per Subs 10
Open Mon 4-6, Tues & Thurs 10-5, Sat 9-12
Friends of the Library Group

LAFAYETTE HILL

P WILLIAM JEANES MEMORIAL LIBRARY*, Nicholas & Athena Karabots Center for Learning, 4051 Joshua Rd, 19444-1400. SAN 314-6723. Tel: 610-828-0441. E-mail: jeanesinfo@mclinc.org. Web Site: jeanesIibrary.org. *Dir,* Lisa Clancy; Tel: 610-828-0441, Ext 108, E-mail: lclancy@mclinc.org; *Ch,* Rachel Fecho; Tel: 610-828-0441, Ext 104, E-mail: rfecho@mclinc.org; *Asst Ch,* Linda Poland; Tel: 610-828-0441, Ext 112, E-mail: lpoland@mclinc.org; *Adult Serv, Ref Librn,* Adam Gilbert-Cole; Tel: 610-828-0441, Ext 103, E-mail: acole@mclinc.org; *Teen Librn,* Sara Huff; Tel: 610-828-0441, Ext 113, E-mail: shuff@mclinc.org; *Circ Mgr,* Karen Wilton; Tel: 610-828-0441, Ext 102, E-mail: kwilton@mclinc.org; *Operations Mgr, Pub Relations Mgr,* Deborah Moore; Tel: 610-828-0441, Ext 107, E-mail: dmoore@mclinc.org; *Tech Serv Mgr,* Maryanne Luthy; Tel: 610-828-0441, Ext 106, E-mail: mluthy@mclinc.org; Staff 20 (MLS 3, Non-MLS 17)
Founded 1933. Pop 17,349; Circ 145,000
Library Holdings: Bk Titles 51,000; Per Subs 210
Subject Interests: Quaker hist
Automation Activity & Vendor Info: (Cataloging) Innovative Interfaces, Inc; (Circulation) Innovative Interfaces, Inc; (OPAC) Innovative Interfaces, Inc
Wireless access
Function: 24/7 Electronic res, 24/7 Online cat, Activity rm, Adult bk club, After school storytime, Art exhibits, Audiobks on Playaways & MP3, Audiobks via web, Bk club(s), Bks on CD, Children's prog, Computer training, Computers for patron use, E-Readers, E-Reserves, Electronic databases & coll, Family literacy, Free DVD rentals, Health sci info serv, Holiday prog, ILL available, Instruction & testing, Internet access, Large print keyboards, Life-long learning prog for all ages, Magazines, Magnifiers for reading, Mail & tel request accepted, Mango lang, Meeting rooms, Movies, Museum passes, Music CDs, Online cat, Online ref, Outreach serv, Outside serv via phone, mail, e-mail & web, OverDrive digital audio bks, Photocopying/Printing, Preschool outreach, Preschool reading prog, Printer for laptops & handheld devices, Prog for adults, Prog for children & young adult, Ref & res, Ref serv available, Scanner, Senior computer classes, Senior outreach, Serves people with intellectual disabilities, Spoken cassettes & CDs, Story hour, Study rm, Summer & winter reading prog, Summer reading prog, Tax forms, Teen prog, Telephone ref, Wheelchair accessible, Winter reading prog, Workshops, Writing prog
Partic in Montgomery County Library & Information Network Consortium
Open Mon 12-8, Tues-Thurs 10-8, Fri & Sat 10-5, Sun 1-5; Mon (Summer) 12-8, Tues-Thurs 10-8, Fri 10-5, Sat 10-2
Friends of the Library Group

LAKE ARIEL

P HAMLIN COMMUNITY LIBRARY, 518 Easton Tpk, 18436-4797. SAN 314-5689. Tel: 570-689-0903. FAX: 570-689-4432. E-mail: hamlin@waynelibraries.org. Web Site: libraryhamlin.org, www.waynelibraries.org/hamlin.html. *Dir,* Lynn A Scramuzza; E-mail: lscramuzza@waynelibraries.org; Staff 3 (Non-MLS 3)
Founded 1969. Pop 9,532
Special Collections: Local History Coll
Wireless access
Function: 24/7 Electronic res, 24/7 Online cat, Adult bk club, Art exhibits, Audio & video playback equip for onsite use, Bk club(s), Bks on CD, CD-ROM, Children's prog, Computer training, Computers for patron use, Digital talking bks, Distance learning, E-Reserves, Electronic databases & coll, Free DVD rentals, Govt ref serv, Holiday prog, Homework prog, ILL available, Instruction & testing, Internet access, Magazines, Mail & tel request accepted, Meeting rooms, Music CDs, Online cat, Online info literacy tutorials on the web & in blackboard, Online ref, OverDrive digital audio bks, Passport agency, Photocopying/Printing, Prog for children & young adult, Scanner, Senior computer classes, Serves people with intellectual disabilities, STEM programs, Story hour, Summer & winter reading prog, Summer reading prog, Wheelchair accessible, Writing prog
Partic in Pennsylvania Library Association
Open Mon-Fri 10-4
Restriction: Free to mem, ID required to use computers (Ltd hrs)

LAKEWOOD

P NORTHERN WAYNE COMMUNITY LIBRARY*, 11 Library Rd, 18439. Tel: 570-798-2444. FAX: 570-798-2444. E-mail: nwcl@nep.net. Web Site: www.waynelibraries.org. *Dir,* Marge Burden; E-mail: burden@waynelibraries.org
Library Holdings: Bks on Deafness & Sign Lang 12; Bk Vols 14,000; Per Subs 35
Automation Activity & Vendor Info: (Cataloging) TLC (The Library Corporation); (Circulation) TLC (The Library Corporation); (OPAC) TLC (The Library Corporation)
Open Tues & Thurs 8:30-6, Wed 6pm-9pm, Fri 9-6, Sat 9-4

LANCASTER

R THE EVANGELICAL & REFORMED HISTORICAL SOCIETY*, 555 W James St, 17603. SAN 314-6758. Tel: 717-290-8734. E-mail: erhs@lancasterseminary.edu. Web Site: www.erhs.info.
Founded 1863
Library Holdings: Bk Titles 7,000
Special Collections: Colonial Coll; Congregations (German Reformed) in Pennsylvania & Surrounding States, church recs; History (William J Hinke Manuscript Coll); Mercersburg Theology Coll; Missionary History (German Reformed Church Manuscript Coll), ms, off doc; Missions (A R Bartholomew Coll); US Church Records of the Reformed Church, the Evangelical & Reformed Church
Function: Archival coll, Art exhibits, Online cat
Publications: Evangelical & Reformed Historical Society (Newsletter)
Restriction: Non-circulating coll

C FRANKLIN & MARSHALL COLLEGE*, Shadek Fackenthal Library, 450 College Ave, 17604. (Mail add: PO Box 3003, 17604-3003), SAN 358-626X. Tel: 717-358-4217. Interlibrary Loan Service Tel: 717-358-4224. FAX: 717-358-4160. E-mail: ask.us@fandm.edu. Web Site: library.fandm.edu. *Col Librn,* Scott Vine; Tel: 717-358-3840, E-mail: scott.vine@fandm.edu; *Assoc Librn, Coll Mgt,* Thomas A Karel; Tel: 717-358-3845, E-mail: tom.karel@fandm.edu; *Assoc Librn, Research Serv,* Lisa Stillwell; Tel: 717-358-3844, E-mail: lisa.stillwell@fandm.edu; Staff 26 (MLS 10, Non-MLS 16)
Founded 1787. Enrl 2,400; Fac 220; Highest Degree: Bachelor
Library Holdings: AV Mats 5,651; CDs 2,671; Bk Titles 491,089; Bk Vols 501,611; Per Subs 2,025; Videos 4,033
Special Collections: German Language Books in America (German American Imprint Coll); Lincoln (W W Griest Coll), photog; Theatre Arts (Anne Figgat Coll); Theatre Memorabilia (Alexander Corbett Coll), photog. US Document Depository
Automation Activity & Vendor Info: (Acquisitions) OCLC Worldshare Management Services; (Cataloging) OCLC Worldshare Management Services; (Circulation) OCLC Worldshare Management Services; (Discovery) OCLC Worldshare Management Services; (ILL) OCLC Worldshare Management Services; (OPAC) OCLC Worldshare Management Services; (Serials) OCLC Worldshare Management Services
Wireless access
Function: Archival coll, Art exhibits, Govt ref serv, Online cat, Online ref, Ref serv available
Partic in Associated College Libraries of Central Pennsylvania; Central Pennsylvania Consortium; Interlibrary Delivery Service of Pennsylvania; OCLC Online Computer Library Center, Inc; Partnership for Academic Library Collaborative & Innovation; The Oberlin Group
Open Mon-Fri 8:30-4:30
Friends of the Library Group
Departmental Libraries:
MARTIN LIBRARY OF THE SCIENCES, Bldg 22, 681 Williamson Way, 17604. (Mail add: PO Box 3003, 17604-3003). Tel: 717-358-4331. *Assoc Librn, Archives & Spec Coll,* Christopher Raab; Tel: 717-358-4225, E-mail: christopher.raab@fandm.edu; *Digital Initiatives Librn,* Brianna Gormly; Tel: 717-358-4206, E-mail: bgormly@fandm.edu; Staff 3 (MLS 1, Non-MLS 2)
Founded 1991
Library Holdings: Bk Titles 33,652; Bk Vols 35,091; Per Subs 109; Videos 52
Subject Interests: Astronomy, Biology, Chem, Computer sci, Geol, Physics, Psychol
Open Mon-Thurs 8-2, Fri 8am-Midnight, Sat 9am-Midnight, Sun 11-2
Friends of the Library Group

J HARRISBURG AREA COMMUNITY COLLEGE*, Lancaster Campus Library, 1641 Old Philadelphia Pike, 17602. Tel: 717-358-2986. Fax: 717-358-2952. E-mail: lanlib@hacc.edu. Web Site: libguides.hacc.edu/home/lancaster. *Dir,* Position Currently Open; Tel: 717-358-2222; *Ref & Instruction Librn,* Lisa J Weigard; Tel: 717-258-2986 E-mail: ejweigar@hacc.edu; *Libr Spec,* Bernadette Lynch; E-mail: blynch@hacc.edu; *Libr Spec,* Mary Wallick; E-mail: mewallick@hacc.edu; Staff 8 (MLS 5.5, Non-MLS 2.5)
Founded 1989. Enrl 21,000; Fac 273; Highest Degree: Associate

Library Holdings: AV Mats 898; Bks on Deafness & Sign Lang 43; Large Print Bks 14; Bk Titles 16,754; Bk Vols 28,199; Per Subs 115
Automation Activity & Vendor Info: (Acquisitions) SirsiDynix; (Cataloging) SirsiDynix; (Circulation) SirsiDynix; (Course Reserve) Docutek; (ILL) SirsiDynix; (Media Booking) SirsiDynix; (OPAC) SirsiDynix; (Serials) SirsiDynix
Wireless access
Open Mon-Thurs (Winter) 7:30am-9:30pm, Fri 7:30-4, Sat 8-2, Sun 12:30-6; Mon-Thurs (Summer) 7:30am-9:30pm
Restriction: Non-circulating to the pub

CR LANCASTER BIBLE COLLEGE*, Charles & Gloria Jones Library, Teague Learning Commons, 901 Eden Rd, 17601-5036. SAN 314-6766. Tel: 717-560-8250. Circulation E-mail: circdesk@lbc.edu. Web Site: www.lbc.edu/library. *Libr Dir,* Clint Banz; *Tech Dir,* Gerald Lincoln; Tel: 717-569-7071, Ext 5362, E-mail: glincoln@lbc.edu; *Assoc Libr Dir,* Deb Hunt; Tel: 717-569-7071, Ext 5349, E-mail: dhunt@lbc.edu; *Head, Tech Serv,* Jocelyn Abel; Tel: 717-569-7071, Ext 5361, E-mail: jabel@lbc.edu; *Acq Asst,* Lisa Swarr; Tel: 717-569-7071, Ext 5385, E-mail: lswarr@lbc.edu; *Circ Asst,* Bethany Fethkenher; Tel: 717-569-7071, Ext 5311, E-mail: bfethkenher@lbc.edu; Staff 6 (MLS 4, Non-MLS 2)
Founded 1933. Enrl 1,525; Fac 58; Highest Degree: Doctorate
Library Holdings: e-books 300,000; e-journals 50,000; Bk Vols 500,000; Per Subs 388
Special Collections: LBC Coll; Lloyd M Perry Coll (Pastoral Theology)
Subject Interests: Bible, Christian educ, Missions, Music, Theol
Automation Activity & Vendor Info: (Acquisitions) Ex Libris Group; (Cataloging) Ex Libris Group; (Circulation) Ex Libris Group; (Discovery) EBSCO Discovery Service; (OPAC) Ex Libris Group; (Serials) Ex Libris Group
Wireless access
Partic in LYRASIS; OCLC Online Computer Library Center, Inc; Southeastern Pennsylvania Theological Library Association
Open Mon-Thurs 7am-11pm, Fri 7am-9pm, Sat 11-9, Sun 2-11
Restriction: Fee for pub use

GL LANCASTER COUNTY LAW LIBRARY*, 50 N Duke St, 17602. (Mail add: PO Box 83480, 17608-3480), SAN 314-6790. Tel: 717-299-8090. FAX: 717-295-2509. Web Site: www.court.co.lancaster.pa.us/146/Law-Library. *Law Librn,* Eleanor Gerlott; E-mail: gerlott@co.lancaster.pa.us; Staff 1 (MLS 1)
Founded 1867
Library Holdings: Bk Vols 27,000; Per Subs 25
Open Mon-Fri 8:30-5
Restriction: Non-circulating to the pub

S LANCASTER COUNTY PRISON LIBRARY*, Law, 625 E King St, 17602-3199. Tel: 717-299-7800, 717-299-7814. FAX: 717-299-7813. *Coordr,* Position Currently Open
Library Holdings: Bk Titles 362; Bk Vols 910; Per Subs 10

P LANCASTER PUBLIC LIBRARY*, 125 N Duke St, 17602. SAN 358-6324. Tel: 717-394-2651. FAX: 717-394-3083. Web Site: lancasterpubliclibrary.org. *Exec Dir,* Heather Sharpe; Tel: 717-394-2651, Ext 108, E-mail: hsharpe@lancasterpubliclibrary.org; *Asst Dir,* Lissa Holland; E-mail: lholland@lancasterpubliclibrary.org; *Dir of Develop,* Lori Dietrich; E-mail: ldietrich@lancasterpubliclibrary.org; *Chief Financial Officer,* Cindy Farley; Tel: 717-394-2651, Ext 130, E-mail: cfarley@lancasterpubliclibrary.org; *Admin Mgr,* Kathy M Leader; Tel: 717-394-2651, Ext 102, E-mail: kleader@lancasterpubliclibrary.org; *Ch Mgr, Teen Serv Mgr,* Coreena Byrnes; E-mail: cbyrnes@lancasterpubliclibrary.org; *Outreach & Vols Coordr,* Leigh Kaliss; Tel: 717-394-2651, Ext 101, E-mail: lkaliss@lancasterpubliclibrary.org
Founded 1759. Pop 221,485; Circ 864,259
Library Holdings: AV Mats 29,190; Bk Vols 249,313; Per Subs 176
Special Collections: Oral History; State Document Depository
Subject Interests: Health, Local hist, Popular lit, Wellness
Wireless access
Mem of Library System of Lancaster County
Partic in OCLC Online Computer Library Center, Inc
Special Services for the Blind - ABE/GED & braille classes for the visually impaired
Open Mon-Thurs 10-8, Fri & Sat 10-5
Friends of the Library Group
Branches: 2
LANCASTER PUBLIC LIBRARY EAST - LEOLA BRANCH, 46 Hillcrest Ave, Leola, 17540, SAN 358-6413. Tel: 717-656-7920. *Asst Dir,* Lissa Holland; E-mail: lholland@lancasterpubliclibrary.org
Founded 1976. Circ 72,054
Library Holdings: Bk Vols 23,635; Per Subs 11
Open Mon & Fri 12-5, Tues & Thurs 10-5, Wed 12-6, Sat 10-1
Friends of the Library Group
LANCASTER PUBLIC LIBRARY WEST - MOUNTVILLE BRANCH, 120 College Ave, Mountville, 17554, SAN 358-6472. Tel: 717-285-3231. *Br Mgr,* Lisa Lane; E-mail: llane@lancasterpubliclibrary.org
Founded 1963. Circ 157,210
Library Holdings: Bk Vols 31,498; Per Subs 9
Open Mon-Thurs 10-8, Fri 10-5, Sat 10-1
Friends of the Library Group

R LANCASTER THEOLOGICAL SEMINARY LIBRARY*, 555 W James St, 17603-9967. SAN 314-6839. Tel: 717-290-8707. E-mail: library@lancasterseminary.edu. Web Site: library.lancasterseminary.edu. *Librn,* Myka Kennedy Stephens; Tel: 717-290-8704, E-mail: mkstephens@lancasterseminary.edu; Staff 3.8 (MLS 2, Non-MLS 1.8)
Founded 1825. Enrl 117; Fac 7; Highest Degree: Doctorate
Special Collections: Church History & Liturgics (Albright Coll)
Subject Interests: Biblical studies, Educ, Hist, Theol
Automation Activity & Vendor Info: (Acquisitions) ByWater Solutions; (Cataloging) ByWater Solutions; (Circulation) ByWater Solutions; (Course Reserve) ByWater Solutions; (Discovery) EBSCO Discovery Service; (ILL) OCLC WorldShare Interlibrary Loan; (OPAC) ByWater Solutions; (Serials) ByWater Solutions
Wireless access
Partic in American Theological Library Association; OCLC Online Computer Library Center, Inc; Southeastern Pennsylvania Theological Library Association

S LANCASTERHISTORY*, 230 N President Ave, 17603-3125. SAN 314-6782. Tel: 717-392-4633. Reference E-mail: research@lancasterhistory.org. Web Site: collections.lancasterhistory.org/en, www.lancasterhistory.org. *Dir, Libr Serv,* Nathan S Pease; E-mail: nathan.pease@lancasterhistory.org; Staff 4 (MLS 1, Non-MLS 3)
Founded 1886
Library Holdings: Microforms 3,000; Bk Titles 15,000; Per Subs 35
Special Collections: 18th & 19th Century Law Library (Judge Jasper Yeates Coll); Lancaster County Archives-Legal Records, 1729-1929; Lancaster History monograph coll; Manuscript groups; Object Coll
Subject Interests: Decorative art, Genealogy, Lancaster County, Penn hist
Automation Activity & Vendor Info: (Cataloging) OCLC
Wireless access
Function: 24/7 Online cat, Archival coll, Internet access, Magnifiers for reading, Microfiche/film & reading machines, Online cat, Photocopying/Printing, Prog for adults, Ref & res, Ref serv available, Res assist avail, Res libr, Wheelchair accessible
Publications: Journal of Lancaster County's Historical Society (Quarterly); The Historian (Online only)
Open Mon-Sat 9:30-5
Restriction: Fee for pub use, Free to mem, In-house use for visitors, Non-circulating, Not a lending libr

S LANCASTERHISTORY RESEARCH CENTER, Library of the Lancaster County Historical Society, (Formerly Lancaster County Historical Society), 230 N President Ave, 17603-3125. Tel: 717-392-4633. E-mail: research@lancasterhistory.org. Web Site: www.lancasterhistory.org/research. *Dir, Libr Serv,* Nathan Pease; Tel: 717-392-4633, Ext 119, E-mail: nathan.pease@lancasterhistory.org
Library Holdings: Bk Vols 175
Wireless access
Restriction: Free to mem, Non-circulating, Not a lending libr

S LANDIS VALLEY VILLAGE & FARM MUSEUM*, Reference Library, 2451 Kissel Hill Rd, 17601. SAN 314-6847. Tel: 717-569-0401. FAX: 717-560-2147. Web Site: www.landisvalleymuseum.org. *Dir,* James McMahon
Founded 1925
Library Holdings: Bk Vols 12,000
Subject Interests: Arts, Folklife, Folklore, Hist, Penn agr hist, Penn rural life & culture, Trade catalogs

P LIBRARY SYSTEM OF LANCASTER COUNTY*, 1866 Colonial Village Lane, Ste 107, 17601. Tel: 717-207-0500. FAX: 717-207-0504. Web Site: www.lancasterlibraries.org. *Exec Dir,* Karla Trout; E-mail: ktrout@lancasterlibraries.org; *IT Mgr,* Mark Sandblade; E-mail: msandblade@lancasterlibraries.org; *Spec Serv Mgr,* Ed Miller; E-mail: emiller@lancasterlibraries.org; *Youth Serv Mgr,* Renee Christiansen; E-mail: rchristiansen@lancasterlibraries.org; *Human Res Coordr, Training & Develop Coordr,* Stephanie Zimmerman; E-mail: szimmerman@lancasterlibraries.org
Founded 1987
Library Holdings: Bk Titles 404,672
Wireless access
Member Libraries: Adamstown Area Library; Columbia Public Library; Eastern Lancaster County Library; Elizabethtown Public Library; Ephrata Public Library; Lancaster Public Library; Lititz Public Library; Manheim Community Library; Manheim Township Public Library; Milanof-Schock Library; Moores Memorial Library; Pequea Valley Public Library;

Quarryville Library; Shuts Environmental Library; Strasburg-Heisler Library
Bookmobiles: 1

P MANHEIM TOWNSHIP PUBLIC LIBRARY*, 595 Granite Run Dr, 17601. Tel: 717-560-6441. FAX: 717-560-0570. E-mail: info@mtpl.info. Web Site: www.mtpl.info. *Exec Dir,* Joyce Sands; E-mail: jsands@mtpl.info; *Adult Serv Mgr,* Karyn Beltle; *Circ Mgr, Tech Mgr,* Alli Walker; *Coll Develop & Tech Serv Mgr,* Katie Keane; *Operations Mgr,* Janet Bailey; *Youth Serv Mgr,* Karin Rezendes
Founded 2007. Pop 38,133; Circ 318,617
Library Holdings: CDs 100; DVDs 2,400; Bk Vols 28,900; Per Subs 59; Talking Bks 1,600
Automation Activity & Vendor Info: (Acquisitions) Innovative Interfaces, Inc; (Cataloging) Innovative Interfaces, Inc; (Circulation) Innovative Interfaces, Inc; (OPAC) Innovative Interfaces, Inc; (Serials) Innovative Interfaces, Inc
Wireless access
Function: Adult bk club, Art exhibits, Audio & video playback equip for onsite use, Audiobks via web, Bi-weekly Writer's Group, Bk club(s), Bks on CD, Chess club, Children's prog, Computer training, Computers for patron use, Digital talking bks, Doc delivery serv, For res purposes, Free DVD rentals, Holiday prog, ILL available, Instruction & testing, Internet access, Magnifiers for reading, Mail & tel request accepted, Museum passes, Music CDs, Online cat, Online info literacy tutorials on the web & in blackboard, Online ref, OverDrive digital audio bks, Photocopying/Printing, Preschool reading prog, Printer for laptops & handheld devices, Prog for adults, Prog for children & young adult, Ref & res, Ref serv available, Scanner, Senior computer classes, Senior outreach, Spanish lang bks, Story hour, Summer reading prog, Tax forms, Teen prog, Telephone ref, Wheelchair accessible, Workshops, Writing prog
Mem of Library System of Lancaster County
Open Mon-Wed 11-7, Thurs & Fri 11-4
Friends of the Library Group

R MENNONITE LIFE*, Archives & Library, (Formerly Lancaster Mennonite Historical Society Library), 2215 Millstream Rd, 17602-1499. SAN 314-6812. Tel: 717-393-9745. FAX: 717-393-8751. Web Site: mennonitelife.org/research/visit-archives-library. *Librn & Archivist,* Steve Ness; E-mail: sness@lmhs.org; Staff 1 (MLS 1)
Founded 1958
Library Holdings: Bk Titles 33,495; Per Subs 256
Special Collections: Anabaptist Archives; Atlantic Coast Conference on Mennonite Church USA Records; Lancaster Mennonite Conference Records
Subject Interests: Amish, Hist, Lancaster County, Mennonite-Anabaptist theol, Mennonites
Automation Activity & Vendor Info: (Cataloging) Follett Software; (Circulation) Follett Software; (OPAC) Follett Software
Wireless access
Function: Archival coll, Computers for patron use, Electronic databases & coll, Internet access, Magazines, Online cat, Photocopying/Printing
Open Tues-Fri 9:30-4
Restriction: Circ to mem only, Fee for pub use, Free to mem

CM PENNSYLVANIA COLLEGE OF HEALTH SCIENCES*, Learning Commons-Health Sciences Library, 850 Greenfield Rd, 17601. SAN 314-6804. Tel: 717-947-6022. FAX: 717-947-6259. E-mail: Library@PACollege.edu. Web Site: pacollege.edu/academics/learning-commons/library/. *Dir, Libr Serv,* Christina Steffy; Tel: 717-947-6142, E-mail: cjsteffy@pacollege.edu; *Educ Librn,* Amy Snyder; Tel: 717-947-6215, E-mail: ansnyder@pacollege.edu; *Acq, Resources Librn,* Scott Denlinger; Tel: 717-947-6128, E-mail: sbdenlinger@pacollege.edu; Staff 3 (MLS 3)
Founded 1926. Highest Degree: Doctorate
Automation Activity & Vendor Info: (Acquisitions) EOS International; (Cataloging) EOS International; (Circulation) EOS International; (Discovery) TDNet; (ILL) SERHOLD; (OPAC) EOS International; (Serials) EOS International
Wireless access
Partic in Associated College Libraries of Central Pennsylvania; Basic Health Sciences Library Network; Central Pennsylvania Health Sciences Library Association; Medical Library Association; National Network of Libraries of Medicine Region 1; Westchester Academic Library Directors Organization

S SHUTS ENVIRONMENTAL LIBRARY, Three Nature's Way, 17602. Tel: 717-295-2055. FAX: 717-295-3688. E-mail: parks@co.lancaster.pa.us. Web Site: www.co.lancaster.pa.us/252/shuts-environmental-library. *Library Contact,* Ann Anderson
Founded 1991
Library Holdings: Bk Titles 4,500
Subject Interests: Environ, Gardening, Health, Native Am, Sci
Wireless access
Mem of Library System of Lancaster County
Open Mon-Wed 9-12 & 1-5

J THADDEUS STEVENS COLLEGE OF TECHNOLOGY*, Kenneth W Schuler Learning Resources Center, 750 E King St, 17602-3198. SAN 370-7539. Tel: 717-299-7753. Administration Tel: 717-299-7754. FAX: 717-396-7186. Web Site: stevenscollege.edu/academics/learning-resources-center. *Dir, Libr & Learning Res,* J J Landis; E-mail: landis@stevenscollege.edu; *Librn,* Tim Creamer; Tel: 717-391-3503, E-mail: creamer@stevenscollege.edu; *Librn,* Suzanne Derr; Tel: 717-396-7176, E-mail: derr@stevenscollege.edu; *Libr Asst,* Erica LaRue; Tel: 717-391-3502, E-mail: larue@stevenscollege.edu; Staff 3 (MLS 3)
Founded 1976. Enrl 1,300; Fac 55; Highest Degree: Associate
Library Holdings: e-books 1,188; Bk Titles 27,000; Per Subs 305
Wireless access
Partic in Health Sciences Libraries Consortium; OCLC Online Computer Library Center, Inc
Open Mon-Thurs 7am-10pm, Fri 7-5, Sun 2-10

LANGHORNE

CR CAIRN UNIVERSITY*, Masland Library, 200 Manor Ave, 19047. SAN 314-9684. Tel: 215-702-4370. Interlibrary Loan Service Tel: 215-702-4520. Reference Tel: 215-702-4225. Administration Tel: 215-702-4376. FAX: 215-702-4374. E-mail: library@cairn.edu. Web Site: library.cairn.edu. *Dir,* Stephanie S Kaceli; E-mail: stephaniekaceli@cairn.edu; Staff 4.3 (MLS 4.3)
Founded 1913. Highest Degree: Master
Library Holdings: AV Mats 12,688; e-books 558,857; e-journals 82,071; Bk Titles 105,341; Bk Vols 138,408; Per Subs 661
Subject Interests: Archives, Biblical studies, Educ, Music, Theol studies
Automation Activity & Vendor Info: (Acquisitions) Innovative Interfaces, Inc - Sierra; (Cataloging) Innovative Interfaces, Inc - Sierra; (Circulation) Innovative Interfaces, Inc - Sierra; (Course Reserve) Innovative Interfaces, Inc - Sierra; (Discovery) EBSCO Discovery Service; (ILL) OCLC WorldShare Interlibrary Loan; (OPAC) Innovative Interfaces, Inc - Sierra; (Serials) Innovative Interfaces, Inc - Sierra
Wireless access
Function: 24/7 Electronic res, 24/7 Online cat, Archival coll, Art exhibits, Audio & video playback equip for onsite use, Computers for patron use, Distance learning, Doc delivery serv, E-Reserves, Electronic databases & coll, For res purposes, ILL available, Internet access, Online cat, Online info literacy tutorials on the web & in blackboard, Online ref, Orientations, Outside serv via phone, mail, e-mail & web, Photocopying/Printing, Printer for laptops & handheld devices, Ref & res, Ref serv available, Res assist avail, Scanner, Study rm, Telephone ref
Partic in LYRASIS; OCLC Online Computer Library Center, Inc; Partnership for Academic Library Collaborative & Innovation; Southeastern Pennsylvania Theological Library Association
Restriction: Badge access after hrs, Borrowing privileges limited to fac & registered students, Circ privileges for students & alumni only, ID required to use computers (Ltd hrs), In-house use for visitors, Open to fac, students & qualified researchers, Open to students, fac, staff & alumni, Photo ID required for access

LANSDALE

P LANSDALE PUBLIC LIBRARY*, 301 Vine St, 19446-3690. SAN 314-6898. Tel: 215-855-3228. FAX: 215-855-6440. E-mail: inforequests@lansdalelibrary.org. Web Site: www.lansdalelibrary.org. *Dir,* Tom Meyer; E-mail: director@lansdalelibrary.org; Staff 4 (MLS 3, Non-MLS 1)
Founded 1928. Pop 16,362; Circ 77,289
Library Holdings: AV Mats 2,532; Bk Titles 42,054; Bk Vols 46,131; Per Subs 168
Subject Interests: Local hist
Automation Activity & Vendor Info: (Cataloging) TLC (The Library Corporation); (Circulation) TLC (The Library Corporation); (OPAC) TLC (The Library Corporation); (Serials) EBSCO Online
Wireless access
Open Mon-Fri 10-9, Sat 10-3

LANSDOWNE

P LANSDOWNE PUBLIC LIBRARY*, 55 S Lansdowne Ave, 19050-2804. SAN 314-691X. Tel: 610-623-0239. FAX: 610-623-6825. E-mail: lansdowne@delcolibraries.org. Web Site: www.lansdownelibrary.org. Staff 10 (MLS 2, Non-MLS 8)
Founded 1898. Pop 11,712; Circ 147,005
Library Holdings: Bk Vols 54,000; Per Subs 75
Wireless access
Mem of Delaware County Libraries
Open Mon-Thurs 9-9, Fri 9-6, Sat 10-4 (10-2 July & Aug)
Friends of the Library Group

LAPORTE

GL SULLIVAN COUNTY LAW LIBRARY, Court House, 245 Muncy St, 18626. (Mail add: PO Box 157, 18626-0157), SAN 375-247X. Tel: 570-946-4053. E-mail: rsimpson@sullivancounty-pa.us. Web Site: www.sullivancounty-pa.us. *Dir,* Jodi Metzger
Library Holdings: Bk Vols 500
Open Mon-Fri 8:30-4

LATROBE

P ADAMS MEMORIAL LIBRARY*, 1112 Ligonier St, 15650. SAN 314-6928. Tel: 724-539-1972. FAX: 724-537-0338. E-mail: library@adamslib.org. Web Site: www.adamslib.org. *Dir,* Tracy Trotter; *Dir, Ch Serv,* Karen Herc; Staff 25 (MLS 5, Non-MLS 20)
Founded 1927. Pop 51,000; Circ 260,000
Library Holdings: Bk Vols 110,000; Per Subs 50
Automation Activity & Vendor Info: (Cataloging) Follett Software; (Circulation) Follett Software; (OPAC) Follett Software
Wireless access
Mem of Westmoreland County Federated Library System
Partic in Monessen District Libr Ctr
Special Services for the Blind - Assistive/Adapted tech devices, equip & products
Open Mon-Thurs 10-7:30, Sat 10-5
Friends of the Library Group
Branches: 2
CALDWELL MEMORIAL LIBRARY, 982 N Chestnut St Extension, Derry, 15627. Tel: 724-694-5765. FAX: 724-694-8546. *Br Mgr,* Aurea Lucas
Library Holdings: Bk Vols 9,731
Open Mon-Thurs 3-8, Sat 10-3
UNITY, 156 Beatty County Rd, 15650. Tel: 724-539-1972. FAX: 724-532-1841.
Library Holdings: Bk Vols 9,323; Per Subs 10
Open Mon & Wed 2-7, Fri 10-3, Sun 1-6
Bookmobiles: 1. In Charge, Darlene Shaw. Bk vols 7,000

M EXCELA HEALTH LATROBE HOSPITAL*, Health Sciences Library, One Mellon Way, 15650-1096. SAN 314-6944. Tel: 724-537-1275. FAX: 724-537-1890. Web Site: www.excelahealth.org/locations/latrobe-hospital. *Mgr,* Marilyn Daniels; Staff 1 (MLS 1)
Founded 1963
Library Holdings: Bk Titles 2,830; Bk Vols 3,052; Per Subs 162
Subject Interests: Allied health, Med, Nursing
Partic in Basic Health Sciences Library Network; National Network of Libraries of Medicine Region 1; Share Westmoreland Consortium
Open Mon-Fri 9:30-6

CR SAINT VINCENT COLLEGE & SEMINARY LIBRARY, Dale P Latimer Library, 300 Fraser Purchase Rd, 15650-2690. SAN 314-6952. Tel: 724-805-2966. Interlibrary Loan Service Tel: 724-805-2484. Reference Tel: 724-805-2370. Administration Tel: 724-805-2307. FAX: 724-805-2905. E-mail: library@stvincent.edu. Web Site: www.stvincent.edu. *Dir,* Brother David Kelly; E-mail: david.kelly@stvincent.edu; *Asst Dir, Circ & ILL, Pub Serv Librn,* Bridget Hornyak; *Access Serv Librn, Coll Develop,* Correne Harkowitch; E-mail: correne.harskowitch@stvincent.edu; *Ser Librn,* Fr Matthias Martinez; E-mail: mathias.martinez@email.stvincent.edu; *Cataloger, Head, Tech Serv, Spec Coll Librn,* Elizabeth DiGiustino; Tel: 724-805-2310, E-mail: elizabeth.digustino@stvincent.edu; Staff 10 (MLS 5, Non-MLS 5)
Founded 1846. Enrl 1,800; Highest Degree: Master
Library Holdings: Bk Titles 382,266; Per Subs 387
Special Collections: Medievalia; Patrology
Subject Interests: Benedictina, Ecclesiastical hist, Hist, Incunabula, Penn, Relig studies, Theol
Automation Activity & Vendor Info: (Acquisitions) ByWater Solutions; (Cataloging) ByWater Solutions; (Circulation) ByWater Solutions; (OPAC) ByWater Solutions
Wireless access
Function: Audio & video playback equip for onsite use, Bks on cassette, Bks on CD, CD-ROM, Computers for patron use, Electronic databases & coll, ILL available, Microfiche/film & reading machines, Music CDs, Online cat, Photocopying/Printing, Ref & res, Ref serv available, Scanner, Spoken cassettes & CDs, Spoken cassettes & DVDs, VHS videos
Partic in LYRASIS; OCLC Online Computer Library Center, Inc
Special Services for the Blind - Reader equip
Open Mon-Thurs 8:15am-11:45pm, Fri 8:15-4:45, Sat 10-4:45, Sun 12-11:45

LAURELDALE

MUHLENBERG COMMUNITY LIBRARY*, 3612 Kutztown Rd, 19605-1842. SAN 314-6960. Tel: 610-929-0589. FAX: 610-929-8165. E-mail: muhlenbergcl@berks.lib.pa.us. Web Site: www.berks.lib.pa.us/muhlenbergcl. *Dir,* Melissa Adams; *Asst Dir,* Lee Cranmer
Founded 1960. Pop 23,753; Circ 150,000
Library Holdings: Bk Vols 28,000; Per Subs 76
Special Collections: Autism Society of Berks; Berks County, PA History Coll
Automation Activity & Vendor Info: (Acquisitions) Horizon; (Cataloging) Horizon; (Circulation) Horizon; (Course Reserve) Horizon; (ILL) Horizon; (Media Booking) Horizon; (OPAC) Horizon; (Serials) Horizon
Wireless access
Mem of Berks County Public Libraries
Open Mon-Thurs 10-8, Fri 10-2, Sat 9-4 (10-2 Summer)

LAURELTON

P WEST END LIBRARY*, 45 Ball Park Rd, 17835. (Mail add: PO Box 111, 17835-0111). Tel: 570-922-4773. FAX: 570-922-1162. E-mail: wellib@westendlibrary.org. Web Site: unioncountylibraries.org. *Dir,* Wendy Rote; Staff 3 (Non-MLS 3)
Founded 1980. Pop 1,735
Library Holdings: Bk Vols 9,194; Per Subs 26
Automation Activity & Vendor Info: (Cataloging) TLC (The Library Corporation); (Circulation) TLC (The Library Corporation); (OPAC) TLC (The Library Corporation)
Mem of Union County Library System
Open Mon & Thurs 10-8, Tues & Fri 9-6, Sat 9-4

LEBANON

J HARRISBURG AREA COMMUNITY COLLEGE*, Pushnik Family Library Lebanon Campus, 735 Cumberland St, 17042. Tel: 717-270-6328. Interlibrary Loan Service Tel: 717-780-2623. Administration Tel: 717-270-6320. Web Site: lib2.hacc.edu. *Libr Dir,* Joseph V McIlhenney; *Automation Syst Coordr,* Michael L Bowden; Tel: 717-780-1936, E-mail: mlbowden@hacc.edu; *Acq,* Kim McGovern; Tel: 717-780-2465, E-mail: kbmcgove@hacc.edu; *ILL,* Diane Wiedemann; E-mail: dlweiden@hacc.edu; Staff 3 (MLS 2, Non-MLS 1)
Founded 1990. Enrl 1,317; Fac 100; Highest Degree: Associate
Library Holdings: AV Mats 364; Bks on Deafness & Sign Lang 17; e-books 2,598; e-journals 2,490; Electronic Media & Resources 82; Bk Titles 15,676; Per Subs 54; Videos 375
Subject Interests: Career, Penn German culture
Automation Activity & Vendor Info: (Acquisitions) SirsiDynix; (Cataloging) SirsiDynix; (Circulation) SirsiDynix; (Course Reserve) Docutek; (ILL) SirsiDynix; (Media Booking) SirsiDynix; (OPAC) SirsiDynix; (Serials) SirsiDynix
Wireless access
Special Services for the Blind - Assistive/Adapted tech devices, equip & products; Large screen computer & software; Low vision equip; Reader equip; Screen enlargement software for people with visual disabilities; Screen reader software; ZoomText magnification & reading software
Open Mon-Thurs 7:30am-9pm, Fri 7:30-4
Restriction: In-house use for visitors, Non-circulating to the pub

M KROHN MEMORIAL LIBRARY, WellSpan Good Samaritan Hospital Medical Library, Fourth & Walnut St, 17042. (Mail add: PO Box 1281, 17042-1281), SAN 371-8719. Tel: 717-270-7826. E-mail: gsh-librarian-1@wellspan.org. *Med Librn,* Georgeanna Ledgerwood; E-mail: gledgerwood@wellspan.org; Staff 1 (MLS 1)
Library Holdings: e-books 102; e-journals 127; Bk Titles 1,033; Per Subs 30
Subject Interests: Clinical med, Hospital admin, Nursing
Automation Activity & Vendor Info: (Cataloging) Professional Software; (Circulation) Professional Software; (Serials) OVID Technologies
Wireless access
Function: Computers for patron use, Doc delivery serv, For res purposes, Health sci info serv, ILL available, Internet access, Online cat, Orientations, Photocopying/Printing, Prof lending libr, Ref serv available, Res libr, Wheelchair accessible
Partic in Basic Health Sciences Library Network; Central Pennsylvania Health Sciences Library Association
Open Mon-Fri 8-4:30
Restriction: Circ limited, Circulates for staff only, Hospital employees & physicians only, In-house use for visitors, Med & health res only, Open to pub for ref only, Prof mat only, Pub use on premises

P LEBANON COMMUNITY LIBRARY, DISTRICT CENTER, 125 N Seventh St, 17046-5000. SAN 320-4189. Tel: 717-273-7624. FAX: 717-273-2719. Web Site: lebanon.lclibs.org. *Libr Dir,* Michelle Hawk; E-mail: hawk@lclibs.org; Staff 19 (MLS 2, Non-MLS 17)
Founded 1925. Pop 60,000
Library Holdings: Audiobooks 4,932; CDs 2,064; DVDs 12,334; e-books 7,922; Large Print Bks 3,038; Bk Titles 84,321; Bk Vols 93,778; Per Subs 120

Special Collections: Spanish Coll
Automation Activity & Vendor Info: (Cataloging) Innovative Interfaces, Inc; (Circulation) Innovative Interfaces, Inc; (ILL) Innovative Interfaces, Inc; (OPAC) Innovative Interfaces, Inc
Wireless access
Function: 24/7 Electronic res, 24/7 Online cat, Adult bk club, Audiobks on Playaways & MP3, Audiobks via web, Bilingual assistance for Spanish patrons, Bk club(s), Bks on CD, Children's prog, Computer training, Computers for patron use, E-Readers, Electronic databases & coll, Equip loans & repairs, Free DVD rentals, Holiday prog, Home delivery & serv to seniorr ctr & nursing homes, Homebound delivery serv, ILL available, Internet access, Life-long learning prog for all ages, Magazines, Meeting rooms, Movies, Music CDs, Online cat, Outreach serv, OverDrive digital audio bks, Photocopying/Printing, Preschool outreach, Preschool reading prog, Prog for adults, Prog for children & young adult, Ref & res, Scanner, Senior computer classes, Senior outreach, Spanish lang bks, STEM programs, Story hour, Summer & winter reading prog, Summer reading prog, Tax forms, Wheelchair accessible, Winter reading prog
Publications: Monthly Newsletter
Mem of Lebanon County Library System
Open Mon-Wed 8-8, Thurs 8-7, Fri & Sat 8-5
Friends of the Library Group

S LEBANON COUNTY HISTORICAL SOCIETY LIBRARY*, Hauck Memorial Archives & Library, 924 Cumberland St, 17042-5186. SAN 314-6979. Tel: 717-272-1473. FAX: 717-272-7474. E-mail: archive@lchsociety.org. Web Site: www.lchsociety.org. *Archivist, Librn,* Adam Bentz, PhD; E-mail: archive@lchsociety.org. Subject Specialists: *Am hist, Mil hist, Political hist,* Adam Bentz, PhD; Staff 1 (Non-MLS 1)
Founded 1898
Library Holdings: Bk Titles 2,000; Bk Vols 2,200; Per Subs 12
Special Collections: Coleman-Cornwall Papers, 1757-1940
Subject Interests: Genealogy, German immigrants in Penn, Lebanon County hist, Lebanon County newspapers, Penn hist
Wireless access
Open Tues-Fri 10-5, Sat 10-2

GL LEBANON COUNTY LAW LIBRARY*, 400 S Eighth St, Rm 305, 17042. SAN 377-1202. Tel: 717-228-4411. FAX: 717-273-7490. Web Site: www.lebcounty.org/law_library/Pages/home.aspx. *Librn,* Luz Rosario; E-mail: lrosario@lebcnty.org; Staff 1 (Non-MLS 1)
Library Holdings: Bk Titles 7,284; Bk Vols 16,191; Per Subs 84
Open Mon-Fri 8:30-4:30

P LEBANON COUNTY LIBRARY SYSTEM, 125 N Seventh St, 17046. SAN 358-6561. Tel: 717-273-7624. FAX: 717-273-2719. Web Site: lclibs.org. *Adminr,* Michelle Hawk; E-mail: hawk@lclibs.org; Staff 1 (MLS 1)
Founded 1969
Automation Activity & Vendor Info: (Acquisitions) Innovative Interfaces, Inc; (Cataloging) Innovative Interfaces, Inc; (Circulation) Innovative Interfaces, Inc; (ILL) Innovative Interfaces, Inc; (OPAC) Innovative Interfaces, Inc; (Serials) Innovative Interfaces, Inc
Wireless access
Member Libraries: Annville Free Library; Lebanon Community Library, District Center; Matthews Public Library; Myerstown Community Library; Palmyra Public Library; Richland Community Library
Restriction: Not a lending libr

G LEBANON VA MEDICAL CENTER LIBRARY*, 1700 S Lincoln Ave, 17042-7597. SAN 314-6987. Tel: 717-272-6621, Ext 4746. Toll Free Tel: 800-409-8771. FAX: 717-228-6069. E-mail: lib.lebvamc@va.gov. Web Site: www.lebanon.va.gov/Services/LibraryPatientEducation.asp. *Librn,* Kristine Scannell; Staff 1 (MLS 1)
Library Holdings: e-journals 8,000; Bk Titles 1,000
Automation Activity & Vendor Info: (Cataloging) EOS International; (Circulation) EOS International
Function: ILL available
Partic in Dept of Vet Affairs Libr Network
Open Mon-Fri 7:30-4
Restriction: Open to pub upon request

LEECHBURG

P LEECHBURG PUBLIC LIBRARY, 139 Market St, 15656. SAN 314-6995. Tel: 724-236-0080. E-mail: leechburgpubliclibrary@yahoo.com. Web Site: www.armstronglibraries.org/leechburg-public-library.
Founded 1926. Circ 3,192
Library Holdings: Bk Vols 13,471; Per Subs 100; Talking Bks 50
Automation Activity & Vendor Info: (Cataloging) Book Systems; (Circulation) Book Systems; (OPAC) Book Systems
Wireless access
Function: 24/7 Electronic res, Adult bk club, After school storytime, Children's prog, Computer training, Computers for patron use, Electronic databases & coll, Family literacy, Holiday prog, Homebound delivery serv, ILL available, Internet access, Magazines, Mango lang, Meeting rooms, Online cat, Online ref, Outreach serv, OverDrive digital audio bks, Photocopying/Printing, Preschool reading prog, Prog for adults, Story hour, Summer reading prog, Tax forms, Wheelchair accessible
Open Tues-Fri 10-7, Sat 9-1
Friends of the Library Group

LEESPORT

P BERKS COUNTY PUBLIC LIBRARIES, 1040 Berk Rd, 19533. (Mail add: PO Box 689, 19533-0689). Tel: 610-378-5260. FAX: 610-378-1525. Web Site: www.berkslibraries.org. *Libr Syst Adminr,* Amy Resh; E-mail: amy.resh@berks.lib.pa.us; *Mgr, Bibliog Serv,* Leslie Gaines; *Outreach Serv Mgr,* Alison Trautmann; E-mail: alison.trautmann@berks.lib.pa.us; *Commun Relations Coordr,* Emily Orischak; *Tech Serv,* Jeff Smilko; Staff (MLS 3, Non-MLS 6)
Founded 1986. Pop 362,483
Library Holdings: Bk Vols 301,654; Per Subs 1,166
Automation Activity & Vendor Info: (Acquisitions) Innovative Interfaces Inc; (Cataloging) Innovative Interfaces, Inc; (Circulation) Innovative Interfaces, Inc; (OPAC) SirsiDynix
Wireless access
Member Libraries: Bernville Area Community Library; Bethel-Tulpehocken Public Library; Boone Area Library; Boyertown Community Library; Brandywine Community Library; Exeter Community Library; Fleetwood Area Public Library; Kutztown Community Library; Mifflin Community Library; Muhlenberg Community Library; Reading Area Community College; Reading Public Library; Robesonia Community Library; Schuylkill Valley Community Library; Sinking Spring Public Library; Spring Township Library; Village Library of Morgantown; Wernersville Public Library; West Lawn-Wyomissing Hills Library; Womelsdorf Community Library
Restriction: Not open to pub
Friends of the Library Group

P SCHUYLKILL VALLEY COMMUNITY LIBRARY*, 1310 Washington Rd, 19533-9708. SAN 370-6842. Tel: 610-926-1555. FAX: 610-926-3710. E-mail: svcl@berks.lib.pa.us. Web Site: www.berkslibraries.org/branch/schuylkill-valley. *Dir,* Christie Brown; *Youth Librn,* Kelly Jacoby; Staff 1 (MLS 1)
Founded 1989. Pop 13,738; Circ 51,013
Library Holdings: Bk Vols 16,156; Per Subs 38
Wireless access
Function: Adult bk club, Audiobks via web, Bks on cassette, Bks on CD, Chess club, Children's prog, Computer training, Computers for patron use, Electronic databases & coll, Free DVD rentals, Holiday prog, ILL available, Internet access, Museum passes, Music CDs, Online cat, OverDrive digital audio bks, Photocopying/Printing, Prog for adults, Prog for children & young adult, Scanner, Spoken cassettes & CDs, Spoken cassettes & DVDs, Story hour, Summer reading prog, Tax forms, VHS videos, Wheelchair accessible
Mem of Berks County Public Libraries
Open Mon-Wed 10-7, Thurs 10-5, Fri 10-2, Sat 9-4
Friends of the Library Group

LEHIGHTON

P LEHIGHTON AREA MEMORIAL LIBRARY*, 124 North St, 18235-1589. SAN 314-7002. Tel: 610-377-2750. FAX: 610-377-5803. E-mail: liblehtn@ptd.net. Web Site: lehightonlibrary.com. *Libr Dir,* Melissa E Hawk; Staff 1 (MLS 1)
Founded 1948. Pop 17,131; Circ 3,500
Library Holdings: AV Mats 1,050; DVDs 200; Large Print Bks 500; Bk Titles 17,800; Bk Vols 18,300; Per Subs 30; Talking Bks 700; Videos 150
Automation Activity & Vendor Info: (Cataloging) TLC (The Library Corporation); (Circulation) TLC (The Library Corporation)
Partic in Lehigh Carbon Library Cooperative
Open Mon 4-7 (Winter), Tues & Thurs 1-7, Wed 10-4, Fri 1-4, Sat 9-3; Mon 1-4 (Summer) Tues & Thurs 1-7, Wed 10-4, Fri 1-4, Sat 9-1

LEHMAN

C PENNSYLVANIA STATE UNIVERSITY, WILKES-BARRE COMMONWEALTH COLLEGE*, Nesbitt Library, PO Box PSU, 18627-0217. SAN 315-3460. Tel: 570-675-9212. Administration Tel: 570-675-9295. Web Site: wilkesbarre.psu.edu/. *Head Librn,* Jennie Levine Knies; Tel: 570-963-2632, E-mail: jak6029@psu.edu; *Info Res & Serv Support Spec,* Chris Burke; E-mail: ccb125@psu.edu; Staff 5 (MLS 2, Non-MLS 3)
Founded 1916. Enrl 825; Fac 88; Highest Degree: Bachelor
Library Holdings: Bk Vols 30,000; Per Subs 100
Subject Interests: Engr
Wireless access
Partic in OCLC Online Computer Library Center, Inc; Research Libraries Information Network

LEWISBURG

C BUCKNELL UNIVERSITY*, Ellen Clarke Bertrand Library, 220 Bertrand Library, One Dent Dr, 17837. SAN 314-7010. Tel: 570-577-1557. Circulation Tel: 570-577-1882. Interlibrary Loan Service Tel: 570-577-1462. FAX: 570-577-3313. E-mail: library@bucknell.edu. Web Site: researchbysubject.bucknell.edu, www.bucknell.edu/azdirectory/library-information-technology. *Exec Dir,* Steven O'Hara; E-mail: stephen.ohara@bucknell.edu; *VPres, Libr & Info Tech,* Param Bedi; E-mail: param.bedi@bucknell.edu; *Head, Spec Coll & Univ Archives,* Isabella O'Neill; Tel: 570-577-3230, E-mail: ioneill@bucknell.edu; *Cat & Metadata, Mgr,* Tam Troup; E-mail: tlt014@bucknell.edu; *Ref Serv Coordr,* Benjamin Hoover; E-mail: bahoover@bucknell.edu; *ILL Spec,* Kay Knapp; E-mail: kay.knapp@bucknell.edu; *Ser Spec,* Kathryn Dalius; E-mail: kathryn.dalius@bucknell.edu; *Acq, Metadata Serv,* Lynda Thaler; E-mail: lyna.thaler@bucknell.edu; *Circ,* Lona Sholly; E-mail: lona.sholly@bucknell.edu; Staff 30 (MLS 10, Non-MLS 20)
Founded 1846. Enrl 3,470; Fac 325; Highest Degree: Master
Special Collections: Fine Presses; Irish Literature. State Document Depository; US Document Depository
Subject Interests: Engr, Liberal arts
Automation Activity & Vendor Info: (Acquisitions) SirsiDynix; (Cataloging) OCLC WorldShare Interlibrary Loan; (Circulation) OCLC WorldShare Interlibrary Loan; (Course Reserve) OCLC WorldShare Interlibrary Loan; (ILL) OCLC ILLiad; (Media Booking) OCLC WorldShare Interlibrary Loan; (OPAC) OCLC WorldShare Interlibrary Loan
Wireless access
Partic in Associated College Libraries of Central Pennsylvania; Coalition for Networked Information; OCLC Online Computer Library Center, Inc; Partnership for Academic Library Collaborative & Innovation
Open Mon-Thurs 7am-2am, Fri 7am-10pm, Sat 9am-10pm, Sun 9am-2am
Friends of the Library Group

P PUBLIC LIBRARY FOR UNION COUNTY*, 255 Reitz Blvd, 17837-9211. SAN 314-7029. Tel: 570-523-1172. FAX: 570-524-7771. Web Site: unioncountylibraries.org. *Dir,* Roberta Greene; E-mail: rgreene@publibuc.org; *Head, Children's Servx,* Mary Harrison; E-mail: mharrison@publibuc.org; Staff 12 (MLS 2, Non-MLS 10)
Founded 1910. Pop 37,000; Circ 220,600
Library Holdings: Bk Vols 108,000; Per Subs 103
Subject Interests: Local hist, Penn hist
Automation Activity & Vendor Info: (Cataloging) TLC (The Library Corporation); (Circulation) TLC (The Library Corporation); (OPAC) TLC (The Library Corporation)
Wireless access
Function: Home delivery & serv to seniorr ctr & nursing homes, Homebound delivery serv, ILL available, Magnifiers for reading, Photocopying/Printing, Prog for adults, Prog for children & young adult, Ref serv available, Summer reading prog, Telephone ref, Wheelchair accessible
Publications: Newsletter (Quarterly)
Mem of Union County Library System
Open Mon, Tues & Thurs 9:30-8:30, Wed, Fri & Sat 9:30-5

S UNION COUNTY HISTORICAL SOCIETY LIBRARY*, Union County Courthouse, 103 S Second St, 17837. SAN 327-618X. Tel: 570-524-8666. FAX: 570-524-8743. E-mail: info@unioncountyhistoricalsociety.org. Web Site: www.unioncountyhistoricalsociety.org, www.unioncountypa.org/departments/historical-society. *Pres,* Bruce Teeple; *Admin Mgr,* Linda Rhoades-Swartz
Founded 1963
Library Holdings: Bk Titles 500
Special Collections: Business & Craftsmen Ledgers (slides & videos). Oral History
Subject Interests: Genealogy
Publications: Union County Heritage
Open Mon-Fri 8:30-12 & 1-4:30

P UNION COUNTY LIBRARY SYSTEM*, 255 Reitz Blvd, 17837-9211. Tel: 570-523-1172. FAX: 570-524-7771. Web Site: unioncountylibraries.org. *Adminr,* Roberta Greene; E-mail: rgreene@publibuc.org; Staff 4 (MLS 2, Non-MLS 2)
Founded 1998. Pop 43,000
Library Holdings: Bk Vols 147,000; Per Subs 219
Automation Activity & Vendor Info: (Cataloging) TLC (The Library Corporation); (Circulation) TLC (The Library Corporation); (OPAC) TLC (The Library Corporation)
Wireless access
Function: Home delivery & serv to seniorr ctr & nursing homes, Homebound delivery serv, ILL available, Magnifiers for reading, Photocopying/Printing, Prog for adults, Prog for children & young adult, Ref serv available, Summer reading prog, Telephone ref, Wheelchair accessible
Member Libraries: Jane I & Annetta M Herr Memorial Library; Public Library for Union County; West End Library
Open Mon, Tues & Thurs 9:30-8:30, Wed, Fri & Sat 9:30-5

LEWISTOWN

S MIFFLIN COUNTY HISTORICAL SOCIETY LIBRARY & MUSEUM*, One W Market St, 17044-1746. SAN 326-9205. Tel: 717-242-1022. FAX: 717-242-3488. E-mail: info@mifflincountyhistory.org. Web Site: www.mifflincountyhistory.org. *Librn,* Jean A Laughlin
Founded 1921
Subject Interests: Genealogy, Local hist
Publications: Notes from Monument Square (Newsletter)
Open Tues & Wed 10-3
Restriction: Open to pub for ref only

P MIFFLIN COUNTY LIBRARY*, 123 N Wayne St, 17044-1794. SAN 358-6626. Tel: 717-242-2391. FAX: 717-242-2825. Web Site: www.mifflincountylibrary.org. *Dir,* Molly Kinney; E-mail: mollykinney@mifcolib.org; *Asst Dir,* Susan Miriello; Tel: 717-242-2391, E-mail: smiriello@mifflincountylibrary.org; Staff 5 (MLS 2, Non-MLS 3)
Founded 1842. Pop 46,486
Jan 2018-Dec 2018 Income (Main & Associated Libraries) $387,000, State $223,000, County $170,000, Locally Generated Income $50,000. Mats Exp $106,928, Books $93,200, Per/Ser (Incl. Access Fees) $3,500, AV Mat $8,228, Electronic Ref Mat (Incl. Access Fees) $2,000. Sal $290,000
Library Holdings: AV Mats 3,870; High Interest/Low Vocabulary Bk Vols 1,815; Bk Titles 65,703; Bk Vols 91,184; Per Subs 159
Automation Activity & Vendor Info: (Cataloging) TLC (The Library Corporation); (Circulation) TLC (The Library Corporation); (OPAC) TLC (The Library Corporation)
Wireless access
Function: 24/7 Electronic res, 24/7 Online cat, Activity rm, Adult bk club, Audiobks on Playaways & MP3, Audiobks via web, Bk club(s), Bks on CD, Children's prog, Computer training, Computers for patron use, E-Readers, E-Reserves, Electronic databases & coll, Family literacy, Home delivery & serv to seniorr ctr & nursing homes, Homebound delivery serv, ILL available, Internet access, Laminating, Life-long learning prog for all ages, Magazines, Mail & tel request accepted, Meeting rooms, Museum passes, Notary serv, Online cat, Outreach serv, OverDrive digital audio bks, Photocopying/Printing, Preschool outreach, Printer for laptops & handheld devices, Prog for adults, Prog for children & young adult, Ref & res, Ref serv available, Scanner, Senior outreach, Story hour, Summer reading prog, Tax forms, Telephone ref, Visual arts prog, Wheelchair accessible
Partic in Cent Pa District
Open Mon, Thurs, Fri & Sat 9-4, Tues & Wed 9-8
Friends of the Library Group
Branches: 1
KISHACOQUILLAS BRANCH, 194 N Penn St, Belleville, 17004. (Mail add: PO Box 996, Belleville, 17004-0996). Tel: 717-935-2880. FAX: 717-935-2880. E-mail: kish@mifflincountylibrary.org. ; Staff 1 (Non-MLS 1)
Founded 1961. Pop 3,913; Circ 20,793
Library Holdings: High Interest/Low Vocabulary Bk Vols 317; Bk Titles 11,564; Bk Vols 11,697; Per Subs 16
Open Mon & Tues 12-4:30 & 5:30-8, Wed & Thurs 9-12:30 & 1:30-5, Sat 9-1

LIGONIER

P LIGONIER VALLEY LIBRARY*, 120 W Main St, 15658-1243. SAN 314-7061. Tel: 724-238-6451. FAX: 724-238-6989. E-mail: library@ligonierlibrary.org. Web Site: www.ligonierlibrary.org. *Dir,* Position Currently Open; *Circ Supvr,* Mary Boyd; *Archivist,* Shirley G Iscrupe; *Ch Serv,* Bobbi McDowell; E-mail: lvlkids@ligonierlibrary.org. Subject Specialists: *City hist, Genealogy, State hist,* Shirley G Iscrupe; Staff 12 (MLS 2, Non-MLS 10)
Founded 1945. Pop 16,644; Circ 130,213
Jan 2014-Dec 2014 Income $526,807, State $65,525, City $1,500, County $6,000, Parent Institution $453,782
Special Collections: Large Print Coll; Ligonier Echo, micro; Newbery-Caldecott Coll; Pennsylvania History (Pennsylvania Room), bks & micro; Writer's Coll
Subject Interests: County hist, Genealogy
Automation Activity & Vendor Info: (Cataloging) Innovative Interfaces, Inc; (Circulation) Innovative Interfaces, Inc; (ILL) OCLC; (OPAC) Innovative Interfaces, Inc
Wireless access
Function: Art exhibits, Bk club(s), Bks on CD, Children's prog, Computers for patron use, Digital talking bks, Electronic databases & coll, Free DVD rentals, Genealogy discussion group, Holiday prog, ILL available, Internet access, Life-long learning prog for all ages, Magazines, Microfiche/film & reading machines, Music CDs, Online cat, OverDrive digital audio bks, Photocopying/Printing, Preschool reading prog, Prog for

adults, Prog for children & young adult, Scanner, Story hour, Study rm, Summer reading prog, Wheelchair accessible
Publications: Happenings (Newsletter)
Mem of Westmoreland County Federated Library System
Partic in Share Westmoreland Consortium
Open Mon-Thurs 10-7, Fri & Sat 10-5

LILLY

P LILLY-WASHINGTON PUBLIC LIBRARY*, 520 Church St, Ste 1, 15938-1118. SAN 314-707X. Tel: 814-886-7543. FAX: 814-886-3925. E-mail: lillywash@cclsys.org. Web Site: www.cclsys.org/lillywash. *Dir,* Brenda Marsh
Founded 1963. Pop 1,162; Circ 14,529. Sal $16,443
Library Holdings: Bk Vols 6,987; Per Subs 21
Automation Activity & Vendor Info: (Circulation) Brodart
Wireless access
Mem of Cambria County Library System & District Center
Open Mon-Wed & Fri (Winter) 10-5, Sat 8:30-3:30; Mon-Wed (Summer) 9-5, Thurs 9-1, Sat 8:30-12:30

LINCOLN UNIVERSITY

C LINCOLN UNIVERSITY, Langston Hughes Memorial Library, 1570 Baltimore Pike, 19352. SAN 314-7096. Tel: 484-365-7367. Reference Tel: 484-365-7365. FAX: 484-365-8106. E-mail: library@lincoln.edu. Web Site: lincoln.edu/departments/langston-hughes-memorial-library. *Interim Libr Dir,* Sophia Sotilleo; Tel: 484-365-7261, E-mail: ssotilleo@lincoln.edu; *Cat & Syst Librn,* Simone Clunie; Tel: 484-365-7357, E-mail: sclunie@lincoln.edu; *Archivist, Spec Coll Librn,* Jessica Garner; Tel: 484-365-7370, E-mail: jgarner@lincoln.edu; *Ref Librn,* Ugochi Nwachuku; Tel: 484-365-7350, E-mail: unwachuku@lincoln.edu; *Libr Serv Spec,* Reachell Chambers; Tel: 484-365-7358, E-mail: rchambers@lincoln.edu; *ILL Tech,* Bonnie Horn; Tel: 484-365-7356, E-mail: bhorn@lincoln.edu; Staff 7 (MLS 6, Non-MLS 1)
Founded 1898. Fac 7; Highest Degree: Master
Library Holdings: e-journals 30,000; Bk Vols 185,000
Special Collections: Africana, bks, per; Langston Hughes Personal Library
Subject Interests: Liberal arts, Presbyterianism lit, Protestant theol, Sci
Wireless access
Publications: Accessions List
Partic in Interlibrary Delivery Service of Pennsylvania; Keystone Library Network; LYRASIS; OCLC Online Computer Library Center, Inc; Tri State Col Libr Coop
Open Mon-Thurs 8-8, Fri 8-5, Sat 9-5, Sun Noon-8

LINESVILLE

P LINESVILLE COMMUNITY PUBLIC LIBRARY*, 111 Penn St, 16424. (Mail add: PO Box 97, 16424-0097), SAN 376-5709. Tel: 814-683-4354. FAX: 814-683-4354. Web Site: linesville.ccfls.org. *Dir,* Telce Varee; Staff 2 (MLS 1, Non-MLS 1)
Founded 1989. Pop 5,661; Circ 10,080
Library Holdings: Bk Titles 18,700; Bk Vols 18,900; Per Subs 61; Talking Bks 434; Videos 172
Wireless access
Mem of Crawford County Federated Library System
Open Mon 9-5, Tues & Thurs 4-8, Wed 9-1 & 4-8, Fri 9-1, Sat 8-12

LITITZ

P LITITZ PUBLIC LIBRARY*, 651 Kissel Hill Rd, 17543. SAN 314-7118. Tel: 717-626-2255. Web Site: www.lititzlibrary.org. *Dir,* Susan Tennant; E-mail: stennant@lititzlibrary.org; *Asst Dir, Ch,* Karen Payonk; E-mail: kpayonk@lititzlibrary.org; *Coordr, Spec Serv,* Linda Skelly; E-mail: lskelly@lititzlibrary.org; Staff 19 (MLS 4, Non-MLS 15)
Founded 1936. Pop 28,337; Circ 279,096
Library Holdings: Bk Vols 54,916; Per Subs 50
Mem of Library System of Lancaster County
Open Mon-Thurs 9-8, Fri 9-6, Sat 9-4
Friends of the Library Group

LOCK HAVEN

C LOCK HAVEN UNIVERSITY OF PENNSYLVANIA*, George B Stevenson Library, 401 N Fairview Ave, 17745-2390. SAN 314-7134. Tel: 570-484-2309. Interlibrary Loan Service Tel: 570-484-2311. Reference Tel: 570-484-2468. Administration Tel: 570-484-2310. Automation Services Tel: 570-484-2466. FAX: 570-484-2506. Web Site: library.lockhaven.edu/stevenson. *Dir, Libr & Info Serv,* Joby Topper; E-mail: jtopper@lhup.edu; Staff 17 (MLS 9, Non-MLS 8)
Founded 1870. Enrl 4,900; Fac 250; Highest Degree: Master
Library Holdings: Bk Titles 238,440; Bk Vols 324,263; Per Subs 218
Special Collections: Eden Phillpotts Coll
Automation Activity & Vendor Info: (Acquisitions) Ex Libris Group; (Cataloging) Ex Libris Group; (Circulation) Ex Libris Group; (Course Reserve) Ex Libris Group; (ILL) Ex Libris Group; (Media Booking) Ex Libris Group; (OPAC) Ex Libris Group; (Serials) Ex Libris Group
Wireless access
Partic in Interlibrary Delivery Service of Pennsylvania; Keystone Library Network; OCLC Online Computer Library Center, Inc; Partnership for Academic Library Collaborative & Innovation
Open Mon-Fri 7:30am-11pm, Sat 9-5, Sun 2-11

P ANNIE HALENBAKE ROSS LIBRARY*, 232 W Main St, 17745-1241. SAN 358-6774. Tel: 570-748-3321. FAX: 570-748-1050. E-mail: ross1@rosslibrary.org. Web Site: www.rosslibrary.org/Annie_Halenbake_Ross_Library. *Libr Dir,* Tammy Garrison; *County Librn,* Joseph Bitner; *Coordr, Youth Serv,* Nancy Antram; Staff 11 (MLS 2, Non-MLS 9)
Founded 1910. Pop 37,914; Circ 126,546. Sal $257,618 (Prof $50,882)
Library Holdings: AV Mats 3,474; CDs 150; DVDs 3,472; Large Print Bks 5,000; Bk Titles 85,763; Bk Vols 121,962; Per Subs 120
Special Collections: Local Genealogical Materials; Pennsylvaniana (Pennsylvania Room), bks, census reports, local photo coll, micro
Automation Activity & Vendor Info: (Cataloging) EOS International; (Circulation) EOS International; (OPAC) EOS International
Wireless access
Function: Art exhibits, Bk club(s), CD-ROM, Computer training, Family literacy, Home delivery & serv to seniorr ctr & nursing homes, ILL available, Internet access, Magnifiers for reading, Photocopying/Printing, Preschool outreach, Prog for adults, Prog for children & young adult, Ref serv available, Senior computer classes, Summer reading prog, Telephone ref, VHS videos, Wheelchair accessible, Workshops
Publications: A Final Peek at the Past; Another Peek at the Past; Clinton County: A Journey Through Time; Flemington Mosaic; Indians of Clinton County; Journal of Travels, Adventures & Remarks of Jerry Church; Maynard's Historical Clinton County; Mountain Folks: Fragments of Central Pennsylvania Folklore; No Rain in Heaven; Old Town: A History of Early Lock Haven; Peek at the Past; Third Peek at the Past
Special Services for the Deaf - Accessible learning ctr; High interest/low vocabulary bks
Special Services for the Blind - BiFolkal kits; Bks on cassette; Bks on CD; Internet workstation with adaptive software; Large print bks; Magnifiers
Open Mon 2-8, Tues & Thurs 10-8, Wed 9-2, Fri & Sat 9-4
Friends of the Library Group
Branches: 2
FRIENDSHIP COMMUNITY LIBRARY, Main St, Beech Creek, 16822. (Mail add: PO Box 478, Beech Creek, 16822-0478). Tel: 570-962-2048. *Library Contact,* Adam Bugaj; Staff 1 (Non-MLS 1)
Founded 1981. Pop 1,727
Library Holdings: Large Print Bks 150; Bk Vols 8,000; Videos 50
Function: AV serv, ILL available, Internet access, Summer reading prog, Wheelchair accessible
Open Mon, Tues & Thurs 3-7
RENOVO AREA LIBRARY, 317 Seventh St, Renovo, 17764, SAN 358-6804. Tel: 570-923-0390. E-mail: renovo@rosslibrary.org. *Br Mgr,* Barbara Rauch; Staff 1 (Non-MLS 1)
Founded 1968. Pop 5,000; Circ 7,729
Library Holdings: AV Mats 63; Large Print Bks 150; Bk Vols 11,405; Per Subs 10
Function: Art exhibits, Children's prog, Computers for patron use, Holiday prog, ILL available, OverDrive digital audio bks, Photocopying/Printing, Preschool reading prog, Prog for children & young adult, Ref serv available, Summer reading prog, Wheelchair accessible
Open Tues 10-12 & 2-8, Wed, Fri & Sat 9-1, Thurs 10-12 & 1-5

LORETTO

CR SAINT FRANCIS UNIVERSITY, Library & Learning Commons, 106 Franciscan Way, 15940. (Mail add: PO Box 600, 15940-0600), SAN 358-6839. Tel: 814-472-3160. Automation Services Tel: 814-472-3163. Information Services Tel: 814-472-3162. FAX: 814-472-3154. E-mail: cirli@francis.edu. Web Site: www.francis.edu/Library. *Dean, Libr Serv,* Sandra A Balough; Tel: 814-472-3153, E-mail: sbalough@francis.edu; *Assoc Dean,* Janie Rager; E-mail: jrager@francis.edu; *Head, Pub Serv,* Carol Stoltz; Tel: 814-472-3165, E-mail: cstoltz@francis.edu; *Head, Tech Serv,* Misti Smith; E-mail: msmith@francis.edu; *Info Serv Librn,* Renee Hoffman; Tel: 814-472-3152, E-mail: rhoffman@francis.edu; *Info Serv Librn,* Marcia Kokus; Tel: 814-472-3161, E-mail: mkokus@francis.edu; *Archivist,* Stephen Rombouts; Tel: 814-472-2761, E-mail: srombouts@francis.edu; Staff 10 (MLS 5, Non-MLS 5)
Founded 1847. Enrl 2,200; Fac 100; Highest Degree: Doctorate
Jul 2020-Jun 2021 Income $935,503. Mats Exp $370,916, Books $590, Per/Ser (Incl. Access Fees) $8,200, Electronic Ref Mat (Incl. Access Fees) $302,467. Sal $439,672 (Prof $299,822)
Library Holdings: CDs 143; DVDs 656; e-books 1,017,161; e-journals 181,927; Bk Titles 50,381; Bk Vols 61,819; Per Subs 7; Videos 73,398
Automation Activity & Vendor Info: (Acquisitions) OCLC Worldshare Management Services; (Cataloging) OCLC Worldshare Management

Services; (Circulation) OCLC Worldshare Management Services; (Course Reserve) OCLC Worldshare Management Services; (Discovery) OCLC Worldshare Management Services; (ILL) OCLC WorldShare Interlibrary Loan; (Media Booking) OCLC Worldshare Management Services; (OPAC) OCLC Worldshare Management Services; (Serials) OCLC Worldshare Management Services
Wireless access
Partic in LYRASIS; Partnership for Academic Library Collaborative & Innovation
Open Mon-Thurs 7:45am-11pm, Fri 7:45-7, Sat 11-9, Sun 12-11

MACUNGIE

P LOWER MACUNGIE LIBRARY, 3450 Brookside Rd, 18062. Tel: 610-966-6864. FAX: 610-965-0384. Web Site: www.lowermaclib.org. *Exec Dir,* Kathee Rhode; E-mail: katheer@lowermaclib.org
Library Holdings: AV Mats 4,290; Bk Vols 35,398; Per Subs 105
Automation Activity & Vendor Info: (Cataloging) Evergreen; (Circulation) Evergreen; (Course Reserve) Evergreen; (ILL) Evergreen; (OPAC) Evergreen
Wireless access
Partic in Lehigh Carbon Library Cooperative
Open Mon & Wed 10-5, Tues & Thurs 10-6, Fri & Sat 10-3
Friends of the Library Group

MAHANOY CITY

P MAHANOY CITY PUBLIC LIBRARY*, 17-19 W Mahanoy St, 17948-2615. SAN 314-7231. Tel: 570-773-1610. FAX: 570-773-0632. E-mail: macitypl@ptd.net. Web Site: www.mahanoylibrary.org. *Dir,* Tom Seiberling
Pop 10,749; Circ 14,162
Library Holdings: Bk Vols 24,000; Per Subs 51
Wireless access
Open Mon 10-7, Tues, Thurs & Fri 10-5, Wed 10-6, Sat 10-2 (9-4 Winter)

MALVERN

P MALVERN PUBLIC LIBRARY*, One E First Ave, Ste 2, 19355-2743. SAN 314-724X. Tel: 610-644-7259. FAX: 610-644-5204. Web Site: www.malvern-library.org. *Dir,* Maggie Stanton; E-mail: mstanton@ccls.org; *Ch,* Meghan Pealer; E-mail: mpealer@ccls.org; Staff 3 (MLS 1, Non-MLS 2)
Founded 1873. Pop 34,222; Circ 51,861
Library Holdings: Bk Titles 37,259; Bk Vols 39,116; Per Subs 94; Talking Bks 2,175; Videos 1,682
Automation Activity & Vendor Info: (Cataloging) Innovative Interfaces, Inc; (Circulation) Innovative Interfaces, Inc; (OPAC) Innovative Interfaces, Inc
Wireless access
Mem of Chester County Library System
Open Mon & Tues 9-8, Wed & Thurs 9-6:30, Fri 9-5, Sat 9-4
Friends of the Library Group

C PENNSYLVANIA STATE UNIVERSITY, Penn State Great Valley Library, 30 E Swedesford Rd, 19355. SAN 314-4593. Tel: 610 648-3228. Circulation Tel: 610-648-3215. Web Site: libraries.psu.edu/greatvalley. *Head Librn,* Billie Walker; E-mail: bew11@psu.edu; Staff 2 (MLS 1, Non-MLS 1)
Highest Degree: Master
Library Holdings: Bk Vols 66,000; Per Subs 100
Wireless access
Function: 24/7 Electronic res, 24/7 Online cat
Open Mon-Thurs 10-9, Fri 10-5, Sat 10-4

C PENNSYLVANIA STATE UNIVERSITY*, Great Valley Library (University Libraries), 30 E Swedesford Rd, 19355. SAN 315-1492. Tel: 610-648-3215. FAX: 610-725-5223. Web Site: libraries.psu.edu/greatvalley. *Head Librn,* Billie Walker; E-mail: bew11@psu.edu; Staff 14 (MLS 3, Non-MLS 11)
Founded 1963. Enrl 1,700; Fac 80; Highest Degree: Master
Library Holdings: Bk Vols 40,000; Per Subs 380
Special Collections: Curriculum; Eric Documents; Psychological Tests; Thesis
Subject Interests: Computer sci, Educ, Engr, Math, Mgt
Automation Activity & Vendor Info: (Cataloging) SirsiDynix; (Circulation) SirsiDynix; (OPAC) SirsiDynix; (Serials) SirsiDynix
Wireless access
Partic in OCLC Online Computer Library Center, Inc; Research Libraries Information Network; Tri State Col Libr Coop
Open Mon-Thurs 9:30-9, Fri 9:30-5, Sat 10-4

MANHEIM

P MANHEIM COMMUNITY LIBRARY*, 15 E High St, 17545-1505. Tel: 717-665-6700. E-mail: info@manheimlibrary.org. Web Site: www.manheimlibrary.org. *Dir,* Jonathan Dunkle; E-mail: jdunkle@manheimlibrary.org; Staff 3 (MLS 1, Non-MLS 2)
Pop 17,091; Circ 32,815
Library Holdings: Bk Vols 33,000; Per Subs 15; Talking Bks 674; Videos 705
Automation Activity & Vendor Info: (Cataloging) Innovative Interfaces, Inc; (Circulation) Innovative Interfaces, Inc; (OPAC) Innovative Interfaces, Inc
Wireless access
Mem of Library System of Lancaster County
Open Mon & Tues 9-8, Wed-Fri 9-5, Sat 9-4
Friends of the Library Group

MANOR

P MANOR PUBLIC LIBRARY*, 44 Main St, 15665. Tel: 724-864-6850. E-mail: manorpublic.library@comcast.net. Web Site: www.manorpubliclibrary.org. *Dir,* Stephanie Capasso; *Library Asst, Children's,* Melissa Paris
Founded 1944
Library Holdings: Bk Vols 14,000; Per Subs 14
Automation Activity & Vendor Info: (Cataloging) Follett Software; (Circulation) Follett Software; (OPAC) Follett Software
Wireless access
Mem of Westmoreland County Federated Library System
Open Mon & Thurs 12-7, Tues, Wed & Sat 10-5

MANSFIELD

P MANSFIELD FREE PUBLIC LIBRARY*, 71 N Main St, 16933. SAN 314-7274. Tel: 570-662-3850. FAX: 570-662-7423. E-mail: mfpl@epix.net. Web Site: www.mansfieldpubliclibrary.com. *Dir,* Elizabeth Kreisler
Founded 1901. Pop 5,929; Circ 20,694
Library Holdings: Audiobooks 250; Bks on Deafness & Sign Lang 5; Braille Volumes 1; DVDs 700; Large Print Bks 300; Bk Vols 17,000; Per Subs 40
Special Collections: Books on tape; Large Print Coll; Pennsylvania & Tioga County
Automation Activity & Vendor Info: (Circulation) EOS International
Wireless access
Mem of Potter-Tioga Library System
Open Mon, Tues & Thurs 1-8, Wed 10-8, Sat 9-4
Friends of the Library Group

C MANSFIELD UNIVERSITY*, North Hall Library, Five Swan St, 16933. SAN 314-7282. Tel: 570-662-4670. Interlibrary Loan Service Tel: 570-662-4690. Administration Tel: 570-662-4689. Information Services Tel: 570-662-4671. FAX: 570-662-4993. E-mail: libref@mansfield.edu. Web Site: lib.mansfield.edu. *Dir,* Scott R DiMarco; E-mail: sdimarco@mansfield.edu; *Coordr, Tech Serv,* Jamey Harris; E-mail: jharris@mansfield.edu; *Electronic Serv, Ref,* Sheila M Kasperek; Tel: 570-662-4675, E-mail: skaspere@mansfield.edu; Staff 12.5 (MLS 4.5, Non-MLS 8)
Founded 1857. Enrl 1,528; Fac 180; Highest Degree: Master
Jul 2018-Jun 2019 Income $1,444,560
Special Collections: Annual Report. Oral History; US Document Depository
Subject Interests: Criminal justice, Educ, Music
Automation Activity & Vendor Info: (Acquisitions) Ex Libris Group; (Cataloging) Ex Libris Group; (Circulation) Ex Libris Group; (ILL) Ex Libris Group; (OPAC) Ex Libris Group; (Serials) Ex Libris Group
Wireless access
Function: 24/7 Electronic res, 24/7 Online cat, Archival coll, Art exhibits, Audio & video playback equip for onsite use, Audiobks on Playaways & MP3, Bks on CD, Computers for patron use, Distance learning, Doc delivery serv, E-Reserves, Electronic databases & coll, Equip loans & repairs, For res purposes, ILL available, Instruction & testing, Internet access, Magazines, Movies, Music CDs, Online cat, Online info literacy tutorials on the web & in blackboard, Online ref, Orientations, Outreach serv, Photocopying/Printing, Printer for laptops & handheld devices, Ref & res, Ref serv available, Res assist avail, Res libr, Scanner, Spanish lang bks, Spoken cassettes & CDs, Spoken cassettes & DVDs, Study rm, Telephone ref, Visual arts prog
Partic in Keystone Library Network; LYRASIS; Partnership for Academic Library Collaborative & Innovation
Special Services for the Deaf - ADA equip

MARCUS HOOK

P MARY M CAMPBELL PUBLIC LIBRARY*, Tenth & Green Sts, 19061-4592. SAN 314-7304. Tel: 610-485-6519. E-mail: marcushook@delcolibraries.org. Web Site:

www.delcolibraries.org/mary-m-campbell-marcus-hook-public-library. *Librn,* Irene H Wallin; Staff 4 (MLS 1, Non-MLS 3)
Founded 1923. Pop 2,314; Circ 11,826
Library Holdings: Bk Vols 23,000; Per Subs 60
Wireless access
Mem of Delaware County Libraries
Open Mon & Wed 10-6, Tues & Thurs 2-8, Sat 10-5
Friends of the Library Group

MARIANNA

P MARIANNA COMMUNITY PUBLIC LIBRARY*, 247 Jefferson Ave, 15345. (Mail add: PO Box 457, 15345-0457), SAN 314-7320. Tel: 724-267-3888. FAX: 724-267-3888. E-mail: mclib@roadlynx.net. Web Site: www.washlibs.org/marianna. *Dir,* Pam Clutter
Founded 1968. Pop 2,486; Circ 8,331
Library Holdings: Bk Vols 8,054; Per Subs 43
Wireless access
Mem of Washington County Library System
Open Mon & Wed 9-5, Tues & Thurs 12-6, Sat 9-4
Friends of the Library Group

MARIENVILLE

P MARIENVILLE AREA LIBRARY, 106 Pine St, 16239. (Mail add: Box 306, 16239-0306), SAN 358-6898. Tel: 814-927-8552. FAX: 814-927-8552. E-mail: contact@marienvillelibrary.org. Web Site: www.marienvillelibrary.org. *Libr Dir,* Jackie McLaughlin; *Libr Asst,* Carole Chenot
Founded 1969. Pop 3,100; Circ 21,000
Library Holdings: DVDs 800; Bk Vols 14,000; Per Subs 37
Automation Activity & Vendor Info: (Cataloging) Evolve; (Circulation) Evolve
Wireless access
Open Mon-Wed 9-5, Thurs 9-8, Sat 9-3
Friends of the Library Group

MARS

P MARS AREA PUBLIC LIBRARY*, 107 Grand Ave, 16046. (Mail add: PO Box 415, 16046-0415), SAN 314-7347. Tel: 724-625-9048. FAX: 724-625-2871. Web Site: www.bcfls.org/mars-area-public-library, www.marsarealibrary.org. *Dir,* Caitlyn Boland; E-mail: cboland@marslibrary.org; Staff 1 (Non-MLS 1)
Founded 1947. Pop 6,000; Circ 48,000
Library Holdings: Bk Titles 32,000; Per Subs 52
Automation Activity & Vendor Info: (Cataloging) TLC (The Library Corporation); (Circulation) TLC (The Library Corporation)
Wireless access
Mem of Butler County Federated Library System
Special Services for the Blind - Audio mat; Large print bks
Open Mon-Thurs 10-7, Fri 10-3, Sat 9-4 (10-2 Summer)
Friends of the Library Group

MARTINSBURG

P MARTINSBURG COMMUNITY LIBRARY*, 201 S Walnut St, 16662-1129. SAN 314-7355. Tel: 814-793-3335. FAX: 814-793-9755. E-mail: mclibrary@atlanticbbn.net. Web Site: www.martinsburgcommunitylibrary.org. *Dir,* Jackie Rhule; Staff 2 (Non-MLS 2)
Founded 1948. Pop 5,270; Circ 21,000
Library Holdings: AV Mats 1,214; Large Print Bks 211; Bk Titles 27,000; Bk Vols 31,684; Per Subs 25; Talking Bks 108; Videos 714
Special Collections: Genealogy (George H Liebegott Coll); Genealogy (John Memorial Coll)
Subject Interests: County hist, Family hist, Town hist
Automation Activity & Vendor Info: (Cataloging) Follett Software; (Circulation) Follett Software; (OPAC) Follett Software
Wireless access
Function: Archival coll
Mem of Blair County Library System
Open Mon, Tues, Thurs & Fri 10-4, Sat 10-2
Friends of the Library Group

MARYSVILLE

P MARYSVILLE-RYE LIBRARY, 198 Overcrest Rd, 17053. SAN 314-7363. Tel: 717-957-2851. Toll Free FAX: 888-823-2616. E-mail: mvpublib@comcast.net. Web Site: pecoinfo.org/library-hours/marysville. *Dir,* Wendy Holler; Staff 2 (MLS 1, Non-MLS 1)
Founded 1966. Pop 6,122; Circ 14,198
Library Holdings: AV Mats 590; Bk Titles 14,272; Bk Vols 16,891; Per Subs 46; Talking Bks 211; Videos 197
Automation Activity & Vendor Info: (Cataloging) TLC (The Library Corporation); (Circulation) TLC (The Library Corporation)
Open Mon & Wed 12-7, Tues 1-8, Thurs 10-8, Sat 9-2
Friends of the Library Group

MASONTOWN

P GERMAN-MASONTOWN PUBLIC LIBRARY*, 104 S Main St, 15461. SAN 314-7371. Tel: 724-583-7030. FAX: 724-583-0979. E-mail: germaslibrary01@yahoo.com. Web Site: german-masontownpubliclibrary.org. *Libr Dir,* Amy Ryan; *Bus Mgr,* Beverly Diamond
Founded 1965. Pop 11,500; Circ 30,779
Library Holdings: Bk Vols 24,328; Per Subs 42
Subject Interests: Local hist
Automation Activity & Vendor Info: (Cataloging) Innovative Interfaces, Inc; (Circulation) Innovative Interfaces, Inc; (OPAC) Innovative Interfaces, Inc; (Serials) Innovative Interfaces, Inc
Wireless access
Function: 24/7 Electronic res, 24/7 Online cat, Activity rm, Adult bk club, After school storytime, Bk club(s), Bks on CD, Children's prog, Computer training, Computers for patron use, Electronic databases & coll, Free DVD rentals, ILL available, Instruction & testing, Internet access, Laminating, Life-long learning prog for all ages, Magazines, Mail & tel request accepted, Meeting rooms, Online cat, Online ref, Outreach serv, Outside serv via phone, mail, e-mail & web, OverDrive digital audio bks, Photocopying/Printing, Preschool outreach, Prog for adults, Prog for children & young adult, Ref & res, Ref serv available, Scanner, Senior computer classes, Story hour, Study rm, Tax forms, Wheelchair accessible
Open Mon 12-6, Tues, Wed & Thurs 10-5, Sat 9-4
Friends of the Library Group

MCCONNELLSBURG

P FULTON COUNTY LIBRARY*, 227 N First St, 17233-1003. SAN 321-5105. Tel: 717-485-5327. FAX: 717-485-5646. Web Site: fultoncountylibrary.org. *Dir,* Jamie Brambley; E-mail: jbrambley@fclspa.org; Staff 6 (MLS 1, Non-MLS 5)
Founded 1975. Pop 14,283; Circ 63,000
Jan 2017-Dec 2017 Income (Main & Associated Libraries) $221,001, State $52,555, City $6,200, County $12,000, Locally Generated Income $150,246. Mats Exp $46,044, Books $28,660, Per/Ser (Incl. Access Fees) $3,319, AV Mat $10,500, Electronic Ref Mat (Incl. Access Fees) $3,565. Sal $156,900
Library Holdings: Audiobooks 1,887; CDs 1,887; DVDs 4,010; Large Print Bks 4,019; Bk Titles 46,645; Per Subs 96; Talking Bks 1,738; Videos 4,010
Special Collections: Handicapped; Special Needs
Subject Interests: Civil War
Automation Activity & Vendor Info: (Cataloging) Brodart; (Circulation) Brodart; (OPAC) Brodart
Wireless access
Function: 24/7 Electronic res, 24/7 Online cat, Activity rm, Adult bk club, Adult literacy prog, Archival coll, Audiobks via web, Bk club(s), Bks on CD, Children's prog, Computer training, Computers for patron use, Digital talking bks, E-Readers, E-Reserves, Electronic databases & coll, Home delivery & serv to seniorr ctr & nursing homes, Homebound delivery serv, ILL available, Internet access, Life-long learning prog for all ages, Magazines, Mail & tel request accepted, Meeting rooms, Microfiche/film & reading machines, Movies, Music CDs, Online cat, Outreach serv, OverDrive digital audio bks, Photocopying/Printing, Preschool outreach, Preschool reading prog, Printer for laptops & handheld devices, Prog for adults, Prog for children & young adult, Ref & res, Ref serv available, Scanner, Senior computer classes, Story hour, Study rm, Summer & winter reading prog, Summer reading prog, Tax forms, Telephone ref, Wheelchair accessible, Workshops
Open Mon & Wed 9-6, Tues & Thurs 9-8, Fri 9-5, Sat 9-4 (10-2 Summer)
Friends of the Library Group
Branches: 1
HUSTONTOWN BRANCH, 313 Pitt St, Ste B, Hustontown, 17229. (Mail add: PO Box 426, Hustontown, 17229-0426), SAN 329-3653. Tel: 717-987-3606. FAX: 717-987-3606. *Br Mgr,* Trudy Fix; E-mail: tfix@fclspa.org; Staff 2 (MLS 1, Non-MLS 1)
Library Holdings: CDs 186; DVDs 1,300; Large Print Bks 703; Bk Titles 11,419; Per Subs 10
Open Mon-Wed & Fri 10-5, Thurs 12-5
Friends of the Library Group

MCDONALD

P HERITAGE PUBLIC LIBRARY*, 52 Fourth St, 15057. SAN 314-7142. Tel: 724-926-8400. FAX: 724-926-4686. Web Site: www.washlibs.org/heritage. *Dir,* April Bailey; E-mail: director@heritagepublibrary.org; Staff 5 (MLS 1, Non-MLS 4)
Founded 1907. Pop 8,500; Circ 27,000
Library Holdings: Bks on Deafness & Sign Lang 20; Large Print Bks 630; Bk Titles 23,000; Per Subs 35; Talking Bks 340

Automation Activity & Vendor Info: (Acquisitions) Follett Software; (Cataloging) Follett Software
Wireless access
Function: 24/7 Electronic res, 24/7 Online cat, Accelerated reader prog, Activity rm, Adult bk club, Archival coll, Art programs, Audiobks via web, Bks on CD, Children's prog, Computers for patron use, Electronic databases & coll, Free DVD rentals, Holiday prog, ILL available, Internet access, Laminating, Magazines, Magnifiers for reading, Movies, Online cat, OverDrive digital audio bks, Photocopying/Printing, Preschool reading prog, Prog for children & young adult, Ref serv available, Scanner, Story hour, Summer reading prog, Tax forms, VHS videos, Wheelchair accessible
Mem of Washington County Library System
Open Mon 4-8, Tues, Wed & Thurs 10-8, Fri 10-2, Sat 9-4
Friends of the Library Group

MCEWENSVILLE

P MONTGOMERY HOUSE LIBRARY*, Warrior Run Area Public, 20 Church St, 17749. (Mail add: PO Box 5, 17749-0005), SAN 314-7150. Tel: 570-538-1381. FAX: 570-538-1381. Web Site: www.montgomeryhouselibrary.org. *Dir,* J A Babay; E-mail: director@montgomeryhouselibrary.org; *Circ Mgr,* Dorothy Wilson; E-mail: dwilson@montgomeryhouselibrary.org; *Cataloger,* Daniel Walz; E-mail: dwalz@montgomeryhouselibrary.org; Staff 1 (MLS 1)
Founded 1967. Pop 9,463; Circ 43,179
Special Collections: Pennsylvania Coll
Subject Interests: Local hist
Automation Activity & Vendor Info: (Acquisitions) LibLime
Wireless access
Open Mon & Thurs 1-8, Tues & Wed 11-7, Fri 10-6, Sat 9-4
Friends of the Library Group

MCKEES ROCKS

P FOR STO-ROX LIBRARY*, 420 Chartiers Ave, 15136. SAN 314-7177. Tel: 412-771-1222. FAX: 412-771-2340. Web Site: www.forstorox.org/programs/ryanarts. *Exec Dir,* Cynthia Haines; E-mail: chaines@forstorox.org; Staff 2 (Non-MLS 2)
Founded 1995. Pop 13,328; Circ 24,848
Library Holdings: Large Print Bks 93; Bk Titles 11,559; Bk Vols 14,162; Per Subs 43; Videos 310
Automation Activity & Vendor Info: (Cataloging) Innovative Interfaces, Inc; (Circulation) Innovative Interfaces, Inc; (OPAC) Innovative Interfaces, Inc; (Serials) Innovative Interfaces, Inc
Mem of Allegheny County Library Association (ACLA)
Open Mon-Thurs 10-8, Fri & Sat 10-5; Mon-Thurs (Winter) 9-6, Fri & Sat 9-5
Friends of the Library Group

MCKEESPORT

P CARNEGIE LIBRARY OF MCKEESPORT*, 1507 Library Ave, 15132-4796. SAN 314-7185. Tel: 412-672-0625. FAX: 412-672-7860. Web Site: www.mckeesportlibrary.org. *Dir,* Colleen Denne; E-mail: dennec@einetwork.net; Staff 3 (MLS 1, Non-MLS 2)
Founded 1902. Pop 63,291; Circ 101,681
Library Holdings: AV Mats 10,811; Large Print Bks 384; Bk Titles 112,658; Bk Vols 114,390; Per Subs 211; Talking Bks 3,742; Videos 4,682
Special Collections: Local History (Western Pennsylvania), bks, pamphlets, pictures; Pennsylvania Archives
Subject Interests: Educ, Hist, Lit
Automation Activity & Vendor Info: (Cataloging) Innovative Interfaces, Inc; (Circulation) Innovative Interfaces, Inc; (OPAC) Innovative Interfaces, Inc; (Serials) Innovative Interfaces, Inc
Wireless access
Mem of Allegheny County Library Association (ACLA)
Open Mon-Wed (Winter) 8-8, Thurs & Fri 8-6:30, Sat 8-4; Mon, Tues, Thurs & Fri (Summer) 10-6, Wed 10-7, Sat 9-1
Friends of the Library Group
Branches: 2
DUQUESNE BRANCH, 300 Kennedy Ave, Duquesne, 15110. Tel: 412-469-9143. *Br Mgr,* Christy Barowich
Open Mon-Thurs 3:45-8, Fri 3:45-6:45; Mon-Fri (Summer) 11-3
WHITE OAK BRANCH, McAllister Lodge, 169 Victoria Dr, White Oak, 15131. Tel: 412-678-2002. *Br Mgr,* Frances Trimble; *Br Coordr,* Mary Jane DeParma; Staff 2 (MLS 1, Non-MLS 1)
Library Holdings: Bk Titles 5,290; Bk Vols 5,460; Per Subs 15
Open Mon & Tues (Winter) 1-5, Wed & Thurs 3-7, Sat 10-2; Mon, Tues & Sat (Summer) 10-2, Wed & Thurs 3-7
Friends of the Library Group

C PENNSYLVANIA STATE UNIVERSITY, GREATER ALLEGHENY, J Clarence Kelly Library, 4000 University Dr, 15132-7698. SAN 314-7207. Tel: 412-675-9110. E-mail: psugalib@psu.edu. Web Site: libraries.psu.edu/greaterallegheny. *Head Librn,* Andrew Marshall; Tel: 412-675-9119, E-mail: adm135@psu.edu; Staff 6 (MLS 2, Non-MLS 4)
Founded 1948. Enrl 878; Fac 59; Highest Degree: Bachelor
Library Holdings: Bk Vols 43,000; Per Subs 70
Automation Activity & Vendor Info: (OPAC) SirsiDynix
Wireless access
Partic in OCLC Online Computer Library Center, Inc; Research Libraries Information Network
Open Mon-Thurs 8-8, Fri 8-5

M UPMC MCKEESPORT*, Health Service Library, 1500 Fifth Ave, 15132. SAN 314-7193. FAX: 412-664-2581. Web Site: www.upmc.com/locations/hospitals/mckeesport. *Librn,* Amy Haugh; Tel: 412-784-4121, E-mail: haughaj@upmc.edu; Staff 1 (Non-MLS 1)
Founded 1975
Library Holdings: Bk Titles 3,811; Bk Vols 4,091; Per Subs 80
Subject Interests: Hospital admin, Med, Nursing
Wireless access
Restriction: Staff use only

MCMURRAY

P PETERS TOWNSHIP PUBLIC LIBRARY*, 616 E McMurray Rd, 15317-3495. SAN 314-7215. Tel: 724-941-9430. FAX: 724-941-9438. E-mail: ptlib@ptlibrary.org. Web Site: www.ptlibrary.org. *Libr Dir,* Myra Oleynik; E-mail: MOleynik@ptlibrary.org; *Asst Libr Dir,* Sue Miller; E-mail: SMiller@ptlibrary.org; *Head, Patron Serv,* Dianne Finnegan; E-mail: FinneganD@ptlibrary.org; *Head, Cat,* Mary Kipling; E-mail: MSKipling@ptlibrary.org; *Head, Circ,* Arlene Henderson; E-mail: CircStaff@ptlibrary.org; *Head, Ref,* Margaret Deitzer; E-mail: MDeitzer@ptlibrary.org; *Head, Youth Serv,* Shannon Pauley; E-mail: SPauley@ptlibrary.org; Staff 22 (MLS 6, Non-MLS 16)
Founded 1957. Pop 17,566; Circ 397,672
Library Holdings: Bk Vols 120,604; Per Subs 200
Special Collections: Oral History; State Document Depository
Automation Activity & Vendor Info: (Cataloging) SirsiDynix; (Circulation) SirsiDynix; (OPAC) SirsiDynix
Wireless access
Mem of Washington County Library System
Open Mon-Thurs 9-9, Fri 9-5, Sat 9-4, Sun (Sept-May) 12-4
Friends of the Library Group

MEADVILLE

C ALLEGHENY COLLEGE*, Library & Information Technology Services (LITS), 520 N Main St, 16335. SAN 314-738X. Tel: 814-332-3768. E-mail: infodesk@allegheny.edu. Web Site: sites.allegheny.edu/lits/library. *Vice Pres, Assessment & Info Serv,* Rick Holmgren; Tel: 814-332-2898, E-mail: rholmgre@allegheny.edu; *Assoc Dir of Libr,* Brian Kern; Tel: 814-332-3792, E-mail: bkern@allegheny.edu; *Dir, Pub Serv,* Aimee Reash; Tel: 814-332-3768, E-mail: areash@allegheny.edu; *Res & Instruction Librn, Spec Coll Librn,* Jane Westenfeld; Tel: 814-332-3769, E-mail: jwestenf@allegheny.edu; *Libr Spec,* Nancy Brenot; Tel: 814-332-3363, E-mail: nbrenot@allegheny.edu; *Libr Spec,* Sherree Byers; Tel: 814-332-2968, E-mail: sbyers@allegheny.edu; *Pub Serv Spec,* William Burlingame; Tel: 814-332-3359, E-mail: wburlingame@allegheny.edu; *Pub Serv Spec,* Linda Ernst; Tel: 814-332-3790, E-mail: lernst@allegheny.edu; *Col Archivist,* Ruth Andel; Tel: 814-332-2398, E-mail: randel@allegheny.edu; *Instructional Technologist, Res,* Helen McCullough; Tel: 814-332-3364, E-mail: hmccull@allegheny.edu; Staff 9 (MLS 7, Non-MLS 2)
Founded 1815. Enrl 2,100; Fac 135; Highest Degree: Bachelor
Library Holdings: AV Mats 8,600; CDs 905; DVDs 936; e-books 150; e-journals 21,750; Electronic Media & Resources 100; Microforms 493,740; Bk Titles 306,660; Bk Vols 796,800; Per Subs 800; Videos 8,612
Special Collections: Atlantic & Great Western Railroad Letters, papers, photog; Ida M Tarbell, letters, ms, bks; Lincoln, bks, pamphlets; Original Library, 1819-23 (Gifts of James Winthrop, Isaiah Thomas & William Bentley). State Document Depository; US Document Depository
Automation Activity & Vendor Info: (Acquisitions) Innovative Interfaces, Inc; (Cataloging) Innovative Interfaces, Inc; (Circulation) Innovative Interfaces, Inc; (ILL) OCLC ILLiad; (Media Booking) Innovative Interfaces, Inc; (OPAC) Innovative Interfaces, Inc; (Serials) Innovative Interfaces, Inc
Wireless access
Partic in Coun of Libr Info Resources; LYRASIS; National Institute for Technology & Liberal Education; Northwest Interlibrary Cooperative of Pennsylvania; OCLC Online Computer Library Center, Inc; Partnership for Academic Library Collaborative & Innovation
Open Mon-Thurs 7:30am-2am, Fri 7:30am-9pm, Sat 9-9, Sun 11am-2am

P CRAWFORD COUNTY FEDERATED LIBRARY SYSTEM, 848 N Main St, 16335-2689. SAN 314-7398. Tel: 814-336-1773. FAX: 814-333-8173. Web Site: www.ccfls.org. *Exec Dir,* John Brice; E-mail: jbrice@ccfls.org; Staff 15 (MLS 4, Non-MLS 11)

Founded 1978. Pop 86,090; Circ 361,028
Library Holdings: AV Mats 11,364; Large Print Bks 701; Bk Titles 103,667; Bk Vols 104,323; Per Subs 261; Talking Bks 3,648; Videos 2,072
Special Collections: Rotating Books on Cassette Coll
Automation Activity & Vendor Info: (Acquisitions) Koha; (Cataloging) Koha; (Circulation) Koha; (Discovery) ByWater Solutions; (ILL) Koha; (Media Booking) Koha; (OPAC) Koha; (Serials) Koha
Wireless access
Member Libraries: Benson Memorial Library; Cambridge Springs Public Library; Cochranton Area Public Library; Linesville Community Public Library; Margaret Shontz Memorial Library; Meadville Public Library; Saegertown Area Library; Springboro Public Library; Stone Memorial Library
Open Mon-Thurs 9-8, Fri & Sat 9-5

S CRAWFORD COUNTY HISTORICAL SOCIETY*, Research Center for Crawford County History, 411 Chestnut St, 16335. (Mail add: PO Box 871, 16335), SAN 314-7401. Tel: 814-724-6080. FAX: 814-724-6080. E-mail: archive@crawfordhistorical.org. Web Site: www.crawfordhistorical.org. *Archivist,* Kim Sherretts; Staff 2 (MLS 1, Non-MLS 1)
Founded 1879
Library Holdings: Bk Vols 2,600; Spec Interest Per Sub 15
Special Collections: Bulen Music Coll; Civil War Coll; Huidekoper, Reynolds & Dick Families; Photograph Coll; Railroad Coll (Erie, Bessemer); Talon Coll. Municipal Document Depository; Oral History
Subject Interests: Crawford County hist
Wireless access
Function: Res libr
Publications: Colorful Crawford County; Crawford County History (Newsletter); European Capital, British Iron & an American Dream: The Story of the Atlantic & Great Western Railroad; Images of America: Meadville; Images of Meadville: Meadville's Architectural Heritage; In French Creek Valley, 1938; Naturalization Abstracts, Crawford County, PA 1800-1906; Place Names of Crawford County, PA; Stories from French Creek Valley; The Diary of William Reynolds; The First 100 Years: Settlement & Growth in Crawford Count, PA; Treads of Tradition: Northwest Pennsylvania Quilts
Open Tues-Fri 9-1, Sat 9-3
Restriction: Non-circulating

M MEADVILLE MEDICAL CENTER*, Winslow Medical Library, 751 Liberty St, 16335. SAN 314-7428. Tel: 814-333-5740. FAX: 814-333-5714.
Library Holdings: Bk Vols 732; Per Subs 154
Subject Interests: Med, Med tech, Nursing
Wireless access
Function: ILL available, Res libr
Partic in National Network of Libraries of Medicine Region 1; Northwest Interlibrary Cooperative of Pennsylvania
Open Mon-Fri 9:30-6
Restriction: Non-circulating to the pub, Pub access by telephone only

P MEADVILLE PUBLIC LIBRARY*, 848 N Main St, 16335. SAN 314-7436. Tel: 814-336-1773. FAX: 814-333-8173. E-mail: info@meadvillelibrary.org. Web Site: meadvillelibrary.org. *Exec Dir,* John J Brice, III; E-mail: jbrice@ccfls.org; *Asst Dir, Ch Serv,* Mary Lee Minnis; E-mail: mlminnis@ccfls.org; Staff 20 (MLS 5, Non-MLS 15)
Founded 1812. Pop 38,911; Circ 248,896
Library Holdings: AV Mats 10,601; Large Print Bks 586; Bk Titles 88,901; Bk Vols 90,142; Per Subs 249; Talking Bks 3,591; Videos 2,079
Special Collections: Crawford County Historical Coll, bks & ms. Oral History
Subject Interests: Hist
Wireless access
Publications: Snippets from the Shelves (Newsletter)
Mem of Crawford County Federated Library System
Partic in LYRASIS; Northwest Interlibrary Cooperative of Pennsylvania
Open Mon-Thurs 9-8, Fri 9-5, Sat 9-1
Friends of the Library Group

MECHANICSBURG

CR MESSIAH UNIVERSITY*, Murray Library, (Formerly Messiah College), One College Ave, Ste 3002, 17055. SAN 358-4941. Tel: 717-691-6006. Circulation Tel: 717-691-6006, Ext 3860. Interlibrary Loan Service Tel: 717-691-6006, Ext 7242. Reference Tel: 717-691-6006, Ext 3910. FAX: 717-691-2356. Web Site: www.messiah.edu/murraylibrary. *Dir,* Linda Poston; Tel: 717-691-6006, Ext 3820, E-mail: poston@messiah.edu; *Circ Supvr,* Deb K Roof; Tel: 717-691-6006, Ext 7293, E-mail: droof@messiah.edu; *ILL Supvr,* Kimberly Steiner; E-mail: ksteiner@messiah.edu; *Coll Develop Coordr,* Sarah K Myers; Tel: 717-691-6006, Ext 3590, E-mail: smyers@messiah.edu; *Electronic Res Coordr,* Michael Rice; Tel: 717-691-6006, Ext 7069, E-mail: mrice@messiah.edu; *Libr Instruction Coordr,* Beth Transue; Tel: 717-691-6006, Ext 3810, E-mail: btransue@messiah.edu; *Pub Serv Coordr,* Lawrie Merz; Tel: 717-691-6006, Ext 3880, E-mail: lmerz@messiah.edu; *Tech Serv Coordr,* Liz Y Kielley; Tel: 717-691-6006, Ext 3850, E-mail: ekielley@messiah.edu; *Acq Tech,* Amanda Flagle; Tel: 717-691-6006, Ext 7073, E-mail: aflagle@messiah.edu; *Archivist,* Glen Pierce; Tel: 717-691-6006, Ext 6048, E-mail: gpierce@messiah.edu; *Ser Tech,* Sharon Berger; Tel: 717-691-6006, Ext 7017, E-mail: sberger@messiah.edu. Subject Specialists: *Hist,* Sarah K Myers; Staff 16 (MLS 6, Non-MLS 10)
Founded 1909. Enrl 3,331; Fac 175; Highest Degree: Doctorate
Special Collections: Artists' Books; Brethren in Christ Archives, bks, ms, micro; Canadian Literature; Ruth E Engle Memorial Coll of Children's Book Illustration; Science & Religion (W Jim Neidhardt Coll)
Subject Interests: Educ, Engr, Nursing
Automation Activity & Vendor Info: (Acquisitions) Ex Libris Group; (Cataloging) Ex Libris Group; (Circulation) Ex Libris Group; (Course Reserve) Ex Libris Group; (ILL) OCLC Online; (OPAC) Ex Libris Group; (Serials) EBSCO Online
Wireless access
Partic in Associated College Libraries of Central Pennsylvania; Partnership for Academic Library Collaborative & Innovation
Open Mon-Thurs (Winter) 7:30am-Midnight, Fri 7:30-6, Sat 10-8, Sun 2-Midnight; Mon & Wed (Summer) 8-8, Tues, Thurs & Fri 8-5
Friends of the Library Group

Departmental Libraries:

BRETHREN IN CHRIST HISTORICAL LIBRARY & ARCHIVES, One College Ave, 17055. (Mail add: PO Box 3002, 17055), SAN 374-9835. Tel: 717-691-6048. FAX: 717-691-6042. E-mail: archives@messiah.edu. Web Site: www.messiah.edu/archives. *Dir,* Glen A Pierce; Staff 1 (Non-MLS 1)
Founded 1952
Library Holdings: Bk Titles 600; Per Subs 20
Special Collections: Anabaptist, Pietist & Wesleyan Studies; Archives of Brethren in Christ Church; Archives of Messiah College; Manuscripts Coll. Oral History
Function: Archival coll
Open Mon-Thurs 9-12 & 1-3

P JOSEPH T SIMPSON PUBLIC LIBRARY*, 16 N Walnut St, 17055-3362. SAN 314-7444. Tel: 717-766-0171. FAX: 717-766-0152. E-mail: mechanicsburg@ccpa.net, simpson@cumberlandcountylibraries.org. Web Site: simpsonlibrary.org. *Dir,* Sue Erdman; E-mail: serdman@ccpa.net; Staff 5 (MLS 5)
Founded 1961. Pop 48,089; Circ 533,735
Jan 2018-Dec 2018 Income $969,202, State $135,848, Locally Generated Income $564,625, Other $268,729. Mats Exp $122,300, Books $73,200, Per/Ser (Incl. Access Fees) $8,600, AV Mat $27,000, Electronic Ref Mat (Incl. Access Fees) $13,500. Sal $545,418
Library Holdings: Audiobooks 4,605; DVDs 14,955; e-books 13,497; Bk Titles 82,386; Per Subs 135
Special Collections: Irving College, Mechanicsburg, Pennsylvania (women's college that closed in 1929)
Automation Activity & Vendor Info: (Acquisitions) Innovative Interfaces, Inc - Sierra; (Cataloging) Innovative Interfaces, Inc - Sierra; (Circulation) Innovative Interfaces, Inc - Sierra; (ILL) Innovative Interfaces, Inc - Sierra; (OPAC) Innovative Interfaces, Inc - Sierra; (Serials) Innovative Interfaces, Inc - Sierra
Wireless access
Function: 24/7 Electronic res, 24/7 Online cat, Activity rm, Adult bk club, Audiobks on Playaways & MP3, Audiobks via web, AV serv, Bk club(s), Bks on CD, CD-ROM, Children's prog, Citizenship assistance, Computer training, Computers for patron use, E-Reserves, Electronic databases & coll, Free DVD rentals, Holiday prog, Home delivery & serv to seniorr ctr & nursing homes, Homebound delivery serv, ILL available, Internet access, Life-long learning prog for all ages, Magazines, Mail & tel request accepted, Meeting rooms, Movies, Music CDs, Online cat, Outreach serv, OverDrive digital audio bks, Photocopying/Printing, Preschool outreach, Preschool reading prog, Printer for laptops & handheld devices, Prog for adults, Prog for children & young adult, Ref & res, Ref serv available, Scanner, Senior computer classes, Senior outreach, STEM programs, Story hour, Study rm, Summer reading prog, Tax forms, Teen prog, Telephone ref, Wheelchair accessible
Mem of Cumberland County Library System
Open Mon-Thurs 10-9, Fri & Sat 10-5, Sun 1-5
Friends of the Library Group

MEDIA

J DELAWARE COUNTY COMMUNITY COLLEGE LIBRARY*, 901 S Media Line Rd, 19063-1094. SAN 314-7452. Tel: 610-359-5149. Reference Tel: 610-359-5146. Administration Tel: 610-359-5150. FAX: 610-359-5272. E-mail: library@dccc.edu. Web Site: library.dccc.edu. *Dean,* Tonya Briggs; *Ref Librn,* Michael LaMagna; E-mail: mlamagna@dccc.edu; *Ref Librn,* Andrea Rodgers; E-mail: arodgers@dccc.edu; *Ref Librn,* Erica Swenson Danowitz; E-mail: edanowitz@dcc.edu; Staff 7.5 (MLS 7.5)
Founded 1967. Enrl 9,589; Highest Degree: Associate

Library Holdings: Audiobooks 188; CDs 554; DVDs 653; e-books 1,374; Bk Vols 23,726; Per Subs 104
Subject Interests: Law, Nursing
Automation Activity & Vendor Info: (Acquisitions) Innovative Interfaces, Inc; (Cataloging) Innovative Interfaces, Inc; (Circulation) Innovative Interfaces, Inc; (Course Reserve) Innovative Interfaces, Inc; (Discovery) EBSCO Discovery Service; (ILL) OCLC; (OPAC) Innovative Interfaces, Inc; (Serials) Innovative Interfaces, Inc
Wireless access
Partic in OCLC Online Computer Library Center, Inc; Tri State Col Libr Coop
Special Services for the Deaf - Assistive tech
Special Services for the Blind - Accessible computers; Assistive/Adapted tech devices, equip & products; Bks on CD; Closed circuit TV magnifier; Digital talking bk machines; Internet workstation with adaptive software; Low vision equip; Scanner for conversion & translation of mats; Screen enlargement software for people with visual disabilities; Screen reader software
Open Mon-Thurs 8am-10pm, Fri 8-5, Sat 9-4
Restriction: Circ privileges for students & alumni only, ID required to use computers (Ltd hrs), In-house use for visitors, Lending libr only via mail, Pub use on premises

P DELAWARE COUNTY LIBRARIES*, Bldg 19, 340 N Middletown Rd, 19063-5597. SAN 320-2267. Tel: 610-891-8622. FAX: 610-891-8641. E-mail: support@delcolibraries.org. Web Site: www.delcolibraries.org. *Dir,* Catherine Bittle; *Asst Dir,* Janis T Stubbs; *IT Dir,* Rene Kelly; *Law Librn,* Harry Brown; *Digital Libr & Ref Coordr,* Diane Arnold; *Tech Serv,* Kristin Suda; Staff 23 (MLS 6, Non-MLS 17)
Founded 1981. Pop 550,000; Circ 2,606,607
Library Holdings: AV Mats 12,000; Bk Titles 16,000; Per Subs 76
Subject Interests: Libr sci
Automation Activity & Vendor Info: (Acquisitions) Innovative Interfaces, Inc; (Cataloging) Innovative Interfaces, Inc; (Circulation) Innovative Interfaces, Inc; (ILL) Innovative Interfaces, Inc; (Media Booking) Innovative Interfaces, Inc; (OPAC) Innovative Interfaces, Inc; (Serials) Innovative Interfaces, Inc
Wireless access
Member Libraries: Aston Public Library; Borough of Folcroft Public Library; Collingdale Public Library; Darby Free Library; Glenolden Library; Haverford Township Free Library; Helen Kate Furness Free Library; J Lewis Crozer Library; Judge Francis J Catania Law Library; Lansdowne Public Library; Marple Public Library; Mary M Campbell Public Library; Media-Upper Providence Free Library; Middletown Free Library; Newtown Public Library; Norwood Public Library; Prospect Park Free Library; Rachel Kohl Community Library; Radnor Memorial Library; Ridley Park Public Library; Ridley Township Public Library; Sharon Hill Public Library; Springfield Township Library; Swarthmore Public Library; Tinicum Memorial Public Library; Upper Darby Township & Sellers Memorial Free Public Library; Yeadon Public Library
Open Mon-Fri 8:30-4:30
Friends of the Library Group

GL JUDGE FRANCIS J CATANIA LAW LIBRARY, Delaware County Courthouse, 201 W Front St, 19063-2778. SAN 314-7460. Tel: 610-891-4462. FAX: 610-891-4480. E-mail: DelcoLawLibrary@co.delaware.pa.us. Web Site: www.delcolibraries.org/francis-j-catania-law-library. Staff 1 (MLS 1)
Founded 1902
Library Holdings: Bk Vols 35,000; Per Subs 2,500
Automation Activity & Vendor Info: (Cataloging) Innovative Interfaces, Inc - Millennium; (OPAC) Innovative Interfaces, Inc - Millennium
Function: 24/7 Online cat, Ref serv available, Res libr
Mem of Delaware County Libraries
Open Mon-Fri 8:30-4:15
Restriction: Not a lending libr, Pub access for legal res only

P MEDIA-UPPER PROVIDENCE FREE LIBRARY*, One E Front St, 19063. SAN 314-7487. Tel: 610-566-1918. Web Site: www.mediauplibrary.org. *Libr Dir,* Sandra Samuel; E-mail: medirector@delcolibraries.org; Staff 11 (MLS 3, Non-MLS 8)
Founded 1901. Pop 15,678
Automation Activity & Vendor Info: (Cataloging) Innovative Interfaces, Inc; (Circulation) Innovative Interfaces, Inc
Wireless access
Mem of Delaware County Libraries
Open Mon-Thurs 10-8, Fri 10-6, Sat 10-4, Sun 1-4

MIDDLETOWN FREE LIBRARY*, 21 N Pennell Rd, 19063. SAN 314-7088. Tel: 610-566-7828. FAX: 610-892-0880. E-mail: middletown@delcolibraries.org. Web Site: www.middletownfreelibrary.org. *Dir,* Mary Glendening; E-mail: midirector@delcolibraries.org; *Ad,* Laura Kuchmay; E-mail: mireference@delcolibraries.org; *Youth Serv Librn,* Jason Fialkovich; E-mail: micsd@delcolibraries.org; Staff 3 (MLS 1, Non-MLS 2)
Founded 1956. Pop 15,807; Circ 143,983
Library Holdings: AV Mats 2,564; DVDs 2,076; Bk Vols 58,257; Per Subs 166
Subject Interests: Civil War
Wireless access
Function: 24/7 Electronic res, 24/7 Online cat, 3D Printer, Activity rm, Adult bk club, Art programs, Audio & video playback equip for onsite use, Audiobks via web, Bk club(s), Bks on CD, Children's prog, Computer training, Computers for patron use, E-Readers, Family literacy, Free DVD rentals, Genealogy discussion group, Holiday prog, ILL available, Internet access, Life-long learning prog for all ages, Magazines, Makerspace, Mango lang, Meeting rooms, Movies, Museum passes, Music CDs, Online cat, Outreach serv, OverDrive digital audio bks, Photocopying/Printing, Preschool outreach, Preschool reading prog, Prog for adults, Prog for children & young adult, Ref serv available, Scanner, Senior outreach, Serves people with intellectual disabilities, STEM programs, Story hour, Summer reading prog, Tax forms, Teen prog, Telephone ref, Visual arts prog, Wheelchair accessible, Workshops
Mem of Delaware County Libraries
Open Mon-Thurs 10-8, Fri 10-5, Sat 11-4, Sun 1-4
Friends of the Library Group

J PENNSYLVANIA INSTITUTE OF TECHNOLOGY LIBRARY*, 800 Manchester Ave, 19063-4098. SAN 328-5839. Tel: 610-892-1524. Toll Free Tel: 800-892-1500. FAX: 610-892-1523. E-mail: library@pit.edu. Web Site: my.pit.edu/Academic-Resources/LibraryOnline.aspx. *Dir, Libr Serv,* Lynea Anderman; E-mail: landerman@pit.edu; Staff 1 (MLS 1)
Founded 1962. Enrl 400; Highest Degree: Associate
Jul 2018-Jun 2019 Income $112,429, Parent Institution $108,929, Other $3,500. Mats Exp $61,338, Books $16,964, Per/Ser (Incl. Access Fees) $24,461, AV Mat $8,269, Electronic Ref Mat (Incl. Access Fees) $11,644. Sal $85,755
Library Holdings: Audiobooks 2; CDs 25; DVDs 844; e-books 99,300; Electronic Media & Resources 15; Bk Titles 11,080; Bk Vols 11,463; Per Subs 78; Videos 200
Special Collections: Architecture & Archaelogy (Hinderliter Coll); Early 20th Century or Earlier Publications (Founder's Coll); Honeywell Technology Coll; Professional Development Coll
Subject Interests: Allied health, Archit, Bus admin, Computer sci, Engr, Tech
Automation Activity & Vendor Info: (Acquisitions) TLC (The Library Corporation); (Cataloging) TLC (The Library Corporation); (Circulation) TLC (The Library Corporation); (ILL) OCLC; (OPAC) TLC (The Library Corporation)
Wireless access
Function: Archival coll, Art exhibits, Audio & video playback equip for onsite use, CD-ROM, Computers for patron use, Electronic databases & coll, Free DVD rentals, ILL available, Internet access, Online cat, Orientations, Outside serv via phone, mail, e-mail & web, Photocopying/Printing, Ref serv available, Res libr, Telephone ref, VHS videos, Workshops
Publications: Off the Shelf (Periodical)
Partic in Health Sciences Libraries Consortium; LYRASIS; OCLC Online Computer Library Center, Inc
Open Mon-Wed 8:30-5, Thurs 9:30-6, Fri 8-4:30
Restriction: Non-circulating coll, Open to pub for ref & circ; with some limitations, Open to students, fac, staff & alumni

MEHOOPANY

P MEHOOPANY AREA LIBRARY*, 310 Schoolhouse Hill Rd, 18629. (Mail add: PO Box 202, 18629-0202). Tel: 570-833-2818. FAX: 570-833-2818. E-mail: mehlib@ptd.net. Web Site: www.mehoopanytwp.org/library. *Board Pres,* Ina Hunter
Founded 1982. Circ 1,052
Library Holdings: AV Mats 68; Large Print Bks 180; Bk Vols 10,395; Talking Bks 216
Special Collections: Accelerated Readers Coll
Function: Summer reading prog
Open Wed-Fri 10:30-5, Sat 10:30-2

MELROSE PARK

C GRATZ COLLEGE*, The Tuttleman Library, 7605 Old York Rd, 19027. SAN 359-0550. Tel: 215-635-7300, Ext 159. FAX: 215-635-7320. E-mail: library@gratz.edu. Web Site: www.gratz.edu/library-and-information-technology-services-lits. *Dir, Libr & Info Tech,* Donna Guerin; E-mail: dguerin@gratz.edu; *IT Spec, Librn,* Andrew Pollak; E-mail: apollak@gratz.edu; Staff 2 (MLS 2)
Founded 1895. Highest Degree: Doctorate
Library Holdings: Bk Titles 93,781; Bk Vols 96,210; Per Subs 181; Videos 792

Special Collections: Anti-Semitica Coll; Archives Coll; Hebraica & Judaica; Holocaust Oral History Archive; Materials for Training Teachers of Hebrew Language & Culture. Oral History
Subject Interests: Bible, Hebrew lang, Hist, Holocaust, Israel studies, Jewish educ, Lit, Music, Rabbinics, Rare bks
Automation Activity & Vendor Info: (Cataloging) TLC (The Library Corporation); (Circulation) TLC (The Library Corporation)
Wireless access
Function: ILL available
Partic in Tri State Col Libr Coop
Open Mon-Thurs 9-5:30, Fri 9-3

MERCER

P MERCER AREA LIBRARY*, 110 E Venango St, 16137-1283. SAN 314-7517. Tel: 724-662-4233. FAX: 724-662-8893. E-mail: mercerarealibrary@gmail.com. Web Site: www.mercerarealibrary.org. *Dir,* Matthew Goldyn; E-mail: director@mercerarealibrary.org
Founded 1916. Pop 11,100; Circ 59,022
Library Holdings: Bk Vols 20,087; Per Subs 51
Special Collections: Video Colls
Automation Activity & Vendor Info: (Acquisitions) Follett Software; (Cataloging) Follett Software; (Circulation) Follett Software; (Course Reserve) Follett Software; (ILL) Follett Software; (Media Booking) Follett Software; (OPAC) Follett Software; (Serials) Follett Software
Wireless access
Partic in Tri County Libr Consortium
Open Tues-Fri 9:30-7, Sat 9-4
Friends of the Library Group

GL MERCER COUNTY LAW LIBRARY*, 305 Mercer County Courthouse, 16137-0123. SAN 327-0653. Tel: 724-662-3800, Ext 2302. Toll Free Tel: 800-711-9124. FAX: 724-662-0620. Web Site: www.mcc.co.mercer.pa.us/library. *Dir,* Jean Heckathorn; Staff 1 (Non-MLS 1)
Founded 1913
Library Holdings: Bk Vols 17,500; Per Subs 30
Function: Res libr
Open Mon-Fri 8:30-4:30
Restriction: Not a lending libr

S STATE REGIONAL CORRECTIONAL FACILITY LIBRARY*, 801 Butler Pike, 16137. SAN 371-6155. Tel: 724-662-1837. FAX: 724-662-1940. *Librn,* Marilyn Fusco; Staff 1 (MLS 1)
Library Holdings: Audiobooks 291; Large Print Bks 82; Bk Titles 13,669; Per Subs 80; Videos 791
Special Collections: Black History; Spanish Coll
Automation Activity & Vendor Info: (Cataloging) Follett Software; (Circulation) Follett Software; (OPAC) Follett Software
Special Services for the Deaf - Bks on deafness & sign lang; High interest/low vocabulary bks
Restriction: Staff & inmates only

MERCERSBURG

P FENDRICK LIBRARY, 20 N Main St, 17236. Tel: 717-328-9233. E-mail: librarian@fendricklibrary.org. Web Site: www.fendricklibrary.org. *Dir,* Cheryl Custer
Library Holdings: Audiobooks 250; DVDs 472; Large Print Bks 100; Bk Vols 50,000; Per Subs 18
Wireless access
Open Mon 2:30-5:30, Wed 10-2, Fri 10-2 & 5-7

MESHOPPEN

P FRANCES E KENNARD PUBLIC LIBRARY*, Auburn & Canal Sts, 18630. (Mail add: PO Box 39, 18630-0039), SAN 314-7568. Tel: 570-833-5060. FAX: 570-833-4238. *Board Pres,* Herbert Smith; *Librn,* Anna Sherwood; Staff 1 (Non-MLS 1)
Founded 1900. Pop 981; Circ 6,500
Library Holdings: Bk Titles 4,681; Bk Vols 4,926; Per Subs 16; Videos 90
Wireless access
Open Mon-Thurs 4-8

MEYERSDALE

P MEYERSDALE PUBLIC LIBRARY, 210 Center St, 15552-1323. (Mail add: PO Box 98, 15552-0098), SAN 314-7576. Tel: 814-634-0512. FAX: 814-634-0512. E-mail: info@meyersdalelibrary.org. Web Site: meyersdalelibrary.org. *Dir,* Terri Foster; Staff 2 (MLS 1, Non-MLS 1)
Founded 1939. Pop 19,000; Circ 30,000
Library Holdings: Bk Vols 31,000; Per Subs 40
Subject Interests: Local hist
Automation Activity & Vendor Info: (Acquisitions) Innovative Interfaces, Inc; (Cataloging) Innovative Interfaces, Inc; (Circulation) Innovative Interfaces, Inc; (Course Reserve) Innovative Interfaces, Inc; (ILL) Innovative Interfaces, Inc; (OPAC) Innovative Interfaces, Inc; (Serials) Innovative Interfaces, Inc
Wireless access
Function: Accelerated reader prog, Adult bk club, Adult literacy prog, Archival coll, Audio & video playback equip for onsite use, Audiobks via web, Bks on cassette, Bks on CD, Children's prog, Citizenship assistance, Computer training, Computers for patron use, Digital talking bks, E-Reserves, Electronic databases & coll, Family literacy, Games & aids for people with disabilities, Genealogy discussion group, Home delivery & serv to seniorr ctr & nursing homes, ILL available, Instruction & testing, Large print keyboards, Learning ctr, Magnifiers for reading, Mail & tel request accepted, Outreach serv, OverDrive digital audio bks, Photocopying/Printing, Preschool outreach, Prog for adults, Prog for children & young adult, Ref serv available, Scanner, Senior outreach, Story hour, Summer reading prog, Tax forms, Telephone ref, Wheelchair accessible
Mem of Somerset County Federated Library System
Open Mon-Fri 10-7, Sat 10-5
Friends of the Library Group

MIDDLEBURG

S SNYDER COUNTY HISTORICAL SOCIETY, INC LIBRARY*, 30 E Market St, 17842-1017. (Mail add: PO Box 276, 17842-0276), SAN 328-8188. Tel: 570-837-6191. FAX: 570-837-4282. E-mail: schs@snydercounty.org. Web Site: snydercountyhistoricalsociety.org. *Librn,* Esther Klinger
Founded 1898
Library Holdings: Bk Titles 3,200
Publications: Snyder Co Historical Society Bulletin
Open Mon & Thurs 10-3:30, Sun 1:30-4

MIDDLETOWN

P MIDDLETOWN PUBLIC LIBRARY*, 20 N Catherine St, 17057-1401. SAN 314-7584. Tel: 717-944-6412. FAX: 717-930-0510. E-mail: info@middletownpubliclib.org. Web Site: middletownpubliclib.org. *Dir,* John Grayshaw; *Librn,* Barbara Scull; Staff 4.5 (MLS 1, Non-MLS 3.5)
Founded 1926. Pop 9,242; Circ 55,108
Special Collections: Interviews from Early 1970s, indexed; Middletown Journal, 1886-present, newsp; Press & Journal Coll. Oral History
Automation Activity & Vendor Info: (Acquisitions) Innovative Interfaces, Inc; (Cataloging) Innovative Interfaces, Inc; (Circulation) Innovative Interfaces, Inc; (OPAC) Innovative Interfaces, Inc
Wireless access
Function: Adult bk club, Audiobks via web, Bks on cassette, Bks on CD, Children's prog, Computers for patron use, Electronic databases & coll, Free DVD rentals, Holiday prog, ILL available, Outreach serv, OverDrive digital audio bks, Photocopying/Printing, Preschool outreach, Prog for adults, Prog for children & young adult, Story hour, Summer & winter reading prog, Summer reading prog, Tax forms, Teen prog, VHS videos, Wheelchair accessible
Partic in Community Libraries Information Consortium
Special Services for the Blind - Audio mat; Bks on cassette; Bks on CD; Large print bks; Playaways (bks on MP3); Recorded bks
Open Mon & Wed 9:30-4, Tues 12-8, Thurs 9:30-8, Sat 9-2
Friends of the Library Group

G PENNSYLVANIA DEPARTMENT OF CONSERVATION & NATURAL RESOURCES, Bureau of Geological Survey Library, 3240 Schoolhouse Rd, 17057-3534. SAN 358-5336. Tel: 717-702-2020. E-mail: ra-pagslibrary@pa.gov. Web Site: www.dcnr.pa.gov/Geology/SurveyLibrary. *Librn,* Jody Smale; E-mail: jsmale@pa.gov; Staff 1 (MLS 1)
Founded 1850
Library Holdings: Bk Titles 11,300; Bk Vols 12,951; Per Subs 65
Special Collections: Aerial Photography, contact prints; Maps (United States Geologic Survey Seven & One Half Minute Maps)
Subject Interests: Earth sci, Geog, Geol
Automation Activity & Vendor Info: (Acquisitions) Ex Libris Group; (Cataloging) Ex Libris Group; (OPAC) Ex Libris Group
Function: 24/7 Electronic res, 24/7 Online cat, Archival coll, Computers for patron use, Ref serv available
Publications: In House Newsletter
Open Mon-Fri 9-12 & 1-4

C PENNSYLVANIA STATE UNIVERSITY-HARRISBURG LIBRARY*, 351 Olmsted Dr, 17057-4850. SAN 314-7592. Tel: 717-948-6070. E-mail: UL-HARRISBURG@lists.psu.edu. Web Site: libraries.psu.edu/harrisburg. *Head Librn,* Glenn McGuigan; Tel: 717-948-6078, E-mail: gxm22@psu.edu; *Humanities Librn,* Heidi Moyer; Tel: 717-948-6056, E-mail: hna2@psu.edu; *Ref Librn,* Bernadette A Lear; Tel: 717-948-6360, E-mail: bal19@psu.edu; *Ref & Instruction Librn,* Emily Reed; Tel: 717-948-6373, E-mail: exr5212@psu.edu; *Info Res,* Alan Mays; Tel:

717-948-6593, E-mail: axm22@psu.edu. Subject Specialists: *Bus, Criminal justice, Pub admin,* Glenn McGuigan; *Am studies, Communications, Humanities,* Heidi Moyer; Staff 15 (MLS 6, Non-MLS 9)
Founded 1966. Enrl 4,800; Fac 250; Highest Degree: Doctorate
Special Collections: Holocaust & Genocide Studies Coll; PA Culture Studies; Women's History Coll
Subject Interests: Am studies, Behav sci, Computer sci, Criminal justice, Educ, Engr, Humanities, Pub affairs
Automation Activity & Vendor Info: (Acquisitions) SirsiDynix; (Cataloging) SirsiDynix; (Circulation) SirsiDynix; (Course Reserve) SirsiDynix; (ILL) OCLC; (OPAC) SirsiDynix; (Serials) SirsiDynix
Wireless access
Function: Archival coll, Art exhibits, Audio & video playback equip for onsite use, E-Reserves, Electronic databases & coll, Equip loans & repairs, Microfiche/film & reading machines, Music CDs, Online cat, Photocopying/Printing, Ref serv available, Scanner, Wheelchair accessible
Special Services for the Deaf - Assistive tech
Special Services for the Blind - Assistive/Adapted tech devices, equip & products
Open Mon-Thurs 7:30am-11pm, Fri 7:30am-9pm, Sat 10-6, Sun 2-11

MIDLAND

P CARNEGIE FREE LIBRARY*, 61 Ninth St, 15059. SAN 314-7606. Tel: 724-643-8980. FAX: 724-643-8985. Web Site: www.beaverlibraries.org/midland.asp. *Dir,* Linda Slopek; E-mail: lslopek@beaverlibraries.org
Founded 1916. Pop 4,684; Circ 22,111
Library Holdings: Audiobooks 841; Large Print Bks 23; Bk Vols 16,576; Per Subs 44; Videos 2,332
Automation Activity & Vendor Info: (Acquisitions) Innovative Interfaces, Inc - Millennium; (Cataloging) Innovative Interfaces, Inc; (Circulation) Innovative Interfaces, Inc; (ILL) Innovative Interfaces, Inc; (OPAC) Innovative Interfaces, Inc
Wireless access
Mem of Beaver County Library System
Open Mon-Thurs 1-7, Sat 10-4

MIFFLINBURG

P JANE I & ANNETTA M HERR MEMORIAL LIBRARY*, 500 Market St, 17844. SAN 314-7614. Tel: 570-966-0831. FAX: 570-966-0106. E-mail: herr@herrlibrary.org. Web Site: www.unioncountylibraries.org. *Dir,* Kelly Walter
Founded 1945. Pop 7,600
Library Holdings: Bk Vols 18,000; Per Subs 35
Automation Activity & Vendor Info: (Circulation) TLC (The Library Corporation)
Wireless access
Mem of Union County Library System
Open Mon & Tues 12-8, Wed & Sat 10-5, Thurs 10-8

MIFFLINTOWN

P JUNIATA COUNTY LIBRARY, 498 Jefferson St, 17059-1424. SAN 358-7010. Tel: 717-436-6378. FAX: 717-436-5053. E-mail: juniatalibrary@juniatalibrary.org. Web Site: www.juniatalibrary.org. *Dir,* Vince Giordano; E-mail: vgiordano@juniatalibrary.org; Staff 1 (MLS 1)
Founded 1966. Pop 25,000; Circ 90,000
Library Holdings: Bk Titles 51,000; Per Subs 70
Subject Interests: Local hist
Automation Activity & Vendor Info: (Cataloging) Evergreen; (Circulation) Evergreen; (OPAC) Evergreen
Wireless access
Open Mon, Tues & Thurs 9-5, Fri 1-7, Sat 9-3
Friends of the Library Group

MILFORD

P PIKE COUNTY PUBLIC LIBRARY*, 119 E Harford St, 18337-1398. SAN 358-707X. Tel: 570-296-8211. FAX: 570-296-8987. Administration E-mail: admin@pcpl.org. Web Site: www.pcpl.org. *Libr Dir,* Rose Chiocchi; E-mail: director@pcpl.org; *Asst Dir,* Linda Krafinski; *Tech Serv Mgr,* Dellana Diovisalvo
Founded 1902. Pop 57,000; Circ 129,000
Library Holdings: Bk Vols 66,547
Automation Activity & Vendor Info: (Cataloging) TLC (The Library Corporation)
Wireless access
Publications: Print & Email Newsletters
Open Mon 10-7, Tues-Thurs 10-6, Fri 10-5, Sat 10-3
Friends of the Library Group
Branches: 1
DINGMAN TOWNSHIP, 100 Bond Ct, 18337-7793. Tel: 570-686-7045. FAX: 570-686-1798. E-mail: dingman@pcpl.org. *Br Mgr,* Nicole Heyer
Open Tues 10-7, Wed & Thurs 2-7, Fri 10-5, Sat 10-3
Friends of the Library Group

MILLERSVILLE

C MILLERSVILLE UNIVERSITY*, Francine G McNairy Library, Nine N George St, 17551. (Mail add: PO Box 1002, 17551-0302), SAN 314-7630. Tel: 717-871-7111. Circulation Tel: 717-872-3612. Administration Tel: 717-871-4146. FAX: 717-871-7957. Web Site: library.millersville.edu. *Dir of Libr Operations,* Andy Welaish; E-mail: Andy.Welaish@millersville.edu; *Cataloging & Metadata Librn,* Teresa Weisser; E-mail: teresa.weisser@millersville.edu; Staff 13 (MLS 13)
Founded 1855. Enrl 7,919; Fac 334; Highest Degree: Master
Library Holdings: AV Mats 13,770; e-books 3,556; Bk Vols 565,281; Per Subs 10,105
Special Collections: Archives of American Industrial Arts Association; The Carl Van Vechten Memorial Coll of Afro American Arts & Letters, bks, photog; Wickersham Coll of 19th Century Textbooks. State Document Depository; US Document Depository
Subject Interests: Educ, Ethnic studies, Holocaust, Local hist
Automation Activity & Vendor Info: (Acquisitions) Ex Libris Group; (Cataloging) Ex Libris Group; (Circulation) Ex Libris Group; (Course Reserve) Docutek; (ILL) Ex Libris Group; (OPAC) Ex Libris Group; (Serials) Ex Libris Group
Wireless access
Partic in Associated College Libraries of Central Pennsylvania; Keystone Library Network; OCLC Online Computer Library Center, Inc; Pa Syst of Higher Educ Libr Coun; Partnership for Academic Library Collaborative & Innovation
Friends of the Library Group

MILLVALE

P MILLVALE COMMUNITY LIBRARY*, 213 Grant Ave, 15209. Tel: 412-822-7081. E-mail: info@millvalelibrary.org. Web Site: www.millvalelibrary.org. *Exec Dir,* Lisa Seel; E-mail: seell@einetwork.net; Staff 3 (MLS 1, Non-MLS 2)
Founded 2007. Pop 3,744
Function: 24/7 Online cat, Activity rm, Adult bk club, Adult literacy prog, Bk club(s), Bks on CD, Children's prog, Computers for patron use, Electronic databases & coll, Equip loans & repairs, Family literacy, Free DVD rentals, Home delivery & serv to seniorr ctr & nursing homes, Homework prog, ILL available, Internet access, Life-long learning prog for all ages, Magazines, Magnifiers for reading, Mail & tel request accepted, Mango lang, Meeting rooms, Movies, Online cat, Online info literacy tutorials on the web & in blackboard, Online ref, Outreach serv, OverDrive digital audio bks, Photocopying/Printing, Preschool outreach, Preschool reading prog, Printer for laptops & handheld devices, Prog for adults, Prog for children & young adult, Ref & res, Scanner, Senior outreach, Story hour, Summer & winter reading prog, Summer reading prog, Tax forms, Visual arts prog, Wheelchair accessible, Winter reading prog, Workshops, Writing prog
Mem of Allegheny County Library Association (ACLA)
Open Tues Noon-8, Wed & Thurs 10-6, Fri 10-2, Sat 10-5

MILTON

P MILTON PUBLIC LIBRARY, 541 Broadway St, 17847. SAN 314-7649. Tel: 570-742-7111. FAX: 570-742-7137. Web Site: miltonpalibrary.org. *Libr Dir,* Kris LaVanish; E-mail: director@miltonpalibrary.org; *Circ,* Kathy Eisley
Founded 1923. Pop 12,000
Special Collections: Milton Daily Standard Newspaper, 1816 to present, micro
Subject Interests: Hist of Milton, Northumberland County
Automation Activity & Vendor Info: (Cataloging) Follett Software; (Circulation) Follett Software; (OPAC) Follett Software
Wireless access
Open Mon-Thurs 10-6, Fri 9-6, Sat 10-2
Friends of the Library Group

MINERSVILLE

P MINERSVILLE PUBLIC LIBRARY ASSOCIATION INC*, Minersville Public Library, 220 S Fourth St, 17954. SAN 314-7657. Tel: 570-544-5196. FAX: 570-544-5196. E-mail: mpl@minersvillelibrary.org. Web Site: www.minersvillelibrary.org. *Libr Dir,* Deborah A Cherrybon
Founded 1934. Pop 4,552; Circ 12,000
Library Holdings: AV Mats 532; DVDs 900; Large Print Bks 525; Bk Vols 16,208; Per Subs 29; Talking Bks 513; Videos 613
Automation Activity & Vendor Info: (Acquisitions) AmLib Library Management System; (Cataloging) AmLib Library Management System;

(Circulation) AmLib Library Management System; (ILL) Fretwell-Downing; (OPAC) AmLib Library Management System
Wireless access
Function: Activity rm, Bks on cassette, Bks on CD, Children's prog, Computers for patron use, Free DVD rentals, Holiday prog, ILL available, Internet access, Laminating, Large print keyboards, Magazines, Mail & tel request accepted, Meeting rooms, Online cat, Photocopying/Printing, Prog for children & young adult, Ref serv available, Scanner, Story hour, Summer & winter reading prog, Summer reading prog, Tax forms, Telephone ref, VHS videos, Wheelchair accessible
Special Services for the Blind - Bks on cassette; Bks on CD; Computer access aids; Copier with enlargement capabilities; Extensive large print coll; Large print & cassettes; Large print bks; Magnifiers
Open Tues & Thurs 12-7, Wed & Fri 12-5, Sat 10-4

MONACA

J COMMUNITY COLLEGE OF BEAVER COUNTY LIBRARY*, One Campus Dr, 15061-2588. SAN 314-7665. Tel: 724-480-3442. Circulation Tel: 724-775-8561, Ext 116. FAX: 724-728-8024. E-mail: library@ccbc.edu. Web Site: ccbc.edu/Library. *Ref Librn,* Terri Gallagher; E-mail: terri.gallagher@ccbc.edu; Staff 1 (MLS 1)
Founded 1967. Enrl 2,545; Fac 41; Highest Degree: Associate
Library Holdings: Bk Titles 46,324; Bk Vols 52,281; Per Subs 89
Subject Interests: Aviation, Law enforcement, Nursing
Automation Activity & Vendor Info: (Cataloging) Innovative Interfaces, Inc; (Circulation) Innovative Interfaces, Inc; (Course Reserve) Innovative Interfaces, Inc; (ILL) Innovative Interfaces, Inc; (OPAC) Innovative Interfaces, Inc
Wireless access
Function: ILL available, Magnifiers for reading, Orientations, Ref serv available
Mem of Beaver County Library System
Open Mon-Thurs 8-6, Fri 8-4

P MONACA PUBLIC LIBRARY*, 998 Indiana Ave, 2nd Flr, 15061. SAN 314-7673. Tel: 724-775-9608. FAX: 724-775-1637. Web Site: www.beaverlibraries.org/monaca.asp. *Dir,* Patricia Smith; E-mail: psmith@beaverlibraries.org
Founded 1973. Pop 7,661; Circ 20,014
Library Holdings: Bk Vols 14,500; Per Subs 26
Automation Activity & Vendor Info: (Cataloging) Innovative Interfaces, Inc; (Circulation) Innovative Interfaces, Inc
Wireless access
Mem of Beaver County Library System
Open Mon-Thurs 1-8, Sat 9-4

C PENNSYLVANIA STATE UNIVERSITY*, Beaver Campus Library, 100 University Dr, 15061. SAN 314-7681. Tel: 724-773-3790. FAX: 724-773-3793. E-mail: UL-BEAVER@lists.psu.edu. Web Site: libraries.psu.edu/beaver. *Head Librn,* Amy Deuink; E-mail: ald120@psu.edu; *Ref Librn,* Beth Seyala; Tel: 724-773-3796, E-mail: elt10@psu.edu; Staff 2 (MLS 2)
Founded 1965. Enrl 900; Fac 63; Highest Degree: Master
Library Holdings: Bk Titles 52,435; Bk Vols 54,614; Per Subs 142; Talking Bks 108; Videos 761
Special Collections: Afro-American Autobiographies
Subject Interests: Steel indust
Wireless access
Partic in OCLC Online Computer Library Center, Inc; Research Libraries Information Network
Open Mon-Thurs (Winter) 8-6, Fri 8-5; Mon-Thurs (Summer) 8-5, Fri 8-4:30

MONESSEN

P MONESSEN PUBLIC LIBRARY*, 326 Donner Ave, 15062. SAN 314-7703. Tel: 724-684-4750. FAX: 724-684-0206. E-mail: Monessen.Public.Library@gmail.com. Web Site: www.monessenlibrary.org. *Dir,* Dave Zilka; E-mail: dzilka@hotmail.com; *Ref Librn,* Allen Feryok; *Ref Librn,* Mary Matovich; *Children's Coordr,* Marsha Adams; *Cat,* Daniel Zyglowicz; Staff 7 (MLS 7)
Founded 1936. Pop 259,824
Library Holdings: High Interest/Low Vocabulary Bk Vols 1,500; Bk Vols 108,900; Per Subs 345
Special Collections: State Document Depository; US Document Depository
Mem of Westmoreland County Federated Library System
Partic in OCLC Online Computer Library Center, Inc
Open Mon-Wed 9-7, Thurs 9-5, Fri 9-4
Friends of the Library Group

MONONGAHELA

P MONONGAHELA AREA LIBRARY*, 813 W Main St, 15063. SAN 314-7711. Tel: 724-258-5409. FAX: 724-258-5440. E-mail: monongahelalib@gmail.com. Web Site: monongahelaarealibrary.com, www.washlibs.org/monongahela. *Dir,* Amy Riegner; E-mail: ariegner@washlibs.org; Staff 1 (Non-MLS 1)
Founded 1905. Pop 17,000; Circ 27,000
Library Holdings: Audiobooks 205; Bks on Deafness & Sign Lang 5; CDs 52; DVDs 168; Large Print Bks 652; Bk Titles 30,764; Per Subs 28
Special Collections: Genealogical Coll; Monongahela Daily Newspapers, 1851-1982 (micro)
Subject Interests: Local hist
Automation Activity & Vendor Info: (Acquisitions) Innovative Interfaces, Inc; (Cataloging) Innovative Interfaces, Inc; (Circulation) Innovative Interfaces, Inc; (Course Reserve) Innovative Interfaces, Inc; (OPAC) Innovative Interfaces, Inc; (Serials) Innovative Interfaces, Inc
Wireless access
Function: Children's prog
Mem of Washington County Library System
Open Mon-Thurs 11-7, Fri 11-5, Sat 10-5
Friends of the Library Group

MONROETON

P MONROETON PUBLIC LIBRARY*, 149 Dalpiaz Dr, 18832. (Mail add: PO Box 145, 18832-0145), SAN 314-772X. Tel: 570-265-2871. FAX: 570-265-7995. E-mail: monroetonlibrary@comcast.net. Web Site: www.monroetonlibrary.org. *Librn,* Karen S Troup; Staff 3 (Non-MLS 3)
Founded 1939. Pop 633; Circ 3,000
Library Holdings: Bk Vols 5,900; Per Subs 15
Automation Activity & Vendor Info: (Cataloging) Follett Software; (Circulation) Follett Software
Mem of Bradford County Library System
Open Mon-Thurs 12-7, Sat 9-4
Friends of the Library Group

MONROEVILLE

J COMMUNITY COLLEGE OF ALLEGHENY COUNTY*, Boyce Campus Library, 595 Beatty Rd, 15146. SAN 358-7134. Tel: 724-325-6798. FAX: 724-325-6696. E-mail: library@ccac.edu. Web Site: ccac.edu/library. *Adjunct Librn,* Katie Wirt; Tel: 724-325-6798, E-mail: kwirt@ccac.edu; Staff 8 (MLS 5, Non-MLS 3)
Founded 1966. Enrl 5,400; Fac 80
Library Holdings: Bk Titles 68,512; Bk Vols 71,910; Per Subs 182; Videos 559
Special Collections: Paralegal Coll
Subject Interests: Allied health, Food serv, Hospitality, Nursing, Paralegal
Automation Activity & Vendor Info: (Cataloging) SirsiDynix; (Circulation) SirsiDynix; (OPAC) SirsiDynix; (Serials) SirsiDynix
Wireless access
Publications: Acquisitions Lists; Bibliographies; Library Handbook; Library Newspaper
Partic in OCLC Online Computer Library Center, Inc; Pittsburgh Regional Libr Consortium
Open Mon-Thurs 8-8, Fri 8-4:30, Sat 9-2

M FORBES REGIONAL HOSPITAL*, Health Sciences Library, 2570 Haymaker Rd, 15146. SAN 314-7746. Tel: 412-858-2000, 412-858-2978.
Founded 1978
Library Holdings: e-books 20; e-journals 900; Electronic Media & Resources 8; Bk Titles 500; Per Subs 80
Special Collections: Forbes History Coll
Subject Interests: Family practice, Gynecology, Obstetrics, Oncology, Pediatrics, Psychiat
Automation Activity & Vendor Info: (OPAC) LibraryWorld, Inc
Partic in Basic Health Sciences Library Network; Pittsburgh Basic Health Sciences Libr Consortium)
Open Mon-Fri 8-3:30

P MONROEVILLE PUBLIC LIBRARY*, 4000 Gateway Campus Blvd, 15146-3381. SAN 314-7770. Tel: 412-372-0500. Circulation Tel: 412-372-0500, Ext 5. Reference Tel: 412-372-0500, Ext 4. Administration Tel: 412-372-0500, Ext 111. FAX: 412-372-1168. Web Site: www.monroevillelibrary.org. *Dir,* Nicole Henline; E-mail: henlinen@einetwork.net; *Asst Dir, Teen Librn,* Pam Bodziock; E-mail: bodziockp@einetwork.net; *Head, Adult Serv,* Tracy Happe; E-mail: happet@einetwork.net; *Head, Children's Servx,* Hope Benson; Tel: 412-372-0500, Ext 127, E-mail: bensonh@einetwork.net; *Head, Tech Serv,* Mark Hudson; Tel: 412-372-0500, Ext 113, E-mail: hudsonm@einetwork.net; Staff 19 (MLS 9, Non-MLS 10)
Founded 1964. Pop 33,162; Circ 221,476
Library Holdings: CDs 6,382; DVDs 5,227; Bk Vols 119,514; Per Subs 219

Special Collections: Local Newspaper 1976-Present, microfilm; New Reader Coll; Newbery & Caldecott Coll; NY Times 1940-Present, microfilm
Subject Interests: Careers, Local hist
Automation Activity & Vendor Info: (Acquisitions) Innovative Interfaces, Inc; (Cataloging) Innovative Interfaces, Inc; (Circulation) Innovative Interfaces, Inc; (OPAC) Innovative Interfaces, Inc
Wireless access
Publications: Program Calendar (Monthly bulletin)
Special Services for the Blind - Accessible computers; Bks & mags in Braille, on rec, tape & cassette; Bks on CD; Large print bks; Ref serv
Open Mon-Thurs 9-9, Fri & Sat 9-5, Sun 12-3
Friends of the Library Group

MONT ALTO

C PENNSYLVANIA STATE UNIVERSITY, Mont Alto Library, One Campus Dr, 17237. SAN 314-7797. Tel: 717-749-6040. Circulation Tel: 717-749-6182. Interlibrary Loan Service Tel: 717-749-6044. Reference Tel: 717-749-6042. FAX: 717-749-6059. Web Site: www.libraries.psu.edu. *Head Librn,* Tom Reinsfelder; E-mail: tlr15@psu.edu; *Ref & Instruction Librn,* Kristi Addleman Ritter; E-mail: kra132@psu.edu; *Info Res & Serv Support Spec,* Sarah Fretz; E-mail: sjf209@psu.edu; Staff 3 (MLS 2, Non-MLS 1)
Founded 1963. Enrl 917; Fac 60
Library Holdings: Bk Vols 30,000
Wireless access
Function: 24/7 Electronic res, 24/7 Online cat, 3D Printer, Archival coll, E-Reserves, Electronic databases & coll, Free DVD rentals, ILL available, Online ref, Ref serv available, Res assist avail, Res libr
Partic in OCLC Online Computer Library Center, Inc; Research Libraries Information Network
Open Mon-Thurs 8am-9pm, Fri 8-4:30, Sat 10-4, Sun Noon-10

MONTGOMERY

P MONTGOMERY AREA PUBLIC LIBRARY*, One S Main St, 17752-1150. SAN 314-7800. Tel: 570-547-6212. FAX: 570-547-0648. E-mail: mapl@jvbrown.edu. Web Site: www.montgomerylib.org. *Librn,* Nicole Loffredo; E-mail: nloffredo@jvbrown.edu; Staff 2 (Non-MLS 2)
Founded 1911. Pop 4,785; Circ 14,995
Library Holdings: Bk Vols 16,000; Per Subs 42
Automation Activity & Vendor Info: (Cataloging) SirsiDynix; (Circulation) SirsiDynix
Open Mon-Wed & Fri 10-6, Thurs 10-4, Sat 9-4

MONTOURSVILLE

P DR W B KONKLE MEMORIAL LIBRARY*, 384 Broad St, 17754-2206. SAN 314-7819. Tel: 570-368-1840. FAX: 570-368-7416. E-mail: konkle@jvbrown.edu. Web Site: www.konklelibrary.org. *Libr Dir,* Canda Fogarty
Founded 1943. Pop 7,694
Library Holdings: Bk Titles 23,000; Per Subs 45
Special Collections: Pennsylvania Coll, bks & pamphlets
Automation Activity & Vendor Info: (Cataloging) Innovative Interfaces, Inc; (Circulation) Innovative Interfaces, Inc; (OPAC) Innovative Interfaces, Inc
Wireless access
Mem of Lycoming County Library System
Open Mon-Thurs 10-7:30, Fri 10-6, Sat 9-4
Friends of the Library Group

MONTROSE

P SUSQUEHANNA COUNTY HISTORICAL SOCIETY & FREE LIBRARY ASSOCIATION*, 458 High School Rd, 18801. SAN 358-7169. Tel: 570-278-1881. FAX: 570-278-9336. E-mail: info@susqcolibrary.org. Web Site: www.susqcolibrary.org. *Adminr, Librn,* Susan Stone; *Asst Librn,* Amy Johnson; *Ch Serv,* Karen Braker-Reed; *Tech Serv,* Aaron Nichols; Staff 14 (MLS 2, Non-MLS 12)
Founded 1907. Pop 42,238; Circ 180,000
Library Holdings: Bk Vols 49,495; Per Subs 159
Special Collections: Genealogy (Census Records), micro; Genealogy (New England Historical & Genealogical Register); Local newspapers, micro
Wireless access
Function: Home delivery & serv to seniorr ctr & nursing homes, Homebound delivery serv, ILL available, Prog for children & young adult, Summer reading prog
Publications: Centennial History of Susquehanna County, Pennsylvania; County Atlas; History of Susquehanna County, Pennsylvania
Open Mon-Thurs 9-8, Sat 9-4
Friends of the Library Group
Branches: 3
FOREST CITY BRANCH, 531 Main St, Forest City, 18421-1421, SAN 358-7193. Tel: 570-785-5590. FAX: 570-785-4822. E-mail: fclib@nep.net. *Librn,* Lisa Spangenberg
Library Holdings: Bk Vols 14,802; Per Subs 57
Open Mon-Wed 9-1 & 2-5, Thurs 9-1 & 2-6, Fri 9-1
HALLSTEAD-GREAT BEND BRANCH LIBRARY, 135 Franklin Ave, Hallstead, 18822, SAN 314-5662. Tel: 570-879-2227. FAX: 570-879-0982. E-mail: hgp@susqcolibrary.org. *Librn,* Angie Hall
Founded 1917. Pop 6,000; Circ 24,631
Library Holdings: Bk Vols 9,089; Per Subs 36
Function: ILL available
Open Mon, Wed & Thurs 9-1 & 2-5, Tues 9-1 & 2-6, Fri 9-1
Friends of the Library Group
SUSQUEHANNA BRANCH, 83 Erie Blvd, Ste C, Susquehanna, 18847, SAN 358-7223. Tel: 570-853-4106. FAX: 570-853-3265. E-mail: sqbrlib@susqcolibrary.org. *Librn,* Laura Nichols
Circ 33,004
Library Holdings: Bk Vols 13,313; Per Subs 55
Open Mon-Wed 9-1 & 2-5, Thurs 9-1 & 2-6, Fri 9-1, Sat 10-1
Friends of the Library Group
Bookmobiles: 1. Librn, Mary Beth Manns

GL SUSQUEHANNA COUNTY LAW LIBRARY*, Court House, 31 Lake Ave, 18801. (Mail add: PO Box 218, 18801-0218), SAN 372-9044. Tel: 570-278-4600. *Dir,* Cathy Hawley; E-mail: chawley@susqco.com
Library Holdings: Bk Vols 12,500
Open Mon-Fri 9-4:30

MOON TOWNSHIP

S MICHAEL BAKER INTERNATIONAL LIBRARY*, 100 Airside Dr, 15108. SAN 314-3007. Tel: 724-495-4021. Toll Free Tel: 800-553-1153. E-mail: library@mbakerintl.com. *Librn,* Regina Hart; Staff 1 (MLS 1)
Founded 1972
Library Holdings: AV Mats 133; CDs 200; Electronic Media & Resources 500; Bk Titles 12,000; Per Subs 140
Subject Interests: Archit, Aviation, Civil, Construction, Design, Energy, Geospatial info tech, Govt, Planning, Railroads, Transportation, Urban develop, Water
Wireless access
Function: Bus archives, Doc delivery serv, Internet access, Ref serv available, Wheelchair accessible
Restriction: Employee & client use only, Open to pub upon request

P MOON TOWNSHIP PUBLIC LIBRARY*, 1700 Beaver Grade Rd, Ste 100, 15108. SAN 378-4231. Tel: 412-269-0334. FAX: 412-269-0136. E-mail: moontwp@einetwork.net. Web Site: www.moonlibrary.org. *Dir,* Anita Greene-Jones; E-mail: greenejonesa@einetwork.net; *Asst Dir, Pub Serv Librn,* Heather Panella; E-mail: panellah@einetwork.net; Staff 4 (MLS 4)
Pop 22,361; Circ 123,633
Library Holdings: Audiobooks 1,000; CDs 800; DVDs 3,000; Bk Vols 50,000; Per Subs 105
Automation Activity & Vendor Info: (Cataloging) Innovative Interfaces, Inc; (Circulation) Innovative Interfaces, Inc; (OPAC) Innovative Interfaces, Inc
Wireless access
Function: Adult bk club, Bks on CD, Chess club, Children's prog, Computer training, Computers for patron use, Electronic databases & coll, Free DVD rentals, Holiday prog, ILL available, Internet access, Magnifiers for reading, Music CDs, Online cat, Photocopying/Printing, Preschool outreach, Prog for adults, Prog for children & young adult, Ref & res, Ref serv available, Senior computer classes, Spoken cassettes & CDs, Spoken cassettes & DVDs, Story hour, Summer reading prog, Tax forms, Teen prog, Telephone ref, Wheelchair accessible
Mem of Allegheny County Library Association (ACLA)
Special Services for the Blind - Bks on CD; Large print bks; Magnifiers
Open Mon-Thurs 10-8, Fri 10-5, Sat 10-5 (10-3 Summer), Sun (Sept-June) 1-5
Friends of the Library Group

C ROBERT MORRIS UNIVERSITY LIBRARY, 6001 University Blvd, 15108-1189. SAN 358-3686. Tel: 412-397-6871. Circulation Tel: 412-397-6882. FAX: 412-397-4288. E-mail: library@rmu.edu. Web Site: sites.google.com/a/rmu.edu/rmu-library. *Dean, Univ Libr,* Tim Schlak; Tel: 412-397-6868, E-mail: schlak@rmu.edu; *Acq,* Emily Paladino; Tel: 412-397-6880, E-mail: paladino@rmu.edu; *Digital Initiatives, Metadata Librn,* Abiodum Ibraheem; Tel: 412-397-6875, E-mail: ibraheem@rmu.edu; *Syst Librn,* David B Bennett; Tel: 412-397-6870, E-mail: bennett@rmu.edu; Staff 18 (MLS 12, Non-MLS 6)
Founded 1962. Enrl 5,358; Fac 183; Highest Degree: Doctorate
Jun 2015-May 2016. Mats Exp $540,195, Books $116,913, Per/Ser (Incl. Access Fees) $119,808, AV Mat $1,030, Electronic Ref Mat (Incl. Access Fees) $302,444. Sal $774,975 (Prof $667,776)

Library Holdings: DVDs 2,615; e-books 130,000; e-journals 500; Bk Titles 87,233; Bk Vols 97,693; Per Subs 270; Videos 930
Automation Activity & Vendor Info: (Cataloging) OCLC; (Course Reserve) OCLC
Wireless access
Function: ILL available
Partic in LYRASIS; OCLC Online Computer Library Center, Inc; Partnership for Academic Library Collaborative & Innovation

MORGAN

P SOUTH FAYETTE TOWNSHIP LIBRARY*, 515 Millers Run Rd, 15064. (Mail add: PO Box 436, 15064). Tel: 412-257-8660. Interlibrary Loan Service Tel: 412-622-3114. FAX: 412-257-8682. E-mail: southfayette@einetwork.net. Web Site: southfayettelibrary.org. *Dir,* Ben Hornfeck; E-mail: hornfeckb@einetwork.net; *Asst Dir,* Erin Weaver; E-mail: weavere@einetwork.net; *Youth Serv Librn,* Nicole Harding; E-mail: hardingn@einetwork.net; Staff 4 (MLS 2, Non-MLS 2)
Founded 1994
Wireless access
Mem of Allegheny County Library Association (ACLA)
Open Mon-Thurs 10-8, Fri & Sat 10-5
Friends of the Library Group

MORGANTOWN

P VILLAGE LIBRARY OF MORGANTOWN*, 207 N Walnut St, 19543. (Mail add: PO Box 797, 19543-0797), SAN 314-7827. Tel: 610-286-1022. FAX: 610-286-1024. E-mail: village.library@villagelibrary.org. Web Site: www.villagelibrary.org. *Dir,* Natasha Donaldson; E-mail: natasha.donaldson@villagelibrary.org; *Ch,* Pam Mohl; E-mail: pam.mohl@villagelibrary.org; Staff 1 (MLS 1)
Founded 1965. Pop 9,216; Circ 78,886
Library Holdings: Per Subs 47
Special Collections: Small Business Coll
Wireless access
Function: 24/7 Electronic res, 24/7 Online cat, Activity rm, After school storytime, AV serv, Bks on cassette, Bks on CD, Children's prog, Computer training, Computers for patron use, Free DVD rentals, Holiday prog, ILL available, Life-long learning prog for all ages, Magazines, Magnifiers for reading, Online cat, Orientations, OverDrive digital audio bks, Photocopying/Printing, Prog for adults, Prog for children & young adult, Scanner, Senior outreach, Story hour, Summer reading prog, Tax forms, Teen prog, Wheelchair accessible, Workshops
Mem of Berks County Public Libraries
Special Services for the Deaf - Closed caption videos
Special Services for the Blind - Audio mat; Bks on cassette; Bks on CD; Large print bks; Magnifiers; Reader equip; Talking bks
Open Mon 9-7, Tues & Thurs 9-5, Wed 9-6, Fri 9-1, Sat 9-4

MORRISVILLE

P MORRISVILLE FREE LIBRARY ASSOCIATION*, 300 N Pennsylvania Ave, 19067-6621. SAN 314-7835. Tel: 215-295-4850. FAX: 267-799-4569. Web Site: www.morrisvillepagov.com/library. *Librn,* Diane Hughes; E-mail: hughesd@buckslib.org; Staff 5 (MLS 1, Non-MLS 4)
Founded 1904. Pop 10,023; Circ 36,911
Library Holdings: AV Mats 1,181; Large Print Bks 171; Bk Titles 26,791; Bk Vols 28,411; Per Subs 73; Talking Bks 265; Videos 391
Automation Activity & Vendor Info: (Cataloging) SirsiDynix; (Circulation) SirsiDynix
Wireless access
Mem of Bucks County Free Library
Open Mon-Thurs 11-8, Sat 10-5
Friends of the Library Group

MOSCOW

P NORTH POCONO PUBLIC LIBRARY, 1315 Church St, 18444. SAN 376-5717. Tel: 570-842-4700. FAX: 570-842-1304. Web Site: lclshome.org/b/north-pocono-public-library. *Dir,* Justine Yeager; E-mail: jyeager@albright.org; Staff 5 (MLS 1, Non-MLS 4)
Founded 1985. Pop 18,835; Circ 62,138
Library Holdings: Bk Titles 35,000; Per Subs 24
Automation Activity & Vendor Info: (Cataloging) Evergreen; (Circulation) Evergreen; (ILL) Evergreen; (OPAC) Evergreen
Wireless access
Mem of Lackawanna County Library System
Open Mon-Thurs 9-7, Fri & Sat 9-5
Friends of the Library Group

MOUNT CARMEL

P MOUNT CARMEL AREA PUBLIC LIBRARY*, 30 S Oak St, 17851-2185. SAN 314-7843. Tel: 570-339-0703. E-mail: mountcarmelpubliclibrary@ptd.net. Web Site: mountcarmelareapubliclibrary.com. *Librn,* Vivian McCracken
Founded 1961. Pop 12,832; Circ 50,000
Library Holdings: Bk Vols 54,000; Per Subs 90
Special Collections: Proceedings Northunderland County, Hist Soc, Local Hist Coll
Subject Interests: Handicrafts, World War II
Wireless access
Open Mon, Tues, Thurs & Fri 8-4, Wed 5-8, Sat 9-1

MOUNT HOLLY SPRINGS

P AMELIA S GIVIN FREE LIBRARY*, 114 N Baltimore Ave, 17065-1201. SAN 314-7851. Tel: 717-486-3688. FAX: 717-486-7170. E-mail: amelia@cumberlandcountylibraries.org. Web Site: www.cumberlandcountylibraries.org/drupal/AME. *Dir,* Cynthia Stratton-Thompson; Staff 5 (MLS 1, Non-MLS 4)
Founded 1889. Pop 9,421; Circ 61,112
Library Holdings: Bk Titles 27,991; Bk Vols 29,411; Per Subs 116; Talking Bks 943; Videos 1,287
Mem of Cumberland County Library System
Open Mon-Thurs 10-8, Fri 10-6, Sat 9-4

MOUNT JEWETT

P MOUNT JEWETT MEMORIAL LIBRARY*, Seven E Main St, 16740. (Mail add: PO Box Y, 16740), SAN 314-786X. Tel: 814-778-5588. FAX: 814-778-5588. E-mail: librarian@mtjewettlibrary.org. Web Site: www.mtjewettlibrary.org. *Dir,* Debbie Deane
Founded 1938. Pop 1,992; Circ 3,966
Library Holdings: Audiobooks 200; e-books 4,000; Bk Vols 16,842; Per Subs 12
Open Mon-Thurs 10-12, 2-5 & 6:30-8, Fri 10-12 & 2-5, Sat 10-2

MOUNT JOY

P MILANOF-SCHOCK LIBRARY, 1184 Anderson Ferry Rd, 17552. SAN 314-7878. Tel: 717-653-1510. FAX: 717-207-0504. E-mail: info@mountjoy.lib.pa.us. Web Site: www.mslibrary.org. *Dir,* Joseph McIlhenney; E-mail: jmcilhenney@mountjoy.lib.pa.us; *Coordr, Ch & Youth Serv,* Jan Betty; E-mail: jbetty@mountjoy.lib.pa.us; *Circ Coordr,* Susan Craine; *Commun Relations Coordr,* Kirstin Rhoads; *Adult Programming,* Kim Beach; E-mail: kbeach@mountjoy.lib.pa.us; Staff 5.7 (MLS 1, Non-MLS 4.7)
Founded 1964. Pop 25,442; Circ 211,148
Library Holdings: Audiobooks 3,290; DVDs 4,954; e-books 6; Large Print Bks 600; Bk Vols 35,881; Per Subs 72
Wireless access
Function: Adult bk club, Adult literacy prog, Bk club(s), Bks on cassette, Bks on CD, Chess club, Children's prog, Computer training, Computers for patron use, E-Reserves, Electronic databases & coll, Free DVD rentals, ILL available, Magnifiers for reading, Museum passes, Music CDs, Notary serv, Online cat, Online ref, Orientations, OverDrive digital audio bks, Passport agency, Photocopying/Printing, Preschool outreach, Prog for adults, Prog for children & young adult, Ref serv available, Senior computer classes, Summer reading prog, Tax forms, Teen prog, Telephone ref, VHS videos, Wheelchair accessible
Mem of Library System of Lancaster County
Open Mon-Thurs 10-8, Sat 9-4
Restriction: Authorized patrons, In-house use for visitors, Lending limited to county residents, Non-resident fee, Pub ref by request, Pub use on premises
Friends of the Library Group

MOUNT PLEASANT

P MOUNT PLEASANT FREE PUBLIC LIBRARY, 120 S Church St, 15666-1879. SAN 314-7886. Tel: 724-547-3850. FAX: 724-547-0324. E-mail: mountpleasant@wlnonline.org. Web Site: www.mountpleasantpalibrary.org. *Dir,* Heidi Leeper; Staff 5 (Non-MLS 5)
Founded 1938. Pop 15,000; Circ 30,000
Library Holdings: AV Mats 270; Large Print Bks 20; Bk Titles 24,700; Per Subs 70; Talking Bks 200
Special Collections: Math Coll; Teen Coll; Whiskey Rebellion
Automation Activity & Vendor Info: (Cataloging) Innovative Interfaces, Inc; (Circulation) Innovative Interfaces, Inc
Mem of Westmoreland County Federated Library System
Partic in Share Westmoreland Consortium
Open Mon-Thurs 10-8, Sat 9-4
Friends of the Library Group

MOUNTAIN TOP

P MARIAN SUTHERLAND KIRBY LIBRARY*, 35 Kirby Ave, 18707. SAN 376-5687. Tel: 570-474-9313. FAX: 570-474-2587. E-mail: info@kirbylib.org. Web Site: www.kirbylib.org. *Dir,* Allison Latagliata; Staff 5 (MLS 1, Non-MLS 4)
Library Holdings: Bk Titles 32,000; Per Subs 80
Wireless access
Mem of Luzerne County Library System
Partic in Pennsylvania Library Association
Open Tues & Wed 9-8:30, Thurs & Fri 9-5, Sat 9-4
Friends of the Library Group

MUNCY

S MUNCY HISTORICAL SOCIETY & MUSEUM OF HISTORY, Historical Library, 40 N Main St, 17756-1004. (Mail add: PO Box 11, 17756-0011), SAN 372-9060. Tel: 570-546-5917. E-mail: muncyhistorical@aol.com. Web Site: www.muncyhistoricalsociety.org.
Library Holdings: Bk Vols 800
Wireless access
Open Mon & Fri Noon-3
Friends of the Library Group

P MUNCY PUBLIC LIBRARY, 108 S Main St, 17756-0119. SAN 314-7916. Tel: 570-546-5014. FAX: 570-546-5014. E-mail: muncy@jvbrown.edu. Web Site: www.muncylibrary.com. *Dir,* Corey Breneisen; E-mail: cbreneisen@jvbrown.edu
Founded 1938. Pop 7,207; Circ 41,624
Library Holdings: AV Mats 1,025; CDs 500; DVDs 600; Large Print Bks 350; Bk Vols 26,000; Per Subs 42; Talking Bks 400; Videos 20
Special Collections: Luminary-Local Newspaper on Microfilm; Pennsylvania History, micro
Wireless access
Mem of Lycoming County Library System
Open Mon, Tues & Thurs 12-8, Wed, Fri & Sat 9-4
Friends of the Library Group

MUNHALL

P CARNEGIE LIBRARY OF HOMESTEAD*, 510 E Tenth Ave, 15120-1910. Tel: 412-462-3444. FAX: 412-462-4669. Web Site: carnegieofhomestead.org. *Dir,* Tara Zins; Staff 2 (MLS 1, Non-MLS 1)
Pop 19,368; Circ 22,350
Library Holdings: Large Print Bks 188; Bk Titles 48,919; Bk Vols 50,191; Per Subs 132; Talking Bks 903; Videos 657
Wireless access
Mem of Allegheny County Library Association (ACLA)
Open Mon-Thurs 10-7, Fri & Sat 10-5

MURRYSVILLE

P MURRYSVILLE COMMUNITY LIBRARY*, 4130 Sardis Rd, 15668. SAN 314-7924. Tel: 724-327-1102. FAX: 724-327-7142. E-mail: murrysville@wlnonline.org. Web Site: www.murrysvillelibrary.org. *Dir,* Ms Jamie Falo; E-mail: jamie.falo@wlnonline.org; *Coordr, Acq, Coordr, Tech Serv,* Susan Lyons; E-mail: susan.lyons@wlnonline.org; *Coordr, Youth Serv,* Carol Siefken; E-mail: carol.siefken@wlnonline.org; Staff 9 (MLS 2, Non-MLS 7)
Founded 1922. Pop 25,940; Circ 149,800
Library Holdings: AV Mats 4,280; Large Print Bks 1,080; Bk Vols 55,500; Per Subs 125
Subject Interests: Local newsp
Automation Activity & Vendor Info: (Acquisitions) Innovative Interfaces, Inc; (Cataloging) Innovative Interfaces, Inc; (Circulation) Innovative Interfaces, Inc; (ILL) Innovative Interfaces, Inc; (OPAC) Innovative Interfaces, Inc; (Serials) Innovative Interfaces, Inc
Wireless access
Mem of Westmoreland County Federated Library System
Open Mon-Wed 9-8:30, Thurs-Sat 9-5

MYERSTOWN

R EVANGELICAL SCHOOL OF THEOLOGY*, Rostad Library, 121 S College St, 17067-1299. SAN 314-7932. Tel: 717-866-5775. FAX: 717-866-4667. E-mail: rostad.library@evangelical.edu. Web Site: www.evangelical.edu/pense-center/rostad-library. *Librn,* Mark Draper; E-mail: mark.draper@evangelical.edu; *Asst Librn,* Julie Miller; E-mail: jmiller@evangelical.edu; Staff 1 (MLS 1)
Founded 1954. Enrl 200; Fac 9; Highest Degree: Master
Library Holdings: Bk Titles 73,490; Bk Vols 76,810; Per Subs 550
Special Collections: Evangelical Association; Evangelical Congregational Church Archives; Pietism
Subject Interests: Biblical studies
Automation Activity & Vendor Info: (Cataloging) TLC (The Library Corporation); (Circulation) TLC (The Library Corporation); (OPAC) TLC (The Library Corporation)
Wireless access
Function: Archival coll, ILL available, Internet access, Photocopying/Printing, Ref serv available
Partic in Southeastern Pennsylvania Theological Library Association

P MYERSTOWN COMMUNITY LIBRARY*, 199 N College St, 17067. (Mail add: PO Box 246, 17067-0246), SAN 314-7940. Tel: 717-866-2800. FAX: 717-866-5898. Web Site: myerstown.lclibs.org. *Dir,* Amy Davis; E-mail: adavis@lclibs.org; Staff 2 (MLS 1, Non-MLS 1)
Founded 1936. Pop 13,341; Circ 72,692
Library Holdings: AV Mats 1,918; Bk Vols 43,367; Per Subs 46
Subject Interests: Local counties, Local genealogies, Penn archives, Penn German Folklore Society, Penn hist
Automation Activity & Vendor Info: (Acquisitions) Baker & Taylor; (Cataloging) Innovative Interfaces, Inc; (Circulation) Innovative Interfaces, Inc; (OPAC) Innovative Interfaces, Inc
Wireless access
Mem of Lebanon County Library System
Open Mon, Wed & Thurs 12-8, Tues 12-6, Fri 9-5, Sat 9-4 (9-1 Summer)

NANTICOKE

J LUZERNE COUNTY COMMUNITY COLLEGE LIBRARY*, 1333 S Prospect St, 18634-3899. SAN 314-7959. Tel: 570-740-0415. Interlibrary Loan Service Tel: 570-740-0424. Reference Tel: 570-740-0661. Toll Free Tel: 800-377-5222, Ext 7415. FAX: 570-735-6130. Web Site: depts.luzerne.edu/library. *Libr Dir,* Katherine Cummings; Tel: 800-377-5222, Ext 7420, E-mail: kcummings@luzerne.edu; *Ref Librn,* Lori Shemanski; E-mail: lshemanski@luzerne.edu; Staff 3 (MLS 3)
Founded 1966. Enrl 3,633; Fac 138; Highest Degree: Associate
Jul 2017-Jun 2018 Income $541,484. Mats Exp $181,163, Books $60,155, Per/Ser (Incl. Access Fees) $11,508, Micro $13,800, AV Mat $14,000, Electronic Ref Mat (Incl. Access Fees) $80,000, Presv $1,700. Sal $130,522 (Prof $197,592)
Library Holdings: Audiobooks 618; AV Mats 2,363; Bks-By-Mail 120; CDs 461; DVDs 520; e-books 143,000; e-journals 2; Electronic Media & Resources 86; Microforms 12,123; Music Scores 406; Bk Titles 56,231; Bk Vols 63,838; Per Subs 96; Videos 772
Automation Activity & Vendor Info: (Acquisitions) SirsiDynix; (Cataloging) SirsiDynix; (Circulation) SirsiDynix; (Course Reserve) SirsiDynix; (ILL) OCLC; (OPAC) SirsiDynix; (Serials) SirsiDynix
Wireless access
Function: 24/7 Electronic res, 24/7 Online cat, Archival coll, Art exhibits, Audio & video playback equip for onsite use, Computers for patron use, Electronic databases & coll, ILL available, Internet access, Magazines, Meeting rooms, Online cat, Online ref, Orientations, Ref & res, Wheelchair accessible
Partic in LYRASIS; OCLC Online Computer Library Center, Inc
Open Mon-Thurs 8-7, Fri 8-5
Restriction: 24-hr pass syst for students only, Access at librarian's discretion, Borrowing requests are handled by ILL, Circ limited, Fee for pub use, Lending limited to county residents, Limited access for the pub

P MILL MEMORIAL LIBRARY*, 495 E Main St, 18634-1897. SAN 314-7967. Tel: 570-735-3030. FAX: 570-735-0340. Web Site: millmemoriallibrary.org. *Dir,* Jim Welch; E-mail: jwelch@luzernelibraries.org; Staff 5 (MLS 1, Non-MLS 4)
Founded 1945. Pop 22,803; Circ 43,910
Library Holdings: Audiobooks 400; DVDs 400; Bk Titles 30,000; Per Subs 43
Automation Activity & Vendor Info: (Cataloging) Innovative Interfaces, Inc; (Circulation) Innovative Interfaces, Inc; (ILL) Innovative Interfaces, Inc; (OPAC) Innovative Interfaces, Inc
Wireless access
Mem of Luzerne County Library System
Open Tues-Thurs 10-8, Fri & Sat 10-5
Friends of the Library Group

NANTY GLO

P NANTY GLO PUBLIC LIBRARY*, 942 Roberts St, 15943-0296. SAN 314-7975. Tel: 814-749-0111. FAX: 814-749-0111. E-mail: nantyglo@cclsys.org. Web Site: cclsys.org/nantyglo. *Librn,* Sharon Gallaher; *Asst Librn,* Janet Llewllyn
Founded 1962. Pop 10,000; Circ 25,000
Library Holdings: Bk Vols 28,000; Per Subs 40
Special Collections: Library of America
Subject Interests: Accelerated readers
Automation Activity & Vendor Info: (Cataloging) Follett Software; (Circulation) Follett Software
Wireless access
Mem of Cambria County Library System & District Center

Special Services for the Blind - Audio mat
Open Mon, Tues & Thurs 1-7, Wed 10-4, Fri 1-5, Sat 9-4 (9-1 Summer)
Friends of the Library Group

NARBERTH

P NARBERTH COMMUNITY LIBRARY*, 80 Windsor Ave, 19072-2296. SAN 314-7991. Tel: 610-664-2878. FAX: 610-667-3245. E-mail: narcirc1@mclinc.org. Web Site: narberthlibrary.org. *Dir,* Brad Ver Ploeg; E-mail: bploeg@mclinc.org; Staff 5.5 (MLS 1.5, Non-MLS 4)
Founded 1921. Pop 4,282; Circ 59,618
Library Holdings: AV Mats 1,420; Large Print Bks 600; Bk Vols 48,760; Per Subs 45
Special Collections: Pennsylvania & Philadelphia Area History (Pennsylvania Coll)
Automation Activity & Vendor Info: (Acquisitions) Innovative Interfaces, Inc; (Cataloging) Innovative Interfaces, Inc; (Circulation) Innovative Interfaces, Inc; (ILL) Innovative Interfaces, Inc; (OPAC) Innovative Interfaces, Inc
Wireless access
Function: Audiobks via web, Bks on cassette, Bks on CD, Children's prog, Computers for patron use, Electronic databases & coll, Free DVD rentals, ILL available, Mail & tel request accepted, Museum passes, Online cat, OverDrive digital audio bks, Photocopying/Printing, Preschool outreach, Prog for adults, Prog for children & young adult, Ref serv available, Story hour, Summer reading prog, Tax forms, Teen prog
Partic in Montgomery County Library & Information Network Consortium
Open Mon-Thurs (Sept-June) 10-8, Fri & Sat 10-5; Sat (July & Aug) 10-2

NATRONA HEIGHTS

M ALLEGHENY VALLEY HOSPITAL*, Medical Library, 1301 Carlisle St, 15065. Tel: 724-226-7092. FAX: 724-226-7303. *Librn,* Craig Arvid Jones
Library Holdings: Bk Vols 700; Per Subs 50
Subject Interests: Med
Function: ILL available
Open Mon-Fri 8:30-12:30

P COMMUNITY LIBRARY OF ALLEGHENY VALLEY*, Harrison Library, 1522 Broadview Blvd, 15065. SAN 378-1674. Tel: 724-226-3491. FAX: 724-226-3821. Web Site: alleghenyvalleylibrary.org. *Dir,* Kathy Firestone; E-mail: firestonek@einetwork.net; Staff 15 (MLS 2, Non-MLS 13)
Founded 1923. Pop 23,284; Circ 153,372
Library Holdings: Audiobooks 2,308; AV Mats 7,152; CDs 521; DVDs 1,150; e-books 24,568; Bk Vols 68,802; Per Subs 83
Automation Activity & Vendor Info: (Acquisitions) Innovative Interfaces, Inc; (Cataloging) Innovative Interfaces, Inc; (Circulation) Innovative Interfaces, Inc; (Course Reserve) Innovative Interfaces, Inc; (ILL) Innovative Interfaces, Inc; (OPAC) Innovative Interfaces, Inc; (Serials) Innovative Interfaces, Inc
Wireless access
Mem of Allegheny County Library Association (ACLA)
Open Mon-Thurs 11-8, Fri 10-3, Sat 9-4
Friends of the Library Group

NAZARETH

P MEMORIAL LIBRARY OF NAZARETH & VICINITY*, 295 E Center St, 18064. SAN 314-8009. Tel: 610-759-4932. FAX: 610-759-9513. E-mail: info@nazarethlibrary.org. Web Site: www.nazarethlibrary.org. *Dir,* Holly Bennett; E-mail: hbennett@nazarethlibrary.org; *Asst Dir, Head, Children's Servx,* Catherine Stewart; E-mail: cstewart@nzarethlibrary.org; Staff 10 (MLS 1, Non-MLS 9)
Founded 1949. Pop 22,690; Circ 139,000
Library Holdings: Audiobooks 1,559; e-books 2,087; Large Print Bks 350; Bk Titles 53,300; Bk Vols 58,764; Per Subs 103; Videos 1,818
Subject Interests: Genealogy, Hist
Automation Activity & Vendor Info: (Cataloging) TLC (The Library Corporation); (Circulation) TLC (The Library Corporation); (Course Reserve) TLC (The Library Corporation); (ILL) TLC (The Library Corporation); (Media Booking) TLC (The Library Corporation); (OPAC) TLC (The Library Corporation); (Serials) TLC (The Library Corporation)
Wireless access
Open Mon & Fri 10-5, Tues-Thurs 10-8, Sat 9-4 (9-1 July & Aug)
Friends of the Library Group

S THE MORAVIAN HISTORICAL SOCIETY, Museum & Library, 214 E Center St, 18064. SAN 374-552X. Tel: 610-759-5070. E-mail: info@moravianhistoricalsociety.org. Web Site: www.moravianhistoricalsociety.org. *Exec Dir,* Susan Ellis; *Curator,* Susan Orr; E-mail: sorr@moravianhistory.org
Founded 1857
Library Holdings: Bk Titles 5,000; Per Subs 10
Function: Res libr
Open Mon-Fri 1-4
Restriction: Not a lending libr

NEW ALEXANDRIA

P NEW ALEXANDRIA PUBLIC LIBRARY*, Keystone Plaza, Rte 22, 15670-9703. (Mail add: PO Box 405, 15670-0405), SAN 314-8025. Tel: 724-668-7747. Web Site: www.newalexlibrary.org. *Dir,* Jennifer Graham; E-mail: jenn.graham@wlnonline.org; Staff 1 (Non-MLS 1)
Founded 1921. Pop 742; Circ 1,081
Library Holdings: Bk Titles 8,462; Bk Vols 10,000; Per Subs 18
Wireless access
Mem of Westmoreland County Federated Library System
Open Mon-Wed 12-5, Thurs 1-6, Sat 10-1
Friends of the Library Group

NEW BETHLEHEM

P REDBANK VALLEY PUBLIC LIBRARY*, 720 Broad St, 16242-1107. SAN 314-8033. Tel: 814-275-2870. FAX: 814-275-2875. E-mail: newbethlehemlibrary@gmail.com. Web Site: www.rvlibrary.org. *Dir,* Janin Strohm; E-mail: newbethdirector@gmail.com; Staff 4 (MLS 1, Non-MLS 3)
Founded 1955. Pop 8,081; Circ 29,796
Library Holdings: AV Mats 800; Bks on Deafness & Sign Lang 35; CDs 230; DVDs 504; Large Print Bks 366; Bk Titles 23,898; Bk Vols 23,921; Per Subs 40; Talking Bks 344
Special Collections: Local Newspaper, microfilm
Automation Activity & Vendor Info: (Cataloging) TLC (The Library Corporation); (Circulation) TLC (The Library Corporation); (OPAC) TLC (The Library Corporation)
Wireless access
Function: Adult bk club, After school storytime, Bks on CD, Children's prog, Computer training, Computers for patron use, Free DVD rentals, Holiday prog, ILL available, Music CDs, Passport agency, Photocopying/Printing, Preschool outreach, Prog for adults, Prog for children & young adult, Story hour, Summer reading prog, Tax forms, Wheelchair accessible
Mem of Oil Creek District Library Center
Special Services for the Deaf - Bks on deafness & sign lang; Closed caption videos; Spec interest per
Special Services for the Blind - Audio mat; Bks on cassette; Bks on CD; Copier with enlargement capabilities; Extensive large print coll; Home delivery serv; Large print bks
Open Mon, Tues & Thurs 10-7, Wed & Fri 9-4, Sat 8-3

NEW BLOOMFIELD

P BLOOMFIELD PUBLIC LIBRARY*, 23 E McClure St, 17068. (Mail add: PO Box 558, 17068-0558). Tel: 717-582-7426. FAX: 717-582-0051. Circulation E-mail: bplcircdesk@gmail.com. Web Site: pecoinfo.org/library-hours/new-bloomfield. *Dir,* Julia McGuigan; E-mail: jmcguigan@gmail.com
Library Holdings: Bks on Deafness & Sign Lang 20; Bk Vols 17,000; Per Subs 25
Automation Activity & Vendor Info: (Cataloging) Follett Software; (Circulation) Follett Software
Wireless access
Open Mon & Fri 1-5, Tues & Thurs 2-7, Wed 9-7, Sat 9-4

L PERRY COUNTY LAW LIBRARY*, Perry County Courthouse, Center Sq, Two E Main St, 17068. (Mail add: PO Box 668, 17068-0668), SAN 372-9079. Tel: 717-582-5143. FAX: 717-582-5144. *Court Adminr,* Christina L Zook
Library Holdings: Bk Vols 100; Per Subs 100
Open Mon-Fri 8-4

S THE PERRY HISTORIANS, Harry W Lenig Library, 763 Dix Hill Rd, 17068. (Mail add: PO Box 73, Newport, 17074-0073), SAN 371-8336. Tel: 717-582-4896. E-mail: staff@theperryhistorians.org. Web Site: www.theperryhistorians.org. *Librn,* Donna Heller Zinn; E-mail: donna@theperryhistorians.org
Founded 1976
Library Holdings: Bk Titles 5,000; Per Subs 25
Special Collections: Court House Records; Land Surveys; Stoneware; Taufscheins
Subject Interests: Genealogy, Local hist
Publications: The Airy View (Newsletter); The Perry Review (Annual)
Open Wed 9-9

NEW BRIGHTON

P NEW BRIGHTON PUBLIC LIBRARY*, 1021 Third Ave, 15066-3011. SAN 314-8041. Tel: 724-846-7991. FAX: 724-846-7995. Web Site: www.beaverlibraries.org/newbrighton.asp. *Libr Dir,* Bernie McKean; E-mail: bmckean@beaverlibraries.org; Staff 1 (MLS 1)

Founded 1975. Pop 8,341; Circ 29,432
Library Holdings: Bk Titles 29,231; Bk Vols 30,908; Per Subs 34; Talking Bks 515; Videos 331
Function: 24/7 Electronic res, 24/7 Online cat, Activity rm, Adult bk club
Mem of Beaver County Library System
Open Tues-Thurs 11-7, Fri 11-5, Sat 9-4

NEW CASTLE

P LAWRENCE COUNTY FEDERATED LIBRARY SYSTEM*, 207 E North St, 16101-3691. Tel: 724-658-6659. FAX: 724-658-7209. Web Site: lawrencecountylibrary.org. *Admin,* Sandra Collins; Tel: 724-658-6659, Ext 113, E-mail: scollins@ncdlc.org; *Outreach Specialist,* Christina Gigliotti; Tel: 724-658-6659, Ext 110, E-mail: cgigliotti@ncdlc.org; Staff 45 (MLS 6, Non-MLS 39)
Founded 1998
Jan 2018-Dec 2018 Income $719,012, State $281,581, County $437,431, Other $564
Library Holdings: e-books 13,116; Bk Titles 110,000; Per Subs 240
Subject Interests: Genealogy
Automation Activity & Vendor Info: (Cataloging) Evergreen; (Circulation) Evergreen; (ILL) OCLC; (OPAC) Evergreen
Wireless access
Function: 24/7 Online cat, Prof lending libr, Ref serv available
Member Libraries: Ellwood City Area Public Library; Frank D Campbell Memorial Library; New Castle Public Library
Bookmobiles: 1. Outreach Spec, Christina Gigliotti. Bk vols 3,000

L LAWRENCE COUNTY LAW LIBRARY*, 430 Court St, 16101. SAN 328-0551. Tel: 724-656-2136. FAX: 724-658-4489. Web Site: co.lawrence.pa.us/courts/law-library. *Law Librn,* JoEllen Thomas; E-mail: jthomas@co.lawrence.pa.us; Staff 1 (MLS 1)
Library Holdings: CDs 15; Bk Vols 25,000; Per Subs 15
Special Collections: State Document Depository
Function: Res libr
Open Mon-Fri 8-4
Restriction: Not a lending libr

P NEW CASTLE PUBLIC LIBRARY, 207 E North St, 16101-3691. SAN 314-8068. Tel: 724-658-6659. FAX: 724-658-7209. Web Site: www.ncdlc.org. *Dir,* Sandra Collins; Tel: 724-658-6659, Ext 113, E-mail: scollins@ncdlc.org; *District Consult Librn,* Amy Geisinger; Tel: 724-658-6659, Ext 124, E-mail: ageisinger@ncdlc.org; *Mgr, Info Tech,* Ron Davis; Tel: 724-658-6659, Ext 130, E-mail: rdavis@ncdlc.org; *Circ Mgr,* Donna Maggie; Tel: 724-658-6659, Ext 107, E-mail: dmaggie@ncdlc.org; *Youth Serv Mgr,* Neva Lilla; Tel: 724-658-6659, Ext 106, E-mail: childrens_director@ncdlc.org; *YA Spec,* Sharon Savage; Tel: 724-658-6659, Ext 111, E-mail: ssavage@ncdlc.org; *Cat,* Jillian Larko; Tel: 724-658-6650, Ext 125, E-mail: jlarko@ncdlc.org; Staff 7 (MLS 6, Non-MLS 1)
Founded 1908. Pop 65,825; Circ 121,300
Jan 2019-Dec 2019. Mats Exp $69,883, Per/Ser (Incl. Access Fees) $4,664, Other Print Mats $1,600, Micro $3,731, AV Mat $4,888, Electronic Ref Mat (Incl. Access Fees) $55,000. Sal $525,492
Library Holdings: AV Mats 2,605; CDs 2,809; DVDs 3,105; e-books 7,796; Electronic Media & Resources 25; Microforms 11,696; Bk Vols 60,013; Per Subs 101
Special Collections: Architecture (Jane Jackson Coll), bks, microflm; Brotherhood (Joshua A Kaplan Coll); Gardening, Landscape (Wylie McCaslin Coll); Judaism (Council Corner Coll); Local History Coll; Pharmacy (Lawrence C Pharmaceutical Coll); Polish Culture (Polish Falcons Coll); Women's World (Federation Coll). State Document Depository; US Document Depository
Subject Interests: Hist
Automation Activity & Vendor Info: (Cataloging) Evergreen; (Circulation) Evergreen; (OPAC) Evergreen
Wireless access
Function: 24/7 Online cat, Adult bk club, Archival coll, Audiobks via web, Bks on CD, Children's prog, Computer training, Computers for patron use, E-Readers, Electronic databases & coll, Equip loans & repairs, Family literacy, Free DVD rentals, Holiday prog, Home delivery & serv to seniorr ctr & nursing homes, Homebound delivery serv, ILL available, Internet access, Large print keyboards, Life-long learning prog for all ages, Magazines, Mail & tel request accepted, Mango lang, Meeting rooms, Microfiche/film & reading machines, Movies, Music CDs, Online cat, Outreach serv, OverDrive digital audio bks, Photocopying/Printing, Preschool outreach, Preschool reading prog, Prog for adults, Prog for children & young adult, Ref & res, Scanner, Senior computer classes, Story hour, Summer reading prog, Tax forms, Teen prog, Telephone ref, Wheelchair accessible
Mem of Lawrence County Federated Library System
Open Mon-Thurs 8:30-8:30, Fri & Sat 8:30-5
Friends of the Library Group
Bookmobiles: 1

NEW CUMBERLAND

P NEW CUMBERLAND PUBLIC LIBRARY*, One Benjamin Plaza, 17070-1597. SAN 314-8084. Tel: 717-774-7820. FAX: 717-774-7824. E-mail: newcumberland@cumberlandcountylibraries.org. Web Site: www.cumberlandcountylibraries.org/NCU. *Dir,* Kate Pursel; E-mail: kpursel@ccpa.net; *Cat,* Denise Shellehamer; *Ch Serv,* Alana Bubnis; Staff 4 (MLS 1, Non-MLS 3)
Founded 1941. Pop 7,665; Circ 192,707
Library Holdings: Bk Titles 57,418; Bk Vols 59,861; Per Subs 131; Talking Bks 491; Videos 3,408
Subject Interests: Local hist
Automation Activity & Vendor Info: (OPAC) SirsiDynix
Wireless access
Mem of Cumberland County Library System
Open Mon-Thurs 10-8, Fri & Sat 10-5
Friends of the Library Group

NEW FLORENCE

P NEW FLORENCE COMMUNITY LIBRARY*, 122 Ligonier St, 15944. SAN 314-8092. Tel: 724-235-2249. FAX: 724-235-2249. E-mail: nflibrary@comcast.net. Web Site: www.newflorencelibrary.org. *Dir,* Margaret Betz; Staff 1 (Non-MLS 1)
Founded 1963. Pop 2,701; Circ 21,000
Library Holdings: Audiobooks 453; DVDs 1,054; Large Print Bks 2,000; Bk Titles 22,591; Bk Vols 23,486; Per Subs 10
Automation Activity & Vendor Info: (OPAC) Innovative Interfaces, Inc
Wireless access
Function: Bks on CD, Children's prog, Computers for patron use, Digital talking bks, Electronic databases & coll, Free DVD rentals, ILL available, Internet access, Magazines, Online cat, Online ref, Outreach serv, OverDrive digital audio bks, Photocopying/Printing, Prog for adults, Prog for children & young adult, Scanner, Story hour, Summer & winter reading prog, Tax forms, Wheelchair accessible
Mem of Westmoreland County Federated Library System
Open Mon & Wed 11-6, Tues 11-8, Thurs & Fri 11-4, Sat 10-5
Restriction: Access at librarian's discretion

NEW HOLLAND

P EASTERN LANCASTER COUNTY LIBRARY*, 11 Chestnut Dr, 17557-9437. SAN 314-8114. Tel: 717-354-0525. FAX: 717-354-7787. Web Site: www.elancolibrary.org. *Libr Dir,* Heather Smith; E-mail: hsmith@elancolibrary.org; Staff 13 (MLS 2, Non-MLS 11)
Pop 22,579; Circ 51,211
Library Holdings: Bk Titles 29,430; Bk Vols 32,611; Per Subs 71; Talking Bks 685; Videos 903
Automation Activity & Vendor Info: (Cataloging) Innovative Interfaces, Inc; (Circulation) Innovative Interfaces, Inc; (ILL) Innovative Interfaces, Inc; (OPAC) Innovative Interfaces, Inc; (Serials) Innovative Interfaces, Inc
Wireless access
Function: Adult bk club, Art exhibits, Audiobks via web, Bks on CD, Children's prog, Computers for patron use, Free DVD rentals, ILL available, Internet access, Magazines, Museum passes, Online cat, OverDrive digital audio bks, Photocopying/Printing, Preschool outreach, Preschool reading prog, Prog for adults, Prog for children & young adult, Story hour, Summer reading prog, Tax forms, Teen prog, VHS videos, Wheelchair accessible
Mem of Library System of Lancaster County
Friends of the Library Group

NEW HOPE

P FREE LIBRARY OF NEW HOPE & SOLEBURY*, 93 W Ferry St, 18938-1332. SAN 314-8122. Tel: 215-862-2330. E-mail: nhspubliclibrary@gmail.com. Web Site: www.nhslibrary.org. *Dir,* Connie Hillman; Staff 1 (MLS 1)
Founded 1894. Pop 9,995; Circ 45,479
Special Collections: New Hope Reference Coll; Performing & Fine Arts Coll
Subject Interests: Archit, Art
Wireless access
Function: Adult bk club, Audiobks via web, Bk club(s), Bks on cassette, Bks on CD, Computers for patron use, Homebound delivery serv, ILL available, Music CDs, Online cat, OverDrive digital audio bks, Photocopying/Printing, Preschool outreach, Prog for adults, Prog for children & young adult, Story hour, Summer reading prog, Tax forms, VHS videos
Mem of Bucks County Free Library
Open Mon-Wed 10-7, Thurs-Sat 10-5
Friends of the Library Group

NEW KENSINGTON

P PEOPLES LIBRARY, New Kensington, 880 Barnes St, 15068. SAN 358-7371. Tel: 724-339-1021. Circulation Tel: 724-339-1021, Ext 10. Interlibrary Loan Service Tel: 724-339-1021, Ext 13. FAX: 724-339-2027. Web Site: www.peopleslibrary.org. *Dir,* David Hrivnak; Tel: 724-339-1021, Ext 12, E-mail: david.hrivnak@wlnonline.org; Staff 15 (MLS 1, Non-MLS 14)
Founded 1928. Pop 46,312; Circ 92,207
Library Holdings: High Interest/Low Vocabulary Bk Vols 134; Bk Titles 35,851; Bk Vols 37,815; Per Subs 36
Subject Interests: Careers, Cookbks, Local hist, Westerns
Automation Activity & Vendor Info: (Acquisitions) Innovative Interfaces, Inc; (Cataloging) Innovative Interfaces, Inc; (Circulation) Innovative Interfaces, Inc; (OPAC) Innovative Interfaces, Inc
Wireless access
Publications: Library Newsletter
Mem of Westmoreland County Federated Library System
Partic in Monessen District Libr Ctr; Share Westmoreland Consortium
Open Mon & Wed 11-6, Tues, Thurs & Sat 9-4
Friends of the Library Group
Branches: 1
LOWER BURRELL, 3052 Wachter Ave, Lower Burrell, 15068, SAN 358-7401. Tel: 724-339-1565. Circulation Tel: 724-339-1565, Ext 10. FAX: 724-339-5132. *Br Mgr,* Andrea Helvling
Library Holdings: Bk Titles 25,251; Bk Vols 26,363
Open Tues & Thurs 1-8, Wed & Fri 9-4, Sat 10-2
Friends of the Library Group

NEW MILFORD

P PRATT MEMORIAL LIBRARY*, 752 Main St, 18834. (Mail add: PO Box 407, 18834), SAN 314-8157. Tel: 570-465-3098. E-mail: prattml@nep.net. *Librn,* Sally Carr
Founded 1903. Pop 3,000; Circ 4,285
Library Holdings: Bk Vols 9,396; Per Subs 23; Talking Bks 125
Wireless access
Open Mon & Sat 2-5, Wed 2-7, Fri 5-7

NEW WILMINGTON

C WESTMINSTER COLLEGE*, McGill Library, S Market St, 16172-0001. SAN 358-7436. Tel: 724-946-6000. Web Site: www.westminster.edu/academics/library. *Assoc Dean, Libr & Info Serv,* Erin T Smith; E-mail: smithet@westminster.edu; *Dir, User Serv,* Stanton Fleming; E-mail: feminsa@westminster.edu; *ILL Spec,* Connie C Davis; E-mail: daviscc@westminster.edu; Staff 4 (MLS 4)
Founded 1852. Enrl 1,350; Fac 100; Highest Degree: Master
Library Holdings: Bk Titles 228,421; Bk Vols 247,000; Per Subs 864
Special Collections: Autographed Books; Bibles in Foreign Languages; James Fenimore Cooper, early eds; K C Constantine, papers
Automation Activity & Vendor Info: (Cataloging) SirsiDynix; (Circulation) SirsiDynix; (OPAC) SirsiDynix
Wireless access
Publications: Friends of the Library Newsletter
Partic in OCLC Online Computer Library Center, Inc; Partnership for Academic Library Collaborative & Innovation; Proquest Dialog
Open Mon-Thurs 7:30am-1am, Fri 7:30am-9pm, Sat 9-5, Sun 1pm-1am
Friends of the Library Group

NEWFOUNDLAND

S CINEMA ARTS, INC*, Motion Picture Archives, 207 Lincoln Green Lane, 18445. (Mail add: PO Box 452, 18445-0452), SAN 323-7206. Tel: 570-676-4145, 570-676-4152. FAX: 570-676-9194. E-mail: jeainc@gmail.com. Web Site: www.allenarchive.com. *VPres,* Beverley Allen; *Acq,* Janice E Allen; *Tech Serv,* Mike Kolvek; Staff 6 (MLS 3, Non-MLS 3)
Founded 1987
Library Holdings: CDs 390; Bk Titles 10,141; Bk Vols 14,961; Per Subs 52; Videos 1,082
Special Collections: Kinograms & Telenews, reels; Posters; Silent Film Coll; Still Photographs
Subject Interests: Educ, Transportation, Travel, World War I, World War II
Restriction: Open by appt only

P NEWFOUNDLAND AREA PUBLIC LIBRARY, 954 Main St, 18445. (Mail add: PO Box 214, 18445-0214), SAN 314-8165. Tel: 570-676-4518. FAX: 570-676-4518. E-mail: napl@waynelibraries.org. Web Site: www.waynelibraries.org/newfoundland. *Dir,* Kristina Russo; E-mail: krusso@waynelibraries.org; *Asst Dir,* Joan Bancroft; E-mail: jbancroft@waynelibraries.org; Staff 3 (MLS 1, Non-MLS 2)
Founded 1967. Pop 4,500; Circ 10,870
Library Holdings: AV Mats 982; Large Print Bks 84; Bk Titles 14,011; Bk Vols 19,981; Per Subs 39; Talking Bks 154; Videos 269
Automation Activity & Vendor Info: (Cataloging) TLC (The Library Corporation); (Circulation) TLC (The Library Corporation)
Wireless access
Open Mon 3-6, Tues & Thurs 10-6, Wed & Fri 10-4, Sat 10-2
Friends of the Library Group

NEWPORT

P NEWPORT PUBLIC LIBRARY*, 316 N Fourth St, 17074-1203. SAN 314-8173. Tel: 717-567-6860. FAX: 717-567-3373. E-mail: nppublib@pa.net. Web Site: pecoinfo.org. *Libr Dir,* Jeanne Heicher; *Asst Dir,* Mary Jane Zentichko; *Ch Serv,* Cheryl Johnson; Staff 3 (Non-MLS 3)
Founded 1914. Pop 9,169
Wireless access
Function: 24/7 Electronic res, 24/7 Online cat, Art exhibits, Audiobks via web, Bks on CD, Computers for patron use, ILL available, Internet access, Laminating, Mail & tel request accepted, Meeting rooms, Music CDs, Online cat, OverDrive digital audio bks, Photocopying/Printing, Prog for children & young adult, Scanner, Story hour, Summer reading prog, Tax forms, Telephone ref, Wheelchair accessible
Open Mon, Wed & Fri 1-8, Tues, Thurs & Sat 10-6
Friends of the Library Group

NEWTOWN

J BUCKS COUNTY COMMUNITY COLLEGE LIBRARY*, 275 Swamp Rd, 18940-0999. SAN 314-8181. Tel: 215-968-8009. Interlibrary Loan Service Tel: 215-504-8555. Reference Tel: 215-968-8013. FAX: 215-968-8148. Web Site: www.bucks.edu/library. *Dir, Libr Serv,* Monica Kuna; Tel: 215-968-8003, E-mail: monica.kuna@bucks.edu; *Coll Mgt Librn,* Marzenna Ostrowski; Tel: 215-504-8619, E-mail: ostrowsk@bucks.edu; *Digital Res Librn,* Brian Johnstone; Tel: 215-504-8554, E-mail: johnston@bucks.edu; *Emerging Tech Librn,* Matthew Seibert; Tel: 215-968-8304, E-mail: seibert@bucks.edu; *Info Literacy Librn,* Margaret Montet; Tel: 215-968-8373, E-mail: montetm@bucks.edu; *New Media Librn,* Paul Proces; Tel: 215-497-8711, E-mail: procesp@bucks.edu; *Learning Tech Liaison,* Jacqueline Burger; Tel: 215-968-8056, E-mail: jacqueline.burger@bucks.edu; Staff 17 (MLS 10, Non-MLS 7)
Founded 1965. Enrl 8,747; Fac 200
Special Collections: US Document Depository
Automation Activity & Vendor Info: (Acquisitions) SirsiDynix; (Cataloging) SirsiDynix; (Circulation) SirsiDynix; (ILL) OCLC; (OPAC) SirsiDynix; (Serials) SirsiDynix
Wireless access
Partic in OCLC Online Computer Library Center, Inc; Pennsylvania Community College Library Consortium; Tri-State College Library Cooperative
Open Mon-Thurs 8am-9pm, Fri 8-3:30, Sat 9-Noon
Friends of the Library Group

S NEWTOWN HISTORIC ASSOCIATION, INC*, Research Center & Barnsley Room of Newtown History, 105 Court St, 18940. (Mail add: PO Box 303, 18940-0303), SAN 326-4289. Tel: 215-968-4004. E-mail: info@newtonhistoric.org. Web Site: www.newtownhistoric.org. *Curator,* Harriet Beckert; Staff 17 (Non-MLS 17)
Founded 1982
Library Holdings: CDs 50; DVDs 20; Bk Vols 1,800; Per Subs 30
Special Collections: Hicks Family (Edward Hicks Coll); New Century Club Records, 1890-present; Newtown (Barnsley Coll), clippings, original doc; Newtown Genealogy Coll; Newtown Records of Local Insurance Company 1831-1989; People & Places in Early Newtown, pictures & postcards; Reading Railroad; Reliance Company Records. Municipal Document Depository
Wireless access
Function: Bus archives, Electronic databases & coll, Mail & tel request accepted, Photocopying/Printing, Ref & res, Res libr
Publications: Half Moon (Newsletter)
Open Tues 9-2, Thurs 7pm-9pm
Restriction: Non-circulating to the pub, Not a lending libr, Open to fac, students & qualified researchers, Open to pub for ref only
Friends of the Library Group

P NEWTOWN LIBRARY CO*, 114 E Centre Ave, 18940. SAN 314-8203. Tel: 215-968-7659. E-mail: librarian@newtownlibrary.com. Web Site: newtownlibrarycompany.org. *Librn,* Karolyn Fisher
Founded 1760
Library Holdings: Bk Vols 21,135; Per Subs 30; Talking Bks 119
Special Collections: Civil War; Old Books for Children (19th Century); P& Local Area Coll; Revolutionary War Coll
Subject Interests: 19th Century, Penn hist
Wireless access
Publications: Newtown Borough Council; Newtown Library Under Two Kings; Newtown's First Library Building

Open Mon-Wed 10-5 & 6:30-8:30, Thurs & Fri 10-5, Sat 10-2:30
Friends of the Library Group

NEWTOWN SQUARE

P NEWTOWN PUBLIC LIBRARY*, 201 Bishop Hollow Rd, 19073. SAN 314-8211. Tel: 610-353-1022. FAX: 610-353-2611. E-mail: newtown@delcolibraries.org. Web Site: newtownlibrary.org. *Dir,* Arlene Caruso; E-mail: nedirector@delcolibraries.org; Staff 1 (MLS 1)
Founded 1974. Pop 11,940; Circ 56,000
Library Holdings: Bk Vols 55,000; Per Subs 90
Special Collections: Nedurian Law Coll
Wireless access
Mem of Delaware County Libraries
Open Mon-Thurs 10-7, Fri & Sat 10-5, Sun 1-5
Friends of the Library Group

NEWVILLE

P JOHN GRAHAM PUBLIC LIBRARY*, Nine Parsonage St, 17241-1399. SAN 314-822X. Tel: 717-776-5900. FAX: 717-776-4408. E-mail: johngraham@ccpa.net. Web Site: www.cumberlandcountylibraries.org/index.php/JGR. *Dir,* Mary Schoedel; E-mail: mschoedel@ccpa.net; Staff 7 (MLS 1, Non-MLS 6)
Founded 1960. Pop 11,115; Circ 62,811
Library Holdings: AV Mats 1,591; Bk Titles 26,811; Bk Vols 27,919; Per Subs 98; Talking Bks 418; Videos 601
Subject Interests: Genealogy, Penn, Relig
Automation Activity & Vendor Info: (Cataloging) Innovative Interfaces, Inc - Sierra; (Circulation) Innovative Interfaces, Inc - Sierra; (OPAC) Innovative Interfaces, Inc - Sierra
Wireless access
Mem of Cumberland County Library System
Open Mon, Tues, Thurs & Fri 10-8, Wed 10-5, Sat 10-2
Friends of the Library Group

NORRISTOWN

GL LAW LIBRARY OF MONTGOMERY COUNTY*, Court House, Two E Airy St, 19404. (Mail add: PO Box 311, 19404-0311), SAN 314-8254. Tel: 610-278-3806. FAX: 610-278-5998. Web Site: www.montcopa.org/325/Law-Library. *Dir, Law Librn,* Jeanne M Ottinger; Tel: 610-278-3806, E-mail: jottinge@montcopa.org; Staff 4 (MLS 3, Non-MLS 1)
Founded 1869
Library Holdings: Bk Vols 70,400; Per Subs 100
Automation Activity & Vendor Info: (Cataloging) Softlink America; (Circulation) Softlink America; (OPAC) Softlink America; (Serials) Softlink America
Open Mon-Fri 8:30-4:15

P MONTGOMERY COUNTY-NORRISTOWN PUBLIC LIBRARY*, 1001 Powell St, 19401-3817. SAN 358-7495. Tel: 610-278-5100. FAX: 610-277-0344. Web Site: mnl.mclinc.org. *Exec Dir,* Kathleen Arnold-Yerger; Tel: 610-278-5100, Ext 140, E-mail: karnold-yerger@mclinc.org; *Hed, Bkmobile Dept, Head, Outreach Serv,* Tom Fluharty; Tel: 610-278-5100, Ext 109; *Head, Circ,* Asha Verma; Tel: 610-278-5100, Ext 112; *Head, Ref,* Loretta Righter; Tel: 610-278-5100, Ext 116; *Head, Tech Serv,* Margaret Walk; Tel: 610-278-5100, Ext 118; *Supvr, ILL,* Valerie Johnson; Tel: 610-278-5100, Ext 121; Staff 92 (MLS 15, Non-MLS 77)
Founded 1794. Pop 313,167; Circ 653,179
Library Holdings: AV Mats 13,833; e-books 22,747; e-journals 3,300; Microforms 53,900; Bk Vols 485,520
Special Collections: Carolyn Wicker Field Coll (autographed children's books & correspondence from children's authors & illustrations); Old Fiction (before 1969-closed bookstacks); Pennsylvania (Steinbright Local History). State Document Depository; US Document Depository
Subject Interests: Penn hist
Automation Activity & Vendor Info: (Cataloging) Innovative Interfaces, Inc; (Circulation) Innovative Interfaces, Inc; (OPAC) Innovative Interfaces, Inc
Wireless access
Function: 24/7 Electronic res, 24/7 Online cat, Activity rm, Adult bk club, After school storytime, Archival coll, Audiobks on Playaways & MP3, Audiobks via web, Bk club(s), Bks on cassette, Bks on CD, Children's prog, Computer training, Computers for patron use, Digital talking bks, Distance learning, E-Readers, Electronic databases & coll, Holiday prog, Home delivery & serv to seniorr ctr & nursing homes, Homebound delivery serv, Homework prog, ILL available, Internet access, Life-long learning prog for all ages, Magazines, Mail & tel request accepted, Mango lang, Meeting rooms, Microfiche/film & reading machines, Movies, Music CDs, Online cat, Online info literacy tutorials on the web & in blackboard, Online ref, Outreach serv, OverDrive digital audio bks, Photocopying/Printing, Preschool outreach, Preschool reading prog, Prog for adults, Prog for children & young adult, Ref & res, Ref serv available, Serves people with intellectual disabilities, Spanish lang bks, Spoken cassettes & CDs, Spoken cassettes & DVDs, STEM programs, Story hour, Summer reading prog, Tax forms, Teen prog, Telephone ref, Wheelchair accessible
Partic in Interlibrary Delivery Service of Pennsylvania; Montgomery County Library & Information Network Consortium; OCLC Online Computer Library Center, Inc; OCLC, Inc through Palinet; Pa Area Libr Network
Special Services for the Deaf - Bks on deafness & sign lang; High interest/low vocabulary bks; Spec interest per
Open Mon-Thurs 9-8, Fri 9-6, Sat 9-5 (10-2 Summer)
Friends of the Library Group
Branches: 4
CONSHOHOCKEN FREE LIBRARY, 301 Fayette St, Conshohocken, 19428, SAN 358-7525. Tel: 610-825-1656. FAX: 610-825-1685. *Br Mgr,* Sydney Mason; E-mail: smason@mclinc.org; Staff 2 (MLS 1, Non-MLS 1)
Circ 46,146
Library Holdings: Bk Titles 21,011
Open Mon & Wed 12-9, Tues & Thurs 10-5, Fri 1-5, Sat 9-12
Friends of the Library Group
PERKIOMEN VALLEY, 290 Second St, Schwenksville, 19473, SAN 376-8074. Tel: 610-287-8360. FAX: 610-287-8360. *Br Mgr,* Aileen Johnson; E-mail: ajohnson@mclinc.org; Staff 1 (Non-MLS 1)
Founded 1930. Pop 33,000; Circ 81,105
Library Holdings: Bk Titles 31,151; Per Subs 27
Function: Adult bk club, After school storytime, Audiobks via web, Bk club(s), Bks on cassette, Bks on CD, Children's prog, Computers for patron use, Digital talking bks, E-Reserves, Electronic databases & coll, Free DVD rentals, Govt ref serv, Holiday prog, Home delivery & serv to seniorr ctr & nursing homes, Homebound delivery serv, ILL available, Internet access, Jail serv, Magnifiers for reading, Mail & tel request accepted, Mail loans to mem, Online cat, Online ref, Outreach serv, OverDrive digital audio bks, Photocopying/Printing, Prog for adults, Prog for children & young adult, Ref & res, Ref serv available, Spoken cassettes & CDs, Spoken cassettes & DVDs, Story hour, Summer reading prog, Tax forms, Teen prog, Telephone ref, Wheelchair accessible
Open Mon & Tues 10-8, Wed & Thurs 12-8, Fri 12-6, Sat 10-2
Friends of the Library Group
ROYERSFORD PUBLIC, 200 S Fourth Ave, Royersford, 19468, SAN 375-4758. Tel: 610-948-7277. FAX: 610-948-7277. *Br Mgr,* Eileen McNamara; E-mail: emcnamara@mclinc.org; Staff 1 (MLS 1)
Pop 31,211; Circ 150,011
Library Holdings: Bk Titles 52,830; Per Subs 46
Open Mon-Thurs 10-8, Fri & Sat 10-2
Friends of the Library Group
UPPER PERKIOMEN VALLEY, 350 Main St, Red Hill, 18076, SAN 358-755X. Tel: 215-679-2020. E-mail: upvlibrary@comcast.net. *Br Mgr,* Jeanne Cove; E-mail: jcove@mclinc.org; Staff 3 (Non-MLS 3)
Founded 1970. Pop 19,327; Circ 81,072
Library Holdings: Bk Vols 31,482; Per Subs 20
Open Mon-Thurs 10-8, Fri 10-5, Sat 10-2
Friends of the Library Group
Bookmobiles: 4. Head, Thomas Fluharty. Bk vols 485,520

S MONTGOMERY COUNTY PLANNING COMMISSION LIBRARY*, One Montgomery Plaza, 425 Swede St, 19401. SAN 314-8262. Tel: 610-278-3722. FAX: 610-278-3941. Web Site: planning.montcopa.org/planning/site/default.asp. *Adminr,* Robin McLean; Tel: 610-278-3726, E-mail: rmclean@montcopa.org; Staff 1 (Non-MLS 1)
Founded 1950
Library Holdings: Bk Titles 4,000; Per Subs 20
Special Collections: 1980 Census of Population & Housing (Computer; 1990 Census; Printouts; Subdivision Files: Maps & Correspondence, micro & flm
Subject Interests: Environ studies, Housing, Land use, Landscape archit, Recreation, Transportation planning
Wireless access
Open Mon-Fri 8:30-4:15

NORTH EAST

P MCCORD MEMORIAL LIBRARY*, 32 W Main St, 16428. SAN 314-8319. Tel: 814-725-4057. FAX: 814-725-3142. E-mail: mccord@ccfls.org. Web Site: www.mccordlibrary.org. *Dir,* Mary Kieffer; *Ch Serv,* Rae Lindsey; Staff 1 (MLS 1)
Founded 1899. Pop 11,214; Circ 79,000
Library Holdings: Bks on Deafness & Sign Lang 37; Bk Titles 32,000; Bk Vols 35,087; Per Subs 93; Spec Interest Per Sub 20
Subject Interests: Agr, Arts & crafts, Genealogy, Local hist, Quilting
Automation Activity & Vendor Info: (Cataloging) Infor Library & Information Solutions; (Circulation) Infor Library & Information Solutions; (OPAC) Infor Library & Information Solutions
Wireless access

Function: Adult literacy prog
Partic in Share NW Consortium
Open Mon-Thurs 10-8, Fri & Sat 10-5
Friends of the Library Group

NORTH VERSAILLES

P NORTH VERSAILLES PUBLIC LIBRARY, 1401 Greensburg Ave, 15227. SAN 314-8270. Tel: 412-823-2222. E-mail: nversailles@einetwork.net. Web Site: www.northversailleslibrary.org. *Dir,* Victoria Lingle; Staff 2 (MLS 1, Non-MLS 1)
Founded 1974. Pop 10,229; Circ 30,709
Library Holdings: Bk Titles 22,250; Bk Vols 24,312; Per Subs 59
Wireless access
Mem of Allegheny County Library Association (ACLA)
Open Mon-Sat 9-4
Friends of the Library Group

NORTH WALES

P NORTH WALES AREA LIBRARY*, 233 S Swartley St, 19454. SAN 314-8297. Tel: 215-699-5410. FAX: 215-699-5901. Web Site: www.northwaleslibrary.org. *Dir,* Jayne Blackledge; E-mail: jayne@northwaleslibrary.org
Founded 1923. Pop 18,781; Circ 114,736
Library Holdings: Audiobooks 983; DVDs 599; e-books 21,571; Large Print Bks 609; Bk Vols 48,842; Per Subs 88; Talking Bks 200; Videos 493
Subject Interests: Bks on CD
Automation Activity & Vendor Info: (Acquisitions) PALS
Wireless access
Function: 24/7 Electronic res, 24/7 Online cat, Activity rm, Adult bk club, Adult literacy prog, Bk club(s), Children's prog, Computers for patron use, E-Reserves, ILL available, Online cat, Photocopying/Printing, Prog for adults, Prog for children & young adult, Story hour, Summer reading prog, Teen prog, Wheelchair accessible, Workshops, Writing prog
Open Mon-Thurs 10-9, Fri 10-4, Sat 10-5
Friends of the Library Group

NORTHAMPTON

P NORTHAMPTON AREA PUBLIC LIBRARY*, 1615 Laubach Ave, 18067-1597. SAN 358-7673. Tel: 610-262-7537. FAX: 610-262-4356. E-mail: info@northamptonapl.org. Web Site: www.northamptonapl.org. *Dir,* Susan Sentz; E-mail: ssentz@northamptonapl.org; *Dir, Operations,* Karen Hein; E-mail: khein@northamptonapl.org; *Ch,* Cheryl DiGiacoma; E-mail: cdigiacoma@northamptonapl.org; Staff 2 (MLS 2)
Founded 1965. Pop 38,251; Circ 133,918
Library Holdings: CDs 3,611; DVDs 5,247; Large Print Bks 1,171; Bk Titles 53,004; Bk Vols 53,761; Per Subs 95; Talking Bks 1,233
Subject Interests: Local hist
Automation Activity & Vendor Info: (Acquisitions) TLC (The Library Corporation); (Cataloging) TLC (The Library Corporation); (Circulation) TLC (The Library Corporation)
Wireless access
Open Mon-Thurs 9-8, Sat 9-4
Friends of the Library Group

NORTHERN CAMBRIA

P NORTHERN CAMBRIA PUBLIC LIBRARY, 4200 Crawford Ave, 15714-1399. Tel: 814-948-8222. FAX: 814-948-2813. E-mail: ncambria@cclsys.org. Web Site: www.cclsys.org/ncambria. *Libr Dir,* Justin Brown; *Asst Dir,* Ayla Reinoehl; *Head, Children's Dept,* Karen Hall
Library Holdings: Bks on Deafness & Sign Lang 12; Bk Titles 15,858; Bk Vols 16,891; Per Subs 38
Automation Activity & Vendor Info: (Cataloging) Follett Software; (Circulation) Follett Software; (OPAC) Follett Software
Wireless access
Mem of Cambria County Library System & District Center
Open Mon-Wed 11-6, Thurs 9-4, Sat 9-1
Friends of the Library Group

NORTHUMBERLAND

P PRIESTLEY FORSYTH MEMORIAL LIBRARY*, 100 King St, 17857-1670. SAN 314-8327. Tel: 570-473-8201. FAX: 570-473-8807. E-mail: pfml@ptd.net. Web Site: www.priestleyforsyth.org. *Dir,* Jeff Johnstonbaugh; Staff 5 (MLS 1, Non-MLS 4)
Founded 1926. Pop 7,400; Circ 52,000
Library Holdings: Bk Vols 27,000; Per Subs 100
Special Collections: Joseph Priestley Coll
Subject Interests: Local hist
Automation Activity & Vendor Info: (Circulation) ComPanion Corp; (OPAC) ComPanion Corp
Friends of the Library Group

NORWOOD

P NORWOOD PUBLIC LIBRARY, 513 Welcome Ave, 19074. SAN 314-8335. Tel: 610-534-0693. FAX: 610-532-8785. E-mail: norwood@delcolibraries.org. Web Site: www.norwoodpubliclibrary.com. *Dir,* Eileen Baker; E-mail: nodirector@delcolibraries.org
Founded 1938. Pop 5,180; Circ 25,698
Library Holdings: Bk Vols 21,800; Per Subs 40
Automation Activity & Vendor Info: (Cataloging) Innovative Interfaces, Inc; (Circulation) Innovative Interfaces, Inc
Wireless access
Function: 24/7 Electronic res, 24/7 Online cat, Audiobks on Playaways & MP3, Audiobks via web, Bks on CD, Children's prog, Computers for patron use, Electronic databases & coll, Free DVD rentals, Homebound delivery serv, ILL available, Internet access, Magazines, Mail & tel request accepted, Museum passes, Music CDs, Online cat, Online ref, Outreach serv, OverDrive digital audio bks, Photocopying/Printing, Preschool outreach, Preschool reading prog, Printer for laptops & handheld devices, Prog for adults, Prog for children & young adult, STEM programs, Story hour, Summer & winter reading prog, Summer reading prog, Tax forms, Teen prog
Mem of Delaware County Libraries
Open Mon 11-6:30, Tues & Thurs 1-6:30, Wed 9:30-6:30, Sat 9-1:30

OAKDALE

J PITTSBURGH TECHNICAL COLLEGE*, Library Resource Center, 1111 McKee Rd, Pittsburgh Technical Library, 15071. SAN 315-0976. Tel: 412-809-5221. FAX: 412-809-5219. E-mail: library@ptcollege.edu. Web Site: www.ptcollege.edu. *Libr Coord,* Mary Fistler; E-mail: fistler.mary@ptcollege.edu; Staff 3 (MLS 1, Non-MLS 2)
Founded 1946. Enrl 2,100; Fac 91; Highest Degree: Associate
Library Holdings: Bk Titles 5,500; Bk Vols 7,500; Per Subs 170
Automation Activity & Vendor Info: (Acquisitions) Innovative Interfaces, Inc - Millennium; (Cataloging) Innovative Interfaces, Inc - Millennium; (Circulation) Innovative Interfaces, Inc; (Course Reserve) Innovative Interfaces, Inc - Millennium; (Media Booking) Innovative Interfaces, Inc - Millennium; (OPAC) Innovative Interfaces, Inc - Millennium; (Serials) Innovative Interfaces, Inc - Millennium
Wireless access
Partic in Health Sciences Libraries Consortium
Open Mon-Thurs 7am-7:30pm, Fri 7-5

P WESTERN ALLEGHENY COMMUNITY LIBRARY, 181 Bateman Rd, 15071-3906. SAN 370-730X. Tel: 724-695-8150. FAX: 724-695-2860. E-mail: westallegheny@einetwork.net. Web Site: westernalleghenylibrary.org. *Libr Dir,* Amy McDonald; E-mail: mcdonalda@einetwork.net; *Head, Libr Serv,* Heather Auman; E-mail: aumanh@einetwork.net; *Youth Serv Mgr,* Becky Proie; E-mail: proieb@einetwork.net; Staff 9 (MLS 4, Non-MLS 5)
Founded 1990. Pop 18,950; Circ 68,027
Library Holdings: AV Mats 1,994; CDs 225; DVDs 297; Large Print Bks 259; Bk Titles 31,467; Bk Vols 34,261; Per Subs 82; Talking Bks 852; Videos 620
Automation Activity & Vendor Info: (Cataloging) Innovative Interfaces, Inc; (Circulation) Innovative Interfaces, Inc; (OPAC) Innovative Interfaces, Inc; (Serials) Innovative Interfaces, Inc
Wireless access
Function: Prog for children & young adult, Ref serv available, Summer reading prog, Wheelchair accessible
Mem of Allegheny County Library Association (ACLA)
Partic in Electronic Info Network
Open Mon-Thurs 9-8, Fri & Sat 9-2, Sun (Sept-May) 1-5
Friends of the Library Group

OAKMONT

P OAKMONT CARNEGIE LIBRARY, 700 Allegheny River Blvd, 15139. SAN 314-8343. Tel: 412-828-9532. FAX: 412-828-5979. E-mail: oakmont@einetwork.net. Web Site: www.oakmontlibrary.org. *Dir,* Beth Ann Mellor; E-mail: mellorb1@einetwork.net; *Archivist/Ref Librn,* Stephanie Zimble; E-mail: zimbles@einetwork.net; *Youth Serv Librn,* Karen Crowell; E-mail: crowellk@einetwork.net; Staff 9 (MLS 2, Non-MLS 7)
Founded 1901. Pop 8,911; Circ 89,000
Library Holdings: CDs 228; DVDs 300; Large Print Bks 100; Bk Vols 38,000; Per Subs 55
Special Collections: Local Geneaology Coll; Local Newspaper (Advance Leader 1917-1945), micro; Local Photography Archive, digitized photog. Oral History
Automation Activity & Vendor Info: (Cataloging) Innovative Interfaces, Inc; (Circulation) Innovative Interfaces, Inc; (OPAC) Innovative Interfaces, Inc; (Serials) Innovative Interfaces, Inc - Sierra
Wireless access
Function: 24/7 Electronic res, 24/7 Online cat, Accelerated reader prog, Activity rm, Adult bk club, Adult literacy prog, Archival coll, Art exhibits

Art programs, Audiobks on Playaways & MP3, Audiobks via web, AV serv, Bk club(s), Bks on CD, CD-ROM, Children's prog, Citizenship assistance, Computer training, E-Reserves, Electronic databases & coll, Family literacy, Free DVD rentals, Games & aids for people with disabilities, Holiday prog, Home delivery & serv to seniorr ctr & nursing homes, Homebound delivery serv, ILL available, Instruction & testing, Internet access, Laminating, Life-long learning prog for all ages, Magazines, Mail & tel request accepted, Mango lang, Meeting rooms, Microfiche/film & reading machines, Movies, Museum passes, Music CDs, Online cat, Online info literacy tutorials on the web & in blackboard, Online ref, Orientations, Outreach serv, Outside serv via phone, mail, e-mail & web, OverDrive digital audio bks, Photocopying/Printing, Preschool outreach, Preschool reading prog, Printer for laptops & handheld devices, Prof lending libr, Prog for adults, Prog for children & young adult, Ref & res, Ref serv available, Res assist avail, Satellite serv, Scanner, Senior outreach, Serves people with intellectual disabilities, Spanish lang bks, STEM programs, Story hour, Study rm, Summer reading prog, Teen prog, Telephone ref, Visual arts prog, Wheelchair accessible, Workshops, Writing prog
Mem of Allegheny County Library Association (ACLA)
Partic in Electronic Info Network
Open Mon & Wed 10-4, Tues & Thurs 10-8, Fri 10-2, Sat 9-4
Restriction: Non-circulating coll
Friends of the Library Group

OIL CITY

P OIL CITY LIBRARY, Two Central Ave, 16301-2795. SAN 314-8378. Tel: 814-678-3072. FAX: 814-676-8028. Web Site: oilregionlibraries.org/locations/oil-city-library. *Dir,* Dan Flaherty; E-mail: director@oilregionlibraries.org; *Cataloger,* Natalie Cubbon; E-mail: ncubbon@oilregionlibraries.org; *Libr Asst,* Kathy Lynch; *Teen Serv,* Daidre Green; E-mail: dgreen@oilregionlibraries.org; Staff 10 (MLS 3, Non-MLS 7)
Founded 1904. Pop 15,206; Circ 153,159
Library Holdings: AV Mats 152; DVDs 800; Large Print Bks 3,000; Bk Vols 103,000; Per Subs 250; Talking Bks 2,000; Videos 3,500
Special Collections: Genealogy (Selden Coll). State Document Depository
Subject Interests: Hist of oil
Automation Activity & Vendor Info: (Cataloging) TLC (The Library Corporation); (Circulation) TLC (The Library Corporation); (OPAC) TLC (The Library Corporation)
Mem of Oil Creek District Library Center
Open Mon-Wed 8:30-8:30, Thurs & Fri 8:30-5, Sat 9-3
Friends of the Library Group

P OIL CREEK DISTRICT LIBRARY CENTER*, Two Central Ave, 16301. Tel: 814-499-1772. FAX: 814-676-0359. Web Site: oilcreek.org. *Adminr,* Dan Flaherty; Tel: 814-678-3071, E-mail: director@oilregionlibraries.org; *ILL Serv,* Debbie Wilson; Tel: 814-678-3054, E-mail: districtloan@oilcitylibrary.org
Wireless access
Member Libraries: Clarion Free Library; Cooperstown Public Library; Eccles-Lesher Memorial Library; Foxburg Free Library; Franklin Public Library; Knox Public Library; Mengle Memorial Library; Oil City Library; Punxsutawney Memorial Library; Rebecca M Arthurs Memorial Library; Redbank Valley Public Library; Reynoldsville Public Library; Summerville Public Library; Sykesville Public Library

C VENANGO COLLEGE OF CLARION UNIVERSITY OF PENNSYLVANIA*, Charles L Suhr Library, 1801 W First St, 16301. SAN 314-836X. Tel: 814-676-6591. Toll Free Tel: 877-836-2646. Web Site: www.clarion.edu/locations/clarion-university-venango/charles_l_suhr_library/index.html. *Dean of Libr,* Terry Latour; *Library Services,* Brenda Sturtz; Tel: 814-393-1244, E-mail: sturtz@clarion.edu; *Library Services,* Sylvia Wiegel; Tel: 814-393-1246, E-mail: swiegel@clarion.edu; Staff 3 (MLS 1, Non-MLS 2)
Founded 1961. Enrl 809; Fac 63; Highest Degree: Master
Library Holdings: Bk Titles 45,691; Bk Vols 48,715; Per Subs 182
Special Collections: Barbara Morgan Harvey Center for the Study of Oil Heritage
Subject Interests: Nursing, Paralegal
Automation Activity & Vendor Info: (Acquisitions) Ex Libris Group; (Cataloging) Ex Libris Group; (Circulation) Ex Libris Group; (Course Reserve) Ex Libris Group; (ILL) OCLC; (Media Booking) Ex Libris Group; (OPAC) Ex Libris Group; (Serials) Ex Libris Group
Wireless access
Open Mon-Thurs 8-8, Fri 8-4

ORANGEVILLE

ORANGEVILLE PUBLIC LIBRARY*, 301 Mill St, 17859-0177. (Mail add: PO Box 268, 17859-0268). Tel: 570-683-5354. E-mail: orangevillelibrary@pa.metrocast.net. Web Site: www.orangevillelibrary.org. *Librn,* Pamela Simpson; *Asst Librn,* Rachel Ford
Founded 1927
Library Holdings: Audiobooks 736; DVDs 1,182; Large Print Bks 180; Bk Titles 14,220; Videos 642
Special Collections: Local Hist (Orangeville, Columbia County, Pennsylvania); Military Fiction; Military Hist
Automation Activity & Vendor Info: (Cataloging) ComPanion Corp; (Circulation) ComPanion Corp; (OPAC) ComPanion Corp
Wireless access
Function: Adult bk club, Bks on cassette, Bks on CD, Children's prog, Computers for patron use, Free DVD rentals, Internet access, Magazines, Photocopying/Printing, Preschool reading prog, Prog for adults, Story hour, Summer reading prog, Wheelchair accessible
Open Mon-Thurs 2-7, Sat 9-Noon

ORWIGSBURG

S ACOPIAN CENTER FOR CONSERVATION LEARNING*, Hawk Mountain Sanctuary Library, 410 Summer Valley Rd, 17961. SAN 375-3638. Tel: 570-943-3411, Ext 101. FAX: 570-943-2284. Web Site: www.hawkmountain.org. *Dir of Educ,* Jamie Dawson; E-mail: dawson@hawkmountain.org; Staff 2 (MLS 1, Non-MLS 1)
Founded 1934
Library Holdings: Bk Titles 5,350; Bk Vols 6,110; Per Subs 61; Videos 72
Special Collections: Oral History
Function: Res libr
Restriction: Mem only, Not a lending libr, Open by appt only, Open to students

P ORWIGSBURG AREA FREE PUBLIC LIBRARY*, 216 E Independent St, 17961-2304. SAN 320-5061. Tel: 570-366-1638. FAX: 570-366-5414. E-mail: orwigsburglibrary@comcast.net. Web Site: www.orwigsburglibrary.org. *Librn,* Claudia Gross; Staff 2 (Non-MLS 2)
Founded 1978. Pop 12,000; Circ 21,000
Library Holdings: Bk Vols 20,000; Per Subs 41
Automation Activity & Vendor Info: (Cataloging) Follett Software; (Circulation) Follett Software; (OPAC) Follett Software
Wireless access
Open Mon-Thurs 10-7, Fri 10-5, Sat 9-4

OXFORD

P OXFORD PUBLIC LIBRARY*, 48 S Second St, 19363-1377. SAN 314-8394. Tel: 610-932-9625. FAX: 610-932-9251. Web Site: oxfordpubliclibrary.org. *Dir,* Carey Bresler; E-mail: cbresler@ccls.org; *Ch Serv Librn,* Faith Dopirak; *Circ Supvr,* Linda Teel; Staff 3 (MLS 1, Non-MLS 2)
Founded 1784. Pop 21,000; Circ 130,000
Library Holdings: AV Mats 2,147; CDs 200; DVDs 950; Large Print Bks 88; Bk Titles 39,410; Bk Vols 40,678; Per Subs 97; Talking Bks 1,027; Videos 388
Special Collections: Local History (Holcombe Coll)
Automation Activity & Vendor Info: (Cataloging) Innovative Interfaces, Inc; (Circulation) Innovative Interfaces, Inc
Wireless access
Function: Adult bk club, Adult literacy prog, After school storytime, Art exhibits, Chess club, Digital talking bks, E-Reserves, Electronic databases & coll, Family literacy, Home delivery & serv to seniorr ctr & nursing homes, Homebound delivery serv, Homework prog, ILL available, Internet access, Magnifiers for reading, Mail & tel request accepted, Music CDs, Online ref, Orientations, Photocopying/Printing, Prog for adults, Prog for children & young adult, Ref & res, Spoken cassettes & CDs, Spoken cassettes & DVDs, Summer reading prog, Telephone ref, VHS videos, Wheelchair accessible, Workshops
Mem of Chester County Library System
Open Mon, Wed & Thurs 9-8, Tues Noon-8, Fri 9-5, Sat 9-4
Friends of the Library Group

PALMERTON

P PALMERTON AREA LIBRARY ASSOCIATION*, 402 Delaware Ave, 18071. SAN 314-8416. Tel: 610-826-3424. FAX: 610-826-6248. E-mail: plapalm@ptd.net. Web Site: www.palmertonarealibrary.com. *Dir,* Diane M Danielson; Staff 1 (Non-MLS 1)
Founded 1928. Pop 12,300; Circ 37,000
Library Holdings: CDs 369; DVDs 225; Music Scores 35; Bk Vols 40,000; Per Subs 55; Talking Bks 1,525; Videos 2,789
Subject Interests: Local hist, Penn hist
Wireless access
Function: Adult bk club, Audiobks via web, Bks on cassette, Bks on CD, Children's prog, Computers for patron use, Free DVD rentals, ILL available, Internet access, Mail & tel request accepted, Music CDs, Online cat, Photocopying/Printing, Senior computer classes, Story hour, Summer reading prog, Tax forms, Teen prog, VHS videos, Wheelchair accessible
Partic in Lehigh Carbon Library Cooperative

Open Mon & Tues 10-8, Wed, Thurs & Fri 10-5, Sat 9-4
Friends of the Library Group

PAOLI

M MAIN LINE HEALTH, PAOLI HOSPITAL*, Robert M White Memorial Library, 255 W Lancaster Ave, 19301. SAN 314-8467. Tel: 484-565-1570. FAX: 484-565-1551. *Librn,* Sarah Hodkinson; Tel: 484-565-1409
Founded 1970
Library Holdings: Bk Titles 800; Per Subs 80
Subject Interests: Allied health, Med, Nursing
Wireless access
Publications: Newsletter
Partic in Basic Health Sciences Library Network; National Network of Libraries of Medicine Region 1
Open Mon & Fri 9-1, Tues & Thurs 9-5

PARKESBURG

P PARKESBURG FREE LIBRARY*, 105 West St, 19365-1499. SAN 314-8475. Tel: 610-857-5165. FAX: 610-857-1193. E-mail: contact@parkesburglibrary.org. Web Site: www.parkesburglibrary.org. *Dir,* Thomas Knecht; E-mail: tknecht@ccls.org; Staff 2 (MLS 1, Non-MLS 1)
Founded 1916. Pop 4,711; Circ 76,394
Library Holdings: DVDs 1,000; Large Print Bks 188; Bk Titles 27,191; Bk Vols 28,420; Per Subs 59; Talking Bks 755; Videos 1,454
Special Collections: Local Historical Files
Automation Activity & Vendor Info: (Circulation) Innovative Interfaces, Inc
Wireless access
Mem of Chester County Library System
Open Mon & Thurs 10-5, Tues & Wed 10-7, Fri 10-4, Sat 9-4 (9-1 Summer)

PATTON

P PATTON PUBLIC LIBRARY*, 444 Magee Ave, 16668-1210. SAN 314-8483. Tel: 814-674-8231. FAX: 814-674-6188. E-mail: patton@cclsys.org. Web Site: www.cclsys.org/patton. *Librn,* Monica Burkhart
Founded 1962. Pop 2,484; Circ 28,920
Library Holdings: Audiobooks 275; DVDs 500; e-books 400; Large Print Bks 643; Microforms 45; Bk Titles 17,365; Per Subs 24; Videos 525
Automation Activity & Vendor Info: (Cataloging) Innovative Interfaces, Inc - Millennium; (Circulation) Innovative Interfaces, Inc - Millennium; (OPAC) Innovative Interfaces, Inc - Millennium
Wireless access
Mem of Cambria County Library System & District Center
Open Mon-Thurs 10-7, Fri & Sat 10-5 (10-2 Summer)
Friends of the Library Group

PECKVILLE

P VALLEY COMMUNITY LIBRARY*, 739 River St, 18452. SAN 328-0578. Tel: 570-489-1765. Web Site: lclshome.org/b/valley-community-library. *Libr Dir,* Michelle Georgetti; E-mail: mgeorgetti@albright.org; *Youth Serv Dir,* Liz Kluesner; E-mail: lkluesner@albright.org; *Head, Circ,* Garren Levi; E-mail: glevi@albright.org; *Ad,* Michelle Georgetti; E-mail: mgeorgetti@albright.org; Staff 6 (MLS 3, Non-MLS 3)
Founded 1985. Pop 33,000; Circ 124,687
Library Holdings: AV Mats 4,790; Bk Vols 32,158; Per Subs 52; Talking Bks 1,840
Special Collections: Joseph McDonald Pearl Harbor Transcripts; Medal of Honor Recipent Gino Merli Memorabilia
Subject Interests: Lackawana County hist, Local hist
Automation Activity & Vendor Info: (Circulation) SirsiDynix
Mem of Lackawanna County Library System
Open Mon-Thurs 10-8, Fri & Sat 10-5
Friends of the Library Group

PENN VALLEY

SR HAR ZION TEMPLE*, Ida & Matthew Rudofker Library, 1500 Hagys Ford Rd, 19072. SAN 327-8662. Tel: 610-667-5000. FAX: 610-667-2032. E-mail: hzt@harziontemple.org. Web Site: www.harziontemple.org. *Librn,* Bill Moody
Library Holdings: Bk Vols 9,000; Per Subs 23
Open Mon-Thurs 3:30-6, Sun 9-1

PENNSBURG

S SCHWENKFELDER LIBRARY & HERITAGE CENTER*, 105 Seminary St, 18073. SAN 314-8491. Tel: 215-679-3103. FAX: 215-679-8175. E-mail: info@schwenkfelder.com. Web Site: www.schwenkfelder.com. *Exec Dir,* Beth A Twiss Houting; Tel: 215-679-3103, Ext 11, E-mail: beth@schwenkfelder.com; *Assoc Dir, Research,* Allen L Viehmeyer; Tel: 215-679-3103, Ext 17, E-mail: allen@schwenkfelder.com; *Archivist,* Hunt Schenkel; Tel: 215-679-3103, Ext 13, E-mail: hunt@schwenkfelder.com; *Curator,* Candace Perry; Tel: 215-679-3103, Ext 12, E-mail: candace@schwenkfelder.com; Staff 5 (Non-MLS 5)
Founded 1884. Pop 20,000
Library Holdings: Bk Titles 25,000
Special Collections: Montgomery County History, bks, ms; Reformation Coll; Schwenkfelder History & Theology, bks, ms; Silesian History Coll
Subject Interests: Hist
Wireless access
Function: Archival coll, Res libr
Open Tues, Wed & Fri 9-4, Thurs 9-8, Sat 10-3, Sun 1-4
Restriction: Non-circulating
Friends of the Library Group

PERRYOPOLIS

P MARY FULLER FRAZIER SCHOOL COMMUNITY LIBRARY*, 142 Constitution St, 15473. SAN 314-8513. Tel: 724-736-8480. FAX: 724-736-8481. E-mail: library.frazier@gmail.com. Web Site: fraziercommunitylibrary.webs.com, perryopolis.com/frazierlibrary. *Librn,* Valerie Madorma; Staff 2 (MLS 2)
Founded 1960. Pop 2,573; Circ 18,000
Library Holdings: Bk Titles 26,114; Bk Vols 28,911; Per Subs 44
Subject Interests: Fayette County hist
Open Mon & Wed 2:30-8, Tues & Thurs 2:30-6, Sat 9-12 (Winter); Mon & Wed 4:30-8, Sat 9-12 (Summer)

PHILADELPHIA

S ACADEMY OF NATURAL SCIENCES OF DREXEL UNIVERSITY*, Ewell Sale Stewart Library & Archives, 1900 Benjamin Franklin Pkwy, 19103-1195. SAN 314-8521. Tel: 215-299-1040. FAX: 215-299-1144. E-mail: archives@ansp.org, library@ansp.org. Web Site: www.ansp.org/research/library. *Dir, Libr & Archives,* Ted Daeschler, PhD; Staff 4 (MLS 3, Non-MLS 1)
Founded 1812
Library Holdings: Bk Titles 250,000
Special Collections: Entomology (Library of the American Entomological Society); Manuscripts (Academy History & Archives); Photograph Coll; Portrait & Drawing Coll; Pre-Linnaean Coll
Subject Interests: Botany, Entomology, Environ res, Evolution, Exploration, Hist of sci, Limnology, Malacology, Ornithology, Systematic biol, Zoology
Automation Activity & Vendor Info: (Acquisitions) Innovative Interfaces, Inc; (Cataloging) Innovative Interfaces, Inc; (OPAC) Innovative Interfaces, Inc; (Serials) Innovative Interfaces, Inc
Function: Archival coll, Art exhibits, Electronic databases & coll, ILL available, Photocopying/Printing, Res libr, Res performed for a fee
Publications: Guide to Microfilm Publication of Academy Minutes & Correspondence; Guide to the Manuscripts Collections of ANSP; Library Catalog; Serial Titles; Wolf Room Rare Book Collection Checklist
Partic in LYRASIS; OCLC Online Computer Library Center, Inc; Philadelphia Area Consortium of Special Collections Libraries
Restriction: Open by appt only, Restricted borrowing privileges
Friends of the Library Group

L AMERICAN LAW INSTITUTE LIBRARY*, 4025 Chestnut St, 19104. SAN 314-8556. Tel: 215-243-1627. Toll Free Tel: 800-253-6397. FAX: 215-243-1636. E-mail: library@ali.org. Web Site: www.ali.org. *Dir,* Richard L Revesz; E-mail: director@ali.org; *Exec Ed,* Marianne M Walker; E-mail: mwalker@ali.org; Staff 1 (MLS 1)
Founded 1965
Library Holdings: Bk Vols 5,500; Per Subs 30
Special Collections: ALI Publications, microfiche; ALI-ABA Materials & Periodicals
Subject Interests: Law

S AMERICAN PHILOSOPHICAL SOCIETY LIBRARY*, 105 S Fifth St, 19106-3386. SAN 314-8564. Tel: 215-440-3400. FAX: 215-440-3423. Reference E-mail: reference@amphilsoc.org. Web Site: www.amphilsoc.org. *Dir & Librn,* Dr Patrick Spero; Tel: 215-440-3403, E-mail: librarian@amphilsoc.org; *Assoc Dir, Coll,* David Gary; E-mail: dgary@amphilsoc.org; *Assoc Librn, Curator of Ms,* Charles B Greifenstein; E-mail: cgreifenstein@amphilsoc.org; *Asst Librn, Head Cataloger,* Marian Christ; E-mail: mchrist@amphilsoc.org; *Head, Conserv,* Anne Downey; E-mail: adowney@amphilsoc.org; *Head, MS Processing,* Valerie-Anne Lutz; E-mail: vlutz@amphilsoc.org; *Asst Head, Cat,* Estelle Markel-Joyet; E-mail: emarkel-joyet@amphilsoc.org; *Asst Head of MS Processing & Library Registrar,* Michael P Miller; *Archivist,* Ann Reinhardt; E-mail: areinhardt@amphilsoc.org; *Curator,* Brian Carpenter; E-mail: bcarpenter@amphilsoc.org. Subject Specialists: *Early Am hist,* Dr Patrick Spero; *Native American,* Brian Carpenter; Staff 20 (MLS 10, Non-MLS 10
Founded 1743

Library Holdings: Bk Titles 275,000; Per Subs 75
Special Collections: American Indian Linguistics (Franz Boas et al Coll); Benjamin Franklin & his Circle; Medical Research (Simon Flexner et al Coll); Stephen Girard Papers, film; Thomas Jefferson
Subject Interests: Am hist to 1840, Biochem, Darwin, Electricity, European background, Evolution, Genetics, Hist of sci in Am, Lewis & Clark expedition, Modern physics, Paleontology, Polar exploration, Quantum physics, Thomas Paine
Wireless access
Publications: Annual Report of the Committee on Library; Mendel Newsletter
Partic in OCLC Research Library Partnership
Open Mon-Fri 9-4:30
Friends of the Library Group

S AMERICAN SWEDISH HISTORICAL MUSEUM LIBRARY, 1900 Pattison Ave, 19145. SAN 314-8580. Tel: 215-389-1776. FAX: 215-389-7701. E-mail: info@americanswedish.org. Web Site: www.americanswedish.org. *Exec Dir,* Tracey Rae Beck; E-mail: tbeck@americanswedish.org
Founded 1926
Library Holdings: Bk Titles 5,000; Per Subs 30
Special Collections: Fredrika Bremer Coll; Jenny Lind Coll; John Ericsson Coll
Subject Interests: Genealogy, Original correspondence, Scandinavian hist, Swedish hist, Swedish-Am hist
Function: Res libr
Publications: Newsletter
Open Tues-Fri 10-4, Sat & Sun 12-4
Restriction: Non-circulating

ARIA HEALTH
M HEALTH SCIENCES LIBRARIES*, Red Lion & Knights Rds, 19114-1436, SAN 324-6302. Tel: 215-612-4135, 215-831-2182. FAX: 215-612-4946. *Dir, Libr Serv,* Gary Jay Christopher; Tel: 215-949-5160, Fax: 215-949-7821, E-mail: gchristopher@ariahealth.org; Staff 3 (Non-MLS 3)
Founded 1950
Library Holdings: Bk Titles 5,121; Bk Vols 5,560; Per Subs 412
Subject Interests: Allied health, Consumer health, Nursing
Function: Prof lending libr
Partic in Basic Health Sciences Library Network; DEVIC
Restriction: Open to pub upon request, Staff use only

M SCHOOL OF NURSING LIBRARY*, Three Neshaminy Interflex, Trevose, 19053, SAN 324-7481. Tel: 215-710-3510, Ext 23523. FAX: 215-710-3543. *Librn,* Sophia Kim; E-mail: skim@ariahealth.org; Staff 1 (MLS 1)
Library Holdings: Bk Vols 2,500; Per Subs 89
Subject Interests: Nursing
Automation Activity & Vendor Info: (Serials) EBSCO Online
Function: Doc delivery serv, ILL available
Partic in DEVIC; National Network of Libraries of Medicine Region 1
Restriction: Access at librarian's discretion, Access for corporate affiliates, Authorized scholars by appt, By permission only, Internal circ only, Open by appt only, Open to fac, students & qualified researchers, Open to pub for ref only, Open to pub upon request, Open to pub with supv only, Open to students, fac & staff, Prof mat only, Pub ref by request

S ATHENAEUM OF PHILADELPHIA, East Washington Sq, 219 S Sixth St, 19106-3794. SAN 314-8610. Tel: 215-925-2688. E-mail: events@athenaonline.org. Web Site: https://www.philageohistory.org/geohistory/, www.philaathenaeum.org, www.philadelphiabuildings.org. *Exec Dir,* Beth Hessel; E-mail: bhessel@PhilaAthenaeum.org; *Dir,* Michael Seneca; E-mail: mseneca@philaathenaeum.org; *Librn,* Jill LeMin Lee; E-mail: jilly@philaathenaeum.org; *Access Serv Librn, Resource Description Mgr,* Lois Reibach; E-mail: lreibach@athenaonline.org; *Curator of Archit,* Bruce Laverty; E-mail: laverty@philaathenaeum.org. Subject Specialists: *Archives, Digital presv,* Michael Seneca; *Bk illustr & design, Genealogy, Rare bks,* Jill LeMin Lee; *Archit, City hist,* Bruce Laverty; Staff 4.5 (MLS 1.5, Non-MLS 3)
Founded 1814
Library Holdings: DVDs 162; e-books 800; Microforms 943; Bk Vols 70,000
Special Collections: Architectural Drawings; Architecture & Design, 1814-1940; Historic Photographs; History of Books, 16th to 20th centuries (Turner Coll)
Subject Interests: Archit, Bk illustr & design, Local hist, Manuscripts
Automation Activity & Vendor Info: (Cataloging) Ex Libris Group; (Circulation) Ex Libris Group; (OPAC) Ex Libris Group
Wireless access
Function: Archival coll, Art exhibits, Bks on CD, Electronic databases & coll, Internet access, Mail loans to mem, Online cat, Prog for adults, Ref & res, Res libr, Scanner
Publications: Athenaeum Newsletter (Online only)
Partic in OCLC Online Computer Library Center, Inc; Philadelphia Area Consortium of Special Collections Libraries
Open Mon,Tues & Thurs 9-4, Wed 10-4, Fri 9-2
Restriction: Circ to mem only, In-house use for visitors, Non-circulating of rare bks, Researchers by appt only

L BALLARD, SPAHR LLP LIBRARY, 1735 Market St, 51st Flr, 19103-7599. SAN 314-8645. Tel: 215-864-8150. FAX: 215-864-8999. *Dir, Research & Intelligence,* John Harbison; E-mail: harbisonj@ballardspahr.com; *Operations Mgr,* Eugenie Tyburski; E-mail: tyburski@ballardspahr.com; Staff 6 (MLS 4, Non-MLS 2)
Library Holdings: Bk Vols 5,000; Per Subs 300
Subject Interests: Law
Automation Activity & Vendor Info: (Circulation) EOS International; (OPAC) EOS International
Wireless access

L THE BEASLEY FIRM, LLC*, Law Library, 1125 Walnut St, 19107. SAN 372-9095. Tel: 215 592-1000. Web Site: www.beasleyfirm.com. *Research Coordr,* Joel Tuckmsn
Restriction: Not open to pub

R CATHOLIC HISTORICAL RESEARCH CENTER OF THE ARCHDIOCESE OF PHILADELPHIA*, Archives & Historical Collections, 6740 Roosevelt Blvd, 19149. SAN 359-0941. Tel: 215-904-8149. E-mail: archives@chrc-phila.org. Web Site: www.chrc-phila.org. *Dir,* Leslie O'Neill; *Curator of Ms, Rec Mgr,* Shawn Weldon; *Asst Archivist,* Patrick Shank
Library Holdings: Bk Vols 8,000
Special Collections: American Catholic Newspapers (19th Century) Religious American Coll; Catechism Coll; Popular Piety Coll
Subject Interests: Archives, Relig
Wireless access
Partic in Philadelphia Area Consortium of Special Collections Libraries
Restriction: Open to pub for ref only

CR CHESTNUT HILL COLLEGE*, Logue Library, 9601 Germantown Ave, 19118-2695. SAN 314-8769. Tel: 215-248-7050. FAX: 215-248-7056. E-mail: librarians@chc.edu. Web Site: library.chc.edu. *Dean of Libr,* Mary Jo Larkin; Tel: 215-248-7055, E-mail: mjlarkin@chc.edu; *Access Serv Librn,* Gail Cathey; Tel: 215-248-7053, E-mail: gcathy@chc.edu; *Circ,* Marian Ehnow; Tel: 215-248-7052, E-mail: methnow@chc.edu; Staff 8 (MLS 5, Non-MLS 3)
Founded 1924. Highest Degree: Doctorate
Library Holdings: Bk Titles 141,260; Bk Vols 144,910; Per Subs 543
Special Collections: Catholic Church Music (Montani Coll); Irish History & Literature Coll
Subject Interests: Educ, Liberal arts, Relig studies
Automation Activity & Vendor Info: (Acquisitions) SirsiDynix; (Cataloging) SirsiDynix; (Circulation) SirsiDynix; (ILL) SirsiDynix; (OPAC) SirsiDynix; (Serials) SirsiDynix
Wireless access
Partic in SEPCHE; Tri-State College Library Cooperative
Open Mon-Thurs 8am-Midnight, Fri 8am-9pm, Sat 9-5, Sun Noon-Midnight

S COLLEGE OF PHYSICIANS OF PHILADELPHIA*, Historical Medical Library, 19 S 22nd St, 19103. SAN 358-7762. Tel: 215-399-2301. FAX: 215-561-6477. E-mail: library@collegeofphysicians.org. Web Site: www.collegeofphysicians.org/library. *Dir,* Robert Hicks; E-mail: rhicks@collegeofphysicians.org; *Col Librn,* Beth Lander; Tel: 215-399-2304, E-mail: blander@collegeofphysicians.org; *Digital Projects Librn,* Tristan Dahn; Tel: 215-399-2307, E-mail: tdahn@collegeofphysicians.org; *Coll, Mgt Librn,* Mary Hanes; E-mail: mhanes@collegeofphysicians.org; *Ref Librn,* Caitlin Angelone; Tel: 215-399-2001, E-mail: cangelone@collegeofphysicians.org; *Archivist,* Christina Perella; Tel: 215-399-3102, E-mail: cperella@collegeofphysicians.org; Staff 5 (MLS 5)
Founded 1788
Library Holdings: Bk Titles 170,000; Bk Vols 350,000; Per Subs 12
Special Collections: Archives of the College of Physicians; Early Printed Books in Medicine, incunables; Gerontology (Joseph T Freeman Coll); Helfand-Radbill Medical Bookplate Coll; Medical Autograph Coll; Medical Portraits Coll; Otto & Gisela Fleischmann Psychoanalytic Coll; Sadoff Library of Forensic Psychiatry & Legal Medicine; Samuel Gross Library of Surgery; Samuel Lewis Curio Coll; Samuel X Radbill Pediatric Historical Library; William Harvey Coll
Subject Interests: Hist of med
Automation Activity & Vendor Info: (Cataloging) SirsiDynix-WorkFlows; (Circulation) SirsiDynix-WorkFlows; (ILL) OCLC; (OPAC) SirsiDynix-Enterprise
Wireless access

Function: Archival coll, Bus archives, Doc delivery serv, For res purposes, ILL available, Online cat, Ref & res, Res libr
Partic in OCLC Online Computer Library Center, Inc; Philadelphia Area Consortium of Special Collections Libraries
Restriction: Authorized patrons, Closed stack, In-house use for visitors, Internal circ only, Open by appt only, Open to pub by appt only, Photo ID required for access, Researchers by appt only, Restricted access
Friends of the Library Group

J COMMUNITY COLLEGE OF PHILADELPHIA LIBRARY*, Mint Bldg, Level 1, 1700 Spring Garden St, 19130. SAN 314-9730. Tel: 215-751-8394. Circulation Tel: 215-751-8383. FAX: 215-751-8762. Web Site: www.myccp.online/library. *Access Serv, Dept Chair,* Michael Krasulski; Tel: 215-751-8397, E-mail: mkrasulski@ccp.edu; *Ref Librn,* Jaroslaw Fedorijczuk; E-mail: jfedorijczuk@ccp.edu; *Electronic Res,* Jalyn Warren; E-mail: jwarren@ccp.edu; *Ref,* Nicole Duncan-Kinard; Tel: 215-751-8407, E-mail: nkinard@ccp.edu; *Ser,* Nicole Karam; Tel: 215-751-8388, E-mail: nkaram@ccp.edu; *Tech Serv,* Jessica Rossi; E-mail: jrossi@ccp.edu; Staff 21 (MLS 10, Non-MLS 11)
Founded 1964. Enrl 22,691; Highest Degree: Associate
Library Holdings: Bk Vols 100,000; Per Subs 300
Automation Activity & Vendor Info: (Acquisitions) Innovative Interfaces, Inc; (Cataloging) Innovative Interfaces, Inc; (Circulation) Innovative Interfaces, Inc; (ILL) OCLC; (OPAC) Innovative Interfaces, Inc; (Serials) Innovative Interfaces, Inc
Wireless access
Partic in LYRASIS
Open Mon-Thurs (Fall-Spring) 7:30am-10pm, Fri 7:30-5, Sat 8-3; Mon-Thurs (Summer) 7:30am-9pm
Restriction: Open to students, fac & staff, Photo ID required for access
Departmental Libraries:
NORTHEAST REGIONAL CENTER LEARNING COMMONS, 12901 Townsend Rd, Rm 127, 19154. Tel: 215-972-6270. *Librn,* Carol Jewett
Open Mon-Thurs (Fall-Spring) 8:30-8, Fri 8:30-5, Sat 10-3; Mon-Thurs (Summer) 8:30-8
NORTHWEST REGIONAL CENTER LIBRARY, 1300 W Godfrey Ave, Rm 117, 19141. Tel: 215-496-6019. *Librn,* Jacquelyn A Bryant
Open Mon-Thurs (Fall-Spring) 8:30-8, Fri 8:30-5, Sat 10-3; Mon-Thurs (Summer) 8:30-8
WEST REGIONAL CENTER LEARNING COMMONS, 4725 Chestnut St, Rm 160, 19139. Tel: 215-299-5848. *Librn,* Michele Belluomini
Open Mon-Thurs (Fall-Spring) 10-2 & 4:30-8, Sat 10-3

GM CORPORAL MICHAEL J CRESCENZ VA MEDICAL CENTER*, Library Service (142D), 3900 Woodland Ave, 19104. SAN 359-2472. Tel: 215-823-5860. FAX: 215-823-5108. E-mail: vhaphilibrarystaff@va.gov. *Chief,* Karla C Kaufman; *Med Librn,* Helena Washington; Staff 2 (MLS 2)
Subject Interests: Behav health, Clinical med, Healthcare mgt, Nursing, Patient educ
Automation Activity & Vendor Info: (Cataloging) CyberTools for Libraries; (Circulation) CyberTools for Libraries; (OPAC) CyberTools for Libraries; (Serials) CyberTools for Libraries
Function: Doc delivery serv, Health sci info serv, ILL available, Ref & res
Publications: New Books (Quarterly); Special Interest Bibliographies
Partic in DEVIC; Veterans Affairs Library Network
Open Mon-Fri 7:30-4:30
Restriction: Lending to staff only, Staff & patient use

L COZEN O'CONNOR*, Law Library, 1650 Market St, Ste 2800, 19103. SAN 372-1965. Tel: 215-665-2000. Interlibrary Loan Service Tel: 215-665-4748. Reference Tel: 215-665-2083. FAX: 215-665-2013. Web Site: www.cozen.com. *Dir, Libr Serv,* Loretta F Orndorff; Tel: 215-665-2136; *Dir, Bus & Legal Intelligence, Dir, Res,* Jill M Poretta; Tel: 215-665-4709, E-mail: jporetta@cozen.com; Staff 10 (MLS 8, Non-MLS 2)
Library Holdings: Bk Titles 6,261
Subject Interests: Legal
Automation Activity & Vendor Info: (Cataloging) Inmagic, Inc.; (OPAC) Inmagic, Inc.; (Serials) Inmagic, Inc.
Partic in Greater Philadelphia Law Library Association
Open Mon-Fri 9-5

S CRITICAL PATH LEARNING CENTER*, AIDS Library, 1233 Locust St, 2nd Flr, 19107. (Mail add: 1233 Locust St, 5th Flr, 19107), SAN 370-7601. Tel: 215-985-4851. FAX: 215-985-4492. TDD: 215-985-0458. E-mail: library@fight.org. Web Site: critpath.org. *Dir,* Caitlin Pratt; E-mail: cpratt@fight.org; *Client Serv Librn, Computer Instrul Serv Librn, Pub Serv,* Sarah Rich; *Coll Mgt Librn,* Allie Fraser; Staff 5 (MLS 2, Non-MLS 3)
Founded 1987
Library Holdings: Bk Titles 2,710; Bk Vols 5,423; Per Subs 131
Function: Adult literacy prog, Art programs, Audio & video playback equip for onsite use, BA reader (adult literacy), Bk club(s), Computer training, Computers for patron use, For res purposes, Health sci info serv, Homebound delivery serv, Instruction & testing, Internet access, Learning ctr, Magazines, Outside serv via phone, mail, e-mail & web, Photocopying/Printing, Prog for adults, Ref serv available, Res libr, Scanner, Telephone ref, VHS videos, Wheelchair accessible, Workshops
Special Services for the Deaf - TDD equip
Open Mon-Fri 1-5

S CURTIS INSTITUTE OF MUSIC*, John de Lancie Library, 1720 Locust St, 19103. (Mail add: 1726 Locust St, 19103), SAN 314-8831. Tel: 215-893-5265. Circulation Tel: 215-717-3156. Administration Tel: 215-717-3121. FAX: 215-717-3170. E-mail: library@curtis.edu. Web Site: www.curtis.edu/academics/library. *Asst Dean,* Emily Waters; Tel: 215-717-3123, E-mail: emily.waters@curtis.edu; *Media Librn, Metadata Librn,* Pete Williams; Tel: 215-717-3147, E-mail: peter.williams@curtis.edu; *Circ Mgr,* Darryl Hartshorne; E-mail: darryl.hartshorne@curtis.edu; *Archivist,* Kristina Wilson; Tel: 215-717-3148, E-mail: kristina.wilson@curtis.edu; *Digital Archivist,* Barbara Benedett; Tel: 215-717-3139, E-mail: barbara.benedett@curtis.edu; Staff 6.3 (MLS 5, Non-MLS 1.3)
Founded 1926. Enrl 163; Fac 107; Highest Degree: Master
Library Holdings: AV Mats 12,041; CDs 18,236; DVDs 1,231; Electronic Media & Resources 3,322; Music Scores 54,523; Bk Titles 7,184; Bk Vols 9,797; Per Subs 70; Videos 1,184
Special Collections: Music Scores
Subject Interests: Music
Automation Activity & Vendor Info: (Cataloging) Innovative Interfaces, Inc; (Circulation) Innovative Interfaces, Inc; (Course Reserve) Innovative Interfaces, Inc; (ILL) OCLC Online; (OPAC) Innovative Interfaces, Inc
Wireless access
Function: 24/7 Electronic res, 24/7 Online cat, Archival coll, Audio & video playback equip for onsite use, Computers for patron use, E-Reserves, Electronic databases & coll, ILL available, Music CDs, Online cat, Photocopying/Printing, Ref & res, Ref serv available, Scanner
Partic in LYRASIS; Philadelphia Area Consortium of Special Collections Libraries
Restriction: Not open to pub, Open to researchers by request, Open to students, fac & staff

S EDWARD M DAVID RESEARCH LIBRARY*, Woodmere Art Museum, 9201 Germantown Ave, 19118. SAN 325-2191. Tel: 215-247-0948. FAX: 215-247-2387. Web Site: www.woodmereartmuseum.org.
Founded 1981
Library Holdings: Bk Titles 2,310; Bk Vols 2,570; Per Subs 16
Special Collections: American 19th Century (Charles Knox Smith Coll), paintings; Philadelphia 20th Century (Woodmere Coll), paintings
Subject Interests: Philadelphia artists
Automation Activity & Vendor Info: (Cataloging) TLC (The Library Corporation); (Circulation) TLC (The Library Corporation)
Undergoing transition (renovation) thru 2019
Restriction: Circ limited, Not open to pub

L DECHERT LLP*, Law Library, Cira Ctr, 2929 Arch St, 19104. SAN 314-8858. Tel: 215-994-4000. FAX: 215-994-2222. Web Site: www.dechert.com. *Library Contact,* Russell Rokicki; E-mail: russell.rokicki@dechert.com; Staff 3 (MLS 3)
Subject Interests: Law
Automation Activity & Vendor Info: (Acquisitions) EOS International; (Cataloging) EOS International; (Circulation) EOS International; (OPAC) EOS International; (Serials) EOS International
Restriction: Staff use only

DREXEL UNIVERSITY LIBRARIES
C HAGERTY LIBRARY*, 33rd & Market Sts, 19104-2875. (Mail add: 3141 Chestnut St, 19104-2875), SAN 314-8912. Tel: 215-895-2750. Circulation Tel: 215-895-2767. Interlibrary Loan Service Tel: 215-895-2769. Reference Tel: 215-895-2755. Toll Free Tel: 888-278-8825. FAX: 215-895-2070. Web Site: www.library.drexel.edu. *Dean, Univ Libr,* Danuta Nitecki; E-mail: dan44@drexel.edu; *Dir, Libr Acad Partnerships,* Elizabeth Ten Have; Tel: 215-895-2751, E-mail: elizabeth.tenhave@drexel.edu; *Dir, Libr Admin Serv,* Lenore Hardy; Tel: 215-895-2758, E-mail: hardy@drexel.edu; *Dir, Libr Serv & Quality Improvement,* John W Wiggins; Tel: 215-895-2773, E-mail: jww@drexel.edu; *Head, Access Serv,* Deirdre Childs; Tel: 215-895-6785, E-mail: dparker@drexel.edu; *Head, Libr Syst,* Peter Ivanick; Tel: 215-895-2090; *Electronic Res Librn,* Noelle Egan; Tel: 215-895-2752, E-mail: nme26@drexel.edu; *Emerging Tech Librn,* Rebekah Kilzer; Tel: 215-895-6783, E-mail: rdk26@drexel.edu; *Ref Librn,* Jay Bhatt; Tel: 215-895-1873, E-mail: bhattjj@drexel.edu; *Ref Librn,* Peggy Dominy; Tel: 215-895-2754, Fax: 215-895-6950, E-mail: dominymf@drexel.edu; *Ref Librn,* Ann Keith Kennedy; Tel: 215-895-2772, E-mail: ann.keith.kennedy@drexel.edu; *Ref Librn,* Larry Milliken; Tel: 215-895-2765, E-mail: larry.milliken@drexel.edu; *Ref Librn,* Emily Missner; Tel: 215-895-6164, E-mail: edm25@drexel.edu; *Ref Librn,* Tim Siftar; Tel: 215-895-2762, E-mail: siftar@drexel.edu; *Evening Ref Librn,* Nancy Bellafante; *Evening Ref Librn,* Steven Bogel; *Evening/Weekend Ref Librn,* Amy Kwasnicki; *Evening/Weekend Ref Librn,* Nancy Thorne;

Evening/Weekend Ref Librn, Katelyn Wolfrom; *Evening/Weekend Supvr,* Joshua Fore; *Evening/Weekend Supvr,* Jimenez Oreste; *Univ Archivist,* Robert Sieczkiewicz; Tel: 215-895-1757, E-mail: robs@drexel.edu; *Webmaster,* Katherine Lynch; Tel: 215-895-1344, E-mail: klynch@drexel.edu. Subject Specialists: *Engr,* Jay Bhatt; *Math, Sciences,* Peggy Dominy; *Media arts & design,* Ann Keith Kennedy; *Humanities, Soc sci,* Larry Milliken; *Bus,* Emily Missner; *Educ, Info sci, Tech,* Tim Siftar; Staff 34 (MLS 12, Non-MLS 22)
Founded 1891. Highest Degree: Doctorate
Library Holdings: AV Mats 2,700; e-books 127,535; e-journals 27,000; Bk Titles 266,821; Bk Vols 323,638; Per Subs 190
Special Collections: A J Drexel & Family; Charles Lukens Huston, Jr Ethics Coll; Drexel Archives; History of the Book
Subject Interests: Art, Design, Libr sci, Sci
Automation Activity & Vendor Info: (Acquisitions) Innovative Interfaces, Inc; (Cataloging) Innovative Interfaces, Inc; (Circulation) Innovative Interfaces, Inc; (Course Reserve) Innovative Interfaces, Inc; (ILL) OCLC ILLiad; (Media Booking) Innovative Interfaces, Inc; (OPAC) Innovative Interfaces, Inc; (Serials) SerialsSolutions
Partic in Health Sciences Libraries Consortium; LYRASIS; Partnership for Academic Library Collaborative & Innovation; Philadelphia Area Consortium of Special Collections Libraries
Open Mon-Fri 8am-Midnight, Sat & Sun 10-10

CM HAHNEMANN LIBRARY*, 245 N 15th St MS 449, 19102-1192, SAN 314-9234. Circulation Tel: 215-762-7631. Interlibrary Loan Service Tel: 215-762-7630. Reference Tel: 215-762-7184. FAX: 215-762-8180. Web Site: www.library.drexel.edu/healthsciences. *Dir, Health Sci Libr, Dir, Libr Admin Serv,* Lenore Hardy; Tel: 215-762-7022; *Assoc Dir, Health Sci Libr,* Linda M Katz; Tel: 215-762-7632, E-mail: linda.katz@drexel.edu; *Access Serv Librn, Evening Supvr,* Katherine Fisher; Tel: 215-762-1069; *Educ Librn,* Gary Childs; *Evening Supvr, Outreach Librn,* Kathleen Turner; *Ref Librn,* Steven Bogel; *Computer Ctr Mgr,* Albert Gerhold; *Evening Supvr,* Paul Hunter; *Evening Supvr,* Elizabeth Warner; *Facilities Coordr, Human Res,* Antonello Dinallo; Tel: 215-762-7186; *ILL Coordr,* Lynda Sadusky; Staff 17 (MLS 7, Non-MLS 10)
Founded 1868. Highest Degree: Doctorate
Library Holdings: AV Mats 1,434; e-books 3,002; e-journals 7,982; Bk Titles 34,734; Bk Vols 36,266; Per Subs 72
Subject Interests: Creative arts therapies, Health sci, Med, Nursing, Pub health
Automation Activity & Vendor Info: (Acquisitions) Innovative Interfaces, Inc; (Cataloging) Innovative Interfaces, Inc; (Circulation) Innovative Interfaces, Inc; (Course Reserve) Innovative Interfaces, Inc; (ILL) OCLC ILLiad; (OPAC) Innovative Interfaces, Inc; (Serials) SerialsSolutions
Partic in LYRASIS; OCLC Online Computer Library Center, Inc
Special Services for the Blind - Assistive/Adapted tech devices, equip & products
Open Mon-Thurs 7:45am-11pm, Fri 7:45-8, Sat & Sun 10-10

CM QUEEN LANE LIBRARY*, 2900 Queen Lane, 19129, SAN 372-8447. Tel: 215-991-8740. FAX: 215-843-0840. Web Site: www.library.drexel.edu/healthsciences. *Circ Librn, Ref Librn,* Adrienne Jenness; E-mail: adrienne.jenness@drexel.edu; *Coordr,* Martha Kirby; E-mail: martha.kirby@drexel.edu; *Circ & ILL,* David Wagner; Staff 5 (MLS 2, Non-MLS 3)
Highest Degree: Doctorate
Library Holdings: AV Mats 628; e-books 127,535; e-journals 27,000; Bk Titles 7,780; Bk Vols 9,911; Per Subs 4
Subject Interests: Anatomy, Biochem, Immunology, Med educ, Microbiology, Neurobiology, Pharmacology, Physiology
Automation Activity & Vendor Info: (Cataloging) Innovative Interfaces, Inc - Millennium; (Circulation) Innovative Interfaces, Inc - Millennium; (ILL) OCLC ILLiad; (OPAC) Innovative Interfaces, Inc - Millennium; (Serials) SerialsSolutions
Partic in LYRASIS; OCLC Online Computer Library Center, Inc
Publications: Queen Lane Library Guide (Library handbook)
Open Mon-Fri 8-5

DRINKER BIDDLE & REATH LLP*, Law Library, One Logan Sq, Ste 2000, 19103-6996. SAN 314-8920. Tel: 215-988-2929. FAX: 215-988-2757. Web Site: www.drinkerbiddle.com. *Dir,* Jennifer Schroth-Tusche; E-mail: jennifer.schroth@dbr.com; *Sr Res Librn,* Janet A Moore; Staff 4 (MLS 3, Non-MLS 1)
Founded 1970
Library Holdings: Bk Titles 4,000; Bk Vols 20,000; Per Subs 350
Special Collections: Historic Patent Model Coll; Rare PA Law Books
Automation Activity & Vendor Info: (Cataloging) SydneyPlus; (Serials) Sydney
Partic in LYRASIS
Restriction: Open by appt only

L DUANE MORRIS LLP LIBRARY*, 30 S 17th St, 19103-4196. SAN 314-8955. Tel: 215-979-1000, 215-979-1720. FAX: 215-979-1020. Web Site: www.duanemorris.com. *Dir, Libr & Res Serv,* Christine Scherzinger; E-mail: CAScherzinger@duanemorris.com; Staff 13 (MLS 9, Non-MLS 4)
Founded 1904
Library Holdings: Bk Vols 9,000
Subject Interests: Law
Automation Activity & Vendor Info: (Acquisitions) SydneyPlus; (Cataloging) SydneyPlus; (OPAC) SydneyPlus; (Serials) SydneyPlus
Wireless access
Partic in OCLC Online Computer Library Center, Inc
Restriction: Not open to pub

S FEDERAL RESERVE BANK OF PHILADELPHIA*, Library & Research Center, 100 N Sixth St, 4th Flr, 19106. (Mail add: Ten Independence Mall, 19106), SAN 314-9021. Tel: 215-574-6540. FAX: 215-574-3847. E-mail: phil.library.mailbox@phil.frb.org. Web Site: www.philadelphiafed.org. *Mgr,* Christine Le; E-mail: christine.le@phil.frb.org; *Info Spec,* Cristine M McCollum; E-mail: cristine.m.mccollum@phil.frb.org; *Cat, Tech Serv Spec,* Beth Paul; E-mail: beth.paul@phil.frb.org; *Archives, E-Publications,* Rebecca Sells; E-mail: becca.sells@phil.frb.org; Staff 4 (MLS 4)
Founded 1922
Library Holdings: Bk Titles 15,000; Bk Vols 30,000; Per Subs 400
Special Collections: Federal Reserve System Publications
Subject Interests: Banking, Econ
Automation Activity & Vendor Info: (Cataloging) Innovative Interfaces, Inc - Sierra; (Circulation) Innovative Interfaces, Inc - Sierra; (ILL) OCLC; (OPAC) Innovative Interfaces, Inc - Sierra; (Serials) Innovative Interfaces, Inc - Sierra
Partic in OCLC Online Computer Library Center, Inc
Restriction: Open by appt only, Open to pub for ref only

GL FIRST JUDICIAL DISTRICT OF PENNSYLVANIA*, Alex Bonavitacola Law Library, City Hall, Rm 600, Broad & Market Sts, 19107. SAN 321-0596. Tel: 215-686-3799. FAX: 215-686-3737. E-mail: FJDLawLibrary@courts.phila.gov. Web Site: www.courts.phila.gov/departments/lawlibrary. *Law Librn,* Stephanie Shepard; E-mail: Stephanie.Shepard@courts.phila.gov
Founded 1970
Library Holdings: Bk Vols 40,000; Per Subs 132
Subject Interests: US law (Penna)
Partic in OCLC Online Computer Library Center, Inc
Open Mon-Fri 8:30-5
Restriction: Open to pub for ref only

L FOX ROTHSCHILD LLP*, Law Library, 2000 Market St, 20th Flr, 19103-3291. SAN 325-965X. Tel: 215-299-2140. FAX: 215-299-2150. Web Site: www.foxrothschild.com. *Chief Innovation Officer, Chief Knowledge Officer,* Catherine M Monte; E-mail: cmonte@foxrothschild.com
Library Holdings: Bk Vols 20,000

S FRANKLIN INSTITUTE LIBRARY*, 222 N 20th St, 19103. SAN 314-9080. Tel: 215-448-1200. FAX: 215-448-1364. Web Site: www.fi.edu. *Asst Dir, Coll, Curator,* Susannah Caroll; Tel: 215-448-1265; Staff 2 (MLS 1, Non-MLS 1)
Founded 1824
Library Holdings: AV Mats 4,000; Bk Titles 19,500; Per Subs 130
Special Collections: Underwater Man Coll; Ware Sugar Coll
Subject Interests: Math, Phys sci, Sci educ
Wireless access
Partic in OCLC Online Computer Library Center, Inc
Restriction: Open by appt only

P FREE LIBRARY OF PHILADELPHIA*, Parkway Central Library & Administrative Offices, 1901 Vine St, 19103. SAN 358-8181. Tel: 215-567-7710, 215-686-5322. Interlibrary Loan Service Tel: 215-686-5360. FAX: 215-567-7850. Web Site: www.freelibrary.org. *Pres & Dir,* Position Currently Open; *Interim Dir,* Leslie M Walker; Staff 841 (MLS 263, Non-MLS 578)
Founded 1891. Pop 1,517,550; Circ 7,419,466
Jul 2013-Jun 2014. Mats Exp $8,242,782, Books $1,620,938, Per/Ser (Incl. Access Fees) $483,011, Manu Arch $156,260, Other Print Mats $846,770, Micro $149,596, AV Mat $1,635,591, Electronic Ref Mat (Incl. Access Fees) $821,833, Presv $23,303
Library Holdings: Audiobooks 47,669; AV Mats 971,389; Bks on Deafness & Sign Lang 1,200; Braille Volumes 64,292; CDs 100,687; DVDs 190,888; e-books 18,871; Electronic Media & Resources 145; Large Print Bks 56,434; Microforms 119,202; Music Scores 36,401; Bk Titles 28,260; Bk Vols 3,477,434; Per Subs 2,383; Talking Bks 791,700; Videos 110,863
Special Collections: US Document Depository
Automation Activity & Vendor Info: (Cataloging) SirsiDynix; (Circulation) SirsiDynix
Wireless access

Partic in OCLC Online Computer Library Center, Inc; Philadelphia Area Consortium of Special Collections Libraries
Special Services for the Deaf - Bks on deafness & sign lang; Captioned film dep; High interest/low vocabulary bks; Spec interest per; TDD equip
Open Mon-Fri Noon-4
Friends of the Library Group
Branches: 74
ANDORRA BRANCH, 705 E Cathedral Rd, 19128-2106, SAN 358-8998. Tel: 215-685-2552. *Br Mgr,* Joanne Woods; Staff 6 (MLS 2, Non-MLS 4)
Founded 1975
Library Holdings: CDs 2,480; DVDs 5,142; Bk Vols 50,741
Function: Wheelchair accessible
Open Mon & Wed 10-6, Tues & Thurs 12-8, Fri 10-5
Friends of the Library Group
ART, 1901 Vine St, Rm 208, 19103-1116. Tel: 215-686-5403. *Head Librn,* Susan Conway; Staff 5 (MLS 4, Non-MLS 1)
Library Holdings: Bk Titles 11,619; Bk Vols 15,085; Per Subs 152
Special Collections: (American Institute of Architects, Philadelphia Chapter Coll); Fine Prints & Print Making; Illustrations (Joseph Pennell Coll); John Frederick Lewis Coll; Old Philadelphia Survey: Restorations & Measured Drawings; Stained Glass (Lawrence Saint Coll & Henry Lee Willet Coll)
Subject Interests: Archit, Costume, Decorative art, Fine arts, Graphic arts
Open Mon-Thurs 9-9, Fri 9-6, Sat 9-5, Sun 1-5
Friends of the Library Group
AUTOMOBILE REFERENCE COLLECTION, 1901 Vine St, 19103-1116. Tel: 215-686-5404. E-mail: erefarc@freelibrary.org. *Curator,* Position Currently Open
Library Holdings: Bk Titles 25,611; Bk Vols 30,910; Per Subs 84
Special Collections: Books & Photographs Tracing the Automobile from 1896 to date; Instruction, Parts & Shop Manuals; Sales Catalogs
Subject Interests: Automobiles
Open Mon-Fri 9-5
Friends of the Library Group
LUCIEN E BLACKWELL WEST PHILADELPHIA REGIONAL, 125 S 52nd St, 19139-3408, SAN 358-8963. Tel: 215-685-7431. FAX: 215-685-7438. *Regional Librn,* Nani Manion; Staff 22 (MLS 7, Non-MLS 15)
Library Holdings: CDs 4,071; DVDs 6,993; Bk Vols 77,820
Function: Wheelchair accessible
Open Tues & Wed 12-8, Thurs 10-6, Fri & Sat 10-5, Sun 1-5
Friends of the Library Group
BUSHROD BRANCH, 6304 Castor Ave, 19149-2731, SAN 358-9021. Tel: 215-685-1471. FAX: 215-685-1079. *Br Mgr,* Mark Wolfe; Staff 8 (MLS 2, Non-MLS 6)
Library Holdings: CDs 2,480; DVDs 5,146; Bk Vols 32,064
Function: Wheelchair accessible
Open Mon & Wed 10-6, Tues & Thurs 12-8, Fri 10-5
Friends of the Library Group
BUSINESS RESOURCE & INNOVATON CENTER, 1901 Vine St, Ground Flr, 19103. Tel: 215-686-8663. E-mail: bric@freelibrary.org. *Admin Librn,* Rebekah Ray
Open Mon-Thurs 9-7, Fri 9-6, Sat 9-5, Sun 1-5
BUSTLETON AVENUE BRANCH, 10199 Bustleton Ave, 19116-3718, SAN 358-9056. Tel: 215-685-0472. FAX: 215-698-8892. *Br Mgr,* Position Currently Open
Library Holdings: CDs 2,349; DVDs 4,520; Bk Vols 40,128
Function: Wheelchair accessible
Open Mon & Wed 12-8, Tues & Thurs 10-6, Fri 10-5
Friends of the Library Group
CENTRAL SENIOR SERVICES, 1901 Vine St, 1st Flr W, 19103. Tel: 215-686-5331. *Mgr,* Lisa Jane Erwin
Function: Homebound delivery serv, Senior outreach
Open Mon-Fri 9-5
CHESTNUT HILL BRANCH, 8711 Germantown Ave, 19118-2716, SAN 358-9080. Tel: 215-685-9290. FAX: 215-685-9291. *Br Mgr,* Prather Egan; Staff 8 (MLS 3, Non-MLS 5)
Library Holdings: CDs 2,934; DVDs 3,760; Bk Vols 44,813
Closed for renovations 2021-
Friends of the Library Group
CHILDREN'S DEPARTMENT, 1901 Vine St, Rm 22, 19103-1116. Tel: 215-686-5369. *Head Librn,* Rebecca Shaknovich; *Curator, Spec Coll,* Christopher Brown. Subject Specialists: *Children's lit,* Christopher Brown; Staff 9.5 (MLS 4, Non-MLS 5.5)
Library Holdings: AV Mats 9,411; Bk Titles 50,119; Bk Vols 52,311; Per Subs 46; Videos 911
Special Collections: Bibliographies; Bibliographies for the Adult Researcher; Children's Books in 60 Different Languages; Children's Literature Research Coll; Folklore Coll; Foreign Language Coll; Historical Bibliography: Books about Children's Literature; Historical Coll of Children's Literature from 1837 to present; Kathrine McAlarney Coll of Illustrated Children's Books; Original Children's Book Illustrations & Manuscripts
Open Mon-Thurs 9-7, Fri 9-6, Sat 9-5, Sun 1-5
Friends of the Library Group
JOSEPH E COLEMAN NORTHWEST REGIONAL, 68 W Chelten Ave, 19144-2795, SAN 358-8939. Tel: 215-685-2151. FAX: 215-848-7790. *Regional Librn,* Robin Manker; Staff 28 (MLS 10, Non-MLS 18)
Library Holdings: AV Mats 1,861; Large Print Bks 209; Bk Titles 38,790; Bk Vols 42,610; Per Subs 79; Videos 410
Function: Wheelchair accessible
Open Tues & Wed 12-8, Thurs 10-6, Fri & Sat 10-5, Sun 1-5
Friends of the Library Group
RAMONITA G DE RODRIGUEZ BRANCH, 600 W Girard Ave, 19123-1311, SAN 358-9897. Tel: 215-686-1768. FAX: 215-686-1769. *Br Mgr,* Lisa Chianese-Lopez; Staff 7 (MLS 2, Non-MLS 5)
Library Holdings: CDs 2,145; DVDs 4,662; Bk Vols 32,149
Open Mon & Wed 11-7, Tues & Thurs 10-6, Fri 10-5
Friends of the Library Group
THOMAS F DONATUCCI SR BRANCH, 1935 Shunk St, 19145-4234, SAN 358-9803. Tel: 215-685-1755. FAX: 215-685-1652. *Br Mgr,* David Mariscotti; Staff 4 (MLS 2, Non-MLS 2)
Library Holdings: CDs 1,858; DVDs 4,364; Bk Vols 32,901
Open Mon & Wed 10-6, Tues & Thurs 12-8, Fri 10-5
Friends of the Library Group
KATHARINE DREXEL BRANCH, 11099 Knights Rd, 19154-3516, SAN 358-9447. Tel: 215-685-9383. FAX: 215-685-9384. *Br Mgr,* Richard Krawczyk; Staff 6 (MLS 2, Non-MLS 4)
Library Holdings: CDs 2,657; DVDs 3,675; Bk Vols 38,173
Function: Wheelchair accessible
Open Mon & Wed 12-8, Tues & Thurs 10-6, Fri 10-5
Friends of the Library Group
CHARLES L DURHAM BRANCH, 3320 Haverford Ave, 19104-2021, SAN 358-9641. Tel: 215-685-7436. FAX: 215-685-7439. *Br Mgr,* Alberto Pagan; Staff 4 (MLS 1, Non-MLS 3)
Library Holdings: CDs 1,860; DVDs 3,011; Bk Vols 26,021
Open Mon & Wed 10-6, Tues & Thurs 10-7, Fri 10-5
Friends of the Library Group
EASTWICK BRANCH, 2851 Island Ave, 19153-2314, SAN 359-0224. Tel: 215-685-4170. FAX: 215-937-0412. *Br Mgr,* Mary Beth Triplett; Staff 5 (MLS 1, Non-MLS 4)
Library Holdings: CDs 2,162; DVDs 3,563; Bk Vols 38,001
Function: Wheelchair accessible
Open Mon & Wed 12-8, Tues & Thurs 10-6, Fri 10-5
Friends of the Library Group
EDUCATION, PHILOSOPHY & RELIGION, 1901 Vine St, Rm 205, 19103-1116. Tel: 215-686-5392. *Head Librn,* Ed Voves; Staff 7 (MLS 6, Non-MLS 1)
Library Holdings: Bk Titles 26,511; Bk Vols 27,291; Per Subs 68
Special Collections: Bibles; Judaica-Hebraica; Moses Marx Coll; The Workplace - Job & Career Information Center
Subject Interests: Educ, Libr, Librarianship, Philos, Psychol, Relig studies
Open Mon-Thurs 9-9, Fri 9-6, Sat 9-5, Sun 1-5
Friends of the Library Group
FALLS OF SCHUYLKILL BRANCH, 3501 Midvale Ave, 19129-1633, SAN 358-920X. Tel: 215-685-2093. FAX: 215-685-2092. *Br Mgr,* Drew Birden; Staff 6 (MLS 2, Non-MLS 4)
Library Holdings: CDs 4,005; DVDs 4,967; Bk Vols 42,401
Function: Wheelchair accessible
Temporarily closed until further notice 2021-
Friends of the Library Group
FICTION & POPULAR CULTURE LIBRARY & CENTRAL CIRCULATION DEPARTMENT, Philbrick Hall, 1901 Vine St, Rm 103, 19103-1116. Tel: 215-686-5320. *Head Librn,* Position Currently Open; *Head, ILL,* Dan Ryan; Staff 24 (MLS 6, Non-MLS 18)
Library Holdings: Bk Titles 11,211; Bk Vols 13,497
Open Mon-Thurs 9-9, Fri 9-6, Sat 9-5, Sun 1-5
Friends of the Library Group
FIELD TEEN CENTER, 1901 Vine St, Ground Flr, 19103. Tel: 215-686-5395. E-mail: teencenter@freelibrary.org. Web Site: libwww.freelibrary.org/teen. *Mgr,* Kris Langlais
Open Mon-Thurs 11-7, Fri 11-6, Sat 9-5, Sun 1-5
FISHTOWN COMMUNITY BRANCH, 1217 E Montgomery Ave, 19125-3445, SAN 358-917X. Tel: 215-685-9990. FAX: 215-685-9989. *Br Mgr,* Sheila O'Steen; Staff 6 (MLS 2, Non-MLS 4)
Library Holdings: CDs 1,381; DVDs 2,881; Bk Vols 15,794
Open Mon & Wed 12-8, Tues & Thurs 10-6, Fri 10-5
Friends of the Library Group
EDWIN A FLEISHER COLLECTION OF ORCHESTRAL MUSIC, 1901 Vine St, Rm 125, 19103-1116. Tel: 215-686-5313. *Curator, Spec Coll,* Gary Galván; E-mail: galvang@freelibrary.org; Staff 5 (MLS 1, Non-MLS 4)
Library Holdings: Bk Titles 16,840; Bk Vols 20,092; Per Subs 76
Special Collections: Archives of American Composers; Conductor's scores & complete instrumental parts for approximately 15,000 orchestra works & approximately 1500 reference scores available for loan on application; Reference files on over 1500 composers; Repository for

discs & cassettes of works from the coll; Repository for tapes of American-International Music Fund's Recording Guarantee Project
Open Mon-Fri 9-5
Friends of the Library Group
FOX CHASE BRANCH, 501 Rhawn St, 19111-2504, SAN 358-9234. Tel: 215-685-0547. FAX: 215-685-0546. *Br Mgr,* Christine Casperson; Staff 8 (MLS 2, Non-MLS 6)
Library Holdings: CDs 2,327; DVDs 4,008; Bk Vols 35,290
Function: Wheelchair accessible
Open Mon & Wed 12-8, Tues & Thurs 10-6, Fri 10-5
Friends of the Library Group
FRANKFORD BRANCH, 4634 Frankford Ave, 19124-5804, SAN 358-9269. Tel: 215-685-1473. FAX: 215-289-6914. *Br Mgr,* LaBae Daniels; Staff 5 (MLS 2, Non-MLS 3)
Library Holdings: CDs 1,867; DVDs 5,321; Bk Vols 40,316
Open Mon & Wed 11-7, Tues & Thurs 10-6, Fri 10-5
Friends of the Library Group
FUMO FAMILY BRANCH, 2437 S Broad St, 19148-3508, SAN 358-9951. Tel: 215-685-1757. *Br Mgr,* Abbe Klebanoff; Staff 5 (MLS 2, Non-MLS 3)
Library Holdings: CDs 1,532; DVDs 3,136; Bk Vols 26,368
Function: Wheelchair accessible
Open Mon & Wed 12-8, Tues & Thurs 10-6, Fri 10-5
Friends of the Library Group
GENERAL INFORMATION DEPARTMENT, 1901 Vine St, Rm 215, 19103-1116. Tel: 215-686-5322. *Head Librn,* Lori Morse; Staff 9 (MLS 1, Non-MLS 8)
Library Holdings: Bk Titles 1,192; Bk Vols 1,794; Per Subs 14
Special Collections: Telephone Directories
Open Mon-Thurs 9-9, Fri 9-6, Sat 9-5, Sun 1-5
Friends of the Library Group
GOVERNMENT PUBLICATIONS, 1901 Vine St, Rm 201, 19103-1116. Tel: 215-686-5330. *Head Librn,* David Ninemire; Staff 8.5 (MLS 6.5, Non-MLS 2)
Library Holdings: Bk Titles 19,801; Bk Vols 21,212; Per Subs 42
Special Collections: US Patent Coll; US Patents. State Document Depository; UN Document Depository; US Document Depository
Open Mon-Thurs 9-9, Fri 9-6, Sat 9-5, Sun 1-5
Friends of the Library Group
GREATER OLNEY BRANCH, 5501 N Fifth St, 19120-2805, SAN 358-9323. Tel: 215-685-2846. FAX: 215-548-2605. *Br Mgr,* Joy Kicinski; Staff 7 (MLS 2, Non-MLS 5)
Library Holdings: CDs 1,727; DVDs 4,093; Bk Vols 33,673
Function: Wheelchair accessible
Open Mon & Wed 12-8, Tues & Thurs 10-6, Fri 10-5
Friends of the Library Group
HADDINGTON BRANCH, 446 N 65th St, 19151-4003, SAN 358-9382. Tel: 215-685-1970. FAX: 215-685-1971. *Br Mgr,* LaKeitha Bellamy Dwyer; Staff 4 (MLS 2, Non-MLS 2)
Library Holdings: CDs 1,086; DVDs 2,806; Bk Vols 24,659
Open Mon & Wed 10-6, Tues & Thurs 11-7, Fri 10-5
Friends of the Library Group
HAVERFORD AVENUE BRANCH, 5543 Haverford Ave, 19139-1432, SAN 358-9390. Tel: 215-685-1964. FAX: 215-685-1966. *Br Mgr,* Marvin DeBose; Staff 4 (MLS 1, Non-MLS 3)
Library Holdings: CDs 2,532; DVDs 3,742; Bk Vols 35,533
Function: Wheelchair accessible
Open Mon & Wed 12-8, Tues & Thurs 10-6, Fri 10-5
Friends of the Library Group
HOLMESBURG BRANCH, 7810 Frankford Ave, 19136-3013, SAN 358-9412. Tel: 215-685-8756. FAX: 215-685-8759. *Br Mgr,* Paul Daka; Staff 6 (MLS 2, Non-MLS 4)
Library Holdings: CDs 1,972; DVDs 3,619; Bk Vols 33,015
Open Mon & Wed 12-8, Tues & Thurs 10-6, Fri 10-5
Friends of the Library Group
INDEPENDENCE BRANCH, 18 S Seventh St, 19106. Tel: 215-685-1633. FAX: 215-685-1844. *Br Mgr,* Marianne Banbor; Staff 9 (MLS 3, Non-MLS 6)
Library Holdings: CDs 3,657; DVDs 6,407; Bk Vols 45,628
Function: Wheelchair accessible
Open Mon & Wed 12-8, Tues & Thurs 10-6, Fri 10-5
Friends of the Library Group
INTERLIBRARY LOAN, 1901 Vine St, 19103-1116. Tel: 215-686-5360. FAX: 215-563-3628. E-mail: ILLrequest@freelibrary.org. *Head Librn,* Dan Ryan; Staff 5.5 (MLS 2, Non-MLS 3.5)
Library Holdings: Bk Vols 304,100
Open Mon-Fri 9-5
Friends of the Library Group
KENSINGTON BRANCH, 104 W Dauphin St, 19133-3701, SAN 358-9471. Tel: 215-685-9996. FAX: 215-685-9997. *Br Mgr,* Sara Palmer; Staff 5 (MLS 2, Non-MLS 3)
Library Holdings: CDs 1,657; DVDs 3,610; Bk Vols 22,725
Function: Wheelchair accessible
Open Mon-Thurs 10-6, Fri 10-5
Friends of the Library Group
KINGSESSING BRANCH, 1201 S 51st, 19143-4353, SAN 358-9501. Tel: 215-685-2690. FAX: 215-685-2691. *Br Mgr,* Ben Remsen; Staff 4 (MLS 2, Non-MLS 2)
Library Holdings: CDs 1,514; DVDs 3,909; Bk Vols 27,414
Open Mon & Wed 10-6, Tues & Thurs 11-7, Fri 10-5
Friends of the Library Group
LAWNCREST BRANCH, 6098 Rising Sun Ave, 19111-6009, SAN 358-9536. Tel: 215-685-0549. FAX: 215-685-0548. *Br Mgr,* Brian Isdell; Staff 6 (MLS 2, Non-MLS 4)
Library Holdings: CDs 2,029; DVDs 3,988; Bk Vols 31,246
Function: Wheelchair accessible
Open Mon & Wed 10-6, Tues & Thurs 12-8, Fri 10-5
Friends of the Library Group
P LIBRARY FOR THE BLIND & PHYSICALLY HANDICAPPED, 1500 Spring Garden St, Ste 230, 19130, SAN 314-9102. Tel: 215-683-3213. Toll Free Tel: 800-222-1754. FAX: 215-683-3211. E-mail: flpblind@freelibrary.org. *Head Librn,* Keri Wilkins; Staff 5 (MLS 5)
Founded 1897. Pop 12,745; Circ 1,125,725
Library Holdings: AV Mats 500; Bk Titles 95,000
Special Collections: Blindness & Handicaps
Function: Wheelchair accessible
Publications: 919 News Insider for Children & Teens (Biannually); 919 News, Reader Newsletter (Quarterly)
Special Services for the Blind - ABE/GED & braille classes for the visually impaired; Braille equip; Braille servs; Closed circuit TV; Info on spec aids & appliances; Magnifiers; Mags & bk reproduction/duplication; Reader equip; Volunteer serv
Open Mon-Fri 9-5
Friends of the Library Group
LITERATURE, 1901 Vine St, Rm 207, 19103-1116. Tel: 215-686-5402. E-mail: ereflit@freelibrary.org. *Head Librn,* Susan Conway; Staff 6 (MLS 5, Non-MLS 1)
Library Holdings: Bk Titles 42,818; Bk Vols 48,908; Per Subs 142
Special Collections: Granger Coll; Ottemiller Coll
Subject Interests: Belles lettres, Folklore, Journalism, Lang arts, Lit
Open Mon-Thurs 9-9, Fri 9-6, Sat 9-5, Sun 1-5
Friends of the Library Group
LOGAN BRANCH, 1333 Wagner Ave, 19141-2916, SAN 358-9595. Tel: 215-685-9156. FAX: 215-456-2285. *Br Mgr,* Lynne Haase; Staff 5 (MLS 2, Non-MLS 3)
Library Holdings: CDs 1,310; DVDs 3,409; Bk Vols 34,174
Function: Wheelchair accessible
Open Mon & Wed 10-6, Tues & Thurs 12-8, Fri 10-5
Friends of the Library Group
LOVETT MEMORIAL BRANCH, 6945 Germantown Ave, 19119-2189, SAN 358-9625. Tel: 215-685-2095. FAX: 215-685-2094. *Br Mgr,* Martha Stender; Staff 6 (MLS 2, Non-MLS 4)
Library Holdings: CDs 3,415; DVDs 4,519; Bk Vols 43,082
Function: Wheelchair accessible
Open Mon & Wed 1-9, Tues & Thurs 10-6, Fri 10-5
Friends of the Library Group
MAP COLLECTION, 1901 Vine St, Rm 201, 19103. Tel: 215-686-5397. E-mail: erefmap@freelibrary.org. *Curator,* Meg MacCall; Staff 1 (MLS 1)
Library Holdings: Bk Titles 9,841; Bk Vols 11,293
Special Collections: 19th & 20th Century Philadelphia Fire Insurance Atlases, suburban atlases; 19th Century Pennsylvania County Atlases; Decorative Maps & Maps of Imaginary Lands; Historical Philadelphia Map Coll; William G Kelzo Coll of Jansson-Visscher Maps of America
Subject Interests: Cartobibliography, Geog, Hist of cartography, Map librarianship
Open Mon-Fri 9-5
Friends of the Library Group
LILLIAN MARRERO BRANCH, 601 W Lehigh Ave, 19133-2228, SAN 358-9560. Tel: 215-685-9794. FAX: 215-685-9689. *Br Mgr,* Mieka Moody; Staff 5 (MLS 2, Non-MLS 3)
Library Holdings: CDs 1,607; DVDs 3,471; Bk Vols 31,823
Function: Wheelchair accessible
Open Mon & Wed 11-7, Tues & Thurs 10-6, Fri 10-5
Friends of the Library Group
MCPHERSON SQUARE BRANCH, 601 E Indiana Ave, 19134-3042, SAN 358-965X. Tel: 215-685-9995. FAX: 215-685-9984. *Br Mgr,* Judi Moore; Staff 5 (MLS 2, Non-MLS 3)
Library Holdings: CDs 1,553; DVDs 3,911; Bk Vols 31,325
Open Mon-Thurs 10-6, Fri 10-5
Friends of the Library Group
CECIL B MOORE BRANCH, 2320 W Cecil B Moore Ave, 19121-2927, SAN 358-9145. Tel: 215-685-2766. FAX: 215-685-3893. *Br Mgr,* James McCain; Staff 9 (MLS 2, Non-MLS 7)
Library Holdings: CDs 1,352; DVDs 3,598; Bk Vols 30,825
Open Mon-Thurs 10-6, Fri 10-5
Friends of the Library Group
MUSIC, 1901 Vine St, Rm 126, 19103-1116. Tel: 215-686-5316. *Head Librn,* Ray Banas; Staff 8 (MLS 5, Non-MLS 3)
Library Holdings: Bk Titles 10,691; Bk Vols 12,510

Special Collections: Coll of Musical Fund Society; Drinker Library of Choral Music; Harvey Husten & Huber Jazz Libraries, rec; Historical Record Coll; Sheet Music (incl Americana)
Subject Interests: Bibliog, Biog, Chamber, Collected works, Criticism, Dance, Essays, Instrumental music, Manuscripts
Open Mon-Thurs 9-9, Fri 9-6, Sat 9-5, Sun 1-5
Friends of the Library Group

NEWSPAPER & MICROFILM CENTER, 1901 Vine St, Rm 214, 19103. Tel: 215-686-5431. FAX: 215-567-0398. *Dept Head,* Jason Malcom; Staff 9 (MLS 5, Non-MLS 4)
Library Holdings: Bk Titles 12,680; Bk Vols 14,310; Per Subs 221
Subject Interests: Current events
Open Mon-Fri 9-6, Sat 9-5, Sun 1-5
Friends of the Library Group

NICETOWN-TIOGA BRANCH, 3720 N Broad St, 19140-3608, SAN 358-9684. Tel: 215-685-9790. FAX: 215-685-9788. *Br Mgr,* Debra E Johnson; Staff 5 (MLS 2, Non-MLS 3)
Library Holdings: CDs 766; DVDs 3,225; Bk Vols 22,078
Open Mon-Thurs 10-6, Fri 10-5
Friends of the Library Group

BLANCHE A NIXON LIBRARY - COBBS CREEK BRANCH, 5800 Cobbs Creek Pkwy, 19143-3036, SAN 358-9110. Tel: 215-685-1973. FAX: 215-685-1974. *Br Mgr,* Christina Holmes; Staff 6 (MLS 2, Non-MLS 4)
Library Holdings: CDs 1,221; DVDs 3,176; Bk Vols 22,078
Open Mon & Wed 12-8, Tues & Thurs 10-6, Fri 10-5
Friends of the Library Group

NORTHEAST REGIONAL, 2228 Cottman Ave, 19149-1297, SAN 358-8904. Tel: 215-685-0522. FAX: 215-742-3225. *Regional Libm,* Peter Lehu; Staff 40 (MLS 15, Non-MLS 25)
Library Holdings: CDs 6,343; DVDs 7,178; Bk Vols 124,416
Open Tues & Wed 12-8, Thurs 10-6, Fri & Sat 10-5, Sun 1-5
Friends of the Library Group

OAK LANE BRANCH, 6614 N 12th St, 19126-3299, SAN 358-9714. Tel: 215-685-2847. *Br Mgr,* Debra Ahrens; Staff 6 (MLS 2, Non-MLS 4)
Library Holdings: CDs 2,019; DVDs 3,640; Bk Vols 31,007
Open Mon & Wed 12-8, Tues & Thurs 10-6, Fri 10-5
Friends of the Library Group

DAVID COHEN OGONTZ LIBRARY, 6017 Ogontz Ave, 19141, SAN 376-8554. Tel: 215-685-3566. FAX: 215-685-3568. *Br Mgr,* Liz Pinder; Staff 4 (MLS 1, Non-MLS 3)
Library Holdings: CDs 1,664; DVDs 3,635; Bk Vols 25,389
Function: Wheelchair accessible
Open Mon & Wed 12-8, Tues & Thurs 10-6, Fri 10-5
Friends of the Library Group

OVERBROOK PARK, 7422 Haverford Ave, 19151-2995, SAN 358-9749. Tel: 215-685-0182. FAX: 215-685-0183. *Br Mgr,* Tamikka Coppin; Staff 6 (MLS 2, Non-MLS 4)
Library Holdings: CDs 1,713; DVDs 3,761; Bk Vols 45,874
Open Mon & Wed 10-6, Tues & Thurs 11-7, Fri 10-5
Friends of the Library Group

PASCHALVILLE BRANCH, 6942 Woodland Ave, 19142-1823, SAN 358-9773. Tel: 215-685-2662. FAX: 215-685-2656. *Br Mgr,* Nyia Morrison; Staff 4 (MLS 2, Non-MLS 2)
Library Holdings: CDs 1,588; DVDs 3,748; Bk Vols 28,617
Open Mon & Wed 10-6, Tues & Thurs 11-7, Fri 10-5
Friends of the Library Group

PHILADELPHIA CITY INSTITUTE, 1905 Locust St, 19103-5730, SAN 358-9838. Tel: 215-685-6621. FAX: 215-685-6622. *Br Mgr,* Erin Hoopes; Staff 9 (MLS 3, Non-MLS 6)
Library Holdings: CDs 4,068; DVDs 6,707; Bk Vols 41,863
Open Mon & Wed 12-8, Tues & Thurs 10-6, Fri 10-5
Friends of the Library Group

PRINT & PICTURE, 1901 Vine St, 2nd Flr, 19103-1116. Tel: 215-686-5405. *Curator,* Laura Straffolino; Staff 2 (MLS 1, Non-MLS 1)
Library Holdings: Bk Titles 20,681; Bk Vols 23,942; Per Subs 51
Special Collections: Centennial Exhibition of 1876 Photographs; Circulating Coll of Pictures on all Subjects; Contemporary Graphic Arts Coll; Greeting Cards; Napoleonica (Carson Coll); Philadelphia Coll; Portrait Prints (Lewis Coll)
Open Mon-Fri 9-5
Friends of the Library Group

QUEEN MEMORIAL BRANCH, 1201 S 23rd St, 19146-4316, SAN 374-7328. Tel: 215-685-1899. FAX: 215-685-1654. *Br Mgr,* Liz Gardner; Staff 4 (MLS 1, Non-MLS 3)
Library Holdings: CDs 1,491; DVDs 3,261; Bk Vols 23,155
Function: Wheelchair accessible
Open Mon-Thurs 10-6, Fri 10-5
Friends of the Library Group

RARE BOOK, 1901 Vine St, 3rd Flr, 19103-1116. Tel: 215-686-5416. E-mail: erefrbd@freelibrary.org. *Head Librn,* Allison Freyemuth; *Curator,* Karin Suni; Staff 5 (MLS 4, Non-MLS 1)
Library Holdings: Bk Titles 41,192; Bk Vols 43,411
Special Collections: A B Frost (C Barton Brewster Coll); A E Newton (Swift Newton Coll) American Pamphlets (Charles J Biddle Coll); Agnes Repplier (Anne Von Moschzisker Coll); American Historical Autographs incl Jay Treaty Papers (Elkins Coll); American Sunday School Union Publications; Americana (William M Elkins Coll); Angling Prints (Evan Randolph Coll); Arthur Rackham (Grace Clark Haskell Coll); Beatrix Potter (Collamore, Cridland, Elkins & Stevens Coll); Bookplates (J Somers Smith Coll); Bret Harte (Edward F R Wood Coll); British Engravers (Lewis Coll); Calligraphy (9th-20th Centuries Coll); Children's Books Printed in America, 1682-1850 (ASW Rosenbach, Emerson Greenaway, Mrs William H Allen, Frederick R Gardner Coll); Christopher Morley Coll; Common Law (Hampton L Carson Coll); Cuneiform Tablets (John Frederick Lewis Coll); Dickens First Editions, Letters & Memoriabilia (Elkins Coll); Dickens Letters (Benoliel Coll); Early Bibles; Edgar Allan Poe (Richard Gimbel Coll); English & Irish Pamphlets; European Manuscripts (Lewis & Widener Coll); Four Folios of Shakespeare (Joseph E Widener Coll); Gift Books; Goldsmith First Editions & Papers (Elkins Coll); Horace (Moncure Biddle Coll); Horn Books (Elisabeth Ball Coll); Howard Pyle & His School (Thornton Oakley Coll); Incunabula (Copinger-Widener Coll); James Branch Cabell (D Jaques Benoliel Coll); John Gilpin (Brewster Coll); Kate Greenaway Coll; Letters of the Presidents (Strouse Coll); Margaret Leaf Coll; Munro Leaf Coll; Oriental Manuscripts & Miniatures (Lewis Coll); Palmer Cox; Pennsylvania German Imprints, Manuscripts & Fraktur (Henry S Borneman & Others Coll); Philadelphia Views (Randolph Coll); Press Books; Robert Lawson (Frederick R Gardner Coll); Theatre Coll; Title Pages & Printer's Marks (John Ashhurst Coll); Wing, Short Title Catalogue Books
Open Mon-Sat 9-5
Friends of the Library Group

REGIONAL FOUNDATION CENTER, 1901 Vine St, 19103-1116. Tel: 215-686-5423. E-mail: nonprofit@freelibrary.org. *Head Librn,* Position Currently Open
Library Holdings: Bk Titles 5,683; Bk Vols 7,981; Per Subs 26
Subject Interests: Fundraising, Info on area foundations, Nat foundations, Nonprofit organization mgt, Philanthropy
Open Mon-Thurs 9-9, Fri 9-6, Sat 9-5, Sun 1-5
Friends of the Library Group

RICHMOND BRANCH, 2987 Almond St, 19134-4955, SAN 358-9927. Tel: 215-685-9992. FAX: 215-291-5312. *Br Mgr,* Amy Thatcher; Staff 5 (MLS 2, Non-MLS 3)
Library Holdings: CDs 1,999; DVDs 4,436; Bk Vols 37,688
Function: Wheelchair accessible
Open Mon & Wed 12-8, Tues & Thurs 10-6, Fri 10-5
Friends of the Library Group

ROXBOROUGH BRANCH, 6245 Ridge Ave, 19128-2630, SAN 358-9986. Tel: 215-685-2550. FAX: 215-685-2551. *Br Mgr,* Eric Woods; Staff 4 (MLS 2, Non-MLS 2)
Library Holdings: CDs 1,999; DVDs 4,436; Bk Vols 37,866
Open Mon & Wed 12-8, Tues & Thurs 10-6, Fri 10-5
Friends of the Library Group

CHARLES SANTORE BRANCH, 932 S Seventh St, 19147-2932, SAN 359-0046. Tel: 215-686-1766. FAX: 215-686-1765. *Br Mgr,* Jeanne Hamann; Staff 6 (MLS 2, Non-MLS 4)
Library Holdings: CDs 2,036; DVDs 5,233; Bk Vols 33,837
Function: Wheelchair accessible
Open Mon & Wed 12-8, Tues & Thurs 10-6, Fri 10-5
Friends of the Library Group

SCIENCE & WELLNESS CENTER, 1901 Vine St, Rm 202, 19103. Tel: 215-686-5394. *Head Librn,* Allen Merry; Staff 7.5 (MLS 6, Non-MLS 1.5)
Library Holdings: Bk Titles 31,412; Bk Vols 34,119; Per Subs 306
Special Collections: Trade Periodical Literature
Subject Interests: Bus, Computers, Consumer info, Philatelic lit
Open Mon-Thurs 9-9, Fri 9-6, Sat 9-5, Sun 1-5
Friends of the Library Group

SOCIAL SCIENCE & HISTORY, 1901 Vine St, Rm 201, 19103-1116. Tel: 215-686-5396. *Head Librn,* David Ninemire; Staff 6 (MLS 4, Non-MLS 2)
Library Holdings: Bk Titles 48,691; Bk Vols 51,408; Per Subs 122
Special Collections: American Imprint Series, micro; American Indian (Wilberforce Eames Coll); Chess (Charles Willing Coll); Confederate Imprints (Simon Gratz Coll); Rowing (Lewis H Kenney Coll)
Subject Interests: Anthrop, Archaeology, Behav sci, Bibliog, Biog, Hist, Intl relations, Polit sci, Soc sci, Sports, Travel
Open Mon-Thurs 9-9, Fri 9-6, Sat 9-5, Sun 1-5
Friends of the Library Group

SOUTH PHILADELPHIA BRANCH, 1700 S Broad St, 19145-2392, SAN 359-0011. Tel: 215-685-1866. FAX: 215-685-1868. *Br Mgr,* Renee Pokorny
Library Holdings: CDs 2,036; DVDs 6,266; Bk Vols 40,498
Function: Wheelchair accessible
Open Mon & Wed 12-8, Tues & Thurs 10-6, Fri 10-5
Friends of the Library Group

TACONY BRANCH, 6742 Torresdale Ave, 19135-2416, SAN 359-0070. Tel: 215-685-8755. FAX: 215-685-8718. *Br Mgr,* Suzin Weber; Staff 6 (MLS 2, Non-MLS 4)
Library Holdings: CDs 2,099; DVDs 5,002; Bk Vols 36,696
Open Mon & Wed 12-8, Tues & Thurs 10-6, Fri 10-5
Friends of the Library Group

TORRESDALE BRANCH, 3079 Holme Ave, 19136-1101, SAN 359-0100. Tel: 215-685-0494. FAX: 215-685-0495. *Br Mgr,* Ann Hornbach; Staff 6 (MLS 2, Non-MLS 4)
Library Holdings: CDs 2,328; DVDs 3,542; Bk Vols 31,097
Open Mon & Wed 12-8, Tues & Thurs 10-6, Fri 10-5
Friends of the Library Group

WADSWORTH AVENUE BRANCH, 1500 Wadsworth Ave, 19150-1699, SAN 359-0135. Tel: 215-685-9293. FAX: 215-685-9293. *Br Mgr,* Andrea Kearny; Staff 5 (MLS 2, Non-MLS 3)
Library Holdings: CDs 1,327; DVDs 2,941; Bk Vols 31,085
Function: Wheelchair accessible
Open Mon & Wed 12-8, Tues & Thurs 10-6, Fri 10-5
Friends of the Library Group

WALNUT STREET WEST BRANCH, 201 S 40th St, 19104, SAN 359-016X. Tel: 215-685-7671. FAX: 215-685-7679. *Br Mgr,* Bruce Siebers; Staff 8 (MLS 3, Non-MLS 5)
Library Holdings: CDs 3,982; DVDs 6,088; Bk Vols 57,648
Function: Wheelchair accessible
Open Mon & Wed 12-8, Tues & Thurs 10-6, Fri 10-5
Friends of the Library Group

WELSH ROAD BRANCH, 9233 Roosevelt Blvd, 19114-2205, SAN 359-0194. Tel: 215-685-0498. FAX: 215-685-0496. *Br Mgr,* Brook Freeman; Staff 7 (MLS 2, Non-MLS 5)
Library Holdings: CDs 2,469; DVDs 5,067; Bk Vols 46,415
Open Mon & Wed 12-8, Tues & Thurs 10-6, Fri 10-5
Friends of the Library Group

WEST OAK LANE BRANCH, 2000 Washington Lane, 19138-1344, SAN 325-4097. Tel: 215-685-2843. FAX: 215-685-2844. *Br Mgr,* Irene Klemas; Staff 6 (MLS 2, Non-MLS 4)
Library Holdings: CDs 2,866; DVDs 3,607; Bk Vols 35,463
Function: Wheelchair accessible
Open Mon & Wed 10-6, Tues & Thurs 12-8, Fri 10-5
Friends of the Library Group

WHITMAN BRANCH, 200 Snyder Ave, 19148-2620, SAN 359-0259. Tel: 215-685-1754. FAX: 215-685-1753. *Br Mgr,* Rachel Solomon; Staff 5 (MLS 2, Non-MLS 3)
Library Holdings: CDs 2,171; DVDs 4,206; Bk Vols 35,963
Function: Wheelchair accessible
Open Mon & Wed 12-8, Tues & Thurs 10-6, Fri 10-5
Friends of the Library Group

WIDENER BRANCH, 2808 W Lehigh Ave, 19132-3296, SAN 359-0283. Tel: 215-685-9799. FAX: 215-685-9716. *Br Mgr,* Titus Moolathara; Staff 5 (MLS 2, Non-MLS 3)
Library Holdings: CDs 1,907; DVDs 4,068; Bk Vols 28,810
Open Mon-Thurs 10-6, Fri 10-5
Friends of the Library Group

WYNNEFIELD BRANCH, 5325 Overbrook Ave, 19131-1498, SAN 359-0313. Tel: 215-685-0298. FAX: 215-685-0294. *Br Mgr,* Susan Ben; Staff 6 (MLS 2, Non-MLS 4)
Library Holdings: CDs 1,947; DVDs 3,692; Bk Vols 37,859
Function: Wheelchair accessible
Open Mon & Wed 12-8, Tues & Thurs 10-6, Fri 10-5
Friends of the Library Group

WYOMING BRANCH, 231 E Wyoming Ave, 19120-4439, SAN 359-0348. Tel: 215-685-9158. FAX: 215-685-9159. *Br Mgr,* Alex Bender; Staff 4 (MLS 1, Non-MLS 3)
Library Holdings: CDs 1,723; DVDs 4,821; Bk Vols 35,220
Open Mon & Wed 11-7, Tues & Thurs 10-6, Fri 10-5
Friends of the Library Group

P FRIENDS FREE LIBRARY OF GERMANTOWN, 5418 Germantown Ave, 19144. SAN 314-9129. Tel: 215-951-2355. FAX: 215-951-2697. E-mail: library@germantownfriends.org. Web Site: www.germantownfriends.org/academics/friends-free-library. *Dir, Libr Serv,* Kate Garrity; E-mail: kgarrity@germantownfriends.org; Staff 6 (MLS 3, Non-MLS 3)
Founded 1845. Circ 27,841
Library Holdings: Bk Titles 61,414; Bk Vols 63,981; Videos 411
Special Collections: Irvin C Poley Theatre Coll 1900-1975
Subject Interests: African-Am studies, Natural sci, Quaker hist
Wireless access

GERMAN SOCIETY OF PENNSYLVANIA*, Joseph Horner Memorial Library, 611 Spring Garden St, 19123. SAN 314-917X. Tel: 215-627-2332. FAX: 215-627-5297. E-mail: librarian@germansociety.org. Web Site: www.germansociety.org/horner-library. *Spec Coll Librn,* Bettina Hess; Staff 2 (MLS 1, Non-MLS 1)
Founded 1817
Library Holdings: Bk Vols 60,000; Per Subs 4; Spec Interest Per Sub 4
Special Collections: Carl Schurz Association Holdings; German American Coll (Printed & Manuscript Coll 18th to 20th Century); German-American Newspapers (19th & Early 20th Century)
Subject Interests: Hist, Lit, Politics
Wireless access
Publications: German Society of Pennsylvania-German Historical Institute Reference Guide 26 (Research guide)
Partic in Philadelphia Area Consortium of Special Collections Libraries
Open Tues & Thurs 10-4
Friends of the Library Group

S GERMANTOWN HISTORICAL SOCIETY*, Pat Henning Library & Archives, 5501 Germantown Ave, 19144-2225. SAN 314-9188. Tel: 215-844-1683. FAX: 215-844-2831. E-mail: library@germantownhistory.org. Web Site: www.germantownhistory.org. *Archivist, Librn,* Alexander Bartlett; Staff 1 (MLS 1)
Founded 1900
Library Holdings: Bk Vols 4,100
Special Collections: African-American Genealogy Archives; German Emigrants Coll; Germantown Hospital Records, 1860s to 1990s; Germantown Industries & Architecture Coll; Horticulture (Edwin C Jellett & Thomas Meehan Coll), bks, graphic works, personal papers; Local History Coll; PG & N Railroad Coll, 1800s to 1900s; Photograph Coll, 1849 to present; Pre-Photographic Images, etchings, paintings, posters; War of the Revolution & Civil War Colls. Oral History
Subject Interests: African-Am hist, Chestnut Hill, Philadelphia, Genealogy, Germantown, Philadelphia, Mount Airy, Philadelphia, Philadelphia hist, 17th-20th Centuries
Wireless access
Function: Archival coll, Art exhibits, Audio & video playback equip for onsite use, Photocopying/Printing, Ref & res, Ref serv available, Res libr, Scanner, Spoken cassettes & CDs
Publications: Germantown Crier (Biannually)
Open Tues 9-1, Thurs 1-5
Restriction: Fee for pub use, In-house use for visitors, Limited access for the pub, Non-circulating, Not a lending libr, Open to pub for ref only, Pub use on premises, Restricted pub use
Friends of the Library Group

GLAXOSMITHKLINE PHARMACEUTICALS

S MARKETING LIBRARY*, One Franklin Plaza, 19101. (Mail add: PO Box 7929 FP 1260, 19101-7929), SAN 359-1271. Tel: 215-751-5576. FAX: 215-751-5509. *Bibliog Instr, Librn, Online Serv,* Doris Shalley; Staff 1 (Non-MLS 1)
Founded 1946
Library Holdings: Bk Titles 2,268; Bk Vols 2,391; Per Subs 216
Publications: Acquisitions Bulletin; Mark Alert (Quarterly)
Open Mon-Fri 8:30-4:30

S RESEARCH & DEVELOPMENT LIBRARY*, UW2322, 709 Swedeland Rd, King of Prussia, 19406-2799. (Mail add: PO Box 1539, King of Prussia, 19406-0939), SAN 359-1247. Tel: 610-270-6400. FAX: 610-270-4127. *Librn,* Robert Guerrero; Staff 12 (MLS 12)
Founded 1947
Library Holdings: Bk Titles 15,856; Bk Vols 17,510; Per Subs 800
Subject Interests: Biochem, Chem, Med, Microbiology, Pharm, Pharmacology
Publications: List of Recent Acquisitions
Restriction: Not open to pub

S GRAND ARMY OF THE REPUBLIC MUSEUM & LIBRARY, 4278 Griscom St, 19124-3954. SAN 372-9176. Tel: 215-289-6484. E-mail: GARMUSLIB1866@gmail.com. Web Site: www.garmuslib.org. *Librn, Pres,* Joseph Perry
Founded 1926
Library Holdings: Bk Vols 6,000
Special Collections: Original copies of Philadelphia Inquirer newspapers published 1861-1865
Subject Interests: Civil War
Function: Res libr
Open Tues 12-4
Restriction: Not a lending libr
Friends of the Library Group

S HISTORICAL SOCIETY OF PENNSYLVANIA*, Library Division, 1300 Locust St, 19107-5699. SAN 314-9250. Tel: 215-732-6200. Interlibrary Loan Service Tel: 215-732-6200, Ext 219. Reference Tel: 215-732-6200, Ext 209. Administration Tel: 215-732-6200, Ext 237. FAX: 215-732-2680. E-mail: library@hsp.org. Reference E-mail: readyref@hsp.org. Web Site: www.hsp.org. *Chief Operating Officer, Sr Dir, Libr & Coll,* Dr Lee Arnold; E-mail: larnold@hsp.org; *Dir, Archives,* Cary Hutto; Tel: 215-732-6200, Ext 301, E-mail: chutto@hsp.org; *Dir, Digital Coll,* Caroline E Hayden; Tel: 215-732-6200, Ext 249, E-mail: chayden@hsp.org; *Dir, Presv & Conserv,* Tara O'Brien; Tel: 215-732-6200, Ext 245, E-mail: tobrien@hsp.org; *Dir, Res Serv,* David Haugaard; E-mail:

dhaugaard@hsp.org; *Asst Dir, Res Serv,* Sarah Heim; Tel: 215-732-6200, Ext 261, E-mail: sheim@hsp.org; *Head, Ref Serv, Historian,* Dr Daniel N Rolph; Tel: 215-732-6200, Ext 203, E-mail: drolph@hsp.org; *Pub Serv Librn, Stacks Mgr,* Steve Smith; Tel: 215-732-6200, Ext 238, E-mail: ssmith@hsp.org; *Cataloger,* Anthony DiGiovanni; Tel: 215-732-6200, Ext 206, E-mail: adigiovanni@hsp.org. Subject Specialists: *Archives, Genealogy, Travel,* Dr Lee Arnold; *Manuscripts,* Cary Hutto; *Copyright, Digital asset mgt,* Caroline E Hayden; *Bk arts, Conserv, Presv,* Tara O'Brien; *Biog, Genealogy, Penn hist,* David Haugaard; *Hist of med, Women's hist,* Sarah Heim; *Civil War, Folklore, Genealogy,* Dr Daniel N Rolph; *Archit,* Steve Smith; *Res, Transcripts,* Anthony DiGiovanni; Staff 16 (MLS 3, Non-MLS 13)
Founded 1824
Library Holdings: AV Mats 1,235; Microforms 28,000; Bk Vols 560,000; Per Subs 2,000; Videos 164
Special Collections: Atlantis National Daily Greek Newspapers; Delaware Valley, architectural drawings & maps, photos, prints; Economic, Social & Political History of Middle Colonies & States, 1650s-present (including Papers of William Penn & the Penn Family, John Dickinson, James Buchanan, George Mifflin Dallas, Jay Cooke, James Logan, Salmon P Chase & Joel R Poinsett); Ethnic & Immigrant Experience in the US since 1877 (Balch Institute Coll), audio rec, bks, newsp, organizational rec, pamphlets, personal papers, photos; Fiorani Radio Production Records; Indian Rights Association Archives; Leonard Covello Papers; Nelson Diaz Papers; Pennsylvania Abolition Society Archives; Scots Thistle Society Coll; Shigezo & Sonoko Iwata Papers; Simon Gratz & Ferdinand J Dreer Autograph Colls
Subject Interests: Genealogical, Hist, Mats dealing with the Delaware Valley region, Original thirteen colonies
Automation Activity & Vendor Info: (Cataloging) OCLC Connexion; (Serials) EBSCO Online
Wireless access
Function: Res libr
Publications: Guide to the Balch Collections (Collection catalog); Guide to the Manuscript Collection of the Historical Society of Pennsylvania (Collection catalog); HSP Sidelights (Newsletter); Pennsylvania Magazine of History & Biography (Quarterly); Serving History in a Changing World by Sally Griffith
Partic in Independent Res Libr Asn; Philadelphia Area Consortium of Special Collections Libraries
Open Tues & Thurs 12:30-5:30, Wed 12:30-8:30, Fri 10-5:30
Restriction: Non-circulating
Friends of the Library Group

CR HOLY FAMILY UNIVERSITY LIBRARY, 9801 Frankford Ave, 19114. SAN 314-9269. Tel: 267-341-3315. FAX: 215-632-8067. E-mail: reference@holyfamily.edu. Web Site: www.holyfamily.edu/academics/library. *Exec Dir,* Shannon Brown; Tel: 267-341-3314, E-mail: sbrown10@holyfamily.edu; *Info Literacy Librn,* Erin Carney; Tel: 267-341-3312, E-mail: ecarney@holyfamily.edu; *Ref Librn,* Robert Ellermeyer; Tel: 267-341-3316, E-mail: rellermeyer@holyfamily.edu; *Ref Librn,* Joe Ward; Tel: 267-341-3584, E-mail: jward@holyfamily.edu; *Syst Librn,* Justin Sewell; Tel: 267-341-3573, E-mail: jsewell2@holyfamily.edu; *Access Services & ILL Coord,* Stephanie Mendes; E-mail: smendes@holyfamily.edu; *Acquisitions & Technical Services Coord,* Gina Palumbo; Tel: 267-341-3311, E-mail: gpalumbo@holyfamily.edu; *Univ Archivist,* Sister Brendan O'Brien; Tel: 267-341-3414, E-mail: srbrendan@holyfamily.edu; Staff 6 (MLS 6)
Founded 1954. Enrl 2,178; Fac 350; Highest Degree: Doctorate
Library Holdings: DVDs 2,930; e-books 17,776; Bk Vols 96,900
Subject Interests: Arts, Bus, Catholicism, Counseling psychol, Criminal justice, Educ, Nursing, Relig, Sciences
Automation Activity & Vendor Info: (Acquisitions) OCLC Worldshare Management Services; (Cataloging) OCLC Worldshare Management Services; (Circulation) OCLC Worldshare Management Services; (Course Reserve) OCLC Worldshare Management Services; (Discovery) OCLC Worldshare Management Services; (ILL) OCLC; (OPAC) OCLC Worldshare Management Services; (Serials) OCLC Worldshare Management Services
Wireless access
Function: Archival coll, Audio & video playback equip for onsite use, Computers for patron use, Electronic databases & coll, ILL available, Online cat, Online info literacy tutorials on the web & in blackboard, Online ref, Orientations, Photocopying/Printing, Ref serv available, Scanner, Telephone ref, Wheelchair accessible, Workshops
Publications: Library & Search Guides (Research guide)
Partic in LYRASIS; OCLC Online Computer Library Center, Inc; Southeastern Pa Consortium for Higher Educ
Open Mon-Thurs 7:30am-9pm, Fri 7:30-6, Sat 9-4

S INDEPENDENCE SEAPORT MUSEUM LIBRARY, 211 S Columbus Blvd, 19106. SAN 314-9781. Tel: 215-413-8640. E-mail: library@phillyseaport.org. Web Site: www.phillyseaport.org/research. *Curatorial Asst,* Pat Weeks; E-mail: pweeks@phillyseaport.org
Founded 1974
Library Holdings: Bk Titles 14,000; Bk Vols 15,000; Per Subs 35
Special Collections: Manuscript Coll; Map & Chart Coll; Philadelphia Area Shipbuilding (NY Shipbuilding Corp, Cramp Shipbuilding Co), vessel registers; Photograph Coll; Rare Book Coll
Subject Interests: Maritime heritage of the Delaware, Naval sci, Port of Philadelphia, S Jersey maritime hist
Function: Archival coll, Art exhibits, Ref & res, Ref serv available, Res libr
Publications: John Lenthall, Naval Architect: A Guide to Plans & Drawings of American Naval & Merchant Vessels 1790-1874; Massachusetts Steam Navigation Company, Salem, Massachusetts Records (1816-1818) & the Newhall Family Business Papers (1809-1852): A Descriptive Guide; Shipbuilding at Cramp & Sons: A History & Guide to Collections of the William Cramp & Sons Ship & Engine Building Company (1830-1927) & the Cramp Shipbuilding Company (1941-46) of Philadelphia
Partic in Philadelphia Area Consortium of Special Collections Libraries
Restriction: Non-circulating, Open by appt only

L JENKINS LAW LIBRARY*, Ten Penn Ctr, 1801 Market St, Ste 900, 19103-6405. SAN 314-9366. Tel: 215-574-7900. Circulation Tel: 215-574-1500. Interlibrary Loan Service Tel: 215-574-7933. Reference Tel: 215-574-1505. FAX: 215-575-9205. E-mail: research@jenkinslaw.org. Circulation E-mail: circulation@jenkinslaw.org. Web Site: www.jenkinslaw.org. *Exec Dir,* Nancy Garner; Tel: 215-574-7944, E-mail: ngarner@jenkinslaw.org; *Exec Dir,* Ida Weingram; Tel: 215-574-7935, E-mail: iweingram@jenkinslaw.org; *Ref Librn,* Thomas Baer; Tel: 215-574-7946, E-mail: tbear@jenkinslaw.org; *Ref Librn,* Michelle Buhalo; Tel: 215-574-7911, E-mail: mbuhalo@jenkinslaw.org; *Ref Librn,* Kristen B Matteucci; Tel: 215 574-7930, E-mail: kmatteucci@jenkinslaw.org; *Educ Serv Mgr,* Dan Giancaterino; Tel: 215-574-7945, E-mail: dgiancaterino@jenkinslaw.org; *Libr Syst Mgr,* Lindsay Braddy; Tel: 215-574-7907; *Res Serv Mgr,* Jenny Hohenstein; Tel: 215-574-7941, E-mail: jhohenstein@jenkinslaw.org; Staff 24 (MLS 13, Non-MLS 11)
Founded 1802
Jan 2017-Dec 2017 Income $5,463,260, Locally Generated Income $1,371,170, Other $4,092,090. Mats Exp $1,524,307, Books $39,336, Per/Ser (Incl. Access Fees) $762,876, Micro $9,917, AV Mat $391, Electronic Ref Mat (Incl. Access Fees) $705,863, Presv $5,924. Sal $1,631,200 (Prof $1,084,800)
Special Collections: Roman & Canon Law (John Marshall Gest Coll). State Document Depository
Automation Activity & Vendor Info: (Acquisitions) Innovative Interfaces, Inc; (Cataloging) Innovative Interfaces, Inc; (Circulation) Innovative Interfaces, Inc; (ILL) OCLC; (OPAC) Innovative Interfaces, Inc; (Serials) SerialsSolutions
Wireless access
Function: 24/7 Electronic res, 24/7 Online cat, Audio & video playback equip for onsite use, Computers for patron use, Distance learning, Doc delivery serv, E-Readers, Electronic databases & coll, ILL available, Internet access, Meeting rooms, Microfiche/film & reading machines, Online cat, Orientations, Photocopying/Printing, Ref & res, Ref serv available, Res assist avail, Res performed for a fee, Scanner, Spoken cassettes & CDs, Spoken cassettes & DVDs, Tax forms, Telephone ref, Wheelchair accessible, Workshops
Publications: Jenkins Flash (Current awareness service)
Partic in OCLC Online Computer Library Center, Inc
Special Services for the Blind - Screen enlargement software for people with visual disabilities
Open Mon, Tues, Thurs & Fri 8:30-6, Wed 8:30-7
Restriction: Circ to mem only, Fee for pub use, Limited access for the pub, Mem only, Non-circulating to the pub, Restricted pub use, Sub libr

C HERBERT D KATZ CENTER FOR ADVANCED JUDAIC STUDIES LIBRARY*, 420 Walnut St, 19106-3703. SAN 314-8939. Tel: 215-746-1290, 215-746-5154. Web Site: www.library.upenn.edu/lkcajs. *Archivist, Pub Serv Librn,* Dr Bruce Nielsen; E-mail: bnielsen@pobox.upenn.edu; *Curator,* Dr Arthur Kiron; E-mail: kiron@pobox.upenn.edu; *Circ,* Josef Gulka; E-mail: jgulka@pobox.upenn.edu; Staff 4 (MLS 2, Non-MLS 2)
Founded 1907
Library Holdings: Bk Titles 162,410; Bk Vols 180,000; Per Subs 92
Special Collections: American-Jewish History, archives; Arabica (Prof Skoss Coll); Bible (Prof Max Margolis Coll); Geniza Fragments; Hebrew Manuscripts; History of Jewish & Oriental Studies; History of Philadelphia Oriental Manuscripts & Papyri; Poland & Hungary Coll; Rare Printed Judaica; USSR Coll
Subject Interests: Biblical studies, Judaica, Near Eastern studies
Automation Activity & Vendor Info: (Acquisitions) Innovative Interfaces Inc; (Cataloging) Innovative Interfaces, Inc; (Circulation) Innovative Interfaces, Inc; (Course Reserve) Innovative Interfaces, Inc; (ILL) Innovative Interfaces, Inc; (Media Booking) Innovative Interfaces, Inc; (OPAC) Innovative Interfaces, Inc; (Serials) Innovative Interfaces, Inc
Wireless access

Publications: The Jewish Quarterly Review
Partic in OCLC Online Computer Library Center, Inc; Research Libraries Information Network
Open Mon-Fri 9-4:30
Restriction: Authorized patrons, Authorized scholars by appt

L KLEHR, HARRISON, HARVEY, BRANZBURG & ELLERS*, Law Library, 1835 Market St, Ste 1400, 19103. SAN 376-1584. Tel: 215-568-6060. FAX: 215-568-6603. Web Site: www.klehr.com. *Librn,* Margaret S Fallon; Tel: 215-569-3091; Staff 3 (MLS 1, Non-MLS 2)
Library Holdings: Bk Titles 12,198; Bk Vols 15,160; Per Subs 32

C LA SALLE UNIVERSITY*, Connelly Library, 1900 W Olney Ave, 19141-1199. SAN 314-9382. Tel: 215-951-1287. Interlibrary Loan Service Tel: 215-951-1862. FAX: 215-951-1595. Web Site: library.lasalle.edu. *Dean & Univ Librn,* Dr Sarah Clark; Tel: 215-951-1286, E-mail: clarks@lasalle.edu; Staff 14 (MLS 10, Non-MLS 4)
Founded 1863. Enrl 4,000; Fac 150; Highest Degree: Doctorate
Library Holdings: Bk Titles 362,819; Bk Vols 365,411; Per Subs 4,789; Videos 1,088
Special Collections: Charles Willson Peale Coll; Germantowniana Coll; Graham Green; Japanese Tea Ceremony; Katherine Ann Porter Coll; Lasalliana; Vietnam War; Walker Percy Coll
Subject Interests: Holocaust, Vietnam War
Wireless access
Function: Res libr
Publications: Connelly Chronicle; Newsletter (Quarterly)
Partic in Partnership for Academic Library Collaborative & Innovation; Philadelphia Area Consortium of Special Collections Libraries
Open Mon-Thurs 8am-Midnight, Fri 8-8, Sat 10-6, Sun Noon-Midnight

S LIBRARY COMPANY OF PHILADELPHIA*, 1314 Locust St, 19107. SAN 314-9404. Tel: 215-546-3181. FAX: 215-546-5167. Web Site: librarycompany.org. *Dir,* Dr Michael J Barsanti; Tel: 215-546-3181, Ext 124, E-mail: mbarsanti@librarycompany.org; *Chief of Ref,* Cornelia S King; E-mail: cking@librarycompany.org; *Chief Cataloger, Digital Initiatives Librn,* Arielle Rambo; E-mail: arambo@librarycompany.org; *Chief Develop Officer,* Raechel Hammer; E-mail: rhammer@librarycompany.org; *Librn,* James N Green; E-mail: jgreen@librarycompany.org; *Curator of Printed Bks,* Rachel D'Agostino; E-mail: rdagostino@librarycompany.org; *Curator, Photog & Prints,* Sarah Weatherwax; E-mail: printroom@librarycompany.org; Staff 18 (MLS 7, Non-MLS 11)
Founded 1731
Library Holdings: Bk Titles 600,000
Special Collections: African American History to 1906; American Imprints to 1880; American Judaica to 1850; American Technology & Business to 1860; Early American Imprints (Zinman Coll); Early American Natural History, Agriculture, Education & Philanthropy; English & American Literature Coll; German Americana to 1830; Libraries of William Byrd, Benjamin Franklin, James Logan, Benjamin Rush & other Early American Book Collectors; Philadelphiana bks, prints; Popular Medicine to 1880; Prints & Photographs of Philadelphia to 1930
Subject Interests: 18th Century med, 18th Century sci, 19th Century women's hist, African-Am, Am archit, Am political hist, Background of Am civilization to 1880, Bookbinding, Early 19th Century med, Early 19th Century sci, Econ hist, Hist, Iconography of Philadelphia to 1930, Women's hist
Automation Activity & Vendor Info: (Cataloging) OCLC Connexion; (OPAC) Ex Libris Group
Wireless access
Publications: Annual Report; Exhibition Catalogues; Newsletter
Partic in Independent Res Libr Asn; OCLC Research Library Partnership; Philadelphia Area Consortium for the History of Science; Philadelphia Area Consortium of Special Collections Libraries
Open Mon-Fri 9-4:45
Friends of the Library Group

R LUTHERAN THEOLOGICAL SEMINARY, Krauth Memorial Library, United Lutheran Seminary, 7301 Germantown Ave, 19119-1794. SAN 314-9412. Tel: 215-248-6329. Interlibrary Loan Service Tel: 215-248-6334. FAX: 215-248-6327. E-mail: request@ltsp.edu. Web Site: www.ltsp.edu/krauth/index.html. *Dir, Archives,* Evan Boyd; Tel: 215-248-6330, E-mail: eboyd@uls.edu; *Acq, ILL Librn,* Ronald Townsend; E-mail: rtownsend@uls.edu; *Archivist,* John Peterson; Tel: 215-248-6383, E-mail: mtairyarchives@ltsp.edu; *Pub Serv Asst,* Sharon Baker; Tel: 215-248-6335, E-mail: sbaker@uls.edu; Staff 4 (MLS 2, Non-MLS 2)
Founded 1864. Enrl 450; Fac 18; Highest Degree: Doctorate
Library Holdings: Bk Titles 200,000; Per Subs 470
Special Collections: Lutheran Archives, Region 7
Subject Interests: Archit, Evangelical Lutheran Church in Am, Liturgy, Lutheran hist, Relig, Relig art, Urban studies, Women
Automation Activity & Vendor Info: (Cataloging) Ex Libris Group; (Circulation) Ex Libris Group; (OPAC) Ex Libris Group
Wireless access
Partic in LYRASIS; OCLC Online Computer Library Center, Inc; Philadelphia Area Consortium of Special Collections Libraries; Southeastern Pennsylvania Theological Library Association
Open Mon-Thurs (Fall & Spring) 8:30am-9pm, Fri 8:30-4:30, Sat 9-3; Mon-Fri (Summer) 8:30-4:30

M MAGEE REHABILITATION HOSPITAL*, Patient Learning Resource Center Library, 1513 Race St, 6th Flr, 19102. SAN 326-1611. Tel: 215-587-3015. FAX: 215-568-3533. Web Site: mageerehab.jeffersonhealth.org/library. *Supvr,* Venus Bradley; Tel: 215-587-3146, E-mail: vbradley@mageerehab.org
Library Holdings: Bk Titles 500; Bk Vols 550; Per Subs 80
Open Mon & Wed 5pm-7pm, Tues 9:30-5, Fri 1-5, Sat 12-4

S THE MASONIC LIBRARY & MUSEUM OF PENNSYLVANIA, Masonic Temple, One N Broad St, 19107-2520. SAN 314-9099. Tel: 215-988-1933. Web Site: pamasonictemple.org/john-wanamaker-resource-center/library. *Dir, Libr & Mus Serv,* Mike Comfort; Tel: 215-988-1977, E-mail: mcomfort@pagrandlodge.org; *Librn,* Catherine L Giaimo; E-mail: clgiaimo@pagrandlodge.org; *Archivist,* Michael Laskowski; E-mail: mlaskowski@pagrandlodge.org; Staff 5 (MLS 2, Non-MLS 3)
Founded 1817
Library Holdings: Bk Vols 75,000; Spec Interest Per Sub 90
Special Collections: General Works on Freemasonry; Masonic Biography & General History; Masonic Manuscript Coll
Subject Interests: Freemasonry, Hist, Philos, Relig
Automation Activity & Vendor Info: (Cataloging) Sydney Enterprise
Wireless access
Function: 24/7 Online cat, Archival coll, Mail loans to mem, Ref serv available
Publications: Grand Lodge Proceedings (Annual); The Pennsylvania Freemason (Quarterly)
Restriction: Circ limited, Closed stack, Non-circulating of rare bks, Non-circulating to the pub

M MERCY PHILADELPHIA HOSPITAL*, Medical Library, 501 S 54th St, 2 Main, Rm 234, 19143. SAN 320-4596. Tel: 610-237-4150. Web Site: www.mercyhealth.org. *Mgr, Libr Serv,* Ellen Abramowitz; Staff 1 (MLS 1)
Founded 1918
Library Holdings: Bk Vols 1,035; Per Subs 85
Subject Interests: Med
Wireless access
Partic in Basic Health Sciences Library Network
Restriction: Staff use only

R MISSIO SEMINARY LIBRARY, 421 N Seventh St, Ste 700, 19123. SAN 314-609X. Tel: 215-368-5000. FAX: 215-368-6906. E-mail: library@missio.edu. Web Site: www.missio.edu/library. *Dir, Libr Serv,* Rachel McConnell; E-mail: rmcconnell@missio.edu; *Tech Serv Coordr,* Lydia Putnam; E-mail: lputnam@missio.edu; Staff 2 (Non-MLS 2)
Founded 1971. Enrl 200; Fac 32; Highest Degree: Doctorate
Library Holdings: Audiobooks 169; AV Mats 2; CDs 33; DVDs 144; e-journals 499; Electronic Media & Resources 11; Large Print Bks 2; Microforms 304; Music Scores 3; Per Subs 87; Videos 22
Special Collections: Biblical Seminary Theses (New York Coll)
Subject Interests: Theol
Automation Activity & Vendor Info: (Acquisitions) OCLC Worldshare Management Services; (Cataloging) OCLC Worldshare Management Services; (Circulation) OCLC Worldshare Management Services; (Course Reserve) OCLC Worldshare Management Services; (Discovery) OCLC; (ILL) OCLC WorldShare Interlibrary Loan; (OPAC) OCLC; (Serials) OCLC Worldshare Management Services
Wireless access
Function: Computers for patron use, Distance learning, Electronic databases & coll
Partic in American Theological Library Association; Southeastern Pennsylvania Theological Library Association; Tri-State College Library Cooperative
Open Tues & Thurs 10-4
Restriction: Open to pub for ref & circ; with some limitations, Open to students, fac, staff & alumni

S MONELL CHEMICAL SENSES CENTER*, Morley R Kare Library, 3500 Market St, 19104-3308. SAN 322-9181. Tel: 215-898-6666. FAX: 215-898-2084. E-mail: library@monell.org. Web Site: www.monell.org/about/library. *Assoc Dir,* Dr Danielle Renee Reed; Tel: 267-280-3248, E-mail: reed@monell.org. Subject Specialists: *Sci,* Dr Danielle Renee Reed; Staff 2 (Non-MLS 2)
Library Holdings: Bk Titles 830; Bk Vols 951; Per Subs 16
Subject Interests: Chem senses, Nutrition
Restriction: Open by appt only

L MONTGOMERY, MCCRACKEN, WALKER & RHOADS LLP LIBRARY, 1735 Market St, 19103. SAN 314-948X. Tel: 215-772-7611. FAX: 215-772-7620. Web Site: www.mmwr.com. *Dir, Libr & Res Serv,* Kathleen Coon; E-mail: kcoon@mmwr.com; *Libr Mgr, Res, Tech,* Joseph Keslar; E-mail: jkeslar@mmwr.com; Staff 3 (MLS 2, Non-MLS 1)
Library Holdings: Bk Titles 8,961; Bk Vols 15,000; Per Subs 162
Subject Interests: Law
Open Mon-Fri 8:30-4:30

C MOORE COLLEGE OF ART & DESIGN*, Connelly Library, Sarah Peter Hall, 1st Flr, 20th St & The Parkway, 19103-1179. SAN 314-9498. Tel: 215-965-4054. FAX: 215-965-8544. E-mail: library@moore.edu. Web Site: library.moore.edu. *Dir,* Kimberly Lesley; E-mail: klesley@moore.edu; *Sr Libr Asst,* Elizabeth Becker; E-mail: ebecker@moore.edu; Staff 6 (MLS 3, Non-MLS 3)
Founded 1848. Enrl 400; Highest Degree: Bachelor
Library Holdings: Bk Vols 40,000; Per Subs 110
Special Collections: Bookworks Coll, artists' books; Joseph Moore Jr Coll; Philadelphia School of Design for Women Archives
Subject Interests: Art hist, Prof, Studio arts, Women's studies in visual arts
Automation Activity & Vendor Info: (Cataloging) Innovative Interfaces, Inc; (Circulation) Innovative Interfaces, Inc; (ILL) Innovative Interfaces, Inc; (OPAC) Innovative Interfaces, Inc; (Serials) Innovative Interfaces, Inc
Wireless access
Partic in OCLC Online Computer Library Center, Inc; Tri State Col Libr Coop
Open Mon-Thurs 8:15am-10pm, Fri 8:15-5, Sat 8:30-4:30

L MORGAN LEWIS & BOCKIUS LLP*, Law Library, 1701 Market St, 13th Flr, 19103-2921. SAN 314-9501. Tel: 215-963-5000. FAX: 215-963-5001. Toll Free FAX: 877-432-9652. Web Site: www.morganlewis.com. *Dir, Libr Serv,* Kristin Foster; E-mail: kristin.foster@morganlewis.com; Staff 8 (MLS 5, Non-MLS 3)
Founded 1873
Library Holdings: Bk Titles 47,890; Bk Vols 49,610; Per Subs 212
Subject Interests: Legal mat, Penn law
Automation Activity & Vendor Info: (Acquisitions) Innovative Interfaces, Inc; (Cataloging) Innovative Interfaces, Inc; (Circulation) Innovative Interfaces, Inc; (OPAC) Innovative Interfaces, Inc; (Serials) Innovative Interfaces, Inc
Wireless access
Restriction: Open to pub upon request, Staff use only

NATIONAL ARCHIVES & RECORDS ADMINISTRATION

G MID ATLANTIC REGION (CENTER CITY PHILADELPHIA)*, 14700 Townsend Rd, 19154. Tel: 215-305-9347. FAX: 215-305-2052. E-mail: philadelphia.archives@nara.gov. Web Site: www.archives.gov/philadelphia. *Archives Dir,* Leslie Simon; E-mail: leslie.simon@nara.gov; *Admin Officer,* Brenda Bernard; Tel: 215-305-2007, E-mail: brenda.bernard@nara.gov
Special Collections: Archival Records of Federal Agencies & Courts in Delaware, Maryland, Pennsylvania, Virginia & West Virginia; Indian Affairs Records, microfilm; Passenger Arrival & Naturalization Records, microfilm; Population Censuses for All States, 1790-1930, microfilm; Pre-Federal & Early Federal History, microfilm; Pre-World War I Military Service Records, microfilm; US Diplomacy Records, microfilm; World War II Fourth Enumeration Draft Cards
Function: Photocopying/Printing
Open Mon-Fri 8-5
Restriction: Ref only to non-staff

G MID ATLANTIC REGION (NORTHEAST PHILADELPHIA)*, 14700 Townsend Rd, 19154-1096, SAN 314-9528. Tel: 215-305-9347. FAX: 215-305-2052. Web Site: www.archives.gov/midatlantic. *Dir,* Leslie Simon; Staff 8 (MLS 3, Non-MLS 5)
Founded 1968
Library Holdings: Bk Titles 350
Special Collections: Genealogy (United States Census Schedules, 1790-1920), micro; United States District Courts Records (Delaware, Maryland, Pennsylvania, Virginia, West Virginia)
Publications: Research Sources in the Archives Branch
Open Mon-Fri 8-4:30

S NATIONAL PARK SERVICE INDEPENDENCE NATIONAL HISTORICAL PARK*, Library & Archives, Merchants Exchange Bldg, 3rd Flr, 143 S Third St, 19106. SAN 314-9536. Tel: 215-597-2069. FAX: 215-597-3969. Web Site: www.nps.gov/inde/learn/historyculture/library-archives.htm. *Archivist, Libr Mgr,* Tyler Love; E-mail: Thadius_Love@nps.gov; Staff 2 (MLS 1, Non-MLS 1)
Founded 1951
Library Holdings: Bk Titles 11,292; Bk Vols 12,631; Per Subs 10
Special Collections: Edwin Owen Lewis Papers, 1927-1974; History & Restoration of Independence Hall (Horace Wells Sellers Coll, 1730-1930); Isidor Ostroff Papers, 1941-1968; National Museum Board of Managers Records, 1873-1918 (collected by William H Staake, Ellen Waln Harrison & Mary B Chew); Philadelphia Bureau of City Property, Independence Hall Records, 1896-1950; The Independence Hall Association Records, 1906-1962; The Morris Family Papers associated with the Deshler-Morris House in Germantown. Oral History
Subject Interests: 18th Century Philadelphia, Am decorative arts of the 18th century, Constitution politics, Hist
Function: Archival coll, Ref serv available
Restriction: Circulates for staff only, In-house use for visitors, Open by appt only

S NEW YEAR SHOOTERS & MUMMERS MUSEUM LIBRARY, 1100 S Second St, 19147. SAN 328-297X. Tel: 215-336-3050. FAX: 215-389-5630. E-mail: info@mummersmuseum.com, mummersmuseum75@aol.com. Web Site: mummersmuseum.com. *Pres,* Rusty Martz; *Curator,* Mark Montanaro
Library Holdings: Per Subs 200
Wireless access
Restriction: Open by appt only
Friends of the Library Group

S DONALD F & MILDRED TOPP OTHMER LIBRARY OF CHEMICAL HISTORY, Science History Institute, 315 Chestnut St, 19106. SAN 326-6885. Tel: 215-873-8205. Circulation Tel: 215-873-5146. Reference Tel: 215-873-8269. Automation Services Tel: 215-873-8257. E-mail: reference@sciencehistory.org. Web Site: guides.othmerlibrary.sciencehistory.org/friendly.php?s=homepage, othmerlib.sciencehistory.org, www.sciencehistory.org/othmer-library. *Libr Dir,* Dr Michelle DiMeo; E-mail: mdimeo@sciencehistory.org; *Head, Ref, Reader Serv,* Ashley Augustniak; E-mail: aaugustyniak@sciencehistory.org; *Digital Coll Librn,* Annabel Pinkney; E-mail: apinkney@sciencehistory.org; *Tech Serv Librn,* Gabriela Zoller; E-mail: gzoller@sciencehistory.org; *Librn,* Caroline McCarthy; E-mail: cmccarthy@sciencehistory.org; *Chief Curator, Archives & Ms,* Patrick Shea; E-mail: PShea@sciencehistory.org; *Curator, Rare Bks,* James Voelkel; E-mail: jvoelkel@sciencehistory.org
Founded 1988
Special Collections: Roy G Neville Historical Chemical Library
Subject Interests: Hist of chem
Automation Activity & Vendor Info: (Acquisitions) Innovative Interfaces, Inc - Sierra; (Cataloging) Innovative Interfaces, Inc - Sierra; (Circulation) Innovative Interfaces, Inc - Sierra; (ILL) Innovative Interfaces, Inc - Sierra; (Media Booking) Innovative Interfaces, Inc - Sierra; (OPAC) Innovative Interfaces, Inc - Sierra; (Serials) Innovative Interfaces, Inc - Sierra
Wireless access
Function: 24/7 Online cat, For res purposes, Microfiche/film & reading machines, Res libr
Publications: Othmeralia (Online only)
Partic in OCLC Online Computer Library Center, Inc; Philadelphia Area Consortium of Special Collections Libraries
Restriction: Closed stack, Non-circulating of rare bks, Open by appt only, Researchers by appt only

C PEIRCE COLLEGE LIBRARY*, 1420 Pine St, 19102. SAN 314-9846. Tel: 215-670-9269. Toll Free Tel: 888-467-3472, Ext 9269. FAX: 215-670-9338. E-mail: library@peirce.edu. Web Site: www.peirce.edu/student-life/our-campus/library. *Dir, Libr Serv,* Kristin Inciardi; Tel: 215-670-9023; Staff 5 (MLS 2, Non-MLS 3)
Founded 1963
Library Holdings: Bk Titles 42,610; Bk Vols 44,190; Per Subs 161
Special Collections: Law Coll
Automation Activity & Vendor Info: (Cataloging) Softlink America; (Circulation) Softlink America; (Course Reserve) Softlink America; (OPAC) Softlink America
Wireless access
Partic in Tri State Col Libr Coop
Open Mon-Thurs 10-8, Fri 10-6, Sat 10-3

S PENNSYLVANIA ACADEMY OF FINE ARTS LIBRARY*, 128 N Broad St, 19102. SAN 314-9617. Tel: 215-972-2030. FAX: 215-569-0153. E-mail: library@pafa.edu. Web Site: www.pafa.org/school/library. *Head Librn,* Brian Duffy; E-mail: bduffy@pafa.edu; Staff 2 (MLS 1, Non-MLS 1)
Library Holdings: Bk Titles 14,500; Per Subs 89
Subject Interests: Visual arts
Wireless access
Partic in Tri State Col Libr Coop
Open Mon-Fri 9-1 & 2-4:30

S PENNSYLVANIA HORTICULTURAL SOCIETY*, McLean Library, 100 N 20th St, 1st Flr, 19103-1495. SAN 314-9641. Tel: 215-988-8800. E-mai PHS-info@pennhort.org. Web Site: phsonline.org/for-gardeners/phs-mclean-library-and-online-resource-center. *Assoc Dir,* Janet Evans; E-mail: jevans@pennhort.org

Founded 1827
Library Holdings: Bk Titles 14,000; Per Subs 200
Special Collections: 15th-20th Century Horticultural Material; Pennsylvania Horticulture, Herbals, Medical Botany, rare bks
Subject Interests: Botany, Early Am horticulture, Landscape design, Specifically Pennsylvania
Partic in LYRASIS; OCLC Online Computer Library Center, Inc; Philadelphia Area Consortium of Special Collections Libraries
Open Mon-Fri 9:30-5

PENNSYLVANIA HOSPITAL
M HISTORIC LIBRARY*, Three Pine Ctr, 800 Spruce St, 19107-6192, SAN 359-0763. Tel: 215-829-5434. FAX: 215-829-7155. Web Site: www.uphs.upenn.edu/paharc/collections/library.html. *Archivist,* Stacey C Peeples; E-mail: peepless@pahosp.com; Staff 1 (Non-MLS 1)
Founded 1762
Library Holdings: Bk Titles 13,681; Bk Vols 15,459; Per Subs 16
Special Collections: Benjamin Smith Barton; Lloyd Zachary; The Meigs Family; Thomas Story Kirkbride; William Byrd of Westover
Subject Interests: Anatomy, Botany, Med texts from 1700 to 1930, Natural hist, Obstetrics, Psychiat, Surgery
Function: Archival coll
Open Mon-Fri 9-4:30
Restriction: Non-circulating
Friends of the Library Group

M MEDICAL LIBRARY*, Three Pine Ctr, 800 Spruce St, 19107-6192, SAN 359-0798. Tel: 215-829-3370. FAX: 215-829-7155. E-mail: libraryservices@pahosp.com. Web Site: www.uphs.upenn.edu/pahedu/library. *Librn,* Lydia Witman; *Archivist, Curator,* Stacey Peeples; E-mail: stacey.peeples@uphs.upenn.edu; *Libr Asst,* Tom Hanley; Staff 3 (MLS 2, Non-MLS 1)
Founded 1940
Library Holdings: Bk Titles 19,782; Bk Vols 22,640; Per Subs 200
Subject Interests: Allied health, Hist of med, Hist of Penn hosp, Hist of psychiat, Med, Nursing, Psychiat, Psychoanalysis
Open Mon-Fri 9-4

S PENNSYLVANIA SCHOOL FOR THE DEAF LIBRARY*, 100 W School House Lane, 19144. SAN 327-0599. Tel: 215-951-4700. FAX: 215-951-4708. E-mail: info@psd.org. Web Site: psd.org/services. *Libr Mgr,* Penny Starr-Ashton; E-mail: pstarrashton@psd.org
Founded 1820
Library Holdings: Bks on Deafness & Sign Lang 4,000; DVDs 600; Bk Vols 24,000; Per Subs 13; Spec Interest Per Sub 5
Wireless access
Special Services for the Deaf - Adult & family literacy prog; Assistive tech; Bks on deafness & sign lang; Closed caption videos; Coll on deaf educ; Deaf publ; Staff with knowledge of sign lang; TDD equip; Video & TTY relay via computer
Open Mon-Fri 8-4

CM PHILADELPHIA COLLEGE OF OSTEOPATHIC MEDICINE*, O J Snyder Memorial Library, 4170 City Ave, 19131-1694. SAN 314-9692. Tel: 215-871-6470. FAX: 215-871-6489. E-mail: library@pcom.edu. Web Site: library.pcom.edu. *Chief Libr Officer,* Stephanie Ferretti; Tel: 215-871-6475, E-mail: stephaniefe@pcom.edu; *Assoc Dir,* PJ Grier; E-mail: pjgrier@pcom.edu; *Asst Dir, Libr Serv,* Skye Bickett; E-mail: skyebi@pcom.edu; *Electronic Res Librn,* Meghan DiRito; *Cat,* Mitzi Killeen; *Circ,* Julia Lewis; *ILL,* Randall Blackwell; Staff 16 (MLS 6, Non-MLS 10)
Founded 1899. Enrl 2,870; Highest Degree: Doctorate
Library Holdings: Bk Titles 18,501; Bk Vols 38,824; Per Subs 525
Special Collections: Archival History of Medicine; First Editions in Osteopathy; Osteopathic Periodicals
Subject Interests: Med, Osteopathic med, Psychol
Publications: Archival Coll; Audio-Visual Coll; Bibliographies; Library Handbook; Library Newsletter; Osteopathic Coll; Osteopathic Colleges & Hospital Libraries Survey Book; Periodicals & Pamphlets; Union List of Osteopathic Literature
Partic in LYRASIS; Partnership for Academic Library Collaborative & Innovation; Philadelphia Area Consortium of Special Collections Libraries; Tri-State College Library Cooperative
Restriction: 24-hr pass syst for students only, Authorized personnel only

PHILADELPHIA CORPORATION FOR AGING LIBRARY*, Wallace Bldg, 642 N Broad St, 19130-3049. SAN 327-0696. Tel: 215-765-9000. FAX: 215-765-9066. E-mail: library@pcaphl.org. Web Site: www.pcacares.org/professionals/research-information. *Librn,* Position Currently Open
Founded 1978
Library Holdings: Bk Titles 4,000; Per Subs 35
Automation Activity & Vendor Info: (Acquisitions) Inmagic, Inc.; (Cataloging) Inmagic, Inc.; (Circulation) Inmagic, Inc.; (ILL) Inmagic, Inc.; (OPAC) Inmagic, Inc.; (Serials) Inmagic, Inc.
Restriction: Open by appt only

S PHILADELPHIA HISTORICAL COMMISSION LIBRARY, One Parkway, 13th Flr, 1515 Arch St, 19102. Tel: 215-686-7660. E-mail: preservation@phila.gov. Web Site: www.phila.gov/departments/philadelphia-historical-commission. *Exec Dir,* Jon Farnham; E-mail: jon.farnham@phila.gov
Library Holdings: Bk Titles 2,500; Bk Vols 3,000; Per Subs 10
Restriction: Staff use only

S PHILADELPHIA MUSEUM OF ART LIBRARY*, Ruth & Raymond G Perelman Bldg, 2525 Pennsylvania Ave, 19130. (Mail add: PO Box 7646, 19101-7646), SAN 314-979X. Tel: 215-684-7650. FAX: 215-236-0534. E-mail: library@philamuseum.org. Web Site: www.philamuseum.org/library. *Dir, Libr & Archive Serv,* Kristen Regina
Founded 1876
Library Holdings: Bk Vols 227,000
Special Collections: Arms & Armor (Kienbusch Coll); Ars Medica; Art Auction Catalogues, 1741-present; European Painting (John G Johnson Coll)
Subject Interests: Am art, Arms, Ceramics, Conserv, Costumes, Decorative art, Drawings, Dutch hist, E Asian art, European painting, Indian arts, Photog, Prints, Sculpture, Textiles
Automation Activity & Vendor Info: (Acquisitions) Ex Libris Group; (Cataloging) Ex Libris Group; (Circulation) Ex Libris Group; (ILL) OCLC; (OPAC) Ex Libris Group; (Serials) Ex Libris Group
Wireless access
Partic in LYRASIS; OCLC Online Computer Library Center, Inc; Partnership for Academic Library Collaborative & Innovation; Philadelphia Area Consortium of Special Collections Libraries
Open Tues-Fri 10-5
Restriction: Non-circulating

S PHILADELPHIA ORCHESTRA LIBRARY*, 300 S Broad St, 14th Flr, 19102-4901. SAN 321-060X. Tel: 215-670-2343. *Principal Librn,* Nicole Jordan; E-mail: njordan@philorch.org; *Librn,* Steven Glanzmann; E-mail: sglanzmann@philorch.org; Staff 3 (MLS 1, Non-MLS 2)
Founded 1900
Library Holdings: Bk Titles 5,000; Bk Vols 10,000
Subject Interests: Orchestra performance, Sheet music
Function: Archival coll
Publications: Marcato (Newsletter)
Restriction: Mem only

SR PHILADELPHIA YEARLY MEETING OF THE RELIGIOUS SOCIETY OF FRIENDS, Henry J Cadbury Library, 1515 Cherry St, 19102. SAN 315-0046. Tel: 215-241-7220. FAX: 215-241-7045, 215-567-2096. E-mail: library@pym.org. Web Site: www.pym.org/library. *Library Contact,* Rita Varley; Tel: 215-241-7219
Founded 1961
Library Holdings: Bk Titles 18,000
Special Collections: Non Violent Alternatives; Peace Education Resources; Quakerism & Quaker History; Religion & Psychology (Dora Wilson Coll), bks & papers
Subject Interests: African-Am, Civil rights, Criminal justice, Environ studies, Family life, Peace, Quaker hist, Quakers, Relig educ, Spiritual life, Women's studies
Automation Activity & Vendor Info: (Cataloging) Follett Software; (Circulation) Follett Software; (OPAC) Follett Software
Wireless access
Restriction: Mem only

L POST & SCHELL, PC*, Law Library, Four Penn Ctr, 1600 JFK Blvd, 19103-2808. SAN 372-1825. Tel: 215-587-1498. FAX: 215-587-1444. Web Site: www.postschell.com. *Chief Info Officer,* Louis J Mazzio; E-mail: lmazzio@postschell.com; Staff 1 (MLS 1)
Founded 1968
Library Holdings: Bk Vols 2,000
Automation Activity & Vendor Info: (Cataloging) SIMA, Inc
Partic in American Association of Law Libraries; Greater Philadelphia Law Library Association

R PRESBYTERIAN HISTORICAL SOCIETY*, 425 Lombard St, 19147-1516. SAN 315-0178. Tel: 215-627-1852. FAX: 215-928-3870. E-mail: refdesk@history.pcusa.org. Web Site: www.history.pcusa.org. *Dir, Prog & Serv,* Nancy Taylor; Staff 12 (MLS 10, Non-MLS 2)
Founded 1852
Library Holdings: Bk Titles 200,000; Per Subs 150
Special Collections: Alaska (Sheldon Jackson Coll); American Indian Missionary Correspondence; American Sunday School Union; Archives of Presbyterian Church (USA) & Predecessor Denominations; Board of Foreign Missions; National & Foreign Missions; National Council of Churches Archives; Religious News Service
Subject Interests: Am Presbyterian hist

Wireless access
Function: Archival coll, Art exhibits, Electronic databases & coll, ILL available, Internet access, Mail & tel request accepted, Online cat, Online ref, Ref serv available, Telephone ref, Wheelchair accessible
Publications: Journal of Presbyterian History; PHS Matters (Monthly newsletter); Presbyterian Heritage (Newsletter)
Partic in OCLC Online Computer Library Center, Inc
Open Mon, Tues, Thurs & Fri 9-4, Wed Noon-7
Restriction: Non-circulating
Friends of the Library Group

S PSYCHOANALYTIC CENTER OF PHILADELPHIA LIBRARY*, Rockland-East Fairmount Park, 3810 Mount Pleasant Dr, 19121-1002. SAN 314-2973. Tel: 215-235-2345. FAX: 215-235-2388. E-mail: pcop@philanalysis.org. Web Site: pcop.pfitinc.com. *Librn,* Zoe Friedberg
Library Holdings: Bk Titles 1,260; Per Subs 12; Videos 13
Subject Interests: Psychoanalysis
Function: ILL available, Ref serv available
Open Mon-Fri 9-5

L REED SMITH LLP, Law Library, Three Logan Sq, 1717 Arch St, Ste 3100, 19103. SAN 372-1701. Tel: 215-851-1413, 215-851-8100. FAX: 215-851-1420. Web Site: www.reedsmith.com. *Law Librn,* Scott DeMaris; E-mail: fdemaris@reedsmith.com
Library Holdings: Bk Vols 8,500; Per Subs 100
Wireless access
Open Mon-Fri 8-5 by appointment

S THE ROSENBACH OF THE FREE LIBRARY OF PHILADELPHIA*, 2010 DeLancey Pl, 19103. SAN 314-9935. Tel: 215-732-1600. Web Site: libwww.freelibrary.org/locations/the-rosenbach, www.rosenbach.org. *Librn,* Elizabeth E Fuller; E-mail: eefuller@rosenbach.org; *Curator,* Judith M Guston; E-mail: jmguston@rosenbach.org; Staff 20 (MLS 1, Non-MLS 19)
Founded 1954
Library Holdings: Bk Vols 30,000
Special Collections: Marianne Moore Coll, bks, drawings, furnishings, ms, photos; Maurice Sendak Coll, bks, drawings, ms; Rosenbach Company Archives, bks, ms; Rush-Williams-Biddle Family Papers, ms
Subject Interests: 20th Century Am lit, Americana, Bk illustr, British lit, Hist of bks, Latin Americana, Printing
Function: Outside serv via phone, mail, e-mail & web, Res libr
Publications: Collection Guides; Exhibition Catalogs; Fine Press & Facsimile Editions of Rare Books & Mss
Partic in Philadelphia Area Consortium of Special Collections Libraries
Restriction: Not a lending libr, Open by appt only
Friends of the Library Group

M ROXBOROUGH MEMORIAL HOSPITAL*, School of Nursing & Medical Libraries, 5800 Ridge Ave, 19128. SAN 325-2868. Tel: 215-487-4345. FAX: 215-487-4350. Web Site: www.roxboroughmemorial.com. *Librn,* Christine Johnson; Staff 1 (MLS 1)
Founded 1945
Library Holdings: CDs 316; Bk Titles 2,000; Per Subs 151; Videos 102
Subject Interests: Allied health, Med, Nursing
Automation Activity & Vendor Info: (Cataloging) New Generation Technologies Inc. (LiBRARYSOFT); (OPAC) New Generation Technologies Inc. (LiBRARYSOFT)
Wireless access
Partic in Basic Health Sciences Library Network
Restriction: Circ limited

S RYERSS MUSEUM & LIBRARY*, Burholme Park, 7370 Central Ave, 19111-3055. SAN 314-9943. Tel: 215-685-0599. E-mail: ryerssmuseum@gmail.com. Web Site: www.ryerssmuseum.org. *Librn,* Beth Atkinson
Founded 1910
Library Holdings: Bk Vols 20,000; Per Subs 10
Special Collections: Local History Coll; Victoriana Coll
Open Fri-Sun 10-4
Friends of the Library Group

M SAINT CHRISTOPHER'S HOSPITAL FOR CHILDREN*, Margery H Nelson Medical Library, 3601 A St, 19134. SAN 329-2940. Tel: 215-427-5374. FAX: 215-427-6872. *Librn,* Brandi DeFields
Library Holdings: Bk Titles 4,400; Per Subs 60
Open Mon-Fri 8:30-5

SAINT JOSEPH'S UNIVERSITY

C CAMPBELL LIBRARY*, Mandeville Hall, 5600 City Ave, 19131. Tel: 610-660-1195. Circulation Tel: 610-660-1197. Reference Tel: 610-660-1196. FAX: 610-660-1604. *Dir,* Sonia Bennett; E-mail: sbennett@sju.edu; Staff 2 (MLS 1, Non-MLS 1)
Founded 1965
Library Holdings: Electronic Media & Resources 1,698; Bk Titles 2,369; Per Subs 200
Special Collections: USDA Yearbooks
Subject Interests: Food mkt
Automation Activity & Vendor Info: (Acquisitions) Innovative Interfaces, Inc; (Cataloging) Innovative Interfaces, Inc; (Circulation) Innovative Interfaces, Inc; (OPAC) Innovative Interfaces, Inc
Partic in LYRASIS
Publications: Subject Bibliographies
Open Mon-Thurs 8:30am-11pm, Fri 8:30-5, Sat 10-6, Sun 1-11

C FRANCIS A DREXEL LIBRARY*, 5600 City Ave, 19131-1395, SAN 359-0976. Tel: 610-660-1905. Circulation Tel: 610-660-1900. Reference Tel: 610-660-1904. Automation Services Tel: 610-660-1914. FAX: 610-660-1916. Web Site: www.sju.edu/libraries/drexel. *Dir, Libr Serv,* Anne Krakow; *Assoc Dir, Res Mgt,* Kristine Mudrick; Tel: 610-660-3215, E-mail: kmudrick@sju.edu; *Cat & Syst Adminr,* Susan Cheney; Tel: 610-660-1976; *Bus Librn,* Cynthia Slater; Tel: 610-660-1139, E-mail: cslater@sju.edu; *Libr Operations Mgr,* Marian Courtney; *Circ Supvr,* Susan Clayton; Tel: 610-660-1926, E-mail: sclayton@sju.edu; *Archives & Ref,* Christopher Dixon; E-mail: cdixon@sju.edu; *Instruction & Outreach,* Stephanie Riley; Tel: 610-660-1913, E-mail: sriley@sju.edu; *Ref Serv,* Naomi Cohen; Tel: 610-660-1057, E-mail: ncohen@sju.edu; Staff 11 (MLS 11)
Founded 1851. Enrl 7,000; Fac 392; Highest Degree: Doctorate
Library Holdings: e-journals 7,480; Bk Titles 206,362; Bk Vols 355,556; Per Subs 1,418
Special Collections: SJU Publications Coll
Subject Interests: Hist, Philos, Theol
Automation Activity & Vendor Info: (Acquisitions) Innovative Interfaces, Inc; (Cataloging) Innovative Interfaces, Inc; (Circulation) Innovative Interfaces, Inc; (ILL) Innovative Interfaces, Inc; (OPAC) Innovative Interfaces, Inc; (Serials) Innovative Interfaces, Inc
Partic in OCLC Online Computer Library Center, Inc; Pa Tri-State Col Libr Coop; Partnership for Academic Library Collaborative & Innovation; Tri State Col Libr Coop
Publications: Library Lines (Newsletter)
Open Mon-Thurs 8:30am-Midnight, Fri 8:30am-9pm, Sat 10-6, Sun Noon-Midnight

L SAUL EWING ARNSTEIN & LEHR*, Law Library, Centre Square West, 1500 Market St, 38th Flr, 19102. SAN 325-9757. Tel: 215-972-7777. FAX: 215-972-1945. Web Site: www.saul.com. *Assoc Libr Dir,* Richard Weston; E-mail: richard.weston@saul.com; Staff 4 (MLS 2, Non-MLS 2)
Library Holdings: Bk Vols 24,500; Per Subs 100
Restriction: Not open to pub

L SCHNADER, HARRISON, SEGAL & LEWIS LIBRARY*, 1600 Market St, Ste 3600, 19103. SAN 315-0011. Tel: 215-751-2000. FAX: 215-751-2205. Web Site: www.schnader.com. *Dir,* Heidi W Heller; Tel: 215-751-2399, E-mail: hheller@schnader.com; Staff 7 (MLS 3, Non-MLS 4)
Library Holdings: Bk Vols 35,000; Per Subs 1,000
Subject Interests: Law
Automation Activity & Vendor Info: (Cataloging) EOS International; (Circulation) EOS International; (OPAC) EOS International; (Serials) EOS International
Partic in OCLC Online Computer Library Center, Inc; Research Libraries Information Network
Restriction: Open to employees & special libr

S SETTLEMENT MUSIC SCHOOL*, Mary Louise Curtis Library, 416 Queen St, 19147. (Mail add: PO Box 63966, 19147-3966), SAN 359-1158. Tel: 215-320-2601. FAX: 215-551-0483. Web Site: settlementmusic.org/about-settlement/branch-locations/mary-louise-curtis. *Br Dir,* Kris Rudzinski; E-mail: kris.rudzinski@settlementmusic.org; Staff 1 (Non-MLS 1)
Founded 1969. Enrl 3,100
Library Holdings: Bk Titles 800
Special Collections: Chamber Music (Mischa Schneider & J Gershon Cohen Coll), scores & parts; Flute Music (William Kincaid Coll), scores & parts
Restriction: Not open to pub

Branches:

GERMANTOWN LIBRARY, 6128 Germantown Ave, 19144, SAN 359-1182. Tel: 215-320-2610. FAX: 215-438-7133. Web Site: settlementmusic.org/about-settlement/branch-locations/germantown. *Br Dir,* Sara Hiner; E-mail: sara.hiner@settlementmusic.org; Staff 1 (Non-MLS 1)
Founded 1959
Library Holdings: Bk Vols 300
Restriction: Not open to pub

KARDON-NORTHEAST - SOL SCHOENBACH LIBRARY, 3745 Clarendon Ave, 19114, SAN 359-1212. Tel: 215-320-2620. FAX: 215-637-8716. Web Site: settlementmusic.org/about-settlement/branch-locations/kardon-northeast.

Br Dir, Matthew Clayton; Tel: 215-320-2622, E-mail: matthew.clayton@settlementmusic.org
Founded 1976
Library Holdings: Bk Titles 1,500
Restriction: Not open to pub

WILLOW GROVE BRANCH LIBRARY, 318 Davisville Rd, Willow Grove, 19090, SAN 328-8501. Tel: 215-320-2630. Web Site: settlementmusic.org/about-settlement/branch-locations/willow-grove. *Br Dir,* Kathleen Krull; E-mail: kathleen.krull@settlementmusic.org; Staff 1 (Non-MLS 1)
Library Holdings: Bk Titles 500
Restriction: Not open to pub

M TALBOT RESEARCH LIBRARY & MEDIA SERVICES*, Fox Chase Cancer Center, 333 Cottman Ave, 3rd Flr, 19111-2497. SAN 314-9323. Tel: 215-728-2710. Reference E-mail: lib_reference@fccc.edu. Web Site: www.foxchase.org/talbot-research-library. *Dir, Libr Serv,* Beth A Lewis; E-mail: beth.lewis@fccc.edu; *Sr Librn,* Andrea Tomlinson; Staff 3 (MLS 3)
Founded 1926
Library Holdings: Bk Vols 5,000; Per Subs 9,819
Subject Interests: Biochem, Cancer, Cell biol, Clinical res, Crystallography, Genetics
Automation Activity & Vendor Info: (Cataloging) ByWater Solutions; (Circulation) ByWater Solutions; (ILL) OCLC; (OPAC) ByWater Solutions; (Serials) SerialsSolutions
Wireless access
Function: Res libr
Partic in Health Sci Libr Asn of NJ; LYRASIS; National Network of Libraries of Medicine Region 1; Northeast Research Libraries Consortium
Open Mon-Fri 9-5
Restriction: Open to pub for ref only

C TEMPLE UNIVERSITY LIBRARIES*, Samuel Paley Library, 1210 W Berks St, 19122-6088. SAN 359-1301. Tel: 215-204-8231. Circulation Tel: 215-204-0744. Reference Tel: 215-204-8212. FAX: 215-204-5201. Web Site: library.temple.edu. *Dean of Libr,* Joe Lucia; E-mail: Joe.Lucia@temple.edu; *Assoc Univ Librn, Learning & Res Serv,* Steven Bell; *Dir, External Libr Serv,* David Washington; E-mail: dwash@temple.edu; *Dir, Health Sci Libr,* Barbara Kuchan; E-mail: bkuchan@temple.edu; *Dir, Libr Admin Serv,* Richard Holland; E-mail: richieh@temple.edu; *Dir, Libr Info Tech, Head, Knowledge Mgt,* David Lacy; E-mail: david.lacy@temple.edu; *Dir, Spec Coll Res Ctr,* Margery Sly; E-mail: msly@temple.edu; *Assoc Dir, Research Strategy,* Nancy B Turner; E-mail: nancy.turner@temple.edu
Founded 1892. Enrl 28,126; Fac 1,045; Highest Degree: Doctorate
Library Holdings: Bk Vols 2,971,988; Per Subs 23,567
Special Collections: Mid 19th Century Philadelphia Urban Planning, Housing Social Welfare, Education & Labor records (Urban Archives); Philadelphia News Photographs from the Philadelphia Inquirer & Bulletin from Individuals & Organizations; Richard Ellis Library, War Posters (Rare Book & Manuscript Coll); Russell H Conwell & Temple University archives, publications, sermons, lectures, faculty & alumni publications, oral history (Cornwellana-Templana Coll); Science Fiction & Fantasy; Small Press & Alternative Press Publications, 1960's-date (Contemporary Culture Coll); Symbolist Literature, 20th Century English Literature, Richard Aldington, Walter de la Mare, 17th Century English History & Religion, Bibles, Herbals & Horticulture, Business & Accounting History, Printing, Publishing & Graphic Arts. Oral History; State Document Depository; US Document Depository
Automation Activity & Vendor Info: (Acquisitions) Ex Libris Group; (Cataloging) Ex Libris Group; (Circulation) Ex Libris Group
Publications: Descriptive Guide to the University Archives; Manuscript Register Series; Monitor; Temple University Libraries Newsletter; Urban Archives Notes
Partic in Association of Research Libraries; Coalition for Networked Information; Northeast Research Libraries Consortium; OCLC Online Computer Library Center, Inc; OCLC Research Library Partnership; Partnership for Academic Library Collaborative & Innovation

Departmental Libraries:

AMBLER CAMPUS LIBRARY, 580 Meetinghouse Rd, Ambler, 19002, SAN 314-2779. Tel: 267-468-8648. FAX: 267-468-8641. *Head of Libr,* Sandra Thompson; Tel: 267-468-8642, E-mail: sandi@temple.edu; Staff 6 (MLS 3, Non-MLS 3)
Highest Degree: Doctorate
Library Holdings: Bk Vols 90,000; Per Subs 446

BLOCKSON AFRO-AMERICAN COLLECTION, Sullivan Hall, 1st Flr, 1330 W Berks St, 19122, SAN 376-2262. Tel: 215-204-6632. FAX: 215-204-5197. *Librn,* Aslaku Berhanu; E-mail: aberhanu@temple.edu
Special Collections: Prints & Photographs; Slave Narrative Coll; Underground Railroad Coll. Oral History

M GINSBURG HEALTH SCIENCES LIBRARY, 3500 N Broad St, 19140, SAN 359-1425. Tel: 215-707-2665. FAX: 215-707-4135. *Dir,* Barbara Kuchan; Tel: 215-707-2402, E-mail: bkuchan@temple.edu
Founded 1901. Enrl 2,282; Highest Degree: Doctorate
Library Holdings: Bk Vols 131,315; Per Subs 1,410
Subject Interests: Allied health, Dentistry, Med, Nursing, Pharm
Friends of the Library Group

CL LAW LIBRARY, Charles Klein Law Bldg, 1719 N Broad St, 19124, SAN 359-145X. Tel: 215-204-7891. FAX: 215-204-1785. Web Site: www.law.temple.edu/resources/library/. *Dir,* Catherine Dunn; Tel: 215-204-4538, E-mail: catherine.dunn@temple.edu; Staff 8 (MLS 5, Non-MLS 3)
Library Holdings: Bk Vols 550,000; Per Subs 850
Special Collections: Historic Trials (Temple University Trials Coll)
Automation Activity & Vendor Info: (Cataloging) Innovative Interfaces, Inc; (Circulation) Innovative Interfaces, Inc; (Course Reserve) Innovative Interfaces, Inc; (ILL) Innovative Interfaces, Inc; (OPAC) Innovative Interfaces, Inc; (Serials) Innovative Interfaces, Inc
Open Mon-Thurs 8am-11pm, Fri 8am-9pm, Sat 9-5, Sun 1-8

CM TEMPLE UNIVERSITY SCHOOL OF PODIATRIC MEDICINE*, Charles E Krausz Library, 148 N Eighth St, 19107. SAN 359-0674. Tel: 215-625-5275. FAX: 215-629-1622. Web Site: podiatry.temple.edu/research/charles-e-krausz-library. *Head Librn,* Carol Vincent; E-mail: cvincent@tuspm.temple.edu; Staff 2 (MLS 1, Non-MLS 1)
Founded 1962. Enrl 445; Fac 114; Highest Degree: Master
Library Holdings: Bk Titles 10,500; Per Subs 150
Special Collections: Anthony Sabatella Coll; Center for the History of Foot Care; Stewart E Reed Coll, bks, prints, per, monographs
Subject Interests: Med, Orthopedics, Podiatry
Automation Activity & Vendor Info: (Acquisitions) Innovative Interfaces, Inc; (Cataloging) Innovative Interfaces, Inc; (Circulation) Innovative Interfaces, Inc; (Course Reserve) Innovative Interfaces, Inc; (ILL) Innovative Interfaces, Inc; (Media Booking) Innovative Interfaces, Inc; (OPAC) Innovative Interfaces, Inc; (Serials) Innovative Interfaces, Inc
Wireless access
Open Mon-Thurs 8am-11:30pm, Fri 8-7, Sat 9-8, Sun Noon-11:30; Mon-Thurs (Summer) 8am-9pm, Fri 8-5

CM THOMAS JEFFERSON UNIVERSITY*, Scott Memorial Library, 1020 Walnut St, 19107. SAN 359-1603. Tel: 215-503-6994. Circulation Tel: 215-503-6995. FAX: 215-923-3203. Web Site: library.jefferson.edu. *Libr Dir,* Anthony Frisby; Tel: 215-503-8848, E-mail: Anthony.Frisby@jefferson.edu; *Dir of Libr Operations,* Rod MacNeil; Tel: 215-503-2827, E-mail: Roderick.MacNeil@jefferson.edu; *Dir, Coll Mgt,* Daphne Hyatt; Tel: 215-503-2829, E-mail: Daphne.Hyatt@jefferson.edu; *Spec Coll Librn & Univ Archivist,* F Michael Angelo; Tel: 215-503-8097, E-mail: Michael.Angelo@jefferson.edu; Staff 26 (MLS 11, Non-MLS 15)
Founded 1896. Enrl 6,987; Fac 1,346; Highest Degree: Doctorate
Library Holdings: e-books 2,873; e-journals 3,377; Electronic Media & Resources 1,115; Bk Titles 48,729
Special Collections: Obstetrics & Gynecology (Bland)
Subject Interests: Med
Wireless access
Partic in LYRASIS; National Network of Libraries of Medicine Region 1; OCLC Online Computer Library Center, Inc
Open Mon-Thurs 8am-Midnight, Fri 8am-10pm, Sat 11-7, Sun 10am-Midnight

C THOMAS JEFFERSON UNIVERSITY-EAST FALLS*, Paul J Gutman Library, 4201 Henry Ave, 19144-5497. SAN 314-9722. Tel: 215-951-2840. Reference Tel: 215-951-2848. FAX: 215-951-2574. Web Site: www.philau.edu/library. *Libr Dir,* Stan Gorski; Tel: 215-951-2581, E-mail: Stanley.Gorski@jefferson.edu; *Cat Librn, Colls Mgr,* Michael DiCamillo; Tel: 215-951-2842, E-mail: Michael.DiCamillo@jefferson.edu; *Electronic Res Librn,* Damien McCaffery; Tel: 215-951-2674, E-mail: Damien.McCaggery@jefferson.edu; *Coll Develop Coordr, Spec Coll Librn,* Sarah Slate; Tel: 215-951-2580, E-mail: Sarah.Slate@jefferson.edu; *Syst Librn,* Daniel Verbit; Tel: 215-951-5365, E-mail: Daniel.Verbit@jefferson.edu; *Circ Supvr,* Meg Leister; Tel: 215-951-2841, E-mail: Meg.Leister@jefferson.edu; *Supvr, Ser,* Max Margulies; Tel: 215-951-5342, E-mail: Max.Margulies@jefferson.edu; *Coordr, Info Literacy,* Teresa Edge; Tel: 215-951-2629, E-mail: Teresa.Edge@jefferson.edu. Subject Specialists: *Fashion, Psychol, Textile hist,* Stan Gorski; Staff 6 (MLS 6)
Founded 1942. Enrl 7,000; Fac 300; Highest Degree: Doctorate
Library Holdings: Bk Vols 120,000; Per Subs 475
Special Collections: Textile History Coll
Subject Interests: Apparel, Archit, Design, Fashion, Hist of textile, Indust, Textiles, Textiles manufacture
Automation Activity & Vendor Info: (Acquisitions) Ex Libris Group; (Cataloging) Ex Libris Group; (Circulation) Ex Libris Group; (Discovery) Ex Libris Group; (ILL) OCLC ILLiad
Wireless access
Function: 24/7 Online cat
Partic in OCLC Online Computer Library Center, Inc; Partnership for Academic Library Collaborative & Innovation; Philadelphia Area

Consortium of Special Collections Libraries; Tri-State College Library Cooperative
Open Mon-Thurs (Fall & Spring) 8am-2am, Fri 8-7:30, Sat 10-5, Sun Noon-2am; Mon–Thurs (Summer) 8am–9pm, Fri 8:30–4:30, Sat 10-5
Restriction: Authorized scholars by appt, Open to students, fac & staff

L TROUTMAN PEPPER*, Law Library, 3000 Two Logan Sq, 18th & Arch Sts, 19103-2799. SAN 314-965X. Tel: 215-981-4000. Web Site: www.troutman.com. *Library Contact,* Nicola Dixon; E-mail: nicola.dixon@troutman.com; Staff 9 (MLS 5, Non-MLS 4)
Library Holdings: Bk Vols 35,000; Per Subs 500
Subject Interests: Law, Med
Automation Activity & Vendor Info: (Acquisitions) Softlink America; (Cataloging) Softlink America; (Circulation) Softlink America; (OPAC) Softlink America; (Serials) Softlink America
Function: For res purposes, ILL available
Partic in Proquest Dialog
Restriction: Access at librarian's discretion, Private libr

S UNION LEAGUE OF PHILADELPHIA LIBRARY*, 140 S Broad St, 19102. SAN 315-0151. Tel: 215-587-5594. FAX: 215-587-5598. E-mail: library@unionleague.org. Web Site: www.unionleague.org. *Exec Dir,* John Meko; Tel: 215-587-5583, E-mail: mekoj@unionleague.org; *Librn,* Beth DeGeorge; Staff 1 (MLS 1)
Founded 1862
Library Holdings: AV Mats 1,500; CDs 200; DVDs 500; Bk Titles 25,000; Bk Vols 26,000; Per Subs 61; Videos 2,000
Special Collections: American Civil War; Lincolniana; Philadelphia & Pennsylvania History Coll
Automation Activity & Vendor Info: (Cataloging) EOS International; (Circulation) EOS International; (OPAC) EOS International
Wireless access
Partic in Philadelphia Area Consortium of Special Collections Libraries
Restriction: Researchers by appt only
Friends of the Library Group

A UNITED STATES ARMY*, Army Corps of Engineers Philadelphia District Library, Wanamaker Bldg, 100 Penn Square E, 19107-3390. SAN 359-1662. Tel: 215-656-6821. FAX: 215-656-6828. Web Site: www.nap.usace.army.mil/library. *Info Spec,* Linda Carnevale Skale; E-mail: linda.c.skale@usace.army.mil; Staff 1 (MLS 1)
Founded 1969
Library Holdings: Bk Vols 9,500; Per Subs 40
Special Collections: Congressional Documents: Rivers & Harbors, from 1933; Transactions of the ASCE, from 1941
Subject Interests: Engr, Sciences
Publications: Accessions List (Monthly); Bibliography Series
Open Mon-Fri 9-5

GL UNITED STATES COURT OF APPEALS*, William H Hastie Library, 1609 United States Courthouse, 601 Market St, 19106-1772. SAN 315-0186. Tel: 267-299-4300. FAX: 267-299-5110. Web Site: www.ca3.uscourts.gov/circuit-libraries. *Circuit Librn,* Judith F Ambler; Staff 12 (MLS 6, Non-MLS 6)
Library Holdings: Bk Vols 100,000; Per Subs 150
Subject Interests: Judicial admin
Automation Activity & Vendor Info: (Acquisitions) SirsiDynix; (Cataloging) SirsiDynix; (Circulation) SirsiDynix; (Serials) SirsiDynix
Open Mon-Fri 8:30-4:30

S US DEPARTMENT OF LABOR*, OSHA Region III Library, Curtis Bldg, Ste 740 W, 170 S Independence Mall W, 19106-3309. SAN 370-2766. Tel: 215-861-4900.
Library Holdings: Bk Vols 2,000
Subject Interests: Occupational health, Occupational safety
Restriction: Not open to pub

G UNITED STATES ENVIRONMENTAL PROTECTION*, Region 3 Library, 1650 Arch St, 2nd Flr, 19103. SAN 314-898X. Tel: 215-814-5254. FAX: 215-814-5253. E-mail: library-reg3@epa.gov. Web Site: www.epa.gov/libraries/region-3-library-services. *Libr Mgr,* Ann Gold; Staff 3 (MLS 3)
Founded 1972
Library Holdings: Bk Titles 9,500; Bk Vols 14,000; Per Subs 200
Subject Interests: Bio-diversity, Ecology, Environ law, Hazardous waste, Pollution control, Toxicology, Wetland ecology
Function: Computers for patron use, ILL available, Ref serv available
Open Mon-Fri 8-5
Restriction: Borrowing requests are handled by ILL

A UNITED STATES NAVY*, Naval Surface Warfare Center Philadelphia Division, 1000 Kittyhawk Ave, Bldg, Rm 307A 77L, 19112-1403. SAN 359-1816. Tel: 215-897-7078. FAX: 215-897-8380. *Tech Info Spec,* ReLinda Fagan; E-mail: relinda.fagan@navy.mil
Founded 1909
Library Holdings: Bk Vols 10,000; Per Subs 40
Special Collections: Navy Technical Manuals
Subject Interests: Chem, Electrical, Marine engr, Mechanical, Metallurgy
Restriction: Not open to pub

C UNIVERSITY OF PENNSYLVANIA LIBRARIES*, Van Pelt Library, 3420 Walnut St, 19104-6206. SAN 359-1840. Tel: 215-898-7556. Circulation Tel: 215-898-7566. Interlibrary Loan Service Tel: 215-898-7559. Information Services Tel: 215-898-7555. FAX: 215-573-0799. E-mail: library@pobox.upenn.edu. Web Site: www.library.upenn.edu/vanpelt. *Vice Provost & Dir,* H Carton Rogers; *Assoc Vice-Provost, Dep Univ Librn,* Jon Shaw; E-mail: jshaw4@upenn.edu; *Assoc Univ Librn,* Richard Griscom; E-mail: griscom@upenn.edu; *Asst Univ Librn, Digital Libr Developer,* Emily Morton-Owens; E-mail: egmowens@upenn.edu; Staff 294 (MLS 118, Non-MLS 176)
Founded 1750. Enrl 20,643; Fac 2,475; Highest Degree: Doctorate
Library Holdings: e-books 508,696; e-journals 79,220; Bk Vols 6,065,122; Videos 19,787
Special Collections: 16th Century Imprints Coll; 18th Century English Fiction (Singer-Mendenhall Coll); American Drama Coll (Clothier, Speiser, Edwin Forrest Library & Manuscripts); Aristotle Texts & Commentaries; Benjamin Franklin Imprints (Curtis Coll); Bibles (Ross & Block Coll); Church History, Spanish Inquisition, Canon Law & Witchcraft (Henry Charles Lea Library); Cryptography (Mendelsohn Coll); Early Americana (Dechert Coll); Elzevier Imprints (Krumbhaar Coll); English Economic History (Colwell Coll, Carey Coll); Eugene Ormandy Archive; Franz Werfel (Alma Mahler Werfel Coll); French Plays of the 18th & 19th Century Coll; French Revolution Pamphlets (McClure Coll); History of Alchemy & Chemistry (Edgar Fahs Smith Library); Indic Manuscripts Coll; Italian Renaissance Literature (Macaulay Coll); James Fenimore Cooper Coll; James T Farrell Coll; Jonathan Swift (Teerink Coll); Leibniz (Schrecker Coll); Lewis Mumford Coll; Marian Anderson Coll; Mark Twain Coll; Neo-Latin Literature (Neufforge Coll); Robert Montgomery Bird Coll; Shakespeariana, Tudor & Stuart Drama (Horace Howard Furness Library); Spanish Golden Age Literature (Rennert & Crawford Coll); Spanish-American Texts, 17th-19th Centuries (Keil Coll); Theodore Dreiser Coll; Van Wyck Brooks Coll; Waldo Frank Coll; Walt Whitman Coll; Washington Irving Coll. UN Document Depository; US Document Depository
Wireless access
Publications: Penn Library Facts; Penn Library News; Penn Library Resource Guide
Partic in Association of Research Libraries; Health Sciences Libraries Consortium; OCLC Online Computer Library Center, Inc; OCLC Research Library Partnership; Partnership for Academic Library Collaborative & Innovation
Friends of the Library Group

Departmental Libraries:

ANNENBERG SCHOOL OF COMMUNICATION, 3620 Walnut St, 19104-6220, SAN 359-1905. Tel: 215-898-7027. FAX: 215-898-5388. Web Site: www.library.upenn.edu/annenberg. *Head of Libr,* Sharon Black; Tel: 215-898-6106, E-mail: sblack@asc.upenn.edu
Founded 1962
Library Holdings: Bk Vols 9,566; Per Subs 305; Videos 500
Special Collections: Faculty Publications; Film (16mm) catalogs; Financial Reports of the Communication Companies & Public TV Stations of the US; Sol Worth Archive; Television Script Archive
Subject Interests: Attitude & opinion res, Communications, Hist & tech of communication, Interpersonal communications, Res in mass media, Theory
Publications: Reference Sources in Communications; Selected Acquisitions

CM STEVEN W ATWOOD VETERINARY MEDICINE LIBRARY, Vernon & Shirley Hill Pavilion, 380 S University Ave, 19104-4539, SAN 359-226X. Tel: 215-898-8895. FAX: 215-573-2007. E-mail: vetlib@pobox.upenn.edu. Web Site: www.library.upenn.edu/vet. *Head of Libr,* Margaret Lindem; Tel: 215-898-8874, E-mail: mlindem@upenn.edu
Library Holdings: Bk Vols 33,777
Special Collections: Fairman Rogers Coll on Equitation & Horsemanship
Open Mon-Fri 8-6, Sat 10-3

CL BIDDLE LAW LIBRARY, 3501 Sansom St, 19104, SAN 359-193X. Tel: 215-898-7488. Circulation Tel: 215-898-9012. Reference Tel: 215-898-7853. FAX: 215-898-6619. E-mail: askbiddle@law.upenn.edu. Web Site: www.law.upenn.edu/library. *Assoc Dean & Dir,* Paul M George; E-mail: pmgeorge@law.upenn.edu; *Assoc Dir, Res Serv,* Timothy C Von Dulm; Tel: 215-898-0844, E-mail: rtvondulm@law.upenn.edu; *Access Serv, Assoc Dir, Res Mgt,* Jeffrey Grillo; Tel: 215-898-7690, E-mail: jgrillo@law.upenn.edu; *Head, Access Serv,* Lori F Rowland; Tel: 215-746-1755, E-mail: lorirowl@law.upenn.edu
Library Holdings: Bk Vols 601,030

Special Collections: 16th Century English Year Books; Anglo-American & Foreign Law, bks, monographs, digests; Early American & English Law Books; Early American Legal, ms; Records & Briefs of Pennsylvania Supreme & Superior Courts, United States Court of Appeals for Third Circuit & United States Supreme Court, micro. US Document Depository
Subject Interests: Admin regulations, Anglo-Am, Canon law, Decisions, Foreign, Intl law, Judicial rpts, Roman law

CM BIOMEDICAL LIBRARY, Johnson Pavilion, 3610 Hamilton Walk, 19104-6060, SAN 359-2111. Tel: 215-898-5818. Interlibrary Loan Service Tel: 215-898-4113. FAX: 215-573-4143. Web Site: www.library.upenn.edu/biomed. *Dir,* Barbara Cavanaugh; E-mail: bbc@upenn.edu
Subject Interests: Biology, Clinical med, Nursing
Partic in RML

CHEMISTRY, Chemistry Laboratories, 1973 Wing, 231 S 34th St, 19104-6323, SAN 359-1964. Tel: 215-898-2177. FAX: 215-898-0741. E-mail: chemlib@pobox.upenn.edu. Web Site: www.library.upenn.edu/chemistry. *Head of Libr,* Judith Currano; E-mail: currano@pobox.upenn.edu
Library Holdings: Bk Vols 39,017
Subject Interests: Biochem, Inorganic, Organic
Open Mon-Fri 9-5

JEAN AUSTIN DUPONT VETERINARY MEDICINE LIBRARY, New Bolton Ctr, Myrin Bldg, Ground Flr, 382 West Street Rd, Kennett Square, 19348-1692. Tel: 610-925-6835. Web Site: guides.library.upenn.edu/NBC. *Asst Librn,* Dee Crandell; E-mail: dcrand@pobox.upenn.edu
Open Mon-Fri 8-6

FISHER FINE ARTS LIBRARY, Furness Bldg, 220 S 34th St, 19104-6308, SAN 359-2022. Tel: 215-898-8325. FAX: 215-573-2066. E-mail: finearts@pobox.upenn.edu. Web Site: www.library.upenn.edu/finearts. *Dir,* Hannah Bennett; E-mail: hbennett@upenn.edu
Library Holdings: Bk Vols 250,000
Special Collections: Rare Architectural Books, 16th to 20th Century; Urban Maps & Views
Subject Interests: Archit, City, Hist of art, Hist presv, Landscape archit, Regional planning, Urban design

KISLAK CENTER FOR SPECIAL COLLECTIONS, RARE BOOKS & MANUSCRIPTS, 3420 Walnut St, 19104. Tel: 215-898-7088. E-mail: kislak@pobox.upenn.edu. Web Site: www.library.upenn.edu/kislak. *Dir,* William Noel; E-mail: wgnoel@upenn.edu; *Curator, Spec Coll,* Lynne Farrington; Tel: 215-746-5828, E-mail: lynne@upenn.edu
Library Holdings: Bk Vols 250,000
Automation Activity & Vendor Info: (Cataloging) Ex Libris Group; (OPAC) Ex Libris Group
Function: Res libr
Partic in Philadelphia Area Consortium of Special Collections Libraries
Restriction: Non-circulating

CM LEON LEVY DENTAL MEDICINE LIBRARY, Evans Bldg, 240 S 40th St, 19104, SAN 359-1999. Tel: 215-898-8969. FAX: 215-898-7985. E-mail: dentlib@pobox.upenn.edu. Web Site: www.library.upenn.edu/dental. *Head of Libr,* Laurel Graham; Tel: 215-898-8978, E-mail: laurelg@upenn.edu
Library Holdings: Bk Vols 59,447
Special Collections: Dental Catalogs; Dental Patents; Foreign Dental Dissertations; Thomas W Evans Historical Documents
Subject Interests: Dentistry, Hist of dent, Oral biol
Partic in RML
Publications: Acquisitions List of Books & Periodicals

LIPPINCOTT-WHARTON SCHOOL, 3420 Walnut St, 19104-3436, SAN 359-2057. Tel: 215-898-5924. FAX: 215-898-2261. E-mail: lippinco@wharton.upenn.edu. Web Site: www.library.upenn.edu/lippincott. *Dir,* Marcella Barnhart; Tel: 215-898-8755, E-mail: bmarcell@wharton.upenn.edu
Library Holdings: Bk Vols 188,976
Special Collections: Corporation Annual Reports; Financial; Investment Sources; Lipman Criminology Coll; New York Stock Exchange & American Stock Exchange, microfiche
Subject Interests: Finance, Labor, Mgt incl acctg, Mkt, Real property, Taxation, Transportation

MATH-PHYSICS-ASTRONOMY LIBRARY, David Rittenhouse Lab, 3N1, 209 S 33rd St, 19104-6317, SAN 359-2081. Tel: 215-898-8173. FAX: 215-573-2009. E-mail: mpalib@pobox.upenn.edu. Web Site: www.library.upenn.edu/mpa. *Head of Libr,* Lauren Gala; E-mail: milaur@upenn.edu
Library Holdings: Bk Vols 52,707
Subject Interests: Astronomy, Math, Physics

MORRIS ARBORETUM LIBRARY, 100 Northwestern Ave, 19118-2697, SAN 359-2359. Tel: 215-247-5777, Ext 115. FAX: 215-248-4439. Web Site: www.morrisarboretum.org. *Librn,* Sandy Hostetter; E-mail: shost@pobox.upenn.edu
Founded 1933
Library Holdings: Bk Vols 6,700; Per Subs 44
Special Collections: 19th Century Historical Botanical Books
Subject Interests: Botany, Conserv, Ecology, Garden design, Hist, Hort, Plant pathology, Urban forestry

MUSEUM LIBRARY, 3260 South St, 19104-6324, SAN 359-2170. Tel: 215-898-4021. FAX: 215-573-7840. E-mail: muselib@pobox.upenn.edu. Web Site: www.library.upenn.edu/museum. *Head of Libr,* Deborah Brown Stewart; E-mail: browndeb@upenn.edu
Library Holdings: Bk Vols 139,864
Special Collections: Aboriginal American Linguistics & Ethnology (Daniel Garrison Brinton Coll); Egyptology
Subject Interests: Anthrop, Archaeology, Ethnology

C UNIVERSITY OF THE ARTS UNIVERSITY LIBRARIES*, Albert M Greenfield Library, Anderson Hall, 1st Flr, 333 S Broad St, 19102. (Mail add: 320 S Broad St, 19102-4994), SAN 359-0828. Tel: 215-717-6280. Interlibrary Loan Service Tel: 215-717-6283. Reference Tel: 215-717-6282. FAX: 215-717-6287. Web Site: library.uarts.edu. *Assoc Provost, Dir, Univ Libr,* Carol H Graney; Tel: 215-717-6281, E-mail: cgraney@uarts.edu; *Access Serv Librn,* Kimberly Lesley; Tel: 215-717-6284; *Digital Initiatives & Syst Librn,* Joshua Roberts; Tel: 215-717-6244, E-mail: joroberts@uarts.edu; *Music Librn,* Dr Mark Germer; Tel: 215-717-6293; *Pub Serv Librn,* Sara J MacDonald; E-mail: smacdonald@uarts.edu; *Ref Librn,* Mary Louise Castaldi; *Tech Serv Librn,* Kathryn Coyle; Tel: 215-717-6285, E-mail: kcoyle@uarts.edu; *Visual Res Librn,* Laura Grutzeck; Tel: 215-717-6294, E-mail: lgrutzeck@uarts.edu; Staff 8 (MLS 8)
Founded 1876. Enrl 2,126; Fac 505; Highest Degree: Master
Library Holdings: CDs 10,476; DVDs 2,804; e-books 90,272; Electronic Media & Resources 43; Microforms 461; Music Scores 19,056; Bk Titles 88,121; Bk Vols 111,872; Per Subs 314; Videos 1,112
Special Collections: Book Arts; Published Works by or about University of the Arts Faculty; Textiles Coll
Subject Interests: Design, Media, Performing arts, Visual arts
Automation Activity & Vendor Info: (Acquisitions) Innovative Interfaces, Inc; (Cataloging) Innovative Interfaces, Inc; (Circulation) Innovative Interfaces, Inc; (Course Reserve) Innovative Interfaces, Inc; (OPAC) Innovative Interfaces, Inc; (Serials) Innovative Interfaces, Inc
Wireless access
Function: ILL available
Partic in Association of Independent Colleges of Art & Design; LYRASIS
Restriction: Researchers by appt only

Departmental Libraries:

MUSIC LIBRARY, Merriam Theater, 3rd Flr, 250 S Broad St, 19102. (Mail add: 320 S Broad St, 19102-4994), SAN 328-7122. Tel: 215-717-6292. FAX: 215-717-6287. *Librn,* Dr Mark Germer; Tel: 215-717-6293; Staff 1 (MLS 1)
Open Mon-Thurs (Winter) 8:15am-8pm, Fri 8:15-6, Sat Noon-5, Sun 4-9; Mon-Thurs (Summer) 9-5, Fri 9-4

VISUAL RESOURCES & SPECIAL COLLECTIONS, Anderson Hall, Mezzanine, 333 S Broad St, 19102. (Mail add: 320 S Broad St, 19102-4994), SAN 359-0852. Tel: 215-717-6290. FAX: 215-717-6287. *Spec Coll Librn, Visual Res,* Laura Grutzeck; Tel: 215-717-6294, E-mail: lgrutzeck@uarts.edu; Staff 1 (MLS 1)
Founded 1958
Open Mon 9-5, Tues-Thurs 9-7, Fri 9-6

C UNIVERSITY OF THE SCIENCES IN PHILADELPHIA*, Joseph W England Library, 4200 Woodland Ave, 19104. SAN 314-9714. Tel: 215-596-8960. Interlibrary Loan Service Tel: 215-596-8969. Reference Tel: 215-596-8967. FAX: 215-596-8760. Web Site: library.usciences.edu. *Dir, Libr & Info Serv,* Charles J Myers; Tel: 215-596-8791, E-mail: c.myers@usciences.edu; *Assoc Libr Dir,* Leslie Bowman; Tel: 215-596-8964, E-mail: l.bowman@usciences.edu; *Access Serv Librn,* Jon Drucker; E-mail: jdrucker@usciences.edu; Staff 20 (MLS 8, Non-MLS 12)
Founded 1822. Enrl 2,600; Fac 150; Highest Degree: Doctorate
Library Holdings: AV Mats 1,236; CDs 169; DVDs 51; e-books 40; e-journals 11,100; Bk Vols 84,403; Per Subs 318; Videos 785
Special Collections: College Archives Coll; Rare Books Coll
Subject Interests: Biology, Chem, Pharm, Pharmacognosy, Pharmacology, Phys therapy, Related health sci, Toxicology
Automation Activity & Vendor Info: (Acquisitions) Ex Libris Group; (Cataloging) Ex Libris Group; (Circulation) Ex Libris Group; (Course Reserve) Docutek; (ILL) OCLC ILLiad; (OPAC) Ex Libris Group; (Serials) Ex Libris Group
Wireless access
Partic in Health Sciences Libraries Consortium; National Network of Libraries of Medicine Region 1; OCLC Online Computer Library Center, Inc; Partnership for Academic Library Collaborative & Innovation
Open Mon-Thurs 8am-Midnight, Fri 8am-10pm, Sat 11-8, Sun Noon-Midnight; Mon-Thurs (Summer) 9-8
Restriction: Limited access for the pub

S WAGNER FREE INSTITUTE OF SCIENCE LIBRARY*, 1700 W Montgomery Ave, 19121. SAN 315-0240. Tel: 215-763-6529, Ext 12. FAX: 215-763-1299. E-mail: library@wagnerfreeinstitute.org. Web Site:

www.wagnerfreeinstitute.org. *Librn,* Lynn Dorwaldt; E-mail: lynnd@wagnerfreeinstitute.org; Staff 2 (MLS 1, Non-MLS 1)
Founded 1855
Library Holdings: Bk Titles 13,000; Bk Vols 45,000; Per Subs 10
Special Collections: 19th Century US & State Geological Surveys; History of Science Coll; Natural Science Coll; Science Education Coll; William Wagner Coll
Subject Interests: Anthrop, Astronomy, Botany, Chem, Geol, Natural sci, Paleontology, Phys sci
Automation Activity & Vendor Info: (Cataloging) Ex Libris Group; (ILL) OCLC; (OPAC) Ex Libris Group
Function: Res libr
Partic in OCLC Online Computer Library Center, Inc; Philadelphia Area Consortium of Special Collections Libraries
Restriction: Non-circulating, Open by appt only

L WHITE & WILLIAMS, LLP*, Law Library, One Liberty Pl, Ste 1800, 1650 Market St, 19103. SAN 329-0484. Tel: 215-864-7000. FAX: 215-864-7123. Web Site: www.whiteandwilliams.com. *Librn Supvr,* Ev Quillen; E-mail: quillene@whiteandwilliams.com; Staff 2 (MLS 1, Non-MLS 1)
Library Holdings: Bk Vols 15,092
Restriction: Not open to pub

S JOHN J WILCOX JR ARCHIVES & LIBRARY*, William Way LGBT Community Ctr, 1315 Spruce St, 19107. SAN 377-2500. Tel: 215-732-2220. FAX: 215-732-0770. E-mail: info@waygay.org. Web Site: www.waygay.org. *Dir,* John Anderies; E-mail: janderies@waygay.org; *Archives, Curator,* Bob Skiba; E-mail: bskiba@waygay.org
Founded 1976
Library Holdings: Bk Titles 6,500; Bk Vols 11,000; Per Subs 10; Spec Interest Per Sub 10
Special Collections: Personal & Organizational Coll related to GLBT people in the Greater Delaware Valley (dating from the early 1960s onward), papers & AV mats; Rare Book Coll (from the late 19th century)
Function: Res libr
Partic in Philadelphia Area Consortium of Special Collections Libraries
Open Mon-Fri 12-9, Sat & Sun 12-5

M WILLS EYE HOSPITAL*, Charles D Kelman Library, 840 Walnut St, 19107. SAN 315-0283. Tel: 215-928-3288. FAX: 215-928-7247. Web Site: www.willseye.org. *Librn,* Gloria Birkett-Parker; E-mail: gparker@willseye.org; Staff 1 (MLS 1)
Founded 1944
Library Holdings: AV Mats 3,165; Electronic Media & Resources 15; Bk Vols 10,000; Videos 150
Special Collections: History of Ophthalmology
Subject Interests: Ophthalmology
Automation Activity & Vendor Info: (Cataloging) SydneyPlus; (Circulation) SydneyPlus; (OPAC) SydneyPlus; (Serials) SydneyPlus
Function: Audio & video playback equip for onsite use, CD-ROM, Doc delivery serv, Health sci info serv, ILL available, Internet access, Orientations, Photocopying/Printing, Res libr, Spoken cassettes & CDs, Telephone ref, VHS videos, Wheelchair accessible
Partic in Association of Vision Science Librarians
Special Services for the Blind - Spec cats
Open Mon-Fri 8:30-6
Restriction: Circulates for staff only, Fee for pub use, Open to pub for ref only, Pub use on premises

S WISTAR INSTITUTE ARCHIVES, 3601 Spruce St, 19104-4268. SAN 320-5851. Tel: 215-898-3700. E-mail: contracts@wistar.org. Web Site: wistar.org/wistar-archives.
Founded 1892
Library Holdings: Bk Vols 2,900; Per Subs 85
Special Collections: Historical Book Coll; Isaac J Ones Wistar Civil War Coll, bks, ephemera & official rec; Wistar Institute & Family Papers
Subject Interests: Biochem, Cell biol, Genetics, Immunology, Oncology, Virology
Automation Activity & Vendor Info: (OPAC) CASPR; (Serials) CASPR
Wireless access

PHOENIXVILLE

R FIRST PRESBYTERIAN CHURCH LIBRARY*, 145 Main St, 19460. SAN 315-0313. Tel: 610-933-8816.
Library Holdings: Bk Vols 2,500
Publications: Christianity Today-Virtue-Concern
Restriction: Mem only

P PHOENIXVILLE PUBLIC LIBRARY*, 183 Second Ave, 19460-3420. SAN 315-0321. Tel: 610-933-3013. Web Site: phoenixvillelibrary.org. *Exec Dir,* Lara Lorenzi; Tel: 610-933-3013, Ext 123, E-mail: llorenzi@ccls.org; *Dir, Adult Serv, Ref Librn,* Mark Pinto; Tel: 610-933-3013, Ext 132, E-mail: mpinto@ccls.org; *Dir, Children & YA,* Rebecca Krause; Tel: 610-933-3013, Ext 127, E-mail: rkrause@ccls.org; *Dir of Develop,* Lauren Coy; Tel: 610-933-3013, Ext 131, E-mail: lcoy@ccls.org; *Circ Mgr/ILL, Mgr, Vols Serv,* Christine Nicholson; Tel: 610-933-3013, Ext 122, E-mail: cnicholson@ccls.org
Founded 1896. Pop 26,500; Circ 138,000
Library Holdings: Bk Vols 70,000; Per Subs 120
Special Collections: Local History
Automation Activity & Vendor Info: (Cataloging) Innovative Interfaces, Inc; (Circulation) Innovative Interfaces, Inc; (OPAC) Innovative Interfaces, Inc
Wireless access
Mem of Chester County Library System
Open Mon, Tues & Thurs 9:30-9, Wed, Fri & Sat 9:30-5
Friends of the Library Group

CR UNIVERSITY OF VALLEY FORGE, Storms Research Center, 1401 Charlestown Rd, 19460. SAN 315-033X. Tel: 610-917-2001. FAX: 610-917-2008. E-mail: research@valleyforge.edu. Web Site: www.valleyforge.edu/academics/library. *Libr Dir,* Julia Patton; Tel: 610-917-2004, E-mail: jgpatton@valleyforge.edu; *Librn,* Melanie Oestreich; Tel: 610-917-2003, E-mail: mroestreich@valleyforge.edu; Staff 2 (MLS 2)
Founded 1939. Enrl 760; Fac 35; Highest Degree: Master
Library Holdings: AV Mats 2,939; Bks on Deafness & Sign Lang 165; CDs 193; DVDs 565; Bk Vols 65,000; Per Subs 47
Special Collections: Valley Forge General Hospital
Subject Interests: Deaf culture, Liberal arts, Theol
Automation Activity & Vendor Info: (Acquisitions) SirsiDynix-WorkFlows; (Cataloging) SirsiDynix-WorkFlows; (Circulation) SirsiDynix-WorkFlows; (Course Reserve) SirsiDynix-WorkFlows; (ILL) OCLC Online; (Media Booking) SirsiDynix-WorkFlows; (OPAC) SirsiDynix-iBistro; (Serials) SirsiDynix-WorkFlows
Wireless access
Partic in Christian Libr Network; LYRASIS; Southeastern Pennsylvania Theological Library Association; Tri-State College Library Cooperative
Special Services for the Deaf - Am sign lang & deaf culture; Bks on deafness & sign lang; Closed caption videos; Sign lang interpreter upon request for prog
Open Mon-Thurs 7:30am-11pm, Fri 7:30-5, Sat 1-9, Sun 6pm-11pm

PIPERSVILLE

P PIPERSVILLE FREE LIBRARY*, 7114 Durham Rd, 18947-9998. (Mail add: PO Box 122, 18947-0122). Tel: 215-766-7880. *Librn,* Dianne Sinovic; E-mail: dsinovic@epix.net
Library Holdings: Bk Vols 12,000
Mem of Bucks County Free Library
Open Mon & Fri 3-5, Tues & Wed 3-5 & 7-9, Thurs 10-12, 3-5 & 7-9

PITTSBURGH

GL ALLEGHENY COUNTY LAW LIBRARY*, 921 City-County Bldg, 414 Grant St, 15219-2543. SAN 315-0356. Tel: 412-350-5353. FAX: 412-350-5889. E-mail: acll@duq.edu. Web Site: acllib.org. *Dir,* Frank Y Liu; Tel: 412-396-5018, E-mail: liu@duq.edu; *Dir, Operations,* Patricia Horvath; E-mail: horvath@duq.edu; *Ref Librn,* Lori Hagen; E-mail: hagenl@duq.edu; *Circ Asst,* Richard Hovis; E-mail: hovisr@duq.edu; *Ref Asst,* Position Currently Open; Staff 4 (MLS 2, Non-MLS 2)
Founded 1867
Library Holdings: Bk Titles 91,462; Bk Vols 110,000; Per Subs 109
Special Collections: US Document Depository
Automation Activity & Vendor Info: (Acquisitions) Innovative Interfaces, Inc - Sierra; (Cataloging) Innovative Interfaces, Inc - Sierra; (Circulation) Innovative Interfaces, Inc - Sierra; (Discovery) Innovative Interfaces, Inc - Sierra; (OPAC) Innovative Interfaces, Inc - Sierra; (Serials) Innovative Interfaces, Inc - Sierra
Wireless access
Function: 24/7 Electronic res, 24/7 Online cat, Computers for patron use, Doc delivery serv, Electronic databases & coll, Internet access, Mail & tel request accepted, Meeting rooms, Microfiche/film & reading machines, Online cat, Photocopying/Printing, Ref serv available, Scanner, Telephone ref
Publications: Allegheny County Law Library Law; History & Genealogy Series
Open Mon-Thur 9-6, Fri 9-5
Restriction: Circ to mem only, Pub access for legal res only

P ALLEGHENY COUNTY LIBRARY ASSOCIATION (ACLA), 22 Wabash St, Ste 202, 15220. Tel: 412-921-1123. FAX: 412-921-0734. Web Site: aclalibraries.org. *Chief Exec Officer,* Marilyn Jenkins; E-mail: jenkinsm@einetwork.net; *Chief Operating Officer,* Kimberley Hrivnak; E-mail: hrivnakk@einetwork.net
Founded 1994
Wireless access

Member Libraries: Andrew Bayne Memorial Library; Andrew Carnegie Free Library & Music Hall; Avalon Public Library; Baldwin Borough Public Library; Bethel Park Public Library; Braddock Carnegie Library; Brentwood Library; Bridgeville Public Library; C C Mellor Memorial Library; Carnegie Free Library of Swissvale; Carnegie Library of Homestead; Carnegie Library of McKeesport; Carnegie Library of Pittsburgh; Clairton Public Library; Community Library of Allegheny Valley; Community Library of Castle Shannon; Cooper-Siegel Community Library; Coraopolis Memorial Library; Crafton Public Library; Dormont Public Library; FOR Sto-Rox Library; Green Tree Public Library; Hampton Community Library; Jefferson Hills Public Library; Millvale Community Library; Moon Township Public Library; Mt Lebanon Public Library; North Versailles Public Library; Northern Tier Regional Library; Northland Public Library; Oakmont Carnegie Library; Penn Hills Library; Pleasant Hills Public Library; Plum Borough Community Library; Robinson Township Library; Scott Township Public Library; Sewickley Public Library; Shaler North Hills Library; South Fayette Township Library; South Park Township Library; Springdale Free Public Library; Upper St Clair Township Library; Western Allegheny Community Library; Whitehall Public Library; Wilkinsburg Public Library
Bookmobiles: 3. Opers Mgr, Charles Arrigo

M ALLEGHENY GENERAL HOSPITAL*, Health Sciences Library, 320 E North Ave, 15212-4772. SAN 315-0364. Tel: 412-359-3040. FAX: 412-359-4420. E-mail: aghlibrary@wpahs.org. Web Site: www.ahn.org.
Founded 1935
Library Holdings: Bk Titles 11,219; Bk Vols 12,684; Per Subs 750
Subject Interests: Anesthesiology, Cancer res, Cardiology, Gynecology, Heart surgery, Internal med, Neurology, Obstetrics, Oncology, Oral surgery, Orthopedics, Pathology, Pediatrics, Rehabilitation, Renal med, Respiratory diseases, Thoracic
Automation Activity & Vendor Info: (Cataloging) EOS International; (Circulation) EOS International
Publications: What's New
Partic in Basic Health Sciences Library Network; Greater NE Regional Med Libr Program; Inc; National Network of Libraries of Medicine Region 1; Proquest Dialog
Open Mon-Fri 8-5:30
Restriction: Circulates for staff only, Non-circulating to the pub

P BALDWIN BOROUGH PUBLIC LIBRARY*, 5230 Wolfe Dr, 15236. SAN 324-3982. Tel: 412-885-2255. FAX: 412-885-5255. E-mail: baldwin@einetwork.net. Web Site: www.baldwinborolibrary.org. *Dir,* Jenny Worley; E-mail: worleyj@einetwork.net; *Adult Serv Coordr,* Nancy Musser; E-mail: mussern@einetwork.net; *Youth Serv Coordr,* Dolores Colarosa; E-mail: colarosad@einetwork.net; Staff 9 (MLS 2, Non-MLS 7)
Founded 1965. Pop 19,997; Circ 81,000
Library Holdings: Bk Titles 33,846; Bk Vols 34,759; Per Subs 142; Talking Bks 1,568; Videos 2,479
Automation Activity & Vendor Info: (Cataloging) Innovative Interfaces, Inc
Wireless access
Mem of Allegheny County Library Association (ACLA)
Open Mon-Thurs 10-8, Fri & Sat 10-5
Friends of the Library Group

P BRENTWOOD LIBRARY*, 3501 Brownsville Rd, 15227. SAN 315-0437. Tel: 412-882-5694. E-mail: brentwood@einetwork.net. Web Site: brentwoodpubliclibrary.org. *Dir,* Dennis Luther; E-mail: lutherd@einetwork.net; Staff 7 (MLS 1, Non-MLS 6)
Founded 1951. Pop 10,466; Circ 134,000
Automation Activity & Vendor Info: (Acquisitions) Innovative Interfaces, Inc; (Cataloging) Innovative Interfaces, Inc; (Circulation) Innovative Interfaces, Inc; (OPAC) Innovative Interfaces, Inc
Wireless access
Mem of Allegheny County Library Association (ACLA)
Open Mon-Thurs 10-8:30, Fri 1-5, Sat 10-3, Sun 12-4
Friends of the Library Group

R BYZANTINE CATHOLIC SEMINARY OF SAINTS CYRIL & METHODIUS LIBRARY*, 3605 Perrysville Ave, 15214-2297. SAN 315-0445. Tel: 412-321-8383. FAX: 412-321-9936. Web Site: www.bcs.edu. *Dir, Informational Serv,* Sandra A Collins; E-mail: scollins@bcs.edu. Subject Specialists: *Byzantine studies, Relig studies, Theol,* Sandra A Collins; Staff 1.5 (MLS 1.5)
Founded 1950. Enrl 20; Fac 12; Highest Degree: Master
Library Holdings: AV Mats 150; CDs 25; DVDs 25; Bk Titles 35,000; Per Subs 70; Videos 25
Special Collections: Church Slavonic Language (Byzantine Catholic Liturgical Books Coll); History of the Byzantine Catholic Church in Carpatho-Ruthenia & in the United States; Ruthenian Cultural Coll; Ruthenian Historical Coll
Subject Interests: Byzantine studies, Eastern Christian theology, Ruthenian studies
Automation Activity & Vendor Info: (Acquisitions) EOS International; (Cataloging) EOS International; (Circulation) EOS International; (Course Reserve) EOS International; (OPAC) EOS International; (Serials) EOS International
Wireless access
Partic in Washington Theological Consortium
Open Mon-Fri 9-9
Restriction: 24-hr pass syst for students only, Access at librarian's discretion, Authorized scholars by appt, Circ limited, Non-circulating of rare bks

CR CARLOW UNIVERSITY*, Grace Library, 3333 Fifth Ave, 15213. SAN 315-0453. Tel: 412-578-6139. FAX: 412-578-6242. E-mail: gracelibrary@carlow.edu. Web Site: www.carlow.edu/Grace_Library.aspx. *Exec Dir,* Michael B Jones, PhD; Tel: 412-578-6378, E-mail: mbjones@carlow.edu; *Cat & Acq,* Karyn L Kwiatkowski; Tel: 412-578-6143, E-mail: klkwiatkowski@carlow.edu; *Pub Serv Librn,* Emily M Szitas; Tel: 412-578-2049, E-mail: emszitas@carlow.edu; *Syst Librn,* Bret Stiffler; Tel: 412-578-6137, E-mail: bstiffler@carlow.edu; *Coordr, Pub Serv,* Carrie Donovan; Tel: 412-578-6142, E-mail: cedonovan@carlow.edu; Staff 7 (MLS 6, Non-MLS 1)
Founded 1929. Enrl 2,310; Fac 280; Highest Degree: Doctorate. Sal $392,721 (Prof $339,035)
Library Holdings: AV Mats 5,625; Bks-By-Mail 2; Bks on Deafness & Sign Lang 173; DVDs 266; e-books 922; e-journals 137; Bk Titles 89,586; Bk Vols 109,371; Per Subs 356; Videos 1,322
Special Collections: African American Studies; Career Resources; Peace Studies
Subject Interests: Early childhood educ, English lit, Irish lit, Theol, Women's studies
Automation Activity & Vendor Info: (Acquisitions) SirsiDynix; (Cataloging) SirsiDynix; (Circulation) SirsiDynix; (Course Reserve) SirsiDynix; (OPAC) SirsiDynix
Wireless access
Publications: Grace Library Student Handbook
Partic in LYRASIS; OCLC Online Computer Library Center, Inc; Partnership for Academic Library Collaborative & Innovation; Pittsburgh Council on Higher Education
Open Mon-Thurs 8am-Midnight, Fri 8-4:30, Sat 9-5, Sun 2-10

P CARNEGIE FREE LIBRARY OF SWISSVALE*, 1800 Monongahela Ave, 15218-2312. SAN 315-2618. Tel: 412-731-2300. FAX: 412-731-6716. E-mail: carnegiefreelibraryofswissvale@gmail.com. Web Site: swissvalelibrary.org. *Dir,* Kate Grannemann; Staff 5 (MLS 2, Non-MLS 3)
Founded 1916. Pop 11,105; Circ 58,386
Automation Activity & Vendor Info: (Cataloging) Innovative Interfaces, Inc - Sierra; (Circulation) Innovative Interfaces, Inc - Sierra; (ILL) Innovative Interfaces, Inc; (OPAC) Innovative Interfaces, Inc
Wireless access
Mem of Allegheny County Library Association (ACLA)
Open Mon, Tues & Thurs 10-8, Wed & Fri 10-4, Sat 9-4
Friends of the Library Group

P CARNEGIE LIBRARY OF PITTSBURGH*, 4400 Forbes Ave, 15213-4007. SAN 359-2561. Tel: 412-622-3114. Interlibrary Loan Service Tel: 412-920-4535. Reference Tel: 412-622-3175. FAX: 412-622-6278. Reference FAX: 412-687-8982. TDD: 412-622-3167. E-mail: info@carnegielibrary.org. Web Site: www.carnegielibrary.org. *Pres & Dir,* Mary Frances Cooper; Tel: 412-622-8874, E-mail: director@carnegielibrary.org; *Dir, Digital Strategy & Tech Integration,* Toby Greenwalt; Staff 104.4 (MLS 104.4)
Founded 1895. Pop 458,597; Circ 3,540,244. Sal $15,497,075
Library Holdings: Bk Vols 1,895,092; Per Subs 3,405
Special Collections: 19th Century American & German Music Journals (Merz Music Library); Architecture & Design (Bernd Coll); Atomic Energy Commission Reports, micro; Cartoons (Cy Hungerford Coll), originals on pasteboard; English Translation of DIN Standards, trade cats; Local History (Isaac Craig Coll, Pittsburgh Newspapers, 1786-date, Pittsburgh Photographic Library); Narratives (Imbrie Memorial Coll); US Government Research Reports (PB Reports incl OTS Translations), micro; US Patents, 1872-date & British Patents, 1617-date, bks, micro; World War I Personal Coll. State Document Depository; US Document Depository
Subject Interests: Archit, Art, Children's lit, Genealogy, Humanities, Indust, Local hist, Music, Natural sci, Soc sci
Automation Activity & Vendor Info: (Acquisitions) Innovative Interfaces, Inc; (Cataloging) Innovative Interfaces, Inc; (Circulation) Innovative Interfaces, Inc; (ILL) Innovative Interfaces, Inc; (OPAC) Innovative Interfaces, Inc; (Serials) Innovative Interfaces, Inc
Wireless access
Publications: A Purchase Guide for Branch & Public Libraries; Science & Technology Desk Reference; The Bridges of Pittsburgh & Allegheny County
Mem of Allegheny County Library Association (ACLA)
Partic in Electronic Info Network; Oakland Library Consortium
Special Services for the Deaf - TDD equip

Open Mon-Thurs 10-8, Fri & Sat 10-5:30, Sun 12-5
Friends of the Library Group
Branches: 18
ALLEGHENY, 1230 Federal St, 15212, SAN 359-2650. Tel: 412-237-1890. FAX: 412-321-3144. Web Site: www.carnegielibrary.org/clp_location/allegheny. *Mgr,* Carlton Stout; E-mail: stoutc@carnegielibrary.org
Library Holdings: Bk Vols 54,245; Per Subs 90
Open Mon-Thurs 10-8, Fri & Sat 10-5, Sun 12-5
Friends of the Library Group
BEECHVIEW, 1910 Broadway Ave, 15216-3130, SAN 359-2685. Tel: 412-563-2900. FAX: 412-563-7530. E-mail: beechview@carnegielibrary.org. Web Site: www.carnegielibrary.org/clp_location/beechview. *Mgr,* Julianne Moore; E-mail: moorej@carnegielibrary.org
Circ 56,153
Library Holdings: Bk Vols 32,983; Per Subs 64
Open Mon, Fri & Sat 10-5, Tues-Thurs 10-8
Friends of the Library Group
BROOKLINE, 708 Brookline Blvd, 15226, SAN 359-2715. Tel: 412-561-1003. FAX: 412-561-1131. E-mail: brookline@carnegielibrary.org. Web Site: www.carnegielibrary.org/clp_location/brookline. *Mgr,* Jessica Clark; E-mail: clarkj2@carnegielibrary.org
Circ 131,039
Library Holdings: Bk Vols 37,837; Per Subs 50
Open Mon-Thurs 10-8, Fri & Sat 10-5
Friends of the Library Group
CARRICK, 1811 Brownsville Rd, 15210-3907, SAN 359-274X. Tel: 412-882-3897. FAX: 412-882-0131. E-mail: carrick@carnegielibrary.org. Web Site: www.carnegielibrary.org/clp_location/carrick. *Mgr,* Julie Kuchta; E-mail: kuchtaj@carnegielibrary.org
Circ 67,647
Library Holdings: Bk Vols 25,733; Per Subs 64
Open Mon, Fri & Sat 10-5, Tues-Thurs 10-8
Friends of the Library Group
DOWNTOWN & BUSINESS, 612 Smithfield St, 15222-2506, SAN 359-2626. Tel: 412-281-7141. FAX: 412-471-1724. E-mail: downtown@carnegielibrary.org. Web Site: www.carnegielibrary.org/clp_location/downtown-business. *Mgr,* Holly Anderton; E-mail: andertonh@carnegielibrary.org
Circ 270,852
Library Holdings: Bk Vols 60,815; Per Subs 145
Special Collections: Industrial & Trade Directories; Pittsburgh Company Index
Subject Interests: Computer sci, Finance, Mkt, Performing arts
Publications: Bibliographies; Pathfinders; What's New
Special Services for the Blind - Computer with voice synthesizer for visually impaired persons
Open Mon-Thurs 8:30-6, Fri 8:30-5, Sat 10-5
Friends of the Library Group
EAST LIBERTY, 130 S Whitfield St, 15206-3806, SAN 359-2804. Tel: 412-363-8232. FAX: 412-363-8272. E-mail: eastliberty@carnegielibrary.org. Web Site: www.carnegielibrary.org/clp_location/east-liberty. *Mgr,* Chris Gmiter; E-mail: gmiter@carnegielibrary.org
Circ 189,177
Library Holdings: Bk Vols 77,268; Per Subs 97
Open Mon-Thurs 10-8, Fri & Sat 10-5
Friends of the Library Group
HAZELWOOD, 5006 Second Ave, 15207-1674, SAN 359-2839. Tel: 412-421-2517. FAX: 412-422-9845. E-mail: hazelwood@carnegielibrary.org. Web Site: www.carnegielibrary.org/clp_location/hazelwood. *Mgr,* Mary Ann McHarg; E-mail: mchargm@carnegielibrary.org
Circ 49,949
Library Holdings: Bk Vols 17,285; Per Subs 40
Open Mon, Fri & Sat 10-5, Tues-Thurs 10-8
Friends of the Library Group
HILL DISTRICT, 2177 Centre Ave, 15219-6316, SAN 359-3134. Tel: 412-281-3753. FAX: 412-281-6272. E-mail: hilldistrict@carnegielibrary.org. Web Site: www.carnegielibrary.org/clp_location/hill-district. *Mgr,* Abby Harwood; E-mail: harwooda@carnegielibrary.org; Staff 5 (MLS 3, Non-MLS 2)
Circ 22,746
Library Holdings: Bk Vols 22,935; Per Subs 34
Open Mon-Wed 10-8, Thurs-Sat 10-5
Friends of the Library Group
HOMEWOOD, 7101 Hamilton Ave, 15208-1052, SAN 359-2863. Tel: 412-731-3080. E-mail: homewood@carnegielibrary.org. Web Site: www.carnegielibrary.org/clp_location/homewood. *Mgr,* Denise Graham; E-mail: grahamd@carnegielibrary.org
Circ 86,648
Library Holdings: Bk Vols 39,056; Per Subs 65
Subject Interests: African-Am culture
Open Mon, Fri & Sat 10-5, Tues-Thurs 10-8
Friends of the Library Group
KNOXVILLE, 400 Brownsville Rd, 15210-2251, SAN 359-2898. Tel: 412-381-6543. FAX: 412-381-9833. E-mail: knoxville@carnegielibrary.org. Web Site: www.carnegielibrary.org/clp_location/knoxville. *Mgr,* Ian Eberhardt; E-mail: eberhardti@carnegielibrary.org
Circ 50,682
Library Holdings: Bk Vols 24,515; Per Subs 56
Open Mon-Wed 10-8, Thurs-Sat 10-5
Friends of the Library Group
LAWRENCEVILLE, 279 Fisk St, 15201-2847, SAN 359-2928. Tel: 412-682-3668. FAX: 412-682-5943. E-mail: lawrenceville@carnegielibrary.org. Web Site: www.carnegielibrary.org/clp_location/lawrenceville. *Mgr,* LeeAnn Anna; E-mail: annal@carnegielibrary.org
Library Holdings: Bk Vols 24,110; Per Subs 38
Open Mon-Wed 10-8, Thurs-Sat 10-5
Friends of the Library Group
P LIBRARY FOR THE BLIND & PHYSICALLY HANDICAPPED, Leonard C Staisey Bldg, 4724 Baum Blvd, 15213-1321, SAN 315-0461. Tel: 412-687-2440. Toll Free Tel: 800-242-0586. FAX: 412-687-2442. E-mail: lbph@carnegielibrary.org. Web Site: www.carnegielibrary.org/clp_location/library-for-the-blind-and-physically-handicapped. *Libr Serv Mgr,* Mark Lee; E-mail: leem@carnegielibrary.org
Special Collections: Materials on Disabilities
Special Services for the Blind - Assistive/Adapted tech devices, equip & products; Bks on cassette; Cassette playback machines; Closed circuit TV; Computer with voice synthesizer for visually impaired persons; Copier with enlargement capabilities; Descriptive video serv (DVS); Digital talking bk; Digital talking bk machines; Large print bks; Large screen computer & software; Newsletter (in large print, Braille or on cassette); Newsline for the Blind; Ref serv; Tel Pioneers equip repair group; Volunteer serv; Web-Braille
Open Mon-Fri 9-5
Friends of the Library Group
MOUNT WASHINGTON, 315 Grandview Ave, 15211-1549, SAN 359-2952. Tel: 412-381-3380. FAX: 412-381-9876. E-mail: mtwashington@carnegielibrary.org. Web Site: www.carnegielibrary.org/clp_location/mt-washington. *Mgr,* Marian Streiff; E-mail: streiffm@carnegielibrary.org
Circ 77,303
Library Holdings: Bk Vols 25,634; Per Subs 68
Open Mon, Fri & Sat 10-5, Tues-Thurs 10-8
Friends of the Library Group
SHERADEN, 720 Sherwood Ave, 15204-1724, SAN 359-2987. Tel: 412-331-1135. E-mail: sheraden@carnegielibrary.org. Web Site: www.carnegielibrary.org/clp_location/sheraden. *Mgr,* Schuyler Hernstrom; E-mail: hernstroms@carnegielibrary.org; Staff 6 (MLS 2, Non-MLS 4)
Circ 42,993
Library Holdings: Bk Vols 22,442; Per Subs 25
Open Mon-Wed 10-8, Thurs-Sat 10-5
Friends of the Library Group
SOUTH SIDE, 2205 E Carson St, 15203, SAN 359-3010. Tel: 412-431-0505. FAX: 412-431-7968. E-mail: southside@carnegielibrary.org. Web Site: www.carnegielibrary.org/clp_location/south-side. *Mgr,* Suzy Waldo; E-mail: waldos@carnegielibrary.org
Circ 74,382
Library Holdings: Bk Vols 27,331; Per Subs 68
Open Mon-Wed 10-8, Thurs-Sat 10-5, Sun 12-5
Friends of the Library Group
SQUIRREL HILL, 5801 Forbes Ave, 15217-1601, SAN 359-3045. Tel: 412-422-9650. FAX: 412-422-5811. E-mail: squirrelhill@carnegielibrary.org. Web Site: www.carnegielibrary.org/clp_location/squirrel-hill. *Mgr,* Jody Bell; E-mail: bellj@carnegielibrary.org
Circ 511,546
Library Holdings: Bk Vols 106,728; Per Subs 147
Special Collections: Jewish History & Culture (Olender Foundation)
Open Mon-Thurs 10-8, Fri & Sat 10-5, Sun 1-5
Friends of the Library Group
WEST END, 47 Wabash St, 15220-5422, SAN 359-307X. Tel: 412-921-1717. FAX: 412-921-3494. E-mail: westend@carnegielibrary.org. Web Site: www.carnegielibrary.org/clp_location/west-end. *Mgr,* Maria Joseph; E-mail: josephm@carnegielibrary.org
Circ 32,983
Library Holdings: Bk Vols 22,307; Per Subs 35
Open Mon, Fri & Sat 10-5, Tues-Thurs 10-8
Friends of the Library Group
WOODS RUN, 1201 Woods Run Ave, 15212-2335, SAN 359-310X. Tel: 412-761-3730. FAX: 412-761-3445. E-mail: woodsrun@carnegielibrary.org. Web Site:

www.carnegielibrary.org/clp_location/woods-run. *Br Mgr,* Martha Honores; E-mail: honoresm@carnegielibrary.org
Circ 100,305
Library Holdings: Bk Vols 32,239; Per Subs 53
Open Mon, Fri & Sat 10-5, Tues-Thurs 10-8
Friends of the Library Group

C CARNEGIE MELLON UNIVERSITY*, University Libraries, Hunt Library, 4909 Frew St, 15213. SAN 359-3193. Tel: 412-268-2444. Reference Tel: 412-268-2442. FAX: 412-268-2793. Reference E-mail: huntref@andrew.cmu.edu. Web Site: www.library.cmu.edu. *Dean, Univ Libr,* Keith G Webster; E-mail: kwebster@andrew.cmu.edu; *Assoc Dean,* Erika Linke; Tel: 412-268-7800, E-mail: linke@cmu.edu; *Head of Acq Serv,* Denise Novak; *Head, Access Serv,* Ona Taylor; *Head, Cat,* Terry Hurlbert; *Head, Library Info Tech, Res & Develop,* Chris Kellen; *Sr Librn,* Kristin Heath; *Acad Librn, Research Librn,* Afeworki Paulos; E-mail: apaulos2@andrew.cmu.edu; *Spec Coll Librn,* Mary Kay Johnsen; *Computer Serv Mgr,* Richard Schall; *Syst Mgr,* Ken Rose; *Syst Mgr,* Rashid Siddiqui; *Ref Serv Supvr,* Precious Jones; *Cat Spec,* Jan Hardy; *Libr Syst Spec,* Jon Singletary; Staff 94 (MLS 26, Non-MLS 68)
Founded 1920. Enrl 8,687; Fac 525; Highest Degree: Doctorate
Library Holdings: Bk Vols 1,021,423; Per Subs 2,945
Special Collections: Architecture Archives; Bookbindings (including Edwards of Halifax); Early Scientific Works; Important Early Printers (Aldus, Plantin & Estienne Coll); Private Presses (Kimscott & Doves Coll); Senator John Heinz III Archives
Automation Activity & Vendor Info: (Acquisitions) SirsiDynix; (Cataloging) SirsiDynix; (Circulation) SirsiDynix; (Course Reserve) SirsiDynix; (ILL) OCLC; (OPAC) SirsiDynix; (Serials) SirsiDynix
Wireless access
Function: ILL available, Photocopying/Printing
Partic in Center for Research Libraries; Digital Libr Fedn; Interlibrary Delivery Service of Pennsylvania; LYRASIS; Oakland Library Consortium; OCLC Online Computer Library Center, Inc; OCLC Research Library Partnership; Partnership for Academic Library Collaborative & Innovation

Departmental Libraries:

HUNT INSTITUTE FOR BOTANICAL DOCUMENTATION, 4909 Frew St, 15213, SAN 315-0739. Tel: 412-268-7301. Reference Tel: 412-268-2436. E-mail: huntinst@andrew.cmu.edu. Web Site: www.huntbotanical.org/library. *Librn,* Charlotte A Tancin; E-mail: ctancin@cmu.edu; *Asst Librn,* Jeannette McDevitt; E-mail: jmcdevit@andrew.cmu.edu; Staff 2 (MLS 2)
Founded 1961
Library Holdings: Bk Titles 29,950; Per Subs 200
Special Collections: 18th Century Taxonomy (Michel Adanson Coll), bks, ms; Linnaeana (Strandell Coll), bks, clippings
Subject Interests: Biog of people in plant sci, Botanical bibliography, Botanical illustration, Hist of bot, Hist of sci
Function: Archival coll, Art exhibits, For res purposes, Mail & tel request accepted, Online cat, Ref & res, Ref serv available, Res libr
Restriction: Closed stack, Non-circulating, Not a lending libr, Restricted loan policy

MELLON INSTITUTE LIBRARY, 4400 Fifth Ave, 4th Flr, 15213, SAN 359-3258. Tel: 412-268-3171. FAX: 412-268-6945. Reference E-mail: sciref@andrew.cmu.edu. Web Site: guides.library.cmu.edu/melloninstitute. *Head, Sci Libr,* Matthew Marsteller; E-mail: matthewm@andrew.cmu.edu
Founded 1911
Subject Interests: Biol sci, Chem
Open Mon-Fri 8:30-5

SORRELLS ENGINEERING & SCIENCE LIBRARY, 4400 Wean Hall, 15213, SAN 359-3223. Tel: 412-268-7217. *Head, Sci Libr,* Matthew Marsteller; *Principal Librn,* G Lynn Berard; E-mail: lberard@andrew.cmu.edu; *Eng Librn,* Donna Beck; E-mail: donnab@andrew.cmu.edu. Subject Specialists: *Math sci, Physics,* Matthew Marsteller; *Civil engr, Environ engr, Mechanical engr,* G Lynn Berard; *Chem engr, Mat sci,* Donna Beck
Founded 1971
Special Collections: Energy & Environment; Robotics & Computer Science
Subject Interests: Computer sci, Energy, Engr, Environ, Math, Physics, Robotics

CARNEGIE MUSEUM OF NATURAL HISTORY LIBRARY, 4400 Forbes Ave, 15213-4080. SAN 315-047X. Tel: 412-622-3284. E-mail: cmnhweb@carnegiemnh.org. Web Site: www.carnegiemnh.org. *Libr Mgr,* Marie Corrado; Tel: 412-622-3264, E-mail: corradom@carnegiemnh.org; Staff 4 (MLS 2, Non-MLS 2)
Founded 1896
Library Holdings: Bk Titles 26,200; Bk Vols 132,000; Per Subs 1,500
Subject Interests: Amphibians, Anthrop, Archaeology, Birds, Botany, Invertebrate paleontology, Invertebrate zool, Mammals, Reptiles, Vertebrate paleontology
Automation Activity & Vendor Info: (Cataloging) Innovative Interfaces, Inc; (OPAC) Innovative Interfaces, Inc; (Serials) Innovative Interfaces, Inc
Wireless access
Function: For res purposes
Open Mon-Fri 9-5

S CDC NATIONAL INSTITUTE FOR OCCUPATIONAL SAFETY & HEALTH, Pittsburgh Library, 626 Cochrans Mill Rd, 15236. (Mail add: PO Box 18070, 15236-8070), SAN 370-2758. Tel: 412-386-4431. FAX: 412-386-4592. Web Site: cdc.gov/niosh. *Librn,* Kathleen Stabryla; E-mail: kis2@cdc.gov; Staff 2 (MLS 2)
Library Holdings: Bk Vols 165,000
Automation Activity & Vendor Info: (OPAC) Ex Libris Group
Wireless access

C CHATHAM COLLEGE*, Jennie King Mellon Library, Woodland Rd, 15232. SAN 315-0496. Tel: 412-365-1670. E-mail: JKMRef@Chatham.edu. Web Site: library.chatham.edu. *Libr Dir,* Jill Ausel; Tel: 412-365-1244, E-mail: jausel@chatham.edu; *Head, Access Serv,* Kate Wenger; Tel: 412-365-1247, E-mail: kwenger@chatham.edu; *Head, Tech Serv,* Dan Nolting; Tel: 412-365-1243, E-mail: dnolting@chatham.edu; *Ref/Outreach Librn,* Jocelyn Codner; Tel: 412-365-1619, E-mail: j.codner@chatham.edu; *Ref & Web Serv Librn,* Dana Mastroinni; Tel: 412-365-1602, E-mail: dmastroinni@chatham.edu; Staff 7 (MLS 4, Non-MLS 3)
Founded 1869. Enrl 1,000; Fac 50; Highest Degree: Master
Library Holdings: Bk Titles 94,000; Bk Vols 97,000; Per Subs 365
Special Collections: African-American (Wray Coll); Mayan Art & Civilization (Snowdon Coll)
Subject Interests: Women studies
Automation Activity & Vendor Info: (Acquisitions) Innovative Interfaces, Inc; (Cataloging) Innovative Interfaces, Inc; (Circulation) Innovative Interfaces, Inc; (Course Reserve) Innovative Interfaces, Inc; (ILL) Innovative Interfaces, Inc; (Media Booking) Innovative Interfaces, Inc; (OPAC) Innovative Interfaces, Inc; (Serials) Innovative Interfaces, Inc
Wireless access
Partic in OCLC Online Computer Library Center, Inc; OhioNET; Partnership for Academic Library Collaborative & Innovation
Open Mon-Thurs 7:45am-Midnight, Fri 7:45-7, Sat 8-7, Sun Noon-Midnight

S CHILDREN'S INSTITUTE LIBRARY*, 1405 Shady Ave, 15217-1350. SAN 315-1115. Tel: 412-420-2247. FAX: 412-420-2510. Web Site: www.amazingkids.org/About/library-services. *Med Librn,* Ann Ferrari; E-mail: afe@the-institute.org; Staff 1 (MLS 1)
Founded 1972
Library Holdings: Bk Vols 2,200; Per Subs 70
Subject Interests: Asthma, Burn injury, Cerebral palsy, Children's lit, Head injury, Learning disabilities, Pediatrics, Prader-Willi, Rehabilitation, Spina bifida, Unusual syndromes (staff libr)
Automation Activity & Vendor Info: (Acquisitions) Innovative Interfaces, Inc; (Cataloging) Innovative Interfaces, Inc; (Circulation) Innovative Interfaces, Inc
Wireless access
Open Mon 2:30-7, Tues-Fri 8:45-2:15

L COHEN & GRIGSBY PC*, Law Library, 625 Liberty Ave, 15222-3152. SAN 374-6224. Tel: 412-297-4870. FAX: 412-209-0672. Web Site: www.cohenlaw.com. *Librn,* Tony Chan; E-mail: achan@cohenlaw.com; Staff 1 (MLS 1)
Library Holdings: Bk Titles 839; Bk Vols 961; Per Subs 160
Subject Interests: Employment, Immigration
Automation Activity & Vendor Info: (Acquisitions) Inmagic, Inc.; (Cataloging) Inmagic, Inc.
Wireless access
Restriction: Open by appt only

COMMUNITY COLLEGE OF ALLEGHENY COUNTY

J ALLEGHENY CAMPUS LIBRARY*, 808 Ridge Ave, 15212-6003, SAN 315-0526. Tel: 412-237-2585. FAX: 412-237-6563. E-mail: library@ccac.edu. Web Site: www.ccac.edu/library. *Dir,* Anne Tanski; *Librn,* Dennis Hennessey; *Librn,* Ruth Byers; *Librn, Web Coordr,* Elora Cunningham; *Librn,* David Mooney; *Archivist,* Pat Moran; Staff 4 (MLS 4)
Founded 1966. Enrl 5,400; Fac 177
Library Holdings: Bk Titles 75,682; Per Subs 294
Automation Activity & Vendor Info: (Cataloging) SirsiDynix; (Circulation) SirsiDynix; (Course Reserve) SirsiDynix; (OPAC) SirsiDynix; (Serials) SirsiDynix
Partic in Knight-Ridder Info, Inc; LYRASIS; OCLC Online Computer Library Center, Inc
Open Mon-Thurs 8-8, Fri 8-4, Sat 9-3

J NORTH CAMPUS LIBRARY & LEARNING SERVICES*, 8701 Perry Hwy, 15237-5372. Tel: 412-369-3681. FAX: 412-369-3626. Web Site: www.ccac.edu/library. *Operations Mgr,* Anne Tanski; E-mail: atanski@ccac.edu; *Dept Head, Librn,* Barbara Thompson; Tel:

412-369-3671, E-mail: bthompson@ccac.edu; Staff 6 (MLS 3, Non-MLS 3)
Highest Degree: Associate
Library Holdings: Bk Titles 20,599; Bk Vols 24,073; Per Subs 167
Automation Activity & Vendor Info: (Cataloging) SirsiDynix; (Circulation) SirsiDynix; (OPAC) SirsiDynix
Open Mon-Thurs 8-9, Fri 8-4, Sat 8-2:30

P COOPER-SIEGEL COMMUNITY LIBRARY*, 403 Fox Chapel Rd, 15238. Tel: 412-828-9520. FAX: 412-828-4960. Web Site: www.coopersiegelcommunitylibrary.org. *Exec Dir*, Jill McConnell; E-mail: mcconnellj@einetwork.net; Staff 8 (MLS 5, Non-MLS 3)
Founded 1986
Library Holdings: e-journals 333; Electronic Media & Resources 41; Per Subs 130
Automation Activity & Vendor Info: (Acquisitions) Innovative Interfaces, Inc; (Cataloging) Innovative Interfaces, Inc; (Circulation) Innovative Interfaces, Inc; (OPAC) Innovative Interfaces, Inc; (Serials) Innovative Interfaces, Inc
Wireless access
Function: 24/7 Electronic res, 24/7 Online cat, 3D Printer, Activity rm, Adult bk club, Adult literacy prog, After school storytime, Art exhibits, Art programs, Audiobks on Playaways & MP3, Audiobks via web, Bi-weekly Writer's Group, Bilingual assistance for Spanish patrons, Bk club(s), Bks on CD, Chess club, Children's prog, Citizenship assistance, Computer training, Computers for patron use, Distance learning, E-Readers, Electronic databases & coll, Free DVD rentals, Genealogy discussion group, Holiday prog, Home delivery & serv to seniorr ctr & nursing homes, Homebound delivery serv, Homework prog, ILL available, Internet access, Life-long learning prog for all ages, Literacy & newcomer serv, Magazines, Mail & tel request accepted, Mango lang, Meeting rooms, Movies, Museum passes, Music CDs, Online cat, Outreach serv, Outside serv via phone, mail, e-mail & web, OverDrive digital audio bks, Photocopying/Printing, Preschool outreach, Preschool reading prog, Printer for laptops & handheld devices, Prog for adults, Prog for children & young adult, Ref & res, Ref serv available, Res assist avail, Res performed for a fee, Scanner, Senior outreach, Spanish lang bks, STEM programs, Story hour, Study rm, Summer & winter reading prog, Summer reading prog, Tax forms, Teen prog, Telephone ref, Visual arts prog, Wheelchair accessible, Winter reading prog, Workshops, Writing prog
Mem of Allegheny County Library Association (ACLA)
Open Mon, Wed & Thurs 10-8, Tues, Fri & Sat 10-5, Sun (Sept-May) 1-5
Branches: 1
SHARPSBURG COMMUNITY LIBRARY, 1212 Main St, 15215. Tel: 412-781-0783. *Br Mgr*, Sara Mariacher; E-mail: mariachers2@einetwork.net; Staff 2 (MLS 1, Non-MLS 1)
Founded 1996
Library Holdings: Bk Vols 12,990
Open Mon & Wed 2-8, Tues & Thurs 10-5, Sat 10-2
Friends of the Library Group

P CRAFTON PUBLIC LIBRARY*, 140 Bradford Ave, 15205. SAN 378-424X. Tel: 412-922-6877. FAX: 412-922-7637. E-mail: craftonlibrarypa@gmail.com. Web Site: www.craftonpubliclibrary.com. *Actg Dir*, Alyssa Zolkiewicz; E-mail: zolkiewicza@einetwork.net; Staff 3.8 (MLS 1.5, Non-MLS 2.3)
Founded 1937. Pop 5,971
Library Holdings: Bk Vols 30,000; Per Subs 75
Automation Activity & Vendor Info: (Cataloging) Innovative Interfaces, Inc; (Circulation) Innovative Interfaces, Inc; (OPAC) Innovative Interfaces, Inc
Wireless access
Mem of Allegheny County Library Association (ACLA)
Partic in Electronic Info Network
Open Mon & Fri 10-6, Tues-Thurs 12-8, Sat 10-5
Friends of the Library Group

P DORMONT PUBLIC LIBRARY*, 2950 W Liberty Ave, 15216-2594. SAN 315-0585. Tel: 412-531-8754. FAX: 412-531-1601. E-mail: dormont@einetwork.net. Web Site: dormontlibrary.org. *Dir*, Cindy D'Agostino; E-mail: DAgostinoc@einetwork.net; Staff 1 (Non-MLS 1)
Founded 1936. Pop 8,600; Circ 43,096
Library Holdings: AV Mats 2,574; e-books 15,073; Electronic Media & Resources 2,376; Bk Vols 26,361; Per Subs 64
Subject Interests: Accelerated readers, Classics, Small bus
Automation Activity & Vendor Info: (Acquisitions) Innovative Interfaces, Inc; (Cataloging) Innovative Interfaces, Inc; (Circulation) Innovative Interfaces, Inc; (Course Reserve) Innovative Interfaces, Inc; (ILL) Innovative Interfaces, Inc; (Media Booking) Innovative Interfaces, Inc; (OPAC) Innovative Interfaces, Inc; (Serials) Innovative Interfaces, Inc
Wireless access
Mem of Allegheny County Library Association (ACLA)
Open Mon-Thurs 9-9, Fri & Sat 9-5

CR DUQUESNE UNIVERSITY*, Gumberg Library, 600 Forbes Ave, 15282. SAN 359-3282. Tel: 412-396-6130. Circulation Tel: 412-396-6131. Interlibrary Loan Service Tel: 412-396-5341. Reference Tel: 412-396-6133. Administration Tel: 412-396-6136. Interlibrary Loan Service FAX: 412-396-1800. Web Site: www.duq.edu/library. *Univ Librn*, Dr Sara Baron; E-mail: barons1@duq.edu; *Asst Univ Librn, Access Serv*, Amy Lee Heinlen; Tel: 412-396-5343, E-mail: heinlena@duq.edu; *Asst Univ Librn, Coll, Metadata Serv*, Tracie Ballock; Tel: 412-396-4560, E-mail: ballockt@duq.edu; *Asst Univ Librn, Res Serv & User Engagement Librn*, Maureen Diana Sasso; Tel: 412-396-5680, E-mail: sasso@duq.edu. Subject Specialists: *Res, Teaching*, Maureen Diana Sasso; Staff 21 (MLS 15, Non-MLS 6)
Founded 1878. Enrl 9,123; Fac 1,009; Highest Degree: Doctorate
Library Holdings: Audiobooks 126; AV Mats 90,953; CDs 10,993; DVDs 5,250; e-books 162,924; e-journals 107,061; Microforms 247,239; Music Scores 17,111; Bk Titles 515,361; Bk Vols 648,583; Per Subs 369; Videos 5,968
Special Collections: Cardinal John Wright Coll; Judge Michael Musmanno Coll; Maureen Sullivan Curriculum Center; Rabbi Herman Hailperin Coll; Simon Silverman Phenomenology Coll
Subject Interests: Catholic studies, Ethics, Philos, Theol
Automation Activity & Vendor Info: (Acquisitions) Innovative Interfaces, Inc - Sierra; (Cataloging) Innovative Interfaces, Inc - Sierra; (Circulation) Innovative Interfaces, Inc - Sierra; (Course Reserve) Innovative Interfaces, Inc - Sierra; (ILL) OCLC ILLiad; (OPAC) Innovative Interfaces, Inc - Sierra; (Serials) Ex Libris Group
Wireless access
Publications: BiblioBrief (Online only)
Partic in Basic Health Sciences Library Network; LYRASIS; National Network of Libraries of Medicine Region 1; Partnership for Academic Library Collaborative & Innovation
Special Services for the Blind - Bks on cassette; Bks on CD; Copier with enlargement capabilities; Duplicating spec requests; Recorded bks; Ref serv; Sound rec; Videos on blindness & physical disabilties
Open Mon-Thurs 7am-1am, Fri 7-9, Sat 10-9, Sun 11am-1am
Departmental Libraries:
CL CENTER FOR LEGAL INFORMATION, 900 Locust St, 15282. (Mail add: Center for Legal Information, 600 Forbes Ave, 15282). Tel: 412-396-5017. Reference Tel: 412-396-1697. FAX: 412-396-6294. E-mail: lawlibrary@duq.edu. Web Site: www.duq.edu/academics/schools/law/law-library. *Dir*, Frank Y Liu; Tel: 412-396-5018, E-mail: liu@duq.edu; *Assoc Dir*, Dittakavi Rao; Tel: 412-396-5014, E-mail: rao@duq.edu; *Asst Dir, Pub Serv*, Tsegaye Beru; Tel: 412-396-4423, E-mail: beru@duq.edu; *Asst Dir, Tech Serv*, Patricia Horvath; Tel: 412-396-5016, E-mail: horvath@duq.edu; *Ref Librn/Circ Syst*, Charles Sprowls; Tel: 412-396-5533, E-mail: sprowlsc@duq.edu; *Mgr, Database Syst/Cat*, Amy Lovell; Tel: 412-396-6292, E-mail: lovell@duq.edu; Staff 11 (MLS 6, Non-MLS 5)
Founded 1911
Library Holdings: Bk Titles 182,390; Bk Vols 265,903; Per Subs 5,126
Special Collections: UN Document Depository; US Document Depository
Automation Activity & Vendor Info: (Acquisitions) Innovative Interfaces, Inc; (Cataloging) Innovative Interfaces, Inc; (Circulation) Innovative Interfaces, Inc; (Course Reserve) Innovative Interfaces, Inc; (ILL) Innovative Interfaces, Inc; (Media Booking) Innovative Interfaces, Inc; (OPAC) Innovative Interfaces, Inc; (Serials) Innovative Interfaces, Inc
Publications: DuqLawWire (Newsletter)
Open Mon-Thurs 7:30 am-Midnight, Fri 7:30am-10pm, Sat 9-9, Sun Noon-Midnight

R EAST LIBERTY PRESBYTERIAN CHURCH LIBRARY*, 116 S Highland Ave, 15206. SAN 315-0615. Tel: 412-441-3800. FAX: 412-441-4422. E-mail: info@cathedralofhope.org. Web Site: www.cathedralofhope.org.
Library Holdings: Bk Titles 2,160; Bk Vols 2,340; Per Subs 7

P GREEN TREE PUBLIC LIBRARY*, Ten W Manilla Ave, 1st Flr, 15220-3310. SAN 315-0666. Tel: 412-921-9292. FAX: 412-921-4004. E-mail: greentree@einetwork.net. Web Site: www.greentreelibrary.org. *Dir*, Adaena Tray; E-mail: traya@einetwork.net; *Asst Dir*, Emily Bryan-Reeder; Staff 8 (MLS 2, Non-MLS 6)
Pop 4,938; Circ 55,000
Library Holdings: AV Mats 2,342; Large Print Bks 710; Bk Titles 35,691 Bk Vols 36,780; Per Subs 92
Automation Activity & Vendor Info: (Acquisitions) Innovative Interfaces Inc; (Cataloging) Innovative Interfaces, Inc; (Circulation) Innovative Interfaces, Inc; (Course Reserve) Innovative Interfaces, Inc; (ILL) Innovative Interfaces, Inc; (Media Booking) Innovative Interfaces, Inc; (OPAC) Innovative Interfaces, Inc; (Serials) Innovative Interfaces, Inc
Wireless access
Publications: Chapter Notes (Newsletter)
Mem of Allegheny County Library Association (ACLA)
Special Services for the Deaf - TDD equip

Special Services for the Blind - Talking bks
Open Mon-Thurs 10-9, Fri & Sat 10-5
Friends of the Library Group

S HISTORICAL SOCIETY OF WESTERN PENNSYLVANIA*, Detre Library & Archives, 1212 Smallman St, 15222. SAN 315-0712. Tel: 412-454-6364. FAX: 412-454-6028. E-mail: library@heinzhistorycenter.org. Web Site: www.heinzhistorycenter.org. *Dir, Archives,* Eric Lidji; Tel: 412-454-6402; *Chief Librn,* Mary Jones; Tel: 412-454-6360, E-mail: mjones@heinzhistorycenter.org; *Chief Archivist,* Matthew Strauss; Tel: 412-454-6362, E-mail: mstrauss@heinzhistorycenter.org; *Acq,* Carly Lough; Tel: 412-454-6367, E-mail: ctlough@heinzhistorycenter.org. Subject Specialists: *Jewish hist,* Eric Lidji; Staff 6 (MLS 3, Non-MLS 3)
Founded 1879
Library Holdings: e-journals 1; Microforms 300; Bk Titles 18,000; Bk Vols 35,000; Per Subs 300; Videos 150
Special Collections: African-American Archives; Business Coll; Italian Archives; Jewish Archives; Polish Archives; Slovak Archives; Steel Coll; Women's Coll
Subject Interests: Genealogy, Hist of Western Penn, Western Penn
Automation Activity & Vendor Info: (Cataloging) OCLC Connexion; (OPAC) EOS International
Wireless access
Function: Archival coll, Res libr
Open Wed-Sat 10-5
Restriction: Non-circulating

S JEFFERSON REGIONAL MEDICAL CENTER*, Behan Health Science Library, 575 Coal Valley Rd, 15236. (Mail add: PO Box 18119, 15236-0119), SAN 371-1625. Tel: 412-469-5000, 412-469-5786. FAX: 412-649-7294. *Library Contact,* Calie Souto; E-mail: calie.souto@ahn.org
Library Holdings: Bk Vols 300; Per Subs 200
Open Mon-Fri 8-4:30

L JONES DAY*, Law Library, 500 Grant St, Ste 4500, 15219. SAN 372-1884. Tel: 412-391-3939. FAX: 412-394-7959. Web Site: www.jonesday.com/pittsburgh. *Dir, Libr & Res Serv,* Ronda Fisch; E-mail: rfisch@jonesday.com
Library Holdings: Bk Vols 15,000

L K&L GATES LIBRARY*, The K&L Gates Ctr, 210 Sixth Ave, 15222. SAN 315-0798. Tel: 412-355-6311. FAX: 412-355-6501. Web Site: www.klgates.com. *Dir, Libr Serv,* Rob Duncan
Founded 1956
Subject Interests: Corp, Securities, Tax

C LA ROCHE UNIVERSITY, John J Wright Library, 9000 Babcock Blvd, 15237. SAN 315-081X. Tel: 412-536-1063. Interlibrary Loan Service Tel: 412 536-1057. Reference Tel: 412 536-1061. Administration Tel: 412 536-1059. FAX: 412-536-1062. E-mail: WrightLibrary@LaRoche.edu. Web Site: library.laroche.edu. *Libr Dir,* Alecia Kerr; E-mail: alecia.kerr@laroche.edu; *Librn,* Brett Giltenboth; E-mail: brett.giltenboth@laroche.edu; *Librn,* Allyssa Yanniello; E-mail: allyssa.yanniello@laroche.edu; *Circ Supvr,* Deborah Brown; E-mail: deborah.brown@laroche.edu; *Resource Sharing Coord,* Caroline Horgan; E-mail: caroline.horgan@laroche.edu; Staff 5 (MLS 3, Non-MLS 2)
Founded 1963. Enrl 1,469; Fac 60; Highest Degree: Master
Library Holdings: Bk Titles 70,000; Per Subs 578
Special Collections: US Document Depository
Automation Activity & Vendor Info: (Acquisitions) Innovative Interfaces, Inc; (Cataloging) Innovative Interfaces, Inc; (Circulation) Innovative Interfaces, Inc; (Course Reserve) Innovative Interfaces, Inc; (ILL) Innovative Interfaces, Inc; (Media Booking) Innovative Interfaces, Inc; (OPAC) Innovative Interfaces, Inc; (Serials) Innovative Interfaces, Inc
Wireless access
Partic in LYRASIS; OCLC Online Computer Library Center, Inc; Partnership for Academic Library Collaborative & Innovation
Open Mon-Thurs 8:30am-Midnight, Fri & Sat 8:30-4:30, Sun 1-Midnight

P MT LEBANON PUBLIC LIBRARY*, 16 Castle Shannon Blvd, 15228-2252. SAN 315-0917. Tel: 412-531-1912. FAX: 412-531-1161. Web Site: www.mtlebanonlibrary.org. *Dir,* Robyn E Vittek; E-mail: vittekr@einetwork.net; Staff 8 (MLS 8)
Founded 1932. Pop 33,137; Circ 554,384
Jan 2013-Dec 2013 Income $2,107,273, State $171,141, City $1,363,791, County $318,794, Locally Generated Income $253,547. Mats Exp $569,976, Books $226,188, Per/Ser (Incl. Access Fees) $14,244, AV Mat $96,948, Electronic Ref Mat (Incl. Access Fees) $62,762, Presv $169,834. Sal $975,395 (Prof $445,089)
Library Holdings: AV Mats 19,864; e-books 82,416; Electronic Media & Resources 20,842; Bk Vols 131,272; Per Subs 269
Special Collections: Local History Coll; Pennsylvania Coll; Special Needs/Disabilities
Subject Interests: Study guides
Automation Activity & Vendor Info: (Cataloging) Innovative Interfaces, Inc; (Circulation) Innovative Interfaces, Inc; (ILL) Innovative Interfaces, Inc; (OPAC) Innovative Interfaces, Inc; (Serials) Innovative Interfaces, Inc
Wireless access
Function: 24/7 Electronic res, Activity rm, Adult bk club, Adult literacy prog, After school storytime, Art exhibits, Audiobks via web, AV serv, Bk club(s), Bks on CD, Chess club, Children's prog, Computer training, Computers for patron use, E-Readers, E-Reserves, Electronic databases & coll, Family literacy, Genealogy discussion group, Holiday prog, Home delivery & serv to seniorr ctr & nursing homes, Homebound delivery serv, ILL available, Large print keyboards, Life-long learning prog for all ages, Literacy & newcomer serv, Magazines, Magnifiers for reading, Mango lang, Microfiche/film & reading machines, Movies, Music CDs, Online cat, Online ref, Outreach serv, OverDrive digital audio bks, Photocopying/Printing, Preschool outreach, Preschool reading prog, Prog for adults, Prog for children & young adult, Scanner, Senior computer classes, Senior outreach, Serves people with intellectual disabilities, Spanish lang bks, Story hour, Study rm, Summer reading prog, Tax forms, Teen prog, Telephone ref, Wheelchair accessible
Publications: More Friends Library Newsletter
Mem of Allegheny County Library Association (ACLA)
Partic in Electronic Info Network
Special Services for the Deaf - Bks on deafness & sign lang; Coll on deaf educ; High interest/low vocabulary bks; TTY equip
Special Services for the Blind - Closed circuit TV magnifier; Computer with voice synthesizer for visually impaired persons; Home delivery serv; Large screen computer & software; Magnifiers; Reader equip; Ref serv
Open Mon-Thurs 9-9, Fri & Sat 9-5, Sun 1-5
Friends of the Library Group

P NORTHLAND PUBLIC LIBRARY*, 300 Cumberland Rd, 15237-5455. SAN 315-0941. Tel: 412-366-8100. FAX: 412-366-2064. E-mail: northland@einetwork.net. Web Site: www.northlandlibrary.org. *Exec Dir,* Amy M Steele; Tel: 412-366-8100, Ext 101, E-mail: steelea@einetwork.net; *Dir of Develop, Found Dir,* Valerie Golik; Tel: 412-366-8100, Ext 104, E-mail: golikv@einetwork.net; *Dir, Support Serv,* Robert Lukitsch; Tel: 412-366-8100, Ext 106, E-mail: lukitschr@einetwork.net; *Dir, Libr Serv,* Kelley Moten; Tel: 412-366-8100, Ext 146, E-mail: motenk2@einetwork.net; *Dir, Mkt & Communications,* Santina Balestreire; Tel: 412-366-8100, Ext 103, E-mail: balestreires@einetwork.net; *Ad/Coll Develop/e-Res,* Mary Lee Hart; Tel: 412-366-8100, Ext 113, E-mail: hartm@einetwork.net; *Mgr, Ad Serv,* Rebecca Munoz; Tel: 412-366-8100, Ext 110, E-mail: munozr@einetwork.net; *Mgr, Children's & YA,* Susan Claus; Tel: 412-366-8100, Ext 120, E-mail: clauss@einetwork.net; *Circ Mgr,* Kim Ann Smith; Tel: 412-366-8100, Ext 115, E-mail: smithk@einetwork.net; *Supvr, Computer Serv,* Adrianne Krings; Tel: 412-366-8100, Ext 144, E-mail: kringsa2@einetwork.net; *Supvr, Tech Serv,* Debra Martin; Tel: 412-366-8100, Ext 166, E-mail: martind@einetwork.net; *ILL,* Karen Wingrove; Tel: 412-366-8100, Ext 119, E-mail: wingrovek@einetwork.net. Subject Specialists: *Computer sci,* Adrianne Krings; Staff 53.6 (MLS 16.6, Non-MLS 37)
Founded 1968. Pop 81,118; Circ 994,544
Jan 2017-Dec 2017 Income $3,452,803, State $294,053, City $2,211,420, County $542,687, Locally Generated Income $404,643. Mats Exp $343,184. Sal $1,645,329
Library Holdings: Audiobooks 7,258; Bks on Deafness & Sign Lang 118; Braille Volumes 4; CDs 4,841; DVDs 14,919; e-books 348,491; e-journals 265; Electronic Media & Resources 42; Large Print Bks 2,925; Music Scores 20; Bk Titles 168,831; Per Subs 217
Special Collections: Northland Historical Image Coll, digitized images
Subject Interests: Genealogy, Local hist
Automation Activity & Vendor Info: (Cataloging) Innovative Interfaces, Inc; (Circulation) Innovative Interfaces, Inc; (OPAC) Innovative Interfaces, Inc
Wireless access
Function: 24/7 Electronic res, 24/7 Online cat, Adult bk club, Adult literacy prog, After school storytime, Art exhibits, Art programs, Audiobks on Playaways & MP3, Audiobks via web, Bk club(s), Bks on CD, CD-ROM, Chess club, Children's prog, Computer training, Computers for patron use, Digital talking bks, Electronic databases & coll, Free DVD rentals, Genealogy discussion group, Govt ref serv, Health sci info serv, Holiday prog, Homebound delivery serv, ILL available, Instruction & testing, Internet access, Life-long learning prog for all ages, Magazines, Magnifiers for reading, Mail & tel request accepted, Mango lang, Meeting rooms, Movies, Music CDs, Online cat, Online info literacy tutorials on the web & in blackboard, Online ref, Outreach serv, OverDrive digital audio bks, Photocopying/Printing, Preschool outreach, Preschool reading prog, Printer for laptops & handheld devices, Prog for adults, Prog for children & young adult, Ref & res, Ref serv available, Satellite serv, Scanner, Senior computer classes, Serves people with intellectual disabilities, Spanish lang bks, STEM programs, Story hour, Study rm, Summer & winter reading prog, Summer reading prog, Tax forms, Teen prog, Telephone ref, Wheelchair accessible, Winter reading prog, Workshops, Writing prog

Publications: Northland News (Newsletter)
Mem of Allegheny County Library Association (ACLA)
Partic in Electronic Info Network
Special Services for the Deaf - Assistive tech; Bks on deafness & sign lang; Closed caption videos
Special Services for the Blind - Aids for in-house use; Assistive/Adapted tech devices, equip & products; Bks on cassette; Bks on CD; Braille bks; Closed circuit TV; Computer with voice synthesizer for visually impaired persons; Digital talking bk; Internet workstation with adaptive software; Large print bks; Low vision equip; Playaways (bks on MP3); Talking bks
Open Mon-Thurs 9-9, Fri 9-6, Sat 9-5, Sun (Winter) 1-5

P PENN HILLS LIBRARY*, 1037 Stotler Rd, 15235-2099. SAN 315-0968. Tel: 412-795-3507. FAX: 412-798-2186. E-mail: phlibrary@einetwork.net. Web Site: www.pennhillslibrary.org. *Interim Dir, Librn,* Mary Ann Zeak; E-mail: zeakm@einetwork.net; Staff 31 (MLS 3, Non-MLS 28)
Founded 1966. Pop 46,807; Circ 278,969
Library Holdings: Bk Titles 112,121; Per Subs 225
Special Collections: Penn Hills Historical Committee Coll
Automation Activity & Vendor Info: (Acquisitions) SirsiDynix; (Cataloging) SirsiDynix; (Circulation) SirsiDynix; (Course Reserve) SirsiDynix; (ILL) SirsiDynix; (Media Booking) SirsiDynix; (OPAC) SirsiDynix; (Serials) SirsiDynix
Wireless access
Publications: The Book Shelf (Newsletter)
Mem of Allegheny County Library Association (ACLA)
Partic in Electronic Info Network
Open Mon-Thurs 9-9, Fri & Sat 9-5, Sun (Sept-May) 1-5
Friends of the Library Group
Branches: 1
LINCOLN PARK SATELLITE, 7300 Ridgeview Ave, 15235. Tel: 412-362-7729. FAX: 412-362-7729. *Br Mgr,* Elaine Gibson; Staff 1 (Non-MLS 1)
Pop 749; Circ 1,256
Library Holdings: Bk Titles 8,190; Bk Vols 9,100; Per Subs 22
Open Mon-Thurs 10-5:30, Fri 10-5
Friends of the Library Group

S PITTSBURGH HISTORY & LANDMARKS FOUNDATION*, James D Van Trump Library, 100 W Station Square Dr, Ste 450, 15219-1134. SAN 315-100X. Tel: 412-471-5808. FAX: 412-471-1633. E-mail: information@phlf.org. Web Site: www.phlf.org. *Hist Coll Dir,* Albert M Tannler; E-mail: al@phlf.org; *Archivist,* Frank Stroker; E-mail: frank@phlf.org
Founded 1964
Library Holdings: Bk Vols 5,000; Per Subs 10
Subject Interests: Archit hist, Pittsburgh hist
Function: Res libr
Restriction: Fee for pub use, Free to mem, Non-circulating, Open by appt only

S PITTSBURGH INSTITUTE OF MORTUARY SCIENCE*, William J Musmanno Memorial Library, 5808 Baum Blvd, 15206. SAN 315-1018. Tel: 412-362-8500. FAX: 412-362-1684. E-mail: librarian@pims.edu. Web Site: pims.edu/library.
Founded 1939. Enrl 130; Fac 20; Highest Degree: Associate
Library Holdings: Audiobooks 1; AV Mats 433; CDs 7; DVDs 107; Bk Vols 2,350; Per Subs 30; Videos 162
Subject Interests: Death care industry
Automation Activity & Vendor Info: (Cataloging) Follett Software; (Circulation) Follett Software
Wireless access
Open Mon-Fri 9-4

S PITTSBURGH POST GAZETTE*, Library, 358 N Shore Dr, 15212. SAN 327-0726. Tel: 412-263-1184. FAX: 412-471-1987. E-mail: library@post-gazette.com. Web Site: www.post-gazette.com. *Head Librn,* Stephen Karlinchak; Tel: 412-263-2585, E-mail: skarlinchak@post-gazette.com; Staff 4 (MLS 1, Non-MLS 3)
Founded 1930
Library Holdings: Electronic Media & Resources 10; Microforms 2,000; Bk Titles 300; Spec Interest Per Sub 5
Special Collections: Photo Files & Digital Photo Archives (both PG & former Pittsburgh Press); Picture Files - Pittsburgh Clipping Files Dating Back to 1930s (both PG & former Pittsburgh Press)
Function: For res purposes, Internet access, Photocopying/Printing, Telephone ref
Special Services for the Blind - Radio reading serv
Restriction: Access at librarian's discretion, Access for corporate affiliates, By permission only, Co libr, Employees & their associates, Non-circulating, Not a lending libr, Not open to pub, Private libr, Pub access by telephone only

R PITTSBURGH THEOLOGICAL SEMINARY*, Clifford E Barbour Library, 616 N Highland Ave, 15206. SAN 315-1042. Tel: 412-924-1354. FAX: 412-362-2329. Reference E-mail: reference@pts.edu. Web Site: www.pts.edu/barbour-library. *Libr Dir,* Michelle Spomer; Tel: 412-924-1408, E-mail: mspomer@pts.edu; *Head, Pub Serv,* Alyson Pope; Tel: 412-924-1356, E-mail: apope@pts.edu; *Head, Tech Serv,* Darlene Veghts; Tel: 412-924-1352, E-mail: dveghts@pts.edu; *Acq Librn,* Mariam Sogoian; Tel: 412-924-1361, E-mail: msogoian@pts.edu; *ILL/Ref Librn,* Mark Russell; Tel: 412-924-1393, E-mail: mcrussell@pts.edu; *Ser Librn,* Diane Faust; Tel: 412-924-1360, E-mail: dfaust@pts.edu; *Circ Supvr,* Ellen Little; Tel: 412-924-1355, E-mail: elittle@pts.edu; *Acq Asst,* Scott Richardson-Eckes; Tel: 412-924-1357, E-mail: srichardson-eckes@pts.edu; Staff 6 (MLS 6)
Founded 1794. Fac 21; Highest Degree: Doctorate
Library Holdings: Microforms 88,311; Bk Vols 296,142; Per Subs 860
Special Collections: Hymnology (Warrington Coll); Reformation Theology (John M Mason Coll)
Subject Interests: Bible, Church hist, Practical theol, Theol
Automation Activity & Vendor Info: (Acquisitions) Innovative Interfaces, Inc; (Cataloging) Innovative Interfaces, Inc; (Circulation) Innovative Interfaces, Inc; (Course Reserve) Innovative Interfaces, Inc; (OPAC) Innovative Interfaces, Inc; (Serials) Innovative Interfaces, Inc
Wireless access
Partic in LYRASIS; OCLC Online Computer Library Center, Inc
Open Mon 8:30-7, Tues-Thurs 8:30-4:30, Fri 8:30-2

S PITTSBURGH TOY LENDING LIBRARY*, c/o First United Methodist Church, 5401 Centre Ave, Rear, 15232. SAN 372-5502. Tel: 412-682-4430. E-mail: ptll@pghtoys.org. Web Site: pghtoys.org. *Pres,* April Merrell; E-mail: ptll@pghtoys.org
Founded 1974
Library Holdings: Bk Titles 100
Special Collections: Parenting; Toys (imaginative & cognitive)
Publications: Networks (Bimonthly); Networks (Newsletter)
Special Services for the Deaf - Bks on deafness & sign lang
Open Mon & Thurs 9:30-12:30 & 4-7, Tues, Wed, Fri & Sat 9:30-12:30
Restriction: Fee for pub use, Mem only

S PITTSBURGH ZOO & PPG AQUARIUM LIBRARY, One Wild Pl, 15206. SAN 370-7113. Tel: 412-665-3640. FAX: 412-665-3661. E-mail: educationinfo@pittsburghzoo.org. Web Site: www.pittsburghzoo.org.
Founded 1983
Library Holdings: Bk Titles 14,000; Per Subs 15
Special Collections: Ciguatera (Inia geoffrensis) Poisoning, research papers; Gambierdiscus toxicus; Platanistidae Dolphins, research papers
Restriction: Staff use only

C POINT PARK UNIVERSITY LIBRARY*, 414 Wood St, 15222. (Mail add: 201 Wood St, 15222). Tel: 412-392-3171. FAX: 412-392-3168. E-mail: library@pointpark.edu. Web Site: www.pointpark.edu/Academics/AcademicResources/library. *Dir,* Elizabeth Evans; Tel: 412-392-3161, E-mail: eevans@pointpark.edu; *Assoc Dir,* Brenton Wilson; Tel: 412-392-3163, E-mail: bwilson@pointpark.edu; *Ref Librn,* Lauren Irvin; Tel: 412-392-3162, E-mail: lirvin@pointpark.edu; *Ref & Instruction Librn,* Robert Stancampiano; Tel: 412-392-3166, E-mail: rstancampiano@pointpark.edu; *Resource Sharing Coord,* Melanie Kirchartz; Tel: 412-392-3165, E-mail: mkirchartz@pointpark.edu; *Tech Serv Coordr,* Margie Stampahar; Tel: 412-392-3167, E-mail: mstampahar@pointpark.edu; *Access Serv, Archives,* Phillip Harrity; E-mail: pharrity@pointpark.edu; Staff 8 (MLS 5, Non-MLS 3)
Enrl 3,523; Highest Degree: Master
Library Holdings: AV Mats 1,439; e-books 30,000; e-journals 17,000; Bk Vols 95,000; Per Subs 270
Special Collections: Plays & Musicals Cores (Performing Arts Coll)
Automation Activity & Vendor Info: (Acquisitions) Koha; (Cataloging) Koha; (Circulation) Koha; (Course Reserve) Koha; (Discovery) EBSCO Discovery Service; (ILL) Koha; (Media Booking) Koha; (OPAC) Koha; (Serials) Koha
Wireless access
Partic in Partnership for Academic Library Collaborative & Innovation; Pittsburgh Council on Higher Education
Special Services for the Blind - Closed circuit TV; ZoomText magnification & reading software
Open Mon-Thurs 8am-Midnight, Fri & Sat 8-7, Sun 12-10

M HOWARD ANDERSON POWER MEMORIAL LIBRARY*, UPMC Magee-Womens Hospital, 300 Halket St, Ste 1205, 15213. SAN 359-4548. Tel: 412-641-4288. FAX: 412-641-4854. E-mail: librarystaff@mail.magee.edu. *Mgr, Libr Serv,* Carrie Everstine; E-mail: everck@upmc.edu; Staff 1.2 (MLS 1, Non-MLS 0.2)
Founded 1965
Library Holdings: e-journals 3; Bk Titles 1,681; Bk Vols 1,799; Per Subs 7
Subject Interests: Med
Wireless access

Function: Computers for patron use, Doc delivery serv, ILL available, Internet access, Photocopying/Printing
Partic in Basic Health Sciences Library Network; National Network of Libraries of Medicine Region 1
Open Mon-Fri 8-4:30
Restriction: Med & nursing staff, patients & families

PPG INDUSTRIES, INC

S CHEMICALS TECHNICAL INFORMATION CENTER*, 440 College Park Dr, Monroeville, 15146, SAN 370-7784. Tel: 724-325-5221. FAX: 724-325-5289. Web Site: www.ppg.com. *Mgr,* Denise Callihan; E-mail: callihan@ppg.com; *Info Spec,* Audrey Anderson; Staff 3 (MLS 1, Non-MLS 2)
Library Holdings: Bk Vols 14,000; Per Subs 120
Subject Interests: Organic chem
Automation Activity & Vendor Info: (Cataloging) SydneyPlus; (Circulation) SydneyPlus; (OPAC) SydneyPlus
Partic in LYRASIS
Publications: Technical Reports Abstract Bulletin
Restriction: Open by appt only

S GLASS TECHNOLOGY CENTER*, Guys Run Rd, Harmar Township, 15238. (Mail add: PO Box 11472, 15238-0472), SAN 359-3673. Tel: 412-820-8568. FAX: 412-820-8696. E-mail: harmarlib@ppg.com. Web Site: www.ppg.com. *Mgr, Libr Serv,* Denise Callihan; *Info Spec,* Audrey Anderson; Tel: 412-820-8517; *Info Spec,* Amy Watson; *Tech Serv,* Beverly Weston; Tel: 412-820-4936; Staff 4 (MLS 2, Non-MLS 2)
Founded 1975
Library Holdings: Bk Titles 25,000; Per Subs 160
Special Collections: Internal Documents Coll
Subject Interests: Ceramics, Chem, Fiber glass, Glass, Mat sci, Physics
Automation Activity & Vendor Info: (ILL) OCLC; (OPAC) Sydney; (Serials) EBSCO Online
Partic in LYRASIS
Publications: Journal List

S TECHNICAL INFORMATION CENTER*, 4325 Rosanna Dr, Allison Park, 15101, SAN 359-3762. Tel: 412-492-5443. FAX: 412-492-5509. Web Site: www.ppg.com. *Dir, Libr Serv,* Denise Callihan; Tel: 724-325-5221, E-mail: callihan@ppg.com; *Assoc Librn,* Cherese Benson; *Info Spec,* Mary Lee Richner; Tel: 412-492-5268; Staff 3 (MLS 2, Non-MLS 1)
Library Holdings: Bk Vols 10,000; Per Subs 200
Subject Interests: Coatings, Paints, Polymers, Resins
Restriction: Co libr, In-house use for visitors, Open by appt only

S PSP METRICS LIBRARY*, The Frick Bldg, 437 Grant St, Ste 1333, 15219-6110. SAN 372-6290. Tel: 412-261-1333. FAX: 412-261-5014. E-mail: info@pspmetrics.com. Web Site: www.pspmetrics.com. *Librn/Communications Spec,* Position Currently Open
Founded 1946
Library Holdings: Bk Titles 500; Per Subs 15
Special Collections: Industrial-Organizational Psychology; Management Development; Work Motivation

L REED SMITH LLP*, Law Library, Reed Smith Ctr, 225 Fifth Ave, 15222. SAN 315-1093. Tel: 412-288-3377. FAX: 412-288-3063. Web Site: www.reedsmith.com. *Librn,* Jeremy Watson; E-mail: jwatson@reedsmith.com; Staff 7 (MLS 3, Non-MLS 4)
Founded 1970
Library Holdings: Bk Titles 10,000; Bk Vols 35,000; Per Subs 2,000
Subject Interests: Penn law
Automation Activity & Vendor Info: (Acquisitions) SirsiDynix; (Cataloging) SirsiDynix; (Circulation) SirsiDynix; (OPAC) SirsiDynix; (Serials) SirsiDynix
Partic in OCLC Online Computer Library Center, Inc
Restriction: Not open to pub

R REFORMED PRESBYTERIAN THEOLOGICAL SEMINARY LIBRARY*, 7418 Penn Ave, 15208. SAN 315-1107. Tel: 412-731-6000. FAX: 412-731-4834. Web Site: rptslibrary.org. *Librn,* Thomas Reid; E-mail: treid@rpts.edu; Staff 1.5 (MLS 1, Non-MLS 0.5)
Founded 1810. Enrl 115; Fac 14; Highest Degree: Doctorate
Jan 2018-Dec 2018 Income $128,355, Parent Institution $125,108, Other $3,247. Mats Exp $34,596, Books $17,546, Per/Ser (Incl. Access Fees) $5,000, Other Print Mats $200, Micro $50, AV Mat $100, Electronic Ref Mat (Incl. Access Fees) $8,500, Presv $3,200. Sal $69,434 (Prof $37,200)
Library Holdings: AV Mats 1,450; Braille Volumes 10; CDs 45; DVDs 80; e-books 263; Electronic Media & Resources 24; Microforms 1,570; Bk Vols 86,800; Per Subs 180
Special Collections: 16th-18th Centuries Rare Theological Works; Reformed Presbyterian Coll
Subject Interests: Bible, Church-state, Theol, Worship
Automation Activity & Vendor Info: (Cataloging) TLC (The Library Corporation); (Circulation) TLC (The Library Corporation); (ILL) TLC (The Library Corporation); (OPAC) TLC (The Library Corporation)
Wireless access
Function: 24/7 Electronic res, 24/7 Online cat, Archival coll, Computers for patron use, Distance learning, Electronic databases & coll, ILL available, Mail & tel request accepted, Mail loans to mem, Microfiche/film & reading machines, Online cat, Online ref, Photocopying/Printing, Ref & res, Ref serv available, Res assist avail, Res libr, Spoken cassettes & CDs, Spoken cassettes & DVDs, VHS videos
Publications: Library Handbook
Partic in OCLC Online Computer Library Center, Inc
Open Mon-Fri 8-4:30
Restriction: Borrowing requests are handled by ILL, In-house use for visitors, Off-site coll in storage - retrieval as requested, Pub use on premises

P ROBINSON TOWNSHIP LIBRARY, 1000 Church Hill Rd, 15205. Tel: 412-787-3906. FAX: 412-787-3910. Web Site: www.robinsonlibrary.org. *Libr Dir,* Sharon Helfrich; E-mail: helfrichs@einetwork.net; Staff 10 (MLS 4, Non-MLS 6)
Founded 2007
Wireless access
Function: 24/7 Electronic res, 24/7 Online cat, Accelerated reader prog, Activity rm, Adult bk club, Adult literacy prog
Mem of Allegheny County Library Association (ACLA)
Open Mon-Thurs 10-8, Fri & Sat 10-5
Friends of the Library Group

S THEATRE HISTORICAL SOCIETY OF AMERICA*, Archive & Research Center, 1221 Penn Ave, 15222. (Mail add: 461 Cochran Rd, Box 144, 15228), SAN 371-5256. Tel: 877-242-9637. Web Site: www.historictheatres.org. *Archives Dir,* Patrick Seymour; Tel: 877-242-9637, Ext 2, E-mail: archivedir@historictheatres.org
Founded 1969
Library Holdings: AV Mats 200; Bk Titles 1,100
Special Collections: Bill Clifford Coll, drawings & sketches; Bill Peterson Coll, photog; Blueprint Coll; Chicago Architectural Photographing Company Coll, theatre building negatives; Michael Miller Coll; Slide Coll; Terry Helgesen Coll
Subject Interests: Cinema, Theatre, Theatre archit
Wireless access
Function: Archival coll, Art exhibits, Mail & tel request accepted, Res libr, Res performed for a fee
Publications: Marquee (Journal)
Restriction: Access at librarian's discretion, Authorized scholars by appt, Closed stack, Fee for pub use, Non-circulating, Not a lending libr, Open by appt only, Open to pub for ref only, Open to researchers by request, Private libr, Pub use on premises, Restricted access

C UNIVERSITY OF PITTSBURGH*, Hillman Library, 3960 Forbes Ave, 15260. SAN 359-3916. Tel: 412-648-3330. FAX: 412-648-7887. Web Site: www.library.pitt.edu/hillman. *Dir of the Univ Libr, Univ Librn,* Kornelia Tancheva; Tel: 412-648-7705, E-mail: tancheva@pitt.edu; *Assoc Univ Librn, Res & Learning,* Rachel Rubin; *Assoc Univ Librn,* Aaron Brenner; Tel: 412-648-5908, E-mail: abrenner@pitt.edu; *Assoc Univ Librn, Coll, Tech Serv,* Fern Brody; Tel: 412-648-7710, E-mail: feb@pitt.edu; *Dir, Info Tech,* Timothy Deliyannides; Tel: 412-648-3254, E-mail: tsd@pitt.edu; *Archives, Assoc Univ Librn, Spec Coll,* Edward Galloway; Tel: 412-648-5901, E-mail: edwardg@pitt.edu; *Dir of Assessment, Dir, Quality Assurance,* Berenika Webster; Tel: 412-624-7209, E-mail: bwebster@pitt.edu; *Dir, Communications, Web Serv,* Jeffrey Wisniewski; Tel: 412-624-4050, E-mail: jeffw@pitt.edu; Staff 260 (MLS 108, Non-MLS 152)
Founded 1873. Enrl 43,347; Fac 1,846
Library Holdings: Bk Vols 1,500,000
Special Collections: 18th & 20th Century historical records & ms including photog, glass plates & negatives of organizations, societies, institutions, businesses, city & county governmental agencies in Southwestern Penn (Archives of Industrial Society); 19th & 20th Century American & English Theatre (Ford & Harriet Curtis Coll); 20th Century Children's Literature (Clifton Fadiman Coll); Archive of Popular Culture; Canadian; Flora & Norman Winkler Coll; Foundation Center Coll; Frank P Ramsey Papers; Hervey Allen Coll, ms, bks; Historical Children's Literature, dating to 18th century, incl Mr Rogers Neighborhood (Elizabeth Nesbitt Room), tv archives, videotapes, puppets, ms; Human Relations Area Files; Izaak Walton's Compleat Angler (Bernard S Horne Coll); John A Nietz Textboook Coll (Early America School Books); Mary Roberts Rinehart Coll, ms, bks; Music & Memorabilia of Stephen Collins Foster (Foster Memorial Library); Pavlowa-Heinrich Ballet Coll; Pennsylvania Industry, Institutions, Ethnic Organizations (Archives of Industrial Society), legis papers, hist rec; Ramon Gomez de la Serna Coll, bks, ms; Rudolf Carnap & Hans Reichenbach Coll, bks, ms; Walter & Martha Leuba Coll; Western Pennsylvania, Early History & Travel (Darlington Memorial Library); William Steinberg Coll. State Document Depository; UN Document Depository; US Document Depository
Subject Interests: Bolivia, Cuba, E Asian, E European, Latin Am, Russia
Automation Activity & Vendor Info: (Cataloging) Ex Libris Group

Wireless access
Publications: Bibliographies; Guide to Libraries
Partic in Association of Research Libraries; Center for Research Libraries; LYRASIS; Northeast Research Libraries Consortium; OCLC Research Library Partnership; Partnership for Academic Library Collaborative & Innovation

Departmental Libraries:

AFRICAN-AMERICAN COLLECTION, Hillman Library, 1st Flr, 15260, SAN 359-3932. Tel: 412-648-7714. FAX: 412-648-7733. Web Site: www.library.pitt.edu/african-american-collection. *Liaison Librn,* Arif Jamal; Tel: 412-648-7759, E-mail: ajamal@pitt.edu

CL BARCO LAW LIBRARY, Law Bldg, 3900 Forbes Ave, 4th Flr, 15260, SAN 359-4513. Tel: 412-648-1325, 412-648-1330. Interlibrary Loan Service Tel: 412-648-1356. FAX: 412-648-1352. Web Site: www.law.pitt.edu/library. *Actg Dir,* Mark Silverman; Tel: 412-648-1376, E-mail: marsil@pitt.edu; *Acq, Ser Librn,* Patricia Roncevich; Tel: 412-648-1321, E-mail: roncevic@pitt.edu; *Syst & Cat Librn,* Chris Todd; Tel: 412-648-1326, E-mail: chris.todd@pitt.edu
Founded 1915
Library Holdings: Bk Vols 185,466; Per Subs 4,674
Partic in OCLC Online Computer Library Center, Inc
Publications: Research Guides; User's Guide
Open Mon-Thurs 7:30am-10pm, Fri 7:30-5, Sat 10-6, Sun 12-8

BEVIER ENGINEERING LIBRARY, G33 Benedum Hall, 15261, SAN 359-4122. Tel: 412-624-9620. FAX: 412-624-8103. Web Site: www.library.pitt.edu/engineering. *Head Librn,* Judith Ann Brink; Tel: 412-624-0859, E-mail: jbrink@pitt.edu

BUHL SOCIAL WORK COLLECTION, Hillman Library, 1st Flr, 3960 Forbes Ave, 15260, SAN 359-3975. Web Site: www.library.pitt.edu/buhl-social-work-collection. *Liaison Librn,* Arif Jamal; Tel: 412-648-7759, E-mail: ajamal@pitt.edu

BUSINESS, 118 Mervis Hall, 15260, SAN 359-436X. Tel: 412-648-1669. FAX: 412-648-1809. *Head Librn,* Position Currently Open
Library Holdings: Bk Vols 15,000; Per Subs 600
Partic in Northeast Research Libraries Consortium

CHEMISTRY, 130 Chevron Science Ctr, 15261, SAN 359-4009. Tel: 412-624-8294. FAX: 412-624-1809. Web Site: www.library.pitt.edu/chemistry. *Head Librn,* Margarete Bower; Tel: 412-624-3714, E-mail: bower@pitt.edu

CM FALK LIBRARY OF THE HEALTH SCIENCES, 200 Scaife Hall, 3550 Terrace St, 15261, SAN 359-4335. Circulation Tel: 412-648-8866. Interlibrary Loan Service Tel: 412-648-2037. FAX: 412-648-9020. E-mail: medlibq@pitt.edu. Web Site: www.hsls.pitt.edu. *Dir,* Barbara A Epstein; E-mail: bepstein@pitt.edu; Staff 24 (MLS 24)
Library Holdings: Bk Vols 447,014; Per Subs 3,182
Special Collections: History of Medicine
Subject Interests: Dentistry, Health, Health & rehabilitation sci, Med, Nursing, Pharm, Pub health
Publications: HSLS Update (Newsletter)
Open Mon-Thurs 7am-Midnight, Fri 7am-10pm, Sat 9:30am-10pm, Sun 11am-Midnight

THEODORE M FINNEY MUSIC LIBRARY, Music Bldg B28, 15260, SAN 359-4246. Tel: 412-624-4130. FAX: 412-624-4180. Web Site: www.library.pitt.edu/music. *Head of Libr,* James P Cassaro; Tel: 412-624-4131, E-mail: cassaro@pitt.edu; Staff 3 (MLS 2, Non-MLS 1)
Founded 1966. Fac 37; Highest Degree: Doctorate
Library Holdings: CDs 30,000; DVDs 900; Microforms 10,000; Music Scores 50,000; Bk Vols 65,000; Per Subs 250; Videos 1,500
Special Collections: Eric Moe Coll, first drafts, ms; Mirskey Coll; Polish Singers Alliance of America Coll
Automation Activity & Vendor Info: (Acquisitions) Ex Libris Group; (Circulation) Ex Libris Group; (Course Reserve) Ex Libris Group; (ILL) OCLC ILLiad; (OPAC) Ex Libris Group
Function: Audio & video playback equip for onsite use, CD-ROM, Computers for patron use, Doc delivery serv, E-Reserves, Electronic databases & coll, ILL available, Music CDs, Online cat, Online info literacy tutorials on the web & in blackboard, Online ref, OverDrive digital audio bks, Photocopying/Printing, Ref serv available, Res libr, Telephone ref, VHS videos, Wheelchair accessible
Restriction: Borrowing privileges limited to fac & registered students, Borrowing requests are handled by ILL, Non-circulating of rare bks, Off-site coll in storage - retrieval as requested, Restricted borrowing privileges

FRICK FINE ARTS LIBRARY, Frick Fine Arts Bldg, 1st Flr, 15260, SAN 359-4157. Tel: 412-648-2410. FAX: 412-648-7568. Web Site: www.library.pitt.edu/fine-arts. *Interim Head Librn,* Kathryn Joranson; Tel: 412-648-2411, E-mail: kmj19@pitt.edu; Staff 4 (MLS 2, Non-MLS 2)
Library Holdings: Bk Vols 85,000; Per Subs 350
Subject Interests: Archit hist, Art hist

HILLMAN LIBRARY-ADMINISTRATIVE OFFICES, 3960 Forbes Ave, Ste 271, 15260, SAN 359-419X. Reference Tel: 412-648-3330. FAX: 412-648-7887. *Dir, Admin Serv,* William Gentz; Tel: 412-648-7748, E-mail: gentz@pitt.edu
Library Holdings: Bk Vols 1,500,000

LANGLEY LIBRARY, 217 Langley Hall, 15260, SAN 359-4181. Tel: 412-624-4490. FAX: 412-624-1809. Web Site: www.library.pitt.edu/langley. *Head of Libr,* Margarete Bower; Tel: 412-624-3714, E-mail: bower@pitt.edu; *Libr Spec,* Laurel Povazan Scholnick; E-mail: laurelp@pitt.edu

M UNIVERSITY OF PITTSBURGH MEDICAL CENTER SHADYSIDE*, Hopwood Library, 5230 Centre Ave, 15232. SAN 315-1166. Tel: 412-623-2620. *Coordr, Libr Serv,* Heidi Patterson; Tel: 412-623-3985; Staff 1 (MLS 1)
Founded 2001
Library Holdings: Bk Vols 8,000; Per Subs 225
Subject Interests: Clinical med, Consumer health info, Nursing
Automation Activity & Vendor Info: (Acquisitions) Ex Libris Group; (Cataloging) Ex Libris Group; (Circulation) Ex Libris Group; (OPAC) Ex Libris Group
Wireless access
Open Mon-Fri 8-5

M UPMC MERCY HOSPITAL OF PITTSBURGH*, Brady Library of the Health Sciences, 1400 Locust St, 15219. SAN 359-3614. Tel: 412-232-7520. FAX: 412-232-8422. Web Site: www.upmc.com/locations/hospitals/mercy/Pages/default.aspx. *Librn,* Olivia Glotfelty; E-mail: glotfeltyo@upmc.edu; *Mgr,* Robert Neumeyer; Staff 3 (MLS 3)
Founded 1922
Library Holdings: Bk Vols 4,500; Per Subs 450
Subject Interests: Gen surgery, Med
Automation Activity & Vendor Info: (Acquisitions) EOS International; (Cataloging) EOS International; (Circulation) EOS International; (OPAC) EOS International; (Serials) EOS International
Wireless access
Function: Archival coll, Doc delivery serv, ILL available, Ref serv available
Partic in Pittsburgh Basic Health Sciences Libr Consortium); Pittsburgh-East Hospital Libr Coop
Restriction: Co libr

M UPMC PASSAVANT - MCCANDLESS*, Medical Library, 9100 Babcock Blvd, 15237-5842. SAN 315-0933. Tel: 412-748-6320. FAX: 412-748-6889. Web Site: www.upmc.com/locations/hospitals/passavant/locations/mccandless. *Med Librn,* Laura Williams; E-mail: williamsl20@upmc.edu
Founded 1971
Special Collections: Consumer Health Pamphlets
Subject Interests: Med, Nursing
Wireless access
Partic in Basic Health Sciences Library Network; National Network of Libraries of Medicine Region 1; Pittsburgh-East Hospital Libr Coop
Open Mon-Thurs 8:30-4

M UPMC ST MARGARET*, Health Sciences Library, 815 Freeport Rd, 15215. SAN 359-3827. Tel: 412-784-4121, 412-784-4238. FAX: 412-784-4989. Web Site: www.upmc.com/locations/hospitals/st-margaret/services/emergency-medicine. *Dir,* Amy Haugh; Staff 2 (MLS 1, Non-MLS 1)
Founded 1951
Library Holdings: Bk Vols 2,500; Per Subs 200
Special Collections: Historical Coll (Harry M Margolis MD)
Subject Interests: Family med, Gerontology, Nursing educ, Occupational therapy, Orthopedics, Rheumatoid arthritis
Partic in Basic Health Sciences Library Network
Open Mon-Fri 8-4:30

G VA PITTSBURGH HEALTHCARE SYSTEM*, Medical Library Highland Drive Div, University Dr C, 15240. SAN 359-4602. Tel: 412-360-3054, 412-822-1748. Web Site: www.pittsburgh.va.gov. *Librn,* Jane Rish; E-mail: jane.rish@va.gov
Founded 1954
Partic in National Network of Libraries of Medicine Region 1
Restriction: Not open to pub

Branches:

MEDICAL LIBRARY HEINZ DIVISION, 1010 Delafield Rd, 15215. (Mail add: Aspinwall Library 142D-A, Delafield Rd, 15240). Tel: 412-784-3747. FAX: 412-784-3508. *Librn,* James R Johnson; E-mail: james.johnson6@va.gov; Staff 1 (MLS 1)
Open Mon-Fri 8-4:30

MEDICAL LIBRARY UNIVERSITY DRIVE DIVISION, University Dr, 15240. Tel: 412-360-3054. FAX: 412-688-6586. *Librn,* Jane Rish; E-mail: jane.rish@va.gov; Staff 1 (MLS 1)
Open Mon-Fri 8-4:30

R WESTMINSTER PRESBYTERIAN CHURCH LIBRARY*, 2040 Washington Rd, Upper St Clair, 15241. SAN 315-1220. Tel: 412-835-6630. FAX: 412-835-5690. Web Site: www.westminster-church.org. *Librn,* Barbara Mauk; E-mail: barbaramauk@gmail.com
Library Holdings: Bk Vols 5,000
Friends of the Library Group

P WHITEHALL PUBLIC LIBRARY*, 100 Borough Park Dr, 15236. SAN 315-1239. Tel: 412-882-6622. FAX: 412-882-9556. E-mail: whitehall@einetwork.net. Web Site: www.whitehallpubliclibrary.org. *Dir,* Paula Kelly
Founded 1963
Library Holdings: Bk Vols 62,000; Per Subs 100
Special Collections: Bks on tapes; Business Coll; College Career Information; Large Print Coll; Parenting Coll; Toddler Board & Cloth Books Coll
Subject Interests: Mysteries, Popular fiction, Popular paperbacks, Travel info
Wireless access
Mem of Allegheny County Library Association (ACLA)
Open Mon-Thurs 9-9, Fri 1-5, Sat 9-5, Sun 12-4
Friends of the Library Group

P WILKINSBURG PUBLIC LIBRARY*, 605 Ross Ave, 15221-2195. SAN 315-1247. Tel: 412-244-2940. FAX: 412-243-6943. Web Site: www.wilkinsburglibrary.org. *Dir,* Bob Metz; E-mail: metzr@einetwork.net; Staff 3 (MLS 3)
Founded 1899. Pop 15,900; Circ 100,000
Library Holdings: AV Mats 6,500; Bks on Deafness & Sign Lang 17; High Interest/Low Vocabulary Bk Vols 150; Large Print Bks 5,000; Bk Titles 73,297; Per Subs 140
Special Collections: Wilkinsburg History Coll, large print coll
Subject Interests: Biographies, Local hist, Mysteries
Automation Activity & Vendor Info: (Cataloging) Innovative Interfaces, Inc; (Circulation) Innovative Interfaces, Inc; (OPAC) Innovative Interfaces, Inc
Wireless access
Mem of Allegheny County Library Association (ACLA)
Open Mon & Wed 10-7, Tues & Thurs 10-6, Fri & Sat 10-5
Friends of the Library Group
Branches: 1
EASTRIDGE, 1900 Graham Blvd, 15235. Tel: 412-342-0056. *Dir,* Joel D Minnigh; *Assoc Librn,* Linda Jennings
Founded 2003
Library Holdings: AV Mats 2,000; Bk Vols 8,000; Per Subs 25
Open Tues & Thurs 10-8, Wed, Fri & Sat 10-5, Sun 1-5
Friends of the Library Group

PITTSTON

S NORTHEASTERN PENNSYLVANIA ALLIANCE*, Northeastern Pennsylvania Nonprofit & Community Assistance Center, 1151 Oak St, 18640-3726. SAN 329-0824. Tel: 570-655-5581. Toll Free Tel: 866-758-1929. FAX: 570-654-5137. E-mail: ncac@nepa-alliance.org. Web Site: www.nepa-alliance.org/community-nonprofit/ncac. *Exec Dir,* Kurt R Bauman; Tel: 570-655-5581, Ext 237, E-mail: kbauman@nepa-alliance.org; *Commun Serv,* Meghan Loftus; E-mail: mloftus@nepa-alliance.org; Staff 2 (MLS 2)
Founded 1980
Library Holdings: Bk Titles 305; Bk Vols 500; Per Subs 35; Spec Interest Per Sub 10; Videos 20
Special Collections: Pennsylvania State Data Center Foundation Library
Wireless access
Publications: Annual Report; Newsletters; Weekly Funding Updates by Email
Open Mon-Fri 10-5
Restriction: Non-circulating

P PITTSTON MEMORIAL LIBRARY*, 47 Broad St, 18640. SAN 315-1255. Tel: 570-654-9565. FAX: 570-654-6078. E-mail: pittstonlibrary@luzernelibraries.org. Web Site: www.pittstonmemoriallibrary.org. *Dir,* Patricia Joyce; E-mail: pjoyce@luzernelibraries.org
Founded 1971. Pop 8,104; Circ 54,435
Library Holdings: AV Mats 3,000; Bk Vols 40,000; Per Subs 75
Automation Activity & Vendor Info: (Cataloging) SirsiDynix; (Circulation) SirsiDynix
Wireless access
Function: Adult bk club, Art exhibits, Audiobks via web, Bk club(s), Bks on cassette, Bks on CD, Children's prog, Computers for patron use, Electronic databases & coll, Free DVD rentals, Holiday prog, ILL available, Photocopying/Printing, Preschool outreach, Prog for adults, Prog for children & young adult, Ref & res, Story hour, Summer reading prog, Tax forms, Teen prog, Telephone ref, Wheelchair accessible
Mem of Luzerne County Library System
Open Mon & Thurs 11-7, Tues, Wed & Fri 9-5, Sat 9-4
Friends of the Library Group

PLEASANT HILLS

P PLEASANT HILLS PUBLIC LIBRARY*, 302 Old Clairton Rd, 15236-4399. SAN 315-1263. Tel: 412-655-2424. FAX: 412-655-2292. E-mail: pleasanthills@einetwork.net. Web Site: www.pleasanthillslibrary.org. *Dir,* Sharon Julian-Milas; E-mail: milass@einetwork.net
Founded 1945. Pop 8,268; Circ 119,585
Library Holdings: Bk Titles 57,800; Per Subs 105
Subject Interests: Lit
Automation Activity & Vendor Info: (Cataloging) Innovative Interfaces, Inc; (Circulation) Innovative Interfaces, Inc
Wireless access
Mem of Allegheny County Library Association (ACLA)
Open Mon-Thurs 10-8:30, Fri 10-4, Sat 9-4 (9-1 Summer)
Friends of the Library Group

PLEASANT MOUNT

P PLEASANT MOUNT PUBLIC LIBRARY, 375 Great Bend Tpk, 18453-4580. (Mail add: PO Box 33, 18453-0033), SAN 320-8389. Tel: 570-448-2573. FAX: 570-448-9713. E-mail: pmpl@waynelibraries.org. Web Site: www.waynelibraries.org/pleasant-mount. *Dir,* Jennifer Snyder; E-mail: jsnyder@waynelibraries.org
Founded 1975. Pop 1,300; Circ 10,500
Library Holdings: CDs 171; DVDs 61; Large Print Bks 123; Bk Titles 7,000; Per Subs 15; Talking Bks 111; Videos 555
Wireless access
Open Tues-Fri 12-5
Friends of the Library Group

PLUM BOROUGH

P PLUM BOROUGH COMMUNITY LIBRARY*, 445 Center-New Texas Rd, 15239. Tel: 412-798-7323. FAX: 412-798-9245. Web Site: www.plumlibrary.org. *Dir,* Marilyn Klingensmith; E-mail: klingensmithm@einetwork.net
Pop 26,940
Library Holdings: AV Mats 3,457; Bk Vols 28,000; Per Subs 75; Videos 3,040
Automation Activity & Vendor Info: (Cataloging) Innovative Interfaces, Inc; (Circulation) Innovative Interfaces, Inc; (OPAC) Innovative Interfaces, Inc
Mem of Allegheny County Library Association (ACLA)
Open Mon-Thurs 10-8, Fri & Sat 10-5
Friends of the Library Group

PLYMOUTH

P PLYMOUTH PUBLIC LIBRARY, 107 W Main St, 18651-2919. SAN 315-128X. Tel: 570-779-4775. FAX: 570-779-5616. E-mail: pplstaff@luzernelibraries.org. Web Site: luzernelibraries.org/plymouth.html. *Exec Dir,* Laura Keller; Staff 1 (MLS 1)
Founded 1938. Pop 10,500; Circ 19,000
Library Holdings: AV Mats 905; High Interest/Low Vocabulary Bk Vols 52; Large Print Bks 450; Bk Titles 42,721; Per Subs 72; Talking Bks 350
Subject Interests: Children's bks, Cookbks, Local hist
Automation Activity & Vendor Info: (Cataloging) Innovative Interfaces, Inc; (Circulation) Innovative Interfaces, Inc; (OPAC) Innovative Interfaces, Inc
Wireless access
Mem of Luzerne County Library System
Open Mon & Wed 10-5, Tues 10-4, Thurs 10-6, Sat 10-2
Friends of the Library Group

PLYMOUTH MEETING

S ECRI INSTITUTE LIBRARY*, 5200 Butler Pike, 19462. SAN 315-1301. Tel: 610-825-6000, Ext 5309. FAX: 610-834-7366. Web Site: www.ecri.org. *Libr Dir,* Amy Stone; Staff 3 (MLS 3)
Founded 1966
Library Holdings: e-journals 604; Bk Titles 6,662; Per Subs 653
Special Collections: Medical & Health Care Related Devices (Health Devices Evaluation Services)
Subject Interests: Med tech
Automation Activity & Vendor Info: (Acquisitions) Inmagic, Inc.; (Cataloging) Inmagic, Inc.; (Circulation) Inmagic, Inc.; (OPAC) Inmagic, Inc.; (Serials) Inmagic, Inc.
Wireless access
Partic in National Network of Libraries of Medicine Region 1
Restriction: Employees only, Limited access based on advanced application

POCONO PINES

P CLYMER LIBRARY, 115 Firehouse Rd, 18350-9705. SAN 324-3974. Tel: 570-646-0826. FAX: 570-646-6181. E-mail: clymer@clymerlibrary.org. Web Site: www.clymerlibrary.org. *Libr Dir,* Becky Wanamaker; E-mail: bwanamaker@clymerlibrary.org; Staff 2 (MLS 1, Non-MLS 1)
Founded 1902. Pop 25,343
Library Holdings: Bk Titles 41,381; Per Subs 50
Automation Activity & Vendor Info: (Circulation) Innovative Interfaces, Inc
Wireless access
Function: 24/7 Online cat, Activity rm, Adult bk club, After school storytime, Art exhibits, Art programs, Audiobks via web, Bk club(s), Bks on CD, Butterfly Garden, Children's prog, Computer training, Computers for patron use, Digital talking bks, E-Readers, E-Reserves, Electronic databases & coll, For res purposes, Free DVD rentals, Games & aids for people with disabilities, Holiday prog, ILL available, Instruction & testing, Internet access, Life-long learning prog for all ages, Magazines, Mail & tel request accepted, Meeting rooms, Movies, Online cat, Online info literacy tutorials on the web & in blackboard, Online ref, Outreach serv, OverDrive digital audio bks, Photocopying/Printing, Preschool outreach, Preschool reading prog, Printer for laptops & handheld devices, Prog for adults, Prog for children & young adult, Ref & res, Ref serv available, Res assist avail, Scanner, Senior outreach, Serves people with intellectual disabilities, STEM programs, Story hour, Study rm, Summer & winter reading prog, Summer reading prog, Tax forms, Teen prog, Telephone ref, Wheelchair accessible, Workshops, Writing prog
Open Mon, Wed, Fri & Sat 10-5, Tues & Thurs 10-8

POINT MARION

P POINT MARION PUBLIC LIBRARY*, 399 Ontario St, 15474. SAN 370-7458. Tel: 724-725-9553. FAX: 724-725-9553. E-mail: pmlibrary@verizon.net. Web Site: www.pointmarionlibrary.com. *Library Contact,* Joyce Dills
Founded 1928. Pop 2,067; Circ 7,675
Library Holdings: Bk Titles 6,550
Open Mon, Wed & Thurs 6pm-9pm, Tues 2-4 & 6-9, Sat 12-2

PORT ALLEGANY

P SAMUEL W SMITH MEMORIAL PUBLIC LIBRARY, 201 E Maple St, 16743. SAN 315-131X. Tel: 814-642-9210. FAX: 814-642-7555. E-mail: swsmith@swsmithlibrary.org. Web Site: www.swsmithlibrary.org. *Dir,* Mary Grace Collier-Kisler; Staff 5 (MLS 1, Non-MLS 4)
Founded 1930. Pop 8,400; Circ 29,900
Automation Activity & Vendor Info: (Circulation) EnvisionWare; (OPAC) EnvisionWare
Wireless access
Function: 24/7 Electronic res, 24/7 Online cat, Accelerated reader prog, Activity rm, Adult bk club, Audiobks via web, Bk club(s), Bks on CD, Children's prog, Computers for patron use, E-Readers, Electronic databases & coll, Family literacy, Free DVD rentals, Holiday prog, ILL available, Internet access, Laminating, Magazines, Magnifiers for reading, Mail & tel request accepted, Mail loans to mem, Meeting rooms, Microfiche/film & reading machines, Movies, Museum passes, Online cat, Online ref, Outreach serv, Outside serv via phone, mail, e-mail & web, OverDrive digital audio bks, Photocopying/Printing, Preschool outreach, Preschool reading prog, Printer for laptops & handheld devices, Prog for adults, Prog for children & young adult, Scanner, Senior outreach, Spanish lang bks, STEM programs, Story hour, Summer & winter reading prog, Summer reading prog, Tax forms, Teen prog, Wheelchair accessible, Winter reading prog
Open Mon, Wed & Fri 9:30-3:30, Tues & Thurs 10:30-6:30
Friends of the Library Group

PORT CARBON

P PORT CARBON PUBLIC LIBRARY*, 111 Pike St, 17965. SAN 315-1328. Tel: 570-622-6115. FAX: 570-622-6115. E-mail: ptclib@wtvaccess.com. Web Site: www2.iu29.org/ptcpl. *Libr Dir,* Jason Abati; Staff 3 (Non-MLS 3)
Pop 2,105
Library Holdings: DVDs 1,000; Bk Titles 14,000; Per Subs 10; Videos 100
Wireless access
Open Mon, Wed & Thurs 1-7, Tues & Fri 1-6

PORTAGE

P PORTAGE PUBLIC LIBRARY*, 704 Main St, 15946-1715. SAN 315-1336. Tel: 814-736-4340. FAX: 814-736-4413. E-mail: portage@cclsys.org. Web Site: www.cclsys.org/portage. *Dir,* Kaytlin Sumner
Founded 1927. Pop 6,879; Circ 31,259
Library Holdings: Large Print Bks 566; Bk Titles 15,147; Bk Vols 15,587; Per Subs 22; Talking Bks 460
Wireless access
Mem of Cambria County Library System & District Center
Open Tues & Thurs 12-7, Wed & Fri 9-4, Sat 9-1 (9-4 Winter)

POTTSTOWN

P POTTSTOWN REGIONAL PUBLIC LIBRARY, 500 E High St, 19464-5656. SAN 315-1344. Tel: 610-970-6551. FAX: 610-970-6553. E-mail: pottstownlibrary@gmail.com. Web Site: pottstownregionalpubliclibrary.org. *Exec Dir,* Melinda Lee M Lipsky; E-mail: mlipsky@mclinc.org; Staff 3 (MLS 3)
Founded 1921. Pop 43,625; Circ 100,950
Jan 2021-Dec 2021 Income $584,531, State $109,422, City $175,500, Locally Generated Income $299,609. Mats Exp $688,800. Sal $400,656
Library Holdings: Bk Vols 67,972; Per Subs 164
Special Collections: Limerick Nuclear Power Plant
Subject Interests: Local hist, Penn hist
Automation Activity & Vendor Info: (Cataloging) Innovative Interfaces, Inc; (Circulation) Innovative Interfaces, Inc; (OPAC) Innovative Interfaces, Inc; (Serials) Innovative Interfaces, Inc
Wireless access
Function: 24/7 Electronic res, 24/7 Online cat, Activity rm, Adult bk club, Audiobks via web, AV serv, Bk club(s), Bks on CD, Children's prog, Computer training, Computers for patron use, Distance learning, E-Reserves, Electronic databases & coll, Free DVD rentals, Holiday prog, Homework prog, ILL available, Internet access, Life-long learning prog for all ages, Magazines, Mango lang, Meeting rooms, Microfiche/film & reading machines, Movies, Museum passes, Music CDs, Online cat, Online ref, Outreach serv, OverDrive digital audio bks, Passport agency, Photocopying/Printing, Preschool outreach, Preschool reading prog, Printer for laptops & handheld devices, Prog for adults, Prog for children & young adult, Ref serv available, Scanner, Senior computer classes, Story hour, Summer reading prog, Teen prog, Telephone ref, Wheelchair accessible
Partic in Montgomery County Library & Information Network Consortium
Open Mon-Wed 10-8, Thurs & Fri 10-6, Sat 9-4
Friends of the Library Group

POTTSVILLE

M LEHIGH VALLEY HEALTH NETWORK, Joseph F McCloskey School of Nursing, 420 S Jackson St, 17901-2798. SAN 372-6215. Tel: 570-621-5033. FAX: 570-621-5351. *Health Sci Librn,* Joan Farrell; E-mail: joan.farrell@lvhn.org
Library Holdings: CDs 24; Videos 50
Subject Interests: Med, Nursing, Pub health
Automation Activity & Vendor Info: (Cataloging) LibraryWorld, Inc; (OPAC) LibraryWorld, Inc
Wireless access
Function: Health sci info serv
Partic in Central Pennsylvania Health Sciences Library Association; National Network of Libraries of Medicine Region 1
Open Mon-Fri 8-4
Restriction: Hospital staff & commun

M JOSEPH F MCCLOSKEY SCHOOL OF NURSING AT LEHIGH VALLEY HOSPITAL - SCHUYLKILL, Medical Library, 420 S Jackson St, 17901. SAN 326-5439. Tel: 570-621-5000, 570-621-5033. Web Site: www.lvhn.org/school_of_nursing. *Librn,* Joan Farrell; E-mail: Joan.Farrell@lvhn.org
Library Holdings: Bk Vols 1,850; Per Subs 15
Subject Interests: Med
Wireless access
Publications: Newsletter (Quarterly)
Restriction: Med staff only

P POTTSVILLE FREE PUBLIC LIBRARY, 215 W Market St, 17901. SAN 315-1379. Tel: 570-622-8105, 570-622-8880. FAX: 570-622-2157. E-mail: potpublib@pottsvillelibrary.org. Web Site: www.pottsvillelibrary.org. *Exec Dir,* Jean Towle; E-mail: jat@pottsvillelibrary.org; *Tech Serv Librn,* William Dreisbach; E-mail: pottech@pottsvillelibrary.org; *Youth Serv Librn,* Darren DeArment; E-mail: potchild@pottsvillelibrary.org; *Circ,* Gina Bensinger; E-mail: potcirc@pottsvillelibrary.org; *ILL,* Danette Reidler; E-mail: potill@pottsvillelibrary.org; *Ref (Info Servs),* Becki White; E-mail: potref@pottsvillelibrary.org; Staff 6 (MLS 6)
Founded 1911. Pop 94,130; Circ 114,350
Library Holdings: AV Mats 15,266; CDs 1,307; DVDs 576; Large Print Bks 4,246; Bk Titles 99,315; Bk Vols 109,980; Per Subs 200; Talking Bks 4,074; Videos 3,128
Special Collections: Anthracite Coll; Lincoln Coll; Molly Maguires Coll. State Document Depository; US Document Depository
Automation Activity & Vendor Info: (Acquisitions) Baker & Taylor; (Cataloging) Evergreen; (Circulation) Evergreen; (ILL) Evergreen; (OPAC) Evergreen

Wireless access
Function: 24/7 Online cat, Adult bk club, Art exhibits, Audiobks via web, Bk club(s), Bks on CD, CD-ROM, Children's prog, Computers for patron use, Doc delivery serv, Electronic databases & coll, Free DVD rentals, Govt ref serv, Health sci info serv, Holiday prog, ILL available, Internet access, Life-long learning prog for all ages, Magazines, Magnifiers for reading, Mail & tel request accepted, Makerspace, Meeting rooms, Microfiche/film & reading machines, Music CDs, Online cat, Photocopying/Printing, Preschool outreach, Preschool reading prog, Prog for adults, Prog for children & young adult, Ref & res, Ref serv available, Spanish lang bks, STEM programs, Story hour, Summer reading prog, Tax forms, Teen prog, Telephone ref, VHS videos, Wheelchair accessible
Open Mon-Thurs 8:30-7:30, Fri & Sat 8:30-5
Friends of the Library Group

GL SCHUYLKILL COUNTY LAW LIBRARY*, Schuylkill County Courthouse, 401 N Second St, 4th Fl, 17901. SAN 315-1395. Tel: 570-628-1235. FAX: 570-628-1017. Web Site: www.co.schuylkill.pa.us/Offices/LawLibrary. *Law Librn,* Charlotte Green; E-mail: cgreen@co.schuylkill.pa.us
Founded 1888
Library Holdings: Bk Vols 30,000; Per Subs 20
Open Mon-Fri 8:30-4:30

PROSPECT

P PROSPECT COMMUNITY LIBRARY, 357 Main St, 16052. SAN 315-1417. Tel: 724-865-9718. FAX: 724-865-9718. E-mail: prospectlibrary@bcfls.org. Web Site: prospectlibrary.org. *Dir,* Bridget Seredey; Staff 1 (Non-MLS 1)
Founded 1922. Pop 3,500; Circ 22,000
Library Holdings: Bk Vols 14,000; Per Subs 20
Subject Interests: Gardening, Genealogy, Local hist
Automation Activity & Vendor Info: (Cataloging) TLC (The Library Corporation); (Circulation) TLC (The Library Corporation); (OPAC) TLC (The Library Corporation)
Wireless access
Function: 24/7 Electronic res, 24/7 Online cat, Adult bk club, Audiobks via web, Bk club(s), Bks on CD, CD-ROM, Children's prog, Computer training, Computers for patron use, Digital talking bks, Electronic databases & coll, Family literacy, Holiday prog, ILL available, Internet access, Magazines, Mango lang, Movies, Music CDs, Online cat, Outreach serv, OverDrive digital audio bks, Photocopying/Printing, Preschool outreach, Preschool reading prog, Prog for adults, Prog for children & young adult, Ref & res, Ref serv available, Scanner, Senior computer classes, STEM programs, Story hour, Summer & winter reading prog, Summer reading prog, Tax forms, Teen prog, Wheelchair accessible
Mem of Butler County Federated Library System
Open Mon & Thurs 1-7, Tues & Wed 10-5, Fri 10-3, Sat 8-3
Friends of the Library Group

PROSPECT PARK

P PROSPECT PARK FREE LIBRARY*, 720 Maryland Ave, 19076. Tel: 610-532-4643. FAX: 610-532-5648. E-mail: prospectpark@delcolibraries.org. Web Site: www.delcolibraries.org/prospect-park-free-library, www.prospectparklibrary.org. *Dir,* Mariann Jennings
Founded 1926. Pop 6,594
Library Holdings: AV Mats 305; Bk Vols 20,000; Per Subs 25
Automation Activity & Vendor Info: (Cataloging) Innovative Interfaces, Inc; (Circulation) Innovative Interfaces, Inc; (OPAC) Innovative Interfaces, Inc
Wireless access
Mem of Delaware County Libraries
Open Mon & Thurs 12-8, Tues & Fri 11-5, Sat 8:30-3:30 (8:30-12:30 Summer)

PUNXSUTAWNEY

PUNXSUTAWNEY MEMORIAL LIBRARY, 301 E Mahoning St, 15767-2198. SAN 315-145X. Tel: 814-938-5020. FAX: 814-938-3180. E-mail: info@punxsutawneylibrary.org. Web Site: www.punxsutawneylibrary.org. *Libr Dir,* Jennifer E Soliday; E-mail: director@punxsutawneylibrary.org
Founded 1916. Pop 16,225; Circ 50,000
Library Holdings: Bk Vols 36,000; Per Subs 50
Automation Activity & Vendor Info: (Cataloging) AmLib Library Management System; (Circulation) AmLib Library Management System; (OPAC) AmLib Library Management System
Wireless access
Mem of Oil Creek District Library Center
Partic in Jefferson County Library System
Open Mon & Wed 10-7, Tues, Thurs & Sat 10-5, Fri Noon-5
Friends of the Library Group

QUARRYVILLE

P QUARRYVILLE LIBRARY, 357 Buck Rd, 17566. Tel: 717-786-1336. FAX: 717-740-2169. E-mail: library@quarryvillelibrary.org. Web Site: www.quarryvillelibrary.org. *Dir,* Susan Eshleman; E-mail: seshleman@quarryvillelibrary.org; *Asst Dir,* Maribeth McMullen
Library Holdings: Audiobooks 900; AV Mats 2,580; Bks on Deafness & Sign Lang 50; Bk Vols 38,515; Per Subs 55
Automation Activity & Vendor Info: (Cataloging) Innovative Interfaces, Inc; (Circulation) Innovative Interfaces, Inc; (OPAC) Innovative Interfaces, Inc
Wireless access
Mem of Library System of Lancaster County
Open Tues-Thurs 10-8, Fri 10-6, Sat 10-2
Friends of the Library Group
Bookmobiles: 1. Spec Servs Coordr, Ed Miller

RADNOR

C CABRINI COLLEGE LIBRARY*, 610 King of Prussia Rd, 19087-3698. SAN 315-1476. Tel: 610-902-8538. FAX: 610-902-8539. E-mail: library@cabrini.edu. Web Site: www.cabrini.edu/library. *Libr Dir,* Anne Schwelm; Tel: 610-902-8536, E-mail: aschwelm@cabrini.edu; *Info Literacy Librn,* Ellie Knickman; Tel: 610-902-8249, E-mail: ellie.knickman@cabrini.edu; *Syst Librn,* Adam Altman; Tel: 610-902-8432, E-mail: adam.altman@cabrini.edu; Staff 7 (MLS 4, Non-MLS 3)
Founded 1957. Enrl 2,256; Fac 71; Highest Degree: Master
Jul 2013-Jun 2014. Mats Exp $248,000, Books $45,000, Per/Ser (Incl. Access Fees) $70,000, Electronic Ref Mat (Incl. Access Fees) $125,000, Presv $8,000. Sal $320,500 (Prof $200,000)
Library Holdings: DVDs 1,000; e-books 600; Bk Titles 76,500; Bk Vols 85,000; Per Subs 340
Special Collections: Cabriniana Coll; Franklin Delano Roosevelt Coll
Subject Interests: Educ, Immigration
Automation Activity & Vendor Info: (Acquisitions) SirsiDynix; (Cataloging) SirsiDynix; (Circulation) SirsiDynix; (OPAC) SirsiDynix; (Serials) SirsiDynix
Wireless access
Function: E-Reserves
Partic in Southeastern Pa Consortium for Higher Educ; Tri State Col Libr Coop
Restriction: Open to students, fac & staff

READING

C ALBRIGHT COLLEGE*, F Wilbur Gingrich Library, 13th & Exeter Sts, 19604. (Mail add: PO Box 15234, 19612-5234), SAN 315-1514. Tel: 610-921-7517. Interlibrary Loan Service Tel: 610-921-7209. Reference Tel: 610-921-7211. FAX: 610-921-7509. Reference E-mail: libraryref@albright.edu. Web Site: library.albright.edu. *Assoc Prof, Coll Mgt Librn, Interim Dir,* Sandra L Stump; Tel: 610-921-7205, E-mail: sstump@albright.edu; *AV,* George E Missonis; Tel: 610-921-7203; *Cat,* Sue Gallagher; Tel: 610-921-7208; *Circ,* Heidi Ziemer; Tel: 610-921-7207; *ILL,* Lindsay Sakmann; E-mail: lsakmann@albright.edu; Staff 14 (MLS 6, Non-MLS 8)
Founded 1856. Enrl 1,753
Library Holdings: e-books 290,000; Bk Vols 202,000; Per Subs 300
Special Collections: Albrightiana; Dick Coll of the Limited Editions Club; Norse-American Coll; Reading & Berks County (J Bennett Nolan Coll)
Subject Interests: Behav sci, Holocaust, Natural sci, Soc sci
Automation Activity & Vendor Info: (Acquisitions) Koha; (Cataloging) Koha; (Circulation) Koha; (OPAC) Koha; (Serials) Koha
Wireless access
Function: ILL available
Publications: eLibris; Library Link (Newsletter); Pathfinders; Serials List; User's Guide
Partic in Associated College Libraries of Central Pennsylvania; Berks County Library Association; LYRASIS; OCLC Online Computer Library Center, Inc; OCLC-LVIS
Open Mon-Thurs 7:30am-Midnight, Fri 7:30-7, Sat 10-7, Sun 10am-Midnight
Friends of the Library Group

C ALVERNIA UNIVERSITY*, Dr Frank A Franco Library Learning Center, 400 St Bernardine St, 19607-1737. SAN 315-1522. Tel: 610-796-8223. Interlibrary Loan Service Tel: 610-796-8224. FAX: 610-796-8347. Web Site: www.alvernia.edu/library. *Libr Dir,* Christina Steffy; E-mail: christina.steffy@alvernia.edu; *Access Serv Librn,* Kathleen Zamietra; Tel: 610-796-5635, E-mail: kathleen.zamietra@alvernia.edu; *Instrul & Ref Librn,* Ronald McColl; Tel: 610-568-1534, E-mail: ronald.mccoll@alvernia.edu; *Tech Serv Librn,* Susan I. Kane; Tel: 610-796-8439, E-mail: susan.kane@alvernia.edu; Staff 12 (MLS 6, Non-MLS 6)
Founded 1958. Enrl 2,215; Highest Degree: Doctorate

Jul 2017-Jun 2018 Income $425,414. Mats Exp $471,934, Books $26,672, Per/Ser (Incl. Access Fees) $87,395, Manu Arch $1,688, Other Print Mats $2,614, AV Mat $724, Electronic Ref Mat (Incl. Access Fees) $218,381. Sal $405,739 (Prof $266,217)
Library Holdings: AV Mats 2,277; CDs 839; DVDs 1,259; e-books 159,300; e-journals 57,785; Bk Titles 73,121; Bk Vols 77,086; Per Subs 150; Videos 2,277
Special Collections: Italian-American Cultural Center; Polish Coll
Subject Interests: Bus, Criminal justice, Nursing, Occupational therapy, Phys therapy
Automation Activity & Vendor Info: (Acquisitions) Innovative Interfaces, Inc; (Cataloging) Innovative Interfaces, Inc; (Circulation) Innovative Interfaces, Inc; (Course Reserve) Innovative Interfaces, Inc; (ILL) Innovative Interfaces, Inc; (OPAC) Innovative Interfaces, Inc; (Serials) Innovative Interfaces, Inc
Wireless access
Partic in Associated College Libraries of Central Pennsylvania; LYRASIS; OCLC Online Computer Library Center, Inc
Open Mon-Thurs 7:30am-Midnight, Fri 7:30-4:30, Sat 9-5, Sun Noon-Midnight

GL BERKS COUNTY LAW LIBRARY, Courthouse, 10th Flr, 633 Court St, 19601-4302. SAN 315-1549. Tel: 610-478-3370. Circulation Tel: 610-478-3370, Ext 3177. Administration Tel: 610-478-6208, Ext 3684. Information Services Tel: 610-478-3370, Ext 3171. FAX: 610-478-6375. E-mail: lawlibrary@countyofberks.com. Web Site: www.co.berks.pa.us/. *Adminr,* Tracy Barlet; Tel: 610-478-6208; *Law Libr Asst,* Melanie Marinaccio; E-mail: mmarinaccio@countyofberks.com; Staff 2 (Non-MLS 2)
Founded 1859
Library Holdings: Bk Titles 4,750; Bk Vols 34,000; Per Subs 1,300
Automation Activity & Vendor Info: (OPAC) Innovative Interfaces, Inc - Millennium
Function: Doc delivery serv
Open Mon-Fri 8:30-4:30
Restriction: Open to pub for ref only, Restricted borrowing privileges

S BERKS HISTORY CENTER, Henry Janssen Library, 160 Spring St, 19601. (Mail add: 940 Centre Ave, 19601), SAN 315-1581. Tel: 610-375-4375. FAX: 610-375-4376. E-mail: library@berkshistory.org. Web Site: www.berkshistory.org/library. *Archivist,* Bradley Smith; E-mail: b.smith@berkshistory.org
Founded 1869
Library Holdings: Bk Titles 16,000
Special Collections: Berks County Family Histories; German & English Newspapers of Reading & Berks County 1797-1907, newsp bd; Iron History of Berks County; Original Manuscripts
Publications: The Historical Review of Berks County
Restriction: Open by appt only

S CARPENTER TECHNOLOGY CORP*, Research & Development Library, 1600 Centre Ave, 19601. (Mail add: PO Box 14662, 19612-4662), SAN 315-1557. Tel: 610-208-2807. E-mail: randdlibrary@cartech.com. *Librn,* Mindy L Peters; E-mail: mpeters@cartech.com; Staff 1 (MLS 1)
Founded 1950
Subject Interests: Mat sci, Metallurgy
Wireless access
Function: Ref & res
Partic in Berks County Library Association
Restriction: Employees only, Open to others by appt, Open to researchers by request

P EXETER COMMUNITY LIBRARY*, 4569 Prestwick Dr, 19606. Tel: 610-406-9431. FAX: 610-406-9415. E-mail: exetercl@berks.lib.pa.us. Web Site: www.berkslibraries.org/branch/exeter. *Exec Dir,* Mallory C Hoffman; *Asst Dir,* Darlene S Mest; *Ch,* Laura C Kauffman; Staff 3 (Non-MLS 3)
Founded 1999. Pop 25,000; Circ 221,158
Library Holdings: CDs 2,489; DVDs 3,625; Bk Vols 18,000; Per Subs 58
Automation Activity & Vendor Info: (Cataloging) SirsiDynix; (Circulation) SirsiDynix; (OPAC) SirsiDynix
Wireless access
Function: Adult bk club, Bk club(s), Electronic databases & coll, ILL available, Mail & tel request accepted, Music CDs, Photocopying/Printing, Prog for adults, Prog for children & young adult, Spoken cassettes & CDs, Summer reading prog, Tax forms, VHS videos, Wheelchair accessible
Mem of Berks County Public Libraries
Open Mon 2-8, Tues & Wed 10-8, Thurs-Sat 10-5
Friends of the Library Group

C PENNSYLVANIA STATE UNIVERSITY*, Thun Library, Berks Campus, Tulpehocken Rd, 19610. (Mail add: PO Box 7009, 19610-7009), SAN 315-1611. Tel: 610-396-6339. FAX: 610-396-6249. E-mail: UL-BERKS@lists.psu.edu. Web Site: www.libraries.psu.edu/berks. *Head Librn,* John Shank; E-mail: jds30@psu.edu; *Ref & Instruction Librn,* Alexandria Chisholm; E-mail: aec67@psu.edu; Staff 4 (MLS 4)
Founded 1958. Enrl 2,400; Fac 100
Library Holdings: Bk Vols 50,000; Per Subs 130
Wireless access
Partic in OCLC Online Computer Library Center, Inc; Research Libraries Information Network
Open Mon-Thurs (Winter) 7:30am-Midnight, Fri 7:30-5, Sat Noon-5, Sun 2-10; Mon-Thurs (Summer) 8am-10pm, Fri 8-5

J READING AREA COMMUNITY COLLEGE, The Yocum Library, 30 S Front St, 19602. (Mail add: PO Box 1706, 19603-1706), SAN 315-1638. Tel: 610-607-6237. Reference Tel: 610-372-4721, Ext 5057. Administration Tel: 610-372-4721, Ext 5061. Toll Free Tel: 800-626-1665, Ext 6237. FAX: 610-607-6254. E-mail: library@racc.edu. Web Site: www.racc.edu/academics/yocum-library. *Assoc Dean, Libr Serv,* Mary Ellen G Heckman; E-mail: mheckman@racc.edu; *Instrul Serv Librn, Ref Serv,* Kim R Stahler; E-mail: kstahler@racc.edu; *Tech Serv Librn,* Brenna Corbit; Tel: 610-372-4721, Ext 5033, E-mail: bcorbit@racc.edu; Staff 5 (MLS 4, Non-MLS 1)
Founded 1971. Enrl 2,951; Fac 60; Highest Degree: Associate
Library Holdings: Bk Vols 32,000; Per Subs 225
Special Collections: Comic Books; Music Score Coll; Schuylkill Navigation Co Maps
Subject Interests: Film, Nursing
Wireless access
Function: ILL available, Magnifiers for reading, Wheelchair accessible
Mem of Berks County Public Libraries
Special Services for the Blind - Aids for in-house use
Open Mon, Thurs & Fri 8:30-5, Tues & Wed 8:30-8, Sat 8:30-1
Restriction: Open to pub for ref & circ; with some limitations

P READING PUBLIC LIBRARY*, 100 S Fifth St, 19602. SAN 359-4963. Tel: 610-655-6350. Administration Tel: 610-655-6365. Administration FAX: 610-478-9035. E-mail: webmaster@reading.lib.pa.us. Web Site: readingpubliclibrary.org. *Exec Dir,* Bronwen Gamble; Tel: 610-655-6355, E-mail: bronwen.gamble@reading.lib.pa.us; *Asst Dir, Syst Adminr,* Mike Najarian; Tel: 610-655-6350, E-mail: mike.najarian@reading.lib.pa.us; *Asst Dir, Pub Serv,* Jennifer Balas Bressler; E-mail: jxbressler@reading.lib.pa.us; *Supvr, Tech Serv,* Pamela Hehr; E-mail: hehr@reading.lib.pa.us
Founded 1763. Pop 382,000; Circ 529,603
Library Holdings: Bk Titles 297,582; Bk Vols 311,785; Per Subs 305
Special Collections: John Updike Coll; Local Imprints, Berks Authors Coll; Pennsylvania German Coll. State Document Depository; US Document Depository
Automation Activity & Vendor Info: (Cataloging) SirsiDynix; (Circulation) SirsiDynix; (OPAC) SirsiDynix
Wireless access
Mem of Berks County Public Libraries
Partic in OCLC Online Computer Library Center, Inc
Open Mon-Wed 9:30-7, Thurs & Fri 9:30-5:30, Sat 9:30-3
Friends of the Library Group
Branches: 3
NORTHEAST, 1348 N 11th St, 19604-1509, SAN 359-4998. Tel: 610-655-6361. FAX: 610-655-6668. E-mail: rplne@reading.lib.pa.us. *Br Mgr,* Betty O'Neil
Library Holdings: Bk Vols 28,336
Open Mon, Tues & Thurs 9:30-5, Wed 12-7:30, Sat 10-3
Friends of the Library Group
NORTHWEST, 901 Schuylkill Ave, 19601, SAN 359-5021. Tel: 610-655-6360. FAX: 610-655-6667. *Br Mgr,* Rob Martin
Founded 1939
Library Holdings: Bk Vols 14,966
Open Tues 12-7:30, Wed (9:30-5 Summer), Thurs 9:30-5, Sat 10-3
SOUTHEAST, 1426 Perkiomen Ave, 19602-2136, SAN 359-5056. Tel: 610-655-6362. FAX: 610-655-6669. E-mail: rplse@reading.lib.pa.us. *Br Mgr,* Emily McNulty
Library Holdings: Bk Vols 23,291
Open Mon 12-7, Tues-Thurs 9:30-5, Sat 10-3
Friends of the Library Group
Bookmobiles: 1

RED LION

P KALTREIDER-BENFER LIBRARY*, 147 S Charles St, 17356. SAN 315-1689. Tel: 717-244-2032. FAX: 717-246-2394. E-mail: kalib@yorklibraries.org. Web Site: www.kaltreider-benfer.org. *Dir,* Don Dellinger; E-mail: ddellinger@yorklibraries.org; Staff 6 (MLS 1, Non-MLS 5)
Founded 1963. Pop 59,157; Circ 215,000
Library Holdings: Bk Titles 51,000; Per Subs 45
Wireless access
Publications: Red Lion Community Directory
Mem of York County Library System

Open Mon-Thurs 10-8, Fri 10-5, Sat 9-4 (10-2 July & Aug)
Friends of the Library Group

REPUBLIC

P REPUBLIC COMMUNITY LIBRARY*, 13 DeGregory Circle, 15475. (Mail add: PO Box 165, 15475-0165). Tel: 724-246-0404. FAX: 724-246-0404. E-mail: rcl1@atlanticbbn.net. *Dir,* Martha Davis
Library Holdings: Bk Vols 10,500
Automation Activity & Vendor Info: (Cataloging) Brodart; (Circulation) Brodart
Open Mon 3-5, Thurs 5-7, Sat 10-1

REYNOLDSVILLE

P REYNOLDSVILLE PUBLIC LIBRARY*, 460 Main St, 15851-1251. SAN 315-1700. Tel: 814-653-9471. FAX: 814-653-9471. E-mail: reylib@comcast.net. Web Site: www.reylib.org.
Founded 1929. Pop 6,870; Circ 35,212
Library Holdings: Bk Vols 12,500; Per Subs 50
Wireless access
Mem of Oil Creek District Library Center
Open Mon-Thurs 1-8, Fri 1-5, Sat 9-4:30

RICHBORO

P FREE LIBRARY OF NORTHAMPTON TOWNSHIP*, 25 Upper Holland Rd, 18954-1514. SAN 315-1719. Tel: 215-357-3050. E-mail: remingtond@buckslib.org. Web Site: www.northamptontownshiplibrary.org. *Dir,* Diana Remington; *Ch,* Christy Lazzarino; *Ref,* Amy Wardle; Staff 5 (MLS 5)
Founded 1970. Pop 39,726; Circ 283,209
Jan 2015-Dec 2015 Income $1,079,258, State $115,914, City $917,354, Locally Generated Income $40,787. Mats Exp $126,088, Books $76,538, Per/Ser (Incl. Access Fees) $9,000, AV Mat $15,605, Electronic Ref Mat (Incl. Access Fees) $19,873, Presv $5,072. Sal $593,247
Library Holdings: Audiobooks 5,678; AV Mats 4,857; Braille Volumes 500; Electronic Media & Resources 7,004,857; Bk Vols 109,026; Per Subs 160
Automation Activity & Vendor Info: (Circulation) SirsiDynix; (OPAC) SirsiDynix
Wireless access
Mem of Bucks County Free Library
Special Services for the Blind - Assistive/Adapted tech devices, equip & products; Children's Braille
Open Mon-Thurs 12-9, Fri & Sat 10-5
Friends of the Library Group

RICHLAND

P RICHLAND COMMUNITY LIBRARY, 111 E Main St, 17087. SAN 315-1727. Tel: 717-866-4939. FAX: 717-866-2661. Web Site: richland.lclibs.org. *Libr Dir,* Mary L Weigley; E-mail: mweigley@lclibs.org. Subject Specialists: *Environ issues, Hist,* Mary L Weigley
Founded 1886. Pop 3,958; Circ 34,467
Library Holdings: Bk Titles 15,000; Per Subs 20
Wireless access
Mem of Lebanon County Library System
Open Mon & Wed 10-5, Tues Noon-7, Thurs 10-6, Fri 10-2, Sat 9-1

RIDGWAY

P RIDGWAY FREE PUBLIC LIBRARY, 329 Center St, 15853. SAN 315-1735. Tel: 814-773-7573. FAX: 814-776-1093. Web Site: www.ridgwaylibrary.org.
Founded 1922. Pop 9,280; Circ 35,286
Automation Activity & Vendor Info: (Acquisitions) Evolve; (Cataloging) Evolve; (Circulation) Evolve; (OPAC) Evolve
Wireless access
Function: ILL available, Internet access, Laminating, Large print keyboards, Magazines, Magnifiers for reading, Music CDs, Online cat, Photocopying/Printing, Prog for children & young adult, Ref serv available, Scanner, Spoken cassettes & CDs, Summer reading prog, Tax forms, VHS videos
Open Mon-Wed 10-6, Thurs-Sat 10-5

RIDLEY PARK

RIDLEY PARK PUBLIC LIBRARY, 107 E Ward St, 19078. SAN 315-1743. Tel: 610-583-7207. FAX: 610-583-2160. E-mail: ridleypark@delcolibraries.org. Web Site: www.delcolibraries.org/ridley-park-public-library. *Dir,* Mary Alice Walsh; E-mail: rpdirector@delcolibraries.org; *Ch Serv,* Mary Ellen Keeney
Founded 1888. Pop 7,000; Circ 26,900
Library Holdings: Bk Vols 18,000; Per Subs 35
Wireless access
Mem of Delaware County Libraries
Open Mon Noon-8:30, Tues & Thurs Noon-5 & 6:30-8:30, Wed 10-8:30, Fri Noon-5, Sat 10-2
Friends of the Library Group

RIEGELSVILLE

P RIEGELSVILLE PUBLIC LIBRARY, 615 Easton Rd, 18077. (Mail add: PO Box 65, 18077-0065), SAN 320-8397. Tel: 610-749-2357. E-mail: riegelsvillelibrary@gmail.com. Web Site: www.riegelsvillelibrary.info. *Libr Dir,* Terri Randolph; E-mail: randolpht@buckslib.org; Staff 2 (MLS 1, Non-MLS 1)
Founded 1886. Pop 2,176; Circ 16,500
Library Holdings: Bk Vols 16,500; Per Subs 31
Special Collections: Riegelsville Historic Room Coll
Wireless access
Function: 24/7 Electronic res, 24/7 Online cat, Adult bk club, Archival coll, Audiobks via web, Bk club(s), Bks on CD, Children's prog, Computers for patron use, Digital talking bks, Free DVD rentals, Holiday prog, ILL available, Internet access, Magazines, Museum passes, Music CDs, Online cat, Photocopying/Printing, Preschool outreach, Prog for adults, Prog for children & young adult, Story hour, Summer reading prog, Tax forms, Wheelchair accessible
Mem of Bucks County Free Library
Open Tues & Wed 9-5, Thurs 9-6, Sat 9-3
Friends of the Library Group

RIMERSBURG

P ECCLES-LESHER MEMORIAL LIBRARY*, 673 Main St, 16248-4817. (Mail add: PO Box 359, 16248-0359), SAN 315-1751. Tel: 814-473-3800. FAX: 814-473-8200. Web Site: www2.youseemore.com/elml. *Dir,* Rachel Campbell; E-mail: director@eccles-lesher.org; *ILL,* Sherri Campbell; E-mail: sherri.campbell@eccles-lesher.org; *Circ,* Linda Bower; Staff 1 (MLS 1)
Founded 1968. Pop 6,003; Circ 29,398
Library Holdings: AV Mats 2,910; Bks on Deafness & Sign Lang 10; DVDs 269; Large Print Bks 375; Bk Titles 25,500; Bk Vols 23,200; Per Subs 52; Talking Bks 641; Videos 2,000
Special Collections: Genealogy Histories of Local Families; Local Newspapers, microfilm
Subject Interests: Fishing, Hunting, Relig studies
Automation Activity & Vendor Info: (Circulation) Follett Software; (OPAC) Follett Software
Wireless access
Publications: Biweekly Newspaper Article
Mem of Oil Creek District Library Center
Open Mon, Tues & Thurs 9-7, Fri 9-5, Sat 9-4
Friends of the Library Group

RINGTOWN

P RINGTOWN AREA LIBRARY*, 132 W Main St, 17967-9538. (Mail add: PO Box 120, 17967), SAN 320-8400. Tel: 570-889-5503. FAX: 570-889-5503. E-mail: ringtownlibrary@epix.net. Web Site: www.ringtownlibrary.org. *Librn,* Tanya Savitsky
Founded 1976. Pop 2,000; Circ 9,450
Library Holdings: Bk Vols 13,205; Per Subs 23
Wireless access
Open Mon & Thurs 11-5, Tues & Wed 12-7, Sat 9-1
Friends of the Library Group

ROARING SPRING

P ROARING SPRING COMMUNITY LIBRARY*, 320 E Main St, 16673-1009. SAN 315-176X. Tel: 814-224-2994. FAX: 814-224-4472. E-mail: info@roaringspringlibrary.org. Web Site: www.roaringspringlibrary.org. *Dir,* Michelle McIntyre; *Asst Dir, Youth Serv Coordr,* Paula Sell
Founded 1959. Pop 6,287; Circ 16,332
Library Holdings: Bk Titles 23,679; Per Subs 88
Automation Activity & Vendor Info: (Cataloging) Follett Software; (Circulation) Follett Software; (OPAC) Follett Software
Function: ILL available
Mem of Blair County Library System
Open Mon & Tues 10-7, Wed & Thurs 10-4
Friends of the Library Group

ROBESONIA

P ROBESONIA COMMUNITY LIBRARY*, 75-A S Brooke St, 19551-1500. SAN 315-1778. Tel: 610-693-3264. FAX: 610-693-6864. E-mail: robesoniacl@berks.lib.pa.us. Web Site: www.berks.lib.pa.us/sro. *Libr Dir,* Abby Brunner; E-mail: robesoniacl@berks.lib.pa.us; Staff 2 (MLS 1, Non-MLS 1)

Founded 1969. Pop 4,995; Circ 59,308
Library Holdings: Bk Titles 22,872
Automation Activity & Vendor Info: (Cataloging) Horizon; (Circulation) Horizon; (OPAC) Horizon
Wireless access
Function: Bks on CD, Children's prog, Computers for patron use, E-Readers, Free DVD rentals, ILL available, Internet access, Magazines, Museum passes, Music CDs, Online cat, Photocopying/Printing, Preschool outreach, Prog for adults, Prog for children & young adult, Summer reading prog, Tax forms
Mem of Berks County Public Libraries
Open Mon-Thurs 9:30-8, Fri & Sat 9-1
Friends of the Library Group

ROCHESTER

P ROCHESTER PUBLIC LIBRARY, 252 Adams St, 15074-2137. SAN 315-1786. Tel: 724-774-7783. FAX: 724-774-9158. Web Site: www.beaverlibraries.org/rochester.asp. *Dir,* Annamae Bolen; E-mail: abolen@beaverlibraries.org
Founded 1922. Pop 4,220; Circ 10,900
Library Holdings: Bk Titles 27,000; Per Subs 25
Wireless access
Mem of Beaver County Library System
Open Mon & Wed 10-5, Tues, Thurs & Fri 10-2

RONKS

S TRAIN COLLECTORS ASSOCIATION*, National Toy Train Library, 300 Paradise Lane, 17572. (Mail add: PO Box 248, Strasburg, 17579-0248), SAN 326-2553. Tel: 717-687-8623, Ext 108. FAX: 717-687-0742. E-mail: ref-library@traincollectors.org. Web Site: www.traincollectors.org. *Librn,* Lori Nyce; *Libr Asst,* Tyler Keck; Staff 2 (MLS 1, Non-MLS 1)
Founded 1982
Library Holdings: Bk Titles 1,500; Per Subs 75
Special Collections: Toy Manufacturers Coll, cats, instruction sheets, advertising & dealer ephemera. Oral History
Wireless access
Publications: National Headquarters News (Newsletter); Train Collectors Quarterly (Periodical)
Restriction: Open to pub for ref only

ROSEMONT

C ROSEMONT COLLEGE LIBRARY*, Gertrude Kistler Memorial Library, 1400 Montgomery Ave, 19010-1631. SAN 315-1794. Tel: 610-527-0200, Ext 2271. Reference Tel: 610-527-0200, Ext 2273. Administration Tel: 610-527-0200, Ext 2973. Web Site: www.rosemont.edu/library. *Exec Dir, Libr Serv,* Brice Peterson; E-mail: brice.peterson@rosemont.edu; *Asst Dir, Libr Serv,* Joseph Tresnan; Tel: 610-527-0200, Ext 2206, E-mail: jtresnan@rosemont.edu; *Head, Access Serv & ILL,* Kathleen Deeming; E-mail: kdeeming@rosemont.edu; *Archives Librn, Ref,* Elena Sisti; Tel: 610-527-0200, Ext 2204, E-mail: elena.sisti@rosemont.edu; Staff 7 (MLS 4, Non-MLS 3)
Founded 1926. Enrl 900; Fac 150; Highest Degree: Master
Library Holdings: AV Mats 2,066; Bks on Deafness & Sign Lang 47; CDs 63; DVDs 1,281; e-books 11,667; e-journals 17,350; Microforms 21,393; Bk Titles 104,049; Bk Vols 138,663
Special Collections: African American Coll; Children's Coll; Homer Coll; Publisher's Binding Coll; Rosemont Coll; Women's Poetry Coll
Subject Interests: Gen liberal arts
Automation Activity & Vendor Info: (Cataloging) SirsiDynix; (Circulation) SirsiDynix; (Course Reserve) SirsiDynix; (OPAC) SirsiDynix
Wireless access
Partic in Interlibrary Delivery Service of Pennsylvania; OCLC Online Computer Library Center, Inc; Southeastern Pa Consortium for Higher Educ; Tri-State College Library Cooperative
Special Services for the Deaf - Staff with knowledge of sign lang
Special Services for the Blind - Assistive/Adapted tech devices, equip & products; Computer with voice synthesizer for visually impaired persons; Dragon Naturally Speaking software; Magnifiers; ZoomText magnification & reading software
Friends of the Library Group

SAEGERTOWN

P SAEGERTOWN AREA LIBRARY*, 325 Broad St, 16433. (Mail add: PO Box 871, 16433-0871), SAN 376-642X. Tel: 814-763-5203. FAX: 814-763-4979. E-mail: sal@ccfls.org. Web Site: saegertown.ccfls.org. *Dir,* Heather J Wakefield; *YA Librn,* Paula Brown
Founded 1984
Library Holdings: DVDs 400; Bk Vols 14,200; Per Subs 30
Automation Activity & Vendor Info: (Cataloging) Follett Software; (Circulation) Follett Software; (OPAC) Follett Software
Wireless access
Mem of Crawford County Federated Library System
Partic in Share NW Consortium
Open Mon-Thurs 12-7, Fri 9-1, Sat 9-2
Friends of the Library Group

SAINT DAVIDS

C EASTERN UNIVERSITY, Warner Memorial Library, 1300 Eagle Rd, 19087-3696. SAN 315-1824. Tel: 610-341-5981. Reference Tel: 610-341-1777. E-mail: reference1777@eastern.edu. Web Site: www.eastern.edu/library. *Dir of the Univ Libr,* Joy Dlugosz; Tel: 610-341-5660, E-mail: jdlugosz@eastern.edu; *Syst Librn,* Chelsea Post; Tel: 610-225-5003, E-mail: cpost@eastern.edu; Staff 5 (MLS 3, Non-MLS 2)
Founded 1952. Enrl 2,516; Fac 110; Highest Degree: Doctorate
Jul 2021-Jun 2022. Mats Exp $375,000, Books $75,000, Per/Ser (Incl. Access Fees) $60,000, AV Mat $3,500, Electronic Ref Mat (Incl. Access Fees) $235,000, Presv $1,500
Library Holdings: Audiobooks 500; e-journals 43,000; Bk Vols 152,000; Per Subs 60; Videos 12,500
Special Collections: Goebel Asian Artifacts; Harry C Goebel Coll on Fine Printing; Mazie Hall; Thomas Edison Artifacts
Automation Activity & Vendor Info: (Acquisitions) TLC (The Library Corporation); (Cataloging) TLC (The Library Corporation); (Circulation) TLC (The Library Corporation); (Course Reserve) TLC (The Library Corporation); (Discovery) EBSCO Discovery Service; (OPAC) TLC (The Library Corporation); (Serials) TLC (The Library Corporation)
Wireless access
Function: 24/7 Online cat, Archival coll, Computers for patron use, Distance learning, Doc delivery serv, Electronic databases & coll, For res purposes, Free DVD rentals, ILL available, Internet access, Magazines, Mail loans to mem, Outside serv via phone, mail, e-mail & web, Photocopying/Printing, Ref & res, Ref serv available, Res assist avail, Res libr, Scanner, Telephone ref, Wheelchair accessible
Partic in Association of Christian Librarians; OCLC Online Computer Library Center, Inc; Partnership for Academic Library Collaborative & Innovation; Tri State Col Libr Coop
Restriction: Authorized patrons, Authorized personnel only, Authorized scholars by appt, Borrowing privileges limited to fac & registered students, Limited access for the pub, Not open to pub, Open to authorized patrons, Open to fac, students & qualified researchers
Friends of the Library Group

SAINT MARYS

P SAINT MARY'S PUBLIC LIBRARY*, 127 Center St, 15857. SAN 315-1859. Tel: 814-834-6141. FAX: 814-834-9814. E-mail: library@stmaryslibrary.org. Web Site: www.stmaryslibrary.org. *Dir,* Leslie Swope; *Ch Serv,* Vicki Miller; *Coll Develop,* Velma Gross; *ILL,* Diana Smith; Staff 7 (MLS 1, Non-MLS 6)
Founded 1921. Pop 13,070
Library Holdings: Bk Titles 38,124; Per Subs 85
Subject Interests: Elk County, St Mary's area hist
Wireless access
Open Mon & Wed 10-8, Tues & Thurs 12-8, Fri 10-5, Sat 9-4 (10-2 July-Aug)
Friends of the Library Group

SAINT THOMAS

P SAINT THOMAS LIBRARY, 30 School House Rd, 17252-9650. Tel: 717-369-4716. FAX: 717-369-4896. Web Site: fclspa.org/locations/st-thomas-library. *Br Mgr,* Deanna Leach; E-mail: dleach@fclspa.org
Founded 1977. Pop 5,775; Circ 12,699
Library Holdings: Bk Vols 9,416; Per Subs 16
Automation Activity & Vendor Info: (Cataloging) AmLib Library Management System; (Circulation) AmLib Library Management System; (OPAC) AmLib Library Management System
Wireless access
Mem of Franklin County Library System
Open Mon & Fri 2-6, Wed 9-2, Sat 9-Noon

SANDY LAKE

P LAKEVIEW AREA PUBLIC LIBRARY*, 56 E Lacock St, 16145. (Mail add: PO Box 622, 16145-0622). Tel: 724-376-4217. FAX: 724-376-2208. E-mail: books@lakeviewarealibrary.org. Web Site: lakeviewarealibrary.org. *Dir,* Wendy Kellogg; E-mail: director@lakeviewarealibrary.org
Wireless access
Open Tues 10-8, Fri 10-6, Sat 10-2

SAXONBURG

P SOUTH BUTLER COMMUNITY LIBRARY*, 240 W Main St, 16056. (Mail add: PO Box 454, 16056-0454), SAN 320-5096. Tel: 724-352-4810. FAX: 724-352-1815. Web Site: www.southbutlerlibrary.org. *Dir,* Michelle Lesniak; E-mail: director@southbutlerlibrary.org; Staff 2 (MLS 2)
Founded 1978. Pop 7,993; Circ 32,028
Library Holdings: Bk Vols 23,000; Per Subs 48; Videos 877
Special Collections: Butler County History
Subject Interests: Cooking, Craft, Gardening
Wireless access
Mem of Butler County Federated Library System
Open Mon & Wed 10-6, Tues & Thurs 10-8, Fri 10-1, Sat 9-4
Friends of the Library Group

SAXTON

P SAXTON COMMUNITY LIBRARY*, 315 Front St, 16678-8612. (Mail add: PO Box 34, 16678-0034), SAN 315-1891. Tel: 814-635-3533. FAX: 814-635-3001. E-mail: books@saxtonlibrary.com. Web Site: www.saxtonlibrary.org. *Libr Dir,* Kristy Williams
Founded 1968. Pop 4,386; Circ 10,269
Library Holdings: Audiobooks 572; DVDs 85; High Interest/Low Vocabulary Bk Vols 14; Large Print Bks 500; Bk Titles 20,715; Per Subs 32
Automation Activity & Vendor Info: (Cataloging) Evergreen; (Circulation) Evergreen
Wireless access
Function: 24/7 Online cat, Activity rm, Adult literacy prog, After school storytime, Bks on CD, Children's prog, Computers for patron use, Free DVD rentals, Holiday prog, Home delivery & serv to seniorr ctr & nursing homes, Homebound delivery serv, ILL available, Internet access, Magazines, Meeting rooms, Online cat, Prog for adults, Prog for children & young adult, STEM programs, Story hour, Summer & winter reading prog, Summer reading prog, Wheelchair accessible, Workshops
Mem of Bedford County Library System
Open Mon & Wed 10-5, Tues & Thurs 11-6, Sat 9-1

SAYRE

M WILLIAM C BECK HEALTH SCIENCE LIBRARY & RESOURCE CENTER*, One Guthrie Sq, 18840. SAN 315-1905. Tel: 570-887-4700, 570-887-4704. Reference Tel: 570-887-4701. FAX: 570-887-4703. Web Site: www.guthrie.org. *Libr Mgr,* Debbie Thompson; E-mail: thompson_debbie@guthrie.org
Founded 1922
Library Holdings: Per Subs 120
Special Collections: Mayock Coll
Subject Interests: Hist, Med, Med ethics, Nursing
Wireless access
Partic in South Central Regional Library Council
Open Mon-Fri 8-5

P SAYRE PUBLIC LIBRARY, INC*, 122 S Elmer Ave, 18840. SAN 315-1913. Tel: 570-888-2256. FAX: 570-888-3355. E-mail: sayre.library@gmail.com. Web Site: sayrepl.org. *Dir,* Holly Bradley; E-mail: director@sayrepl.org; Staff 2 (Non-MLS 2)
Founded 1936. Pop 5,813; Circ 6,483
Library Holdings: AV Mats 1,525; Large Print Bks 655; Bk Titles 25,663; Per Subs 45; Talking Bks 510
Subject Interests: Local hist
Automation Activity & Vendor Info: (Cataloging) Biblionix; (Circulation) Biblionix
Wireless access
Mem of Bradford County Library System
Open Tues & Thurs 10-7:30, Wed, Fri & Sat 10-5
Friends of the Library Group

SCHNECKSVILLE

LEHIGH CARBON COMMUNITY COLLEGE LIBRARY*, Rothrock Library, 4750 Orchard Rd, 18078. SAN 315-1921. Tel: 610-799-1150. Interlibrary Loan Service Tel: 610-799-1160. FAX: 610-779-1159. Web Site: www.lccc.edu. *Dean, Libr Serv,* Dr Richard Wilt; Tel: 610-799-1164; *Coordr, Ref (Info Servs),* Rick Paterick; E-mail: rpaterick@lccc.edu; *Acq,* Rose Boettger; E-mail: rboettger@lccc.edu; *Cat,* Jane Yagerhofer; E-mail: jyagerhofer@lccc.edu; *Circ,* Barbara Hoffman; E-mail: bhoffman@lccc.edu; *Info Serv,* Corinne Betz; E-mail: cbetz@lccc.edu; *Ser,* Darlene Coleman; E-mail: dcoleman@lccc.edu; Staff 19 (MLS 7, Non-MLS 12)
Founded 1967. Enrl 6,400; Fac 80; Highest Degree: Associate
Library Holdings: Bk Titles 42,293; Bk Vols 50,834; Per Subs 550
Special Collections: College Archives; New York Times, 1851-present, micro
Subject Interests: Allied health, Criminal justice
Automation Activity & Vendor Info: (Acquisitions) Innovative Interfaces, Inc; (Cataloging) Innovative Interfaces, Inc; (Circulation) Innovative Interfaces, Inc; (Course Reserve) Innovative Interfaces, Inc; (ILL) Innovative Interfaces, Inc; (Media Booking) Innovative Interfaces, Inc; (OPAC) Innovative Interfaces, Inc; (Serials) Innovative Interfaces, Inc
Wireless access
Publications: Library Skills Workbook (Research guide)
Partic in ARIEL; Interlibrary Delivery Service of Pennsylvania; LYRASIS
Open Mon-Thurs 7:30am-9:45pm, Fri 7:30-5, Sat (Fall-Spring) 8:30-1:30

SCHUYLKILL HAVEN

C PENNSYLVANIA STATE UNIVERSITY, SCHUYLKILL CAMPUS*, Ciletti Memorial Library, 240 University Dr, 17972-2210. SAN 315-193X. Tel: 570-385-6234. FAX: 570-385-6232. E-mail: UL-SCHUYKILL@psulist.psu.edu. Web Site: libraries.psu.edu/schuylkill. *Head Libn,* Matthew Wayman; E-mail: mjw13@psu.edu; Staff 6 (MLS 2, Non-MLS 4)
Founded 1934. Enrl 1,124; Fac 45
Library Holdings: CDs 300; DVDs 800; Bk Vols 44,000; Per Subs 170
Special Collections: County Coll (Pennsylvania German & Dutch Materials, Coal Industry); O'Hara Coll (materials by & on John O'Hara); Richter Coll (materials by & on Conrad Richter); Treasure Coll (Jones' family bks & recs)
Automation Activity & Vendor Info: (Acquisitions) SirsiDynix; (Cataloging) SirsiDynix; (Circulation) SirsiDynix; (Course Reserve) SirsiDynix; (OPAC) SirsiDynix
Wireless access
Partic in OCLC Online Computer Library Center, Inc; Research Libraries Information Network
Open Mon-Thurs 7:45am-10pm, Fri 7:45-5, Sat 9-2, Sun 1-9

P SCHUYLKILL HAVEN FREE PUBLIC LIBRARY*, 104 Saint John St, 17972. SAN 315-1948. Tel: 570-385-0542. FAX: 570-385-2523. E-mail: sch@iu29.org. Web Site: www.haven.k12.pa.us/community/schuylkill_haven_public_library. *Dir,* Lynette Moyer; Staff 2 (MLS 1, Non-MLS 1)
Founded 1934. Pop 8,200; Circ 34,356
Library Holdings: Audiobooks 400; DVDs 2,000; Large Print Bks 706; Bk Titles 30,735; Per Subs 47; Talking Bks 200; Videos 12
Automation Activity & Vendor Info: (Cataloging) Follett Software; (Circulation) Follett Software
Open Mon & Tues 11-8, Wed & Fri 10-5, Thurs 11-7, Sat 9-1 (9-4 Winter)

SCOTT TOWNSHIP

P SCOTT TOWNSHIP PUBLIC LIBRARY, 301 Lindsay Rd, 15106-4206. Tel: 412-429-5380. FAX: 412-429-5370. E-mail: scottcomments@einetwork.net. Web Site: www.scottlibrary.org. *Dir & Libn,* Gina Leone; Staff 5 (MLS 2, Non-MLS 3)
Founded 2001. Pop 46,900; Circ 87,500
Library Holdings: Bk Vols 30,000
Automation Activity & Vendor Info: (Cataloging) Innovative Interfaces, Inc; (Circulation) Innovative Interfaces, Inc; (OPAC) Innovative Interfaces, Inc
Wireless access
Mem of Allegheny County Library Association (ACLA)
Special Services for the Deaf - Adult & family literacy prog; Bks on deafness & sign lang; Closed caption videos
Open Mon-Thurs 10-8, Fri 12-5, Sat 10-5 (10-2 Summer)
Friends of the Library Group

SCOTTDALE

P SCOTTDALE PUBLIC LIBRARY, 106 Spring St, 15683-1711. SAN 315-1956. Tel: 724-887-6140. FAX: 724-887-6140. E-mail: scottdalepubliclibrary@gmail.com. Web Site: scottdalelibrary.com. *Dir,* Patricia E Miller
Founded 1910. Pop 5,833; Circ 26,294
Library Holdings: Bk Vols 30,000; Per Subs 61
Automation Activity & Vendor Info: (Cataloging) Innovative Interfaces, Inc. - Polaris; (Circulation) Innovative Interfaces, Inc. - Polaris; (OPAC) Innovative Interfaces, Inc. - Polaris
Mem of Westmoreland County Federated Library System
Open Mon & Wed 9-5, Tues & Thurs 1-6, Fri 10-2, Sat 9-3
Friends of the Library Group

SCRANTON

J JOHNSON COLLEGE LIBRARY*, 3427 N Main Ave, 18508-1995. SAN 315-1999. Tel: 570-702-8953. FAX: 570-348-2181. Web Site: www.johnson.edu/current-students/student-resources/library. *Dir,* Ronald Krysiewski; E-mail: rkrysiewski@johnson.edu; Staff 2 (MLS 1, Non-MLS 1)
Founded 1969. Enrl 349; Fac 21
Library Holdings: Bk Titles 4,410; Bk Vols 5,217; Per Subs 118

Wireless access
Open Mon-Thurs 7:30am-9pm, Fri 8-4

J LACKAWANNA COLLEGE*, Seeley Memorial Library, 406 N Washington Ave, 18503. SAN 359-5145. Tel: 570-961-7831. E-mail: library@lackawanna.edu. Web Site: lackawanna.edu/academics/library. *Libr Dir,* Mary Beth Roche; Tel: 570-504-1589, E-mail: rochem@lackawanna.edu; *Colls Librn,* Gene Berger; Tel: 570-961-1590, E-mail: bergerg@lackawanna.edu. Subject Specialists: *Media,* Gene Berger; Staff 5 (MLS 3, Non-MLS 2)
Founded 1965. Enrl 1,269; Fac 20; Highest Degree: Associate
Library Holdings: Electronic Media & Resources 12; Large Print Bks 14; Bk Titles 15,356; Bk Vols 18,674; Per Subs 46; Spec Interest Per Sub 12; Videos 683
Automation Activity & Vendor Info: (Cataloging) Follett Software; (Circulation) Follett Software; (Course Reserve) Follett Software; (OPAC) Follett Software; (Serials) Follett Software
Open Mon-Thurs (Fall & Spring) 7am-9pm, Fri 7-4, Sun 3-9; Mon-Fri (Summer) 8-4

L LACKAWANNA COUNTY LAW LIBRARY*, Courthouse, Ground Flr, 200 N Washington Ave, 18503. SAN 315-2006. Tel: 570-963-6712. FAX: 570-963-6713. *Librn,* Donna V Gower; E-mail: dgower@albright.org; Staff 1 (Non-MLS 1)
Founded 1879
Library Holdings: Electronic Media & Resources 2; Bk Titles 5,000
Subject Interests: Law
Wireless access
Open Mon-Fri 9-3
Restriction: Non-circulating to the pub

P LACKAWANNA COUNTY LIBRARY SYSTEM*, 520 Vine St, 18509-3298. SAN 324-8062. Tel: 570-348-3003. Interlibrary Loan Service Tel: 570-348-3000, Ext 3029. FAX: 570-348-3028. Web Site: www.lclshome.org. *Adminr,* Mary Garm; E-mail: garm@albright.org; Staff 98 (MLS 17, Non-MLS 81)
Founded 1983. Pop 213,385; Circ 1,320,801
Library Holdings: Bk Titles 521,107; Per Subs 690
Automation Activity & Vendor Info: (Acquisitions) Evergreen; (Cataloging) Evergreen; (Circulation) Evergreen; (OPAC) Evergreen; (Serials) Evergreen
Wireless access
Member Libraries: Abington Community Library; Carbondale Public Library; Dalton Community Library; North Pocono Public Library; Scranton Public Library; Taylor Community Library; Valley Community Library
Open Mon-Fri 9-5
Bookmobiles: 1

S LACKAWANNA HISTORICAL SOCIETY LIBRARY*, 232 Monroe Ave, 18510. SAN 315-2014. Tel: 570-344-3841. E-mail: lackawannahistory@gmail.com. Web Site: www.lackawannahistory.org. *Exec Dir,* Mary Ann Savakinus Moran; *Asst Dir,* Sarah Piccini
Founded 1886
Library Holdings: Bk Vols 3,500
Special Collections: Lackawanna County & Pennsylvania History; Scranton History, ms, photog & newsp files bd
Subject Interests: Antiques, Archit, Coal mining, Ethnic hist, Family hist, Local hist, Transportation
Publications: Lackawana Historical Society Journal (Quarterly)

C MARYWOOD UNIVERSITY LIBRARY & LEARNING COMMONS*, 2300 Adams Ave, 18509. SAN 315-2022. Tel: 570-961-4707. Interlibrary Loan Service Tel: 570-348-6205. Reference Tel: 570-961-4714. FAX: 570-961-4769. E-mail: libraryhelp@maryu.marywood.edu. Web Site: www.marywood.edu/library. *Libr Dir,* Zhong Ming Geng; E-mail: geng@maryu.marywood.edu; *Head, Continuing & E-Res,* Michelle Sitko; E-mail: sitko@maryu.marywood.edu; *Coll Develop Librn,* Jim Frutchey; E-mail: frutchey@maryu.marywood.edu; *Info Literacy Librn,* Annette Fisher; E-mail: fisher@maryu.marywood.edu; *Outreach Librn,* Amanda Avery; E-mail: aavery@maryu.marywood.edu; *Res & Instruction Librn,* Hong Miao; E-mail: hongm@maryu.marywood.edu; *User Serv Librn,* Leslie Christianson; E-mail: lchristianson@maryu.marywood.edu; Staff 8 (MLS 8)
Founded 1915. Enrl 2,926; Fac 168; Highest Degree: Doctorate
Subject Interests: Art, Behav sci, Educ, Music, Nutrition, Relig studies, Soc sci, Soc work
Automation Activity & Vendor Info: (Acquisitions) SirsiDynix; (Cataloging) SirsiDynix; (Circulation) SirsiDynix; (Course Reserve) SirsiDynix; (ILL) OCLC; (OPAC) SirsiDynix; (Serials) SirsiDynix
Wireless access
Partic in LYRASIS; OCLC Online Computer Library Center, Inc; Partnership for Academic Library Collaborative & Innovation
Open Mon-Thurs 7:30am-2am, Fri 7:30-7, Sat 8:30-7, Sun 11am-2am

P SCRANTON PUBLIC LIBRARY*, Albright Memorial Library, 500 Vine St, 18509-3298. SAN 359-5269. Tel: 570-348-3000. Circulation Tel: 570-348-3000, Ext 3002. Reference Tel: 570-348-3000, Ext 3008. Administration Tel: 570-348-3000, Ext 5000. FAX: 570-348-3020. Web Site: lclshome.org/b/albright-memorial-library. *Chief Exec Officer,* Scott Thomas; Tel: 570-348-3000, Ext 3011, E-mail: sthomas@albright.org; *Head, Circ,* Christina Thomas; Tel: 570-348-3000, Ext 3001, E-mail: cthomas@albright.org; *Head, Ref Serv,* Martina Soden; Tel: 570-348-3000, Ext 3051, E-mail: msoden@albright.org; Staff 15 (MLS 7, Non-MLS 8)
Founded 1893. Pop 213,000; Circ 415,000
Jan 2019-Dec 2019 Income (Main & Associated Libraries) $3,406,082, State $987,748, City $37,205, County $2,115,542, Other $265,587. Mats Exp $349,443, Books $162,416, Per/Ser (Incl. Access Fees) $10,010, AV Mat $37,436, Electronic Ref Mat (Incl. Access Fees) $139,581. Sal $1,875,908 (Prof $540,701)
Library Holdings: Audiobooks 8,341; Bks on Deafness & Sign Lang 39; CDs 4,289; DVDs 32,211; e-books 15,992; Electronic Media & Resources 24,576; Large Print Bks 14,905; Microforms 8,407; Bk Titles 152,604; Bk Vols 180,000; Per Subs 213; Videos 105
Special Collections: State Document Depository; US Document Depository
Subject Interests: Local hist
Automation Activity & Vendor Info: (Acquisitions) Evergreen; (Cataloging) Evergreen; (Circulation) Evergreen; (OPAC) Evergreen; (Serials) Evergreen
Wireless access
Function: 24/7 Electronic res, 24/7 Online cat, 3D Printer, Accelerated reader prog, Adult bk club, Adult literacy prog, Archival coll, Art exhibits, Art programs, Audio & video playback equip for onsite use, Audiobks on Playaways & MP3, Audiobks via web, AV serv, Bk club(s), Bk reviews (Group), Bus archives, Computer training, Computers for patron use, Digital talking bks, Doc delivery serv, Electronic databases & coll, Equip loans & repairs, Family literacy, For res purposes, Free DVD rentals, Games & aids for people with disabilities, Genealogy discussion group, Govt ref serv, Health sci info serv, Holiday prog, Home delivery & serv to seniorr ctr & nursing homes, Homebound delivery serv, Homework prog, ILL available, Instruction & testing, Internet access, Large print keyboards, Learning ctr, Life-long learning prog for all ages, Literacy & newcomer serv, Magazines, Magnifiers for reading, Mail & tel request accepted, Meeting rooms, Microfiche/film & reading machines, Movies, Museum passes, Music CDs, Online cat, Online info literacy tutorials on the web & in blackboard, Online ref, Outreach serv, OverDrive digital audio bks, Photocopying/Printing, Printer for laptops & handheld devices, Prof lending libr, Prog for adults, Prog for children & young adult, Ref & res, Ref serv available, Res assist avail, Res performed for a fee, Scanner, Senior computer classes, Senior outreach, Serves people with intellectual disabilities, Spanish lang bks, Spoken cassettes & CDs, STEM programs, Tax forms, Teen prog, Telephone ref, Visual arts prog, Wheelchair accessible, Winter reading prog, Workshops
Mem of Lackawanna County Library System
Open Mon-Thurs 10-7, Fri & Sat 10-5
Restriction: Borrowing requests are handled by ILL, Non-circulating of rare bks
Friends of the Library Group
Branches: 3
NANCY KAY HOLMES BRANCH, 1032 Green Ridge St at Wyoming Ave, 18509, SAN 359-5293. Tel: 570-207-0764. Web Site: lclshome.org/b/nancy-kay-holmes-branch-library. *Actg Br Mgr,* Diane Demko; E-mail: ddemko@albright.org; Staff 4 (MLS 2, Non-MLS 2)
Founded 1915
Library Holdings: Bk Vols 8,700; Per Subs 25
Function: 24/7 Electronic res, 24/7 Online cat, Art programs, Audiobks on Playaways & MP3, Audiobks via web, Bks on CD, Children's prog, Computers for patron use, Digital talking bks, Electronic databases & coll, Free DVD rentals, Holiday prog, ILL available, Internet access, Magazines, Movies, Museum passes, Music CDs, Online cat, Online ref, Outreach serv, OverDrive digital audio bks, Photocopying/Printing, Preschool outreach, Preschool reading prog, Printer for laptops & handheld devices, Prog for children & young adult, STEM programs, Story hour, Summer & winter reading prog, Summer reading prog, Teen prog, Winter reading prog
Open Mon-Thurs 11-6, Fri 11-5:30
LACKAWANNA COUNTY CHILDREN'S LIBRARY, 520 Vine St, 18509-3298. Tel: 570-348-3000, Ext 3015. FAX: 570-348-3020. Web Site: www.lclshome.org/b/lackawanna-county-childrens-library. *Head, Children's Servx,* Laureen O'Handley; Tel: 570-348-3000, Ext 3027, E-mail: lohandley@albright.org; Staff 3 (MLS 1, Non-MLS 2)
Founded 1985
Function: 24/7 Electronic res, 24/7 Online cat, 3D Printer, Accelerated reader prog, Activity rm, After school storytime, Art programs, Audiobk on Playaways & MP3, Audiobks via web, Bilingual assistance for Spanish patrons, Bk club(s), Bks on CD, Children's prog, Computer training, Computers for patron use, Digital talking bks, Electronic databases & coll, Family literacy, Free DVD rentals, Holiday prog,

Homework prog, ILL available, Internet access, Laminating, Learning ctr, Life-long learning prog for all ages, Literacy & newcomer serv, Magazines, Meeting rooms, Movies, Museum passes, Music CDs, Online cat, Online info literacy tutorials on the web & in blackboard, Online ref, Outreach serv, Outside serv via phone, mail, e-mail & web, OverDrive digital audio bks, Photocopying/Printing, Preschool outreach, Preschool reading prog, Printer for laptops & handheld devices, Prog for children & young adult, Spanish lang bks, STEM programs, Story hour, Summer & winter reading prog, Summer reading prog, Visual arts prog, Wheelchair accessible, Winter reading prog, Workshops, Writing prog
Open Mon-Thurs 10-7, Fri & Sat 10-5
Bookmobiles: 1

S SCRANTON TIMES-TRIBUNE*, Reference Library, 149 Penn Ave, 18503. SAN 315-2030. Tel: 570-348-9140. Toll Free Tel: 800-228-4637, Ext 9140. FAX: 570-348-9135. E-mail: Library@Timesshamrock.com. Web Site: thetimes-tribune.com. *Libr Mgr,* Brian Fulton
Founded 1920
Library Holdings: Bk Vols 3,200
Subject Interests: Anthracite mining, Coal, Govt, Local hist, Railroads
Restriction: Open by appt only

CR UNIVERSITY OF SCRANTON, Harry & Jeanette Weinberg Memorial Library, 800 Linden St, 18510-4634. SAN 315-2049. Tel: 570-941-4000. Circulation Tel: 570-941-7524. Interlibrary Loan Service Tel: 570-941-4003. FAX: 570-941-7817. Web Site: www.scranton.edu/academics/wml. *Interim Dean of Libr, Research & Scholarly Servs Coord,* George J Aulisio; Tel: 570-941-7816, E-mail: george.aulisio@scranton.edu; *Assoc Dean of Libr,* Jean Lenville; Tel: 570-941-4009, E-mail: nancy-jean.lenville@scranton.edu; *Archives & Spec Coll Librn,* Michael Knies; Tel: 570-941-6341, E-mail: michael.knies@scranton.edu; *Cataloging & Metadata Librn,* Marleen Cloutier; Tel: 570-941-7482, E-mail: marleen.cloutier@scranton.edu; *Coll & Res Librn,* Sylvia Orner; Tel: 570-941-7811, E-mail: sylvia.orner@scranton.edu; *Digital Serv Librn,* Colleen Farry; Tel: 570-941-4831, E-mail: colleen.farry@scranton.edu; *Research & Instruction Librarian for Health Sciences,* Ian O'Hara; Tel: 570-941-7802, E-mail: ian.ohara@scranton.edu; *Research & Instruction Librarian for Student Success,* Kelly Banyas; Tel: 570-941-6373, E-mail: kelly.banyas@scranton.edu; *Learning Commons Coord, Research & Instruction Librarian for Technology & Outreach,* Sheli Pratt-McHugh; Tel: 570-941-4006, E-mail: sheli.pratt-mchugh@scranton.edu; *Circ Serv Coordr,* Patricia A Savitts; Tel: 570-941-6139, E-mail: patricia.savitts@scranton.edu; *Information Literacy Coord,* Donna Witek; Tel: 570-941-7801, E-mail: donna.witek@scranton.edu; *ILL Coordr,* Kevin Kocur; Tel: 570-941-4003, E-mail: kevin.kocur@scranton.edu; *Libr Syst Coordr,* Mary Kovalcin; Tel: 570-941-6135, E-mail: mary.kovalcin@scranton.edu; *Media Res Coordr,* Sharon A Finnerty; Tel: 570-941-6330, E-mail: sharon.finnerty@scranton.edu; Staff 38 (MLS 14, Non-MLS 24)
Founded 1888. Enrl 4,326; Fac 376; Highest Degree: Doctorate
Library Holdings: AV Mats 23,688; e-books 629,484; e-journals 67,360; Electronic Media & Resources 116,159; Microforms 26,567; Bk Vols 331,245; Per Subs 2,494
Special Collections: Congressman Joseph McDade Coll; Early Printed Books & Manuscripts Medieval Manuscripts; International Correspondence School; Jesuitica; Joseph Polakoff Coll, papers; Passionist Congregation Historical Archives; University Archives Coll; Zaner-Bloser
Automation Activity & Vendor Info: (Acquisitions) Innovative Interfaces, Inc - Sierra; (Cataloging) Innovative Interfaces, Inc - Sierra; (Circulation) Innovative Interfaces, Inc - Sierra; (Course Reserve) Innovative Interfaces, Inc - Sierra; (Discovery) Innovative Interfaces, Inc; (ILL) OCLC ILLiad; (OPAC) Innovative Interfaces, Inc - Sierra; (Serials) Innovative Interfaces, Inc - Sierra
Wireless access
Function: 24/7 Online cat, Archival coll, Audio & video playback equip for onsite use, Computers for patron use, Magazines, Microfiche/film & reading machines, Online ref, Photocopying/Printing, Printer for laptops & handheld devices, Ref serv available, Res libr, Scanner, Telephone ref
Publications: A Modern Renaissance Library: 200 Selections from the Collection of Edward R Leahy; Faculty & Student Guides; Newsletters; Reference Bibliographies; Weinberg Memorial Library Information Update (Newsletter); William Morris & the Kelmscott Press Exhibition Catalog
Partic in Interlibrary Delivery Service of Pennsylvania; LYRASIS; OCLC Online Computer Library Center, Inc; Partnership for Academic Library Collaborative & Innovation; Westchester Academic Library Directors Organization
Open Mon-Thurs 8am-11:30pm, Fri 8am-10pm, Sat Noon-8, Sun Noon-11:30
Friends of the Library Group

SELINSGROVE

P SNYDER COUNTY LIBRARIES*, Rudy Gelnett Memorial Library, One North High St, 17870-1548. SAN 359-5382. Tel: 570-374-7163. FAX: 570-374-2120. Web Site: www.snydercountylibraries.org. *Exec Dir,* Pam Ross; E-mail: scldir@ptd.net; Staff 10 (MLS 1, Non-MLS 9)
Founded 1976. Pop 37,546; Circ 103,488
Library Holdings: Bk Titles 66,148; Bk Vols 75,000; Per Subs 172
Automation Activity & Vendor Info: (Acquisitions) EOS International; (Cataloging) EOS International; (Circulation) EOS International; (OPAC) EOS International
Wireless access
Open Mon-Thurs 10-8, Fri & Sat 10-5
Friends of the Library Group
Branches: 3
BEAVERTOWN COMMUNITY LIBRARY, 111 W Walnut St, Beavertown, 17813, SAN 359-5412. Tel: 570-658-3437. FAX: 570-658-3437. E-mail: beavertownlibrary@pdt.net. *Br Mgr,* Sherri Sellers; Staff 2 (Non-MLS 2)
Founded 1977
Library Holdings: Bk Vols 4,384; Per Subs 19
Open Mon & Tues 2-7, Thurs 12-5, Fri 2-5, Sat 10-Noon
Friends of the Library Group
MCCLURE COMMUNITY LIBRARY, Four Library Lane, McClure, 17841. (Mail add: PO Box 370, McClure, 17841-0370), SAN 359-5447. Tel: 570-658-7700. FAX: 570-658-7700. E-mail: mcclurelibrary@nmax.net. *Br Mgr,* Joe Hall; Staff 1 (Non-MLS 1)
Founded 1977
Library Holdings: Bk Vols 4,562; Per Subs 28
Open Mon & Thurs 2-7, Tues 12-5, Fri 2-5, Sat 10-12
Friends of the Library Group
MIDDLEBURG COMMUNITY LIBRARY, 13 N Main St, Middleburg, 17842. (Mail add: PO Box 43, Middleburg, 17842-0043), SAN 359-5471. Tel: 570-837-5931. FAX: 570-837-5931. E-mail: midduser@ptd.net. *Br Mgr,* Shirley Carroll; *Librn,* Chris Snyder; Staff 2 (Non-MLS 2)
Founded 1982
Library Holdings: Bk Titles 6,607; Per Subs 34
Open Mon-Thurs 2-7, Fri 1-5, Sat 10-1
Friends of the Library Group

C SUSQUEHANNA UNIVERSITY*, Blough-Weis Library, 514 University Ave, 17870-1050. SAN 315-2065. Tel: 570-372-4319. Circulation Tel: 570-372-4022. Interlibrary Loan Service Tel: 570-372-4016. Reference Tel: 570-372-4160. FAX: 570-372-4310. Web Site: www.susqu.edu/library. *Univ Librn/Libr Dir,* Katherine Furlong; Tel: 570-372-4320; *Digital Librn, Instrul Serv,* Rob Sieczkiewicz; Tel: 570-372-4329, E-mail: sieczkiewicz@susqu.edu; *Info Literacy Librn,* Kathleen Dalton; Tel: 570-372-4301, E-mail: dalton@susqu.edu; *Coll Develop, Outreach Librn,* Ryan Ake; Tel: 570-372-4324, E-mail: ake@susqu.edu; *Spec Coll Librn,* Meg Garnett; Tel: 570-372-4327, E-mail: garnett@susqu.edu; *Syst Librn,* Robert Gessner; Tel: 570-372-4322, E-mail: gessnerr@susqu.edu; *Pub Serv,* Cindy Whitmoyer; Tel: 570-372-4459; Staff 8 (MLS 6, Non-MLS 2)
Founded 1858. Enrl 2,100; Fac 180; Highest Degree: Bachelor
Library Holdings: Bk Titles 202,682; Bk Vols 367,146; Per Subs 50,390
Special Collections: Jane Apple Shakespeare Coll; Music (Wilt Coll); Pennsylvania Coll
Subject Interests: Bus, Environ studies, Music
Automation Activity & Vendor Info: (Acquisitions) SirsiDynix; (Cataloging) SirsiDynix; (Circulation) SirsiDynix; (Course Reserve) SirsiDynix; (ILL) OCLC; (Media Booking) SirsiDynix; (OPAC) SirsiDynix; (Serials) SirsiDynix
Wireless access
Function: Res libr
Partic in Associated College Libraries of Central Pennsylvania; Partnership for Academic Library Collaborative & Innovation
Open Mon-Thurs 8am-1am, Fri 8-8, Sat 10-8, Sun 11am-1am

SEWICKLEY

P SEWICKLEY PUBLIC LIBRARY*, 500 Thorn St, 15143. SAN 315-2081. Tel: 412-741-6920. FAX: 412-741-6099. E-mail: sewickley@einetwork.net. Web Site: sewickleylibrary.org. *Exec Dir,* Carolyn Toth; E-mail: tothc@einetwork.net; *Head, Adult Serv,* Lynne Schneider; E-mail: schneiderl@einetwork.net
Founded 1873. Pop 14,089; Circ 183,443
Library Holdings: Bk Vols 89,400; Per Subs 220
Subject Interests: Western Penn hist
Automation Activity & Vendor Info: (Cataloging) Innovative Interfaces, Inc; (Circulation) Innovative Interfaces, Inc; (OPAC) Innovative Interfaces, Inc
Wireless access
Publications: Newsletter
Mem of Allegheny County Library Association (ACLA)
Partic in Electronic Info Network

Open Mon-Thurs 9-9, Fri 9-6, Sat 9-5, Sun 1-5
Friends of the Library Group

SHAMOKIN

P SHAMOKIN & COAL TOWNSHIP PUBLIC LIBRARY, INC*, 210 E Independence St, 17872-6888. SAN 315-209X. Tel: 570-648-3202. FAX: 570-648-4255. E-mail: shamokinlibrary@gmail.com. Web Site: sctplibrary.com. *Libr Dir,* Victoria Ryan; Staff 5 (MLS 1, Non-MLS 4)
Founded 1941. Pop 20,092; Circ 54,153
Special Collections: History of Pennsylvania, Northcumberland County & Shamokin (Pennsylvania Coll)
Automation Activity & Vendor Info: (Cataloging) Evergreen; (Circulation) Evergreen; (OPAC) Evergreen
Wireless access
Open Mon & Thurs 9:30-6, Tues, Wed & Fri 9:30-5, Sat 10-2

SHARON

P COMMUNITY LIBRARY OF SHENANGO VALLEY*, 11 N Sharpsville Ave, 16146. SAN 315-2103. Tel: 724-981-4360. FAX: 724-981-5208. E-mail: clshenangovalley@gmail.com. Web Site: www.clsv.net. *Dir,* Mrs Robin Pundzak; E-mail: rpundzak@clsv.net; *Teen Serv Coordr,* Kira Conner; *Adult Serv,* Charissa Senteney; *Ch Serv,* Stephanie Messina; Staff 11 (MLS 3, Non-MLS 8)
Founded 1923. Pop 32,813; Circ 80,000
Library Holdings: Bk Vols 60,000; Per Subs 125
Special Collections: Ekker Sports Coll. State Document Depository
Subject Interests: Genealogy, Local hist
Automation Activity & Vendor Info: (Acquisitions) Evolve; (Cataloging) Evolve; (Circulation) Evolve; (OPAC) Evolve
Wireless access
Publications: The Bookmark (Quarterly); The Bookmark (Newsletter)
Open Mon-Thurs 10-8, Fri & Sat 10-5
Friends of the Library Group

C PENN STATE SHENANGO*, Lartz Memorial Library, 177 Vine Ave, 16146. SAN 315-2111. Tel: 724-983-2876. FAX: 724-983-2820. Web Site: www.libraries.psu.edu/shenango. *Head Librn,* Amy Deuink; E-mail: ald120@psu.edu; Staff 4 (MLS 2, Non-MLS 2)
Founded 1965. Enrl 600; Fac 28; Highest Degree: Bachelor
Library Holdings: CDs 50; DVDs 300; Bk Vols 35,000; Per Subs 35
Automation Activity & Vendor Info: (Acquisitions) SirsiDynix; (Cataloging) SirsiDynix; (Circulation) SirsiDynix; (Course Reserve) SirsiDynix; (ILL) Atlas Systems; (OPAC) SirsiDynix; (Serials) SirsiDynix
Wireless access
Function: 24/7 Electronic res, Bi-weekly Writer's Group, E-Reserves, Electronic databases & coll, Internet access, Learning ctr, Magazines, Music CDs, Online cat, Online ref, Photocopying/Printing, Study rm, Wheelchair accessible
Partic in Health Sciences Libraries Consortium; OCLC Online Computer Library Center, Inc; Research Libraries Information Network
Open Mon-Thurs (Fall & Spring) 8-8, Fri 8-5; Mon-Thurs (Summer) 8-5, Fri 8-4

SHARON HILL

P SHARON HILL PUBLIC LIBRARY*, 246 Sharon Ave, 19079. SAN 315-2138. Tel: 610-586-3993. FAX: 610-586-8233. Web Site: www.sharonhillpubliclibrary.org. *Dir,* Betty Wilson; E-mail: SHDirector@Delcolibraries.org
Founded 1938. Pop 7,464; Circ 14,426
Library Holdings: AV Mats 112; Bk Vols 16,594; Per Subs 20; Talking Bks 200
Wireless access
Mem of Delaware County Libraries
Open Mon, Wed & Thurs 1-7, Tues 10-7, Fri 10-5, Sat 10-5 (10-2 July-Aug)
Friends of the Library Group

SHEFFIELD

P SHEFFIELD TOWNSHIP LIBRARY*, 20 Leather St, 16347. (Mail add: PO Box 607, 16347). SAN 315-2146. Tel: 814-968-3439. FAX: 814-968-5761. E-mail: librarian@sheffieldlibrary.org. Web Site: sheffieldlibrary.org. *Dir,* Alexis Lee McAvoy; E-mail: librarian@sheffieldlibrary.org
Founded 1922. Pop 2,793; Circ 4,127
Library Holdings: Bk Vols 11,000; Per Subs 33
Wireless access
Function: 24/7 Online cat, Bks on CD, Children's prog, Computers for patron use, Electronic databases & coll, Free DVD rentals, ILL available, Internet access, Online cat, Online ref, OverDrive digital audio bks, Photocopying/Printing, Summer reading prog, Tax forms
Open Tues-Thurs 10-7, Sat 9-3
Restriction: Lending limited to county residents

SHENANDOAH

P SHENANDOAH AREA FREE PUBLIC LIBRARY, 15 W Washington St, 17976-1708. SAN 315-2154. Tel: 570-462-9829. E-mail: shenfpl@ptd.net. Web Site: www.iu29.org/shenandoahpl. *Libr Dir,* Dalton Babcock; Staff 1 (Non-MLS 1)
Founded 1975. Pop 5,624; Circ 15,416
Library Holdings: DVDs 248; Large Print Bks 166; Bk Vols 11,519; Per Subs 23; Videos 453
Automation Activity & Vendor Info: (Acquisitions) PALS; (Cataloging) PALS; (Circulation) PALS
Wireless access
Special Services for the Deaf - Adult & family literacy prog
Open Mon & Fri 11-5, Tues & Thurs 11-2 & 4-7, Wed 11-7, Sat 9-2

SHILLINGTON

P MIFFLIN COMMUNITY LIBRARY*, Six Philadelphia Ave, 19607. Tel: 610-777-3911. FAX: 610-777-5516. E-mail: mifflincl@berks.lib.pa.us. Web Site: www.berks.lib.pa.us/mifflincl. *Libr Dir,* Patricia Reichl; Staff 10 (MLS 2, Non-MLS 8)
Founded 1998
Library Holdings: Audiobooks 974; CDs 1,160; DVDs 3,165; Large Print Bks 1,180; Bk Vols 28,022; Per Subs 60
Automation Activity & Vendor Info: (Acquisitions) Innovative Interfaces, Inc; (Cataloging) Innovative Interfaces, Inc; (Circulation) Innovative Interfaces, Inc; (OPAC) Innovative Interfaces, Inc; (Serials) Innovative Interfaces, Inc
Wireless access
Function: 24/7 Online cat, Activity rm, Adult bk club, After school storytime
Mem of Berks County Public Libraries
Open Mon, Tues & Thurs 9-8, Wed 9-5, Fri 9-1, Sat 9-4 (9-1 Summer)
Friends of the Library Group

SHINGLEHOUSE

P OSWAYO VALLEY MEMORIAL LIBRARY*, 103 N Pleasant St, 16748. (Mail add: PO Box 188, 16748-0188), SAN 315-2162. Tel: 814-697-6691. FAX: 814-697-6691. E-mail: ovmlibrary@gmail.com. Web Site: oswayovml.edublogs.org. *Dir,* Rhonda Duell
Founded 1915. Pop 3,568; Circ 29,411
Library Holdings: Bk Vols 18,000; Per Subs 35
Wireless access
Mem of Potter-Tioga Library System
Open Tues 12-7, Wed & Thurs 10-5, Fri & Sat 8-3

SHIPPENSBURG

P SHIPPENSBURG PUBLIC LIBRARY*, 73 W King St, 17257-1299. SAN 315-2170. Tel: 717-532-4508. FAX: 717-532-2454. E-mail: shippensburg@cumberlandcountylibraries.org. Web Site: www.shippensburglibrary.org. *Dir,* Jody Cole; Staff 15 (MLS 2, Non-MLS 13)
Founded 1933. Pop 30,881; Circ 225,446
Library Holdings: Bk Vols 62,901; Per Subs 107
Automation Activity & Vendor Info: (Cataloging) Innovative Interfaces, Inc; (Circulation) Innovative Interfaces, Inc
Wireless access
Mem of Cumberland County Library System
Open Mon-Thurs 9-8, Fri 9-5, Sat 9-5 (9-1 Summer)
Friends of the Library Group

C SHIPPENSBURG UNIVERSITY*, Ezra Lehman Memorial Library, 1871 Old Main Dr, 17257. SAN 359-5560. Tel: 717-477-1461. Circulation Tel: 717-477-1465. Reference Tel: 717-477-1474. FAX: 717-477-1389. E-mail: librarian@ship.edu. Web Site: library.ship.edu. *Dean, Libr & Media Serv,* Dr Michelle Foreman; Tel: 717-477-1475, E-mail: mtforeman@ship.edu; *Instruction & Assessment Librn,* Josefine Smith; Tel: 717-477-1634, E-mail: jmsmith@ship.edu; *Pub Serv Librn, Research Coordr,* Kirk Moll; Tel: 717-477-1473, E-mail: kamoll@ship.edu; *Scholarly Communications, E-Res & Web Librn,* Aaron Dobbs; Tel: 717-477-1018, E-mail: awdobbs@ship.edu; *Spec Coll & Archives Librn,* Christy Fic; Tel: 717-477-1516, E-mail: cmfic@ship.edu; *Mgr, Libr Serv,* Sara Pike; Tel: 717-477-1027, E-mail: slpike@ship.edu; *Libr Tech,* Melanie Reed; Tel: 717-477-1325, E-mail: mareed@ship.edu; *Libr Tech,* Karen Thomas; Tel: 717-477-1469, E-mail: kjthom@ship.edu; *Libr Asst II,* Susan Hockenberry; E-mail: sehockenberry@ship.edu; *Pub Serv Asst,* Denise Weitry; Tel: 717-477-1289, E-mail: dweitry@ship.edu; Staff 22 (MLS 9, Non-MLS 13)
Founded 1871. Enrl 7,500; Fac 360; Highest Degree: Master
Library Holdings: Bk Vols 449,125; Per Subs 1,243
Special Collections: University Archives. US Document Depository
Subject Interests: Criminal justice, Curric, Educ, Media
Automation Activity & Vendor Info: (Acquisitions) Ex Libris Group; (Cataloging) Ex Libris Group; (Circulation) Ex Libris Group; (Course

Reserve) Ex Libris Group; (Media Booking) Ex Libris Group; (OPAC) Ex Libris Group; (Serials) Ex Libris Group
Wireless access
Partic in Associated College Libraries of Central Pennsylvania; Keystone Library Network; LYRASIS; OCLC Online Computer Library Center, Inc; Pa Syst of Higher Educ Libr Coun; Partnership for Academic Library Collaborative & Innovation

SHREWSBURY

P PAUL SMITH LIBRARY OF SOUTHERN YORK COUNTY*, 80 Constitution Ave, 17361-1710. Tel: 717-235-4313. E-mail: sycstaff@yorklibraries.org. Web Site: www.yorklibraries.org/shrewsbury-paul-smith. *Dir,* Michele Lefler; E-mail: mlefler@yorklibraries.org
Founded 2003
Library Holdings: Bk Vols 48,000; Per Subs 54
Automation Activity & Vendor Info: (Acquisitions) Innovative Interfaces, Inc; (Cataloging) Innovative Interfaces, Inc; (Circulation) Innovative Interfaces, Inc; (OPAC) Innovative Interfaces, Inc
Wireless access
Function: 24/7 Electronic res, 24/7 Online cat, Activity rm, Adult bk club, Adult literacy prog, Archival coll, Audiobks on Playaways & MP3, Audiobks via web, Bk club(s), Bks on CD, Children's prog, Computer training, Computers for patron use, Digital talking bks, Electronic databases & coll, Health sci info serv, Holiday prog, ILL available, Instruction & testing, Internet access, Life-long learning prog for all ages, Magazines, Meeting rooms, Movies, Music CDs, Online cat, OverDrive digital audio bks, Photocopying/Printing, Prog for adults, Prog for children & young adult, Ref & res, Ref serv available, Scanner, Serves people with intellectual disabilities, Spanish lang bks, Story hour, Study rm, Summer reading prog, Tax forms, Teen prog, Telephone ref, Wheelchair accessible, Workshops, Writing prog
Mem of York County Library System
Open Mon-Wed 10-8, Thurs-Sat 10-5 (10-2 Summer)
Friends of the Library Group

SINKING SPRING

P SINKING SPRING PUBLIC LIBRARY*, 3940 Penn Ave, 19608. SAN 315-2189. Tel: 610-678-4311. FAX: 610-670-4826. E-mail: sspl@berks.lib.pa.us. Web Site: www.berks.lib.pa.us/sss. *Dir,* John Nelka; *Children & Teen Librn,* Christine Weida
Founded 1965. Pop 8,467; Circ 27,070
Library Holdings: Bk Titles 10,000; Per Subs 40
Wireless access
Mem of Berks County Public Libraries
Open Mon-Thurs 10-8, Fri 10-3, Sat (Summer) 10-3
Friends of the Library Group

SLATINGTON

P SLATINGTON PUBLIC LIBRARY, 650 Main St, 18080. SAN 315-2197. Tel: 610-767-6461. FAX: 610-767-2732. E-mail: slatlib@ptd.net. Web Site: sites.google.com/view/slatingtonlibrary. *Libr Dir,* Rosanne Pugh
Founded 1962. Pop 13,395; Circ 20,310
Library Holdings: Bk Vols 24,027
Partic in Lehigh Carbon Library Cooperative
Open Mon, Wed & Fri 9-5, Tues 9-3, Sat 8-Noon

S WILDLIFE INFORMATION CENTER*, Donald S Heintzelman Wildlife Library, 8844 Paint Mill Rd, 18080. (Mail add: PO Box 198, 18080-0198), SAN 375-1864. Tel: 610-760-8889. FAX: 610-760-8889. E-mail: mail@lgnc.org. Web Site: www.lgnc.org. *Exec Dir,* Dan R Kunkle
Founded 1986
Library Holdings: Bk Titles 5,000; Per Subs 125
Subject Interests: Conserv, Ecology, Ornithology, Wildlife
Restriction: Open by appt only

SLIPPERY ROCK

P SLIPPERY ROCK COMMUNITY LIBRARY, 465 N Main St, 16057. (Mail add: PO Box 25, 16057-0025). Tel: 724-738-9179. E-mail: srcl@bcfls.org. Web Site: www.slipperyrocklibrary.org. *Dir & Librn,* Karen Pierce
Founded 2005
Library Holdings: Audiobooks 50; Bk Titles 5,000; Per Subs 10
Automation Activity & Vendor Info: (Cataloging) TLC (The Library Corporation); (Circulation) TLC (The Library Corporation)
Wireless access
Function: 24/7 Electronic res, 24/7 Online cat, Activity rm, Adult bk club, After school storytime
Mem of Butler County Federated Library System
Open Mon-Thurs 10-6:30, Sat 10-2:30 (Summer); Mon & Thurs 10-6:30, Tues & Wed 10-5, Sat 10-2
Friends of the Library Group

C SLIPPERY ROCK UNIVERSITY OF PENNSYLVANIA, Bailey Library, 109 Campus Loop, 16057. SAN 315-2219. Tel: 724-738-2058. Circulation Tel: 724-738-2637. Interlibrary Loan Service Tel: 724-738-2580. Information Services Tel: 724-738-2641. FAX: 724-738-2661. Web Site: www.sru.edu/academics/bailey-library. *Chair, Libr Serv,* Jessica Jordan; Tel: 724-738-2663, E-mail: jessica.jordan@sru.edu; *Acq Librn,* Heather Getsay; Tel: 724-738-2665, E-mail: heather.getsay@sru.edu; *Health Sci Librn,* Alessia Zanin-Yost; E-mail: alessia.zanin-yost@sru.edu; *Librn,* Allison Brungard; E-mail: allison.brungard@sru.edu; *Archivist, Performing Arts Librn,* Judy Silva; E-mail: judith.silva@sru.edu; *Tech Serv Librn,* Aiping Chen-Gaffey; Tel: 724-738-2660, E-mail: aiping.chen-gaffey@sru.edu; *User Experience Librn,* Rocco Cremonese; E-mail: rocco.cremonese@sru.edu; *Evening Supvr,* Karen Mason; *Outreach Coordr, Syst,* Deepam Mistery; *Archives,* Jared Negley; *Circ,* Kathy Manning; *ILL,* Ellen Pontius. Subject Specialists: *Educ,* Jessica Jordan; *Nursing, Occupational therapy, Phys therapy, Psychol,* Alessia Zanin-Yost; *STEM,* Allison Brungard; *Art, Dance, Theatre,* Judy Silva; *Modern lang, Music,* Aiping Chen-Gaffey; *Bus,* Rocco Cremonese; Staff 17 (MLS 7, Non-MLS 10)
Founded 1889. Enrl 8,700; Fac 400; Highest Degree: Doctorate
Library Holdings: Bk Vols 400,000; Per Subs 820
Special Collections: Italy, bks, flm, micro; Japan, bks, flm, micro; Physical Education, Recreation & Sports, bks, flm, micro. Oral History; State Document Depository; US Document Depository
Automation Activity & Vendor Info: (Acquisitions) Ex Libris Group; (Cataloging) Ex Libris Group; (Circulation) Ex Libris Group; (Course Reserve) Docutek; (ILL) OCLC; (Media Booking) Ex Libris Group; (OPAC) Ex Libris Group; (Serials) Ex Libris Group
Wireless access
Publications: Japanese Collection; Japanese Collection Supplement
Partic in Interlibrary Delivery Service of Pennsylvania; Keystone Library Network; OCLC Online Computer Library Center, Inc; Partnership for Academic Library Collaborative & Innovation
Open Mon-Thurs 7:30am-10pm, Fri 7:30-5, Sun Noon-10
Friends of the Library Group

SMETHPORT

P HAMLIN MEMORIAL LIBRARY*, 123 S Mechanic St, 16749. (Mail add: PO Box 422, 16749-0422), SAN 315-2235. Tel: 814-887-9262. FAX: 814-887-9234. E-mail: library@hamlinlibrary.org. Web Site: www.hamlinlibrary.org. *Dir,* Lorine Rounsville; Staff 1 (Non-MLS 1)
Founded 1967. Pop 5,933; Circ 22,605
Library Holdings: AV Mats 1,143; Large Print Bks 970; Bk Vols 25,429; Per Subs 42; Talking Bks 1,116
Subject Interests: Automotive hist, Civil War
Open Mon & Tues 12-5 & 7-9, Wed 10-5, Thurs 7pm-9pm, Fri 12-5, Sat 9-1
Friends of the Library Group

SMITHFIELD

P SMITHFIELD PUBLIC LIBRARY, 14 Water St, 15478. (Mail add: PO Box 497, 15478-0497). Tel: 724-569-1777. E-mail: smithfieldpubliclibrary@atlanticbbn.net. *Librn,* Jean Kennedy
Library Holdings: Bk Vols 10,000
Wireless access
Open Tues & Thurs 12-5

SMITHTON

P SMITHTON PUBLIC LIBRARY*, Center & Second St, 15479. (Mail add: PO Box 382, 15479-0382), SAN 315-2243. Tel: 724-872-0701. FAX: 724-872-0701. E-mail: smithtonpubliclibrary@yahoo.com. *Libr Dir,* Ken Ofslager
Founded 1959. Pop 552; Circ 6,884
Library Holdings: Bk Vols 6,000; Per Subs 15
Mem of Westmoreland County Federated Library System
Special Services for the Blind - Bks on cassette; Bks on CD
Open Mon & Thurs 4:30-8, Sat 10-1

SOMERSET

P MARY S BIESECKER PUBLIC LIBRARY*, 230 S Rosina Ave, 15501. SAN 315-2251. Tel: 814-445-4011. FAX: 814-443-0725. E-mail: info@maryslibrary.com. Web Site: www.maryslibrary.com. *Dir,* Lee Ann Schrock; Staff 5 (Non-MLS 5)
Founded 1914. Pop 6,762; Circ 31,117
Library Holdings: Bk Titles 29,641; Bk Vols 34,250
Special Collections: Civil War; Geneaology; Local & Pennsylvania History; Somerset County Newspapers, microfilms
Automation Activity & Vendor Info: (Cataloging) Follett Software; (Circulation) Follett Software
Wireless access

Function: 24/7 Online cat, Adult bk club, Bk club(s), Bks on CD, Children's prog, Computer training, Computers for patron use, ILL available, Internet access, Magazines, Magnifiers for reading, Microfiche/film & reading machines, Movies, Music CDs, Online cat, OverDrive digital audio bks, Photocopying/Printing, Preschool reading prog, Printer for laptops & handheld devices, Prog for adults, Prog for children & young adult, Ref serv available, Spoken cassettes & CDs, Spoken cassettes & DVDs, Summer reading prog, VHS videos, Wheelchair accessible
Mem of Cambria County Library System & District Center
Partic in Pennsylvania Library Association
Open Mon-Fri 10-6, Sat 9-4

P SOMERSET COUNTY FEDERATED LIBRARY SYSTEM*, 6022 Glades Pike, Ste 120, 15501-0043. Tel: 814-445-5907. Administration Tel: 814-445-2556. FAX: 814-443-0650. E-mail: somerset@somersetcountypalibraries.org. Web Site: www.scfls.org. *Adminr,* Cheryl A Morgan; E-mail: cmorgan@somersetcountypalibraries.org; Staff 2 (MLS 2)
Library Holdings: Bk Vols 143,757; Per Subs 297
Automation Activity & Vendor Info: (Cataloging) Evergreen; (Circulation) Evergreen; (OPAC) Evergreen
Wireless access
Function: Audiobks via web, Bks on cassette, Bks on CD, Computer training, Computers for patron use, Electronic databases & coll, Free DVD rentals, Games & aids for people with disabilities, Home delivery & serv to seniorr ctr & nursing homes, Homebound delivery serv, ILL available, Internet access, Mail & tel request accepted, Online ref, OverDrive digital audio bks, Photocopying/Printing, Preschool outreach, Ref serv available, Serves people with intellectual disabilities, Story hour, Summer reading prog, Tax forms, Telephone ref, VHS videos, Wheelchair accessible
Member Libraries: Meyersdale Public Library; Somerset County Library; Windber Public Library
Special Services for the Blind - Bks on CD; Cassettes; Large print & cassettes; Large print bks; Large screen computer & software
Bookmobiles: 1. Bk vols 7,427

GL SOMERSET COUNTY LAW LIBRARY*, Court House, 111 E Union St, Ste 50, 15501. SAN 315-2278. Tel: 814-445-1510. FAX: 814-445-1455. Web Site: www.co.somerset.pa.us/department.asp?deptnum=99. *Library Contact,* Kyle Watson
Library Holdings: Bk Vols 21,785; Per Subs 75
Open Mon-Fri 8:30-4

P SOMERSET COUNTY LIBRARY*, 6022 Glades Pike, Ste 120, 15501-4300. SAN 315-2286. Tel: 814-445-5907. Administration Tel: 814-445-2556. FAX: 814-443-0650. E-mail: somerset@somersetcountypalibraries.org. Web Site: somersetcolibrary.org. *Dir,* Cheryl Morgan; E-mail: cmorgan@somersetcountypalibraries.org; Staff 7 (MLS 2, Non-MLS 5)
Founded 1947. Pop 39,320; Circ 116,435
Library Holdings: Bk Titles 60,339; Bk Vols 100,361; Per Subs 176; Talking Bks 2,309; Videos 3,670
Automation Activity & Vendor Info: (Cataloging) Evergreen; (Circulation) Evergreen; (OPAC) Evergreen
Wireless access
Function: 24/7 Electronic res, Audiobks via web, Bk club(s), Bks on cassette, Bks on CD, Children's prog, Computers for patron use, Electronic databases & coll, Free DVD rentals, Games & aids for people with disabilities, Home delivery & serv to seniorr ctr & nursing homes, ILL available, Internet access, Large print keyboards, Magazines, Magnifiers for reading, Mail & tel request accepted, Online cat, Online ref, Outreach serv, OverDrive digital audio bks, Photocopying/Printing, Preschool outreach, Preschool reading prog, Ref serv available, Scanner, Senior outreach, Serves people with intellectual disabilities, Story hour, Summer reading prog, Tax forms, Telephone ref, VHS videos, Wheelchair accessible
Mem of Somerset County Federated Library System
Special Services for the Blind - Low vision equip
Open Mon-Thurs 8-8, Fri 8-5, Sat 8-4
Friends of the Library Group
Bookmobiles: 1. In Charge, Christine Bowser

STATE CORRECTIONAL INSTITUTION
S LAUREL HIGHLANDS LIBRARY*, 5706 Glades Pike, 15501. (Mail add: PO Box 631, 15501-0631). Tel: 814-445-6501. FAX: 814-443-0208. *Corrections Librn,* Sandra Pletcher; *Libr Asst II,* Margaret Foreback; Staff 2 (MLS 1, Non-MLS 1)
Library Holdings: Audiobooks 906; Bk Vols 13,900; Per Subs 57; Videos 261
Automation Activity & Vendor Info: (Acquisitions) Follett Software; (Cataloging) Follett Software; (Circulation) Follett Software; (ILL) Follett Software; (OPAC) Follett Software
Open Mon 1-9, Tues-Thurs 7am-9pm, Fri-Sun 7-3

S SOMERSET LIBRARY*, 1590 Walters Mill Rd, 15510-0001. Tel: 814-443-8100. FAX: 814-443-8157. *Librn,* Marcia Roman
Library Holdings: Bk Vols 15,000; Per Subs 70
Automation Activity & Vendor Info: (Cataloging) Follett Software; (Circulation) Follett Software; (OPAC) Follett Software
Open Mon-Fri 8:30-8, Sat & Sun 8:30-3:30

SOUDERTON

P ZION MENNONITE CHURCH & PUBLIC LIBRARY*, 149 Cherry Lane, 18964. SAN 320-7285. Tel: 215-723-3592. FAX: 215-723-0573. E-mail: contact@zionmennonite.org. Web Site: www.zionmennonite.org. *Head Librn,* Laura Martin
Founded 1945
Library Holdings: Bk Vols 5,500; Per Subs 15
Subject Interests: Bibles, Mennonite hist
Publications: Christianity Today; Mennonite Weekly Review
Open Mon-Fri 9-4

SOUTH CANAAN

R SAINT TIKHON'S ORTHODOX THEOLOGICAL SEMINARY*, Patriarch Saint Tikhon Library, St Tikhon's Rd, 18459. (Mail add: PO Box 130, 18459-0130), SAN 315-2316. Tel: 570-561-1818, Ext 111. E-mail: library@stots.edu. Web Site: www.stots.edu/library.htm. *Head Librn,* Sergei Arhipov; Tel: 570-561-1818, Ext 5, E-mail: sergei.arhipov@stots.edu; *Asst Librn,* Michael Juk; Tel: 570-561-1818, Ext 8; Staff 4 (MLS 2, Non-MLS 2)
Founded 1938. Highest Degree: Master
Library Holdings: Bk Vols 36,000; Per Subs 230
Special Collections: Russian & Church Slavic Theological & Literature Coll
Subject Interests: Orthodox Eastern Church, Orthodox theol
Automation Activity & Vendor Info: (Serials) Gateway
Partic in Southeastern Pennsylvania Theological Library Association
Open Mon 8:30-12:15 & 8pm-9pm, Tues-Thurs 1:30-4 & 7:30-9, Fri 8:30-12:15, 1-3:30 & 7:30-9, Sat 1:30-3, Sun 8pm-9pm

SOUTH FORK

P SOUTH FORK PUBLIC LIBRARY*, 320 Main St, 15956-9998. SAN 315-2324. Tel: 814-495-4812. FAX: 814-495-7369. E-mail: southforklibrary@comcast.net. *Dir,* Joy Bailey
Pop 928; Circ 6,324
Library Holdings: Bk Vols 11,000; Per Subs 12
Wireless access
Mem of Cambria County Library System & District Center
Open Mon-Fri (Summer) 10-4, Sat 9-1; Mon-Fri (Winter) 11-5, Sat 9-4
Friends of the Library Group

SOUTH PARK

P SOUTH PARK TOWNSHIP LIBRARY*, 2575 Brownsville Rd, 15129-8527. SAN 314-7053. Tel: 412-833-5585. FAX: 412-833-7368. E-mail: southpark@einetwork.net. Web Site: www.southparklibrary.org. *Dir,* Amanda DeKnight; *Ch,* Tami Pauline; E-mail: paulinet@einetwork.net; *Tech Serv Librn,* Jeff Connelly; *Adult Serv Coordr,* Donna Neiport; Staff 3 (MLS 3)
Founded 1970. Pop 14,251; Circ 60,000
Library Holdings: Bk Titles 36,000; Bk Vols 50,000; Per Subs 70
Wireless access
Mem of Allegheny County Library Association (ACLA)
Partic in Electronic Info Network
Open Mon & Thurs 1-9, Tues & Wed 10-9, Sat 10-5
Friends of the Library Group

SOUTHAMPTON

P SOUTHAMPTON FREE LIBRARY*, 947 Street Rd, 18966. SAN 315-2332. Tel: 215-322-1415. FAX: 215-396-9375. E-mail: info@southamptonfreelibrary.org. Web Site: www.southamptonfreelibrary.org/. *Dir,* Kim Ingram; E-mail: ingramk@buckslib.org; *Head, Children's Servx,* Lora Terifay; *Head, Circ,* Debbie Stroup; *Head, Ref (Info Serv),* Jeannie Kim; Staff 6 (MLS 3, Non-MLS 3)
Founded 1921. Pop 15,764; Circ 175,000
Library Holdings: Bk Vols 80,000; Per Subs 85
Automation Activity & Vendor Info: (Acquisitions) SirsiDynix; (Cataloging) SirsiDynix; (Circulation) SirsiDynix; (OPAC) SirsiDynix
Wireless access
Mem of Bucks County Free Library
Open Mon-Thurs 10-8, Fri & Sat 10-5
Friends of the Library Group

SPRING CITY

P SPRING CITY FREE PUBLIC LIBRARY*, 245 Broad St, 19475-1702. SAN 315-2367. Tel: 610-948-4130. FAX: 610-948-9478. Web Site: springcitylibrary.org. *Exec Dir,* Julie Wiant; E-mail: jwiant@ccls.org
Founded 1910. Pop 8,798; Circ 33,611
Library Holdings: Bk Vols 16,500; Per Subs 54
Automation Activity & Vendor Info: (Cataloging) Innovative Interfaces, Inc; (Circulation) Innovative Interfaces, Inc; (OPAC) Innovative Interfaces, Inc
Wireless access
Function: ILL available, Photocopying/Printing
Mem of Chester County Library System
Open Mon, Wed, Fri & Sat 10-5, Tues & Thurs 10-8

SPRING GROVE

P GLATFELTER MEMORIAL LIBRARY, 101 Glenview Rd, 17362. SAN 315-2383. Tel: 717-225-3220. E-mail: glatfelterlibrary@yorklibraries.org. Web Site: www.yorklibraries.org/spring-grove-glatfelter. *Libr Mgr,* Shaina Dampier; E-mail: sdampier@yorklibraries.org; Staff 6 (MLS 1, Non-MLS 5)
Founded 1937. Pop 20,309; Circ 78,422
Library Holdings: Bk Vols 35,423
Wireless access
Mem of York County Library System
Open Mon & Thurs 1-8, Tues, Wed, Fri & Sat 10-2
Friends of the Library Group

SPRINGBORO

P SPRINGBORO PUBLIC LIBRARY*, 110 S Main St, 16435-1108. (Mail add: PO Box 51, 16435-0051), SAN 315-2391. Tel: 814-587-3901. FAX: 814-587-3901. E-mail: springboropl@ccfls.org. Web Site: springboro.ccfls.org. *Dir,* Joy Post
Pop 2,800; Circ 10,000
Library Holdings: Bk Vols 10,000; Per Subs 15
Wireless access
Mem of Crawford County Federated Library System
Open Mon-Thurs 12:30-7:30, Sat 9-4 (9-1 Summer)

SPRINGDALE

P SPRINGDALE FREE PUBLIC LIBRARY*, 331 School St, 15144. SAN 315-2405. Tel: 724-274-9729. FAX: 724-274-6125. E-mail: springdale@einetwork.net. Web Site: www.springdalepubliclibrary.org. *Dir,* Janet Tyree; E-mail: tyreej@einetwork.net; Staff 1 (Non-MLS 1)
Founded 1933. Pop 9,798; Circ 43,740
Library Holdings: Bk Titles 35,000; Per Subs 50
Wireless access
Function: Adult bk club, Adult literacy prog, After school storytime, Art exhibits, Audiobks via web, Bi-weekly Writer's Group, Bk club(s), Bk reviews (Group), Bks on CD, Computer training, Computers for patron use, Doc delivery serv, E-Reserves, Electronic databases & coll, Family literacy, Free DVD rentals, Genealogy discussion group, Health sci info serv, Holiday prog, Home delivery & serv to seniorr ctr & nursing homes, Homebound delivery serv, Homework prog, ILL available, Internet access, Learning ctr, Magnifiers for reading, Mail & tel request accepted, Mail loans to mem, Online cat, Outreach serv, OverDrive digital audio bks, Photocopying/Printing, Preschool outreach, Preschool reading prog, Printer for laptops & handheld devices, Prog for adults, Prog for children & young adult, Ref serv available, Senior computer classes, Senior outreach, Spoken cassettes & DVDs, Story hour, Summer & winter reading prog, Tax forms, Teen prog, Telephone ref, VHS videos, Wheelchair accessible, Workshops, Writing prog
Mem of Allegheny County Library Association (ACLA)
Open Mon, Wed & Thurs 12-8, Tues & Fri 10-5, Sat 9-4
Friends of the Library Group

SPRINGFIELD

P SPRINGFIELD TOWNSHIP LIBRARY*, 70 Powell Rd, 19064-2446. SAN 315-2421. Tel: 610-543-2113. FAX: 610-543-1356. E-mail: springfield@delcolibraries.org. Web Site: www.delcolibraries.org/springfield-township-library, www.springfieldtwplib.org. *Dir,* Christine Rushton; *Youth Serv Librn,* Alicia Nestor; E-mail: splib112@comcast.net; *Pub Serv Mgr,* Harold N Boyer; E-mail: clioguyme@yahoo.com; *Tech Serv,* Christine M Rushton; Tel: 610-543-2113, Ext104, E-mail: springfieldlibrary104@comcast.net; Staff 14.3 (MLS 4, Non-MLS 10.3)
Founded 1937. Pop 24,211; Circ 179,167
Jan 2016-Dec 2016 Income (Main Library Only) $830,348, State $75,452, County $6,774, Locally Generated Income $29,198, Parent Institution $718,924. Mats Exp $114,263, Books $80,051, Per/Ser (Incl. Access Fees) $17,923, AV Mat $14,115, Presv $2,174. Sal $503,928
Library Holdings: Audiobooks 5,191; AV Mats 6,833; Bks-By-Mail 11,174; CDs 3,114; DVDs 6,800; e-books 21,879; e-journals 219; High Interest/Low Vocabulary Bk Vols 2,180; Bk Vols 112,884; Per Subs 86; Videos 6,862
Special Collections: Genealogy Coll; Local History Coll
Automation Activity & Vendor Info: (Cataloging) Innovative Interfaces, Inc; (Circulation) Innovative Interfaces, Inc; (Course Reserve) Innovative Interfaces, Inc; (ILL) Innovative Interfaces, Inc; (Media Booking) Innovative Interfaces, Inc; (OPAC) Innovative Interfaces, Inc; (Serials) Innovative Interfaces, Inc
Wireless access
Function: Audiobks via web, AV serv, Bks on CD, Children's prog, Home delivery & serv to seniorr ctr & nursing homes, ILL available, Internet access, Magazines, Magnifiers for reading, Mail & tel request accepted, Mango lang, Microfiche/film & reading machines, Music CDs, OverDrive digital audio bks, Photocopying/Printing, Preschool outreach, Preschool reading prog, Ref serv available, Scanner, Spoken cassettes & CDs, Spoken cassettes & DVDs, Study rm, Summer & winter reading prog, Telephone ref, Wheelchair accessible
Mem of Delaware County Libraries
Open Mon-Thurs 9-9, Fri 9-6, Sat 9-4, Sun 1-4
Friends of the Library Group

STATE COLLEGE

S INTERNATIONAL INSTITUTE FOR SPORT HISTORY LIBRARY, IISOH Library, c/o Harvey Abrams, 237 S Fraser, Ste 732, 16804. (Mail add: c/o Harvey Abrams, PO Box 732, 16804-0732). Tel: 814-321-4018. Web Site: www.sportlibrary.org. *Pres,* Harvey Abrams; E-mail: HAbrams@iisoh.org. Subject Specialists: *Hist of sport, Olympic games, Phys educ,* Harvey Abrams; Staff 1 (Non-MLS 1)
Founded 2001
Library Holdings: Bk Vols 10,000
Special Collections: History of Dance Coll; History of Recreation Coll; History of Sport Coll; Olympic Games Coll; Physical Education & Recreation Coll; Sport in Art Coll; Sports Organization & Federation Documents. Oral History
Subject Interests: Dance, Hist of sport, Olympic games, Phys educ, Recreation
Function: Res libr
Publications: Newsletter (Quarterly)
Restriction: Non-circulating
Friends of the Library Group

G PENNSYLVANIA FISH & BOAT COMMISSION*, Benner Spring Fish Research Station Library, 1735 Shiloh Rd, 16801-8495. SAN 314-3090. Tel: 814-355-4837. FAX: 814-355-8264. *Head, Res Serv,* Brian Niewinski; E-mail: bniewinski@pa.gov; Staff 2 (Non-MLS 2)
Founded 1953
Library Holdings: Bk Titles 510; Bk Vols 680; Per Subs 59
Special Collections: Fisheries & fisheries related texts, journals & reprints
Open Mon-Fri 8-3:30

S PENNSYLVANIA STATE UNIVERSITY*, Applied Research Laboratory Information Services, N Atherton St, 16801. (Mail add: PO Box 30, 16804-0030), SAN 315-2464. Tel: 814-863-9940. FAX: 814-863-5568. E-mail: library@arl.psu.edu. Web Site: www.arl.psu.edu. *Dept Head,* Patricia G Hayes; E-mail: pgh1@psu.edu; *Tech Libr Spec,* Richard W Brown; *Libr Asst,* Wanda Andrews; Staff 3 (Non-MLS 3)
Founded 1945
Library Holdings: Bk Titles 4,580; Bk Vols 4,790; Per Subs 30
Special Collections: Children's Diversity Coll; Eric Walker Coll. Oral History
Subject Interests: Applied math, Computers, Electronics, Engr, Manufacturing engr, Oceanography, Physics
Automation Activity & Vendor Info: (Acquisitions) Inmagic, Inc.; (Cataloging) Inmagic, Inc.; (Circulation) Inmagic, Inc.; (Serials) Inmagic, Inc.
Partic in DTIC
Restriction: Authorized personnel only, Circ limited, Internal use only, Not open to pub, Researchers only, Secured area only open to authorized personnel
Friends of the Library Group

P SCHLOW CENTRE REGION LIBRARY*, 211 S Allen St, 16801-4806. SAN 315-2472. Tel: 814-237-6236. Circulation Tel: 814-235-7815. Reference Tel: 814-235-7816. Administration Tel: 814-235-7814. FAX: 814-238-8508. E-mail: refdesk@schlowlibrary.org. Web Site: www.schlowlibrary.org. *Dir,* Catherine Alloway; E-mail: calloway@schlowlibrary.org; *Head, Adult Serv,* Maria Burchill; *Head, Children's Servx,* Paula Bannon; *Head, Info Tech,* Nathaniel Rasmussen; Staff 24 (MLS 5, Non-MLS 19)
Founded 1957. Pop 79,406; Circ 591,851
Library Holdings: AV Mats 13,052; Bk Vols 109,691; Per Subs 202
Special Collections: Oral History

Automation Activity & Vendor Info: (Acquisitions) SirsiDynix; (Cataloging) SirsiDynix; (Circulation) SirsiDynix; (OPAC) SirsiDynix
Wireless access
Function: Art exhibits, Chess club, Free DVD rentals, ILL available, Internet access, Music CDs, Online ref, Prog for adults, Prog for children & young adult, Senior computer classes, Spoken cassettes & DVDs, Summer reading prog, Tax forms, Telephone ref, Wheelchair accessible
Partic in Centre County Fed of Pub Librs; LYRASIS; OCLC Online Computer Library Center, Inc
Open Mon-Wed 9-9, Thurs 12-9, Fri 9-6, Sat 9-5, Sun (Sept-May) 1-5
Friends of the Library Group

STEWARTSTOWN

P MASON-DIXON PUBLIC LIBRARY*, 250 Bailey Dr, 17363. SAN 315-2499. Tel: 717-993-2404. FAX: 717-993-9210. Web Site: www.yorklibraries.org/stewartstown-mason-dixon. *Libr Dir,* Carol Stampler; E-mail: cstampler@yorklibraries.org; Staff 1 (MLS 1)
Founded 1961. Pop 12,731; Circ 60,885
Library Holdings: CDs 119; Bk Vols 35,000; Per Subs 103; Talking Bks 382; Videos 254
Wireless access
Mem of York County Library System
Open Mon & Wed 10-8, Tues & Thurs 12-8, Fri 10-5, Sat 9-4
Friends of the Library Group

STRAFFORD

P TREDYFFRIN PUBLIC LIBRARY*, 582 Upper Gulph Rd, 19087-2096. SAN 315-2502. Tel: 610-688-7092. FAX: 610-688-2014. E-mail: tpl@ccls.org. Web Site: www.tredyffrinlibraries.org. *Libr Dir,* Chris Kibler; E-mail: ckibler@ccls.org; *Asst Dir, Head, Tech Serv,* Valerie Green; E-mail: vgreen@ccls.org; *Dir, Ref, Dir, Technology,* Catherine Boyle; E-mail: cboyle@ccls.org; Staff 8 (MLS 6, Non-MLS 2)
Founded 1965. Pop 34,067; Circ 464,914
Library Holdings: e-books 38; Bk Titles 86,185; Bk Vols 90,962; Per Subs 412
Subject Interests: Local hist
Automation Activity & Vendor Info: (Circulation) Innovative Interfaces, Inc; (OPAC) Innovative Interfaces, Inc
Wireless access
Mem of Chester County Library System
Partic in OCLC Online Computer Library Center, Inc
Open Mon, Tues & Thurs 9:30-9, Fri 9:30-6, Sat 9:30-5, Sun 1-5
Friends of the Library Group
Branches: 1
PAOLI BRANCH, 18 Darby Rd, Paoli, 19301-1416, SAN 321-8708. Tel: 610-296-7996. FAX: 610-296-9708. *Br Mgr,* Beverly Michaels; Staff 11 (MLS 1, Non-MLS 10)
Pop 34,067; Circ 106,279
Library Holdings: Bk Titles 24,692; Bk Vols 25,991; Per Subs 72
Subject Interests: Local hist
Open Mon-Thurs 9:30-8, Fri 9:30-6, Sat 9:30-5, Sun 1-5
Friends of the Library Group

STRASBURG

P STRASBURG-HEISLER LIBRARY*, 143 Precision Ave, 17579, SAN 376-6055. Tel: 717-687-8969. FAX: 717-740-2188. E-mail: staff@strasburglibrary.org. Web Site: strasburglibrary.org. *Dir,* Kristin Fernitz; E-mail: kfernitz@strasburglibrary.org; *Circ,* Gwen Barrows; E-mail: gbarrows@strasburglibrary.org; *Circ,* Ms Chris Hess; E-mail: chess@strasburglibrary.org; *Circ,* Lisa Kilheffer; E-mail: lkilheffer@strasburglibrary.org
Library Holdings: Bk Titles 16,000; Bk Vols 18,000; Per Subs 25
Wireless access
Mem of Library System of Lancaster County
Open Mon, Tues & Thurs 10-7, Wed & Fri 10-5, Sat 10-2
Friends of the Library Group

STROUDSBURG

P EASTERN MONROE PUBLIC LIBRARY*, 1002 N Ninth St, 18360. SAN 315-2529. Tel: 570-421-0800. Circulation Tel: 570-421-0800, Ext 301. Interlibrary Loan Service Tel: 570-421-0800, Ext 310. Reference Tel: 570-421-0800, Ext 316. FAX: 570-421-0212. E-mail: reference@monroepl.org. Web Site: monroepl.org. *Dir,* Susan Lyons; Tel: 570-421-0800, Ext 304, E-mail: slyons@monroepl.org; *Dept Head, Adult Serv,* Mary Stewart Erm; *Head, Circ,* Linda Crooks; E-mail: lcrooks@monroepl.org; *Head, Tech Serv,* Linnae Cintron; *Admin Serv Mgr,* Rose Hewitt; E-mail: rhewitt@monroepl.org; *Ch Serv,* Julie Bonser; *ILL,* Cheryl Brice; *IT Librn,* Chen-Fang Cheng; Staff 20 (MLS 10, Non-MLS 10)
Founded 1916. Pop 89,000; Circ 493,285
Jan 2017-Dec 2017 Income (Main & Associated Libraries) $1,878,436, State $407,404, County $1,271,032, Locally Generated Income $200,000. Mats Exp $256,813. Sal $10,867,881
Special Collections: Monroe County History Coll
Subject Interests: Local hist
Automation Activity & Vendor Info: (Acquisitions) Baker & Taylor; (Cataloging) Evergreen; (Circulation) Evergreen; (ILL) OCLC; (OPAC) Evergreen
Wireless access
Function: 24/7 Electronic res, 24/7 Online cat, Adult bk club, Adult literacy prog, Art exhibits, Audiobks on Playaways & MP3, Audiobks via web, Children's prog, Citizenship assistance, Computer training, Computers for patron use, Electronic databases & coll, Family literacy, Free DVD rentals, Genealogy discussion group, Govt ref serv, Health sci info serv, Holiday prog, Home delivery & serv to seniorr ctr & nursing homes, ILL available, Internet access, Jail serv, Literacy & newcomer serv, Magazines, Mango lang, Meeting rooms, Microfiche/film & reading machines, Movies, Music CDs, Online cat, Outreach serv, OverDrive digital audio bks, Photocopying/Printing, Printer for laptops & handheld devices, Prog for adults, Prog for children & young adult, Ref & res, Ref serv available, Res assist avail, Scanner, Senior computer classes, Serves people with intellectual disabilities, Spanish lang bks, Spoken cassettes & CDs, STEM programs, Story hour, Study rm, Summer reading prog, Tax forms, Teen prog, Telephone ref, Wheelchair accessible, Workshops
Special Services for the Deaf - Assistive tech
Special Services for the Blind - Assistive/Adapted tech devices, equip & products
Friends of the Library Group
Branches: 2
POCONO TOWNSHIP BRANCH, Municipal Bldg, Rte 611, Tannersville, 18372. (Mail add: 1002 N Ninth St, 18360-1210), SAN 320-8370. Tel: 570-629-5858. E-mail: ptl@monroepl.org. *Br Librn,* Suzanne Campbell; Staff 1 (Non-MLS 1)
Founded 1987. Circ 24,765
Library Holdings: Audiobooks 281; AV Mats 1,626; CDs 134; DVDs 1,096; High Interest/Low Vocabulary Bk Vols 50; Large Print Bks 393; Bk Vols 13,287; Per Subs 21; Videos 115
Open Mon 9-1 & 2-6, Tues & Fri 1-6, Wed 3-7, Thurs 9-2, Sat 10-2
Friends of the Library Group
SMITHFIELDS BRANCH, RGB Plaza, Rte 209, 507 Seven Bridges Rd, East Stroudsburg, 18301. (Mail add: 507 Seven Bridges Rd, Ste 102, East Stroudsburg, 18301), SAN 371-9308. Tel: 570-223-1881. E-mail: smf@monroepl.org. *Br Librn,* C Sue Young; Staff 2 (MLS 1, Non-MLS 1)
Founded 1991. Circ 34,197
Library Holdings: Audiobooks 529; AV Mats 2,272; CDs 196; DVDs 1,131; High Interest/Low Vocabulary Bk Vols 69; Large Print Bks 913; Bk Vols 16,476; Per Subs 35; Videos 416
Automation Activity & Vendor Info: (Cataloging) SirsiDynix; (Circulation) SirsiDynix; (OPAC) SirsiDynix-WorkFlows
Open Mon-Thurs 10-7, Fri & Sat 10-4
Friends of the Library Group
Bookmobiles: 1

S MONROE COUNTY HISTORICAL ASSOCIATION*, Elizabeth D Walters Research Library, 900 Main St, 18360-1604. SAN 325-5344. Tel: 570-421-7703. FAX: 570-421-9199. E-mail: librarian@monroehistorical.org. Web Site: monroehistorical.org. *Exec Dir,* Amy Leiser; *Research Librn,* Tania Shelton
Founded 1921
Library Holdings: Bk Titles 5,000; Bk Vols 10,000; Per Subs 17
Special Collections: Monroe County History & Genealogy Coll, bks, docs, ms, photogs. Oral History
Wireless access
Function: Res libr
Publications: Fanlight
Open Tues-Fri 10-4

L MONROE COUNTY LAW LIBRARY*, Court House, 610 Monroe St, 18360. SAN 327-0866. Tel: 570-517-3332. Web Site: www.monroepacourts.us. *Librn,* Joseph Sciabica; E-mail: jsciabica@monroepacourts.us; Staff 1 (Non-MLS 1)
Library Holdings: Bk Vols 7,000; Per Subs 12
Open Mon-Fri 8:30-4:30

SUGAR GROVE

P SUGAR GROVE FREE LIBRARY*, 22 Harmon St, 16350. (Mail add: PO Box 313, 16350-0313), SAN 315-2537. Tel: 814-489-7872. FAX: 814-489-7872. E-mail: sgfreelibrary@gmail.com. Web Site: www.sgfreelibrary.org. *Libr Dir,* Daniel H Nickerson; *Libr Asst,* Karla LoPresti; Staff 1 (Non-MLS 1)
Founded 1936. Pop 5,720
Library Holdings: Bk Titles 19,136; Per Subs 50
Special Collections: Artist Coll, bks

Subject Interests: Early oil industry, Gardening, Relig
Automation Activity & Vendor Info: (Cataloging) Innovative Interfaces, Inc; (Circulation) Innovative Interfaces, Inc; (OPAC) Innovative Interfaces, Inc
Wireless access
Function: Adult bk club, Audio & video playback equip for onsite use, Audiobks via web, Bks on CD, Children's prog, Computer training, Computers for patron use, Distance learning, E-Readers, Electronic databases & coll, Equip loans & repairs, Free DVD rentals, Holiday prog, Home delivery & serv to seniorr ctr & nursing homes, Homebound delivery serv, ILL available, Instruction & testing, Internet access, Magazines, Movies, Music CDs, Online cat, Outside serv via phone, mail, e-mail & web, OverDrive digital audio bks, Photocopying/Printing, Preschool outreach, Prog for children & young adult, Ref serv available, Scanner, Senior computer classes, Story hour, Summer reading prog, Tax forms, Teen prog, Telephone ref, Wheelchair accessible, Workshops
Partic in Warren County Libr Syst
Open Mon, Tues & Wed 10-7, Thurs 10-3, Sat 9-3

SUMMERDALE

C CENTRAL PENN COLLEGE*, Charles T Jones Library, 600 Valley Rd, 17093. (Mail add: PO Box 309, 17093). Tel: 717-728-2500. Web Site: www.centralpenn.edu/library. *Libr Dir,* Diane Porterfield; E-mail: dianeporterfield@centralpenn.edu; Staff 3.5 (MLS 3.5)
Founded 2002. Enrl 1,000; Highest Degree: Bachelor
Automation Activity & Vendor Info: (Acquisitions) Innovative Interfaces, Inc; (Cataloging) Innovative Interfaces, Inc; (Circulation) Innovative Interfaces, Inc; (Course Reserve) Innovative Interfaces, Inc; (OPAC) Innovative Interfaces, Inc; (Serials) Innovative Interfaces, Inc
Wireless access
Restriction: Open to students, fac, staff & alumni

SUMMERVILLE

P SUMMERVILLE PUBLIC LIBRARY*, 114 Second Ave, 15864. (Mail add: PO Box 301, 15864-0301), SAN 315-2545. Tel: 814-856-3169. FAX: 814-856-3169. E-mail: sumlibrary@gmail.com. Web Site: www.summervillelibrary.org. *Dir,* Jennifer Coleman
Founded 1932. Pop 1,897; Circ 6,000
Library Holdings: High Interest/Low Vocabulary Bk Vols 80; Bk Titles 12,000; Bk Vols 16,000; Per Subs 46
Special Collections: Oral History
Subject Interests: Cookery, Local hist
Automation Activity & Vendor Info: (Acquisitions) Evolve; (Cataloging) Evolve; (ILL) Auto-Graphics, Inc; (OPAC) Evolve
Wireless access
Mem of Oil Creek District Library Center
Open Mon-Thurs 11-6:30, Sat 9-3

SUNBURY

P DEGENSTEIN COMMUNITY LIBRARY, 40 S Fifth St, 17801. SAN 315-2553. Tel: 570-286-2461. FAX: 570-286-4203. E-mail: info@degensteinlibrary.org. Web Site: degensteinlibrary.org. *Libr Dir,* Melissa A Rowse; E-mail: mrowse@degensteinlibrary.org; Staff 2 (MLS 1, Non-MLS 1)
Founded 1937. Pop 18,267; Circ 34,553
Jan 2020-Dec 2020 Income $67,984, State $54,251, City $13,733
Library Holdings: Bk Vols 64,000; Per Subs 98
Special Collections: Pennsylvania History Room. State Document Depository; UN Document Depository; US Document Depository
Subject Interests: Local hist
Automation Activity & Vendor Info: (Circulation) Innovative Interfaces, Inc
Wireless access
Open Mon & Thurs 1-7, Tues, Wed & Fri 11-6, Sat 9-1
Friends of the Library Group

GL NORTHUMBERLAND COUNTY LAW LIBRARY*, Court House, 201 Market St, 17801-3471. SAN 315-2561. Tel: 570-988-4167. FAX: 570-988-4497.
Founded 1886
Special Collections: Municipal Document Depository; State Document Depository
Function: Res libr
Open Mon 9-5, Tues-Fri 9-4:30
Restriction: Open to pub for ref only

SWARTHMORE

SWARTHMORE COLLEGE*, McCabe Library, 500 College Ave, 19081. SAN 359-5773. Tel: 610-328-8489. Circulation Tel: 610-328-8477. Interlibrary Loan Service Tel: 610-328-7822. Reference Tel: 610-328-8493. FAX: 610-328-7329. E-mail: librarian@swarthmore.edu. Circulation E-mail: circ@swarthmore.edu. Web Site: www.swarthmore.edu/libraries. *Col Librn,* Peggy Seiden; Tel: 610-328-8553, E-mail: pseiden1@swarthmore.edu; *Assoc Col Librn, Coll Mgt, Discovery Serv,* Barb Weir; Tel: 610-328-8443, E-mail: bweir1@swarthmore.edu; *Assoc Col Librn, Info & Res Serv,* Pam Harris; Tel: 610-690-2056, E-mail: pharris1@swarthmore.edu; *Performing Arts Librn,* Donna Fournier; Tel: 610-328-8231, E-mail: dfourni1@swarthmore.edu; *Sci Librn,* Andrea Baruzzi; Tel: 610-328-7685, E-mail: abaruzzi1@swarthmore.edu; *Soc Sci Librn,* Sarah Elichko; Tel: 610-690-5786, E-mail: selichk1@swarthmore.edu; *Access Serv, Supvr, User Serv,* Alison Masterpasqua; Tel: 610-328-8478, E-mail: amaster1@swarthmore.edu. Subject Specialists: *Dance, Music,* Donna Fournier; Staff 18 (MLS 11.7, Non-MLS 6.3)
Founded 1864. Enrl 1,514; Fac 180; Highest Degree: Bachelor
Library Holdings: e-journals 15,164; Bk Vols 860,000; Per Subs 1,174; Videos 11,604
Special Collections: British Writings on Travel in America (British Americana Coll); History of Technology (Bathe Coll); Private Press (Charles B Shaw Coll); Recorded Literature (Potter Coll); Romantic Poetry (Wells Wordsworth & Thomson Coll); W H Auden Coll. State Document Depository; US Document Depository
Subject Interests: Humanities, Soc sci
Wireless access
Partic in LYRASIS; OCLC Online Computer Library Center, Inc; OCLC Research Library Partnership; Partnership for Academic Library Collaborative & Innovation; Tri-College Consortium
Open Mon-Fri 8-8, Sat 10-6, Sun 10-8
Restriction: Open to students, fac & staff
Friends of the Library Group

Departmental Libraries:

CORNELL SCIENCE & ENGINEERING, 500 College Ave, 19081. Tel: 610-328-7685. FAX: 610-690-5776. Web Site: www.swarthmore.edu/libraries/cornell-science-library. *Sci Librn,* Andrea Baruzzi; E-mail: abaruzz1@swarthmore.edu; *Access Serv, Lending Servs,* Joanne McCole; Tel: 610-328-8267, E-mail: mccole1@swarthmorecollege.edu
Library Holdings: Bk Vols 92,575
Open Mon-Thurs 8:15am-1am, Fri 8:15am-11pm, Sat 10-10, Sun 11am-1am

S FRIENDS HISTORICAL LIBRARY, 500 College Ave, 19081, SAN 315-2588. Tel: 610-328-8496. FAX: 610-690-5728. E-mail: friends@swarthmore.edu. Web Site: www.swarthmore.edu/friends-historical-library. *Archivist,* Celia Caust-Ellenbogen; Tel: 610-328-8498, E-mail: ccauste1@swarthmore.edu; *Archivist,* Susanna Morikawa; Tel: 610-328-8542, E-mail: smorika1@swarthmore.edu; Staff 2 (Non-MLS 2)
Founded 1871
Library Holdings: Bk Vols 45,000; Per Subs 212
Special Collections: Archival Records of Swarthmore College; Archives of Philadelphia Yearly Meeting, New York Yearly Meeting, Baltimore Yearly Meeting & other Quaker Meetings; Papers of Quakers including Lucretia Mott, Elias Hicks, John Woolman & John G Whittier; Records of Quaker Organizations including Friends General Conference; Society of Friends Coll, bks, per, printed mat
Subject Interests: Quaker hist
Partic in Interlibrary Delivery Service of Pennsylvania; OCLC, Inc through Palinet; Philadelphia Area Consortium of Special Collections Libraries
Publications: Catalog of the Book & Serials Collections of the Friends Historical Library; Guide to the Manuscript Collections of Friends Historical Library of Swarthmore College; Guide to the Records of Philadelphia Yearly Meeting
Open Mon-Fri 8:30-4:30

DANIEL UNDERHILL MUSIC & DANCE, Six Whittier Pl, 19081. Tel: 610-328-8232. Web Site: www.swarthmore.edu/libraries/underhill-music-dance-library. *Librn,* Donna Fournier; Tel: 610-328-8231, E-mail: dfourni1@swarthmore.edu
Library Holdings: Bk Vols 40,936
Open Mon-Thurs 9am-1am, Fri 9-6, Sat 10-6, Sun 11:30am-1am

P SWARTHMORE PUBLIC LIBRARY*, Borough Hall, 121 Park Ave, 19081-1536. SAN 315-260X. Tel: 610-543-0436, 610-543-3171. FAX: 610-328-6699. E-mail: Swarthmore@delcolibraries.org. Web Site: www.delcolibraries.org, www.swarthmorepubliclibrary.org. *Dir,* Amber Osborne; Staff 4 (MLS 2, Non-MLS 2)
Founded 1929. Pop 6,157; Circ 115,000
Library Holdings: Per Subs 96
Automation Activity & Vendor Info: (Circulation) Innovative Interfaces, Inc
Wireless access
Function: ILL available
Mem of Delaware County Libraries
Open Mon-Thurs 9:30-8, Fri 9:30-7, Sat 10-3, Sun 1-5
Friends of the Library Group

SYKESVILLE

P SYKESVILLE PUBLIC LIBRARY*, 21 E Main St, 15865-0021. SAN 315-2626. Tel: 814-894-5243. FAX: 814-894-5243. E-mail: sykeslibrary@comcast.net. *Librn,* Ruth Sackash
Founded 1968. Pop 2,973; Circ 7,025
Library Holdings: Bk Titles 10,625; Bk Vols 9,000; Per Subs 35
Mem of Oil Creek District Library Center

TAMAQUA

P TAMAQUA PUBLIC LIBRARY*, 30 S Railroad St, 18252. SAN 315-2642. Tel: 570-668-4660. FAX: 570-668-3047. E-mail: tamaquapubliclibrary@hotmail.com. Web Site: www.tamaquapl.com, www.tamaquapubliclibrary.com. *Libr Dir,* Gayle R Heath
Founded 1934. Pop 17,144
Library Holdings: Bk Titles 39,000; Per Subs 52
Wireless access
Open Mon 10-8, Tues & Wed 10-5, Thurs 10-2, Fri 12-5, Sat 9:30-4:30 (10-2 Summer)

TAYLOR

P TAYLOR COMMUNITY LIBRARY, 710 S Main St, 18517-1774. SAN 315-2677. Tel: 570-562-1234. FAX: 570-562-1539. E-mail: tayadim@albright.org. Web Site: taylorborough.com/community/taylor-community-library, www.lclshome.org/b/taylor-community-library. *Dir,* Jeanie Sluck; E-mail: jeanie@albright.org
Founded 1953. Pop 7,200
Library Holdings: Bk Vols 40,500; Per Subs 16
Automation Activity & Vendor Info: (Cataloging) SirsiDynix; (Circulation) SirsiDynix; (OPAC) SirsiDynix
Wireless access
Mem of Lackawanna County Library System
Open Mon-Thurs 9-9, Fri 9-5, Sat 9-4

TELFORD

P INDIAN VALLEY PUBLIC LIBRARY, 100 E Church Ave, 18969. SAN 315-2685. Tel: 215-723-9109. FAX: 215-723-0583. Web Site: www.ivpl.org. *Dir,* Margie Stern; E-mail: mstern@ivpl.org; *Outreach Serv, Teen Librn,* Nicole Husbands; E-mail: nhusbands@ivpl.org; *Adult Serv,* DeAnne O'Brien; E-mail: dobrien@ivpl.org; *Ch Serv,* Angela Buckley; E-mail: abuckley@ivpl.org; *Ref Serv,* Melanie Ford; E-mail: mford@ivpl.org; *Tech Serv,* Mary Porter; E-mail: mporter@ivpl.org; Staff 22 (MLS 6, Non-MLS 16)
Founded 1963. Pop 41,000; Circ 520,000
Library Holdings: AV Mats 9,450; Large Print Bks 925; Bk Vols 130,000; Per Subs 130
Special Collections: Charles Price Genealogy Coll; Chinese Culture Coll; Local Newspaper 1881-date; Pennsylvania Archives
Automation Activity & Vendor Info: (Cataloging) OpenAccess Software, Inc; (Circulation) OpenAccess Software, Inc
Wireless access
Open Mon-Thurs 9-9, Fri 10-9, Sat 10-5, Sun 1-5
Friends of the Library Group

TIDIOUTE

P TIDIOUTE PUBLIC LIBRARY, 197 Main St, 16351. (Mail add: PO Box T, 16351-0225), SAN 315-2693. Tel: 814-484-3581. FAX: 814-484-3581. E-mail: librarian@tidioutelibrary.org. Web Site: tidioutelibrary.org. *Dir,* Elizabeth Nicholson
Founded 1921. Pop 939; Circ 10,815
Library Holdings: Bk Vols 12,000; Per Subs 45
Wireless access
Open Mon & Wed 12-7, Fri & Sat 9-3
Friends of the Library Group

TIONESTA

P SARAH STEWART BOVARD MEMORIAL LIBRARY, 156 Elm St, 16353. (Mail add: PO Box 127, 16353-0127), SAN 315-2707. Tel: 814-755-4454. FAX: 814-755-4333. E-mail: ssbml@zoominternet.net. Web Site: www.tionestalibrary.org. *Dir,* Carla Woodside; E-mail: librarydirector@zoominternet.net; Staff 1 (Non-MLS 1)
Founded 1942. Pop 5,072; Circ 14,000
Library Holdings: Bk Titles 19,000; Per Subs 47
Special Collections: Artifacts (Forest County Logging & Boat Building Tools Coll); Forest County History & Geography, bks, pamphlets, photog, etc
Automation Activity & Vendor Info: (Cataloging) Evolve; (Circulation) Evolve; (OPAC) Evolve
Wireless access
Function: 24/7 Electronic res, 24/7 Online cat, Adult bk club, Archival coll, Audio & video playback equip for onsite use, Audiobks on Playaways & MP3, Audiobks via web, Bk club(s), Bks on CD, Computers for patron use, Electronic databases & coll, Equip loans & repairs, Free DVD rentals, ILL available, Internet access, Laminating, Magazines, Meeting rooms, Movies, Online cat, OverDrive digital audio bks, Photocopying/Printing, Printer for laptops & handheld devices, Scanner, Tax forms, Wheelchair accessible
Open Mon, Fri & Sat 10-2, Tues & Thurs 10-4, Wed 2-6
Friends of the Library Group

TITUSVILLE

P BENSON MEMORIAL LIBRARY, 213 N Franklin St, 16354-1788. SAN 315-2715. Tel: 814-827-2913. FAX: 814-827-9836. E-mail: bensonml@ccfls.org. Web Site: bensonlibrary.org. *Exec Dir,* Jessica Hilburn; E-mail: jessica.hilburn@bensonlibrary.org; Staff 6 (MLS 1, Non-MLS 5)
Founded 1902. Pop 14,050; Circ 78,076
Library Holdings: Audiobooks 1,060; CDs 105; DVDs 2,308; e-books 1,511; Electronic Media & Resources 150; Large Print Bks 706; Bk Titles 38,259; Per Subs 119
Subject Interests: Early petroleum indust, Genealogy, Local hist
Automation Activity & Vendor Info: (Acquisitions) Baker & Taylor; (Cataloging) Koha; (Circulation) Koha; (Discovery) ByWater Solutions; (ILL) Auto-Graphics, Inc; (OPAC) ByWater Solutions; (Serials) EBSCO Online
Wireless access
Function: 24/7 Electronic res, 24/7 Online cat, 3D Printer, Adult bk club, Archival coll, Audio & video playback equip for onsite use, Audiobks on Playaways & MP3, Audiobks via web, AV serv, Bk club(s), Bks on CD, Butterfly Garden, CD-ROM, Children's prog, Computers for patron use, Digital talking bks, Electronic databases & coll, Family literacy, For res purposes, Free DVD rentals, Games & aids for people with disabilities, Holiday prog, Home delivery & serv to seniorr ctr & nursing homes, Homebound delivery serv, ILL available, Internet access, Life-long learning prog for all ages, Magazines, Magnifiers for reading, Mail loans to mem, Makerspace, Meeting rooms, Microfiche/film & reading machines, Movies, Music CDs, Online cat, Online ref, Outreach serv, OverDrive digital audio bks, Photocopying/Printing, Preschool outreach, Prog for adults, Prog for children & young adult, Ref & res, Ref serv available, Res assist avail, Scanner, STEM programs, Story hour, Summer & winter reading prog, Summer reading prog, Tax forms, Teen prog, Telephone ref, Wheelchair accessible, Winter reading prog
Mem of Crawford County Federated Library System
Open Mon & Wed 11-7, Tues, Thurs & Fri 9-5, Sat 9-2
Restriction: Non-resident fee

S PENNSYLVANIA HISTORICAL & MUSEUM COMMISSION*, Drake Well Museum Library, 202 Museum Lane, 16354-8902. SAN 315-2723. Tel: 814-827-2797. FAX: 814-827-4888. E-mail: drakewell@verizon.net. Web Site: www.drakewell.org. *Dir,* Melissa Mann; E-mail: mmann@pa.gov
Founded 1934
Library Holdings: CDs 150; Microforms 40; Music Scores 10; Bk Titles 4,000; Bk Vols 4,500; Spec Interest Per Sub 16
Special Collections: Ida M Tarbell; National Fuel Gas; National Transit Company; Pennsylvania Petroleum Industry; Roberts Torpedo Coll. Oral History
Subject Interests: Hist of region, Petroleum indust
Function: Res libr
Open Tues-Sat (March-Dec) 9-5, Sun 12-5
Restriction: Not a lending libr
Friends of the Library Group

C UNIVERSITY OF PITTSBURGH AT TITUSVILLE*, Haskell Memorial Library, 504 E Main St, 16354. SAN 315-2731. Tel: 814-827-4439. FAX: 814-827-4449. Web Site: www.library.pitt.edu/titusville. *Head of Libr,* Marc Ross; Tel: 814-827-4452, E-mail: marcross@pitt.edu; *Libr Spec,* Ann Lucas; Tel: 814-827-4439, E-mail: annlu@pitt.edu
Founded 1963
Library Holdings: Bk Vols 47,200; Per Subs 90
Automation Activity & Vendor Info: (Circulation) Ex Libris Group; (OPAC) Ex Libris Group; (Serials) Ex Libris Group
Wireless access
Partic in OCLC Online Computer Library Center, Inc
Open Mon-Fri 9-4:45

TOBYHANNA

P POCONO MOUNTAIN PUBLIC LIBRARY*, Coolbaugh Township Municipal Ctr, 5500 Municipal Dr, 18466. SAN 372-7289. Tel: 570-894-8860. FAX: 570-894-8852. E-mail: pmpl_library@yahoo.com. Web Site: www.poconomountpl.org. *Dir,* Ann Shincovich; E-mail: anndirector_pmpl@yahoo.com; *Cat Librn,* Kathryn Ritter-Vicich; *Ch,* Susanne Mocerino; *ILL Librn, Purchasing,* Bev Abel; *YA Librn,* Mary Ar

Lewis; *Ch Serv, Circ,* Sarah Rieder; *Coll,* Jo Collins; *Pub Serv,* Linda Fernandez; *Pub Serv,* Linda Salmon; Staff 8 (MLS 1, Non-MLS 7)
Founded 1975. Pop 17,947; Circ 160,962
Library Holdings: Bk Titles 31,458; Bk Vols 38,000; Per Subs 100
Automation Activity & Vendor Info: (Cataloging) Follett Software; (Circulation) Follett Software; (OPAC) Follett Software
Wireless access
Open Mon & Wed 10-8, Tues & Thurs 10-5, Fri & Sat 12-4
Friends of the Library Group

A UNITED STATES ARMY*, Tobyhanna Army Depot Post Library, 11 Hap Arnold Blvd, 18466-5099. Tel: 570-615-8851. *Library Contact,* Kathy Fabricatore; E-mail: kathleen.fabricatore.nat@mail.mil
Founded 1959
Library Holdings: DVDs 1,000; Bk Vols 500; Per Subs 28
Partic in OCLC Online Computer Library Center, Inc
Restriction: Not open to pub

TOPTON

P BRANDYWINE COMMUNITY LIBRARY*, 60 Tower Dr, 19562-1301. SAN 323-9411. Tel: 610-682-7115. FAX: 610-682-7385. E-mail: brandywinecl@berks.lib.pa.us. Web Site: berkslibraries.org/branch/brandywine. *Libr Dir,* Heather Wicke; *Youth Serv Coordr,* Yvonne Albright; Staff 1 (Non-MLS 1)
Founded 1989. Pop 12,770; Circ 82,092
Library Holdings: AV Mats 5,323; Large Print Bks 1,086; Bk Titles 21,608; Per Subs 81; Talking Bks 1,821
Automation Activity & Vendor Info: (Acquisitions) Innovative Interfaces, Inc; (Cataloging) Innovative Interfaces, Inc; (Circulation) Innovative Interfaces, Inc; (Course Reserve) Innovative Interfaces, Inc; (ILL) Innovative Interfaces, Inc; (Media Booking) Innovative Interfaces, Inc; (OPAC) Innovative Interfaces, Inc; (Serials) Innovative Interfaces, Inc
Wireless access
Mem of Berks County Public Libraries

TOWANDA

P TOWANDA PUBLIC LIBRARY*, 104 Main St, 18848. SAN 315-2758. Tel: 570-265-2470. FAX: 570-265-7212. E-mail: towandapublib@gmail.com. Web Site: www.towandapubliclibrary.org. *Ch, Dir,* Katie Patton; E-mail: kpatton.tpl@gmail.com; Staff 5 (MLS 1, Non-MLS 4)
Founded 1880. Pop 10,461; Circ 48,100
Library Holdings: Bk Vols 30,000; Per Subs 76
Special Collections: Local History Coll
Subject Interests: Civil War
Automation Activity & Vendor Info: (Acquisitions) Evergreen
Wireless access
Mem of Bradford County Library System
Open Mon-Thurs 10-8, Fri & Sat 10-5
Friends of the Library Group

TOWER CITY

P TOWER-PORTER COMMUNITY LIBRARY*, 230 E Grand Ave, 17980-1124. SAN 315-2766. Tel: 717-647-4900. E-mail: toweport@comcast.net. Web Site: www2.iu29.org/towpl. *Pres of Board,* Deb Welker; *Libr Dir,* Thomas Houtz
Pop 4,185
Library Holdings: Bk Vols 8,500; Per Subs 10
Wireless access
Open Mon-Thurs 1-8, Sat 9-4

TRAFFORD

P TRAFFORD COMMUNITY PUBLIC LIBRARY*, 416 Brinton Ave, 15085. (Mail add: PO Box 173, 15085-0173), SAN 315-2774. Tel: 412-372-5115. FAX: 412-372-0993. E-mail: traffordcpl@comcast.net. Web Site: www.traffordlibrary.org. *Dir,* Jessica Beichler; Staff 2 (MLS 1, Non-MLS 1)
Pop 3,662; Circ 12,715
Library Holdings: Bk Vols 12,000; Per Subs 25
Special Collections: Trafford Historical Society Coll, holdings
Wireless access
Function: 24/7 Online cat, Archival coll, Bk club(s), Bks on CD, Children's prog, Computers for patron use, Electronic databases & coll, Free DVD rentals, Holiday prog, ILL available, Internet access, Magazines, Mail & tel request accepted, Online cat, Online ref, Outreach serv, Outside serv via phone, mail, e-mail & web, Photocopying/Printing, Prog for adults, Ref & res, Res assist avail, Scanner, STEM programs, Story hour, Summer reading prog, Tax forms, Workshops
Mem of Westmoreland County Federated Library System
Open Mon 10-6, Tues-Thurs 10-7, Fri 10-2, Sat 9-4

TREMONT

P TREMONT AREA FREE PUBLIC LIBRARY*, 19 N Pine St, 17981-1410. (Mail add: PO Box 54, 17981-0054), SAN 315-2782. Tel: 570-695-3325. E-mail: tafpl@epix.net. *Libr Dir,* Bonnie Wiscount
Pop 1,796; Circ 4,000
Library Holdings: Bk Vols 12,600; Per Subs 15
Wireless access
Open Mon & Wed 11-5, Tues & Thurs 11-2 & 6-8, Fri 10-4, Sat 8-Noon

TREVOSE

S SUEZ WATER TECHNOLOGIES & SOLUTIONS*, Technology Library, 4636 Somerton Rd, 19053. SAN 315-2790. Tel: 215-355-3300. Web Site: www.suezwatertechnologies.com. *Librn,* Dianne E Rose; Staff 1 (MLS 1)
Founded 1925
Library Holdings: Electronic Media & Resources 50; Bk Titles 4,500; Bk Vols 5,500; Per Subs 200
Subject Interests: Corrosion, Indust wastes, Water pollution, Water treatment
Publications: Acquisitions List
Restriction: Access at librarian's discretion

TROY

P BRADFORD COUNTY LIBRARY SYSTEM*, 16093 Rte 6, 16947. SAN 315-2812. Tel: 570-297-2436. FAX: 570-297-4197. E-mail: bclibrary@bradfordco.org. Web Site: bradfordcountylibrary.org. *Dir,* Jeffrey Singer; E-mail: singerj@bradfordco.org; *ILL,* Theresa Fritchman; E-mail: fritchmant@bradfordco.org; Staff 11 (MLS 3, Non-MLS 8)
Founded 1941. Pop 75,000; Circ 144,069
Library Holdings: Bk Vols 47,000
Subject Interests: Local hist
Automation Activity & Vendor Info: (Acquisitions) Brodart; (Cataloging) Biblionix; (Circulation) Follett Software
Wireless access
Member Libraries: Allen F Pierce Free Library; Green Free Library; Mather Memorial Library; Monroeton Public Library; New Albany Community Library; Sayre Public Library, Inc; Spalding Memorial Library; Towanda Public Library; Wyalusing Public Library
Open Mon-Thurs 8-8, Fri 8-6, Sat 8-3
Friends of the Library Group
Bookmobiles: 1. In Charge, Rosemary Wynott

P ALLEN F PIERCE FREE LIBRARY*, 34 Fenner Ave, 16947-1125. SAN 315-2820. Tel: 570-297-2745. FAX: 570-297-2394. Web Site: piercefl.edublogs.org. *Dir,* Susan Wolfe; E-mail: s16@epix.net; Staff 2 (MLS 1, Non-MLS 1)
Founded 1912. Pop 5,197; Circ 8,312
Library Holdings: Bk Titles 17,219; Bk Vols 18,100; Per Subs 53; Talking Bks 100; Videos 63
Automation Activity & Vendor Info: (Circulation) Follett Software; (Course Reserve) Follett Software; (OPAC) Follett Software
Wireless access
Mem of Bradford County Library System
Open Tues & Thurs 1-7, Wed & Fri 9-5, Sat 8-3

TUNKHANNOCK

P TUNKHANNOCK PUBLIC LIBRARY, 220 W Tioga St, 18657-6611. SAN 315-2839. Tel: 570-836-1677. FAX: 570-836-2148. Web Site: www.tunkhannocklibrary.org. *Exec Dir,* Dellana Diovisalvo; E-mail: tunkhannocklibrarydirector@gmail.com; Staff 1 (MLS 1)
Founded 1890. Pop 28,276; Circ 135,974
Library Holdings: Audiobooks 1,533; DVDs 2,714; e-books 1,050; e-journals 100; Large Print Bks 3,394; Bk Vols 35,425; Per Subs 53
Automation Activity & Vendor Info: (Acquisitions) Brodart; (Cataloging) Brodart; (Circulation) Evergreen; (ILL) Evergreen; (OPAC) Evergreen
Wireless access
Function: 24/7 Electronic res, 24/7 Online cat, Activity rm, Adult literacy prog, Audiobks via web, Bk club(s), Bks on CD, Children's prog, Computer training, Computers for patron use, Electronic databases & coll, Games & aids for people with disabilities, ILL available, Internet access, Jail serv, Life-long learning prog for all ages, Magazines, Mail & tel request accepted, Mango lang, Meeting rooms, Movies, Online cat, Outreach serv, Preschool outreach, Prog for adults, Prog for children & young adult, Ref serv available, Satellite serv, Scanner, Senior computer classes, Serves people with intellectual disabilities, Story hour, Summer & winter reading prog, Tax forms, Wheelchair accessible, Workshops
Open Mon, Tues & Thurs 10-5, Wed & Fri 10-6, Sat 10-4 (10-2 Summer)

TYRONE

P TYRONE-SNYDER PUBLIC LIBRARY, 1000 Pennsylvania Ave, 16686. SAN 315-2847. Tel: 814-684-1133. FAX: 814-684-1878. E-mail: director@tyronelibrary.org. Web Site: www.tyronelibrary.org. *Dir,* Jennifer Powell; *Asst Dir,* Lana Conrad
Founded 1964. Circ 23,828
Library Holdings: Bk Vols 25,146; Per Subs 42
Special Collections: Local history
Automation Activity & Vendor Info: (Cataloging) Evergreen; (Circulation) Evergreen; (OPAC) Evergreen
Wireless access
Function: 24/7 Electronic res, 24/7 Online cat, 3D Printer, Activity rm, Adult bk club, Art programs, Bk club(s), Bks on CD, Children's prog, Computers for patron use, Electronic databases & coll, ILL available, Internet access, Laminating, Life-long learning prog for all ages, Magazines, Magnifiers for reading, Meeting rooms, Movies, Museum passes, Online cat, Photocopying/Printing, Preschool reading prog, Printer for laptops & handheld devices, Prog for adults, Prog for children & young adult, Ref serv available, Res assist avail, Scanner, Senior computer classes, Serves people with intellectual disabilities, STEM programs, Story hour, Summer & winter reading prog, Summer reading prog, Tax forms, Teen prog, Wheelchair accessible, Workshops
Mem of Blair County Library System
Open Wed & Fri 10-5, Tues 10-6, Thurs 12-7, Sat 10-2
Friends of the Library Group

ULSTER

P MATHER MEMORIAL LIBRARY*, 23866 Rte 220, 18850. (Mail add: PO Box 230, 18850-0230), SAN 315-2855. Tel: 570-358-3595. FAX: 570-358-3595. E-mail: matherpl@epix.net. Web Site: www.matherlibrary.org. *Librn,* Deneen Roach
Founded 1920. Pop 2,685; Circ 13,787
Library Holdings: Audiobooks 248; DVDs 427; Large Print Bks 398; Bk Vols 13,830; Per Subs 33; Videos 194
Automation Activity & Vendor Info: (Circulation) Biblionix
Wireless access
Function: Bks on CD, Computers for patron use, ILL available, Magazines, Mango lang, Online cat, OverDrive digital audio bks, Photocopying/Printing, Preschool reading prog, Story hour, Summer reading prog
Mem of Bradford County Library System
Open Tues 9-6, Wed & Thurs 10-6, Fri 2-6, Sat 9-4

ULYSSES

P ULYSSES LIBRARY ASSOCIATION*, 401 N Main St, 16948. (Mail add: PO Box 316, 16948-0316), SAN 315-2863. Tel: 814-848-7226. FAX: 814-848-7226. E-mail: ulylib@verizon.net. Web Site: www.ulysseslibrary.com. *Librn,* Sheri Graves; *Asst Librn,* Bonnie Merkey
Founded 1916. Pop 1,375; Circ 11,547
Library Holdings: Bk Vols 15,824; Per Subs 15
Automation Activity & Vendor Info: (Acquisitions) Brodart; (Cataloging) Brodart; (Circulation) Brodart
Wireless access
Function: Summer reading prog
Mem of Potter-Tioga Library System
Open Tues, Thurs & Fri 1-7, Wed 9-6, Sat 9-5

UNION CITY

P UNION CITY PUBLIC LIBRARY*, S Main & Stranahan Sts, 16438. SAN 315-2871. Tel: 814-438-3209. FAX: 814-438-8031. Interlibrary Loan Service E-mail: unioncitypl@gmail.com. Web Site: www.ucpl.org. *Librn,* Christine Slocum
Founded 1908. Pop 6,491; Circ 7,111
Library Holdings: Bk Titles 24,678; Per Subs 46
Special Collections: Local Newspaper, micro
Automation Activity & Vendor Info: (Circulation) Follett Software; (OPAC) Follett Software
Wireless access
Open Mon & Thurs 9-7:30, Tues & Fri 9-5:30, Sat 9-4 (10-2 Summer)
Friends of the Library Group

UNIONTOWN

GL FAYETTE COUNTY LAW LIBRARY*, Court House, 61 E Main St, Ste D, 15401-3514. SAN 315-288X. Tel: 724-430-1228. FAX: 724-430-4886. E-mail: falawlib@fayettepa.org. Web Site: www.fayettecountypa.org/403/Law-Library. *Law Librn,* Eric Harvey; Staff 2 (MLS 1, Non-MLS 1)
Founded 1927
Library Holdings: Bk Vols 25,000
Open Mon-Fri 8-4:30
Restriction: Non-circulating

C PENNSYLVANIA STATE UNIVERSITY*, Fayette Library, 2201 University Dr, 15456. (Mail add: PO Box 519, 15401-0519), SAN 315-2898. Tel: 724-430-4155. FAX: 724-430-4152. E-mail: ul-fayette@lists.psu.edu. Web Site: www.libraries.psu.edu/fayette. *Head Librn,* Emma Beaver; Tel: 724-430-4156, E-mail: ehb5131@psu.edu; *Info Res Spec,* Meghan Hill; Tel: 724-430-4153, E-mail: mmh5481@psu.edu; Staff 2 (MLS 1, Non-MLS 1)
Founded 1965. Enrl 994; Fac 48
Library Holdings: Bk Vols 50,000; Per Subs 125
Wireless access
Partic in OCLC Online Computer Library Center, Inc; Research Libraries Information Network
Open Mon-Thurs 8-6, Fri 8-5

M UNIONTOWN HOSPITAL*, Professional Library, 500 W Berkeley St, 15401. SAN 327-084X. Tel: 724-430-5178. FAX: 724-430-3349. Web Site: www.uniontownhospital.com. *Librn,* Debra Mancini; E-mail: mancini@utwn.org; Staff 1 (MLS 1)
Jul 2012-Jun 2013. Mats Exp $25,900, Books $2,000, Per/Ser (Incl. Access Fees) $5,900, Electronic Ref Mat (Incl. Access Fees) $18,000
Library Holdings: e-books 80; Bk Titles 268; Bk Vols 270; Per Subs 22
Partic in Basic Health Sciences Library Network; National Network of Libraries of Medicine Region 1; Pittsburgh Basic Health Sciences Libr Consortium)
Open Tues & Thurs 8:30-4

P UNIONTOWN PUBLIC LIBRARY, 24 Jefferson St, 15401-3602. SAN 315-2901. Tel: 724-437-1165. FAX: 724-439-5689. E-mail: upl@uniontownlib.org. Web Site: uniontownlib.org. *Libr Dir,* Christy Fusco; E-mail: cfusco@uniontownlib.org; Staff 8 (MLS 1, Non-MLS 7)
Founded 1928. Pop 10,372; Circ 70,070. Sal $184,556
Library Holdings: Bk Vols 98,673; Per Subs 75
Special Collections: Pennsylvania Room. Oral History
Subject Interests: Local hist
Automation Activity & Vendor Info: (Cataloging) Innovative Interfaces, Inc; (Circulation) Innovative Interfaces, Inc; (ILL) Innovative Interfaces, Inc; (OPAC) Innovative Interfaces, Inc
Wireless access
Function: Adult bk club, Archival coll, Art exhibits, Bks on CD, Children's prog, Computers for patron use, E-Reserves, Free DVD rentals, ILL available, Learning ctr, Magnifiers for reading, Mail & tel request accepted, Microfiche/film & reading machines, Online cat, OverDrive digital audio bks, Photocopying/Printing, Prog for adults, Prog for children & young adult, Ref serv available, Serves people with intellectual disabilities, Story hour, Summer reading prog, Wheelchair accessible
Special Services for the Blind - Audio mat; Bks on CD; Copier with enlargement capabilities; Large print bks; Low vision equip; Magnifiers; Recorded bks; Sec-Tec enlarger
Open Mon 9:30-6, Tues-Fri 9:30-5
Friends of the Library Group

UNIVERSITY PARK

CL PENNSYLVANIA STATE UNIVERSITY - DICKINSON SCHOOL OF LAW*, The H Laddie Montague, Jr Law Library, 214 Lewis Katz Bldg, 16802. SAN 314-383X. Tel: 814-865-8861. Web Site: pennstatelaw.psu.edu/library. *Assoc Dean, Libr & Info Serv, Dir, Law Libr,* Steven Hinckley; Tel: 814-867-0390, E-mail: sdh14@psu.edu; *Assoc Dir, Law Librn,* Theresa K Tarves; Tel: 814-863-6861, E-mail: tkb115@psu.edu; *Head, Coll Serv, Ref Librn,* Lauren Gluckman; Tel: 814-865-2298, E-mail: lig2@psu.edu; *Head, Fac Serv,* Rebecca A Mattsen; Tel: 814-867-2239, E-mail: ram6023@psu.edu; *Head, Instrul Serv,* Andrew J Tig Wartluft; Tel: 814-865-8875, E-mail: ajw5743@psu.edu; *Ref & Info Serv Librn,* Jenny Ham; Tel: 814-863-0885, E-mail: juh1421@psu.edu; Staff 14 (MLS 6, Non-MLS 8)
Founded 1834. Enrl 620; Fac 35; Highest Degree: Doctorate
Library Holdings: Bk Titles 103,610; Bk Vols 451,196; Per Subs 1,482
Special Collections: US Document Depository
Subject Interests: European commun law, Intl human rights
Wireless access
Function: ILL available, Prof lending libr, Ref & res, VHS videos
Partic in Interlibrary Delivery Service of Pennsylvania; OCLC Online Computer Library Center, Inc
Open Mon-Fri 8-5

C PENNSYLVANIA STATE UNIVERSITY LIBRARIES*, Pattee Library & Paterno Library, 510 Paterno Library, 16802. SAN 359-601X. Tel: 814-865-0401. FAX: 814-865-3665. Web Site: www.libraries.psu.edu. *Dean of Univ Libr & Scholarly Communications,* Barbara I Dewey; E-mail: bid1@psu.edu; *Dir of Develop,* Bob Darrah; Tel: 814-865-2258, E-mail: rjd18@psu.edu; *Head, Access Serv, Head, User Serv,* Ann Snowman; Tel: 814-863-1362, E-mail: ams32@psu.edu; *Head, Cat & Metadata Serv,* Ann Copeland; Tel: 814-865-2259, E-mail: auc1@psu.edu; *Head, Conserv, Head, Digitization & Presv Dept,* L Suzanne Kellerman; Tel:

814-863-4696, E-mail: lsk3@psu.edu; *Head, Research Informatics & Publishing,* Cynthia Hudson-Vitale; Tel: 814-865-2095, E-mail: cuv185@psu.edu; *Mgr, Pub Relations & Mkt,* Jill Shockey; Tel: 814-863-4240, E-mail: jss140@psu.edu; Staff 531 (MLS 161, Non-MLS 370)
Founded 1857. Enrl 91,061; Fac 5,625; Highest Degree: Doctorate
Library Holdings: Bk Vols 5,365,489; Per Subs 99,091
Special Collections: Ambit Magazine Archives; American Literature (Hay & Pattee Coll); Amy Bonner Coll; Australiana (Moody & Sutherland Coll), bks & pictures; Barbara Hackman Franklin Papers; Be Glad Then America, opera recs & papers; Bibles (Plumb Coll); Black Literature Coll; Boal Family Papers; Christopher Logue Papers; Conrad Richter Coll, ms; Edward Lucie-Smith Papers; Eric A Walker Papers; Erwin Mueller Papers; Eugene Wettstone Coll; Evan Pugh Coll & Papers; Fay S Lincoln Photography Coll; Fred L Pattee Papers; Fred Waring Archives & Music Library; George M Rhodes Papers; George W Atherton Papers; German-American Literature (Allison-Shelley Coll), bks, ms; Glass Bottle Blowers Association Archives; Henry M Shoemaker Coll; I W Abel Papers; Jacques Brunius Coll; John C Griffiths Papers; John O'Hara Coll; Joseph Priestley Coll; Kenneth Burke Coll; Maurice Goddard Papers; National Committee for Citizens in Education Archives; Noran Kersta Television History Coll; Pennsylvania AFL-CIO Archives; Pennsylvania Art Education Association Archives; Pennsylvania German Imprints (Ammon Stapleton Coll); Pennsylvania Imprints; Peter Porter Coll; Ramon del Valle-Inclan Coll; Richard Henry Stoddard & Elizabeth Drew Barstow Stoddard Coll, ms; Roxburghe Club Coll; Russell E Marker Papers; Science Fiction Coll; Sebastian Martorana Papers; United Wallpaper Craftsmen of North America Archives; Vance Packard Papers; Warren S Smith Papers; William C Darrah Cartes de Visite Coll; William Frear Papers; William G Waring Papers
Subject Interests: Agr, Archit, Art, Behav sci, Commonwealth, Feminism, Hist, Latin Am lit, Natural sci, Soc sci
Wireless access
Function: Archival coll, AV serv, Distance learning, Doc delivery serv, E-Reserves, Electronic databases & coll, Family literacy, Homebound delivery serv, ILL available, Online info literacy tutorials on the web & in blackboard, Photocopying/Printing, Ref serv available
Publications: Guide to the University Libraries; Library Bibliographical Series; The Library (Newsletter)
Partic in Association of Research Libraries; OCLC Online Computer Library Center, Inc; OCLC Research Library Partnership; Partnership for Academic Library Collaborative & Innovation
Special Services for the Blind - Assistive/Adapted tech devices, equip & products; Low vision equip; Reader equip; Reading & writing aids; ZoomText magnification & reading software

Departmental Libraries:

ARCHITECTURE & LANDSCAPE ARCHITECTURE, 111 Stuckeman Family Bldg, 16802-1912, SAN 359-6044. Tel: 814-865-3614. E-mail: UL-ARCH@lists.psu.edu. Web Site: libraries.psu.edu/architecture. *Head Librn,* Henry Pisciotta; Tel: 814-865-6778, E-mail: hap10@psu.edu; *Librn,* Tara Murray; Tel: 814-865-0660, E-mail: tem10@psu.edu. Subject Specialists: *German (Lang), Lit, Slavic (Lang),* Tara Murray; Staff 4 (MLS 1, Non-MLS 3)
Open Mon-Thurs 7:45am-11pm, Fri 7:45-6, Sat 1-6, Sun Noon-11

FLETCHER L BYROM EARTH & MINERAL SCIENCES LIBRARY, 105 Deike Bldg, 16802, SAN 359-6079. Tel: 814-865-9517. E-mail: EMSL@psu.edu. Web Site: libraries.psu.edu/ems. *Distinguished Librn, Head of Libr,* Linda Musser; Tel: 814-863-7073, E-mail: lrm4@psu.edu; *Librn,* Elise D Gowen; Tel: 814-863-7324, E-mail: edg16@psu.edu. Subject Specialists: *Earth sci, Mineral sci,* Elise D Gowen; Staff 4 (MLS 2, Non-MLS 2)
Founded 1931. Highest Degree: Doctorate
Subject Interests: Earth sci, Geog, Mat sci, Meteorology, Mining
Open Mon-Thurs 7:45am-11pm, Fri 7:45-6, Sat 1-5, Sun 1-11

EBERLY FAMILY SPECIAL COLLECTIONS LIBRARY, 104 Paterno Library, 16802-1808. Tel: 814-865-1793, 814-865-7931. E-mail: spcollections@psu.edu. Web Site: libraries.psu.edu/specialcollections. *Head of Libr,* Jennifer Meehan; E-mail: jim6012@psu.edu; *Head, Hist Coll & Labor Archives,* James Quigel; Tel: 814-863-3181, E-mail: jpq1@psu.edu; *Curator, Exhibitions Coordr,* Clara Drummond; E-mail: cjd86@psu.edu; Staff 21 (MLS 4, Non-MLS 17)
Founded 1904. Highest Degree: Doctorate
Library Holdings: Bk Vols 200,000
Subject Interests: Archives, Manuscripts, Rare bks
Open Mon-Fri 9-5, Sun 1-5
Restriction: Non-circulating

ENGINEERING, 325 Hammond Bldg, 16802, SAN 359-6109. Tel: 814-865-3451. E-mail: UL-ENGR@lists.psu.edu. Web Site: www.libraries.psu.edu/engineering. *Head, Eng Libr,* Beth Thomsett-Scott; Tel: 814-865-3697, E-mail: ect9@psu.edu; *Eng Librn,* Paul J Mcmonigle; Tel: 814-865-7005, E-mail: pmj201@psu.edu; Staff 7 (MLS 3, Non-MLS 4)
Open Mon-Thurs 7:45am-11pm, Fri 7:45-6, Sat Noon-5, Sun Noon-11

DONALD W HAMER CENTER FOR MAPS & GEOSPATIAL INFORMATION, One Central Pattee Library, Lower Level, 16802-1807. Tel: 814-863-0094. E-mail: ul-maps@lists.psu.edu. Web Site: libraries.psu.edu/maps. *Librn,* Nathan Piekielek; Tel: 814-865-3703, E-mail: nbp104@psu.edu; Staff 3 (MLS 1, Non-MLS 2)
Open Mon-Fri 9-7, Sun 10-7

LIBRARY LEARNING SERVICES, 216 Pattee Tower, 16802-1803. Tel: 814-865-9257. FAX: 814-865-3665. E-mail: ul-instruct@psu.edu. Web Site: libraries.psu.edu/about/departments/library-learning-services. *Head, Learning Serv,* Rebecca K Miller Waltz; Tel: 814-865-3064, E-mail: rkm17@psu.edu; *Open Education Librn,* Amanda Larson; Tel: 814-863-3305, E-mail: acl49@psu.edu; *Student Engagement Coord,* Hailley Fargo; Tel: 814-865-1850, E-mail: hmf14@psu.edu; *Info Literacy Librn,* Anne Behler; Tel: 814-863-3832, E-mail: acb10@psu.edu; *Info Literacy Librn,* Glenn N Masuchika; Tel: 814-867-2229, E-mail: gnm1@psu.edu; *Info Literacy Librn, Learning Technologies Coordr,* Emily Rimland; Tel: 814-863-7355, E-mail: elf113@psu.edu; *Online Learning Librn,* Victoria Raish; Tel: 814-863-9750, E-mail: vrc112@psu.edu; *Ref & Instruction Librn,* Dawn Amsberry; Tel: 814-865-5093, E-mail: dua4@psu.edu; Staff 10 (MLS 6, Non-MLS 4)

LIFE SCIENCES, 408 Paterno Library, 16802-1811. Tel: 814-865-7056. E-mail: UL-LIFE-SCI@psu.edu. Web Site: libraries.psu.edu/lifesciences. *Head Librn,* Amy Paster; Tel: 814-865-3708, E-mail: alp4@psu.edu; *Agr Sci Librn,* Helen Smith; Tel: 814-865-3706, E-mail: hfs1@psu.edu; *Biological Sci Librn,* Janet Hughes; Tel: 814-865-3705, E-mail: jah19@psu.edu; *Health Sci Librn, Liaison Librn,* Dr Christina L Wissinger, PhD; Tel: 814-863-1359, E-mail: clw68@psu.edu; *Nursing Librn,* Kat Phillips; Tel: 814-865-7313, E-mail: kec5013@psu.edu. Subject Specialists: *Entomology, Mycology, Turfgrass,* Amy Paster; *Allied health,* Kat Phillips; Staff 7 (MLS 5, Non-MLS 2)
Founded 1888. Highest Degree: Doctorate
Special Collections: Kneebone Mushroom Reference Library
Open Mon-Thurs 7:30am-2am, Fri 7:30-7, Sat 10-7, Sun 10am-2am

MARY M & BERTIL E LOFSTROM LIBRARY, 76 University Dr, Hazleton, 18202, SAN 314-6146. Tel: 570-450-3170. FAX: 570-450-3128. E-mail: UL-HAZLETON@lists.psu.edu. Web Site: libraries.psu.edu/hazleton. *Head Librn,* Valerie A Lynn; Tel: 570-450-3172, E-mail: vag3@psu.edu; *Ref & Instruction Librn,* Shannon G Richie; Tel: 570-450-3562, E-mail: sgr1@psu.edu; *Info Res & Serv Support Spec,* Eric Angel; Tel: 570-450-3171, E-mail: ema33@psu.edu; *Info Res & Serv Support Spec,* Lisa Hartz; Tel: 570-450-3127, E-mail: lah41@psu.edu; Staff 6 (MLS 2, Non-MLS 4)
Founded 1934. Enrl 1,316; Fac 69
Library Holdings: Bk Vols 80,500; Per Subs 230
Partic in Big Ten Academic Alliance; OCLC Online Computer Library Center, Inc; Research Libraries Information Network
Open Mon-Thurs 7:30am-10pm, Fri 7:30-5, Sun 2-8

MICROFORMS & GOVERNMENT INFORMATION, 208 Paterno Library, 2nd Flr, 16802-1804. Tel: 814-863-0377. E-mail: ul-microgov@psu.edu. Web Site: www.libraries.psu.edu/microgov. *Librn,* Eric Novotny; Tel: 814-865-1014, E-mail: enc1@psu.edu. Subject Specialists: *Hist,* Eric Novotny; Staff 4 (MLS 1, Non-MLS 3)
Open Mon-Fri 8-7, Sat & Sun 10-5

GEORGE & SHERRY MIDDLEMAS ARTS & HUMANITIES LIBRARY, Pennsylvania State University, W 337 Pattee Library, 16802-1801. Tel: 814-863-4547. FAX: 814-863-7502. E-mail: artshumslib@psu.edu. Web Site: libraries.psu.edu/artshumanities. *Music Librn,* Amanda Maple; Tel: 814-863-1401, E-mail: alm8@psu.edu; *Librn,* Jade Atwill, PhD; Tel: 814-863-0738, E-mail: yya2@psu.edu; *Librn,* Tara Murray; Tel: 814-865-0660, E-mail: tem10@psu.edu; *Librn,* Manuel Ostos; Tel: 814-865-3693, E-mail: muo16@psu.edu; *Archit/Art Librn,* Henry Pisciotta; Tel: 814-865-6778, E-mail: hap10@psu.edu; *Paterno Family Librn for Lit,* William Brockman; Tel: 814-865-9718, E-mail: uxb5@psu.edu; *Tombros Librn for Classics & Humanities,* Charles E Jones; Tel: 814-867-4872, E-mail: cej14@psu.edu. Subject Specialists: *Asian studies,* Jade Atwill, PhD; *German (Lang), Lit, Slavic (Lang),* Tara Murray; *Lit, Romance langs,* Manuel Ostos; Staff 10 (MLS 8, Non-MLS 2)
Open Mon-Thurs 7:30am-2am, Fri 7:30-7, Sat 10-7, Sun 10am-2am

PHYSICAL & MATHEMATICAL SCIENCES, 201 Davey Lab, 16802-6301, SAN 359-6168. Tel: 814-865-7617. FAX: 814-865-2565. E-mail: ul-pams@psu.edu. Web Site: libraries.psu.edu/pams. *Head of Libr,* Nan Butkovich; Tel: 814-865-3716, E-mail: njb2@psu.edu; *Head, STEM for Engagement & Outreach,* John J Meier; Tel: 814-867-1448, E-mail: jjm38@psu.edu; Staff 4 (MLS 2, Non-MLS 2)
Founded 2005
Special Collections: US Patent Depository
Subject Interests: Astronomy, Astrophysics, Chem, Math, Physics, Statistics
Open Mon-Thurs 7:45am-Midnight, Fri 7:45am-8pm, Sat Noon-7, Sun Noon-Midnight

WILLIAM & JOAN SCHREYER BUSINESS LIBRARY, 309 Paterno Library, 3rd Flr, 16802-1810. FAX: 814-863-6370. Reference E-mail: ul-buslib@lists.psu.edu. Web Site: libraries.psu.edu/business. *Head of Libr, Librn,* Diane W Zabel; Tel: 814-865-1013, E-mail: dxz2@psu.edu;

Bus Librn, Kevin Harwell; Tel: 814-865-0141, E-mail: krh7@psulias.psu.edu; *Bus Liaison Librn,* Carmen Cole; Tel: 814-865-6493, E-mail: ccc143@psu.edu; *Bus Liaison Librn,* Lauren Reiter; Tel: 814-865-4414, E-mail: lmr29@psu.edu; *Foster Communications Librn,* Jeff A Knapp; Tel: 814-867-6501, E-mail: jak47@psu.edu. Subject Specialists: *Info sci,* Carmen Cole; Staff 6 (MLS 4, Non-MLS 2)
Open Mon-Thurs 7:30am-2am, Fri 7:30-7, Sat 10-7, Sun 10am-2am

SOCIAL SCIENCES & EDUCATION, 208 Paterno Library, 2nd & 5th Flrs, 16802-1809. Tel: 814-865-4547. E-mail: UL-ssed@lists.psu.edu. Web Site: libraries.psu.edu/ssed. *Interim Head of Libr,* Nonny Schlotzhauer; Tel: 814-863-4644, E-mail: vxs120@psu.edu; *Data Spec, Govt Info Spec, Librn,* Stephen Woods; Tel: 814-865-0665, E-mail: sjw31@psu.edu; *Soc Sci Librn,* Andrew Dudash; Tel: 814-867-1629, E-mail: amd846@psu.edu; *Soc Sci Librn,* Sylvia A Owiny, PhD; Tel: 814-865-8864, E-mail: san17@psu.edu; Staff 8 (MLS 6, Non-MLS 2)
Library Holdings: Per Subs 1,200
Open Mon-Thurs 7:30am-2am, Fri 7:30-7, Sat 10-7, Sun 10-2

VAIRO LIBRARY, Brandywine Campus, 25 Yearsley Mill Rd, Media, 19063-5596, SAN 314-7495. Tel: 610-892-1380. E-mail: UL-BRANDYWINE@lists.psu.edu. Web Site: libraries.psu.edu/brandywine. *Head Librn,* Teresa Slobuski; E-mail: sut477@psu.edu; Staff 4 (MLS 2, Non-MLS 2)
Founded 1967. Enrl 1,734; Fac 75
Library Holdings: Bk Vols 75,000; Per Subs 100
Partic in OCLC Online Computer Library Center, Inc; Research Libraries Information Network
Open Mon-Thurs 7:30am-9pm, Fri 7:30-5, Sun 3-7

UPPER BURRELL

C PENNSYLVANIA STATE UNIVERSITY, NEW KENSINGTON*, Elisabeth S Blissell Library, 3550 Seventh St Rd, Rte 780, 15068-1798. SAN 314-8149. Tel: 724-334-6071. FAX: 724-334-6113. E-mail: UL-NEW-KEN@lists.psu.edu. Web Site: libraries.psu.edu/newkensington. *Head Librn,* Jennifer R Gilley; Tel: 724-334-6076, E-mail: jrg15@psu.edu; *Ref Librn,* Amy Rustic; Tel: 724-334-6072, E-mail: aer123@psu.edu; Staff 2 (Non-MLS 2)
Founded 1958. Enrl 983; Fac 40
Library Holdings: Bk Vols 36,000; Per Subs 100
Wireless access
Partic in OCLC Online Computer Library Center, Inc; Research Libraries Information Network

UPPER DARBY

P UPPER DARBY TOWNSHIP & SELLERS MEMORIAL FREE PUBLIC LIBRARY*, 76 S State Rd, 19082. SAN 359-6192. Tel: 610-789-4440. Reference FAX: 610-789-6363. Administration FAX: 610-789-5319. E-mail: upperdarby@delcolibraries.org. Web Site: www.udlibraries.org. *Dir,* Jennifer Stock; E-mail: uddirector@delcolibraries.org; *Asst Dir, Tech Serv,* Elaine Irwin; E-mail: techservices@udlibraries.org; *Head, Adult Serv,* Maria Polymenakos; E-mail: circservices@udlibraries.org; *Head, Children's Servx, Head, Youth Serv,* Charlotte Ryan; Staff 22 (MLS 9, Non-MLS 13)
Founded 1930. Pop 81,831; Circ 293,318
Library Holdings: Bk Vols 122,050; Per Subs 251
Subject Interests: Local hist
Automation Activity & Vendor Info: (Circulation) Innovative Interfaces, Inc
Wireless access
Function: Homebound delivery serv, ILL available, Prog for adults, Prog for children & young adult, Ref serv available, Summer reading prog
Mem of Delaware County Libraries
Open Mon-Fri 9-9, Sat 9-5, Sun (Sept-May) 1:30-5
Friends of the Library Group
Branches: 2
MUNICIPAL, 501 Bywood Ave, 19082, SAN 359-6222. Tel: 610-734-7649. FAX: 610-734-5781. *Br Librn,* Karen Healy
Library Holdings: Bk Titles 23,504; Per Subs 44
Open Mon & Tues 10-9, Wed & Thurs 10-6, Fri 10-5, Sat 10-3
Friends of the Library Group
PRIMOS BRANCH, 409 Ashland Ave, Secane, 19018, SAN 359-6249. Tel: 610-622-8091. FAX: 484-461-9026. *Br Librn,* Position Currently Open
Library Holdings: Bk Vols 30,260; Per Subs 53
Open Mon-Thurs 9-9, Fri 9-5, Sat 10-3
Friends of the Library Group

UPPER ST CLAIR

P UPPER ST CLAIR TOWNSHIP LIBRARY*, 1820 McLaughlin Run Rd, 15241-2397. SAN 315-1204. Tel: 412-835-5540. FAX: 412-835-6763. Web Site: www.twpusc.org/library/library-home. *Dir,* Helen Palascak; E-mail: palascakh@einetwork.net; *Head, Children's Servx,* Debra Conn; *Head, Tech Serv,* Maureen Case; *Circ Coordr,* Vanessa Ryzner; Staff 11 (MLS 11)
Founded 1957. Pop 20,053; Circ 394,641
Jul 2018-Jun 2019. Mats Exp $1,154,973, Books $79,733, Per/Ser (Incl. Access Fees) $8,811, AV Mat $25,344. Sal $718,619
Library Holdings: Audiobooks 4,682; DVDs 5,006; Bk Titles 57,149; Per Subs 94
Automation Activity & Vendor Info: (Acquisitions) Innovative Interfaces, Inc - Millennium; (Cataloging) Innovative Interfaces, Inc - Millennium; (Circulation) Innovative Interfaces, Inc - Millennium; (OPAC) Innovative Interfaces, Inc - Millennium; (Serials) Innovative Interfaces, Inc - Millennium
Wireless access
Function: 24/7 Electronic res, 24/7 Online cat, 3D Printer, Activity rm, Adult bk club, After school storytime, Art programs, Audiobks on Playaways & MP3, Audiobks via web, Bi-weekly Writer's Group, Bk club(s), Bk reviews (Group), Bks on CD, Chess club, Children's prog, Computer training, Computers for patron use, Digital talking bks, E-Reserves, Electronic databases & coll, Free DVD rentals, Genealogy discussion group, Holiday prog, Home delivery & serv to seniorr ctr & nursing homes, Homebound delivery serv, ILL available, Internet access, Large print keyboards, Life-long learning prog for all ages, Magazines, Magnifiers for reading, Mail & tel request accepted, Mango lang, Meeting rooms, Movies, Music CDs, Online cat, OverDrive digital audio bks, Photocopying/Printing, Preschool outreach, Printer for laptops & handheld devices, Prog for adults, Prog for children & young adult, Ref serv available, Scanner, Serves people with intellectual disabilities, STEM programs, Story hour, Study rm, Summer & winter reading prog, Tax forms, Teen prog, Wheelchair accessible, Workshops
Mem of Allegheny County Library Association (ACLA)
Open Mon-Thurs 9:30-9, Fri & Sat 9:30-5, Sun (Sept-May) 1-5
Friends of the Library Group

VANDERGRIFT

P VANDERGRIFT PUBLIC LIBRARY ASSOCIATION*, 128C Washington Ave, 15690-1214. SAN 315-2952. Tel: 724-568-2212. FAX: 724-568-3862. E-mail: vandergriftpubliclibrary@comcast.net. Web Site: www.vandergriftpubliclibrary.org/wordpress. *Dir,* Vanessa Groholski
Founded 1901. Pop 5,904; Circ 23,963
Library Holdings: Bk Titles 19,000; Per Subs 40
Wireless access
Mem of Westmoreland County Federated Library System
Open Mon, Tues & Thurs 1-8, Wed 10-8, Fri 10-5, Sat 8-3

VILLANOVA

S DEVEREUX, Advanced Behavioral Health Library, 444 Devereux Dr, 19085. SAN 321-6349. Tel: 610-542-3051. Web Site: www.devereux.org. *Library Liaison,* Kara Krissel; E-mail: kkrissel@devereux.org
Founded 1957
Library Holdings: Bk Titles 2,100; Per Subs 50
Special Collections: Mental Health (ICTR Coll), A-tapes; Psychology (ICTR Psychodiagnostic Test Coll)
Subject Interests: Psychiat, Spec educ
Automation Activity & Vendor Info: (OPAC) Sydney
Wireless access
Partic in DEVIC; National Network of Libraries of Medicine Region 1; OCLC Online Computer Library Center, Inc; Proquest Dialog
Open Mon-Fri 9-5

C VILLANOVA UNIVERSITY*, Falvey Memorial Library, 800 Lancaster Ave, 19085. SAN 359-6346. Tel: 610-519-4270. Web Site: library.villanova.edu. *Univ Librn,* Millicent Gaskell; Tel: 610-519-4290, E-mail: millicent.gaskell@villanova.edu; *Assoc Univ Librn for Colls & Stewardship,* Jee Davis; Tel: 610-519-7821, E-mail: jeehyun.davis@villanova.edu; Staff 32 (MLS 22, Non-MLS 10)
Founded 1842. Enrl 10,000; Fac 500; Highest Degree: Doctorate
Special Collections: Digital Library; Dime Novel Coll; Elbert G Hubbard Coll; Irish American History & Literature (Joseph McGarrity Coll); Mendel Coll; Saint Augustine Coll; Sherman-Thackara Coll; Smith Antique Map Coll
Automation Activity & Vendor Info: (Acquisitions) Ex Libris Group; (Cataloging) Ex Libris Group; (Circulation) Ex Libris Group
Wireless access
Partic in LYRASIS; OCLC Online Computer Library Center, Inc; Partnership for Academic Library Collaborative & Innovation; Philadelphia Area Consortium of Special Collections Libraries
Departmental Libraries:
CL LAW LIBRARY, Villanova University Charles Widger School of Law, 299 N Spring Mill Rd, 19085, SAN 359-6370. Tel: 610-519-7020. *Asst Dean, Libr & Info Serv, Asst Prof of Law,* Amy Emerson; Tel: 610-519-7023; *Assoc Dir, Res & Info Serv,* Amy Spare; Tel: 610-519-7188, E-mail: spare@law.villanova.edu; *Assoc Dir, Coll Mgt,* Steve Elkins; Tel: 610-519-7780, E-mail: elkins@law.villanova.edu; Staff 23 (MLS 10, Non-MLS 13)
Founded 1953. Enrl 750; Fac 35; Highest Degree: Doctorate

Library Holdings: Microforms 1,121,935; Bk Titles 146,361; Bk Vols 337,075; Per Subs 3,703
Special Collections: Church & State Coll. US Document Depository
Subject Interests: Tax law
Automation Activity & Vendor Info: (Acquisitions) Innovative Interfaces, Inc; (Cataloging) Innovative Interfaces, Inc; (Circulation) Innovative Interfaces, Inc; (ILL) OCLC; (OPAC) Innovative Interfaces, Inc; (Serials) Innovative Interfaces, Inc
Publications: New Aquisitions

WALLINGFORD

P HELEN KATE FURNESS FREE LIBRARY*, 100 N Providence Rd, 19086. SAN 315-3002. Tel: 610-566-9331. FAX: 610-566-9337. E-mail: furnesslibrary@delcolibraries.org. Web Site: www.hkflibrary.org. *Libr Dir,* Jennifer Stock; Tel: 610-566-9331, E-mail: fsdirector@delcolibraries.org; *Ch,* Lori L Friedgen-Veitch; *Evening Ref Librn,* Meg Hawkins; *Evening Ref Librn,* Molly Deutsch; *Tech Serv Librn,* Maricela Ayala; Staff 7 (MLS 6, Non-MLS 1)
Founded 1902. Pop 15,000; Circ 76,500
Library Holdings: Bk Titles 44,400; Per Subs 90; Talking Bks 392
Wireless access
Mem of Delaware County Libraries
Open Mon-Thurs 10-5 & 7-9, Fri 10-5, Sat 10-3, Sun 1-4

R OHEV SHALOM SYNAGOGUE*, Ray Doblitz Memorial Library, Two Chester Rd, 19086. SAN 315-3010. Tel: 610-874-1465. FAX: 610-874-1466. E-mail: library@ohev.net. Web Site: www.ohev.net. *Librn,* Amy Graham
Founded 1955
Library Holdings: Bk Titles 5,300; Bk Vols 5,500; Per Subs 14
Subject Interests: Judaica
Automation Activity & Vendor Info: (Cataloging) JayWil Software Development, Inc
Wireless access

R PENDLE HILL LIBRARY*, 338 Plush Mill Rd, 19086. SAN 372-9281. Tel: 610-566-4507. Toll Free Tel: 800-742-3150. FAX: 610-566-3679. E-mail: info@pendlehill.org. Web Site: www.pendlehill.org/explore/community-life/library. *Exec Dir,* Jennifer Karsten; E-mail: jkarsten@pendlehill.org
Library Holdings: Bk Vols 12,000; Per Subs 20
Subject Interests: Quakers, Relig
Wireless access

WARMINSTER

P WARMINSTER TOWNSHIP FREE LIBRARY*, 1076 Emma Lane, 18974. SAN 315-3053. Tel: 215-672-4362. FAX: 215-672-3604. E-mail: hellowa@buckslib.org. Web Site: warminstertownship.org/library. *Dir,* Tracey Reed; E-mail: reedt@buckslib.org; *Ad,* Heather Lipinski; E-mail: lipinskih@buckslib.org; *Youth Serv Librn,* Ann Duffy; E-mail: duffya@buckslib.org; *Children's & Teen Serv,* Katie Hansen; E-mail: hansenk@buckslib.org; Staff 12 (MLS 3.4, Non-MLS 8.6)
Founded 1960. Pop 31,875; Circ 221,485
Library Holdings: AV Mats 5,720; Bk Vols 100,936; Per Subs 91
Automation Activity & Vendor Info: (Circulation) SirsiDynix-WorkFlows; (OPAC) SirsiDynix-iBistro
Wireless access
Function: Bk club(s), Bks on cassette, Bks on CD, Children's prog, Computers for patron use, E-Reserves, Electronic databases & coll, ILL available, Internet access, Music CDs, Online cat, OverDrive digital audio bks, Photocopying/Printing, Prog for adults, Prog for children & young adult, Spoken cassettes & CDs, Spoken cassettes & DVDs, Summer reading prog, Tax forms, Teen prog, VHS videos
Publications: Newsletter
Mem of Bucks County Free Library
Open Mon-Wed 10-8, Thurs & Sat 10-5, Fri 12-5, Sun 12-4
Friends of the Library Group

CM WON INSTITUTE OF GRADUATE STUDIES LIBRARY, 800 Jacksonville Rd, 18974. Tel: 215-884-8942, Ext 208. Web Site: woninstitute.edu/graduate-studies/resources-for/current-students/library. *Librn,* Linda Jones; E-mail: librarian@woninstitute.edu
Subject Interests: Acupuncture, Buddhism, Christian studies, Cross-cultural studies, Hist of relig, Psychol, Traditional Chinese med
Wireless access
Partic in Tri-State College Library Cooperative
Open Mon-Fri 9-5:30

WARREN

WARREN COUNTY HISTORICAL SOCIETY*, Library & Archives, 210 Fourth Ave, 16365. (Mail add: PO Box 427, 16365-0427), SAN 327-0459. Tel: 814-723-1795. FAX: 814-723-1795. E-mail: warrencountyhistory@aol.com. Web Site: www.warrenhistory.org. *Managing Dir,* Michelle Gray; *Prog Coordr,* Casey Ferry; *Curator,* Dr Ruth Barnes Shaw; Staff 3 (Non-MLS 3)
Founded 1900
Library Holdings: Bk Vols 2,200
Special Collections: Allegheny River Travel & History; Chief Cornplanter & the Seneca Indians; Historic Images 1900-2000; Horton Genealogy Coll; Lieutenant Governor Stone Coll
Subject Interests: Local hist
Publications: Cavalcade-Warren County's Second Century; Stepping Stones Magazine, 1955-Present
Open Mon-Fri 8:30-4:30
Restriction: Not a lending libr

M WARREN GENERAL HOSPITAL*, Health Sciences Library, Two Crescent Park W, 16365. SAN 370-6931. Tel: 814-723-4973, Ext 1825. FAX: 814-723-3785. E-mail: wghlibrary@gmail.com. *Libr Supvr,* Nancy Bean; Staff 1 (Non-MLS 1)
Library Holdings: Bk Titles 800; Per Subs 100
Partic in National Network of Libraries of Medicine Region 1
Restriction: Staff use only

P WARREN LIBRARY ASSOCIATION*, Warren Public Library, 205 Market St, 16365. SAN 315-3061. Tel: 814-723-4650. FAX: 814-723-4521. E-mail: wla@westpa.net. Web Site: www.warrenlibrary.org. *Dir,* Kelli Knapp; E-mail: kknapp@warrenlibrary.org; *IT & Security Mgr,* Dale Aikens; E-mail: daikens@warrenlibrary.org; *Adult Serv,* Jennifer Franklin; E-mail: jfranklin@warrenlibrary.org; *Cat,* Jenna Derr; E-mail: jderr@warrenlibrary.org; *Ch Serv,* Susan Slater; E-mail: sslater@warrenlibrary.org; *Extn Serv,* Leslie LaBarte; E-mail: llabarte@warrenlibrary.org; *ILL,* Julie Miller; E-mail: jmiller@warrenlibrary.org; *Ref (Info Servs),* Beverly Leonhardt; E-mail: bleonhardt@warrenlibrary.org; Staff 30 (MLS 7, Non-MLS 23)
Founded 1873. Pop 41,815; Circ 349,765
Library Holdings: Bk Vols 167,257; Per Subs 242
Special Collections: Local History; Local Newspapers 1824-current; Petroleum History Coll, bks, maps, pamphlets; Sheet Music, Popular Show Tunes, 1834-1955 (Robertson Music Coll). State Document Depository; US Document Depository
Automation Activity & Vendor Info: (Cataloging) Innovative Interfaces, Inc; (Circulation) Innovative Interfaces, Inc; (OPAC) Innovative Interfaces, Inc
Wireless access
Function: 24/7 Electronic res, 24/7 Online cat, Adult bk club, Archival coll, Art exhibits, Audiobks on Playaways & MP3, Audiobks via web, AV serv, Bks on CD, CD-ROM, Children's prog, Computer training, Computers for patron use, E-Readers, Electronic databases & coll, For res purposes, Free DVD rentals, Govt ref serv, Health sci info serv, Holiday prog, ILL available, Internet access, Life-long learning prog for all ages, Magazines, Mail & tel request accepted, Meeting rooms, Microfiche/film & reading machines, Movies, Music CDs, Online cat, Online ref, Outreach serv, Outside serv via phone, mail, e-mail & web, OverDrive digital audio bks, Photocopying/Printing, Preschool outreach, Printer for laptops & handheld devices, Prof lending libr, Prog for adults, Prog for children & young adult, Ref & res, Ref serv available, Res assist avail, Res libr, Scanner, Serves people with intellectual disabilities, Story hour, Study rm, Summer reading prog, Tax forms, Telephone ref, VHS videos, Wheelchair accessible, Workshops
Open Mon-Thurs 10-8, Fri & Sat 10-5
Restriction: Borrowing requests are handled by ILL, ID required to use computers (Ltd hrs), Non-circulating coll, Non-circulating of rare bks, Non-resident fee
Friends of the Library Group

WASHINGTON

P CITIZENS LIBRARY*, 55 S College St, 15301. SAN 315-3088. Tel: 724-222-2400. FAX: 724-222-2606. E-mail: citlib@citlib.org. Web Site: www.washlibs.org/Citizens. *Dir,* Diane L Ambrose; E-mail: dambrose@citlib.org; *Asst Dir, District Consult Librn,* Melinda Tanner; E-mail: mtanner@citlib.org; *Genealogy Librn,* Ella Hatfield; E-mail: ehatfield@citlib.org; *Ch Mgr,* Rebecca Smiley; E-mail: rsmiley@citlib.org; *Circ Serv Mgr,* Kathy Pienkowski; E-mail: kpien@citlib.org; *Coll Develop Mgr,* Carol Levy; E-mail: clevy@citlib.org; *Circ Asst,* Taryn King; E-mail: tking@citlib.org; Staff 7 (MLS 7)
Founded 1870. Pop 54,519; Circ 170,024
Special Collections: Genealogy & Local History (Iams Coll), ms. State Document Depository
Automation Activity & Vendor Info: (Acquisitions) Innovative Interfaces, Inc; (Cataloging) Innovative Interfaces, Inc; (Circulation) Innovative Interfaces, Inc; (OPAC) Innovative Interfaces, Inc
Wireless access
Function: Archival coll, ILL available
Mem of Washington County Library System
Partic in Asn for Libr Info; OCLC Online Computer Library Center, Inc

Special Services for the Deaf - Bks on deafness & sign lang; High interest/low vocabulary bks; Spec interest per; TDD equip
Open Mon-Thurs 10-8, Fri & Sat 10-5:30
Friends of the Library Group

J PENN COMMERCIAL BUSINESS/TECHNICAL SCHOOL*, 242 Oak Spring Rd, 15301. Tel: 724-222-5330. Toll Free Tel: 888-309-7484. FAX: 724-222-4722. Web Site: www.penncommercial.net. *Librn,* Position Currently Open
Founded 1929
Library Holdings: Bk Titles 2,120; Bk Vols 2,350; Per Subs 29
Open Mon-Fri 8-5

C WASHINGTON & JEFFERSON COLLEGE LIBRARY*, Clark Family Library, 60 S Lincoln St, 15301. SAN 315-310X. Tel: 724-223-6070. Reference Tel: 724-223-6072. Administration Tel: 724-223-6071. FAX: 724-223-5272. Web Site: libguides.washjeff.edu. *Dir, Libr Serv,* Ronalee Ciocco; Tel: 724-503-1001, Ext 3039, E-mail: rciocco@washjeff.edu; *Librn,* John Henderson; Tel: 724-503-1001, Ext 3032, E-mail: jhenderson@washjeff.edu; *Colls Librn, Research Librn,* Samantha Martin; Tel: 724-503-1001, Ext 3127, E-mail: smartin@washjeff.edu; *Copyright Librn,* Beth Miller; Tel: 724-223-6069, E-mail: bmiller@washjeff.edu; *Syst Librn,* Jacqueline Laick; Tel: 724-223-6539, E-mail: jlaick@washjeff.edu; *ILL Mgr, Supvr, User Serv,* Rachael Bolden; E-mail: rbolden@washjeff.edu; *Supvr, User Serv,* Jayne Silfee; E-mail: jsilfee@washjeff.edu; *Archivist,* Kelly Helm; Tel: 724-223-6048, E-mail: khelm@washjeff.edu; *Acq, Spec Projects,* Cheri L Duball; Tel: 724-223-6104, E-mail: cduball@washjeff.edu; *Ser,* Carla V Myers; Tel: 724-223-6547, E-mail: cmyers@washjeff.edu; Staff 10 (MLS 5.5, Non-MLS 4.5)
Founded 1781
Library Holdings: AV Mats 8,484; e-books 13,000; Bk Titles 153,257; Bk Vols 161,130; Per Subs 522
Special Collections: College History; Washington County (Historical); Western Pennsylvania & Upper Ohio Valley, ms
Subject Interests: Behav sci, Hist, Natural sci, Soc sci
Automation Activity & Vendor Info: (Acquisitions) SirsiDynix; (Cataloging) SirsiDynix; (Circulation) SirsiDynix; (Course Reserve) SirsiDynix; (OPAC) SirsiDynix; (Serials) SirsiDynix
Wireless access
Partic in LYRASIS; OCLC Online Computer Library Center, Inc; OhioNET; Partnership for Academic Library Collaborative & Innovation
Open Mon-Thurs 8am-2am, Fri 8am-9pm, Sat 9-6, Sun 11am-2am

S WASHINGTON COUNTY HISTORICAL SOCIETY*, Norma K Grimes Research Library, 49 E Maiden St, 15301. SAN 327-0637. Tel: 724-225-6740. FAX: 724-225-8495. Interlibrary Loan Service E-mail: wchs@wchspa.org. Web Site: www.wchspa.org/grimes. *Exec Dir,* Clay Kilgore; E-mail: clay@wchspa.net; *Research Librn,* Chuck Edgar; E-mail: research@wchspa.net
Founded 1900
Library Holdings: Bk Titles 1,847
Special Collections: Military History of Washington County
Open Tues-Fri 11-4

GL WASHINGTON COUNTY LAW LIBRARY*, One S Main St, Ste G004, 15301. SAN 315-3118. Tel: 724-228-6747. Web Site: www.washingtoncourts.us/pages/lawLibrary.aspx. *Law Librn,* Jamie Yancich; E-mail: jamie.yancich@washingtoncourts.us; *Asst Law Librn,* Suzanne McCord; Tel: 724-250-4026, E-mail: suzanne.mccord@washingtoncourts.us; Staff 2 (MLS 1, Non-MLS 1)
Founded 1867
Library Holdings: Bk Titles 1,250; Bk Vols 15,000; Per Subs 20; Spec Interest Per Sub 19
Subject Interests: Legal res, Local hist
Open Mon-Fri 9-4:30
Restriction: Non-circulating to the pub

P WASHINGTON COUNTY LIBRARY SYSTEM, 55 S College St, 15301. Tel: 724-222-2400, Ext 231. Web Site: washlibs.org. *Exec Dir,* Jessica Miller; E-mail: jmiller@citlib.org
Member Libraries: Avella Area Public Library; Bentleyville Public Library; Burgettstown Community Library; California Area Public Library; Charleroi Area Public Library; Chartiers-Houston Community Library; Citizens Library; Donora Public Library; Frank Sarris Public Library; Fredericktown Area Public Library; Heritage Public Library; Marianna Community Public Library; Monongahela Area Library; Peters Township Public Library

M WASHINGTON HOSPITAL*, Health Sciences Libraries, 155 Wilson Ave, 15301-3398. SAN 315-3126. Tel: 724-223-3144. FAX: 724-223-4096. Web Site: whs.org. *Dir,* Jamie Golden; E-mail: jgolden@whs.org; Staff 4 (MLS 1, Non-MLS 3)
Founded 1927
Subject Interests: Family practice, Internal med, Med, Nursing
Open Mon-Fri 7-3:30

WATERFORD

P WATERFORD PUBLIC LIBRARY*, 24 S Park Row, 16441. (Mail add: PO Box 820, 16441-0820), SAN 315-3150. Tel: 814-796-4729. FAX: 814-796-4729. E-mail: wpl@waterfordlibrary.org. Web Site: www.waterfordlibrary.org. *Librn,* Susan Osborn; Staff 1 (MLS 1)
Founded 1936. Pop 1,517; Circ 20,373
Jul 2014-Jun 2015 Income $34,760, State $3,742, City $15,875, County $7,047, Locally Generated Income $8,096. Mats Exp $7,578. Sal $13,851
Library Holdings: Audiobooks 260; Bk Vols 18,470; Per Subs 33
Automation Activity & Vendor Info: (Circulation) SirsiDynix; (OPAC) SirsiDynix
Wireless access
Open Mon & Fri 1-5, Tues 10-2, Wed 11-5, Thurs 7pm-9pm, Sat 9-3

WAVERLY

P WAVERLY MEMORIAL LIBRARY*, 1115 N Abington Rd, 18471. (Mail add: PO Box 142, 18471-0142), SAN 315-3169. Tel: 570-586-8191. FAX: 570-586-0185. E-mail: info@waverlycomm.org. Web Site: www.waverlycomm.com. *Exec Dir,* Maria Wilson
Pop 1,800; Circ 4,100
Library Holdings: Bk Vols 3,000
Subject Interests: Children's bks, Fiction
Open Mon-Fri 8-7

WAYMART

S STATE CORRECTIONAL INSTITUTION*, Waymart Library, PO Box 256, 18472-0256. Tel: 570-488-5811, Ext 3459. FAX: 570-488-2609. Web Site: www.cor.pa.gov/Facilities/StatePrisons/Pages/Waymart.aspx. *Librn,* Maria Suhadolnik; E-mail: msuhadolni@pa.gov
Library Holdings: Bk Vols 11,500; Per Subs 40
Automation Activity & Vendor Info: (Cataloging) Follett Software; (Circulation) Follett Software
Restriction: Not open to pub

WAYNE

P RADNOR MEMORIAL LIBRARY, 114 W Wayne Ave, 19087. Tel: 610-687-1124. E-mail: RML@radnorlibrary.org. Web Site: www.radnorlibrary.org. *Exec Dir,* Joyce Platfoot; E-mail: jplatfoot@radnorlibrary.org; *Head, Children's Servx,* Carrie Sturgill; E-mail: csturgill@radnorlibrary.org; *Head, Info Serv,* Joanne Iantorno; E-mail: jiantorno@radnorlibrary.org; Staff 14 (MLS 11, Non-MLS 3)
Founded 1892. Pop 31,531; Circ 156,790
Library Holdings: AV Mats 9,155; e-books 32,126; e-journals 174; Electronic Media & Resources 47; Bk Vols 115,302; Per Subs 111
Special Collections: Pennsylvania History; Reader Development Coll. Oral History
Subject Interests: Archit, Art, Drama, Foreign lang, Hist, Lit
Automation Activity & Vendor Info: (Acquisitions) Innovative Interfaces, Inc - Sierra; (Cataloging) Innovative Interfaces, Inc - Sierra; (Circulation) Innovative Interfaces, Inc - Sierra; (Course Reserve) Innovative Interfaces, Inc - Sierra; (ILL) Innovative Interfaces, Inc - Sierra; (Media Booking) Innovative Interfaces, Inc - Sierra; (OPAC) Innovative Interfaces, Inc - Sierra; (Serials) Innovative Interfaces, Inc - Sierra
Wireless access
Mem of Delaware County Libraries
Open Mon-Fri 9-9, Sat 9-5, Sun 1-5
Friends of the Library Group

J VALLEY FORGE MILITARY ACADEMY & COLLEGE*, May H Baker Memorial Library, 1001 Eagle Rd, 19087-3695. SAN 315-3193. Tel: 610-989-1359, 610-989-1364. Web Site: www.library.vfmac.edu. *Col Librn, Dir, Libr Serv,* Dana J Kerrigan; E-mail: dkerrigan@vfmac.edu; *Academy Librn,* Deborah Parsons; Tel: 610-989-1438, E-mail: dparsons@vfmac.edu; Staff 4 (MLS 2, Non-MLS 2)
Founded 1928. Enrl 535; Fac 72; Highest Degree: Associate
Library Holdings: AV Mats 500; Electronic Media & Resources 17; High Interest/Low Vocabulary Bk Vols 200; Bk Titles 50,000; Bk Vols 80,000; Per Subs 60
Special Collections: Military & Naval History Coll
Subject Interests: Classical lit, Govt, Mil sci, World hist
Automation Activity & Vendor Info: (Cataloging) Mandarin Library Automation; (Circulation) Mandarin Library Automation; (OPAC) Mandarin Library Automation
Wireless access
Publications: Competency Handbook; Faculty Library Partnership Project; How to Effectively Use the Library Information; Library Policies & Procedures; PathFinders; Strategic Developmental Plan for Library Services, Plans & Operations; Webs of the Week
Partic in Tri State Col Libr Coop

Open Mon-Thurs 8am-9:30pm, Fri 8-4, Sun 6:30pm-9:30pm
Restriction: Badge access after hrs

R WAYNE PRESBYTERIAN CHURCH LIBRARY, 125 E Lancaster Ave, 19087. SAN 315-3207. Tel: 610-688-8700. FAX: 610-688-8743. Web Site: waynepres.org. *Librn,* Pamela Jensen; E-mail: jens0581@umn.edu
Founded 1957
Library Holdings: Bk Vols 6,000; Per Subs 10
Wireless access
Open Mon-Fri 8:30-4:30

WAYNESBORO

P ALEXANDER HAMILTON MEMORIAL FREE LIBRARY, 45 E Main St, 17268-1691. SAN 315-3215. Tel: 717-762-3335. E-mail: staff@ahmfl.org. Web Site: www.ahmfl.org. *Exec Dir,* Linda May; E-mail: lindamay@ahmfl.org; Staff 1 (MLS 1)
Founded 1921. Pop 24,500; Circ 139,400
Library Holdings: Bk Titles 57,000; Bk Vols 78,000; Per Subs 91
Subject Interests: Civil War, Genealogy, Penn hist
Automation Activity & Vendor Info: (Cataloging) Follett Software; (Circulation) Follett Software
Wireless access
Mem of Franklin County Library System
Open Mon-Thurs 11-7, Fri 9-5, Sat 10-3
Friends of the Library Group

WAYNESBURG

P EVA K BOWLBY PUBLIC LIBRARY*, 311 N West St, 15370-1238. SAN 359-6559. Tel: 724-627-9776. FAX: 724-852-1900. Reference E-mail: reference@evakbowlby.org. Web Site: www.evakbowlby.org. *Exec Dir,* Kathy McClure; Tel: 724-727-9776, Ext 15; Staff 13 (MLS 1, Non-MLS 12)
Founded 1943. Pop 40,476; Circ 71,573
Library Holdings: Bk Vols 55,000; Per Subs 100
Special Collections: Local History Coll, rare bks; W & W Railroad (Roach Coll), photog
Subject Interests: Agr
Automation Activity & Vendor Info: (Acquisitions) Follett Software; (Cataloging) Follett Software; (Circulation) Follett Software; (Course Reserve) Follett Software; (ILL) Follett Software; (OPAC) Follett Software
Publications: Newsletter (Quarterly)
Mem of Greene County Library System
Partic in OCLC Online Computer Library Center, Inc
Open Mon & Wed 10-8, Tues & Thurs 10-7, Fri & Sat 9:30-4:30; Mon-Thurs (Summer) 10-7, Fri & Sat 9:30-3:30

GL GREENE COUNTY LAW LIBRARY*, Greene County Courthouse, Ste 218, 10 E High St, 15370. SAN 315-3223. Tel: 724-852-5212. FAX: 724-627-4716. Web Site: www.co.greene.pa.us/secured/gc2/depts/lo/judges/law-library.htm. *Court Adminr,* Sheila S Rode
Library Holdings: Bk Vols 1,250
Open Mon-Fri 8:30-4:30

P GREENE COUNTY LIBRARY SYSTEM*, 311 N West St, 15370. SAN 359-6613. Tel: 724-627-9776, Ext 410. Web Site: www.greenecolib.org. *Syst Adminr,* Kathy McClure; Staff 1 (MLS 1)
Founded 1976. Pop 40,476; Circ 101,969
Special Collections: Local History Coll. Municipal Document Depository; State Document Depository
Automation Activity & Vendor Info: (Cataloging) Innovative Interfaces, Inc; (Circulation) Innovative Interfaces, Inc
Wireless access
Member Libraries: Eva K Bowlby Public Library; Flenniken Public Library
Special Services for the Blind - Bks on cassette; Bks on CD; Cassettes; Large print bks; Recorded bks
Open Mon-Thurs 9:30-4

C WAYNESBURG COLLEGE*, Eberly Library, 51 W College St, 15370. SAN 315-3231. Tel: 724-852-3278. Web Site: waynesburg.libguides.com/eberly. *Libr Dir,* Rea Andrew Redd; Tel: 724-852-3419, E-mail: rredd@waynesburg.edu; *Syst Librn,* John Walters Thompson; Tel: 724-852-7668, E-mail: jthompso@waynesburg.edu; *Cat,* Beth Boehm; Tel: 724-852-7640, E-mail: bboehm@waynesburg.edu; Staff 7 (MLS 5, Non-MLS 2)
Founded 1849. Enrl 2,159; Fac 141; Highest Degree: Master
Library Holdings: AV Mats 2,070; CDs 709; DVDs 439; Bk Titles 83,893; Bk Vols 86,702; Per Subs 395; Talking Bks 582; Videos 1,747
Special Collections: Western Pennsylvania History (Trans-Appalachian Coll)
Subject Interests: Criminal justice, Educ, Nursing
Automation Activity & Vendor Info: (Cataloging) OCLC; (Circulation) Innovative Interfaces, Inc; (Course Reserve) Innovative Interfaces, Inc; (ILL) OCLC; (OPAC) Innovative Interfaces, Inc; (Serials) EBSCO Online
Wireless access
Function: Adult literacy prog, AV serv, Distance learning, ILL available, Photocopying/Printing, Res libr, Satellite serv
Publications: Library Brochure
Partic in OCLC Online Computer Library Center, Inc; OhioNET; Pittsburgh Regional Libr Consortium
Open Mon-Thurs 7:30am-Midnight, Fri 7:30-5, Sat 10-4, Sun 2-Midnight
Restriction: Open to fac, students & qualified researchers
Friends of the Library Group

WEATHERLY

P WEATHERLY AREA COMMUNITY LIBRARY*, 1518 Brenkman Dr, 18255. (Mail add: PO Box 141, 18255). Tel: 570-427-5085. E-mail: wacl1518@pa.metrocast.net. Web Site: weatherlylibrary.org. *Pres,* Susie Gerhard
Founded 1995
Library Holdings: DVDs 10; Large Print Bks 200; Bk Vols 20,000; Per Subs 10; Talking Bks 203; Videos 103
Special Collections: Municipal Document Depository
Wireless access
Special Services for the Blind - Talking bks
Open Mon-Wed 2-5, Thurs 10-12 & 7-9, Fri 10-12 & 3-5, Sat 9-12

WELLSBORO

P GREEN FREE LIBRARY, 134 Main St, 16901. SAN 315-324X. Tel: 570-724-4876. FAX: 570-724-7605. E-mail: frontdesk@greenfreelibrary.org. Web Site: www.greenfreelibrary.org. *Dir,* Leslie A Wishard; Staff 6 (MLS 1, Non-MLS 5)
Founded 1911. Pop 11,900; Circ 45,000
Library Holdings: AV Mats 1,100; Large Print Bks 1,300; Bk Titles 37,200; Per Subs 50
Subject Interests: Civil War, Genealogy, Local hist
Automation Activity & Vendor Info: (Cataloging) Innovative Interfaces, Inc; (Circulation) Innovative Interfaces, Inc; (OPAC) Innovative Interfaces, Inc
Wireless access
Function: ILL available
Mem of Potter-Tioga Library System
Open Mon-Thurs 9-7, Fri-Sun 10-3
Friends of the Library Group

WERNERSVILLE

P WERNERSVILLE PUBLIC LIBRARY*, 100 N Reber St, 19565-1412. SAN 315-3266. Tel: 610-678-8771. FAX: 610-678-3025. E-mail: wernersvillepl@berks.lib.pa.us. Web Site: www.berkslibraries.org/branch/wernersville. *Dir,* Leigh-Anne Yacovelli; Staff 1 (MLS 1)
Founded 1906. Pop 15,278; Circ 51,227
Jan 2019-Dec 2019 Income $190,950, State $48,061, City $52,730, County $40,244, Locally Generated Income $49,915. Mats Exp $31,921. Sal $112,103
Library Holdings: DVDs 3,956; e-books 9,930; Per Subs 51
Subject Interests: Local hist
Wireless access
Function: 24/7 Electronic res, 24/7 Online cat, 3D Printer, Adult bk club, Audiobks via web, Bk club(s), Bks on CD, Children's prog, Computers for patron use, Electronic databases & coll, Free DVD rentals, Holiday prog, Home delivery & serv to seniorr ctr & nursing homes, Homebound delivery serv, ILL available, Internet access, Life-long learning prog for all ages, Magazines, Mail & tel request accepted, Mail loans to mem, Meeting rooms, Movies, Museum passes, Music CDs, Online cat, Outreach serv, OverDrive digital audio bks, Photocopying/Printing, Preschool outreach, Preschool reading prog, Prog for adults, Prog for children & young adult, Ref serv available, Scanner, Senior outreach, Serves people with intellectual disabilities, Spoken cassettes & CDs, Spoken cassettes & DVDs, STEM programs, Story hour, Study rm, Summer reading prog, Tax forms, Teen prog, Telephone ref, Wheelchair accessible, Workshops
Mem of Berks County Public Libraries
Open Mon & Fri 12-7, Tues-Thurs 10-8, Sat 9-4
Friends of the Library Group

WEST CHESTER

G CHESTER COUNTY ARCHIVES & RECORDS SERVICES LIBRARY*, 601 Westtown Rd, Ste 080, 19382-4958. (Mail add: PO Box 2747, 19380-0990), SAN 323-5181. Tel: 610-344-6760. FAX: 610-344-5616. E-mail: ccarchives@chesco.org. Web Site: www.chesco.org/192/Archives-Records. *Dir,* Laurie A Rofini; Staff 3 (MLS 1, Non-MLS 2)
Founded 1982

Special Collections: Municipal Document Depository
Subject Interests: Hist of Chester county
Function: Archival coll
Open Mon-Fri 9-4

S CHESTER COUNTY HISTORICAL SOCIETY LIBRARY*, 225 N High St, 19380. SAN 315-3304. Tel: 610-692-4800, Ext 221. FAX: 610-692-4357. E-mail: library@chestercohistorical.org. Web Site: www.chestercohistorical.org/library. *Librn,* Jasmine Smith; *Asst Librn,* Margaret Baillie; Staff 2 (MLS 2)
Founded 1893
Library Holdings: Bk Vols 10,000; Per Subs 50
Special Collections: Chester County Newspapers; Chester County School Records; Photograph Coll; Postal History Coll; William Penn (Albert Cook Myers Coll)
Subject Interests: Decorative art, Genealogy, Hist of Chester county, Local family hist, Local hist
Wireless access
Partic in OCLC Online Computer Library Center, Inc
Open Tues-Sat 9:30-4:30
Restriction: Non-circulating

M CHESTER COUNTY HOSPITAL LIBRARY*, Health Care Library, 701 E Marshall St, 19380. SAN 329-7063. Tel: 610-431-5204. FAX: 610-696-8411. *Med Librn,* John Mokonyama; E-mail: john.mokonyama@pennmedicine.upenn.edu; Staff 1 (MLS 1)
Library Holdings: CDs 100; DVDs 50; e-books 1,500; Bk Titles 1,600; Per Subs 30
Special Collections: Diversity Coll; Medical Ethics Coll
Automation Activity & Vendor Info: (Cataloging) EOS International; (Media Booking) EOS International
Wireless access
Partic in Basic Health Sciences Library Network
Open Mon-Fri 8-4:30

L CHESTER COUNTY LAW LIBRARY*, 201 W Market St, Ste 2400, 19380-0989. SAN 315-3290. Tel: 610-344-6166. FAX: 610-344-6994. E-mail: lawlibrary@chesco.org. Web Site: www.chesco.org/572/law-library. *Libr Asst,* Ritza Hazen; *Libr Asst,* Judith Roccaro
Founded 1862
Library Holdings: Bk Titles 31,611; Bk Vols 33,190; Per Subs 40
Subject Interests: Penn law
Open Mon-Fri 8:30-4:30
Restriction: Open to pub for ref only

R GROVE UNITED METHODIST CHURCH LIBRARY*, 490 W Boot Rd, 19380. SAN 315-3320. Tel: 610-696-2663. FAX: 610-696-5625. Web Site: www.grovechurch.org. *Dir,* Eva Johnson; E-mail: pastoreva@grovechurch.org; *Librn,* Linda S Seybold; E-mail: linsey33@verizon.net; Staff 2 (MLS 1, Non-MLS 1)
Founded 1976
Library Holdings: Bk Titles 1,116; Bk Vols 1,208
Subject Interests: Bible, Christianity, Methodism
Wireless access
Open Mon-Fri 10-3

SR SWEDENBORG FOUNDATION LIBRARY, 320 N Church St, 19380. SAN 327-0319. Tel: 610-430-3222. Toll Free Tel: 800-355-3222. FAX: 610-430-7982. E-mail: info@swedenborg.com. Web Site: www.swedenborg.com. *Library Contact,* Jeanne Chiquoine; E-mail: jchiquoine@swedenborg.com
Founded 1874
Library Holdings: Bk Vols 1,500
Restriction: Open by appt only

P WEST CHESTER PUBLIC LIBRARY, 415 N Church St, 19380-2401. SAN 315-3339. Tel: 610-696-1721. FAX: 610-429-1077. E-mail: wcpl@ccls.org. Web Site: wcpubliclibrary.org. *Exec Dir,* Victoria E Dow; E-mail: vdow@ccls.org; *Ad, Asst Dir,* Hannah Siegele; E-mail: hsiegele@ccls.org; *Youth Serv Librn,* Clara Kelly; E-mail: ckelly@ccls.org; Staff 13 (MLS 2, Non-MLS 11)
Founded 1872. Pop 60,000; Circ 155,000
Library Holdings: Bk Titles 46,000; Per Subs 110
Special Collections: Cake Pans - specialty; Mobile hotspots - rental
Subject Interests: Local hist
Automation Activity & Vendor Info: (Circulation) Innovative Interfaces, Inc; (OPAC) Innovative Interfaces, Inc
Wireless access
Function: 24/7 Electronic res, 24/7 Online cat, Adult bk club, Adult literacy prog, Bks on CD, Chess club, Children's prog, Computers for patron use, ILL available, Internet access, Life-long learning prog for all ages, Magazines, Mango lang, Meeting rooms, Museum passes, Online cat, OverDrive digital audio bks, Photocopying/Printing, Preschool reading prog, Prog for adults, Prog for children & young adult, Ref serv available, Scanner, Spanish lang bks, STEM programs, Story hour, Summer reading prog, Teen prog, Wheelchair accessible
Publications: WCPLNews (Online only)
Mem of Chester County Library System
Open Mon-Thurs 10-7, Fri & Sat 10-5

C WEST CHESTER UNIVERSITY*, Francis Harvey Green Library, 25 W Rosedale Ave, 19383. SAN 359-6672. Tel: 610-436-2747. Circulation Tel: 610-436-2946. Interlibrary Loan Service Tel: 610-436-3454. Reference Tel: 610-436-2453. Interlibrary Loan Service FAX: 610-636-2251. Administration FAX: 610-738-0554. Circulation E-mail: libcirc@wcupa.edu. Reference E-mail: refdesk@wcupa.edu. Administration E-mail: Libadmin@wcupa.edu. Web Site: www.library.wcupa.edu. *Dean of Libr,* Mary Page; E-mail: libadmin@wcupa.edu; *Assoc Dean of Libr,* Amy Ward; Tel: 610-436-2263, E-mail: award@wcupa.edu; *Rare Bks, Spec Coll Librn,* Ron McColl; Tel: 610-436-3456, E-mail: rmccoll@wcupa.edu; *Bus Operations Mgr,* Nancy Shipe; Tel: 610-436-3311, E-mail: nshipe@wcupa.edu; *Access Serv,* Deidre Childs; Tel: 610 738-0480, E-mail: dchilds@wcupa.edu; *Electronic Res,* Kerry Walton; Tel: 610-436-3453, E-mail: kwalton2@wcupa.edu; *Info Literacy,* Dr Rachel McMullin; Tel: 610-738-0510; *Music,* Tim Sestrick; Tel: 610-436-2379, E-mail: tsestrick@wcupa.edu; *Outreach Serv,* Danielle Skaggs; Tel: 610 436-2401, E-mail: dskaggs@wcupa.edu; Staff 47 (MLS 15, Non-MLS 32)
Founded 1871. Fac 914; Highest Degree: Doctorate
Special Collections: Anthony Wayne Letters (Rare Book), bks, letters; History of County (Chester County Coll, incl Darlington Coll of Rare Scientific & Botanical); Holocaust Studies (Frejdowicz Coll); John Sanderson's Biographies of the Signers of the Declaration of Independence; Philips Coll of Autographed Books & Letters; Physical Education (Ehinger Coll); Shakespeare Folios; Stanley Weintraub Coll, ms & related mats
Subject Interests: Art, Educ, Health, Humanities, Kinesiology, Music, Nursing
Automation Activity & Vendor Info: (Acquisitions) Ex Libris Group; (Cataloging) Ex Libris Group; (Circulation) Ex Libris Group; (Course Reserve) Atlas Systems; (Discovery) Ex Libris Group; (ILL) OCLC ILLiad; (OPAC) Ex Libris Group; (Serials) Ex Libris Group
Wireless access
Partic in Keystone Library Network; LYRASIS; OCLC Online Computer Library Center, Inc; Partnership for Academic Library Collaborative & Innovation; Westchester Academic Library Directors Organization
Special Services for the Blind - Accessible computers
Friends of the Library Group

Departmental Libraries:

PRESSER MUSIC LIBRARY, School of Music & Performing Arts Ctr, 19383. Tel: 610-436-2379, 610-436-2430. FAX: 610-436-2873. *Music Librn,* Tim Sestrick; E-mail: tsestrick@wcupa.edu; *Music Libr Supvr,* Hunter King; E-mail: tking@wcupa.edu; *Music Libr Tech,* Lucille Stroud; E-mail: lstroud@wcupa.edu
Library Holdings: AV Mats 43,459; CDs 12,872; DVDs 79; Music Scores 34,604; Bk Titles 10,452
Automation Activity & Vendor Info: (ILL) Ex Libris Group
Open Mon-Thurs (Fall & Spring) 8am-10pm, Fri 8-6, Sat 10-6, Sun 2-10; Mon-Fri (Summer) 8-4
Friends of the Library Group

WEST GROVE

P AVON GROVE LIBRARY*, 117 Rosehill Ave, 19390. SAN 315-3355. Tel: 610-869-2004. FAX: 610-869-2957. Web Site: www.avongrovelibrary.org, www.ccls.org. *Dir,* Lori Schwabenbauer; E-mail: lschwabenbauer@ccls.org; Staff 7 (MLS 1, Non-MLS 6)
Founded 1874. Pop 30,080; Circ 148,175
Library Holdings: Audiobooks 1,178; CDs 1,036; DVDs 2,683; e-books 37,366; e-journals 79; Large Print Bks 1,200; Bk Titles 35,493; Bk Vols 38,952; Per Subs 125
Special Collections: Local History
Wireless access
Function: 24/7 Electronic res, 24/7 Online cat, Adult bk club, Art exhibits, Audiobks via web, Bk club(s), Bks on CD, Children's prog, Computers for patron use, Electronic databases & coll, Holiday prog, Homebound delivery serv, ILL available, Internet access, Life-long learning prog for all ages, Magazines, Mail & tel request accepted, Mango lang, Movies, Music CDs, Online cat, Outreach serv, Outside serv via phone, mail, e-mail & web, OverDrive digital audio bks, Photocopying/Printing, Prog for adults, Prog for children & young adult, Ref serv available, Scanner, Spanish lang bks, STEM programs, Story hour, Summer reading prog, Teen prog, Wheelchair accessible, Workshops, Writing prog
Mem of Chester County Library System
Open Mon-Thurs 10-8, Fri & Sat 10-5
Friends of the Library Group

WEST LAWN

P WEST LAWN-WYOMISSING HILLS LIBRARY*, 101 Woodside Ave, 19609. SAN 315-3363. Tel: 610-678-4888. FAX: 610-678-9210. E-mail: wlwhl@berks.lib.pa.us. Web Site: www.berks.lib.pa.us/swl. *Br Mgr,* John Duffy; Staff 4 (Non-MLS 4)
Founded 1937. Pop 10,000
Library Holdings: Bk Vols 9,000; Per Subs 25
Wireless access
Mem of Berks County Public Libraries
Open Mon-Thurs 10-8, Fri 10-4, Sat 9-4
Friends of the Library Group

WEST MIFFLIN

J COMMUNITY COLLEGE OF ALLEGHENY COUNTY*, South Campus Library, 1750 Clairton Rd, 15122-3097. SAN 315-3371. Tel: 412-469-6295. FAX: 412-469-6370. E-mail: library@ccac.edu. Web Site: www.ccac.edu/library. *Librn,* Irene Grimm; Tel: 412-469-4322, E-mail: igrimm@ccac.edu; *Librn,* Dawn Diehl; Tel: 412-469-6294, E-mail: ddiehl@ccac.edu; Staff 11 (MLS 6, Non-MLS 5)
Founded 1967
Library Holdings: Bk Vols 42,126; Per Subs 144
Subject Interests: Allied health, Nursing
Automation Activity & Vendor Info: (Cataloging) SirsiDynix; (Circulation) SirsiDynix; (Course Reserve) SirsiDynix; (ILL) OCLC; (OPAC) SirsiDynix; (Serials) SirsiDynix
Wireless access
Special Services for the Blind - Assistive/Adapted tech devices, equip & products
Open Mon-Thurs 8-8, Fri 8-4:30, Sat 9-2

J PITTSBURGH INSTITUTE OF AERONAUTICS*, Clifford Ball Learning Resource Center, Five Allegheny County Airport, 15122-2674. (Mail add: PO Box 10897, Pittsburgh, 15236). Tel: 412-346-2100, 412-462-9011. Toll Free Tel: 800-444-1440. FAX: 412-466-0513. E-mail: info@pia.edu. Web Site: pia.edu/campuses/pittsburgh. *Dean, Acad Support,* Jason Pfarr; E-mail: jpfarr@pia.edu
Founded 1929. Fac 20; Highest Degree: Associate
Library Holdings: Bk Vols 8,000; Per Subs 20
Open Mon-Fri 7:15-8 & 2:30-3:30

WEST NEWTON

P WEST NEWTON PUBLIC LIBRARY*, 124 N Water St, 15089. SAN 370-7474. Tel: 724-633-0798. Web Site: www.westnewtonlibrary.com. *Dir,* Robin Matty
Founded 1939. Circ 3,250
Library Holdings: AV Mats 468; Large Print Bks 311; Bk Titles 9,992; Bk Vols 10,091; Per Subs 12; Talking Bks 137; Videos 322
Subject Interests: Civil War
Automation Activity & Vendor Info: (Cataloging) Follett Software; (Circulation) Follett Software
Wireless access
Mem of Westmoreland County Federated Library System
Open Mon & Thurs 12-5, Wed 12-8, Sat 10-2

WEST PITTSTON

P WEST PITTSTON LIBRARY, 200 Exeter Ave, 18643-2442. SAN 315-3398. Tel: 570-654-9847. FAX: 570-654-8037. E-mail: wplibrary@luzernelibraries.org. Web Site: www.wplibrary.org. *Dir,* David J Bauman
Founded 1873. Pop 5,000
Library Holdings: Bk Vols 26,000; Per Subs 32
Wireless access
Mem of Luzerne County Library System
Special Services for the Blind - Reader equip; Talking bks
Open Mon-Thurs 12-8, Fri 10-4, Sat 10-2
Friends of the Library Group

WEST SUNBURY

P NORTH TRAILS PUBLIC LIBRARY, 1553 W Sunbury Rd, 16061-1211. Tel: 724-476-1006. FAX: 724-637-2700. Web Site: www.northtrailslibrary.org. *Dir, Extn Serv,* Kathy D Kline; E-mail: kkline@bcfls.org; Staff 3 (MLS 2, Non-MLS 1)
Founded 2004. Pop 30,000; Circ 330,000
Jan 2021-Dec 2021 Income $82,000, County $77,000, Locally Generated Income $5,000
Automation Activity & Vendor Info: (Acquisitions) OCLC CatExpress; (Cataloging) TLC (The Library Corporation); (Circulation) TLC (The Library Corporation)
Wireless access
Function: 24/7 Electronic res, 24/7 Online cat, Activity rm, Adult bk club, Bk club(s), Bks on CD, Computer training, Computers for patron use, Digital talking bks, E-Reserves, Electronic databases & coll, Holiday prog, ILL available, Internet access, Life-long learning prog for all ages, Magazines, Mail & tel request accepted, Meeting rooms, Movies, Music CDs, Online cat, Outreach serv, OverDrive digital audio bks, Photocopying/Printing, Preschool outreach, Preschool reading prog, Prof lending libr, Prog for adults, Prog for children & young adult, Ref & res, Ref serv available, Res assist avail, Spoken cassettes & CDs, STEM programs, Story hour, Summer reading prog, Tax forms, Wheelchair accessible
Mem of Butler County Federated Library System
Open Mon 10-5, Tues & Wed 1-7, Thurs 10-7
Friends of the Library Group

WESTFIELD

P WESTFIELD PUBLIC LIBRARY*, 147 Maple St, 16950-1616. SAN 315-3401. Tel: 814-367-5411. FAX: 814-367-5411. E-mail: wpublibrary@gmail.com. Web Site: www.westfieldpubliclibrary.com. *Libr Dir,* Rebecca Nagy
Pop 2,441; Circ 26,000
Library Holdings: Bk Vols 12,900; Per Subs 23
Mem of Potter-Tioga Library System
Open Tues & Wed 12-7, Thurs 9-5, Fri 1-7, Sat 8-3

WHITE HAVEN

P WHITE HAVEN AREA COMMUNITY LIBRARY*, 121 Towanda St, 18661. Tel: 570-443-8776. E-mail: Whacl.Library@yahoo.com. Web Site: www.whitehavenlibrary.com. *Chairperson,* Charlotte Carter
Library Holdings: Bk Vols 6,000; Per Subs 10
Wireless access

WHITEHALL

P WHITEHALL TOWNSHIP PUBLIC LIBRARY*, 3700 Mechanicsville Rd, 18052. SAN 315-341X. Tel: 610-432-4339. FAX: 610-432-9387. E-mail: whitehallpl@cliu.org. Web Site: www.whitehallpl.org. *Dir,* Patty J Vahey; E-mail: vahey.p@whitehallpl.org; *Youth Serv,* Lorraine Santaliz; Staff 6 (MLS 2, Non-MLS 4)
Founded 1964. Pop 26,768
Library Holdings: Bk Vols 103,933; Per Subs 131
Special Collections: Adult Easy Readers Coll; Braille Bible Coll; Juvenile Braille Picture Books Coll
Subject Interests: Local hist, Songbooks
Automation Activity & Vendor Info: (Cataloging) Evergreen; (Circulation) Evergreen; (OPAC) Evergreen
Wireless access
Function: Accelerated reader prog, Adult bk club, Art exhibits, Audiobks via web, AV serv, Bks on cassette, Bks on CD, Children's prog, Computer training, Computers for patron use, E-Reserves, Electronic databases & coll, ILL available, Large print keyboards, Microfiche/film & reading machines, Music CDs, Online cat, OverDrive digital audio bks, Photocopying/Printing, Preschool outreach, Preschool reading prog, Prog for adults, Prog for children & young adult, Ref serv available, Senior computer classes, Spoken cassettes & CDs, Spoken cassettes & DVDs, Story hour, Summer & winter reading prog, Summer reading prog, Tax forms, Teen prog, Telephone ref, VHS videos
Publications: Brochure for New Members; Monthly Bibliography of New Acquisitions
Partic in Lehigh Carbon Library Cooperative
Open Mon-Thurs 9-9, Fri & Sat 9-5
Friends of the Library Group

WILCOX

P WILCOX PUBLIC LIBRARY, 105 Clarion St, 15870. (Mail add: PO Box 58, 15870-0058), SAN 315-3428. Tel: 814-929-5639. FAX: 814-929-9934. E-mail: wilcoxlibrary@windstream.net. Web Site: www.wilcoxlibrary.org. *Libr Dir,* Barbara DePonceau
Founded 1963. Pop 1,781; Circ 4,600
Library Holdings: Bk Vols 7,720; Per Subs 10
Automation Activity & Vendor Info: (OPAC) Follett Software
Wireless access
Function: 24/7 Electronic res, 24/7 Online cat, Accelerated reader prog, Audio & video playback equip for onsite use, Audiobks via web, Bks on CD, Children's prog, Computers for patron use, Electronic databases & coll, Family literacy, Free DVD rentals, ILL available, Internet access, Magazines, Movies, Online cat, OverDrive digital audio bks, Preschool reading prog, Scanner, Story hour, Summer reading prog
Open Mon-Thurs 10-4

WILKES-BARRE

GM DEPARTMENT OF VETERANS AFFAIRS*, Medical Center Library, 1111 E End Blvd, 18711. SAN 315-3479. Tel: 570-824-3521, Ext 4297. FAX: 570-821-7264. Web Site:

www.wilkes-barre.va.gov/patients/patiented.asp. *Coordr,* Sandy Dompkosky; Staff 1 (Non-MLS 1)
Founded 1950
Library Holdings: Bk Titles 4,500; Bk Vols 5,200; Per Subs 280
Subject Interests: Med
Restriction: Staff & mem only

M GEISINGER WYOMING VALLEY MEDICAL CENTER*, Health Sciences Library, 1000 E Mountain Dr, 18711. SAN 372-7939. Tel: 570-808-7809. FAX: 570-806-7682. E-mail: hsl@geisinger.edu. Web Site: www.geisinger.org/patient-care/for-professionals/professional-resources/health-sciences-library. *Libr Spec,* Alison Tompkins; Staff 2 (MLS 1, Non-MLS 1)
Founded 1981
Library Holdings: Bk Titles 2,160; Bk Vols 2,780; Per Subs 25
Subject Interests: Pub health
Function: Doc delivery serv, ILL available, Photocopying/Printing, Ref serv available, Res libr
Special Services for the Deaf - Bks on deafness & sign lang; TTY equip
Open Mon-Fri 8-3:30

L HON MAX ROSENN MEMORIAL LAW LIBRARY*, Wilkes-Barre Law & Library Association, 200 N River St, Rm 23, 18711-1001. SAN 315-3509. Tel: 570-822-6712. FAX: 570-822-8210. E-mail: law.library@luzernecounty.org. Web Site: luzernecountybar.com/site/law-library. *Dir & Law Librn-in-Chief,* Joseph Paul Justice Burke, III; E-mail: JoeatWBLLA@aol.com
Founded 1855
Library Holdings: Bk Vols 40,000; Per Subs 40
Open Mon-Fri 9-4

C KING'S COLLEGE*, D Leonard Corgan Library, 14 W Jackson St, 18701-2010. SAN 315-3436. Tel: 570-208-5840. FAX: 570-208-6022. Web Site: www.kings.edu. *Dir,* Dr Terrence Mech; Tel: 570-208-5943, E-mail: terrencemech@kings.edu; *Asst Tech Prof, Electronic Res & Syst Librn,* Adam Balcziunas; *Asst Tech Prof, Instruction & Ref Librn,* Marianne Sodoski; *Asst Tech Prof, Instruction & Ref Librn,* Rebecca Thompson; *Asst Tech Prof, Instrul & Ref Serv Coordr,* Jordana Shane; *Circ Supvr,* Emily Sisk; Staff 5 (MLS 5)
Founded 1946. Enrl 2,128; Fac 151; Highest Degree: Master
Jul 2015-Jun 2016 Income $1,203,432. Mats Exp $507,141, Books $75,459, Per/Ser (Incl. Access Fees) $94,894, Micro $4,645, AV Mat $1,541, Electronic Ref Mat (Incl. Access Fees) $271,268, Presv $1,290. Sal $515,467 (Prof $342,124)
Library Holdings: AV Mats 2,097; CDs 469; DVDs 930; Electronic Media & Resources 52; Microforms 13,985; Bk Vols 185,069; Per Subs 181; Videos 2,089
Special Collections: Public & Private Papers of Honorable Daniel J Flood, MC; Public & Private Papers of The Honorable James L Nelligan
Automation Activity & Vendor Info: (Acquisitions) Innovative Interfaces, Inc; (Cataloging) Innovative Interfaces, Inc; (Circulation) Innovative Interfaces, Inc; (OPAC) Innovative Interfaces, Inc
Wireless access
Publications: Daniel J Flood Collection Register; Edward Welles Catalog of Artists
Partic in LYRASIS; OCLC Online Computer Library Center, Inc

S LUZERNE COUNTY HISTORICAL SOCIETY*, Bishop Memorial Library, 49 S Franklin St, 18701. SAN 315-3517. Tel: 570-823-6244. FAX: 570-823-9011. Web Site: www.luzernehistory.org. *Archivist, Librn,* Amanda Fontenova; Tel: 570-823-6244, Ext 2
Founded 1858
Special Collections: Local Newspapers on Microfilm, 1800s to early 1900s; Manuscripts of Personal & Family Papers of Prominent Wyoming Valley Individuals
Subject Interests: County hist, Genealogy, Hist of Wyoming Valley
Wireless access
Function: Archival coll, Res libr, Res performed for a fee
Open Wed & Fri 12-5, Thurs 12-6, Sat 10-2
Restriction: Fee for pub use, Free to mem, Non-circulating

P LUZERNE COUNTY LIBRARY SYSTEM*, 71 S Franklin St, 18701. Tel: 570-823-0156, Ext 234. FAX: 570-823-7325. Administration E-mail: administrator@luzernelibraries.org. Web Site: www.luzernelibraries.org.
Member Libraries: Back Mountain Memorial Library; Hazleton Area Public Library; Hoyt Library; Marian Sutherland Kirby Library; Mill Memorial Library; Osterhout Free Library; Pittston Memorial Library; Plymouth Public Library; West Pittston Library; Wyoming Free Library

P OSTERHOUT FREE LIBRARY*, 71 S Franklin St, 18701. SAN 359-6850. Tel: 570-823-0156. FAX: 570-823-5477. Reference E-mail: reference@luzernelibraries.org. Web Site: osterhout.info. *Exec Dir,* Richard Miller; E-mail: rmiller@luzernelibraries.org; *Head, Youth Serv,* Elaine Rash; E-mail: erash@luzernelibraries.org; *Coord, Ad Serv,* Liz Caputo; Staff 33 (MLS 5, Non-MLS 28)
Founded 1889. Pop 154,707; Circ 258,489
Library Holdings: Bk Vols 200,000; Per Subs 300
Subject Interests: Local hist
Wireless access
Function: 24/7 Electronic res, 24/7 Online cat, Accelerated reader prog, Activity rm, Adult bk club, Adult literacy prog, After school storytime, Archival coll, Art exhibits, Audiobks on Playaways & MP3, Audiobks via web, AV serv, Bilingual assistance for Spanish patrons, Bk club(s), Bks on CD, CD-ROM, Children's prog, Citizenship assistance, Computer training, Computers for patron use, Digital talking bks, Distance learning, E-Readers, E-Reserves, Electronic databases & coll, Family literacy, For res purposes, Free DVD rentals, Genealogy discussion group, Holiday prog, Homebound delivery serv, ILL available, Internet access, Life-long learning prog for all ages, Literacy & newcomer serv, Magazines, Mail & tel request accepted, Mail loans to mem, Mango lang, Meeting rooms, Microfiche/film & reading machines, Music CDs, Online cat, Online ref, Outreach serv, Photocopying/Printing, Preschool outreach, Preschool reading prog, Prog for adults, Prog for children & young adult, Ref & res, Ref serv available, Res assist avail, Res performed for a fee, Scanner, Senior outreach, Spanish lang bks, Spoken cassettes & CDs, Spoken cassettes & DVDs, STEM programs, Story hour, Summer & winter reading prog, Summer reading prog, Tax forms, Teen prog, Telephone ref, Wheelchair accessible, Winter reading prog, Words travel prog, Workshops
Publications: Osterhout Free Library Newsletter (Quarterly)
Mem of Luzerne County Library System
Partic in Northeastern Pennsylvania Library Network
Special Services for the Deaf - Bks on deafness & sign lang; High interest/low vocabulary bks
Open Mon-Thurs 9-8, Fri 9-5, Sat 9-4 (10-2 July & Aug)
Friends of the Library Group
Branches: 3
NORTH, 28 Oliver St, 18705, SAN 359-6885. Tel: 570-822-4660. FAX: 570-822-4660. *Supvr,* Joanne Austin; E-mail: jaustin@luzernelibraries.org; Staff 2 (Non-MLS 2)
Library Holdings: Bk Titles 15,659; Bk Vols 17,818; Per Subs 23; Talking Bks 88; Videos 219
Open Mon 1-7:30, Tues & Wed 1:30-5:30, Thurs 1-5:30, Fri 1-5
Friends of the Library Group
PLAINS TOWNSHIP, 126 N Main St, Plains, 18705, SAN 359-6915. Tel: 570-824-1862. FAX: 570-824-1862. *Library Contact,* David Bauman; E-mail: dbauman@luzernelibraries.org; Staff 1 (Non-MLS 1)
Library Holdings: Large Print Bks 78; Bk Titles 13,691; Bk Vols 15,081; Per Subs 29; Talking Bks 219; Videos 179
Open Mon-Wed 12:30-5:30, Thurs 1:30-6:30
SOUTH, Two Airy St, 18702, SAN 359-694X. Tel: 570-823-5544. FAX: 570-823-5544. *Library Contact,* Rebecca Schmitt; E-mail: rschmitt@luzernelibraries.org; Staff 1 (Non-MLS 1)
Library Holdings: Large Print Bks 116; Bk Titles 9,690; Bk Vols 10,115; Per Subs 29; Talking Bks 189; Videos 209
Open Mon & Tues 12:30-5:30, Thurs 12:30-6:30, Fri 1-5
Friends of the Library Group

M WILKES-BARRE GENERAL HOSPITAL*, Library Services, 575 N River St, 18764. SAN 315-3495. Tel: 570-552-1175. FAX: 570-552-1183. E-mail: library@commonwealthhealth.net. *Mgr,* Rosemarie Kazda Taylor; Staff 1 (MLS 1)
Founded 1935
Library Holdings: e-books 150; e-journals 18,000; Bk Vols 3,500; Per Subs 58
Special Collections: Health Resource Center, Consumer Health Coll
Subject Interests: Med, Nursing
Automation Activity & Vendor Info: (Cataloging) Professional Software; (Circulation) Professional Software; (OPAC) Professional Software; (Serials) Professional Software
Wireless access
Partic in Basic Health Sciences Library Network; Middle Atlantic Regional Med Libr Prog
Open Mon-Fri 7-3:30

C WILKES UNIVERSITY, Farley Library, 84 W South St, 18766. Tel: 570-408-3212. Interlibrary Loan Service Tel: 570-408-4256. Reference Tel: 570-408-3215. Administration Tel: 570-408-4255. FAX: 570-408-7823. E-mail: ask.librarian@wilkes.edu. Web Site: www.wilkes.edu/library. *Dean,* John Stachacz; Tel: 570-408-4254, E-mail: john.stachacz@wilkes.edu; *Head, Pub Serv,* Brian Sacolic; Tel: 570-408-3206, E-mail: brian.sacolic@wilkes.edu; *Archivist, Pub Serv Librn,* Suzanne Calev; Tel: 570-408-2012, E-mail: suzanne.calev@wilkes.edu; Staff 19 (MLS 5, Non-MLS 14)
Founded 1933. Enrl 3,010; Fac 188; Highest Degree: Doctorate
Library Holdings: e-journals 53,000; Bk Vols 170,000; Per Subs 1,800
Special Collections: Admiral Howard Stark Coll; McClintock Room, mss Northeast Pennsylvania History; Poland, Culture & History (Polish Room
Wireless access

Publications: Library News Brief
Partic in Northeastern Pennsylvania Library Network; OCLC Online Computer Library Center, Inc
Open Mon-Thurs 8am-Midnight, Fri 8-5, Sat 11-6, Sun 3pm-11pm
Restriction: In-house use for visitors, Open to students, fac & staff

WILLIAMSBURG

P WILLIAMSBURG PUBLIC LIBRARY*, 511 W Second St, 16693. SAN 315-3525. Tel: 814-832-3367. FAX: 814-832-3845. E-mail: library@williamsburgpl.net. Web Site: williamsburg.blaircountylibraries.org/. *Dir,* Roane Lytle; E-mail: rlytle@williamsburgpl.net; Staff 1 (MLS 1)
Founded 1950. Pop 6,344; Circ 9,288
Library Holdings: Bk Vols 17,370; Per Subs 50
Subject Interests: Penn hist
Automation Activity & Vendor Info: (Cataloging) Follett Software; (Circulation) Follett Software; (OPAC) Follett Software
Wireless access
Mem of Blair County Library System
Open Mon, Tues & Thurs 1-8, Wed 10-5

WILLIAMSPORT

P JAMES V BROWN LIBRARY OF WILLIAMSPORT & LYCOMING COUNTY, 19 E Fourth St, 17701. SAN 359-7067. Tel: 570-326-0536. Reference Tel: 570-327-2954. FAX: 570-326-1671. E-mail: jvbrown@jvbrown.edu. Web Site: www.jvbrown.edu. *Dir,* Barbara S McGary; E-mail: bmcgary@jvbrown.edu; *Youth Serv Coordr,* Nina White; *Tech Serv,* Laura Spencer; Staff 36 (MLS 6, Non-MLS 30)
Founded 1905. Pop 84,702; Circ 561,942
Library Holdings: Audiobooks 8,318; DVDs 21,060; e-books 3,469; Bk Titles 120,043; Per Subs 198
Special Collections: Pennsylvania Coll
Subject Interests: Adoption, Parenting coll
Automation Activity & Vendor Info: (Cataloging) Innovative Interfaces, Inc; (Circulation) Innovative Interfaces, Inc; (OPAC) Innovative Interfaces, Inc
Wireless access
Mem of Lycoming County Library System
Special Services for the Blind - Closed circuit TV magnifier; Reader equip
Open Mon-Fri 10-6, Sat 9-2
Friends of the Library Group
Bookmobiles: 2

C LYCOMING COLLEGE*, John G Snowden Memorial Library, 700 College Pl, 17701. SAN 315-355X. Tel: 570-321-4053. Interlibrary Loan Service Tel: 570-321-4091. Reference Tel: 570-321-4086. FAX: 570-321-4090. Web Site: www.lycoming.edu/library. *Assoc Dean, Dir, Libr Serv,* Paige Flanagan; Tel: 570-321-4082; *Head, Coll Mgt,* Susan K Beidler; Tel: 570-321-4084, E-mail: beidler@lycoming.edu; *Instrul Serv Librn & Coordr of Ref & Assessment,* Mary Broussard; Tel: 570-321-4068, E-mail: brouss@lycoming.edu; *Circ Supvr, Libr Tech,* Kim Moerschbacher; Tel: 570-321-4053, E-mail: moerschbacher@lycoming.edu; *Archive Spec,* Janet McNeil Hurlbert; Tel: 570-321-4350, E-mail: hurlbjan@lycoming.edu; *Asst to the Dir, Libr Tech,* Tami Hutson; E-mail: hutson@lycoming.edu; Staff 12 (MLS 5, Non-MLS 7)
Founded 1812. Enrl 1,450; Fac 92; Highest Degree: Bachelor
Library Holdings: e-books 2,500; Bk Vols 186,000; Per Subs 1,140
Special Collections: Religion (Central Pennsylvania Conference of the United Methodist Church Archives). US Document Depository
Subject Interests: Psychol, Relig studies, Sociol
Automation Activity & Vendor Info: (Acquisitions) TLC (The Library Corporation); (Cataloging) TLC (The Library Corporation); (Circulation) TLC (The Library Corporation); (OPAC) TLC (The Library Corporation); (Serials) TLC (The Library Corporation)
Wireless access
Partic in Associated College Libraries of Central Pennsylvania; Partnership for Academic Library Collaborative & Innovation
Open Mon-Thurs (Winter) 7:30am-1am, Fri 7:30am-9pm, Sat 10-9, Sun 1-1; Mon-Fri (Summer) 8-4:30
Friends of the Library Group

LYCOMING COUNTY LIBRARY SYSTEM*, 19 E Fourth St, 17701. Tel: 570-326-0536. Web Site: www.lycolibrary.org. *Exec Dir,* Barbara McGary; Tel: 570-326-0536, E-mail: bmcgary@jvbrown.edu
Wireless access
Member Libraries: Dr W B Konkle Memorial Library; Hughesville Area Public Library; James V Brown Library of Williamsport & Lycoming County; Jersey Shore Public Library; Muncy Public Library
Open Mon-Fri 10-6, Sat 9-2

PENNSYLVANIA COLLEGE OF TECHNOLOGY*, Roger & Peggy Madigan Library, 999 Hagan Way, 17701. (Mail add: One College Ave, DIF No 69, 17701), SAN 315-3576. Tel: 570-327-4523. Interlibrary Loan Service Tel: 570-320-2400, Ext 7788. Reference Tel: 570-320-2409. Administration Tel: 570-320-2400, Ext 7104. Toll Free Tel: 800-367-9222. FAX: 570-327-4503. E-mail: library@pct.edu. Reference E-mail: refdesk@pct.edu. Web Site: www.pct.edu/library. *Dir,* Tracey Amey; E-mail: tamey@pct.edu; *Asst Dir, Libr Serv,* Joann Eichenlaub; E-mail: jeichenl@pct.edu; *Info Tech, Librn,* Jessica Oberlin; E-mail: juo1@pct.edu; *Librn, Archives & Digital Coll Initiatives,* Nicole Warner; E-mail: nwarner@pct.edu; *Librn, Cat & Metadata Initiatives,* Helen Yoas; E-mail: hyoas@pct.edu; *Librn, Info Literacy Initiatives,* Judith Zebrowski; E-mail: jzebrows@pct.edu; *Acq & Tech Serv Mgr,* Diana Worth; E-mail: dworth@pct.edu; *Libr Operations & Pub Serv Mgr,* Jean Bremigen; E-mail: jbremige@pct.edu; *Ref & Res Initiative,* Georgia Laudenslager; E-mail: glaudens@pct.edu. Subject Specialists: *Budgeting, Coll & resource mgt,* Tracey Amey; *Communications, Humanities,* Nicole Warner; *Natural res mgt, Transportation tech,* Helen Yoas; *Bus, Hospitality,* Judith Zebrowski; *Civil engr, Indust tech, Plastics,* Georgia Laudenslager; Staff 18 (MLS 6, Non-MLS 12)
Founded 1965. Enrl 6,000; Highest Degree: Master
Library Holdings: AV Mats 8,000; e-books 18,000; e-journals 36,000; Electronic Media & Resources 85; Microforms 800; Bk Titles 102,000; Bk Vols 131,136; Per Subs 800
Special Collections: Sloan Art Coll; Williamsport Technical Institute 1914-1965 black & white photographs & other information. State Document Depository
Subject Interests: Archit, Art, Aviation, Civil engr, Construction, Culinary arts, Health sci, Natural res conservation, Tech
Automation Activity & Vendor Info: (Acquisitions) OCLC Worldshare Management Services; (Cataloging) OCLC Worldshare Management Services; (Circulation) OCLC Worldshare Management Services; (ILL) OCLC ILLiad; (OPAC) OCLC; (Serials) OCLC Worldshare Management Services
Wireless access
Partic in Associated College Libraries of Central Pennsylvania; Interlibrary Delivery Service of Pennsylvania; LYRASIS; OCLC Online Computer Library Center, Inc
Special Services for the Deaf - Assistive tech; Closed caption videos; High interest/low vocabulary bks; Sorenson video relay syst
Special Services for the Blind - Assistive/Adapted tech devices, equip & products

M SUSQUEHANNA HEALTH MEDICAL LIBRARY*, Williamsport Regional Medical Ctr, 700 High St, 3rd Flr, 17701. SAN 315-3584. Tel: 570-321-2266. E-mail: medical_library@susquehannahealth.org. Web Site: www.susquehannahealth.org/medical-professionals/medical-library. *Coordr,* Donna Mitchell; E-mail: dmitchell@susquehannahealth.org; Staff 2 (MLS 1, Non-MLS 1)
Founded 1951
Library Holdings: Bk Vols 4,300; Per Subs 130
Subject Interests: Allied health, Med, Nursing
Automation Activity & Vendor Info: (Cataloging) AmLib Library Management System; (Circulation) AmLib Library Management System; (OPAC) AmLib Library Management System
Wireless access
Function: Audio & video playback equip for onsite use, AV serv, Computer training, Doc delivery serv, Electronic databases & coll, Health sci info serv
Open Mon-Fri 8-4:30
Restriction: Hospital staff & commun, Open to pub for ref only, Pub use on premises

WILLOW GROVE

P UPPER MORELAND FREE PUBLIC LIBRARY, 109 Park Ave, 19090-3277. SAN 315-3630. Tel: 215-659-0741. E-mail: uppermoreland@mclinc.org. Web Site: www.uppermorelandlibrary.org. *Exec Dir,* Margie Peters; *Pub Serv Dir,* Cathy Gilmore; *Dir, Staff Develop, Tech,* Katie Fitzpatrick; *Pub Serv Librn,* Alex King; *Youth Librn,* Becky Tkacs; Staff 5 (MLS 4, Non-MLS 1)
Founded 1959. Pop 24,015; Circ 215,972
Jan 2013-Dec 2013 Income $821,633. Mats Exp $92,590, Books $46,866, Per/Ser (Incl. Access Fees) $10,121, AV Mat $16,949, Electronic Ref Mat (Incl. Access Fees) $18,654. Sal $485,385 (Prof $252,889)
Library Holdings: Audiobooks 3,449; AV Mats 11,889; Bks on Deafness & Sign Lang 58; CDs 1,053; DVDs 10,476; e-books 12,248; e-journals 110; Electronic Media & Resources 14; High Interest/Low Vocabulary Bk Vols 40; Large Print Bks 2,899; Music Scores 39; Bk Titles 59,613; Per Subs 111
Subject Interests: English as a second lang, Graphic novels, Local hist
Automation Activity & Vendor Info: (Cataloging) Innovative Interfaces, Inc; (Circulation) Innovative Interfaces, Inc; (OPAC) Innovative Interfaces, Inc; (Serials) Innovative Interfaces, Inc
Wireless access
Function: 24/7 Electronic res, Adult bk club, Art exhibits, Audiobks on Playaways & MP3, Audiobks via web, Bk club(s), Bks on CD, Children's prog, Computer training, Computers for patron use, E-Readers, E-Reserves,

Electronic databases & coll, Family literacy, Free DVD rentals, ILL available, Instruction & testing, Internet access, Life-long learning prog for all ages, Magazines, Mail & tel request accepted, Mango lang, Movies, Museum passes, Music CDs, Online cat, Online ref, OverDrive digital audio bks, Photocopying/Printing, Preschool outreach, Preschool reading prog, Prog for adults, Prog for children & young adult, Ref serv available, Res assist avail, Scanner, Spoken cassettes & CDs, Spoken cassettes & DVDs, STEM programs, Story hour, Study rm, Summer & winter reading prog, Summer reading prog, Tax forms, Teen prog, Telephone ref, Wheelchair accessible, Winter reading prog, Writing prog
Partic in Montgomery County Library & Information Network Consortium
Special Services for the Deaf - Pocket talkers
Special Services for the Blind - Large screen computer & software
Open Mon-Thurs 10-9, Fri & Sat 10-5, Sun 1-5
Friends of the Library Group

WINDBER

P WINDBER PUBLIC LIBRARY*, 1909 Graham Ave, 15963-2011. SAN 315-3665. Tel: 814-467-4950. FAX: 814-467-0960. E-mail: windlib@scfls.org. *Dir,* Susan Brandau; E-mail: sbrandau@somersetcountypalibraries.org; Staff 1 (Non-MLS 1)
Founded 1918. Pop 13,137; Circ 12,060
Library Holdings: Bk Vols 24,402
Automation Activity & Vendor Info: (Cataloging) Evergreen; (Circulation) Evergreen; (OPAC) Evergreen
Wireless access
Function: 24/7 Online cat, Accelerated reader prog, Activity rm, ILL available, Outside serv via phone, mail, e-mail & web, Photocopying/Printing, Prog for adults, Prog for children & young adult, Summer reading prog, VHS videos, Wheelchair accessible
Mem of Somerset County Federated Library System
Open Mon-Thurs 10-6, Fri 10-4, Sat 10-5 (10-2 July & Aug)

WOMELSDORF

P WOMELSDORF COMMUNITY LIBRARY*, 203 W High St, 19567-1307. Tel: 610-589-1424. FAX: 610-589-5022. E-mail: womelsdorfcl@berks.lib.pa.us. Web Site: www.berks.lib.pa.us/womelsdorfcl. *Dir,* Nina Meister
Founded 1978. Circ 21,700
Library Holdings: AV Mats 500; Bk Vols 7,770; Per Subs 36
Automation Activity & Vendor Info: (Acquisitions) SirsiDynix; (Cataloging) SirsiDynix; (ILL) SirsiDynix; (OPAC) SirsiDynix
Wireless access
Mem of Berks County Public Libraries
Open Mon 10-8, Tues 10-7, Wed 10-4, Thurs 11-8, Sat 9-4
Friends of the Library Group

WORTHINGTON

P WORTHINGTON WEST FRANKLIN COMMUNITY LIBRARY*, 214 E Main St, Ste 1, 16262. SAN 370-7326. Tel: 724-297-3762. FAX: 724-297-3762. E-mail: wwlibrary@comcast.net. Web Site: www.armstronglibraries.org/worthington. *Libr Dir,* Dalton Good; Staff 1 (MLS 1)
Founded 1985. Pop 2,500
Library Holdings: Audiobooks 96; CDs 33; DVDs 92; Large Print Bks 628; Bk Titles 18,300; Per Subs 50; Videos 459
Automation Activity & Vendor Info: (Cataloging) Follett Software; (Circulation) Follett Software; (OPAC) Follett Software
Wireless access
Function: Art exhibits, Bks on cassette, Bks on CD, Children's prog, Computers for patron use, Distance learning, Electronic databases & coll, ILL available, Mail & tel request accepted, Music CDs, Online cat, Photocopying/Printing, Prog for adults, Scanner, Story hour, Summer reading prog, Tax forms, Telephone ref, VHS videos, Wheelchair accessible
Special Services for the Blind - Cassettes; Large print bks; Sound rec
Open Tues 1-5, Wed 12-5, Thurs & Fri 10:30-6, Sat 10:30-4:30

WRIGHTSTOWN

P VILLAGE LIBRARY OF WRIGHTSTOWN*, 727 Penns Park Rd, 18940-9605. SAN 315-3681. Tel: 215-598-3322. Web Site: www.wrightstownlibrary.org. *Libr Dir,* Rebecca Hone; E-mail: honer@buckslib.org
Founded 1958. Pop 2,839; Circ 25,281
Library Holdings: Bk Titles 18,000; Per Subs 59
Wireless access
Function: 24/7 Electronic res, 24/7 Online cat, Activity rm, Adult bk club
Publications: Newsletter (Monthly)
Mem of Bucks County Free Library
Open Mon, Tues & Fri 9-5, Wed & Thurs 9-7, Sat 10-1, Sun 1-5

WYALUSING

P WYALUSING PUBLIC LIBRARY*, 115 Church St, 18853. (Mail add: PO Box 98, 18853-0098), SAN 315-369X. Tel: 570-746-1711. FAX: 570-746-1674. E-mail: wyalusingpl@gmail.com. Web Site: wyalusinglibrary.org. *Dir,* Cathy Brady; *Circ Librn,* Morgan Clinton; *Circ Librn,* Amy Girven; *Circ Librn,* Ruth Parsons
Founded 1902. Pop 1,927; Circ 11,987
Library Holdings: Bk Vols 13,000; Per Subs 28
Subject Interests: Local hist
Mem of Bradford County Library System
Open Mon, Wed, & Fri 10-8, Tues & Thurs 3-6, Sat 9-4

WYNCOTE

CR RECONSTRUCTIONIST RABBINICAL COLLEGE LIBRARY*, Mordecai M Kaplan Library, 1299 Church Rd, 19095. SAN 314-9900. Tel: 215-576-0800, Ext 232. Administration Tel: 215-576-0800, Ext 234. FAX: 215-576-6143. E-mail: kaplanlibrary@rrc.edu. Web Site: www.rrc.edu. *Dir,* Alan LaPayover; E-mail: alapayover@rrc.edu; Staff 1 (Non-MLS 1)
Founded 1968. Enrl 42; Fac 10; Highest Degree: Master
Library Holdings: Electronic Media & Resources 10; Bk Vols 47,000; Per Subs 120
Subject Interests: Jewish studies, Rabbinics
Automation Activity & Vendor Info: (Cataloging) SirsiDynix; (Circulation) SirsiDynix; (ILL) OCLC; (OPAC) SirsiDynix; (Serials) SirsiDynix
Wireless access
Partic in Asn of Jewish Librs; Southeastern Pennsylvania Theological Library Association
Open Mon-Thurs 9-5, Fri 9-4

WYNDMOOR

P FREE LIBRARY OF SPRINGFIELD TOWNSHIP*, 8900 Hawthorne Lane, 19038. SAN 372-7726. Tel: 215-836-5300. FAX: 215-836-2404. E-mail: springfieldlibrary@mclinc.org. Web Site: freelibraryofspringfieldtownship.org. *Dir,* Marycatherine McGarvey; E-mail: mmcgarvey@mclinc.org; *Asst Dir, Acq,* Joy Utz; E-mail: jutz@mclinc.org; *Head, Ref Serv,* Stephanie Renne; E-mail: srenne@mclinc.org; *Ch Serv,* Amy Anbler; *Circ,* Kathy Lenahen; E-mail: klenahen@mclinc.org; *ILL,* Marylou Hughes; E-mail: mlhughes@mclinc.org; *YA Serv,* Marie Keissling; E-mail: mkiessling@mclinc.org; Staff 17.5 (MLS 6.5, Non-MLS 11)
Founded 1965. Pop 19,450; Circ 226,278
Automation Activity & Vendor Info: (Acquisitions) Innovative Interfaces, Inc; (Cataloging) Innovative Interfaces, Inc; (Circulation) Innovative Interfaces, Inc; (Course Reserve) Innovative Interfaces, Inc; (ILL) Innovative Interfaces, Inc; (Media Booking) Innovative Interfaces, Inc; (OPAC) Innovative Interfaces, Inc; (Serials) Innovative Interfaces, Inc
Wireless access
Function: 24/7 Electronic res, 24/7 Online cat, Accelerated reader prog, Activity rm, Adult bk club, Adult literacy prog, After school storytime, Art exhibits, Art programs, Audio & video playback equip for onsite use, Audiobks on Playaways & MP3, AV serv, Bk club(s), Bk reviews (Group), Bks on CD, Chess club, Children's prog, Citizenship assistance, Computer training, Computers for patron use, Digital talking bks, Doc delivery serv, E-Reserves, Electronic databases & coll, Family literacy, Free DVD rentals, Games & aids for people with disabilities, Genealogy discussion group, Govt ref serv, Health sci info serv, Holiday prog, Home delivery & serv to seniorr ctr & nursing homes, Homebound delivery serv, ILL available, Internet access, Learning ctr, Life-long learning prog for all ages, Magazines, Magnifiers for reading, Mail & tel request accepted, Mail loans to mem, Makerspace, Mango lang, Meeting rooms, Movies, Museum passes, Music CDs, Online cat, Online ref, Orientations, Outreach serv, Outside serv via phone, mail, e-mail & web, OverDrive digital audio bks, Photocopying/Printing, Preschool outreach, Preschool reading prog, Printer for laptops & handheld devices, Prof lending libr, Prog for adults, Prog for children & young adult, Ref & res, Ref serv available, Res assist avail, Scanner, Senior computer classes, Serves people with intellectual disabilities, Spoken cassettes & CDs, Spoken cassettes & DVDs, STEM programs, Story hour, Study rm, Summer & winter reading prog, Summer reading prog, Tax forms, Teen prog, Telephone ref, Visual arts prog, Wheelchair accessible, Winter reading prog, Words travel prog, Workshops, Writing prog
Partic in Montgomery County Library & Information Network Consortium
Open Mon-Thurs (Winter) 9-9, Fri 9-5, Sat 10-5, Sun 1-4; Mon-Thurs (Summer) 9-9, Fri 9-5, Sat 10-2
Friends of the Library Group

WYNNEWOOD

R ANTHONY CARDINAL BEVILACQUA THEOLOGICAL RESEARCH CENTER*, Ryan Memorial Library, 100 E Wynnewood Rd, 19096. SAN 359-0917. Tel: 610-785-6274. FAX: 610-664-7913. Web Site: www.scs.edu/library. *Vice Pres, Assessment & Info Serv,* Cait Kokolus;

E-mail: ckokolus@scs.edu; *Dir,* James Humble; E-mail: jhumble@scs.edu; Staff 5 (MLS 3, Non-MLS 2)
Founded 1832. Enrl 250; Fac 35; Highest Degree: Master
Library Holdings: AV Mats 16,021; e-journals 2,000; Electronic Media & Resources 36; Bk Titles 87,000; Bk Vols 94,000; Per Subs 215
Special Collections: Nineteenth Century Devotional Literature; Pre-Vatican II Liturgical Books; Rare Books
Subject Interests: Catholic theol, Patristics, Philos, Scripture studies
Automation Activity & Vendor Info: (Acquisitions) Ex Libris Group; (Cataloging) Ex Libris Group; (Circulation) Ex Libris Group; (Course Reserve) Ex Libris Group; (ILL) Ex Libris Group; (OPAC) Ex Libris Group; (Serials) Ex Libris Group
Wireless access
Partic in Southeastern Pennsylvania Theological Library Association; Tri-State College Library Cooperative
Open Mon-Thurs 8:30am-10pm, Fri 8:30-4:30, Sat 9:30-4:30, Sun 1-10

M LANKENAU HOSPITAL*, Medical Library, 100 Lancaster Ave, 19096. SAN 359-0615. Tel: 484-476-2000. FAX: 610-645-3425. *Dir,* Mazen Hassan; *Librn,* Kary Heller; *Librn,* Maria Panoc; Staff 2 (MLS 2)
Founded 1860
Library Holdings: Bk Titles 6,281; Bk Vols 6,419; Per Subs 321
Special Collections: Collected Papers of the Lankenau Research Center
Subject Interests: Gen med, Surgery
Wireless access
Partic in National Network of Libraries of Medicine Region 1; Regional Med Libr Network
Open Mon-Fri 8-5
Friends of the Library Group

R MAIN LINE REFORM TEMPLE*, Beth Elohim Library, 410 Montgomery Ave, 19096. SAN 315-3711. Tel: 610-649-7800. FAX: 610-642-6338. Web Site: www.mlrt.org. *Librn,* Sally Brown; E-mail: sbrown@mlrt.org; Staff 2 (MLS 1, Non-MLS 1)
Founded 1961
Library Holdings: Bk Titles 10,184; Bk Vols 14,990; Per Subs 23; Talking Bks 25
Special Collections: Young Adult (Steven Berman Memorial Coll)
Subject Interests: Jewish hist, Judaica
Open Mon-Thurs 10-3, Sun 10-1

P PENN WYNNE LIBRARY*, 130 Overbrook Pkwy, 19096-3211. SAN 314-9609. Tel: 610-642-7844. FAX: 610-642-2761. E-mail: pennwynnelibrary@lmls.org. Web Site: www.lmls.org. *Head Librn,* Judy Soret; Staff 5 (MLS 2, Non-MLS 3)
Founded 1929
Library Holdings: Audiobooks 1,334; CDs 1,290; DVDs 3,737; Large Print Bks 1,030; Bk Vols 44,170; Per Subs 30
Special Collections: Cake pan coll (circulating); Judaica
Automation Activity & Vendor Info: (Acquisitions) Innovative Interfaces, Inc; (Cataloging) Innovative Interfaces, Inc; (Circulation) Innovative Interfaces, Inc; (OPAC) Innovative Interfaces, Inc
Wireless access
Function: 24/7 Electronic res, 24/7 Online cat, Bks on CD, Children's prog, Computers for patron use, Free DVD rentals, ILL available, Magazines, Mail & tel request accepted, Mango lang, Meeting rooms, Museum passes, Online cat, OverDrive digital audio bks, Photocopying/Printing, Printer for laptops & handheld devices, Prog for adults, Prog for children & young adult, Story hour, Summer reading prog, Tax forms, Telephone ref, Wheelchair accessible
Mem of Lower Merion Library System
Partic in Montgomery County Library & Information Network Consortium
Open Mon-Thurs 10-9, Fri & Sat 10-5

WYOMING

P WYOMING FREE LIBRARY*, 358 Wyoming Ave, 18644-1822. SAN 315-372X. Tel: 570-693-1364. FAX: 570-693-0189. Web Site: wyomingfreelibrary.com. *Libr Dir,* John Roberts; E-mail: jroberts@osterhout.lib.pa.us
Library Holdings: Bk Vols 21,500; Per Subs 15
Wireless access
Mem of Luzerne County Library System
Open Mon & Fri 10-6, Tues-Thurs 9-5, Sat 9-4

WYOMISSING

SPRING TOWNSHIP LIBRARY*, 78C Commerce Dr, 19610. Tel: 610-373-9888. FAX: 610-373-0334. E-mail: springtwp@berks.lib.pa.us. Web Site: www.berks.lib.pa.us/springtwp. *Dir,* Donna Eby; *Ch,* Andrea Hunter; Staff 2 (MLS 1, Non-MLS 1)
Founded 2004. Pop 25,000; Circ 82,000
Library Holdings: Bk Vols 15,171; Per Subs 34
Automation Activity & Vendor Info: (Cataloging) Horizon; (Circulation) Horizon; (OPAC) Horizon; (Serials) Horizon
Wireless access
Function: Art exhibits, Bks on cassette, Bks on CD, Children's prog, Computer training, Computers for patron use, Digital talking bks, Electronic databases & coll, Free DVD rentals, ILL available, Internet access, Mail & tel request accepted, Museum passes, Music CDs, Online cat, Orientations, Outreach serv, Outside serv via phone, mail, e-mail & web, OverDrive digital audio bks, Photocopying/Printing, Preschool outreach, Prog for adults, Prog for children & young adult, Senior computer classes, Spoken cassettes & CDs, Spoken cassettes & DVDs, Story hour, Summer reading prog, Tax forms, Teen prog, Telephone ref, VHS videos, Wheelchair accessible
Mem of Berks County Public Libraries
Open Mon-Thurs 9-8, Fri 9-2, Sat 9-4
Friends of the Library Group

P WYOMISSING PUBLIC LIBRARY*, Nine Reading Blvd, 19610-2084. SAN 315-3738. Tel: 610-374-2385. FAX: 610-374-8424. Web Site: wyopublib.org. *Dir,* Colleen Stamm; E-mail: colleen@wyopublib.org
Founded 1913. Pop 11,155; Circ 83,470
Library Holdings: Bk Vols 33,000; Per Subs 57
Automation Activity & Vendor Info: (Cataloging) Evergreen; (Circulation) Evergreen; (OPAC) Evergreen
Wireless access
Open Mon-Thurs 9-8, Fri 9-5, Sat 9-4

YEADON

P YEADON PUBLIC LIBRARY*, 809 Longacre Blvd, 19050. SAN 315-3762. Tel: 610-623-4090. E-mail: yeadonlibrary@comcast.net. Web Site: www.yeadonlibrary.org. *Dir,* Richard Ashby, Jr; *Asst Dir,* Darlene Walker; *Circ & ILL Mgr,* Ja'Nelle Schretzenmaire; Staff 4 (Non-MLS 4)
Founded 1937. Pop 11,727
Library Holdings: Bk Vols 38,000; Per Subs 100
Special Collections: African-American Cultural Center; Brodie/Johnson African-American Cultural Center for Children; Fifty-Plus Center; Parenting Center
Wireless access
Mem of Delaware County Libraries
Open Mon-Thurs 10-9, Fri 10-6, Sat 10-5
Friends of the Library Group

YORK

R FIRST CHURCH OF THE BRETHREN LIBRARY*, 2710 Kingston Rd, 17402-3799. SAN 315-3797. Tel: 717-755-0307. *Librn,* Helen Lehman; Staff 1 (Non-MLS 1)
Founded 1966
Library Holdings: Bk Titles 7,280; Bk Vols 7,500; Per Subs 26
Special Collections: Church of the Brethren Coll
Subject Interests: Biog, Family studies, Fiction, Inspiration, Recreation, Relig studies
Restriction: Mem only

J HARRISBURG AREA COMMUNITY COLLEGE*, York Campus Library, 2010 Pennsylvania Ave, 17404. Tel: 717-801-3220. FAX: 717-718-8967. E-mail: yorklib@hacc.edu. Web Site: libguides.hacc.edu/home/york. *Campus Librn,* Laura Wukovitz; Tel: 717-801-3335; *Adjunct Librn,* Diane Appelt; E-mail: dappelt@hacc.edu; *Adjunct Librn,* Jill Carew; E-mail: jbcarew@hacc.edu; *Ref & Instruction Librn,* Allyson Valentine; Tel: 717-718-3256, E-mail: afvalent@hacc.edu; *Libr Spec,* Kathleen Frederick; E-mail: kofreder@hacc.edu; *Libr Tech,* Becky Anstine; E-mail: rcanstin@hacc.edu; Staff 4.9 (MLS 3.4, Non-MLS 1.5)
Founded 2005. Enrl 3,157; Fac 140; Highest Degree: Associate
Library Holdings: AV Mats 96; Bks on Deafness & Sign Lang 1; DVDs 100; Large Print Bks 2; Bk Vols 4,000; Per Subs 72; Talking Bks 1; Videos 57
Automation Activity & Vendor Info: (Acquisitions) SirsiDynix; (Cataloging) SirsiDynix; (Circulation) SirsiDynix; (Course Reserve) Docutek; (ILL) SirsiDynix; (Media Booking) SirsiDynix; (OPAC) SirsiDynix; (Serials) SirsiDynix
Wireless access
Open Mon-Thurs (Fall & Spring) 7:30am-9pm, Fri 7:30-4, Sat 8:30am-12:30pm; Mon-Thurs (Summer) 7:30am-9pm

P MARTIN MEMORIAL LIBRARY*, 159 E Market St, 17401-1269. SAN 315-3819. Tel: 717-846-5300. FAX: 717-849-6998. Web Site: www.yorklibraries.org/york-martin. *Libr Dir,* Mina Edmondson; E-mail: medmondson@yorklibraries.org; *Ad, Info Serv Librn,* Sarah Fretz; *Ch Mgr,* Trish Bissett; *ILL Mgr,* Bob Rambo; Staff 54 (MLS 8, Non-MLS 46)
Founded 1935. Pop 112,500; Circ 585,300
Library Holdings: Bk Vols 150,000; Per Subs 200
Automation Activity & Vendor Info: (Circulation) SirsiDynix
Wireless access
Mem of York County Library System

Open Mon-Thurs 10-7, Fri & Sat 10-5, Sun 1-5
Friends of the Library Group

C PENN STATE UNIVERSITY YORK*, Lee R Glatfelter Library, 1031 Edgecomb Ave, 17403. SAN 315-3835. Tel: 717-771-4020. FAX: 717-771-4022. E-mail: ul-york@lists.psu.edu. Web Site: www.libraries.psu.edu/york. *Head Librn,* Barbara Eshbach; Tel: 717-771-4023, E-mail: bee11@psu.edu; *Ref & Instruction Librn,* Joel Burkholder; Tel: 717-771-4024, E-mail: jmb7609@psu.edu; *Info Res, Libr Serv Mgr,* Dawn Oswald; Tel: 717-777-4021, E-mail: djo10@psu.edu; *Info Res & Serv Support Spec,* Deborah Martin; Tel: 717-777-4198, E-mail: dem164@psu.edu; Staff 3.5 (MLS 1, Non-MLS 2.5)
Enrl 1,329; Fac 110; Highest Degree: Master
Library Holdings: CDs 500; DVDs 2,000; Bk Vols 65,000; Per Subs 150
Automation Activity & Vendor Info: (Circulation) SirsiDynix-WorkFlows; (Course Reserve) SirsiDynix-WorkFlows; (OPAC) SirsiDynix
Wireless access
Function: Art exhibits, E-Reserves, Electronic databases & coll, Free DVD rentals, Music CDs, Online cat, Online info literacy tutorials on the web & in blackboard, Photocopying/Printing, Ref serv available, Wheelchair accessible
Partic in OCLC Online Computer Library Center, Inc; Research Libraries Information Network
Open Mon-Thurs (Winter) 8am-9pm, Fri 8-5, Sat 10-4, Sun 1-6; Mon-Thurs (Summer) 8-8, Fri 8-5, Sat 11-4
Restriction: Open to pub for ref & circ; with some limitations, Open to students, fac & staff

M WELLSPAN YORK HOSPITAL*, Philip A Hoover MD Library, 1001 S George St, 17405-7198. SAN 315-3878. Tel: 717-851-2495. FAX: 717-851-2487. E-mail: libserv@wellspan.org. Web Site: www.wellspan.org/offices-locations/wellspan-york-hospital. *Dir, Libr Serv,* Catherine Kelly; Tel: 717-851-2495, E-mail: ckelly3@wellspan.org; Staff 5 (MLS 2, Non-MLS 3)
Founded 1929
Library Holdings: e-journals 2,000; Bk Titles 7,000; Bk Vols 31,300; Per Subs 375
Subject Interests: Clinical med, Nursing
Automation Activity & Vendor Info: (Acquisitions) SirsiDynix; (Cataloging) SirsiDynix; (Circulation) SirsiDynix; (ILL) OCLC; (OPAC) SirsiDynix-iLink; (Serials) EBSCO Online
Wireless access
Function: Res libr
Partic in Basic Health Sciences Library Network
Open Mon-Fri 7:30-4:30

C YORK COLLEGE OF PENNSYLVANIA*, Schmidt Library, 441 Country Club Rd, 17403-3651. SAN 315-3843. Tel: 717-815-1304. Interlibrary Loan Service Tel: 717-815-1485. Reference Tel: 717-815-1356. Administration Tel: 717-815-1577. FAX: 717-849-1608. E-mail: library@ycp.edu. Information Services E-mail: infoservices@ycp.edu. Web Site: library.ycp.edu. *Libr Dir,* Jim Kapoun; Tel: 717-815-1353, E-mail: jkapoun@ycp.edu; *Dir, Info Literacy,* Trenton Bankert; Tel: 717-815-1480, E-mail: tbankert2@ycp.edu; *Content Dev,* Beth Jacoby; Tel: 717-815-1950, E-mail: bjacoby@ycp.edu; *Instrul Media,* Patricia Poet; Tel: 717-815-1458, E-mail: ppoet@ycp.edu; *Pub Serv,* Zehao Zhou; Tel: 717-815-1518, E-mail: zzhou@ycp.edu; *Syst,* Vickie Kline; Tel: 717-815-1459, E-mail: vkline@ycp.edu; Staff 14 (MLS 5, Non-MLS 9)
Founded 1787. Enrl 4,300; Fac 543; Highest Degree: Doctorate
Library Holdings: CDs 2,527; DVDs 5,069; e-books 104,757; e-journals 11,122; Electronic Media & Resources 11,708; Music Scores 527; Bk Titles 117,576; Videos 1,708
Special Collections: Lincoln Coll
Subject Interests: Bus admin, Educ, Nursing
Automation Activity & Vendor Info: (Acquisitions) SirsiDynix-Unicorn; (Cataloging) SirsiDynix; (Circulation) SirsiDynix; (Course Reserve) Docutek; (ILL) Relais International; (OPAC) SirsiDynix; (Serials) SerialsSolutions
Wireless access
Partic in Associated College Libraries of Central Pennsylvania; LYRASIS; OCLC Online Computer Library Center, Inc; Partnership for Academic Library Collaborative & Innovation
Open Mon-Thurs 8am-2am, Fri 8-8, Sat 10-6, Sun Noon-2am

S YORK COUNTY HISTORY CENTER*, Historical Society of York County Library & Archives, 250 E Market St, 17403. SAN 315-3800. Tel: 717-848-1587. FAX: 717-812-1204. E-mail: nsmith@yorkhistorycenter.org. Web Site: yorkhistorycenter.org. *Dir, Libr & Archive Serv,* Nicole Smith; E-mail: nsmith@yorkhistorycenter.org; *Asst Dir, Archives & Libr,* Adam Bentz; E-mail: abentz@yorkhistorycenter.org; *Registrar,* Bryan Bailey; E-mail: bbailey@yorkhistorycenter.org; Staff 2 (Non-MLS 2)
Founded 1895
Library Holdings: Bk Vols 35,000; Per Subs 50
Special Collections: Art (Lewis Miller Folk Drawing Coll), ms; Folk Coll; Genealogy of York & Adams County (York County Genealogical Coll), bks, ms; General Jacob Devers Coll; Governmental Archives (Archives of York City & York County), ms; History (York County Historical Coll), bks, ms; James Shettel Circus & Theater in America Coll, broadsides, ms, photog; Local Newspapers Coll, 1789 to present, micro; York Gazette & Daily, 1815-1970, micro
Subject Interests: Decorative art, Fine arts, Genealogy, Local hist
Wireless access
Function: Ref & res
Open Tues-Sat 9-5
Restriction: Non-circulating to the pub

P YORK COUNTY LIBRARY SYSTEM*, 159 E Market St, 3rd Flr, 17401. SAN 315-386X. Administration Tel: 717-849-6969. FAX: 717-849-6999. Web Site: www.yorklibraries.org. *Pres,* Robert Lambert; E-mail: rlambert@yorklibraries.org
Pop 381,751; Circ 1,553,057
Library Holdings: Bk Vols 453,646; Per Subs 661
Wireless access
Member Libraries: Arthur Hufnagel Public Library of Glen Rock; Dillsburg Area Public Library; Glatfelter Memorial Library; Guthrie Memorial Library; Kaltreider-Benfer Library; Martin Memorial Library; Mason-Dixon Public Library; Paul Smith Library of Southern York County
Branches: 5

COLLINSVILLE COMMUNITY LIBRARY, 2632 Delta Rd, Brogue, 17309, SAN 324-007X. Tel: 717-927-9014. FAX: 717-927-9664. Web Site: www.yorklibraries.org/brogue-collinsville. *Librn,* Ellen Helfrick; E-mail: ehelfrick@yorklibraries.org; Staff 3 (MLS 1, Non-MLS 2)
Pop 14,025; Circ 38,575
Library Holdings: Bk Vols 13,600; Per Subs 30
Open Mon & Wed 10-4, Tues 3-8, Thurs 2-6, Fri 1-5, Sat 9-1
Friends of the Library Group

DOVER AREA COMMUNITY LIBRARY, 3700-3 Davidsburg Rd, Dover, 17315, SAN 377-7154. Tel: 717-292-6814. FAX: 717-292-9774. Web Site: www.yorklibraries.org/dover. *Librn,* Ray Van de Castle; E-mail: rvandecastle@yorklibraries.org; Staff 1 (MLS 1)
Pop 22,349; Circ 88,585
Library Holdings: Bk Titles 17,505; Bk Vols 19,126; Per Subs 24
Open Mon 12-8, Tues 10-2, Wed 10-8, Thurs-Sat 10-1
Friends of the Library Group

KREUTZ CREEK VALLEY LIBRARY, 66 Walnut Springs Rd, Hellam, 17406, SAN 377-7170. Tel: 717-252-4080. FAX: 717-252-0283. Web Site: www.yorklibraries.org/kreutz-creek. *Br Mgr,* Susan Nenstiel; E-mail: snenstiel@yorklibraries.org; Staff 1 (MLS 1)
Pop 10,363; Circ 49,245
Library Holdings: Bk Titles 13,008; Bk Vols 13,803
Open Mon, Wed & Fri 10-3, Tues & Thurs 2-8, Sat 10-1
Friends of the Library Group

RED LAND COMMUNITY LIBRARY, 70 Newberry Commons, Etters, 17319, SAN 324-0088. Tel: 717-938-5599. Web Site: www.yorklibraries.org/red-land. *Libr Mgr,* Karen Hostetter; E-mail: khostetter@yorklibraries.org; Staff 1 (MLS 1)
Pop 44,865; Circ 62,783
Library Holdings: Bk Titles 22,241; Bk Vols 25,595; Per Subs 18
Open Mon 10-5, Tues 1-8, Thurs 10-8, Fri 10-1
Friends of the Library Group

VILLAGE LIBRARY, 35-C N Main St, Jacobus, 17407, SAN 324-3184. Tel: 717-428-1034. FAX: 717-428-3869. Web Site: www.yorklibraries.org/village. *Librn,* Becky Shives; E-mail: rshives@yorklibraries.org; Staff 4 (Non-MLS 4)
Pop 7,514; Circ 82,000
Library Holdings: Bk Vols 18,000; Per Subs 26
Open Mon & Wed 10-4, Tues 12-4, Thurs 12-8, Fri 10-2, Sat 10-12
Friends of the Library Group

YORK HAVEN

P YORK HAVEN COMMUNITY LIBRARY*, Two N Front St, 17370. SAN 315-3886. Tel: 717-266-4712. *Dir,* Cynthia Owad
Library Holdings: Bk Titles 10,009; Per Subs 17
Wireless access
Open Tues & Wed 4:30-6:30

YOUNGSVILLE

P YOUNGSVILLE PUBLIC LIBRARY, 100 Broad St, 16371. SAN 315-3894. Tel: 814-563-7670. FAX: 814-563-7670. E-mail: youngsvillepubliclibrary@gmail.com. Web Site: www.youngsvillelibrary.org. *Libr Dir,* Kristy Wallace
Founded 1931. Pop 5,000; Circ 15,000
Library Holdings: Bk Titles 13,000; Per Subs 30
Wireless access
Open Mon & Tues 12-7:30, Wed 10-5, Fri 12-4
Friends of the Library Group

YOUNGWOOD

J WESTMORELAND COUNTY COMMUNITY COLLEGE LIBRARY*, Founders Hall, Youngwood Campus, 145 Pavilion Lane, 15697-1814. SAN 315-3908. Tel: 724-925-4100. Interlibrary Loan Service Tel: 724-925-6956. Reference Tel: 724-925-4102. Administration Tel: 724-925-4097. Toll Free Tel: 800-262-2103, Ext 4100. FAX: 724-925-1150. E-mail: library@westmoreland.edu. Web Site: westmoreland.edu/pages/current-students/library. *Dir,* Annette G Boyer; E-mail: boyera@westmoreland.edu; *Digital Serv Librn, Instrul Serv Librn,* Raeanna Paterson; E-mail: patersonr@westmoreland.edu; *Tech Serv Librn,* Belinda Sedlak; Tel: 724-925-4096, E-mail: sedlakb@westmoreland.edu; Staff 7 (MLS 4, Non-MLS 3)
Founded 1970. Enrl 3,300; Fac 88; Highest Degree: Associate
Library Holdings: DVDs 4,855; Electronic Media & Resources 24; Bk Vols 42,000; Per Subs 71
Automation Activity & Vendor Info: (Acquisitions) SirsiDynix; (Cataloging) SirsiDynix; (Circulation) SirsiDynix; (Course Reserve) SirsiDynix; (Discovery) EBSCO Discovery Service; (ILL) SirsiDynix; (OPAC) SirsiDynix; (Serials) SirsiDynix
Wireless access
Partic in LYRASIS; OCLC Online Computer Library Center, Inc
Open Mon-Thurs 8-8, Fri 8-2, Sat 9-1

ZELIENOPLE

P ZELIENOPLE AREA PUBLIC LIBRARY*, 227 S High St, 16063. SAN 315-3916. Tel: 724-452-9330. FAX: 724-452-9318. E-mail: zaplib@bcfls.org. Web Site: bcfls.org/zelienople-area-public-library. *Dir,* Maggie Boylan; *Adult Serv,* Amy Kellner; Staff 3 (MLS 1, Non-MLS 2)
Founded 1919. Pop 11,500; Circ 95,000
Library Holdings: Audiobooks 355; AV Mats 1,500; CDs 300; DVDs 750; e-books 50; Large Print Bks 825; Bk Titles 6,500; Per Subs 75; Talking Bks 250; Videos 75
Special Collections: Preschool AV Coll, puppets, teaching devices, videos
Automation Activity & Vendor Info: (Cataloging) TLC (The Library Corporation); (Circulation) TLC (The Library Corporation); (ILL) TLC (The Library Corporation); (OPAC) TLC (The Library Corporation)
Wireless access
Function: Adult bk club, Audiobks via web, Bk club(s), Bks on CD, Children's prog, Computer training, Computers for patron use, E-Reserves, Electronic databases & coll, Family literacy, Free DVD rentals, Holiday prog, ILL available, Music CDs, Online cat, Online ref, OverDrive digital audio bks, Preschool reading prog, Prog for adults, Prog for children & young adult, Ref serv available, Senior computer classes, Story hour, Summer reading prog, Tax forms, Teen prog, Telephone ref, Wheelchair accessible
Mem of Butler County Federated Library System
Special Services for the Deaf - TTY equip
Special Services for the Blind - Bks on cassette; Bks on CD; Large print bks; Playaways (bks on MP3)
Open Mon-Thurs 10-7, Fri 9-2, Sat 10-5
Restriction: Use of others with permission of librn
Friends of the Library Group